Peterson's Four-Year Colleges 2018

PETERSON'S®

PETERSON'S®

About Peterson's®

Peterson's® provides the accurate, dependable, high-quality education content and guidance you need to succeed. No matter where you are on your academic or professional path, you can rely on Peterson's publications and its online information at **www.petersons.com** for the most up-to-date education exploration data, expert test-prep tools, and top-notch career success resources—everything you need to achieve your goals.

For more information, contact Peterson's, 3 Columbia Circle, Suite 205, Albany, NY 12203-5158;
800-338-3282 Ext. 54229; or visit us online at **www.petersons.com**.

Previous editions published as *Peterson's Annual Guide to Undergraduate Study* © 1970, 1971, 1972, 1973, 1974, 1975, 1976, 1977, 1978, 1979, 1980, 1981, 1982 and as *Peterson's Four-Year Colleges* © 1983, 1984, 1985, 1986, 1987, 1988, 1989, 1990, 1991, 1992, 1993, 1994, 1995, 1996, 1997, 1998, 1999, 2000, 2001, 2002, 2003, 2004, 2005, 2006, 2007, 2008, 2009, 2010, 2011, 2012, 2013, 2014, 2015. 2016

ISSN 1544-2330
ISBN 978-0-7689-4123-4

Printed in the United States of America

10 9 8 7 6 5 4 3 2 1 19 18 17

Forty-eighth Edition

Contents

A Note from the Peterson's® Editors

For over fifty years, Peterson's® has given students and parents the most comprehensive, up-to-date information on undergraduate institutions in the United States and Canada. *Peterson's® Four-Year Colleges 2018* features advice and tips on the college search and selection process, such as how to consider the factors that truly make a difference during your search, how to understand the application process, and how to get financial aid. Each year, Peterson's® researches the data published in *Peterson's® Four-Year Colleges*. The information is furnished by the colleges and is accurate at the time of publishing.

Opportunities abound for students, and this guide can help you find what you want in a number of ways:

- For application and admissions advice and guidance, just head to **THE ADVICE CENTER.** The "College Admissions Countdown Calendar" outlines pertinent month-by-month milestones. "Choosing Your Top Ten Colleges" gets you started on putting together the most important Top Ten list you have ever made. You'll find some excellent advice in the article, "Planning is Essential on the Road to College," by Sarah E. Gibbs, Director of Admissions at Grove City College. Next, "Surviving Standardized Tests" describes frequently used tests and what you need to know to succeed on them. Of course, part of the college selection process involves visiting the schools themselves, and "The Whys and Whats of College Visits" is the planner you need to make those trips well worth your while. Be sure to check out the articles on specific institutions and programs that may be just right for you, including "Honors Programs and Colleges: Smart Choices for an Undergraduate Education," "Public and Private Colleges and Universities—How to Choose," "Distance Education—It's Closer than You Think," and "Why Not Women's Colleges?" Next, "Applying 101" provides advice on how best to approach the application phase of the process. If you can't make sense out of the early decision/early action conundrum, "The 'Early Decision' Decision" may help clarify it for you. The article "Coming to America: Tips for International Students Considering Study in the U.S." offers helpful information and expert tips from professionals who work with international students at colleges and universities throughout the United States. For essential information on how to meet your education expenses, you'll find the "Financial Aid Countdown Calendar" followed by the articles "Who's Paying for This? Financial Aid Basics" and "Middle Income Families: Making the Financial Aid Process Work." Finally, you'll want to read through the "How to Use This Guide" section, which explains the information presented for each individual college, how Peterson's collects its data, and how Peterson's determines eligibility for inclusion in this guide.
- Next up is the **PROFILES** section. Here you'll find our unparalleled college profiles, arranged alphabetically by state, U.S. territories, and by country. They provide need-to-know information about accredited four-year colleges—including entrance difficulty, campus setting, total enrollment, student-faculty ratio, application deadlines, expenses, most frequently chosen baccalaureate fields, and academic programs. The contact information appears at the conclusion of each college profile. Display ads, which appear near some of the institutions' profiles, have been provided and paid for by those colleges or universities that wished to supplement their profile data with additional information about their institution. A star ★ next to the name of a school signifies that the school also has an expanded profile on Peterson's website at www.petersons.com.
- Nearly 200 two-page narrative descriptions appear as **COLLEGE CLOSE-UPS**—descriptions written by admissions or college officials that provide great detail about each school. They are edited to provide a consistent format across entries for your ease of comparison.
- If you already have specifics in mind, such as a particular major or institution, turn to the **INDEXES** section. Here you can search for a school based on major, entrance difficulty, cost ranges, and geography. If you already have colleges in mind that pique your interest, you can use the "Alphabetical Listing of Colleges and Universities" to search for these schools. Page numbers referring to all information presented about a college are conveniently referenced.

Peterson's® publishes a full line of books—college and grad guides, education exploration, test preparation, financial aid, and career preparation. Peterson's® publications can be found at high school guidance offices, college libraries and career centers, and your local bookstore and library. Peterson's® books are also available at www.petersonsbooks.com.

We welcome any comments or suggestions you may have about this publication. Your feedback will help us make educational dreams possible for you—and others like you.

Colleges will be pleased to know that Peterson's® helped you in your selection. Admissions staff members are more than happy to answer questions, address specific problems, and help in any way they can. The editors at Peterson's® wish you great success in your college search!

NOTICE: Certain portions of or information contained in this book have been submitted and paid for by the educational institution identified, and such institutions take full responsibility for the accuracy, timeliness, completeness and functionality of such content. Such portions or information include (i) each display ad in the "Profiles" section from pages 55 through 1272 that comprises a half or full page of information covering a single educational institution, and (ii) each two-page description in the "College Close-Up" section from pages 1274 through 1603.

The Advice Center

College Admissions Countdown Calendar

This practical month-by-month calendar is designed to help you stay on top of the process of applying to college. For most students, the process begins in September of the junior year of high school and ends in June of the senior year. You may want to begin considering financial aid options, reviewing your academic schedule, and attending college fairs before your junior year.

JUNIOR YEAR

September

- Check with your counselor to make sure your course credits will meet college requirements.
- Be sure you are involved in one or two extracurricular activities.
- Begin building your personal list of colleges.

October

- Register for and take the PSAT/NMSQT®.

November

- Strive to get the best grades you can. A serious effort will provide you with the most options during the application process.

December

- Get involved in a community service activity.
- Begin to read newspapers and a weekly news magazine.
- Buy *Peterson's® SAT® Prep Guide*, or *Peterson's ACT® Prep Guide* and begin to study for the tests.

January

- With your school counselor, decide when to take the ACT®, SAT®, and SAT Subject Tests™ (and which Subject Tests to take). If English is not your primary language and you are planning on attending a college in North America, decide when to take the TOEFL®.
- Keep your grades up!

February

- Plan a challenging schedule of classes for your senior year.
- Think about which teachers you will ask to write recommendations.
- Check http://www.nacacnet.org/ and click on "College Fairs" for up-to-date schedules and locations of college fairs.

March

- Register for the tests you will take in the spring (ACT®, SAT®, SAT Subject Tests™, or the TOEFL®).
- Meet with your school counselor to discuss college choices.
- Review your transcript and test scores with your counselor to determine how competitive your range of choices should be.
- Develop a preliminary list of fifteen to twenty colleges and universities.
- Start scheduling campus visits. The best time is when school is in session (but never during final exams). Summers are OK but will not show you what the college is really like. If possible, save your top college choices for the fall. Be aware, however, that fall is the busiest visit season, and you will need advance planning. Don't forget to write thank you letters to your interviewers.

April

- Take any standardized tests for which you have registered.
- Create a list of your potential college choices and begin to record personal and academic information that can be transferred later to your college applications.

May

- Plan college visits and make appointments.
- Structure your summer plans to include advanced academic work, travel, volunteer work, or a job.
- Confirm your academic schedule for the fall.

Summer

- Write to any colleges on your list that do not accept the Common Application to request application forms.
- Begin working on your application essays.

SENIOR YEAR

September

- Register for the ACT®, SAT®, SAT Subject Tests™, or the TOEFL®, as necessary.
- Check with your school counselor for the fall visiting schedule of college reps.
- Ask appropriate teachers if they would write recommendations for you. Don't forget to write thank you letters when they accept.
- Meet with your counselor to compile your final list of colleges.

October

- Mail or send early applications electronically after carefully checking them to be sure they are completely filled out.
- Photocopy or print extra copies of your applications to use as a backup.
- Take the tests for which you have registered.
- Don't be late! Keep track of all deadlines for transcripts, recommendations, financial aid, etc.

November

- Be sure that you have requested your ACT® and SAT® scores be sent to your colleges of choice.
- Complete and submit all applications. Print or photocopy an extra copy for your records.

December

- Take any necessary tests: ACT®, SAT®, SAT Subject Tests™, or the TOEFL®.
- Meet with your counselor to verify that all is in order and that transcripts were sent to colleges.

January

- Prepare the Free Application for Federal Student Aid (FAFSA®), available at www.fafsa.ed.gov or through your school counseling office. An estimated income tax statement (which can be corrected later) can be used. The sooner you apply for financial aid, the better your chances.

February

- Submit your FAFSA® either online or via U.S. mail.
- Be sure your midyear report has gone out to the colleges to which you've applied.
- Let colleges know of any new honors or accomplishments that were not in your original application.

March

- Register for any Advanced Placement® (AP®) tests you might take.
- Be sure you have received a FAFSA® acknowledgment.

April

- Review the acceptances and financial aid offers you receive.
- Go back to visit one or two of your top-choice colleges.
- Notify your college of choice that you have accepted its offer (and send in a deposit by May 1).
- Notify the colleges you have chosen not to attend of your decision.

May

- Take AP® tests.

June

- Graduate! Congratulations and best of luck.

Choosing Your Top Ten Colleges

By using all the information in the various sections of this guide, you will find colleges worthy of the most important top-ten list on the planet—yours.

The first thing you will need to do is decide what type of institution of higher learning you want to attend. Each of the thousands of four-year colleges and universities in the United States is as unique as the people applying to it. Although listening to the voices and media hype around you can make it sound as though there are only a few elite schools worth attending, this simply is not true. By considering some of the following criteria, you will soon find that the large pool of interesting colleges can be narrowed down to a more reasonable number.

SIZE AND CATEGORY

Schools come in all shapes and sizes, from tiny rural colleges of 400 students to massive state university systems serving 100,000 students or more. If you are coming from a small high school, a college with 3,500 students may seem large to you. If you are currently attending a high school with 3,000 students, selecting a college of a similar size may not feel like a new enough experience. Some students coming from very large impersonal high schools are looking for a place where they will be recognized from the beginning and offered a more personal approach. If you don't have a clue about what size might feel right to you, try visiting a couple of nearby colleges of varying sizes. You do not have to be seriously interested in them; just feel what impact the number of students on campus has on you.

Large Universities

Large universities offer a wide range of educational, athletic, and social experiences. Universities offer a full scope of undergraduate majors and award master's and doctoral degrees as well. Universities are usually composed of several smaller colleges. Depending on your interest in a major field or area of study, you would likely apply to a specific college within the university. Each college has the flexibility to set its own standards for admission, which may differ from the overall average of the university. The colleges within a university system also set their own course requirements for earning a degree.

Universities may be public or private. Some large private universities, such as Harvard, Yale, Princeton, University of Pennsylvania, New York University, Northwestern, and Stanford, are well-known for their high entrance standards, the excellence of their education, and the success rates of their graduates. These institutions place a great deal of emphasis on research and compete aggressively for grants from the federal government to fund these projects. Large public universities, such as the State University of New York (SUNY) System, University of Michigan, University of Texas, University of Illinois, University of Washington, and University of North Carolina, also support excellent educational programs, compete for and win research funding, and have successful graduates. Public universities usually offer substantially lower tuition rates to in-state students, although their tuition rates for out-of-state residents are often comparable to those of private institutions.

At many large universities, sports play a major role on campus. Athletics can dominate the calendar and set the tone year-round at some schools. Alumni travel from far and wide to attend their alma mater's football or basketball games, and the campus—and frequently the entire town—grinds to a halt when there is a home game. Athletes are heroes and dominate campus social life.

What are some other features of life on a university campus? Every kind of club imaginable, from literature to bioengineering and chorus to politics, can be found on most college campuses. You will be able to play the intramural version of almost every sport in which the university fields interscholastic teams and join fraternities, sororities, and groups dedicated to social action. You can become a member of a band, an orchestra, or perhaps a chamber music group or work on the newspaper, the literary magazine, or the website. The list can go on and on. You may want to try out a new interest or two or pursue what you have always been interested in and make like-minded friends along the way.

Take a look at the size of the classrooms in the larger universities and envision yourself sitting in that atmosphere. Would this offer a learning environment that would benefit you?

Liberal Arts Colleges

If you have considered large universities and come to the conclusion that all that action could be a distraction, a small liberal arts college might be right for you. Ideally tucked away on a picture-perfect campus, a liberal arts college generally has fewer than 5,000 students. The mission of most liberal arts schools is learning for the sake of learning, with a strong emphasis on creating lifelong learners who will be able to apply their education to any number of careers. This contrasts with objectives of the profession-based preparation of specialized colleges.

Liberal arts colleges cannot offer the breadth of courses provided by the large universities. As a result, liberal arts colleges try to create a niche for themselves. For instance, a college may place its emphasis on its humanities departments, whose professors are all well-known published authors and international presenters in their areas of expertise. A college may highlight its science departments by providing state-of-the-art-facilities where undergraduates conduct research side by side with top-notch professors and copublish their findings in the most prestigious scientific journals in the country. The personal approach is very important at liberal arts colleges. Whether in advisement, course selection, athletic programs tailored to students' interests, or dinner with the department head at her home, liberal arts colleges emphasize that they get to know their students.

If they are so perfect, why doesn't everyone choose a liberal arts college? Well, the small size limits options. Fewer people may mean less diversity. The fact that many of these colleges encourage a study-abroad option (a student elects to spend a semester or a year studying in another country) reduces the number of students on campus even further. Some liberal arts colleges have a certain reputation that does not appeal to some students. You should ask yourself questions about the campus life that most appeals to you. Will you fit in with the campus culture? Will the small size mean that you go through your social options quickly? Check out the activities listed on the Student Center bulletin board. Does the student body look diverse enough for you? Will what is happening keep you busy and interested? Do the students have input into decision making? Do they create the social climate of the school?

Small Universities

Smaller universities often combine stringent admissions policies, handpicked faculty members, and attractive scholarship packages. These institutions generally have undergraduate enrollments of about 4,000 students. Some are more famous for their graduate and professional schools but have also established strong undergraduate colleges. Smaller universities balance the great majors options of large universities with a smaller campus community. They offer choices but not to the same extent as large universities. On the other hand, by limiting admissions and enrollment, they manage to cultivate some of the characteristics of a liberal arts college. Like a liberal arts college, a small university may emphasize a particular program and go out of its way to draw strong candidates in a specific area, such as premed, to its campus. Universities such as The Johns Hopkins University, University of Notre Dame, Vanderbilt University, Washington University in St. Louis, and Wesleyan University in Connecticut are a few examples of this category.

Technical or Specialized Colleges

Another alternative to the liberal arts college or large university is the technical or otherwise specialized college. Its goal is to offer a specialized and saturated experience in a particular field of study. Such an institution might limit its course offerings to engineering and science, the performing or fine arts, or business. Schools such as California Institute of Technology, Carnegie Mellon University, Massachusetts Institute of Technology, and Rensselaer Polytechnic Institute concentrate on attracting the finest math and science students in the country. At other schools, like Bentley College in Massachusetts or Bryant College in Rhode Island, students eat, sleep, and breathe business. These institutions are purists at heart and strong believers in the necessity of focused, specialized study to produce excellence in their graduates' achievements. If you are certain about your chosen path in life and want to immerse yourself in subjects such as math, music, or business, you will fit right in.

Religious Colleges

Many private colleges have religious origins, and many of these have become secular institutions with virtually no trace of their religious roots. Others remain dedicated to a religious way of education. What sets religious colleges apart is the way they combine faith, learning, and student life. Faculty members and administrators are hired with faith as a criterion as much as their academic credentials.

Single-Gender Colleges

There are strong arguments that being able to pursue one's education without the distraction, competition, and stress caused by the presence of the opposite sex helps a student evolve a stronger sense of her or his self-worth; achieve more academically; have a more fulfilling, less pressured social schedule; and achieve more later in life. For various historic, social, and psychological reasons, there are many more all-women than all-men colleges. A strict single-sex environment is rare. Even though the undergraduate day college adheres to an all-female or all-male admissions policy, coeducational evening classes or graduate programs and coordinate facilities and classes shared with nearby coed or opposite-sex institutions can result in a good number of students of the opposite sex being found on campus. If you want to concentrate on your studies and hone your leadership qualities, a single-gender school is an option.

LOCATION

Location and distance from home are two other important considerations. If you have always lived in the suburbs, choosing an urban campus can be an adventure, but after a week of the urban experience, will you long for a grassy campus and open space? On the other hand, if you choose a college in a rural area, will you run screaming into the Student Center some night looking for noise, lights, and people? The location—urban, rural, or suburban—can directly affect how easy or how difficult adjusting to college life will be for you.

Don't forget to factor in distance from home. Everyone going off to college wants to think he or she won't be homesick, but sometimes it's nice to get a home-cooked meal or to do the laundry in a place that does not require quarters. Even your kid sister may seem like less of a nuisance after a couple of months away.

Here are some questions you might ask yourself as you go through the selection process: In what part of the country do I want to be? How far away from home do I want to be? What is the cost of returning home? Do I need to be close to a city? How close? How large of a city? Would city life distract me? Would I concentrate better in a setting that is more rural or more suburban?

ENTRANCE DIFFICULTY

Many students will look at a college's entrance difficulty as an indicator of whether or not they will be admitted. For instance, if you have an excellent academic record, you might wish to primarily consider those colleges that are highly competitive. Although entrance difficulty does not translate directly to quality of education, it indicates which colleges are attracting large numbers of high-achieving students. A high-achieving student body usually translates into prestige for the college and its graduates. Prestige has some advantages but should definitely be viewed as a secondary factor that might tip the scales when all the other important factors are equal. Never base your decision on prestige alone!

The other principle to keep in mind when considering this factor is to not sell yourself short. If everything else tells you that a college might be right for you, but your numbers just miss that college's average range, apply there anyway. Your numbers—grades and test scores—are undeniably important in the admissions decision, but there are other considerations. First, lower grades in honors or AP® courses will impress colleges more than top grades in regular-track courses because they demonstrate that you are the kind of student willing to accept challenges. Second, admissions directors are looking for different qualities in students that can be combined to create a multifaceted class. For example, if you did poorly in your freshman and sophomore years but made a great improvement in your grades in later years, this usually will impress a college. If you are likely to contribute to your class because of your special personal qualities, a strong sense of commitment and purpose, unusual and valuable experiences, or special interests and talents, these factors can outweigh numbers that are weaker than average. Nevertheless, be practical. Overreach yourself in a few applications, but put the bulk of your effort into gaining admission to colleges where you have a realistic chance for admission.

THE PRICE OF AN EDUCATION

The price tag for higher education continues to rise, and it has become an increasingly important factor for people. While it is necessary to consider your family's resources when choosing a list of colleges to which you might apply, never eliminate a college solely because of cost. There are many ways to pay for college, including loans, and a college education will never depreciate in value, unlike other purchases. It is an investment in yourself and will pay back the expense many times over in your lifetime.

Surviving Standardized Tests

WHAT ARE STANDARDIZED TESTS?

Colleges and universities in the United States use tests to help evaluate applicants' readiness for admission or to place them in appropriate courses. The tests that are most frequently used by colleges are the ACT® Exam and the College Board's SAT® Exam. In addition, the Educational Testing Service (ETS) offers the TOEFL® test, which evaluates the English-language proficiency of nonnative speakers. The tests are offered at designated testing centers located at high schools and colleges throughout the United States and U.S. territories and at testing centers in various countries throughout the world.

Upon request, special accommodations for students with documented visual, hearing, physical, or learning disabilities are available. Examples of special accommodations include tests in Braille or large print and such aids as a reader, recorder, magnifying glass, or sign language interpreter. Additional testing time may be allowed in some instances. Contact the appropriate testing program or your guidance counselor for details on how to request special accommodations.

THE ACT® Exam

The ACT® exam is a standardized college entrance examination that measures knowledge and skills in English, mathematics, reading comprehension, and science reasoning and the application of these skills to future academic tasks. The ACT® exam consists of four multiple-choice tests. The four tests and the content covered in each is as follows:

English Test (75 questions; 45 minutes)

- Usage and mechanics
- Rhetorical skills

Mathematics Test (60 questions; 60 minutes)

- Pre-algebra
- Elementary algebra
- Intermediate algebra
- Coordinate geometry
- Plane geometry
- Trigonometry

Reading Test (40 questions; 35 minutes)

- Literary narrative/Prose fiction
- Humanities
- Social studies
- Natural sciences

Science (40 questions; 35 minutes)

- Data representation
- Research summaries
- Conflicting viewpoints

Each section is scored from 1 to 36 and is scaled for slight variations in difficulty. Students are not penalized for incorrect responses. The composite score is the average of the four scaled scores. The ACT® Plus Writing includes the four multiple-choice tests and the 40-minute Writing Test, which measures writing skills emphasized in high school English classes and in entry-level college composition courses.

To prepare for the ACT® Exam, ask your guidance counselor for a free guidebook, *Preparing for the ACT® Test*, or download it at www.act.org/content/dam/act/unsecured/documents/Preparing-for-the-ACT.pdf. Besides providing general test-preparation information and additional test-taking strategies, this guidebook provides a full-length practice exam including the Writing Test, instructions for taking the Writing Test, test-preparation strategies, and what to expect on test day.

DON'T FORGET TO . . .

- ❑ Take the SAT® Exam or ACT® Exam before application deadlines.
- ❑ Note that test registration deadlines precede test dates by about six weeks.
- ❑ Register to take the TOEFL® test if English is not your native language and you are planning on studying at a North American college.
- ❑ Contact the College Board or ACT, Inc., in advance if you need special accommodations when taking tests.

The SAT® has these sections: Evidence-Based Reading and Writing, Math, and the SAT® Essay. It is based on 1600 points—the top scores for the Math section and the Evidence-Based Reading and Writing section will be 800, and the SAT® Essay score is reported separately.

Reading Test (52 questions; 65 minutes)

Passages in U.S. and world literature, history/social studies, and science are used to test the following skills:

- Command of Evidence
- Words in Context
- Analysis in History/Social Studies and in Science

Writing and Language Test (44 questions; 35 minutes)

Passages in careers, history/social studies, humanities, and science are used to test the following skills:

- Command of Evidence
- Words in Context
- Analysis in History/Social Studies and in Science
- Expression of ideas
- Standard English conventions

Math Test (58 questions; 80 minutes)

This test is divided into two sections: the no-calculator section (25 minutes) and the calculator section (55 minutes).

- Content includes algebra, problem solving and data analysis, advanced math, area and volume calculations, trigonometric functions, and lines, triangles, and circles using theorems.

SAT® Essay (Optional)

* 50 minutes

- Argument passage written for a general audience
- Analysis of argument in passage using text evidence
- Score: 3–12 (Reading: 1–4 scale, Analysis: 1–4 scale, Writing: 1–4 scale)

According to the College Board's website, the following are the "Key Content Features" of the SAT® exam:

- **Relevant Words in Context:** Students need to interpret the meaning of words based on the context of the passage in which they appear. The focus is on "relevant" words—not obscure ones.
- **Command of Evidence:** In addition to demonstrating writing skills, students need to show that they're able to interpret, synthesize, and use evidence found in a wide range of sources.
- **Essay Analyzing a Source:** Students read a passage and explain how the author builds an argument, and supports their claims with actual data from the passage.
- **Math Focused on Three Key Areas:** Problem Solving and Data Analysis (using ratios, percentages, and proportional reasoning to solve problems in science, social science, and career contexts), the Heart of Algebra (mastery of linear equations and systems), and Passport to Advanced Math (more complex equations and the manipulation they require).
- **Problems Grounded in Real-World Contexts:** All of the questions are grounded in the real world, directly related to work performed in college.
- **Analysis in Science and in Social Studies:** Students need to apply reading, writing, language, and math skills to answer questions in contexts of science, history, and social studies.
- **Founding Documents and Great Global Conversation:** Students will find an excerpt from one of the Founding Documents—such as the Declaration of Independence, the Constitution, and the Bill of Rights—or a text from the "Great Global Conversation" about freedom, justice, and human dignity.
- **No Penalty for Wrong Answers:** Students earn points for the questions they answer correctly.

Check out the College Board's website at https://collegereadiness.collegeboard.org/sat-subject-tests/about/at-a-glance for the most up-to-date information.

Top 10 Ways Not to Take the Test

10. Cramming the night before the test.
9. Not becoming familiar with the directions before you take the test.
8. Not becoming familiar with the format of the test before you take it.
7. Not knowing how the test is graded.
6. Spending too much time on any one question.
5. Second-guessing yourself.
4. Not checking spelling, grammar, and sentence structure in essays.
3. Writing a one-paragraph essay.
2. Forgetting to take a deep breath to keep from—
1. Losing It!

SAT SUBJECT TESTS™

SAT Subject Tests™ are required by some institutions for admission and/or placement in freshman-level courses. Each Subject Test measures one's knowledge of a specific subject and the ability to apply that knowledge. Students should check with each institution for its specific requirements. In general, students are required to take three Subject Tests (one English, one mathematics, and one of their choice).

Subject Tests are given in the following areas: biology, chemistry, Chinese, French, German, Italian, Japanese, Korean, Latin, literature, mathematics, modern Hebrew, physics, Spanish, U.S. history, and world history. These tests are 1 hour long and are primarily multiple-choice tests. Three Subject Tests may be taken on one test date.

On the subject tests, students gain a point for each correct answer and lose a fraction of a point for each incorrect answer. The raw scores are then converted to scaled scores that range from 200 to 800 For more details about SAT Subject Tests™, visit https://collegereadiness.collegeboard.org/sat-subject-tests/about/at-a-glance.

THE TOEFL(IBT)® INTERNET-BASED TEST

The Test of English as a Foreign Language Internet-Based Test (TOEFL iBT®) is designed to help assess a student's grasp of English if it is not the student's first language. Performance on the TOEFL® test may help interpret scores on the critical reading sections of the SAT® exam. The test consists of four integrated sections: speaking, listening, reading, and writing. The TOEFL iBT® emphasizes integrated skills. The paper-based versions of the TOEFL® test will continue to be administered in certain countries where the Internet-based version has not yet been introduced. For further information, visit www.ets.org/toefl.

WHAT OTHER TESTS SHOULD I KNOW ABOUT?

The AP® Program

The AP® program allows high school students to try college-level work and build valuable skills and study habits in the process. Subject matter is explored in more depth in AP courses than in other high school classes. A qualifying score on an AP test—which varies from school to school—can earn you college credit or advanced placement. Getting qualifying grades on enough exams can even earn you a full year's credit and sophomore standing at more than 1,500 higher-education institutions. There are more than thirty AP courses across multiple subject areas, including art history, biology, and computer science. Speak to your guidance counselor for information about your school's offerings. For more information about the AP® program, visit https://apstudent.collegeboard.org/home.

College-Level Examination Program (CLEP®)

The CLEP® exam enables students to earn college credit for what they already know, whether it was learned in school, through independent study, or through other experiences outside of the classroom. More than 2,900 colleges and universities now award credit for qualifying scores on one or more of the 33 CLEP exams. The exams, which are 90 minutes in length and are primarily multiple choice, are administered at participating colleges and universities.

For more information, check out the website at https://clep.collegeboard.org.

WHAT CAN I DO TO PREPARE FOR THESE TESTS?

Know what to expect. Get familiar with how the tests are structured, how much time is allowed, and the directions for each type of question. Get plenty of rest the night before the test and eat breakfast that morning.

There are a variety of products, from books to software to videos, available to help you prepare for most standardized tests. Find the learning style that suits you best. As for which products to buy, there are two major categories—those created by the test-makers and those created by private companies. The best approach is to talk to someone who has been through the process and find out which product or products he or she recommends.

Some students report significant increases in scores after participating in coaching programs. Longer-term programs (40 hours) seem to raise scores more than short-term programs (20 hours), but beyond 40 hours, score gains are minor. Math scores appear to benefit more from coaching than critical reading scores.

Resources

There is a variety of ways to prepare for standardized tests—find a method that fits your schedule and your budget—but you should definitely prepare. Far too many students walk into these tests cold, either because they find standardized tests frightening or annoying or they just haven't found the time to study. The key is that these exams are standardized. That means these tests are largely the same from administration to administration; they always test the same concepts. They have to, or else you couldn't compare the scores of people who took the tests on different dates. The numbers or words may change, but the underlying content doesn't.

So how do you prepare? At the very least, you should review relevant material, such as math formulas and commonly used vocabulary words, and know the directions for each question type or test section. You should take at least one practice test and review your mistakes so you don't make them again on the test day. Beyond that, you know best how much preparation you need. You'll also find lots of material in libraries or bookstores to help you: books and software from the test-makers and from other publishers (including Peterson's) or live courses that range from national test-preparation companies to teachers at your high school who offer classes.

Planning is Essential on the Road to College

Sarah E. Gibbs, Director of Admissions
Grove City College

The road to college is much like an expedition. It can appear overwhelming, exciting, and at times too far away to be tangible. However, much like planning a trip out of town or across the globe, there is preparation involved, and it is always best to start that planning early. First, you must figure out where you want to go, then how you want to get there, and finally, what you want to do once you arrive. Each decision will require a different route—a route that may or may not look the same as that of your friends.

The same is true when considering college planning. If you start early—making short-term and long-term goals—it will help you determine your next steps. For instance, if you start your freshman year determining you want to graduate with a certain GPA, that decision will dictate your next steps, like studying, choosing to take harder curriculum, and prioritizing your involvement in activities.

Once you establish your short-term and long-term goals, you need to make wise decisions about those goals. For instance, if you do not do well in a certain class, don't make a rash decision to withdraw from that subject area. You may want to continue in that subject knowing that you may need to seek out help or tutors to help you achieve your goal.

In addition to thinking through your academic goals, you must also consider your personal interests and activities. Your interests may determine the type of college you would like to attend. Decide early on what your passion(s) are, and invest your time wisely in those pursuits. If you know those activities are ones you want to pursue in college, then visit college campuses that fulfill your desire to march in the band, compete in a varsity or intramural sport, or participate in a service organization.

Ask yourself the question that most students do not: Am I ready for college? If the answer is no, then ask yourself what you need to do to be ready, and work towards that goal.

When looking at applicants, most private colleges will look holistically at the student, taking into consideration his or her commitment, dedication, and character. These attributes, along with academic performance and specific major pursuit, indicate whether the student may succeed at a campus. Also, make sure you participate in any interview process through an admissions office. Interviewing with an Admission Counselor allows him/her to get to know you and become your advocate.

Ultimately, the sooner you start planning, the better prepared you will be for the journey you are about to take. Not only will you be prepared for the college planning process, you will be well equipped for attending college and achieving your goals and dreams for a successful future.

Sarah E. Gibbs has spent seventeen years serving families in higher education. She is currently the Director of Admission at Grove City College in Grove City, Pennsylvania.

The Whys and Whats of College Visits

Dawn B. Sova, Ph.D.

The campus visit should not be a passive activity for you and your parents. Take the initiative and gather information beyond that provided in the official tour. You will see many important indicators during your visit that will tell you more about the true character of a college and its students than the tour guide will reveal. Know what to look for and how to assess the importance of such indicators.

WHAT SHOULD YOU ASK AND WHAT SHOULD YOU LOOK FOR?

Your first stop on a campus visit is the visitor center or admissions office, where you will probably have to wait to meet with a counselor. Colleges usually plan to greet visitors later than the appointed time in order to give them the opportunity to review some of the campus information that is liberally scattered throughout the visitor waiting room. Take advantage of the time to become even more familiar with the college by arriving 15 to 30 minutes before your appointment to observe the behavior of staff members and to browse through the yearbooks and student newspapers that will be available.

If you prepare in advance, you will have already reviewed the college catalog and map of the campus. These materials familiarize you with the academic offerings and the physical layout of the campus, but the true character of the college and its students emerges in other ways.

Begin your investigation with the visitor center staff members. As a student's first official contact with the college, they should make every effort to welcome prospective students and project a friendly image.

- How do they treat you and other prospective students who are waiting? Are they friendly and willing to speak with you, or do they try their hardest to avoid eye contact and conversation?
- Are they friendly with each other and with students who enter the office, or are they curt and unwilling to help?
- Does the waiting room have a friendly feeling or is it cold and sterile?

If the visitor center staff members seem indifferent to prospective students, there is little reason to believe that they will be warm and welcoming to current students. View such behavior as a warning to watch very carefully the interaction of others with you during the tour. An indifferent or unfriendly reception in the admissions office may be simply the first of many signs that attending this college will not be a pleasant experience.

Look through several yearbooks and see the types of activities that are actually photographed, as opposed to the activities that colleges promise in their promotional literature. Some questions are impossible to answer if the college is very large, but for small and moderately sized colleges the yearbook is a good indicator of campus activity.

- Has the number of clubs and organizations increased or decreased in the past five years?
- Do the same students appear repeatedly in activities?
- Do sororities and fraternities dominate campus activities?
- Are participants limited to one sex or one ethnic group, or is there diversity?
- Are all activities limited to the campus, or are students involved in activities in the community?

Use what you observe in the yearbooks as a means of forming a more complete understanding of the college, but don't base your entire impression on just one facet. If time permits, look through several copies of the school newspaper, which should reflect the major concerns and interests of the students. The paper is also a good way to learn about the campus social life.

- Does the paper contain a mix of national and local news?
- What products or services are advertised?
- How assertive are the editorials?
- With what topics are the columnists concerned?
- Are movies and concerts that meet your tastes advertised or reviewed?
- What types of ads appear in the classified section?

The newspaper should be a public forum for students, and, as such, should reflect the character of the campus and of the student body. A paper that deals only with seemingly safe and well-edited topics on the editorial page and in regular feature columns might indicate administrative censorship. A lack of ads for restaurants might indicate either a lack of good places to eat or that area restaurants do not welcome student business. A limited mention of movies, concerts, or other entertainment might reveal a severely limited campus social life. Even if ads and reviews are included, you should still balance how such activities reflect your tastes.

You will have only a limited amount of time to ask questions during your initial meeting with the admissions counselor, for very few schools include a formal interview in the initial campus visit or tour. Instead, this brief meeting is often just a nicety that allows the admissions office to begin a file for the student and to record some initial impressions. Save your questions for the tour guide and for students on campus you meet along the way.

HOW CAN YOU ASSESS THE TRUE CHARACTER OF A COLLEGE AND ITS STUDENTS?

Colleges do not train their tour guides to deceive prospective students, but they do caution guides to avoid unflattering topics and campus sites. Does this mean that you will see only a sugarcoated version of life on a particular college campus? Not at all, especially not if you are observant.

Most organized campus visits include such campus facilities as dormitories, dining halls, libraries, student activity and recreation centers, and the health and student services centers. Some may only be pointed out, while you will walk through others. Either way, you will find that many signs of the true character of the college emerge if you keep your eyes open.

Bulletin boards in dormitories and student centers contain a wealth of information about campus activities, student concerns, and campus groups. Read the posters, notices, and messages to learn what *really* interests students. Unlike ads in the school newspaper, posters put up by students advertise both on-and off-campus events, so they will give you an idea of what is also available in the surrounding community.

Review the notices, which may cover either campuswide events or events that concern only small groups of students. The catalog may not mention a performance group, but an individual dormitory with its own small theater may offer regular productions. Poetry readings, jam sessions, writers' groups, and other activities may be announced and show diversity of student interests.

Even the brief bulletin board messages offering objects for sale and noting objects that people want to purchase reveal a lot about a campus. Are most of the items computer related? Or do the messages specify audio equipment or musical instruments? Are offers to trade goods or services posted? Don't ignore the "ride wanted" messages. Students who want to share rides home during a break may specify widely diverse geographical locations. If so, then you know that the student body is not limited to only the immediate area or one locale. Other messages can also enhance your knowledge of the true character of the campus and its students.

As you walk through various buildings, examine their condition carefully.

- Is the paint peeling, and do the exteriors look worn?
- Are the exteriors and interiors of the building clean?
- Is the equipment in the classrooms up-to-date or outdated?

Pay particular attention to the residence halls, especially to factors that might affect your safety. Observe the appearance of the structure, and ask about the security measures in and around the residence halls.

- Are the residence halls noisy or quiet?
- Do they seem crowded?
- How good is the lighting around each residence hall?
- Are the residence halls spread throughout the campus or are they clustered in one main area?
- Who has access to the residence halls in addition to students?
- How secure are the means by which students enter and leave the residence hall?

While you are on the subject of dormitory safety, you should also ask about campus safety. Don't expect that the guide will rattle off a list of crimes that have been committed in the past year. To obtain that information, access the recent year of issues of *The Chronicle of Higher Education* and locate its yearly report on campus crime. Also ask the guide about safety measures that the campus police take and those that students have initiated.

- Can students request escorts to their residences late at night?
- Do campus shuttle buses run at frequent intervals all night?
- Are "blue-light" telephones liberally placed throughout the campus for students to use to call for help?
- Do the campus police patrol the campus regularly?

If the guide does not answer your questions satisfactorily, wait until after the tour to contact the campus police or traffic office for answers.

Campus tours usually just point out the health services center without taking the time to walk through. Even if you don't see the inside of the building, you should take a close look at the location of the health services center and ask the guide questions about services.

- How far is the health center from the residence halls?
- Is a doctor always on call?
- Does the campus transport sick students from their dormitories or must they walk?
- What are the operating hours of the health center?
- Does the health center refer students to a nearby hospital?

If the guide can't answer your questions, visit the health center later and ask someone there.

Most campus tours take pride in showing students their activities centers, which may contain snack bars, game rooms, workout facilities, and other means of entertainment. Should you scrutinize this building as carefully as the rest? Of course. Outdated and poorly maintained activity equipment contributes to your total impression of the college. You should also ask about the hours, availability, and cost (no, the activities are usually not free) of using the bowling alleys, pool tables, air hockey tables, and other amenities.

As you walk through campus with the tour, also look carefully at the appearance of the students who pass. The way in which both men and women groom themselves, the way they dress, and even their physical bearing communicate a lot more than any guidebook can. If everyone seems to conform to the same look, you might feel that you would be uncomfortable at the college, however nonconformist that look might be. On the other hand, you might not feel comfortable on a campus that stresses diversity of dress and behavior, and your observations now can save you discomfort later.

- Does every student seem to wear a sorority or fraternity t-shirt or jacket?
- Is everyone of your sex sporting the latest fad haircut?
- Do all of the men or the women seem to be wearing expensive name-brand clothes?
- Do most of the students seem to be working hard to look outrageous with regards to clothing, hair color, and body art?
- Would you feel uncomfortable in a room full of these students?

Is appearance important to you? If it is, then you should consider very seriously if you answer yes to any of the above questions. You don't have to be the same as everyone else on campus, but standing out too much may make you unhappy.

As you observe the physical appearance of the students, also listen to their conversations as you pass them. What are they talking about? How are they speaking? Are their voices and accents all the same, or do you hear diversity in their speech? Are you offended by their language? Think how you will feel if surrounded by the same speech habits and patterns for four years.

WHERE SHOULD YOU VISIT ON YOUR OWN?

Your campus visit is not over when the tour ends because you will probably have many questions yet to be answered and many places to still be seen. Where you go depends upon the extent to which the organized tour covers the campus. Your tour should take you to view residential halls, health and student services centers, the gymnasium or field house, dining halls, the library, and recreational centers. If any of the facilities on this list have been omitted, visit them on your own and ask questions of the students and staff members you meet. In addition, you should step off campus and gain an impression of the surrounding community. You will probably become bored with life on campus and spend at least some time off campus. Make certain that you know what the surrounding area is like.

The campus tour leaves little time to ask impromptu questions of current students, but you can do so after the tour. Eat lunch in one of the dining halls. Most will allow visitors to pay cash to experience a typical student meal. Food may not be important to you now while you are living at home and can simply take anything you want from the refrigerator at any time, but it will be when you are away at college with only a meal ticket to feed you.

- How clean is the dining hall? Consider serving tables, floors, and seating.
- What is the quality of the food?
- How big are the portions?
- How much variety do students have at each meal?
- How healthy are the food choices?

While you are eating, try to strike up a conversation with students and tell them that you are considering attending their college. Their reactions and advice can be eye-opening. Ask them questions about the academic atmosphere and the professors.

- Are the classes large or small?
- Do the majority of the professors only lecture or are tutorials and seminars common?
- Is the emphasis of the faculty career-oriented or abstract?
- Are the teaching methods innovative and stimulating or boring and dull?
- Is the academic atmosphere pressured, lax, or somewhere in between?
- Which are the strong majors? The weak majors?
- Is the emphasis on grades or social life or a mix of both at the college?
- How hard do students have to work to receive high grades?

Current students can also give you the inside line on the true nature of the college social life. You may gain some idea through looking in the yearbook, in the newspaper, and on the bulletin boards, but students will reveal the true highs and lows of campus life. Ask them about drug use, partying, dating, drinking, and anything else that may affect your life as a student.

- Which are the most popular club activities?
- What do students do on weekends? Do most go home?
- How frequently do concerts occur on campus? Who has recently performed?
- How can you become involved in specific activities (name them)?
- How strictly are campus rules enforced and how severe are penalties?
- What counseling services are available?
- Are academic tutoring services available?
- Do they feel that the faculty really cares about students, especially freshmen?

You will receive the most valuable information from current students, but you will only be able to speak with them after the tour is over. And you might have to risk rejection as you try to initiate conversations with students who might not want to reveal how they feel about the campus. Still, the value of this information is worth the chance.

If you have the time, you should also visit the library to see just how accessible research materials are and to observe the physical layout. The catalog usually specifies the days and hours of operation, as well as the number of volumes contained in the library and the number of periodicals to which it subscribes. A library also requires accessibility, good lighting, an adequate number of study carrels, and lounge areas for students. Many colleges have created 24-hour study lounges for students who find the residence halls too noisy for studying, although most colleges claim that they designate areas of the residences as "quiet study" areas. You may not be interested in any of this information, but when you are a student you will have to make frequent use of the campus library so you should know what is available. You should at least ask how extensive their holdings are in your proposed major area. If they have virtually nothing, you will have to spend a lot of time ordering items via interlibrary loan or making copies, which can become expensive. The ready answer of students that they will obtain their information from the Internet is unpleasantly countered by professors who demand journal articles with documentation.

Make a point of at least driving through the community surrounding the college because you will be spending time there shopping, dining, working in a part-time job, or attending events. Even the largest and best-stocked campus will not meet all of your social and personal needs. If you can spare the time, stop in several stores to see if they welcome college students.

- Is the surrounding community suburban, urban, or rural?
- Does the community offer stores of interest, such as bookstores, craft shops, and boutiques?
- Do the businesses employ college students?
- Does the community have a movie or stage theater?
- Are there several types of interesting restaurants?
- Do there seem to be any clubs that court a college clientele?
- Is the center of activity easy to walk to, or do you need other transportation?

You might feel that a day is not enough to answer all of your questions, but even answering some questions will provide you with a stronger basis for choosing a college. Many students visit a college campus several times before making their decision. Keep in mind that for the rest of your life you will be associated with the college that you attend. You will spend four years of your life at this college. The effort of spending several days to obtain the information to make your decision is worthwhile.

Dawn B. Sova, Ph.D., is a former newspaper reporter and columnist, as well as the author of more than eight books and numerous magazine articles. She teaches creative and research writing, as well as scientific and technical writing, newswriting, and journalism.

Honors Programs and Colleges: Smart Choices for an Undergraduate Education

Dr. Joan Digby

In general, students and their parents are guided toward a narrow selection of colleges and universities based on reputation, conversations with friends, or promotional material. Few people think to approach the college search focused on honors opportunities. As a result, students with extraordinary talents and interests miss out on a rich variety of untapped financial resources and exciting college experiences.

The smarter approach is to seek out a distinctive education that caters to students' great diversity of intellectual and creative strengths. If you are a strong student filled with ideas, longing for creative expression and ready to take on career-shaping challenges, then an honors education is just for you. Honors programs and colleges offer some of the finest undergraduate degrees available at U.S. colleges and do it with students in mind. The essence of honors is personal attention, top faculty, enlightening seminars, illuminating study-travel experiences, research options, and career-building internships—all designed to enhance a classic education and prepare you for life achievements. And here is an eye-opening bonus: Honors programs and colleges may reward your past academic performance by giving you scholarships that will help you pay for your higher education!

Take your choice of institutions: community college, state or private, two- or four-year, college or large research university. There are honors opportunities in each. What they share is an unqualified commitment to academic excellence. Honors education teaches students to think and write clearly, be excited by ideas, and become independent, creative, self-confident learners. It prepares exceptional students for professional choices in every imaginable sphere of life: arts and sciences, engineering, business, health, education, medicine, theater, music, film, journalism, media, law, politics—invent your own professional goal and honors will guide you to it! Whichever honors program or college you choose, you can be sure to enjoy an extraordinarily fulfilling undergraduate education.

WHO ARE HONORS STUDENTS?

Who are you? Perhaps a high school junior filling out your first college application, a community college student seeking to transfer to a four-year college, or possibly a four-year college student doing better than you had expected. You might be an international student, a varsity athlete, captain of the debate team, or second violin in the orchestra. Whether you are the first person in your family to attend college or an adult with a grown family seeking a new career, honors might well be right for you. Honors programs admit students with every imaginable background and educational goal.

How does honors satisfy students and give them something special? Read what students in some honors programs and colleges say. Although they refer to particular honors colleges or programs, their experiences are typical of what students find exciting about honors education on hundreds of campuses around the country.

> "Being an honors program student has been a life-changing experience for me. I have gained tremendously in knowledge, experience, and self-esteem. I have learned so much more in the program than any textbook could teach about the value of encouraging support and positive thinking."
>
> —*Cheri, Mount Wachusett Community College*

> "I've been in a healing ceremony in Ecuador and have performed music on stage. I've guided my peers and Navajo children, hiked the Grand Canyon, and so much more. Sometimes, experience speaks for itself; always, it creates paths, opens eyes, and helps us find our places. Thanks to my honors program, I've experienced these wonders and accomplishments. Now I know that there are no greater lessons than how to learn and love discovery."
>
> —*April, University of North Florida*

> "The Honors College has been my home away from home. In the midst of a diverse, fairly large university, it has provided me with the intimacy that I needed... My freshman-year living situation on the honors floor... allowed me to find like-minded students early in my college career."
>
> —*Brian, Davidson Honors College, University of Montana*

"I was able to transition from an honors program at a two-year institution into an honors program at a four-year institution without any reservations or tribulations."

—Rachel, Harrisburg Area Community College

"Every single professor is in love with what they do and it shows in their research, their amazing teaching, and their interaction with students outside of the classroom. The undergraduate journey can be very difficult at times, but as an Honors College student, you're sure to have plenty of support every step of the way."

—Walteria, Wilkes Honors College, Florida Atlantic University

"The class size is perfect and I've been able to make some of my closest relationships with students and teachers through the program. The majority of honors faculty I have encountered have been overwhelmingly helpful... and my favorite courses have been honors classes."

—Ellen, Eastern Illinois University

"Our professor met us at a local restaurant the last evening of class, and we shared a wonderful dinner. It had such a familiar feel to it because these are students I have known throughout my four years in the program."

—Betsy, University of La Verne

"For the last two years, I have investigated new synthetic methods under the direction of a professor emeritus. Through the University Honors College, I am able to pursue this interest in chemistry and other academic endeavors... that have allowed me to develop my academic potential and contribute to the scientific body of knowledge."

—Justin, University of Pittsburgh

"The most rewarding part of being a member of the honors program is the joy of doing creative, meaningful projects with faculty I love."

—Meleia, Hartwick College

"I would... like to add a word of praise for the way the curriculum is structured. It has deepened and enriched my thinking and helped me develop tools to negotiate the complex world we live in."

—Monideepa, Southeastern Louisiana University

"We have a better time... our discussions get rather heated. In a lot of classes, only one or two students will speak up, but in the honors classes, it's a free-for-all."

—Jonathan, Reinhardt College

"My internship at a major international bank gave me an in-depth look into the world of investment and accounting. Funded by the Honors College, I was able to study business and culture in Shanghai, China, for a month. These valuable experiences are helping me to develop professionally, academically, and personally."

—Jenny, Honors College, The College of Staten Island, CUNY

"The honors thesis was the key factor during the selection process at my future employer.... It helped me to get the job and have an advantage over others. It is a lot of work but, in the end, it is worth it."

—Olgierd, Lee Honors College, Western Michigan University

These portraits don't tell the whole story, but they should give you a sense of what it means to be part of an honors program or college. One of the great strengths of honors programs and colleges is that they are nurturing environments that encourage students to be well-rounded and help students make life choices.

WHAT IS AN HONORS PROGRAM?

An honors program is a sequence of courses designed specifically to encourage independent and creative learning. For more than half a century, honors education—given definition by the National Collegiate Honors Council—has been an institution on U.S. campuses. Although honors programs have many different designs, there are typical components. At two-year colleges, the programs often concentrate on special versions of general education courses and may have individual capstone projects that come out of students' special interests. At four-year colleges and universities, honors programs are generally designed for students of almost every major in every college on campus. In growing numbers, they are given additional prominence as honors colleges. Whether a program or a college, honors often includes a general education or "core" component followed by advanced courses (often called colloquia or seminars). Some programs have honors contracts that shape existing courses into honors components to suit the needs of individual students. Many have interdisciplinary or collaborative seminars that bring students of different majors together to discuss a complex topic with faculty members from different disciplines. A good number have final thesis, capstone, or creative projects, which may or may not be in the departmental major. Almost always, honors curriculum is incorporated within whatever number of credits is required of every student for graduation. Honors very rarely requires students to take additional credits. Students who complete an honors program or honors college curriculum frequently receive transcript and diploma notations as well as certificates, medallions, or other citations at graduation ceremonies.

In every case, catering to the student as an individual plays a central role in honors course design. Most honors classes are small (fewer than 20 students); most are discussion-oriented, giving students a chance to present their own interpretations of ideas and even teach a part of the course. Many classes are interdisciplinary, which means they are taught by faculty members from two or more departments, providing different perspectives on a subject. All honors classes help students develop and articulate their own perspectives by cultivating both verbal and written style. They help students mature intellectually, preparing them to engage in their own explorations and research. Some programs even extend the options for self-growth to study abroad and internships in science, government, the arts, or business related to the major. Other programs encourage or require community service as part of the honors experience. In every case, honors is an experiential education that deepens classroom learning and extends far beyond.

Despite their individual differences, all honors programs and honors colleges rely on faculty members who enjoy working with bright, independent students. The ideal honors faculty members are open-minded, encouraging master teachers. They want to see their students achieve at their highest capacity and are glad to spend time with students in discussions and laboratories, on field trips and at conferences, or online in e-mail. They often influence career decisions, are inspiring role models, and remain friends long after they have served as thesis advisers.

WHERE ARE HONORS PROGRAMS AND HONORS COLLEGES LOCATED?

Because honors programs and honors colleges include students from many different departments or colleges, they usually have their own offices and space on campus. Some have their own buildings. Most programs have honors centers or lounges, where students gather together for informal conversations, luncheons, discussions, lectures, and special projects.

Many honors students have cultivated strong personal interests that have nothing to do with classes. They may be multilingual; they may be fine artists or poets, musicians or racing car enthusiasts, mothers or fathers. Some volunteer in hospitals or do landscape gardening to pay for college. Many work in retail stores and in catering. Some are avid sports enthusiasts, while others collect antiques. When they get together in honors lounges, there is always an interesting mixture of ideas!

In the honors center, you will also find the honors director or dean. The honors director often serves as a personal adviser to all of the students in the program. Many programs also have peer counselors and mentors who are upperclass honors students and know the ropes from a student's perspective and experience. Some have specially assigned honors advisers who guide honors students through their degrees, assist in registration, and answer every imaginable question. The honors office area usually is a good place to meet people, ask questions, and solve problems.

In general, honors provides an environment in which students feel free to talk about their passionate interests and ideas knowing that they will find good listeners and, sometimes, even arguers. There is no end to conversations among honors students. Like many students in honors, you may feel a great relief in finding a sympathetic group that respects your intelligence and creativity. In honors, you can be eccentric; you can be yourself! Some lifelong friendships, even marriages, are the result of social relationships developed in honors programs.

ARE YOU READY FOR HONORS?

Admission to honors programs and honors colleges is generally based on a combination of several factors: high school or previous college grades, experience taking AP or IB courses, SAT or ACT scores, personal essay, and extracurricular achievements. To stay in honors, students need to maintain a certain grade point average (GPA) and show progress toward the completion of the specific honors program or college requirements. Since you have probably exceeded admissions standards all along, maintaining your GPA will not be as big a problem as it sounds. Your professors and your honors director are there to help you succeed in the program. Most honors programs have very low attrition rates because students enjoy classes and do well.

Of course, you must be careful about how you budget your time for studying. Honors encourages well-rounded, diversified students, so you should play a sport, work at the radio station, join clubs of interest, or pledge a sorority or fraternity. You might find a job in the student center or library that will help you pay for your car expenses and that also is reasonable. But remember, each activity takes time, and you must strike the balance that leaves you enough time to do your homework, write papers, prepare for seminar discussions, do your research, and do well on exams. Choose the jobs and activities that attract you, but never let them overshadow your primary purpose—which is to be a student.

Sometimes even the very best students who apply for admission into an honors program or college are frightened by the thought of speaking in front of a group, giving seminar papers, or writing a thesis. But if you understand how the programs work, you will see that there is nothing to fear. The basis of honors is confidence in the student and building the student's self-confidence. Admittance to an honors program means you have already demonstrated your academic achievement in high school or college classes. Once in the honors environment, you learn how to formulate and structure ideas so that you can apply critical judgment to sets of facts and opinions. In small seminar classes, you practice discussion and arguments, so by the time you come to the senior thesis or project, the method is second nature. For most honors students, the senior thesis, performance, or portfolio presentation is the project that gives them the greatest fulfillment and pride. In many honors programs and colleges, students present their work either to other students or to faculty members in their major departments. Students often present their work at regional and national honors conferences. Some students even publish their work jointly with their faculty mentors. These are great achievements, and they come naturally with the training. There is nothing to fear. Honors will prepare you for life.

Dr. Joan Digby is Director of the Honors Program and Professor of English at Long Island University, C.W. Post Campus. She was also President of the National Collegiate Honors Council from 1999 to 2000.

Public and Private Colleges and Universities—How to Choose

Debra Humphreys

As you survey the thousands of four-year colleges in the country and weigh the options before you, it is important to be aware of how colleges differ and what kind of educational experience each college offers you. In every state in the country, you will find both public and private colleges and universities. What are the differences between public and private colleges, and how should you approach the decision to attend one or the other? What are some common misconceptions regarding both public and private colleges that you should know about before you eliminate an entire category of institution from your list of prospective schools?

WHAT ARE THE BASIC CHARACTERISTICS OF PUBLIC AND PRIVATE INSTITUTIONS?

Over the course of the nation's history, what began as a small group of mostly church-affiliated colleges has grown in both size and complexity. Over the years, education in the United States became increasingly democratized, and more and more state-sponsored institutions and state systems of higher education emerged. These included small colleges, sometimes called "normal schools," designed to train school teachers for the expanding public school system; land-grant colleges and universities brought into existence with federal support in the mid-nineteenth century in order to prepare workers to expand the nation's agricultural and technological capacity; and large state systems that evolved in the twentieth century and now include two-year colleges, basic four-year institutions, and large research universities, all supported at least in part by state revenues.

While there are some clear distinctions to be made, even some of the core characteristics of public and private colleges vary from state to state. In general, a public institution receives at least part of its operating budget from state tax revenues, operates with a mandate and mission from the state where it is located, and is accountable to the elected officials of that state. Most private colleges and universities are independent, not-for-profit institutions. They operate with revenues from tuition; income from endowments; private gifts and bequests; and federal, private, or corporate foundation grants. These institutions are primarily accountable to a board of trustees, usually made up of local or national business and community leaders and esteemed alumni.

There are also a small but growing number of for-profit colleges whose operating revenues include tuition dollars but also might include investor financing. Some of these colleges are owned and operated by publicly traded corporations. Most of the following generalizations about private institutions however refer to the more familiar not-for-profit independent college previously described.

While the distinction between public and private institutions might seem clear at first, these two kinds of colleges and universities actually share many characteristics. All accredited colleges and universities in the country—whether public or private, for profit or not—are entitled to receive public funds from the federal government in the form of direct grants and loans for eligible students, support for student work-study programs, and competitive grants to support research or campus programs. In exchange for this federal support, all schools undergo a peer-reviewed accreditation process by a regional accreditor authorized by the federal government's Department of Education.

Whether a college is public or private, you should know if it is accredited and therefore an institution whose students are eligible for all available federal financial aid. Accreditation status also provides you with assurance that the school operates in a fiscally responsible manner and that its academic programs have been deemed sound by an outside group of educators from its peer institutions.

HOW ARE PUBLIC AND PRIVATE COLLEGES AND UNIVERSITIES RUN?

In many ways, your experience as a student will not differ significantly based on what type of governance system a college or university uses. However, some knowledge of this might be useful in making choices among the various options. Private colleges and universities tend to have more independence and autonomy in how they are run, with boards of trustees that oversee financial and other programs and life on campus at these schools. Public colleges and universities often have more complex governing structures with boards of regents or other types of oversight committees made up of politically appointed or elected officials exercising more or less oversight and intrusion into their day-to-day operations. New York, for instance, has a board of regents that oversees the system's campuses and is more actively involved in reviewing and revising curricular requirements that apply to institutions throughout the system. Other states have multiple public colleges, each with its own board overseeing each campus' operations with more or less intrusion into day-to-day operations.

Whether an institution is public or private, you will want to ask lots of questions about campus climate and academic programs in order to help you determine if a school is right for you. Being aware of some facts about public and private institutions will help you frame these questions to get truly useful answers.

ARE ALL PUBLIC COLLEGES AND UNIVERSITIES BIG AND IMPERSONAL?

Like private institutions, public colleges come in all shapes and sizes. Some are large institutions offering multiple degrees and majors to both undergraduate and graduate students alike. These institutions offer students many curricular options as well as access to leading scholars and an environment where cutting-edge academic research is conducted. While an institution of this size and scope might seem intimidating at first, remember that there are large institutions that do take very seriously their undergraduate programs. While you may receive less customized attention at a larger institution, many large public and private research universities offer options such as smaller honors programs, academic learning communities with smaller cohorts of students, or theme residence halls that can minimize the potential that you will get lost in the crowd.

If you are considering a large research institution— whether it is public or private—you should ask questions about the undergraduate program. What is the student-faculty ratio for undergraduates? What is the average class size, especially for introductory first-year courses? How many courses are taught by graduate students, and what sort of teacher training do those students receive? Are there opportunities for undergraduate students to participate in research projects with university faculty members?

In addition to the large, public research universities, there are many other smaller, state-funded regional institutions that still offer a wide range of both liberal arts and sciences fields as well as professional fields of study. Many states also offer small, public liberal arts colleges that share many of the defining characteristics of traditional, private liberal arts colleges. In 1987, some of these institutions formed the Council of Public Liberal Arts Colleges (COPLAC). COPLAC schools pride themselves on providing students of high ability and from all backgrounds access to a quality liberal education. These colleges and universities have been nationally recognized as outstanding in many ways. They offer small classes, innovations in teaching, personal interactions with faculty members, opportunities for faculty-supervised research, and supportive atmospheres. Most of them are located on campuses in rural or small-town settings. In addition to offering rigorous and well-integrated undergraduate programs, these institutions often charge far less tuition than many private colleges do. More information can be found at http://www.coplac.org.

These public liberal arts colleges, along with more traditional private liberal arts institutions, do offer unique learning environments that research suggests often lead to higher levels of student achievement. Liberal arts colleges tend to offer a high degree of student-faculty interaction, high levels of student engagement with both in-class and out-of-class experiences, and lots of opportunities for collaborative and innovative learning practices. Businesses are also increasingly asking for exactly the set of skills and capacities that a liberal education provides, whether offered in a traditional liberal arts college setting or within a larger university that grants degrees in both liberal arts and other fields. Many public liberal arts and more comprehensive colleges and universities also now offer students a rigorous liberal education while integrating liberal learning into professional degree programs, for instance in health sciences, engineering, or education.

ARE PUBLIC COLLEGES CHEAPER THAN PRIVATE COLLEGES?

The cost of college is not easy to calculate and is not limited simply to the advertised price of tuition. It is absolutely not the case that attending a public college will always cost a student less money than attending a private institution. It is true that the basic tuition for in-state or out-of-state students attending public colleges is on average less expensive than the advertised tuition rate at private institutions. It is very important, however, to note that many private colleges and universities offer significant amounts of financial aid—often beyond the basic federal loans and grants available to all students. Many, but not all, private colleges have large endowments that allow them to effectively discount the standard, published tuition rates for a great number of their students. The National Association of College and University Business Officers sampled a small group of private colleges and discovered that only 10 percent of entering students were paying the full, advertised tuition. Ninety percent of their students received price discounts in the form of scholarships or financial aid. In other words, don't write off a college simply because its tuition looks extremely high relative to other institutions.

Both private and public institutions, however, have been fiscally stressed in recent years because of declining values of stock portfolios in endowments or because of declining state revenues resulting from the deteriorating economy. It is safe to say that for many students in the coming years, it will become increasingly difficult to get large amounts of financial aid. Many institutions, however, remain committed to widening access to more students from less economically privileged backgrounds. In addition, students demonstrating high levels of academic achievement are being rewarded at both private and public institutions—both in terms of admission and financial aid.

It is important to look carefully at the tuition and the financial aid requirements and availability at each school you are considering, private or public. In-state and out-of-state tuitions and the difference between them varies substantially from state to state. Out-of-state tuition also varies from state to state but still tends to be lower than average private tuition levels.

Policies vary as well for determining state residency status. In many states, the policy for dependent students requires that their parents must have lived in the state for at least twelve months prior to attendance in order to qualify for in-state tuition. For independent students, the requirement of twelve months residence prior to enrollment applies to the student. Independent status must be verified and generally entails proof that a student receives no support from parents or other relatives living in or out of the state in question. As budgets have increasingly tightened, states have over the past several years made it increasingly difficult to establish in-state residence after matriculating at a school. Exceptions are sometimes made, however, for students from migrant, refugee, or military families.

IS IT EASIER TO GAIN ADMISSION TO A PUBLIC INSTITUTION ESPECIALLY AS A STATE RESIDENT?

Few public colleges and universities automatically admit students who graduate from a public high school in their state. Many, however, give preference in admissions and financial assistance to in-state residents. Moreover, some states have implemented policies that guarantee admission to at least one of the state's public institutions for all students graduating in a top percentage of their high school classes.

There are, indeed, more highly selective private than public institutions. Many public colleges and universities, however, do admit very few applicants. These highly selective institutions might draw their students from a national pool of applicants and can be among the most selective in the country. However, the national universities and liberal arts colleges with the lowest acceptance rates in the country are mostly all private institutions.

While some public institutions offer virtually open admissions to state residents, it is important for all prospective students to realize that even an open-admission institution will require incoming students to meet certain academic standards before being admitted to credit-bearing courses. In most cases, public and private institutions give incoming students a series of placement exams that determines at what level the student can begin his or her course work. Depending on the results of these exams, a student may be required to take and pass one or more remedial courses before being admitted to courses that will actually count towards a degree.

Since each state's requirements are different and shift often, you should not assume that, regardless of your academic background, admission is automatic to your local state college. In the current climate—with costs rising and competition across systems tightening—admission rates are dropping at many public institutions.

IS THE CLIMATE ON A PUBLIC COLLEGE CAMPUS SIGNIFICANTLY DIFFERENT THAN THAT ON A PRIVATE COLLEGE CAMPUS?

The social and academic climate at colleges and universities varies substantially, and public institutions do not necessarily offer a distinctively different climate than private institutions do. You can find, at some public institutions, the small, residential environment traditionally associated with private liberal arts colleges. You will also find the presence of fraternities and sororities at both public and private institutions. You should look carefully at whether a school in which you are interested has fraternities and sororities and how much influence the Greek system has on college life. At some institutions, fraternities and sororities dominate the entire social life of the campus.

One campus environment that can only be found at a private institution is a highly religious environment. Many early colleges and universities were founded by churches or religious orders. Some of these institutions no longer retain a strong affiliation with one church or denomination. Others do retain a strong affiliation, and church traditions can heavily influence the climate of these institutions. Usually, these campuses will admit a student from any religious background, but they may require students to attend chapel services and/or take religion or theology courses to graduate. In addition, some college missions and curricula are influenced by their religious affiliations. For instance, many Catholic institutions have a strong commitment to community service and social justice. Students may find, at these institutions, curricula related to social justice issues and requirements that they complete a community-service learning activity or course to graduate. Institutions with a strong mission are also often able to develop more coherent, cohesive, and innovative curricula for their students.

Finally, other important climate factors to consider include whether a college or university is in an urban or rural setting; what the diversity of the student body is in terms of geographic, religious, or racial/ethnic background; if most students live on campus or commute from home; and finally if the college dominates the life of the community in which it is located. Each of these options has advantages and disadvantages you will want to weigh in making your decisions.

ARE PRIVATE COLLEGES MORE ACADEMICALLY RIGOROUS THAN PUBLIC COLLEGES?

Private colleges and universities are not necessarily more academically rigorous than public institutions. You will find rigorous, intellectually challenging, and innovative academic programs at both private and public institutions. There is also a common misconception that schools that are more highly selective have the most effective or engaging academic programs. Research suggests that there is no connection between the selectivity of an institution and the presence of effective or innovative teaching and learning practices. There is, however, preliminary research that suggests that the academic quality of

Questions to Ask as You Evaluate Prospective Colleges and Universities

- Does the college offer a distinctive first-year experience?
- Does the college offer a small-size freshman seminar for all students?
- Are all students required to complete a senior project or assignment that allows them to integrate all that they have learned and demonstrate acquired skills and knowledge?
- Are students encouraged or required to complete internships and/or service learning courses?
- Are students encouraged to study abroad? Is support for study abroad provided to all students and are study abroad experiences integrated into a student's overall curricula?
- Does the college offer learning communities, especially in the student's early years?
- Are students required to complete rigorous writing courses not only in the freshman year but also across the curriculum in whatever major he or she chooses to pursue?
- Are there opportunities for students to pursue independent research or creative projects under the supervision of a senior faculty member?

one's peers does seem to have an impact on the grade point averages of fellow students.

Nothing could be more important in your decision-making process than evaluating the nature of academic programs at prospective colleges or universities. Across both public and private institutions, there have been exciting and important changes in how colleges and universities are organizing undergraduate curricula. Many promising programs have been proven to result in higher levels of student retention, graduation, satisfaction, and academic achievement.

Many colleges and universities also now participate in the National Survey of Student Engagement. This survey asks students in both their first and last years about a series of effective educational practices and the degree to which they are engaged in the academic life of their school. Issues that are examined in the survey include the level of academic challenge, active and collaborative learning opportunities, the nature of student-faculty interactions, the number of enriching educational experiences available, and the supportive nature of the campus environment. Ask if the school you are considering participates in this survey and if you can see the results from recent classes of students.

THE PRIVATE/PUBLIC CHOICE

While there are distinct differences between public and private colleges and universities you should not limit your choice—whatever your background—to only one type of institution. There are wonderful opportunities at many different kinds of schools. The availability of many kinds of financial aid may bring private institutions with high-tuition levels within reach for you, whatever your financial background. Whether a school is highly selective or has open admissions, you should also be able to find a college or university that will challenge you academically and provide you with a supportive environment in which to live, learn, and pursue a college degree of lasting value.

Debra Humphreys is Senior Vice President for Academic Planning and Public Engagement for the Association of American Colleges and Universities.

Distance Education— It's Closer Than You Think

You may not realize it, but as an incoming college student, you are joining a revolution that is radically changing education. It's called distance learning. From kindergarten up to postgraduate degrees, distance learning is fast becoming an essential teaching tool. Most of the colleges and universities you are considering for a bachelor's degree offer distance learning in one form or another. Most likely you will be a distance learner at some point, whether during college or graduate school or throughout your career.

In case you're not familiar with distance learning—or asynchronous learning, online learning, or distance education—it means you don't sit in a classroom facing a teacher. You can be hundreds of miles or minutes from the teacher and other students. Most often you connect through the Internet to the teacher, fellow students, and study materials. However, increasingly sophisticated technologies, such as virtual laboratories, simulations, and interactive multimedia, are also used. You may run across the term "blended learning." Many institutions incorporate online learning into their face-to-face classes. In fact, a number of colleges require that a part of all classes is online.

FROM SNAIL-MAIL COURSES TO LEADING-EDGE TECHNOLOGY

Talk about change. Distance education began in the late 1800s, when schools mailed correspondence courses to farmers who wanted to learn how to grow better crops. Since technology came along, distance learning has become accessible and widespread. At first educators were skeptical, but as name-plate universities began to incorporate it into their teaching methodology, distance education became accepted.

When brick-and-mortar colleges and universities first considered distance education, the goal was to make it as good as face-to-face education. Now, says Ray Schroeder, Professor Emeritus of Communication and Director of the Center for Online Learning, Research, and Service (COLRS), at the University of Illinois at Springfield, "Field research shows that online learning technologies are better than face-to-face learning in a number of ways." Having taught online, he has seen firsthand how students participate more in discussions and learn from one another. Peg Miller, Ph.D., former Coordinator of Academic Support for Distributed Learning, University of Central Florida, cites a survey she conducted every other semester that compares face-to-face and distance learners at her institution. She has found that students from face-to-face and online classes were almost identical in the grades they earned and in their satisfaction with the classes.

ON THE UPSWING

Many reasons have caused the phenomenal growth of distance education. It's convenient and user-friendly, plus the scope of classes is stunning. Not that you'll likely begin your college years with classes in forensics or grading diamonds, but they are offered and indicate the enormous variety of courses. Along with many others in education, Michael P. Lambert, former executive director of the Distance Education Training Council, feels that online learning has transformed how people learn. "You no longer sit in a box with 35 other people where you might never raise your hand," he says. Adds Gerald Heeger, former President of the University of Maryland University College (UMUC), "Online learning gets rid of the limitations of geography and time. And as bandwidth increases, we will do more and more."

PROCEED WITH CAUTION

Now that you're convinced that distance education sounds great, and you're ready to day "sign me up," it's only fair to warn you that perhaps you shouldn't start your bachelor's degree totally online. Distance learning changes how you study, respond to your teachers, participate in class discussions, and take exams. If you're not prepared for the differences, you can easily fall behind and even fail. Though the age of online students continues to drop, most are older, have had some life experience since graduating from high school, and have the self-discipline, maturity, and self-motivation, that distance education demands. The average age of distance students is in the mid-30s, and 95 percent of them work full-time. They know what they want from college and are willing to meet the rigors of online learning, which are considerable.

Of course, some students straight from high school do successfully start college as distance learners because they've already had some online learning experience. Some take online classes in high school or advanced-placement and college courses. At Stevens Institute of Technology's Web Campus, incoming freshmen brush up on math and precalculus online before their first fall semester. At first, Nathan Kahl, former instructor for the Euclid Program at Stevens Institute of Technology Web Campus, was skeptical that high school graduates could succeed in the online courses he taught, but he saw that "everyone quickly got into the swing of things." He admits that he underestimated the students' ability to learn online. Heeger agrees "There's no reason why a bright junior in high school who is ready to take college freshmen courses can't do it."

The University of Phoenix Online (parent company: Apollo Group, Inc.) has developed a bachelor's degree program specifically for incoming freshmen of any age—including those just out of high school. In today's job market, a college education is a necessity, yet many students have life situations that prevent them from attending. Notes former president of Apollo Group, Inc., Brian Mueller about the accommodations their program makes for students who are new to higher education, "It is our experience that if you create an online classroom, it must have all the features that incoming students need, which are small, highly interactive, and collaborative classes." Their freshman classes average 15 and require that the instructor has consistent contact with the students. New freshmen also get a tremendous amount of support in writing, math, and online research skills and have the help of an academic counselor who closely tracks them for ten weeks into their first semester. "We think there are more students coming out of high school who must have jobs, so we took the model for working adults and created an environment for traditional students that combines education and work," says Mueller.

However, not all educators have the same experience with incoming freshmen. Jimmy Reeves, Ph.D., Professor of Chemistry and Coordinator of the Tablet PC Initiative at the University of North Carolina at Wilmington, teaches both online and face-to-face classes and knows how students can react. Freshmen who fail his face-to-face class sometimes ask to take his class online. He says no because the discipline required is rare among 19-year-old students. "Junior and senior college students do well, but it has more to do with their level of maturity and the reasons why they're in college," he says, referring to the fact that many incoming college students want to experiment or come because their parents demand it. "Without any real desire to learn or sense of why they're in college, it's easy to get distracted in online classes," he notes. You can't hide in the back of a lecture hall half asleep on Monday morning and hope for the best on multiple-choice questions. In online classes, your active participation is noticed and taken into account for final grades.

Attending college isn't just about acquiring knowledge in a particular field in order to get a job. It's also about learning social skills and meeting people with different ideas from diverse backgrounds. "If you want to live in a dorm and have bull sessions on the meaning of life with the kids down the hall, then being a fully online freshman student isn't for you," advises Cynthia Davis, Acting Vice Provost and Dean of the Undergraduate School at the University of Maryland University College (UMUC). She adds that sometimes students mistakenly think getting a bachelor's degree online will take less time than physically attending classes or won't require as much work. But as she points out, online classes demand the same amount of effort, if not more, than face-to-face classes.

WHAT'S IT GOING TO BE LIKE?

Blended learning or mixed-mode classes, combining face-to-face and online instruction, are becoming a permanent fixture in higher education. Students might sit in a classroom on Monday but take the remaining two classes for that week online. Professors routinely post the syllabus, class calendar, or PowerPoint lectures. Reeves says that it's rare to see college classes without some Web-based materials. Davis comments that UMUC routinely Web-enhances all of its face-to-face classes with companion Web classrooms. Students can have optional online discussions or print copies of class materials.

"We find more students use online technology to enhance their studies and get better grades," comments Schroeder. Educators see a trend of students enrolling in one university and taking courses from other institutions. For instance, say you're in an art class but want to study German cathedral architecture, which your university doesn't have but another one offers online. It's only a matter of time before this will be a standard option for college students.

LOTS TO LOOK FOR, LOTS TO AVOID, LOTS TO ASK

Though much of distance education depends on the Internet, you can't just type in "distance education" and see what comes up in a search for a college. You must seriously research and do background checks to make sure a diploma mill doesn't hand you a bachelor's degree that isn't credible. There are plenty of places to get information. Petersons.com offers a database of colleges and universities that have online courses, as well as totally online distance education providers. "You have to be a good consumer," recommends Heeger. "It's no different from getting a loan. You don't borrow money from people you never heard of. You shouldn't get degrees from people you never heard of." Schroeder suggests checking the course completion of online programs, their enrollment, and growth of programs. "Just as one checks with friends and colleagues about the quality of consumer services, such as computers and cars, one should check with students who are enrolled in online programs," he advises.

Is the Institution Accredited by a Valid Accrediting Body?

There are several kinds of accrediting organizations:

- The six regional accrediting agencies recognized by the U.S. Department of Education
- The Council for Higher Education Accreditation (www.chea.org)
- Other institutional accrediting agencies, such as the Accrediting Council for Independent Colleges and Schools and the Distance Education and Training Council
- Specialized accrediting agencies that cover schools offering everything from acupuncture to veterinary medicine
- Other discipline-based accrediting organizations, such as those for law and business schools

Can You Transfer Credits Received Online from One Institution to Another?

Policies vary greatly among universities and colleges. Though distance education is widely accepted, there are so many places where students can take bogus online courses that institutions are justifiably cautious. If students do decide they want to get a bachelor's degree completely online, they need to be sure the campus-based program and distance education program offer the same degree. At most institutions, both on-campus and online degrees are the same, but others do differ-

Test-Drive an Online Class

Just like face-to-face instruction, online classes are different, depending on the course material and how each teacher chooses to structure the course, but here's a typical scenario of what it's like to be a distance learner.

Getting started. First you'll want to get to the general information page for the class, which you'll visit often. The professor's contact information, the class calendar, the syllabus, and announcements on quizzes and tests or links to other pages on which you'll find posted discussion questions may be found here. Some teachers will ask you to tell something about yourself to the other students in the class. Be sure to read the syllabus, which will outline the course and tell you when assignments are due and how grades are determined.

Responding to discussion questions. Those students who never raised their hands will get a shock in online courses. Responding with thoughtful answers to online discussion groups is mandatory. Usually the teacher will assign reading material and then post a discussion question. The material might be from your textbook or websites. You must respond to the question and possibly to the postings of other students in the class. Teachers will gauge your participation in the class and how well you learn the material.

Interacting with fellow students and your teacher. Ray Schroeder, Professor Emeritus of Communication and Director of the Center for Online Learning, Research, and Service (COLRS) at the University of Illinois at Springfield, gives talks about distance education. Often he'll ask his audience to recall their favorite class from elementary school up to college and what made it so memorable. Was it the textbook? The actual classroom? The view out the window? When he asks if it was the interaction among students and with the teacher, the audience realizes that's what made the class good. "Both in person and online, learning takes place in the interaction," says Schroeder. "Otherwise, we would do just as well to read a book or watch a video to learn." In online classes, interaction between you and the professor and other students is an enormous part of your success.

Nathan Kahl, former instructor for the Euclid Program at Stevens Institute of Technology Web Campus, explains, "Distance students expect that their teachers will be online at least as much as they are." The level of interaction expected from you will vary by school and course, but you should know that in online courses, you must be an active participant. On the flip side, teachers carefully monitor discussions to make sure the more talkative students don't dominate. Keith W. Miller, Professor of Computer Science at the University of Illinois at Springfield, interacts with his students in a variety of ways. "I make announcements to the whole class on the homepage. I send e-mails to the whole class. I enter into the electronic discussions on the bulletin board forums, and post daily reminders and assignments to the course calendar. The students interact with me using e-mail, notes in their assignments, and via the bulletin boards. Now and then someone calls me at my office on the phone, but that's rare." He likes to answer his e-mails at least once a day, which means that his students get much more feedback than they would if he were physically in a classroom with them.

As do most online teachers, Cynthia Davis, Associate Dean of Academic Affairs in the School of Undergraduate Studies at the University of Maryland University College, gets students to participate with a weekly discussion topic. "If we're reading a novel," she says, "I ask them to discuss the role of the narrator or analyze a passage. The students respond individually and then respond to other students' comments."

Attending virtual lectures. Some online courses allow you to hear and see the professor or other guest speakers who are also online. If you want to ask a question, there's a button to indicate you want to speak. Everyone else can hear you as if you all were in the same room. Other professors add voice to PowerPoint lectures, which you can view when you want to, not at some prearranged time.

Taking quizzes and tests. No more waiting weeks to get your tests back. Online technology in some courses instantly zaps back the corrected test and notes that you missed question six and need to study page 54 of the textbook. Just like in face-to-face classes, you have an allotted amount of time to take the quiz. Some online courses may have automated components, such as instant quizzes and animated and interactive practice sessions. Others have mandatory proctored exams at a nearby community college or learning center for students who are off campus.

entiate in the degrees conferred, and it will show up on your diploma.

What Kind of Refund Policy Does the University Have for Distance Learners?

It might become painfully apparent for students that online learning is not for them, and they want to drop out. Find out ahead of time about the refund policy for online classes. What happens if you're ill during an online class? How can you make up the work? Even before taking any classes, you should find out if you're suited for online learning. Many institutions offer self-assessment tests on their websites.

What Online Services Does the College Provide?

Is the dorm wired? Can you get an e-mail address from the university? What about browsers and computer compatibility? Ask how the Internet is part of face-to-face classes. To what extent is the library online, and is it available 24/7 for research? Ask about writing and math labs and help-desk support. Look for online tutorials that show students how to use the school's specific software. Is there a tech fee?

IF YOU'RE LEARNING ONLINE, YOU BETTER HAVE THESE

Since online learning is part of college, it's helpful to know what to expect ahead of time, rather than three weeks into the class, when you feel like throwing your laptop out the window and would happily settle for sitting in the back row of the nearest classroom. Here are the five skills and abilities that successful online students must have:

1. You must have the self-discipline to do things you don't want to do when you don't want to do them.

If you're a procrastinator, you'll find the catch-up tactics that served you well in face-to-face classes won't work online. "Students get the idea they can whiz by without studying, or they came from high schools where they weren't pushed," cautions Heeger. "Maybe they never got Fs in high school, but they do here." That's because they don't realize they're responsible for learning the material on their own. The burden is on you to keep up with the homework. It doesn't take long to fall far behind in online classes.

Typically, students in face-to-face and online classes need 2 hours for work outside of class for every hour in class. But online students often forget to add that hour. For every hour they would have to sit in a traditional classroom, they should be listening, studying, thinking, writing, responding to discussions, and getting ready for tests, plus the 2 hours outside of class. Three classes a week—that's 9 to 10 hours for one class. Online teachers keep students on track with weekly quizzes and homework assignments. If students start lagging, they're likely to get an e-mail from the professor asking what's going on. Claudine SchWeber, Ph.D., Chair of the Doctor of Management Program at the University of Maryland University College, has taught online for years and states, "My classes are structured by weekly readings, activities, and discussions. Students can't decide to get around to doing the work when they feel like it. It must be done at the instructor's pace. The first shot of online can be a shock to their system."

2. You must have the ability to manage your time without anyone telling you do your homework NOW.

In high school, students usually can put off studying until the weekend. "That doesn't work in college. You can't write complex papers the night before," says Karen L. Kirkendall, Ph.D., Associate Professor of Liberal and Integrative Studies and Director of the Capitol Scholars Honors Program at the University of Illinois at Springfield. She teaches both online and face-to-face classes and has seen first-time online students who have never failed before start to slip and suddenly realize they are in big trouble. "My online classes are extraordinarily structured so I pretty much know when students aren't engaged, which I monitor by seeing how much they participate in online discussions," she notes.

Distance Learning Myths

As distance education becomes more accepted, people will readily discard some of the myths on this list. But for now, they persist.

Distance learning is for people on ranches 200 miles from the nearest freeway. Geography is not a factor. Many distance learners who are located across the campus or a few miles away just don't want to deal with the commute or have a work schedule that conflicts with being in a class at a certain time. They appreciate the flexibility that distance education gives them.

Distance learning is easier than face-to-face classes. Once you start an online class, you'll knock that myth off the list. Still, some students think it will be easier. When they realize they must not only respond to discussion questions but also comment on the responses from other students, they wonder why they ever thought distance education was going to be easy. Online teachers normally keep track of how their students progress with frequent monitoring and quizzes.

I'll get a better education in face-to-face classes. Much research has been conducted comparing the two and consistently, online learning is equivalent or better. Teachers of online courses now have plenty of precedents to follow, training and research to help them teach better, and technology to prepare for classes and keep up with their students' progress.

I'll talk to a computer all day. Yes, you are in front of a computer as a distance learner, but you also interact with professors and other students much more than you ever would in a core freshman class of 200. Teachers have sophisticated software to facilitate interaction. Even though you don't physically see your teachers, they put a great deal of effort into class preparation and reading e-mails. Some get as many as 3,000 e-mails in a ten-week class. Distance learners often get to know fellow students much more easily online than they would walking in and out of a class.

I need to be a computer geek. If you can handle the simplest maneuvers around a computer, such as attaching documents to e-mails or going to a specified Web address, you can be a distance learner. And you'll have tech support to help out if you run into problems.

Distance education is cheaper than face-to-face. Too bad this is a myth. It costs the same as a traditional college if you attend a recognized institution. Most students pay for distance education through student loans.

3. You must have the skills to communicate your thoughts in writing.

"Online participation in class discussions isn't instant messaging. You are what you write in online classes," advises SchWeber. Most of the work in online classes is written, whether it's participation in discussions, homework, quizzes, papers, or tests.

Since you'll communicate by e-mail and post your thoughts, netiquette is essential. You need to think differently online than when speaking on the phone or face-to-face. "You can't write a report that sounds like you are hanging out with friends," advises SchWeber. "When you are totally online, the only image people (including your professor) have of you is how you write." Kirkendall has reprimanded students who sent e-mails showing disrespect to the teacher because they were upset about something. Probably they would never respond that way if face-to-face. "Never hit the submit button when you're angry," Kirkendall cautions.

4. You must have the ability to research worthwhile information on the Web.

You need to know what's junk and what's reliable. In addition, professors take plagiarism very seriously, especially because it's so easy to do.

5. You must have some computer skills and know sc computer-speak.

Those who design the software and set up how a dista learning class is taught are careful to make sure the technol doesn't get in the way of learning; however, you should kr the basics. "In some classes, certain downloads are requi such as Adobe Acrobat, but in general, the skills are beyond the abilities used daily by most elementary sch children," says Schroeder, pointing out that if distance p grams use expensive or exotic technology, they defeat purpose. He reports that most computers that are five years have the speed, memory, and capability to support on learning. Some classes might require a microphone. should be familiar with some of the computer jargon so tha you're asked to post something or use a drop box, add attachment, or take part in a threaded discussion, you'll kn what you need to do. Just about every distance learning p vider has online tutorials to familiarize you with their p ticular online software. If you run into technical proble help-desk support is available.

Why Not Women's Colleges?

Before we start talking about the many advantages that women's colleges offer, let's get some myths out of the way. It is almost certain that the minute you hear "women's colleges" in the same sentence with "choosing colleges" you immediately think: no boys, no fun, no way!

Maybe that is why some girls who visit Joan Jaffe's office at Mills College in San Francisco, California, rush in to tell her that they just saw some guys on the campus of this women's college. Jaffe, Associate Dean of Admission, frequently gets this reaction from the young women who visit the campus. That's because many think that if they go to a women's college they are never going to see a guy within 2 miles of the campus gates, which, by the way, will clang shut behind them, leaving them secluded inside a heavily guarded male-free zone.

KISS MYTH NUMBER ONE GOOD-BYE

Forget iron gates. The first myth to get rid of is the one that assumes attending a women's college means kissing your social life good-bye. In fact, as Patricia Gibbs, Vice President for Student Affairs, Dean of Students at Wesleyan College in Macon, Georgia, points out, "If you were a guy looking for a date, where would you go?" Not only that, the majority of women's colleges are near, if not next to, coed campuses. Most share activities with other colleges and universities, and many have reciprocal agreements so that guys can take classes at the women's college and vice versa.

When it comes to dating, women's colleges offer the best of both worlds. You can hang out with guys when you want to and then retreat to your own lovely environment (women's dorms usually are beautiful) and hang out with the girls. Julie Binder, who transferred from the University of Wisconsin to all-women's Barnard College in New York City, notes that there is open registration with Columbia University, which just happens to be right next door. "Campus life is shared. Sports are shared," she says.

As you dig deeper into this myth, you will find that attending a women's college is not about isolation, it's about options. You get to choose if you want to be in classes, clubs, and organizations only with women or mingle with the men.

SCRATCH MYTH NUMBER TWO

Myth Number Two: Women's colleges are just a bunch of catty, competitive females waiting for the right moment to claw each other's eyes out. Scratch that myth, too. Instead, women's colleges cultivate an environment of sisterhood—women who look out for one another. Most women's colleges encourage women in the upper-level classes to help their younger classmates. Talking to their "big sisters," newcomers can find out what classes to take and which professors are best, and they find a sympathetic ear for the problems that most first-year college students face.

The Rich Traditions in Women's Colleges

Tradition plays an important part of the experience women have in women's colleges. They run the gamut from solemn ceremonies of passing along the bond of sisterhood to the fun of secret surprises. "Women's colleges have a strong sense of tradition," says Amy Shaver, former Academic Dean at Stephens College in Columbia, Missouri. It's also a wonderful way to help women from all social, economic, religious, and ethnic backgrounds to share a common experience and pass it on to the next generation of students. "Traditions bond women over the generations," says Jennifer Rickard, former Dean of Admissions and Financial Aid at Bryn Mawr College, who notes that it's not unusual at all to have students today singing songs and participating in ceremonies that the class of 1945 did and which will be the same when today's students have their twenty-year reunion.

Here's a sampling of the many traditions you'll find on women's college campuses:

Lantern Night At Bryn Mawr's Lantern Night, women gather around a fountain on campus. Each woman is given a lantern as a symbol of knowledge and learning. Each class has a color, and as the lanterns are passed from the sophomores to the first-year students, songs are sung in Greek that are the same as the ones sung 100 years ago around the same fountain.

Senior Paint Night Mills College seniors get the okay to paint the campus in their class color. Along with brushes and cans of paint, they are given a few guidelines as to what can and cannot be painted, but the rest is up to them.

The Crossing of the Bridge As women students come to Stephens to begin their college education, they cross over a bridge on campus in a ceremony symbolizing their entrance into the world of academia. At graduation, they cross over another bridge on campus and are welcomed into the alumnae society.

Candlelight Induction Ceremony Spelman students dressed in white dresses and black shoes light candles and hear the charge to be the best they can be. While the candles are still lit, they sing the Spelman hymn.

Midnight Breakfast At Barnard, the night before finals, the president of the college, deans, and professors make breakfast for the students.

"The sense of community is very strong at women's colleges," observes Fran Samuels, former Director of College Counseling at The Master's School in Dobbs Ferry, New York. "The myth is that a women's college will be cliquish. In truth, the women are supportive of each other." The strong bonds of sisterhood that naturally develop connect students to their college, its history, and its students—past, present, and future. Many women's colleges designate a rotating color for each incoming class. For example, if the freshman class you enter is dubbed the golden hearts, by the time you graduate, you are connected to all the golden hearts who graduated ahead of you and all the golden hearts who will graduate after you.

TOSS MYTH NUMBER THREE

Another myth that should be tossed out is that women's colleges don't prepare you for the "real world." Well, try saying that to the 12 women members of Congress who graduated from women's colleges. Or to the 15 women on *Business Week*'s list of the rising stars in corporate America. Although you are not in a totally coed situation, on the other hand you are in an environment in which you can gain skills to think critically and learn to meet challenges. Becky Marsh, Director of Communications and Marketing at Whitfield School, in St. Louis, Missouri, points out that when you first ride a bike, training wheels allow you to learn how to balance. Once you are ready to race down the street, you take them off. Same with women's colleges. The focus is on your education and your strengths, and who you are. You graduate ready to take on the obstacles of the real world. "In high school, I had the feeling that boys were given more opportunities to share their knowledge. It was harder and more intimidating for me to share my opinions in a coed class," says Brittany Johnson, from Spelman College in Atlanta, Georgia. "Now I feel like I can do anything."

Graduates of women's colleges feel empowered and willing to confront any limits to their abilities. While in college, they have many opportunities to assume leadership roles and see women in leadership positions as professors and deans. "They don't doubt whether they can do anything. Instead, they ask, 'Why can't I do it now?'" reports Amy Shaver, former Academic Dean at Stephens College in Columbia, Missouri. Women can find their own voices and establish their own ways of approaching things that will ultimately make them successful in a male-dominated world. They learn from seeing other women students and professors engaged in the intellectual process.

THE ADVANTAGES

As more young women find out about the advantages that women's colleges offer them, they like what they see. Maybe that is why attendance at women's colleges is growing. Learning leadership skills tops the list of advantages. Says Shaver, "Women in a same-sex environment are more likely to take risks and speak up in class. They are more willing to stand up and voice an opinion." If you think about it, students get plenty of practice at a women's college because all the leadership roles go to women. From day one on a women's campus, you will see women leading the entire college or involved in interesting and significant research. You get more exposure to what leadership is and what to expect as a leader. "Leadership becomes ingrained," notes Jennifer Fondiller, Dean of Enrollment Management at Barnard College in New York City.

You might not realize it, but women react differently in classrooms with all women. They tend to speak up with confidence and test their ideas more readily when they are not competing with men. Researchers find that even as early as the fifth grade, girls are taught differently than boys. Teachers call on boys more frequently and don't ask girls the more thought-provoking questions or to critically analyze problems. In coed situations, the more aggressive and competitive guys take over, whereas in all-female classes, research indicates there is much more give-and-take and exchange of ideas.

Coming from a coed public school, Johnson realized that more attention was given to the guys in her classes, but at Spelman, she says, "Everyone is on the same path." Arlene Cash, former Vice President for Enrollment Management at Spelman, notes that women don't have to vie for attention or retreat into the intellectual background in all-women classes. In a coed class, the environment becomes more adversarial. "Women feel they have to perform. In women's colleges they become more academically involved and interact with faculty members more frequently," says Debbie Greenberg, former College Counselor at Whitfield School. Speaking of the rich interaction that occurs in her classes at Barnard, Binder says, "The diversity of experience around the discussion table is unparalleled."

YOU CAN SUCCEED

Shaver characterizes the environment in women's colleges as one in which there is no fear of failing when the social pressures and dynamics of men and women are removed from the classroom. Women's colleges give women the opportunity to explore different avenues without the fear of failing. "We challenge them to become what they want to become," says Gibbs from Wesleyan. "No one says, 'You can't do that because you are a woman.'" At the same time, you are interacting with other women who have the same goals as you, which reinforces who you are. Or, as Jennifer Rickard, former Dean of Admissions and Financial Aid at Bryn Mawr College, in Bryn Mawr, Pennsylvania, points out, women are not just sitting in classes to do well on exams and get good grades. They also are figuring out what they want to do with their education. "There's less expectation to conform to an external measure," she says.

Many women's colleges foster self-government and give their students responsibilities they might not find in a coed institution. At Bryn Mawr, for instance, students pay a self-government association fee as part of their tuition. This is put into a fund that is controlled by a student government that takes ownership of how the students want to govern themselves. "This isn't student government making only recommendations to the administration as to how to allocate the budget to the different student groups vying for funds," notes Rickard. "You have students dealing with real-world management issues, such as resource allocation."

Since women's colleges are smaller than big coed universities, women receive all the benefits that students get from a small liberal arts college in addition to the advantages that only a women's college offers. A big plus is interaction with professors and staff, which is hard to achieve when you are one of 200 students in a lecture hall taught by a graduate student.

What Made You Choose a Women's College?

When she got to the point of choosing which college to attend, Wisambi Loundu had plenty of options. Coming from San Diego, the California universities were a logical choice. Women's colleges were not on her list. In fact, she hardly knew they existed. Her first thought when someone suggested a women's college to her was, "I'm not going to a school full of girls minus boys." Her second thought was just as negative. "If it's all girls, they will always be fighting." The third and fourth thoughts assumed that a women's college wouldn't prepare her for the real world, plus she would be isolated.

But then her math teacher's daughter told her about Bryn Mawr, and as Wisambi started exploring the possibility, the advantages of a women's college started lining up. However, it wasn't until she visited Bryn Mawr that she really began to see herself there. "I fell in love with the campus," says Wisambi. "It was like nothing I'd ever seen before." Her stay in the dorm added to her steadily growing thoughts that Bryn Mawr might be it. "The girls I stayed with in the dorm were so friendly. At first I was suspicious, but I saw it was not a front. Plus, there were girls from all over the world."

But Wisambi didn't make her final decision just yet. She decided to look at other schools, like Wellesley and the University of California schools, as well as Stanford. Meanwhile, her friend told her more about Bryn Mawr. "She said I'd make lasting friends and she talked about how the academics would train me for the outside world even if there were no men on campus. Bryn Mawr would build my identity as a woman."

She still wasn't convinced and made a second visit, along with visits to Wellesley and Stanford, which she says were nice, but too big. It would be too hard to make friends there, she thought. When the time came to make her final selection, she chose Bryn Mawr.

Now at Bryn Mawr, how does Wisambi feel about her choice? The academics are more challenging than she anticipated but doable, and she is excited about the internships she will be able to access. She also finds that the staff and teachers at Bryn Mawr go out of their way to make her feel at home. "They match us up with a mentor and professor," she says.

How about dating? Since Bryn Mawr is part of a tri-college community, guys are around, though Wisambi says you have to make an effort to meet people on other campuses.

Talking to seniors who are getting ready to head out to the "real world," Wisambi can see that they are full of confidence and don't think for a minute that they won't do well. "And that's a positive," she says.

Women's colleges tend to foster seminar-style classes taught by full professors, many of them women. "You have an expert teaching you," says Gibbs. Faculty members get to know their students and can challenge them intellectually on an individual basis. "Within two days, all my teachers knew my name," recalls Johnson, who says she was given each professor's e-mail address, home phone number, and all the contact information she needed and was encouraged to reach out to them.

Women are encouraged to achieve their intellectual goals. Professors often will point out specific programs that they know suit the student's interests. Add to this the opportunities to conduct research with a professor, and in many cases actually present research findings to a professional society, and you can see why women graduate with a terrific resume before they even start their careers. Rickard mentions the opportunity that Bryn Mawr students have to work on funded projects with professors during the summer and then present the results along with them at conferences. "It's a window into the academic world and the world of the intellectual," she notes. It's no surprise that women in women's colleges major in math and science at a higher national average than women in coed institutions.

Paid and unpaid internships, too, are more available for women at women's colleges, mainly because of the network of women graduates in business and industry who want to help their "sisters" at their alma maters. "I'm getting my professional edge now," says Binder, who is interested in TV production and had a paid internship as a production assistant while a sophomore at Barnard. "You will have an amazing resume by the time you graduate," she says.

Peggy Hock, Ph.D., former College Counselor at Notre Dame High School in San Jose, California, points out that colleges naturally rely on their alumni to come forward with networking opportunities for students; however, the alumnae of women's colleges tend to be more loyal and willing to give of their time. This translates into many more opportunities for internships, mentoring, and job possibilities. At Barnard, for example, the career office has an alumna mentor network. Students can call, ask questions, and get advice about career choices. At alumnae events, current students mix with the graduates. Binder takes full advantage of the Web log of women who are working all over the world and willing to spend time online with Barnard students. She applied for a job at a public relations firm in New York after contacting a fellow Barnard graduate working there. She met with her and subsequently got a letter of recommendation.

HOW TO CHOOSE

Choosing a women's college isn't any different from choosing a coed college. You should definitely visit the campus and don't be afraid to ask lots of questions—even the ones that might make you uncomfortable. Because women's colleges are similar to small coed liberal arts colleges, make sure that you don't compare a women's campus to a big university.

Janet Ashley, former Interim Director for Admissions at Spelman College, advises high school women to ask what a women's college can give them academically. "Their choice depends on what their goals are," she says.

If you're worried about the dating scene, ask about the levels of interaction with guys and how close the relationships are with neighboring institutions.

"Look at the individuality of each women's college," suggests Rickard, "because each has its own personality."

Look at the school before looking at the fact that it's a women's college, and on the flip side, don't rule out a school just because it is a women's college. "So many students make quick decisions about where to apply," warns Fondiller, noting that sometimes the decision hinges on what schools a friend is applying to rather than if that institution really fits the student. Many women's colleges specialize in certain fields like science, math, or theater.

Famous Firsts from Women's Colleges

Quick, from which college did the first woman to be named Secretary of State graduate? Or the woman scientist who identified the Hong Kong flu? Or the first woman executive vice president of the American Stock Exchange? Here's a big clue. They were all graduates of women's colleges.

SENATOR

- Barbara Mikulski (MD)—Mount Saint Agnes College

REPRESENTATIVES (Current and Former)

- Tammy Baldwin (WI)—Smith College
- Donna Christian-Christensen (VI)—St. Mary's College
- Rosa DeLauro (CT)—Marymount College
- Jane Harman (CA)—Smith College
- Gabrielle Giffords (AZ, 2007–12)—Scripps College
- Eddie Bernice Johnson (TX)—Saint Mary's College
- Barbara Lee (CA)—Mills College
- Nita Lowey (NY)—Mount Holyoke College
- Betty McCollum (MN)—College of Saint Catherine
- Nancy Pelosi (CA), first woman elected as Speaker of the House of Representatives—Trinity College
- Allyson Schwartz (PA)—Simmons College

FORMER SECRETARY OF STATE

- Hillary Rodham Clinton (NY)—Wellesley College

OTHER FAMOUS WOMEN FIRSTS

- Madeleine Albright, first woman to be named Secretary of State in the United States, appointed in 1997—Wellesley College
- Jane Amsterdam, first woman editor, the New York Post—Cedar Crest College
- Emily Green Balch, first woman to receive the Nobel Peace Prize in 1946—Bryn Mawr College
- Catherine Brewer Benson, first woman to receive a college bachelor's degree—Wesleyan College
- Earla Biekert, first scientist to identify the Hong Kong flu virus—Wesleyan College
- Cathleen Black, first woman leader of the American Newspaper Publishers Association—Trinity Washington University
- Sarah Porter Boehmler, first woman executive vice president of American Stock Exchange—Sweet Briar College
- Jane Matilda Bolin, first African American woman judge in the United States—Wellesley College
- Dorothy L. Brown, first African American woman general surgeon in the South—Bennett College for Women
- Pearl S. Buck, first American woman to win the Nobel Prize in Literature—Randolph-Macon Woman's College
- Ila Burdett, Georgia's first female Rhodes Scholar—Agnes Scott College
- Dorothy Vredenburgh Bush, first woman secretary of the Democratic National Party—Mississippi University for Women
- Hon. Audrey J. S. Carrion, first Hispanic woman judge Circuit Court for Baltimore City—College of Notre Dame of Maryland
- Rachel Carson, first environmentalist who awakened public consciousness through her book, *Silent Spring*—Chatham University
- Barbara Cassani, first woman CEO of a commercial airline—Mount Holyoke College
- Elaine L. Chao, U.S. Secretary of Labor, 2001; First Asian American woman appointed to a President's cabinet—Mount Holyoke College

Adapted from the website of the Women's College Coalition at http://www.womenscolleges.org.

Applying 101

The words "applying yourself" have several important meanings in the college application process. One meaning refers to the fact that you need to keep focused during this important time in your life, keep your priorities straight, and know the dates that your applications are due so you can apply on time. The phrase might also refer to the person who is really responsible for your application—you.

You are the only person who should compile your college application. You need to take ownership of this process. The guidance counselor is not responsible for completing your applications, and neither are your parents. College applications must be completed in addition to your normal workload at school, college visits, and SAT®, ACT®, or TOEFL® testing.

THE APPLICATION

The application is your way of introducing yourself to a college admissions office. As with any introduction, you want to make a good first impression. The first thing you should do in presenting your application is to find out what the college or university needs from you. Read the application carefully to find out the application fee and deadline, required standardized tests, number of essays, interview requirements, and anything else you can do or submit to help improve your chances for acceptance.

FOLLOW THESE TIPS WHEN FILLING OUT YOUR APPLICATIONS

- **Follow the directions to the letter.** You don't want to be in a position to ask an admissions officer for exceptions due to your inattentiveness.
- **Proofread all parts of your application,** including your essay. Again, the final product indicates to the admissions staff how meticulous and careful you are in your work.
- **Submit your application as early as possible,** provided all of the pieces are available. If there is a problem with your application, this will allow you to work through it with the admissions staff in plenty of time. If you wait until the last minute, it not only takes away that cushion but also reflects poorly on your sense of priorities.
- **Keep a copy of the completed application,** whether it is a photocopy or a copy saved on your computer.

Completing college applications yourself helps you learn more about the schools to which you are applying. The information a college asks for in its application can tell you much about the school. State university applications often tell you how they are going to view their applicants. Usually, they select students based on GPAs and test scores. Colleges that request an interview, ask you to respond to a few open-ended questions, or require an essay are interested in a more personal approach to the application process and may be looking for different types of students than those sought by a state school.

In addition to submitting the actual application, there are several other items that are commonly required. You will be responsible for ensuring that your standardized test scores and your high school transcript arrive at the colleges to which you apply. Most colleges will ask that you submit teacher recommendations as well. Select teachers who know you and your abilities well and allow them plenty of time to complete the recommendations. When all portions of the application have been completed and sent in, whether electronically or by mail, make sure you follow up with the college to ensure their receipt.

THE APPLICATION ESSAY

Whereas the other portions of your application—your transcript, test scores, and involvement in extracurricular activities—are a reflection of what you've accomplished up to this point, your application essay is an opportunity to present yourself in the here and now. The essay shows your originality and verbal skills and how you approach a topic or problem and express your opinion.

Some colleges may request one essay or a combination of essays and short-answer topics to learn more about who you are and how well you can communicate your thoughts. Common essay topics cover such simple themes as writing about yourself and your experiences or why you want to attend that particular school. Other colleges will ask that you show your imaginative or creative side by writing about a favorite author, for instance, or commenting on a hypothetical situation. In such cases, they will be looking at your thought processes and level of creativity.

Admissions officers, particularly those at small or mid-size colleges, use the essay to determine how you, as a student, will fit into life at that college. The essay, therefore, is a critical component of the application process. Here are some tips for writing a winning essay:

- Colleges are looking for an honest representation of who you are and what you think. Make sure that the tone of the essay reflects enthusiasm, maturity, creativity, the ability to communicate, talent, and your leadership skills.
- Be sure you set aside enough time to write the essay, revise it, and revise it *again*. Running "spell check" will only detect a fraction of the errors you probably made on your first pass at writing it. Take a break and then come back to it and reread it. You will probably notice other style, content, and grammar problems—and ways that you can improve the essay overall.

- Always answer the question that is being asked, making sure that you are specific, clear, and true to your personality.

- Enlist the help of reviewers who know you well— friends, parents, teachers—since they are likely to be the most honest and will keep you on track in the presentation of your true self.

THE PERSONAL INTERVIEW

Although it is relatively rare that a personal interview is required, many colleges recommend that you take this opportunity for a face-to-face discussion with a member of the admissions staff. Read through the application materials to determine whether or not a college places great emphasis on the interview. If they strongly recommend that you have one, it may work against you to forego it.

In contrast to a group interview and some alumni interviews, which are intended to provide information about a college, the personal interview is viewed both as an information session and as further evaluation of your skills and strengths. You will meet with a member of the admissions staff who will be assessing your personal qualities, high school preparation, and your capacity to contribute to undergraduate life at the institution. On average, these meetings last about 45 minutes—a relatively short amount of time in which to gather information and leave the desired impression—so here are some suggestions on how to make the most of it.

Scheduling Your Visit

Generally, students choose to visit campuses in the summer or fall of their senior year. Both times have their advantages. A summer visit, when the campus is not in session, generally allows for a less hectic visit and interview. Visiting in the fall, on the other hand, provides the opportunity to see what campus life is like in full swing. If you choose the fall, consider arranging an overnight trip so that you can stay in one of the college dormitories. At the very least, you should make your way around campus to take part in classes, athletic events, and social activities. Always make an appointment and avoid scheduling more than two college interviews on any given day. Multiple interviews in a single day hinder your chances of making a good impression, and your impressions of the colleges will blur into each other as you hurriedly make your way from place to place.

Preparation

Know the basics about the college before going for your interview. Read the college catalog and website in addition to this guide. You will be better prepared to ask questions that are not answered in the literature and that will give you a better understanding of what the college has to offer. You should also spend some time thinking about your strengths and weaknesses and, in particular, what you are looking for in a college education. You will find that as you get a few interviews under your belt, they will get easier. You might consider starting with a college that is not a top contender on your list, so that the stakes are not as high.

Asking Questions

Inevitably, your interviewer will ask you, “Do you have any questions?” Not having one may suggest that you’re unprepared or, even worse, not interested. When you do ask questions, make sure that they are ones that matter to you and that have a bearing on your decision about whether or not to attend that college. The questions that you ask will give the interviewer some insight into your personality and priorities. Avoid asking questions that are answered in the college literature—again, a sign of unpreparedness. Although the interviewer will undoubtedly pose questions to you, the interview should not be viewed merely as a question-and-answer session. If a conversation evolves out of a particular question, so much the better. Your interviewer can learn a great deal about you from how you sustain a conversation. Similarly, you will be able to learn a great deal about the college in a conversational format.

Separate the Interview from the Interviewer

Many students base their feelings about a college solely on their impressions of the interviewer. Try not to characterize a college based only on your personal reaction, however, since your impressions can be skewed by whether you and your interviewer hit it off. Pay lots of attention to everything else that you see, hear, and learn about a college. Once on campus, you may never see your interviewer again.

In the end, remember to relax and be yourself. Your interviewer will expect you to be somewhat nervous, which will relieve some of the pressure. Don’t drink jitters-producing caffeinated beverages prior to the interview, and suppress nervous fidgets like leg-wagging, finger-drumming, or bracelet jangling. Consider your interview an opportunity to put forth your best effort and to enhance everything that the college knows about you up to this point.

THE FINAL DECISION

Once you have received your acceptance letters, it is time to go back and look at the whole picture. Provided you received more than one acceptance, you are now in a position to compare your options. The best way to do this is to compare your original list of important college-ranking criteria with what you’ve discovered about each college along the way. In addition, you and your family will need to factor in the financial aid component. You will need to look beyond these cost issues and the quantifiable pros and cons of each college, however, and know that you have a good feeling about your final choice. Before sending off your acceptance letter, you need to feel confident that the college will feel like home for the next four years. Once the choice is made, the only hard part will be waiting for an entire summer before heading off to college!

The "Early Decision" Decision

Maybe a senior you knew last year didn't get into the college he wanted. He said it was because he didn't apply "early decision". Maybe your friend's mom told your mom that unless students apply early decision, their chances of getting into top schools are slim to none, even though they have great grades and spectacular essays. Maybe you figure you'd better get in on the early decision action.

All of the above are true—well, sort of—because many students applying to college get the term "early decision" backwards. High school guidance and college counselors run into this kind of thinking all the time and suggest putting "decision" before "early"—as in making a wise decision about committing to a college before applying early. For some students, early decision is a great option. For others, early decision is loaded with pitfalls and dangers.

"When students come back in the fall of their senior year, I often hear 'I know I want to apply early. Can you help me choose the school?'" says Kathy Cleaver, Co-Director of College Counseling at Durham Academy in Durham, North Carolina. She compares that to saying, "I know I want to get married, please help me pick the man." Continues Cleaver, "First you have to fall in love with the school and know it's your first choice and then join the circus for early decision." She's referring to the media hype flying around high school halls about early decision—it's easy to fall prey to the early decision madness. Hot competition to get into "top" schools creates early decision anxiety. Michael "Mickey" Gilbert, Guidance Counselor at Passaic High School in Passaic, New Jersey, throws out some scary numbers that confirm that, yes, the competition for admittance to top schools is white-hot. There are about 30,000 high schools in the United States, and although the majority of high school seniors apply to institutions in their own states, there are still limited spaces in the "top" schools and the eight Ivy League schools. "No wonder kids think that early decision is the way to go," speculates Gilbert. Early decision panic sets in because students are convinced that if they get their applications in early, they have an edge. Sometimes early decision might make the difference, but there are many issues to consider before taking the early decision leap.

EARLY THIS, EARLY THAT

With all the buzz about early decision, do you really know what it means along with all the other early options, such as early action and early notification? And what about the variations of early decision? Each institution can have its own version of early decision, meaning that deadlines and criteria are different. There's the early decision that notifies students by December, there's the early decision round two, and then there is the early action/single choice.

Seeing the confusion, the National Association for College Admission Counseling (NACAC) developed a standard set of definitions. NACAC is an education association of secondary school counselors, college and university admissions and financial aid officers, counselors, and other individuals who work with students as they transition from high school to college. While each institution has its own variations of each early option, an understanding of the basic differences can help. The list that follows was adapted from the definitions found on the NACAC website (www.nacacnet.org).

Early Decision

- Early decision is the application process in which students make a commitment to a first-choice institution where, if admitted, they definitely will enroll. Should a student who applies for financial aid not be offered an award that makes attendance possible, the student may decline the offer of admission and be released from the early decision commitment.
- While pursuing admission under an early decision plan, students may apply to other institutions, but may have only one early decision application pending at any time.
- The institution must notify the applicant of the decision within a reasonable and clearly stated period of time after the early decision deadline. Usually, a nonrefundable deposit must be made well in advance of May 1.
- A student applying for financial aid must adhere to institutional early decision aid application deadlines.
- The institution will respond to an application for financial aid at or near the time of an offer of admission.
- The early decision application supercedes all other applications. Immediately upon acceptance of an offer of admission, a student must withdraw all other applications and make no subsequent applications.
- The application form will include a request for a parent and a counselor signature, in addition to the student's signature, indicating an understanding of the early decision commitment and agreement to abide by its terms.

Early Action

- Early action is the application process in which students make application to an institution of preference and receive a decision well in advance of the institution's regular response date. Students who are admitted under early action are not obligated to accept the institution's offer of admission or to submit a deposit until the regular reply date (not prior to May 1).

- A student may apply to other colleges without restriction.
- The institution must notify the applicant of the decision within a reasonable and clearly stated period of time after the early action deadline.
- A student applying for financial aid must adhere to institutional aid application deadlines.
- A student admitted under an early action plan may not be required to make a commitment prior to May 1, but may be encouraged to do so as soon as a final college choice is made. Colleges that solicit commitments to offers of early action admission and/or financial assistance prior to May 1 may do so provided those offers include a clear statement that written requests for extensions until May 1 will be granted, and that such requests will not jeopardize a student's status for admission or financial aid.

Regular Decision

- Regular decision is the application process in which a student submits an application to an institution by a specified date and receives a decision within a reasonable and clearly stated period of time, but not later than April 15.
- A student may apply to other colleges without restriction.
- The institution will state a deadline for completion of applications and will respond to completed applications by a specified date.
- A student applying for financial aid must adhere to institutional aid application deadlines.
- A student admitted under a regular decision plan may not be required to make a commitment prior to May 1, but may be encouraged to do so as soon as a final college choice is made. Colleges that solicit commitments to offers of admission and/or financial assistance prior to May 1 may do so provided those offers include a clear statement that written requests for extensions until May 1 will be granted, and that such requests will not jeopardize a student's status for admission or financial aid.

Rolling Admission

- Rolling admission is the application process in which an institution reviews applications as they are completed and renders admission decisions to students throughout the admission cycle.
- A student may apply to other colleges without restriction.
- The institution will respond to completed applications in a timely manner.
- A student applying for financial aid must adhere to institutional aid application deadlines.
- A student admitted under a rolling admission plan may not be required to make a commitment prior to May 1, but may be encouraged to do so as soon as a final college choice is made. Colleges that solicit commitments to offers of admission and/or financial assistance prior to May 1 may do so provided those offers include a clear statement that written requests for extensions until May 1 will be granted, and that such requests will not jeopardize a student's status for admission or financial aid.

Wait List

- Wait list is an admission decision option utilized by institutions to protect against shortfalls in enrollment. Wait lists are sometimes made necessary because of the uncertainty of the admission process, as students submit applications for admission to multiple institutions and may receive several offers of admission. By placing a student on the wait list, an institution does not initially offer or deny admission, but extends to a candidate the possibility of admission in the future before the institution's admission cycle is concluded.
- The institution will ensure that a wait list, if necessary, is of reasonable length and is maintained for a reasonable period of time, but never later than August 1.
- In the letter offering a wait list position, the institution should provide a past wait list history, which describes the number of students placed on the wait list(s), the number offered admission from the wait list, and the availability of financial aid. Students should be given an indication of when they can expect to be notified of a final admission decision.
- An institution must resolve final status and notify wait list candidates as soon after May 1 as possible.
- The institution will not require students to submit deposits to remain on a wait list or pressure students for a commitment to enroll prior to sending an official offer of admission in writing.

There is one more option, called early action/single choice (EASC), that some highly selective schools such as Harvard, Yale, Princeton, and Stanford have begun using. Early action/single choice is a nonbinding early admission option for freshman applicants that replaces early decision. With this change, students learn about their admission decision in December without being required to reply until May 1. This option allows students to apply to as many colleges as they want under a regular admission time frame. The difference is that the early action/single choice option does not allow a candidate to apply to other schools under any type of early action, early decision, or early notification program. Students are asked to sign a statement in their application agreeing to file only one early application.

Each of these options has variations, depending on the institution using them. Some schools have a November 1 deadline for early decision round one. Smaller schools have a deadline of November 15, while others have a December 1 deadline. Then there's an early decision round two. To make matters even more complicated, some schools with early decision say that students can't apply to other institutions if they've sent in an early decision application to their admissions office. Others say it's okay to apply to other schools at the same time you're applying early decision to them, but if they send you an acceptance, you must withdraw the other applications.

PARENTS, SOME ADVICE FOR YOU

Though guidance counselors stress that high school students should make the final decision about which college to attend, they also say that parents are a very important part of the decision equation. Parents can help as organizers of all the information and provide the support needed to make a good choice. "Little things like setting up file folders and keeping track of deadlines can keep a student on track," advises David Gibson, former College Advisor at St. Mary's Parish in Annapolis, Maryland.

Along with their children, parents also need to understand the basics of early option terminology as it applies to each institution being considered. Five different colleges might have five different early decision criteria. Read the fine print, and make note of deadlines.

What really will help—you, your child, and your wallet—is to understand the basics about financial aid. Says Shawn Leftwich, Director of Undergraduate Admissions at Wheaton College in Illinois, "Have an in-depth discussion with the financial aid officer so that you are aware of the ramifications, restrictions, and implications of the financial aid offer."

If possible, make an appointment to visit with a financial aid officer at the college while your child is visiting the campus. Bring your tax forms and discuss the prospects of financial aid. "Financial aid people are straight shooters. It's not in their best interest to tell you one thing to get your foot in the door and then turn around and pull the rug out from under you," says Bill McClintick, Dean of College Relations and Outreach at Mercerburg Academy. "Parents might not like the answer they get from the financial aid officer, but they will get a candid assessment of their eligibility for financial aid."

Leftwich suggests having an honest discussion with your child early in the college selection process. Talk about what you can realistically afford, what colleges will appropriately challenge him or her, if location is a factor, and what kind of environment best suits your child. Whichever option your child uses to apply, you both will know the decision is an informed one.

Just because two institutions have an application process called early decision or early action doesn't mean that their policies are identical. "There is no common terminology, even among the colleges that have early decision," says Christoph Guttentag, Dean of Undergraduate Admissions at Duke University in Durham, North Carolina. He also points out that just when you think you've got the definitions figured out, institutions change them. "Colleges are always balancing the needs of their institution and the needs of students," he comments.

EARLY DECISION: A MATCHMAKING TOOL OR A CLEVER STRATEGY?

Despite the differences in what actually constitutes early decision, it has become more of a strategy than a matchmaking tool, according to Bill McClintick, Director of College Relations and Outreach at Mercersburg Academy in Mercersburg, Pennsylvania. He also chairs the national steering committee on admissions standards for NACAC. The focus of early decision used to be on matching the student with the college and letting the admissions office know that that institution is where the student wants to be above all others. Today, early decision is misunderstood and misused. High school seniors think that they must use the early decision tactic to get an edge. The result, says McClintick is "at many of the top places, early decision applications have gone through the roof."

Though high school students may have exaggerated ideas of how much early decision can really help them, it is true that it does give a small segment of students applying at highly selective schools an advantage. Generally, the more selective the institution, the more small differences matter. "Even if it's a small increase, you need everything you can get," states John Latting, Ph.D., Emory University's Assistant Vice Provost for Undergraduate Enrollment and Dean of Admission.

"Remember," cautions McClintick, "we're only talking about a small slice of kids in the grand scheme of things." He mentions 5 percent of high school seniors nationally who aspire to the "top" institutions. State colleges and universities fill a much lower percentage of their freshman class with early decision applications. "I don't believe that more kids are chasing the same number of spots," says Jon Reider, Director of College Counseling at San Francisco University High School in San Francisco, California. "Students are applying to more and more schools, even with the early decision option on the side. This is inflating the selectivity of some colleges beyond what it used to be." In reality, 90 percent of students apply regular admission. Interest in early decision comes from a relatively small segment of the college applicant pool.

THE BENEFITS OF EARLY DECISION

There are clear benefits for students who apply for early decision. Aside from the fact that early decision does play a role in acceptance rates for a relatively small percentage of students at a small number of schools, early decision is a good option. The caveat is that students must know, without a shred of doubt, that one institution, above all others, is the best match for their goals and their likes and dislikes, and that based on grades and test scores, they solidly match the institution's criteria for admission. The option to go early decision should be taken after extensive research, multiple visits to the campus, and talking to a lot of people. "Early decision is for those who can put their hearts and souls into one application," advises Cleaver.

There are other advantages. You have to make only one choice, and you will know by December if you've been accepted. You have to fill out only one application. You are not chewing your nails over your list of possibilities during the Christmas holiday. Instead, you know where you're going and can sit back and enjoy the rest of your senior year, while others in your class are madly filling out applications, writing essays, and agonizing over the thin envelopes that arrive in the mail. Says Guttentag, "The advantage of having that challenging process over with is not insignificant."

Early decision is helpful for admissions officers at selective colleges because it allows them to make decisions between well-qualified students and select those who really want to be at their institution. As Shawn Leftwich, Director of Undergraduate Admissions at Wheaton College in Illinois, points out, early decision is for the students who are strongly committed. "We like you. You like us. We know you're coming, and we can fill our freshman class." However, on the flip side, she adds that some students aren't so sure about which college they want to attend, and early decision only makes the process more stressful.

Before you decide to go with early decision, consider early action. Many high school counselors lean toward early action, which is another good option. With early action you're able to apply later in the process. This means you will be able to take the SATs again. Your first-semester grades and AP classes taken in the first semester of your senior year can be used to evaluate your eligibility. You have September and October to visit several campuses while they are in session and plenty of time to do the research to put more than one school on your list.

THE PITFALLS OF EARLY DECISION

Though early decision has benefits, before you jump into it, look at the ramifications of that option. Advises Gilbert, "Early decision might give you an edge, but the tradeoff is not so great."

Perhaps the most compelling reason why students should seriously examine early decision before jumping at it is because they are bound by an agreement to attend that school if accepted. Students sign a pledge to attend that institution and are required to withdraw applications from all other schools. They also are obligated to accept the financial aid award that the institution gives them. An early decision is a binding decision. "Regardless," advises David Gibson, of David Gibson College Advising, LLC, in Annapolis, Maryland, "students don't learn about their financial aid awards until March or April, and if the award funding is not at all acceptable because the family's financial need was not met, they need to decline the offer and begin searching for a new college. March or April is not a good time to start applying to new colleges."

How binding is binding? Though no school can force a student to attend if they've signed an early decision agreement, students who decide not to attend that school hurt others with that decision. High school counselors have to sign the binding agreement, along with parents, and must state that they will not send out transcripts to other institutions. Many institutions will not accept the application of a student who applied early decision elsewhere and backed out of the agreement. Admissions officers may find out in May that an early decision student is not coming, so they'll call the counselor and ask if the student applied to another school. If so, often a phone call to the other institution is made and acceptance denied. Sometimes the counselor loses a good reputation with that institution, putting applicants who follow in subsequent years at a disadvantage.

QUESTIONS TO ASK YOURSELF BEFORE APPLYING EARLY DECISION

What if you don't get accepted early decision—then what? Speaking from the experience of seeing students deal with early decision rejection letters, Reider says, "Some of your friends are getting acceptance letters, and you get one thin envelope and the pain of rejection. You've given the early decision institution your best shot and you lost." Cleaver has seen kids in her high school end up thinking they won't get in anywhere. "This is the first time they've faced a big rejection and news they don't want to hear," she says, noting that because of the timetable of early decision, letters often come right around exam time in December.

When students apply regular decision, meaning they wait until well into their senior year and apply to several different institutions, it's "all or some," quips Latting. "With early decision, it's all or nothing." Many application deadlines for regular decision are in January. If you get that rejection letter from the school you were counting on, that doesn't give you much time to apply to other schools, much less visit them.

Are you ready to make such a drastic decision so early in your senior year? A lot can change in how you think about your future between the beginning of your senior year and graduation. With six or seven months behind you as a senior, you might be in a better position to compare colleges in April than you were back in September. Think about it—you're making the decision about where you want to spend the next four years of your life in early October of your senior year!

Have you given yourself enough time to pick one college above all others? If you want to apply early decision, you should start making plans to do so in your junior year. In order to apply early decision, you must have your ACTs or SATs taken, campus visits done, a final choice made, a dynamite essay written, a stellar application filled out, and teacher recommendation letters collected. That's a lot to cram into the end of your junior year and a few months into your senior year.

Have you given an admissions office enough information to make a decision about you? The more information the admissions office has about grades and classes you took and activities and leadership positions you held, the better they can decide if you're a good match for them. Do you really want decisions being made about you based on sophomore and junior grades and activities? What happens to that AP English class you finally felt ready to take the beginning of your senior year? What about that calculus class you aced in the first semester of your senior year? Admissions won't be able to assess that on an early decision application.

After the consequences of signing a binding agreement, the financial aspect of early decision is the next biggest pitfall. "You can't compare financial aid offers," says Latting. "You have only one offer." Students won't know if they're eligible for Pell grants or merit scholarships. Government FAFSA forms are not submitted until January, and students might not find out how much aid they can get until March or April, long after the early decision agreement was signed and sealed. "This means that if they are accepted, they are then obligated to a college that might not fund them to the level of their financial need," says Gibson. Students who apply early action or regular decision are in a better position to negotiate financial aid packages.

EARLY DECISION REJECTION

In case you haven't heard, "fat" is good, "thin" is bad. Thin envelopes from college admissions offices usually mean a single-page letter saying good luck, we wish you the best, but you're not going to be attending our school next fall. However stated, it's hard to be rejected, especially when you've applied early decision, which states to the college and to yourself that this is the college you've decided is the only one you really, really want to attend above all others.

But thin envelopes don't mean the end of the world. Cleaver advises to not let early decision get control of you. "There are too many choices of colleges for you not to get into college. You might not get into Princeton, but there are many other wonderful schools if you do the research to look for a good match. Early decision is a tool to use to apply, but it is not always the best tool."

Objecting to the term "perfect match," Reider asks, "Does it really matter what kind of car you drive? There are twenty different colleges that can get you where you want to go. You'll be successful in most places."

HOW TO DO EARLY DECISION THE RIGHT WAY

Taking the early decision option requires more than gathering information, filling out an application, writing an essay, and waiting for an envelope to come in the mail or an e-mail to hit your Inbox. If you're going to be serious about early decision, the time to start is in your junior year.

Research the institutions at the top of your list. Think through what you want out of college—not just in terms of a future career, but also factors such as location, size, distance from home, sports, and other activities. Think about who you want to be. "It has to be a love connection," says Cleaver. Tune out all the early decision talk and do your homework about each college. Then ask yourself if one stands out above all the others you've researched. Is this the one to which you can commit to a binding agreement? Are you in the competition to be admitted? Will you have the funds to attend this college?

"Admissions can tell if your application is from the heart," Cleaver cautions. Students ask her how to make their applications "look like they want to go there." She replies that what they put on an application and in an essay has to pour out of their hearts. Students who visit the campus and sit in on a class or a campus organization have the edge if something really clicked with them. They will write a convincing application. Perhaps they'll tell about how exciting the professor they heard was or how wonderful it is that the college has a chess club. Cleaver observes that kids usually write about an institution's sports team or about the ivy-covered walls of the campus on their application essay instead of writing about some interesting aspect of the university that spoke to them, which takes research, time, and reflection. "Don't make the mistake of chasing a name and not being a good consumer," cautions McClintick. Part of being a good consumer is to make sure you are a reasonably competitive applicant. This means looking at the school's admission criteria and statistics. What percentage of the freshman class is filled with early decision and early action students? If it's a high percentage, then you might want to reconsider where that school falls on your wish list. How many students return for their sophomore year? If more than 10 percent leave after their freshman year, that should tell you something about student satisfaction—and ultimately yours.

One of the most important ways to choose the right school is to visit the campus, perhaps multiple times and preferably with students on campus. "Campus visits are a critical time to talk with undergraduates and to find out what the academic, social, and physical climate is like," advises Guttentag. If you're staying in a dorm on Tuesday night during a visit, you can tell how serious kids are about their work. What kinds of conversations are they having? "Are these the kind of kids you want to spend four years of your life with?" asks McClintick.

After you've thoroughly investigated all the aspects of a college and decided it's at the absolute top of your list, after you are familiar with the early decision requirements at that institution, and after you've determined that you have a good chance of getting into that institution, then you can say early decision is for you. For those who are not so sure, fortunately, colleges and universities have plenty of other options for admission.

Coming to America: Tips for International Students Considering Study in the U.S.

Introduction: Why Study in the United States?

Are you thinking about going to a college or university in the United States? If you're looking at this book, you probably are! All around the world, students like you, pursuing higher education, are considering that possibility. They envision themselves on modern, high-tech campuses in well-known cities, surrounded by American students, taking classes and having fun. A degree from a U.S. school would certainly lead to success and fortune, either back in your home country or perhaps even in the United States, wouldn't it?

It can be done—but becoming a student at a college or university in the U.S. requires academic talent, planning, time, effort, and money. While there may be only a small number of institutions of higher learning in your country, there are more than 2,900 four-year colleges and universities in the United States. Choosing one, being accepted, and then traveling and becoming a student in America is a big undertaking.

If this is your dream, here is some helpful information and expert tips from professionals who work with international students at colleges and universities throughout the United States.

Timing and Planning

The journey to a college or university in the U.S. often starts years in advance. Most international students choose to study in the U.S. because of the high quality of academics. Your family may also have a lot of input on this decision, too.

"We always tell students they should be looking in the sophomore year, visiting in the junior year, and applying in the senior year," says Father Francis E. Chambers, OSA, D.Min., Associate Director of International Admission at Villanova University. He stresses that prospective students need to be taking challenging courses in the years leading up to college. "We want to see academic rigor. Most admission decisions are based on the first six semesters—senior year is too late."

Heidi Gregori-Gahan, Assistant Provost for International Programs at the University of Southern Indiana agrees that it's important to start early. "Plan ahead and do your homework. There is so much to choose from—so many schools, programs, degrees, and experiences. It can be overwhelming."

While students in some countries may pay an agent to help them get into a school in the United States, Gregori-Gahan often directs potential international students to EducationUSA (http://educationusa.state.gov), a U.S. State Department network of over 400 international student advising centers in more than 170 countries. "They are there to provide unbiased information about studying in the United States and help you understand the process and what you need to do."

Two to three years of advance planning is also recommended by Daphne Durham, who has been an international student adviser at Harvard, Suffolk University, Valdosta State University, and the University of Georgia. She points out that the academic schedule in other countries is often different than that of the United States, so you need to synchronize your calendar accordingly.

You will have to take several tests in order to gain admission to a U.S. school, so it's important to know when those tests are given in your country, then register and take them so your scores will be available when you apply. Even if you have taken English in school, you will probably have to take The Test of English as a Foreign Language (TOEFL®), but some schools also accept the International English Language Testing Sytem (IELTS). You will probably also have to take the SAT® or ACT® tests, which are achievement or aptitude tests, and are usually required of all students applying for admission, not just international students.

"Make sure you understand how the international admissions process works at the school or schools you want to attend," says Durham. "What test scores are needed and when? Does the school have a fixed calendar or rolling admissions?" Those are just some of the many factors that can impact your application and could make a difference in when you are able to start school.

"Every university is unique in what's required and what they need to do. Even navigating each school's different website can be challenging," explains Gregori-Gahan.

Searching for Schools

This book contains information on thousands of four-year colleges and universities, and it will be a valuable resource for you in your search and application process. But with so many options, how do you decide which school you should attend?

"Where I find a big difference with international students is if their parents don't recognize the school, they don't apply to the school," says Fr. Chambers. "They could be overlooking a lot of great schools. They have to look outside the box."

The school Gregori-Gahan represents is in Evansville, Indiana, and it probably isn't familiar to students abroad. "Not many people have heard of anything beyond New York and California and maybe Florida. I like to tell students that this is 'real America.' But happy international students on our campus have recruited others to come here."

She points out that Internet technology has made a huge difference in the search process for international students. Websites full of information, live chat, webinars, virtual tours, and admission interviews via Skype have made it easier for potential students to connect with U.S. institutions, get more information, and be better able to visualize the campus.

One thing than will help narrow your search for a school is knowing specifically what you want to study. You need to know what the course of study is called in the United States, what it means, and what is required in order to study that subject. You also need to consider your future plans. What are your goals and objectives? What do you plan to do after earning your degree?

"If you're going to overcome the hurdles and get to a U.S. school, you have to have a directed path chosen," says Durham.

The other thing that could help your search process is finding a school that is a good fit.

Fit Is Important

You want your clothing and shoes to fit you properly and be comfortable, so a place where you will spend four or more years of your life studying should also be comfortable and appropriate for you. So how can you determine if a particular school is a good fit?

"We really recommend international students visit first. Yes, there are websites and virtual tours, but there's still nothing that beats an in-person visit," says Fr. Chambers. He estimates that 50 to 60 percent of Villanova's international students visited the campus before enrolling.

"It can be hard to get a sense of a place—you're so far away and you're probably not going to set foot on campus until you arrive," says Gregori-Gahan. "There is a high potential for culture shock."

You need to ask yourself what is important to you in a campus environment, then do some homework to ensure that the schools you are considering meet those needs. Here are some things to consider when it comes to fit:

- **Location:** Is it important for you to be in a well-known city or is a part of the United States that is unfamiliar a possibility? "Look at geographic areas, but also cost of living," recommends Durham. "Be sure to factor in transportation costs also, especially if you plan to return to your home country regularly."
- **Student population:** Some small schools have just 1,000 students while larger ones may have 30,000 students or more.
- **Familiar faces:** Is it important for you to be at a school with others from your home nation or region?
- **Climate:** Some students want a climate similar to where they live now, but others are open and curious about seasons and weather conditions they may not have ever experienced. "We do have four seasons here," says Gregori-Gahan. "Sometimes students who come here from tropical regions are concerned about the winters. The first snow is so exciting, but after that, students may not be aware of how cold it really is."
- **Amenities:** Do you want to find your own housing or choose a school where the majority of students live on campus? Is there public transportation available or is it necessary to walk or have a bicycle or car? Does the school or community have access to things that are important to you culturally and meet the traditions you want to follow?
- **Campus size:** Some campuses are tightly compacted into a few city blocks, but others cover hundreds of acres of land. "International students are amazed by how green and spacious our campus is, with blooming flowers, trees, and lots of grass," says Gregori-Gahan.
- **Academic offerings:** Does this school offer the program you want to study? Can you complete it in four years or perhaps sooner? What sort of internship and career services are available?
- **Finances:** Can you afford to attend this school? Is there any sort of financial assistance available for international students?
- **Support services:** Durham suggests students look carefully at each school's offerings for international students. "Does the school have online guidance for getting your visa? Is ESL tutoring available? Does the school offer host family or community friend programs?" She also suggests you look for campus support groups for students from your country or region.

Looking at the listings and reading the in-depth descriptions in this book can help you search for a school that is a good fit for you.

Government Requirements

The one thing that every international student must have in order to study in the United States is a student visa. Having accurate advice and following all the necessary steps regarding the visa process is essential to being able to enter this country and start school.

As you schedule your tests and application deadlines, you must also consider how long it will take to get your visa. This varies depending on where you live; in some countries, extensive background checks are required. The subject you plan to study can also impact your visa status; it does help to have a major rather than be undeclared. The U.S. State Department website, http://travel.state.gov/content/visas/english/study-exchange.html, can give you an idea of how long it will take.

In addition to the visa, you will also need a Form I-20, which is a U.S. government immigration form. You must have that form when you get to the United States.

"It's very different from being a tourist. You need to be prepared to meet with an immigration officer and be interviewed about your college," explains Durham. "Where you are going, why you are going, where the school is located, what you are studying, and so on."

You also need to keep in mind that there are reporting requirements once you are a student in the U.S. Every semester, your adviser has to report to the government to confirm that you are enrolled in and attending school in order for you to stay in the United States.

Finances

Part of the visa process includes having the funds to pay for the cost of your schooling and support yourself. Finances are a huge hurdle in the process of becoming a college student in the United States.

"It's crucial. So many foreign systems offer 'free' higher education to students. How is your family going to handle the ongoing expense of attending college for four years or longer in the United States?" Durham reiterates that planning ahead is key because there are so many details. Student loans require a U.S.-based cosigner. Each school has its own financial aid deadlines. You have to factor in your own government's requirements, such currency exchange and fund transfers.

The notion that abundant funds are available to assist international students is not true. Sometimes state schools may offer diversity waivers or there may be special scholarship opportunities for international students. But attending school in the U.S. is still a costly venture.

"We do offer financial aid to international students, but they still have to be able to handle a large portion of the costs. Full-need scholarships are not likely," explained Fr. Chambers. "Sometimes students think that once they get here, it will all work out and the funds will be there. But the scenario for the first year has to be repeated each year they are on campus.

Once You Arrive...

You've taken your tests, researched schools, found a good fit, applied, got accepted, arranged the financing, gotten your visa and I-20, and made it to the campus in the United States. Now what?

You can expect the school where you have enrolled to be welcoming and helpful, but within reason. If you arrive on a weekend, or at a time outside of the time when international students are scheduled to arrive, the assistance you need may not be available to you.

Every school offers different levels of assistance to international students. For instance, Villanova offers a full-service office that can assist students with everything from visas, to employment, to finding a place for students to stay over breaks.

Fr. Chambers attends the international student orientation session to greet the students he's worked with through the recruitment and application process. "But I rarely see an international student after that. I think that bodes well for them being integrated into the entire university."

"Those of us who work with international students are really working to help them adjust," says Gregori-Gahan. "International students get here well before school starts so they can get over jet lag. We have orientation sessions and pair them with peer advisers who help them navigate the first few days, and we assure them that we are there for them."

Students should be open to their new setting, but they should be prepared that things may not be at all how they had envisioned during their planning and searching process. "While you may think you'll meet lots of Americans, don't underestimate the importance of community with your traditional home culture and people," says Durham.

Don't Make These Mistakes

The journey to college attendance in the United States is a long one, with many steps. The experts warn about mistakes to avoid along the way.

"Not reading through everything thoroughly and not understanding what the program of study really is and what will it cost. You have to be really clear on the important details," says Gregori-Gahan.

"Every school does things differently," cautions Fr. Chambers. "International students must be aware of that as they are applying."

Durham stresses that going to school in the United States is too big a decision to leave to someone else. "Students need to know about their school—they have to be in charge of their application."

"It involves a lot of work to be successful and happy and not surprised by too many things," Gregori-Gahan says.

Hopefully now, you are more informed and better prepared to pursue your dream of studying at a college or university in the United States.

Financial Aid Countdown Calendar

JUNIOR YEAR

Fall

Now is the time to get serious about the colleges in which you are interested. Meet with your guidance counselor to help you narrow down your choices. Hopefully by the spring, your list will have five to ten solid choices. College visits are always a great idea—remember this will be the place you will call home for four years, so start your campus visits soon!

- ❑ Register for the PSAT/NMSQT®.
- ❑ Check out local financial aid nights in the area. Be sure to attend these valuable sessions, especially if this is the first time your family is sending someone off to college. Try to become familiar with common financial aid terms. Start reviewing the literature available and begin to familiarize yourself with the various programs. A good booklet is published by the U.S. Department of Education, "Funding Your Education: The Guide to Federal Student Aid" and is available at any financial aid office or on the web at https://studentaid.ed.gov/sa/sites/default/files/funding-your-education.pdf.
- ❑ In October, take the PSAT/NMSQT®.
- ❑ Do some web browsing! There are many free scholarship search engines, such as Petersons.com. Also, head to the bookstore or library and pick up a copy of *Peterson's® Scholarships, Grants & Prizes,* which features details on aid from private sources, or *Best Scholarships for the Best Students,* which offers great info on scholarships, fellowships, and experiential learning programs for top students.
- ❑ Ask your parents to contact their employers, unions, and any religious and fraternal organizations with which they have a connection to learn about possible scholarship opportunities.
- ❑ Check with your high school guidance counselor for the qualifications and deadlines of local scholarship awards. Many guidance counselors report that there are few applicants for these awards.

Winter

- ❑ Keep checking for scholarships! Remember that this is the one area over which you have control. The harder you work, the better your chances for success!
- ❑ Register and study for the ACT® or SAT® and SAT Subject Tests™.

Spring

- ❑ Spring Break—a great time to visit colleges. Remember your top ten list? Time to start narrowing it down.
- ❑ Review the requirements for local scholarships. What can you do now and over the summer to improve your chances?
- ❑ Take the ACT® or SAT®. Good luck!
- ❑ Look for a summer job, especially one that ties in with your college plans. For example, if you want to major in premed, why not try to get a job at a hospital or with a laboratory?

Summer

- ❑ College visit time! Ask: Is this where I see myself getting my undergraduate degree? Can I adjust to the seasons, the town surrounding the campus, the distance from home, the college size? Does this school feel right for me?
- ❑ Why not get a jump on college (and maybe save some money!) and enroll for a college course at the local community college? Or, better yet, do some extra prep work for the ACT® or SAT®!

SENIOR YEAR

Fall

How's the college list coming? Can you get your list down to five or six choices? Your guidance counselor can help with this process. Once you have your top choices, make a list of what each college requires for admission and financial aid. Be sure your list includes all deadlines. Attend a financial aid night presentation with your parents. Some of these sessions offer help in completing forms; others offer a broader view of the process. Contact the presenter (usually a local college financial aid professional) to be sure you are getting the information you need.

- ❑ Do any of these colleges require the CSS/Financial Aid PROFILE® financial aid application? Many private colleges use this form for institutional aid. You need to file this comprehensive form in late September or early October. For more information or to find out which colleges use this supplemental form, go to https://student.collegeboard.org/css-financial-aid-profile. (Website registration is free; however, PROFILE® is a fee-based application).
- ❑ Starting with the 2017–18 FAFSA® application cycle, Students can file as early as Oct. 1, 2016, rather than beginning on Jan. 1, 2017. The earlier submission date will be a permanent change, enabling students to complete and submit a FAFSA® as early as October 1 every year. (There is NO CHANGE to the 2016–17 schedule. The FAFSA® was available on January 1, 2016 as in previous years.)
- ❑ Don't falter now in your scholarship search. Get the applications filed by the published deadlines.
- ❑ Register now if you are planning to retake the SAT®.
- ❑ Most important, start completing your college applications—the earlier, the better! If you are interested in early decision or early action, now is the time! Remember, accuracy and completeness are a must!

Winter

- ❑ Ensure all college applications are completed.
- ❑ Do you have some questions? Call the local financial aid office. Many states have special toll-free call-in programs in January and February, Financial Aid Awareness Month. Be sure that you have completed each school's required forms.
- ❑ As the letters of admission start to arrive, the financial aid award letters should be right behind them. Important question for parents: What is the bottom line? Remember, aid at a lower-cost state school will be less than a higher-cost private college. But what will you be required to pay? This can be confusing, so consider gift aid (scholarships and grants), student loans, and parent loans. The school with the lowest sticker price (tuition, fees, and room and board) might not be the best bargain when you look at the overall financial aid package.

Spring

- ❑ Still not sure where to go? The financial aid package at your top choice just not enough? Call the financial aid office and the admissions office. Talk it over. While schools don't like to bargain, they are usually willing to take a second look. Is there something unusual about your family's financial situation that might impact your parents' ability to pay?
- ❑ By May 1, you must make your final decision. Notify your chosen college and find out what you need to do next. Tell the other colleges you are not accepting their offers of admission and financial aid.

Summer

- ❑ Time to crunch the numbers. Parents, get information from the college on the total charges for the coming fall term. Deduct the aid package and then plan for how the balance will be paid. Contact the college financial aid office for the best parental loan program. If you want to arrange for a payment plan, contact the business office for further information. Most schools have deferred payment plans available for a nominal fee.

Congratulations! Remember that you need to reapply for aid every year!

Who's Paying for This? Financial Aid Basics

A college education can be expensive—costing more than $150,000 for four years at some of the higher priced private colleges and universities. Even at the lower-cost state colleges and universities, the cost of a four-year education can approach $60,000. Determining how you and your family will come up with the necessary funds to pay for your education requires planning, perseverance, and learning as much as you can about the options that are available to you. But before you get discouraged, College Board statistics show that 53 percent of full-time students attend four-year public and private colleges with tuition and fees less than $9,000, while 20 percent attend colleges that have tuition and fees more than $36,000. College costs tend to be less in the western states and higher in New England.

Paying for college should not be looked at as a four-year financial commitment. For many families, paying the total cost of a student's college education out of current income and savings is usually not realistic. For families that have planned ahead and have financial savings established for higher education, the burden is a lot easier. But for most, meeting the cost of college requires the pooling of current income and assets and investing in longer-term loan options. These family resources, together with financial assistance from state, federal, and institutional sources, enable millions of students each year to attend the institution of their choice.

FINANCIAL AID PROGRAMS

There are three types of financial aid:

1. Gift-aid—Scholarships and grants are funds that do not have to be repaid.
2. Loans—Loans must be repaid, usually after graduation; the amount you have to pay back is the total you've borrowed plus any accrued interest. This is considered a source of self-help aid.
3. Student employment—Student employment is a job arranged for you by the financial aid office. This is another source of self-help aid.

The federal government has four major grant programs—the Federal Pell Grant, the Federal Supplemental Educational Opportunity Grant, Academic Competitiveness Grants (ACG), and National SMART (Science and Mathematics Access to Retain Talent) grants. ACG and SMART grants are limited to students who qualify for a Pell Grant and are awarded to a select group of students. Overall, these grants are targeted to low-to-moderate income families with significant financial need. The federal government also sponsors a student employment program called the Federal Work-Study Program, which offers jobs both on and off campus, and several loan programs, including those for students and for parents of undergraduate students.

There are two types of student loan programs: subsidized and unsubsidized. The subsidized Federal Direct Loan and the Federal Perkins Loan are need-based, government-subsidized loans. Students who borrow through these programs do not have to pay interest on the loan until after they graduate or leave school. The unsubsidized Federal Direct Loan and the Federal Direct PLUS Loan Program are not based on need, and borrowers are responsible for the interest while the student is in school. These loans are administered by different methods. Once you choose your college, the financial aid office will guide you through this process.

After you've submitted your financial aid application and you've been accepted for admission, each college will send you a letter describing your financial aid award. Most award letters show estimated college costs, how much you and your family are expected to contribute, and the amount and types of aid you have been awarded. Most students are awarded aid from a combination of sources and programs. Hence, your award is often called a financial aid "package."

SOURCES OF FINANCIAL AID

Millions of students and families apply for financial aid each year. Financial aid from all sources exceeds $143 billion per year. The largest single source of aid is the federal government, which will award more than $100 billion this year.

The next largest source of financial aid is found in the college and university community. Most of this aid is awarded to students who have a demonstrated need based on the Federal Methodology. Some institutions use a different formula, the Institutional Methodology (IM), to award their own funds in conjunction with other forms of aid. Institutional aid may be either need-based or non-need based. Aid that is not based on need is usually awarded for a student's academic performance (merit awards), specific talents or abilities, or to attract the type of students a college seeks to enroll.

Another source of financial aid is from state government. All states offer grant and/or scholarship aid, most of which is need-based. However, more and more states are offering substantial merit-based aid programs. Most state programs award aid only to students attending college in their home state.

Other sources of financial aid include:

- Private agencies
- Foundations
- Corporations
- Clubs

- Fraternal and service organizations
- Civic associations
- Unions
- Religious groups that award grants, scholarships, and low-interest loans
- Employers that provide tuition reimbursement benefits for employees and their children

More information about these different sources of aid is available from high school guidance offices, public libraries, college financial aid offices, directly from the sponsoring organizations, and online at www.petersons.com/college-search/scholarship-search.aspx.

HOW NEED-BASED FINANCIAL AID IS AWARDED

When you apply for aid, your family's financial situation is analyzed using a government-approved formula called the Federal Methodology. This formula looks at five items:

1. Demographic information of the family
2. Income of the parents
3. Assets of the parents
4. Income of the student
5. Assets of the student

This analysis determines the amount you and your family are expected to contribute toward your college expenses, called your Expected Family Contribution, or EFC. If the EFC is equal to or more than the cost of attendance at a particular college, then you do not demonstrate financial need. However, even if you don't have financial need, you may still qualify for aid, as there are grants, scholarships, and loan programs that are not need-based.

If the cost of your education is greater than your EFC, then you do demonstrate financial need and qualify for assistance. The amount of your financial need that can be met varies from school to school. Some are able to meet your full need, while others can only cover a certain percentage of need. Here's the formula:

Cost of Attendance
− Expected Family Contribution
= Financial Need

The EFC remains constant, but your need will vary according to the costs of attendance at a particular college. In general, the higher the tuition and fees at a particular college, the higher the cost of attendance will be. Expenses for books and supplies, room and board, transportation, and other miscellaneous items are included in the overall cost of attendance. It is important to remember that you do not have to be low-income to qualify for financial aid. Many middle and upper-middle income families qualify for need-based financial aid.

APPLYING FOR FINANCIAL AID

Every student must complete the Free Application for Federal Student Aid (FAFSA) to be considered for financial aid. The FAFSA is available from your high school guidance office, many public libraries, colleges in your area, or directly from the U.S. Department of Education.

Students are encouraged to apply for federal student aid on the Web. The electronic version of the FAFSA can be accessed at http://www.fafsa.ed.gov.

The NEW Federal Student Aid ID

In order for a student to complete the online FAFSA®, he or she will need a Federal Student Aid (FSA) ID. You can get this online at https://fsaid.ed.gov/npas/index.htm. Since May 2015, the FSA ID has replaced the previously used PIN system. Parents of dependent students also need to obtain their own FSA ID in order to sign their child's FAFSA® electronically online.

The FSA ID can be used to access several federal aid-related websites, including FAFSA.gov and StudentLoans.gov. It consists of a username and password and can be used to electronically sign Federal Student Aid documents, access your personal records, and make binding legal obligations. The FSA ID is beneficial in several ways:

- It removes your personal identifiable information (PII), such as your Social Security number, from your log-in credentials.
- It creates a more secure and efficient way to verify your information when you log in to access to your federal student aid information online.
- It gives you the ability to easily update your personal information.
- It allows you to easily retrieve your username and password by requesting a secure code be sent to your e-mail address or by answering challenge questions.

It's relatively simple to create an FSA ID and should only take a few minutes. In addition, you will have an opportunity to link your current Federal Student Aid PIN (if you already have one) to your FSA ID. The final step is to confirm your e-mail address. You will receive a secure code to the e-mail address you provided when you set up your FSA ID. Once you retrieve the code from your e-mail account and enter it—to confirm your e-mail address is valid—you will be able to use this e-mail address instead of your username to log in to any of the federal aid-related websites, making the log-in process EVEN simpler for you and your parents.

When you initially create your FSA ID, your information will need to be verified with the Social Security Administration. This process can take anywhere from one to three days. For that reason, it's a good idea to take care of setting up your FSA ID as early as possible, so it will be all set when you are ready to begin completing your FAFSA.

IMPORTANT NOTE: Since your FSA ID provides access to your personal information and is used to sign online documents, it's imperative that you protect this ID. Don't share it with *anyone* or write it down in an insecure location—you could place yourself at great risk for identify theft.

If Every College You're Applying to for Fall 2018 Requires the FAFSA

. . . then it's pretty simple: Complete the FAFSA after October 1, 2017, being certain to send it in before any college-imposed deadlines. (Students will now be permitted to send in the

2018–19 FAFSA before January 1, 2018.) Beginning with the 2018–19 FAFSA, students will be required to report income information from an earlier tax year. For example, on the 2017–18 FAFSA, students (and parents, as appropriate) will report their 2016 income information, rather than their 2017 income information.

After you send in your FAFSA, you'll receive a Student Aid Report (SAR) that includes all of the information you reported and shows your EFC. If you provided an e-mail address, the SAR is sent to you electronically; otherwise, you will receive a SAR or SAR Acknowledgment in the mail, which lists your FAFSA information but may require you to make any corrections on the FAFSA website. Be sure to review the SAR, checking to see if the information you reported is accurately represented. If you used estimated numbers to complete the FAFSA, you may have to resubmit the SAR with any corrections to the data. The college(s) you have designated on the FAFSA will receive the information you reported and will use that data to make their decision.

The CSS/Financial Aid PROFILE®

To award their own funds, some colleges require an additional application, the CSS/Financial Aid PROFILE® form. The PROFILE asks supplemental questions that some colleges and awarding agencies feel provide a more accurate assessment of the family's ability to pay for college. It is up to the college to decide whether it will use only the FAFSA or both the FAFSA and the PROFILE. PROFILE applications are available from the high school guidance office and on the Web. Both the paper application and the website list those colleges and programs that require the PROFILE application.

If a College Requires the PROFILE

Step 1: Register for the CSS/Financial Aid PROFILE in the fall of your senior year in high school. You can apply for the PROFILE online at http://profileonline.collegeboard.com/prf/index.jsp. Registration information with a list of the colleges that require the PROFILE is available in most high school guidance offices. There is a fee for using the Financial Aid PROFILE application ($25 for the first college, which includes the $9 application fee, and $16 for each additional college). You must pay for the service by credit card when you register. If you do not have a credit card, you will be billed. A limited number of fee waivers are automatically granted to first-time applicants based on the financial information provided on the PROFILE.

Step 2: Fill out your customized CSS/Financial Aid PROFILE. Once you register, your application will be immediately available online and will have questions that all students must complete, questions which must be completed by the student's parents (unless the student is independent and the colleges or programs selected do not require parental information), and *may* have supplemental questions needed by one or more of your schools or programs. If required, those will be found in Section Q of the application.

In addition to the PROFILE application you complete online, you may also be required to complete a Business/ Farm Supplement via traditional paper format. Completion of this form is not a part of the online process. If this form is required, instructions on how to download and print the supplemental form are provided. If your biological or adoptive parents are separated or divorced and your colleges and programs require it, your noncustodial parent may be asked to complete the Noncustodial PROFILE.

Once you complete and submit your PROFILE application, it will be processed and sent directly to your requested colleges and programs.

IF YOU DON'T QUALIFY FOR NEED-BASED AID

If you are not eligible for need-based aid, you can still find ways to lessen your burden.

Here are some suggestions:

- Search for merit scholarships. You can start at the initial stages of your application process. College merit awards are increasingly important as more and more colleges award these to students they especially want to attract. As a result, applying to a college at which your qualifications put you at the top of the entering class may give you a larger merit award. Another source of aid to look for is private scholarships that are given for special skills and talents. Additional information can be found at www.finaid.org.
- Seek employment during the summer and the academic year. The student employment office at your college can help you locate a school-year job. Many colleges and local businesses have vacancies remaining after they have hired students who are receiving Federal Work-Study Program financial aid.
- Borrow through the unsubsidized Federal Direct Loan program. This is generally available to all students. The terms and conditions are similar to the subsidized loans. The biggest difference is that the borrower is responsible for the interest while still in college, although the government permits students to delay paying the interest right away and add the accrued interest to the total amount owed. You must file the FAFSA to be considered.
- After you've secured what you can through scholarships, working, and borrowing, you and your parents will be expected to meet your share of the college bill (the Expected Family Contribution). Many colleges offer monthly payment plans that spread the cost over the academic year. If the monthly payments are too high, parents can borrow through the Federal Direct PLUS Loan Program, through one of the many private education loan programs available, or through home equity loans and lines of credit. Families seeking assistance in financing college expenses should inquire at the financial aid office about what programs are available at the college. Some families seek the advice of professional financial advisers and tax consultants.

How to Use This Guide

PROFILES

The **PROFILES** section contains basic data in capsule form for quick review and comparison. Organized by state, more than 2,700 colleges and universities are listed alphabetically, followed by their city and state and website URL. Those schools that offer a special, detailed listing at www.petersons.com, will also have a ★ next to their name.

The following outline of the format shows the section headings and the items that each section covers. Any item that does not apply to a particular college or for which no information was supplied is omitted from that college's listing. Display ads, which appear near some of the institutions' profiles, have been provided and paid for by those colleges and universities that chose to supplement their profile with additional information.

Category Overviews

Type of Institution

Private institutions are designated as *independent* (nonprofit), *proprietary* (profit-making), or *independent with a specific religious denomination or affiliation*. Nondenominational or interdenominational religious orientation is possible and would be indicated. Public institutions are designated by the source of funding. Designations include *federal, state, province, commonwealth* (Puerto Rico), *territory* (U.S. territories), *county, district* (an educational administrative unit often having boundaries different from units of local government), *city, state and local* (local may refer to county, district, or city), or *state-related* (funded primarily by the state but administratively autonomous). *Religious affiliation* may follow, along with year founded. Each institution is classified as one of the following:

- Primarily two-year: Awards baccalaureate degrees but majority of students are enrolled in two-year programs.
- Four-year: Awards baccalaureate degrees; may also award associate degrees; does not award graduate (postbaccalaureate) degrees.
- Five-year: Awards a five-year baccalaureate in a professional field such as architecture or pharmacy; does not award graduate degrees.
- Upper-level: Awards baccalaureate degrees, but entering students must have at least two years of previous college-level credit; may also offer graduate degrees.
- Comprehensive: Awards baccalaureate degrees; may also award associate degrees; offers graduate degree programs, primarily at the master's, specialist's, or professional level, although one or two doctoral programs may be offered.
- University: Offers four years of undergraduate work, plus graduate degrees through the doctorate in more than two academic or professional fields.

Setting

Designated as *urban* (located within a major city), *suburban* (a residential area within commuting distance of a major city), *small town* (a small but compactly settled area not within commuting distance of a major city), or *rural* (a remote and sparsely populated area).

Endowment

The total dollar value of funds and/or property donated to the institution or the multicampus educational system of which the institution is a part.

Student body

An institution is *coed* (coeducational—admits men and women), *primarily* (80 percent or more) *women, primarily men, women only,* or *men only.* A few schools are designated as *undergraduate: women only; graduate: coed* or *undergraduate: men only; graduate: coed.*

Entrance

The five levels of entrance difficulty *(most difficult, very difficult, moderately difficult, minimally difficult,* and *noncompetitive)* are based on the percentage of applicants who were accepted for fall 2016 freshman admission (or, in the case of upper-level schools, for entering-class admission) and on the high school class rank and standardized test scores of the accepted freshmen who actually enrolled in fall 2016. The colleges were asked to select the level that most closely corresponds to their entrance difficulty, according to these guidelines.

UNDERGRAD STUDENTS

Number of full-time or part-time undergraduates. Number of states and territories that students come from; percentages of undergraduates who are out-of-state; live on campus; Black or African American, non-Hispanic/Latino; Hispanic/Latino; Asian, non-Hispanic/Latino; Native Hawaiian or other Pacific Islander, non-Hispanic/Latino; American Indian or Alaska Native, non-Hispanic/Latino American Indian or Alaska Native, non-Hispanic/Latino; two or more races, non-Hispanic/Latino; race/ethnicity unknown; international; and percentage of students who transferred in are given.

Freshmen

Admission: Figures are given for the number of students who applied for fall 2016 admission, the number of those who were admitted, and the number who enrolled. *Average high school GPA:* Freshman statistics include the average high school GPA. *Test scores:* Percentage of freshmen who took the SAT® (not the Redesigned SAT) and received critical reading, math, and writing scores above 500, above 600, and above 700; as well as percentage of freshmen taking the ACT® who received a composite score of 18 or higher, 24 or higher, and 30 or higher.

Retention: The percentage of full-time freshmen who returned the following year for the fall semester/term.

FACULTY

Total: The total number of faculty members; percentage of full-time faculty members as of fall 2016; and percentage of total faculty members who hold terminal degrees. *Student/faculty ratio:* School's estimate of the ratio of matriculated undergraduate students to faculty members teaching undergraduate courses.

ACADEMICS

Calendar: Most colleges indicate one of the following: 4-1-4, 4-4-1, or a similar arrangement (two terms of equal length plus an abbreviated winter or spring term, with the numbers referring to months); semesters; trimesters; quarters; 3-3 (three courses for each of three terms); modular (the academic year is divided into small blocks of time; courses of varying lengths are assembled according to individual programs); or standard year (for most Canadian institutions). *Degrees:* This names the full range of levels of certificates, diplomas, and degrees, including prebaccalaureate, baccalaureate, graduate, and professional, that are offered by this institution.

Special study options: Details on study options available at each college, such as accelerated degree program, academic remediation for entering students, Advanced Placement credit, cooperative education programs, distance learning, double majors, English as a second language (ESL), and external degree programs. *ROTC:* Army, Naval, or Air Force Reserve Officers' Training Corps programs offered either on campus, at a branch campus [designated by a (b)], or at a cooperating host institution [designated by (c)].

Unusual degree programs: Information is offered here on any unique programs at the institution, such as 3-2 engineering, computer science, or business administration programs.

Computers: Information is provided on the numbers of computers/terminals available on campus for general student use, what computer technology is accessible to students, and availability of a campuswide network and wireless campus network.

STUDENT LIFE

Housing options: Institution's policy about whether students are permitted to live off-campus or are required to live on campus for a specified period; whether freshmen only, coed, single-sex, cooperative, and disabled student housing options are available; whether campus housing is leased by the school and/or provided by a third party; whether freshman applicants are given priority for college housing. "College housing not available" indicates that no college-owned or -operated housing facilities are provided for undergraduates and that noncommuting students must arrange for their own accommodations.

Activities and organizations: Information on clubs and organizations, including sororities and fraternities.

Athletics: Membership in one or more of the following athletic associations is indicated by initials: NCAA: National Collegiate Athletic Association; NAIA: National Association of Intercollegiate Athletics; NCCAA: National Christian College Athletic Association; USCAA: United States Collegiate Athletic Association; and CIS: Canadian Interuniversity Sport. The overall NCAA division in which all or most intercollegiate teams compete is designated by I, II, or III. All teams that do not compete in this division are listed as exceptions.

Sports offered by the college are divided into two groups: *Intercollegiate* ("M" or "W" following the name of each sport indicates that it is offered for men or women) and *Intramural.* An "s" in parentheses following an "M" or "W" for an intercollegiate sport indicates that athletic scholarships (or grants-in-aid) are offered for men or women in that sport, and a "c" indicates a club team as opposed to a varsity team.

Campus security: Campus safety measures including 24-hour emergency response devices (phones and alarms) and patrols by trained security personnel, student patrols, late-night transport-escort service, and controlled dormitory access (key, security card, etc.).

Student services: Information indicates services offered to students by the college, such as legal services, health clinics, personal-psychological counseling, and women's centers.

COSTS & FINANCIAL AID

Costs: Costs are given for the 2017–18 academic year or for the 2016–17 academic year if 2017–18 figures were not yet available. *Tuition:* Annual expenses may be expressed as a comprehensive fee (including full-time tuition, mandatory fees, and college room and board) or as separate figures for full-time tuition, fees, room and board, or room only. For public institutions where tuition differs according to residence, separate figures are given for area or state residents and for nonresidents. Part-time tuition is expressed in terms of a per-unit rate (per credit, per semester hour, etc.).

The tuition structure at some institutions is complex in that freshmen and sophomores may be charged a different rate from that for juniors and seniors, a professional or vocational division may have a different fee structure from the liberal arts division of the same institution, or part-time tuition may be prorated on a sliding scale according to the number of credit hours taken. Tuition and fees may vary according to academic program, campus/location, class time (day, evening, weekend), course/credit load, course level, degree level, reciprocity agreements, and student level. *Room and board* charges are reported as an average for one academic year and may vary according to the board plan selected, campus/location, type of housing facility, or student level. *Payment plans* may include tuition prepayment, installment payments, and deferred payment. A tuition prepayment plan gives a student the option of locking in the current tuition rate for the entire term of enrollment by paying the full amount in advance rather than year by year. *Waivers:* availability of full or partial undergraduate tuition waivers to minority students, children of alumni, employees or their children, adult students, and senior citizens may be listed.

Financial Aid: This information represents aid awarded to undergraduates for the available academic year. Figures are given for the number of undergraduates who applied for aid, the number who were judged to have need, and the number who had their need met. The number of Federal Work-Study Programs and/or part-time jobs and average earnings are listed, as well as the number of non-need-based awards. The *Average percent of need met* for those determined to have need, *Average financial aid package* awarded to undergraduates (the amount of scholarships, grants, work-study payments, or loans in the institutionally administered financial aid package divided by the number of students who received any financial aid-amounts used to pay the officially designated Expected Family Contribution (EFC), *Average need-based loan, Average need-based gift aid,* and *Average non-need-based aid* are given. *Average indebtedness upon graduation,* which is the average per-borrower indebtedness of the last graduating undergraduate class from amounts borrowed at this institution through any loan programs, excluding parent loans, is listed last.

APPLYING

Standardized Tests

The most commonly required standardized tests are the ACT®, SAT®, and SAT Subject Tests™. These and other standardized tests may be used for selective admission, as a basis for counseling or course placement, or for both purposes. This section notes if a test is used for admission or placement and whether it is required, required for some, or recommended. In addition to the ACT and SAT, the following standardized entrance and placement examinations are referred to by their initials: ABLE (Adult Basic Learning Examination); ACT ASSET (ACT Assessment of Skills for Successful Entry and Transfer); ACT PEP (ACT Proficiency Examination Program); CAT (California Achievement Tests); CELT (Comprehensive English Language Test); CPAt (Career Programs Assessment); CPT (Computerized Placement Test); DAT (Differential Aptitude Test); LSAT (Law School Admission Test); MAPS (Multiple Assessment Program Service); MCAT (Medical College Admission Test); MMPI (Minnesota Multiphasic Personality Inventory); OAT (Optometry Admission Test); PAA (Prueba de Aptitud Académica—Spanish-language version of SAT); PCAT (Pharmacy College Admission Test); PSAT/NMSQT® (Preliminary SAT/National Merit Scholarship Qualifying Test); SCAT (Scholastic College Aptitude Test); TABE (Test of Adult Basic Education); TASP (Texas Academic Skills Program); TOEFL® (Test of English as a Foreign Language); WPCT (Washington Pre-College Test).

Options: This includes the following: Early admission—(highly qualified students may matriculate before graduating from high school); Early action—admission plan that allows students to apply and be notified of an admission decision well in advance of the regular notification dates (if accepted, the candidate is not committed to enroll; students may reply to the offer under the college's regular reply policy); Deferred entrance—practice of permitting accepted students to postpone enrollment, usually for a period of one academic term or year; Early decision deadline—plan that permits students to apply and be notified of an admission decision (and financial aid offer, if applicable) well in advance of the regular notification date, and applicants agree to accept an offer of admission and to withdraw their applications from other colleges.

Application fee: The fee required with an application is noted.

Required, Required for some, and Recommended: Other application requirements are grouped into three categories and may include an essay, standardized test scores, a high school transcript, a minimum high school grade point average (expressed as a number on a scale of 0 to 4.0, where 4.0 equals A, 3.0 equals B, etc.), letters of recommendation, an interview on campus or with local alumni, and, for certain types of schools or programs, special requirements such as a musical audition or an art portfolio.

Application deadlines and notification: Admission application deadlines and dates for notification of acceptance or rejection are given either as specific dates or as rolling and continuous. Rolling means that applications are processed as they are received, and qualified students are accepted as long as there are openings. Continuous means that applicants are notified of acceptance or rejection as applications are processed up until the date indicated or the actual beginning of classes. The application deadline and the notification date for transfers are given if they differ from the dates for freshmen. Early decision and early action application deadlines and notification dates are also indicated when relevant.

CONTACT

The name, title, mailing address, and phone number of the person to contact for further information are given at the end of the profile. The fax number and e-mail address may also be provided.

Additional Information

Each school that has a College Close-Up and a half-page display in this guide will have a cross-reference with the page numbers of the half-page display and Close-Up.

COLLEGE CLOSE-UPS

The nearly 175 two-page descriptions provide an inside look at colleges and universities. The descriptions provide a wealth of information that is crucial in the college decision-making process—components such as tuition, financial aid, and major fields of study. Prepared exclusively by college officials, the descriptions are designed to help give students a better sense of the individuality of each institution, in terms that include campus environment, student activities, and lifestyle. The absence of any college or university does not constitute an editorial decision on the part of Peterson's. In essence, these descriptions are an open forum for colleges and universities, on a voluntary basis, to communicate their particular message to prospective college students. The colleges included have paid a fee to Peterson's to provide this information. The College Close-Ups are edited to provide a consistent format across entries for your ease of comparison.

INDEXES

Here you'll find easy-to-use breakdowns of schools' majors, entrance difficulty, and cost ranges. In addition, you'll find an "Advertisers Index," a "Geographical Listing of College Close-Ups," and an "Alphabetical Listing of Colleges and Universities."

ajors

his listing presents hundreds of undergraduate fields of study at are currently offered, according to the colleges' responses ı *Peterson's® Annual Survey of Undergraduate Institutions*. he majors appear in alphabetical order, each followed by an phabetical list of the schools that offer a bachelor's-level ogram in that particular field. Liberal Arts and Sciences/ iberal Studies indicates a general program with no specified ajor.

he terms used are those of the U.S. Department of Education lassification of Instructional Programs (CIP). Many institu- ons, however, use different terms. Although the term major used in this guide, some colleges may use other terms, such concentration, program of study, or field.

ntrance Difficulty

his listing groups colleges by their own assessment of their trance difficulty level. The colleges were asked to select the vel that most closely corresponds to their entrance difficulty. stitutions for which high school class rank and/or stan- ardized test scores do not apply as admission criteria were ked to select the level that best indicates their entrance diffi- ılty as compared to other institutions.

ost Ranges

olleges are grouped into ten price ranges, from under $2000 $30,000 and over.

ATA COLLECTION PROCEDURES

he data contained in the **PROFILES** and **INDEXES** sec- ons were researched between winter 2016 and spring 2017 rough *Peterson's® Annual Survey of Undergraduate Institu- ons*. Questionnaires were sent to the more than 4,500 col- ges and universities that met the outlined inclusion criteria. ll data included in this edition have been submitted by offi- ials (usually admissions and financial aid officers, registrars, institutional research personnel) at the colleges. Some of e institutions that submitted data were contacted directly by e Peterson's research staff to verify unusual figures, resolve iscrepancies, or obtain additional data. All usable infor- ation received in time for publication has been included. The mission of any particular item from the **PROFILES** and **NDEXES** sections signifies that the information is either not pplicable to that institution or not available. Because of eterson's comprehensive editorial review and because all aterial comes directly from college officials, we believe that e information presented is accurate. You should check with a pecific college or university at the time of application to verify such figures as tuition and fees, which may have changed since this guide's publication.

CRITERIA FOR INCLUSION IN THIS BOOK

The term "four-year college" is the commonly used designation for institutions that grant the baccalaureate degree. Four years is the expected amount of time required to earn this degree, although some bachelor's degree programs may be completed in three years, others require five years, and part-time programs may take considerably longer. Upper-level institutions offer only the junior and senior years and accept only students with two years of college-level credit. Therefore, "four-year college" is a conventional term that accurately describes most of the institutions included in this guide, but should not be taken literally in all cases.

To be included in this guide, an institution must have full accreditation or be a candidate for accreditation (preaccreditation) status by an institutional or specialized accrediting body recognized by the U.S. Department of Education or the Council for Higher Education Accreditation (CHEA). Institutional accrediting bodies, which review each institution as a whole, include the six regional associations of schools and colleges (Middle States, New England, North Central, Northwest, Southern, and Western), each of which is responsible for a specified portion of the United States and its territories. Other institutional accrediting bodies are national in scope and accredit specific kinds of institutions (e.g., Bible colleges, independent colleges, and rabbinical and Talmudic schools). Program registration by the New York State Board of Regents is considered to be the equivalent of institutional accreditation, since the board requires that all programs offered by an institution meet its standards before recognition is granted. A Canadian institution must be chartered and authorized to grant degrees by the provincial government, affiliated with a chartered institution, or accredited by a recognized U.S. accrediting body. This guide also includes institutions outside the United States that are accredited by these U.S. accrediting bodies. There are recognized specialized or professional accrediting bodies in more than forty different fields, each of which is authorized to accredit institutions or specific programs in its particular field. For specialized institutions that offer programs in one field only, we designate this to be the equivalent of institutional accreditation. A full explanation of the accrediting process and complete information on recognized, institutional (regional and national) and specialized accrediting bodies can be found online at www.chea.org or at www2.ed.gov/admins/finaid/accred/index.html.

NOTICE: Certain portions of or information contained in this book have been submitted and paid for by the educational institution identified, and such institutions take full responsibility for the accuracy, timeliness, completeness and functionality of such content. Such portions or information include (i) each display ad in the "Profiles" section from pages 55 through 1272 that comprises a half or full page of information covering a single educational institution, and (ii) each two-page description in the "College Close-Up" section from pages 1273 through 1606.

Institutional Changes Since *Peterson's®* *Four-Year Colleges* 2017

The following is an alphabetical listing of institutions that have closed, merged with other institutions, or changed their names or status since *Peterson's®* *Four-Year Colleges 2017*.

Alliant International University–México City (Mexico City, Mexico): *closed.*
Allied American University (Laguna Hills, CA): *closed.*
American National University (Canton, OH): *closed.*
American National University (Cincinnati, OH): *closed.*
American National University (Cleveland, OH): *closed.*
American National University (Columbus, OH): *closed.*
American National University (Stow, OH): *closed.*
Argosy University, Washington DC (Arlington, VA): *name changed to Argosy University, Northern Virginia.*
The Art Institute of Charlotte, a campus of South University (Charlotte, NC): *name changed to The Art Institute of Charlotte, a branch of Miami International University of Art & Design.*
The Art Institute of Dallas, a campus of South University (Dallas, TX): *name changed to The Art Institute of Dallas, a branch of Miami International University of Art & Design.*
The Art Institute of Raleigh-Durham, a campus of South University (Durham, NC): *name changed to The Art Institute of Raleigh-Durham, a branch of Miami International University of Art & Design.*
The Art Institutes International Minnesota (Minneapolis, MN): *closed.*
Berkeley College (Woodland Park, NJ): *name changed to Berkeley College–Woodland Park Campus.*
Blessing-Rieman College of Nursing (Quincy, IL): *name changed to Blessing-Rieman College of Nursing & Health Sciences.*
Broadview University–Boise (Meridian, ID): *closed.*
Broadview University–Layton (Layton, UT): *closed.*
Brooks Institute (Ventura, CA): *closed.*
Brown Mackie College–Birmingham (Birmingham, AL): *closed.*
Brown Mackie College–Dallas/Ft. Worth (Bedford, TX): *closed.*
Brown Mackie College–San Antonio (San Antonio, TX): *closed.*
Burlington College (Burlington, VT): *closed.*
Cabrini College (Radnor, PA): *name changed to Cabrini University.*
California Maritime Academy (Vallejo, CA): *name changed to California State University Maritime Academy.*
Calvary Bible College and Theological Seminary (Kansas City, MO): *name changed to Calvary University.*
Career Point College (San Antonio, TX): *closed.*
Castleton State College (Castleton, VT): *name changed to Castleton University.*
Centenary College (Hackettstown, NJ): *name changed to Centenary University.*
Colorado Heights University (Denver, CO): *closed.*
Colorado Technical University Denver South (Aurora, CO): *name changed to Colorado Technical University Aurora.*
The Criswell College (Dallas, TX): *name changed to Criswell College.*
Daniel Webster College (Nashua, NH): *merged into Southern New Hampshire University (Manchester, NH).*
DeVry College of New York (New York, NY): *name changed to DeVry College of New York–Midtown Manhattan Campus.*
DeVry University (Mesa, AZ): *now a DeVry University center and no longer profiled separately.*
DeVry University (Phoenix, AZ): *name changed to DeVry University–Phoenix Campus.*
DeVry University (Alhambra, CA): *closed.*
DeVry University (Anaheim, CA): *now a DeVry University center and no longer profiled separately.*
DeVry University (Bakersfield, CA): *now a DeVry University center and no longer profiled separately.*
DeVry University (Fremont, CA): *name changed to DeVry University–Fremont Campus.*
DeVry University (Long Beach, CA): *name changed to DeVry University–Long Beach Campus.*
DeVry University (Oakland, CA): *now a DeVry University center and no longer profiled separately.*
DeVry University (Oxnard, CA): *closed.*
DeVry University (Palmdale, CA): *now a DeVry University center and no longer profiled separately.*
DeVry University (Pomona, CA): *name changed to DeVry University–Pomona Campus.*
DeVry University (San Diego, CA): *name changed to DeVry University–San Diego Campus.*
DeVry University (Sherman Oaks, CA): *name changed to DeVry University–Sherman Oaks Campus.*
DeVry University (Colorado Springs, CO): *now a DeVry University center and no longer profiled separately.*
DeVry University (Westminster, CO): *name changed to DeVry University–Westminster Campus.*
DeVry University (Jacksonville, FL): *name changed to DeVry University–Jacksonville Campus.*
DeVry University (Miramar, FL): *name changed to DeVry University–Miramar Campus.*
DeVry University (Orlando, FL): *name changed to DeVry University–Orlando Campus.*
DeVry University (Alpharetta, GA): *name changed to DeVry University–Alpharetta Campus.*
DeVry University (Atlanta, GA): *now a DeVry University center and no longer profiled separately.*
DeVry University (Decatur, GA): *name changed to DeVry University–Decatur Campus.*
DeVry University (Duluth, GA): *now a DeVry University center and no longer profiled separately.*
DeVry University (Addison, IL): *name changed to DeVry University–Addison Campus.*
DeVry University (Chicago, IL): *name changed to DeVry University–Chicago Campus.*
DeVry University (Downers Grove, IL): *now a DeVry University center and no longer profiled separately.*
DeVry University (Elgin, IL): *now a DeVry University center and no longer profiled separately.*
DeVry University (Gurnee, IL): *now a DeVry University center and no longer profiled separately.*
DeVry University (Naperville, IL): *now a DeVry University center and no longer profiled separately.*
DeVry University (Tinley Park, IL): *name changed to DeVry University–Tinley Park Campus.*
DeVry University (Merrillville, IN): *now a DeVry University center and no longer profiled separately.*
DeVry University (Bethesda, MD): *closed.*
DeVry University (Kansas City, MO): *name changed to DeVry University–Kansas City Campus.*
DeVry University (Charlotte, NC): *name changed to DeVry University–Charlotte Campus.*

Institutional Changes Since Peterson's® Four-Year Colleges 2017

DeVry University (North Brunswick, NJ): *name changed to DeVry University–North Brunswick Campus.*

DeVry University (Paramus, NJ): *now a DeVry University center and no longer profiled separately.*

DeVry University (Henderson, NV): *name changed to DeVry University–Henderson Campus.*

DeVry University (Columbus, OH): *name changed to DeVry University–Columbus Campus.*

DeVry University (Seven Hills, OH): *name changed to DeVry University–Seven Hills Campus.*

DeVry University (Oklahoma City, OK): *name changed to DeVry University–Oklahoma City Campus.*

DeVry University (Fort Washington, PA): *name changed to DeVry University–Ft. Washington Campus.*

DeVry University (King of Prussia, PA): *closed.*

DeVry University (Philadelphia, PA): *now a DeVry University center and no longer profiled separately.*

DeVry University (Nashville, TN): *name changed to DeVry University–Nashville Campus.*

DeVry University (Austin, TX): *name changed toDeVry University–Austin Campus.*

DeVry University (Irving, TX): *name changed to DeVry University–Irving Campus.*

DeVry University (San Antonio, TX): *name changed to DeVry University–San Antonio Campus.*

DeVry University (Sandy, UT): *closed.*

DeVry University (Arlington, VA): *name changed to DeVry University–Arlington Campus.*

DeVry University (Chesapeake, VA): *name changed to DeVry University–Chesapeake Campus.*

DeVry University (Manassas, VA): *closed.*

Doane College (Crete, NE): *name changed to Doane University.*

Dowling College (Oakdale, NY): *closed.*

ECPI University (Lake Mary, FL): *merged into a single entry for ECPI University (Virginia Beach, VA).*

ECPI University (Raleigh, NC): *merged into a single entry for ECPI University (Virginia Beach, VA).*

ECPI University (Glen Allen, VA): *merged into a single entry for ECPI University (Virginia Beach, VA).*

ECPI University (Manassas, VA): *merged into a single entry for ECPI University (Virginia Beach, VA).*

ECPI University (Newport News, VA): *merged into a single entry for ECPI University (Virginia Beach, VA).*

Ellis University (Oakbrook Terrace, IL): *closed.*

Everest University (Jacksonville, FL): *closed.*

Everest University (Lakeland, FL): *closed.*

Everest University (Largo, FL): *closed.*

Everest University (Melbourne, FL): *closed.*

Everest University (Orlando, FL): *closed.*

Everest University (Pompano Beach, FL): *closed.*

Ex'pression College for Digital Arts (Emeryville, CA): *name changed to SAE Expression College.*

Globe Institute of Technology (New York, NY): *closed.*

Globe University–Appleton (Grand Chute, WI): *closed.*

Globe University–Eau Claire (Eau Claire, WI): *closed.*

Globe University–Green Bay (Bellevue, WI): *closed.*

Globe University–La Crosse (Onalaska, WI): *closed.*

Globe University–Madison East (Madison, WI): *closed.*

Globe University–Madison West (Middleton, WI): *closed.*

Globe University–Sioux Falls (Sioux Falls, SD): *closed.*

Globe University–Wausau (Rothschild, WI): *closed.*

Hillsdale Free Will Baptist College (Moore, OK): *name changed to Randall University.*

Iowa Wesleyan College (Mount Pleasant, IA): *name changed to Iowa Wesleyan University.*

ITT Technical Institute (Tempe, AZ): *closed.*

ITT Technical Institute (Clovis, CA): *closed.*

ITT Technical Institute (Concord, CA): *closed.*

ITT Technical Institute (Corona, CA): *closed.*

ITT Technical Institute (Deerfield Beach, FL): *closed.*

ITT Technical Institute (West Palm Beach, FL): *closed.*

ITT Technical Institute (Douglasville, GA): *closed.*

ITT Technical Institute (Springfield, IL): *closed.*ITT Technical Institute (Indianapolis, IN): *closed.*

ITT Technical Institute (Lexington, KY): *closed.*

ITT Technical Institute (Hanover, MD): *closed.*

ITT Technical Institute (Madison, MS): *closed.*

ITT Technical Institute (Charlotte, NC): *closed.*

ITT Technical Institute (Durham, NC): *closed.*

ITT Technical Institute (Oklahoma City, OK): *closed.*

ITT Technical Institute (Salem, OR): *closed.*

Lakehead University–Orillia (Orillia, ON, Canada): *merged into a single entry for Lakehead University (Thunder Bay, ON) by request from the institution.*

Lakeland College (Sheboygan, WI): *name changed to Lakeland University.*

Laurel University (High Point, NC): *name changed to John Wesley University.*

Mary Baldwin College (Staunton, VA): *name changed to Mary Baldwin University.*

The Master's College and Seminary (Santa Clarita, CA): *name changed to The Master's University.*

Mater Ecclesiae College (Greenville, RI): *closed.*

Minnesota School of Business–Blaine (Blaine, MN): *closed.*

Minnesota School of Business–Elk River (Elk River, MN): *closed.*

Minnesota School of Business–Lakeville (Lakeville, MN): *closed.*

Minnesota School of Business–Richfield (Richfield, MN): *closed.*

Minnesota School of Business–Rochester (Rochester, MN): *closed.*

Minnesota School of Business–St. Cloud (Waite Park, MN): *closed.*

National American University (Denver, CO): *closed.*

Northwood University, Texas Campus (Cedar Hill, TX): *merged into a single entry for Northwood University, Michigan Campus (Midland, MI) by request from the institution.*

Oregon College of Art & Craft (Portland, OR): *name changed to Oregon College of Art and Craft.*

Our Lady of Holy Cross College (New Orleans, LA): *name changed to University of Holy Cross.*

Pioneer Pacific College–Eugene/Springfield Branch (Springfield, OR): *merged into a single entry for Pioneer Pacific College (Wilsonville, OR).*

Purdue University Northwest (Westville, IN): *merged into a single entry for Purdue University Northwest (Hammond, IN) by request from the institution.*

Rasmussen College Appleton (Appleton, WI): *merged into Rasmussen College Green Bay (Green Bay, WI).*

St. Catharine College (St. Catharine, KY): *closed.*

Saint Joseph's College (Rensselaer, IN): *closed.*

Santa Fe University of Art and Design (Santa Fe, NM): *closed.*

School of the Museum of Fine Arts, Boston (Boston, MA): *merged as a unit into Tufts University (Medford, MA).*

Skyline College (Roanoke, VA): *closed.*

Summit University (Clarks Summit, PA): *name changed to Clarks Summit University.*

Tennessee Wesleyan College (Athens, TN): *name changed to Tennessee Wesleyan University.*

Truett-McConnell College (Cleveland, GA): *name changed to Truett McConnell University.*

The University of Montana (Missoula, MT): *name changed to University of Montana.*

Waldorf College (Forest City, IA): *name changed to Waldorf University.*

Profiles

NOTICE: Certain portions of or information contained in this book have been submitted and paid for by the educational institution identified, and such institutions take full responsibility for the accuracy, timeliness, completeness and functionality of such content. Such portions or information include (i) each display ad in the "Profiles" section from pages 55 through 1271 that comprises a half or full page of information covering a single educational institution, and (ii) each two-page description in the "College Close-Up" section from pages 1273 through 1610.

A ★ indicates that the school has detailed information with a Premium Profile on Petersons.com.

U.S. AND U.S. TERRITORIES

ALABAMA

Alabama Agricultural and Mechanical University

Huntsville, Alabama

http://www.aamu.edu/

CONTACT
Dr. Evelyn Ellis, Interim Director of Admissions, Alabama Agricultural and Mechanical University, 4900 Meridian Street, Huntsville, AL 35811. *Phone:* 256-372-5245. *Toll-free phone:* 800-553-0816. *Fax:* 256-851-9747.

Alabama State University

Montgomery, Alabama

http://www.alasu.edu/

- **State-supported** comprehensive, founded 1867, part of Alabama Commission on Higher Education
- **Urban** 172-acre campus
- **Endowment** $86.5 million
- **Coed** 4,727 undergraduate students, 92% full-time, 62% women, 38% men
- **Minimally difficult** entrance level, 46% of applicants were admitted

UNDERGRAD STUDENTS
4,368 full-time, 359 part-time. Students come from 40 states and territories; 26 other countries; 34% are from out of state; 93% Black or African American, non-Hispanic/Latino; 1% Hispanic/Latino; 0.3% Asian, non-Hispanic/Latino; 0.1% American Indian or Alaska Native, non-Hispanic/Latino; 1% Two or more races, non-Hispanic/Latino; 1% Race/ethnicity unknown; 2% international; 3% transferred in; 34% live on campus.

Freshmen:
Admission: 9,053 applied, 4,155 admitted, 1,163 enrolled. ***Average high school GPA:*** 2.8. ***Test scores:*** SAT critical reading scores over 500: 13%; SAT math scores over 500: 17%; ACT scores over 18: 46%; SAT critical reading scores over 600: 3%; SAT math scores over 600: 4%; ACT scores over 24: 8%.
Retention: 62% of full-time freshmen returned.

FACULTY
Total: 403, 62% full-time, 47% with terminal degrees.
Student/faculty ratio: 17:1.

ACADEMICS
Calendar: semesters. *Degrees:* certificates, bachelor's, master's, doctoral, post-master's, and postbachelor's certificates.
Special study options: academic remediation for entering students, advanced placement credit, cooperative education, distance learning, double majors, freshman honors college, honors programs, independent study, internships, part-time degree program, student-designed majors, summer session for credit. ***ROTC:*** Army (c), Air Force (b).
Computers: 541 computers/terminals and 1,082 ports are available on campus for general student use. Students can access the following: computer help desk, free student e-mail accounts, online (class) grades, online (class) registration, online (class) schedules. Campuswide network is available. Wireless service is available via entire campus.
Library: Levi Watkins Learning Center plus 1 other. *Books:* 435,092 (physical), 69,699 (digital/electronic); *Serial titles:* 1,607 (physical), 4,986 (digital/electronic); *Databases:* 171. Weekly public service hours: 50; study areas open 24 hours, 5-7 days a week; students can reserve study rooms.

STUDENT LIFE
Housing options: men-only, women-only, special housing for students with disabilities. Campus housing is university owned.
Activities and organizations: drama/theater group, student-run newspaper, radio station, choral group, marching band, Alpha Kappa Alpha Sorority Inc, Empower Ministry, Nu Alpha Nu Service Fraternity Inc, Gamma Sigma Sigma National Service Sorority Inc, Delta Sigma Theta Sorority Inc, national fraternities, national sororities.
Athletics Member NCAA. All Division I. ***Intercollegiate sports:*** baseball M(s), basketball M(s)/W(s), bowling W(s), cheerleading M(s)/W(s), cross-country running M(s)/W(s), football M(s), golf M(s)/W(s), soccer W(s), softball W(s), tennis M(s)/W(s), track and field M(s)/W(s), volleyball W(s). ***Intramural sports:*** basketball M, football M.
Campus security: 24-hour emergency response devices and patrols, late-night transport/escort service, self-defense education, well-lit campus.
Student services: health clinic, personal/psychological counseling.

COSTS & FINANCIAL AID
Costs (2017–18) ***One-time required fee:*** $150. ***Tuition:*** state resident $6936 full-time, $289 per credit hour part-time; nonresident $13,872 full-time, $578 per credit hour part-time. Full-time tuition and fees vary according to class time, course level, course load, degree level, program, and student level. Part-time tuition and fees vary according to class time, course level, course load, degree level, program, and student level. ***Required fees:*** $2284 full-time, $446 per credit hour part-time. ***Room and board:*** $5422; room only: $3346. Room and board charges vary according to board plan and housing facility. ***Payment plan:*** deferred payment. ***Waivers:*** employees or children of employees.
Financial Aid Of all full-time matriculated undergraduates who enrolled in 2016, 4,206 applied for aid, 4,095 were judged to have need, 1,975 had their need fully met. 570 Federal Work-Study jobs (averaging $1896). 506 state and other part-time jobs (averaging $649). In 2016, 88 non-need-based awards were made. ***Average percent of need met:*** 81. ***Average financial aid package:*** $19,409. ***Average need-based loan:*** $3976. ***Average need-based gift aid:*** $5114. ***Average non-need-based aid:*** $8833. ***Average indebtedness upon graduation:*** $32,487.

APPLYING
Standardized Tests *Required:* SAT or ACT (for admission).
Options: electronic application, early admission, deferred entrance.
Application fee: $25.
Required: high school transcript, minimum 2.0 GPA.
Recommended: essay or personal statement, interview.
Application deadlines: 7/31 (freshmen), 7/31 (transfers).
Notification: continuous (freshmen), continuous (transfers).

CONTACT
Dr. William E. Smith, Director of Admissions and Recruitment, Alabama State University, 915 South Jackson Street, Montgomery, AL 36101-0271. *Phone:* 334-229-4291. *Toll-free phone:* 800-253-5037. *Fax:* 334-229-4984. *E-mail:* wesmith@alasu.edu.

Amridge University

Montgomery, Alabama

http://www.amridgeuniversity.edu/

- **Independent** university, founded 1967, affiliated with Church of Christ
- **Urban** 10-acre campus
- **Endowment** $2.1 million
- **Coed** 315 undergraduate students, 54% full-time, 57% women, 43% men
- **Minimally difficult** entrance level

UNDERGRAD STUDENTS
171 full-time, 144 part-time. Students come from 48 states and territories; 50% are from out of state; 39% Black or African American, non-Hispanic/Latino; 2% Hispanic/Latino; 0.3% Asian, non-Hispanic/Latino; 0.3% Native Hawaiian or other Pacific Islander, non-Hispanic/Latino; 0.6% American Indian or Alaska Native, non-Hispanic/Latino; 25% Race/ethnicity unknown.

Freshmen:
Admission: 7 enrolled.

FACULTY
Total: 64, 59% full-time, 70% with terminal degrees.
Student/faculty ratio: 10:1.

ACADEMICS
Calendar: semesters. *Degrees:* associate, bachelor's, master's, and doctoral.
Special study options: academic remediation for entering students, accelerated degree program, adult/continuing education programs, advanced placement credit, distance learning, double majors, external degree program, independent study, internships, part-time degree program, services for LD students, summer session for credit.
Computers: 5 computers/terminals are available on campus for general student use. Students can access the following: computer help desk, free student e-mail accounts, online (class) grades, online (class) registration, online (class) schedules. Campuswide network is available. Wireless service is available via entire campus.
Library: Southern Christian University Library.

STUDENT LIFE
Housing options: college housing not available.
Activities and organizations: Amridge University Student Advisory Committee.
Campus security: 24-hour emergency response devices, security guards.

COSTS & FINANCIAL AID
Costs (2016–17) ***Tuition:*** $9960 full-time, $430 per semester hour part-time. Full-time tuition and fees vary according to course load, program, and student level. Part-time tuition and fees vary according to course load, program, and student level. No tuition increase for student's term of enrollment. ***Required fees:*** $900 full-time, $40 per semester hour part-time, $110 per term part-time. ***Payment plans:*** tuition prepayment, installment. ***Waivers:*** employees or children of employees.
Financial Aid Of all full-time matriculated undergraduates who enrolled in 2016, 131 applied for aid, 129 were judged to have need, 96 had their need fully met. ***Average financial aid package:*** $9097. ***Average need-based loan:*** $5280. ***Average need-based gift aid:*** $2804. ***Average indebtedness upon graduation:*** $11,179.

APPLYING
Standardized Tests *Required for some:* SAT or ACT (for admission).
Options: electronic application, early admission.
Application fee: $50.
Required: high school transcript, minimum 2.0 GPA.
Application deadlines: rolling (freshmen), rolling (transfers).

CONTACT
Amridge University, 1200 Taylor Road, Montgomery, AL 36117.
Phone: 334-387-3877 Ext. 7528. *Toll-free phone:* 888-790-8080.

See page 1278 for the College Close-Up.

Athens State University

Athens, Alabama

http://www.athens.edu/

- **State-supported** upper-level, founded 1822
- **Small-town** 45-acre campus
- **Coed** 3,025 undergraduate students, 40% full-time, 66% women, 34% men
- **Noncompetitive** entrance level

UNDERGRAD STUDENTS
1,212 full-time, 1,813 part-time. Students come from 23 states and territories; 1 other country; 4% are from out of state; 13% Black or African American, non-Hispanic/Latino; 2% Hispanic/Latino; 0.8% Asian, non-Hispanic/Latino; 0.1% Native Hawaiian or other Pacific Islander, non-Hispanic/Latino; 1% American Indian or Alaska Native, non-Hispanic/Latino; 2% Two or more races, non-Hispanic/Latino; 3% Race/ethnicity unknown; 0.1% international; 21% transferred in.

FACULTY
Total: 184, 44% full-time, 34% with terminal degrees.
Student/faculty ratio: 17:1.

ACADEMICS
Calendar: semesters. *Degrees:* certificates, bachelor's, and master's.
Special study options: adult/continuing education programs, advanced placement credit, cooperative education, distance learning, double majors, independent study, internships, off-campus study, part-time degree program, study abroad, summer session for credit.
Computers: 210 computers/terminals are available on campus for general student use. Students can access the following: online (class) grades, online (class) schedules, transcripts, e-mail. Campuswide network is available. Wireless service is available via entire campus.
Library: Athens State University Library.

STUDENT LIFE
Housing options: college housing not available.
Activities and organizations: drama/theater group, student-run newspaper, national sororities.
Student services: personal/psychological counseling.

COSTS & FINANCIAL AID
Costs (2016–17) ***Tuition:*** state resident $5730 full-time; nonresident $11,460 full-time. ***Required fees:*** $750 full-time. ***Payment plan:*** installment. ***Waivers:*** senior citizens and employees or children of employees.
Financial Aid Of all full-time matriculated undergraduates who enrolled in 2015, 1,073 applied for aid, 978 were judged to have need, 21 had their need fully met. In 2015, 3 non-need-based awards were made. ***Average percent of need met:*** 2. ***Average financial aid package:*** $8599. ***Average need-based loan:*** $2925. ***Average need-based gift aid:*** $2976. ***Average non-need-based aid:*** $2060.

APPLYING
Options: electronic application, deferred entrance.
Application fee: $30.
Notification: continuous (transfers).

CONTACT
Athens State University, 300 North Beaty Street, Athens, AL 35611.
Phone: 256-233-8151. *Toll-free phone:* 800-522-0272.

Auburn University

Auburn University, Alabama

http://www.auburn.edu/

- **State-supported** university, founded 1856
- **Small-town** 1875-acre campus with easy access to Atlanta, Birmingham
- **Endowment** $627.7 million
- **Coed** 22,658 undergraduate students, 90% full-time, 49% women, 51% men
- **Moderately difficult** entrance level, 81% of applicants were admitted

UNDERGRAD STUDENTS
20,396 full-time, 2,262 part-time. Students come from 51 states and territories; 62 other countries; 34% are from out of state; 7% Black or African American, non-Hispanic/Latino; 3% Hispanic/Latino; 2% Asian, non-Hispanic/Latino; 0.5% American Indian or Alaska Native, non-Hispanic/Latino; 1% Two or more races, non-Hispanic/Latino; 0.6% Race/ethnicity unknown; 5% international; 5% transferred in; 20% live on campus.

Freshmen:
Admission: 18,256 applied, 14,704 admitted, 4,529 enrolled. ***Average high school GPA:*** 3.85. ***Test scores:*** SAT critical reading scores over 500: 89%; SAT math scores over 500: 89%; SAT writing scores over 500: 82%; ACT scores over 18: 100%; SAT critical reading scores over 600: 35%; SAT math scores over 600: 44%; SAT writing scores over 600: 30%; ACT scores over 24: 84%; SAT critical reading scores over 700: 8%; SAT math scores over 700: 12%; SAT writing scores over 700: 5%; ACT scores over 30: 32%.
Retention: 91% of full-time freshmen returned.

FACULTY
Total: 1,448, 87% full-time, 88% with terminal degrees.
Student/faculty ratio: 19:1.

ACADEMICS
Calendar: semesters. *Degrees:* bachelor's, master's, doctoral, post-master's, and postbachelor's certificates.

Special study options: accelerated degree program, adult/continuing education programs, advanced placement credit, cooperative education, distance learning, double majors, English as a second language, freshman honors college, honors programs, independent study, internships, off-campus study, part-time degree program, services for LD students, study abroad, summer session for credit. ***ROTC:*** Army (b), Navy (b), Air Force (b).

Unusual degree programs: 3-2 engineering.

Computers: 1,722 computers/terminals are available on campus for general student use. Students can access the following: computer help desk, free student e-mail accounts, online (class) grades, online (class) registration, bursar payments, course materials. Campuswide network is available. 100% of college-owned or -operated housing units are wired for high-speed Internet access. Wireless service is available via entire campus.

Library: R. B. Draughon Library plus 3 others. *Books:* 4.5 million (physical), 998,420 (digital/electronic); *Serial titles:* 76,117 (physical), 81,492 (digital/electronic). Study areas open 24 hours, 5-7 days a week.

STUDENT LIFE
Housing options: coed, men-only, women-only, special housing for students with disabilities. Campus housing is university owned.

Activities and organizations: drama/theater group, student-run newspaper, radio and television station, choral group, marching band, Student Government Association, University Program Council, IMPACT (volunteer opportunities), International Student Organization, student media (AU Plainsman newspaper, WEGL radio, Glomerata yearbook, Eagle Eye television, AU Circle literary journal), national fraternities, national sororities.

Athletics Member NCAA. All Division I except football (Division I-A). ***Intercollegiate sports:*** baseball M(s), basketball M(s)/W(s), cheerleading M/W, cross-country running M(s)/W(s), equestrian sports W(s), golf M(s)/W(s), gymnastics W(s), soccer W(s), softball W(s), swimming and diving M(s)/W(s), tennis M(s)/W(s), track and field M(s)/W(s), volleyball W(s). ***Intramural sports:*** basketball M/W, crew M(c)/W(c), football M, golf M/W, ice hockey M(c)/W(c), lacrosse M(c)/W(c), racquetball M/W, rugby M(c), sailing M(c)/W(c), sand volleyball M(c)/W(c), skiing (downhill) M(c)/W(c), soccer M/W, softball M/W, swimming and diving M/W, table tennis M/W, tennis M/W, track and field M/W, ultimate Frisbee M/W, volleyball M/W, water polo M(c)/W(c), wrestling M(c)/W(c).

Campus security: 24-hour emergency response devices and patrols, late-night transport/escort service, controlled dormitory access.

Student services: health clinic, personal/psychological counseling.

COSTS & FINANCIAL AID
Costs (2016–17) ***Tuition:*** state resident $9072 full-time, $378 per semester hour part-time; nonresident $27,216 full-time, $1134 per semester hour part-time. Full-time tuition and fees vary according to program and reciprocity agreements. Part-time tuition and fees vary according to course load, program, and reciprocity agreements. ***Required fees:*** $1624 full-time, $812 per term part-time. ***Room and board:*** $12,898; room only: $7538. Room and board charges vary according to board plan and housing facility. ***Payment plan:*** installment. ***Waivers:*** employees or children of employees.

Financial Aid Of all full-time matriculated undergraduates who enrolled in 2015, 12,895 applied for aid, 7,074 were judged to have need, 893 had their need fully met. 189 Federal Work-Study jobs (averaging $4115). In 2015, 4270 non-need-based awards were made. ***Average percent of need met:*** 45. ***Average financial aid package:*** $10,411. ***Average need-based loan:*** $4594. ***Average need-based gift aid:*** $7690. ***Average non-need-based aid:*** $7083. ***Average indebtedness upon graduation:*** $28,170.

APPLYING
Standardized Tests *Required:* SAT or ACT (for admission).

Options: electronic application, early admission, early action.

Application fee: $50.

Required: essay or personal statement, high school transcript, minimum 2.0 GPA. ***Required for some:*** minimum 3.0 GPA. ***Recommended:*** minimum 3.0 GPA.

Application deadlines: 1/15 (freshmen), 6/1 (transfers), 10/1 (early action).

Notification: 2/1 (freshmen), 2/1 (out-of-state freshmen), continuous (transfers), 10/15 (early action).

CONTACT
Ms. Cindy Singley, Director, University Recruitment, Auburn University, Auburn University, AL 36849. *Phone:* 334-844-4080. *Toll-free phone:* 800-AUBURN9. *E-mail:* admissions@auburn.edu.

Auburn University at Montgomery
Montgomery, Alabama
http://www.aum.edu/

- **State-supported** comprehensive, founded 1967, part of Auburn University
- **Urban** 500-acre campus
- **Coed** 4,273 undergraduate students, 72% full-time, 64% women, 36% men
- **Moderately difficult** entrance level, 77% of applicants were admitted

UNDERGRAD STUDENTS
3,095 full-time, 1,178 part-time. Students come from 33 states and territories; 38 other countries; 6% are from out of state; 36% Black or African American, non-Hispanic/Latino; 1% Hispanic/Latino; 2% Asian, non-Hispanic/Latino; 0.1% Native Hawaiian or other Pacific Islander, non-Hispanic/Latino; 0.6% American Indian or Alaska Native, non-Hispanic/Latino; 3% Two or more races, non-Hispanic/Latino; 0.6% Race/ethnicity unknown; 4% international; 11% transferred in; 24% live on campus.

Freshmen:
Admission: 2,905 applied, 2,225 admitted, 594 enrolled. ***Average high school GPA:*** 3.3. ***Test scores:*** ACT scores over 18: 100%; ACT scores over 24: 26%.

Retention: 66% of full-time freshmen returned.

FACULTY
Total: 320, 68% full-time.

Student/faculty ratio: 15:1.

ACADEMICS
Calendar: semesters. *Degrees:* bachelor's, master's, doctoral, and post-master's certificates.

Special study options: academic remediation for entering students, advanced placement credit, cooperative education, distance learning, double majors, English as a second language, honors programs, independent study, internships, off-campus study, part-time degree program, services for LD students, study abroad, summer session for credit. ***ROTC:*** Army (b), Air Force (c).

Computers: 600 computers/terminals are available on campus for general student use. Students can access the following: computer help desk, free student e-mail accounts, online (class) grades, online (class) registration, online (class) schedules. Campuswide network is available. 100% of college-owned or -operated housing units are wired for high-speed Internet access. Wireless service is available via entire campus.

Library: Auburn University at Montgomery Library. *Books:* 340,819 (physical). Weekly public service hours: 86; students can reserve study rooms.

STUDENT LIFE
Housing options: coed, special housing for students with disabilities. Campus housing is university owned.

Activities and organizations: drama/theater group, student-run newspaper, television station, choral group, Student Government Association, Campus Activities Board, Panhellenic Association, Accounting Club, national fraternities, national sororities.

Athletics Member NCAA. All Division II. ***Intercollegiate sports:*** baseball M(s), basketball M(s)/W(s), cheerleading M(s)/W(s), cross-country running M(s)/W(s), soccer M(s)/W(s), softball W(s), tennis M(s)/W(s). ***Intramural sports:*** archery M(c)/W(c), badminton M/W, basketball M/W, football M/W, golf M(c)/W(c), soccer M/W, softball M/W, table tennis M/W, tennis M/W, ultimate Frisbee M/W, volleyball M/W.

Campus security: 24-hour emergency response devices and patrols, student patrols, late-night transport/escort service, controlled dormitory access, personal safety and emergency preparedness seminars.

Student services: health clinic, personal/psychological counseling.

COSTS & FINANCIAL AID

Costs (2016–17) ***Tuition:*** state resident $8880 full-time, $296 per credit hour part-time; nonresident $19,950 full-time, $665 per credit hour part-time. Full-time tuition and fees vary according to course load and degree level. Part-time tuition and fees vary according to course load and degree level. ***Required fees:*** $760 full-time, $10 per credit hour part-time, $230 per term part-time. ***Room and board:*** $5650; room only: $4450. Room and board charges vary according to housing facility. ***Payment plan:*** installment. ***Waivers:*** senior citizens and employees or children of employees.

Financial Aid Of all full-time matriculated undergraduates who enrolled in 2015, 2,340 applied for aid, 2,049 were judged to have need, 243 had their need fully met. In 2015, 229 non-need-based awards were made. ***Average financial aid package:*** $6970. ***Average need-based loan:*** $3934. ***Average need-based gift aid:*** $4538. ***Average non-need-based aid:*** $6485. ***Average indebtedness upon graduation:*** $30,454.

APPLYING

Standardized Tests *Required:* SAT or ACT (for admission).

Options: electronic application, deferred entrance.

Required: high school transcript.

Application deadlines: rolling (freshmen), rolling (transfers).

Notification: continuous (freshmen), continuous (out-of-state freshmen), continuous (transfers).

CONTACT

Mr. Rahmel Cowen, Director of Admissions and Recruiting, Auburn University at Montgomery, PO Box 244023, Montgomery, AL 36124. *Phone:* 334-244-3615. *Toll-free phone:* 800-227-2649. *Fax:* 334-244-3795. *E-mail:* admissions@aum.edu.

★ Birmingham-Southern College

Birmingham, Alabama

http://www.bsc.edu/

CONTACT

Ms. Jennifer Waters, Director of Admission, Birmingham-Southern College, Box 549008, Birmingham, AL 35254. *Phone:* 205-226-4696. *Toll-free phone:* 800-523-5793. *Fax:* 205-226-3074. *E-mail:* jwaters@bsc.edu.

Columbia Southern University

Orange Beach, Alabama

http://www.columbiasouthern.edu/

- **Proprietary** comprehensive, founded 1993
- **Small-town** campus
- **Coed** 15,573 undergraduate students, 57% full-time, 37% women, 63% men
- **Noncompetitive** entrance level

UNDERGRAD STUDENTS

8,937 full-time, 6,636 part-time. Students come from 63 states and territories; 41 other countries; 93% are from out of state; 22% Black or African American, non-Hispanic/Latino; 7% Hispanic/Latino; 2% Asian, non-Hispanic/Latino; 0.2% Native Hawaiian or other Pacific Islander, non-Hispanic/Latino; 1% American Indian or Alaska Native, non-Hispanic/Latino; 3% Two or more races, non-Hispanic/Latino; 6% Race/ethnicity unknown; 13% transferred in.

Freshmen:

Admission: 351 enrolled.

FACULTY

Total: 458, 29% full-time, 62% with terminal degrees.

Student/faculty ratio: 70:1.

ACADEMICS

Calendar: Non-standard Term: 9-weeks of instruction, LifePace Learning: 10-week courses that are self-paced. *Degrees:* certificates, associate, bachelor's, master's, doctoral, and postbachelor's certificates (offers only distance learning degree programs).

Special study options: academic remediation for entering students, adult/continuing education programs, distance learning, off-campus study, part-time degree program, services for LD students.

Computers: Students can access the following: computer help desk, online (class) grades, online (class) registration, online (class) schedules, student portals for learning modules, policy updates, and other institutional information.

Library: CSU Online Library.

STUDENT LIFE

Housing options: college housing not available.

Activities and organizations: Student Veteran Association, American Criminal Justice Association, Delta Epsilon Tou (DET) - Alumni Honor Society.

COSTS

Costs (2017–18) ***One-time required fee:*** $135. ***Tuition:*** $5040 full-time, $220 per credit hour part-time. Full-time tuition and fees vary according to course load. Part-time tuition and fees vary according to course load. ***Payment plan:*** installment. ***Waivers:*** employees or children of employees.

APPLYING

Options: electronic application.

Required for some: high school transcript.

Application deadlines: rolling (freshmen), rolling (transfers).

CONTACT

Director of Admissions, Columbia Southern University, 21982 University Lane, Orange Beach, AL 36561. *Phone:* 251-981-3771. *Toll-free phone:* 800-977-8449. *Fax:* 251-224-0540. *E-mail:* admissions@columbiasouthern.edu.

Concordia College Alabama

Selma, Alabama

http://www.ccal.edu/

- **Independent Lutheran** 4-year, founded 1922, part of Concordia University System
- **Small-town** 59-acre campus with easy access to Birmingham
- **Coed**
- **Moderately difficult** entrance level

FACULTY

Student/faculty ratio: 19:1.

ACADEMICS

Calendar: semesters. *Degrees:* associate and bachelor's.

Library: Ellwinger-Hunt Learning Resource Center.

STUDENT LIFE

Housing options: coed. Campus housing is university owned. Freshman applicants given priority for college housing.

Activities and organizations: drama/theater group, student-run newspaper, choral group, marching band, Music Ensemble, Rotaract, Phi Theta Kappa, Spiritual Life, Red Cross, national fraternities.

Campus security: 24-hour patrols.

Student services: personal/psychological counseling.

FINANCIAL AID

Financial Aid Of all full-time matriculated undergraduates who enrolled in 2008, 800 applied for aid, 782 were judged to have need, 487 had their need fully met. 86 Federal Work-Study jobs (averaging $600). In 2008, 22 non-need-based awards were made. ***Average percent of need met:*** 92. ***Average financial aid package:*** $4410. ***Average need-based gift aid:*** $1500. ***Average non-need-based aid:*** $500. ***Average indebtedness upon graduation:*** $5500.

APPLYING

Standardized Tests *Recommended:* SAT or ACT (for admission).

Options: electronic application, deferred entrance.

Application fee: $10.

Required: high school transcript, minimum 2.0 GPA.

CONTACT
Ms. Phyllis Richardson, Director, STARRS, Concordia College Alabama, 1712 Broad Street, PO Box 2470-36702, Selma, AL 36701. *Phone:* 334-874-5700 Ext. 102. *Fax:* 334-874-5755. *E-mail:* prichardson@ccal.edu.

Faulkner University
Montgomery, Alabama
http://www.faulkner.edu/

- **Independent** university, founded 1942, affiliated with Church of Christ
- **Urban** 75-acre campus with easy access to Montgomery
- **Endowment** $18.9 million
- **Coed** 2,583 undergraduate students, 69% full-time, 60% women, 40% men
- **Minimally difficult** entrance level, 45% of applicants were admitted

UNDERGRAD STUDENTS
1,779 full-time, 804 part-time. Students come from 29 states and territories; 30 other countries; 13% are from out of state; 45% Black or African American, non-Hispanic/Latino; 2% Hispanic/Latino; 0.6% Asian, non-Hispanic/Latino; 0.2% Native Hawaiian or other Pacific Islander, non-Hispanic/Latino; 0.5% American Indian or Alaska Native, non-Hispanic/Latino; 2% Two or more races, non-Hispanic/Latino; 1% Race/ethnicity unknown; 2% international; 22% transferred in; 25% live on campus.

Freshmen:
Admission: 2,446 applied, 1,110 admitted, 314 enrolled. ***Average high school GPA:*** 3.23. ***Test scores:*** SAT critical reading scores over 500: 44%; SAT math scores over 500: 39%; SAT writing scores over 500: 39%; ACT scores over 18: 85%; SAT critical reading scores over 600: 17%; SAT math scores over 600: 22%; ACT scores over 24: 23%; SAT math scores over 700: 6%; ACT scores over 30: 6%.
Retention: 55% of full-time freshmen returned.

FACULTY
Total: 305, 39% full-time, 46% with terminal degrees.
Student/faculty ratio: 11:1.

ACADEMICS
Calendar: semesters. *Degrees:* associate, bachelor's, master's, and doctoral.
Special study options: academic remediation for entering students, accelerated degree program, adult/continuing education programs, advanced placement credit, distance learning, double majors, English as a second language, freshman honors college, honors programs, independent study, internships, off-campus study, part-time degree program, services for LD students, study abroad, summer session for credit. ***ROTC:*** Army (c), Air Force (c).
Computers: 496 computers/terminals and 4,205 ports are available on campus for general student use. Students can access the following: campus intranet, computer help desk, free student e-mail accounts, online (class) grades, online (class) registration, online (class) schedules, student account access. Campuswide network is available. 100% of college-owned or -operated housing units are wired for high-speed Internet access. Wireless service is available via entire campus.
Library: Gus Nichols Library System plus 4 others. *Books:* 282,460 (physical), 223,809 (digital/electronic); *Serial titles:* 1,563 (physical); *Databases:* 128. Weekly public service hours: 74.

STUDENT LIFE
Housing options: on-campus residence required through junior year; men-only, women-only, special housing for students with disabilities. Campus housing is university owned. Freshman campus housing is guaranteed.
Activities and organizations: drama/theater group, student-run newspaper, choral group, marching band, Student Government, Marching Band, Dinner Theatre, Acappella Chorus, Phi Lambda/Kappa Social Clubs.
Athletics Member NAIA. ***Intercollegiate sports:*** baseball M(s), basketball M(s)/W(s), cheerleading M(s)(c)/W(s)(c), football M(s), golf M(s)/W(s), soccer M(s)/W(s), softball W(s), volleyball W(s). ***Intramural sports:*** basketball M/W, bowling M/W, golf M/W, racquetball M/W, soccer M/W, softball M/W, table tennis M/W, ultimate Frisbee M/W, volleyball M/W.
Campus security: 24-hour emergency response devices and patrols, late-night transport/escort service, controlled dormitory access.
Student services: health clinic, personal/psychological counseling.

COSTS & FINANCIAL AID
Costs (2017–18) ***Comprehensive fee:*** $28,840 includes full-time tuition ($18,780), mandatory fees ($1810), and room and board ($8250). Full-time tuition and fees vary according to class time, course load, location, and program. Part-time tuition: $635 per semester hour. Part-time tuition and fees vary according to class time, course load, location, and program. ***Required fees:*** $320 per term part-time. ***College room only:*** $4300. Room and board charges vary according to board plan and housing facility. ***Payment plans:*** installment, deferred payment. ***Waivers:*** adult students and employees or children of employees.
Financial Aid Of all full-time matriculated undergraduates who enrolled in 2015, 253 applied for aid, 236 were judged to have need, 27 had their need fully met. In 2015, 24 non-need-based awards were made. ***Average percent of need met:*** 61. ***Average financial aid package:*** $14,006. ***Average need-based loan:*** $3064. ***Average need-based gift aid:*** $11,587. ***Average non-need-based aid:*** $6113. ***Average indebtedness upon graduation:*** $29,000. ***Financial aid deadline:*** 8/1.

APPLYING
Standardized Tests *Required for some:* SAT or ACT (for admission).
Options: electronic application, early admission, deferred entrance.
Required: high school transcript, minimum 2.0 GPA. ***Recommended:*** essay or personal statement, 2 letters of recommendation, interview.
Application deadlines: rolling (freshmen), rolling (transfers).
Notification: continuous (freshmen), continuous (transfers).

CONTACT
Mr. Neil Scott, Director of Admissions, Faulkner University, 5345 Atlanta Highway, Montgomery, AL 36109-3398. *Phone:* 334-386-7200. *Toll-free phone:* 800-879-9816. *Fax:* 334-386-7137. *E-mail:* nscott@faulkner.edu.

Heritage Christian University
Florence, Alabama
http://www.hcu.edu/

CONTACT
Mr. Brad McKinnon, Dean of Students, Heritage Christian University, PO Box HCU, Florence, AL 35630. *Phone:* 256-766-6610 Ext. 305. *Toll-free phone:* 800-367-3565. *Fax:* 256-766-9289. *E-mail:* bmckinnon@hcu.edu.

Herzing University
Birmingham, Alabama
http://www.herzing.edu/birmingham/

CONTACT
Ms. Tess Anderson, Admissions Coordinator, Herzing University, 280 West Valley Avenue, Birmingham, AL 35209. *Phone:* 205-916-2800. *Toll-free phone:* 800-596-0724. *E-mail:* admiss@bhm.herzing.edu.

Huntingdon College
Montgomery, Alabama
http://www.huntingdon.edu/

- **Independent United Methodist** 4-year, founded 1854
- **Suburban** 71-acre campus with easy access to Birmingham
- **Endowment** $47.0 million
- **Coed** 1,148 undergraduate students, 77% full-time, 49% women, 51% men

UNDERGRAD STUDENTS
881 full-time, 267 part-time. Students come from 21 states and territories; 3 other countries; 19% are from out of state; 21% Black or African American, non-Hispanic/Latino; 4% Hispanic/Latino; 0.3% Asian, non-Hispanic/Latino; 0.1% Native Hawaiian or other Pacific Islander, non-Hispanic/Latino; 0.9% American Indian or Alaska Native, non-Hispanic/Latino; 4% Two or more races, non-Hispanic/Latino; 5% Race/ethnicity unknown; 0.2% international; 11% transferred in; 62% live on campus.

Freshmen:
Admission: 277 enrolled. ***Average high school GPA:*** 3.38. ***Test scores:*** SAT critical reading scores over 500: 42%; SAT math scores over 500: 40%; ACT scores over 18: 89%; SAT critical reading scores over 600: 5%; SAT math scores over 600: 7%; ACT scores over 24: 26%; ACT scores over 30: 2%.

Retention: 62% of full-time freshmen returned.

FACULTY
Total: 109, 42% full-time, 54% with terminal degrees.

Student/faculty ratio: 14:1.

ACADEMICS
Calendar: semesters. *Degree:* bachelor's.

Special study options: adult/continuing education programs, advanced placement credit, distance learning, double majors, freshman honors college, honors programs, independent study, internships, off-campus study, part-time degree program, services for LD students, student-designed majors, study abroad, summer session for credit. ***ROTC:*** Army (c), Air Force (c).

Computers: 9 computers/terminals are available on campus for general student use. Students can access the following: campus intranet, computer help desk, free student e-mail accounts, online (class) grades, online (class) registration, online (class) schedules, student Web hosting. Campuswide network is available. 100% of college-owned or -operated housing units are wired for high-speed Internet access. Wireless service is available via classrooms, dorm rooms, learning centers, libraries, student centers.

Library: Houghton Memorial Library. *Books:* 97,616 (physical), 75,767 (digital/electronic); *Serial titles:* 190 (physical), 18,006 (digital/electronic); *Databases:* 110. Students can reserve study rooms.

STUDENT LIFE
Housing options: on-campus residence required through junior year; coed, men-only, women-only, special housing for students with disabilities. Campus housing is university owned. Freshman campus housing is guaranteed.

Activities and organizations: drama/theater group, student-run newspaper, choral group, marching band, Student Government Association, Campus Activities Board, Voice of Justice, Freshman Forum, Exchange Club, national fraternities, national sororities.

Athletics Member NCAA. All Division III. ***Intercollegiate sports:*** baseball M, basketball M/W, football M, golf M/W, lacrosse M/W, sand volleyball W, soccer M/W, softball W, tennis M/W, volleyball W, wrestling M. ***Intramural sports:*** baseball W(c), basketball M/W, cheerleading M(c)/W(c), football M/W, sand volleyball M/W, soccer M/W, softball M/W, table tennis M/W, tennis M/W, volleyball M/W.

Campus security: 24-hour emergency response devices and patrols, late-night transport/escort service, controlled dormitory access, electronic video surveillance, weather alert broadcasts.

Student services: health clinic, personal/psychological counseling.

COSTS & FINANCIAL AID
Costs (2017–18) ***Comprehensive fee:*** $35,900 includes full-time tuition ($24,900), mandatory fees ($1500), and room and board ($9500). Full-time tuition and fees vary according to course load, program, and student level. Part-time tuition: $1040 per credit hour. Part-time tuition and fees vary according to course load and program. No tuition increase for student's term of enrollment. ***Room and board:*** Room and board charges vary according to housing facility. ***Payment plans:*** installment, deferred payment. ***Waivers:*** children of alumni and employees or children of employees.

Financial Aid Of all full-time matriculated undergraduates who enrolled in 2016, 757 applied for aid, 671 were judged to have need, 96 had their need fully met. 147 Federal Work-Study jobs (averaging $901). In 2016, 199 non-need-based awards were made. ***Average percent of need met:*** 68. ***Average financial aid package:*** $18,551. ***Average need-based loan:*** $4023. ***Average need-based gift aid:*** $15,171. ***Average non-need-based aid:*** $11,209. ***Average indebtedness upon graduation:*** $33,503.

APPLYING
Standardized Tests *Required:* SAT or ACT (for admission).

Required: high school transcript. ***Required for some:*** essay or personal statement, 3 letters of recommendation, interview, audition for music, portfolio for art.

CONTACT
Office of Admission, Huntingdon College, 1500 East Fairview Avenue, Montgomery, AL 36106-2148. *Phone:* 334-833-4497. *Toll-free phone:* 800-763-0313. *Fax:* 334-833-4347.
E-mail: admiss@hawks.huntingdon.edu.

Huntsville Bible College

Huntsville, Alabama

http://www.hbc1.edu/

CONTACT
Huntsville Bible College, 904 Oakwood Avenue, Huntsville, AL 35811-1632.

Jacksonville State University

Jacksonville, Alabama

http://www.jsu.edu/

- **State-supported** comprehensive, founded 1883
- **Small-town** 459-acre campus with easy access to Birmingham
- **Coed** 7,561 undergraduate students, 72% full-time, 57% women, 43% men
- **Moderately difficult** entrance level, 53% of applicants were admitted

UNDERGRAD STUDENTS
5,480 full-time, 2,081 part-time. 16% are from out of state; 18% Black or African American, non-Hispanic/Latino; 1% Hispanic/Latino; 0.7% Asian, non-Hispanic/Latino; 0.1% Native Hawaiian or other Pacific Islander, non-Hispanic/Latino; 0.7% American Indian or Alaska Native, non-Hispanic/Latino; 4% Race/ethnicity unknown; 2% international; 8% transferred in; 16% live on campus.

Freshmen:
Admission: 4,979 applied, 2,643 admitted, 1,320 enrolled. ***Average high school GPA:*** 3.35. ***Test scores:*** SAT critical reading scores over 500: 46%; SAT math scores over 500: 50%; ACT scores over 18: 96%; SAT critical reading scores over 600: 16%; SAT math scores over 600: 8%; ACT scores over 24: 45%; SAT critical reading scores over 700: 2%; SAT math scores over 700: 1%; ACT scores over 30: 8%.

Retention: 78% of full-time freshmen returned.

FACULTY
Total: 473, 67% full-time.

Student/faculty ratio: 18:1.

ACADEMICS
Calendar: semesters. *Degrees:* bachelor's, master's, doctoral, post-master's, and postbachelor's certificates.

Special study options: academic remediation for entering students, accelerated degree program, adult/continuing education programs, advanced placement credit, cooperative education, distance learning, double majors, English as a second language, freshman honors college, honors programs, independent study, internships, part-time degree program, services for LD students, study abroad, summer session for credit. ***ROTC:*** Army (b).

Computers: 350 computers/terminals are available on campus for general student use. Students can access the following: computer help desk, free student e-mail accounts, online (class) grades, online (class) registration, online (class) schedules. Campuswide network is available. Wireless service is available via entire campus.

Library: Houston Cole Library. *Books:* 711,815 (physical), 32,128 (digital/electronic); *Databases:* 307. Weekly public service hours: 87.

STUDENT LIFE
Housing options: on-campus residence required for freshman year; coed, men-only, women-only, special housing for students with disabilities. Campus housing is university owned.

Activities and organizations: drama/theater group, student-run newspaper, radio and television station, choral group, marching band, Student Government Association, Archaeology Club, Campus Fellowship

Clubs, Computer Science Club, Biology Club, national fraternities, national sororities.

Athletics Member NCAA. All Division I except football (Division I-AA). ***Intercollegiate sports:*** baseball M(s), basketball M(s)/W(s), cross-country running M(s)/W(s), golf M(s)/W(s), riflery M(s)/W(s), soccer W(s), softball W(s), tennis M(s)/W(s), volleyball W(s). ***Intramural sports:*** badminton M(c)/W(c), basketball M(c)/W(c), bowling M(c)/W(c), football M(c), golf M(c)/W(c), racquetball M(c)/W(c), soccer M(c)/W(c), softball M(c)/W(c), table tennis M(c)/W(c), tennis M(c)/W(c), volleyball M(c)/W(c).

Campus security: 24-hour emergency response devices and patrols, student patrols, late-night transport/escort service, controlled dormitory access, night security officer in female residence halls.

Student services: health clinic, personal/psychological counseling.

COSTS & FINANCIAL AID

Costs (2016–17) ***Tuition:*** state resident $9135 full-time, $300 per credit hour part-time; nonresident $18,270 full-time, $600 per credit hour part-time. ***Required fees:*** $525 full-time, $525 per year part-time, $525 per year part-time. ***Room and board:*** $7128. Room and board charges vary according to board plan and housing facility. ***Payment plan:*** installment. ***Waivers:*** employees or children of employees.

Financial Aid Of all full-time matriculated undergraduates who enrolled in 2015, 4,849 applied for aid, 4,761 were judged to have need. ***Average financial aid package:*** $9592. ***Average need-based loan:*** $992. ***Average need-based gift aid:*** $4558.

APPLYING

Standardized Tests *Required:* SAT or ACT (for admission).

Options: electronic application, early admission, deferred entrance.

Application fee: $35.

Required: high school transcript.

Application deadlines: rolling (freshmen), rolling (transfers).

Notification: continuous (freshmen), continuous (transfers).

CONTACT

Mr. Andrew Green, Director of Admission, Jacksonville State University, 700 Pelham Road North, Jacksonville, AL 36265. *Phone:* 256-782-5363. *Toll-free phone:* 800-231-5291. *Fax:* 256-782-5291. *E-mail:* info@jsu.edu.

Judson College

Marion, Alabama

http://www.judson.edu/

- **Independent Baptist** 4-year, founded 1838
- **Rural** 118-acre campus with easy access to Birmingham
- **Endowment** $15.4 million
- **Coed, primarily women**
- **Moderately difficult** entrance level

FACULTY

Student/faculty ratio: 8:1.

ACADEMICS

Calendar: semesters plus 2-month term in May and June. *Degrees:* associate and bachelor's.

Library: Bowling Library. *Books:* 62,633 (physical), 145,000 (digital/electronic); *Serial titles:* 60 (physical), 44,447 (digital/electronic); *Databases:* 93. Weekly public service hours: 63; students can reserve study rooms.

STUDENT LIFE

Housing options: on-campus residence required through senior year; women-only. Campus housing is university owned. Freshman campus housing is guaranteed.

Activities and organizations: drama/theater group, student-run newspaper, choral group, Student Government Association, Campus Ministries, Faith-Based Service Learning Activities, Ambassadors, Science Club.

Athletics Member NCCAA.

Campus security: 24-hour emergency response devices and patrols, late-night transport/escort service, controlled dormitory access.

Student services: personal/psychological counseling.

COSTS

Costs (2016–17) ***Comprehensive fee:*** $27,354 includes full-time tuition ($16,248), mandatory fees ($1128), and room and board ($9978). Full-time tuition and fees vary according to course load, degree level, and program. Part-time tuition: $550 per credit hour. Part-time tuition and fees vary according to course load, degree level, and program. ***Required fees:*** $564 per term part-time. ***College room only:*** $5616. Room and board charges vary according to board plan. ***Payment plans:*** installment, deferred payment.

APPLYING

Standardized Tests *Required:* SAT or ACT (for admission).

Options: electronic application, early admission, deferred entrance.

Application fee: $42.

Required: high school transcript, minimum 2.0 GPA.

CONTACT

Ms. Layne Hoggle, Executive Director of Enrollment Services, Judson College, 302 Bibb Street, Marion, AL 36756. *Phone:* 334-683-5110. *Toll-free phone:* 800-447-9472. *Fax:* 334-683-5282. *E-mail:* admissions@judson.edu.

Miles College

Fairfield, Alabama

http://www.miles.edu/

CONTACT

Mr. Christopher Robertson, Director of Admissions and Recruitment, Miles College, 5500 Myron Massey Boulevard, Bell Building, Fairfield, AL 35064. *Phone:* 205-929-1657. *Toll-free phone:* 800-445-0708. *Fax:* 205-929-1627. *E-mail:* admissions@miles.edu.

Oakwood University

Huntsville, Alabama

http://www.oakwood.edu/

CONTACT

Mr. Jason McCracken, Director of Enrollment Management, Oakwood University, 7000 Adventist Boulevard, NW, Huntsville, AL 35896. *Phone:* 256-726-7354. *Toll-free phone:* 800-824-5312. *Fax:* 256-726-7154. *E-mail:* admission@oakwood.edu.

Remington College–Mobile Campus

Mobile, Alabama

http://www.remingtoncollege.edu/

CONTACT

Remington College–Mobile Campus, 828 Downtowner Loop West, Mobile, AL 36609. *Phone:* 251-343-8200. *Toll-free phone:* 800-323-8122.

★ Samford University

Birmingham, Alabama

http://www.samford.edu/

- **Independent Baptist** university, founded 1841
- **Suburban** 247-acre campus
- **Endowment** $270.8 million
- **Coed** 3,341 undergraduate students, 96% full-time, 65% women, 35% men
- **Moderately difficult** entrance level, 91% of applicants were admitted

UNDERGRAD STUDENTS

3,207 full-time, 134 part-time. Students come from 47 states and territories; 21 other countries; 67% are from out of state; 7% Black or African American, non-Hispanic/Latino; 4% Hispanic/Latino; 1% Asian, non-Hispanic/Latino; 0.2% American Indian or Alaska Native, non-Hispanic/Latino; 2% Two or more races, non-Hispanic/Latino; 0.7% Race/ethnicity unknown; 2% international; 3% transferred in; 70% live on campus.

A ★ indicates that the school has detailed information with a Premium Profile on Petersons.com.

Freshmen:
Admission: 3,446 applied, 3,149 admitted, 916 enrolled. ***Average high school GPA:*** 3.64. ***Test scores:*** SAT critical reading scores over 500: 84%; SAT math scores over 500: 77%; SAT writing scores over 500: 81%; ACT scores over 18: 99%; SAT critical reading scores over 600: 39%; SAT math scores over 600: 33%; SAT writing scores over 600: 32%; ACT scores over 24: 72%; SAT critical reading scores over 700: 8%; SAT math scores over 700: 5%; SAT writing scores over 700: 4%; ACT scores over 30: 18%.

Retention: 89% of full-time freshmen returned.

FACULTY
Total: 532, 66% full-time, 74% with terminal degrees.
Student/faculty ratio: 12:1.

ACADEMICS
Calendar: 4-1-4. *Degrees:* certificates, bachelor's, master's, doctoral, post-master's, and postbachelor's certificates.

Special study options: accelerated degree program, adult/continuing education programs, distance learning, double majors, English as a second language, honors programs, independent study, internships, off-campus study, part-time degree program, services for LD students, study abroad, summer session for credit. ***ROTC:*** Army (c), Air Force (b).

Unusual degree programs: 3-2 engineering with The University of Alabama at Birmingham, Auburn University, Mercer University.

Computers: 330 computers/terminals and 400 ports are available on campus for general student use. Students can access the following: campus intranet, computer help desk, free student e-mail accounts, online (class) grades, online (class) registration, online (class) schedules, free online storage and tech support. Campuswide network is available. 100% of college-owned or -operated housing units are wired for high-speed Internet access. Wireless service is available via entire campus.

Library: University Library plus 2 others. *Books:* 636,268 (physical), 196,223 (digital/electronic); *Serial titles:* 5,960 (physical), 117,223 (digital/electronic); *Databases:* 291. Weekly public service hours: 99; students can reserve study rooms.

STUDENT LIFE
Housing options: on-campus residence required through sophomore year; men-only, women-only. Campus housing is university owned. Freshman campus housing is guaranteed.

Activities and organizations: drama/theater group, student-run newspaper, radio station, choral group, marching band, College Panhellenic, Interfraternity Council, Chi Omega, Alpha Delta Pi, Phi Mu, national fraternities, national sororities.

Athletics Member NCAA. All Division I except football (Division I-AA). ***Intercollegiate sports:*** baseball M(s), basketball M(s)/W(s), cross-country running M(s)/W(s), golf M(s)/W(s), soccer W(s), softball W(s), tennis M(s)/W(s), track and field M(s)/W(s), volleyball W(s). ***Intramural sports:*** basketball M/W, crew M(c)/W(c), football M/W, golf M(c)/W(c), lacrosse M(c)/W(c), rugby M(c), sand volleyball M/W, soccer M, softball M/W, swimming and diving M(c)/W(c), table tennis M/W, tennis M/W, ultimate Frisbee M/W, volleyball M/W.

Campus security: 24-hour emergency response devices and patrols, late-night transport/escort service, blue-light emergency phones, lighted sidewalks, nighttime campus access control gate.

Student services: health clinic, personal/psychological counseling.

COSTS & FINANCIAL AID
Costs (2017–18) ***Comprehensive fee:*** $40,770 includes full-time tuition ($29,640), mandatory fees ($850), and room and board ($10,280). Full-time tuition and fees vary according to course load and program. Part-time tuition and fees vary according to course load and program. ***College room only:*** $5416. Room and board charges vary according to board plan and housing facility. ***Payment plan:*** installment. ***Waivers:*** employees or children of employees.

Financial Aid Of all full-time matriculated undergraduates who enrolled in 2015, 1,762 applied for aid, 1,264 were judged to have need, 281 had their need fully met. 433 Federal Work-Study jobs (averaging $1964). 717 state and other part-time jobs (averaging $1648). In 2015, 1357 non-need-based awards were made. ***Average percent of need met:*** 70. ***Average financial aid package:*** $19,005. ***Average need-based loan:*** $3843. ***Average need-based gift aid:*** $15,072. ***Average non-need-based aid:*** $10,222. ***Average indebtedness upon graduation:*** $29,292.

APPLYING
Standardized Tests *Required:* SAT or ACT (for admission).

Options: electronic application, early admission, deferred entrance.

Application fee: $40.

Required: essay or personal statement, high school transcript, 1 letter of recommendation. ***Required for some:*** interview.

Notification: continuous until 11/7 (freshmen).

CONTACT
Mr. Brian L. Kennedy, Director of Recruitment, Samford University, 800 Lakeshore Drive, Samford Hall, Birmingham, AL 35229-0002. *Phone:* 205-726-4176. *Toll-free phone:* 800-888-7218. *E-mail:* blkenned@samford.edu.

Selma University

Selma, Alabama

http://www.selmauniversity.edu/

CONTACT
Selma University, 1501 Lapsley Street, Selma, AL 36701-5299. *Phone:* 334-872-2533 Ext. 116.

Southeastern Bible College

Birmingham, Alabama

http://www.sebc.edu/

- **Independent nondenominational** 4-year, founded 1935
- **Suburban** 22-acre campus
- **Coed** 143 undergraduate students, 74% full-time, 41% women, 59% men
- **Noncompetitive** entrance level, 100% of applicants were admitted

UNDERGRAD STUDENTS
106 full-time, 37 part-time. Students come from 9 states and territories; 1 other country; 12% are from out of state; 35% Black or African American, non-Hispanic/Latino; 0.7% Hispanic/Latino; 1% Race/ethnicity unknown; 0.7% international; 29% live on campus.

Freshmen:
Admission: 18 applied, 18 admitted. ***Test scores:*** ACT scores over 18: 82%; ACT scores over 24: 18%.

Retention: 67% of full-time freshmen returned.

FACULTY
Total: 25, 32% full-time, 44% with terminal degrees.
Student/faculty ratio: 8:1.

ACADEMICS
Calendar: semesters. *Degrees:* diplomas, associate, and bachelor's.

Special study options: academic remediation for entering students, adult/continuing education programs, advanced placement credit, double majors, internships, part-time degree program, services for LD students, study abroad, summer session for credit.

Computers: 24 computers/terminals are available on campus for general student use. Students can access the following: free student e-mail accounts. 100% of college-owned or -operated housing units are wired for high-speed Internet access. Wireless service is available via entire campus.

Library: Gannett-Estes Library. *Books:* 39,373 (physical), 42,621 (digital/electronic); *Serial titles:* 85 (physical), 340 (digital/electronic). Weekly public service hours: 66.

STUDENT LIFE
Housing options: men-only, women-only. Campus housing is university owned.

Activities and organizations: choral group, Student Council, Student Missions Fellowship.

Campus security: student patrols, controlled dormitory access.

COSTS
Costs (2016–17) ***Comprehensive fee:*** $16,040 includes full-time tuition ($11,340), mandatory fees ($450), and room and board ($4250). Full-time tuition and fees vary according to program. Part-time tuition: $405 per credit hour. Part-time tuition and fees vary according to program.

Required fees: $225 per term part-time. ***Payment plan:*** installment. ***Waivers:*** employees or children of employees.

APPLYING

Standardized Tests *Required:* SAT or ACT (for admission).

Options: electronic application, deferred entrance.

Application fee: $30.

Required: essay or personal statement, high school transcript, minimum 1.5 GPA, 1 letter of recommendation, interview.

CONTACT

Mr. Josh Scott, Admissions Counselor, Southeastern Bible College, 2545 Valleydale Road, Birmingham, AL 35244. *Phone:* 205-970-9241. *Toll-free phone:* 800-749-8878. *Fax:* 205-970-9207. *E-mail:* jscott@sebc.edu.

South University

Montgomery, Alabama

http://www.southuniversity.edu/montgomery/

CONTACT

South University, 5355 Vaughn Road, Montgomery, AL 36116-1120. *Phone:* 334-395-8800. *Toll-free phone:* 866-629-2962.

Spring Hill College

Mobile, Alabama

http://www.shc.edu/

- **Independent Roman Catholic (Jesuit)** comprehensive, founded 1830
- **Suburban** 450-acre campus
- **Coed** 1,396 undergraduate students, 99% full-time, 63% women, 37% men
- **Moderately difficult** entrance level, 44% of applicants were admitted

UNDERGRAD STUDENTS

1,382 full-time, 14 part-time. Students come from 32 states and territories; 21 other countries; 61% are from out of state; 14% Black or African American, non-Hispanic/Latino; 3% Hispanic/Latino; 1% Asian, non-Hispanic/Latino; 0.4% Native Hawaiian or other Pacific Islander, non-Hispanic/Latino; 0.6% American Indian or Alaska Native, non-Hispanic/Latino; 3% Two or more races, non-Hispanic/Latino; 5% Race/ethnicity unknown; 3% international; 3% transferred in; 75% live on campus.

Freshmen:

Admission: 8,534 applied, 3,715 admitted, 392 enrolled. ***Average high school GPA:*** 3.61. ***Test scores:*** SAT critical reading scores over 500: 80%; SAT math scores over 500: 78%; ACT scores over 18: 100%; SAT critical reading scores over 600: 31%; SAT math scores over 600: 18%; ACT scores over 24: 57%; SAT critical reading scores over 700: 2%; SAT math scores over 700: 2%; ACT scores over 30: 8%.

Retention: 76% of full-time freshmen returned.

FACULTY

Total: 132, 67% full-time, 73% with terminal degrees.

Student/faculty ratio: 14:1.

ACADEMICS

Calendar: semesters. *Degrees:* certificates, bachelor's, master's, post-master's, and postbachelor's certificates.

Special study options: academic remediation for entering students, accelerated degree program, adult/continuing education programs, advanced placement credit, distance learning, double majors, honors programs, independent study, internships, off-campus study, part-time degree program, services for LD students, student-designed majors, study abroad, summer session for credit. ***ROTC:*** Army (c), Air Force (c).

Unusual degree programs: 3-2 engineering with Marquette University, University of Alabama at Birmingham, University of Florida, Auburn University, Texas A&M University, University of South Alabama.

Computers: Students can access the following: campus intranet, computer help desk, free student e-mail accounts, online (class) grades, online (class) registration, online (class) schedules. Campuswide network is available. 100% of college-owned or -operated housing units are wired for high-speed Internet access. Wireless service is available via computer centers, computer labs, dorm rooms, libraries, student centers.

Library: Marnie and John Burke Memorial Library plus 1 other.

STUDENT LIFE

Housing options: on-campus residence required through senior year; coed. Campus housing is university owned. Freshman campus housing is guaranteed.

Activities and organizations: drama/theater group, student-run newspaper, choral group, Fraternities and sororities, SHAPe, National Society of Leadership and Success, Peer One Project, Chemistry Club, national fraternities, national sororities.

Athletics Member NCAA. All Division II. ***Intercollegiate sports:*** baseball M(s), basketball M(s)/W(s), cross-country running M(s)/W(s), golf M(s)/W(s), soccer M(s)/W(s), softball W(s), tennis M(s)/W(s), track and field M(s)/W(s), volleyball W(s). ***Intramural sports:*** basketball M/W, bowling M(c)/W(c), football M/W, racquetball M/W, rugby M(c)/W(c), soccer M/W, ultimate Frisbee M/W, volleyball M/W.

Campus security: 24-hour emergency response devices and patrols, late-night transport/escort service, controlled dormitory access.

Student services: health clinic, personal/psychological counseling.

COSTS & FINANCIAL AID

Costs (2016–17) ***Comprehensive fee:*** $48,488 includes full-time tuition ($33,634), mandatory fees ($2164), and room and board ($12,690). Full-time tuition and fees vary according to course load. Part-time tuition: $1024 per credit hour. Part-time tuition and fees vary according to course load. ***Required fees:*** $53 per credit hour part-time. ***College room only:*** $6700. Room and board charges vary according to board plan and housing facility. ***Payment plan:*** installment. ***Waivers:*** employees or children of employees.

Financial Aid Of all full-time matriculated undergraduates who enrolled in 2016, 1,088 applied for aid, 968 were judged to have need, 236 had their need fully met. In 2016, 357 non-need-based awards were made. ***Average percent of need met:*** 79. ***Average financial aid package:*** $32,092. ***Average need-based loan:*** $4530. ***Average need-based gift aid:*** $25,089. ***Average non-need-based aid:*** $21,065.

APPLYING

Standardized Tests *Required:* SAT or ACT (for admission).

Options: electronic application, early admission, deferred entrance.

Application fee: $25.

Required: essay or personal statement, high school transcript, 1 letter of recommendation. ***Recommended:*** minimum 2.5 GPA, interview.

Application deadlines: 7/15 (freshmen), rolling (transfers).

Notification: continuous (freshmen), continuous (out-of-state freshmen), continuous (transfers).

CONTACT

Ms. Britney Finley, Admissions Counselor, Spring Hill College, 4000 Dauphin Street, Mobile, AL 36608-1791. *Phone:* 251-380-3032. *Toll-free phone:* 800-SHC-6704. *Fax:* 251-460-2186. *E-mail:* bfinley@shc.edu.

Stillman College

Tuscaloosa, Alabama

http://www.stillman.edu/

CONTACT

Stillman College, PO Drawer 1430, 3600 Stillman Boulevard, Tuscaloosa, AL 35403-9990. *Phone:* 205-366-8837. *Toll-free phone:* 800-841-5722.

Strayer University–Birmingham Campus

Birmingham, Alabama

http://www.strayer.edu/alabama/birmingham/

CONTACT

Strayer University–Birmingham Campus, 3570 Grandview Parkway, Suite 200, Birmingham, AL 35243.

Strayer University–Huntsville Campus

Huntsville, Alabama

http://www.strayer.edu/alabama/huntsville/

CONTACT
Strayer University–Huntsville Campus, 4955 Corporate Drive, NW, Suite 200, Huntsville, AL 35805.

Talladega College

Talladega, Alabama

http://www.talladega.edu/

- **Independent** 4-year, founded 1867
- **Small-town** 130-acre campus with easy access to Birmingham
- **Endowment** $3.1 million
- **Coed** 989 undergraduate students, 86% full-time, 47% women, 53% men
- **Moderately difficult** entrance level, 15% of applicants were admitted

UNDERGRAD STUDENTS
846 full-time, 143 part-time. Students come from 30 states and territories; 3 other countries; 39% are from out of state; 89% Black or African American, non-Hispanic/Latino; 4% Hispanic/Latino; 0.2% Asian, non-Hispanic/Latino; 3% Race/ethnicity unknown; 6% transferred in; 65% live on campus.

Freshmen:
Admission: 2,047 applied, 312 admitted, 350 enrolled. ***Average high school GPA:*** 2.8.
Retention: 59% of full-time freshmen returned.

FACULTY
Total: 64, 61% full-time, 47% with terminal degrees.
Student/faculty ratio: 20:1.

ACADEMICS
Calendar: semesters. *Degrees:* associate and bachelor's.
Special study options: accelerated degree program, adult/continuing education programs, distance learning, double majors, English as a second language, independent study, internships, off-campus study, part-time degree program, services for LD students, study abroad, summer session for credit.
Computers: 186 computers/terminals and 240 ports are available on campus for general student use. Students can access the following: computer help desk, free student e-mail accounts, online (class) grades, online (class) registration, online (class) schedules. Campuswide network is available. 100% of college-owned or -operated housing units are wired for high-speed Internet access. Wireless service is available via entire campus.
Library: Savery Library. *Books:* 13,000 (physical); *Serial titles:* 1,922 (digital/electronic); *Databases:* 147. Weekly public service hours: 65.

STUDENT LIFE
Housing options: men-only, women-only. Campus housing is university owned. Freshman campus housing is guaranteed.
Activities and organizations: choral group, marching band, Student Government Association, Crimson Ambassadors, Students in Free Enterprise (SIFE), Talladega College Choir, Social Work Club, national fraternities, national sororities.
Athletics Member NAIA. ***Intercollegiate sports:*** baseball M, basketball M, golf M, softball W, tennis W. ***Intramural sports:*** baseball M, basketball M/W, cheerleading M/W, football M, tennis M/W, volleyball W.
Campus security: 24-hour patrols, late-night transport/escort service, campus police.
Student services: health clinic, personal/psychological counseling.

COSTS & FINANCIAL AID
Costs (2016–17) ***Comprehensive fee:*** $18,844 includes full-time tuition ($11,192), mandatory fees ($1148), and room and board ($6504). Full-time tuition and fees vary according to course load. Part-time tuition: $466 per credit hour. ***Required fees:*** $659 per contact hour part-time. ***College room only:*** $3020. ***Payment plans:*** tuition prepayment, installment. ***Waivers:*** employees or children of employees.
Financial Aid Of all full-time matriculated undergraduates who enrolled in 2003, 407 applied for aid, 375 were judged to have need, 100 had their need fully met. 141 Federal Work-Study jobs (averaging $691). ***Average percent of need met:*** 90. ***Average financial aid package:*** $5000. ***Average need-based loan:*** $5335. ***Average need-based gift aid:*** $3025. ***Average non-need-based aid:*** $5774. ***Average indebtedness upon graduation:*** $12,790. ***Financial aid deadline:*** 6/30.

APPLYING
Standardized Tests *Required:* SAT or ACT (for admission).
Options: electronic application, early admission.
Application fee: $25.
Required: high school transcript, minimum 2.0 GPA.
Application deadlines: rolling (freshmen), rolling (transfers).
Notification: continuous (freshmen), continuous (transfers).

CONTACT
Talladega College, 627 West Battle Street, Talladega, AL 35160-2354.
Phone: 256-761-6175. *Toll-free phone:* 866-540-3956.

Troy University

Troy, Alabama

http://www.troy.edu/

- **State-supported** comprehensive, founded 1887, part of Troy University System
- **Small-town** 906-acre campus
- **Endowment** $97.2 million
- **Coed** 14,243 undergraduate students, 63% full-time, 60% women, 40% men
- **Moderately difficult** entrance level, 90% of applicants were admitted

UNDERGRAD STUDENTS
9,040 full-time, 5,203 part-time. Students come from 42 states and territories; 62 other countries; 33% are from out of state; 30% Black or African American, non-Hispanic/Latino; 3% Hispanic/Latino; 3% Asian, non-Hispanic/Latino; 0.2% Native Hawaiian or other Pacific Islander, non-Hispanic/Latino; 0.6% American Indian or Alaska Native, non-Hispanic/Latino; 3% Two or more races, non-Hispanic/Latino; 5% Race/ethnicity unknown; 5% international; 10% transferred in; 32% live on campus.

Freshmen:
Admission: 6,565 applied, 5,938 admitted, 1,834 enrolled. ***Test scores:*** SAT critical reading scores over 500: 43%; SAT math scores over 500: 49%; SAT writing scores over 500: 50%; ACT scores over 18: 89%; SAT critical reading scores over 600: 10%; SAT math scores over 600: 18%; SAT writing scores over 600: 27%; ACT scores over 24: 38%; SAT critical reading scores over 700: 2%; SAT math scores over 700: 10%; SAT writing scores over 700: 3%; ACT scores over 30: 5%.
Retention: 74% of full-time freshmen returned.

FACULTY
Total: 1,097, 48% full-time.
Student/faculty ratio: 15:1.

ACADEMICS
Calendar: semesters. *Degrees:* associate, bachelor's, master's, doctoral, and post-master's certificates.
Special study options: academic remediation for entering students, accelerated degree program, advanced placement credit, distance learning, double majors, English as a second language, honors programs, independent study, internships, part-time degree program, services for LD students, summer session for credit. ***ROTC:*** Army (b), Air Force (b).
Computers: 1,435 computers/terminals and 21,221 ports are available on campus for general student use. Students can access the following: campus intranet, computer help desk, free student e-mail accounts, online (class) grades, online (class) registration, online (class) schedules. Campuswide network is available. Wireless service is available via classrooms, dorm rooms, libraries.
Library: Lurleen B. Wallace Library (Troy Campus) plus 2 others. *Books:* 624,347 (physical), 120,402 (digital/electronic); *Serial titles:* 37,650 (physical), 22,415 (digital/electronic); *Databases:* 192.

STUDENT LIFE
Housing options: on-campus residence required for freshman year; coed, men-only, women-only. Campus housing is university owned. Freshman campus housing is guaranteed.

Activities and organizations: drama/theater group, student-run newspaper, television station, choral group, marching band, T-Day/Athletic Events (Homecoming), Activities Council, Pep Rallies, national fraternities, national sororities.

Athletics Member NCAA. All Division I except football (Division I-A). ***Intercollegiate sports:*** baseball M(s), basketball M(s)/W(s), cross-country running M(s)/W(s), golf M(s)/W(s), soccer W(s), softball W(s), tennis M(s)/W(s), track and field M(s)/W(s), volleyball W(s). ***Intramural sports:*** basketball M/W, bowling M/W, cross-country running M/W, football M, golf M/W, soccer W, softball W, tennis M/W, track and field M/W, volleyball W.

Campus security: 24-hour emergency response devices and patrols, student patrols, late-night transport/escort service, controlled dormitory access.

Student services: health clinic, personal/psychological counseling.

COSTS & FINANCIAL AID
Costs (2016–17) ***Tuition:*** state resident $9632 full-time, $301 per credit hour part-time; nonresident $19,264 full-time, $602 per credit hour part-time. Full-time tuition and fees vary according to location and program. Part-time tuition and fees vary according to location and program. ***Required fees:*** $1567 full-time, $39 per credit hour part-time, $50 per term part-time. ***Room and board:*** $7853; room only: $4635. Room and board charges vary according to board plan and housing facility. ***Payment plan:*** installment. ***Waivers:*** employees or children of employees.

Financial Aid Of all full-time matriculated undergraduates who enrolled in 2016, 6,455 applied for aid, 6,397 were judged to have need. 4 Federal Work-Study jobs (averaging $2876). In 2016, 4767 non-need-based awards were made. ***Average financial aid package:*** $4394. ***Average need-based loan:*** $4340. ***Average need-based gift aid:*** $4675. ***Average non-need-based aid:*** $7108. ***Average indebtedness upon graduation:*** $5475.

APPLYING
Standardized Tests *Required:* SAT or ACT (for admission).

Options: electronic application, deferred entrance.

Application fee: $30.

Required: high school transcript. ***Recommended:*** interview.

Application deadlines: rolling (freshmen), rolling (transfers).

CONTACT
Mr. Buddy Starling, Associate Vice Chancellor for Enrollment Management, Troy University, University Avenue, Troy, AL 36082. *Phone:* 334-670-3243. *Toll-free phone:* 800-551-9716. *Fax:* 334-670-3733. *E-mail:* bstar@troy.edu.

Tuskegee University

Tuskegee, Alabama

http://www.tuskegee.edu/

- **Independent** comprehensive, founded 1881
- **Small-town** 5000-acre campus
- **Endowment** $113.7 million
- **Coed**
- **Moderately difficult** entrance level

FACULTY
Student/faculty ratio: 14:1.

ACADEMICS
Calendar: semesters. *Degrees:* bachelor's, master's, and doctoral.
Library: Hollis B. Frissell Library plus 3 others. *Books:* 370,430 (physical), 2,330 (digital/electronic); *Serial titles:* 1,810 (physical), 836 (digital/electronic); *Databases:* 175. Students can reserve study rooms.

STUDENT LIFE
Housing options: on-campus residence required through sophomore year; coed, men-only, women-only. Campus housing is university owned. Freshman applicants given priority for college housing.

Activities and organizations: drama/theater group, student-run newspaper, television station, choral group, marching band, Student Government, Marching Band, State Clubs, Fraternities, Sororities, national fraternities, national sororities.

Athletics Member NCAA. All Division II.

Campus security: 24-hour emergency response devices and patrols, late-night transport/escort service.

Student services: health clinic, personal/psychological counseling.

COSTS & FINANCIAL AID
Costs (2016–17) ***Comprehensive fee:*** $29,640 includes full-time tuition ($18,560), mandatory fees ($1760), and room and board ($9320). Full-time tuition and fees vary according to course load. Part-time tuition: $5135 per term. Part-time tuition and fees vary according to course load. ***College room only:*** $4300. Room and board charges vary according to board plan and housing facility.

Financial Aid Of all full-time matriculated undergraduates who enrolled in 2015, 2,328 applied for aid, 2,195 were judged to have need, 1,269 had their need fully met. 625 Federal Work-Study jobs (averaging $2610). 395 state and other part-time jobs (averaging $4500). In 2015, 611 non-need-based awards were made. ***Average percent of need met:*** 85. ***Average financial aid package:*** $20,500. ***Average need-based loan:*** $6000. ***Average need-based gift aid:*** $950. ***Average non-need-based aid:*** $6500. ***Average indebtedness upon graduation:*** $26,500.

APPLYING
Standardized Tests *Required:* SAT or ACT (for admission). *Recommended:* SAT (for admission).

Options: electronic application, early admission.

Application fee: $25.

Required: high school transcript, minimum 3.0 GPA.

CONTACT
Hon. Courtney L. Griffin, Executive Director of Enrollment Management, Tuskegee University, 1200 Old Montgomery Road, Margaret Murray Hall - Admissions, Tuskegee, AL 36088. *Phone:* 334-724-4828. *Toll-free phone:* 800-622-6531. *Fax:* 334-727-5750. *E-mail:* cgriffin@mytu.tuskegee.edu.

United States Sports Academy

Daphne, Alabama

http://www.ussa.edu/

- **Independent** upper-level, founded 1972
- **Suburban** 10-acre campus
- **Endowment** $1.0 million
- **Coed** 270 undergraduate students, 100% full-time, 21% women, 79% men

UNDERGRAD STUDENTS
270 full-time. Students come from 23 states and territories; 16% Black or African American, non-Hispanic/Latino; 9% Hispanic/Latino; 4% Asian, non-Hispanic/Latino; 0.7% Native Hawaiian or other Pacific Islander, non-Hispanic/Latino; 2% Two or more races, non-Hispanic/Latino; 13% Race/ethnicity unknown; 100% transferred in.

FACULTY
Total: 34, 21% full-time, 79% with terminal degrees.

Student/faculty ratio: 12:1.

ACADEMICS
Calendar: continuous. *Degrees:* certificates, diplomas, bachelor's, master's, doctoral, and post-master's certificates.

Special study options: distance learning.

Computers: 1 computer/terminal is available on campus for general student use. Students can access the following: computer help desk, free student e-mail accounts, online (class) grades, online (class) registration, online (class) schedules. Campuswide network is available.
Library: United States Sports Academy Library plus 1 other. *Books:* 4,000 (digital/electronic).

STUDENT LIFE
Activities and organizations: Alumni Association.

Campus security: electronically operated building entrances.

COSTS & FINANCIAL AID
Costs (2017–18) ***One-time required fee:*** $50. ***Tuition:*** $9480 full-time. ***Required fees:*** $800 full-time. ***Payment plan:*** installment. ***Waivers:*** employees or children of employees.

Financial Aid Of all full-time matriculated undergraduates who enrolled in 2016, 31 applied for aid, 31 were judged to have need, 25 had their need fully met. ***Average percent of need met:*** 29. ***Average financial aid package:*** $4748. ***Average need-based loan:*** $4758. ***Average need-based gift aid:*** $3978.

APPLYING
Options: electronic application.

Application fee: $50.

Notification: continuous (transfers).

CONTACT
United States Sports Academy, One Academy Drive, Daphne, AL 36526-7055. *Phone:* 251-626-3303 Ext. 7147. *Toll-free phone:* 800-223-2668.

The University of Alabama

Tuscaloosa, Alabama

http://www.ua.edu/

- **State-supported** university, founded 1831, part of University of Alabama System
- **Suburban** 1026-acre campus with easy access to Birmingham
- **Endowment** $672.4 million
- **Coed** 32,563 undergraduate students, 90% full-time, 56% women, 44% men
- **Moderately difficult** entrance level, 53% of applicants were admitted

UNDERGRAD STUDENTS
29,220 full-time, 3,343 part-time. Students come from 51 states and territories; 59 other countries; 57% are from out of state; 10% Black or African American, non-Hispanic/Latino; 4% Hispanic/Latino; 1% Asian, non-Hispanic/Latino; 0.1% Native Hawaiian or other Pacific Islander, non-Hispanic/Latino; 0.4% American Indian or Alaska Native, non-Hispanic/Latino; 3% Two or more races, non-Hispanic/Latino; 0.3% Race/ethnicity unknown; 2% international; 5% transferred in; 26% live on campus.

Freshmen:
Admission: 38,237 applied, 20,107 admitted, 7,559 enrolled. ***Average high school GPA:*** 3.69. ***Test scores:*** SAT critical reading scores over 500: 70%; SAT math scores over 500: 72%; SAT writing scores over 500: 67%; ACT scores over 18: 100%; SAT critical reading scores over 600: 29%; SAT math scores over 600: 30%; SAT writing scores over 600: 25%; ACT scores over 24: 72%; SAT critical reading scores over 700: 10%; SAT math scores over 700: 12%; SAT writing scores over 700: 6%; ACT scores over 30: 40%.

Retention: 86% of full-time freshmen returned.

FACULTY
Total: 1,829, 73% full-time, 73% with terminal degrees.
Student/faculty ratio: 23:1.

ACADEMICS
Calendar: semesters. *Degrees:* bachelor's, master's, doctoral, and post-master's certificates.

Special study options: academic remediation for entering students, accelerated degree program, adult/continuing education programs, advanced placement credit, cooperative education, distance learning, double majors, English as a second language, external degree program, freshman honors college, honors programs, independent study, internships, off-campus study, part-time degree program, services for LD students, student-designed majors, study abroad, summer session for credit. ***ROTC:*** Army (b), Air Force (b).

Computers: 2,500 computers/terminals and 10,000 ports are available on campus for general student use. Students can access the following: campus intranet, computer help desk, free student e-mail accounts, online (class) grades, online (class) registration, online (class) schedules. Campuswide network is available. 100% of college-owned or -operated housing units are wired for high-speed Internet access. Wireless service is available via entire campus.

Library: Amelia Gayle Gorgas Library plus 8 others. *Books:* 3.3 million (physical), 1.5 million (digital/electronic); *Serial titles:* 727 (physical), 127,820 (digital/electronic); *Databases:* 905. Weekly public service hours: 146; study areas open 24 hours, 5-7 days a week; students can reserve study rooms.

STUDENT LIFE
Housing options: on-campus residence required for freshman year; coed, men-only, women-only, special housing for students with disabilities. Campus housing is university owned and leased by the school. Freshman campus housing is guaranteed.

Activities and organizations: drama/theater group, student-run newspaper, radio station, choral group, marching band, ABXY Gaming Network, Association of Residence Communities, International Student Association, Student Government Association, Black Student Union, national fraternities, national sororities.

Athletics Member NCAA. All Division I except football (Division I-A). ***Intercollegiate sports:*** badminton M(c)/W(c), baseball M(s), basketball M(s)/W(s), bowling M(c)/W(c), cheerleading M(s)/W(s), crew M(c)/W(s), cross-country running M(s)/W(s), equestrian sports M(c)/W(c), field hockey W(c), golf M(s)/W(s), gymnastics W(s), ice hockey M(c), lacrosse M(c)/W(c), racquetball M(c)/W(c), rugby M(c)/W(c), soccer M(c)/W(s), softball W(s), swimming and diving M(s)/W(s), table tennis M(c)/W(c), tennis M(s)/W(s), track and field M(s)/W(s), triathlon M(c)/W(c), ultimate Frisbee M(c)/W(c), volleyball M(c)/W(s), wrestling M(c). ***Intramural sports:*** basketball M/W, soccer M/W, tennis M/W, ultimate Frisbee M/W, volleyball M/W.

Campus security: 24-hour emergency response devices and patrols, late-night transport/escort service, controlled dormitory access, 24-hour patrols by University of Alabama Police (UAPD), certified law enforcement personnel.

Student services: health clinic, personal/psychological counseling, women's center, legal services.

COSTS & FINANCIAL AID
Costs (2016–17) ***Tuition:*** state resident $10,470 full-time; nonresident $26,950 full-time. ***Room and board:*** $9550; room only: $6000. Room and board charges vary according to board plan, housing facility, and location.

Financial Aid Of all full-time matriculated undergraduates who enrolled in 2015, 15,770 applied for aid, 12,380 were judged to have need, 2,409 had their need fully met. 618 Federal Work-Study jobs (averaging $2725). In 2015, 6853 non-need-based awards were made. ***Average percent of need met:*** 53. ***Average financial aid package:*** $13,656. ***Average need-based loan:*** $4256. ***Average need-based gift aid:*** $11,597. ***Average non-need-based aid:*** $14,770. ***Average indebtedness upon graduation:*** $33,816.

APPLYING
Standardized Tests *Required:* SAT or ACT (for admission).

Options: electronic application, early admission.

Application fee: $40.

Required: high school transcript, minimum 3.0 GPA. ***Required for some:*** essay or personal statement, 2 letters of recommendation, interview.

Application deadlines: 5/1 (freshmen), 3/1 (transfers).

Notification: continuous (freshmen), continuous (transfers).

CONTACT
Ms. Mary K. Spiegel, Executive Director of Undergraduate Admissions, The University of Alabama, Box 870132, Tuscaloosa, AL 35487. *Phone:* 205-348-5666. *Toll-free phone:* 800-933-BAMA. *Fax:* 205-348-9046. *E-mail:* admissions@ua.edu.

The University of Alabama at Birmingham

Birmingham, Alabama

http://www.uab.edu/

- **State-supported** university, founded 1969, part of University of Alabama System
- **Urban** 323-acre campus with easy access to Birmingham
- **Endowment** $424.5 million
- **Coed** 12,369 undergraduate students, 73% full-time, 59% women, 41% men
- **Moderately difficult** entrance level, 89% of applicants were admitted

UNDERGRAD STUDENTS

8,971 full-time, 3,398 part-time. Students come from 45 states and territories; 50 other countries; 11% are from out of state; 26% Black or African American, non-Hispanic/Latino; 3% Hispanic/Latino; 6% Asian, non-Hispanic/Latino; 0.3% American Indian or Alaska Native, non-Hispanic/Latino; 4% Two or more races, non-Hispanic/Latino; 0.8% Race/ethnicity unknown; 2% international; 13% transferred in; 22% live on campus.

Freshmen:

Admission: 5,838 applied, 5,212 admitted, 2,021 enrolled. ***Average high school GPA:*** 3.65. ***Test scores:*** ACT scores over 18: 100%; ACT scores over 24: 59%; ACT scores over 30: 18%.

Retention: 82% of full-time freshmen returned.

FACULTY

Total: 961, 89% full-time, 85% with terminal degrees.

Student/faculty ratio: 18:1.

ACADEMICS

Calendar: semesters. *Degrees:* certificates, bachelor's, master's, doctoral, post-master's, and postbachelor's certificates.

Special study options: academic remediation for entering students, accelerated degree program, adult/continuing education programs, advanced placement credit, cooperative education, distance learning, double majors, English as a second language, freshman honors college, honors programs, independent study, internships, off-campus study, part-time degree program, services for LD students, student-designed majors, study abroad, summer session for credit. ***ROTC:*** Army (b), Air Force (c).

Unusual degree programs: 3-2 engineering; biology, computer science.

Computers: Students can access the following: campus intranet, computer help desk, free student e-mail accounts, online (class) grades, online (class) registration, online (class) schedules, transcript requests. Campuswide network is available. 100% of college-owned or -operated housing units are wired for high-speed Internet access. Wireless service is available via classrooms, computer centers, computer labs, dorm rooms, learning centers, libraries, student centers.

Library: Mervyn Sterne Library plus 2 others. *Books:* 1.3 million (physical). Students can reserve study rooms.

STUDENT LIFE

Housing options: coed, special housing for students with disabilities. Campus housing is university owned and is provided by a third party. Freshman applicants given priority for college housing.

Activities and organizations: drama/theater group, student-run newspaper, radio station, choral group, marching band, campus ministries, service-oriented groups, sports-affiliated groups, national fraternities, national sororities.

Athletics Member NCAA. All Division I. ***Intercollegiate sports:*** baseball M(s), basketball M(s)/W(s), bowling W(s), cross-country running W(s), football M(s), golf M(s)/W(s), riflery W(s), soccer M(s)/W(s), softball W(s), tennis M(s)/W(s), track and field W(s), volleyball W(s). ***Intramural sports:*** badminton M(c)/W(c), basketball M/W, football M/W, lacrosse M(c)/W(c), rugby M(c), soccer M/W, softball M/W, table tennis M(c)/W(c), tennis M(c)/W(c), ultimate Frisbee M/W, wrestling M(c).

Campus security: 24-hour emergency response devices and patrols, late-night transport/escort service, controlled dormitory access.

Student services: health clinic, personal/psychological counseling, women's center.

COSTS & FINANCIAL AID

Costs (2016–17) ***Tuition:*** state resident $9936 full-time, $305 per credit hour part-time; nonresident $22,844 full-time, $717 per contact hour part-time. Full-time tuition and fees vary according to course load, degree level, program, and reciprocity agreements. Part-time tuition and fees vary according to course load, degree level, program, and reciprocity agreements. ***Room and board:*** $9980; room only: $6020. Room and board charges vary according to board plan and housing facility. ***Payment plan:*** installment. ***Waivers:*** employees or children of employees.

Financial Aid Of all full-time matriculated undergraduates who enrolled in 2016, 6,626 applied for aid, 5,464 were judged to have need, 535 had their need fully met. In 2016, 1755 non-need-based awards were made. ***Average percent of need met:*** 50. ***Average financial aid package:*** $10,369. ***Average need-based loan:*** $4574. ***Average need-based gift aid:*** $5052. ***Average non-need-based aid:*** $7582. ***Average indebtedness upon graduation:*** $34,950.

APPLYING

Standardized Tests *Required:* SAT or ACT (for admission).

Options: electronic application, early admission, deferred entrance.

Application fee: $30.

Required: high school transcript.

Application deadlines: 6/1 (freshmen), 6/1 (transfers).

Notification: continuous (freshmen), continuous (transfers).

CONTACT

Mr. Tyler Peterson, Director of Undergraduate Admissions, The University of Alabama at Birmingham, 1701 11th Avenue South, Birmingham, AL 35294-4412. *Phone:* 205-934-8221. *Toll-free phone:* 800-421-8743. *Fax:* 205-975-7114. *E-mail:* chooseuab@uab.edu.

The University of Alabama in Huntsville

Huntsville, Alabama

http://www.uah.edu/

- **State-supported** university, founded 1950, part of University of Alabama System
- **Suburban** 400-acre campus
- **Endowment** $66.9 million
- **Coed** 6,507 undergraduate students, 81% full-time, 42% women, 58% men
- **Moderately difficult** entrance level, 76% of applicants were admitted

UNDERGRAD STUDENTS

5,257 full-time, 1,250 part-time. 16% are from out of state; 11% Black or African American, non-Hispanic/Latino; 4% Hispanic/Latino; 4% Asian, non-Hispanic/Latino; 1% American Indian or Alaska Native, non-Hispanic/Latino; 2% Two or more races, non-Hispanic/Latino; 3% Race/ethnicity unknown; 3% international; 12% transferred in; 21% live on campus.

Freshmen:

Admission: 4,545 applied, 3,467 admitted, 1,213 enrolled. ***Average high school GPA:*** 3.79. ***Test scores:*** SAT critical reading scores over 500: 87%; SAT math scores over 500: 83%; ACT scores over 18: 100%; SAT critical reading scores over 600: 61%; SAT math scores over 600: 52%; ACT scores over 24: 79%; SAT critical reading scores over 700: 17%; SAT math scores over 700: 15%; ACT scores over 30: 37%.

Retention: 83% of full-time freshmen returned.

FACULTY

Total: 542, 60% full-time, 47% with terminal degrees.

Student/faculty ratio: 17:1.

ACADEMICS

Calendar: semesters. *Degrees:* certificates, bachelor's, master's, doctoral, post-master's, and postbachelor's certificates.

Special study options: academic remediation for entering students, advanced placement credit, cooperative education, distance learning, double majors, English as a second language, freshman honors college, honors programs, independent study, internships, off-campus study, part-time degree program, services for LD students, student-designed majors, study abroad, summer session for credit. ***ROTC:*** Army (c).

Unusual degree programs: 3-2 engineering with Oakwood College, Morehouse College, Clark Atlanta University, Spelman College.

Computers: 1,227 computers/terminals and 5,330 ports are available on campus for general student use. Students can access the following: campus intranet, computer help desk, free student e-mail accounts, online (class) grades, online (class) registration, online (class) schedules. Campuswide network is available. 100% of college-owned or -operated housing units are wired for high-speed Internet access. Wireless service is available via classrooms, computer centers, computer labs, dorm rooms, learning centers, libraries, student centers.

Library: Louis Salmon Library. *Books:* 239,503 (physical), 387,481 (digital/electronic); *Serial titles:* 3,441 (physical), 42,868 (digital/electronic); *Databases:* 133.

STUDENT LIFE

Housing options: on-campus residence required through sophomore year; coed, cooperative, special housing for students with disabilities. Campus housing is university owned. Freshman campus housing is guaranteed.

Activities and organizations: drama/theater group, student-run newspaper, choral group, Student Government Association, Student Run Sports, International Student Association, CRU, Blue Crew, national fraternities, national sororities.

Athletics Member NCAA. All Division II except ice hockey (Division I). ***Intercollegiate sports:*** baseball M(s), basketball M(s)/W(s), cheerleading M(s)/W(s), crew M(c)/W(c), cross-country running M(s)/W(s), ice hockey M(s), lacrosse M(c)/W(c), soccer M(s)/W(s), softball W(s), tennis M(s)/W(s), track and field M(s)/W(s), volleyball W(s). ***Intramural sports:*** basketball M/W, football M/W, racquetball M/W, soccer M/W, softball M/W, tennis M/W, ultimate Frisbee M/W, volleyball M/W.

Campus security: 24-hour emergency response devices and patrols, late-night transport/escort service, controlled dormitory access, 24/7 dispatch center, community policing efforts.

Student services: health clinic, personal/psychological counseling.

COSTS & FINANCIAL AID

Costs (2016–17) ***Tuition:*** state resident $8996 full-time, $382 per credit hour part-time; nonresident $19,766 full-time, $841 per credit hour part-time. Full-time tuition and fees vary according to course load and program. Part-time tuition and fees vary according to course load and program. ***Required fees:*** $846 full-time. ***Room and board:*** $9603; room only: $6553. Room and board charges vary according to board plan and housing facility. ***Payment plan:*** installment. ***Waivers:*** employees or children of employees.

Financial Aid Of all full-time matriculated undergraduates who enrolled in 2016, 5,231 applied for aid, 2,650 were judged to have need, 456 had their need fully met. 66 Federal Work-Study jobs (averaging $3904). In 2016, 1403 non-need-based awards were made. ***Average percent of need met:*** 61. ***Average financial aid package:*** $10,713. ***Average need-based loan:*** $7218. ***Average need-based gift aid:*** $7486. ***Average non-need-based aid:*** $8507. ***Average indebtedness upon graduation:*** $35,009. ***Financial aid deadline:*** 7/31.

APPLYING

Standardized Tests *Required:* SAT or ACT (for admission).

Options: electronic application, deferred entrance.

Application fee: $30.

Required: high school transcript.

Application deadlines: 8/17 (freshmen), 8/17 (transfers).

Notification: continuous (freshmen), continuous (out-of-state freshmen), continuous (transfers).

CONTACT

Ms. Peggy Masters, Director of Undergraduate Admissions, The University of Alabama in Huntsville, Enrollment Services, 301 Sparkman Drive, Huntsville, AL 35899. *Phone:* 256-824-2771. *Toll-free phone:* 800-UAH-CALL. *Fax:* 256-824-4539. *E-mail:* uahadmissions@uah.edu.

University of Mobile

Mobile, Alabama

http://www.umobile.edu/

- **Independent Southern Baptist** comprehensive, founded 1961
- **Suburban** 880-acre campus
- **Endowment** $23.2 million
- **Coed** 1,376 undergraduate students, 90% full-time, 63% women, 37% men
- **Moderately difficult** entrance level, 62% of applicants were admitted

UNDERGRAD STUDENTS

1,241 full-time, 135 part-time. Students come from 30 states and territories; 21 other countries; 18% are from out of state; 19% Black or African American, non-Hispanic/Latino; 3% Hispanic/Latino; 0.6% Asian, non-Hispanic/Latino; 0.1% Native Hawaiian or other Pacific Islander, non-Hispanic/Latino; 0.8% American Indian or Alaska Native, non-Hispanic/Latino; 3% Two or more races, non-Hispanic/Latino; 16% Race/ethnicity unknown; 4% international; 7% transferred in; 55% live on campus.

Freshmen:

Admission: 935 applied, 579 admitted, 225 enrolled. ***Average high school GPA:*** 3.54. ***Test scores:*** SAT critical reading scores over 500: 50%; SAT math scores over 500: 100%; ACT scores over 18: 89%; SAT critical reading scores over 600: 25%; SAT math scores over 600: 50%; ACT scores over 24: 27%; ACT scores over 30: 3%.

Retention: 71% of full-time freshmen returned.

FACULTY

Total: 150, 53% full-time, 49% with terminal degrees.

Student/faculty ratio: 13:1.

ACADEMICS

Calendar: semesters. *Degrees:* associate, bachelor's, and master's.

Special study options: academic remediation for entering students, accelerated degree program, adult/continuing education programs, advanced placement credit, distance learning, double majors, honors programs, independent study, internships, part-time degree program, services for LD students, summer session for credit. ***ROTC:*** Army (c), Air Force (c).

Unusual degree programs: 3-2 engineering with University of South Alabama.

Computers: 119 computers/terminals are available on campus for general student use. Students can access the following: campus intranet, computer help desk, free student e-mail accounts, online (class) grades, online (class) registration, online (class) schedules. Campuswide network is available. 100% of college-owned or -operated housing units are wired for high-speed Internet access. Wireless service is available via entire campus.

Library: J. L. Bedsole Library. *Books:* 66,089 (physical), 157,420 (digital/electronic); *Serial titles:* 153 (physical), 151,115 (digital/electronic); *Databases:* 80.

STUDENT LIFE

Housing options: on-campus residence required through sophomore year; men-only, women-only. Campus housing is university owned. Freshman campus housing is guaranteed.

Activities and organizations: drama/theater group, choral group, Campus Activity Board, Campus Ministry, Student Government Association, Student Nurse Organization.

Athletics Member NAIA. ***Intercollegiate sports:*** baseball M(s), basketball M(s)/W(s), cheerleading M/W(s), cross-country running M(s)/W(s), golf M(s)/W(s), soccer M(s)/W(s), softball W(s), tennis M(s)/W(s), track and field M(s)/W(s), volleyball W(s). ***Intramural sports:*** basketball M/W, golf M/W, soccer M/W, softball M/W, tennis M/W, track and field M/W, volleyball M/W.

Campus security: 24-hour emergency response devices and patrols, controlled dormitory access, text alerts.

Student services: personal/psychological counseling.

COSTS & FINANCIAL AID

Costs (2016–17) ***Comprehensive fee:*** $31,000 includes full-time tuition ($20,200), mandatory fees ($1200), and room and board ($9600). Full-time tuition and fees vary according to course load. Part-time tuition: $720 per credit hour. Part-time tuition and fees vary according to course load. ***Required fees:*** $400 per year part-time. ***College room only:*** $5400. Room and board charges vary according to housing facility. ***Payment plan:*** installment. ***Waivers:*** employees or children of employees.

Financial Aid Of all full-time matriculated undergraduates who enrolled in 2016, 970 applied for aid, 888 were judged to have need, 887 had their need fully met. 55 Federal Work-Study jobs (averaging $1575). In 2016, 163 non-need-based awards were made. ***Average percent of need met:*** 66. ***Average financial aid package:*** $17,739. ***Average need-based loan:*** $2175. ***Average need-based gift aid:*** $5279. ***Average non-need-based aid:*** $10,158. ***Average indebtedness upon graduation:*** $30,029.

APPLYING

Standardized Tests *Required:* SAT or ACT (for admission).

Options: electronic application, deferred entrance.

Application fee: $25.

Required: high school transcript, minimum 2.8 GPA.

Application deadlines: rolling (freshmen), rolling (transfers).

Notification: continuous (freshmen), continuous (transfers).

CONTACT

Mrs. Charity Wittner, Vice President, University of Mobile, 5735 College Parkway, Mobile, AL 36613-2842. *Phone:* 251-442-22222. *Toll-free phone:* 800-946-7267. *E-mail:* cwittner@umobile.edu.

University of Montevallo

Montevallo, Alabama

http://www.montevallo.edu/

- **State-supported** comprehensive, founded 1896
- **Small-town** 160-acre campus with easy access to Birmingham
- **Endowment** $18.1 million
- **Coed** 2,409 undergraduate students, 90% full-time, 68% women, 32% men
- **Moderately difficult** entrance level, 65% of applicants were admitted

UNDERGRAD STUDENTS

2,178 full-time, 231 part-time. Students come from 31 states and territories; 19 other countries; 9% are from out of state; 15% Black or African American, non-Hispanic/Latino; 4% Hispanic/Latino; 0.9% Asian, non-Hispanic/Latino; 0.4% American Indian or Alaska Native, non-Hispanic/Latino; 3% Two or more races, non-Hispanic/Latino; 4% Race/ethnicity unknown; 1% international; 48% live on campus.

Freshmen:

Admission: 2,334 applied, 1,527 admitted, 477 enrolled. ***Average high school GPA:*** 3.44. ***Test scores:*** SAT critical reading scores over 500: 59%; SAT math scores over 500: 61%; SAT writing scores over 500: 44%; ACT scores over 18: 98%; SAT critical reading scores over 600: 31%; SAT math scores over 600: 15%; SAT writing scores over 600: 31%; ACT scores over 24: 48%; SAT critical reading scores over 700: 13%; SAT writing scores over 700: 6%; ACT scores over 30: 10%.

Retention: 73% of full-time freshmen returned.

FACULTY

Total: 221, 69% full-time, 73% with terminal degrees.

Student/faculty ratio: 14:1.

ACADEMICS

Calendar: semesters. *Degrees:* bachelor's, master's, and post-master's certificates.

Special study options: academic remediation for entering students, accelerated degree program, advanced placement credit, distance learning, double majors, honors programs, independent study, internships, part-time degree program, services for LD students, study abroad, summer session for credit. ***ROTC:*** Army (c), Air Force (c).

Unusual degree programs: 3-2 engineering with Auburn University, University of Alabama at Birmingham.

Computers: 340 computers/terminals are available on campus for general student use. Students can access the following: campus intranet, computer help desk, free student e-mail accounts, online (class) grades, online (class) registration, online (class) schedules. Campuswide network is available. 100% of college-owned or -operated housing units are wired for high-speed Internet access. Wireless service is available via classrooms, computer centers, computer labs, dorm rooms, libraries, student centers.

Library: Carmichael Library. Students can reserve study rooms.

STUDENT LIFE

Housing options: on-campus residence required for freshman year; coed, men-only, women-only. Campus housing is university owned. Freshman campus housing is guaranteed.

Activities and organizations: drama/theater group, student-run newspaper, television station, choral group, Student Government Association, University Programming Council, Campus Ministries, Greek Life, Environmental Club, national fraternities, national sororities.

Athletics Member NCAA. All Division II. ***Intercollegiate sports:*** baseball M(s), basketball M(s)/W(s), cheerleading W, cross-country running M/W, golf M(s)/W(s), lacrosse W, soccer M(s)/W(s), softball W, tennis W(s), track and field M/W, volleyball W(s). ***Intramural sports:*** basketball M/W, bowling M, football M, golf M, tennis M/W, volleyball M/W.

Campus security: 24-hour emergency response devices and patrols, late-night transport/escort service, controlled dormitory access.

Student services: health clinic, personal/psychological counseling.

COSTS & FINANCIAL AID

Costs (2016–17) ***Tuition:*** state resident $11,370 full-time, $379 per credit hour part-time; nonresident $23,640 full-time, $788 per credit hour part-time. ***Required fees:*** $670 full-time. ***Room and board:*** $7462; room only: $4762. Room and board charges vary according to housing facility. ***Payment plan:*** installment. ***Waivers:*** employees or children of employees.

Financial Aid Of all full-time matriculated undergraduates who enrolled in 2016, 1,657 applied for aid, 1,431 were judged to have need, 300 had their need fully met. 134 Federal Work-Study jobs (averaging $1649). In 2016, 517 non-need-based awards were made. ***Average percent of need met:*** 57. ***Average financial aid package:*** $11,100. ***Average need-based loan:*** $4010. ***Average need-based gift aid:*** $8588. ***Average non-need-based aid:*** $10,337. ***Average indebtedness upon graduation:*** $28,848.

APPLYING

Standardized Tests *Required:* SAT or ACT (for admission).

Options: electronic application, early admission, deferred entrance.

Application fee: $30.

Required: high school transcript, minimum 2.0 GPA. ***Recommended:*** interview.

Application deadlines: 8/15 (freshmen), rolling (transfers).

Notification: 9/1 (freshmen).

CONTACT

Audrey Crawford, Director of Admissions, University of Montevallo, University of Montevallo, Office of Admissions, Station 6030, Montevallo, AL 35115-6030. *Phone:* 205-665-6030. *Toll-free phone:* 800-292-4349. *Fax:* 205-665-6032. *E-mail:* admissions@montevallo.edu.

University of North Alabama

Florence, Alabama

http://www.una.edu/

- **State-supported** comprehensive, founded 1830
- **Urban** 200-acre campus with easy access to Huntsville
- **Endowment** $32.6 million
- **Coed** 6,313 undergraduate students, 82% full-time, 59% women, 41% men
- **Minimally difficult** entrance level, 52% of applicants were admitted

UNDERGRAD STUDENTS

5,163 full-time, 1,150 part-time. Students come from 38 states and territories; 40 other countries; 18% are from out of state; 14% Black or African American, non-Hispanic/Latino; 3% Hispanic/Latino; 0.6% Asian, non-Hispanic/Latino; 0.1% Native Hawaiian or other Pacific Islander, non-Hispanic/Latino; 1% American Indian or Alaska Native, non-Hispanic/Latino; 3% Two or more races, non-Hispanic/Latino; 5% Race/ethnicity unknown; 4% international; 9% transferred in; 19% live on campus.

Freshmen:

Admission: 4,761 applied, 2,457 admitted, 1,196 enrolled. ***Average high school GPA:*** 3.26. ***Test scores:*** SAT critical reading scores over 500: 38%; SAT math scores over 500: 41%; ACT scores over 18: 89%; SAT critical reading scores over 600: 6%; SAT math scores over 600: 6%; ACT scores over 24: 39%; ACT scores over 30: 3%.

Retention: 75% of full-time freshmen returned.

FACULTY

Total: 430, 57% full-time, 58% with terminal degrees.

Student/faculty ratio: 21:1.

ACADEMICS

Calendar: semesters. *Degrees:* bachelor's, master's, post-master's, and postbachelor's certificates.

Special study options: academic remediation for entering students, accelerated degree program, advanced placement credit, cooperative education, distance learning, double majors, English as a second language, external degree program, honors programs, independent study, internships, off-campus study, part-time degree program, services for LD students, student-designed majors, study abroad, summer session for credit. ***ROTC:*** Army (b).

Unusual degree programs: 3-2 business administration; engineering with The University of Alabama; nursing; social work.

Computers: 925 computers/terminals are available on campus for general student use. Students can access the following: campus intranet, computer help desk, free student e-mail accounts, online (class) grades, online (class) registration, online (class) schedules. Campuswide network is available. 100% of college-owned or -operated housing units are wired for high-speed Internet access. Wireless service is available via entire campus.

Library: Collier Library plus 3 others. *Books:* 224,081 (physical), 421,886 (digital/electronic); *Serial titles:* 4,086 (physical), 54,780 (digital/electronic); *Databases:* 150. Weekly public service hours: 98; students can reserve study rooms.

STUDENT LIFE

Housing options: on-campus residence required for freshman year; coed, men-only, women-only. Campus housing is university owned and is provided by a third party. Freshman campus housing is guaranteed.

Activities and organizations: drama/theater group, student-run newspaper, choral group, marching band, Phi Mu, Alpha Gamma Delta, Zeta Tau Alpha, Alpha Delta Pi, Student Government Association, national fraternities, national sororities.

Athletics Member NCAA. All Division II. ***Intercollegiate sports:*** baseball M(s), basketball M(s)/W(s), cheerleading M(s)/W(s), cross-country running M(s)/W(s), football M(s), golf M(s), soccer W(s), softball W(s), tennis M(s)/W(s), track and field W(s), volleyball W(s). ***Intramural sports:*** badminton M/W, basketball M/W, bowling M/W, equestrian sports W, football M/W, rugby M, soccer M/W, swimming and diving M/W, table tennis M/W, ultimate Frisbee M/W, volleyball M/W, weight lifting M/W.

Campus security: 24-hour emergency response devices and patrols, student patrols, late-night transport/escort service, controlled dormitory access.

Student services: health clinic, personal/psychological counseling, women's center.

COSTS & FINANCIAL AID

Costs (2016–17) ***Tuition:*** state resident $7920 full-time, $264 per credit hour part-time; nonresident $15,840 full-time, $528 per credit hour part-time. Full-time tuition and fees vary according to course load, program, and student level. Part-time tuition and fees vary according to course load and program. ***Required fees:*** $2000 full-time, $237 per credit hour part-time. ***Room and board:*** $7284. Room and board charges vary according to board plan, housing facility, and student level. ***Payment plan:*** installment. ***Waivers:*** senior citizens and employees or children of employees.

Financial Aid Of all full-time matriculated undergraduates who enrolled in 2015, 2,893 applied for aid, 2,567 were judged to have need, 235 had their need fully met. 160 Federal Work-Study jobs (averaging $2016). 536 state and other part-time jobs (averaging $1759). In 2015, 325 non-need-based awards were made. ***Average percent of need met:*** 54. ***Average financial aid package:*** $7972. ***Average need-based loan:*** $3646. ***Average need-based gift aid:*** $4254. ***Average non-need-based aid:*** $4946.

APPLYING

Standardized Tests *Required:* SAT or ACT (for admission).

Options: electronic application, early admission, deferred entrance.

Application fee: $25.

Required: high school transcript, minimum 2.0 GPA, 13 approved units from high school academic core.

Application deadlines: rolling (freshmen), rolling (transfers).

Notification: continuous (freshmen), continuous (transfers).

CONTACT

Mrs. Julie Taylor, Interim Director of Admissions, University of North Alabama, One Harrison Plaza, Florence, AL 35632-0001. *Phone:* 256-765-4680. *Toll-free phone:* 800-TALK-UNA. *Fax:* 256-765-4329. *E-mail:* admissions@una.edu.

University of South Alabama

Mobile, Alabama

http://www.southalabama.edu/

- **State-supported** university, founded 1963
- **Suburban** 1225-acre campus
- **Endowment** $135.8 million
- **Coed** 11,761 undergraduate students, 82% full-time, 54% women, 46% men
- **Moderately difficult** entrance level, 80% of applicants were admitted

UNDERGRAD STUDENTS

9,604 full-time, 2,151 part-time. Students come from 45 states and territories; 73 other countries; 18% are from out of state; 22% Black or African American, non-Hispanic/Latino; 3% Hispanic/Latino; 3% Asian, non-Hispanic/Latino; 0.1% Native Hawaiian or other Pacific Islander, non-Hispanic/Latino; 0.7% American Indian or Alaska Native, non-Hispanic/Latino; 3% Two or more races, non-Hispanic/Latino; 2% Race/ethnicity unknown; 9% international; 7% transferred in; 27% live on campus.

Freshmen:

Admission: 6,401 applied, 5,097 admitted, 1,997 enrolled. ***Average high school GPA:*** 3.48. ***Test scores:*** SAT critical reading scores over 500: 58%; SAT math scores over 500: 58%; SAT writing scores over 500: 48%; ACT scores over 18: 99%; SAT critical reading scores over 600: 21%; SAT math scores over 600: 18%; SAT writing scores over 600: 14%; ACT scores over 24: 48%; SAT critical reading scores over 700: 2%; SAT writing scores over 700: 1%; ACT scores over 30: 8%.

Retention: 73% of full-time freshmen returned.

FACULTY

Total: 1,047, 56% full-time, 43% with terminal degrees.

Student/faculty ratio: 20:1.

ACADEMICS

Calendar: semesters. *Degrees:* certificates, bachelor's, master's, doctoral, post-master's, and postbachelor's certificates.

Special study options: academic remediation for entering students, accelerated degree program, adult/continuing education programs, advanced placement credit, cooperative education, distance learning, double majors, English as a second language, freshman honors college, honors programs, independent study, internships, part-time degree program, services for LD students, student-designed majors, study abroad, summer session for credit. ***ROTC:*** Army (b), Air Force (b).

Computers: Students can access the following: campus intranet, computer help desk, free student e-mail accounts, online (class) grades, online (class) registration, online (class) schedules. Campuswide network is available. 100% of college-owned or -operated housing units are wired for high-speed Internet access. Wireless service is available via entire campus.

Library: Marx Library plus 5 others. *Books:* 703,077 (physical), 34,645 (digital/electronic); *Serial titles:* 4,077 (physical), 1.2 million (digital/electronic); *Databases:* 32.

STUDENT LIFE

Housing options: coed, special housing for students with disabilities. Campus housing is university owned and is provided by a third party.

Activities and organizations: drama/theater group, student-run newspaper, radio and television station, choral group, marching band, Student Government Association, African American Student Association, Council of International Student Organizations, Alpha Epsilon Delta Pre-Health Professions, Panhellenic Council, national fraternities, national sororities.

Athletics Member NCAA. All Division I. ***Intercollegiate sports:*** baseball M(s), basketball M(s)/W(s), cross-country running M(s)/W(s), football M(s), golf M(s)/W(s), soccer W(s), softball W(s), tennis M(s)/W(s), track and field M(s)/W(s), volleyball W(s). ***Intramural sports:*** basketball M/W, rock climbing M(c)/W(c), rugby M(c)/W(c), sailing M(c)/W(c), soccer M/W, softball M/W, ultimate Frisbee M(c)/W(c), volleyball M/W, water polo M/W.

Campus security: 24-hour emergency response devices and patrols, late-night transport/escort service.

Student services: health clinic, personal/psychological counseling, women's center, legal services.

COSTS & FINANCIAL AID

Costs (2016–17) ***Tuition:*** state resident $9060 full-time, $302 per credit hour part-time; nonresident $18,120 full-time, $604 per credit hour part-time. Full-time tuition and fees vary according to course load and program. Part-time tuition and fees vary according to course load and program. ***Room and board:*** $7340; room only: $3850. Room and board charges vary according to board plan and housing facility. ***Payment plan:*** installment. ***Waivers:*** employees or children of employees.

Financial Aid Of all full-time matriculated undergraduates who enrolled in 2015, 7,167 applied for aid, 5,829 were judged to have need, 487 had their need fully met. In 2015, 1146 non-need-based awards were made. ***Average percent of need met:*** 50. ***Average financial aid package:*** $9708. ***Average need-based loan:*** $4348. ***Average need-based gift aid:*** $6606. ***Average non-need-based aid:*** $5321.

APPLYING

Standardized Tests *Required for some:* SAT or ACT (for admission).

Options: electronic application, early admission, deferred entrance.

Application fee: $45.

Required: high school transcript. ***Required for some:*** essay or personal statement, minimum 3.5 GPA, 1 letter of recommendation, minimum high school GPA of 3.0 for Accelerated College Enrollment Program, minimum high school GPA of 3.5 for Early Admission. ***Recommended:*** minimum 2.5 GPA.

Application deadlines: 7/15 (freshmen), 7/15 (transfers).

Notification: continuous (freshmen), continuous (out-of-state freshmen), continuous (transfers).

CONTACT

Mr. T. Scott Henne, Director, New Student Recruitment, University of South Alabama, Mobile, AL 36688-0002. *Phone:* 251-460-7834. *Toll-free phone:* 800-872-5247. *Fax:* 251-460-7876. *E-mail:* recruitment@southalabama.edu.

The University of West Alabama

Livingston, Alabama

http://www.uwa.edu/

- **State-supported** comprehensive, founded 1835
- **Small-town** 514-acre campus
- **Endowment** $32,355
- **Coed** 1,978 undergraduate students, 87% full-time, 55% women, 45% men
- **Minimally difficult** entrance level, 53% of applicants were admitted

UNDERGRAD STUDENTS

1,722 full-time, 256 part-time. Students come from 30 states and territories; 24 other countries; 20% are from out of state; 41% Black or African American, non-Hispanic/Latino; 2% Hispanic/Latino; 0.2% Asian, non-Hispanic/Latino; 0.1% Native Hawaiian or other Pacific Islander, non-Hispanic/Latino; 0.3% American Indian or Alaska Native, non-Hispanic/Latino; 2% Two or more races, non-Hispanic/Latino; 4% Race/ethnicity unknown; 6% international; 13% transferred in; 44% live on campus.

Freshmen:

Admission: 1,032 applied, 548 admitted, 377 enrolled. ***Test scores:*** ACT scores over 18: 78%; ACT scores over 24: 20%; ACT scores over 30: 1%. ***Retention:*** 65% of full-time freshmen returned.

FACULTY

Total: 282, 46% full-time, 65% with terminal degrees.

Student/faculty ratio: 12:1.

ACADEMICS

Calendar: semesters. *Degrees:* certificates, associate, bachelor's, master's, and post-master's certificates.

Special study options: academic remediation for entering students, accelerated degree program, advanced placement credit, cooperative education, distance learning, double majors, English as a second language, freshman honors college, honors programs, independent study, internships, part-time degree program, services for LD students, study abroad, summer session for credit. ***ROTC:*** Air Force (c).

Unusual degree programs: 3-2 engineering with Auburn University, The University of Alabama at Birmingham, Mississippi State University, The University of Alabama; forestry with Auburn University; social work with University of Alabama; wildlife with Auburn University.

Computers: 600 computers/terminals are available on campus for general student use. Students can access the following: campus intranet, computer help desk, free student e-mail accounts, online (class) grades, online (class) registration, online (class) schedules. Campuswide network is available. 100% of college-owned or -operated housing units are wired for high-speed Internet access. Wireless service is available via entire campus.

Library: Julia Tutwiler Library. *Books:* 166,174 (physical), 1,789 (digital/electronic); *Serial titles:* 36 (physical), 96,027 (digital/electronic); *Databases:* 177. Weekly public service hours: 94; students can reserve study rooms.

STUDENT LIFE

Housing options: on-campus residence required for freshman year; coed. Campus housing is university owned. Freshman campus housing is guaranteed.

Activities and organizations: drama/theater group, student-run newspaper, television station, choral group, marching band, The UWA Band, The Student Government Association, UWA Ambassadors, Phi Mu, Blue Key, national fraternities, national sororities.

Athletics Member NCAA. All Division II. ***Intercollegiate sports:*** baseball M(s), basketball M(s)/W(s), cross-country running M(s)/W(s), football M(s), golf M(s)/W(s), soccer M(s)/W(s), softball W(s), tennis M(s)/W(s), track and field M(s)/W(s), triathlon W(s), volleyball W(s). ***Intramural sports:*** basketball M/W, bowling M/W, football M/W, soccer M/W, softball M/W, table tennis M/W, tennis M/W, ultimate Frisbee M/W, volleyball M/W.

Campus security: 24-hour emergency response devices and patrols, student patrols, late-night transport/escort service, controlled dormitory access.

Student services: health clinic, personal/psychological counseling.

COSTS & FINANCIAL AID

Costs (2017–18) ***Tuition:*** state resident $7286 full-time, $310 per hour part-time; nonresident $14,572 full-time, $620 per hour part-time. Full-time tuition and fees vary according to course load. Part-time tuition and fees vary according to course load. ***Required fees:*** $1590 full-time. ***Room and board:*** $6640; room only: $4040. Room and board charges vary according to board plan, housing facility, and student level. ***Payment plan:*** installment. ***Waivers:*** employees or children of employees.

Financial Aid Of all full-time matriculated undergraduates who enrolled in 2015, 1,472 applied for aid, 1,288 were judged to have need, 90 had their need fully met. 99 Federal Work-Study jobs (averaging $3338). 45 state and other part-time jobs (averaging $2300). In 2015, 68 non-need-based awards were made. ***Average percent of need met:*** 23. ***Average financial aid package:*** $10,833. ***Average need-based gift aid:*** $5123. ***Average non-need-based aid:*** $4844. ***Average indebtedness upon graduation:*** $24,449.

APPLYING
Standardized Tests *Required:* SAT or ACT (for admission).
Options: electronic application, deferred entrance.
Application fee: $40.
Required: high school transcript, minimum 2.0 GPA.
Application deadlines: rolling (freshmen), rolling (transfers).
Notification: continuous (freshmen), continuous (transfers).

CONTACT
Mrs. Brenda Edwards, Coordinator of Admissions Operations, The University of West Alabama, Station 4, Livingston, AL 35470. *Phone:* 205-652-3699. *Toll-free phone:* 888-636-8800. *Fax:* 205-652-3881. *E-mail:* belliott@uwa.edu.

Virginia College in Birmingham
Birmingham, Alabama
http://www.vc.edu/

CONTACT
Director of Admissions, Virginia College in Birmingham, 488 Palisades Boulevard, Birmingham, AL 35209. *Phone:* 205-802-1200.

Virginia College in Huntsville
Huntsville, Alabama
http://www.vc.edu/

CONTACT
Director of Admission, Virginia College in Huntsville, 2021 Drake Avenue SW, Huntsville, AL 35801. *Phone:* 256-533-7387. *Fax:* 256-533-7785.

ALASKA

Alaska Bible College
Palmer, Alaska
http://www.akbible.edu/

- **Independent nondenominational** 4-year, founded 1966
- **Small-town** 2-acre campus with easy access to Anchorage, AK
- **Coed** 50 undergraduate students, 58% full-time, 32% women, 68% men
- **Minimally difficult** entrance level

UNDERGRAD STUDENTS
29 full-time, 21 part-time. Students come from 7 states and territories; 10% are from out of state; 2% Black or African American, non-Hispanic/Latino; 4% Hispanic/Latino; 4% American Indian or Alaska Native, non-Hispanic/Latino; 4% Two or more races, non-Hispanic/Latino; 40% transferred in; 25% live on campus.

Freshmen:
Admission: 6 enrolled.
Retention: 20% of full-time freshmen returned.

FACULTY
Total: 12, 25% full-time, 8% with terminal degrees.
Student/faculty ratio: 4:1.

ACADEMICS
Calendar: semesters. *Degrees:* certificates, associate, and bachelor's.
Special study options: academic remediation for entering students, advanced placement credit, distance learning, double majors, independent study, internships, off-campus study, part-time degree program.
Computers: 2 computers/terminals are available on campus for general student use. Students can access the following: campus intranet, computer help desk, free student e-mail accounts, online (class) grades, online (class) registration, online (class) schedules. Campuswide network is available. 4% of college-owned or -operated housing units are wired for high-speed Internet access. Wireless service is available via entire campus.
Library: Alaska Bible College Ball Memorial Library. *Books:* 32,000 (physical); *Serial titles:* 46 (physical). Weekly public service hours: 40.

STUDENT LIFE
Housing options: men-only, women-only. Campus housing is university owned. Freshman applicants given priority for college housing.

COSTS
Costs (2017–18) ***Comprehensive fee:*** $12,000 includes full-time tuition ($9000), mandatory fees ($300), and room and board ($2700). Part-time tuition: $375 per credit hour. ***Waivers:*** senior citizens and employees or children of employees.

APPLYING
Standardized Tests *Required:* SAT or ACT (for admission).
Options: electronic application, deferred entrance.
Application fee: $35.
Required: essay or personal statement, high school transcript, minimum 2.0 GPA, 3 letters of recommendation.
Application deadlines: 7/1 (freshmen), 7/1 (transfers).
Notification: continuous until 7/15 (freshmen), continuous until 7/15 (transfers).

CONTACT
Justin Archuletta, Director of Admissions, Alaska Bible College, 248 E Elmwood Ave, Palmer, AK 99645. *Phone:* 907-745-3201 Ext. 111. *Toll-free phone:* 800-478-7884. *Fax:* 907-745-3210. *E-mail:* admissions@akbible.edu.

Alaska Pacific University
Anchorage, Alaska
http://www.alaskapacific.edu/

- **Independent** comprehensive, founded 1959
- **Urban** 170-acre campus
- **Coed** 294 undergraduate students, 71% full-time, 63% women, 37% men
- **Minimally difficult** entrance level, 55% of applicants were admitted

UNDERGRAD STUDENTS
209 full-time, 85 part-time. Students come from 2 other countries; 4% Black or African American, non-Hispanic/Latino; 1% Hispanic/Latino; 3% Asian, non-Hispanic/Latino; 0.7% Native Hawaiian or other Pacific Islander, non-Hispanic/Latino; 14% American Indian or Alaska Native, non-Hispanic/Latino; 12% Two or more races, non-Hispanic/Latino; 10% Race/ethnicity unknown; 19% transferred in; 26% live on campus.

Freshmen:
Admission: 474 applied, 261 admitted, 41 enrolled. ***Average high school GPA:*** 3.22.
Retention: 46% of full-time freshmen returned.

FACULTY
Total: 82, 34% full-time, 34% with terminal degrees.
Student/faculty ratio: 7:1.

ACADEMICS
Calendar: semesters. *Degrees:* certificates, associate, bachelor's, master's, doctoral, and postbachelor's certificates.
Special study options: academic remediation for entering students, accelerated degree program, adult/continuing education programs, advanced placement credit, distance learning, double majors, independent study, internships, part-time degree program, services for LD students, student-designed majors, study abroad, summer session for credit. ***ROTC:*** Air Force (c).
Unusual degree programs: 3-2 environmental science.
Computers: 105 computers/terminals and 480 ports are available on campus for general student use. Students can access the following: campus intranet, computer help desk, free student e-mail accounts, online (class) grades, online (class) registration, online (class) schedules. Campuswide network is available. 100% of college-owned or -operated housing units are wired for high-speed Internet access. Wireless service is available via entire campus.
Library: Consortium Library. Students can reserve study rooms.

STUDENT LIFE
Housing options: on-campus residence required through sophomore year; coed. Campus housing is university owned. Freshman campus housing is guaranteed.
Activities and organizations: drama/theater group, student-run newspaper, choral group, ASAPU (Associated Students of Alaska Pacific University), Photography Club, Dive Club, Basketball club, Spectrum Club.
Athletics ***Intramural sports:*** basketball M/W, skiing (cross-country) M/W, soccer M/W, volleyball M/W.
Campus security: 24-hour emergency response devices, student patrols, late-night transport/escort service, controlled dormitory access.
Student services: personal/psychological counseling.

COSTS & FINANCIAL AID
Costs (2017–18) ***Comprehensive fee:*** $27,970 includes full-time tuition ($20,350), mandatory fees ($480), and room and board ($7140). Full-time tuition and fees vary according to course load, degree level, program, and reciprocity agreements. Part-time tuition: $848 per semester hour. Part-time tuition and fees vary according to course load, degree level, and program. ***Required fees:*** $130 per term part-time. ***Room and board:*** Room and board charges vary according to board plan and housing facility. ***Payment plans:*** installment, deferred payment. ***Waivers:*** employees or children of employees.
Financial Aid Of all full-time matriculated undergraduates who enrolled in 2015, 147 applied for aid, 129 were judged to have need, 30 had their need fully met. In 2015, 36 non-need-based awards were made. ***Average percent of need met:*** 39. ***Average financial aid package:*** $10,522. ***Average need-based loan:*** $4128. ***Average need-based gift aid:*** $5973. ***Average non-need-based aid:*** $4635. ***Average indebtedness upon graduation:*** $8922.

APPLYING
Options: electronic application, deferred entrance.
Application fee: $25.
Required: high school transcript, minimum 2.5 GPA.
Application deadlines: 8/1 (freshmen), 8/1 (transfers).
Notification: continuous (freshmen), continuous (out-of-state freshmen), continuous (transfers).

CONTACT
Ms. Kate Miller, Director of Admissions, Alaska Pacific University, 4101 University Drive, Anchorage, AK 99508. *Phone:* 907-564-8300. *Toll-free phone:* 800-252-7528. *Fax:* 907-564-8317. *E-mail:* admissions@alaskapacific.edu.

Charter College
Anchorage, Alaska
http://www.chartercollege.edu/

CONTACT
Ms. Lily Sirianni, Vice President, Charter College, 2221 East Northern Lights Boulevard, Suite 120, Anchorage, AK 99508. *Phone:* 907-277-1000. *Toll-free phone:* 888-200-9942.

University of Alaska Anchorage
Anchorage, Alaska
http://www.uaa.alaska.edu/

CONTACT
Enrollment Services, University of Alaska Anchorage, PO Box 141629, 3901 Old Seward Highway, Anchorage, AK 99508-8046. *Phone:* 907-786-1480. *Fax:* 907-786-4888. *E-mail:* enroll@uaa.alaska.edu.

University of Alaska Anchorage, Kenai Peninsula College
Soldotna, Alaska
http://www.kpc.alaska.edu/

- **State-supported** primarily 2-year, founded 1964, part of University of Alaska System
- **Rural** 360-acre campus
- **Coed**
- **Noncompetitive** entrance level

ACADEMICS
Calendar: semesters. *Degrees:* certificates, associate, and bachelor's.
Library: Kenai Peninsula College Library.

STUDENT LIFE
Housing options: coed. Campus housing is university owned.
Campus security: 24-hour emergency response devices.
Student services: health clinic.

COSTS
Costs (2016–17) ***Tuition:*** state resident $4608 full-time, $194 per credit part-time; nonresident $16,344 full-time, $681 per credit part-time. Full-time tuition and fees vary according to course load, degree level, location, and program. Part-time tuition and fees vary according to course load, degree level, location, and program. ***Required fees:*** $1176 full-time. ***Room and board:*** $10,868; room only: $6918. Room and board charges vary according to board plan.

APPLYING
Standardized Tests *Required:* ACT, SAT or ACCUPLACER (for admission).
Options: electronic application.
Application fee: $40.
Required: high school transcript.

CONTACT
Mrs. Julie Cotterell, Admission and Student Records Coordinator, University of Alaska Anchorage, Kenai Peninsula College, 156 College Road, Soldotna, AK 99669-9798. *Phone:* 907-262-0311. *Toll-free phone:* 877-262-0330. *E-mail:* jmcotterell@kpc.alaska.edu.

University of Alaska Fairbanks
Fairbanks, Alaska
http://www.uaf.edu/

- **State-supported** university, founded 1917, part of University of Alaska System
- **Small-town** 2250-acre campus
- **Endowment** $80.1 million
- **Coed** 7,239 undergraduate students, 44% full-time, 57% women, 43% men
- **Minimally difficult** entrance level, 73% of applicants were admitted

UNDERGRAD STUDENTS
3,189 full-time, 4,050 part-time. Students come from 50 states and territories; 34 other countries; 14% are from out of state; 2% Black or African American, non-Hispanic/Latino; 7% Hispanic/Latino; 1% Asian, non-Hispanic/Latino; 0.4% Native Hawaiian or other Pacific Islander, non-Hispanic/Latino; 14% American Indian or Alaska Native, non-Hispanic/Latino; 4% Two or more races, non-Hispanic/Latino; 27% Race/ethnicity unknown; 1% international; 5% transferred in; 37% live on campus.

Freshmen:
Admission: 1,557 applied, 1,144 admitted, 846 enrolled. ***Average high school GPA:*** 3.33. ***Test scores:*** SAT critical reading scores over 500: 69%; SAT math scores over 500: 65%; SAT writing scores over 500: 58%; ACT scores over 18: 84%; SAT critical reading scores over 600: 26%; SAT math scores over 600: 27%; SAT writing scores over 600: 19%; ACT scores over 24: 41%; SAT critical reading scores over 700: 4%; SAT math scores over 700: 5%; SAT writing scores over 700: 2%; ACT scores over 30: 7%.
Retention: 75% of full-time freshmen returned.

FACULTY
Total: 909, 36% full-time, 58% with terminal degrees.
Student/faculty ratio: 10:1.

ACADEMICS
Calendar: semesters. *Degrees:* certificates, associate, bachelor's, master's, doctoral, and postbachelor's certificates.

Special study options: academic remediation for entering students, accelerated degree program, advanced placement credit, cooperative education, distance learning, double majors, English as a second language, external degree program, honors programs, independent study, internships, off-campus study, part-time degree program, services for LD students, student-designed majors, study abroad, summer session for credit. ***ROTC:*** Army (b).

Unusual degree programs: 3-2 engineering; computer science.

Computers: 125 computers/terminals and 22 ports are available on campus for general student use. Students can access the following: campus intranet, computer help desk, free student e-mail accounts, online (class) grades, online (class) registration, online (class) schedules, university portal. Campuswide network is available. 100% of college-owned or -operated housing units are wired for high-speed Internet access. Wireless service is available via entire campus.

Library: Rasmuson Library plus 2 others. Weekly public service hours: 87; students can reserve study rooms.

STUDENT LIFE
Housing options: coed, special housing for students with disabilities. Campus housing is university owned. Freshman applicants given priority for college housing.

Activities and organizations: drama/theater group, student-run newspaper, radio station, choral group, Chi Alpha, Yoga Club, Aurora Aerial Arts, Festival of Native Arts, Gender and Sexuality Alliance, national fraternities, national sororities.

Athletics Member NCAA. All Division II except ice hockey (Division I). ***Intercollegiate sports:*** basketball M(s)/W(s), cross-country running M(s)/W(s), ice hockey M(s), riflery M(s)/W(s), skiing (cross-country) M(s)/W(s), swimming and diving W(s), volleyball W(s). ***Intramural sports:*** badminton M(c)/W(c), basketball M/W, cross-country running M(c)/W(c), fencing M(c)/W(c), ice hockey M/W, soccer M/W, ultimate Frisbee M/W, volleyball M/W.

Campus security: 24-hour emergency response devices and patrols, student patrols, late-night transport/escort service, controlled dormitory access, ID check at door of residence halls, crime prevention and safety workshops.

Student services: health clinic, personal/psychological counseling, women's center, legal services.

COSTS & FINANCIAL AID
Costs (2017–18) ***Tuition:*** state resident $6690 full-time, $202 per credit hour part-time; nonresident $22,080 full-time, $715 per credit hour part-time. Full-time tuition and fees vary according to course level, course load, location, program, and reciprocity agreements. Part-time tuition and fees vary according to course level, course load, location, program, and reciprocity agreements. ***Required fees:*** $1454 full-time. ***Room and board:*** $8530; room only: $4140. Room and board charges vary according to board plan, housing facility, and location. ***Payment plans:*** installment, deferred payment. ***Waivers:*** children of alumni, senior citizens, and employees or children of employees.

Financial Aid Of all full-time matriculated undergraduates who enrolled in 2015, 2,741 applied for aid, 1,739 were judged to have need, 213 had their need fully met. 35 Federal Work-Study jobs (averaging $4210). In 2015, 499 non-need-based awards were made. ***Average percent of need met:*** 53. ***Average financial aid package:*** $8074. ***Average need-based loan:*** $3793. ***Average need-based gift aid:*** $6744. ***Average non-need-based aid:*** $3929. ***Average indebtedness upon graduation:*** $25,344. ***Financial aid deadline:*** 7/1.

APPLYING
Standardized Tests *Required:* SAT or ACT (for admission).
Options: electronic application, deferred entrance.
Application fee: $50.
Required: high school transcript, minimum 2.5 GPA.
Application deadlines: 6/15 (freshmen), 6/15 (transfers).
Notification: continuous (freshmen), continuous (out-of-state freshmen), continuous (transfers).

CONTACT
Ms. Mary Kreta, Director of Admissions, University of Alaska Fairbanks, PO Box 757480, Fairbanks, AK 99775-7480. *Phone:* 907-474-7500. *Toll-free phone:* 800-478-1823. *Fax:* 907-474-7097.
E-mail: admissions@uaf.edu.

See previous page for display ad and page 1540 for the College Close-Up.

University of Alaska Southeast

Juneau, Alaska

http://www.uas.alaska.edu/

CONTACT
Ms. Deema Ferguson, Admissions Clerk, University of Alaska Southeast, 11120 Glacier Highway, Juneau, AK 99801-8625. *Phone:* 907-796-6294 Ext. 6100. *Toll-free phone:* 877-465-4827. *Fax:* 907-796-6365. *E-mail:* admissions@uas.alaska.edu.

University of Alaska Southeast, Sitka Campus

Sitka, Alaska

http://www.uas.alaska.edu/

CONTACT
Ms. Teal Gordon, Admissions Representative, University of Alaska Southeast, Sitka Campus, UAS Sitka, 1332 Seward Avenue, Sitka, AK 99835. *Phone:* 907-747-7726. *Toll-free phone:* 800-478-6653.
Fax: 907-747-7731. *E-mail:* ktgordon@uas.alaska.edu.

ARIZONA

Argosy University, Phoenix

Phoenix, Arizona

http://www.argosy.edu/phoenix-arizona/default.aspx

CONTACT
Argosy University, Phoenix, 2233 West Dunlap Avenue, Phoenix, AZ 85021. *Phone:* 602-216-2600. *Toll-free phone:* 866-216-2777.

Arizona Christian University

Phoenix, Arizona

http://arizonachristian.edu/

- **Independent Conservative Baptist** 4-year, founded 1960
- **Urban** 19-acre campus with easy access to Phoenix
- **Coed** 820 undergraduate students, 80% full-time, 42% women, 58% men

UNDERGRAD STUDENTS
656 full-time, 164 part-time. Students come from 29 states and territories; 17 other countries; 27% are from out of state; 13% Black or African American, non-Hispanic/Latino; 18% Hispanic/Latino; 1% Asian, non-Hispanic/Latino; 0.6% Native Hawaiian or other Pacific Islander, non-Hispanic/Latino; 0.9% American Indian or Alaska Native, non-Hispanic/Latino; 6% Two or more races, non-Hispanic/Latino; 6% Race/ethnicity unknown; 2% international; 16% transferred in; 29% live on campus.

Freshmen:
Admission: 129 enrolled. ***Average high school GPA:*** 3.22. ***Test scores:*** SAT critical reading scores over 500: 38%; SAT math scores over 500: 49%; ACT scores over 18: 81%; SAT critical reading scores over 600: 10%; SAT math scores over 600: 12%; ACT scores over 24: 18%; SAT critical reading scores over 700: 3%; ACT scores over 30: 2%.
Retention: 52% of full-time freshmen returned.

FACULTY
Total: 97, 15% full-time.
Student/faculty ratio: 16:1.

ACADEMICS
Calendar: 4-4-1. *Degrees:* associate and bachelor's.
Special study options: academic remediation for entering students, adult/continuing education programs, advanced placement credit, distance learning, double majors, independent study, internships, part-time degree program, services for LD students, study abroad, summer session for credit. ***ROTC:*** Air Force (c).
Computers: 37 computers/terminals are available on campus for general student use. Students can access the following: free student e-mail accounts, online (class) grades, online (class) registration, online (class) schedules. 100% of college-owned or -operated housing units are wired for high-speed Internet access. Wireless service is available via entire campus.
Library: R. S. Beal Library. *Books:* 28,886 (physical), 19,792 (digital/electronic); *Serial titles:* 2,255 (physical); *Databases:* 23. Weekly public service hours: 86.

STUDENT LIFE
Housing options: on-campus residence required through sophomore year; coed. Campus housing is university owned. Freshman campus housing is guaranteed.
Activities and organizations: choral group, Joseph Story Pre-Law Society, International Student Association, Pre-Medicine Club, Flock Council and Flock Leaders, Reason and Religion.
Athletics Member NAIA, NCCAA. ***Intercollegiate sports:*** baseball M(s), basketball M(s)/W(s), cross-country running M(s)/W(s), football M(s), golf M(s)/W(s), soccer M(s)/W(s), softball W(s), swimming and diving W(s), tennis M(s)/W(s), track and field M(s)/W(s), volleyball W(s). ***Intramural sports:*** basketball M/W, bowling M(c)/W(c), cheerleading W(c), soccer M/W, table tennis M/W, volleyball M/W.
Campus security: 24-hour emergency response devices, student patrols, late-night transport/escort service, controlled dormitory access, 20-hour patrol with a guard on call on weekdays, 24-hour patrol by trained security personnel on weekends.
Student services: personal/psychological counseling.

COSTS & FINANCIAL AID
Costs (2017–18) ***Comprehensive fee:*** $34,306 includes full-time tuition ($23,972) and room and board ($10,334). Full-time tuition and fees vary according to class time, course load, and program. Part-time tuition and fees vary according to class time, course load, and program. ***Required fees:*** $493 per term part-time. ***College room only:*** $5310. Room and board charges vary according to board plan. ***Payment plan:*** installment. ***Waivers:*** employees or children of employees.
Financial Aid Of all full-time matriculated undergraduates who enrolled in 2014, 503 applied for aid, 446 were judged to have need. In 2014, 52 non-need-based awards were made. ***Average financial aid package:*** $15,811. ***Average need-based loan:*** $3705. ***Average need-based gift aid:*** $13,195. ***Average non-need-based aid:*** $5414. ***Average indebtedness upon graduation:*** $26,228. ***Financial aid deadline:*** 6/5.

APPLYING
Standardized Tests *Required:* SAT or ACT (for admission).
Required: essay or personal statement, high school transcript, minimum 2.0 GPA, 1 letter of recommendation.

CONTACT
Lambert Cruz, Registrar and Asst Dir Enrollment Mgmt, Arizona Christian University, 2625 E Cactus Road, Phoenix, AZ 85032.
Phone: 602-386-4160. *Toll-free phone:* 800-247-2697.
Fax: 602-4042159. *E-mail:* lambert.cruz@arizonachristian.edu.

Arizona College–Mesa

Mesa, Arizona

http://www.arizonacollege.edu/

CONTACT
Arizona College–Mesa, 163 N Dobson Road, Mesa, AZ 85201.

Arizona State University at the Downtown Phoenix campus

Phoenix, Arizona

http://campus.asu.edu/downtown/

- **State-supported** university, founded 2006
- **Urban** 18-acre campus with easy access to Phoenix
- **Coed** 9,238 undergraduate students, 89% full-time, 66% women, 34% men
- **Moderately difficult** entrance level, 77% of applicants were admitted

UNDERGRAD STUDENTS
8,238 full-time, 1,000 part-time. Students come from 50 states and territories; 38 other countries; 27% are from out of state; 6% Black or African American, non-Hispanic/Latino; 29% Hispanic/Latino; 5% Asian, non-Hispanic/Latino; 0.2% Native Hawaiian or other Pacific Islander, non-Hispanic/Latino; 2% American Indian or Alaska Native, non-Hispanic/Latino; 4% Two or more races, non-Hispanic/Latino; 0.7% Race/ethnicity unknown; 2% international; 15% live on campus.

Freshmen:
Admission: 5,224 applied, 4,007 admitted. ***Average high school GPA:*** 3.48. ***Test scores:*** SAT critical reading scores over 500: 70%; SAT math scores over 500: 68%; ACT scores over 18: 95%; SAT critical reading scores over 600: 24%; SAT math scores over 600: 24%; ACT scores over 24: 49%; SAT critical reading scores over 700: 2%; SAT math scores over 700: 3%; ACT scores over 30: 7%.

Retention: 84% of full-time freshmen returned.

FACULTY
Total: 628, 84% full-time, 66% with terminal degrees.

Student/faculty ratio: 20:1.

ACADEMICS
Calendar: semesters (15 weeks) and sessions (7.5 weeks). *Degrees:* certificates, bachelor's, master's, doctoral, post-master's, and postbachelor's certificates.

Special study options: accelerated degree program, advanced placement credit, cooperative education, distance learning, double majors, freshman honors college, honors programs, independent study, internships, off-campus study, part-time degree program, services for LD students, student-designed majors, study abroad, summer session for credit. ***ROTC:*** Army (c), Navy (c), Air Force (c).

Computers: 486 computers/terminals are available on campus for general student use. Students can access the following: campus intranet, computer help desk, free student e-mail accounts, online (class) grades, online (class) registration, online (class) schedules. Campuswide network is available. 100% of college-owned or -operated housing units are wired for high-speed Internet access. Wireless service is available via classrooms, computer centers, computer labs, dorm rooms, learning centers, libraries, student centers.

Library: Downtown Phoenix campus Library. *Books:* 3.0 million (physical), 881,323 (digital/electronic); *Serial titles:* 72,161 (physical), 75,943 (digital/electronic); *Databases:* 630. Weekly public service hours: 149; study areas open 24 hours, 5-7 days a week; students can reserve study rooms.

STUDENT LIFE
Housing options: on-campus residence required for freshman year; coed, special housing for students with disabilities. Campus housing is leased by the school and is provided by a third party. Freshman campus housing is guaranteed.

Activities and organizations: drama/theater group, student-run newspaper, radio and television station, Student Nurses Association, American Medical Student Association, Exercise and Wellness Organization, Student Nutrition Council, Physical Therapy Club.

Athletics Member NCAA. All Division I. ***Intercollegiate sports:*** baseball M(s), basketball M(s)/W(s), cross-country running M(s)/W(s), football M(s), golf M(s)/W(s), gymnastics W(s), ice hockey M(s), lacrosse W(s), sand volleyball W(s), soccer W(s), softball W(s), swimming and diving M(s)/W(s), tennis M(s)/W(s), track and field M(s)/W(s), triathlon W(s), volleyball W(s), water polo W(s), wrestling M(s). ***Intramural sports:*** baseball M(c), basketball M/W, cheerleading M(c)/W(c), crew M(c), equestrian sports M(c)/W(c), fencing M(c)/W(c), golf M(c), gymnastics M(c), ice hockey M(c)/W(c), lacrosse M(c)/W(c), racquetball M(c)/W(c), rowing M(c), rugby M(c)/W(c), sailing M(c)/W(c), soccer M(c)/W(c), softball M/W, tennis M(c)/W(c), triathlon M(c)/W(c), ultimate Frisbee M(c)/W(c), volleyball M(c)/W(c), water polo M(c)/W(c).

Campus security: 24-hour emergency response devices and patrols, late-night transport/escort service, controlled dormitory access, LiveSafe smart phone application, surveillance camera in some residence halls.

Student services: health clinic, personal/psychological counseling.

COSTS & FINANCIAL AID
Costs (2016–17) ***Tuition:*** state resident $9684 full-time, $692 per credit hour part-time; nonresident $25,784 full-time, $1074 per credit hour part-time. Full-time tuition and fees vary according to program. Part-time tuition and fees vary according to program. ***Required fees:*** $686 full-time. ***Room and board:*** $13,310; room only: $8710. Room and board charges vary according to board plan and housing facility. ***Payment plan:*** installment. ***Waivers:*** employees or children of employees.

Financial Aid Of all full-time matriculated undergraduates who enrolled in 2015, 6,689 applied for aid, 5,763 were judged to have need, 935 had their need fully met. 396 Federal Work-Study jobs (averaging $2613). 1,252 state and other part-time jobs (averaging $3393). In 2015, 1117 non-need-based awards were made. ***Average percent of need met:*** 57. ***Average financial aid package:*** $13,859. ***Average need-based loan:*** $4109. ***Average need-based gift aid:*** $9607. ***Average non-need-based aid:*** $7886. ***Average indebtedness upon graduation:*** $25,342.

APPLYING
Standardized Tests *Required for some:* SAT or ACT (for admission), SAT Subject Tests (for admission). *Recommended:* SAT or ACT (for admission).

Options: electronic application, deferred entrance.

Application fee: $50.

Required: high school transcript, minimum 3.0 GPA. ***Required for some:*** essay or personal statement, letters of recommendation, additional requirements for Honors College and certain majors.

Application deadlines: rolling (freshmen), rolling (transfers).

Notification: continuous until 9/1 (freshmen), continuous (transfers).

CONTACT
Admission Services, Arizona State University, Arizona State University at the Downtown Phoenix campus, PO Box 870112, Tempe, AZ 85287-0112. *Phone:* 480-965-7788. *Fax:* 480-965-3610.
E-mail: admissions@asu.edu.

Arizona State University at the Polytechnic campus

Mesa, Arizona

http://campus.asu.edu/polytechnic

- **State-supported** university, founded 1996
- **Suburban** 575-acre campus with easy access to Phoenix
- **Coed** 3,869 undergraduate students, 87% full-time, 29% women, 71% men
- **Moderately difficult** entrance level, 76% of applicants were admitted

UNDERGRAD STUDENTS
3,354 full-time, 515 part-time. Students come from 47 states and territories; 45 other countries; 22% are from out of state; 4% Black or African American, non-Hispanic/Latino; 20% Hispanic/Latino; 6% Asian, non-Hispanic/Latino; 0.4% Native Hawaiian or other Pacific Islander, non-Hispanic/Latino; 1% American Indian or Alaska Native, non-Hispanic/Latino; 4% Two or more races, non-Hispanic/Latino; 0.7% Race/ethnicity unknown; 8% international; 23% live on campus.

Freshmen:
Admission: 1,974 applied, 1,502 admitted. ***Average high school GPA:*** 3.41. ***Test scores:*** SAT critical reading scores over 500: 74%; SAT math scores over 500: 83%; ACT scores over 18: 97%; SAT critical reading scores over 600: 29%; SAT math scores over 600: 45%; ACT scores over 24: 62%; SAT critical reading scores over 700: 9%; SAT math scores over 700: 10%; ACT scores over 30: 16%.

Retention: 85% of full-time freshmen returned.

FACULTY
Total: 209, 95% full-time, 75% with terminal degrees.

Student/faculty ratio: 20:1.

ACADEMICS
Calendar: semesters (15 weeks) and sessions (7.5 weeks). *Degrees:* certificates, bachelor's, master's, and doctoral.

Special study options: accelerated degree program, advanced placement credit, cooperative education, distance learning, double majors, freshman honors college, honors programs, independent study, internships, off-campus study, part-time degree program, services for LD students, student-designed majors, study abroad, summer session for credit. ***ROTC:*** Army (c), Navy (c), Air Force (c).

Computers: 535 computers/terminals are available on campus for general student use. Students can access the following: campus intranet, computer help desk, free student e-mail accounts, online (class) grades, online (class) registration, online (class) schedules. Campuswide network is available. 100% of college-owned or -operated housing units are wired for high-speed Internet access. Wireless service is available via classrooms, computer centers, computer labs, dorm rooms, learning centers, libraries, student centers.

Library: Polytechnic campus Library. *Books:* 3.0 million (physical), 881,323 (digital/electronic); *Serial titles:* 72,161 (physical), 75,943 (digital/electronic); *Databases:* 630. Weekly public service hours: 149; study areas open 24 hours, 5-7 days a week; students can reserve study rooms.

STUDENT LIFE
Housing options: on-campus residence required for freshman year; coed, special housing for students with disabilities. Campus housing is university owned and is provided by a third party. Freshman campus housing is guaranteed.

Activities and organizations: student-run newspaper, Pre-Health Club, AIGA Polytechnic, Environmental Resource Management Club, Computer Science, Disc Golf Club.

Athletics Member NCAA. All Division I. ***Intercollegiate sports:*** baseball M(s), basketball M(s)/W(s), cross-country running M(s)/W(s), football M(s), golf M(s)/W(s), gymnastics W(s), ice hockey M(s), lacrosse W(s), sand volleyball W(s), soccer W(s), softball W(s), swimming and diving M(s)/W(s), tennis M(s)/W(s), track and field M(s)/W(s), triathlon W(s), volleyball W(s), water polo W(s), wrestling M(s). ***Intramural sports:*** baseball M(c), basketball M/W, cheerleading M(c)/W(c), crew M(c), equestrian sports M(c)/W(c), fencing M(c)/W(c), golf M(c), gymnastics M(c), ice hockey M(c)/W(c), lacrosse M(c)/W(c), racquetball M(c)/W(c), rowing M(c), rugby M(c)/W(c), sailing M(c)/W(c), soccer M(c)/W(c), softball M/W, tennis M(c)/W(c), triathlon M(c)/W(c), ultimate Frisbee M(c)/W(c), volleyball M(c)/W(c), water polo M(c)/W(c).

Campus security: 24-hour emergency response devices and patrols, late-night transport/escort service, controlled dormitory access, LiveSafe smart phone application, surveillance camera in some residence halls.

Student services: health clinic, personal/psychological counseling.

COSTS & FINANCIAL AID
Costs (2016–17) ***Tuition:*** state resident $9200 full-time, $692 per credit hour part-time; nonresident $24,495 full-time, $1074 per credit hour part-time. Full-time tuition and fees vary according to program. Part-time tuition and fees vary according to program. ***Required fees:*** $686 full-time. ***Room and board:*** $11,474; room only: $6874. Room and board charges vary according to board plan and housing facility. ***Payment plan:*** installment. ***Waivers:*** employees or children of employees.

Financial Aid Of all full-time matriculated undergraduates who enrolled in 2015, 2,385 applied for aid, 2,052 were judged to have need, 401 had their need fully met. 150 Federal Work-Study jobs (averaging $3016). 742 state and other part-time jobs (averaging $3963). In 2015, 388 non-need-based awards were made. ***Average percent of need met:*** 57. ***Average financial aid package:*** $14,073. ***Average need-based loan:*** $4315. ***Average need-based gift aid:*** $8984. ***Average non-need-based aid:*** $6849. ***Average indebtedness upon graduation:*** $26,925.

APPLYING
Standardized Tests *Required for some:* SAT or ACT (for admission), SAT Subject Tests (for admission). *Recommended:* SAT or ACT (for admission).

Options: electronic application, deferred entrance.

Application fee: $50.

Required: high school transcript, minimum 3.0 GPA. ***Required for some:*** essay or personal statement, letters of recommendation, additional requirements for Honors College and certain majors.

Application deadlines: rolling (freshmen), rolling (transfers).

Notification: continuous until 9/1 (freshmen), continuous (transfers).

CONTACT
Admission Services, Arizona State University, Arizona State University at the Polytechnic campus, PO Box 870112, Tempe, AZ 85287-0112. *Phone:* 480-965-7788. *Fax:* 480-965-3610. *E-mail:* admissions@asu.edu.

Arizona State University at the Tempe campus

Tempe, Arizona

http://www.asu.edu/

- **State-supported** university, founded 1885
- **Urban** 661-acre campus with easy access to Phoenix
- **Coed** 42,477 undergraduate students, 92% full-time, 43% women, 57% men
- **Moderately difficult** entrance level, 83% of applicants were admitted

UNDERGRAD STUDENTS
38,946 full-time, 3,531 part-time. Students come from 51 states and territories; 111 other countries; 26% are from out of state; 4% Black or African American, non-Hispanic/Latino; 20% Hispanic/Latino; 7% Asian, non-Hispanic/Latino; 0.2% Native Hawaiian or other Pacific Islander, non-Hispanic/Latino; 1% American Indian or Alaska Native, non-Hispanic/Latino; 4% Two or more races, non-Hispanic/Latino; 0.7% Race/ethnicity unknown; 13% international; 8% transferred in; 21% live on campus.

Freshmen:
Admission: 24,764 applied, 20,431 admitted, 8,230 enrolled. ***Average high school GPA:*** 3.49. ***Test scores:*** SAT critical reading scores over 500: 78%; SAT math scores over 500: 84%; ACT scores over 18: 98%; SAT critical reading scores over 600: 37%; SAT math scores over 600: 45%; ACT scores over 24: 66%; SAT critical reading scores over 700: 9%; SAT math scores over 700: 11%; ACT scores over 30: 17%.

Retention: 86% of full-time freshmen returned.

FACULTY
Total: 2,201, 93% full-time, 88% with terminal degrees.

Student/faculty ratio: 23:1.

ACADEMICS
Calendar: semesters (15 weeks) and sessions (7.5 weeks). *Degrees:* certificates, bachelor's, master's, doctoral, post-master's, and postbachelor's certificates (profile includes data for the West, Polytechnic and Downtown Phoenix campuses).

Special study options: accelerated degree program, advanced placement credit, cooperative education, distance learning, double majors, English as a second language, freshman honors college, honors programs, independent study, internships, off-campus study, part-time degree program, services for LD students, student-designed majors, study abroad, summer session for credit. ***ROTC:*** Army (b), Navy (b), Air Force (b).

Computers: 2,421 computers/terminals are available on campus for general student use. Students can access the following: campus intranet, computer help desk, free student e-mail accounts, online (class) grades, online (class) registration, online (class) schedules. Campuswide network is available. 100% of college-owned or -operated housing units are wired for high-speed Internet access. Wireless service is available via classrooms, computer centers, computer labs, dorm rooms, learning centers, libraries, student centers.

Library: Hayden Library plus 3 others. *Books:* 3.0 million (physical), 881,323 (digital/electronic); *Serial titles:* 72,161 (physical), 75,943 (digital/electronic); *Databases:* 630. Weekly public service hours: 149; study areas open 24 hours, 5-7 days a week; students can reserve study rooms.

STUDENT LIFE
Housing options: on-campus residence required for freshman year; coed, special housing for students with disabilities. Campus housing is

university owned, leased by the school and is provided by a third party. Freshman campus housing is guaranteed.

Activities and organizations: drama/theater group, student-run newspaper, choral group, marching band, Resource for Animal Welfare and Rescues at ASU, AstroDevils: ASU Astronomy Club, Society of Women Engineers, Software Developers Association, Actuary Club, national fraternities, national sororities.

Athletics Member NCAA. All Division I except football (Division I-A). ***Intercollegiate sports:*** baseball M(s), basketball M(s)/W(s), cross-country running M(s)/W(s), golf M(s)/W(s), gymnastics M(c)/W(s), ice hockey M(s), lacrosse W(s), sand volleyball W(s), soccer W(s), softball W(s), swimming and diving M(s)/W(s), tennis M(s)/W(s), track and field M(s)/W(s), triathlon W(s), volleyball W(s), water polo W(s), wrestling M(s). ***Intramural sports:*** badminton M/W, baseball M(c), basketball M/W, cheerleading M(c)/W(c), crew M(c), equestrian sports M(c)/W(c), fencing M(c)/W(c), golf M(c), ice hockey M(c)/W(c), lacrosse M(c)/W(c), racquetball M(c)/W(c), rowing M(c), rugby M(c)/W(c), sailing M(c)/W(c), sand volleyball M/W, soccer M(c)/W(c), softball M/W, tennis M(c)/W(c), triathlon M(c)/W(c), ultimate Frisbee M(c)/W(c), volleyball M(c)/W(c), water polo M(c)/W(c).

Campus security: 24-hour emergency response devices and patrols, late-night transport/escort service, controlled dormitory access, LiveSafe smart phone application, surveillance cameras in some residence halls.

Student services: health clinic, personal/psychological counseling.

COSTS & FINANCIAL AID

Costs (2016–17) ***Tuition:*** state resident $9684 full-time, $692 per credit hour part-time; nonresident $25,784 full-time, $1074 per credit hour part-time. Full-time tuition and fees vary according to program. Part-time tuition and fees vary according to program. ***Required fees:*** $686 full-time. ***Room and board:*** $11,386; room only: $6786. Room and board charges vary according to board plan and housing facility. ***Payment plan:*** installment. ***Waivers:*** employees or children of employees.

Financial Aid Of all full-time matriculated undergraduates who enrolled in 2015, 25,678 applied for aid, 20,889 were judged to have need, 4,052 had their need fully met. 1,279 Federal Work-Study jobs (averaging $2402). 6,103 state and other part-time jobs (averaging $3284). In 2015, 8072 non-need-based awards were made. ***Average percent of need met:*** 61. ***Average financial aid package:*** $14,528. ***Average need-based loan:*** $4060. ***Average need-based gift aid:*** $10,074. ***Average non-need-based aid:*** $7968. ***Average indebtedness upon graduation:*** $22,903.

APPLYING

Standardized Tests *Required for some:* SAT or ACT (for admission), SAT Subject Tests (for admission). *Recommended:* SAT or ACT (for admission).

Options: electronic application, deferred entrance.

Application fee: $50.

Required: high school transcript, minimum 3.0 GPA. ***Required for some:*** essay or personal statement, letters of recommendation, additional requirements for Honors College and certain majors.

Application deadlines: rolling (freshmen), rolling (transfers).

Notification: continuous until 9/1 (freshmen), continuous (transfers).

CONTACT

Admission Services, Arizona State University, Arizona State University at the Tempe campus, PO Box 870112, Tempe, AZ 85287-0112.
Phone: 480-965-7788. *Fax:* 480-965-3610. *E-mail:* admissions@asu.edu.

Arizona State University at the West campus

Glendale, Arizona

http://campus.asu.edu/west

- **State-supported** comprehensive, founded 1984
- **Urban** 278-acre campus with easy access to Phoenix
- **Coed** 3,264 undergraduate students, 83% full-time, 59% women, 41% men
- **Moderately difficult** entrance level, 78% of applicants were admitted

UNDERGRAD STUDENTS

2,698 full-time, 566 part-time. Students come from 45 states and territories; 26 other countries; 15% are from out of state; 6% Black or African American, non-Hispanic/Latino; 31% Hispanic/Latino; 5% Asian, non-Hispanic/Latino; 0.2% Native Hawaiian or other Pacific Islander, non-Hispanic/Latino; 1% American Indian or Alaska Native, non-Hispanic/Latino; 4% Two or more races, non-Hispanic/Latino; 0.8% Race/ethnicity unknown; 4% international; 13% live on campus.

Freshmen:

Admission: 1,504 applied, 1,171 admitted. ***Average high school GPA:*** 3.49. ***Test scores:*** SAT critical reading scores over 500: 66%; SAT math scores over 500: 69%; ACT scores over 18: 94%; SAT critical reading scores over 600: 22%; SAT math scores over 600: 19%; ACT scores over 24: 45%; SAT critical reading scores over 700: 4%; SAT math scores over 700: 1%; ACT scores over 30: 7%.

Retention: 87% of full-time freshmen returned.

FACULTY

Total: 293, 91% full-time, 78% with terminal degrees.

Student/faculty ratio: 12:1.

ACADEMICS

Calendar: semesters (15 weeks) and sessions (7.5 weeks). *Degrees:* certificates, bachelor's, master's, doctoral, and postbachelor's certificates.

Special study options: accelerated degree program, advanced placement credit, cooperative education, distance learning, double majors, freshman honors college, honors programs, independent study, internships, off-campus study, part-time degree program, services for LD students, student-designed majors, study abroad, summer session for credit. ***ROTC:*** Army (c), Navy (c), Air Force (c).

Computers: 612 computers/terminals are available on campus for general student use. Students can access the following: campus intranet, computer help desk, free student e-mail accounts, online (class) grades, online (class) registration, online (class) schedules. Campuswide network is available. 100% of college-owned or -operated housing units are wired for high-speed Internet access. Wireless service is available via classrooms, computer centers, computer labs, dorm rooms, learning centers, libraries, student centers.

Library: Fletcher Library at the West campus. *Books:* 3.0 million (physical), 881,323 (digital/electronic); *Serial titles:* 72,161 (physical), 75,943 (digital/electronic); *Databases:* 630. Weekly public service hours: 149; study areas open 24 hours, 5-7 days a week; students can reserve study rooms.

STUDENT LIFE

Housing options: on-campus residence required for freshman year; coed, special housing for students with disabilities. Campus housing is university owned and is provided by a third party. Freshman campus housing is guaranteed.

Activities and organizations: drama/theater group, student-run newspaper, choral group, Hispanic Honor Society, Teachers of the Future, Business to Business, W. P. Carey MBA Association, American Medical Student Association.

Athletics Member NCAA. All Division I. ***Intercollegiate sports:*** baseball M(s), basketball M(s)/W(s), cross-country running M(s)/W(s), football M(s), golf M(s)/W(s), gymnastics W(s), ice hockey M(s), lacrosse W(s), sand volleyball W(s), soccer W(s), softball W(s), swimming and diving M(s)/W(s), tennis M(s)/W(s), track and field M(s)/W(s), triathlon W(s), volleyball W(s), water polo W(s), wrestling M(s). ***Intramural sports:*** baseball M(c), basketball M/W, cheerleading M(c)/W(c), crew M(c), equestrian sports M(c)/W(c), fencing M(c)/W(c), golf M(c), gymnastics M(c), ice hockey M(c)/W(c), lacrosse M(c)/W(c), racquetball M(c)/W(c), rowing M(c), rugby M(c)/W(c), sailing M(c)/W(c), sand volleyball M/W, soccer M(c)/W(c), softball M/W, tennis M(c)/W(c), triathlon M(c)/W(c), ultimate Frisbee M(c)/W(c), volleyball M(c)/W(c), water polo M(c)/W(c).

Campus security: 24-hour emergency response devices and patrols, late-night transport/escort service, controlled dormitory access, LiveSafe smart phone application, surveillance camera in some residence halls.

Student services: health clinic, personal/psychological counseling.

COSTS & FINANCIAL AID

Costs (2016–17) ***Tuition:*** state resident $9200 full-time, $692 per credit hour part-time; nonresident $24,495 full-time, $1074 per credit hour part-time. Full-time tuition and fees vary according to program. Part-time tuition and fees vary according to program. ***Required fees:*** $686 full-time. ***Room and board:*** $10,754; room only: $6154. Room and board charges vary according to board plan and housing facility. ***Payment plan:*** installment. ***Waivers:*** employees or children of employees.

Financial Aid Of all full-time matriculated undergraduates who enrolled in 2015, 2,239 applied for aid, 2,004 were judged to have need, 325 had their need fully met. 125 Federal Work-Study jobs (averaging $2613). 498 state and other part-time jobs (averaging $3541). In 2015, 216 non-need-based awards were made. ***Average percent of need met:*** 59. ***Average financial aid package:*** $12,783. ***Average need-based loan:*** $4420. ***Average need-based gift aid:*** $8605. ***Average non-need-based aid:*** $6689. ***Average indebtedness upon graduation:*** $22,251.

APPLYING

Standardized Tests *Required for some:* SAT or ACT (for admission), SAT Subject Tests (for admission). *Recommended:* SAT or ACT (for admission).

Options: electronic application, deferred entrance.

Application fee: $50.

Required: high school transcript, minimum 3.0 GPA. ***Required for some:*** essay or personal statement, letters of recommendation, additional requirements for Honors College and certain majors.

Application deadlines: rolling (freshmen), rolling (transfers).

Notification: continuous until 9/1 (freshmen), continuous (transfers).

CONTACT

Arizona State University at the West campus, PO Box 870112, Tempe, AZ 85287-0112. *Phone:* 480-965-7788. *Fax:* 480-965-3610.
E-mail: admissions@asu.edu.

The Art Institute of Phoenix

Phoenix, Arizona

http://www.artinstitutes.edu/phoenix/

CONTACT

The Art Institute of Phoenix, 2233 West Dunlap Avenue, Phoenix, AZ 85021-2859. *Phone:* 602-331-7500. *Toll-free phone:* 800-474-2479.

The Art Institute of Tucson

Tucson, Arizona

http://www.artinstitutes.edu/tucson/

CONTACT

The Art Institute of Tucson, 5099 East Grant Road, Suite 100, Tucson, AZ 85712. *Phone:* 520-318-2700. *Toll-free phone:* 866-690-8850.

Brookline College

Phoenix, Arizona

http://brooklinecollege.edu/

CONTACT

Ms. Theresa Dean, Director of Admissions, Brookline College, 2445 West Dunlap Avenue, Suite 100, Phoenix, AZ 85021. *Phone:* 602-242-6265. *Toll-free phone:* 800-793-2428. *Fax:* 602-973-2572.
E-mail: tdean@brooklinecollege.edu.

Brookline College

Tempe, Arizona

http://brooklinecollege.edu/

CONTACT

Ms. Cheryl Kindred, Campus Director, Brookline College, 1140-1150 South Priest Drive, Tempe, AZ 85281. *Phone:* 480-545-8755. *Toll-free phone:* 888-886-2428. *Fax:* 480-926-1371.
E-mail: ckindred@brooklinecollege.edu.

Brookline College

Tucson, Arizona

http://brooklinecollege.edu/

CONTACT

Ms. Leigh Anne Pechota, Campus Director, Brookline College, 5441 East 22nd Street, Suite 125, Tucson, AZ 85711. *Phone:* 520-748-9799. *Toll-free phone:* 888-292-2428. *Fax:* 520-748-9355.
E-mail: lpechota@brooklinecollege.edu.

Chamberlain College of Nursing

Phoenix, Arizona

http://www.chamberlain.edu/

- **Proprietary** 4-year
- **Coed**

FACULTY

Student/faculty ratio: 12:1.

ACADEMICS

Calendar: semesters. *Degree:* bachelor's.

STUDENT LIFE

Housing options: college housing not available.

COSTS

Costs (2016–17) ***Tuition:*** $18,900 full-time, $675 per credit hour part-time. ***Required fees:*** $600 full-time.

APPLYING

Standardized Tests *Required:* SAT or ACT (for admission).

Options: deferred entrance.

Application fee: $95.

CONTACT

Admissions, Chamberlain College of Nursing, 2149 West Dunlap Avenue, Phoenix, AZ 85021. *Phone:* 602-331-2720.
oll-free phone: 877-751-5783.

CollegeAmerica–Flagstaff

Flagstaff, Arizona

http://www.collegeamerica.edu/

CONTACT

CollegeAmerica–Flagstaff, 399 South Malpais Lane, Flagstaff, AZ 86001. *Phone:* 928-213-6060 Ext. 1402. *Toll-free phone:* 800-622-2894.

CollegeAmerica–Phoenix

Phoenix, Arizona

http://www.collegeamerica.edu/

CONTACT

CollegeAmerica–Phoenix, 9801 North Metro Parkway East, Phoenix, AZ 85051. *Toll-free phone:* 800-622-2894.

DeVry University–Phoenix Campus

Phoenix, Arizona

http://www.devry.edu/

- **Proprietary** comprehensive, founded 1967, part of DeVry University
- **Urban** campus
- **Coed**
- **Minimally difficult** entrance level

FACULTY

Student/faculty ratio: 13:1.

ACADEMICS

Calendar: semesters. *Degrees:* associate, bachelor's, master's, and postbachelor's certificates.
Library: Learning Resource Center.

STUDENT LIFE

Housing options: college housing not available.

COSTS
Costs (2016–17) ***Tuition:*** $17,052 full-time, $609 per credit hour part-time. ***Required fees:*** $460 full-time.

APPLYING
Options: deferred entrance.

Application fee: $30.

Required: high school transcript, interview.

CONTACT
DeVry University–Phoenix Campus, 2149 West Dunlap Avenue, Phoenix, AZ 85021. *Phone:* 602-870-9222. *Toll-free phone:* 866-338-7934.

Dunlap-Stone University

Phoenix, Arizona

http://www.dunlap-stone.edu/

CONTACT
Dunlap-Stone University, 19820 North 7th Street, Suite #100, Phoenix, AZ 85024. *Phone:* 602-648-5750. *Toll-free phone:* 800-474-8013.

★ Embry-Riddle Aeronautical University–Prescott

Prescott, Arizona

http://www.embryriddle.edu/

- **Independent** comprehensive, founded 1978
- **Small-town** 547-acre campus with easy access to Phoenix
- **Endowment** $111.2 million
- **Coed** 2,205 undergraduate students, 94% full-time, 23% women, 77% men
- **Moderately difficult** entrance level, 79% of applicants were admitted

UNDERGRAD STUDENTS
2,082 full-time, 123 part-time. Students come from 47 states and territories; 97 other countries; 77% are from out of state; 2% Black or African American, non-Hispanic/Latino; 4% Hispanic/Latino; 5% Asian, non-Hispanic/Latino; 0.6% Native Hawaiian or other Pacific Islander, non-Hispanic/Latino; 0.5% American Indian or Alaska Native, non-Hispanic/Latino; 10% Two or more races, non-Hispanic/Latino; 9% Race/ethnicity unknown; 10% international; 5% transferred in; 41% live on campus.

Freshmen:
Admission: 1,908 applied, 1,510 admitted, 583 enrolled. ***Average high school GPA:*** 3.61. ***Test scores:*** SAT critical reading scores over 500: 74%; SAT math scores over 500: 83%; SAT writing scores over 500: 65%; ACT scores over 18: 96%; SAT critical reading scores over 600: 28%; SAT math scores over 600: 50%; SAT writing scores over 600: 23%; ACT scores over 24: 69%; SAT critical reading scores over 700: 4%; SAT math scores over 700: 5%; SAT writing scores over 700: 2%; ACT scores over 30: 16%.

Retention: 77% of full-time freshmen returned.

ACADEMICS
Calendar: semesters. *Degrees:* certificates, bachelor's, and master's.

Special study options: advanced placement credit, cooperative education, double majors, English as a second language, honors programs, internships, part-time degree program, services for LD students, study abroad, summer session for credit. ***ROTC:*** Army (b), Air Force (b).

Computers: 730 computers/terminals are available on campus for general student use. Students can access the following: campus intranet, computer help desk, free student e-mail accounts, online (class) grades, online (class) registration, online (class) schedules. Campuswide network is available. 100% of college-owned or -operated housing units are wired for high-speed Internet access. Wireless service is available via entire campus.

Library: Christine & Steven F. Udvar-Hazy Library & Learning Center.

STUDENT LIFE
Housing options: on-campus residence required for freshman year; coed. Campus housing is university owned. Freshman campus housing is guaranteed.

Activities and organizations: student-run newspaper, choral group, Hawaii Club, Strike Eagles, Theta XI, American Institute of Aeronautics and Astronautics (AIAA), Arnold Air Society, national fraternities, national sororities.

Athletics Member NCAA, NAIA. All NCAA Division II. ***Intercollegiate sports:*** basketball M(s)/W(s), cross-country running M(s)/W(s), golf M(s)/W(s), soccer M(s)/W(s), softball W(s), track and field M(s)/W(s), volleyball W(s), wrestling M(s). ***Intramural sports:*** archery M(c)/W(c), baseball M(c), basketball M/W, bowling M(c)/W(c), field hockey M(c)/W(c), football M/W, ice hockey M(c), racquetball M/W, rock climbing M/W, rugby M(c)/W(c), skiing (cross-country) M(c)/W(c), soccer M(c)/W(c), softball W(c), table tennis M/W, tennis M/W, ultimate Frisbee M(c)/W(c), volleyball M(c)/W(c).

Campus security: 24-hour emergency response devices and patrols, student patrols, late-night transport/escort service.

Student services: health clinic, personal/psychological counseling.

COSTS & FINANCIAL AID
Costs (2017–18) ***Comprehensive fee:*** $45,130 includes full-time tuition ($33,408), mandatory fees ($1254), and room and board ($10,468). Full-time tuition and fees vary according to course load. Part-time tuition: $1392 per credit hour. Part-time tuition and fees vary according to course load. ***Required fees:*** $627 per term part-time. ***College room only:*** $5860. Room and board charges vary according to board plan, housing facility, location, and student level. ***Waivers:*** employees or children of employees.

Financial Aid Of all full-time matriculated undergraduates who enrolled in 2016, 1,552 applied for aid, 1,350 were judged to have need. 40 Federal Work-Study jobs (averaging $1793). 1,213 state and other part-time jobs (averaging $1024). In 2016, 372 non-need-based awards were made. ***Average financial aid package:*** $18,769. ***Average need-based loan:*** $4507. ***Average need-based gift aid:*** $15,121. ***Average non-need-based aid:*** $13,125.

APPLYING
Standardized Tests *Recommended:* SAT and SAT Subject Tests or ACT (for admission).

Options: electronic application, deferred entrance.

Application fee: $50.

Required: high school transcript, minimum 2.0 GPA, 2 letters of recommendation, medical examination for flight students. ***Recommended:*** essay or personal statement, minimum 3.0 GPA, interview.

Application deadlines: rolling (freshmen), rolling (out-of-state freshmen), rolling (transfers).

Notification: continuous (freshmen), continuous (out-of-state freshmen), continuous (transfers).

CONTACT
Embry-Riddle Aeronautical University–Prescott, 3700 Willow Creek Road, Prescott, AZ 863013720. *Phone:* 800-888-3728. *Toll-free phone:* 800-888-3728. *Fax:* 928-777-6606. *E-mail:* pradmit@erau.edu.

See next page for display ad and page 1344 for the College Close-Up.

Grand Canyon University

Phoenix, Arizona

http://www.gcu.edu/

CONTACT
Enrollment, Grand Canyon University, 3300 West Camelback Road, PO Box 11097, Phoenix, AZ 86017-3030. *Phone:* 800-486-7085. *Toll-free phone:* 800-800-9776. *E-mail:* admissionsonline@gcu.edu.

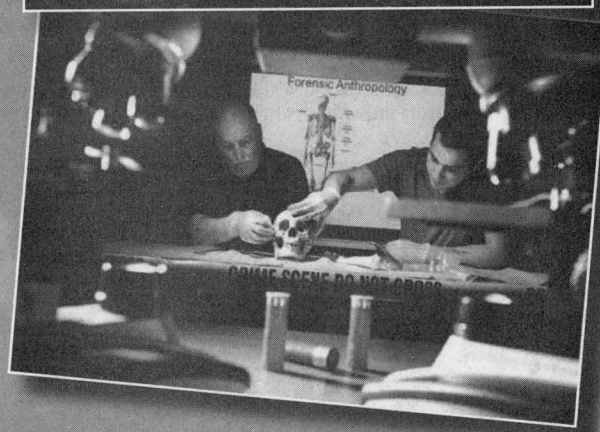

Harrison Middleton University

Tempe, Arizona

http://www.hmu.edu/

- **Independent** comprehensive, founded 1998
- **Suburban** campus with easy access to Phoenix
- **Coed** 10 undergraduate students, 100% full-time, 50% women, 50% men
- 100% of applicants were admitted

UNDERGRAD STUDENTS
10 full-time. 100% are from out of state.

Freshmen:
Admission: 1 applied, 1 admitted.

FACULTY
Total: 23, 74% full-time, 43% with terminal degrees.
Student/faculty ratio: 1:1.

ACADEMICS
Calendar: continuous. *Degree:* diplomas, master's, and doctoral.
Special study options: advanced placement credit, distance learning, double majors, independent study, student-designed majors, summer session for credit.
Library: William Speight Harrison Athenaeum Online LIbrary.

STUDENT LIFE
Housing options: college housing not available.

COSTS
Costs (2016–17) ***One-time required fee:*** $400. ***Tuition:*** $5400 full-time, $300 per credit hour part-time. ***Payment plan:*** installment.

APPLYING
Options: electronic application.
Application fee: $50.
Required: high school transcript, interview.
Application deadlines: rolling (freshmen), rolling (transfers).
Notification: continuous (freshmen), continuous (transfers).

CONTACT
Harrison Middleton University, 1105 East Broadway, Tempe, AZ 85282. *Phone:* 877-248.6724. *Toll-free phone:* 877-248-6724.

International Baptist College and Seminary

Chandler, Arizona

http://www.ibcs.edu/

CONTACT
Director of Admissions, International Baptist College and Seminary, 2211 West Germann Road, Chandler, AZ 85286. *Phone:* 480-245-7970. *Toll-free phone:* 800-422-4858. *E-mail:* admissions@ibconline.edu.

National Paralegal College

Phoenix, Arizona

http://nationalparalegal.edu/

- **Proprietary** comprehensive
- **Coed** 939 undergraduate students, 95% full-time, 89% women, 11% men
- 88% of applicants were admitted

UNDERGRAD STUDENTS
895 full-time, 44 part-time. Students come from 54 states and territories; 2 other countries; 97% are from out of state; 8% Black or African American, non-Hispanic/Latino; 5% Hispanic/Latino; 1% Asian, non-Hispanic/Latino; 0.2% Native Hawaiian or other Pacific Islander, non-Hispanic/Latino; 0.5% American Indian or Alaska Native, non-Hispanic/Latino; 0.2% Two or more races, non-Hispanic/Latino; 44% Race/ethnicity unknown; 19% transferred in.

Freshmen:
Admission: 2,679 applied, 2,351 admitted, 71 enrolled.
Retention: 36% of full-time freshmen returned.

FACULTY
Total: 33, 15% full-time, 97% with terminal degrees.

ACADEMICS
Calendar: continuous new session each month. *Degrees:* certificates, associate, bachelor's, and master's.

Special study options: academic remediation for entering students, accelerated degree program, distance learning, part-time degree program, summer session for credit.

Unusual degree programs: legal and paralegal studies, taxation studies.

Computers: Students can access the following: online (class) grades, online (class) schedules.
Library: Jones eGlobal Library.

COSTS
Costs (2017–18) ***One-time required fee:*** $195. ***Tuition:*** $7800 full-time, $325 per credit hour part-time. No tuition increase for student's term of enrollment. ***Payment plans:*** tuition prepayment, installment. ***Waivers:*** employees or children of employees.

APPLYING
Options: electronic application.

Required for some: high school transcript. ***Recommended:*** essay or personal statement, interview.

Application deadlines: rolling (freshmen), rolling (transfers).

Notification: continuous (freshmen), continuous (transfers).

CONTACT
Admissions Office, National Paralegal College, 717 East Maryland Avenue, Suite 115, Phoenix, AZ 85014. *Phone:* 845-371-9101. *Toll-free phone:* 800-371-6105. *Fax:* 866-347-2744. *E-mail:* info@nationalparalegal.edu.

Northern Arizona University

Flagstaff, Arizona

http://www.nau.edu/

- **State-supported** university, founded 1899, part of Arizona University System
- **Small-town** 708-acre campus
- **Coed** 26,506 undergraduate students, 81% full-time, 59% women, 41% men
- **Moderately difficult** entrance level, 78% of applicants were admitted

UNDERGRAD STUDENTS
21,494 full-time, 5,012 part-time. Students come from 51 states and territories; 78 other countries; 29% are from out of state; 3% Black or African American, non-Hispanic/Latino; 23% Hispanic/Latino; 2% Asian, non-Hispanic/Latino; 0.3% Native Hawaiian or other Pacific Islander, non-Hispanic/Latino; 3% American Indian or Alaska Native, non-Hispanic/Latino; 6% Two or more races, non-Hispanic/Latino; 1% Race/ethnicity unknown; 4% international; 11% transferred in; 43% live on campus.

Freshmen:
Admission: 36,511 applied, 28,495 admitted, 5,607 enrolled. ***Average high school GPA:*** 3.6. ***Test scores:*** SAT critical reading scores over 500: 61%; SAT math scores over 500: 63%; SAT writing scores over 500: 53%; ACT scores over 18: 89%; SAT critical reading scores over 600: 19%; SAT math scores over 600: 19%; SAT writing scores over 600: 13%; ACT scores over 24: 41%; SAT critical reading scores over 700: 2%; SAT math scores over 700: 2%; SAT writing scores over 700: 1%; ACT scores over 30: 5%.

Retention: 76% of full-time freshmen returned.

FACULTY
Total: 1,650, 66% full-time.

Student/faculty ratio: 18:1.

ACADEMICS
Calendar: semesters. *Degrees:* certificates, bachelor's, master's, doctoral, post-master's, and postbachelor's certificates.

Special study options: accelerated degree program, advanced placement credit, cooperative education, distance learning, double majors, English as a second language, freshman honors college, honors programs, independent study, internships, off-campus study, part-time degree program, services for LD students, study abroad, summer session for credit. ***ROTC:*** Army (b), Air Force (b).

Unusual degree programs: 3-2 business administration; engineering; forestry; social work; sustainable communities, criminology, climate science solutions, career and technical education, applied geospatial sciences, psychological sciences; law with The University of Arizona.

Computers: 1,600 ports are available on campus for general student use. Students can access the following: campus intranet, computer help desk, free student e-mail accounts, online (class) grades, online (class) registration, online (class) schedules, computer repair service available on campus. Campuswide network is available. 100% of college-owned or -operated housing units are wired for high-speed Internet access. Wireless service is available via entire campus.

Library: Cline Library plus 1 other. *Books:* 574,723 (physical), 232,571 (digital/electronic); *Serial titles:* 6,264 (physical), 88,412 (digital/electronic); *Databases:* 141. Weekly public service hours: 117; students can reserve study rooms.

STUDENT LIFE

Housing options: coed, men-only, women-only, cooperative, special housing for students with disabilities. Campus housing is university owned and is provided by a third party. Freshman applicants given priority for college housing.

Activities and organizations: drama/theater group, student-run newspaper, radio and television station, choral group, marching band, national fraternities, national sororities.

Athletics Member NCAA. All Division I. ***Intercollegiate sports:*** basketball M(s)/W(s), cross-country running M(s)/W(s), football M(s), golf W(s), soccer W(s), swimming and diving W(s), tennis M(s)/W(s), track and field M(s)/W(s), volleyball W(s). ***Intramural sports:*** archery M(c)/W(c), badminton M/W, baseball M(c)/W(c), basketball M/W, cheerleading M(c)/W(c), fencing M(c)/W(c), football M(c)/W(c), gymnastics M(c)/W(c), ice hockey M(c)/W(c), lacrosse M(c)/W(c), racquetball M/W, rock climbing M(c)/W(c), rugby M(c)/W(c), soccer M/W, softball M(c)/W(c), tennis M(c)/W(c), triathlon M(c)/W(c), ultimate Frisbee M(c)/W(c), volleyball M/W, water polo M(c)/W(c), wrestling M(c)/W(c).

Campus security: 24-hour emergency response devices and patrols, late-night transport/escort service, controlled dormitory access.

Student services: health clinic, personal/psychological counseling, legal services.

COSTS & FINANCIAL AID

Costs (2016–17) ***Tuition:*** state resident $9746 full-time, $696 per credit hour part-time; nonresident $23,126 full-time, $964 per credit hour part-time. Full-time tuition and fees vary according to course load, location, and reciprocity agreements. Part-time tuition and fees vary according to course load, location, and reciprocity agreements. No tuition increase for student's term of enrollment. ***Required fees:*** $1018 full-time, $336 per credit hour part-time. ***Room and board:*** $9482; room only: $5128. Room and board charges vary according to board plan and housing facility. ***Payment plan:*** installment. ***Waivers:*** employees or children of employees.

Financial Aid Of all full-time matriculated undergraduates who enrolled in 2016, 15,323 applied for aid, 12,736 were judged to have need, 1,282 had their need fully met. In 2016, 2769 non-need-based awards were made. ***Average percent of need met:*** 60. ***Average financial aid package:*** $11,505. ***Average need-based loan:*** $4253. ***Average need-based gift aid:*** $6784. ***Average non-need-based aid:*** $6483. ***Average indebtedness upon graduation:*** $26,279.

APPLYING

Standardized Tests *Recommended:* SAT (for admission), ACT (for admission), SAT or ACT (for admission), SAT and SAT Subject Tests or ACT (for admission), SAT Subject Tests (for admission).

Options: electronic application, deferred entrance.

Application fee: $25.

Required: high school transcript, minimum 3.0 GPA, 16 college preparatory courses with minimum 2.0 in each subject area.

Application deadlines: rolling (freshmen), rolling (transfers).

Notification: continuous (freshmen), continuous (transfers).

CONTACT

Undergraduate Admissions, Northern Arizona University, Box 4084, Flagstaff, AZ 86011. *Phone:* 928-523-5511. *Toll-free phone:* 888-628-2968. *Fax:* 928-523-6023. *E-mail:* admissions@nau.edu.

See previous page for display ad and page 1444 for the College Close-Up.

Penn Foster College

Scottsdale, Arizona

http://www.pennfostercollege.edu/

- **Proprietary** primarily 2-year
- **Coed**

ACADEMICS

Calendar: continuous. *Degrees:* certificates, associate, and bachelor's.

Library: Penn Foster College Online Library.

STUDENT LIFE

Housing options: college housing not available.

Activities and organizations: Online Community-Hosted Academic Interest Groups.

COSTS

Costs (2016–17) ***Tuition:*** $79 per credit part-time. Part-time tuition and fees vary according to course load and program.

APPLYING

Options: electronic application.

Application fee: $75.

Required: high school transcript, computer with Internet access.

CONTACT

Admissions, Penn Foster College, 14300 North Northsight Boulevard, Suite 120, Scottsdale, AZ 85260. *Phone:* 888-427-1000. *Toll-free phone:* 800-471-3232.

Pima Medical Institute

Mesa, Arizona

http://www.pmi.edu/

CONTACT

Admissions Office, Pima Medical Institute, 957 South Dobson Road, Mesa, AZ 85202. *Phone:* 480-644-0267 Ext. 225. *Toll-free phone:* 800-477-PIMA.

Pima Medical Institute

Tucson, Arizona

http://www.pmi.edu/

CONTACT

Admissions Office, Pima Medical Institute, 3350 East Grant Road, Tucson, AZ 85716. *Phone:* 520-326-1600 Ext. 5112. *Toll-free phone:* 800-477-PIMA.

Prescott College

Prescott, Arizona

http://www.prescott.edu/

- **Independent** comprehensive, founded 1966
- **Small-town** 13-acre campus
- **Endowment** $1.5 million
- **Coed** 356 undergraduate students, 75% full-time, 60% women, 40% men
- **Moderately difficult** entrance level, 80% of applicants were admitted

UNDERGRAD STUDENTS

267 full-time, 89 part-time. Students come from 47 states and territories; 10 other countries; 90% are from out of state; 1% Black or African American, non-Hispanic/Latino; 7% Hispanic/Latino; 1% Asian, non-Hispanic/Latino; 4% American Indian or Alaska Native, non-Hispanic/Latino; 7% Two or more races, non-Hispanic/Latino; 8% Race/ethnicity unknown; 0.8% international; 29% transferred in; 16% live on campus.

Freshmen:
Admission: 167 applied, 133 admitted, 47 enrolled. ***Average high school GPA:*** 3.2. ***Test scores:*** SAT critical reading scores over 500: 70%; SAT math scores over 500: 48%; SAT writing scores over 500: 56%; ACT scores over 18: 84%; SAT critical reading scores over 600: 35%; SAT math scores over 600: 13%; SAT writing scores over 600: 17%; ACT scores over 24: 52%; SAT critical reading scores over 700: 9%; ACT scores over 30: 5%.

Retention: 79% of full-time freshmen returned.

FACULTY
Total: 115, 57% full-time, 43% with terminal degrees.

Student/faculty ratio: 9:1.

ACADEMICS
Calendar: semesters (4-week blocks followed by 10-week terms for each quarter). *Degrees:* bachelor's, master's, doctoral, post-master's, and postbachelor's certificates.

Special study options: adult/continuing education programs, advanced placement credit, distance learning, double majors, external degree program, independent study, internships, off-campus study, services for LD students, student-designed majors, study abroad, summer session for credit.

Computers: 100 computers/terminals and 20 ports are available on campus for general student use. Students can access the following: campus intranet, computer help desk, free student e-mail accounts, online (class) grades, online (class) schedules, learning management system, free e-portfolios. Campuswide network is available. 100% of college-owned or -operated housing units are wired for high-speed Internet access. Wireless service is available via entire campus.
Library: Prescott College Library.

STUDENT LIFE
Housing options: on-campus residence required for freshman year; coed. Campus housing is university owned. Freshman campus housing is guaranteed.

Activities and organizations: drama/theater group, choral group, Student Union, Catalyst, WEB (Women's Empowerment Breakthrough), HUB (Helping Understand Bikes), Aztlan Center.

Campus security: 24-hour emergency response devices, late-night transport/escort service, controlled dormitory access.

Student services: personal/psychological counseling.

COSTS & FINANCIAL AID
Costs (2017–18) ***Comprehensive fee:*** $37,266 includes full-time tuition ($28,976), mandatory fees ($590), and room and board ($7700). ***College room only:*** $6900. Room and board charges vary according to board plan. ***Payment plan:*** installment. ***Waivers:*** employees or children of employees.

Financial Aid Of all full-time matriculated undergraduates who enrolled in 2016, 218 applied for aid, 187 were judged to have need, 16 had their need fully met. In 2016, 76 non-need-based awards were made. ***Average percent of need met:*** 64. ***Average financial aid package:*** $20,132. ***Average need-based loan:*** $4576. ***Average need-based gift aid:*** $15,202. ***Average non-need-based aid:*** $6575. ***Average indebtedness upon graduation:*** $27,130.

APPLYING
Standardized Tests *Required:* SAT or ACT (for admission).

Options: electronic application, early decision, deferred entrance.

Required: essay or personal statement, high school transcript, 1 letter of recommendation. ***Required for some:*** interview.

Application deadlines: 8/15 (freshmen), 8/15 (transfers).

Early decision deadline: 12/1.

Notification: continuous (freshmen), continuous (out-of-state freshmen), continuous (transfers), 12/15 (early decision).

CONTACT
Nancy Simmons, Admissions Coordinator, Prescott College, 220 Grove Avenue, Prescott, AZ 86301. *Phone:* 928-350-2100. *Toll-free phone:* 877-350-2100. *Fax:* 928-776-5242. *E-mail:* admissions@prescott.edu.

Southwest University of Visual Arts

Tucson, Arizona

http://www.suva.edu/

- **Proprietary** comprehensive, founded 1983
- **Suburban** campus with easy access to Tucson
- **Coed**

ACADEMICS
Calendar: semester with a full summer program. *Degrees:* bachelor's and master's.
Library: Southwest University of Visual Arts Library plus 1 other. *Books:* 6,013 (physical); *Serial titles:* 85 (physical), 28 (digital/electronic); *Databases:* 62. Weekly public service hours: 65.

STUDENT LIFE
Housing options: college housing not available.

COSTS
Costs (2016–17) ***Tuition:*** $22,944 full-time, $5736 per term part-time. Full-time tuition and fees vary according to course load and location. Part-time tuition and fees vary according to course load and location. ***Required fees:*** $125 full-time.

APPLYING
Standardized Tests *Required for some:* ACT ASSET.

Required: essay or personal statement, high school transcript, interview.

CONTACT
Robert Mairs, Director of Admissions, Southwest University of Visual Arts, 2525 North Country Club Road, Tucson, AZ 85716-2505. *Phone:* 520-325-0123. *Toll-free phone:* 800-825-8753. *Fax:* 520-325-5535.

Trine University

Peoria, Arizona

http://www.trine.edu/peoria/

CONTACT
Trine University, 14100 North 83rd. Avenue, Suite 100, Peoria, AZ 85381.

University of Advancing Technology

Tempe, Arizona

http://www.uat.edu/

- **Proprietary** comprehensive, founded 1983
- **Urban** campus with easy access to Phoenix, AZ
- **Coed, primarily men** 1,013 undergraduate students, 100% full-time, 8% women, 92% men

UNDERGRAD STUDENTS
1,013 full-time. 7% Black or African American, non-Hispanic/Latino; 7% Hispanic/Latino; 3% Asian, non-Hispanic/Latino; 0.3% Native Hawaiian or other Pacific Islander, non-Hispanic/Latino; 0.7% American Indian or Alaska Native, non-Hispanic/Latino; 6% Two or more races, non-Hispanic/Latino; 14% Race/ethnicity unknown; 2% international; 22% live on campus.

Freshmen:
Admission: 140 enrolled. ***Average high school GPA:*** 2.5.

FACULTY
Total: 60, 52% full-time, 10% with terminal degrees.

Student/faculty ratio: 13:1.

ACADEMICS
Calendar: semesters. *Degrees:* associate, bachelor's, and master's.

Special study options: cooperative education, distance learning, double majors, independent study, internships, summer session for credit.

Computers: 400 computers/terminals and 300 ports are available on campus for general student use. Students can access the following: campus intranet, free student e-mail accounts, online (class) grades, online (class) registration, online (class) schedules. Campuswide network is available. 100% of college-owned or -operated housing units are wired for high-speed Internet access. Wireless service is available via entire campus.
Library: University of Advancing Computer Technology Library.

STUDENT LIFE

Housing options: on-campus residence required for freshman year; coed. Campus housing is university owned, leased by the school and is provided by a third party.

Activities and organizations: student-run newspaper, television station, Web Club, Gaming Club, Animation Club, Video Club, Student Government.

Athletics ***Intramural sports:*** fencing M/W, softball M/W.

Campus security: 24-hour patrols.

COSTS & FINANCIAL AID

Costs (2016–17) ***Comprehensive fee:*** $33,450 includes full-time tuition ($23,150), mandatory fees ($600), and room and board ($9700). ***College room only:*** $6635. Room and board charges vary according to board plan. ***Payment plans:*** tuition prepayment, installment. ***Waivers:*** employees or children of employees.

Financial Aid Of all full-time matriculated undergraduates who enrolled in 2010, 799 applied for aid, 747 were judged to have need. ***Average financial aid package:*** $10,343. ***Average need-based loan:*** $5512. ***Average need-based gift aid:*** $6767.

APPLYING

Standardized Tests *Required for some:* SAT or ACT (for admission).

Options: electronic application.

Required: essay or personal statement, high school transcript. ***Required for some:*** minimum 2.5 GPA.

CONTACT

Admissions Office, University of Advancing Technology, 2625 West Baseline Road, Tempe, AZ 85283-1042. *Phone:* 602-383-8228. *Toll-free phone:* 800-658-5744. *Fax:* 602-383-8222. *E-mail:* admissions@uat.edu.

The University of Arizona

Tucson, Arizona

http://www.arizona.edu/

- **State-supported** university, founded 1885, part of Arizona Board of Regents
- **Urban** 392-acre campus
- **Endowment** $754.4 million
- **Coed** 34,072 undergraduate students, 86% full-time, 52% women, 48% men
- **Moderately difficult** entrance level, 79% of applicants were admitted

UNDERGRAD STUDENTS

29,341 full-time, 4,731 part-time. Students come from 112 other countries; 32% are from out of state; 4% Black or African American, non-Hispanic/Latino; 26% Hispanic/Latino; 5% Asian, non-Hispanic/Latino; 0.3% Native Hawaiian or other Pacific Islander, non-Hispanic/Latino; 1% American Indian or Alaska Native, non-Hispanic/Latino; 4% Two or more races, non-Hispanic/Latino; 0.8% Race/ethnicity unknown; 7% international; 6% transferred in; 20% live on campus.

Freshmen:

Admission: 36,166 applied, 28,433 admitted, 7,753 enrolled. ***Average high school GPA:*** 3.48. ***Test scores:*** SAT critical reading scores over 500: 68%; SAT math scores over 500: 73%; SAT writing scores over 500: 63%; ACT scores over 18: 92%; SAT critical reading scores over 600: 28%; SAT math scores over 600: 32%; SAT writing scores over 600: 21%; ACT scores over 24: 55%; SAT critical reading scores over 700: 5%; SAT math scores over 700: 6%; SAT writing scores over 700: 4%; ACT scores over 30: 13%.

Retention: 81% of full-time freshmen returned.

FACULTY

Total: 1,956, 85% full-time, 85% with terminal degrees.

Student/faculty ratio: 22:1.

ACADEMICS

Calendar: semesters. *Degrees:* certificates, bachelor's, master's, doctoral, post-master's, and postbachelor's certificates.

Special study options: accelerated degree program, adult/continuing education programs, advanced placement credit, cooperative education, distance learning, double majors, English as a second language, external degree program, freshman honors college, honors programs, independent study, internships, off-campus study, part-time degree program, services for LD students, student-designed majors, study abroad, summer session for credit. ***ROTC:*** Army (b), Navy (b), Air Force (b).

Computers: Students can access the following: campus intranet, computer help desk, free student e-mail accounts, online (class) grades, online (class) registration, online (class) schedules. Campuswide network is available. Wireless service is available via classrooms, computer centers, computer labs, dorm rooms, learning centers, libraries, student centers.

Library: University of Arizona Main Library plus 4 others. *Books:* 3.1 million (physical), 1.8 million (digital/electronic); *Serial titles:* 6.3 million (physical), 101,171 (digital/electronic); *Databases:* 835. Study areas open 24 hours, 5-7 days a week; students can reserve study rooms.

STUDENT LIFE

Housing options: coed, women-only, special housing for students with disabilities. Campus housing is university owned and leased by the school. Freshman applicants given priority for college housing.

Activities and organizations: drama/theater group, student-run newspaper, radio and television station, choral group, marching band, national fraternities, national sororities.

Athletics Member NCAA. All Division I except football (Division I-A). ***Intercollegiate sports:*** badminton M(c)/W(c), baseball M(s), basketball M(s)/W(s), cheerleading M(c)/W(c), cross-country running M(s)/W(s), golf M(s)/W(s), gymnastics W(s), ice hockey M(c), lacrosse M(c)/W(c), racquetball M(c)/W(c), rugby M(c)/W(c), soccer M(c)/W(s), softball W(s), swimming and diving M(s)/W(s), tennis M(s)/W(s), track and field M(s)/W(s), ultimate Frisbee M(c)/W(c), volleyball M(c)/W(s), water polo M(c)/W(c). ***Intramural sports:*** basketball M/W, football M/W, racquetball M/W, soccer M/W, table tennis M/W, tennis M/W, ultimate Frisbee M/W, volleyball M/W, water polo M/W, wrestling M(c)/W(c).

Campus security: 24-hour patrols, student patrols, late-night transport/escort service, emergency telephones.

Student services: health clinic, personal/psychological counseling, women's center, legal services.

COSTS & FINANCIAL AID

Costs (2016–17) ***Tuition:*** state resident $10,160 full-time, $768 per credit hour part-time; nonresident $30,759 full-time, $1415 per credit hour part-time. Full-time tuition and fees vary according to class time, course level, course load, degree level, location, program, reciprocity agreements, and student level. Part-time tuition and fees vary according to class time, course level, course load, degree level, location, program, reciprocity agreements, and student level. No tuition increase for student's term of enrollment. ***Required fees:*** $1017 full-time, $88 per credit hour part-time. ***Room and board:*** $11,300; room only: $7300. Room and board charges vary according to board plan and housing facility. ***Payment plan:*** installment. ***Waivers:*** employees or children of employees.

Financial Aid Of all full-time matriculated undergraduates who enrolled in 2015, 18,907 applied for aid, 15,304 were judged to have need, 1,580 had their need fully met. In 2015, 6353 non-need-based awards were made. ***Average percent of need met:*** 56. ***Average financial aid package:*** $12,707. ***Average need-based loan:*** $4146. ***Average need-based gift aid:*** $10,109. ***Average non-need-based aid:*** $8164. ***Average indebtedness upon graduation:*** $23,273.

APPLYING

Standardized Tests *Recommended:* SAT or ACT (for admission).

Options: electronic application, early admission.

Application fee: $50.

Required: essay or personal statement, high school transcript. ***Required for some:*** minimum 3.0 GPA, interview.

Application deadlines: 5/1 (freshmen), rolling (transfers).

Notification: continuous (freshmen).

CONTACT

The University of Arizona, Tucson, AZ 85721. *Phone:* 520-621-3705.

University of Phoenix–Online Campus

Phoenix, Arizona

http://www.phoenix.edu/

CONTACT

Marc Booker, Sr. Director, Office of Admissions and Evaluation, University of Phoenix–Online Campus, 4035 South Riverpoint Parkway, Mail Stop CF-L101, Phoenix, AZ 85040. *Phone:* 602-557-4609. *Toll-free phone:* 866-766-0766. *Fax:* 480-643-1156.

University of Phoenix–Phoenix Campus

Tempe, Arizona

http://www.phoenix.edu/

CONTACT

Marc Booker, Sr. Director, Office of Admissions and Evaluation, University of Phoenix–Phoenix Campus, 4035 South Riverpoint Parkway, Mail Stop CF-L101, Phoenix, AZ 85040. *Phone:* 602-557-4609. *Toll-free phone:* 866-766-0766. *Fax:* 480-643-1156.

University of Phoenix–Southern Arizona Campus

Tucson, Arizona

http://www.phoenix.edu/

CONTACT

Marc Booker, Sr. Director, Office of Admissions and Evaluation, University of Phoenix–Southern Arizona Campus, 4035 South Riverpoint Parkway, Mail Stop CF-L101, Phoenix, AZ 85040-1958. *Phone:* 602-557-4609. *Toll-free phone:* 866-766-0766. *Fax:* 480-643-1156.

Western International University

Tempe, Arizona

http://www.west.edu/

- **Proprietary** comprehensive, founded 1978, part of Apollo Global and Apollo Group
- **Urban** 4-acre campus with easy access to Phoenix
- **Coed** 2,322 undergraduate students, 100% full-time, 64% women, 36% men
- 100% of applicants were admitted

UNDERGRAD STUDENTS

2,322 full-time. Students come from 59 states and territories; 10 other countries; 0.3% transferred in.

Freshmen:

Admission: 1,142 applied, 1,142 admitted, 20 enrolled.

FACULTY

Total: 233, 3% full-time, 36% with terminal degrees.

ACADEMICS

Calendar: continuous. *Degrees:* associate, bachelor's, master's, and postbachelor's certificates.

Special study options: academic remediation for entering students, accelerated degree program, adult/continuing education programs, advanced placement credit, distance learning, double majors, independent study, summer session for credit.

Computers: Students can access the following: campus intranet, computer help desk, free student e-mail accounts, online (class) grades, online (class) registration, online (class) schedules. Campuswide network is available. Wireless service is available via entire campus.

Library: Learning Resource Center.

STUDENT LIFE

Housing options: college housing not available.

Campus security: 24-hour emergency response devices and patrols, late-night transport/escort service.

COSTS & FINANCIAL AID

Costs (2017–18) ***Tuition:*** $6000 full-time, $250 per semester hour part-time. ***Payment plan:*** deferred payment. ***Waivers:*** employees or children of employees.

Financial Aid ***Average financial aid package:*** $3321. ***Average indebtedness upon graduation:*** $5285.

APPLYING

Options: electronic application, deferred entrance.

Application fee: $25.

Required: high school transcript, minimum 2.5 GPA.

Application deadlines: rolling (freshmen), rolling (transfers).

Notification: continuous (freshmen), continuous (transfers), rolling (early decision plan 1), rolling (early decision plan 2), rolling (early action).

CONTACT

Ken Costello, VP Operations and BIRT, Western International University, 1601 W Fountainhead Parkway, Tempe, AZ 85382. *Phone:* 602-943-2311. *Toll-free phone:* 866-948-4636. *E-mail:* ken.costello@west.edu.

ARKANSAS

Arkansas Baptist College

Little Rock, Arkansas

http://www.arkansasbaptist.edu/

CONTACT

Arkansas Baptist College, 1621 Dr. Martin Luther King, Jr. Drive, Little Rock, AR 72202-6067. *Phone:* 501-244-5104 Ext. 5124.

Arkansas State University

Jonesboro, Arkansas

http://www.astate.edu/

- **State-supported** comprehensive, founded 1909, part of Arkansas State University System
- **Small-town** 1376-acre campus with easy access to Memphis
- **Endowment** $54.9 million
- **Coed**
- **Moderately difficult** entrance level

FACULTY

Student/faculty ratio: 17:1.

ACADEMICS

Calendar: semesters. *Degrees:* associate, bachelor's, master's, doctoral, post-master's, and postbachelor's certificates.

Library: Dean B. Ellis Library. *Books:* 386,049 (physical), 452,194 (digital/electronic); *Serial titles:* 353 (physical), 40,469 (digital/electronic); *Databases:* 163. Weekly public service hours: 103; students can reserve study rooms.

STUDENT LIFE

Housing options: on-campus residence required for freshman year; coed, men-only, women-only. Campus housing is university owned.

Activities and organizations: drama/theater group, student-run newspaper, radio and television station, choral group, marching band, Honors College, Volunteer A-State, Baptist Collegiate Ministry, Black Student Association, Student Activities Board, national fraternities, national sororities.

Athletics Member NCAA. All Division I except football (Division I-A).

Campus security: 24-hour emergency response devices and patrols, student patrols, late-night transport/escort service, controlled dormitory access, check-in desk, video surveillance cameras.

Student services: health clinic, personal/psychological counseling.

COSTS & FINANCIAL AID

Costs (2016–17) ***Tuition:*** state resident $6060 full-time, $202 per credit hour part-time; nonresident $12,120 full-time, $404 per credit hour part-time. Full-time tuition and fees vary according to course load, location, and program. Part-time tuition and fees vary according to course load, location, and program. ***Required fees:*** $2140 full-time, $69 per credit hour part-time, $35 per term part-time. ***Room and board:*** $8540. Room and board charges vary according to board plan, housing facility, and student level.

Financial Aid Of all full-time matriculated undergraduates who enrolled in 2015, 6,564 applied for aid, 6,304 were judged to have need, 3,463 had their need fully met. 190 Federal Work-Study jobs (averaging $3500). 380 state and other part-time jobs (averaging $3900). In 2015, 748 non-need-based awards were made. ***Average percent of need met:*** 51. ***Average financial aid package:*** $10,500. ***Average need-based loan:*** $8200. ***Average need-based gift aid:*** $10,000. ***Average non-need-based aid:*** $5600. ***Average indebtedness upon graduation:*** $27,400. ***Financial aid deadline:*** 7/1.

APPLYING

Standardized Tests *Required:* SAT or ACT (for admission). *Required for some:* ACT ASSET; ACT Compass; TOEFL, IELTS, PTE, iTEP, or Proof of English Proficiency for international students. *Recommended:* ACT (for admission).

Options: electronic application, early admission.

Application fee: $15.

Required: high school transcript, minimum 2.8 GPA, minimum ACT composite score of 21, immunization, Selective Service.

CONTACT

Ms. Tracy Finch, Director of Admissions, Records, and Registration, Arkansas State University, PO Box 1570, State University, AR 72467. *Phone:* 870-972-2031. *Toll-free phone:* 800-382-3030. *Fax:* 870-972-3406. *E-mail:* admissions@astate.edu.

Arkansas Tech University

Russellville, Arkansas

http://www.atu.edu/

- **State-supported** comprehensive, founded 1909
- **Small-town** 559-acre campus
- **Endowment** $23.2 million
- **Coed** 11,053 undergraduate students, 61% full-time, 55% women, 45% men
- **Moderately difficult** entrance level, 64% of applicants were admitted

UNDERGRAD STUDENTS

6,785 full-time, 4,268 part-time. Students come from 38 states and territories; 45 other countries; 4% are from out of state; 7% Black or African American, non-Hispanic/Latino; 7% Hispanic/Latino; 1% Asian, non-Hispanic/Latino; 0.8% American Indian or Alaska Native, non-Hispanic/Latino; 3% Two or more races, non-Hispanic/Latino; 3% international; 5% transferred in; 32% live on campus.

Freshmen:

Admission: 5,232 applied, 3,344 admitted, 1,892 enrolled. ***Average high school GPA:*** 3.25. ***Test scores:*** SAT critical reading scores over 500: 21%; SAT math scores over 500: 67%; ACT scores over 18: 84%; SAT critical reading scores over 600: 4%; SAT math scores over 600: 21%; ACT scores over 24: 38%; SAT math scores over 700: 4%; ACT scores over 30: 4%.

Retention: 69% of full-time freshmen returned.

FACULTY

Total: 608, 60% full-time, 42% with terminal degrees.

Student/faculty ratio: 19:1.

ACADEMICS

Calendar: semesters. *Degrees:* certificates, associate, bachelor's, master's, doctoral, and post-master's certificates.

Special study options: academic remediation for entering students, accelerated degree program, adult/continuing education programs, advanced placement credit, distance learning, double majors, English as a second language, honors programs, independent study, internships, off-campus study, part-time degree program, services for LD students, study abroad, summer session for credit. ***ROTC:*** Army (c).

Computers: 1,124 computers/terminals are available on campus for general student use. Students can access the following: campus intranet, computer help desk, free student e-mail accounts, online (class) grades, online (class) registration, online (class) schedules. Campuswide network is available. 100% of college-owned or -operated housing units are wired for high-speed Internet access. Wireless service is available via classrooms, computer centers, computer labs, dorm rooms, learning centers, libraries, student centers.

Library: Ross Pendergraft Library and Technology Center. *Books:* 313,011 (physical), 47,410 (digital/electronic); *Databases:* 259. Students can reserve study rooms.

STUDENT LIFE

Housing options: on-campus residence required through sophomore year; coed, men-only, women-only, special housing for students with disabilities. Campus housing is university owned. Freshman campus housing is guaranteed.

Activities and organizations: drama/theater group, student-run newspaper, radio and television station, choral group, marching band, national fraternities, national sororities.

Athletics Member NCAA. All Division II. ***Intercollegiate sports:*** baseball M(s), basketball M(s)/W(s), cheerleading M(s)/W(s), cross-country running W(s), football M(s), golf M(s)/W(s), softball W(s), tennis W(s), volleyball W(s). ***Intramural sports:*** basketball M/W, bowling M/W, golf M(c)/W(c), racquetball M/W, soccer M/W, softball M/W, table tennis M/W, tennis M/W, ultimate Frisbee M/W, volleyball M/W.

Campus security: 24-hour emergency response devices and patrols, student patrols, late-night transport/escort service, controlled dormitory access.

Student services: health clinic, personal/psychological counseling.

COSTS & FINANCIAL AID

Costs (2016–17) ***Tuition:*** state resident $6570 full-time, $219 per credit hour part-time; nonresident $13,140 full-time, $438 per credit hour part-time. Full-time tuition and fees vary according to course load and location. Part-time tuition and fees vary according to course load and location. ***Required fees:*** $1710 full-time, $57 per credit hour part-time. ***Room and board:*** $7036; room only: $4296. Room and board charges vary according to board plan, housing facility, and location. ***Payment plans:*** installment, deferred payment. ***Waivers:*** senior citizens and employees or children of employees.

Financial Aid Of all full-time matriculated undergraduates who enrolled in 2015, 6,343 applied for aid, 4,857 were judged to have need, 307 had their need fully met. In 2015, 861 non-need-based awards were made. ***Average percent of need met:*** 58. ***Average financial aid package:*** $9302. ***Average need-based loan:*** $3640. ***Average need-based gift aid:*** $4458. ***Average non-need-based aid:*** $6804. ***Average indebtedness upon graduation:*** $27,156.

APPLYING

Standardized Tests *Required:* SAT or ACT (for admission).

Options: electronic application, early action, deferred entrance.

Required: high school transcript, minimum 2.0 GPA.

Notification: continuous (freshmen), continuous (transfers).

CONTACT

Ms. Shauna Donnell, Director of Enrollment Management, Arkansas Tech University, Doc Bryan Student Services Building, Suite 141, Russellville, AR 72801. *Phone:* 479-968-0343. *Toll-free phone:* 800-582-6953. *Fax:* 479-964-0522. *E-mail:* tech.enroll@atu.edu.

Central Baptist College

Conway, Arkansas

http://www.cbc.edu/

- **Independent Baptist** 4-year, founded 1952
- **Small-town** 11-acre campus
- **Coed** 832 undergraduate students, 79% full-time, 47% women, 53% men
- **Minimally difficult** entrance level, 62% of applicants were admitted

UNDERGRAD STUDENTS

658 full-time, 174 part-time. Students come from 19 states and territories; 12 other countries; 26% are from out of state; 19% Black or African American, non-Hispanic/Latino; 3% Hispanic/Latino; 0.1% Asian, non-Hispanic/Latino; 2% Native Hawaiian or other Pacific Islander, non-Hispanic/Latino; 1% American Indian or Alaska Native, non-Hispanic/Latino; 0.4% Two or more races, non-Hispanic/Latino; 0.6% Race/ethnicity unknown; 2% international; 9% transferred in.

Freshmen:
Admission: 318 applied, 197 admitted, 126 enrolled. ***Test scores:*** SAT critical reading scores over 500: 9%; SAT math scores over 500: 27%; SAT writing scores over 500: 18%; ACT scores over 18: 86%; ACT scores over 24: 32%; ACT scores over 30: 1%.

Retention: 73% of full-time freshmen returned.

FACULTY
Total: 87, 34% full-time, 28% with terminal degrees.

Student/faculty ratio: 12:1.

ACADEMICS
Calendar: semesters. *Degrees:* associate and bachelor's.

Special study options: academic remediation for entering students, adult/continuing education programs, advanced placement credit, distance learning, independent study, internships, part-time degree program, services for LD students, summer session for credit. ***ROTC:*** Army (c).

Computers: 70 computers/terminals are available on campus for general student use. Students can access the following: computer help desk, free student e-mail accounts, online (class) grades, online (class) registration, online (class) schedules. Campuswide network is available. Wireless service is available via entire campus.
Library: Story Library. Students can reserve study rooms.

STUDENT LIFE
Housing options: on-campus residence required through senior year; coed.

Activities and organizations: drama/theater group, student-run newspaper, radio station, choral group.

Athletics Member NCCAA. ***Intercollegiate sports:*** baseball M, basketball M/W, golf M/W, soccer M/W, softball W, volleyball W, wrestling M. ***Intramural sports:*** table tennis M/W.

Campus security: controlled dormitory access.

Student services: personal/psychological counseling.

COSTS
Costs (2017–18) ***Comprehensive fee:*** $23,250 includes full-time tuition ($14,250), mandatory fees ($1500), and room and board ($7500). Full-time tuition and fees vary according to program. Part-time tuition: $475 per credit hour. Part-time tuition and fees vary according to program. ***Room and board:*** Room and board charges vary according to board plan and housing facility. ***Payment plan:*** installment. ***Waivers:*** senior citizens and employees or children of employees.

APPLYING
Standardized Tests *Required:* SAT or ACT (for admission).

Options: electronic application, early admission.

Required: high school transcript.

Application deadlines: 8/15 (freshmen), 8/15 (transfers).

CONTACT
Central Baptist College, 1501 College Avenue, Conway, AR 72032.
Toll-free phone: 800-205-6872.

Ecclesia College

Springdale, Arkansas

http://www.ecollege.edu/

- **Independent Christian** comprehensive, founded 1995
- **Small-town** 200-acre campus with easy access to Northwest Arkansas
- **Coed** 246 undergraduate students, 78% full-time, 41% women, 59% men
- **Noncompetitive** entrance level, 31% of applicants were admitted

UNDERGRAD STUDENTS
191 full-time, 55 part-time. 75% live on campus.

Freshmen:
Admission: 211 applied, 65 admitted, 66 enrolled.

Retention: 57% of full-time freshmen returned.

FACULTY
Total: 75, 24% full-time, 36% with terminal degrees.

Student/faculty ratio: 10:1.

ACADEMICS
Calendar: semesters. *Degrees:* associate, bachelor's, and master's.

Special study options: distance learning, double majors, English as a second language, independent study, internships.

Computers: Students can access the following: campus intranet, computer help desk, free student e-mail accounts, online (class) grades, online (class) schedules. Campuswide network is available. 90% of college-owned or -operated housing units are wired for high-speed Internet access. Wireless service is available via entire campus.
Library: Ecclesia College Library.

STUDENT LIFE
Housing options: on-campus residence required through senior year; men-only, women-only. Campus housing is university owned. Freshman campus housing is guaranteed.

Activities and organizations: drama/theater group, choral group, Service Learning, Student Council, Worship Team, Missions.

Athletics Member NCCAA. ***Intercollegiate sports:*** baseball M(s), basketball M(s)/W(s), cross-country running M(s)/W(s), soccer M(s)/W(s), softball W(s).

Campus security: student patrols.

Student services: personal/psychological counseling.

COSTS
Costs (2017–18) ***Comprehensive fee:*** $20,150 includes full-time tuition ($14,250), mandatory fees ($890), and room and board ($5010). Part-time tuition: $475 per credit hour. Part-time tuition and fees vary according to course load. ***Room and board:*** Room and board charges vary according to housing facility. ***Payment plan:*** installment. ***Waivers:*** employees or children of employees.

APPLYING
Standardized Tests *Required:* SAT or ACT (for admission).

Options: electronic application.

Application fee: $35.

Required: essay or personal statement, high school transcript, minimum 2.0 GPA, 1 letter of recommendation, interview.

Application deadlines: rolling (freshmen), rolling (transfers).

Notification: continuous (freshmen), continuous (transfers).

CONTACT
Ecclesia College, 9653 Nations Drive, Springdale, AR 72762.
Phone: 479-248-7236 Ext. 223.

Harding University

Searcy, Arkansas

http://www.harding.edu/

- **Independent** university, founded 1924, affiliated with Church of Christ
- **Small-town** 350-acre campus with easy access to Little Rock
- **Endowment** $119.2 million
- **Coed** 4,419 undergraduate students, 94% full-time, 56% women, 44% men
- **Moderately difficult** entrance level, 70% of applicants were admitted

UNDERGRAD STUDENTS
4,143 full-time, 276 part-time. Students come from 54 states and territories; 49 other countries; 71% are from out of state; 4% Black or African American, non-Hispanic/Latino; 3% Hispanic/Latino; 0.7% Asian, non-Hispanic/Latino; 0.7% American Indian or Alaska Native, non-Hispanic/Latino; 2% Two or more races, non-Hispanic/Latino; 0.3% Race/ethnicity unknown; 6% international; 4% transferred in; 74% live on campus.

Freshmen:
Admission: 2,217 applied, 1,556 admitted, 1,019 enrolled. ***Average high school GPA:*** 3.61. ***Test scores:*** SAT critical reading scores over 500: 74%; SAT math scores over 500: 70%; ACT scores over 18: 96%; SAT critical reading scores over 600: 32%; SAT math scores over 600: 33%; ACT scores over 24: 60%; SAT critical reading scores over 700: 9%; SAT math scores over 700: 8%; ACT scores over 30: 16%.

Retention: 82% of full-time freshmen returned.

FACULTY
Total: 523, 60% full-time, 52% with terminal degrees.

Student/faculty ratio: 14:1.

ACADEMICS
Calendar: semesters. *Degrees:* bachelor's, master's, doctoral, and post-master's certificates.

Special study options: academic remediation for entering students, accelerated degree program, adult/continuing education programs, advanced placement credit, cooperative education, distance learning, double majors, English as a second language, freshman honors college, honors programs, independent study, internships, part-time degree program, services for LD students, student-designed majors, study abroad, summer session for credit.

Computers: 512 computers/terminals and 3,200 ports are available on campus for general student use. Students can access the following: campus intranet, computer help desk, free student e-mail accounts, online (class) grades, online (class) registration, online (class) schedules. Campuswide network is available. 100% of college-owned or -operated housing units are wired for high-speed Internet access. Wireless service is available via entire campus.

Library: Brackett Library plus 1 other. *Books:* 190,355 (physical), 129,853 (digital/electronic); *Serial titles:* 510 (physical), 81,906 (digital/electronic); *Databases:* 170. Students can reserve study rooms.

STUDENT LIFE
Housing options: on-campus residence required through senior year; men-only, women-only, special housing for students with disabilities. Campus housing is university owned. Freshman campus housing is guaranteed.

Activities and organizations: drama/theater group, student-run newspaper, radio and television station, choral group, marching band, Bisons for Christ, Harding in Action, Spring Break Campaigns, HUmanity.

Athletics Member NCAA. All Division II. ***Intercollegiate sports:*** baseball M(s), basketball M(s)/W(s), cheerleading W, cross-country running M(s)/W(s), football M(s), golf M(s)/W(s), lacrosse M(c), rugby M(c), soccer M(s)/W(s), tennis M(s)/W(s), track and field M(s)/W(s), ultimate Frisbee M(c)/W(c), volleyball W(s). ***Intramural sports:*** basketball M/W, cross-country running M/W, football M/W, golf M/W, racquetball M/W, soccer M/W, softball M/W, swimming and diving M/W, table tennis M/W, tennis M/W, track and field M/W, ultimate Frisbee M/W, volleyball M/W, weight lifting M/W.

Campus security: 24-hour emergency response devices and patrols, student patrols, late-night transport/escort service, controlled dormitory access.

Student services: health clinic, personal/psychological counseling.

COSTS & FINANCIAL AID
Costs (2016–17) ***Comprehensive fee:*** $25,196 includes full-time tuition ($17,940), mandatory fees ($500), and room and board ($6756). Full-time tuition and fees vary according to course load. Part-time tuition: $598 per credit hour. Part-time tuition and fees vary according to course load. ***Required fees:*** $25 per credit hour part-time. ***College room only:*** $3266. Room and board charges vary according to board plan and housing facility. ***Payment plans:*** tuition prepayment, installment. ***Waivers:*** senior citizens and employees or children of employees.

Financial Aid Of all full-time matriculated undergraduates who enrolled in 2015, 3,163 applied for aid, 2,534 were judged to have need, 929 had their need fully met. 544 Federal Work-Study jobs (averaging $1069). 1,488 state and other part-time jobs (averaging $1201). In 2015, 528 non-need-based awards were made. ***Average percent of need met:*** 78. ***Average financial aid package:*** $17,723. ***Average need-based loan:*** $8010. ***Average need-based gift aid:*** $7147. ***Average non-need-based aid:*** $6574. ***Average indebtedness upon graduation:*** $30,570.

APPLYING
Standardized Tests *Required:* SAT or ACT (for admission).

Options: electronic application, early admission, early action, deferred entrance.

Application fee: $50.

Required: essay or personal statement, high school transcript, 3 letters of recommendation.

Application deadlines: rolling (freshmen), rolling (transfers).
Notification: continuous (freshmen), continuous (transfers).

CONTACT
Mr. Glenn Dillard, Assistant Vice President for Enrollment Management, Harding University, 915 E. Market Avenue, Box 12255, Searcy, AR 72149-5615. *Phone:* 501-279-4407. *Toll-free phone:* 800-477-4407. *Fax:* 501-279-4129. *E-mail:* admissions@harding.edu.

See previous page for display ad and page 1372 for the College Close-Up.

Henderson State University

Arkadelphia, Arkansas

http://www.hsu.edu/

- **State-supported** comprehensive, founded 1890
- **Small-town** 151-acre campus with easy access to Little Rock
- **Coed** 3,066 undergraduate students, 91% full-time, 57% women, 43% men
- **Moderately difficult** entrance level, 66% of applicants were admitted

UNDERGRAD STUDENTS
2,791 full-time, 275 part-time. Students come from 27 states and territories; 26 other countries; 14% are from out of state; 23% Black or African American, non-Hispanic/Latino; 4% Hispanic/Latino; 0.8% Asian, non-Hispanic/Latino; 0.1% Native Hawaiian or other Pacific Islander, non-Hispanic/Latino; 0.4% American Indian or Alaska Native, non-Hispanic/Latino; 3% Two or more races, non-Hispanic/Latino; 0.2% Race/ethnicity unknown; 1% international; 7% transferred in; 43% live on campus.

Freshmen:
Admission: 4,072 applied, 2,692 admitted, 746 enrolled. ***Average high school GPA:*** 3.23. ***Test scores:*** SAT critical reading scores over 500: 42%; SAT math scores over 500: 51%; ACT scores over 18: 85%; SAT critical reading scores over 600: 21%; SAT math scores over 600: 21%; ACT scores over 24: 35%; SAT critical reading scores over 700: 3%; SAT math scores over 700: 3%; ACT scores over 30: 5%.
Retention: 60% of full-time freshmen returned.

FACULTY
Total: 257, 69% full-time, 51% with terminal degrees.
Student/faculty ratio: 15:1.

ACADEMICS
Calendar: semesters. *Degrees:* certificates, bachelor's, master's, post-master's, and postbachelor's certificates.
Special study options: academic remediation for entering students, advanced placement credit, distance learning, double majors, freshman honors college, honors programs, internships, off-campus study, part-time degree program, services for LD students, study abroad, summer session for credit. ***ROTC:*** Army (c).
Computers: 125 computers/terminals are available on campus for general student use. Students can access the following: campus intranet, computer help desk, free student e-mail accounts, online (class) grades, online (class) registration, online (class) schedules. Campuswide network is available. 100% of college-owned or -operated housing units are wired for high-speed Internet access. Wireless service is available via classrooms, computer centers, computer labs, dorm rooms, libraries, student centers.
Library: Huie Library plus 1 other. *Books:* 225,859 (physical), 142,000 (digital/electronic); *Databases:* 223. Weekly public service hours: 80; students can reserve study rooms.

STUDENT LIFE
Housing options: on-campus residence required through sophomore year; coed, men-only, women-only. Campus housing is university owned and is provided by a third party. Freshman applicants given priority for college housing.
Activities and organizations: drama/theater group, student-run newspaper, radio and television station, choral group, marching band, Heart and Key, Student Government Association, Residence Hall Association, national fraternities, national sororities.
Athletics Member NCAA. All Division II. ***Intercollegiate sports:*** baseball M(s), basketball M(s)/W(s), cross-country running W(s), football M(s), golf M(s)/W(s), softball W(s), swimming and diving M(s)/W(s), tennis W(s), volleyball W(s). ***Intramural sports:*** basketball M/W, football M, soccer M.
Campus security: 24-hour emergency response devices and patrols, late-night transport/escort service, controlled dormitory access, Reddie Rides offered at night.
Student services: health clinic, personal/psychological counseling.

COSTS & FINANCIAL AID
Costs (2016–17) ***Tuition:*** state resident $6450 full-time, $215 per credit hour part-time; nonresident $13,290 full-time, $443 per credit hour part-time. Full-time tuition and fees vary according to course load. Part-time tuition and fees vary according to course load. ***Required fees:*** $1666 full-time. ***Room and board:*** $7082. Room and board charges vary according to board plan and housing facility. ***Payment plan:*** installment. ***Waivers:*** children of alumni, senior citizens, and employees or children of employees.
Financial Aid Of all full-time matriculated undergraduates who enrolled in 2014, 2,703 applied for aid, 2,424 were judged to have need, 265 had their need fully met. In 2014, 138 non-need-based awards were made. ***Average percent of need met:*** 57. ***Average financial aid package:*** $11,778. ***Average need-based loan:*** $3714. ***Average need-based gift aid:*** $4572. ***Average non-need-based aid:*** $5730. ***Average indebtedness upon graduation:*** $23,641.

APPLYING
Standardized Tests *Required:* SAT or ACT (for admission). *Recommended:* ACT (for admission).
Options: electronic application, deferred entrance.
Required: high school transcript. ***Required for some:*** essay or personal statement, 3 letters of recommendation. ***Recommended:*** minimum 2.5 GPA.
Application deadlines: 7/15 (freshmen), rolling (transfers).
Notification: continuous (freshmen), continuous (transfers).

CONTACT
Dr. Brandie Benton, Associate Provost Enrollment Services & Admissions, Henderson State University, 1100 Henderson Street, PO Box 7560, Arkadelphia, AR 71999-0001. *Phone:* 870-230-5203. *Toll-free phone:* 800-228-7333. *Fax:* 870-230-5066. *E-mail:* bentonb@hsu.edu.

Hendrix College

Conway, Arkansas

http://www.hendrix.edu/

- **Independent United Methodist** comprehensive, founded 1876
- **Suburban** 180-acre campus with easy access to Little Rock
- **Endowment** $185.5 million
- **Coed** 1,321 undergraduate students, 99% full-time, 53% women, 47% men
- **Very difficult** entrance level, 77% of applicants were admitted

UNDERGRAD STUDENTS
1,314 full-time, 7 part-time. Students come from 36 states and territories; 28 other countries; 46% are from out of state; 6% Black or African American, non-Hispanic/Latino; 5% Hispanic/Latino; 5% Asian, non-Hispanic/Latino; 0.6% American Indian or Alaska Native, non-Hispanic/Latino; 3% Two or more races, non-Hispanic/Latino; 0.5% Race/ethnicity unknown; 4% international; 0.5% transferred in; 94% live on campus.

Freshmen:
Admission: 1,830 applied, 1,411 admitted, 351 enrolled. ***Average high school GPA:*** 3.94. ***Test scores:*** SAT critical reading scores over 500: 91%; SAT math scores over 500: 91%; ACT scores over 18: 100%; SAT critical reading scores over 600: 55%; SAT math scores over 600: 46%; ACT scores over 24: 89%; SAT critical reading scores over 700: 22%; SAT math scores over 700: 13%; ACT scores over 30: 41%.
Retention: 87% of full-time freshmen returned.

FACULTY
Total: 138, 78% full-time, 72% with terminal degrees.
Student/faculty ratio: 11:1.

ACADEMICS
Calendar: semesters. *Degrees:* bachelor's and master's.

Special study options: advanced placement credit, cooperative education, double majors, English as a second language, independent study, internships, off-campus study, services for LD students, student-designed majors, study abroad. ***ROTC:*** Army (c).

Unusual degree programs: 3-2 engineering with Columbia University, Vanderbilt University, Washington University in St. Louis; public health with University of Arkansas.

Computers: 75 computers/terminals are available on campus for general student use. Students can access the following: campus intranet, computer help desk, free student e-mail accounts, online (class) grades, online (class) registration, online (class) schedules. Campuswide network is available. 100% of college-owned or -operated housing units are wired for high-speed Internet access. Wireless service is available via entire campus.

Library: Olin C. and Marjorie H. Bailey Library plus 1 other. *Books:* 234,623 (physical), 31,614 (digital/electronic); *Serial titles:* 409 (physical), 74,279 (digital/electronic); *Databases:* 58. Study areas open 24 hours, 5-7 days a week.

STUDENT LIFE

Housing options: on-campus residence required through senior year; coed, men-only, women-only, special housing for students with disabilities. Campus housing is university owned. Freshman campus housing is guaranteed.

Activities and organizations: drama/theater group, student-run newspaper, radio station, choral group, Environmental Concerns Committee, student government, Music ensembles, Unity, Social Committee.

Athletics Member NCAA. All Division III. ***Intercollegiate sports:*** baseball M, basketball M/W, cross-country running M/W, field hockey W, football M, golf M/W, lacrosse M/W, soccer M/W, softball W, swimming and diving M/W, tennis M/W, track and field M/W, volleyball W. ***Intramural sports:*** basketball M/W, cheerleading M/W, football M/W, racquetball M/W, soccer M/W, softball M/W, table tennis M/W, tennis M/W, ultimate Frisbee M/W.

Campus security: 24-hour emergency response devices and patrols, late-night transport/escort service, controlled dormitory access.

Student services: health clinic, personal/psychological counseling.

COSTS & FINANCIAL AID

Costs (2017–18) ***Comprehensive fee:*** $55,996 includes full-time tuition ($43,720), mandatory fees ($350), and room and board ($11,926). Full-time tuition and fees vary according to course load. Part-time tuition: $5261 per course. Part-time tuition and fees vary according to course load. ***College room only:*** $6140. Room and board charges vary according to board plan and housing facility. ***Payment plan:*** installment. ***Waivers:*** employees or children of employees.

Financial Aid Of all full-time matriculated undergraduates who enrolled in 2016, 1,099 applied for aid, 902 were judged to have need, 355 had their need fully met. 579 Federal Work-Study jobs (averaging $1911). 328 state and other part-time jobs (averaging $1684). In 2016, 378 non-need-based awards were made. ***Average percent of need met:*** 85. ***Average financial aid package:*** $35,223. ***Average need-based loan:*** $3675. ***Average need-based gift aid:*** $31,309. ***Average non-need-based aid:*** $25,907. ***Average indebtedness upon graduation:*** $30,213.

APPLYING

Standardized Tests *Required:* SAT or ACT (for admission).

Options: electronic application, early action.

Application fee: $40.

Required: essay or personal statement, high school transcript. ***Required for some:*** interview. ***Recommended:*** 1 letter of recommendation.

Application deadlines: 6/1 (freshmen), 7/1 (transfers), 11/15 (early action).

Notification: continuous (freshmen), continuous (transfers), 12/15 (early action).

CONTACT

Hendrix College, 1600 Washington Avenue, Conway, AR 72032. *Phone:* 501-450-1362. *Toll-free phone:* 800-277-9017. *Fax:* 501-450-3843. *E-mail:* adm@hendrix.edu.

John Brown University

Siloam Springs, Arkansas

http://www.jbu.edu/

- **Independent interdenominational** comprehensive, founded 1919
- **Small-town** 200-acre campus
- **Endowment** $101.5 million
- **Coed** 2,017 undergraduate students, 75% full-time, 58% women, 42% men
- **Moderately difficult** entrance level, 77% of applicants were admitted

UNDERGRAD STUDENTS

1,521 full-time, 496 part-time. Students come from 40 states and territories; 37 other countries; 47% are from out of state; 3% Black or African American, non-Hispanic/Latino; 6% Hispanic/Latino; 2% Asian, non-Hispanic/Latino; 0.1% Native Hawaiian or other Pacific Islander, non-Hispanic/Latino; 2% American Indian or Alaska Native, non-Hispanic/Latino; 3% Two or more races, non-Hispanic/Latino; 3% Race/ethnicity unknown; 5% international; 9% transferred in; 71% live on campus.

Freshmen:

Admission: 1,206 applied, 930 admitted, 322 enrolled. ***Average high school GPA:*** 3.7. ***Test scores:*** SAT critical reading scores over 500: 82%; SAT math scores over 500: 71%; SAT writing scores over 500: 78%; ACT scores over 18: 97%; SAT critical reading scores over 600: 51%; SAT math scores over 600: 28%; SAT writing scores over 600: 30%; ACT scores over 24: 72%; SAT critical reading scores over 700: 10%; SAT math scores over 700: 5%; SAT writing scores over 700: 4%; ACT scores over 30: 19%.

Retention: 85% of full-time freshmen returned.

FACULTY

Total: 263, 29% full-time, 44% with terminal degrees.

Student/faculty ratio: 13:1.

ACADEMICS

Calendar: semesters. *Degrees:* associate, bachelor's, master's, and post-master's certificates.

Special study options: accelerated degree program, adult/continuing education programs, distance learning, double majors, English as a second language, external degree program, honors programs, independent study, internships, services for LD students, study abroad. ***ROTC:*** Army (c), Air Force (c).

Computers: 250 computers/terminals are available on campus for general student use. Students can access the following: campus intranet, computer help desk, free student e-mail accounts, online (class) grades, online (class) registration, online (class) schedules. Campuswide network is available. 100% of college-owned or -operated housing units are wired for high-speed Internet access. Wireless service is available via entire campus.

Library: Arutunoff Learning Resource Center plus 4 others. *Books:* 104,100 (physical), 317,000 (digital/electronic); *Serial titles:* 1,000 (physical), 65,600 (digital/electronic); *Databases:* 134. Weekly public service hours: 110; students can reserve study rooms.

STUDENT LIFE

Housing options: on-campus residence required through junior year; coed, men-only, women-only, special housing for students with disabilities. Campus housing is university owned. Freshman campus housing is guaranteed.

Activities and organizations: drama/theater group, student-run newspaper, radio and television station, choral group, Student Government Association, Student Ministries Organization, Student Activities Club, Student Missionary Fellowship, Enactus.

Athletics Member NAIA. ***Intercollegiate sports:*** basketball M(s)/W(s), cross-country running M(s)/W(s), rugby M(c)/W(c), soccer M(s)/W(s), tennis M(s)/W(s), ultimate Frisbee M(c)/W(c), volleyball W(s). ***Intramural sports:*** basketball M/W, football M/W, racquetball M/W, soccer M/W, softball M/W, table tennis M/W, tennis M/W, volleyball M/W.

Campus security: 24-hour emergency response devices and patrols, late-night transport/escort service, controlled dormitory access.

Student services: health clinic, personal/psychological counseling.

COSTS & FINANCIAL AID

Costs (2016–17) ***Comprehensive fee:*** $34,164 includes full-time tuition ($24,218), mandatory fees ($1106), and room and board ($8840). Full-time tuition and fees vary according to course load. Part-time tuition: $807 per credit hour. Part-time tuition and fees vary according to course load. ***Required fees:*** $277 per term part-time. ***Room and board:*** Room and board charges vary according to board plan and housing facility. ***Payment plan:*** installment. ***Waivers:*** employees or children of employees.

Financial Aid Of all full-time matriculated undergraduates who enrolled in 2015, 1,227 applied for aid, 818 were judged to have need, 9 had their need fully met. In 2015, 628 non-need-based awards were made. ***Average percent of need met:*** 59. ***Average financial aid package:*** $18,587. ***Average need-based loan:*** $4523. ***Average need-based gift aid:*** $13,803. ***Average non-need-based aid:*** $15,006. ***Average indebtedness upon graduation:*** $26,651.

APPLYING

Standardized Tests *Required for some:* SAT or ACT (for admission).

Options: electronic application, deferred entrance.

Application fee: $25.

Required: essay or personal statement, high school transcript, minimum 2.5 GPA, 2 letters of recommendation. ***Recommended:*** interview.

Application deadlines: rolling (freshmen), rolling (transfers).

Notification: continuous (freshmen), continuous (transfers).

CONTACT

Mr. Jared Burgess, Director of Visitation Program, John Brown University, 2000 West University, Siloam Springs, AR 72761. *Phone:* 479-524-7190. *Toll-free phone:* 877-JBU-INFO. *Fax:* 479-524-4196. *E-mail:* jburgess@jbu.edu.

Lyon College

Batesville, Arkansas

http://www.lyon.edu/

- **Independent Presbyterian** 4-year, founded 1872
- **Small-town** 136-acre campus
- **Coed** 715 undergraduate students, 98% full-time, 48% women, 52% men
- **Moderately difficult** entrance level, 59% of applicants were admitted

UNDERGRAD STUDENTS

698 full-time, 17 part-time. 29% are from out of state; 6% Black or African American, non-Hispanic/Latino; 7% Hispanic/Latino; 2% Asian, non-Hispanic/Latino; 2% American Indian or Alaska Native, non-Hispanic/Latino; 6% Race/ethnicity unknown; 2% international; 6% transferred in; 74% live on campus.

Freshmen:

Admission: 1,607 applied, 950 admitted, 211 enrolled. ***Average high school GPA:*** 3.63. ***Test scores:*** SAT critical reading scores over 500: 78%; SAT math scores over 500: 70%; SAT writing scores over 500: 93%; ACT scores over 18: 99%; SAT critical reading scores over 600: 26%; SAT math scores over 600: 22%; SAT writing scores over 600: 56%; ACT scores over 24: 55%; SAT critical reading scores over 700: 4%; SAT math scores over 700: 4%; SAT writing scores over 700: 7%; ACT scores over 30: 14%.

Retention: 64% of full-time freshmen returned.

FACULTY

Total: 82, 51% full-time, 57% with terminal degrees.

ACADEMICS

Calendar: semesters. *Degree:* bachelor's.

Special study options: accelerated degree program, advanced placement credit, double majors, independent study, internships, off-campus study, part-time degree program, student-designed majors, study abroad, summer session for credit.

Unusual degree programs: 3-2 engineering with Missouri University of Science and Technology, University of Arkansas, University of Minnesota.

Computers: Students can access the following: campus intranet, computer help desk, free student e-mail accounts, online (class) grades, online (class) registration, online (class) schedules. Campuswide network is available. 100% of college-owned or -operated housing units are wired for high-speed Internet access. Wireless service is available via entire campus.

Library: Mabee-Simpson Library.

STUDENT LIFE

Housing options: on-campus residence required through junior year; coed. Campus housing is university owned. Freshman campus housing is guaranteed.

Activities and organizations: drama/theater group, student-run newspaper, choral group, Wesley Fellowship, Gay-Straight Alliance, Alpha Xi Delta Sorority, Fellowship of Christian Athletes, Young Democrats/Japanese Culture Club, national fraternities, national sororities.

Athletics Member NAIA. ***Intercollegiate sports:*** baseball M(s), basketball M(s)/W(s), cross-country running M(s)/W(s), football M(s), golf M(s)/W(s), soccer M(s)/W(s), softball W(s), volleyball W(s), wrestling M(s)/W(s). ***Intramural sports:*** badminton M/W, basketball M/W, football M/W, softball M/W, table tennis M/W, tennis M/W, ultimate Frisbee M/W, volleyball M/W.

Campus security: 24-hour patrols, late-night transport/escort service, controlled dormitory access.

Student services: health clinic, personal/psychological counseling.

COSTS & FINANCIAL AID

Costs (2016–17) ***Comprehensive fee:*** $34,730 includes full-time tuition ($26,050), mandatory fees ($240), and room and board ($8440). Full-time tuition and fees vary according to course load. Part-time tuition: $860 per credit hour. ***Room and board:*** Room and board charges vary according to board plan and housing facility. ***Payment plan:*** installment. ***Waivers:*** employees or children of employees.

Financial Aid Of all full-time matriculated undergraduates who enrolled in 2016, 569 applied for aid, 507 were judged to have need, 115 had their need fully met. 142 Federal Work-Study jobs (averaging $963). 7 state and other part-time jobs (averaging $857). In 2016, 101 non-need-based awards were made. ***Average percent of need met:*** 71. ***Average financial aid package:*** $21,210. ***Average need-based loan:*** $3992. ***Average need-based gift aid:*** $18,345. ***Average non-need-based aid:*** $14,205. ***Average indebtedness upon graduation:*** $22,321.

APPLYING

Standardized Tests *Required:* SAT or ACT (for admission), SAT and SAT Subject Tests or ACT (for admission).

Options: electronic application, early admission, deferred entrance.

Application fee: $25.

Required: high school transcript, minimum 2.5 GPA. ***Required for some:*** essay or personal statement, 2 letters of recommendation.

Application deadlines: rolling (freshmen), rolling (transfers).

Notification: continuous (freshmen), continuous (transfers).

CONTACT

Office of Enrollment Services, Lyon College, 2300 Highland Road, Batesville, AR 72501. *Phone:* 870-307-7250. *Toll-free phone:* 800-423-2542. *Fax:* 870-307-7542. *E-mail:* admissions@lyon.edu.

Ouachita Baptist University

Arkadelphia, Arkansas

http://www.obu.edu/

- **Independent Baptist** 4-year, founded 1886
- **Small-town** 200-acre campus with easy access to Little Rock
- **Endowment** $93.3 million
- **Coed** 1,494 undergraduate students, 98% full-time, 53% women, 47% men
- **Moderately difficult** entrance level, 67% of applicants were admitted

UNDERGRAD STUDENTS

1,469 full-time, 25 part-time. Students come from 31 states and territories; 30 other countries; 34% are from out of state; 8% Black or African American, non-Hispanic/Latino; 4% Hispanic/Latino; 0.9% Asian, non-Hispanic/Latino; 0.1% Native Hawaiian or other Pacific Islander, non-Hispanic/Latino; 0.7% American Indian or Alaska Native, non-Hispanic/Latino; 0.1% Two or more races, non-Hispanic/Latino; 2% international; 4% transferred in; 96% live on campus.

Freshmen:
Admission: 1,712 applied, 1,145 admitted, 396 enrolled. ***Average high school GPA:*** 3.55. ***Test scores:*** SAT critical reading scores over 500: 68%; SAT math scores over 500: 67%; ACT scores over 18: 94%; SAT critical reading scores over 600: 33%; SAT math scores over 600: 24%; ACT scores over 24: 54%; SAT critical reading scores over 700: 4%; SAT math scores over 700: 1%; ACT scores over 30: 16%.

Retention: 81% of full-time freshmen returned.

FACULTY
Total: 159, 67% full-time, 66% with terminal degrees.

Student/faculty ratio: 12:1.

ACADEMICS
Calendar: semesters. *Degrees:* associate and bachelor's.

Special study options: academic remediation for entering students, accelerated degree program, advanced placement credit, cooperative education, distance learning, double majors, English as a second language, honors programs, independent study, internships, off-campus study, part-time degree program, study abroad, summer session for credit. ***ROTC:*** Army (b).

Unusual degree programs: 3-2 engineering with University of Arkansas.

Computers: 275 computers/terminals and 1,375 ports are available on campus for general student use. Students can access the following: campus intranet, computer help desk, free student e-mail accounts, online (class) grades, online (class) schedules, student Web portal. Campuswide network is available. 100% of college-owned or -operated housing units are wired for high-speed Internet access. Wireless service is available via entire campus.

Library: Riley-Hickingbotham Library plus 2 others. *Books:* 176,669 (physical), 5,279 (digital/electronic). Weekly public service hours: 80; students can reserve study rooms.

STUDENT LIFE
Housing options: on-campus residence required through senior year; men-only, women-only, special housing for students with disabilities. Campus housing is university owned and leased by the school. Freshman campus housing is guaranteed.

Activities and organizations: drama/theater group, student-run newspaper, television station, choral group, marching band, Phi Beta Lambda, Campus Activities Board, Student Education Association, Student Foundation, International Club.

Athletics Member NCAA. All Division II. ***Intercollegiate sports:*** baseball M(s), basketball M(s)/W(s), cheerleading M/W, cross-country running W(s), football M(s), soccer M(s)/W(s), softball W(s), swimming and diving M(s)/W(s), tennis M(s)/W(s), volleyball W(s), wrestling M(s). ***Intramural sports:*** basketball M/W, football M/W, soccer M, softball M/W, table tennis M/W.

Campus security: 24-hour emergency response devices and patrols, controlled dormitory access.

Student services: health clinic, personal/psychological counseling.

COSTS & FINANCIAL AID
Costs (2017–18) ***Comprehensive fee:*** $33,500 includes full-time tuition ($25,300), mandatory fees ($570), and room and board ($7630). Full-time tuition and fees vary according to degree level. Part-time tuition: $700 per semester hour. Part-time tuition and fees vary according to degree level. ***Room and board:*** Room and board charges vary according to housing facility. ***Payment plans:*** installment, deferred payment. ***Waivers:*** employees or children of employees.

Financial Aid Of all full-time matriculated undergraduates who enrolled in 2016, 1,136 applied for aid, 903 were judged to have need, 320 had their need fully met. In 2016, 534 non-need-based awards were made. ***Average percent of need met:*** 84. ***Average financial aid package:*** $22,754. ***Average need-based loan:*** $3872. ***Average need-based gift aid:*** $17,433. ***Average non-need-based aid:*** $10,861. ***Average indebtedness upon graduation:*** $29,298. ***Financial aid deadline:*** 5/1.

APPLYING
Standardized Tests *Required:* SAT or ACT (for admission).

Options: deferred entrance.

Required: high school transcript, minimum 2.8 GPA. ***Recommended:*** interview.

Application deadlines: 8/15 (freshmen), 8/15 (transfers).

Notification: continuous (freshmen), continuous (transfers).

CONTACT
Mrs. Lori Motl, Director of Admissions Counseling, Ouachita Baptist University, OBU Box 3776, Arkadelphia, AR 71998-0001. *Phone:* 870-245-5110. *Toll-free phone:* 800-342-5628. *Fax:* 870-245-5500. *E-mail:* motll@obu.edu.

Philander Smith College

Little Rock, Arkansas

http://www.philander.edu/

- **Independent United Methodist** 4-year, founded 1877
- **Urban** 25-acre campus
- **Coed** 567 undergraduate students, 92% full-time, 64% women, 36% men
- **Minimally difficult** entrance level, 52% of applicants were admitted

UNDERGRAD STUDENTS
521 full-time, 46 part-time. 50% are from out of state; 90% Black or African American, non-Hispanic/Latino; 0.4% Hispanic/Latino; 0.5% Asian, non-Hispanic/Latino; 0.2% Native Hawaiian or other Pacific Islander, non-Hispanic/Latino; 0.2% American Indian or Alaska Native, non-Hispanic/Latino; 2% Two or more races, non-Hispanic/Latino; 6% international; 9% transferred in; 40% live on campus.

Freshmen:
Admission: 3,330 applied, 1,730 admitted, 112 enrolled. ***Average high school GPA:*** 2.88. ***Test scores:*** SAT critical reading scores over 500: 33%; SAT math scores over 500: 38%; ACT scores over 18: 65%; SAT critical reading scores over 600: 10%; SAT math scores over 600: 24%; ACT scores over 24: 14%; ACT scores over 30: 1%.

FACULTY
Total: 56, 82% full-time, 54% with terminal degrees.

Student/faculty ratio: 11:1.

ACADEMICS
Calendar: semesters. *Degree:* bachelor's.

Special study options: academic remediation for entering students, accelerated degree program, adult/continuing education programs, advanced placement credit, cooperative education, double majors, independent study, internships, part-time degree program, services for LD students, study abroad, summer session for credit. ***ROTC:*** Army (c).

Unusual degree programs: 3-2 engineering.

Computers: Students can access the following: campus intranet, computer help desk, free student e-mail accounts, online (class) grades, online (class) registration, online (class) schedules. Campuswide network is available. 100% of college-owned or -operated housing units are wired for high-speed Internet access. Wireless service is available via entire campus.

Library: D. W. Reynolds Library & Technology Center.

STUDENT LIFE
Housing options: on-campus residence required for freshman year; coed. Campus housing is university owned.

Activities and organizations: drama/theater group, choral group, Student Government Association, Panther Programming Council, Panther Dolls, Panther Newscast, Religious Life Council, national fraternities, national sororities.

Athletics Member NAIA. ***Intercollegiate sports:*** basketball M(s)/W(s), track and field M(s)/W(s), volleyball W(s).

Campus security: 24-hour emergency response devices and patrols, student patrols, controlled dormitory access.

Student services: health clinic, personal/psychological counseling.

FINANCIAL AID
Financial Aid Of all full-time matriculated undergraduates who enrolled in 2014, 483 applied for aid, 468 were judged to have need, 27 had their need fully met. 77 Federal Work-Study jobs (averaging $2600). In 2014, 39 non-need-based awards were made. ***Average percent of need met:*** 53. ***Average financial aid package:*** $13,375. ***Average need-based loan:*** $3936. ***Average need-based gift aid:*** $10,033. ***Average non-need-based aid:*** $15,503. ***Average indebtedness upon graduation:*** $41,565.

APPLYING
Standardized Tests *Required:* SAT or ACT (for admission).
Options: electronic application, deferred entrance.
Application fee: $25.
Required: high school transcript.

CONTACT
Ms. Bertha Owens, Recruitment Admissions and Registrar, Philander Smith College, 900 West Daisy Bates Drive, Little Rock, AR 72202. *Phone:* 501-370-5303. *Toll-free phone:* 800-446-6772. *Fax:* 501-370-5385.

Southern Arkansas University–Magnolia

Magnolia, Arkansas

http://www.saumag.edu/

- **State-supported** comprehensive, founded 1909, part of Southern Arkansas University System
- **Small-town** 1390-acre campus
- **Endowment** $30.0 million
- **Coed** 3,286 undergraduate students, 86% full-time, 55% women, 45% men
- **Moderately difficult** entrance level, 69% of applicants were admitted

UNDERGRAD STUDENTS
2,834 full-time, 452 part-time. Students come from 30 states and territories; 30 other countries; 22% are from out of state; 27% Black or African American, non-Hispanic/Latino; 3% Hispanic/Latino; 0.8% Asian, non-Hispanic/Latino; 0.8% Native Hawaiian or other Pacific Islander, non-Hispanic/Latino; 0.6% American Indian or Alaska Native, non-Hispanic/Latino; 3% international; 6% transferred in; 54% live on campus.

Freshmen:
Admission: 3,460 applied, 2,392 admitted, 854 enrolled. ***Average high school GPA:*** 3.28. ***Test scores:*** SAT critical reading scores over 500: 44%; SAT math scores over 500: 40%; ACT scores over 18: 80%; SAT critical reading scores over 600: 4%; SAT math scores over 600: 4%; ACT scores over 24: 33%; SAT critical reading scores over 700: 4%; SAT math scores over 700: 4%; ACT scores over 30: 3%.
Retention: 66% of full-time freshmen returned.

FACULTY
Total: 281, 56% full-time, 46% with terminal degrees.
Student/faculty ratio: 19:1.

ACADEMICS
Calendar: semesters. *Degrees:* certificates, associate, bachelor's, and master's.
Special study options: academic remediation for entering students, accelerated degree program, adult/continuing education programs, advanced placement credit, distance learning, double majors, English as a second language, freshman honors college, honors programs, independent study, internships, part-time degree program, services for LD students, study abroad, summer session for credit.
Computers: 199 computers/terminals and 199 ports are available on campus for general student use. Students can access the following: campus intranet, computer help desk, free student e-mail accounts, online (class) grades, online (class) registration, online (class) schedules. Campuswide network is available. 100% of college-owned or -operated housing units are wired for high-speed Internet access. Wireless service is available via computer centers, computer labs, dorm rooms, libraries, student centers.
Library: Magale Library. *Books:* 176,437 (physical), 7,779 (digital/electronic); *Serial titles:* 301 (physical), 80 (digital/electronic); *Databases:* 155. Weekly public service hours: 87.

STUDENT LIFE
Housing options: on-campus residence required through sophomore year; coed, men-only, women-only. Campus housing is university owned and is provided by a third party. Freshman campus housing is guaranteed.
Activities and organizations: drama/theater group, student-run newspaper, radio station, choral group, marching band, Student Government Association, Student Activities Board, Resident Hall Association, Residential College, International Student Association, national fraternities, national sororities.
Athletics Member NCAA. All Division II. ***Intercollegiate sports:*** baseball M(s), basketball M(s)/W(s), cheerleading M(s)(c)/W(s)(c), cross-country running M(s)/W(s), football M(s), golf M/W, softball W(s), tennis W(s), track and field M(s)/W(s), volleyball W(s). ***Intramural sports:*** badminton M/W, basketball M/W, football M, golf M/W, soccer M/W, softball M/W, swimming and diving M/W, table tennis M/W, tennis M/W, ultimate Frisbee M/W, volleyball M/W.
Campus security: 24-hour emergency response devices, student patrols, late-night transport/escort service, controlled dormitory access.
Student services: health clinic, personal/psychological counseling.

FINANCIAL AID
Financial Aid Of all full-time matriculated undergraduates who enrolled in 2015, 2,368 applied for aid, 2,105 were judged to have need, 721 had their need fully met. 529 Federal Work-Study jobs (averaging $1749). 481 state and other part-time jobs (averaging $2626). In 2015, 423 non-need-based awards were made. ***Average percent of need met:*** 78. ***Average financial aid package:*** $11,880. ***Average need-based loan:*** $3790. ***Average need-based gift aid:*** $4713. ***Average non-need-based aid:*** $5066. ***Average indebtedness upon graduation:*** $5998.

APPLYING
Standardized Tests *Required:* SAT or ACT (for admission). *Recommended:* ACT (for admission).
Options: electronic application, early admission, deferred entrance.
Required: high school transcript. ***Required for some:*** interview.
Application deadlines: 8/27 (freshmen), 8/27 (transfers).

CONTACT
Southern Arkansas University–Magnolia, 100 East University, Magnolia, AR 71753. *Phone:* 870-235-4040. *Toll-free phone:* 800-332-7286.

Strayer University–Little Rock Campus

Little Rock, Arkansas

http://www.strayer.edu/arkansas/little-rock/

CONTACT
Strayer University–Little Rock Campus, 10825 Financial Centre Parkway, Suite 131, Little Rock, AR 72211.

University of Arkansas

Fayetteville, Arkansas

http://www.uark.edu/

- **State-supported** university, founded 1871, part of University of Arkansas System
- **Urban** 718-acre campus
- **Coed** 22,548 undergraduate students, 88% full-time, 53% women, 47% men
- **Moderately difficult** entrance level, 63% of applicants were admitted

UNDERGRAD STUDENTS
19,853 full-time, 2,695 part-time. Students come from 51 states and territories; 83 other countries; 44% are from out of state; 5% Black or African American, non-Hispanic/Latino; 8% Hispanic/Latino; 2% Asian, non-Hispanic/Latino; 0.1% Native Hawaiian or other Pacific Islander, non-Hispanic/Latino; 1% American Indian or Alaska Native, non-Hispanic/Latino; 3% Two or more races, non-Hispanic/Latino; 0.5% Race/ethnicity unknown; 3% international; 6% transferred in; 26% live on campus.

Freshmen:
Admission: 21,539 applied, 13,613 admitted, 4,967 enrolled. ***Average high school GPA:*** 3.68. ***Test scores:*** SAT critical reading scores over 500: 77%; SAT math scores over 500: 81%; ACT scores over 18: 100%; SAT critical reading scores over 600: 28%; SAT math scores over 600: 36%; ACT scores over 24: 73%; SAT critical reading scores over 700: 4%; SAT math scores over 700: 5%; ACT scores over 30: 20%.
Retention: 82% of full-time freshmen returned.

FACULTY
Total: 1,353, 87% full-time, 78% with terminal degrees.
Student/faculty ratio: 19:1.

ACADEMICS
Calendar: semesters. *Degrees:* certificates, bachelor's, master's, doctoral, post-master's, and postbachelor's certificates.
Special study options: academic remediation for entering students, accelerated degree program, advanced placement credit, cooperative education, distance learning, double majors, English as a second language, freshman honors college, honors programs, independent study, internships, off-campus study, part-time degree program, services for LD students, student-designed majors, study abroad, summer session for credit. ***ROTC:*** Army (b), Air Force (b).
Unusual degree programs: 3-2 business administration; law.
Computers: 675 computers/terminals and 24 ports are available on campus for general student use. Students can access the following: computer help desk, free student e-mail accounts, online (class) grades, online (class) registration, online (class) schedules. Campuswide network is available. 100% of college-owned or -operated housing units are wired for high-speed Internet access. Wireless service is available via entire campus.
Library: David W. Mullins Library plus 4 others. *Books:* 1.9 million (physical), 570,318 (digital/electronic); *Serial titles:* 3,154 (physical), 63,090 (digital/electronic); *Databases:* 318. Weekly public service hours: 109; students can reserve study rooms.

STUDENT LIFE
Housing options: on-campus residence required for freshman year; coed, women-only, special housing for students with disabilities. Campus housing is university owned. Freshman campus housing is guaranteed.
Activities and organizations: drama/theater group, student-run newspaper, radio and television station, choral group, marching band, Associated Student Government, Catholic Campus Ministry, Chinese Students and Scholars, Alpha Lambda Delta, Student Alumni Association, national fraternities, national sororities.
Athletics Member NCAA. All Division I except football (Division I-A). ***Intercollegiate sports:*** baseball M(s), basketball M(s)/W(s), cross-country running M(s)/W(s), golf M(s)/W(s), gymnastics W(s), soccer W(s), softball W(s), swimming and diving W(s), tennis M(s)/W(s), track and field M(s)/W(s), volleyball W(s). ***Intramural sports:*** badminton M/W, baseball M(c), basketball M/W, bowling M/W, golf M/W, ice hockey M(c), lacrosse M(c)/W(c), racquetball M/W, riflery M(c)/W(c), rugby M(c)/W(c), sand volleyball M/W, soccer M/W, softball M/W, swimming and diving M(c)/W(c), table tennis M/W, tennis M/W, triathlon M(c)/W(c), ultimate Frisbee M(c)/W(c), volleyball M/W.
Campus security: 24-hour emergency response devices and patrols, student patrols, late-night transport/escort service, controlled dormitory access, RAD (Rape Aggression Defense program); tornado siren; self-defense seminars; Defibrillators; 24 hr police dispatch.
Student services: health clinic, personal/psychological counseling, women's center, legal services.

COSTS & FINANCIAL AID
Costs (2016–17) ***One-time required fee:*** $140. ***Tuition:*** state resident $7204 full-time, $240 per credit hour part-time; nonresident $21,552 full-time, $718 per credit hour part-time. Full-time tuition and fees vary according to course load, location, and program. Part-time tuition and fees vary according to course load, location, and program. ***Required fees:*** $1616 full-time, $54 per credit hour part-time. ***Room and board:*** $10,332; room only: $6620. Room and board charges vary according to board plan, housing facility, and location. ***Payment plan:*** installment. ***Waivers:*** senior citizens and employees or children of employees.
Financial Aid Of all full-time matriculated undergraduates who enrolled in 2016, 12,366 applied for aid, 8,401 were judged to have need, 1,001 had their need fully met. 1,020 Federal Work-Study jobs (averaging $2778). In 2016, 2791 non-need-based awards were made. ***Average percent of need met:*** 56. ***Average financial aid package:*** $9440. ***Average need-based loan:*** $5059. ***Average need-based gift aid:*** $7025. ***Average non-need-based aid:*** $5035. ***Average indebtedness upon graduation:*** $24,182.

APPLYING
Standardized Tests *Required:* SAT or ACT (for admission).
Options: electronic application, early action.
Application fee: $40.
Required: high school transcript, minimum 3.0 GPA, minimum ACT Composite score of 20 or SAT total (math and critical reading only) of 930, completion of 16 core academic units. ***Required for some:*** essay or personal statement.
Application deadlines: 8/1 (freshmen), 8/1 (transfers), 11/1 (early action).
Notification: continuous until 9/1 (freshmen), continuous (transfers), 12/15 (early action).

CONTACT
Cliff Murphy, Senior Associate Director of Admissions, University of Arkansas, 232 Silas H. Hunt Hall, Office of Admissions, Fayetteville, AR 72701-1201. *Phone:* 479-575-6870. *Toll-free phone:* 800-377-8632. *Fax:* 479-575-7515. *E-mail:* uofa@uark.edu.

University of Arkansas at Little Rock
Little Rock, Arkansas
http://www.ualr.edu/

CONTACT
Ms. Tammy Harrison, Director of Admissions, University of Arkansas at Little Rock, 2801 South University Avenue, Little Rock, AR 72204-1099. *Phone:* 501-569-3127. *Toll-free phone:* 800-482-8892. *Fax:* 501-569-8956. *E-mail:* twharrison@ualn.edu.

University of Arkansas at Monticello
Monticello, Arkansas
http://www.uamont.edu/

CONTACT
Ms. Mary Whiting, Director of Admissions, University of Arkansas at Monticello, Monticello, AR 71656. *Phone:* 870-460-1026. *Toll-free phone:* 800-844-1826. *E-mail:* admissions@uamont.edu.

University of Arkansas at Pine Bluff
Pine Bluff, Arkansas
http://www.uapb.edu/

- **State-supported** comprehensive, founded 1873, part of University of Arkansas System
- **Urban** 327-acre campus
- **Endowment** $3.5 million
- **Coed**
- 46% of applicants were admitted

FACULTY
Student/faculty ratio: 15:1.

ACADEMICS
Calendar: semesters. *Degrees:* certificates, associate, bachelor's, master's, and doctoral.
Library: John Brown Watson Memorial Library plus 4 others.

STUDENT LIFE
Housing options: men-only, women-only. Campus housing is university owned.
Activities and organizations: drama/theater group, student-run newspaper, choral group, marching band, Union Programming Board, Student Government Association, Pan Hellenic Council, Lion Year Book, Arkansawyer Newspaper, national fraternities, national sororities.
Athletics Member NCAA, NAIA. All NCAA Division I except football (Division I-AA).
Campus security: 24-hour emergency response devices and patrols.
Student services: health clinic, personal/psychological counseling.

FINANCIAL AID
Financial Aid Of all full-time matriculated undergraduates who enrolled in 2005, 2,825 applied for aid, 2,825 were judged to have need, 1,200 had their need fully met. 328 Federal Work-Study jobs (averaging $1000).

Average percent of need met: 70. ***Average financial aid package:*** $8121. ***Average need-based loan:*** $4500. ***Average need-based gift aid:*** $1000.

APPLYING

Standardized Tests *Required:* SAT or ACT (for admission).

Options: electronic application, early admission, deferred entrance.

Required: high school transcript, minimum 2.0 GPA.

CONTACT

University of Arkansas at Pine Bluff, 1200 North University Drive, Pine Bluff, AR 71601-2799. *Phone:* 870-575-8492.
Toll-free phone: 800-264-6585.

University of Arkansas for Medical Sciences

Little Rock, Arkansas

http://www.uams.edu/

- **State-supported** university, founded 1879, part of University of Arkansas System
- **Urban** 5-acre campus with easy access to Little Rock
- **Endowment** $29.5 million
- **Coed** 774 undergraduate students, 74% full-time, 80% women, 20% men
- 29% of applicants were admitted

UNDERGRAD STUDENTS

575 full-time, 199 part-time. 62% are from out of state; 11% Black or African American, non-Hispanic/Latino; 5% Hispanic/Latino; 2% Asian, non-Hispanic/Latino; 0.8% American Indian or Alaska Native, non-Hispanic/Latino; 3% Two or more races, non-Hispanic/Latino; 2% Race/ethnicity unknown; 0.8% international.

Freshmen:

Admission: 4,285 applied, 1,258 admitted.

FACULTY

Total: 516, 90% full-time.

ACADEMICS

Calendar: semesters. *Degrees:* certificates, associate, bachelor's, master's, doctoral, and postbachelor's certificates (bachelor's degree is upper-level).

Special study options: part-time degree program, services for LD students. ***ROTC:*** Army (c).

Computers: Students can access the following: campus intranet, computer help desk, free student e-mail accounts, online (class) grades. Campuswide network is available. 100% of college-owned or -operated housing units are wired for high-speed Internet access. Wireless service is available via entire campus.

Library: Medical Sciences Library.

STUDENT LIFE

Housing options: coed. Campus housing is university owned.

Athletics ***Intercollegiate sports:*** ultimate Frisbee M/W, volleyball M/W. ***Intramural sports:*** basketball M/W, football M, golf M, ultimate Frisbee M/W, volleyball M/W.

Campus security: 24-hour emergency response devices and patrols, late-night transport/escort service, controlled dormitory access.

Student services: health clinic, personal/psychological counseling.

COSTS & FINANCIAL AID

Costs (2016–17) ***Tuition:*** state resident $7035 full-time, $263 per semester hour part-time; nonresident $15,999 full-time, $597 per semester hour part-time. Full-time tuition and fees vary according to course load, location, program, and reciprocity agreements. Part-time tuition and fees vary according to course load, location, program, and reciprocity agreements. ***Required fees:*** $1577 full-time, $1577 per term part-time. ***Room only:*** $7560. Room and board charges vary according to housing facility. ***Waivers:*** senior citizens and employees or children of employees.

Financial Aid ***Average indebtedness upon graduation:*** $7000.

CONTACT

University of Arkansas for Medical Sciences, 4301 West Markham, Little Rock, AR 72205-7199.

University of Arkansas–Fort Smith

Fort Smith, Arkansas

http://uafs.edu/

CONTACT

Ms. Kelly Westeen, Director of Admissions, University of Arkansas–Fort Smith, 5210 Grand Avenue, PO Box 3649, Fort Smith, AR 72913-3649. *Phone:* 479-788-7106. *Toll-free phone:* 888-512-5466. *Fax:* 479-424-6106. *E-mail:* kelly.westeen@uafortsmith.edu.

University of Central Arkansas

Conway, Arkansas

http://www.uca.edu/

- **State-supported** university, founded 1907
- **Small-town** 356-acre campus
- **Coed** 9,616 undergraduate students, 83% full-time, 59% women, 41% men
- **Moderately difficult** entrance level, 90% of applicants were admitted

UNDERGRAD STUDENTS

8,010 full-time, 1,606 part-time. Students come from 43 states and territories; 73 other countries; 8% are from out of state; 17% Black or African American, non-Hispanic/Latino; 5% Hispanic/Latino; 2% Asian, non-Hispanic/Latino; 0.1% Native Hawaiian or other Pacific Islander, non-Hispanic/Latino; 0.5% American Indian or Alaska Native, non-Hispanic/Latino; 3% Two or more races, non-Hispanic/Latino; 0.6% Race/ethnicity unknown; 6% international; 7% transferred in.

Freshmen:

Admission: 4,922 applied, 4,419 admitted, 1,880 enrolled. ***Average high school GPA:*** 3.48. ***Test scores:*** ACT scores over 18: 97%; ACT scores over 24: 52%; ACT scores over 30: 12%.

Retention: 73% of full-time freshmen returned.

FACULTY

Total: 725, 75% full-time.

ACADEMICS

Calendar: semesters. *Degrees:* bachelor's, master's, doctoral, post-master's, and postbachelor's certificates.

Special study options: academic remediation for entering students, accelerated degree program, advanced placement credit, cooperative education, distance learning, double majors, English as a second language, freshman honors college, honors programs, independent study, internships, part-time degree program, services for LD students, study abroad, summer session for credit. ***ROTC:*** Army (b).

Unusual degree programs: 3-2 engineering with Arkansas Tech University in Russellville.

Computers: 610 computers/terminals are available on campus for general student use. Students can access the following: campus intranet, computer help desk, free student e-mail accounts, online (class) grades, online (class) registration, online (class) schedules. Campuswide network is available. 100% of college-owned or -operated housing units are wired for high-speed Internet access. Wireless service is available via entire campus.

Library: Torreyson Library plus 1 other. *Books:* 431,575 (physical), 31,048 (digital/electronic); *Serial titles:* 79,229 (physical), 43,328 (digital/electronic); *Databases:* 84. Study areas open 24 hours, 5-7 days a week; students can reserve study rooms.

STUDENT LIFE

Housing options: on-campus residence required for freshman year; coed, men-only, women-only, special housing for students with disabilities. Campus housing is university owned and leased by the school. Freshman campus housing is guaranteed.

Activities and organizations: drama/theater group, student-run newspaper, radio and television station, choral group, marching band, Bears Den, Greek Organizations, national fraternities, national sororities.

Athletics Member NCAA. All Division I. ***Intercollegiate sports:*** baseball M(s), basketball M(s)/W(s), cheerleading M(s)(c)/W(s)(c), cross-country running M(s)/W(s), football M(s), golf M(s)/W(s), soccer M(s)/W(s), softball W(s), tennis W(s), track and field M(s)/W(s), volleyball W(s).

Intramural sports: basketball M/W, soccer M/W, softball M/W, tennis W, track and field M/W, volleyball M/W.

Campus security: 24-hour emergency response devices and patrols, student patrols, late-night transport/escort service, controlled dormitory access.

Student services: health clinic, personal/psychological counseling, women's center.

COSTS & FINANCIAL AID

Costs (2016–17) ***Tuition:*** state resident $6223 full-time, $207 per credit hour part-time; nonresident $12,446 full-time, $415 per credit hour part-time. Full-time tuition and fees vary according to course load. Part-time tuition and fees vary according to course load. ***Required fees:*** $2001 full-time. ***Room and board:*** $6248. Room and board charges vary according to board plan and housing facility. ***Payment plan:*** installment. ***Waivers:*** senior citizens and employees or children of employees.

Financial Aid ***Financial aid deadline:*** 7/1.

APPLYING

Standardized Tests *Required:* SAT or ACT (for admission).

Options: electronic application, early admission, deferred entrance.

Application fee: $25.

Required: high school transcript. ***Required for some:*** minimum 2.75 GPA, minimum ACT score of 21 or SAT score of 1450.

Application deadlines: rolling (freshmen), rolling (transfers).

Notification: continuous (freshmen), continuous (transfers).

CONTACT

Admissions Office, University of Central Arkansas, 201 Donaghey Avenue, Bernard 100, Conway, AR 72035. *Phone:* 501-450-3120. *Toll-free phone:* 800-243-8245. *Fax:* 501-450-5228. *E-mail:* admissions@uca.edu.

University of the Ozarks

Clarksville, Arkansas

http://www.ozarks.edu/

CONTACT

Ms. Jana Hart, Dean of Admission and Financial Aid, University of the Ozarks, 415 North College Avenue, Clarksville, AR 72830-2880. *Phone:* 479-979-1227. *Toll-free phone:* 800-264-8636. *Fax:* 479-979-1417. *E-mail:* admiss@ozarks.edu.

Williams Baptist College

Walnut Ridge, Arkansas

http://www.wbcoll.edu/

- **Independent Southern Baptist** comprehensive, founded 1941
- **Rural** 180-acre campus
- **Coed** 469 undergraduate students, 90% full-time, 50% women, 50% men
- **Minimally difficult** entrance level, 60% of applicants were admitted

UNDERGRAD STUDENTS

423 full-time, 46 part-time. Students come from 23 states and territories; 7 other countries; 29% are from out of state; 9% Black or African American, non-Hispanic/Latino; 3% Hispanic/Latino; 0.2% American Indian or Alaska Native, non-Hispanic/Latino; 1% Two or more races, non-Hispanic/Latino; 6% international; 7% transferred in; 65% live on campus.

Freshmen:

Admission: 665 applied, 402 admitted, 113 enrolled. ***Average high school GPA:*** 3.2. ***Test scores:*** ACT scores over 18: 83%; ACT scores over 24: 22%; ACT scores over 30: 4%.

FACULTY

Total: 50, 52% full-time, 38% with terminal degrees.

Student/faculty ratio: 14:1.

ACADEMICS

Calendar: semesters. *Degrees:* associate, bachelor's, and master's.

Special study options: adult/continuing education programs, advanced placement credit, double majors, independent study, internships, off-campus study, part-time degree program, services for LD students, student-designed majors, study abroad, summer session for credit. ***ROTC:*** Army (c).

Computers: 70 computers/terminals are available on campus for general student use. Students can access the following: campus intranet, computer help desk, free student e-mail accounts, online (class) grades, online (class) registration, online (class) schedules. Campuswide network is available. Wireless service is available via entire campus.

Library: Felix Goodson Library plus 1 other. *Books:* 60,000 (physical), 100,000 (digital/electronic); *Serial titles:* 17 (physical), 5 (digital/electronic); *Databases:* 102. Weekly public service hours: 87; students can reserve study rooms.

STUDENT LIFE

Housing options: on-campus residence required through sophomore year; men-only, women-only. Campus housing is university owned. Freshman campus housing is guaranteed.

Activities and organizations: drama/theater group, choral group, Student Government, Student Activties Board, Bancroft Society, Cultural Awareness, International Student Society.

Athletics Member NAIA. ***Intercollegiate sports:*** baseball M(s), basketball M(s)/W(s), cross-country running M(s)/W(s), golf M(s)/W(s), soccer M(s)/W(s), softball W(s), swimming and diving M(s)/W(s), track and field M(s)/W(s), volleyball W(s), wrestling M(s). ***Intramural sports:*** basketball M/W, cheerleading W(c), football M, racquetball M/W, softball M/W, table tennis M/W, tennis M/W, ultimate Frisbee M(c)/W(c), volleyball M/W.

Campus security: 24-hour emergency response devices and patrols, student patrols, late-night transport/escort service, controlled dormitory access.

Student services: health clinic, personal/psychological counseling.

COSTS & FINANCIAL AID

Costs (2017–18) ***Comprehensive fee:*** $24,920 includes full-time tuition ($16,200), mandatory fees ($1120), and room and board ($7600). Part-time tuition: $675 per credit hour. Part-time tuition and fees vary according to course load. ***Required fees:*** $81 per term part-time. ***Room and board:*** Room and board charges vary according to board plan. ***Payment plan:*** installment. ***Waivers:*** employees or children of employees.

Financial Aid Of all full-time matriculated undergraduates who enrolled in 2015, 432 applied for aid, 326 were judged to have need. 181 Federal Work-Study jobs (averaging $1417). 20 state and other part-time jobs (averaging $1571). ***Average financial aid package:*** $19,240. ***Average need-based loan:*** $3789. ***Average need-based gift aid:*** $4656. ***Average indebtedness upon graduation:*** $19,295.

APPLYING

Standardized Tests *Required:* SAT or ACT (for admission).

Options: electronic application, early admission.

Required: high school transcript, minimum 2.6 GPA. ***Required for some:*** essay or personal statement, 2 letters of recommendation, interview.

Application deadlines: rolling (freshmen), rolling (transfers).

CONTACT

Mr. Andrew Watson, Director of Admissions, Williams Baptist College, PO Box 3737, Walnut Ridge, AR 72476. *Phone:* 870-759-4118. *Toll-free phone:* 800-722-4434. *Fax:* 870-759-4163. *E-mail:* awatson@wbcoll.edu.

CALIFORNIA

★ Academy of Art University

San Francisco, California

http://www.academyart.edu/

- **Proprietary** comprehensive, founded 1929
- **Urban** 3-acre campus
- **Coed** 8,303 undergraduate students, 58% full-time, 57% women, 43% men
- **Noncompetitive** entrance level, 100% of applicants were admitted

UNDERGRAD STUDENTS

4,827 full-time, 3,476 part-time. Students come from 50 states and territories; 103 other countries; 41% are from out of state; 7% Black or African American, non-Hispanic/Latino; 12% Hispanic/Latino; 7% Asian, non-Hispanic/Latino; 0.7% Native Hawaiian or other Pacific Islander, non-Hispanic/Latino; 0.5% American Indian or Alaska Native, non-Hispanic/Latino; 3% Two or more races, non-Hispanic/Latino; 22% Race/ethnicity unknown; 29% international; 9% transferred in; 15% live on campus.

Freshmen:
Admission: 2,761 applied, 2,761 admitted, 1,064 enrolled.
Retention: 71% of full-time freshmen returned.

FACULTY
Total: 1,404, 19% full-time, 21% with terminal degrees.
Student/faculty ratio: 14:1.

ACADEMICS
Calendar: semesters. *Degrees:* certificates, associate, bachelor's, master's, and postbachelor's certificates.
Special study options: academic remediation for entering students, adult/continuing education programs, distance learning, English as a second language, independent study, internships, part-time degree program, services for LD students, study abroad, summer session for credit.
Computers: 900 computers/terminals are available on campus for general student use. Students can access the following: free student e-mail accounts, online (class) grades, online (class) registration, online (class) schedules, support for students taking online courses. Campuswide network is available. 100% of college-owned or -operated housing units are wired for high-speed Internet access. Wireless service is available via entire campus.
Library: Academy of Art University Library. *Books:* 36,000 (physical), 9,000 (digital/electronic); *Serial titles:* 197 (physical), 400,000 (digital/electronic); *Databases:* 20. Weekly public service hours: 83; students can reserve study rooms.

STUDENT LIFE
Housing options: coed, men-only, women-only. Campus housing is university owned and leased by the school. Freshman campus housing is guaranteed.
Activities and organizations: drama/theater group, student-run newspaper, radio and television station, choral group, Tea Time Animation, Beyond the Front Row, Children's Book Club, Comic Book Club, Empower, national fraternities, national sororities.
Athletics Member NCAA. All Division II. ***Intercollegiate sports:*** baseball M(s), basketball M(s)/W(s), cross-country running M(s)/W(s), golf M(s)/W(s), soccer M(s)/W(s), softball W(s), tennis W(s), track and field M(s)/W(s), volleyball W(s).
Campus security: 24-hour emergency response devices and patrols, late-night transport/escort service, controlled dormitory access, ID check at all buildings.

COSTS & FINANCIAL AID
Costs (2017–18) ***Comprehensive fee:*** $42,282 includes full-time tuition ($26,190), mandatory fees ($300), and room and board ($15,792). Full-time tuition and fees vary according to course load. Part-time tuition: $873 per unit. Part-time tuition and fees vary according to course load. ***Room and board:*** Room and board charges vary according to board plan and housing facility. ***Payment plan:*** installment.
Financial Aid Of all full-time matriculated undergraduates who enrolled in 2015, 2,411 applied for aid, 2,225 were judged to have need, 40 had their need fully met. 107 Federal Work-Study jobs (averaging $4370). In 2015, 49 non-need-based awards were made. ***Average percent of need met:*** 34. ***Average financial aid package:*** $11,209. ***Average need-based loan:*** $3887. ***Average need-based gift aid:*** $10,316. ***Average non-need-based aid:*** $8742. ***Average indebtedness upon graduation:*** $27,020.

APPLYING
Options: electronic application, early admission, deferred entrance.
Application fee: $50.
Required: high school transcript. ***Recommended:*** interview.
Application deadlines: rolling (freshmen), rolling (transfers).
Notification: continuous (freshmen), continuous (transfers).

CONTACT
Admissions, Academy of Art University, 79 New Montgomery Street, San Francisco, CA 94105. *Phone:* 800-544-2787.
Toll-free phone: 800-544-ARTS. *Fax:* 415-618-6287.
E-mail: info@academyart.edu.

See below for display ad and page 1274 for the College Close-Up.

Alliant International University–San Diego

San Diego, California

http://www.alliant.edu/

- **Independent** university, founded 1952, part of Alliant International University
- **Suburban** 60-acre campus with easy access to San Diego
- **Coed** 163 undergraduate students, 86% full-time, 48% women, 52% men
- **Minimally difficult** entrance level

UNDERGRAD STUDENTS
140 full-time, 23 part-time. Students come from 24 states and territories; 4 other countries; 37% are from out of state.

FACULTY
Total: 520.
Student/faculty ratio: 12:1.

ACADEMICS
Calendar: semesters. *Degrees:* certificates, bachelor's, master's, doctoral, and postbachelor's certificates.
Special study options: academic remediation for entering students, advanced placement credit, distance learning, English as a second language, honors programs, independent study, internships, part-time degree program, services for LD students, summer session for credit.
Computers: 100 computers/terminals are available on campus for general student use. Students can access the following: campus intranet, computer help desk, free student e-mail accounts, online (class) grades, online (class) registration, online (class) schedules. Campuswide network is available. Wireless service is available via entire campus.
Library: Walter Library.

STUDENT LIFE
Housing options: college housing not available.
Activities and organizations: Residence Hall Association, Latino Students Association, Finance Club, Student Government, Sigma Iota Epsilon.
Campus security: 24-hour patrols.
Student services: health clinic, personal/psychological counseling.

COSTS & FINANCIAL AID
Costs (2016–17) ***Tuition:*** $21,000 full-time, $700 per credit hour part-time. ***Required fees:*** $220 full-time, $70 per term part-time. ***Payment plan:*** deferred payment. ***Waivers:*** children of alumni and employees or children of employees.
Financial Aid Of all full-time matriculated undergraduates who enrolled in 2015, 118 applied for aid, 118 were judged to have need, 7 had their need fully met. 33 Federal Work-Study jobs (averaging $4000). In 2015, 118 non-need-based awards were made. ***Average percent of need met:*** 62. ***Average financial aid package:*** $16,815. ***Average need-based loan:*** $5025. ***Average need-based gift aid:*** $14,315. ***Average non-need-based aid:*** $4000.

APPLYING
Options: electronic application, deferred entrance.
Application fee: $65.
Required: high school transcript, minimum 2.0 GPA.
Notification: continuous (transfers).

CONTACT
Ms. Ashley Carter, Director of Admissions, Alliant International University–San Diego, 10455 Pomerado Road, San Diego, CA 92131-1799. *Phone:* 866-825-5426. *Toll-free phone:* 866-825-5426. *E-mail:* admissions@alliant.edu.

American Jewish University

Bel Air, California

http://www.aju.edu/

CONTACT
Mr. Yosef Funke, Director of Undergraduate Admissions, American Jewish University, Familian Campus, 15600 Mulholland Drive, Los Angeles, CA 90077-1599. *Phone:* 310-440-1250. *Toll-free phone:* 888-853-6763. *Fax:* 310-471-3657. *E-mail:* admissions@aju.edu.

American Musical and Dramatic Academy, Los Angeles

Los Angeles, California

http://www.amda.edu/

CONTACT
Ms. Karen Jackson, Director of Admission, American Musical and Dramatic Academy, Los Angeles, 6305 Yucca Street, Los Angeles, CA 90028. *Phone:* 323-469-3300. *Toll-free phone:* 888-474-9444. *Fax:* 323-469-5246. *E-mail:* kjackson@amda.edu.

American University of Health Sciences

Signal Hill, California

http://www.auhs.edu/

CONTACT
American University of Health Sciences, 1600 East Hill Street, Building #1, Signal Hill, CA 90755.

Angeles College

Los Angeles, California

http://www.angelescollege.edu/

CONTACT
Angeles College, 3440 Wilshire Boulevard, Suite 310, Los Angeles, CA 90010.

★ Antioch University Los Angeles

Culver City, California

http://www.antiochla.edu/

- **Independent** upper-level, founded 1972, part of Antioch University
- **Urban** 1-acre campus with easy access to Los Angeles
- **Coed** 132 undergraduate students, 25% full-time, 69% women, 31% men
- **Moderately difficult** entrance level

UNDERGRAD STUDENTS
33 full-time, 99 part-time. Students come from 6 states and territories; 1 other country; 1% are from out of state.

ACADEMICS
Calendar: quarters. *Degrees:* bachelor's, master's, doctoral, post-master's, and postbachelor's certificates.
Special study options: academic remediation for entering students, accelerated degree program, adult/continuing education programs, advanced placement credit, cooperative education, distance learning, double majors, independent study, internships, part-time degree program, services for LD students, student-designed majors, summer session for credit.
Computers: Students can access the following: computer help desk, free student e-mail accounts, online (class) registration. Campuswide network is available. Wireless service is available via classrooms, computer labs, libraries.

STUDENT LIFE
Housing options: college housing not available.
Activities and organizations: student-run newspaper, radio and television station.
Campus security: 24-hour emergency response devices, late-night transport/escort service.
Student services: personal/psychological counseling.

COSTS
Costs (2016–17) ***Tuition:*** $26,256 full-time. Full-time tuition and fees vary according to course load and program. Part-time tuition and fees vary according to course load and program. ***Required fees:*** $400 full-time. ***Payment plan:*** installment. ***Waivers:*** employees or children of employees.

APPLYING

Options: electronic application, deferred entrance.

Application fee: $60.

Notification: continuous until 10/1 (transfers).

CONTACT

Admissions, Antioch University Los Angeles, 400 Corporate Pointe, Culver City, CA 90230. *Phone:* 310-578-1080 Ext. 100. *Toll-free phone:* 800-726-8462. *Fax:* 310-822-4824. *E-mail:* admissions@antiochla.edu.

Antioch University Santa Barbara

Santa Barbara, California

http://www.antiochsb.edu/

- **Independent** upper-level, founded 1977, part of Antioch University
- **Urban** campus
- **Coed** 128 undergraduate students
- **Moderately difficult** entrance level

UNDERGRAD STUDENTS

Students come from 3 states and territories; 1% are from out of state; 2% Black or African American, non-Hispanic/Latino; 16% Hispanic/Latino; 0.8% Asian, non-Hispanic/Latino; 41% Race/ethnicity unknown; 16% international.

FACULTY

Total: 78, 12% full-time.

ACADEMICS

Calendar: quarters. *Degrees:* certificates, bachelor's, master's, and doctoral.

Special study options: academic remediation for entering students, accelerated degree program, cooperative education, distance learning, external degree program, independent study, internships, off-campus study, part-time degree program, services for LD students, student-designed majors, summer session for credit.

Computers: 16 computers/terminals are available on campus for general student use. Students can access the following: computer help desk, free student e-mail accounts, online (class) grades, online (class) registration, online (class) schedules. Campuswide network is available. Wireless service is available via entire campus.

Library: Sage Library.

STUDENT LIFE

Housing options: college housing not available.

Activities and organizations: student-run newspaper.

Campus security: late-night transport/escort service.

COSTS

Costs (2016–17) ***Tuition:*** $17,820 full-time, $495 per credit part-time. Full-time tuition and fees vary according to course load, degree level, and program. Part-time tuition and fees vary according to course load, degree level, and program. ***Required fees:*** $300 full-time. ***Payment plan:*** installment. ***Waivers:*** employees or children of employees.

APPLYING

Standardized Tests *Required for some:* TOEFL for international students.

Options: electronic application, deferred entrance.

Application fee: $60.

Notification: continuous (transfers).

CONTACT

Jessica Grater, Research Analyst, Antioch University Santa Barbara, 602 Anacapa Street, Santa Barbara, CA 93101-1581. *Phone:* 407-967-6547. *Toll-free phone:* 866-526-8462. *E-mail:* jgrater@antioch.edu.

Argosy University, Inland Empire

Ontario, California

http://www.argosy.edu/locations/inland-empire/

CONTACT

Argosy University, Inland Empire, 3401 Centre Lake Drive, Suite 200, Ontario, CA 91761. *Phone:* 909-472-0800. *Toll-free phone:* 866-217-9075.

Argosy University, Los Angeles

Santa Monica, California

http://www.argosy.edu/locations/los-angeles/

CONTACT

Argosy University, Los Angeles, 5230 Pacific Concourse, Suite 200, Santa Monica, CA 90045. *Phone:* 310-531-9700. *Toll-free phone:* 866-505-0332.

Argosy University, Orange County

Orange, California

http://www.argosy.edu/locations/los-angeles-orange-county/

CONTACT

Argosy University, Orange County, 601 South Lewis Street, Orange, CA 92868. *Phone:* 714-620-3700. *Toll-free phone:* 800-716-9598.

Argosy University, San Diego

San Diego, California

http://www.argosy.edu/locations/san-diego/

CONTACT

Argosy University, San Diego, 1615 Murray Canyon Road, Suite 100, San Diego, CA 92108. *Phone:* 619-321-3000. *Toll-free phone:* 866-505-0333.

Argosy University, San Francisco Bay Area

Alameda, California

http://www.argosy.edu/locations/san-francisco/

CONTACT

Argosy University, San Francisco Bay Area, 1005 Atlantic Avenue, Alameda, CA 94501. *Phone:* 510-217-4700. *Toll-free phone:* 866-215-2777.

Art Center College of Design

Pasadena, California

http://www.artcenter.edu/

- **Independent** comprehensive, founded 1930
- **Suburban** 163-acre campus with easy access to Los Angeles
- **Coed**
- **Very difficult** entrance level

ACADEMICS

Calendar: semesters. *Degrees:* bachelor's and master's.

Library: James Lemont Fogg Memorial Library. *Books:* 93,839 (physical), 4,117 (digital/electronic); *Serial titles:* 420 (physical), 25,266 (digital/electronic); *Databases:* 38. Weekly public service hours: 75.

STUDENT LIFE

Housing options: college housing not available.

Activities and organizations: ACSG, Christian Fellowship, Stop Motion Club, Art Center Business Club, Fine Art Society.

Campus security: 24-hour emergency response devices and patrols, late-night transport/escort service.

Student services: personal/psychological counseling.

COSTS & FINANCIAL AID

Costs (2016–17) ***Tuition:*** $40,046 full-time, $1669 per credit part-time. ***Required fees:*** $550 full-time.

Financial Aid ***Average financial aid package:*** $17,803. ***Average need-based loan:*** $10,169. ***Average need-based gift aid:*** $14,627.

APPLYING

Standardized Tests *Required for some:* SAT (for admission), ACT (for admission), SAT or ACT (for admission).

Options: electronic application, deferred entrance.

Application fee: $50.

Required: essay or personal statement, high school transcript, portfolio.

CONTACT
Ms. Kit Baron, Vice President, Admissions and Enrollment Management, Art Center College of Design, 1700 Lida Street, Pasadena, CA 91103.
Phone: 626-396-2322. *Fax:* 626-795-0578.
E-mail: kit.baron@artcenter.edu.

The Art Institute of California–Hollywood, a campus of Argosy University

North Hollywood, California

http://www.artinstitutes.edu/hollywood/

CONTACT
The Art Institute of California–Hollywood, a campus of Argosy University, 5250 Lankershim Boulevard, North Hollywood, CA 91601.
Phone: 818-299-5100. *Toll-free phone:* 877-468-6232.

The Art Institute of California–Inland Empire, a campus of Argosy University

San Bernardino, California

http://www.artinstitutes.edu/inlandempire/

CONTACT
The Art Institute of California–Inland Empire, a campus of Argosy University, 674 East Brier Drive, San Bernardino, CA 92408.
Phone: 909-915-2100. *Toll-free phone:* 800-353-0812.

The Art Institute of California–Los Angeles, a campus of Argosy University

Santa Monica, California

http://www.artinstitutes.edu/losangeles/

CONTACT
The Art Institute of California–Los Angeles, a campus of Argosy University, 2900 31st Street, Santa Monica, CA 90405-3035.
Phone: 310-752-4700. *Toll-free phone:* 888-646-4610.

The Art Institute of California–Orange County, a campus of Argosy University

Santa Ana, California

http://www.artinstitutes.edu/orangecounty/

CONTACT
The Art Institute of California–Orange County, a campus of Argosy University, 3601 West Sunflower Avenue, Santa Ana, CA 92704.
Phone: 714-830-0200. *Toll-free phone:* 888-549-3055.

The Art Institute of California–Sacramento, a campus of Argosy University

Sacramento, California

http://www.artinstitutes.edu/sacramento/

CONTACT
The Art Institute of California–Sacramento, a campus of Argosy University, 2850 Gateway Oaks Drive, Suite 100, Sacramento, CA 95833.
Phone: 916-830-6320. *Toll-free phone:* 800-477-1957.

The Art Institute of California–San Diego, a campus of Argosy University

San Diego, California

http://www.artinstitutes.edu/sandiego/

CONTACT
The Art Institute of California–San Diego, a campus of Argosy University, 7650 Mission Valley Road, San Diego, CA 92108.
Phone: 858-598-1200. *Toll-free phone:* 866-275-2422.

The Art Institute of California–San Francisco, a campus of Argosy University

San Francisco, California

http://www.artinstitutes.edu/sanfrancisco/

CONTACT
The Art Institute of California–San Francisco, a campus of Argosy University, 10 United Nations Plaza, San Francisco, CA 94102-4928.
Phone: 415-865-0198. *Toll-free phone:* 888-493-3261.

Ashford University

San Diego, California

http://www.ashford.edu/

CONTACT
Ms. Waunita M. Sullivan, Director of Enrollment, Ashford University, 8620 Spectrum Center Boulevard, San Diego, CA 92123.
Phone: 563-242-4023 Ext. 3401. *Toll-free phone:* 866-711-1700.
E-mail: admissns@tfu.edu.

Azusa Pacific University

Azusa, California

http://www.apu.edu/

- **Independent nondenominational** university, founded 1899
- **Suburban** 60-acre campus with easy access to Los Angeles
- **Endowment** $60.7 million
- **Coed** 5,883 undergraduate students, 91% full-time, 65% women, 35% men
- **Moderately difficult** entrance level, 81% of applicants were admitted

UNDERGRAD STUDENTS
5,356 full-time, 527 part-time. 18% are from out of state; 5% Black or African American, non-Hispanic/Latino; 29% Hispanic/Latino; 9% Asian, non-Hispanic/Latino; 1% Native Hawaiian or other Pacific Islander, non-Hispanic/Latino; 0.1% American Indian or Alaska Native, non-Hispanic/Latino; 8% Two or more races, non-Hispanic/Latino; 2% Race/ethnicity unknown; 2% international; 9% transferred in; 62% live on campus.

Freshmen:
Admission: 6,084 applied, 4,922 admitted, 1,192 enrolled. ***Average high school GPA:*** 3.68. ***Test scores:*** SAT critical reading scores over 500: 68%; SAT math scores over 500: 66%; ACT scores over 18: 96%; SAT critical reading scores over 600: 23%; SAT math scores over 600: 23%; ACT scores over 24: 54%; SAT critical reading scores over 700: 3%; SAT math scores over 700: 2%; ACT scores over 30: 10%.
Retention: 88% of full-time freshmen returned.

FACULTY
Total: 1,181, 39% full-time, 26% with terminal degrees.
Student/faculty ratio: 12:1.

ACADEMICS
Calendar: semesters. *Degrees:* certificates, bachelor's, master's, doctoral, post-master's, and postbachelor's certificates.
Special study options: academic remediation for entering students, accelerated degree program, adult/continuing education programs, advanced placement credit, cooperative education, distance learning,

double majors, English as a second language, freshman honors college, honors programs, independent study, internships, off-campus study, part-time degree program, services for LD students, study abroad, summer session for credit. ***ROTC:*** Army (b), Air Force (c).

Unusual degree programs: 3-2 business administration.

Computers: Students can access the following: campus intranet, computer help desk, free student e-mail accounts, online (class) grades, online (class) registration, online (class) schedules. Campuswide network is available. Wireless service is available via entire campus.

Library: Marshburn Memorial Library plus 3 others. *Books:* 372,625 (physical), 122,986 (digital/electronic); *Databases:* 119. Study areas open 24 hours, 5-7 days a week; students can reserve study rooms.

STUDENT LIFE

Housing options: on-campus residence required through sophomore year; coed, men-only, women-only. Campus housing is university owned and leased by the school. Freshman applicants given priority for college housing.

Activities and organizations: drama/theater group, student-run newspaper, radio and television station, choral group, marching band.

Athletics Member NCAA, NAIA. All NCAA Division II. ***Intercollegiate sports:*** baseball M(s), basketball M(s)/W(s), cross-country running M(s)/W(s), football M(s), gymnastics W(s), soccer M(s)/W(s), softball W(s), swimming and diving W(s), tennis M(s)/W(s), track and field M(s)/W(s), volleyball W(s), water polo W. ***Intramural sports:*** basketball M/W, cheerleading W(c), rugby M(c), skiing (downhill) M/W, soccer M/W, softball M/W, tennis M/W, ultimate Frisbee M/W, volleyball M/W.

Campus security: 24-hour emergency response devices and patrols, student patrols, late-night transport/escort service, controlled dormitory access.

Student services: health clinic, personal/psychological counseling, women's center.

COSTS & FINANCIAL AID

Costs (2016–17) ***Tuition:*** $35,540 full-time, $1481 per credit hour part-time. Full-time tuition and fees vary according to course load and degree level. Part-time tuition and fees vary according to course load and degree level. ***Required fees:*** $580 full-time. ***Room only:*** $5576. Room and board charges vary according to board plan and housing facility. ***Payment plan:*** installment.

Financial Aid Of all full-time matriculated undergraduates who enrolled in 2015, 5,149 applied for aid, 4,052 were judged to have need, 1,690 had their need fully met. In 2015, 532 non-need-based awards were made. ***Average percent of need met:*** 64. ***Average financial aid package:*** $7071. ***Average need-based loan:*** $4800. ***Average need-based gift aid:*** $3604. ***Average non-need-based aid:*** $8198. ***Average indebtedness upon graduation:*** $24,338.

APPLYING

Standardized Tests *Required:* SAT or ACT (for admission).

Options: electronic application, early action.

Application fee: $45.

Application deadlines: 6/1 (freshmen), 6/1 (transfers), 11/15 (early action).

Notification: continuous until 10/1 (freshmen), continuous (transfers), 1/15 (early action).

CONTACT

Ms. Lynnette Barnes, Processing Coordinator, Azusa Pacific University, 901 East Alosta Avenue, PO Box 7000, Undergraduate Admissions, 7221, Azusa, CA 91702-7000. *Phone:* 626-815-6000 Ext. 3419. *Toll-free phone:* 800-TALK-APU. *E-mail:* admissions@apu.edu.

Bergin University of Canine Studies

Rohnert Park, California

http://www.berginu.edu/

CONTACT

Bergin University of Canine Studies, 5860 Labath Avenue, Rohnert Park, CA 94928.

Bethesda University

Anaheim, California

http://www.buc.edu/

CONTACT

Jacquie Ha, Director of Admission, Bethesda University, 730 North Euclid Street, Anaheim, CA 92801. *Phone:* 714-517-1945. *Fax:* 714-517-1948. *E-mail:* admission@bcu.edu.

Beverly Hills Design Institute

Beverly Hills, California

http://www.bhdi.edu/

- **Proprietary** primarily 2-year
- **Urban** campus with easy access to Los Angeles
- **Coed**
- **Noncompetitive** entrance level

ACADEMICS

Degrees: associate and bachelor's.

Library: Main Library plus 1 other.

STUDENT LIFE

Housing options: college housing not available.

Campus security: 24-hour emergency response devices and patrols.

COSTS

Costs (2016–17) ***One-time required fee:*** $100. ***Tuition:*** $19,998 full-time, $621 per credit part-time. Full-time tuition and fees vary according to class time, course level, course load, degree level, location, program, reciprocity agreements, and student level. Part-time tuition and fees vary according to class time, course level, course load, degree level, location, program, reciprocity agreements, and student level. No tuition increase for student's term of enrollment. ***Required fees:*** $2340 full-time. ***Payment plans:*** tuition prepayment, installment.

APPLYING

Standardized Tests *Recommended:* SAT or ACT (for admission).

Options: electronic application, early admission.

Application fee: $40.

Required: essay or personal statement, interview. ***Required for some:*** high school transcript.

CONTACT

Beverly Hills Design Institute, 8484 Wilshire Boulevard, Suite 730, Beverly Hills, CA 90211. *Phone:* 310-360-8888.

Biola University

La Mirada, California

http://www.biola.edu/

- **Independent interdenominational** university, founded 1908
- **Suburban** 95-acre campus with easy access to Los Angeles
- **Coed** 4,091 undergraduate students, 96% full-time, 64% women, 36% men
- **Moderately difficult** entrance level, 69% of applicants were admitted

UNDERGRAD STUDENTS

3,947 full-time, 144 part-time. 26% are from out of state; 2% Black or African American, non-Hispanic/Latino; 20% Hispanic/Latino; 17% Asian, non-Hispanic/Latino; 0.3% Native Hawaiian or other Pacific Islander, non-Hispanic/Latino; 0.2% American Indian or Alaska Native, non-Hispanic/Latino; 6% Two or more races, non-Hispanic/Latino; 3% Race/ethnicity unknown; 3% international; 6% transferred in; 65% live on campus.

Freshmen:

Admission: 3,941 applied, 2,706 admitted, 872 enrolled. ***Average high school GPA:*** 3.32. ***Test scores:*** SAT critical reading scores over 500: 74%; SAT math scores over 500: 74%; SAT writing scores over 500: 73%; ACT scores over 18: 97%; SAT critical reading scores over 600: 32%; SAT math scores over 600: 30%; SAT writing scores over 600: 30%; ACT scores over 24: 56%; SAT critical reading scores over 700: 5%; SAT math scores over 700: 5%; SAT writing scores over 700: 5%; ACT scores over 30: 12%.

Retention: 84% of full-time freshmen returned.

FACULTY
Total: 536, 51% full-time, 43% with terminal degrees.
Student/faculty ratio: 15:1.

ACADEMICS
Calendar: 4-1-4. *Degrees:* diplomas, bachelor's, master's, doctoral, post-master's, and postbachelor's certificates.

Special study options: adult/continuing education programs, advanced placement credit, cooperative education, distance learning, double majors, English as a second language, honors programs, independent study, internships, off-campus study, part-time degree program, services for LD students, study abroad, summer session for credit. ***ROTC:*** Army (c), Air Force (c).

Unusual degree programs: 3-2 engineering.

Computers: Students can access the following: campus intranet, computer help desk, free student e-mail accounts, online (class) grades, online (class) registration, online (class) schedules. Campuswide network is available. 100% of college-owned or -operated housing units are wired for high-speed Internet access. Wireless service is available via entire campus.

Library: Biola University Library plus 1 other. *Books:* 550,000 (physical); *Databases:* 259. Weekly public service hours: 100; students can reserve study rooms.

STUDENT LIFE
Housing options: coed, women-only, special housing for students with disabilities. Campus housing is university owned. Freshman campus housing is guaranteed.

Activities and organizations: drama/theater group, student-run newspaper, radio and television station, choral group, Adventure Club, Guerilla Film Society, Biola Cross-Fit, Xopoc Dance Team, Lacrosse Club.

Athletics Member NCAA, NAIA. All NCAA Division II. ***Intercollegiate sports:*** baseball M(s), basketball M(s)/W(s), cross-country running M(s)/W(s), golf M(s)/W(s), soccer M(s)/W(s), softball W(s), swimming and diving M(s)/W(s), tennis M(s)/W(s), track and field M(s)/W(s), volleyball W(s). ***Intramural sports:*** archery M(c)/W(c), basketball M/W, bowling M/W, cheerleading W(c), football M/W, lacrosse M(c)/W(c), rugby M(c), soccer M/W, softball M/W, tennis M/W, ultimate Frisbee M/W, volleyball M(c)/W, water polo M(c)/W(c).

Campus security: 24-hour emergency response devices and patrols, late-night transport/escort service, controlled dormitory access.

Student services: health clinic, personal/psychological counseling.

COSTS & FINANCIAL AID
Costs (2017–18) ***One-time required fee:*** $60. ***Tuition:*** Full-time tuition and fees vary according to course load and degree level. Part-time tuition and fees vary according to course load and degree level. ***Room and board:*** $10,560; room only: $5784. Room and board charges vary according to board plan and housing facility. ***Payment plan:*** installment. ***Waivers:*** employees or children of employees.

Financial Aid Of all full-time matriculated undergraduates who enrolled in 2014, 3,256 applied for aid, 2,878 were judged to have need, 168 had their need fully met. 453 Federal Work-Study jobs (averaging $1175). In 2014, 977 non-need-based awards were made. ***Average percent of need met:*** 49. ***Average financial aid package:*** $18,943. ***Average need-based loan:*** $3958. ***Average need-based gift aid:*** $13,487. ***Average non-need-based aid:*** $7392. ***Average indebtedness upon graduation:*** $35,630.

APPLYING
Standardized Tests *Required:* SAT or ACT (for admission).

Options: electronic application, early decision, early action, deferred entrance.

Application fee: $45.

Required: essay or personal statement, high school transcript. ***Required for some:*** interview. ***Recommended:*** minimum 3.0 GPA.

Application deadlines: 3/1 (freshmen), 3/1 (transfers), 11/15 (early action).

Notification: 4/1 (freshmen), 4/1 (out-of-state freshmen), 4/1 (transfers), 1/15 (early action).

CONTACT
Mrs. Michelle Reider, Associate Director of Undergraduate Admissions, Biola University, 13800 Biola Avenue, La Mirada, CA 90639. *Phone:* 562-903-4752. *Toll-free phone:* 800-652-4652.
E-mail: admissions@biola.edu.

Brandman University

Irvine, California

http://www.brandman.edu/irvine/

- **Independent** comprehensive, founded 1958
- **Suburban** campus with easy access to Greater Los Angeles Area
- **Coed** 3,577 undergraduate students, 32% full-time, 61% women, 39% men

UNDERGRAD STUDENTS
1,140 full-time, 2,437 part-time. Students come from 45 states and territories; 1 other country; 18% are from out of state; 10% Black or African American, non-Hispanic/Latino; 24% Hispanic/Latino; 4% Asian, non-Hispanic/Latino; 2% Native Hawaiian or other Pacific Islander, non-Hispanic/Latino; 0.9% American Indian or Alaska Native, non-Hispanic/Latino; 4% Two or more races, non-Hispanic/Latino; 9% Race/ethnicity unknown; 17% transferred in.

Freshmen:
Admission: 50 enrolled.

ACADEMICS
Calendar: trimesters. *Degrees:* certificates, associate, bachelor's, master's, doctoral, post-master's, and postbachelor's certificates.

Special study options: academic remediation for entering students, accelerated degree program, adult/continuing education programs, advanced placement credit, cooperative education, distance learning, double majors, independent study, internships, off-campus study, part-time degree program, services for LD students, summer session for credit.

Computers: 837 computers/terminals are available on campus for general student use. Students can access the following: campus intranet, computer help desk, free student e-mail accounts, online (class) grades, online (class) registration, online (class) schedules. Campuswide network is available. Wireless service is available via entire campus.

Library: Leatherby Library plus 1 other.

STUDENT LIFE
Campus security: late-night transport/escort service.
Student services: personal/psychological counseling.

COSTS
Costs (2016–17) ***Tuition:*** $18,000 full-time, $500 per credit hour part-time. Full-time tuition and fees vary according to degree level. Part-time tuition and fees vary according to degree level. ***Required fees:*** $450 full-time, $75 per term part-time.

APPLYING
Required: high school transcript, minimum 2.0 GPA. ***Required for some:*** 3 letters of recommendation, 3 letters of recommendation, CPR certification, immunizations, professional liability insurance, RN licensure, and prerequisite coursework for RN-BSN program.

CONTACT
Admissions Office, Brandman University, 16355 Laguna Canyon Drive, Irvine, CA 92618. *Phone:* 800-7460082 Ext. 39847. *Toll-free phone:* 800-746-0082. *E-mail:* apply@brandman.edu.

Bristol University

Anaheim, California

http://bristoluniversity.edu/

CONTACT
Bristol University, 2390 Orangewood Avenue, Suite 485, Anaheim, CA 92806.

California Baptist University

Riverside, California

http://www.calbaptist.edu/

- **Independent Southern Baptist** comprehensive, founded 1950
- **Suburban** 160-acre campus with easy access to Los Angeles
- **Endowment** $16.8 million
- **Coed** 6,937 undergraduate students, 85% full-time, 63% women, 37% men
- **Moderately difficult** entrance level, 64% of applicants were admitted

UNDERGRAD STUDENTS

5,885 full-time, 1,052 part-time. Students come from 46 states and territories; 24 other countries; 7% are from out of state; 8% Black or African American, non-Hispanic/Latino; 36% Hispanic/Latino; 5% Asian, non-Hispanic/Latino; 1% Native Hawaiian or other Pacific Islander, non-Hispanic/Latino; 0.6% American Indian or Alaska Native, non-Hispanic/Latino; 6% Two or more races, non-Hispanic/Latino; 4% Race/ethnicity unknown; 2% international; 11% transferred in; 39% live on campus.

Freshmen:

Admission: 4,971 applied, 3,181 admitted, 1,146 enrolled. ***Average high school GPA:*** 3.4. ***Test scores:*** SAT critical reading scores over 500: 46%; SAT math scores over 500: 55%; SAT writing scores over 500: 42%; ACT scores over 18: 84%; SAT critical reading scores over 600: 14%; SAT math scores over 600: 18%; SAT writing scores over 600: 8%; ACT scores over 24: 32%; SAT critical reading scores over 700: 1%; SAT math scores over 700: 1%; ACT scores over 30: 3%.

Retention: 75% of full-time freshmen returned.

FACULTY

Total: 704, 45% full-time, 45% with terminal degrees.

Student/faculty ratio: 18:1.

ACADEMICS

Calendar: 2-4-4-2. *Degrees:* associate, bachelor's, master's, and doctoral.

Special study options: academic remediation for entering students, accelerated degree program, adult/continuing education programs, advanced placement credit, distance learning, double majors, English as a second language, honors programs, internships, off-campus study, part-time degree program, services for LD students, study abroad, summer session for credit. ***ROTC:*** Army (b), Air Force (c).

Computers: 279 computers/terminals are available on campus for general student use. Students can access the following: campus intranet, computer help desk, free student e-mail accounts, online (class) grades, online (class) registration, online (class) schedules, online course evaluations. Campuswide network is available. 70% of college-owned or -operated housing units are wired for high-speed Internet access. Wireless service is available via entire campus.

Library: Annie Gabriel Library. *Books:* 130,837 (physical), 190,918 (digital/electronic); *Serial titles:* 59,915 (physical), 21,548 (digital/electronic); *Databases:* 83. Weekly public service hours: 101; students can reserve study rooms.

STUDENT LIFE

Housing options: on-campus residence required for freshman year; men-only, women-only, cooperative. Campus housing is university owned. Freshman applicants given priority for college housing.

Activities and organizations: drama/theater group, student-run newspaper, choral group, International Service Projects, United States Service Projects, CBU Crazies (Campus Spirit), Summer of Service, Associated Students of California Baptist University (government and leadership).

Athletics Member NCAA. All Division II. ***Intercollegiate sports:*** baseball M(s), basketball M(s)/W(s), cheerleading W(s), cross-country running M(s)/W(s), golf M(s)/W(s), soccer M(s)/W(s), softball W(s), swimming and diving M(s)/W(s), track and field M(s)/W(s), volleyball M(s)/W(s), water polo M(s)/W(s), wrestling M(s). ***Intramural sports:*** basketball M/W, bowling M/W, football M/W, golf M/W, rock climbing M/W, soccer M/W, softball W, table tennis M/W, ultimate Frisbee M/W, volleyball M/W.

Campus security: 24-hour emergency response devices and patrols, late-night transport/escort service, controlled dormitory access.

Student services: health clinic, personal/psychological counseling.

COSTS & FINANCIAL AID

Costs (2017–18) ***One-time required fee:*** $310. ***Comprehensive fee:*** $44,106 includes full-time tuition ($30,446), mandatory fees ($2120), and room and board ($11,540). Full-time tuition and fees vary according to course load, location, and program. Part-time tuition: $1171 per unit. Part-time tuition and fees vary according to course load, location, and program. ***Required fees:*** $175 per term part-time. ***College room only:*** $5630. Room and board charges vary according to board plan and housing facility. ***Payment plan:*** installment. ***Waivers:*** employees or children of employees.

Financial Aid Of all full-time matriculated undergraduates who enrolled in 2016, 5,293 applied for aid, 5,086 were judged to have need, 361 had their need fully met. 255 Federal Work-Study jobs (averaging $1400). In 2016, 309 non-need-based awards were made. ***Average percent of need met:*** 56. ***Average financial aid package:*** $17,879. ***Average need-based loan:*** $4686. ***Average need-based gift aid:*** $14,409. ***Average non-need-based aid:*** $9129. ***Average indebtedness upon graduation:*** $20,693.

APPLYING

Standardized Tests *Required:* SAT or ACT (for admission). *Recommended:* SAT and SAT Subject Tests or ACT (for admission).

Options: electronic application, deferred entrance.

Application fee: $45.

Required: essay or personal statement, minimum 2.0 GPA, 2 letters of recommendation. ***Required for some:*** high school transcript.

Application deadlines: rolling (freshmen), rolling (transfers).

Notification: continuous (freshmen), continuous (transfers).

CONTACT

Mr. Taylor Neece, Director of Undergraduate Admissions, California Baptist University, 8432 Magnolia Avenue, Riverside, CA 92504-3297. *Phone:* 951-343-4212. *Toll-free phone:* 877-228-8866. *Fax:* 951-343-4525. *E-mail:* admissions@calbaptist.edu.

California Christian College

Fresno, California

http://www.calchristiancollege.edu/

- **Independent Free Will Baptist** 4-year
- **Urban** campus
- **Endowment** $166,018
- **Coed** 18 undergraduate students, 61% full-time, 22% women, 78% men
- **Noncompetitive** entrance level, 100% of applicants were admitted

UNDERGRAD STUDENTS

11 full-time, 7 part-time. Students come from 2 states and territories; 0.2% are from out of state; 6% Black or African American, non-Hispanic/Latino; 61% Hispanic/Latino; 6% American Indian or Alaska Native, non-Hispanic/Latino; 11% Two or more races, non-Hispanic/Latino; 28% transferred in; 25% live on campus.

Freshmen:

Admission: 2 applied, 2 admitted, 2 enrolled.

FACULTY

Total: 4, 25% full-time, 50% with terminal degrees.

Student/faculty ratio: 12:1.

ACADEMICS

Calendar: semesters. *Degrees:* associate and bachelor's.

Special study options: academic remediation for entering students, cooperative education, distance learning, independent study, part-time degree program.

Computers: 12 computers/terminals and 5 ports are available on campus for general student use. Students can access the following: free student e-mail accounts, online (class) grades. Campuswide network is available. 100% of college-owned or -operated housing units are wired for high-speed Internet access. Wireless service is available via entire campus.

Library: Cortese Library. Weekly public service hours: 15.

STUDENT LIFE

Housing options: on-campus residence required through sophomore year; men-only, women-only. Campus housing is leased by the school.

Student services: personal/psychological counseling.

COSTS & FINANCIAL AID
Costs (2016–17) ***Comprehensive fee:*** $13,940 includes full-time tuition ($8400), mandatory fees ($590), and room and board ($4950). Part-time tuition: $350 per unit. ***Payment plan:*** installment.

Financial Aid Of all full-time matriculated undergraduates who enrolled in 2015, 10 applied for aid, 9 were judged to have need. 3 Federal Work-Study jobs (averaging $1623). ***Average percent of need met:*** 55. ***Average financial aid package:*** $12,138. ***Average need-based loan:*** $4277. ***Average need-based gift aid:*** $5228.

APPLYING
Standardized Tests *Required:* standardized Bible content tests (for admission). *Recommended:* SAT or ACT (for admission).

Options: electronic application.

Application fee: $40.

Required: essay or personal statement, high school transcript, minimum 2.0 GPA, 2 letters of recommendation, statement of faith, moral/ethical statement. ***Recommended:*** interview.

Application deadlines: rolling (freshmen), rolling (transfers).

Notification: continuous (freshmen), continuous (transfers).

CONTACT
Mr. Trent Walley, Admissions Director, California Christian College, 5364 E. Belmont Avenue, Fresno, CA 93727. *Phone:* 559-251-4215 Ext. 1002. *Fax:* 559-385-2329. *E-mail:* twalley@calchristiancollege.edu.

California Coast University

Santa Ana, California

http://www.calcoast.edu/

CONTACT
California Coast University, 925 North Spurgeon Street, Santa Ana, CA 92701. *Phone:* 714-547-9625. *Toll-free phone:* 888-CCU-UNIV.

California College of the Arts

San Francisco, California

http://www.cca.edu/

- **Independent** comprehensive, founded 1907
- **Urban** 4-acre campus with easy access to San Francisco, Oakland
- **Endowment** $30.3 million
- **Coed** 1,528 undergraduate students, 94% full-time, 64% women, 36% men

UNDERGRAD STUDENTS
1,442 full-time, 86 part-time. Students come from 49 states and territories; 53 other countries; 32% are from out of state; 6% Black or African American, non-Hispanic/Latino; 12% Hispanic/Latino; 18% Asian, non-Hispanic/Latino; 0.8% Native Hawaiian or other Pacific Islander, non-Hispanic/Latino; 0.2% American Indian or Alaska Native, non-Hispanic/Latino; 6% Race/ethnicity unknown; 35% international; 9% transferred in; 22% live on campus.

Freshmen:
Admission: 256 enrolled. ***Average high school GPA:*** 3.34.
Retention: 82% of full-time freshmen returned.

FACULTY
Total: 485, 21% full-time, 56% with terminal degrees.
Student/faculty ratio: 9:1.

ACADEMICS
Calendar: semesters. *Degrees:* bachelor's and master's.

Special study options: academic remediation for entering students, advanced placement credit, double majors, English as a second language, external degree program, independent study, internships, off-campus study, part-time degree program, services for LD students, student-designed majors, study abroad, summer session for credit.

Computers: 400 computers/terminals and 80 ports are available on campus for general student use. Students can access the following: campus intranet, computer help desk, free student e-mail accounts, online (class) grades, online (class) registration, online (class) schedules, online course evaluations, learning management system, media applications, software training, print payments. Campuswide network is available. 100% of college-owned or -operated housing units are wired for high-speed Internet access. Wireless service is available via classrooms, computer centers, computer labs, dorm rooms, learning centers, libraries, student centers.

Library: Meyer Library plus 1 other.

STUDENT LIFE
Housing options: coed, special housing for students with disabilities. Campus housing is university owned and leased by the school. Freshman applicants given priority for college housing.

Activities and organizations: student-run radio station, Student of Color Coalition, International Student Alliance, Chimera Council, Animation Resource Center, MyChina, national fraternities, national sororities.

Campus security: 24-hour emergency response devices and patrols, late-night transport/escort service, controlled dormitory access.

Student services: personal/psychological counseling.

COSTS & FINANCIAL AID
Costs (2017–18) ***Tuition:*** $44,976 full-time. Full-time tuition and fees vary according to degree level. Part-time tuition and fees vary according to degree level. ***Required fees:*** $490 full-time. ***Room only:*** $9370. Room and board charges vary according to housing facility. ***Payment plan:*** installment. ***Waivers:*** employees or children of employees.

Financial Aid Of all full-time matriculated undergraduates who enrolled in 2016, 774 applied for aid, 720 were judged to have need, 31 had their need fully met. 675 Federal Work-Study jobs (averaging $3000). 114 state and other part-time jobs (averaging $3000). In 2016, 344 non-need-based awards were made. ***Average percent of need met:*** 59. ***Average financial aid package:*** $30,706. ***Average need-based loan:*** $4776. ***Average need-based gift aid:*** $25,984. ***Average non-need-based aid:*** $11,043. ***Average indebtedness upon graduation:*** $32,434.

APPLYING
Required: essay or personal statement, minimum 2.0 GPA, 1 letter of recommendation, portfolio of creative work. ***Required for some:*** high school transcript, interview.

CONTACT
Mr. Arnold Icasiano, Director of Admissions, California College of the Arts, 1111 Eighth Street, San Francisco, CA 94107. *Phone:* 415-703-9523 Ext. 9532. *Toll-free phone:* 800-447-1ART. *Fax:* 415-703-9539. *E-mail:* enroll@cca.edu.

California College San Diego

National City, California

http://www.cc-sd.edu/

CONTACT
California College San Diego, 700 Bay Marina Drive, Suite 100, National City, CA 91950. *Toll-free phone:* 800-622-3188.

California College San Diego

San Diego, California

http://www.cc-sd.edu/

CONTACT
Tana Sanderson, Director of Admission, California College San Diego, 6602 Convoy Court, Suite 100, San Diego, CA 92111. *Phone:* 619-295-5785. *Toll-free phone:* 800-622-3188. *E-mail:* tana.sanderson@cc-sd.edu.

California College San Diego

San Marcos, California

http://www.cc-sd.edu/

CONTACT
California College San Diego, 277 Rancheros Drive, Suite 200, San Marcos, CA 92069. *Toll-free phone:* 800-622-3188.

California Institute of Integral Studies
San Francisco, California
http://www.ciis.edu/

- **Independent** upper-level, founded 1968
- **Urban** campus with easy access to San Francisco
- **Endowment** $1.4 million
- **Coed** 102 undergraduate students, 85% full-time, 81% women, 19% men
- **Minimally difficult** entrance level

UNDERGRAD STUDENTS
87 full-time, 15 part-time. 8% Black or African American, non-Hispanic/Latino; 20% Hispanic/Latino; 5% Asian, non-Hispanic/Latino; 1% Native Hawaiian or other Pacific Islander, non-Hispanic/Latino; 1% American Indian or Alaska Native, non-Hispanic/Latino; 9% Two or more races, non-Hispanic/Latino; 3% Race/ethnicity unknown; 3% international; 54% transferred in.

FACULTY
Total: 231, 29% full-time.
Student/faculty ratio: 11:1.

ACADEMICS
Calendar: semesters. *Degrees:* bachelor's, master's, doctoral, and postbachelor's certificates.
Special study options: adult/continuing education programs, external degree program.
Computers: 25 computers/terminals are available on campus for general student use. Students can access the following: campus intranet, free student e-mail accounts, online (class) grades, online (class) registration, online (class) schedules. Campuswide network is available. Wireless service is available via classrooms, libraries, student centers.
Library: The Laurance S. Rockefeller Library plus 1 other.

STUDENT LIFE
Housing options: college housing not available.
Activities and organizations: drama/theater group, Student Alliance, People of Color, Queer@CIIS, International Students and Friends, AWARE - Awaking to Whiteness and Racism Everywhere.
Student services: personal/psychological counseling.

COSTS & FINANCIAL AID
Costs (2017–18) ***Tuition:*** $19,724 full-time, $809 per unit part-time. ***Required fees:*** $480 full-time, $160 per term part-time. ***Payment plan:*** installment. ***Waivers:*** employees or children of employees.
Financial Aid Of all full-time matriculated undergraduates who enrolled in 2015, 86 applied for aid, 86 were judged to have need, 4 had their need fully met. 6 Federal Work-Study jobs (averaging $3208). ***Average percent of need met:*** 22. ***Average financial aid package:*** $18,625. ***Average need-based loan:*** $5799. ***Average need-based gift aid:*** $6193.

APPLYING
Options: electronic application.
Application fee: $65.

CONTACT
Admissions Counselor, California Institute of Integral Studies, 1453 Mission Street, San Francisco, CA 94103. *Phone:* 415-575-6156. *Fax:* 415-575-1268. *E-mail:* admissions@ciis.edu.

California Institute of Technology
Pasadena, California
http://www.caltech.edu/

- **Independent** university, founded 1891
- **Suburban** 124-acre campus with easy access to Los Angeles
- **Endowment** $2.2 billion
- **Coed** 979 undergraduate students, 100% full-time, 41% women, 59% men
- **Most difficult** entrance level, 8% of applicants were admitted

UNDERGRAD STUDENTS
979 full-time. Students come from 47 states and territories; 25 other countries; 66% are from out of state; 1% Black or African American, non-Hispanic/Latino; 12% Hispanic/Latino; 43% Asian, non-Hispanic/Latino; 6% Two or more races, non-Hispanic/Latino; 9% international; 0.4% transferred in; 86% live on campus.

Freshmen:
Admission: 6,855 applied, 553 admitted, 235 enrolled. ***Test scores:*** SAT critical reading scores over 500: 100%; SAT math scores over 500: 100%; SAT writing scores over 500: 100%; ACT scores over 18: 100%; SAT critical reading scores over 600: 100%; SAT math scores over 600: 100%; SAT writing scores over 600: 100%; ACT scores over 24: 100%; SAT critical reading scores over 700: 92%; SAT math scores over 700: 99%; SAT writing scores over 700: 92%; ACT scores over 30: 100%.
Retention: 98% of full-time freshmen returned.

FACULTY
Total: 369, 91% full-time, 94% with terminal degrees.
Student/faculty ratio: 3:1.

ACADEMICS
Calendar: 3 10-week terms. *Degrees:* bachelor's, master's, doctoral, and post-master's certificates.
Special study options: cooperative education, double majors, English as a second language, independent study, off-campus study, services for LD students, student-designed majors, study abroad. ***ROTC:*** Army (c), Air Force (c).
Unusual degree programs: 3-2 engineering with Bowdoin College, Bryn Mawr College, Grinnell College, Haverford College, Mt. Holyoke College, Oberlin College, Occidental College, Ohio Wesleyan University, Pomona College, Reed College, Spelman College, Wesleyan University, Whitman College.
Computers: 75 computers/terminals and 1,250 ports are available on campus for general student use. Students can access the following: campus intranet, computer help desk, free student e-mail accounts, online (class) grades, online (class) registration, online (class) schedules. Campuswide network is available. 100% of college-owned or -operated housing units are wired for high-speed Internet access. Wireless service is available via entire campus.
Library: Sherman Fairchild Library plus 6 others. *Books:* 297,949 (physical), 69,296 (digital/electronic); *Serial titles:* 9,987 (physical), 6,330 (digital/electronic); *Databases:* 211. Weekly public service hours: 168; study areas open 24 hours, 5-7 days a week; students can reserve study rooms.

STUDENT LIFE
Housing options: on-campus residence required for freshman year; coed, special housing for students with disabilities. Campus housing is university owned. Freshman campus housing is guaranteed.
Activities and organizations: drama/theater group, student-run newspaper, choral group, Instrumental music groups, Entrepreneur's Club, Glee Club, Theater arts, Ultimate Disc Club.
Athletics Member NCAA. All Division III. ***Intercollegiate sports:*** baseball M, basketball M/W, cross-country running M/W, fencing M/W, soccer M/W, swimming and diving M/W, tennis M/W, track and field M/W, volleyball W, water polo M/W. ***Intramural sports:*** badminton M(c)/W(c), basketball M/W, soccer M/W, table tennis M/W, ultimate Frisbee M(c)/W(c), volleyball M/W.
Campus security: 24-hour emergency response devices and patrols, late-night transport/escort service, controlled dormitory access.
Student services: health clinic, personal/psychological counseling, women's center.

COSTS & FINANCIAL AID
Costs (2016–17) ***Comprehensive fee:*** $61,677 includes full-time tuition ($45,846), mandatory fees ($1731), and room and board ($14,100). ***College room only:*** $7914. Room and board charges vary according to housing facility. ***Payment plans:*** installment, deferred payment. ***Waivers:*** employees or children of employees.
Financial Aid Of all full-time matriculated undergraduates who enrolled in 2016, 587 applied for aid, 500 were judged to have need, 500 had their need fully met. 267 Federal Work-Study jobs (averaging $3207). 44 state and other part-time jobs (averaging $2580). In 2016, 2 non-need-based awards were made. ***Average percent of need met:*** 100. ***Average financial aid package:*** $46,095. ***Average need-based loan:*** $3449. ***Average need-based gift aid:*** $41,901. ***Average non-need-based aid:*** $5000. ***Average indebtedness upon graduation:*** $18,219.

APPLYING

Standardized Tests *Required:* SAT or ACT (for admission), SAT and SAT Subject Tests or ACT (for admission).

Options: electronic application, early admission, early action, deferred entrance.

Application fee: $75.

Required: essay or personal statement, high school transcript, 2 letters of recommendation.

Application deadlines: 1/3 (freshmen), 2/15 (transfers), 11/1 (early action).

Notification: 4/1 (freshmen), 5/1 (transfers), 12/15 (early action).

CONTACT

Mr. Jarrid James Whitney, Executive Director of Admissions, California Institute of Technology, 383 South Hill Avenue, Mail Code 10-90, Pasadena, CA 91125. *Phone:* 626-395-6341. *Fax:* 626-683-3026.

California Institute of the Arts

Valencia, California

http://www.calarts.edu/

- **Independent** comprehensive, founded 1961
- **Suburban** 60-acre campus with easy access to Los Angeles
- **Endowment** $101.6 million
- **Coed**
- **Very difficult** entrance level

FACULTY

Student/faculty ratio: 7:1.

ACADEMICS

Calendar: semesters. *Degrees:* bachelor's, master's, doctoral, and postbachelor's certificates.

Library: Division of Library and Information Resources.

STUDENT LIFE

Housing options: coed, special housing for students with disabilities. Campus housing is university owned.

Activities and organizations: drama/theater group, student-run radio and television station, choral group, Student Council, FISK - Graphic Arts Club, Soccer Club, Korean Bible Study, Black Student Union.

Campus security: 24-hour emergency response devices and patrols, late-night transport/escort service, controlled dormitory access.

Student services: health clinic, personal/psychological counseling.

COSTS & FINANCIAL AID

Costs (2016–17) ***Tuition:*** $45,030 full-time.

Financial Aid Of all full-time matriculated undergraduates who enrolled in 2016, 637 applied for aid, 553 were judged to have need, 64 had their need fully met. 280 Federal Work-Study jobs (averaging $2188). In 2016, 78 non-need-based awards were made. ***Average percent of need met:*** 75. ***Average financial aid package:*** $35,000. ***Average need-based loan:*** $10,500. ***Average need-based gift aid:*** $17,500. ***Average non-need-based aid:*** $8800. ***Average indebtedness upon graduation:*** $31,293.

APPLYING

Options: electronic application.

Application fee: $70.

Required: essay or personal statement, high school transcript, 2 letters of recommendation, portfolio or audition. ***Required for some:*** 3 letters of recommendation, interview.

CONTACT

Molly Ryan, Director of Admissions, California Institute of the Arts, 24700 McBean Parkway, Valencia, CA 91355-2340. *Phone:* 661-255-1050. *Toll-free phone:* 800-545-2787. *Fax:* 661-253-7710. *E-mail:* admiss@calarts.edu.

California Intercontinental University

Irvine, California

http://caluniversity.edu/

CONTACT

John Ramsay, Director of Admission, California Intercontinental University, 17310 Red Hill Avenue, #200, Irvine, CA 92614. *Phone:* 909-396-6090. *Toll-free phone:* 866-687-2258. *Fax:* 909-804-5151. *E-mail:* admissions@caluniversity.com.

California Lutheran University

Thousand Oaks, California

http://www.callutheran.edu/

- **Independent Lutheran** comprehensive, founded 1959
- **Suburban** 290-acre campus with easy access to Los Angeles
- **Endowment** $92.9 million
- **Coed** 2,892 undergraduate students, 96% full-time, 57% women, 43% men
- **Moderately difficult** entrance level, 64% of applicants were admitted

UNDERGRAD STUDENTS

2,768 full-time, 124 part-time. Students come from 22 states and territories; 26 other countries; 15% are from out of state; 3% Black or African American, non-Hispanic/Latino; 29% Hispanic/Latino; 5% Asian, non-Hispanic/Latino; 0.4% Native Hawaiian or other Pacific Islander, non-Hispanic/Latino; 0.2% American Indian or Alaska Native, non-Hispanic/Latino; 7% Two or more races, non-Hispanic/Latino; 4% Race/ethnicity unknown; 3% international; 9% transferred in; 52% live on campus.

Freshmen:

Admission: 6,013 applied, 3,860 admitted, 639 enrolled. ***Average high school GPA:*** 3.7. ***Test scores:*** SAT critical reading scores over 500: 75%; SAT math scores over 500: 78%; ACT scores over 18: 98%; SAT critical reading scores over 600: 24%; SAT math scores over 600: 30%; ACT scores over 24: 61%; SAT critical reading scores over 700: 1%; SAT math scores over 700: 3%; ACT scores over 30: 9%.

Retention: 85% of full-time freshmen returned.

FACULTY

Total: 437, 44% full-time, 58% with terminal degrees.

Student/faculty ratio: 14:1.

ACADEMICS

Calendar: semesters. *Degrees:* certificates, bachelor's, master's, doctoral, post-master's, and postbachelor's certificates.

Special study options: accelerated degree program, adult/continuing education programs, advanced placement credit, cooperative education, double majors, honors programs, independent study, internships, off-campus study, part-time degree program, services for LD students, student-designed majors, study abroad, summer session for credit. ***ROTC:*** Army (c), Air Force (c).

Unusual degree programs: 3-2 computer science, political public policy and administration.

Computers: 334 computers/terminals are available on campus for general student use. Students can access the following: campus intranet, computer help desk, free student e-mail accounts, online (class) grades, online (class) registration, online (class) schedules. Campuswide network is available. 100% of college-owned or -operated housing units are wired for high-speed Internet access. Wireless service is available via entire campus.

Library: Pearson Library. *Books:* 133,915 (physical), 194,230 (digital/electronic); *Serial titles:* 152 (physical); *Databases:* 179. Students can reserve study rooms.

STUDENT LIFE

Housing options: on-campus residence required through junior year; coed, special housing for students with disabilities. Campus housing is university owned. Freshman campus housing is guaranteed.

Activities and organizations: drama/theater group, student-run newspaper, radio and television station, choral group, Student Government, recreation, sports fan, or club sports related, service organizations, campus ministry or other religiously affiliated organization, multicultural organizations.

Athletics Member NCAA. All Division III. ***Intercollegiate sports:*** baseball M, basketball M/W, cheerleading M/W, cross-country running M/W, football M, golf M/W, soccer M/W, softball W, swimming and diving M/W, tennis M/W, track and field M/W, volleyball M/W, water polo M/W. ***Intramural sports:*** basketball M(c)/W(c), football M(c)/W(c), lacrosse M(c)/W(c), rugby M(c)/W(c), soccer M(c)/W(c), softball M(c)/W(c), tennis M(c)/W(c), volleyball M(c)/W(c), water polo M(c)/W(c).

Campus security: 24-hour emergency response devices and patrols, late-night transport/escort service, controlled dormitory access, escort service, shuttle service.

Student services: health clinic, personal/psychological counseling, women's center.

COSTS & FINANCIAL AID

Costs (2016–17) ***Comprehensive fee:*** $52,840 includes full-time tuition ($39,310), mandatory fees ($470), and room and board ($13,060). Part-time tuition: $1265 per unit. ***College room only:*** $7010. Room and board charges vary according to board plan and housing facility. ***Payment plan:*** installment.

Financial Aid Of all full-time matriculated undergraduates who enrolled in 2016, 2,509 applied for aid, 1,813 were judged to have need, 182 had their need fully met. 261 Federal Work-Study jobs (averaging $2500). In 2016, 782 non-need-based awards were made. ***Average percent of need met:*** 72. ***Average financial aid package:*** $30,415. ***Average need-based loan:*** $4739. ***Average need-based gift aid:*** $26,191. ***Average non-need-based aid:*** $17,885. ***Average indebtedness upon graduation:*** $32,030.

APPLYING

Standardized Tests *Required:* SAT or ACT (for admission).

Options: electronic application, early action, deferred entrance.

Application fee: $25.

Required: essay or personal statement, high school transcript, minimum 2.8 GPA, 1 letter of recommendation. ***Recommended:*** minimum 3.0 GPA, interview.

Application deadlines: 1/1 (freshmen), 6/1 (transfers), 11/1 (early action).

Notification: 4/1 (freshmen), continuous (transfers), 1/15 (early action).

CONTACT

Dr. Michael Elgarico, Dean of Undergraduate Enrollment, California Lutheran University, Office of Admission, #1350, Thousand Oaks, CA 91360. *Phone:* 805-493-3135. *Toll-free phone:* 877-258-3678. *Fax:* 805-493-3114. *E-mail:* cluadm@clunet.edu.

California Miramar University

San Diego, California

http://www.calmu.edu/

CONTACT

Jean Van Slyke, Director of Admissions, California Miramar University, 3550 Camino Del Rio North, Suite 208, San Diego, CA 92108. *Phone:* 858-653-3000. *Toll-free phone:* 877-570-5678. *Fax:* 858-653-6786. *E-mail:* admissions@calmu.edu.

California National University for Advanced Studies

Northridge, California

http://www.cnuas.edu/

CONTACT

Ms. Stephanie Smith, Registrar, California National University for Advanced Studies, Admissions, 8550 Balboa Boulevard, Suite 210, Northridge, CA 91325. *Phone:* 818-830-2411. *Toll-free phone:* 800-782-2422. *Fax:* 818-830-2418. *E-mail:* cnuadms@mail.cnuas.edu.

California Polytechnic State University, San Luis Obispo

San Luis Obispo, California

http://www.calpoly.edu/

- **State-supported** comprehensive, founded 1901, part of California State University System
- **Suburban** 6000-acre campus
- **Coed** 20,426 undergraduate students, 96% full-time, 47% women, 53% men
- **Moderately difficult** entrance level, 29% of applicants were admitted

UNDERGRAD STUDENTS

19,703 full-time, 723 part-time. 14% are from out of state; 0.7% Black or African American, non-Hispanic/Latino; 16% Hispanic/Latino; 13% Asian, non-Hispanic/Latino; 0.1% Native Hawaiian or other Pacific Islander, non-Hispanic/Latino; 0.1% American Indian or Alaska Native, non-Hispanic/Latino; 7% Two or more races, non-Hispanic/Latino; 5% Race/ethnicity unknown; 2% international; 4% transferred in; 35% live on campus.

Freshmen:

Admission: 48,162 applied, 14,202 admitted, 4,341 enrolled. ***Average high school GPA:*** 3.92. ***Test scores:*** SAT critical reading scores over 500: 94%; SAT math scores over 500: 99%; ACT scores over 18: 100%; SAT critical reading scores over 600: 58%; SAT math scores over 600: 72%; ACT scores over 24: 91%; SAT critical reading scores over 700: 14%; SAT math scores over 700: 25%; ACT scores over 30: 41%.

Retention: 95% of full-time freshmen returned.

FACULTY

Total: 1,439, 63% full-time, 58% with terminal degrees.

Student/faculty ratio: 19:1.

ACADEMICS

Calendar: quarters. *Degrees:* bachelor's, master's, and postbachelor's certificates.

Special study options: academic remediation for entering students, advanced placement credit, cooperative education, distance learning, double majors, English as a second language, honors programs, internships, off-campus study, part-time degree program, services for LD students, study abroad, summer session for credit. ***ROTC:*** Army (b).

Computers: Students can access the following: campus intranet, free student e-mail accounts, online (class) grades, online (class) registration, online (class) schedules. Campuswide network is available. Wireless service is available via classrooms, computer centers, computer labs, dorm rooms, learning centers, libraries, student centers.

Library: Robert E. Kennedy Library.

STUDENT LIFE

Housing options: on-campus residence required for freshman year; coed, special housing for students with disabilities. Campus housing is university owned.

Activities and organizations: drama/theater group, student-run newspaper, radio and television station, choral group, marching band, national fraternities, national sororities.

Athletics Member NCAA. All Division I except football (Division I-AA). ***Intercollegiate sports:*** baseball M(s), basketball M(s)/W(s), cross-country running M(s)/W(s), golf M(s)/W(s), soccer M(s)/W(s), softball W(s), swimming and diving M(s)/W(s), tennis M(s)/W(s), track and field M(s)/W(s), volleyball W(s), wrestling M(s). ***Intramural sports:*** badminton M/W, basketball M/W, football M/W, racquetball M/W, soccer M/W, softball M/W, table tennis M/W, tennis M/W, volleyball M/W.

Campus security: 24-hour emergency response devices and patrols, student patrols, late-night transport/escort service.

Student services: health clinic, personal/psychological counseling, women's center, legal services.

COSTS & FINANCIAL AID

Costs (2017–18) ***Tuition:*** state resident $5472 full-time, $3174 per year part-time; nonresident $16,632 full-time, $7638 per year part-time. Full-time tuition and fees vary according to course load, degree level, and program. Part-time tuition and fees vary according to course load, degree level, and program. ***Required fees:*** $3603 full-time, $3141 per year part-time. ***Room and board:*** $12,507; room only: $7360. Room and board charges vary according to housing facility. ***Payment plan:*** installment. ***Waivers:*** employees or children of employees.

Financial Aid Of all full-time matriculated undergraduates who enrolled in 2015, 12,054 applied for aid, 8,043 were judged to have need, 630 had their need fully met. In 2015, 2447 non-need-based awards were made. ***Average percent of need met:*** 57. ***Average financial aid package:*** $10,141. ***Average need-based loan:*** $3995. ***Average need-based gift aid:*** $3524. ***Average non-need-based aid:*** $1890. ***Average indebtedness upon graduation:*** $22,413.

APPLYING

Standardized Tests *Required:* SAT or ACT (for admission).

Options: electronic application, early admission, early decision.

Application fee: $55.

Required: high school transcript.

Application deadlines: 11/30 (freshmen), 11/30 (transfers).

Early decision deadline: 10/31.

Notification: 4/1 (freshmen), 4/1 (transfers), 12/15 (early decision).

CONTACT

Mr. James Maraviglia, Associate Vice Provost for Marketing and Enrollment Development, California Polytechnic State University, San Luis Obispo, Admissions Office, 1 Grand Avenue, San Luis Obispo, CA 93407-0031. *Phone:* 805-756-2311. *Fax:* 805-756-5911. *E-mail:* admissions@calpoly.edu.

California State Polytechnic University, Pomona

Pomona, California

http://www.cpp.edu/

- **State-supported** comprehensive, founded 1938, part of California State University System
- **Urban** 1400-acre campus with easy access to Los Angeles
- **Endowment** $85.6 million
- **Coed** 23,733 undergraduate students, 89% full-time, 45% women, 55% men
- **Moderately difficult** entrance level, 59% of applicants were admitted

UNDERGRAD STUDENTS

21,148 full-time, 2,585 part-time. Students come from 36 states and territories; 107 other countries; 1% are from out of state; 3% Black or African American, non-Hispanic/Latino; 42% Hispanic/Latino; 23% Asian, non-Hispanic/Latino; 0.2% Native Hawaiian or other Pacific Islander, non-Hispanic/Latino; 0.2% American Indian or Alaska Native, non-Hispanic/Latino; 4% Two or more races, non-Hispanic/Latino; 4% Race/ethnicity unknown; 6% international; 14% transferred in; 10% live on campus.

Freshmen:

Admission: 32,920 applied, 19,474 admitted, 4,204 enrolled. ***Average high school GPA:*** 3.45. ***Test scores:*** SAT critical reading scores over 500: 50%; SAT math scores over 500: 64%; ACT scores over 18: 89%; SAT critical reading scores over 600: 16%; SAT math scores over 600: 27%; ACT scores over 24: 48%; SAT critical reading scores over 700: 2%; SAT math scores over 700: 5%; ACT scores over 30: 10%.

Retention: 89% of full-time freshmen returned.

FACULTY

Total: 1,221, 50% full-time, 56% with terminal degrees.

Student/faculty ratio: 23:1.

ACADEMICS

Calendar: quarters. *Degrees:* bachelor's, master's, and doctoral.

Special study options: academic remediation for entering students, adult/continuing education programs, advanced placement credit, cooperative education, distance learning, double majors, English as a second language, freshman honors college, honors programs, internships, off-campus study, part-time degree program, services for LD students, study abroad, summer session for credit. ***ROTC:*** Army (b).

Computers: 2,117 computers/terminals and 3,588 ports are available on campus for general student use. Students can access the following: campus intranet, computer help desk, free student e-mail accounts, online (class) grades, online (class) schedules. Campuswide network is available. 100% of college-owned or -operated housing units are wired for high-speed Internet access. Wireless service is available via entire campus.

Library: University Library. *Books:* 577,476 (physical), 14,408 (digital/electronic); *Serial titles:* 277,642 (physical), 13,362 (digital/electronic); *Databases:* 143. Weekly public service hours: 92; study areas open 24 hours, 5-7 days a week; students can reserve study rooms.

STUDENT LIFE

Housing options: on-campus residence required for freshman year; coed, special housing for students with disabilities. Campus housing is university owned and is provided by a third party. Freshman applicants given priority for college housing.

Activities and organizations: drama/theater group, student-run newspaper, choral group, Rose Float Club, Mexican American Student Association (MASA), Barkada - Filipino American Student Association, American Marketing Association, Cal Poly Society of Accountants, national fraternities, national sororities.

Athletics Member NCAA. All Division II. ***Intercollegiate sports:*** baseball M(s), basketball M(s)/W(s), cross-country running M(s)/W(s), soccer M(s)/W(s), track and field M(s)/W(s), volleyball W(s). ***Intramural sports:*** basketball M/W, bowling M/W, football M/W, softball M/W, volleyball M/W.

Campus security: 24-hour emergency response devices and patrols, student patrols, late-night transport/escort service, controlled dormitory access, video camera surveillance.

Student services: health clinic, personal/psychological counseling, women's center.

COSTS & FINANCIAL AID

Costs (2017–18) ***Tuition:*** state resident $5472 full-time; nonresident $16,632 full-time, $248 per credit hour part-time. Full-time tuition and fees vary according to course load, degree level, and program. Part-time tuition and fees vary according to course load, degree level, and program. ***Required fees:*** $1555 full-time. ***Room and board:*** $14,514; room only: $9027. Room and board charges vary according to board plan and housing facility. ***Payment plans:*** installment, deferred payment. ***Waivers:*** employees or children of employees.

Financial Aid Of all full-time matriculated undergraduates who enrolled in 2016, 16,552 applied for aid, 14,460 were judged to have need, 813 had their need fully met. 393 Federal Work-Study jobs (averaging $2477). In 2016, 12 non-need-based awards were made. ***Average percent of need met:*** 55. ***Average financial aid package:*** $11,105. ***Average need-based loan:*** $4722. ***Average need-based gift aid:*** $9805. ***Average non-need-based aid:*** $1262. ***Average indebtedness upon graduation:*** $22,404.

APPLYING

Standardized Tests *Required:* SAT or ACT (for admission).

Options: electronic application.

Application fee: $55.

Required: high school transcript, minimum 2.0 GPA.

Application deadlines: 11/30 (freshmen), 11/30 (transfers).

Notification: continuous (freshmen), 5/1 (transfers).

CONTACT

Mr. Andrew M. Wright, Director of Admissions, California State Polytechnic University, Pomona, 3801 West Temple Avenue, Bldg. 98-T2, Room 6, Pomona, CA 91768-2557. *Phone:* 909-869-3130. *Fax:* 909-869-4529. *E-mail:* awright@cpp.edu.

California State University, Bakersfield

Bakersfield, California

http://www.csub.edu/

- **State-supported** comprehensive, founded 1970, part of California State University System
- **Urban** 575-acre campus
- **Coed** 8,025 undergraduate students, 83% full-time, 61% women, 39% men
- **Moderately difficult** entrance level, 100% of applicants were admitted

UNDERGRAD STUDENTS
6,655 full-time, 1,370 part-time. 1% are from out of state; 7% Black or African American, non-Hispanic/Latino; 55% Hispanic/Latino; 7% Asian, non-Hispanic/Latino; 0.1% Native Hawaiian or other Pacific Islander, non-Hispanic/Latino; 0.6% American Indian or Alaska Native, non-Hispanic/Latino; 3% Two or more races, non-Hispanic/Latino; 4% Race/ethnicity unknown; 4% international.

Freshmen:
Admission: 5,796 applied, 5,796 admitted, 1,462 enrolled. ***Average high school GPA:*** 3.2. ***Test scores:*** SAT critical reading scores over 500: 23%; SAT math scores over 500: 34%; ACT scores over 18: 57%; SAT critical reading scores over 600: 3%; SAT math scores over 600: 5%; ACT scores over 24: 14%.
Retention: 77% of full-time freshmen returned.

FACULTY
Total: 473, 58% full-time, 47% with terminal degrees.
Student/faculty ratio: 28:1.

ACADEMICS
Calendar: quarters. *Degrees:* bachelor's and master's.
Special study options: adult/continuing education programs, external degree program, part-time degree program.
Computers: Students can access the following: online (class) registration. Campuswide network is available.
Library: Walter W. Stiern Library.

STUDENT LIFE
Housing options: coed, special housing for students with disabilities.
Athletics Member NCAA. All Division II except wrestling (Division I). ***Intercollegiate sports:*** basketball M(s), golf M(s), soccer M(s), softball W(s), swimming and diving M(s)/W(s), tennis W(s), track and field M(s)/W(s), volleyball W(s), water polo W(s), wrestling M(s). ***Intramural sports:*** archery M/W, badminton M/W, baseball M/W, basketball M/W, fencing M/W, football M/W, golf M/W, gymnastics M/W, racquetball M/W, riflery M/W, soccer M, softball M/W, swimming and diving M/W, tennis W, volleyball M/W, weight lifting M/W, wrestling M/W.
Campus security: 24-hour emergency response devices and patrols, late-night transport/escort service.

COSTS & FINANCIAL AID
Costs (2016–17) ***Tuition:*** state resident $5472 full-time, $3174 per year part-time; nonresident $16,632 full-time, $12,102 per year part-time. Full-time tuition and fees vary according to course load and degree level. Part-time tuition and fees vary according to course load and degree level. ***Required fees:*** $2777 full-time, $1389 per year part-time. ***Room and board:*** Room and board charges vary according to board plan and housing facility. ***Waivers:*** senior citizens and employees or children of employees.
Financial Aid Of all full-time matriculated undergraduates who enrolled in 2016, 6,591 applied for aid, 5,895 were judged to have need, 859 had their need fully met. ***Average percent of need met:*** 15. ***Average financial aid package:*** $4278. ***Average need-based loan:*** $1410. ***Average need-based gift aid:*** $3397. ***Average indebtedness upon graduation:*** $11,437.

APPLYING
Standardized Tests *Required for some:* SAT or ACT (for admission).
Options: electronic application, deferred entrance.
Application fee: $55.
Required: high school transcript.

CONTACT
Debra Blowers, Assistant Director, Admissions and Evaluations, California State University, Bakersfield, 9001 Stockdale Highway, Balersfield, CA 93311-1099. *Phone:* 661-664-3036. *Toll-free phone:* 800-788-2782. *E-mail:* admissions@csub.edu.

California State University Channel Islands

Camarillo, California

http://www.csuci.edu/

CONTACT
Ms. Ginger Reyes, California State University Channel Islands, One University Drive, Camarillo, CA 93012. *Phone:* 805-437-8520. *Fax:* 805-437-8519. *E-mail:* prospective.student@csuci.edu.

California State University, Chico

Chico, California

http://www.csuchico.edu/

- **State-supported** comprehensive, founded 1887, part of California State University System
- **Small-town** 119-acre campus
- **Endowment** $54.8 million
- **Coed** 16,471 undergraduate students, 90% full-time, 53% women, 47% men
- **Moderately difficult** entrance level, 67% of applicants were admitted

UNDERGRAD STUDENTS
14,819 full-time, 1,652 part-time. 11% are from out of state; 2% Black or African American, non-Hispanic/Latino; 31% Hispanic/Latino; 6% Asian, non-Hispanic/Latino; 0.2% Native Hawaiian or other Pacific Islander, non-Hispanic/Latino; 0.6% American Indian or Alaska Native, non-Hispanic/Latino; 5% Two or more races, non-Hispanic/Latino; 8% Race/ethnicity unknown; 4% international; 9% transferred in; 13% live on campus.

Freshmen:
Admission: 23,124 applied, 15,393 admitted, 2,762 enrolled. ***Average high school GPA:*** 3.3. ***Test scores:*** SAT critical reading scores over 500: 49%; SAT math scores over 500: 51%; ACT scores over 18: 83%; SAT critical reading scores over 600: 11%; SAT math scores over 600: 12%; ACT scores over 24: 29%; SAT critical reading scores over 700: 1%; SAT math scores over 700: 1%; ACT scores over 30: 2%.
Retention: 86% of full-time freshmen returned.

FACULTY
Total: 996, 51% full-time, 58% with terminal degrees.
Student/faculty ratio: 24:1.

ACADEMICS
Calendar: semesters. *Degrees:* certificates, bachelor's, master's, post-master's, and postbachelor's certificates.
Special study options: academic remediation for entering students, adult/continuing education programs, advanced placement credit, cooperative education, distance learning, double majors, English as a second language, external degree program, honors programs, independent study, internships, off-campus study, part-time degree program, services for LD students, student-designed majors, study abroad, summer session for credit.
Computers: 243 computers/terminals and 243 ports are available on campus for general student use. Students can access the following: campus intranet, computer help desk, free student e-mail accounts, online (class) grades, online (class) registration, online (class) schedules, student account information, calendar, transcripts. Campuswide network is available. 100% of college-owned or -operated housing units are wired for high-speed Internet access. Wireless service is available via entire campus.
Library: Meriam Library plus 1 other. *Books:* 923,470 (physical), 180,505 (digital/electronic); *Serial titles:* 660 (physical). Study areas open 24 hours, 5-7 days a week; students can reserve study rooms.

STUDENT LIFE
Housing options: coed, women-only, special housing for students with disabilities. Campus housing is university owned. Freshman applicants given priority for college housing.
Activities and organizations: drama/theater group, student-run newspaper, radio station, choral group, Pre-Medical Association, Health Professionals Association (HPA), Audio Engineering Society, Student

Association Of Social Work SASW (Undergraduate), Recreation Hospitality and Parks Society (RHAPS), national fraternities, national sororities.

Athletics Member NCAA. All Division II. ***Intercollegiate sports:*** baseball M(s), basketball M(s)/W(s), cross-country running M(s)/W(s), golf M(s)/W(s), soccer M(s)/W(s), softball W(s), track and field M(s)/W(s), volleyball W(s). ***Intramural sports:*** badminton M/W, basketball M/W, football M/W, golf M/W, soccer M/W, softball M/W, track and field M/W, volleyball W.

Campus security: 24-hour emergency response devices and patrols, student patrols, late-night transport/escort service, controlled dormitory access, crime prevention workshops, RAD self-defense program, Chico Safe Rides, blue light emergency phones, freshmen safety orientation.

Student services: health clinic, personal/psychological counseling, women's center, legal services.

COSTS & FINANCIAL AID

Costs (2016–17) ***Tuition:*** state resident $7044 full-time; nonresident $18,204 full-time. Full-time tuition and fees vary according to degree level. Part-time tuition and fees vary according to course load and degree level. ***Required fees:*** $5472 full-time. ***Room and board:*** $12,824. Room and board charges vary according to board plan and housing facility. ***Payment plans:*** installment, deferred payment. ***Waivers:*** senior citizens and employees or children of employees.

Financial Aid Of all full-time matriculated undergraduates who enrolled in 2015, 12,000 applied for aid, 10,261 were judged to have need, 1,576 had their need fully met. In 2015, 445 non-need-based awards were made. ***Average percent of need met:*** 76. ***Average financial aid package:*** $16,081. ***Average need-based loan:*** $4534. ***Average need-based gift aid:*** $9941. ***Average non-need-based aid:*** $1226.

APPLYING

Standardized Tests *Required:* SAT or ACT (for admission).

Options: electronic application, deferred entrance.

Application fee: $55.

Required: high school transcript, GPA from 10th/11th grade college preparatory courses.

Application deadlines: 11/30 (freshmen), 11/30 (transfers).

Notification: 3/1 (freshmen), 3/1 (transfers).

CONTACT

Admissions Counselor, California State University, Chico, 400 West First Street, Chico, CA 95929-0722. *Phone:* 530-898-6322. *Toll-free phone:* 800-542-4426. *Fax:* 530-898-6456. *E-mail:* info@csuchico.edu.

California State University, Dominguez Hills

Carson, California

http://www.csudh.edu/

- **State-supported** comprehensive, founded 1960, part of California State University System
- **Urban** 350-acre campus with easy access to Los Angeles
- **Endowment** $10.1 million
- **Coed** 12,562 undergraduate students, 73% full-time, 63% women, 37% men
- **Moderately difficult** entrance level, 58% of applicants were admitted

UNDERGRAD STUDENTS

9,172 full-time, 3,390 part-time. Students come from 15 states and territories; 37 other countries; 13% Black or African American, non-Hispanic/Latino; 59% Hispanic/Latino; 9% Asian, non-Hispanic/Latino; 0.3% Native Hawaiian or other Pacific Islander, non-Hispanic/Latino; 0.1% American Indian or Alaska Native, non-Hispanic/Latino; 3% Two or more races, non-Hispanic/Latino; 4% Race/ethnicity unknown; 3% international; 22% transferred in; 5% live on campus.

Freshmen:

Admission: 4,615 applied, 2,672 admitted, 1,305 enrolled. ***Average high school GPA:*** 3.13. ***Test scores:*** SAT critical reading scores over 500: 15%; SAT math scores over 500: 19%; SAT writing scores over 500: 14%; ACT scores over 18: 42%; SAT critical reading scores over 600: 2%; SAT math scores over 600: 3%; SAT writing scores over 600: 1%; ACT scores over 24: 6%.

Retention: 82% of full-time freshmen returned.

FACULTY

Total: 966, 30% full-time, 44% with terminal degrees.

Student/faculty ratio: 23:1.

ACADEMICS

Calendar: semesters. *Degrees:* bachelor's, master's, post-master's, and postbachelor's certificates.

Special study options: academic remediation for entering students, accelerated degree program, advanced placement credit, cooperative education, distance learning, double majors, external degree program, honors programs, independent study, internships, off-campus study, part-time degree program, services for LD students, student-designed majors, study abroad, summer session for credit. ***ROTC:*** Army (b), Air Force (c).

Computers: 1,100 computers/terminals and 1,100 ports are available on campus for general student use. Students can access the following: campus intranet, computer help desk, free student e-mail accounts, online (class) grades, online (class) registration, online (class) schedules. Campuswide network is available. 100% of college-owned or -operated housing units are wired for high-speed Internet access. Wireless service is available via entire campus.

Library: Leo F. Cain Educational Resource Center. *Books:* 457,885 (physical), 300,523 (digital/electronic); *Serial titles:* 6,542 (physical), 75,366 (digital/electronic); *Databases:* 94. Weekly public service hours: 81; students can reserve study rooms.

STUDENT LIFE

Housing options: men-only, women-only, special housing for students with disabilities. Campus housing is university owned. Freshman applicants given priority for college housing.

Activities and organizations: drama/theater group, student-run newspaper, radio station, choral group, American Marketing Association, Phi Sigma Sigma, Organization of African Studies, Latino Student Business Association, Circle K, national fraternities, national sororities.

Athletics Member NCAA. All Division II. ***Intercollegiate sports:*** baseball M(s), basketball M(s)/W(s), golf M(s), soccer M(s)/W(s), softball W(s), track and field W(s), volleyball W(s). ***Intramural sports:*** basketball M/W, football M/W, soccer M/W, softball M/W, swimming and diving M/W, tennis M/W, volleyball M/W, weight lifting M/W.

Campus security: 24-hour emergency response devices and patrols, student patrols, late-night transport/escort service.

Student services: health clinic, personal/psychological counseling, women's center.

COSTS & FINANCIAL AID

Costs (2016–17) ***Tuition:*** state resident $5472 full-time, $3174 per year part-time; nonresident $16,632 full-time, $372 per unit part-time. ***Required fees:*** $946 full-time, $946 per year part-time. ***Room and board:*** Room and board charges vary according to housing facility. ***Payment plan:*** installment. ***Waivers:*** senior citizens and employees or children of employees.

Financial Aid Of all full-time matriculated undergraduates who enrolled in 2015, 6,989 applied for aid, 6,700 were judged to have need, 109 had their need fully met. 194 Federal Work-Study jobs (averaging $1424). In 2015, 182 non-need-based awards were made. ***Average percent of need met:*** 34. ***Average financial aid package:*** $6320. ***Average need-based loan:*** $2354. ***Average need-based gift aid:*** $5240. ***Average non-need-based aid:*** $4022. ***Average indebtedness upon graduation:*** $16,370. ***Financial aid deadline:*** 5/15.

APPLYING

Standardized Tests *Required for some:* SAT or ACT (for admission).

Options: electronic application.

Application fee: $55.

Required: high school transcript.

Application deadlines: rolling (freshmen), rolling (transfers).

Notification: continuous (freshmen), continuous (transfers).

CONTACT
Information Center, California State University, Dominguez Hills, 1000 East Victoria Street, Carson, CA 90747-0001. *Phone:* 310-243-3696. *E-mail:* info@csudh.edu.

California State University, East Bay

Hayward, California

http://www.csueastbay.edu/

- **State-supported** comprehensive, founded 1957, part of California State University System
- **Suburban** 343-acre campus with easy access to San Francisco Bay Area
- **Endowment** $10.7 million
- **Coed** 13,008 undergraduate students, 85% full-time, 61% women, 39% men
- **Moderately difficult** entrance level, 74% of applicants were admitted

UNDERGRAD STUDENTS
11,110 full-time, 1,898 part-time. Students come from 27 states and territories; 59 other countries; 1% are from out of state; 11% Black or African American, non-Hispanic/Latino; 31% Hispanic/Latino; 24% Asian, non-Hispanic/Latino; 1% Native Hawaiian or other Pacific Islander, non-Hispanic/Latino; 0.3% American Indian or Alaska Native, non-Hispanic/Latino; 6% Two or more races, non-Hispanic/Latino; 4% Race/ethnicity unknown; 6% international; 17% transferred in.

Freshmen:
Admission: 14,776 applied, 10,938 admitted, 1,787 enrolled. ***Average high school GPA:*** 3.1. ***Test scores:*** SAT critical reading scores over 500: 25%; SAT math scores over 500: 30%; SAT writing scores over 500: 23%; ACT scores over 18: 58%; SAT critical reading scores over 600: 4%; SAT math scores over 600: 6%; SAT writing scores over 600: 3%; ACT scores over 24: 11%; SAT math scores over 700: 1%.

Retention: 80% of full-time freshmen returned.

FACULTY
Total: 839, 42% full-time.
Student/faculty ratio: 23:1.

ACADEMICS
Calendar: quarters. *Degrees:* certificates, bachelor's, master's, doctoral, and postbachelor's certificates.

Special study options: academic remediation for entering students, accelerated degree program, adult/continuing education programs, advanced placement credit, cooperative education, distance learning, double majors, English as a second language, honors programs, independent study, internships, off-campus study, part-time degree program, services for LD students, student-designed majors, study abroad, summer session for credit.

Computers: 700 computers/terminals are available on campus for general student use. Students can access the following: campus intranet, computer help desk, free student e-mail accounts, online (class) grades, online (class) registration, online (class) schedules. Campuswide network is available. 100% of college-owned or -operated housing units are wired for high-speed Internet access. Wireless service is available via entire campus.

Library: Hayward Campus Library.

STUDENT LIFE
Housing options: coed, special housing for students with disabilities. Campus housing is university owned.

Activities and organizations: drama/theater group, student-run newspaper, radio and television station, choral group, Vietnamese Student Association, Accounting Association, Filipino-American Students Association, Movimiento Estudiantil Chicano, Hayward Orientation Team, national fraternities, national sororities.

Athletics Member NCAA, NAIA. All NCAA Division III. ***Intercollegiate sports:*** baseball M, basketball M/W, cross-country running M/W, soccer M/W, softball W, swimming and diving W, volleyball W, water polo W. ***Intramural sports:*** badminton M/W, basketball M/W, golf M/W, gymnastics M, racquetball M/W, soccer M/W, softball M/W, swimming and diving M/W, tennis M/W, volleyball M/W, weight lifting M/W.

Campus security: 24-hour emergency response devices and patrols, late-night transport/escort service.

Student services: health clinic, personal/psychological counseling, legal services.

COSTS & FINANCIAL AID
Costs (2017–18) ***Tuition:*** state resident $6834 full-time; nonresident $18,714 full-time, $264 per credit hour part-time. Full-time tuition and fees vary according to course load, program, and reciprocity agreements. Part-time tuition and fees vary according to course load, program, and reciprocity agreements. ***Required fees:*** $1093 full-time. ***Room and board:*** $14,184. Room and board charges vary according to board plan and housing facility. ***Payment plan:*** installment. ***Waivers:*** senior citizens and employees or children of employees.

Financial Aid Of all full-time matriculated undergraduates who enrolled in 2016, 7,847 applied for aid, 7,676 were judged to have need, 189 had their need fully met. 1,358 Federal Work-Study jobs (averaging $2400). ***Average percent of need met:*** 55. ***Average financial aid package:*** $16,778. ***Average need-based loan:*** $6352. ***Average need-based gift aid:*** $8545. ***Average indebtedness upon graduation:*** $19,149.

APPLYING
Standardized Tests *Required for some:* SAT or ACT (for admission).
Options: electronic application.
Application fee: $55.
Required: high school transcript, minimum 2.0 GPA, California State University eligibility index.
Application deadlines: 11/30 (freshmen), 11/11 (transfers).
Notification: continuous (freshmen), continuous (transfers).

CONTACT
Dave Vasques, Associate Director for Admissions, California State University, East Bay, 25800 Carlos Bee Boulevard, Hayward, CA 94542-3000. *Phone:* 510-885-2029. *E-mail:* dave.vasquez@csueastbay.edu.

California State University, Fresno

Fresno, California

http://www.csufresno.edu/

- **State-supported** comprehensive, founded 1911, part of California State University System
- **Urban** 1399-acre campus
- **Coed** 21,482 undergraduate students, 83% full-time, 57% women, 43% men
- **Minimally difficult** entrance level, 52% of applicants were admitted

UNDERGRAD STUDENTS
17,806 full-time, 3,676 part-time. 1% are from out of state; 3% Black or African American, non-Hispanic/Latino; 48% Hispanic/Latino; 15% Asian, non-Hispanic/Latino; 0.2% Native Hawaiian or other Pacific Islander, non-Hispanic/Latino; 0.3% American Indian or Alaska Native, non-Hispanic/Latino; 3% Two or more races, non-Hispanic/Latino; 4% Race/ethnicity unknown; 5% international; 8% transferred in; 5% live on campus.

Freshmen:
Admission: 19,935 applied, 10,404 admitted, 3,563 enrolled. ***Test scores:*** SAT critical reading scores over 500: 26%; SAT math scores over 500: 29%; SAT writing scores over 500: 22%; ACT scores over 18: 55%; SAT critical reading scores over 600: 5%; SAT math scores over 600: 5%; SAT writing scores over 600: 3%; ACT scores over 24: 13%; SAT critical reading scores over 700: 1%; ACT scores over 30: 1%.

Retention: 83% of full-time freshmen returned.

FACULTY
Total: 1,307, 50% full-time.
Student/faculty ratio: 22:1.

ACADEMICS
Calendar: semesters. *Degrees:* bachelor's, master's, doctoral, post-master's, and postbachelor's certificates.

Special study options: academic remediation for entering students, accelerated degree program, adult/continuing education programs, advanced placement credit, cooperative education, distance learning, double majors, English as a second language, freshman honors college, honors programs, independent study, internships, off-campus study, part-time degree program, services for LD students, student-designed majors, study abroad, summer session for credit. ***ROTC:*** Army (b), Air Force (b).

Computers: Students can access the following: campus intranet, computer help desk, free student e-mail accounts, online (class) grades, online (class) registration, online (class) schedules. Campuswide network is available. Wireless service is available via classrooms, computer centers, computer labs, learning centers, libraries, student centers.
Library: Henry Madden Library.

STUDENT LIFE
Housing options: coed, men-only, women-only. Campus housing is university owned.

Activities and organizations: drama/theater group, student-run newspaper, radio station, choral group, marching band, national fraternities, national sororities.

Athletics Member NCAA. All Division I except football (Division I-A). ***Intercollegiate sports:*** baseball M(s), basketball M(s)/W(s), cross-country running M(s)/W(s), equestrian sports W(s), golf M(s)/W(s), lacrosse W(s), soccer W(s), softball W(s), swimming and diving W(s), tennis M(s)/W(s), track and field M(s)/W(s), volleyball W(s). ***Intramural sports:*** archery M/W, badminton M/W, baseball M, basketball M/W, bowling M/W, cross-country running M/W, equestrian sports W, fencing M/W, golf M/W, gymnastics M/W, racquetball M/W, tennis M/W, volleyball M/W.

Campus security: 24-hour emergency response devices and patrols, late-night transport/escort service, controlled dormitory access.

Student services: health clinic, personal/psychological counseling, women's center.

FINANCIAL AID
Financial Aid Of all full-time matriculated undergraduates who enrolled in 2016, 15,326 applied for aid, 14,165 were judged to have need, 685 had their need fully met. 182 Federal Work-Study jobs (averaging $4821). In 2016, 427 non-need-based awards were made. ***Average percent of need met:*** 70. ***Average financial aid package:*** $10,923. ***Average need-based loan:*** $4152. ***Average need-based gift aid:*** $10,108. ***Average non-need-based aid:*** $2546. ***Average indebtedness upon graduation:*** $18,221.

APPLYING
Standardized Tests *Required:* SAT or ACT (for admission).

Options: electronic application.

Application fee: $55.

Required: high school transcript, minimum 2.0 GPA.

CONTACT
Mr. Andy Hernandez, Admissions Officer, California State University, Fresno, 5150 North Maple Avenue, Fresno, CA 93740-8026. *Phone:* 559-278-6115. *Fax:* 559-278-4812. *E-mail:* andyhe@csufresno.edu.

California State University, Fullerton

Fullerton, California

http://www.fullerton.edu/

- **State-supported** comprehensive, founded 1957, part of California State University System
- **Suburban** 236-acre campus with easy access to Los Angeles
- **Endowment** $52.6 million
- **Coed** 34,576 undergraduate students, 81% full-time, 56% women, 44% men
- **Moderately difficult** entrance level, 48% of applicants were admitted

UNDERGRAD STUDENTS
27,994 full-time, 6,582 part-time. Students come from 65 other countries; 1% are from out of state; 2% Black or African American, non-Hispanic/Latino; 42% Hispanic/Latino; 21% Asian, non-Hispanic/Latino; 0.2% Native Hawaiian or other Pacific Islander, non-Hispanic/Latino; 0.1% American Indian or Alaska Native, non-Hispanic/Latino; 4% Two or more races, non-Hispanic/Latino; 4% Race/ethnicity unknown; 6% international; 12% transferred in; 6% live on campus.

Freshmen:
Admission: 44,493 applied, 21,459 admitted, 4,426 enrolled.
Average high school GPA: 3.58.
Retention: 89% of full-time freshmen returned.

FACULTY
Total: 2,044, 46% full-time, 53% with terminal degrees.
Student/faculty ratio: 25:1.

ACADEMICS
Calendar: semesters. *Degrees:* bachelor's, master's, doctoral, post-master's, and postbachelor's certificates.

Special study options: academic remediation for entering students, adult/continuing education programs, advanced placement credit, cooperative education, distance learning, double majors, honors programs, independent study, internships, off-campus study, part-time degree program, services for LD students, student-designed majors, study abroad, summer session for credit. ***ROTC:*** Army (b).

Computers: 2,000 computers/terminals are available on campus for general student use. Students can access the following: campus intranet, computer help desk, free student e-mail accounts, online (class) grades, online (class) registration, online (class) schedules. Campuswide network is available. Wireless service is available via entire campus.
Library: Pollak Library.

STUDENT LIFE
Housing options: coed. Campus housing is university owned. Freshman applicants given priority for college housing.

Activities and organizations: drama/theater group, student-run newspaper, radio station, choral group, Pan-Hellenic Council, American Marketing Association, Lacrosse Club, Samaritans (volunteer service club), Human Services Student Association, national fraternities, national sororities.

Athletics Member NCAA. All Division I. ***Intercollegiate sports:*** archery M(c)/W(c), baseball M(s), basketball M(s)/W(s), bowling M(c)/W(c), cross-country running M(s)/W(s), equestrian sports M(c)/W(c), golf M(s)/W(s), ice hockey M(c)/W(c), lacrosse M(c)/W(c), rugby M(c)/W(c), sailing M(c)/W(c), skiing (downhill) M(c)/W(c), soccer M(s)/W(s), softball W(s), tennis W(s), track and field M(s)/W(s), ultimate Frisbee M(c)/W(c), volleyball M(c)/W(s), water polo M(c)/W(c). ***Intramural sports:*** badminton M/W, basketball M/W, bowling M/W, football M/W, racquetball M/W, soccer M/W, softball M/W, volleyball M/W.

Campus security: 24-hour emergency response devices and patrols, student patrols, late-night transport/escort service, controlled dormitory access.

Student services: health clinic, personal/psychological counseling, women's center, legal services.

COSTS & FINANCIAL AID
Costs (2016–17) ***Tuition:*** state resident $5472 full-time, $3174 per year part-time; nonresident $16,632 full-time, $7638 per year part-time. Full-time tuition and fees vary according to course load, degree level, and program. Part-time tuition and fees vary according to course load, degree level, and program. ***Required fees:*** $1088 full-time, $1088 per year part-time. ***Room and board:*** $15,642. Room and board charges vary according to board plan and housing facility. ***Payment plans:*** installment, deferred payment. ***Waivers:*** senior citizens and employees or children of employees.

Financial Aid Of all full-time matriculated undergraduates who enrolled in 2015, 18,107 applied for aid, 16,042 were judged to have need, 12,072 had their need fully met. 387 Federal Work-Study jobs (averaging $1273). In 2015, 97 non-need-based awards were made. ***Average percent of need met:*** 75. ***Average financial aid package:*** $7772. ***Average need-based loan:*** $2208. ***Average need-based gift aid:*** $3897. ***Average non-need-based aid:*** $1683. ***Average indebtedness upon graduation:*** $14,965.

APPLYING
Options: electronic application.

Application fee: $55.

Required: high school transcript, minimum 2.0 GPA.

Application deadlines: 11/30 (freshmen), 11/30 (transfers).

Notification: continuous (freshmen), continuous (transfers).

CONTACT
Ms. Nancy J. Dority, Assistant Vice President of Enrollment Services, California State University, Fullerton, Office of Admissions and Records, PO Box 34080, Fullerton, CA 92834-9480. *Phone:* 657-278-2370. *Fax:* 657-278-2356. *E-mail:* admissions@fullerton.edu.

California State University, Long Beach

Long Beach, California

http://www.csulb.edu/

- **State-supported** comprehensive, founded 1949, part of California State University System
- **Suburban** 320-acre campus with easy access to Los Angeles
- **Endowment** $57.0 million
- **Coed** 32,246 undergraduate students, 84% full-time, 56% women, 44% men
- **Moderately difficult** entrance level, 32% of applicants were admitted

UNDERGRAD STUDENTS

26,942 full-time, 5,304 part-time. Students come from 40 states and territories; 90 other countries; 1% are from out of state; 7% Black or African American, non-Hispanic/Latino; 40% Hispanic/Latino; 22% Asian, non-Hispanic/Latino; 0.2% Native Hawaiian or other Pacific Islander, non-Hispanic/Latino; 0.2% American Indian or Alaska Native, non-Hispanic/Latino; 5% Two or more races, non-Hispanic/Latino; 3% Race/ethnicity unknown; 7% international; 30% live on campus.

Freshmen:

Admission: 60,732 applied, 19,711 admitted. ***Average high school GPA:*** 3.53. ***Test scores:*** SAT critical reading scores over 500: 58%; SAT math scores over 500: 65%; ACT scores over 18: 88%; SAT critical reading scores over 600: 17%; SAT math scores over 600: 24%; ACT scores over 24: 47%; SAT critical reading scores over 700: 2%; SAT math scores over 700: 3%; ACT scores over 30: 6%.

Retention: 91% of full-time freshmen returned.

FACULTY

Total: 2,305, 43% full-time, 58% with terminal degrees.

Student/faculty ratio: 26:1.

ACADEMICS

Calendar: semesters. *Degrees:* bachelor's, master's, doctoral, and postbachelor's certificates.

Special study options: academic remediation for entering students, accelerated degree program, adult/continuing education programs, advanced placement credit, distance learning, double majors, English as a second language, honors programs, independent study, internships, off-campus study, part-time degree program, services for LD students, student-designed majors, study abroad, summer session for credit. ***ROTC:*** Army (b), Air Force (c).

Computers: 2,000 computers/terminals are available on campus for general student use. Students can access the following: campus intranet, computer help desk, free student e-mail accounts, online (class) grades, online (class) registration, online (class) schedules. Campuswide network is available. Wireless service is available via entire campus.

Library: CSULB University Library. *Books:* 746,820 (physical), 764,807 (digital/electronic); *Serial titles:* 16,579 (physical), 69,287 (digital/electronic); *Databases:* 227. Weekly public service hours: 97.

STUDENT LIFE

Housing options: coed.

Activities and organizations: drama/theater group, student-run newspaper, radio and television station, choral group, national fraternities, national sororities.

Athletics Member NCAA. All Division I. ***Intercollegiate sports:*** archery M(c)/W(c), baseball M(s), basketball M(s)/W(s), bowling M(c)/W(c), cheerleading M(c)/W(c), crew M(c)/W(c), cross-country running M(s)/W(s), golf M(s)/W(s), rugby M(c)/W(c), sailing M(c)/W(c), sand volleyball W, skiing (downhill) M(c)/W(c), soccer M/W(s), softball W(s), tennis M/W(s), track and field M(s)/W(s), triathlon M(c)/W(c), ultimate Frisbee M(c)/W(c), volleyball M(s)/W(s), water polo M(s)/W(s), weight lifting M(c)/W(c), wrestling M(c)/W(c). ***Intramural sports:*** basketball M/W, cheerleading M/W, racquetball M/W, sand volleyball W, softball W, tennis W.

Campus security: 24-hour emergency response devices and patrols, student patrols, late-night transport/escort service, controlled dormitory access.

Student services: health clinic, personal/psychological counseling, women's center, legal services.

COSTS & FINANCIAL AID

Costs (2016–17) ***Tuition:*** state resident $5472 full-time, $3174 per year part-time; nonresident $15,144 full-time. Full-time tuition and fees vary according to degree level and program. Part-time tuition and fees vary according to course load, degree level, and program. ***Required fees:*** $988 full-time. ***Room and board:*** $12,398. Room and board charges vary according to board plan. ***Payment plan:*** installment. ***Waivers:*** senior citizens and employees or children of employees.

Financial Aid Of all full-time matriculated undergraduates who enrolled in 2016, 24,042 applied for aid, 21,513 were judged to have need, 9,948 had their need fully met. ***Average percent of need met:*** 80. ***Average financial aid package:*** $13,529. ***Average need-based loan:*** $3877. ***Average need-based gift aid:*** $6517. ***Average indebtedness upon graduation:*** $15,917.

APPLYING

Standardized Tests *Required:* SAT or ACT (for admission).

Options: electronic application.

Application fee: $55.

Required: high school transcript. ***Required for some:*** minimum 2.0 GPA.

Application deadlines: 11/30 (freshmen), 11/30 (transfers).

Notification: continuous (freshmen), continuous (transfers).

CONTACT

Mrs. Janice Miller, Director, Admin Ops and Policy, ES Admissions, California State University, Long Beach, Brotman Hall, 1250 Bellflower Boulevard, Long Beach, CA 90840. *Phone:* 562-985-7827. *E-mail:* janice.miller@csulb.edu.

California State University, Los Angeles

Los Angeles, California

http://www.calstatela.edu/

CONTACT

Vince Lopez, Director of Outreach and Recruitment, California State University, Los Angeles, 5151 State University Drive, Los Angeles, CA 90032-8530. *Phone:* 323-343-3839. *E-mail:* admission@calstatela.edu.

California State University Maritime Academy

Vallejo, California

http://www.csum.edu/

- **State-supported** comprehensive, founded 1929, part of California State University System
- **Suburban** 64-acre campus with easy access to San Francisco
- **Coed** 1,075 undergraduate students, 97% full-time, 15% women, 85% men
- **Moderately difficult** entrance level, 82% of applicants were admitted

UNDERGRAD STUDENTS

1,038 full-time, 37 part-time. 15% are from out of state; 2% Black or African American, non-Hispanic/Latino; 17% Hispanic/Latino; 10% Asian, non-Hispanic/Latino; 0.1% Native Hawaiian or other Pacific Islander, non-Hispanic/Latino; 0.2% American Indian or Alaska Native, non-Hispanic/Latino; 11% Two or more races, non-Hispanic/Latino; 6% Race/ethnicity unknown; 1% international; 9% transferred in; 67% live on campus.

Freshmen:

Admission: 1,206 applied, 983 admitted, 223 enrolled. ***Average high school GPA:*** 3.3. ***Test scores:*** SAT critical reading scores over 500: 72%; SAT math scores over 500: 83%; ACT scores over 18: 96%; SAT critical reading scores over 600: 28%; SAT math scores over 600: 35%; ACT scores over 24: 58%; SAT critical reading scores over 700: 2%; SAT math scores over 700: 2%; ACT scores over 30: 5%.

Retention: 82% of full-time freshmen returned.

FACULTY

Total: 90, 71% full-time, 62% with terminal degrees.

Student/faculty ratio: 15:1.

ACADEMICS
Calendar: semesters. *Degrees:* bachelor's and master's.

Special study options: academic remediation for entering students, advanced placement credit, internships, study abroad, summer session for credit. ***ROTC:*** Navy (c), Air Force (c).

Computers: 75 computers/terminals are available on campus for general student use. Students can access the following: campus intranet, computer help desk, free student e-mail accounts, online (class) grades, online (class) registration, online (class) schedules. Campuswide network is available. 100% of college-owned or -operated housing units are wired for high-speed Internet access. Wireless service is available via entire campus.

STUDENT LIFE
Housing options: on-campus residence required through senior year; coed. Campus housing is university owned. Freshman campus housing is guaranteed.

Activities and organizations: student-run newspaper, choral group, Sailing Club, Dive Club, drill team.

Athletics Member NAIA. ***Intercollegiate sports:*** basketball M(s)/W(s), crew M/W, golf M(s)/W, rugby M, sailing M/W, soccer M(s), volleyball W(s), water polo M/W. ***Intramural sports:*** baseball M, basketball M/W, football M/W, golf M/W, racquetball M/W, rugby M, sailing M/W, softball M/W, tennis M/W, volleyball M/W.

Campus security: 24-hour patrols, student patrols.

Student services: health clinic, personal/psychological counseling.

COSTS & FINANCIAL AID
Costs (2017–18) ***Tuition:*** state resident $5472 full-time; nonresident $11,160 full-time, $372 per credit hour part-time. Full-time tuition and fees vary according to course load and reciprocity agreements. Part-time tuition and fees vary according to course load and reciprocity agreements. ***Required fees:*** $2888 full-time. ***Room and board:*** $12,807. Room and board charges vary according to board plan. ***Payment plan:*** installment. ***Waivers:*** employees or children of employees.

Financial Aid Of all full-time matriculated undergraduates who enrolled in 2016, 575 applied for aid, 526 were judged to have need, 42 had their need fully met. ***Average need-based loan:*** $4588. ***Average need-based gift aid:*** $8575. ***Average indebtedness upon graduation:*** $24,052.

APPLYING
Standardized Tests *Required:* SAT or ACT (for admission).

Options: electronic application.

Application fee: $55.

Required: high school transcript, minimum 2.0 GPA, health form.

Notification: continuous (freshmen), continuous (transfers).

CONTACT
California State University Maritime Academy, 200 Maritime Academy Drive, Vallejo, CA 94590. *Phone:* 707-654-1330. *Toll-free phone:* 800-561-1945.

California State University, Monterey Bay

Seaside, California

http://www.csumb.edu/

- **State-supported** comprehensive, founded 1994, part of California State University System
- **Small-town** 1387-acre campus with easy access to San Jose
- **Coed** 6,657 undergraduate students, 93% full-time, 62% women, 38% men
- **Moderately difficult** entrance level, 49% of applicants were admitted

UNDERGRAD STUDENTS
6,171 full-time, 486 part-time. 2% are from out of state; 7% Black or African American, non-Hispanic/Latino; 36% Hispanic/Latino; 6% Asian, non-Hispanic/Latino; 1% Native Hawaiian or other Pacific Islander, non-Hispanic/Latino; 0.9% American Indian or Alaska Native, non-Hispanic/Latino; 7% Two or more races, non-Hispanic/Latino; 4% Race/ethnicity unknown; 4% international; 12% transferred in; 46% live on campus.

Freshmen:
Admission: 15,561 applied, 7,576 admitted, 1,052 enrolled. ***Average high school GPA:*** 3.32. ***Test scores:*** SAT critical reading scores over 500: 47%; SAT math scores over 500: 45%; SAT writing scores over 500: 41%; ACT scores over 18: 74%; SAT critical reading scores over 600: 11%; SAT math scores over 600: 11%; SAT writing scores over 600: 8%; ACT scores over 24: 24%; SAT critical reading scores over 700: 1%; SAT math scores over 700: 1%; ACT scores over 30: 2%.

Retention: 82% of full-time freshmen returned.

FACULTY
Total: 497, 31% full-time, 48% with terminal degrees.

Student/faculty ratio: 25:1.

ACADEMICS
Calendar: semesters. *Degrees:* bachelor's and master's.

Special study options: academic remediation for entering students, accelerated degree program, advanced placement credit, cooperative education, distance learning, double majors, independent study, internships, off-campus study, part-time degree program, services for LD students, student-designed majors, study abroad, summer session for credit.

Computers: Students can access the following: campus intranet, computer help desk, free student e-mail accounts, online (class) grades, online (class) registration, online (class) schedules. Campuswide network is available. 100% of college-owned or -operated housing units are wired for high-speed Internet access. Wireless service is available via entire campus.

Library: The Tanimura & Antle Family Memorial Library.

STUDENT LIFE
Housing options: on-campus residence required through sophomore year; coed, special housing for students with disabilities. Campus housing is university owned. Freshman applicants given priority for college housing.

Activities and organizations: drama/theater group, student-run newspaper, radio station, choral group, Asian Pacific Islander Association, Black Students United, MEChA, Rugby Sports Club, Psi Chi/Psychology Society, national fraternities, national sororities.

Athletics Member NCAA. All Division II. ***Intercollegiate sports:*** baseball M(s), basketball M(s)/W(s), cross-country running M(s)/W(s), golf M(s)/W(s), sailing M/W, soccer M(s)/W(s), softball W(s), volleyball W(s), water polo W(s). ***Intramural sports:*** basketball M/W, football M, soccer M/W, softball M/W, ultimate Frisbee M/W, volleyball M/W.

Campus security: 24-hour emergency response devices and patrols, student patrols, late-night transport/escort service, controlled dormitory access.

Student services: health clinic, personal/psychological counseling, women's center.

FINANCIAL AID
Financial Aid Of all full-time matriculated undergraduates who enrolled in 2015, 4,840 applied for aid, 4,213 were judged to have need, 510 had their need fully met. In 2015, 39 non-need-based awards were made. ***Average percent of need met:*** 71. ***Average financial aid package:*** $11,069. ***Average need-based loan:*** $4355. ***Average need-based gift aid:*** $9670. ***Average non-need-based aid:*** $2669. ***Average indebtedness upon graduation:*** $20,806. ***Financial aid deadline:*** 6/1.

APPLYING
Standardized Tests *Required:* SAT or ACT (for admission).

Options: electronic application, deferred entrance.

Application fee: $55.

Required: high school transcript, minimum 2.0 GPA.

CONTACT
Mr. John Larsen, Assistant Director of Recruitment, California State University, Monterey Bay, 100 Campus Center, Seaside, CA 93955. *Phone:* 831-582-3738. *Fax:* 831-582-3783. *E-mail:* admissions@csumb.edu.

California State University, Northridge

Northridge, California

http://www.csun.edu/

- **State-supported** comprehensive, founded 1958, part of California State University System
- **Urban** 356-acre campus with easy access to Los Angeles
- **Coed** 35,552 undergraduate students, 81% full-time, 54% women, 46% men
- **Moderately difficult** entrance level, 48% of applicants were admitted

UNDERGRAD STUDENTS

28,969 full-time, 6,583 part-time. 5% Black or African American, non-Hispanic/Latino; 46% Hispanic/Latino; 11% Asian, non-Hispanic/Latino; 0.1% Native Hawaiian or other Pacific Islander, non-Hispanic/Latino; 0.1% American Indian or Alaska Native, non-Hispanic/Latino; 3% Two or more races, non-Hispanic/Latino; 4% Race/ethnicity unknown; 9% international.

Freshmen:

Admission: 32,913 applied, 15,876 admitted, 4,499 enrolled. ***Average high school GPA:*** 3.24. ***Test scores:*** SAT critical reading scores over 500: 29%; SAT math scores over 500: 33%; SAT critical reading scores over 600: 6%; SAT math scores over 600: 8%; SAT critical reading scores over 700: 1%; SAT math scores over 700: 1%.

Retention: 77% of full-time freshmen returned.

FACULTY

Total: 2,125, 42% full-time, 50% with terminal degrees.

Student/faculty ratio: 27:1.

ACADEMICS

Calendar: semesters. *Degrees:* bachelor's, master's, and doctoral.

Special study options: academic remediation for entering students, adult/continuing education programs, advanced placement credit, distance learning, double majors, English as a second language, independent study, internships, off-campus study, part-time degree program, services for LD students, student-designed majors, study abroad, summer session for credit. ***ROTC:*** Army (c), Air Force (c).

Computers: Students can access the following: online (class) registration. Campuswide network is available.

Library: Oviatt Library plus 1 other. Students can reserve study rooms.

STUDENT LIFE

Activities and organizations: drama/theater group, student-run newspaper, radio station, choral group, national fraternities, national sororities.

Athletics Member NCAA. All Division I except football (Division II). ***Intercollegiate sports:*** baseball M(s), basketball M(s)/W(s), cross-country running M(s)/W(s), football M(s), golf M(s), soccer M(s), softball W(s), swimming and diving M(s)/W(s), tennis W(s), track and field M(s)/W(s), volleyball M(s)/W(s). ***Intramural sports:*** baseball M, basketball M/W, bowling M(c)/W(c), cross-country running M/W, football M/W, golf M, ice hockey M(c), racquetball M/W, rugby M(c), sailing M(c)/W(c), skiing (downhill) M(c)/W(c), soccer M/W, softball W, swimming and diving M/W, table tennis M(c)/W(c), tennis W, track and field M/W, volleyball M/W.

Campus security: 24-hour emergency response devices, late-night transport/escort service.

Student services: health clinic, personal/psychological counseling, women's center.

COSTS & FINANCIAL AID

Costs (2016–17) ***Tuition:*** state resident $5472 full-time; nonresident $16,632 full-time, $372 per credit hour part-time. ***Required fees:*** $1115 full-time. ***Room and board:*** $10,272. Room and board charges vary according to board plan and housing facility. ***Payment plan:*** installment. ***Waivers:*** senior citizens and employees or children of employees.

Financial Aid Of all full-time matriculated undergraduates who enrolled in 2016, 24,211 applied for aid, 23,468 were judged to have need. In 2016, 5236 non-need-based awards were made. ***Average financial aid package:*** $18,142. ***Average need-based loan:*** $5893. ***Average need-based gift aid:*** $15,987. ***Average non-need-based aid:*** $1693. ***Average indebtedness upon graduation:*** $16,956.

APPLYING

Standardized Tests *Required:* SAT or ACT (for admission).

Options: electronic application.

Application fee: $55.

Required: high school transcript.

Notification: continuous (freshmen), continuous (transfers).

CONTACT

Juana Maria Valdivia, Director, Student Outreach and Recruitment, California State University, Northridge, Bayramian Hall 19, 18111 Nordhoff Street, Northridge, CA 91330-8212. *Phone:* 818-677-2967. *E-mail:* outreach.recruitment@csun.edu.

California State University, Sacramento

Sacramento, California

http://www.csus.edu/

- **State-supported** comprehensive, founded 1947, part of California State University System
- **Urban** 300-acre campus
- **Coed** 26,648 undergraduate students, 74% full-time, 56% women, 44% men
- **Moderately difficult** entrance level, 100% of applicants were admitted

UNDERGRAD STUDENTS

19,812 full-time, 6,836 part-time. 1% are from out of state; 6% Black or African American, non-Hispanic/Latino; 23% Hispanic/Latino; 21% Asian, non-Hispanic/Latino; 1% Native Hawaiian or other Pacific Islander, non-Hispanic/Latino; 0.8% American Indian or Alaska Native, non-Hispanic/Latino; 6% Two or more races, non-Hispanic/Latino; 5% Race/ethnicity unknown; 2% international; 13% transferred in; 4% live on campus.

Freshmen:

Admission: 3,694 applied, 3,694 admitted, 3,695 enrolled. ***Average high school GPA:*** 3.27. ***Test scores:*** SAT math scores over 500: 41%; SAT writing scores over 500: 34%; ACT scores over 18: 69%; SAT math scores over 600: 10%; SAT writing scores over 600: 7%; ACT scores over 24: 17%; SAT math scores over 700: 1%; SAT writing scores over 700: 1%; ACT scores over 30: 1%.

Retention: 82% of full-time freshmen returned.

FACULTY

Total: 1,491, 44% full-time.

Student/faculty ratio: 26:1.

ACADEMICS

Calendar: semesters. *Degrees:* bachelor's, master's, and doctoral.

Special study options: off-campus study, part-time degree program. ***ROTC:*** Army (c), Air Force (b).

Computers: Students can access the following: computer help desk, free student e-mail accounts, online (class) grades, online (class) registration, online (class) schedules, online transcripts. Campuswide network is available. Wireless service is available via entire campus.

Library: California State University, Sacramento Library.

STUDENT LIFE

Housing options: coed, special housing for students with disabilities. Campus housing is university owned.

Athletics Member NCAA. All Division I except football (Division I-AA). ***Intercollegiate sports:*** baseball M(s), basketball M(s)/W(s), bowling M(c)/W(c), cheerleading M/W, crew M(s)/W(s), cross-country running M(s)/W(s), golf M(s)/W, gymnastics W(s), ice hockey M(c), lacrosse M(c)/W(c), racquetball M(c)/W(c), rugby M(c), skiing (downhill) M(c)/W(c), soccer M(s)/W(s), softball W(s), tennis M(s)/W(s), track and field M(s)/W(s), volleyball M(c)/W(s). ***Intramural sports:*** basketball M/W, crew M/W, football M/W, golf M/W, ice hockey M, skiing (downhill) M/W, soccer M/W, softball M/W, table tennis M/W, tennis M/W, volleyball M/W, water polo M/W, weight lifting M/W.

Campus security: 24-hour emergency response devices and patrols, student patrols, late-night transport/escort service, controlled dormitory access.

COSTS & FINANCIAL AID

Costs (2017–18) ***Tuition:*** state resident $5742 full-time; nonresident $17,622 full-time, $372 per credit hour part-time. ***Required fees:*** $1462 full-time. ***Room and board:*** $11,856; room only: $7226. Room and board charges vary according to board plan and housing facility.

Financial Aid Of all full-time matriculated undergraduates who enrolled in 2015, 18,515 applied for aid, 16,719 were judged to have need, 1,729 had their need fully met. In 2015, 30 non-need-based awards were made. ***Average percent of need met:*** 60. ***Average financial aid package:*** $10,618. ***Average need-based loan:*** $4221. ***Average need-based gift aid:*** $8469. ***Average non-need-based aid:*** $1497. ***Average indebtedness upon graduation:*** $18,985.

APPLYING

Standardized Tests *Required for some:* SAT or ACT (for admission).

Options: electronic application, early decision, early action, deferred entrance.

Application fee: $55.

Required: minimum 2.0 GPA. ***Required for some:*** high school transcript.

CONTACT

Mr. Emiliano Diaz, Director of University Outreach Services, California State University, Sacramento, 6000 J Street, Lassen Hall, Sacramento, CA 95819-6048. *Phone:* 916-278-3901. *Fax:* 916-278-5603. *E-mail:* admissions@csus.edu.

California State University, San Bernardino

San Bernardino, California

http://www.csusb.edu/

- **State-supported** comprehensive, founded 1965, part of California State University System
- **Suburban** 430-acre campus with easy access to Los Angeles
- **Coed** 18,453 undergraduate students, 89% full-time, 60% women, 40% men
- **Moderately difficult** entrance level, 58% of applicants were admitted

UNDERGRAD STUDENTS

16,474 full-time, 1,979 part-time. Students come from 30 states and territories; 79 other countries; 0.4% are from out of state; 6% Black or African American, non-Hispanic/Latino; 63% Hispanic/Latino; 6% Asian, non-Hispanic/Latino; 0.2% Native Hawaiian or other Pacific Islander, non-Hispanic/Latino; 0.2% American Indian or Alaska Native, non-Hispanic/Latino; 3% Two or more races, non-Hispanic/Latino; 4% Race/ethnicity unknown; 7% international; 14% transferred in; 8% live on campus.

Freshmen:

Admission: 15,740 applied, 9,152 admitted, 2,791 enrolled. ***Average high school GPA:*** 3.25. ***Test scores:*** SAT critical reading scores over 500: 21%; SAT math scores over 500: 25%; SAT writing scores over 500: 19%; ACT scores over 18: 49%; SAT critical reading scores over 600: 3%; SAT math scores over 600: 4%; SAT writing scores over 600: 2%; ACT scores over 24: 5%.

Retention: 85% of full-time freshmen returned.

FACULTY

Total: 998, 46% full-time, 47% with terminal degrees.

Student/faculty ratio: 28:1.

ACADEMICS

Calendar: quarters. *Degrees:* certificates, bachelor's, master's, doctoral, and postbachelor's certificates.

Special study options: academic remediation for entering students, accelerated degree program, advanced placement credit, cooperative education, distance learning, double majors, honors programs, independent study, internships, off-campus study, part-time degree program, services for LD students, student-designed majors, study abroad, summer session for credit. ***ROTC:*** Army (b), Air Force (b).

Computers: Students can access the following: computer help desk, free student e-mail accounts, online (class) grades, online (class) registration, online (class) schedules. Campuswide network is available. Wireless service is available via entire campus.

Library: Pfau Library.

STUDENT LIFE

Housing options: coed, women-only, special housing for students with disabilities. Campus housing is university owned and is provided by a third party. Freshman applicants given priority for college housing.

Activities and organizations: drama/theater group, student-run newspaper, radio and television station, choral group, national fraternities, national sororities.

Athletics Member NCAA. All Division II. ***Intercollegiate sports:*** baseball M(s), basketball M(s)/W(s), cross-country running W, golf M(s), soccer M(s)/W(s), softball W(s), track and field W, volleyball W(s).

Campus security: 24-hour emergency response devices and patrols, student patrols, late-night transport/escort service, residence staff on call 24 hours.

Student services: health clinic, personal/psychological counseling, women's center, legal services.

COSTS & FINANCIAL AID

Costs (2017–18) ***Tuition:*** state resident $5472 full-time; nonresident $11,160 full-time, $248 per credit hour part-time. ***Required fees:*** $1129 full-time. ***Room and board:*** $12,966. Room and board charges vary according to board plan and housing facility. ***Payment plan:*** installment. ***Waivers:*** senior citizens and employees or children of employees.

Financial Aid Of all full-time matriculated undergraduates who enrolled in 2016, 14,696 applied for aid, 13,868 were judged to have need, 1,298 had their need fully met. 326 Federal Work-Study jobs (averaging $4073). In 2016, 35 non-need-based awards were made. ***Average percent of need met:*** 64. ***Average financial aid package:*** $9430. ***Average need-based loan:*** $4165. ***Average need-based gift aid:*** $9944. ***Average non-need-based aid:*** $3690. ***Average indebtedness upon graduation:*** $22,452.

APPLYING

Standardized Tests *Recommended:* SAT or ACT (for admission).

Options: electronic application, early admission, early action.

Application fee: $55.

Required: high school transcript, minimum 2.0 GPA.

Application deadlines: rolling (freshmen), rolling (transfers).

Notification: continuous (freshmen), continuous (transfers).

CONTACT

Julie Rogers, Assistant Director of Admissions and Evaluations, California State University, San Bernardino, 5500 University Parkway, University Hall, Room 115, San Bernardino, CA 92407-2397. *Phone:* 909-537-5211. *Fax:* 909-537-7034. *E-mail:* moreinfo@mail.csusb.edu.

California State University, San Marcos

San Marcos, California

http://www.csusm.edu/

- **State-supported** comprehensive, founded 1990, part of California State University System
- **Suburban** 304-acre campus with easy access to San Diego
- **Coed** 12,562 undergraduate students, 83% full-time, 61% women, 39% men
- **Moderately difficult** entrance level, 73% of applicants were admitted

UNDERGRAD STUDENTS

10,466 full-time, 2,096 part-time. 3% Black or African American, non-Hispanic/Latino; 42% Hispanic/Latino; 10% Asian, non-Hispanic/Latino; 0.3% Native Hawaiian or other Pacific Islander, non-Hispanic/Latino; 0.3% American Indian or Alaska Native, non-Hispanic/Latino; 5% Two or more races, non-Hispanic/Latino; 5% Race/ethnicity unknown; 5% international; 17% transferred in; 80% live on campus.

Freshmen:

Admission: 12,872 applied, 9,402 admitted, 2,152 enrolled. ***Average high school GPA:*** 3.31. ***Test scores:*** SAT math scores over 500: 43%; SAT writing scores over 500: 38%; ACT scores over 18: 79%; SAT math scores over 600: 7%; SAT writing scores over 600: 7%; ACT scores over 24: 22%; ACT scores over 30: 1%.

Retention: 81% of full-time freshmen returned.

FACULTY
Total: 802, 33% full-time.
Student/faculty ratio: 26:1.

ACADEMICS
Calendar: semesters. *Degrees:* bachelor's and master's.
Special study options: academic remediation for entering students, adult/continuing education programs, advanced placement credit, distance learning, double majors, English as a second language, independent study, internships, off-campus study, part-time degree program, services for LD students, student-designed majors, study abroad, summer session for credit. ***ROTC:*** Army (b), Navy (c), Air Force (c).
Computers: Students can access the following: computer help desk, free student e-mail accounts, online (class) registration. Campuswide network is available.
Library: Kellogg Library. *Books:* 215,402 (physical), 268,189 (digital/electronic); *Serial titles:* 3,130 (physical), 81,643 (digital/electronic); *Databases:* 100. Weekly public service hours: 100; students can reserve study rooms.

STUDENT LIFE
Housing options: special housing for students with disabilities. Campus housing is provided by a third party.
Activities and organizations: drama/theater group, student-run newspaper, choral group, national fraternities, national sororities.
Athletics Member NCAA. All Division II. ***Intercollegiate sports:*** baseball M, basketball M/W, cross-country running M/W, golf M/W, soccer M/W, softball W, track and field M/W, volleyball W.
Campus security: 24-hour emergency response devices and patrols, student patrols, late-night transport/escort service.
Student services: health clinic, personal/psychological counseling, women's center.

COSTS & FINANCIAL AID
Costs (2016–17) ***Tuition:*** state resident $0 full-time; nonresident $16,292 full-time, $372 per unit part-time. Part-time tuition and fees vary according to course load. ***Required fees:*** $7364 full-time, $2433 per term part-time. ***Room and board:*** $13,240. Room and board charges vary according to housing facility. ***Waivers:*** senior citizens and employees or children of employees.
Financial Aid Of all full-time matriculated undergraduates who enrolled in 2015, 8,037 applied for aid, 7,025 were judged to have need, 636 had their need fully met. In 2015, 14 non-need-based awards were made. ***Average percent of need met:*** 46. ***Average financial aid package:*** $10,677. ***Average need-based loan:*** $4061. ***Average need-based gift aid:*** $8873. ***Average non-need-based aid:*** $1669. ***Average indebtedness upon graduation:*** $22,736.

APPLYING
Standardized Tests *Required:* SAT or ACT (for admission).
Options: electronic application.
Application fee: $65.
Required: high school transcript.
Application deadlines: 11/30 (freshmen), 11/30 (transfers).
Notification: continuous (freshmen), continuous (transfers).

CONTACT
Scott Hagg, Director of Admissions, California State University, San Marcos, 333 South Twin Oaks Valley Road, San Marcos, CA 92096-0001. *Phone:* 760-750-4848. *Fax:* 760-750-3248. *E-mail:* apply@csusm.edu.

California State University, Stanislaus

Turlock, California

http://www.csustan.edu/

- **State-supported** comprehensive, founded 1957, part of California State University System
- **Suburban** 228-acre campus
- **Endowment** $12.1 million
- **Coed** 8,099 undergraduate students, 84% full-time, 64% women, 36% men
- **Moderately difficult** entrance level, 61% of applicants were admitted

UNDERGRAD STUDENTS
6,781 full-time, 1,318 part-time. Students come from 17 states and territories; 17 other countries; 1% are from out of state; 11% transferred in; 8% live on campus.

Freshmen:
Admission: 3,160 applied, 1,943 admitted, 1,270 enrolled. ***Average high school GPA:*** 3.31. ***Test scores:*** SAT critical reading scores over 500: 28%; SAT math scores over 500: 30%; SAT writing scores over 500: 27%; ACT scores over 18: 61%; SAT critical reading scores over 600: 5%; SAT math scores over 600: 6%; SAT writing scores over 600: 4%; ACT scores over 24: 13%; SAT critical reading scores over 700: 1%; ACT scores over 30: 2%.
Retention: 82% of full-time freshmen returned.

FACULTY
Total: 549, 49% full-time, 54% with terminal degrees.
Student/faculty ratio: 20:1.

ACADEMICS
Calendar: semesters. *Degrees:* bachelor's, master's, doctoral, and post-master's certificates.
Special study options: academic remediation for entering students, advanced placement credit, cooperative education, distance learning, double majors, English as a second language, honors programs, independent study, internships, off-campus study, part-time degree program, services for LD students, student-designed majors, study abroad, summer session for credit.
Computers: 200 computers/terminals are available on campus for general student use. Students can access the following: computer help desk, free student e-mail accounts, online (class) grades, online (class) registration, online (class) schedules. Campuswide network is available. 100% of college-owned or -operated housing units are wired for high-speed Internet access. Wireless service is available via entire campus.
Library: Vasche Library. *Books:* 507,271 (physical), 8,555 (digital/electronic); *Serial titles:* 63,246 (physical), 62,246 (digital/electronic); *Databases:* 167. Weekly public service hours: 90.

STUDENT LIFE
Housing options: coed. Campus housing is university owned and leased by the school.
Activities and organizations: drama/theater group, student-run newspaper, radio station, choral group, Alpha Xi Delta, Phi Sigma Sigma, Kappa Sigma, Tau Kappa Epsilon, Theta Chi, national fraternities, national sororities.
Athletics Member NCAA. All Division II. ***Intercollegiate sports:*** baseball M(s), basketball M(s)/W(s), cross-country running M(s)/W(s), golf M(s), soccer M(s)/W(s), softball W(s), tennis W(s), track and field M(s)/W(s), volleyball W(s). ***Intramural sports:*** basketball M/W, cheerleading M(c)/W(c), football M/W, soccer M/W, ultimate Frisbee M/W, volleyball M/W.
Campus security: 24-hour emergency response devices and patrols, student patrols, late-night transport/escort service, controlled dormitory access.
Student services: health clinic, personal/psychological counseling, women's center.

COSTS & FINANCIAL AID
Costs (2016–17) ***Tuition:*** state resident $5472 full-time; nonresident $16,632 full-time. Full-time tuition and fees vary according to reciprocity agreements. Part-time tuition and fees vary according to reciprocity agreements. ***Required fees:*** $1256 full-time. ***Room and board:*** $8567; room only: $6467. Room and board charges vary according to board plan and housing facility. ***Payment plan:*** installment. ***Waivers:*** employees or children of employees.
Financial Aid Of all full-time matriculated undergraduates who enrolled in 2015, 5,709 applied for aid, 5,296 were judged to have need, 1,326 had their need fully met. 193 Federal Work-Study jobs (averaging $3815). In 2015, 41 non-need-based awards were made. ***Average percent of need met:*** 89. ***Average financial aid package:*** $16,098. ***Average need-based loan:*** $4114. ***Average need-based gift aid:*** $9530. ***Average non-need-based aid:*** $1559.

APPLYING
Standardized Tests *Required for some:* SAT or ACT (for admission).

Options: electronic application.

Application fee: $55.

Required for some: high school transcript. ***Recommended:*** minimum 3.3 GPA.

Application deadlines: 11/30 (freshmen), 11/30 (transfers).

Notification: continuous (freshmen), continuous (transfers).

CONTACT

Student Outreach, California State University, Stanislaus, One University Circle, Turlock, CA 95382. *Phone:* 209-667-3070.
Toll-free phone: 800-300-7420. *Fax:* 209-667-3394.
E-mail: outreach_help_desk@csustan.edu.

California University of Management and Sciences

Anaheim, California

http://www.calums.edu/

CONTACT

California University of Management and Sciences, 721 North Euclid Street, Anaheim, CA 92801.

Chapman University

Orange, California

http://www.chapman.edu/

- **Independent** comprehensive, founded 1861, affiliated with Christian Church (Disciples of Christ)
- **Suburban** 78-acre campus with easy access to Los Angeles
- **Endowment** $301.3 million
- **Coed** 6,410 undergraduate students, 96% full-time, 60% women, 40% men
- **Very difficult** entrance level, 54% of applicants were admitted

UNDERGRAD STUDENTS

6,130 full-time, 280 part-time. Students come from 49 states and territories; 56 other countries; 32% are from out of state; 2% Black or African American, non-Hispanic/Latino; 15% Hispanic/Latino; 11% Asian, non-Hispanic/Latino; 0.3% Native Hawaiian or other Pacific Islander, non-Hispanic/Latino; 0.2% American Indian or Alaska Native, non-Hispanic/Latino; 7% Two or more races, non-Hispanic/Latino; 4% Race/ethnicity unknown; 4% international; 6% transferred in; 34% live on campus.

Freshmen:
Admission: 12,821 applied, 6,927 admitted, 1,492 enrolled. ***Average high school GPA:*** 3.71. ***Test scores:*** SAT critical reading scores over 500: 93%; SAT math scores over 500: 94%; SAT writing scores over 500: 94%; ACT scores over 18: 99%; SAT critical reading scores over 600: 53%; SAT math scores over 600: 56%; SAT writing scores over 600: 56%; ACT scores over 24: 84%; SAT critical reading scores over 700: 11%; SAT math scores over 700: 10%; SAT writing scores over 700: 12%; ACT scores over 30: 26%.
Retention: 89% of full-time freshmen returned.

FACULTY

Total: 956, 48% full-time.

Student/faculty ratio: 14:1.

ACADEMICS

Calendar: 4-1-4. *Degrees:* bachelor's, master's, and doctoral.

Special study options: academic remediation for entering students, adult/continuing education programs, advanced placement credit, distance learning, double majors, honors programs, independent study, internships, off-campus study, part-time degree program, services for LD students, student-designed majors, study abroad, summer session for credit. ***ROTC:*** Army (c), Air Force (c).

Unusual degree programs: 3-2 business administration; engineering with University of California, Irvine.

Computers: Students can access the following: campus intranet, computer help desk, free student e-mail accounts, online (class) grades, online (class) registration, online (class) schedules. Campuswide network is available. 100% of college-owned or -operated housing units are wired for high-speed Internet access. Wireless service is available via entire campus.

Library: Leatherby Libraries plus 1 other. *Books:* 334,330 (physical), 16,370 (digital/electronic); *Serial titles:* 326 (physical), 67,937 (digital/electronic); *Databases:* 274. Weekly public service hours: 127; students can reserve study rooms.

STUDENT LIFE

Housing options: coed, special housing for students with disabilities. Campus housing is university owned. Freshman campus housing is guaranteed.

Activities and organizations: drama/theater group, student-run newspaper, radio station, choral group, national fraternities, national sororities.

Athletics Member NCAA. All Division III. ***Intercollegiate sports:*** baseball M, basketball M/W, cheerleading W(c), crew M(c)/W(c), cross-country running M/W, equestrian sports W(c), football M, golf M, ice hockey M(c), lacrosse M(c)/W, soccer M/W, softball W, swimming and diving M/W, tennis M/W, track and field M/W, volleyball M(c)/W, water polo M/W. ***Intramural sports:*** basketball M/W, soccer M/W, ultimate Frisbee M/W, volleyball M/W.

Campus security: 24-hour emergency response devices and patrols, late-night transport/escort service, controlled dormitory access, full safety education program.

Student services: health clinic, personal/psychological counseling.

COSTS & FINANCIAL AID

Costs (2017–18) ***Comprehensive fee:*** $65,504 includes full-time tuition ($50,210), mandatory fees ($384), and room and board ($14,910). Part-time tuition: $1560 per credit hour. Part-time tuition and fees vary according to course load. ***College room only:*** $10,176. Room and board charges vary according to board plan and housing facility. ***Payment plans:*** tuition prepayment, installment, deferred payment. ***Waivers:*** employees or children of employees.

Financial Aid Of all full-time matriculated undergraduates who enrolled in 2015, 3,917 applied for aid, 3,435 were judged to have need, 299 had their need fully met. 2,964 Federal Work-Study jobs (averaging $2700). In 2015, 384 non-need-based awards were made. ***Average percent of need met:*** 66. ***Average financial aid package:*** $30,329. ***Average need-based loan:*** $4568. ***Average need-based gift aid:*** $16,243. ***Average non-need-based aid:*** $16,367. ***Average indebtedness upon graduation:*** $25,959.

APPLYING

Standardized Tests *Required:* SAT or ACT (for admission). *Recommended:* SAT Subject Tests (for admission).

Options: electronic application, early action.

Application fee: $70.

Required: essay or personal statement, high school transcript, 1 letter of recommendation. ***Required for some:*** audition for music, dance, and theatre majors; portfolio for art and film majors; supplemental application for all talent-based majors.

Application deadlines: 1/15 (freshmen), 2/15 (transfers), 11/1 (early action).

Notification: 3/15 (freshmen), 4/15 (transfers), 1/10 (early action).

CONTACT

Ms. Marcela Mejia-Martinez, Director of Undergraduate Admission, Chapman University, One University Drive, Orange, CA 92866.
Phone: 714-997-6711. *Toll-free phone:* 888-CUAPPLY.
Fax: 714-997-6713. *E-mail:* admit@chapman.edu.

Charles R. Drew University of Medicine and Science

Los Angeles, California

http://www.cdrewu.edu/

CONTACT

Ms. Yvette Lane, Associate Director, Student Service, Charles R. Drew University of Medicine and Science, 1731 East 120th Street, Los Angeles, CA 90059. *Phone:* 323-563-4922. *Fax:* 323-563-4923.
E-mail: yvettelane@cdrewu.edu.

Claremont McKenna College

Claremont, California

http://www.claremontmckenna.edu/

- **Independent** comprehensive, founded 1946
- **Suburban** 69-acre campus with easy access to Los Angeles
- **Endowment** $733.9 million
- **Coed** 1,347 undergraduate students, 100% full-time, 49% women, 51% men
- **Most difficult** entrance level, 9% of applicants were admitted

UNDERGRAD STUDENTS

1,346 full-time, 1 part-time. Students come from 46 states and territories; 38 other countries; 56% are from out of state; 5% Black or African American, non-Hispanic/Latino; 14% Hispanic/Latino; 10% Asian, non-Hispanic/Latino; 0.1% Native Hawaiian or other Pacific Islander, non-Hispanic/Latino; 0.1% American Indian or Alaska Native, non-Hispanic/Latino; 6% Two or more races, non-Hispanic/Latino; 6% Race/ethnicity unknown; 17% international; 1% transferred in; 97% live on campus.

Freshmen:

Admission: 6,342 applied, 599 admitted, 321 enrolled. ***Test scores:*** SAT critical reading scores over 500: 100%; SAT math scores over 500: 100%; SAT writing scores over 500: 100%; ACT scores over 18: 100%; SAT critical reading scores over 600: 100%; SAT math scores over 600: 98%; SAT writing scores over 600: 96%; ACT scores over 24: 100%; SAT critical reading scores over 700: 50%; SAT math scores over 700: 53%; SAT writing scores over 700: 61%; ACT scores over 30: 81%.

Retention: 93% of full-time freshmen returned.

FACULTY

Total: 162, 88% full-time, 97% with terminal degrees.

Student/faculty ratio: 9:1.

ACADEMICS

Calendar: semesters. *Degrees:* bachelor's and master's.

Special study options: advanced placement credit, double majors, honors programs, independent study, internships, off-campus study, services for LD students, student-designed majors, study abroad. ***ROTC:*** Army (b), Air Force (c).

Unusual degree programs: 3-2 engineering with Columbia University, Harvey Mudd College.

Computers: 220 computers/terminals are available on campus for general student use. Students can access the following: campus intranet, computer help desk, free student e-mail accounts, online (class) grades, online (class) registration, online (class) schedules. Campuswide network is available. 100% of college-owned or -operated housing units are wired for high-speed Internet access. Wireless service is available via entire campus.

Library: Claremont Colleges Library plus 2 others. *Books:* 986,527 (physical), 884,518 (digital/electronic); *Serial titles:* 16,450 (physical), 70,795 (digital/electronic); *Databases:* 493. Weekly public service hours: 111; students can reserve study rooms.

STUDENT LIFE

Housing options: on-campus residence required for freshman year; coed, special housing for students with disabilities. Campus housing is university owned. Freshman campus housing is guaranteed.

Activities and organizations: drama/theater group, student-run newspaper, radio station, choral group, The Forum - student newspaper, ASCMC - student government, Debate/Forensics Club, SOURCE, Rotaract.

Athletics Member NCAA. All Division III. ***Intercollegiate sports:*** archery M(c)/W(c), baseball M, basketball M/W, cheerleading M(c)/W(c), cross-country running M/W, equestrian sports M(c)/W(c), fencing M(c)/W(c), field hockey M(c)/W(c), football M, golf M/W, lacrosse M(c)/W, rugby M(c)/W(c), sailing M(c)/W(c), skiing (downhill) M(c)/W(c), soccer M/W, softball W, swimming and diving M/W, tennis M/W, track and field M/W, volleyball M(c)/W, water polo M/W. ***Intramural sports:*** basketball M/W, bowling M/W, crew M/W, football M, soccer M/W, squash M/W, table tennis M/W, tennis M/W, ultimate Frisbee M/W, volleyball M/W, water polo M/W, weight lifting M/W.

Campus security: 24-hour emergency response devices and patrols, student patrols, late-night transport/escort service, controlled dormitory access.

Student services: health clinic, personal/psychological counseling.

COSTS & FINANCIAL AID

Costs (2016–17) ***One-time required fee:*** $500. ***Comprehensive fee:*** $66,690 includes full-time tuition ($50,700), mandatory fees ($250), and room and board ($15,740). Part-time tuition: $8450 per course. Part-time tuition and fees vary according to course load. ***College room only:*** $8470. Room and board charges vary according to board plan and housing facility. ***Payment plan:*** installment. ***Waivers:*** employees or children of employees.

Financial Aid Of all full-time matriculated undergraduates who enrolled in 2016, 643 applied for aid, 531 were judged to have need, 531 had their need fully met. In 2016, 78 non-need-based awards were made. ***Average percent of need met:*** 100. ***Average financial aid package:*** $46,129. ***Average need-based loan:*** $4266. ***Average need-based gift aid:*** $42,445. ***Average non-need-based aid:*** $15,744. ***Average indebtedness upon graduation:*** $23,375. ***Financial aid deadline:*** 2/1.

APPLYING

Standardized Tests *Required:* SAT or ACT (for admission). *Required for some:* SAT Subject Tests (for admission), TOEFL or IELTS for students for whom English is not their first language and the primary language of instruction in high school was not English.

Options: electronic application, early decision, deferred entrance.

Application fee: $70.

Required: essay or personal statement, high school transcript, 3 letters of recommendation. ***Required for some:*** interview.

Application deadlines: 1/1 (freshmen), 4/1 (transfers).

Early decision deadline: 11/1 (for plan 1), 1/1 (for plan 2).

Notification: 4/1 (freshmen), 5/15 (transfers), 12/15 (early decision plan 1), 2/15 (early decision plan 2).

CONTACT

Ms. Jennifer Sandoval-Dancs, Director of Admission, Claremont McKenna College, Office of Admission and Financial Aid, 888 Columbia Avenue, Claremont, CA 91711. *Phone:* 909-621-8088. *Fax:* 909-621-8516. *E-mail:* jennifer.sandoval@cmc.edu.

Cogswell Polytechnical College

San Jose, California

http://www.cogswell.edu/

- **Proprietary** comprehensive, founded 1887
- **Suburban** 2-acre campus with easy access to San Francisco, San Jose
- **Coed** 633 undergraduate students, 83% full-time, 27% women, 73% men
- **Moderately difficult** entrance level, 61% of applicants were admitted

UNDERGRAD STUDENTS

528 full-time, 105 part-time. Students come from 13 states and territories; 2 other countries; 11% are from out of state; 4% Black or African American, non-Hispanic/Latino; 18% Hispanic/Latino; 16% Asian, non-Hispanic/Latino; 2% Native Hawaiian or other Pacific Islander, non-Hispanic/Latino; 0.6% American Indian or Alaska Native, non-Hispanic/Latino; 9% Two or more races, non-Hispanic/Latino; 7% Race/ethnicity unknown; 1% international; 6% transferred in; 30% live on campus.

Freshmen:

Admission: 349 applied, 212 admitted, 110 enrolled. ***Average high school GPA:*** 2.99. ***Test scores:*** SAT critical reading scores over 500: 76%; SAT math scores over 500: 82%; SAT writing scores over 500: 68%; ACT scores over 18: 100%; SAT critical reading scores over 600: 26%; SAT math scores over 600: 29%; SAT writing scores over 600: 15%; ACT scores over 24: 29%.

Retention: 78% of full-time freshmen returned.

FACULTY

Total: 91, 19% full-time, 13% with terminal degrees.

Student/faculty ratio: 13:1.

ACADEMICS

Calendar: semesters. *Degrees:* bachelor's and master's.

Special study options: academic remediation for entering students, advanced placement credit, cooperative education, distance learning, double majors, internships, part-time degree program, student-designed majors, summer session for credit.

Computers: 224 computers/terminals are available on campus for general student use. Students can access the following: computer help desk, free student e-mail accounts, online (class) grades, online (class) registration, online (class) schedules. Campuswide network is available. Wireless service is available via entire campus.
Library: Cogswell College Library.

STUDENT LIFE
Housing options: coed. Campus housing is provided by a third party. Freshman campus housing is guaranteed.

Activities and organizations: choral group, ASB, Game Development club, Audio Production and Engineering club, Comic Club, Women's club.

Campus security: 24-hour emergency response devices.

Student services: personal/psychological counseling.

COSTS & FINANCIAL AID
Costs (2016–17) ***Tuition:*** $18,096 full-time, $754 per credit part-time. Full-time tuition and fees vary according to course load, degree level, and program. Part-time tuition and fees vary according to course load, degree level, and program. ***Required fees:*** $1000 full-time. ***Room only:*** $8000. Room and board charges vary according to housing facility. ***Payment plan:*** deferred payment. ***Waivers:*** employees or children of employees.
Financial Aid Of all full-time matriculated undergraduates who enrolled in 2011, 14 Federal Work-Study jobs (averaging $1900).

APPLYING
Standardized Tests *Recommended:* SAT or ACT (for admission).

Options: electronic application, deferred entrance.

Required: essay or personal statement, high school transcript, minimum 2.0 GPA, letters of recommendation. ***Required for some:*** portfolio for digital art and animation, digital audio technology and digital media management majors. ***Recommended:*** minimum 2.7 GPA, interview.

Application deadlines: rolling (freshmen), rolling (out-of-state freshmen), rolling (transfers).

Notification: continuous (freshmen), continuous (out-of-state freshmen), continuous (transfers).

CONTACT
Aaron Kark, Executive Director of Enrollment Services, Cogswell Polytechnical College, 191 Baypointe Parkway, San Jose, CA 95134. *Phone:* 408-498-5156. *Toll-free phone:* 800-264-7955. *Fax:* 408-747-0764. *E-mail:* akark@cogswell.edu.

The Colburn School Conservatory of Music

Los Angeles, California

http://www.colburnschool.edu/

- **Independent** comprehensive, founded 1980
- **Urban** campus with easy access to Los Angeles
- **Coed**
- **Most difficult** entrance level

FACULTY
Student/faculty ratio: 3:1.

ACADEMICS
Calendar: semesters. *Degrees:* certificates, diplomas, bachelor's, master's, and postbachelor's certificates.
Library: Colburn School Library.

STUDENT LIFE
Housing options: on-campus residence required through junior year; coed. Campus housing is university owned. Freshman campus housing is guaranteed.

Campus security: 24-hour emergency response devices and patrols, controlled dormitory access.

Student services: personal/psychological counseling.

COSTS & FINANCIAL AID
Costs (2016–17) ***Comprehensive fee:*** includes mandatory fees ($3000). Full scholarships covering tuition, room and board are awarded to all students enrolled in the Conservatory (to the extent that this amount is not underwritten by outside scholarships).

Financial Aid Of all full-time matriculated undergraduates who enrolled in 2016, 19 applied for aid, 18 were judged to have need. ***Average percent of need met:*** 92. ***Average financial aid package:*** $2667. ***Average need-based gift aid:*** $2667. ***Financial aid deadline:*** 9/1.

APPLYING
Standardized Tests *Recommended:* SAT or ACT (for admission).

Options: electronic application, deferred entrance.

Application fee: $120.

Required: essay or personal statement, high school transcript, 2 letters of recommendation, interview, pre-screening DVD, in-person audition by invitation.

CONTACT
Ms. Jessica Cameron, Manager of Admissions, The Colburn School Conservatory of Music, 200 South Grand Avenue, Los Angeles, CA 90012. *Phone:* 213-621-4534. *Fax:* 213-625-0371. *E-mail:* admissions@colburnschool.edu.

Coleman University

San Diego, California

http://www.coleman.edu/

CONTACT
Admissions Department, Coleman University, 7380 Parkway Drive, La Mesa, CA 91942-1532. *Phone:* 619-465-3990. *Toll-free phone:* 800-430-2030. *E-mail:* jschafer@cts.com.

Columbia College Hollywood

Tarzana, California

http://www.columbiacollege.edu/

CONTACT
Carmen Munoz, Admissions Director, Columbia College Hollywood, 18618 Oxnard Street, Tarzana, CA 91356. *Phone:* 818-345-8414 Ext. 203. *Toll-free phone:* 800-785-0585. *Fax:* 818-345-9053. *E-mail:* admissions@columbiacollege.edu.

Concordia University Irvine

Irvine, California

http://www.cui.edu/

- **Independent** comprehensive, founded 1972, affiliated with Lutheran Church–Missouri Synod, part of The Concordia University System
- **Suburban** 70-acre campus with easy access to Los Angeles
- **Endowment** $26.6 million
- **Coed** 1,925 undergraduate students, 92% full-time, 64% women, 36% men
- **Moderately difficult** entrance level, 65% of applicants were admitted

UNDERGRAD STUDENTS
1,777 full-time, 148 part-time. Students come from 39 states and territories; 26 other countries; 15% are from out of state; 4% Black or African American, non-Hispanic/Latino; 23% Hispanic/Latino; 7% Asian, non-Hispanic/Latino; 0.3% Native Hawaiian or other Pacific Islander, non-Hispanic/Latino; 0.4% American Indian or Alaska Native, non-Hispanic/Latino; 5% Two or more races, non-Hispanic/Latino; 7% Race/ethnicity unknown; 4% international; 8% transferred in; 51% live on campus.

Freshmen:
Admission: 3,839 applied, 2,497 admitted, 407 enrolled. ***Average high school GPA:*** 3.44. ***Test scores:*** SAT critical reading scores over 500: 57%; SAT math scores over 500: 58%; SAT writing scores over 500: 56%; ACT scores over 18: 91%; SAT critical reading scores over 600: 22%; SAT math scores over 600: 21%; SAT writing scores over 600: 17%; ACT scores over 24: 45%; SAT critical reading scores over 700: 5%; SAT math scores over 700: 3%; SAT writing scores over 700: 2%; ACT scores over 30: 7%.

Retention: 78% of full-time freshmen returned.

FACULTY

Total: 425, 21% full-time, 33% with terminal degrees.

Student/faculty ratio: 18:1.

ACADEMICS

Calendar: semesters. *Degrees:* associate, bachelor's, master's, and doctoral (associate's degree for international students only).

Special study options: academic remediation for entering students, accelerated degree program, adult/continuing education programs, advanced placement credit, distance learning, double majors, honors programs, independent study, internships, off-campus study, part-time degree program, services for LD students, study abroad, summer session for credit.

Computers: 64 computers/terminals are available on campus for general student use. Students can access the following: computer help desk, free student e-mail accounts, online (class) grades, online (class) registration, online (class) schedules. Campuswide network is available. 100% of college-owned or -operated housing units are wired for high-speed Internet access. Wireless service is available via entire campus.

Library: Concordia University Library.

STUDENT LIFE

Housing options: coed, women-only, special housing for students with disabilities. Campus housing is university owned. Freshman campus housing is guaranteed.

Activities and organizations: drama/theater group, student-run newspaper, choral group, intramurals, Screaming Eagles, Lacrosse, Abbey West, LEAD Student Activities.

Athletics Member NCAA. All Division II. ***Intercollegiate sports:*** baseball M(s), basketball M(s)/W(s), cross-country running M(s)/W(s), lacrosse M(s)(c)/W(s)(c), soccer M(s)/W(s), softball W(s), swimming and diving M(s)/W(s), tennis M(s)/W(s), track and field M(s)/W(s), volleyball M(s)/W(s), water polo M(s)/W(s). ***Intramural sports:*** basketball M/W, bowling M/W, cheerleading M(c)/W(c), football M/W, soccer M/W, softball M/W, track and field M/W, ultimate Frisbee M/W, volleyball M/W.

Campus security: 24-hour emergency response devices and patrols, student patrols, late-night transport/escort service, lighted walkways, 24-hour dispatch.

Student services: health clinic, personal/psychological counseling.

COSTS & FINANCIAL AID

Costs (2017–18) ***Comprehensive fee:*** $44,860 includes full-time tuition ($33,400), mandatory fees ($700), and room and board ($10,760). Full-time tuition and fees vary according to course load. Part-time tuition: $995 per unit. Part-time tuition and fees vary according to course load. ***College room only:*** $6200. Room and board charges vary according to board plan and housing facility. ***Payment plan:*** installment. ***Waivers:*** employees or children of employees.

Financial Aid Of all full-time matriculated undergraduates who enrolled in 2016, 1,443 applied for aid, 1,266 were judged to have need, 185 had their need fully met. 55 Federal Work-Study jobs (averaging $2320). In 2016, 275 non-need-based awards were made. ***Average percent of need met:*** 62. ***Average financial aid package:*** $21,103. ***Average need-based loan:*** $4513. ***Average need-based gift aid:*** $18,100. ***Average non-need-based aid:*** $10,880. ***Average indebtedness upon graduation:*** $31,747. ***Financial aid deadline:*** 3/2.

APPLYING

Standardized Tests *Required:* SAT or ACT (for admission).

Options: electronic application, early action, deferred entrance.

Application fee: $50.

Required: high school transcript. ***Recommended:*** essay or personal statement, minimum 2.8 GPA, 1 letter of recommendation, interview.

Application deadlines: rolling (freshmen), rolling (transfers), 12/1 (early action).

Notification: continuous (freshmen), continuous (transfers), 12/15 (early action).

CONTACT

Mr. Doug Wible, Director of Undergraduate Admissions, Concordia University Irvine, 1530 Concordia West, Irvine, CA 92612-3299. *Phone:* 800-229-1200. *Toll-free phone:* 800-229-1200. *Fax:* 949-214-3520. *E-mail:* admission@cui.edu.

Design Institute of San Diego

San Diego, California

http://www.disd.edu/

- **Proprietary** 4-year, founded 1977
- **Urban** campus with easy access to San Diego
- **Coed** 143 undergraduate students, 62% full-time, 90% women, 10% men

UNDERGRAD STUDENTS

89 full-time, 54 part-time. Students come from 30 states and territories; 6 other countries; 5% Black or African American, non-Hispanic/Latino; 17% Hispanic/Latino; 11% Asian, non-Hispanic/Latino; 0.7% Native Hawaiian or other Pacific Islander, non-Hispanic/Latino; 0.7% American Indian or Alaska Native, non-Hispanic/Latino; 0.7% Two or more races, non-Hispanic/Latino; 8% international; 61% transferred in.

Freshmen:

Admission: 5 enrolled.

Retention: 71% of full-time freshmen returned.

FACULTY

Total: 27, 19% full-time.

Student/faculty ratio: 9:1.

ACADEMICS

Calendar: semesters. *Degree:* bachelor's.

Special study options: adult/continuing education programs, internships, part-time degree program, services for LD students, student-designed majors, study abroad, summer session for credit.

Computers: 61 computers/terminals are available on campus for general student use. Students can access the following: campus intranet, free student e-mail accounts, computer lab tutors and support from the IT Department. Campuswide network is available. Wireless service is available via classrooms, computer centers, computer labs, libraries.

Library: DISD Library. *Books:* 5,992 (physical); *Serial titles:* 197 (physical).

STUDENT LIFE

Housing options: college housing not available.

Activities and organizations: ASID Student Chapter, IIDA Student Chapter, A Bridge for Kids non-profit organization Community Service Event, Student Mentor Program.

Campus security: security guard patrols during the semester from 5:30 - 10:30 pm Monday - Thursday. No classes on Friday past 5:00 pm.

COSTS

Costs (2017–18) ***Tuition:*** $21,450 full-time, $719 per unit part-time. Full-time tuition and fees vary according to class time, course load, and program. Part-time tuition and fees vary according to class time, course load, and program. ***Required fees:*** $10 full-time, $10 per year part-time. ***Payment plans:*** installment, deferred payment. ***Waivers:*** employees or children of employees.

APPLYING

Required: essay or personal statement, high school transcript, 2 letters of recommendation. ***Required for some:*** official transcripts from all colleges attended. ***Recommended:*** minimum 2.0 GPA, interview.

CONTACT

Mr. Christopher Pfeil, Admissions, Design Institute of San Diego, 8555 Commerce Avenue, San Diego, CA 92121. *Phone:* 858-566-1200 Ext. 1025. *Toll-free phone:* 800-619-4337. *Fax:* 858-566-2711. *E-mail:* admissions@disd.edu.

DeVry University–Folsom Campus

Folsom, California

http://www.devry.edu/

CONTACT

DeVry University–Folsom Campus, 950 Iron Point Road, Folsom, CA 95630. *Toll-free phone:* 866-338-7934.

DeVry University–Fremont Campus

Fremont, California

http://www.devry.edu/

CONTACT
Admissions Office, DeVry University–Fremont Campus, 6600 Dumbarton Circle, Fremont, CA 94555. *Phone:* 510-574-1200. *Toll-free phone:* 866-338-7934.

DeVry University–Long Beach Campus

Long Beach, California

http://www.devry.edu/

CONTACT
Admissions Office, DeVry University–Long Beach Campus, 3880 Kilroy Airport Way, Long Beach, CA 90806. *Phone:* 562-427-0861. *Toll-free phone:* 866-338-7934.

DeVry University–Pomona Campus

Pomona, California

http://www.devry.edu/

- **Proprietary** comprehensive, founded 1983, part of DeVry University
- **Urban** campus
- **Coed**
- **Minimally difficult** entrance level

FACULTY
Student/faculty ratio: 24:1.

ACADEMICS
Calendar: semesters. *Degrees:* associate, bachelor's, master's, and postbachelor's certificates.

STUDENT LIFE
Housing options: college housing not available.

COSTS
Costs (2016–17) ***Tuition:*** $17,052 full-time, $609 per credit hour part-time. ***Required fees:*** $460 full-time.

APPLYING
Options: deferred entrance.

Application fee: $30.

Required: high school transcript, interview.

CONTACT
DeVry University–Pomona Campus, 901 Corporate Center Drive, Pomona, CA 91768. *Phone:* 909-622-8866. *Toll-free phone:* 866-338-7934.

DeVry University–San Diego Campus

San Diego, California

http://www.devry.edu/

CONTACT
Admissions Office, DeVry University–San Diego Campus, 2655 Camino Del Rio North, Suite 350, San Diego, CA 92108-1633. *Phone:* 619-683-2446. *Toll-free phone:* 866-338-7934.

DeVry University–Sherman Oaks Campus

Sherman Oaks, California

http://www.devry.edu/

CONTACT
Admissions Office, DeVry University–Sherman Oaks Campus, 15301 Ventura Boulevard, D-100, Sherman Oaks, CA 91403. *Phone:* 818-713-8111. *Toll-free phone:* 866-338-7934.

Dominican University of California

San Rafael, California

http://www.dominican.edu/

- **Independent** comprehensive, founded 1890, affiliated with Roman Catholic Church
- **Suburban** 85-acre campus with easy access to San Francisco
- **Endowment** $28.3 million
- **Coed** 1,391 undergraduate students, 88% full-time, 73% women, 27% men
- **Moderately difficult** entrance level, 78% of applicants were admitted

UNDERGRAD STUDENTS
1,225 full-time, 166 part-time. Students come from 27 states and territories; 13 other countries; 9% are from out of state; 5% Black or African American, non-Hispanic/Latino; 20% Hispanic/Latino; 23% Asian, non-Hispanic/Latino; 1% Native Hawaiian or other Pacific Islander, non-Hispanic/Latino; 0.7% American Indian or Alaska Native, non-Hispanic/Latino; 7% Two or more races, non-Hispanic/Latino; 8% Race/ethnicity unknown; 1% international; 4% transferred in; 35% live on campus.

Freshmen:
Admission: 2,049 applied, 1,593 admitted, 269 enrolled. ***Average high school GPA:*** 3.5. ***Test scores:*** SAT critical reading scores over 500: 52%; SAT math scores over 500: 59%; SAT writing scores over 500: 54%; ACT scores over 18: 95%; SAT critical reading scores over 600: 17%; SAT math scores over 600: 15%; SAT writing scores over 600: 12%; ACT scores over 24: 40%; SAT critical reading scores over 700: 2%; SAT writing scores over 700: 2%; ACT scores over 30: 4%.

Retention: 87% of full-time freshmen returned.

FACULTY
Total: 325, 31% full-time, 42% with terminal degrees.

Student/faculty ratio: 9:1.

ACADEMICS
Calendar: semesters. *Degrees:* bachelor's and master's.

Special study options: accelerated degree program, adult/continuing education programs, distance learning, double majors, external degree program, honors programs, independent study, internships, off-campus study, part-time degree program, student-designed majors, study abroad.

Unusual degree programs: 3-2 occupational therapy.

Computers: 195 computers/terminals and 700 ports are available on campus for general student use. Students can access the following: computer help desk, free student e-mail accounts, online (class) grades, online (class) registration, online (class) schedules, office software. Campuswide network is available. 100% of college-owned or -operated housing units are wired for high-speed Internet access. Wireless service is available via entire campus.

Library: Archbishop Alemany Library. *Books:* 110,523 (physical); *Databases:* 84.

STUDENT LIFE
Housing options: coed, special housing for students with disabilities. Campus housing is university owned. Freshman applicants given priority for college housing.

Activities and organizations: drama/theater group, student-run newspaper, radio station, choral group, Filipino Cultural Club, BSU, Perceptions, Global Ambassadors, Intramural Club/Programming.

Athletics Member NCAA. All Division II. ***Intercollegiate sports:*** basketball M(s)/W(s), cross-country running M(s)/W(s), golf M(s)/W(s), lacrosse M(s), soccer M(s)/W(s), softball W(s), tennis W(s), volleyball W(s). ***Intramural sports:*** badminton M/W, bowling M/W, cheerleading W, sailing M/W, skiing (downhill) M/W, soccer M/W, softball M/W, table tennis M/W, tennis M/W, ultimate Frisbee M/W, volleyball M/W, weight lifting M/W.

Campus security: 24-hour patrols, late-night transport/escort service, controlled dormitory access.

Student services: health clinic, personal/psychological counseling.

COSTS & FINANCIAL AID
Costs (2017–18) ***Comprehensive fee:*** $58,750 includes full-time tuition ($44,240), mandatory fees ($450), and room and board ($14,060). Full-time tuition and fees vary according to course load. Part-time tuition:

$1850 per credit hour. Part-time tuition and fees vary according to course load. ***Required fees:*** $150 per term part-time. ***College room only:*** $8280. Room and board charges vary according to board plan. ***Payment plan:*** installment. ***Waivers:*** employees or children of employees.

Financial Aid Of all full-time matriculated undergraduates who enrolled in 2015, 973 applied for aid, 901 were judged to have need, 105 had their need fully met. 223 Federal Work-Study jobs (averaging $1516). 12 state and other part-time jobs (averaging $13,380). In 2015, 217 non-need-based awards were made. ***Average percent of need met:*** 66. ***Average financial aid package:*** $27,874. ***Average need-based loan:*** $4692. ***Average need-based gift aid:*** $22,862. ***Average non-need-based aid:*** $14,866. ***Average indebtedness upon graduation:*** $35,369.

APPLYING

Standardized Tests *Required:* SAT or ACT (for admission).

Options: electronic application, deferred entrance.

Required: essay or personal statement, high school transcript, minimum 2.0 GPA, 1 letter of recommendation. ***Recommended:*** interview.

Application deadlines: 2/1 (freshmen), 2/1 (transfers).

Notification: continuous until 10/15 (freshmen), continuous (transfers).

CONTACT

Mr. Rich Toledo, Asst. Vice President, Undergraduate Admissions, Dominican University of California, 50 Acacia Avenue, San Rafael, CA 94901-2298. *Phone:* 415-485-3206. *Toll-free phone:* 888-323-6763. *Fax:* 415-485-3287. *E-mail:* rich.toledo@dominican.edu.

See below for display ad and page 1334 for the College Close-Up.

Epic Bible College

Sacramento, California

http://epic.edu/

CONTACT

Ms. Sheila Knoll, Assistant Director of Records, Epic Bible College, 4330 Auburn Boulevard, Sacramento, CA 95841. *Phone:* 916-348-4689. *E-mail:* kclarke@tlbc.edu.

Feather River College

Quincy, California

http://www.frc.edu/

- **District-supported** primarily 2-year, founded 1968, part of California Community College System
- **Rural** 240-acre campus
- **Endowment** $48,148
- **Coed** 1,663 undergraduate students, 29% full-time, 47% women, 52% men
- **Noncompetitive** entrance level

UNDERGRAD STUDENTS

481 full-time, 1,173 part-time. Students come from 28 states and territories; 6 other countries; 10% are from out of state; 12% Black or African American, non-Hispanic/Latino; 25% Hispanic/Latino; 4% Asian, non-Hispanic/Latino; 1% Native Hawaiian or other Pacific Islander, non-Hispanic/Latino; 3% American Indian or Alaska Native, non-Hispanic/Latino; 6% Race/ethnicity unknown; 1% international; 14% transferred in; 42% live on campus.

Freshmen:

Admission: 528 enrolled.

FACULTY

Total: 105, 24% full-time, 10% with terminal degrees.

Student/faculty ratio: 17:1.

ACADEMICS

Calendar: semesters plus summer and winter terms. *Degrees:* certificates, diplomas, associate, and bachelor's.

Special study options: academic remediation for entering students, adult/continuing education programs, advanced placement credit, cooperative education, distance learning, double majors, English as a second language, independent study, part-time degree program, services for LD students, summer session for credit.

Computers: 111 computers/terminals and 111 ports are available on campus for general student use. Students can access the following: computer help desk, free student e-mail accounts, online (class) grades,

online (class) registration, online (class) schedules. Campuswide network is available. Wireless service is available via entire campus.
Library: Feather River College Library. *Books:* 23,852 (physical), 130,000 (digital/electronic); *Serial titles:* 98 (physical), 28,376 (digital/electronic); *Databases:* 35. Weekly public service hours: 61; students can reserve study rooms.

STUDENT LIFE
Housing options: coed. Campus housing is provided by a third party.
Activities and organizations: drama/theater group, Phi Theta Kappa Honor Society, International Cultural Club, Horse Show Team, Student Environmental Association, Student Alliance for Equity.
Athletics ***Intercollegiate sports:*** baseball M, basketball M/W, cross-country running W, equestrian sports M(s)/W(s), football M, sand volleyball W, soccer M/W, softball W, track and field W, volleyball W.
Campus security: student patrols, part-time private security company patrols.
Student services: health clinic, personal/psychological counseling.

COSTS & FINANCIAL AID
Costs (2016–17) ***Tuition:*** state resident $1380 full-time, $46 per credit part-time; nonresident $7740 full-time, $258 per credit part-time. Full-time tuition and fees vary according to course load. Part-time tuition and fees vary according to course load. ***Required fees:*** $81 full-time, $2 per credit part-time, $18 per term part-time. ***Room only:*** $5350. Room and board charges vary according to housing facility. ***Payment plan:*** installment.
Financial Aid Of all full-time matriculated undergraduates who enrolled in 2015, 22 Federal Work-Study jobs (averaging $750). 103 state and other part-time jobs (averaging $1504).

APPLYING
Standardized Tests *Recommended:* ACCUPLACER.
Options: electronic application.

CONTACT
Mrs. Leslie Mikesell, Director of Admissions and Records, Feather River College, 570 Golden Eagle Avenue, Quincy, CA 95971. *Phone:* 530-283-0202 Ext. 285. *Toll-free phone:* 800-442-9799. *E-mail:* info@frc.edu.

★ FIDM/Fashion Institute of Design & Merchandising, Los Angeles Campus

Los Angeles, California
http://www.fidm.edu/

- **Proprietary** 4-year, founded 1969, part of FIDM/Fashion Institute of Design & Merchandising
- **Urban** campus with easy access to Los Angeles
- **Coed** 2,715 undergraduate students, 87% full-time, 89% women, 11% men
- **Moderately difficult** entrance level, 41% of applicants were admitted

UNDERGRAD STUDENTS
2,349 full-time, 366 part-time. Students come from 49 states and territories; 58 other countries; 48% are from out of state; 7% Black or African American, non-Hispanic/Latino; 22% Hispanic/Latino; 6% Asian, non-Hispanic/Latino; 1% Native Hawaiian or other Pacific Islander, non-Hispanic/Latino; 0.8% American Indian or Alaska Native, non-Hispanic/Latino; 5% Two or more races, non-Hispanic/Latino; 7% Race/ethnicity unknown; 14% international; 9% transferred in.

Freshmen:
Admission: 1,503 applied, 623 admitted, 398 enrolled. ***Average high school GPA:*** 2.9.
Retention: 93% of full-time freshmen returned.

FACULTY
Total: 314, 34% full-time.
Student/faculty ratio: 14:1.

ACADEMICS
Calendar: quarters. *Degrees:* associate and bachelor's (also includes Orange County Campus).
Special study options: academic remediation for entering students, accelerated degree program, adult/continuing education programs, advanced placement credit, cooperative education, distance learning, English as a second language, independent study, internships, off-campus study, part-time degree program, services for LD students, study abroad, summer session for credit.
Computers: 433 computers/terminals and 20 ports are available on campus for general student use. Students can access the following: campus intranet, computer help desk, free student e-mail accounts, online (class) grades, online (class) registration, online (class) schedules. Campuswide network is available. Wireless service is available via computer centers, computer labs, learning centers, libraries, student centers.
Library: FIDM Los Angeles Campus Library. *Books:* 48,534 (physical), 2,778 (digital/electronic); *Serial titles:* 548 (physical); *Databases:* 39. Students can reserve study rooms.

STUDENT LIFE
Housing options: college housing not available.
Activities and organizations: Cross-Cultural Student Alliance, Fashion Industry Club, Phi Theta Kappa Honor Society, Student Council, FIDM MODE Magazine.
Campus security: 24-hour emergency response devices and patrols, late-night transport/escort service.
Student services: personal/psychological counseling.

COSTS & FINANCIAL AID
Costs (2017–18) ***Tuition:*** $30,575 full-time. Full-time tuition and fees vary according to course load and program. Part-time tuition and fees vary according to course load and program. ***Required fees:*** $1185 full-time. ***Payment plan:*** installment. ***Waivers:*** employees or children of employees.
Financial Aid Of all full-time matriculated undergraduates who enrolled in 2015, 88 Federal Work-Study jobs (averaging $2935).

APPLYING
Standardized Tests *Recommended:* SAT and SAT Subject Tests or ACT (for admission).
Options: electronic application, deferred entrance.
Application fee: $225.
Required: essay or personal statement, high school transcript, minimum 2.5 GPA, 3 letters of recommendation, interview, major-determined project.
Application deadlines: rolling (freshmen), rolling (transfers).

CONTACT
Ms. Susan Aronson, Executive Director of Admissions, FIDM/Fashion Institute of Design & Merchandising, Los Angeles Campus, 919 South Grand Avenue, Los Angeles, CA 90015. *Phone:* 213-624-1200 Ext. 5400. *Toll-free phone:* 800-624-1200. *E-mail:* saronson@fidm.edu.

FIDM/Fashion Institute of Design & Merchandising, San Francisco Campus

San Francisco, California
http://www.fidm.edu/

- **Proprietary** 4-year, founded 1973, part of FIDM/Fashion Institute of Design & Merchandising
- **Urban** campus with easy access to San Francisco
- **Coed** 332 undergraduate students, 86% full-time, 91% women, 9% men
- **Moderately difficult** entrance level, 36% of applicants were admitted

UNDERGRAD STUDENTS
285 full-time, 47 part-time. Students come from 15 states and territories; 13 other countries; 6% are from out of state; 5% Black or African American, non-Hispanic/Latino; 23% Hispanic/Latino; 18% Asian, non-Hispanic/Latino; 3% Native Hawaiian or other Pacific Islander, non-Hispanic/Latino; 1% American Indian or Alaska Native, non-Hispanic/Latino; 3% Two or more races, non-Hispanic/Latino; 5% Race/ethnicity unknown; 7% international; 17% transferred in.

Freshmen:
Admission: 201 applied, 73 admitted, 52 enrolled. ***Average high school GPA:*** 2.9.
Retention: 96% of full-time freshmen returned.

FACULTY
Total: 51, 14% full-time.
Student/faculty ratio: 14:1.

ACADEMICS
Calendar: quarters. *Degrees:* associate and bachelor's.
Special study options: academic remediation for entering students, accelerated degree program, adult/continuing education programs, advanced placement credit, cooperative education, distance learning, English as a second language, honors programs, independent study, internships, off-campus study, part-time degree program, services for LD students, study abroad, summer session for credit.
Computers: 135 computers/terminals are available on campus for general student use. Students can access the following: campus intranet, computer help desk, free student e-mail accounts, online (class) grades, online (class) registration, online (class) schedules. Campuswide network is available. Wireless service is available via classrooms, computer centers, computer labs, libraries, student centers.
Library: FIDM San Francisco Library. Students can reserve study rooms.

STUDENT LIFE
Housing options: college housing not available.
Activities and organizations: Cross-Cultural Student Alliance, Fashion Industry Club, Phi Theta Kappa- National Honor Society, Student Council, FIDM MODE Magazine.
Campus security: 24-hour emergency response devices and patrols, security escorts.
Student services: personal/psychological counseling.

COSTS
Costs (2017–18) ***Tuition:*** $30,575 full-time, $680 per credit hour part-time. Full-time tuition and fees vary according to program. Part-time tuition and fees vary according to program. ***Required fees:*** $1185 full-time. ***Payment plan:*** installment. ***Waivers:*** employees or children of employees.

APPLYING
Standardized Tests *Recommended:* SAT or ACT (for admission).
Options: electronic application, deferred entrance.
Application fee: $225.
Required: essay or personal statement, high school transcript, minimum 2.5 GPA, 3 letters of recommendation, interview, major-determined project.
Application deadlines: rolling (freshmen), rolling (transfers).

CONTACT
Ms. Sheryl Badalamenti, Director of Admissions, FIDM/Fashion Institute of Design & Merchandising, San Francisco Campus, 55 Stockton Street, San Francisco, CA 94108-5829. *Phone:* 415-433-6691 Ext. 1550. *Toll-free phone:* 800-422-3436. *E-mail:* sbadalamenti@fidm.edu.

Fremont College
Cerritos, California
http://www.fremont.edu/

CONTACT
Natasha Dawson, Director of Admissions, Fremont College, 18000 Studebaker Road, Suite 900A, Cerritos, CA 90703. *Phone:* 562-809-5100. *Toll-free phone:* 800-373-6668. *Fax:* 562-809-5100. *E-mail:* info@fremont.edu.

Fresno Pacific University
Fresno, California
http://www.fresno.edu/

- **Independent** comprehensive, founded 1944, affiliated with Mennonite Brethren Church
- **Suburban** 50-acre campus with easy access to Fresno
- **Coed** 2,439 undergraduate students, 85% full-time, 71% women, 29% men
- **Moderately difficult** entrance level, 68% of applicants were admitted

UNDERGRAD STUDENTS
2,077 full-time, 362 part-time. 3% are from out of state; 8% Black or African American, non-Hispanic/Latino; 28% Hispanic/Latino; 7% Asian, non-Hispanic/Latino; 0.9% Native Hawaiian or other Pacific Islander, non-Hispanic/Latino; 2% American Indian or Alaska Native, non-Hispanic/Latino; 1% Two or more races, non-Hispanic/Latino; 6% Race/ethnicity unknown; 0.8% international; 21% transferred in; 45% live on campus.

Freshmen:
Admission: 644 applied, 441 admitted, 201 enrolled. ***Average high school GPA:*** 3.54. ***Test scores:*** SAT critical reading scores over 500: 40%; SAT math scores over 500: 40%; SAT writing scores over 500: 26%; ACT scores over 18: 81%; SAT critical reading scores over 600: 8%; SAT math scores over 600: 4%; SAT writing scores over 600: 1%; ACT scores over 24: 25%; SAT critical reading scores over 700: 1%; ACT scores over 30: 5%.
Retention: 83% of full-time freshmen returned.

FACULTY
Total: 479, 17% full-time, 33% with terminal degrees.
Student/faculty ratio: 13:1.

ACADEMICS
Calendar: semesters. *Degrees:* certificates, associate, bachelor's, master's, and postbachelor's certificates.
Special study options: accelerated degree program, adult/continuing education programs, advanced placement credit, cooperative education, distance learning, double majors, English as a second language, honors programs, independent study, internships, off-campus study, part-time degree program, services for LD students, student-designed majors, study abroad, summer session for credit.
Computers: Students can access the following: campus intranet, computer help desk, free student e-mail accounts, online (class) grades, online (class) registration, online (class) schedules. Campuswide network is available. Wireless service is available via entire campus.
Library: Hiebert Library.

STUDENT LIFE
Housing options: on-campus residence required through junior year; men-only, women-only, special housing for students with disabilities. Campus housing is university owned and leased by the school. Freshman campus housing is guaranteed.
Activities and organizations: drama/theater group, student-run newspaper, choral group.
Athletics Member NCAA. All Division II. ***Intercollegiate sports:*** baseball M(s), basketball M(s)/W(s), cheerleading W(c), cross-country running M(s)/W(s), soccer M(s)/W(s), swimming and diving M(s)/W(s), track and field M(s)/W(s), volleyball M(c)/W(s), water polo M(s)/W(s). ***Intramural sports:*** basketball M/W, bowling M/W, football M/W, soccer M/W, ultimate Frisbee M/W, volleyball M/W.
Campus security: 24-hour emergency response devices and patrols, student patrols, late-night transport/escort service, controlled dormitory access, 24-hour monitored closed-circuit security cameras.
Student services: health clinic, personal/psychological counseling.

FINANCIAL AID
Financial Aid Of all full-time matriculated undergraduates who enrolled in 2016, 1,892 applied for aid, 1,784 were judged to have need, 146 had their need fully met. In 2016, 178 non-need-based awards were made. ***Average percent of need met:*** 50. ***Average financial aid package:*** $21,383. ***Average need-based loan:*** $8159. ***Average need-based gift aid:*** $8362. ***Average non-need-based aid:*** $10,883.

APPLYING
Standardized Tests *Required:* SAT or ACT (for admission).
Options: electronic application, early admission, deferred entrance.
Application fee: $40.
Required: essay or personal statement, high school transcript, 1 letter of recommendation. ***Required for some:*** interview. ***Recommended:*** minimum 3.1 GPA.

CONTACT
Andy Johnson, Director of Undergraduate Admissions, Fresno Pacific University, 1717 South Chestnut Avenue, Fresno, CA 93727. *Phone:* 559-453-2000. *Toll-free phone:* 800-660-6089. *Fax:* 559-453-2007. *E-mail:* andy.johnson@fresno.edu.

Golden Gate University
San Francisco, California
http://www.ggu.edu/

- **Independent** university, founded 1901
- **Urban** campus with easy access to San Francisco Bay Area
- **Endowment** $29.8 million
- **Coed**
- **Moderately difficult** entrance level

FACULTY
Student/faculty ratio: 16:1.

ACADEMICS
Calendar: trimesters. *Degrees:* certificates, associate, bachelor's, master's, doctoral, and postbachelor's certificates.
Library: Golden Gate University Library plus 1 other.

STUDENT LIFE
Housing options: college housing not available.
Activities and organizations: student-run newspaper, American Marketing Association, Korean Student Association, Japanese Student Association, Thai Student Association, Computing Society.
Campus security: late-night transport/escort service.
Student services: personal/psychological counseling.

COSTS & FINANCIAL AID
Costs (2016–17) ***Tuition:*** $15,120 full-time. Full-time tuition and fees vary according to course load, degree level, and program. Part-time tuition and fees vary according to course load and program. ***Payment plans:*** installment, deferred payment.
Financial Aid Of all full-time matriculated undergraduates who enrolled in 2013, 299 applied for aid, 239 were judged to have need, 49 had their need fully met. 18 Federal Work-Study jobs (averaging $5000). In 2013, 49 non-need-based awards were made. ***Average percent of need met:*** 20. ***Average financial aid package:*** $10,350. ***Average need-based loan:*** $5500. ***Average need-based gift aid:*** $3750. ***Average non-need-based aid:*** $3750.

APPLYING
Options: electronic application, deferred entrance.
Application fee: $55.
Required: high school transcript, minimum 2.0 GPA. ***Required for some:*** minimum 3.2 GPA, interview. ***Recommended:*** essay or personal statement, minimum 3.0 GPA.

CONTACT
Mr. Louis D. Riccardi Jr., Director of Enrollment Services, Golden Gate University, 536 Mission Street, San Francisco, CA 94105-2968. *Phone:* 415-442-7800. *Toll-free phone:* 800-448-3381. *Fax:* 415-442-7807. *E-mail:* info@ggu.edu.

Grace Mission University
Fullerton, California
http://www.gm.edu/

CONTACT
Grace Mission University, 1645 West Valencia Drive, Fullerton, CA 92833.

Gurnick Academy of Medical Arts
San Mateo, California
http://www.gurnick.edu/

CONTACT
Gurnick Academy of Medical Arts, 2121 South El Camino Real, Building C 2000, San Mateo, CA 94403.

Harvey Mudd College
Claremont, California
http://www.hmc.edu/

- **Independent** 4-year, founded 1955, part of The Claremont Colleges Consortium
- **Suburban** 33-acre campus with easy access to Los Angeles
- **Endowment** $277.0 million
- **Coed** 829 undergraduate students, 100% full-time, 46% women, 54% men
- **Most difficult** entrance level, 13% of applicants were admitted

UNDERGRAD STUDENTS
829 full-time. Students come from 43 states and territories; 27 other countries; 56% are from out of state; 3% Black or African American, non-Hispanic/Latino; 16% Hispanic/Latino; 19% Asian, non-Hispanic/Latino; 0.4% Native Hawaiian or other Pacific Islander, non-Hispanic/Latino; 0.4% American Indian or Alaska Native, non-Hispanic/Latino; 10% Two or more races, non-Hispanic/Latino; 5% Race/ethnicity unknown; 11% international; 0.2% transferred in; 99% live on campus.

Freshmen:
Admission: 4,180 applied, 538 admitted, 214 enrolled. ***Test scores:*** SAT critical reading scores over 500: 100%; SAT math scores over 500: 100%; SAT writing scores over 500: 100%; ACT scores over 18: 100%; SAT critical reading scores over 600: 98%; SAT math scores over 600: 100%; SAT writing scores over 600: 93%; ACT scores over 24: 100%; SAT critical reading scores over 700: 71%; SAT math scores over 700: 90%; SAT writing scores over 700: 63%; ACT scores over 30: 97%.
Retention: 98% of full-time freshmen returned.

FACULTY
Total: 103, 96% full-time, 100% with terminal degrees.
Student/faculty ratio: 8:1.

ACADEMICS
Calendar: semesters. *Degree:* bachelor's.
Special study options: double majors, internships, off-campus study, services for LD students, student-designed majors, study abroad. ***ROTC:*** Army (c), Air Force (b).
Unusual degree programs: 3-2 engineering; economics/engineering with Claremont McKenna College, Scripps College.
Computers: Students can access the following: campus intranet, computer help desk, free student e-mail accounts, online (class) grades, online (class) registration, online (class) schedules. Campuswide network is available. 100% of college-owned or -operated housing units are wired for high-speed Internet access. Wireless service is available via entire campus.
Library: Claremont Colleges Library plus 1 other.

STUDENT LIFE
Housing options: on-campus residence required for freshman year; coed. Campus housing is university owned. Freshman campus housing is guaranteed.
Activities and organizations: drama/theater group, student-run newspaper, radio station, choral group, Claremont Colleges Ballroom Dance Company, Science Bus, Society of Women Engineers (SWE), Intervarsity Christian Fellowship, Gonzo Unicycle Madness (Unicycle Club).
Athletics Member NCAA. All Division III. ***Intercollegiate sports:*** baseball M, basketball M/W, cross-country running M/W, football M, golf M/W, lacrosse W, soccer M/W, softball W, swimming and diving M/W, tennis M/W, track and field M/W, volleyball W, water polo M/W. ***Intramural sports:*** basketball M/W, bowling M/W, equestrian sports M(c)/W(c), fencing M(c)/W(c), field hockey M(c)/W(c), football M/W, lacrosse M(c), rugby M(c)/W(c), soccer M/W(c), table tennis M/W, tennis M(c)/W(c), ultimate Frisbee M(c)/W(c), volleyball M(c)/W(c), water polo M/W.

Campus security: 24-hour emergency response devices and patrols, late-night transport/escort service, controlled dormitory access.

Student services: health clinic, personal/psychological counseling, women's center.

COSTS & FINANCIAL AID

Costs (2016–17) ***One-time required fee:*** $250. ***Comprehensive fee:*** $69,717 includes full-time tuition ($52,383), mandatory fees ($283), and room and board ($17,051). Part-time tuition: $1637 per unit. Part-time tuition and fees vary according to course load. ***College room only:*** $9209. Room and board charges vary according to board plan. ***Payment plan:*** installment. ***Waivers:*** employees or children of employees.

Financial Aid Of all full-time matriculated undergraduates who enrolled in 2015, 478 applied for aid, 414 were judged to have need, 414 had their need fully met. 133 Federal Work-Study jobs (averaging $652). 25 state and other part-time jobs (averaging $7678). In 2015, 170 non-need-based awards were made. ***Average percent of need met:*** 100. ***Average financial aid package:*** $42,799. ***Average need-based loan:*** $5259. ***Average need-based gift aid:*** $39,799. ***Average non-need-based aid:*** $11,822. ***Average indebtedness upon graduation:*** $25,412. ***Financial aid deadline:*** 2/1.

APPLYING

Standardized Tests *Required:* SAT or ACT (for admission), SAT Subject Tests (for admission).

Options: electronic application, early admission, early decision, deferred entrance.

Application fee: $70.

Required: essay or personal statement, high school transcript, 3 letters of recommendation. ***Recommended:*** interview.

Application deadlines: 1/5 (freshmen), 4/1 (transfers).

Early decision deadline: 11/15 (for plan 1), 1/5 (for plan 2).

Notification: 4/1 (freshmen), 5/15 (transfers), 12/15 (early decision plan 1), 2/15 (early decision plan 2).

CONTACT

Peter Osgood, Director of Admission, Harvey Mudd College, 301 Platt Boulevard, Claremont, CA 91711. *Phone:* 909-621-8011. *Fax:* 909-607-7046. *E-mail:* posgood@hmc.edu.

Henley-Putnam University
San Jose, California
http://www.henley-putnam.edu/

CONTACT

Henley-Putnam University, 2107 N. First Street, Suite 210, San Jose, CA 95131. *Phone:* 408-453-9900 Ext. 9928. *Toll-free phone:* 888-852-8746.

Holy Names University
Oakland, California
http://www.hnu.edu/

- **Independent Roman Catholic** comprehensive, founded 1868
- **Urban** 60-acre campus with easy access to San Francisco
- **Coed** 526 undergraduate students, 87% full-time, 65% women, 35% men
- **Moderately difficult** entrance level, 49% of applicants were admitted

UNDERGRAD STUDENTS

455 full-time, 71 part-time. Students come from 11 states and territories; 15 other countries; 7% are from out of state; 21% Black or African American, non-Hispanic/Latino; 42% Hispanic/Latino; 10% Asian, non-Hispanic/Latino; 2% Native Hawaiian or other Pacific Islander, non-Hispanic/Latino; 0.4% American Indian or Alaska Native, non-Hispanic/Latino; 2% Two or more races, non-Hispanic/Latino; 2% Race/ethnicity unknown; 4% international; 9% transferred in; 51% live on campus.

Freshmen:

Admission: 972 applied, 472 admitted, 130 enrolled. ***Average high school GPA:*** 3.23. ***Test scores:*** SAT critical reading scores over 500: 21%; SAT math scores over 500: 27%; SAT writing scores over 500: 19%; ACT scores over 18: 54%; SAT critical reading scores over 600: 2%; SAT math scores over 600: 2%; ACT scores over 24: 8%; SAT math scores over 700: 1%.

Retention: 75% of full-time freshmen returned.

FACULTY

Total: 152, 28% full-time.

Student/faculty ratio: 13:1.

ACADEMICS
Calendar: semesters. *Degrees:* certificates, bachelor's, master's, post-master's, and postbachelor's certificates.

Special study options: academic remediation for entering students, accelerated degree program, adult/continuing education programs, advanced placement credit, distance learning, double majors, English as a second language, honors programs, independent study, internships, part-time degree program, services for LD students, student-designed majors, study abroad, summer session for credit. ***ROTC:*** Army (c), Air Force (c).

Unusual degree programs: 3-2 business administration.

Computers: 92 computers/terminals are available on campus for general student use. Students can access the following: computer help desk, free student e-mail accounts, online (class) grades, online (class) registration, online (class) schedules. Campuswide network is available. 100% of college-owned or -operated housing units are wired for high-speed Internet access. Wireless service is available via entire campus.

Library: Cushing Library. *Books:* 41,811 (physical), 137,046 (digital/electronic); *Databases:* 49. Students can reserve study rooms.

STUDENT LIFE
Housing options: coed. Campus housing is university owned. Freshman campus housing is guaranteed.

Activities and organizations: drama/theater group, choral group, Drama Club, Latinos Unidos, Black Student Union, Biology Club, Hiking Club.

Athletics Member NCAA. All Division II. ***Intercollegiate sports:*** baseball M(s), basketball M(s)/W(s), cross-country running M(s)/W(s), golf M(s)/W(s), soccer M(s)/W(s), softball W(s), tennis M(s)/W(s), volleyball M(s)/W(s).

Campus security: 24-hour emergency response devices, late-night transport/escort service, controlled dormitory access, 24-hour security main gate.

Student services: personal/psychological counseling.

COSTS & FINANCIAL AID
Costs (2017–18) ***Comprehensive fee:*** $50,996 includes full-time tuition ($37,672), mandatory fees ($516), and room and board ($12,808). Full-time tuition and fees vary according to course level, course load, degree level, program, and reciprocity agreements. Part-time tuition: $1292 per unit. Part-time tuition and fees vary according to course level, course load, degree level, program, and reciprocity agreements. ***Required fees:*** $258 per term part-time. ***College room only:*** $6614. Room and board charges vary according to board plan and housing facility. ***Payment plan:*** installment. ***Waivers:*** employees or children of employees.

Financial Aid Of all full-time matriculated undergraduates who enrolled in 2006, 373 applied for aid, 247 were judged to have need, 58 had their need fully met. 50 Federal Work-Study jobs (averaging $1699). 53 state and other part-time jobs (averaging $1750). In 2006, 77 non-need-based awards were made. ***Average percent of need met:*** 43. ***Average financial aid package:*** $15,554. ***Average need-based loan:*** $4154. ***Average need-based gift aid:*** $13,258. ***Average non-need-based aid:*** $10,557. ***Average indebtedness upon graduation:*** $10,500. ***Financial aid deadline:*** 6/30.

APPLYING
Standardized Tests *Required:* SAT or ACT (for admission).

Options: electronic application, deferred entrance.

Application fee: $20.

Required: essay or personal statement, high school transcript, 1 letter of recommendation, minimum 1 recommendation. ***Required for some:*** interview.

Application deadlines: rolling (freshmen), rolling (transfers).

Notification: continuous (freshmen), continuous (transfers).

CONTACT
Holy Names University, 3500 Mountain Boulevard, Oakland, CA 94619. *Phone:* 510-436-1351. *Toll-free phone:* 800-430-1321. *Fax:* 510-436-1325. *E-mail:* admissions@hnu.edu.

See previous page for display ad and page 1380 for the College Close-Up.

Hope International University
Fullerton, California
http://www.hiu.edu/

- **Independent** comprehensive, founded 1928, affiliated with Christian Churches and Churches of Christ
- **Suburban** 16-acre campus with easy access to Los Angeles
- **Coed** 875 undergraduate students, 72% full-time, 54% women, 46% men
- **Moderately difficult** entrance level, 34% of applicants were admitted

UNDERGRAD STUDENTS
634 full-time, 241 part-time. 7% Black or African American, non-Hispanic/Latino; 21% Hispanic/Latino; 3% Asian, non-Hispanic/Latino; 0.7% Native Hawaiian or other Pacific Islander, non-Hispanic/Latino; 0.6% American Indian or Alaska Native, non-Hispanic/Latino; 11% Two or more races, non-Hispanic/Latino; 15% Race/ethnicity unknown; 0.4% international; 13% transferred in; 42% live on campus.

Freshmen:

Admission: 1,051 applied, 360 admitted, 121 enrolled. ***Average high school GPA:*** 3.11. ***Test scores:*** SAT critical reading scores over 500: 28%; SAT math scores over 500: 39%; SAT writing scores over 500: 29%; ACT scores over 18: 63%; SAT critical reading scores over 600: 4%; SAT math scores over 600: 2%; SAT writing scores over 600: 3%; ACT scores over 24: 16%; SAT math scores over 700: 1%.

Retention: 78% of full-time freshmen returned.

FACULTY
Total: 252, 17% full-time, 35% with terminal degrees.

Student/faculty ratio: 9:1.

ACADEMICS
Calendar: 4-1-4. *Degrees:* certificates, associate, bachelor's, master's, and post-master's certificates.

Special study options: academic remediation for entering students, adult/continuing education programs, advanced placement credit, distance learning, double majors, English as a second language, independent study, internships, off-campus study, part-time degree program, services for LD students, study abroad. ***ROTC:*** Army (c).

Computers: Students can access the following: computer help desk, free student e-mail accounts, online (class) grades, online (class) registration, online (class) schedules, 30 Internet hotspots on campus. Campuswide network is available. 100% of college-owned or -operated housing units are wired for high-speed Internet access. Wireless service is available via entire campus.

Library: Darling Library.

STUDENT LIFE
Housing options: on-campus residence required through sophomore year; men-only, women-only, special housing for students with disabilities. Campus housing is university owned. Freshman campus housing is guaranteed.

Activities and organizations: drama/theater group, student-run newspaper, choral group, Campus Ministries, International Student Organization, Musical Theater, Student Government, Student Publications.

Athletics Member NAIA, NCCAA. ***Intercollegiate sports:*** basketball M(s)/W(s), cheerleading M/W, cross-country running M(s)/W(s), golf M(s)/W(s), soccer M(s)/W(s), softball W(s), tennis M(s)/W(s), track and field M(s)/W(s), volleyball M(s)/W(s). ***Intramural sports:*** table tennis M/W, ultimate Frisbee M/W, volleyball M/W.

Campus security: 24-hour emergency response devices and patrols, late-night transport/escort service, controlled dormitory access.

Student services: personal/psychological counseling.

COSTS & FINANCIAL AID
Costs (2017–18) ***Comprehensive fee:*** $41,730 includes full-time tuition ($30,700), mandatory fees ($1100), and room and board ($9930). Full-time tuition and fees vary according to course level, course load, degree level, location, program, and reciprocity agreements. Part-time tuition: $1395 per credit hour. Part-time tuition and fees vary according to course level, course load, degree level, location, program, and reciprocity agreements. ***College room only:*** $4900. Room and board charges vary according to board plan. ***Payment plan:*** installment. ***Waivers:*** employees or children of employees.

Financial Aid Of all full-time matriculated undergraduates who enrolled in 2015, 355 applied for aid, 323 were judged to have need, 7 had their need fully met. 61 Federal Work-Study jobs (averaging $2000). 97 state and other part-time jobs (averaging $2000). In 2015, 14 non-need-based awards were made. ***Average percent of need met:*** 42. ***Average financial aid package:*** $20,029. ***Average need-based loan:*** $4819. ***Average need-based gift aid:*** $15,971. ***Average non-need-based aid:*** $9407. ***Average indebtedness upon graduation:*** $28,438.

APPLYING

Standardized Tests *Required:* SAT or ACT (for admission).

Options: electronic application.

Application fee: $40.

Required: essay or personal statement, high school transcript, minimum 2.5 GPA, 2 letters of recommendation, rank in upper 50% of high school class. ***Required for some:*** interview.

Application deadlines: rolling (freshmen), rolling (out-of-state freshmen), rolling (transfers).

Notification: continuous (freshmen), continuous (out-of-state freshmen), continuous (transfers).

CONTACT

Ms. Midge Madden, Office Manager, Hope International University, 2500 East Nutwood Avenue, Fullerton, CA 92831-3138. *Phone:* 714-879-3901 Ext. 2240. *Toll-free phone:* 866-722-HOPE. *Fax:* 714-681-7423. *E-mail:* mfmadden@hiu.edu.

Horizon University

San Diego, California

http://www.horizonuniversity.edu/

CONTACT

Horizon University, 5331 Mt. Alifan Drive, San Diego, CA 92111. *Toll-free phone:* 800-553-HORIZON.

Humboldt State University

Arcata, California

http://www.humboldt.edu/

- **State-supported** comprehensive, founded 1913, part of California State University System
- **Rural** 161-acre campus
- **Endowment** $33.0 million
- **Coed** 7,968 undergraduate students, 94% full-time, 56% women, 44% men
- **Moderately difficult** entrance level, 76% of applicants were admitted

UNDERGRAD STUDENTS

7,492 full-time, 476 part-time. Students come from 49 states and territories; 21 other countries; 7% are from out of state; 3% Black or African American, non-Hispanic/Latino; 35% Hispanic/Latino; 3% Asian, non-Hispanic/Latino; 0.2% Native Hawaiian or other Pacific Islander, non-Hispanic/Latino; 1% American Indian or Alaska Native, non-Hispanic/Latino; 7% Two or more races, non-Hispanic/Latino; 6% Race/ethnicity unknown; 1% international; 11% transferred in; 25% live on campus.

Freshmen:

Admission: 12,967 applied, 9,895 admitted, 1,295 enrolled. ***Average high school GPA:*** 3.22. ***Test scores:*** SAT critical reading scores over 500: 52%; SAT math scores over 500: 47%; SAT writing scores over 500: 41%; ACT scores over 18: 81%; SAT critical reading scores over 600: 14%; SAT math scores over 600: 10%; SAT writing scores over 600: 8%; ACT scores over 24: 32%; SAT critical reading scores over 700: 2%; SAT math scores over 700: 1%; SAT writing scores over 700: 1%; ACT scores over 30: 2%.

Retention: 71% of full-time freshmen returned.

FACULTY

Total: 578, 42% full-time, 56% with terminal degrees.

Student/faculty ratio: 23:1.

ACADEMICS

Calendar: semesters. *Degrees:* bachelor's, master's, post-master's, and postbachelor's certificates.

Special study options: academic remediation for entering students, adult/continuing education programs, advanced placement credit, cooperative education, distance learning, double majors, English as a second language, honors programs, independent study, internships, off-campus study, part-time degree program, services for LD students, student-designed majors, study abroad, summer session for credit.

Computers: 1,098 computers/terminals are available on campus for general student use. Students can access the following: computer help desk, free student e-mail accounts, online (class) grades, online (class) registration, online (class) schedules. Campuswide network is available. 100% of college-owned or -operated housing units are wired for high-speed Internet access. Wireless service is available via entire campus.

Library: Humbolot State University Library.

STUDENT LIFE

Housing options: coed. Campus housing is university owned. Freshman applicants given priority for college housing.

Activities and organizations: drama/theater group, student-run newspaper, radio station, choral group, marching band, Bicycle Learning Center, Campus Center for Appropriate Technology (CCAT), Youth Educational Services, HOLA, MECHA, national fraternities, national sororities.

Athletics Member NCAA. All Division II. ***Intercollegiate sports:*** basketball M(s)/W(s), cheerleading W(c), crew M(c)/W, cross-country running M(s)/W(s), football M(s), lacrosse M(c), soccer M(s)/W(s), softball W(s), track and field M(s)/W(s), volleyball W(s). ***Intramural sports:*** baseball M(c), basketball M/W, fencing M(c)/W(c), rugby M(c)/W(c), soccer M/W, ultimate Frisbee M(c)/W(c), volleyball M(c), water polo M(c).

Campus security: 24-hour emergency response devices and patrols, late-night transport/escort service, controlled dormitory access.

Student services: health clinic, personal/psychological counseling, women's center.

COSTS & FINANCIAL AID

Costs (2017–18) ***Tuition:*** state resident $5472 full-time, $3174 per year part-time; nonresident $16,632 full-time, $372 per credit hour part-time. Full-time tuition and fees vary according to degree level. Part-time tuition and fees vary according to course load and degree level. ***Required fees:*** $1740 full-time, $1306 per year part-time. ***Room and board:*** $12,638; room only: $7726. Room and board charges vary according to board plan and housing facility. ***Payment plan:*** installment. ***Waivers:*** employees or children of employees.

Financial Aid Of all full-time matriculated undergraduates who enrolled in 2016, 6,547 applied for aid, 5,857 were judged to have need, 393 had their need fully met. 309 Federal Work-Study jobs (averaging $2040). In 2016, 289 non-need-based awards were made. ***Average percent of need met:*** 68. ***Average financial aid package:*** $13,650. ***Average need-based loan:*** $7074. ***Average need-based gift aid:*** $8692. ***Average non-need-based aid:*** $722. ***Average indebtedness upon graduation:*** $24,337.

APPLYING

Standardized Tests *Required for some:* SAT or ACT (for admission).

Options: electronic application.

Application fee: $55.

Required: high school transcript, minimum 2.0 GPA.

Application deadlines: 12/1 (freshmen), 12/1 (transfers).

Notification: continuous (freshmen), continuous (out-of-state freshmen), continuous (transfers).

CONTACT

Mr. Steven Ladwig, Associate Director of Admissions, Humboldt State University, 1 Harpst Street, Arcata, CA 95521. *Phone:* 707-826-4402. *Toll-free phone:* 866-850-9556. *Fax:* 707-826-6190. *E-mail:* hsuinfo@humboldt.edu.

Humphreys College

Stockton, California

http://www.humphreys.edu/

- **Independent** comprehensive, founded 1896
- **Suburban** 10-acre campus with easy access to San Francisco
- **Coed**
- **Noncompetitive** entrance level

ACADEMICS
Calendar: quarters. *Degrees:* associate, bachelor's, master's, and doctoral.
Library: Humphreys College Library plus 1 other.

STUDENT LIFE
Housing options: coed.
Activities and organizations: Business Club, Paralegal Club, Student Council, Collegiate Secretaries International.
Campus security: 24-hour patrols, late-night transport/escort service.

COSTS
Costs (2016–17) ***Tuition:*** $14,004 full-time, $389 per credit hour part-time. Full-time tuition and fees vary according to course load. Part-time tuition and fees vary according to course load.

APPLYING
Options: early admission, deferred entrance.
Application fee: $35.
Required: high school transcript, minimum 2.0 GPA. ***Recommended:*** interview.

CONTACT
Humphreys College, 6650 Inglewood Avenue, Stockton, CA 95207-3896. *Phone:* 209-235-2901.

Interior Designers Institute
Newport Beach, California
http://www.idi.edu/

CONTACT
Interior Designers Institute, 1061 Camelback Road, Newport Beach, CA 92660.

John F. Kennedy University
Pleasant Hill, California
http://www.jfku.edu/

CONTACT
Ms. Jen Miller-Hogg, Director of Admissions, John F. Kennedy University, 100 Ellinwood Way, Pleasant Hill, CA 94523-4817.
Phone: 925-969-3584. *Toll-free phone:* 800-696-JFKU.
E-mail: jmhogg@jfku.edu.

John Paul the Great Catholic University
Escondido, California
http://www.jpcatholic.com/

- **Independent** comprehensive, founded 2006, affiliated with Roman Catholic Church
- **Urban** 3-acre campus with easy access to San Diego
- **Coed** 227 undergraduate students, 93% full-time, 47% women, 53% men
- **Moderately difficult** entrance level, 98% of applicants were admitted

UNDERGRAD STUDENTS
210 full-time, 17 part-time. Students come from 39 states and territories; 53% are from out of state; 0.4% Black or African American, non-Hispanic/Latino; 23% Hispanic/Latino; 4% Asian, non-Hispanic/Latino; 0.4% Native Hawaiian or other Pacific Islander, non-Hispanic/Latino; 0.4% American Indian or Alaska Native, non-Hispanic/Latino; 4% Two or more races, non-Hispanic/Latino; 13% Race/ethnicity unknown; 12% transferred in; 79% live on campus.

Freshmen:
Admission: 204 applied, 200 admitted, 74 enrolled. ***Average high school GPA:*** 3.47. ***Test scores:*** SAT critical reading scores over 500: 73%; SAT math scores over 500: 51%; SAT writing scores over 500: 71%; ACT scores over 18: 92%; SAT critical reading scores over 600: 31%; SAT math scores over 600: 22%; SAT writing scores over 600: 27%; ACT scores over 24: 73%; SAT critical reading scores over 700: 9%; SAT math scores over 700: 2%; SAT writing scores over 700: 2%; ACT scores over 30: 12%.
Retention: 71% of full-time freshmen returned.

FACULTY
Total: 35, 23% full-time, 29% with terminal degrees.
Student/faculty ratio: 17:1.

ACADEMICS
Calendar: quarters. *Degrees:* bachelor's, master's, and postbachelor's certificates.
Special study options: advanced placement credit, distance learning, double majors, independent study, internships, part-time degree program, study abroad, summer session for credit.
Computers: Campuswide network is available. 100% of college-owned or -operated housing units are wired for high-speed Internet access. Wireless service is available via entire campus.
Library: John Paul the Great Catholic University Library.

STUDENT LIFE
Housing options: on-campus residence required through senior year; men-only, women-only. Campus housing is leased by the school. Freshman campus housing is guaranteed.
Activities and organizations: drama/theater group, student-run newspaper, choral group, Student government, Knights of Columbus, Flag football, Swing dance club, Gaming club.
Campus security: student patrols, leased campus housing provides their own security.
Student services: personal/psychological counseling.

COSTS & FINANCIAL AID
Costs (2016–17) ***Tuition:*** $24,000 full-time, $667 per credit part-time. Full-time tuition and fees vary according to degree level. Part-time tuition and fees vary according to degree level. No tuition increase for student's term of enrollment. ***Required fees:*** $900 full-time. ***Room only:*** $8100. Room and board charges vary according to housing facility.
Financial Aid Of all full-time matriculated undergraduates who enrolled in 2015, 172 applied for aid, 143 were judged to have need, 11 had their need fully met. In 2015, 15 non-need-based awards were made. ***Average percent of need met:*** 34. ***Average financial aid package:*** $13,005. ***Average need-based loan:*** $7115. ***Average need-based gift aid:*** $12,678. ***Average non-need-based aid:*** $8564. ***Financial aid deadline:*** 4/15.

APPLYING
Standardized Tests *Required for some:* SAT or ACT (for admission).
Options: electronic application, deferred entrance.
Application fee: $50.
Required: essay or personal statement, high school transcript, minimum 2.6 GPA. ***Recommended:*** interview.
Application deadlines: rolling (freshmen), rolling (transfers).
Notification: continuous (freshmen), continuous (transfers).

CONTACT
Mr. Martin Harold, Vice President of Admissions, John Paul the Great Catholic University, 220 W. Grand Avenue, Escondido, CA 92025.
Phone: 858-653-6740 Ext. 1101. *Fax:* 858-653-3791.
E-mail: mharold@jpcatholic.com.

Laguna College of Art & Design
Laguna Beach, California
http://www.lcad.edu/

- **Independent** comprehensive, founded 1962
- **Small-town** 9-acre campus with easy access to Los Angeles
- **Endowment** $1.7 million
- **Coed** 567 undergraduate students, 87% full-time, 63% women, 37% men
- **Very difficult** entrance level, 39% of applicants were admitted

UNDERGRAD STUDENTS
495 full-time, 72 part-time. Students come from 32 states and territories; 13 other countries; 42% are from out of state; 2% Black or African American, non-Hispanic/Latino; 19% Hispanic/Latino; 18% Asian, non-Hispanic/Latino; 0.7% Native Hawaiian or other Pacific Islander, non-Hispanic/Latino; 0.5% American Indian or Alaska Native, non-Hispanic/Latino; 3% Two or more races, non-Hispanic/Latino; 4% Race/ethnicity unknown; 2% international; 12% transferred in; 11% live on campus.

Freshmen:
Admission: 472 applied, 185 admitted, 88 enrolled. ***Average high school GPA:*** 3.25. ***Test scores:*** SAT critical reading scores over 500: 88%; SAT math scores over 500: 80%; ACT scores over 18: 100%; SAT critical reading scores over 600: 66%; SAT math scores over 600: 32%; ACT scores over 24: 80%; SAT critical reading scores over 700: 16%; SAT math scores over 700: 10%; ACT scores over 30: 10%.

Retention: 97% of full-time freshmen returned.

FACULTY
Total: 146, 12% full-time, 42% with terminal degrees.

Student/faculty ratio: 12:1.

ACADEMICS
Calendar: semesters. *Degrees:* certificates, bachelor's, master's, and postbachelor's certificates.

Special study options: double majors, independent study, internships, off-campus study, part-time degree program, services for LD students.

Computers: 85 computers/terminals are available on campus for general student use. Students can access the following: campus intranet, computer help desk, free student e-mail accounts, online (class) grades, online (class) registration, online (class) schedules. Campuswide network is available. 100% of college-owned or -operated housing units are wired for high-speed Internet access. Wireless service is available via entire campus.

Library: Dennis and Leslie Power Library plus 1 other. *Books:* 20,000 (physical); *Serial titles:* 82 (physical); *Databases:* 12. Weekly public service hours: 54.

STUDENT LIFE
Housing options: coed. Campus housing is leased by the school. Freshman applicants given priority for college housing.

Campus security: late-night transport/escort service.

Student services: personal/psychological counseling.

COSTS & FINANCIAL AID
Costs (2017–18) ***Tuition:*** $29,800 full-time, $1242 per unit part-time. Full-time tuition and fees vary according to course load and degree level. Part-time tuition and fees vary according to course load and degree level. ***Room only:*** $9500. ***Payment plan:*** installment. ***Waivers:*** employees or children of employees.

Financial Aid Of all full-time matriculated undergraduates who enrolled in 2015, 38 Federal Work-Study jobs (averaging $1483). ***Average indebtedness upon graduation:*** $38,000.

APPLYING
Standardized Tests *Recommended:* SAT or ACT (for admission).

Options: early admission, deferred entrance.

Application fee: $45.

Required: essay or personal statement, high school transcript, minimum 2.5 GPA, portfolio. ***Required for some:*** 2 letters of recommendation, interview.

Application deadlines: rolling (freshmen), rolling (transfers).

Notification: continuous (freshmen), continuous (transfers).

CONTACT
Madison Keyes, Admissions Coordinator, Laguna College of Art & Design, 2222 Laguna Canyon Road, Laguna Beach, CA 92651. *Phone:* 949-376-6000 Ext. 248. *Toll-free phone:* 800-255-0762. *E-mail:* mkeyes@lcad.edu.

La Sierra University
Riverside, California
http://www.lasierra.edu/

- **Independent Seventh-day Adventist** comprehensive, founded 1922, part of Seventh-Day Adventist Education System
- **Suburban** 100-acre campus with easy access to Los Angeles
- **Endowment** $16.6 million
- **Coed**
- **Minimally difficult** entrance level

FACULTY
Student/faculty ratio: 15:1.

ACADEMICS
Calendar: quarters. *Degrees:* certificates, bachelor's, master's, doctoral, post-master's, and postbachelor's certificates.

Library: University Library plus 1 other. *Books:* 216,387 (physical), 115,868 (digital/electronic); *Serial titles:* 386,353 (physical); *Databases:* 79. Weekly public service hours: 76; students can reserve study rooms.

STUDENT LIFE
Housing options: on-campus residence required for freshman year; men-only, women-only, cooperative. Campus housing is university owned. Freshman campus housing is guaranteed.

Activities and organizations: drama/theater group, student-run newspaper, choral group, Student Association of LSU, Korean Student Association, Enactus (SIFE), Ol Club, Black Student Association.

Athletics Member NAIA.

Campus security: 24-hour emergency response devices and patrols, student patrols, late-night transport/escort service.

Student services: health clinic, personal/psychological counseling, women's center.

COSTS & FINANCIAL AID
Costs (2016–17) ***Comprehensive fee:*** $40,680 includes full-time tuition ($31,590), mandatory fees ($990), and room and board ($8100). Full-time tuition and fees vary according to course load, degree level, and location. Part-time tuition: $850 per quarter hour. Part-time tuition and fees vary according to course load, degree level, and location. ***Room and board:*** Room and board charges vary according to board plan and housing facility.

Financial Aid Of all full-time matriculated undergraduates who enrolled in 2014, 1,617 applied for aid, 1,524 were judged to have need, 114 had their need fully met. In 2014, 330 non-need-based awards were made. ***Average percent of need met:*** 69. ***Average financial aid package:*** $22,616. ***Average need-based loan:*** $5264. ***Average need-based gift aid:*** $20,429. ***Average non-need-based aid:*** $8262. ***Average indebtedness upon graduation:*** $36,251. ***Financial aid deadline:*** 8/15.

APPLYING
Standardized Tests *Required:* SAT or ACT (for admission).

Options: electronic application, deferred entrance.

Required: essay or personal statement, high school transcript, minimum 2.0 GPA, 2 letters of recommendation, Eligibility Index Table (combination of GPA and test scores). ***Required for some:*** interview.

CONTACT
Ms. Ivy Teheda, Associate Director of Admissions, La Sierra University, 4500 Riverwalk Parkway, Riverside, CA 92515. *Phone:* 951-785-2957. *Toll-free phone:* 800-874-5587. *Fax:* 951-7852447. *E-mail:* iteheda@lasierra.edu.

Life Pacific College
San Dimas, California
http://www.lifepacific.edu/

CONTACT
Ms. Dorienne Elston, Director of Admissions, Life Pacific College, 1100 Covina Boulevard, San Dimas, CA 91773-3298. *Phone:* 909-599-5433 Ext. 314. *Toll-free phone:* 877-886-5433 Ext. 314. *Fax:* 909-706-3070. *E-mail:* adm@lifepacific.edu.

Lincoln University
Oakland, California
http://www.lincolnuca.edu/

- **Independent** comprehensive, founded 1919
- **Urban** campus
- **Coed** 252 undergraduate students, 62% full-time, 47% women, 53% men
- **Minimally difficult** entrance level, 81% of applicants were admitted

UNDERGRAD STUDENTS
157 full-time, 95 part-time. Students come from 19 other countries; 0.7% Black or African American, non-Hispanic/Latino; 1% Hispanic/Latino; 10% Asian, non-Hispanic/Latino; 1% Native Hawaiian or other Pacific Islander, non-Hispanic/Latino; 83% international.

Freshmen:
Admission: 276 applied, 223 admitted. *Average high school GPA:* 2.5.

FACULTY
Total: 32, 44% full-time, 84% with terminal degrees.

Student/faculty ratio: 17:1.

ACADEMICS
Calendar: semesters. *Degrees:* certificates, bachelor's, master's, and doctoral.

Special study options: advanced placement credit, double majors, English as a second language, summer session for credit.

Computers: 39 computers/terminals are available on campus for general student use. Students can access the following: computer help desk, free student e-mail accounts, online (class) schedules. Campuswide network is available. Wireless service is available via entire campus.
Library: Lincoln University Library. *Books:* 14,400 (physical), 128,000 (digital/electronic); *Serial titles:* 350 (physical), 5,050 (digital/electronic); *Databases:* 19.

STUDENT LIFE
Housing options: college housing not available.

Campus security: 24-hour emergency response devices.

Student services: personal/psychological counseling.

COSTS
Costs (2016–17) *Tuition:* $10,200 full-time, $425 per unit part-time. Full-time tuition and fees vary according to course level, course load, degree level, and program. Part-time tuition and fees vary according to course level, course load, degree level, and program. *Required fees:* $425 full-time, $400 per year part-time. *Payment plan:* installment.

APPLYING
Options: electronic application, deferred entrance.

Application fee: $75.

Required: high school transcript, minimum 2.0 GPA. *Required for some:* essay or personal statement, letters of recommendation, interview.

Application deadlines: 6/17 (freshmen), 8/7 (transfers).

CONTACT
Mr. Sunny Saggi, Admissions Officer, Lincoln University, 401 15th Street, Oakland, CA 94612. *Phone:* 510-628-8010 Ext. 8011. *Toll-free phone:* 888-810-9998. *Fax:* 510-628-8012.
E-mail: admissions@lincolnuca.edu.

Loma Linda University
Loma Linda, California
http://www.llu.edu/

CONTACT
Admissions Office, Loma Linda University, Loma Linda, CA 92350. *Phone:* 909-558-1000. *Toll-free phone:* 800-422-4558.

Los Angeles Film School
Hollywood, California
http://www.lafilm.edu/

- **Proprietary** 4-year
- **Urban** campus with easy access to Hollywood
- **Coed** 1,358 undergraduate students, 100% full-time, 24% women, 76% men
- **Noncompetitive** entrance level, 85% of applicants were admitted

UNDERGRAD STUDENTS
1,358 full-time. Students come from 48 states and territories; 16 other countries; 32% are from out of state.

Freshmen:
Admission: 1,505 applied, 1,272 admitted.

FACULTY
Total: 116, 89% full-time, 9% with terminal degrees.

ACADEMICS
Calendar: continuous. *Degrees:* associate and bachelor's.

Special study options: accelerated degree program, adult/continuing education programs, advanced placement credit, cooperative education, distance learning, services for LD students.

Computers: 8 computers/terminals are available on campus for general student use. Students can access the following: campus intranet, computer help desk, free student e-mail accounts, online (class) grades, online (class) schedules. Campuswide network is available. Wireless service is available via classrooms, computer centers, computer labs, libraries, student centers.
Library: Main Library plus 1 other.

STUDENT LIFE
Housing options: college housing not available.

Campus security: 24-hour patrols.

COSTS
Costs (2016–17) *Tuition:* $79,000 per degree program part-time. Full-time tuition and fees vary according to course load, degree level, location, and program. No tuition increase for student's term of enrollment.
Payment plan: installment.

APPLYING
Options: electronic application.

Application fee: $75.

Required: essay or personal statement, high school transcript, interview.

CONTACT
Los Angeles Film School, 6363 Sunset Boulevard, Hollywood, CA 90028. *Toll-free phone:* 877-952-3456.

Loyola Marymount University
Los Angeles, California
http://www.lmu.edu/

- **Independent Roman Catholic** comprehensive, founded 1911
- **Suburban** 142-acre campus with easy access to Los Angeles
- **Endowment** $418.9 million
- **Coed** 6,261 undergraduate students, 97% full-time, 56% women, 44% men

UNDERGRAD STUDENTS
6,044 full-time, 217 part-time. Students come from 53 states and territories; 75 other countries; 26% are from out of state; 6% Black or African American, non-Hispanic/Latino; 21% Hispanic/Latino; 11% Asian, non-Hispanic/Latino; 0.2% Native Hawaiian or other Pacific Islander, non-Hispanic/Latino; 0.1% American Indian or Alaska Native, non-Hispanic/Latino; 8% Two or more races, non-Hispanic/Latino; 10% international; 6% transferred in; 52% live on campus.

Freshmen:
Admission: 1,331 enrolled. *Average high school GPA:* 3.74. *Test scores:* SAT critical reading scores over 500: 93%; SAT math scores over 500: 95%; SAT writing scores over 500: 93%; ACT scores over 18: 100%; SAT critical reading scores over 600: 54%; SAT math scores over 600: 61%; SAT writing scores over 600: 56%; ACT scores over 24: 95%; SAT critical reading scores over 700: 14%; SAT math scores over 700: 15%; SAT writing scores over 700: 13%; ACT scores over 30: 33%.
Retention: 88% of full-time freshmen returned.

ACADEMICS
Calendar: semesters. *Degrees:* bachelor's, master's, doctoral, post-master's, and postbachelor's certificates.

Special study options: academic remediation for entering students, accelerated degree program, advanced placement credit, distance learning, double majors, English as a second language, honors programs, independent study, internships, part-time degree program, services for LD students, student-designed majors, study abroad, summer session for credit. *ROTC:* Army (c), Air Force (b).

Unusual degree programs: 3-2 engineering.

Computers: 820 computers/terminals and 2,000 ports are available on campus for general student use. Students can access the following: campus intranet, computer help desk, free student e-mail accounts, online (class) grades, online (class) registration, online (class) schedules. Campuswide network is available. 100% of college-owned or -operated housing units are wired for high-speed Internet access. Wireless service is available via entire campus.

Library: William H. Hannon Library. *Books:* 516,463 (physical), 491,084 (digital/electronic); *Serial titles:* 974 (physical), 44,816 (digital/electronic); *Databases:* 275. Weekly public service hours: 146; study areas open 24 hours, 5-7 days a week; students can reserve study rooms.

STUDENT LIFE

Housing options: coed, men-only, women-only, special housing for students with disabilities. Campus housing is university owned. Freshman applicants given priority for college housing.

Activities and organizations: drama/theater group, student-run newspaper, radio and television station, choral group, Entrepreneurship Society, Ignatians, Tri Beta National Honor Society, Sursum Corda Service Organization, Creare Service Organization, national fraternities, national sororities.

Athletics Member NCAA. All Division I. ***Intercollegiate sports:*** baseball M(s), basketball M(s)/W(s), cheerleading M/W, crew M/W(s), cross-country running M(s)/W(s), golf M(s), soccer M(s)/W(s), softball W(s), swimming and diving W(s), tennis M(s)/W(s), track and field M/W, volleyball W(s), water polo M(s)/W(s). ***Intramural sports:*** baseball M(c), basketball M/W(c), football M/W, ice hockey M(c), lacrosse M(c)/W(c), rugby M(c), sand volleyball M/W, skiing (downhill) M(c)/W(c), soccer M(c)/W(c), table tennis M/W, tennis M(c)/W(c), volleyball M(c)/W(c).

Campus security: 24-hour emergency response devices and patrols, late-night transport/escort service, controlled dormitory access, personal property engraving program, lighted pathways/sidewalks, shuttle buses, self-defense education, and emergency preparedness.

Student services: health clinic, personal/psychological counseling.

COSTS & FINANCIAL AID

Costs (2016–17) ***One-time required fee:*** $250. ***Comprehensive fee:*** $58,715 includes full-time tuition ($43,526), mandatory fees ($704), and room and board ($14,485). Full-time tuition and fees vary according to reciprocity agreements. Part-time tuition: $1816 per credit hour. Part-time tuition and fees vary according to course load. ***Required fees:*** $8 per unit part-time, $64 per term part-time. ***College room only:*** $10,085. Room and board charges vary according to board plan and housing facility. ***Payment plans:*** installment, deferred payment. ***Waivers:*** employees or children of employees.

Financial Aid Of all full-time matriculated undergraduates who enrolled in 2015, 4,462 applied for aid, 3,324 were judged to have need, 660 had their need fully met. 1,426 Federal Work-Study jobs (averaging $1848). 2,300 state and other part-time jobs (averaging $2440). In 2015, 1515 non-need-based awards were made. ***Average percent of need met:*** 66. ***Average financial aid package:*** $29,049. ***Average need-based loan:*** $6041. ***Average need-based gift aid:*** $20,440. ***Average non-need-based aid:*** $10,085. ***Average indebtedness upon graduation:*** $30,698.

APPLYING

Standardized Tests *Required:* SAT or ACT (for admission).

Required: essay or personal statement, high school transcript, 1 letter of recommendation.

CONTACT

Loyola Marymount University, One LMU Drive, Los Angeles, CA 90045-2659. *Phone:* 310-338-2750. *Toll-free phone:* 800-LMU-INFO.

Marymount California University

Rancho Palos Verdes, California

http://www.marymountcalifornia.edu/

- **Independent Roman Catholic** comprehensive, founded 1932
- **Suburban** 26-acre campus with easy access to Los Angeles
- **Endowment** $9.5 million
- **Coed** 942 undergraduate students, 94% full-time, 50% women, 50% men
- **Minimally difficult** entrance level, 76% of applicants were admitted

UNDERGRAD STUDENTS

882 full-time, 60 part-time. Students come from 26 states and territories; 33 other countries; 10% are from out of state; 8% Black or African American, non-Hispanic/Latino; 39% Hispanic/Latino; 5% Asian, non-Hispanic/Latino; 0.1% Native Hawaiian or other Pacific Islander, non-Hispanic/Latino; 0.4% American Indian or Alaska Native, non-Hispanic/Latino; 2% Two or more races, non-Hispanic/Latino; 7% Race/ethnicity unknown; 18% international; 11% transferred in; 32% live on campus.

Freshmen:

Admission: 1,755 applied, 1,337 admitted, 219 enrolled. ***Average high school GPA:*** 3.01. ***Test scores:*** SAT critical reading scores over 500: 24%; SAT math scores over 500: 27%; SAT writing scores over 500: 23%; ACT scores over 18: 74%; SAT critical reading scores over 600: 2%; SAT math scores over 600: 6%; SAT writing scores over 600: 2%; ACT scores over 24: 10%; SAT math scores over 700: 1%; ACT scores over 30: 2%.

Retention: 62% of full-time freshmen returned.

FACULTY

Total: 120, 24% full-time, 35% with terminal degrees.

Student/faculty ratio: 16:1.

ACADEMICS

Calendar: semesters. *Degrees:* associate, bachelor's, and master's.

Special study options: academic remediation for entering students, accelerated degree program, adult/continuing education programs, advanced placement credit, cooperative education, distance learning, English as a second language, honors programs, independent study, internships, off-campus study, part-time degree program, services for LD students, study abroad, summer session for credit.

Unusual degree programs: 3-2 business administration.

Computers: 210 computers/terminals are available on campus for general student use. Students can access the following: campus intranet, computer help desk, free student e-mail accounts, online (class) grades, online (class) registration, online (class) schedules. Campuswide network is available. 100% of college-owned or -operated housing units are wired for high-speed Internet access. Wireless service is available via entire campus.

Library: College Library plus 1 other. *Books:* 23,246 (physical), 135,971 (digital/electronic); *Serial titles:* 255 (physical), 30,329 (digital/electronic); *Databases:* 51. Weekly public service hours: 60; students can reserve study rooms.

STUDENT LIFE

Housing options: coed. Campus housing is university owned. Freshman applicants given priority for college housing.

Activities and organizations: drama/theater group, choral group, Latinos Unidos, Student Veterans Organization, Marymount Pride, Black Student Union, Society for Advancement of Management (SAM).

Athletics Member NAIA. ***Intercollegiate sports:*** baseball M(s), golf M(s)/W(s), lacrosse M(s)/W(s), soccer M(s)/W(s), track and field M(s). ***Intramural sports:*** basketball M/W, golf M/W, lacrosse M/W, soccer M/W, softball M/W, swimming and diving M/W, track and field M/W, volleyball M/W.

Campus security: 24-hour emergency response devices and patrols, late-night transport/escort service, controlled dormitory access.

Student services: health clinic, personal/psychological counseling.

COSTS & FINANCIAL AID

Costs (2017–18) ***One-time required fee:*** $300. ***Comprehensive fee:*** $50,296 includes full-time tuition ($34,134), mandatory fees ($1750), and room and board ($14,412). Full-time tuition and fees vary according to location. Part-time tuition: $1475 per credit hour. Part-time tuition and fees vary according to location. ***Required fees:*** $600 per year part-time. ***College room only:*** $9004. Room and board charges vary according to board plan and housing facility. ***Payment plan:*** installment. ***Waivers:*** senior citizens and employees or children of employees.

Financial Aid Of all full-time matriculated undergraduates who enrolled in 2016, 607 applied for aid, 598 were judged to have need, 146 had their need fully met. 7 Federal Work-Study jobs (averaging $4000). In 2016, 85 non-need-based awards were made. ***Average percent of need met:*** 91. ***Average financial aid package:*** $34,529. ***Average need-based loan:*** $4351. ***Average need-based gift aid:*** $22,320. ***Average non-need-based aid:*** $14,914. ***Average indebtedness upon graduation:*** $32,470. ***Financial aid deadline:*** 2/15.

APPLYING

Standardized Tests *Recommended:* SAT or ACT (for admission).

Options: electronic application, early admission, deferred entrance.

Application fee: $50.

Required: high school transcript. ***Required for some:*** essay or personal statement, interview. ***Recommended:*** minimum 2.0 GPA.

Application deadlines: 8/15 (freshmen), 8/15 (transfers).

Notification: continuous until 9/1 (freshmen), continuous until 9/1 (transfers).

CONTACT

Ms. Melissa Bettis, Admissions Counselor, Marymount California University, 30800 Palos Verdes Drive East, Rancho Palos Verdes, CA 90275. *Phone:* 310-303-7311. *Fax:* 310-303-7698.
E-mail: admissions@marymountcalifornia.edu.

The Master's University

Santa Clarita, California

http://www.masters.edu/

- **Independent nondenominational** comprehensive, founded 1927
- **Suburban** 110-acre campus with easy access to Los Angeles
- **Coed** 1,390 undergraduate students, 68% full-time, 47% women, 53% men
- **Moderately difficult** entrance level, 83% of applicants were admitted

UNDERGRAD STUDENTS

952 full-time, 438 part-time. Students come from 42 states and territories; 21 other countries; 30% are from out of state; 3% Black or African American, non-Hispanic/Latino; 8% Hispanic/Latino; 6% Asian, non-Hispanic/Latino; 0.4% Native Hawaiian or other Pacific Islander, non-Hispanic/Latino; 6% Two or more races, non-Hispanic/Latino; 7% Race/ethnicity unknown; 4% international; 6% transferred in; 82% live on campus.

Freshmen:

Admission: 446 applied, 371 admitted, 173 enrolled. ***Average high school GPA:*** 3.65. ***Test scores:*** SAT math scores over 500: 60%; SAT writing scores over 500: 63%; ACT scores over 18: 95%; SAT math scores over 600: 22%; SAT writing scores over 600: 29%; ACT scores over 24: 52%; SAT math scores over 700: 3%; SAT writing scores over 700: 5%; ACT scores over 30: 13%.

Retention: 88% of full-time freshmen returned.

FACULTY

Total: 238, 28% full-time, 38% with terminal degrees.

Student/faculty ratio: 10:1.

ACADEMICS

Calendar: semesters. *Degrees:* bachelor's, master's, and doctoral.

Special study options: academic remediation for entering students, accelerated degree program, adult/continuing education programs, advanced placement credit, cooperative education, distance learning, double majors, external degree program, independent study, internships, part-time degree program, services for LD students, study abroad, summer session for credit. ***ROTC:*** Army (c), Air Force (c).

Computers: 57 computers/terminals are available on campus for general student use. Students can access the following: campus intranet, computer help desk, free student e-mail accounts, online (class) grades, online (class) registration, online (class) schedules. Campuswide network is available. 100% of college-owned or -operated housing units are wired for high-speed Internet access. Wireless service is available via entire campus.

Library: Robert L. Powell Library plus 1 other. *Books:* 115,518 (physical), 290,100 (digital/electronic); *Serial titles:* 3,077 (physical), 45,429 (digital/electronic); *Databases:* 79.

STUDENT LIFE

Housing options: on-campus residence required through junior year; men-only, women-only. Campus housing is university owned. Freshman campus housing is guaranteed.

Activities and organizations: drama/theater group, choral group, University Singers Choir, Summer Missions, Intramural Sports, Church Ministries, Theatre Arts Group.

Athletics Member NAIA. ***Intercollegiate sports:*** baseball M(s), basketball M(s)/W(s), cross-country running M(s)/W(s), golf M(s), soccer M(s)/W(s), track and field M(s)/W(s), volleyball W(s). ***Intramural sports:*** basketball M/W, soccer M/W, volleyball M/W.

Campus security: 24-hour patrols.

Student services: health clinic, personal/psychological counseling.

COSTS & FINANCIAL AID

Costs (2017–18) ***Comprehensive fee:*** $43,870 includes full-time tuition ($32,600), mandatory fees ($420), and room and board ($10,850). Full-time tuition and fees vary according to class time, course load, location, and program. Part-time tuition: $1370 per credit hour. Part-time tuition and fees vary according to class time, course load, location, and program. ***College room only:*** $5950. Room and board charges vary according to board plan. ***Payment plan:*** installment. ***Waivers:*** employees or children of employees.

Financial Aid Of all full-time matriculated undergraduates who enrolled in 2015, 878 applied for aid, 758 were judged to have need, 101 had their need fully met. 60 Federal Work-Study jobs (averaging $2577). 174 state and other part-time jobs (averaging $1904). In 2015, 143 non-need-based awards were made. ***Average percent of need met:*** 66. ***Average financial aid package:*** $22,088. ***Average need-based loan:*** $4249. ***Average need-based gift aid:*** $18,112. ***Average non-need-based aid:*** $9865. ***Average indebtedness upon graduation:*** $29,133.

APPLYING

Standardized Tests *Required:* SAT or ACT (for admission).

Options: electronic application, early admission, early action, deferred entrance.

Application fee: $40.

Required: essay or personal statement, high school transcript, minimum 2.8 GPA, 2 letters of recommendation. ***Recommended:*** interview.

Application deadlines: 9/1 (freshmen), 9/1 (transfers), 11/15 (early action).

Notification: 3/15 (freshmen), 3/15 (transfers), 12/22 (early action).

CONTACT

Mr. Madison Currie, Director of Admissions, The Master's University, 21726 Placerita Canyon Road, Santa Clarita, CA 91321. *Phone:* 661-362-2601. *Toll-free phone:* 800-568-6248. *Fax:* 661-362-2718.
E-mail: admissions@masters.edu.

Menlo College

Atherton, California

http://www.menlo.edu/

- **Independent** 4-year, founded 1927
- **Small-town** 45-acre campus with easy access to San Francisco
- **Endowment** $25.6 million
- **Coed** 777 undergraduate students, 98% full-time, 45% women, 55% men
- **Moderately difficult** entrance level, 41% of applicants were admitted

UNDERGRAD STUDENTS

758 full-time, 19 part-time. Students come from 26 states and territories; 35 other countries; 19% are from out of state; 6% Black or African American, non-Hispanic/Latino; 23% Hispanic/Latino; 10% Asian, non-Hispanic/Latino; 2% Native Hawaiian or other Pacific Islander, non-Hispanic/Latino; 0.5% American Indian or Alaska Native, non-Hispanic/Latino; 9% Two or more races, non-Hispanic/Latino; 10% Race/ethnicity unknown; 14% international; 12% transferred in; 60% live on campus.

Freshmen:

Admission: 2,195 applied, 897 admitted, 158 enrolled. ***Average high school GPA:*** 3.2.

Retention: 77% of full-time freshmen returned.

FACULTY

Total: 101, 30% full-time, 53% with terminal degrees.

Student/faculty ratio: 14:1.

ACADEMICS

Calendar: semesters. *Degree:* bachelor's.

Special study options: academic remediation for entering students, accelerated degree program, adult/continuing education programs, advanced placement credit, double majors, English as a second language, independent study, internships, part-time degree program, services for LD students, student-designed majors, study abroad, summer session for credit. ***ROTC:*** Air Force (c).

Computers: 220 computers/terminals are available on campus for general student use. Students can access the following: campus intranet, computer help desk, free student e-mail accounts, online (class) grades, online (class) registration, online (class) schedules. Campuswide network is available. 100% of college-owned or -operated housing units are wired for high-speed Internet access. Wireless service is available via entire campus.
Library: Bowman Library. *Books:* 47,340 (physical), 17,379 (digital/electronic); *Serial titles:* 76 (physical); *Databases:* 42. Weekly public service hours: 95; students can reserve study rooms.

STUDENT LIFE
Housing options: on-campus residence required through sophomore year; coed, men-only, women-only. Campus housing is university owned.
Activities and organizations: student-run newspaper, International Club, Student Government, SERV, Finance Club, Hawaiian Club.
Athletics Member NAIA. ***Intercollegiate sports:*** baseball M(s), basketball M(s)/W(s), cross-country running M(s)/W(s), golf M(s)/W(s), soccer M(s)/W(s), softball W(s), track and field M(s)/W(s), volleyball M(s)/W(s), wrestling M(s)/W(s). ***Intramural sports:*** basketball M(c)/W(c), cheerleading W(c), rugby M(c), ultimate Frisbee M(c).
Campus security: 24-hour emergency response devices and patrols, controlled dormitory access.
Student services: personal/psychological counseling, women's center.

COSTS & FINANCIAL AID
Costs (2017–18) ***Comprehensive fee:*** $55,030 includes full-time tuition ($40,625), mandatory fees ($725), and room and board ($13,680). Part-time tuition: $1693 per credit. ***Room and board:*** Room and board charges vary according to housing facility. ***Payment plan:*** installment. ***Waivers:*** employees or children of employees.
Financial Aid Of all full-time matriculated undergraduates who enrolled in 2014, 522 applied for aid, 478 were judged to have need, 54 had their need fully met. 345 Federal Work-Study jobs (averaging $1024). In 2014, 168 non-need-based awards were made. ***Average percent of need met:*** 66. ***Average financial aid package:*** $28,874. ***Average need-based loan:*** $3741. ***Average need-based gift aid:*** $25,073. ***Average non-need-based aid:*** $12,737. ***Average indebtedness upon graduation:*** $29,943.

APPLYING
Standardized Tests *Required:* SAT or ACT (for admission).
Options: electronic application, early admission, early action, deferred entrance.
Application fee: $40.
Required: essay or personal statement, high school transcript, 1 letter of recommendation. ***Recommended:*** minimum 2.5 GPA, interview.
Application deadlines: 4/1 (freshmen), 6/1 (transfers), 11/15 (early action).
Notification: continuous (transfers), 1/15 (early action).

CONTACT
Priscila DeSouza, Associate Dean of Enrollment Management, Menlo College, 1000 El Camino Real, Atherton, CA 94027. *Phone:* 650-543-3786. *Toll-free phone:* 800-556-3656. *Fax:* 650-543-4496.
E-mail: admissions@menlo.edu.

Mills College
Oakland, California
http://www.mills.edu/

- **Independent** comprehensive, founded 1852
- **Urban** 135-acre campus with easy access to San Francisco
- **Endowment** $182.8 million
- **Undergraduate: women only; graduate: coed** 819 undergraduate students, 95% full-time, 100% women
- **Moderately difficult** entrance level, 84% of applicants were admitted

UNDERGRAD STUDENTS
775 full-time, 44 part-time. Students come from 37 states and territories; 8 other countries; 19% are from out of state; 9% Black or African American, non-Hispanic/Latino; 27% Hispanic/Latino; 9% Asian, non-Hispanic/Latino; 0.2% Native Hawaiian or other Pacific Islander, non-Hispanic/Latino; 0.5% American Indian or Alaska Native, non-Hispanic/Latino; 8% Two or more races, non-Hispanic/Latino; 0.9% Race/ethnicity unknown; 1% international; 12% transferred in; 60% live on campus.

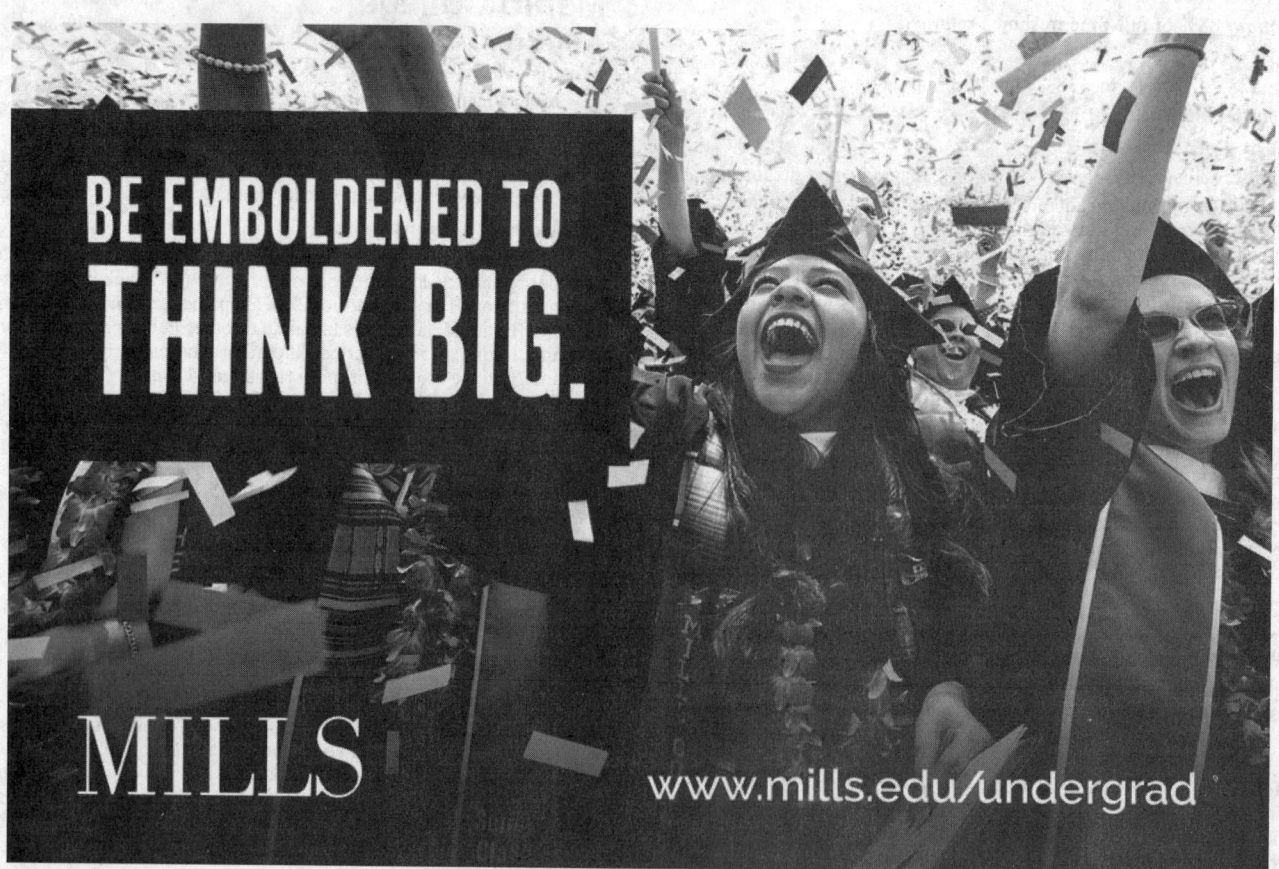

Freshmen:
Admission: 1,052 applied, 888 admitted, 170 enrolled. ***Average high school GPA:*** 3.62.
Retention: 78% of full-time freshmen returned.

FACULTY
Total: 183, 50% full-time, 77% with terminal degrees.
Student/faculty ratio: 10:1.

ACADEMICS
Calendar: semesters. *Degrees:* certificates, bachelor's, master's, doctoral, and postbachelor's certificates.
Special study options: accelerated degree program, adult/continuing education programs, advanced placement credit, cooperative education, double majors, independent study, internships, off-campus study, part-time degree program, services for LD students, student-designed majors, study abroad, summer session for credit. ***ROTC:*** Army (c).
Unusual degree programs: 3-2 engineering with University of Southern California; education, public policy, infant mental health, mathematics.
Computers: 335 computers/terminals are available on campus for general student use. Students can access the following: campus intranet, computer help desk, free student e-mail accounts, online (class) grades, online (class) registration, online (class) schedules, online degree audit. Campuswide network is available. 100% of college-owned or -operated housing units are wired for high-speed Internet access. Wireless service is available via entire campus.
Library: F. W. Olin Library. *Books:* 188,132 (physical), 136,684 (digital/electronic); *Serial titles:* 166 (physical), 46,007 (digital/electronic); *Databases:* 97. Weekly public service hours: 89; students can reserve study rooms.

STUDENT LIFE
Housing options: coed, women-only, cooperative, special housing for students with disabilities. Campus housing is university owned. Freshman campus housing is guaranteed.
Activities and organizations: student-run newspaper, choral group, Associated Students of Mills College, The Campanil, The Mills Choir, Mujeres Unidas, Asian Pacific Islander Student Association.
Athletics Member NCAA. All Division III. ***Intercollegiate sports:*** crew W, cross-country running W, rowing W, soccer W, swimming and diving W, tennis W, volleyball W. ***Intramural sports:*** basketball W, cheerleading W(c), soccer W, softball W(c), track and field W(c), volleyball W.
Campus security: 24-hour emergency response devices and patrols, late-night transport/escort service, controlled dormitory access.
Student services: health clinic, personal/psychological counseling, women's center.

COSTS & FINANCIAL AID
Costs (2016–17) ***Comprehensive fee:*** $59,163 includes full-time tuition ($44,322), mandatory fees ($1313), and room and board ($13,528). Full-time tuition and fees vary according to course load. Part-time tuition: $1847 per credit. Part-time tuition and fees vary according to course load. ***College room only:*** $6926. Room and board charges vary according to board plan and housing facility. ***Payment plan:*** installment. ***Waivers:*** employees or children of employees.
Financial Aid Of all full-time matriculated undergraduates who enrolled in 2016, 697 applied for aid, 652 were judged to have need, 95 had their need fully met. 318 Federal Work-Study jobs (averaging $2667). 315 state and other part-time jobs (averaging $3376). In 2016, 33 non-need-based awards were made. ***Average percent of need met:*** 81. ***Average financial aid package:*** $42,502. ***Average need-based loan:*** $7141. ***Average need-based gift aid:*** $35,497. ***Average non-need-based aid:*** $20,894. ***Average indebtedness upon graduation:*** $33,327. ***Financial aid deadline:*** 2/15.

APPLYING
Options: electronic application, early admission, early action, deferred entrance.
Application fee: $50.
Required: essay or personal statement, high school transcript, 1 letter of recommendation, any previous college transcripts. ***Recommended:*** interview.
Application deadlines: 1/15 (freshmen), 3/1 (transfers), 11/15 (early action).
Notification: 3/30 (freshmen), 4/1 (transfers), 12/1 (early action).

CONTACT
Mrs. Robynne Royster, Director of Undergraduate Admissions, Mills College, 5000 MacArthur Boulevard, Oakland, CA 94613-1301. *Phone:* 510-430-2135. *Toll-free phone:* 800-87-MILLS. *Fax:* 510-430-3314. *E-mail:* admission@mills.edu.

See previous page for display ad and page 1420 for the College Close-Up.

Mount Saint Mary's University
Los Angeles, California
http://www.msmu.edu/

- **Independent Roman Catholic** comprehensive, founded 1925
- **Urban** 56-acre campus with easy access to Los Angeles
- **Endowment** $124.0 million
- **Coed, primarily women** 2,831 undergraduate students, 77% full-time, 93% women, 7% men

UNDERGRAD STUDENTS
2,184 full-time, 647 part-time. Students come from 22 states and territories; 2% are from out of state; 6% Black or African American, non-Hispanic/Latino; 62% Hispanic/Latino; 15% Asian, non-Hispanic/Latino; 0.5% Native Hawaiian or other Pacific Islander, non-Hispanic/Latino; 0.4% American Indian or Alaska Native, non-Hispanic/Latino; 2% Two or more races, non-Hispanic/Latino; 4% Race/ethnicity unknown; 0.7% international; 3% transferred in; 22% live on campus.

Freshmen:
Admission: 572 enrolled. ***Average high school GPA:*** 3.33. ***Test scores:*** SAT critical reading scores over 500: 30%; SAT math scores over 500: 32%; SAT writing scores over 500: 26%; ACT scores over 18: 65%; SAT critical reading scores over 600: 5%; SAT math scores over 600: 5%; SAT writing scores over 600: 5%; ACT scores over 24: 13%; ACT scores over 30: 1%.
Retention: 79% of full-time freshmen returned.

FACULTY
Total: 521, 24% full-time, 45% with terminal degrees.
Student/faculty ratio: 11:1.

ACADEMICS
Calendar: semesters. *Degrees:* associate, bachelor's, master's, doctoral, and post-master's certificates.
Special study options: academic remediation for entering students, accelerated degree program, advanced placement credit, cooperative education, distance learning, double majors, English as a second language, honors programs, independent study, internships, off-campus study, part-time degree program, services for LD students, student-designed majors, study abroad, summer session for credit.
Computers: 170 computers/terminals are available on campus for general student use. Students can access the following: campus intranet, computer help desk, free student e-mail accounts, online (class) grades, online (class) registration, online (class) schedules. Campuswide network is available. 100% of college-owned or -operated housing units are wired for high-speed Internet access. Wireless service is available via entire campus.
Library: Charles Willard Coe Library plus 2 others. *Books:* 310,130 (physical), 363,514 (digital/electronic); *Serial titles:* 615 (physical), 37,727 (digital/electronic); *Databases:* 217. Weekly public service hours: 89; study areas open 24 hours, 5-7 days a week.

STUDENT LIFE
Housing options: men-only, women-only. Campus housing is university owned. Freshman applicants given priority for college housing.
Activities and organizations: drama/theater group, student-run newspaper, choral group, California Nursing Student Association (CNSA), Pangkat Pilipino, Scholar Mentor Club, Mount Movement, Na Pua O Ka'Aina (NPOKA), national sororities.
Athletics ***Intramural sports:*** basketball M/W, soccer M/W, softball M/W, swimming and diving M/W, tennis M/W, volleyball M/W.
Campus security: 24-hour emergency response devices and patrols, late-night transport/escort service, controlled dormitory access.
Student services: health clinic, personal/psychological counseling, women's center.

COSTS & FINANCIAL AID

Costs (2016–17) ***Comprehensive fee:*** $49,173 includes full-time tuition ($36,682), mandatory fees ($1040), and room and board ($11,451). Full-time tuition and fees vary according to course load, degree level, and program. Part-time tuition: $1528 per unit. Part-time tuition and fees vary according to course load, degree level, and program. ***College room only:*** $6870. Room and board charges vary according to board plan and housing facility. ***Payment plan:*** installment. ***Waivers:*** employees or children of employees.

Financial Aid Of all full-time matriculated undergraduates who enrolled in 2016, 2,002 applied for aid, 1,826 were judged to have need, 56 had their need fully met. In 2016, 259 non-need-based awards were made. ***Average percent of need met:*** 53. ***Average financial aid package:*** $27,165. ***Average need-based loan:*** $4634. ***Average need-based gift aid:*** $17,115. ***Average non-need-based aid:*** $9786. ***Average indebtedness upon graduation:*** $32,805.

APPLYING

Standardized Tests *Required for some:* SAT or ACT (for admission).

Required: essay or personal statement, high school transcript, minimum 2.5 GPA, 1 letter of recommendation. ***Recommended:*** 2 letters of recommendation, interview.

CONTACT

Erika Yamasaki, Director of Admissions, Mount Saint Mary's University, 12001 Chalon Road, Los Angeles, CA 90049-1599. *Phone:* 800-999-9893. *Toll-free phone:* 800-999-9893. *Fax:* 310-954-4259. *E-mail:* admissions@msmu.edu.

Mt. Sierra College

Monrovia, California

http://www.mtsierra.edu/

CONTACT

Mt. Sierra College, 101 East Huntington Drive, Monrovia, CA 91016. *Phone:* 888-486-9818. *Toll-free phone:* 888-828-8000.

Musicians Institute

Hollywood, California

http://www.mi.edu/

CONTACT

Musicians Institute, 1655 North McCadden Place, Hollywood, CA 90028. *Phone:* 323-860-4345. *Toll-free phone:* 800-255-PLAY.

National University

La Jolla, California

http://www.nu.edu/

- **Independent** comprehensive, founded 1971, part of National University System
- **Urban** campus with easy access to San Diego
- **Coed** 8,314 undergraduate students, 36% full-time, 55% women, 45% men
- **Noncompetitive** entrance level

UNDERGRAD STUDENTS

3,026 full-time, 5,288 part-time. Students come from 49 states and territories; 33 other countries; 9% are from out of state; 10% Black or African American, non-Hispanic/Latino; 27% Hispanic/Latino; 10% Asian, non-Hispanic/Latino; 1% Native Hawaiian or other Pacific Islander, non-Hispanic/Latino; 0.5% American Indian or Alaska Native, non-Hispanic/Latino; 5% Two or more races, non-Hispanic/Latino; 7% Race/ethnicity unknown; 2% international; 42% transferred in.

Freshmen:

Admission: 117 enrolled.

FACULTY

Total: 1,325, 22% full-time, 45% with terminal degrees.

Student/faculty ratio: 17:1.

ACADEMICS

Calendar: continuous. *Degrees:* certificates, associate, bachelor's, master's, post-master's, and postbachelor's certificates.

Special study options: academic remediation for entering students, accelerated degree program, adult/continuing education programs, advanced placement credit, cooperative education, distance learning, double majors, English as a second language, independent study, internships, off-campus study, part-time degree program, services for LD students, study abroad, summer session for credit. ***ROTC:*** Army (c), Air Force (c).

Computers: 2,800 computers/terminals are available on campus for general student use. Students can access the following: computer help desk, free student e-mail accounts, online (class) grades, online (class) registration, online (class) schedules. Campuswide network is available. Wireless service is available via entire campus.

Library: National University Library. *Books:* 216,574 (physical), 289,279 (digital/electronic); *Serial titles:* 1,630 (physical), 77,230 (digital/electronic); *Databases:* 190. Weekly public service hours: 72; students can reserve study rooms.

STUDENT LIFE

Housing options: college housing not available.

Campus security: 24-hour emergency response devices and patrols, late-night transport/escort service.

COSTS & FINANCIAL AID

Costs (2017–18) ***One-time required fee:*** $60. ***Tuition:*** $13,032 full-time, $362 per unit part-time. ***Payment plan:*** deferred payment. ***Waivers:*** employees or children of employees.

Financial Aid Of all full-time matriculated undergraduates who enrolled in 2015, 4,546 applied for aid, 3,863 were judged to have need, 235 had their need fully met. In 2015, 21 non-need-based awards were made. ***Average percent of need met:*** 48. ***Average financial aid package:*** $7768. ***Average need-based loan:*** $5505. ***Average need-based gift aid:*** $3240. ***Average non-need-based aid:*** $2076. ***Average indebtedness upon graduation:*** $52,986.

APPLYING

Options: electronic application, deferred entrance.

Application fee: $60.

Required: high school transcript, minimum 2.0 GPA, interview. ***Required for some:*** essay or personal statement.

Application deadlines: rolling (freshmen), rolling (transfers).

Notification: continuous (freshmen), continuous (transfers).

CONTACT

National University, 11255 North Torrey Pines Road, La Jolla, CA 92037-1011. *Toll-free phone:* 800-628-8648.

NewSchool of Architecture and Design

San Diego, California

http://www.newschoolarch.edu/

- **Proprietary** comprehensive, founded 1980
- **Urban** 1-acre campus
- **Coed, primarily men**
- **Moderately difficult** entrance level

FACULTY

Student/faculty ratio: 9:1.

ACADEMICS

Calendar: quarters. *Degrees:* bachelor's and master's.

Library: Richard Welsh Library at NewSchool of Architecture and Design. *Books:* 15,502 (physical), 123 (digital/electronic); *Serial titles:* 52 (physical); *Databases:* 8. Weekly public service hours: 68.

STUDENT LIFE

Activities and organizations: student-run newspaper, American Institute of Architects student chapter, Student Council, Night Owls, Alpha Rho Chi - Numisius Chapter, CMSA.

Campus security: 24-hour emergency response devices.

Student services: personal/psychological counseling.

FINANCIAL AID

Financial Aid Of all full-time matriculated undergraduates who enrolled in 2000, 71 applied for aid. 6 Federal Work-Study jobs (averaging $1544).

In 2000, 6 non-need-based awards were made. ***Average percent of need met:*** 90. ***Average financial aid package:*** $9700. ***Average non-need-based aid:*** $5000. ***Average indebtedness upon graduation:*** $40,000.

APPLYING
Standardized Tests *Recommended:* SAT or ACT (for admission).

Options: electronic application, early decision.

Application fee: $75.

Required: essay or personal statement, minimum 2.5 GPA. ***Required for some:*** high school transcript, portfolio. ***Recommended:*** letters of recommendation.

CONTACT
Kirk Nielson, Director of Enrollment and Field Recruitment, NewSchool of Architecture and Design, 1249 F Street, San Diego, CA 92101. *Phone:* 619-684-8841. *Toll-free phone:* 800-490-7081.
E-mail: knielson@newschoolarch.edu.

New York Film Academy
Burbank, California
http://https://www.nyfa.edu/

- **Independent** comprehensive, founded 1992
- **Suburban** campus with easy access to Los Angeles, New York, Miami
- **Coed**

Freshmen:
Average high school GPA: 2.5.

ACADEMICS
Degrees: certificates, associate, bachelor's, and master's.

COSTS
Costs (2016–17) ***Tuition:*** $40,000 full-time. Full-time tuition and fees vary according to course level, course load, degree level, program, and reciprocity agreements. ***Required fees:*** $2000 full-time. ***Room only:*** $1600. Room and board charges vary according to location.

APPLYING
Standardized Tests *Required:* SAT or ACT (for admission).

Application fee: $50.

Required: essay or personal statement, high school transcript, 2 letters of recommendation, portfolio.

CONTACT
Admissions Office, New York Film Academy, 3300 Riverside Drive, Burbank, CA 91505. *Phone:* 818-333-3558. *Fax:* 818-333 3557. *E-mail:* studios@nyfa.edu.

Northcentral University
San Diego, California
http://www.ncu.edu/

- **Proprietary** upper-level
- **Coed** 133 undergraduate students, 9% full-time, 65% women, 35% men
- **Minimally difficult** entrance level

UNDERGRAD STUDENTS
12 full-time, 121 part-time. Students come from 36 states and territories; 1 other country; 16% Black or African American, non-Hispanic/Latino; 12% Hispanic/Latino; 2% Asian, non-Hispanic/Latino; 0.8% American Indian or Alaska Native, non-Hispanic/Latino; 2% Two or more races, non-Hispanic/Latino; 27% Race/ethnicity unknown.

FACULTY
Total: 478, 19% full-time, 100% with terminal degrees.

ACADEMICS
Calendar: continuous. *Degrees:* bachelor's, master's, doctoral, post-master's, and postbachelor's certificates (offers only distance learning programs).

Special study options: accelerated degree program, distance learning, part-time degree program, services for LD students.

Computers: Students can access the following: free student e-mail accounts, online (class) grades, online (class) registration.
Library: Northcentral University Library (Virtual).

COSTS
Costs (2017–18) ***One-time required fee:*** $450. ***Tuition:*** $10,680 full-time, $1335 per course part-time. ***Payment plans:*** tuition prepayment, installment. ***Waivers:*** employees or children of employees.

APPLYING
Options: electronic application.
Notification: continuous (transfers).

CONTACT
Northcentral University, 2488 Historic Decatur Road, Suite 100, San Diego, CA 92106. *Phone:* 866-776-0331. *Toll-free phone:* 866-776-0331.

Northwestern Polytechnic University
Fremont, California
http://www.npu.edu/

CONTACT
Mr. Michael Tang, Admission Officer, Northwestern Polytechnic University, 47671 Westinghouse Drive, Fremont, CA 94539. *Phone:* 510-592-9688 Ext. 15. *Fax:* 510-657-8975. *E-mail:* admission@npu.edu.

Notre Dame de Namur University
Belmont, California
http://www.ndnu.edu/

CONTACT
Notre Dame de Namur University, 1500 Ralston Avenue, Belmont, CA 94002-1908. *Phone:* 650-508-3600. *Toll-free phone:* 800-263-0545.

Occidental College
Los Angeles, California
http://www.oxy.edu/

- **Independent** comprehensive, founded 1887
- **Urban** 120-acre campus with easy access to Los Angeles
- **Endowment** $371.7 million
- **Coed** 2,062 undergraduate students, 99% full-time, 57% women, 43% men
- **Very difficult** entrance level, 46% of applicants were admitted

UNDERGRAD STUDENTS
2,045 full-time, 17 part-time. Students come from 48 states and territories; 31 other countries; 52% are from out of state; 5% Black or African American, non-Hispanic/Latino; 15% Hispanic/Latino; 14% Asian, non-Hispanic/Latino; 0.1% Native Hawaiian or other Pacific Islander, non-Hispanic/Latino; 8% Two or more races, non-Hispanic/Latino; 2% Race/ethnicity unknown; 7% international; 2% transferred in; 79% live on campus.

Freshmen:
Admission: 6,409 applied, 2,936 admitted, 502 enrolled. ***Average high school GPA:*** 3.64. ***Test scores:*** SAT critical reading scores over 500: 99%; SAT math scores over 500: 99%; SAT writing scores over 500: 99%; ACT scores over 18: 100%; SAT critical reading scores over 600: 77%; SAT math scores over 600: 76%; SAT writing scores over 600: 78%; ACT scores over 24: 99%; SAT critical reading scores over 700: 25%; SAT math scores over 700: 30%; SAT writing scores over 700: 25%; ACT scores over 30: 52%.

Retention: 91% of full-time freshmen returned.

FACULTY
Total: 276, 65% full-time.
Student/faculty ratio: 10:1.

ACADEMICS
Calendar: semesters. *Degrees:* diplomas, bachelor's, and master's.

Special study options: advanced placement credit, double majors, honors programs, independent study, internships, off-campus study, services for LD students, student-designed majors, study abroad. ***ROTC:*** Army (c), Air Force (c).

Unusual degree programs: 3-2 engineering with California Institute of Technology, Columbia University; law with Columbia University, biotechnology with Keck Graduate Institute.

Computers: 200 computers/terminals are available on campus for general student use. Students can access the following: campus intranet, computer help desk, free student e-mail accounts, online (class) grades, online (class) registration, online (class) schedules. Campuswide network is available. 98% of college-owned or -operated housing units are wired for high-speed Internet access. Wireless service is available via entire campus.
Library: Mary Norton Clapp Library and Academic Commons plus 2 others. Study areas open 24 hours, 5-7 days a week; students can reserve study rooms.

STUDENT LIFE
Housing options: on-campus residence required through junior year; coed, women-only. Campus housing is university owned. Freshman campus housing is guaranteed.
Activities and organizations: drama/theater group, student-run newspaper, radio station, choral group, Dance Production, Greek Council, Vagina Monologues, Oxypreneurship, La Raza Coalition, national fraternities, national sororities.
Athletics Member NCAA. All Division III. ***Intercollegiate sports:*** baseball M, basketball M/W, cross-country running M/W, football M, golf M/W, lacrosse M(c)/W, rugby M(c)/W(c), soccer M/W, softball W, swimming and diving M/W, tennis M/W, track and field M/W, ultimate Frisbee M(c)/W(c), volleyball W, water polo M/W. ***Intramural sports:*** basketball M/W, soccer M/W.
Campus security: 24-hour emergency response devices and patrols, late-night transport/escort service, controlled dormitory access.
Student services: health clinic, personal/psychological counseling, women's center.

COSTS & FINANCIAL AID
Costs (2016–17) ***Comprehensive fee:*** $65,530 includes full-time tuition ($50,492), mandatory fees ($578), and room and board ($14,460). Part-time tuition: $2104 per unit. Part-time tuition and fees vary according to course load. ***Required fees:*** $578 per year part-time. ***College room only:*** $8230. Room and board charges vary according to board plan. ***Payment plans:*** tuition prepayment, installment. ***Waivers:*** employees or children of employees.
Financial Aid Of all full-time matriculated undergraduates who enrolled in 2015, 1,331 applied for aid, 1,147 were judged to have need, 1,145 had their need fully met. 800 Federal Work-Study jobs (averaging $2713). 181 state and other part-time jobs (averaging $1481). In 2015, 258 non-need-based awards were made. ***Average percent of need met:*** 100. ***Average financial aid package:*** $46,791. ***Average need-based loan:*** $6124. ***Average need-based gift aid:*** $36,889. ***Average non-need-based aid:*** $11,219. ***Average indebtedness upon graduation:*** $29,940. ***Financial aid deadline:*** 1/15.

APPLYING
Standardized Tests *Required:* SAT or ACT (for admission). *Recommended:* SAT Subject Tests (for admission).
Options: electronic application, early admission, early decision, deferred entrance.
Application fee: $65.
Required: essay or personal statement, high school transcript, 2 letters of recommendation. ***Recommended:*** interview.
Application deadlines: 1/15 (freshmen), 4/1 (transfers).
Early decision deadline: 11/15 (for plan 1), 1/1 (for plan 2).
Notification: 3/25 (freshmen), 5/1 (transfers), 12/15 (early decision plan 1), 2/1 (early decision plan 2).

CONTACT
Mr. Vince Cuseo, Vice President of Enrollment and Dean of the College, Occidental College, 1600 Campus Road, Los Angeles, CA 90041. *Phone:* 323-259-2700. *Toll-free phone:* 800-825-5262. *Fax:* 323-341-4875. *E-mail:* admission@oxy.edu.

Otis College of Art and Design
Los Angeles, California
http://www.otis.edu/

CONTACT
Otis College of Art and Design, 9045 Lincoln Boulevard, Los Angeles, CA 90045-9785. *Phone:* 310-665-2577. *Toll-free phone:* 800-527-OTIS.

Pacific College
Costa Mesa, California
http://www.pacific-college.edu/

CONTACT
Pacific College, 3160 Red Hill Avenue, Costa Mesa, CA 92626.

Pacific Oaks College
Pasadena, California
http://www.pacificoaks.edu/

CONTACT
Ms. Augusta Pickens, Office of Admissions, Pacific Oaks College, 5 Westmoreland Place, Pasadena, CA 91103. *Phone:* 626-397-1349. *Toll-free phone:* 877-314-2380. *Fax:* 626-666-1220. *E-mail:* admissions@pacificoaks.edu.

Pacific States University
Los Angeles, California
http://www.psuca.edu/

- **Independent** comprehensive, founded 1928
- **Urban** 1-acre campus
- **Coed** 19 undergraduate students, 100% full-time, 37% women, 63% men
- **Noncompetitive** entrance level

UNDERGRAD STUDENTS
19 full-time. Students come from 1 other state; 6 other countries; 16% Asian, non-Hispanic/Latino; 79% international; 21% transferred in.

Freshmen:
Admission: 1 enrolled.
Retention: 90% of full-time freshmen returned.

FACULTY
Total: 34, 21% full-time, 35% with terminal degrees.
Student/faculty ratio: 5:1.

ACADEMICS
Calendar: quarters. *Degrees:* certificates, diplomas, bachelor's, master's, doctoral, and postbachelor's certificates.
Special study options: academic remediation for entering students, accelerated degree program, adult/continuing education programs, distance learning, double majors, English as a second language, independent study.
Computers: 50 computers/terminals are available on campus for general student use. Students can access the following: online (class) schedules. Campuswide network is available. 90% of college-owned or -operated housing units are wired for high-speed Internet access. Wireless service is available via classrooms, computer labs, dorm rooms, libraries, student centers.
Library: University Library plus 1 other. Students can reserve study rooms.

STUDENT LIFE
Housing options: coed. Campus housing is university owned.
Campus security: patrols by trained security personnel during campus hours.

APPLYING
Standardized Tests *Required for some:* TOEFL or IELTS. *Recommended:* SAT or ACT (for admission).
Options: electronic application, deferred entrance.
Application fee: $100.
Required: high school transcript, minimum 2.5 GPA. ***Recommended:*** essay or personal statement.
Application deadlines: rolling (freshmen), rolling (transfers).
Notification: continuous (freshmen), continuous (transfers).

CONTACT
Mr. Maawiya Ayeva, Director of Admissions, Pacific States University, 3424 Wilshire Boulevard, 12th Floor, Los Angeles, CA 90010. *Phone:* 323-731-2383 Ext. 202. *Toll-free phone:* 888-200-0383. *Fax:* 323-731-7276. *E-mail:* admissions@psuca.edu.

Pacific Union College
Angwin, California
http://www.puc.edu/

- **Independent Seventh-day Adventist** comprehensive, founded 1882
- **Rural** 200-acre campus with easy access to San Francisco Bay Area
- **Coed**
- **Moderately difficult** entrance level

FACULTY
Student/faculty ratio: 13:1.

ACADEMICS
Calendar: quarters. *Degrees:* certificates, associate, bachelor's, and master's.
Library: W.E. Nelson Memorial Library.

STUDENT LIFE
Housing options: on-campus residence required through senior year; men-only, women-only. Campus housing is university owned.

Activities and organizations: drama/theater group, student-run newspaper, choral group, Student Association, Business Club, Asian Student Association, Korean Adventist Student Association, Student Organization of Latinos.

Athletics Member NAIA.

Campus security: 24-hour emergency response devices and patrols, late-night transport/escort service.

Student services: health clinic, personal/psychological counseling, women's center.

COSTS & FINANCIAL AID
Costs (2016–17) ***Comprehensive fee:*** $36,456 includes full-time tuition ($27,999), mandatory fees ($630), and room and board ($7827). Part-time tuition: $810 per unit. ***College room only:*** $4632.

Financial Aid Of all full-time matriculated undergraduates who enrolled in 2016, 1,282 applied for aid, 1,049 were judged to have need, 39 had their need fully met. In 2016, 240 non-need-based awards were made. ***Average percent of need met:*** 57. ***Average financial aid package:*** $25,507. ***Average need-based loan:*** $4745. ***Average need-based gift aid:*** $17,219. ***Average non-need-based aid:*** $12,335. ***Average indebtedness upon graduation:*** $40,263.

APPLYING
Standardized Tests *Required:* SAT or ACT (for admission).

Options: electronic application, deferred entrance.

Application fee: $30.

Required: high school transcript, minimum 2.3 GPA, 3 letters of recommendation.

CONTACT
Mr. Craig Philpott, Associate Director, Admissions, Pacific Union College, Enrollment Services, One Angwin Avenue, Angwin, CA 94508. *Phone:* 800-862-7080. *Toll-free phone:* 800-862-7080. *Fax:* 707-965-6671. *E-mail:* enroll@puc.edu.

Palo Alto University
Palo Alto, California
http://www.paloaltou.edu/

- **Independent** upper-level
- **Rural** campus with easy access to San Francisco Bay Area/Silicon Valley
- **Endowment** $1.4 million
- **Coed**

ACADEMICS
Calendar: quarters. *Degrees:* bachelor's, master's, and doctoral.

COSTS
Costs (2016–17) ***Tuition:*** $17,112 full-time. Full-time tuition and fees vary according to class time and program. No tuition increase for student's term of enrollment. ***Required fees:*** $5196 full-time.

CONTACT
Mr. Michael Teodosio, Assistant Director of Undergraduate Admissions, Palo Alto University, 1791 Arastradero Road, Palo Alto, CA 94304. *Phone:* 650-417-2050. *Toll-free phone:* 800-818-6136. *E-mail:* undergrad@paloaltou.edu.

Patten University
Oakland, California
http://patten.edu/

CONTACT
Ms. Kim Guerra, Director of Admissions, Patten University, 2433 Coolidge Avenue, Oakland, CA 94601-2699. *Phone:* 510-261-8500 Ext. 7763. *Toll-free phone:* 877-4PATTEN. *Fax:* 510-534-4344.

Pepperdine University
Malibu, California
http://www.pepperdine.edu/

- **Independent** university, founded 1937, affiliated with Church of Christ
- **Suburban** 830-acre campus with easy access to Los Angeles
- **Endowment** $781.3 million
- **Coed** 3,542 undergraduate students, 91% full-time, 59% women, 41% men
- **Very difficult** entrance level, 37% of applicants were admitted

UNDERGRAD STUDENTS
3,222 full-time, 320 part-time. Students come from 53 states and territories; 68 other countries; 16% are from out of state; 5% Black or African American, non-Hispanic/Latino; 14% Hispanic/Latino; 11% Asian, non-Hispanic/Latino; 0.2% Native Hawaiian or other Pacific Islander, non-Hispanic/Latino; 0.3% American Indian or Alaska Native, non-Hispanic/Latino; 5% Two or more races, non-Hispanic/Latino; 5% Race/ethnicity unknown; 11% international; 3% transferred in; 56% live on campus.

Freshmen:
Admission: 11,111 applied, 4,097 admitted, 743 enrolled. ***Average high school GPA:*** 3.64. ***Test scores:*** SAT critical reading scores over 500: 92%; SAT math scores over 500: 93%; SAT writing scores over 500: 91%; ACT scores over 18: 100%; SAT critical reading scores over 600: 51%; SAT math scores over 600: 59%; SAT writing scores over 600: 57%; ACT scores over 24: 89%; SAT critical reading scores over 700: 11%; SAT math scores over 700: 17%; SAT writing scores over 700: 10%; ACT scores over 30: 35%.

Retention: 90% of full-time freshmen returned.

FACULTY
Total: 681, 55% full-time, 74% with terminal degrees.

Student/faculty ratio: 14:1.

ACADEMICS
Calendar: semesters. *Degrees:* bachelor's, master's, and doctoral.

Special study options: adult/continuing education programs, advanced placement credit, distance learning, double majors, honors programs, independent study, internships, part-time degree program, student-designed majors, study abroad, summer session for credit. ***ROTC:*** Army (c), Air Force (c).

Unusual degree programs: 3-2 engineering with University of Southern California, Washington University in St. Louis.

Computers: 218 computers/terminals and 139 ports are available on campus for general student use. Students can access the following: campus intranet, computer help desk, free student e-mail accounts, online (class) grades, online (class) registration, online (class) schedules. Campuswide network is available. 100% of college-owned or -operated housing units are wired for high-speed Internet access. Wireless service is available via entire campus.

Library: Payson Library plus 5 others. *Books:* 348,364 (physical), 237,133 (digital/electronic); *Serial titles:* 411 (physical), 61,042 (digital/electronic); *Databases:* 150. Weekly public service hours: 112; students can reserve study rooms.

STUDENT LIFE

Housing options: on-campus residence required through sophomore year; men-only, women-only, special housing for students with disabilities. Campus housing is university owned. Freshman campus housing is guaranteed.

Activities and organizations: drama/theater group, student-run newspaper, radio and television station, choral group, Latino Student Association, Black Student Union, Panhellenic Council, Interfraternity Council, International Justice Mission, national fraternities, national sororities.

Athletics Member NCAA. All Division I. ***Intercollegiate sports:*** baseball M(s), basketball M(s)/W(s), cross-country running M(s)/W(s), golf M(s)/W(s), soccer M(c)/W(s), swimming and diving W(s), tennis M(s)/W(s), track and field M(s)/W(s), triathlon W, volleyball M(s)/W(s), water polo M(s). ***Intramural sports:*** basketball M/W, football M/W, golf M(c)/W(c), lacrosse M(c)/W(c), rugby M(c), soccer M/W, tennis M(c)/W(c), ultimate Frisbee M(c)/W(c), volleyball M/W.

Campus security: 24-hour emergency response devices and patrols, student patrols, late-night transport/escort service, controlled dormitory access, front gate security, 24-hour security in residence halls, controlled access, crime prevention programs.

Student services: health clinic, personal/psychological counseling.

COSTS & FINANCIAL AID

Costs (2016–17) ***Comprehensive fee:*** $64,352 includes full-time tuition ($49,770), mandatory fees ($252), and room and board ($14,330). Part-time tuition: $1565 per credit hour. ***Room and board:*** Room and board charges vary according to board plan and housing facility. ***Payment plan:*** installment. ***Waivers:*** employees or children of employees.

Financial Aid Of all full-time matriculated undergraduates who enrolled in 2016, 3,176 applied for aid, 1,647 were judged to have need, 305 had their need fully met. 901 Federal Work-Study jobs (averaging $1217). 230 state and other part-time jobs (averaging $1029). In 2016, 815 non-need-based awards were made. ***Average percent of need met:*** 75. ***Average financial aid package:*** $39,927. ***Average need-based loan:*** $5877. ***Average need-based gift aid:*** $36,283. ***Average non-need-based aid:*** $18,084. ***Average indebtedness upon graduation:*** $29,640.

APPLYING

Standardized Tests *Required:* SAT or ACT (for admission).

Options: electronic application.

Application fee: $65.

Required: essay or personal statement, high school transcript, 2 letters of recommendation.

Application deadlines: 1/5 (freshmen), 1/5 (transfers).

Notification: 4/1 (freshmen), 4/1 (transfers).

CONTACT

Ms. Wolf Hayley, Director of Admission, Enrollment Management, Pepperdine University, 24255 Pacific Coast Highway, Malibu, CA 90263. *Phone:* 310-506-4392. *E-mail:* hayley.wolf@pepperdine.edu.

See below for display ad and page 1458 for the College Close-Up.

Pima Medical Institute

Chula Vista, California

http://www.pmi.edu/

CONTACT

Admissions Office, Pima Medical Institute, 780 Bay Boulevard, Chula Vista, CA 91910. *Phone:* 619-425-3200. *Toll-free phone:* 800-477-PIMA.

Pitzer College

Claremont, California

http://www.pitzer.edu/

- **Independent** 4-year, founded 1963, part of The Claremont Colleges Consortium
- **Suburban** 35-acre campus with easy access to Los Angeles
- **Endowment** $127.0 million
- **Coed** 1,089 undergraduate students, 97% full-time, 56% women, 44% men
- **Very difficult** entrance level, 14% of applicants were admitted

UNDERGRAD STUDENTS
1,056 full-time, 33 part-time. Students come from 44 states and territories; 17 other countries; 52% are from out of state; 5% Black or African American, non-Hispanic/Latino; 15% Hispanic/Latino; 9% Asian, non-Hispanic/Latino; 0.5% American Indian or Alaska Native, non-Hispanic/Latino; 9% Two or more races, non-Hispanic/Latino; 6% Race/ethnicity unknown; 11% international; 0.9% transferred in; 73% live on campus.

Freshmen:
Admission: 4,142 applied, 569 admitted, 268 enrolled. ***Average high school GPA:*** 3.82. ***Test scores:*** SAT critical reading scores over 500: 100%; SAT math scores over 500: 100%; SAT critical reading scores over 600: 93%; SAT math scores over 600: 93%; ACT scores over 24: 100%; SAT critical reading scores over 700: 49%; SAT math scores over 700: 44%; ACT scores over 30: 66%.
Retention: 94% of full-time freshmen returned.

FACULTY
Total: 116, 71% full-time, 100% with terminal degrees.
Student/faculty ratio: 11:1.

ACADEMICS
Calendar: semesters. *Degree:* bachelor's.
Special study options: adult/continuing education programs, advanced placement credit, cooperative education, double majors, English as a second language, honors programs, independent study, internships, off-campus study, part-time degree program, services for LD students, student-designed majors, study abroad, summer session for credit. ***ROTC:*** Army (c), Air Force (c).
Unusual degree programs: 3-2 business administration; public administration, mathematics, psychology with Claremont Graduate University.
Computers: Students can access the following: campus intranet, computer help desk, free student e-mail accounts, online (class) grades, online (class) registration, online (class) schedules. Campuswide network is available. 100% of college-owned or -operated housing units are wired for high-speed Internet access. Wireless service is available via entire campus.
Library: Honnold Library plus 3 others. Students can reserve study rooms.

STUDENT LIFE
Housing options: on-campus residence required for freshman year; coed, cooperative, special housing for students with disabilities. Campus housing is university owned. Freshman campus housing is guaranteed.
Activities and organizations: drama/theater group, student-run newspaper, radio station, choral group, Student Senate, The Other Side, Without A Box, Residence Hall Association, PAct (Pitzer Activities).
Athletics Member NCAA. All Division III. ***Intercollegiate sports:*** baseball M, basketball M/W, cross-country running M/W, football M, golf M/W, lacrosse W, soccer M/W, softball W, swimming and diving M/W, tennis M/W, track and field M/W, volleyball W, water polo M/W. ***Intramural sports:*** badminton M(c)/W(c), basketball M/W, equestrian sports M(c)/W(c), fencing M(c)/W(c), field hockey M(c)/W(c), football M, ice hockey M(c)/W(c), lacrosse M(c), rugby M(c)/W(c), soccer M/W(c), tennis M(c)/W(c), ultimate Frisbee M(c)/W(c), volleyball M(c)/W(c).
Campus security: 24-hour emergency response devices and patrols, late-night transport/escort service, controlled dormitory access, LiveSafe App, CUC and Campus Safety Emergency RSS Feed.
Student services: health clinic, personal/psychological counseling, women's center.

FINANCIAL AID
Financial Aid Of all full-time matriculated undergraduates who enrolled in 2016, 492 applied for aid, 414 were judged to have need, 406 had their need fully met. In 2016, 12 non-need-based awards were made. ***Average percent of need met:*** 100. ***Average financial aid package:*** $45,338. ***Average need-based loan:*** $4101. ***Average need-based gift aid:*** $40,447. ***Average non-need-based aid:*** $6187. ***Average indebtedness upon graduation:*** $21,569. ***Financial aid deadline:*** 2/1.

APPLYING
Standardized Tests *Required for some:* SAT or ACT (for admission).
Options: electronic application, early decision, deferred entrance.
Application fee: $70.
Required: essay or personal statement, high school transcript, minimum 2.0 GPA, 3 letters of recommendation. ***Recommended:*** interview.
Application deadlines: 1/1 (freshmen), 4/1 (transfers).
Early decision deadline: 11/15 (for plan 1), 1/1 (for plan 2).
Notification: 4/1 (freshmen), 5/15 (transfers), 12/18 (early decision plan 1), 2/12 (early decision plan 2).

CONTACT
Ms. Yvonne Berumen, Vice President for Admission and Financial Aid, Pitzer College, 1050 North Mills Avenue, Claremont, CA 91711-6101. *Phone:* 909-621-8129. *Toll-free phone:* 800-748-9371. *Fax:* 909-621-8770. *E-mail:* admission@pitzer.edu.

Platt College
Alhambra, California
http://www.plattcollege.edu/

CONTACT
Mr. Detroit Whiteside, Director of Admissions, Platt College, 1000 South Fremont A9W, Alhambra, CA 91803. *Phone:* 323-258-8050. *Toll-free phone:* 888-866-6697 (in-state); 888-80-PLATT (out-of-state).

Platt College
Ontario, California
http://www.plattcollege.edu/

CONTACT
Ms. Jennifer Abandonato, Director of Admissions, Platt College, 3700 Inland Empire Boulevard, Ontario, CA 91764. *Phone:* 909-941-9410. *Toll-free phone:* 888-80-PLATT.

Platt College
Riverside, California
http://www.plattcollege.edu/

CONTACT
Platt College, 6465 Sycamore Canyon Boulevard, Suite 100, Riverside, CA 92507. *Toll-free phone:* 888-807-5288.

Platt College San Diego
San Diego, California
http://www.platt.edu/

CONTACT
Ms. Kimberly Harbert, Director of Admissions, Platt College San Diego, 6250 El Cajon Boulevard, San Diego, CA 92115-3919. *Phone:* 619-265-0107. *Toll-free phone:* 866-752-8826. *Fax:* 619-265-8655. *E-mail:* kharbert@platt.edu.

See next page for display ad and page 1462 for the College Close-Up.

Point Loma Nazarene University
San Diego, California
http://www.pointloma.edu/

- **Independent Nazarene** comprehensive, founded 1902
- **Suburban** 93-acre campus with easy access to San Diego
- **Coed** 3,053 undergraduate students, 85% full-time, 65% women, 35% men
- **Moderately difficult** entrance level, 69% of applicants were admitted

UNDERGRAD STUDENTS
2,592 full-time, 461 part-time. Students come from 40 states and territories; 10 other countries; 17% are from out of state; 2% Black or African American, non-Hispanic/Latino; 24% Hispanic/Latino; 6% Asian, non-Hispanic/Latino; 1% Native Hawaiian or other Pacific Islander, non-Hispanic/Latino; 0.4% American Indian or Alaska Native, non-Hispanic/Latino; 7% Two or more races, non-Hispanic/Latino; 2% Race/ethnicity unknown; 1% international; 12% transferred in; 56% live on campus.

Freshmen:
Admission: 3,162 applied, 2,195 admitted, 594 enrolled. ***Average high school GPA:*** 3.81. ***Test scores:*** SAT critical reading scores over 500: 83%; SAT math scores over 500: 84%; SAT writing scores over 500: 78%; ACT scores over 18: 99%; SAT critical reading scores over 600: 36%; SAT math scores over 600: 37%; SAT writing scores over 600: 31%; ACT scores over 24: 73%; SAT critical reading scores over 700: 4%; SAT math scores over 700: 5%; SAT writing scores over 700: 4%; ACT scores over 30: 16%.

Retention: 86% of full-time freshmen returned.

FACULTY

Total: 418, 32% full-time, 44% with terminal degrees.

Student/faculty ratio: 15:1.

ACADEMICS

Calendar: semesters. *Degrees:* certificates, bachelor's, master's, and post-master's certificates.

Special study options: academic remediation for entering students, accelerated degree program, adult/continuing education programs, advanced placement credit, distance learning, double majors, external degree program, honors programs, independent study, internships, off-campus study, part-time degree program, services for LD students, study abroad, summer session for credit. ***ROTC:*** Army (c), Navy (c), Air Force (c).

Computers: 346 computers/terminals and 5,320 ports are available on campus for general student use. Students can access the following: campus intranet, computer help desk, free student e-mail accounts, online (class) grades, online (class) registration, online (class) schedules. Campuswide network is available. 100% of college-owned or -operated housing units are wired for high-speed Internet access. Wireless service is available via entire campus.

Library: Ryan Library.

STUDENT LIFE

Housing options: on-campus residence required for freshman year; men-only, women-only, special housing for students with disabilities. Campus housing is university owned. Freshman campus housing is guaranteed.

Activities and organizations: drama/theater group, student-run newspaper, radio and television station, choral group.

Athletics Member NCAA. All Division II. ***Intercollegiate sports:*** baseball M(s), basketball M(s)/W(s), cross-country running W(s), golf W(s), soccer M(s)/W(s), tennis M(s)/W(s), track and field W(s), volleyball W(s). ***Intramural sports:*** basketball M/W, cheerleading M(c)/W(c), football M/W, rugby M(c)/W(c), soccer M/W, softball M/W, tennis M/W, volleyball M/W.

Campus security: 24-hour patrols, student patrols, late-night transport/escort service.

Student services: health clinic, personal/psychological counseling, women's center.

COSTS & FINANCIAL AID

Costs (2017–18) ***Comprehensive fee:*** $44,750 includes full-time tuition ($34,000), mandatory fees ($600), and room and board ($10,150). Full-time tuition and fees vary according to course load and program. Part-time tuition: $1417 per credit hour. Part-time tuition and fees vary according to course load and program. ***Room and board:*** Room and board charges vary according to board plan. ***Payment plan:*** installment. ***Waivers:*** senior citizens and employees or children of employees.

Financial Aid Of all full-time matriculated undergraduates who enrolled in 2015, 2,022 applied for aid, 1,714 were judged to have need, 241 had their need fully met. In 2015, 480 non-need-based awards were made. ***Average percent of need met:*** 61. ***Average financial aid package:*** $22,624. ***Average need-based loan:*** $4792. ***Average need-based gift aid:*** $17,325. ***Average non-need-based aid:*** $10,270. ***Average indebtedness upon graduation:*** $34,844.

APPLYING

Standardized Tests *Required:* SAT or ACT (for admission). *Recommended:* SAT (for admission), ACT (for admission).

Options: electronic application, early action.

Application fee: $55.

Required: essay or personal statement, high school transcript, minimum 2.8 GPA, 2 letters of recommendation.

Application deadlines: 2/15 (freshmen), 11/15 (early action).

Notification: 4/1 (freshmen), 12/21 (early action).

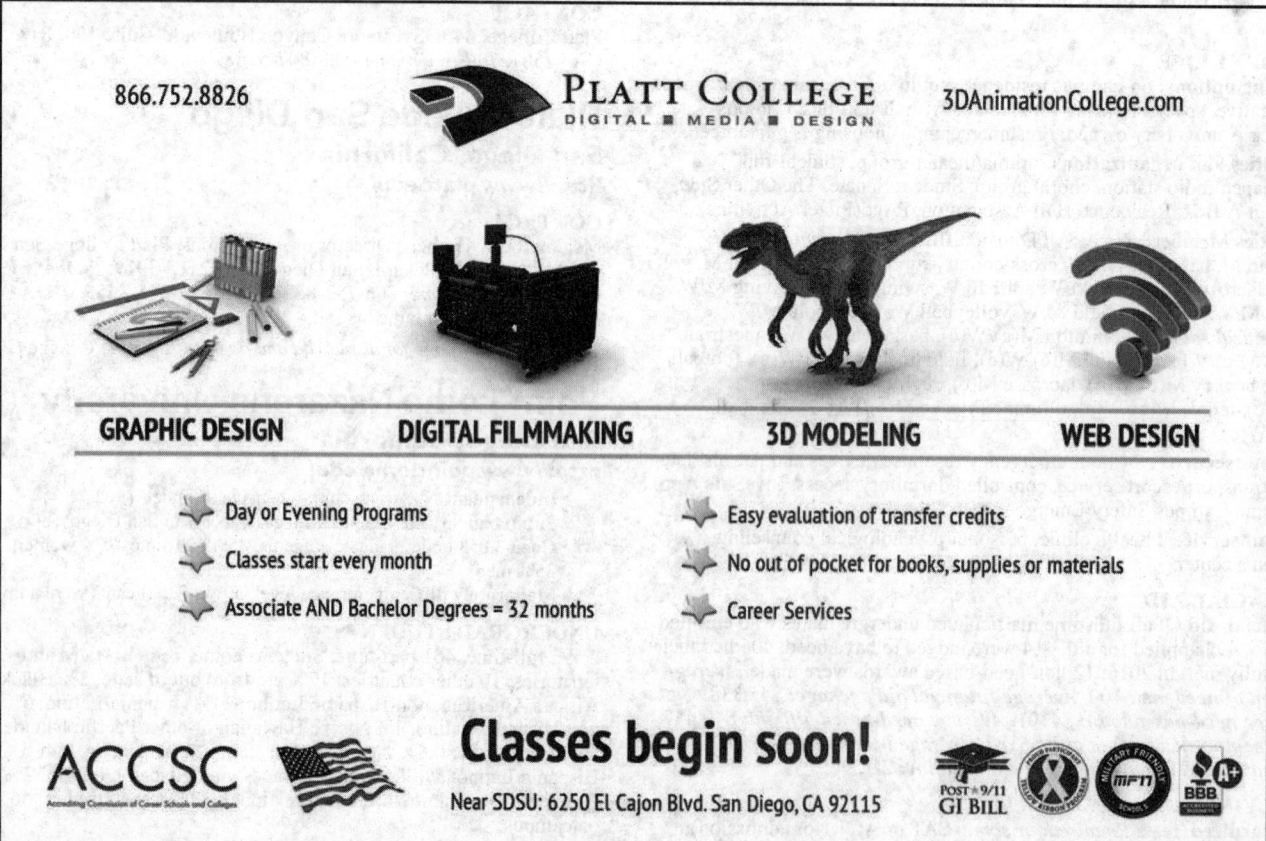

CONTACT
Shannon Hutchison, Director of Undergraduate Admissions, Point Loma Nazarene University, 3900 Lomaland Drive, San Diego, CA 92106.
Phone: 619-849-2541. *Toll-free phone:* 800-733-7770.
Fax: 619-849-2601. *E-mail:* admissions@pointloma.edu.

Pomona College

Claremont, California

http://www.pomona.edu/

- **Independent** 4-year, founded 1887
- **Suburban** 140-acre campus with easy access to Los Angeles
- **Endowment** $2.0 billion
- **Coed** 1,660 undergraduate students, 99% full-time, 51% women, 49% men
- **Most difficult** entrance level, 9% of applicants were admitted

UNDERGRAD STUDENTS
1,651 full-time, 9 part-time. Students come from 49 states and territories; 63 other countries; 70% are from out of state; 8% Black or African American, non-Hispanic/Latino; 15% Hispanic/Latino; 14% Asian, non-Hispanic/Latino; 0.1% Native Hawaiian or other Pacific Islander, non-Hispanic/Latino; 0.4% American Indian or Alaska Native, non-Hispanic/Latino; 7% Two or more races, non-Hispanic/Latino; 5% Race/ethnicity unknown; 11% international; 0.5% transferred in; 99% live on campus.

Freshmen:
Admission: 8,102 applied, 765 admitted, 411 enrolled. ***Test scores:*** SAT critical reading scores over 500: 100%; SAT math scores over 500: 100%; SAT writing scores over 500: 100%; ACT scores over 18: 100%; SAT critical reading scores over 600: 94%; SAT math scores over 600: 94%; SAT writing scores over 600: 94%; ACT scores over 24: 99%; SAT critical reading scores over 700: 63%; SAT math scores over 700: 65%; SAT writing scores over 700: 67%; ACT scores over 30: 82%.
Retention: 97% of full-time freshmen returned.

FACULTY
Total: 241, 78% full-time, 94% with terminal degrees.
Student/faculty ratio: 8:1.

ACADEMICS
Calendar: semesters. *Degree:* bachelor's.
Special study options: advanced placement credit, double majors, independent study, internships, off-campus study, services for LD students, student-designed majors, study abroad. ***ROTC:*** Army (c), Air Force (c).
Unusual degree programs: 3-2 engineering with California Institute of Technology, Washington University in St. Louis, Dartmouth College.
Computers: 180 computers/terminals are available on campus for general student use. Students can access the following: computer help desk, free student e-mail accounts, online (class) grades, online (class) registration, online (class) schedules. Campuswide network is available. 100% of college-owned or -operated housing units are wired for high-speed Internet access. Wireless service is available via entire campus.
Library: Honnold/Mudd Library plus 4 others.

STUDENT LIFE
Housing options: on-campus residence required for freshman year; coed. Campus housing is university owned. Freshman campus housing is guaranteed.
Activities and organizations: drama/theater group, student-run newspaper, radio station, choral group, Student Government, music/choral organizations, service organizations, intramural sports, outdoor activities club.
Athletics Member NCAA. All Division III. ***Intercollegiate sports:*** baseball M, basketball M/W, cross-country running M/W, football M, golf M/W, lacrosse W, soccer M/W, softball W, swimming and diving M/W, tennis M/W, track and field M/W, ultimate Frisbee M(c)/W(c), volleyball M(c)/W, water polo M/W. ***Intramural sports:*** badminton M(c)/W(c), basketball M/W, crew W(c), cross-country running M/W, equestrian sports M(c)/W(c), fencing M/W, field hockey M(c)/W(c), football M, golf M/W, lacrosse M(c), racquetball M/W, rock climbing M/W, skiing (cross-country) M(c)/W(c), skiing (downhill) M(c)/W(c), soccer M/W, softball M/W, squash M/W, swimming and diving M/W, tennis M/W, track and field M/W, ultimate Frisbee M, volleyball M/W, water polo M/W.
Campus security: 24-hour emergency response devices and patrols, late-night transport/escort service, controlled dormitory access.
Student services: health clinic, personal/psychological counseling, women's center.

COSTS & FINANCIAL AID
Costs (2016–17) ***Comprehensive fee:*** $64,957 includes full-time tuition ($49,005), mandatory fees ($347), and room and board ($15,605). ***Room and board:*** Room and board charges vary according to board plan. ***Payment plan:*** installment. ***Waivers:*** employees or children of employees.
Financial Aid Of all full-time matriculated undergraduates who enrolled in 2015, 1,148 applied for aid, 917 were judged to have need, 917 had their need fully met. 153 Federal Work-Study jobs (averaging $1566). 676 state and other part-time jobs (averaging $2300). In 2015, 2 non-need-based awards were made. ***Average percent of need met:*** 100. ***Average financial aid package:*** $48,034. ***Average need-based gift aid:*** $46,039. ***Average non-need-based aid:*** $5000. ***Average indebtedness upon graduation:*** $18,738. ***Financial aid deadline:*** 3/1.

APPLYING
Standardized Tests *Required:* SAT or ACT (for admission).
Options: electronic application, early admission, early decision, deferred entrance.
Application fee: $70.
Required: essay or personal statement, high school transcript, 2 letters of recommendation. ***Recommended:*** interview, supplemental forms for visual and performing arts and science research.
Application deadlines: 1/1 (freshmen), 2/15 (transfers).
Early decision deadline: 11/1 (for plan 1), 1/1 (for plan 2).
Notification: 4/1 (freshmen), 4/1 (transfers), 12/15 (early decision plan 1), 2/15 (early decision plan 2).

CONTACT
Mr. C. Seth Allen, Vice President for Enrollment and Dean of Admissions and Financial Aid, Pomona College, 333 North College Way, Claremont, CA 91711. *Phone:* 909-621-8134. *Fax:* 909-621-8952.
E-mail: admissions@pomona.edu.

Providence Christian College

Pasadena, California

http://www.providencecc.edu/

CONTACT
Providence Christian College, 1539 East Howard Street, Pasadena, CA 91124.

SAE Expression College

Emeryville, California

http://www.sae.edu/

CONTACT
SAE Expression College, 6601 Shellmound Street, Emeryville, CA 94608. *Toll-free phone:* 877-833-8800.

Saint Katherine College

San Marcos, California

http://www.stkath.org/

- **Independent Christian** 4-year
- **Suburban** 2-acre campus with easy access to San Diego, CA
- **Endowment** $32,123
- **Coed**
- 62% of applicants were admitted

FACULTY
Student/faculty ratio: 9:1.

ACADEMICS
Calendar: semesters. *Degree:* bachelor's.
Library: Saint Katherine College Library plus 1 other. *Books:* 12,500 (physical); *Serial titles:* 10 (physical); *Databases:* 5.

STUDENT LIFE

Housing options: men-only, women-only. Campus housing is leased by the school. Freshman applicants given priority for college housing.

Activities and organizations: student-run newspaper, Fellowship of Christian Athletes, Orthodox Christian Fellowship.

Athletics Member NCCAA.

Student services: personal/psychological counseling.

COSTS

Costs (2016–17) ***One-time required fee:*** $200. ***Comprehensive fee:*** $28,000 includes full-time tuition ($19,500), mandatory fees ($400), and room and board ($8100). Full-time tuition and fees vary according to course load and program. Part-time tuition: $14,625 per year. Part-time tuition and fees vary according to course load and program. ***Required fees:*** $200 per term part-time. ***Payment plans:*** tuition prepayment, installment, deferred payment.

APPLYING

Standardized Tests *Required:* SAT or ACT (for admission).

Options: electronic application.

Required: essay or personal statement, high school transcript, minimum 2.5 GPA, 2 letters of recommendation, interview.

CONTACT

Dean Marina Karavokiris, Dean of Admissions and Registrar, Saint Katherine College, 1637 Capalina Road, San Marcos, CA 92069. *Phone:* 760-471-1316 Ext. 307. *Fax:* 760-471.1314. *E-mail:* admissions@stkath.org.

Saint Mary's College of California

Moraga, California

http://www.stmarys-ca.edu/

- **Independent Roman Catholic** upper-level, founded 1863
- **Suburban** 420-acre campus with easy access to San Francisco
- **Endowment** $143.9 million
- **Coed** 2,802 undergraduate students, 93% full-time, 60% women, 40% men
- **Moderately difficult** entrance level, 80% of applicants were admitted

UNDERGRAD STUDENTS

2,597 full-time, 205 part-time. Students come from 35 states and territories; 26 other countries; 11% are from out of state; 4% Black or African American, non-Hispanic/Latino; 26% Hispanic/Latino; 12% Asian, non-Hispanic/Latino; 1% Native Hawaiian or other Pacific Islander, non-Hispanic/Latino; 0.4% American Indian or Alaska Native, non-Hispanic/Latino; 7% Two or more races, non-Hispanic/Latino; 3% Race/ethnicity unknown; 2% international; 5% transferred in; 55% live on campus.

Freshmen:

Admission: 4,711 applied, 3,787 admitted.

FACULTY

Total: 512, 42% full-time.

Student/faculty ratio: 11:1.

ACADEMICS

Calendar: 4-1-4. *Degrees:* bachelor's, master's, and doctoral.

Special study options: adult/continuing education programs, advanced placement credit, double majors, honors programs, independent study, internships, off-campus study, part-time degree program, services for LD students, student-designed majors, study abroad, summer session for credit. ***ROTC:*** Army (c), Air Force (c).

Unusual degree programs: 3-2 engineering with Washington University in St. Louis, University of Southern California in Los Angeles; education.

Computers: 244 computers/terminals and 1,800 ports are available on campus for general student use. Students can access the following: campus intranet, computer help desk, free student e-mail accounts, online (class) grades, online (class) registration, online (class) schedules, student accounts. Campuswide network is available. 100% of college-owned or -operated housing units are wired for high-speed Internet access. Wireless service is available via entire campus.

Library: St. Albert Hall Library. *Books:* 177,000 (physical), 170,000 (digital/electronic); *Serial titles:* 47,000 (digital/electronic); *Databases:* 229. Students can reserve study rooms.

STUDENT LIFE

Housing options: coed, men-only, women-only, special housing for students with disabilities. Campus housing is university owned. Freshman campus housing is guaranteed.

Activities and organizations: drama/theater group, student-run newspaper, radio and television station, choral group, Gael Force, Campus Activities Board, LASA-Latin American Student Association-Black Student Union, La Hermandad, Asian Pacific American Student Association.

Athletics Member NCAA. All Division I. ***Intercollegiate sports:*** baseball M(s), basketball M(s)/W(s), cheerleading W, crew M(c)/W(s), cross-country running M(s)/W(s), golf M(s), lacrosse M(c)/W(s), rugby M(c), soccer M(s)/W(s), softball W(s), tennis M(s)/W(s), track and field M(s)/W(s), volleyball W(s), water polo M(c)/W(c). ***Intramural sports:*** badminton M/W, baseball M(c), basketball M/W, football M/W, soccer M(c)/W(c), softball M/W, tennis M(c)/W(c), volleyball M(c)/W(c).

Campus security: 24-hour emergency response devices and patrols, late-night transport/escort service.

Student services: health clinic, personal/psychological counseling, women's center.

COSTS & FINANCIAL AID

Costs (2017–18) ***Comprehensive fee:*** $61,056 includes full-time tuition ($45,536), mandatory fees ($150), and room and board ($15,370). Part-time tuition: $5706 per course. ***Required fees:*** $75 per term part-time. ***Room and board:*** Room and board charges vary according to board plan and housing facility. ***Waivers:*** employees or children of employees.

Financial Aid Of all full-time matriculated undergraduates who enrolled in 2015, 2,134 applied for aid, 1,932 were judged to have need, 163 had their need fully met. In 2015, 406 non-need-based awards were made. ***Average percent of need met:*** 62. ***Average financial aid package:*** $27,902. ***Average need-based loan:*** $4702. ***Average need-based gift aid:*** $23,119. ***Average non-need-based aid:*** $15,766. ***Average indebtedness upon graduation:*** $31,203.

APPLYING

Standardized Tests *Required:* SAT or ACT (for admission).

Options: electronic application, early action, deferred entrance.

Application fee: $60.

Application deadlines: 7/1 (transfers), 11/15 (early action).

Notification: continuous (transfers), 1/15 (early action).

CONTACT

Mr. Michael McKeon, Dean of Admissions, Saint Mary's College of California, 1928 St. Marys Road, P.M.B. 4800, Moraga, CA 94575-4800. *Phone:* 925-631-4224. *Toll-free phone:* 800-800-4SMC. *Fax:* 925-376-7193. *E-mail:* smcadmit@stmarys-ca.edu.

★ Samuel Merritt University

Oakland, California

http://www.samuelmerritt.edu/

- **Independent** upper-level, founded 1909
- **Urban** 1-acre campus with easy access to San Francisco
- **Endowment** $42.7 million
- **Coed, primarily women** 738 undergraduate students, 71% full-time, 83% women, 17% men

UNDERGRAD STUDENTS

521 full-time, 217 part-time. Students come from 2 states and territories; 0.2% are from out of state; 4% Black or African American, non-Hispanic/Latino; 20% Hispanic/Latino; 25% Asian, non-Hispanic/Latino; 0.8% Native Hawaiian or other Pacific Islander, non-Hispanic/Latino; 0.2% American Indian or Alaska Native, non-Hispanic/Latino; 6% Two or more races, non-Hispanic/Latino; 7% Race/ethnicity unknown; 29% transferred in.

FACULTY

Total: 333, 47% full-time, 42% with terminal degrees.

Student/faculty ratio: 9:1.

ACADEMICS
Calendar: trimesters. *Degrees:* bachelor's, master's, doctoral, and post-master's certificates (bachelor's degree offered jointly with Saint Mary's College of California).

Special study options: academic remediation for entering students, accelerated degree program, advanced placement credit, cooperative education, distance learning, independent study, internships, off-campus study, part-time degree program, services for LD students.

Computers: 160 computers/terminals are available on campus for general student use. Students can access the following: campus intranet, computer help desk, free student e-mail accounts, online (class) grades, online (class) registration, online (class) schedules. Campuswide network is available. Wireless service is available via entire campus.
Library: John A. Graziano Memorial Library. *Books:* 11,777 (physical), 242 (digital/electronic); *Serial titles:* 719 (physical), 16,204 (digital/electronic); *Databases:* 24. Weekly public service hours: 86; students can reserve study rooms.

STUDENT LIFE
Housing options: college housing not available.

Activities and organizations: Student Body Association, California Podiatric Medical Students' Association (CPMSA), International Healthcare Club, Community Service Honor Society, Scholars in Service.

Campus security: 24-hour emergency response devices and patrols, late-night transport/escort service, 24-hour controlled access.

Student services: health clinic, personal/psychological counseling.

FINANCIAL AID
Financial Aid Of all full-time matriculated undergraduates who enrolled in 2015, 714 applied for aid, 700 were judged to have need. 147 Federal Work-Study jobs (averaging $1354). ***Average percent of need met:*** 18. ***Average financial aid package:*** $11,358. ***Average need-based loan:*** $5534. ***Average need-based gift aid:*** $12,120.

APPLYING
Options: electronic application, deferred entrance.

Application fee: $45.

CONTACT
Samuel Merritt University, 3100 Telegraph Avenue, Oakland, CA 94609-3108. *Phone:* 510-869-1508. *Toll-free phone:* 800-607-6377.

San Diego Christian College

Santee, California

http://www.sdcc.edu/

- **Independent nondenominational** comprehensive, founded 1970
- **Suburban** 10-acre campus with easy access to San Diego
- **Endowment** $656,599
- **Coed**
- **Minimally difficult** entrance level

FACULTY
Student/faculty ratio: 17:1.

ACADEMICS
Calendar: semesters. *Degrees:* associate, bachelor's, master's, and postbachelor's certificates.
Library: San Diego Christian College. *Books:* 64,247 (physical), 338,731 (digital/electronic); *Serial titles:* 257 (physical), 24,477 (digital/electronic); *Databases:* 106. Weekly public service hours: 75; students can reserve study rooms.

STUDENT LIFE
Housing options: on-campus residence required through sophomore year; men-only, women-only. Campus housing is leased by the school. Freshman campus housing is guaranteed.

Activities and organizations: drama/theater group, choral group, ASB - Student Government, Service and Community Engagement, Ministry Teams, Flight team, Intramurals.

Athletics Member NAIA.

Campus security: 24-hour emergency response devices, late-night transport/escort service.

Student services: health clinic, personal/psychological counseling.

COSTS & FINANCIAL AID
Costs (2016–17) ***Comprehensive fee:*** $40,524 includes full-time tuition ($28,100), mandatory fees ($1450), and room and board ($10,974). Full-time tuition and fees vary according to course load, location, and program. Part-time tuition: $1210 per credit. Part-time tuition and fees vary according to course load, location, and program. ***Required fees:*** $290 per term part-time. ***Room and board:*** Room and board charges vary according to board plan and student level.

Financial Aid Of all full-time matriculated undergraduates who enrolled in 2016, 650 applied for aid, 615 were judged to have need, 150 had their need fully met. 65 Federal Work-Study jobs (averaging $2400). 29 state and other part-time jobs (averaging $2400). In 2016, 18 non-need-based awards were made. ***Average financial aid package:*** $24,561. ***Average need-based loan:*** $3505. ***Average need-based gift aid:*** $4516. ***Average non-need-based aid:*** $10,369. ***Average indebtedness upon graduation:*** $19,212. ***Financial aid deadline:*** 7/1.

APPLYING
Standardized Tests *Required for some:* SAT or ACT (for admission).

Options: electronic application, deferred entrance.

Application fee: $25.

Required: essay or personal statement, high school transcript, 1 letter of recommendation. ***Required for some:*** interview. ***Recommended:*** minimum 2.8 GPA.

CONTACT
Christine Roberts, Admissions Director, San Diego Christian College, 200 Riverview Parkway, Santee, CA 92017. *Phone:* 619-201-8760. *Toll-free phone:* 800-676-2242. *Fax:* 619-201-8749. *E-mail:* christine.roberts@sdcc.edu.

San Diego State University

San Diego, California

http://www.sdsu.edu/

- **State-supported** university, founded 1897, part of California State University System
- **Urban** 283-acre campus with easy access to San Diego
- **Endowment** $223.2 million
- **Coed** 29,853 undergraduate students, 90% full-time, 54% women, 46% men
- **Moderately difficult** entrance level, 35% of applicants were admitted

UNDERGRAD STUDENTS
26,788 full-time, 3,065 part-time. Students come from 52 states and territories; 115 other countries; 9% are from out of state; 4% Black or African American, non-Hispanic/Latino; 31% Hispanic/Latino; 14% Asian, non-Hispanic/Latino; 0.2% Native Hawaiian or other Pacific Islander, non-Hispanic/Latino; 0.3% American Indian or Alaska Native, non-Hispanic/Latino; 7% Two or more races, non-Hispanic/Latino; 4% Race/ethnicity unknown; 7% international; 12% transferred in; 15% live on campus.

Freshmen:
Admission: 60,691 applied, 20,943 admitted, 5,077 enrolled. ***Average high school GPA:*** 3.67. ***Test scores:*** SAT critical reading scores over 500: 75%; SAT math scores over 500: 81%; SAT writing scores over 500: 70%; ACT scores over 18: 97%; SAT critical reading scores over 600: 28%; SAT math scores over 600: 37%; SAT writing scores over 600: 24%; ACT scores over 24: 69%; SAT critical reading scores over 700: 3%; SAT math scores over 700: 4%; SAT writing scores over 700: 2%; ACT scores over 30: 13%.

Retention: 90% of full-time freshmen returned.

FACULTY
Total: 1,783, 49% full-time, 61% with terminal degrees.

Student/faculty ratio: 27:1.

ACADEMICS
Calendar: semesters. *Degrees:* bachelor's, master's, doctoral, and postbachelor's certificates.

Special study options: academic remediation for entering students, advanced placement credit, distance learning, double majors, English as a second language, external degree program, freshman honors college, honors programs, independent study, internships, off-campus study, services for LD students, student-designed majors, study abroad, summer session for credit. ***ROTC:*** Army (b), Navy (b), Air Force (b).

Computers: 2,000 computers/terminals are available on campus for general student use. Students can access the following: computer help desk, free student e-mail accounts, online (class) grades, online (class) registration, online (class) schedules, learning management system. Campuswide network is available. 100% of college-owned or -operated housing units are wired for high-speed Internet access. Wireless service is available via entire campus.

Library: Malcolm A. Love Library. *Books:* 2.2 million (physical), 776,490 (digital/electronic); *Databases:* 130. Weekly public service hours: 99; study areas open 24 hours, 5-7 days a week; students can reserve study rooms.

STUDENT LIFE

Housing options: on-campus residence required for freshman year; coed, special housing for students with disabilities. Campus housing is university owned. Freshman applicants given priority for college housing.

Activities and organizations: drama/theater group, student-run newspaper, radio and television station, choral group, marching band, AB Samahan, Asian Pacific Student Alliance, Enviro-Business Society, M.E.Ch.A de SDSU, Social fraternities and sororities, including both general and culturally based organizations, national fraternities, national sororities.

Athletics Member NCAA. All Division I. ***Intercollegiate sports:*** baseball M(s), basketball M(s)/W(s), cross-country running W(s), football M(s), golf M(s)/W(s), lacrosse W(s), rowing W(s), soccer M(s)/W(s), softball W(s), swimming and diving W(s), tennis M(s)/W(s), track and field W(s), volleyball W(s), water polo W(s). ***Intramural sports:*** basketball M/W, bowling M/W, football M/W, ice hockey M(c), lacrosse M(c)/W(c), racquetball M/W, rowing M(c)/W(c), rugby M(c), skiing (downhill) M(c)/W(c), soccer M(c)/W(c), softball M/W, tennis M(c)/W(c), triathlon M(c)/W(c), ultimate Frisbee M(c)/W(c), volleyball M(c)/W(c), water polo M(c)/W(c).

Campus security: 24-hour emergency response devices and patrols, student patrols, late-night transport/escort service.

Student services: health clinic, personal/psychological counseling, women's center.

COSTS & FINANCIAL AID

Costs (2016–17) ***Tuition:*** state resident $5472 full-time; nonresident $16,632 full-time. Full-time tuition and fees vary according to course load, degree level, and location. Part-time tuition and fees vary according to course load, degree level, and location. ***Required fees:*** $1612 full-time. ***Room and board:*** $14,812. Room and board charges vary according to board plan and housing facility. ***Payment plan:*** installment. ***Waivers:*** employees or children of employees.

Financial Aid Of all full-time matriculated undergraduates who enrolled in 2016, 18,000 applied for aid, 14,800 were judged to have need, 4,400 had their need fully met. 660 Federal Work-Study jobs (averaging $2200). In 2016, 1000 non-need-based awards were made. ***Average percent of need met:*** 69. ***Average financial aid package:*** $11,400. ***Average need-based loan:*** $4300. ***Average need-based gift aid:*** $9600. ***Average non-need-based aid:*** $2500. ***Average indebtedness upon graduation:*** $19,969. ***Financial aid deadline:*** 3/2.

APPLYING

Standardized Tests *Required:* SAT or ACT (for admission).

Options: electronic application.

Application fee: $55.

Required: high school transcript.

Application deadlines: 11/30 (freshmen), 11/30 (transfers).

Notification: 3/1 (freshmen), 3/1 (transfers).

CONTACT

Office of Admissions, San Diego State University, 5500 Campanile Drive, San Diego, CA 92182-7455. *Phone:* 619-594-6336. *Toll-free phone:* 855-594-6336 (in-state); 855-594-3983 (out-of-state). *E-mail:* admissions@sdsu.edu.

San Diego State University–Imperial Valley Campus

Calexico, California

http://www.ivcampus.sdsu.edu/

CONTACT

Aracely Bororquez, Admissions Department, San Diego State University–Imperial Valley Campus, 720 Heber Avenue, Calexico, CA 92231. *Phone:* 760-768-5506. *Fax:* 760-768-5589. *E-mail:* transfer@mail.sdsu.edu.

San Francisco Art Institute

San Francisco, California

http://www.sfai.edu/

- **Independent** comprehensive, founded 1871
- **Urban** 4-acre campus with easy access to San Francisco
- **Endowment** $8.8 million
- **Coed** 338 undergraduate students, 92% full-time, 62% women, 38% men
- **Moderately difficult** entrance level, 38% of applicants were admitted

UNDERGRAD STUDENTS

312 full-time, 26 part-time. Students come from 34 states and territories; 22 other countries; 41% are from out of state; 4% Black or African American, non-Hispanic/Latino; 16% Hispanic/Latino; 5% Asian, non-Hispanic/Latino; 0.9% American Indian or Alaska Native, non-Hispanic/Latino; 9% Two or more races, non-Hispanic/Latino; 3% Race/ethnicity unknown; 20% international; 10% transferred in; 34% live on campus.

Freshmen:

Admission: 492 applied, 186 admitted, 62 enrolled. ***Average high school GPA:*** 2.97. ***Test scores:*** SAT critical reading scores over 500: 72%; SAT math scores over 500: 64%; SAT writing scores over 500: 77%; ACT scores over 18: 100%; SAT critical reading scores over 600: 43%; SAT math scores over 600: 21%; SAT writing scores over 600: 23%; ACT scores over 24: 50%; SAT math scores over 700: 7%.

Retention: 49% of full-time freshmen returned.

FACULTY

Total: 110, 23% full-time, 80% with terminal degrees.

Student/faculty ratio: 9:1.

ACADEMICS

Calendar: semesters. *Degrees:* bachelor's, master's, and postbachelor's certificates.

Special study options: academic remediation for entering students, distance learning, English as a second language, external degree program, honors programs, independent study, internships, off-campus study, services for LD students, study abroad, summer session for credit.

Computers: 150 computers/terminals are available on campus for general student use. Students can access the following: computer help desk, free student e-mail accounts, online (class) grades, online (class) registration, online (class) schedules. Campuswide network is available. 100% of college-owned or -operated housing units are wired for high-speed Internet access. Wireless service is available via entire campus.

Library: Anne Bremer Memorial Library plus 1 other. *Books:* 31,831 (physical); *Serial titles:* 126 (physical), 791 (digital/electronic); *Databases:* 6. Weekly public service hours: 59.

STUDENT LIFE

Housing options: on-campus residence required for freshman year; coed. Campus housing is leased by the school and is provided by a third party. Freshman applicants given priority for college housing.

Activities and organizations: student-run newspaper, radio station, SFAEYE, Student Union, LOGS (Legion of Graduate Students), Tea and Heresies, TWR (Radio Station).

Campus security: 24-hour patrols, security cameras.

Student services: personal/psychological counseling.

COSTS & FINANCIAL AID

Costs (2016–17) ***Comprehensive fee:*** $58,505 includes full-time tuition ($42,220), mandatory fees ($870), and room and board ($15,415). Full-time tuition and fees vary according to degree level. Part-time tuition: $1849 per unit. Part-time tuition and fees vary according to degree level.

College room only: $11,500. Room and board charges vary according to housing facility. ***Payment plan:*** installment. ***Waivers:*** employees or children of employees.

Financial Aid Of all full-time matriculated undergraduates who enrolled in 2016, 200 applied for aid, 171 were judged to have need, 17 had their need fully met. In 2016, 128 non-need-based awards were made. ***Average percent of need met:*** 53. ***Average financial aid package:*** $15,441. ***Average need-based loan:*** $2318. ***Average need-based gift aid:*** $5918. ***Average non-need-based aid:*** $5583. ***Average indebtedness upon graduation:*** $32,515.

APPLYING

Standardized Tests *Recommended:* SAT or ACT (for admission).

Options: electronic application, early action, deferred entrance.

Application fee: $75.

Required: essay or personal statement, high school transcript, 1 letter of recommendation. ***Required for some:*** portfolio and artist statement for BFA applicants, critical essay for BA applicants. ***Recommended:*** minimum 2.5 GPA, interview.

Application deadlines: rolling (freshmen), rolling (transfers).

Notification: continuous (freshmen), continuous (transfers).

CONTACT

Office of Admissions, San Francisco Art Institute, 800 Chestnut Street, San Francisco, CA 94133. *Phone:* 415-749-4500. *Toll-free phone:* 800-345-SFAI. *Fax:* 415-749-4592. *E-mail:* admissions@sfai.edu.

San Francisco Conservatory of Music

San Francisco, California

http://www.sfcm.edu/

- **Independent** comprehensive, founded 1917
- **Urban** 2-acre campus with easy access to San Francisco Bay Area
- **Endowment** $37.1 million
- **Coed** 188 undergraduate students, 99% full-time, 45% women, 55% men

UNDERGRAD STUDENTS

186 full-time, 2 part-time. Students come from 26 states and territories; 14 other countries; 48% are from out of state; 4% Black or African American, non-Hispanic/Latino; 6% Hispanic/Latino; 7% Asian, non-Hispanic/Latino; 1% American Indian or Alaska Native, non-Hispanic/Latino; 11% Two or more races, non-Hispanic/Latino; 6% Race/ethnicity unknown; 34% international; 10% transferred in; 61% live on campus.

Freshmen:

Admission: 54 enrolled.

Retention: 100% of full-time freshmen returned.

FACULTY

Total: 145, 22% full-time, 10% with terminal degrees.

Student/faculty ratio: 6:1.

ACADEMICS

Calendar: semesters. *Degrees:* diplomas, bachelor's, master's, post-master's, and postbachelor's certificates.

Special study options: academic remediation for entering students, advanced placement credit, cooperative education, English as a second language, independent study, internships, services for LD students.

Computers: 12 computers/terminals and 350 ports are available on campus for general student use. Students can access the following: campus intranet, computer help desk, free student e-mail accounts, online (class) grades, online (class) registration, online (class) schedules. Campuswide network is available. 100% of college-owned or -operated housing units are wired for high-speed Internet access. Wireless service is available via entire campus.

Library: San Francisco Conservatory of Music Library. *Books:* 22,873 (physical), 3,073 (digital/electronic); *Serial titles:* 70 (physical), 374 (digital/electronic); *Databases:* 13. Weekly public service hours: 72.

STUDENT LIFE

Housing options: on-campus residence required through sophomore year; coed. Campus housing is leased by the school and is provided by a third party. Freshman campus housing is guaranteed.

Activities and organizations: drama/theater group, choral group, Yoga Group, Student Counsel.

Campus security: 24-hour emergency response devices and patrols, controlled dormitory access, resident assistant on-call for residential hall residents, after hours on-call mental health counceling.

Student services: personal/psychological counseling.

COSTS & FINANCIAL AID

Costs (2016–17) ***One-time required fee:*** $50. ***Comprehensive fee:*** $59,110 includes full-time tuition ($42,400), mandatory fees ($1010), and room and board ($15,700). Part-time tuition: $1868 per credit. Part-time tuition and fees vary according to course load. ***Required fees:*** $1010 per year part-time. ***College room only:*** $12,100. Room and board charges vary according to board plan and housing facility. ***Payment plan:*** installment. ***Waivers:*** employees or children of employees.

Financial Aid Of all full-time matriculated undergraduates who enrolled in 2016, 157 applied for aid, 126 were judged to have need, 98 had their need fully met. 25 Federal Work-Study jobs (averaging $2500). 4 state and other part-time jobs (averaging $2500). In 2016, 34 non-need-based awards were made. ***Average percent of need met:*** 46. ***Average financial aid package:*** $35,305. ***Average need-based loan:*** $5200. ***Average need-based gift aid:*** $17,754. ***Average non-need-based aid:*** $15,900. ***Average indebtedness upon graduation:*** $36,113. ***Financial aid deadline:*** 3/1.

APPLYING

Required: essay or personal statement, high school transcript, minimum 2.5 GPA, 2 letters of recommendation, audition, pre-screen recording in select areas. ***Required for some:*** interview.

CONTACT

Ms. Melissa Cocco-Mitten, Director of Admissions, San Francisco Conservatory of Music, 50 Oak Street, San Francisco, CA 94102. *Phone:* 415-503-6231. *Fax:* 415-503-6299. *E-mail:* admit@sfcm.edu.

San Francisco State University

San Francisco, California

http://www.sfsu.edu/

- **State-supported** university, founded 1899, part of California State University System
- **Urban** 142-acre campus
- **Endowment** $72.2 million
- **Coed** 25,945 undergraduate students, 83% full-time, 56% women, 44% men
- **Moderately difficult** entrance level, 68% of applicants were admitted

UNDERGRAD STUDENTS

21,515 full-time, 4,430 part-time. 1% are from out of state; 5% Black or African American, non-Hispanic/Latino; 30% Hispanic/Latino; 27% Asian, non-Hispanic/Latino; 0.5% Native Hawaiian or other Pacific Islander, non-Hispanic/Latino; 0.2% American Indian or Alaska Native, non-Hispanic/Latino; 6% Two or more races, non-Hispanic/Latino; 5% Race/ethnicity unknown; 7% international; 11% transferred in; 15% live on campus.

Freshmen:

Admission: 36,223 applied, 24,704 admitted, 3,642 enrolled. ***Average high school GPA:*** 3.23. ***Test scores:*** SAT critical reading scores over 500: 45%; SAT math scores over 500: 48%; ACT scores over 18: 79%; SAT critical reading scores over 600: 12%; SAT math scores over 600: 11%; ACT scores over 24: 28%; SAT critical reading scores over 700: 1%; SAT math scores over 700: 1%; ACT scores over 30: 3%.

Retention: 80% of full-time freshmen returned.

ACADEMICS

Calendar: semesters. *Degrees:* certificates, bachelor's, master's, doctoral, post-master's, and postbachelor's certificates.

Special study options: academic remediation for entering students, accelerated degree program, adult/continuing education programs, advanced placement credit, cooperative education, distance learning, double majors, English as a second language, honors programs, independent study, internships, off-campus study, part-time degree program, services for LD students, student-designed majors, study abroad, summer session for credit. ***ROTC:*** Army (c), Air Force (c).

Computers: 2,000 computers/terminals and 800 ports are available on campus for general student use. Students can access the following: campus intranet, computer help desk, free student e-mail accounts, online (class) grades, online (class) registration, online (class) schedules. Campuswide network is available. 100% of college-owned or -operated housing units are wired for high-speed Internet access. Wireless service is available via entire campus.

Library: J. Paul Leonard Library. Study areas open 24 hours, 5-7 days a week; students can reserve study rooms.

STUDENT LIFE

Housing options: coed, women-only, special housing for students with disabilities. Campus housing is university owned. Freshman applicants given priority for college housing.

Activities and organizations: drama/theater group, student-run newspaper, radio and television station, choral group, national fraternities, national sororities.

Athletics Member NCAA. All Division II. ***Intercollegiate sports:*** baseball M(s), basketball M(s)/W(s), cross-country running M(s)/W(s), soccer M(s)/W(s), softball W(s), track and field W(s), volleyball W(s), wrestling M(s). ***Intramural sports:*** basketball M/W, cheerleading M(c)/W(c), rugby M(c)/W(c), soccer M/W, tennis M/W, volleyball M/W, water polo M(c)/W(c).

Campus security: 24-hour emergency response devices and patrols, student patrols, late-night transport/escort service, controlled dormitory access.

Student services: health clinic, personal/psychological counseling, women's center, legal services.

COSTS & FINANCIAL AID

Costs (2016–17) ***Tuition:*** state resident $5472 full-time, $1587 per term part-time; nonresident $16,632 full-time, $3819 per term part-time. Full-time tuition and fees vary according to course load. Part-time tuition and fees vary according to course load. ***Required fees:*** $1012 full-time, $506 per term part-time. ***Room and board:*** $12,698; room only: $8330. Room and board charges vary according to board plan and housing facility. ***Payment plan:*** installment. ***Waivers:*** senior citizens and employees or children of employees.

Financial Aid Of all full-time matriculated undergraduates who enrolled in 2016, 16,565 applied for aid, 14,832 were judged to have need, 3,509 had their need fully met. In 2016, 265 non-need-based awards were made. ***Average percent of need met:*** 70. ***Average financial aid package:*** $15,082. ***Average need-based loan:*** $4495. ***Average need-based gift aid:*** $9103. ***Average non-need-based aid:*** $1850. ***Average indebtedness upon graduation:*** $20,716.

APPLYING

Standardized Tests *Required:* SAT or ACT (for admission).

Options: electronic application.

Application fee: $55.

Required: high school transcript.

Application deadlines: 11/30 (freshmen), 11/30 (transfers).

Notification: 12/1 (freshmen), 12/1 (transfers).

CONTACT

Admissions Officer, San Francisco State University, 1600 Holloway Avenue, San Francisco, CA 94132-1722. *Phone:* 415-338-1113. *Fax:* 415-338-7196. *E-mail:* ugadmit@sfsu.edu.

San Jose State University

San Jose, California

http://www.sjsu.edu/

- **State-supported** comprehensive, founded 1857, part of California State University System
- **Urban** 152-acre campus
- **Coed**
- **Very difficult** entrance level

FACULTY

Student/faculty ratio: 28:1.

ACADEMICS

Calendar: semesters. *Degrees:* bachelor's and master's.

Library: Dr. Martin Luther King Jr. Library plus 1 other.

STUDENT LIFE

Housing options: on-campus residence required for freshman year; coed, men-only, women-only, cooperative, special housing for students with disabilities. Freshman applicants given priority for college housing.

Activities and organizations: drama/theater group, student-run newspaper, radio and television station, choral group, marching band, national fraternities, national sororities.

Athletics Member NCAA. All Division I except football (Division I-A).

Campus security: 24-hour emergency response devices and patrols, student patrols, late-night transport/escort service.

Student services: health clinic, personal/psychological counseling, women's center.

COSTS & FINANCIAL AID

Costs (2016–17) ***Tuition:*** state resident $5472 full-time, $1587 per term part-time; nonresident $14,400 full-time, $3819 per term part-time. ***Required fees:*** $1945 full-time, $1945 per year part-time. ***Room and board:*** $14,867; room only: $9467. Room and board charges vary according to board plan, housing facility, and location. ***Payment plans:*** installment, deferred payment.

Financial Aid Of all full-time matriculated undergraduates who enrolled in 2016, 15,319 applied for aid, 13,543 were judged to have need, 9,906 had their need fully met. In 2016, 36 non-need-based awards were made. ***Average percent of need met:*** 86. ***Average financial aid package:*** $18,142. ***Average need-based loan:*** $4229. ***Average need-based gift aid:*** $10,957. ***Average non-need-based aid:*** $1519. ***Average indebtedness upon graduation:*** $19,797. ***Financial aid deadline:*** 4/28.

APPLYING

Standardized Tests *Required:* SAT or ACT (for admission).

Options: electronic application.

Application fee: $55.

Required: high school transcript.

CONTACT

Admissions Office, San Jose State University, One Washington Square, San Jose, CA 95192-0001. *Phone:* 408-283-7500. *Fax:* 408-924-2050. *E-mail:* admissions@sjsu.edu.

Santa Barbara Business College

Bakersfield, California

http://www.sbbcollege.edu/

CONTACT

Santa Barbara Business College, 5300 California Avenue, Bakersfield, CA 93309.

Santa Barbara Business College

Santa Maria, California

http://www.sbbcollege.edu/

CONTACT

Santa Barbara Business College, 303 East Plaza Drive, Santa Maria, CA 93454.

Santa Barbara Business College

Ventura, California

http://www.sbbcollege.edu/

CONTACT

Santa Barbara Business College, 4839 Market Street, Ventura, CA 93003.

Santa Clara University

Santa Clara, California

http://www.scu.edu/

- **Independent Roman Catholic (Jesuit)** university, founded 1851
- **Suburban** 106-acre campus with easy access to San Francisco, San Jose
- **Endowment** $840.7 million
- **Coed** 5,438 undergraduate students, 98% full-time, 50% women, 50% men
- **Very difficult** entrance level, 48% of applicants were admitted

UNDERGRAD STUDENTS
5,353 full-time, 85 part-time. Students come from 50 states and territories; 46 other countries; 28% are from out of state; 3% Black or African American, non-Hispanic/Latino; 17% Hispanic/Latino; 17% Asian, non-Hispanic/Latino; 0.1% Native Hawaiian or other Pacific Islander, non-Hispanic/Latino; 0.1% American Indian or Alaska Native, non-Hispanic/Latino; 7% Two or more races, non-Hispanic/Latino; 3% Race/ethnicity unknown; 4% international; 2% transferred in; 55% live on campus.

Freshmen:
Admission: 15,834 applied, 7,648 admitted, 1,317 enrolled. ***Average high school GPA:*** 3.67. ***Test scores:*** SAT critical reading scores over 500: 98%; SAT math scores over 500: 99%; ACT scores over 18: 100%; SAT critical reading scores over 600: 73%; SAT math scores over 600: 83%; ACT scores over 24: 98%; SAT critical reading scores over 700: 21%; SAT math scores over 700: 31%; ACT scores over 30: 53%.

Retention: 96% of full-time freshmen returned.

FACULTY
Total: 904, 60% full-time, 82% with terminal degrees.

Student/faculty ratio: 11:1.

ACADEMICS
Calendar: quarters. *Degrees:* bachelor's, master's, doctoral, post-master's, and postbachelor's certificates.

Special study options: advanced placement credit, cooperative education, double majors, honors programs, independent study, internships, off-campus study, services for LD students, student-designed majors, study abroad, summer session for credit. ***ROTC:*** Army (b), Air Force (c).

Computers: Students can access the following: campus intranet, computer help desk, free student e-mail accounts, online (class) grades, online (class) registration, online (class) schedules. Campuswide network is available. 100% of college-owned or -operated housing units are wired for high-speed Internet access. Wireless service is available via entire campus.

Library: University Library plus 1 other. *Books:* 603,388 (physical), 612,072 (digital/electronic); *Serial titles:* 15,262 (physical), 77,789 (digital/electronic); *Databases:* 373. Weekly public service hours: 121; students can reserve study rooms.

STUDENT LIFE
Housing options: coed, special housing for students with disabilities. Campus housing is university owned. Freshman applicants given priority for college housing.

Activities and organizations: drama/theater group, student-run newspaper, radio station, choral group, marching band.

Athletics Member NCAA. All Division I. ***Intercollegiate sports:*** baseball M(s), basketball M(s)/W(s), cross-country running M(s)/W(s), equestrian sports M(c)/W(c), field hockey W(c), golf M(s)/W(s), ice hockey M(c), lacrosse M(c)/W(c), rowing M/W, rugby M(c)/W(c), sailing M(c)/W(c), sand volleyball W, soccer M(s)/W(s), softball W(s), swimming and diving M(c)/W(c), tennis M(s)/W(s), track and field M(s)/W(s), triathlon M(c)/W(c), ultimate Frisbee M(c)/W(c), volleyball M(c)/W(s), water polo M(s)/W(s). ***Intramural sports:*** badminton M/W, basketball M/W, football M/W, soccer M/W, softball M/W, table tennis M/W, tennis M/W, volleyball M/W.

Campus security: 24-hour emergency response devices and patrols, late-night transport/escort service, controlled dormitory access.

Student services: health clinic, personal/psychological counseling.

COSTS & FINANCIAL AID
Costs (2016–17) ***Comprehensive fee:*** $61,077 includes full-time tuition ($47,112) and room and board ($13,965). Part-time tuition: $1309 per unit. Part-time tuition and fees vary according to course load. ***Room and board:*** Room and board charges vary according to board plan and housing facility. ***Payment plan:*** installment. ***Waivers:*** employees or children of employees.

Financial Aid Of all full-time matriculated undergraduates who enrolled in 2016, 3,103 applied for aid, 2,435 were judged to have need, 758 had their need fully met. 306 Federal Work-Study jobs (averaging $2965). In 2016, 1417 non-need-based awards were made. ***Average percent of need met:*** 76. ***Average financial aid package:*** $34,298. ***Average need-based loan:*** $4976. ***Average need-based gift aid:*** $27,281. ***Average non-need-based aid:*** $14,378. ***Average indebtedness upon graduation:*** $27,385.

APPLYING
Standardized Tests *Required:* SAT or ACT (for admission).

Options: electronic application, early admission, early decision, early action, deferred entrance.

Application fee: $60.

Required: essay or personal statement, high school transcript, 1 letter of recommendation.

Application deadlines: 1/7 (freshmen), 4/1 (transfers), 11/1 (early action).

Early decision deadline: 11/1.

Notification: 4/1 (freshmen), continuous (transfers), 12/23 (early decision), 12/23 (early action).

CONTACT
Mrs. Eva Blanco, Dean of Undergraduate Admissions, Santa Clara University, 500 El Camino Real, Santa Clara, CA 95053.
Phone: 408-554-4700. *Fax:* 408-554-5255. *E-mail:* admission@scu.edu.

Scripps College

Claremont, California

http://www.scrippscollege.edu/

- **Independent** 4-year, founded 1926
- **Suburban** 37-acre campus with easy access to Los Angeles
- **Women only** 1,039 undergraduate students, 99% full-time
- **Very difficult** entrance level, 30% of applicants were admitted

UNDERGRAD STUDENTS
1,030 full-time, 9 part-time. Students come from 42 states and territories; 22 other countries; 53% are from out of state; 4% Black or African American, non-Hispanic/Latino; 11% Hispanic/Latino; 15% Asian, non-Hispanic/Latino; 0.1% Native Hawaiian or other Pacific Islander, non-Hispanic/Latino; 6% Two or more races, non-Hispanic/Latino; 6% Race/ethnicity unknown; 5% international; 2% transferred in; 100% live on campus.

Freshmen:
Admission: 3,032 applied, 903 admitted, 270 enrolled. ***Average high school GPA:*** 4.01. ***Test scores:*** SAT critical reading scores over 500: 101%; SAT math scores over 500: 99%; SAT writing scores over 500: 100%; ACT scores over 18: 100%; SAT critical reading scores over 600: 97%; SAT math scores over 600: 87%; SAT writing scores over 600: 96%; ACT scores over 24: 98%; SAT critical reading scores over 700: 55%; SAT math scores over 700: 29%; SAT writing scores over 700: 53%; ACT scores over 30: 63%.

Retention: 92% of full-time freshmen returned.

FACULTY
Total: 122, 75% full-time, 93% with terminal degrees.

Student/faculty ratio: 11:1.

ACADEMICS
Calendar: semesters. *Degrees:* bachelor's and postbachelor's certificates.

Special study options: accelerated degree program, advanced placement credit, double majors, independent study, internships, off-campus study, services for LD students, student-designed majors, study abroad. ***ROTC:*** Army (c), Air Force (c).

Unusual degree programs: 3-2 business administration with Claremont Graduate University; engineering with Harvey Mudd College, Columbia University; American politics, economics, philosophy, public policy, international studies, religion with Claremont Graduate University.

Computers: 151 computers/terminals and 320 ports are available on campus for general student use. Students can access the following: campus intranet, computer help desk, free student e-mail accounts, online (class) grades, online (class) registration, online (class) schedules, 2 ports per dorm room. Campuswide network is available. 100% of college-owned or -operated housing units are wired for high-speed Internet access. Wireless service is available via entire campus.

Library: Honnold Library plus 2 others. Students can reserve study rooms.

STUDENT LIFE

Housing options: on-campus residence required for freshman year; women-only, special housing for students with disabilities. Campus housing is university owned. Freshman campus housing is guaranteed.

Activities and organizations: drama/theater group, student-run newspaper, radio station, choral group, Scripps Associated Students.

Athletics Member NCAA. All Division III. ***Intercollegiate sports:*** basketball W, cross-country running W, equestrian sports W(c), fencing W(c), golf W, lacrosse W, rugby W(c), skiing (downhill) W(c), soccer W, softball W, swimming and diving W, tennis W, track and field W, ultimate Frisbee W(c), volleyball W, water polo W. ***Intramural sports:*** basketball W, soccer W, softball W, volleyball W, water polo W.

Campus security: 24-hour emergency response devices and patrols, late-night transport/escort service, controlled dormitory access.

Student services: health clinic, personal/psychological counseling, women's center.

COSTS & FINANCIAL AID

Costs (2016–17) ***Comprehensive fee:*** $66,664 includes full-time tuition ($50,766), mandatory fees ($216), and room and board ($15,682). Full-time tuition and fees vary according to course load and degree level. Part-time tuition: $6346 per course. Part-time tuition and fees vary according to course load and degree level. ***College room only:*** $8538. Room and board charges vary according to board plan. ***Payment plans:*** tuition prepayment, installment. ***Waivers:*** employees or children of employees.

Financial Aid Of all full-time matriculated undergraduates who enrolled in 2015, 472 applied for aid, 371 were judged to have need, 371 had their need fully met. In 2015, 35 non-need-based awards were made. ***Average percent of need met:*** 100. ***Average financial aid package:*** $42,513. ***Average need-based loan:*** $4329. ***Average need-based gift aid:*** $37,361. ***Average non-need-based aid:*** $10,993. ***Average indebtedness upon graduation:*** $20,205. ***Financial aid deadline:*** 2/1.

APPLYING

Standardized Tests *Required:* SAT or ACT (for admission).

Options: electronic application, early admission, early decision, deferred entrance.

Application fee: $60.

Required: essay or personal statement, high school transcript, 2 letters of recommendation, school report completed by the student's secondary school counselor. ***Recommended:*** minimum 3.0 GPA.

Application deadlines: 1/1 (freshmen), 4/1 (transfers).

Early decision deadline: 11/15 (for plan 1), 1/1 (for plan 2).

Notification: 4/1 (freshmen), 4/1 (out-of-state freshmen), 5/15 (transfers), 12/15 (early decision plan 1), 2/15 (early decision plan 2).

CONTACT

Laura Stratton, Director of Admission, Scripps College, 1030 Columbia Avenue, Claremont, CA 91711. *Phone:* 909-621-8149. *Toll-free phone:* 800-770-1333. *Fax:* 909-607-7508.
E-mail: admission@scrippscollege.edu.

Shasta Bible College

Redding, California

http://www.shasta.edu/

CONTACT

Connie Barton, Registrar, Shasta Bible College, 2951 Goodwater Avenue, Redding, CA 96002. *Phone:* 530-221-4275 Ext. 26. *Toll-free phone:* 800-800-4SBC. *Fax:* 530-221-6929. *E-mail:* registrar@shasta.edu.

Shepherd University

Los Angeles, California

http://www.shepherduniversity.edu/

CONTACT

Shepherd University, 3200 North San Fernando Road, Los Angeles, CA 90065.

Silicon Valley University

San Jose, California

http://www.svuca.edu/

CONTACT

Luna Liu, Admissions Office, Silicon Valley University, 2160 Lundy Avenue, Suite 110, San Jose, CA 95131. *Phone:* 408-435-8989 Ext. 111.
E-mail: admission-office@svuca.edu.

Simpson University

Redding, California

http://www.simpsonu.edu/

- **Independent** comprehensive, founded 1921, affiliated with The Christian and Missionary Alliance
- **Suburban** 100-acre campus
- **Endowment** $5.9 million
- **Coed** 790 undergraduate students, 94% full-time, 66% women, 34% men
- **Moderately difficult** entrance level, 52% of applicants were admitted

UNDERGRAD STUDENTS

741 full-time, 49 part-time. Students come from 23 states and territories; 9 other countries; 12% are from out of state; 4% Black or African American, non-Hispanic/Latino; 16% Hispanic/Latino; 4% Asian, non-Hispanic/Latino; 0.5% Native Hawaiian or other Pacific Islander, non-Hispanic/Latino; 3% American Indian or Alaska Native, non-Hispanic/Latino; 3% Two or more races, non-Hispanic/Latino; 9% Race/ethnicity unknown; 1% international; 9% transferred in; 41% live on campus.

Freshmen:

Admission: 627 applied, 327 admitted, 118 enrolled. ***Average high school GPA:*** 3.4. ***Test scores:*** SAT critical reading scores over 500: 48%; SAT math scores over 500: 47%; SAT writing scores over 500: 40%; ACT scores over 18: 83%; SAT critical reading scores over 600: 15%; SAT math scores over 600: 16%; SAT writing scores over 600: 10%; ACT scores over 24: 33%; SAT critical reading scores over 700: 2%; SAT math scores over 700: 1%; SAT writing scores over 700: 1%.

Retention: 82% of full-time freshmen returned.

FACULTY

Total: 139, 31% full-time, 39% with terminal degrees.

Student/faculty ratio: 11:1.

ACADEMICS

Calendar: semesters. *Degrees:* certificates, associate, bachelor's, master's, post-master's, and postbachelor's certificates.

Special study options: academic remediation for entering students, accelerated degree program, adult/continuing education programs, advanced placement credit, distance learning, double majors, honors programs, independent study, internships, off-campus study, part-time degree program, services for LD students, student-designed majors, study abroad, summer session for credit.

Computers: 50 computers/terminals are available on campus for general student use. Students can access the following: campus intranet, computer help desk, free student e-mail accounts, online (class) grades, online (class) registration, online (class) schedules. Campuswide network is available. 100% of college-owned or -operated housing units are wired for high-speed Internet access. Wireless service is available via entire campus.

Library: Start-Kilgour Memorial Library. *Books:* 103,721 (physical), 369,714 (digital/electronic); *Serial titles:* 340 (physical), 28,286 (digital/electronic); *Databases:* 54. Weekly public service hours: 93; students can reserve study rooms.

STUDENT LIFE

Housing options: on-campus residence required through junior year; men-only, women-only, special housing for students with disabilities. Campus housing is university owned. Freshman campus housing is guaranteed.

Activities and organizations: drama/theater group, student-run newspaper, choral group, Summer Missions Trips, Biology Club, Boxing Club.

Athletics Member NAIA, NCCAA. ***Intercollegiate sports:*** baseball M(s), basketball M(s)/W(s), cross-country running M(s)/W(s), golf M(s)/W(s), soccer M(s)/W(s), softball W(s), volleyball W(s), wrestling M(s). ***Intramural sports:*** basketball M/W, soccer M/W, ultimate Frisbee M/W, volleyball M/W.

Campus security: 24-hour emergency response devices and patrols, student patrols, late-night transport/escort service, controlled dormitory access, emergency whistle program and monthly campus safety meetings.

Student services: health clinic, personal/psychological counseling.

COSTS & FINANCIAL AID

Costs (2017–18) ***Comprehensive fee:*** $35,700 includes full-time tuition ($27,250), mandatory fees ($100), and room and board ($8350). Full-time tuition and fees vary according to course load. Part-time tuition: $1150 per credit hour. Part-time tuition and fees vary according to course load. ***Room and board:*** Room and board charges vary according to board plan and housing facility. ***Payment plan:*** deferred payment. ***Waivers:*** employees or children of employees.

Financial Aid Of all full-time matriculated undergraduates who enrolled in 2016, 702 applied for aid, 628 were judged to have need, 70 had their need fully met. 58 Federal Work-Study jobs (averaging $1229). In 2016, 29 non-need-based awards were made. ***Average percent of need met:*** 59. ***Average financial aid package:*** $17,174. ***Average need-based loan:*** $4556. ***Average need-based gift aid:*** $11,606. ***Average non-need-based aid:*** $10,039. ***Average indebtedness upon graduation:*** $26,938.

APPLYING

Standardized Tests *Required:* SAT or ACT (for admission). *Recommended:* SAT and SAT Subject Tests or ACT (for admission).

Options: electronic application, early action, deferred entrance.

Application fee: $35.

Required: essay or personal statement, high school transcript, minimum 3.0 GPA, 1 letter of recommendation, Christian commitment. ***Required for some:*** interview.

Application deadlines: 8/1 (freshmen), 8/1 (transfers), 12/1 (early action).

Notification: continuous (freshmen), continuous (transfers).

CONTACT

Mr. Molly McKeever, Director of Undergraduate Admissions, Simpson University, 2211 College View Drive, Redding, CA 96003-8606. *Phone:* 530-226-5600. *Toll-free phone:* 888-9-SIMPSON. *Fax:* 530-226-4861. *E-mail:* admissions@simpsonu.edu.

Soka University of America

Aliso Viejo, California

http://www.soka.edu/

- **Independent** comprehensive, founded 1987
- **Suburban** 103-acre campus with easy access to Los Angeles, San Diego
- **Endowment** $1.2 billion
- **Coed** 419 undergraduate students, 100% full-time, 62% women, 38% men
- **Most difficult** entrance level, 38% of applicants were admitted

UNDERGRAD STUDENTS

417 full-time, 2 part-time. 46% are from out of state; 4% Black or African American, non-Hispanic/Latino; 10% Hispanic/Latino; 15% Asian, non-Hispanic/Latino; 0.5% Native Hawaiian or other Pacific Islander, non-Hispanic/Latino; 0.5% American Indian or Alaska Native, non-Hispanic/Latino; 5% Two or more races, non-Hispanic/Latino; 4% Race/ethnicity unknown; 43% international; 99% live on campus.

Freshmen:

Admission: 500 applied, 192 admitted, 104 enrolled. ***Average high school GPA:*** 3.91. ***Test scores:*** SAT critical reading scores over 500: 75%; SAT math scores over 500: 99%; SAT writing scores over 500: 92%; ACT scores over 18: 100%; SAT critical reading scores over 600: 40%; SAT math scores over 600: 73%; SAT writing scores over 600: 53%; ACT scores over 24: 100%; SAT critical reading scores over 700: 13%; SAT math scores over 700: 38%; SAT writing scores over 700: 13%; ACT scores over 30: 29%.

Retention: 94% of full-time freshmen returned.

FACULTY

Total: 69, 68% full-time, 88% with terminal degrees.

Student/faculty ratio: 8:1.

ACADEMICS

Calendar: semesters. *Degrees:* bachelor's and master's.

Special study options: cooperative education, independent study, internships, off-campus study, services for LD students, study abroad.

Computers: 100 computers/terminals and 100 ports are available on campus for general student use. Students can access the following: campus intranet, computer help desk, free student e-mail accounts, online (class) grades, online (class) registration, online (class) schedules, course and administrative applications. Campuswide network is available. 100% of college-owned or -operated housing units are wired for high-speed Internet access. Wireless service is available via entire campus.

Library: Daisaku and Kaneko Ikeda Library. Study areas open 24 hours, 5-7 days a week; students can reserve study rooms.

STUDENT LIFE

Housing options: on-campus residence required through senior year; coed, men-only, women-only, cooperative, special housing for students with disabilities. Campus housing is university owned. Freshman campus housing is guaranteed.

Activities and organizations: choral group, Josho Daiko (Japanese Drum Club), Rhythmission (Hip Hop Dance Club), Sualseros (Salsa Dance Club), Ka Pilina Ho'olokahi (Hawaiian Dance Club), Soul Wings (Choir).

Athletics Member NAIA. ***Intercollegiate sports:*** cross-country running M(s)/W(s), golf W, soccer M(s)/W(s), swimming and diving M(s)/W(s), track and field M(s)/W(s). ***Intramural sports:*** badminton M/W, baseball M(c), basketball M/W, cheerleading M(c)/W(c), football M/W, golf M(c), racquetball M(c)/W(c), soccer M(c)/W(c), softball M/W, tennis M/W, volleyball M(c)/W(c), water polo M/W, weight lifting M/W.

Campus security: 24-hour emergency response devices and patrols, student patrols, late-night transport/escort service, controlled dormitory access.

Student services: health clinic, personal/psychological counseling.

COSTS & FINANCIAL AID

Costs (2017–18) ***Comprehensive fee:*** $43,942 includes full-time tuition ($30,106), mandatory fees ($1670), and room and board ($12,166). Full-time tuition and fees vary according to class time, course level, course load, and program. Part-time tuition: $1255 per credit hour. Part-time tuition and fees vary according to class time, course level, course load, and program. ***Room and board:*** Room and board charges vary according to board plan. ***Payment plans:*** installment, deferred payment. ***Waivers:*** employees or children of employees.

Financial Aid Of all full-time matriculated undergraduates who enrolled in 2016, 417 applied for aid, 361 were judged to have need, 321 had their need fully met. 77 Federal Work-Study jobs (averaging $2000). In 2016, 22 non-need-based awards were made. ***Average percent of need met:*** 72. ***Average financial aid package:*** $34,969. ***Average need-based loan:*** $6959. ***Average need-based gift aid:*** $26,236. ***Average non-need-based aid:*** $11,409. ***Average indebtedness upon graduation:*** $22,409. ***Financial aid deadline:*** 3/2.

APPLYING

Standardized Tests *Required:* SAT or ACT (for admission).

Options: electronic application, early admission, early action, deferred entrance.

Application fee: $45.

Required: essay or personal statement, high school transcript, 2 letters of recommendation, IERF evaluation for course work completed abroad. ***Recommended:*** interview.

Application deadlines: 1/15 (freshmen), 11/1 (early action).

Notification: 3/1 (freshmen), 3/1 (out-of-state freshmen), 12/1 (early action).

CONTACT

Maura Grainger, Admission Operations Coordinator, Soka University of America, Enrollment Services, 1 University Drive, Aliso Viejo, CA 92656. *Phone:* 949-480-4151 Ext. 4151. *Toll-free phone:* 888-600-SOKA. *Fax:* 949-480-4151. *E-mail:* mgrainger@soka.edu.

Sonoma State University
Rohnert Park, California
http://www.sonoma.edu/

- **State-supported** comprehensive, founded 1960, part of California State University System
- **Small-town** 280-acre campus with easy access to San Francisco
- **Endowment** $44.0 million
- **Coed** 8,606 undergraduate students, 91% full-time, 63% women, 37% men
- **Moderately difficult** entrance level, 76% of applicants were admitted

UNDERGRAD STUDENTS
7,795 full-time, 811 part-time. 2% Black or African American, non-Hispanic/Latino; 31% Hispanic/Latino; 5% Asian, non-Hispanic/Latino; 0.2% Native Hawaiian or other Pacific Islander, non-Hispanic/Latino; 0.4% American Indian or Alaska Native, non-Hispanic/Latino; 6% Two or more races, non-Hispanic/Latino; 7% Race/ethnicity unknown; 2% international; 9% transferred in; 23% live on campus.

Freshmen:
Admission: 16,487 applied, 12,575 admitted, 1,806 enrolled. ***Average high school GPA:*** 3.23. ***Test scores:*** SAT critical reading scores over 500: 49%; SAT math scores over 500: 48%; SAT writing scores over 500: 44%; ACT scores over 18: 84%; SAT critical reading scores over 600: 11%; SAT math scores over 600: 9%; SAT writing scores over 600: 7%; ACT scores over 24: 32%; SAT critical reading scores over 700: 1%; SAT math scores over 700: 1%; SAT writing scores over 700: 1%; ACT scores over 30: 2%.
Retention: 79% of full-time freshmen returned.

FACULTY
Total: 582, 41% full-time, 61% with terminal degrees.
Student/faculty ratio: 24:1.

ACADEMICS
Calendar: semesters. *Degrees:* bachelor's and master's.
Special study options: academic remediation for entering students, accelerated degree program, adult/continuing education programs, advanced placement credit, cooperative education, distance learning, double majors, English as a second language, honors programs, independent study, internships, off-campus study, part-time degree program, services for LD students, student-designed majors, study abroad, summer session for credit. ***ROTC:*** Army (c), Air Force (c).
Computers: Students can access the following: computer help desk, free student e-mail accounts, online (class) grades, online (class) registration, online (class) schedules. Campuswide network is available. 100% of college-owned or -operated housing units are wired for high-speed Internet access. Wireless service is available via entire campus.
Library: Jean and Charles Schultz Information Center plus 1 other. *Books:* 790,148 (physical), 168,724 (digital/electronic); *Serial titles:* 44,834 (physical). Students can reserve study rooms.

STUDENT LIFE
Housing options: coed, special housing for students with disabilities. Campus housing is university owned. Freshman applicants given priority for college housing.
Activities and organizations: drama/theater group, student-run newspaper, radio station, choral group, national fraternities, national sororities.
Athletics Member NCAA. All Division II. ***Intercollegiate sports:*** baseball M(s), basketball M(s)/W(s), cross-country running W, golf M/W, soccer M(s)/W(s), softball W(s), tennis M(s)/W(s), track and field W, volleyball W(s), water polo W. ***Intramural sports:*** archery M(c)/W(c), basketball M/W, cheerleading M/W, crew M/W, cross-country running M, fencing M/W, football M/W, lacrosse M(c)/W(c), rock climbing M/W, rowing M/W, soccer M/W, ultimate Frisbee M(c)/W(c), volleyball M(c)/W(c).
Campus security: 24-hour emergency response devices and patrols, student patrols, late-night transport/escort service, controlled dormitory access.
Student services: health clinic, personal/psychological counseling, women's center, legal services.

COSTS & FINANCIAL AID
Costs (2017–18) ***Tuition:*** state resident $5472 full-time; nonresident $16,632 full-time. Full-time tuition and fees vary according to course load and degree level. Part-time tuition and fees vary according to course load and degree level. ***Required fees:*** $1858 full-time. ***Room and board:*** $13,146. Room and board charges vary according to board plan and housing facility. ***Payment plan:*** installment. ***Waivers:*** employees or children of employees.
Financial Aid Of all full-time matriculated undergraduates who enrolled in 2015, 5,589 applied for aid, 4,522 were judged to have need, 221 had their need fully met. 212 Federal Work-Study jobs (averaging $2214). In 2015, 198 non-need-based awards were made. ***Average percent of need met:*** 54. ***Average financial aid package:*** $10,085. ***Average need-based loan:*** $4056. ***Average need-based gift aid:*** $9968. ***Average non-need-based aid:*** $936. ***Average indebtedness upon graduation:*** $20,797.

APPLYING
Standardized Tests *Required:* SAT or ACT (for admission).
Options: electronic application, early admission.
Application fee: $55.
Required: high school transcript.
Application deadlines: rolling (freshmen), rolling (transfers).
Notification: continuous (freshmen), continuous (transfers).

CONTACT
Ms. Natalie Kalogiannis, Director of Admissions, Sonoma State University, 1801 East Cotati Avenue, Rohnert Park, CA 94928-3609. *Phone:* 707-664-2874. *E-mail:* natalie.kalogiannis@sonoma.edu.

Southern California Institute of Architecture
Los Angeles, California
http://www.sciarc.edu/

- **Independent** comprehensive, founded 1972
- **Urban** campus with easy access to Los Angeles
- **Coed**
- **Moderately difficult** entrance level

FACULTY
Student/faculty ratio: 12:1.

ACADEMICS
Calendar: semesters. *Degrees:* bachelor's and master's.
Library: Kappe Library plus 1 other. *Books:* 30,177 (physical), 127,353 (digital/electronic); *Serial titles:* 76 (physical), 8 (digital/electronic); *Databases:* 19.

STUDENT LIFE
Housing options: college housing not available.
Activities and organizations: Student Union.
Campus security: 24-hour emergency response devices and patrols, electronically operated school entrances 24/7.
Student services: personal/psychological counseling.

COSTS & FINANCIAL AID
Costs (2016–17) ***Tuition:*** $41,800 full-time. Full-time tuition and fees vary according to course load. ***Required fees:*** $1100 full-time.
Financial Aid Of all full-time matriculated undergraduates who enrolled in 2016, 78 applied for aid, 75 were judged to have need, 1 had their need fully met. In 2016, 18 non-need-based awards were made. ***Average percent of need met:*** 31. ***Average financial aid package:*** $19,661. ***Average need-based loan:*** $4553. ***Average need-based gift aid:*** $17,745. ***Average non-need-based aid:*** $20,452. ***Average indebtedness upon graduation:*** $39,287.

APPLYING
Standardized Tests *Required:* SAT or ACT (for admission).
Options: electronic application, deferred entrance.
Application fee: $85.
Required: essay or personal statement, high school transcript, 3 letters of recommendation, portfolio of creative visual work, resumé, statement of purpose. ***Required for some:*** interview. ***Recommended:*** minimum 3.0 GPA.

CONTACT
Jamie Black, Admissions Counselor, Southern California Institute of Architecture, 960 East Third Street, Los Angeles, CA 90013. *Phone:* 213-356-5320. *Fax:* 213-613-2260. *E-mail:* admissions@sciarc.edu.

Southern California Institute of Technology
Anaheim, California
http://www.scitech.edu/

CONTACT
Mrs. Sam Rokni, Southern California Institute of Technology, 525 N Muller Street, Anaheim, CA 92801. *Phone:* 714-300-0300 Ext. 227. *Fax:* 714-300-0311. *E-mail:* admissions@scitech.edu.

Southern California Seminary
El Cajon, California
http://www.socalsem.edu/

- **Independent interdenominational** comprehensive, founded 1946
- **Suburban** 15-acre campus with easy access to San Diego, CA
- **Endowment** $115,260
- **Coed**
- **Moderately difficult** entrance level

ACADEMICS
Calendar: trimesters. *Degrees:* diplomas, associate, bachelor's, master's, and doctoral.
Library: SCS Library. *Books:* 22,304 (physical), 338,731 (digital/electronic); *Serial titles:* 74 (physical), 24 (digital/electronic); *Databases:* 106. Weekly public service hours: 60.

STUDENT LIFE
Housing options: men-only, women-only. Campus housing is university owned.
Campus security: 24-hour emergency response devices and patrols.

COSTS
Costs (2016–17) ***Tuition:*** $13,860 full-time, $36 per credit part-time. Full-time tuition and fees vary according to course load, location, program, and reciprocity agreements. Part-time tuition and fees vary according to course load, location, program, and reciprocity agreements. ***Required fees:*** $384 full-time. ***Room only:*** $6205.

APPLYING
Options: electronic application, early admission, deferred entrance.
Application fee: $37.
Required: essay or personal statement, high school transcript, minimum 2.0 GPA, 2 letters of recommendation, interview.

CONTACT
Southern California Seminary, 2075 East Madison Avenue, El Cajon, CA 92019. *Phone:* 619-201-8959. *Toll-free phone:* 888-389-7244.

Stanbridge College
Irvine, California
http://www.stanbridge.edu/

CONTACT
Stanbridge College, 2041 Business Center Drive, Irvine, CA 92612.

Stanford University
Stanford, California
http://www.stanford.edu/

- **Independent** university, founded 1891
- **Suburban** 8180-acre campus with easy access to San Francisco, San Jose
- **Coed** 7,034 undergraduate students, 100% full-time, 49% women, 51% men
- **Most difficult** entrance level, 5% of applicants were admitted

UNDERGRAD STUDENTS
7,034 full-time. Students come from 52 states and territories; 76 other countries; 58% are from out of state; 6% Black or African American, non-Hispanic/Latino; 16% Hispanic/Latino; 21% Asian, non-Hispanic/Latino; 0.3% Native Hawaiian or other Pacific Islander, non-Hispanic/Latino; 1% American Indian or Alaska Native, non-Hispanic/Latino; 10% Two or more races, non-Hispanic/Latino; 0.2% Race/ethnicity unknown; 9% international; 0.6% transferred in; 93% live on campus.

Freshmen:
Admission: 43,997 applied, 2,118 admitted, 1,738 enrolled. ***Average high school GPA:*** 3.94. ***Test scores:*** SAT critical reading scores over 500: 99%; SAT math scores over 500: 100%; SAT writing scores over 500: 99%; ACT scores over 18: 100%; SAT critical reading scores over 600: 94%; SAT math scores over 600: 97%; SAT writing scores over 600: 95%; ACT scores over 24: 99%; SAT critical reading scores over 700: 68%; SAT math scores over 700: 75%; SAT writing scores over 700: 72%; ACT scores over 30: 87%.
Retention: 98% of full-time freshmen returned.

FACULTY
Total: 1,637, 99% full-time, 99% with terminal degrees.
Student/faculty ratio: 4:1.

ACADEMICS
Calendar: quarters. *Degrees:* bachelor's, master's, doctoral, and postbachelor's certificates.
Special study options: advanced placement credit, distance learning, double majors, English as a second language, honors programs, independent study, internships, off-campus study, services for LD students, student-designed majors, study abroad, summer session for credit. ***ROTC:*** Army (c), Navy (c), Air Force (c).
Computers: 1,000 computers/terminals are available on campus for general student use. Students can access the following: campus intranet, computer help desk, free student e-mail accounts, online (class) grades, online (class) registration, online (class) schedules. Campuswide network is available. 100% of college-owned or -operated housing units are wired for high-speed Internet access. Wireless service is available via entire campus.
Library: Green Library plus 20 others. *Books:* 9.5 million (physical), 1.5 million (digital/electronic); *Serial titles:* 77,000 (physical). Study areas open 24 hours, 5-7 days a week; students can reserve study rooms.

STUDENT LIFE
Housing options: on-campus residence required for freshman year; coed, women-only, cooperative, special housing for students with disabilities. Campus housing is university owned. Freshman campus housing is guaranteed.
Activities and organizations: drama/theater group, student-run newspaper, radio and television station, choral group, marching band, Ram's Head (theatre club), Axe Committee (athletic support), Business Association of Stanford Entrepreneurial Students, Asian-American Student Association, Stanford Daily, national fraternities, national sororities.
Athletics Member NCAA, NAIA. All NCAA Division I. ***Intercollegiate sports:*** archery M(c)/W(c), badminton M(c)/W(c), baseball M(s), basketball M(s)/W(s), cheerleading M(c)/W(c), crew M(s)/W(s), cross-country running M(s)/W(s), equestrian sports M(c)/W(c), fencing M(s)/W(s), field hockey W(s), football M(s), golf M(s)/W(s), gymnastics M(s)/W(s), ice hockey M(c), lacrosse M(c)/W(s), racquetball M(c)/W(c), rock climbing M(c)/W(c), rowing M(s)/W(s), rugby M(c)/W(c), sailing M/W, sand volleyball W, skiing (downhill) M(c)/W(c), soccer M(s)/W(s), softball W(s), squash M(c)/W(s), swimming and diving M(s)/W(s), tennis M(s)/W(s), track and field M(s)/W(s), triathlon M(c)/W(c), ultimate Frisbee M(c)/W(c), volleyball M(s)/W(s), water polo M(s)/W(s), wrestling M(s). ***Intramural sports:*** badminton M/W, baseball M(c), basketball M(c)/W(c), bowling M/W, cross-country running M(c)/W(c), football M/W, golf M(c)/W(c), lacrosse W(c), racquetball M/W, rock climbing M/W, sand volleyball M/W, soccer M(c)/W(c), softball M/W, swimming and diving M(c)/W(c), table tennis M(c)/W(c), tennis M(c)/W(c), track and field M/W, ultimate Frisbee M/W, volleyball M/W, water polo M/W.
Campus security: 24-hour emergency response devices and patrols, late-night transport/escort service, controlled dormitory access.
Student services: health clinic, personal/psychological counseling, women's center, legal services.

COSTS & FINANCIAL AID
Costs (2017–18) ***Comprehensive fee:*** $62,541 includes full-time tuition ($47,331), mandatory fees ($609), and room and board ($14,601). ***College room only:*** $8712. Room and board charges vary according to board plan. ***Payment plan:*** installment. ***Waivers:*** employees or children of employees.

Financial Aid Of all full-time matriculated undergraduates who enrolled in 2015, 3,730 applied for aid, 3,324 were judged to have need, 2,998 had their need fully met. 558 Federal Work-Study jobs (averaging $2360). 1,776 state and other part-time jobs (averaging $2249). In 2015, 20 non-need-based awards were made. ***Average percent of need met:*** 100. ***Average financial aid package:*** $49,124. ***Average need-based loan:*** $3231. ***Average need-based gift aid:*** $45,318. ***Average non-need-based aid:*** $13,697. ***Average indebtedness upon graduation:*** $21,987.

APPLYING
Standardized Tests *Required:* SAT or ACT (for admission). *Recommended:* SAT Subject Tests (for admission).

Options: electronic application, early action, deferred entrance.

Application fee: $90.

Required: essay or personal statement, high school transcript, 2 letters of recommendation.

Application deadlines: 1/3 (freshmen), 3/15 (transfers), 11/1 (early action).

Notification: 4/1 (freshmen), 5/15 (transfers), 12/15 (early action).

CONTACT
Rick Shaw, Dean of Undergraduate Admission and Financial Aid, Stanford University, Montag Hall, 355 Galvez Street, Stanford, CA 94305-3020. *Phone:* 650-723-2091. *Fax:* 650-725-2846. *E-mail:* admission@stanford.edu.

SUM Bible College & Theological Seminary

Oakland, California

http://www.sum.edu/

CONTACT
Admissions, SUM Bible College & Theological Seminary, 735 105th Avenue, Oakland, CA 94603. *Phone:* 510-567-6174. *Toll-free phone:* 888-567-6174. *Fax:* 510-568-1024.

Thomas Aquinas College

Santa Paula, California

http://www.thomasaquinas.edu/

- **Independent Roman Catholic** 4-year, founded 1971
- **Rural** 131-acre campus with easy access to Los Angeles
- **Endowment** $16.8 million
- **Coed** 377 undergraduate students, 100% full-time, 50% women, 50% men
- **Very difficult** entrance level, 75% of applicants were admitted

UNDERGRAD STUDENTS
377 full-time. Students come from 37 states and territories; 8 other countries; 58% are from out of state; 0.3% Black or African American, non-Hispanic/Latino; 15% Hispanic/Latino; 1% Asian, non-Hispanic/Latino; 7% Two or more races, non-Hispanic/Latino; 2% Race/ethnicity unknown; 3% international; 99% live on campus.

Freshmen:
Admission: 189 applied, 142 admitted, 79 enrolled. ***Average high school GPA:*** 3.82. ***Test scores:*** SAT critical reading scores over 500: 100%; SAT math scores over 500: 98%; SAT writing scores over 500: 97%; ACT scores over 18: 100%; SAT critical reading scores over 600: 86%; SAT math scores over 600: 51%; SAT writing scores over 600: 68%; ACT scores over 24: 88%; SAT critical reading scores over 700: 30%; SAT math scores over 700: 12%; SAT writing scores over 700: 27%; ACT scores over 30: 35%.

Retention: 94% of full-time freshmen returned.

FACULTY
Total: 36, 89% full-time, 86% with terminal degrees.

Student/faculty ratio: 11:1.

ACADEMICS
Calendar: semesters. *Degree:* bachelor's.

Special study options: cooperative education.

Computers: 20 computers/terminals and 16 ports are available on campus for general student use. Students can access the following: computer help desk, free student e-mail accounts. Campuswide network is available.

Library: St. Bernardine Library. *Books:* 56,978 (physical); *Serial titles:* 140 (physical). Students can reserve study rooms.

STUDENT LIFE
Housing options: on-campus residence required through senior year; men-only, women-only. Campus housing is university owned. Freshman campus housing is guaranteed.

Activities and organizations: drama/theater group, choral group, Musical Groups (Choir, Chamber Orchestra), Theatre Groups, Language Clubs, Pro-Life Ministry, Religious groups.

Athletics ***Intramural sports:*** basketball M/W, football M, soccer M/W, softball M/W, table tennis M/W, tennis M/W, ultimate Frisbee M/W, volleyball M/W.

Campus security: daily security patrol.

Student services: personal/psychological counseling.

COSTS & FINANCIAL AID
Costs (2017–18) ***Comprehensive fee:*** $32,450 includes full-time tuition ($24,500) and room and board ($7950). Part-time tuition: $681 per credit hour. ***Payment plan:*** installment.

Financial Aid Of all full-time matriculated undergraduates who enrolled in 2016, 298 applied for aid, 290 were judged to have need, 290 had their need fully met. 272 state and other part-time jobs (averaging $4632). ***Average percent of need met:*** 100. ***Average financial aid package:*** $20,738. ***Average need-based loan:*** $4424. ***Average need-based gift aid:*** $14,225. ***Average indebtedness upon graduation:*** $16,901. ***Financial aid deadline:*** 3/2.

APPLYING
Standardized Tests *Required:* SAT or ACT (for admission).

Options: electronic application.

Required: essay or personal statement, high school transcript, 3 letters of recommendation. ***Required for some:*** interview. ***Recommended:*** minimum 3.0 GPA.

Application deadlines: rolling (freshmen), rolling (out-of-state freshmen).

Notification: continuous (freshmen), continuous (out-of-state freshmen).

CONTACT
Mr. Jonathan P. Daly, Director of Admissions, Thomas Aquinas College, 10000 Ojai Road, Santa Paula, CA 93060-9621. *Phone:* 805-525-4417 Ext. 5901. *Toll-free phone:* 800-634-9797. *Fax:* 805-421-5905. *E-mail:* admissions@thomasaquinas.edu.

Touro College Los Angeles

West Hollywood, California

http://www.touro.edu/losangeles/

CONTACT
Touro College Los Angeles, 1317 North Crescent Heights Boulevard, West Hollywood, CA 90046.

Touro University Worldwide

Los Alamitos, California

http://www.tuw.edu/

CONTACT
Touro University Worldwide, 10601 Calle Lee, Suite 179, Los Alamitos, CA 90720.

Trident University International

Cypress, California

http://www.trident.edu/

CONTACT
Trident University International, 5757 Plaza Drive, Suite 100, Cypress, CA 90630. *Phone:* 800-579-3197.

United States University

San Diego, California

http://www.usuniversity.edu/

CONTACT
Admissions, United States University, 7675 Mission Valley Road, San Diego, CA 92108. *Phone:* 619-477-6310. *Toll-free phone:* 888-422-3381. *Fax:* 619-477-7340.

University of Antelope Valley

Lancaster, California

http://www.uav.edu/

CONTACT
University of Antelope Valley, 44055 North Sierra Highway, Lancaster, CA 93534.

University of California, Berkeley

Berkeley, California

http://www.berkeley.edu/

- **State-supported** university, founded 1868, part of University of California System
- **Urban** 1232-acre campus with easy access to San Francisco
- **Coed**
- 15% of applicants were admitted

FACULTY
Student/faculty ratio: 17:1.

ACADEMICS
Calendar: semesters. *Degrees:* bachelor's, master's, doctoral, and postbachelor's certificates.
Library: Doe Library.

STUDENT LIFE
Housing options: coed, men-only, women-only, cooperative, special housing for students with disabilities. Campus housing is university owned and is provided by a third party. Freshman campus housing is guaranteed.

Activities and organizations: drama/theater group, student-run newspaper, radio and television station, choral group, marching band, national fraternities, national sororities.

Athletics Member NCAA. All Division I.

Campus security: 24-hour emergency response devices and patrols, late-night transport/escort service, controlled dormitory access, Office of Emergency Preparedness.

Student services: health clinic, personal/psychological counseling, women's center, legal services.

COSTS & FINANCIAL AID
Costs (2016–17) ***Tuition:*** state resident $11,220 full-time; nonresident $37,902 full-time. ***Required fees:*** $2289 full-time. ***Room and board:*** $16,042. Room and board charges vary according to board plan and housing facility.

Financial Aid Of all full-time matriculated undergraduates who enrolled in 2015, 14,400 applied for aid, 12,942 were judged to have need, 2,972 had their need fully met. In 2015, 1477 non-need-based awards were made. ***Average percent of need met:*** 81. ***Average financial aid package:*** $22,288. ***Average need-based loan:*** $6310. ***Average need-based gift aid:*** $19,087. ***Average non-need-based aid:*** $5637. ***Average indebtedness upon graduation:*** $17,869. ***Financial aid deadline:*** 3/2.

APPLYING
Standardized Tests *Required:* SAT or ACT (for admission). *Recommended:* SAT Subject Tests (for admission).

Options: electronic application.

Application fee: $70.

Required: essay or personal statement.

CONTACT
University of California, Berkeley, Berkeley, CA 94720-1500.

University of California, Davis

Davis, California

http://www.ucdavis.edu/

- **State-supported** university, founded 1905, part of University of California System
- **Suburban** 5300-acre campus with easy access to San Francisco
- **Coed** 28,384 undergraduate students, 99% full-time, 59% women, 41% men
- **Very difficult** entrance level, 38% of applicants were admitted

UNDERGRAD STUDENTS
27,966 full-time, 418 part-time. 4% are from out of state; 2% Black or African American, non-Hispanic/Latino; 19% Hispanic/Latino; 32% Asian, non-Hispanic/Latino; 0.5% Native Hawaiian or other Pacific Islander, non-Hispanic/Latino; 0.2% American Indian or Alaska Native, non-Hispanic/Latino; 5% Two or more races, non-Hispanic/Latino; 2% Race/ethnicity unknown; 11% international; 10% transferred in; 25% live on campus.

Freshmen:
Admission: 64,510 applied, 24,614 admitted, 5,385 enrolled. ***Average high school GPA:*** 4. ***Test scores:*** SAT critical reading scores over 500: 80%; SAT math scores over 500: 89%; SAT writing scores over 500: 84%; ACT scores over 18: 99%; SAT critical reading scores over 600: 41%; SAT math scores over 600: 65%; SAT writing scores over 600: 51%; ACT scores over 24: 81%; SAT critical reading scores over 700: 10%; SAT math scores over 700: 29%; SAT writing scores over 700: 13%; ACT scores over 30: 33%.

Retention: 92% of full-time freshmen returned.

FACULTY
Total: 1,830, 90% full-time, 98% with terminal degrees.
Student/faculty ratio: 18:1.

ACADEMICS
Calendar: quarters. *Degrees:* bachelor's, master's, doctoral, post-master's, and postbachelor's certificates.

Special study options: academic remediation for entering students, adult/continuing education programs, advanced placement credit, double majors, English as a second language, freshman honors college, honors programs, independent study, internships, part-time degree program, services for LD students, student-designed majors, study abroad, summer session for credit. ***ROTC:*** Army (b), Navy (c), Air Force (c).

Computers: Students can access the following: campus intranet, computer help desk, free student e-mail accounts, online (class) grades, online (class) registration, online (class) schedules, software packages. Campuswide network is available. 100% of college-owned or -operated housing units are wired for high-speed Internet access. Wireless service is available via classrooms, libraries.

Library: Peter J. Shields Library plus 6 others. *Books:* 4.6 million (physical), 832,007 (digital/electronic).

STUDENT LIFE
Housing options: coed, women-only, cooperative, special housing for students with disabilities. Campus housing is university owned, leased by the school and is provided by a third party. Freshman campus housing is guaranteed.

Activities and organizations: drama/theater group, student-run newspaper, radio and television station, choral group, marching band, national fraternities, national sororities.

Athletics Member NCAA. All Division I except football (Division I-AA). ***Intercollegiate sports:*** baseball M(s), basketball M(s)/W(s), cross-country running M(s)/W(s), field hockey W(s), golf M(s)/W(s), gymnastics W(s), lacrosse W(s), soccer M(s)/W(s), softball W(s), swimming and diving

W(s), tennis M(s)/W(s), track and field M(s)/W(s), volleyball W(s), water polo M(s)/W(s). ***Intramural sports:*** archery M(c)/W(c), badminton M(c)/W(c), basketball M/W, crew M(c)/W(c), equestrian sports M(c)/W(c), fencing M(c)/W(c), football M/W, golf M/W, gymnastics M(c), ice hockey M(c)/W, lacrosse M(c)/W(c), racquetball M(c)/W(c), riflery M(c)/W(c), rugby M(c), sailing M(c)/W(c), skiing (cross-country) M(c)/W(c), skiing (downhill) M(c)/W(c), soccer M/W, softball M/W, swimming and diving W(c), table tennis M/W, tennis M/W, volleyball M(c)/W, water polo W(c).

Campus security: 24-hour emergency response devices and patrols, student patrols, late-night transport/escort service, controlled dormitory access, Campus Violence Prevention Program (CVPP).

Student services: health clinic, personal/psychological counseling, women's center, legal services.

COSTS & FINANCIAL AID

Costs (2017–18) ***Tuition:*** state resident $11,220 full-time; nonresident $39,516 full-time. ***Required fees:*** $2880 full-time. ***Room and board:*** $16,136. Room and board charges vary according to board plan.

Financial Aid Of all full-time matriculated undergraduates who enrolled in 2016, 20,393 applied for aid, 17,572 were judged to have need, 2,977 had their need fully met. In 2016, 1097 non-need-based awards were made. ***Average percent of need met:*** 79. ***Average financial aid package:*** $21,194. ***Average need-based loan:*** $5558. ***Average need-based gift aid:*** $18,271. ***Average non-need-based aid:*** $5643. ***Average indebtedness upon graduation:*** $19,276.

APPLYING

Standardized Tests *Required:* SAT or ACT (for admission).

Options: electronic application.

Application fee: $70.

Required: essay or personal statement, high school transcript, minimum 2.8 GPA, high school subject requirements.

Application deadlines: 11/30 (freshmen), 11/30 (transfers).

Notification: 3/15 (freshmen), continuous until 3/15 (transfers).

CONTACT

University of California, Davis, CA. *E-mail:* undergraduateadmissions@ucdavis.edu.

University of California, Irvine

Irvine, California

http://www.uci.edu/

- **State-supported** university, founded 1965, part of University of California System
- **Suburban** 1477-acre campus with easy access to Los Angeles
- **Coed** 27,331 undergraduate students, 98% full-time, 53% women, 47% men
- **Very difficult** entrance level, 41% of applicants were admitted

UNDERGRAD STUDENTS

26,889 full-time, 442 part-time. Students come from 46 states and territories; 71 other countries; 3% are from out of state; 2% Black or African American, non-Hispanic/Latino; 26% Hispanic/Latino; 36% Asian, non-Hispanic/Latino; 0.1% Native Hawaiian or other Pacific Islander, non-Hispanic/Latino; 4% Two or more races, non-Hispanic/Latino; 2% Race/ethnicity unknown; 16% international; 9% transferred in; 41% live on campus.

Freshmen:

Admission: 77,810 applied, 31,631 admitted, 6,552 enrolled. ***Average high school GPA:*** 3.97. ***Test scores:*** SAT critical reading scores over 500: 76%; SAT math scores over 500: 92%; SAT writing scores over 500: 84%; SAT critical reading scores over 600: 37%; SAT math scores over 600: 64%; SAT writing scores over 600: 40%; SAT critical reading scores over 700: 11%; SAT math scores over 700: 27%; SAT writing scores over 700: 8%.

Retention: 92% of full-time freshmen returned.

FACULTY

Total: 1,596, 79% full-time, 98% with terminal degrees.

Student/faculty ratio: 19:1.

ACADEMICS

Calendar: quarters. *Degrees:* bachelor's, master's, doctoral, and postbachelor's certificates.

Special study options: accelerated degree program, advanced placement credit, distance learning, double majors, English as a second language, honors programs, independent study, internships, off-campus study, services for LD students, study abroad, summer session for credit. ***ROTC:*** Army (b), Air Force (c).

Computers: 1,500 computers/terminals are available on campus for general student use. Students can access the following: campus intranet, computer help desk, free student e-mail accounts, online (class) grades, online (class) registration, online (class) schedules. Campuswide network is available. 100% of college-owned or -operated housing units are wired for high-speed Internet access. Wireless service is available via entire campus.

Library: Langson Library plus 4 others. *Books:* 2.0 million (physical), 1.2 million (digital/electronic); *Serial titles:* 4,826 (physical), 145,231 (digital/electronic); *Databases:* 1,274. Study areas open 24 hours, 5-7 days a week; students can reserve study rooms.

STUDENT LIFE

Housing options: coed, men-only, women-only, special housing for students with disabilities. Campus housing is university owned and is provided by a third party. Freshman campus housing is guaranteed.

Activities and organizations: drama/theater group, student-run newspaper, radio station, choral group, marching band, national fraternities, national sororities.

Athletics Member NCAA. All Division I. ***Intercollegiate sports:*** archery M(c)/W(c), badminton M(c)/W(c), baseball M(s), basketball M(s)/W(s), crew M(c)/W(c), cross-country running M(s)/W(s), fencing M(c)/W(c), golf M(s)/W(s), lacrosse M(c)/W(c), rugby M(c)/W(c), sailing M(c)/W(c), soccer M(s)/W(s), table tennis M(c)/W(c), tennis M(s)/W(s), track and field M(s)/W(s), ultimate Frisbee M(c)/W(c), volleyball M(s)/W(s), water polo M(s)/W(s), wrestling M(c)/W(c). ***Intramural sports:*** basketball M/W, bowling M/W, football M/W, racquetball M/W, soccer M/W, softball M/W, swimming and diving M/W, table tennis M/W, tennis M/W, track and field M/W, ultimate Frisbee M/W, volleyball M/W, water polo M/W, wrestling M/W.

Campus security: 24-hour emergency response devices and patrols, student patrols, late-night transport/escort service, controlled dormitory access.

Student services: health clinic, personal/psychological counseling.

COSTS & FINANCIAL AID

Costs (2016–17) ***Tuition:*** state resident $11,220 full-time; nonresident $37,902 full-time. ***Required fees:*** $3815 full-time. ***Room and board:*** $13,661. Room and board charges vary according to board plan and housing facility. ***Payment plan:*** installment. ***Waivers:*** employees or children of employees.

Financial Aid Of all full-time matriculated undergraduates who enrolled in 2015, 18,674 applied for aid, 16,641 were judged to have need, 2,965 had their need fully met. In 2015, 520 non-need-based awards were made. ***Average percent of need met:*** 81. ***Average financial aid package:*** $22,203. ***Average need-based loan:*** $6890. ***Average need-based gift aid:*** $18,593. ***Average non-need-based aid:*** $8242. ***Average indebtedness upon graduation:*** $20,628. ***Financial aid deadline:*** 6/26.

APPLYING

Standardized Tests *Required:* SAT or ACT (for admission). *Recommended:* SAT Subject Tests (for admission).

Options: electronic application.

Application fee: $70.

Required: essay or personal statement, high school transcript.

Application deadlines: 11/30 (freshmen), 11/30 (transfers).

Notification: 3/31 (freshmen), 4/30 (transfers).

CONTACT

University of California, Irvine, UC IRVINE Office of Admissions and Relations with Schools, 260 Aldrich Hall, Irvine, CA 92697-1075. *Phone:* 949-824-6703. *Fax:* 949-824-2951. *E-mail:* admissions@uci.edu.

University of California, Los Angeles

Los Angeles, California

http://www.ucla.edu/

- **State-supported** university, founded 1919, part of University of California System
- **Urban** 419-acre campus with easy access to Los Angeles
- **Endowment** $3.6 billion
- **Coed** 30,873 undergraduate students, 98% full-time, 57% women, 43% men
- **Very difficult** entrance level, 18% of applicants were admitted

UNDERGRAD STUDENTS

30,343 full-time, 530 part-time. Students come from 55 states and territories; 116 other countries; 13% are from out of state; 3% Black or African American, non-Hispanic/Latino; 22% Hispanic/Latino; 29% Asian, non-Hispanic/Latino; 0.3% Native Hawaiian or other Pacific Islander, non-Hispanic/Latino; 0.2% American Indian or Alaska Native, non-Hispanic/Latino; 5% Two or more races, non-Hispanic/Latino; 2% Race/ethnicity unknown; 12% international; 11% transferred in; 46% live on campus.

Freshmen:

Admission: 97,121 applied, 17,474 admitted, 6,545 enrolled. ***Average high school GPA:*** 4.33. ***Test scores:*** SAT critical reading scores over 500: 91%; SAT math scores over 500: 92%; SAT writing scores over 500: 92%; ACT scores over 18: 99%; SAT critical reading scores over 600: 65%; SAT math scores over 600: 72%; SAT writing scores over 600: 68%; ACT scores over 24: 86%; SAT critical reading scores over 700: 27%; SAT math scores over 700: 42%; SAT writing scores over 700: 32%; ACT scores over 30: 57%.

Retention: 97% of full-time freshmen returned.

FACULTY

Total: 2,706, 58% full-time, 92% with terminal degrees.

Student/faculty ratio: 17:1.

ACADEMICS

Calendar: quarters. *Degrees:* bachelor's, master's, and doctoral.

Special study options: accelerated degree program, advanced placement credit, double majors, freshman honors college, independent study, internships, off-campus study, services for LD students, student-designed majors, study abroad, summer session for credit. ***ROTC:*** Army (b), Navy (b), Air Force (b).

Computers: 4,000 computers/terminals are available on campus for general student use. Students can access the following: campus intranet, computer help desk, free student e-mail accounts, online (class) grades, online (class) registration, online (class) schedules, 24/7 Chat with a Librarian. Campuswide network is available. 100% of college-owned or -operated housing units are wired for high-speed Internet access. Wireless service is available via entire campus.

Library: Charles E. Young Research Library plus 13 others. *Books:* 13.8 million (physical), 2.1 million (digital/electronic); *Serial titles:* 9,543 (physical), 99,598 (digital/electronic); *Databases:* 1,794. Weekly public service hours: 104; study areas open 24 hours, 5-7 days a week; students can reserve study rooms.

STUDENT LIFE

Housing options: coed, special housing for students with disabilities. Campus housing is university owned. Freshman campus housing is guaranteed.

Activities and organizations: drama/theater group, student-run newspaper, radio and television station, choral group, marching band, national fraternities, national sororities.

Athletics Member NCAA. All Division I except football (Division I-A). ***Intercollegiate sports:*** baseball M(s), basketball M(s)/W(s), crew W(s), cross-country running M(s)/W(s), golf M(s)/W(s), gymnastics W(s), soccer M(s)/W(s), softball W(s), swimming and diving W(s), tennis M(s)/W(s), track and field M(s)/W(s), volleyball M(s)/W(s), water polo M(s)/W(s). ***Intramural sports:*** archery M/W, badminton M/W, basketball M/W, bowling M/W, crew M/W, cross-country running M/W, fencing M/W, field hockey W, football M/W, golf M/W, gymnastics M/W, ice hockey M/W, lacrosse M/W, racquetball M/W, riflery M/W, rugby M/W, sailing M/W, skiing (cross-country) M/W, skiing (downhill) M/W, soccer M/W, softball M/W, squash M/W, swimming and diving M/W, table tennis M/W, tennis M/W, track and field M/W, ultimate Frisbee M/W, volleyball M/W, water polo M/W.

Campus security: 24-hour emergency response devices and patrols, student patrols, late-night transport/escort service, controlled dormitory access.

Student services: health clinic, personal/psychological counseling, women's center, legal services.

FINANCIAL AID

Financial Aid Of all full-time matriculated undergraduates who enrolled in 2016, 18,067 applied for aid, 16,580 were judged to have need, 4,211 had their need fully met. 2,828 Federal Work-Study jobs (averaging $2158). 55 state and other part-time jobs (averaging $2487). In 2016, 930 non-need-based awards were made. ***Average percent of need met:*** 83. ***Average financial aid package:*** $22,998. ***Average need-based loan:*** $7242. ***Average need-based gift aid:*** $19,577. ***Average non-need-based aid:*** $5000. ***Average indebtedness upon graduation:*** $21,323.

APPLYING

Standardized Tests *Required:* SAT or ACT (for admission).

Options: electronic application.

Application fee: $70.

Required: essay or personal statement, high school transcript.

Application deadlines: 11/30 (freshmen), 11/30 (transfers).

Notification: 3/31 (freshmen), 4/30 (transfers).

CONTACT

University of California, Los Angeles, 405 Hilgard Avenue, Los Angeles, CA 90095. *Phone:* 310-825-3101.

University of California, Merced

Merced, California

http://www.ucmerced.edu/

- **State-supported** university, part of University of California System
- **Small-town** 815-acre campus with easy access to Fresno
- **Endowment** $38,592
- **Coed**
- **Moderately difficult** entrance level

FACULTY

Student/faculty ratio: 18:1.

ACADEMICS

Degrees: bachelor's, master's, and doctoral.

Library: Kolligian Library. Students can reserve study rooms.

STUDENT LIFE

Housing options: coed, special housing for students with disabilities. Campus housing is university owned. Freshman campus housing is guaranteed.

Activities and organizations: drama/theater group, student-run newspaper, radio station, choral group, marching band, Philipino American Alliance, Vietnamese Student Association, Intervarsity Christian Fellowship, Latino Associated Students, Hip Hop Movement, national fraternities, national sororities.

Athletics Member NAIA.

Campus security: 24-hour emergency response devices and patrols, student patrols, late-night transport/escort service, controlled dormitory access.

Student services: health clinic, personal/psychological counseling, women's center, legal services.

COSTS & FINANCIAL AID

Costs (2016–17) ***Tuition:*** state resident $11,784 full-time, $2496 per term part-time; nonresident $35,808 full-time, $8952 per term part-time. Full-time tuition and fees vary according to course load. Part-time tuition and fees vary according to course load. ***Required fees:*** $1988 full-time, $1988 per year part-time. ***Room and board:*** $15,646. Room and board charges vary according to board plan.

Financial Aid Of all full-time matriculated undergraduates who enrolled in 2015, 5,752 applied for aid, 5,349 were judged to have need, 1,503 had their need fully met. In 2015, 63 non-need-based awards were made. ***Average percent of need met:*** 84. ***Average financial aid package:*** $23,468. ***Average need-based loan:*** $5281. ***Average need-based gift aid:***

$19,426. ***Average non-need-based aid:*** $11,136. ***Average indebtedness upon graduation:*** $21,180.

APPLYING
Standardized Tests *Required:* SAT or ACT (for admission).

Options: electronic application.

Application fee: $70.

Required: essay or personal statement, high school transcript, minimum 3.0 high school GPA for California residents.

CONTACT
Mr. Ruben Lubers, Assistant Director, Admissions and Outreach, University of California, Merced, 5200 North Lake Road, Merced, CA 95343. *Phone:* 209-228-4241. *E-mail:* admissions@ucmerced.edu.

University of California, Riverside

Riverside, California

http://www.ucr.edu/

- **State-supported** university, founded 1954, part of University of California System
- **Urban** 1200-acre campus with easy access to Los Angeles
- **Endowment** $138.8 million
- **Coed** 19,799 undergraduate students, 99% full-time, 54% women, 46% men
- **Very difficult** entrance level, 66% of applicants were admitted

UNDERGRAD STUDENTS
19,544 full-time, 255 part-time. Students come from 30 states and territories; 41 other countries; 0.6% are from out of state; 4% Black or African American, non-Hispanic/Latino; 41% Hispanic/Latino; 34% Asian, non-Hispanic/Latino; 0.2% Native Hawaiian or other Pacific Islander, non-Hispanic/Latino; 0.1% American Indian or Alaska Native, non-Hispanic/Latino; 6% Two or more races, non-Hispanic/Latino; 1% Race/ethnicity unknown; 2% international; 6% transferred in; 34% live on campus.

Freshmen:
Admission: 42,629 applied, 28,280 admitted, 5,358 enrolled. ***Average high school GPA:*** 3.65. ***Test scores:*** SAT critical reading scores over 500: 60%; SAT math scores over 500: 69%; SAT writing scores over 500: 61%; ACT scores over 18: 97%; SAT critical reading scores over 600: 18%; SAT math scores over 600: 30%; SAT writing scores over 600: 18%; ACT scores over 24: 54%; SAT critical reading scores over 700: 2%; SAT math scores over 700: 6%; SAT writing scores over 700: 2%; ACT scores over 30: 11%.

Retention: 91% of full-time freshmen returned.

FACULTY
Student/faculty ratio: 22:1.

ACADEMICS
Calendar: quarters. *Degrees:* bachelor's, master's, doctoral, and postbachelor's certificates.

Special study options: accelerated degree program, adult/continuing education programs, advanced placement credit, distance learning, double majors, honors programs, independent study, internships, off-campus study, part-time degree program, services for LD students, study abroad, summer session for credit. ***ROTC:*** Army (c), Air Force (c).

Unusual degree programs: 3-2 engineering.

Computers: 556 computers/terminals are available on campus for general student use. Students can access the following: campus intranet, computer help desk, free student e-mail accounts, online (class) grades, online (class) registration, online (class) schedules, online viewing of financial information. Campuswide network is available. 100% of college-owned or -operated housing units are wired for high-speed Internet access. Wireless service is available via entire campus.
Library: Tomas Rivera Library plus 4 others.

STUDENT LIFE
Housing options: coed, special housing for students with disabilities. Campus housing is university owned and is provided by a third party. Freshman campus housing is guaranteed.

Activities and organizations: drama/theater group, student-run newspaper, radio station, choral group, American Red Cross at University of California Riverside, American Medical Student Association, Running Club At UCR, Katipunan Pilipino Student Organization, Circle K International, national fraternities, national sororities.

Athletics Member NCAA. All Division I. ***Intercollegiate sports:*** baseball M(s), basketball M(s)/W(s), cross-country running M(s)/W(s), golf M(s), soccer M(s)/W(s), softball W(s), tennis M/W, volleyball W(s). ***Intramural sports:*** badminton M/W, basketball M/W, racquetball M/W, rugby M(c)/W(c), soccer M/W, softball M/W, table tennis M(c)/W(c), tennis M/W, volleyball M/W, wrestling M(c).

Campus security: 24-hour emergency response devices and patrols, student patrols, late-night transport/escort service, controlled dormitory access.

Student services: health clinic, personal/psychological counseling, women's center, legal services.

COSTS & FINANCIAL AID
Costs (2016–17) ***Tuition:*** state resident $11,220 full-time, $5610 per year part-time; nonresident $37,902 full-time, $18,951 per year part-time. Full-time tuition and fees vary according to course load. Part-time tuition and fees vary according to course load. ***Required fees:*** $2361 full-time. ***Room and board:*** $16,400. Room and board charges vary according to board plan and housing facility. ***Payment plan:*** deferred payment.

Financial Aid Of all full-time matriculated undergraduates who enrolled in 2016, 17,057 applied for aid, 15,552 were judged to have need, 2,859 had their need fully met. 3,196 Federal Work-Study jobs (averaging $1540). In 2016, 283 non-need-based awards were made. ***Average percent of need met:*** 78. ***Average financial aid package:*** $22,301. ***Average need-based loan:*** $6634. ***Average need-based gift aid:*** $18,289. ***Average non-need-based aid:*** $5269. ***Average indebtedness upon graduation:*** $21,838. ***Financial aid deadline:*** 3/2.

APPLYING
Standardized Tests *Required:* SAT or ACT (for admission). *Recommended:* SAT Subject Tests (for admission).

Options: electronic application.

Application fee: $70.

Required: essay or personal statement, high school transcript, minimum 3.0 GPA.

Application deadlines: 11/30 (freshmen), 11/30 (transfers).

Notification: continuous until 2/1 (freshmen), continuous until 3/1 (transfers).

CONTACT
Ms. Emily D. Engelschall, Director, Undergraduate Admissions, University of California, Riverside, 3221 Student Services, 900 University Avenue, Riverside, CA 92521. *Phone:* 951-827-3986. *Fax:* 951-827-6346. *E-mail:* discover@ucr.edu.

University of California, San Diego

La Jolla, California

http://www.ucsd.edu/

- **State-supported** university, founded 1959, part of University of California System
- **Suburban** 1976-acre campus with easy access to San Diego
- **Coed** 28,127 undergraduate students, 98% full-time, 48% women, 52% men
- **Very difficult** entrance level, 36% of applicants were admitted

UNDERGRAD STUDENTS
27,698 full-time, 429 part-time. Students come from 52 states and territories; 93 other countries; 6% are from out of state; 2% Black or African American, non-Hispanic/Latino; 16% Hispanic/Latino; 39% Asian, non-Hispanic/Latino; 0.2% Native Hawaiian or other Pacific Islander, non-Hispanic/Latino; 4% American Indian or Alaska Native, non-Hispanic/Latino; 3% Race/ethnicity unknown; 19% international; 10% transferred in; 43% live on campus.

Freshmen:
Admission: 84,209 applied, 30,273 admitted, 5,748 enrolled. ***Average high school GPA:*** 4. ***Test scores:*** SAT critical reading scores over 500: 90%; SAT math scores over 500: 94%; SAT writing scores over 500: 91%; ACT scores over 18: 98%; SAT critical reading scores over 600: 58%; SAT math scores over 600: 74%; SAT writing scores over 600: 64%; ACT scores over 24: 84%; SAT critical reading scores over 700: 18%; SAT

math scores over 700: 41%; SAT writing scores over 700: 22%; ACT scores over 30: 47%.

Retention: 95% of full-time freshmen returned.

FACULTY

Total: 1,213, 83% full-time, 98% with terminal degrees.

Student/faculty ratio: 19:1.

ACADEMICS

Calendar: quarters. *Degrees:* bachelor's, master's, and doctoral.

Special study options: accelerated degree program, advanced placement credit, cooperative education, double majors, English as a second language, freshman honors college, honors programs, independent study, internships, off-campus study, services for LD students, student-designed majors, study abroad, summer session for credit. ***ROTC:*** Army (c), Navy (c), Air Force (c).

Computers: Students can access the following: campus intranet, computer help desk, free student e-mail accounts, online (class) grades, online (class) registration, online (class) schedules. Campuswide network is available. 100% of college-owned or -operated housing units are wired for high-speed Internet access. Wireless service is available via entire campus.

Library: Geisel Library plus 1 other. *Books:* 3.5 million (physical), 958,000 (digital/electronic). Study areas open 24 hours, 5-7 days a week; students can reserve study rooms.

STUDENT LIFE

Housing options: coed, special housing for students with disabilities. Campus housing is university owned. Freshman campus housing is guaranteed.

Activities and organizations: drama/theater group, student-run newspaper, radio and television station, choral group, marching band, national fraternities, national sororities.

Athletics Member NCAA. All Division II. ***Intercollegiate sports:*** baseball M, basketball M/W, crew M/W, cross-country running M/W, fencing M/W, golf M, soccer M/W, softball W, swimming and diving M/W, tennis M/W, track and field M/W, volleyball M/W, water polo M/W. ***Intramural sports:*** basketball M/W, bowling M/W, equestrian sports M(c)/W(c), football M(c)/W(c), ice hockey M, lacrosse M(c)/W(c), racquetball M/W, sailing M(c)/W(c), skiing (downhill) M(c)/W(c), soccer M/W, softball M/W, table tennis M/W, tennis M/W, ultimate Frisbee M(c)/W(c), volleyball M/W, water polo M/W.

Campus security: 24-hour emergency response devices and patrols, student patrols, late-night transport/escort service, crime prevention programs.

Student services: health clinic, personal/psychological counseling, women's center, legal services.

COSTS & FINANCIAL AID

Costs (2016–17) ***One-time required fee:*** $165. ***Tuition:*** state resident $11,220 full-time; nonresident $37,902 full-time. ***Required fees:*** $2425 full-time. ***Room and board:*** Room and board charges vary according to board plan and housing facility.

Financial Aid Of all full-time matriculated undergraduates who enrolled in 2016, 17,287 applied for aid, 15,003 were judged to have need, 4,952 had their need fully met. In 2016, 548 non-need-based awards were made. ***Average percent of need met:*** 86. ***Average financial aid package:*** $22,499. ***Average need-based loan:*** $5880. ***Average need-based gift aid:*** $18,412. ***Average non-need-based aid:*** $11,001. ***Average indebtedness upon graduation:*** $21,830.

APPLYING

Standardized Tests *Required:* SAT or ACT (for admission), SAT and SAT Subject Tests or ACT (for admission), ACT Assessment with Writing or SAT Reasoning Test, plus two SAT Subject Tests (for admission).

Options: electronic application.

Application fee: $60.

Required: essay or personal statement, high school transcript, minimum 2.8 GPA. ***Required for some:*** minimum 3.4 GPA.

Notification: 3/31 (freshmen).

CONTACT

Ms. Adele Brumfield, Assistant Vice Chancellor, Enrollment Management, University of California, San Diego, 9500 Gilman Drive, 0021, La Jolla, CA 92093-0021. *Phone:* 858-534-3156.
E-mail: admissionsreply@ucsd.edu.

See below for display ad and page 1544 for the College Close-Up.

University of California, Santa Barbara

Santa Barbara, California

http://www.ucsb.edu/

- **State-supported** university, founded 1909, part of University of California System
- **Suburban** 989-acre campus
- **Endowment** $155.0 million
- **Coed** 21,574 undergraduate students, 98% full-time, 53% women, 47% men
- **Very difficult** entrance level, 36% of applicants were admitted

UNDERGRAD STUDENTS

21,198 full-time, 376 part-time. Students come from 51 states and territories; 81 other countries; 5% are from out of state; 2% Black or African American, non-Hispanic/Latino; 26% Hispanic/Latino; 21% Asian, non-Hispanic/Latino; 0.4% Native Hawaiian or other Pacific Islander, non-Hispanic/Latino; 0.2% American Indian or Alaska Native, non-Hispanic/Latino; 6% Two or more races, non-Hispanic/Latino; 1% Race/ethnicity unknown; 8% international; 9% transferred in; 39% live on campus.

Freshmen:

Admission: 77,098 applied, 27,580 admitted, 4,996 enrolled. ***Average high school GPA:*** 4.02. ***Test scores:*** SAT critical reading scores over 500: 93%; SAT math scores over 500: 94%; SAT writing scores over 500: 95%; ACT scores over 18: 99%; SAT critical reading scores over 600: 62%; SAT math scores over 600: 72%; SAT writing scores over 600: 68%; ACT scores over 24: 84%; SAT critical reading scores over 700: 17%; SAT math scores over 700: 31%; SAT writing scores over 700: 22%; ACT scores over 30: 39%.

Retention: 92% of full-time freshmen returned.

FACULTY

Total: 1,089, 85% full-time, 100% with terminal degrees.

Student/faculty ratio: 18:1.

ACADEMICS

Calendar: quarters plus 6-week summer term. *Degrees:* bachelor's, master's, doctoral, post-master's, and postbachelor's certificates.

Special study options: accelerated degree program, advanced placement credit, cooperative education, double majors, English as a second language, honors programs, independent study, internships, off-campus study, services for LD students, student-designed majors, study abroad, summer session for credit. ***ROTC:*** Army (b), Air Force (c).

Computers: 700 computers/terminals are available on campus for general student use. Students can access the following: computer help desk, free student e-mail accounts, online (class) grades, online (class) registration, online (class) schedules. Campuswide network is available. 100% of college-owned or -operated housing units are wired for high-speed Internet access. Wireless service is available via classrooms, computer labs, dorm rooms, libraries, student centers.

Library: Davidson Library plus 1 other. *Books:* 3.2 million (physical), 773,673 (digital/electronic); *Serial titles:* 75,015 (physical); *Databases:* 717. Weekly public service hours: 96; study areas open 24 hours, 5-7 days a week; students can reserve study rooms.

STUDENT LIFE

Housing options: coed, cooperative. Campus housing is university owned and is provided by a third party. Freshman applicants given priority for college housing.

Activities and organizations: drama/theater group, student-run newspaper, radio and television station, choral group, national fraternities, national sororities.

Athletics Member NCAA. All Division I. ***Intercollegiate sports:*** baseball M(s), basketball M(s)/W(s), bowling M(c)/W(c), crew M(c)/W(c), cross-country running M(s)/W(s), equestrian sports M(c)/W(c), fencing M(c)/W(c), field hockey W(c), golf M(s), gymnastics M(s)/W(s), lacrosse M(c)/W(c), rugby M(c), sailing M(c)/W(c), skiing (downhill) M(c)/W(c), soccer M(s)/W(s), softball W(s), swimming and diving M(s)/W(s), tennis M(s)/W(s), track and field M(s)/W(s), ultimate Frisbee M(c)/W(c), volleyball M(s)/W(s), water polo M(s)/W(s). ***Intramural sports:*** badminton M/W, basketball M/W, bowling M/W, cross-country running M/W, football M/W, golf M/W, gymnastics M/W, racquetball M/W, soccer M/W, softball M/W, squash M/W, tennis M/W, ultimate Frisbee M/W, volleyball M/W, water polo M/W.

Campus security: 24-hour emergency response devices and patrols, student patrols, late-night transport/escort service, controlled dormitory access.

Student services: health clinic, personal/psychological counseling, women's center, legal services.

COSTS & FINANCIAL AID

Costs (2016–17) ***Tuition:*** state resident $11,220 full-time; nonresident $37,902 full-time. ***Required fees:*** $2849 full-time. ***Room and board:*** $13,605. Room and board charges vary according to board plan and housing facility. ***Payment plan:*** installment.

Financial Aid Of all full-time matriculated undergraduates who enrolled in 2016, 14,954 applied for aid, 12,705 were judged to have need, 2,286 had their need fully met. In 2016, 428 non-need-based awards were made. ***Average percent of need met:*** 79. ***Average financial aid package:*** $22,544. ***Average need-based loan:*** $6477. ***Average need-based gift aid:*** $18,999. ***Average non-need-based aid:*** $7952. ***Average indebtedness upon graduation:*** $21,001.

APPLYING

Standardized Tests *Required:* SAT or ACT (for admission). *Recommended:* SAT Subject Tests (for admission).

Options: electronic application.

Application fee: $70.

Required: essay or personal statement, high school transcript. ***Required for some:*** interview.

Application deadlines: 11/30 (freshmen), 11/30 (transfers).

Notification: 3/15 (freshmen), 5/1 (transfers).

CONTACT

Office of Admissions, University of California, Santa Barbara, 1210 Cheadle Hall, Santa Barbara, CA 93106-2014. *Phone:* 805-893-2881. *Fax:* 805-893-2676. *E-mail:* admissions@sa.ucsb.edu.

University of California, Santa Cruz

Santa Cruz, California

http://www.ucsc.edu/

- **State-supported** university, founded 1965, part of University of California System
- **Small-town** 2000-acre campus with easy access to San Francisco, San Jose
- **Endowment** $162.2 million
- **Coed**
- **Very difficult** entrance level

ACADEMICS

Calendar: quarters. *Degrees:* bachelor's, master's, doctoral, and postbachelor's certificates.

Library: UCSC Library. *Books:* 1.5 million (physical), 865,233 (digital/electronic); *Serial titles:* 722 (physical), 60,280 (digital/electronic); *Databases:* 390. Weekly public service hours: 98; students can reserve study rooms.

STUDENT LIFE

Housing options: coed, men-only, women-only, cooperative. Campus housing is university owned. Freshman campus housing is guaranteed.

Activities and organizations: drama/theater group, student-run newspaper, radio and television station, choral group, Filipino Student Association, Movimiento Estudiantil Chicano de Aztlan, CSA (Chinese Student Association), A/BSA (African/Black Student Alliance), SEC (Student Environmental Center), national fraternities, national sororities.

Athletics Member NCAA. All Division III.

Campus security: 24-hour emergency response devices and patrols, late-night transport/escort service, controlled dormitory access, evening main gate security, campus police force and fire station.

Student services: health clinic, personal/psychological counseling, women's center.

FINANCIAL AID

Financial Aid Of all full-time matriculated undergraduates who enrolled in 2016, 12,677 applied for aid, 10,730 were judged to have need, 2,705 had their need fully met. 1,086 Federal Work-Study jobs (averaging $2649). In 2016, 1172 non-need-based awards were made. ***Average percent of need met:*** 84. ***Average financial aid package:*** $24,821. ***Average need-based loan:*** $6551. ***Average need-based gift aid:*** $20,041. ***Average non-need-based aid:*** $5064. ***Average indebtedness upon graduation:*** $22,582. ***Financial aid deadline:*** 3/2.

APPLYING

Standardized Tests *Required:* SAT or ACT (for admission).

Options: electronic application.

Application fee: $70.

Required: essay or personal statement, high school transcript, minimum high school GPA of 3.0 for California residents, 3.4 for non-residents.

CONTACT

Michael McCawley, Director, Admissions, University of California, Santa Cruz, 1156 High Street, Santa Cruz, CA 95064. *Phone:* 831-459-2374. *Fax:* 831-459-4163. *E-mail:* admissions@ucsc.edu.

See this page for display ad and page 1546 for the College Close-Up.

University of La Verne

La Verne, California

http://www.laverne.edu/

- **Independent** university, founded 1891
- **Suburban** 66-acre campus with easy access to Los Angeles
- **Coed** 2,809 undergraduate students, 97% full-time, 58% women, 42% men
- **Moderately difficult** entrance level, 48% of applicants were admitted

UNDERGRAD STUDENTS

2,715 full-time, 94 part-time. Students come from 22 states and territories; 28 other countries; 4% are from out of state; 5% Black or African American, non-Hispanic/Latino; 53% Hispanic/Latino; 6% Asian, non-Hispanic/Latino; 0.7% Native Hawaiian or other Pacific Islander, non-Hispanic/Latino; 0.1% American Indian or Alaska Native, non-Hispanic/Latino; 5% Two or more races, non-Hispanic/Latino; 2% Race/ethnicity unknown; 6% international; 6% transferred in; 29% live on campus.

Freshmen:

Admission: 8,072 applied, 3,879 admitted, 555 enrolled. ***Average high school GPA:*** 3.46. ***Test scores:*** SAT critical reading scores over 500: 55%; SAT math scores over 500: 63%; SAT writing scores over 500: 56%; ACT scores over 18: 96%; SAT critical reading scores over 600: 12%; SAT math scores over 600: 17%; SAT writing scores over 600: 10%; ACT scores over 24: 45%; SAT critical reading scores over 700: 1%; SAT math scores over 700: 3%; ACT scores over 30: 7%.

Retention: 88% of full-time freshmen returned.

FACULTY

Total: 470, 48% full-time, 29% with terminal degrees.

Student/faculty ratio: 13:1.

ACADEMICS

Calendar: 4-1-4. *Degrees:* certificates, bachelor's, master's, and doctoral (also offers continuing education program with significant enrollment not reflected in profile).

Special study options: academic remediation for entering students, adult/continuing education programs, advanced placement credit, distance learning, double majors, English as a second language, freshman honors college, honors programs, independent study, internships, off-campus study, part-time degree program, services for LD students, student-designed majors, study abroad, summer session for credit.

ROTC: Army (c).

Computers: Students can access the following: computer help desk, free student e-mail accounts, online (class) grades, online (class) registration, online (class) schedules, MyLaVerne (online). Campuswide network is available. 100% of college-owned or -operated housing units are wired for high-speed Internet access. Wireless service is available via entire campus.

Library: Wilson Library. Students can reserve study rooms.

STUDENT LIFE
Housing options: coed, men-only, women-only. Campus housing is university owned.

Activities and organizations: drama/theater group, student-run newspaper, radio and television station, choral group, Associated Students of La Verne, Latino Student Forum, Black Student Union, Psi Chi, Voices in Action, national fraternities, national sororities.

Athletics Member NCAA. All Division III. ***Intercollegiate sports:*** baseball M, basketball M/W, cross-country running M/W, football M, golf M, soccer M/W, softball W, swimming and diving M/W, tennis M/W, track and field M/W, volleyball W, water polo M/W.

Campus security: 24-hour emergency response devices and patrols, late-night transport/escort service, controlled dormitory access.

Student services: health clinic, personal/psychological counseling.

COSTS & FINANCIAL AID
Costs (2017–18) ***Comprehensive fee:*** $54,590 includes full-time tuition ($39,916), mandatory fees ($1534), and room and board ($13,140). Full-time tuition and fees vary according to location. Part-time tuition: $1166 per credit hour. Part-time tuition and fees vary according to location. ***College room only:*** $7030. Room and board charges vary according to board plan and housing facility. ***Payment plans:*** installment, deferred payment. ***Waivers:*** employees or children of employees.

Financial Aid Of all full-time matriculated undergraduates who enrolled in 2016, 2,376 applied for aid, 2,264 were judged to have need, 197 had their need fully met. 281 Federal Work-Study jobs (averaging $2530). In 2016, 393 non-need-based awards were made. ***Average percent of need met:*** 46. ***Average financial aid package:*** $31,389. ***Average need-based loan:*** $4859. ***Average need-based gift aid:*** $14,146. ***Average non-need-based aid:*** $21,784. ***Average indebtedness upon graduation:*** $31,445.

APPLYING
Standardized Tests *Required:* SAT or ACT (for admission).

Options: electronic application, deferred entrance.

Application fee: $50.

Required: essay or personal statement, high school transcript, 2 letters of recommendation.

Application deadlines: 2/1 (freshmen), 4/1 (transfers).

Notification: continuous (freshmen), continuous (transfers).

CONTACT
Mr. Erasmo Fuentes, Associate Director of Admission, University of La Verne, 1950 Third Street, La Verne, CA 91750. *Phone:* 800-876-4858. *Toll-free phone:* 800-876-4858. *Fax:* 909-392-2714. *E-mail:* admissions@ulv.edu.

University of Phoenix–Bay Area Campus

San Jose, California

http://www.phoenix.edu/

CONTACT
Marc Booker, Sr. Director, Office of Admissions and Evaluation, University of Phoenix–Bay Area Campus, 4035 South Riverpoint Parkway, Mail Stop CF-L101, Phoenix, AZ 85040-1958. *Phone:* 602-557-4609. *Toll-free phone:* 866-766-0766. *Fax:* 480-643-1156.

University of Phoenix–Central Valley Campus

Fresno, California

http://www.phoenix.edu/

CONTACT
Marc Booker, Sr. Director, Office of Admissions and Evaluation, University of Phoenix–Central Valley Campus, 4035 South Riverpoint Parkway, Mail Stop CF-L101, Phoenix, AZ 85040. *Phone:* 602-557-4609. *Toll-free phone:* 866-766-0766. *Fax:* 480-643-1156.

University of Phoenix–Sacramento Valley Campus

Sacramento, California

http://www.phoenix.edu/

CONTACT
Marc Booker, Sr. Director, Office of Admissions and Evaluation, University of Phoenix–Sacramento Valley Campus, 4035 South Riverpoint Parkway, Mail Stop CF-L101, Phoenix, AZ 85040. *Phone:* 602-557-4609. *Toll-free phone:* 866-766-0766. *Fax:* 480-643-1156.

University of Phoenix–San Diego Campus

San Diego, California

http://www.phoenix.edu/

CONTACT
Marc Booker, Sr. Director, Office of Admissions and Evaluation, University of Phoenix–San Diego Campus, 4035 South Riverpoint Parkway, Mail Stop CF-L101, Phoenix, AZ 85040. *Phone:* 602-557-4609. *Toll-free phone:* 866-766-0766. *Fax:* 480-643-1156.

University of Phoenix–Southern California Campus

Costa Mesa, California

http://www.phoenix.edu/

CONTACT
Marc Booker, Sr. Director, Office of Admissions and Evaluation, University of Phoenix–Southern California Campus, 4035 South Riverpoint Parkway, Mail Stop CF-L101, Phoenix, AZ 85040. *Phone:* 602-557-4609. *Toll-free phone:* 866-766-0766. *Fax:* 480-643-1156.

University of Redlands

Redlands, California

http://www.redlands.edu/

- **Independent** comprehensive, founded 1907
- **Small-town** 140-acre campus with easy access to Los Angeles
- **Endowment** $110.8 million
- **Coed**
- **Moderately difficult** entrance level

ACADEMICS
Calendar: 4-4-1. *Degrees:* certificates, diplomas, bachelor's, master's, doctoral, post-master's, and postbachelor's certificates.

Library: Armacost Library.

STUDENT LIFE
Housing options: on-campus residence required through senior year; coed, men-only, women-only, cooperative, special housing for students with disabilities. Campus housing is university owned. Freshman campus housing is guaranteed.

Activities and organizations: drama/theater group, student-run newspaper, radio station, choral group, Associated Students, service organizations, cultural organizations, social awareness groups.

Athletics Member NCAA. All Division III.

Campus security: 24-hour emergency response devices and patrols, student patrols, late-night transport/escort service, controlled dormitory access.

Student services: health clinic, personal/psychological counseling, women's center.

COSTS & FINANCIAL AID
Costs (2016–17) ***One-time required fee:*** $150. ***Comprehensive fee:*** $60,050 includes full-time tuition ($46,220), mandatory fees ($350), and room and board ($13,480). Part-time tuition: $1445 per credit hour. Part-time tuition and fees vary according to course load. ***Required fees:*** $116 per year part-time. ***Room and board:*** Room and board charges vary according to board plan and housing facility.

Financial Aid Of all full-time matriculated undergraduates who enrolled in 2015, 2,342 applied for aid, 2,024 were judged to have need, 972 had their need fully met. In 2015, 532 non-need-based awards were made. ***Average percent of need met:*** 83. ***Average financial aid package:*** $33,187. ***Average need-based loan:*** $6467. ***Average need-based gift aid:*** $27,847. ***Average non-need-based aid:*** $15,733. ***Average indebtedness upon graduation:*** $32,662.

APPLYING

Standardized Tests *Required:* SAT or ACT (for admission).

Options: electronic application, early action, deferred entrance.

Application fee: $30.

Required: essay or personal statement, high school transcript, 2 letters of recommendation. ***Recommended:*** interview.

CONTACT

Ms. Belinda Sandoval Zazueta, Director of Undergraduate Admission, University of Redlands, 1200 East Colton Avenue, PO Box 3080, Redlands, CA 92373-0999. *Phone:* 909-748-8159. *Toll-free phone:* 800-455-5064. *E-mail:* belinda_sandoval@redlands.edu.

See this page for display ad and page 1576 for the College Close-Up.

University of San Diego

San Diego, California

http://www.sandiego.edu/

- **Independent Roman Catholic** university, founded 1949
- **Urban** 180-acre campus with easy access to San Diego
- **Endowment** $449.8 million
- **Coed** 5,711 undergraduate students, 96% full-time, 54% women, 46% men
- **Very difficult** entrance level, 51% of applicants were admitted

UNDERGRAD STUDENTS

5,499 full-time, 212 part-time. Students come from 49 states and territories; 62 other countries; 38% are from out of state; 3% Black or African American, non-Hispanic/Latino; 19% Hispanic/Latino; 7% Asian, non-Hispanic/Latino; 0.4% Native Hawaiian or other Pacific Islander, non-Hispanic/Latino; 0.4% American Indian or Alaska Native, non-Hispanic/Latino; 6% Two or more races, non-Hispanic/Latino; 3% Race/ethnicity unknown; 9% international; 6% transferred in; 44% live on campus.

Freshmen:

Admission: 14,413 applied, 7,406 admitted, 1,133 enrolled. ***Average high school GPA:*** 3.85. ***Test scores:*** SAT critical reading scores over 500: 89%; SAT math scores over 500: 94%; SAT writing scores over 500: 90%; ACT scores over 18: 99%; SAT critical reading scores over 600: 54%; SAT math scores over 600: 60%; SAT writing scores over 600: 54%; ACT scores over 24: 90%; SAT critical reading scores over 700: 9%; SAT math scores over 700: 9%; SAT writing scores over 700: 9%; ACT scores over 30: 33%.

Retention: 87% of full-time freshmen returned.

FACULTY

Total: 906, 49% full-time, 81% with terminal degrees.

Student/faculty ratio: 14:1.

ACADEMICS

Calendar: 4-1-4. *Degrees:* bachelor's, master's, doctoral, and postbachelor's certificates.

Special study options: advanced placement credit, double majors, English as a second language, honors programs, independent study, internships, part-time degree program, services for LD students, study abroad, summer session for credit. ***ROTC:*** Army (c), Navy (b), Air Force (c).

Computers: 951 computers/terminals and 4,250 ports are available on campus for general student use. Students can access the following: campus intranet, computer help desk, free student e-mail accounts, online (class) grades, online (class) registration, online (class) schedules. Campuswide network is available. 100% of college-owned or -operated housing units are wired for high-speed Internet access. Wireless service is available via entire campus.

Library: Helen K. and James S. Copley Library plus 1 other. *Books:* 713,623 (physical), 817,563 (digital/electronic); *Serial titles:* 15,789 (physical), 975 (digital/electronic). Weekly public service hours: 116; students can reserve study rooms.

STUDENT LIFE

Housing options: on-campus residence required through sophomore year; coed, men-only, women-only, special housing for students with disabilities. Campus housing is university owned. Freshman campus housing is guaranteed.

Activities and organizations: drama/theater group, student-run newspaper, radio and television station, choral group, marching band, Torero Ambassador's Club, International Student Organization, International Buddy Program, USD Chapter American Marketing Association, Entrepreneurship Club, national fraternities, national sororities.

Athletics Member NCAA. All Division I except football (Division I-AA). ***Intercollegiate sports:*** baseball M(s), basketball M(s)/W(s), crew M/W(s), cross-country running M(s)/W(s), equestrian sports M(c)/W(c), golf M(s), lacrosse M(c)/W(c), rock climbing M(c)/W(c), rugby M(c), soccer M(s)/W(s), softball W(s), swimming and diving W(s), tennis M(s)/W(s), track and field W(s), ultimate Frisbee M(c)/W(c), volleyball M(c)/W(s). ***Intramural sports:*** baseball M(c), basketball M/W, football M/W, golf M(c), soccer M(c)/W(c), softball M/W, tennis M/W, ultimate Frisbee M/W, volleyball M/W(c), water polo M(c).

Campus security: 24-hour emergency response devices and patrols, late-night transport/escort service, controlled dormitory access.

Student services: health clinic, personal/psychological counseling, women's center, legal services.

COSTS & FINANCIAL AID

Costs (2017–18) ***Comprehensive fee:*** $60,338 includes full-time tuition ($47,100), mandatory fees ($608), and room and board ($12,630). Part-time tuition: $1625 per unit. Part-time tuition and fees vary according to course load. ***Required fees:*** $524 per year part-time. ***Room and board:*** Room and board charges vary according to board plan and housing facility. ***Payment plan:*** installment. ***Waivers:*** employees or children of employees.

Financial Aid Of all full-time matriculated undergraduates who enrolled in 2015, 3,283 applied for aid, 2,868 were judged to have need, 379 had their need fully met. 514 Federal Work-Study jobs (averaging $2098). In 2015, 914 non-need-based awards were made. ***Average percent of need met:*** 70. ***Average financial aid package:*** $32,292. ***Average need-based loan:*** $7061. ***Average need-based gift aid:*** $25,655. ***Average non-need-based aid:*** $14,502. ***Average indebtedness upon graduation:*** $29,646.

APPLYING

Standardized Tests *Required:* SAT or ACT (for admission).

Options: electronic application, deferred entrance.

Application fee: $55.

Required: essay or personal statement, high school transcript, 1 letter of recommendation.

Application deadlines: 12/15 (freshmen), 3/1 (transfers).

Notification: 4/1 (freshmen), continuous until 6/30 (transfers).

CONTACT

Ms. Minh-Ha Hoang, Director of Admissions, University of San Diego, 5998 Alcala Park, San Diego, CA 92110. *Phone:* 619-260-4506. *Toll-free phone:* 800-248-4873. *Fax:* 619-260-6836. *E-mail:* admissions@sandiego.edu.

★ University of San Francisco

San Francisco, California

http://www.usfca.edu/

- **Independent Roman Catholic (Jesuit)** university, founded 1855
- **Urban** 55-acre campus
- **Endowment** $311.6 million
- **Coed** 6,782 undergraduate students, 95% full-time, 62% women, 38% men
- **Moderately difficult** entrance level, 64% of applicants were admitted

UNDERGRAD STUDENTS

6,448 full-time, 334 part-time. Students come from 52 states and territories; 71 other countries; 21% are from out of state; 3% Black or African American, non-Hispanic/Latino; 20% Hispanic/Latino; 21% Asian, non-Hispanic/Latino; 0.6% Native Hawaiian or other Pacific Islander, non-Hispanic/Latino; 0.3% American Indian or Alaska Native,

non-Hispanic/Latino; 7% Two or more races, non-Hispanic/Latino; 2% Race/ethnicity unknown; 20% international; 8% transferred in; 35% live on campus.

Freshmen:
Admission: 15,462 applied, 9,951 admitted, 1,267 enrolled. ***Average high school GPA:*** 3.63. ***Test scores:*** SAT critical reading scores over 500: 86%; SAT math scores over 500: 90%; SAT writing scores over 500: 85%; ACT scores over 18: 100%; SAT critical reading scores over 600: 36%; SAT math scores over 600: 46%; SAT writing scores over 600: 38%; ACT scores over 24: 76%; SAT critical reading scores over 700: 5%; SAT math scores over 700: 8%; SAT writing scores over 700: 6%; ACT scores over 30: 17%.
Retention: 83% of full-time freshmen returned.

FACULTY
Total: 1,245, 40% full-time.

Student/faculty ratio: 14:1.

ACADEMICS
Calendar: 4-1-4. *Degrees:* bachelor's, master's, doctoral, post-master's, and postbachelor's certificates.

Special study options: accelerated degree program, adult/continuing education programs, advanced placement credit, cooperative education, distance learning, double majors, English as a second language, external degree program, honors programs, independent study, internships, off-campus study, part-time degree program, services for LD students, student-designed majors, study abroad, summer session for credit. ***ROTC:*** Army (b), Air Force (c).

Unusual degree programs: 3-2 engineering with University of Southern California; physics.

Computers: 265 computers/terminals are available on campus for general student use. Students can access the following: campus intranet, computer help desk, free student e-mail accounts, online (class) grades, online (class) registration, online (class) schedules. Campuswide network is available. Wireless service is available via classrooms, computer centers, computer labs, dorm rooms, learning centers, libraries, student centers.

Library: Gleeson Library plus 2 others. *Books:* 738,947 (physical), 407,670 (digital/electronic); *Serial titles:* 924 (physical), 144,845 (digital/electronic); *Databases:* 240. Study areas open 24 hours, 5-7 days a week; students can reserve study rooms.

STUDENT LIFE
Housing options: on-campus residence required for freshman year; coed, women-only. Campus housing is university owned and leased by the school. Freshman campus housing is guaranteed.

Activities and organizations: drama/theater group, student-run newspaper, radio and television station, choral group, marching band, national fraternities, national sororities.

Athletics Member NCAA. All Division I. ***Intercollegiate sports:*** baseball M(s), basketball M(s)/W(s), cross-country running M(s)/W(s), golf M(s)/W(s), soccer M(s)/W(s), softball M(c)/W(c), tennis M(s)/W(s), track and field M/W(s), volleyball M(c)/W(s). ***Intramural sports:*** basketball M/W, bowling M/W, fencing M(c)/W(c), football M/W, golf M(c)/W(c), lacrosse M(c), racquetball M/W, rugby M(c)/W(c), skiing (cross-country) M(c)/W(c), soccer M/W, softball M/W, swimming and diving M/W, table tennis M/W, tennis M/W, volleyball M/W.

Campus security: 24-hour emergency response devices and patrols, student patrols, late-night transport/escort service, controlled dormitory access.

Student services: health clinic, personal/psychological counseling, women's center.

COSTS & FINANCIAL AID
Costs (2017–18) ***Comprehensive fee:*** $60,580 includes full-time tuition ($45,760), mandatory fees ($490), and room and board ($14,330). Full-time tuition and fees vary according to course load, degree level, location, program, and reciprocity agreements. Part-time tuition and fees vary according to course load, degree level, location, program, and reciprocity agreements. ***College room only:*** $9630. Room and board charges vary according to board plan and housing facility. ***Payment plan:*** installment. ***Waivers:*** employees or children of employees.

Financial Aid Of all full-time matriculated undergraduates who enrolled in 2016, 3,971 applied for aid, 3,540 were judged to have need, 2,140 had their need fully met. 941 Federal Work-Study jobs (averaging $4890). 1,850 state and other part-time jobs (averaging $5361). In 2016, 1018 non-need-based awards were made. ***Average percent of need met:*** 77. ***Average financial aid package:*** $35,963. ***Average need-based loan:*** $4925. ***Average need-based gift aid:*** $21,451. ***Average non-need-based aid:*** $13,208. ***Average indebtedness upon graduation:*** $34,114. ***Financial aid deadline:*** 2/15.

APPLYING
Standardized Tests *Required:* SAT or ACT (for admission). *Required for some:* TOEFL, IELTS or PTE Academic if English is not the student's native language.

Options: electronic application, early admission, early decision, early action, deferred entrance.

Application fee: $65.

Required: essay or personal statement, high school transcript, 1 letter of recommendation. ***Recommended:*** minimum 3.0 GPA.

Application deadlines: 1/15 (freshmen), rolling (transfers), 11/15 (early action).

Early decision deadline: 11/15.

Notification: continuous until 4/1 (freshmen), continuous until 8/15 (transfers), 1/1 (early decision), 1/1 (early action).

CONTACT
Mr. Michael Hughes, Associate Dean and Director, Admission, University of San Francisco, 2130 Fulton Street, San Francisco, CA 94117-1080.
Phone: 415-422-6563. *Toll-free phone:* 800-CALL-USF.
E-mail: admissions@usfca.edu.

See previous page for display ad and page 1578 for the College Close-Up.

University of Southern California
Los Angeles, California
http://www.usc.edu/

- **Independent** university, founded 1880
- **Urban** 229-acre campus with easy access to Los Angeles
- **Endowment** $4.6 billion
- **Coed** 18,794 undergraduate students, 97% full-time, 52% women, 48% men
- **Most difficult** entrance level, 17% of applicants were admitted

UNDERGRAD STUDENTS
18,195 full-time, 599 part-time. Students come from 56 states and territories; 111 other countries; 33% are from out of state; 4% Black or African American, non-Hispanic/Latino; 14% Hispanic/Latino; 21% Asian, non-Hispanic/Latino; 0.2% Native Hawaiian or other Pacific Islander, non-Hispanic/Latino; 0.1% American Indian or Alaska Native, non-Hispanic/Latino; 5% Two or more races, non-Hispanic/Latino; 2% Race/ethnicity unknown; 14% international; 8% transferred in; 30% live on campus.

Freshmen:
Admission: 54,280 applied, 9,022 admitted, 3,068 enrolled. ***Average high school GPA:*** 3.73. ***Test scores:*** SAT critical reading scores over 500: 98%; SAT math scores over 500: 98%; SAT writing scores over 500: 98%; ACT scores over 18: 100%; SAT critical reading scores over 600: 84%; SAT math scores over 600: 89%; SAT writing scores over 600: 88%; ACT scores over 24: 96%; SAT critical reading scores over 700: 36%; SAT math scores over 700: 57%; SAT writing scores over 700: 50%; ACT scores over 30: 75%.
Retention: 96% of full-time freshmen returned.

FACULTY
Total: 3,455, 60% full-time, 81% with terminal degrees.

Student/faculty ratio: 8:1.

ACADEMICS
Calendar: semesters. *Degrees:* bachelor's, master's, doctoral, post-master's, and postbachelor's certificates.

Special study options: accelerated degree program, advanced placement credit, cooperative education, distance learning, double majors, English as a second language, freshman honors college, honors programs, independent study, internships, off-campus study, part-time degree program, services for LD students, study abroad, summer session for credit. ***ROTC:*** Army (b), Navy (b), Air Force (b).

Unusual degree programs: 3-2 engineering.

Computers: Students can access the following: campus intranet, computer help desk, free student e-mail accounts, online (class) grades, online (class) registration, online (class) schedules, online degree progress, financial aid applications, document sharing, calendars, personal Web space, customizable Web portal, course management systems. Campuswide network is available. 100% of college-owned or -operated housing units are wired for high-speed Internet access. Wireless service is available via entire campus.
Library: Doheny Memorial Library plus 23 others.

STUDENT LIFE
Housing options: coed, special housing for students with disabilities. Campus housing is university owned and is provided by a third party. Freshman campus housing is guaranteed.

Activities and organizations: drama/theater group, student-run newspaper, radio and television station, choral group, marching band, national fraternities, national sororities.

Athletics Member NCAA. All Division I except football (Division I-A). ***Intercollegiate sports:*** archery M(c)/W(c), badminton M(c)/W(c), baseball M(s), basketball M(s)/W(s), cheerleading M(c)/W(c), crew M(c)/W(s), cross-country running M(s)/W(s), equestrian sports W(c), fencing W(c), field hockey W(c), golf M(s)/W(s), gymnastics W(c), ice hockey M(c)/W(c), lacrosse M(c)/W(s), racquetball M(c)/W(c), rock climbing M(c)/W(c), rugby M(c)/W(c), sailing W(c), skiing (downhill) M(c)/W(c), soccer M(c)/W(s), softball W(c), squash M(c)/W(c), swimming and diving M(s)/W(s), tennis M(s)/W(s), track and field M(s)/W(s), ultimate Frisbee M(c)/W(c), volleyball M(s)/W(s), water polo M(s)/W(s). ***Intramural sports:*** badminton M/W, basketball M/W, cross-country running M/W, football M/W, golf M/W, racquetball M/W, soccer M/W, softball M/W, tennis M/W, ultimate Frisbee M/W, volleyball M/W.

Campus security: 24-hour emergency response devices and patrols, student patrols, late-night transport/escort service, controlled dormitory access.

Student services: health clinic, personal/psychological counseling, women's center, legal services.

COSTS & FINANCIAL AID
Costs (2016–17) ***One-time required fee:*** $350. ***Comprehensive fee:*** $67,340 includes full-time tuition ($52,217), mandatory fees ($775), and room and board ($14,348). Full-time tuition and fees vary according to program. Part-time tuition: $1733 per unit. Part-time tuition and fees vary according to course load and program. ***College room only:*** $8648. Room and board charges vary according to board plan and housing facility. ***Payment plans:*** tuition prepayment, installment. ***Waivers:*** employees or children of employees.

Financial Aid Of all full-time matriculated undergraduates who enrolled in 2015, 9,013 applied for aid, 6,720 were judged to have need, 5,248 had their need fully met. In 2015, 3489 non-need-based awards were made. ***Average percent of need met:*** 100. ***Average financial aid package:*** $48,399. ***Average need-based loan:*** $6548. ***Average need-based gift aid:*** $35,011. ***Average non-need-based aid:*** $19,665. ***Average indebtedness upon graduation:*** $27,882.

APPLYING
Standardized Tests *Required:* SAT or ACT (for admission).

Options: electronic application, deferred entrance.

Application fee: $80.

Required: essay or personal statement, high school transcript.

Application deadlines: 1/15 (freshmen), 2/1 (transfers).

Notification: 4/1 (freshmen), 4/1 (out-of-state freshmen), 6/1 (transfers).

CONTACT
Timothy Brunold, Dean of Admission, University of Southern California, University Park Campus, Los Angeles, CA 90089. *Phone:* 213-740-1111. *Fax:* 213-821-0200. *E-mail:* admitusc@usc.edu.

University of the Pacific

Stockton, California

http://www.pacific.edu/

- **Independent** university, founded 1851
- **Suburban** 175-acre campus with easy access to Sacramento
- **Coed** 3,735 undergraduate students, 97% full-time, 52% women, 48% men
- **Moderately difficult** entrance level, 65% of applicants were admitted

UNDERGRAD STUDENTS
3,636 full-time, 99 part-time. 7% are from out of state; 3% Black or African American, non-Hispanic/Latino; 18% Hispanic/Latino; 35% Asian, non-Hispanic/Latino; 0.6% Native Hawaiian or other Pacific Islander, non-Hispanic/Latino; 0.4% American Indian or Alaska Native, non-Hispanic/Latino; 6% Two or more races, non-Hispanic/Latino; 4% Race/ethnicity unknown; 7% international; 5% transferred in; 46% live on campus.

Freshmen:
Admission: 14,449 applied, 9,328 admitted, 937 enrolled. ***Average high school GPA:*** 3.45. ***Test scores:*** SAT critical reading scores over 500: 74%; SAT math scores over 500: 82%; SAT writing scores over 500: 72%; ACT scores over 18: 97%; SAT critical reading scores over 600: 35%; SAT math scores over 600: 50%; SAT writing scores over 600: 34%; ACT scores over 24: 68%; SAT critical reading scores over 700: 6%; SAT math scores over 700: 16%; SAT writing scores over 700: 11%; ACT scores over 30: 23%.

Retention: 85% of full-time freshmen returned.

FACULTY
Total: 768, 56% full-time, 80% with terminal degrees.

Student/faculty ratio: 13:1.

ACADEMICS
Calendar: semesters. *Degrees:* bachelor's, master's, and doctoral.

Special study options: academic remediation for entering students, accelerated degree program, advanced placement credit, cooperative education, double majors, English as a second language, honors programs, independent study, internships, part-time degree program, services for LD students, student-designed majors, summer session for credit. ***ROTC:*** Air Force (c).

Computers: Students can access the following: campus intranet, computer help desk, free student e-mail accounts, online (class) grades, online (class) registration, online (class) schedules. Campuswide network is available. Wireless service is available via entire campus.
Library: University of the Pacific Library plus 1 other.

STUDENT LIFE
Housing options: on-campus residence required through sophomore yearCampus housing is university owned. Freshman campus housing is guaranteed.

Activities and organizations: drama/theater group, student-run newspaper, radio station, choral group, national fraternities, national sororities.

Athletics Member NCAA. All Division I. ***Intercollegiate sports:*** baseball M(s), basketball M(s)/W(s), cross-country running W(s), field hockey W(s), golf M(s), soccer W(s), softball W(s), swimming and diving M(s)/W(s), tennis M(s)/W(s), volleyball M(s)/W(s), water polo M(s)/W(s). ***Intramural sports:*** badminton M(c)/W(c), basketball M/W, bowling M/W, football M/W, golf M, lacrosse M(c)/W(c), rugby M(c), soccer M(c)/W(c), tennis M/W, volleyball W.

Campus security: 24-hour emergency response devices and patrols, late-night transport/escort service, controlled dormitory access.

Student services: health clinic, personal/psychological counseling, legal services.

COSTS & FINANCIAL AID
Costs (2016–17) ***Comprehensive fee:*** $57,446 includes full-time tuition ($44,068), mandatory fees ($520), and room and board ($12,858). Part-time tuition: $1520 per credit hour. Part-time tuition and fees vary according to course load. ***Room and board:*** Room and board charges vary according to board plan and housing facility. ***Payment plan:*** deferred payment. ***Waivers:*** employees or children of employees.

Financial Aid Of all full-time matriculated undergraduates who enrolled in 2016, 2,530 applied for aid, 2,325 were judged to have need, 310 had their need fully met. In 2016, 586 non-need-based awards were made. ***Average percent of need met:*** 55. ***Average financial aid package:*** $32,595. ***Average need-based loan:*** $9224. ***Average need-based gift aid:*** $25,217. ***Average non-need-based aid:*** $12,181. ***Average indebtedness upon graduation:*** $28,810.

APPLYING
Standardized Tests *Required:* SAT or ACT (for admission). *Recommended:* SAT and SAT Subject Tests or ACT (for admission).

Options: electronic application, early action.

Application fee: $35.

Required: essay or personal statement, high school transcript.

Application deadlines: 1/15 (freshmen), 6/1 (transfers), 11/15 (early action).

Notification: continuous (freshmen), continuous (transfers), 1/15 (early action).

CONTACT
Mr. Rich Toledo, Director of Admissions, University of the Pacific, 3601 Pacific Avenue, Stockton, CA 95211-0197. *Phone:* 209-946-2211. *Fax:* 209-946-2413. *E-mail:* admissions@pacific.edu.

★ University of the West
Rosemead, California
http://www.uwest.edu/

- **Independent** comprehensive, founded 1991
- **Suburban** 10-acre campus with easy access to Los Angeles, Pasadena, Long Beach
- **Coed** 106 undergraduate students, 93% full-time, 55% women, 45% men
- **Minimally difficult** entrance level, 85% of applicants were admitted

UNDERGRAD STUDENTS
99 full-time, 7 part-time. Students come from 5 states and territories; 10 other countries; 4% are from out of state; 0.9% Black or African American, non-Hispanic/Latino; 45% Hispanic/Latino; 8% Asian, non-Hispanic/Latino; 2% American Indian or Alaska Native, non-Hispanic/Latino; 2% Two or more races, non-Hispanic/Latino; 37% international; 15% transferred in; 36% live on campus.

Freshmen:
Admission: 235 applied, 200 admitted, 19 enrolled. ***Average high school GPA:*** 2.43.
Retention: 83% of full-time freshmen returned.

FACULTY
Total: 55, 25% full-time, 53% with terminal degrees.

Student/faculty ratio: 10:1.

ACADEMICS
Calendar: semesters. *Degrees:* certificates, diplomas, bachelor's, master's, doctoral, post-master's, and postbachelor's certificates.

Special study options: academic remediation for entering students, accelerated degree program, adult/continuing education programs, cooperative education, double majors, English as a second language, independent study, internships, part-time degree program, summer session for credit.

Computers: 501 computers/terminals are available on campus for general student use. Students can access the following: computer help desk, free student e-mail accounts, online (class) grades, online (class) registration, online (class) schedules. Campuswide network is available. 100% of college-owned or -operated housing units are wired for high-speed Internet access. Wireless service is available via entire campus.
Library: University of the West Library plus 1 other. Students can reserve study rooms.

STUDENT LIFE
Housing options: coed, special housing for students with disabilities. Campus housing is university owned. Freshman campus housing is guaranteed.

Activities and organizations: Buddhawest Club, Music Club, Explorer Club, Badminton Club, Chaplaincy Club.

Campus security: 24-hour emergency response devices and patrols, controlled dormitory access.

Student services: personal/psychological counseling.

COSTS & FINANCIAL AID
Costs (2017–18) ***One-time required fee:*** $50. ***Comprehensive fee:*** $21,584 includes full-time tuition ($13,800), mandatory fees ($900), and room and board ($6884). Full-time tuition and fees vary according to course load, degree level, and program. Part-time tuition: $460 per credit hour. Part-time tuition and fees vary according to course load, degree level, and program. ***Required fees:*** $640 per year part-time. ***Room and board:*** Room and board charges vary according to board plan. ***Payment plan:*** installment. ***Waivers:*** employees or children of employees.

Financial Aid Of all full-time matriculated undergraduates who enrolled in 2003, 30 applied for aid, 18 were judged to have need. 20 state and other part-time jobs.

APPLYING
Options: electronic application, deferred entrance.

Application fee: $50.

Required: essay or personal statement, high school transcript, minimum 2.0 GPA, 3 letters of recommendation. ***Required for some:*** interview.

Application deadlines: 6/15 (freshmen), 6/15 (transfers).

Notification: 7/15 (freshmen), 7/15 (out-of-state freshmen), 7/15 (transfers).

CONTACT
University of the West, 1409 Walnut Grove Avenue, Rosemead, CA 91770. *Phone:* 626-571-8811 Ext. 311.

Vanguard University of Southern California
Costa Mesa, California
http://www.vanguard.edu/

- **Independent** comprehensive, founded 1920, affiliated with Assemblies of God
- **Suburban** 38-acre campus with easy access to Los Angeles
- **Coed**
- **Moderately difficult** entrance level

FACULTY
Student/faculty ratio: 15:1.

ACADEMICS
Calendar: semesters. *Degrees:* certificates, associate, bachelor's, and master's.
Library: O. Cope Budge Library.

STUDENT LIFE
Housing options: on-campus residence required through sophomore year; coed, men-only, women-only, special housing for students with disabilities. Campus housing is university owned. Freshman campus housing is guaranteed.

Activities and organizations: drama/theater group, student-run newspaper, choral group, local outreach, Global Missions, student organizations/clubs, choral groups.

Athletics Member NAIA.

Campus security: 24-hour emergency response devices and patrols, student patrols, late-night transport/escort service, controlled dormitory access.

Student services: health clinic, personal/psychological counseling, women's center.

COSTS & FINANCIAL AID
Costs (2016–17) ***Tuition:*** $1290 per credit hour part-time. Full-time tuition and fees vary according to course load, location, and program. Part-time tuition and fees vary according to course load and program. ***Room only:*** Room and board charges vary according to board plan and housing facility.

Financial Aid Of all full-time matriculated undergraduates who enrolled in 2014, 1,397 applied for aid, 1,275 were judged to have need, 156 had their need fully met. In 2014, 105 non-need-based awards were made. ***Average percent of need met:*** 33. ***Average financial aid package:***

$13,017. ***Average need-based gift aid:*** $6070. ***Average non-need-based aid:*** $6850. ***Financial aid deadline:*** 3/2.

APPLYING

Standardized Tests *Required:* SAT or ACT (for admission).

Options: electronic application, early admission, early action, deferred entrance.

Application fee: $45.

Required: essay or personal statement, high school transcript, minimum 2.8 GPA, 2 letters of recommendation. ***Required for some:*** interview.

CONTACT

Kristi Pruett, Undergraduate Admissions, Vanguard University of Southern California, 55 Fair Drive, Costa Mesa, CA 92626. *Phone:* 800-722-6279 Ext. 4107. *Toll-free phone:* 800-722-6279. *Fax:* 714-966-5471. *E-mail:* admissions@vanguard.edu.

West Coast Ultrasound Institute

Beverly Hills, California

http://wcui.edu/

CONTACT

West Coast Ultrasound Institute, 291 S. La Cienega Boulevard, Suite 500, Beverly Hills, CA 90211.

West Coast University

Anaheim, California

http://westcoastuniversity.edu/

CONTACT

West Coast University, 1477 S. Manchester Avenue, Anaheim, CA 92802.

West Coast University

North Hollywood, California

http://www.westcoastuniversity.edu/

CONTACT

Mr. Roger A. Miller, Dean of Admissions and Registrar, West Coast University, 12215 Victory Boulevard, North Hollywood, CA 91606. *Phone:* 213-427-4400. *Toll-free phone:* 866-508-2684. *E-mail:* info@katz.wcula.edu.

West Coast University

Ontario, California

http://westcoastuniversity.edu/

CONTACT

West Coast University, 2855 E. Guasti Road, Ontario, CA 91761.

Westmont College

Santa Barbara, California

http://www.westmont.edu/

- **Independent nondenominational** 4-year, founded 1937
- **Suburban** 113-acre campus with easy access to Los Angeles
- **Endowment** $75.0 million
- **Coed** 1,298 undergraduate students, 99% full-time, 61% women, 39% men
- **Moderately difficult** entrance level, 83% of applicants were admitted

UNDERGRAD STUDENTS

1,291 full-time, 7 part-time. Students come from 39 states and territories; 20 other countries; 25% are from out of state; 2% Black or African American, non-Hispanic/Latino; 16% Hispanic/Latino; 8% Asian, non-Hispanic/Latino; 0.4% Native Hawaiian or other Pacific Islander, non-Hispanic/Latino; 0.5% American Indian or Alaska Native, non-Hispanic/Latino; 6% Two or more races, non-Hispanic/Latino; 3% Race/ethnicity unknown; 3% international; 4% transferred in; 86% live on campus.

Freshmen:
Admission: 2,001 applied, 1,656 admitted, 347 enrolled. ***Average high school GPA:*** 3.79. ***Test scores:*** SAT critical reading scores over 500: 82%; SAT math scores over 500: 86%; SAT writing scores over 500: 82%; ACT scores over 18: 99%; SAT critical reading scores over 600: 47%; SAT math scores over 600: 42%; SAT writing scores over 600: 42%; ACT scores over 24: 70%; SAT critical reading scores over 700: 14%; SAT math scores over 700: 8%; SAT writing scores over 700: 9%; ACT scores over 30: 25%.

Retention: 81% of full-time freshmen returned.

FACULTY
Total: 157, 60% full-time, 67% with terminal degrees.

Student/faculty ratio: 11:1.

ACADEMICS
Calendar: semesters. *Degrees:* bachelor's and postbachelor's certificates.

Special study options: academic remediation for entering students, accelerated degree program, advanced placement credit, double majors, honors programs, internships, off-campus study, services for LD students, student-designed majors, study abroad, summer session for credit. ***ROTC:*** Army (c), Air Force (c).

Unusual degree programs: 3-2 engineering with Washington University in St. Louis; Boston University; University of Southern California; University of California, Berkeley, Los Angeles, and Santa Barbara; California Polytechnic State University; Stanford University.

Computers: 100 computers/terminals are available on campus for general student use. Students can access the following: campus intranet, computer help desk, free student e-mail accounts, online (class) grades, online (class) registration, online (class) schedules. Campuswide network is available. 100% of college-owned or -operated housing units are wired for high-speed Internet access. Wireless service is available via entire campus.

Library: Roger John Voskuyl Library. *Books:* 134,000 (physical), 158,000 (digital/electronic); *Databases:* 100. Weekly public service hours: 100; study areas open 24 hours, 5-7 days a week; students can reserve study rooms.

STUDENT LIFE
Housing options: on-campus residence required through sophomore year; coed, cooperative, special housing for students with disabilities. Campus housing is university owned. Freshman campus housing is guaranteed.

Activities and organizations: drama/theater group, student-run newspaper, choral group, Student Ministries, Student Government, Competitive Athletics, Music, Art and Theater ensembles, Intramural Sports.

Athletics Member NAIA. ***Intercollegiate sports:*** baseball M(s), basketball M(s)/W(s), cross-country running M(s)/W(s), equestrian sports M(c), rugby M(c), soccer M(s)/W(s), tennis M(s)/W(s), track and field M(s)/W(s), volleyball M(c)/W(s). ***Intramural sports:*** badminton M/W, basketball M/W, bowling M/W, cross-country running M/W, football M/W, golf M/W, racquetball M/W, soccer M(c)/W, softball M/W, table tennis M/W, tennis M/W, ultimate Frisbee M(c), volleyball M/W, water polo M/W.

Campus security: 24-hour emergency response devices and patrols, late-night transport/escort service, controlled dormitory access.

Student services: health clinic, personal/psychological counseling, women's center.

COSTS & FINANCIAL AID
Costs (2017–18) ***One-time required fee:*** $300. ***Comprehensive fee:*** $57,930 includes full-time tuition ($42,890), mandatory fees ($1154), and room and board ($13,886). ***College room only:*** $8610. Room and board charges vary according to board plan and housing facility. ***Payment plan:*** installment. ***Waivers:*** employees or children of employees.

Financial Aid Of all full-time matriculated undergraduates who enrolled in 2016, 929 applied for aid, 853 were judged to have need, 179 had their need fully met. 349 Federal Work-Study jobs (averaging $1806). In 2016, 327 non-need-based awards were made. ***Average percent of need met:*** 79. ***Average financial aid package:*** $32,102. ***Average need-based loan:*** $5312. ***Average need-based gift aid:*** $24,806. ***Average non-need-based aid:*** $14,186. ***Average indebtedness upon graduation:*** $31,609.

APPLYING
Standardized Tests *Required:* SAT or ACT (for admission).

Options: electronic application, early action.

Application fee: $50.

Required: essay or personal statement, high school transcript, 1 letter of recommendation. ***Required for some:*** interview. ***Recommended:*** interview.

Application deadlines: 2/15 (freshmen), 3/1 (transfers), 11/15 (early action).

Notification: continuous until 3/1 (freshmen), continuous until 3/15 (transfers), 12/15 (early action).

CONTACT
Mr. Silvio E. Vazquez, Dean of Admissions, Westmont College, 955 La Paz Road, Santa Barbara, CA 93108. *Phone:* 805-565-6200. *Toll-free phone:* 800-777-9011. *Fax:* 805-565-6234.
E-mail: admissions@westmont.edu.

See previous page for display ad and page 1596 for the College Close-Up.

Whittier College
Whittier, California
http://www.whittier.edu/

- **Independent** comprehensive, founded 1887
- **Suburban** 95-acre campus with easy access to Los Angeles
- **Endowment** $97.3 million
- **Coed** 1,650 undergraduate students, 98% full-time, 56% women, 44% men
- **Moderately difficult** entrance level, 63% of applicants were admitted

UNDERGRAD STUDENTS
1,623 full-time, 27 part-time. Students come from 36 states and territories; 27 other countries; 16% are from out of state; 5% Black or African American, non-Hispanic/Latino; 44% Hispanic/Latino; 10% Asian, non-Hispanic/Latino; 0.1% Native Hawaiian or other Pacific Islander, non-Hispanic/Latino; 0.5% American Indian or Alaska Native, non-Hispanic/Latino; 4% Two or more races, non-Hispanic/Latino; 0.7% Race/ethnicity unknown; 4% international; 4% transferred in; 50% live on campus.

Freshmen:
Admission: 5,192 applied, 3,251 admitted, 442 enrolled. ***Average high school GPA:*** 3.51. ***Test scores:*** SAT critical reading scores over 500: 60%; SAT math scores over 500: 61%; SAT writing scores over 500: 61%; ACT scores over 18: 94%; SAT critical reading scores over 600: 18%; SAT math scores over 600: 20%; SAT writing scores over 600: 19%; ACT scores over 24: 41%; SAT critical reading scores over 700: 3%; SAT math scores over 700: 3%; SAT writing scores over 700: 1%; ACT scores over 30: 4%.

Retention: 80% of full-time freshmen returned.

FACULTY
Total: 188, 62% full-time, 70% with terminal degrees.

Student/faculty ratio: 12:1.

ACADEMICS
Calendar: 4-1-4. *Degrees:* bachelor's, master's, and doctoral.

Special study options: academic remediation for entering students, accelerated degree program, adult/continuing education programs, advanced placement credit, distance learning, double majors, independent study, internships, off-campus study, services for LD students, student-designed majors, study abroad, summer session for credit. ***ROTC:*** Army (c).

Unusual degree programs: 3-2 engineering with University of Southern California, University of Minnesota.

Computers: 175 computers/terminals are available on campus for general student use. Students can access the following: campus intranet, computer help desk, free student e-mail accounts, online (class) grades, online (class) registration, online (class) schedules. Campuswide network is available. 100% of college-owned or -operated housing units are wired for high-speed Internet access. Wireless service is available via entire campus.

Library: Bonnie Bell Wardman Library plus 1 other.

STUDENT LIFE

Housing options: on-campus residence required through junior year; coed, special housing for students with disabilities. Campus housing is university owned. Freshman campus housing is guaranteed.

Activities and organizations: drama/theater group, student-run newspaper, radio and television station, choral group, Hispanic Students Association, Hawaiian Islander Club, Black Student Union, Asian Students Association, Environment and Sustainability.

Athletics Member NCAA. All Division III. ***Intercollegiate sports:*** baseball M, basketball M/W, cross-country running M/W, football M, golf M/W, lacrosse M/W, soccer M/W, softball W, swimming and diving M/W, tennis M/W, track and field M/W, volleyball W, water polo M/W. ***Intramural sports:*** basketball M/W, softball M/W, volleyball M/W.

Campus security: 24-hour emergency response devices and patrols, late-night transport/escort service, controlled dormitory access.

Student services: health clinic, personal/psychological counseling.

COSTS & FINANCIAL AID

Costs (2017–18) ***Comprehensive fee:*** $59,438 includes full-time tuition ($45,720), mandatory fees ($390), and room and board ($13,328). Full-time tuition and fees vary according to course load. Part-time tuition: $1905 per semester hour. Part-time tuition and fees vary according to course load. ***College room only:*** $7198. Room and board charges vary according to board plan. ***Payment plan:*** installment. ***Waivers:*** employees or children of employees.

Financial Aid Of all full-time matriculated undergraduates who enrolled in 2016, 1,319 applied for aid, 1,227 were judged to have need, 192 had their need fully met. 146 Federal Work-Study jobs (averaging $2374). 572 state and other part-time jobs (averaging $1977). In 2016, 274 non-need-based awards were made. ***Average percent of need met:*** 77. ***Average financial aid package:*** $35,665. ***Average need-based loan:*** $5676. ***Average need-based gift aid:*** $32,434. ***Average non-need-based aid:*** $22,431. ***Average indebtedness upon graduation:*** $31,826. ***Financial aid deadline:*** 6/30.

APPLYING

Standardized Tests *Required:* SAT or ACT (for admission). *Recommended:* SAT Subject Tests (for admission).

Options: electronic application, early action, deferred entrance.

Application fee: $50.

Required: essay or personal statement, high school transcript, minimum 2.0 GPA, 2 letters of recommendation. ***Required for some:*** minimum 3.5 GPA. ***Recommended:*** minimum 2.5 GPA, interview.

Application deadlines: rolling (freshmen), rolling (transfers), 11/15 (early action).

Notification: continuous (freshmen), 3/1 (transfers), 12/31 (early action).

CONTACT

Mr. Kieron Miller, Director of Admission, Whittier College, Office of Admission, 13406 East Philadelphia Street, Whittier, CA 90608-0634. *Phone:* 562-907-4238. *Fax:* 562-907-4870. *E-mail:* admission@whittier.edu.

See below for display ad and page 1602 for the College Close-Up.

William Jessup University

Rocklin, California

http://www.jessup.edu/

- **Independent nondenominational** comprehensive, founded 1939
- **Suburban** 126-acre campus with easy access to Sacramento
- **Coed**
- **Moderately difficult** entrance level

FACULTY

Student/faculty ratio: 11:1.

ACADEMICS

Calendar: semesters. *Degrees:* certificates, associate, bachelor's, master's, and postbachelor's certificates.

Library: Paul Nystrom Library plus 1 other.

STUDENT LIFE

Housing options: on-campus residence required through junior year; men-only, women-only. Campus housing is university owned and is provided by a third party. Freshman campus housing is guaranteed.

Activities and organizations: drama/theater group, choral group.

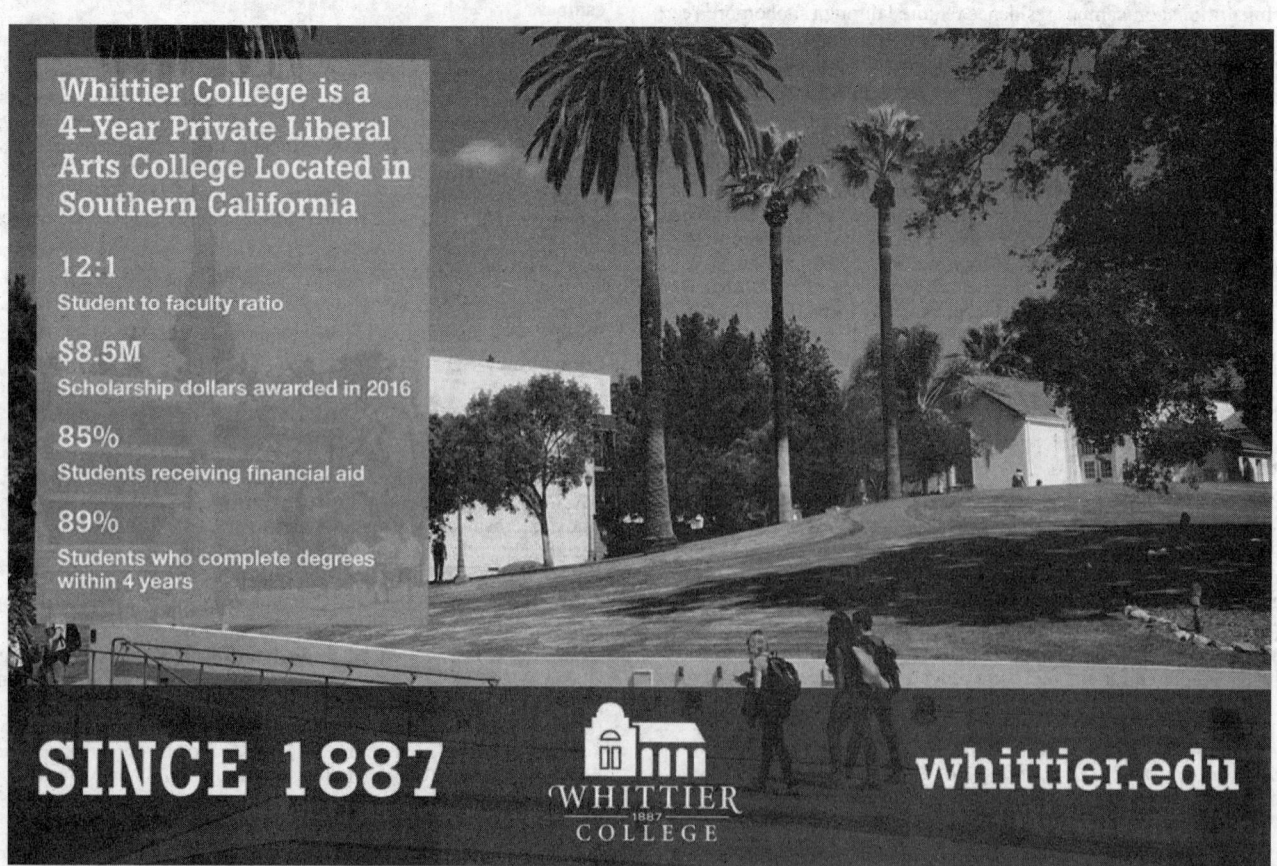

Athletics Member NAIA.

Campus security: 24-hour patrols, student patrols, late-night transport/escort service, controlled dormitory access, day and evening patrols by trained security personnel.

Student services: personal/psychological counseling.

COSTS & FINANCIAL AID

Costs (2016–17) ***Comprehensive fee:*** $39,350 includes full-time tuition ($28,300), mandatory fees ($400), and room and board ($10,650). Full-time tuition and fees vary according to course load. Part-time tuition: $1190 per credit. Part-time tuition and fees vary according to course load. ***Room and board:*** Room and board charges vary according to board plan and housing facility.

Financial Aid Of all full-time matriculated undergraduates who enrolled in 2016, 899 applied for aid, 824 were judged to have need, 114 had their need fully met. 148 Federal Work-Study jobs (averaging $2313). 125 state and other part-time jobs (averaging $2179). In 2016, 140 non-need-based awards were made. ***Average percent of need met:*** 65. ***Average financial aid package:*** $21,232. ***Average need-based loan:*** $4520. ***Average need-based gift aid:*** $17,973. ***Average non-need-based aid:*** $9109. ***Average indebtedness upon graduation:*** $24,656.

APPLYING

Standardized Tests *Required:* SAT or ACT (for admission).

Options: electronic application.

Application fee: $45.

Required: essay or personal statement, high school transcript, minimum 2.0 GPA. ***Required for some:*** 1 letter of recommendation, interview. ***Recommended:*** 1 letter of recommendation, interview.

CONTACT

Traditional Undergraduate Admission, William Jessup University, 2121 University Avenue, Rocklin, CA 95765. *Phone:* 916-577-2222. *Fax:* 916-577-2220. *E-mail:* admissions@jessup.edu.

Woodbury University

Burbank, California

http://www.woodbury.edu/

- **Independent** comprehensive, founded 1884
- **Suburban** 22-acre campus with easy access to Los Angeles
- **Coed** 1,135 undergraduate students, 86% full-time, 48% women, 52% men
- **Moderately difficult** entrance level, 66% of applicants were admitted

UNDERGRAD STUDENTS

973 full-time, 162 part-time. 5% are from out of state; 3% Black or African American, non-Hispanic/Latino; 28% Hispanic/Latino; 8% Asian, non-Hispanic/Latino; 0.7% Native Hawaiian or other Pacific Islander, non-Hispanic/Latino; 0.4% American Indian or Alaska Native, non-Hispanic/Latino; 2% Two or more races, non-Hispanic/Latino; 0.8% Race/ethnicity unknown; 23% international; 13% transferred in.

Freshmen:

Admission: 1,487 applied, 985 admitted, 137 enrolled. ***Average high school GPA:*** 3.4. ***Test scores:*** SAT critical reading scores over 500: 47%; SAT math scores over 500: 48%; ACT scores over 18: 81%; SAT critical reading scores over 600: 17%; SAT math scores over 600: 12%; ACT scores over 24: 44%; SAT critical reading scores over 700: 2%; SAT math scores over 700: 2%; ACT scores over 30: 11%.

Retention: 78% of full-time freshmen returned.

FACULTY

Total: 240, 35% full-time, 43% with terminal degrees.

Student/faculty ratio: 8:1.

ACADEMICS

Calendar: semesters. *Degrees:* bachelor's and master's.

Special study options: academic remediation for entering students, adult/continuing education programs, advanced placement credit, double majors, independent study, internships, part-time degree program, services for LD students, student-designed majors, study abroad, summer session for credit.

Computers: Students can access the following: campus intranet, computer help desk, free student e-mail accounts, online (class) grades, online (class) registration, online (class) schedules. Campuswide network is available. 100% of college-owned or -operated housing units are wired for high-speed Internet access. Wireless service is available via classrooms, computer centers, computer labs, learning centers, libraries, student centers.

Library: Los Angeles Times Library.

STUDENT LIFE

Housing options: coed. Campus housing is university owned and is provided by a third party. Freshman applicants given priority for college housing.

Activities and organizations: national fraternities, national sororities.

Campus security: 24-hour patrols, late-night transport/escort service, controlled dormitory access.

Student services: health clinic, personal/psychological counseling.

COSTS & FINANCIAL AID

Costs (2016–17) ***Comprehensive fee:*** $49,042 includes full-time tuition ($36,882), mandatory fees ($1024), and room and board ($11,136). Full-time tuition and fees vary according to course load, degree level, and program. Part-time tuition: $1201 per credit hour. Part-time tuition and fees vary according to course load, degree level, and program. ***Required fees:*** $500 per term part-time. ***College room only:*** $6868. Room and board charges vary according to board plan, housing facility, and location. ***Payment plan:*** deferred payment. ***Waivers:*** employees or children of employees.

Financial Aid Of all full-time matriculated undergraduates who enrolled in 2016, 639 applied for aid, 607 were judged to have need, 11 had their need fully met. In 2016, 102 non-need-based awards were made. ***Average percent of need met:*** 51. ***Average financial aid package:*** $23,976. ***Average need-based loan:*** $4465. ***Average need-based gift aid:*** $19,919. ***Average non-need-based aid:*** $11,133. ***Average indebtedness upon graduation:*** $41,211. ***Financial aid deadline:*** 2/1.

APPLYING

Standardized Tests *Recommended:* SAT or ACT (for admission).

Options: electronic application, deferred entrance.

Application fee: $75.

Required: high school transcript, minimum 2.0 GPA. ***Recommended:*** essay or personal statement, minimum 3.0 GPA, 2 letters of recommendation.

Application deadlines: rolling (freshmen), rolling (transfers).

Notification: continuous (freshmen), continuous (transfers).

CONTACT

Woodbury University, 7500 Glenoaks Boulevard, Burbank, CA 91510-7846. *Phone:* 818-252-5225. *Toll-free phone:* 800-784-WOOD. *E-mail:* info@woodbury.edu.

World Mission University

Los Angeles, California

http://www.wmu.edu/

CONTACT

World Mission University, 500 Shatto Place, Suite 600, Los Angeles, CA 90020.

Yeshiva Ohr Elchonon Chabad/West Coast Talmudical Seminary

Los Angeles, California

http://www.yoec.edu/

CONTACT

Rabbi Ezra Binyomin Schochet, Dean, Yeshiva Ohr Elchonon Chabad/West Coast Talmudical Seminary, 7215 Waring Avenue, Los Angeles, CA 90046-7660. *Phone:* 323-937-3763. *E-mail:* roshyeshiva@yoec.edu.

COLLEGES AT-A-GLANCE

Zaytuna College

Berkeley, California

http://www.zaytuna.edu/

CONTACT
Yusuf Samara, Admissions, Zaytuna College, 2401 Le Conte Avenue, Berkeley, CA 94709. *Phone:* 510-900-3156. *E-mail:* admissions@zaytuna.org.

COLORADO

Adams State University

Alamosa, Colorado

http://www.adams.edu/

- **State-supported** comprehensive, founded 1921
- **Small-town** 90-acre campus with easy access to Pueblo
- **Endowment** $64,882
- **Coed** 2,002 undergraduate students, 81% full-time, 49% women, 51% men
- **Moderately difficult** entrance level, 99% of applicants were admitted

UNDERGRAD STUDENTS
1,631 full-time, 371 part-time. 7% Black or African American, non-Hispanic/Latino; 35% Hispanic/Latino; 0.8% Asian, non-Hispanic/Latino; 0.6% Native Hawaiian or other Pacific Islander, non-Hispanic/Latino; 1% American Indian or Alaska Native, non-Hispanic/Latino; 4% Two or more races, non-Hispanic/Latino; 4% Race/ethnicity unknown; 1% international; 11% transferred in; 53% live on campus.

Freshmen:
Admission: 1,957 applied, 1,929 admitted, 462 enrolled. ***Average high school GPA:*** 3.11. ***Test scores:*** ACT scores over 18: 64%; ACT scores over 24: 15%; ACT scores over 30: 1%.
Retention: 62% of full-time freshmen returned.

FACULTY
Total: 235, 47% full-time, 30% with terminal degrees.
Student/faculty ratio: 14:1.

ACADEMICS
Calendar: semesters. *Degrees:* associate, bachelor's, master's, and doctoral.
Special study options: academic remediation for entering students, accelerated degree program, adult/continuing education programs, advanced placement credit, cooperative education, distance learning, double majors, external degree program, independent study, internships, off-campus study, part-time degree program, services for LD students, student-designed majors, study abroad, summer session for credit.
Computers: 322 computers/terminals are available on campus for general student use. Students can access the following: campus intranet, computer help desk, free student e-mail accounts, online (class) grades, online (class) registration, online (class) schedules. Campuswide network is available. 100% of college-owned or -operated housing units are wired for high-speed Internet access. Wireless service is available via classrooms, computer centers, computer labs, dorm rooms, learning centers, libraries, student centers.
Library: Nielsen Library. *Books:* 252 (physical), 891 (digital/electronic); *Serial titles:* 102 (physical), 372 (digital/electronic); *Databases:* 60. Weekly public service hours: 84.

STUDENT LIFE
Housing options: on-campus residence required through sophomore year; coed, men-only, women-only. Campus housing is university owned. Freshman campus housing is guaranteed.
Activities and organizations: drama/theater group, student-run newspaper, radio station, choral group, marching band, Student Programming Board, Student government, Semillas de la Tierra, Newman Club, Fellowship of Christian Athletes.
Athletics Member NCAA. All Division II. ***Intercollegiate sports:*** baseball M(s), basketball M(s)/W(s), cross-country running M(s)/W(s), football M(s), golf M(s)/W(s), lacrosse M(s)/W(s), soccer M(s)/W(s), softball W(s), swimming and diving M(s)/W(s), track and field M(s)/W(s), volleyball W(s), wrestling M(s). ***Intramural sports:*** basketball M/W, bowling M/W, cheerleading M(c)/W(c), football M/W, golf M(c)/W(c), racquetball M/W, rock climbing M/W, rugby M(c)/W(c), skiing (cross-country) M/W, skiing (downhill) M/W, soccer M/W, softball M/W, swimming and diving M/W, volleyball M/W, water polo M/W.
Campus security: 24-hour emergency response devices and patrols, student patrols, late-night transport/escort service, controlled dormitory access.
Student services: personal/psychological counseling.

COSTS & FINANCIAL AID
Costs (2016–17) ***Tuition:*** state resident $5736 full-time, $239 per credit hour part-time; nonresident $16,752 full-time, $698 per credit hour part-time. Full-time tuition and fees vary according to course load. Part-time tuition and fees vary according to course load. No tuition increase for student's term of enrollment. ***Required fees:*** $3417 full-time, $138 per credit hour part-time. ***Room and board:*** $8550; room only: $4000. Room and board charges vary according to board plan and housing facility. ***Payment plans:*** installment, deferred payment. ***Waivers:*** senior citizens and employees or children of employees.
Financial Aid Of all full-time matriculated undergraduates who enrolled in 2016, 1,629 applied for aid, 1,282 were judged to have need, 66 had their need fully met. ***Average percent of need met:*** 62. ***Average financial aid package:*** $13,050. ***Average need-based loan:*** $3907. ***Average need-based gift aid:*** $8356. ***Average indebtedness upon graduation:*** $17,808.

APPLYING
Standardized Tests *Required:* SAT or ACT (for admission).
Options: electronic application, early admission, deferred entrance.
Application fee: $30.
Required: high school transcript, minimum 2.0 GPA. ***Required for some:*** essay or personal statement, audition for music majors, portfolio for art majors.
Application deadlines: rolling (freshmen), rolling (transfers).
Notification: continuous (freshmen), continuous (transfers).

CONTACT
ASU One Stop, Adams State University, 208 Edgemont Boulevard, Alamosa, CO 81101. *Phone:* 719-587-7306. *Toll-free phone:* 800-824-6494. *Fax:* 719-587-7366. *E-mail:* onestop@adams.edu.

American Sentinel University

Aurora, Colorado

http://www.americansentinel.edu/

CONTACT
Natalie Nixon, Vice President of Admission, American Sentinel University, 2260 South Xanadu Way, Suite 310, Aurora, CO 80014. *Phone:* 800-729-2427. *Toll-free phone:* 800-729-2427. *Fax:* 866-505-2450. *E-mail:* natalie.nixon@AmericanSentinel.edu.

Argosy University, Denver

Denver, Colorado

http://www.argosy.edu/locations/denver/

CONTACT
Argosy University, Denver, 7600 East Eastman Avenue, Denver, CO 80231. *Phone:* 303-923-4110. *Toll-free phone:* 866-431-5981.

The Art Institute of Colorado

Denver, Colorado

http://www.artinstitutes.edu/denver/

CONTACT
The Art Institute of Colorado, 1200 Lincoln Street, Denver, CO 80203. *Phone:* 303-837-0825. *Toll-free phone:* 800-275-2420.

Aspen University
Denver, Colorado
http://www.aspen.edu/

CONTACT
Aspen University, 720 South Colorado Boulevard, Suite 1150N, Denver, CO 80246-1930. *Phone:* 303-333-4224. *Toll-free phone:* 800-441-4746.

CollegeAmerica–Colorado Springs
Colorado Springs, Colorado
http://www.collegeamerica.edu/

CONTACT
CollegeAmerica–Colorado Springs, 2020 North Academy Boulevard, Colorado Springs, CO 80909. *Phone:* 719-637-0600. *Toll-free phone:* 800-622-2894.

CollegeAmerica–Denver
Denver, Colorado
http://www.collegeamerica.edu/

- **Independent** primarily 2-year, founded 1962
- **Urban** campus
- **Coed**
- **Noncompetitive** entrance level

FACULTY
Student/faculty ratio: 15:1.

ACADEMICS
Calendar: continuous. *Degrees:* associate and bachelor's.

STUDENT LIFE
Housing options: college housing not available.

CONTACT
Admissions Office, CollegeAmerica–Denver, 1385 South Colorado Boulevard, Denver, CO 80222. *Phone:* 303-300-8740 Ext. 7020. *Toll-free phone:* 800-622-2894.

CollegeAmerica–Fort Collins
Fort Collins, Colorado
http://www.collegeamerica.edu/

- **Independent** primarily 2-year, founded 1962
- **Suburban** campus
- **Coed** 120 undergraduate students
- **Minimally difficult** entrance level

ACADEMICS
Calendar: continuous. *Degrees:* associate and bachelor's.
Special study options: cooperative education, distance learning, honors programs, independent study, internships.
Computers: Students can access the following: campus intranet, computer help desk. Campuswide network is available. Wireless service is available via entire campus.

STUDENT LIFE
Housing options: college housing not available.

APPLYING
Required: essay or personal statement, high school transcript, interview. ***Recommended:*** minimum 2.0 GPA.
Notification: continuous (freshmen), continuous (transfers).

CONTACT
CollegeAmerica–Fort Collins, 4601 South Mason Street, Fort Collins, CO 80525. *Phone:* 970-223-6060 Ext. 8002. *Toll-free phone:* 800-622-2894.

Colorado Christian University
Lakewood, Colorado
http://www.ccu.edu/

- **Independent interdenominational** comprehensive, founded 1914
- **Suburban** 26-acre campus with easy access to Denver
- **Coed** 1,306 undergraduate students
- **Moderately difficult** entrance level, 63% of applicants were admitted

UNDERGRAD STUDENTS
32% are from out of state; 55% live on campus.

Freshmen:
Admission: 1,917 applied, 1,213 admitted. ***Average high school GPA:*** 3.61.
Retention: 94% of full-time freshmen returned.

ACADEMICS
Calendar: semesters. *Degrees:* associate, bachelor's, and master's.
Special study options: academic remediation for entering students, accelerated degree program, adult/continuing education programs, advanced placement credit, cooperative education, distance learning, double majors, honors programs, independent study, internships, off-campus study, part-time degree program, services for LD students, student-designed majors, study abroad, summer session for credit. ***ROTC:*** Army (c).
Computers: Students can access the following: online (class) registration. Campuswide network is available. 100% of college-owned or -operated housing units are wired for high-speed Internet access. Wireless service is available via classrooms, computer centers, computer labs, dorm rooms, learning centers, libraries, student centers.
Library: Clifton Fowler Library plus 1 other.

STUDENT LIFE
Housing options: on-campus residence required through sophomore year; men-only, women-only, special housing for students with disabilities. Campus housing is university owned and leased by the school. Freshman campus housing is guaranteed.
Activities and organizations: drama/theater group, choral group.
Athletics Member NCAA. All Division II. ***Intercollegiate sports:*** baseball M(s), basketball M(s)/W(s), cross-country running M(s)/W(s), golf M(s)/W(s), soccer M(s)/W(s), softball W(s), tennis M(s)/W(s), track and field M(s)/W(s), volleyball W(s).
Campus security: 24-hour emergency response devices and patrols, student patrols.
Student services: health clinic, personal/psychological counseling, women's center.

COSTS & FINANCIAL AID
Costs (2016–17) ***Comprehensive fee:*** $39,676 includes full-time tuition ($28,860), mandatory fees ($500), and room and board ($10,316). ***College room only:*** $2815.
Financial Aid Of all full-time matriculated undergraduates who enrolled in 2004, 750 applied for aid, 615 were judged to have need, 55 had their need fully met. 16 Federal Work-Study jobs (averaging $2000). In 2004, 252 non-need-based awards were made. ***Average percent of need met:*** 54. ***Average financial aid package:*** $8931. ***Average need-based loan:*** $3946. ***Average need-based gift aid:*** $6056. ***Average non-need-based aid:*** $12,655. ***Average indebtedness upon graduation:*** $18,633.

APPLYING
Standardized Tests *Required:* SAT or ACT (for admission).
Options: electronic application, early admission, deferred entrance.
Application fee: $30.
Required: essay or personal statement, high school transcript, 2 letters of recommendation, interview, Spiritual Recommendation. ***Required for some:*** minimum 2.8 GPA, 3 letters of recommendation, interview.
Application deadlines: 8/1 (freshmen), 8/1 (transfers).
Notification: continuous (transfers).

CONTACT
Jo Leda Martin, Director of Admissions, Colorado Christian University, 8787 West Alameda, Lakewood, CO 80226. *Phone:* 303-963-3206. *Toll-*

free phone: 800-44-FAITH. *Fax:* 303-963-3201. *E-mail:* jomartin@ccu.edu.

The Colorado College

Colorado Springs, Colorado

http://www.coloradocollege.edu/

- **Independent** comprehensive, founded 1874
- **Urban** 90-acre campus with easy access to Denver
- **Endowment** $683.2 million
- **Coed** 2,101 undergraduate students, 99% full-time, 54% women, 46% men
- **Very difficult** entrance level, 16% of applicants were admitted

UNDERGRAD STUDENTS

2,084 full-time, 17 part-time. Students come from 52 states and territories; 55 other countries; 83% are from out of state; 3% Black or African American, non-Hispanic/Latino; 9% Hispanic/Latino; 4% Asian, non-Hispanic/Latino; 0.5% American Indian or Alaska Native, non-Hispanic/Latino; 9% Two or more races, non-Hispanic/Latino; 1% Race/ethnicity unknown; 8% international; 1% transferred in; 75% live on campus.

Freshmen:

Admission: 7,894 applied, 1,262 admitted, 533 enrolled. ***Test scores:*** SAT critical reading scores over 500: 97%; SAT math scores over 500: 99%; SAT writing scores over 500: 96%; ACT scores over 18: 100%; SAT critical reading scores over 600: 78%; SAT math scores over 600: 85%; SAT writing scores over 600: 84%; ACT scores over 24: 98%; SAT critical reading scores over 700: 40%; SAT math scores over 700: 32%; SAT writing scores over 700: 28%; ACT scores over 30: 65%.

Retention: 96% of full-time freshmen returned.

FACULTY

Total: 232, 80% full-time, 91% with terminal degrees.

Student/faculty ratio: 10:1.

ACADEMICS

Calendar: 8 blocks of 3 1/2 week courses. *Degrees:* bachelor's, master's, and postbachelor's certificates (master's degree in education only).

Special study options: advanced placement credit, double majors, English as a second language, independent study, internships, off-campus study, services for LD students, student-designed majors, study abroad, summer session for credit. ***ROTC:*** Army (c).

Unusual degree programs: 3-2 engineering with Rensselaer Polytechnic Institute, Washington University in St. Louis, University of Southern California, Columbia University.

Computers: 396 computers/terminals are available on campus for general student use. Students can access the following: campus intranet, computer help desk, free student e-mail accounts, online (class) grades, online (class) registration, online (class) schedules. Campuswide network is available. 100% of college-owned or -operated housing units are wired for high-speed Internet access. Wireless service is available via entire campus.

Library: Tutt Library plus 1 other. *Books:* 419,811 (physical), 344,607 (digital/electronic); *Serial titles:* 4,322 (physical), 73,232 (digital/electronic); *Databases:* 320. Students can reserve study rooms.

STUDENT LIFE

Housing options: on-campus residence required through junior year; coed, men-only, women-only. Campus housing is university owned. Freshman campus housing is guaranteed.

Activities and organizations: drama/theater group, student-run newspaper, choral group, national fraternities, national sororities.

Athletics Member NCAA. All Division III except ice hockey (Division I), soccer (Division I). ***Intercollegiate sports:*** baseball M(c), basketball M/W, cross-country running M/W, equestrian sports M(c)/W(c), ice hockey M(s)/W(c), lacrosse M/W, rugby M(c)/W(c), skiing (downhill) M(c)/W(c), soccer M/W(s), softball W(c), swimming and diving M/W, tennis M/W, track and field M/W, ultimate Frisbee M(c)/W(c), volleyball W, water polo W(c). ***Intramural sports:*** basketball M/W, football M, ice hockey M/W, racquetball M/W, soccer M/W, softball M/W, table tennis M/W, ultimate Frisbee M/W, volleyball M/W.

Campus security: 24-hour emergency response devices and patrols, late-night transport/escort service, controlled dormitory access, whistle program, student escort service, good campus lighting.

Student services: health clinic, personal/psychological counseling.

COSTS & FINANCIAL AID

Costs (2016–17) ***One-time required fee:*** $150. ***Comprehensive fee:*** $62,560 includes full-time tuition ($50,472), mandatory fees ($420), and room and board ($11,668). Part-time tuition: $8482 per course. Part-time tuition and fees vary according to course load. ***Required fees:*** $2121 per credit hour part-time. ***College room only:*** $6902. Room and board charges vary according to board plan and housing facility. ***Payment plan:*** installment. ***Waivers:*** employees or children of employees.

Financial Aid Of all full-time matriculated undergraduates who enrolled in 2016, 808 applied for aid, 679 were judged to have need, 679 had their need fully met. 333 Federal Work-Study jobs (averaging $1930). 206 state and other part-time jobs (averaging $2017). In 2016, 144 non-need-based awards were made. ***Average percent of need met:*** 100. ***Average financial aid package:*** $46,024. ***Average need-based loan:*** $5267. ***Average need-based gift aid:*** $42,451. ***Average non-need-based aid:*** $10,193. ***Average indebtedness upon graduation:*** $20,742. ***Financial aid deadline:*** 2/15.

APPLYING

Standardized Tests *Required for some:* SAT or ACT (for admission).

Options: electronic application, early decision, early action, deferred entrance.

Application fee: $60.

Required: essay or personal statement, high school transcript, 2 letters of recommendation. ***Recommended:*** interview.

Application deadlines: 1/15 (freshmen), 3/1 (transfers), 11/10 (early action).

Early decision deadline: 11/10 (for plan 1), 1/15 (for plan 2).

Notification: 4/1 (freshmen), 5/1 (transfers), 12/15 (early decision plan 1), 2/10 (early decision plan 2), 12/20 (early action).

CONTACT

Mr. Carlos Jiminez, Director of Admission - Outreach and Recruitment, The Colorado College, 14 East Cache La Poudre Street, Colorado Springs, CO 80903-3294. *Phone:* 719-389-6344. *Toll-free phone:* 800-542-7214. *Fax:* 719-389-6816. *E-mail:* admission@coloradocollege.edu.

Colorado Mesa University

Grand Junction, Colorado

http://www.coloradomesa.edu/

- **State-supported** comprehensive, founded 1925
- **Small-town** 86-acre campus
- **Endowment** $24.6 million
- **Coed** 9,595 undergraduate students, 76% full-time, 54% women, 46% men
- **Minimally difficult** entrance level, 83% of applicants were admitted

UNDERGRAD STUDENTS

7,277 full-time, 2,318 part-time. Students come from 47 states and territories; 14% are from out of state; 2% Black or African American, non-Hispanic/Latino; 18% Hispanic/Latino; 2% Asian, non-Hispanic/Latino; 0.5% Native Hawaiian or other Pacific Islander, non-Hispanic/Latino; 0.7% American Indian or Alaska Native, non-Hispanic/Latino; 4% Two or more races, non-Hispanic/Latino; 2% Race/ethnicity unknown; 1% international; 7% transferred in; 23% live on campus.

Freshmen:

Admission: 7,152 applied, 5,918 admitted, 2,023 enrolled. ***Average high school GPA:*** 3.11. ***Test scores:*** SAT critical reading scores over 500: 40%; SAT math scores over 500: 43%; ACT scores over 18: 78%; SAT critical reading scores over 600: 12%; SAT math scores over 600: 13%; ACT scores over 24: 26%; SAT critical reading scores over 700: 1%; SAT math scores over 700: 1%; ACT scores over 30: 3%.

Retention: 74% of full-time freshmen returned.

FACULTY

Total: 552, 53% full-time.

Student/faculty ratio: 21:1.

ACADEMICS
Calendar: semesters. *Degrees:* certificates, associate, bachelor's, master's, doctoral, and postbachelor's certificates.

Special study options: academic remediation for entering students, accelerated degree program, advanced placement credit, distance learning, double majors, honors programs, internships, off-campus study, part-time degree program, services for LD students, study abroad, summer session for credit.

Computers: 525 computers/terminals are available on campus for general student use. Students can access the following: campus intranet, computer help desk, free student e-mail accounts, online (class) grades, online (class) registration, online (class) schedules. Campuswide network is available. 100% of college-owned or -operated housing units are wired for high-speed Internet access. Wireless service is available via entire campus.
Library: John U. Tomlinson Library. *Books:* 354,788 (physical), 43,611 (digital/electronic). Study areas open 24 hours, 5-7 days a week; students can reserve study rooms.

STUDENT LIFE
Housing options: on-campus residence required for freshman year; coed, special housing for students with disabilities. Campus housing is university owned. Freshman applicants given priority for college housing.

Activities and organizations: drama/theater group, student-run newspaper, radio and television station, choral group, marching band, Environmental Club, Student Body Association, KMSA radio station, Rodeo Club, Campus Residents Association, national fraternities, national sororities.

Athletics Member NCAA. All Division II. ***Intercollegiate sports:*** baseball M(s), basketball M(s)/W(s), cheerleading M/W, cross-country running M(s)/W(s), football M(s), golf M(s)/W(s), lacrosse M(s)/W(s), rugby M(c)/W(c), sand volleyball W(s), skiing (cross-country) M(c)/W(c), skiing (downhill) M(c)/W(c), soccer M(s)/W(s), softball W(s), swimming and diving M(s)/W(s), tennis M(s)/W(s), track and field M(s)/W(s), volleyball W(s), wrestling M(s). ***Intramural sports:*** badminton M/W, basketball M/W, bowling M(c)/W(c), equestrian sports M/W, football M/W, racquetball M/W, soccer M/W, softball M/W, tennis M/W, ultimate Frisbee M/W, volleyball M/W, water polo M/W.

Campus security: 24-hour emergency response devices and patrols, late-night transport/escort service, controlled dormitory access.

Student services: health clinic, personal/psychological counseling, legal services.

COSTS & FINANCIAL AID
Costs (2016–17) ***Tuition:*** state resident $7572 full-time, $252 per credit hour part-time; nonresident $19,530 full-time, $651 per credit hour part-time. Full-time tuition and fees vary according to course load. Part-time tuition and fees vary according to course load. ***Required fees:*** $823 full-time, $27 per credit hour part-time. ***Room and board:*** $10,560; room only: $5850. Room and board charges vary according to board plan and housing facility. ***Payment plan:*** installment. ***Waivers:*** employees or children of employees.

Financial Aid Of all full-time matriculated undergraduates who enrolled in 2015, 5,876 applied for aid, 4,614 were judged to have need, 870 had their need fully met. In 2015, 488 non-need-based awards were made. ***Average percent of need met:*** 65. ***Average financial aid package:*** $9026. ***Average need-based loan:*** $3790. ***Average need-based gift aid:*** $6813. ***Average non-need-based aid:*** $3641. ***Average indebtedness upon graduation:*** $27,902.

APPLYING
Standardized Tests *Required:* SAT or ACT (for admission).

Options: electronic application, deferred entrance.

Application fee: $30.

Required: high school transcript. ***Recommended:*** 2 letters of recommendation.

Application deadlines: rolling (freshmen), rolling (transfers).

Notification: continuous (freshmen), continuous (transfers).

CONTACT
Admissions, Colorado Mesa University, 1100 North Avenue, Grand Junction, CO 81501. *Phone:* 970-248-1875. *Toll-free phone:* 800-982-MESA. *Fax:* 970-248-1973. *E-mail:* admissions@coloradomeas.edu.

Colorado Mountain College
Glenwood Springs, Colorado
http://www.coloradomtn.edu/

- **District-supported** 4-year, founded 1965, part of Colorado Mountain College District System
- **Rural** 680-acre campus
- **Coed**
- **Noncompetitive** entrance level

FACULTY
Student/faculty ratio: 13:1.

ACADEMICS
Calendar: semesters. *Degrees:* certificates, associate, and bachelor's.
Library: Quigley Library.

STUDENT LIFE
Housing options: on-campus residence required for freshman year; coed, special housing for students with disabilities. Campus housing is university owned. Freshman applicants given priority for college housing.

Activities and organizations: drama/theater group, student-run newspaper, Student Government, Outdoor activities, World Awareness Society, Peer Mentors, Student Activities Board.

Athletics Member NCAA, NJCAA. All NCAA Division I.

Campus security: 24-hour emergency response devices, student patrols, controlled dormitory access.

Student services: health clinic, personal/psychological counseling.

COSTS & FINANCIAL AID
Costs (2016–17) ***Tuition:*** $62 per credit hour part-time; state resident $127 per credit hour part-time; nonresident $429 per credit hour part-time.

Financial Aid In 2015, 316 non-need-based awards were made. ***Average need-based gift aid:*** $1680. ***Average non-need-based aid:*** $1241.

APPLYING
Standardized Tests *Recommended:* SAT or ACT (for admission).

Options: electronic application, early admission, deferred entrance.

Required: high school transcript.

CONTACT
Vicky Butler, Admissions Assistant, Colorado Mountain College, 3000 CR 114, Glenwood Springs, CO 81601. *Phone:* 970-947-8276. *Toll-free phone:* 800-621-8559. *E-mail:* vvalentine@coloradomtn.edu.

Colorado Mountain College
Leadville, Colorado
http://www.coloradomtn.edu/

CONTACT
Ms. Mary Laing, Admissions Assistant, Colorado Mountain College, 901South Highway 24, Leadville, CO 80461. *Phone:* 719-486-4292. *Toll-free phone:* 800-621-8559. *E-mail:* joinus@coloradomtn.edu.

Colorado Mountain College
Steamboat Springs, Colorado
http://www.coloradomtn.edu/

- **District-supported** 4-year, founded 1965, part of Colorado Mountain College District System
- **Small-town** 10-acre campus
- **Coed**
- **Noncompetitive** entrance level

FACULTY
Student/faculty ratio: 12:1.

ACADEMICS
Calendar: semesters. *Degrees:* certificates, associate, and bachelor's.
Library: Main Library plus 1 other.

STUDENT LIFE
Housing options: on-campus residence required for freshman year; coed, special housing for students with disabilities. Campus housing is university owned.

Activities and organizations: student-run newspaper, Student Government, Sky Club, Ski Club, International Club, Phi Theta Kappa.

Athletics Member NCAA, NJCAA. All NCAA Division I.

Campus security: 24-hour emergency response devices, student patrols, controlled dormitory access.

Student services: health clinic, personal/psychological counseling.

COSTS

Costs (2016–17) ***Tuition:*** $62 per credit part-time; state resident $127 per credit part-time; nonresident $429 per credit part-time.
Room and board: $8572.

APPLYING

Standardized Tests *Recommended:* SAT or ACT (for admission).

Options: electronic application, early admission, deferred entrance.

Required: high school transcript.

CONTACT

Ms. Jackie Brazill, Admissions Assistant, Colorado Mountain College, 1275 Crawford Avenue, Steamboat Springs, CO 80487. *Phone:* 970-870-4417 Ext. 4417. *Toll-free phone:* 800-621-8559.
E-mail: jbrazill@coloradomtn.edu.

Colorado School of Mines

Golden, Colorado

http://www.mines.edu/

- **State-supported** university, founded 1874
- **Small-town** 499-acre campus with easy access to Denver, Boulder, Colorado Springs
- **Endowment** $234.2 million
- **Coed** 4,612 undergraduate students, 95% full-time, 28% women, 72% men
- **Very difficult** entrance level, 40% of applicants were admitted

UNDERGRAD STUDENTS

4,397 full-time, 215 part-time. Students come from 50 states and territories; 42 other countries; 38% are from out of state; 1% Black or African American, non-Hispanic/Latino; 7% Hispanic/Latino; 5% Asian, non-Hispanic/Latino; 0.1% Native Hawaiian or other Pacific Islander, non-Hispanic/Latino; 0.2% American Indian or Alaska Native, non-Hispanic/Latino; 5% Two or more races, non-Hispanic/Latino; 0.6% Race/ethnicity unknown; 7% international; 3% transferred in; 28% live on campus.

Freshmen:

Admission: 12,284 applied, 4,957 admitted, 977 enrolled. ***Average high school GPA:*** 3.8. ***Test scores:*** SAT critical reading scores over 500: 99%; SAT math scores over 500: 100%; SAT writing scores over 500: 94%; ACT scores over 18: 100%; SAT critical reading scores over 600: 78%; SAT math scores over 600: 95%; SAT writing scores over 600: 58%; ACT scores over 24: 99%; SAT critical reading scores over 700: 23%; SAT math scores over 700: 47%; SAT writing scores over 700: 11%; ACT scores over 30: 67%.

Retention: 92% of full-time freshmen returned.

FACULTY

Total: 532, 54% full-time, 52% with terminal degrees.

Student/faculty ratio: 15:1.

ACADEMICS

Calendar: semesters. *Degrees:* bachelor's, master's, doctoral, and post-master's certificates.

Special study options: accelerated degree program, advanced placement credit, cooperative education, double majors, honors programs, independent study, internships, off-campus study, services for LD students, study abroad, summer session for credit. ***ROTC:*** Army (b), Air Force (b).

Computers: 1,000 computers/terminals are available on campus for general student use. Students can access the following: campus intranet, computer help desk, free student e-mail accounts, online (class) grades, online (class) registration, online (class) schedules. Campuswide network is available. 100% of college-owned or -operated housing units are wired for high-speed Internet access. Wireless service is available via entire campus.

Library: Arthur Lakes Library. *Books:* 503,801 (physical), 134,211 (digital/electronic); *Serial titles:* 578 (physical), 104,424 (digital/electronic); *Databases:* 128. Weekly public service hours: 107; students can reserve study rooms.

STUDENT LIFE

Housing options: on-campus residence required for freshman year; coed. Campus housing is university owned and is provided by a third party. Freshman campus housing is guaranteed.

Activities and organizations: drama/theater group, student-run newspaper, radio station, choral group, marching band, Society of Women Engineers, Residence Hall Association, Associated Students of Colorado School of Mines, Student Professional Societies/ and/ Religious Organizations, Multicultural Engineering Program, national fraternities, national sororities.

Athletics Member NCAA. All Division II. ***Intercollegiate sports:*** baseball M(s), basketball M(s)/W(s), bowling M(c)/W(c), cross-country running M(s)/W(s), football M(s), golf M(s), ice hockey M(c)/W(c), lacrosse M(c)/W(c), rugby M(c)/W(c), soccer M(s)/W(s), softball W(s), swimming and diving M(s)/W(s), track and field M(s)/W(s), volleyball W(s), wrestling M(s). ***Intramural sports:*** badminton M/W, basketball M/W, bowling M/W, cross-country running M/W, equestrian sports M/W, field hockey M/W, football M/W, golf M/W, lacrosse M, racquetball M/W, skiing (downhill) M/W, soccer M/W, softball M/W, swimming and diving M/W, table tennis M/W, tennis M/W, track and field M/W, ultimate Frisbee M/W, volleyball M/W, wrestling M.

Campus security: 24-hour emergency response devices and patrols, late-night transport/escort service, controlled dormitory access, fully trained police officers.

Student services: health clinic, personal/psychological counseling, women's center.

COSTS & FINANCIAL AID

Costs (2016–17) ***Tuition:*** state resident $15,690 full-time, $523 per credit hour part-time; nonresident $34,020 full-time, $1134 per credit hour part-time. Full-time tuition and fees vary according to course load. ***Required fees:*** $2152 full-time. ***Room and board:*** $11,477. Room and board charges vary according to board plan and housing facility. ***Payment plan:*** installment. ***Waivers:*** employees or children of employees.

Financial Aid Of all full-time matriculated undergraduates who enrolled in 2015, 2,842 applied for aid, 2,027 were judged to have need, 358 had their need fully met. 395 Federal Work-Study jobs (averaging $1787). 1,719 state and other part-time jobs (averaging $2417). In 2015, 1282 non-need-based awards were made. ***Average percent of need met:*** 56. ***Average financial aid package:*** $14,039. ***Average need-based loan:*** $4661. ***Average need-based gift aid:*** $5478. ***Average non-need-based aid:*** $8182. ***Average indebtedness upon graduation:*** $32,901.

APPLYING

Standardized Tests *Required:* SAT or ACT (for admission).

Options: electronic application, deferred entrance.

Application fee: $45.

Required: high school transcript. ***Required for some:*** essay or personal statement, interview. ***Recommended:*** minimum 3.8 GPA, rank in upper quartile of high school class.

Application deadlines: 4/1 (freshmen), 4/1 (transfers).

Notification: continuous until 10/1 (freshmen), continuous until 10/1 (transfers).

CONTACT

Mrs. Marisa Garcia, Assistant Director of Enrollment Management, Colorado School of Mines, Admissions Office, Starzer Welcome Center, 1812 Illinois Street, Golden, CO 80401. *Phone:* 303-273-3220. *Toll-free phone:* 800-446-9488 Ext. 3220. *Fax:* 303-273-3509. *E-mail:* admissions@mines.edu.

Colorado State University

Fort Collins, Colorado

http://www.colostate.edu/

- **State-supported** university, founded 1870, part of Colorado State University System
- **Urban** 586-acre campus with easy access to Denver
- **Endowment** $286.3 million
- **Coed** 25,688 undergraduate students, 90% full-time, 52% women, 48% men
- **Moderately difficult** entrance level, 78% of applicants were admitted

UNDERGRAD STUDENTS
22,993 full-time, 2,695 part-time. Students come from 54 states and territories; 78 other countries; 23% are from out of state; 2% Black or African American, non-Hispanic/Latino; 12% Hispanic/Latino; 3% Asian, non-Hispanic/Latino; 0.1% Native Hawaiian or other Pacific Islander, non-Hispanic/Latino; 0.5% American Indian or Alaska Native, non-Hispanic/Latino; 3% Two or more races, non-Hispanic/Latino; 3% Race/ethnicity unknown; 4% international; 7% transferred in; 29% live on campus.

Freshmen:
Admission: 21,759 applied, 16,963 admitted, 4,956 enrolled. ***Average high school GPA:*** 3.61. ***Test scores:*** SAT critical reading scores over 500: 80%; SAT math scores over 500: 82%; ACT scores over 18: 99%; SAT critical reading scores over 600: 38%; SAT math scores over 600: 39%; ACT scores over 24: 65%; SAT critical reading scores over 700: 6%; SAT math scores over 700: 6%; ACT scores over 30: 14%.
Retention: 86% of full-time freshmen returned.

FACULTY
Total: 1,046, 98% full-time, 100% with terminal degrees.
Student/faculty ratio: 18:1.

ACADEMICS
Calendar: semesters. *Degrees:* bachelor's, master's, doctoral, and postbachelor's certificates.
Special study options: accelerated degree program, adult/continuing education programs, advanced placement credit, cooperative education, distance learning, double majors, English as a second language, honors programs, independent study, internships, off-campus study, part-time degree program, services for LD students, study abroad, summer session for credit. ***ROTC:*** Army (b), Air Force (b).
Unusual degree programs: 3-2 engineering.
Computers: 1,700 computers/terminals and 3,000 ports are available on campus for general student use. Students can access the following: campus intranet, computer help desk, free student e-mail accounts, online (class) grades, online (class) registration, online (class) schedules, personalized portal services including transcripts and financials (billing, financial aid). Campuswide network is available. 100% of college-owned or -operated housing units are wired for high-speed Internet access. Wireless service is available via classrooms, computer centers, computer labs, dorm rooms, learning centers, libraries, student centers.
Library: William E. Morgan Library plus 2 others. *Books:* 1.2 million (physical), 534,252 (digital/electronic); *Serial titles:* 53,973 (physical), 84,523 (digital/electronic); *Databases:* 343. Weekly public service hours: 108; study areas open 24 hours, 5-7 days a week; students can reserve study rooms.

STUDENT LIFE
Housing options: on-campus residence required for freshman year; coed, special housing for students with disabilities. Campus housing is university owned. Freshman campus housing is guaranteed.
Activities and organizations: drama/theater group, student-run newspaper, radio and television station, choral group, marching band, Associated Students of CSU (ASCSU Student Government), Esports, Campus Feminist Alliance, Council of International Student Affairs, Snowriders, national fraternities, national sororities.
Athletics Member NCAA. All Division I except football (Division I-A). ***Intercollegiate sports:*** baseball M(c), basketball M(s)/W(s), crew M(c)/W(c), cross-country running M(s)/W(s), field hockey M(c)/W(c), golf M(s)/W(s), ice hockey M(c)/W(c), lacrosse M(c)/W(c), rock climbing M(c)/W(c), rowing M(c)/W(c), rugby M(c)/W(c), skiing (downhill) M(c)/W(c), soccer M(c)/W(s), softball W(s), swimming and diving M(c)/W(s), table tennis M(c)/W(c), tennis W(s), track and field M(s)/W(s), triathlon M(c)/W(c), ultimate Frisbee M(c)/W(c), volleyball M(c)/W(s), water polo M(c)/W(c), weight lifting M(c)/W(c), wrestling M(c)/W(c). ***Intramural sports:*** badminton M/W, basketball M/W, bowling M/W, golf M/W, racquetball M/W, soccer M/W, softball M/W, table tennis M/W, tennis M/W, ultimate Frisbee M/W, volleyball M/W, water polo M/W, wrestling M/W.
Campus security: 24-hour emergency response devices and patrols, student patrols, late-night transport/escort service, controlled dormitory access.
Student services: health clinic, personal/psychological counseling, women's center, legal services.

COSTS & FINANCIAL AID
Costs (2016–17) ***Tuition:*** state resident $8716 full-time, $396 per credit hour part-time; nonresident $26,010 full-time, $1301 per credit hour part-time. Full-time tuition and fees vary according to course level, course load, program, and student level. Part-time tuition and fees vary according to course level, course load, program, and student level. ***Required fees:*** $2336 full-time, $57 per credit hour part-time, $285 per term part-time. ***Room and board:*** $11,110; room only: $5416. Room and board charges vary according to board plan, housing facility, and location. ***Waivers:*** employees or children of employees.
Financial Aid Of all full-time matriculated undergraduates who enrolled in 2014, 14,934 applied for aid, 10,890 were judged to have need, 2,518 had their need fully met. 434 Federal Work-Study jobs (averaging $2185). 1,026 state and other part-time jobs (averaging $2297). In 2014, 2585 non-need-based awards were made. ***Average percent of need met:*** 82. ***Average financial aid package:*** $10,906. ***Average need-based loan:*** $6687. ***Average need-based gift aid:*** $7162. ***Average non-need-based aid:*** $4158. ***Average indebtedness upon graduation:*** $23,347.

APPLYING
Standardized Tests *Required:* SAT or ACT (for admission).
Options: electronic application, early action, deferred entrance.
Application fee: $50.
Required: essay or personal statement, high school transcript, 1 letter of recommendation.
Application deadlines: 5/1 (freshmen), 6/1 (transfers), 12/1 (early action).
Notification: continuous until 9/15 (freshmen), continuous (transfers), 2/1 (early action).

CONTACT
Kelly Nolin, Associate Director of Admission, Recruitment and Outreach, Colorado State University, Ammons Hall (1062), Fort Collins, CO 80523-1062. *Phone:* 970-491-6909. *Fax:* 970-491-7799.
E-mail: admissions@colostate.edu.

Colorado State University–Global Campus

Greenwood Village, Colorado

http://csuglobal.edu/

CONTACT
Colorado State University–Global Campus, 8000 E. Maplewood Avenue, Greenwood Village, CO 80111. *Toll-free phone:* 800-920-6723.

Colorado State University–Pueblo

Pueblo, Colorado

http://www.csupueblo.edu/

- **State-supported** comprehensive, founded 1933, part of Colorado State University System
- **Small-town** 275-acre campus with easy access to Colorado Springs
- **Endowment** $15.8 million
- **Coed**
- **Moderately difficult** entrance level

FACULTY
Student/faculty ratio: 16:1.

ACADEMICS
Calendar: semesters. *Degrees:* bachelor's and master's.
Library: CSU-Pueblo University Library plus 1 other. *Books:* 307,896 (physical), 84,011 (digital/electronic); *Serial titles:* 166 (physical), 404 (digital/electronic); *Databases:* 100. Weekly public service hours: 93; students can reserve study rooms.

STUDENT LIFE
Housing options: on-campus residence required through sophomore year; coed, special housing for students with disabilities. Campus housing is university owned. Freshman campus housing is guaranteed.
Activities and organizations: student-run newspaper, radio and television station, choral group, marching band, Fellowship of Christian Athletes, Latino Student Union, I Am That Girl, CSU-Pueblo International Student Association, Gaming Club, national fraternities, national sororities.
Athletics Member NCAA. All Division II.
Campus security: 24-hour emergency response devices and patrols, student patrols, late-night transport/escort service, controlled dormitory access, parking and building checks.
Student services: health clinic, personal/psychological counseling.

COSTS & FINANCIAL AID
Costs (2016–17) ***One-time required fee:*** $85. ***Tuition:*** state resident $7269 full-time, $242 per credit hour part-time; nonresident $21,851 full-time, $728 per credit hour part-time. Full-time tuition and fees vary according to course load, degree level, location, program, and reciprocity agreements. Part-time tuition and fees vary according to course load, degree level, location, program, and reciprocity agreements. ***Required fees:*** $2250 full-time, $75 per credit hour part-time. ***Room and board:*** $9910; room only: $5660. Room and board charges vary according to board plan and housing facility. ***Payment plans:*** installment, deferred payment.
Financial Aid Of all full-time matriculated undergraduates who enrolled in 2015, 2,933 applied for aid, 2,521 were judged to have need, 168 had their need fully met. 686 Federal Work-Study jobs (averaging $3000). 1,109 state and other part-time jobs (averaging $3000). In 2015, 333 non-need-based awards were made. ***Average percent of need met:*** 51. ***Average financial aid package:*** $9865. ***Average need-based loan:*** $3723. ***Average need-based gift aid:*** $7340. ***Average non-need-based aid:*** $3361. ***Average indebtedness upon graduation:*** $28,914.

APPLYING
Standardized Tests *Required:* SAT or ACT (for admission).
Options: electronic application, deferred entrance.
Application fee: $25.
Required: high school transcript, minimum 2.0 GPA. ***Required for some:*** essay or personal statement.

CONTACT
Ms. Tiffany Kingrey, Assistant Director of Admissions, Colorado State University–Pueblo, 2200 Bonforte Boulevard, Pueblo, CO 81001-4901. *Phone:* 719-549-2629. *Fax:* 719-549-2419.
E-mail: tiffany.kingrey@csupueblo.edu.

Colorado Technical University Aurora

Aurora, Colorado

http://www.coloradotech.edu/

CONTACT
Rosaland Giboney, Associate Director of Admissions, Colorado Technical University Aurora, 3151 South Vaughn Way, Aurora, CO 80014.
Phone: 888-404-7555. *Toll-free phone:* 888-309-6555.
E-mail: rgiboney@coloradotech.edu.

Colorado Technical University Colorado Springs

Colorado Springs, Colorado

http://www.coloradotech.edu/

CONTACT
Beth Braaten, Vice President of Admissions, Colorado Technical University Colorado Springs, 4435 North Chestnut Street, Colorado Springs, CO 80907. *Phone:* 888-404-7555. *Toll-free phone:* 866-942-6555. *E-mail:* bbraaten@coloradotech.edu.

Colorado Technical University Online

Colorado Springs, Colorado

http://www.coloradotech.edu/

CONTACT
William Beckley, Chief Admission Officer, Colorado Technical University Online, 4435 North Chestnut Street, Colorado Springs, CO 80907. *Phone:* 888-404-7555. *Toll-free phone:* 866-813-1836.

Denver School of Nursing

Denver, Colorado

http://www.denverschoolofnursing.edu/

CONTACT
Denver School of Nursing, 1401 19th Street, Denver, CO 80202.
Toll-free phone: 888-479-5550.

DeVry University–Westminster Campus

Westminster, Colorado

http://www.devry.edu/

- **Proprietary** comprehensive, founded 1945
- **Urban** campus
- **Coed**

FACULTY
Student/faculty ratio: 12:1.

ACADEMICS
Calendar: semesters. *Degrees:* associate, bachelor's, master's, and postbachelor's certificates.

COSTS & FINANCIAL AID
Costs (2016–17) ***Tuition:*** $17,052 full-time, $609 per credit hour part-time. ***Required fees:*** $460 full-time.
Financial Aid Of all full-time matriculated undergraduates who enrolled in 2007, 148 applied for aid, 136 were judged to have need, 6 had their need fully met. In 2007, 17 non-need-based awards were made. ***Average percent of need met:*** 37. ***Average financial aid package:*** $11,971. ***Average need-based loan:*** $8024. ***Average need-based gift aid:*** $6094. ***Average non-need-based aid:*** $13,350. ***Average indebtedness upon graduation:*** $11,071.

APPLYING
Options: deferred entrance.
Application fee: $30.

CONTACT
Admissions Office, DeVry University–Westminster Campus, 1870 West 122nd Avenue, Westminster, CO 80234-2010. *Phone:* 303-280-7400.
Toll-free phone: 866-338-7934.

Ecotech Institute

Aurora, Colorado

http://www.ecotechinstitute.com/

CONTACT
Ecotech Institute, 1400 South Abilene Street, Aurora, CO 80012.

Fort Lewis College

Durango, Colorado

http://www.fortlewis.edu/

- **State-supported** comprehensive, founded 1911
- **Small-town** 350-acre campus
- **Endowment** $8.0 million
- **Coed** 3,679 undergraduate students, 92% full-time, 51% women, 49% men
- **Moderately difficult** entrance level, 86% of applicants were admitted

UNDERGRAD STUDENTS

3,393 full-time, 286 part-time. Students come from 49 states and territories; 22 other countries; 50% are from out of state; 1% Black or African American, non-Hispanic/Latino; 11% Hispanic/Latino; 0.7% Asian, non-Hispanic/Latino; 0.2% Native Hawaiian or other Pacific Islander, non-Hispanic/Latino; 25% American Indian or Alaska Native, non-Hispanic/Latino; 7% Two or more races, non-Hispanic/Latino; 2% Race/ethnicity unknown; 1% international; 10% transferred in; 40% live on campus.

Freshmen:

Admission: 3,105 applied, 2,669 admitted, 814 enrolled. ***Average high school GPA:*** 3.25. ***Test scores:*** SAT critical reading scores over 500: 57%; SAT math scores over 500: 55%; SAT writing scores over 500: 40%; ACT scores over 18: 89%; SAT critical reading scores over 600: 11%; SAT math scores over 600: 17%; SAT writing scores over 600: 9%; ACT scores over 24: 33%; SAT critical reading scores over 700: 2%; SAT math scores over 700: 1%; SAT writing scores over 700: 1%; ACT scores over 30: 4%.

Retention: 63% of full-time freshmen returned.

FACULTY

Total: 252, 69% full-time, 71% with terminal degrees.

Student/faculty ratio: 17:1.

ACADEMICS

Calendar: semesters modified trimesters. *Degrees:* bachelor's, master's, and postbachelor's certificates.

Special study options: academic remediation for entering students, advanced placement credit, double majors, honors programs, independent study, internships, services for LD students, student-designed majors, study abroad, summer session for credit.

Unusual degree programs: 3-2 social work with University of Denver.

Computers: 825 computers/terminals are available on campus for general student use. Students can access the following: campus intranet, computer help desk, free student e-mail accounts, online (class) grades, online (class) registration, online (class) schedules. Campuswide network is available. 100% of college-owned or -operated housing units are wired for high-speed Internet access. Wireless service is available via entire campus.

Library: John F. Reed Library plus 1 other. *Books:* 148,329 (physical), 173,600 (digital/electronic); *Serial titles:* 170 (physical), 150,831 (digital/electronic); *Databases:* 84. Weekly public service hours: 80; study areas open 24 hours, 5-7 days a week; students can reserve study rooms.

STUDENT LIFE

Housing options: on-campus residence required for freshman year; coed, special housing for students with disabilities. Campus housing is university owned. Freshman applicants given priority for college housing.

Activities and organizations: drama/theater group, student-run newspaper, radio station, KDUR - Campus/community radio, Environmental Center, Student Union Productions, Dance Co-Motion, Master Plan Ministries.

Athletics Member NCAA. All Division II. ***Intercollegiate sports:*** baseball M(c), basketball M(s)/W(s), cheerleading M(c)/W(c), cross-country running M(s)/W(s), fencing M(c)/W(c), football M(s), golf M(s), ice hockey M(c)/W(c), lacrosse M(c)/W(s), rock climbing M(c)/W(c), rugby M(c)/W(c), skiing (cross-country) M(c)/W(c), skiing (downhill) M(c)/W(c), soccer M(s)/W(s), softball W(s), ultimate Frisbee M(c)/W(c), volleyball W(s), wrestling M(c)/W(c). ***Intramural sports:*** badminton M/W, basketball M/W, football M/W, golf M/W, racquetball M/W, soccer M/W, softball M/W, ultimate Frisbee M/W, volleyball M/W.

Campus security: 24-hour emergency response devices and patrols, late-night transport/escort service, controlled dormitory access.

Student services: health clinic, personal/psychological counseling, legal services.

COSTS & FINANCIAL AID

Costs (2016–17) ***Tuition:*** state resident $6360 full-time, $265 per credit hour part-time; nonresident $16,072 full-time, $670 per credit hour part-time. Full-time tuition and fees vary according to course load and reciprocity agreements. Part-time tuition and fees vary according to course load and reciprocity agreements. ***Required fees:*** $1745 full-time, $58 per credit hour part-time. ***Room and board:*** $9328; room only: $4620. Room and board charges vary according to board plan and housing facility. ***Payment plan:*** installment. ***Waivers:*** minority students and employees or children of employees.

Financial Aid Of all full-time matriculated undergraduates who enrolled in 2015, 2,572 applied for aid, 2,161 were judged to have need, 354 had their need fully met. 147 Federal Work-Study jobs (averaging $1832). 257 state and other part-time jobs (averaging $1810). In 2015, 641 non-need-based awards were made. ***Average percent of need met:*** 93. ***Average financial aid package:*** $15,959. ***Average need-based loan:*** $4113. ***Average need-based gift aid:*** $5029. ***Average non-need-based aid:*** $4476. ***Average indebtedness upon graduation:*** $22,265.

APPLYING

Standardized Tests *Required:* SAT or ACT (for admission).

Options: electronic application, early action, deferred entrance.

Application fee: $40.

Required: high school transcript. ***Required for some:*** interview. ***Recommended:*** essay or personal statement, 2 letters of recommendation.

CONTACT

Fort Lewis College, 1000 Rim Drive, Durango, CO 81301-3999.
Phone: 970-247-7184. *Toll-free phone:* 877-FLC-COLO.

Johnson & Wales University

Denver, Colorado

http://www.jwu.edu/denver/

- **Independent** comprehensive, founded 1993
- **Small-town** campus
- **Coed**
- **Moderately difficult** entrance level

FACULTY

Student/faculty ratio: 16:1.

ACADEMICS

Calendar: quarters. *Degrees:* associate, bachelor's, and master's.

Library: Johnson & Wales University Library.

STUDENT LIFE

Housing options: on-campus residence required for freshman year; coed, special housing for students with disabilities. Campus housing is university owned. Freshman campus housing is guaranteed.

Activities and organizations: drama/theater group, student-run newspaper.

Athletics Member NAIA.

Campus security: 24-hour emergency response devices and patrols, student patrols, late-night transport/escort service.

COSTS & FINANCIAL AID

Costs (2016–17) ***Tuition:*** $30,396 full-time. ***Required fees:*** $350 full-time. ***Room only:*** $8268.

Financial Aid Of all full-time matriculated undergraduates who enrolled in 2015, 1,191 applied for aid, 943 were judged to have need, 156 had their need fully met. In 2015, 212 non-need-based awards were made. ***Average percent of need met:*** 72. ***Average financial aid package:*** $22,575. ***Average need-based loan:*** $4773. ***Average need-based gift aid:*** $8763. ***Average non-need-based aid:*** $7937.

APPLYING

Standardized Tests *Required for some:* SAT or ACT (for admission).

Options: electronic application, early admission, deferred entrance.

Required: high school transcript. ***Required for some:*** essay or personal statement, minimum 2.8 GPA, interview. ***Recommended:*** minimum 2.0 GPA.

CONTACT
Kim Medina, Director of Admissions, Johnson & Wales University, 7150 Montview Boulevard, Denver, CO 80220. *Phone:* 303-256-9300. *Toll-free phone:* 877-598-3368. *Fax:* 303-598-3368.
E-mail: den@admissions.jwu.edu.

Metropolitan State University of Denver

Denver, Colorado

http://www.msudenver.edu/

- **State-supported** comprehensive, founded 1963
- **Urban** 175-acre campus with easy access to Denver
- **Coed** 20,186 undergraduate students, 61% full-time, 53% women, 47% men
- **Minimally difficult** entrance level, 65% of applicants were admitted

UNDERGRAD STUDENTS
12,313 full-time, 7,873 part-time. 3% are from out of state; 6% Black or African American, non-Hispanic/Latino; 22% Hispanic/Latino; 4% Asian, non-Hispanic/Latino; 0.3% Native Hawaiian or other Pacific Islander, non-Hispanic/Latino; 0.6% American Indian or Alaska Native, non-Hispanic/Latino; 4% Two or more races, non-Hispanic/Latino; 4% Race/ethnicity unknown; 0.5% international; 10% transferred in.

Freshmen:
Admission: 5,995 applied, 3,913 admitted, 1,983 enrolled. ***Average high school GPA:*** 2.9. ***Test scores:*** SAT critical reading scores over 500: 46%; SAT math scores over 500: 49%; ACT scores over 18: 81%; SAT critical reading scores over 600: 12%; SAT math scores over 600: 14%; ACT scores over 24: 21%; SAT math scores over 700: 3%; ACT scores over 30: 2%.
Retention: 70% of full-time freshmen returned.

FACULTY
Total: 1,418, 39% full-time.
Student/faculty ratio: 18:1.

ACADEMICS
Calendar: semesters. *Degrees:* bachelor's, master's, and post-master's certificates.
Special study options: accelerated degree program, adult/continuing education programs, advanced placement credit, cooperative education, distance learning, double majors, external degree program, honors programs, independent study, internships, off-campus study, part-time degree program, services for LD students, student-designed majors, study abroad, summer session for credit. ***ROTC:*** Army (b), Air Force (c).
Computers: 808 computers/terminals are available on campus for general student use. Students can access the following: computer help desk, free student e-mail accounts, online (class) grades, online (class) registration, online (class) schedules. Campuswide network is available. Wireless service is available via entire campus.
Library: Auraria Library.

STUDENT LIFE
Housing options: college housing not available.
Activities and organizations: drama/theater group, student-run newspaper, radio and television station, choral group, national fraternities, national sororities.
Athletics Member NCAA. All Division II. ***Intercollegiate sports:*** baseball M(s), basketball M(s)/W(s), cross-country running M/W, soccer M(s)/W(s), softball W(s), tennis M(s)/W(s), track and field M/W, volleyball W(s). ***Intramural sports:*** baseball M(c)/W(c), cheerleading M(c)/W(c), fencing M(c)/W(c), football M(c), ice hockey M(c), lacrosse M(c), rugby M(c), soccer M(c), squash M(c)/W, swimming and diving M(c)/W(c), ultimate Frisbee M(c)/W(c), volleyball M(c)/W(c).
Campus security: 24-hour emergency response devices and patrols, late-night transport/escort service.
Student services: health clinic, personal/psychological counseling, women's center, legal services.

COSTS & FINANCIAL AID
Costs (2016–17) ***Tuition:*** state resident $5693 full-time; nonresident $18,859 full-time. Full-time tuition and fees vary according to course load and location. Part-time tuition and fees vary according to course load and location. ***Required fees:*** $1237 full-time. ***Payment plans:*** installment, deferred payment. ***Waivers:*** senior citizens.
Financial Aid Of all full-time matriculated undergraduates who enrolled in 2015, 9,425 applied for aid, 7,988 were judged to have need, 247 had their need fully met. 153 Federal Work-Study jobs (averaging $3585). 687 state and other part-time jobs (averaging $3388). In 2015, 2575 non-need-based awards were made. ***Average percent of need met:*** 57. ***Average financial aid package:*** $8590. ***Average need-based loan:*** $4013. ***Average need-based gift aid:*** $6515. ***Average non-need-based aid:*** $2380. ***Average indebtedness upon graduation:*** $28,380.

APPLYING
Standardized Tests *Required:* SAT or ACT (for admission). *Required for some:* SAT (for admission), ACT (for admission).
Options: electronic application, deferred entrance.
Application fee: $25.
Required: high school transcript. ***Recommended:*** minimum 2.0 GPA.
Application deadlines: 7/1 (freshmen), rolling (transfers).
Notification: continuous (freshmen), continuous (transfers).

CONTACT
Ms. Michelle Brown, Associate Director of Admissions, Metropolitan State University of Denver, 890 Auraria Parkway, Denver, CO 80204.
Phone: 303-556-2615.

Naropa University

Boulder, Colorado

http://www.naropa.edu/

- **Independent** comprehensive, founded 1974
- **Urban** 12-acre campus with easy access to Denver
- **Endowment** $7.0 million
- **Coed**
- **Moderately difficult** entrance level

FACULTY
Student/faculty ratio: 14:1.

ACADEMICS
Calendar: semesters. *Degrees:* bachelor's and master's.
Library: Allen Ginsberg Library plus 2 others. *Books:* 34,909 (physical), 150,000 (digital/electronic); *Serial titles:* 47 (physical), 12 (digital/electronic); *Databases:* 29. Weekly public service hours: 69.

STUDENT LIFE
Housing options: on-campus residence required for freshman year; coed. Campus housing is university owned. Freshman campus housing is guaranteed.
Activities and organizations: drama/theater group, choral group, Student Union of Naropa, ROOT: Reconnecting on Outdoor Terrain, Team Tapas (yoga club), Community of Color and Allies, Naropa Zazen.
Campus security: late-night transport/escort service, controlled dormitory access, foot and vehicle patrol 4:30 pm to midnight, 24 hour on-call Safety and Security Manager.
Student services: personal/psychological counseling.

COSTS & FINANCIAL AID
Costs (2016–17) ***Comprehensive fee:*** $41,135 includes full-time tuition ($31,000), mandatory fees ($170), and room and board ($9965). Full-time tuition and fees vary according to course load. Part-time tuition: $995 per credit. Part-time tuition and fees vary according to course load. ***Required fees:*** $335 per term part-time.
Financial Aid Of all full-time matriculated undergraduates who enrolled in 2015, 272 applied for aid, 251 were judged to have need, 1 had their need fully met. 168 Federal Work-Study jobs (averaging $3077). 11 state and other part-time jobs (averaging $2455). In 2015, 15 non-need-based awards were made. ***Average percent of need met:*** 90. ***Average financial aid package:*** $37,077. ***Average need-based loan:*** $11,519. ***Average need-based gift aid:*** $24,862. ***Average non-need-based aid:*** $6858. ***Average indebtedness upon graduation:*** $38,199.

APPLYING
Options: electronic application, deferred entrance.
Application fee: $50.

Required: essay or personal statement, high school transcript, 1 letter of recommendation. ***Required for some:*** interview.

CONTACT

Ms. Karen Wills, Assistant Dean of Undergraduate Admissions, Naropa University, 2130 Arapahoe Avenue, Boulder, CO 80302. *Phone:* 303-245-4693. *Toll-free phone:* 800-772-6951. *Fax:* 303-546-3536. *E-mail:* kwills@naropa.edu.

National American University

Centennial, Colorado

http://www.national.edu/

CONTACT

National American University, 8242 South University Boulevard, Suite 100, Centennial, CO 80122. *Toll-free phone:* 877-628-5211.

National American University

Colorado Springs, Colorado

http://www.national.edu/

CONTACT

National American University, 1079 Space Center Drive, Suite 140, Colorado Springs, CO 80915. *Toll-free phone:* 855-369-9397.

National American University

Colorado Springs, Colorado

http://www.national.edu/

CONTACT

Director of Admissions, National American University, 1915 Jamboree Drive, Suite 185, Colorado Springs, CO 80920. *Phone:* 719-590-8300. *Toll-free phone:* 855-369-9397. *E-mail:* csadmissions@national.edu.

Nazarene Bible College

Colorado Springs, Colorado

http://www.nbc.edu/

- **Independent** 4-year, founded 1967, affiliated with Church of the Nazarene
- **Urban** 64-acre campus with easy access to Colorado Springs
- **Coed** 769 undergraduate students, 12% full-time, 39% women, 61% men
- **Noncompetitive** entrance level, 14% of applicants were admitted

UNDERGRAD STUDENTS

89 full-time, 680 part-time. Students come from 48 states and territories; 14 other countries; 89% are from out of state; 7% Black or African American, non-Hispanic/Latino; 9% Hispanic/Latino; 2% Asian, non-Hispanic/Latino; 0.5% Native Hawaiian or other Pacific Islander, non-Hispanic/Latino; 0.9% American Indian or Alaska Native, non-Hispanic/Latino; 3% Two or more races, non-Hispanic/Latino; 12% transferred in.

Freshmen:
Admission: 129 applied, 18 admitted, 18 enrolled.

FACULTY

Total: 148, 6% full-time, 53% with terminal degrees.
Student/faculty ratio: 6:1.

ACADEMICS

Calendar: trimesters. *Degrees:* certificates, diplomas, associate, and bachelor's.

Special study options: academic remediation for entering students, accelerated degree program, advanced placement credit, distance learning, double majors, independent study, internships, part-time degree program, summer session for credit.

Computers: 10 computers/terminals are available on campus for general student use. Students can access the following: free student e-mail accounts, online (class) grades, online (class) schedules. Campuswide network is available. Wireless service is available via entire campus.

Library: Trimble Library. *Books:* 47,287 (physical), 1,502 (digital/electronic); *Serial titles:* 285 (physical), 3,145 (digital/electronic); *Databases:* 14. Weekly public service hours: 51.

STUDENT LIFE

Housing options: college housing not available.

Campus security: 24-hour security personnel on campus.

Student services: personal/psychological counseling.

COSTS & FINANCIAL AID

Costs (2017–18) ***Tuition:*** $10,360 full-time, $370 per credit hour part-time. Full-time tuition and fees vary according to program and reciprocity agreements. Part-time tuition and fees vary according to program and reciprocity agreements. ***Required fees:*** $840 full-time, $30 per credit hour part-time. ***Payment plan:*** installment. ***Waivers:*** employees or children of employees.

Financial Aid Of all full-time matriculated undergraduates who enrolled in 2014, 122 applied for aid, 89 were judged to have need, 84 had their need fully met. ***Average percent of need met:*** 96. ***Average financial aid package:*** $7695. ***Average need-based loan:*** $3337. ***Average need-based gift aid:*** $4527. ***Average indebtedness upon graduation:*** $33,289.

APPLYING

Options: electronic application, deferred entrance.

Required: official transcripts from all prior colleges. ***Required for some:*** high school transcript.

Application deadlines: rolling (freshmen), rolling (transfers).

Notification: continuous (freshmen), continuous (transfers).

CONTACT

Scott McConnaughey, Director of Admissions/Admissions Counselor, Nazarene Bible College, 1111 Academy Park Loop, Colorado Springs, CO 80910-3704. *Phone:* 719-884-5062. *Toll-free phone:* 800-873-3873. *Fax:* 719-884-5039. *E-mail:* semcconnaughey@nbc.edu.

Pima Medical Institute

Denver, Colorado

http://www.pmi.edu/

CONTACT

Admissions Office, Pima Medical Institute, 7475 Dakin Street, Denver, CO 80221. *Phone:* 303-426-1800. *Toll-free phone:* 800-477-PIMA.

Platt College

Aurora, Colorado

http://www.plattcolorado.edu/

CONTACT

Admissions Office, Platt College, 3100 South Parker Road, Suite 200, Aurora, CO 80014-3141. *Phone:* 303-369-5151.

Pueblo Community College

Pueblo, Colorado

http://www.pueblocc.edu/

- **State-supported** primarily 2-year, founded 1933, part of Colorado Community College System
- **Urban** 35-acre campus
- **Endowment** $1.1 million
- **Coed** 5,562 undergraduate students, 65% full-time, 59% women, 41% men
- **Noncompetitive** entrance level, 100% of applicants were admitted

UNDERGRAD STUDENTS

3,634 full-time, 1,928 part-time. Students come from 20 states and territories; 1 other country; 1% are from out of state; 3% Black or African American, non-Hispanic/Latino; 15% Hispanic/Latino; 0.8% Asian, non-Hispanic/Latino; 0.1% Native Hawaiian or other Pacific Islander, non-Hispanic/Latino; 2% American Indian or Alaska Native, non-Hispanic/Latino; 19% Two or more races, non-Hispanic/Latino; 0.5% Race/ethnicity unknown; 0.6% international; 6% transferred in.

Freshmen:
Admission: 1,685 applied, 1,685 admitted, 1,387 enrolled.
Retention: 55% of full-time freshmen returned.

FACULTY
Total: 427, 26% full-time.
Student/faculty ratio: 16:1.

ACADEMICS
Calendar: semesters. *Degrees:* certificates, associate, and bachelor's.
Special study options: academic remediation for entering students, accelerated degree program, advanced placement credit, cooperative education, distance learning, double majors, English as a second language, honors programs, independent study, internships, part-time degree program, services for LD students, summer session for credit.
Computers: 1,180 computers/terminals are available on campus for general student use. Students can access the following: campus intranet, computer help desk, free student e-mail accounts, online (class) grades, online (class) registration, online (class) schedules. Campuswide network is available. Wireless service is available via classrooms, computer centers, computer labs, learning centers, libraries, student centers.
Library: PCC Library. *Books:* 19,162 (physical), 33,004 (digital/electronic); *Serial titles:* 695 (physical), 7,707 (digital/electronic); *Databases:* 12. Weekly public service hours: 60.

STUDENT LIFE
Housing options: college housing not available.
Activities and organizations: drama/theater group, choral group, Phi Theta Kappa, Welding Club, Culinary Arts Club, Performing Arts Club, Art Club.
Campus security: 24-hour emergency response devices and patrols, late-night transport/escort service.
Student services: health clinic, personal/psychological counseling.

COSTS & FINANCIAL AID
Costs (2017–18) ***Tuition:*** state resident $6216 full-time, $164 per credit hour part-time; nonresident $14,585 full-time, $569 per credit hour part-time. Full-time tuition and fees vary according to degree level, location, program, and reciprocity agreements. Part-time tuition and fees vary according to degree level, location, program, and reciprocity agreements. ***Required fees:*** $905 full-time, $20 per credit hour part-time, $57 per term part-time. ***Payment plans:*** installment, deferred payment. ***Waivers:*** employees or children of employees.
Financial Aid Of all full-time matriculated undergraduates who enrolled in 2013, 84 Federal Work-Study jobs (averaging $3500). 254 state and other part-time jobs (averaging $3500). ***Average financial aid package:*** $5647.

APPLYING
Options: electronic application, early admission, deferred entrance.
Application deadlines: rolling (freshmen), rolling (transfers).
Notification: continuous until 9/1 (freshmen), continuous until 9/1 (transfers).

CONTACT
Mrs. Barbara Benedict, Director of Admissions and Records, Pueblo Community College, 900 West Orman Avenue, Pueblo, CO 81004.
Phone: 719-549-3039. *Toll-free phone:* 888-642-6017.
Fax: 719-549-3012. *E-mail:* barbara.benedict@pueblocc.edu.

Regis University

Denver, Colorado

http://www.regis.edu/

- **Independent Roman Catholic (Jesuit)** comprehensive, founded 1877
- **Suburban** 90-acre campus with easy access to Denver
- **Endowment** $55.8 million
- **Coed** 4,499 undergraduate students, 54% full-time, 61% women, 39% men
- **Moderately difficult** entrance level, 66% of applicants were admitted

UNDERGRAD STUDENTS
2,419 full-time, 2,080 part-time. Students come from 46 states and territories; 3 other countries; 46% are from out of state; 5% Black or African American, non-Hispanic/Latino; 19% Hispanic/Latino; 5% Asian, non-Hispanic/Latino; 0.1% Native Hawaiian or other Pacific Islander, non-Hispanic/Latino; 0.6% American Indian or Alaska Native, non-Hispanic/Latino; 4% Two or more races, non-Hispanic/Latino; 7% Race/ethnicity unknown; 1% international; 9% transferred in.

Freshmen:
Admission: 5,493 applied, 3,609 admitted, 545 enrolled. ***Average high school GPA:*** 3.52. ***Test scores:*** SAT critical reading scores over 500: 68%; SAT math scores over 500: 65%; SAT writing scores over 500: 66%; ACT scores over 18: 98%; SAT critical reading scores over 600: 22%; SAT math scores over 600: 23%; SAT writing scores over 600: 16%; ACT scores over 24: 55%; SAT critical reading scores over 700: 3%; SAT math scores over 700: 2%; SAT writing scores over 700: 5%; ACT scores over 30: 10%.
Retention: 79% of full-time freshmen returned.

FACULTY
Total: 803, 34% full-time, 52% with terminal degrees.
Student/faculty ratio: 14:1.

ACADEMICS
Calendar: semesters. *Degrees:* certificates, bachelor's, master's, doctoral, post-master's, and postbachelor's certificates.
Special study options: academic remediation for entering students, accelerated degree program, adult/continuing education programs, advanced placement credit, cooperative education, distance learning, double majors, external degree program, freshman honors college, honors programs, independent study, internships, off-campus study, part-time degree program, services for LD students, student-designed majors, study abroad, summer session for credit. ***ROTC:*** Army (c), Navy (c), Air Force (c).
Unusual degree programs: 3-2 engineering with Washington University in St. Louis.
Computers: 600 computers/terminals and 24 ports are available on campus for general student use. Students can access the following: campus intranet, computer help desk, free student e-mail accounts, online (class) grades, online (class) registration, online (class) schedules. Campuswide network is available. 100% of college-owned or -operated housing units are wired for high-speed Internet access. Wireless service is available via entire campus.
Library: Dayton Memorial Library. *Books:* 393,000 (physical), 118,000 (digital/electronic); *Databases:* 248. Weekly public service hours: 101; students can reserve study rooms.

STUDENT LIFE
Housing options: on-campus residence required through sophomore year; coed, special housing for students with disabilities. Campus housing is university owned. Freshman applicants given priority for college housing.
Activities and organizations: drama/theater group, student-run newspaper, radio station, choral group.
Athletics Member NCAA. All Division II. ***Intercollegiate sports:*** baseball M(s), basketball M(s)/W(s), cross-country running M(s)/W(s), golf M(s), lacrosse W(s), soccer M(s)/W(s), softball W(s), volleyball W(s). ***Intramural sports:*** basketball M/W, lacrosse M, rugby M/W, soccer M/W, tennis M/W, ultimate Frisbee M/W, volleyball M/W.
Campus security: 24-hour emergency response devices and patrols, student patrols, late-night transport/escort service, controlled dormitory access.
Student services: health clinic, personal/psychological counseling.

COSTS & FINANCIAL AID
Costs (2017–18) ***Comprehensive fee:*** $45,095 includes full-time tuition ($34,100), mandatory fees ($575), and room and board ($10,420). Full-time tuition and fees vary according to class time, course level, course load, degree level, location, program, reciprocity agreements, and student level. Part-time tuition: $1066 per credit hour. Part-time tuition and fees vary according to class time, course level, course load, degree level, location, program, reciprocity agreements, and student level. ***College room only:*** $5600. Room and board charges vary according to board plan and housing facility. ***Payment plans:*** installment, deferred payment. ***Waivers:*** employees or children of employees.
Financial Aid Of all full-time matriculated undergraduates who enrolled in 2015, 1,871 applied for aid, 1,661 were judged to have need, 261 had their need fully met. 366 Federal Work-Study jobs (averaging $1726). 508 state and other part-time jobs (averaging $1785). In 2015, 519 non-need-based awards were made. ***Average percent of need met:*** 76. ***Average financial aid package:*** $27,284. ***Average need-based loan:*** $4437. ***Average need-based gift aid:*** $17,582. ***Average non-need-based aid:*** $12,827. ***Average indebtedness upon graduation:*** $28,153.

APPLYING
Standardized Tests *Required:* SAT or ACT (for admission).
Options: electronic application, deferred entrance.
Required: essay or personal statement, high school transcript. ***Required for some:*** 1 letter of recommendation, interview.
Application deadlines: 4/15 (freshmen), 8/1 (transfers).
Notification: continuous (freshmen), continuous (transfers).

CONTACT
Ms. Sarah Engel, Director of Admissions, Regis University, 3333 Regis Boulevard, Mail Code A-12, Denver, CO 80221. *Phone:* 303-458-4938. *Toll-free phone:* 800-388-2366 Ext. 4900. *Fax:* 303-964-5534. *E-mail:* sengel@regis.edu.

Rocky Mountain College of Art + Design

Lakewood, Colorado

http://www.rmcad.edu/

- **Proprietary** comprehensive, founded 1963
- **Urban** 23-acre campus with easy access to Denver
- **Coed**
- **Moderately difficult** entrance level

FACULTY
Student/faculty ratio: 9:1.

ACADEMICS
Calendar: semesters. *Degrees:* certificates, bachelor's, and master's.
Library: Rocky Mountain College of Art and Design Library plus 1 other. *Books:* 15,325 (physical), 189,000 (digital/electronic); *Serial titles:* 1,842 (physical), 3,293 (digital/electronic); *Databases:* 36. Weekly public service hours: 76; students can reserve study rooms.

STUDENT LIFE
Housing options: college housing not available.
Activities and organizations: The American Institute of Graphic Arts (AIGA), The American Society of Interior Designers (ASID), Gay-Straight Alliance, Game Art + Design Club, Animation Club.
Campus security: 24-hour emergency response devices, late-night transport/escort service, patrols by trained security personnel during campus hours.
Student services: personal/psychological counseling.

COSTS & FINANCIAL AID
Costs (2016–17) ***Tuition:*** $15,870 full-time, $594 per credit part-time. Full-time tuition and fees vary according to course load, degree level, and location. Part-time tuition and fees vary according to course load, degree level, and location. ***Required fees:*** $525 full-time.
Financial Aid ***Average indebtedness upon graduation:*** $29,156.

APPLYING
Options: electronic application.
Application fee: $50.
Required: essay or personal statement, high school transcript, minimum 2.0 GPA, interview, portfolio.

CONTACT
Mr. Marc Abraham, Director of Admissions, Rocky Mountain College of Art + Design, 1600 Pierce Street, Lakewood, CO 80214. *Phone:* 321-256-9223. *Toll-free phone:* 800-888-ARTS. *E-mail:* mabraham@rmcad.edu.

United States Air Force Academy

Colorado Springs, Colorado

http://www.usafa.edu/

- **Federally supported** 4-year, founded 1954
- **Suburban** 18,000-acre campus with easy access to Colorado Springs, Denver
- **Endowment** $106.7 million
- **Coed** 4,237 undergraduate students, 100% full-time, 25% women, 75% men
- **Most difficult** entrance level, 15% of applicants were admitted

UNDERGRAD STUDENTS
4,237 full-time. Students come from 54 states and territories; 23 other countries; 88% are from out of state; 6% Black or African American, non-Hispanic/Latino; 11% Hispanic/Latino; 5% Asian, non-Hispanic/Latino; 0.7% Native Hawaiian or other Pacific Islander, non-Hispanic/Latino; 0.3% American Indian or Alaska Native, non-Hispanic/Latino; 7% Two or more races, non-Hispanic/Latino; 7% Race/ethnicity unknown; 1% international; 100% live on campus.

Freshmen:
Admission: 9,894 applied, 1,492 admitted, 1,115 enrolled. ***Average high school GPA:*** 3.87. ***Test scores:*** SAT critical reading scores over 500: 99%; SAT math scores over 500: 100%; ACT scores over 18: 100%; SAT critical reading scores over 600: 77%; SAT math scores over 600: 90%; ACT scores over 24: 99%; SAT critical reading scores over 700: 23%; SAT math scores over 700: 31%; ACT scores over 30: 59%.
Retention: 88% of full-time freshmen returned.

FACULTY
Total: 502, 100% full-time, 60% with terminal degrees.
Student/faculty ratio: 9:1.

ACADEMICS
Calendar: semesters. *Degree:* bachelor's.
Special study options: academic remediation for entering students, advanced placement credit, English as a second language, honors programs, independent study, internships, off-campus study, study abroad, summer session for credit.
Computers: 5,000 ports are available on campus for general student use. Students can access the following: campus intranet, computer help desk, free student e-mail accounts, online (class) grades, online (class) registration, online (class) schedules. Campuswide network is available. 100% of college-owned or -operated housing units are wired for high-speed Internet access. Wireless service is available via entire campus.
Library: McDermott Library plus 1 other. *Books:* 463,745 (physical), 74,225 (digital/electronic); *Serial titles:* 229 (physical), 325 (digital/electronic); *Databases:* 36. Weekly public service hours: 83.

STUDENT LIFE
Housing options: on-campus residence required through senior year; coed. Campus housing is university owned. Freshman campus housing is guaranteed.
Activities and organizations: drama/theater group, student-run radio station, choral group, marching band, Recreational Ski Club, Men's and Women's Rugby Club, Cycling Club, Aviation Club, Drum and Bugle Corps.
Athletics Member NCAA. All Division I. ***Intercollegiate sports:*** archery M(c)/W(c), baseball M, basketball M/W, cheerleading M/W, cross-country running M/W, equestrian sports M(c)/W(c), fencing M/W, football M, golf M/W(c), gymnastics M/W, ice hockey M, lacrosse M/W(c), racquetball M(c)/W(c), riflery M/W, rock climbing M(c)/W(c), skiing (cross-country) M(c)/W(c), skiing (downhill) M(c)/W(c), soccer M/W, softball W(c), swimming and diving M/W, tennis M/W, track and field M/W, triathlon M(c)/W(c), ultimate Frisbee M(c)/W(c), volleyball M(c)/W, water polo M/W(c), weight lifting M(c)/W(c), wrestling M. ***Intramural sports:*** basketball M/W, cross-country running M/W, racquetball M/W, rugby M(c)/W(c), soccer M/W, softball M/W, ultimate Frisbee M/W, volleyball M/W, wrestling M.
Campus security: 24-hour emergency response devices and patrols, late-night transport/escort service, controlled dormitory access, self-defense education, well-lit campus, Charge of Quarters.
Student services: health clinic, personal/psychological counseling, women's center, legal services.

COSTS
Costs (2016–17) ***Comprehensive fee:*** Tuition, room and board, and medical and dental care are provided by the US government. Each cadet receives a salary from which to pay for uniforms, supplies, and personal expenses.

APPLYING
Standardized Tests *Required:* SAT or ACT (for admission).
Options: electronic application.

Required: essay or personal statement, high school transcript, 1 letter of recommendation, interview, authorized nomination, Candidate Fitness Assessment, medical examination.

Application deadlines: 12/31 (freshmen), 12/31 (transfers).

Notification: continuous until 10/15 (freshmen), continuous until 10/15 (transfers).

CONTACT

Dr. Phillip Prosseda, CHIEF, Selections Division, United States Air Force Academy, HQ USAFA/RRS, 2304 Cadet Drive, Suite 2400, USAF Academy, CO 80840-5025. *Phone:* 800-443-9266. *Toll-free phone:* 800-443-9266. *Fax:* 719-333-3012.

University of Colorado Boulder

Boulder, Colorado

http://www.colorado.edu/

- **State-supported** university, founded 1876, part of University of Colorado System
- **Suburban** 600-acre campus with easy access to Denver
- **Endowment** $514.0 million
- **Coed** 27,846 undergraduate students, 92% full-time, 44% women, 56% men
- **Moderately difficult** entrance level, 77% of applicants were admitted

UNDERGRAD STUDENTS

25,727 full-time, 2,119 part-time. Students come from 52 states and territories; 122 other countries; 41% are from out of state; 2% Black or African American, non-Hispanic/Latino; 11% Hispanic/Latino; 5% Asian, non-Hispanic/Latino; 0.1% Native Hawaiian or other Pacific Islander, non-Hispanic/Latino; 0.2% American Indian or Alaska Native, non-Hispanic/Latino; 5% Two or more races, non-Hispanic/Latino; 0.7% Race/ethnicity unknown; 7% international; 4% transferred in; 29% live on campus.

Freshmen:

Admission: 34,047 applied, 26,087 admitted, 6,439 enrolled. ***Average high school GPA:*** 3.65. ***Test scores:*** SAT critical reading scores over 500: 84%; SAT math scores over 500: 92%; ACT scores over 18: 99%; SAT critical reading scores over 600: 45%; SAT math scores over 600: 56%; ACT scores over 24: 83%; SAT critical reading scores over 700: 11%; SAT math scores over 700: 14%; ACT scores over 30: 29%.

Retention: 87% of full-time freshmen returned.

FACULTY

Total: 2,054, 73% full-time, 78% with terminal degrees.

Student/faculty ratio: 17:1.

ACADEMICS

Calendar: semesters. *Degrees:* bachelor's, master's, doctoral, and post-master's certificates.

Special study options: accelerated degree program, adult/continuing education programs, advanced placement credit, cooperative education, distance learning, double majors, English as a second language, freshman honors college, honors programs, independent study, internships, off-campus study, part-time degree program, services for LD students, student-designed majors, study abroad, summer session for credit. ***ROTC:*** Army (b), Navy (b), Air Force (b).

Computers: 1,804 computers/terminals are available on campus for general student use. Students can access the following: campus intranet, computer help desk, free student e-mail accounts, online (class) grades, online (class) registration, online (class) schedules, training, tutorials, workshops, seminars, standard and academic software, student government voting. Campuswide network is available. 100% of college-owned or -operated housing units are wired for high-speed Internet access. Wireless service is available via entire campus.

Library: Norlin Library plus 5 others. *Books:* 664,601 (physical), 984,952 (digital/electronic); *Databases:* 594. Students can reserve study rooms.

STUDENT LIFE

Housing options: on-campus residence required for freshman year; coed, special housing for students with disabilities. Campus housing is university owned and is provided by a third party. Freshman campus housing is guaranteed.

Activities and organizations: drama/theater group, student-run newspaper, radio station, choral group, marching band, Student Government, Environmental Center, Ski and Snowboard Club, AIESEC

(international leadership organization), Program Council, national fraternities, national sororities.

Athletics Member NCAA. All Division I except football (Division I-A). ***Intercollegiate sports:*** baseball M(c)/W(c), basketball M(s)/W(s), cheerleading M/W, crew M(c)/W(c), cross-country running M(s)/W(s), equestrian sports M(c)/W(c), fencing M(c)/W(c), field hockey M(c)/W(c), golf M(s)/W(s), ice hockey M(c)/W(c), lacrosse M(c)/W(s), racquetball M(c)/W(c), rugby M(c)/W(c), skiing (cross-country) M(s)/W(s), skiing (downhill) M(s)/W(s), soccer M(c)/W(s), softball W(c), swimming and diving M(c)/W(c), tennis M(c)/W(s), track and field M(s)/W(s), triathlon M(c)/W(c), ultimate Frisbee M(c)/W(c), volleyball M(c)/W(s), water polo M(c)/W(c), wrestling M(c)/W(c). ***Intramural sports:*** badminton M/W, basketball M/W, ice hockey M/W, soccer M/W, tennis M/W, ultimate Frisbee M/W, volleyball M/W, water polo M/W.

Campus security: 24-hour patrols, student patrols, late-night transport/escort service, controlled dormitory access, University police department, LifeLine Response app connecting to police dispatch center.

Student services: health clinic, personal/psychological counseling, women's center, legal services.

COSTS & FINANCIAL AID

Costs (2017–18) ***One-time required fee:*** $182. ***Tuition:*** state resident $9768 full-time; nonresident $32,346 full-time. Full-time tuition and fees vary according to program. Part-time tuition and fees vary according to course load and program. No tuition increase for student's term of enrollment. ***Required fees:*** $1763 full-time. ***Room and board:*** $13,590. Room and board charges vary according to board plan, housing facility, and location. ***Payment plan:*** deferred payment. ***Waivers:*** senior citizens and employees or children of employees.

Financial Aid Of all full-time matriculated undergraduates who enrolled in 2016, 12,537 applied for aid, 9,046 were judged to have need, 3,570 had their need fully met. 797 Federal Work-Study jobs (averaging $1768). 1,014 state and other part-time jobs (averaging $2327). In 2016, 6869 non-need-based awards were made. ***Average percent of need met:*** 81. ***Average financial aid package:*** $16,838. ***Average need-based loan:*** $6490. ***Average need-based gift aid:*** $11,026. ***Average non-need-based aid:*** $9205. ***Average indebtedness upon graduation:*** $27,405.

APPLYING

Standardized Tests *Required:* SAT or ACT (for admission).

Options: electronic application, early action, deferred entrance.

Application fee: $50.

Required: essay or personal statement, high school transcript, 1 letter of recommendation. ***Required for some:*** audition for music program. ***Recommended:*** minimum 3.0 GPA.

Application deadlines: 1/15 (freshmen), 3/1 (transfers), 11/15 (early action).

Notification: 4/1 (freshmen), continuous until 3/1 (transfers), 2/1 (early action).

CONTACT

Admissions Office, University of Colorado Boulder, Regent Administrative Center 125, 552 UCB, Boulder, CO 80309. *Phone:* 303-492-6301. *Fax:* 303-735-2501. *E-mail:* apply@colorado.edu.

See previous page for display ad and page 1550 for the College Close-Up.

University of Colorado Colorado Springs

Colorado Springs, Colorado

http://www.uccs.edu/

- **State-supported** university, founded 1965, part of University of Colorado System
- **Urban** 532-acre campus with easy access to Colorado Springs
- **Coed** 10,414 undergraduate students, 76% full-time, 52% women, 48% men
- **Moderately difficult** entrance level, 93% of applicants were admitted

UNDERGRAD STUDENTS

7,927 full-time, 2,487 part-time. Students come from 50 states and territories; 44 other countries; 12% are from out of state; 4% Black or African American, non-Hispanic/Latino; 17% Hispanic/Latino; 3% Asian, non-Hispanic/Latino; 0.3% Native Hawaiian or other Pacific Islander, non-Hispanic/Latino; 0.4% American Indian or Alaska Native, non-Hispanic/Latino; 7% Two or more races, non-Hispanic/Latino; 2% Race/ethnicity unknown; 1% international; 11% transferred in; 16% live on campus.

Freshmen:

Admission: 9,664 applied, 8,972 admitted, 2,085 enrolled. ***Average high school GPA:*** 3.36. ***Test scores:*** SAT critical reading scores over 500: 67%; SAT math scores over 500: 68%; ACT scores over 18: 93%; SAT critical reading scores over 600: 25%; SAT math scores over 600: 24%; ACT scores over 24: 45%; SAT critical reading scores over 700: 4%; SAT math scores over 700: 4%; ACT scores over 30: 6%.

Retention: 69% of full-time freshmen returned.

FACULTY

Total: 813.

Student/faculty ratio: 18:1.

ACADEMICS

Calendar: semesters. *Degrees:* bachelor's, master's, doctoral, post-master's, and postbachelor's certificates.

Special study options: accelerated degree program, advanced placement credit, cooperative education, distance learning, double majors, English as a second language, honors programs, independent study, internships, off-campus study, part-time degree program, services for LD students, student-designed majors, study abroad, summer session for credit. ***ROTC:*** Army (b).

Unusual degree programs: 3-2 business administration; engineering; nursing; chemistry, criminal justice.

Computers: Students can access the following: campus intranet, computer help desk, free student e-mail accounts, online (class) grades, online (class) registration, online (class) schedules, student portal, learning management system. Campuswide network is available. 100% of college-owned or -operated housing units are wired for high-speed Internet access. Wireless service is available via entire campus.

Library: Kraemer Family Library. Students can reserve study rooms.

STUDENT LIFE

Housing options: on-campus residence required for freshman year; coed. Campus housing is university owned. Freshman applicants given priority for college housing.

Activities and organizations: drama/theater group, student-run newspaper, radio and television station, choral group, Fans Initiating Growth Honor and Tradition (spirit club), Pi Beta Phi, Sustainability Club, Gamers (computing), El Circulo, national fraternities, national sororities.

Athletics Member NCAA. All Division II. ***Intercollegiate sports:*** baseball M(s), basketball M(s)/W(s), cross-country running M(s)/W(s), golf M(s)/W(s), lacrosse W(s), soccer M(s)/W(s), softball W(s), track and field M(s)/W(s), volleyball W(s).

Campus security: 24-hour emergency response devices and patrols, student patrols, late-night transport/escort service, controlled dormitory access, emergency text messaging, state-authorized campus police and public safety department.

Student services: health clinic, personal/psychological counseling.

COSTS & FINANCIAL AID

Costs (2016–17) ***One-time required fee:*** $140. ***Tuition:*** state resident $8280 full-time, $276 per credit hour part-time; nonresident $21,690 full-time, $723 per credit hour part-time. Full-time tuition and fees vary according to course load, degree level, location, program, reciprocity agreements, and student level. Part-time tuition and fees vary according to course load, degree level, location, program, reciprocity agreements, and student level. ***Required fees:*** $1583 full-time. ***Room and board:*** $9800. Room and board charges vary according to board plan, housing facility, and student level. ***Payment plan:*** installment. ***Waivers:*** employees or children of employees.

Financial Aid Of all full-time matriculated undergraduates who enrolled in 2015, 6,113 applied for aid, 4,682 were judged to have need, 137 had their need fully met. 205 Federal Work-Study jobs (averaging $2758). 306 state and other part-time jobs (averaging $3532). In 2015, 388 non-need-based awards were made. ***Average percent of need met:*** 44. ***Average financial aid package:*** $8749. ***Average need-based loan:*** $4252. ***Average need-based gift aid:*** $6497. ***Average non-need-based aid:*** $2135. ***Average indebtedness upon graduation:*** $22,228.

APPLYING
Standardized Tests *Required:* SAT or ACT (for admission).
Options: electronic application, deferred entrance.
Application fee: $50.
Required: high school transcript.
Application deadlines: rolling (freshmen), rolling (transfers).
Notification: continuous (freshmen), continuous (transfers).

CONTACT
Mr. Chris Beiswanger, Director of Student Recruitment and Admissions Counseling, University of Colorado Colorado Springs, 1420 Austin Bluffs Parkway, Colorado Springs, CO 80918. *Phone:* 719-255-3088. *Toll-free phone:* 800-990-8227 Ext. 3383. *E-mail:* cbeiswan@uccs.edu.

University of Colorado Denver
Denver, Colorado
http://www.ucdenver.edu/

- **State-supported** university, founded 1912, part of University of Colorado System
- **Urban** 171-acre campus with easy access to Denver, CO
- **Endowment** $428.7 million
- **Coed** 14,622 undergraduate students
- **Moderately difficult** entrance level, 61% of applicants were admitted

UNDERGRAD STUDENTS
Students come from 49 states and territories; 41 other countries; 9% are from out of state; 5% Black or African American, non-Hispanic/Latino; 20% Hispanic/Latino; 10% Asian, non-Hispanic/Latino; 0.1% Native Hawaiian or other Pacific Islander, non-Hispanic/Latino; 0.4% American Indian or Alaska Native, non-Hispanic/Latino; 5% Two or more races, non-Hispanic/Latino; 2% Race/ethnicity unknown; 8% international.

Freshmen:
Admission: 12,252 applied, 7,415 admitted. ***Average high school GPA:*** 3.4. ***Test scores:*** SAT critical reading scores over 500: 68%; SAT math scores over 500: 67%; ACT scores over 18: 95%; SAT critical reading scores over 600: 23%; SAT math scores over 600: 25%; ACT scores over 24: 45%; SAT critical reading scores over 700: 4%; SAT math scores over 700: 3%; ACT scores over 30: 7%.
Retention: 71% of full-time freshmen returned.

FACULTY
Total: 4,448, 85% full-time, 61% with terminal degrees.
Student/faculty ratio: 16:1.

ACADEMICS
Calendar: semesters. *Degrees:* bachelor's, master's, doctoral, post-master's, and postbachelor's certificates.
Special study options: accelerated degree program, advanced placement credit, cooperative education, distance learning, double majors, English as a second language, honors programs, independent study, internships, off-campus study, part-time degree program, services for LD students, student-designed majors, study abroad, summer session for credit. ***ROTC:*** Army (c), Air Force (c).
Unusual degree programs: 3-2 criminal justice.
Computers: 750 computers/terminals are available on campus for general student use. Students can access the following: campus intranet, computer help desk, free student e-mail accounts, online (class) grades, online (class) registration, online (class) schedules. Campuswide network is available. 100% of college-owned or -operated housing units are wired for high-speed Internet access. Wireless service is available via entire campus.
Library: Auraria Library plus 1 other. *Books:* 632,468 (physical), 716,415 (digital/electronic); *Serial titles:* 6,521 (physical), 89,954 (digital/electronic); *Databases:* 298. Weekly public service hours: 85; students can reserve study rooms.

STUDENT LIFE
Housing options: college housing not available.
Activities and organizations: drama/theater group, student-run newspaper, choral group, Veterans Student Organization (Service), Golden Key Honor Society (Academic), Minority Association for Pre-Health Students (Health), Future Doctors of Denver, Intercultural Club Beijing (Cultural and Social).
Athletics ***Intramural sports:*** basketball M(c)/W(c), cheerleading M(c)/W(c), cross-country running M(c)/W(c), golf M(c)/W(c), ice hockey M(c), lacrosse M(c)/W(c), soccer M(c)/W(c), tennis M(c)/W(c), ultimate Frisbee M(c)/W(c), volleyball W(c).
Campus security: 24-hour emergency response devices and patrols, student patrols, late-night transport/escort service.
Student services: health clinic, personal/psychological counseling, women's center.

COSTS & FINANCIAL AID
Costs (2017–18) ***Tuition:*** state resident $9420 full-time, $314 per credit hour part-time; nonresident $29,040 full-time, $968 per credit hour part-time. Full-time tuition and fees vary according to course level, course load, degree level, location, program, reciprocity agreements, and student level. Part-time tuition and fees vary according to course level, course load, degree level, location, program, reciprocity agreements, and student level. ***Required fees:*** $1299 full-time, $1299 per year part-time. ***Room and board:*** Room and board charges vary according to board plan. ***Payment plans:*** installment, deferred payment. ***Waivers:*** employees or children of employees.
Financial Aid Of all full-time matriculated undergraduates who enrolled in 2015, 4,707 applied for aid, 4,077 were judged to have need, 104 had their need fully met. 382 Federal Work-Study jobs (averaging $3614). 377 state and other part-time jobs (averaging $4358). In 2015, 405 non-need-based awards were made. ***Average percent of need met:*** 53. ***Average financial aid package:*** $9995. ***Average need-based loan:*** $3914. ***Average need-based gift aid:*** $7497. ***Average non-need-based aid:*** $2564. ***Average indebtedness upon graduation:*** $19,378.

APPLYING
Standardized Tests *Required:* SAT or ACT (for admission).
Options: electronic application, deferred entrance.
Application fee: $50.
Required: minimum 2.5 GPA. ***Required for some:*** minimum 3.0 GPA, audition, portfolio, entrance exam.
Application deadlines: 8/1 (freshmen), rolling (out-of-state freshmen), 8/1 (transfers).
Notification: continuous (freshmen), continuous (out-of-state freshmen), continuous (transfers).

CONTACT
Catherine Wilson, Office of Admissions, University of Colorado Denver, PO Box 173364, Campus Box 167, Denver, CO 80217. *Phone:* 303-315-2601. *E-mail:* admissions@ucdenver.edu.

University of Denver
Denver, Colorado
http://www.du.edu/

- **Independent** university, founded 1864
- **Urban** 125-acre campus with easy access to Denver
- **Endowment** $607.4 million
- **Coed** 5,754 undergraduate students, 95% full-time, 54% women, 46% men
- **Moderately difficult** entrance level, 53% of applicants were admitted

UNDERGRAD STUDENTS
5,491 full-time, 263 part-time. Students come from 55 states and territories; 59 other countries; 62% are from out of state; 2% Black or African American, non-Hispanic/Latino; 10% Hispanic/Latino; 4% Asian, non-Hispanic/Latino; 0.1% Native Hawaiian or other Pacific Islander, non-Hispanic/Latino; 0.3% American Indian or Alaska Native, non-Hispanic/Latino; 4% Two or more races, non-Hispanic/Latino; 2% Race/ethnicity unknown; 8% international; 2% transferred in; 45% live on campus.

Freshmen:
Admission: 20,322 applied, 10,867 admitted, 1,399 enrolled. ***Average high school GPA:*** 3.72. ***Test scores:*** SAT critical reading scores over 500: 89%; SAT math scores over 500: 93%; SAT writing scores over 500: 82%; ACT scores over 18: 100%; SAT critical reading scores over 600: 55%; SAT math scores over 600: 58%; SAT writing scores over 600: 36%; ACT

scores over 24: 90%; SAT critical reading scores over 700: 13%; SAT math scores over 700: 9%; SAT writing scores over 700: 4%; ACT scores over 30: 37%.

Retention: 87% of full-time freshmen returned.

FACULTY
Total: 1,276, 57% full-time, 61% with terminal degrees.

Student/faculty ratio: 11:1.

ACADEMICS
Calendar: quarters semesters for law school. *Degrees:* certificates, bachelor's, master's, doctoral, post-master's, and postbachelor's certificates.

Special study options: accelerated degree program, adult/continuing education programs, advanced placement credit, cooperative education, distance learning, double majors, English as a second language, freshman honors college, honors programs, independent study, internships, off-campus study, part-time degree program, services for LD students, student-designed majors, study abroad, summer session for credit. ***ROTC:*** Army (c), Air Force (c).

Unusual degree programs: 3-2 business administration; engineering; social work; art history, public policy, accounting, international studies, education, environmental science, geography.

Computers: 150 computers/terminals and 36,000 ports are available on campus for general student use. Students can access the following: campus intranet, computer help desk, free student e-mail accounts, online (class) grades, online (class) registration, online (class) schedules. Campuswide network is available. 95% of college-owned or -operated housing units are wired for high-speed Internet access. Wireless service is available via entire campus.

Library: Anderson Academic Commons plus 1 other. *Books:* 1.7 million (physical), 2.3 million (digital/electronic); *Serial titles:* 553,655 (physical), 127,847 (digital/electronic); *Databases:* 1,273. Weekly public service hours: 145; study areas open 24 hours, 5-7 days a week; students can reserve study rooms.

STUDENT LIFE
Housing options: on-campus residence required through sophomore year; coed, cooperative. Campus housing is university owned. Freshman campus housing is guaranteed.

Activities and organizations: drama/theater group, student-run newspaper, radio station, choral group, marching band, Club Sports Council, Alpine Club, DU Programs Board, Greek Life Council, Residence Hall Association, national fraternities, national sororities.

Athletics Member NCAA. All Division I. ***Intercollegiate sports:*** baseball M(c), basketball M(s)/W(s), cross-country running M(c)/W(c), equestrian sports M(c)/W(c), golf M(s)/W(s), gymnastics W(s), ice hockey M(s)/W(c), lacrosse M(s)/W(s), racquetball M(c)/W(c), skiing (cross-country) M(s)/W(s), skiing (downhill) M(s)/W(s), soccer M(s)/W(s), softball W(c), swimming and diving M(s)/W(s), tennis M(s)/W(s), volleyball W(s), water polo M(c)/W(c). ***Intramural sports:*** basketball M/W, field hockey M(c)/W(c), football M/W, golf M(c)/W(c), gymnastics W(c), ice hockey M(c)/W(c), lacrosse M(c)/W(c), racquetball M(c)/W(c), rock climbing M(c)/W(c), rowing M(c), rugby M(c)/W(c), skiing (downhill) M(c)/W(c), soccer M(c)/W(c), softball M/W, swimming and diving M(c)/W(c), table tennis M/W, tennis M(c)/W(c), ultimate Frisbee M(c)/W(c), volleyball M(c)/W(c).

Campus security: 24-hour emergency response devices and patrols, late-night transport/escort service, controlled dormitory access, 24-hour locked residence hall entrances.

Student services: health clinic, personal/psychological counseling, women's center.

COSTS & FINANCIAL AID
Costs (2017–18) ***Comprehensive fee:*** $61,281 includes full-time tuition ($47,520), mandatory fees ($1149), and room and board ($12,612). Full-time tuition and fees vary according to course load and program. Part-time tuition: $1320 per credit hour. Part-time tuition and fees vary according to course load and program. ***College room only:*** $7806. Room and board charges vary according to board plan and housing facility. ***Payment plans:*** installment, deferred payment. ***Waivers:*** senior citizens and employees or children of employees.

Financial Aid Of all full-time matriculated undergraduates who enrolled in 2016, 2,923 applied for aid, 2,220 were judged to have need, 788 had their need fully met. 398 Federal Work-Study jobs (averaging $2929). 181 state and other part-time jobs (averaging $2920). In 2016, 2202 non-need-based awards were made. ***Average percent of need met:*** 84. ***Average financial aid package:*** $37,109. ***Average need-based loan:*** $4260. ***Average need-based gift aid:*** $30,824. ***Average non-need-based aid:*** $16,702. ***Average indebtedness upon graduation:*** $31,077.

APPLYING

Standardized Tests *Required:* SAT or ACT (for admission).

Options: electronic application, early admission, early decision, early action, deferred entrance.

Application fee: $65.

Required: essay or personal statement, high school transcript, 1 letter of recommendation. ***Recommended:*** 2 letters of recommendation, interview.

Application deadlines: 1/15 (freshmen), rolling (transfers), 11/1 (early action).

Notification: 3/15 (freshmen), continuous (transfers), 1/15 (early action).

CONTACT

Mr. Todd R. Rinehart, Associate Vice Chancellor for Enrollment, University of Denver, 2197 South University Boulevard, Denver, CO 80208. *Phone:* 303-871-3125. *Toll-free phone:* 800-525-9495. *Fax:* 303-871-3301. *E-mail:* admission@du.edu.

See previous page for display ad and page 1552 for the College Close-Up.

University of Northern Colorado

Greeley, Colorado

http://www.unco.edu/

- **State-supported** university, founded 1890
- **Suburban** 243-acre campus with easy access to Denver
- **Endowment** $76.9 million
- **Coed** 9,503 undergraduate students, 88% full-time, 64% women, 36% men
- **Moderately difficult** entrance level, 90% of applicants were admitted

UNDERGRAD STUDENTS

8,331 full-time, 1,172 part-time. Students come from 50 states and territories; 38 other countries; 15% are from out of state; 4% Black or African American, non-Hispanic/Latino; 19% Hispanic/Latino; 2% Asian, non-Hispanic/Latino; 0.2% Native Hawaiian or other Pacific Islander, non-Hispanic/Latino; 0.4% American Indian or Alaska Native, non-Hispanic/Latino; 4% Two or more races, non-Hispanic/Latino; 11% Race/ethnicity unknown; 2% international; 8% transferred in; 37% live on campus.

Freshmen:

Admission: 6,784 applied, 6,124 admitted, 2,079 enrolled. ***Average high school GPA:*** 3.33. ***Test scores:*** SAT critical reading scores over 500: 58%; SAT math scores over 500: 61%; ACT scores over 18: 90%; SAT critical reading scores over 600: 22%; SAT math scores over 600: 15%; ACT scores over 24: 36%; SAT critical reading scores over 700: 3%; SAT math scores over 700: 1%; ACT scores over 30: 5%.

Retention: 70% of full-time freshmen returned.

FACULTY

Total: 744, 66% full-time.

Student/faculty ratio: 18:1.

ACADEMICS

Calendar: semesters. *Degrees:* bachelor's, master's, and doctoral.

Special study options: academic remediation for entering students, accelerated degree program, adult/continuing education programs, advanced placement credit, cooperative education, distance learning, double majors, English as a second language, external degree program, honors programs, independent study, internships, off-campus study, part-time degree program, services for LD students, student-designed majors, study abroad, summer session for credit. ***ROTC:*** Army (b), Air Force (b).

Computers: 1,723 computers/terminals and 825 ports are available on campus for general student use. Students can access the following: computer help desk, free student e-mail accounts, online (class) grades, online (class) registration, online (class) schedules. Campuswide network is available. 100% of college-owned or -operated housing units are wired for high-speed Internet access. Wireless service is available via entire campus.

Library: James A. Michener Library plus 2 others. *Books:* 1.3 million (physical), 170,533 (digital/electronic); *Serial titles:* 19,826 (physical), 65,044 (digital/electronic); *Databases:* 199. Weekly public service hours: 97; students can reserve study rooms.

STUDENT LIFE

Housing options: on-campus residence required for freshman year; coed, women-only, special housing for students with disabilities. Campus housing is university owned. Freshman campus housing is guaranteed.

Activities and organizations: drama/theater group, student-run newspaper, radio station, choral group, marching band, Fraternities and Sororities, Club Sports, Campus Religious/Spiritual Organizations, Academic Clubs, Services Clubs, national fraternities, national sororities.

Athletics Member NCAA. All Division I. ***Intercollegiate sports:*** baseball M(s), basketball M(s)/W(s), cross-country running M(s)/W(s), football M(s), golf M(s)/W(s), soccer W(s), softball W(s), swimming and diving W(s), tennis M(s)/W(s), track and field M(s)/W(s), volleyball W(s), wrestling M(s). ***Intramural sports:*** badminton M(c)/W(c), baseball M(c), cross-country running M(c)/W(c), fencing M(c)/W(c), golf M(c)/W(c), ice hockey M(c), lacrosse M(c)/W(c), rock climbing M(c)/W(c), rugby M(c)/W(c), soccer M/W, softball W, swimming and diving M(c)/W(c), tennis M(c)/W(c), volleyball W, wrestling M.

Campus security: 24-hour emergency response devices and patrols, student patrols, late-night transport/escort service, controlled dormitory access.

Student services: health clinic, personal/psychological counseling, women's center, legal services.

COSTS & FINANCIAL AID

Costs (2017–18) ***One-time required fee:*** $250. ***Tuition:*** state resident $6906 full-time, $275 per credit hour part-time; nonresident $18,492 full-time, $736 per credit hour part-time. Full-time tuition and fees vary according to location and program. Part-time tuition and fees vary according to location and program. ***Required fees:*** $1982 full-time, $92 per credit hour part-time. ***Room and board:*** $10,770; room only: $5100. Room and board charges vary according to board plan and housing facility. ***Payment plan:*** installment. ***Waivers:*** employees or children of employees.

Financial Aid Of all full-time matriculated undergraduates who enrolled in 2015, 6,570 applied for aid, 5,008 were judged to have need, 1,578 had their need fully met. 197 Federal Work-Study jobs (averaging $2206). 579 state and other part-time jobs (averaging $2589). In 2015, 1049 non-need-based awards were made. ***Average percent of need met:*** 75. ***Average financial aid package:*** $10,831. ***Average need-based loan:*** $3938. ***Average need-based gift aid:*** $7102. ***Average non-need-based aid:*** $5930. ***Average indebtedness upon graduation:*** $27,393.

APPLYING

Standardized Tests *Required:* SAT or ACT (for admission).

Options: electronic application, deferred entrance.

Application fee: $45.

Required: high school transcript. ***Required for some:*** essay or personal statement.

Application deadlines: 8/1 (freshmen), 8/1 (transfers).

Notification: continuous (freshmen), continuous (transfers).

CONTACT

Sean Broghammer, Director of Admissions, University of Northern Colorado, Campus Box 10, Carter Hall 3006, Greeley, CO 80639. *Phone:* 970-351-2881. *Toll-free phone:* 888-700-4UNC. *Fax:* 970-351-2984. *E-mail:* admissions@unco.edu.

University of Phoenix–Colorado Campus

Lone Tree, Colorado

http://www.phoenix.edu/

CONTACT

Marc Booker, Sr. Director, Office of Admissions and Evaluation, University of Phoenix–Colorado Campus, 4035 South Riverpoint Parkway, Mail Stop CF-L101, Phoenix, AZ 85040. *Phone:* 602-557-4609. *Toll-free phone:* 866-766-0766. *Fax:* 480-643-1156.

University of Phoenix–Colorado Springs Downtown Campus

Colorado Springs, Colorado

http://www.phoenix.edu/

CONTACT

Marc Booker, Sr. Director, Office of Admissions and Evaluation, University of Phoenix–Colorado Springs Downtown Campus, 4035 South Riverpoint Parkway, Mail Stop CF-L101, Phoenix, AZ 85040. *Phone:* 602-557-4609. *Toll-free phone:* 866-766-0766. *Fax:* 480-643-1156.

Western State Colorado University

Gunnison, Colorado

http://www.western.edu/

- **State-supported** comprehensive, founded 1901
- **Rural** 381-acre campus
- **Coed** 2,495 undergraduate students, 78% full-time, 42% women, 58% men
- **Moderately difficult** entrance level, 92% of applicants were admitted

UNDERGRAD STUDENTS

1,939 full-time, 556 part-time. Students come from 50 states and territories; 8 other countries; 30% are from out of state; 3% Black or African American, non-Hispanic/Latino; 11% Hispanic/Latino; 0.7% Asian, non-Hispanic/Latino; 0.4% Native Hawaiian or other Pacific Islander, non-Hispanic/Latino; 0.7% American Indian or Alaska Native, non-Hispanic/Latino; 4% Two or more races, non-Hispanic/Latino; 7% Race/ethnicity unknown; 0.4% international; 7% transferred in; 45% live on campus.

Freshmen:

Admission: 2,191 applied, 2,013 admitted, 469 enrolled. ***Average high school GPA:*** 3.03. ***Test scores:*** SAT critical reading scores over 500: 57%; SAT math scores over 500: 47%; ACT scores over 18: 87%; SAT critical reading scores over 600: 14%; SAT math scores over 600: 16%; ACT scores over 24: 34%; SAT critical reading scores over 700: 3%; SAT math scores over 700: 2%; ACT scores over 30: 5%.

Retention: 69% of full-time freshmen returned.

FACULTY

Total: 166, 70% full-time, 70% with terminal degrees.

Student/faculty ratio: 19:1.

ACADEMICS

Calendar: semesters. *Degrees:* bachelor's, master's, and postbachelor's certificates.

Special study options: academic remediation for entering students, adult/continuing education programs, advanced placement credit, double majors, honors programs, independent study, internships, off-campus study, part-time degree program, services for LD students, study abroad, summer session for credit.

Computers: 181 computers/terminals and 600 ports are available on campus for general student use. Students can access the following: computer help desk, free student e-mail accounts, online (class) grades, online (class) registration, online (class) schedules. Campuswide network is available. 100% of college-owned or -operated housing units are wired for high-speed Internet access. Wireless service is available via entire campus.

Library: Leslie J. Savage Library plus 1 other. *Books:* 157,404 (physical), 116,731 (digital/electronic); *Serial titles:* 69 (physical), 45 (digital/electronic); *Databases:* 117. Weekly public service hours: 101; students can reserve study rooms.

STUDENT LIFE

Housing options: on-campus residence required through sophomore year; coed, men-only, women-only. Campus housing is university owned. Freshman campus housing is guaranteed.

Activities and organizations: drama/theater group, student-run newspaper, radio and television station, choral group, Mountain Search and Rescue Team, Student Government Association, Rodeo Club, wilderness pursuits, Peak Productions.

Athletics Member NCAA. All Division II. ***Intercollegiate sports:*** baseball M(c), basketball M(s)/W(s), cheerleading M(c)/W(c), cross-country running M(s)/W(s), football M(s), ice hockey M(c), lacrosse M(c)/W(c), rock climbing M(c)/W(c), rugby M(c)/W(c), skiing (cross-country) M(c)/W(c), skiing (downhill) M(c)/W(c), soccer M(c)/W(s), swimming and diving W(s), track and field M(s)/W(s), volleyball M(c)/W(s), wrestling M(s)/W(c). ***Intramural sports:*** basketball M/W, football M/W, golf M/W, soccer M/W, softball M/W, table tennis M/W, tennis M/W, ultimate Frisbee M/W, volleyball M/W.

Campus security: 24-hour emergency response devices and patrols, student patrols, late-night transport/escort service, controlled dormitory access.

Student services: health clinic, personal/psychological counseling.

COSTS & FINANCIAL AID

Costs (2016–17) ***Tuition:*** state resident $6312 full-time, $263 per credit hour part-time; nonresident $17,616 full-time, $734 per credit hour part-time. Full-time tuition and fees vary according to course load and reciprocity agreements. Part-time tuition and fees vary according to course load and reciprocity agreements. ***Required fees:*** $2881 full-time. ***Room and board:*** $9446; room only: $4930. Room and board charges vary according to board plan and housing facility. ***Payment plans:*** installment, deferred payment. ***Waivers:*** senior citizens and employees or children of employees.

Financial Aid Of all full-time matriculated undergraduates who enrolled in 2016, 1,715 applied for aid, 1,085 were judged to have need, 73 had their need fully met. 105 Federal Work-Study jobs (averaging $1200). 150 state and other part-time jobs (averaging $1050). In 2016, 472 non-need-based awards were made. ***Average percent of need met:*** 61. ***Average financial aid package:*** $9806. ***Average need-based loan:*** $3846. ***Average need-based gift aid:*** $7399. ***Average non-need-based aid:*** $4311. ***Average indebtedness upon graduation:*** $25,589.

APPLYING

Standardized Tests *Required:* SAT or ACT (for admission).

Options: electronic application, deferred entrance.

Application fee: $30.

Required: essay or personal statement, high school transcript, interview. ***Recommended:*** minimum 2.5 GPA.

Notification: continuous until 11/15 (freshmen), continuous (transfers).

CONTACT

Western State Colorado University, 600 North Adams Street, Gunnison, CO 81231. *Phone:* 970-943-2211. *Toll-free phone:* 800-876-5309. *E-mail:* admissions@western.edu.

Yeshiva Toras Chaim Talmudical Seminary

Denver, Colorado

CONTACT

Rabbi Israel Kagan, Dean, Yeshiva Toras Chaim Talmudical Seminary, 1555 Stuart Street, Denver, CO 80204-1415. *Phone:* 303-629-8200. *Fax:* 303-623-5949.

CONNECTICUT

Albertus Magnus College

New Haven, Connecticut

http://www.albertus.edu/

- **Independent Roman Catholic** comprehensive, founded 1925
- **Suburban** 50-acre campus
- **Coed** 1,220 undergraduate students, 85% full-time, 67% women, 33% men
- **Moderately difficult** entrance level, 67% of applicants were admitted

UNDERGRAD STUDENTS

1,034 full-time, 186 part-time. Students come from 10 states and territories; 3 other countries; 5% are from out of state; 34% Black or African American, non-Hispanic/Latino; 18% Hispanic/Latino; 0.5%

Asian, non-Hispanic/Latino; 0.2% American Indian or Alaska Native, non-Hispanic/Latino; 0.9% Two or more races, non-Hispanic/Latino; 8% Race/ethnicity unknown; 2% international; 9% transferred in; 40% live on campus.

Freshmen:
Admission: 780 applied, 519 admitted, 135 enrolled. ***Average high school GPA:*** 2.6. ***Test scores:*** SAT critical reading scores over 500: 38%; SAT math scores over 500: 37%; SAT writing scores over 500: 47%; ACT scores over 18: 91%; SAT critical reading scores over 600: 13%; SAT math scores over 600: 9%; SAT writing scores over 600: 12%; ACT scores over 24: 53%; SAT critical reading scores over 700: 2%; SAT writing scores over 700: 2%; ACT scores over 30: 5%.
Retention: 84% of full-time freshmen returned.

FACULTY
Total: 134, 39% full-time, 51% with terminal degrees.
Student/faculty ratio: 14:1.

ACADEMICS
Calendar: semesters. *Degrees:* certificates, diplomas, associate, bachelor's, master's, post-master's, and postbachelor's certificates.
Special study options: academic remediation for entering students, accelerated degree program, adult/continuing education programs, advanced placement credit, distance learning, double majors, English as a second language, freshman honors college, honors programs, independent study, internships, part-time degree program, services for LD students, student-designed majors, study abroad, summer session for credit.
Unusual degree programs: 3-2 business administration; social work.
Computers: 117 computers/terminals are available on campus for general student use. Students can access the following: campus intranet, computer help desk, free student e-mail accounts, online (class) grades, online (class) registration, online (class) schedules, online class sessions. Campuswide network is available. 100% of college-owned or -operated housing units are wired for high-speed Internet access. Wireless service is available via entire campus.
Library: Rosary Hall. *Books:* 38,339 (physical), 148,500 (digital/electronic); *Databases:* 88.

STUDENT LIFE
Housing options: coed, women-only. Campus housing is university owned. Freshman applicants given priority for college housing.
Activities and organizations: drama/theater group, choral group, Student Alumni Association, Student Government Association, M.A.L.E.S Club, Service Club, Honors Club.
Athletics Member NCAA. All Division III. ***Intercollegiate sports:*** baseball M, basketball M/W, golf M/W, lacrosse M/W, soccer M/W, softball W, swimming and diving W, tennis M/W, volleyball M/W. ***Intramural sports:*** basketball M/W, soccer M/W.
Campus security: 24-hour emergency response devices and patrols, late-night transport/escort service, controlled dormitory access.
Student services: health clinic, personal/psychological counseling.

COSTS & FINANCIAL AID
Costs (2017–18) ***Comprehensive fee:*** $45,506 includes full-time tuition ($31,000), mandatory fees ($490), and room and board ($14,016). Full-time tuition and fees vary according to program. Part-time tuition and fees vary according to program. ***Room and board:*** Room and board charges vary according to board plan. ***Payment plan:*** installment. ***Waivers:*** senior citizens and employees or children of employees.
Financial Aid Of all full-time matriculated undergraduates who enrolled in 2016, 944 applied for aid, 910 were judged to have need, 43 had their need fully met. In 2016, 33 non-need-based awards were made. ***Average percent of need met:*** 50. ***Average financial aid package:*** $15,110. ***Average need-based loan:*** $4270. ***Average need-based gift aid:*** $12,459. ***Average non-need-based aid:*** $5033. ***Average indebtedness upon graduation:*** $38,376.

APPLYING
Standardized Tests *Required:* SAT or ACT (for admission). *Recommended:* SAT Subject Tests (for admission).
Options: electronic application, deferred entrance.
Application fee: $35.
Required: high school transcript, minimum 2.0 GPA, 1 letter of recommendation. ***Required for some:*** essay or personal statement, interview.
Application deadlines: rolling (freshmen), rolling (transfers).
Notification: continuous (freshmen), continuous (transfers).

CONTACT
Anthony Reich, Director of Admission, Albertus Magnus College, 700 Prospect Street, New Haven, CT 06511-1189. *Phone:* 203-773-5032 Ext. 5032. *Toll-free phone:* 800-578-9160. *E-mail:* admissions@albertus.edu.

Bais Binyomin Academy
Stamford, Connecticut

CONTACT
Director of Admissions, Bais Binyomin Academy, 132 Prospect Street, Stamford, CT 06901-1202. *Phone:* 203-325-4351.

Central Connecticut State University
New Britain, Connecticut
http://www.ccsu.edu/

- **State-supported** comprehensive, founded 1849, part of Connecticut State Colleges & Universities (CSCU)
- **Suburban** 314-acre campus
- **Endowment** $62.7 million
- **Coed** 9,538 undergraduate students, 79% full-time, 46% women, 54% men
- **Moderately difficult** entrance level, 60% of applicants were admitted

UNDERGRAD STUDENTS
7,539 full-time, 1,999 part-time. Students come from 30 states and territories; 16 other countries; 4% are from out of state; 12% Black or African American, non-Hispanic/Latino; 14% Hispanic/Latino; 4% Asian, non-Hispanic/Latino; 0.1% Native Hawaiian or other Pacific Islander, non-Hispanic/Latino; 0.1% American Indian or Alaska Native, non-Hispanic/Latino; 3% Two or more races, non-Hispanic/Latino; 3% Race/ethnicity unknown; 2% international; 11% transferred in; 24% live on campus.

Freshmen:
Admission: 7,810 applied, 4,687 admitted, 1,269 enrolled. ***Average high school GPA:*** 3.07. ***Test scores:*** SAT critical reading scores over 500: 51%; SAT math scores over 500: 55%; SAT writing scores over 500: 50%; ACT scores over 18: 89%; SAT critical reading scores over 600: 10%; SAT math scores over 600: 13%; SAT writing scores over 600: 9%; ACT scores over 24: 27%; SAT critical reading scores over 700: 1%; SAT math scores over 700: 1%; SAT writing scores over 700: 1%; ACT scores over 30: 7%.
Retention: 78% of full-time freshmen returned.

FACULTY
Total: 935, 48% full-time, 55% with terminal degrees.
Student/faculty ratio: 15:1.

ACADEMICS
Calendar: semesters. *Degrees:* certificates, bachelor's, master's, doctoral, post-master's, and postbachelor's certificates.
Special study options: academic remediation for entering students, adult/continuing education programs, advanced placement credit, cooperative education, distance learning, double majors, English as a second language, honors programs, independent study, internships, off-campus study, part-time degree program, services for LD students, student-designed majors, study abroad, summer session for credit. ***ROTC:*** Army (c), Air Force (c).
Computers: 750 computers/terminals are available on campus for general student use. Students can access the following: campus intranet, computer help desk, free student e-mail accounts, online (class) grades, online (class) registration, online (class) schedules. Campuswide network is available. 100% of college-owned or -operated housing units are wired for high-speed Internet access. Wireless service is available via entire campus.

Library: Elihu Burritt Library plus 1 other. *Books:* 572,464 (physical), 160,771 (digital/electronic); *Serial titles:* 3,957 (physical), 57,143 (digital/electronic); *Databases:* 105. Weekly public service hours: 84.

STUDENT LIFE
Housing options: coed, women-only, special housing for students with disabilities. Campus housing is university owned.

Activities and organizations: drama/theater group, student-run newspaper, radio and television station, choral group, Inter-Residence Council, student radio station, Program Boad (C.A.N.), Student Government Association, A Cappella Society, national fraternities, national sororities.

Athletics Member NCAA. All Division I except football (Division I-AA). ***Intercollegiate sports:*** baseball M(s), basketball M(s)/W(s), cross-country running M(s)/W(s), golf M(s)/W(s), lacrosse W(s), soccer M(s)/W(s), softball W(s), swimming and diving W(s), track and field M(s)/W(s), volleyball W(s). ***Intramural sports:*** basketball M/W, fencing M(c)/W(c), field hockey W(c), football M, gymnastics W, lacrosse M(c), rugby M(c)/W(c), soccer M/W, softball W, volleyball W.

Campus security: 24-hour emergency response devices and patrols, student patrols, late-night transport/escort service, controlled dormitory access.

Student services: health clinic, personal/psychological counseling, women's center.

COSTS & FINANCIAL AID
Costs (2016–17) ***Tuition:*** state resident $5216 full-time, $217 per credit part-time; nonresident $16,882 full-time, $223 per credit part-time. Full-time tuition and fees vary according to course level, course load, and program. Part-time tuition and fees vary according to course level, course load, and program. ***Required fees:*** $4525 full-time, $265 per credit part-time, $58 per term part-time. ***Room and board:*** $11,462; room only: $6636. Room and board charges vary according to board plan and housing facility. ***Payment plan:*** installment. ***Waivers:*** senior citizens and employees or children of employees.

Financial Aid Of all full-time matriculated undergraduates who enrolled in 2016, 6,792 applied for aid, 5,814 were judged to have need, 314 had their need fully met. 269 Federal Work-Study jobs (averaging $1500). In 2016, 325 non-need-based awards were made. ***Average percent of need met:*** 64. ***Average financial aid package:*** $9350. ***Average need-based loan:*** $4291. ***Average need-based gift aid:*** $5725. ***Average non-need-based aid:*** $3075. ***Average indebtedness upon graduation:*** $28,016. ***Financial aid deadline:*** 9/15.

APPLYING
Standardized Tests *Required:* SAT or ACT (for admission).

Options: electronic application.

Application fee: $50.

Required: essay or personal statement, high school transcript, minimum 2.0 GPA, 2 letters of recommendation. ***Required for some:*** high school class rank. ***Recommended:*** minimum 3.0 GPA.

Application deadlines: 5/1 (freshmen), 5/1 (transfers).

Notification: continuous until 10/15 (freshmen), continuous until 10/15 (transfers).

CONTACT
Central Connecticut State University, 1615 Stanley Street, New Britain, CT 06050. *Phone:* 860-832-2285. *Toll-free phone:* 888-733-2278. *Fax:* 860-832-2522. *E-mail:* admissions@ccsu.edu.

Charter Oak State College

New Britain, Connecticut

http://www.charteroak.edu/

- **State-supported** comprehensive, founded 1973, part of Connecticut State Colleges & Universities (CSCU)
- **Suburban** campus
- **Coed** 1,533 undergraduate students, 20% full-time, 68% women, 32% men
- **Noncompetitive** entrance level

UNDERGRAD STUDENTS
313 full-time, 1,220 part-time. Students come from 43 states and territories; 20% are from out of state; 16% Black or African American, non-Hispanic/Latino; 14% Hispanic/Latino; 1% Asian, non-Hispanic/Latino; 0.1% Native Hawaiian or other Pacific Islander, non-Hispanic/Latino; 0.7% American Indian or Alaska Native, non-Hispanic/Latino; 2% Two or more races, non-Hispanic/Latino; 8% Race/ethnicity unknown; 1% international.

FACULTY
Total: 186, 56% with terminal degrees.

Student/faculty ratio: 12:1.

ACADEMICS
Calendar: semesters. *Degrees:* certificates, associate, bachelor's, and master's (offers only external degree programs).

Special study options: accelerated degree program, adult/continuing education programs, advanced placement credit, distance learning, double majors, external degree program, independent study, off-campus study, part-time degree program, services for LD students, student-designed majors, summer session for credit.

Computers: Students can access the following: computer help desk, free student e-mail accounts, online (class) grades, online (class) registration, online (class) schedules. Campuswide network is available. Wireless service is available via entire campus.

STUDENT LIFE
Housing options: college housing not available.

COSTS & FINANCIAL AID
Costs (2016–17) ***Tuition:*** state resident $8610 full-time, $287 per credit part-time; nonresident $11,310 full-time, $377 per credit part-time. Full-time tuition and fees vary according to course load. Part-time tuition and fees vary according to course load. ***Required fees:*** $783 full-time, $261 per term part-time. ***Payment plan:*** installment.

Financial Aid Of all full-time matriculated undergraduates who enrolled in 2015, 261 applied for aid, 241 were judged to have need, 8 had their need fully met. In 2015, 1 non-need-based awards were made. ***Average percent of need met:*** 47. ***Average financial aid package:*** $7454. ***Average need-based loan:*** $4280. ***Average need-based gift aid:*** $4406. ***Average non-need-based aid:*** $922.

APPLYING
Options: electronic application, deferred entrance.

Application fee: $75.

Required: 9 college-level credits, 16 years of age.

Notification: continuous (transfers).

CONTACT
Charter Oak State College, CT. *Phone:* 860-515-3858.

Connecticut College

New London, Connecticut

http://www.conncoll.edu/

- **Independent** comprehensive, founded 1911
- **Small-town** 750-acre campus with easy access to Providence, RI
- **Endowment** $273.6 million
- **Coed** 1,865 undergraduate students, 98% full-time, 63% women, 37% men
- **Very difficult** entrance level, 35% of applicants were admitted

UNDERGRAD STUDENTS
1,819 full-time, 46 part-time. Students come from 43 states and territories; 42 other countries; 81% are from out of state; 4% Black or African American, non-Hispanic/Latino; 9% Hispanic/Latino; 4% Asian, non-Hispanic/Latino; 0.1% Native Hawaiian or other Pacific Islander, non-Hispanic/Latino; 0.1% American Indian or Alaska Native, non-Hispanic/Latino; 3% Two or more races, non-Hispanic/Latino; 3% Race/ethnicity unknown; 7% international; 1% transferred in; 97% live on campus.

Freshmen:
Admission: 5,879 applied, 2,065 admitted, 472 enrolled. ***Test scores:*** SAT critical reading scores over 500: 100%; SAT math scores over 500: 98%; SAT writing scores over 500: 100%; ACT scores over 18: 100%; SAT critical reading scores over 600: 81%; SAT math scores over 600: 87%; SAT writing scores over 600: 84%; ACT scores over 24: 99%; SAT

critical reading scores over 700: 26%; SAT math scores over 700: 29%; SAT writing scores over 700: 29%; ACT scores over 30: 54%.
Retention: 89% of full-time freshmen returned.

FACULTY
Total: 245, 72% full-time, 80% with terminal degrees.
Student/faculty ratio: 9:1.

ACADEMICS
Calendar: semesters. *Degrees:* bachelor's and master's.
Special study options: accelerated degree program, adult/continuing education programs, advanced placement credit, double majors, independent study, internships, off-campus study, part-time degree program, services for LD students, student-designed majors, study abroad.
Unusual degree programs: 3-2 engineering with Washington University in St. Louis.
Computers: Students can access the following: campus intranet, computer help desk, free student e-mail accounts, online (class) grades, online (class) registration, online (class) schedules, learning management system. Campuswide network is available. 100% of college-owned or -operated housing units are wired for high-speed Internet access. Wireless service is available via classrooms, computer centers, computer labs, dorm rooms, learning centers, libraries, student centers.
Library: Charles Shain Library plus 1 other.

STUDENT LIFE
Housing options: on-campus residence required through junior year; coed. Campus housing is university owned. Freshman campus housing is guaranteed.
Activities and organizations: drama/theater group, student-run newspaper, radio station, choral group, Active Minds, Eclipse, Habitat for Humanity, Connecticut College Law Society, Connecticut College Democrats.
Athletics Member NCAA. All Division III. ***Intercollegiate sports:*** basketball M/W, crew M/W, cross-country running M/W, field hockey W, ice hockey M/W, lacrosse M/W, sailing M/W, soccer M/W, squash M/W, swimming and diving M/W, tennis M/W, track and field M/W, volleyball W, water polo M/W. ***Intramural sports:*** basketball M/W, racquetball M/W, soccer M/W, softball M/W, squash M/W, tennis M/W, volleyball M/W.
Campus security: 24-hour emergency response devices and patrols, late-night transport/escort service, controlled dormitory access.
Student services: health clinic, personal/psychological counseling, women's center.

COSTS & FINANCIAL AID
Costs (2016–17) ***Comprehensive fee:*** $65,000 includes full-time tuition ($50,620), mandatory fees ($320), and room and board ($14,060). Part-time tuition: $1508 per credit hour. ***College room only:*** $8115. ***Payment plan:*** installment. ***Waivers:*** employees or children of employees.
Financial Aid Of all full-time matriculated undergraduates who enrolled in 2016, 1,125 applied for aid, 1,036 were judged to have need, 1,036 had their need fully met. ***Average percent of need met:*** 100. ***Average financial aid package:*** $40,891. ***Average need-based loan:*** $4497. ***Average need-based gift aid:*** $37,745. ***Average indebtedness upon graduation:*** $27,514.

APPLYING
Options: electronic application, early decision, deferred entrance.
Application fee: $60.
Required: essay or personal statement, high school transcript, 2 letters of recommendation. ***Recommended:*** interview.
Application deadlines: 1/1 (freshmen), 4/1 (transfers).
Early decision deadline: 11/15 (for plan 1), 1/1 (for plan 2).
Notification: 3/31 (freshmen), 5/15 (transfers), 12/15 (early decision plan 1), 2/15 (early decision plan 2).

CONTACT
Andrew Strickler, Dean of Admission and Financial Aid, Connecticut College, 270 Mohegan Avenue, New London, CT 06320. *Phone:* 860-439-2200. *E-mail:* admission@conncoll.edu.

Eastern Connecticut State University
Willimantic, Connecticut
http://www.easternct.edu/

- **State-supported** comprehensive, founded 1889, part of Connecticut State Colleges & Universities (CSCU)
- **Small-town** 182-acre campus with easy access to Hartford
- **Endowment** $13.3 million
- **Coed**
- **Moderately difficult** entrance level

FACULTY
Student/faculty ratio: 16:1.

ACADEMICS
Calendar: semesters. *Degrees:* associate, bachelor's, and master's.
Library: J. Eugene Smith Library.

STUDENT LIFE
Housing options: coed. Campus housing is university owned. Freshman campus housing is guaranteed.
Activities and organizations: drama/theater group, student-run newspaper, radio and television station, choral group, Repertory Dance Troupe, Rugby Club, Biology Club, Education Club, Psychology Club.
Athletics Member NCAA. All Division III.
Campus security: 24-hour emergency response devices and patrols, student patrols, late-night transport/escort service, controlled dormitory access.
Student services: health clinic, personal/psychological counseling, women's center.

COSTS & FINANCIAL AID
Costs (2016–17) ***Tuition:*** state resident $5216 full-time, $490 per credit hour part-time; nonresident $16,882 full-time, $496 per credit hour part-time. Part-time tuition and fees vary according to course load. ***Required fees:*** $5284 full-time, $80 per year part-time. ***Room and board:*** $12,559; room only: $7172. Room and board charges vary according to board plan and housing facility.
Financial Aid Of all full-time matriculated undergraduates who enrolled in 2015, 3,535 applied for aid, 2,863 were judged to have need, 299 had their need fully met. 85 Federal Work-Study jobs (averaging $2198). In 2015, 312 non-need-based awards were made. ***Average percent of need met:*** 61. ***Average financial aid package:*** $9669. ***Average need-based loan:*** $4301. ***Average need-based gift aid:*** $5743. ***Average non-need-based aid:*** $3726. ***Average indebtedness upon graduation:*** $30,566.

APPLYING
Options: electronic application, deferred entrance.
Application fee: $50.
Required: high school transcript. ***Required for some:*** interview. ***Recommended:*** essay or personal statement, rank in upper 50% of high school class.

CONTACT
Eastern Connecticut State University, CT. *Phone:* 860-465-4381.

Fairfield University
Fairfield, Connecticut
http://www.fairfield.edu/

- **Independent Roman Catholic (Jesuit)** comprehensive, founded 1942
- **Suburban** 200-acre campus with easy access to New York City
- **Endowment** $309.8 million
- **Coed** 4,032 undergraduate students, 94% full-time, 61% women, 39% men
- **Very difficult** entrance level, 61% of applicants were admitted

UNDERGRAD STUDENTS
3,803 full-time, 229 part-time. Students come from 35 states and territories; 47 other countries; 71% are from out of state; 2% Black or African American, non-Hispanic/Latino; 8% Hispanic/Latino; 2% Asian, non-Hispanic/Latino; 0.1% Native Hawaiian or other Pacific Islander, non-Hispanic/Latino; 1% Two or more races, non-Hispanic/Latino; 6% Race/ethnicity unknown; 3% international; 1% transferred in; 72% live on campus.

Freshmen:
Admission: 11,055 applied, 6,795 admitted, 1,056 enrolled. ***Average high school GPA:*** 3.48. ***Test scores:*** SAT critical reading scores over 500: 93%; SAT math scores over 500: 95%; SAT writing scores over 500: 94%; ACT scores over 18: 100%; SAT critical reading scores over 600: 46%; SAT math scores over 600: 56%; SAT writing scores over 600: 51%; ACT scores over 24: 91%; SAT critical reading scores over 700: 4%; SAT math scores over 700: 6%; SAT writing scores over 700: 6%; ACT scores over 30: 15%.

Retention: 89% of full-time freshmen returned.

FACULTY
Total: 597, 45% full-time, 66% with terminal degrees.

Student/faculty ratio: 12:1.

ACADEMICS
Calendar: semesters. *Degrees:* bachelor's, master's, doctoral, post-master's, and postbachelor's certificates.

Special study options: accelerated degree program, adult/continuing education programs, advanced placement credit, distance learning, double majors, honors programs, independent study, internships, off-campus study, part-time degree program, services for LD students, student-designed majors, study abroad, summer session for credit. ***ROTC:*** Army (c), Air Force (c).

Computers: 68 computers/terminals are available on campus for general student use. Students can access the following: campus intranet, computer help desk, free student e-mail accounts, online (class) grades, online (class) registration, online (class) schedules. Campuswide network is available. 100% of college-owned or -operated housing units are wired for high-speed Internet access. Wireless service is available via entire campus.

Library: DiMenna-Nyselius Library. *Books:* 376,704 (physical), 898,580 (digital/electronic); *Serial titles:* 152 (physical), 36,383 (digital/electronic); *Databases:* 148. Weekly public service hours: 105; study areas open 24 hours, 5-7 days a week; students can reserve study rooms.

STUDENT LIFE
Housing options: coed, special housing for students with disabilities. Campus housing is university owned. Freshman campus housing is guaranteed.

Activities and organizations: drama/theater group, student-run newspaper, radio and television station, choral group, Fairfield University Student Association, Intramural/Club Sports, Commuter Student Association, Fairfield United, Campus Ministry.

Athletics Member NCAA. All Division I. ***Intercollegiate sports:*** baseball M(s), basketball M(s)/W(s), crew M(s)/W(s), cross-country running M(s)/W(s), field hockey W(s), golf M(s)/W(s), lacrosse M(s)/W(s), soccer M(s)/W(s), softball W(s), swimming and diving M(s)/W(s), tennis M(s)(c)/W(s), volleyball W(s). ***Intramural sports:*** baseball M(c), basketball M/W, cheerleading M(c)/W(c), cross-country running M(c)/W(c), equestrian sports M(c)/W(c), field hockey W(c), golf M/W, ice hockey M(c), lacrosse M(c)/W(c), rugby M(c)/W(c), sailing M(c)/W(c), skiing (downhill) M(c)/W(c), soccer M/W, softball M/W, table tennis M/W, tennis M/W, ultimate Frisbee M(c)/W(c), volleyball M/W.

Campus security: 24-hour emergency response devices and patrols, late-night transport/escort service, controlled dormitory access, bicycle patrols, security/safety software app, emergency alert system.

Student services: health clinic, personal/psychological counseling.

COSTS & FINANCIAL AID
Costs (2016–17) ***One-time required fee:*** $280. ***Comprehensive fee:*** $59,860 includes full-time tuition ($45,350), mandatory fees ($650), and room and board ($13,860). Full-time tuition and fees vary according to class time, course level, course load, degree level, and program. Part-time tuition: $725 per credit hour. Part-time tuition and fees vary according to class time, course level, course load, degree level, and program. ***Required fees:*** $60 per term part-time. ***College room only:*** $8490. Room and board charges vary according to board plan and housing facility. ***Payment plan:*** installment. ***Waivers:*** employees or children of employees.

Financial Aid Of all full-time matriculated undergraduates who enrolled in 2016, 2,470 applied for aid, 1,739 were judged to have need, 550 had their need fully met. 508 Federal Work-Study jobs (averaging $1091). In 2016, 1079 non-need-based awards were made. ***Average percent of need met:*** 82. ***Average financial aid package:*** $33,012. ***Average need-based loan:*** $4654. ***Average need-based gift aid:*** $26,170. ***Average non-need-based aid:*** $14,445. ***Average indebtedness upon graduation:*** $37,910. ***Financial aid deadline:*** 1/15.

APPLYING
Options: electronic application, early admission, early decision, early action, deferred entrance.

Application fee: $60.

Required: essay or personal statement, high school transcript, 1 letter of recommendation. ***Recommended:*** interview.

Application deadlines: 1/15 (freshmen), 5/1 (transfers), 11/1 (early action).

Early decision deadline: 11/15 (for plan 1), 1/15 (for plan 2).

Notification: 4/1 (freshmen), 12/15 (early decision plan 1), 2/15 (early decision plan 2), 12/20 (early action).

CONTACT
Alison Hildenbrand, Director of Admission, Fairfield University, 1073 North Benson Road, Fairfield, CT 06824. *Phone:* 203-254-4100. *Fax:* 203-254-4199. *E-mail:* admis@fairfield.edu.

Goodwin College
East Hartford, Connecticut
http://www.goodwin.edu/

CONTACT
Mr. Nicholas Lentino, Assistant Vice President for Admissions, Goodwin College, One Riverside Drive, East Hartford, CT 06118. *Phone:* 860-727-6765. *Toll-free phone:* 800-889-3282. *Fax:* 860-291-9550. *E-mail:* nlentino@goodwin.edu.

Holy Apostles College and Seminary
Cromwell, Connecticut
http://www.holyapostles.edu/

- **Independent Roman Catholic** comprehensive, founded 1956
- **Suburban** 17-acre campus with easy access to Hartford, New Haven
- **Coed**
- **Noncompetitive** entrance level

FACULTY
Student/faculty ratio: 2:1.

ACADEMICS
Calendar: semesters. *Degrees:* certificates, associate, bachelor's, master's, post-master's, and postbachelor's certificates.
Library: Holy Apostles College and Seminary Library.

STUDENT LIFE
Housing options: college housing not available.
Activities and organizations: Pro-Life Organization.

COSTS
Costs (2016–17) ***One-time required fee:*** $50. ***Tuition:*** $9600 full-time, $960 per course part-time. ***Required fees:*** $70 full-time, $35 per term part-time.

APPLYING
Standardized Tests *Recommended:* SAT (for admission).

Options: deferred entrance.

Application fee: $50.

Required: high school transcript. ***Required for some:*** interview.

CONTACT
Fr. Peter Samuel Kucer, Academic Dean, Holy Apostles College and Seminary, 33 Prospect Hill Road, Cromwell, CT 06416. *Phone:* 860-632-3063. *Fax:* 860-632-3030. *E-mail:* pkucer@holyapostles.edu.

Lincoln College of New England

Southington, Connecticut

http://www.lincolncollegene.edu/

- **Proprietary** 4-year, founded 1966
- **Small-town** 32-acre campus with easy access to Hartford
- **Coed** 536 undergraduate students, 57% full-time, 81% women, 19% men
- **Minimally difficult** entrance level

UNDERGRAD STUDENTS
304 full-time, 232 part-time. 11% are from out of state; 20% Black or African American, non-Hispanic/Latino; 14% Hispanic/Latino; 2% Asian, non-Hispanic/Latino; 0.4% American Indian or Alaska Native, non-Hispanic/Latino; 8% Two or more races, non-Hispanic/Latino; 8% Race/ethnicity unknown; 15% transferred in.

Freshmen:
Admission: 86 enrolled.

Retention: 56% of full-time freshmen returned.

FACULTY
Total: 66, 33% full-time, 9% with terminal degrees.

Student/faculty ratio: 13:1.

ACADEMICS
Calendar: semesters. *Degrees:* certificates, associate, and bachelor's.

Special study options: academic remediation for entering students, adult/continuing education programs, advanced placement credit, distance learning, independent study, internships, part-time degree program, services for LD students, summer session for credit.

Computers: 54 computers/terminals are available on campus for general student use. Students can access the following: free student e-mail accounts, online (class) grades, online (class) schedules.
Library: Pupillo Library. *Books:* 13,097 (physical), 133,718 (digital/electronic); *Serial titles:* 13,516 (physical), 133,791 (digital/electronic); *Databases:* 73.

STUDENT LIFE
Housing options: coed, special housing for students with disabilities. Campus housing is university owned. Freshman applicants given priority for college housing.

Activities and organizations: student-run radio station, Student Government Association, Student Ambassador Club, Criminal Justice Club, Mortuary Science, Dental.

Campus security: 24-hour patrols, late-night transport/escort service.

Student services: personal/psychological counseling.

COSTS & FINANCIAL AID
Costs (2017–18) ***Comprehensive fee:*** $24,550 includes full-time tuition ($18,780), mandatory fees ($1270), and room and board ($4500). Part-time tuition: $710 per credit hour. Part-time tuition and fees vary according to course load. ***Required fees:*** $635 per term part-time. ***College room only:*** $6800. Room and board charges vary according to board plan. ***Payment plan:*** installment. ***Waivers:*** employees or children of employees.

Financial Aid Of all full-time matriculated undergraduates who enrolled in 2015, 92 Federal Work-Study jobs (averaging $2000). 30 state and other part-time jobs.

APPLYING
Options: electronic application.

Application fee: $25.

Required: high school transcript. ***Required for some:*** essay or personal statement, interview. ***Recommended:*** essay or personal statement.

Application deadlines: rolling (freshmen), rolling (out-of-state freshmen), rolling (transfers).

Notification: continuous (freshmen), continuous (out-of-state freshmen), continuous (transfers).

CONTACT
Mr. Edward Lizotte, Director of Admissions, Lincoln College of New England, 2279 Mount Vernon Road, Southington, CT 06489. *Phone:* 860-628-4751 Ext. 41905. *Toll-free phone:* 800-825-0087. *Fax:* 860-628-6444. *E-mail:* alizotte@lincolncollegene.edu.

Mitchell College

New London, Connecticut

http://www.mitchell.edu/

- **Independent** 4-year, founded 1938
- **Suburban** 67-acre campus with easy access to Hartford, CT and Providence RI
- **Endowment** $8.8 million
- **Coed**
- **Minimally difficult** entrance level

FACULTY
Student/faculty ratio: 14:1.

ACADEMICS
Calendar: semesters. *Degrees:* associate and bachelor's.
Library: Mitchell College Library. *Books:* 33,182 (physical), 8,168 (digital/electronic); *Databases:* 46. Weekly public service hours: 81.

STUDENT LIFE
Housing options: coed, men-only, women-only. Campus housing is university owned. Freshman applicants given priority for college housing.

Activities and organizations: drama/theater group, student-run radio station, choral group, Mitchell College Drama Society, Sigma Alpha Pi Leadership Society, Behavioral Science, Early Childhood, Gaming Club.

Athletics Member NCAA. All Division III.

Campus security: 24-hour emergency response devices and patrols, student patrols, late-night transport/escort service, controlled dormitory access.

Student services: health clinic, personal/psychological counseling.

FINANCIAL AID
Financial Aid Of all full-time matriculated undergraduates who enrolled in 2004, 491 applied for aid, 414 were judged to have need. 44 Federal Work-Study jobs (averaging $1000). In 2004, 70 non-need-based awards were made. ***Average percent of need met:*** 89. ***Average financial aid package:*** $16,357. ***Average need-based loan:*** $2904. ***Average need-based gift aid:*** $8058. ***Average non-need-based aid:*** $2890.

APPLYING
Options: electronic application, early admission, early decision, deferred entrance.

Application fee: $30.

Required: essay or personal statement, high school transcript, minimum 2.0 GPA, 1 letter of recommendation. ***Recommended:*** interview.

CONTACT
Mr. Bob Martin, Director of Admissions, Mitchell College, 437 Pequot Avenue, New London, CT 06320. *Phone:* 860-701-5178. *Toll-free phone:* 800-443-2811. *Fax:* 860-444-1209. *E-mail:* admissions@mitchell.edu.

Paier College of Art, Inc.

Hamden, Connecticut

http://www.paiercollegeofart.edu/

- **Proprietary** 4-year, founded 1946
- **Suburban** 3-acre campus with easy access to New York City
- **Coed**

FACULTY
Student/faculty ratio: 4:1.

ACADEMICS
Calendar: semesters plus 1 summer session. *Degree:* certificates, diplomas, and bachelor's.
Library: Adele K. Paier Memorial Library.

STUDENT LIFE
Housing options: college housing not available.

Activities and organizations: student-run newspaper, Student Council, School Newspaper.

COSTS & FINANCIAL AID
Costs (2016–17) ***Tuition:*** $15,000 full-time, $500 per credit part-time. Part-time tuition and fees vary according to course load and degree level. ***Required fees:*** $450 full-time, $160 per semester part-time.

Financial Aid Of all full-time matriculated undergraduates who enrolled in 1999, 102 applied for aid, 92 were judged to have need, 1 had their need fully met. ***Average percent of need met:*** 62. ***Average financial aid package:*** $6717. ***Average need-based loan:*** $3446. ***Average need-based gift aid:*** $3460. ***Average indebtedness upon graduation:*** $13,536.

APPLYING
Standardized Tests *Required:* SAT or ACT (for admission).

Required: high school transcript, minimum 2.0 GPA, 2 letters of recommendation, interview, portfolio, interview. ***Recommended:*** essay or personal statement.

CONTACT
Mrs. Lynn Pascale, Admissions Secretary, Paier College of Art, Inc., 20 Gorham Avenue, Hamden, CT 06514 . *Phone:* 203-287-3031. *Fax:* 203-287-3021. *E-mail:* paier.admission@snet.net.

★ Post University
Waterbury, Connecticut
http://www.post.edu/

- **Independent** comprehensive, founded 1890
- **Suburban** 70-acre campus with easy access to Hartford
- **Coed**
- **Moderately difficult** entrance level

FACULTY
Student/faculty ratio: 12:1.

ACADEMICS
Calendar: semesters modular courses offered in the evening and on weekends. *Degrees:* certificates, associate, bachelor's, master's, and postbachelor's certificates.
Library: Trauriq Library and Resource Center. *Books:* 12,933 (physical), 150,000 (digital/electronic); *Serial titles:* 300 (physical), 27,257 (digital/electronic); *Databases:* 25. Weekly public service hours: 75.

STUDENT LIFE
Housing options: coed, special housing for students with disabilities. Campus housing is university owned.

Activities and organizations: drama/theater group, choral group, Equine Club, Newman Club, GSA, Accounting Club, Choir.

Athletics Member NCAA. All Division II.

Campus security: 24-hour emergency response devices and patrols, late-night transport/escort service, controlled dormitory access, annual and semi-annual emergency preparedness training for students and staff.

Student services: health clinic, personal/psychological counseling.

COSTS & FINANCIAL AID
Costs (2016–17) ***Comprehensive fee:*** $40,150 includes full-time tuition ($28,250), mandatory fees ($1300), and room and board ($10,600). Full-time tuition and fees vary according to class time, course load, degree level, location, and program. Part-time tuition: $945 per credit. Part-time tuition and fees vary according to class time, course load, degree level, location, and program. ***Room and board:*** Room and board charges vary according to housing facility. ***Payment plans:*** tuition prepayment, installment.

Financial Aid Of all full-time matriculated undergraduates who enrolled in 2014, 619 applied for aid, 595 were judged to have need, 87 had their need fully met. In 2014, 12 non-need-based awards were made. ***Average percent of need met:*** 58. ***Average financial aid package:*** $19,829. ***Average need-based loan:*** $4023. ***Average need-based gift aid:*** $15,866. ***Average non-need-based aid:*** $9807. ***Average indebtedness upon graduation:*** $20,246.

APPLYING
Standardized Tests *Required:* SAT or ACT (for admission).

Options: electronic application, deferred entrance.

Required: high school transcript, minimum 2.0 GPA, 1 letter of recommendation. ***Recommended:*** essay or personal statement, interview.

CONTACT
Ms. Kathryn Reilly, Director of Admissions, Main Campus, Post University, PO Box 2540, Waterbury, CT 06723. *Phone:* 203-596-4555. *Toll-free phone:* 800-345-2562. *Fax:* 203-756-5810. *E-mail:* admissions@post.edu.

★ Quinnipiac University
Hamden, Connecticut
http://www.qu.edu/

- **Independent** comprehensive, founded 1929
- **Suburban** 600-acre campus with easy access to New Haven, Hartford
- **Endowment** $388.0 million
- **Coed** 7,099 undergraduate students, 96% full-time, 61% women, 39% men
- **Moderately difficult** entrance level, 76% of applicants were admitted

UNDERGRAD STUDENTS
6,784 full-time, 315 part-time. Students come from 32 states and territories; 30 other countries; 70% are from out of state; 5% Black or African American, non-Hispanic/Latino; 9% Hispanic/Latino; 3% Asian, non-Hispanic/Latino; 0.2% American Indian or Alaska Native, non-Hispanic/Latino; 2% Two or more races, non-Hispanic/Latino; 3% Race/ethnicity unknown; 2% international; 3% transferred in; 80% live on campus.

Freshmen:
Admission: 23,492 applied, 17,957 admitted, 1,910 enrolled. ***Average high school GPA:*** 3.4. ***Test scores:*** SAT critical reading scores over 500: 70%; SAT math scores over 500: 75%; SAT writing scores over 500: 72%; ACT scores over 18: 96%; SAT critical reading scores over 600: 21%; SAT math scores over 600: 29%; SAT writing scores over 600: 21%; ACT scores over 24: 62%; SAT critical reading scores over 700: 2%; SAT math scores over 700: 3%; SAT writing scores over 700: 2%; ACT scores over 30: 8%.

Retention: 90% of full-time freshmen returned.

FACULTY
Total: 1,028, 39% full-time, 55% with terminal degrees.

Student/faculty ratio: 16:1.

ACADEMICS
Calendar: semesters. *Degrees:* bachelor's, master's, doctoral, post-master's, and postbachelor's certificates.

Special study options: accelerated degree program, advanced placement credit, distance learning, double majors, honors programs, independent study, internships, part-time degree program, services for LD students, study abroad, summer session for credit. ***ROTC:*** Army (c), Air Force (c).

Computers: 600 computers/terminals and 2,500 ports are available on campus for general student use. Students can access the following: campus intranet, computer help desk, free student e-mail accounts, online (class) grades, online (class) registration, online (class) schedules, e-commerce and "Q"; card for local merchants, food service, dorm card access. Campuswide network is available. 100% of college-owned or -operated housing units are wired for high-speed Internet access. Wireless service is available via entire campus.
Library: Arnold Bernhard Library plus 3 others. *Books:* 135,000 (physical), 500,000 (digital/electronic); *Databases:* 190. Weekly public service hours: 93; study areas open 24 hours, 5-7 days a week; students can reserve study rooms.

STUDENT LIFE
Housing options: coed. Campus housing is university owned. Freshman campus housing is guaranteed.

Activities and organizations: drama/theater group, student-run newspaper, radio and television station, choral group, Student Government, Social Programming Board, Drama Club, Chronicle (student newspaper), dance company, national fraternities, national sororities.

Athletics Member NCAA. All Division I. ***Intercollegiate sports:*** baseball M(s), basketball M(s)/W(s), cross-country running M(s)/W(s), field hockey W(s), golf W(s), gymnastics W(s), ice hockey M(s)/W(s), lacrosse M(s)/W(s), rugby W(s), soccer M(s)/W(s), softball W(s), tennis M(s)/W(s), track and field W(s), volleyball W(s). ***Intramural sports:*** baseball M, basketball M/W, bowling M/W, field hockey W, soccer M/W, softball W, tennis M/W, volleyball M/W.

Campus security: 24-hour emergency response devices and patrols, late-night transport/escort service, controlled dormitory access, text message emergency notification system.

Student services: health clinic, personal/psychological counseling, women's center.

COSTS & FINANCIAL AID

Costs (2017–18) ***Comprehensive fee:*** $60,290 includes full-time tuition ($44,420), mandatory fees ($1680), and room and board ($14,190). Part-time tuition: $1020 per credit. Part-time tuition and fees vary according to class time and course load. ***Required fees:*** $40 per credit part-time. ***Room and board:*** Room and board charges vary according to housing facility. ***Payment plan:*** installment. ***Waivers:*** employees or children of employees.

Financial Aid Of all full-time matriculated undergraduates who enrolled in 2016, 4,968 applied for aid, 4,248 were judged to have need, 663 had their need fully met. 1,448 Federal Work-Study jobs (averaging $2053). In 2016, 1701 non-need-based awards were made. ***Average percent of need met:*** 65. ***Average financial aid package:*** $27,228. ***Average need-based loan:*** $4438. ***Average need-based gift aid:*** $21,612. ***Average non-need-based aid:*** $16,502. ***Average indebtedness upon graduation:*** $47,217.

APPLYING

Standardized Tests *Required for some:* SAT or ACT (for admission).

Options: electronic application, early decision, deferred entrance.

Application fee: $65.

Required: essay or personal statement, high school transcript, 1 letter of recommendation. ***Required for some:*** minimum 3.0 GPA. ***Recommended:*** minimum 3.0 GPA, interview.

Application deadlines: 2/1 (freshmen), 4/1 (transfers).

Early decision deadline: 11/1.

Notification: continuous (freshmen), continuous (out-of-state freshmen), continuous (transfers).

CONTACT

Ms. Joan Isaac-Mohr, Vice President for Admissions and Financial Aid, Quinnipiac University, 275 Mount Carmel Avenue, Hamden, CT 06518. *Phone:* 203-582-8600. *Toll-free phone:* 800-462-1944. *Fax:* 203-582-8906. *E-mail:* admissions@qu.edu.

See below for display ad and page 1466 for the College Close-Up.

Sacred Heart University

Fairfield, Connecticut

http://www.sacredheart.edu/

- **Independent Roman Catholic** comprehensive, founded 1963
- **Suburban** 300-acre campus with easy access to New York City
- **Endowment** $141.8 million
- **Coed** 5,428 undergraduate students, 88% full-time, 64% women, 36% men
- **Moderately difficult** entrance level, 57% of applicants were admitted

UNDERGRAD STUDENTS

4,794 full-time, 634 part-time. Students come from 44 states and territories; 24 other countries; 63% are from out of state; 4% Black or African American, non-Hispanic/Latino; 10% Hispanic/Latino; 2% Asian, non-Hispanic/Latino; 0.1% Native Hawaiian or other Pacific Islander, non-Hispanic/Latino; 0.1% American Indian or Alaska Native, non-Hispanic/Latino; 2% Two or more races, non-Hispanic/Latino; 8% Race/ethnicity unknown; 1% international; 2% transferred in; 51% live on campus.

Freshmen:

Admission: 10,017 applied, 5,731 admitted, 1,322 enrolled. ***Average high school GPA:*** 3.46.

Retention: 81% of full-time freshmen returned.

FACULTY

Total: 802, 35% full-time, 45% with terminal degrees.

Student/faculty ratio: 15:1.

ACADEMICS

Calendar: semesters. *Degrees:* bachelor's, master's, doctoral, and post-master's certificates (also offers part-time program with significant enrollment not reflected in profile).

Special study options: academic remediation for entering students, accelerated degree program, adult/continuing education programs, advanced placement credit, cooperative education, distance learning, double majors, English as a second language, honors programs, independent study, internships, part-time degree program, services for LD

students, student-designed majors, study abroad, summer session for credit. ***ROTC:*** Air Force (c).

Unusual degree programs: 3-2 engineering with Columbia University, Rensselaer Polytechnic Institute; health professions.

Computers: 424 computers/terminals are available on campus for general student use. Students can access the following: computer help desk, free student e-mail accounts, online (class) grades, online (class) registration. Campuswide network is available. 100% of college-owned or -operated housing units are wired for high-speed Internet access. Wireless service is available via entire campus.

Library: Ryan Matura Library plus 1 other. *Books:* 122,977 (physical), 183,824 (digital/electronic); *Serial titles:* 436 (physical), 51,535 (digital/electronic); *Databases:* 132. Weekly public service hours: 119; students can reserve study rooms.

STUDENT LIFE

Housing options: on-campus residence required through sophomore year; coed, special housing for students with disabilities. Campus housing is university owned and leased by the school. Freshman campus housing is guaranteed.

Activities and organizations: drama/theater group, student-run newspaper, radio and television station, choral group, marching band, Student Nurses Association, Habitat for Humanity, Pre-PT Club, Student Events Team, Concert Choir, national fraternities, national sororities.

Athletics Member NCAA. All Division I except football (Division I-AA). ***Intercollegiate sports:*** baseball M(s), basketball M(s)/W(s), bowling W(s), cheerleading W(c), crew W, cross-country running M(s)/W(s), equestrian sports W, fencing M/W, field hockey W(s), golf M(s)/W(s), ice hockey M(s)/W, lacrosse M(s)/W(s), rugby W, soccer M(s)/W(s), softball W(s), swimming and diving W(s), tennis M(s)/W(s), track and field M(s)/W(s), volleyball M/W(s), wrestling M(s). ***Intramural sports:*** baseball M(c), basketball M(c)/W(c), bowling M(c), cross-country running M(c)/W(c), field hockey W(c), golf M(c)/W(c), gymnastics W(c), ice hockey M(c), lacrosse M(c)/W(c), rugby M(c), sailing M(c)/W(c), soccer M(c)/W(c), softball W, tennis M(c)/W(c), volleyball M(c)/W(c), weight lifting W(c).

Campus security: 24-hour emergency response devices and patrols, late-night transport/escort service, controlled dormitory access, Bystander Intervention, Personal Safety Escort Program, Silent Witness Program, crime prevention announcements, SHU Safe App.

Student services: health clinic, personal/psychological counseling.

COSTS & FINANCIAL AID

Costs (2016–17) ***Comprehensive fee:*** $52,750 includes full-time tuition ($38,050), mandatory fees ($250), and room and board ($14,450). Part-time tuition: $600 per credit hour. Part-time tuition and fees vary according to course load. ***Required fees:*** $115 per term part-time. ***College room only:*** $10,000. Room and board charges vary according to board plan and housing facility. ***Payment plan:*** installment. ***Waivers:*** employees or children of employees.

Financial Aid Of all full-time matriculated undergraduates who enrolled in 2016, 3,895 applied for aid, 3,214 were judged to have need, 571 had their need fully met. 888 Federal Work-Study jobs (averaging $1450). 514 state and other part-time jobs (averaging $1141). In 2016, 1439 non-need-based awards were made. ***Average percent of need met:*** 58. ***Average financial aid package:*** $20,275. ***Average need-based loan:*** $4953. ***Average need-based gift aid:*** $16,046. ***Average non-need-based aid:*** $12,067. ***Average indebtedness upon graduation:*** $40,240.

APPLYING

Options: electronic application, early admission, early decision, early action, deferred entrance.

Application fee: $50.

Required: high school transcript, 1 letter of recommendation. ***Required for some:*** interview, interview for Early Decision candidates. ***Recommended:*** essay or personal statement.

Application deadlines: rolling (freshmen), 12/15 (early action).

Early decision deadline: 12/1.

Notification: continuous (freshmen), continuous (transfers), 12/15 (early decision), 1/31 (early action).

CONTACT

Mr. Kevin O'Sullivan, Executive Director of Undergraduate Admissions, Sacred Heart University, 5151 Park Avenue, Fairfield, CT 06825. *Phone:* 203-371-7880. *Fax:* 203-365-7607. *E-mail:* enroll@sacredheart.edu.

St. Vincent's College

Bridgeport, Connecticut

http://www.stvincentscollege.edu/

- **Independent** primarily 2-year, founded 1991, affiliated with Roman Catholic Church
- **Urban** campus with easy access to New York City
- **Endowment** $4.1 million
- **Coed** 763 undergraduate students, 9% full-time, 85% women, 15% men

UNDERGRAD STUDENTS

65 full-time, 698 part-time. Students come from 12 states and territories; 2% are from out of state; 15% Black or African American, non-Hispanic/Latino; 15% Hispanic/Latino; 2% Asian, non-Hispanic/Latino; 0.3% American Indian or Alaska Native, non-Hispanic/Latino; 21% Race/ethnicity unknown; 28% transferred in.

Freshmen:

Admission: 33 enrolled.

FACULTY

Total: 67, 27% full-time.

Student/faculty ratio: 14:1.

ACADEMICS

Calendar: semesters. *Degrees:* certificates, associate, and bachelor's.

Special study options: academic remediation for entering students, adult/continuing education programs, advanced placement credit, distance learning, internships, part-time degree program, summer session for credit.

Computers: 32 computers/terminals are available on campus for general student use. Students can access the following: campus intranet, computer help desk, free student e-mail accounts, online (class) grades, online (class) registration, online (class) schedules. Campuswide network is available. Wireless service is available via entire campus.

Library: Daniel T. Banks Health Science Library. *Books:* 1,500 (physical), 84,000 (digital/electronic); *Serial titles:* 81 (physical); *Databases:* 5. Weekly public service hours: 40; students can reserve study rooms.

STUDENT LIFE

Housing options: college housing not available.

Activities and organizations: Radiography Club, Student Nurses Association, SALUTE (veterans national honor society), Phi Theta Kappa (honor society).

Campus security: 24-hour emergency response devices and patrols, late-night transport/escort service.

COSTS & FINANCIAL AID

Costs (2016–17) ***Tuition:*** $14,520 full-time, $605 per credit hour part-time. Full-time tuition and fees vary according to course load. Part-time tuition and fees vary according to course load. ***Required fees:*** $350 full-time, $350 per year part-time. ***Payment plan:*** installment. ***Waivers:*** employees or children of employees.

Financial Aid Of all full-time matriculated undergraduates who enrolled in 2014, 64 applied for aid, 58 were judged to have need, 7 had their need fully met. ***Average percent of need met:*** 40. ***Average financial aid package:*** $8235. ***Average need-based loan:*** $3883. ***Average need-based gift aid:*** $4765. ***Average indebtedness upon graduation:*** $18,805.

APPLYING

Standardized Tests *Recommended:* SAT or ACT (for admission).

Required: high school transcript. ***Recommended:*** minimum 2.0 GPA.

CONTACT

St. Vincent's College, 2800 Main Street, Bridgeport, CT 06606-4292. *Toll-free phone:* 800-873-1013.

Southern Connecticut State University

New Haven, Connecticut

http://www.southernct.edu/

- **State-supported** comprehensive, founded 1893, part of Connecticut State Colleges & Universities (CSCU)
- **Suburban** 168-acre campus with easy access to New York City
- **Coed** 7,963 undergraduate students, 86% full-time, 62% women, 38% men
- **Moderately difficult** entrance level, 64% of applicants were admitted

UNDERGRAD STUDENTS

6,830 full-time, 1,133 part-time. Students come from 29 states and territories; 9 other countries; 4% are from out of state; 17% Black or African American, non-Hispanic/Latino; 14% Hispanic/Latino; 4% Asian, non-Hispanic/Latino; 0.1% Native Hawaiian or other Pacific Islander, non-Hispanic/Latino; 0.3% American Indian or Alaska Native, non-Hispanic/Latino; 3% Two or more races, non-Hispanic/Latino; 7% Race/ethnicity unknown; 0.6% international; 9% transferred in; 33% live on campus.

Freshmen:
Admission: 8,625 applied, 5,479 admitted, 1,404 enrolled. ***Average high school GPA:*** 3. ***Test scores:*** SAT critical reading scores over 500: 58%; SAT math scores over 500: 61%; SAT writing scores over 500: 57%; ACT scores over 18: 79%; SAT critical reading scores over 600: 10%; SAT math scores over 600: 15%; SAT writing scores over 600: 9%; ACT scores over 24: 25%; SAT math scores over 700: 1%; ACT scores over 30: 1%.

Retention: 77% of full-time freshmen returned.

FACULTY

Total: 964, 44% full-time, 48% with terminal degrees.

Student/faculty ratio: 14:1.

ACADEMICS

Calendar: semesters. *Degrees:* bachelor's, master's, doctoral, post-master's, and postbachelor's certificates.

Special study options: academic remediation for entering students, accelerated degree program, advanced placement credit, cooperative education, distance learning, double majors, freshman honors college, honors programs, independent study, internships, off-campus study, part-time degree program, services for LD students, student-designed majors, study abroad, summer session for credit. ***ROTC:*** Army (c), Air Force (c).

Computers: 1,000 computers/terminals are available on campus for general student use. Students can access the following: computer help desk, free student e-mail accounts, online (class) grades, online (class) registration, online (class) schedules. Campuswide network is available. 100% of college-owned or -operated housing units are wired for high-speed Internet access. Wireless service is available via entire campus.
Library: Hilton C. Buley Library. *Books:* 478,191 (physical), 135,134 (digital/electronic); *Serial titles:* 14,528 (physical), 158 (digital/electronic); *Databases:* 203. Students can reserve study rooms.

STUDENT LIFE

Housing options: coed, special housing for students with disabilities. Campus housing is university owned. Freshman campus housing is guaranteed.

Activities and organizations: drama/theater group, student-run newspaper, radio and television station, choral group, marching band, Student Government Association, Psychology Club, Habitat for Humanity, Crescent Players, Black Student Union, national fraternities, national sororities.

Athletics Member NCAA. All Division II. ***Intercollegiate sports:*** baseball M(s), basketball M(s)/W(s), cheerleading M(c)/W(c), cross-country running M(s)/W(s), field hockey W(s), football M(s), gymnastics W(s), lacrosse W(s), rugby M(c)/W(c), soccer M(s)/W(s), softball W(s), swimming and diving M(s)/W(s), track and field M(s)/W(s), ultimate Frisbee M(c)/W(c), volleyball W(s). ***Intramural sports:*** badminton M/W, basketball M/W, football M/W, ice hockey M(c)/W(c), soccer M/W, softball M/W, tennis M/W, volleyball M/W.

Campus security: 24-hour emergency response devices and patrols, late-night transport/escort service, controlled dormitory access.

Student services: health clinic, personal/psychological counseling, women's center.

COSTS & FINANCIAL AID

Costs (2016–17) ***Tuition:*** state resident $5216 full-time, $519 per credit hour part-time; nonresident $16,882 full-time, $535 per credit hour part-time. Full-time tuition and fees vary according to course load and reciprocity agreements. Part-time tuition and fees vary according to course load. ***Required fees:*** $4838 full-time, $55 per term part-time. ***Room and board:*** $11,870; room only: $6594. Room and board charges vary according to board plan and housing facility. ***Payment plans:*** installment, deferred payment. ***Waivers:*** senior citizens and employees or children of employees.

Financial Aid Of all full-time matriculated undergraduates who enrolled in 2016, 5,412 applied for aid, 4,582 were judged to have need, 1,145 had their need fully met. 96 Federal Work-Study jobs (averaging $4196). In 2016, 210 non-need-based awards were made. ***Average percent of need met:*** 68. ***Average financial aid package:*** $14,501. ***Average need-based loan:*** $4359. ***Average need-based gift aid:*** $6639. ***Average non-need-based aid:*** $4636. ***Average indebtedness upon graduation:*** $28,370. ***Financial aid deadline:*** 3/9.

APPLYING

Standardized Tests *Required:* SAT or ACT (for admission).

Options: electronic application, deferred entrance.

Application fee: $50.

Required: essay or personal statement, high school transcript.

Application deadlines: rolling (freshmen), 8/1 (transfers).

Notification: continuous (freshmen), continuous (transfers).

CONTACT

Mrs. Alexis S. Haakonsen, Director of Admissions, Southern Connecticut State University, Admissions House, 131 Farnham Avenue, New Haven, CT 06515-1202. *Phone:* 203-392-5652. *Fax:* 203-392-5727. *E-mail:* haakonsena1@southernct.edu.

Trinity College

Hartford, Connecticut

http://www.trincoll.edu/

- **Independent** comprehensive, founded 1823
- **Urban** 100-acre campus
- **Endowment** $551.8 million
- **Coed**
- **Most difficult** entrance level

FACULTY

Student/faculty ratio: 10:1.

ACADEMICS

Calendar: semesters. *Degrees:* bachelor's and master's.
Library: Trinity College Library plus 1 other.

STUDENT LIFE

Housing options: on-campus residence required for freshman year; coed, special housing for students with disabilities. Campus housing is university owned. Freshman campus housing is guaranteed.

Activities and organizations: drama/theater group, student-run newspaper, radio station, choral group, Friends Active in Community Engagement and Service (FACES), The Mill, Student Government Association, Relay for Life, Multi-Cultural Affairs Council, national fraternities, national sororities.

Athletics Member NCAA. All Division III.

Campus security: 24-hour emergency response devices and patrols, late-night transport/escort service, controlled dormitory access.

Student services: health clinic, personal/psychological counseling, women's center.

COSTS & FINANCIAL AID

Costs (2016–17) ***One-time required fee:*** $50. ***Comprehensive fee:*** $66,440 includes full-time tuition ($50,350), mandatory fees ($2410), and room and board ($13,680). Full-time tuition and fees vary according to course load and program. Part-time tuition and fees vary according to course load and program. ***College room only:*** $8900. Room and board charges vary according to board plan.

Financial Aid Of all full-time matriculated undergraduates who enrolled in 2015, 1,010 applied for aid, 947 were judged to have need, 947 had their need fully met. 797 Federal Work-Study jobs (averaging $1788). In 2015, 75 non-need-based awards were made. ***Average percent of need met:*** 100. ***Average financial aid package:*** $45,859. ***Average need-based loan:*** $4526. ***Average need-based gift aid:*** $42,969. ***Average non-need-based aid:*** $26,799. ***Average indebtedness upon graduation:*** $30,609. ***Financial aid deadline:*** 3/1.

APPLYING

Options: electronic application, early admission, early decision, deferred entrance.

Application fee: $60.

Required: essay or personal statement, high school transcript, 3 letters of recommendation. ***Recommended:*** interview.

CONTACT

Trinity College, 300 Summit Street, Hartford, CT 06106-3100.
Phone: 860-297-2180.

United States Coast Guard Academy

New London, Connecticut

http://www.uscga.edu/

- **Federally supported** 4-year, founded 1876
- **Suburban** 103-acre campus with easy access to Providence, Hartford
- **Endowment** $26.9 million
- **Coed** 986 undergraduate students, 100% full-time, 36% women, 64% men
- **Very difficult** entrance level, 15% of applicants were admitted

UNDERGRAD STUDENTS

986 full-time. Students come from 52 states and territories; 12 other countries; 95% are from out of state; 6% Black or African American, non-Hispanic/Latino; 9% Hispanic/Latino; 6% Asian, non-Hispanic/Latino; 0.1% Native Hawaiian or other Pacific Islander, non-Hispanic/Latino; 0.2% American Indian or Alaska Native, non-Hispanic/Latino; 9% Two or more races, non-Hispanic/Latino; 1% Race/ethnicity unknown; 2% international; 100% live on campus.

Freshmen:

Admission: 2,026 applied, 304 admitted, 291 enrolled. ***Average high school GPA:*** 3.81. ***Test scores:*** SAT critical reading scores over 500: 94%; SAT math scores over 500: 98%; SAT writing scores over 500: 92%; ACT scores over 18: 99%; SAT critical reading scores over 600: 65%; SAT math scores over 600: 83%; SAT writing scores over 600: 54%; ACT scores over 24: 88%; SAT critical reading scores over 700: 11%; SAT math scores over 700: 21%; SAT writing scores over 700: 6%; ACT scores over 30: 34%.

Retention: 89% of full-time freshmen returned.

FACULTY

Total: 147, 86% full-time, 53% with terminal degrees.

Student/faculty ratio: 7:1.

ACADEMICS

Calendar: semesters. *Degree:* bachelor's.

Special study options: academic remediation for entering students, advanced placement credit, double majors, honors programs, independent study, internships, off-campus study, summer session for credit.

Computers: 280 computers/terminals are available on campus for general student use. Students can access the following: campus intranet, computer help desk, free student e-mail accounts, online (class) grades, online (class) schedules. Campuswide network is available. 100% of college-owned or -operated housing units are wired for high-speed Internet access. Wireless service is available via classrooms, dorm rooms, libraries, student centers.

Library: USCG Academy Library. Students can reserve study rooms.

STUDENT LIFE

Housing options: on-campus residence required through senior year; coed. Campus housing is university owned. Freshman campus housing is guaranteed.

Activities and organizations: drama/theater group, choral group, marching band, Club Sports, Musical activities, Multicultural Club, Officers Christian Fellowship, International Dance Club.

Athletics Member NCAA. All Division III. ***Intercollegiate sports:*** baseball M, basketball M/W, cheerleading W(c), crew M/W, cross-country running M/W, football M, ice hockey M(c)/W(c), lacrosse M(c)/W(c), riflery M/W, rugby M(c)/W(c), sailing M/W, soccer M/W, softball W, swimming and diving M/W, tennis M, track and field M/W, volleyball W, water polo M(c)/W(c), wrestling M. ***Intramural sports:*** basketball M/W, bowling M/W, equestrian sports M(c)/W(c), fencing M(c)/W(c), football M, golf M/W, racquetball M/W, sailing M/W, skiing (downhill) M/W, soccer M/W, softball M/W, table tennis M/W, track and field M/W, ultimate Frisbee M/W, volleyball M/W, water polo M/W, weight lifting M/W, wrestling M.

Campus security: 24-hour patrols, late-night transport/escort service, controlled dormitory access, cadets staff a 24-hour Watch Office.

Student services: health clinic, personal/psychological counseling, legal services.

COSTS

Costs (2016–17) ***Comprehensive fee:*** Tuition, room and board, and medical and dental care are provided by the US government. Each cadet receives a salary from which to pay for uniforms, supplies, and personal expenses.

APPLYING

Standardized Tests *Required:* SAT or ACT (for admission).

Options: electronic application, early action, deferred entrance.

Required: essay or personal statement, high school transcript, 3 letters of recommendation, medical examination, physical fitness examination. ***Recommended:*** interview.

Application deadlines: 2/1 (freshmen), rolling (out-of-state freshmen), 2/1 (transfers), 11/15 (early action).

Notification: continuous until 4/15 (freshmen), continuous until 4/15 (out-of-state freshmen), continuous until 4/15 (transfers), 2/1 (early action).

CONTACT

Mr. Daniel V. Pinch, Associate Director of Admissions for Outreach, United States Coast Guard Academy, 31 Mohegan Avenue, New London, CT 06320-4195. *Phone:* 860-701-6327. *Toll-free phone:* 800-883-8724. *Fax:* 860-701-6700. *E-mail:* daniel.v.pinch@uscga.edu.

University of Bridgeport

Bridgeport, Connecticut

http://www.bridgeport.edu/

- **Independent** comprehensive, founded 1927
- **Urban** 86-acre campus with easy access to New York City
- **Endowment** $34.1 million
- **Coed** 2,941 undergraduate students, 73% full-time, 63% women, 37% men
- **Moderately difficult** entrance level, 58% of applicants were admitted

UNDERGRAD STUDENTS

2,140 full-time, 801 part-time. Students come from 39 states and territories; 41 other countries; 37% are from out of state; 34% Black or African American, non-Hispanic/Latino; 20% Hispanic/Latino; 3% Asian, non-Hispanic/Latino; 0.3% Native Hawaiian or other Pacific Islander, non-Hispanic/Latino; 1% American Indian or Alaska Native, non-Hispanic/Latino; 3% Two or more races, non-Hispanic/Latino; 14% international; 10% transferred in; 44% live on campus.

Freshmen:

Admission: 6,969 applied, 4,027 admitted, 487 enrolled. ***Average high school GPA:*** 2.99. ***Test scores:*** SAT critical reading scores over 500: 31%; SAT math scores over 500: 31%; ACT scores over 18: 82%; SAT critical reading scores over 600: 6%; SAT math scores over 600: 5%; ACT scores over 24: 21%; SAT math scores over 700: 1%.

Retention: 64% of full-time freshmen returned.

FACULTY

Total: 503, 26% full-time.

Student/faculty ratio: 16:1.

ACADEMICS

Calendar: semesters. *Degrees:* certificates, associate, bachelor's, master's, doctoral, post-master's, and postbachelor's certificates.

Special study options: academic remediation for entering students, accelerated degree program, adult/continuing education programs, advanced placement credit, cooperative education, distance learning, double majors, English as a second language, honors programs, independent study, internships, off-campus study, part-time degree program, services for LD students, student-designed majors, study abroad, summer session for credit.

Computers: 300 computers/terminals and 300 ports are available on campus for general student use. Students can access the following: computer help desk, free student e-mail accounts, online (class) grades, online (class) registration, online (class) schedules. Campuswide network is available. 100% of college-owned or -operated housing units are wired for high-speed Internet access. Wireless service is available via classrooms, computer centers, computer labs, dorm rooms, learning centers, libraries, student centers.

Library: Wahlstrom Library. *Books:* 166,320 (physical), 6,078 (digital/electronic). Weekly public service hours: 90.

STUDENT LIFE

Housing options: on-campus residence required through sophomore year; coed. Campus housing is university owned. Freshman campus housing is guaranteed.

Activities and organizations: student-run newspaper, choral group, Student Congress, International Relations Club, Black Students Alliance, Latin America Club, Martial Arts Club, national fraternities, national sororities.

Athletics Member NCAA. All Division II. ***Intercollegiate sports:*** baseball M(s), basketball M(s)/W(s), cross-country running M(s)/W(s), gymnastics W(s), lacrosse W(s), soccer M(s)/W(s), softball W(s), swimming and diving M(s)/W(s), volleyball W(s). ***Intramural sports:*** basketball M/W, football M/W, golf M/W, racquetball M/W, soccer M/W, softball M/W, tennis M/W.

Campus security: 24-hour emergency response devices and patrols, student patrols, late-night transport/escort service, controlled dormitory access.

Student services: health clinic, personal/psychological counseling.

COSTS & FINANCIAL AID

Costs (2016–17) ***Comprehensive fee:*** $44,950 includes full-time tuition ($29,550), mandatory fees ($2080), and room and board ($13,320). Full-time tuition and fees vary according to course load and program. Part-time tuition: $985 per credit hour. Part-time tuition and fees vary according to course load and program. ***Required fees:*** $210 per term part-time. ***Room and board:*** Room and board charges vary according to board plan and housing facility. ***Payment plans:*** installment, deferred payment. ***Waivers:*** senior citizens and employees or children of employees.

Financial Aid Of all full-time matriculated undergraduates who enrolled in 2014, 1,774 applied for aid, 1,711 were judged to have need, 59 had their need fully met. In 2014, 275 non-need-based awards were made. ***Average percent of need met:*** 60. ***Average financial aid package:*** $26,304. ***Average need-based loan:*** $4308. ***Average need-based gift aid:*** $5738. ***Average non-need-based aid:*** $11,500. ***Average indebtedness upon graduation:*** $21,200.

APPLYING

Standardized Tests *Required:* SAT or ACT (for admission).

Options: electronic application, early admission, deferred entrance.

Application fee: $25.

Required: essay or personal statement, high school transcript, minimum 2.0 GPA. ***Required for some:*** 2 letters of recommendation, interview, portfolio, audition. ***Recommended:*** 1 letter of recommendation, interview.

Application deadlines: rolling (freshmen), rolling (transfers).

Notification: continuous (freshmen), continuous (transfers).

CONTACT

Ms. Jessica N. Crowley Goddu, Director of Undergraduate Admissions, University of Bridgeport, 126 Park Avenue, Bridgeport, CT 06604. *Phone:* 203-576-4812. *Toll-free phone:* 800-EXCEL-UB. *Fax:* 203-576-4941. *E-mail:* admit@bridgeport.edu.

University of Connecticut

Storrs, Connecticut

http://www.uconn.edu/

CONTACT

Nathan Fuerst, Director of Undergraduate Admissions, University of Connecticut, 2131 Hillside Road, U-88, Storrs, CT 06269. *Phone:* 860-486-3137. *Fax:* 860-486-1476. *E-mail:* beahusky@uconn.edu.

★ University of Hartford

West Hartford, Connecticut

http://www.hartford.edu/

- **Independent** comprehensive, founded 1877
- **Suburban** 320-acre campus with easy access to Hartford
- **Endowment** $145.5 million
- **Coed** 5,150 undergraduate students, 88% full-time, 51% women, 49% men
- **Moderately difficult** entrance level, 72% of applicants were admitted

UNDERGRAD STUDENTS

4,508 full-time, 642 part-time. Students come from 46 states and territories; 49 other countries; 51% are from out of state; 15% Black or African American, non-Hispanic/Latino; 12% Hispanic/Latino; 3% Asian, non-Hispanic/Latino; 0.1% Native Hawaiian or other Pacific Islander, non-Hispanic/Latino; 0.3% American Indian or Alaska Native, non-Hispanic/Latino; 3% Two or more races, non-Hispanic/Latino; 7% Race/ethnicity unknown; 6% international; 5% transferred in; 65% live on campus.

Freshmen:

Admission: 15,526 applied, 11,168 admitted, 1,301 enrolled. ***Average high school GPA:*** 3.04. ***Test scores:*** SAT critical reading scores over 500: 58%; SAT math scores over 500: 60%; ACT scores over 18: 93%; SAT critical reading scores over 600: 18%; SAT math scores over 600: 21%; ACT scores over 24: 45%; SAT critical reading scores over 700: 2%; SAT math scores over 700: 2%; ACT scores over 30: 10%.

Retention: 75% of full-time freshmen returned.

FACULTY

Total: 880, 42% full-time.

Student/faculty ratio: 9:1.

ACADEMICS

Calendar: semesters. *Degrees:* certificates, diplomas, associate, bachelor's, master's, doctoral, post-master's, and postbachelor's certificates.

Special study options: academic remediation for entering students, adult/continuing education programs, advanced placement credit, cooperative education, distance learning, double majors, English as a second language, honors programs, independent study, internships, off-campus study, part-time degree program, services for LD students, student-designed majors, study abroad, summer session for credit. ***ROTC:*** Army (c), Air Force (c).

Computers: 400 computers/terminals are available on campus for general student use. Students can access the following: campus intranet, computer help desk, free student e-mail accounts, online (class) grades, online (class) registration, online (class) schedules, student Web pages. Campuswide network is available. 100% of college-owned or -operated housing units are wired for high-speed Internet access. Wireless service is available via entire campus.

Library: Mortensen Library plus 1 other. *Books:* 266,863 (physical); *Serial titles:* 2,921 (physical), 55,898 (digital/electronic); *Databases:* 228. Weekly public service hours: 104.

STUDENT LIFE

Housing options: coed, women-only, special housing for students with disabilities. Campus housing is university owned and leased by the school. Freshman campus housing is guaranteed.

Activities and organizations: drama/theater group, student-run newspaper, radio and television station, choral group, Program Council, Brothers and Sisters United, Hillel, Student Government Association, Residence Hall Association, national fraternities, national sororities.

Athletics Member NCAA. All Division I. ***Intercollegiate sports:*** badminton M(c)/W(c), baseball M(s), basketball M(s)/W(s), cross-country running M(s)/W(s), golf M(s)/W(s), lacrosse M(s), racquetball M(c)/W(c), rugby M(c)/W(c), soccer M(s)/W(s), softball W(s), track and field M/W, volleyball M(c)/W(s). ***Intramural sports:*** badminton M/W, basketball M/W, football M/W, racquetball M/W, soccer M/W, softball M/W, tennis M/W, ultimate Frisbee M/W, volleyball M/W.

Campus security: 24-hour emergency response devices and patrols, late-night transport/escort service, controlled dormitory access, bicycle patrols.

Student services: health clinic, personal/psychological counseling, women's center, legal services.

COSTS & FINANCIAL AID

Costs (2017–18) ***Comprehensive fee:*** $51,316 includes full-time tuition ($36,088), mandatory fees ($2882), and room and board ($12,346). Full-time tuition and fees vary according to program. Part-time tuition: $556 per credit hour. Part-time tuition and fees vary according to course load and program. ***College room only:*** $8008. Room and board charges vary according to board plan and housing facility. ***Payment plans:*** tuition prepayment, installment. ***Waivers:*** senior citizens and employees or children of employees.

Financial Aid Of all full-time matriculated undergraduates who enrolled in 2016, 3,602 applied for aid, 3,298 were judged to have need, 476 had their need fully met. 449 Federal Work-Study jobs (averaging $1472). In 2016, 837 non-need-based awards were made. ***Average percent of need met:*** 68. ***Average financial aid package:*** $25,950. ***Average need-based loan:*** $4557. ***Average need-based gift aid:*** $20,600. ***Average non-need-based aid:*** $15,431.

APPLYING

Standardized Tests *Required:* SAT or ACT (for admission).

Options: electronic application, early admission, early action, deferred entrance.

Application fee: $35.

Required: high school transcript. ***Recommended:*** essay or personal statement, 2 letters of recommendation, interview.

Application deadlines: rolling (freshmen), rolling (transfers).

Notification: continuous (freshmen), continuous (transfers).

CONTACT

Mr. Richard Zeiser, Dean of Admissions, University of Hartford, 200 Bloomfield Avenue, West Hartford, CT 06117. *Phone:* 860-768-4296. *Toll-free phone:* 800-947-4303. *Fax:* 860-768-4961. *E-mail:* admissions@hartford.edu.

See below for display ad and page 1558 for the College Close-Up.

★ University of New Haven

West Haven, Connecticut

http://www.newhaven.edu/

- **Independent** comprehensive, founded 1920
- **Suburban** 82-acre campus with easy access to New Haven
- **Coed** 4,936 undergraduate students, 92% full-time, 50% women, 50% men
- **Moderately difficult** entrance level, 81% of applicants were admitted

UNDERGRAD STUDENTS

4,552 full-time, 384 part-time. Students come from 39 states and territories; 31 other countries; 57% are from out of state; 11% Black or African American, non-Hispanic/Latino; 10% Hispanic/Latino; 3% Asian, non-Hispanic/Latino; 0.2% Native Hawaiian or other Pacific Islander, non-Hispanic/Latino; 0.2% American Indian or Alaska Native, non-Hispanic/Latino; 2% Two or more races, non-Hispanic/Latino; 6% Race/ethnicity unknown; 7% international; 5% transferred in; 57% live on campus.

Freshmen:

Admission: 10,720 applied, 8,633 admitted, 1,128 enrolled. ***Average high school GPA:*** 3.38. ***Test scores:*** SAT critical reading scores over 500: 59%; SAT math scores over 500: 62%; SAT writing scores over 500: 54%; ACT scores over 18: 92%; SAT critical reading scores over 600: 17%; SAT math scores over 600: 17%; SAT writing scores over 600: 12%; ACT scores over 24: 46%; SAT critical reading scores over 700: 2%; SAT math scores over 700: 1%; SAT writing scores over 700: 1%; ACT scores over 30: 6%.

Retention: 80% of full-time freshmen returned.

FACULTY
Total: 644, 41% full-time, 59% with terminal degrees.
Student/faculty ratio: 16:1.

ACADEMICS
Calendar: 4-1-4. *Degrees:* certificates, associate, bachelor's, master's, doctoral, post-master's, and postbachelor's certificates.
Special study options: academic remediation for entering students, accelerated degree program, adult/continuing education programs, advanced placement credit, cooperative education, distance learning, double majors, English as a second language, honors programs, independent study, internships, off-campus study, part-time degree program, services for LD students, study abroad, summer session for credit. ***ROTC:*** Army (b), Air Force (c).
Computers: Students can access the following: campus intranet, computer help desk, free student e-mail accounts, online (class) grades, online (class) registration, online (class) schedules, computer repair services. Campuswide network is available. Wireless service is available via entire campus.
Library: Marvin K. Peterson Library.

STUDENT LIFE
Housing options: coed, special housing for students with disabilities. Campus housing is university owned and leased by the school. Freshman applicants given priority for college housing.
Activities and organizations: student-run newspaper, radio and television station, marching band, national fraternities, national sororities.
Athletics Member NCAA. All Division II. ***Intercollegiate sports:*** baseball M(s), basketball M(s)/W(s), cross-country running M(s)/W(s), football M(s), ice hockey M(c), lacrosse M(c)/W(s), rugby M(c), soccer M(s)/W(s), softball W(s), tennis W(s), track and field M(s)/W(s), ultimate Frisbee M(c)/W(c), volleyball M(c)/W(s), wrestling M(c). ***Intramural sports:*** basketball M/W, cheerleading M/W, racquetball M/W, soccer M/W, softball M/W, tennis M/W, volleyball M/W.
Campus security: 24-hour emergency response devices and patrols, student patrols, late-night transport/escort service, controlled dormitory access, vehicle, bicycle and foot patrols, crime prevention programs.
Student services: health clinic, personal/psychological counseling.

COSTS & FINANCIAL AID
Costs (2016–17) ***Comprehensive fee:*** $52,190 includes full-time tuition ($35,700), mandatory fees ($1360), and room and board ($15,130). Full-time tuition and fees vary according to course load, location, and program. Part-time tuition: $1190 per credit hour. Part-time tuition and fees vary according to class time, course load, location, and program. ***Required fees:*** $65 per term part-time. ***College room only:*** $9580. Room and board charges vary according to board plan, housing facility, and location. ***Payment plan:*** installment. ***Waivers:*** senior citizens and employees or children of employees.
Financial Aid Of all full-time matriculated undergraduates who enrolled in 2016, 3,697 applied for aid, 3,408 were judged to have need, 538 had their need fully met. In 2016, 639 non-need-based awards were made. ***Average percent of need met:*** 60. ***Average financial aid package:*** $22,746. ***Average need-based loan:*** $4392. ***Average need-based gift aid:*** $19,147. ***Average non-need-based aid:*** $14,358. ***Average indebtedness upon graduation:*** $46,449.

APPLYING
Standardized Tests *Required:* SAT or ACT (for admission).
Options: electronic application, early decision, early action.
Application fee: $50.
Required: essay or personal statement, high school transcript, 1 letter of recommendation. ***Recommended:*** interview.
Application deadlines: rolling (freshmen), rolling (transfers), 12/15 (early action).
Early decision deadline: 12/1.
Notification: continuous (freshmen), continuous (transfers), 12/15 (early decision), 1/15 (early action).

CONTACT
Mr. Jason Riendeau, Director of Undergraduate Admissions, University of New Haven, Bayer Hall, 300 Boston Post Road, West Haven, CT 06516.
Phone: 203-932-2920. *Toll-free phone:* 800-342-5864.
E-mail: jriendeau@newhaven.edu.

See below for display ad and page 1570 for the College Close-Up.

University of Saint Joseph

West Hartford, Connecticut

http://www.usj.edu/

- **Independent Roman Catholic** comprehensive, founded 1932
- **Suburban** 90-acre campus with easy access to Hartford
- **Coed, primarily women** 894 undergraduate students, 81% full-time, 97% women, 3% men
- **Moderately difficult** entrance level, 87% of applicants were admitted

UNDERGRAD STUDENTS

726 full-time, 168 part-time. 4% are from out of state; 15% Black or African American, non-Hispanic/Latino; 16% Hispanic/Latino; 5% Asian, non-Hispanic/Latino; 0.2% Native Hawaiian or other Pacific Islander, non-Hispanic/Latino; 0.2% American Indian or Alaska Native, non-Hispanic/Latino; 1% Two or more races, non-Hispanic/Latino; 9% Race/ethnicity unknown; 1% international; 9% transferred in; 61% live on campus.

Freshmen:

Admission: 743 applied, 647 admitted, 126 enrolled. ***Average high school GPA:*** 3.39. ***Test scores:*** SAT critical reading scores over 500: 43%; SAT math scores over 500: 45%; SAT writing scores over 500: 54%; ACT scores over 18: 88%; SAT critical reading scores over 600: 13%; SAT math scores over 600: 9%; SAT writing scores over 600: 12%; ACT scores over 24: 29%.

Retention: 75% of full-time freshmen returned.

FACULTY

Total: 301, 45% full-time.

Student/faculty ratio: 10:1.

ACADEMICS

Calendar: semesters. *Degrees:* certificates, bachelor's, master's, doctoral, post-master's, and postbachelor's certificates.

Special study options: accelerated degree program, adult/continuing education programs, advanced placement credit, distance learning, double majors, honors programs, independent study, internships, off-campus study, part-time degree program, services for LD students, student-designed majors, study abroad, summer session for credit.

Computers: 72 computers/terminals are available on campus for general student use. Students can access the following: campus intranet, computer help desk, free student e-mail accounts, online (class) grades, online (class) registration, online (class) schedules. Campuswide network is available. 100% of college-owned or -operated housing units are wired for high-speed Internet access. Wireless service is available via classrooms, computer centers, computer labs, dorm rooms, libraries, student centers.

Library: Pope Pius XII Library.

STUDENT LIFE

Housing options: women-only, special housing for students with disabilities. Campus housing is university owned.

Activities and organizations: drama/theater group, choral group.

Athletics Member NCAA. All Division III. ***Intercollegiate sports:*** basketball W, cross-country running W, lacrosse W, soccer W, softball W, swimming and diving W, tennis W, volleyball W. ***Intramural sports:*** badminton M/W, basketball M/W, cross-country running M(c)/W(c), field hockey W(c).

Campus security: 24-hour emergency response devices and patrols, late-night transport/escort service, controlled dormitory access.

Student services: health clinic, personal/psychological counseling.

COSTS & FINANCIAL AID

Costs (2017–18) ***Comprehensive fee:*** $49,128 includes full-time tuition ($36,273), mandatory fees ($1760), and room and board ($11,095). Full-time tuition and fees vary according to course load, degree level, location, program, and student level. Part-time tuition: $818 per credit hour. Part-time tuition and fees vary according to course load, degree level, location, program, and student level. ***Required fees:*** $58 per credit hour part-time. ***College room only:*** $6250. Room and board charges vary according to board plan and housing facility. ***Payment plan:*** installment. ***Waivers:*** employees or children of employees.

Financial Aid Of all full-time matriculated undergraduates who enrolled in 2015, 722 applied for aid, 676 were judged to have need, 65 had their need fully met. In 2015, 71 non-need-based awards were made. ***Average percent of need met:*** 66. ***Average financial aid package:*** $25,201. ***Average need-based loan:*** $4670. ***Average need-based gift aid:*** $20,487. ***Average non-need-based aid:*** $13,258. ***Average indebtedness upon graduation:*** $35,144.

APPLYING

Standardized Tests *Required for some:* SAT or ACT (for admission).

Options: electronic application, deferred entrance.

Application fee: $50.

Required: high school transcript, 1 letter of recommendation. ***Recommended:*** essay or personal statement, interview.

Application deadlines: rolling (freshmen), rolling (transfers).

Notification: continuous (freshmen), continuous (transfers).

CONTACT

Office of Admissions, University of Saint Joseph, 1678 Asylum Avenue, West Hartford, CT 06117. *Phone:* 860-231-5216. *Toll-free phone:* 866-442-8752. *Fax:* 860-231-5744. *E-mail:* admissions@usj.edu.

Wesleyan University

Middletown, Connecticut

http://www.wesleyan.edu/

- **Independent** university, founded 1831
- **Suburban** 316-acre campus with easy access to Hartford, CT and New Haven, CT
- **Endowment** $802.2 million
- **Coed** 2,971 undergraduate students, 98% full-time, 54% women, 46% men
- **Most difficult** entrance level, 18% of applicants were admitted

UNDERGRAD STUDENTS

2,918 full-time, 53 part-time. Students come from 52 states and territories; 53 other countries; 92% are from out of state; 7% Black or African American, non-Hispanic/Latino; 10% Hispanic/Latino; 7% Asian, non-Hispanic/Latino; 0.2% Native Hawaiian or other Pacific Islander, non-Hispanic/Latino; 0.1% American Indian or Alaska Native, non-Hispanic/Latino; 5% Two or more races, non-Hispanic/Latino; 5% Race/ethnicity unknown; 10% international; 2% transferred in; 98% live on campus.

Freshmen:

Admission: 11,928 applied, 2,129 admitted, 774 enrolled. ***Test scores:*** SAT critical reading scores over 500: 97%; SAT math scores over 500: 100%; SAT writing scores over 500: 98%; ACT scores over 18: 100%; SAT critical reading scores over 600: 84%; SAT math scores over 600: 85%; SAT writing scores over 600: 87%; ACT scores over 24: 98%; SAT critical reading scores over 700: 49%; SAT math scores over 700: 43%; SAT writing scores over 700: 49%; ACT scores over 30: 77%.

Retention: 94% of full-time freshmen returned.

FACULTY

Total: 450, 83% full-time, 86% with terminal degrees.

Student/faculty ratio: 8:1.

ACADEMICS

Calendar: semesters. *Degrees:* bachelor's, master's, doctoral, and post-master's certificates.

Special study options: accelerated degree program, adult/continuing education programs, advanced placement credit, double majors, honors programs, independent study, internships, off-campus study, services for LD students, student-designed majors, study abroad, summer session for credit. ***ROTC:*** Air Force (c).

Unusual degree programs: 3-2 engineering with Columbia University, California Institute of Technology, Dartmouth College.

Computers: 1,600 computers/terminals and 6,000 ports are available on campus for general student use. Students can access the following: campus intranet, computer help desk, free student e-mail accounts, online (class) grades, online (class) registration, online (class) schedules, electronic portfolio, course drop/add, learning management system, software training. Campuswide network is available. 100% of college-owned or -operated housing units are wired for high-speed Internet access. Wireless service is available via entire campus.

Library: Olin Memorial Library plus 1 other. *Books:* 1.2 million (physical), 502,915 (digital/electronic); *Serial titles:* 999 (physical), 74,957 (digital/electronic); *Databases:* 213. Weekly public service hours: 113.

STUDENT LIFE

Housing options: on-campus residence required through senior year; coed, men-only, women-only, special housing for students with disabilities. Campus housing is university owned. Freshman campus housing is guaranteed.

Activities and organizations: drama/theater group, student-run newspaper, radio station, choral group, Espwesso, First Class, Long Lane Farm, Ujamaa, Terpsichore, national fraternities.

Athletics Member NCAA. All Division III. ***Intercollegiate sports:*** baseball M, basketball M/W, crew M/W, cross-country running M/W, equestrian sports M(c)/W(c), field hockey W, football M, golf M, ice hockey M/W, lacrosse M/W, rugby M(c)/W(c), sailing M(c)/W(c), skiing (cross-country) M(c)/W(c), skiing (downhill) M(c)/W(c), soccer M/W, softball W, squash M/W, swimming and diving M/W, tennis M/W, track and field M/W, volleyball M(c)/W, water polo M(c), wrestling M. ***Intramural sports:*** basketball M/W, ice hockey M/W, soccer M/W, softball M/W, squash M/W, ultimate Frisbee M/W, water polo M/W.

Campus security: 24-hour emergency response devices and patrols, late-night transport/escort service, controlled dormitory access, Self-defense classes offered by certified instructors.

Student services: health clinic, personal/psychological counseling.

COSTS & FINANCIAL AID

Costs (2017–18) ***Comprehensive fee:*** $66,940 includes full-time tuition ($52,174), mandatory fees ($300), and room and board ($14,466). ***Room and board:*** Room and board charges vary according to board plan and student level. ***Payment plan:*** installment.

Financial Aid Of all full-time matriculated undergraduates who enrolled in 2016, 1,336 applied for aid, 1,293 were judged to have need, 1,293 had their need fully met. 1,008 Federal Work-Study jobs (averaging $2513). 156 state and other part-time jobs (averaging $2419). In 2016, 18 non-need-based awards were made. ***Average percent of need met:*** 100. ***Average financial aid package:*** $47,077. ***Average need-based loan:*** $4153. ***Average need-based gift aid:*** $42,457. ***Average non-need-based aid:*** $31,571. ***Average indebtedness upon graduation:*** $22,495. ***Financial aid deadline:*** 2/15.

APPLYING

Standardized Tests *Required for some:* SAT and SAT Subject Tests or ACT (for admission).

Options: electronic application, early admission, early decision, deferred entrance.

Application fee: $55.

Required: essay or personal statement, high school transcript, 2 letters of recommendation. ***Required for some:*** interview. ***Recommended:*** interview.

Application deadlines: 1/1 (freshmen), 3/15 (transfers).

Early decision deadline: 11/15 (for plan 1), 1/1 (for plan 2).

Notification: 4/1 (freshmen), 5/15 (transfers), 12/15 (early decision plan 1), 2/15 (early decision plan 2).

CONTACT

Ms. Nancy Hargrave Meislahn, Dean of Admission and Financial Aid, Wesleyan University, Stewart M. Reid House, Admission Office, 70 Wyllys Avenue, Middletown, CT 06459. *Phone:* 860-685-3000. *Fax:* 860-685-3001. *E-mail:* admission@wesleyan.edu.

★ Western Connecticut State University

Danbury, Connecticut

http://www.wcsu.edu/

- **State-supported** comprehensive, founded 1903, part of Connecticut State Colleges & Universities (CSCU)
- **Urban** 340-acre campus with easy access to New York City
- **Endowment** $18.4 million
- **Coed** 5,181 undergraduate students, 79% full-time, 52% women, 48% men
- **Moderately difficult** entrance level, 67% of applicants were admitted

UNDERGRAD STUDENTS

4,116 full-time, 1,065 part-time. Students come from 18 states and territories; 7 other countries; 6% are from out of state; 11% Black or African American, non-Hispanic/Latino; 18% Hispanic/Latino; 4% Asian, non-Hispanic/Latino; 0.1% Native Hawaiian or other Pacific Islander, non-Hispanic/Latino; 0.1% American Indian or Alaska Native, non-Hispanic/Latino; 3% Two or more races, non-Hispanic/Latino; 3% Race/ethnicity unknown; 0.2% international; 10% transferred in; 32% live on campus.

Freshmen:

Admission: 5,484 applied, 3,665 admitted, 836 enrolled. ***Average high school GPA:*** 3. ***Test scores:*** SAT critical reading scores over 500: 47%; SAT math scores over 500: 45%; SAT writing scores over 500: 46%; SAT critical reading scores over 600: 11%; SAT math scores over 600: 11%; SAT writing scores over 600: 11%; SAT critical reading scores over 700: 2%; SAT math scores over 700: 2%; SAT writing scores over 700: 1%.

Retention: 73% of full-time freshmen returned.

FACULTY

Total: 637, 35% full-time, 30% with terminal degrees.

Student/faculty ratio: 12:1.

ACADEMICS

Calendar: semesters. *Degrees:* associate, bachelor's, master's, doctoral, and post-master's certificates.

Special study options: advanced placement credit, cooperative education, distance learning, honors programs, independent study, internships, part-time degree program, services for LD students, student-designed majors, study abroad, summer session for credit. ***ROTC:*** Army (c), Air Force (c).

Computers: 666 computers/terminals and 1,065 ports are available on campus for general student use. Students can access the following: computer help desk, free student e-mail accounts, online (class) grades, online (class) registration, online (class) schedules, online payment. Campuswide network is available. 100% of college-owned or -operated housing units are wired for high-speed Internet access. Wireless service is available via entire campus.

Library: Ruth Haas Library plus 2 others. *Books:* 199,945 (physical), 231,262 (digital/electronic); *Serial titles:* 300 (physical), 47,000 (digital/electronic); *Databases:* 102. Weekly public service hours: 144; students can reserve study rooms.

STUDENT LIFE

Housing options: coed. Campus housing is university owned.

Activities and organizations: drama/theater group, student-run newspaper, radio station, choral group, National Society of Collegiate Scholars, Criminology Club, Jazz Club, American Marketing Club, Meteorology, national fraternities, national sororities.

Athletics Member NCAA. All Division III. ***Intercollegiate sports:*** baseball M, basketball M/W, cheerleading W(c), field hockey W, football M, lacrosse M/W, soccer M/W, softball W, swimming and diving W, tennis M/W, volleyball W. ***Intramural sports:*** basketball M/W, football M, ice hockey M(c), rock climbing M(c)/W(c), soccer M/W, softball W.

Campus security: 24-hour emergency response devices and patrols, student patrols, late-night transport/escort service, controlled dormitory access.

Student services: health clinic, personal/psychological counseling.

COSTS & FINANCIAL AID

Costs (2016–17) ***Tuition:*** state resident $5216 full-time, $217 per credit hour part-time; nonresident $16,882 full-time, $223 per credit hour part-time. Full-time tuition and fees vary according to course load, program, and reciprocity agreements. ***Required fees:*** $4801 full-time, $256 per credit hour part-time. ***Room and board:*** $11,884; room only: $6829. Room and board charges vary according to board plan and housing facility. ***Payment plan:*** installment. ***Waivers:*** senior citizens and employees or children of employees.

Financial Aid Of all full-time matriculated undergraduates who enrolled in 2015, 3,436 applied for aid, 2,891 were judged to have need, 223 had their need fully met. 81 Federal Work-Study jobs (averaging $2478). In 2015, 31 non-need-based awards were made. ***Average percent of need met:*** 45. ***Average financial aid package:*** $8426. ***Average need-based loan:*** $4234. ***Average need-based gift aid:*** $5251. ***Average non-need-based aid:*** $10,195. ***Average indebtedness upon graduation:*** $31,229. ***Financial aid deadline:*** 3/15.

APPLYING

Standardized Tests *Recommended:* SAT or ACT (for admission).

Options: electronic application, deferred entrance.

Application fee: $50.

Required: high school transcript. ***Required for some:*** essay or personal statement, interview.

Application deadlines: rolling (freshmen), rolling (transfers).

Notification: continuous (freshmen), continuous (transfers).

CONTACT

Office of University Admissions, Western Connecticut State University, 181 White Street, Danbury, CT 06810. *Phone:* 203-837-9000. *Toll-free phone:* 877-837-WCSU. *Fax:* 203-837-8338.
E-mail: admissions@wcsu.edu.

See this page for display ad and page 1594 for the College Close-Up.

Yale University

New Haven, Connecticut

http://www.yale.edu/

- **Independent** university, founded 1701
- **Urban** 342-acre campus with easy access to New York City
- **Endowment** $25.6 billion
- **Coed**
- **Most difficult** entrance level

FACULTY

Student/faculty ratio: 6:1.

ACADEMICS

Calendar: semesters. *Degrees:* bachelor's, master's, doctoral, and post-master's certificates.

Library: Sterling Memorial Library plus 15 others. *Books:* 13.8 million (physical), 1.8 million (digital/electronic). Weekly public service hours: 93; students can reserve study rooms.

STUDENT LIFE

Housing options: on-campus residence required through sophomore year; coed, special housing for students with disabilities. Campus housing is university owned. Freshman campus housing is guaranteed.

Activities and organizations: drama/theater group, student-run newspaper, radio station, choral group, marching band, national fraternities, national sororities.

Athletics Member NCAA. All Division I except football (Division I-AA).

Campus security: 24-hour emergency response devices and patrols, late-night transport/escort service, controlled dormitory access.

Student services: health clinic, personal/psychological counseling, women's center.

COSTS & FINANCIAL AID

Costs (2016–17) ***Comprehensive fee:*** $64,650 includes full-time tuition ($49,480) and room and board ($15,170). ***College room only:*** $8520. Room and board charges vary according to board plan.

Financial Aid Of all full-time matriculated undergraduates who enrolled in 2015, 2,940 applied for aid, 2,727 were judged to have need, 2,727 had their need fully met. ***Average percent of need met:*** 100.

Average financial aid package: $50,380. ***Average need-based loan:*** $2885. ***Average need-based gift aid:*** $47,960. ***Average indebtedness upon graduation:*** $15,521. ***Financial aid deadline:*** 3/1.

APPLYING

Standardized Tests *Required:* SAT or ACT (for admission). *Recommended:* SAT Subject Tests (for admission).

Options: electronic application, early admission, early action, deferred entrance.

Application fee: $80.

Required: essay or personal statement, high school transcript, 3 letters of recommendation. ***Recommended:*** interview.

CONTACT

Undergraduate Admissions, Yale University, Yale University, PO Box 208234, New Haven, CT 06520. *Phone:* 203-432-9300. *E-mail:* student.questions@yale.edu.

DELAWARE

Delaware State University

Dover, Delaware

http://www.desu.edu/

- **State-supported** university, founded 1891, part of Delaware Higher Education Commission
- **Small-town** 400-acre campus
- **Coed**
- **Moderately difficult** entrance level

FACULTY

Student/faculty ratio: 15:1.

ACADEMICS

Calendar: semesters. *Degrees:* bachelor's, master's, and doctoral. **Library:** William C. Jason Library.

STUDENT LIFE

Housing options: coed, men-only, women-only, special housing for students with disabilities. Campus housing is university owned. Freshman applicants given priority for college housing.

Activities and organizations: drama/theater group, student-run newspaper, radio and television station, choral group, marching band, SGA, NPHC, Women's Senate, RHA, Men's Council, national fraternities, national sororities.

Athletics Member NCAA. All Division I except football (Division I-AA).

Campus security: 24-hour emergency response devices and patrols, student patrols, late-night transport/escort service, controlled dormitory access.

Student services: health clinic, personal/psychological counseling, women's center.

COSTS & FINANCIAL AID

Costs (2016–17) ***Tuition:*** state resident $7523 full-time, $280 per credit hour part-time; nonresident $16,138 full-time, $638 per credit hour part-time. Full-time tuition and fees vary according to course load and reciprocity agreements. Part-time tuition and fees vary according to course load and reciprocity agreements. ***Required fees:*** $300 per term part-time. ***Room and board:*** $10,936; room only: $6976. Room and board charges vary according to board plan and housing facility. ***Payment plans:*** installment, deferred payment.

Financial Aid Of all full-time matriculated undergraduates who enrolled in 2014, 3,171 applied for aid, 2,880 were judged to have need, 432 had their need fully met. In 2014, 45 non-need-based awards were made. ***Average percent of need met:*** 68. ***Average financial aid package:*** $11,631. ***Average need-based loan:*** $5617. ***Average need-based gift aid:*** $5367. ***Average non-need-based aid:*** $16,110. ***Average indebtedness upon graduation:*** $32,589.

APPLYING

Standardized Tests *Required:* SAT or ACT (for admission).

Options: electronic application, early admission, early action.

Application fee: $35.

Required: high school transcript, minimum 2.0 GPA.

CONTACT

Mrs. Erin Hill, Executive Director for Admissions, Delaware State University, 1200 North DuPont Highway, Dover, DE 19901-2277. *Phone:* 302-857-6351. *Toll-free phone:* 800-845-2544. *Fax:* 302-857-6352. *E-mail:* ehill@desu.edu.

Goldey-Beacom College

Wilmington, Delaware

http://www.gbc.edu/

CONTACT

Mr. Larry Eby, Director of Admissions, Goldey-Beacom College, 4701 Limestone Road, Wilmington, DE 19808. *Phone:* 302-225-6289. *Toll-free phone:* 800-833-4877. *Fax:* 302-996-5408. *E-mail:* admissions@gbc.edu.

Strayer University–Christiana Campus

Newark, Delaware

http://www.strayer.edu/delaware/christiana/

CONTACT

Strayer University–Christiana Campus, 240 Continental Drive, Suite 108, Newark, DE 19713.

University of Delaware

Newark, Delaware

http://www.udel.edu/

- **State-related** university, founded 1743
- **Small-town** 1000-acre campus with easy access to Philadelphia, Baltimore
- **Coed** 18,322 undergraduate students, 92% full-time, 58% women, 42% men
- **Moderately difficult** entrance level, 63% of applicants were admitted

UNDERGRAD STUDENTS

16,812 full-time, 1,510 part-time. 61% are from out of state; 5% Black or African American, non-Hispanic/Latino; 7% Hispanic/Latino; 5% Asian, non-Hispanic/Latino; 0.1% Native Hawaiian or other Pacific Islander, non-Hispanic/Latino; 0.1% American Indian or Alaska Native, non-Hispanic/Latino; 3% Two or more races, non-Hispanic/Latino; 0.8% Race/ethnicity unknown; 4% international; 2% transferred in; 43% live on campus.

Freshmen:

Admission: 24,881 applied, 15,567 admitted, 4,098 enrolled. ***Average high school GPA:*** 3.7. ***Test scores:*** SAT critical reading scores over 500: 94%; SAT math scores over 500: 94%; SAT writing scores over 500: 92%; ACT scores over 18: 99%; SAT critical reading scores over 600: 53%; SAT math scores over 600: 61%; SAT writing scores over 600: 51%; ACT scores over 24: 84%; SAT critical reading scores over 700: 14%; SAT math scores over 700: 13%; SAT writing scores over 700: 8%; ACT scores over 30: 20%.

Retention: 92% of full-time freshmen returned.

FACULTY

Total: 1,655, 71% full-time, 77% with terminal degrees.

Student/faculty ratio: 13:1.

ACADEMICS

Calendar: 4-1-4. *Degrees:* associate, bachelor's, master's, and doctoral.

Special study options: academic remediation for entering students, accelerated degree program, adult/continuing education programs, advanced placement credit, distance learning, double majors, English as a second language, honors programs, independent study, internships, off-campus study, part-time degree program, services for LD students, student-designed majors, study abroad, summer session for credit. ***ROTC:*** Army (b), Air Force (b).

Computers: Students can access the following: campus intranet, computer help desk, free student e-mail accounts, online (class) grades,

online (class) registration, online (class) schedules, personal Web page. Campuswide network is available. 100% of college-owned or -operated housing units are wired for high-speed Internet access. Wireless service is available via entire campus.
Library: Hugh Morris Library.

STUDENT LIFE
Housing options: on-campus residence required for freshman year; coed, women-only, special housing for students with disabilities. Campus housing is university owned. Freshman campus housing is guaranteed.

Activities and organizations: drama/theater group, student-run newspaper, radio station, choral group, marching band, national fraternities, national sororities.

Athletics Member NCAA. All Division I except football (Division I-AA). ***Intercollegiate sports:*** baseball M(s), basketball M(s)/W(s), bowling M(c)/W(c), cheerleading M(s)/W(s), crew M(c)/W(s), cross-country running M(c)/W(s), equestrian sports M(c)/W(c), field hockey W(s), golf M(s)/W(s), ice hockey M(c)/W(c), lacrosse M(s)/W(s), rugby M(c)/W(c), sailing M(c)/W(c), soccer M(s)/W(s), softball W(s), swimming and diving M/W(s), tennis M(s)/W(s), track and field M(c)/W(s), volleyball W(s), wrestling M(c). ***Intramural sports:*** badminton M/W, basketball M/W, field hockey W(c), football M/W, golf M/W, lacrosse M(c)/W(c), racquetball M/W, rock climbing M(c)/W(c), soccer M(c)/W(c), softball M/W, squash M/W, swimming and diving M/W, table tennis M/W, tennis M/W, track and field M/W, ultimate Frisbee M/W, volleyball M(c)/W(c), water polo M/W.

Campus security: 24-hour emergency response devices and patrols, student patrols, late-night transport/escort service, controlled dormitory access.

Student services: health clinic, personal/psychological counseling, women's center.

COSTS & FINANCIAL AID
Costs (2016–17) ***Tuition:*** state resident $11,540 full-time, $481 per credit hour part-time; nonresident $30,960 full-time, $1290 per credit hour part-time. ***Required fees:*** $1290 full-time. ***Room and board:*** $12,068; room only: $7316. Room and board charges vary according to board plan and housing facility. ***Payment plan:*** installment. ***Waivers:*** senior citizens and employees or children of employees.

Financial Aid Of all full-time matriculated undergraduates who enrolled in 2015, 11,547 applied for aid, 8,117 were judged to have need, 885 had their need fully met. In 2015, 3427 non-need-based awards were made. ***Average percent of need met:*** 56. ***Average financial aid package:*** $12,963. ***Average need-based loan:*** $4580. ***Average need-based gift aid:*** $9280. ***Average non-need-based aid:*** $7568. ***Average indebtedness upon graduation:*** $33,150. ***Financial aid deadline:*** 3/15.

APPLYING
Standardized Tests *Required:* SAT or ACT (for admission). *Required for some:* SAT Subject Tests (for admission). *Recommended:* SAT Subject Tests (for admission).

Options: electronic application, early admission, deferred entrance.

Application fee: $75.

Required: essay or personal statement, high school transcript, 1 letter of recommendation.

CONTACT
Dr. Jose Aviles, Director of Admissions, University of Delaware, 122 University Visitors Center, Newark, DE 19716. *Phone:* 302-831-8123. *Fax:* 302-831-6905. *E-mail:* admissions@udel.edu.

Wesley College

Dover, Delaware

http://www.wesley.edu/

CONTACT
Mr. Christopher Jester, Assistant Director of Undergraduate Admissions, Wesley College, 120 North State Street, Dover, DE 19901-3875. *Phone:* 302-736-2468. *Toll-free phone:* 800-937-5398. *E-mail:* christopher.jester@wesley.edu.

Wilmington University

New Castle, Delaware

http://www.wilmu.edu/

- **Independent** university, founded 1967
- **Suburban** 17-acre campus with easy access to Philadelphia
- **Endowment** $73.9 million
- **Coed** 8,873 undergraduate students, 40% full-time, 65% women, 35% men
- **Noncompetitive** entrance level, 100% of applicants were admitted

UNDERGRAD STUDENTS
3,570 full-time, 5,303 part-time. Students come from 41 states and territories; 74 other countries; 34% are from out of state; 25% Black or African American, non-Hispanic/Latino; 3% Hispanic/Latino; 2% Asian, non-Hispanic/Latino; 0.3% Native Hawaiian or other Pacific Islander, non-Hispanic/Latino; 2% American Indian or Alaska Native, non-Hispanic/Latino; 0.1% Two or more races, non-Hispanic/Latino; 13% Race/ethnicity unknown; 2% international; 70% transferred in.

Freshmen:
Admission: 3,299 applied, 3,296 admitted, 672 enrolled.
Retention: 64% of full-time freshmen returned.

FACULTY
Total: 3,093, 9% full-time, 13% with terminal degrees.
Student/faculty ratio: 17:1.

ACADEMICS
Calendar: semesters. *Degrees:* certificates, associate, bachelor's, master's, doctoral, post-master's, and postbachelor's certificates.

Special study options: academic remediation for entering students, accelerated degree program, adult/continuing education programs, cooperative education, distance learning, double majors, English as a second language, external degree program, independent study, internships, part-time degree program, study abroad, summer session for credit. ***ROTC:*** Army (c), Air Force (c).

Computers: 600 computers/terminals are available on campus for general student use. Students can access the following: free student e-mail accounts, online (class) grades, online (class) registration, online (class) schedules. Campuswide network is available. Wireless service is available via entire campus.
Library: Robert C. and Dorothy M. Peoples Library plus 1 other.

STUDENT LIFE
Housing options: college housing not available.

Activities and organizations: Student Government Association, Green Team, Photography Club, WU Student United Way, Wildcat Cheerleaders.

Athletics Member NCAA. All Division II. ***Intercollegiate sports:*** baseball M(s), basketball M(s)/W(s), bowling W(s), cross-country running M(s)/W(s), softball W(s), volleyball W(s).

Campus security: 24-hour emergency response devices and patrols, late-night transport/escort service.

COSTS & FINANCIAL AID
Costs (2016–17) ***Tuition:*** $8496 full-time, $354 per credit part-time. Full-time tuition and fees vary according to location. Part-time tuition and fees vary according to location. ***Required fees:*** $50 full-time, $25 per term part-time. ***Payment plan:*** installment. ***Waivers:*** employees or children of employees.

Financial Aid Of all full-time matriculated undergraduates who enrolled in 2004, 1,217 applied for aid, 900 were judged to have need. 25 Federal Work-Study jobs (averaging $2000). In 2004, 74 non-need-based awards were made. ***Average percent of need met:*** 48. ***Average financial aid package:*** $5770. ***Average need-based loan:*** $3889. ***Average need-based gift aid:*** $2464. ***Average non-need-based aid:*** $1100. ***Average indebtedness upon graduation:*** $17,486.

APPLYING
Options: early admission, deferred entrance.

Application fee: $25.

Required: high school transcript. ***Recommended:*** interview.

Application deadlines: rolling (freshmen), rolling (transfers).

Notification: continuous (freshmen), continuous (transfers).

CONTACT
Ms. Laura Morris, Director of Admissions, Wilmington University, 320 North DuPont Highway, New Castle, DE 19720-6491. *Phone:* 302-295-1179. *Toll-free phone:* 877-967-5464.
E-mail: undergradadmissions@wilmu.edu.

DISTRICT OF COLUMBIA

American University
Washington, District of Columbia
http://www.american.edu/

- **Independent Methodist** university, founded 1893
- **Suburban** 84-acre campus with easy access to Washington, DC
- **Endowment** $558.1 million
- **Coed** 7,901 undergraduate students, 95% full-time, 63% women, 37% men
- **Very difficult** entrance level, 26% of applicants were admitted

UNDERGRAD STUDENTS
7,545 full-time, 356 part-time. Students come from 54 states and territories; 98 other countries; 82% are from out of state; 7% Black or African American, non-Hispanic/Latino; 13% Hispanic/Latino; 7% Asian, non-Hispanic/Latino; 0.1% American Indian or Alaska Native, non-Hispanic/Latino; 5% Two or more races, non-Hispanic/Latino; 3% Race/ethnicity unknown; 7% international; 3% transferred in.

Freshmen:
Admission: 19,325 applied, 5,008 admitted, 1,679 enrolled. ***Test scores:*** SAT critical reading scores over 500: 96%; SAT math scores over 500: 95%; SAT writing scores over 500: 97%; ACT scores over 18: 100%; SAT critical reading scores over 600: 71%; SAT math scores over 600: 57%; SAT writing scores over 600: 64%; ACT scores over 24: 94%; SAT critical reading scores over 700: 23%; SAT math scores over 700: 9%; SAT writing scores over 700: 15%; ACT scores over 30: 38%.
Retention: 90% of full-time freshmen returned.

FACULTY
Total: 1,436, 55% full-time, 52% with terminal degrees.
Student/faculty ratio: 12:1.

ACADEMICS
Calendar: semesters. *Degrees:* certificates, associate, bachelor's, master's, doctoral, and postbachelor's certificates.
Special study options: accelerated degree program, advanced placement credit, cooperative education, distance learning, double majors, English as a second language, honors programs, independent study, internships, off-campus study, part-time degree program, services for LD students, student-designed majors, study abroad, summer session for credit. ***ROTC:*** Army (c), Air Force (c).
Unusual degree programs: 3-2 engineering with University of Maryland, College Park.
Computers: 700 computers/terminals and 7,000 ports are available on campus for general student use. Students can access the following: campus intranet, computer help desk, free student e-mail accounts, online (class) grades, online (class) registration, online (class) schedules, online e-support through learning management system. Campuswide network is available. 100% of college-owned or -operated housing units are wired for high-speed Internet access. Wireless service is available via entire campus.
Library: Bender Library plus 1 other. *Books:* 700,000 (physical), 300,000 (digital/electronic); *Serial titles:* 650 (physical), 125,000 (digital/electronic); *Databases:* 300. Study areas open 24 hours, 5-7 days a week; students can reserve study rooms.

STUDENT LIFE
Housing options: coed, special housing for students with disabilities. Campus housing is university owned and leased by the school. Freshman campus housing is guaranteed.
Activities and organizations: drama/theater group, student-run newspaper, radio and television station, choral group, Kennedy Political Union, Habitat for Humanity, Student government, Amnesty International, Multiple Ethnic and religious organizations, national fraternities, national sororities.
Athletics Member NCAA. All Division I. ***Intercollegiate sports:*** basketball M(s)/W(s), cross-country running M(s)/W(s), field hockey W(s), lacrosse W(s), soccer M(s)/W(s), swimming and diving M/W, track and field M(s)/W(s), volleyball W(s), wrestling M(s). ***Intramural sports:*** baseball M(c)/W(c), basketball M/W, crew M(c)/W(c), equestrian sports M(c)/W(c), field hockey M(c)/W(c), football M/W, golf M(c)/W(c), gymnastics M(c)/W(c), ice hockey M(c)/W(c), lacrosse M(c)/W(c), rugby M(c)/W(c), sailing M(c)/W(c), soccer M/W, table tennis M/W, tennis M/W, track and field M/W, ultimate Frisbee M(c)/W(c), volleyball M/W, water polo M/W, weight lifting M.
Campus security: 24-hour emergency response devices and patrols, late-night transport/escort service, controlled dormitory access, e-mail and text emergency notification system, special events security, safe ride home program, self defense training.
Student services: health clinic, personal/psychological counseling, women's center.

COSTS & FINANCIAL AID
Costs (2016–17) ***Comprehensive fee:*** $59,379 includes full-time tuition ($44,046), mandatory fees ($807), and room and board ($14,526). Full-time tuition and fees vary according to course load. Part-time tuition: $1467 per credit hour. ***Required fees:*** $100 per term part-time. ***College room only:*** $9800. Room and board charges vary according to board plan, housing facility, and location. ***Payment plans:*** tuition prepayment, installment. ***Waivers:*** employees or children of employees.
Financial Aid Of all full-time matriculated undergraduates who enrolled in 2016, 4,316 applied for aid, 3,711 were judged to have need, 710 had their need fully met. In 2016, 630 non-need-based awards were made. ***Average percent of need met:*** 70. ***Average financial aid package:*** $31,064. ***Average need-based loan:*** $4693. ***Average need-based gift aid:*** $25,024. ***Average non-need-based aid:*** $14,579. ***Financial aid deadline:*** 1/10.

APPLYING
Options: electronic application, early admission, early decision, deferred entrance.
Application fee: $70.
Required: essay or personal statement, high school transcript. ***Recommended:*** 2 letters of recommendation.
Application deadlines: 1/10 (freshmen), 3/1 (transfers).
Early decision deadline: 11/10 (for plan 1), 1/10 (for plan 2).
Notification: 4/1 (freshmen), continuous (transfers), 12/31 (early decision plan 1), 2/15 (early decision plan 2).

CONTACT
Mr. Jeremy Lowe, Acting Asst Vice Provost, Undergraduate Admissions, American University, 4400 Massachusetts Avenue, NW, Washington, DC 20016-8001. *Phone:* 202-885-6000. *E-mail:* admissions@american.edu.

The Catholic University of America
Washington, District of Columbia
http://www.cua.edu/

- **Independent** university, founded 1887, affiliated with Roman Catholic Church
- **Urban** 176-acre campus with easy access to Washington DC
- **Coed** 3,241 undergraduate students, 95% full-time, 54% women, 45% men

UNDERGRAD STUDENTS
3,094 full-time, 144 part-time. Students come from 48 states and territories; 27 other countries; 96% are from out of state; 5% Black or African American, non-Hispanic/Latino; 13% Hispanic/Latino; 4% Asian, non-Hispanic/Latino; 0.2% American Indian or Alaska Native, non-Hispanic/Latino; 5% Two or more races, non-Hispanic/Latino; 3% Race/ethnicity unknown; 5% international; 2% transferred in; 57% live on campus.

Freshmen:
Admission: 723 enrolled. ***Average high school GPA:*** 3.36. ***Test scores:*** SAT critical reading scores over 500: 82%; SAT math scores over 500: 81%; ACT scores over 18: 97%; SAT critical reading scores over 600:

39%; SAT math scores over 600: 36%; ACT scores over 24: 70%; SAT critical reading scores over 700: 8%; SAT math scores over 700: 6%; ACT scores over 30: 20%.

Retention: 84% of full-time freshmen returned.

FACULTY

Total: 736, 56% full-time, 53% with terminal degrees.

Student/faculty ratio: 7:1.

ACADEMICS

Calendar: semesters. *Degrees:* certificates, bachelor's, master's, doctoral, post-master's, and postbachelor's certificates.

Special study options: accelerated degree program, adult/continuing education programs, advanced placement credit, cooperative education, distance learning, double majors, English as a second language, honors programs, independent study, internships, off-campus study, part-time degree program, services for LD students, study abroad, summer session for credit. ***ROTC:*** Army (c), Navy (c), Air Force (c).

Unusual degree programs: 3-2 engineering; nursing; architecture, accounting, education, psychology.

Computers: 542 computers/terminals and 13,403 ports are available on campus for general student use. Students can access the following: campus intranet, computer help desk, free student e-mail accounts, online (class) grades, online (class) registration, online (class) schedules. Campuswide network is available. 100% of college-owned or -operated housing units are wired for high-speed Internet access. Wireless service is available via entire campus.

Library: Mullen Library plus 7 others. *Books:* 739,107 (physical), 216,309 (digital/electronic); *Serial titles:* 338,081 (physical), 87,846 (digital/electronic); *Databases:* 418. Weekly public service hours: 102.

STUDENT LIFE

Housing options: on-campus residence required through sophomore year; men-only, women-only. Campus housing is university owned. Freshman campus housing is guaranteed.

Activities and organizations: drama/theater group, student-run newspaper, radio station, choral group, College Republicans, Habitat for Humanity, Student Nurse's Association, Cardinals for Life, College Democrats, national fraternities, national sororities.

Athletics Member NCAA. All Division III. ***Intercollegiate sports:*** baseball M, basketball M/W, cross-country running M/W, field hockey W, football M, lacrosse M/W, soccer M/W, softball W, swimming and diving M/W, tennis M/W, track and field M/W, volleyball W. ***Intramural sports:*** badminton M/W, basketball M/W, cheerleading M(c)/W(c), crew M(c)/W(c), football M/W, ice hockey M(c)/W(c), lacrosse M(c), racquetball M/W, rowing M(c)/W(c), rugby M(c)/W(c), sailing M(c)/W(c), soccer M/W, softball M/W, tennis M/W, ultimate Frisbee M(c)/W(c), volleyball M/W.

Campus security: 24-hour emergency response devices and patrols, late-night transport/escort service, controlled dormitory access, controlled access of academic buildings.

Student services: health clinic, personal/psychological counseling, legal services.

COSTS & FINANCIAL AID

Costs (2016–17) ***One-time required fee:*** $425. ***Comprehensive fee:*** $56,356 includes full-time tuition ($41,800), mandatory fees ($736), and room and board ($13,820). Full-time tuition and fees vary according to program. Part-time tuition: $1655 per credit hour. Part-time tuition and fees vary according to course load and program. ***Required fees:*** $420 per year part-time. ***Room and board:*** Room and board charges vary according to board plan and housing facility. ***Payment plan:*** installment. ***Waivers:*** children of alumni and employees or children of employees.

Financial Aid Of all full-time matriculated undergraduates who enrolled in 2016, 2,014 applied for aid, 1,705 were judged to have need, 733 had their need fully met. 407 Federal Work-Study jobs (averaging $1914). In 2016, 1016 non-need-based awards were made. ***Average percent of need met:*** 80. ***Average financial aid package:*** $29,024. ***Average need-based loan:*** $5245. ***Average need-based gift aid:*** $24,944. ***Average non-need-based aid:*** $18,038. ***Average indebtedness upon graduation:*** $46,779. ***Financial aid deadline:*** 4/10.

APPLYING

Required: essay or personal statement, high school transcript, 1 letter of recommendation. ***Recommended:*** minimum 3.0 GPA, interview.

CONTACT
Dr. Christopher Lydon, Dean, University Admissions, The Catholic University of America, 102 McMahon Hall, 620 Michigan Avenue, NE, Washington, DC 20064. *Phone:* 202-319-5305. *Toll-free phone:* 800-673-2772. *Fax:* 202-319-6533. *E-mail:* cua-admissions@cua.edu.

See previous page for display ad and page 1314 for the College Close-Up.

Gallaudet University

Washington, District of Columbia

http://www.gallaudet.edu/

- **Independent** university, founded 1864
- **Urban** 99-acre campus
- **Coed** 1,121 undergraduate students, 97% full-time, 52% women, 48% men
- **Moderately difficult** entrance level, 66% of applicants were admitted

UNDERGRAD STUDENTS
1,082 full-time, 39 part-time. Students come from 50 states and territories; 21 other countries; 97% are from out of state; 16% Black or African American, non-Hispanic/Latino; 10% Hispanic/Latino; 4% Asian, non-Hispanic/Latino; 0.5% Native Hawaiian or other Pacific Islander, non-Hispanic/Latino; 0.6% American Indian or Alaska Native, non-Hispanic/Latino; 3% Two or more races, non-Hispanic/Latino; 6% Race/ethnicity unknown; 7% international; 10% transferred in; 82% live on campus.

Freshmen:
Admission: 511 applied, 338 admitted, 245 enrolled. ***Average high school GPA:*** 3.15. ***Test scores:*** SAT critical reading scores over 500: 40%; SAT math scores over 500: 36%; ACT scores over 18: 38%; SAT critical reading scores over 600: 11%; SAT math scores over 600: 11%; ACT scores over 24: 14%; SAT critical reading scores over 700: 4%; ACT scores over 30: 1%.

Retention: 80% of full-time freshmen returned.

FACULTY
Total: 271, 67% full-time, 50% with terminal degrees.

Student/faculty ratio: 7:1.

ACADEMICS
Calendar: semesters. *Degrees:* bachelor's, master's, doctoral, post-master's, and postbachelor's certificates (Undergraduate programs are open primarily to the students with hearing-impairments).

Special study options: academic remediation for entering students, adult/continuing education programs, advanced placement credit, distance learning, double majors, English as a second language, honors programs, independent study, internships, off-campus study, part-time degree program, services for LD students, student-designed majors, study abroad, summer session for credit.

Computers: 400 computers/terminals are available on campus for general student use. Students can access the following: campus intranet, computer help desk, free student e-mail accounts, online (class) grades, online (class) registration, online (class) schedules. Campuswide network is available. 100% of college-owned or -operated housing units are wired for high-speed Internet access. Wireless service is available via entire campus.

Library: Merrill Learning Center. *Books:* 121,359 (physical), 547,506 (digital/electronic); *Serial titles:* 4,142 (physical), 71,930 (digital/electronic); *Databases:* 79. Weekly public service hours: 90; students can reserve study rooms.

STUDENT LIFE
Housing options: coed, special housing for students with disabilities. Campus housing is university owned.

Activities and organizations: drama/theater group, student-run newspaper, television station, Student Body Government, The Buff and Blue, Rainbow Society, Green Grow, national fraternities, national sororities.

Athletics Member NCAA. All Division III. ***Intercollegiate sports:*** baseball M, basketball M/W, cheerleading M(c)/W(c), cross-country running M/W, football M, soccer M/W, softball W, swimming and diving M/W, track and field M/W, volleyball W. ***Intramural sports:*** basketball M/W, football M/W, table tennis M/W, ultimate Frisbee M/W, volleyball M/W.

Campus security: 24-hour emergency response devices and patrols, late-night transport/escort service, controlled dormitory access.

Student services: health clinic, personal/psychological counseling.

COSTS & FINANCIAL AID
Costs (2017–18) ***Comprehensive fee:*** $30,596 includes full-time tuition ($16,032), mandatory fees ($526), and room and board ($14,038). Full-time tuition and fees vary according to course load. Part-time tuition: $668 per credit hour. Part-time tuition and fees vary according to course load. ***College room only:*** $7658. Room and board charges vary according to board plan. ***Payment plans:*** installment, deferred payment. ***Waivers:*** employees or children of employees.

Financial Aid Of all full-time matriculated undergraduates who enrolled in 2014, 901 applied for aid, 842 were judged to have need, 79 had their need fully met. In 2014, 29 non-need-based awards were made. ***Average percent of need met:*** 71. ***Average financial aid package:*** $20,705. ***Average need-based loan:*** $4070. ***Average need-based gift aid:*** $18,699. ***Average non-need-based aid:*** $8949. ***Average indebtedness upon graduation:*** $18,643.

APPLYING
Standardized Tests *Required:* SAT or ACT (for admission). *Recommended:* ACT (for admission).

Options: electronic application, deferred entrance.

Application fee: $50.

Required: essay or personal statement, high school transcript, 2 letters of recommendation, audiogram. ***Required for some:*** interview.

Notification: continuous (freshmen), continuous (transfers).

CONTACT
Gallaudet University, 800 Florida Avenue, NE, Washington, DC 20002-3625. *Phone:* 202-651-5750. *Toll-free phone:* 800-995-0550.

Georgetown University

Washington, District of Columbia

http://www.georgetown.edu/

- **Independent Roman Catholic (Jesuit)** university, founded 1789
- **Urban** 104-acre campus with easy access to Washington, DC
- **Coed** 7,453 undergraduate students, 95% full-time, 56% women, 44% men
- **Most difficult** entrance level, 17% of applicants were admitted

UNDERGRAD STUDENTS
7,056 full-time, 397 part-time. Students come from 52 states and territories; 100 other countries; 96% are from out of state; 6% Black or African American, non-Hispanic/Latino; 8% Hispanic/Latino; 9% Asian, non-Hispanic/Latino; 0.1% Native Hawaiian or other Pacific Islander, non-Hispanic/Latino; 4% Two or more races, non-Hispanic/Latino; 3% Race/ethnicity unknown; 14% international; 2% transferred in; 78% live on campus.

Freshmen:
Admission: 19,997 applied, 3,369 admitted, 1,574 enrolled. ***Test scores:*** SAT critical reading scores over 500: 100%; SAT math scores over 500: 99%; ACT scores over 18: 100%; SAT critical reading scores over 600: 91%; SAT math scores over 600: 92%; ACT scores over 24: 98%; SAT critical reading scores over 700: 60%; SAT math scores over 700: 57%; ACT scores over 30: 79%.

Retention: 96% of full-time freshmen returned.

FACULTY
Total: 1,618, 63% full-time, 64% with terminal degrees.

Student/faculty ratio: 11:1.

ACADEMICS
Calendar: semesters. *Degrees:* certificates, bachelor's, master's, doctoral, post-master's, and postbachelor's certificates.

Special study options: academic remediation for entering students, adult/continuing education programs, advanced placement credit, distance learning, double majors, English as a second language, honors programs, independent study, internships, off-campus study, part-time degree program, services for LD students, student-designed majors, study abroad, summer session for credit. ***ROTC:*** Army (b), Navy (c), Air Force (c).

Unusual degree programs: 3-2 foreign service.

Computers: 450 computers/terminals and 1,000 ports are available on campus for general student use. Students can access the following: computer help desk, free student e-mail accounts, online (class) grades, online (class) registration, online (class) schedules. Campuswide network is available. 100% of college-owned or -operated housing units are wired for high-speed Internet access. Wireless service is available via classrooms, computer centers, computer labs, dorm rooms, learning centers, libraries, student centers.
Library: Joseph Mark Lauinger Memorial Library plus 6 others. *Books:* 2.9 million (physical), 1.9 million (digital/electronic); *Serial titles:* 48,099 (physical), 304,023 (digital/electronic); *Databases:* 1,339. Weekly public service hours: 100; study areas open 24 hours, 5-7 days a week; students can reserve study rooms.

STUDENT LIFE
Housing options: on-campus residence required through sophomore year; coed, special housing for students with disabilities. Campus housing is university owned. Freshman campus housing is guaranteed.

Activities and organizations: drama/theater group, student-run newspaper, radio and television station, choral group, Georgetown University Student Association (Student Government), International Relations Club, College Democrats, Georgetown University Grilling Society, Black Student Alliance.

Athletics Member NCAA. All Division I except football (Division I-AA). ***Intercollegiate sports:*** baseball M(s), basketball M(s)/W(s), crew M(s)/W(s), cross-country running M(s)/W(s), field hockey W(s), golf M(s)/W(s), ice hockey M(c), lacrosse M(s)/W(s), rugby M(c)/W(c), sailing M/W, soccer M(s)/W(s), softball W(s), swimming and diving M/W(s), tennis M/W(s), track and field M(s)/W(s), ultimate Frisbee M(c)/W(c), volleyball M(c)/W(s), water polo M(c). ***Intramural sports:*** basketball M/W, cross-country running M/W, football M/W, golf M/W, racquetball M/W, soccer M/W, softball M/W, squash M/W, table tennis M/W, tennis M/W, track and field M/W, ultimate Frisbee M, volleyball M/W.

Campus security: 24-hour emergency response devices and patrols, late-night transport/escort service, controlled dormitory access, student guards at residence halls and academic facilities.

Student services: health clinic, personal/psychological counseling, women's center.

COSTS & FINANCIAL AID
Costs (2016–17) ***Comprehensive fee:*** $66,115 includes full-time tuition ($49,968), mandatory fees ($579), and room and board ($15,568). Full-time tuition and fees vary according to course load and program. Part-time tuition: $2082 per credit hour. Part-time tuition and fees vary according to course load and program. ***College room only:*** $10,726. Room and board charges vary according to board plan and housing facility. ***Payment plan:*** installment.

Financial Aid Of all full-time matriculated undergraduates who enrolled in 2016, 4,003 applied for aid, 2,728 were judged to have need, 2,728 had their need fully met. 2,520 Federal Work-Study jobs (averaging $2866). ***Average percent of need met:*** 100. ***Average financial aid package:*** $48,999. ***Average need-based loan:*** $4076. ***Average need-based gift aid:*** $40,252. ***Average indebtedness upon graduation:*** $23,412. ***Financial aid deadline:*** 2/1.

APPLYING
Standardized Tests *Required:* SAT or ACT (for admission). *Recommended:* SAT Subject Tests (for admission).

Options: electronic application, early action, deferred entrance.

Application fee: $75.

Required: essay or personal statement, high school transcript, 2 letters of recommendation, interview.

Application deadlines: 1/10 (freshmen), 3/1 (transfers), 11/1 (early action).

Notification: 4/1 (freshmen), 6/1 (transfers), 12/15 (early action).

CONTACT
Dean Charles A. Deacon, Dean of Undergraduate Admissions, Georgetown University, 37th and O Street, NW, Washington, DC 20057. *Phone:* 202-687-3600. *Fax:* 202-687-5084.

The George Washington University
Washington, District of Columbia
http://www.gwu.edu/

- **Independent** university, founded 1821
- **Urban** 36-acre campus
- **Coed** 11,157 undergraduate students, 91% full-time, 56% women, 44% men
- **Very difficult** entrance level, 46% of applicants were admitted

UNDERGRAD STUDENTS
10,163 full-time, 994 part-time. Students come from 54 states and territories; 87 other countries; 97% are from out of state; 6% Black or African American, non-Hispanic/Latino; 8% Hispanic/Latino; 10% Asian, non-Hispanic/Latino; 0.1% Native Hawaiian or other Pacific Islander, non-Hispanic/Latino; 0.1% American Indian or Alaska Native, non-Hispanic/Latino; 4% Two or more races, non-Hispanic/Latino; 5% Race/ethnicity unknown; 10% international; 5% transferred in; 62% live on campus.

Freshmen:
Admission: 19,837 applied, 9,216 admitted, 2,589 enrolled. ***Test scores:*** SAT critical reading scores over 500: 96%; SAT math scores over 500: 98%; SAT writing scores over 500: 99%; ACT scores over 18: 100%; SAT critical reading scores over 600: 71%; SAT math scores over 600: 78%; SAT writing scores over 600: 77%; ACT scores over 24: 96%; SAT critical reading scores over 700: 23%; SAT math scores over 700: 26%; SAT writing scores over 700: 25%; ACT scores over 30: 50%.

Retention: 94% of full-time freshmen returned.

FACULTY
Total: 2,487, 44% full-time.

Student/faculty ratio: 13:1.

ACADEMICS
Calendar: semesters. *Degrees:* certificates, associate, bachelor's, master's, doctoral, post-master's, and postbachelor's certificates.

Special study options: accelerated degree program, adult/continuing education programs, advanced placement credit, cooperative education, distance learning, double majors, honors programs, independent study, internships, off-campus study, part-time degree program, services for LD students, student-designed majors, study abroad, summer session for credit. ***ROTC:*** Army (c), Navy (b), Air Force (c).

Unusual degree programs: 3-2 business administration; engineering; chemical toxicology, art therapy, economics, engineering economics, operations research.

Computers: Campuswide network is available.
Library: Gelman Library.

STUDENT LIFE
Housing options: on-campus residence required through sophomore year; coed, women-only. Campus housing is university owned. Freshman campus housing is guaranteed.

Activities and organizations: drama/theater group, student-run newspaper, radio and television station, choral group, marching band, Program Board, Student Association, Residence Hall Association, College Democrats, College Republicans, national fraternities, national sororities.

Athletics Member NCAA. All Division I. ***Intercollegiate sports:*** baseball M(s), basketball M(s)/W(s), crew M(s)/W(s), cross-country running M(s)/W(s), golf M(s), gymnastics W(s), soccer M(s)/W(s), swimming and diving M(s)/W(s), tennis M(s)/W(s), volleyball W(s), water polo M(s). ***Intramural sports:*** badminton M(c)/W(c), basketball M/W, bowling M(c)/W(c), equestrian sports M(c)/W(c), fencing M(c)/W(c), football M/W, lacrosse M(c), racquetball M/W, rugby M(c), sailing M(c)/W(c), soccer M/W, softball M/W, squash M(c)/W, swimming and diving M/W, tennis M/W, volleyball M(c)/W, water polo M/W.

Campus security: 24-hour emergency response devices and patrols, late-night transport/escort service, controlled dormitory access.

Student services: health clinic, personal/psychological counseling, legal services.

COSTS & FINANCIAL AID
Costs (2017–18) ***Comprehensive fee:*** $66,518 includes full-time tuition ($53,435), mandatory fees ($83), and room and board ($13,000). Full-

time tuition and fees vary according to student level. Part-time tuition: $1520 per credit hour. Part-time tuition and fees vary according to course load. No tuition increase for student's term of enrollment. ***College room only:*** $8900. Room and board charges vary according to housing facility. ***Payment plan:*** installment. ***Waivers:*** employees or children of employees.

Financial Aid Of all full-time matriculated undergraduates who enrolled in 2015, 5,607 applied for aid, 4,611 were judged to have need, 2,171 had their need fully met. In 2015, 2718 non-need-based awards were made. ***Average percent of need met:*** 87. ***Average financial aid package:*** $43,674. ***Average need-based loan:*** $5809. ***Average need-based gift aid:*** $29,433. ***Average non-need-based aid:*** $19,541. ***Average indebtedness upon graduation:*** $33,305. ***Financial aid deadline:*** 2/1.

APPLYING

Standardized Tests *Required for some:* SAT or ACT (for admission), SAT and SAT Subject Tests or ACT (for admission).

Options: electronic application, early admission, early decision, deferred entrance.

Application fee: $75.

Required: essay or personal statement, high school transcript, 2 letters of recommendation. ***Recommended:*** interview.

Application deadlines: 1/1 (freshmen), rolling (transfers).

Early decision deadline: 11/1 (for plan 1), 1/1 (for plan 2).

Notification: 4/1 (freshmen), continuous (transfers), 12/15 (early decision plan 1), 2/1 (early decision plan 2).

CONTACT

The George Washington University, 2121 I Street, NW, Washington, DC 20052. *Phone:* 202-994-6040.

Howard University

Washington, District of Columbia

http://www.howard.edu/

- **Independent** university, founded 1867
- **Urban** 256-acre campus with easy access to Washington
- **Endowment** $590.7 million
- **Coed**
- **Moderately difficult** entrance level

FACULTY

Student/faculty ratio: 10:1.

ACADEMICS

Calendar: semesters. *Degrees:* certificates, bachelor's, master's, doctoral, and post-master's certificates.

Library: Howard University Libraries plus 7 others. Study areas open 24 hours, 5-7 days a week; students can reserve study rooms.

STUDENT LIFE

Housing options: on-campus residence required through sophomore year; coed, men-only, women-only, special housing for students with disabilities. Campus housing is university owned. Freshman applicants given priority for college housing.

Activities and organizations: drama/theater group, student-run newspaper, radio and television station, choral group, marching band, Howard University Student Association, Undergraduate Student Assembly, Campus Pals, International Student Organization, Entrepreneurial Society, Howard University, national fraternities, national sororities.

Athletics Member NCAA. All Division I except football (Division I-AA).

Campus security: 24-hour emergency response devices and patrols, student patrols, late-night transport/escort service, controlled dormitory access, security lighting.

Student services: health clinic, personal/psychological counseling.

FINANCIAL AID

Financial Aid Of all full-time matriculated undergraduates who enrolled in 2015, 5,598 applied for aid, 5,253 were judged to have need, 475 had their need fully met. 522 Federal Work-Study jobs (averaging $4656). 273 state and other part-time jobs (averaging $4872). In 2015, 460 non-need-based awards were made. ***Average percent of need met:*** 71. ***Average financial aid package:*** $16,451. ***Average need-based loan:*** $5061. ***Average need-based gift aid:*** $8165. ***Average non-need-based aid:*** $25,040. ***Average indebtedness upon graduation:*** $32,071. ***Financial aid deadline:*** 5/1.

APPLYING

Standardized Tests *Required:* SAT or ACT (for admission).

Options: electronic application, early admission, early action, deferred entrance.

Application fee: $45.

Required: essay or personal statement, high school transcript. ***Required for some:*** 2 letters of recommendation.

CONTACT

Tammy McCants, Associate Director of Admissions, Howard University, 2400 Sixth Street N.W., Suite 111, Washington, DC 20059. *Phone:* 202-806-2763. *Toll-free phone:* 800-822-6363. *Fax:* 202-806-4465. *E-mail:* admission@howard.edu.

Strayer University–Takoma Park Campus

Washington, District of Columbia

http://www.strayer.edu/district-columbia/takoma-park/

CONTACT

Strayer University–Takoma Park Campus, 6830 Laurel Street, NW, Washington, DC 20012.

Strayer University–Washington Campus

Washington, District of Columbia

http://www.strayer.edu/district-columbia/washington/

CONTACT

Strayer University–Washington Campus, 1133 15th Street, NW, Washington, DC 20025.

Trinity Washington University

Washington, District of Columbia

http://www.trinitydc.edu/

CONTACT

Director of Admissions, Trinity Washington University, 125 Michigan Avenue, NE, Washington, DC 20017-1094. *Phone:* 800-492-6882. *Toll-free phone:* 800-IWANTTC. *E-mail:* admissions@trinitydc.edu.

University of Phoenix–Washington D.C. Campus

Washington, District of Columbia

http://www.phoenix.edu/

CONTACT

Mr. Marc Booker, Sr. Director, Office of Admissions and Evaluation, University of Phoenix–Washington D.C. Campus, 4035 South Riverpoint Parkway, Mail Stop CF-L101, Phoenix, AZ 85040. *Phone:* 602-557-4609. *Toll-free phone:* 866-766-0766. *Fax:* 480-643-1156.

University of the District of Columbia

Washington, District of Columbia

http://www.udc.edu/

CONTACT

Ms. Nicole L. Daniels, Director of Undergraduate Recruitment and Admissions, University of the District of Columbia, 4200 Connecticut Avenue NW, Washington, DC 20008. *Phone:* 202-274-6430. *Fax:* 202-274-5553. *E-mail:* nicole.daniels@udc.edu.

University of the Potomac

Washington, District of Columbia

http://www.potomac.edu/

- **Proprietary** comprehensive, founded 1991
- **Urban** campus with easy access to Washington DC; Tysons, VA
- **Coed** 165 undergraduate students, 95% full-time, 32% women, 68% men
- **Noncompetitive** entrance level

UNDERGRAD STUDENTS
157 full-time, 8 part-time. Students come from 48 states and territories; 38 other countries; 60% are from out of state; 44% Black or African American, non-Hispanic/Latino; 3% Hispanic/Latino; 4% Asian, non-Hispanic/Latino; 0.6% Native Hawaiian or other Pacific Islander, non-Hispanic/Latino; 2% American Indian or Alaska Native, non-Hispanic/Latino; 4% Two or more races, non-Hispanic/Latino; 6% Race/ethnicity unknown; 19% international; 2% transferred in.

Freshmen:
Admission: 30 enrolled.
Retention: 76% of full-time freshmen returned.

FACULTY
Total: 79, 6% full-time, 41% with terminal degrees.
Student/faculty ratio: 7:1.

ACADEMICS
Calendar: 6 8-week terms. *Degrees:* certificates, associate, bachelor's, and master's.
Special study options: adult/continuing education programs, distance learning, external degree program, honors programs, part-time degree program, services for LD students.
Computers: 28 computers/terminals are available on campus for general student use. Students can access the following: campus intranet, free student e-mail accounts, online (class) grades, online (class) schedules, student portal, access to learning management system. Campuswide network is available. Wireless service is available via entire campus.
Library: Learning Resource Center - Washington Campus plus 1 other. *Books:* 4,500 (physical); *Serial titles:* 20 (physical), 5 (digital/electronic); *Databases:* 5. Weekly public service hours: 35.

STUDENT LIFE
Housing options: college housing not available.
Campus security: late-night transport/escort service.

COSTS
Costs (2017–18) ***Tuition:*** $12,984 full-time, $541 per credit hour part-time. No tuition increase for student's term of enrollment. ***Required fees:*** $900 full-time, $450 per term part-time.

APPLYING
Options: electronic application.
Required: interview.
Application deadlines: rolling (freshmen), rolling (transfers).
Notification: continuous (freshmen), continuous (transfers).

CONTACT
Nerissa Conn-Kulling, Director of Admissions, University of the Potomac, 1401 H Street N.W. Suite 100, Washington, DC 20005. *Phone:* 202-274-2338. *Toll-free phone:* 888-686-0876.
E-mail: nerissa.coon-kulling@potomac.edu.

FLORIDA

Adventist University of Health Sciences

Orlando, Florida

http://www.adu.edu/

- **Independent** comprehensive, founded 1992
- **Urban** 9-acre campus with easy access to Orlando
- **Endowment** $7.4 million
- **Coed** 1,659 undergraduate students, 34% full-time, 80% women, 20% men
- **Minimally difficult** entrance level, 76% of applicants were admitted

UNDERGRAD STUDENTS
565 full-time, 1,094 part-time. Students come from 43 states and territories; 12 other countries; 25% are from out of state; 16% Black or African American, non-Hispanic/Latino; 27% Hispanic/Latino; 7% Asian, non-Hispanic/Latino; 0.7% Native Hawaiian or other Pacific Islander, non-Hispanic/Latino; 0.4% American Indian or Alaska Native, non-Hispanic/Latino; 2% Two or more races, non-Hispanic/Latino; 6% Race/ethnicity unknown; 0.7% international; 10% transferred in; 10% live on campus.

Freshmen:
Admission: 329 applied, 251 admitted, 92 enrolled.
Retention: 68% of full-time freshmen returned.

FACULTY
Total: 260, 32% full-time, 30% with terminal degrees.
Student/faculty ratio: 8:1.

ACADEMICS
Calendar: trimesters. *Degrees:* certificates, associate, bachelor's, master's, doctoral, and postbachelor's certificates.
Special study options: academic remediation for entering students, distance learning, double majors, independent study, internships, services for LD students, summer session for credit.
Computers: 47 computers/terminals are available on campus for general student use. Students can access the following: campus intranet, computer help desk, free student e-mail accounts, online (class) grades, online (class) registration, online (class) schedules. Campuswide network is available. Wireless service is available via entire campus.
Library: The R. A. Williams Library. *Books:* 11,559 (physical), 19,921 (digital/electronic); *Serial titles:* 34 (physical), 37,041 (digital/electronic); *Databases:* 74. Weekly public service hours: 65; students can reserve study rooms.

STUDENT LIFE
Housing options: coed. Campus housing is leased by the school.
Activities and organizations: drama/theater group, choral group, Student Nursing Association, Student Occupational Therapy Association, Pre Physician Assistant, Pre Medical School, Campus Ministries.
Campus security: 24-hour emergency response devices and patrols, late-night transport/escort service, controlled dormitory access.
Student services: personal/psychological counseling.

COSTS & FINANCIAL AID
Costs (2017–18) ***Tuition:*** $13,650 full-time, $455 per credit hour part-time. ***Required fees:*** $600 full-time, $300 per term part-time. ***Room only:*** $4200. ***Payment plans:*** installment, deferred payment. ***Waivers:*** employees or children of employees.
Financial Aid ***Financial aid deadline:*** 7/22.

APPLYING
Standardized Tests *Required for some:* SAT or ACT (for admission), TOEFL.
Options: electronic application, early admission, early action.
Application fee: $20.
Required: minimum 2.5 GPA. ***Required for some:*** essay or personal statement, high school transcript, 2 letters of recommendation, interview.
Application deadlines: 7/1 (freshmen), 7/1 (transfers), 6/1 (early action).

Notification: continuous until 7/15 (freshmen), continuous until 7/15 (transfers).

CONTACT
Adventist University of Health Sciences, 671 Winyah Drive, Orlando, FL 32803. *Phone:* 407-303-7742. *Toll-free phone:* 800-500-7747.

American College for Medical Careers
Orlando, Florida
http://www.acmc.edu/

CONTACT
American College for Medical Careers, 5959 Lake Ellenor Drive, Orlando, FL 32809. *Toll-free phone:* 888-599-7887.

Argosy University, Sarasota
Sarasota, Florida
http://www.argosy.edu/locations/sarasota/

CONTACT
Argosy University, Sarasota, 5250 17th Street, Sarasota, FL 34235. *Phone:* 941-379-0404. *Toll-free phone:* 800-331-5995.

Argosy University, Tampa
Tampa, Florida
http://www.argosy.edu/locations/tampa/

CONTACT
Argosy University, Tampa, 1403 North Howard Avenue, Tampa, FL 33607. *Phone:* 813-393-5290. *Toll-free phone:* 800-850-6488.

The Art Institute of Fort Lauderdale
Fort Lauderdale, Florida
http://www.artinstitutes.edu/fortlauderdale/

CONTACT
The Art Institute of Fort Lauderdale, 1799 Southeast 17th Street, Fort Lauderdale, FL 33316. *Phone:* 954-463-3000. *Toll-free phone:* 800-275-7603.

The Art Institute of Tampa, a branch of Miami International University of Art & Design
Tampa, Florida
http://www.artinstitutes.edu/tampa/

CONTACT
The Art Institute of Tampa, a branch of Miami International University of Art & Design, Parkside at Tampa Bay Park, 4401 North Himes Avenue, Suite 150, Tampa, FL 33614. *Phone:* 813-873-2112. *Toll-free phone:* 866-703-3277.

Ave Maria University
Ave Maria, Florida
http://www.avemaria.edu/

- **Independent Roman Catholic** comprehensive, founded 2002
- **Small-town** 790-acre campus
- **Endowment** $2.5 million
- **Coed**
- **Moderately difficult** entrance level

FACULTY
Student/faculty ratio: 14:1.

ACADEMICS
Calendar: semesters. *Degrees:* bachelor's, master's, and doctoral.
Library: Canizaro Library.

STUDENT LIFE
Housing options: on-campus residence required through senior year; men-only, women-only. Campus housing is university owned. Freshman campus housing is guaranteed.

Activities and organizations: drama/theater group, student-run newspaper, choral group, Students for Life, Drama Club, Student Government Association, Intercollegiate Studies Institute, Faith in Action Ministry.

Athletics Member NAIA.

Campus security: 24-hour patrols, controlled dormitory access, County Sheriff workstation on campus with deputy patrols.

Student services: health clinic, personal/psychological counseling.

FINANCIAL AID
Financial Aid Of all full-time matriculated undergraduates who enrolled in 2016, 721 applied for aid, 603 were judged to have need, 146 had their need fully met. 90 Federal Work-Study jobs (averaging $1459). 3 state and other part-time jobs (averaging $2087). In 2016, 379 non-need-based awards were made. ***Average percent of need met:*** 76. ***Average financial aid package:*** $17,812. ***Average need-based loan:*** $3986. ***Average need-based gift aid:*** $13,683. ***Average non-need-based aid:*** $8957. ***Average indebtedness upon graduation:*** $25,962.

APPLYING
Standardized Tests *Required:* SAT or ACT (for admission).

Options: electronic application, deferred entrance.

Required: high school transcript, minimum 2.8 GPA, activities list. ***Required for some:*** essay or personal statement, 2 letters of recommendation, interview.

CONTACT
Ave Maria University, 5050 Ave Maria Boulevard, Ave Maria, FL 34142. *Phone:* 239-280-2487. *Toll-free phone:* 877-283-8648. *Fax:* 239-280-2559.

★ The Baptist College of Florida
Graceville, Florida
http://www.baptistcollege.edu/

- **Independent Southern Baptist** comprehensive, founded 1943
- **Small-town** 250-acre campus
- **Endowment** $6.6 million
- **Coed** 440 undergraduate students, 62% full-time, 35% women, 65% men
- **Noncompetitive** entrance level, 60% of applicants were admitted

UNDERGRAD STUDENTS
274 full-time, 166 part-time. Students come from 16 states and territories; 31% are from out of state; 8% Black or African American, non-Hispanic/Latino; 3% Hispanic/Latino; 0.5% Asian, non-Hispanic/Latino; 0.5% Native Hawaiian or other Pacific Islander, non-Hispanic/Latino; 0.5% American Indian or Alaska Native, non-Hispanic/Latino; 3% Two or more races, non-Hispanic/Latino; 5% Race/ethnicity unknown; 15% transferred in; 39% live on campus.

Freshmen:
Admission: 119 applied, 71 admitted, 34 enrolled.
Retention: 72% of full-time freshmen returned.

FACULTY
Total: 67, 37% full-time, 49% with terminal degrees.
Student/faculty ratio: 10:1.

ACADEMICS
Calendar: semesters. *Degrees:* associate, bachelor's, and master's.

Special study options: academic remediation for entering students, advanced placement credit, distance learning, double majors, independent study, internships, part-time degree program, services for LD students, summer session for credit.

Computers: 25 computers/terminals are available on campus for general student use. Students can access the following: free student e-mail accounts, online (class) grades, online (class) registration. Campuswide network is available. Wireless service is available via entire campus.
Library: Ida J. MacMillan Library plus 1 other. *Books:* 90,006 (physical), 88,931 (digital/electronic); *Serial titles:* 5,602 (physical), 5,602 (digital/electronic); *Databases:* 16. Weekly public service hours: 66.

STUDENT LIFE
Housing options: on-campus residence required through sophomore year; men-only, women-only, special housing for students with disabilities. Campus housing is university owned. Freshman campus housing is guaranteed.

Activities and organizations: drama/theater group, choral group, Baptist Collegiate Ministry, College Choir, AACC.

Athletics ***Intramural sports:*** basketball M/W, fencing M/W, football M/W, soccer M/W, softball M/W, ultimate Frisbee M/W, volleyball M/W.

Campus security: student patrols, patrols by police officers 11 pm to 7 am.

Student services: personal/psychological counseling.

COSTS & FINANCIAL AID
Costs (2017–18) ***Comprehensive fee:*** $15,238 includes full-time tuition ($10,200), mandatory fees ($900), and room and board ($4138). Full-time tuition and fees vary according to location and program. Part-time tuition: $340 per credit hour. Part-time tuition and fees vary according to location and program. ***Required fees:*** $30 per credit part-time. ***Room and board:*** Room and board charges vary according to board plan and housing facility. ***Waivers:*** employees or children of employees.

Financial Aid Of all full-time matriculated undergraduates who enrolled in 2016, 336 applied for aid, 295 were judged to have need, 9 had their need fully met. 24 Federal Work-Study jobs (averaging $2163). In 2016, 20 non-need-based awards were made. ***Average percent of need met:*** 41. ***Average financial aid package:*** $8517. ***Average need-based loan:*** $3520. ***Average need-based gift aid:*** $5993. ***Average non-need-based aid:*** $1872. ***Average indebtedness upon graduation:*** $24,444. ***Financial aid deadline:*** 4/15.

APPLYING
Standardized Tests *Required:* SAT or ACT (for admission).

Options: electronic application, deferred entrance.

Application fee: $25.

Required: essay or personal statement, high school transcript, minimum 2.5 GPA, 2 letters of recommendation, Christian/church member for 1 year minimum. ***Recommended:*** interview.

Application deadlines: 8/11 (freshmen), 8/11 (transfers).

Notification: continuous (freshmen), continuous (transfers).

CONTACT
The Baptist College of Florida, 5400 College Drive, Graceville, FL 32440-1898. *Phone:* 850-263-3261 Ext. 460.
Toll-free phone: 800-328-2660 Ext. 460.

★ Barry University

Miami Shores, Florida

http://www.barry.edu/

- **Independent Roman Catholic** university, founded 1940
- **Suburban** 122-acre campus with easy access to Miami
- **Coed** 3,541 undergraduate students, 83% full-time, 61% women, 39% men
- **Moderately difficult** entrance level, 62% of applicants were admitted

UNDERGRAD STUDENTS
2,924 full-time, 617 part-time. 21% are from out of state; 29% Black or African American, non-Hispanic/Latino; 31% Hispanic/Latino; 0.8% Asian, non-Hispanic/Latino; 0.2% Native Hawaiian or other Pacific Islander, non-Hispanic/Latino; 0.2% American Indian or Alaska Native, non-Hispanic/Latino; 2% Two or more races, non-Hispanic/Latino; 9% Race/ethnicity unknown; 8% international; 30% live on campus.

Freshmen:
Admission: 4,982 applied, 3,070 admitted, 480 enrolled. ***Test scores:*** SAT critical reading scores over 500: 29%; SAT math scores over 500: 25%; ACT scores over 18: 81%; SAT critical reading scores over 600: 2%; SAT math scores over 600: 4%; ACT scores over 24: 10%; ACT scores over 30: 1%.

Retention: 65% of full-time freshmen returned.

ACADEMICS
Calendar: semesters. *Degrees:* certificates, bachelor's, master's, doctoral, post-master's, and postbachelor's certificates.

Special study options: academic remediation for entering students, accelerated degree program, adult/continuing education programs, advanced placement credit, distance learning, double majors, English as a second language, honors programs, independent study, internships, off-campus study, part-time degree program, services for LD students, study abroad, summer session for credit. ***ROTC:*** Army (c), Air Force (c).

Unusual degree programs: 3-2 engineering with University of Miami.

Computers: 368 computers/terminals are available on campus for general student use. Students can access the following: campus intranet, computer help desk, free student e-mail accounts, online (class) grades, online (class) registration, online (class) schedules, learning management system. Campuswide network is available. Wireless service is available via computer centers, computer labs, learning centers, student centers.

Library: Monsignor William Barry Memorial Library plus 1 other.

STUDENT LIFE
Housing options: on-campus residence required for freshman year; coed, men-only, women-only, special housing for students with disabilities. Campus housing is university owned.

Activities and organizations: drama/theater group, student-run newspaper, radio and television station, choral group, Student Government Association, Campus Activities Board, SCUBA Society, Caribbean Students Association, Jamaican Association, national fraternities, national sororities.

Athletics Member NCAA. All Division II. ***Intercollegiate sports:*** baseball M(s), basketball M(s)/W(s), crew W(s), golf M(s)/W(s), soccer M(s)/W(s), softball W(s), tennis M(s)/W(s), volleyball W(s). ***Intramural sports:*** basketball M/W, football M/W, golf M/W, soccer M/W, softball M/W, volleyball M/W.

Campus security: 24-hour emergency response devices and patrols, late-night transport/escort service.

Student services: health clinic, personal/psychological counseling.

COSTS & FINANCIAL AID
Costs (2017–18) ***Comprehensive fee:*** $39,600 includes full-time tuition ($28,800) and room and board ($10,800). Part-time tuition: $865 per credit hour. Part-time tuition and fees vary according to course load. ***Room and board:*** Room and board charges vary according to housing facility. ***Payment plans:*** installment, deferred payment. ***Waivers:*** employees or children of employees.

Financial Aid Of all full-time matriculated undergraduates who enrolled in 2016, 2,319 applied for aid, 2,226 were judged to have need, 69 had their need fully met. In 2016, 354 non-need-based awards were made. ***Average percent of need met:*** 52. ***Average financial aid package:*** $20,983. ***Average need-based loan:*** $4488. ***Average need-based gift aid:*** $8811. ***Average non-need-based aid:*** $8629. ***Average indebtedness upon graduation:*** $39,255.

APPLYING
Standardized Tests *Required:* SAT or ACT (for admission).

Options: electronic application, early admission, deferred entrance.

Application fee: $30.

Required: high school transcript, minimum 2.0 GPA. ***Required for some:*** essay or personal statement. ***Recommended:*** interview.

Application deadlines: rolling (freshmen), rolling (transfers).

Notification: continuous (freshmen), continuous (transfers).

CONTACT
Barry University, 11300 Northeast Second Avenue, Miami Shores, FL 33161-6695. *Phone:* 305-899-3394. *Toll-free phone:* 800-695-2279.

Beacon College

Leesburg, Florida

http://www.beaconcollege.edu/

- **Independent** 4-year, founded 1989
- **Small-town** 19-acre campus with easy access to Orlando
- **Endowment** $74,955
- **Coed** 314 undergraduate students, 98% full-time, 43% women, 57% men
- **Moderately difficult** entrance level, 48% of applicants were admitted

UNDERGRAD STUDENTS
307 full-time, 7 part-time. Students come from 38 states and territories; 8 other countries; 70% are from out of state; 16% Black or African

American, non-Hispanic/Latino; 5% Hispanic/Latino; 3% Asian, non-Hispanic/Latino; 0.3% Native Hawaiian or other Pacific Islander, non-Hispanic/Latino; 1% American Indian or Alaska Native, non-Hispanic/Latino; 4% Two or more races, non-Hispanic/Latino; 3% international; 12% transferred in; 80% live on campus.

Freshmen:
Admission: 236 applied, 114 admitted, 66 enrolled. ***Average high school GPA:*** 2.87.
Retention: 88% of full-time freshmen returned.

FACULTY
Total: 34, 68% full-time, 50% with terminal degrees.
Student/faculty ratio: 12:1.

ACADEMICS
Calendar: semesters. *Degrees:* associate and bachelor's.
Special study options: academic remediation for entering students, adult/continuing education programs, advanced placement credit, cooperative education, double majors, honors programs, independent study, internships, services for LD students, study abroad, summer session for credit.
Computers: 150 computers/terminals and 450 ports are available on campus for general student use. Students can access the following: campus intranet, computer help desk, free student e-mail accounts, online (class) grades, online (class) schedules. Campuswide network is available. 100% of college-owned or -operated housing units are wired for high-speed Internet access. Wireless service is available via entire campus.
Library: Beacon College Library. *Books:* 14,147 (physical), 147,563 (digital/electronic); *Serial titles:* 38 (physical); *Databases:* 67. Weekly public service hours: 76; students can reserve study rooms.

STUDENT LIFE
Housing options: coed, special housing for students with disabilities. Campus housing is university owned and leased by the school. Freshman campus housing is guaranteed.
Activities and organizations: drama/theater group, student-run radio station, Gamma Beta Phi, Performance Club, Human Services and Psychology Club, Nerd Culture Club, Campus Activities Board, national fraternities, national sororities.
Campus security: 24-hour emergency response devices and patrols, student patrols, late-night transport/escort service.
Student services: health clinic, personal/psychological counseling.

COSTS & FINANCIAL AID
Costs (2016–17) ***Comprehensive fee:*** $46,862 includes full-time tuition ($36,172) and room and board ($10,690). Part-time tuition: $1210 per credit. Part-time tuition and fees vary according to course load. ***College room only:*** $6794. Room and board charges vary according to housing facility. ***Payment plan:*** installment. ***Waivers:*** employees or children of employees.
Financial Aid Of all full-time matriculated undergraduates who enrolled in 2015, 137 applied for aid, 118 were judged to have need. In 2015, 67 non-need-based awards were made. ***Average financial aid package:*** $12,366. ***Average need-based loan:*** $3438. ***Average need-based gift aid:*** $18,625. ***Average non-need-based aid:*** $4470. ***Average indebtedness upon graduation:*** $27,000.

APPLYING
Options: electronic application, early admission, deferred entrance.
Application fee: $50.
Required: high school transcript, 3 letters of recommendation, psycho-educational evaluation showing diagnosed learning disability or ADHD. ***Recommended:*** minimum 2.0 GPA, interview.
Application deadlines: rolling (freshmen), rolling (transfers).
Notification: 8/1 (freshmen), 8/1 (transfers).

CONTACT
Ms. Dale Herold, VP of Admissions and Enrollment Management, Beacon College, 105 East Main Street, Leesburg, FL 34748. *Phone:* 352-638-9778. *Fax:* 352-787-0796. *E-mail:* dherold@beaconcollege.edu.

Belhaven University
Orlando, Florida
http://orlando.belhaven.edu/

CONTACT
Jeremy Couch, Director of Admission, Belhaven University, 5200 Vineland Road, Suite 100, Orlando, FL 32811. *Phone:* 407-804-1424. *Toll-free phone:* 877-804-1424. *Fax:* 407-661-1732. *E-mail:* orlando@belhaven.edu.

Bethune-Cookman University
Daytona Beach, Florida
http://www.cookman.edu/

- **Independent Methodist** comprehensive, founded 1904
- **Urban** 60-acre campus with easy access to Orlando
- **Coed** 3,796 undergraduate students, 94% full-time, 53% women, 47% men
- **Minimally difficult** entrance level, 53% of applicants were admitted

UNDERGRAD STUDENTS
3,584 full-time, 212 part-time. Students come from 39 states and territories; 37 other countries; 27% are from out of state; 78% Black or African American, non-Hispanic/Latino; 3% Hispanic/Latino; 0.1% American Indian or Alaska Native, non-Hispanic/Latino; 2% Two or more races, non-Hispanic/Latino; 13% Race/ethnicity unknown; 2% international; 3% transferred in; 66% live on campus.

Freshmen:
Admission: 13,007 applied, 6,878 admitted, 1,167 enrolled. ***Average high school GPA:*** 2.91.
Retention: 63% of full-time freshmen returned.

FACULTY
Total: 316, 70% full-time, 36% with terminal degrees.
Student/faculty ratio: 15:1.

ACADEMICS
Calendar: semesters. *Degrees:* bachelor's and master's.
Special study options: academic remediation for entering students, accelerated degree program, adult/continuing education programs, advanced placement credit, cooperative education, distance learning, double majors, honors programs, independent study, internships, part-time degree program, study abroad, summer session for credit. ***ROTC:*** Army (c), Air Force (c).
Unusual degree programs: 3-2 engineering with Tuskegee University, University of Florida, Florida Atlantic University, Florida Agricultural and Mechanical University, University of Central Florida.
Computers: 611 computers/terminals and 1,471 ports are available on campus for general student use. Students can access the following: campus intranet, computer help desk, free student e-mail accounts, online (class) grades, online (class) registration, online (class) schedules. Campuswide network is available. 100% of college-owned or -operated housing units are wired for high-speed Internet access. Wireless service is available via entire campus.
Library: Carl S. Swisher Library plus 1 other. *Books:* 68,225 (physical), 105,811 (digital/electronic); *Serial titles:* 18 (physical), 36,000 (digital/electronic); *Databases:* 34. Weekly public service hours: 92; study areas open 24 hours, 5-7 days a week; students can reserve study rooms.

STUDENT LIFE
Housing options: on-campus residence required through sophomore year; coed, men-only, women-only. Campus housing is university owned. Freshman campus housing is guaranteed.
Activities and organizations: drama/theater group, student-run newspaper, radio station, choral group, marching band, National Council of Negro Women, Gamma Sigma Sigma Sorority, Black Male Think Tank, What's Next Dance Company, NAACP, national fraternities, national sororities.
Athletics Member NCAA, NAIA. All NCAA Division I except football (Division I-AA). ***Intercollegiate sports:*** baseball M(s), basketball M(s)/W(s), bowling W(s), cheerleading W, cross-country running M(s)/W(s), golf M(s)/W(s), softball W(s), tennis M(s)/W(s), track and

field M(s)/W(s), volleyball W(s). ***Intramural sports:*** basketball M/W, bowling M/W, football M, racquetball W, soccer M/W, table tennis W.

Campus security: 24-hour emergency response devices and patrols, student patrols, late-night transport/escort service.

Student services: health clinic, personal/psychological counseling.

COSTS & FINANCIAL AID

Costs (2016–17) ***Comprehensive fee:*** $23,120 includes full-time tuition ($13,440), mandatory fees ($970), and room and board ($8710). Full-time tuition and fees vary according to course load and degree level. Part-time tuition: $560 per credit hour. Part-time tuition and fees vary according to course load and degree level. ***Required fees:*** $50 per credit hour part-time. ***College room only:*** $6710. Room and board charges vary according to housing facility. ***Payment plan:*** installment. ***Waivers:*** employees or children of employees.

Financial Aid Of all full-time matriculated undergraduates who enrolled in 2016, 3,436 applied for aid, 3,332 were judged to have need, 181 had their need fully met. 200 Federal Work-Study jobs (averaging $2500). 100 state and other part-time jobs (averaging $2000). In 2016, 73 non-need-based awards were made. ***Average percent of need met:*** 48. ***Average financial aid package:*** $13,302. ***Average need-based loan:*** $4027. ***Average need-based gift aid:*** $9982. ***Average non-need-based aid:*** $10,915. ***Average indebtedness upon graduation:*** $35,082.

APPLYING

Standardized Tests *Required:* SAT or ACT (for admission).

Options: electronic application, early admission, deferred entrance.

Application fee: $25.

Required: high school transcript, minimum 2.3 GPA, 1 letter of recommendation, medical history. ***Required for some:*** interview. ***Recommended:*** essay or personal statement.

Application deadlines: 6/30 (freshmen), 6/30 (transfers).

Notification: continuous (freshmen), continuous (transfers).

CONTACT

Treran Porter, Director of Recruitment, Bethune-Cookman University, FL. *Phone:* 386-481-2603. *Toll-free phone:* 800-448-0228. *E-mail:* portert@cookman.edu.

Broward College

Fort Lauderdale, Florida

http://www.broward.edu/

CONTACT

Mr. Willie J. Alexander, Associate Vice President for Student Affairs/College Registrar, Broward College, 225 East Las Olas Boulevard, Fort Lauderdale, FL 33301. *Phone:* 954-201-7471. *Fax:* 954-201-7466. *E-mail:* walexand@broward.edu.

Carlos Albizu University, Miami Campus

Miami, Florida

http://www.albizu.edu/

- **Independent** comprehensive, founded 1980, part of Carlos Albizu University
- **Urban** 18-acre campus
- **Coed**
- **Moderately difficult** entrance level

FACULTY

Student/faculty ratio: 11:1.

ACADEMICS

Calendar: trimesters. *Degrees:* certificates, diplomas, bachelor's, master's, and doctoral.

Library: Albizu Library. *Books:* 27,760 (physical), 22,900 (digital/electronic); *Serial titles:* 295 (physical), 17,034 (digital/electronic); *Databases:* 73. Weekly public service hours: 66.

STUDENT LIFE

Housing options: college housing not available.

Activities and organizations: student-run newspaper, Student Council, Psi Chi, Kappa Delta Pi, Military Psychology Chapter, Neuropsychology Club.

Campus security: 24-hour emergency response devices and patrols, late-night transport/escort service.

COSTS & FINANCIAL AID

Costs (2016–17) ***Tuition:*** $11,628 full-time, $323 per credit part-time. Full-time tuition and fees vary according to course load, degree level, and program. Part-time tuition and fees vary according to course load, degree level, and program. ***Required fees:*** $756 full-time, $252 per term part-time.

Financial Aid Of all full-time matriculated undergraduates who enrolled in 2015, 137 applied for aid, 137 were judged to have need. ***Average percent of need met:*** 52. ***Average financial aid package:*** $7837. ***Average need-based loan:*** $4250. ***Average need-based gift aid:*** $4720.

APPLYING

Options: electronic application.

Application fee: $25.

Required: high school transcript, minimum 2.0 GPA, 2 letters of recommendation, interview.

CONTACT

Ms. Maria Elena Torres, Admissions Officer, Carlos Albizu University, Miami Campus, 2173 NW 99 Avenue, Miami, FL 33172. *Phone:* 305-593-1223 Ext. 3134. *Toll-free phone:* 888-GO-TO-CAU (in-state); 800-GO-TO-CAU (out-of-state). *Fax:* 305-593-1854. *E-mail:* matorres@albizu.edu.

Chamberlain College of Nursing

Jacksonville, Florida

http://www.chamberlain.edu/

- **Proprietary** 4-year
- **Coed**

FACULTY

Student/faculty ratio: 13:1.

ACADEMICS

Calendar: semesters. *Degree:* bachelor's.

STUDENT LIFE

Housing options: college housing not available.

COSTS

Costs (2016–17) ***Tuition:*** $18,900 full-time, $675 per credit hour part-time. ***Required fees:*** $600 full-time.

APPLYING

Standardized Tests *Required:* SAT or ACT (for admission).

Options: deferred entrance.

Application fee: $95.

CONTACT

Admissions, Chamberlain College of Nursing, 5200 Belfort Road, Jacksonville, FL 32256. *Phone:* 904-251-8100. *Toll-free phone:* 877-751-5783.

Chamberlain College of Nursing

Miramar, Florida

http://www.chamberlain.edu/

- **Proprietary** 4-year
- **Coed**
- **Moderately difficult** entrance level

FACULTY

Student/faculty ratio: 11:1.

ACADEMICS

Degree: bachelor's.

STUDENT LIFE

Housing options: college housing not available.

COSTS
Costs (2016–17) ***Tuition:*** $18,900 full-time, $675 per credit hour part-time. ***Required fees:*** $600 full-time.

APPLYING
Standardized Tests *Required:* SAT or ACT (for admission).
Options: deferred entrance.
Application fee: $95.

CONTACT
Director of Recruitment, Chamberlain College of Nursing, 2300 SW 145th Avenue, Miramar, FL 33027. *Phone:* 954-885-3510. *Toll-free phone:* 877-751-5783.

Chipola College
Marianna, Florida
http://www.chipola.edu/

- **State-supported** primarily 2-year, founded 1947
- **Rural** 105-acre campus
- **Coed**
- **Noncompetitive** entrance level

FACULTY
Student/faculty ratio: 24:1.

ACADEMICS
Calendar: semesters. *Degrees:* certificates, associate, and bachelor's.
Library: Chipola Library.

STUDENT LIFE
Housing options: college housing not available.
Activities and organizations: drama/theater group, student-run newspaper, choral group.
Athletics Member NJCAA.
Campus security: night security personnel.

APPLYING
Options: early admission.
Required: high school transcript.

CONTACT
Mrs. Kathy L. Rehberg, Registrar, Chipola College, 3094 Indian Circle, Marianna, FL 32446-3065. *Phone:* 850-718-2233. *Fax:* 850-718-2287. *E-mail:* rehbergk@chipola.edu.

City College
Altamonte Springs, Florida
http://www.citycollege.edu/

CONTACT
Ms. Kimberly Bowden, Director of Admissions, City College, 177 Montgomery Road, Altamonte Springs, FL 32714. *Phone:* 352-335-4000. *Fax:* 352-335-4303. *E-mail:* kbowden@citycollege.edu.

City College
Fort Lauderdale, Florida
http://www.citycollege.edu/

CONTACT
City College, 2000 West Commercial Boulevard, Suite 200, Fort Lauderdale, FL 33309. *Phone:* 954-492-5353. *Toll-free phone:* 866-314-5681.

City College
Gainesville, Florida
http://www.citycollege.edu/

CONTACT
Admissions Office, City College, 7001 Northwest 4th Boulevard, Gainesville, FL 32607. *Phone:* 352-335-4000.

City College
Hollywood, Florida
http://www.citycollege.edu/

CONTACT
City College, 6565 Taft Street, Hollywood, FL 33024. *Toll-free phone:* 866-314-5681.

City College
Miami, Florida
http://www.citycollege.edu/

CONTACT
Admissions Office, City College, 9300 South Dadeland Boulevard, Suite PH, Miami, FL 33156. *Phone:* 305-666-9242. *Fax:* 305-666-9243.

College of Business and Technology–Main Campus
Miami, Florida
http://www.cbt.edu/

- **Proprietary** primarily 2-year, founded 1988
- **Urban** campus
- **Coed** 10 undergraduate students, 100% full-time, 80% women, 20% men
- **Minimally difficult** entrance level

UNDERGRAD STUDENTS
10 full-time. Students come from 1 other state; 100% Hispanic/Latino.

Freshmen:
Admission: 10 enrolled.

FACULTY
Total: 1, 100% full-time.
Student/faculty ratio: 10:1.

ACADEMICS
Calendar: semesters. *Degrees:* certificates, diplomas, associate, and bachelor's.
Special study options: academic remediation for entering students, adult/continuing education programs, cooperative education, English as a second language, independent study.
Computers: 15 computers/terminals are available on campus for general student use. Students can access the following: campus intranet, computer help desk, free student e-mail accounts, online (class) grades, online (class) schedules. Campuswide network is available. Wireless service is available via entire campus.
Library: CBT College-Miami Branch Library (Use Flagler). *Books:* 1,520 (physical); *Serial titles:* 10 (physical); *Databases:* 60.

STUDENT LIFE
Housing options: college housing not available.
Campus security: security guard posted at main entrance, local police department.

COSTS
Costs (2017–18) ***Tuition:*** $11,952 full-time. ***Required fees:*** $1400 full-time. ***Payment plan:*** installment.

APPLYING
Options: electronic application.
Application fee: $25.
Required: high school transcript, interview.

CONTACT
College of Business and Technology–Main Campus, 8700 West Flagler Street, Suite 420, Miami, FL 33174. *Phone:* 305-273-4499 Ext. 1100.

College of Business and Technology–Miami Gardens

Miami Gardens, Florida

http://www.cbt.edu/

- **Proprietary** primarily 2-year
- **Urban** campus with easy access to Miami
- **Coed** 113 undergraduate students, 100% full-time, 48% women, 52% men
- **Minimally difficult** entrance level

UNDERGRAD STUDENTS
113 full-time. Students come from 1 other state; 1 other country; 27% Black or African American, non-Hispanic/Latino; 65% Hispanic/Latino; 3% Race/ethnicity unknown; 2% international.

Freshmen:
Admission: 11 enrolled.

FACULTY
Total: 19, 16% full-time, 37% with terminal degrees.
Student/faculty ratio: 18:1.

ACADEMICS
Calendar: semesters. *Degrees:* certificates, diplomas, associate, and bachelor's.
Special study options: academic remediation for entering students, adult/continuing education programs, cooperative education, independent study, services for LD students.
Computers: 50 computers/terminals are available on campus for general student use. Students can access the following: campus intranet, computer help desk, free student e-mail accounts, online (class) grades, online (class) schedules. Campuswide network is available. Wireless service is available via entire campus.
Library: CBT College–Miami Gardens Library. *Books:* 1,034 (physical); *Serial titles:* 15 (physical); *Databases:* 60.

STUDENT LIFE
Housing options: college housing not available.
Campus security: security guard posted at main entrance, local police department.

COSTS
Costs (2017–18) ***Tuition:*** $11,952 full-time. ***Required fees:*** $1400 full-time. ***Payment plan:*** installment.

APPLYING
Options: electronic application.
Application fee: $25.
Required: high school transcript, interview.

CONTACT
College of Business and Technology–Miami Gardens, 5190 NW 167 Street, Miami Gardens, FL 33014. *Phone:* 305-273-4499 Ext. 1100.

College of Central Florida

Ocala, Florida

http://www.cf.edu/

- **State and locally supported** primarily 2-year, founded 1957, part of Florida Community College System
- **Small-town** 139-acre campus
- **Endowment** $65.4 million
- **Coed** 7,931 undergraduate students, 38% full-time, 63% women, 37% men
- **Noncompetitive** entrance level, 55% of applicants were admitted

UNDERGRAD STUDENTS
3,036 full-time, 4,895 part-time. 16% are from out of state.

Freshmen:
Admission: 4,416 applied, 2,430 admitted, 1,503 enrolled.

FACULTY
Total: 374, 37% full-time, 10% with terminal degrees.

ACADEMICS
Calendar: semesters. *Degrees:* certificates, diplomas, associate, and bachelor's.
Special study options: academic remediation for entering students, adult/continuing education programs, advanced placement credit, cooperative education, distance learning, English as a second language, freshman honors college, honors programs, independent study, internships, part-time degree program, services for LD students, summer session for credit.
Computers: 2,500 computers/terminals are available on campus for general student use. Students can access the following: campus intranet, computer help desk, online (class) grades, online (class) registration, online (class) schedules. Campuswide network is available. Wireless service is available via classrooms, computer centers, computer labs, learning centers, libraries, student centers.
Library: Clifford B. Stearns Learning Resources Center. *Books:* 75,935 (physical), 43,910 (digital/electronic); *Databases:* 152. Students can reserve study rooms.

STUDENT LIFE
Housing options: college housing not available.
Activities and organizations: drama/theater group, student-run newspaper, choral group, Inspirational Choir, Model United Nations, Performing Arts, Phi Theta Kappa (PTK), Student Nurses Association.
Athletics Member NJCAA. ***Intercollegiate sports:*** baseball M(s), basketball M(s)/W(s), softball W(s), volleyball W(s). ***Intramural sports:*** bowling M/W.
Campus security: 24-hour emergency response devices and patrols, student patrols, late-night transport/escort service.
Student services: personal/psychological counseling.

COSTS
Costs (2016–17) ***Tuition:*** state resident $107 per credit hour part-time; nonresident $422 per credit hour part-time. Full-time tuition and fees vary according to course level, degree level, program, and student level. Part-time tuition and fees vary according to course level, degree level, program, and student level. ***Waivers:*** employees or children of employees.

APPLYING
Options: electronic application, early admission.
Application fee: $30.
Required: high school transcript.
Application deadlines: rolling (freshmen), rolling (transfers).
Notification: continuous (freshmen), continuous (transfers).

CONTACT
Ms. Devona Sewell, Registrar, Admission and Records, College of Central Florida, 3001 SW College Road, Ocala, FL 34474. *Phone:* 352-237-2111 Ext. 1398. *Fax:* 352-873-5882. *E-mail:* sewelld@cf.edu.

Daytona State College

Daytona Beach, Florida

http://www.daytonastate.edu/

- **State-supported** primarily 2-year, founded 1958, part of Florida Community College System
- **Suburban** 100-acre campus with easy access to Orlando
- **Endowment** $11.4 million
- **Coed** 12,807 undergraduate students, 38% full-time, 61% women, 39% men
- **Noncompetitive** entrance level

UNDERGRAD STUDENTS
4,830 full-time, 7,977 part-time. 3% are from out of state; 13% Black or African American, non-Hispanic/Latino; 17% Hispanic/Latino; 2% Asian, non-Hispanic/Latino; 0.2% Native Hawaiian or other Pacific Islander, non-Hispanic/Latino; 0.2% American Indian or Alaska Native, non-Hispanic/Latino; 3% Two or more races, non-Hispanic/Latino; 0.7% Race/ethnicity unknown; 0.7% international; 4% transferred in.

Freshmen:
Admission: 1,340 admitted, 1,340 enrolled.

FACULTY
Total: 853, 34% full-time, 17% with terminal degrees.

ACADEMICS
Calendar: semesters. *Degrees:* certificates, diplomas, associate, bachelor's, and postbachelor's certificates.

Special study options: academic remediation for entering students, adult/continuing education programs, advanced placement credit, cooperative education, distance learning, double majors, English as a second language, external degree program, freshman honors college, honors programs, independent study, internships, off-campus study, part-time degree program, services for LD students, study abroad, summer session for credit. ***ROTC:*** Army (c), Air Force (c).

Computers: 3,230 computers/terminals are available on campus for general student use. Students can access the following: campus intranet, computer help desk, free student e-mail accounts, online (class) grades, online (class) registration, online (class) schedules. Campuswide network is available. Wireless service is available via entire campus.

Library: Mary Karl Memorial Learning Resources Center plus 1 other. *Books:* 35,000 (physical), 170,000 (digital/electronic); *Serial titles:* 250 (physical); *Databases:* 100. Weekly public service hours: 68; students can reserve study rooms.

STUDENT LIFE
Housing options: college housing not available.

Activities and organizations: drama/theater group, student-run newspaper, choral group, Phi Theta Kappa International Honors Society, Student Government Association, Student Occupational Therapy Club, Massage Therapy Club, Student Paralegal Club, national fraternities, national sororities.

Athletics Member NJCAA. ***Intercollegiate sports:*** baseball M(s), basketball M(s)/W(s), golf W(s), soccer M/W, softball W(s), volleyball W(s). ***Intramural sports:*** basketball M/W, football M/W, soccer M/W, table tennis M/W, tennis M/W.

Campus security: 24-hour emergency response devices and patrols, late-night transport/escort service.

Student services: personal/psychological counseling, women's center.

FINANCIAL AID
Financial Aid *Average need-based gift aid:* $1813.

APPLYING
Options: electronic application, early admission, deferred entrance.

Required: high school transcript.

Application deadlines: rolling (freshmen), rolling (transfers).

Notification: continuous (freshmen), continuous (transfers).

CONTACT
Dr. Karen Sanders, Director of Admissions and Recruitment, Daytona State College, 1200 International Speedway Boulevard, Daytona Beach, FL 32114. *Phone:* 386-506-3050. *E-mail:* sanderk@daytonastate.edu.

DeVry University–Jacksonville Campus

Jacksonville, Florida

http://www.devry.edu/

CONTACT
Admissions Office, DeVry University–Jacksonville Campus, 5200 Belfort Road, Suite 175, Jacksonville, FL 32256-6040. *Phone:* 904-367-4942. *Toll-free phone:* 866-338-7934.

DeVry University–Miramar Campus

Miramar, Florida

http://www.devry.edu/

- **Proprietary** comprehensive, founded 2002, part of DeVry University
- **Coed**
- **Minimally difficult** entrance level

FACULTY
Student/faculty ratio: 25:1.

ACADEMICS
Calendar: semesters. *Degrees:* associate, bachelor's, master's, and postbachelor's certificates.

STUDENT LIFE
Housing options: college housing not available.

COSTS & FINANCIAL AID
Costs (2016–17) *Tuition:* $17,052 full-time, $609 per credit hour part-time. ***Required fees:*** $460 full-time.

Financial Aid Of all full-time matriculated undergraduates who enrolled in 2007, 204 applied for aid, 197 were judged to have need, 2 had their need fully met. In 2007, 35 non-need-based awards were made. ***Average percent of need met:*** 38. ***Average financial aid package:*** $12,172. ***Average need-based loan:*** $7414. ***Average need-based gift aid:*** $7044. ***Average non-need-based aid:*** $12,256. ***Average indebtedness upon graduation:*** $51,131.

APPLYING
Options: deferred entrance.

Application fee: $30.

Required: high school transcript, interview.

CONTACT
DeVry University–Miramar Campus, 2300 Southwest 145th Avenue, Miramar, FL 33027. *Phone:* 954-499-9775. *Toll-free phone:* 866-338-7934.

DeVry University–Orlando Campus

Orlando, Florida

http://www.devry.edu/

- **Proprietary** comprehensive, founded 2000, part of DeVry University
- **Urban** campus
- **Coed**
- **Minimally difficult** entrance level

FACULTY
Student/faculty ratio: 37:1.

ACADEMICS
Calendar: semesters. *Degrees:* associate, bachelor's, master's, and postbachelor's certificates.

Library: Learning Resource Center.

STUDENT LIFE
Housing options: college housing not available.

COSTS & FINANCIAL AID
Costs (2016–17) *Tuition:* $17,502 full-time, $609 per credit hour part-time. ***Required fees:*** $460 full-time.

Financial Aid Of all full-time matriculated undergraduates who enrolled in 2007, 314 applied for aid, 294 were judged to have need, 2 had their need fully met. In 2007, 35 non-need-based awards were made. ***Average percent of need met:*** 33. ***Average financial aid package:*** $10,774. ***Average need-based loan:*** $7062. ***Average need-based gift aid:*** $5608. ***Average non-need-based aid:*** $18,240. ***Average indebtedness upon graduation:*** $23,511.

APPLYING
Options: deferred entrance.

Application fee: $30.

Required: high school transcript, interview.

CONTACT
DeVry University–Orlando Campus, 7352 Greenbriar Parkway, Orlando, FL 32819. *Phone:* 407-345-2800. *Toll-free phone:* 866-338-7934.

Eastern Florida State College

Cocoa, Florida

http://www.easternflorida.edu/

CONTACT
Ms. Stephanie Burnette, Registrar, Eastern Florida State College, 1519 Clearlake Road, Cocoa, FL 32922-6597. *Phone:* 321-433-7271. *Fax:* 321-433-7172. *E-mail:* cocoaadmissions@brevardcc.edu.

Eckerd College

St. Petersburg, Florida

http://www.eckerd.edu/

- **Independent Presbyterian** 4-year, founded 1958
- **Suburban** 188-acre campus with easy access to Tampa
- **Endowment** $54.5 million
- **Coed** 1,789 undergraduate students, 98% full-time, 62% women, 38% men
- **Moderately difficult** entrance level, 73% of applicants were admitted

UNDERGRAD STUDENTS

1,748 full-time, 41 part-time. Students come from 48 states and territories; 40 other countries; 77% are from out of state; 3% Black or African American, non-Hispanic/Latino; 9% Hispanic/Latino; 2% Asian, non-Hispanic/Latino; 0.2% Native Hawaiian or other Pacific Islander, non-Hispanic/Latino; 0.3% American Indian or Alaska Native, non-Hispanic/Latino; 3% Two or more races, non-Hispanic/Latino; 1% Race/ethnicity unknown; 5% international; 4% transferred in; 87% live on campus.

Freshmen:

Admission: 4,135 applied, 3,016 admitted, 488 enrolled. ***Average high school GPA:*** 3.38. ***Test scores:*** SAT critical reading scores over 500: 76%; SAT math scores over 500: 78%; ACT scores over 18: 98%; SAT critical reading scores over 600: 31%; SAT math scores over 600: 29%; ACT scores over 24: 70%; SAT critical reading scores over 700: 4%; SAT math scores over 700: 2%; ACT scores over 30: 16%.

Retention: 81% of full-time freshmen returned.

FACULTY

Total: 168, 68% full-time, 81% with terminal degrees.

Student/faculty ratio: 13:1.

ACADEMICS

Calendar: 4-1-4. *Degree:* bachelor's.

Special study options: accelerated degree program, adult/continuing education programs, advanced placement credit, double majors, external degree program, honors programs, independent study, internships, off-campus study, part-time degree program, services for LD students, student-designed majors, study abroad, summer session for credit. ***ROTC:*** Army (c), Air Force (c).

Unusual degree programs: 3-2 engineering with Columbia University.

Computers: 300 computers/terminals and 2,000 ports are available on campus for general student use. Students can access the following: campus intranet, computer help desk, free student e-mail accounts, online (class) grades, online (class) registration, online (class) schedules, free computer repair shop. Campuswide network is available. 100% of college-owned or -operated housing units are wired for high-speed Internet access. Wireless service is available via entire campus.

Library: Peter Armacost Library.

STUDENT LIFE

Housing options: on-campus residence required for freshman year; coed, women-only. Campus housing is university owned. Freshman campus housing is guaranteed.

Activities and organizations: drama/theater group, student-run newspaper, radio and television station, choral group, Earth Society, Water Search and Rescue Team, The Current (student newspaper), College Choir, Organization of Students.

Athletics Member NCAA. All Division II. ***Intercollegiate sports:*** baseball M(s), basketball M(s)/W(s), golf M(s)/W(s), sailing M/W, soccer M(s)/W(s), softball W(s), tennis M(s)/W(s), volleyball W(s). ***Intramural sports:*** baseball M, basketball M/W, bowling M/W, cheerleading M(c)/W(c), equestrian sports M(c)/W(c), field hockey M(c)/W(c), football M(c)/W(c), golf M(c)/W(c), lacrosse M(c)/W(c), rugby M(c)/W(c), sailing M/W, soccer M(c)/W(c), softball M/W, swimming and diving M(c)/W(c), table tennis M/W, tennis M(c)/W(c), ultimate Frisbee M(c)/W(c), volleyball M/W.

Campus security: 24-hour emergency response devices and patrols, student patrols, late-night transport/escort service, controlled dormitory access.

Student services: health clinic, personal/psychological counseling, women's center.

COSTS & FINANCIAL AID

Costs (2017–18) ***Comprehensive fee:*** $54,490 includes full-time tuition ($42,428), mandatory fees ($356), and room and board ($11,706). Part-time tuition: $5092 per course. ***College room only:*** $5906. Room and board charges vary according to board plan and housing facility. ***Payment plan:*** installment. ***Waivers:*** employees or children of employees.

Financial Aid Of all full-time matriculated undergraduates who enrolled in 2016, 1,253 applied for aid, 1,090 were judged to have need, 493 had their need fully met. 767 Federal Work-Study jobs (averaging $2000). 13 state and other part-time jobs (averaging $2000). In 2016, 530 non-need-based awards were made. ***Average percent of need met:*** 86. ***Average financial aid package:*** $34,291. ***Average need-based loan:*** $4626. ***Average need-based gift aid:*** $24,086. ***Average non-need-based aid:*** $16,207. ***Average indebtedness upon graduation:*** $33,979.

APPLYING

Standardized Tests *Required:* SAT or ACT (for admission). *Recommended:* SAT Subject Tests (for admission).

Options: electronic application, early action, deferred entrance.

Application fee: $40.

Required: essay or personal statement, high school transcript. ***Recommended:*** interview.

Application deadlines: rolling (freshmen), rolling (transfers), 11/15 (early action).

Notification: continuous (freshmen), continuous (transfers), 12/15 (early action).

CONTACT

Ms. Lucille Lopez, Eckerd College, 4200 54th Avenue South, St. Petersburg, FL 33711. *Phone:* 727-864-8331. *Toll-free phone:* 800-456-9009. *Fax:* 727-866-2304. *E-mail:* admissions@eckerd.edu.

Edward Waters College

Jacksonville, Florida

http://www.ewc.edu/

CONTACT

Edward Waters College, 1658 Kings Road, Jacksonville, FL 32209-6199. *Phone:* 904-470-8202. *Toll-free phone:* 888-898-3191.

Embry-Riddle Aeronautical University–Daytona

Daytona Beach, Florida

http://www.daytonabeach.erau.edu/

- **Independent** university, founded 1926
- **Suburban** 185-acre campus with easy access to Orlando
- **Endowment** $111.2 million
- **Coed** 5,278 undergraduate students, 92% full-time, 19% women, 81% men
- **Moderately difficult** entrance level, 69% of applicants were admitted

UNDERGRAD STUDENTS

4,876 full-time, 402 part-time. Students come from 52 states and territories; 99 other countries; 63% are from out of state; 6% Black or African American, non-Hispanic/Latino; 4% Hispanic/Latino; 4% Asian, non-Hispanic/Latino; 0.2% Native Hawaiian or other Pacific Islander, non-Hispanic/Latino; 0.3% American Indian or Alaska Native, non-Hispanic/Latino; 8% Two or more races, non-Hispanic/Latino; 9% Race/ethnicity unknown; 14% international; 5% transferred in; 37% live on campus.

Freshmen:

Admission: 4,588 applied, 3,160 admitted, 1,275 enrolled. ***Average high school GPA:*** 3.66. ***Test scores:*** SAT critical reading scores over 500: 73%; SAT math scores over 500: 84%; SAT writing scores over 500: 65%; ACT scores over 18: 96%; SAT critical reading scores over 600: 27%; SAT math scores over 600: 44%; SAT writing scores over 600: 22%; ACT scores over 24: 65%; SAT critical reading scores over 700: 4%; SAT math scores over 700: 10%; SAT writing scores over 700: 2%; ACT scores over 30: 15%.

Retention: 77% of full-time freshmen returned.

ACADEMICS
Calendar: semesters. *Degrees:* associate, bachelor's, master's, and doctoral.

Special study options: academic remediation for entering students, accelerated degree program, advanced placement credit, cooperative education, distance learning, double majors, English as a second language, honors programs, internships, services for LD students, study abroad, summer session for credit. ***ROTC:*** Army (b), Navy (b), Air Force (b).

Computers: 1,049 computers/terminals are available on campus for general student use. Students can access the following: campus intranet, computer help desk, free student e-mail accounts, online (class) grades, online (class) registration, online (class) schedules. Campuswide network is available. 100% of college-owned or -operated housing units are wired for high-speed Internet access. Wireless service is available via entire campus.

Library: Jack R. Hunt Memorial Library.

STUDENT LIFE
Housing options: on-campus residence required for freshman year; coed. Campus housing is university owned. Freshman campus housing is guaranteed.

Activities and organizations: drama/theater group, student-run newspaper, radio station, choral group, Eagle Wing, Future Professional Pilots Association, African Student Association, Caribbean Student Association, Sigma Gamma Tau, national fraternities, national sororities.

Athletics Member NCAA, NAIA. All NCAA Division II except golf (Division I). ***Intercollegiate sports:*** baseball M(s), basketball M(s)/W(s), cheerleading M/W, cross-country running M(s)/W(s), golf M(s)/W(s), lacrosse M(s)/W(s), rowing M(s)/W(s), soccer M(s)/W(s), softball W(s), tennis M(s)/W(s), track and field M(s)/W(s), volleyball W(s). ***Intramural sports:*** archery M(c)/W(c), basketball M(c)/W(c), equestrian sports M(c)/W(c), football M/W, golf M/W, ice hockey M(c), lacrosse M(c), racquetball M(c)/W(c), rowing M(c)/W(c), rugby M(c), soccer M/W, softball M/W, swimming and diving M(c)/W(c), table tennis M/W, tennis M/W, ultimate Frisbee M(c)/W(c), volleyball M/W.

Campus security: 24-hour emergency response devices and patrols, student patrols, late-night transport/escort service, controlled dormitory access.

Student services: health clinic, personal/psychological counseling, women's center.

COSTS & FINANCIAL AID
Costs (2017–18) ***Comprehensive fee:*** $45,922 includes full-time tuition ($33,408), mandatory fees ($1414), and room and board ($11,100). Part-time tuition: $1392 per credit hour. ***Required fees:*** $707 per term part-time. ***College room only:*** $6660. Room and board charges vary according to board plan, housing facility, and location. ***Payment plan:*** installment. ***Waivers:*** employees or children of employees.

Financial Aid Of all full-time matriculated undergraduates who enrolled in 2016, 3,373 applied for aid, 3,041 were judged to have need. 171 Federal Work-Study jobs (averaging $1849). 1,243 state and other part-time jobs (averaging $2999). In 2016, 564 non-need-based awards were made. ***Average financial aid package:*** $17,938. ***Average need-based loan:*** $4742. ***Average need-based gift aid:*** $14,290. ***Average non-need-based aid:*** $12,930.

APPLYING
Standardized Tests *Recommended:* SAT or ACT (for admission).

Options: electronic application, deferred entrance.

Application fee: $50.

Required: high school transcript, minimum 2.0 GPA, 2 letters of recommendation. ***Required for some:*** medical examination for flight students. ***Recommended:*** essay or personal statement, minimum 3.0 GPA, 3 letters of recommendation.

Application deadlines: rolling (freshmen), rolling (out-of-state freshmen), 6/1 (transfers).

Notification: continuous (freshmen), continuous (out-of-state freshmen), continuous (transfers).

CONTACT
Embry-Riddle Aeronautical University–Daytona, 600 South Clyde Morris Boulevard, Daytona Beach, FL 32114-3900. *Phone:* 386-226-6100. *Toll-free phone:* 800-862-2416. *Fax:* 386-226-7070. *E-mail:* dbadmit@erau.edu.

See below for display ad and page 1342 for the College Close-Up.

Embry-Riddle Aeronautical University–Worldwide

Daytona Beach, Florida

http://www.worldwide.erau.edu/

- **Independent** comprehensive, founded 1970
- **Endowment** $111.2 million
- **Coed** 10,544 undergraduate students, 29% full-time, 11% women, 89% men
- **Minimally difficult** entrance level, 67% of applicants were admitted

UNDERGRAD STUDENTS
3,046 full-time, 7,498 part-time.

Freshmen:
Admission: 1,015 applied, 676 admitted, 497 enrolled.

ACADEMICS
Calendar: 5 9-week terms with monthly starts. *Degrees:* certificates, associate, bachelor's, master's, and doctoral (programs offered at 100 military bases worldwide).

Special study options: accelerated degree program, advanced placement credit, cooperative education, distance learning, double majors, external degree program, independent study, off-campus study, part-time degree program, services for LD students, study abroad, summer session for credit.

Computers: Students can access the following: free student e-mail accounts, online (class) grades, online (class) registration, online (class) schedules.

Library: Jack R. Hunt Memorial Library.

STUDENT LIFE
Housing options: college housing not available.

COSTS & FINANCIAL AID
Costs (2017–18) ***Tuition:*** $9000 full-time, $375 per credit hour part-time. Full-time tuition and fees vary according to program. Part-time tuition and fees vary according to program. ***Required fees:*** $76 full-time. ***Room only:*** Room and board charges vary according to location. ***Waivers:*** employees or children of employees.

Financial Aid Of all full-time matriculated undergraduates who enrolled in 2016, 1,175 applied for aid, 1,033 were judged to have need. ***Average financial aid package:*** $6114. ***Average need-based loan:*** $4481. ***Average need-based gift aid:*** $4562.

APPLYING
Standardized Tests *Required for some:* SAT or ACT (for admission).

Options: electronic application, deferred entrance.

Application fee: $50.

Required for some: essay or personal statement, high school transcript, minimum 2.0 GPA, 2 letters of recommendation.

Application deadlines: rolling (freshmen), rolling (transfers).

Notification: continuous (freshmen), continuous (transfers).

CONTACT
Embry-Riddle Aeronautical University–Worldwide, 600 South Clyde Morris Boulevard, Daytona Beach, FL 32114-3900. *Phone:* 800-522-6787. *Toll-free phone:* 800-522-6787. *Fax:* 386-226-6984. *E-mail:* worldwide@erau.edu.

Everest University

Orange Park, Florida

http://www.everest.edu/

CONTACT
Admissions Office, Everest University, 805 Wells Road, Orange Park, FL 32073. *Phone:* 904-264-9122.

Everest University

Tampa, Florida

http://www.everest.edu/

CONTACT
Everest University, 3319 West Hillsborough Avenue, Tampa, FL 33614. *Phone:* 813-879-6000 Ext. 129.

Everglades University

Boca Raton, Florida

http://www.evergladesuniversity.edu/

- **Independent** comprehensive, founded 1989
- **Suburban** campus with easy access to Fort Lauderdale
- **Coed**
- **Noncompetitive** entrance level

FACULTY
Student/faculty ratio: 10:1.

ACADEMICS
Calendar: semesters. *Degrees:* bachelor's and master's.
Library: Everglades University Library. *Books:* 19,974 (physical), 122,000 (digital/electronic); *Serial titles:* 48 (physical), 5,180 (digital/electronic); *Databases:* 55. Weekly public service hours: 6.

STUDENT LIFE
Housing options: college housing not available.

Campus security: 24-hour emergency response devices and patrols, late-night transport/escort service.

COSTS
Costs (2016–17) ***One-time required fee:*** $145. ***Tuition:*** $15,048 full-time, $627 per credit part-time. ***Required fees:*** $1600 full-time, $100 per term part-time.

APPLYING
Standardized Tests *Required for some:* SAT or ACT (for admission).

Options: electronic application.

Application fee: $50.

Required: high school transcript, University entrance examination (minimum score of 15) or ACT/SAT scores (minimum composite score of 17 ACT or a combined score of 1200 on SAT).

CONTACT
Everglades University, 5002 T-Rex Avenue, Suite 100, Boca Raton, FL 33431. *Phone:* 561-912-1211. *Toll-free phone:* 888-772-6077.

Everglades University

Maitland, Florida

http://www.evergladesuniversity.edu/

- **Independent** comprehensive
- **Suburban** campus with easy access to Orlando
- **Coed**
- **Noncompetitive** entrance level

FACULTY
Student/faculty ratio: 10:1.

ACADEMICS
Calendar: semesters. *Degrees:* bachelor's and master's.
Library: Everglades University Library. *Books:* 19,974 (physical), 122,000 (digital/electronic); *Serial titles:* 48 (physical), 5,180 (digital/electronic); *Databases:* 55. Weekly public service hours: 6.

STUDENT LIFE
Housing options: college housing not available.

Campus security: 24-hour emergency response devices and patrols, late-night transport/escort service.

COSTS & FINANCIAL AID
Costs (2016–17) ***One-time required fee:*** $145. ***Tuition:*** $15,048 full-time, $627 per credit hour part-time. ***Required fees:*** $1600 full-time, $100 per term part-time.

Financial Aid Of all full-time matriculated undergraduates who enrolled in 2014, 117 applied for aid, 103 were judged to have need, 16 had their need fully met. In 2014, 1 non-need-based awards were made. ***Average percent of need met:*** 68. ***Average financial aid package:*** $11,755. ***Average need-based loan:*** $5736. ***Average need-based gift aid:*** $5645. ***Average non-need-based aid:*** $1208. ***Average indebtedness upon graduation:*** $50,999.

APPLYING

Options: electronic application.

Application fee: $50.

Required: high school transcript, University entrance examination (minimum score of 15) or ACT/SAT scores (minimum composite score of 17 ACT or a combined score of 1200 on SAT).

CONTACT

Everglades University, 850 Trafalgar Court, Suite 100, Maitland, FL 32751. *Phone:* 407-277-0311. *Toll-free phone:* 866-289-1078.

Everglades University

Sarasota, Florida

http://www.evergladesuniversity.edu/

- **Independent** comprehensive, founded 2003
- **Urban** campus with easy access to Sarasota
- **Coed**
- **Noncompetitive** entrance level

FACULTY

Student/faculty ratio: 10:1.

ACADEMICS

Calendar: semesters. *Degrees:* bachelor's and master's.

Library: Everglades University Library. *Books:* 19,974 (physical), 122,000 (digital/electronic); *Serial titles:* 48 (physical), 5,180 (digital/electronic); *Databases:* 55. Weekly public service hours: 6.

STUDENT LIFE

Housing options: college housing not available.

Campus security: 24-hour emergency response devices and patrols, late-night transport/escort service.

COSTS

Costs (2016–17) ***One-time required fee:*** $145. ***Tuition:*** $15,048 full-time, $627 per credit hour part-time. ***Required fees:*** $1600 full-time, $100 per term part-time.

APPLYING

Options: electronic application.

Application fee: $50.

Required: high school transcript, University entrance examination (minimum score of 15) or ACT/SAT scores (minimum composite score of 17 ACT or a combined score of 1200 on SAT).

CONTACT

Everglades University, 6001 Lake Osprey Drive #110, Sarasota, FL 34240. *Phone:* 866-289-1078. *Toll-free phone:* 888-854-8308.

Flagler College

St. Augustine, Florida

http://www.flagler.edu/

- **Independent** comprehensive, founded 1968
- **Small-town** 49-acre campus with easy access to Jacksonville
- **Endowment** $49.0 million
- **Coed** 2,614 undergraduate students, 97% full-time, 63% women, 37% men
- 55% of applicants were admitted

UNDERGRAD STUDENTS

2,539 full-time, 75 part-time. Students come from 46 states and territories; 44 other countries; 59% are from out of state; 0.3% Black or African American, non-Hispanic/Latino; 5% Hispanic/Latino; 0.1% Asian, non-Hispanic/Latino; 78% Native Hawaiian or other Pacific Islander, non-Hispanic/Latino; 4% American Indian or Alaska Native, non-Hispanic/Latino; 2% Two or more races, non-Hispanic/Latino; 6% Race/ethnicity unknown; 3% international; 6% transferred in; 38% live on campus.

Freshmen:

Admission: 4,794 applied, 2,639 admitted, 600 enrolled. ***Average high school GPA:*** 3.43. ***Test scores:*** SAT critical reading scores over 500: 74%; SAT math scores over 500: 59%; SAT writing scores over 500: 68%; ACT scores over 18: 100%; SAT critical reading scores over 600: 23%; SAT math scores over 600: 15%; SAT writing scores over 600: 17%; ACT scores over 24: 53%; SAT critical reading scores over 700: 3%; SAT math scores over 700: 1%; SAT writing scores over 700: 2%; ACT scores over 30: 6%.

Retention: 71% of full-time freshmen returned.

FACULTY

Total: 239, 49% full-time, 49% with terminal degrees.

Student/faculty ratio: 17:1.

ACADEMICS

Calendar: semesters. *Degrees:* bachelor's and master's.

Special study options: academic remediation for entering students, adult/continuing education programs, advanced placement credit, cooperative education, distance learning, double majors, honors programs, independent study, internships, part-time degree program, services for LD students, study abroad, summer session for credit.

Computers: 343 computers/terminals are available on campus for general student use. Students can access the following: campus intranet, computer help desk, free student e-mail accounts, online (class) grades, online (class) registration, online (class) schedules, local and remote printing to campus printers, remote access to intranet files. Campuswide network is available. 100% of college-owned or -operated housing units are wired for high-speed Internet access. Wireless service is available via entire campus.

Library: Proctor Library. *Books:* 102,047 (physical), 212,689 (digital/electronic); *Serial titles:* 630 (physical), 44,000 (digital/electronic); *Databases:* 60. Weekly public service hours: 100; students can reserve study rooms.

STUDENT LIFE

Housing options: men-only, women-only. Campus housing is university owned. Freshman campus housing is guaranteed.

Activities and organizations: drama/theater group, student-run newspaper, radio station, choral group, Student Government Association, Inter-Varsity, International Student Club, Flagler College Volunteers, Phi Alpha Omega (women's service club).

Athletics Member NCAA. All Division II. ***Intercollegiate sports:*** baseball M(s), basketball M(s)/W(s), cheerleading W, cross-country running M(s)/W(s), golf M(s)/W(s), soccer M(s)/W(s), softball M/W(s), tennis M(s)/W(s), track and field M(s)/W(s), volleyball W(s). ***Intramural sports:*** badminton M/W, basketball M/W, bowling M/W, football M/W, golf M/W, lacrosse M(c), soccer M/W, softball W, swimming and diving M/W, table tennis M/W, tennis M/W, volleyball M/W, weight lifting M/W.

Campus security: 24-hour emergency response devices and patrols, student patrols, late-night transport/escort service, controlled dormitory access, transport/escort service is provided from 6:00 pm until 6:00 am daily.

Student services: health clinic, personal/psychological counseling.

COSTS & FINANCIAL AID

Costs (2017–18) ***Comprehensive fee:*** $28,988 includes full-time tuition ($18,200), mandatory fees ($100), and room and board ($10,688). Full-time tuition and fees vary according to location. Part-time tuition: $620 per credit hour. Part-time tuition and fees vary according to location. ***College room only:*** $5350. Room and board charges vary according to board plan and housing facility. ***Payment plan:*** installment. ***Waivers:*** employees or children of employees.

Financial Aid Of all full-time matriculated undergraduates who enrolled in 2016, 1,941 applied for aid, 1,553 were judged to have need, 216 had their need fully met. 261 Federal Work-Study jobs (averaging $1400). 57 state and other part-time jobs (averaging $1400). In 2016, 452 non-need-based awards were made. ***Average percent of need met:*** 57. ***Average financial aid package:*** $12,151. ***Average need-based loan:*** $4047. ***Average need-based gift aid:*** $8522. ***Average non-need-based aid:*** $2573. ***Average indebtedness upon graduation:*** $29,267.

APPLYING

Standardized Tests *Required:* SAT or ACT (for admission).

Options: electronic application, early admission, early decision.

Application fee: $50.

Required: essay or personal statement, high school transcript, 1 letter of recommendation. ***Required for some:*** interview, interview for early admission. ***Recommended:*** minimum 2.5 GPA.

Application deadlines: 3/1 (freshmen), 3/1 (transfers).

Early decision deadline: 11/1.

Notification: 3/31 (freshmen), 3/31 (transfers), 12/15 (early decision).

CONTACT

Ms. Rachel Branch, Director of Admissions, Flagler College, 74 King Street, St. Augustine, FL 32085. *Phone:* 904-819-6294. *Toll-free phone:* 800-304-4208. *Fax:* 904-819-6466. *E-mail:* rbranch@flagler.edu.

Flagler College–Tallahassee

Tallahassee, Florida

http://www.flagler.edu/

CONTACT

Flagler College–Tallahassee, 444 Appleyard Drive, Tallahassee, FL 32304.

★ Florida Agricultural and Mechanical University

Tallahassee, Florida

http://www.famu.edu/

- **State-supported** university, founded 1887, part of State University System of Florida
- **Urban** 419-acre campus with easy access to Jacksonville
- **Endowment** $100.3 million
- **Coed** 7,769 undergraduate students, 85% full-time, 65% women, 35% men
- **Moderately difficult** entrance level, 31% of applicants were admitted

UNDERGRAD STUDENTS

6,623 full-time, 1,146 part-time. Students come from 40 states and territories; 58 other countries; 13% are from out of state; 90% Black or African American, non-Hispanic/Latino; 2% Hispanic/Latino; 0.5% Asian, non-Hispanic/Latino; 0.1% American Indian or Alaska Native, non-Hispanic/Latino; 3% Two or more races, non-Hispanic/Latino; 0.9% international; 6% transferred in; 28% live on campus.

Freshmen:

Admission: 6,988 applied, 2,174 admitted, 1,328 enrolled. ***Average high school GPA:*** 3.47. ***Test scores:*** SAT critical reading scores over 500: 47%; SAT math scores over 500: 46%; SAT writing scores over 500: 37%; ACT scores over 18: 93%; SAT critical reading scores over 600: 13%; SAT math scores over 600: 9%; SAT writing scores over 600: 10%; ACT scores over 24: 32%; SAT critical reading scores over 700: 2%; SAT math scores over 700: 1%; SAT writing scores over 700: 1%; ACT scores over 30: 3%.

Retention: 83% of full-time freshmen returned.

FACULTY

Total: 674, 81% full-time, 60% with terminal degrees.

Student/faculty ratio: 15:1.

ACADEMICS

Calendar: semesters. *Degrees:* associate, bachelor's, master's, doctoral, and post-master's certificates.

Special study options: academic remediation for entering students, accelerated degree program, adult/continuing education programs, advanced placement credit, cooperative education, distance learning, double majors, honors programs, independent study, internships, off-campus study, part-time degree program, services for LD students, study abroad, summer session for credit. ***ROTC:*** Army (b), Navy (b), Air Force (c).

Unusual degree programs: 3-2 business administration; occupational therapy, architecture.

Computers: 4,000 computers/terminals and 8,000 ports are available on campus for general student use. Students can access the following: campus intranet, computer help desk, free student e-mail accounts, online (class) grades, online (class) registration, online (class) schedules. Campuswide network is available. 100% of college-owned or -operated housing units are wired for high-speed Internet access. Wireless service is available via classrooms, computer centers, computer labs, dorm rooms, learning centers, libraries, student centers.

Library: Samuel H. Coleman Memorial Library plus 4 others. *Books:* 1.0 million (physical), 449,805 (digital/electronic); *Serial titles:* 16,025 (physical), 225,391 (digital/electronic); *Databases:* 320. Weekly public service hours: 141; study areas open 24 hours, 5-7 days a week; students can reserve study rooms.

STUDENT LIFE

Housing options: on-campus residence required for freshman year; coed, men-only, women-only, special housing for students with disabilities. Campus housing is university owned. Freshman applicants given priority for college housing.

Activities and organizations: drama/theater group, student-run newspaper, radio and television station, choral group, marching band, National Council of Negro Women, FAMU Chapter, American Society of Mechanical Engineers, Psi Chi International Honor Society, Caribbean Student Association, Academy of Student Pharmacists/Student National Pharmaceutical Association, national fraternities, national sororities.

Athletics Member NCAA. All Division I except football (Division I-AA). ***Intercollegiate sports:*** baseball M(s), basketball M(s)/W(s), bowling W(s), cheerleading M/W, cross-country running M(s)/W(s), golf M(s)/W(s), softball W(s), swimming and diving M(s)/W(s), tennis M(s)/W(s), track and field M(s)/W(s), volleyball W(s). ***Intramural sports:*** badminton M/W, basketball M/W, bowling M/W, cheerleading W, football M, golf M/W, gymnastics M/W, racquetball M/W, skiing (downhill) M/W, soccer M/W, softball M/W, swimming and diving M/W, table tennis M/W, tennis M/W, track and field M/W, ultimate Frisbee M/W, volleyball M/W, weight lifting M/W, wrestling M/W.

Campus security: 24-hour emergency response devices and patrols, late-night transport/escort service, controlled dormitory access.

Student services: health clinic, personal/psychological counseling.

COSTS & FINANCIAL AID

Costs (2017–18) ***Tuition:*** state resident $5645 full-time, $188 per credit hour part-time; nonresident $17,585 full-time, $586 per credit hour part-time. ***Required fees:*** $140 full-time. ***Room and board:*** $10,058; room only: $5780. Room and board charges vary according to board plan and housing facility. ***Payment plan:*** tuition prepayment. ***Waivers:*** senior citizens and employees or children of employees.

Financial Aid Of all full-time matriculated undergraduates who enrolled in 2015, 6,672 applied for aid, 5,872 were judged to have need, 830 had their need fully met. 194 Federal Work-Study jobs (averaging $2123). In 2015, 134 non-need-based awards were made. ***Average percent of need met:*** 70. ***Average financial aid package:*** $13,113. ***Average need-based loan:*** $3902. ***Average need-based gift aid:*** $5817. ***Average non-need-based aid:*** $6521. ***Average indebtedness upon graduation:*** $33,568.

APPLYING

Standardized Tests *Required:* SAT or ACT (for admission).

Options: electronic application, early admission.

Application fee: $30.

Required: essay or personal statement, high school transcript, minimum 2.5 GPA, 3 letters of recommendation. ***Required for some:*** interview, audition for music major applicants. ***Recommended:*** minimum 3.0 GPA.

Application deadlines: 5/15 (freshmen), 5/15 (transfers).

Notification: continuous (freshmen), continuous (out-of-state freshmen), continuous (transfers).

CONTACT

Ms. Barbara R. Cox, Director, Admissions, Florida Agricultural and Mechanical University, Office of Admissions, Florida A & M University, Tallahassee, FL 32307. *Phone:* 850-599-3796. *Toll-free phone:* 866-642-1198. *Fax:* 850-599-3069. *E-mail:* ugrdadmissions@famu.edu.

Florida Atlantic University

Boca Raton, Florida

http://www.fau.edu/

- **State-supported** university, founded 1961, part of State University System of Florida
- **Suburban** 850-acre campus with easy access to Miami, Fort Lauderdale, West Palm Beach
- **Endowment** $257.9 million
- **Coed** 25,400 undergraduate students, 63% full-time, 56% women, 44% men
- **Moderately difficult** entrance level, 60% of applicants were admitted

UNDERGRAD STUDENTS

16,092 full-time, 9,308 part-time. Students come from 48 states and territories; 125 other countries; 5% are from out of state; 20% Black or African American, non-Hispanic/Latino; 26% Hispanic/Latino; 4% Asian, non-Hispanic/Latino; 0.1% Native Hawaiian or other Pacific Islander, non-Hispanic/Latino; 0.2% American Indian or Alaska Native, non-Hispanic/Latino; 4% Two or more races, non-Hispanic/Latino; 0.7% Race/ethnicity unknown; 3% international; 10% transferred in; 17% live on campus.

Freshmen:

Admission: 15,907 applied, 9,509 admitted, 3,180 enrolled. ***Average high school GPA:*** 4.01. ***Test scores:*** SAT critical reading scores over 500: 67%; SAT math scores over 500: 64%; SAT writing scores over 500: 59%; ACT scores over 18: 98%; SAT critical reading scores over 600: 18%; SAT math scores over 600: 18%; SAT writing scores over 600: 12%; ACT scores over 24: 39%; SAT critical reading scores over 700: 3%; SAT math scores over 700: 2%; SAT writing scores over 700: 1%; ACT scores over 30: 5%.

Retention: 77% of full-time freshmen returned.

FACULTY

Total: 1,315, 61% full-time, 62% with terminal degrees.

Student/faculty ratio: 23:1.

ACADEMICS

Calendar: semesters. *Degrees:* certificates, associate, bachelor's, master's, doctoral, and post-master's certificates.

Special study options: accelerated degree program, adult/continuing education programs, advanced placement credit, cooperative education, distance learning, double majors, English as a second language, freshman honors college, honors programs, independent study, internships, off-campus study, part-time degree program, services for LD students, study abroad, summer session for credit. ***ROTC:*** Army (b), Air Force (c).

Unusual degree programs: 3-2 business administration; engineering; nursing; architecture, mathematics.

Computers: 1,350 computers/terminals are available on campus for general student use. Students can access the following: campus intranet, computer help desk, free student e-mail accounts, online (class) grades, online (class) registration, online (class) schedules. Campuswide network is available. 100% of college-owned or -operated housing units are wired for high-speed Internet access. Wireless service is available via entire campus.

Library: S. E. Wimberly Library plus 2 others. *Books:* 1.4 million (physical), 1.3 million (digital/electronic); *Serial titles:* 649 (physical), 106,566 (digital/electronic); *Databases:* 492. Study areas open 24 hours, 5-7 days a week.

STUDENT LIFE

Housing options: on-campus residence required for freshman year; coed, women-only. Campus housing is university owned. Freshman campus housing is guaranteed.

Activities and organizations: drama/theater group, student-run newspaper, radio and television station, choral group, marching band, American Society of Civil Engineers, Dive Club, Pre-Law Society, Submarine Club, American Criminal Justice Society, national fraternities, national sororities.

Athletics Member NCAA. All Division I. ***Intercollegiate sports:*** baseball M(s), basketball M(s)/W(s), cheerleading M/W, cross-country running M/W, football M(s), golf M(s)/W(s), soccer M/W, softball W(s), swimming and diving M/W, tennis M/W, track and field W, volleyball W(s). ***Intramural sports:*** baseball M/W, bowling M/W, football M, ice hockey M(c)/W(c), lacrosse M(c), rock climbing M(c)/W(c), rugby M(c)/W(c), sailing M(c)/W(c), soccer M/W, softball W, table tennis M/W, ultimate Frisbee M/W, volleyball M/W, weight lifting M(c), wrestling M(c).

Campus security: 24-hour emergency response devices and patrols, student patrols, late-night transport/escort service, controlled dormitory access.

Student services: health clinic, personal/psychological counseling, women's center.

COSTS & FINANCIAL AID

Costs (2017–18) ***Tuition:*** state resident $6039 full-time, $105 per credit hour part-time; nonresident $21,595 full-time, $599 per credit hour part-time. Full-time tuition and fees vary according to course load. Part-time tuition and fees vary according to course load. ***Required fees:*** $96 per credit hour part-time. ***Room and board:*** $12,050. Room and board charges vary according to board plan and housing facility. ***Payment plans:*** tuition prepayment, installment, deferred payment. ***Waivers:*** senior citizens and employees or children of employees.

Financial Aid Of all full-time matriculated undergraduates who enrolled in 2016, 11,501 applied for aid, 9,587 were judged to have need, 1,193 had their need fully met. 226 Federal Work-Study jobs (averaging $2230). 6 state and other part-time jobs (averaging $2329). In 2016, 239 non-need-based awards were made. ***Average percent of need met:*** 63. ***Average financial aid package:*** $13,345. ***Average need-based loan:*** $7236. ***Average need-based gift aid:*** $6604. ***Average non-need-based aid:*** $3483. ***Average indebtedness upon graduation:*** $22,648.

APPLYING

Standardized Tests *Required:* SAT or ACT (for admission).

Options: electronic application, early admission, deferred entrance.

Application fee: $30.

Required: high school transcript.

Application deadlines: 5/1 (freshmen), 5/1 (transfers).

Notification: continuous (freshmen), continuous (transfers).

CONTACT

Ms. Mary Edmunds, Associate Director, Florida Atlantic University, 777 Glades Road, PO Box 3091, Boca Raton, FL 33431-0991. *Phone:* 561-297-3040. *Fax:* 561-297-2758. *E-mail:* recruitment@fau.edu.

Florida College

Temple Terrace, Florida

http://www.floridacollege.edu/

- **Independent** 4-year, founded 1944
- **Small-town** 95-acre campus with easy access to Tampa
- **Endowment** $11.9 million
- **Coed** 533 undergraduate students, 97% full-time, 51% women, 49% men
- **Moderately difficult** entrance level, 79% of applicants were admitted

UNDERGRAD STUDENTS

517 full-time, 16 part-time. Students come from 34 states and territories; 5 other countries; 63% are from out of state; 6% Black or African American, non-Hispanic/Latino; 7% Hispanic/Latino; 0.4% Asian, non-Hispanic/Latino; 1% American Indian or Alaska Native, non-Hispanic/Latino; 5% Two or more races, non-Hispanic/Latino; 1% Race/ethnicity unknown; 4% international; 81% live on campus.

Freshmen:

Admission: 284 applied, 223 admitted, 150 enrolled. ***Test scores:*** SAT critical reading scores over 500: 65%; SAT math scores over 500: 52%; ACT scores over 18: 92%; SAT critical reading scores over 600: 38%; SAT math scores over 600: 21%; ACT scores over 24: 52%; SAT critical reading scores over 700: 13%; SAT math scores over 700: 6%; ACT scores over 30: 15%.

FACULTY

Total: 34.

Student/faculty ratio: 13:1.

ACADEMICS

Calendar: semesters. *Degrees:* associate and bachelor's.

Special study options: academic remediation for entering students, advanced placement credit, independent study, summer session for credit. ***ROTC:*** Army (c), Air Force (c).

Computers: 36 computers/terminals are available on campus for general student use. Students can access the following: campus intranet, computer help desk, free student e-mail accounts, online (class) grades, online (class) schedules. Campuswide network is available. 100% of college-owned or -operated housing units are wired for high-speed Internet access. Wireless service is available via classrooms, computer centers, computer labs, dorm rooms, libraries, student centers.

Library: Chatlos Library.

STUDENT LIFE

Housing options: on-campus residence required through sophomore year; men-only, women-only. Campus housing is university owned. Freshman campus housing is guaranteed.

Activities and organizations: drama/theater group, choral group, Co-ed Societies, ROTARACT CLUB, NAFME, SBGA, Footlighters.

Athletics Member USCAA. ***Intercollegiate sports:*** basketball M(s)/W, cheerleading W, cross-country running M/W, soccer M(s)/W(s), volleyball W(s). ***Intramural sports:*** basketball M/W, football M/W, soccer M/W, softball M/W, ultimate Frisbee M/W, volleyball M/W.

Campus security: controlled dormitory access, evening patrols by trained security personnel.

Student services: health clinic, personal/psychological counseling.

COSTS & FINANCIAL AID

Costs (2016–17) ***Comprehensive fee:*** $24,780 includes full-time tuition ($15,670), mandatory fees ($880), and room and board ($8230). Part-time tuition: $618 per credit hour. Part-time tuition and fees vary according to course load. ***College room only:*** $4180. Room and board charges vary according to board plan and housing facility. ***Payment plan:*** installment. ***Waivers:*** employees or children of employees.

Financial Aid Of all full-time matriculated undergraduates who enrolled in 2014, 452 applied for aid, 387 were judged to have need, 33 had their need fully met. 33 Federal Work-Study jobs (averaging $708). In 2014, 120 non-need-based awards were made. ***Average percent of need met:*** 60. ***Average financial aid package:*** $10,640. ***Average need-based loan:*** $3932. ***Average need-based gift aid:*** $6563. ***Average non-need-based aid:*** $4213.

APPLYING

Standardized Tests *Required:* SAT or ACT (for admission).

Options: electronic application.

Application fee: $40.

Required: high school transcript, minimum 2.0 GPA, 2 letters of recommendation. ***Required for some:*** essay for international students.

Application deadlines: 8/1 (freshmen), 8/1 (transfers).

Notification: continuous (freshmen), continuous (transfers).

CONTACT

Mrs. Colleen Engel, Assistant Director of Admissions, Florida College, 119 North Glen Arven Avenue, Temple Terrace, FL 33617. *Phone:* 813-988-5131 Ext. 152. *Fax:* 813-899-6772. *E-mail:* admissions@floridacollege.edu.

Florida Gateway College

Lake City, Florida

http://www.fgc.edu/

CONTACT

Admissions, Florida Gateway College, 149 SE College Place, Lake City, FL 32025-8703. *Phone:* 386-755-4236. *E-mail:* admissions@fgc.edu.

Florida Gulf Coast University

Fort Myers, Florida

http://www.fgcu.edu/

- **State-supported** comprehensive, founded 1991, part of State University System of Florida
- **Suburban** 760-acre campus
- **Endowment** $72.9 million
- **Coed** 13,711 undergraduate students, 79% full-time, 56% women, 44% men
- **Moderately difficult** entrance level, 56% of applicants were admitted

UNDERGRAD STUDENTS

10,810 full-time, 2,901 part-time. Students come from 45 states and territories; 82 other countries; 11% are from out of state; 7% Black or African American, non-Hispanic/Latino; 20% Hispanic/Latino; 2% Asian, non-Hispanic/Latino; 0.1% Native Hawaiian or other Pacific Islander, non-Hispanic/Latino; 0.2% American Indian or Alaska Native, non-Hispanic/Latino; 3% Two or more races, non-Hispanic/Latino; 1% Race/ethnicity unknown; 2% international; 8% transferred in; 35% live on campus.

Freshmen:

Admission: 15,152 applied, 8,508 admitted, 2,652 enrolled. ***Average high school GPA:*** 3.83. ***Test scores:*** SAT critical reading scores over 500: 76%; SAT math scores over 500: 70%; SAT writing scores over 500: 67%; ACT scores over 18: 99%; SAT critical reading scores over 600: 18%; SAT math scores over 600: 15%; SAT writing scores over 600: 12%; ACT scores over 24: 48%; SAT critical reading scores over 700: 2%; SAT math scores over 700: 1%; SAT writing scores over 700: 1%; ACT scores over 30: 4%.

Retention: 79% of full-time freshmen returned.

FACULTY

Total: 834, 56% full-time, 41% with terminal degrees.

Student/faculty ratio: 21:1.

ACADEMICS

Calendar: semesters. *Degrees:* certificates, associate, bachelor's, master's, and doctoral.

Special study options: academic remediation for entering students, accelerated degree program, advanced placement credit, cooperative education, distance learning, double majors, honors programs, independent study, internships, off-campus study, part-time degree program, services for LD students, study abroad, summer session for credit.

Computers: 1,029 computers/terminals are available on campus for general student use. Students can access the following: computer help desk, free student e-mail accounts, online (class) registration, online (class) schedules, online admissions and advising. Campuswide network is available. 100% of college-owned or -operated housing units are wired for high-speed Internet access. Wireless service is available via entire campus.

Library: Library Services plus 1 other. *Books:* 242,131 (physical), 73,000 (digital/electronic); *Serial titles:* 128,865 (digital/electronic); *Databases:* 389. Students can reserve study rooms.

STUDENT LIFE

Housing options: coed. Campus housing is university owned.

Activities and organizations: drama/theater group, student-run newspaper, Student Government, Ignite (Religious Organization), International Club, Martial Arts Club, Physical Therapy Association, national fraternities, national sororities.

Athletics Member NCAA. All Division I. ***Intercollegiate sports:*** baseball M(s), basketball M(s)/W(s), cheerleading W, cross-country running M(s)/W(s), golf M(s)/W(s), soccer M(s)/W(s), softball W(s), swimming and diving W(s), tennis M(s)/W(s), volleyball W(s). ***Intramural sports:*** basketball M/W, cross-country running M(c)/W(c), fencing M(c)/W(c), football M/W, ice hockey M(c), lacrosse M(c)/W(c), sailing M(c)/W(c), skiing (downhill) M(c)/W(c), soccer M/W, softball M/W, swimming and diving M(c)/W(c), table tennis M/W, tennis M(c)/W(c), ultimate Frisbee M/W, volleyball M/W, water polo M/W, weight lifting M(c)/W(c), wrestling M(c)/W(c).

Campus security: 24-hour emergency response devices and patrols, late-night transport/escort service.

Student services: health clinic, personal/psychological counseling.

FINANCIAL AID

Financial Aid Of all full-time matriculated undergraduates who enrolled in 2015, 7,883 applied for aid, 5,285 were judged to have need, 451 had their need fully met. In 2015, 308 non-need-based awards were made. ***Average percent of need met:*** 56. ***Average financial aid package:*** $9585. ***Average need-based loan:*** $7128. ***Average need-based gift aid:*** $5299. ***Average non-need-based aid:*** $3888. ***Average indebtedness upon graduation:*** $24,763. ***Financial aid deadline:*** 6/30.

APPLYING

Standardized Tests *Required:* SAT or ACT (for admission).

Options: electronic application, deferred entrance.

Application fee: $30.

Required: high school transcript, minimum 2.0 GPA.

Application deadlines: 5/1 (freshmen), 7/1 (transfers).

Notification: continuous (freshmen), continuous (transfers).

CONTACT

Florida Gulf Coast University, 10501 FGCU Boulevard South, Fort Myers, FL 33965-6565. *Phone:* 239-590-7878. *Toll-free phone:* 888-889-1095.

Florida Institute of Technology

Melbourne, Florida

http://www.fit.edu/

- **Independent** university, founded 1958
- **Small-town** 130-acre campus with easy access to Orlando
- **Endowment** $62.1 million
- **Coed** 3,629 undergraduate students, 91% full-time, 30% women, 70% men
- **Moderately difficult** entrance level, 61% of applicants were admitted

UNDERGRAD STUDENTS

3,286 full-time, 343 part-time. Students come from 50 states and territories; 107 other countries; 49% are from out of state; 6% Black or African American, non-Hispanic/Latino; 7% Hispanic/Latino; 2% Asian, non-Hispanic/Latino; 0.3% Native Hawaiian or other Pacific Islander, non-Hispanic/Latino; 0.2% American Indian or Alaska Native, non-Hispanic/Latino; 2% Two or more races, non-Hispanic/Latino; 5% Race/ethnicity unknown; 35% international; 6% transferred in; 45% live on campus.

Freshmen:

Admission: 9,503 applied, 5,828 admitted, 761 enrolled. ***Average high school GPA:*** 3.67. ***Test scores:*** SAT critical reading scores over 500: 81%; SAT math scores over 500: 96%; ACT scores over 18: 100%; SAT critical reading scores over 600: 32%; SAT math scores over 600: 52%; ACT scores over 24: 77%; SAT critical reading scores over 700: 4%; SAT math scores over 700: 10%; ACT scores over 30: 21%.

Retention: 83% of full-time freshmen returned.

FACULTY

Total: 772, 40% full-time, 59% with terminal degrees.

Student/faculty ratio: 14:1.

ACADEMICS

Calendar: semesters. *Degrees:* bachelor's, master's, doctoral, and post-master's certificates.

Special study options: academic remediation for entering students, accelerated degree program, adult/continuing education programs, advanced placement credit, cooperative education, distance learning, double majors, English as a second language, independent study, internships, part-time degree program, services for LD students, student-designed majors, study abroad, summer session for credit.

ROTC: Army (b).

Computers: 254 computers/terminals and 100 ports are available on campus for general student use. Students can access the following: campus intranet, computer help desk, free student e-mail accounts, online (class) grades, online (class) registration, online (class) schedules. Campuswide network is available. 100% of college-owned or -operated housing units are wired for high-speed Internet access. Wireless service is available via classrooms, computer centers, computer labs, dorm rooms, learning centers, libraries, student centers.

Library: Evans Library. *Books:* 131,973 (physical), 164,272 (digital/electronic); *Serial titles:* 1,548 (physical), 44,772 (digital/electronic); *Databases:* 172. Weekly public service hours: 96; students can reserve study rooms.

STUDENT LIFE

Housing options: on-campus residence required through sophomore year; coed. Campus housing is university owned. Freshman campus housing is guaranteed.

Activities and organizations: drama/theater group, student-run newspaper, radio and television station, choral group, Florida Institute of Technology Society for Science Fiction and Fantasy (FITSSFF), International Student Services Organization (ISSO), Student Government Association (SGA), Surf Club, Campus Activities Board, national fraternities, national sororities.

Athletics Member NCAA. All Division II. ***Intercollegiate sports:*** baseball M(s), basketball M(s)/W(s), crew M(s)/W(s), cross-country running M(s)/W(s), football M(s), golf M(s)/W(s), lacrosse M(s)/W(s), soccer M(s)/W(s), softball W(s), swimming and diving M(s)/W(s), tennis M(s)/W(s), track and field M(s)/W(s), volleyball W(s), water polo M(c)/W(c). ***Intramural sports:*** badminton M/W, baseball M(c)/W(c), basketball M/W, bowling M/W, football M/W, ice hockey M(c)/W(c), racquetball M/W, rugby M/W, sailing M/W, soccer M/W, softball W, tennis M/W, ultimate Frisbee M/W, volleyball M/W.

Campus security: 24-hour emergency response devices and patrols, late-night transport/escort service, controlled dormitory access.

Student services: health clinic, personal/psychological counseling, women's center.

COSTS & FINANCIAL AID

Costs (2017–18) ***Comprehensive fee:*** $54,120 includes full-time tuition ($40,490), mandatory fees ($750), and room and board ($12,880). Full-time tuition and fees vary according to course load and program. Part-time tuition: $1170 per credit hour. ***College room only:*** $7000. Room and board charges vary according to board plan and housing facility. ***Payment plan:*** installment. ***Waivers:*** senior citizens and employees or children of employees.

Financial Aid Of all full-time matriculated undergraduates who enrolled in 2016, 1,845 applied for aid, 1,666 were judged to have need, 642 had their need fully met. 634 Federal Work-Study jobs (averaging $2294). 423 state and other part-time jobs (averaging $6315). In 2016, 1074 non-need-based awards were made. ***Average percent of need met:*** 86. ***Average financial aid package:*** $36,720. ***Average need-based loan:*** $5059. ***Average need-based gift aid:*** $25,435. ***Average non-need-based aid:*** $15,123. ***Average indebtedness upon graduation:*** $36,678.

APPLYING

Standardized Tests *Required:* SAT or ACT (for admission).

Options: electronic application, deferred entrance.

Required: essay or personal statement, high school transcript, minimum 2.6 GPA, 1 letter of recommendation. ***Recommended:*** minimum 3.3 GPA, interview.

Application deadlines: rolling (freshmen), rolling (transfers).

Notification: continuous (freshmen), continuous (transfers).

CONTACT

Michael J. Perry, Director of Undergraduate Admission, Florida Institute of Technology, 150 West University Boulevard, Melbourne, FL 32901-6975. *Phone:* 321-674-8030. *Toll-free phone:* 800-888-4348. *Fax:* 321-723-9468. *E-mail:* admission@fit.edu.

Florida International University

Miami, Florida

http://www.fiu.edu/

- **State-supported** university, founded 1965, part of State University System of Florida
- **Urban** 582-acre campus with easy access to Miami
- **Endowment** $174.1 million
- **Coed** 45,813 undergraduate students, 57% full-time, 56% women, 44% men
- **Moderately difficult** entrance level, 49% of applicants were admitted

UNDERGRAD STUDENTS

26,335 full-time, 19,478 part-time. Students come from 48 states and territories; 146 other countries; 3% are from out of state; 12% Black or African American, non-Hispanic/Latino; 67% Hispanic/Latino; 2% Asian, non-Hispanic/Latino; 0.1% Native Hawaiian or other Pacific Islander, non-Hispanic/Latino; 0.1% American Indian or Alaska Native, non-Hispanic/Latino; 3% Two or more races, non-Hispanic/Latino; 0.7% Race/ethnicity unknown; 5% international; 11% transferred in; 8% live on campus.

Freshmen:

Admission: 17,218 applied, 8,498 admitted, 4,551 enrolled. ***Average high school GPA:*** 3.94. ***Test scores:*** SAT critical reading scores over 500: 89%; SAT math scores over 500: 86%; SAT writing scores over 500: 85%; ACT scores over 18: 100%; SAT critical reading scores over 600: 31%; SAT math scores over 600: 26%; SAT writing scores over 600: 24%; ACT scores over 24: 64%; SAT critical reading scores over 700: 4%; SAT math scores over 700: 2%; SAT writing scores over 700: 2%; ACT scores over 30: 8%.

Retention: 88% of full-time freshmen returned.

FACULTY

Total: 2,356, 54% full-time, 66% with terminal degrees.

Student/faculty ratio: 26:1.

ACADEMICS

Calendar: semesters. *Degrees:* bachelor's, master's, doctoral, and postbachelor's certificates.

Special study options: accelerated degree program, adult/continuing education programs, advanced placement credit, cooperative education, distance learning, double majors, freshman honors college, honors programs, independent study, internships, off-campus study, part-time degree program, services for LD students, study abroad, summer session for credit. ***ROTC:*** Army (b), Air Force (b).

Computers: Students can access the following: computer help desk, free student e-mail accounts, online (class) grades, online (class) registration, online (class) schedules, online financial and cashier's information; financial, campus maps information available on cell phones. Campuswide network is available. 100% of college-owned or -operated housing units are wired for high-speed Internet access. Wireless service is available via entire campus.

Library: Steven and Dorothea Green Library plus 4 others. *Books:* 1.5 million (physical), 287,899 (digital/electronic); *Serial titles:* 59,593 (physical), 106,720 (digital/electronic); *Databases:* 790. Weekly public service hours: 112; students can reserve study rooms.

STUDENT LIFE

Housing options: coed. Campus housing is university owned.

Activities and organizations: drama/theater group, student-run newspaper, radio station, choral group, marching band, Students for Community Service, Black Student Leadership Council, Hospitality Management Student Club, Hispanic Students Association, Haitian Students Organization, national fraternities, national sororities.

Athletics Member NCAA. All Division I. ***Intercollegiate sports:*** baseball M(s), basketball M(s)/W(s), cross-country running M(s)/W(s), football M(s), golf W(s), soccer M(s)/W(s), softball W(s), swimming and diving W(s), tennis W(s), track and field M(s)/W(s), volleyball W(s). ***Intramural sports:*** badminton M(c)/W(c), baseball M(c), basketball M/W, crew M(c)/W(c), cross-country running M(c)/W(c), equestrian sports M(c)/W(c), football M/W, golf W, lacrosse M(c)/W(c), racquetball M/W, rugby M(c)/W(c), sailing M/W, soccer M/W, softball M/W, swimming and diving M(c)/W(c), table tennis M/W, tennis M(c)/W(c), ultimate Frisbee M/W, volleyball M/W, weight lifting M/W, wrestling M(c)/W(c).

Campus security: 24-hour emergency response devices and patrols, late-night transport/escort service, controlled dormitory access.

Student services: health clinic, personal/psychological counseling, women's center.

COSTS & FINANCIAL AID

Costs (2017–18) ***Tuition:*** state resident $6168 full-time, $206 per credit hour part-time; nonresident $18,566 full-time, $619 per credit hour part-time. ***Required fees:*** $390 full-time. ***Room and board:*** $10,846; room only: $6487. Room and board charges vary according to board plan and housing facility. ***Payment plan:*** installment. ***Waivers:*** employees or children of employees.

Financial Aid Of all full-time matriculated undergraduates who enrolled in 2014, 18,764 applied for aid, 18,460 were judged to have need, 2,580 had their need fully met. In 2014, 1251 non-need-based awards were made. ***Average percent of need met:*** 22. ***Average financial aid package:*** $8483. ***Average need-based loan:*** $3778. ***Average need-based gift aid:*** $5989. ***Average non-need-based aid:*** $2267. ***Average indebtedness upon graduation:*** $18,918. ***Financial aid deadline:*** 5/15.

APPLYING

Standardized Tests *Required:* SAT or ACT (for admission). *Required for some:* TOEFL for applicants whose native language is not English.

Options: electronic application.

Application fee: $30.

Required: high school transcript. ***Required for some:*** portfolio or audition.

Application deadlines: 11/1 (freshmen), rolling (out-of-state freshmen), rolling (transfers).

Notification: continuous (freshmen), continuous (out-of-state freshmen), continuous (transfers).

CONTACT

Ms. Luisa Havens, Vice President of Enrollment Services, Florida International University, 11200 SW Eighth Street, PC 140, Miami, FL 33199. *Phone:* 305-348-2363. *Fax:* 305-348-3648. *E-mail:* admiss@fiu.edu.

Florida Keys Community College

Key West, Florida

http://www.fkcc.edu/

- **State-supported** primarily 2-year, founded 1965, part of Florida College System
- **Small-town** 20-acre campus
- **Coed** 1,023 undergraduate students, 37% full-time, 58% women, 42% men
- **Noncompetitive** entrance level

UNDERGRAD STUDENTS

377 full-time, 646 part-time. 8% Black or African American, non-Hispanic/Latino; 25% Hispanic/Latino; 1% Asian, non-Hispanic/Latino; 0.3% Native Hawaiian or other Pacific Islander, non-Hispanic/Latino; 0.1% American Indian or Alaska Native, non-Hispanic/Latino; 2% Two or more races, non-Hispanic/Latino; 8% Race/ethnicity unknown; 0.6% international.

Freshmen:

Admission: 195 enrolled.

ACADEMICS

Calendar: trimesters. *Degrees:* certificates, associate, and bachelor's.

Special study options: academic remediation for entering students, adult/continuing education programs, advanced placement credit, cooperative education, distance learning, double majors, English as a second language, independent study, internships, part-time degree program, services for LD students, student-designed majors, summer session for credit.

Computers: Students can access the following: campus intranet, computer help desk, free student e-mail accounts, online (class) grades, online (class) registration, online (class) schedules. Campuswide network is available. 100% of college-owned or -operated housing units are wired for high-speed Internet access. Wireless service is available via entire campus.

Library: Florida Keys Community College Library. Students can reserve study rooms.

STUDENT LIFE

Housing options: coed.

Activities and organizations: choral group.

Campus security: 24-hour patrols.

Student services: personal/psychological counseling.

COSTS & FINANCIAL AID

Costs (2016–17) ***Tuition:*** state resident $2483 full-time, $109 per credit hour part-time; nonresident $9933 full-time, $439 per credit hour part-time. Full-time tuition and fees vary according to course load. Part-time tuition and fees vary according to course load. ***Required fees:*** $793 full-time. ***Room and board:*** $11,650; room only: $9620. ***Payment plan:*** installment. ***Waivers:*** employees or children of employees.

Financial Aid Of all full-time matriculated undergraduates who enrolled in 2015, 30 Federal Work-Study jobs (averaging $2000).

APPLYING

Options: electronic application, early admission, deferred entrance.

Application fee: $20.

Required for some: high school transcript.

Application deadlines: rolling (freshmen), rolling (transfers).

Notification: continuous (freshmen), continuous (transfers).

CONTACT

Florida Keys Community College, 5901 College Road, Key West, FL 33040-4397. *Phone:* 305-296-9081 Ext. 237.

Florida Memorial University

Miami-Dade, Florida

http://www.fmuniv.edu/

CONTACT

Mrs. Peggy Murray Martin, Director of Admissions and International Student Advisor, Florida Memorial University, 15800 NW 42nd Avenue, Miami-Dade, FL 33054. *Phone:* 305-626-3147. *Toll-free phone:* 800-822-1362.

★ Florida National University

Hialeah, Florida

http://www.fnu.edu/

- **Proprietary** comprehensive, founded 1982
- **Urban** 4-acre campus with easy access to Miami
- **Coed** 3,191 undergraduate students, 79% full-time, 73% women, 27% men
- **Moderately difficult** entrance level, 99% of applicants were admitted

UNDERGRAD STUDENTS

2,517 full-time, 674 part-time. Students come from 20 states and territories; 26 other countries; 2% are from out of state; 3% Black or African American, non-Hispanic/Latino; 82% Hispanic/Latino; 0.4% Asian, non-Hispanic/Latino; 0.1% American Indian or Alaska Native, non-Hispanic/Latino; 0.6% Two or more races, non-Hispanic/Latino; 0.8% Race/ethnicity unknown; 12% international; 7% transferred in.

Freshmen:

Admission: 1,566 applied, 1,556 admitted, 644 enrolled.

Retention: 83% of full-time freshmen returned.

FACULTY

Total: 123, 53% full-time, 17% with terminal degrees.

Student/faculty ratio: 31:1.

ACADEMICS

Calendar: semesters. *Degrees:* certificates, diplomas, associate, bachelor's, master's, post-master's, and postbachelor's certificates.

Special study options: academic remediation for entering students, accelerated degree program, adult/continuing education programs, advanced placement credit, cooperative education, distance learning, English as a second language, independent study, internships, part-time degree program, services for LD students, summer session for credit.

Computers: 300 computers/terminals are available on campus for general student use. Students can access the following: computer help desk, free student e-mail accounts, online (class) grades, online (class) registration, online (class) schedules. Campuswide network is available. Wireless service is available via entire campus.

Library: Hialeah Campus Library plus 1 other. *Books:* 23,301 (physical), 144,218 (digital/electronic); *Serial titles:* 56 (physical), 196,357 (digital/electronic); *Databases:* 32. Weekly public service hours: 69; students can reserve study rooms.

STUDENT LIFE

Housing options: college housing not available.

Activities and organizations: student-run newspaper, Student Government Association, Bible Club, Salsa Club, W.I.C.S (Women Community Service), Criminal Justice Society, national fraternities.

Athletics Member USCAA. ***Intercollegiate sports:*** basketball M(s), soccer M(s), volleyball W(s).

Campus security: 24-hour emergency response devices.

COSTS & FINANCIAL AID

Costs (2016–17) ***Tuition:*** $12,600 full-time, $525 per credit part-time. No tuition increase for student's term of enrollment. ***Required fees:*** $650 full-time. ***Payment plans:*** tuition prepayment, installment. ***Waivers:*** employees or children of employees.

Financial Aid Of all full-time matriculated undergraduates who enrolled in 2015, 2,376 applied for aid, 2,257 were judged to have need. 42 Federal Work-Study jobs (averaging $8320). ***Average need-based gift aid:*** $5750.

APPLYING

Standardized Tests *Required:* SAT or ACT (for admission).

Options: electronic application, deferred entrance.

Required: high school transcript, interview.

Application deadlines: rolling (freshmen), rolling (transfers).

Notification: continuous (freshmen), continuous (transfers).

CONTACT

Mr. Robert Lopez, Director of Admissions, Florida National University, 4425 W. Jose Regueiro (20th) Avenue, Hialeah, FL 33012. *Phone:* 305-821-3333. *Fax:* 305-362-0595. *E-mail:* rlopez@fnu.edu.

★ Florida Southern College

Lakeland, Florida

http://www.flsouthern.edu/

- **Independent** comprehensive, founded 1885, affiliated with United Methodist Church
- **Suburban** 113-acre campus with easy access to Tampa, Orlando
- **Endowment** $71.7 million
- **Coed** 2,386 undergraduate students, 97% full-time, 63% women, 37% men
- **Moderately difficult** entrance level, 46% of applicants were admitted

UNDERGRAD STUDENTS

2,319 full-time, 67 part-time. Students come from 46 states and territories; 52 other countries; 37% are from out of state; 4% Black or African American, non-Hispanic/Latino; 11% Hispanic/Latino; 2% Asian, non-Hispanic/Latino; 0.1% Native Hawaiian or other Pacific Islander, non-Hispanic/Latino; 0.7% American Indian or Alaska Native, non-Hispanic/Latino; 2% Two or more races, non-Hispanic/Latino; 1% Race/ethnicity unknown; 4% international; 3% transferred in; 87% live on campus.

Freshmen:

Admission: 6,192 applied, 2,820 admitted, 648 enrolled. ***Average high school GPA:*** 3.73. ***Test scores:*** SAT critical reading scores over 500: 81%; SAT math scores over 500: 88%; SAT writing scores over 500: 68%; ACT scores over 18: 99%; SAT critical reading scores over 600: 29%; SAT math scores over 600: 32%; SAT writing scores over 600: 18%; ACT scores over 24: 71%; SAT critical reading scores over 700: 5%; SAT math scores over 700: 4%; SAT writing scores over 700: 3%; ACT scores over 30: 12%.

Retention: 81% of full-time freshmen returned.

FACULTY

Total: 286, 53% full-time, 55% with terminal degrees.

Student/faculty ratio: 14:1.

ACADEMICS

Calendar: semesters. *Degrees:* bachelor's, master's, and doctoral.

Special study options: accelerated degree program, adult/continuing education programs, advanced placement credit, distance learning, double majors, external degree program, honors programs, independent study, internships, off-campus study, part-time degree program, student-designed majors, study abroad, summer session for credit. ***ROTC:*** Army (b), Air Force (c).

Unusual degree programs: 3-2 business administration; engineering with Washington University in St. Louis; environmental science with Duke University, accounting/accountancy with Florida Southern College, medicine with Lake Erie College of Osteopathic Medicine.

Computers: 490 computers/terminals and 65 ports are available on campus for general student use. Students can access the following: campus intranet, computer help desk, free student e-mail accounts, online (class) grades, online (class) registration, online (class) schedules, campus portal. Campuswide network is available. 100% of college-owned or -operated housing units are wired for high-speed Internet access. Wireless service is available via entire campus.

Library: Roux Library plus 1 other. *Books:* 160,667 (physical), 167,731 (digital/electronic); *Serial titles:* 22 (physical), 97,772 (digital/electronic); *Databases:* 118. Weekly public service hours: 104; students can reserve study rooms.

STUDENT LIFE

Housing options: on-campus residence required through senior year; coed, men-only, women-only, special housing for students with disabilities. Campus housing is university owned. Freshman campus housing is guaranteed.

Activities and organizations: drama/theater group, student-run newspaper, television station, choral group, National Society for Leadership and Success, Association of Campus Entertainment, Association of Honors Students, Beyond (Campus Ministry), Multicultural Student Council, national fraternities, national sororities.

Athletics Member NCAA. All Division II. ***Intercollegiate sports:*** baseball M(s), basketball M(s)/W(s), cheerleading W(c), cross-country running M(s)/W(s), equestrian sports W(c), golf M(s)/W(s), lacrosse M(s)/W(s), soccer M(s)/W(s), softball W(s), swimming and diving M(s)/W(s), tennis M(s)/W(s), track and field M/W, volleyball W(s). ***Intramural sports:*** basketball M/W, bowling M/W, football M/W, soccer M/W, softball M/W, swimming and diving M/W, tennis M/W, ultimate Frisbee M/W, volleyball M/W, water polo M/W.

Campus security: 24-hour emergency response devices and patrols, student patrols, late-night transport/escort service, controlled dormitory access.

Student services: health clinic, personal/psychological counseling.

COSTS & FINANCIAL AID

Costs (2016–17) ***Comprehensive fee:*** $43,830 includes full-time tuition ($32,450), mandatory fees ($700), and room and board ($10,680). Part-time tuition: $936 per credit hour. Part-time tuition and fees vary according to class time and course load. ***College room only:*** $6330. Room and board charges vary according to board plan and housing facility. ***Payment plan:*** installment. ***Waivers:*** children of alumni and employees or children of employees.

Financial Aid Of all full-time matriculated undergraduates who enrolled in 2016, 1,830 applied for aid, 1,553 were judged to have need, 385 had their need fully met. In 2016, 742 non-need-based awards were made. ***Average percent of need met:*** 73. ***Average financial aid package:*** $26,342. ***Average need-based loan:*** $5776. ***Average need-based gift aid:*** $20,145. ***Average non-need-based aid:*** $19,947. ***Average indebtedness upon graduation:*** $26,637. ***Financial aid deadline:*** 7/1.

APPLYING

Standardized Tests *Required:* SAT or ACT (for admission).

Options: electronic application, early admission, early decision, deferred entrance.

Application fee: $30.

Required: high school transcript, minimum 2.0 GPA, 1 letter of recommendation. ***Recommended:*** essay or personal statement, interview.

Application deadlines: 3/1 (freshmen), rolling (transfers).

Early decision deadline: 12/1.

Notification: continuous (freshmen), continuous (transfers), 12/15 (early decision).

CONTACT
Florida Southern College, 111 Lake Hollingsworth Drive, Lakeland, FL 33801-5698. *Phone:* 863-680-4131. *Toll-free phone:* 800-274-4131.

See previous page for display ad and page 1356 for the College Close-Up.

Florida SouthWestern State College

Fort Myers, Florida

http://www.fsw.edu/

- **State and locally supported** primarily 2-year, founded 1962, part of Florida College System
- **Urban** 413-acre campus
- **Endowment** $731,365
- **Coed** 16,616 undergraduate students, 34% full-time, 61% women, 39% men
- **Noncompetitive** entrance level, 81% of applicants were admitted

UNDERGRAD STUDENTS
5,708 full-time, 10,908 part-time. Students come from 46 states and territories; 27 other countries; 4% are from out of state; 10% Black or African American, non-Hispanic/Latino; 28% Hispanic/Latino; 2% Asian, non-Hispanic/Latino; 0.2% Native Hawaiian or other Pacific Islander, non-Hispanic/Latino; 0.4% American Indian or Alaska Native, non-Hispanic/Latino; 2% Two or more races, non-Hispanic/Latino; 6% Race/ethnicity unknown; 2% international; 4% transferred in; 2% live on campus.

Freshmen:
Admission: 5,769 applied, 4,663 admitted, 3,257 enrolled. ***Average high school GPA:*** 2.96.

Retention: 66% of full-time freshmen returned.

FACULTY
Total: 536, 35% full-time, 24% with terminal degrees.
Student/faculty ratio: 31:1.

ACADEMICS
Calendar: semesters. *Degrees:* certificates, associate, and bachelor's.
Special study options: academic remediation for entering students, accelerated degree program, advanced placement credit, cooperative education, distance learning, double majors, English as a second language, honors programs, independent study, internships, off-campus study, part-time degree program, services for LD students, study abroad, summer session for credit.
Computers: 2,700 computers/terminals are available on campus for general student use. Students can access the following: computer help desk, free student e-mail accounts, online (class) grades, online (class) registration, online (class) schedules. Campuswide network is available. 100% of college-owned or -operated housing units are wired for high-speed Internet access. Wireless service is available via entire campus.
Library: Richard H. Rush Library. *Books:* 45,355 (physical), 28,410 (digital/electronic); *Databases:* 128. Weekly public service hours: 79.

STUDENT LIFE
Housing options: coed. Campus housing is university owned.
Activities and organizations: drama/theater group, choral group.
Athletics Member NJCAA. ***Intercollegiate sports:*** baseball M, softball W. ***Intramural sports:*** basketball M/W, soccer M/W, volleyball M/W.
Campus security: 24-hour emergency response devices and patrols, late-night transport/escort service, controlled dormitory access, Rave Guardian app for students, faculty, and staff.

COSTS & FINANCIAL AID
Costs (2016–17) ***Tuition:*** state resident $2436 full-time, $81 per credit hour part-time; nonresident $9750 full-time, $325 per credit hour part-time. Full-time tuition and fees vary according to degree level. Part-time tuition and fees vary according to degree level. ***Required fees:*** $965 full-time. ***Room and board:*** $8860. Room and board charges vary according to board plan. ***Payment plan:*** installment. ***Waivers:*** employees or children of employees.
Financial Aid Of all full-time matriculated undergraduates who enrolled in 2014, 3,887 applied for aid, 3,311 were judged to have need, 68 had their need fully met. In 2014, 166 non-need-based awards were made. ***Average percent of need met:*** 47. ***Average financial aid package:*** $6172. ***Average need-based loan:*** $3461. ***Average need-based gift aid:*** $5119. ***Average non-need-based aid:*** $2588.

APPLYING
Options: electronic application, early admission, deferred entrance.
Application fee: $30.
Required: high school transcript.
Application deadlines: 8/17 (freshmen), 8/17 (transfers).
Notification: continuous (freshmen), continuous (transfers).

CONTACT
FSW Admissions, Florida SouthWestern State College, 8099 College Parkway, Fort Myers, FL 33919. *Phone:* 239-489-9054. *Fax:* 239-489-9094. *E-mail:* admissions@fsw.edu.

Florida State College at Jacksonville

Jacksonville, Florida

http://www.fscj.edu/

CONTACT
Dr. Peter Biegel, Registrar, Florida State College at Jacksonville, 501 West State Street, Jacksonville, FL 32202. *Phone:* 904-632-5112. *Toll-free phone:* 888-873-1145. *E-mail:* pbiegel@fscj.edu.

Florida State University

Tallahassee, Florida

http://www.fsu.edu/

- **State-supported** university, founded 1851, part of State University System of Florida
- **Suburban** 451-acre campus
- **Endowment** $584.5 million
- **Coed** 32,929 undergraduate students, 89% full-time, 55% women, 45% men
- **Very difficult** entrance level, 58% of applicants were admitted

UNDERGRAD STUDENTS
29,282 full-time, 3,647 part-time. Students come from 52 states and territories; 50 other countries; 10% are from out of state; 8% Black or African American, non-Hispanic/Latino; 20% Hispanic/Latino; 2% Asian, non-Hispanic/Latino; 0.1% Native Hawaiian or other Pacific Islander, non-Hispanic/Latino; 0.3% American Indian or Alaska Native, non-Hispanic/Latino; 3% Two or more races, non-Hispanic/Latino; 1% Race/ethnicity unknown; 1% international; 6% transferred in; 18% live on campus.

Freshmen:
Admission: 29,027 applied, 16,840 admitted, 6,277 enrolled. ***Average high school GPA:*** 3.95. ***Test scores:*** SAT critical reading scores over 500: 97%; SAT math scores over 500: 95%; SAT writing scores over 500: 96%; ACT scores over 18: 100%; SAT critical reading scores over 600: 54%; SAT math scores over 600: 52%; SAT writing scores over 600: 49%; ACT scores over 24: 93%; SAT critical reading scores over 700: 9%; SAT math scores over 700: 7%; SAT writing scores over 700: 6%; ACT scores over 30: 21%.

Retention: 93% of full-time freshmen returned.

FACULTY
Total: 1,762, 81% full-time.
Student/faculty ratio: 26:1.

ACADEMICS
Calendar: semesters. *Degrees:* certificates, associate, bachelor's, master's, doctoral, post-master's, and postbachelor's certificates.
Special study options: accelerated degree program, advanced placement credit, cooperative education, distance learning, double majors, English as a second language, honors programs, independent study, internships, off-campus study, part-time degree program, services for LD students, study abroad, summer session for credit. ***ROTC:*** Army (b), Navy (c), Air Force (b).
Unusual degree programs: 3-2 engineering; education, criminology, mathematics, computer science.

Computers: 1,100 computers/terminals are available on campus for general student use. Students can access the following: computer help desk, free student e-mail accounts, online (class) grades, online (class) registration, online (class) schedules, course home pages, course search, online fee payment. Campuswide network is available. 100% of college-owned or -operated housing units are wired for high-speed Internet access. Wireless service is available via entire campus.

Library: Robert Manning Strozier Library plus 8 others. *Books:* 3.4 million (physical), 1.6 million (digital/electronic); *Serial titles:* 60,740 (physical), 2.7 million (digital/electronic); *Databases:* 1,144. Weekly public service hours: 134; study areas open 24 hours, 5-7 days a week; students can reserve study rooms.

STUDENT LIFE

Housing options: coed, women-only, special housing for students with disabilities. Campus housing is university owned. Freshman applicants given priority for college housing.

Activities and organizations: drama/theater group, student-run newspaper, radio and television station, choral group, marching band, Student Government, honors program, Golden Key Honor Society, Marching Chiefs, intramural sports, national fraternities, national sororities.

Athletics Member NCAA. All Division I except football (Division I-A). ***Intercollegiate sports:*** baseball M(s), basketball M(s)/W(s), bowling M(c)/W(c), cheerleading M/W, cross-country running M(s)/W(s), golf M(s)/W(s), rugby M(c)/W(c), sand volleyball W, soccer M(c)/W(s), softball W(s), swimming and diving M(s)/W(s), table tennis M(c)/W(c), tennis M(s)/W(s), track and field M(s)/W(s), volleyball M(c)/W(s), wrestling M(c)/W(c). ***Intramural sports:*** badminton M(c)/W(c), baseball M(c), basketball M/W, bowling M/W, crew M(c)/W(c), equestrian sports M(c)/W(c), fencing M(c)/W(c), field hockey W(c), football M/W, golf M/W, gymnastics W(c), ice hockey M(c)/W(c), lacrosse M(c)/W(c), racquetball M/W, sailing M(c)/W(c), soccer M/W, softball M/W, squash M(c)/W(c), swimming and diving M/W, table tennis M/W, tennis M/W, track and field M/W, ultimate Frisbee M(c)/W(c), volleyball M/W, water polo M(c)/W(c), weight lifting M/W, wrestling M/W.

Campus security: 24-hour emergency response devices and patrols, late-night transport/escort service, controlled dormitory access.

Student services: health clinic, personal/psychological counseling, women's center, legal services.

COSTS & FINANCIAL AID

Costs (2016–17) ***Tuition:*** state resident $4640 full-time, $216 per credit hour part-time; nonresident $19,806 full-time, $721 per credit hour part-time. Full-time tuition and fees vary according to course load, degree level, and location. Part-time tuition and fees vary according to course load, degree level, and location. ***Required fees:*** $1867 full-time. ***Room and board:*** $10,304; room only: $6256. Room and board charges vary according to board plan and housing facility. ***Payment plans:*** tuition prepayment, installment. ***Waivers:*** senior citizens and employees or children of employees.

Financial Aid Of all full-time matriculated undergraduates who enrolled in 2015, 20,930 applied for aid, 14,394 were judged to have need, 986 had their need fully met. 780 Federal Work-Study jobs (averaging $2400). 34 state and other part-time jobs (averaging $2400). In 2015, 4229 non-need-based awards were made. ***Average percent of need met:*** 62. ***Average financial aid package:*** $11,761. ***Average need-based loan:*** $4363. ***Average need-based gift aid:*** $9000. ***Average non-need-based aid:*** $3831. ***Average indebtedness upon graduation:*** $23,679.

APPLYING

Standardized Tests *Required:* SAT or ACT (for admission).

Options: electronic application, early admission, deferred entrance.

Application fee: $30.

Required: high school transcript. ***Recommended:*** essay or personal statement.

Application deadlines: 2/7 (freshmen), 6/1 (transfers).

Notification: 3/29 (freshmen), continuous (transfers).

CONTACT

Florida State University, 600 West College Avenue, Tallahassee, FL 32306. *Phone:* 850-644-1389.

Fortis College

Cutler Bay, Florida

http://www.fortis.edu/

CONTACT

Fortis College, 19600 South Dixie Highway, Suite B, Cutler Bay, FL 33157. *Toll-free phone:* 855-4-FORTIS.

Full Sail University

Winter Park, Florida

http://www.fullsail.edu/

CONTACT

Ms. Mary Beth Plank, Director of Admissions, Full Sail University, 3300 University Boulevard, Winter Park, FL 32792-7437. *Phone:* 407-679-6333. *Toll-free phone:* 800-226-7625. *E-mail:* admissions@fullsail.com.

Gulf Coast State College

Panama City, Florida

http://www.gulfcoast.edu/

- **State-supported** primarily 2-year, founded 1957, part of Florida College System
- **Urban** 80-acre campus
- **Endowment** $30.5 million
- **Coed** 5,483 undergraduate students, 34% full-time, 61% women, 39% men
- **Noncompetitive** entrance level

UNDERGRAD STUDENTS

1,850 full-time, 3,633 part-time. Students come from 17 states and territories; 3% are from out of state; 12% Black or African American, non-Hispanic/Latino; 6% Hispanic/Latino; 3% Asian, non-Hispanic/Latino; 1% American Indian or Alaska Native, non-Hispanic/Latino; 4% Two or more races, non-Hispanic/Latino; 3% Race/ethnicity unknown; 0.4% international; 3% transferred in.

Freshmen:

Admission: 913 enrolled.

FACULTY

Total: 320, 47% full-time.

Student/faculty ratio: 19:1.

ACADEMICS

Calendar: semesters. *Degrees:* certificates, associate, and bachelor's.

Special study options: academic remediation for entering students, accelerated degree program, adult/continuing education programs, advanced placement credit, cooperative education, distance learning, double majors, English as a second language, external degree program, honors programs, independent study, off-campus study, part-time degree program, services for LD students, study abroad, summer session for credit.

Computers: 1,000 computers/terminals are available on campus for general student use. Students can access the following: computer help desk, free student e-mail accounts, online (class) grades, online (class) registration, online (class) schedules. Campuswide network is available. Wireless service is available via entire campus.

Library: Gulf Coast State College Library. *Books:* 44,254 (physical), 58,468 (digital/electronic); *Databases:* 152.

STUDENT LIFE

Housing options: college housing not available.

Activities and organizations: drama/theater group, student-run newspaper, radio and television station, choral group.

Athletics Member NJCAA. ***Intercollegiate sports:*** baseball M(s), basketball M(s)/W(s), softball W(s), volleyball W(s).

Campus security: 24-hour patrols, late-night transport/escort service, patrols by trained security personnel during campus hours.

Student services: personal/psychological counseling.

COSTS & FINANCIAL AID

Costs (2016–17) ***Tuition:*** state resident $2370 full-time, $99 per credit hour part-time; nonresident $8635 full-time, $360 per credit hour part-time. Full-time tuition and fees vary according to degree level. Part-time tuition and fees vary according to degree level. ***Required fees:*** $620 full-time, $26 per credit hour part-time.

Financial Aid Of all full-time matriculated undergraduates who enrolled in 2015, 145 Federal Work-Study jobs (averaging $3200). 60 state and other part-time jobs (averaging $2600).

APPLYING

Options: electronic application, early admission, deferred entrance.

Application fee: $20.

Required: high school transcript.

Application deadlines: rolling (freshmen), rolling (transfers).

Notification: continuous (freshmen).

CONTACT

Mrs. Sam Wagner, Application Process Specialist, Gulf Coast State College, 5230 West U.S. Highway 98, Panama City, FL 32401. *Phone:* 850-769-1551 Ext. 2936. *Fax:* 850-913-3308. *E-mail:* swagner1@gulfcoast.edu.

Herzing University

Winter Park, Florida

http://www.herzing.edu/orlando

CONTACT

Herzing University, 1865 SR 436, Winter Park, FL 32792. *Toll-free phone:* 800-596-0724.

Hobe Sound Bible College

Hobe Sound, Florida

http://www.hsbc.edu/

- **Independent nondenominational** 4-year, founded 1960
- **Small-town** 84-acre campus
- **Coed**
- **Noncompetitive** entrance level

ACADEMICS

Calendar: semesters. *Degrees:* certificates, associate, and bachelor's.

Special study options: academic remediation for entering students, advanced placement credit, distance learning, double majors, English as a second language, external degree program, independent study, internships, summer session for credit.

Library: College Library.

STUDENT LIFE

Housing options: on-campus residence required through senior year; men-only, women-only.

Activities and organizations: choral group.

Campus security: student patrols, late-night transport/escort service, controlled dormitory access.

COSTS & FINANCIAL AID

Costs (2017–18) ***Comprehensive fee:*** $12,320 includes full-time tuition ($5600), mandatory fees ($720), and room and board ($6000). Part-time tuition: $300 per credit hour. Part-time tuition and fees vary according to course load. ***Required fees:*** $720 per year part-time. ***College room only:*** $2300. ***Payment plans:*** installment, deferred payment. ***Waivers:*** employees or children of employees.

Financial Aid ***Average financial aid package:*** $3550. ***Average indebtedness upon graduation:*** $7000.

APPLYING

Standardized Tests *Required:* SAT or ACT (for admission).

Options: early admission.

Application fee: $25.

Required: essay or personal statement, high school transcript, 3 letters of recommendation, photograph, medical report.

Application deadlines: rolling (freshmen), rolling (transfers).

Notification: continuous until 8/30 (freshmen), continuous until 8/30 (transfers).

CONTACT

Mrs. Pamela S. Davis, Director of Admissions, Hobe Sound Bible College, PO Box 1065, Hobe Sound, FL 33475-1065. *Phone:* 772-545-1400 Ext. 1019. *E-mail:* pamdavis@hsbc.edu.

Hodges University

Naples, Florida

http://www.hodges.edu/

- **Independent** comprehensive, founded 1990
- **Suburban** 31-acre campus with easy access to Miami
- **Endowment** $2.8 million
- **Coed**
- **Minimally difficult** entrance level

FACULTY

Student/faculty ratio: 5:1.

ACADEMICS

Calendar: trimesters. *Degrees:* certificates, associate, bachelor's, and master's.

Library: Terry P. McMahan Libraries plus 1 other.

STUDENT LIFE

Housing options: college housing not available.

Activities and organizations: Ambassadors, Paralegal Club, Institute of Managerial Accountants, Sports club, Entrepreneurial Club.

Campus security: late-night transport/escort service, building security.

Student services: personal/psychological counseling.

COSTS & FINANCIAL AID

Costs (2016–17) ***Tuition:*** $13,200 full-time, $550 per credit hour part-time. ***Required fees:*** $500 full-time.

Financial Aid Of all full-time matriculated undergraduates who enrolled in 2015, 965 applied for aid, 937 were judged to have need, 291 had their need fully met. 60 Federal Work-Study jobs (averaging $4370). In 2015, 31 non-need-based awards were made. ***Average percent of need met:*** 79. ***Average financial aid package:*** $10,095. ***Average need-based loan:*** $3200. ***Average need-based gift aid:*** $3050. ***Average non-need-based aid:*** $300. ***Average indebtedness upon graduation:*** $17,775.

APPLYING

Standardized Tests *Required for some:* CPAT.

Options: electronic application, deferred entrance.

Application fee: $20.

Required: essay or personal statement, high school transcript, interview. ***Required for some:*** 2 letters of recommendation.

CONTACT

Hodges University, 2655 Northbrooke Drive, Naples, FL 34119. *Phone:* 239-513-1122 Ext. 6104. *Toll-free phone:* 800-466-8017.

Indian River State College

Fort Pierce, Florida

http://www.irsc.edu/

CONTACT

Mr. Eileen Storck, Dean of Educational Services, Indian River State College, 3209 Virginia Avenue, Fort Pierce, FL 34981-5596. *Phone:* 772-462-7361. *Toll-free phone:* 866-792-4772. *E-mail:* estrock@irsc.edu.

Jacksonville University

Jacksonville, Florida

http://www.ju.edu/

- **Independent** comprehensive, founded 1934
- **Suburban** 260-acre campus with easy access to Jacksonville, Saint Augustine
- **Endowment** $37.4 million
- **Coed** 2,889 undergraduate students, 73% full-time, 62% women, 38% men
- **Moderately difficult** entrance level, 49% of applicants were admitted

UNDERGRAD STUDENTS
2,113 full-time, 776 part-time. Students come from 52 states and territories; 51 other countries; 33% are from out of state; 15% Black or African American, non-Hispanic/Latino; 9% Hispanic/Latino; 3% Asian, non-Hispanic/Latino; 0.5% Native Hawaiian or other Pacific Islander, non-Hispanic/Latino; 1% American Indian or Alaska Native, non-Hispanic/Latino; 17% Race/ethnicity unknown; 6% international; 5% transferred in; 37% live on campus.

Freshmen:
Admission: 5,506 applied, 2,708 admitted, 504 enrolled. ***Average high school GPA:*** 3.18. ***Test scores:*** SAT critical reading scores over 500: 51%; SAT math scores over 500: 51%; SAT writing scores over 500: 40%; ACT scores over 18: 89%; SAT critical reading scores over 600: 14%; SAT math scores over 600: 16%; SAT writing scores over 600: 16%; ACT scores over 24: 37%; SAT critical reading scores over 700: 3%; SAT math scores over 700: 2%; ACT scores over 30: 4%.
Retention: 65% of full-time freshmen returned.

FACULTY
Total: 346, 64% full-time, 59% with terminal degrees.
Student/faculty ratio: 11:1.

ACADEMICS
Calendar: semesters. *Degrees:* bachelor's, master's, doctoral, and post-master's certificates.
Special study options: academic remediation for entering students, accelerated degree program, adult/continuing education programs, advanced placement credit, cooperative education, distance learning, double majors, English as a second language, freshman honors college, honors programs, independent study, internships, off-campus study, part-time degree program, services for LD students, student-designed majors, study abroad, summer session for credit. ***ROTC:*** Army (b), Navy (b).
Unusual degree programs: 3-2 business administration; engineering; nursing; mathematics.
Computers: 400 computers/terminals and 1,205 ports are available on campus for general student use. Students can access the following: campus intranet, computer help desk, free student e-mail accounts, online (class) grades, online (class) registration, online (class) schedules, learning management systems. Campuswide network is available. 100% of college-owned or -operated housing units are wired for high-speed Internet access. Wireless service is available via entire campus.
Library: Carl S. Swisher Library. *Books:* 156,688 (physical), 148,457 (digital/electronic); *Serial titles:* 183,530 (physical); *Databases:* 2. Weekly public service hours: 88; students can reserve study rooms.

STUDENT LIFE
Housing options: on-campus residence required through junior year; coed, men-only, women-only, special housing for students with disabilities. Campus housing is university owned. Freshman campus housing is guaranteed.
Activities and organizations: drama/theater group, student-run newspaper, radio and television station, choral group, marching band, Student Veterans of America - Special Interest, Pi Kappa Alpha - Fraternity, Honor Student Association - Academic, Dolphin Divers - Special Interest, Alpha Delta Pi - Sorority, national fraternities, national sororities.
Athletics Member NCAA. All Division I except football (Division I-AA). ***Intercollegiate sports:*** baseball M(s), basketball M(s)/W(s), crew M(s)/W(s), cross-country running M/W(s), golf M(s)/W(s), lacrosse M(s)/W(s), sand volleyball W, soccer M(s)/W(s), softball W(s), track and field W(s), volleyball W(s). ***Intramural sports:*** basketball M/W, cheerleading M(c)/W(c), football M/W, riflery M(c)/W(c), sailing M(c)/W(c), sand volleyball M/W, soccer M/W, softball M/W, ultimate Frisbee M/W, volleyball M/W.
Campus security: 24-hour emergency response devices and patrols, student patrols, late-night transport/escort service, controlled dormitory access, trained security patrols during evening hours.
Student services: health clinic, personal/psychological counseling.

COSTS & FINANCIAL AID
Costs (2016–17) ***Comprehensive fee:*** $47,480 includes full-time tuition ($33,930) and room and board ($13,550). Full-time tuition and fees vary according to course level, course load, degree level, and program. Part-time tuition: $1130 per credit hour. Part-time tuition and fees vary according to course level, course load, degree level, and program. ***Required fees:*** $560 per credit hour part-time. ***College room only:*** $9150. Room and board charges vary according to board plan and housing facility. ***Payment plan:*** deferred payment. ***Waivers:*** employees or children of employees.
Financial Aid Of all full-time matriculated undergraduates who enrolled in 2016, 2,087 applied for aid, 1,811 were judged to have need, 515 had their need fully met. 158 Federal Work-Study jobs (averaging $1763). 164 state and other part-time jobs (averaging $425). In 2016, 175 non-need-based awards were made. ***Average percent of need met:*** 87. ***Average financial aid package:*** $22,584. ***Average need-based loan:*** $3015. ***Average need-based gift aid:*** $16,212. ***Average non-need-based aid:*** $12,264.

APPLYING
Standardized Tests *Recommended:* SAT or ACT (for admission), SAT and SAT Subject Tests or ACT (for admission).
Options: electronic application, early admission, deferred entrance.
Application fee: $30.
Required: high school transcript, minimum 2.0 GPA. ***Required for some:*** essay or personal statement, 2 letters of recommendation, audition for music, dance, and theater majors; portfolio for art, computer art, and design majors; interview for the Honors Program. ***Recommended:*** interview.
Application deadlines: rolling (freshmen), rolling (transfers).
Notification: continuous (freshmen), continuous (transfers).

CONTACT
Mrs. Allana Forte, Director of Admissions and Recruitment, Jacksonville University, 2800 University Boulevard North, Office of Admissions, Jacksonville, FL 32211. *Phone:* 904-256-7000.
Toll-free phone: 800-225-2027. *Fax:* 904-256-7012.
E-mail: admissions@ju.edu.

Johnson & Wales University
North Miami, Florida
http://www.jwu.edu/northmiami/

- **Independent** 4-year, founded 1992
- **Suburban** 8-acre campus with easy access to Miami
- **Coed**
- **Moderately difficult** entrance level

FACULTY
Student/faculty ratio: 25:1.

ACADEMICS
Calendar: quarters. *Degrees:* associate and bachelor's.
Library: Florida Campus Library.

STUDENT LIFE
Housing options: on-campus residence required for freshman year; coed. Campus housing is university owned and leased by the school. Freshman campus housing is guaranteed.
Activities and organizations: national fraternities, national sororities.
Athletics Member NAIA.
Campus security: 24-hour emergency response devices and patrols, video camera surveillance throughout campus.
Student services: personal/psychological counseling.

COSTS & FINANCIAL AID
Costs (2016–17) ***Comprehensive fee:*** $39,014 includes full-time tuition ($30,396), mandatory fees ($350), and room and board ($8268).
Financial Aid Of all full-time matriculated undergraduates who enrolled in 2015, 1,524 applied for aid, 1,242 were judged to have need, 131 had their need fully met. In 2015, 213 non-need-based awards were made. ***Average percent of need met:*** 70. ***Average financial aid package:*** $23,531. ***Average need-based loan:*** $5350. ***Average need-based gift aid:*** $9591. ***Average non-need-based aid:*** $7433.

APPLYING
Standardized Tests *Required for some:* SAT or ACT (for admission).
Options: early admission, deferred entrance.

Required: high school transcript. ***Required for some:*** essay or personal statement, interview. ***Recommended:*** minimum 2.0 GPA.

CONTACT
Jeff Greenip, Director of Admissions, Johnson & Wales University, 1701 Northeast 127th Street, North Miami, FL 33181. *Phone:* 305-892-7600. *Toll-free phone:* 866-598-3567. *Fax:* 305-892-7020.
E-mail: mia@admissions.jwu.edu.

Johnson University Florida

Kissimmee, Florida

http://www.johnsonu.edu/

- **Independent** 4-year, founded 1976, affiliated with Christian Churches and Churches of Christ
- **Small-town** 40-acre campus with easy access to Orlando
- **Coed** 185 undergraduate students, 87% full-time, 51% women, 49% men
- **Minimally difficult** entrance level, 62% of applicants were admitted

UNDERGRAD STUDENTS
161 full-time, 24 part-time. Students come from 11 states and territories; 1 other country; 14% are from out of state; 12% Black or African American, non-Hispanic/Latino; 13% Hispanic/Latino; 0.5% Asian, non-Hispanic/Latino; 2% Two or more races, non-Hispanic/Latino; 0.5% Race/ethnicity unknown; 1% international; 5% transferred in; 72% live on campus.

Freshmen:
Admission: 232 applied, 143 admitted, 36 enrolled.
Retention: 55% of full-time freshmen returned.

FACULTY
Total: 31, 48% full-time, 58% with terminal degrees.
Student/faculty ratio: 12:1.

ACADEMICS
Calendar: semesters. *Degree:* diplomas and bachelor's.
Special study options: adult/continuing education programs, advanced placement credit, distance learning, double majors, independent study, internships, part-time degree program, study abroad, summer session for credit.
Computers: 10 computers/terminals are available on campus for general student use. Students can access the following: computer help desk, free student e-mail accounts, online (class) grades, online (class) registration, online (class) schedules. Campuswide network is available. 100% of college-owned or -operated housing units are wired for high-speed Internet access. Wireless service is available via entire campus.
Library: Library. *Books:* 52,392 (physical), 245,630 (digital/electronic); *Serial titles:* 4,653 (physical), 27 (digital/electronic); *Databases:* 125. Weekly public service hours: 69.

STUDENT LIFE
Housing options: men-only, women-only. Campus housing is university owned.
Activities and organizations: choral group, Student Government Association, Harvesters (Missions), SunRunners club, Timothy club (preachers), Indoor Soccer.
Athletics Member NCCAA. ***Intercollegiate sports:*** basketball M, soccer M, volleyball W. ***Intramural sports:*** field hockey M(c), ultimate Frisbee M(c).
Campus security: controlled dormitory access, late night trained security patrol.
Student services: personal/psychological counseling.

FINANCIAL AID
Financial Aid Of all full-time matriculated undergraduates who enrolled in 2005, 186 applied for aid, 186 were judged to have need, 5 had their need fully met. 38 Federal Work-Study jobs (averaging $1103). In 2005, 10 non-need-based awards were made. ***Average percent of need met:*** 46. ***Average financial aid package:*** $5947. ***Average need-based loan:*** $3418. ***Average need-based gift aid:*** $2788. ***Average non-need-based aid:*** $2000. ***Average indebtedness upon graduation:*** $15,353. ***Financial aid deadline:*** 7/15.

APPLYING
Standardized Tests *Required:* SAT or ACT (for admission).
Options: electronic application, early admission, early decision, deferred entrance.
Application fee: $35.
Required: essay or personal statement, high school transcript, minimum 2.5 GPA, 3 letters of recommendation. ***Required for some:*** interview.
Application deadlines: 7/15 (freshmen), 7/15 (transfers).
Early decision deadline: 7/15 (for plan 1), 7/15 (for plan 2).
Notification: continuous until 8/15 (freshmen), continuous until 8/15 (transfers), 8/15 (early decision plan 1), 8/15 (early decision plan 2).

CONTACT
Kirsys Asenjo, Director of Admissions, Johnson University Florida, 1011 Bill Beck Blvd., Kissimmee, FL 34744. *Phone:* 407-569-1380. *Toll-free phone:* 888-468-6322. *Fax:* 321-206-2007.
E-mail: kasenjo@johnsonu.edu.

Jones College

Jacksonville, Florida

http://www.jones.edu/

- **Independent** 4-year, founded 1918
- **Urban** 3-acre campus
- **Coed**
- **Noncompetitive** entrance level

ACADEMICS
Calendar: trimesters. *Degrees:* associate and bachelor's.
Library: James V. Forrestal Library plus 1 other.

STUDENT LIFE
Housing options: college housing not available.
Campus security: late-night transport/escort service, emergency notification system through email/texting/phones.

COSTS
Costs (2016–17) ***Tuition:*** $7560 full-time, $315 per credit hour part-time. Full-time tuition and fees vary according to course load. Part-time tuition and fees vary according to course load. ***Required fees:*** $90 full-time, $45 per term part-time. ***Room only:*** Room and board charges vary according to housing facility.

APPLYING
Standardized Tests *Required for some:* CPAt/ACCUPLACER.
Options: electronic application.
Required: interview. ***Required for some:*** high school transcript.

CONTACT
Jones College, 5353 Arlington Expressway, Jacksonville, FL 32211-5588. *Phone:* 904-743-1122. *Toll-free phone:* 800-331-0176.

Jose Maria Vargas University

Pembroke Pines, Florida

http://www.jmvu.edu/

CONTACT
Jose Maria Vargas University, 10131 Pines Boulevard, Pembroke Pines, FL 33026.

Keiser University

Fort Lauderdale, Florida

http://www.keiseruniversity.edu/

CONTACT
Keiser University, 1500 NW 49th Street, Fort Lauderdale, FL 33309. *Phone:* 954-275-1569. *Toll-free phone:* 888-534-7379.

Lincoln Culinary Institute

West Palm Beach, Florida

http://www.lincolnedu.com/campus/west-palm-beach-culinary-fl

CONTACT
Lincoln Culinary Institute, 2410 Metrocentre Boulevard, West Palm Beach, FL 33407. *Phone:* 561-842-8324 Ext. 202.

Lynn University

Boca Raton, Florida

http://www.lynn.edu/

- **Independent** comprehensive, founded 1962
- **Suburban** 123-acre campus with easy access to Fort Lauderdale
- **Endowment** $24.0 million
- **Coed** 2,095 undergraduate students, 93% full-time, 49% women, 51% men
- **Moderately difficult** entrance level, 82% of applicants were admitted

UNDERGRAD STUDENTS
1,950 full-time, 145 part-time. Students come from 45 states and territories; 95 other countries; 53% are from out of state; 9% Black or African American, non-Hispanic/Latino; 16% Hispanic/Latino; 1% Asian, non-Hispanic/Latino; 0.1% Native Hawaiian or other Pacific Islander, non-Hispanic/Latino; 0.3% American Indian or Alaska Native, non-Hispanic/Latino; 1% Two or more races, non-Hispanic/Latino; 7% Race/ethnicity unknown; 21% international; 8% transferred in; 46% live on campus.

Freshmen:
Admission: 3,514 applied, 2,872 admitted, 566 enrolled. ***Average high school GPA:*** 3.03. ***Test scores:*** SAT critical reading scores over 500: 43%; SAT math scores over 500: 42%; SAT writing scores over 500: 37%; ACT scores over 18: 91%; SAT critical reading scores over 600: 9%; SAT math scores over 600: 6%; SAT writing scores over 600: 8%; ACT scores over 24: 27%; SAT critical reading scores over 700: 1%; SAT math scores over 700: 1%; SAT writing scores over 700: 1%; ACT scores over 30: 1%. ***Retention:*** 68% of full-time freshmen returned.

FACULTY
Total: 176, 60% full-time, 46% with terminal degrees.
Student/faculty ratio: 21:1.

ACADEMICS
Calendar: semesters plus 3 summer sessions. *Degrees:* bachelor's, master's, doctoral, post-master's, and postbachelor's certificates.
Special study options: academic remediation for entering students, accelerated degree program, advanced placement credit, cooperative education, distance learning, double majors, English as a second language, independent study, internships, part-time degree program, services for LD students, student-designed majors, study abroad, summer session for credit. ***ROTC:*** Air Force (c).
Computers: 150 computers/terminals are available on campus for general student use. Students can access the following: campus intranet, computer help desk, free student e-mail accounts, online (class) grades, online (class) schedules, online registration with advisor approval for juniors, seniors and MBA students. Campuswide network is available. 100% of college-owned or -operated housing units are wired for high-speed Internet access.
Library: Eugene M. and Christine E. Lynn Library. *Books:* 58,957 (physical), 186,437 (digital/electronic); *Serial titles:* 209 (physical), 36,193 (digital/electronic); *Databases:* 109. Weekly public service hours: 96.

STUDENT LIFE
Housing options: on-campus residence required through sophomore year; coed, special housing for students with disabilities. Campus housing is university owned. Freshman campus housing is guaranteed.
Activities and organizations: drama/theater group, student-run newspaper, radio and television station, Knights of the Round Table, intramural groups, student newspaper, Student Activities Board, Greek Life, national fraternities, national sororities.
Athletics Member NCAA. All Division II. ***Intercollegiate sports:*** baseball M(s), basketball M(s)/W(s), cross-country running W(s), golf M(s)/W(s), lacrosse M(s), soccer M(s)/W(s), softball W(s), swimming and diving W(s), tennis M(s)/W(s), volleyball W(s). ***Intramural sports:*** basketball M/W, cheerleading W(c), football M/W, golf M/W, soccer M/W, tennis M/W, ultimate Frisbee M/W, volleyball M(c).
Campus security: 24-hour emergency response devices and patrols, late-night transport/escort service, controlled dormitory access, video monitor at residence entrances.
Student services: health clinic, personal/psychological counseling, women's center.

COSTS & FINANCIAL AID
Costs (2017–18) ***One-time required fee:*** $1000. ***Comprehensive fee:*** $49,480 includes full-time tuition ($35,260), mandatory fees ($2250), and room and board ($11,970). Full-time tuition and fees vary according to class time, degree level, and program. Part-time tuition: $1020 per credit hour. Part-time tuition and fees vary according to class time, course load, and program. ***Room and board:*** Room and board charges vary according to board plan and housing facility. ***Payment plans:*** installment, deferred payment. ***Waivers:*** employees or children of employees.
Financial Aid Of all full-time matriculated undergraduates who enrolled in 2016, 1,613 applied for aid, 833 were judged to have need, 826 had their need fully met. 183 Federal Work-Study jobs (averaging $2039). 34 state and other part-time jobs (averaging $7435). In 2016, 516 non-need-based awards were made. ***Average percent of need met:*** 55. ***Average financial aid package:*** $22,404. ***Average need-based loan:*** $4572. ***Average need-based gift aid:*** $9991. ***Average non-need-based aid:*** $10,739. ***Average indebtedness upon graduation:*** $33,689.

APPLYING
Standardized Tests *Recommended:* SAT or ACT (for admission).
Options: electronic application, early admission, early action, deferred entrance.
Application fee: $45.
Required: essay or personal statement, high school transcript. ***Required for some:*** audition for Conservatory of Music. ***Recommended:*** interview.
Application deadlines: 3/1 (freshmen), rolling (transfers), 11/15 (early action).
Notification: continuous until 12/15 (freshmen), continuous (transfers), 12/15 (early action).

CONTACT
Stefano Papaleo, Director of Undergraduate Admission, Lynn University, Admission, 3601 North Military Trail, Boca Raton, FL 33431. *Phone:* 561-237-7831. *Toll-free phone:* 800-888-5966. *Fax:* 561-237-7100. *E-mail:* spapaleo@lynn.edu.

Marconi International University

Pembroke Pines, Florida

http://www.marconiinternationaluniversity.edu/

CONTACT
Admissions, Marconi International University, 1806 Flamingo Road, Suite 120, Pembroke Pines, FL 33028. *Phone:* 954-374-4701. *E-mail:* info@marconiinternational.org.

Miami Dade College

Miami, Florida

http://www.mdc.edu/

- **State and locally supported** primarily 2-year, founded 1960, part of Florida College System
- **Urban** campus
- **Endowment** $137.1 million
- **Coed** 55,206 undergraduate students, 38% full-time, 57% women, 43% men
- **Noncompetitive** entrance level, 100% of applicants were admitted

UNDERGRAD STUDENTS
21,075 full-time, 34,131 part-time. Students come from 42 states and territories; 164 other countries; 0.4% are from out of state; 14% Black or African American, non-Hispanic/Latino; 69% Hispanic/Latino; 1% Asian, non-Hispanic/Latino; 0.1% Native Hawaiian or other Pacific Islander,

non-Hispanic/Latino; 0.1% American Indian or Alaska Native, non-Hispanic/Latino; 0.5% Two or more races, non-Hispanic/Latino; 3% Race/ethnicity unknown; 6% international; 0.5% transferred in.

Freshmen:
Admission: 44,910 applied, 44,910 admitted, 11,610 enrolled.

FACULTY
Total: 2,453, 30% full-time, 25% with terminal degrees.
Student/faculty ratio: 24:1.

ACADEMICS
Calendar: 16-16-6-6. *Degrees:* certificates, associate, bachelor's, and postbachelor's certificates.

Special study options: academic remediation for entering students, accelerated degree program, adult/continuing education programs, advanced placement credit, cooperative education, distance learning, English as a second language, freshman honors college, honors programs, independent study, internships, off-campus study, part-time degree program, services for LD students, study abroad, summer session for credit. ***ROTC:*** Army (b), Air Force (c).

Computers: 9,655 computers/terminals and 1,500 ports are available on campus for general student use. Students can access the following: campus intranet, computer help desk, free student e-mail accounts, online (class) grades, online (class) registration, online (class) schedules, admissions, student feedback of faculty, financial aid. Campuswide network is available. Wireless service is available via entire campus.
Library: Miami Dade College Learning Resources plus 9 others. *Books:* 187,729 (physical), 59,920 (digital/electronic); *Serial titles:* 68,309 (physical), 40,849 (digital/electronic); *Databases:* 125. Weekly public service hours: 69; students can reserve study rooms.

STUDENT LIFE
Housing options: college housing not available.

Activities and organizations: drama/theater group, student-run newspaper, radio and television station, choral group, Student Government Association, Phi Theta Kappa, Phi Beta Lambda (business), Future Educators of America Professional, Kappa Delta Pi Honor Society (education), national fraternities.

Athletics Member NCAA, NJCAA. All NCAA Division I.
Intercollegiate sports: baseball M(s), basketball M(s)/W(s), softball W(s), volleyball W(s).

Campus security: 24-hour emergency response devices and patrols, student patrols, late-night transport/escort service, Emergency Mass Notification System (EMNS), campus sirens and public address systems, LiveSafe mobile safety App for Students/Employees..

Student services: health clinic, personal/psychological counseling.

COSTS & FINANCIAL AID
Costs (2016–17) ***One-time required fee:*** $30. ***Tuition:*** state resident $1987 full-time, $83 per credit hour part-time; nonresident $7947 full-time, $331 per credit hour part-time. Full-time tuition and fees vary according to course load, degree level, and program. Part-time tuition and fees vary according to course load, degree level, and program. ***Required fees:*** $851 full-time, $35 per credit hour part-time. ***Waivers:*** employees or children of employees.

Financial Aid Of all full-time matriculated undergraduates who enrolled in 2015, 800 Federal Work-Study jobs (averaging $5000). 125 state and other part-time jobs (averaging $5000).

APPLYING
Options: electronic application, early admission.

Application fee: $30.

Required: high school transcript.

Application deadlines: rolling (freshmen), rolling (transfers).

Notification: continuous (freshmen), continuous (transfers).

CONTACT
Ms. Ferne Creary, Interim College Registrar, Miami Dade College, 11011 SW 104th Street, Miami, FL 33176. *Phone:* 305-237-2206. *Fax:* 305-237-2532. *E-mail:* fcreary@mdc.edu.

Miami International University of Art & Design
Miami, Florida
http://www.artinstitutes.edu/miami/

CONTACT
Miami International University of Art & Design, 1501 Biscayne Boulevard, Suite 100, Miami, FL 33132-1418. *Phone:* 305-428-5700. *Toll-free phone:* 800-225-9023.

Miami Regional University
Miami Springs, Florida
http://www.mru.edu/

CONTACT
Miami Regional University, 700 South Royal Poinciana Boulevard, Miami Springs, FL 33166.

Millennia Atlantic University
Doral, Florida
http://www.maufl.edu/

CONTACT
Millennia Atlantic University, 3801 NW 97th Avenue, Doral, FL 33178.

New College of Florida
Sarasota, Florida
http://www.ncf.edu/

- **State-supported** comprehensive, founded 1960, part of State University System of Florida
- **Suburban** 119-acre campus with easy access to Tampa-St. Petersburg
- **Endowment** $37.8 million
- **Coed** 861 undergraduate students, 100% full-time, 62% women, 38% men
- **Very difficult** entrance level, 71% of applicants were admitted

UNDERGRAD STUDENTS
861 full-time. Students come from 39 states and territories; 22 other countries; 15% are from out of state; 3% Black or African American, non-Hispanic/Latino; 18% Hispanic/Latino; 3% Asian, non-Hispanic/Latino; 4% Two or more races, non-Hispanic/Latino; 2% Race/ethnicity unknown; 2% international; 4% transferred in; 77% live on campus.

Freshmen:
Admission: 1,417 applied, 1,010 admitted, 231 enrolled. ***Average high school GPA:*** 4. ***Test scores:*** SAT critical reading scores over 500: 99%; SAT math scores over 500: 96%; SAT writing scores over 500: 94%; ACT scores over 18: 100%; SAT critical reading scores over 600: 77%; SAT math scores over 600: 54%; SAT writing scores over 600: 60%; ACT scores over 24: 89%; SAT critical reading scores over 700: 30%; SAT math scores over 700: 10%; SAT writing scores over 700: 9%; ACT scores over 30: 35%.

Retention: 84% of full-time freshmen returned.

FACULTY
Total: 108, 70% full-time, 92% with terminal degrees.
Student/faculty ratio: 10:1.

ACADEMICS
Calendar: 4-1-4. *Degrees:* bachelor's and master's.

Special study options: accelerated degree program, double majors, freshman honors college, honors programs, independent study, internships, off-campus study, services for LD students, student-designed majors, study abroad, summer session for credit.

Computers: 105 computers/terminals and 1,256 ports are available on campus for general student use. Students can access the following: campus intranet, computer help desk, free student e-mail accounts, online (class) grades, online (class) registration, online (class) schedules. Campuswide network is available. 100% of college-owned or -operated housing units are wired for high-speed Internet access. Wireless service is available via classrooms, computer labs, dorm rooms, learning centers, libraries, student centers.

Library: Jane Bancroft Cook Library. *Books:* 223,507 (physical), 5,464 (digital/electronic); *Serial titles:* 1,408 (digital/electronic); *Databases:* 168. Weekly public service hours: 96.

STUDENT LIFE

Housing options: on-campus residence required through senior year; coed, special housing for students with disabilities. Campus housing is university owned. Freshman campus housing is guaranteed.

Activities and organizations: drama/theater group, student-run newspaper, choral group, Dance Collective, Queery, New College Student Alliance, Generation Action, NCF Democrats.

Athletics ***Intercollegiate sports:*** sailing M/W. ***Intramural sports:*** basketball M/W, fencing M/W, golf M/W, racquetball M/W, sailing M(c)/W(c), soccer M(c)/W(c), softball M(c)/W(c), swimming and diving M(c)/W(c), table tennis M(c)/W(c), tennis M(c)/W(c), triathlon M(c)/W(c), ultimate Frisbee M(c)/W(c), weight lifting M/W, wrestling M/W.

Campus security: 24-hour emergency response devices and patrols, student patrols, controlled dormitory access, campus police are state certified police officers and available 24/7.

Student services: health clinic, personal/psychological counseling.

COSTS & FINANCIAL AID

Costs (2017–18) ***Tuition:*** state resident $6916 full-time; nonresident $29,944 full-time. ***Room and board:*** $9264; room only: $6602. Room and board charges vary according to board plan and housing facility. ***Payment plan:*** installment.

Financial Aid Of all full-time matriculated undergraduates who enrolled in 2016, 689 applied for aid, 472 were judged to have need, 168 had their need fully met. 29 Federal Work-Study jobs (averaging $1071). In 2016, 314 non-need-based awards were made. ***Average percent of need met:*** 81. ***Average financial aid package:*** $13,458. ***Average need-based loan:*** $3714. ***Average need-based gift aid:*** $8832. ***Average non-need-based aid:*** $2454. ***Average indebtedness upon graduation:*** $15,173.

APPLYING

Standardized Tests *Required:* SAT or ACT (for admission).

Options: electronic application, early admission, early action, deferred entrance.

Application fee: $30.

Required: essay or personal statement, high school transcript, 1 letter of recommendation. ***Recommended:*** minimum 3.0 GPA.

Application deadlines: 4/15 (freshmen), 4/15 (transfers), 11/1 (early action).

Notification: 4/25 (freshmen), 4/25 (transfers), 4/1 (early action).

CONTACT

Office of Admissions, New College of Florida, 5800 Bay Shore Road, Sarasota, FL 34243-2109. *Phone:* 941-487-5000. *Fax:* 941-487-5010. *E-mail:* admissions@ncf.edu.

See page 1438 for the College Close-Up.

New World School of the Arts

Miami, Florida

http://www.mdc.edu/nwsa/

CONTACT

Recruitment and Admissions Coordinator, New World School of the Arts, 300 NE Second Avenue, Miami, FL 33132. *Phone:* 305-237-7408. *Fax:* 305-237-3794. *E-mail:* nwsaadm@mdc.edu.

Northwest Florida State College

Niceville, Florida

http://www.nwfsc.edu/

CONTACT

Ms. Karen Cooper, Director of Admissions, Northwest Florida State College, 100 College Boulevard, Niceville, FL 32578. *Phone:* 850-729-4901. *Fax:* 850-729-5206. *E-mail:* cooperk@nwfsc.edu.

Nova Southeastern University

Fort Lauderdale, Florida

http://www.nova.edu/

- **Independent** university, founded 1964
- **Suburban** 314-acre campus
- **Endowment** $104.5 million
- **Coed** 4,295 undergraduate students, 71% full-time, 70% women, 30% men
- **Moderately difficult** entrance level, 52% of applicants were admitted

UNDERGRAD STUDENTS

3,051 full-time, 1,244 part-time. Students come from 49 states and territories; 68 other countries; 18% are from out of state; 16% Black or African American, non-Hispanic/Latino; 30% Hispanic/Latino; 10% Asian, non-Hispanic/Latino; 0.1% Native Hawaiian or other Pacific Islander, non-Hispanic/Latino; 0.3% American Indian or Alaska Native, non-Hispanic/Latino; 2% Two or more races, non-Hispanic/Latino; 4% Race/ethnicity unknown; 6% international; 14% transferred in; 25% live on campus.

Freshmen:

Admission: 6,532 applied, 3,421 admitted, 659 enrolled. ***Average high school GPA:*** 3.98. ***Test scores:*** SAT critical reading scores over 500: 75%; SAT math scores over 500: 77%; ACT scores over 18: 99%; SAT critical reading scores over 600: 33%; SAT math scores over 600: 33%; ACT scores over 24: 63%; SAT critical reading scores over 700: 3%; SAT math scores over 700: 8%; ACT scores over 30: 16%.

Retention: 75% of full-time freshmen returned.

FACULTY

Total: 1,543, 54% full-time, 74% with terminal degrees.

Student/faculty ratio: 17:1.

ACADEMICS

Calendar: trimesters. *Degrees:* certificates, associate, bachelor's, master's, doctoral, post-master's, and postbachelor's certificates.

Special study options: academic remediation for entering students, adult/continuing education programs, advanced placement credit, distance learning, double majors, freshman honors college, honors programs, independent study, internships, off-campus study, part-time degree program, services for LD students, study abroad, summer session for credit.

Unusual degree programs: 3-2 business administration; computer science, criminal justice, education, humanities and social sciences.

Computers: 3,000 computers/terminals and 6,000 ports are available on campus for general student use. Students can access the following: campus intranet, computer help desk, free student e-mail accounts, online (class) grades, online (class) registration, online (class) schedules. Campuswide network is available. 100% of college-owned or -operated housing units are wired for high-speed Internet access. Wireless service is available via entire campus.

Library: Alvin Sherman Library, Research, and Information Technology Center plus 4 others. *Books:* 498,823 (physical), 379,928 (digital/electronic); *Serial titles:* 6,035 (physical), 20,738 (digital/electronic); *Databases:* 577. Study areas open 24 hours, 5-7 days a week; students can reserve study rooms.

STUDENT LIFE

Housing options: on-campus residence required through sophomore year; coed, special housing for students with disabilities. Campus housing is university owned. Freshman campus housing is guaranteed.

Activities and organizations: drama/theater group, student-run newspaper, radio and television station, choral group, Delta Epsilon Iota, Make-a Meal Service Organization, Pre-Med, HOSA: Future Health Professionals, Student Government Association, national fraternities, national sororities.

Athletics Member NCAA. All Division II. ***Intercollegiate sports:*** baseball M(s), basketball M(s)/W(s), cheerleading W, crew W(s), cross-country running M(s)/W(s), golf M(s)/W(s), soccer M(s)/W(s), softball W(s), swimming and diving M(s)/W(s), tennis W(s), track and field M(s)/W(s), volleyball W(s). ***Intramural sports:*** badminton M/W, basketball M/W, racquetball M/W, rowing W, soccer M/W, softball W, ultimate Frisbee M/W, volleyball M/W, water polo M/W.

Campus security: 24-hour emergency response devices and patrols, late-night transport/escort service, controlled dormitory access, shuttle bus service.

Student services: health clinic, personal/psychological counseling.

COSTS & FINANCIAL AID

Costs (2016–17) ***Comprehensive fee:*** $40,276 includes full-time tuition ($27,986), mandatory fees ($750), and room and board ($11,540). Full-time tuition and fees vary according to class time and program. Part-time tuition: $933 per credit hour. Part-time tuition and fees vary according to class time, course load, and program. ***College room only:*** $8550. Room and board charges vary according to board plan and housing facility. ***Payment plans:*** installment, deferred payment. ***Waivers:*** employees or children of employees.

Financial Aid Of all full-time matriculated undergraduates who enrolled in 2016, 2,566 applied for aid, 2,258 were judged to have need, 305 had their need fully met. 1,198 Federal Work-Study jobs (averaging $6462). 412 state and other part-time jobs (averaging $1232). In 2016, 593 non-need-based awards were made. ***Average percent of need met:*** 68. ***Average financial aid package:*** $28,480. ***Average need-based loan:*** $3873. ***Average need-based gift aid:*** $15,156. ***Average non-need-based aid:*** $10,813. ***Average indebtedness upon graduation:*** $34,763.

APPLYING

Standardized Tests *Required:* SAT or ACT (for admission).

Options: electronic application, early decision, early action, deferred entrance.

Application fee: $50.

Required: minimum 3.0 GPA. ***Recommended:*** high school transcript.

Application deadlines: rolling (freshmen), rolling (transfers).

Notification: continuous (freshmen), continuous (transfers).

CONTACT

Ms. Mensima Biney, Director of Undergraduate Admissions, Nova Southeastern University, Enrollment Processing Services, 3301 College Avenue, Ft. Lauderdale, FL 33329-9905. *Phone:* 954-262-8004. *Toll-free phone:* 800-541-NOVA. *Fax:* 954-262-3811. *E-mail:* nsuinfo@nova.edu.

Palm Beach Atlantic University

West Palm Beach, Florida

http://www.pba.edu/

- **Independent nondenominational** comprehensive, founded 1968
- **Urban** 100-acre campus with easy access to Miami-Dade County
- **Endowment** $77.1 million
- **Coed** 2,926 undergraduate students, 79% full-time, 65% women, 35% men
- **Moderately difficult** entrance level, 93% of applicants were admitted

UNDERGRAD STUDENTS

2,300 full-time, 626 part-time. Students come from 45 states and territories; 39 other countries; 34% are from out of state; 10% Black or African American, non-Hispanic/Latino; 15% Hispanic/Latino; 2% Asian, non-Hispanic/Latino; 0.2% Native Hawaiian or other Pacific Islander, non-Hispanic/Latino; 0.5% American Indian or Alaska Native, non-Hispanic/Latino; 3% Two or more races, non-Hispanic/Latino; 3% Race/ethnicity unknown; 4% international; 9% transferred in; 49% live on campus.

Freshmen:

Admission: 1,449 applied, 1,353 admitted, 505 enrolled. ***Average high school GPA:*** 3.6. ***Test scores:*** SAT critical reading scores over 500: 65%; SAT math scores over 500: 55%; SAT writing scores over 500: 57%; ACT scores over 18: 82%; SAT critical reading scores over 600: 27%; SAT math scores over 600: 18%; SAT writing scores over 600: 20%; ACT scores over 24: 52%; SAT critical reading scores over 700: 5%; SAT math scores over 700: 4%; SAT writing scores over 700: 3%; ACT scores over 30: 3%.

Retention: 75% of full-time freshmen returned.

FACULTY

Total: 381, 46% full-time, 62% with terminal degrees.

Student/faculty ratio: 12:1.

ACADEMICS

Calendar: semesters. *Degrees:* bachelor's, master's, and doctoral.

Special study options: academic remediation for entering students, accelerated degree program, adult/continuing education programs, advanced placement credit, distance learning, double majors, honors programs, independent study, internships, off-campus study, part-time degree program, services for LD students, student-designed majors, study abroad, summer session for credit. ***ROTC:*** Army (c).

Unusual degree programs: 3-2 divinity.

Computers: 350 computers/terminals are available on campus for general student use. Students can access the following: campus intranet, computer help desk, free student e-mail accounts, online (class) grades, online (class) registration, online (class) schedules. Campuswide network is available. 100% of college-owned or -operated housing units are wired for high-speed Internet access. Wireless service is available via entire campus.

Library: Warren Library plus 1 other. *Books:* 141,300 (physical), 123,825 (digital/electronic); *Serial titles:* 142 (physical), 133,086 (digital/electronic); *Databases:* 90. Weekly public service hours: 97; students can reserve study rooms.

STUDENT LIFE

Housing options: on-campus residence required through sophomore year; coed, men-only, women-only. Campus housing is university owned and leased by the school. Freshman campus housing is guaranteed.

Activities and organizations: drama/theater group, student-run newspaper, choral group, Impact Leadership Team, Nursing Student Association, Nurses Christian Fellowship, Student Government, Sigma Alpha Omega, national fraternities, national sororities.

Athletics Member NCAA. All Division II. ***Intercollegiate sports:*** baseball M(s), basketball M(s)/W(s), cheerleading M(c)/W(c), crew M(c)/W(c), cross-country running W(s), golf M(s)/W(s), lacrosse M(c)/W(c), soccer M(s)/W(s), softball W(s), tennis M(s)/W(s), volleyball W(s). ***Intramural sports:*** basketball M/W, sand volleyball M/W, soccer M(c)/W, softball M/W, ultimate Frisbee M/W, volleyball M/W.

Campus security: 24-hour emergency response devices and patrols, late-night transport/escort service, controlled dormitory access, lighted pathways/sidewalks, self-defense education, closed-circuit television system.

Student services: health clinic, personal/psychological counseling.

COSTS & FINANCIAL AID

Costs (2017–18) ***Comprehensive fee:*** $39,490 includes full-time tuition ($29,510), mandatory fees ($440), and room and board ($9540). Full-time tuition and fees vary according to course load, location, and program. Part-time tuition and fees vary according to course load, location, and program. ***College room only:*** $5030. Room and board charges vary according to board plan and housing facility. ***Payment plan:*** installment. ***Waivers:*** children of alumni and employees or children of employees.

Financial Aid Of all full-time matriculated undergraduates who enrolled in 2016, 1,883 applied for aid, 1,629 were judged to have need, 307 had their need fully met. 194 Federal Work-Study jobs (averaging $2898). 8 state and other part-time jobs (averaging $2335). In 2016, 612 non-need-based awards were made. ***Average percent of need met:*** 63. ***Average financial aid package:*** $20,358. ***Average need-based loan:*** $3940. ***Average need-based gift aid:*** $17,448. ***Average non-need-based aid:*** $11,954. ***Average indebtedness upon graduation:*** $28,862.

APPLYING

Standardized Tests *Required:* SAT or ACT (for admission).

Options: electronic application, early admission, early action, deferred entrance.

Application fee: $50.

Required: essay or personal statement, high school transcript. ***Required for some:*** interview.

Application deadlines: rolling (freshmen), rolling (transfers), 3/31 (early action).

Notification: continuous (freshmen), continuous (transfers), 4/15 (early action).

CONTACT

Mr. Joseph Bryan, Assistant Vice President for Admissions, Palm Beach Atlantic University, 901 South Flagler Drive, PO Box 24708, West Palm

Beach, FL 33416-4708. *Phone:* 561-803-2102. *Toll-free phone:* 888-GO-TO-PBA. *Fax:* 561-803-2115. *E-mail:* joseph_bryan@pba.edu.

Palm Beach State College

Lake Worth, Florida

http://www.palmbeachstate.edu/

- **State-supported** 4-year, founded 1933, part of Florida College System
- **Urban** 150-acre campus with easy access to West Palm Beach
- **Endowment** $31.0 million
- **Coed**
- **Noncompetitive** entrance level

FACULTY

Student/faculty ratio: 49:1.

ACADEMICS

Calendar: semesters. *Degrees:* certificates, diplomas, associate, and bachelor's.

Library: Harold C. Manor Library plus 3 others.

STUDENT LIFE

Housing options: college housing not available.

Activities and organizations: drama/theater group, student-run newspaper, choral group, Student Government, Phi Theta Kappa, Students for International Understanding, Black Student Union, Drama Club, national fraternities.

Athletics Member NJCAA.

Campus security: 24-hour emergency response devices and patrols.

Student services: health clinic, women's center.

APPLYING

Standardized Tests *Recommended:* SAT and SAT Subject Tests or ACT (for admission).

Options: electronic application, early admission, deferred entrance.

Application fee: $30.

Required: high school transcript.

CONTACT

Ms. Anne Guiler, Coordinator of Distance Learning, Palm Beach State College, Lake Worth, FL 33461. *Phone:* 561-868-3032. *Fax:* 561-868-3584. *E-mail:* enrollmt@palmbeachstate.edu.

Pasco-Hernando State College

New Port Richey, Florida

http://www.phsc.edu/

CONTACT

Ms. Estela Carrion, Director of Admissions and Student Records, Pasco-Hernando State College, 10230 Ridge Road, New Port Richey, FL 34654-5199. *Phone:* 727-816-3261. *Toll-free phone:* 877-TRY-PHSC. *Fax:* 727-816-3389. *E-mail:* carrioe@phsc.edu.

Pensacola Christian College

Pensacola, Florida

http://www.pcci.edu/

CONTACT

Pensacola Christian College, 250 Brent Lane, Pensacola, FL 32503-2267. *Toll-free phone:* 800-722-4636.

Pensacola State College

Pensacola, Florida

http://www.pensacolastate.edu/

- **State-supported** primarily 2-year, founded 1948, part of Florida College System
- **Urban** 130-acre campus
- **Coed** 9,643 undergraduate students, 37% full-time, 61% women, 39% men
- **Noncompetitive** entrance level, 100% of applicants were admitted

UNDERGRAD STUDENTS

3,576 full-time, 6,067 part-time. 15% Black or African American, non-Hispanic/Latino; 7% Hispanic/Latino; 3% Asian, non-Hispanic/Latino; 0.5% Native Hawaiian or other Pacific Islander, non-Hispanic/Latino; 0.8% American Indian or Alaska Native, non-Hispanic/Latino; 5% Two or more races, non-Hispanic/Latino; 2% Race/ethnicity unknown; 0.3% international.

Freshmen:

Admission: 3,608 applied, 3,608 admitted, 1,544 enrolled.

FACULTY

Total: 573, 30% full-time, 12% with terminal degrees.

Student/faculty ratio: 18:1.

ACADEMICS

Calendar: semesters. *Degrees:* certificates, diplomas, associate, and bachelor's.

Special study options: academic remediation for entering students, adult/continuing education programs, advanced placement credit, cooperative education, distance learning, double majors, English as a second language, external degree program, honors programs, independent study, part-time degree program, services for LD students, summer session for credit. ***ROTC:*** Army (b).

Computers: 1,700 computers/terminals are available on campus for general student use. Students can access the following: campus intranet, computer help desk, free student e-mail accounts, online (class) grades, online (class) registration, online (class) schedules. Campuswide network is available. Wireless service is available via entire campus.

Library: Edward M. Chadbourne Library plus 3 others.

STUDENT LIFE

Housing options: college housing not available.

Activities and organizations: drama/theater group, student-run newspaper, choral group, Student Government Association, Health Occupations Students of America (HOSA), SkillsUSA, African-American Student Association, Forestry Club.

Athletics Member NJCAA. ***Intercollegiate sports:*** baseball M(s), basketball M(s)/W(s), softball W(s), volleyball W. ***Intramural sports:*** archery M/W, badminton M/W, basketball M/W, bowling M/W, cross-country running M/W, gymnastics M/W, racquetball M/W, sailing M/W, swimming and diving M/W, tennis M/W, track and field M/W, volleyball M/W, weight lifting M/W, wrestling M.

Campus security: 24-hour emergency response devices and patrols, late-night transport/escort service.

Student services: health clinic, personal/psychological counseling.

COSTS & FINANCIAL AID

Costs (2016–17) ***One-time required fee:*** $30. ***Tuition:*** $105 per credit hour part-time; state resident $2510 full-time, $105 per credit hour part-time; nonresident $10,075 full-time, $420 per credit hour part-time. Full-time tuition and fees vary according to course level and degree level. Part-time tuition and fees vary according to course level and degree level. ***Payment plan:*** deferred payment. ***Waivers:*** senior citizens and employees or children of employees.

Financial Aid Of all full-time matriculated undergraduates who enrolled in 2015, 120 Federal Work-Study jobs (averaging $3000).

APPLYING

Options: electronic application, early admission.

Application fee: $30.

Required: high school transcript.

Application deadlines: 8/30 (freshmen), 8/30 (transfers).

Notification: continuous until 8/30 (freshmen), continuous until 8/30 (transfers).

CONTACT

Ms. Susan Desbrow, Registrar, Pensacola State College, 1000 College Boulevard, Pensacola, FL 32504. *Phone:* 850-484-1605. *Fax:* 850-484-1020. *E-mail:* kdutremble@pensacolastate.edu.

Polk State College
Winter Haven, Florida
http://www.polk.edu/

- **State-supported** 4-year, founded 1964, part of Florida College System
- **Suburban** 98-acre campus with easy access to Orlando, Tampa
- **Coed** 11,364 undergraduate students, 31% full-time, 63% women, 37% men
- **Noncompetitive** entrance level

UNDERGRAD STUDENTS
3,529 full-time, 7,835 part-time. Students come from 9 states and territories; 1 other country; 1% are from out of state; 16% Black or African American, non-Hispanic/Latino; 21% Hispanic/Latino; 2% Asian, non-Hispanic/Latino; 0.1% Native Hawaiian or other Pacific Islander, non-Hispanic/Latino; 0.2% American Indian or Alaska Native, non-Hispanic/Latino; 3% Two or more races, non-Hispanic/Latino; 4% Race/ethnicity unknown; 1% international; 5% transferred in.

Freshmen:
Admission: 1,589 enrolled.

FACULTY
Total: 389, 42% full-time, 21% with terminal degrees.
Student/faculty ratio: 26:1.

ACADEMICS
Calendar: semesters 16-16-6-6. *Degrees:* certificates, diplomas, associate, and bachelor's.
Special study options: academic remediation for entering students, accelerated degree program, adult/continuing education programs, advanced placement credit, cooperative education, distance learning, double majors, English as a second language, honors programs, independent study, internships, off-campus study, part-time degree program, services for LD students, study abroad, summer session for credit. ***ROTC:*** Army (c), Air Force (c).
Computers: 800 computers/terminals are available on campus for general student use. Students can access the following: computer help desk, free student e-mail accounts, online (class) grades, online (class) registration, online (class) schedules. Campuswide network is available. Wireless service is available via entire campus.
Library: Polk State College Libraries plus 1 other. *Books:* 82,640 (physical), 110,114 (digital/electronic).

STUDENT LIFE
Housing options: college housing not available.
Activities and organizations: drama/theater group, choral group, Florida Student Nursing Association, Honors Program Student Council, Phi Theta Kappa (PTK), Student Government Association, SALO (Student Activities and Leadership Office).
Athletics Member NJCAA. ***Intercollegiate sports:*** baseball M(s), basketball M(s), sand volleyball W, soccer W(s), softball W(s), volleyball W(s). ***Intramural sports:*** basketball M/W, bowling M/W, cheerleading M/W, football M/W, sand volleyball W, table tennis M/W, volleyball W.
Campus security: 24-hour emergency response devices and patrols.
Student services: personal/psychological counseling, legal services.

COSTS
Costs (2017–18) ***Tuition:*** state resident $3367 full-time, $112 per credit hour part-time; nonresident $12,272 full-time, $409 per credit hour part-time. Full-time tuition and fees vary according to course level, course load, and degree level. Part-time tuition and fees vary according to course level, course load, and degree level. ***Waivers:*** employees or children of employees.

APPLYING
Options: electronic application, early admission, deferred entrance.
Required: high school transcript.
Application deadlines: rolling (freshmen), rolling (transfers).
Notification: continuous (freshmen), continuous (transfers).

CONTACT
Polk State College, 999 Avenue H, NE, Winter Haven, FL 33881-4299. *Phone:* 863-297-1021.

Polytechnic University of Puerto Rico, Miami Campus
Miami, Florida
http://www.pupr.edu/miami/

CONTACT
Admissions Department, Polytechnic University of Puerto Rico, Miami Campus, 8180 Northwest 36th Street, Suite 401, Miami, FL 33166. *Phone:* 305-418-4220. *Toll-free phone:* 888-729-7659. *Fax:* 305-418-4325.

Polytechnic University of Puerto Rico, Orlando Campus
Orlando, Florida
http://www.pupr.edu/orlando/

CONTACT
Teresa Cardona, Director of Recruitment and Admission, Polytechnic University of Puerto Rico, Orlando Campus, 550 North Econlockhatchee Trail, Orlando, FL 32825. *Phone:* 407-677-7000. *Toll-free phone:* 888-577-POLY. *Fax:* 407-677-5082.

Rasmussen College Fort Myers
Fort Myers, Florida
http://www.rasmussen.edu/

- **Proprietary** 4-year, part of Rasmussen College System
- **Suburban** campus
- **Coed** 423 undergraduate students, 61% full-time, 74% women, 26% men
- **Minimally difficult** entrance level, 96% of applicants were admitted

UNDERGRAD STUDENTS
260 full-time, 163 part-time.

Freshmen:
Admission: 45 applied, 43 admitted, 43 enrolled.

FACULTY
Total: 59, 17% full-time.
Student/faculty ratio: 22:1.

ACADEMICS
Calendar: quarters. *Degrees:* certificates, diplomas, associate, and bachelor's.
Special study options: academic remediation for entering students, accelerated degree program, adult/continuing education programs, distance learning, double majors, internships, part-time degree program, summer session for credit.
Computers: 129 computers/terminals are available on campus for general student use. Students can access the following: computer help desk, free student e-mail accounts, online (class) grades, online (class) schedules. Campuswide network is available. Wireless service is available via entire campus.
Library: Rasmussen College Library - Fort Myers.

STUDENT LIFE
Housing options: college housing not available.

COSTS
Costs (2017–18) ***Tuition:*** $11,055 full-time. Full-time tuition and fees vary according to course level, course load, degree level, location, and program. Part-time tuition and fees vary according to course level, course load, degree level, location, and program. No tuition increase for student's term of enrollment. ***Required fees:*** $1695 full-time. ***Payment plans:*** installment, deferred payment. ***Waivers:*** employees or children of employees.

APPLYING
Standardized Tests *Required:* institutional exam (for admission).
Options: electronic application, early admission, deferred entrance.
Required: high school transcript, minimum 2.0 GPA. ***Required for some:*** interview.
Application deadlines: rolling (freshmen), rolling (transfers).

CONTACT
Ms. Susan Hammerstrom, Director of Admissions, Rasmussen College Fort Myers, 9160 Forum Corporate Parkway, Suite 100, Fort Myers, FL 33905. *Phone:* 239-477-2100. *Toll-free phone:* 888-549-6755. *E-mail:* susan.hammerstrom@rasmussen.edu.

Rasmussen College Land O' Lakes

Land O' Lakes, Florida

http://www.rasmussen.edu/

- **Proprietary** 4-year, part of Rasmussen College System
- **Suburban** campus
- **Coed** 207 undergraduate students, 39% full-time, 63% women, 37% men
- **Minimally difficult** entrance level, 100% of applicants were admitted

UNDERGRAD STUDENTS
80 full-time, 127 part-time.

Freshmen:
Admission: 8 applied, 8 admitted, 8 enrolled.

FACULTY
Total: 33, 12% full-time.
Student/faculty ratio: 22:1.

ACADEMICS
Calendar: quarters. *Degrees:* certificates, diplomas, associate, and bachelor's.
Special study options: academic remediation for entering students, accelerated degree program, adult/continuing education programs, distance learning, double majors, internships, part-time degree program, summer session for credit.
Computers: 61 computers/terminals are available on campus for general student use. Students can access the following: computer help desk, free student e-mail accounts, online (class) grades, online (class) schedules. Campuswide network is available. Wireless service is available via entire campus.
Library: Rasmussen College Library - Land O' Lakes.

STUDENT LIFE
Housing options: college housing not available.

COSTS
Costs (2017–18) ***Tuition:*** $11,055 full-time. Full-time tuition and fees vary according to course level, course load, degree level, location, and program. Part-time tuition and fees vary according to course level, course load, degree level, location, and program. No tuition increase for student's term of enrollment. ***Required fees:*** $1695 full-time. ***Payment plans:*** installment, deferred payment. ***Waivers:*** employees or children of employees.

APPLYING
Standardized Tests *Required:* institutional exam (for admission).
Options: electronic application, early admission, deferred entrance.
Required: high school transcript, minimum 2.0 GPA. ***Required for some:*** interview.
Application deadlines: rolling (freshmen), rolling (transfers).

CONTACT
Ms. Susan Hammerstrom, Director of Admissions, Rasmussen College Land O' Lakes, 18600 Fernview Street, Land O' Lakes, FL 34638. *Phone:* 813-435-3601. *Toll-free phone:* 888-549-6755. *E-mail:* susan.hammerstrom@rasmussen.edu.

Rasmussen College New Port Richey

New Port Richey, Florida

http://www.rasmussen.edu/

- **Proprietary** 4-year, part of Rasmussen College System
- **Suburban** campus
- **Coed** 370 undergraduate students, 55% full-time, 75% women, 25% men
- **Minimally difficult** entrance level, 90% of applicants were admitted

UNDERGRAD STUDENTS
204 full-time, 166 part-time.

Freshmen:
Admission: 20 applied, 18 admitted, 18 enrolled.

FACULTY
Total: 36, 47% full-time.
Student/faculty ratio: 22:1.

ACADEMICS
Calendar: quarters. *Degrees:* certificates, diplomas, associate, and bachelor's.
Special study options: academic remediation for entering students, accelerated degree program, adult/continuing education programs, distance learning, double majors, internships, part-time degree program, summer session for credit.
Computers: 118 computers/terminals are available on campus for general student use. Students can access the following: computer help desk, free student e-mail accounts, online (class) grades, online (class) schedules. Campuswide network is available. Wireless service is available via entire campus.
Library: Rasmussen College Library - New Port Richey.

STUDENT LIFE
Housing options: college housing not available.

COSTS & FINANCIAL AID
Costs (2017–18) ***Tuition:*** $11,055 full-time. Full-time tuition and fees vary according to course level, course load, degree level, location, and program. Part-time tuition and fees vary according to course level, course load, degree level, location, and program. No tuition increase for student's term of enrollment. ***Required fees:*** $1695 full-time. ***Payment plans:*** installment, deferred payment. ***Waivers:*** employees or children of employees.
Financial Aid Of all full-time matriculated undergraduates who enrolled in 2015, 6 Federal Work-Study jobs.

APPLYING
Standardized Tests *Required:* institutional exam (for admission).
Options: electronic application, early admission, deferred entrance.
Required: high school transcript, minimum 2.0 GPA. ***Required for some:*** interview.
Application deadlines: rolling (freshmen), rolling (transfers).

CONTACT
Susan Hammerstrom, Director of Admissions, Rasmussen College New Port Richey, 8661 Citizens Drive, New Port Richey, FL 34654. *Phone:* 727-942-0069. *Toll-free phone:* 888-549-6755. *E-mail:* susan.hammerstrom@rasmussen.edu.

Rasmussen College Ocala

Ocala, Florida

http://www.rasmussen.edu/

- **Proprietary** 4-year, founded 1984, part of Rasmussen College System
- **Suburban** campus with easy access to Orlando
- **Coed** 719 undergraduate students, 58% full-time, 76% women, 24% men
- **Minimally difficult** entrance level, 80% of applicants were admitted

UNDERGRAD STUDENTS
414 full-time, 305 part-time.

Freshmen:
Admission: 79 applied, 63 admitted, 63 enrolled.

FACULTY
Total: 44, 23% full-time.
Student/faculty ratio: 22:1.

ACADEMICS
Calendar: quarters. *Degrees:* certificates, diplomas, associate, and bachelor's.
Special study options: academic remediation for entering students, accelerated degree program, adult/continuing education programs, distance learning, double majors, internships, part-time degree program, summer session for credit.
Computers: 124 computers/terminals are available on campus for general student use. Students can access the following: computer help desk, free

student e-mail accounts, online (class) grades, online (class) schedules. Campuswide network is available. Wireless service is available via entire campus.
Library: Rasmussen College Library - Ocala.

STUDENT LIFE
Housing options: college housing not available.

COSTS
Costs (2017–18) ***Tuition:*** $11,055 full-time. Full-time tuition and fees vary according to course level, course load, degree level, location, and program. Part-time tuition and fees vary according to course level, course load, degree level, location, and program. No tuition increase for student's term of enrollment. ***Required fees:*** $1695 full-time. ***Payment plans:*** installment, deferred payment. ***Waivers:*** employees or children of employees.

APPLYING
Standardized Tests *Required:* institutional exam (for admission).
Options: electronic application, early admission, deferred entrance.
Required: high school transcript, minimum 2.0 GPA.
Required for some: interview.
Application deadlines: rolling (freshmen), rolling (transfers).

CONTACT
Susan Hammerstrom, Director of Admissions, Rasmussen College Ocala, 4755 SW 46th Court, Ocala, FL 34474. *Phone:* 352-629-1941.
Toll-free phone: 888-549-6755.
E-mail: susan.hammerstrom@rasmussen.edu.

Rasmussen College Ocala School of Nursing

Ocala, Florida

http://www.rasmussen.edu/

- **Proprietary** 4-year, part of Rasmussen College System
- **Suburban** campus
- **Coed** 4,326 undergraduate students, 48% full-time, 85% women, 15% men
- **Minimally difficult** entrance level, 92% of applicants were admitted

UNDERGRAD STUDENTS
2,058 full-time, 2,268 part-time.

Freshmen:
Admission: 107 applied, 98 admitted, 98 enrolled.

FACULTY
Total: 43, 40% full-time.
Student/faculty ratio: 22:1.

ACADEMICS
Calendar: quarters. *Degrees:* associate and bachelor's.
Special study options: academic remediation for entering students, accelerated degree program, adult/continuing education programs, distance learning, double majors, internships, part-time degree program, summer session for credit.
Computers: Students can access the following: computer help desk, free student e-mail accounts, online (class) grades, online (class) schedules. Campuswide network is available. Wireless service is available via entire campus.
Library: Rasmussen College Library - Ocala.

STUDENT LIFE
Housing options: college housing not available.

COSTS
Costs (2017–18) ***Tuition:*** $11,055 full-time. ***Required fees:*** $1695 full-time.

APPLYING
Standardized Tests *Required:* institutional exam (for admission).
Options: electronic application, early admission, deferred entrance.
Required: high school transcript, minimum 2.0 GPA. ***Required for some:*** interview.
Application deadlines: rolling (freshmen), rolling (transfers).

CONTACT
Ms. Susan Hammerstrom, Director of Admissions, Rasmussen College Ocala School of Nursing, 2100 SW 22nd Place, Ocala, FL 34471.
Phone: 352-291-8560. *Toll-free phone:* 888-549-6755.
E-mail: susan.hammerstrom@rasmussen.edu.

Rasmussen College Tampa/Brandon

Tampa, Florida

http://www.rasmussen.edu/

- **Proprietary** 4-year, part of Rasmussen College System
- **Suburban** campus
- **Coed** 358 undergraduate students, 40% full-time, 72% women, 28% men
- **Minimally difficult** entrance level, 97% of applicants were admitted

UNDERGRAD STUDENTS
143 full-time, 215 part-time.

Freshmen:
Admission: 33 applied, 32 admitted, 32 enrolled.

FACULTY
Total: 62, 15% full-time.
Student/faculty ratio: 22:1.

ACADEMICS
Calendar: quarters. *Degrees:* certificates, diplomas, associate, and bachelor's.
Special study options: academic remediation for entering students, accelerated degree program, adult/continuing education programs, distance learning, double majors, internships, part-time degree program, summer session for credit.
Computers: 47 computers/terminals are available on campus for general student use. Students can access the following: computer help desk, free student e-mail accounts, online (class) grades, online (class) schedules. Campuswide network is available. Wireless service is available via entire campus.
Library: Rasmussen College Library - Tampa.

STUDENT LIFE
Housing options: college housing not available.

COSTS
Costs (2017–18) ***Tuition:*** $11,055 full-time. Full-time tuition and fees vary according to course level, course load, degree level, location, and program. Part-time tuition and fees vary according to course level, course load, degree level, location, and program. No tuition increase for student's term of enrollment. ***Required fees:*** $1695 full-time. ***Payment plans:*** installment, deferred payment. ***Waivers:*** employees or children of employees.

APPLYING
Standardized Tests *Required:* institutional exam (for admission).
Options: electronic application, early admission, deferred entrance.
Required: high school transcript, minimum 2.0 GPA. ***Required for some:*** interview.
Application deadlines: rolling (freshmen), rolling (transfers).

CONTACT
Ms. Susan Hammerstrom, Director of Admissions, Rasmussen College Tampa/Brandon, 4042 Park Oaks Boulevard, Suite 100, Tampa, FL 33610. *Phone:* 813-246-7600. *Toll-free phone:* 888-549-6755.
E-mail: susan.hammerstrom@rasmussen.edu.

Ringling College of Art and Design

Sarasota, Florida

http://www.ringling.edu/

- **Independent** 4-year, founded 1931
- **Urban** 49-acre campus with easy access to Tampa-St. Petersburg
- **Endowment** $42.1 million
- **Coed** 1,341 undergraduate students, 95% full-time, 65% women, 35% men
- **Moderately difficult** entrance level, 78% of applicants were admitted

UNDERGRAD STUDENTS
1,270 full-time, 71 part-time. Students come from 46 states and territories; 57 other countries; 55% are from out of state; 3% Black or African American, non-Hispanic/Latino; 16% Hispanic/Latino; 8% Asian, non-Hispanic/Latino; 0.2% Native Hawaiian or other Pacific Islander, non-Hispanic/Latino; 0.8% American Indian or Alaska Native, non-Hispanic/Latino; 3% Two or more races, non-Hispanic/Latino; 6% Race/ethnicity unknown; 16% international; 7% transferred in; 72% live on campus.

Freshmen:
Admission: 1,752 applied, 1,369 admitted, 355 enrolled. ***Average high school GPA:*** 3.27.

Retention: 87% of full-time freshmen returned.

FACULTY
Total: 160, 64% full-time, 53% with terminal degrees.

Student/faculty ratio: 11:1.

ACADEMICS
Calendar: semesters. *Degree:* bachelor's.

Special study options: academic remediation for entering students, advanced placement credit, English as a second language, independent study, internships, off-campus study, part-time degree program, services for LD students, study abroad, summer session for credit.

Computers: 1,000 computers/terminals are available on campus for general student use. Students can access the following: campus intranet, computer help desk, free student e-mail accounts, online (class) grades, online (class) registration, online (class) schedules, central file storage, high performance computing labs. Campuswide network is available. 100% of college-owned or -operated housing units are wired for high-speed Internet access. Wireless service is available via entire campus.

Library: Alfred R. Goldstein Library. *Books:* 64,331 (physical), 129,469 (digital/electronic); *Databases:* 36. Weekly public service hours: 90; study areas open 24 hours, 5-7 days a week; students can reserve study rooms.

STUDENT LIFE
Housing options: coed, men-only, women-only. Campus housing is university owned. Freshman applicants given priority for college housing.

Activities and organizations: drama/theater group, student-run television station, choral group, Student Government Association, Digital Painting Sketch Club, Resident Student Association, MOSAIC, Quidditch Team.

Athletics ***Intramural sports:*** football M(c)/W(c).

Campus security: 24-hour emergency response devices and patrols, late-night transport/escort service, controlled dormitory access, lighted campus.

Student services: health clinic, personal/psychological counseling, legal services.

COSTS & FINANCIAL AID
Costs (2016–17) ***Comprehensive fee:*** $57,430 includes full-time tuition ($39,510), mandatory fees ($3530), and room and board ($14,390). Full-time tuition and fees vary according to course load, program, and student level. Part-time tuition: $1840 per credit hour. Part-time tuition and fees vary according to program and student level. ***College room only:*** $7750. Room and board charges vary according to board plan and housing facility. ***Payment plan:*** installment. ***Waivers:*** employees or children of employees.

Financial Aid Of all full-time matriculated undergraduates who enrolled in 2016, 935 applied for aid, 863 were judged to have need, 44 had their need fully met. In 2016, 314 non-need-based awards were made. ***Average percent of need met:*** 48. ***Average financial aid package:*** $24,503. ***Average need-based loan:*** $7807. ***Average need-based gift aid:*** $15,839. ***Average non-need-based aid:*** $11,663. ***Average indebtedness upon graduation:*** $44,384.

APPLYING
Options: electronic application, early action, deferred entrance.

Application fee: $70.

Required: essay or personal statement, high school transcript, minimum 2.0 GPA, 2 letters of recommendation, portfolio, resumé. ***Recommended:*** interview.

Application deadlines: rolling (freshmen), rolling (transfers), 11/1 (early action).

Notification: continuous (freshmen), continuous (transfers), 12/15 (early action).

CONTACT
Ringling College of Art and Design, 2700 North Tamiami Trail, Sarasota, FL 34234-5895. *Phone:* 941-359-7523. *Toll-free phone:* 800-255-7695. *E-mail:* admissions@ringling.edu.

Rollins College

Winter Park, Florida

http://www.rollins.edu/

- **Independent** comprehensive, founded 1885
- **Suburban** 80-acre campus with easy access to Orlando
- **Endowment** $339.7 million
- **Coed** 1,942 undergraduate students, 100% full-time, 60% women, 40% men
- **Moderately difficult** entrance level, 61% of applicants were admitted

UNDERGRAD STUDENTS
1,935 full-time, 7 part-time. Students come from 41 states and territories; 57 other countries; 42% are from out of state; 3% Black or African American, non-Hispanic/Latino; 14% Hispanic/Latino; 3% Asian, non-Hispanic/Latino; 0.3% American Indian or Alaska Native, non-Hispanic/Latino; 3% Two or more races, non-Hispanic/Latino; 3% Race/ethnicity unknown; 10% international; 3% transferred in; 61% live on campus.

Freshmen:
Admission: 5,445 applied, 3,301 admitted, 538 enrolled. ***Average high school GPA:*** 3.32. ***Test scores:*** SAT critical reading scores over 500: 97%; SAT math scores over 500: 97%; SAT writing scores over 500: 91%; ACT scores over 18: 100%; SAT critical reading scores over 600: 56%; SAT math scores over 600: 56%; SAT writing scores over 600: 47%; ACT scores over 24: 92%; SAT critical reading scores over 700: 10%; SAT math scores over 700: 9%; SAT writing scores over 700: 6%; ACT scores over 30: 35%.

Retention: 83% of full-time freshmen returned.

FACULTY
Total: 235, 100% full-time, 89% with terminal degrees.

Student/faculty ratio: 10:1.

ACADEMICS
Calendar: semesters. *Degrees:* bachelor's, master's, and doctoral.

Special study options: academic remediation for entering students, accelerated degree program, adult/continuing education programs, advanced placement credit, double majors, honors programs, independent study, internships, off-campus study, part-time degree program, services for LD students, student-designed majors, study abroad, summer session for credit.

Unusual degree programs: 3-2 business administration with Crummer Graduate School of Business, Rollins College; engineering with Columbia University, Washington University in St. Louis, Auburn University; environmental management with Duke University.

Computers: 254 computers/terminals are available on campus for general student use. Students can access the following: campus intranet, computer help desk, free student e-mail accounts, online (class) grades, online (class) registration, online (class) schedules. Campuswide network is available. 100% of college-owned or -operated housing units are wired for high-speed Internet access. Wireless service is available via entire campus.

Library: Olin Library. *Books:* 259,302 (physical), 200,491 (digital/electronic); *Serial titles:* 2,358 (physical), 134,353 (digital/electronic); *Databases:* 80. Study areas open 24 hours, 5-7 days a week; students can reserve study rooms.

STUDENT LIFE
Housing options: on-campus residence required through sophomore year; coed, men-only, women-only, special housing for students with disabilities. Campus housing is university owned. Freshman campus housing is guaranteed.

Activities and organizations: drama/theater group, student-run newspaper, radio and television station, choral group, Black Student

Union, Student Government Association, Eco-Rollins, Spectrum, WPRK 91.5, national fraternities, national sororities.

Athletics Member NCAA. All Division II. ***Intercollegiate sports:*** baseball M(s), basketball M(s)/W(s), crew M/W, cross-country running M/W, golf M(s)/W(s), lacrosse M/W, sailing M/W, skiing (downhill) M/W, soccer M(s)/W(s), softball W(s), swimming and diving M/W, tennis M(s)/W(s), volleyball W(s). ***Intramural sports:*** baseball M, basketball M/W, bowling M/W, equestrian sports W(c), ice hockey M(c), soccer M/W, softball M/W, table tennis M/W, tennis M/W, ultimate Frisbee M/W, volleyball M/W.

Campus security: 24-hour emergency response devices and patrols, late-night transport/escort service, controlled dormitory access.

Student services: health clinic, personal/psychological counseling, women's center.

COSTS & FINANCIAL AID

Costs (2017–18) ***Comprehensive fee:*** $63,065 includes full-time tuition ($48,335) and room and board ($14,730). ***College room only:*** $8715. Room and board charges vary according to housing facility. ***Payment plan:*** installment. ***Waivers:*** employees or children of employees.

Financial Aid Of all full-time matriculated undergraduates who enrolled in 2016, 1,104 applied for aid, 986 were judged to have need, 269 had their need fully met. 232 Federal Work-Study jobs (averaging $1251). 3 state and other part-time jobs (averaging $4000). In 2016, 551 non-need-based awards were made. ***Average percent of need met:*** 78. ***Average financial aid package:*** $39,204. ***Average need-based loan:*** $4557. ***Average need-based gift aid:*** $31,145. ***Average non-need-based aid:*** $20,042. ***Average indebtedness upon graduation:*** $32,208.

APPLYING

Standardized Tests *Required:* Selection of Test Score Waived Option (TSWO) or official SAT/ACT scores (for admission).

Options: electronic application, early admission, early decision, deferred entrance.

Application fee: $50.

Required: essay or personal statement, high school transcript, 1 letter of recommendation. ***Recommended:*** minimum 2.0 GPA, interview.

Application deadlines: 2/15 (freshmen), 4/15 (transfers).

Early decision deadline: 11/15 (for plan 1), 1/15 (for plan 2).

Notification: 4/1 (freshmen), continuous (transfers), 12/15 (early decision plan 1), 2/1 (early decision plan 2).

CONTACT

Ms. Faye Tydlaska, VP Enrollment Mgmt & Marketing, Rollins College, 1000 Holt Avenue, Campus Box 2720, Winter Park, FL 32789. *Phone:* 407-646-2000 Ext. 2161. *E-mail:* admissions@rollins.edu.

St. John Vianney College Seminary

Miami, Florida

http://www.sjvcs.edu/

CONTACT

Br. Edward Van Merrienboer, Academic Dean, St. John Vianney College Seminary, 2900 Southwest 87th Avenue, Miami, FL 33165-3244. *Phone:* 305-223-4561 Ext. 13.

Saint Leo University

Saint Leo, Florida

http://www.saintleo.edu/

- **Independent Roman Catholic** comprehensive, founded 1889
- **Rural** 280-acre campus with easy access to Tampa, Orlando
- **Endowment** $58.1 million
- **Coed** 2,264 undergraduate students, 97% full-time, 57% women, 43% men
- **Moderately difficult** entrance level, 70% of applicants were admitted

UNDERGRAD STUDENTS

2,192 full-time, 72 part-time. Students come from 47 states and territories; 63 other countries; 30% are from out of state; 14% Black or African American, non-Hispanic/Latino; 19% Hispanic/Latino; 2% Asian, non-Hispanic/Latino; 0.3% American Indian or Alaska Native, non-Hispanic/Latino; 2% Two or more races, non-Hispanic/Latino; 7% Race/ethnicity unknown; 12% international; 6% transferred in; 67% live on campus.

Freshmen:

Admission: 4,501 applied, 3,139 admitted, 610 enrolled. ***Average high school GPA:*** 3.5. ***Test scores:*** SAT critical reading scores over 500: 48%; SAT math scores over 500: 54%; SAT writing scores over 500: 36%; ACT scores over 18: 97%; SAT critical reading scores over 600: 13%; SAT math scores over 600: 11%; SAT writing scores over 600: 8%; ACT scores over 24: 38%; SAT math scores over 700: 1%; SAT writing scores over 700: 1%; ACT scores over 30: 7%.

Retention: 72% of full-time freshmen returned.

FACULTY

Total: 211, 61% full-time, 64% with terminal degrees.

Student/faculty ratio: 14:1.

ACADEMICS

Calendar: semesters. *Degrees:* certificates, associate, bachelor's, master's, doctoral, and postbachelor's certificates.

Special study options: academic remediation for entering students, accelerated degree program, adult/continuing education programs, advanced placement credit, distance learning, double majors, English as a second language, honors programs, independent study, internships, part-time degree program, services for LD students, study abroad, summer session for credit. ***ROTC:*** Army (b), Air Force (b).

Computers: 150 computers/terminals are available on campus for general student use. Students can access the following: campus intranet, computer help desk, free student e-mail accounts, online (class) grades, online (class) registration, online (class) schedules. Campuswide network is available. 100% of college-owned or -operated housing units are wired for high-speed Internet access. Wireless service is available via classrooms, computer centers, computer labs, dorm rooms, learning centers, libraries, student centers.

Library: Cannon Memorial Library plus 1 other. *Books:* 97,155 (physical), 403,383 (digital/electronic); *Serial titles:* 265 (physical), 170,845 (digital/electronic); *Databases:* 72. Weekly public service hours: 119.

STUDENT LIFE

Housing options: on-campus residence required through junior year; coed, men-only, women-only, special housing for students with disabilities. Campus housing is university owned. Freshman applicants given priority for college housing.

Activities and organizations: drama/theater group, student-run newspaper, choral group, Caribbean Student Association, Alpha Phi Omega, Intercultural Student Association, Opus Fides, Pacioli Accounting Club, national fraternities, national sororities.

Athletics Member NCAA. All Division II. ***Intercollegiate sports:*** baseball M(s), basketball M(s)/W(s), cross-country running M(s)/W(s), golf M(s)/W(s), lacrosse M(s)/W(s), soccer M(s)/W(s), softball W(s), swimming and diving M(s)/W(s), tennis M(s)/W(s), track and field M(s)/W(s), volleyball W(s). ***Intramural sports:*** basketball M/W, bowling M/W, field hockey M/W, football M/W, sand volleyball M/W, soccer M/W, ultimate Frisbee M/W.

Campus security: 24-hour emergency response devices and patrols, late-night transport/escort service, controlled dormitory access, surveillance cameras in parking lots.

Student services: health clinic, personal/psychological counseling.

COSTS & FINANCIAL AID

Costs (2017–18) ***Comprehensive fee:*** $32,540 includes full-time tuition ($21,600), mandatory fees ($370), and room and board ($10,570). ***College room only:*** $5620. Room and board charges vary according to board plan and housing facility. ***Payment plans:*** installment, deferred payment. ***Waivers:*** employees or children of employees.

Financial Aid Of all full-time matriculated undergraduates who enrolled in 2016, 1,804 applied for aid, 1,559 were judged to have need, 249 had their need fully met. 334 Federal Work-Study jobs (averaging $4313). 6 state and other part-time jobs (averaging $3903). In 2016, 578 non-need-based awards were made. ***Average percent of need met:*** 70. ***Average financial aid package:*** $20,298. ***Average need-based loan:*** $4088. ***Average need-based gift aid:*** $15,376. ***Average non-need-based aid:*** $7073. ***Average indebtedness upon graduation:*** $28,542.

APPLYING
Standardized Tests *Recommended:* SAT or ACT (for admission).
Options: electronic application, early admission, deferred entrance.
Application fee: $40.
Required: high school transcript, 1 letter of recommendation. *Recommended:* interview.
Application deadlines: rolling (freshmen), rolling (transfers).
Notification: continuous (freshmen), continuous (transfers).

CONTACT
Saint Leo University, MC 2008, PO Box 6665, Saint Leo, FL 33574-6665. *Phone:* 352-588-8283. *Toll-free phone:* 800-334-5532. *Fax:* 352-588-8257. *E-mail:* admissions@saintleo.edu.

St. Petersburg College

St. Petersburg, Florida

http://www.spcollege.edu/

- **State and locally supported** 4-year, founded 1927
- **Suburban** 410-acre campus with easy access to Tampa
- **Coed** 31,767 undergraduate students, 29% full-time, 60% women, 40% men
- **Noncompetitive** entrance level, 25% of applicants were admitted

UNDERGRAD STUDENTS
9,301 full-time, 22,466 part-time. 4% are from out of state; 14% Black or African American, non-Hispanic/Latino; 13% Hispanic/Latino; 3% Asian, non-Hispanic/Latino; 0.2% Native Hawaiian or other Pacific Islander, non-Hispanic/Latino; 0.4% American Indian or Alaska Native, non-Hispanic/Latino; 3% Two or more races, non-Hispanic/Latino; 2% Race/ethnicity unknown; 0.7% international.

Freshmen:
Admission: 5,264 applied, 1,339 admitted, 4,254 enrolled.

FACULTY
Total: 1,780, 21% full-time.
Student/faculty ratio: 22:1.

ACADEMICS
Calendar: semesters. *Degrees:* certificates, diplomas, associate, and bachelor's.
Special study options: academic remediation for entering students, accelerated degree program, adult/continuing education programs, advanced placement credit, cooperative education, distance learning, English as a second language, freshman honors college, honors programs, internships, off-campus study, part-time degree program, services for LD students, study abroad, summer session for credit. ***ROTC:*** Army (c).
Computers: Students can access the following: campus intranet, computer help desk, free student e-mail accounts, online (class) grades, online (class) registration, online (class) schedules. Campuswide network is available. Wireless service is available via entire campus.
Library: M. M. Bennett Library.

STUDENT LIFE
Housing options: college housing not available.
Activities and organizations: drama/theater group, student-run newspaper, choral group.
Athletics Member NJCAA. ***Intercollegiate sports:*** baseball M(s), basketball M(s)/W(s), softball W(s), tennis W(s), volleyball W(s).
Campus security: late-night transport/escort service.
Student services: women's center.

COSTS
Costs (2017–18) ***Tuition:*** state resident $2428 full-time, $113 per credit hour part-time; nonresident $9717 full-time, $389 per credit hour part-time. ***Required fees:*** $957 full-time.

APPLYING
Options: electronic application, early admission.
Application fee: $30.
Required: high school transcript.
Notification: continuous (freshmen).

CONTACT
Ms. Susan Fell, Director of Admissions and Records, St. Petersburg College, PO Box 13489, St. Petersburg, FL 33733-3489. *Phone:* 727-341-3166. *E-mail:* information@spcollege.edu.

St. Thomas University

Miami Gardens, Florida

http://www.stu.edu/

- **Independent Roman Catholic** university, founded 1961
- **Suburban** 140-acre campus with easy access to Miami, FL
- **Endowment** $24.9 million
- **Coed** 2,752 undergraduate students, 29% full-time, 58% women, 42% men

UNDERGRAD STUDENTS
811 full-time, 1,941 part-time. Students come from 30 states and territories; 38 other countries; 11% are from out of state; 20% Black or African American, non-Hispanic/Latino; 46% Hispanic/Latino; 0.2% Asian, non-Hispanic/Latino; 0.1% Native Hawaiian or other Pacific Islander, non-Hispanic/Latino; 0.1% American Indian or Alaska Native, non-Hispanic/Latino; 3% Two or more races, non-Hispanic/Latino; 3% Race/ethnicity unknown; 17% international; 3% transferred in; 39% live on campus.

Freshmen:
Admission: 195 enrolled. ***Average high school GPA:*** 3.25. ***Test scores:*** SAT critical reading scores over 500: 35%; SAT math scores over 500: 42%; SAT writing scores over 500: 31%; ACT scores over 18: 72%; SAT critical reading scores over 600: 3%; SAT math scores over 600: 5%; SAT writing scores over 600: 3%; ACT scores over 24: 7%; ACT scores over 30: 1%.
Retention: 70% of full-time freshmen returned.

FACULTY
Total: 84.
Student/faculty ratio: 12:1.

ACADEMICS
Calendar: semesters. *Degrees:* certificates, bachelor's, master's, doctoral, post-master's, and postbachelor's certificates.
Special study options: academic remediation for entering students, accelerated degree program, adult/continuing education programs, advanced placement credit, distance learning, double majors, English as a second language, external degree program, honors programs, independent study, internships, part-time degree program, services for LD students, study abroad, summer session for credit.
Computers: 100 computers/terminals and 20 ports are available on campus for general student use. Students can access the following: campus intranet, computer help desk, free student e-mail accounts, online (class) grades, online (class) registration, online (class) schedules. Campuswide network is available. 100% of college-owned or -operated housing units are wired for high-speed Internet access. Wireless service is available via entire campus.
Library: St. Thomas University Library plus 1 other. *Books:* 154,000 (physical), 221,000 (digital/electronic); *Serial titles:* 393 (physical), 226 (digital/electronic); *Databases:* 137. Weekly public service hours: 101; students can reserve study rooms.

STUDENT LIFE
Housing options: coed. Campus housing is university owned.
Activities and organizations: choral group, marching band, Psychology Club, National Society of Leadership and Success (NSLS), Criminal Justice, Kreyol Nation, Gay Strait Alliance (GSA).
Athletics Member NAIA. ***Intercollegiate sports:*** baseball M(s), basketball M(s)/W(s), cheerleading W(s), cross-country running M(s)/W(s), golf M(s)/W(s), sand volleyball W(s), soccer M(s)/W(s), softball W(s), tennis M(s)/W(s), track and field M(s)/W(s), volleyball W(s). ***Intramural sports:*** badminton M/W, baseball M, basketball M/W, cross-country running M/W, football M/W, golf M/W, racquetball M/W, sand volleyball M/W, soccer M/W, softball M/W, table tennis M/W, tennis M/W, volleyball M/W.

Campus security: 24-hour emergency response devices and patrols, late-night transport/escort service, controlled dormitory access.

Student services: health clinic, personal/psychological counseling.

COSTS

Costs (2016–17) ***Comprehensive fee:*** $40,500 includes full-time tuition ($28,800) and room and board ($11,700). Full-time tuition and fees vary according to course load. Part-time tuition: $576 per credit hour. Part-time tuition and fees vary according to course load. ***College room only:*** $7200. Room and board charges vary according to board plan and housing facility. ***Payment plans:*** installment, deferred payment. ***Waivers:*** employees or children of employees.

APPLYING

Standardized Tests *Recommended:* SAT or ACT (for admission).

Required: high school transcript, minimum 2.5 GPA. ***Required for some:*** interview. ***Recommended:*** essay or personal statement, 1 letter of recommendation.

CONTACT

Mr. Anthony Noriega, Associate Director of Admissions, St. Thomas University, 16401 Northwest 37th Avenue, Miami Gardens, FL 33054-6459. *Phone:* 305-628-6617. *Toll-free phone:* 800-367-9010. *E-mail:* ajnoriega@stu.edu.

Santa Fe College

Gainesville, Florida

http://www.sfcollege.edu/

CONTACT

Santa Fe College, 3000 Northwest 83rd Street, Gainesville, FL 32606. *Phone:* 352-395-4177.

Schiller International University

Largo, Florida

http://www.schiller.edu/

CONTACT

Admissions Officer, Schiller International University, Largo, FL 33770. *Toll-free phone:* 800-261-9571 (in-state); 800-261-9751 (out-of-state). *Fax:* 727-738-6376. *E-mail:* admissions@schiller.edu.

Seminole State College of Florida

Sanford, Florida

http://www.seminolestate.edu/

- **State and locally supported** primarily 2-year, founded 1966
- **Small-town** 200-acre campus with easy access to Orlando
- **Endowment** $24.6 million
- **Coed** 17,906 undergraduate students, 34% full-time, 55% women, 45% men
- **Noncompetitive** entrance level, 64% of applicants were admitted

UNDERGRAD STUDENTS

6,137 full-time, 11,769 part-time. Students come from 21 states and territories; 68 other countries; 3% are from out of state; 16% Black or African American, non-Hispanic/Latino; 24% Hispanic/Latino; 3% Asian, non-Hispanic/Latino; 0.3% Native Hawaiian or other Pacific Islander, non-Hispanic/Latino; 0.3% American Indian or Alaska Native, non-Hispanic/Latino; 3% Two or more races, non-Hispanic/Latino; 3% Race/ethnicity unknown; 2% international; 7% transferred in.

Freshmen:

Admission: 4,587 applied, 2,941 admitted, 2,670 enrolled.

Retention: 52% of full-time freshmen returned.

FACULTY

Total: 798, 26% full-time, 22% with terminal degrees.

Student/faculty ratio: 26:1.

ACADEMICS

Calendar: semesters. *Degrees:* certificates, diplomas, associate, bachelor's, and postbachelor's certificates.

Special study options: academic remediation for entering students, accelerated degree program, adult/continuing education programs, advanced placement credit, cooperative education, distance learning, double majors, English as a second language, external degree program, honors programs, independent study, internships, part-time degree program, services for LD students, study abroad, summer session for credit. ***ROTC:*** Army (b).

Computers: 300 computers/terminals are available on campus for general student use. Students can access the following: campus intranet, computer help desk, free student e-mail accounts, online (class) grades, online (class) registration, online (class) schedules, online syllabi. Campuswide network is available. Wireless service is available via entire campus.

Library: Seminole State Library at Sanford Lake Mary plus 3 others. *Books:* 67,023 (physical), 145,374 (digital/electronic); *Serial titles:* 520 (physical), 18,003 (digital/electronic); *Databases:* 130. Weekly public service hours: 60; students can reserve study rooms.

STUDENT LIFE

Housing options: college housing not available.

Activities and organizations: drama/theater group, student-run newspaper, choral group, Phi Beta Lambda, Phi Theta Kappa, Student Government Association, Sigma Phi Gamma, Hispanic Student Association.

Athletics Member NJCAA. ***Intercollegiate sports:*** baseball M(s), golf W(s), softball W(s).

Campus security: 24-hour emergency response devices and patrols, late-night transport/escort service.

Student services: personal/psychological counseling.

COSTS

Costs (2017–18) ***Tuition:*** state resident $3597 full-time, $104 per credit hour part-time; nonresident $12,739 full-time, $382 per credit hour part-time. Full-time tuition and fees vary according to course level, course load, degree level, and program. Part-time tuition and fees vary according to course level, course load, degree level, and program. ***Payment plan:*** deferred payment. ***Waivers:*** senior citizens and employees or children of employees.

APPLYING

Options: electronic application, early admission, deferred entrance.

Required: high school transcript, minimum 2.0 GPA.

Application deadlines: rolling (freshmen), rolling (transfers).

Notification: continuous (freshmen), continuous (transfers).

CONTACT

Ms. Pamela Mennechey, Associate Vice President - Student Recruitment and Enrollment, Seminole State College of Florida, Sanford, FL 32773-6199. *Phone:* 407-708-2050. *Fax:* 407-708-2395. *E-mail:* admissions@scc-fl.edu.

Southeastern University

Lakeland, Florida

http://www.seu.edu/

- **Independent** comprehensive, founded 1935, affiliated with Assemblies of God
- **Suburban** 87-acre campus with easy access to Tampa, Orlando
- **Endowment** $8.9 million
- **Coed** 5,055 undergraduate students, 77% full-time, 57% women, 43% men
- **Minimally difficult** entrance level, 46% of applicants were admitted

UNDERGRAD STUDENTS

3,888 full-time, 1,167 part-time. Students come from 49 states and territories; 47 other countries; 37% are from out of state; 15% Black or African American, non-Hispanic/Latino; 19% Hispanic/Latino; 2% Asian, non-Hispanic/Latino; 0.6% Native Hawaiian or other Pacific Islander, non-Hispanic/Latino; 0.4% American Indian or Alaska Native, non-Hispanic/Latino; 0.1% Two or more races, non-Hispanic/Latino; 5% Race/ethnicity unknown; 2% international; 13% transferred in; 57% live on campus.

Freshmen:

Admission: 4,061 applied, 1,862 admitted, 1,071 enrolled. ***Average high school GPA:*** 3.23. ***Test scores:*** SAT critical reading scores over 500: 49%; SAT math scores over 500: 39%; SAT writing scores over 500: 39%; ACT scores over 18: 78%; SAT critical reading scores over 600: 13%;

SAT math scores over 600: 10%; SAT writing scores over 600: 11%; ACT scores over 24: 30%; SAT critical reading scores over 700: 2%; SAT math scores over 700: 1%; ACT scores over 30: 4%.

Retention: 70% of full-time freshmen returned.

FACULTY

Total: 414, 36% full-time, 39% with terminal degrees.

Student/faculty ratio: 20:1.

ACADEMICS

Calendar: semesters. *Degrees:* certificates, associate, bachelor's, master's, doctoral, and postbachelor's certificates.

Special study options: academic remediation for entering students, adult/continuing education programs, advanced placement credit, cooperative education, distance learning, double majors, honors programs, independent study, internships, off-campus study, part-time degree program, services for LD students, study abroad, summer session for credit. ***ROTC:*** Army (c).

Computers: 156 computers/terminals are available on campus for general student use. Students can access the following: campus intranet, computer help desk, free student e-mail accounts, online (class) grades, online (class) registration, online (class) schedules, network programs. Campuswide network is available. 100% of college-owned or -operated housing units are wired for high-speed Internet access. Wireless service is available via entire campus.

Library: Steelman Library. *Books:* 81,194 (physical), 169,763 (digital/electronic).

STUDENT LIFE

Housing options: on-campus residence required through sophomore year; men-only, women-only. Campus housing is university owned. Freshman campus housing is guaranteed.

Activities and organizations: drama/theater group, student-run newspaper, radio and television station, choral group.

Athletics Member NAIA. ***Intercollegiate sports:*** baseball M(s), basketball M(s)/W(s), cheerleading M/W, cross-country running M(s)/W(s), football M(s), golf M(s)/W(s), soccer M(s)/W(s), softball W(s), tennis M(s)/W(s), volleyball W(s), wrestling M(s). ***Intramural sports:*** basketball M/W, football M/W, soccer M/W, softball M/W, ultimate Frisbee M/W, volleyball M/W.

Campus security: 24-hour emergency response devices and patrols, late-night transport/escort service, controlled dormitory access.

Student services: health clinic, personal/psychological counseling.

COSTS & FINANCIAL AID

Costs (2017–18) ***Comprehensive fee:*** $33,610 includes full-time tuition ($23,160), mandatory fees ($1000), and room and board ($9450). Full-time tuition and fees vary according to class time, degree level, location, and reciprocity agreements. Part-time tuition: $965 per hour. Part-time tuition and fees vary according to class time, course load, degree level, location, and reciprocity agreements. ***Room and board:*** Room and board charges vary according to board plan and housing facility. ***Payment plan:*** installment. ***Waivers:*** employees or children of employees.

Financial Aid Of all full-time matriculated undergraduates who enrolled in 2016, 3,458 applied for aid, 3,047 were judged to have need, 375 had their need fully met. 75 Federal Work-Study jobs (averaging $2208). In 2016, 686 non-need-based awards were made. ***Average percent of need met:*** 63. ***Average financial aid package:*** $15,184. ***Average need-based loan:*** $3935. ***Average need-based gift aid:*** $6089. ***Average non-need-based aid:*** $9400. ***Average indebtedness upon graduation:*** $29,224.

APPLYING

Standardized Tests *Required:* SAT or ACT (for admission).

Options: electronic application, early admission, deferred entrance.

Application fee: $40.

Required: essay or personal statement, high school transcript, 2 letters of recommendation. ***Required for some:*** interview.

Application deadlines: 5/1 (freshmen), 7/1 (transfers).

Notification: 6/1 (freshmen), continuous (transfers).

CONTACT

Ms. Sarah Clark, Director of Admissions, Southeastern University, 1000 Longfellow Blvd, Lakeland, FL 33801. *Phone:* 863-667-5018. *Toll-free phone:* 800-500-8760. *E-mail:* admission@seu.edu.

Southern Technical College

Fort Myers, Florida

http://www.southerntech.edu/locations/ft-myers/

CONTACT

Ms. Tiffany Quinlan, Director of Admissions, Southern Technical College, 1685 Medical Lane, Fort Myers, FL 33907. *Phone:* 239-939-4766. *Toll-free phone:* 877-347-5492. *Fax:* 239-936-4040. *E-mail:* tquinlan@southerntech.edu.

Southern Technical College

Tampa, Florida

http://www.southerntech.edu/locations/tampa/

CONTACT

Admissions, Southern Technical College, 3910 Riga Boulevard, Tampa, FL 33619. *Phone:* 813-630-4401. *Toll-free phone:* 877-347-5492.

South Florida Bible College and Theological Seminary

Deerfield Beach, Florida

http://www.sfbc.edu/

CONTACT

South Florida Bible College and Theological Seminary, 1100 South Federal Highway, Deerfield Beach, FL 33441.

South Florida State College

Avon Park, Florida

http://www.southflorida.edu/

- **State-supported** primarily 2-year, founded 1965, part of Florida State College System
- **Rural** 228-acre campus with easy access to Tampa, St. Petersburg, Orlando
- **Endowment** $6.1 million
- **Coed** 2,722 undergraduate students, 35% full-time, 62% women, 38% men
- **Noncompetitive** entrance level, 80% of applicants were admitted

UNDERGRAD STUDENTS

945 full-time, 1,777 part-time. 3% are from out of state; 11% Black or African American, non-Hispanic/Latino; 35% Hispanic/Latino; 2% Asian, non-Hispanic/Latino; 0.3% Native Hawaiian or other Pacific Islander, non-Hispanic/Latino; 0.4% American Indian or Alaska Native, non-Hispanic/Latino; 3% Two or more races, non-Hispanic/Latino; 2% Race/ethnicity unknown; 1% international; 4% transferred in.

Freshmen:

Admission: 485 applied, 389 admitted, 440 enrolled. ***Average high school GPA:*** 3.

FACULTY

Total: 148, 41% full-time, 18% with terminal degrees.

Student/faculty ratio: 16:1.

ACADEMICS

Calendar: semesters. *Degrees:* certificates, diplomas, associate, and bachelor's.

Special study options: academic remediation for entering students, adult/continuing education programs, advanced placement credit, cooperative education, distance learning, English as a second language, independent study, internships, part-time degree program, services for LD students, summer session for credit.

Computers: 85 computers/terminals are available on campus for general student use. Students can access the following: campus intranet, computer help desk, free student e-mail accounts, online (class) grades, online (class) registration, online (class) schedules. Campuswide network is available. 100% of college-owned or -operated housing units are wired for high-speed Internet access. Wireless service is available via classrooms, computer centers, computer labs, learning centers, libraries, student centers.

Library: Library Services.

STUDENT LIFE
Housing options: Campus housing is provided by a third party.
Activities and organizations: Phi Theta Kappa, Phi Beta Lambda, Art Club, Anime and Gaming Club, Basketball Club.
Athletics Member NJCAA. ***Intercollegiate sports:*** baseball M(s), cross-country running W(s), softball W(s), volleyball W(s). ***Intramural sports:*** basketball M(c)/W(c), soccer M(c)/W(c).
Campus security: 24-hour emergency response devices and patrols, late-night transport/escort service.
Student services: personal/psychological counseling.

COSTS
Costs (2017–18) ***One-time required fee:*** $15. ***Tuition:*** state resident $2593 full-time, $105 per credit hour part-time; nonresident $11,087 full-time, $394 per credit hour part-time. Full-time tuition and fees vary according to course level, course load, degree level, and program. Part-time tuition and fees vary according to course level, course load, degree level, and program. ***Room and board:*** $5920; room only: $2000. ***Payment plan:*** installment. ***Waivers:*** employees or children of employees.

APPLYING
Options: electronic application, early admission, deferred entrance.
Application fee: $15.
Required: high school transcript.
Notification: continuous (freshmen).

CONTACT
Ms. Mary Puckorius, Admissions Coordinator, South Florida State College, 600 West College Drive, Avon Park, FL 33825. *Phone:* 863-784-7416.

South University
Royal Palm Beach, Florida
http://www.southuniversity.edu/west-palm-beach/

CONTACT
South University, University Centre, 9801 Belvedere Road, Royal Palm Beach, FL 33411. *Phone:* 561-273-6500. *Toll-free phone:* 866-629-2902.

South University
Tampa, Florida
http://www.southuniversity.edu/tampa/

CONTACT
South University, 4401 North Himes Avenue, Suite 175, Tampa, FL 33614. *Phone:* 813-393-3800. *Toll-free phone:* 800-846-1472.

State College of Florida Manatee-Sarasota
Bradenton, Florida
http://www.scf.edu/

- **State-supported** 4-year, founded 1957, part of Florida Community College System
- **Suburban** 100-acre campus with easy access to Tampa-St. Petersburg
- **Coed** 9,073 undergraduate students, 40% full-time, 61% women, 39% men
- **Noncompetitive** entrance level, 100% of applicants were admitted

UNDERGRAD STUDENTS
3,659 full-time, 5,414 part-time. Students come from 30 states and territories; 39 other countries; 4% are from out of state; 7% transferred in.

Freshmen:
Admission: 2,935 applied, 2,935 admitted, 1,601 enrolled. ***Test scores:*** SAT critical reading scores over 500: 25%; SAT math scores over 500: 26%; SAT writing scores over 500: 31%; ACT scores over 18: 57%; SAT math scores over 600: 4%; SAT writing scores over 600: 5%; ACT scores over 24: 16%; ACT scores over 30: 3%.

FACULTY
Total: 444, 36% full-time.

ACADEMICS
Calendar: semesters. *Degrees:* certificates, associate, and bachelor's.
Special study options: academic remediation for entering students, advanced placement credit, cooperative education, distance learning, double majors, English as a second language, external degree program, honors programs, independent study, part-time degree program, services for LD students, summer session for credit.
Computers: 1,000 computers/terminals are available on campus for general student use. Students can access the following: campus intranet, computer help desk, free student e-mail accounts, online (class) registration, online (class) schedules. Campuswide network is available. Wireless service is available via entire campus.
Library: Sara Harlee Library. *Books:* 129,690 (physical), 731,905 (digital/electronic); *Databases:* 140.

STUDENT LIFE
Housing options: college housing not available.
Activities and organizations: drama/theater group, student-run newspaper, choral group, Student Government Association, Phi Theta Kappa, American Chemical Society Student Affiliate, Campus Ministry, Medical Community Club.
Athletics Member NJCAA. ***Intercollegiate sports:*** baseball M(s), basketball M(s), softball W(s), volleyball W(s). ***Intramural sports:*** basketball M/W, softball M/W, volleyball M/W, weight lifting M/W.
Campus security: 24-hour emergency response devices and patrols, late-night transport/escort service.

COSTS & FINANCIAL AID
Costs (2016–17) ***One-time required fee:*** $40. ***Tuition:*** state resident $3074 full-time, $102 per credit part-time; nonresident $11,596 full-time, $387 per credit part-time. Full-time tuition and fees vary according to degree level. Part-time tuition and fees vary according to degree level. ***Payment plan:*** deferred payment. ***Waivers:*** employees or children of employees.
Financial Aid Of all full-time matriculated undergraduates who enrolled in 2015, 82 Federal Work-Study jobs (averaging $2800). ***Financial aid deadline:*** 8/15.

APPLYING
Options: electronic application, early admission.
Required: high school transcript.
Application deadlines: 8/20 (freshmen), 8/20 (transfers).
Notification: continuous (freshmen), continuous (transfers).

CONTACT
Ms. MariLynn Lewy, AVP of Student Services, State College of Florida Manatee-Sarasota, Bradenton, FL 34206. *Phone:* 941-752-5384. *Fax:* 941-727-6380. *E-mail:* lewym@scf.edu.

Stetson University
DeLand, Florida
http://www.stetson.edu/

- **Independent** comprehensive, founded 1883
- **Small-town** 159-acre campus with easy access to Orlando
- **Endowment** $208.9 million
- **Coed**
- **Moderately difficult** entrance level

FACULTY
Student/faculty ratio: 13:1.

ACADEMICS
Calendar: semesters. *Degrees:* bachelor's, master's, doctoral, and post-master's certificates.
Library: duPont-Ball Library plus 1 other. *Books:* 454,022 (physical), 1.6 million (digital/electronic); *Serial titles:* 311 (physical), 114,491 (digital/electronic); *Databases:* 130. Weekly public service hours: 99; students can reserve study rooms.

STUDENT LIFE
Housing options: on-campus residence required through junior year; coed, men-only, women-only. Campus housing is university owned and leased by the school. Freshman campus housing is guaranteed.

Activities and organizations: drama/theater group, student-run newspaper, radio station, choral group, Caribbean Student Association, Fellowship of Christian Athletes, Kaleidoscope (promotes inclusivity), Enactus (social action), Model United Nations, national fraternities, national sororities.

Athletics Member NCAA. All Division I.

Campus security: 24-hour emergency response devices and patrols, late-night transport/escort service, controlled dormitory access.

Student services: health clinic, personal/psychological counseling.

COSTS & FINANCIAL AID

Costs (2016–17) ***Comprehensive fee:*** $55,566 includes full-time tuition ($42,890), mandatory fees ($350), and room and board ($12,326). Part-time tuition: $4445 per course. Part-time tuition and fees vary according to course load. ***College room only:*** $7094. Room and board charges vary according to board plan and housing facility.

Financial Aid Of all full-time matriculated undergraduates who enrolled in 2016, 2,338 applied for aid, 2,104 were judged to have need, 404 had their need fully met. 558 Federal Work-Study jobs (averaging $2459). 69 state and other part-time jobs (averaging $3687). In 2016, 753 non-need-based awards were made. ***Average percent of need met:*** 74. ***Average financial aid package:*** $34,778. ***Average need-based loan:*** $4899. ***Average need-based gift aid:*** $28,073. ***Average non-need-based aid:*** $22,185. ***Average indebtedness upon graduation:*** $31,457.

APPLYING

Standardized Tests *Required for some:* SAT or ACT (for admission).

Options: electronic application, deferred entrance.

Application fee: $50.

Required: essay or personal statement, high school transcript, 1 letter of recommendation. ***Recommended:*** interview.

CONTACT

Director of Admissions, Stetson University, 421 N Woodland Boulevard, Unit 8378, DeLand, FL 32723. *Phone:* 386-822-7100. *Toll-free phone:* 800-688-0101. *Fax:* 386-822-7112. *E-mail:* admissions@stetson.edu.

Strayer University–Baymeadows Campus

Jacksonville, Florida

http://www.strayer.edu/florida/baymeadows/

CONTACT

Strayer University–Baymeadows Campus, 8375 Dix Ellis Trail, Suite 200, Jacksonville, FL 32256.

Strayer University–Brickell Campus

Miami, Florida

http://www.strayer.edu/florida/brickell/

CONTACT

Strayer University–Brickell Campus, 1201 Brickell Avenue, Suite 700, Miami, FL 33131.

Strayer University–Coral Springs Campus

Pompano Beach, Florida

http://www.strayer.edu/florida/coral-springs/

CONTACT

Strayer University–Coral Springs Campus, 5830 Coral Ridge Drive, Suite 300, Pompano Beach, FL 33076.

Strayer University–Doral Campus

Miami, Florida

http://www.strayer.edu/florida/doral/

CONTACT

Strayer University–Doral Campus, 11430 Northwest 20th Street, Suite 150, Miami, FL 33172.

Strayer University–Fort Lauderdale Campus

Fort Lauderdale, Florida

http://www.strayer.edu/florida/fort-lauderdale/

CONTACT

Strayer University–Fort Lauderdale Campus, 2307 West Broward Boulevard, Suite 100, Fort Lauderdale, FL 33312.

Strayer University–Maitland Campus

Maitland, Florida

http://www.strayer.edu/florida/maitland/

CONTACT

Strayer University–Maitland Campus, 850 Trafalgar Court, Suite 360, Maitland, FL 32751.

Strayer University–Miramar Campus

Miramar, Florida

http://www.strayer.edu/florida/miramar/

CONTACT

Strayer University–Miramar Campus, 15620 Southwest 29th Street, Miramar, FL 33027.

Strayer University–Orlando East Campus

Orlando, Florida

http://www.strayer.edu/florida/orlando-east/

CONTACT

Strayer University–Orlando East Campus, 2200 North Alafaya Trail, Suite 500, Orlando, FL 32826.

Strayer University–Palm Beach Gardens Campus

West Palm Beach, Florida

http://www.strayer.edu/florida/palm-beach-gardens/

CONTACT

Strayer University–Palm Beach Gardens Campus, 11025 RCA Center Drive, Suite 200, West Palm Beach, FL 33410.

Strayer University–Sand Lake Campus

Orlando, Florida

http://www.strayer.edu/florida/sand-lake/

CONTACT

Strayer University–Sand Lake Campus, 8541 South Park Circle, Building 900, Orlando, FL 32819.

Strayer University–Tampa East Campus

Tampa, Florida

http://www.strayer.edu/florida/tampa-east/

CONTACT

Strayer University–Tampa East Campus, 5650 Breckenridge Park Drive, Suite 300, Tampa, FL 33610.

Strayer University–Tampa Westshore Campus

Tampa, Florida

http://www.strayer.edu/florida/tampa-westshore/

CONTACT
Strayer University–Tampa Westshore Campus, 4902 Eisenhower Boulevard, Suite 100, Tampa, FL 33634.

Tallahassee Community College

Tallahassee, Florida

http://www.tcc.fl.edu/

- **State and locally supported** primarily 2-year, founded 1966, part of Florida College System
- **Suburban** 214-acre campus
- **Endowment** $10.0 million
- **Coed** 12,200 undergraduate students, 47% full-time, 53% women, 47% men
- **Noncompetitive** entrance level

UNDERGRAD STUDENTS
5,744 full-time, 6,456 part-time. Students come from 24 states and territories; 79 other countries; 3% are from out of state; 30% Black or African American, non-Hispanic/Latino; 12% Hispanic/Latino; 1% Asian, non-Hispanic/Latino; 0.1% Native Hawaiian or other Pacific Islander, non-Hispanic/Latino; 0.2% American Indian or Alaska Native, non-Hispanic/Latino; 4% Two or more races, non-Hispanic/Latino; 2% Race/ethnicity unknown; 1% international; 8% transferred in.

Freshmen:
Admission: 2,270 admitted, 2,270 enrolled.
Retention: 58% of full-time freshmen returned.

FACULTY
Total: 568, 33% full-time, 72% with terminal degrees.
Student/faculty ratio: 21:1.

ACADEMICS
Calendar: semesters. *Degrees:* certificates, associate, and bachelor's.
Special study options: academic remediation for entering students, accelerated degree program, adult/continuing education programs, advanced placement credit, distance learning, English as a second language, external degree program, honors programs, independent study, off-campus study, part-time degree program, services for LD students, study abroad, summer session for credit. ***ROTC:*** Army (c), Navy (c), Air Force (c).
Computers: 1,733 computers/terminals are available on campus for general student use. Students can access the following: campus intranet, computer help desk, free student e-mail accounts, online (class) grades, online (class) registration, online (class) schedules. Campuswide network is available. Wireless service is available via entire campus.
Library: Tallahassee Community College Library. Weekly public service hours: 68; students can reserve study rooms.

STUDENT LIFE
Housing options: college housing not available.
Activities and organizations: drama/theater group, student-run newspaper, choral group, Student Government Association, International Student Organization, Phi Theta Kappa, Model United Nations, Honors Council.
Athletics Member NJCAA. ***Intercollegiate sports:*** baseball M(s), basketball M(s)/W(s), softball W(s). ***Intramural sports:*** basketball M/W, football M/W, soccer M/W, softball M/W, volleyball M/W.
Campus security: 24-hour emergency response devices and patrols, late-night transport/escort service.
Student services: personal/psychological counseling.

COSTS & FINANCIAL AID
Costs (2016–17) ***Tuition:*** state resident $3025 full-time, $101 per credit hour part-time; nonresident $11,288 full-time, $387 per credit hour part-time. Full-time tuition and fees vary according to course load. Part-time tuition and fees vary according to course load. ***Payment plans:*** installment, deferred payment. ***Waivers:*** employees or children of employees.
Financial Aid Of all full-time matriculated undergraduates who enrolled in 2015, 4,359 applied for aid, 3,384 were judged to have need. 110 Federal Work-Study jobs (averaging $2172). ***Average financial aid package:*** $3507. ***Average need-based gift aid:*** $3733.

APPLYING
Options: electronic application, early admission, deferred entrance.
Required: high school transcript.
Application deadlines: 8/1 (freshmen), 8/1 (transfers).

CONTACT
Student Success Center, Tallahassee Community College, 444 Appleyard Drive, Tallahassee, FL 32304-2895. *Phone:* 850-201-8555.
E-mail: admissions@tcc.fl.edu.

Talmudic University

Miami Beach, Florida

http://www.talmudicu.edu/

CONTACT
Rabbi Yeshaya Greenberg, Dean of Students, Talmudic University, 4000 Alton Road, Miami Beach, FL 33140. *Phone:* 305-534-7050.
Fax: 305-534-8444. *E-mail:* yandtg@gmail.com.

Trinity Baptist College

Jacksonville, Florida

http://www.tbc.edu/

- **Independent Baptist** comprehensive, founded 1974
- **Urban** 148-acre campus with easy access to Jacksonville
- **Coed** 268 undergraduate students
- **Moderately difficult** entrance level, 51% of applicants were admitted

UNDERGRAD STUDENTS
Students come from 21 states and territories; 4 other countries; 23% are from out of state.

Freshmen:
Admission: 350 applied, 179 admitted.

ACADEMICS
Calendar: semesters. *Degrees:* associate, bachelor's, and master's.
Special study options: academic remediation for entering students, accelerated degree program, adult/continuing education programs, advanced placement credit, distance learning, double majors, independent study, internships, part-time degree program, services for LD students, summer session for credit.
Computers: 21 computers/terminals are available on campus for general student use. Students can access the following: campus intranet, computer help desk, free student e-mail accounts, online (class) grades, online (class) registration, online (class) schedules. Campuswide network is available. Wireless service is available via entire campus.

STUDENT LIFE
Housing options: on-campus residence required through junior year; men-only, women-only. Campus housing is university owned. Freshman campus housing is guaranteed.
Activities and organizations: drama/theater group, student-run newspaper, choral group.
Athletics Member NCCAA. ***Intercollegiate sports:*** baseball M, basketball M/W, cheerleading W, soccer M/W, volleyball W. ***Intramural sports:*** baseball M, basketball M/W, football M, softball M/W.
Campus security: 24-hour emergency response devices and patrols, controlled dormitory access.
Student services: health clinic, personal/psychological counseling.

COSTS & FINANCIAL AID
Costs (2017–18) ***Comprehensive fee:*** $18,040 includes full-time tuition ($10,490), mandatory fees ($1150), and room and board ($6400). Full-time tuition and fees vary according to course load, location, and program. Part-time tuition: $438 per credit hour. Part-time tuition and fees vary according to course load, location, and program. ***College room only:***

$3163. Room and board charges vary according to board plan and housing facility. ***Waivers:*** children of alumni and employees or children of employees.

Financial Aid ***Financial aid deadline:*** 4/15.

APPLYING

Standardized Tests *Required for some:* SAT or ACT (for admission).

Options: electronic application, early admission.

Application fee: $35.

Required: essay or personal statement, high school transcript, 2 letters of recommendation. ***Required for some:*** interview.

Application deadlines: rolling (freshmen), rolling (transfers).

Notification: continuous until 8/15 (freshmen), continuous until 8/15 (transfers).

CONTACT

Melissa Gibson, Trinity Baptist College, 800 Hammond Blvd, Jacksonville, FL 32219. *Phone:* 904-596-2307. *Toll-free phone:* 800-786-2206. *E-mail:* mgibson@tbc.edu.

Trinity College of Florida

Trinity, Florida

http://www.trinitycollege.edu/

- **Independent nondenominational** 4-year, founded 1932
- **Small-town** 40-acre campus with easy access to Tampa
- **Endowment** $713,306
- **Coed** 202 undergraduate students, 83% full-time, 43% women, 57% men
- **Noncompetitive** entrance level, 71% of applicants were admitted

UNDERGRAD STUDENTS

168 full-time, 34 part-time. Students come from 19 states and territories; 2 other countries; 10% are from out of state; 29% Black or African American, non-Hispanic/Latino; 17% Hispanic/Latino; 1% Asian, non-Hispanic/Latino; 0.5% Two or more races, non-Hispanic/Latino; 9% Race/ethnicity unknown; 1% international; 16% transferred in; 29% live on campus.

Freshmen:

Admission: 75 applied, 53 admitted, 26 enrolled. ***Average high school GPA:*** 2.98. ***Test scores:*** SAT critical reading scores over 500: 22%; SAT math scores over 500: 17%; SAT writing scores over 500: 17%; ACT scores over 18: 48%; SAT math scores over 600: 6%; ACT scores over 24: 10%; ACT scores over 30: 5%.

Retention: 54% of full-time freshmen returned.

FACULTY

Total: 25, 32% full-time, 40% with terminal degrees.

Student/faculty ratio: 9:1.

ACADEMICS

Calendar: semesters. *Degrees:* certificates, associate, and bachelor's.

Special study options: academic remediation for entering students, accelerated degree program, adult/continuing education programs, advanced placement credit, cooperative education, distance learning, double majors, honors programs, independent study, off-campus study, part-time degree program, services for LD students, summer session for credit.

Computers: 17 computers/terminals and 144 ports are available on campus for general student use. Students can access the following: computer help desk, free student e-mail accounts, online (class) grades, online (class) registration. Campuswide network is available. 100% of college-owned or -operated housing units are wired for high-speed Internet access. Wireless service is available via entire campus.

Library: Raymond H. Center, M.D. Library. *Books:* 33,116 (physical), 165,300 (digital/electronic); *Serial titles:* 38 (physical); *Databases:* 9. Weekly public service hours: 60.

STUDENT LIFE

Housing options: men-only, women-only, special housing for students with disabilities. Campus housing is university owned and leased by the school. Freshman campus housing is guaranteed.

Activities and organizations: choral group, SGA, GCMF, Prayer Group, Trinity Against Trafficking.

Athletics Member NCCAA. ***Intercollegiate sports:*** basketball M/W, soccer M, volleyball W.

Campus security: student patrols.

Student services: personal/psychological counseling.

COSTS & FINANCIAL AID

Costs (2017–18) ***Comprehensive fee:*** $22,140 includes full-time tuition ($14,850), mandatory fees ($840), and room and board ($6450). Full-time tuition and fees vary according to course load and program. Part-time tuition: $495 per credit hour. Part-time tuition and fees vary according to course load and program. ***Required fees:*** $420 per term part-time. ***Payment plan:*** installment. ***Waivers:*** senior citizens and employees or children of employees.

Financial Aid Of all full-time matriculated undergraduates who enrolled in 2016, 154 applied for aid, 144 were judged to have need, 46 had their need fully met. 27 Federal Work-Study jobs (averaging $2599). 1 state and other part-time job (averaging $3622). In 2016, 8 non-need-based awards were made. ***Average percent of need met:*** 74. ***Average financial aid package:*** $13,874. ***Average need-based loan:*** $9138. ***Average need-based gift aid:*** $5348. ***Average non-need-based aid:*** $3262. ***Average indebtedness upon graduation:*** $21,510.

APPLYING

Standardized Tests *Required:* SAT or ACT (for admission).

Options: electronic application, deferred entrance.

Application fee: $35.

Required: essay or personal statement, high school transcript, 2 letters of recommendation. ***Required for some:*** interview. ***Recommended:*** minimum 2.2 GPA.

Application deadlines: 7/31 (freshmen), 7/31 (transfers).

Notification: continuous (freshmen), continuous (out-of-state freshmen), continuous (transfers).

CONTACT

Mr. Alton Shady, Admissions Representative, Trinity College of Florida, 2430 Welbilt Boulevard, Trinity, FL 34655. *Phone:* 727-376-6911 Ext. 309. *Toll-free phone:* 800-388-0869. *Fax:* 727-569-1410. *E-mail:* ashady@trinitycollege.edu.

University of Central Florida

Orlando, Florida

http://www.ucf.edu/

- **State-supported** university, founded 1963, part of State University System of Florida
- **Suburban** 1415-acre campus with easy access to Orlando
- **Endowment** $144.9 million
- **Coed** 55,776 undergraduate students, 69% full-time, 55% women, 45% men
- **Moderately difficult** entrance level, 50% of applicants were admitted

UNDERGRAD STUDENTS

38,454 full-time, 17,322 part-time. Students come from 50 states and territories; 141 other countries; 6% are from out of state; 11% Black or African American, non-Hispanic/Latino; 25% Hispanic/Latino; 6% Asian, non-Hispanic/Latino; 0.2% Native Hawaiian or other Pacific Islander, non-Hispanic/Latino; 0.2% American Indian or Alaska Native, non-Hispanic/Latino; 4% Two or more races, non-Hispanic/Latino; 0.6% Race/ethnicity unknown; 1% international; 12% transferred in; 19% live on campus.

Freshmen:

Admission: 34,886 applied, 17,441 admitted, 6,403 enrolled. ***Average high school GPA:*** 3.92. ***Test scores:*** SAT critical reading scores over 500: 92%; SAT math scores over 500: 92%; SAT writing scores over 500: 81%; ACT scores over 18: 100%; SAT critical reading scores over 600: 44%; SAT math scores over 600: 48%; SAT writing scores over 600: 29%; ACT scores over 24: 78%; SAT critical reading scores over 700: 8%; SAT math scores over 700: 8%; SAT writing scores over 700: 4%; ACT scores over 30: 17%.

Retention: 89% of full-time freshmen returned.

FACULTY
Total: 2,012, 75% full-time, 70% with terminal degrees.

Student/faculty ratio: 30:1.

ACADEMICS
Calendar: semesters. *Degrees:* certificates, associate, bachelor's, master's, doctoral, post-master's, and postbachelor's certificates.

Special study options: accelerated degree program, adult/continuing education programs, advanced placement credit, cooperative education, distance learning, double majors, English as a second language, freshman honors college, honors programs, independent study, internships, off-campus study, part-time degree program, services for LD students, study abroad, summer session for credit. ***ROTC:*** Army (b), Air Force (b).

Unusual degree programs: 3-2 engineering; nursing; history, communicative sciences and disorders, computer science, law.

Computers: 4,154 computers/terminals and 500 ports are available on campus for general student use. Students can access the following: campus intranet, computer help desk, free student e-mail accounts, online (class) grades, online (class) registration, online (class) schedules. Campuswide network is available. 100% of college-owned or -operated housing units are wired for high-speed Internet access. Wireless service is available via entire campus.

Library: University Library plus 1 other. *Books:* 1.5 million (physical), 156,190 (digital/electronic); *Serial titles:* 838 (physical), 52,337 (digital/electronic); *Databases:* 365. Weekly public service hours: 106; students can reserve study rooms.

STUDENT LIFE
Housing options: coed, men-only, women-only, special housing for students with disabilities. Campus housing is university owned and is provided by a third party. Freshman applicants given priority for college housing.

Activities and organizations: drama/theater group, student-run newspaper, radio and television station, choral group, marching band, Volunteer UCF, RWC Intramural Sports, Fraternity and Sorority Life, Multicultural Student Center and Organizations, Knight-thon Dance Marathon, national fraternities, national sororities.

Athletics Member NCAA. All Division I except football (Division I-A). ***Intercollegiate sports:*** baseball M(s), basketball M(s)/W(s), crew W(s), cross-country running W(s), golf M(s)/W(s), soccer M(s)/W(s), softball W(s), tennis M(s)/W(s), track and field W(s), volleyball W(s). ***Intramural sports:*** badminton M/W, baseball M, basketball M/W, bowling M(c)/W(c), crew M(c), equestrian sports M(c)/W(c), fencing M(c), golf M/W, ice hockey M(c), lacrosse M(c)/W(c), racquetball M/W, rock climbing M(c)/W(c), rugby M(c)/W(c), soccer M/W, softball W(c), swimming and diving M(c)/W(c), table tennis M(c)/W(c), tennis M/W, ultimate Frisbee M(c)/W(c), volleyball M/W, water polo M(c)/W(c), wrestling M(c)/W(c).

Campus security: 24-hour emergency response devices and patrols, late-night transport/escort service, controlled dormitory access.

Student services: health clinic, personal/psychological counseling, women's center, legal services.

COSTS & FINANCIAL AID
Costs (2016–17) ***Tuition:*** state resident $6368 full-time, $212 per credit hour part-time; nonresident $22,467 full-time, $749 per credit hour part-time. Full-time tuition and fees vary according to course load. Part-time tuition and fees vary according to course load. ***Room and board:*** $9554; room only: $5400. Room and board charges vary according to board plan and housing facility. ***Payment plans:*** tuition prepayment, deferred payment. ***Waivers:*** senior citizens and employees or children of employees.

Financial Aid Of all full-time matriculated undergraduates who enrolled in 2015, 30,093 applied for aid, 23,776 were judged to have need, 1,646 had their need fully met. 719 Federal Work-Study jobs (averaging $3529). In 2015, 1524 non-need-based awards were made. ***Average percent of need met:*** 56. ***Average financial aid package:*** $8744. ***Average need-based loan:*** $4667. ***Average need-based gift aid:*** $5656. ***Average non-need-based aid:*** $4180. ***Average indebtedness upon graduation:*** $21,911. ***Financial aid deadline:*** 6/30.

APPLYING
Standardized Tests *Required:* SAT or ACT (for admission).

Options: electronic application, early admission.

Application fee: $30.

Required: high school transcript, minimum 2.5 GPA. ***Recommended:*** essay or personal statement.

Application deadlines: 5/1 (freshmen), 7/1 (transfers).

Notification: continuous (freshmen), continuous (transfers).

CONTACT

Dr. Gordon Chavis Jr., Associate Vice President, Undergraduate Admissions, Student Financial Assistance and Outreach Programs, University of Central Florida, PO Box 160111, Orlando, FL 32816-0111. *Phone:* 407-823-3000. *Fax:* 407-823-5625. *E-mail:* admission@ucf.edu.

See previous page for display ad and page 1548 for the College Close-Up.

University of Florida

Gainesville, Florida

http://www.ufl.edu/

- **State-supported** university, founded 1853, part of Board of Trustees
- **Suburban** 2000-acre campus with easy access to Jacksonville
- **Endowment** $1.6 billion
- **Coed** 34,554 undergraduate students, 90% full-time, 55% women, 45% men
- **Very difficult** entrance level, 46% of applicants were admitted

UNDERGRAD STUDENTS

31,014 full-time, 3,540 part-time. Students come from 51 states and territories; 127 other countries; 6% are from out of state; 6% Black or African American, non-Hispanic/Latino; 21% Hispanic/Latino; 8% Asian, non-Hispanic/Latino; 0.5% Native Hawaiian or other Pacific Islander, non-Hispanic/Latino; 0.2% American Indian or Alaska Native, non-Hispanic/Latino; 3% Two or more races, non-Hispanic/Latino; 3% Race/ethnicity unknown; 2% international; 5% transferred in; 24% live on campus.

Freshmen:

Admission: 30,118 applied, 13,835 admitted, 6,833 enrolled. ***Test scores:*** SAT critical reading scores over 500: 98%; SAT math scores over 500: 98%; SAT writing scores over 500: 97%; ACT scores over 18: 100%; SAT critical reading scores over 600: 72%; SAT math scores over 600: 76%; SAT writing scores over 600: 69%; ACT scores over 24: 97%; SAT critical reading scores over 700: 21%; SAT math scores over 700: 26%; SAT writing scores over 700: 18%; ACT scores over 30: 51%.

ACADEMICS

Calendar: semesters. *Degrees:* certificates, associate, bachelor's, master's, doctoral, post-master's, and postbachelor's certificates.

Special study options: accelerated degree program, adult/continuing education programs, advanced placement credit, cooperative education, distance learning, double majors, English as a second language, external degree program, honors programs, independent study, internships, off-campus study, part-time degree program, services for LD students, student-designed majors, study abroad, summer session for credit. ***ROTC:*** Army (b), Navy (b), Air Force (b).

Unusual degree programs: 3-2 business administration; engineering; forestry.

Computers: 1,685 computers/terminals and 245 ports are available on campus for general student use. Students can access the following: campus intranet, computer help desk, free student e-mail accounts, online (class) grades, online (class) registration, online (class) schedules, course management system. Campuswide network is available. 100% of college-owned or -operated housing units are wired for high-speed Internet access. Wireless service is available via entire campus.

Library: George A. Smathers Libraries plus 7 others. *Books:* 4.3 million (physical), 1.4 million (digital/electronic); *Serial titles:* 4,357 (physical), 162,542 (digital/electronic); *Databases:* 1,574. Weekly public service hours: 168; study areas open 24 hours, 5-7 days a week; students can reserve study rooms.

STUDENT LIFE

Housing options: coed, special housing for students with disabilities. Campus housing is university owned and is provided by a third party. Freshman applicants given priority for college housing.

Activities and organizations: drama/theater group, student-run newspaper, radio and television station, choral group, marching band, VISA - Volunteers for International Student Affairs, Fellowship of Christian Athletes, Black Student Union, Hispanic Student Association, Asian American Student Union, national fraternities, national sororities.

Athletics Member NCAA. All Division I. ***Intercollegiate sports:*** baseball M(s), basketball M(s)/W(s), bowling M(c)/W(c), cheerleading M(s)/W(s), cross-country running M(s)/W(s), football M(s), golf M(s)/W(s), gymnastics W(s), lacrosse W(s), racquetball M(c)/W(c), soccer M/W(s), softball W(s), swimming and diving M(s)/W(s), table tennis M(c)/W(c), tennis M(s)/W(s), track and field M(s)/W(s), ultimate Frisbee M(c)/W(c), volleyball M/W(s). ***Intramural sports:*** archery M(c)/W(c), badminton M(c)/W(c), baseball M(c), basketball M/W, bowling M/W, cheerleading W(c), crew M(c)/W(c), cross-country running M(c)/W(c), equestrian sports M(c)/W(c), fencing M(c)/W(c), field hockey M(c)/W(c), football M/W, golf M/W, gymnastics W(c), ice hockey M(c), lacrosse M(c)/W(c), racquetball M/W, rock climbing M(c)/W(c), rugby M(c)/W(c), sailing M(c)/W(c), sand volleyball M/W, soccer M/W, softball M/W, swimming and diving M/W, table tennis M/W, tennis M/W, track and field M/W, ultimate Frisbee M/W, volleyball M/W, water polo M(c)/W(c), weight lifting M(c)/W(c), wrestling M(c)/W(c).

Campus security: 24-hour emergency response devices and patrols, student patrols, late-night transport/escort service, controlled dormitory access, crime and rape prevention programs.

Student services: health clinic, personal/psychological counseling, legal services.

COSTS & FINANCIAL AID

Costs (2016–17) ***Tuition:*** state resident $4477 full-time, $149 per credit hour part-time; nonresident $26,755 full-time, $856 per credit hour part-time. ***Required fees:*** $1904 full-time. ***Room and board:*** $9910; room only: $5440.

Financial Aid Of all full-time matriculated undergraduates who enrolled in 2015, 22,004 applied for aid, 16,068 were judged to have need, 4,018 had their need fully met. 1,027 Federal Work-Study jobs (averaging $2478). 4,720 state and other part-time jobs (averaging $1817). In 2015, 1707 non-need-based awards were made. ***Average percent of need met:*** 99. ***Average financial aid package:*** $12,494. ***Average need-based loan:*** $4540. ***Average need-based gift aid:*** $7083. ***Average non-need-based aid:*** $2531. ***Average indebtedness upon graduation:*** $21,645.

APPLYING

Standardized Tests *Required:* SAT or ACT (for admission). *Required for some:* SAT Subject Tests (for admission).

Options: electronic application.

Application fee: $30.

Required: essay or personal statement, high school transcript.

Application deadlines: 11/1 (freshmen), rolling (transfers).

Notification: 2/12 (freshmen), continuous (transfers).

CONTACT

Office of Admissions, University of Florida, PO Box 114000, Gainesville, FL 32611-4000. *Phone:* 352-392-1365.

University of Fort Lauderdale

Lauderhill, Florida

http://uftl.edu/

CONTACT

University of Fort Lauderdale, 4093 NW 16th Street, Lauderhill, FL 33313.

University of Miami

Coral Gables, Florida

http://www.miami.edu/

- **Independent** university, founded 1925
- **Suburban** 239-acre campus with easy access to Miami
- **Coed** 11,122 undergraduate students, 94% full-time, 51% women, 49% men
- **Very difficult** entrance level, 38% of applicants were admitted

UNDERGRAD STUDENTS

10,481 full-time, 641 part-time. 57% are from out of state; 8% Black or African American, non-Hispanic/Latino; 22% Hispanic/Latino; 6% Asian, non-Hispanic/Latino; 0.1% Native Hawaiian or other Pacific Islander, non-Hispanic/Latino; 0.1% American Indian or Alaska Native, non-Hispanic/Latino; 3% Two or more races, non-Hispanic/Latino; 4% Race/ethnicity unknown; 14% international; 5% transferred in; 37% live on campus.

Freshmen:
Admission: 33,415 applied, 12,624 admitted, 2,080 enrolled. ***Average high school GPA:*** 3.6. ***Test scores:*** SAT critical reading scores over 500: 98%; SAT math scores over 500: 97%; SAT writing scores over 500: 94%; ACT scores over 18: 100%; SAT critical reading scores over 600: 74%; SAT math scores over 600: 81%; SAT writing scores over 600: 69%; ACT scores over 24: 98%; SAT critical reading scores over 700: 21%; SAT math scores over 700: 29%; SAT writing scores over 700: 19%; ACT scores over 30: 60%.
Retention: 92% of full-time freshmen returned.

FACULTY
Total: 1,549, 73% full-time, 78% with terminal degrees.
Student/faculty ratio: 12:1.

ACADEMICS
Calendar: semesters. *Degrees:* certificates, bachelor's, master's, doctoral, post-master's, and postbachelor's certificates.
Special study options: academic remediation for entering students, accelerated degree program, advanced placement credit, cooperative education, distance learning, double majors, English as a second language, honors programs, independent study, internships, off-campus study, part-time degree program, services for LD students, student-designed majors, study abroad, summer session for credit. ***ROTC:*** Army (b), Air Force (b).
Computers: Students can access the following: campus intranet, computer help desk, free student e-mail accounts, online (class) grades, online (class) registration, online (class) schedules, online bill payment, online housing registration. Campuswide network is available. 100% of college-owned or -operated housing units are wired for high-speed Internet access. Wireless service is available via entire campus.
Library: Otto G. Richter Library.

STUDENT LIFE
Housing options: on-campus residence required for freshman year; coed, special housing for students with disabilities. Campus housing is university owned. Freshman campus housing is guaranteed.
Activities and organizations: drama/theater group, student-run newspaper, radio and television station, choral group, marching band, Association of Greek Letter Organizations, Federation of Cuban Students, Association of Commuter Students, United Black Students, Chinese Students and Scholars Association, national fraternities, national sororities.
Athletics Member NCAA. All Division I except football (Division I-A). ***Intercollegiate sports:*** baseball M(s), basketball M(s)/W(s), cheerleading M/W, crew W(s), cross-country running M(s)/W(s), golf W(s), soccer W(s), swimming and diving M(s)/W(s), tennis M(s)/W(s), track and field M(s)/W(s), volleyball W(s). ***Intramural sports:*** badminton M(c)/W(c), baseball M(c), basketball M/W, cross-country running M(c)/W(c), equestrian sports M(c)/W(c), fencing M(c)/W(c), field hockey W(c), football M/W, golf M(c)/W(c), ice hockey M(c), lacrosse M(c)/W(c), racquetball M(c)/W(c), rock climbing M(c)/W(c), rugby M(c)/W(c), sailing M(c)/W(c), soccer M(c)/W(c), softball M/W, squash M(c)/W(c), swimming and diving M(c)/W(c), table tennis M(c)/W(c), tennis M(c)/W(c), ultimate Frisbee M(c)/W(c), volleyball M(c)/W(c), water polo M(c)/W(c), weight lifting M/W, wrestling M(c)/W(c).
Campus security: 24-hour emergency response devices and patrols, student patrols, late-night transport/escort service, controlled dormitory access, programs, seminars, activities, classes and publications are available to students, faculty, staff, parents and friends.
Student services: health clinic, personal/psychological counseling, women's center.

COSTS & FINANCIAL AID
Costs (2016–17) ***Comprehensive fee:*** $60,314 includes full-time tuition ($45,600), mandatory fees ($1404), and room and board ($13,310). Full-time tuition and fees vary according to course load. Part-time tuition: $1900 per credit hour. Part-time tuition and fees vary according to course load and program. ***College room only:*** $7720. Room and board charges vary according to board plan and housing facility. ***Payment plan:*** installment. ***Waivers:*** employees or children of employees.
Financial Aid Of all full-time matriculated undergraduates who enrolled in 2016, 5,247 applied for aid, 4,521 were judged to have need, 4,164 had their need fully met. In 2016, 1052 non-need-based awards were made. ***Average percent of need met:*** 90. ***Average financial aid package:*** $40,549. ***Average need-based loan:*** $4527. ***Average need-based gift aid:*** $10,616. ***Average non-need-based aid:*** $18,480. ***Average indebtedness upon graduation:*** $21,500. ***Financial aid deadline:*** 4/15.

APPLYING
Standardized Tests *Required:* SAT or ACT (for admission). *Required for some:* SAT and SAT Subject Tests or ACT (for admission).
Options: electronic application, early admission, early decision, early action, deferred entrance.
Application fee: $70.
Required: essay or personal statement, 1 letter of recommendation. ***Required for some:*** high school transcript, interview, college transcript(s) and statement of good standing from prior institution(s).
Application deadlines: 1/1 (freshmen), 7/1 (transfers), 11/1 (early action).
Early decision deadline: 11/1 (for plan 1), 1/1 (for plan 2).
Notification: 4/15 (freshmen), 4/1 (transfers), 12/20 (early decision plan 1), 2/16 (early decision plan 2), 1/20 (early action).

CONTACT
Ms. Deanna Lynn Voss, Executive Director of Undergraduate Admission, University of Miami, PO Box 248025, Coral Gables, FL 33124. *Phone:* 305-284-4323. *Fax:* 305-284-6605. *E-mail:* admission@miami.edu.

University of North Florida
Jacksonville, Florida
http://www.unf.edu/

- **State-supported** comprehensive, founded 1965, part of State University System of Florida
- **Urban** 1300-acre campus with easy access to Jacksonville, FL
- **Endowment** $96.5 million
- **Coed** 13,846 undergraduate students, 70% full-time, 56% women, 44% men
- **Moderately difficult** entrance level, 65% of applicants were admitted

UNDERGRAD STUDENTS
9,702 full-time, 4,144 part-time. Students come from 46 states and territories; 55 other countries; 4% are from out of state; 10% Black or African American, non-Hispanic/Latino; 11% Hispanic/Latino; 4% Asian, non-Hispanic/Latino; 0.1% Native Hawaiian or other Pacific Islander, non-Hispanic/Latino; 0.1% American Indian or Alaska Native, non-Hispanic/Latino; 5% Two or more races, non-Hispanic/Latino; 0.4% Race/ethnicity unknown; 2% international; 12% transferred in; 25% live on campus.

Freshmen:
Admission: 11,346 applied, 7,322 admitted, 1,978 enrolled. ***Average high school GPA:*** 3.82. ***Test scores:*** SAT critical reading scores over 500: 89%; SAT math scores over 500: 85%; SAT writing scores over 500: 73%; ACT scores over 18: 100%; SAT critical reading scores over 600: 36%; SAT math scores over 600: 29%; SAT writing scores over 600: 20%; ACT scores over 24: 48%; SAT critical reading scores over 700: 6%; SAT math scores over 700: 2%; SAT writing scores over 700: 1%; ACT scores over 30: 7%.
Retention: 80% of full-time freshmen returned.

FACULTY
Total: 890, 61% full-time, 60% with terminal degrees.
Student/faculty ratio: 19:1.

ACADEMICS
Calendar: semesters. *Degrees:* associate, bachelor's, master's, doctoral, post-master's, and postbachelor's certificates (doctoral degree in education only).
Special study options: accelerated degree program, adult/continuing education programs, advanced placement credit, cooperative education, distance learning, double majors, English as a second language, honors

programs, independent study, internships, off-campus study, part-time degree program, services for LD students, study abroad, summer session for credit. ***ROTC:*** Army (b), Navy (c).

Unusual degree programs: 3-2 computer science.

Computers: 700 computers/terminals are available on campus for general student use. Students can access the following: campus intranet, computer help desk, free student e-mail accounts, online (class) grades, online (class) registration, online (class) schedules, reduced prices for students on certain business and design software. Campuswide network is available. 100% of college-owned or -operated housing units are wired for high-speed Internet access. Wireless service is available via entire campus.

Library: Thomas G. Carpenter Library. *Books:* 860,144 (physical), 269,885 (digital/electronic); *Serial titles:* 16,185 (physical), 44,772 (digital/electronic); *Databases:* 271. Weekly public service hours: 137; students can reserve study rooms.

STUDENT LIFE

Housing options: coed, special housing for students with disabilities. Campus housing is university owned. Freshman campus housing is guaranteed.

Activities and organizations: drama/theater group, student-run newspaper, radio and television station, choral group, Student Government Association, African American Student Association, International Student Association, Filipino Student Association, National Education Association, national fraternities, national sororities.

Athletics Member NCAA. All Division I. ***Intercollegiate sports:*** baseball M(s), basketball M(s)/W(s), cross-country running M(s)/W(s), golf M(s)/W, soccer M(s)/W(s), softball W(s), swimming and diving W(s), tennis M(s)/W(s), track and field M(s)/W(s), volleyball W(s). ***Intramural sports:*** badminton M/W, basketball M/W, bowling M/W, fencing M(c)/W(c), football M/W, golf M/W, lacrosse M(c)/W(c), racquetball M(c)/W(c), rugby M(c), sailing M(c)/W(c), soccer M/W, swimming and diving M/W, table tennis M/W, track and field M/W, ultimate Frisbee M(c)/W(c), volleyball M(c)/W(c).

Campus security: 24-hour emergency response devices and patrols, late-night transport/escort service, controlled dormitory access, electronic parking lot security.

Student services: health clinic, personal/psychological counseling, women's center.

COSTS & FINANCIAL AID

Costs (2016–17) ***Tuition:*** state resident $4281 full-time, $143 per credit hour part-time; nonresident $17,999 full-time, $600 per credit hour part-time. Full-time tuition and fees vary according to course load. Part-time tuition and fees vary according to course load. ***Required fees:*** $2113 full-time, $70 per credit hour part-time. ***Room and board:*** $9772. Room and board charges vary according to board plan and housing facility. ***Payment plan:*** installment. ***Waivers:*** senior citizens and employees or children of employees.

Financial Aid Of all full-time matriculated undergraduates who enrolled in 2016, 6,673 applied for aid, 5,121 were judged to have need, 607 had their need fully met. 138 Federal Work-Study jobs (averaging $3418). In 2016, 1355 non-need-based awards were made. ***Average percent of need met:*** 89. ***Average financial aid package:*** $8050. ***Average need-based loan:*** $4236. ***Average need-based gift aid:*** $5850. ***Average non-need-based aid:*** $3331. ***Average indebtedness upon graduation:*** $18,685.

APPLYING

Standardized Tests *Required:* SAT or ACT (for admission).

Options: electronic application, deferred entrance.

Application fee: $30.

Required: high school transcript, minimum 2.5 GPA, minimum SAT scores of 460 critical reading and math, 440 writing or minimum ACT scores of 19 reading and math, 18 ACT English/writing. ***Required for some:*** essay or personal statement. ***Recommended:*** minimum 3.0 GPA.

Application deadlines: rolling (freshmen), 5/10 (transfers).

Notification: continuous (freshmen), continuous (transfers).

CONTACT

Ms. Karen Lucas, Director of Admissions, University of North Florida, 1 UNF Drive, Jacksonville, FL 32224. *Phone:* 904-620-5252. *Fax:* 904-620-2014. *E-mail:* admissions@unf.edu.

University of Phoenix–Central Florida Campus

Orlando, Florida

http://www.phoenix.edu/

CONTACT

Marc Booker, Sr. Director, Office of Admissions and Evaluation, University of Phoenix–Central Florida Campus, 4035 South Riverpoint Parkway, Mail Stop CF-L101, Phoenix, AZ 85040. *Phone:* 602-557-4609. *Toll-free phone:* 866-766-0766. *Fax:* 480-643-1156.

University of Phoenix–North Florida Campus

Jacksonville, Florida

http://www.phoenix.edu/

CONTACT

Marc Booker, Sr. Director, Office of Admissions and Evaluation, University of Phoenix–North Florida Campus, 4035 South Riverpoint Parkway, Mail Stop CF-L101, Phoenix, AZ 85040. *Phone:* 602-557-4609. *Toll-free phone:* 866-766-0766. *Fax:* 480-643-1156.

University of Phoenix–South Florida Campus

Miramar, Florida

http://www.phoenix.edu/

CONTACT

Marc Booker, Sr. Director, Office of Admissions and Evaluation, University of Phoenix–South Florida Campus, 4035 South Riverpoint Parkway, Mail Stop CF-L101, Phoenix, AZ 85040. *Phone:* 602-557-4609. *Toll-free phone:* 866-766-0766. *Fax:* 480-643-1156.

University of South Florida

Tampa, Florida

http://www.usf.edu/

- **State-supported** university, founded 1956, part of State University System of Florida
- **Urban** 1562-acre campus
- **Endowment** $417.4 million
- **Coed** 31,111 undergraduate students, 77% full-time, 55% women, 45% men
- **Moderately difficult** entrance level, 45% of applicants were admitted

UNDERGRAD STUDENTS

24,088 full-time, 7,023 part-time. Students come from 50 states and territories; 139 other countries; 5% are from out of state; 11% Black or African American, non-Hispanic/Latino; 21% Hispanic/Latino; 6% Asian, non-Hispanic/Latino; 0.2% Native Hawaiian or other Pacific Islander, non-Hispanic/Latino; 0.2% American Indian or Alaska Native, non-Hispanic/Latino; 4% Two or more races, non-Hispanic/Latino; 1% Race/ethnicity unknown; 6% international; 11% transferred in; 21% live on campus.

Freshmen:

Admission: 30,386 applied, 13,563 admitted, 4,133 enrolled. ***Average high school GPA:*** 3.94. ***Test scores:*** SAT critical reading scores over 500: 91%; SAT math scores over 500: 93%; SAT writing scores over 500: 83%; ACT scores over 18: 100%; SAT critical reading scores over 600: 40%; SAT math scores over 600: 48%; SAT writing scores over 600: 30%; ACT scores over 24: 82%; SAT critical reading scores over 700: 6%; SAT math scores over 700: 8%; SAT writing scores over 700: 3%; ACT scores over 30: 16%.

Retention: 88% of full-time freshmen returned.

FACULTY

Total: 1,734, 70% full-time, 69% with terminal degrees.

Student/faculty ratio: 24:1.

ACADEMICS
Calendar: semesters. *Degrees:* associate, bachelor's, master's, and doctoral.

Special study options: academic remediation for entering students, accelerated degree program, adult/continuing education programs, advanced placement credit, cooperative education, distance learning, double majors, freshman honors college, honors programs, internships, off-campus study, part-time degree program, services for LD students, study abroad, summer session for credit. ***ROTC:*** Army (b), Navy (b), Air Force (b).

Computers: 825 computers/terminals and 2,000 ports are available on campus for general student use. Students can access the following: campus intranet, computer help desk, free student e-mail accounts, online (class) grades, online (class) registration, online (class) schedules. Campuswide network is available. 100% of college-owned or -operated housing units are wired for high-speed Internet access. Wireless service is available via entire campus.

Library: Tampa Campus Library plus 5 others. *Books:* 1.8 million (physical), 652,513 (digital/electronic); *Serial titles:* 537 (physical), 58,975 (digital/electronic); *Databases:* 930. Weekly public service hours: 116; study areas open 24 hours, 5-7 days a week; students can reserve study rooms.

STUDENT LIFE
Housing options: on-campus residence required for freshman year; coed, women-only, cooperative, special housing for students with disabilities. Campus housing is university owned. Freshman campus housing is guaranteed.

Activities and organizations: drama/theater group, student-run newspaper, radio and television station, choral group, marching band, Student Government, Campus Activities Board, USF Ambassadors, Student Admissions Representatives, national fraternities, national sororities.

Athletics Member NCAA. All Division I except football (Division I-A). ***Intercollegiate sports:*** badminton M(c)/W(c), baseball M(s), basketball W(s), bowling M(c)/W(c), crew M(c)/W(c), cross-country running M(s)/W(s), fencing M(c)/W(c), golf M(s)/W(s), gymnastics M(c)/W(c), rugby M(c)/W(c), soccer M(s)/W(s), softball W(s), tennis M(s)/W(s), track and field M(s)/W(s), volleyball M(c)/W(s). ***Intramural sports:*** badminton M/W, basketball M/W, bowling M/W, football M, golf M/W, racquetball M/W, soccer M/W, swimming and diving M/W, tennis M/W, track and field M/W, volleyball M/W, weight lifting M.

Campus security: 24-hour emergency response devices and patrols, student patrols, late-night transport/escort service, controlled dormitory access, residence hall lobby personnel 8 pm to 6 am.

Student services: health clinic, personal/psychological counseling, women's center, legal services.

COSTS & FINANCIAL AID
Costs (2017–18) ***Tuition:*** state resident $6336 full-time, $211 per credit hour part-time; nonresident $17,250 full-time, $575 per credit hour part-time. ***Required fees:*** $74 full-time. ***Room and board:*** $9700. ***Payment plan:*** deferred payment.

Financial Aid Of all full-time matriculated undergraduates who enrolled in 2015, 21,860 applied for aid, 18,151 were judged to have need, 1,808 had their need fully met. 773 Federal Work-Study jobs (averaging $3213). 286 state and other part-time jobs (averaging $1611). In 2015, 2480 non-need-based awards were made. ***Average percent of need met:*** 59. ***Average financial aid package:*** $11,240. ***Average need-based loan:*** $6579. ***Average need-based gift aid:*** $7202. ***Average non-need-based aid:*** $2684. ***Average indebtedness upon graduation:*** $22,276.

APPLYING
Standardized Tests *Required:* SAT or ACT (for admission).

Options: electronic application, early admission, deferred entrance.

Application fee: $30.

Required: minimum 2.0 GPA. ***Required for some:*** high school transcript, 1 letter of recommendation.

Application deadlines: 3/1 (freshmen), 3/1 (transfers).

Notification: continuous (freshmen), continuous (transfers).

CONTACT
University of South Florida, Office of Undergraduate Admissions, 4202 East Fowler Avenue, Tampa, FL 33620-9951. *Phone:* 813-974-3350. *Fax:* 813-974-9689. *E-mail:* admissions@usf.edu.

University of South Florida, St. Petersburg

St. Petersburg, Florida

http://www.stpt.usf.edu/

- **State-supported** comprehensive, founded 1965, part of University of South Florida System
- **Urban** 48-acre campus with easy access to Tampa
- **Endowment** $19.1 million
- **Coed** 4,203 undergraduate students, 65% full-time, 62% women, 38% men

UNDERGRAD STUDENTS
2,735 full-time, 1,468 part-time. Students come from 26 states and territories; 28 other countries; 3% are from out of state; 8% Black or African American, non-Hispanic/Latino; 16% Hispanic/Latino; 4% Asian, non-Hispanic/Latino; 0.2% Native Hawaiian or other Pacific Islander, non-Hispanic/Latino; 0.2% American Indian or Alaska Native, non-Hispanic/Latino; 4% Two or more races, non-Hispanic/Latino; 2% Race/ethnicity unknown; 0.7% international; 4% transferred in; 16% live on campus.

Freshmen:
Admission: 648 enrolled.

Retention: 70% of full-time freshmen returned.

FACULTY
Total: 301, 52% full-time, 58% with terminal degrees.

Student/faculty ratio: 16:1.

ACADEMICS
Calendar: semesters. *Degrees:* certificates, bachelor's, and master's.

Special study options: distance learning, double majors, freshman honors college, honors programs, independent study, internships, services for LD students, study abroad, summer session for credit. ***ROTC:*** Army (b).

Computers: 125 computers/terminals and 350 ports are available on campus for general student use. Students can access the following: computer help desk, free student e-mail accounts, online (class) grades, online (class) registration, online (class) schedules. Campuswide network is available. 100% of college-owned or -operated housing units are wired for high-speed Internet access. Wireless service is available via entire campus.

Library: Nelson Poynter Memorial Library. *Books:* 199,210 (physical), 652,513 (digital/electronic); *Serial titles:* 7,817 (physical), 57,570 (digital/electronic); *Databases:* 930. Weekly public service hours: 79; students can reserve study rooms.

STUDENT LIFE
Housing options: on-campus residence required for freshman year; coed. Campus housing is university owned and is provided by a third party. Freshman applicants given priority for college housing.

Activities and organizations: drama/theater group, student-run newspaper, radio station, Student Government, Harborside Activities Board, Delta Sigma Pi, Multicultural Activities Council, HERD Step Team.

Athletics ***Intercollegiate sports:*** baseball M(c), sailing W(c). ***Intramural sports:*** basketball M/W, football M/W, sailing M/W, soccer M/W, volleyball M/W.

Campus security: 24-hour emergency response devices and patrols, late-night transport/escort service, controlled dormitory access.

Student services: health clinic, personal/psychological counseling.

COSTS
Costs (2017–18) ***Tuition:*** state resident $5820 full-time, $194 per credit hour part-time; nonresident $16,736 full-time, $558 per credit hour part-time. ***Required fees:*** $10 full-time. ***Room and board:*** $9250. Room and board charges vary according to board plan and housing facility. ***Payment plan:*** installment. ***Waivers:*** employees or children of employees.

APPLYING

Standardized Tests *Required:* SAT or ACT (for admission).

Required: high school transcript, minimum 2.5 GPA.

CONTACT

Ms. Holly Kickliter, Director, Enrollment Services, University of South Florida, St. Petersburg, 140 Seventh Avenue South, St. Petersburg, FL 33701. *Phone:* 727-873-4142. *Fax:* 727-873-4525. *E-mail:* admissions@usfsp.edu.

University of South Florida Sarasota-Manatee

Sarasota, Florida

http://www.usfsm.edu/

- **State-supported** comprehensive, founded 1956, part of University of South Florida System
- **Urban** 31-acre campus with easy access to Tampa
- **Endowment** $9.2 million
- **Coed** 1,873 undergraduate students, 54% full-time, 60% women, 40% men

UNDERGRAD STUDENTS

1,016 full-time, 857 part-time. Students come from 23 states and territories; 11 other countries; 3% are from out of state; 5% Black or African American, non-Hispanic/Latino; 14% Hispanic/Latino; 3% Asian, non-Hispanic/Latino; 0.1% Native Hawaiian or other Pacific Islander, non-Hispanic/Latino; 0.4% American Indian or Alaska Native, non-Hispanic/Latino; 2% Two or more races, non-Hispanic/Latino; 2% Race/ethnicity unknown; 2% international; 18% transferred in.

Freshmen:

Admission: 87 enrolled. ***Average high school GPA:*** 3.75. ***Test scores:*** SAT critical reading scores over 500: 82%; SAT math scores over 500: 65%; ACT scores over 18: 98%; SAT critical reading scores over 600: 33%; SAT math scores over 600: 19%; ACT scores over 24: 53%; SAT math scores over 700: 1%; ACT scores over 30: 4%.

Retention: 84% of full-time freshmen returned.

FACULTY

Total: 140, 58% full-time, 66% with terminal degrees.

Student/faculty ratio: 14:1.

ACADEMICS

Calendar: semesters. *Degrees:* certificates, associate, bachelor's, master's, and post-master's certificates.

Special study options: advanced placement credit, distance learning, double majors, honors programs, independent study, internships, part-time degree program, services for LD students, study abroad, summer session for credit. ***ROTC:*** Army (c), Navy (c), Air Force (c).

Computers: 46 computers/terminals are available on campus for general student use. Students can access the following: campus intranet, computer help desk, free student e-mail accounts, online (class) grades, online (class) registration, online (class) schedules. Campuswide network is available. Wireless service is available via entire campus.

Library: USF Libraries. *Books:* 1,266 (physical), 652,513 (digital/electronic); *Serial titles:* 139 (physical), 58,975 (digital/electronic); *Databases:* 930. Weekly public service hours: 96; students can reserve study rooms.

STUDENT LIFE

Housing options: college housing not available.

Activities and organizations: Box Office Bulls, Criminology Club, Gamers' Club, Recreational Events Club, Student Veteran Society.

Campus security: 24-hour emergency response devices and patrols, late-night transport/escort service.

Student services: health clinic, personal/psychological counseling.

COSTS

Costs (2016–17) ***Tuition:*** state resident $4206 full-time, $186 per credit hour part-time; nonresident $15,120 full-time, $549 per credit hour part-time. Full-time tuition and fees vary according to course load and program. Part-time tuition and fees vary according to course load and program. ***Required fees:*** $1381 full-time, $5 per term part-time. ***Waivers:*** employees or children of employees.

APPLYING

Standardized Tests *Required:* SAT or ACT (for admission). *Recommended:* SAT Subject Tests (for admission).

Required: high school transcript, minimum 3.3 GPA. ***Required for some:*** minimum 3.3 GPA, interview. ***Recommended:*** essay or personal statement, minimum 3.3 GPA, 2 letters of recommendation.

CONTACT

Mr. Andy Telatovich, Director, Admissions, University of South Florida Sarasota-Manatee, 8350 N. Tamiami Trail, C107, Sarasota, FL 34232. *Phone:* 941-359-4330. *Fax:* 941-359-4236. *E-mail:* atelatovich@sar.usf.edu.

The University of Tampa

Tampa, Florida

http://www.ut.edu/

- **Independent** comprehensive, founded 1931
- **Urban** 110-acre campus with easy access to Tampa-St. Petersburg, Clearwater
- **Coed** 7,382 undergraduate students, 97% full-time, 58% women, 42% men
- **Moderately difficult** entrance level, 48% of applicants were admitted

UNDERGRAD STUDENTS

7,124 full-time, 258 part-time. Students come from 50 states and territories; 140 other countries; 66% are from out of state; 5% Black or African American, non-Hispanic/Latino; 12% Hispanic/Latino; 2% Asian, non-Hispanic/Latino; 0.2% American Indian or Alaska Native, non-Hispanic/Latino; 3% Two or more races, non-Hispanic/Latino; 7% Race/ethnicity unknown; 11% international; 8% transferred in; 52% live on campus.

Freshmen:

Admission: 19,947 applied, 9,634 admitted, 1,877 enrolled. ***Average high school GPA:*** 3.4. ***Test scores:*** SAT critical reading scores over 500: 74%; SAT math scores over 500: 78%; SAT writing scores over 500: 69%; ACT scores over 18: 99%; SAT critical reading scores over 600: 18%; SAT math scores over 600: 21%; SAT writing scores over 600: 16%; ACT scores over 24: 62%; SAT critical reading scores over 700: 1%; SAT math scores over 700: 2%; SAT writing scores over 700: 1%; ACT scores over 30: 9%.

Retention: 75% of full-time freshmen returned.

FACULTY

Total: 732, 42% full-time, 58% with terminal degrees.

Student/faculty ratio: 17:1.

ACADEMICS

Calendar: semesters. *Degrees:* certificates, bachelor's, master's, and post-master's certificates.

Special study options: academic remediation for entering students, adult/continuing education programs, advanced placement credit, cooperative education, double majors, English as a second language, honors programs, independent study, internships, part-time degree program, services for LD students, study abroad, summer session for credit. ***ROTC:*** Army (b), Navy (c), Air Force (c).

Unusual degree programs: 3-2 chemistry/business administration.

Computers: 802 computers/terminals and 8,000 ports are available on campus for general student use. Students can access the following: campus intranet, computer help desk, free student e-mail accounts, online (class) grades, online (class) registration, online (class) schedules. Campuswide network is available. 100% of college-owned or -operated housing units are wired for high-speed Internet access. Wireless service is available via entire campus.

Library: Macdonald Kelce Library. *Books:* 195,067 (physical), 145,016 (digital/electronic); *Serial titles:* 1,214 (physical), 190,560 (digital/electronic); *Databases:* 214. Weekly public service hours: 100; students can reserve study rooms.

STUDENT LIFE

Housing options: coed, special housing for students with disabilities. Campus housing is university owned and leased by the school. Freshman applicants given priority for college housing.

Activities and organizations: drama/theater group, student-run newspaper, radio and television station, choral group, Greek Life, student government, PEACE (volunteer organization), Student Productions, Minaret, national fraternities, national sororities.

Athletics Member NCAA. All Division II except lacrosse (Division I), track and field (Division I). ***Intercollegiate sports:*** baseball M(s), basketball M(s)/W(s), crew W(s), cross-country running M(s)/W(s), golf M(s)/W(s), lacrosse M(s)/W(s), soccer M(s)/W(s), softball W(s), swimming and diving M(s)/W(s), tennis W(s), track and field M(s)/W(s), volleyball W(s). ***Intramural sports:*** basketball M/W, cheerleading W(c), crew M(c), equestrian sports W(c), field hockey M(c)/W(c), football M/W, golf M/W, ice hockey M(c), soccer M/W, softball M/W, swimming and diving M/W, tennis M(c)/W(c), ultimate Frisbee M/W, volleyball M/W.

Campus security: 24-hour emergency response devices and patrols, student patrols, late-night transport/escort service, controlled dormitory access.

Student services: health clinic, personal/psychological counseling, women's center.

COSTS & FINANCIAL AID

Costs (2016–17) ***One-time required fee:*** $85. ***Comprehensive fee:*** $37,936 includes full-time tuition ($25,858), mandatory fees ($1882), and room and board ($10,196). Full-time tuition and fees vary according to class time, course load, and program. Part-time tuition: $550 per credit hour. Part-time tuition and fees vary according to class time, course load, and program. ***Required fees:*** $40 per term part-time. ***College room only:*** $5384. Room and board charges vary according to board plan and housing facility. ***Payment plan:*** installment. ***Waivers:*** employees or children of employees.

Financial Aid Of all full-time matriculated undergraduates who enrolled in 2016, 5,133 applied for aid, 4,222 were judged to have need, 363 had their need fully met. 308 Federal Work-Study jobs (averaging $2000). 212 state and other part-time jobs (averaging $2000). In 2016, 2053 non-need-based awards were made. ***Average percent of need met:*** 61. ***Average financial aid package:*** $17,011. ***Average need-based loan:*** $4358. ***Average need-based gift aid:*** $13,377. ***Average non-need-based aid:*** $7885. ***Average indebtedness upon graduation:*** $31,448.

APPLYING

Standardized Tests *Required:* SAT or ACT (for admission).

Options: electronic application, early admission, early action, deferred entrance.

Application fee: $40.

Required: essay or personal statement, high school transcript, minimum 2.0 GPA. ***Required for some:*** 1 letter of recommendation. ***Recommended:*** interview.

Application deadlines: rolling (freshmen), rolling (transfers), 11/15 (early action).

Notification: continuous until 10/1 (freshmen), continuous (transfers), 12/15 (early action).

CONTACT

Mr. Dennis Nostrand, Vice President for Enrollment, The University of Tampa, 401 West Kennedy Boulevard, Tampa, FL 33606-1480. *Phone:* 813-257-1808. *Toll-free phone:* 888-646-2738 (in-state); 888-MINARET (out-of-state). *Fax:* 813-258-7398. *E-mail:* admissions@ut.edu.

University of West Florida

Pensacola, Florida

http://www.uwf.edu/

- **State-supported** comprehensive, founded 1963, part of State University System of Florida
- **Suburban** 1600-acre campus
- **Endowment** $62.8 million
- **Coed**
- **Moderately difficult** entrance level

FACULTY

Student/faculty ratio: 21:1.

ACADEMICS

Calendar: semesters. *Degrees:* associate, bachelor's, master's, doctoral, and post-master's certificates.

Library: John C. Pace Library plus 2 others. *Books:* 834,298 (physical), 163,625 (digital/electronic); *Serial titles:* 288 (physical), 80,370 (digital/electronic); *Databases:* 167. Weekly public service hours: 107.

STUDENT LIFE

Housing options: coed. Campus housing is university owned.

Activities and organizations: drama/theater group, student-run newspaper, choral group, National Society of Leadership and Service, Baptist Collegiate Ministries, Alpha Chi Omega, Alpha Delta Pi, Student Alumni Association, national fraternities, national sororities.

Athletics Member NCAA. All Division II.

Campus security: 24-hour emergency response devices and patrols, student patrols, late-night transport/escort service, controlled dormitory access.

Student services: health clinic, personal/psychological counseling.

COSTS & FINANCIAL AID

Costs (2016–17) ***Tuition:*** state resident $6360 full-time, $212 per credit hour part-time; nonresident $19,260 full-time, $642 per credit hour part-time. Full-time tuition and fees vary according to location and reciprocity agreements. Part-time tuition and fees vary according to location and reciprocity agreements. ***Room and board:*** $9580; room only: $5800. Room and board charges vary according to board plan, housing facility, and student level. ***Payment plans:*** tuition prepayment, deferred payment.

Financial Aid Of all full-time matriculated undergraduates who enrolled in 2014, 5,843 applied for aid, 4,881 were judged to have need, 566 had their need fully met. 241 Federal Work-Study jobs (averaging $1027). In 2014, 453 non-need-based awards were made. ***Average percent of need met:*** 46. ***Average financial aid package:*** $8411. ***Average need-based loan:*** $4097. ***Average need-based gift aid:*** $6184. ***Average non-need-based aid:*** $2257.

APPLYING

Standardized Tests *Required:* SAT or ACT (for admission), SAT and SAT Subject Tests or ACT (for admission).

Options: electronic application, early admission, deferred entrance.

Application fee: $30.

Required: high school transcript, minimum 2.5 GPA.

CONTACT

Katie Condon, Director of Admissions, University of West Florida, Admissions, 11000 University Parkway, Pensacola, FL 32514. *Phone:* 850-474-2230. *Toll-free phone:* 800-263-1074. *Fax:* 850-474-3460. *E-mail:* admissions@uwf.edu.

Valencia College

Orlando, Florida

http://valenciacollege.edu/

- **State-supported** 4-year, founded 1967, part of Florida College System
- **Urban** 654-acre campus with easy access to Orlando
- **Endowment** $63.7 million
- **Coed** 44,515 undergraduate students, 36% full-time, 56% women, 44% men
- 99% of applicants were admitted

UNDERGRAD STUDENTS

16,176 full-time, 28,339 part-time. Students come from 20 states and territories; 122 other countries; 3% are from out of state; 16% Black or African American, non-Hispanic/Latino; 35% Hispanic/Latino; 4% Asian, non-Hispanic/Latino; 0.4% Native Hawaiian or other Pacific Islander, non-Hispanic/Latino; 0.3% American Indian or Alaska Native, non-Hispanic/Latino; 2% Two or more races, non-Hispanic/Latino; 11% Race/ethnicity unknown; 3% international; 7% transferred in.

Freshmen:

Admission: 10,778 applied, 10,640 admitted, 8,874 enrolled.

FACULTY

Total: 1,808, 31% full-time, 23% with terminal degrees.

Student/faculty ratio: 25:1.

ACADEMICS

Calendar: semesters. *Degrees:* certificates, diplomas, associate, and bachelor's.

Special study options: academic remediation for entering students, accelerated degree program, adult/continuing education programs, advanced placement credit, cooperative education, distance learning, double majors, English as a second language, external degree program, freshman honors college, honors programs, independent study, internships, part-time degree program, services for LD students, study abroad, summer session for credit. ***ROTC:*** Army (c), Navy (c).

Computers: Students can access the following: campus intranet, computer help desk, free student e-mail accounts, online (class) grades, online (class) registration, online (class) schedules, education plans, &"what-if"; degree plan, view and print unofficial transcripts, order official transcripts, career exploration. Campuswide network is available. Wireless service is available via entire campus.

Library: Learning Resources Center plus 4 others. *Books:* 176,369 (physical), 174,255 (digital/electronic); *Serial titles:* 15,416 (physical), 34,167 (digital/electronic); *Databases:* 210. Weekly public service hours: 85; students can reserve study rooms.

STUDENT LIFE

Housing options: college housing not available.

Activities and organizations: drama/theater group, student-run newspaper, choral group, National Society for Leadership and Success, PTK, Honors, Gay-Straight Alliance, Valencia Hospitality.

Athletics ***Intramural sports:*** basketball M/W, soccer M/W, volleyball M/W.

Campus security: 24-hour emergency response devices and patrols, late-night transport/escort service, video monitoring for certain areas.

Student services: personal/psychological counseling.

COSTS & FINANCIAL AID

Costs (2017–18) ***Tuition:*** state resident $2474 full-time, $103 per credit hour part-time; nonresident $9383 full-time, $391 per credit hour part-time. Full-time tuition and fees vary according to degree level. Part-time tuition and fees vary according to degree level. ***Payment plan:*** installment. ***Waivers:*** senior citizens and employees or children of employees.

Financial Aid Of all full-time matriculated undergraduates who enrolled in 2010, 21,366 applied for aid, 17,532 were judged to have need, 485 had their need fully met. 242 Federal Work-Study jobs (averaging $2608). 27 state and other part-time jobs (averaging $2738). In 2010, 93 non-need-based awards were made. ***Average percent of need met:*** 46. ***Average financial aid package:*** $7383. ***Average need-based loan:*** $3242. ***Average need-based gift aid:*** $3430. ***Average non-need-based aid:*** $642.

APPLYING

Options: electronic application, early admission, deferred entrance.

Application fee: $35.

Required for some: high school transcript, professional license for some allied health bachelors programs.

Application deadlines: rolling (freshmen), rolling (transfers).

CONTACT

Dr. Linda K. Herlocker, Assistant Vice President of Admissions and Records, Valencia College, West Campus, MC 4-8, 1800 S. Kirkman Rd, SSB 104-D, Orlando, FL 32811-2302. *Phone:* 407-582-1511. *Fax:* 407-582-1866. *E-mail:* lherlocker@valenciacollege.edu.

Warner University

Lake Wales, Florida

http://www.warner.edu/

CONTACT

Mr. Jason Roe, Director of Admissions, Warner University, Warner Southern Center, 13895 Highway 27, Lake Wales, FL 33859. *Phone:* 863-638-7212 Ext. 7213. *Toll-free phone:* 800-309-9563. *Fax:* 863-638-1472. *E-mail:* admissions@warner.edu.

Webber International University

Babson Park, Florida

http://www.webber.edu/

- **Independent** comprehensive, founded 1927
- **Small-town** 110-acre campus with easy access to Orlando
- **Coed** 654 undergraduate students, 95% full-time, 31% women, 69% men
- **Moderately difficult** entrance level, 50% of applicants were admitted

UNDERGRAD STUDENTS

620 full-time, 34 part-time. Students come from 24 states and territories; 37 other countries; 13% are from out of state; 26% Black or African American, non-Hispanic/Latino; 14% Hispanic/Latino; 0.2% Asian, non-Hispanic/Latino; 0.5% Native Hawaiian or other Pacific Islander, non-Hispanic/Latino; 0.3% American Indian or Alaska Native, non-Hispanic/Latino; 22% international; 11% transferred in; 53% live on campus.

Freshmen:

Admission: 713 applied, 354 admitted, 177 enrolled. ***Average high school GPA:*** 2.83. ***Test scores:*** SAT critical reading scores over 500: 23%; SAT math scores over 500: 36%; ACT scores over 18: 73%; SAT critical reading scores over 600: 4%; SAT math scores over 600: 13%; ACT scores over 24: 7%; SAT math scores over 700: 1%.

Retention: 43% of full-time freshmen returned.

FACULTY

Total: 41, 49% full-time, 54% with terminal degrees.

Student/faculty ratio: 23:1.

ACADEMICS

Calendar: semesters. *Degrees:* associate, bachelor's, and master's.

Special study options: academic remediation for entering students, accelerated degree program, adult/continuing education programs, advanced placement credit, cooperative education, distance learning, double majors, English as a second language, honors programs, internships, part-time degree program, services for LD students, study abroad, summer session for credit.

Computers: 92 computers/terminals are available on campus for general student use. Students can access the following: campus intranet, computer help desk, free student e-mail accounts, online (class) grades, online (class) registration, online (class) schedules. Campuswide network is available. 100% of college-owned or -operated housing units are wired for high-speed Internet access. Wireless service is available via entire campus.

Library: Grace and Roger Babson Library. *Books:* 1,041 (physical); *Databases:* 127. Weekly public service hours: 70; students can reserve study rooms.

STUDENT LIFE

Housing options: on-campus residence required for freshman year; coed, men-only, women-only. Campus housing is university owned. Freshman campus housing is guaranteed.

Activities and organizations: student-run newspaper, marching band, Student Leadership Association, Phi Beta Lambda, Society of International Students, Fellowship of Christian Athletes, Rotaract.

Athletics Member NAIA. ***Intercollegiate sports:*** baseball M(s), basketball M(s)/W(s), bowling M(s)/W(s), cheerleading M(s)/W(s), cross-country running M(s)/W(s), football M(s), golf M(s)/W(s), sand volleyball M(s)/W(s), soccer M(s)/W(s), softball W(s), tennis M(s)/W(s), track and field M(s)/W(s), triathlon M(s)/W(s), volleyball M(s)/W(s).

Campus security: 24-hour emergency response devices and patrols, late-night transport/escort service, controlled dormitory access.

Student services: health clinic, personal/psychological counseling.

COSTS & FINANCIAL AID

Costs (2017–18) ***Comprehensive fee:*** $34,052 includes full-time tuition ($22,770), mandatory fees ($2588), and room and board ($8694). Full-time tuition and fees vary according to class time, course load, and program. Part-time tuition: $335 per credit hour. Part-time tuition and fees vary according to class time, course load, and program. ***College room only:*** $5512. Room and board charges vary according to board plan, gender, and housing facility. ***Payment plan:*** installment. ***Waivers:*** children of alumni, adult students, senior citizens, and employees or children of employees.

Financial Aid Of all full-time matriculated undergraduates who enrolled in 2016, 475 applied for aid, 456 were judged to have need, 35 had their need fully met. 35 Federal Work-Study jobs (averaging $59,636). 40 state and other part-time jobs (averaging $49,866). In 2016, 131 non-need-based awards were made. ***Average percent of need met:*** 60. ***Average financial aid package:*** $19,825. ***Average need-based loan:*** $4208. ***Average need-based gift aid:*** $16,287. ***Average non-need-based aid:*** $10,851. ***Average indebtedness upon graduation:*** $25,135. ***Financial aid deadline:*** 8/1.

APPLYING

Standardized Tests *Required for some:* SAT or ACT (for admission).

Options: electronic application.

Application fee: $35.

Required: high school transcript, minimum 2.0 GPA. ***Required for some:*** interview. ***Recommended:*** essay or personal statement, letters of recommendation.

Application deadlines: 8/1 (freshmen), 8/1 (transfers), rolling (early action).

Early decision deadline: rolling (for plan 1), rolling (for plan 2).

Notification: continuous (freshmen), continuous (transfers), rolling (early decision plan 1), rolling (early decision plan 2), rolling (early action).

CONTACT

Office of Admissions, Webber International University, PO Box 96, Babson Park, FL 33827. *Phone:* 863-638-2910. *Toll-free phone:* 800-741-1844. *Fax:* 863-638-1591. *E-mail:* admissions@webber.edu.

West Coast University

Doral, Florida

http://westcoastuniversity.edu/

CONTACT

West Coast University, 9250 NW 36th Street, Doral, FL 33178.

Yeshiva Gedolah Rabbinical College

Miami Beach, Florida

CONTACT

Yeshiva Gedolah Rabbinical College, 1140 Alton Road, Miami Beach, FL 33139.

GEORGIA

Abraham Baldwin Agricultural College

Tifton, Georgia

http://www.abac.edu/

CONTACT

Mrs. Donna Webb, Director of Enrollment Services, Abraham Baldwin Agricultural College, Box 4, 2802 Moore Highway, Tifton, GA 31793-2601. *Phone:* 229-391-5004. *Toll-free phone:* 800-733-3653. *Fax:* 229-391-5002. *E-mail:* dwebb@abac.edu.

Agnes Scott College

Decatur, Georgia

http://www.agnesscott.edu/

- **Independent** 4-year, founded 1889, affiliated with Presbyterian Church (U.S.A.)
- **Urban** 100-acre campus with easy access to Atlanta
- **Endowment** $241.2 million
- **Women only** 927 undergraduate students, 99% full-time
- **Moderately difficult** entrance level, 65% of applicants were admitted

UNDERGRAD STUDENTS

917 full-time, 10 part-time. Students come from 44 states and territories; 34 other countries; 52% are from out of state; 30% Black or African American, non-Hispanic/Latino; 10% Hispanic/Latino; 8% Asian, non-Hispanic/Latino; 0.1% Native Hawaiian or other Pacific Islander, non-Hispanic/Latino; 0.2% American Indian or Alaska Native, non-Hispanic/Latino; 6% Two or more races, non-Hispanic/Latino; 2% Race/ethnicity unknown; 9% international; 1% transferred in; 86% live on campus.

Freshmen:

Admission: 1,399 applied, 905 admitted, 272 enrolled. ***Average high school GPA:*** 3.83. ***Test scores:*** SAT critical reading scores over 500: 93%; SAT math scores over 500: 87%; SAT writing scores over 500: 93%; ACT scores over 18: 100%; SAT critical reading scores over 600: 59%; SAT math scores over 600: 38%; SAT writing scores over 600: 53%; ACT scores over 24: 81%; SAT critical reading scores over 700: 18%; SAT math scores over 700: 9%; SAT writing scores over 700: 9%; ACT scores over 30: 26%.

Retention: 84% of full-time freshmen returned.

FACULTY

Total: 113, 69% full-time, 85% with terminal degrees.

Student/faculty ratio: 10:1.

ACADEMICS

Calendar: semesters. *Degree:* bachelor's.

Special study options: accelerated degree program, adult/continuing education programs, advanced placement credit, distance learning, double majors, independent study, internships, off-campus study, part-time degree program, services for LD students, student-designed majors, study abroad, summer session for credit. ***ROTC:*** Army (c), Air Force (c).

Unusual degree programs: 3-2 engineering with Georgia Institute of Technology; nursing with Emory University; computer science with Emory University.

Computers: 450 computers/terminals are available on campus for general student use. Students can access the following: campus intranet, computer help desk, free student e-mail accounts, online (class) grades, online (class) registration, online (class) schedules. Campuswide network is available. 100% of college-owned or -operated housing units are wired for high-speed Internet access. Wireless service is available via entire campus.

Library: McCain Library. *Books:* 239,270 (physical), 57,182 (digital/electronic); *Databases:* 417. Weekly public service hours: 104; study areas open 24 hours, 5-7 days a week.

STUDENT LIFE

Housing options: on-campus residence required through senior year; women-only. Campus housing is university owned. Freshman campus housing is guaranteed.

Activities and organizations: drama/theater group, student-run newspaper, radio station, choral group, marching band.

Athletics Member NCAA. All Division III. ***Intercollegiate sports:*** basketball W, cross-country running W, soccer W, softball W, tennis W, volleyball W. ***Intramural sports:*** archery W, badminton W, cheerleading W(c), lacrosse W(c), swimming and diving W(c), tennis W.

Campus security: 24-hour emergency response devices and patrols, late-night transport/escort service, controlled dormitory access, security systems in apartments, public safety facility, surveillance equipment, key required for residence hall entry.

Student services: health clinic, personal/psychological counseling.

COSTS & FINANCIAL AID

Costs (2017–18) ***Comprehensive fee:*** $51,930 includes full-time tuition ($39,720), mandatory fees ($240), and room and board ($11,970). Part-time tuition: $1655 per credit. Part-time tuition and fees vary according to course load. ***Room and board:*** Room and board charges vary according to board plan and housing facility. ***Payment plan:*** installment. ***Waivers:*** employees or children of employees.

Financial Aid Of all full-time matriculated undergraduates who enrolled in 2016, 724 applied for aid, 655 were judged to have need, 163 had their need fully met. In 2016, 228 non-need-based awards were made. ***Average percent of need met:*** 84. ***Average financial aid package:*** $35,349. ***Average need-based loan:*** $4391. ***Average need-based gift aid:*** $28,811. ***Average non-need-based aid:*** $26,029. ***Average indebtedness upon graduation:*** $34,022. ***Financial aid deadline:*** 5/1.

APPLYING
Standardized Tests *Required for some:* SAT or ACT (for admission), SAT and SAT Subject Tests or ACT (for admission).
Options: electronic application, early admission, early decision, early action, deferred entrance.
Required: essay or personal statement, high school transcript. *Recommended:* interview.
Application deadlines: 5/1 (freshmen), 6/1 (transfers), 11/15 (early action).
Early decision deadline: 11/1.
Notification: 4/15 (freshmen), continuous (transfers), 12/1 (early decision), 1/15 (early action).
CONTACT
Agnes Scott College, 141 East College Avenue, Decatur, GA 30030-3797. *Phone:* 404-471-6285. *Toll-free phone:* 800-868-8602.

Albany State University
Albany, Georgia
http://www.asurams.edu/

- **State-supported** comprehensive, founded 1903, part of University System of Georgia
- **Urban** 232-acre campus
- **Endowment** $1.8 million
- **Coed** 3,316 undergraduate students, 84% full-time, 67% women, 33% men
- **Minimally difficult** entrance level, 47% of applicants were admitted

UNDERGRAD STUDENTS
2,780 full-time, 536 part-time. 2% are from out of state; 90% Black or African American, non-Hispanic/Latino; 1% Hispanic/Latino; 0.1% Asian, non-Hispanic/Latino; 0.2% American Indian or Alaska Native, non-Hispanic/Latino; 1% Two or more races, non-Hispanic/Latino; 2% Race/ethnicity unknown; 0.4% international.

Freshmen:
Admission: 2,381 applied, 1,126 admitted, 426 enrolled. ***Average high school GPA:*** 2.92. ***Test scores:*** SAT critical reading scores over 500: 16%; SAT math scores over 500: 13%; ACT scores over 18: 55%; SAT critical reading scores over 600: 1%; SAT math scores over 600: 1%; ACT scores over 24: 2%.
Retention: 69% of full-time freshmen returned.

FACULTY
Total: 220, 89% full-time.
Student/faculty ratio: 16:1.

ACADEMICS
Calendar: semesters. *Degrees:* bachelor's, master's, and post-master's certificates.
Special study options: academic remediation for entering students, adult/continuing education programs, advanced placement credit, cooperative education, distance learning, double majors, honors programs, independent study, internships, off-campus study, part-time degree program, services for LD students, study abroad, summer session for credit. ***ROTC:*** Army (b).
Unusual degree programs: 3-2 engineering with Georgia Institute of Technology.
Computers: Students can access the following: campus intranet, computer help desk, free student e-mail accounts, online (class) grades, online (class) registration, online (class) schedules, academic advising tools, online payment, and campus one stop portal. Campuswide network is available. 100% of college-owned or -operated housing units are wired for high-speed Internet access. Wireless service is available via entire campus.
Library: James Pendergrast Memorial Library.

STUDENT LIFE
Housing options: on-campus residence required for freshman year; coed, men-only, women-only. Campus housing is university owned. Freshman applicants given priority for college housing.
Activities and organizations: drama/theater group, student-run newspaper, radio and television station, choral group, marching band, ASU Anointed Gospel Choir, ASU Pan-Hellenic Council (Greeks), Peer Educators, SIFE (Students In Free Enterprise), Student Government Association, national fraternities, national sororities.
Athletics Member NCAA. All Division II. ***Intercollegiate sports:*** baseball M(s), basketball M(s)/W(s), cheerleading M/W, cross-country running M(s)/W(s), football M(s), softball W(s), tennis W(s), track and field M(s)/W(s), volleyball W(s). ***Intramural sports:*** basketball M/W, football M.
Campus security: 24-hour emergency response devices and patrols, late-night transport/escort service, controlled dormitory access, ConnectED Emergency E-mail, Emergency sirens, Active Shooter Team, Certified Police Officers.
Student services: health clinic, personal/psychological counseling.

COSTS & FINANCIAL AID
Costs (2017–18) ***Tuition:*** state resident $4858 full-time, $162 per credit hour part-time; nonresident $17,678 full-time, $589 per credit hour part-time. ***Required fees:*** $1602 full-time. ***Room and board:*** $7788; room only: $4940.
Financial Aid Of all full-time matriculated undergraduates who enrolled in 2014, 2,729 applied for aid, 2,616 were judged to have need, 234 had their need fully met. In 2014, 1 non-need-based awards were made. ***Average percent of need met:*** 71. ***Average financial aid package:*** $5164. ***Average need-based loan:*** $2402. ***Average need-based gift aid:*** $2595. ***Average non-need-based aid:*** $1500. ***Average indebtedness upon graduation:*** $39,014. ***Financial aid deadline:*** 6/30.

APPLYING
Standardized Tests *Required:* SAT or ACT (for admission).
Options: electronic application, early admission, deferred entrance.
Application fee: $25.
Required: high school transcript, minimum 2.2 GPA.
Application deadlines: 6/1 (freshmen), 6/1 (transfers).
Notification: continuous (freshmen), continuous (out-of-state freshmen), continuous (transfers).
CONTACT
Interim Director, Enrollment Services, Albany State University, 504 College Drive, Albany, GA 31705-2717. *Phone:* 229-430-4646. *Toll-free phone:* 800-822-7267. *Fax:* 229-430-4105. *E-mail:* enrollmentservices@asurams.edu.

American InterContinental University Atlanta
Atlanta, Georgia
http://www.aiuniv.edu/

CONTACT
American InterContinental University Atlanta, 6600 Peachtree-Dunwoody Road, 500 Embassy Row, Atlanta, GA 30328. *Phone:* 877-564-6248. *Toll-free phone:* 800-353-1744. *Fax:* 877-564-6248.

Argosy University, Atlanta
Atlanta, Georgia
http://www.argosy.edu/locations/atlanta/

CONTACT
Argosy University, Atlanta, 980 Hammond Drive, Suite 100, Atlanta, GA 30328. *Phone:* 770-671-1200. *Toll-free phone:* 888-671-4777.

Armstrong State University
Savannah, Georgia
http://www.armstrong.edu/

- **State-supported** comprehensive, founded 1935, part of University System of Georgia
- **Suburban** 267-acre campus
- **Endowment** $12.2 million
- **Coed** 6,397 undergraduate students, 74% full-time, 66% women, 34% men

UNDERGRAD STUDENTS
4,737 full-time, 1,660 part-time. Students come from 44 states and territories; 63 other countries; 8% are from out of state; 26% Black or African American, non-Hispanic/Latino; 8% Hispanic/Latino; 4% Asian, non-Hispanic/Latino; 0.3% Native Hawaiian or other Pacific Islander, non-Hispanic/Latino; 0.3% American Indian or Alaska Native, non-Hispanic/Latino; 5% Two or more races, non-Hispanic/Latino; 0.2% Race/ethnicity unknown; 1% international; 9% transferred in; 21% live on campus.

Freshmen:
Admission: 1,010 enrolled. ***Average high school GPA:*** 3.2. ***Test scores:*** SAT critical reading scores over 500: 50%; SAT math scores over 500: 41%; SAT writing scores over 500: 37%; ACT scores over 18: 90%; SAT critical reading scores over 600: 13%; SAT math scores over 600: 6%; SAT writing scores over 600: 6%; ACT scores over 24: 22%; SAT critical reading scores over 700: 2%; SAT writing scores over 700: 1%; ACT scores over 30: 1%.
Retention: 74% of full-time freshmen returned.

FACULTY
Total: 468, 61% full-time.
Student/faculty ratio: 17:1.

ACADEMICS
Calendar: semesters. *Degrees:* certificates, associate, bachelor's, master's, doctoral, post-master's, and postbachelor's certificates.
Special study options: academic remediation for entering students, adult/continuing education programs, advanced placement credit, cooperative education, distance learning, double majors, honors programs, independent study, internships, off-campus study, part-time degree program, services for LD students, study abroad, summer session for credit. ***ROTC:*** Army (b), Navy (c).
Computers: 300 computers/terminals are available on campus for general student use. Students can access the following: campus intranet, computer help desk, free student e-mail accounts, online (class) grades, online (class) registration, online (class) schedules. Campuswide network is available. 100% of college-owned or -operated housing units are wired for high-speed Internet access. Wireless service is available via entire campus.
Library: Lane Library plus 1 other. *Books:* 207,421 (physical), 215,400 (digital/electronic); *Serial titles:* 500 (physical), 2,000 (digital/electronic); *Databases:* 300. Weekly public service hours: 108; students can reserve study rooms.

STUDENT LIFE
Housing options: on-campus residence required for freshman year; coed. Campus housing is leased by the school and is provided by a third party. Freshman applicants given priority for college housing.
Activities and organizations: drama/theater group, student-run newspaper, choral group, Hispanic Outreach and Leadership at Armstrong (HOLA), Student Government Association, Campus Union Board, Gay Straight Alliance, Collegiate 100, national fraternities, national sororities.
Athletics Member NCAA. All Division II. ***Intercollegiate sports:*** baseball M(s), basketball M(s)/W(s), cross-country running M/W(s), golf M(s)/W(s), soccer W(s), softball W(s), tennis M(s)/W(s), volleyball W(s). ***Intramural sports:*** archery M(c)/W(c), baseball M(c), basketball M(c)/W(c), fencing M/W, football M, rugby M(c), sand volleyball M/W, soccer M(c)/W(c), softball M/W, table tennis M/W, tennis M(c)/W(c), ultimate Frisbee M(c)/W(c), volleyball M/W.
Campus security: 24-hour emergency response devices and patrols, student patrols, late-night transport/escort service, controlled dormitory access, personal safety app.
Student services: health clinic, personal/psychological counseling.

COSTS & FINANCIAL AID
Costs (2016–17) ***Tuition:*** state resident $4858 full-time, $162 per credit hour part-time; nonresident $17,678 full-time, $589 per credit hour part-time. Full-time tuition and fees vary according to course load, location, and program. Part-time tuition and fees vary according to course load, location, and program. ***Required fees:*** $1474 full-time, $612 per term part-time. ***Room and board:*** $10,750; room only: $6592. Room and board charges vary according to board plan and housing facility. ***Payment plan:*** installment. ***Waivers:*** senior citizens and employees or children of employees.
Financial Aid Of all full-time matriculated undergraduates who enrolled in 2014, 4,016 applied for aid, 3,211 were judged to have need. 71 Federal Work-Study jobs (averaging $2000). In 2014, 112 non-need-based awards were made. ***Average financial aid package:*** $8625. ***Average need-based loan:*** $4750. ***Average need-based gift aid:*** $1500. ***Average non-need-based aid:*** $1500. ***Financial aid deadline:*** 4/20.

APPLYING
Standardized Tests *Required:* SAT or ACT (for admission). *Required for some:* SAT Subject Tests (for admission).
Required: high school transcript, minimum 2.5 GPA.

CONTACT
Tobe Frierson, Director of Admissions, Armstrong State University, 11935 Abercorn St, Savannah, GA 31419. *Phone:* 912-344-2503. *Toll-free phone:* 800-633-2349. *Fax:* 912-344-3417.
E-mail: admissions.info@armstrong.edu.

The Art Institute of Atlanta
Atlanta, Georgia
http://www.artinstitutes.edu/atlanta/

CONTACT
The Art Institute of Atlanta, 6600 Peachtree Dunwoody Road, NE, 100 Embassy Row, Atlanta, GA 30328. *Phone:* 770-394-8300.
Toll-free phone: 800-275-4242.

Ashworth College
Norcross, Georgia
http://www.ashworthcollege.edu/

CONTACT
Mr. Eric Ryall, Registrar, Ashworth College, 6625 The Corners Parkway, Suite 500, Norcross, GA 30092. *Phone:* 770-729-8400 Ext. 5297. *Toll-free phone:* 800-957-5412.

Augusta University
Augusta, Georgia
http://www.augusta.edu/

- **State-supported** comprehensive, founded 1828, part of University System of Georgia
- **Urban** 670-acre campus
- **Endowment** $9.4 million
- **Coed** 5,224 undergraduate students, 78% full-time, 64% women, 36% men

UNDERGRAD STUDENTS
4,077 full-time, 1,147 part-time. 25% Black or African American, non-Hispanic/Latino; 5% Hispanic/Latino; 0.8% Asian, non-Hispanic/Latino; 0.5% Native Hawaiian or other Pacific Islander, non-Hispanic/Latino; 0.4% American Indian or Alaska Native, non-Hispanic/Latino; 4% Two or more races, non-Hispanic/Latino; 6% Race/ethnicity unknown; 1% international.

Freshmen:
Admission: 745 enrolled.
Retention: 70% of full-time freshmen returned.

FACULTY
Total: 1,482, 65% full-time, 97% with terminal degrees.

ACADEMICS
Calendar: semesters. *Degrees:* associate, bachelor's, master's, doctoral, post-master's, and postbachelor's certificates.
Special study options: academic remediation for entering students, adult/continuing education programs, advanced placement credit, cooperative education, distance learning, double majors, honors programs, independent study, internships, off-campus study, services for LD students, study abroad, summer session for credit. ***ROTC:*** Army (b).
Computers: Students can access the following: campus intranet, computer help desk, free student e-mail accounts, online (class) grades, online (class) registration, online (class) schedules. Campuswide network is available. 100% of college-owned or -operated housing units are wired

for high-speed Internet access. Wireless service is available via classrooms, computer centers, computer labs, dorm rooms, learning centers, libraries, student centers.
Library: Main Library plus 2 others.

STUDENT LIFE
Housing options: coed. Campus housing is university owned.
Activities and organizations: drama/theater group, student-run newspaper, choral group, national fraternities, national sororities.
Athletics Member NCAA. All Division II except men's and women's golf (Division I). ***Intercollegiate sports:*** baseball M(s), basketball M(s)/W(s), cross-country running M(s)/W(s), golf M(s)/W(s), softball W(s), tennis M(s)/W(s), track and field M/W. ***Intramural sports:*** badminton M/W, basketball M/W, football M/W, racquetball M/W, soccer M/W, softball M/W, table tennis M/W, volleyball M/W.
Campus security: 24-hour emergency response devices and patrols, late-night transport/escort service.
Student services: health clinic, personal/psychological counseling.

COSTS & FINANCIAL AID
Costs (2017–18) ***Tuition:*** state resident $6592 full-time, $220 per credit hour part-time; nonresident $21,300 full-time, $710 per credit hour part-time. Full-time tuition and fees vary according to course load, location, and program. Part-time tuition and fees vary according to course load, location, and program. ***Required fees:*** $1690 full-time. ***Room and board:*** $13,200. Room and board charges vary according to board plan and housing facility. ***Payment plan:*** installment. ***Waivers:*** senior citizens and employees or children of employees.
Financial Aid Of all full-time matriculated undergraduates who enrolled in 2015, 2,981 applied for aid, 2,355 were judged to have need, 258 had their need fully met. In 2015, 39 non-need-based awards were made. ***Average financial aid package:*** $2210. ***Average need-based loan:*** $2063. ***Average need-based gift aid:*** $2118. ***Average non-need-based aid:*** $1353. ***Financial aid deadline:*** 3/1.

APPLYING
Options: electronic application.
Application fee: $50.

CONTACT
Augusta University, 1120 15th Street, Augusta, GA 30912. *Phone:* 706-737-1632. *Toll-free phone:* 800-519-3388.

Bainbridge State College

Bainbridge, Georgia

http://www.bainbridge.edu/

- **State-supported** primarily 2-year, founded 1972, part of University System of Georgia
- **Small-town** 160-acre campus
- **Coed** 2,459 undergraduate students, 32% full-time, 70% women, 30% men
- **Noncompetitive** entrance level

UNDERGRAD STUDENTS
792 full-time, 1,667 part-time. Students come from 6 states and territories; 5 other countries; 4% are from out of state; 47% Black or African American, non-Hispanic/Latino; 2% Hispanic/Latino; 1% Asian, non-Hispanic/Latino; 0.2% American Indian or Alaska Native, non-Hispanic/Latino; 0.6% Two or more races, non-Hispanic/Latino; 0.5% Race/ethnicity unknown; 0.3% international.

Freshmen:
Admission: 616 admitted.

FACULTY
Total: 123, 48% full-time, 28% with terminal degrees.

ACADEMICS
Calendar: semesters. *Degrees:* certificates, diplomas, associate, and bachelor's.
Special study options: academic remediation for entering students, advanced placement credit, distance learning, double majors, honors programs, independent study, part-time degree program, services for LD students, study abroad, summer session for credit.
Computers: 650 computers/terminals and 650 ports are available on campus for general student use. Students can access the following: free student e-mail accounts, online (class) grades, online (class) registration, online (class) schedules. Campuswide network is available. Wireless service is available via entire campus.
Library: Bainbridge State College Library. *Books:* 44,125 (physical), 31,917 (digital/electronic); *Serial titles:* 179 (physical), 2,052 (digital/electronic); *Databases:* 282. Weekly public service hours: 50; students can reserve study rooms.

STUDENT LIFE
Housing options: college housing not available.
Activities and organizations: student-run newspaper, choral group, Adult Learners Student Organization, BANS, LPN Club, Honors, Student Government Association.
Campus security: 24-hour emergency response devices and patrols, late-night transport/escort service, police patrols and electronically-controlled building access.
Student services: personal/psychological counseling.

COSTS
Costs (2016–17) ***Tuition:*** state resident $2181 full-time, $91 per credit hour part-time; nonresident $8256 full-time, $344 per credit hour part-time. Full-time tuition and fees vary according to course load and program. Part-time tuition and fees vary according to course load and program. ***Required fees:*** $1046 full-time, $523 per term part-time. ***Waivers:*** senior citizens and employees or children of employees.

APPLYING
Standardized Tests *Required for some:* SAT or ACT (for admission), ACT Compass.
Options: electronic application, early admission.
Required for some: high school transcript, minimum 1.8 GPA, 3 letters of recommendation, interview, immunizations/waivers, medical records, criminal background check.
Application deadlines: rolling (freshmen), rolling (transfers).
Notification: continuous (freshmen), continuous (transfers).

CONTACT
Mr. Spencer Stewart, Associate Dean of Student Affairs, Bainbridge State College, 2500 East Shotwell Street, Bainbridge, GA 39819. *Phone:* 229-243-6030. *Toll-free phone:* 866-825-1715 (in-state); 888-825-1715 (out-of-state). *Fax:* 229-248-2848. *E-mail:* sstewart@bainbridge.edu.

Berry College

Mount Berry, Georgia

http://www.berry.edu/

- **Independent interdenominational** comprehensive, founded 1902
- **Suburban** 27,000-acre campus with easy access to Atlanta
- **Endowment** $944.4 million
- **Coed** 2,073 undergraduate students, 99% full-time, 60% women, 40% men
- **Moderately difficult** entrance level, 62% of applicants were admitted

UNDERGRAD STUDENTS
2,050 full-time, 23 part-time. Students come from 42 states and territories; 9 other countries; 33% are from out of state; 4% Black or African American, non-Hispanic/Latino; 7% Hispanic/Latino; 1% Asian, non-Hispanic/Latino; 0.3% American Indian or Alaska Native, non-Hispanic/Latino; 3% Two or more races, non-Hispanic/Latino; 3% Race/ethnicity unknown; 0.6% international; 2% transferred in; 86% live on campus.

Freshmen:
Admission: 3,477 applied, 2,159 admitted, 534 enrolled. ***Average high school GPA:*** 3.74. ***Test scores:*** SAT critical reading scores over 500: 87%; SAT math scores over 500: 90%; SAT writing scores over 500: 80%; ACT scores over 18: 100%; SAT critical reading scores over 600: 43%; SAT math scores over 600: 39%; SAT writing scores over 600: 29%; ACT scores over 24: 76%; SAT critical reading scores over 700: 8%; SAT math scores over 700: 5%; SAT writing scores over 700: 5%; ACT scores over 30: 20%.
Retention: 85% of full-time freshmen returned.

FACULTY
Total: 228, 73% full-time, 78% with terminal degrees.

Student/faculty ratio: 12:1.

ACADEMICS
Calendar: semesters. *Degrees:* bachelor's and master's.

Special study options: adult/continuing education programs, advanced placement credit, double majors, honors programs, independent study, internships, part-time degree program, services for LD students, student-designed majors, study abroad, summer session for credit.

Unusual degree programs: 3-2 engineering with Georgia Institute of Technology, Kennesaw State University; nursing with Emory University.

Computers: 200 computers/terminals and 80 ports are available on campus for general student use. Students can access the following: campus intranet, computer help desk, free student e-mail accounts, online (class) grades, online (class) registration, online (class) schedules. Campuswide network is available. 100% of college-owned or -operated housing units are wired for high-speed Internet access. Wireless service is available via classrooms, computer centers, computer labs, dorm rooms, learning centers, libraries, student centers.

Library: Memorial Library plus 1 other. *Books:* 213,724 (physical), 375,698 (digital/electronic); *Serial titles:* 9,234 (physical), 52,975 (digital/electronic); *Databases:* 266. Weekly public service hours: 106; students can reserve study rooms.

STUDENT LIFE
Housing options: on-campus residence required through senior year; coed, men-only, women-only. Campus housing is university owned. Freshman campus housing is guaranteed.

Activities and organizations: drama/theater group, student-run newspaper, choral group, Student Government Association, Campus Outreach, Block-n-Bridle, Allied Health, Athletes Bettering the Community.

Athletics Member NCAA. All Division III. ***Intercollegiate sports:*** baseball M, basketball M/W, cross-country running M/W, equestrian sports W, football M, golf M/W, lacrosse M/W, soccer M/W, softball W, swimming and diving M/W, tennis M/W, track and field M/W, volleyball W. ***Intramural sports:*** basketball M/W, cheerleading M(c)/W(c), crew M(c)/W(c), racquetball M/W, rowing M(c)/W(c), soccer M/W, softball M/W, swimming and diving M/W, tennis M/W, ultimate Frisbee M/W, volleyball M/W.

Campus security: 24-hour emergency response devices and patrols, controlled dormitory access, lighted pathways, gated campus, mobile police patrols, identification of valuables, limited access to campus, on-campus police officers.

Student services: health clinic, personal/psychological counseling.

COSTS & FINANCIAL AID
Costs (2016–17) ***Comprehensive fee:*** $45,286 includes full-time tuition ($33,330), mandatory fees ($226), and room and board ($11,730). Part-time tuition: $1111 per credit hour. ***College room only:*** $6630. Room and board charges vary according to board plan and housing facility. ***Payment plan:*** installment. ***Waivers:*** senior citizens and employees or children of employees.

Financial Aid Of all full-time matriculated undergraduates who enrolled in 2016, 1,756 applied for aid, 1,426 were judged to have need, 413 had their need fully met. 358 Federal Work-Study jobs (averaging $2270). 91 state and other part-time jobs (averaging $6294). In 2016, 612 non-need-based awards were made. ***Average percent of need met:*** 83. ***Average financial aid package:*** $27,248. ***Average need-based loan:*** $4976. ***Average need-based gift aid:*** $22,585. ***Average non-need-based aid:*** $13,767. ***Average indebtedness upon graduation:*** $26,449.

APPLYING
Standardized Tests *Required:* SAT or ACT (for admission).

Options: electronic application, early admission, early decision, early action.

Required: essay or personal statement, high school transcript, 1 letter of recommendation. ***Required for some:*** 2 letters of recommendation. ***Recommended:*** interview.

Application deadlines: 7/21 (freshmen), 7/21 (transfers).

Notification: continuous (freshmen), continuous (transfers).

CONTACT
Mr. Timothy Tarpley, Director of Operations, Enrollment Management, Berry College, PO Box 490159, 2277 Martha Berry Highway, NW, Mount Berry, GA 30149-0159. *Phone:* 706-236-2215. *Toll-free phone:* 800-237-7942. *E-mail:* admissions@berry.edu.

Beulah Heights University

Atlanta, Georgia

http://www.beulah.org/

- **Independent Pentecostal** comprehensive, founded 1918
- **Urban** 10-acre campus with easy access to Atlanta
- **Coed**
- **Noncompetitive** entrance level

FACULTY
Student/faculty ratio: 8:1.

ACADEMICS
Calendar: semesters. *Degrees:* associate, bachelor's, master's, and doctoral.

Library: Barth Memorial Library. *Books:* 50,000 (physical). Weekly public service hours: 65.

STUDENT LIFE
Housing options: men-only, women-only. Campus housing is university owned.

Activities and organizations: student-run newspaper, choral group, Chapel Choir, Student Government Association, Club Give.

Campus security: 24-hour emergency response devices and patrols.

Student services: personal/psychological counseling.

COSTS & FINANCIAL AID
Costs (2016–17) ***Tuition:*** $9090 full-time, $303 per credit hour part-time. Full-time tuition and fees vary according to course load. ***Required fees:*** $300 full-time. ***Room only:*** $6000. Room and board charges vary according to housing facility. ***Payment plans:*** installment, deferred payment.

Financial Aid Of all full-time matriculated undergraduates who enrolled in 2009, 113 applied for aid, 113 were judged to have need. 13 Federal Work-Study jobs (averaging $4335). ***Average percent of need met:*** 75. ***Average financial aid package:*** $5619. ***Average need-based loan:*** $2250. ***Average need-based gift aid:*** $3500. ***Average indebtedness upon graduation:*** $40,000.

APPLYING
Standardized Tests *Required for some:* TOEFL for international students. *Recommended:* SAT or ACT (for admission).

Options: electronic application, early admission.

Application fee: $30.

Required: essay or personal statement, high school transcript, minimum 2.0 GPA, 2 letters of recommendation, Statement of Faith. ***Recommended:*** interview.

CONTACT
Willie Marcellin, Admissions Coordinator, Beulah Heights University, 892 Berne Street, SE, Atlanta, GA 30316. *Phone:* 404-627-2681 Ext. 158. *Toll-free phone:* 888-777-BHBC. *E-mail:* arthur.breland@beulah.edu.

Brenau University

Gainesville, Georgia

http://www.brenau.edu/

- **Independent** comprehensive, founded 1878
- **Small-town** 57-acre campus with easy access to Atlanta
- **Coed, primarily women** 1,653 undergraduate students, 63% full-time, 90% women, 10% men
- **Moderately difficult** entrance level, 36% of applicants were admitted

UNDERGRAD STUDENTS
1,038 full-time, 615 part-time. Students come from 37 states and territories; 16 other countries; 5% are from out of state; 33% Black or African American, non-Hispanic/Latino; 9% Hispanic/Latino; 2% Asian, non-Hispanic/Latino; 0.1% Native Hawaiian or other Pacific Islander, non-Hispanic/Latino; 0.2% American Indian or Alaska Native, non-

Hispanic/Latino; 3% Two or more races, non-Hispanic/Latino; 2% Race/ethnicity unknown; 3% international; 26% transferred in; 24% live on campus.

Freshmen:
Admission: 1,975 applied, 704 admitted, 177 enrolled.
Retention: 71% of full-time freshmen returned.

FACULTY
Total: 326, 34% full-time, 54% with terminal degrees.
Student/faculty ratio: 11:1.

ACADEMICS
Calendar: semesters. *Degrees:* associate, bachelor's, master's, doctoral, post-master's, and postbachelor's certificates (also offers coed evening and weekend programs with significant enrollment not reflected in profile).

Special study options: academic remediation for entering students, advanced placement credit, distance learning, double majors, honors programs, independent study, internships, part-time degree program, services for LD students, study abroad, summer session for credit.

Computers: 190 computers/terminals are available on campus for general student use. Students can access the following: campus intranet, computer help desk, free student e-mail accounts, online (class) grades, online (class) registration, online (class) schedules. Campuswide network is available. 100% of college-owned or -operated housing units are wired for high-speed Internet access. Wireless service is available via entire campus.

Library: Brenau Trustee Library plus 1 other. *Books:* 82,609 (physical), 385,040 (digital/electronic); *Serial titles:* 194 (physical), 94,068 (digital/electronic); *Databases:* 119. Weekly public service hours: 89; students can reserve study rooms.

STUDENT LIFE
Housing options: on-campus residence required through junior year; men-only, women-only, special housing for students with disabilities. Campus housing is university owned. Freshman campus housing is guaranteed.

Activities and organizations: drama/theater group, student-run newspaper, radio station, choral group, Sigma Alpha Pi Leadership Society, Student Government Association/Student Activities Board, Circle K, Silhouettes, International Club, national sororities.

Athletics Member NAIA. ***Intercollegiate sports:*** basketball W(s), cheerleading W(s), crew W(c), cross-country running W(s), golf W(s), soccer W(s), softball W(s), swimming and diving W(s), tennis W(s), track and field W(s), volleyball W(s).

Campus security: 24-hour emergency response devices and patrols, late-night transport/escort service.

Student services: health clinic, personal/psychological counseling, women's center.

COSTS & FINANCIAL AID
Costs (2016–17) ***Comprehensive fee:*** $39,570 includes full-time tuition ($26,752), mandatory fees ($400), and room and board ($12,418). Full-time tuition and fees vary according to course load, location, and program. Part-time tuition: $892 per credit hour. Part-time tuition and fees vary according to course load, location, and program. ***Required fees:*** $200 per term part-time. ***Payment plan:*** installment. ***Waivers:*** employees or children of employees.

Financial Aid Of all full-time matriculated undergraduates who enrolled in 2016, 922 applied for aid, 851 were judged to have need, 91 had their need fully met. 134 Federal Work-Study jobs (averaging $1852). In 2016, 116 non-need-based awards were made. ***Average percent of need met:*** 73. ***Average financial aid package:*** $21,389. ***Average need-based loan:*** $8830. ***Average need-based gift aid:*** $13,418. ***Average non-need-based aid:*** $11,759. ***Average indebtedness upon graduation:*** $33,375.

APPLYING
Options: electronic application, deferred entrance.

Required: high school transcript. ***Recommended:*** essay or personal statement, interview.

Application deadlines: rolling (freshmen), rolling (transfers).
Notification: continuous (freshmen), continuous (transfers).

CONTACT
Ann Johnston, Brenau University, Admissions, 500 Washington Street, SE, Gainesville, GA 30501. *Phone:* 770-534-6100. *Toll-free phone:* 800-252-5119. *Fax:* 770-538-4701. *E-mail:* ajohnston5@brenau.edu.

Brewton-Parker College

Mt. Vernon, Georgia

http://www.bpc.edu/

- **Independent Southern Baptist** 4-year, founded 1904
- **Rural** 280-acre campus
- **Coed** 666 undergraduate students, 64% full-time, 43% women, 57% men
- **Minimally difficult** entrance level

UNDERGRAD STUDENTS
423 full-time, 243 part-time. Students come from 20 states and territories; 10 other countries; 13% are from out of state; 26% Black or African American, non-Hispanic/Latino; 6% Hispanic/Latino; 0.5% Asian, non-Hispanic/Latino; 0.2% Native Hawaiian or other Pacific Islander, non-Hispanic/Latino; 0.3% American Indian or Alaska Native, non-Hispanic/Latino; 2% Two or more races, non-Hispanic/Latino; 22% Race/ethnicity unknown; 3% international; 3% transferred in; 55% live on campus.

Freshmen:
Admission: 293 applied, 186 enrolled. ***Average high school GPA:*** 3.04.
Test scores: SAT critical reading scores over 500: 35%; SAT math scores over 500: 35%; SAT writing scores over 500: 38%; ACT scores over 18: 54%; SAT critical reading scores over 600: 6%; SAT math scores over 600: 6%; SAT writing scores over 600: 7%; ACT scores over 24: 7%; SAT critical reading scores over 700: 1%; ACT scores over 30: 4%.
Retention: 56% of full-time freshmen returned.

FACULTY
Total: 85, 36% full-time, 40% with terminal degrees.
Student/faculty ratio: 15:1.

ACADEMICS
Calendar: semesters. *Degrees:* associate and bachelor's.

Special study options: academic remediation for entering students, accelerated degree program, advanced placement credit, cooperative education, honors programs, independent study, internships, part-time degree program, services for LD students, summer session for credit.

Computers: 104 computers/terminals are available on campus for general student use. Students can access the following: campus intranet, computer help desk, free student e-mail accounts, online (class) grades, online (class) registration, online (class) schedules. Campuswide network is available. 100% of college-owned or -operated housing units are wired for high-speed Internet access. Wireless service is available via classrooms, computer centers, computer labs, dorm rooms, learning centers, libraries, student centers.

Library: Fountain-New Library. *Books:* 88,734 (physical); *Serial titles:* 6,729 (physical); *Databases:* 290.

STUDENT LIFE
Housing options: on-campus residence required through junior year; men-only, women-only. Campus housing is university owned. Freshman campus housing is guaranteed.

Activities and organizations: drama/theater group, student-run newspaper, Council of Intramural Activities, Student Activities Council, Student Government Association, Circle K, Baptist Student Union.

Athletics Member NAIA. ***Intercollegiate sports:*** baseball M(s), basketball M(s)/W(s), cheerleading M(s)/W(s), cross-country running M(s)/W(s), soccer M(s)/W(s), softball W(s), volleyball W(s), wrestling M(s). ***Intramural sports:*** basketball M/W, football M/W, golf M, softball M/W, table tennis M/W, tennis M/W, ultimate Frisbee M/W, volleyball M/W, wrestling M/W.

Campus security: 24-hour emergency response devices, controlled dormitory access, campus security is provided from 6 pm to 6 am.

Student services: personal/psychological counseling.

COSTS & FINANCIAL AID
Costs (2017–18) ***One-time required fee:*** $200. ***Comprehensive fee:*** $26,360 includes full-time tuition ($17,740), mandatory fees ($900), and room and board ($7720). Full-time tuition and fees vary according to

course load, location, and program. Part-time tuition: $435 per credit hour. Part-time tuition and fees vary according to course load, location, and program. ***Required fees:*** $650 per year part-time. ***College room only:*** $3300. Room and board charges vary according to board plan and housing facility. ***Payment plan:*** installment. ***Waivers:*** senior citizens and employees or children of employees.

Financial Aid Of all full-time matriculated undergraduates who enrolled in 2009, 819 applied for aid, 736 were judged to have need, 118 had their need fully met. 170 Federal Work-Study jobs (averaging $676). 114 state and other part-time jobs (averaging $466). In 2009, 96 non-need-based awards were made. ***Average percent of need met:*** 71. ***Average financial aid package:*** $11,736. ***Average need-based loan:*** $3436. ***Average need-based gift aid:*** $9011. ***Average non-need-based aid:*** $3915. ***Average indebtedness upon graduation:*** $28,231. ***Financial aid deadline:*** 5/1.

APPLYING

Standardized Tests *Required:* SAT or ACT (for admission).

Options: electronic application.

Application fee: $35.

Required: high school transcript, minimum 2.0 GPA.

Application deadlines: 8/1 (freshmen), rolling (transfers).

Notification: continuous (freshmen), continuous (transfers).

CONTACT

Ms. Tiffany Quarterman, Admissions Office Manager, Brewton-Parker College, PO Box 197, Mount Vernon, GA 30445. *Phone:* 912-583-3247. *Toll-free phone:* 800-342-1087. *Fax:* 912-583-3598. *E-mail:* admissions@bpc.edu.

Carver College

Atlanta, Georgia

http://www.carver.edu/

- **Independent nondenominational** 4-year, founded 1943
- **Urban** 16-acre campus with easy access to Atlanta
- **Coed** 104 undergraduate students, 60% full-time, 33% women, 67% men
- **Noncompetitive** entrance level, 100% of applicants were admitted

UNDERGRAD STUDENTS

62 full-time, 42 part-time. Students come from 4 states and territories; 4 other countries; 1% are from out of state; 65% Black or African American, non-Hispanic/Latino; 1% Asian, non-Hispanic/Latino; 34% international; 36% live on campus.

Freshmen:

Admission: 49 applied, 49 admitted, 34 enrolled.

Average high school GPA: 2.

Retention: 56% of full-time freshmen returned.

FACULTY

Total: 19, 11% full-time.

Student/faculty ratio: 6:1.

ACADEMICS

Calendar: semesters. *Degrees:* certificates, associate, and bachelor's.

Special study options: academic remediation for entering students, adult/continuing education programs, cooperative education, double majors, off-campus study, part-time degree program, summer session for credit.

Computers: 7 computers/terminals are available on campus for general student use. Students can access the following: campus intranet, computer help desk, free student e-mail accounts, online (class) grades, online (class) schedules. Campuswide network is available. Wireless service is available via entire campus.

Library: Carver Bible College Library plus 1 other. Study areas open 24 hours, 5-7 days a week; students can reserve study rooms.

STUDENT LIFE

Housing options: men-only, women-only. Campus housing is leased by the school.

Activities and organizations: drama/theater group, choral group, Student Government Association, Student Missions Organization, Carver Praise Team, Thespian Club.

Athletics Member NCCAA. ***Intercollegiate sports:*** basketball M(s)/W(s).

Campus security: 24-hour patrols, late-night transport/escort service.

Student services: personal/psychological counseling.

APPLYING

Application fee: $35.

Required: essay or personal statement, high school transcript, minimum 2.0 GPA, 2 letters of recommendation. ***Required for some:*** interview. ***Recommended:*** interview.

Application deadlines: 8/1 (freshmen), 8/1 (transfers).

CONTACT

Bertha Mack, Admissions Officer, Carver College, 3870 Cascade Road SW, Atlanta, GA 30331. *Phone:* 404-527-4520 Ext. 209. *Fax:* 404-527-4524. *E-mail:* info@carver.edu.

Chamberlain College of Nursing

Atlanta, Georgia

http://www.chamberlain.edu/

- **Proprietary** 4-year
- **Coed**

FACULTY

Student/faculty ratio: 13:1.

ACADEMICS

Degree: bachelor's.

STUDENT LIFE

Housing options: college housing not available.

COSTS

Costs (2016–17) ***Tuition:*** $18,900 full-time, $675 per credit hour part-time. ***Required fees:*** $600 full-time.

APPLYING

Standardized Tests *Required:* SAT or ACT (for admission).

Options: deferred entrance.

Application fee: $95.

CONTACT

Chamberlain College of Nursing, 5775 Peachtree Dunwoody Road NE, Suite A-100, Atlanta, GA 30342. *Toll-free phone:* 877-751-5783.

Clark Atlanta University

Atlanta, Georgia

http://www.cau.edu/

- **Independent United Methodist** university, founded 1865
- **Urban** 126-acre campus
- **Endowment** $62.2 million
- **Coed** 3,093 undergraduate students, 97% full-time, 71% women, 29% men
- **Moderately difficult** entrance level, 72% of applicants were admitted

UNDERGRAD STUDENTS

2,986 full-time, 107 part-time. Students come from 43 states and territories; 10 other countries; 65% are from out of state; 83% Black or African American, non-Hispanic/Latino; 0.2% Hispanic/Latino; 0.2% Asian, non-Hispanic/Latino; 0.1% American Indian or Alaska Native, non-Hispanic/Latino; 12% Race/ethnicity unknown; 4% international; 4% transferred in; 62% live on campus.

Freshmen:

Admission: 10,733 applied, 7,711 admitted, 999 enrolled. ***Average high school GPA:*** 3. ***Test scores:*** SAT critical reading scores over 500: 24%; SAT math scores over 500: 21%; SAT critical reading scores over 600: 2%; SAT math scores over 600: 2%.

Retention: 67% of full-time freshmen returned.

FACULTY

Total: 276, 64% full-time, 71% with terminal degrees.

Student/faculty ratio: 19:1.

ACADEMICS

Calendar: semesters. *Degrees:* bachelor's, master's, doctoral, post-master's, and postbachelor's certificates.

Special study options: academic remediation for entering students, accelerated degree program, adult/continuing education programs, advanced placement credit, cooperative education, double majors, honors programs, independent study, internships, off-campus study, part-time degree program, services for LD students, study abroad, summer session for credit. ***ROTC:*** Army (c), Navy (c).

Unusual degree programs: 3-2 engineering with Georgia Institute of Technology, Boston University, North Carolina Agricultural and Technical State University.

Computers: 741 computers/terminals and 2,000 ports are available on campus for general student use. Students can access the following: computer help desk, free student e-mail accounts, online (class) grades, online (class) registration, online (class) schedules. Campuswide network is available. 100% of college-owned or -operated housing units are wired for high-speed Internet access. Wireless service is available via entire campus.

Library: Robert W. Woodruff Library.

STUDENT LIFE

Housing options: on-campus residence required through sophomore year; coed, men-only, women-only. Campus housing is university owned and is provided by a third party. Freshman applicants given priority for college housing.

Activities and organizations: drama/theater group, student-run newspaper, radio and television station, choral group, marching band, Spirit Boosters, Pre-Alumni Council, Campus Activities Board, Orientation Guides, National Association for the Advancement of Colored People, national fraternities, national sororities.

Athletics Member NCAA. All Division II. ***Intercollegiate sports:*** baseball M(s), basketball M(s)/W(s), cross-country running M(s)/W(s), football M(s), softball W(s), tennis W(s), track and field M(s)/W(s), volleyball W(s). ***Intramural sports:*** basketball M/W, football M, softball W, tennis W, track and field M/W, volleyball M/W.

Campus security: 24-hour emergency response devices and patrols, late-night transport/escort service, controlled dormitory access.

Student services: health clinic, personal/psychological counseling.

COSTS & FINANCIAL AID

Costs (2016–17) ***Comprehensive fee:*** $33,196 includes full-time tuition ($19,880), mandatory fees ($2516), and room and board ($10,800). Part-time tuition: $828 per credit hour. ***Required fees:*** $1162 per term part-time. ***Room and board:*** Room and board charges vary according to board plan and housing facility. ***Payment plan:*** installment. ***Waivers:*** employees or children of employees.

Financial Aid Of all full-time matriculated undergraduates who enrolled in 2015, 2,537 applied for aid, 2,405 were judged to have need, 954 had their need fully met. 191 Federal Work-Study jobs (averaging $1733). In 2015, 14 non-need-based awards were made. ***Average percent of need met:*** 38. ***Average financial aid package:*** $7062. ***Average need-based loan:*** $2390. ***Average need-based gift aid:*** $4601. ***Average non-need-based aid:*** $10,331. ***Average indebtedness upon graduation:*** $40,815.

APPLYING

Standardized Tests *Required:* SAT or ACT (for admission).

Options: electronic application, early admission, deferred entrance.

Application fee: $35.

Required: essay or personal statement, high school transcript, minimum 2.5 GPA, 2 letters of recommendation. ***Required for some:*** interview.

Application deadlines: 6/1 (freshmen), 6/1 (transfers).

Notification: continuous (freshmen), continuous (out-of-state freshmen), continuous (transfers).

CONTACT

Ms. Lorri Rice, Director of Recruitment and Admissions, Clark Atlanta University, 223 James P. Brawley Drive, SW, Atlanta, GA 30314. *Phone:* 404-880-8043. *Toll-free phone:* 800-688-3228. *Fax:* 404-880-6174. *E-mail:* cauadmissions@cau.edu.

Clayton State University

Morrow, Georgia

http://www.clayton.edu/

- **State-supported** comprehensive, founded 1969, part of University System of Georgia
- **Suburban** 163-acre campus with easy access to Atlanta
- **Coed** 6,555 undergraduate students, 55% full-time, 69% women, 31% men
- **Minimally difficult** entrance level, 41% of applicants were admitted

UNDERGRAD STUDENTS

3,636 full-time, 2,919 part-time. Students come from 26 states and territories; 21 other countries; 3% are from out of state; 66% Black or African American, non-Hispanic/Latino; 5% Hispanic/Latino; 5% Asian, non-Hispanic/Latino; 0.1% Native Hawaiian or other Pacific Islander, non-Hispanic/Latino; 0.2% American Indian or Alaska Native, non-Hispanic/Latino; 3% Two or more races, non-Hispanic/Latino; 3% Race/ethnicity unknown; 1% international; 11% transferred in; 18% live on campus.

Freshmen:

Admission: 2,295 applied, 939 admitted, 588 enrolled. ***Average high school GPA:*** 3.03. ***Test scores:*** SAT critical reading scores over 500: 37%; SAT math scores over 500: 30%; ACT scores over 18: 82%; SAT critical reading scores over 600: 5%; SAT math scores over 600: 4%; ACT scores over 24: 13%; SAT critical reading scores over 700: 1%.

Retention: 71% of full-time freshmen returned.

FACULTY

Total: 366, 64% full-time, 66% with terminal degrees.

Student/faculty ratio: 18:1.

ACADEMICS

Calendar: semesters. *Degrees:* certificates, associate, bachelor's, and master's.

Special study options: academic remediation for entering students, adult/continuing education programs, advanced placement credit, cooperative education, distance learning, double majors, English as a second language, freshman honors college, honors programs, independent study, internships, off-campus study, part-time degree program, services for LD students, student-designed majors, study abroad, summer session for credit. ***ROTC:*** Army (c), Navy (c), Air Force (c).

Computers: 3,500 computers/terminals are available on campus for general student use. Students can access the following: computer help desk, free student e-mail accounts, online (class) grades, online (class) registration, online (class) schedules. Campuswide network is available. 100% of college-owned or -operated housing units are wired for high-speed Internet access. Wireless service is available via entire campus.

Library: Clayton State University Library.

STUDENT LIFE

Housing options: on-campus residence required for freshman year; coed. Campus housing is university owned. Freshman applicants given priority for college housing.

Activities and organizations: drama/theater group, student-run newspaper, radio station, choral group, national fraternities, national sororities.

Athletics Member NCAA. All Division II. ***Intercollegiate sports:*** basketball M(s)/W(s), cheerleading W(s)(c), cross-country running M(s)/W(s), golf M(s), soccer M(s)/W(s), tennis W(s), track and field M(s)/W(s). ***Intramural sports:*** bowling M/W, softball M/W, table tennis M/W, volleyball M/W.

Campus security: 24-hour emergency response devices and patrols, late-night transport/escort service, controlled dormitory access, lighted pathways.

Student services: health clinic, personal/psychological counseling.

COSTS & FINANCIAL AID

Costs (2016–17) ***Tuition:*** state resident $4858 full-time, $162 per credit hour part-time; nonresident $17,678 full-time, $589 per credit hour part-time. Full-time tuition and fees vary according to course load. Part-time tuition and fees vary according to course load. ***Required fees:*** $1454 full-time, $727 per term part-time. ***Room and board:*** $10,156. Room and board charges vary according to board plan and housing facility. ***Waivers:*** senior citizens and employees or children of employees.

Financial Aid Of all full-time matriculated undergraduates who enrolled in 2016, 3,224 applied for aid, 3,002 were judged to have need, 83 had their need fully met. 73 Federal Work-Study jobs (averaging $4071). In 2016, 27 non-need-based awards were made. ***Average percent of need met:*** 44. ***Average financial aid package:*** $9259. ***Average need-based loan:*** $4233. ***Average need-based gift aid:*** $6156. ***Average non-need-based aid:*** $1862. ***Average indebtedness upon graduation:*** $30,423.

APPLYING

Standardized Tests *Required:* SAT or ACT (for admission).

Options: electronic application, early admission, deferred entrance.

Application fee: $40.

Required: high school transcript, proof of immunization.

Notification: continuous (freshmen), continuous (transfers).

CONTACT

Admissions, Clayton State University, 2000 Clayton State Boulevard, Morrow, GA 30260-0285. *Phone:* 678-466-4115. *Fax:* 678-466-4149. *E-mail:* csc-info@clayton.edu.

College of Coastal Georgia

Brunswick, Georgia

http://www.ccga.edu/

- **State-supported** 4-year, founded 1961, part of University System of Georgia
- **Small-town** 193-acre campus with easy access to Jacksonville
- **Endowment** $8.0 million
- **Coed** 3,529 undergraduate students, 61% full-time, 66% women, 34% men
- **Minimally difficult** entrance level, 53% of applicants were admitted

UNDERGRAD STUDENTS

2,165 full-time, 1,364 part-time. Students come from 42 states and territories; 35 other countries; 7% are from out of state; 19% Black or African American, non-Hispanic/Latino; 6% Hispanic/Latino; 1% Asian, non-Hispanic/Latino; 0.1% Native Hawaiian or other Pacific Islander, non-Hispanic/Latino; 0.2% American Indian or Alaska Native, non-Hispanic/Latino; 4% Two or more races, non-Hispanic/Latino; 3% Race/ethnicity unknown; 0.9% international; 6% transferred in; 18% live on campus.

Freshmen:

Admission: 2,109 applied, 1,110 admitted, 861 enrolled. ***Average high school GPA:*** 2.96. ***Test scores:*** SAT critical reading scores over 500: 30%; SAT math scores over 500: 24%; ACT scores over 18: 60%; SAT critical reading scores over 600: 6%; SAT math scores over 600: 2%; ACT scores over 24: 14%; ACT scores over 30: 2%.

Retention: 57% of full-time freshmen returned.

FACULTY

Total: 214, 49% full-time, 43% with terminal degrees.

Student/faculty ratio: 19:1.

ACADEMICS

Calendar: semesters. *Degrees:* associate and bachelor's.

Special study options: academic remediation for entering students, advanced placement credit, distance learning, double majors, honors programs, internships, part-time degree program, services for LD students, study abroad, summer session for credit.

Computers: 395 computers/terminals and 300 ports are available on campus for general student use. Students can access the following: computer help desk, free student e-mail accounts, online (class) grades, online (class) registration, online (class) schedules. Campuswide network is available. 100% of college-owned or -operated housing units are wired for high-speed Internet access. Wireless service is available via entire campus.

Library: Clara Wood Gould Memorial Library. *Books:* 52,423 (physical), 144,111 (digital/electronic); *Serial titles:* 513 (physical), 6,636 (digital/electronic); *Databases:* 350. Weekly public service hours: 77; students can reserve study rooms.

STUDENT LIFE

Housing options: on-campus residence required for freshman year; coed. Campus housing is university owned, leased by the school and is provided by a third party. Freshman campus housing is guaranteed.

Activities and organizations: student-run newspaper, International Association, Coastal Georgia Association of Nursing Students, Urban Gaming Club, Association of Coastal Educators, CCGA Biology Club.

Athletics Member NAIA. ***Intercollegiate sports:*** basketball M(s)/W(s), golf M(s)/W(s), softball W(s), tennis M(s)/W(s), volleyball W(s). ***Intramural sports:*** baseball M(c), basketball M/W, bowling M, cheerleading W(c), football M/W, golf M/W, lacrosse W(c), sailing M(c)/W(c), soccer M/W, softball M/W, ultimate Frisbee M/W.

Campus security: 24-hour emergency response devices and patrols, late-night transport/escort service, controlled dormitory access.

Student services: health clinic, personal/psychological counseling.

COSTS & FINANCIAL AID

Costs (2017–18) ***Tuition:*** state resident $3064 full-time, $102 per semester hour part-time; nonresident $11,322 full-time, $377 per semester hour part-time. Full-time tuition and fees vary according to course load. Part-time tuition and fees vary according to course load. ***Required fees:*** $1370 full-time, $685 per term part-time. ***Room and board:*** $8458; room only: $5008. Room and board charges vary according to board plan, housing facility, and location. ***Payment plan:*** installment. ***Waivers:*** senior citizens and employees or children of employees.

Financial Aid Of all full-time matriculated undergraduates who enrolled in 2015, 1,627 applied for aid, 1,379 were judged to have need, 654 had their need fully met. 29 Federal Work-Study jobs (averaging $3900). ***Average percent of need met:*** 38. ***Average financial aid package:*** $9875. ***Average need-based loan:*** $3500. ***Average need-based gift aid:*** $7875. ***Average indebtedness upon graduation:*** $25,455. ***Financial aid deadline:*** 6/1.

APPLYING

Standardized Tests *Required:* SAT or ACT (for admission).

Options: electronic application, early admission, deferred entrance.

Application fee: $25.

Required: high school transcript, minimum 2.0 GPA, immunization records, proof of residency.

Application deadlines: 8/24 (freshmen), 8/24 (transfers).

Notification: continuous (freshmen), continuous (transfers).

CONTACT

Ms. Aerial Dickerson, Associate Director of Admissions, College of Coastal Georgia, One College Drive, Brunswick, GA 31520. *Phone:* 912-279-5730. *Toll-free phone:* 800-675-7235. *Fax:* 912-262-3072. *E-mail:* admiss@ccga.edu.

Columbus State University

Columbus, Georgia

http://www.columbusstate.edu/

- **State-supported** comprehensive, founded 1958, part of University System of Georgia
- **Suburban** 132-acre campus with easy access to Atlanta
- **Coed** 6,789 undergraduate students, 71% full-time, 59% women, 41% men
- **Minimally difficult** entrance level, 56% of applicants were admitted

UNDERGRAD STUDENTS

4,834 full-time, 1,955 part-time. 16% are from out of state; 37% Black or African American, non-Hispanic/Latino; 6% Hispanic/Latino; 2% Asian, non-Hispanic/Latino; 0.1% Native Hawaiian or other Pacific Islander, non-Hispanic/Latino; 0.4% American Indian or Alaska Native, non-Hispanic/Latino; 2% Two or more races, non-Hispanic/Latino; 1% international; 10% transferred in; 20% live on campus.

Freshmen:

Admission: 3,157 applied, 1,758 admitted, 926 enrolled. ***Average high school GPA:*** 3.1. ***Test scores:*** SAT critical reading scores over 500: 46%; SAT math scores over 500: 42%; SAT writing scores over 500: 37%; ACT scores over 18: 80%; SAT critical reading scores over 600: 12%; SAT math scores over 600: 10%; SAT writing scores over 600: 9%; ACT

scores over 24: 19%; SAT critical reading scores over 700: 1%; SAT math scores over 700: 1%; ACT scores over 30: 2%.
Retention: 74% of full-time freshmen returned.

FACULTY
Total: 544, 53% full-time, 52% with terminal degrees.
Student/faculty ratio: 17:1.

ACADEMICS
Calendar: semesters. *Degrees:* certificates, associate, bachelor's, master's, doctoral, post-master's, and postbachelor's certificates.
Special study options: academic remediation for entering students, adult/continuing education programs, advanced placement credit, cooperative education, distance learning, double majors, English as a second language, freshman honors college, honors programs, independent study, internships, off-campus study, part-time degree program, services for LD students, study abroad, summer session for credit.
ROTC: Army (b).
Unusual degree programs: 3-2 engineering with Georgia Institute of Technology.
Computers: Students can access the following: campus intranet, computer help desk, free student e-mail accounts, online (class) grades, online (class) registration, online (class) schedules. Campuswide network is available. 100% of college-owned or -operated housing units are wired for high-speed Internet access. Wireless service is available via entire campus.
Library: Simon Schwob Memorial Library plus 1 other. *Books:* 383,649 (physical).

STUDENT LIFE
Housing options: on-campus residence required for freshman year; coed, men-only, women-only, special housing for students with disabilities. Campus housing is university owned. Freshman applicants given priority for college housing.
Activities and organizations: drama/theater group, student-run newspaper, choral group, Student Government Association, Student Activities Council, Campus Ministry Association, African Students Association, SABER Student Newspaper, national fraternities, national sororities.
Athletics Member NCAA. All Division II. ***Intercollegiate sports:*** baseball M(s), basketball M(s)/W(s), cross-country running M(s)/W(s), golf M(s)/W(s), soccer W(s), softball W(s), tennis M(s)/W(s), track and field M(s)/W(s), volleyball W(s). ***Intramural sports:*** baseball M, basketball M/W, cross-country running M/W, football M, lacrosse M(c), racquetball M/W, riflery M(c)/W(c), skiing (downhill) M/W, soccer M/W, softball W, ultimate Frisbee M/W, volleyball M/W, wrestling M(c).
Campus security: 24-hour emergency response devices and patrols, late-night transport/escort service, controlled dormitory access.
Student services: health clinic, personal/psychological counseling.

COSTS & FINANCIAL AID
Costs (2016–17) ***Tuition:*** state resident $5226 full-time, $174 per credit hour part-time; nonresident $18,444 full-time, $615 per credit hour part-time. Full-time tuition and fees vary according to course load, degree level, and program. Part-time tuition and fees vary according to course load, degree level, and program. ***Required fees:*** $1850 full-time, $925 per term part-time. ***Room and board:*** $10,198; room only: $6344. Room and board charges vary according to board plan and housing facility.
Financial Aid Of all full-time matriculated undergraduates who enrolled in 2015, 4,208 applied for aid, 3,521 were judged to have need, 581 had their need fully met. In 2015, 205 non-need-based awards were made. ***Average percent of need met:*** 70. ***Average financial aid package:*** $9235. ***Average need-based loan:*** $4239. ***Average need-based gift aid:*** $4904. ***Average non-need-based aid:*** $2011. ***Average indebtedness upon graduation:*** $29,844.

APPLYING
Standardized Tests *Required:* SAT or ACT (for admission).
Options: electronic application, early admission, deferred entrance.
Application fee: $40.
Required: high school transcript, minimum 2.4 GPA, proof of immunization.
Application deadlines: 6/30 (freshmen), 6/30 (transfers).
Notification: continuous (freshmen), continuous (transfers).

CONTACT
Columbus State University, 4225 University Avenue, Columbus, GA 31907-5645. *Phone:* 706-507-8808. *Toll-free phone:* 866-264-2035.

Covenant College
Lookout Mountain, Georgia
http://www.covenant.edu/

- **Independent** comprehensive, founded 1955, affiliated with Presbyterian Church in America
- **Suburban** 350-acre campus
- **Coed**
- **Moderately difficult** entrance level

FACULTY
Student/faculty ratio: 13:1.

ACADEMICS
Calendar: semesters. *Degrees:* bachelor's and master's (master's degree in education only).
Library: Kresge Memorial Library.

STUDENT LIFE
Housing options: on-campus residence required through junior year; coed. Campus housing is university owned. Freshman campus housing is guaranteed.
Activities and organizations: drama/theater group, student-run newspaper, radio station, choral group.
Athletics Member NCAA, NAIA, NCCAA. All NCAA Division III.
Campus security: controlled dormitory access, night security guards.
Student services: health clinic, personal/psychological counseling, women's center.

COSTS & FINANCIAL AID
Costs (2016–17) ***Comprehensive fee:*** $41,860 includes full-time tuition ($31,320), mandatory fees ($910), and room and board ($9630). Full-time tuition and fees vary according to course load. Part-time tuition: $1340 per credit hour. Part-time tuition and fees vary according to course load. ***Room and board:*** Room and board charges vary according to board plan and housing facility.
Financial Aid Of all full-time matriculated undergraduates who enrolled in 2014, 762 applied for aid, 652 were judged to have need, 192 had their need fully met. In 2014, 305 non-need-based awards were made. ***Average percent of need met:*** 80. ***Average financial aid package:*** $24,369. ***Average need-based loan:*** $6660. ***Average need-based gift aid:*** $17,976. ***Average non-need-based aid:*** $11,875. ***Average indebtedness upon graduation:*** $24,895.

APPLYING
Standardized Tests *Required:* SAT or ACT (for admission).
Options: electronic application, early admission, deferred entrance.
Application fee: $35.
Required: essay or personal statement, high school transcript, minimum 2.5 GPA, 2 letters of recommendation, interview.

CONTACT
Mr. Philip Howlett, Assistant Director of Admissions, Covenant College, 14049 Scenic Highway, Lookout Mountain, GA 30750. *Phone:* 706-419-1145. *Toll-free phone:* 888-451-2683. *Fax:* 706-820-0893. *E-mail:* admissions@covenant.edu.

Dalton State College
Dalton, Georgia
http://www.daltonstate.edu/

- **State-supported** 4-year, founded 1963, part of University System of Georgia
- **Small-town** 144-acre campus
- **Endowment** $33.6 million
- **Coed** 5,188 undergraduate students, 64% full-time, 60% women, 40% men
- **Noncompetitive** entrance level, 36% of applicants were admitted

UNDERGRAD STUDENTS
3,334 full-time, 1,854 part-time. Students come from 13 states and territories; 53 other countries; 3% are from out of state; 4% Black or African American, non-Hispanic/Latino; 23% Hispanic/Latino; 1% Asian, non-Hispanic/Latino; 0.1% Native Hawaiian or other Pacific Islander, non-Hispanic/Latino; 0.3% American Indian or Alaska Native, non-Hispanic/Latino; 2% Two or more races, non-Hispanic/Latino; 4% Race/ethnicity unknown; 3% international; 4% live on campus.

Freshmen:
Admission: 1,414 applied, 515 admitted, 1,059 enrolled. ***Average high school GPA:*** 3.1. ***Test scores:*** SAT critical reading scores over 500: 37%; SAT math scores over 500: 30%; ACT scores over 18: 72%; SAT critical reading scores over 600: 6%; SAT math scores over 600: 4%; ACT scores over 24: 14%; ACT scores over 30: 1%.
Retention: 73% of full-time freshmen returned.

FACULTY
Total: 271, 64% full-time, 38% with terminal degrees.
Student/faculty ratio: 19:1.

ACADEMICS
Calendar: semesters. *Degrees:* certificates, associate, and bachelor's.
Special study options: academic remediation for entering students, adult/continuing education programs, advanced placement credit, cooperative education, distance learning, double majors, English as a second language, independent study, internships, off-campus study, part-time degree program, services for LD students, student-designed majors, study abroad, summer session for credit.
Computers: 730 computers/terminals are available on campus for general student use. Students can access the following: free student e-mail accounts, online (class) grades, online (class) registration, online (class) schedules. Campuswide network is available. Wireless service is available via computer centers, computer labs, learning centers, libraries, student centers.
Library: Derrell C. Roberts Library. *Books:* 143,415 (physical), 99,973 (digital/electronic); *Databases:* 72. Students can reserve study rooms.

STUDENT LIFE
Housing options: coed, special housing for students with disabilities. Campus housing is university owned.
Activities and organizations: Lambda Alpha Eplison (Criminal Justice), Rotaract, College Republicans, Beta Chi Nu (Biology), LASO (Latin American Student Organization), national fraternities, national sororities.
Athletics Member NAIA. ***Intercollegiate sports:*** basketball M/W(c), cheerleading M(c)/W(c), cross-country running M(c)/W(c), golf M(c)/W(c), soccer M(c)/W(c), tennis M(c)/W(c), track and field M(c)/W(c), volleyball W(c). ***Intramural sports:*** basketball M, football M, lacrosse M(c), softball M/W, table tennis M/W, tennis M/W, ultimate Frisbee M/W, volleyball M/W.
Campus security: 24-hour emergency response devices and patrols.

COSTS & FINANCIAL AID
Costs (2017–18) ***One-time required fee:*** $200. ***Tuition:*** state resident $3064 full-time, $102 per credit hour part-time; nonresident $11,322 full-time, $377 per credit hour part-time. Full-time tuition and fees vary according to course load and program. Part-time tuition and fees vary according to course load and program. ***Required fees:*** $1052 full-time, $365 per year part-time, $365 per term part-time. ***Room and board:*** $7970; room only: $4972. Room and board charges vary according to board plan. ***Payment plan:*** installment. ***Waivers:*** senior citizens and employees or children of employees.
Financial Aid Of all full-time matriculated undergraduates who enrolled in 2014, 2,154 applied for aid, 1,874 were judged to have need, 978 had their need fully met. In 2014, 813 non-need-based awards were made. ***Average percent of need met:*** 84. ***Average financial aid package:*** $2850. ***Average need-based loan:*** $4750. ***Average need-based gift aid:*** $3500. ***Average non-need-based aid:*** $895. ***Average indebtedness upon graduation:*** $3000. ***Financial aid deadline:*** 7/1.

APPLYING
Standardized Tests *Required:* SAT or ACT (for admission).
Options: electronic application, deferred entrance.
Application fee: $30.
Required: high school transcript.
Application deadlines: 7/1 (freshmen), 7/1 (transfers).
Notification: continuous (freshmen).

CONTACT
Katherine Logan, Director of Admissions, Dalton State College, 650 College Drive, Dalton, GA 30720-3797. *Phone:* 706-272-4524. *Toll-free phone:* 800-829-4436. *Fax:* 706-272-2530. *E-mail:* klogan@daltonstate.edu.

DeVry University–Alpharetta Campus
Alpharetta, Georgia
http://www.devry.edu/

CONTACT
Admissions Office, DeVry University–Alpharetta Campus, 2555 Northwinds Parkway, Alpharetta, GA 30009. *Phone:* 770-619-3600. *Toll-free phone:* 866-338-7934.

DeVry University–Decatur Campus
Decatur, Georgia
http://www.devry.edu/

- **Proprietary** comprehensive, founded 1969, part of DeVry University
- **Suburban** campus
- **Coed**
- **Minimally difficult** entrance level

FACULTY
Student/faculty ratio: 26:1.

ACADEMICS
Calendar: semesters. *Degrees:* associate, bachelor's, master's, and postbachelor's certificates.
Library: Learning Resource Center.

STUDENT LIFE
Housing options: college housing not available.

COSTS
Costs (2016–17) ***Tuition:*** $17,052 full-time, $609 per credit hour part-time. ***Required fees:*** $460 full-time.

APPLYING
Options: deferred entrance.
Application fee: $30.
Required: high school transcript, interview.

CONTACT
DeVry University–Decatur Campus, 1 West Court Square, Suite 100, Decatur, GA 30030. *Phone:* 404-270-2700. *Toll-free phone:* 866-338-7934.

East Georgia State College
Swainsboro, Georgia
http://www.ega.edu/

- **State-supported** primarily 2-year, founded 1973, part of University System of Georgia
- **Rural** 207-acre campus
- **Coed** 3,001 undergraduate students, 77% full-time, 59% women, 41% men
- **Minimally difficult** entrance level

UNDERGRAD STUDENTS
2,308 full-time, 693 part-time. Students come from 5 states and territories; 1 other country; 0.2% are from out of state; 44% Black or African American, non-Hispanic/Latino; 4% Hispanic/Latino; 0.9% Asian, non-Hispanic/Latino; 0.1% Native Hawaiian or other Pacific Islander, non-Hispanic/Latino; 0.2% American Indian or Alaska Native, non-Hispanic/Latino; 3% Two or more races, non-Hispanic/Latino; 0.9% Race/ethnicity unknown; 0.3% international; 9% transferred in; 12% live on campus.

Freshmen:
Admission: 1,148 enrolled.
Retention: 1% of full-time freshmen returned.

FACULTY
Student/faculty ratio: 26:1.

ACADEMICS
Calendar: semesters. *Degrees:* certificates, associate, and bachelor's.
Special study options: academic remediation for entering students, adult/continuing education programs, advanced placement credit, distance learning, honors programs, independent study, off-campus study, part-time degree program, services for LD students, study abroad, summer session for credit.
Computers: Students can access the following: computer help desk, free student e-mail accounts, online (class) grades, online (class) registration, online (class) schedules. Campuswide network is available. 100% of college-owned or -operated housing units are wired for high-speed Internet access. Wireless service is available via entire campus.
Library: East Georgia College Library. Students can reserve study rooms.

STUDENT LIFE
Housing options: coed. Campus housing is provided by a third party.
Activities and organizations: drama/theater group, student-run newspaper, choral group.
Athletics Member NJCAA. ***Intercollegiate sports:*** baseball M(s), basketball M(s)/W(s), softball W. ***Intramural sports:*** basketball M/W, cheerleading M(c)/W(c), football M/W, softball M/W.
Campus security: 24-hour patrols, late-night transport/escort service, controlled dormitory access.
Student services: health clinic, personal/psychological counseling.

COSTS & FINANCIAL AID
Costs (2017–18) ***One-time required fee:*** $35. ***Tuition:*** state resident $2726 full-time, $91 per credit hour part-time; nonresident $10,320 full-time, $344 per credit hour part-time. Full-time tuition and fees vary according to class time, course load, location, and student level. Part-time tuition and fees vary according to class time, course load, location, and student level. ***Required fees:*** $886 full-time, $443 per term part-time. ***Room and board:*** $8504; room only: $5960. Room and board charges vary according to location. ***Payment plan:*** installment. ***Waivers:*** senior citizens.
Financial Aid Of all full-time matriculated undergraduates who enrolled in 2015, 43 Federal Work-Study jobs (averaging $1560).

APPLYING
Options: early admission, deferred entrance.
Application fee: $20.
Required: high school transcript.
Application deadlines: rolling (freshmen), rolling (transfers).
Notification: continuous (freshmen), continuous (transfers).

CONTACT
East Georgia State College, 131 College Circle, Swainsboro, GA 30401-2699. *Phone:* 478-289-2112.

Emmanuel College
Franklin Springs, Georgia
http://www.ec.edu/

- **Independent** 4-year, founded 1919, affiliated with Pentecostal Holiness Church
- **Rural** 90-acre campus with easy access to Atlanta, GA
- **Endowment** $3.7 million
- **Coed** 920 undergraduate students, 87% full-time, 48% women, 52% men
- **Minimally difficult** entrance level, 41% of applicants were admitted

UNDERGRAD STUDENTS
796 full-time, 124 part-time. Students come from 30 states and territories; 20 other countries; 25% are from out of state; 13% Black or African American, non-Hispanic/Latino; 6% Hispanic/Latino; 0.8% Asian, non-Hispanic/Latino; 0.7% Native Hawaiian or other Pacific Islander, non-Hispanic/Latino; 0.2% American Indian or Alaska Native, non-Hispanic/Latino; 3% Two or more races, non-Hispanic/Latino; 5% international; 7% transferred in; 59% live on campus.

Freshmen:
Admission: 1,386 applied, 562 admitted, 238 enrolled. ***Average high school GPA:*** 3.25.
Retention: 55% of full-time freshmen returned.

FACULTY
Total: 89, 52% full-time, 43% with terminal degrees.
Student/faculty ratio: 14:1.

ACADEMICS
Calendar: semesters. *Degrees:* associate and bachelor's.
Special study options: academic remediation for entering students, advanced placement credit, distance learning, honors programs, independent study, internships, part-time degree program, services for LD students, study abroad, summer session for credit.
Unusual degree programs: 3-2 psychology with Richmont University.
Computers: 80 computers/terminals are available on campus for general student use. Students can access the following: campus intranet, computer help desk, free student e-mail accounts, online (class) grades, online (class) registration, online (class) schedules. Campuswide network is available. 100% of college-owned or -operated housing units are wired for high-speed Internet access. Wireless service is available via entire campus.
Library: Shaw-Leslie Library plus 1 other. *Books:* 41,206 (physical), 50,364 (digital/electronic); *Serial titles:* 99 (physical); *Databases:* 124. Weekly public service hours: 84.

STUDENT LIFE
Housing options: on-campus residence required through sophomore year; men-only, women-only. Campus housing is university owned. Freshman campus housing is guaranteed.
Activities and organizations: drama/theater group, choral group, Students in Free Enterprise (SIFE), Fellowship of Christian Athletes, SOS, BSU, International Students Club.
Athletics Member NCAA, NCCAA. All NCAA Division II. ***Intercollegiate sports:*** archery M(s)/W(s), baseball M(s), basketball M(s)/W(s), bowling M(s)/W(s), cross-country running M(s)/W(s), golf M(s)/W(s), lacrosse M(s)/W(s), riflery M(s)/W(s), soccer M(s)/W(s), softball W(s), swimming and diving M(s)/W(s), tennis M(s)/W(s), track and field M(s)/W(s), volleyball M(s)/W(s), wrestling M(s)/W(s). ***Intramural sports:*** basketball M/W, football M/W, golf M/W, soccer M/W, tennis M/W, track and field M/W, volleyball M/W, weight lifting M/W.
Campus security: 24-hour patrols.
Student services: personal/psychological counseling.

COSTS & FINANCIAL AID
Costs (2016–17) ***Comprehensive fee:*** $26,730 includes full-time tuition ($18,990), mandatory fees ($340), and room and board ($7400). Part-time tuition: $795 per credit hour. ***Room and board:*** Room and board charges vary according to housing facility. ***Payment plan:*** installment. ***Waivers:*** senior citizens and employees or children of employees.
Financial Aid Of all full-time matriculated undergraduates who enrolled in 2016, 626 applied for aid, 543 were judged to have need, 109 had their need fully met. 102 Federal Work-Study jobs (averaging $839). 135 state and other part-time jobs (averaging $842). In 2016, 94 non-need-based awards were made. ***Average percent of need met:*** 69. ***Average financial aid package:*** $15,574. ***Average need-based loan:*** $3737. ***Average need-based gift aid:*** $12,270. ***Average non-need-based aid:*** $4388. ***Average indebtedness upon graduation:*** $25,609. ***Financial aid deadline:*** 6/15.

APPLYING
Standardized Tests *Required:* SAT or ACT (for admission).
Options: electronic application, early admission, deferred entrance.
Application fee: $25.
Required: essay or personal statement, high school transcript. ***Required for some:*** interview.
Application deadlines: 8/1 (freshmen), 8/1 (transfers).
Notification: continuous until 8/1 (freshmen), continuous until 8/1 (transfers).

CONTACT
Mrs. Kay Clifton, Director of Admissions, Emmanuel College, PO Box 129, 181 Spring Street, Franklin Springs, GA 30639-0129. *Phone:* 706-245-7226 Ext. 2814. *Toll-free phone:* 800-860-8800.
E-mail: admissions@ec.edu.

Emory University

Atlanta, Georgia

http://www.emory.edu/

- **Independent Methodist** university, founded 1836
- **Suburban** 634-acre campus with easy access to Atlanta
- **Endowment** $6.7 billion
- **Coed** 6,861 undergraduate students, 98% full-time, 59% women, 41% men
- **Most difficult** entrance level, 25% of applicants were admitted

UNDERGRAD STUDENTS
6,714 full-time, 147 part-time. Students come from 54 states and territories; 72 other countries; 79% are from out of state; 9% Black or African American, non-Hispanic/Latino; 9% Hispanic/Latino; 18% Asian, non-Hispanic/Latino; 0.1% American Indian or Alaska Native, non-Hispanic/Latino; 4% Two or more races, non-Hispanic/Latino; 2% Race/ethnicity unknown; 16% international; 1% transferred in; 64% live on campus.

Freshmen:
Admission: 19,924 applied, 5,039 admitted, 1,358 enrolled. ***Average high school GPA:*** 3.72. ***Test scores:*** SAT critical reading scores over 500: 100%; SAT math scores over 500: 100%; SAT writing scores over 500: 100%; ACT scores over 18: 100%; SAT critical reading scores over 600: 89%; SAT math scores over 600: 94%; SAT writing scores over 600: 93%; ACT scores over 24: 100%; SAT critical reading scores over 700: 41%; SAT math scores over 700: 61%; SAT writing scores over 700: 51%; ACT scores over 30: 78%.

Retention: 94% of full-time freshmen returned.

FACULTY
Total: 1,178, 87% full-time, 92% with terminal degrees.

Student/faculty ratio: 8:1.

ACADEMICS
Calendar: semesters. *Degrees:* bachelor's, master's, doctoral, post-master's, and postbachelor's certificates (enrollment figures include Emory University, Oxford College; application data for main campus only).

Special study options: advanced placement credit, cooperative education, double majors, English as a second language, honors programs, independent study, internships, off-campus study, services for LD students, study abroad, summer session for credit. ***ROTC:*** Army (c), Navy (c), Air Force (c).

Unusual degree programs: 3-2 business administration; engineering with Georgia Institute of Technology; nursing.

Computers: Students can access the following: campus intranet, computer help desk, free student e-mail accounts, online (class) grades, online (class) registration, online (class) schedules, computer repair system. Campuswide network is available. 100% of college-owned or -operated housing units are wired for high-speed Internet access. Wireless service is available via entire campus.

Library: Robert W. Woodruff Library plus 8 others. *Books:* 3.5 million (physical), 704,535 (digital/electronic); *Databases:* 874.

STUDENT LIFE
Housing options: on-campus residence required through sophomore year; coed. Campus housing is university owned. Freshman campus housing is guaranteed.

Activities and organizations: drama/theater group, student-run newspaper, radio and television station, choral group, Volunteer Emory, music/theater, Student Government, Outdoor Emory, Hillel, national fraternities, national sororities.

Athletics Member NCAA. All Division III. ***Intercollegiate sports:*** badminton M(c)/W(c), baseball M, basketball M/W, crew M(c)/W(c), cross-country running M/W, equestrian sports M(c)/W(c), fencing M(c)/W(c), field hockey M(c)/W(c), golf M(c)/W(c), gymnastics W(c), lacrosse M(c)/W(c), rock climbing M(c)/W(c), rugby M(c), sailing M(c)/W(c), soccer M/W, softball W, squash M(c)/W(c), swimming and diving M/W, tennis M/W, track and field M/W, ultimate Frisbee M(c)/W(c), volleyball M/W, water polo M(c)/W(c), weight lifting M(c)/W(c). ***Intramural sports:*** basketball M/W, football M/W, golf M, soccer M/W, softball W, swimming and diving M/W, table tennis M/W, tennis M/W, volleyball W.

Campus security: 24-hour emergency response devices and patrols, student patrols, late-night transport/escort service, controlled dormitory access.

Student services: health clinic, personal/psychological counseling, women's center, legal services.

COSTS & FINANCIAL AID
Costs (2017–18) ***Comprehensive fee:*** $63,286 includes full-time tuition ($48,690), mandatory fees ($702), and room and board ($13,894). Full-time tuition and fees vary according to degree level and location. Part-time tuition: $2029 per credit hour. ***College room only:*** $8072. Room and board charges vary according to board plan, housing facility, and student level. ***Payment plan:*** installment. ***Waivers:*** employees or children of employees.

Financial Aid Of all full-time matriculated undergraduates who enrolled in 2016, 2,798 applied for aid, 2,422 were judged to have need, 2,351 had their need fully met. 1,238 Federal Work-Study jobs (averaging $2378). In 2016, 270 non-need-based awards were made. ***Average percent of need met:*** 100. ***Average financial aid package:*** $44,168. ***Average need-based loan:*** $4747. ***Average need-based gift aid:*** $40,816. ***Average non-need-based aid:*** $25,962. ***Average indebtedness upon graduation:*** $29,217. ***Financial aid deadline:*** 3/1.

APPLYING
Standardized Tests *Required:* SAT or ACT (for admission).

Options: electronic application, early admission, early decision, deferred entrance.

Application fee: $75.

Required: essay or personal statement, high school transcript, 2 letters of recommendation.

Application deadlines: 1/1 (freshmen), 3/15 (transfers).

Early decision deadline: 11/1 (for plan 1), 1/1 (for plan 2).

Notification: 4/1 (freshmen), 4/30 (transfers), 12/15 (early decision plan 1), 2/15 (early decision plan 2).

CONTACT
Dr. John Latting, Dean of Admission, Emory University, 1390 Oxford Road NE, 3rd Floor, Atlanta, GA 30322-1100. *Phone:* 404-727-6036. *Toll-free phone:* 800-727-6036. *Fax:* 404-727-4303.
E-mail: admiss@emory.edu.

Fort Valley State University

Fort Valley, Georgia

http://www.fvsu.edu/

CONTACT
Mr. Donald Moore, Director of Admissions and Recruitment, Fort Valley State University, 1005 State University Drive, Fort Valley, GA 31030. *Phone:* 478-825-6307. *Toll-free phone:* 877-462-3878. *Fax:* 478-825-6169. *E-mail:* admissap@fvsu.edu.

Georgia Christian University

Atlanta, Georgia

http://www.gcuniv.edu/

CONTACT
Georgia Christian University, 6789 Peachtree Industrial Boulevard, Atlanta, GA 30360.

Georgia College & State University

Milledgeville, Georgia

http://www.gcsu.edu/

- **State-supported** comprehensive, founded 1889, part of University System of Georgia
- **Small-town** 602-acre campus
- **Endowment** $35.3 million
- **Coed** 6,047 undergraduate students, 92% full-time, 61% women, 39% men
- **Moderately difficult** entrance level, 85% of applicants were admitted

UNDERGRAD STUDENTS
5,555 full-time, 492 part-time. Students come from 22 states and territories; 39 other countries; 1% are from out of state; 5% Black or African American, non-Hispanic/Latino; 5% Hispanic/Latino; 2% Asian, non-Hispanic/Latino; 0.0% Native Hawaiian or other Pacific Islander, non-Hispanic/Latino; 0.2% American Indian or Alaska Native, non-Hispanic/Latino; 3% Two or more races, non-Hispanic/Latino; 0.3% Race/ethnicity unknown; 1% international; 5% transferred in; 33% live on campus.

Freshmen:
Admission: 3,980 applied, 3,364 admitted, 1,381 enrolled. ***Average high school GPA:*** 3.47. ***Test scores:*** SAT critical reading scores over 500: 84%; SAT math scores over 500: 83%; SAT writing scores over 500: 76%; ACT scores over 18: 96%; SAT critical reading scores over 600: 33%; SAT math scores over 600: 33%; SAT writing scores over 600: 24%; ACT scores over 24: 58%; SAT critical reading scores over 700: 3%; SAT math scores over 700: 2%; SAT writing scores over 700: 3%; ACT scores over 30: 2%.

Retention: 85% of full-time freshmen returned.

FACULTY
Total: 421, 80% full-time, 67% with terminal degrees.

Student/faculty ratio: 17:1.

ACADEMICS
Calendar: semesters. *Degrees:* bachelor's, master's, doctoral, and post-master's certificates.

Special study options: accelerated degree program, advanced placement credit, distance learning, double majors, English as a second language, external degree program, freshman honors college, honors programs, independent study, internships, part-time degree program, services for LD students, student-designed majors, study abroad, summer session for credit. ***ROTC:*** Army (c).

Unusual degree programs: 3-2 engineering with Georgia Institute of Technology.

Computers: 900 computers/terminals and 6,295 ports are available on campus for general student use. Students can access the following: campus intranet, computer help desk, free student e-mail accounts, online (class) grades, online (class) registration, online (class) schedules. Campuswide network is available. 100% of college-owned or -operated housing units are wired for high-speed Internet access. Wireless service is available via entire campus.

Library: Ina Dillard Russell Library plus 1 other. *Books:* 184,103 (physical), 597,074 (digital/electronic); *Serial titles:* 5,556 (physical), 162,750 (digital/electronic); *Databases:* 376. Weekly public service hours: 102; students can reserve study rooms.

STUDENT LIFE
Housing options: on-campus residence required for freshman year; coed, special housing for students with disabilities. Campus housing is university owned and leased by the school. Freshman campus housing is guaranteed.

Activities and organizations: drama/theater group, student-run newspaper, radio station, choral group, Wesley foundation Ministries, Gardening Club, Beta Beta Beta, Literary Guild, Bobcats Against Hunger, national fraternities, national sororities.

Athletics Member NCAA. All Division II. ***Intercollegiate sports:*** baseball M(s), basketball M(s)/W(s), cheerleading M/W, cross-country running M(s)/W(s), golf M(s), soccer W(s), softball W(s), tennis M(s)/W(s), volleyball W(s). ***Intramural sports:*** baseball M(c), basketball M/W, equestrian sports W(c), football M/W, golf M(c), ice hockey M(c), lacrosse M(c)/W(c), rugby M(c)/W(c), soccer M(c)/W(c), softball M(c)/W(c), swimming and diving W(c), tennis M(c)/W(c), ultimate Frisbee M(c)/W(c), volleyball M/W(c), water polo M(c)/W(c).

Campus security: 24-hour emergency response devices and patrols, student patrols, late-night transport/escort service, controlled dormitory access.

Student services: health clinic, personal/psychological counseling, women's center.

COSTS & FINANCIAL AID
Costs (2016–17) ***Tuition:*** state resident $7180 full-time; nonresident $25,528 full-time. Full-time tuition and fees vary according to course load, location, and program. Part-time tuition and fees vary according to course load, location, and program. ***Required fees:*** $2022 full-time. ***Room and board:*** $11,946; room only: $6400. Room and board charges vary according to board plan and housing facility. ***Payment plan:*** installment. ***Waivers:*** senior citizens and employees or children of employees.

Financial Aid Of all full-time matriculated undergraduates who enrolled in 2016, 4,133 applied for aid, 2,736 were judged to have need, 514 had their need fully met. In 2016, 205 non-need-based awards were made. ***Average percent of need met:*** 58. ***Average financial aid package:*** $10,428. ***Average need-based loan:*** $4569. ***Average need-based gift aid:*** $4309. ***Average non-need-based aid:*** $2069. ***Average indebtedness upon graduation:*** $29,138.

APPLYING
Standardized Tests *Required:* SAT or ACT (for admission). *Required for some:* SAT Subject Tests (for admission).

Options: electronic application, early admission, early action, deferred entrance.

Application fee: $40.

Required: proof of immunization. ***Required for some:*** essay or personal statement, high school transcript.

Application deadlines: 4/1 (freshmen), rolling (out-of-state freshmen), 7/1 (transfers), 11/1 (early action).

Notification: continuous (freshmen), continuous (out-of-state freshmen), continuous (transfers).

CONTACT
Mr. Ramon Blakley, Director of Admissions, Georgia College & State University, CPO Box 023, Milledgeville, GA 31061. *Phone:* 478-445-1283. *Toll-free phone:* 800-342-0471. *Fax:* 478-445-3653. *E-mail:* admissions@gcsu.edu.

Georgia Gwinnett College

Lawrenceville, Georgia

http://www.ggc.edu/

- **State-supported** 4-year, part of University System of Georgia
- **Suburban** 260-acre campus with easy access to Atlanta
- **Coed** 12,052 undergraduate students, 68% full-time, 56% women, 44% men
- **Noncompetitive** entrance level, 89% of applicants were admitted

UNDERGRAD STUDENTS
8,154 full-time, 3,898 part-time. Students come from 39 states and territories; 133 other countries; 1% are from out of state; 33% Black or African American, non-Hispanic/Latino; 17% Hispanic/Latino; 10% Asian, non-Hispanic/Latino; 0.1% Native Hawaiian or other Pacific Islander, non-Hispanic/Latino; 0.2% American Indian or Alaska Native, non-Hispanic/Latino; 4% Two or more races, non-Hispanic/Latino; 0.9% Race/ethnicity unknown; 2% international; 6% transferred in; 6% live on campus.

Freshmen:
Admission: 3,705 applied, 3,293 admitted, 2,437 enrolled. ***Average high school GPA:*** 2.79. ***Test scores:*** SAT critical reading scores over 500: 32%; SAT math scores over 500: 35%; SAT writing scores over 500: 24%; ACT scores over 18: 60%; SAT critical reading scores over 600: 6%; SAT math scores over 600: 6%; SAT writing scores over 600: 3%; ACT scores over 24: 14%; SAT critical reading scores over 700: 1%; ACT scores over 30: 1%.

Retention: 69% of full-time freshmen returned.

FACULTY
Total: 687, 64% full-time, 67% with terminal degrees.

Student/faculty ratio: 18:1.

ACADEMICS

Calendar: semesters. *Degrees:* associate and bachelor's.

Special study options: academic remediation for entering students, advanced placement credit, double majors, English as a second language, honors programs, internships, part-time degree program, services for LD students, study abroad, summer session for credit. ***ROTC:*** Army (b).

Computers: 243 computers/terminals are available on campus for general student use. Students can access the following: campus intranet, computer help desk, free student e-mail accounts, online (class) grades, online (class) registration, online (class) schedules. Campuswide network is available. 100% of college-owned or -operated housing units are wired for high-speed Internet access. Wireless service is available via entire campus.

Library: Daniel J. Kaufman Library and Learning Center. *Books:* 76,355 (physical), 118,119 (digital/electronic); *Serial titles:* 141 (physical), 5,119 (digital/electronic); *Databases:* 112. Weekly public service hours: 79; students can reserve study rooms.

STUDENT LIFE

Housing options: coed. Campus housing is university owned. Freshman campus housing is guaranteed.

Athletics Member NAIA. ***Intercollegiate sports:*** baseball M, soccer M/W, softball W, tennis M/W.

Campus security: 24-hour emergency response devices and patrols, student patrols, late-night transport/escort service, controlled dormitory access.

Student services: health clinic, personal/psychological counseling.

COSTS

Costs (2016–17) ***Tuition:*** state resident $3844 full-time, $128 per credit hour part-time; nonresident $14,348 full-time, $478 per credit hour part-time. Full-time tuition and fees vary according to course load and reciprocity agreements. Part-time tuition and fees vary according to course load and reciprocity agreements. ***Required fees:*** $852 full-time, $602 per term part-time. ***Room and board:*** Room and board charges vary according to board plan and housing facility. ***Payment plans:*** installment, deferred payment. ***Waivers:*** senior citizens and employees or children of employees.

APPLYING

Standardized Tests *Required:* SAT or ACT (for admission). *Recommended:* SAT or ACT (for admission).

Options: electronic application, deferred entrance.

Application fee: $20.

Required: high school transcript, minimum 2.0 GPA.

Application deadlines: 6/1 (freshmen), rolling (transfers).

CONTACT

Admissions Office, Georgia Gwinnett College, 1000 University Center Lane, Lawrenceville, GA 30043. *Phone:* 678-407-5313. *Toll-free phone:* 877-704-4422. *E-mail:* ggcadmissions@ggc.edu.

Georgia Highlands College

Rome, Georgia

http://www.highlands.edu/

- **State-supported** primarily 2-year, founded 1970, part of University System of Georgia
- **Suburban** 226-acre campus with easy access to Atlanta
- **Endowment** $37,568
- **Coed** 5,994 undergraduate students, 47% full-time, 64% women, 36% men
- **Noncompetitive** entrance level, 69% of applicants were admitted

UNDERGRAD STUDENTS

2,789 full-time, 3,205 part-time. Students come from 27 states and territories; 49 other countries; 1% are from out of state; 17% Black or African American, non-Hispanic/Latino; 13% Hispanic/Latino; 1% Asian, non-Hispanic/Latino; 0.0% Native Hawaiian or other Pacific Islander, non-Hispanic/Latino; 0.2% American Indian or Alaska Native, non-Hispanic/Latino; 3% Two or more races, non-Hispanic/Latino; 0.4% Race/ethnicity unknown; 7% transferred in.

Freshmen:

Admission: 4,467 applied, 3,095 admitted, 1,415 enrolled. ***Average high school GPA:*** 3.

Retention: 69% of full-time freshmen returned.

FACULTY

Total: 287, 43% full-time, 12% with terminal degrees.

Student/faculty ratio: 21:1.

ACADEMICS

Calendar: semesters. *Degrees:* associate and bachelor's.

Special study options: academic remediation for entering students, advanced placement credit, cooperative education, distance learning, double majors, honors programs, independent study, part-time degree program, services for LD students, study abroad, summer session for credit.

Computers: 1,690 computers/terminals are available on campus for general student use. Students can access the following: campus intranet, free student e-mail accounts, online (class) grades, online (class) registration, online (class) schedules, Campus-wide wifi is available to all students. Campuswide network is available. Wireless service is available via entire campus.

Library: Georgia Highlands College Library–Floyd Campus plus 4 others. *Books:* 72,257 (physical), 136,290 (digital/electronic); *Serial titles:* 54 (physical), 20 (digital/electronic); *Databases:* 349. Weekly public service hours: 58; students can reserve study rooms.

STUDENT LIFE

Housing options: college housing not available.

Activities and organizations: student-run newspaper, Highlands Association of Nursing Students, Green Highlands, Brother 2 Brother, Student Government Association, Phi Theta Kappa.

Athletics Member NJCAA. ***Intercollegiate sports:*** baseball M(s), basketball M(s)/W(s), softball W(s). ***Intramural sports:*** basketball M/W, cheerleading M/W, football M/W, golf M/W, skiing (downhill) M/W, table tennis M/W, tennis M/W, ultimate Frisbee M/W, volleyball M/W, weight lifting M/W.

Campus security: 24-hour emergency response devices and patrols, emergency phone/email alert system.

Student services: personal/psychological counseling.

COSTS & FINANCIAL AID

Costs (2017–18) ***One-time required fee:*** $30. ***Tuition:*** state resident $2181 full-time, $91 per credit hour part-time; nonresident $8256 full-time, $344 per credit hour part-time. Full-time tuition and fees vary according to course load. Part-time tuition and fees vary according to course load. ***Required fees:*** $1064 full-time, $412 per term part-time. ***Payment plan:*** installment. ***Waivers:*** senior citizens.

Financial Aid Of all full-time matriculated undergraduates who enrolled in 2015, 50 Federal Work-Study jobs (averaging $3500).

APPLYING

Options: electronic application, deferred entrance.

Application fee: $30.

Required: high school transcript, minimum 2.0 GPA.

Application deadlines: 7/15 (freshmen), 7/15 (transfers).

Notification: continuous (freshmen), continuous (transfers).

CONTACT

Charlene Graham, Assistant Director of Admissions, Georgia Highlands College, 3175 Cedartown Highway, Rome, GA 30161. *Phone:* 706-295-6339. *Toll-free phone:* 800-332-2406. *Fax:* 706-295-6341. *E-mail:* cgraham@highlands.edu.

Georgia Institute of Technology
Atlanta, Georgia
http://www.gatech.edu/

- **State-supported** university, founded 1885, part of University System of Georgia
- **Urban** 400-acre campus
- **Endowment** $1.8 billion
- **Coed** 15,489 undergraduate students, 89% full-time, 37% women, 63% men
- 26% of applicants were admitted

UNDERGRAD STUDENTS
13,815 full-time, 1,674 part-time. Students come from 54 states and territories; 127 other countries; 34% are from out of state; 7% Black or African American, non-Hispanic/Latino; 7% Hispanic/Latino; 20% Asian, non-Hispanic/Latino; 4% Two or more races, non-Hispanic/Latino; 3% Race/ethnicity unknown; 10% international; 4% transferred in; 53% live on campus.

Freshmen:
Admission: 30,528 applied, 7,868 admitted, 2,877 enrolled. ***Average high school GPA:*** 4.03. ***Test scores:*** SAT critical reading scores over 500: 99%; SAT math scores over 500: 99%; SAT writing scores over 500: 98%; ACT scores over 18: 100%; SAT critical reading scores over 600: 90%; SAT math scores over 600: 96%; SAT writing scores over 600: 89%; ACT scores over 24: 98%; SAT critical reading scores over 700: 45%; SAT math scores over 700: 66%; SAT writing scores over 700: 46%; ACT scores over 30: 83%.
Retention: 97% of full-time freshmen returned.

FACULTY
Total: 1,190, 90% full-time, 78% with terminal degrees.
Student/faculty ratio: 20:1.

ACADEMICS
Calendar: semesters. *Degrees:* bachelor's, master's, and doctoral.
Special study options: academic remediation for entering students, accelerated degree program, advanced placement credit, cooperative education, distance learning, English as a second language, honors programs, independent study, internships, off-campus study, part-time degree program, services for LD students, student-designed majors, study abroad, summer session for credit. ***ROTC:*** Army (b), Navy (b), Air Force (b).
Unusual degree programs: 3-2 engineering with Georgia Institute of Technology.
Computers: 2,500 computers/terminals and 22,981 ports are available on campus for general student use. Students can access the following: campus intranet, computer help desk, free student e-mail accounts, online (class) grades, online (class) registration, online (class) schedules, constant access to a virtual lab environment from a personal device or GT computer. Campuswide network is available. 100% of college-owned or -operated housing units are wired for high-speed Internet access. Wireless service is available via entire campus.
Library: Georgia Institute of Technology Library plus 1 other. *Books:* 931,886 (physical), 632,320 (digital/electronic); *Serial titles:* 361 (physical), 27,533 (digital/electronic); *Databases:* 314. Weekly public service hours: 168; study areas open 24 hours, 5-7 days a week; students can reserve study rooms.

STUDENT LIFE
Housing options: coed, men-only, women-only, special housing for students with disabilities. Campus housing is university owned. Freshman campus housing is guaranteed.
Activities and organizations: drama/theater group, student-run newspaper, radio and television station, choral group, marching band, national fraternities, national sororities.
Athletics Member NCAA. All Division I. ***Intercollegiate sports:*** baseball M(s), basketball M(s)/W(s), cheerleading M/W, cross-country running M(s)/W(s), football M(s), golf M(s), softball W(s), swimming and diving M(s)/W(s), tennis M(s)/W(s), track and field M(s)/W(s), volleyball W(s). ***Intramural sports:*** archery M(c)/W(c), badminton M(c)/W(c), baseball M(c)/W(c), basketball M/W, bowling M/W, crew M(c)/W(c), equestrian sports M(c)/W(c), fencing M(c)/W(c), field hockey M(c)/W(c), golf M(c)/W(c), gymnastics M(c)/W(c), ice hockey M(c)/W(c), lacrosse M(c)/W(c), racquetball M, rowing M(c)/W(c), rugby M(c)/W(c), sailing M(c)/W(c), soccer M/W, softball M, swimming and diving M(c)/W(c), tennis M(c)/W(c), ultimate Frisbee M, volleyball M/W, water polo M(c)/W(c), wrestling M(c).
Campus security: 24-hour emergency response devices and patrols, late-night transport/escort service, controlled dormitory access, lighted pathways/sidewalks, emergency notification system, self-defense education, emergency telephones, shuttle buses, video cameras.
Student services: health clinic, personal/psychological counseling, women's center, legal services.

COSTS & FINANCIAL AID
Costs (2016–17) ***Tuition:*** state resident $9812 full-time, $2916 per term part-time; nonresident $30,004 full-time, $8903 per term part-time. Part-time tuition and fees vary according to course load. ***Required fees:*** $2400 full-time, $1200 per term part-time. ***Room and board:*** $13,640; room only: $8940. Room and board charges vary according to board plan, housing facility, and student level. ***Payment plan:*** deferred payment. ***Waivers:*** senior citizens and employees or children of employees.
Financial Aid Of all full-time matriculated undergraduates who enrolled in 2015, 8,991 applied for aid, 5,673 were judged to have need, 874 had their need fully met. 395 Federal Work-Study jobs (averaging $1831). In 2015, 1560 non-need-based awards were made. ***Average percent of need met:*** 52. ***Average financial aid package:*** $13,171. ***Average need-based loan:*** $5007. ***Average need-based gift aid:*** $11,070. ***Average non-need-based aid:*** $11,275. ***Average indebtedness upon graduation:*** $32,169. ***Financial aid deadline:*** 1/31.

APPLYING
Standardized Tests *Required:* SAT or ACT (for admission).
Options: electronic application, early admission, early action, deferred entrance.
Application fee: $75.
Required: essay or personal statement, high school transcript.
Application deadlines: 1/1 (freshmen), 3/1 (transfers), 10/15 (early action).
Notification: 3/14 (freshmen), 6/15 (transfers), 1/10 (early action).

CONTACT
Mr. Rick A. Clark Jr., Director of Undergraduate Admissions, Georgia Institute of Technology, Office of Undergraduate Admission, Atlanta, GA 30332-0320. *Phone:* 404-894-4154. *Fax:* 404-894-9511.
E-mail: admission@gatech.edu.

Georgia Military College
Milledgeville, Georgia
http://www.gmc.edu/

- **Public** primarily 2-year, founded 1879
- **Small-town** campus
- **Endowment** $1.5 million
- **Coed** 8,234 undergraduate students, 56% full-time, 60% women, 40% men
- **Noncompetitive** entrance level

UNDERGRAD STUDENTS
4,587 full-time, 3,647 part-time. Students come from 35 states and territories; 5 other countries; 4% are from out of state; 44% Black or African American, non-Hispanic/Latino; 7% Hispanic/Latino; 2% Asian, non-Hispanic/Latino; 0.4% Native Hawaiian or other Pacific Islander, non-Hispanic/Latino; 2% American Indian or Alaska Native, non-Hispanic/Latino; 0.4% Two or more races, non-Hispanic/Latino; 3% Race/ethnicity unknown; 0.3% international; 8% transferred in; 3% live on campus.

Freshmen:
Admission: 1,700 enrolled.
Retention: 53% of full-time freshmen returned.

FACULTY
Total: 564, 23% full-time.
Student/faculty ratio: 21:1.

ACADEMICS
Calendar: quarters. *Degrees:* associate and bachelor's.

Special study options: academic remediation for entering students, advanced placement credit, cooperative education, distance learning, double majors, independent study, off-campus study, part-time degree program, services for LD students, student-designed majors, study abroad, summer session for credit. ***ROTC:*** Army (b).

Computers: 835 computers/terminals are available on campus for general student use. Students can access the following: campus intranet, computer help desk, free student e-mail accounts, online (class) grades, online (class) registration, online (class) schedules. Campuswide network is available. 100% of college-owned or -operated housing units are wired for high-speed Internet access. Wireless service is available via entire campus.

Library: Sibley Cone Library plus 1 other. *Books:* 38,125 (physical), 57,769 (digital/electronic); *Serial titles:* 52 (physical); *Databases:* 331. Weekly public service hours: 68.

STUDENT LIFE

Housing options: on-campus residence required through sophomore year; coed. Campus housing is university owned. Freshman campus housing is guaranteed.

Activities and organizations: drama/theater group, student-run newspaper, choral group, Student Government Association, Alpha Phi Omega National Service Fraternity, Phi Theta Kappa, Drama Club, Biology Club.

Athletics Member NJCAA. ***Intercollegiate sports:*** cross-country running M/W, football M(s), golf M/W, riflery M/W, soccer M(s)/W(s), softball W(s). ***Intramural sports:*** badminton M/W, basketball M/W, golf M/W, softball M/W, tennis M/W, volleyball M/W.

Campus security: 24-hour emergency response devices and patrols, controlled dormitory access.

Student services: health clinic.

COSTS & FINANCIAL AID

Costs (2017–18) ***Tuition:*** state resident $5445 full-time, $122 per credit hour part-time; nonresident $5445 full-time, $122 per credit hour part-time. Full-time tuition and fees vary according to location. Part-time tuition and fees vary according to location. ***Required fees:*** $683 full-time, $30 per credit hour part-time, $30 per credit hour part-time. ***Room and board:*** Room and board charges vary according to location. ***Waivers:*** employees or children of employees.

Financial Aid Of all full-time matriculated undergraduates who enrolled in 2012, 6,554 applied for aid, 6,132 were judged to have need, 282 had their need fully met. 121 Federal Work-Study jobs (averaging $1614). In 2012, 61 non-need-based awards were made. ***Average percent of need met:*** 47. ***Average financial aid package:*** $9567. ***Average need-based loan:*** $3189. ***Average need-based gift aid:*** $4626. ***Average non-need-based aid:*** $2226.

APPLYING

Options: electronic application, early admission, deferred entrance.

Application fee: $35.

Required for some: high school transcript, interview.

Application deadlines: rolling (freshmen), rolling (transfers).

CONTACT

Georgia Military College, 201 East Greene Street, Old Capitol Building, Milledgeville, GA 31061-3398. *Phone:* 478-387-4890. *Toll-free phone:* 800-342-0413.

Georgia Southern University

Statesboro, Georgia

http://www.georgiasouthern.edu/

- **State-supported** university, founded 1906, part of University System of Georgia
- **Small-town** 900-acre campus
- **Endowment** $44.4 million
- **Coed** 18,005 undergraduate students, 89% full-time, 51% women, 49% men
- **Moderately difficult** entrance level, 65% of applicants were admitted

UNDERGRAD STUDENTS

15,976 full-time, 2,029 part-time. Students come from 49 states and territories; 73 other countries; 4% are from out of state; 25% Black or African American, non-Hispanic/Latino; 5% Hispanic/Latino; 2% Asian, non-Hispanic/Latino; 0.1% Native Hawaiian or other Pacific Islander, non-Hispanic/Latino; 0.4% American Indian or Alaska Native, non-Hispanic/Latino; 2% Two or more races, non-Hispanic/Latino; 1% Race/ethnicity unknown; 2% international; 6% transferred in; 27% live on campus.

Freshmen:

Admission: 9,834 applied, 6,348 admitted, 3,600 enrolled. ***Average high school GPA:*** 3.33. ***Test scores:*** SAT critical reading scores over 500: 87%; SAT math scores over 500: 85%; SAT writing scores over 500: 67%; ACT scores over 18: 100%; SAT critical reading scores over 600: 24%; SAT math scores over 600: 26%; SAT writing scores over 600: 16%; ACT scores over 24: 45%; SAT critical reading scores over 700: 2%; SAT math scores over 700: 2%; SAT writing scores over 700: 1%; ACT scores over 30: 5%.

Retention: 81% of full-time freshmen returned.

FACULTY

Total: 866, 90% full-time, 81% with terminal degrees.

Student/faculty ratio: 21:1.

ACADEMICS

Calendar: semesters. *Degrees:* bachelor's, master's, doctoral, post-master's, and postbachelor's certificates.

Special study options: academic remediation for entering students, accelerated degree program, adult/continuing education programs, advanced placement credit, cooperative education, distance learning, double majors, English as a second language, honors programs, independent study, internships, off-campus study, part-time degree program, services for LD students, student-designed majors, study abroad, summer session for credit. ***ROTC:*** Army (b).

Unusual degree programs: 3-2 engineering with Georgia Institute of Technology; nursing.

Computers: 3,743 computers/terminals and 5,200 ports are available on campus for general student use. Students can access the following: campus intranet, computer help desk, free student e-mail accounts, online (class) grades, online (class) registration, online (class) schedules, online degree audit, online career services, and online healthcare. Campuswide network is available. 100% of college-owned or -operated housing units are wired for high-speed Internet access. Wireless service is available via entire campus.

Library: Henderson Library. *Books:* 657,965 (physical), 30,602 (digital/electronic); *Serial titles:* 435 (physical), 84,081 (digital/electronic); *Databases:* 369. Weekly public service hours: 143; study areas open 24 hours, 5-7 days a week; students can reserve study rooms.

STUDENT LIFE

Housing options: on-campus residence required for freshman year; coed, special housing for students with disabilities. Campus housing is university owned. Freshman applicants given priority for college housing.

Activities and organizations: drama/theater group, student-run newspaper, radio station, choral group, marching band, Residence Hall Association, Campus Religious Ministries, Student Government Association, Club Sports and Recreation, Greek Life, national fraternities, national sororities.

Athletics Member NCAA. All Division I. ***Intercollegiate sports:*** baseball M(s), basketball M(s)/W(s), cheerleading M/W, cross-country running W(s), football M(s), golf M(s), riflery M/W(s), soccer M(s)/W(s), softball W(s), swimming and diving W(s), tennis M(s)/W(s), track and field W(s), volleyball W(s). ***Intramural sports:*** archery M/W, baseball M, basketball M/W, bowling M/W, cheerleading M(c)/W(c), cross-country running M(c)/W(c), equestrian sports M(c)/W(c), fencing M/W, football M/W, golf M/W, gymnastics M/W, lacrosse M/W, riflery M/W, rugby M/W, soccer M/W, softball W, swimming and diving M/W, tennis M/W, track and field M(c)/W(c), ultimate Frisbee M/W, volleyball M/W, water polo M(c)/W(c), weight lifting M/W, wrestling M(c).

Campus security: 24-hour emergency response devices and patrols, student patrols, late-night transport/escort service, controlled dormitory access, bike police and services.

Student services: health clinic, personal/psychological counseling, women's center, legal services.

COSTS & FINANCIAL AID
Costs (2016–17) ***Tuition:*** state resident $4704 full-time, $174 per credit hour part-time; nonresident $16,600 full-time, $615 per credit hour part-time. Full-time tuition and fees vary according to course load, degree level, location, and program. Part-time tuition and fees vary according to course load, degree level, location, and program. ***Required fees:*** $2092 full-time, $1046 per term part-time. ***Room and board:*** $9650; room only: $5900. Room and board charges vary according to board plan and housing facility. ***Payment plan:*** installment. ***Waivers:*** senior citizens and employees or children of employees.

Financial Aid Of all full-time matriculated undergraduates who enrolled in 2015, 14,342 applied for aid, 10,601 were judged to have need, 982 had their need fully met. 219 Federal Work-Study jobs (averaging $1814). In 2015, 340 non-need-based awards were made. ***Average percent of need met:*** 51. ***Average financial aid package:*** $9952. ***Average need-based loan:*** $4952. ***Average need-based gift aid:*** $6864. ***Average non-need-based aid:*** $1695. ***Average indebtedness upon graduation:*** $28,098.

APPLYING
Standardized Tests *Required:* SAT or ACT (for admission).

Options: electronic application, early admission, deferred entrance.

Application fee: $30.

Required: minimum 2.0 GPA. ***Required for some:*** high school transcript.

Application deadlines: 5/1 (freshmen), 8/1 (transfers).

Notification: continuous (freshmen), continuous (transfers).

CONTACT
Miss Amy Smith, Director, Georgia Southern University, PO Box 8024, Statesboro, GA 30460. *Phone:* 912-478-5391. *Fax:* 912-478-7240. *E-mail:* admissions@georgiasouthern.edu.

★ Georgia Southwestern State University

Americus, Georgia

http://www.gsw.edu/

- **State-supported** comprehensive, founded 1906, part of University System of Georgia
- **Small-town** 250-acre campus
- **Endowment** $31.2 million
- **Coed** 2,558 undergraduate students, 69% full-time, 62% women, 38% men
- **Moderately difficult** entrance level, 68% of applicants were admitted

UNDERGRAD STUDENTS
1,769 full-time, 789 part-time. Students come from 25 states and territories; 29 other countries; 4% are from out of state; 27% Black or African American, non-Hispanic/Latino; 4% Hispanic/Latino; 1% Asian, non-Hispanic/Latino; 0.2% Native Hawaiian or other Pacific Islander, non-Hispanic/Latino; 0.3% American Indian or Alaska Native, non-Hispanic/Latino; 2% Two or more races, non-Hispanic/Latino; 0.3% Race/ethnicity unknown; 2% international; 11% transferred in; 32% live on campus.

Freshmen:
Admission: 1,389 applied, 947 admitted, 485 enrolled. ***Average high school GPA:*** 3.27. ***Test scores:*** SAT critical reading scores over 500: 43%; SAT math scores over 500: 38%; ACT scores over 18: 90%; SAT critical reading scores over 600: 7%; SAT math scores over 600: 7%; ACT scores over 24: 23%; SAT math scores over 700: 1%; ACT scores over 30: 2%.

Retention: 70% of full-time freshmen returned.

FACULTY
Total: 161, 70% full-time, 59% with terminal degrees.

Student/faculty ratio: 18:1.

ACADEMICS
Calendar: semesters. *Degrees:* bachelor's, master's, post-master's, and postbachelor's certificates.

Special study options: academic remediation for entering students, accelerated degree program, advanced placement credit, distance learning, double majors, English as a second language, honors programs, internships, part-time degree program, services for LD students, study abroad, summer session for credit.

Unusual degree programs: engineering with Georgia Institute of Technology.

Computers: 260 computers/terminals are available on campus for general student use. Students can access the following: free student e-mail accounts, online (class) grades, online (class) registration, online (class) schedules. Campuswide network is available. 100% of college-owned or -operated housing units are wired for high-speed Internet access. Wireless service is available via dorm rooms, learning centers, libraries, student centers.

Library: James Earl Carter Library. *Books:* 207,635 (physical), 68,397 (digital/electronic); *Serial titles:* 76 (physical), 81 (digital/electronic); *Databases:* 277. Weekly public service hours: 72; students can reserve study rooms.

STUDENT LIFE
Housing options: on-campus residence required through sophomore year; coed. Campus housing is university owned. Freshman campus housing is guaranteed.

Activities and organizations: drama/theater group, student-run newspaper, choral group, National sororities and fraternities, African Student Association, Enactus, Humanitarian Society, International Student Association, national fraternities, national sororities.

Athletics Member NCAA. All Division II. ***Intercollegiate sports:*** baseball M(s), basketball M(s)/W(s), cross-country running W(s), golf M(s), soccer M(s)/W(s), softball W(s), tennis M(s)/W(s). ***Intramural sports:*** basketball M/W, racquetball M/W, ultimate Frisbee M/W, volleyball M/W.

Campus security: 24-hour emergency response devices and patrols, late-night transport/escort service, controlled dormitory access.

Student services: health clinic, personal/psychological counseling.

COSTS & FINANCIAL AID
Costs (2016–17) ***Tuition:*** state resident $4858 full-time, $162 per credit hour part-time; nonresident $17,678 full-time, $589 per credit hour part-time. Full-time tuition and fees vary according to course load, location, and program. Part-time tuition and fees vary according to course load, location, and program. ***Required fees:*** $1376 full-time, $670 per term part-time. ***Room and board:*** $8952; room only: $5130. Room and board charges vary according to board plan and housing facility. ***Waivers:*** senior citizens.

Financial Aid Of all full-time matriculated undergraduates who enrolled in 2016, 1,577 applied for aid, 1,288 were judged to have need, 164 had their need fully met. 56 Federal Work-Study jobs (averaging $2207). In 2016, 124 non-need-based awards were made. ***Average percent of need met:*** 60. ***Average financial aid package:*** $9480. ***Average need-based loan:*** $3984. ***Average need-based gift aid:*** $4902. ***Average non-need-based aid:*** $1977. ***Average indebtedness upon graduation:*** $28,469. ***Financial aid deadline:*** 6/15.

APPLYING
Standardized Tests *Required:* SAT or ACT (for admission).

Options: electronic application, early admission, deferred entrance.

Application fee: $25.

Required: high school transcript, minimum 2.0 GPA, college preparatory curriculum; standardized test scores. ***Recommended:*** interview.

Application deadlines: 7/21 (freshmen), 7/21 (transfers).

Notification: continuous (freshmen), continuous (transfers).

CONTACT
Mr. David Jenkins, Assistant Director of Admissions, Georgia Southwestern State University, Americus, GA 31709. *Phone:* 229-928-1273. *Toll-free phone:* 800-338-0082. *Fax:* 229-931-2983. *E-mail:* admissions@gsw.edu.

Georgia State University

Atlanta, Georgia

http://www.gsu.edu/

- **State-supported** university, founded 1913, part of University System of Georgia
- **Urban** 72-acre campus with easy access to Atlanta
- **Endowment** $139.8 million
- **Coed** 25,455 undergraduate students, 76% full-time, 59% women, 41% men
- **Moderately difficult** entrance level, 53% of applicants were admitted

UNDERGRAD STUDENTS

19,371 full-time, 6,084 part-time. Students come from 53 states and territories; 140 other countries; 5% are from out of state; 42% Black or African American, non-Hispanic/Latino; 10% Hispanic/Latino; 13% Asian, non-Hispanic/Latino; 0.1% Native Hawaiian or other Pacific Islander, non-Hispanic/Latino; 0.1% American Indian or Alaska Native, non-Hispanic/Latino; 6% Two or more races, non-Hispanic/Latino; 1% Race/ethnicity unknown; 2% international; 7% transferred in; 21% live on campus.

Freshmen:

Admission: 17,467 applied, 9,212 admitted, 3,975 enrolled. ***Average high school GPA:*** 3.4. ***Test scores:*** SAT critical reading scores over 500: 69%; SAT math scores over 500: 64%; SAT writing scores over 500: 60%; ACT scores over 18: 96%; SAT critical reading scores over 600: 23%; SAT math scores over 600: 22%; SAT writing scores over 600: 16%; ACT scores over 24: 44%; SAT critical reading scores over 700: 3%; SAT math scores over 700: 4%; SAT writing scores over 700: 1%; ACT scores over 30: 6%.

Retention: 83% of full-time freshmen returned.

FACULTY

Total: 1,691, 73% full-time, 83% with terminal degrees.

Student/faculty ratio: 19:1.

ACADEMICS

Calendar: semesters. *Degrees:* certificates, associate, bachelor's, master's, doctoral, post-master's, and postbachelor's certificates.

Special study options: advanced placement credit, cooperative education, distance learning, double majors, English as a second language, honors programs, independent study, internships, part-time degree program, services for LD students, study abroad, summer session for credit. ***ROTC:*** Army (b), Navy (c), Air Force (c).

Computers: 1,431 computers/terminals and 20,500 ports are available on campus for general student use. Students can access the following: computer help desk, free student e-mail accounts, online (class) grades, online (class) registration, online (class) schedules. Campuswide network is available. 100% of college-owned or -operated housing units are wired for high-speed Internet access. Wireless service is available via entire campus.

Library: University Library plus 1 other. *Books:* 1.7 million (physical), 645,924 (digital/electronic); *Serial titles:* 14,284 (digital/electronic). Students can reserve study rooms.

STUDENT LIFE

Housing options: coed, special housing for students with disabilities. Campus housing is university owned and leased by the school. Freshman applicants given priority for college housing.

Activities and organizations: drama/theater group, student-run newspaper, radio and television station, choral group, marching band, Spotlight Programs Board, Fraternities/Sororities, Service Organizations, Academic Organizations, Sports Clubs, national fraternities, national sororities.

Athletics Member NCAA. All Division I. ***Intercollegiate sports:*** baseball M(s), basketball M(s)/W(s), crew M(c)/W(c), cross-country running W(s), equestrian sports M(c)/W(c), football M(s), golf M(s)/W(s), ice hockey M(c), lacrosse M(c), rugby M(c), soccer M(s)/W(s), softball W(s), squash M(c)/W(c), swimming and diving M(c)/W(c), table tennis M(c)/W(c), tennis M(s)/W(s), track and field W(s), ultimate Frisbee M(c)/W(c), volleyball W(s). ***Intramural sports:*** badminton M/W, basketball M/W, bowling M/W, crew M(c)/W(c), equestrian sports M(c)/W(c), football M/W, golf M/W, racquetball M/W, rock climbing M(c)/W(c), soccer M/W, table tennis M/W, ultimate Frisbee M/W, volleyball M/W, wrestling M(c)/W(c).

Campus security: 24-hour emergency response devices and patrols, late-night transport/escort service, controlled dormitory access, Emergency Notification System.

Student services: health clinic, personal/psychological counseling.

COSTS & FINANCIAL AID

Costs (2016–17) ***Tuition:*** state resident $8558 full-time, $285 per credit hour part-time; nonresident $26,768 full-time, $892 per credit hour part-time. Part-time tuition and fees vary according to course load. ***Required fees:*** $2128 full-time, $1064 per term part-time. ***Room and board:*** $14,084; room only: $10,252. Room and board charges vary according to board plan and housing facility. ***Waivers:*** senior citizens and employees or children of employees.

Financial Aid Of all full-time matriculated undergraduates who enrolled in 2015, 16,980 applied for aid, 14,777 were judged to have need, 1,170 had their need fully met. ***Average percent of need met:*** 59. ***Average financial aid package:*** $11,461. ***Average need-based gift aid:*** $4997. ***Average indebtedness upon graduation:*** $29,959. ***Financial aid deadline:*** 4/1.

APPLYING

Standardized Tests *Required:* SAT or ACT (for admission).

Options: electronic application, early admission, early action, deferred entrance.

Application fee: $60.

Required: essay or personal statement, high school transcript, minimum 2.8 GPA, 1 letter of recommendation, college preparatory curriculum as specified by the University System of Georgia Board of Regents, combined SAT of 830, minimum Freshman Index of 2500.

Application deadlines: 3/1 (freshmen), 8/1 (transfers), 11/16 (early action).

Notification: 5/1 (freshmen), continuous (transfers), 1/30 (early action).

CONTACT

Scott Burke, Director of Admissions, Georgia State University, PO Box 4009, Atlanta, GA 30302-4009. *Phone:* 404-413-2500. *Fax:* 404-413-2002. *E-mail:* onestopshop@gsu.edu.

Gordon State College

Barnesville, Georgia

http://www.gordonstate.edu/

- **State-supported** primarily 2-year, founded 1852, part of University System of Georgia
- **Small-town** 235-acre campus with easy access to Atlanta
- **Coed** 3,901 undergraduate students, 64% full-time, 66% women, 34% men
- 41% of applicants were admitted

UNDERGRAD STUDENTS

2,492 full-time, 1,409 part-time. 0.7% are from out of state; 37% Black or African American, non-Hispanic/Latino; 3% Hispanic/Latino; 0.9% Asian, non-Hispanic/Latino; 0.1% Native Hawaiian or other Pacific Islander, non-Hispanic/Latino; 3% Two or more races, non-Hispanic/Latino; 0.4% Race/ethnicity unknown; 0.2% international; 6% transferred in.

Freshmen:

Admission: 2,718 applied, 1,122 admitted, 881 enrolled.

FACULTY

Total: 199, 60% full-time, 52% with terminal degrees.

Student/faculty ratio: 21:1.

ACADEMICS

Calendar: semesters. *Degrees:* associate and bachelor's.

Special study options: academic remediation for entering students, accelerated degree program, adult/continuing education programs, advanced placement credit, cooperative education, distance learning, double majors, honors programs, internships, off-campus study, part-time degree program, services for LD students, study abroad, summer session for credit.

Computers: 466 computers/terminals and 1,000 ports are available on campus for general student use. Students can access the following: campus intranet, computer help desk, free student e-mail accounts, online (class) grades, online (class) registration, online (class) schedules. Campuswide network is available. 100% of college-owned or -operated housing units are wired for high-speed Internet access. Wireless service is available via entire campus.

Library: DOROTHY W. HIGHTOWER COLLABORATIVE LEARNING CENTER & LIBRARY. *Books:* 103,423 (physical), 35,999 (digital/electronic); *Serial titles:* 401 (physical), 87,985 (digital/electronic); *Databases:* 325. Weekly public service hours: 73.

STUDENT LIFE

Housing options: on-campus residence required for freshman year; coed. Campus housing is university owned. Freshman applicants given priority for college housing.

Activities and organizations: drama/theater group, student-run newspaper, choral group, Campus Activity Board, Student Government Association, Earth Wind Fire (science club), Student African American Brotherhood (SAAB), Swazi Step Team.

Athletics Member NJCAA. ***Intercollegiate sports:*** baseball M, basketball M, soccer M/W, softball W.

Campus security: 24-hour emergency response devices and patrols, student patrols, controlled dormitory access, Resident Assistants and Resident Directors in housing, parking patrol.

Student services: health clinic, personal/psychological counseling.

COSTS & FINANCIAL AID

Costs (2017–18) ***Tuition:*** state resident $3064 full-time, $103 per credit hour part-time; nonresident $11,322 full-time, $378 per credit hour part-time. ***Required fees:*** $1100 full-time, $550 per term part-time. ***Room and board:*** $8101. Room and board charges vary according to board plan and housing facility. ***Payment plan:*** installment.

Financial Aid Of all full-time matriculated undergraduates who enrolled in 2015, 75 Federal Work-Study jobs (averaging $1850).

APPLYING

Standardized Tests *Required:* SAT or ACT (for admission).

Options: electronic application, early admission, deferred entrance.

Application fee: $30.

Required: high school transcript.

Application deadlines: rolling (freshmen), rolling (transfers).

CONTACT

Gordon State College, 419 College Drive, Barnesville, GA 30204-1762. *Phone:* 678-359-5021. *Toll-free phone:* 800-282-6504.

Herzing University

Atlanta, Georgia

http://www.herzing.edu/atlanta/

CONTACT

Herzing University, 3393 Peachtree Road, NE, Suite 1003, Atlanta, GA 30326. *Toll-free phone:* 800-596-0724.

Kennesaw State University

Kennesaw, Georgia

http://www.kennesaw.edu/

- **State-supported** comprehensive, founded 1963, part of University System of Georgia
- **Suburban** 602-acre campus with easy access to Atlanta
- **Endowment** $37.2 million
- **Coed** 32,166 undergraduate students, 76% full-time, 48% women, 52% men
- **Moderately difficult** entrance level, 59% of applicants were admitted

UNDERGRAD STUDENTS

24,412 full-time, 7,754 part-time. Students come from 54 states and territories; 134 other countries; 10% are from out of state; 21% Black or African American, non-Hispanic/Latino; 9% Hispanic/Latino; 5% Asian, non-Hispanic/Latino; 0.1% Native Hawaiian or other Pacific Islander, non-Hispanic/Latino; 0.2% American Indian or Alaska Native, non-Hispanic/Latino; 4% Two or more races, non-Hispanic/Latino; 2% Race/ethnicity unknown; 2% international; 9% transferred in; 15% live on campus.

Freshmen:

Admission: 15,122 applied, 8,847 admitted, 5,347 enrolled. ***Average high school GPA:*** 3.31. ***Test scores:*** SAT critical reading scores over 500: 79%; SAT math scores over 500: 79%; SAT writing scores over 500: 64%; ACT scores over 18: 99%; SAT critical reading scores over 600: 25%; SAT math scores over 600: 25%; SAT writing scores over 600: 15%; ACT scores over 24: 43%; SAT critical reading scores over 700: 3%; SAT math scores over 700: 3%; SAT writing scores over 700: 1%; ACT scores over 30: 5%.

Retention: 80% of full-time freshmen returned.

FACULTY

Total: 1,948, 57% full-time, 60% with terminal degrees.

Student/faculty ratio: 20:1.

ACADEMICS

Calendar: semesters. *Degrees:* certificates, bachelor's, master's, doctoral, post-master's, and postbachelor's certificates.

Special study options: adult/continuing education programs, advanced placement credit, cooperative education, distance learning, double majors, English as a second language, freshman honors college, honors programs, internships, off-campus study, part-time degree program, services for LD students, study abroad, summer session for credit. ***ROTC:*** Army (c), Air Force (c).

Computers: 4,201 computers/terminals and 25,000 ports are available on campus for general student use. Students can access the following: campus intranet, computer help desk, free student e-mail accounts, online (class) grades, online (class) registration, online (class) schedules. Campuswide network is available. 100% of college-owned or -operated housing units are wired for high-speed Internet access. Wireless service is available via classrooms, computer centers, computer labs, dorm rooms, learning centers, libraries, student centers.

Library: KSU Library System plus 1 other. *Books:* 483,694 (physical), 412,308 (digital/electronic); *Serial titles:* 1,599 (physical), 101,202 (digital/electronic); *Databases:* 396. Weekly public service hours: 95; students can reserve study rooms.

STUDENT LIFE

Housing options: coed. Campus housing is provided by a third party. Freshman applicants given priority for college housing.

Activities and organizations: drama/theater group, student-run newspaper, radio station, choral group, marching band, African American Student Alliance, American Medical Student Association, International Student Association, Kennesaw Activities Board, Graduate Student Association, national fraternities, national sororities.

Athletics Member NCAA. All Division I except football (Division I-AA). ***Intercollegiate sports:*** baseball M(s), basketball M(s)/W(s), cross-country running M(s)/W(s), golf M(s)/W(s), lacrosse W(s), soccer W(s), softball W(s), tennis M(s)/W(s), track and field M(s)/W(s), volleyball W(s). ***Intramural sports:*** archery M(c)/W(c), badminton M(c)/W(c), baseball M(c), basketball M/W, bowling M/W, cheerleading M(c)/W(c), cross-country running M(c)/W(c), equestrian sports M(c)/W(c), fencing M(c)/W(c), football M/W, golf M/W, gymnastics M(c)/W(c), ice hockey M(c), lacrosse M(c)/W(c), racquetball M/W, rugby M(c)/W(c), sand volleyball M/W, soccer M/W, softball M/W, swimming and diving M(c)/W(c), table tennis M(c)/W(c), tennis M/W, ultimate Frisbee M/W, volleyball M/W, weight lifting M(c)/W(c), wrestling M(c).

Campus security: 24-hour emergency response devices and patrols, student patrols, late-night transport/escort service, controlled dormitory access, campus advisory Web page; early notification system; sirens; rapid email, text, and phone messages to all staff and students.

Student services: health clinic, personal/psychological counseling.

COSTS & FINANCIAL AID

Costs (2016–17) ***Tuition:*** state resident $5320 full-time, $177 per credit hour part-time; nonresident $18,776 full-time, $626 per credit hour part-time. Full-time tuition and fees vary according to course load, degree level, location, program, and student level. Part-time tuition and fees vary according to course load, degree level, location, program, and student level. ***Required fees:*** $2956 full-time, $1478 per term part-time. ***Room and board:*** $11,467. Room and board charges vary according to board plan, housing facility, and student level. ***Payment plan:*** deferred payment. ***Waivers:*** senior citizens and employees or children of employees.

Financial Aid Of all full-time matriculated undergraduates who enrolled in 2016, 21,674 applied for aid, 17,780 were judged to have need, 698 had their need fully met. In 2016, 189 non-need-based awards were made. ***Average percent of need met:*** 38. ***Average financial aid package:*** $8426. ***Average need-based loan:*** $3475. ***Average need-based gift aid:*** $4654. ***Average non-need-based aid:*** $1229. ***Average indebtedness upon graduation:*** $25,613.

APPLYING

Standardized Tests *Required:* SAT or ACT (for admission). *Required for some:* SAT Subject Tests (for admission).

Options: electronic application, early admission, deferred entrance.

Application fee: $40.

Required: high school transcript, minimum 2.5 GPA.

Application deadlines: 5/5 (freshmen), 6/16 (transfers).

Notification: continuous (freshmen), continuous (transfers).

CONTACT

Admissions Office, Kennesaw State University, 3391 Town Point Drive, Suite 1000, Mail Drop #9111, Kennesaw, GA 30144. *Phone:* 770-423-6300. *Fax:* 470-578-9169. *E-mail:* ksuadmit@kennesaw.edu.

LaGrange College

LaGrange, Georgia

http://www.lagrange.edu/

- **Independent United Methodist** comprehensive, founded 1831
- **Small-town** 120-acre campus with easy access to Atlanta
- **Endowment** $49.0 million
- **Coed** 906 undergraduate students, 94% full-time, 49% women, 51% men
- **Moderately difficult** entrance level, 58% of applicants were admitted

UNDERGRAD STUDENTS

854 full-time, 52 part-time. Students come from 18 states and territories; 7 other countries; 17% are from out of state; 23% Black or African American, non-Hispanic/Latino; 1% Hispanic/Latino; 1% Asian, non-Hispanic/Latino; 0.2% American Indian or Alaska Native, non-Hispanic/Latino; 2% Two or more races, non-Hispanic/Latino; 0.1% Race/ethnicity unknown; 0.8% international; 10% transferred in; 62% live on campus.

Freshmen:

Admission: 1,568 applied, 905 admitted, 240 enrolled. ***Average high school GPA:*** 3.44. ***Test scores:*** SAT critical reading scores over 500: 53%; ACT scores over 18: 95%; SAT critical reading scores over 600: 16%; ACT scores over 24: 30%; SAT critical reading scores over 700: 3%; ACT scores over 30: 1%.

Retention: 66% of full-time freshmen returned.

FACULTY

Total: 110, 67% full-time, 68% with terminal degrees.

Student/faculty ratio: 11:1.

ACADEMICS

Calendar: 4-1-4. *Degrees:* bachelor's and master's.

Special study options: accelerated degree program, adult/continuing education programs, advanced placement credit, distance learning, double majors, independent study, internships, part-time degree program, services for LD students, student-designed majors, study abroad, summer session for credit.

Unusual degree programs: 3-2 engineering with Georgia Institute of Technology, Auburn University.

Computers: 116 computers/terminals and 960 ports are available on campus for general student use. Students can access the following: campus intranet, free student e-mail accounts, online (class) grades, online (class) registration, online (class) schedules. Campuswide network is available. 100% of college-owned or -operated housing units are wired for high-speed Internet access. Wireless service is available via entire campus.

Library: Frank and Laura Lewis Library. *Books:* 98,264 (physical), 419,828 (digital/electronic); *Serial titles:* 92 (physical), 44 (digital/electronic); *Databases:* 195. Weekly public service hours: 84; study areas open 24 hours, 5-7 days a week; students can reserve study rooms.

STUDENT LIFE

Housing options: on-campus residence required through senior year; coed, men-only, women-only, special housing for students with disabilities. Campus housing is university owned. Freshman campus housing is guaranteed.

Activities and organizations: drama/theater group, student-run newspaper, choral group, marching band, Student Government Association, Greek Life, Baptist Collegiate Ministries, Wesley Fellowship, Fellowship of Christian Athletes, national fraternities, national sororities.

Athletics Member NCAA. All Division III. ***Intercollegiate sports:*** baseball M, basketball M/W, cheerleading W, cross-country running M/W, football M, golf M, lacrosse W, soccer M/W, softball W, swimming and diving M/W, tennis M/W, volleyball W. ***Intramural sports:*** basketball M/W, softball M/W, table tennis M/W, water polo M/W.

Campus security: 24-hour patrols, controlled dormitory access, mass notification system (e2Campus) to send emergency messages to students and employees.

Student services: health clinic, personal/psychological counseling.

COSTS & FINANCIAL AID

Costs (2016–17) ***One-time required fee:*** $150. ***Comprehensive fee:*** $39,930 includes full-time tuition ($28,160), mandatory fees ($330), and room and board ($11,440). Full-time tuition and fees vary according to class time, course load, and program. Part-time tuition: $1160 per credit hour. Part-time tuition and fees vary according to class time, course load, and program. ***College room only:*** $6310. Room and board charges vary according to board plan and housing facility. ***Payment plan:*** installment. ***Waivers:*** senior citizens and employees or children of employees.

Financial Aid Of all full-time matriculated undergraduates who enrolled in 2015, 815 applied for aid, 743 were judged to have need, 139 had their need fully met. In 2015, 71 non-need-based awards were made. ***Average percent of need met:*** 71. ***Average financial aid package:*** $24,242. ***Average need-based loan:*** $4218. ***Average need-based gift aid:*** $6878. ***Average non-need-based aid:*** $11,088. ***Average indebtedness upon graduation:*** $29,301.

APPLYING

Standardized Tests *Required:* SAT or ACT (for admission). *Required for some:* SAT (for admission), ACT (for admission).

Options: electronic application, deferred entrance.

Required: essay or personal statement, high school transcript. ***Required for some:*** minimum 2.5 GPA, 3 letters of recommendation, interview.

Application deadlines: rolling (freshmen), rolling (transfers).

Notification: continuous (freshmen), continuous (transfers).

CONTACT

Ms. Holly Phillips, Administrative Coordinator, LaGrange College, 601 Broad Street, LaGrange, GA 30240-2999. *Phone:* 706-880-8005. *Toll-free phone:* 800-593-2885. *Fax:* 706-880-8010. *E-mail:* hphillips@lagrange.edu.

Life University

Marietta, Georgia

http://www.life.edu/

- **Independent** comprehensive, founded 1974
- **Suburban** 96-acre campus
- **Coed** 718 undergraduate students, 74% full-time, 55% women, 45% men
- **Minimally difficult** entrance level, 92% of applicants were admitted

UNDERGRAD STUDENTS

531 full-time, 187 part-time. Students come from 53 states and territories; 55% are from out of state; 26% Black or African American, non-Hispanic/Latino; 13% Hispanic/Latino; 2% Asian, non-Hispanic/Latino; 3% American Indian or Alaska Native, non-Hispanic/Latino; 8% Race/ethnicity unknown; 5% international; 10% live on campus.

Freshmen:

Admission: 280 applied, 258 admitted, 128 enrolled. ***Average high school GPA:*** 3.12.

Retention: 63% of full-time freshmen returned.

FACULTY
Total: 183, 70% full-time, 80% with terminal degrees.
Student/faculty ratio: 12:1.

ACADEMICS
Calendar: quarters. *Degrees:* certificates, associate, bachelor's, master's, and doctoral.

Special study options: academic remediation for entering students, accelerated degree program, advanced placement credit, cooperative education, distance learning, double majors, English as a second language, independent study, internships, off-campus study, part-time degree program, services for LD students, student-designed majors, study abroad, summer session for credit.

Computers: Students can access the following: campus intranet, computer help desk, free student e-mail accounts, online (class) grades, online (class) registration. Campuswide network is available. 100% of college-owned or -operated housing units are wired for high-speed Internet access. Wireless service is available via entire campus.
Library: Library & Learning Services. *Books:* 35,643 (physical), 363,658 (digital/electronic); *Serial titles:* 61 (physical), 31,104 (digital/electronic); *Databases:* 25. Weekly public service hours: 98; students can reserve study rooms.

STUDENT LIFE
Housing options: coed. Campus housing is university owned.

Activities and organizations: student-run newspaper, Student Ambassadors, Jewish Life, Student Nutrition and Dietetics Association, Gay Straight Alliance, Hispanic Club.

Athletics Member NAIA. ***Intercollegiate sports:*** basketball M(s)/W(s), cross-country running W(s), ice hockey M(s), rugby M(s)/W(s), soccer M(s)/W(s), swimming and diving W(s), track and field W(s), volleyball W(s), wrestling M(s)/W(s). ***Intramural sports:*** basketball M/W, cross-country running M/W, rugby M/W, soccer M, softball M/W, table tennis M, tennis M/W, volleyball M/W, weight lifting M/W.

Campus security: 24-hour emergency response devices and patrols, controlled dormitory access.

Student services: health clinic, personal/psychological counseling.

COSTS & FINANCIAL AID
Costs (2017–18) ***Comprehensive fee:*** $25,620 includes full-time tuition ($10,170), mandatory fees ($1050), and room and board ($14,400). Full-time tuition and fees vary according to course load. Part-time tuition: $226 per credit hour. ***College room only:*** $5100. Room and board charges vary according to housing facility. ***Payment plan:*** installment. ***Waivers:*** employees or children of employees.

Financial Aid Of all full-time matriculated undergraduates who enrolled in 2014, 490 applied for aid, 444 were judged to have need, 1 had their need fully met. 51 Federal Work-Study jobs (averaging $2100). ***Average financial aid package:*** $9900. ***Average need-based loan:*** $4500. ***Average need-based gift aid:*** $5500. ***Average indebtedness upon graduation:*** $36,200.

APPLYING
Standardized Tests *Recommended:* SAT or ACT (for admission).
Options: electronic application.
Application fee: $50.
Required: high school transcript, minimum 2.0 GPA.
Notification: continuous (freshmen), continuous (transfers).

CONTACT
Miss Robyn Stanley, Executive Director Enrollment Management, Life University, 1269 Barclay Circle, Marietta, GA 30060. *Phone:* 770-426 Ext. 2877. *Toll-free phone:* 800-543-3202. *Fax:* 770-426-2895. *E-mail:* robyn.stanley@life.edu.

Luther Rice College & Seminary
Lithonia, Georgia
http://www.lutherrice.edu/

- **Independent Baptist** comprehensive, founded 1962
- **Suburban** 5-acre campus with easy access to Atlanta
- **Endowment** $532,584
- **Coed** 351 undergraduate students, 17% full-time, 30% women, 70% men
- **Noncompetitive** entrance level, 76% of applicants were admitted

UNDERGRAD STUDENTS
58 full-time, 293 part-time. Students come from 29 states and territories; 2 other countries; 42% are from out of state; 43% Black or African American, non-Hispanic/Latino; 1% Hispanic/Latino; 0.6% Asian, non-Hispanic/Latino; 0.3% American Indian or Alaska Native, non-Hispanic/Latino; 0.6% Race/ethnicity unknown; 48% transferred in.

Freshmen:
Admission: 34 applied, 26 admitted, 17 enrolled. ***Average high school GPA:*** 2.55.

Retention: 50% of full-time freshmen returned.

FACULTY
Total: 32, 47% full-time, 72% with terminal degrees.
Student/faculty ratio: 31:1.

ACADEMICS
Calendar: semesters. *Degrees:* bachelor's, master's, and doctoral.
Special study options: adult/continuing education programs, cooperative education, distance learning, independent study, part-time degree program, summer session for credit.
Computers: 13 computers/terminals are available on campus for general student use. Students can access the following: free student e-mail accounts, online (class) grades, online (class) registration, online (class) schedules. Campuswide network is available. Wireless service is available via entire campus.
Library: Smith Library. *Books:* 60,384 (physical), 429,353 (digital/electronic); *Serial titles:* 90 (physical), 38,398 (digital/electronic); *Databases:* 115. Weekly public service hours: 41.

STUDENT LIFE
Housing options: college housing not available.
Activities and organizations: SGA - Student Government Association.
Campus security: 24-hour emergency response devices.
Student services: personal/psychological counseling.

COSTS
Costs (2017–18) ***Tuition:*** $264 per credit hour part-time. ***Required fees:*** $90 per course part-time. ***Payment plan:*** installment. ***Waivers:*** employees or children of employees.

APPLYING
Options: electronic application.
Application fee: $50.
Required: essay or personal statement, high school transcript, letters of recommendation, Bible Exam.
Application deadlines: rolling (freshmen), rolling (transfers).

CONTACT
Mr. Steve Pray, Director of Student Development, Luther Rice College & Seminary, 3038 Evans Mill Road, Lithonia, GA 30038.
Phone: 770-484-1204. *Toll-free phone:* 800-442-1577.
E-mail: studentservices@LutherRice.edu.

Mercer University
Macon, Georgia
http://www.mercer.edu/

- **Independent Baptist** university, founded 1833
- **Urban** 150-acre campus with easy access to Atlanta
- **Coed** 3,046 undergraduate students, 98% full-time, 51% women, 49% men
- **Moderately difficult** entrance level, 69% of applicants were admitted

UNDERGRAD STUDENTS
2,998 full-time, 48 part-time. Students come from 39 states and territories; 36 other countries; 19% are from out of state; 19% Black or African American, non-Hispanic/Latino; 5% Hispanic/Latino; 8% Asian, non-Hispanic/Latino; 0.2% Native Hawaiian or other Pacific Islander, non-Hispanic/Latino; 0.2% American Indian or Alaska Native, non-Hispanic/Latino; 4% Two or more races, non-Hispanic/Latino; 3% Race/ethnicity unknown; 3% international; 3% transferred in; 78% live on campus.

Freshmen:
Admission: 4,836 applied, 3,354 admitted, 828 enrolled. ***Average high school GPA:*** 3.82. ***Test scores:*** SAT critical reading scores over 500: 95%; SAT math scores over 500: 98%; ACT scores over 18: 100%; SAT critical reading scores over 600: 49%; SAT math scores over 600: 55%; ACT scores over 24: 86%; SAT critical reading scores over 700: 10%; SAT math scores over 700: 11%; ACT scores over 30: 23%.

Retention: 87% of full-time freshmen returned.

FACULTY
Total: 745, 52% full-time, 75% with terminal degrees.

Student/faculty ratio: 13:1.

ACADEMICS
Calendar: semesters. *Degrees:* certificates, bachelor's, master's, doctoral, and post-master's certificates.

Special study options: accelerated degree program, adult/continuing education programs, advanced placement credit, cooperative education, distance learning, double majors, English as a second language, honors programs, independent study, internships, off-campus study, part-time degree program, services for LD students, student-designed majors, study abroad, summer session for credit. ***ROTC:*** Army (b).

Unusual degree programs: 3-2 engineering; nursing; pharmacy, physical therapy, physicians assistant.

Computers: Students can access the following: campus intranet, computer help desk, free student e-mail accounts, online (class) grades, online (class) registration, online (class) schedules. Campuswide network is available. 100% of college-owned or -operated housing units are wired for high-speed Internet access. Wireless service is available via entire campus.

Library: Jack Tarver Library plus 3 others. *Books:* 668,465 (physical), 40,482 (digital/electronic); *Serial titles:* 20,131 (physical), 40,707 (digital/electronic); *Databases:* 225. Study areas open 24 hours, 5-7 days a week.

STUDENT LIFE
Housing options: on-campus residence required through sophomore year; coed, men-only, women-only, special housing for students with disabilities. Campus housing is university owned and is provided by a third party. Freshman campus housing is guaranteed.

Activities and organizations: drama/theater group, student-run newspaper, radio and television station, choral group, marching band, national fraternities, national sororities.

Athletics Member NCAA. All Division I. ***Intercollegiate sports:*** baseball M(s), basketball M(s)/W(s), cross-country running M(s)/W(s), football M(s), golf M(s)/W(s), lacrosse M(s)/W(s), sand volleyball W(s), soccer M(s)/W(s), softball W(s), tennis M(s)/W(s), track and field W(s), volleyball W(s). ***Intramural sports:*** basketball M/W, cheerleading M/W, equestrian sports W(c), golf M/W, sand volleyball M/W, soccer M/W, softball M/W, swimming and diving M(c)/W(c), table tennis M/W, tennis M/W, volleyball M/W, wrestling M(c).

Campus security: 24-hour emergency response devices and patrols, student patrols, late-night transport/escort service, controlled dormitory access, patrols by police officers.

Student services: health clinic, personal/psychological counseling.

COSTS & FINANCIAL AID
Costs (2016–17) ***Comprehensive fee:*** $47,046 includes full-time tuition ($34,830), mandatory fees ($300), and room and board ($11,916). Full-time tuition and fees vary according to location. Part-time tuition: $1161 per credit hour. Part-time tuition and fees vary according to course load and location. ***Required fees:*** $10 per credit hour part-time. ***College room only:*** $5978. Room and board charges vary according to board plan, housing facility, location, and student level. ***Payment plan:*** installment. ***Waivers:*** employees or children of employees.

Financial Aid Of all full-time matriculated undergraduates who enrolled in 2015, 2,940 applied for aid, 2,016 were judged to have need, 836 had their need fully met. In 2015, 842 non-need-based awards were made. ***Average percent of need met:*** 86. ***Average financial aid package:*** $34,952. ***Average need-based loan:*** $10,046. ***Average need-based gift aid:*** $24,409. ***Average non-need-based aid:*** $19,813. ***Average indebtedness upon graduation:*** $28,194.

APPLYING
Standardized Tests *Required:* SAT or ACT (for admission).

Options: electronic application, early action, deferred entrance.

Application fee: $50.

Required: essay or personal statement, high school transcript, minimum 3.0 GPA, 1 letter of recommendation. ***Required for some:*** interview. ***Recommended:*** interview.

Application deadlines: 7/1 (freshmen), rolling (transfers), 3/1 (early action).

Notification: continuous (freshmen), continuous (transfers), rolling (early action).

CONTACT
Ms. Kelly L. Holloway, Director of Freshman Admissions, Mercer University, 1501 Mercer University Drive, Macon, GA 31207-0003. *Phone:* 478-301-5125. *Toll-free phone:* 800-MERCER-U. *Fax:* 478-301-2828. *E-mail:* holloway_kl@mercer.edu.

Middle Georgia State University

Macon, Georgia

http://www.mga.edu/

- **State-supported** comprehensive, founded 2015, part of University System of Georgia
- **Urban** 419-acre campus with easy access to Atlanta
- **Endowment** $874,853
- **Coed**
- **Minimally difficult** entrance level

FACULTY
Student/faculty ratio: 21:1.

ACADEMICS
Calendar: semesters. *Degrees:* certificates, associate, bachelor's, and master's.

Library: Macon State University Library. *Books:* 143,214 (physical), 164,854 (digital/electronic); *Serial titles:* 4,554 (physical), 23,764 (digital/electronic); *Databases:* 138. Weekly public service hours: 23; students can reserve study rooms.

STUDENT LIFE
Housing options: on-campus residence required for freshman year; coed. Campus housing is university owned.

Activities and organizations: drama/theater group, student-run newspaper, television station, choral group, marching band, national fraternities, national sororities.

Athletics Member NAIA.

Campus security: 24-hour emergency response devices and patrols, late-night transport/escort service.

Student services: health clinic, personal/psychological counseling.

COSTS & FINANCIAL AID
Costs (2016–17) ***Tuition:*** state resident $3260 full-time, $109 per hour part-time; nonresident $12,046 full-time, $402 per hour part-time. ***Required fees:*** $1282 full-time. ***Room and board:*** $7870. Room and board charges vary according to board plan, housing facility, and location.

Financial Aid Of all full-time matriculated undergraduates who enrolled in 2015, 7,540 applied for aid, 7,540 were judged to have need. 87 Federal Work-Study jobs (averaging $2385). ***Average financial aid package:*** $4309. ***Average need-based loan:*** $3520. ***Average need-based gift aid:*** $4091. ***Average non-need-based aid:*** $1000.

APPLYING
Standardized Tests *Required:* SAT or ACT (for admission).

Options: electronic application, early admission.

Application fee: $30.

Required: high school transcript, minimum 2.0 GPA.

CONTACT
Ms. Margo Woodham, Director of Admissions, Middle Georgia State University, 100 University Parkway, Macon, GA 31206. *Phone:* 478-471-2700. *Toll-free phone:* 800-272-7619. *Fax:* 478-471-5343. *E-mail:* admissions@mga.edu.

Morehouse College

Atlanta, Georgia

http://www.morehouse.edu/

- **Independent** 4-year, founded 1867
- **Urban** 66-acre campus with easy access to Atlanta, Georgia
- **Endowment** $132.3 million
- **Men only** 2,108 undergraduate students, 96% full-time
- **Moderately difficult** entrance level, 66% of applicants were admitted

UNDERGRAD STUDENTS
2,020 full-time, 88 part-time. Students come from 44 states and territories; 15 other countries; 71% are from out of state; 95% Black or African American, non-Hispanic/Latino; 0.9% Hispanic/Latino; 0.1% Asian, non-Hispanic/Latino; 0.2% American Indian or Alaska Native, non-Hispanic/Latino; 0.4% Two or more races, non-Hispanic/Latino; 2% Race/ethnicity unknown; 2% international; 3% transferred in; 74% live on campus.

Freshmen:
Admission: 3,186 applied, 2,105 admitted, 611 enrolled. ***Average high school GPA:*** 3.22. ***Test scores:*** SAT critical reading scores over 500: 45%; SAT math scores over 500: 45%; SAT writing scores over 500: 37%; ACT scores over 18: 81%; SAT critical reading scores over 600: 11%; SAT math scores over 600: 12%; SAT writing scores over 600: 7%; ACT scores over 24: 30%; SAT critical reading scores over 700: 2%; SAT math scores over 700: 1%; ACT scores over 30: 6%.
Retention: 76% of full-time freshmen returned.

FACULTY
Total: 204, 76% full-time, 71% with terminal degrees.
Student/faculty ratio: 12:1.

ACADEMICS
Calendar: semesters. *Degree:* bachelor's.

Special study options: academic remediation for entering students, advanced placement credit, cooperative education, double majors, honors programs, independent study, internships, off-campus study, part-time degree program, services for LD students, study abroad, summer session for credit. ***ROTC:*** Army (b), Navy (b), Air Force (c).

Unusual degree programs: 3-2 engineering with Auburn University, Clarkson University, Columbia University, Dartmouth College, Georgia Institute of Technology, Indiana University–Purdue University Indianapolis, Notre Dame University, North Carolina Agricultural and Technical State University.

Computers: 1,158 computers/terminals are available on campus for general student use. Students can access the following: campus intranet, computer help desk, free student e-mail accounts, online (class) grades, online (class) registration, online (class) schedules, on-campus computer repair service, computer helpline. Campuswide network is available. 100% of college-owned or -operated housing units are wired for high-speed Internet access. Wireless service is available via entire campus.
Library: Atlanta University Center Robert R. Woodruff Library. *Books:* 364,010 (physical), 82,075 (digital/electronic); *Serial titles:* 7,877 (physical), 92,245 (digital/electronic); *Databases:* 302. Students can reserve study rooms.

STUDENT LIFE
Housing options: on-campus residence required through junior year; men-only. Campus housing is university owned. Freshman campus housing is guaranteed.

Activities and organizations: drama/theater group, student-run newspaper, choral group, marching band, Morehouse College Glee Club, Morehouse Business Association, SGA, Morehouse Public Health Association, Pre-Law Society, national fraternities.

Athletics Member NCAA. All Division II. ***Intercollegiate sports:*** baseball M(s), basketball M(s), cross-country running M(s), football M(s), golf M, tennis M(s), track and field M(s). ***Intramural sports:*** basketball M, golf M, lacrosse M, rugby M, soccer M, softball M, swimming and diving M, table tennis M(c), tennis M, volleyball M, wrestling M(c).

Campus security: 24-hour emergency response devices and patrols, late-night transport/escort service, controlled dormitory access.

Student services: health clinic, personal/psychological counseling.

COSTS & FINANCIAL AID
Costs (2017–18) ***One-time required fee:*** $1013. ***Comprehensive fee:*** $40,835 includes full-time tuition ($25,055), mandatory fees ($2223), and room and board ($13,557). Full-time tuition and fees vary according to course load. Part-time tuition: $1013 per credit hour. Part-time tuition and fees vary according to course load. ***College room only:*** $7510. Room and board charges vary according to board plan and housing facility. ***Payment plan:*** installment. ***Waivers:*** employees or children of employees.

Financial Aid Of all full-time matriculated undergraduates who enrolled in 2015, 1,888 applied for aid, 1,651 were judged to have need, 198 had their need fully met. 182 Federal Work-Study jobs (averaging $3906). 137 state and other part-time jobs (averaging $3039). In 2015, 157 non-need-based awards were made. ***Average percent of need met:*** 53. ***Average financial aid package:*** $20,054. ***Average need-based loan:*** $4306. ***Average need-based gift aid:*** $16,971. ***Average non-need-based aid:*** $18,154. ***Average indebtedness upon graduation:*** $32,627.

APPLYING
Standardized Tests *Required:* SAT or ACT (for admission). *Recommended:* SAT and SAT Subject Tests or ACT (for admission).

Options: electronic application, early admission, early decision, early action, deferred entrance.

Application fee: $50.

Required: essay or personal statement, high school transcript, interview. ***Recommended:*** minimum 3.0 GPA.

Application deadlines: 2/1 (freshmen), 2/1 (transfers), 11/1 (early action).

Notification: 3/15 (freshmen), 3/15 (transfers), 12/15 (early action).

CONTACT
Morehouse College, 830 Westview Drive, SW, Atlanta, GA 30314. *Phone:* 470-639-0391. *Toll-free phone:* 800-851-1254.

Oglethorpe University

Atlanta, Georgia

http://www.oglethorpe.edu/

- **Independent** 4-year, founded 1835
- **Suburban** 102-acre campus with easy access to Atlanta
- **Endowment** $19.7 million
- **Coed**
- **Very difficult** entrance level

FACULTY
Student/faculty ratio: 15:1.

ACADEMICS
Calendar: semesters. *Degree:* bachelor's.
Library: Philip Weltner Library.

STUDENT LIFE
Housing options: on-campus residence required through sophomore year; coed. Campus housing is university owned. Freshman campus housing is guaranteed.

Activities and organizations: drama/theater group, student-run newspaper, choral group, national fraternities, national sororities.

Athletics Member NCAA. All Division III.

Campus security: 24-hour emergency response devices and patrols, late-night transport/escort service, controlled dormitory access.

Student services: health clinic, personal/psychological counseling.

COSTS & FINANCIAL AID
Costs (2016–17) ***Comprehensive fee:*** $48,135 includes full-time tuition ($35,000), mandatory fees ($425), and room and board ($12,710). Full-time tuition and fees vary according to degree level. Part-time tuition: $1467 per credit hour. Part-time tuition and fees vary according to class time, course load, and degree level. ***College room only:*** $4050. Room and

board charges vary according to housing facility and location. ***Payment plans:*** tuition prepayment, installment.

Financial Aid Of all full-time matriculated undergraduates who enrolled in 2015, 824 applied for aid, 748 were judged to have need, 113 had their need fully met. In 2015, 320 non-need-based awards were made. ***Average percent of need met:*** 72. ***Average financial aid package:*** $28,986. ***Average need-based loan:*** $4259. ***Average need-based gift aid:*** $24,206. ***Average non-need-based aid:*** $17,571. ***Average indebtedness upon graduation:*** $23,212.

APPLYING

Standardized Tests *Required:* SAT or ACT (for admission).

Options: electronic application, early admission, early action, deferred entrance.

Application fee: $50.

Required: essay or personal statement, high school transcript, 1 letter of recommendation. ***Required for some:*** interview. ***Recommended:*** minimum 2.5 GPA, interview.

CONTACT

Ms. Lucy Leusch, Vice President for Enrollment and Financial Aid, Oglethorpe University, 4484 Peachtree Road, NE, Atlanta, GA 30319. *Phone:* 404-364-8307. *Toll-free phone:* 800-428-4484. *Fax:* 404-364-8491. *E-mail:* admission@oglethorpe.edu.

Paine College

Augusta, Georgia

http://www.paine.edu/

- **Independent Methodist** 4-year, founded 1882
- **Urban** 65-acre campus with easy access to Columbia, SC
- **Endowment** $8.4 million
- **Coed** 502 undergraduate students
- **Minimally difficult** entrance level, 25% of applicants were admitted

UNDERGRAD STUDENTS

Students come from 18 states and territories; 7 other countries; 17% are from out of state; 77% Black or African American, non-Hispanic/Latino; 2% Hispanic/Latino; 0.2% Asian, non-Hispanic/Latino; 0.6% American Indian or Alaska Native, non-Hispanic/Latino; 1% Two or more races, non-Hispanic/Latino; 14% Race/ethnicity unknown; 2% international; 42% live on campus.

Freshmen:

Admission: 3,964 applied, 977 admitted. ***Average high school GPA:*** 2.58. ***Test scores:*** SAT critical reading scores over 500: 2%; SAT math scores over 500: 6%; ACT scores over 18: 22%; SAT critical reading scores over 600: 2%; SAT math scores over 600: 2%; ACT scores over 24: 1%.

Retention: 35% of full-time freshmen returned.

FACULTY

Total: 47, 66% full-time, 70% with terminal degrees.

Student/faculty ratio: 10:1.

ACADEMICS

Calendar: semesters. *Degree:* bachelor's.

Special study options: academic remediation for entering students, accelerated degree program, adult/continuing education programs, advanced placement credit, distance learning, double majors, honors programs, independent study, internships, off-campus study, part-time degree program, services for LD students, study abroad, summer session for credit. ***ROTC:*** Army (c).

Unusual degree programs: engineering with Tuskegee University.

Computers: 130 computers/terminals and 696 ports are available on campus for general student use. Students can access the following: campus intranet, computer help desk, free student e-mail accounts, online (class) grades, online (class) registration, online (class) schedules. Campuswide network is available. 100% of college-owned or -operated housing units are wired for high-speed Internet access. Wireless service is available via entire campus.

Library: Collins-Callaway Library. *Books:* 70,791 (physical), 137,762 (digital/electronic); *Serial titles:* 205 (physical). Weekly public service hours: 83; students can reserve study rooms.

STUDENT LIFE

Housing options: men-only, women-only. Campus housing is university owned. Freshman applicants given priority for college housing.

Activities and organizations: drama/theater group, student-run newspaper, choral group, Wesley Fellowship, Alpha Kappa Mu National Honor Society, International Student Association, National Association for the Advancement of Colored People, Creme de la Creme Models, national fraternities, national sororities.

Athletics Member NCAA. All Division II. ***Intercollegiate sports:*** baseball M(s), basketball M(s)/W(s), cross-country running M(s)/W(s), golf M(s), softball W(s), track and field M(s)/W(s), volleyball W(s). ***Intramural sports:*** baseball M, basketball M/W, cheerleading M/W, soccer M/W, softball M/W, table tennis M/W, tennis M/W, track and field M/W, volleyball M/W, weight lifting M/W.

Campus security: 24-hour emergency response devices and patrols, late-night transport/escort service.

Student services: personal/psychological counseling.

COSTS & FINANCIAL AID

Costs (2016–17) ***Comprehensive fee:*** $20,886 includes full-time tuition ($12,705), mandatory fees ($1519), and room and board ($6662). Full-time tuition and fees vary according to class time, course load, and location. Part-time tuition: $529 per credit hour. Part-time tuition and fees vary according to class time, course load, and location. ***College room only:*** $3136. Room and board charges vary according to housing facility. ***Payment plans:*** installment, deferred payment. ***Waivers:*** children of alumni and employees or children of employees.

Financial Aid ***Average indebtedness upon graduation:*** $2304.

APPLYING

Standardized Tests *Required:* SAT or ACT (for admission).

Options: electronic application, early admission, deferred entrance.

Application fee: $25.

Required: high school transcript, minimum 2.0 GPA, 2 letters of recommendation. ***Required for some:*** score of 500 on each Georgia high school exit exam.

Application deadlines: 7/1 (freshmen), 7/1 (transfers).

Notification: continuous (freshmen), continuous (out-of-state freshmen), continuous (transfers).

CONTACT

Mr. R. Wayne Woodson, Dean of Students, Paine College, 1235 15th Street, Augusta, GA 30901-3182. *Phone:* 706-821-8320. *Toll-free phone:* 800-476-7703. *Fax:* 706-821-8691. *E-mail:* rwoodson@paine.edu.

Piedmont College

Demorest, Georgia

http://www.piedmont.edu/

- **Independent** comprehensive, founded 1897, affiliated with United Church of Christ
- **Rural** 186-acre campus with easy access to Atlanta
- **Endowment** $52.9 million
- **Coed** 1,295 undergraduate students, 91% full-time, 64% women, 36% men
- **Moderately difficult** entrance level, 57% of applicants were admitted

UNDERGRAD STUDENTS

1,177 full-time, 118 part-time. Students come from 21 states and territories; 4 other countries; 8% are from out of state; 9% Black or African American, non-Hispanic/Latino; 7% Hispanic/Latino; 2% Asian, non-Hispanic/Latino; 0.2% Native Hawaiian or other Pacific Islander, non-Hispanic/Latino; 0.6% American Indian or Alaska Native, non-Hispanic/Latino; 3% Two or more races, non-Hispanic/Latino; 10% Race/ethnicity unknown; 0.1% international; 9% transferred in; 68% live on campus.

Freshmen:

Admission: 1,335 applied, 763 admitted, 274 enrolled. ***Average high school GPA:*** 3.47. ***Test scores:*** SAT critical reading scores over 500: 47%; SAT math scores over 500: 42%; ACT scores over 18: 89%; SAT critical reading scores over 600: 11%; SAT math scores over 600: 10%; ACT scores over 24: 31%; SAT critical reading scores over 700: 1%; SAT math scores over 700: 1%; ACT scores over 30: 4%.

Retention: 68% of full-time freshmen returned.

FACULTY
Total: 279, 45% full-time, 72% with terminal degrees.

Student/faculty ratio: 11:1.

ACADEMICS
Calendar: semesters. *Degrees:* certificates, bachelor's, master's, doctoral, and post-master's certificates.

Special study options: accelerated degree program, adult/continuing education programs, advanced placement credit, cooperative education, distance learning, double majors, honors programs, independent study, internships, off-campus study, part-time degree program, services for LD students, student-designed majors, study abroad, summer session for credit.

Unusual degree programs: 3-2 engineering with Georgia Institute of Technology.

Computers: 150 computers/terminals are available on campus for general student use. Students can access the following: campus intranet, computer help desk, free student e-mail accounts, online (class) grades, online (class) registration, online (class) schedules. Campuswide network is available. Wireless service is available via classrooms, computer centers, computer labs, dorm rooms, learning centers, libraries, student centers.
Library: Arrendale Library plus 2 others. *Books:* 99,693 (physical), 416,680 (digital/electronic); *Serial titles:* 24,272 (digital/electronic). Students can reserve study rooms.

STUDENT LIFE
Housing options: on-campus residence required through sophomore year; coed, men-only, women-only, special housing for students with disabilities. Campus housing is university owned. Freshman campus housing is guaranteed.

Activities and organizations: drama/theater group, student-run newspaper, radio and television station, choral group, Campus Activity Board, Student Government Association, Team Piedmont, National Society of Leadership and Success, American Marketing Association-Piedmont Chapter.

Athletics Member NCAA. All Division III. ***Intercollegiate sports:*** baseball M, basketball M/W, cross-country running M/W, golf M/W, lacrosse M/W, soccer M/W, softball W, tennis M/W, track and field M/W, volleyball W. ***Intramural sports:*** cheerleading W.

Campus security: 24-hour emergency response devices and patrols, late-night transport/escort service.

Student services: personal/psychological counseling.

COSTS & FINANCIAL AID
Costs (2017–18) ***Comprehensive fee:*** $34,338 includes full-time tuition ($24,268), mandatory fees ($200), and room and board ($9870). Full-time tuition and fees vary according to course load, degree level, location, and program. Part-time tuition: $1011 per credit hour. Part-time tuition and fees vary according to course load, degree level, location, and program. ***College room only:*** $5502. Room and board charges vary according to board plan. ***Payment plan:*** installment. ***Waivers:*** adult students and employees or children of employees.

Financial Aid Of all full-time matriculated undergraduates who enrolled in 2016, 1,047 applied for aid, 950 were judged to have need, 179 had their need fully met. 76 Federal Work-Study jobs (averaging $2103). 324 state and other part-time jobs (averaging $2033). In 2016, 184 non-need-based awards were made. ***Average percent of need met:*** 70. ***Average financial aid package:*** $19,224. ***Average need-based loan:*** $4064. ***Average need-based gift aid:*** $15,294. ***Average non-need-based aid:*** $11,511. ***Average indebtedness upon graduation:*** $30,187.

APPLYING
Standardized Tests *Required:* SAT or ACT (for admission).

Options: electronic application, early admission, deferred entrance.

Required: high school transcript. ***Required for some:*** interview. ***Recommended:*** essay or personal statement.

Application deadlines: 7/1 (freshmen), 7/1 (transfers).

CONTACT
Ms. Brenda Boonstra, Director of Undergraduate Admissions, Piedmont College, PO Box 10, 165 Central Avenue, Demorest, GA 30535. *Phone:* 706-776-0103 Ext. 1188. *Toll-free phone:* 800-277-7020. *Fax:* 706-776-6635. *E-mail:* bboonstra@piedmont.edu.

Point University
West Point, Georgia
http://point.edu/

- **Independent Christian** comprehensive, founded 1937
- **Small-town** campus with easy access to Atlanta, GA and Montgomery, AL
- **Coed** 1,954 undergraduate students, 70% full-time, 53% women, 47% men
- **Moderately difficult** entrance level, 51% of applicants were admitted

UNDERGRAD STUDENTS
1,366 full-time, 588 part-time. Students come from 13 other countries; 37% are from out of state; 30% Black or African American, non-Hispanic/Latino; 4% Hispanic/Latino; 0.6% Asian, non-Hispanic/Latino; 0.2% Native Hawaiian or other Pacific Islander, non-Hispanic/Latino; 0.2% American Indian or Alaska Native, non-Hispanic/Latino; 6% Two or more races, non-Hispanic/Latino; 6% Race/ethnicity unknown; 2% international; 8% transferred in; 41% live on campus.

Freshmen:
Admission: 1,184 applied, 609 admitted, 321 enrolled. ***Average high school GPA:*** 3.22. ***Test scores:*** SAT critical reading scores over 500: 22%; SAT math scores over 500: 33%; ACT scores over 18: 62%; SAT critical reading scores over 600: 4%; SAT math scores over 600: 5%; ACT scores over 24: 15%.
Retention: 68% of full-time freshmen returned.

FACULTY
Total: 186, 22% full-time, 33% with terminal degrees.

Student/faculty ratio: 18:1.

ACADEMICS
Calendar: semesters. *Degrees:* certificates, associate, bachelor's, and master's.

Special study options: accelerated degree program, adult/continuing education programs, advanced placement credit, distance learning, double majors, independent study, part-time degree program, services for LD students, summer session for credit.

Computers: 115 computers/terminals and 50 ports are available on campus for general student use. Students can access the following: campus intranet, computer help desk, free student e-mail accounts, online (class) grades, online (class) registration, online (class) schedules. Campuswide network is available. 100% of college-owned or -operated housing units are wired for high-speed Internet access. Wireless service is available via entire campus.
Library: Point University Library.

STUDENT LIFE
Housing options: on-campus residence required through sophomore year; men-only, women-only. Campus housing is leased by the school. Freshman applicants given priority for college housing.

Activities and organizations: choral group, marching band, Student Government Association, Community Concert Band, Campus Life Ministers, Campus Activities Board, Fellowship of Christian Athletes (FCA).

Athletics Member NAIA, NCCAA. ***Intercollegiate sports:*** baseball M(s), basketball M(s)/W(s), cheerleading M(s)/W(s), cross-country running M(s)/W(s), football M(s), golf M(s)/W(s), lacrosse M(s)/W(s), soccer M(s)/W(s), softball W(s), swimming and diving M(s)/W(s), tennis M(s)/W(s), volleyball W(s). ***Intramural sports:*** basketball M/W, football M/W, sand volleyball M/W, softball M/W, table tennis M/W, ultimate Frisbee M/W, volleyball M/W.

Campus security: 24-hour patrols.

Student services: personal/psychological counseling.

COSTS
Costs (2016–17) ***Comprehensive fee:*** $26,900 includes full-time tuition ($18,100), mandatory fees ($1100), and room and board ($7700). Full-time tuition and fees vary according to course load. Part-time tuition and fees vary according to course load. ***College room only:*** $4500. ***Payment plan:*** installment. ***Waivers:*** employees or children of employees.

APPLYING
Standardized Tests *Required for some:* SAT or ACT (for admission).

Options: electronic application, deferred entrance.

Required: minimum 2.0 GPA, 1 letter of recommendation. ***Required for some:*** essay or personal statement, high school transcript, college transcript. ***Recommended:*** high school transcript.

Application deadlines: 8/1 (freshmen), rolling (out-of-state freshmen), 8/1 (transfers).

Notification: continuous (freshmen), continuous (out-of-state freshmen), continuous (transfers).

CONTACT

Ms. Hannah Blount, Assistant Director of Admission, Point University, 507 West 10th Street, West Point, GA 31833. *Phone:* 706-385-1022. *Toll-free phone:* 855-37-POINT. *Fax:* 706-645-9473. *E-mail:* admissions@point.edu.

Reinhardt University

Waleska, Georgia

http://www.reinhardt.edu/

CONTACT

Ms. Julie Fleming, Director of Admissions, Reinhardt University, 7300 Reinhardt College Circle, Waleska, GA 30183-0128. *Phone:* 770-720-5526. *Fax:* 770-720-5602. *E-mail:* admissions@mail.reinhardt.edu.

Savannah College of Art and Design

Savannah, Georgia

http://www.scad.edu/

- **Independent** comprehensive, founded 1978
- **Urban** campus
- **Coed** 10,573 undergraduate students, 83% full-time, 67% women, 33% men
- **Moderately difficult** entrance level, 71% of applicants were admitted

UNDERGRAD STUDENTS

8,825 full-time, 1,748 part-time. Students come from 54 states and territories; 102 other countries; 79% are from out of state; 10% Black or African American, non-Hispanic/Latino; 8% Hispanic/Latino; 5% Asian, non-Hispanic/Latino; 0.4% Native Hawaiian or other Pacific Islander, non-Hispanic/Latino; 0.5% American Indian or Alaska Native, non-Hispanic/Latino; 3% Race/ethnicity unknown; 21% international; 6% transferred in; 42% live on campus.

Freshmen:

Admission: 11,723 applied, 8,329 admitted, 2,345 enrolled. ***Average high school GPA:*** 3.51. ***Test scores:*** SAT critical reading scores over 500: 72%; SAT math scores over 500: 60%; SAT writing scores over 500: 62%; ACT scores over 18: 94%; SAT critical reading scores over 600: 30%; SAT math scores over 600: 18%; SAT writing scores over 600: 21%; ACT scores over 24: 53%; SAT critical reading scores over 700: 4%; SAT math scores over 700: 1%; SAT writing scores over 700: 2%; ACT scores over 30: 12%.

Retention: 85% of full-time freshmen returned.

FACULTY

Total: 686, 78% full-time, 80% with terminal degrees.

Student/faculty ratio: 19:1.

ACADEMICS

Calendar: quarters. *Degrees:* certificates, bachelor's, master's, and postbachelor's certificates.

Special study options: accelerated degree program, advanced placement credit, cooperative education, distance learning, double majors, English as a second language, independent study, internships, off-campus study, part-time degree program, services for LD students, study abroad, summer session for credit.

Computers: 3,450 computers/terminals are available on campus for general student use. Students can access the following: campus intranet, computer help desk, free student e-mail accounts, online (class) grades, online (class) registration, online (class) schedules. Campuswide network is available. 100% of college-owned or -operated housing units are wired for high-speed Internet access. Wireless service is available via entire campus.

Library: Jen Library plus 4 others. *Books:* 260,652 (physical), 191,604 (digital/electronic); *Serial titles:* 936 (physical), 45,815 (digital/electronic); *Databases:* 92. Weekly public service hours: 105; students can reserve study rooms.

STUDENT LIFE

Housing options: coed, women-only, special housing for students with disabilities. Campus housing is university owned and leased by the school. Freshman applicants given priority for college housing.

Activities and organizations: drama/theater group, student-run newspaper, radio station, choral group.

Athletics Member NAIA. ***Intercollegiate sports:*** bowling M(s)/W(s), cross-country running M(s)/W(s), equestrian sports M(s)/W(s), golf M(s)/W(s), lacrosse M(s)/W(s), soccer M(s)/W(s), swimming and diving M(s)/W(s), tennis M(s)/W(s), track and field M/W. ***Intramural sports:*** badminton M/W, basketball M/W, fencing M(c)/W(c), sand volleyball M/W, soccer M/W, table tennis M/W, volleyball M/W.

Campus security: 24-hour emergency response devices and patrols, student patrols, late-night transport/escort service, controlled dormitory access, video camera surveillance.

Student services: health clinic, personal/psychological counseling.

COSTS & FINANCIAL AID

Costs (2017–18) ***One-time required fee:*** $500. ***Tuition:*** Full-time tuition and fees vary according to course load and degree level. Part-time tuition and fees vary according to course load and degree level. ***Room and board:*** $14,244. Room and board charges vary according to board plan, housing facility, and location. ***Payment plan:*** installment. ***Waivers:*** employees or children of employees.

Financial Aid Of all full-time matriculated undergraduates who enrolled in 2016, 5,099 applied for aid, 4,337 were judged to have need, 461 had their need fully met. In 2016, 4479 non-need-based awards were made. ***Average percent of need met:*** 43. ***Average financial aid package:*** $17,805. ***Average need-based loan:*** $4523. ***Average need-based gift aid:*** $13,710. ***Average non-need-based aid:*** $7938. ***Average indebtedness upon graduation:*** $37,390.

APPLYING

Standardized Tests *Required:* SAT or ACT (for admission).

Options: electronic application, early admission, deferred entrance.

Application fee: $70.

Required for some: essay or personal statement, high school transcript, interview, portfolio/audition for performing arts, riding, writing, or visual arts. ***Recommended:*** essay or personal statement, interview.

Application deadlines: rolling (freshmen), rolling (transfers).

Notification: continuous (freshmen), continuous (transfers).

CONTACT

Ms. Rina Gaitonde Le Blanc, Executive Director of Admissions Operations, Savannah College of Art and Design, 342 Bull Street, PO Box 3146, Savannah, GA 31402-3146. *Phone:* 912-525-5100. *Toll-free phone:* 800-869-7223. *E-mail:* admission@scad.edu.

Savannah State University

Savannah, Georgia

http://www.savannahstate.edu/

- **State-supported** comprehensive, founded 1890, part of University System of Georgia
- **Suburban** 173-acre campus
- **Endowment** $5.4 million
- **Coed**
- **Minimally difficult** entrance level

FACULTY

Student/faculty ratio: 21:1.

ACADEMICS

Calendar: semesters. *Degrees:* certificates, associate, bachelor's, master's, and postbachelor's certificates.

Library: Asa H. Gordon Library. *Books:* 108,766 (physical), 185,056 (digital/electronic); *Serial titles:* 217 (physical), 2,000 (digital/electronic); *Databases:* 298. Weekly public service hours: 84.

STUDENT LIFE
Housing options: coed, men-only, women-only. Campus housing is university owned.
Activities and organizations: drama/theater group, student-run newspaper, radio and television station, choral group, marching band, Marching band, Wesleyan Gospel Choir, Residence Hall Association, Student Government Association, Tiger Ambassadors, national fraternities, national sororities.
Athletics Member NCAA. All Division I.
Campus security: 24-hour emergency response devices and patrols, late-night transport/escort service, controlled dormitory access.
Student services: health clinic, personal/psychological counseling, women's center.

COSTS & FINANCIAL AID
Costs (2016–17) ***Tuition:*** state resident $4858 full-time, $162 per credit hour part-time; nonresident $17,678 full-time, $589 per credit hour part-time. Full-time tuition and fees vary according to course load, program, and reciprocity agreements. Part-time tuition and fees vary according to course load, program, and reciprocity agreements. ***Required fees:*** $1758 full-time, $879 per term part-time. ***Room and board:*** Room and board charges vary according to board plan and housing facility.
Financial Aid ***Financial aid deadline:*** 7/31.

APPLYING
Standardized Tests *Required:* SAT or ACT (for admission). *Required for some:* SAT Subject Tests (for admission). *Recommended:* SAT (for admission).
Options: electronic application, early admission, deferred entrance.
Required: high school transcript, minimum 2.3 GPA. ***Required for some:*** essay or personal statement, interview.

CONTACT
Mr. Descatur Potier, Assistant Vice President of Academic Affairs for Enrollment Services/Director of Admission, Savannah State University, PO Box 20209, 3219 College Street, Savannah, GA 31404. *Phone:* 912-358-4014. *Toll-free phone:* 800-788-0478. *Fax:* 912-650-8009. *E-mail:* potierd@savannahstate.edu.

Shorter University

Rome, Georgia

http://www.shorter.edu/

- **Independent Baptist** comprehensive, founded 1873
- **Small-town** 155-acre campus with easy access to Atlanta
- **Endowment** $14.8 million
- **Coed** 1,377 undergraduate students, 88% full-time, 57% women, 43% men
- **Moderately difficult** entrance level, 63% of applicants were admitted

UNDERGRAD STUDENTS
1,205 full-time, 172 part-time. Students come from 35 states and territories; 23 other countries; 14% are from out of state; 24% Black or African American, non-Hispanic/Latino; 5% Hispanic/Latino; 1% Asian, non-Hispanic/Latino; 0.2% Native Hawaiian or other Pacific Islander, non-Hispanic/Latino; 0.4% American Indian or Alaska Native, non-Hispanic/Latino; 2% Two or more races, non-Hispanic/Latino; 1% Race/ethnicity unknown; 4% international; 12% transferred in; 54% live on campus.

Freshmen:
Admission: 1,622 applied, 1,020 admitted, 262 enrolled. ***Average high school GPA:*** 3.35. ***Test scores:*** SAT critical reading scores over 500: 37%; SAT math scores over 500: 41%; SAT writing scores over 500: 39%; ACT scores over 18: 81%; SAT critical reading scores over 600: 9%; SAT math scores over 600: 9%; SAT writing scores over 600: 9%; ACT scores over 24: 26%; SAT critical reading scores over 700: 1%; ACT scores over 30: 2%.
Retention: 58% of full-time freshmen returned.

FACULTY
Total: 145, 68% full-time, 56% with terminal degrees.
Student/faculty ratio: 12:1.

ACADEMICS
Calendar: semesters. *Degrees:* associate, bachelor's, and master's.
Special study options: academic remediation for entering students, adult/continuing education programs, advanced placement credit, double majors, honors programs, independent study, internships, off-campus study, part-time degree program, services for LD students, student-designed majors, study abroad, summer session for credit.
Computers: 100 computers/terminals are available on campus for general student use. Students can access the following: campus intranet, computer help desk, free student e-mail accounts, online (class) grades, online (class) registration, online (class) schedules. Campuswide network is available. 100% of college-owned or -operated housing units are wired for high-speed Internet access. Wireless service is available via classrooms, computer centers, computer labs, dorm rooms, learning centers, libraries, student centers.
Library: Livingston Library. *Books:* 124,378 (physical), 321,000 (digital/electronic); *Databases:* 186. Students can reserve study rooms.

STUDENT LIFE
Housing options: men-only, women-only. Campus housing is university owned. Freshman applicants given priority for college housing.
Activities and organizations: drama/theater group, student-run newspaper, radio and television station, choral group, marching band, Baptist Collegiate Ministries, Student Government Association, Fellowship of Christian Athletes, Habitat for Humanity, SAVE (Students Advocating Volunteer Efforts), national fraternities, national sororities.
Athletics Member NAIA. ***Intercollegiate sports:*** baseball M(s), basketball M(s)/W(s), cheerleading M(s)/W(s), cross-country running M(s)/W(s), football M(s), golf M(s)/W(s), soccer M(s)/W(s), softball W(s), tennis M(s)/W(s), track and field M(s)/W(s), volleyball W(s). ***Intramural sports:*** basketball M/W, bowling M/W, soccer M/W, table tennis M/W, tennis M/W, ultimate Frisbee M/W, volleyball W.
Campus security: 24-hour emergency response devices and patrols.
Student services: health clinic, personal/psychological counseling.

COSTS & FINANCIAL AID
Costs (2017–18) ***Comprehensive fee:*** $31,130 includes full-time tuition ($21,300), mandatory fees ($430), and room and board ($9400). Full-time tuition and fees vary according to course load, location, and program. Part-time tuition: $550 per credit hour. Part-time tuition and fees vary according to location and program. ***Required fees:*** $8 per credit hour part-time. ***College room only:*** $5000. Room and board charges vary according to board plan and housing facility. ***Payment plan:*** installment. ***Waivers:*** senior citizens and employees or children of employees.
Financial Aid Of all full-time matriculated undergraduates who enrolled in 2012, 1,198 applied for aid, 1,078 were judged to have need, 197 had their need fully met. In 2012, 124 non-need-based awards were made. ***Average percent of need met:*** 61. ***Average financial aid package:*** $16,335. ***Average need-based loan:*** $4164. ***Average need-based gift aid:*** $12,863. ***Average non-need-based aid:*** $5371.

APPLYING
Standardized Tests *Required:* SAT or ACT (for admission).
Options: electronic application, early admission, deferred entrance.
Application fee: $25.
Required: essay or personal statement, high school transcript. ***Required for some:*** interview, audition for music and theater programs. ***Recommended:*** minimum 2.0 GPA, 1 letter of recommendation, interview.
Application deadlines: 8/25 (freshmen), 8/25 (transfers).
Notification: continuous (freshmen), continuous (transfers).

CONTACT
Shorter University, 315 Shorter Avenue, Rome, GA 30165. *Phone:* 706-233-7342. *Toll-free phone:* 800-868-6980.

South Georgia State College

Douglas, Georgia

http://www.sgc.edu/

CONTACT
South Georgia State College, 100 West College Park Drive, Douglas, GA 31533-5098. *Phone:* 912-260-4409. *Toll-free phone:* 800-342-6364.

South University
Savannah, Georgia
http://www.southuniversity.edu/savannah/

CONTACT
South University, 709 Mall Boulevard, Savannah, GA 31406.
Phone: 912-201-8000. *Toll-free phone:* 866-629-2901.

Spelman College
Atlanta, Georgia
http://www.spelman.edu/

- **Independent** 4-year, founded 1881
- **Urban** 39-acre campus with easy access to Atlanta
- **Endowment** $347.0 million
- **Women only** 2,125 undergraduate students, 97% full-time
- **Very difficult** entrance level, 36% of applicants were admitted

UNDERGRAD STUDENTS
2,061 full-time, 64 part-time. Students come from 41 states and territories; 7 other countries; 72% are from out of state; 96% Black or African American, non-Hispanic/Latino; 0.2% Hispanic/Latino; 0.1% Asian, non-Hispanic/Latino; 1% American Indian or Alaska Native, non-Hispanic/Latino; 1% Two or more races, non-Hispanic/Latino; 0.8% international; 1% transferred in; 67% live on campus.

Freshmen:
Admission: 7,864 applied, 2,810 admitted, 533 enrolled. ***Average high school GPA:*** 3.46. ***Test scores:*** SAT critical reading scores over 500: 76%; SAT math scores over 500: 68%; SAT writing scores over 500: 73%; ACT scores over 18: 99%; SAT critical reading scores over 600: 25%; SAT math scores over 600: 19%; SAT writing scores over 600: 20%; ACT scores over 24: 43%; SAT critical reading scores over 700: 4%; SAT math scores over 700: 1%; SAT writing scores over 700: 2%; ACT scores over 30: 6%.

Retention: 91% of full-time freshmen returned.

FACULTY
Total: 248, 69% full-time.
Student/faculty ratio: 11:1.

ACADEMICS
Calendar: semesters. *Degree:* bachelor's.
Special study options: adult/continuing education programs, advanced placement credit, cooperative education, double majors, honors programs, independent study, internships, off-campus study, part-time degree program, services for LD students, student-designed majors, study abroad. ***ROTC:*** Army (c), Navy (c), Air Force (c).
Unusual degree programs: 3-2 engineering with North Carolina Agricultural and Technical State University, Rensselaer Polytechnic Institute, Georgia Institute of Technology, Boston University, The University of Alabama in Huntsville, Auburn University.
Computers: 700 computers/terminals and 1,500 ports are available on campus for general student use. Students can access the following: computer help desk, free student e-mail accounts, online (class) grades, online (class) registration, online (class) schedules. Campuswide network is available. 100% of college-owned or -operated housing units are wired for high-speed Internet access. Wireless service is available via entire campus.
Library: Robert Woodruff Library plus 1 other. *Books:* 76,329 (digital/electronic). Study areas open 24 hours, 5-7 days a week; students can reserve study rooms.

STUDENT LIFE
Housing options: on-campus residence required through sophomore year; women-only. Campus housing is university owned and leased by the school. Freshman applicants given priority for college housing.
Activities and organizations: drama/theater group, student-run newspaper, choral group, Glee Club, Theater Program, Student Government, Honors Program, Religious Groups, national sororities.
Campus security: 24-hour emergency response devices and patrols, late-night transport/escort service, controlled dormitory access, lighted pathways/sidewalks.
Student services: health clinic, personal/psychological counseling, women's center.

COSTS & FINANCIAL AID
Costs (2016–17) ***Comprehensive fee:*** $39,001 includes full-time tuition ($22,827), mandatory fees ($3811), and room and board ($12,363). Full-time tuition and fees vary according to course load. Part-time tuition and fees vary according to course load. ***Required fees:*** $950 per credit hour part-time. ***Room and board:*** Room and board charges vary according to board plan and housing facility. ***Payment plans:*** installment, deferred payment. ***Waivers:*** employees or children of employees.
Financial Aid Of all full-time matriculated undergraduates who enrolled in 2016, 1,853 applied for aid, 1,700 were judged to have need, 14 had their need fully met. In 2016, 15 non-need-based awards were made. ***Average percent of need met:*** 33. ***Average financial aid package:*** $16,900. ***Average need-based loan:*** $5013. ***Average need-based gift aid:*** $12,410. ***Average non-need-based aid:*** $35,697. ***Average indebtedness upon graduation:*** $38,430.

APPLYING
Standardized Tests *Required:* SAT or ACT (for admission).
Options: electronic application, early admission, early decision, early action, deferred entrance.
Application fee: $35.
Required: essay or personal statement, high school transcript, minimum 2.0 GPA, 2 letters of recommendation. ***Required for some:*** interview.
Application deadlines: 2/1 (freshmen), 4/1 (transfers), 11/15 (early action).
Early decision deadline: 11/1.
Notification: 4/1 (freshmen), 5/1 (transfers), 12/15 (early decision), 12/31 (early action).

CONTACT
Ms. Tiffany Nelson, Director of Admissions, Spelman College, 350 Spelman Lane, SW, Atlanta, GA 30314-4399. *Phone:* 800-982-2411. *Toll-free phone:* 800-982-2411. *Fax:* 404-270-5201. *E-mail:* admiss@spelman.edu.

Strayer University–Augusta Campus
Augusta, Georgia
http://www.strayer.edu/georgia/augusta/

CONTACT
Strayer University–Augusta Campus, 1330 Augusta West Parkway, Augusta, GA 30909.

Strayer University–Chamblee Campus
Atlanta, Georgia
http://www.strayer.edu/georgia/chamblee/

CONTACT
Strayer University–Chamblee Campus, 3355 Northeast Expressway, Suite 100, Atlanta, GA 30341.

Strayer University–Cobb County Campus
Atlanta, Georgia
http://www.strayer.edu/georgia/cobb-county/

CONTACT
Strayer University–Cobb County Campus, 3101 Towercreek Parkway, SE, Suite 700, Atlanta, GA 30339-3256.

Strayer University–Columbus Campus

Columbus, Georgia

http://www.strayer.edu/georgia/columbus/

CONTACT
Strayer University–Columbus Campus, 6003 Veterans Parkway, Suite 100, Columbus, GA 31909.

Strayer University–Douglasville Campus

Douglasville, Georgia

http://www.strayer.edu/georgia/douglasville/

CONTACT
Strayer University–Douglasville Campus, 4655 Timber Ridge Drive, Douglasville, GA 30135.

Strayer University–Lithonia Campus

Lithonia, Georgia

http://www.strayer.edu/georgia/lithonia/

CONTACT
Strayer University–Lithonia Campus, 3120 Stonecrest Boulevard, Suite 200, Lithonia, GA 30038.

Strayer University–Morrow Campus

Morrow, Georgia

http://www.strayer.edu/georgia/morrow/

CONTACT
Strayer University–Morrow Campus, 3000 Corporate Center Drive, Suite 100, Morrow, GA 30260.

Strayer University–Roswell Campus

Roswell, Georgia

http://www.strayer.edu/georgia/roswell/

CONTACT
Strayer University–Roswell Campus, 100 Mansell Court East, Suite 100, Roswell, GA 30076.

Strayer University–Savannah Campus

Savannah, Georgia

http://www.strayer.edu/georgia/savannah/

CONTACT
Strayer University–Savannah Campus, 20 Martin Court, Savannah, GA 31419.

Thomas University

Thomasville, Georgia

http://www.thomasu.edu/

- **Independent** comprehensive, founded 1950
- **Small-town** 24-acre campus
- **Endowment** $4.2 million
- **Coed** 769 undergraduate students, 60% full-time, 55% women, 45% men
- **Minimally difficult** entrance level, 47% of applicants were admitted

UNDERGRAD STUDENTS
465 full-time, 304 part-time. Students come from 14 states and territories; 10 other countries; 35% are from out of state; 26% transferred in; 9% live on campus.

Freshmen:
Admission: 416 applied, 197 admitted, 106 enrolled.

FACULTY
Total: 53, 96% full-time, 70% with terminal degrees.

Student/faculty ratio: 6:1.

ACADEMICS
Calendar: semesters. *Degrees:* associate, bachelor's, master's, post-master's, and postbachelor's certificates.

Special study options: academic remediation for entering students, accelerated degree program, adult/continuing education programs, advanced placement credit, cooperative education, distance learning, double majors, independent study, internships, part-time degree program, services for LD students, study abroad, summer session for credit.

Computers: 80 computers/terminals are available on campus for general student use. Students can access the following: campus intranet, computer help desk, free student e-mail accounts, online (class) grades, online (class) registration, online (class) schedules. Campuswide network is available. 100% of college-owned or -operated housing units are wired for high-speed Internet access. Wireless service is available via entire campus.

Library: Thomas University Library plus 1 other. Weekly public service hours: 60.

STUDENT LIFE
Housing options: on-campus residence required through sophomore year; coed. Campus housing is university owned. Freshman applicants given priority for college housing.

Activities and organizations: drama/theater group, student-run newspaper, choral group, Student Government Association, Professional Management Association, National Society for Leadership and Success.

Athletics Member NAIA. ***Intercollegiate sports:*** baseball M(s), golf M(s)/W, soccer M(s)/W(s), softball W(s). ***Intramural sports:*** football M/W, table tennis M/W, tennis M/W, volleyball M/W.

Campus security: late-night transport/escort service, controlled dormitory access, evening security guards.

Student services: personal/psychological counseling.

COSTS
Costs (2017–18) ***Tuition:*** $15,940 full-time, $630 per credit hour part-time. ***Required fees:*** $1000 full-time, $550 per year part-time. ***Room only:*** $4800. Room and board charges vary according to housing facility. ***Payment plan:*** installment.

APPLYING
Options: electronic application, early admission, deferred entrance.

Application fee: $25.

Required: high school transcript.

Application deadlines: rolling (freshmen), rolling (transfers).

Notification: continuous (freshmen), continuous (transfers).

CONTACT
Mrs. Rita Gagliano, Office of Admission, Thomas University, 1501 Millpond Road, Thomasville, GA 31792. *Phone:* 229-227-6942. *Toll-free phone:* 800-538-9784. *Fax:* 229-227-6919. *E-mail:* rgagliano@thomasu.edu.

Toccoa Falls College

Toccoa Falls, Georgia

http://www.tfc.edu/

- **Independent interdenominational** 4-year, founded 1907
- **Small-town** 1100-acre campus with easy access to Atlanta, GA metro area
- **Endowment** $2.7 million
- **Coed** 1,254 undergraduate students, 63% full-time, 57% women, 43% men
- **Moderately difficult** entrance level, 54% of applicants were admitted

UNDERGRAD STUDENTS
793 full-time, 461 part-time. Students come from 31 states and territories; 8 other countries; 23% are from out of state; 6% Black or African American, non-Hispanic/Latino; 3% Hispanic/Latino; 7% Asian, non-Hispanic/Latino; 0.2% Native Hawaiian or other Pacific Islander, non-Hispanic/Latino; 0.5% American Indian or Alaska Native, non-Hispanic/Latino; 2% Two or more races, non-Hispanic/Latino; 16%

Race/ethnicity unknown; 1% international; 4% transferred in; 39% live on campus.

Freshmen:
Admission: 881 applied, 477 admitted, 216 enrolled. ***Average high school GPA:*** 3.45. ***Test scores:*** SAT critical reading scores over 500: 48%; SAT math scores over 500: 39%; ACT scores over 18: 76%; SAT critical reading scores over 600: 12%; SAT math scores over 600: 8%; ACT scores over 24: 25%; SAT critical reading scores over 700: 1%; ACT scores over 30: 4%.
Retention: 72% of full-time freshmen returned.

FACULTY
Total: 112, 38% full-time, 38% with terminal degrees.
Student/faculty ratio: 14:1.

ACADEMICS
Calendar: 4-1-4. *Degrees:* certificates, associate, and bachelor's.
Special study options: advanced placement credit, distance learning, double majors, independent study, internships, part-time degree program, services for LD students, study abroad, summer session for credit.
Computers: 42 computers/terminals and 20 ports are available on campus for general student use. Students can access the following: campus intranet, computer help desk, free student e-mail accounts, online (class) grades, online (class) registration, online (class) schedules. Campuswide network is available. 95% of college-owned or -operated housing units are wired for high-speed Internet access. Wireless service is available via entire campus.
Library: Seby Jones Library plus 1 other. *Books:* 61,023 (physical), 371,350 (digital/electronic); *Serial titles:* 87 (physical), 73,000 (digital/electronic); *Databases:* 280. Weekly public service hours: 104; students can reserve study rooms.

STUDENT LIFE
Housing options: on-campus residence required through junior year; men-only, women-only. Campus housing is university owned. Freshman campus housing is guaranteed.
Activities and organizations: drama/theater group, student-run newspaper, radio station, choral group, Outdoor Club, Hmong Student Fellowship, The Justice Campaign, Toccoa Falls for Life, Theatrical Society.
Athletics Member NCCAA. ***Intercollegiate sports:*** baseball M, basketball M/W, cross-country running M/W, soccer M/W, volleyball W. ***Intramural sports:*** basketball M/W, football M/W, soccer M/W, softball M/W, ultimate Frisbee M/W, volleyball M/W.
Campus security: student patrols.
Student services: health clinic, personal/psychological counseling.

COSTS & FINANCIAL AID
Costs (2017–18) ***Comprehensive fee:*** $29,968 includes full-time tuition ($21,334), mandatory fees ($700), and room and board ($7934). Full-time tuition and fees vary according to location. Part-time tuition: $889 per credit hour. Part-time tuition and fees vary according to location. ***Required fees:*** $700 per year part-time. ***Room and board:*** Room and board charges vary according to board plan. ***Payment plan:*** installment. ***Waivers:*** employees or children of employees.
Financial Aid Of all full-time matriculated undergraduates who enrolled in 2015, 593 applied for aid, 547 were judged to have need, 60 had their need fully met. In 2015, 65 non-need-based awards were made. ***Average percent of need met:*** 69. ***Average financial aid package:*** $18,438. ***Average need-based loan:*** $3581. ***Average need-based gift aid:*** $14,244. ***Average non-need-based aid:*** $9409. ***Average indebtedness upon graduation:*** $27,593.

APPLYING
Standardized Tests *Required:* SAT or ACT (for admission).
Options: electronic application, early admission, deferred entrance.
Application fee: $25.
Required: essay or personal statement, high school transcript, minimum 2.0 GPA, 1 letter of recommendation. ***Required for some:*** interview.
Application deadlines: rolling (freshmen), rolling (transfers).
Notification: continuous (freshmen), continuous (transfers).

CONTACT
Mr. Ronnie Stewart, Toccoa Falls College, 107 Kincaid Drive, MSC 899, Toccoa Falls, GA 30598. *Phone:* 706-886-6831 Ext. 5378. *Toll-free phone:* 888-785-5624. *Fax:* 706-282-6012. *E-mail:* rstewart@tfc.edu.

Truett McConnell University
Cleveland, Georgia
http://www.truett.edu/

- **Independent Baptist** comprehensive, founded 1946
- **Rural** 200-acre campus with easy access to Atlanta
- **Coed** 2,152 undergraduate students, 34% full-time, 56% women, 44% men
- **Minimally difficult** entrance level, 91% of applicants were admitted

UNDERGRAD STUDENTS
740 full-time, 1,412 part-time. Students come from 17 states and territories; 15 other countries; 9% are from out of state; 8% Black or African American, non-Hispanic/Latino; 6% Hispanic/Latino; 0.4% Asian, non-Hispanic/Latino; 0.1% American Indian or Alaska Native, non-Hispanic/Latino; 2% Race/ethnicity unknown; 2% international; 2% transferred in.

Freshmen:
Admission: 543 applied, 492 admitted, 222 enrolled. ***Average high school GPA:*** 3.36. ***Test scores:*** SAT critical reading scores over 500: 41%; SAT math scores over 500: 42%; SAT writing scores over 500: 35%; ACT scores over 18: 66%; SAT critical reading scores over 600: 12%; SAT math scores over 600: 6%; SAT writing scores over 600: 10%; ACT scores over 24: 13%; SAT critical reading scores over 700: 2%; SAT writing scores over 700: 2%; ACT scores over 30: 1%.
Retention: 63% of full-time freshmen returned.

FACULTY
Total: 52.
Student/faculty ratio: 15:1.

ACADEMICS
Calendar: semesters. *Degrees:* bachelor's and master's.
Special study options: academic remediation for entering students, accelerated degree program, advanced placement credit, distance learning, double majors, services for LD students, summer session for credit.
Computers: 40 computers/terminals are available on campus for general student use. Students can access the following: computer help desk, free student e-mail accounts, online (class) grades, online (class) registration, online (class) schedules. Campuswide network is available. 100% of college-owned or -operated housing units are wired for high-speed Internet access. Wireless service is available via entire campus.
Library: Cofer Library.

STUDENT LIFE
Housing options: on-campus residence required through senior year; men-only, women-only. Campus housing is university owned.
Activities and organizations: choral group.
Athletics Member NAIA. ***Intercollegiate sports:*** baseball M(s), basketball M(s)/W(s), cross-country running M(s)/W(s), golf M(s)/W(s), lacrosse W(s), soccer M(s)/W(s), softball W(s), volleyball W(s), wrestling M(s). ***Intramural sports:*** football M/W.
Campus security: 24-hour weekday patrols, 10-hour weekend patrols by trained security personnel.

COSTS & FINANCIAL AID
Costs (2017–18) ***Comprehensive fee:*** $26,630 includes full-time tuition ($18,570), mandatory fees ($660), and room and board ($7400). Full-time tuition and fees vary according to course load, degree level, location, and program. Part-time tuition: $619 per credit hour. Part-time tuition and fees vary according to course load, degree level, location, and program. ***Required fees:*** $330 per term part-time. ***Room and board:*** Room and board charges vary according to housing facility. ***Payment plan:*** installment. ***Waivers:*** employees or children of employees.
Financial Aid Of all full-time matriculated undergraduates who enrolled in 2016, 644 applied for aid, 574 were judged to have need, 124 had their need fully met. 45 Federal Work-Study jobs (averaging $1039). In 2016, 100 non-need-based awards were made. ***Average percent of need met:*** 68. ***Average financial aid package:*** $15,321. ***Average need-based loan:***

$4753. ***Average need-based gift aid:*** $11,975. ***Average non-need-based aid:*** $6299. ***Average indebtedness upon graduation:*** $15,542.

APPLYING

Standardized Tests *Required:* SAT or ACT (for admission).

Options: electronic application, early admission, deferred entrance.

Required: high school transcript, minimum 2.0 GPA. ***Required for some:*** essay or personal statement, 1 letter of recommendation, interview.

Application deadlines: 8/1 (freshmen), 8/1 (transfers).

Notification: continuous (freshmen), continuous (transfers).

CONTACT

Truett McConnell University, 100 Alumni Drive, Cleveland, GA 30528. *Phone:* 706-865-2134 Ext. 4301. *Toll-free phone:* 800-226-8621.

University of Georgia

Athens, Georgia

http://www.uga.edu/

- **State-supported** comprehensive, founded 1785, part of University System of Georgia
- **Suburban** 767-acre campus with easy access to Atlanta
- **Endowment** $1.0 billion
- **Coed** 27,951 undergraduate students, 94% full-time, 57% women, 43% men
- **Moderately difficult** entrance level, 54% of applicants were admitted

UNDERGRAD STUDENTS

26,328 full-time, 1,623 part-time. Students come from 54 states and territories; 124 other countries; 8% are from out of state; 8% Black or African American, non-Hispanic/Latino; 6% Hispanic/Latino; 10% Asian, non-Hispanic/Latino; 0.1% Native Hawaiian or other Pacific Islander, non-Hispanic/Latino; 0.1% American Indian or Alaska Native, non-Hispanic/Latino; 4% Two or more races, non-Hispanic/Latino; 0.8% Race/ethnicity unknown; 2% international; 4% transferred in; 32% live on campus.

Freshmen:

Admission: 22,694 applied, 12,232 admitted, 5,433 enrolled. ***Average high school GPA:*** 3.98. ***Test scores:*** SAT critical reading scores over 500: 95%; SAT math scores over 500: 96%; SAT writing scores over 500: 94%; ACT scores over 18: 100%; SAT critical reading scores over 600: 62%; SAT math scores over 600: 66%; SAT writing scores over 600: 59%; ACT scores over 24: 93%; SAT critical reading scores over 700: 15%; SAT math scores over 700: 17%; SAT writing scores over 700: 13%; ACT scores over 30: 42%.

Retention: 95% of full-time freshmen returned.

FACULTY

Total: 2,268, 89% full-time, 91% with terminal degrees.

Student/faculty ratio: 18:1.

ACADEMICS

Calendar: semesters. *Degrees:* certificates, bachelor's, master's, doctoral, post-master's, and postbachelor's certificates.

Special study options: academic remediation for entering students, accelerated degree program, adult/continuing education programs, advanced placement credit, cooperative education, distance learning, double majors, external degree program, honors programs, independent study, internships, off-campus study, part-time degree program, services for LD students, student-designed majors, study abroad, summer session for credit. ***ROTC:*** Army (b), Air Force (b).

Computers: Students can access the following: campus intranet, computer help desk, free student e-mail accounts, online (class) grades, online (class) registration, online (class) schedules. Campuswide network is available. 100% of college-owned or -operated housing units are wired for high-speed Internet access. Wireless service is available via classrooms, computer centers, computer labs, dorm rooms, learning centers, libraries, student centers.

Library: Ilah Dunlap Little Memorial Library plus 4 others. *Books:* 5.2 million (digital/electronic). Students can reserve study rooms.

STUDENT LIFE

Housing options: on-campus residence required for freshman year; coed, women-only, special housing for students with disabilities. Campus housing is university owned. Freshman campus housing is guaranteed.

Activities and organizations: drama/theater group, student-run newspaper, radio station, choral group, marching band, Intramural Sports, Recreational sports program, Communiversity, University Union, Red Coat Band, national fraternities, national sororities.

Athletics Member NCAA. All Division I except football (Division I-A). ***Intercollegiate sports:*** badminton M(c)/W(c), baseball M(s), basketball M(s)/W(s), cheerleading M(c)/W(c), crew M(c)/W(c), cross-country running M(s)/W(s), equestrian sports M(c)/W(s), fencing M(c)/W(c), golf M(s)/W(s), gymnastics M(c)/W(s), ice hockey M(c), lacrosse M(c)/W(c), racquetball M(c)/W(c), rugby M(c)/W(c), sailing M(c)/W(c), soccer M(c)/W(s), softball W(s), swimming and diving M(s)/W(s), tennis M(s)/W(s), track and field M(s)/W(s), ultimate Frisbee M(c)/W(c), volleyball M(c)/W(s), water polo M(c)/W(c), wrestling M(c). ***Intramural sports:*** badminton M/W, basketball M/W, football M/W, golf M/W, racquetball M/W, soccer M/W, softball M/W, tennis M/W, ultimate Frisbee M/W, volleyball M/W, water polo M/W.

Campus security: 24-hour emergency response devices and patrols, late-night transport/escort service, controlled dormitory access.

Student services: health clinic, personal/psychological counseling, women's center, legal services.

COSTS & FINANCIAL AID

Costs (2016–17) ***Tuition:*** state resident $9364 full-time; nonresident $27,574 full-time. Full-time tuition and fees vary according to course load, location, and program. Part-time tuition and fees vary according to course load, location, and program. ***Required fees:*** $2270 full-time. ***Room and board:*** $9616; room only: $5660. Room and board charges vary according to board plan and housing facility. ***Waivers:*** senior citizens.

Financial Aid Of all full-time matriculated undergraduates who enrolled in 2016, 18,463 applied for aid, 11,593 were judged to have need, 2,552 had their need fully met. 382 Federal Work-Study jobs (averaging $2410). In 2016, 1204 non-need-based awards were made. ***Average percent of need met:*** 71. ***Average financial aid package:*** $11,997. ***Average need-based loan:*** $4232. ***Average need-based gift aid:*** $9116. ***Average non-need-based aid:*** $2418. ***Average indebtedness upon graduation:*** $21,730.

APPLYING

Standardized Tests *Required:* SAT or ACT (for admission).

Options: electronic application, early admission, early action, deferred entrance.

Application fee: $60.

Required: high school transcript, counselor evaluation. ***Recommended:*** essay or personal statement, minimum 2.0 GPA.

Application deadlines: 1/15 (freshmen), 4/1 (transfers), 10/15 (early action).

Notification: 4/1 (freshmen), continuous (transfers), 12/1 (early action).

CONTACT

Mr. Charles Carabello, Associate Director for Enrollment Management, University of Georgia, Terrell Hall, Athens, GA 30602. *Phone:* 706-542-8776. *Fax:* 706-542-1466. *E-mail:* admproc@uga.edu.

University of North Georgia

Dahlonega, Georgia

http://www.ung.edu/

- **State-supported** comprehensive, founded 1873, part of University System of Georgia
- **Small-town** 1077-acre campus with easy access to Atlanta
- **Endowment** $53.6 million
- **Coed** 17,704 undergraduate students, 71% full-time, 56% women, 44% men
- **Moderately difficult** entrance level, 66% of applicants were admitted

UNDERGRAD STUDENTS

12,567 full-time, 5,137 part-time. Students come from 51 states and territories; 98 other countries; 5% are from out of state; 4% Black or African American, non-Hispanic/Latino; 11% Hispanic/Latino; 3% Asian, non-Hispanic/Latino; 0.1% Native Hawaiian or other Pacific Islander, non-Hispanic/Latino; 0.2% American Indian or Alaska Native, non-Hispanic/Latino; 3% Two or more races, non-Hispanic/Latino; 1% Race/ethnicity unknown; 2% international; 3% transferred in; 15% live on campus.

Freshmen:
Admission: 5,634 applied, 3,736 admitted, 3,958 enrolled. ***Average high school GPA:*** 3.55. ***Test scores:*** SAT critical reading scores over 500: 83%; SAT math scores over 500: 74%; SAT writing scores over 500: 65%; ACT scores over 18: 99%; SAT critical reading scores over 600: 28%; SAT math scores over 600: 22%; SAT writing scores over 600: 16%; ACT scores over 24: 58%; SAT critical reading scores over 700: 4%; SAT math scores over 700: 2%; SAT writing scores over 700: 1%; ACT scores over 30: 5%.

Retention: 79% of full-time freshmen returned.

FACULTY
Total: 897, 69% full-time, 54% with terminal degrees.
Student/faculty ratio: 21:1.

ACADEMICS
Calendar: semesters. *Degrees:* certificates, associate, bachelor's, master's, doctoral, post-master's, and postbachelor's certificates.
Special study options: academic remediation for entering students, accelerated degree program, advanced placement credit, cooperative education, distance learning, double majors, English as a second language, freshman honors college, honors programs, independent study, internships, part-time degree program, services for LD students, study abroad, summer session for credit. ***ROTC:*** Army (b).
Unusual degree programs: 3-2 engineering with Georgia Institute of Technology, Clemson University.
Computers: 2,443 computers/terminals are available on campus for general student use. Students can access the following: campus intranet, computer help desk, free student e-mail accounts, online (class) grades, online (class) registration, online (class) schedules. Campuswide network is available. 100% of college-owned or -operated housing units are wired for high-speed Internet access. Wireless service is available via classrooms, computer centers, computer labs, dorm rooms, learning centers, libraries, student centers.
Library: Library Technology Center plus 4 others. *Books:* 270,623 (physical), 291,155 (digital/electronic); *Serial titles:* 115,466 (physical); *Databases:* 240. Students can reserve study rooms.

STUDENT LIFE
Housing options: on-campus residence required through sophomore year; coed, men-only, women-only. Campus housing is university owned. Freshman applicants given priority for college housing.
Activities and organizations: drama/theater group, student-run newspaper, radio station, choral group, marching band, Student Government Association, Commuter Council, Graduate Student Senate, Student Activities Board, Greek organizations, national fraternities, national sororities.
Athletics Member NCAA. All Division II. ***Intercollegiate sports:*** baseball M(s), basketball M(s)/W(s), cheerleading M/W, cross-country running M(c)/W(s), equestrian sports W(c), golf M(s)/W(s), lacrosse M(c)/W(c), riflery M(s)/W(s), soccer M(s)/W(s), softball W(s), tennis M(s)/W(s), wrestling M(c). ***Intramural sports:*** basketball M/W, football M/W, golf M(c)/W(c), rugby M/W, soccer M/W, softball M/W, table tennis M/W, ultimate Frisbee M/W, volleyball M/W, water polo M/W.
Campus security: 24-hour emergency response devices and patrols, late-night transport/escort service, controlled dormitory access.
Student services: health clinic, personal/psychological counseling.

COSTS & FINANCIAL AID
Costs (2017–18) ***Tuition:*** state resident $5352 full-time, $178 per credit hour part-time; nonresident $18,894 full-time, $630 per credit hour part-time. Full-time tuition and fees vary according to course load, degree level, and location. Part-time tuition and fees vary according to course load, degree level, and location. ***Required fees:*** $1876 full-time. ***Room and board:*** $9680; room only: $5360. Room and board charges vary according to board plan and housing facility. ***Payment plan:*** installment. ***Waivers:*** senior citizens and employees or children of employees.
Financial Aid Of all full-time matriculated undergraduates who enrolled in 2015, 11,355 applied for aid, 7,489 were judged to have need, 4,562 had their need fully met. 94 Federal Work-Study jobs (averaging $2425). In 2015, 553 non-need-based awards were made. ***Average percent of need met:*** 62. ***Average financial aid package:*** $13,962. ***Average need-based loan:*** $5189. ***Average need-based gift aid:*** $5803. ***Average non-need-based aid:*** $1292. ***Average indebtedness upon graduation:*** $10,062.

APPLYING
Standardized Tests *Required:* SAT or ACT (for admission).
Options: electronic application, early admission.
Application fee: $30.
Required: high school transcript, minimum 2.0 GPA, proof of immunization.
Application deadlines: 7/1 (freshmen), rolling (transfers).
Notification: continuous (freshmen), continuous (transfers).

CONTACT
Molly Potts, Director of Admissions, University of North Georgia, Admissions Center, 3820 Mundy Mill Road, Oakwood, GA 30566. *Phone:* 678-717-3849. *Toll-free phone:* 800-498-9581.
E-mail: molly.potts@ung.edu.

University of Phoenix–Atlanta Campus

Sandy Springs, Georgia

http://www.phoenix.edu/

CONTACT
Marc Booker, Sr. Director, Office of Admissions and Evaluation, University of Phoenix–Atlanta Campus, 4035 South Riverpoint Parkway, Mail Stop CF-L101, Phoenix, AZ 85040. *Phone:* 602-557-4609. *Toll-free phone:* 866-766-0766. *Fax:* 480-643-1156.

University of Phoenix–Augusta Campus

Augusta, Georgia

http://www.phoenix.edu/

CONTACT
University of Phoenix–Augusta Campus, 3150 Perimeter Parkway, Augusta, GA 30909-4583. *Toll-free phone:* 866-766-0766.

University of Phoenix–Columbus Georgia Campus

Columbus, Georgia

http://www.phoenix.edu/

CONTACT
Marc Booker, Sr. Director, Office of Admissions and Evaluation, University of Phoenix–Columbus Georgia Campus, 4035 South Riverpoint Parkway, Mail Stop CF-L101, Phoenix, AZ 85040. *Phone:* 602-557-4609. *Toll-free phone:* 866-766-0766. *Fax:* 480-643-1156.

University of West Georgia

Carrollton, Georgia

http://www.westga.edu/

- **State-supported** comprehensive, founded 1933, part of University System of Georgia
- **Rural** 645-acre campus with easy access to Atlanta
- **Endowment** $27.3 million
- **Coed** 11,155 undergraduate students, 81% full-time, 64% women, 36% men
- **Moderately difficult** entrance level, 59% of applicants were admitted

UNDERGRAD STUDENTS
9,084 full-time, 2,071 part-time. Students come from 31 states and territories; 66 other countries; 4% are from out of state; 38% Black or African American, non-Hispanic/Latino; 5% Hispanic/Latino; 1% Asian, non-Hispanic/Latino; 0.1% Native Hawaiian or other Pacific Islander, non-Hispanic/Latino; 0.1% American Indian or Alaska Native, non-

Hispanic/Latino; 4% Two or more races, non-Hispanic/Latino; 1% Race/ethnicity unknown; 1% international; 7% transferred in; 29% live on campus.

Freshmen:
Admission: 8,131 applied, 4,801 admitted, 2,434 enrolled. ***Average high school GPA:*** 3.15. ***Test scores:*** SAT critical reading scores over 500: 34%; SAT math scores over 500: 29%; SAT writing scores over 500: 27%; ACT scores over 18: 84%; SAT critical reading scores over 600: 7%; SAT math scores over 600: 5%; SAT writing scores over 600: 3%; ACT scores over 24: 16%; SAT critical reading scores over 700: 1%; ACT scores over 30: 1%.
Retention: 72% of full-time freshmen returned.

FACULTY
Total: 715, 59% full-time, 61% with terminal degrees.
Student/faculty ratio: 21:1.

ACADEMICS
Calendar: semesters. *Degrees:* bachelor's, master's, doctoral, post-master's, and postbachelor's certificates.
Special study options: accelerated degree program, advanced placement credit, cooperative education, distance learning, double majors, external degree program, freshman honors college, honors programs, independent study, internships, off-campus study, part-time degree program, services for LD students, study abroad, summer session for credit. ***ROTC:*** Air Force (c).
Unusual degree programs: 3-2 engineering with Georgia Institute of Technology, Auburn University, Mercer University.
Computers: 1,200 computers/terminals are available on campus for general student use. Students can access the following: campus intranet, computer help desk, free student e-mail accounts, online (class) grades, online (class) registration, online (class) schedules. Campuswide network is available. 100% of college-owned or -operated housing units are wired for high-speed Internet access. Wireless service is available via entire campus.
Library: Irvine Sullivan Ingram Library plus 1 other. Weekly public service hours: 137; study areas open 24 hours, 5-7 days a week; students can reserve study rooms.

STUDENT LIFE
Housing options: on-campus residence required for freshman year; coed, women-only, special housing for students with disabilities. Campus housing is university owned and leased by the school. Freshman campus housing is guaranteed.
Activities and organizations: drama/theater group, student-run newspaper, radio and television station, choral group, marching band, Black Student Alliance, Student Activities Council, Baptist Collegiate Ministries, Campus Outreach, United Voices Gospel Choir, national fraternities, national sororities.
Athletics Member NCAA. All Division II. ***Intercollegiate sports:*** baseball M(s), basketball M(s)/W(s), cheerleading W(s), cross-country running M(s)/W(s), football M(s), golf M(s)/W(s), soccer W(s), softball W(s), tennis W(s), track and field W(s), volleyball W(s). ***Intramural sports:*** baseball M(c), basketball M(c)/W(c), equestrian sports W(c), golf M/W, lacrosse M(c), rock climbing M(c)/W(c), soccer M(c), ultimate Frisbee M/W, wrestling M(c).
Campus security: 24-hour emergency response devices and patrols, student patrols, late-night transport/escort service, controlled dormitory access.
Student services: health clinic, personal/psychological counseling.

COSTS & FINANCIAL AID
Costs (2017–18) ***Tuition:*** state resident $5226 full-time, $174 per semester hour part-time; nonresident $18,444 full-time, $615 per semester hour part-time. Full-time tuition and fees vary according to course load, degree level, location, and program. Part-time tuition and fees vary according to course load, degree level, location, and program. ***Required fees:*** $1962 full-time. ***Room and board:*** $9652; room only: $5300. Room and board charges vary according to board plan and housing facility. ***Payment plan:*** installment. ***Waivers:*** senior citizens and employees or children of employees.
Financial Aid Of all full-time matriculated undergraduates who enrolled in 2016, 8,162 applied for aid, 6,852 were judged to have need, 3,680 had their need fully met. In 2016, 518 non-need-based awards were made. ***Average percent of need met:*** 47. ***Average financial aid package:*** $8852. ***Average need-based loan:*** $4058. ***Average need-based gift aid:*** $4965. ***Average non-need-based aid:*** $2334. ***Average indebtedness upon graduation:*** $26,874. ***Financial aid deadline:*** 7/1.

APPLYING
Standardized Tests *Required:* SAT or ACT (for admission).
Options: electronic application, early admission, deferred entrance.
Application fee: $40.
Required: minimum 2.6 GPA, proof of immunization. ***Required for some:*** high school transcript.
Application deadlines: rolling (freshmen), rolling (transfers).
Notification: continuous (freshmen), continuous (transfers).

CONTACT
Ms. Ketty Ballard, Associate Director (Recruiting), University of West Georgia, 1601 Maple Street, Carrollton, GA 30118. *Phone:* 678-839-5600. *Fax:* 678-839-4747. *E-mail:* admiss@westga.edu.

Valdosta State University
Valdosta, Georgia
http://www.valdosta.edu/

- **State-supported** university, founded 1906, part of University System of Georgia
- **Small-town** 180-acre campus
- **Endowment** $7.5 million
- **Coed** 8,780 undergraduate students, 82% full-time, 60% women, 40% men
- **Moderately difficult** entrance level, 65% of applicants were admitted

UNDERGRAD STUDENTS
7,185 full-time, 1,595 part-time. Students come from 47 states and territories; 65 other countries; 10% are from out of state; 37% Black or African American, non-Hispanic/Latino; 6% Hispanic/Latino; 1% Asian, non-Hispanic/Latino; 0.1% Native Hawaiian or other Pacific Islander, non-Hispanic/Latino; 0.2% American Indian or Alaska Native, non-Hispanic/Latino; 4% Two or more races, non-Hispanic/Latino; 0.8% Race/ethnicity unknown; 3% international; 9% transferred in; 27% live on campus.

Freshmen:
Admission: 5,108 applied, 3,327 admitted, 1,458 enrolled. ***Average high school GPA:*** 3.18. ***Test scores:*** SAT critical reading scores over 500: 49%; SAT math scores over 500: 39%; SAT writing scores over 500: 36%; ACT scores over 18: 94%; SAT critical reading scores over 600: 9%; SAT math scores over 600: 7%; SAT writing scores over 600: 5%; ACT scores over 24: 19%; SAT critical reading scores over 700: 1%; SAT math scores over 700: 1%; ACT scores over 30: 1%.
Retention: 71% of full-time freshmen returned.

FACULTY
Total: 603, 69% full-time, 63% with terminal degrees.
Student/faculty ratio: 20:1.

ACADEMICS
Calendar: semesters. *Degrees:* certificates, associate, bachelor's, master's, doctoral, post-master's, and postbachelor's certificates.
Special study options: accelerated degree program, adult/continuing education programs, advanced placement credit, cooperative education, distance learning, double majors, English as a second language, external degree program, honors programs, independent study, internships, off-campus study, part-time degree program, services for LD students, study abroad, summer session for credit. ***ROTC:*** Air Force (b).
Unusual degree programs: 3-2 engineering with Georgia Institute of Technology.
Computers: 1,691 computers/terminals are available on campus for general student use. Students can access the following: campus intranet, computer help desk, free student e-mail accounts, online (class) grades, online (class) registration, online (class) schedules. Campuswide network is available. 100% of college-owned or -operated housing units are wired for high-speed Internet access. Wireless service is available via entire campus.

Library: Odum Library. *Books:* 573,723 (physical), 184,929 (digital/electronic); *Serial titles:* 10,852 (physical), 46,502 (digital/electronic); *Databases:* 225. Students can reserve study rooms.

STUDENT LIFE
Housing options: on-campus residence required for freshman year; coed, special housing for students with disabilities. Campus housing is university owned. Freshman applicants given priority for college housing.
Activities and organizations: drama/theater group, student-run newspaper, radio and television station, choral group, marching band, Black Student League, Enactus, Psychology Club, Collegiate women of VSU, College Republican Society, national fraternities, national sororities.
Athletics Member NCAA. All Division II. ***Intercollegiate sports:*** baseball M(s), basketball M(s)/W(s), cheerleading M/W, cross-country running M(s)/W(s), football M(s), golf M(s), soccer W(s), softball W(s), tennis M(s)/W(s), volleyball W(s). ***Intramural sports:*** basketball M/W, bowling M/W, football M/W, golf M/W, lacrosse M(c)/W(c), rugby M(c), sand volleyball M/W, soccer M(c)/W(c), softball M/W, swimming and diving M(c)/W(c), table tennis M(c)/W(c), tennis M/W, track and field M(c)/W(c), ultimate Frisbee M/W, volleyball M/W.
Campus security: 24-hour emergency response devices and patrols, late-night transport/escort service, controlled dormitory access, bicycle patrols, security cameras, mobile security app.
Student services: health clinic, personal/psychological counseling.

COSTS & FINANCIAL AID
Costs (2017–18) ***Tuition:*** state resident $4181 full-time; nonresident $14,755 full-time. Full-time tuition and fees vary according to course load, location, program, and reciprocity agreements. Part-time tuition and fees vary according to course load, location, program, and reciprocity agreements. ***Required fees:*** $2116 full-time. ***Room and board:*** $7900; room only: $4060. Room and board charges vary according to board plan and housing facility. ***Payment plan:*** installment. ***Waivers:*** employees or children of employees.
Financial Aid Of all full-time matriculated undergraduates who enrolled in 2015, 6,194 applied for aid, 5,323 were judged to have need, 781 had their need fully met. In 2015, 77 non-need-based awards were made. ***Average percent of need met:*** 78. ***Average financial aid package:*** $15,919. ***Average need-based loan:*** $3464. ***Average need-based gift aid:*** $6361. ***Average non-need-based aid:*** $2478. ***Average indebtedness upon graduation:*** $29,607.

APPLYING
Standardized Tests *Required:* SAT or ACT (for admission).
Options: electronic application, deferred entrance.
Application fee: $40.
Required: high school transcript.
Application deadlines: 6/15 (freshmen), rolling (out-of-state freshmen), 6/15 (transfers).
Notification: continuous until 9/1 (freshmen), continuous until 8/1 (out-of-state freshmen), continuous until 8/1 (transfers).

CONTACT
Mr. Ryan M. Hogan, Director of Admissions, Valdosta State University, Office of Admissions, 1500 North Patterson Street, Valdosta, GA 31698. *Phone:* 229-333-5791. *Toll-free phone:* 800-618-1878. *Fax:* 229-333-5482. *E-mail:* admissions@valdosta.edu.

Wesleyan College
Macon, Georgia
http://www.wesleyancollege.edu/

- **Independent United Methodist** comprehensive, founded 1836
- **Suburban** 200-acre campus with easy access to Atlanta
- **Endowment** $58.6 million
- **Undergraduate: women only; graduate: coed** 635 undergraduate students, 78% full-time, 99% women, 1% men
- **Moderately difficult** entrance level, 38% of applicants were admitted

UNDERGRAD STUDENTS
494 full-time, 141 part-time. Students come from 15 states and territories; 20 other countries; 11% are from out of state; 26% Black or African American, non-Hispanic/Latino; 5% Hispanic/Latino; 3% Asian, non-Hispanic/Latino; 0.2% Native Hawaiian or other Pacific Islander, non-Hispanic/Latino; 3% Two or more races, non-Hispanic/Latino; 1% Race/ethnicity unknown; 19% international; 3% transferred in; 60% live on campus.

Freshmen:
Admission: 842 applied, 317 admitted, 104 enrolled. ***Average high school GPA:*** 3.39. ***Test scores:*** SAT critical reading scores over 500: 68%; SAT math scores over 500: 51%; SAT writing scores over 500: 42%; ACT scores over 18: 90%; SAT critical reading scores over 600: 22%; SAT math scores over 600: 11%; SAT writing scores over 600: 11%; ACT scores over 24: 39%; SAT critical reading scores over 700: 4%; SAT math scores over 700: 1%; SAT writing scores over 700: 1%; ACT scores over 30: 3%.
Retention: 71% of full-time freshmen returned.

FACULTY
Total: 83, 69% full-time, 59% with terminal degrees.
Student/faculty ratio: 15:1.

ACADEMICS
Calendar: semesters. *Degrees:* bachelor's and master's.
Special study options: adult/continuing education programs, advanced placement credit, cooperative education, distance learning, double majors, honors programs, independent study, internships, off-campus study, part-time degree program, services for LD students, student-designed majors, study abroad, summer session for credit. ***ROTC:*** Army (c).
Unusual degree programs: 3-2 engineering with Georgia Institute of Technology, Auburn University, Mercer University.
Computers: 63 computers/terminals are available on campus for general student use. Students can access the following: campus intranet, computer help desk, free student e-mail accounts, online (class) grades, online (class) registration, online (class) schedules, online payment. Campuswide network is available. 100% of college-owned or -operated housing units are wired for high-speed Internet access. Wireless service is available via entire campus.
Library: Willet Memorial Library. Study areas open 24 hours, 5-7 days a week; students can reserve study rooms.

STUDENT LIFE
Housing options: women-only, special housing for students with disabilities. Campus housing is university owned. Freshman campus housing is guaranteed.
Activities and organizations: drama/theater group, student-run newspaper, choral group, Student Government Association (SGA), Black Student Alliance (BSA), A.X.I.S. (Association of eXemplary International Students), GLBAL (Gay, Lesbian, Bi-sexual ALliance), Campus Activities Board (CAB).
Athletics Member NCAA. All Division III. ***Intercollegiate sports:*** basketball W, equestrian sports W, soccer W, softball W, tennis W, volleyball W.
Campus security: 24-hour emergency response devices and patrols, late-night transport/escort service.
Student services: health clinic, personal/psychological counseling, women's center.

COSTS & FINANCIAL AID
Costs (2017–18) ***One-time required fee:*** $250. ***Comprehensive fee:*** $31,940 includes full-time tuition ($21,370), mandatory fees ($1000), and room and board ($9570). Full-time tuition and fees vary according to class time, course load, program, and reciprocity agreements. Part-time tuition: $510 per semester hour. Part-time tuition and fees vary according to class time, course load, and reciprocity agreements. ***Required fees:*** $40 per semester hour part-time. ***Room and board:*** Room and board charges vary according to housing facility. ***Payment plan:*** installment. ***Waivers:*** employees or children of employees.
Financial Aid Of all full-time matriculated undergraduates who enrolled in 2016, 345 applied for aid, 320 were judged to have need, 61 had their need fully met. In 2016, 85 non-need-based awards were made. ***Average percent of need met:*** 74. ***Average financial aid package:*** $20,567. ***Average need-based loan:*** $5880. ***Average need-based gift aid:*** $15,880. ***Average non-need-based aid:*** $10,742. ***Average indebtedness upon graduation:*** $35,392. ***Financial aid deadline:*** 6/1.

APPLYING
Standardized Tests *Required:* SAT or ACT (for admission).

Options: electronic application, early admission, early decision, early action, deferred entrance.

Application fee: $30.

Required: high school transcript, minimum 2.0 GPA, 1 letter of recommendation. ***Required for some:*** interview. ***Recommended:*** essay or personal statement, 2 letters of recommendation.

Application deadlines: 1/15 (freshmen), 7/17 (transfers), 11/15 (early action).

Early decision deadline: 11/15.

Notification: 2/15 (freshmen), continuous (transfers), 12/15 (early decision), 12/15 (early action).

CONTACT
Ms. Danielle Lodge, Executive Director of Enrollment, Wesleyan College, 4760 Forsyth Road, Macon, GA 31210-4462. *Phone:* 478-757-5206. *Toll-free phone:* 800-447-6610. *Fax:* 478-757-4030.
E-mail: admissions@wesleyancollege.edu.

Young Harris College

Young Harris, Georgia

http://www.yhc.edu/

- **Independent United Methodist** 4-year, founded 1886
- **Small-town** 800-acre campus
- **Endowment** $93.7 million
- **Coed**
- **Moderately difficult** entrance level

FACULTY
Student/faculty ratio: 12:1.

ACADEMICS
Calendar: semesters. *Degree:* bachelor's.
Library: Duckworth Library. *Databases:* 72. Study areas open 24 hours, 5-7 days a week.

STUDENT LIFE
Housing options: on-campus residence required through senior year; coed, men-only, women-only, special housing for students with disabilities. Campus housing is university owned. Freshman campus housing is guaranteed.

Activities and organizations: drama/theater group, student-run newspaper, choral group, Greek life, religious organizations/Bible study, intramural sports, Student Government Association, Campus Activities Board, national fraternities, national sororities.

Athletics Member NCAA. All Division II.

Campus security: 24-hour emergency response devices and patrols, student patrols, late-night transport/escort service, controlled dormitory access.

Student services: health clinic, personal/psychological counseling.

FINANCIAL AID
Financial Aid Of all full-time matriculated undergraduates who enrolled in 2015, 931 applied for aid, 814 were judged to have need, 158 had their need fully met. 116 Federal Work-Study jobs (averaging $836). 377 state and other part-time jobs (averaging $1078). In 2015, 336 non-need-based awards were made. ***Average percent of need met:*** 73. ***Average financial aid package:*** $23,364. ***Average need-based loan:*** $3709. ***Average need-based gift aid:*** $20,363. ***Average non-need-based aid:*** $19,650. ***Average indebtedness upon graduation:*** $27,173.

APPLYING
Standardized Tests *Required:* SAT or ACT (for admission).

Options: electronic application.

Required: high school transcript.

CONTACT
Mr. Clinton G. Hobbs, Vice President for Enrollment Management, Young Harris College, PO Box 116, Young Harris, GA 30582-0098. *Phone:* 706-379-3111. *Toll-free phone:* 800-241-3754. *Fax:* 706-379-3108.
E-mail: admissions@yhc.edu.

HAWAII

Argosy University, Hawai`i

Honolulu, Hawaii

http://www.argosy.edu/locations/hawaii/

CONTACT
Argosy University, Hawai`i, 1001 Bishop Street, Suite 400, Honolulu, HI 96813. *Phone:* 808-536-5555. *Toll-free phone:* 888-323-2777.

Brigham Young University–Hawaii

Laie, Hawaii

http://www.byuh.edu/

CONTACT
Mr. Arapata P. Meha, Brigham Young University–Hawaii, 55-220 Kulanui Street, Laie, HI 96762-1294. *Phone:* 808-675-3731.
Fax: 808-675-3741. *E-mail:* admissions@byuh.edu.

Chaminade University of Honolulu

Honolulu, Hawaii

http://www.chaminade.edu/

- **Independent Roman Catholic** comprehensive, founded 1955
- **Urban** 62-acre campus with easy access to Honolulu
- **Endowment** $14.1 million
- **Coed** 1,183 undergraduate students, 97% full-time, 71% women, 29% men
- **Moderately difficult** entrance level, 91% of applicants were admitted

UNDERGRAD STUDENTS
1,150 full-time, 33 part-time. Students come from 35 states and territories; 13 other countries; 30% are from out of state; 3% Black or African American, non-Hispanic/Latino; 5% Hispanic/Latino; 39% Asian, non-Hispanic/Latino; 21% Native Hawaiian or other Pacific Islander, non-Hispanic/Latino; 0.5% American Indian or Alaska Native, non-Hispanic/Latino; 13% Two or more races, non-Hispanic/Latino; 4% Race/ethnicity unknown; 1% international; 6% transferred in; 24% live on campus.

Freshmen:
Admission: 842 applied, 769 admitted, 256 enrolled. ***Average high school GPA:*** 3.43. ***Test scores:*** SAT critical reading scores over 500: 37%; SAT math scores over 500: 49%; ACT scores over 18: 86%; SAT critical reading scores over 600: 8%; SAT math scores over 600: 9%; ACT scores over 24: 20%; SAT math scores over 700: 1%; ACT scores over 30: 2%.
Retention: 74% of full-time freshmen returned.

FACULTY
Total: 143, 65% full-time.
Student/faculty ratio: 11:1.

ACADEMICS
Calendar: semesters. *Degrees:* associate, bachelor's, master's, and postbachelor's certificates.

Special study options: academic remediation for entering students, accelerated degree program, adult/continuing education programs, advanced placement credit, distance learning, double majors, independent study, internships, off-campus study, part-time degree program, study abroad, summer session for credit. ***ROTC:*** Army (c), Air Force (c).

Computers: 200 computers/terminals are available on campus for general student use. Students can access the following: computer help desk, free student e-mail accounts, online (class) grades, online (class) registration, online (class) schedules. Campuswide network is available. 100% of college-owned or -operated housing units are wired for high-speed Internet access. Wireless service is available via entire campus.
Library: Sullivan Library. *Books:* 51,328 (physical), 133,447 (digital/electronic); *Serial titles:* 11,276 (physical), 144,925 (digital/electronic); *Databases:* 82.

STUDENT LIFE
Housing options: coed, women-only, special housing for students with disabilities. Campus housing is university owned and leased by the school.

Activities and organizations: drama/theater group, student-run newspaper, radio station, choral group, Lumana O Samoa (Samoan Club), Kaimi Lalakea (Hawaiian Club), Rotaract, Residence Hall Association, Chaminade Student Government Association.

Athletics Member NCAA. All Division II. ***Intercollegiate sports:*** basketball M(s)/W(s), cross-country running M(s)/W(s), golf M(s), soccer M(s)/W(s), softball W(s), tennis W(s), volleyball W(s). ***Intramural sports:*** basketball M/W.

Campus security: 24-hour emergency response devices and patrols, late-night transport/escort service, controlled dormitory access.

Student services: personal/psychological counseling.

COSTS & FINANCIAL AID
Costs (2017–18) ***One-time required fee:*** $180. ***Comprehensive fee:*** $37,614 includes full-time tuition ($24,400), mandatory fees ($114), and room and board ($13,100). Full-time tuition and fees vary according to course load, location, and program. Part-time tuition: $813 per credit. Part-time tuition and fees vary according to course load, location, and program. ***Room and board:*** Room and board charges vary according to board plan and housing facility. ***Payment plan:*** installment. ***Waivers:*** employees or children of employees.

Financial Aid Of all full-time matriculated undergraduates who enrolled in 2015, 951 applied for aid, 839 were judged to have need, 118 had their need fully met. In 2015, 316 non-need-based awards were made. ***Average percent of need met:*** 66. ***Average financial aid package:*** $19,111. ***Average need-based loan:*** $4234. ***Average need-based gift aid:*** $4943. ***Average non-need-based aid:*** $7827. ***Average indebtedness upon graduation:*** $31,145.

APPLYING
Standardized Tests *Required:* SAT or ACT (for admission), TOEFL for international students (for admission).

Options: electronic application, deferred entrance.

Application fee: $50.

Required: essay or personal statement, high school transcript, minimum 2.5 GPA. ***Required for some:*** minimum 2.8 GPA, 2 letters of recommendation, interview. ***Recommended:*** minimum 3.0 GPA.

Application deadlines: rolling (freshmen), rolling (transfers).

Notification: continuous (freshmen), continuous (transfers).

CONTACT
Office of Admissions, Chaminade University of Honolulu, 3140 Waialae Avenue, Honolulu, HI 96816-1578. *Phone:* 808-735-4735. *Toll-free phone:* 800-735-3733. *Fax:* 808-739-4647.
E-mail: admissions@chaminade.edu.

Hawai`i Pacific University

Honolulu, Hawaii

http://www.hpu.edu/

- **Independent** comprehensive, founded 1965
- **Urban** 140-acre campus
- **Endowment** $52.5 million
- **Coed** 3,436 undergraduate students, 74% full-time, 58% women, 42% men
- **Moderately difficult** entrance level, 75% of applicants were admitted

UNDERGRAD STUDENTS
2,553 full-time, 883 part-time. Students come from 55 states and territories; 64 other countries; 44% are from out of state; 5% Black or African American, non-Hispanic/Latino; 14% Hispanic/Latino; 14% Asian, non-Hispanic/Latino; 2% Native Hawaiian or other Pacific Islander, non-Hispanic/Latino; 0.5% American Indian or Alaska Native, non-Hispanic/Latino; 12% Two or more races, non-Hispanic/Latino; 22% Race/ethnicity unknown; 11% international; 11% transferred in; 13% live on campus.

Freshmen:
Admission: 5,452 applied, 4,109 admitted, 478 enrolled. ***Average high school GPA:*** 3.43. ***Test scores:*** SAT critical reading scores over 500: 52%; SAT math scores over 500: 51%; SAT writing scores over 500: 44%; ACT scores over 18: 87%; SAT critical reading scores over 600: 14%; SAT math scores over 600: 15%; SAT writing scores over 600: 9%; ACT scores over 24: 31%; SAT critical reading scores over 700: 2%; SAT math scores over 700: 2%; ACT scores over 30: 6%.

Retention: 65% of full-time freshmen returned.

FACULTY
Total: 468, 48% full-time.

Student/faculty ratio: 12:1.

ACADEMICS
Calendar: semesters. *Degrees:* certificates, associate, bachelor's, master's, post-master's, and postbachelor's certificates.

Special study options: academic remediation for entering students, accelerated degree program, adult/continuing education programs, advanced placement credit, cooperative education, distance learning, double majors, English as a second language, freshman honors college, honors programs, independent study, internships, off-campus study, part-time degree program, services for LD students, student-designed majors, study abroad, summer session for credit. ***ROTC:*** Army (c), Air Force (c).

Unusual degree programs: 3-2 engineering with Washington University in St. Louis, University of Southern California.

Computers: 200 computers/terminals are available on campus for general student use. Students can access the following: campus intranet, computer help desk, free student e-mail accounts, online (class) grades, online (class) registration, online (class) schedules. Campuswide network is available. Wireless service is available via entire campus.

Library: Meader Library plus 2 others. *Books:* 103,021 (physical), 191,075 (digital/electronic); *Serial titles:* 64 (physical), 4,520 (digital/electronic); *Databases:* 101. Students can reserve study rooms.

STUDENT LIFE
Housing options: coed. Campus housing is university owned. Freshman applicants given priority for college housing.

Activities and organizations: drama/theater group, student-run newspaper, choral group, Student Government Association, Campus Activities Board, Student Nurses Association, Travel Industry Management Student Organization, Christian Student Organization.

Athletics Member NCAA. All Division II. ***Intercollegiate sports:*** baseball M(s), basketball M(s)/W(s), cross-country running M(s)/W(s), golf M(s)/W(s), gymnastics W(s), soccer M(s)/W(s), softball W(s), tennis M(s)/W(s), volleyball W(s). ***Intramural sports:*** basketball M/W, soccer M/W, tennis M/W, volleyball M/W.

Campus security: 24-hour emergency response devices and patrols, late-night transport/escort service, controlled dormitory access, emergency notification, patrol system and emergency exit alarms in residence halls.

Student services: personal/psychological counseling.

COSTS
Costs (2017–18) ***Comprehensive fee:*** $38,704 includes full-time tuition ($24,200), mandatory fees ($300), and room and board ($14,204). Full-time tuition and fees vary according to course level, course load, degree level, location, program, and student level. Part-time tuition: $810 per credit. Part-time tuition and fees vary according to course level, course load, degree level, location, program, and student level. ***Required fees:*** $25 per term part-time. ***College room only:*** $7830. Room and board charges vary according to board plan, housing facility, and location. ***Payment plan:*** installment. ***Waivers:*** employees or children of employees.

APPLYING
Standardized Tests *Required:* SAT or ACT (for admission). *Required for some:* TOEFL or IELTS.

Options: electronic application, deferred entrance.

Application fee: $50.

Required: high school transcript, minimum 2.5 GPA. ***Required for some:*** interview. ***Recommended:*** essay or personal statement, 2 letters of recommendation.

Application deadlines: rolling (freshmen), rolling (transfers).

Notification: continuous (transfers).

CONTACT
Marissa Bratton, Director of Admissions, Hawai`i Pacific University, 1 Aloha Tower Drive, Honolulu, HI 96813. *Phone:* 808-544-0238. *Toll-free phone:* 866-225-5478. *Fax:* 808-544-1136. *E-mail:* admissions@hpu.edu.

Pacific Rim Christian University

Honolulu, Hawaii

http://www.pacrim.edu/

CONTACT
Pacific Rim Christian University, 2223 Ho'one'e Place, Honolulu, HI 96819.

Remington College–Honolulu Campus

Honolulu, Hawaii

http://www.remingtoncollege.edu/

CONTACT
Louis LaMair, Director of Recruitment, Remington College–Honolulu Campus, 1111 Bishop Street, Suite 400, Honolulu, HI 96813. *Phone:* 808-942-1000. *Toll-free phone:* 800-323-8122. *Fax:* 808-533-3064. *E-mail:* louis.lamair@remingtoncollege.edu.

University of Hawaii at Hilo

Hilo, Hawaii

http://hilo.hawaii.edu/

CONTACT
University of Hawaii at Hilo, Admissions, 200 W. Kawili Street, Hilo, HI 96720. *Phone:* 808-932-7446. *Toll-free phone:* 800-897-4456. *Fax:* 808-932-7459. *E-mail:* uhhadm@hawaii.edu.

★ University of Hawaii at Manoa

Honolulu, Hawaii

http://manoa.hawaii.edu/

- **State-supported** university, founded 1907, part of University of Hawaii System
- **Urban** 320-acre campus with easy access to Honolulu
- **Coed** 13,132 undergraduate students, 83% full-time, 56% women, 44% men
- **Moderately difficult** entrance level, 80% of applicants were admitted

UNDERGRAD STUDENTS
10,871 full-time, 2,261 part-time. Students come from 50 states and territories; 67 other countries; 26% are from out of state; 2% Black or African American, non-Hispanic/Latino; 2% Hispanic/Latino; 41% Asian, non-Hispanic/Latino; 17% Native Hawaiian or other Pacific Islander, non-Hispanic/Latino; 0.4% American Indian or Alaska Native, non-Hispanic/Latino; 16% Two or more races, non-Hispanic/Latino; 0.2% Race/ethnicity unknown; 3% international; 12% transferred in; 25% live on campus.

Freshmen:
Admission: 7,861 applied, 6,296 admitted, 1,972 enrolled. ***Average high school GPA:*** 3.5. ***Test scores:*** SAT critical reading scores over 500: 66%; SAT math scores over 500: 74%; SAT writing scores over 500: 60%; ACT scores over 18: 96%; SAT critical reading scores over 600: 21%; SAT math scores over 600: 30%; SAT writing scores over 600: 17%; ACT scores over 24: 48%; SAT critical reading scores over 700: 3%; SAT math scores over 700: 5%; SAT writing scores over 700: 2%; ACT scores over 30: 8%.
Retention: 77% of full-time freshmen returned.

FACULTY
Total: 1,406, 82% full-time, 91% with terminal degrees.
Student/faculty ratio: 10:1.

ACADEMICS
Calendar: semesters. *Degrees:* bachelor's, master's, doctoral, and postbachelor's certificates.
Special study options: accelerated degree program, advanced placement credit, cooperative education, distance learning, double majors, English as a second language, honors programs, independent study, internships, off-campus study, part-time degree program, services for LD students, student-designed majors, study abroad, summer session for credit. ***ROTC:*** Army (b), Air Force (b).
Computers: 117 computers/terminals and 6 ports are available on campus for general student use. Students can access the following: campus intranet, computer help desk, free student e-mail accounts, online (class) grades, online (class) registration, online (class) schedules. Campuswide network is available. 100% of college-owned or -operated housing units are wired for high-speed Internet access. Wireless service is available via entire campus.
Library: Hamilton Library plus 6 others. *Books:* 263,139 (physical), 356,688 (digital/electronic); *Serial titles:* 21,291 (physical), 62,291 (digital/electronic); *Databases:* 304. Weekly public service hours: 132; study areas open 24 hours, 5-7 days a week; students can reserve study rooms.

STUDENT LIFE
Housing options: coed, special housing for students with disabilities. Campus housing is university owned. Freshman applicants given priority for college housing.
Activities and organizations: drama/theater group, student-run newspaper, radio station, choral group, marching band, Biology Club, Pre-Medical Association, International Student Association, Katipunan, Timpuyog, national fraternities, national sororities.
Athletics Member NCAA. All Division I except football (Division I-A). ***Intercollegiate sports:*** baseball M(s), basketball M(s)/W(s), cheerleading M/W, cross-country running W, golf M(s)/W(s), sailing W, soccer W(s), softball W(s), swimming and diving M(s)/W(s), tennis M(s)/W(s), track and field W(s), volleyball M(s)/W(s), water polo W(s). ***Intramural sports:*** badminton M/W, basketball M/W, crew M/W, cross-country running M/W, golf M/W, rugby M, sailing W, soccer M, softball M, swimming and diving M/W, table tennis M/W, tennis M/W, track and field M/W, ultimate Frisbee M/W, volleyball M/W, weight lifting M/W, wrestling M/W.
Campus security: 24-hour emergency response devices and patrols, student patrols, late-night transport/escort service, controlled dormitory access.
Student services: health clinic, personal/psychological counseling, women's center.

COSTS & FINANCIAL AID
Costs (2017–18) ***Tuition:*** state resident $10,872 full-time, $453 per credit hour part-time; nonresident $32,904 full-time, $1371 per credit hour part-time. Full-time tuition and fees vary according to class time, course level, course load, degree level, program, reciprocity agreements, and student level. Part-time tuition and fees vary according to class time, course level, course load, degree level, program, reciprocity agreements, and student level. ***Required fees:*** $860 full-time, $430 per term part-time. ***Room and board:*** Room and board charges vary according to board plan and housing facility. ***Payment plan:*** installment. ***Waivers:*** minority students, adult students, senior citizens, and employees or children of employees.
Financial Aid Of all full-time matriculated undergraduates who enrolled in 2016, 8,704 applied for aid, 5,956 were judged to have need, 1,772 had their need fully met. 553 Federal Work-Study jobs (averaging $2317). In 2016, 2358 non-need-based awards were made. ***Average percent of need met:*** 70. ***Average financial aid package:*** $14,840. ***Average need-based loan:*** $4601. ***Average need-based gift aid:*** $9779. ***Average non-need-based aid:*** $12,779. ***Average indebtedness upon graduation:*** $24,665.

APPLYING
Standardized Tests *Required:* SAT or ACT (for admission). *Recommended:* SAT (for admission), ACT (for admission).
Options: electronic application.
Application fee: $70.
Required: minimum 2.8 GPA. ***Required for some:*** high school transcript.
Application deadlines: 3/1 (freshmen), 3/1 (transfers).
Notification: continuous (transfers).

A ★ indicates that the school has detailed information with a Premium Profile on Petersons.com.

CONTACT
Ms. Lisa Buto, Student Services Specialist, University of Hawaii at Manoa, 2600 Campus Road, Room 001, Honolulu, HI 96822. *Phone:* 808-956-8975. *Toll-free phone:* 800-823-9771. *Fax:* 808-956-4148. *E-mail:* uhmanoa.admissions@hawaii.edu.

University of Hawaii Maui College
Kahului, Hawaii
http://maui.hawaii.edu/

CONTACT
Mr. Stephen Kameda, Director of Admissions and Records, University of Hawaii Maui College, 310 Kaahumanu Avenue, Kahului, HI 96732. *Phone:* 808-984-3267. *Toll-free phone:* 800-479-6692. *Fax:* 808-984-3872. *E-mail:* skameda@hawaii.edu.

University of Hawaii–West Oahu
Kapolei, Hawaii
http://www.uhwo.hawaii.edu/

- **State-supported** 4-year, founded 1976, part of University of Hawaii System
- **Small-town** campus with easy access to Honolulu
- **Coed**
- **Moderately difficult** entrance level

FACULTY
Student/faculty ratio: 24:1.

ACADEMICS
Calendar: semesters. *Degree:* certificates and bachelor's.
Library: University of Hawaii-West Oahu Library.

STUDENT LIFE
Housing options: college housing not available.
Campus security: 24-hour emergency response devices and patrols, late-night transport/escort service.
Student services: personal/psychological counseling.

COSTS & FINANCIAL AID
Costs (2016–17) ***Tuition:*** state resident $7200 full-time, $300 per credit part-time; nonresident $20,160 full-time, $840 per credit part-time. ***Required fees:*** $240 full-time, $240 per term part-time.
Financial Aid Of all full-time matriculated undergraduates who enrolled in 2014, 678 applied for aid, 678 were judged to have need. ***Average percent of need met:*** 50. ***Average financial aid package:*** $5150. ***Average need-based loan:*** $1768. ***Average need-based gift aid:*** $2610.

APPLYING
Standardized Tests *Required for some:* SAT (for admission), ACT (for admission), SAT or ACT (for admission).
Options: deferred entrance.
Application fee: $50.
Required: minimum 2.7 GPA. ***Required for some:*** high school transcript, 2 letters of recommendation, college transcripts.

CONTACT
Mr. Craig Morimoto, University of Hawaii–West Oahu, HI. *Phone:* 808-689-2916. *Toll-free phone:* 866-299-8656. *E-mail:* uhwoadm@hawaii.edu.

University of Phoenix–Hawaii Campus
Honolulu, Hawaii
http://www.phoenix.edu/

CONTACT
Marc Booker, Sr. Director, Office of Admissions and Evaluation, University of Phoenix–Hawaii Campus, 4035 South Riverpoint Parkway, Mail Stop CF-L101, Phoenix, AZ 85040. *Phone:* 602-557-4609. *Toll-free phone:* 866-766-0766. *Fax:* 480-643-1156.

IDAHO

Boise Bible College
Boise, Idaho
http://www.boisebible.edu/

CONTACT
Russell Grove, Director of Admissions, Boise Bible College, 8695 West Marigold Street, Boise, ID 83714-1220. *Phone:* 208-376-7731. *Toll-free phone:* 800-893-7755. *Fax:* 208-376-7743. *E-mail:* rgrove@boisebible.edu.

Boise State University
Boise, Idaho
http://www.boisestate.edu/

- **State-supported** university, founded 1932, part of Idaho System of Higher Education
- **Urban** 285-acre campus
- **Endowment** $96.7 million
- **Coed** 20,209 undergraduate students, 61% full-time, 54% women, 46% men
- **Moderately difficult** entrance level, 82% of applicants were admitted

UNDERGRAD STUDENTS
12,375 full-time, 7,834 part-time. Students come from 50 states and territories; 58 other countries; 28% are from out of state; 2% Black or African American, non-Hispanic/Latino; 12% Hispanic/Latino; 2% Asian, non-Hispanic/Latino; 0.4% Native Hawaiian or other Pacific Islander, non-Hispanic/Latino; 0.5% American Indian or Alaska Native, non-Hispanic/Latino; 4% Two or more races, non-Hispanic/Latino; 2% Race/ethnicity unknown; 3% international; 7% transferred in; 17% live on campus.

Freshmen:
Admission: 8,330 applied, 6,808 admitted, 2,627 enrolled. ***Average high school GPA:*** 3.43. ***Test scores:*** SAT critical reading scores over 500: 57%; SAT math scores over 500: 59%; SAT writing scores over 500: 49%; ACT scores over 18: 92%; SAT critical reading scores over 600: 17%; SAT math scores over 600: 19%; SAT writing scores over 600: 11%; ACT scores over 24: 43%; SAT critical reading scores over 700: 2%; SAT math scores over 700: 2%; SAT writing scores over 700: 1%; ACT scores over 30: 6%.
Retention: 78% of full-time freshmen returned.

FACULTY
Total: 1,320, 55% full-time, 44% with terminal degrees.
Student/faculty ratio: 18:1.

ACADEMICS
Calendar: semesters. *Degrees:* associate, bachelor's, master's, doctoral, and postbachelor's certificates.
Special study options: academic remediation for entering students, adult/continuing education programs, advanced placement credit, cooperative education, distance learning, double majors, English as a second language, freshman honors college, honors programs, independent study, internships, off-campus study, part-time degree program, services for LD students, student-designed majors, study abroad, summer session for credit. ***ROTC:*** Army (b).
Computers: 900 computers/terminals are available on campus for general student use. Students can access the following: campus intranet, computer help desk, free student e-mail accounts, online (class) grades, online (class) registration, online (class) schedules. Campuswide network is available. 100% of college-owned or -operated housing units are wired for high-speed Internet access. Wireless service is available via classrooms, computer centers, computer labs, dorm rooms, learning centers, libraries, student centers.
Library: Albertsons Library plus 1 other. *Books:* 800,205 (physical), 60,977 (digital/electronic); *Serial titles:* 112,213 (digital/electronic); *Databases:* 303. Weekly public service hours: 115; study areas open 24 hours, 5-7 days a week; students can reserve study rooms.

STUDENT LIFE
Housing options: coed, men-only, women-only. Campus housing is university owned. Freshman applicants given priority for college housing.

Activities and organizations: drama/theater group, student-run newspaper, radio station, choral group, marching band, Latter-Day Saints Student Association, Residence Hall Association, Organization of Student Social Workers, Marching Band Association, Teacher Education Association, national fraternities, national sororities.

Athletics Member NCAA. All Division I except football (Division I-A). ***Intercollegiate sports:*** basketball M(s)/W(s), cross-country running M(s)/W(s), golf M(s)/W(s), gymnastics W(s), soccer W(s), softball W(s), swimming and diving W(s), tennis M(s)/W(s), track and field M(s)/W(s), volleyball W(s), wrestling M(s). ***Intramural sports:*** baseball M, basketball M/W, golf M/W, lacrosse M(c)/W(c), rugby M(c)/W(c), soccer M(c)/W(c), softball W(c), swimming and diving M/W, track and field M/W, triathlon M/W, ultimate Frisbee M(c)/W(c), volleyball M(c)/W(c), water polo M/W.

Campus security: 24-hour emergency response devices and patrols, late-night transport/escort service, controlled dormitory access.

Student services: health clinic, personal/psychological counseling, women's center, legal services.

COSTS & FINANCIAL AID

Costs (2016–17) ***One-time required fee:*** $175. ***Tuition:*** state resident $4872 full-time, $200 per credit hour part-time; nonresident $19,322 full-time, $470 per credit hour part-time. Full-time tuition and fees vary according to course load, program, and reciprocity agreements. Part-time tuition and fees vary according to course load and program. ***Required fees:*** $2208 full-time, $97 per credit hour part-time. ***Room and board:*** $7076; room only: $3756. Room and board charges vary according to board plan and housing facility. ***Payment plan:*** installment. ***Waivers:*** senior citizens and employees or children of employees.

Financial Aid Of all full-time matriculated undergraduates who enrolled in 2015, 7,360 applied for aid, 7,185 were judged to have need, 864 had their need fully met. 256 Federal Work-Study jobs (averaging $2126). 213 state and other part-time jobs (averaging $2289). In 2015, 284 non-need-based awards were made. ***Average percent of need met:*** 57. ***Average financial aid package:*** $9361. ***Average need-based loan:*** $4408. ***Average need-based gift aid:*** $5116. ***Average non-need-based aid:*** $1919. ***Average indebtedness upon graduation:*** $28,127. ***Financial aid deadline:*** 6/30.

APPLYING

Standardized Tests *Required for some:* SAT or ACT (for admission).

Options: electronic application.

Application fee: $50.

Required for some: high school transcript.

Application deadlines: rolling (freshmen), rolling (transfers).

Notification: continuous (freshmen), continuous (transfers).

CONTACT

Ms. Kelly Talbert, Director/Admissions, Boise State University, 1910 University Drive, Boise, ID 83725. *Phone:* 208-426-3844. *T oll-free phone:* 800-824-7017. *E-mail:* bsuinfo@boisestate.edu.

Brigham Young University–Idaho

Rexburg, Idaho

http://www.byui.edu/

- **Independent** 4-year, founded 1888, affiliated with The Church of Jesus Christ of Latter-day Saints
- **Small-town** 255-acre campus
- **Coed** 32,458 undergraduate students, 51% full-time, 58% women, 42% men
- **Moderately difficult** entrance level, 96% of applicants were admitted

UNDERGRAD STUDENTS

16,538 full-time, 15,920 part-time. Students come from 53 states and territories; 116 other countries; 78% are from out of state; 0.6% Black or African American, non-Hispanic/Latino; 3% Hispanic/Latino; 1% Asian, non-Hispanic/Latino; 0.7% Native Hawaiian or other Pacific Islander, non-Hispanic/Latino; 0.3% American Indian or Alaska Native, non-Hispanic/Latino; 6% Two or more races, non-Hispanic/Latino; 2% Race/ethnicity unknown; 9% international; 8% transferred in.

Freshmen:

Admission: 8,034 applied, 7,699 admitted, 4,188 enrolled. ***Test scores:*** SAT math scores over 500: 50%; SAT writing scores over 500: 55%; ACT scores over 18: 91%; SAT math scores over 600: 11%; SAT writing scores over 600: 14%; ACT scores over 24: 39%; SAT math scores over 700: 1%; SAT writing scores over 700: 1%; ACT scores over 30: 3%.

Retention: 71% of full-time freshmen returned.

FACULTY

Total: 792, 61% full-time.

Student/faculty ratio: 25:1.

ACADEMICS

Calendar: semesters. *Degrees:* associate and bachelor's.

Special study options: academic remediation for entering students, accelerated degree program, adult/continuing education programs, advanced placement credit, honors programs, internships, part-time degree program, services for LD students, summer session for credit. ***ROTC:*** Army (b).

Computers: Students can access the following: online (class) registration. Campuswide network is available. Wireless service is available via entire campus.

Library: David O. McKay Library. Students can reserve study rooms.

STUDENT LIFE

Housing options: men-only, women-only. Campus housing is university owned.

Activities and organizations: drama/theater group, student-run newspaper, radio station, choral group, national fraternities, national sororities.

Campus security: 24-hour emergency response devices and patrols, late-night transport/escort service.

Student services: health clinic, personal/psychological counseling, legal services.

COSTS & FINANCIAL AID

Costs (2016–17) ***Comprehensive fee:*** $3422 includes full-time tuition ($1960), mandatory fees ($14), and room and board ($1448). Part-time tuition: $163 per credit hour. ***Room and board:*** Room and board charges vary according to housing facility and location. ***Waivers:*** employees or children of employees.

Financial Aid Of all full-time matriculated undergraduates who enrolled in 2015, 2,400 state and other part-time jobs.

APPLYING

Standardized Tests *Required:* SAT or ACT (for admission).

Options: electronic application.

Application fee: $35.

Required: essay or personal statement, high school transcript, interview.

Application deadlines: 2/15 (freshmen), 3/15 (transfers).

Notification: 4/1 (freshmen), 3/15 (transfers).

CONTACT

Brigham Young University–Idaho, 525 South Center Street, Rexburg, ID 83460. *Phone:* 208-496-1310.

The College of Idaho

Caldwell, Idaho

http://www.collegeofidaho.edu/

- **Independent** comprehensive, founded 1891
- **Suburban** 50-acre campus
- **Endowment** $100.5 million
- **Coed** 962 undergraduate students, 95% full-time, 50% women, 50% men
- **Moderately difficult** entrance level, 85% of applicants were admitted

UNDERGRAD STUDENTS

918 full-time, 44 part-time. Students come from 28 states and territories; 49 other countries; 28% are from out of state; 2% Black or African American, non-Hispanic/Latino; 13% Hispanic/Latino; 2% Asian, non-Hispanic/Latino; 0.8% Native Hawaiian or other Pacific Islander, non-Hispanic/Latino; 0.5% American Indian or Alaska Native, non-Hispanic/Latino; 4% Two or more races, non-Hispanic/Latino; 5% Race/ethnicity unknown; 7% international; 4% transferred in; 58% live on campus.

Freshmen:
Admission: 975 applied, 827 admitted, 238 enrolled. ***Average high school GPA:*** 3.59. ***Test scores:*** SAT critical reading scores over 500: 55%; SAT math scores over 500: 51%; SAT writing scores over 500: 43%; ACT scores over 18: 92%; SAT critical reading scores over 600: 15%; SAT math scores over 600: 13%; SAT writing scores over 600: 10%; ACT scores over 24: 40%; SAT critical reading scores over 700: 4%; SAT math scores over 700: 2%; SAT writing scores over 700: 1%; ACT scores over 30: 6%.

Retention: 70% of full-time freshmen returned.

FACULTY
Total: 138, 63% full-time, 58% with terminal degrees.

Student/faculty ratio: 9:1.

ACADEMICS
Calendar: 12-6-12 week calendar. *Degrees:* bachelor's and master's.

Special study options: academic remediation for entering students, advanced placement credit, cooperative education, double majors, English as a second language, honors programs, independent study, internships, off-campus study, part-time degree program, services for LD students, study abroad, summer session for credit. ***ROTC:*** Army (c).

Unusual degree programs: 3-2 engineering with Washington University in St. Louis, Columbia University; nursing with Idaho State University.

Computers: 475 computers/terminals are available on campus for general student use. Students can access the following: campus intranet, computer help desk, free student e-mail accounts, online (class) grades, online (class) registration, online (class) schedules, online course syllabi, course assignments, course discussion. Campuswide network is available. 100% of college-owned or -operated housing units are wired for high-speed Internet access. Wireless service is available via entire campus.

Library: Terteling Library. *Books:* 132,423 (physical), 17,119 (digital/electronic); *Serial titles:* 4,026 (physical), 17,180 (digital/electronic); *Databases:* 61.

STUDENT LIFE
Housing options: on-campus residence required through junior year; coed, special housing for students with disabilities. Campus housing is university owned. Freshman campus housing is guaranteed.

Activities and organizations: drama/theater group, student-run newspaper, choral group, marching band, ISO- International Student Organization, ALAS- Association of Latino American Students, Potter's Clay, GSCA- Gay-Straight Campus Alliance, AFRO- Africans Friends Relatives and Others, national fraternities, national sororities.

Athletics Member NAIA. ***Intercollegiate sports:*** baseball M(s), basketball M(s)/W(s), cross-country running M(s)/W(s), golf M(s)/W(s), lacrosse M(c)/W(c), skiing (cross-country) M/W, skiing (downhill) M(s)/W(s), soccer M(s)/W(s), softball W(s), swimming and diving M(s)/W(s), tennis W(s), track and field M(s)/W(s), volleyball W(s). ***Intramural sports:*** badminton M/W, basketball M/W, football M/W, soccer M/W, softball M/W, ultimate Frisbee M/W, volleyball M/W.

Campus security: 24-hour emergency response devices and patrols, student patrols, late-night transport/escort service, controlled dormitory access.

Student services: health clinic, personal/psychological counseling, women's center.

COSTS & FINANCIAL AID
Costs (2017–18) ***Comprehensive fee:*** $38,089 includes full-time tuition ($28,000), mandatory fees ($755), and room and board ($9334). Part-time tuition: $1165 per credit. ***Room and board:*** Room and board charges vary according to board plan and housing facility. ***Payment plan:*** installment. ***Waivers:*** employees or children of employees.

Financial Aid Of all full-time matriculated undergraduates who enrolled in 2016, 607 applied for aid, 607 were judged to have need, 133 had their need fully met. In 2016, 310 non-need-based awards were made. ***Average percent of need met:*** 77. ***Average financial aid package:*** $29,373. ***Average need-based loan:*** $4767. ***Average need-based gift aid:*** $5038. ***Average non-need-based aid:*** $13,324. ***Average indebtedness upon graduation:*** $7270.

APPLYING
Options: electronic application, early admission, early action, deferred entrance.

Required: essay or personal statement, high school transcript, 1 letter of recommendation. ***Recommended:*** interview, class rank, extracurricular resumé.

Application deadlines: 8/1 (freshmen), 8/1 (transfers), 11/15 (early action).

Notification: continuous (freshmen), continuous (transfers), 11/15 (early action).

CONTACT
Lorna Hunter, Vice President of Enrollment Management, The College of Idaho, 2112 Cleveland Boulevard, Caldwell, ID 83605-4432.
Phone: 208-459-5319. *Toll-free phone:* 800-244-3246.
Fax: 208-459-5415.
E-mail: admission@collegeofidaho.edu.

Idaho State University

Pocatello, Idaho

http://www.isu.edu/

- **State-supported** university, founded 1901
- **Urban** 1100-acre campus
- **Coed** 11,087 undergraduate students, 59% full-time, 54% women, 46% men
- **Minimally difficult** entrance level, 100% of applicants were admitted

UNDERGRAD STUDENTS
6,555 full-time, 4,532 part-time. Students come from 40 states and territories; 57 other countries; 9% are from out of state; 1% Black or African American, non-Hispanic/Latino; 11% Hispanic/Latino; 1% Asian, non-Hispanic/Latino; 0.2% Native Hawaiian or other Pacific Islander, non-Hispanic/Latino; 1% American Indian or Alaska Native, non-Hispanic/Latino; 3% Two or more races, non-Hispanic/Latino; 3% Race/ethnicity unknown; 7% international; 4% transferred in; 11% live on campus.

Freshmen:
Admission: 2,950 applied, 2,941 admitted, 1,342 enrolled. ***Average high school GPA:*** 3.27. ***Test scores:*** SAT critical reading scores over 500: 41%; SAT math scores over 500: 39%; SAT writing scores over 500: 31%; ACT scores over 18: 83%; SAT critical reading scores over 600: 10%; SAT math scores over 600: 13%; SAT writing scores over 600: 5%; ACT scores over 24: 38%; SAT critical reading scores over 700: 1%; SAT math scores over 700: 1%; ACT scores over 30: 7%.

Retention: 71% of full-time freshmen returned.

FACULTY
Total: 813, 74% full-time, 39% with terminal degrees.

Student/faculty ratio: 15:1.

ACADEMICS
Calendar: semesters. *Degrees:* certificates, bachelor's, master's, doctoral, post-master's, and postbachelor's certificates.

Special study options: academic remediation for entering students, accelerated degree program, adult/continuing education programs, advanced placement credit, cooperative education, distance learning, double majors, English as a second language, honors programs, independent study, internships, off-campus study, part-time degree program, services for LD students, student-designed majors, study abroad, summer session for credit. ***ROTC:*** Army (b).

Computers: 250 computers/terminals and 10 ports are available on campus for general student use. Students can access the following: computer help desk, free student e-mail accounts, online (class) grades, online (class) registration, online (class) schedules. Campuswide network is available. 100% of college-owned or -operated housing units are wired for high-speed Internet access. Wireless service is available via entire campus.

Library: Eli M. Oboler Library. *Books:* 1.3 million (physical), 192,366 (digital/electronic); *Databases:* 1,727. Weekly public service hours: 103; students can reserve study rooms.

STUDENT LIFE
Housing options: coed, men-only, women-only, special housing for students with disabilities. Campus housing is university owned.

Activities and organizations: drama/theater group, student-run newspaper, radio and television station, choral group, marching band,

Latter Day Saint Student Association, Saudi Student Association, University Honors, Academy of Students of Pharmacy, Greek Clubs, national fraternities, national sororities.

Athletics Member NCAA. All Division I except football (Division I-AA). ***Intercollegiate sports:*** basketball M(s)/W(s), cross-country running M(s)/W(s), golf W(s), soccer W(s), softball W(s), tennis M(s)/W(s), track and field M(s)/W(s), volleyball W(s). ***Intramural sports:*** basketball M/W, cross-country running M/W, football M, golf W, rock climbing M(c)/W(c), soccer M/W, softball M/W, tennis M/W, track and field M/W, volleyball M/W.

Campus security: 24-hour emergency response devices and patrols, late-night transport/escort service, controlled dormitory access.

Student services: health clinic, personal/psychological counseling, women's center.

COSTS & FINANCIAL AID

Costs (2017–18) ***Tuition:*** state resident $5243 full-time, $348 per credit hour part-time; nonresident $19,310 full-time, $576 per credit hour part-time. Full-time tuition and fees vary according to course load, program, and reciprocity agreements. Part-time tuition and fees vary according to course load. No tuition increase for student's term of enrollment. ***Required fees:*** $1713 full-time. ***Room and board:*** $6663; room only: $2875. Room and board charges vary according to board plan, housing facility, and location. ***Payment plan:*** installment. ***Waivers:*** senior citizens and employees or children of employees.

Financial Aid Of all full-time matriculated undergraduates who enrolled in 2015, 4,967 applied for aid, 4,333 were judged to have need, 199 had their need fully met. In 2015, 518 non-need-based awards were made. ***Average percent of need met:*** 46. ***Average financial aid package:*** $8494. ***Average need-based loan:*** $3834. ***Average need-based gift aid:*** $4686. ***Average non-need-based aid:*** $2251. ***Average indebtedness upon graduation:*** $30,617.

APPLYING

Standardized Tests *Required:* SAT or ACT (for admission). *Recommended:* ACT (for admission).

Options: electronic application, early admission, deferred entrance.

Application fee: $50.

Required: high school transcript, minimum 2.0 GPA.

Application deadlines: rolling (freshmen), rolling (transfers).

Notification: continuous (freshmen), continuous (transfers).

CONTACT

Admissions Office, Idaho State University, 921 South 8th, Stop 8270, Pocatello, ID 83209-8270. *Phone:* 208-282-2475. *Fax:* 208-282-4511. *E-mail:* admiss@isu.edu.

Lewis-Clark State College

Lewiston, Idaho

http://www.lcsc.edu/

- **State-supported** 4-year, founded 1893
- **Small-town** 44-acre campus
- **Coed**
- **Minimally difficult** entrance level

FACULTY

Student/faculty ratio: 14:1.

ACADEMICS

Calendar: semesters. *Degrees:* certificates, associate, and bachelor's.

Library: Lewis-Clark State College Library.

STUDENT LIFE

Housing options: coed. Campus housing is university owned, leased by the school and is provided by a third party.

Athletics Member NAIA.

Campus security: 24-hour emergency response devices and patrols, student patrols, late-night transport/escort service.

COSTS & FINANCIAL AID

Costs (2016–17) ***Tuition:*** state resident $6000 full-time, $307 per credit hour part-time; nonresident $17,000 full-time, $307 per credit hour part-time. Full-time tuition and fees vary according to course load and reciprocity agreements. ***Required fees:*** $1224 full-time. ***Room and board:*** $6570; room only: $3570. Room and board charges vary according to board plan and housing facility.

Financial Aid Of all full-time matriculated undergraduates who enrolled in 2015, 2,265 applied for aid, 1,869 were judged to have need, 527 had their need fully met. 66 Federal Work-Study jobs (averaging $1584). 98 state and other part-time jobs (averaging $1306). In 2015, 360 non-need-based awards were made. ***Average percent of need met:*** 77. ***Average financial aid package:*** $10,773. ***Average need-based loan:*** $3671. ***Average need-based gift aid:*** $4386. ***Average non-need-based aid:*** $4350. ***Average indebtedness upon graduation:*** $27,370.

APPLYING

Standardized Tests *Required for some:* SAT or ACT (for admission).

Options: electronic application, deferred entrance.

Required: high school transcript, minimum 2.0 GPA. ***Required for some:*** interview.

CONTACT

Soo Lee Bruce-Smith, Coordinator of New Student Recruitment, Lewis-Clark State College, 500 Eighth Avenue, Lewiston, ID 83501-2698. *Phone:* 208-792-2210. *Toll-free phone:* 800-933-5272. *Fax:* 208-792-2876. *E-mail:* admissions@lcsc.edu.

New Saint Andrews College

Moscow, Idaho

http://www.nsa.edu/

- **Independent Christian** comprehensive, founded 1993
- **Small-town** campus
- **Coed** 140 undergraduate students, 91% full-time, 58% women, 42% men
- **Moderately difficult** entrance level, 93% of applicants were admitted

UNDERGRAD STUDENTS

128 full-time, 12 part-time. Students come from 28 states and territories; 5 other countries; 93% are from out of state; 4% Hispanic/Latino; 2% Asian, non-Hispanic/Latino; 0.8% American Indian or Alaska Native, non-Hispanic/Latino; 0.8% Two or more races, non-Hispanic/Latino; 8% Race/ethnicity unknown; 7% international.

Freshmen:

Admission: 68 applied, 63 admitted, 31 enrolled. ***Test scores:*** SAT critical reading scores over 500: 92%; SAT math scores over 500: 71%; ACT scores over 18: 99%; SAT critical reading scores over 600: 69%; SAT math scores over 600: 37%; ACT scores over 24: 81%; SAT critical reading scores over 700: 31%; SAT math scores over 700: 3%; ACT scores over 30: 36%.

Retention: 76% of full-time freshmen returned.

FACULTY

Total: 18, 33% full-time, 50% with terminal degrees.

Student/faculty ratio: 12:1.

ACADEMICS

Calendar: 4 8-week terms. *Degrees:* associate, bachelor's, master's, and postbachelor's certificates.

Special study options: advanced placement credit, independent study, part-time degree program, summer session for credit.

Computers: 4 computers/terminals are available on campus for general student use. Students can access the following: campus intranet, free student e-mail accounts, online (class) grades, online (class) registration, online (class) schedules. Campuswide network is available. Wireless service is available via entire campus.

Library: Tyndale Library plus 1 other.

STUDENT LIFE

Housing options: college housing not available.

Activities and organizations: drama/theater group, choral group, Students for the Relief of the Oppressed, Nursing Home Visits and Elderly Assistance (snow and leaf removal, firewood distribution), Blood Drives, Fall Carnival, St. Andrews Day Food Bank Drive.

Athletics ***Intramural sports:*** rugby M(c), soccer M(c), volleyball W(c).

Campus security: 24-hour emergency response devices.

Student services: personal/psychological counseling.

COSTS
Costs (2016–17) ***Tuition:*** $12,100 full-time, $950 per course part-time. Full-time tuition and fees vary according to program. Part-time tuition and fees vary according to program. No tuition increase for student's term of enrollment. ***Payment plan:*** installment. ***Waivers:*** employees or children of employees.

APPLYING
Standardized Tests *Required:* SAT or ACT (for admission).
Options: electronic application, deferred entrance.
Application fee: $40.
Required: essay or personal statement, high school transcript, 2 letters of recommendation. ***Required for some:*** interview.
Application deadlines: 2/15 (freshmen), 2/15 (transfers).
Notification: 3/15 (freshmen), 3/15 (transfers).

CONTACT
Mr. John Sawyer, Director of Student Recruitment, New Saint Andrews College, PO Box 9025, Moscow, ID 83843. *Phone:* 208-882-1566 Ext. 100. *Fax:* 208-882-4293. *E-mail:* info@nsa.edu.

Northwest Nazarene University

Nampa, Idaho

http://www.nnu.edu/

- **Independent** comprehensive, founded 1913, affiliated with Church of the Nazarene
- **Small-town** 85-acre campus with easy access to Boise
- **Coed**
- **Moderately difficult** entrance level

FACULTY
Student/faculty ratio: 15:1.

ACADEMICS
Calendar: semesters. *Degrees:* associate, bachelor's, master's, doctoral, and post-master's certificates.
Library: John E. Riley Library.

STUDENT LIFE
Housing options: on-campus residence required through sophomore year; men-only, women-only, special housing for students with disabilities. Campus housing is university owned. Freshman campus housing is guaranteed.
Activities and organizations: drama/theater group, student-run newspaper, choral group, Students in Free Enterprise (SIFE), Student Government Association, Fellowship of Christian Athletes, The Crusader newspaper, The Oasis yearbook.
Athletics Member NCAA. All Division II.
Campus security: 24-hour emergency response devices and patrols, student patrols, late-night transport/escort service, controlled dormitory access, residence hall check-in system, on-campus police hub.
Student services: health clinic, personal/psychological counseling.

COSTS & FINANCIAL AID
Costs (2016–17) ***Comprehensive fee:*** $35,450 includes full-time tuition ($28,150), mandatory fees ($500), and room and board ($6800). Full-time tuition and fees vary according to class time, course load, degree level, location, program, and reciprocity agreements. Part-time tuition: $1200 per credit hour. Part-time tuition and fees vary according to class time, location, and program. ***College room only:*** $3200. Room and board charges vary according to board plan.
Financial Aid Of all full-time matriculated undergraduates who enrolled in 2015, 1,014 applied for aid, 931 were judged to have need, 194 had their need fully met. 132 Federal Work-Study jobs (averaging $702). In 2015, 169 non-need-based awards were made. ***Average percent of need met:*** 72. ***Average financial aid package:*** $25,366. ***Average need-based loan:*** $4944. ***Average need-based gift aid:*** $5770. ***Average non-need-based aid:*** $9418. ***Average indebtedness upon graduation:*** $31,318.

APPLYING
Standardized Tests *Required:* SAT or ACT (for admission).
Options: electronic application, early action, deferred entrance.
Application fee: $40.
Required: essay or personal statement, high school transcript, minimum 2.5 GPA, 2 letters of recommendation. ***Required for some:*** interview.

CONTACT
Northwest Nazarene University, 623 S. University Boulevard, Nampa, ID 83686-5897. *Phone:* 208-467-8950. *Toll-free phone:* 877-668-4968.

Stevens-Henager College

Boise, Idaho

http://www.stevenshenager.edu/

- **Independent** 4-year, founded 2004
- **Coed**

ACADEMICS
Degrees: associate and bachelor's.

FINANCIAL AID
Financial Aid Of all full-time matriculated undergraduates who enrolled in 2010, 650 applied for aid, 553 were judged to have need, 55 had their need fully met. In 2010, 10 non-need-based awards were made. ***Average percent of need met:*** 60. ***Average financial aid package:*** $8850. ***Average need-based loan:*** $3500. ***Average need-based gift aid:*** $5350. ***Average non-need-based aid:*** $7500. ***Average indebtedness upon graduation:*** $11,500.

CONTACT
David Breck, Director of Admission, Stevens-Henager College, 1444 South Entertainment Avenue, Boise, ID 83709. *Phone:* 208-383-4540. *Toll-free phone:* 800-622-2670 (in-state); 800-622-2640 (out-of-state). *Fax:* 208-345-6999.

Stevens-Henager College

Idaho Falls, Idaho

http://www.stevenshenager.edu/

CONTACT
Stevens-Henager College, 901 Pier View Drive, Suite 105, Idaho Falls, ID 83402. *Toll-free phone:* 800-622-2640.

University of Idaho

Moscow, Idaho

http://www.uidaho.edu/

- **State-supported** university, founded 1889
- **Small-town** 810-acre campus
- **Endowment** $235.2 million
- **Coed** 9,586 undergraduate students, 76% full-time, 49% women, 51% men
- **Moderately difficult** entrance level, 76% of applicants were admitted

UNDERGRAD STUDENTS
7,269 full-time, 2,317 part-time. Students come from 51 states and territories; 51 other countries; 22% are from out of state; 1% Black or African American, non-Hispanic/Latino; 10% Hispanic/Latino; 2% Asian, non-Hispanic/Latino; 0.3% Native Hawaiian or other Pacific Islander, non-Hispanic/Latino; 0.6% American Indian or Alaska Native, non-Hispanic/Latino; 4% Two or more races, non-Hispanic/Latino; 6% Race/ethnicity unknown; 4% international; 6% transferred in; 36% live on campus.

Freshmen:
Admission: 5,953 applied, 4,518 admitted, 1,660 enrolled. ***Average high school GPA:*** 3.41. ***Test scores:*** SAT critical reading scores over 500: 64%; SAT math scores over 500: 59%; SAT writing scores over 500: 53%; ACT scores over 18: 94%; SAT critical reading scores over 600: 24%; SAT math scores over 600: 20%; SAT writing scores over 600: 14%; ACT scores over 24: 51%; SAT critical reading scores over 700: 4%; SAT math scores over 700: 3%; SAT writing scores over 700: 2%; ACT scores over 30: 11%.
Retention: 77% of full-time freshmen returned.

FACULTY
Total: 725, 82% full-time, 73% with terminal degrees.
Student/faculty ratio: 16:1.

ACADEMICS

Calendar: semesters. *Degrees:* certificates, bachelor's, master's, doctoral, post-master's, and postbachelor's certificates.

Special study options: academic remediation for entering students, accelerated degree program, adult/continuing education programs, advanced placement credit, cooperative education, distance learning, double majors, English as a second language, honors programs, independent study, internships, off-campus study, part-time degree program, services for LD students, study abroad, summer session for credit. ***ROTC:*** Army (b), Navy (b), Air Force (c).

Unusual degree programs: architecture.

Computers: 510 computers/terminals are available on campus for general student use. Students can access the following: campus intranet, computer help desk, free student e-mail accounts, online (class) grades, online (class) registration, online (class) schedules. Campuswide network is available. 100% of college-owned or -operated housing units are wired for high-speed Internet access. Wireless service is available via entire campus.

Library: University of Idaho Library plus 1 other. *Books:* 1.4 million (physical), 552,875 (digital/electronic); *Serial titles:* 43,777 (physical), 78,174 (digital/electronic).

STUDENT LIFE

Housing options: on-campus residence required for freshman year; coed, men-only, women-only, cooperative, special housing for students with disabilities. Campus housing is university owned. Freshman campus housing is guaranteed.

Activities and organizations: drama/theater group, student-run newspaper, radio and television station, choral group, marching band, Student Alumni Relations Board (SARB), Associate Students University of Idaho (ASUI), Vandal Volunteers Club, Earth Club, Gender and Sexuality Alliance, national fraternities, national sororities.

Athletics Member NCAA. All Division I except football (Division I-A). ***Intercollegiate sports:*** basketball M(s)/W(s), cross-country running M(s)/W(s), golf M(s)/W(s), soccer W(s), swimming and diving W(s), tennis M(s)/W(s), track and field M(s)/W(s), volleyball W(s). ***Intramural sports:*** badminton M/W, baseball M, basketball M/W, cheerleading M, equestrian sports M(c)/W(c), football M, golf M/W, ice hockey M(c)/W(c), lacrosse M(c)/W(c), racquetball M/W, rock climbing M(c)/W(c), rugby M(c)/W(c), sand volleyball M/W, skiing (cross-country) M/W, skiing (downhill) M(c)/W(c), soccer M/W, softball M/W, swimming and diving M/W, table tennis M/W, tennis M/W, track and field M/W, ultimate Frisbee M/W, volleyball M/W, water polo M(c)/W(c), weight lifting M/W, wrestling M.

Campus security: 24-hour emergency response devices and patrols, late-night transport/escort service, controlled dormitory access, contracted services with the city of Moscow police department.

Student services: health clinic, personal/psychological counseling, women's center.

COSTS & FINANCIAL AID

Costs (2016–17) ***Tuition:*** state resident $5162 full-time, $302 per credit hour part-time; nonresident $19,970 full-time, $1042 per credit hour part-time. Full-time tuition and fees vary according to course load, program, and reciprocity agreements. Part-time tuition and fees vary according to program and reciprocity agreements. ***Required fees:*** $2070 full-time, $60 per credit hour part-time, $60 per credit hour part-time. ***Room and board:*** $8354. Room and board charges vary according to board plan. ***Payment plan:*** installment. ***Waivers:*** employees or children of employees.

Financial Aid Of all full-time matriculated undergraduates who enrolled in 2015, 6,228 applied for aid, 5,088 were judged to have need, 1,563 had their need fully met. 457 Federal Work-Study jobs (averaging $1247). 157 state and other part-time jobs (averaging $1463). In 2015, 1533 non-need-based awards were made. ***Average percent of need met:*** 76. ***Average financial aid package:*** $13,811. ***Average need-based loan:*** $6842. ***Average need-based gift aid:*** $4768. ***Average non-need-based aid:*** $5058. ***Average indebtedness upon graduation:*** $26,539.

APPLYING

Standardized Tests *Required:* SAT or ACT (for admission).

Options: electronic application, deferred entrance.

Application fee: $60.

Required: high school transcript, minimum 2.2 GPA. ***Required for some:*** essay or personal statement.

Application deadlines: 8/1 (freshmen), rolling (transfers).

Notification: continuous (freshmen), continuous (transfers).

CONTACT

Ms. Melissa Goodwin, Associate Director, Admissions, University of Idaho, 875 Perimeter Drive, MS 4264, Moscow, ID 83844-4264. *Phone:* 208-885-6326. *Toll-free phone:* 888-884-3246. *Fax:* 208-885-9119. *E-mail:* admissions@uidaho.edu.

ILLINOIS

Ambria College of Nursing

Hoffman Estates, Illinois

http://www.ambria.edu/

CONTACT

Ambria College of Nursing, 5210 Trillium Boulevard, Hoffman Estates, IL 60192.

American Academy of Art

Chicago, Illinois

http://www.aaart.edu/

- **Independent** 4-year, founded 1923
- **Urban** campus with easy access to Chicago
- **Coed** 297 undergraduate students, 73% full-time, 60% women, 40% men
- **Moderately difficult** entrance level

UNDERGRAD STUDENTS

217 full-time, 80 part-time. Students come from 6 states and territories; 16% are from out of state; 7% Black or African American, non-Hispanic/Latino; 33% Hispanic/Latino; 5% Asian, non-Hispanic/Latino; 0.7% Native Hawaiian or other Pacific Islander, non-Hispanic/Latino; 0.3% American Indian or Alaska Native, non-Hispanic/Latino; 3% Two or more races, non-Hispanic/Latino; 3% transferred in.

Freshmen:

Admission: 74 enrolled.

Retention: 78% of full-time freshmen returned.

FACULTY

Total: 25, 100% full-time, 64% with terminal degrees.

Student/faculty ratio: 10:1.

ACADEMICS

Calendar: semesters. *Degree:* bachelor's.

Special study options: academic remediation for entering students, accelerated degree program, adult/continuing education programs, independent study, internships, part-time degree program, study abroad, summer session for credit.

Library: Irving Shapiro Library.

STUDENT LIFE

Campus security: 24-hour emergency response devices.

FINANCIAL AID

Financial Aid ***Average percent of need met:*** 70.

APPLYING

Options: electronic application.

Application fee: $25.

Required: high school transcript, interview.

Application deadlines: rolling (freshmen), rolling (transfers).

CONTACT

Mr. Stuart Rosenbloom, Director of Admissions, American Academy of Art, 332 South Michigan Avenue, Suite 300, Chicago, IL 60604-4302. *Phone:* 312-461-0600 Ext. 129. *Toll-free phone:* 888-461-0600. *E-mail:* srosenbloom@aaart.edu.

American InterContinental University Online

Schaumburg, Illinois

http://www.aiuniv.edu/

CONTACT

Jennifer Ziegenmier, Senior Vice President of Admissions and Marketing, American InterContinental University Online, 231 N. Martingale Road, 6th Floor, Schaumburg, IL 60173. *Phone:* 877-564-6248. *Toll-free phone:* 877-701-3800. *E-mail:* jziegenmier@aiuonline.edu.

Argosy University, Chicago

Chicago, Illinois

http://www.argosy.edu/chicago-illinois/default.aspx

CONTACT

Argosy University, Chicago, 225 North Michigan Avenue, Suite 1300, Chicago, IL 60601. *Phone:* 312-777-7600. *Toll-free phone:* 800-626-4123.

Argosy University, Schaumburg

Schaumburg, Illinois

http://www.argosy.edu/locations/chicago-schaumburg/

CONTACT

Argosy University, Schaumburg, 999 North Plaza Drive, Suite 111, Schaumburg, IL 60173-5403. *Phone:* 847-969-4900. *Toll-free phone:* 866-290-2777.

Augustana College

Rock Island, Illinois

http://www.augustana.edu/

- **Independent** 4-year, founded 1860, affiliated with Evangelical Lutheran Church in America
- **Suburban** 115-acre campus
- **Endowment** $148.0 million
- **Coed** 2,537 undergraduate students, 99% full-time, 57% women, 43% men
- **Moderately difficult** entrance level, 52% of applicants were admitted

UNDERGRAD STUDENTS

2,523 full-time, 14 part-time. Students come from 35 states and territories; 42 other countries; 15% are from out of state; 4% Black or African American, non-Hispanic/Latino; 10% Hispanic/Latino; 2% Asian, non-Hispanic/Latino; 0.1% Native Hawaiian or other Pacific Islander, non-Hispanic/Latino; 3% Two or more races, non-Hispanic/Latino; 1% Race/ethnicity unknown; 5% international; 2% transferred in; 71% live on campus.

Freshmen:

Admission: 6,587 applied, 3,400 admitted, 697 enrolled. ***Average high school GPA:*** 3.3. ***Test scores:*** SAT critical reading scores over 500: 78%; SAT math scores over 500: 88%; SAT writing scores over 500: 78%; ACT scores over 18: 99%; SAT critical reading scores over 600: 31%; SAT math scores over 600: 44%; SAT writing scores over 600: 34%; ACT scores over 24: 68%; SAT critical reading scores over 700: 6%; SAT math scores over 700: 15%; SAT writing scores over 700: 6%; ACT scores over 30: 14%.

Retention: 89% of full-time freshmen returned.

FACULTY

Total: 262, 73% full-time, 77% with terminal degrees.

Student/faculty ratio: 12:1.

ACADEMICS

Calendar: quarters. *Degree:* bachelor's.

Special study options: advanced placement credit, double majors, English as a second language, honors programs, independent study, internships, off-campus study, part-time degree program, services for LD students, student-designed majors, study abroad, summer session for credit.

Unusual degree programs: 3-2 engineering with Washington University in St. Louis, Northern Illinois University; forestry with Duke University; nursing with Trinity College; accounting with Wake Forest University, occupational therapy and/or physical therapy with Washington University in St. Louis, landscape architecture and veterinary medicine with University of Illinois, optometry with Illinois College of Optometry, pre-Law with Capital University.

Computers: 600 computers/terminals and 1,800 ports are available on campus for general student use. Students can access the following: campus intranet, computer help desk, free student e-mail accounts, online (class) grades, online (class) registration, online (class) schedules. Campuswide network is available. 100% of college-owned or -operated housing units are wired for high-speed Internet access. Wireless service is available via entire campus.

Library: Thomas Tredway Library plus 1 other. *Books:* 131,497 (physical), 133 (digital/electronic); *Serial titles:* 171 (physical), 122,827 (digital/electronic); *Databases:* 115. Weekly public service hours: 100.

STUDENT LIFE

Housing options: on-campus residence required through junior year; coed. Campus housing is university owned. Freshman campus housing is guaranteed.

Activities and organizations: drama/theater group, student-run newspaper, radio station, choral group, College Union Board of Managers, Student Government Association, student newspaper, student radio station, service organizations (APO, Dance Marathon committee).

Athletics Member NCAA. All Division III. ***Intercollegiate sports:*** baseball M, basketball M/W, cheerleading W(c), crew M(c)/W(c), cross-country running M/W, equestrian sports M(c)/W(c), fencing M(c)/W(c), football M, golf M/W, ice hockey M(c), lacrosse M/W, soccer M/W, softball W, swimming and diving M/W, tennis M/W, track and field M/W, ultimate Frisbee M(c)/W(c), volleyball M(c)/W, water polo M(c)/W(c), wrestling M. ***Intramural sports:*** badminton M/W, basketball M/W, bowling M/W, cross-country running M/W, football M/W, golf M/W, racquetball M/W, rugby M, skiing (cross-country) M/W, skiing (downhill) M/W, soccer M/W, softball M/W, swimming and diving M/W, table tennis M/W, tennis M/W, track and field M/W, ultimate Frisbee M/W, volleyball M/W, wrestling M.

Campus security: 24-hour emergency response devices and patrols, late-night transport/escort service, controlled dormitory access.

Student services: personal/psychological counseling.

COSTS & FINANCIAL AID

Costs (2017–18) ***Comprehensive fee:*** $51,222 includes full-time tuition ($39,690), mandatory fees ($1218), and room and board ($10,314). Part-time tuition: $1755 per credit. Part-time tuition and fees vary according to course load. ***College room only:*** $5220. Room and board charges vary according to board plan and housing facility. ***Payment plans:*** tuition prepayment, installment. ***Waivers:*** employees or children of employees.

Financial Aid Of all full-time matriculated undergraduates who enrolled in 2015, 2,216 applied for aid, 1,885 were judged to have need, 416 had their need fully met. 1,281 Federal Work-Study jobs (averaging $2364). In 2015, 550 non-need-based awards were made. ***Average percent of need met:*** 85. ***Average financial aid package:*** $29,389. ***Average need-based loan:*** $4732. ***Average need-based gift aid:*** $23,444. ***Average non-need-based aid:*** $19,404. ***Average indebtedness upon graduation:*** $33,547.

APPLYING

Standardized Tests *Recommended:* SAT or ACT (for admission).

Options: electronic application, early admission, early decision, early action, deferred entrance.

Required: high school transcript. ***Required for some:*** essay or personal statement, interview. ***Recommended:*** essay or personal statement, 1 letter of recommendation, interview.

Application deadlines: rolling (freshmen), rolling (transfers), 11/1 (early action).

Early decision deadline: 11/1.

Notification: continuous (freshmen), continuous (transfers), 11/15 (early decision), 12/1 (early action).

CONTACT
W. Kent Barnds, Vice President of Enrollment Management, Augustana College, 639 38th Street, Rock Island, IL 61201. *Phone:* 309-794-7662. *Toll-free phone:* 800-798-8100. *Fax:* 309-794-8797. *E-mail:* admissions@augustana.edu.

Aurora University

Aurora, Illinois

http://www.aurora.edu/

- **Independent** comprehensive, founded 1893
- **Suburban** 32-acre campus with easy access to Chicago
- **Endowment** $40.6 million
- **Coed** 3,796 undergraduate students, 87% full-time, 65% women, 35% men
- **Moderately difficult** entrance level, 88% of applicants were admitted

UNDERGRAD STUDENTS
3,302 full-time, 494 part-time. Students come from 39 states and territories; 5 other countries; 16% are from out of state; 8% Black or African American, non-Hispanic/Latino; 27% Hispanic/Latino; 2% Asian, non-Hispanic/Latino; 0.1% Native Hawaiian or other Pacific Islander, non-Hispanic/Latino; 0.3% American Indian or Alaska Native, non-Hispanic/Latino; 3% Two or more races, non-Hispanic/Latino; 5% Race/ethnicity unknown; 0.2% international; 15% transferred in; 25% live on campus.

Freshmen:
Admission: 2,615 applied, 2,294 admitted, 654 enrolled. ***Average high school GPA:*** 3.32. ***Test scores:*** SAT critical reading scores over 500: 38%; SAT math scores over 500: 41%; ACT scores over 18: 93%; SAT critical reading scores over 600: 7%; SAT math scores over 600: 7%; ACT scores over 24: 25%; ACT scores over 30: 1%.

Retention: 68% of full-time freshmen returned.

FACULTY
Total: 488, 32% full-time.

Student/faculty ratio: 17:1.

ACADEMICS
Calendar: semesters. *Degrees:* bachelor's, master's, doctoral, post-master's, and postbachelor's certificates.

Special study options: academic remediation for entering students, accelerated degree program, adult/continuing education programs, advanced placement credit, distance learning, double majors, independent study, internships, off-campus study, part-time degree program, services for LD students, student-designed majors, study abroad, summer session for credit. ***ROTC:*** Army (c).

Computers: 287 computers/terminals are available on campus for general student use. Students can access the following: campus intranet, computer help desk, free student e-mail accounts, online (class) grades, online (class) registration, online (class) schedules, learning management system. Campuswide network is available. 100% of college-owned or -operated housing units are wired for high-speed Internet access. Wireless service is available via classrooms, computer labs, dorm rooms, learning centers, libraries, student centers.

Library: Charles B. Phillips Library plus 1 other. *Books:* 38,404 (physical), 160,012 (digital/electronic); *Serial titles:* 62 (physical), 46,444 (digital/electronic); *Databases:* 61. Weekly public service hours: 97; students can reserve study rooms.

STUDENT LIFE
Housing options: coed. Campus housing is university owned. Freshman applicants given priority for college housing.

Activities and organizations: drama/theater group, student-run newspaper, radio station, choral group, Latin American Student Organization, American Marketing Association, Student Nursing Association, Phi Eta Sigma, Spartan Athletic Training Student Organization, national fraternities, national sororities.

Athletics Member NCAA. All Division III. ***Intercollegiate sports:*** baseball M, basketball M/W, bowling W, cross-country running M/W, football M, golf M/W, ice hockey M/W, lacrosse M/W, soccer M/W, softball W, tennis M/W, track and field M/W, volleyball W. ***Intramural sports:*** badminton M/W, basketball M/W, cheerleading W(c), football M/W, ice hockey M(c), racquetball M/W, soccer M/W, softball M/W, table tennis M/W, ultimate Frisbee M/W, volleyball M/W.

Campus security: 24-hour emergency response devices and patrols, late-night transport/escort service, controlled dormitory access.

Student services: health clinic, personal/psychological counseling.

COSTS & FINANCIAL AID
Costs (2017–18) ***Comprehensive fee:*** $34,990 includes full-time tuition ($23,260), mandatory fees ($260), and room and board ($11,470). Full-time tuition and fees vary according to course load, location, and program. Part-time tuition: $670 per semester hour. Part-time tuition and fees vary according to course load, location, and program. ***Room and board:*** Room and board charges vary according to board plan, housing facility, and location. ***Payment plans:*** installment, deferred payment. ***Waivers:*** children of alumni and employees or children of employees.

Financial Aid Of all full-time matriculated undergraduates who enrolled in 2016, 2,869 applied for aid, 2,612 were judged to have need, 252 had their need fully met. 1,890 Federal Work-Study jobs (averaging $1960). 35 state and other part-time jobs (averaging $9535). In 2016, 592 non-need-based awards were made. ***Average percent of need met:*** 79. ***Average financial aid package:*** $20,413. ***Average need-based loan:*** $3682. ***Average need-based gift aid:*** $14,405. ***Average non-need-based aid:*** $9570. ***Average indebtedness upon graduation:*** $27,578.

APPLYING
Standardized Tests *Required:* SAT or ACT (for admission).

Options: electronic application, deferred entrance.

Required: high school transcript, minimum 2.0 GPA. ***Required for some:*** essay or personal statement, 2 letters of recommendation, interview.

Application deadlines: rolling (freshmen), rolling (transfers).

Notification: continuous (freshmen), continuous (transfers).

CONTACT
Mr. James Lancaster, Assistant Vice President for Enrollment, Aurora University, 347 South Gladstone Avenue, Aurora, IL 60506-4892. *Phone:* 630-844-5533. *Toll-free phone:* 800-742-5281. *Fax:* 630-844-5535. *E-mail:* admission@aurora.edu.

Benedictine University

Lisle, Illinois

http://www.ben.edu/

- **Independent Roman Catholic** comprehensive, founded 1887
- **Suburban** 108-acre campus with easy access to Chicago
- **Coed**
- **Moderately difficult** entrance level

FACULTY
Student/faculty ratio: 12:1.

ACADEMICS
Calendar: semesters. *Degrees:* certificates, diplomas, associate, bachelor's, master's, doctoral, and postbachelor's certificates.
Library: Benedictine Library.

STUDENT LIFE
Housing options: coed, men-only, women-only, special housing for students with disabilities. Campus housing is university owned and is provided by a third party. Freshman campus housing is guaranteed.

Activities and organizations: student-run newspaper, television station, choral group, Student Senate, MSA-Muslim Student Association, AMSA-American Medical Student Association, The Candor-Student Newspaper, Programming Board.

Athletics Member NCAA. All Division III.

Campus security: 24-hour emergency response devices and patrols, late-night transport/escort service, controlled dormitory access.

Student services: health clinic, personal/psychological counseling.

FINANCIAL AID
Financial Aid Of all full-time matriculated undergraduates who enrolled in 2016, 2,292 applied for aid, 2,159 were judged to have need. In 2016, 396 non-need-based awards were made. ***Average financial aid package:*** $21,842. ***Average need-based loan:*** $4698. ***Average need-based gift aid:*** $7892. ***Average non-need-based aid:*** $12,106. ***Average indebtedness upon graduation:*** $29,070.

APPLYING
Standardized Tests *Required:* SAT or ACT (for admission).
Options: electronic application, deferred entrance.
Application fee: $40.
Required: essay or personal statement, high school transcript. ***Required for some:*** interview. ***Recommended:*** rank in upper 50% of high school class.

CONTACT
Ms. Kari Gibbons, Dean of Enrollment, Benedictine University, 5700 College Road, Lisle, IL 60532-0900. *Phone:* 630-829-6300. *Toll-free phone:* 888-829-6363. *Fax:* 630-829-6301. *E-mail:* admissions@ben.edu.

Blackburn College

Carlinville, Illinois

http://www.blackburn.edu/

- **Independent Presbyterian** 4-year, founded 1837
- **Small-town** 80-acre campus with easy access to St. Louis
- **Endowment** $18.8 million
- **Coed** 596 undergraduate students, 96% full-time, 54% women, 46% men
- **Moderately difficult** entrance level, 52% of applicants were admitted

UNDERGRAD STUDENTS
572 full-time, 24 part-time. Students come from 22 states and territories; 4 other countries; 11% are from out of state; 12% Black or African American, non-Hispanic/Latino; 3% Hispanic/Latino; 0.9% Asian, non-Hispanic/Latino; 0.2% Native Hawaiian or other Pacific Islander, non-Hispanic/Latino; 0.2% American Indian or Alaska Native, non-Hispanic/Latino; 4% Two or more races, non-Hispanic/Latino; 2% Race/ethnicity unknown; 1% international; 7% transferred in; 69% live on campus.

Freshmen:
Admission: 1,001 applied, 517 admitted, 170 enrolled. ***Average high school GPA:*** 3.26. ***Test scores:*** ACT scores over 18: 78%; ACT scores over 24: 21%; ACT scores over 30: 2%.
Retention: 65% of full-time freshmen returned.

FACULTY
Total: 68, 47% full-time, 47% with terminal degrees.
Student/faculty ratio: 13:1.

ACADEMICS
Calendar: semesters. *Degree:* bachelor's.
Special study options: advanced placement credit, cooperative education, double majors, honors programs, independent study, internships, off-campus study, services for LD students, student-designed majors, study abroad, summer session for credit.
Unusual degree programs: 3-2 engineering with Washington University in St. Louis, University of Missouri–Kansas City; nursing with St. John's College (Springfield).
Computers: 202 computers/terminals are available on campus for general student use. Students can access the following: computer help desk, free student e-mail accounts, online (class) grades, online (class) registration, online (class) schedules. Campuswide network is available. 100% of college-owned or -operated housing units are wired for high-speed Internet access. Wireless service is available via entire campus.
Library: Lumpkin Learning Commons. *Books:* 62,000 (physical); *Serial titles:* 40 (physical); *Databases:* 21. Weekly public service hours: 80; students can reserve study rooms.

STUDENT LIFE
Housing options: on-campus residence required through junior year; coed, women-only. Campus housing is university owned. Freshman campus housing is guaranteed.
Activities and organizations: drama/theater group, student-run newspaper, radio station, choral group, Habitat for Humanity, Pre-Health Professions, Running Club, Trading Card Games, Spectrum.
Athletics Member NCAA. All Division III. ***Intercollegiate sports:*** baseball M, basketball M/W, cross-country running M/W, golf M, soccer M/W, softball W, tennis W, volleyball W. ***Intramural sports:*** badminton M/W, basketball M/W, football M/W, golf M/W, racquetball M/W, soccer M/W, softball M/W, table tennis M/W, tennis M/W, ultimate Frisbee M/W, volleyball M/W.
Campus security: student patrols, late-night transport/escort service.
Student services: personal/psychological counseling.

COSTS & FINANCIAL AID
Costs (2017–18) ***Comprehensive fee:*** $29,652 includes full-time tuition ($21,582), mandatory fees ($410), and room and board ($7660). Full-time tuition and fees vary according to student level. Part-time tuition: $720 per credit hour. Part-time tuition and fees vary according to student level. ***Required fees:*** $190 per year part-time. ***College room only:*** $4448. Room and board charges vary according to board plan. ***Payment plan:*** installment. ***Waivers:*** employees or children of employees.
Financial Aid Of all full-time matriculated undergraduates who enrolled in 2009, 581 applied for aid, 502 were judged to have need, 194 had their need fully met. 388 Federal Work-Study jobs (averaging $2653). 113 state and other part-time jobs (averaging $2337). In 2009, 62 non-need-based awards were made. ***Average percent of need met:*** 80. ***Average financial aid package:*** $13,873. ***Average need-based loan:*** $4107. ***Average need-based gift aid:*** $11,209. ***Average non-need-based aid:*** $5163. ***Average indebtedness upon graduation:*** $20,077.

APPLYING
Standardized Tests *Required:* SAT or ACT (for admission).
Options: electronic application, deferred entrance.
Required: high school transcript, minimum 2.0 GPA. ***Required for some:*** essay or personal statement, 3 letters of recommendation, interview. ***Recommended:*** minimum 2.5 GPA.
Application deadlines: rolling (freshmen), rolling (transfers).
Notification: continuous (freshmen), continuous (transfers).

CONTACT
Mrs. Alisha Kapp, Director of Admission, Blackburn College, 700 College Avenue, Carlinville, IL 62626. *Phone:* 217-854-5110. *Toll-free phone:* 800-233-3550. *E-mail:* alisha.kapp@blackburn.edu.

Blessing-Rieman College of Nursing & Health Sciences

Quincy, Illinois

http://www.brcn.edu/

- **Independent** comprehensive, founded 1985
- **Small-town** 1-acre campus
- **Endowment** $7.0 million
- **Coed, primarily women**
- **Moderately difficult** entrance level

FACULTY
Student/faculty ratio: 12:1.

ACADEMICS
Calendar: semesters. *Degrees:* bachelor's and master's.
Library: Blessing Health Professions Library plus 1 other.

STUDENT LIFE
Housing options: on-campus residence required through sophomore year; coed. Campus housing is university owned. Freshman campus housing is guaranteed.
Activities and organizations: drama/theater group, student-run newspaper, radio station, choral group, Student Nurses Organization, national fraternities, national sororities.
Campus security: 24-hour patrols, late-night transport/escort service, controlled dormitory access.
Student services: health clinic, personal/psychological counseling.

COSTS & FINANCIAL AID
Costs (2016–17) ***Tuition:*** $22,900 full-time, $763 per credit hour part-time. Full-time tuition and fees vary according to course load, degree level, program, and student level. Part-time tuition and fees vary according to course load, degree level, program, and student level. ***Required fees:*** $680 full-time. ***Room only:*** Room and board charges vary according to student level.
Financial Aid Of all full-time matriculated undergraduates who enrolled in 2015, 105 applied for aid, 105 were judged to have need, 105 had their

need fully met. ***Average percent of need met:*** 100. ***Average financial aid package:*** $14,625. ***Average need-based gift aid:*** $3631.

APPLYING
Standardized Tests *Required:* SAT or ACT (for admission).

Options: electronic application, deferred entrance.

Required: high school transcript, minimum 3.0 GPA. ***Recommended:*** essay or personal statement, interview.

CONTACT
Ms. Heather Mutter, Admissions Counselor, Blessing-Rieman College of Nursing & Health Sciences, Broadway at 11th Street, POB 7005, Quincy, IL 62305-7005. *Phone:* 217-228-5520 Ext. 6979. *Toll-free phone:* 800-877-9140. *Fax:* 217-223-4661. *E-mail:* admissions@brcn.edu.

★ Bradley University
Peoria, Illinois
http://www.bradley.edu/

- **Independent** comprehensive, founded 1897
- **Suburban** 85-acre campus
- **Endowment** $274.5 million
- **Coed** 4,473 undergraduate students, 96% full-time, 51% women, 49% men
- **Moderately difficult** entrance level, 70% of applicants were admitted

UNDERGRAD STUDENTS
4,278 full-time, 195 part-time. Students come from 39 states and territories; 30 other countries; 17% are from out of state; 5% Black or African American, non-Hispanic/Latino; 7% Hispanic/Latino; 3% Asian, non-Hispanic/Latino; 0.1% Native Hawaiian or other Pacific Islander, non-Hispanic/Latino; 0.2% American Indian or Alaska Native, non-Hispanic/Latino; 2% Two or more races, non-Hispanic/Latino; 25% Race/ethnicity unknown; 1% international; 5% transferred in; 62% live on campus.

Freshmen:
Admission: 9,786 applied, 6,832 admitted, 1,023 enrolled. ***Average high school GPA:*** 3.67. ***Test scores:*** SAT critical reading scores over 500: 62%; SAT math scores over 500: 71%; SAT writing scores over 500: 65%; ACT scores over 18: 99%; SAT critical reading scores over 600: 32%; SAT math scores over 600: 33%; SAT writing scores over 600: 19%; ACT scores over 24: 63%; SAT critical reading scores over 700: 6%; SAT math scores over 700: 7%; SAT writing scores over 700: 1%; ACT scores over 30: 15%.
Retention: 87% of full-time freshmen returned.

FACULTY
Total: 582, 59% full-time, 49% with terminal degrees.

Student/faculty ratio: 12:1.

ACADEMICS
Calendar: semesters. *Degrees:* bachelor's, master's, doctoral, post-master's, and postbachelor's certificates.

Special study options: accelerated degree program, advanced placement credit, cooperative education, distance learning, double majors, honors programs, independent study, internships, off-campus study, part-time degree program, services for LD students, student-designed majors, study abroad, summer session for credit. ***ROTC:*** Army (b).

Computers: 103 computers/terminals are available on campus for general student use. Students can access the following: computer help desk, free student e-mail accounts, online (class) grades, online (class) registration, online (class) schedules, online directory, catalog and other resources. Campuswide network is available. 100% of college-owned or -operated housing units are wired for high-speed Internet access. Wireless service is available via entire campus.

Library: Cullom-Davis Library. *Books:* 446,041 (physical), 43,242 (digital/electronic); *Serial titles:* 280 (physical), 57,963 (digital/electronic); *Databases:* 54. Weekly public service hours: 108; students can reserve study rooms.

STUDENT LIFE
Housing options: on-campus residence required through sophomore year; coed. Campus housing is university owned, leased by the school and is provided by a third party. Freshman campus housing is guaranteed.

Activities and organizations: drama/theater group, student-run newspaper, radio and television station, choral group, Activities Council of Bradley University, CRU (Campus Christian group), Fraternity/Sorority Life, Service on Saturday, Up 'Til Dawn, national fraternities, national sororities.

Athletics Member NCAA. All Division I. ***Intercollegiate sports:*** baseball M(s), basketball M(s)/W(s), cheerleading M/W, cross-country running M(s)/W(s), golf M(s)/W(s), soccer M(s), softball W(s), table tennis M(c), tennis W(s), track and field M(s)/W(s), volleyball M(c)/W(s), wrestling M(c). ***Intramural sports:*** badminton M/W, baseball M(c), basketball M/W, bowling M/W, fencing M(c)/W(c), football M/W, golf M/W, ice hockey M(c), lacrosse M(c)/W(c), racquetball M/W, rock climbing M(c)/W(c), soccer M(c)/W(c), softball M/W(c), swimming and diving M/W, table tennis M/W, tennis M/W, triathlon M(c)/W(c), ultimate Frisbee M(c)/W(c), volleyball M/W, water polo M(c), wrestling M/W.

Campus security: 24-hour emergency response devices and patrols, student patrols, late-night transport/escort service, controlled dormitory access, emergency text messaging, mass notification/emergency communication system in 20 academic buildings.

Student services: health clinic, personal/psychological counseling.

COSTS & FINANCIAL AID
Costs (2016–17) ***One-time required fee:*** $200. ***Comprehensive fee:*** $42,130 includes full-time tuition ($31,740), mandatory fees ($380), and room and board ($10,010). Full-time tuition and fees vary according to course load and program. Part-time tuition: $850 per credit hour. Part-time tuition and fees vary according to course load and program. ***Required fees:*** $380 per year part-time. ***College room only:*** $5790. Room and board charges vary according to board plan and housing facility. ***Payment plans:*** installment, deferred payment. ***Waivers:*** senior citizens and employees or children of employees.

Financial Aid Of all full-time matriculated undergraduates who enrolled in 2016, 3,505 applied for aid, 2,972 were judged to have need, 436 had their need fully met. 290 Federal Work-Study jobs (averaging $1953). In 2016, 1271 non-need-based awards were made. ***Average percent of need met:*** 70. ***Average financial aid package:*** $22,141. ***Average need-based loan:*** $6662. ***Average need-based gift aid:*** $17,049. ***Average non-need-based aid:*** $11,042. ***Average indebtedness upon graduation:*** $25,725.

APPLYING
Standardized Tests *Required:* SAT or ACT (for admission).

Options: electronic application, deferred entrance.

Application fee: $35.

Required: essay or personal statement, high school transcript. ***Required for some:*** audition required of music majors and recommended for theatre majors, portfolio recommended for art majors. ***Recommended:*** minimum 2.8 GPA, 1 letter of recommendation, interview.

Application deadlines: rolling (freshmen), rolling (transfers).

Notification: continuous (freshmen), continuous (transfers).

CONTACT
Dr. Justin Ball, Vice President for Enrollment Management, Bradley University, 1501 W. Bradley Avenue, Peoria, IL 61625. *Phone:* 309-677-1000. *Toll-free phone:* 800-447-6460. *Fax:* 309-677-2797.
E-mail: admissions@bradley.edu.

Chamberlain College of Nursing
Addison, Illinois
http://www.chamberlain.edu/

- **Proprietary** 4-year
- **Coed**

FACULTY
Student/faculty ratio: 24:1.

ACADEMICS
Calendar: semesters. *Degrees:* bachelor's, master's, doctoral, and post-master's certificates.

STUDENT LIFE
Housing options: college housing not available.

COSTS
Costs (2016–17) ***Tuition:*** $18,900 full-time, $675 per credit hour part-time. ***Required fees:*** $600 full-time.

APPLYING
Standardized Tests *Required:* SAT or ACT (for admission).

Options: deferred entrance.

Application fee: $95.

CONTACT
Admissions, Chamberlain College of Nursing, 1221 North Swift Road, Addison, IL 60101. *Phone:* 630-953-3680. *Toll-free phone:* 877-751-5783.

Chamberlain College of Nursing
Chicago, Illinois
http://www.chamberlain.edu/

- **Proprietary** 4-year
- **Coed**

FACULTY
Student/faculty ratio: 13:1.

ACADEMICS
Calendar: semesters. *Degree:* bachelor's.

STUDENT LIFE
Housing options: college housing not available.

COSTS
Costs (2016–17) ***Tuition:*** $18,900 full-time, $675 per credit hour part-time. ***Required fees:*** $600 full-time.

APPLYING
Standardized Tests *Required:* SAT or ACT (for admission).

Options: deferred entrance.

Application fee: $95.

CONTACT
Admissions, Chamberlain College of Nursing, 3300 North Campbell Avenue, Chicago, IL 60618. *Phone:* 773-961-3000. *Toll-free phone:* 877-751-5783.

Chamberlain College of Nursing
Tinley Park, Illinois
http://www.chamberlain.edu/

- **Proprietary** 4-year
- **Coed**

FACULTY
Student/faculty ratio: 14:1.

ACADEMICS
Degree: bachelor's.

STUDENT LIFE
Housing options: college housing not available.

COSTS
Costs (2016–17) ***Tuition:*** $18,900 full-time, $675 per credit hour part-time. ***Required fees:*** $600 full-time.

APPLYING
Standardized Tests *Required:* SAT or ACT (for admission).

Options: deferred entrance.

Application fee: $95.

CONTACT
Chamberlain College of Nursing, 18624 West Creek Drive, Tinley Park, IL 60477. *Toll-free phone:* 877-751-5783.

Chicago State University
Chicago, Illinois
http://www.csu.edu/

CONTACT
Mr. John Martinez, Associate Director of Admissions, Chicago State University, 95th Street at King Drive, ADM 200, Chicago, IL 60628. *Phone:* 773-995-3578. *Fax:* 773-995-3820. *E-mail:* jmarti21@csu.edu.

Christian Life College
Mount Prospect, Illinois
http://www.christianlifecollege.edu/

CONTACT
Christian Life College, 400 East Gregory Street, Mount Prospect, IL 60056. *Phone:* 847-259-1840 Ext. 100.

Columbia College Chicago
Chicago, Illinois
http://www.colum.edu/

- **Independent** comprehensive, founded 1890
- **Urban** campus with easy access to Chicago
- **Coed** 7,809 undergraduate students, 91% full-time, 58% women, 42% men
- **Moderately difficult** entrance level, 88% of applicants were admitted

UNDERGRAD STUDENTS
7,142 full-time, 667 part-time. Students come from 58 states and territories; 31 other countries; 42% are from out of state; 14% Black or African American, non-Hispanic/Latino; 13% Hispanic/Latino; 3% Asian, non-Hispanic/Latino; 0.1% Native Hawaiian or other Pacific Islander, non-Hispanic/Latino; 0.2% American Indian or Alaska Native, non-Hispanic/Latino; 5% Two or more races, non-Hispanic/Latino; 6% Race/ethnicity unknown; 3% international; 9% transferred in; 31% live on campus.

Freshmen:
Admission: 8,325 applied, 7,330 admitted, 1,555 enrolled. ***Average high school GPA:*** 3.13. ***Test scores:*** ACT scores over 18: 87%; ACT scores over 24: 42%; ACT scores over 30: 8%.
Retention: 71% of full-time freshmen returned.

FACULTY
Total: 1,158, 27% full-time.

Student/faculty ratio: 13:1.

ACADEMICS
Calendar: semesters. *Degrees:* bachelor's, master's, and postbachelor's certificates.

Special study options: academic remediation for entering students, adult/continuing education programs, advanced placement credit, cooperative education, distance learning, double majors, English as a second language, honors programs, independent study, internships, off-campus study, part-time degree program, services for LD students, study abroad, summer session for credit.

Computers: Students can access the following: campus intranet, computer help desk, free student e-mail accounts, online (class) grades, online (class) registration, online (class) schedules. Campuswide network is available. 100% of college-owned or -operated housing units are wired for high-speed Internet access. Wireless service is available via entire campus.

Library: Columbia College Chicago Library. Students can reserve study rooms.

STUDENT LIFE
Housing options: coed. Campus housing is university owned and leased by the school. Freshman applicants given priority for college housing.

Activities and organizations: drama/theater group, student-run newspaper, radio and television station, choral group.

Athletics ***Intramural sports:*** baseball M, basketball M/W, football M/W, tennis M/W, volleyball M/W.

Campus security: 24-hour emergency response devices and patrols, late-night transport/escort service, controlled dormitory access.

Student services: health clinic, personal/psychological counseling.

COSTS & FINANCIAL AID
Costs (2017–18) ***Tuition:*** $25,580 full-time. Full-time tuition and fees vary according to course load. Part-time tuition and fees vary according to course load. ***Payment plan:*** installment. ***Waivers:*** employees or children of employees.

Financial Aid Of all full-time matriculated undergraduates who enrolled in 2015, 6,354 applied for aid.

APPLYING
Options: electronic application, deferred entrance.

Application fee: $35.

Required: essay or personal statement, high school transcript, 1 letter of recommendation. ***Required for some:*** portfolio/audition. ***Recommended:*** minimum 2.0 GPA, interview.

CONTACT
Mr. Derek Brinkley, Director of Admissions & Recruitment, Columbia College Chicago, 600 South Michigan Avenue, Room 301-B, Chicago, IL 60605-1996. *Phone:* 312-369-7493. *E-mail:* dbrinkley@colum.edu.

Concordia University Chicago

River Forest, Illinois

http://www.cuchicago.edu/

- **Independent** comprehensive, founded 1864, affiliated with Lutheran Church–Missouri Synod, part of Concordia University System
- **Suburban** 40-acre campus with easy access to Chicago
- **Coed** 1,530 undergraduate students, 89% full-time, 57% women, 43% men
- **Moderately difficult** entrance level, 50% of applicants were admitted

UNDERGRAD STUDENTS
1,357 full-time, 173 part-time. Students come from 35 states and territories; 3 other countries; 24% are from out of state; 12% Black or African American, non-Hispanic/Latino; 26% Hispanic/Latino; 2% Asian, non-Hispanic/Latino; 0.1% Native Hawaiian or other Pacific Islander, non-Hispanic/Latino; 0.2% American Indian or Alaska Native, non-Hispanic/Latino; 3% Two or more races, non-Hispanic/Latino; 5% Race/ethnicity unknown; 2% international; 7% transferred in; 34% live on campus.

Freshmen:
Admission: 4,802 applied, 2,386 admitted, 356 enrolled. ***Average high school GPA:*** 3.05. ***Test scores:*** SAT critical reading scores over 500: 58%; SAT math scores over 500: 67%; ACT scores over 18: 93%; SAT critical reading scores over 600: 11%; SAT math scores over 600: 16%; ACT scores over 24: 32%; SAT math scores over 700: 2%; ACT scores over 30: 5%.

Retention: 65% of full-time freshmen returned.

FACULTY
Total: 481, 56% full-time, 57% with terminal degrees.

Student/faculty ratio: 10:1.

ACADEMICS
Calendar: semesters. *Degrees:* certificates, diplomas, bachelor's, master's, doctoral, post-master's, and postbachelor's certificates.

Special study options: accelerated degree program, adult/continuing education programs, distance learning, double majors, honors programs, independent study, internships, part-time degree program, student-designed majors, study abroad.

Computers: Students can access the following: campus intranet, computer help desk, free student e-mail accounts, online (class) grades, online (class) registration, online (class) schedules. Campuswide network is available. 100% of college-owned or -operated housing units are wired for high-speed Internet access. Wireless service is available via entire campus.

Library: Klinck Memorial Library. *Books:* 160,000 (physical); *Databases:* 80. Weekly public service hours: 89; students can reserve study rooms.

STUDENT LIFE
Housing options: coed. Campus housing is university owned. Freshman campus housing is guaranteed.

Activities and organizations: drama/theater group, student-run newspaper, radio and television station, choral group, Campus Ministry, College Life, Student Government Association, Campus Activities Board, Art Club.

Athletics Member NCAA. All Division III. ***Intercollegiate sports:*** basketball M/W, cheerleading W, cross-country running M/W, football M, lacrosse M/W, soccer M/W, tennis M/W, track and field M/W, volleyball W. ***Intramural sports:*** baseball M(c), basketball M(c)/W(c), soccer M(c)/W(c), softball W(c), ultimate Frisbee M(c)/W(c), volleyball M(c)/W(c).

Campus security: 24-hour emergency response devices and patrols, student patrols, late-night transport/escort service, controlled dormitory access, emergency call boxes.

Student services: health clinic, personal/psychological counseling.

COSTS & FINANCIAL AID
Costs (2017–18) ***Comprehensive fee:*** $41,010 includes full-time tuition ($30,656), mandatory fees ($906), and room and board ($9448). Full-time tuition and fees vary according to course load, degree level, and reciprocity agreements. Part-time tuition: $924 per credit hour. Part-time tuition and fees vary according to course load, degree level, and reciprocity agreements. ***College room only:*** $5948. Room and board charges vary according to board plan and housing facility. ***Payment plan:*** installment. ***Waivers:*** children of alumni, senior citizens, and employees or children of employees.

Financial Aid Of all full-time matriculated undergraduates who enrolled in 2014, 1,321 applied for aid, 1,204 were judged to have need, 200 had their need fully met. In 2014, 150 non-need-based awards were made. ***Average percent of need met:*** 76. ***Average financial aid package:*** $20,524. ***Average need-based loan:*** $4268. ***Average need-based gift aid:*** $15,829. ***Average non-need-based aid:*** $12,728. ***Average indebtedness upon graduation:*** $29,103. ***Financial aid deadline:*** 6/1.

APPLYING
Standardized Tests *Required:* SAT or ACT (for admission).

Options: electronic application, early admission, deferred entrance.

Required: high school transcript, minimum 2.0 GPA, 1 letter of recommendation. ***Required for some:*** essay or personal statement, interview.

Application deadlines: rolling (freshmen), rolling (transfers).

CONTACT
Ms. Gwen Kanelos, Director of Admission, Concordia University Chicago, 7400 Augusta Street, River Forest, IL 60305. *Phone:* 708-209-3101. *Toll-free phone:* 800-285-2668. *Fax:* 708-209-3473. *E-mail:* Gwen.Kanelos@cuchicago.edu.

DePaul University

Chicago, Illinois

http://www.depaul.edu/

- **Independent Roman Catholic** university, founded 1898
- **Urban** 38-acre campus with easy access to Chicago
- **Endowment** $438.2 million
- **Coed**
- **Moderately difficult** entrance level

FACULTY
Student/faculty ratio: 16:1.

ACADEMICS
Calendar: quarters College of Law on semester system. *Degrees:* certificates, bachelor's, master's, doctoral, post-master's, and postbachelor's certificates.

Library: John T. Richardson Library plus 5 others. *Books:* 1.1 million (physical), 288,465 (digital/electronic); *Serial titles:* 12,000 (physical), 69,693 (digital/electronic). Students can reserve study rooms.

STUDENT LIFE
Housing options: coed, special housing for students with disabilities. Campus housing is university owned, leased by the school and is provided by a third party. Freshman applicants given priority for college housing.

Activities and organizations: drama/theater group, student-run newspaper, radio station, choral group, DePaul Activities Board (DAB), DePaul Community Service Association (DCSA), DePaul Fundamental Research in Academic Gaming, DePaul's Voices for the Animals, National Society of Collegiate Scholars (NSCS), national fraternities, national sororities.

Athletics Member NCAA. All Division I.

Campus security: 24-hour emergency response devices and patrols, late-night transport/escort service, controlled dormitory access, security lighting, prevention/awareness programs, on-campus police officers, video cameras, smoke detectors in residence halls.

Student services: health clinic, personal/psychological counseling, women's center, legal services.

COSTS & FINANCIAL AID

Costs (2016–17) ***Comprehensive fee:*** $51,013 includes full-time tuition ($37,020), mandatory fees ($606), and room and board ($13,387). Full-time tuition and fees vary according to course load and program. Part-time tuition: $600 per credit hour. Part-time tuition and fees vary according to course load and program. ***College room only:*** $9640. Room and board charges vary according to board plan, housing facility, and location. ***Payment plans:*** installment, deferred payment.

Financial Aid Of all full-time matriculated undergraduates who enrolled in 2015, 10,668 applied for aid, 9,395 were judged to have need, 859 had their need fully met. 579 Federal Work-Study jobs (averaging $3499). 2,343 state and other part-time jobs (averaging $2868). In 2015, 2578 non-need-based awards were made. ***Average percent of need met:*** 61. ***Average financial aid package:*** $22,627. ***Average need-based loan:*** $4353. ***Average need-based gift aid:*** $11,848. ***Average non-need-based aid:*** $13,981. ***Average indebtedness upon graduation:*** $29,829.

APPLYING

Standardized Tests *Recommended:* SAT or ACT (for admission).

Options: electronic application, early action, deferred entrance.

Required: high school transcript, minimum 2.0 GPA. ***Required for some:*** minimum 3.0 GPA, interview, audition/interview for School of Music and Theatre. ***Recommended:*** essay or personal statement, minimum 2.8 GPA.

CONTACT

Carlene Klaas-Kennelly, Dean of Undergraduate Admission, DePaul University, 1 East Jackson Boulevard, Suite 900, Chicago, IL 60604. *Phone:* 312-362-8300. *Toll-free phone:* 800-4DE-PAUL. *E-mail:* admission@depaul.edu.

DeVry University–Addison Campus

Addison, Illinois

http://www.devry.edu/

CONTACT

Admissions Office, DeVry University–Addison Campus, 1221 North Swift Road, Addison, IL 60101-6106. *Phone:* 630-953-1300. *Toll-free phone:* 866-338-7934.

DeVry University–Chicago Campus

Chicago, Illinois

http://www.devry.edu/

- **Proprietary** comprehensive, founded 1931, part of DeVry University
- **Urban** campus
- **Coed**
- **Minimally difficult** entrance level

FACULTY

Student/faculty ratio: 18:1.

ACADEMICS

Calendar: semesters. *Degrees:* associate, bachelor's, master's, and postbachelor's certificates.

Library: Learning Resource Center.

STUDENT LIFE

Housing options: college housing not available.

COSTS & FINANCIAL AID

Costs (2016–17) ***Tuition:*** $17,052 full-time, $609 per credit hour part-time. ***Required fees:*** $460 full-time.

Financial Aid Of all full-time matriculated undergraduates who enrolled in 2007, 479 applied for aid, 467 were judged to have need, 5 had their need fully met. In 2007, 14 non-need-based awards were made. ***Average percent of need met:*** 48. ***Average financial aid package:*** $16,145. ***Average need-based loan:*** $8033. ***Average need-based gift aid:*** $8371. ***Average non-need-based aid:*** $11,220. ***Average indebtedness upon graduation:*** $49,157.

APPLYING

Application fee: $30.

Required: high school transcript, interview.

CONTACT

DeVry University–Chicago Campus, 3300 North Campbell Avenue, Chicago, IL 60618. *Phone:* 773-929-8500. *Toll-free phone:* 866-338-7934.

DeVry University Online

Addison, Illinois

http://www.devry.edu/

- **Proprietary** comprehensive, founded 2000
- **Coed**

FACULTY

Student/faculty ratio: 13:1.

ACADEMICS

Calendar: semesters. *Degrees:* associate, bachelor's, master's, and postbachelor's certificates.

STUDENT LIFE

Housing options: college housing not available.

COSTS & FINANCIAL AID

Costs (2016–17) ***Tuition:*** $17,052 full-time, $609 per credit hour part-time. ***Required fees:*** $460 full-time.

Financial Aid Of all full-time matriculated undergraduates who enrolled in 2006, 810 applied for aid, 785 were judged to have need, 9 had their need fully met. In 2006, 146 non-need-based awards were made. ***Average percent of need met:*** 36. ***Average financial aid package:*** $10,560. ***Average need-based loan:*** $6201. ***Average need-based gift aid:*** $7114. ***Average non-need-based aid:*** $10,591. ***Average indebtedness upon graduation:*** $35,423.

APPLYING

Options: deferred entrance.

Application fee: $30.

Required: high school transcript, interview.

CONTACT

DeVry University Online, 1221 North Swift Road, Addison, IL 60101. *Phone:* 877-496-9050. *Toll-free phone:* 866-338-7934.

DeVry University–Tinley Park Campus

Tinley Park, Illinois

http://www.devry.edu/

CONTACT

Admissions Office, DeVry University–Tinley Park Campus, 18624 West Creek Drive, Tinley Park, IL 60477 . *Phone:* 708-342-3300. *Toll-free phone:* 866-338-7934.

Dominican University

River Forest, Illinois

http://www.dom.edu/

- **Independent Roman Catholic** comprehensive, founded 1901
- **Suburban** 30-acre campus with easy access to Chicago
- **Endowment** $28.7 million
- **Coed** 2,306 undergraduate students, 91% full-time, 67% women, 33% men
- **Moderately difficult** entrance level, 64% of applicants were admitted

UNDERGRAD STUDENTS
2,105 full-time, 201 part-time. Students come from 31 states and territories; 10 other countries; 6% are from out of state; 7% Black or African American, non-Hispanic/Latino; 48% Hispanic/Latino; 3% Asian, non-Hispanic/Latino; 0.2% Native Hawaiian or other Pacific Islander, non-Hispanic/Latino; 0.2% American Indian or Alaska Native, non-Hispanic/Latino; 0.7% Two or more races, non-Hispanic/Latino; 2% Race/ethnicity unknown; 3% international; 7% transferred in; 26% live on campus.

Freshmen:
Admission: 4,568 applied, 2,911 admitted, 495 enrolled. ***Average high school GPA:*** 3.7. ***Test scores:*** SAT critical reading scores over 500: 67%; SAT math scores over 500: 58%; SAT writing scores over 500: 41%; ACT scores over 18: 96%; SAT critical reading scores over 600: 25%; SAT math scores over 600: 33%; SAT writing scores over 600: 16%; ACT scores over 24: 36%; SAT critical reading scores over 700: 8%; SAT math scores over 700: 8%; SAT writing scores over 700: 8%; ACT scores over 30: 2%.
Retention: 72% of full-time freshmen returned.

FACULTY
Total: 369, 45% full-time, 65% with terminal degrees.
Student/faculty ratio: 11:1.

ACADEMICS
Calendar: semesters. *Degrees:* certificates, bachelor's, master's, doctoral, post-master's, and postbachelor's certificates.
Special study options: academic remediation for entering students, accelerated degree program, adult/continuing education programs, advanced placement credit, distance learning, double majors, English as a second language, honors programs, independent study, internships, off-campus study, part-time degree program, services for LD students, student-designed majors, study abroad, summer session for credit.
Unusual degree programs: 3-2 business administration; engineering with Illinois Institute of Technology; nursing; social work; library science, pharmacy with Midwestern University.
Computers: 550 computers/terminals and 4,000 ports are available on campus for general student use. Students can access the following: campus intranet, computer help desk, free student e-mail accounts, online (class) grades, online (class) registration, online (class) schedules. Campuswide network is available. 100% of college-owned or -operated housing units are wired for high-speed Internet access. Wireless service is available via entire campus.
Library: Rebecca Crown Library. *Books:* 247,967 (physical), 9,389 (digital/electronic); *Serial titles:* 280 (physical), 53,047 (digital/electronic); *Databases:* 114. Weekly public service hours: 100; students can reserve study rooms.

STUDENT LIFE
Housing options: coed, women-only, special housing for students with disabilities. Campus housing is university owned and leased by the school. Freshman applicants given priority for college housing.
Activities and organizations: drama/theater group, student-run newspaper, choral group, Polish Club, Commuter Student Association, Nutrition Club, Organization of Latin American Students, Fashion Club.
Athletics Member NCAA. All Division III. ***Intercollegiate sports:*** baseball M, basketball M/W, cross-country running M/W, golf M, soccer M/W, softball W, tennis M/W, volleyball M/W. ***Intramural sports:*** basketball M/W, bowling M/W, football M/W, racquetball M/W, soccer M/W, ultimate Frisbee M/W, volleyball M/W.
Campus security: 24-hour emergency response devices and patrols, student patrols, late-night transport/escort service, controlled dormitory access, door alarms.
Student services: health clinic, personal/psychological counseling.

COSTS & FINANCIAL AID
Costs (2017–18) ***One-time required fee:*** $150. ***Comprehensive fee:*** $42,472 includes full-time tuition ($32,160), mandatory fees ($370), and room and board ($9942). Full-time tuition and fees vary according to course load, program, and reciprocity agreements. Part-time tuition: $1072 per credit hour. Part-time tuition and fees vary according to course load, program, and reciprocity agreements. ***Required fees:*** $90 per term part-time. ***Room and board:*** Room and board charges vary according to board plan and housing facility. ***Payment plan:*** deferred payment. ***Waivers:*** employees or children of employees.
Financial Aid Of all full-time matriculated undergraduates who enrolled in 2015, 1,745 applied for aid, 1,646 were judged to have need, 164 had their need fully met. In 2015, 172 non-need-based awards were made. ***Average percent of need met:*** 71. ***Average financial aid package:*** $23,256. ***Average need-based loan:*** $4268. ***Average need-based gift aid:*** $19,183. ***Average non-need-based aid:*** $8321. ***Average indebtedness upon graduation:*** $28,533.

APPLYING
Standardized Tests *Required:* SAT or ACT (for admission).
Options: electronic application, deferred entrance.
Application fee: $25.
Required: high school transcript. ***Required for some:*** interview. ***Recommended:*** essay or personal statement, minimum 2.5 GPA.
Application deadlines: rolling (freshmen), rolling (transfers).
Notification: continuous (freshmen), continuous (transfers).

CONTACT
Mr. Glenn Hamilton, Assistant Vice President, Enrollment Management, Dominican University, 7900 West Division Street, River Forest, IL 60305. *Phone:* 708-524-6800. *Toll-free phone:* 800-828-8475. *Fax:* 708-524-6864. *E-mail:* domadmis@dom.edu.

Eastern Illinois University

Charleston, Illinois

http://www.eiu.edu/

- **State-supported** comprehensive, founded 1895
- **Small-town** 320-acre campus
- **Endowment** $76.9 million
- **Coed** 5,957 undergraduate students, 86% full-time, 61% women, 39% men
- **Moderately difficult** entrance level, 47% of applicants were admitted

UNDERGRAD STUDENTS
5,133 full-time, 824 part-time. Students come from 35 states and territories; 30 other countries; 6% are from out of state; 19% Black or African American, non-Hispanic/Latino; 7% Hispanic/Latino; 1% Asian, non-Hispanic/Latino; 0.1% Native Hawaiian or other Pacific Islander, non-Hispanic/Latino; 0.3% American Indian or Alaska Native, non-Hispanic/Latino; 2% Two or more races, non-Hispanic/Latino; 2% Race/ethnicity unknown; 2% international; 9% transferred in; 38% live on campus.

Freshmen:
Admission: 8,420 applied, 3,947 admitted, 772 enrolled. ***Average high school GPA:*** 3.08. ***Test scores:*** ACT scores over 18: 85%; ACT scores over 24: 27%; ACT scores over 30: 4%.
Retention: 71% of full-time freshmen returned.

FACULTY
Total: 527, 80% full-time, 65% with terminal degrees.
Student/faculty ratio: 14:1.

ACADEMICS
Calendar: semesters. *Degrees:* bachelor's, master's, post-master's, and postbachelor's certificates.
Special study options: academic remediation for entering students, accelerated degree program, adult/continuing education programs, advanced placement credit, distance learning, double majors, English as a second language, freshman honors college, honors programs, independent study, internships, off-campus study, part-time degree program, services for LD students, study abroad, summer session for credit. ***ROTC:*** Army (b).
Unusual degree programs: 3-2 engineering with University of Illinois at Urbana–Champaign, Southern Illinois University at Carbondale.
Computers: 706 computers/terminals and 10,000 ports are available on campus for general student use. Students can access the following: computer help desk, free student e-mail accounts, online (class) grades, online (class) registration, online (class) schedules. Campuswide network is available. 100% of college-owned or -operated housing units are wired for high-speed Internet access. Wireless service is available via

classrooms, computer centers, computer labs, dorm rooms, learning centers, libraries, student centers.
Library: Booth Library. *Books:* 1.0 million (physical), 1.3 million (digital/electronic); *Serial titles:* 161 (physical), 45,276 (digital/electronic); *Databases:* 244. Weekly public service hours: 98.

STUDENT LIFE
Housing options: on-campus residence required for freshman year; coed, men-only, women-only. Campus housing is university owned. Freshman campus housing is guaranteed.
Activities and organizations: drama/theater group, student-run newspaper, radio and television station, choral group, marching band, Greek Organizations, Black Student Union, Intramural Sports, University Board, Religious Student Organizations, national fraternities, national sororities.
Athletics Member NCAA. All Division I except football (Division I-AA). ***Intercollegiate sports:*** baseball M(s), basketball M(s)/W(s), cross-country running M(s)/W(s), golf M(s)/W(s), ice hockey M(c), racquetball M(c)/W(c), soccer M(s)/W(s), softball W(s), swimming and diving M(s)/W(s), tennis M(s)/W(s), track and field M(s)/W(s), ultimate Frisbee M(c)/W(c), volleyball W(s), water polo M(c)/W(c), wrestling M(c)/W(c). ***Intramural sports:*** badminton M/W, baseball M(c), basketball M/W, bowling M/W, racquetball M/W, rugby M(c), soccer M/W, softball M/W, table tennis M/W, tennis M/W, volleyball M/W.
Campus security: 24-hour emergency response devices and patrols, student patrols, controlled dormitory access, AlertEIU and warning sirens, self-defense education, shuttle buses, lighted pathways and sidewalks.
Student services: health clinic, personal/psychological counseling, women's center, legal services.

COSTS & FINANCIAL AID
Costs (2016–17) ***Tuition:*** state resident $8670 full-time, $289 per credit hour part-time; nonresident $10,830 full-time, $361 per credit hour part-time. Full-time tuition and fees vary according to course load and student level. Part-time tuition and fees vary according to course load and student level. No tuition increase for student's term of enrollment. ***Required fees:*** $2910 full-time, $106 per credit hour part-time. ***Room and board:*** $9546. Room and board charges vary according to board plan and housing facility. ***Payment plan:*** installment. ***Waivers:*** senior citizens and employees or children of employees.
Financial Aid Of all full-time matriculated undergraduates who enrolled in 2016, 4,747 applied for aid, 3,437 were judged to have need, 345 had their need fully met. 204 Federal Work-Study jobs (averaging $889). 1,807 state and other part-time jobs (averaging $1633). In 2016, 631 non-need-based awards were made. ***Average percent of need met:*** 67. ***Average financial aid package:*** $9187. ***Average need-based loan:*** $4363. ***Average need-based gift aid:*** $7608. ***Average non-need-based aid:*** $2808. ***Average indebtedness upon graduation:*** $31,382.

APPLYING
Standardized Tests *Required:* SAT or ACT (for admission).
Options: electronic application, deferred entrance.
Application fee: $30.
Required: high school transcript, minimum 2.3 GPA. ***Required for some:*** essay or personal statement, 1 letter of recommendation, audition for music program.
Application deadlines: rolling (freshmen), rolling (transfers).
Notification: continuous (freshmen), continuous (transfers).

CONTACT
Denise Lee, Assistant Director of Admissions, Eastern Illinois University, 600 Lincoln Avenue, Charleston, IL 61920. *Phone:* 217-581-7975. *Toll-free phone:* 877-581-2348. *Fax:* 217-581-7060. *E-mail:* dalee@eiu.edu.

East-West University
Chicago, Illinois
http://www.eastwest.edu/

CONTACT
Bryan Lambert, Director of Enrollment, East-West University, 816 South Michigan Avenue, Chicago, IL 60605-2103. *Phone:* 312-939-0112 Ext. 1701.

Elmhurst College
Elmhurst, Illinois
http://www.elmhurst.edu/

- **Independent** comprehensive, founded 1871, affiliated with United Church of Christ
- **Suburban** 38-acre campus with easy access to Chicago
- **Endowment** $91.8 million
- **Coed**
- **Moderately difficult** entrance level

FACULTY
Student/faculty ratio: 14:1.

ACADEMICS
Calendar: 4-1-4. *Degrees:* bachelor's and master's.
Library: Buehler Library.

STUDENT LIFE
Housing options: coed. Campus housing is university owned, leased by the school and is provided by a third party. Freshman applicants given priority for college housing.
Activities and organizations: drama/theater group, student-run newspaper, radio station, choral group, Programming Board and Student Government, theater and music groups, Black Student Union, residence life groups, Hablamos, national fraternities, national sororities.
Athletics Member NCAA. All Division III.
Campus security: 24-hour emergency response devices and patrols, late-night transport/escort service, controlled dormitory access.
Student services: health clinic, personal/psychological counseling.

COSTS & FINANCIAL AID
Costs (2016–17) ***Comprehensive fee:*** $45,578 includes full-time tuition ($35,250), mandatory fees ($250), and room and board ($10,078). Part-time tuition: $997 per semester hour. Part-time tuition and fees vary according to course load. ***College room only:*** $6152. Room and board charges vary according to board plan and housing facility.
Financial Aid Of all full-time matriculated undergraduates who enrolled in 2016, 2,290 applied for aid, 2,097 were judged to have need, 424 had their need fully met. 347 Federal Work-Study jobs (averaging $1055). 246 state and other part-time jobs (averaging $1622). In 2016, 514 non-need-based awards were made. ***Average percent of need met:*** 79. ***Average financial aid package:*** $26,073. ***Average need-based loan:*** $4492. ***Average need-based gift aid:*** $22,024. ***Average non-need-based aid:*** $15,289. ***Average indebtedness upon graduation:*** $28,246.

APPLYING
Standardized Tests *Required:* SAT or ACT (for admission).
Options: electronic application, deferred entrance.
Required: high school transcript. ***Required for some:*** essay or personal statement, interview. ***Recommended:*** essay or personal statement, interview.

CONTACT
Mrs. Stephanie Levenson, Executive Director of Admission, Elmhurst College, Elmhurst College, Admission Office, 190 South Prospect Avenue, Elmhurst, IL 60126-3296. *Phone:* 630-617-3400. *Toll-free phone:* 800-697-1871. *Fax:* 630-617-5501. *E-mail:* admit@elmhurst.edu.

See page 1340 for the College Close-Up.

Eureka College
Eureka, Illinois
http://www.eureka.edu/

- **Independent** 4-year, founded 1855, affiliated with Christian Church (Disciples of Christ)
- **Small-town** 64-acre campus
- **Endowment** $25.3 million
- **Coed** 672 undergraduate students, 96% full-time, 51% women, 49% men
- **Minimally difficult** entrance level, 65% of applicants were admitted

UNDERGRAD STUDENTS
645 full-time, 27 part-time. Students come from 8 states and territories; 2 other countries; 6% are from out of state; 5% Black or African American, non-Hispanic/Latino; 3% Hispanic/Latino; 0.6% Asian, non-

Hispanic/Latino; 0.6% American Indian or Alaska Native, non-Hispanic/Latino; 3% Two or more races, non-Hispanic/Latino; 2% Race/ethnicity unknown; 1% international; 13% transferred in; 66% live on campus.

Freshmen:
Admission: 1,046 applied, 675 admitted, 153 enrolled. ***Average high school GPA:*** 3.19. ***Test scores:*** SAT critical reading scores over 500: 50%; SAT math scores over 500: 50%; SAT writing scores over 500: 50%; ACT scores over 18: 91%; SAT critical reading scores over 600: 25%; SAT writing scores over 600: 25%; ACT scores over 24: 33%; SAT writing scores over 700: 25%; ACT scores over 30: 4%.

Retention: 69% of full-time freshmen returned.

FACULTY
Total: 74, 55% full-time, 55% with terminal degrees.

Student/faculty ratio: 13:1.

ACADEMICS
Calendar: semesters 4 8-week terms. *Degree:* bachelor's.

Special study options: advanced placement credit, cooperative education, double majors, honors programs, independent study, internships, services for LD students, student-designed majors, study abroad, summer session for credit.

Unusual degree programs: 3-2 physical science with University of Missouri–Kansas City, psychology/occupational therapy with Washington University in St. Louis.

Computers: 82 computers/terminals and 50 ports are available on campus for general student use. Students can access the following: campus intranet, computer help desk, free student e-mail accounts, online (class) grades, online (class) registration, online (class) schedules, bill payments, tax information. Campuswide network is available. 100% of college-owned or -operated housing units are wired for high-speed Internet access. Wireless service is available via classrooms, computer centers, computer labs, dorm rooms, learning centers, libraries, student centers.

Library: Melick Library. *Books:* 81,371 (physical), 7,171 (digital/electronic); *Serial titles:* 532 (physical), 919 (digital/electronic); *Databases:* 11. Weekly public service hours: 70; students can reserve study rooms.

STUDENT LIFE
Housing options: on-campus residence required through senior year; coed, men-only, women-only. Campus housing is university owned. Freshman campus housing is guaranteed.

Activities and organizations: drama/theater group, student-run newspaper, choral group, Student Senate, Campus Activities Board (CAB), Alpha Phi Omega, Student Alliance for Greener Environments (SAGE), Multicultural Student Union (MCSU), national fraternities, national sororities.

Athletics Member NCAA. All Division III. ***Intercollegiate sports:*** baseball M, basketball M/W, cross-country running M/W, football M, golf M/W, soccer M/W, softball W, swimming and diving M/W, tennis M/W, track and field M/W, volleyball W. ***Intramural sports:*** cheerleading M(c)/W(c).

Campus security: 24-hour emergency response devices, late-night transport/escort service, controlled dormitory access, late night patrols.

Student services: health clinic, personal/psychological counseling.

COSTS & FINANCIAL AID
Costs (2017–18) ***Comprehensive fee:*** $34,760 includes full-time tuition ($25,150), mandatory fees ($240), and room and board ($9370). Full-time tuition and fees vary according to course load and program. Part-time tuition: $700 per semester hour. Part-time tuition and fees vary according to course load and program. ***Required fees:*** $120 per semester part-time. ***College room only:*** $4490. Room and board charges vary according to board plan and housing facility. ***Payment plan:*** installment. ***Waivers:*** senior citizens and employees or children of employees.

Financial Aid Of all full-time matriculated undergraduates who enrolled in 2016, 462 applied for aid, 455 were judged to have need, 42 had their need fully met. 107 Federal Work-Study jobs (averaging $1967). 47 state and other part-time jobs (averaging $1149). In 2016, 162 non-need-based awards were made. ***Average percent of need met:*** 71. ***Average financial aid package:*** $18,087. ***Average need-based loan:*** $4444. ***Average need-based gift aid:*** $11,281. ***Average non-need-based aid:*** $7719. ***Average indebtedness upon graduation:*** $40,681.

APPLYING
Standardized Tests *Required:* SAT or ACT (for admission).

Options: electronic application.

Required: high school transcript, minimum 2.3 GPA, 1 letter of recommendation. ***Required for some:*** essay or personal statement. ***Recommended:*** essay or personal statement, interview.

Application deadlines: 8/1 (freshmen), 8/15 (transfers).

Notification: continuous (freshmen), continuous (transfers).

CONTACT
Mr. Mike Murtagh, Vice President of Institutional Advancement, Eureka College, 300 East College Avenue, Eureka, IL 61530. *Phone:* 309-467-6315. *Toll-free phone:* 888-4-EUREKA. *E-mail:* mmurtagh@eureka.edu.

Governors State University

University Park, Illinois

http://www.govst.edu/

- **State-supported** university, founded 1969
- **Suburban** 742-acre campus with easy access to Chicago
- **Endowment** $2.0 million
- **Coed** 3,517 undergraduate students, 55% full-time, 64% women, 36% men
- **Moderately difficult** entrance level, 42% of applicants were admitted

UNDERGRAD STUDENTS
1,925 full-time, 1,592 part-time. Students come from 21 states and territories; 18 other countries; 3% are from out of state; 39% Black or African American, non-Hispanic/Latino; 12% Hispanic/Latino; 1% Asian, non-Hispanic/Latino; 0.1% Native Hawaiian or other Pacific Islander, non-Hispanic/Latino; 0.2% American Indian or Alaska Native, non-Hispanic/Latino; 2% Two or more races, non-Hispanic/Latino; 10% Race/ethnicity unknown; 1% international; 24% transferred in; 7% live on campus.

Freshmen:
Admission: 1,176 applied, 499 admitted, 200 enrolled. ***Average high school GPA:*** 2.83. ***Test scores:*** ACT scores over 18: 66%; ACT scores over 24: 10%; ACT scores over 30: 1%.

Retention: 53% of full-time freshmen returned.

FACULTY
Total: 481, 45% full-time, 43% with terminal degrees.

Student/faculty ratio: 13:1.

ACADEMICS
Calendar: semesters. *Degrees:* certificates, bachelor's, master's, doctoral, post-master's, and postbachelor's certificates.

Special study options: adult/continuing education programs, advanced placement credit, distance learning, double majors, English as a second language, external degree program, honors programs, independent study, internships, off-campus study, part-time degree program, services for LD students, student-designed majors, study abroad, summer session for credit.

Computers: 112 computers/terminals and 500 ports are available on campus for general student use. Students can access the following: campus intranet, computer help desk, free student e-mail accounts, online (class) grades, online (class) registration, online (class) schedules, student portal. Campuswide network is available. 100% of college-owned or -operated housing units are wired for high-speed Internet access. Wireless service is available via entire campus.

Library: University Library. *Books:* 296,238 (physical), 319,423 (digital/electronic); *Serial titles:* 2,187 (physical), 92,506 (digital/electronic); *Databases:* 176. Weekly public service hours: 75; students can reserve study rooms.

STUDENT LIFE
Housing options: coed. Campus housing is university owned.

Activities and organizations: drama/theater group, student-run newspaper, choral group, Computer Technology Club, Student Leadership Institute, Tau Sigma National Honor Society, Dual Degree Program, National Student Speech Language and Hearing Association.

Athletics Member NAIA. ***Intercollegiate sports:*** basketball M(s)/W(s), cross-country running M(s)/W(s), golf M(s)/W(s), volleyball M(s)/W(s). ***Intramural sports:*** basketball M/W, table tennis M/W.

Campus security: 24-hour emergency response devices and patrols, late-night transport/escort service, controlled dormitory access.

Student services: health clinic, personal/psychological counseling.

COSTS & FINANCIAL AID

Costs (2016–17) ***Tuition:*** state resident $8160 full-time, $272 per credit hour part-time; nonresident $16,320 full-time, $544 per credit hour part-time. Full-time tuition and fees vary according to course load, degree level, reciprocity agreements, and student level. Part-time tuition and fees vary according to course load, degree level, reciprocity agreements, and student level. No tuition increase for student's term of enrollment. ***Required fees:*** $2356 full-time, $76 per credit hour part-time, $38 per term part-time. ***Room and board:*** $9868; room only: $7868. Room and board charges vary according to board plan and housing facility. ***Payment plans:*** installment, deferred payment. ***Waivers:*** senior citizens and employees or children of employees.

Financial Aid Of all full-time matriculated undergraduates who enrolled in 2016, 1,719 applied for aid, 1,498 were judged to have need, 330 had their need fully met. 103 Federal Work-Study jobs (averaging $188,154). In 2016, 201 non-need-based awards were made. ***Average percent of need met:*** 51. ***Average financial aid package:*** $10,462. ***Average need-based loan:*** $4429. ***Average need-based gift aid:*** $4348. ***Average non-need-based aid:*** $2825. ***Financial aid deadline:*** 10/1.

APPLYING

Standardized Tests *Required:* SAT and SAT Subject Tests or ACT (for admission).

Options: electronic application, early admission, early decision, deferred entrance.

Application fee: $25.

Required: high school transcript, minimum 2.5 GPA. ***Recommended:*** essay or personal statement.

Early decision deadline: 11/15.

Notification: 1/31 (early decision).

CONTACT

Ms. Yakeea Daniels, Assistant Vice President for Enrollment Services and Admissions, Governors State University, One University Parkway, University Park, IL 60484. *Phone:* 708-534-4510. *Toll-free phone:* 800-478-8478. *Fax:* 708-235-7455. *E-mail:* ydaniels@govst.edu.

Greenville College

Greenville, Illinois

http://www.greenville.edu/

- **Independent Free Methodist** comprehensive, founded 1892
- **Small-town** 50-acre campus with easy access to St. Louis
- **Endowment** $16.3 million
- **Coed** 994 undergraduate students, 92% full-time, 50% women, 50% men
- **Moderately difficult** entrance level, 58% of applicants were admitted

UNDERGRAD STUDENTS

919 full-time, 75 part-time. Students come from 36 states and territories; 14 other countries; 32% are from out of state; 11% Black or African American, non-Hispanic/Latino; 5% Hispanic/Latino; 1% Asian, non-Hispanic/Latino; 0.1% Native Hawaiian or other Pacific Islander, non-Hispanic/Latino; 0.3% American Indian or Alaska Native, non-Hispanic/Latino; 0.7% Two or more races, non-Hispanic/Latino; 10% Race/ethnicity unknown; 3% international; 9% transferred in; 73% live on campus.

Freshmen:

Admission: 1,093 applied, 632 admitted, 200 enrolled. ***Average high school GPA:*** 3.3. ***Test scores:*** SAT critical reading scores over 500: 34%; SAT math scores over 500: 36%; SAT writing scores over 500: 23%; ACT scores over 18: 84%; SAT critical reading scores over 600: 7%; SAT math scores over 600: 9%; SAT writing scores over 600: 1%; ACT scores over 24: 32%; ACT scores over 30: 6%.

Retention: 67% of full-time freshmen returned.

FACULTY

Total: 164, 35% full-time, 40% with terminal degrees.

Student/faculty ratio: 14:1.

ACADEMICS

Calendar: 4-1-4. *Degrees:* bachelor's and master's.

Special study options: academic remediation for entering students, accelerated degree program, adult/continuing education programs, advanced placement credit, cooperative education, distance learning, double majors, external degree program, honors programs, independent study, internships, off-campus study, part-time degree program, student-designed majors, study abroad, summer session for credit.

Unusual degree programs: 3-2 engineering with University of Illinois at Urbana–Champaign, Washington University in St. Louis; nursing with St. John's College, Southern Illinois University Edwardsville, Mennonite College of Nursing; chiropractic with Logan College of Chiropractic.

Computers: 50 computers/terminals are available on campus for general student use. Students can access the following: campus intranet, computer help desk, free student e-mail accounts, online (class) grades, online (class) registration, online (class) schedules. Campuswide network is available. 100% of college-owned or -operated housing units are wired for high-speed Internet access. Wireless service is available via entire campus.

Library: Ruby E. Dare Library. *Books:* 131,047 (physical), 7,408 (digital/electronic). Students can reserve study rooms.

STUDENT LIFE

Housing options: on-campus residence required through senior year; men-only, women-only. Campus housing is university owned. Freshman campus housing is guaranteed.

Activities and organizations: drama/theater group, student-run newspaper, radio station, choral group, marching band, Campus Activity Board, Panther Corps Marching Band, Greenville College Student Association, Habitat for Humanity, Music and Entertainment Industry Student Association.

Athletics Member NCAA, NCCAA. All NCAA Division III. ***Intercollegiate sports:*** baseball M, basketball M/W, cross-country running M/W, football M, golf M/W, soccer M/W, softball W, tennis M/W, track and field M/W, volleyball M/W. ***Intramural sports:*** basketball M/W, cheerleading W, football M/W, softball M/W, ultimate Frisbee M/W, volleyball M/W.

Campus security: 24-hour emergency response devices and patrols, late-night transport/escort service, controlled dormitory access.

Student services: personal/psychological counseling.

COSTS & FINANCIAL AID

Costs (2017–18) ***Comprehensive fee:*** $35,678 includes full-time tuition ($26,124), mandatory fees ($232), and room and board ($9322). Full-time tuition and fees vary according to degree level. Part-time tuition and fees vary according to course load and degree level. ***College room only:*** $4918. Room and board charges vary according to housing facility. ***Waivers:*** senior citizens and employees or children of employees.

Financial Aid Of all full-time matriculated undergraduates who enrolled in 2015, 925 applied for aid, 837 were judged to have need, 123 had their need fully met. In 2015, 145 non-need-based awards were made. ***Average percent of need met:*** 76. ***Average financial aid package:*** $20,443. ***Average need-based loan:*** $4337. ***Average need-based gift aid:*** $16,716. ***Average non-need-based aid:*** $9594. ***Average indebtedness upon graduation:*** $32,860.

APPLYING

Standardized Tests *Required:* SAT or ACT (for admission).

Options: electronic application, early admission, deferred entrance.

Required: essay or personal statement, high school transcript, minimum 2.3 GPA, agreement to lifestyle statement. ***Required for some:*** interview.

Application deadlines: rolling (freshmen), rolling (transfers).

Notification: continuous (freshmen), continuous (transfers).

CONTACT

Mr. Karl Hatton, Dean of Admissions, Greenville College, 315 East College Avenue, Greenville, IL 62246. *Phone:* 618-664-7100. *Toll-free phone:* 800-345-4440. *Fax:* 618-664-9841. *E-mail:* admissions@greenville.edu.

Hebrew Theological College

Skokie, Illinois

http://www.htc.edu/

CONTACT

Rabbi Berish Cardash, Hebrew Theological College, 7135 North Carpenter Road, Skokie, IL 60077-3263. *Phone:* 847-982-2500.

Illinois College

Jacksonville, Illinois

http://www.ic.edu/

- **Independent interdenominational** comprehensive, founded 1829
- **Small-town** 62-acre campus with easy access to St. Louis
- **Coed** 952 undergraduate students, 100% full-time, 52% women, 48% men
- **Moderately difficult** entrance level, 61% of applicants were admitted

UNDERGRAD STUDENTS

948 full-time, 4 part-time. 16% are from out of state; 12% Black or African American, non-Hispanic/Latino; 10% Hispanic/Latino; 1% Asian, non-Hispanic/Latino; 0.1% Native Hawaiian or other Pacific Islander, non-Hispanic/Latino; 0.2% American Indian or Alaska Native, non-Hispanic/Latino; 4% Two or more races, non-Hispanic/Latino; 0.7% Race/ethnicity unknown; 4% international; 5% transferred in; 84% live on campus.

Freshmen:

Admission: 2,431 applied, 1,471 admitted, 240 enrolled. ***Average high school GPA:*** 3.52. ***Test scores:*** SAT critical reading scores over 500: 47%; SAT math scores over 500: 58%; SAT writing scores over 500: 53%; ACT scores over 18: 80%; SAT critical reading scores over 600: 16%; SAT math scores over 600: 37%; SAT writing scores over 600: 11%; ACT scores over 24: 37%; ACT scores over 30: 5%.

Retention: 79% of full-time freshmen returned.

FACULTY

Total: 104, 81% full-time, 73% with terminal degrees.

Student/faculty ratio: 11:1.

ACADEMICS

Calendar: semesters. *Degrees:* bachelor's and master's.

Computers: Students can access the following: computer help desk, free student e-mail accounts, online (class) grades, online (class) registration, online (class) schedules. Campuswide network is available. Wireless service is available via entire campus.

Library: Schewe Library.

STUDENT LIFE

Housing options: on-campus residence required through sophomore year; coed, men-only, women-only. Campus housing is university owned. Freshman campus housing is guaranteed.

Athletics Member NCAA. All Division III. ***Intercollegiate sports:*** baseball M, cheerleading W, cross-country running M/W, football M, golf M/W, soccer M/W, softball W, swimming and diving M/W, tennis M/W, track and field M/W, volleyball W. ***Intramural sports:*** badminton M/W, basketball M/W, fencing M/W, football M, racquetball M/W, softball M/W, swimming and diving M/W, volleyball M/W, water polo M/W, weight lifting M/W.

Campus security: 24-hour emergency response devices and patrols, late-night transport/escort service, controlled dormitory access.

COSTS & FINANCIAL AID

Costs (2017–18) ***Comprehensive fee:*** $41,330 includes full-time tuition ($31,590), mandatory fees ($550), and room and board ($9190). Part-time tuition: $970 per credit hour. Part-time tuition and fees vary according to course load. ***Room and board:*** Room and board charges vary according to board plan and housing facility. ***Payment plan:*** installment. ***Waivers:*** employees or children of employees.

Financial Aid Of all full-time matriculated undergraduates who enrolled in 2015, 849 applied for aid, 792 were judged to have need, 161 had their need fully met. In 2015, 141 non-need-based awards were made. ***Average percent of need met:*** 87. ***Average financial aid package:*** $27,778. ***Average need-based loan:*** $5289. ***Average need-based gift aid:*** $22,176. ***Average non-need-based aid:*** $17,939. ***Average indebtedness upon graduation:*** $32,000.

APPLYING

Options: electronic application, early admission, early action, deferred entrance.

Required: high school transcript, 1 letter of recommendation. ***Required for some:*** essay or personal statement. ***Recommended:*** essay or personal statement, minimum 2.5 GPA, interview.

CONTACT

Mr. Rick Bystry, Associate Director of Admission, Illinois College, 1101 West College, Jacksonville, IL 62650. *Phone:* 217-245-3030. *Toll-free phone:* 866-464-5265. *Fax:* 217-245-3034. *E-mail:* admissions@ic.edu.

The Illinois Institute of Art–Chicago

Chicago, Illinois

http://www.artinstitutes.edu/chicago/

CONTACT

The Illinois Institute of Art–Chicago, 350 North Orleans Street, Chicago, IL 60654. *Phone:* 312-280-3500. *Toll-free phone:* 800-351-3450.

The Illinois Institute of Art–Schaumburg

Schaumburg, Illinois

http://www.artinstitutes.edu/schaumburg/

CONTACT

The Illinois Institute of Art–Schaumburg, 1000 North Plaza Drive, Suite 100, Schaumburg, IL 60173. *Phone:* 847-619-3450. *Toll-free phone:* 800-314-3450.

Illinois Institute of Technology

Chicago, Illinois

http://www.iit.edu/

- **Independent** university, founded 1890
- **Urban** 120-acre campus with easy access to Chicago
- **Endowment** $235.5 million
- **Coed**
- **Moderately difficult** entrance level

FACULTY

Student/faculty ratio: 13:1.

ACADEMICS

Calendar: semesters. *Degrees:* bachelor's, master's, doctoral, post-master's, and postbachelor's certificates.

Library: Paul V. Galvin Library plus 5 others. *Books:* 1.7 million (physical), 99,658 (digital/electronic); *Serial titles:* 895 (physical); *Databases:* 464. Study areas open 24 hours, 5-7 days a week; students can reserve study rooms.

STUDENT LIFE

Housing options: on-campus residence required for freshman year; coed. Campus housing is university owned and is provided by a third party. Freshman applicants given priority for college housing.

Activities and organizations: drama/theater group, student-run newspaper, radio station, choral group, Union Board, International Students Association, Student Government Association, Greek Council, Commuter Student Associate, national fraternities, national sororities.

Athletics Member NCAA. All Division III.

Campus security: 24-hour emergency response devices and patrols, late-night transport/escort service, controlled dormitory access.

Student services: health clinic, personal/psychological counseling, women's center, legal services.

COSTS & FINANCIAL AID

Costs (2016–17) ***One-time required fee:*** $330. ***Comprehensive fee:*** $59,141 includes full-time tuition ($43,500), mandatory fees ($2823), and room and board ($12,818). Full-time tuition and fees vary according to student level. Part-time tuition: $1359 per credit hour. Part-time tuition and fees vary according to course load and student level. ***Required fees:***

$40 per course part-time, $155 per term part-time. ***College room only:*** $6062. Room and board charges vary according to board plan and housing facility.

Financial Aid Of all full-time matriculated undergraduates who enrolled in 2015, 1,685 applied for aid, 1,611 were judged to have need, 194 had their need fully met. In 2015, 1051 non-need-based awards were made. ***Average percent of need met:*** 76. ***Average financial aid package:*** $36,732. ***Average need-based loan:*** $5011. ***Average need-based gift aid:*** $31,201. ***Average non-need-based aid:*** $23,056. ***Average indebtedness upon graduation:*** $30,569.

APPLYING

Standardized Tests *Required:* SAT or ACT (for admission).

Options: electronic application, early admission, deferred entrance.

Required: essay or personal statement, high school transcript, 1 letter of recommendation. ***Recommended:*** interview.

CONTACT

Ms. Toni Riley, Director, Undergraduate Admissions Office, Illinois Institute of Technology, Office of Undergraduate Admission, Perlstein 101, 10 West 33rd Street, Chicago, IL 60616. *Phone:* 312-567-5239. *Toll-free phone:* 800-448-2329. *E-mail:* admission@iit.edu.

Illinois State University

Normal, Illinois

http://www.illinoisstate.edu/

- **State-supported** university, founded 1857
- **Urban** 490-acre campus
- **Coed** 18,643 undergraduate students, 94% full-time, 55% women, 45% men
- **Moderately difficult** entrance level, 89% of applicants were admitted

UNDERGRAD STUDENTS

17,457 full-time, 1,186 part-time. Students come from 39 states and territories; 35 other countries; 2% are from out of state; 8% Black or African American, non-Hispanic/Latino; 10% Hispanic/Latino; 2% Asian, non-Hispanic/Latino; 0.1% Native Hawaiian or other Pacific Islander, non-Hispanic/Latino; 0.2% American Indian or Alaska Native, non-Hispanic/Latino; 3% Two or more races, non-Hispanic/Latino; 0.3% Race/ethnicity unknown; 0.6% international; 11% transferred in; 32% live on campus.

Freshmen:

Admission: 12,078 applied, 10,735 admitted, 3,694 enrolled. ***Average high school GPA:*** 3.36. ***Test scores:*** ACT scores over 18: 100%; ACT scores over 24: 46%; ACT scores over 30: 6%.

Retention: 81% of full-time freshmen returned.

FACULTY

Total: 1,210, 73% full-time, 66% with terminal degrees.

Student/faculty ratio: 18:1.

ACADEMICS

Calendar: semesters. *Degrees:* bachelor's, master's, doctoral, post-master's, and postbachelor's certificates.

Special study options: academic remediation for entering students, accelerated degree program, adult/continuing education programs, advanced placement credit, cooperative education, distance learning, double majors, English as a second language, honors programs, independent study, internships, off-campus study, part-time degree program, services for LD students, student-designed majors, study abroad, summer session for credit. ***ROTC:*** Army (b).

Unusual degree programs: 3-2 engineering with University of Illinois, Bradley University.

Computers: 2,500 computers/terminals and 2,500 ports are available on campus for general student use. Students can access the following: campus intranet, computer help desk, free student e-mail accounts, online (class) grades, online (class) registration, online (class) schedules. Campuswide network is available. 100% of college-owned or -operated housing units are wired for high-speed Internet access. Wireless service is available via entire campus.

Library: Milner Library.

STUDENT LIFE

Housing options: on-campus residence required through sophomore year; coed, special housing for students with disabilities. Campus housing is university owned. Freshman campus housing is guaranteed.

Activities and organizations: drama/theater group, student-run newspaper, radio and television station, choral group, marching band, national fraternities, national sororities.

Athletics Member NCAA. All Division I except football (Division I-AA). ***Intercollegiate sports:*** baseball M(s), basketball M(s)/W(s), cross-country running M(s)/W(s), golf M(s)/W(s), gymnastics W(s), soccer W(s), softball W(s), swimming and diving W(s), tennis M(s)/W(s), track and field M(s)/W(s), volleyball W(s). ***Intramural sports:*** badminton M(c)/W(c), baseball M(c), basketball M/W(c), cheerleading W(c), cross-country running M(c)/W(c), equestrian sports M(c)/W(c), fencing M(c)/W(c), golf M(c)/W(c), ice hockey M(c), lacrosse M(c)/W(c), rugby M(c)/W(c), soccer M(c)/W(c), softball M(c)/W(c), table tennis M(c)/W(c), tennis M(c)/W(c), triathlon M(c)/W(c), ultimate Frisbee M(c)/W(c), volleyball M(c)/W(c), water polo M(c)/W(c), wrestling M(c)/W(c).

Campus security: 24-hour emergency response devices and patrols, student patrols, late-night transport/escort service, controlled dormitory access.

Student services: health clinic, personal/psychological counseling, women's center, legal services.

COSTS & FINANCIAL AID

Costs (2016–17) ***Tuition:*** state resident $11,108 full-time, $370 per credit hour part-time; nonresident $22,215 full-time, $741 per credit hour part-time. Full-time tuition and fees vary according to degree level. Part-time tuition and fees vary according to degree level. No tuition increase for student's term of enrollment. ***Required fees:*** $2953 full-time, $82 per credit hour part-time. ***Room and board:*** $9850; room only: $5334. Room and board charges vary according to board plan and housing facility. ***Payment plan:*** installment. ***Waivers:*** minority students, senior citizens, and employees or children of employees.

Financial Aid Of all full-time matriculated undergraduates who enrolled in 2014, 13,132 applied for aid, 11,013 were judged to have need, 3,119 had their need fully met. 307 Federal Work-Study jobs (averaging $2034). 51 state and other part-time jobs (averaging $2462). In 2014, 866 non-need-based awards were made. ***Average percent of need met:*** 72. ***Average financial aid package:*** $10,482. ***Average need-based loan:*** $4517. ***Average need-based gift aid:*** $9785. ***Average non-need-based aid:*** $2706. ***Average indebtedness upon graduation:*** $30,373.

APPLYING

Standardized Tests *Required:* SAT or ACT (for admission).

Options: electronic application.

Application fee: $50.

Required for some: interview. ***Recommended:*** essay or personal statement, high school transcript.

Application deadlines: 4/1 (freshmen), rolling (transfers).

Notification: continuous (freshmen), continuous (out-of-state freshmen), continuous (transfers).

CONTACT

Mr. Jeff Mavros, Director of Admissions, Illinois State University, Campus Box 2200, Normal, IL 61790-2200. *Phone:* 309-438-2181. *Toll-free phone:* 800-366-2478. *Fax:* 309-438-3932. *E-mail:* admissions@ilstu.edu.

Illinois Wesleyan University

Bloomington, Illinois

http://www.iwu.edu/

- **Independent** 4-year, founded 1850
- **Suburban** 85-acre campus
- **Endowment** $224.2 million
- **Coed** 1,842 undergraduate students, 99% full-time, 56% women, 44% men
- **Very difficult** entrance level, 62% of applicants were admitted

UNDERGRAD STUDENTS

1,828 full-time, 14 part-time. 13% are from out of state; 4% Black or African American, non-Hispanic/Latino; 7% Hispanic/Latino; 4% Asian, non-Hispanic/Latino; 0.1% Native Hawaiian or other Pacific Islander, non-Hispanic/Latino; 0.1% American Indian or Alaska Native, non-Hispanic/Latino; 3% Two or more races, non-Hispanic/Latino; 2% Race/ethnicity unknown; 9% international; 1% transferred in; 70% live on campus.

Freshmen:
Admission: 3,744 applied, 2,318 admitted, 450 enrolled. ***Average high school GPA:*** 3.73. ***Test scores:*** ACT scores over 18: 100%; ACT scores over 24: 85%; ACT scores over 30: 26%.

Retention: 93% of full-time freshmen returned.

FACULTY
Total: 213, 70% full-time, 82% with terminal degrees.

Student/faculty ratio: 11:1.

ACADEMICS
Calendar: 4-4-1. *Degree:* bachelor's.

Special study options: advanced placement credit, distance learning, double majors, English as a second language, honors programs, independent study, internships, off-campus study, services for LD students, student-designed majors, study abroad. ***ROTC:*** Army (c).

Unusual degree programs: 3-2 engineering with Case Western Reserve University, Northwestern University, Washington University in St. Louis, Dartmouth College, University of Illinois; forestry with Duke University; occupational therapy.

Computers: Students can access the following: campus intranet, computer help desk, free student e-mail accounts, online (class) grades, online (class) registration, online (class) schedules. Campuswide network is available. Wireless service is available via entire campus.
Library: The Ames Library.

STUDENT LIFE
Housing options: on-campus residence required through sophomore year; coed, special housing for students with disabilities. Campus housing is university owned. Freshman campus housing is guaranteed.

Athletics Member NCAA. All Division III. ***Intercollegiate sports:*** baseball M, basketball M/W, cheerleading M(c)/W(c), cross-country running M/W, football M, golf M/W, lacrosse M/W, soccer M/W, softball W, swimming and diving M/W, tennis M/W, track and field M/W, ultimate Frisbee M(c)/W(c), volleyball M(c)/W, water polo M(c). ***Intramural sports:*** badminton M/W, basketball M/W, football M/W, golf M/W, racquetball M/W, soccer M/W, softball M/W, tennis M/W, volleyball M/W.

Campus security: 24-hour emergency response devices and patrols, late-night transport/escort service, controlled dormitory access, emergency response team.

COSTS & FINANCIAL AID
Costs (2017–18) ***Comprehensive fee:*** $56,430 includes full-time tuition ($45,654), mandatory fees ($202), and room and board ($10,574). Part-time tuition: $1427 per credit hour. ***College room only:*** $6622. Room and board charges vary according to housing facility. ***Payment plan:*** installment. ***Waivers:*** employees or children of employees.

Financial Aid Of all full-time matriculated undergraduates who enrolled in 2016, 1,342 applied for aid, 1,101 were judged to have need, 463 had their need fully met. In 2016, 625 non-need-based awards were made. ***Average percent of need met:*** 86. ***Average financial aid package:*** $32,607. ***Average need-based loan:*** $5616. ***Average need-based gift aid:*** $25,892. ***Average non-need-based aid:*** $18,240. ***Average indebtedness upon graduation:*** $34,999.

APPLYING
Standardized Tests *Required:* SAT or ACT (for admission).

Options: electronic application, early admission, early action, deferred entrance.

Required: essay or personal statement, high school transcript, minimum 2.0 GPA, 1 letter of recommendation. ***Recommended:*** minimum 3.0 GPA, 2 letters of recommendation, interview.

CONTACT
Mr. Bob Geraty, Interim Dean of Admissions, Illinois Wesleyan University, PO Box 2900, Bloomington, IL 61702-2900. *Phone:* 309-556-3031. *Toll-free phone:* 800-332-2498. *Fax:* 309-556-3820.
E-mail: iwuadmit@iwu.edu.

Judson University
Elgin, Illinois
http://www.judsonu.edu/

- **Independent Baptist** comprehensive, founded 1963
- **Suburban** 90-acre campus with easy access to Chicago
- **Endowment** $11.2 million
- **Coed** 1,123 undergraduate students, 69% full-time, 59% women, 41% men
- **Moderately difficult** entrance level, 75% of applicants were admitted

UNDERGRAD STUDENTS
777 full-time, 346 part-time. Students come from 30 states and territories; 25 other countries; 16% are from out of state; 10% Black or African American, non-Hispanic/Latino; 17% Hispanic/Latino; 2% Asian, non-Hispanic/Latino; 0.3% Native Hawaiian or other Pacific Islander, non-Hispanic/Latino; 0.3% American Indian or Alaska Native, non-Hispanic/Latino; 2% Two or more races, non-Hispanic/Latino; 12% Race/ethnicity unknown; 4% international; 7% transferred in; 65% live on campus.

Freshmen:
Admission: 676 applied, 506 admitted, 192 enrolled. ***Average high school GPA:*** 3.28. ***Test scores:*** SAT critical reading scores over 500: 50%; SAT math scores over 500: 69%; ACT scores over 18: 88%; SAT critical reading scores over 600: 28%; SAT math scores over 600: 34%; ACT scores over 24: 32%; SAT critical reading scores over 700: 3%; SAT math scores over 700: 3%; ACT scores over 30: 7%.

Retention: 79% of full-time freshmen returned.

FACULTY
Total: 200, 31% full-time, 26% with terminal degrees.

Student/faculty ratio: 10:1.

ACADEMICS
Calendar: semesters. *Degrees:* certificates, associate, bachelor's, master's, and doctoral.

Special study options: academic remediation for entering students, accelerated degree program, adult/continuing education programs, advanced placement credit, distance learning, double majors, honors programs, independent study, internships, off-campus study, part-time degree program, services for LD students, student-designed majors, study abroad, summer session for credit. ***ROTC:*** Army (c).

Computers: 181 computers/terminals are available on campus for general student use. Students can access the following: campus intranet, computer help desk, free student e-mail accounts, online (class) grades, online (class) registration, online (class) schedules. Campuswide network is available. 100% of college-owned or -operated housing units are wired for high-speed Internet access. Wireless service is available via entire campus.
Library: Benjamin P. Browne Library. *Books:* 120,524 (physical), 2,243 (digital/electronic); *Serial titles:* 291 (physical), 46,254 (digital/electronic); *Databases:* 57. Weekly public service hours: 83; students can reserve study rooms.

STUDENT LIFE
Housing options: on-campus residence required through senior year; coed, men-only, women-only, special housing for students with disabilities. Campus housing is university owned. Freshman campus housing is guaranteed.

Activities and organizations: drama/theater group, choral group, Judson Student Organization, University Ministries, Judson Choir, Fellowship of Christian Athletes, Judson Business Society.

Athletics Member NAIA, NCCAA. ***Intercollegiate sports:*** baseball M(s), basketball M(s)/W(s), bowling M(s)/W(s), cheerleading M(s)/W(s), cross-country running M(s)/W(s), golf M(s)/W(s), lacrosse M(s), soccer M(s)/W(s), softball W(s), tennis M(s)/W(s), track and field M(s)/W(s), volleyball W(s). ***Intramural sports:*** basketball M/W, soccer M/W, volleyball M/W.

Campus security: 24-hour emergency response devices and patrols, controlled dormitory access.

Student services: health clinic, personal/psychological counseling.

COSTS & FINANCIAL AID
Costs (2017–18) ***One-time required fee:*** $100. ***Comprehensive fee:*** $39,274 includes full-time tuition ($28,408), mandatory fees ($1026), and room and board ($9840). Full-time tuition and fees vary according to course load and program. Part-time tuition: $1145 per credit. Part-time tuition and fees vary according to course load and program. ***Room and board:*** Room and board charges vary according to board plan. ***Payment plan:*** deferred payment. ***Waivers:*** adult students, senior citizens, and employees or children of employees.

Financial Aid Of all full-time matriculated undergraduates who enrolled in 2013, 615 applied for aid, 615 were judged to have need, 88 had their need fully met. 100 Federal Work-Study jobs (averaging $1075). In 2013, 38 non-need-based awards were made. ***Average percent of need met:*** 55. ***Average financial aid package:*** $18,828. ***Average need-based loan:*** $4993. ***Average need-based gift aid:*** $8976. ***Average non-need-based aid:*** $8514. ***Average indebtedness upon graduation:*** $33,921. ***Financial aid deadline:*** 8/1.

APPLYING
Standardized Tests *Required:* SAT or ACT (for admission).

Options: electronic application.

Application fee: $50.

Required: high school transcript, minimum 2.5 GPA, minimum ACT score of 21, lifestyle statement. ***Required for some:*** essay or personal statement, 1 letter of recommendation.

Application deadlines: rolling (freshmen), rolling (transfers).

Notification: continuous (freshmen), continuous (transfers).

CONTACT
Mrs. Nancy Binger, Executive Director of Enrollment Services, Judson University, 1151 North State Street, Elgin, IL 60123. *Phone:* 847-628-2512. *Toll-free phone:* 800-879-5376. *Fax:* 847-628-2526. *E-mail:* nbinger@judsonu.edu.

Kendall College

Chicago, Illinois

http://www.kendall.edu/

- **Proprietary** 4-year, founded 1934, part of Laureate International Universities
- **Urban** campus with easy access to Chicago
- **Coed** 1,200 undergraduate students, 60% full-time, 75% women, 26% men
- **Minimally difficult** entrance level, 84% of applicants were admitted

UNDERGRAD STUDENTS
717 full-time, 483 part-time. Students come from 34 states and territories; 39 other countries; 13% are from out of state; 16% Black or African American, non-Hispanic/Latino; 16% Hispanic/Latino; 3% Asian, non-Hispanic/Latino; 0.4% Native Hawaiian or other Pacific Islander, non-Hispanic/Latino; 0.3% American Indian or Alaska Native, non-Hispanic/Latino; 2% Two or more races, non-Hispanic/Latino; 1% Race/ethnicity unknown; 19% international; 12% transferred in.

Freshmen:
Admission: 154 applied, 129 admitted, 58 enrolled. ***Average high school GPA:*** 2.93.

Retention: 54% of full-time freshmen returned.

FACULTY
Total: 279, 12% full-time.

Student/faculty ratio: 8:1.

ACADEMICS
Calendar: quarters. *Degrees:* associate and bachelor's.

Special study options: academic remediation for entering students, accelerated degree program, advanced placement credit, distance learning, English as a second language, independent study, internships, off-campus study, part-time degree program, services for LD students, study abroad, summer session for credit.

Computers: 60 computers/terminals are available on campus for general student use. Students can access the following: campus intranet, computer help desk, free student e-mail accounts, online (class) grades, online (class) registration, online (class) schedules. Campuswide network is available. Wireless service is available via entire campus.

Library: Iva Freeman Library. *Books:* 11,484 (physical); *Serial titles:* 56 (physical); *Databases:* 23. Weekly public service hours: 61.

STUDENT LIFE
Housing options: coed. Campus housing is leased by the school.

Activities and organizations: International Club, SEED Club, Soccer Club, Meditation Club, Kendall Cares Community Service.

Campus security: 24-hour emergency response devices and patrols, controlled dormitory access, 24-hour security at dorms.

Student services: personal/psychological counseling.

COSTS & FINANCIAL AID
Costs (2016–17) ***Comprehensive fee:*** $30,913 includes full-time tuition ($18,793), mandatory fees ($1035), and room and board ($11,085). Full-time tuition and fees vary according to course load and program. Part-time tuition and fees vary according to course load and program. ***College room only:*** $10,500. ***Payment plan:*** installment. ***Waivers:*** employees or children of employees.

Financial Aid Of all full-time matriculated undergraduates who enrolled in 2010, 941 applied for aid, 840 were judged to have need, 13 had their need fully met. In 2010, 23 non-need-based awards were made. ***Average percent of need met:*** 28. ***Average financial aid package:*** $9732. ***Average need-based loan:*** $4521. ***Average need-based gift aid:*** $6690. ***Average non-need-based aid:*** $2379.

APPLYING
Standardized Tests *Required for some:* SAT or ACT (for admission).

Options: electronic application, deferred entrance.

Application fee: $25.

Required: essay or personal statement, high school transcript, interview. ***Recommended:*** minimum 2.0 GPA.

Application deadlines: rolling (freshmen), rolling (transfers).

Notification: continuous (freshmen), continuous (transfers).

CONTACT
Ms. Angela Batchelor, Manager of Enrollment, Kendall College, 900 North Branch Street, Chicago, IL 60642. *Toll-free phone:* 888-90-KENDALL. *E-mail:* info@kendall.edu.

Knox College

Galesburg, Illinois

http://www.knox.edu/

- **Independent** 4-year, founded 1837
- **Small-town** 82-acre campus with easy access to Peoria, Quad Cities
- **Endowment** $123.7 million
- **Coed** 1,357 undergraduate students, 98% full-time, 59% women, 41% men
- **Very difficult** entrance level, 65% of applicants were admitted

UNDERGRAD STUDENTS
1,327 full-time, 30 part-time. Students come from 43 states and territories; 43 other countries; 44% are from out of state; 8% Black or African American, non-Hispanic/Latino; 14% Hispanic/Latino; 6% Asian, non-Hispanic/Latino; 5% Two or more races, non-Hispanic/Latino; 3% Race/ethnicity unknown; 14% international; 2% transferred in; 90% live on campus.

Freshmen:
Admission: 3,514 applied, 2,292 admitted, 347 enrolled. ***Test scores:*** SAT critical reading scores over 500: 76%; SAT math scores over 500: 83%; SAT writing scores over 500: 82%; ACT scores over 18: 99%; SAT critical reading scores over 600: 38%; SAT math scores over 600: 61%; SAT writing scores over 600: 32%; ACT scores over 24: 77%; SAT critical reading scores over 700: 10%; SAT math scores over 700: 18%; SAT writing scores over 700: 7%; ACT scores over 30: 30%.

Retention: 87% of full-time freshmen returned.

FACULTY
Total: 135, 83% full-time, 87% with terminal degrees.
Student/faculty ratio: 11:1.

ACADEMICS
Calendar: trimesters. *Degree:* bachelor's.
Special study options: advanced placement credit, double majors, English as a second language, honors programs, independent study, internships, off-campus study, part-time degree program, services for LD students, student-designed majors, study abroad.
Unusual degree programs: 3-2 engineering with University of Illinois at Urbana–Champaign, Washington University in St. Louis, Columbia University, Rensselaer Polytechnic Institute; forestry with Duke University; nursing with Rush University.
Computers: 275 computers/terminals are available on campus for general student use. Students can access the following: campus intranet, computer help desk, free student e-mail accounts, online (class) grades, online (class) registration, online (class) schedules, transcripts, learning management system. Campuswide network is available. 100% of college-owned or -operated housing units are wired for high-speed Internet access. Wireless service is available via entire campus.
Library: Henry M. Seymour Library plus 1 other. *Books:* 338,946 (physical), 10,259 (digital/electronic); *Serial titles:* 125 (physical), 15,640 (digital/electronic); *Databases:* 79. Weekly public service hours: 106; students can reserve study rooms.

STUDENT LIFE
Housing options: on-campus residence required through sophomore year; coed, men-only, women-only, special housing for students with disabilities. Campus housing is university owned. Freshman campus housing is guaranteed.
Activities and organizations: drama/theater group, student-run newspaper, radio station, choral group, Student-Run Radio Station (WVKC), International Club, Student Newspaper (The Knox Student), Common Ground, Terpsichore (Dance Collective), national fraternities, national sororities.
Athletics Member NCAA. All Division III. ***Intercollegiate sports:*** baseball M, basketball M/W, cross-country running M/W, football M, golf M/W, soccer M/W, softball W, swimming and diving M/W, tennis M/W, track and field M/W, volleyball W. ***Intramural sports:*** basketball M/W, soccer M/W, ultimate Frisbee M(c)/W(c), volleyball M/W, water polo M(c)/W(c).
Campus security: 24-hour emergency response devices and patrols, late-night transport/escort service.
Student services: health clinic, personal/psychological counseling.

COSTS & FINANCIAL AID
Costs (2017–18) ***Comprehensive fee:*** $54,624 includes full-time tuition ($44,191), mandatory fees ($767), and room and board ($9666). Full-time tuition and fees vary according to course load. Part-time tuition and fees vary according to course load. ***College room only:*** $4854. Room and board charges vary according to housing facility. ***Payment plan:*** installment. ***Waivers:*** employees or children of employees.
Financial Aid Of all full-time matriculated undergraduates who enrolled in 2016, 1,122 applied for aid, 1,042 were judged to have need, 269 had their need fully met. In 2016, 275 non-need-based awards were made. ***Average percent of need met:*** 87. ***Average financial aid package:*** $36,532. ***Average need-based loan:*** $5250. ***Average need-based gift aid:*** $31,006. ***Average non-need-based aid:*** $19,121. ***Average indebtedness upon graduation:*** $30,368.

APPLYING
Standardized Tests *Required for some:* SAT or ACT (for admission).
Options: electronic application, early admission, early decision, early action, deferred entrance.
Application fee: $50.
Required: essay or personal statement, high school transcript, 2 letters of recommendation. ***Recommended:*** interview.
Application deadlines: 1/15 (freshmen), 4/1 (transfers), 12/1 (early action).
Early decision deadline: 11/1.
Notification: 3/15 (freshmen), 5/1 (transfers), 11/15 (early decision), 1/15 (early action).

CONTACT
Mr. Paul Steenis, Dean of Admission, Knox College, 2 East South Street, Campus Box148, Galesburg, IL 61401. *Phone:* 309-341-7100. *Toll-free phone:* 800-678-KNOX. *Fax:* 309-341-7070.
E-mail: admission@knox.edu.

Lake Forest College

Lake Forest, Illinois

http://www.lakeforest.edu/

- **Independent** comprehensive, founded 1857
- **Suburban** 107-acre campus with easy access to Chicago
- **Endowment** $83.9 million
- **Coed** 1,540 undergraduate students, 99% full-time, 57% women, 43% men
- **Moderately difficult** entrance level, 57% of applicants were admitted

UNDERGRAD STUDENTS
1,524 full-time, 16 part-time. Students come from 44 states and territories; 71 other countries; 36% are from out of state; 6% Black or African American, non-Hispanic/Latino; 16% Hispanic/Latino; 5% Asian, non-Hispanic/Latino; 0.3% American Indian or Alaska Native, non-Hispanic/Latino; 3% Two or more races, non-Hispanic/Latino; 4% Race/ethnicity unknown; 8% international; 4% transferred in; 73% live on campus.

Freshmen:
Admission: 4,227 applied, 2,407 admitted, 360 enrolled. ***Average high school GPA:*** 3.62. ***Test scores:*** SAT critical reading scores over 500: 86%; SAT math scores over 500: 84%; SAT writing scores over 500: 80%; ACT scores over 18: 100%; SAT critical reading scores over 600: 30%; SAT math scores over 600: 28%; SAT writing scores over 600: 27%; ACT scores over 24: 75%; SAT critical reading scores over 700: 4%; SAT math scores over 700: 2%; SAT writing scores over 700: 4%; ACT scores over 30: 25%.
Retention: 83% of full-time freshmen returned.

FACULTY
Total: 186, 52% full-time, 73% with terminal degrees.
Student/faculty ratio: 12:1.

ACADEMICS
Calendar: semesters. *Degrees:* bachelor's, master's, and postbachelor's certificates.
Special study options: accelerated degree program, advanced placement credit, double majors, honors programs, independent study, internships, off-campus study, part-time degree program, services for LD students, student-designed majors, study abroad, summer session for credit.
Unusual degree programs: 3-2 engineering with Washington University in St. Louis.
Computers: 300 computers/terminals and 2,000 ports are available on campus for general student use. Students can access the following: campus intranet, computer help desk, free student e-mail accounts, online (class) grades, online (class) registration, online (class) schedules, file storage. Campuswide network is available. 100% of college-owned or -operated housing units are wired for high-speed Internet access. Wireless service is available via entire campus.
Library: Donnelley and Lee Library. *Books:* 294,734 (physical), 169,997 (digital/electronic); *Serial titles:* 49,666 (physical), 68,879 (digital/electronic); *Databases:* 72. Weekly public service hours: 91; study areas open 24 hours, 5-7 days a week; students can reserve study rooms.

STUDENT LIFE
Housing options: on-campus residence required through junior year; coed. Campus housing is university owned. Freshman applicants given priority for college housing.
Activities and organizations: drama/theater group, student-run newspaper, radio station, choral group, Student Government, Athletic Council, United Black Association, Alpha Phi, PRIDE, national fraternities, national sororities.
Athletics Member NCAA. All Division III. ***Intercollegiate sports:*** archery M(c)/W(c), basketball M/W, cheerleading M(c)/W(c), cross-country running M/W, equestrian sports M(c)/W(c), fencing M(c)/W(c), football M, golf M/W, ice hockey M/W, lacrosse M(c)/W(c), rugby M(c)/W(c), sailing M(c)/W(c), soccer M/W, softball W, swimming and

diving M/W, tennis M/W, track and field M(c)/W(c), ultimate Frisbee M(c)/W(c), volleyball W, water polo M(c)/W(c). ***Intramural sports:*** badminton M/W, basketball M/W, ice hockey M/W, soccer M/W, table tennis M/W, volleyball M/W.

Campus security: 24-hour emergency response devices and patrols, student patrols, late-night transport/escort service, controlled dormitory access.

Student services: health clinic, personal/psychological counseling.

COSTS & FINANCIAL AID

Costs (2017–18) ***Comprehensive fee:*** $55,600 includes full-time tuition ($44,824), mandatory fees ($724), and room and board ($10,052). ***College room only:*** $4800. Room and board charges vary according to board plan and housing facility. ***Payment plan:*** installment. ***Waivers:*** employees or children of employees.

Financial Aid ***Financial aid deadline:*** 5/1.

APPLYING

Standardized Tests *Recommended:* SAT or ACT (for admission).

Options: electronic application, early decision, early action, deferred entrance.

Required: essay or personal statement, high school transcript, 1 letter of recommendation. ***Recommended:*** interview.

Application deadlines: 2/15 (freshmen), 1/1 (transfers), 11/15 (early action).

Early decision deadline: 11/15.

Notification: continuous until 3/10 (freshmen), 12/15 (early decision), 12/15 (early action).

CONTACT

Christopher Ellertson, Vice President for Enrollment, Lake Forest College, 555 North Sheridan Road, Lake Forest, IL 60045-2338. *Phone:* 847-735-5000. *Toll-free phone:* 800-828-4751. *Fax:* 847-735-6271. *E-mail:* admissions@lakeforest.edu.

Lakeview College of Nursing

Danville, Illinois

http://www.lakeviewcol.edu/

- **Independent** upper-level, founded 1987
- **Small-town** 1-acre campus
- **Coed, primarily women** 236 undergraduate students, 84% full-time, 82% women, 18% men
- **Moderately difficult** entrance level

UNDERGRAD STUDENTS

199 full-time, 37 part-time. Students come from 1 other state; 9% Black or African American, non-Hispanic/Latino; 3% Hispanic/Latino; 6% Asian, non-Hispanic/Latino; 0.4% Native Hawaiian or other Pacific Islander, non-Hispanic/Latino; 1% Two or more races, non-Hispanic/Latino; 0.4% Race/ethnicity unknown.

FACULTY

Total: 29, 69% full-time.

Student/faculty ratio: 12:1.

ACADEMICS

Calendar: semesters. *Degree:* bachelor's.

Special study options: academic remediation for entering students, accelerated degree program, off-campus study, part-time degree program, services for LD students, summer session for credit. ***ROTC:*** Army (c), Air Force (c).

Computers: 61 computers/terminals are available on campus for general student use. Students can access the following: free student e-mail accounts, online (class) grades, online (class) schedules. Campuswide network is available. Wireless service is available via classrooms, computer centers, computer labs, libraries, student centers.

Library: Lakeview College of Nursing Library plus 1 other.

STUDENT LIFE

Housing options: college housing not available.

Campus security: 24-hour emergency response devices and patrols.

COSTS & FINANCIAL AID

Costs (2017–18) ***Tuition:*** $14,080 full-time, $440 per credit hour part-time. Full-time tuition and fees vary according to course level, course load, and location. Part-time tuition and fees vary according to course level, course load, and location. ***Required fees:*** $2080 full-time, $65 per credit hour part-time. ***Payment plan:*** installment. ***Waivers:*** employees or children of employees.

Financial Aid Of all full-time matriculated undergraduates who enrolled in 2014, 419 applied for aid, 386 were judged to have need. In 2014, 6 non-need-based awards were made. ***Average percent of need met:*** 80. ***Average financial aid package:*** $22,950. ***Average need-based loan:*** $5500. ***Average need-based gift aid:*** $5730. ***Average non-need-based aid:*** $500.

APPLYING

Standardized Tests *Required:* Nursing Admission Test (for admission).

Options: early admission.

Application fee: $100.

CONTACT

Admissions Office, Lakeview College of Nursing, 903 North Logan Avenue, Danville, IL 61832. *Phone:* 217-709-0920. *Fax:* 217-709-0953. *E-mail:* admission@lakeviewcol.edu.

Lewis University

Romeoville, Illinois

http://www.lewisu.edu/

- **Independent** comprehensive, founded 1932, affiliated with Roman Catholic Church
- **Suburban** 410-acre campus with easy access to Chicago
- **Endowment** $61.6 million
- **Coed** 4,553 undergraduate students, 82% full-time, 53% women, 47% men
- **Moderately difficult** entrance level, 59% of applicants were admitted

UNDERGRAD STUDENTS

3,744 full-time, 809 part-time. Students come from 35 states and territories; 24 other countries; 8% are from out of state; 6% Black or African American, non-Hispanic/Latino; 19% Hispanic/Latino; 4% Asian, non-Hispanic/Latino; 0.1% Native Hawaiian or other Pacific Islander, non-Hispanic/Latino; 0.1% American Indian or Alaska Native, non-Hispanic/Latino; 3% Two or more races, non-Hispanic/Latino; 5% Race/ethnicity unknown; 1% international; 11% transferred in; 24% live on campus.

Freshmen:

Admission: 6,199 applied, 3,669 admitted, 642 enrolled. ***Average high school GPA:*** 3.4. ***Test scores:*** SAT critical reading scores over 500: 55%; SAT math scores over 500: 75%; ACT scores over 18: 97%; SAT critical reading scores over 600: 25%; SAT math scores over 600: 30%; ACT scores over 24: 42%; SAT critical reading scores over 700: 5%; SAT math scores over 700: 5%; ACT scores over 30: 6%.

Retention: 79% of full-time freshmen returned.

FACULTY

Total: 657, 35% full-time, 40% with terminal degrees.

Student/faculty ratio: 13:1.

ACADEMICS

Calendar: semesters. *Degrees:* certificates, associate, bachelor's, master's, doctoral, post-master's, and postbachelor's certificates.

Special study options: academic remediation for entering students, accelerated degree program, adult/continuing education programs, advanced placement credit, distance learning, double majors, English as a second language, honors programs, independent study, internships, off-campus study, part-time degree program, services for LD students, student-designed majors, study abroad, summer session for credit. ***ROTC:*** Army (c), Air Force (c).

Computers: 600 computers/terminals are available on campus for general student use. Students can access the following: campus intranet, computer help desk, free student e-mail accounts, online (class) grades, online (class) registration, online (class) schedules, online help, online billing, online financial aid, online payments, online housing application, online application for graduation, course management system. Campuswide network is available. 100% of college-owned or -operated housing units are wired for high-speed Internet access. Wireless service is available via entire campus.

Library: Lewis University Library. *Books:* 141,150 (physical), 204,209 (digital/electronic); *Serial titles:* 13,419 (physical), 140,108 (digital/electronic); *Databases:* 121. Weekly public service hours: 102; students can reserve study rooms.

STUDENT LIFE

Housing options: coed. Campus housing is university owned. Freshman campus housing is guaranteed.

Activities and organizations: drama/theater group, student-run newspaper, radio and television station, choral group, Student Governing Board, Student Nurses Association, Latin American Student Organization, Theta Kappa Pi Sorority, Delta Sigma Pi (business fraternity), national fraternities, national sororities.

Athletics Member NCAA. All Division II except volleyball (Division I). ***Intercollegiate sports:*** baseball M(s), basketball M(s)/W(s), cheerleading W(s)(c), cross-country running M(s)/W(s), golf M(s)/W(s), ice hockey M(c), lacrosse M(c)/W(c), rugby M(c)/W(c), skiing (downhill) M(c)/W(c), soccer M(s)/W(s), softball W(s), swimming and diving M(s)/W(s), tennis M(s)/W(s), track and field M(s)/W(s), ultimate Frisbee M(c)/W(c), volleyball M(s)/W(s), water polo M(c)/W(c). ***Intramural sports:*** badminton M/W, baseball M(c), basketball M/W, bowling M/W, football M/W, rugby M/W, soccer M(c)/W(c), softball M/W, table tennis M/W, volleyball M(c)/W.

Campus security: 24-hour emergency response devices and patrols, student patrols, late-night transport/escort service, controlled dormitory access.

Student services: health clinic, personal/psychological counseling.

COSTS & FINANCIAL AID

Costs (2017–18) ***Comprehensive fee:*** $41,710 includes full-time tuition ($31,100), mandatory fees ($150), and room and board ($10,460). Full-time tuition and fees vary according to course load, location, and program. Part-time tuition: $913 per credit. Part-time tuition and fees vary according to course load, location, and program. ***Required fees:*** $75 per term part-time. ***College room only:*** $6560. Room and board charges vary according to board plan and housing facility. ***Payment plan:*** installment. ***Waivers:*** children of alumni, adult students, and employees or children of employees.

Financial Aid Of all full-time matriculated undergraduates who enrolled in 2016, 3,212 applied for aid, 2,865 were judged to have need, 552 had their need fully met. In 2016, 609 non-need-based awards were made. ***Average percent of need met:*** 85. ***Average financial aid package:*** $24,080. ***Average need-based loan:*** $4430. ***Average need-based gift aid:*** $14,923. ***Average non-need-based aid:*** $10,919. ***Average indebtedness upon graduation:*** $36,073. ***Financial aid deadline:*** 5/1.

APPLYING

Standardized Tests *Required:* SAT or ACT (for admission).

Options: electronic application, deferred entrance.

Application fee: $40.

Required: high school transcript, minimum 2.0 GPA. ***Required for some:*** interview.

Application deadlines: 8/1 (freshmen), rolling (transfers).

Notification: continuous (freshmen), continuous (transfers).

CONTACT

Mr. Ryan Cockerill, Director of Admission, Lewis University, Unit #297, One University Parkway, Romeoville, IL 60446. *Phone:* 815-836-5237. *Toll-free phone:* 800-897-9000. *Fax:* 815-836-5002. *E-mail:* cockerry@lewisu.edu.

Lincoln Christian University

Lincoln, Illinois

http://www.lincolnchristian.edu/

- **Independent** comprehensive, founded 1944, affiliated with Christian Churches and Churches of Christ
- **Small-town** 100-acre campus
- **Endowment** $5.0 million
- **Coed** 528 undergraduate students, 79% full-time, 46% women, 54% men
- **Moderately difficult** entrance level, 56% of applicants were admitted

UNDERGRAD STUDENTS

417 full-time, 111 part-time. Students come from 23 states and territories; 4 other countries; 29% are from out of state; 9% Black or African American, non-Hispanic/Latino; 4% Hispanic/Latino; 1% Asian, non-Hispanic/Latino; 1% American Indian or Alaska Native, non-Hispanic/Latino; 2% Two or more races, non-Hispanic/Latino; 0.2% Race/ethnicity unknown; 3% international; 5% transferred in; 51% live on campus.

Freshmen:

Admission: 234 applied, 130 admitted, 91 enrolled. ***Average high school GPA:*** 2.8. ***Test scores:*** SAT critical reading scores over 500: 25%; SAT math scores over 500: 50%; SAT writing scores over 500: 25%; ACT scores over 18: 87%; SAT math scores over 600: 25%; SAT writing scores over 600: 25%; ACT scores over 24: 28%; ACT scores over 30: 7%.

Retention: 65% of full-time freshmen returned.

FACULTY

Total: 91, 37% full-time, 44% with terminal degrees.

Student/faculty ratio: 15:1.

ACADEMICS

Calendar: semesters. *Degrees:* associate, bachelor's, master's, and doctoral.

Special study options: academic remediation for entering students, adult/continuing education programs, advanced placement credit, cooperative education, distance learning, double majors, external degree program, honors programs, independent study, internships, off-campus study, part-time degree program, services for LD students, study abroad, summer session for credit.

Computers: 51 computers/terminals are available on campus for general student use. Students can access the following: campus intranet, computer help desk, free student e-mail accounts, online (class) grades, online (class) registration, online (class) schedules. Campuswide network is available. 100% of college-owned or -operated housing units are wired for high-speed Internet access. Wireless service is available via entire campus.

Library: Jessie Eury Library. *Books:* 92,813 (physical), 55,082 (digital/electronic); *Serial titles:* 719 (physical), 15,442 (digital/electronic); *Databases:* 52. Weekly public service hours: 82.

STUDENT LIFE

Housing options: on-campus residence required through senior year; men-only, women-only. Campus housing is university owned. Freshman campus housing is guaranteed.

Activities and organizations: drama/theater group, choral group, Chorale, Student Cabinet, American Association of Christian Counselors (AACC) - Student Chapter, Cheerleading.

Athletics Member NAIA, NCCAA. ***Intercollegiate sports:*** baseball M(s), basketball M(s)/W(s), soccer M(s)/W(s), volleyball W(s). ***Intramural sports:*** badminton M/W, basketball M/W, soccer M/W, ultimate Frisbee M/W, volleyball M/W.

Campus security: 24-hour emergency response devices, student patrols, controlled dormitory access, 24-hour emergency alert hotline.

Student services: personal/psychological counseling.

COSTS & FINANCIAL AID

Costs (2017–18) ***Comprehensive fee:*** $20,584 includes full-time tuition ($13,020) and room and board ($7564). Part-time tuition: $434 per credit hour. ***College room only:*** $3600. ***Payment plan:*** installment. ***Waivers:*** senior citizens and employees or children of employees.

Financial Aid Of all full-time matriculated undergraduates who enrolled in 2015, 392 applied for aid, 349 were judged to have need, 22 had their need fully met. 60 Federal Work-Study jobs (averaging $1945). 120 state and other part-time jobs (averaging $1910). In 2015, 64 non-need-based awards were made. ***Average percent of need met:*** 52. ***Average financial aid package:*** $10,199. ***Average need-based loan:*** $3805. ***Average need-based gift aid:*** $7018. ***Average non-need-based aid:*** $2866. ***Average indebtedness upon graduation:*** $32,138.

APPLYING

Standardized Tests *Required:* SAT or ACT (for admission).

Options: electronic application, deferred entrance.

Required: essay or personal statement, high school transcript, 3 letters of recommendation. ***Required for some:*** interview.

Application deadlines: rolling (freshmen), rolling (transfers).

Notification: continuous (freshmen), continuous (transfers).

CONTACT

Mrs. Mary K. Davis, Admissions Office Manager, Lincoln Christian University, 100 Campus View Drive, Lincoln, IL 62656. *Phone:* 217-732-3168 Ext. 2251. *Toll-free phone:* 888-522-5228. *Fax:* 217-732-4199. *E-mail:* enroll@lincolnchristian.edu.

Lincoln College

Lincoln, Illinois

http://www.lincolncollege.edu/

- **Independent** primarily 2-year, founded 1865
- **Small-town** 42-acre campus
- **Coed** 1,304 undergraduate students
- **Minimally difficult** entrance level, 68% of applicants were admitted

UNDERGRAD STUDENTS

4% are from out of state.

Freshmen:

Admission: 1,537 applied, 1,045 admitted.

FACULTY

Student/faculty ratio: 15:1.

ACADEMICS

Calendar: semesters. *Degrees:* associate and bachelor's.

Special study options: academic remediation for entering students, accelerated degree program, freshman honors college, honors programs, independent study, part-time degree program, summer session for credit.

Computers: Students can access the following: campus intranet, computer help desk, free student e-mail accounts, online (class) grades, online (class) schedules. Campuswide network is available. Wireless service is available via entire campus.

Library: McKinstry Library.

STUDENT LIFE

Housing options: on-campus residence required through sophomore year; men-only, women-only. Campus housing is university owned. Freshman campus housing is guaranteed.

Activities and organizations: drama/theater group, student-run radio and television station, choral group, Black Student Union, Phi Theta Kappa, Purple Pulse, Student Activities Board, Woment of Worth.

Athletics Member NJCAA. ***Intercollegiate sports:*** baseball M(s), basketball M(s)/W(s), cheerleading M(s)(c)/W(s)(c), cross-country running M(s)/W(s), golf M(s)/W(s), soccer M(s)/W(s), softball W(s), swimming and diving M(s)/W(s), track and field M(s)/W(s), volleyball M(s)(c)/W(s), wrestling M(s). ***Intramural sports:*** basketball M/W, football M/W, sand volleyball M/W, softball M/W, table tennis M/W.

Campus security: 24-hour emergency response devices and patrols, controlled dormitory access.

Student services: health clinic, personal/psychological counseling.

COSTS & FINANCIAL AID

Costs (2017–18) ***One-time required fee:*** $50. ***Tuition:*** $300 per credit hour part-time. No tuition increase for student's term of enrollment. ***Room only:*** Room and board charges vary according to housing facility. ***Payment plan:*** installment.

Financial Aid Of all full-time matriculated undergraduates who enrolled in 2015, 200 Federal Work-Study jobs (averaging $900).

APPLYING

Standardized Tests *Required:* SAT or ACT (for admission).

Options: electronic application, early admission, deferred entrance.

Required: high school transcript, minimum 2.0 GPA. ***Required for some:*** essay or personal statement, 2 letters of recommendation, interview.

Application deadlines: rolling (freshmen), rolling (out-of-state freshmen), rolling (transfers).

CONTACT

Lincoln College, 300 Keokuk Street, Lincoln, IL 62656-1699. *Phone:* 217-735-7251 Ext. 7251. *Toll-free phone:* 800-569-0558.

Lincoln College–Normal

Normal, Illinois

http://www.lincolncollege.edu/normal/

- **Independent** 4-year, founded 1865
- **Suburban** 10-acre campus with easy access to Bloomington, Normal, IL
- **Coed** 527 undergraduate students, 55% full-time, 52% women, 48% men
- **Minimally difficult** entrance level, 72% of applicants were admitted

UNDERGRAD STUDENTS

290 full-time, 237 part-time. Students come from 9 states and territories; 1 other country; 2% are from out of state.

Freshmen:

Admission: 1,417 applied, 1,017 admitted. ***Average high school GPA:*** 2.3. ***Test scores:*** ACT scores over 18: 31%; ACT scores over 24: 3%.

FACULTY

Total: 58, 16% full-time.

Student/faculty ratio: 14:1.

ACADEMICS

Calendar: some programs are semester; some are continuous. *Degrees:* certificates, associate, and bachelor's.

Special study options: academic remediation for entering students, accelerated degree program, adult/continuing education programs, cooperative education, distance learning, honors programs, independent study, internships, part-time degree program, summer session for credit.

Computers: 63 computers/terminals and 187 ports are available on campus for general student use. Students can access the following: computer help desk, free student e-mail accounts, online (class) grades, online (class) schedules. Campuswide network is available. 100% of college-owned or -operated housing units are wired for high-speed Internet access. Wireless service is available via entire campus.

Library: Milner Library at Illinois State University.

STUDENT LIFE

Housing options: college housing not available.

Activities and organizations: Residence Hall Association, MCC Student Government, Black Student Union, BACCHUS.

Campus security: controlled dormitory access.

FINANCIAL AID

Financial Aid Of all full-time matriculated undergraduates who enrolled in 2014, 612 applied for aid, 589 were judged to have need, 32 had their need fully met. 127 Federal Work-Study jobs (averaging $1074). In 2014, 50 non-need-based awards were made. ***Average percent of need met:*** 61. ***Average financial aid package:*** $18,824. ***Average need-based loan:*** $3773. ***Average need-based gift aid:*** $14,985. ***Average non-need-based aid:*** $4650.

APPLYING

Standardized Tests *Required for some:* SAT or ACT (for admission).

Options: electronic application, deferred entrance.

Application fee: $25.

Required: high school transcript. ***Required for some:*** essay or personal statement, 1 letter of recommendation, interview. ***Recommended:*** minimum 2.0 GPA.

Application deadlines: 9/1 (freshmen), rolling (out-of-state freshmen), 9/1 (transfers).

Notification: continuous (freshmen), continuous (out-of-state freshmen), continuous (transfers).

CONTACT

Mr. Steve Puck, Director of Admissions, Lincoln College–Normal, 715 West Raab Road, Normal, IL 61761. *Phone:* 309-268-4314. *Toll-free phone:* 800-569-0558. *Fax:* 309-862-3352. *E-mail:* spuck@lincolncollege.edu.

Loyola University Chicago

Chicago, Illinois

http://www.luc.edu/

- **Independent Roman Catholic (Jesuit)** university, founded 1870
- **Urban** 105-acre campus
- **Endowment** $533.6 million
- **Coed** 11,129 undergraduate students, 93% full-time, 66% women, 34% men
- **Moderately difficult** entrance level, 73% of applicants were admitted

UNDERGRAD STUDENTS
10,362 full-time, 767 part-time. Students come from 52 states and territories; 106 other countries; 35% are from out of state; 5% Black or African American, non-Hispanic/Latino; 15% Hispanic/Latino; 12% Asian, non-Hispanic/Latino; 0.3% Native Hawaiian or other Pacific Islander, non-Hispanic/Latino; 0.1% American Indian or Alaska Native, non-Hispanic/Latino; 4% Two or more races, non-Hispanic/Latino; 1% Race/ethnicity unknown; 5% international; 5% transferred in; 40% live on campus.

Freshmen:
Admission: 22,712 applied, 16,482 admitted, 2,622 enrolled. ***Average high school GPA:*** 3.65. ***Test scores:*** SAT critical reading scores over 500: 83%; SAT math scores over 500: 82%; SAT writing scores over 500: 80%; ACT scores over 18: 100%; SAT critical reading scores over 600: 43%; SAT math scores over 600: 38%; SAT writing scores over 600: 39%; ACT scores over 24: 78%; SAT critical reading scores over 700: 9%; SAT math scores over 700: 6%; SAT writing scores over 700: 7%; ACT scores over 30: 21%.

Retention: 82% of full-time freshmen returned.

FACULTY
Total: 1,513, 53% full-time.
Student/faculty ratio: 14:1.

ACADEMICS
Calendar: semesters. *Degrees:* certificates, associate, bachelor's, master's, doctoral, post-master's, and postbachelor's certificates (also offers adult part-time program with significant enrollment not reflected in profile).

Special study options: accelerated degree program, adult/continuing education programs, advanced placement credit, cooperative education, distance learning, double majors, English as a second language, freshman honors college, honors programs, independent study, internships, off-campus study, part-time degree program, services for LD students, study abroad, summer session for credit. ***ROTC:*** Army (b), Navy (c), Air Force (c).

Unusual degree programs: 3-2 business administration; engineering; social work; political science, sociology, psychology/applied social psychology, computers, biology, accounting, information technology, criminal justice and criminology.

Computers: 1,300 computers/terminals are available on campus for general student use. Students can access the following: campus intranet, computer help desk, free student e-mail accounts, online (class) grades, online (class) registration, online (class) schedules. Campuswide network is available. 100% of college-owned or -operated housing units are wired for high-speed Internet access. Wireless service is available via entire campus.

Library: Cudahy Library plus 7 others. *Books:* 1.2 million (physical), 669,326 (digital/electronic); *Serial titles:* 2,310 (physical), 57,961 (digital/electronic); *Databases:* 534. Weekly public service hours: 144; study areas open 24 hours, 5-7 days a week; students can reserve study rooms.

STUDENT LIFE
Housing options: on-campus residence required through sophomore year; coed, special housing for students with disabilities. Campus housing is university owned. Freshman campus housing is guaranteed.

Activities and organizations: drama/theater group, student-run newspaper, radio station, Panhellenic Council, National Society of Collegiate Scholars, Vegetarian and Vegan Society, Interfraternity Council, American Medical Student Association, national fraternities, national sororities.

Athletics Member NCAA. All Division I. ***Intercollegiate sports:*** basketball M(s)/W(s), cross-country running M(s)/W(s), golf M(s)/W(s), soccer M(s)/W(s), softball W(s), track and field M(s)/W(s), volleyball M(s)/W(s). ***Intramural sports:*** badminton M/W, baseball M(c), basketball M/W, cross-country running M(c)/W(c), field hockey W(c), football M(c)/W(c), golf M(c)/W(c), ice hockey M(c)/W(c), lacrosse M(c)/W(c), racquetball M/W, rugby M(c)/W(c), soccer M(c)/W(c), softball W(c), swimming and diving M(c)/W(c), table tennis M/W, tennis M(c)/W(c), ultimate Frisbee M(c)/W(c), volleyball M(c)/W(c), water polo M(c)/W(c).

Campus security: 24-hour emergency response devices, late-night transport/escort service, controlled dormitory access, Loyola Alert (special service to provide personalized, time-sensitive alerts to students, faculty, staff and other personnel).

Student services: health clinic, personal/psychological counseling, women's center.

COSTS & FINANCIAL AID
Costs (2017–18) ***Comprehensive fee:*** $56,908 includes full-time tuition ($41,470), mandatory fees ($1358), and room and board ($14,080). Full-time tuition and fees vary according to degree level, location, program, and student level. Part-time tuition: $770 per credit. Part-time tuition and fees vary according to course load. ***Required fees:*** $350 per year part-time. ***College room only:*** $8800. Room and board charges vary according to board plan, housing facility, and location. ***Payment plans:*** installment, deferred payment. ***Waivers:*** senior citizens and employees or children of employees.

Financial Aid Of all full-time matriculated undergraduates who enrolled in 2016, 7,715 applied for aid, 6,795 were judged to have need, 966 had their need fully met. 5,014 Federal Work-Study jobs (averaging $2780). In 2016, 2799 non-need-based awards were made. ***Average percent of need met:*** 80. ***Average financial aid package:*** $33,514. ***Average need-based loan:*** $4521. ***Average need-based gift aid:*** $20,311. ***Average non-need-based aid:*** $15,184. ***Average indebtedness upon graduation:*** $33,319.

APPLYING
Standardized Tests *Required:* SAT or ACT (for admission).
Options: electronic application.
Required: essay or personal statement, high school transcript, minimum 2.0 GPA. ***Recommended:*** letters of recommendation, interview.
Notification: continuous (freshmen), continuous (transfers).

CONTACT
Ms. Erin Moriarty, Director of Undergraduate Admissions, Loyola University Chicago, 1032 West Sheridan Road, Chicago, IL 60660.
Phone: 773-508-3079. *Toll-free phone:* 800-262-2373.
E-mail: admission@luc.edu.

MacMurray College

Jacksonville, Illinois

http://www.mac.edu/

- **Independent United Methodist** 4-year, founded 1846
- **Small-town** 60-acre campus
- **Endowment** $13.5 million
- **Coed** 552 undergraduate students, 97% full-time, 50% women, 50% men
- **Moderately difficult** entrance level, 54% of applicants were admitted

UNDERGRAD STUDENTS
536 full-time, 16 part-time. Students come from 25 states and territories; 15% are from out of state; 10% Black or African American, non-Hispanic/Latino; 6% Hispanic/Latino; 0.2% Asian, non-Hispanic/Latino; 0.4% Native Hawaiian or other Pacific Islander, non-Hispanic/Latino; 3% Two or more races, non-Hispanic/Latino; 5% Race/ethnicity unknown; 0.2% international; 7% transferred in; 56% live on campus.

Freshmen:
Admission: 1,076 applied, 584 admitted, 147 enrolled. ***Average high school GPA:*** 3.33. ***Test scores:*** SAT critical reading scores over 500: 25%; SAT math scores over 500: 25%; ACT scores over 18: 87%; SAT critical reading scores over 600: 8%; ACT scores over 24: 12%; ACT scores over 30: 2%.

Retention: 67% of full-time freshmen returned.

ACADEMICS
Calendar: 4-1-4. *Degrees:* associate and bachelor's.

Special study options: academic remediation for entering students, accelerated degree program, advanced placement credit, distance learning, double majors, independent study, internships, off-campus study, part-time degree program, services for LD students, study abroad, summer session for credit.

Computers: 100 computers/terminals are available on campus for general student use. Students can access the following: campus intranet, computer help desk, free student e-mail accounts, online (class) grades, online (class) registration, online (class) schedules. Campuswide network is available. 100% of college-owned or -operated housing units are wired for high-speed Internet access. Wireless service is available via entire campus.

Library: Henry Pfeiffer Library. *Books:* 87,300 (physical), 4,591 (digital/electronic); *Serial titles:* 893 (physical), 13,638 (digital/electronic); *Databases:* 42. Weekly public service hours: 85.

STUDENT LIFE

Housing options: on-campus residence required through junior year; coed. Campus housing is university owned. Freshman campus housing is guaranteed.

Activities and organizations: drama/theater group, choral group, Campus Activity Board, MacMurray Student Association, Helping Hands, Belles Lettres, Phi Nu.

Athletics Member NCAA. All Division III. ***Intercollegiate sports:*** baseball M, basketball M/W, cheerleading W(c), football M, golf M/W, soccer M/W, softball W, volleyball W, wrestling M/W. ***Intramural sports:*** basketball M/W.

Campus security: 24-hour emergency response devices and patrols, student patrols, late-night transport/escort service, controlled dormitory access.

Student services: health clinic, personal/psychological counseling.

COSTS & FINANCIAL AID

Costs (2017–18) ***Comprehensive fee:*** $35,025 includes full-time tuition ($25,340), mandatory fees ($760), and room and board ($8925). Full-time tuition and fees vary according to course load and location. Part-time tuition: $780 per credit hour. Part-time tuition and fees vary according to course load and location. ***Required fees:*** $40 per credit hour part-time, $10 per term part-time. ***Room and board:*** Room and board charges vary according to housing facility. ***Payment plan:*** deferred payment. ***Waivers:*** children of alumni, senior citizens, and employees or children of employees.

Financial Aid Of all full-time matriculated undergraduates who enrolled in 2016, 512 applied for aid, 481 were judged to have need, 98 had their need fully met. 313 Federal Work-Study jobs (averaging $1510). In 2016, 43 non-need-based awards were made. ***Average percent of need met:*** 80. ***Average financial aid package:*** $21,509. ***Average need-based loan:*** $5134. ***Average need-based gift aid:*** $16,287. ***Average non-need-based aid:*** $11,288. ***Average indebtedness upon graduation:*** $36,877.

APPLYING

Standardized Tests *Required:* SAT or ACT (for admission).

Options: electronic application, early admission.

Required: high school transcript, minimum 2.5 GPA. ***Required for some:*** essay or personal statement.

Application deadlines: rolling (freshmen), rolling (transfers).

Notification: continuous (freshmen), continuous (transfers).

CONTACT

Kristen Chenoweth, Associate Director of Admissions, MacMurray College, 447 East College Avenue, Jacksonville, IL 62650.
Phone: 217-479-7063. *Toll-free phone:* 800-252-7485.
Fax: 217-291-0702.
E-mail: kristen.chenoweth@mac.edu.

McKendree University
Lebanon, Illinois
http://www.mckendree.edu/

- **Independent** comprehensive, founded 1828, affiliated with United Methodist Church
- **Suburban** 235-acre campus with easy access to St. Louis, MO; Belleville, IL
- **Endowment** $37.0 million
- **Coed** 2,290 undergraduate students, 80% full-time, 54% women, 46% men
- **Moderately difficult** entrance level, 68% of applicants were admitted

UNDERGRAD STUDENTS

1,823 full-time, 467 part-time. Students come from 36 states and territories; 32 other countries; 27% are from out of state; 14% Black or African American, non-Hispanic/Latino; 5% Hispanic/Latino; 0.9% Asian, non-Hispanic/Latino; 0.9% Native Hawaiian or other Pacific Islander, non-Hispanic/Latino; 0.7% American Indian or Alaska Native, non-Hispanic/Latino; 3% Two or more races, non-Hispanic/Latino; 8% Race/ethnicity unknown; 3% international; 5% transferred in; 78% live on campus.

Freshmen:

Admission: 2,283 applied, 1,556 admitted, 458 enrolled. ***Average high school GPA:*** 3.44. ***Test scores:*** SAT critical reading scores over 500: 68%; SAT math scores over 500: 71%; SAT writing scores over 500: 49%; ACT scores over 18: 93%; SAT critical reading scores over 600: 39%; SAT math scores over 600: 12%; SAT writing scores over 600: 19%; ACT scores over 24: 34%; SAT critical reading scores over 700: 10%; ACT scores over 30: 2%.

Retention: 76% of full-time freshmen returned.

FACULTY

Total: 296, 34% full-time, 39% with terminal degrees.

Student/faculty ratio: 14:1.

ACADEMICS

Calendar: semesters. *Degrees:* associate, bachelor's, master's, doctoral, and post-master's certificates.

Special study options: academic remediation for entering students, accelerated degree program, adult/continuing education programs, advanced placement credit, cooperative education, distance learning, double majors, honors programs, independent study, internships, off-campus study, part-time degree program, services for LD students, student-designed majors, study abroad, summer session for credit. ***ROTC:*** Army (c), Air Force (c).

Unusual degree programs: 3-2 engineering with Missouri University of Science and Technology; occupational therapy with Washington University in St. Louis.

Computers: 205 computers/terminals and 1,096 ports are available on campus for general student use. Students can access the following: campus intranet, computer help desk, free student e-mail accounts, online (class) grades, online (class) registration, online (class) schedules. Campuswide network is available. 100% of college-owned or -operated housing units are wired for high-speed Internet access. Wireless service is available via entire campus.

Library: Holman Library. *Books:* 76,806 (physical), 11,853 (digital/electronic); *Serial titles:* 5,099 (physical), 7,229 (digital/electronic); *Databases:* 59. Students can reserve study rooms.

STUDENT LIFE

Housing options: on-campus residence required through junior year; coed, special housing for students with disabilities. Campus housing is university owned and leased by the school. Freshman campus housing is guaranteed.

Activities and organizations: drama/theater group, student-run newspaper, radio station, choral group, marching band, Center for Public Service, Wonders of Wellness, Campus Ministries, APO, Debate, national fraternities, national sororities.

Athletics Member NCAA. All Division II except volleyball (Division I). ***Intercollegiate sports:*** baseball M(s), basketball M(s)/W(s), bowling M(c)/W(s), cheerleading M(s)(c)/W(s)(c), cross-country running M(s)/W(s), fencing M(c)/W(c), football M(s), golf M(s)/W(s), ice hockey M(c)/W(c), lacrosse W(s), soccer M(s)/W(s), softball W(s), swimming and diving M(s)/W(s), tennis M(s)/W(s), track and field M(s)/W(s), volleyball M(s)/W(s), water polo M(s)/W(s), weight lifting M(c)/W(c), wrestling M(s)/W(s)(c). ***Intramural sports:*** basketball M/W, football M/W, softball M/W, ultimate Frisbee M/W, volleyball M/W.

Campus security: 24-hour emergency response devices and patrols, student patrols, late-night transport/escort service, controlled dormitory access.

Student services: health clinic, personal/psychological counseling.

COSTS & FINANCIAL AID

Costs (2017–18) ***Comprehensive fee:*** $38,990 includes full-time tuition ($28,560), mandatory fees ($1080), and room and board ($9350). Full-time tuition and fees vary according to course load, degree level, and location. Part-time tuition: $935 per credit hour. Part-time tuition and fees vary according to course load, degree level, and location. ***College room only:*** $5020. Room and board charges vary according to board plan and housing facility. ***Payment plans:*** installment, deferred payment. ***Waivers:*** children of alumni and employees or children of employees.

Financial Aid Of all full-time matriculated undergraduates who enrolled in 2016, 1,577 applied for aid, 1,428 were judged to have need, 283 had their need fully met. 881 Federal Work-Study jobs (averaging $1785). 67 state and other part-time jobs (averaging $1138). In 2016, 320 non-need-based awards were made. ***Average percent of need met:*** 73. ***Average financial aid package:*** $21,543. ***Average need-based loan:*** $4027. ***Average need-based gift aid:*** $17,864. ***Average non-need-based aid:*** $11,556. ***Average indebtedness upon graduation:*** $30,029.

APPLYING

Standardized Tests *Required:* SAT or ACT (for admission).

Options: electronic application, deferred entrance.

Required: essay or personal statement, high school transcript, minimum 2.5 GPA, 1 letter of recommendation, rank in upper 50% of high school class, minimum ACT score of 20. ***Required for some:*** interview.

Application deadlines: rolling (freshmen), rolling (transfers).

Notification: continuous (freshmen), continuous (transfers).

CONTACT

Mrs. Josie Blasdel, Director of Undergraduate Admission, McKendree University, 701 College Road, Lebanon, IL 62254. *Phone:* 618-537-6836. *Toll-free phone:* 800-232-7228. *E-mail:* jlblasdel@mckendree.edu.

Methodist College

Peoria, Illinois

http://www.methodistcol.edu/

CONTACT

Methodist College, 415 St. Mark Court, Peoria, IL 61603.

Midstate College

Peoria, Illinois

http://www.midstate.edu/

CONTACT

Ms. Jessica Hancock, Director of Admissions, Midstate College, 411 West Northmoor Road, Peoria, IL 61614. *Phone:* 309-692-4092. *Toll-free phone:* 800-251-4299. *Fax:* 309-692-3893. *E-mail:* jhancock2@midstate.edu.

Millikin University

Decatur, Illinois

http://www.millikin.edu/

- **Independent** comprehensive, founded 1901, affiliated with Presbyterian Church (U.S.A.)
- **Suburban** 75-acre campus
- **Endowment** $115.2 million
- **Coed** 1,971 undergraduate students, 93% full-time, 58% women, 42% men
- **Moderately difficult** entrance level, 64% of applicants were admitted

UNDERGRAD STUDENTS

1,825 full-time, 146 part-time. Students come from 33 states and territories; 24 other countries; 16% are from out of state; 14% Black or African American, non-Hispanic/Latino; 6% Hispanic/Latino; 1% Asian, non-Hispanic/Latino; 0.2% American Indian or Alaska Native, non-Hispanic/Latino; 4% Two or more races, non-Hispanic/Latino; 1% Race/ethnicity unknown; 2% international; 6% transferred in; 58% live on campus.

Freshmen:

Admission: 3,608 applied, 2,302 admitted, 448 enrolled. ***Average high school GPA:*** 3.35. ***Test scores:*** SAT critical reading scores over 500: 66%; SAT math scores over 500: 29%; SAT writing scores over 500: 48%; ACT scores over 18: 92%; SAT critical reading scores over 600: 19%; SAT math scores over 600: 10%; SAT writing scores over 600: 16%; ACT scores over 24: 40%; ACT scores over 30: 8%.

Retention: 72% of full-time freshmen returned.

FACULTY

Total: 266, 55% full-time, 50% with terminal degrees.

Student/faculty ratio: 11:1.

ACADEMICS

Calendar: semesters. *Degrees:* certificates, bachelor's, master's, and doctoral.

Special study options: accelerated degree program, adult/continuing education programs, advanced placement credit, distance learning, double majors, English as a second language, honors programs, independent study, internships, off-campus study, part-time degree program, services for LD students, student-designed majors, study abroad, summer session for credit.

Unusual degree programs: 3-2 engineering with Washington University in St. Louis, University of Missouri–Kansas City; occupational therapy with Washington University, pharmacy with Midwestern University.

Computers: 255 computers/terminals and 318 ports are available on campus for general student use. Students can access the following: computer help desk, free student e-mail accounts, online (class) grades, online (class) registration, online (class) schedules, online degree audit, online financials (view and pay bills, financial aid). Campuswide network is available. 100% of college-owned or -operated housing units are wired for high-speed Internet access. Wireless service is available via classrooms, computer centers, computer labs, dorm rooms, learning centers, libraries, student centers.

Library: Staley Library. *Books:* 167,802 (physical), 22,272 (digital/electronic); *Serial titles:* 1,000 (physical), 53,000 (digital/electronic); *Databases:* 133. Weekly public service hours: 89.

STUDENT LIFE

Housing options: on-campus residence required for freshman year; coed, special housing for students with disabilities. Campus housing is university owned, leased by the school and is provided by a third party. Freshman campus housing is guaranteed.

Activities and organizations: drama/theater group, student-run newspaper, radio station, choral group, University Center Board, Multicultural Student Council, Student Housing Council, Panhellenic Council, Interfraternity Council, national fraternities, national sororities.

Athletics Member NCAA. All Division III. ***Intercollegiate sports:*** baseball M, basketball M/W, cheerleading M/W, cross-country running M/W, football M, golf M/W, soccer M/W, softball W, swimming and diving M/W, tennis W, track and field M/W, volleyball W, wrestling M. ***Intramural sports:*** basketball M/W, bowling M/W, football M, soccer M/W, softball M/W, volleyball M/W.

Campus security: 24-hour emergency response devices and patrols, late-night transport/escort service, controlled dormitory access, emergency notification program.

Student services: health clinic, personal/psychological counseling, women's center.

COSTS & FINANCIAL AID

Costs (2016–17) ***Comprehensive fee:*** $42,159 includes full-time tuition ($31,032), mandatory fees ($792), and room and board ($10,335). Part-time tuition: $449 per credit hour. ***Required fees:*** $22 per credit hour part-time. ***College room only:*** $8035. Room and board charges vary according to board plan, housing facility, and student level. ***Payment plan:*** installment. ***Waivers:*** employees or children of employees.

Financial Aid Of all full-time matriculated undergraduates who enrolled in 2015, 1,815 applied for aid, 1,600 were judged to have need, 728 had their need fully met. 458 Federal Work-Study jobs (averaging $957). 420 state and other part-time jobs (averaging $756). In 2015, 184 non-need-based awards were made. ***Average percent of need met:*** 89. ***Average financial aid package:*** $23,593. ***Average need-based loan:*** $4626. ***Average need-based gift aid:*** $8748. ***Average non-need-based aid:*** $14,219. ***Average indebtedness upon graduation:*** $32,924.

APPLYING
Standardized Tests *Required:* SAT or ACT (for admission).

Options: electronic application, deferred entrance.

Required: high school transcript, minimum 2.0 GPA, 2 letters of recommendation. ***Required for some:*** audition for music/theatre, art portfolio review. ***Recommended:*** interview.

Application deadlines: rolling (freshmen), rolling (transfers).

Notification: continuous (freshmen), continuous (transfers).

CONTACT
Mr. Kevin McIntyre, Dean of Admission, Millikin University, 1184 West Main Street, Decatur, IL 62522-2084. *Phone:* 217-424-6210. *Toll-free phone:* 800-373-7733. *Fax:* 217-425-4669. *E-mail:* admis@millikin.edu.

Monmouth College

Monmouth, Illinois

http://www.monmouthcollege.edu/

- **Independent** 4-year, founded 1853, affiliated with Presbyterian Church
- **Small-town** 112-acre campus
- **Endowment** $100.4 million
- **Coed** 1,147 undergraduate students, 98% full-time, 52% women, 48% men
- **Moderately difficult** entrance level, 52% of applicants were admitted

UNDERGRAD STUDENTS
1,128 full-time, 19 part-time. Students come from 30 states and territories; 30 other countries; 11% are from out of state; 10% Black or African American, non-Hispanic/Latino; 11% Hispanic/Latino; 2% Asian, non-Hispanic/Latino; 0.4% American Indian or Alaska Native, non-Hispanic/Latino; 3% Two or more races, non-Hispanic/Latino; 5% Race/ethnicity unknown; 7% international; 3% transferred in; 92% live on campus.

Freshmen:
Admission: 3,248 applied, 1,690 admitted, 285 enrolled. ***Average high school GPA:*** 3.3. ***Test scores:*** ACT scores over 18: 94%; ACT scores over 24: 35%; ACT scores over 30: 6%.

Retention: 72% of full-time freshmen returned.

FACULTY
Total: 116, 76% full-time, 74% with terminal degrees.

Student/faculty ratio: 12:1.

ACADEMICS
Calendar: semesters. *Degree:* bachelor's.

Special study options: academic remediation for entering students, advanced placement credit, double majors, English as a second language, honors programs, independent study, internships, off-campus study, part-time degree program, services for LD students, student-designed majors, study abroad. ***ROTC:*** Army (c).

Unusual degree programs: 3-2 engineering with Case Western Reserve University, University of Southern California, Illinois Institute of Technology; nursing with Rush University; architecture with Washington University in St. Louis, occupational therapy, medical technology with Rush University.

Computers: 140 computers/terminals are available on campus for general student use. Students can access the following: campus intranet, computer help desk, free student e-mail accounts, online (class) grades, online (class) registration, online (class) schedules. Campuswide network is available. 100% of college-owned or -operated housing units are wired for high-speed Internet access. Wireless service is available via entire campus.

Library: Hewes Library. *Books:* 206,954 (physical), 33,996 (digital/electronic); *Serial titles:* 3,400 (physical), 28,190 (digital/electronic); *Databases:* 115. Weekly public service hours: 96; students can reserve study rooms.

STUDENT LIFE
Housing options: on-campus residence required through senior year; coed, men-only, women-only, special housing for students with disabilities. Campus housing is university owned. Freshman campus housing is guaranteed.

Activities and organizations: drama/theater group, student-run newspaper, radio and television station, choral group, marching band, Fighting Scots Marching Band and Jazz Band, Associated Students of Monmouth College, Crimson Masque (theatre), Alternative Spring Break, Coalition for Ethnic Awareness, national fraternities, national sororities.

Athletics Member NCAA. All Division III. ***Intercollegiate sports:*** baseball M, basketball M/W, cross-country running M/W, football M, golf M/W, lacrosse M/W, soccer M/W, softball W, swimming and diving M/W, tennis M/W, track and field M/W, volleyball W, water polo M/W. ***Intramural sports:*** archery M/W, badminton M/W, baseball M, cheerleading W(c), soccer M/W, swimming and diving M/W, table tennis M/W, tennis M/W, ultimate Frisbee M/W, volleyball M/W, water polo M(c)/W(c), wrestling M.

Campus security: 24-hour emergency response devices and patrols, late-night transport/escort service, controlled dormitory access, full-time Director of Campus Security.

Student services: personal/psychological counseling.

COSTS & FINANCIAL AID
Costs (2017–18) ***Comprehensive fee:*** $45,020 includes full-time tuition ($36,400) and room and board ($8620). Full-time tuition and fees vary according to course load. Part-time tuition: $4552 per course. ***College room only:*** $4860. Room and board charges vary according to housing facility. ***Payment plan:*** installment. ***Waivers:*** employees or children of employees.

Financial Aid Of all full-time matriculated undergraduates who enrolled in 2016, 991 applied for aid, 931 were judged to have need, 201 had their need fully met. 496 Federal Work-Study jobs (averaging $1442). In 2016, 198 non-need-based awards were made. ***Average percent of need met:*** 87. ***Average financial aid package:*** $31,972. ***Average need-based loan:*** $4802. ***Average need-based gift aid:*** $26,314. ***Average non-need-based aid:*** $21,021. ***Average indebtedness upon graduation:*** $31,037.

APPLYING
Standardized Tests *Required:* SAT or ACT (for admission).

Options: electronic application, deferred entrance.

Required: high school transcript. ***Required for some:*** interview. ***Recommended:*** essay or personal statement, minimum 2.7 GPA, letters of recommendation, interview.

Application deadlines: rolling (freshmen), rolling (transfers).

Notification: continuous (freshmen), continuous (transfers).

CONTACT
Mr. Nick Spaeth, Assoc VP of Admissions, Monmouth College, 700 East Broadway, Monmouth, IL 61462-1988. *Phone:* 309-457-2143. *Toll-free phone:* 800-747-2687. *Fax:* 309-457-2141.
E-mail: admissions@monmouthcollege.edu.

Moody Bible Institute

Chicago, Illinois

http://www.moody.edu/

CONTACT
Ms. Jacqueline Holman, Admissions Office, Moody Bible Institute, 820 North LaSalle Boulevard, Chicago, IL 60610. *Phone:* 312-329-4307. *Toll-free phone:* 800-967-4MBI. *Fax:* 312-329-8987.
E-mail: admissions@moody.edu.

Morthland College

West Frankfort, Illinois

http://www.morthland.edu/

CONTACT
Morthland College, 202 East Oak Street, West Frankfort, IL 62896.

National Louis University

Chicago, Illinois

http://www.nl.edu/

- **Independent** university, founded 1886
- **Urban** 12-acre campus
- **Coed** 1,463 undergraduate students, 62% full-time, 75% women, 25% men
- **Minimally difficult** entrance level, 80% of applicants were admitted

UNDERGRAD STUDENTS
903 full-time, 560 part-time. Students come from 18 states and territories; 3% are from out of state; 36% Black or African American, non-Hispanic/Latino; 39% Hispanic/Latino; 2% Asian, non-Hispanic/Latino; 0.1% Native Hawaiian or other Pacific Islander, non-Hispanic/Latino; 0.2% American Indian or Alaska Native, non-Hispanic/Latino; 2% Two or more races, non-Hispanic/Latino; 2% Race/ethnicity unknown; 0.7% international; 22% transferred in.

Freshmen:
Admission: 401 applied, 319 admitted, 315 enrolled. ***Average high school GPA:*** 2.6.
Retention: 73% of full-time freshmen returned.

FACULTY
Total: 437, 30% full-time.
Student/faculty ratio: 12:1.

ACADEMICS
Calendar: quarters. *Degrees:* bachelor's, master's, doctoral, post-master's, and postbachelor's certificates.
Special study options: academic remediation for entering students, accelerated degree program, adult/continuing education programs, advanced placement credit, distance learning, English as a second language, independent study, internships, services for LD students, summer session for credit.
Computers: Students can access the following: campus intranet, computer help desk, free student e-mail accounts, online (class) grades, online (class) registration, online (class) schedules. Campuswide network is available. Wireless service is available via entire campus.
Library: NLU Library.

STUDENT LIFE
Housing options: college housing not available.
Campus security: 24-hour emergency response devices and patrols.
Student services: personal/psychological counseling.

COSTS & FINANCIAL AID
Costs (2017–18) ***Tuition:*** $12,456 full-time, $470 per credit hour part-time. Full-time tuition and fees vary according to course load and degree level. Part-time tuition and fees vary according to course load and degree level. ***Required fees:*** $390 full-time.
Financial Aid Of all full-time matriculated undergraduates who enrolled in 2011, 772 applied for aid, 736 were judged to have need, 10 had their need fully met. 66 Federal Work-Study jobs (averaging $3890). In 2011, 52 non-need-based awards were made. ***Average percent of need met:*** 43. ***Average financial aid package:*** $12,225. ***Average need-based loan:*** $4426. ***Average need-based gift aid:*** $8302. ***Average non-need-based aid:*** $5605. ***Average indebtedness upon graduation:*** $29,900.

APPLYING
Standardized Tests *Required for some:* SAT or ACT (for admission).
Options: electronic application, deferred entrance.
Required: high school transcript, minimum 2.0 GPA. ***Required for some:*** 2 letters of recommendation. ***Recommended:*** interview.
Application deadlines: rolling (freshmen), rolling (transfers).
Notification: continuous (freshmen), continuous (transfers).

CONTACT
National Louis University, 1000 Capitol Drive, Wheeling, IL 60090.
Phone: 888-NLU-TODAY. *Toll-free phone:* 888-658-8632.

North Central College

Naperville, Illinois

http://www.northcentralcollege.edu/

- **Independent United Methodist** comprehensive, founded 1861
- **Suburban** 65-acre campus with easy access to Chicago
- **Endowment** $98.7 million
- **Coed** 2,716 undergraduate students, 93% full-time, 53% women, 47% men
- **Moderately difficult** entrance level, 59% of applicants were admitted

UNDERGRAD STUDENTS
2,534 full-time, 182 part-time. Students come from 30 states and territories; 35 other countries; 7% are from out of state; 4% Black or African American, non-Hispanic/Latino; 13% Hispanic/Latino; 3% Asian, non-Hispanic/Latino; 0.1% Native Hawaiian or other Pacific Islander, non-Hispanic/Latino; 0.2% American Indian or Alaska Native, non-Hispanic/Latino; 3% Two or more races, non-Hispanic/Latino; 6% Race/ethnicity unknown; 2% international; 10% transferred in; 56% live on campus.

Freshmen:
Admission: 6,860 applied, 4,072 admitted, 589 enrolled. ***Average high school GPA:*** 3.58. ***Test scores:*** ACT scores over 18: 99%; ACT scores over 24: 58%; ACT scores over 30: 10%.
Retention: 78% of full-time freshmen returned.

FACULTY
Total: 266, 53% full-time, 66% with terminal degrees.
Student/faculty ratio: 15:1.

ACADEMICS
Calendar: quarters. *Degrees:* bachelor's, master's, and postbachelor's certificates.
Special study options: academic remediation for entering students, accelerated degree program, advanced placement credit, double majors, English as a second language, honors programs, independent study, internships, off-campus study, part-time degree program, services for LD students, student-designed majors, study abroad, summer session for credit. ***ROTC:*** Army (c), Air Force (c).
Unusual degree programs: 3-2 engineering with Washington University in St. Louis; University of Illinois at Urbana–Champaign; Marquette University; University of Minnesota, Twin Cities Campus.
Computers: 350 computers/terminals are available on campus for general student use. Students can access the following: campus intranet, computer help desk, free student e-mail accounts, online (class) grades, online (class) registration, online (class) schedules, software packages. Campuswide network is available. 100% of college-owned or -operated housing units are wired for high-speed Internet access. Wireless service is available via classrooms, computer centers, computer labs, dorm rooms, learning centers, libraries, student centers.
Library: Oesterle Library. *Books:* 124,616 (physical), 77,180 (digital/electronic); *Databases:* 214.

STUDENT LIFE
Housing options: on-campus residence required through sophomore year; coed, men-only, women-only, special housing for students with disabilities. Campus housing is university owned. Freshman applicants given priority for college housing.
Activities and organizations: drama/theater group, student-run newspaper, radio station, choral group, College Union Activities Board, WONC (student radio station), Cardinals in Action (service group), ENACTUS (Students in Free Enterprise SIFE), Residence Hall Association.
Athletics Member NCAA. All Division III. ***Intercollegiate sports:*** baseball M, basketball M/W, bowling W, cheerleading W, cross-country running M/W, football M, golf M/W, lacrosse M/W, soccer M/W, softball W, swimming and diving M/W, tennis M/W, track and field M/W, triathlon W, volleyball M/W, wrestling M. ***Intramural sports:*** badminton M/W, basketball M/W, football M/W, golf M/W, racquetball M/W, soccer M/W, softball M/W, ultimate Frisbee M/W, volleyball M/W.
Campus security: 24-hour emergency response devices and patrols, late-night transport/escort service, controlled dormitory access.
Student services: health clinic, personal/psychological counseling.

COSTS & FINANCIAL AID
Costs (2016–17) ***Comprehensive fee:*** $47,010 includes full-time tuition ($36,474), mandatory fees ($180), and room and board ($10,356). Part-time tuition: $1013 per credit hour. Part-time tuition and fees vary according to course load. ***Required fees:*** $20 per term part-time. ***College room only:*** $7173. Room and board charges vary according to housing facility. ***Payment plan:*** installment. ***Waivers:*** senior citizens and employees or children of employees.

Financial Aid Of all full-time matriculated undergraduates who enrolled in 2016, 2,207 applied for aid, 1,993 were judged to have need, 364 had their need fully met. 1,423 Federal Work-Study jobs (averaging $248). In 2016, 530 non-need-based awards were made. ***Average percent of need met:*** 78. ***Average financial aid package:*** $24,522. ***Average need-based loan:*** $4481. ***Average need-based gift aid:*** $20,954. ***Average non-need-based aid:*** $17,057. ***Average indebtedness upon graduation:*** $34,911.

APPLYING
Standardized Tests *Required:* SAT or ACT (for admission). *Recommended:* ACT (for admission).

Options: electronic application, deferred entrance.

Application fee: $25.

Required: high school transcript, minimum 2.5 GPA. ***Required for some:*** interview. ***Recommended:*** essay or personal statement, 1 letter of recommendation.

Application deadlines: rolling (freshmen), rolling (transfers).

Notification: continuous (freshmen), continuous (transfers).

CONTACT
Ms. Martha Stolze, Dean of Admission, North Central College, 30 North Brainard Street, PO Box 3063, Naperville, IL 60566-7063.
Phone: 630-637-5800. *Toll-free phone:* 800-411-1861.
Fax: 630-637-5819.
E-mail: admissions@noctrl.edu.

Northeastern Illinois University

Chicago, Illinois

http://www.neiu.edu/

- **State-supported** comprehensive, founded 1961
- **Urban** 67-acre campus with easy access to Chicago
- **Endowment** $768,031
- **Coed** 8,095 undergraduate students, 56% full-time, 56% women, 44% men
- **Minimally difficult** entrance level, 67% of applicants were admitted

UNDERGRAD STUDENTS
4,502 full-time, 3,593 part-time. Students come from 7 states and territories; 45 other countries; 1% are from out of state; 10% Black or African American, non-Hispanic/Latino; 37% Hispanic/Latino; 9% Asian, non-Hispanic/Latino; 0.3% Native Hawaiian or other Pacific Islander, non-Hispanic/Latino; 0.2% American Indian or Alaska Native, non-Hispanic/Latino; 2% Two or more races, non-Hispanic/Latino; 3% Race/ethnicity unknown; 5% international; 16% transferred in.

Freshmen:
Admission: 4,499 applied, 3,016 admitted, 749 enrolled. ***Average high school GPA:*** 2.8. ***Test scores:*** ACT scores over 18: 52%; ACT scores over 24: 9%.

Retention: 61% of full-time freshmen returned.

FACULTY
Total: 625, 60% full-time, 64% with terminal degrees.
Student/faculty ratio: 14:1.

ACADEMICS
Calendar: semesters. *Degrees:* bachelor's and master's.

Special study options: academic remediation for entering students, adult/continuing education programs, advanced placement credit, cooperative education, distance learning, double majors, English as a second language, external degree program, honors programs, independent study, internships, off-campus study, part-time degree program, services for LD students, study abroad, summer session for credit. ***ROTC:*** Army (c), Air Force (c).

Computers: 560 computers/terminals are available on campus for general student use. Students can access the following: computer help desk, free student e-mail accounts, online (class) grades, online (class) registration, online (class) schedules, productivity software. Campuswide network is available. Wireless service is available via classrooms, computer centers, computer labs, learning centers, libraries, student centers.

Library: Ronald Williams Library plus 3 others. *Books:* 688,147 (physical), 156,705 (digital/electronic); *Serial titles:* 742 (physical), 86,898 (digital/electronic); *Databases:* 188.
Weekly public service hours: 92.

STUDENT LIFE
Housing options: Campus housing is provided by a third party.

Activities and organizations: drama/theater group, student-run newspaper, radio station, choral group, Student Government Association, United Greek Council, ASSW - Association of Student Social Workers, Accounting Associates, Computer Science Society, national fraternities, national sororities.

Athletics ***Intramural sports:*** badminton M/W, baseball M(c), basketball M(c)/W(c), crew M/W, cross-country running M/W, football M/W, ice hockey M/W, racquetball M/W, rock climbing M/W, soccer M(c)/W(c), softball M/W, table tennis M/W, tennis M/W, volleyball M(c)/W(c), weight lifting M/W.

Campus security: 24-hour emergency response devices and patrols, late-night transport/escort service, controlled dormitory access.

Student services: health clinic, personal/psychological counseling, women's center.

COSTS & FINANCIAL AID
Costs (2017–18) ***Tuition:*** state resident $11,320 full-time, $377 per credit hour part-time; nonresident $22,639 full-time, $755 per credit hour part-time. Full-time tuition and fees vary according to course load and degree level. Part-time tuition and fees vary according to course load and degree level. No tuition increase for student's term of enrollment. ***Required fees:*** $1681 full-time. ***Room and board:*** $11,424; room only: $8424. Room and board charges vary according to housing facility. ***Payment plan:*** deferred payment. ***Waivers:*** senior citizens and employees or children of employees.

Financial Aid Of all full-time matriculated undergraduates who enrolled in 2016, 3,473 applied for aid, 2,897 were judged to have need, 117 had their need fully met. In 2016, 80 non-need-based awards were made. ***Average percent of need met:*** 17. ***Average financial aid package:*** $8549. ***Average need-based loan:*** $4277. ***Average need-based gift aid:*** $6882. ***Average non-need-based aid:*** $1936. ***Average indebtedness upon graduation:*** $16,247.

APPLYING
Standardized Tests *Required:* SAT or ACT (for admission).

Options: electronic application, deferred entrance.

Application fee: $30.

Required: high school transcript.

Application deadlines: 7/1 (freshmen), 7/1 (transfers).

Notification: 9/1 (freshmen), continuous (transfers).

CONTACT
Ms. Zarrin Kerwell, Admissions Counselor, Northeastern Illinois University, 5500 North St. Louis Avenue, Chicago, IL 60625.
Phone: 773-442-4026. *Fax:* 773-794-6243. *E-mail:* admrec@neiu.edu.

Northern Illinois University

De Kalb, Illinois

http://www.niu.edu/

- **State-supported** university, founded 1895
- **Small-town** 650-acre campus with easy access to Chicago
- **Endowment** $3.4 million
- **Coed** 14,079 undergraduate students, 88% full-time, 49% women, 51% men
- **Moderately difficult** entrance level, 52% of applicants were admitted

UNDERGRAD STUDENTS
12,343 full-time, 1,736 part-time. Students come from 42 states and territories; 47 other countries; 3% are from out of state; 16% Black or African American, non-Hispanic/Latino; 17% Hispanic/Latino; 5% Asian,

non-Hispanic/Latino; 0.1% Native Hawaiian or other Pacific Islander, non-Hispanic/Latino; 0.1% American Indian or Alaska Native, non-Hispanic/Latino; 4% Two or more races, non-Hispanic/Latino; 0.5% Race/ethnicity unknown; 2% international; 12% transferred in; 26% live on campus.

Freshmen:
Admission: 14,980 applied, 7,766 admitted, 1,802 enrolled. ***Average high school GPA:*** 3.26. ***Test scores:*** ACT scores over 18: 87%; ACT scores over 24: 35%; ACT scores over 30: 5%.

Retention: 73% of full-time freshmen returned.

FACULTY
Total: 1,081, 77% full-time, 74% with terminal degrees.

Student/faculty ratio: 15:1.

ACADEMICS
Calendar: semesters. *Degrees:* bachelor's, master's, and doctoral.

Special study options: accelerated degree program, adult/continuing education programs, advanced placement credit, cooperative education, double majors, honors programs, independent study, internships, off-campus study, part-time degree program, services for LD students, student-designed majors, study abroad, summer session for credit. ***ROTC:*** Army (b), Air Force (c).

Computers: 1,500 computers/terminals are available on campus for general student use. Students can access the following: computer help desk, free student e-mail accounts, online (class) grades, online (class) registration, online (class) schedules. Campuswide network is available. 100% of college-owned or -operated housing units are wired for high-speed Internet access. Wireless service is available via entire campus.

Library: Founders Memorial Library plus 4 others. *Books:* 1.8 million (physical), 471,409 (digital/electronic); *Serial titles:* 600 (physical), 76,936 (digital/electronic); *Databases:* 318. Students can reserve study rooms.

STUDENT LIFE
Housing options: on-campus residence required through senior year; coed. Campus housing is university owned. Freshman applicants given priority for college housing.

Activities and organizations: drama/theater group, student-run newspaper, radio station, choral group, marching band, American Marketing Association, Delta Sigma Pi, Pi Sigma Epsilon, Black Choir, Student Volunteer Choir, national fraternities, national sororities.

Athletics Member NCAA. All Division I except football (Division I-A). ***Intercollegiate sports:*** baseball M(s), basketball M(s)/W(s), cross-country running W, golf M(s)/W(s), gymnastics W(s), soccer M(s)/W(s), softball W(s), swimming and diving M(s)/W(s), tennis M(s)/W(s), volleyball W(s), wrestling M(s). ***Intramural sports:*** archery M(c)/W(c), badminton M/W, basketball M/W, bowling M(c)/W(c), cross-country running W, football M/W, golf M/W, ice hockey M(c)/W(c), lacrosse M(c)/W(c), racquetball M/W, rugby M(c)/W(c), skiing (downhill) M(c)/W(c), soccer M/W, softball M/W, table tennis M/W, tennis M/W, track and field M(c)/W(c), volleyball M/W, water polo M(c)/W(c), weight lifting M(c)/W(c).

Campus security: 24-hour emergency response devices and patrols, student patrols, late-night transport/escort service, controlled dormitory access.

Student services: health clinic, personal/psychological counseling, women's center, legal services.

COSTS & FINANCIAL AID
Costs (2016–17) ***Tuition:*** state resident $9466 full-time; nonresident $18,931 full-time. Part-time tuition and fees vary according to course load and location. ***Required fees:*** $2746 full-time, $94 per credit hour part-time, $125 per term part-time. ***Room and board:*** $10,776. Room and board charges vary according to student level. ***Payment plan:*** installment. ***Waivers:*** senior citizens and employees or children of employees.

Financial Aid Of all full-time matriculated undergraduates who enrolled in 2015, 11,615 applied for aid, 10,142 were judged to have need, 685 had their need fully met. 6,183 Federal Work-Study jobs (averaging $2644). In 2015, 1242 non-need-based awards were made. ***Average percent of need met:*** 59. ***Average financial aid package:*** $12,366. ***Average need-based loan:*** $4455. ***Average need-based gift aid:*** $7955. ***Average non-need-based aid:*** $4207. ***Average indebtedness upon graduation:*** $34,714.

APPLYING
Standardized Tests *Required:* SAT or ACT (for admission).

Options: electronic application.

Application fee: $40.

Required: high school transcript, high school class rank.

Application deadlines: 8/1 (freshmen), 8/1 (transfers).

Notification: continuous (freshmen), continuous (transfers).

CONTACT
Katy Saalfeld, Acting Director of Admissions, Northern Illinois University, Student Affairs & Enrollment Management, DeKalb, IL 60115-2857. *Phone:* 815-753-0446. *Toll-free phone:* 800-892-3050. *E-mail:* admissions@niu.edu.

North Park University

Chicago, Illinois

http://www.northpark.edu/

CONTACT
Office of Admissions, North Park University, 3225 West Foster Avenue, Chicago, IL 60625-4895. *Phone:* 773-244-5500. *Toll-free phone:* 800-888-NPC8. *Fax:* 773-583-0858. *E-mail:* afao@northpark.edu.

Northwestern University

Evanston, Illinois

http://www.northwestern.edu/

- **Independent** university, founded 1851
- **Suburban** 250-acre campus with easy access to Chicago
- **Coed** 8,353 undergraduate students, 98% full-time, 50% women, 50% men
- **Most difficult** entrance level, 11% of applicants were admitted

UNDERGRAD STUDENTS
8,216 full-time, 137 part-time. Students come from 75 other countries; 67% are from out of state; 6% Black or African American, non-Hispanic/Latino; 12% Hispanic/Latino; 17% Asian, non-Hispanic/Latino; 0.1% American Indian or Alaska Native, non-Hispanic/Latino; 5% Two or more races, non-Hispanic/Latino; 2% Race/ethnicity unknown; 10% international; 1% transferred in; 99% live on campus.

Freshmen:
Admission: 35,100 applied, 3,743 admitted, 1,985 enrolled. ***Test scores:*** SAT critical reading scores over 500: 100%; SAT math scores over 500: 100%; ACT scores over 18: 100%; SAT critical reading scores over 600: 96%; SAT math scores over 600: 98%; ACT scores over 24: 99%; SAT critical reading scores over 700: 70%; SAT math scores over 700: 80%; ACT scores over 30: 87%.

Retention: 98% of full-time freshmen returned.

FACULTY
Total: 1,731, 85% full-time, 100% with terminal degrees.

Student/faculty ratio: 7:1.

ACADEMICS
Calendar: quarters. *Degrees:* certificates, bachelor's, master's, doctoral, and post-master's certificates.

Special study options: accelerated degree program, adult/continuing education programs, advanced placement credit, cooperative education, double majors, honors programs, independent study, internships, part-time degree program, services for LD students, student-designed majors, study abroad, summer session for credit. ***ROTC:*** Army (c), Navy (b), Air Force (c).

Computers: Students can access the following: campus intranet, computer help desk, free student e-mail accounts, online (class) grades, online (class) registration, online (class) schedules. Campuswide network is available. 100% of college-owned or -operated housing units are wired for high-speed Internet access. Wireless service is available via entire campus.

Library: University Library plus 6 others.

STUDENT LIFE

Housing options: coed, men-only, women-only. Campus housing is university owned. Freshman campus housing is guaranteed.

Activities and organizations: drama/theater group, student-run newspaper, radio and television station, choral group, marching band, national fraternities, national sororities.

Athletics Member NCAA. All Division I.

Campus security: 24-hour emergency response devices and patrols, late-night transport/escort service, controlled dormitory access.

Student services: health clinic, personal/psychological counseling, women's center.

COSTS & FINANCIAL AID

Costs (2016–17) ***Comprehensive fee:*** $66,344 includes full-time tuition ($50,424), mandatory fees ($431), and room and board ($15,489). ***Room and board:*** Room and board charges vary according to board plan and housing facility. ***Payment plan:*** installment.

Financial Aid Of all full-time matriculated undergraduates who enrolled in 2016, 3,997 applied for aid, 3,612 were judged to have need, 3,612 had their need fully met. In 2016, 348 non-need-based awards were made. ***Average percent of need met:*** 100. ***Average financial aid package:*** $45,505. ***Average need-based loan:*** $4652. ***Average need-based gift aid:*** $39,409. ***Average non-need-based aid:*** $4006. ***Average indebtedness upon graduation:*** $20,308. ***Financial aid deadline:*** 3/5.

APPLYING

Standardized Tests *Required:* SAT or ACT (for admission). *Required for some:* SAT Subject Tests (for admission).

Options: electronic application, early admission, early decision, deferred entrance.

Application fee: $75.

Required: essay or personal statement, high school transcript, 1 letter of recommendation. ***Required for some:*** audition for music program.

Application deadlines: 1/1 (freshmen), 3/15 (transfers).

Early decision deadline: 11/1.

Notification: 4/1 (freshmen), continuous (transfers), 12/15 (early decision).

CONTACT

Mr. Christopher Watson, Dean of Undergraduate Admission, Northwestern University, PO Box 3060, Evanston, IL 60208. *Phone:* 847-491-7271. *E-mail:* ug-admission@northwestern.edu.

★ Olivet Nazarene University

Bourbonnais, Illinois

http://www.olivet.edu/

- **Independent** comprehensive, founded 1907, affiliated with Church of the Nazarene
- **Small-town** 275-acre campus with easy access to Chicago
- **Endowment** $2.8 million
- **Coed** 3,358 undergraduate students, 90% full-time, 60% women, 40% men
- **Minimally difficult** entrance level, 78% of applicants were admitted

UNDERGRAD STUDENTS

3,019 full-time, 339 part-time. Students come from 44 states and territories; 23 other countries; 36% are from out of state; 8% Black or African American, non-Hispanic/Latino; 7% Hispanic/Latino; 2% Asian, non-Hispanic/Latino; 0.1% Native Hawaiian or other Pacific Islander, non-Hispanic/Latino; 0.1% American Indian or Alaska Native, non-Hispanic/Latino; 2% Two or more races, non-Hispanic/Latino; 0.1% Race/ethnicity unknown; 1% international; 8% transferred in; 70% live on campus.

Freshmen:

Admission: 4,305 applied, 3,345 admitted, 704 enrolled. ***Average high school GPA:*** 3.54.

Retention: 75% of full-time freshmen returned.

ACADEMICS

Calendar: semesters. *Degrees:* associate, bachelor's, master's, and doctoral.

Special study options: academic remediation for entering students, adult/continuing education programs, advanced placement credit, cooperative education, distance learning, double majors, honors programs, independent study, internships, off-campus study, part-time degree

program, services for LD students, student-designed majors, study abroad, summer session for credit. ***ROTC:*** Army (b).

Computers: Students can access the following: campus intranet, computer help desk, free student e-mail accounts, online (class) grades, online (class) registration, online (class) schedules. Campuswide network is available. Wireless service is available via entire campus.

Library: Benner Library. *Books:* 159,187 (physical), 169,095 (digital/electronic); *Serial titles:* 3,565 (physical), 8,882 (digital/electronic); *Databases:* 189.

STUDENT LIFE

Housing options: on-campus residence required through senior year; men-only, women-only. Campus housing is university owned. Freshman campus housing is guaranteed.

Activities and organizations: drama/theater group, student-run newspaper, radio station, choral group, marching band, Fellowship of Christian Athletes, C.A.U.S.E. (College and University Serving and Enabling), Diakonia, Student Education Association, Women's Residence Association.

Athletics Member NAIA, NCCAA. ***Intercollegiate sports:*** baseball M(s), basketball M(s)/W(s), cheerleading M(s)/W(s), cross-country running M(s)/W(s), football M(s), golf M(s), soccer M(s)/W(s), softball W(s), tennis M(s)/W(s), track and field M(s)/W(s), volleyball W(s). ***Intramural sports:*** baseball M, basketball M/W, football M/W, golf M/W, racquetball M/W, soccer M/W, softball M/W, table tennis M/W, tennis M/W, track and field M/W, volleyball M/W.

Campus security: 24-hour patrols, late-night transport/escort service.

Student services: health clinic, personal/psychological counseling.

COSTS & FINANCIAL AID

Costs (2016–17) ***Comprehensive fee:*** $42,380 includes full-time tuition ($33,490), mandatory fees ($990), and room and board ($7900). Full-time tuition and fees vary according to course load. Part-time tuition: $1373 per semester hour. Part-time tuition and fees vary according to course load. ***Room and board:*** Room and board charges vary according to board plan. ***Payment plan:*** installment. ***Waivers:*** employees or children of employees.

Financial Aid Of all full-time matriculated undergraduates who enrolled in 2015, 2,666 applied for aid, 2,441 were judged to have need, 619 had their need fully met. 350 Federal Work-Study jobs (averaging $845). 1,032 state and other part-time jobs (averaging $1657). In 2015, 556 non-need-based awards were made. ***Average percent of need met:*** 80. ***Average financial aid package:*** $25,369. ***Average need-based loan:*** $3203. ***Average need-based gift aid:*** $20,623. ***Average non-need-based aid:*** $13,320. ***Average indebtedness upon graduation:*** $32,754.

APPLYING

Standardized Tests *Required:* SAT or ACT (for admission).

Options: electronic application, deferred entrance.

Application fee: $25.

Required: high school transcript, minimum 2.0 GPA, 2 letters of recommendation. ***Recommended:*** essay or personal statement, interview.

Application deadlines: rolling (freshmen), rolling (transfers).

Notification: continuous (freshmen), continuous (transfers).

CONTACT

Jordan Gerstenberger, Director of Recruitment, Olivet Nazarene University, One University Avenue, Bourbonnais, IL 60914. *Phone:* 815-928-5595. *Toll-free phone:* 800-648-1463.

See previous page for display ad and page 1454 for the College Close-Up.

Principia College

Elsah, Illinois

http://www.principiacollege.edu/

- **Independent Christian Science** 4-year, founded 1910
- **Rural** 2600-acre campus with easy access to St. Louis
- **Endowment** $662.2 million
- **Coed** 479 undergraduate students, 96% full-time, 51% women, 49% men
- **Moderately difficult** entrance level, 91% of applicants were admitted

UNDERGRAD STUDENTS

462 full-time, 17 part-time. Students come from 36 states and territories; 29 other countries; 87% are from out of state; 2% Black or African American, non-Hispanic/Latino; 4% Hispanic/Latino; 2% Asian, non-Hispanic/Latino; 0.2% Native Hawaiian or other Pacific Islander, non-Hispanic/Latino; 0.2% American Indian or Alaska Native, non-Hispanic/Latino; 1% Two or more races, non-Hispanic/Latino; 0.6% Race/ethnicity unknown; 17% international; 3% transferred in; 99% live on campus.

Freshmen:

Admission: 165 applied, 150 admitted, 112 enrolled. ***Average high school GPA:*** 3.41. ***Test scores:*** SAT critical reading scores over 500: 75%; SAT math scores over 500: 67%; SAT writing scores over 500: 61%; ACT scores over 18: 98%; SAT critical reading scores over 600: 35%; SAT math scores over 600: 28%; SAT writing scores over 600: 23%; ACT scores over 24: 71%; SAT critical reading scores over 700: 7%; SAT math scores over 700: 3%; SAT writing scores over 700: 2%; ACT scores over 30: 16%.

Retention: 91% of full-time freshmen returned.

FACULTY

Total: 80, 76% full-time, 58% with terminal degrees.

Student/faculty ratio: 7:1.

ACADEMICS

Calendar: semesters. *Degree:* bachelor's.

Special study options: advanced placement credit, double majors, independent study, internships, off-campus study, part-time degree program, student-designed majors, study abroad, summer session for credit.

Unusual degree programs: 3-2 engineering with University of Minnesota, Southern Illinois University Edwardsville.

Computers: 100 computers/terminals are available on campus for general student use. Students can access the following: campus intranet, computer help desk, free student e-mail accounts, online (class) grades, online (class) registration, online (class) schedules. Campuswide network is available. 100% of college-owned or -operated housing units are wired for high-speed Internet access. Wireless service is available via classrooms, computer centers, computer labs, dorm rooms, libraries, student centers.

Library: Marshall Brooks Library plus 1 other. *Books:* 172,556 (physical), 332,742 (digital/electronic); *Serial titles:* 239 (physical), 73,070 (digital/electronic); *Databases:* 100. Weekly public service hours: 90; students can reserve study rooms.

STUDENT LIFE

Housing options: on-campus residence required through senior year; coed, men-only, women-only. Campus housing is university owned. Freshman campus housing is guaranteed.

Activities and organizations: drama/theater group, student-run newspaper, radio and television station, choral group, Christian Science Organization, Community Service Team, International Students Association (Friendship Around the World), Rugby, Student Government.

Athletics Member NCAA. All Division III. ***Intercollegiate sports:*** baseball M, basketball M/W, cross-country running M/W, lacrosse W(c), rugby M(c), soccer M/W, softball W, swimming and diving M/W, tennis M/W, track and field M/W, volleyball W. ***Intramural sports:*** basketball M/W, soccer M/W, softball M/W.

Campus security: 24-hour emergency response devices and patrols, controlled dormitory access.

Student services: health clinic.

COSTS & FINANCIAL AID

Costs (2017–18) ***Comprehensive fee:*** $40,350 includes full-time tuition ($28,320), mandatory fees ($600), and room and board ($11,430). Full-time tuition and fees vary according to course load. Part-time tuition: $916 per credit hour. Part-time tuition and fees vary according to course load. ***Required fees:*** $300 per term part-time. ***College room only:*** $5430. Room and board charges vary according to board plan. ***Payment plan:*** installment. ***Waivers:*** employees or children of employees.

Financial Aid Of all full-time matriculated undergraduates who enrolled in 2016, 345 applied for aid, 335 were judged to have need, 184 had their need fully met. In 2016, 133 non-need-based awards were made. ***Average percent of need met:*** 95. ***Average financial aid package:*** $31,415. ***Average need-based loan:*** $5580. ***Average need-based gift aid:*** $27,447. ***Average non-need-based aid:*** $23,301. ***Average indebtedness upon graduation:*** $21,260.

APPLYING
Standardized Tests *Required:* SAT or ACT (for admission).

Options: electronic application, deferred entrance.

Required: essay or personal statement, high school transcript, minimum 2.4 GPA, 3 letters of recommendation, Christian Science commitment. ***Required for some:*** interview. ***Recommended:*** interview.

Application deadlines: rolling (freshmen), rolling (transfers).

Notification: continuous (freshmen), continuous (transfers).

CONTACT
Ms. Tami Gavaletz, Director of Admissions and Financial Aid, Principia College, 1 Maybeck Place, Elsah, IL 62028. *Phone:* 618-374-5187. *Toll-free phone:* 800-277-4648 Ext. 2804.

Quincy University

Quincy, Illinois

http://www.quincy.edu/

- **Independent Roman Catholic** comprehensive, founded 1860
- **Small-town** 70-acre campus
- **Endowment** $18.1 million
- **Coed**
- **Moderately difficult** entrance level

FACULTY
Student/faculty ratio: 14:1.

ACADEMICS
Calendar: semesters. *Degrees:* associate, bachelor's, and master's.
Library: Brenner Library.

STUDENT LIFE
Housing options: on-campus residence required through junior year; coed, special housing for students with disabilities. Campus housing is university owned. Freshman campus housing is guaranteed.

Activities and organizations: drama/theater group, student-run newspaper, choral group, marching band, Student Senate, Kappa Kappa Psi, Student Programming Board, Minority Student Association, Students in Free Enterprise (SIFE), national fraternities, national sororities.

Athletics Member NCAA. All Division II except volleyball (Division I).

Campus security: 24-hour emergency response devices and patrols, student patrols, late-night transport/escort service, controlled dormitory access, self-defense education, shuttle buses, lighted pathways/sidewalks.

Student services: health clinic, personal/psychological counseling.

COSTS & FINANCIAL AID
Costs (2016–17) ***Comprehensive fee:*** $37,628 includes full-time tuition ($25,998), mandatory fees ($1130), and room and board ($10,500). Part-time tuition: $710 per semester hour. Part-time tuition and fees vary according to course load. ***Required fees:*** $30 per semester hour part-time. ***College room only:*** $5500. Room and board charges vary according to board plan, housing facility, and student level.

Financial Aid Of all full-time matriculated undergraduates who enrolled in 2015, 938 applied for aid, 851 were judged to have need, 232 had their need fully met. 250 Federal Work-Study jobs (averaging $1794). 107 state and other part-time jobs (averaging $1580). In 2015, 97 non-need-based awards were made. ***Average percent of need met:*** 88. ***Average financial aid package:*** $24,970. ***Average need-based loan:*** $5820. ***Average need-based gift aid:*** $17,839. ***Average non-need-based aid:*** $11,165. ***Average indebtedness upon graduation:*** $28,607.

APPLYING
Standardized Tests *Required:* SAT or ACT (for admission).

Options: electronic application, deferred entrance.

Application fee: $25.

Required: essay or personal statement, high school transcript, minimum 2.5 GPA. ***Required for some:*** 1 letter of recommendation, audition for music majors, portfolio recommended for art majors. ***Recommended:*** interview.

CONTACT
Ms. Abby Wayman, Associate Director, Admissions, Quincy University, Admissions Office, 1800 College Avenue, Quincy, IL 62301-2699. *Phone:* 217-228-5432 Ext. 3414. *Toll-free phone:* 800-688-4295. *E-mail:* admissions@quincy.edu.

Rasmussen College Aurora

Aurora, Illinois

http://www.rasmussen.edu/

- **Proprietary** 4-year, part of Rasmussen College System
- **Suburban** campus
- **Coed** 410 undergraduate students, 67% full-time, 77% women, 23% men
- **Minimally difficult** entrance level, 96% of applicants were admitted

UNDERGRAD STUDENTS
273 full-time, 137 part-time.

Freshmen:
Admission: 23 applied, 22 admitted, 29 enrolled.

FACULTY
Total: 15, 20% full-time.
Student/faculty ratio: 22:1.

ACADEMICS
Calendar: quarters. *Degrees:* certificates, diplomas, associate, and bachelor's.

Special study options: academic remediation for entering students, accelerated degree program, adult/continuing education programs, distance learning, double majors, internships, part-time degree program, summer session for credit.

Computers: 87 computers/terminals are available on campus for general student use. Students can access the following: computer help desk, free student e-mail accounts, online (class) grades, online (class) schedules. Campuswide network is available. Wireless service is available via entire campus.
Library: Rasmussen College Library - Aurora.

STUDENT LIFE
Housing options: college housing not available.

COSTS
Costs (2017–18) ***Tuition:*** $11,055 full-time. Full-time tuition and fees vary according to course level, course load, degree level, location, and program. Part-time tuition and fees vary according to course level, course load, degree level, location, and program. No tuition increase for student's term of enrollment. ***Required fees:*** $1695 full-time. ***Payment plans:*** installment, deferred payment. ***Waivers:*** employees or children of employees.

APPLYING
Standardized Tests *Required:* institutional exam (for admission).

Options: electronic application, early admission, deferred entrance.

Required: high school transcript, minimum 2.0 GPA. ***Required for some:*** interview.

Application deadlines: rolling (freshmen), rolling (transfers).

CONTACT
Ms. Susan Hammerstrom, Director of Admissions, Rasmussen College Aurora, 2363 Sequoia Drive, Aurora, IL 60506. *Phone:* 630-888-3500. *Toll-free phone:* 888-549-6755. *E-mail:* susan.hammerstrom@rasmussen.edu.

Rasmussen College Mokena/Tinley Park

Mokena, Illinois

http://www.rasmussen.edu/

- **Proprietary** 4-year, part of Rasmussen College System
- **Suburban** campus
- **Coed** 396 undergraduate students, 49% full-time, 84% women, 16% men
- **Minimally difficult** entrance level, 96% of applicants were admitted

UNDERGRAD STUDENTS
195 full-time, 201 part-time.

Freshmen:
Admission: 26 applied, 25 admitted, 25 enrolled.

FACULTY
Total: 25, 4% full-time.
Student/faculty ratio: 22:1.

ACADEMICS
Calendar: quarters. *Degrees:* certificates, diplomas, associate, and bachelor's.

Special study options: academic remediation for entering students, accelerated degree program, adult/continuing education programs, distance learning, double majors, internships, part-time degree program, summer session for credit.

Computers: 73 computers/terminals are available on campus for general student use. Students can access the following: computer help desk, free student e-mail accounts, online (class) grades, online (class) schedules. Campuswide network is available. Wireless service is available via entire campus.
Library: Rasmussen College Library - Mokena.

STUDENT LIFE
Housing options: college housing not available.

COSTS
Costs (2017–18) ***Tuition:*** $11,055 full-time. Full-time tuition and fees vary according to course level, course load, degree level, location, and program. Part-time tuition and fees vary according to course level, course load, degree level, location, and program. No tuition increase for student's term of enrollment. ***Required fees:*** $1695 full-time. ***Payment plans:*** installment, deferred payment. ***Waivers:*** employees or children of employees.

APPLYING
Standardized Tests *Required:* institutional exam (for admission).

Options: electronic application, early admission, deferred entrance.

Required: high school transcript, minimum 2.0 GPA.
Required for some: interview.

Application deadlines: rolling (freshmen), rolling (transfers).

CONTACT
Ms. Susan Hammerstrom, Director of Admissions, Rasmussen College Mokena/Tinley Park, 8650 West Spring Lake Road, Mokena, IL 60448.
Phone: 815-534-3300. *Toll-free phone:* 888-549-6755.

Rasmussen College Rockford

Rockford, Illinois

http://www.rasmussen.edu/

- **Proprietary** 4-year, part of Rasmussen College System
- **Suburban** campus
- **Coed** 431 undergraduate students, 52% full-time, 77% women, 23% men
- **Minimally difficult** entrance level, 90% of applicants were admitted

UNDERGRAD STUDENTS
222 full-time, 209 part-time.

Freshmen:
Admission: 29 applied, 26 admitted, 26 enrolled.

FACULTY
Total: 54, 22% full-time.

Student/faculty ratio: 22:1.

ACADEMICS
Calendar: quarters. *Degrees:* certificates, diplomas, associate, and bachelor's.

Special study options: academic remediation for entering students, accelerated degree program, adult/continuing education programs, distance learning, double majors, internships, part-time degree program, summer session for credit.

Computers: 103 computers/terminals are available on campus for general student use. Students can access the following: computer help desk, free student e-mail accounts, online (class) grades, online (class) schedules. Campuswide network is available. Wireless service is available via entire campus.
Library: Rasmussen College Library - Rockford.

STUDENT LIFE
Housing options: college housing not available.

COSTS
Costs (2017–18) ***Tuition:*** $11,055 full-time. Full-time tuition and fees vary according to course level, course load, degree level, location, and program. Part-time tuition and fees vary according to course level, course load, degree level, location, and program. No tuition increase for student's term of enrollment. ***Required fees:*** $1695 full-time. ***Payment plans:*** installment, deferred payment. ***Waivers:*** employees or children of employees.

APPLYING
Standardized Tests *Required:* institutional exam (for admission).

Options: electronic application, early admission, deferred entrance.

Required: high school transcript, minimum 2.0 GPA. ***Required for some:*** interview.

Application deadlines: rolling (freshmen), rolling (transfers).

CONTACT
Ms. Susan Hammerstrom, Director of Admissions, Rasmussen College Rockford, 6000 East State Street, Fourth Floor, Rockford, IL 61108.
Phone: 815-316-4800. *Toll-free phone:* 888-549-6755.
E-mail: susan.hammerstrom@rasmussen.edu.

Rasmussen College Romeoville/Joliet

Romeoville, Illinois

http://www.rasmussen.edu/

- **Proprietary** 4-year, part of Rasmussen College System
- **Suburban** campus
- **Coed** 542 undergraduate students, 48% full-time, 79% women, 21% men
- **Minimally difficult** entrance level, 91% of applicants were admitted

UNDERGRAD STUDENTS
262 full-time, 280 part-time.

Freshmen:
Admission: 35 applied, 32 admitted, 32 enrolled.

FACULTY
Total: 58, 22% full-time.

Student/faculty ratio: 22:1.

ACADEMICS
Calendar: quarters. *Degrees:* certificates, diplomas, associate, and bachelor's.

Special study options: academic remediation for entering students, accelerated degree program, adult/continuing education programs, distance learning, double majors, internships, part-time degree program, summer session for credit.

Computers: 87 computers/terminals are available on campus for general student use. Students can access the following: computer help desk, free student e-mail accounts, online (class) grades, online (class) schedules. Campuswide network is available. Wireless service is available via entire campus.
Library: Rasmussen College Library - Romeoville.

STUDENT LIFE
Housing options: college housing not available.

COSTS
Costs (2017–18) ***Tuition:*** $11,055 full-time. Full-time tuition and fees vary according to course level, course load, degree level, location, and program. Part-time tuition and fees vary according to course level, course load, degree level, location, and program. No tuition increase for student's term of enrollment. ***Required fees:*** $1695 full-time. ***Payment plans:*** installment, deferred payment. ***Waivers:*** employees or children of employees.

APPLYING
Standardized Tests *Required:* institutional exam (for admission).

Options: electronic application, early admission, deferred entrance.

Required: high school transcript, minimum 2.0 GPA. ***Required for some:*** interview.

Application deadlines: rolling (freshmen), rolling (transfers).

CONTACT
Ms. Susan Hammerstrom, Director of Admissions, Rasmussen College Romeoville/Joliet, 1400 West Normantown Road, Romeoville, IL 60446.
Phone: 815-306-2600. *Toll-free phone:* 888-549-6755.
E-mail: susan.hammerstrom@rasmussen.edu.

Resurrection University

Chicago, Illinois

http://www.resu.edu/

- **Independent** upper-level, founded 1982
- **Urban** 10-acre campus with easy access to Chicago
- **Endowment** $1.5 million
- **Coed** 609 undergraduate students, 68% full-time, 78% women, 22% men
- **Moderately difficult** entrance level

UNDERGRAD STUDENTS
416 full-time, 193 part-time. Students come from 9 states and territories; 1% are from out of state; 15% Black or African American, non-Hispanic/Latino; 21% Hispanic/Latino; 16% Asian, non-Hispanic/Latino; 0.5% Native Hawaiian or other Pacific Islander, non-Hispanic/Latino; 0.7% American Indian or Alaska Native, non-Hispanic/Latino; 6% Two or more races, non-Hispanic/Latino; 6% Race/ethnicity unknown; 34% transferred in.

FACULTY
Total: 59, 44% full-time, 10% with terminal degrees.
Student/faculty ratio: 7:1.

ACADEMICS
Calendar: semesters. *Degrees:* certificates, bachelor's, and master's.
Special study options: academic remediation for entering students, accelerated degree program, advanced placement credit, independent study, part-time degree program, summer session for credit.
Computers: 36 computers/terminals are available on campus for general student use. Students can access the following: campus intranet, computer help desk, free student e-mail accounts, online (class) grades, online (class) registration, online (class) schedules. Campuswide network is available. Wireless service is available via entire campus.
Library: Resurrection University Library.

STUDENT LIFE
Housing options: college housing not available.
Campus security: 24-hour emergency response devices and patrols, late-night transport/escort service.
Student services: personal/psychological counseling.

FINANCIAL AID
Financial Aid Of all full-time matriculated undergraduates who enrolled in 2016, 434 applied for aid, 434 were judged to have need, 98 had their need fully met. In 2016, 6 non-need-based awards were made. ***Average percent of need met:*** 80. ***Average financial aid package:*** $18,775. ***Average need-based loan:*** $5500. ***Average need-based gift aid:*** $5000. ***Average non-need-based aid:*** $2000.

APPLYING
Standardized Tests *Required for some:* TEAS.
Options: electronic application, deferred entrance.
Application fee: $50.
Notification: 5/15 (transfers).

CONTACT
Resurrection University, 1431 N. Claremont Avenue, Chicago, IL 60622.

Robert Morris University Illinois

Chicago, Illinois

http://www.robertmorris.edu/

- **Independent** comprehensive, founded 1913
- **Urban** campus with easy access to Chicago
- **Endowment** $30.7 million
- **Coed** 2,352 undergraduate students, 96% full-time, 46% women, 54% men
- **Minimally difficult** entrance level, 23% of applicants were admitted

UNDERGRAD STUDENTS
2,253 full-time, 99 part-time. Students come from 39 states and territories; 10 other countries; 12% are from out of state; 25% Black or African American, non-Hispanic/Latino; 31% Hispanic/Latino; 3% Asian, non-Hispanic/Latino; 0.2% Native Hawaiian or other Pacific Islander, non-Hispanic/Latino; 0.2% American Indian or Alaska Native, non-Hispanic/Latino; 2% Two or more races, non-Hispanic/Latino; 3% Race/ethnicity unknown; 0.7% international; 15% transferred in; 10% live on campus.

Freshmen:
Admission: 2,732 applied, 632 admitted, 551 enrolled. ***Average high school GPA:*** 2.81. ***Test scores:*** ACT scores over 18: 64%; ACT scores over 24: 19%; ACT scores over 30: 1%.
Retention: 48% of full-time freshmen returned.

FACULTY
Total: 209, 39% full-time, 22% with terminal degrees.
Student/faculty ratio: 20:1.

ACADEMICS
Calendar: 5 10-week academic sessions per year. *Degrees:* associate, bachelor's, and master's.
Special study options: accelerated degree program, adult/continuing education programs, advanced placement credit, double majors, honors programs, internships, part-time degree program, services for LD students, study abroad, summer session for credit. ***ROTC:*** Army (c).
Computers: 1,360 computers/terminals are available on campus for general student use. Students can access the following: computer help desk, free student e-mail accounts, online (class) grades, online (class) registration, online (class) schedules, online credentials, online payments, online student accounts, online degree audit. Campuswide network is available. 100% of college-owned or -operated housing units are wired for high-speed Internet access. Wireless service is available via entire campus.
Library: Information Technology Library. *Books:* 163,851 (physical), 62,525 (digital/electronic); *Databases:* 40. Weekly public service hours: 74; students can reserve study rooms.

STUDENT LIFE
Housing options: coed. Campus housing is leased by the school. Freshman applicants given priority for college housing.
Activities and organizations: drama/theater group, student-run newspaper, choral group, marching band, Eagle Newspaper, Warriors to Scholars, Culinary Society, UNA-USA, Student Council.
Athletics Member NAIA, USCAA. ***Intercollegiate sports:*** baseball M(s), basketball M(s)/W(s), bowling M(s)/W(s), cheerleading M(s)/W(s), cross-country running M(s)/W(s), football M(s), golf M(s)/W(s), ice hockey M/W, lacrosse M(s)/W(s), soccer M(s)/W(s), softball W(s), track and field M(s)/W(s), volleyball M(s)/W(s). ***Intramural sports:*** bowling M/W, cross-country running M/W, softball M/W, volleyball M/W.
Campus security: late-night transport/escort service, controlled dormitory access, Urban campus has multiple security officers at all times who are off-duty Chicago police officers.
Student services: personal/psychological counseling.

COSTS & FINANCIAL AID
Costs (2017–18) ***Comprehensive fee:*** $40,380 includes full-time tuition ($26,700), mandatory fees ($480), and room and board ($13,200). Part-time tuition: $742 per quarter hour. Part-time tuition and fees vary according to course load. ***Payment plan:*** installment. ***Waivers:*** employees or children of employees.
Financial Aid Of all full-time matriculated undergraduates who enrolled in 2016, 2,081 applied for aid, 1,968 were judged to have need, 111 had their need fully met. 114 Federal Work-Study jobs (averaging $1099). In 2016, 81 non-need-based awards were made. ***Average percent of need met:*** 48. ***Average financial aid package:*** $17,131. ***Average need-based loan:*** $4303. ***Average need-based gift aid:*** $13,701. ***Average non-need-based aid:*** $13,002. ***Average indebtedness upon graduation:*** $30,985.

APPLYING
Standardized Tests *Required for some:* SAT or ACT (for admission), ACT for nursing and surgical technology programs.
Options: electronic application, deferred entrance.
Application fee: $20.
Required for some: high school transcript. ***Recommended:*** interview.
Application deadlines: rolling (freshmen), rolling (out-of-state freshmen), rolling (transfers).
Notification: continuous (freshmen), continuous (out-of-state freshmen), continuous (transfers).

CONTACT
Admissions Office, Robert Morris University Illinois, 401 South State Street, Chicago, IL 60605. *Phone:* 312-935-4400. *Toll-free phone:* 800-762-5960. *Fax:* 312-935-4182. *E-mail:* enroll@robertmorris.edu.

Rockford University

Rockford, Illinois

http://www.rockford.edu/

- **Independent** comprehensive, founded 1847
- **Suburban** 150-acre campus with easy access to Chicago
- **Coed** 1,086 undergraduate students, 87% full-time, 57% women, 43% men

UNDERGRAD STUDENTS
945 full-time, 141 part-time. 11% are from out of state; 10% Black or African American, non-Hispanic/Latino; 14% Hispanic/Latino; 2% Asian, non-Hispanic/Latino; 0.1% American Indian or Alaska Native, non-Hispanic/Latino; 3% Two or more races, non-Hispanic/Latino; 0.7% Race/ethnicity unknown; 3% international; 14% transferred in; 37% live on campus.

Freshmen:
Admission: 162 enrolled. ***Average high school GPA:*** 3.23. ***Test scores:*** ACT scores over 18: 94%; ACT scores over 24: 35%; ACT scores over 30: 5%.
Retention: 58% of full-time freshmen returned.

FACULTY
Total: 155, 49% full-time, 48% with terminal degrees.
Student/faculty ratio: 10:1.

ACADEMICS
Calendar: semesters. *Degrees:* bachelor's, master's, and postbachelor's certificates.
Special study options: academic remediation for entering students, accelerated degree program, adult/continuing education programs, advanced placement credit, distance learning, double majors, English as a second language, honors programs, independent study, internships, off-campus study, part-time degree program, services for LD students, study abroad, summer session for credit.
Computers: 94 computers/terminals and 4 ports are available on campus for general student use. Students can access the following: campus intranet, computer help desk, free student e-mail accounts, online (class) grades, online (class) registration, online (class) schedules, online bill payment. Campuswide network is available. 100% of college-owned or -operated housing units are wired for high-speed Internet access. Wireless service is available via entire campus.
Library: Howard Colman Library. *Books:* 134,831 (physical), 140,140 (digital/electronic); *Serial titles:* 157 (physical), 23,000 (digital/electronic); *Databases:* 27. Weekly public service hours: 85; students can reserve study rooms.

STUDENT LIFE
Housing options: coed, special housing for students with disabilities. Campus housing is university owned.
Activities and organizations: drama/theater group, student-run newspaper, radio station, choral group, Campus Activities Board, Multicultural Club, Student Government Association, Nursing Student Organization, Alpha Helix.
Athletics Member NCAA. All Division III. ***Intercollegiate sports:*** baseball M, basketball M/W, cross-country running M/W, football M, soccer M/W, softball W, track and field M/W, volleyball W. ***Intramural sports:*** basketball M/W, football M/W, volleyball M/W.
Campus security: 24-hour emergency response devices and patrols, student patrols, late-night transport/escort service, controlled dormitory access.
Student services: health clinic, personal/psychological counseling.

COSTS & FINANCIAL AID
Costs (2017–18) ***Comprehensive fee:*** $38,470 includes full-time tuition ($29,920), mandatory fees ($130), and room and board ($8420). Full-time tuition and fees vary according to course load. Part-time tuition: $785 per credit hour. Part-time tuition and fees vary according to course load. ***College room only:*** $4570. Room and board charges vary according to board plan and housing facility. ***Payment plan:*** installment. ***Waivers:*** employees or children of employees.
Financial Aid Of all full-time matriculated undergraduates who enrolled in 2015, 851 applied for aid, 806 were judged to have need, 99 had their need fully met. 130 Federal Work-Study jobs (averaging $727). 164 state and other part-time jobs (averaging $859). In 2015, 82 non-need-based awards were made. ***Average percent of need met:*** 64. ***Average financial aid package:*** $18,757. ***Average need-based loan:*** $5046. ***Average need-based gift aid:*** $14,176. ***Average non-need-based aid:*** $10,221. ***Average indebtedness upon graduation:*** $40,313.

APPLYING
Standardized Tests *Required:* SAT or ACT (for admission).
Required: high school transcript. ***Required for some:*** essay or personal statement, minimum 2.7 GPA, 2 letters of recommendation. ***Recommended:*** minimum 2.7 GPA.

CONTACT
Ms. Jennifer Nordstrom, Associate Vice President for Undergraduate Admission, Rockford University, 5050 East State Street, Rockford, IL 61108-2393. *Phone:* 815-226-4050. *Toll-free phone:* 800-892-2984. *Fax:* 815-226-2822. *E-mail:* admissions@rockford.edu.

Roosevelt University

Chicago, Illinois

http://www.roosevelt.edu/

- **Independent** comprehensive, founded 1945
- **Urban** campus with easy access to Chicago
- **Endowment** $84.8 million
- **Coed**
- **Moderately difficult** entrance level

FACULTY
Student/faculty ratio: 11:1.

ACADEMICS
Calendar: semesters. *Degrees:* bachelor's, master's, doctoral, and postbachelor's certificates.
Library: Murray-Green Library plus 4 others.

STUDENT LIFE
Housing options: on-campus residence required through sophomore year; coed. Campus housing is university owned, leased by the school and is provided by a third party. Freshman campus housing is guaranteed.
Activities and organizations: student-run newspaper, radio station, International Student Union, RU Proud, Association of Latin Americans (ALAS), Student Government, Residence Hall Council, national fraternities, national sororities.
Athletics Member NAIA.
Campus security: 24-hour emergency response devices and patrols, late-night transport/escort service, controlled dormitory access.
Student services: personal/psychological counseling.

COSTS & FINANCIAL AID
Costs (2016–17) ***Comprehensive fee:*** $40,919 includes full-time tuition ($28,119) and room and board ($12,800). Full-time tuition and fees vary according to program. Part-time tuition: $759 per credit. Part-time tuition and fees vary according to program. ***Required fees:*** $288 per term part-time. ***Room and board:*** Room and board charges vary according to board plan and housing facility.
Financial Aid Of all full-time matriculated undergraduates who enrolled in 2014, 2,812 applied for aid, 2,397 were judged to have need, 169 had their need fully met. In 2014, 500 non-need-based awards were made. ***Average percent of need met:*** 75. ***Average financial aid package:*** $22,318. ***Average need-based loan:*** $8800. ***Average need-based gift aid:*** $9000. ***Average non-need-based aid:*** $7000.

APPLYING
Standardized Tests *Required:* SAT or ACT (for admission).
Options: electronic application, deferred entrance.
Application fee: $25.
Required: high school transcript, minimum 2.5 GPA, audition for music and theater programs. ***Required for some:*** essay or personal statement, interview. ***Recommended:*** essay or personal statement.

CONTACT
Director of Admission, Roosevelt University, IL. *Phone:* 312-341-2107. *Toll-free phone:* 877-APPLYRU. *Fax:* 312-341-3253. *E-mail:* admission@roosevelt.edu.

Rush University

Chicago, Illinois

http://www.rushu.rush.edu/

CONTACT
Rush University, 600 South Paulina, Chicago, IL 60612-3832. *Phone:* 312-942-7100.

Saint Anthony College of Nursing

Rockford, Illinois

http://www.sacn.edu/

- **Independent Roman Catholic** upper-level, founded 1915
- **Suburban** 7-acre campus with easy access to Chicago
- **Coed, primarily women** 238 undergraduate students, 70% full-time, 89% women, 11% men
- **Moderately difficult** entrance level

UNDERGRAD STUDENTS
167 full-time, 71 part-time. Students come from 2 states and territories; 10% are from out of state; 2% Black or African American, non-Hispanic/Latino; 13% Hispanic/Latino; 5% Asian, non-Hispanic/Latino; 0.4% Native Hawaiian or other Pacific Islander, non-Hispanic/Latino; 2% Two or more races, non-Hispanic/Latino; 0.4% Race/ethnicity unknown; 24% transferred in.

FACULTY
Total: 39, 59% full-time, 38% with terminal degrees.

Student/faculty ratio: 7:1.

ACADEMICS
Calendar: semesters. *Degrees:* bachelor's, master's, doctoral, and post-master's certificates.

Special study options: advanced placement credit, independent study, internships, part-time degree program, services for LD students, summer session for credit.

Computers: 104 computers/terminals are available on campus for general student use. Students can access the following: computer help desk, free student e-mail accounts, online (class) grades, online (class) registration, online (class) schedules. Campuswide network is available. Wireless service is available via entire campus.

Library: Sister Mary Linus Learning Resource Center. Students can reserve study rooms.

STUDENT LIFE
Housing options: college housing not available.

Activities and organizations: Student Organization.

Campus security: 24-hour patrols.

Student services: health clinic, personal/psychological counseling, legal services.

FINANCIAL AID
Financial Aid Of all full-time matriculated undergraduates who enrolled in 2015, 154 applied for aid, 145 were judged to have need, 3 had their need fully met. In 2015, 1 non-need-based awards were made. ***Average percent of need met:*** 38. ***Average financial aid package:*** $9203. ***Average need-based loan:*** $4268. ***Average need-based gift aid:*** $7100. ***Average non-need-based aid:*** $4000.

APPLYING
Options: electronic application.

Application fee: $75.

Notification: 3/21 (transfers).

CONTACT
Ms. April Lipnitzky, Enrollment Management Coordinator, Saint Anthony College of Nursing, 5658 East State Street, Rockford, IL 61108-2468. *Phone:* 815-227-2141. *Fax:* 815-227-2730. *E-mail:* admissions@sacn.edu.

St. Augustine College

Chicago, Illinois

http://www.staugustine.edu/

CONTACT
Ms. Gloria Quiroz, Director of Admissions, St. Augustine College, 1333-1345 West Argyle, Chicago, IL 60640-3501. *Phone:* 773-878-3256. *Fax:* 773-878-0937. *E-mail:* info@staugustine.edu.

Saint Francis Medical Center College of Nursing

Peoria, Illinois

http://www.sfmccon.edu/

- **Independent Roman Catholic** upper-level, founded 1986
- **Urban** campus
- **Coed, primarily women** 392 undergraduate students, 77% full-time, 90% women, 10% men
- 72% of applicants were admitted

UNDERGRAD STUDENTS
301 full-time, 91 part-time. Students come from 3 states and territories; 3 other countries; 1% are from out of state; 3% Black or African American, non-Hispanic/Latino; 3% Hispanic/Latino; 2% Asian, non-Hispanic/Latino; 1% Two or more races, non-Hispanic/Latino; 0.8% Race/ethnicity unknown; 0.8% international; 21% transferred in; 18% live on campus.

Freshmen:
Admission: 223 applied, 161 admitted.

FACULTY
Total: 53, 68% full-time, 21% with terminal degrees.

Student/faculty ratio: 9:1.

ACADEMICS
Calendar: semesters. *Degrees:* bachelor's, master's, doctoral, and post-master's certificates.

Special study options: academic remediation for entering students, accelerated degree program, adult/continuing education programs, advanced placement credit, distance learning, independent study, part-time degree program, summer session for credit.

Computers: 62 computers/terminals and 53 ports are available on campus for general student use. Students can access the following: computer help desk, online (class) grades, online (class) registration, online (class) schedules. Campuswide network is available. 100% of college-owned or -operated housing units are wired for high-speed Internet access. Wireless service is available via entire campus.

Library: Sister Mary Ludgera Pieperbeck Learning and Resource Center plus 1 other. *Books:* 4,054 (physical), 298 (digital/electronic); *Serial titles:* 126 (physical); *Databases:* 57. Students can reserve study rooms.

STUDENT LIFE
Housing options: coed. Campus housing is university owned.

Activities and organizations: Student Senate, SNAI, Minority Student Association, Tau Omicron.

Campus security: 24-hour emergency response devices and patrols, controlled dormitory access.

Student services: health clinic, personal/psychological counseling.

COSTS & FINANCIAL AID
Costs (2017–18) ***Tuition:*** $19,734 full-time, $598 per semester hour part-time. Full-time tuition and fees vary according to course load, degree level, program, and student level. Part-time tuition and fees vary according to course load, degree level, program, and student level. ***Required fees:*** $1120 full-time, $90 per course part-time. ***Room only:*** $3600. ***Payment plan:*** installment. ***Waivers:*** employees or children of employees.

Financial Aid Of all full-time matriculated undergraduates who enrolled in 2016, 249 applied for aid, 218 were judged to have need, 14 had their need fully met. In 2016, 22 non-need-based awards were made. ***Average percent of need met:*** 40. ***Average financial aid package:*** $9152. ***Average need-based loan:*** $5450. ***Average need-based gift aid:*** $6840. ***Average non-need-based aid:*** $2123.

APPLYING
Options: deferred entrance.
Application fee: $50.
Notification: 10/15 (transfers).

CONTACT
Saint Francis Medical Center College of Nursing, 511 Northeast Greenleaf Street, Peoria, IL 61603-3783. *Phone:* 309-624-8980.

St. John's College

Springfield, Illinois

http://www.stjohnscollegespringfield.edu/

CONTACT
St. John's College, 729 East Carpenter Street, Springfield, IL 62702. *Phone:* 217-525-5628.

Saint Xavier University

Chicago, Illinois

http://www.sxu.edu/

CONTACT
Dr. Kathleen Carlson, Vice President, Saint Xavier University, 3700 West 103rd Street, Chicago, IL 60655-3105. *Phone:* 773-298-3305. *Toll-free phone:* 800-462-9288. *E-mail:* carlson@sxu.edu.

School of the Art Institute of Chicago

Chicago, Illinois

http://www.saic.edu/

- **Independent** comprehensive, founded 1866
- **Urban** 1-acre campus with easy access to Chicago
- **Coed** 2,849 undergraduate students, 94% full-time, 73% women, 27% men
- **Very difficult** entrance level, 59% of applicants were admitted

UNDERGRAD STUDENTS
2,681 full-time, 168 part-time. Students come from 48 other countries; 3% Black or African American, non-Hispanic/Latino; 11% Hispanic/Latino; 11% Asian, non-Hispanic/Latino; 0.1% Native Hawaiian or other Pacific Islander, non-Hispanic/Latino; 0.2% American Indian or Alaska Native, non-Hispanic/Latino; 3% Two or more races, non-Hispanic/Latino; 5% Race/ethnicity unknown; 32% international; 7% transferred in; 17% live on campus.

Freshmen:
Admission: 5,244 applied, 3,111 admitted, 634 enrolled. ***Average high school GPA:*** 3.51.
Retention: 81% of full-time freshmen returned.

FACULTY
Total: 731, 24% full-time, 68% with terminal degrees.
Student/faculty ratio: 11:1.

ACADEMICS
Calendar: semesters. *Degrees:* bachelor's, master's, and postbachelor's certificates.
Special study options: academic remediation for entering students, advanced placement credit, cooperative education, double majors, English as a second language, independent study, internships, off-campus study, part-time degree program, services for LD students, student-designed majors, study abroad, summer session for credit.
Computers: 300 computers/terminals and 945 ports are available on campus for general student use. Students can access the following: campus intranet, computer help desk, free student e-mail accounts, online (class) grades, online (class) registration, online (class) schedules. Campuswide network is available. 100% of college-owned or -operated housing units are wired for high-speed Internet access. Wireless service is available via entire campus.
Library: The John M. Flaxman Library plus 1 other. *Books:* 110,287 (physical), 203,725 (digital/electronic); *Serial titles:* 19,541 (physical), 204,634 (digital/electronic); *Databases:* 177.

STUDENT LIFE
Housing options: coed, special housing for students with disabilities. Campus housing is university owned.
Activities and organizations: drama/theater group, student-run newspaper, radio and television station, Student Association/Student Union Galleries, Korean Student Association, InterVarsity, Curatorial Community, Good 'Ol Futbol.
Campus security: 24-hour emergency response devices and patrols, late-night transport/escort service, controlled dormitory access.
Student services: health clinic, personal/psychological counseling.

COSTS & FINANCIAL AID
Costs (2016–17) ***Comprehensive fee:*** $60,940 includes full-time tuition ($44,910), mandatory fees ($840), and room and board ($15,190). Full-time tuition and fees vary according to course load, degree level, and program. Part-time tuition: $1497 per credit hour. Part-time tuition and fees vary according to course load, degree level, and program. ***Required fees:*** $285 per term part-time. ***College room only:*** $11,600. Room and board charges vary according to board plan and housing facility. ***Payment plan:*** installment. ***Waivers:*** employees or children of employees.
Financial Aid Of all full-time matriculated undergraduates who enrolled in 2015, 1,320 applied for aid, 1,163 were judged to have need, 106 had their need fully met. In 2015, 1243 non-need-based awards were made. ***Average percent of need met:*** 60. ***Average financial aid package:*** $34,730. ***Average need-based loan:*** $5178. ***Average need-based gift aid:*** $18,949. ***Average non-need-based aid:*** $9363. ***Average indebtedness upon graduation:*** $35,455.

APPLYING
Standardized Tests *Required:* SAT or ACT (for admission).
Options: electronic application, early action, deferred entrance.
Application fee: $65.
Required: essay or personal statement, high school transcript. ***Recommended:*** interview.
Application deadlines: 11/15 (freshmen), 3/15 (transfers).
Notification: continuous until 1/30 (freshmen), continuous (transfers).

CONTACT
Ms. Asia Mitchell, Director, Undergraduate Admissions, School of the Art Institute of Chicago, 36 South Wabash, Chicago, IL 60603. *Phone:* 312-629-6100. *Toll-free phone:* 800-232-SAIC. *Fax:* 312-629-6101. *E-mail:* ugadmiss@saic.edu.

Shimer College

Chicago, Illinois

http://www.shimer.edu/

CONTACT
Ms. Amy Pritts, Director of Admission, Shimer College, 3424 South State Street, Chicago, IL 60616. *Phone:* 312-235-3504. *Toll-free phone:* 800-215-7173. *Fax:* 888-808-3133. *E-mail:* admission@shimer.edu.

Southern Illinois University Carbondale

Carbondale, Illinois

http://www.siu.edu/

- **State-supported** university, founded 1869, part of Southern Illinois Univelrsity
- **Rural** 1136-acre campus with easy access to St. Louis
- **Coed**
- **Moderately difficult** entrance level

UNDERGRAD STUDENTS
Students come from 53 states and territories; 57 other countries.

ACADEMICS
Calendar: semesters plus 8-week summer session. *Degrees:* certificates, associate, bachelor's, master's, doctoral, and postbachelor's certificates.
Special study options: academic remediation for entering students, accelerated degree program, adult/continuing education programs, advanced placement credit, cooperative education, distance learning, double majors, English as a second language, honors programs,

independent study, internships, off-campus study, part-time degree program, services for LD students, student-designed majors, study abroad, summer session for credit. ***ROTC:*** Army (b), Air Force (b).

Computers: 1,900 computers/terminals are available on campus for general student use. Students can access the following: campus intranet, computer help desk, free student e-mail accounts, online (class) grades, online (class) registration, online (class) schedules. Campuswide network is available. 100% of college-owned or -operated housing units are wired for high-speed Internet access. Wireless service is available via classrooms, computer centers, computer labs, dorm rooms, learning centers, libraries, student centers.

Library: Morris Library plus 1 other. *Books:* 310,152 (physical), 307,707 (digital/electronic); *Serial titles:* 309 (physical), 49,681 (digital/electronic); *Databases:* 171. Weekly public service hours: 100; students can reserve study rooms.

STUDENT LIFE

Housing options: on-campus residence required for freshman year; coed, men-only, women-only, special housing for students with disabilities. Campus housing is university owned. Freshman campus housing is guaranteed.

Activities and organizations: drama/theater group, student-run newspaper, radio and television station, choral group, marching band, Inter-Greek Council, Black Affairs Council, Residence Hall Association, Collegiate FFA, Equestrian Club, national fraternities, national sororities.

Athletics Member NCAA. All Division I except football (Division I-AA). ***Intercollegiate sports:*** baseball M(s), basketball M(s)/W(s), cheerleading M/W, cross-country running M(s)/W(s), golf M(s)/W(s), softball W(s), swimming and diving M(s)/W(s), tennis M(s)/W(s), track and field M(s)/W(s), volleyball W(s). ***Intramural sports:*** archery M(c)/W(c), badminton M(c)/W(c), baseball M(c), basketball M/W, bowling M(c)/W(c), equestrian sports M(c)/W(c), fencing M(c)/W(c), gymnastics M(c)/W(c), lacrosse M(c), racquetball M/W, rock climbing M(c)/W(c), rugby M(c)/W(c), sailing M(c)/W(c), soccer M(c)/W(c), softball W(c), swimming and diving W, table tennis M(c)/W(c), tennis M(c)/W(c), triathlon M(c)/W(c), ultimate Frisbee M(c)/W(c), volleyball M(c)/W(c), water polo M(c)/W(c), weight lifting M(c)/W(c), wrestling M(c)/W(c).

Campus security: 24-hour emergency response devices and patrols, student patrols, late-night transport/escort service, controlled dormitory access, well-lit pathways, night safety vans, student transit system.

Student services: health clinic, personal/psychological counseling, women's center, legal services.

COSTS & FINANCIAL AID

Costs (2016–17) ***Tuition:*** state resident $9099 full-time, $303 per credit hour part-time; nonresident $22,748 full-time, $758 per credit hour part-time. Full-time tuition and fees vary according to course load, location, program, reciprocity agreements, and student level. Part-time tuition and fees vary according to course load, location, program, reciprocity agreements, and student level. No tuition increase for student's term of enrollment. ***Required fees:*** $4382 full-time, $951 per credit hour part-time. ***Room and board:*** $10,186. Room and board charges vary according to board plan and housing facility. ***Payment plan:*** installment. ***Waivers:*** children of alumni, senior citizens, and employees or children of employees.

Financial Aid Of all full-time matriculated undergraduates who enrolled in 2016, 8,475 applied for aid, 7,386 were judged to have need, 623 had their need fully met. 1,495 Federal Work-Study jobs (averaging $1039). In 2016, 482 non-need-based awards were made. ***Average percent of need met:*** 60. ***Average financial aid package:*** $14,946. ***Average need-based loan:*** $4439. ***Average need-based gift aid:*** $7533. ***Average non-need-based aid:*** $6788. ***Average indebtedness upon graduation:*** $33,218.

APPLYING

Standardized Tests *Required:* SAT or ACT (for admission).

Options: electronic application, deferred entrance.

Application fee: $40.

Required: high school transcript.

Application deadlines: rolling (freshmen), rolling (out-of-state freshmen), rolling (transfers).

Notification: continuous until 9/1 (freshmen), continuous until 9/1 (out-of-state freshmen), continuous (transfers).

CONTACT
Tamora Workman, Director of the Registrar's Office, Southern Illinois University Carbondale, Office of Registrar, 1263 Lincoln Drive MC 4701, Carbondale, IL 62901. *Phone:* 618-453-2963. *Fax:* 618-453-2915. *E-mail:* regstrar@siu.edu.

See previous page for display ad and page 1510 for the College Close-Up.

Southern Illinois University Edwardsville

Edwardsville, Illinois

http://www.siue.edu/

- **State-supported** comprehensive, founded 1957, part of Southern Illinois University
- **Suburban** 2660-acre campus with easy access to St. Louis
- **Endowment** $19.2 million
- **Coed** 11,720 undergraduate students, 85% full-time, 53% women, 47% men
- **Moderately difficult** entrance level, 89% of applicants were admitted

UNDERGRAD STUDENTS
9,908 full-time, 1,812 part-time. Students come from 41 states and territories; 39 other countries; 12% are from out of state; 14% Black or African American, non-Hispanic/Latino; 4% Hispanic/Latino; 2% Asian, non-Hispanic/Latino; 0.1% Native Hawaiian or other Pacific Islander, non-Hispanic/Latino; 0.3% American Indian or Alaska Native, non-Hispanic/Latino; 3% Two or more races, non-Hispanic/Latino; 1% Race/ethnicity unknown; 1% international; 12% transferred in; 26% live on campus.

Freshmen:
Admission: 7,274 applied, 6,496 admitted, 1,932 enrolled. *Average high school GPA:* 3.43. *Test scores:* ACT scores over 18: 96%; ACT scores over 24: 44%; ACT scores over 30: 7%.

Retention: 74% of full-time freshmen returned.

FACULTY
Total: 861, 69% full-time, 68% with terminal degrees.

Student/faculty ratio: 20:1.

ACADEMICS
Calendar: semesters. *Degrees:* bachelor's, master's, doctoral, post-master's, and postbachelor's certificates.

Special study options: academic remediation for entering students, accelerated degree program, advanced placement credit, cooperative education, distance learning, double majors, English as a second language, external degree program, honors programs, independent study, internships, off-campus study, part-time degree program, services for LD students, student-designed majors, study abroad, summer session for credit. *ROTC:* Army (b), Air Force (c).

Unusual degree programs: 3-2 engineering.

Computers: 315 computers/terminals are available on campus for general student use. Students can access the following: campus intranet, computer help desk, free student e-mail accounts, online (class) grades, online (class) registration, online (class) schedules, online job finder. Campuswide network is available. 100% of college-owned or -operated housing units are wired for high-speed Internet access. Wireless service is available via entire campus.

Library: Lovejoy Library. *Books:* 735,524 (physical), 53,922 (digital/electronic); *Serial titles:* 226 (physical), 33,821 (digital/electronic). Students can reserve study rooms.

STUDENT LIFE
Housing options: coed, special housing for students with disabilities. Campus housing is university owned. Freshman applicants given priority for college housing.

Activities and organizations: drama/theater group, student-run newspaper, radio and television station, choral group, Fraternity and Sorority Life, Campus Activities Board, Sports Clubs/Intramurals, Dance Marathon, Student Government, national fraternities, national sororities.

Athletics Member NCAA. All Division I. *Intercollegiate sports:* baseball M(s), basketball M(s)/W(s), cross-country running M(s)/W(s), golf M(s), soccer M(s)/W(s), softball W(s), tennis W(s), track and field M(s)/W(s), volleyball W(s), wrestling M(s). *Intramural sports:* archery M/W, badminton M/W, basketball M/W, bowling M/W, cheerleading M/W, fencing M/W, football M, ice hockey M, racquetball M/W, rock climbing M/W, soccer M/W, softball M/W, swimming and diving M/W, table tennis M/W, tennis M/W, ultimate Frisbee M/W, volleyball M/W, water polo M/W, weight lifting M/W.

Campus security: 24-hour emergency response devices and patrols, student patrols, late-night transport/escort service, controlled dormitory access, 24-hour ID check at residence hall entrances, emergency call boxes located throughout campus.

Student services: health clinic, personal/psychological counseling, legal services.

COSTS & FINANCIAL AID
Costs (2017–18) *Tuition:* state resident $8772 full-time, $292 per credit hour part-time; nonresident $8772 full-time, $731 per credit hour part-time. Full-time tuition and fees vary according to course load, degree level, location, and program. Part-time tuition and fees vary according to course load, degree level, location, and program. No tuition increase for student's term of enrollment. ***Required fees:*** $2721 full-time. ***Room and board:*** $9481. Room and board charges vary according to board plan, housing facility, and student level. ***Payment plan:*** installment. ***Waivers:*** senior citizens and employees or children of employees.

Financial Aid Of all full-time matriculated undergraduates who enrolled in 2015, 8,167 applied for aid, 6,499 were judged to have need, 2,442 had their need fully met. In 2015, 521 non-need-based awards were made. ***Average percent of need met:*** 60. ***Average financial aid package:*** $11,223. ***Average need-based loan:*** $4496. ***Average need-based gift aid:*** $7760. ***Average non-need-based aid:*** $5113. ***Average indebtedness upon graduation:*** $22,277.

APPLYING
Standardized Tests *Required:* SAT or ACT (for admission).

Options: electronic application, deferred entrance.

Application fee: $40.

Required: high school transcript. ***Recommended:*** minimum 2.5 GPA.

Notification: continuous (freshmen), continuous (transfers).

CONTACT
Mr. Todd Burrell, Director of Admissions, Southern Illinois University Edwardsville, Campus Box 1600, Rendleman Hall, Edwardsville, IL 62026-1600. *Phone:* 618-650-3705. *Toll-free phone:* 800-447-SIUE. *Fax:* 618-650-5013. *E-mail:* admissions@siue.edu.

Telshe Yeshiva–Chicago

Chicago, Illinois

CONTACT
Rosh Hayeshiva, Telshe Yeshiva–Chicago, 3535 West Foster Avenue, Chicago, IL 60625-5598. *Phone:* 773-463-7738.

Trinity Christian College

Palos Heights, Illinois

http://www.trnty.edu/

- **Independent Christian Reformed** comprehensive, founded 1959
- **Suburban** 53-acre campus with easy access to Chicago
- **Endowment** $10.8 million
- **Coed** 1,193 undergraduate students, 80% full-time, 67% women, 33% men
- **Moderately difficult** entrance level, 70% of applicants were admitted

UNDERGRAD STUDENTS
955 full-time, 238 part-time. Students come from 29 states and territories; 10 other countries; 30% are from out of state; 9% Black or African American, non-Hispanic/Latino; 12% Hispanic/Latino; 1% Asian, non-Hispanic/Latino; 0.1% Native Hawaiian or other Pacific Islander, non-Hispanic/Latino; 0.3% American Indian or Alaska Native, non-Hispanic/Latino; 2% Two or more races, non-Hispanic/Latino; 4% Race/ethnicity unknown; 8% international; 6% transferred in; 45% live on campus.

Freshmen:
Admission: 884 applied, 619 admitted, 160 enrolled. *Average high school GPA:* 3.46. *Test scores:* SAT critical reading scores over 500: 60%; ACT

scores over 18: 92%; SAT critical reading scores over 600: 40%; ACT scores over 24: 43%; SAT critical reading scores over 700: 10%; ACT scores over 30: 9%.

Retention: 83% of full-time freshmen returned.

FACULTY

Total: 156, 45% full-time, 45% with terminal degrees.

Student/faculty ratio: 10:1.

ACADEMICS

Calendar: semesters plus 2 week interim term. *Degrees:* bachelor's and master's.

Special study options: academic remediation for entering students, accelerated degree program, adult/continuing education programs, advanced placement credit, cooperative education, distance learning, double majors, English as a second language, honors programs, independent study, internships, off-campus study, part-time degree program, services for LD students, study abroad, summer session for credit.

Computers: 170 computers/terminals are available on campus for general student use. Students can access the following: campus intranet, computer help desk, free student e-mail accounts, online (class) grades, online (class) registration, online (class) schedules. Campuswide network is available. 100% of college-owned or -operated housing units are wired for high-speed Internet access. Wireless service is available via entire campus.

Library: Jennie Huizenga Memorial Library plus 1 other. *Books:* 72,833 (physical), 6,060 (digital/electronic); *Serial titles:* 62 (physical), 24 (digital/electronic); *Databases:* 44. Weekly public service hours: 84; students can reserve study rooms.

STUDENT LIFE

Housing options: coed. Campus housing is university owned. Freshman campus housing is guaranteed.

Activities and organizations: drama/theater group, student-run newspaper, choral group, Student Association, Student ministries, Campus newspaper, Pro-Life Task Force, PACE (prison tutoring program).

Athletics Member NAIA, NCCAA. ***Intercollegiate sports:*** baseball M(s), basketball M(s)/W(s), cross-country running M(s)/W(s), golf M(s)/W, soccer M(s)/W(s), softball W(s), track and field M(s)/W(s), volleyball M/W(s). ***Intramural sports:*** badminton M/W, basketball M/W, football M/W, soccer M/W, volleyball M/W.

Campus security: 24-hour emergency response devices and patrols, student patrols, late-night transport/escort service, controlled dormitory access, security cameras, Code Blue Emergency Phones.

Student services: personal/psychological counseling.

COSTS & FINANCIAL AID

Costs (2016–17) ***One-time required fee:*** $225. ***Comprehensive fee:*** $37,030 includes full-time tuition ($27,200), mandatory fees ($250), and room and board ($9580). Full-time tuition and fees vary according to course load and degree level. Part-time tuition: $908 per credit hour. Part-time tuition and fees vary according to course load and degree level. ***Room and board:*** Room and board charges vary according to board plan and housing facility. ***Payment plan:*** installment. ***Waivers:*** employees or children of employees.

Financial Aid Of all full-time matriculated undergraduates who enrolled in 2016, 772 applied for aid, 708 were judged to have need, 100 had their need fully met. In 2016, 121 non-need-based awards were made. ***Average percent of need met:*** 70. ***Average financial aid package:*** $19,593. ***Average need-based loan:*** $4640. ***Average need-based gift aid:*** $15,990. ***Average non-need-based aid:*** $9420. ***Average indebtedness upon graduation:*** $31,321.

APPLYING

Standardized Tests *Required:* SAT or ACT (for admission).

Options: electronic application, deferred entrance.

Application fee: $30.

Required: essay or personal statement, high school transcript, minimum 2.5 GPA, interview. ***Required for some:*** 1 letter of recommendation, minimum ACT composite score of 19 or combined SAT of 910.

Application deadlines: rolling (freshmen), rolling (transfers).

Notification: continuous (freshmen), continuous (transfers).

CONTACT

Jeremy Klyn, Director of Admissions, Trinity Christian College, 6601 West College Drive, Palos Heights, IL 60463. *Phone:* 708-293-4712. *Toll-free phone:* 866-TRIN-4-ME. *Fax:* 708-239-4826. *E-mail:* admissions@trnty.edu.

Trinity College of Nursing and Health Sciences

Rock Island, Illinois

http://www.trinitycollegeqc.edu/

CONTACT

Ms. Lori Perez, Admissions Representative, Trinity College of Nursing and Health Sciences, 2122 - 25th Avenue, Rock Island, IL 61201. *Phone:* 309-779-7700. *Fax:* 309-779-7748. *E-mail:* perezlj@ihs.org.

Trinity International University

Deerfield, Illinois

http://www.tiu.edu/

CONTACT

Mr. Aaron Mahl, Director of Undergraduate Admissions, Trinity International University, 2065 Half Day Road, Deerfield, IL 60015-1284. *Phone:* 847-317-7000. *Toll-free phone:* 800-822-3225. *Fax:* 847-317-8097. *E-mail:* tcadmissions@tiu.edu.

University of Chicago

Chicago, Illinois

http://www.uchicago.edu/

- **Independent** university, founded 1890
- **Urban** 217-acre campus with easy access to Chicago
- **Endowment** $7.2 billion
- **Coed** 5,941 undergraduate students, 100% full-time, 48% women, 52% men
- **Most difficult** entrance level, 8% of applicants were admitted

UNDERGRAD STUDENTS

5,918 full-time, 23 part-time. Students come from 50 states and territories; 70 other countries; 81% are from out of state; 5% Black or African American, non-Hispanic/Latino; 11% Hispanic/Latino; 18% Asian, non-Hispanic/Latino; 0.2% American Indian or Alaska Native, non-Hispanic/Latino; 4% Two or more races, non-Hispanic/Latino; 6% Race/ethnicity unknown; 12% international; 0.4% transferred in; 56% live on campus.

Freshmen:

Admission: 31,484 applied, 2,499 admitted, 1,591 enrolled. ***Average high school GPA:*** 4.15. ***Test scores:*** SAT critical reading scores over 500: 100%; SAT math scores over 500: 100%; SAT writing scores over 500: 100%; ACT scores over 18: 100%; SAT critical reading scores over 600: 99%; SAT math scores over 600: 100%; SAT writing scores over 600: 98%; ACT scores over 24: 100%; SAT critical reading scores over 700: 84%; SAT math scores over 700: 87%; SAT writing scores over 700: 79%; ACT scores over 30: 96%.

Retention: 99% of full-time freshmen returned.

FACULTY

Total: 1,828, 72% full-time, 87% with terminal degrees.

Student/faculty ratio: 5:1.

ACADEMICS

Calendar: quarters. *Degrees:* bachelor's, master's, and doctoral.

Special study options: accelerated degree program, advanced placement credit, double majors, English as a second language, independent study, internships, off-campus study, services for LD students, student-designed majors, study abroad, summer session for credit. ***ROTC:*** Army (c), Air Force (c).

Unusual degree programs: 3-2 social work; public policy, social sciences, international relations.

Computers: 300 computers/terminals are available on campus for general student use. Students can access the following: campus intranet, computer help desk, free student e-mail accounts, online (class) grades, online

(class) registration, online (class) schedules. Campuswide network is available. Wireless service is available via entire campus.
Library: Joseph Regenstein Library plus 5 others. *Books:* 9.6 million (physical), 1.4 million (digital/electronic); *Databases:* 1,337.

STUDENT LIFE
Housing options: on-campus residence required for freshman year; coed, special housing for students with disabilities. Campus housing is university owned. Freshman campus housing is guaranteed.

Activities and organizations: drama/theater group, student-run newspaper, radio station, choral group, University Theatre, Model United Nations, Council on University Programming, South Asian Students Association, Splash, national fraternities, national sororities.

Athletics Member NCAA. All Division III. ***Intercollegiate sports:*** baseball M, basketball M/W, cross-country running M/W, football M, soccer M/W, softball W, swimming and diving M/W, tennis M/W, track and field M/W, volleyball W, wrestling M. ***Intramural sports:*** badminton M/W, basketball M/W, bowling M/W, football M/W, racquetball M/W, sailing W(c), soccer M/W, softball M/W, swimming and diving M/W, table tennis M/W, tennis M/W, track and field M/W, ultimate Frisbee M/W, volleyball M/W.

Campus security: 24-hour emergency response devices and patrols, student patrols, late-night transport/escort service, controlled dormitory access.

Student services: health clinic, personal/psychological counseling, women's center.

COSTS & FINANCIAL AID
Costs (2016–17) ***One-time required fee:*** $1158. ***Comprehensive fee:*** $67,584 includes full-time tuition ($50,997), mandatory fees ($1494), and room and board ($15,093). Full-time tuition and fees vary according to course load. Part-time tuition and fees vary according to course load. ***Room and board:*** Room and board charges vary according to board plan and housing facility. ***Payment plan:*** installment. ***Waivers:*** employees or children of employees.

Financial Aid Of all full-time matriculated undergraduates who enrolled in 2016, 3,058 applied for aid, 2,527 were judged to have need, 2,527 had their need fully met. ***Average percent of need met:*** 100. ***Average financial aid package:*** $49,967. ***Average need-based loan:*** $3858. ***Average need-based gift aid:*** $43,792. ***Average indebtedness upon graduation:*** $23,852.

APPLYING
Standardized Tests *Required:* SAT or ACT (for admission).

Options: electronic application, early admission, early decision, early action, deferred entrance.

Application fee: $75.

Required: essay or personal statement, high school transcript, 2 letters of recommendation.

Application deadlines: 1/1 (freshmen), 3/1 (transfers), 11/1 (early action).

Notification: 4/1 (freshmen), 5/9 (transfers), 12/17 (early action).

CONTACT
Mr. James G. Nondorf, Vice President for Enrollment and Student Advancement and Dean of Admissions and Financial Aid, University of Chicago, Rosenwald Hall, 1101 East 58th Street, Suite 105, Chicago, IL 60637. *Phone:* 773-702-8650. *Fax:* 773-702-4199.
E-mail: collegeadmissions@uchicago.edu.

University of Illinois at Chicago

Chicago, Illinois

http://www.uic.edu/

- **State-supported** university, founded 1946, part of University of Illinois System
- **Urban** 240-acre campus with easy access to Chicago
- **Endowment** $287.2 million
- **Coed** 17,959 undergraduate students, 92% full-time, 50% women, 50% men
- **Moderately difficult** entrance level, 74% of applicants were admitted

UNDERGRAD STUDENTS
16,517 full-time, 1,442 part-time. Students come from 47 states and territories; 92 other countries; 3% are from out of state; 8% Black or African American, non-Hispanic/Latino; 31% Hispanic/Latino; 22% Asian, non-Hispanic/Latino; 0.1% Native Hawaiian or other Pacific Islander, non-Hispanic/Latino; 0.1% American Indian or Alaska Native, non-Hispanic/Latino; 3% Two or more races, non-Hispanic/Latino; 0.8% Race/ethnicity unknown; 3% international; 11% transferred in; 16% live on campus.

Freshmen:
Admission: 17,931 applied, 13,196 admitted, 3,307 enrolled. ***Average high school GPA:*** 3.32. ***Test scores:*** SAT critical reading scores over 500: 66%; SAT math scores over 500: 79%; SAT writing scores over 500: 64%; ACT scores over 18: 97%; SAT critical reading scores over 600: 23%; SAT math scores over 600: 48%; SAT writing scores over 600: 21%; ACT scores over 24: 53%; SAT critical reading scores over 700: 6%; SAT math scores over 700: 16%; SAT writing scores over 700: 6%; ACT scores over 30: 9%.
Retention: 80% of full-time freshmen returned.

FACULTY
Total: 1,601, 72% full-time, 82% with terminal degrees.

Student/faculty ratio: 18:1.

ACADEMICS
Calendar: semesters. *Degrees:* bachelor's, master's, doctoral, post-master's, and postbachelor's certificates.

Special study options: academic remediation for entering students, accelerated degree program, advanced placement credit, cooperative education, distance learning, double majors, freshman honors college, honors programs, independent study, internships, off-campus study, part-time degree program, services for LD students, student-designed majors, study abroad, summer session for credit. ***ROTC:*** Army (b), Navy (c), Air Force (c).

Computers: 1,052 computers/terminals are available on campus for general student use. Students can access the following: campus intranet, computer help desk, free student e-mail accounts, online (class) grades, online (class) registration, online (class) schedules. Campuswide network is available. 100% of college-owned or -operated housing units are wired for high-speed Internet access. Wireless service is available via classrooms, computer centers, computer labs, dorm rooms, learning centers, libraries, student centers.
Library: Richard J. Daley Library plus 2 others. *Books:* 2.3 million (physical), 532,279 (digital/electronic); *Serial titles:* 61,000 (digital/electronic); *Databases:* 1,000. Weekly public service hours: 132; study areas open 24 hours, 5-7 days a week; students can reserve study rooms.

STUDENT LIFE
Housing options: coed. Campus housing is university owned.

Activities and organizations: drama/theater group, student-run newspaper, radio station, choral group, Muslim Student Association, Alternative Spring Break, Filipinos in Alliance, Society of Future Physicians, Ski and Snowboard Club, national fraternities, national sororities.

Athletics Member NCAA. All Division I. ***Intercollegiate sports:*** baseball M(s), basketball M(s)/W(s), cross-country running M(s)/W(s), gymnastics M(s)/W(s), soccer M(s), softball W(s), swimming and diving M(s)/W(s), tennis M(s)/W(s), track and field M(s)/W(s), volleyball W(s). ***Intramural sports:*** badminton M/W, basketball M/W, bowling M/W, fencing M(c)/W(c), field hockey W, football M/W, golf M/W, racquetball M/W, rugby M(c)/W(c), soccer M/W, softball M/W, squash M/W, table tennis M/W, tennis M/W, volleyball M(c)/W, water polo M(c)/W(c), wrestling M.

Campus security: 24-hour emergency response devices and patrols, student patrols, late-night transport/escort service, controlled dormitory access, housing ID stickers, guest escort policy, 24-hour closed circuit videos for exits and entrances, security screen for first floor.

Student services: health clinic, personal/psychological counseling, women's center, legal services.

COSTS & FINANCIAL AID
Costs (2016–17) ***Tuition:*** state resident $10,584 full-time; nonresident $23,440 full-time. Full-time tuition and fees vary according to degree level and program. Part-time tuition and fees vary according to course load, degree level, and program. No tuition increase for student's term of

enrollment. ***Required fees:*** $3080 full-time. ***Room and board:*** $10,882; room only: $7891. Room and board charges vary according to board plan and housing facility. ***Payment plan:*** installment. ***Waivers:*** senior citizens and employees or children of employees.

Financial Aid Of all full-time matriculated undergraduates who enrolled in 2015, 13,536 applied for aid, 12,260 were judged to have need, 1,104 had their need fully met. 883 Federal Work-Study jobs (averaging $2500). 3,225 state and other part-time jobs (averaging $2500). In 2015, 550 non-need-based awards were made. ***Average percent of need met:*** 61. ***Average financial aid package:*** $14,546. ***Average need-based loan:*** $4311. ***Average need-based gift aid:*** $13,099. ***Average non-need-based aid:*** $5564. ***Average indebtedness upon graduation:*** $24,601.

APPLYING

Standardized Tests *Required:* SAT or ACT (for admission).

Options: electronic application, early admission, early action.

Application fee: $50.

Required: essay or personal statement, high school transcript. ***Required for some:*** audition for music and theater majors, portfolio for art majors.

Application deadlines: 1/15 (freshmen), 3/31 (transfers).

Notification: continuous until 11/30 (freshmen), continuous (transfers).

CONTACT

Ms. Maureen Woods, Associate Director, Admissions Undergraduate, University of Illinois at Chicago, Chicago. *Phone:* 312-996-4111. *Fax:* 312-413-7628. *E-mail:* uic.admit@uic.edu.

University of Illinois at Springfield

Springfield, Illinois

http://www.uis.edu/

- **State-supported** comprehensive, founded 1969, part of University of Illinois System
- **Suburban** 746-acre campus
- **Endowment** $15.7 million
- **Coed** 2,959 undergraduate students, 65% full-time, 51% women, 49% men
- **Moderately difficult** entrance level, 65% of applicants were admitted

UNDERGRAD STUDENTS

1,913 full-time, 1,046 part-time. Students come from 46 states and territories; 24 other countries; 13% are from out of state; 14% Black or African American, non-Hispanic/Latino; 8% Hispanic/Latino; 4% Asian, non-Hispanic/Latino; 0.2% Native Hawaiian or other Pacific Islander, non-Hispanic/Latino; 0.2% American Indian or Alaska Native, non-Hispanic/Latino; 3% Two or more races, non-Hispanic/Latino; 2% Race/ethnicity unknown; 5% international; 20% transferred in; 30% live on campus.

Freshmen:

Admission: 1,467 applied, 958 admitted, 300 enrolled. ***Average high school GPA:*** 3.43. ***Test scores:*** ACT scores over 18: 92%; ACT scores over 24: 48%; ACT scores over 30: 9%.

Retention: 74% of full-time freshmen returned.

FACULTY

Total: 392, 56% full-time, 60% with terminal degrees.

Student/faculty ratio: 14:1.

ACADEMICS

Calendar: semesters. *Degrees:* bachelor's, master's, doctoral, post-master's, and postbachelor's certificates.

Special study options: academic remediation for entering students, advanced placement credit, cooperative education, distance learning, English as a second language, honors programs, independent study, internships, off-campus study, part-time degree program, services for LD students, study abroad, summer session for credit.

Computers: 550 computers/terminals and 39 ports are available on campus for general student use. Students can access the following: campus intranet, computer help desk, free student e-mail accounts, online (class) grades, online (class) registration, online (class) schedules. Campuswide network is available. 100% of college-owned or -operated housing units are wired for high-speed Internet access. Wireless service is available via entire campus.

Library: Norris L Brookens Library plus 1 other. *Books:* 467,511 (physical), 171,279 (digital/electronic); *Serial titles:* 10,567 (physical), 14,463 (digital/electronic); *Databases:* 135. Weekly public service hours: 90; students can reserve study rooms.

STUDENT LIFE

Housing options: on-campus residence required for freshman year; coed, special housing for students with disabilities. Campus housing is university owned. Freshman campus housing is guaranteed.

Activities and organizations: drama/theater group, student-run newspaper, radio station, choral group, Student Activities Committee, Black Student Union, Christian Student Fellowship, Dance Marathon, Club Dodgeball, national fraternities, national sororities.

Athletics Member NCAA. All Division II. ***Intercollegiate sports:*** baseball M(s), basketball M(s)/W(s), cheerleading M(s)/W(s), cross-country running M(s)/W(s), golf M(s)/W(s), soccer M(s)/W(s), softball W(s), tennis M(s)/W(s), track and field M(s)/W(s), volleyball W(s). ***Intramural sports:*** badminton M(c)/W(c), basketball M/W, football M/W, racquetball M/W, sand volleyball M/W, soccer M(c)/W, softball M/W, squash M(c)/W(c), table tennis M/W, tennis M/W, ultimate Frisbee M/W, volleyball M(c)/W(c).

Campus security: 24-hour emergency response devices and patrols, late-night transport/escort service, controlled dormitory access.

Student services: health clinic, personal/psychological counseling, women's center.

COSTS & FINANCIAL AID

Costs (2017–18) ***Tuition:*** state resident $9405 full-time, $314 per credit hour part-time; nonresident $18,930 full-time, $631 per credit hour part-time. Full-time tuition and fees vary according to course load. Part-time tuition and fees vary according to course load. No tuition increase for student's term of enrollment. ***Required fees:*** $3204 full-time, $18 per credit hour part-time, $1107 per term part-time. ***Room and board:*** $11,600; room only: $7460. Room and board charges vary according to board plan and housing facility. ***Payment plan:*** installment. ***Waivers:*** senior citizens and employees or children of employees.

Financial Aid Of all full-time matriculated undergraduates who enrolled in 2015, 1,527 applied for aid, 1,270 were judged to have need, 183 had their need fully met. In 2015, 295 non-need-based awards were made. ***Average percent of need met:*** 69. ***Average financial aid package:*** $13,364. ***Average need-based loan:*** $4264. ***Average need-based gift aid:*** $10,582. ***Average non-need-based aid:*** $7788. ***Average indebtedness upon graduation:*** $24,652. ***Financial aid deadline:*** 11/15.

APPLYING

Standardized Tests *Required:* SAT or ACT (for admission).

Options: electronic application, deferred entrance.

Application fee: $50.

Required: high school transcript.

Application deadlines: rolling (freshmen), rolling (transfers).

Notification: continuous (transfers).

CONTACT

Fernando Planas, Director of Admissions, University of Illinois at Springfield, One University Plaza, MS UHB 1080, Springfield, IL 62703-5407. *Phone:* 217-206-4847. *Toll-free phone:* 888-977-4847. *E-mail:* admissions@uis.edu.

University of Illinois at Urbana–Champaign

Champaign, Illinois

http://www.illinois.edu/

CONTACT

Stacey Kostell, Director of Admissions, University of Illinois at Urbana–Champaign, 901 West Illinois, Urbana, IL 61801. *Phone:* 217-333-0302. *Fax:* 217-244-4614. *E-mail:* ugradadmissions@uiuc.edu.

University of St. Francis

Joliet, Illinois

http://www.stfrancis.edu/

- **Independent Roman Catholic** comprehensive, founded 1920
- **Suburban** 34-acre campus with easy access to Chicago
- **Endowment** $16.5 million
- **Coed** 1,362 undergraduate students, 96% full-time, 62% women, 38% men
- **Moderately difficult** entrance level, 49% of applicants were admitted

UNDERGRAD STUDENTS
1,301 full-time, 61 part-time. Students come from 20 states and territories; 7 other countries; 5% are from out of state; 8% Black or African American, non-Hispanic/Latino; 20% Hispanic/Latino; 2% Asian, non-Hispanic/Latino; 0.2% Native Hawaiian or other Pacific Islander, non-Hispanic/Latino; 0.4% American Indian or Alaska Native, non-Hispanic/Latino; 3% Two or more races, non-Hispanic/Latino; 0.4% Race/ethnicity unknown; 3% international; 13% transferred in; 28% live on campus.

Freshmen:
Admission: 1,560 applied, 768 admitted, 215 enrolled. ***Average high school GPA:*** 3.44. ***Test scores:*** SAT critical reading scores over 500: 50%; SAT math scores over 500: 62%; SAT writing scores over 500: 37%; ACT scores over 18: 97%; SAT math scores over 600: 12%; SAT writing scores over 600: 12%; ACT scores over 24: 43%; ACT scores over 30: 3%.
Retention: 82% of full-time freshmen returned.

FACULTY
Total: 277, 35% full-time, 45% with terminal degrees.
Student/faculty ratio: 12:1.

ACADEMICS
Calendar: semesters. *Degrees:* certificates, bachelor's, master's, doctoral, post-master's, and postbachelor's certificates.
Special study options: academic remediation for entering students, accelerated degree program, adult/continuing education programs, advanced placement credit, distance learning, double majors, English as a second language, honors programs, independent study, internships, off-campus study, part-time degree program, services for LD students, student-designed majors, study abroad, summer session for credit. ***ROTC:*** Army (c).
Computers: 560 computers/terminals and 2,000 ports are available on campus for general student use. Students can access the following: campus intranet, computer help desk, free student e-mail accounts, online (class) grades, online (class) registration, online (class) schedules, billing/payment. Campuswide network is available. 100% of college-owned or -operated housing units are wired for high-speed Internet access. Wireless service is available via entire campus.
Library: Brown Library. *Books:* 113,077 (physical), 4,118 (digital/electronic); *Serial titles:* 605 (physical), 113 (digital/electronic); *Databases:* 76. Weekly public service hours: 74; students can reserve study rooms.

STUDENT LIFE
Housing options: coed, special housing for students with disabilities. Campus housing is university owned. Freshman campus housing is guaranteed.
Activities and organizations: drama/theater group, student-run newspaper, radio and television station, choral group, Justice League, Unidos Vamos Alcanzar (UVA), International Club, Student Nurses Association, Student Activities Board, national sororities.
Athletics Member NAIA. ***Intercollegiate sports:*** baseball M(s), basketball M(s)/W(s), bowling M(s)/W(s), cheerleading M(s)/W(s), cross-country running M(s)/W(s), football M(s), golf M(s)/W(s), soccer M(s)/W(s), softball W(s), tennis M(s)/W(s), track and field M(s)/W(s), volleyball W(s). ***Intramural sports:*** basketball M/W, bowling M/W, table tennis M/W, volleyball M/W.
Campus security: 24-hour emergency response devices and patrols, student patrols, late-night transport/escort service, controlled dormitory access, First Response trained security personnel.
Student services: health clinic, personal/psychological counseling.

COSTS & FINANCIAL AID
Costs (2016–17) ***Comprehensive fee:*** $39,924 includes full-time tuition ($30,520), mandatory fees ($320), and room and board ($9084). Full-time tuition and fees vary according to degree level, location, and program. Part-time tuition: $825 per credit hour. Part-time tuition and fees vary according to degree level and program. ***Required fees:*** $125 per term part-time. ***Room and board:*** Room and board charges vary according to housing facility. ***Payment plans:*** installment, deferred payment. ***Waivers:*** children of alumni and employees or children of employees.
Financial Aid Of all full-time matriculated undergraduates who enrolled in 2016, 1,197 applied for aid, 1,102 were judged to have need, 397 had their need fully met. 156 Federal Work-Study jobs (averaging $2484). 300 state and other part-time jobs (averaging $2500). In 2016, 87 non-need-based awards were made. ***Average percent of need met:*** 80. ***Average financial aid package:*** $22,637. ***Average need-based loan:*** $4649. ***Average need-based gift aid:*** $18,534. ***Average non-need-based aid:*** $10,115. ***Average indebtedness upon graduation:*** $31,506.

APPLYING
Standardized Tests *Required:* SAT or ACT (for admission).
Options: electronic application, deferred entrance.
Required: high school transcript, minimum 2.5 GPA. ***Required for some:*** essay or personal statement, 2 letters of recommendation, interview.
Notification: continuous (freshmen), continuous (transfers).

CONTACT
Mr. Eric Ruiz, Director of Freshman Admissions, University of St. Francis, 500 North Wilcox Street, Joliet, IL 60435-6188. *Phone:* 800-735-7500. *Toll-free phone:* 800-735-7500. *Fax:* 815-740-5070. *E-mail:* eruiz@stfrancis.edu.

VanderCook College of Music

Chicago, Illinois

http://www.vandercook.edu/

- **Independent** comprehensive, founded 1909
- **Urban** campus
- **Endowment** $864,660
- **Coed**

FACULTY
Student/faculty ratio: 6:1.

ACADEMICS
Calendar: semesters. *Degrees:* bachelor's and master's.
Library: Harry Ruppel Memorial Library plus 1 other. *Books:* 16,576 (physical); *Serial titles:* 5,681 (physical). Weekly public service hours: 72; study areas open 24 hours, 5-7 days a week.

STUDENT LIFE
Housing options: coed, special housing for students with disabilities. Campus housing is provided by a third party.
Activities and organizations: student-run radio station, choral group, NAfME (National Association for Music Education), ACDA (American Choral Directors Association), NBA (National Band Association), ASTA (American String Teachers Association), national fraternities, national sororities.
Campus security: 24-hour emergency response devices and patrols, late-night transport/escort service, controlled dormitory access.
Student services: health clinic, personal/psychological counseling.

COSTS & FINANCIAL AID
Costs (2016–17) ***Comprehensive fee:*** $39,078 includes full-time tuition ($25,440), mandatory fees ($1740), and room and board ($11,898). Full-time tuition and fees vary according to course level, course load, and program. Part-time tuition: $1075 per semester hour. Part-time tuition and fees vary according to course level, course load, and program. ***Required fees:*** $1380 per year part-time. ***College room only:*** $6062. Room and board charges vary according to board plan and housing facility.
Financial Aid Of all full-time matriculated undergraduates who enrolled in 2014, 105 applied for aid, 93 were judged to have need, 24 Federal Work-Study jobs (averaging $516). 11 state and other part-time jobs (averaging $1297). In 2014, 16 non-need-based awards were made. ***Average financial aid package:*** $17,160. ***Average need-based loan:***

$4378. ***Average need-based gift aid:*** $9168. ***Average non-need-based aid:*** $6822. ***Average indebtedness upon graduation:*** $27,232.

APPLYING

Standardized Tests *Required:* SAT or ACT (for admission).

Required: essay or personal statement, high school transcript, 3 letters of recommendation, interview, audition on the applicant's primary instrument or voice. ***Required for some:*** minimum 3.0 GPA. ***Recommended:*** minimum 3.0 GPA.

CONTACT

Mrs. LeeAnn L. Meyer, Director of Admissions and Retention, VanderCook College of Music, 3140 South Federal Street, Chicago, IL 60616. *Phone:* 312-788-1120 Ext. 230. *Fax:* 312-225-5211. *E-mail:* lmeyer@vandercook.edu.

Western Illinois University

Macomb, Illinois

http://www.wiu.edu/

- **State-supported** comprehensive, founded 1899
- **Small-town** 1050-acre campus with easy access to Quad Cities; Peoria, IL; Springfield, IL
- **Endowment** $41.4 million
- **Coed** 8,543 undergraduate students, 88% full-time, 51% women, 49% men
- **Moderately difficult** entrance level, 59% of applicants were admitted

UNDERGRAD STUDENTS

7,482 full-time, 1,061 part-time. Students come from 40 states and territories; 63 other countries; 12% are from out of state; 21% Black or African American, non-Hispanic/Latino; 12% Hispanic/Latino; 0.9% Asian, non-Hispanic/Latino; 0.1% American Indian or Alaska Native, non-Hispanic/Latino; 3% Two or more races, non-Hispanic/Latino; 2% Race/ethnicity unknown; 2% international; 11% transferred in; 45% live on campus.

Freshmen:

Admission: 10,191 applied, 6,059 admitted, 1,527 enrolled. ***Average high school GPA:*** 3.2. ***Test scores:*** ACT scores over 18: 82%; ACT scores over 24: 22%; ACT scores over 30: 4%.

Retention: 69% of full-time freshmen returned.

FACULTY

Total: 615, 92% full-time, 69% with terminal degrees.

Student/faculty ratio: 15:1.

ACADEMICS

Calendar: semesters. *Degrees:* bachelor's, master's, doctoral, and postbachelor's certificates.

Special study options: academic remediation for entering students, adult/continuing education programs, advanced placement credit, distance learning, double majors, English as a second language, external degree program, freshman honors college, honors programs, independent study, internships, off-campus study, part-time degree program, services for LD students, student-designed majors, study abroad, summer session for credit. ***ROTC:*** Army (b).

Unusual degree programs: 3-2 engineering with University of Iowa, University of Illinois; arts and sciences/clinical laboratory science; general studies/chiropractic with Palmer College of Chiropractic.

Computers: 632 computers/terminals and 1,012 ports are available on campus for general student use. Students can access the following: computer help desk, free student e-mail accounts, online (class) grades, online (class) registration, online (class) schedules. Campuswide network is available. 100% of college-owned or -operated housing units are wired for high-speed Internet access. Wireless service is available via entire campus.

Library: Leslie Malpass Library plus 4 others. *Books:* 1.0 million (physical), 50,866 (digital/electronic); *Databases:* 126.

STUDENT LIFE

Housing options: on-campus residence required through sophomore year; coed, men-only, women-only, special housing for students with disabilities. Campus housing is university owned. Freshman campus housing is guaranteed.

Activities and organizations: drama/theater group, student-run newspaper, radio and television station, choral group, marching band, Student Government Association, Black Student Association, University Union Board, Western's All Volunteer Effort (WAVE), Inter Hall Council, national fraternities, national sororities.

Athletics Member NCAA. All Division I except football (Division I-AA). ***Intercollegiate sports:*** baseball M(s), basketball M(s)/W(s), cross-country running M(s)/W(s), golf M(s)/W, soccer M(s)/W(s), softball W(s), swimming and diving M(s)/W(s), tennis W(s), track and field M(s)/W(s), volleyball W(s). ***Intramural sports:*** badminton M(c)/W(c), baseball M(c), basketball M/W, bowling M(c), cheerleading M/W, cross-country running M/W, equestrian sports M(c)/W(c), fencing M(c)/W(c), football M/W, golf M/W, ice hockey M(c), lacrosse M(c), racquetball M/W, rugby M/W, sand volleyball M/W, soccer M/W, softball M/W, swimming and diving M/W, table tennis M/W, tennis M/W, ultimate Frisbee M(c)/W(c), volleyball M/W, water polo M/W, wrestling M.

Campus security: 24-hour emergency response devices and patrols, student patrols, late-night transport/escort service, controlled dormitory access.

Student services: health clinic, personal/psychological counseling, women's center, legal services.

COSTS & FINANCIAL AID

Costs (2016–17) ***Tuition:*** state resident $8541 full-time, $285 per credit hour part-time; nonresident $12,812 full-time, $427 per credit hour part-time. Full-time tuition and fees vary according to course load, location, and student level. Part-time tuition and fees vary according to course load, location, and student level. No tuition increase for student's term of enrollment. ***Required fees:*** $2704 full-time, $90 per credit hour part-time. ***Room and board:*** $9580; room only: $5880. Room and board charges vary according to board plan, housing facility, and student level. ***Payment plan:*** installment. ***Waivers:*** senior citizens and employees or children of employees.

Financial Aid Of all full-time matriculated undergraduates who enrolled in 2016, 6,376 applied for aid, 5,609 were judged to have need, 1,509 had their need fully met. 183 Federal Work-Study jobs (averaging $2508). 1,498 state and other part-time jobs (averaging $1528). In 2016, 286 non-need-based awards were made. ***Average percent of need met:*** 59. ***Average financial aid package:*** $11,646. ***Average need-based loan:*** $4269. ***Average need-based gift aid:*** $8952. ***Average non-need-based aid:*** $3072. ***Average indebtedness upon graduation:*** $30,721.

APPLYING

Standardized Tests *Required:* SAT or ACT (for admission).

Options: electronic application, deferred entrance.

Application fee: $30.

Required: high school transcript, minimum 2.5 GPA.

Application deadlines: 5/15 (freshmen), rolling (transfers).

Notification: continuous (freshmen), continuous (transfers).

CONTACT

Western Illinois University, 1 University Circle, Macomb, IL 61455-1390. *Phone:* 309-298-3157. *Toll-free phone:* 877-742-5948.

Wheaton College

Wheaton, Illinois

http://www.wheaton.edu/

- **Independent nondenominational** comprehensive, founded 1860
- **Suburban** 80-acre campus with easy access to Chicago
- **Endowment** $388.0 million
- **Coed** 2,456 undergraduate students, 98% full-time, 53% women, 47% men
- **Very difficult** entrance level, 79% of applicants were admitted

UNDERGRAD STUDENTS

2,400 full-time, 56 part-time. Students come from 50 states and territories; 39 other countries; 73% are from out of state; 3% Black or African American, non-Hispanic/Latino; 6% Hispanic/Latino; 9% Asian, non-Hispanic/Latino; 0.1% American Indian or Alaska Native, non-Hispanic/Latino; 4% Two or more races, non-Hispanic/Latino; 0.1% Race/ethnicity unknown; 3% international; 2% transferred in; 88% live on campus.

Freshmen:
Admission: 1,850 applied, 1,455 admitted, 588 enrolled. ***Average high school GPA:*** 3.7. ***Test scores:*** SAT critical reading scores over 500: 96%; SAT math scores over 500: 94%; SAT writing scores over 500: 95%; ACT scores over 18: 100%; SAT critical reading scores over 600: 74%; SAT math scores over 600: 70%; SAT writing scores over 600: 69%; ACT scores over 24: 93%; SAT critical reading scores over 700: 32%; SAT math scores over 700: 23%; SAT writing scores over 700: 21%; ACT scores over 30: 51%.

Retention: 95% of full-time freshmen returned.

FACULTY
Total: 317, 68% full-time, 80% with terminal degrees.

Student/faculty ratio: 11:1.

ACADEMICS
Calendar: semesters. *Degrees:* bachelor's, master's, doctoral, and postbachelor's certificates.

Special study options: advanced placement credit, double majors, independent study, internships, off-campus study, services for LD students, student-designed majors, study abroad, summer session for credit. ***ROTC:*** Army (b), Air Force (c).

Unusual degree programs: 3-2 engineering with Illinois Institute of Technology, University of Minnesota, University of Illinois-Chicago; nursing with Emory University, Vanderbilt University.

Computers: 325 computers/terminals and 3,500 ports are available on campus for general student use. Students can access the following: campus intranet, computer help desk, free student e-mail accounts, online (class) grades, online (class) registration, online (class) schedules, financial information, degree requirements evaluation. Campuswide network is available. 100% of college-owned or -operated housing units are wired for high-speed Internet access. Wireless service is available via entire campus.

Library: Buswell Memorial Library. *Books:* 518,164 (physical), 226,974 (digital/electronic); *Serial titles:* 389 (physical), 6,182 (digital/electronic); *Databases:* 249. Weekly public service hours: 94; students can reserve study rooms.

STUDENT LIFE
Housing options: on-campus residence required through senior year; coed, men-only, women-only, cooperative, special housing for students with disabilities. Campus housing is university owned. Freshman campus housing is guaranteed.

Activities and organizations: drama/theater group, student-run newspaper, choral group, Discipleship small groups, intramurals, Club Sports, Christian Service Council, New Student Orientation.

Athletics Member NCAA. All Division III. ***Intercollegiate sports:*** baseball M, basketball M/W, cheerleading W(c), crew M(c)/W(c), cross-country running M/W, football M, golf M/W, ice hockey M(c), lacrosse M(c)/W(c), soccer M/W, softball W, swimming and diving M/W, tennis M/W, track and field M/W, volleyball W, wrestling M. ***Intramural sports:*** basketball M/W, golf M/W, soccer M/W, softball M, ultimate Frisbee M/W, volleyball M/W.

Campus security: 24-hour emergency response devices and patrols, student patrols, late-night transport/escort service, controlled dormitory access.

Student services: health clinic, personal/psychological counseling.

COSTS & FINANCIAL AID
Costs (2016–17) ***Comprehensive fee:*** $43,610 includes full-time tuition ($34,050) and room and board ($9560). Full-time tuition and fees vary according to program. Part-time tuition: $1419 per credit hour. Part-time tuition and fees vary according to course load and program. ***College room only:*** $5650. Room and board charges vary according to board plan and housing facility. ***Payment plans:*** installment, deferred payment.

Financial Aid Of all full-time matriculated undergraduates who enrolled in 2016, 1,504 applied for aid, 1,314 were judged to have need, 296 had their need fully met. 157 Federal Work-Study jobs (averaging $1336). In 2016, 531 non-need-based awards were made. ***Average percent of need met:*** 85. ***Average financial aid package:*** $24,946. ***Average need-based loan:*** $4929. ***Average need-based gift aid:*** $20,622. ***Average non-need-based aid:*** $6343. ***Average indebtedness upon graduation:*** $27,354.

APPLYING
Standardized Tests *Required:* SAT or ACT (for admission).

Options: electronic application, early action, deferred entrance.

Application fee: $50.

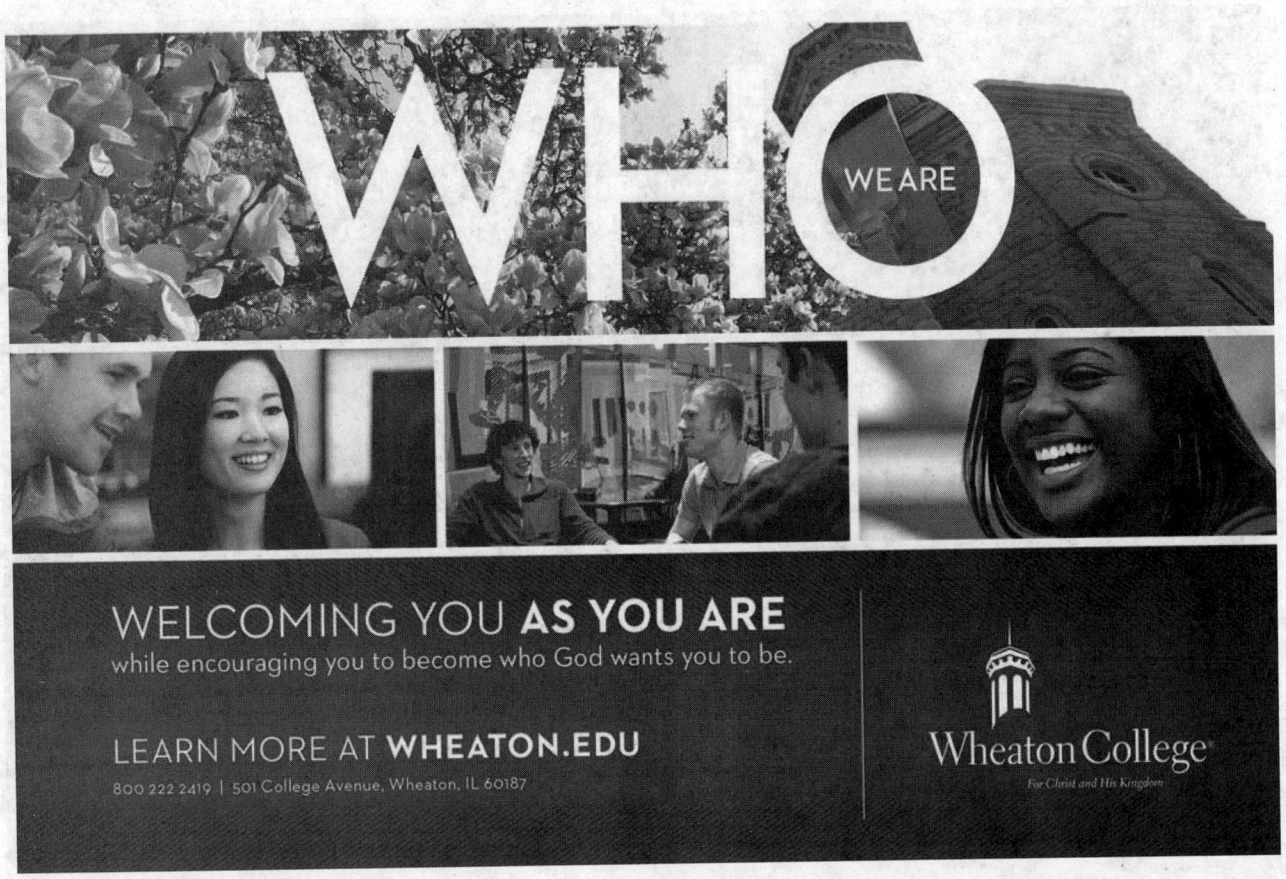

Required: essay or personal statement, high school transcript, 2 letters of recommendation. ***Recommended:*** interview.

Application deadlines: 1/10 (freshmen), 3/1 (transfers), 11/1 (early action).

Notification: 4/1 (freshmen), 4/1 (transfers), 12/31 (early action).

CONTACT

Ms. Shawn Wynne, Director of Admissions, Wheaton College, 501 College Avenue, Wheaton, IL 60187-5593. *Phone:* 630-752-5011. *Toll-free phone:* 800-222-2419. *Fax:* 630-752-5285. *E-mail:* admissions@wheaton.edu.

See previous page for display ad and page 1600 for the College Close-Up.

INDIANA

Anderson University

Anderson, Indiana

http://www.anderson.edu/

- **Independent** comprehensive, founded 1917, affiliated with Church of God
- **Suburban** 163-acre campus with easy access to Indianapolis
- **Endowment** $29.9 million
- **Coed** 1,883 undergraduate students, 84% full-time, 60% women, 40% men
- **Moderately difficult** entrance level, 66% of applicants were admitted

UNDERGRAD STUDENTS

1,591 full-time, 292 part-time. Students come from 39 states and territories; 18 other countries; 24% are from out of state; 13% Black or African American, non-Hispanic/Latino; 2% Hispanic/Latino; 2% Asian, non-Hispanic/Latino; 0.3% Native Hawaiian or other Pacific Islander, non-Hispanic/Latino; 1% American Indian or Alaska Native, non-Hispanic/Latino; 0.3% Two or more races, non-Hispanic/Latino; 3% Race/ethnicity unknown; 2% international; 419% transferred in; 63% live on campus.

Freshmen:

Admission: 2,650 applied, 1,760 admitted, 425 enrolled. ***Average high school GPA:*** 3.4. ***Test scores:*** SAT critical reading scores over 500: 52%; SAT math scores over 500: 57%; ACT scores over 18: 83%; SAT critical reading scores over 600: 15%; SAT math scores over 600: 13%; ACT scores over 24: 41%; SAT critical reading scores over 700: 2%; SAT math scores over 700: 1%; ACT scores over 30: 3%.

Retention: 78% of full-time freshmen returned.

FACULTY

Total: 277, 42% full-time, 36% with terminal degrees.

Student/faculty ratio: 12:1.

ACADEMICS

Calendar: semesters. *Degrees:* associate, bachelor's, master's, and doctoral.

Special study options: academic remediation for entering students, accelerated degree program, adult/continuing education programs, advanced placement credit, distance learning, double majors, honors programs, independent study, internships, off-campus study, part-time degree program, services for LD students, student-designed majors, study abroad, summer session for credit.

Unusual degree programs: 3-2 engineering with Purdue University.

Computers: 300 computers/terminals are available on campus for general student use. Students can access the following: campus intranet, computer help desk, free student e-mail accounts, online (class) grades, online (class) registration, online (class) schedules, microcomputer software. Campuswide network is available. 100% of college-owned or -operated housing units are wired for high-speed Internet access. Wireless service is available via entire campus.

Library: Robert A. Nicholson Library. *Books:* 204,415 (physical), 2.4 million (digital/electronic); *Serial titles:* 457 (physical); *Databases:* 199. Weekly public service hours: 95; study areas open 24 hours, 5-7 days a week; students can reserve study rooms.

STUDENT LIFE

Housing options: on-campus residence required through junior year; men-only, women-only. Campus housing is university owned. Freshman campus housing is guaranteed.

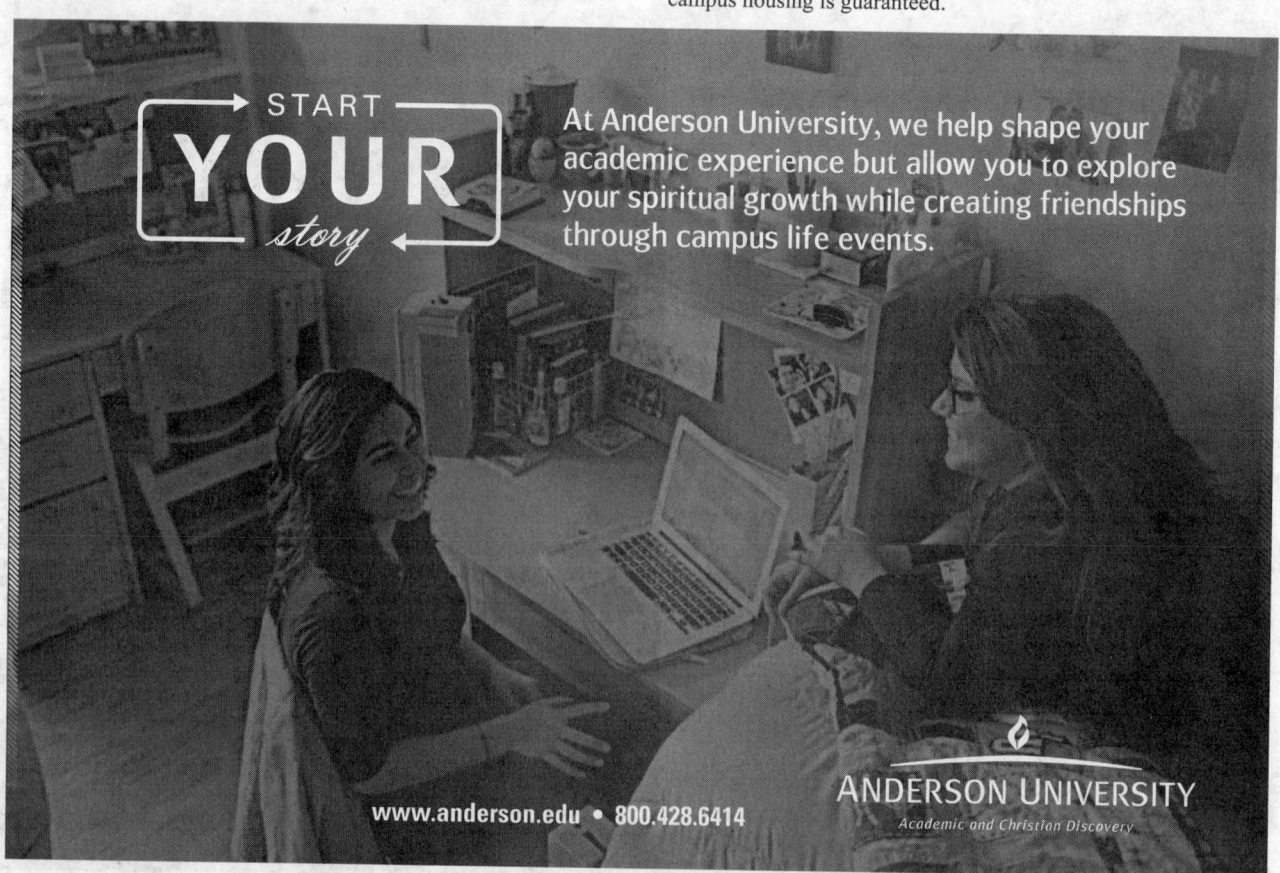

Activities and organizations: drama/theater group, student-run newspaper, radio station, choral group, Adult and Continuing Education Students Association, Multicultural Student Union, Campus Ministries.

Athletics Member NCAA. All Division III. ***Intercollegiate sports:*** baseball M, basketball M/W, cross-country running M/W, football M, golf M/W, soccer M/W, softball W, tennis M/W, track and field M/W, volleyball W. ***Intramural sports:*** badminton M/W, basketball M/W, bowling M/W, cheerleading M(c)/W(c), rugby M(c), soccer M/W, softball M/W, tennis M/W, volleyball M/W.

Campus security: 24-hour emergency response devices and patrols, student patrols, late-night transport/escort service, controlled dormitory access, 24-hour crime line.

Student services: health clinic, personal/psychological counseling.

COSTS & FINANCIAL AID

Costs (2017–18) ***Comprehensive fee:*** $39,450 includes full-time tuition ($29,210), mandatory fees ($500), and room and board ($9740). Part-time tuition: $1218 per semester hour. Part-time tuition and fees vary according to course load. ***College room only:*** $6120. Room and board charges vary according to board plan and housing facility. ***Payment plan:*** installment. ***Waivers:*** employees or children of employees.

Financial Aid Of all full-time matriculated undergraduates who enrolled in 2014, 1,549 applied for aid, 1,410 were judged to have need, 604 had their need fully met. In 2014, 307 non-need-based awards were made. ***Average percent of need met:*** 88. ***Average financial aid package:*** $23,905. ***Average need-based loan:*** $10,011. ***Average need-based gift aid:*** $15,932. ***Average non-need-based aid:*** $14,313.

APPLYING

Standardized Tests *Required:* SAT or ACT (for admission).

Options: electronic application, deferred entrance.

Application fee: $25.

Required: high school transcript, minimum 2.0 GPA, 2 letters of recommendation, lifestyle statement. ***Required for some:*** interview. ***Recommended:*** essay or personal statement.

Application deadlines: 7/1 (freshmen), rolling (transfers).

Notification: 9/1 (freshmen), continuous until 9/1 (transfers).

CONTACT

Ms. Kynan Simison, Director of Admissions, Anderson University, 1100 East 5th Street, Anderson, IN 46012-3495. *Phone:* 765-641-4076. *Toll-free phone:* 800-428-6414. *Fax:* 765-641-3851.
E-mail: info@anderson.edu.

See previous page for display ad and page 1280 for the College Close-Up.

The Art Institute of Indianapolis

Indianapolis, Indiana

http://www.artinstitutes.edu/indianapolis/

CONTACT

The Art Institute of Indianapolis, 3500 Depauw Boulevard, Suite 1010, Indianapolis, IN 46268. *Phone:* 317-613-4800. *Toll-free phone:* 866-441-9031.

Ball State University

Muncie, Indiana

http://www.bsu.edu/

- **State-supported** university, founded 1918
- **Suburban** 1140-acre campus with easy access to Indianapolis
- **Endowment** $182.4 million
- **Coed** 17,011 undergraduate students, 89% full-time, 60% women, 40% men

UNDERGRAD STUDENTS

15,110 full-time, 1,901 part-time. Students come from 44 states and territories; 40 other countries; 14% are from out of state; 8% Black or African American, non-Hispanic/Latino; 4% Hispanic/Latino; 1% Asian, non-Hispanic/Latino; 0.1% Native Hawaiian or other Pacific Islander, non-Hispanic/Latino; 3% Two or more races, non-Hispanic/Latino; 2% Race/ethnicity unknown; 2% international; 5% transferred in; 43% live on campus.

Freshmen:

Admission: 3,877 enrolled. ***Average high school GPA:*** 3.45. ***Test scores:*** SAT critical reading scores over 500: 63%; SAT math scores over 500: 62%; SAT writing scores over 500: 54%; ACT scores over 18: 97%; SAT critical reading scores over 600: 17%; SAT math scores over 600: 14%; SAT writing scores over 600: 10%; ACT scores over 24: 38%; SAT critical reading scores over 700: 2%; SAT math scores over 700: 1%; SAT writing scores over 700: 1%; ACT scores over 30: 5%.

Retention: 81% of full-time freshmen returned.

FACULTY

Total: 1,268, 80% full-time, 69% with terminal degrees.

Student/faculty ratio: 14:1.

ACADEMICS

Calendar: semesters. *Degrees:* certificates, bachelor's, master's, doctoral, post-master's, and postbachelor's certificates.

Special study options: accelerated degree program, adult/continuing education programs, advanced placement credit, cooperative education, distance learning, double majors, English as a second language, external degree program, freshman honors college, honors programs, independent study, internships, part-time degree program, services for LD students, student-designed majors, study abroad, summer session for credit. ***ROTC:*** Army (b).

Computers: 532 computers/terminals and 8,721 ports are available on campus for general student use. Students can access the following: campus intranet, computer help desk, free student e-mail accounts, online (class) grades, online (class) registration, online (class) schedules, room reservations, testing and test results, manage and pay tuition, order/buy textbooks, request room repairs, order transcripts, manage meal plan, manage and prepay long distance service, undergraduate degree progress report. Campuswide network is available. 100% of college-owned or -operated housing units are wired for high-speed Internet access. Wireless service is available via entire campus.

Library: Bracken Library plus 2 others. *Books:* 814,042 (physical), 14,201 (digital/electronic); *Serial titles:* 13,653 (physical), 92,865 (digital/electronic); *Databases:* 286. Weekly public service hours: 123; students can reserve study rooms.

STUDENT LIFE

Housing options: on-campus residence required for freshman year; coed, men-only, women-only, special housing for students with disabilities. Campus housing is university owned. Freshman campus housing is guaranteed.

Activities and organizations: drama/theater group, student-run newspaper, radio and television station, choral group, marching band, Student Voluntary Services, Catholic Student Union, Dance Marathon, Black Student Association, Spectrum, national fraternities, national sororities.

Athletics Member NCAA. All Division I except football (Division I-A). ***Intercollegiate sports:*** baseball M(s)/W(c), basketball M(s)/W(s), bowling M(c)/W(c), cheerleading M/W, cross-country running W(s), equestrian sports M(c)/W(c), fencing M(c)/W(c), field hockey W(s), golf M(s)/W(s), gymnastics W(s), lacrosse M(c)/W(c), racquetball M(c)/W(c), rock climbing M(c)/W(c), rugby M(c)/W(c), soccer M(c)/W(s), softball W(s), swimming and diving M(s)/W(s), tennis M(s)/W(s), track and field W(s), triathlon M(c)/W(c), ultimate Frisbee M(c)/W(c), volleyball M(s)/W(s), water polo M(c)/W(c), wrestling M(c). ***Intramural sports:*** archery M(c)/W(c), badminton M/W, basketball M/W, bowling M/W, golf M/W, gymnastics W(c), ice hockey M(c), racquetball M/W, soccer M/W, softball M/W, swimming and diving M/W, table tennis M/W, tennis M/W, track and field M/W, ultimate Frisbee M/W, volleyball M/W.

Campus security: 24-hour emergency response devices and patrols, late-night transport/escort service, controlled dormitory access.

Student services: health clinic, personal/psychological counseling, women's center, legal services.

COSTS & FINANCIAL AID

Costs (2017–18) ***Tuition:*** state resident $9172 full-time, $302 per credit hour part-time; nonresident $25,262 full-time, $1000 per credit hour part-time. Full-time tuition and fees vary according to program and reciprocity agreements. Part-time tuition and fees vary according to course load, program, and reciprocity agreements. ***Required fees:*** $676 full-time. ***Room and board:*** $10,038. Room and board charges vary according to board plan and housing facility. ***Payment plan:*** installment. ***Waivers:*** senior citizens and employees or children of employees.

Financial Aid Of all full-time matriculated undergraduates who enrolled in 2016, 12,927 applied for aid, 10,181 were judged to have need, 4,150 had their need fully met. 748 Federal Work-Study jobs (averaging $2500). In 2016, 1966 non-need-based awards were made. ***Average percent of need met:*** 68. ***Average financial aid package:*** $12,659. ***Average need-based loan:*** $4434. ***Average need-based gift aid:*** $5742. ***Average non-need-based aid:*** $8386. ***Average indebtedness upon graduation:*** $27,617.

APPLYING

Standardized Tests *Required for some:* SAT or ACT (for admission).

Required: high school transcript. ***Required for some:*** essay or personal statement.

CONTACT

Ball State University, 2000 West University Avenue, Muncie, IN 47306. *Phone:* 765-285-8287. *Toll-free phone:* 800-482-4BSU.

Bethel College

Mishawaka, Indiana

http://www.bethelcollege.edu/

- **Independent** comprehensive, founded 1947, affiliated with Missionary Church
- **Suburban** 80-acre campus
- **Endowment** $11.2 million
- **Coed** 1,388 undergraduate students, 81% full-time, 64% women, 36% men
- **Minimally difficult** entrance level, 98% of applicants were admitted

UNDERGRAD STUDENTS

1,128 full-time, 260 part-time. Students come from 27 states and territories; 11 other countries; 28% are from out of state; 11% Black or African American, non-Hispanic/Latino; 7% Hispanic/Latino; 2% Asian, non-Hispanic/Latino; 0.3% American Indian or Alaska Native, non-Hispanic/Latino; 5% Two or more races, non-Hispanic/Latino; 0.8% Race/ethnicity unknown; 1% international; 9% transferred in; 52% live on campus.

Freshmen:

Admission: 1,168 applied, 1,142 admitted, 243 enrolled. ***Average high school GPA:*** 3.47. ***Test scores:*** SAT critical reading scores over 500: 53%; SAT math scores over 500: 56%; SAT writing scores over 500: 47%; ACT scores over 18: 92%; SAT critical reading scores over 600: 12%; SAT math scores over 600: 22%; SAT writing scores over 600: 10%; ACT scores over 24: 43%; SAT critical reading scores over 700: 3%; SAT math scores over 700: 2%; SAT writing scores over 700: 1%; ACT scores over 30: 4%.

Retention: 76% of full-time freshmen returned.

FACULTY

Total: 192, 37% full-time, 31% with terminal degrees.

Student/faculty ratio: 12:1.

ACADEMICS

Calendar: semesters. *Degrees:* associate, bachelor's, and master's.

Special study options: academic remediation for entering students, accelerated degree program, adult/continuing education programs, advanced placement credit, distance learning, double majors, external degree program, honors programs, independent study, internships, off-campus study, part-time degree program, services for LD students, student-designed majors, study abroad, summer session for credit. ***ROTC:*** Army (c), Air Force (c).

Unusual degree programs: 3-2 engineering with University of Notre Dame, Trine University.

Computers: 160 computers/terminals and 440 ports are available on campus for general student use. Students can access the following: campus intranet, computer help desk, free student e-mail accounts, online (class) grades, online (class) schedules. Campuswide network is available. 100% of college-owned or -operated housing units are wired for high-speed Internet access. Wireless service is available via entire campus.

Library: Otis and Elizabeth Bowen Library. *Books:* 95,315 (physical), 159,582 (digital/electronic); *Serial titles:* 825 (physical), 53,615 (digital/electronic); *Databases:* 90. Weekly public service hours: 83.

STUDENT LIFE

Housing options: on-campus residence required through sophomore year; men-only, women-only. Campus housing is university owned.

Activities and organizations: drama/theater group, student-run newspaper, radio station, choral group, Student Government, Psychology Club, Education Club, American Sign Language Club.

Athletics Member NAIA, NCCAA. ***Intercollegiate sports:*** baseball M(s), basketball M(s)/W(s), cheerleading M(s)/W(s), cross-country running M(s)/W(s), golf M(s)/W(s), lacrosse W(s), rugby M(s), soccer M(s)/W(s), softball W(s), tennis M(s)/W(s), track and field M(s)/W(s), volleyball W(s). ***Intramural sports:*** basketball M/W, football M, soccer M/W, softball M/W, volleyball M/W.

Campus security: 24-hour emergency response devices and patrols, late-night transport/escort service, controlled dormitory access.

Student services: health clinic, personal/psychological counseling.

COSTS & FINANCIAL AID

Costs (2017–18) ***Comprehensive fee:*** $36,730 includes full-time tuition ($27,580), mandatory fees ($350), and room and board ($8800). Full-time tuition and fees vary according to program. Part-time tuition: $880 per credit hour. Part-time tuition and fees vary according to course load and program. ***Required fees:*** $150 per year part-time. ***College room only:*** $4160. Room and board charges vary according to board plan and housing facility. ***Payment plan:*** installment. ***Waivers:*** employees or children of employees.

Financial Aid In 2016, 92 non-need-based awards were made. ***Average non-need-based aid:*** $11,697. ***Average indebtedness upon graduation:*** $34,148. ***Financial aid deadline:*** 3/10.

APPLYING

Standardized Tests *Required:* SAT or ACT (for admission).

Options: electronic application, early admission, deferred entrance.

Required: high school transcript, minimum 2.0 GPA. ***Recommended:*** essay or personal statement, minimum 2.5 GPA, interview.

Application deadlines: 8/15 (freshmen), 8/16 (out-of-state freshmen), 8/15 (transfers).

Notification: continuous (freshmen), continuous (out-of-state freshmen), continuous (transfers).

CONTACT

Dr. Toni Pauls, Vice President for Enrollment, Bethel College, 1001 Bethel Circle, Mishawaka, IN 46545. *Phone:* 574-807-7600. *Toll-free phone:* 800-422-4101. *Fax:* 574-807-7650. *E-mail:* admissions@bethelcollege.edu.

See next page for display ad and page 1302 for the College Close-Up.

Butler University

Indianapolis, Indiana

http://www.butler.edu/

- **Independent** comprehensive, founded 1855
- **Suburban** 295-acre campus with easy access to Indianapolis
- **Endowment** $174.5 million
- **Coed** 4,290 undergraduate students, 98% full-time, 60% women, 40% men
- **Moderately difficult** entrance level, 73% of applicants were admitted

UNDERGRAD STUDENTS

4,199 full-time, 91 part-time. Students come from 49 states and territories; 59 other countries; 53% are from out of state; 4% Black or African American, non-Hispanic/Latino; 4% Hispanic/Latino; 3% Asian, non-Hispanic/Latino; 0.2% American Indian or Alaska Native, non-Hispanic/Latino; 3% Two or more races, non-Hispanic/Latino; 3% Race/ethnicity unknown; 0.8% international; 2% transferred in; 53% live on campus.

Freshmen:

Admission: 12,937 applied, 9,406 admitted, 1,256 enrolled. ***Average high school GPA:*** 3.79. ***Test scores:*** SAT critical reading scores over 500: 87%; SAT math scores over 500: 88%; SAT writing scores over 500: 83%;

ACT scores over 18: 100%; SAT critical reading scores over 600: 38%; SAT math scores over 600: 42%; SAT writing scores over 600: 31%; ACT scores over 24: 85%; SAT critical reading scores over 700: 5%; SAT math scores over 700: 6%; SAT writing scores over 700: 2%; ACT scores over 30: 26%.

Retention: 92% of full-time freshmen returned.

FACULTY

Total: 530, 68% full-time.

Student/faculty ratio: 11:1.

ACADEMICS

Calendar: semesters. *Degrees:* bachelor's, master's, doctoral, and postbachelor's certificates.

Special study options: accelerated degree program, advanced placement credit, cooperative education, distance learning, double majors, honors programs, independent study, internships, off-campus study, services for LD students, student-designed majors, study abroad, summer session for credit. ***ROTC:*** Army (c), Air Force (c).

Unusual degree programs: 3-2 engineering with Indiana University–Purdue University Indianapolis.

Computers: 490 computers/terminals are available on campus for general student use. Students can access the following: campus intranet, computer help desk, free student e-mail accounts, online (class) grades, online (class) registration, online (class) schedules. Campuswide network is available. 100% of college-owned or -operated housing units are wired for high-speed Internet access. Wireless service is available via entire campus.

Library: Irwin Library plus 2 others. *Books:* 196,295 (physical), 293,303 (digital/electronic); *Serial titles:* 18,930 (physical), 44,712 (digital/electronic); *Databases:* 243. Weekly public service hours: 106; students can reserve study rooms.

STUDENT LIFE

Housing options: on-campus residence required through junior year; coed, women-only. Campus housing is university owned. Freshman campus housing is guaranteed.

Activities and organizations: drama/theater group, student-run newspaper, radio and television station, choral group, marching band, Answers for Autism (Butler University chapter), Pre-Pharmacy Club, Engineering Dual Degree Club (EDDC), Delta Delta Delta, Delta Tau Delta, national fraternities, national sororities.

Athletics Member NCAA. All Division I except football (Division I-AA). ***Intercollegiate sports:*** baseball M(s), basketball M(s)/W(s), crew M(c)/W(c), cross-country running M(s)/W(s), equestrian sports W(c), golf M(s)/W(s), ice hockey M(c), lacrosse M(c)/W(s), rugby M(c), soccer M(s)/W(s), softball W(s), swimming and diving M(c)/W, tennis M(s)/W(s), track and field M(s)/W(s), ultimate Frisbee M(c)/W(c), volleyball M(c)/W(s). ***Intramural sports:*** badminton M/W, baseball M, basketball M/W, bowling M/W, football M, soccer M/W, softball M/W, swimming and diving M/W, table tennis M/W, tennis M/W, track and field M/W, volleyball M/W, weight lifting M/W.

Campus security: 24-hour emergency response devices and patrols, late-night transport/escort service, controlled dormitory access.

Student services: health clinic, personal/psychological counseling.

COSTS & FINANCIAL AID

Costs (2017–18) ***Comprehensive fee:*** $52,935 includes full-time tuition ($38,900), mandatory fees ($1005), and room and board ($13,030). Full-time tuition and fees vary according to course level, course load, degree level, and program. Part-time tuition: $1558 per credit hour. Part-time tuition and fees vary according to course level, course load, degree level, and program. ***College room only:*** $6740. Room and board charges vary according to board plan and housing facility. ***Payment plan:*** installment. ***Waivers:*** employees or children of employees.

Financial Aid Of all full-time matriculated undergraduates who enrolled in 2016, 4,172 applied for aid, 2,686 were judged to have need, 315 had their need fully met. 153 Federal Work-Study jobs (averaging $925). In 2016, 1451 non-need-based awards were made. ***Average percent of need met:*** 67. ***Average financial aid package:*** $24,536. ***Average need-based loan:*** $5124. ***Average need-based gift aid:*** $20,022. ***Average non-need-based aid:*** $13,570. ***Average indebtedness upon graduation:*** $35,730.

APPLYING

Standardized Tests *Required:* SAT or ACT (for admission).

Options: electronic application, early action, deferred entrance.

Required: essay or personal statement, high school transcript. ***Required for some:*** audition, interview, portfolio; 4 years of math and science strongly recommended for COPHS majors and natural sciences.

Application deadlines: 2/1 (freshmen), 8/15 (transfers), 11/1 (early action).

Notification: continuous (freshmen), continuous (transfers), 12/20 (early action).

CONTACT

Mr. Delorean Menifee, Director of Admission, Butler University, 4600 Sunset Avenue, Indianapolis, IN 46208-3485. *Phone:* 317-940-8100. *Toll-free phone:* 888-940-8100. *Fax:* 317-940-8150. *E-mail:* admission@butler.edu.

Calumet College of Saint Joseph

Whiting, Indiana

http://www.ccsj.edu/

- **Independent Roman Catholic** comprehensive, founded 1951
- **Urban** 25-acre campus with easy access to Chicago
- **Endowment** $3.9 million
- **Coed** 784 undergraduate students, 62% full-time, 45% women, 55% men
- **Noncompetitive** entrance level, 30% of applicants were admitted

UNDERGRAD STUDENTS

489 full-time, 295 part-time. Students come from 26 states and territories; 17 other countries; 49% are from out of state; 22% Black or African American, non-Hispanic/Latino; 30% Hispanic/Latino; 1% Asian, non-Hispanic/Latino; 0.1% Native Hawaiian or other Pacific Islander, non-Hispanic/Latino; 0.4% American Indian or Alaska Native, non-Hispanic/Latino; 1% Two or more races, non-Hispanic/Latino; 5% Race/ethnicity unknown; 14% transferred in.

Freshmen:

Admission: 628 applied, 191 admitted, 113 enrolled. ***Average high school GPA:*** 2.63. ***Test scores:*** SAT critical reading scores over 500: 29%; SAT writing scores over 500: 20%; ACT scores over 18: 58%; SAT critical reading scores over 600: 2%; SAT writing scores over 600: 4%; ACT scores over 24: 10%; SAT writing scores over 700: 2%.

Retention: 53% of full-time freshmen returned.

FACULTY

Total: 136, 22% full-time, 40% with terminal degrees.

Student/faculty ratio: 11:1.

ACADEMICS

Calendar: semesters. *Degrees:* certificates, associate, bachelor's, and master's.

Special study options: academic remediation for entering students, accelerated degree program, adult/continuing education programs, advanced placement credit, cooperative education, distance learning, double majors, external degree program, honors programs, independent study, internships, part-time degree program, services for LD students, summer session for credit.

Computers: 241 computers/terminals are available on campus for general student use. Students can access the following: computer help desk, free student e-mail accounts, online (class) grades, online (class) schedules. Campuswide network is available. Wireless service is available via entire campus.

Library: Mary Gorman Specker Memorial Library. *Books:* 100,500 (physical), 7,132 (digital/electronic); *Serial titles:* 2 (physical); *Databases:* 31. Weekly public service hours: 63.

STUDENT LIFE

Housing options: college housing not available.

Activities and organizations: drama/theater group, student-run newspaper, Student Government, Los Amigos Hispanic Club, Criminal Justice Club, Drama Club, GIVE.

Athletics Member NAIA. ***Intercollegiate sports:*** baseball M(s), basketball M(s)/W(s), bowling M(s)/W(s), cross-country running M(s)/W(s), golf M(s)/W(s), soccer M(s)/W(s), softball W(s), tennis M(s)/W(s), track and field M(s)/W(s), volleyball M(s)/W(s), wrestling M(s).

Campus security: day and night security, emergency alert system.

Student services: personal/psychological counseling.

COSTS & FINANCIAL AID

Costs (2017–18) ***Tuition:*** $17,650 full-time, $560 per credit hour part-time. Full-time tuition and fees vary according to course load and program. Part-time tuition and fees vary according to course load and program. No tuition increase for student's term of enrollment. ***Required fees:*** $270 full-time, $135 per term part-time. ***Payment plan:*** deferred payment. ***Waivers:*** children of alumni, senior citizens, and employees or children of employees.

Financial Aid Of all full-time matriculated undergraduates who enrolled in 2014, 503 applied for aid, 454 were judged to have need, 41 had their need fully met. 15 Federal Work-Study jobs (averaging $3923). 1 state and other part-time job (averaging $1928). In 2014, 16 non-need-based awards were made. ***Average percent of need met:*** 62. ***Average financial aid package:*** $12,564. ***Average need-based loan:*** $3822. ***Average need-based gift aid:*** $7787. ***Average non-need-based aid:*** $3283. ***Average indebtedness upon graduation:*** $23,465.

APPLYING

Standardized Tests *Required:* ACCUPLACER (for admission). *Recommended:* SAT or ACT (for admission).

Options: electronic application, deferred entrance.

Required: high school transcript. ***Required for some:*** essay or personal statement, 1 letter of recommendation. ***Recommended:*** minimum 2.0 GPA, interview.

Application deadlines: rolling (freshmen), rolling (transfers).

Notification: continuous (freshmen), continuous (transfers).

CONTACT

Mr. Andy Marks, Director of Enrollment, Calumet College of Saint Joseph, 2400 New York Avenue, Whiting, IN 46394. *Phone:* 219-473-4295. *Toll-free phone:* 877-700-9100. *Fax:* 219-473-4336. *E-mail:* admissions@ccsj.edu.

Chamberlain College of Nursing

Indianapolis, Indiana

http://www.chamberlain.edu/

- **Proprietary** 4-year
- **Coed**

FACULTY

Student/faculty ratio: 14:1.

ACADEMICS

Degree: bachelor's.

COSTS

Costs (2016–17) ***Tuition:*** $18,900 full-time, $675 per credit hour part-time. ***Required fees:*** $600 full-time.

APPLYING

Standardized Tests *Required:* SAT or ACT (for admission).

Options: deferred entrance.

Application fee: $95.

CONTACT

Chamberlain College of Nursing, 9100 Keystone Crossing, Indianapolis, IN 46240. *Toll-free phone:* 877-751-5783.

Crossroads Bible College

Indianapolis, Indiana

http://www.crossroads.edu/

CONTACT

Michael Garrison, Admissions Counselor, Crossroads Bible College, 601 North Shortridge Road, Indianapolis, IN 46219. *Phone:* 317-789-8266. *Toll-free phone:* 800-822-3119. *E-mail:* admissions@crossroads.edu.

DePauw University

Greencastle, Indiana

http://www.depauw.edu/

- **Independent** 4-year, founded 1837, affiliated with United Methodist Church
- **Small-town** 655-acre campus with easy access to Indianapolis
- **Endowment** $614.6 million
- **Coed** 2,225 undergraduate students, 98% full-time, 53% women, 47% men
- **Moderately difficult** entrance level, 65% of applicants were admitted

UNDERGRAD STUDENTS

2,190 full-time, 35 part-time. Students come from 43 states and territories; 42 other countries; 63% are from out of state; 6% Black or African American, non-Hispanic/Latino; 5% Hispanic/Latino; 3% Asian, non-Hispanic/Latino; 0.3% American Indian or Alaska Native, non-Hispanic/Latino; 6% Two or more races, non-Hispanic/Latino; 2% Race/ethnicity unknown; 8% international; 0.7% transferred in; 97% live on campus.

Freshmen:

Admission: 4,845 applied, 3,167 admitted, 559 enrolled. ***Average high school GPA:*** 3.81. ***Test scores:*** SAT critical reading scores over 500: 80%; SAT math scores over 500: 90%; SAT writing scores over 500: 83%; ACT scores over 18: 99%; SAT critical reading scores over 600: 37%; SAT math scores over 600: 52%; SAT writing scores over 600: 39%; ACT scores over 24: 77%; SAT critical reading scores over 700: 6%; SAT math scores over 700: 15%; SAT writing scores over 700: 6%; ACT scores over 30: 19%.

Retention: 92% of full-time freshmen returned.

FACULTY

Total: 266, 86% full-time, 93% with terminal degrees.

Student/faculty ratio: 9:1.

ACADEMICS

Calendar: 4-1-4. *Degree:* bachelor's.

Special study options: advanced placement credit, cooperative education, double majors, English as a second language, honors programs, independent study, internships, off-campus study, part-time degree program, services for LD students, student-designed majors, study abroad. ***ROTC:*** Army (c), Air Force (c).

Unusual degree programs: 3-2 engineering with Columbia University, Washington University in St. Louis.

Computers: Students can access the following: campus intranet, computer help desk, free student e-mail accounts, online (class) grades, online (class) registration, online (class) schedules. Campuswide network is available. 100% of college-owned or -operated housing units are wired for high-speed Internet access. Wireless service is available via entire campus.

Library: Roy O. West Library plus 2 others. Study areas open 24 hours, 5-7 days a week; students can reserve study rooms.

STUDENT LIFE

Housing options: on-campus residence required through senior year; coed, special housing for students with disabilities. Campus housing is university owned. Freshman campus housing is guaranteed.

Activities and organizations: drama/theater group, student-run newspaper, radio and television station, choral group, national fraternities, national sororities.

Athletics Member NCAA. All Division III. ***Intercollegiate sports:*** baseball M, basketball M/W, cheerleading M(c)/W(c), crew M(c)/W(c), cross-country running M/W, field hockey W, football M, golf M/W, lacrosse M/W, rugby M(c), soccer M/W, softball W, swimming and diving M/W, tennis M/W, track and field M/W, volleyball W. ***Intramural sports:*** badminton M/W, basketball M/W, bowling M/W, football M/W, golf M, racquetball M/W, soccer M/W, softball M/W, table tennis M/W, tennis M/W, ultimate Frisbee M/W, volleyball M/W.

Campus security: 24-hour emergency response devices and patrols, student patrols, late-night transport/escort service, controlled dormitory access.

Student services: health clinic, personal/psychological counseling, women's center.

COSTS & FINANCIAL AID

Costs (2017–18) ***Comprehensive fee:*** $60,367 includes full-time tuition ($47,026), mandatory fees ($812), and room and board ($12,529). Part-time tuition: $1470 per credit hour. ***Room and board:*** Room and board charges vary according to board plan. ***Payment plan:*** installment. ***Waivers:*** employees or children of employees.

Financial Aid Of all full-time matriculated undergraduates who enrolled in 2016, 1,487 applied for aid, 1,305 were judged to have need, 349 had their need fully met. In 2016, 840 non-need-based awards were made. ***Average percent of need met:*** 89. ***Average financial aid package:*** $39,790. ***Average need-based loan:*** $4920. ***Average need-based gift aid:*** $34,859. ***Average non-need-based aid:*** $17,350. ***Average indebtedness upon graduation:*** $22,770. ***Financial aid deadline:*** 2/1.

APPLYING

Standardized Tests *Required:* SAT or ACT (for admission).

Options: electronic application, early admission, early decision, early action, deferred entrance.

Required: essay or personal statement, high school transcript, 1 letter of recommendation. ***Recommended:*** interview.

Application deadlines: 2/1 (freshmen), 3/1 (transfers), 12/1 (early action).

Early decision deadline: 11/1.

Notification: continuous until 12/15 (freshmen), continuous (out-of-state freshmen), 4/1 (transfers), 12/1 (early decision), 1/15 (early action).

CONTACT

Ms. Rachel Schmidtke, Director of Recruitment, DePauw University, 204 East Seminary Street, Greencastle, IN 46135. *Phone:* 765-658-4104. *Toll-free phone:* 800-447-2495. *Fax:* 765-658-4007.
E-mail: rachelschmidtke@depauw.edu.

Earlham College

Richmond, Indiana

http://www.earlham.edu/

- **Independent** comprehensive, founded 1847, affiliated with Society of Friends
- **Small-town** 800-acre campus with easy access to Cincinnati, Indianapolis, Dayton
- **Endowment** $384.1 million
- **Coed** 1,031 undergraduate students, 99% full-time, 56% women, 44% men
- **Very difficult** entrance level, 58% of applicants were admitted

UNDERGRAD STUDENTS

1,024 full-time, 7 part-time. Students come from 45 states and territories; 59 other countries; 84% are from out of state; 12% Black or African American, non-Hispanic/Latino; 7% Hispanic/Latino; 6% Asian, non-Hispanic/Latino; 0.1% Native Hawaiian or other Pacific Islander, non-Hispanic/Latino; 0.5% American Indian or Alaska Native, non-Hispanic/Latino; 0.3% Two or more races, non-Hispanic/Latino; 2% Race/ethnicity unknown; 23% international; 1% transferred in; 96% live on campus.

Freshmen:

Admission: 2,917 applied, 1,681 admitted, 355 enrolled. ***Average high school GPA:*** 3.67. ***Test scores:*** SAT critical reading scores over 500: 95%; SAT math scores over 500: 90%; SAT writing scores over 500: 89%; ACT scores over 18: 99%; SAT critical reading scores over 600: 63%; SAT math scores over 600: 59%; SAT writing scores over 600: 51%; ACT scores over 24: 87%; SAT critical reading scores over 700: 20%; SAT math scores over 700: 24%; SAT writing scores over 700: 18%; ACT scores over 30: 35%.

Retention: 80% of full-time freshmen returned.

FACULTY

Total: 106, 95% full-time, 95% with terminal degrees.

Student/faculty ratio: 10:1.

ACADEMICS

Calendar: semesters. *Degrees:* bachelor's and master's.

Special study options: accelerated degree program, advanced placement credit, double majors, English as a second language, independent study, internships, off-campus study, services for LD students, student-designed majors, study abroad.

Unusual degree programs: 3-2 engineering with Columbia University, University of Minnesota, Rensselaer Polytechnic Institute.

Computers: 165 computers/terminals are available on campus for general student use. Students can access the following: campus intranet, computer help desk, free student e-mail accounts, online (class) grades, online (class) registration, online (class) schedules. Campuswide network is available. 100% of college-owned or -operated housing units are wired for high-speed Internet access. Wireless service is available via entire campus.

Library: Lilly Library plus 2 others. Study areas open 24 hours, 5-7 days a week; students can reserve study rooms.

STUDENT LIFE

Housing options: on-campus residence required through senior year; coed, men-only, women-only, special housing for students with disabilities. Campus housing is university owned. Freshman campus housing is guaranteed.

Activities and organizations: drama/theater group, student-run newspaper, radio station, choral group, Gospel Revelations Chorus, Dance Alloy, club sports, Student Government, Black Student Union.

Athletics Member NCAA. All Division III. ***Intercollegiate sports:*** baseball M, basketball M/W, cheerleading W(c), cross-country running M/W, equestrian sports W(c), field hockey W, football M, golf M/W, lacrosse M(c)/W(c), rugby M(c)/W(c), soccer M/W, tennis M/W, track and field M/W, ultimate Frisbee M(c)/W(c), volleyball M(c)/W. ***Intramural sports:*** basketball M/W, bowling M/W, football M, racquetball M/W, rock climbing M/W, soccer M/W, ultimate Frisbee M/W.

Campus security: 24-hour emergency response devices and patrols, student patrols, late-night transport/escort service, controlled dormitory access.

Student services: health clinic, personal/psychological counseling, women's center.

COSTS & FINANCIAL AID

Costs (2016–17) ***Comprehensive fee:*** $54,870 includes full-time tuition ($44,370), mandatory fees ($930), and room and board ($9570). Part-time tuition: $1479 per credit hour. ***College room only:*** $4950. Room and board charges vary according to board plan. ***Payment plans:*** tuition prepayment, installment, deferred payment. ***Waivers:*** employees or children of employees.

Financial Aid Of all full-time matriculated undergraduates who enrolled in 2015, 891 applied for aid, 774 were judged to have need, 243 had their need fully met. In 2015, 108 non-need-based awards were made. ***Average percent of need met:*** 93. ***Average financial aid package:*** $40,987. ***Average need-based loan:*** $5230. ***Average need-based gift aid:*** $34,097. ***Average non-need-based aid:*** $17,183. ***Average indebtedness upon graduation:*** $25,784. ***Financial aid deadline:*** 3/1.

APPLYING

Standardized Tests *Recommended:* SAT or ACT (for admission).

Options: electronic application, early admission, early decision, early action, deferred entrance.

Required: essay or personal statement, high school transcript, minimum 3.0 GPA, 2 letters of recommendation. ***Recommended:*** interview.

Application deadlines: 2/15 (freshmen), 4/1 (transfers), 12/1 (early action).

Early decision deadline: 11/1.

Notification: 4/1 (freshmen), continuous until 4/15 (transfers), 12/1 (early decision), 2/1 (early action).

CONTACT

Josh Stevens, Director of Admissions, Earlham College, 801 National Road West, Richmond, IN 47374. *Phone:* 765-983-1600. *Toll-free phone:* 800-327-5426. *Fax:* 765-983-1560. *E-mail:* admission@earlham.edu.

Franklin College

Franklin, Indiana

http://www.franklincollege.edu/

- **Independent** comprehensive, founded 1834, affiliated with American Baptist Churches in the U.S.A.
- **Suburban** 207-acre campus with easy access to Indianapolis
- **Endowment** $80.1 million
- **Coed** 1,075 undergraduate students, 94% full-time, 54% women, 46% men
- **Moderately difficult** entrance level, 60% of applicants were admitted

UNDERGRAD STUDENTS

1,008 full-time, 67 part-time. Students come from 19 states and territories; 14 other countries; 11% are from out of state; 4% Black or African American, non-Hispanic/Latino; 2% Hispanic/Latino; 0.6% Asian, non-Hispanic/Latino; 0.2% American Indian or Alaska Native, non-Hispanic/Latino; 3% Two or more races, non-Hispanic/Latino; 4% Race/ethnicity unknown; 2% international; 2% transferred in; 76% live on campus.

Freshmen:

Admission: 2,221 applied, 1,333 admitted, 328 enrolled. ***Average high school GPA:*** 3.4. ***Test scores:*** SAT critical reading scores over 500: 54%; SAT math scores over 500: 59%; SAT writing scores over 500: 46%; ACT scores over 18: 90%; SAT critical reading scores over 600: 11%; SAT math scores over 600: 15%; SAT writing scores over 600: 8%; ACT scores over 24: 28%; ACT scores over 30: 4%.

Retention: 79% of full-time freshmen returned.

FACULTY

Total: 109, 71% full-time, 59% with terminal degrees.

Student/faculty ratio: 12:1.

ACADEMICS

Calendar: 4-1-4. *Degrees:* bachelor's and master's.

Special study options: academic remediation for entering students, advanced placement credit, cooperative education, double majors, English as a second language, independent study, internships, off-campus study, part-time degree program, services for LD students, student-designed majors, study abroad, summer session for credit. ***ROTC:*** Army (c).

Unusual degree programs: 3-2 engineering with Indiana University–Purdue University Indianapolis.

Computers: 150 computers/terminals are available on campus for general student use. Students can access the following: campus intranet, computer help desk, free student e-mail accounts, online (class) grades, online (class) registration, online (class) schedules. Campuswide network is available. 100% of college-owned or -operated housing units are wired for high-speed Internet access. Wireless service is available via classrooms, computer centers, computer labs, dorm rooms, learning centers, libraries, student centers.

Library: Hamilton Library.

STUDENT LIFE

Housing options: on-campus residence required through junior year; coed. Campus housing is university owned. Freshman campus housing is guaranteed.

Activities and organizations: drama/theater group, student-run newspaper, radio and television station, choral group, FLOW, FC Volunteers, Student Entertainment Board, Student Congress, national fraternities, national sororities.

Athletics Member NCAA. All Division III. ***Intercollegiate sports:*** baseball M, basketball M/W, cheerleading W(c), cross-country running M/W, football M, golf M/W, lacrosse W, soccer M/W, softball W, swimming and diving M/W, tennis M/W, track and field M/W, volleyball W. ***Intramural sports:*** basketball M/W, softball W, volleyball W.

Campus security: 24-hour emergency response devices and patrols, late-night transport/escort service.

Student services: health clinic, personal/psychological counseling.

COSTS & FINANCIAL AID

Costs (2017–18) ***Comprehensive fee:*** $39,946 includes full-time tuition ($30,586), mandatory fees ($185), and room and board ($9175). Full-time tuition and fees vary according to course load and degree level. Part-time tuition and fees vary according to course load and degree level. ***Required***

fees: $430 per credit hour part-time. ***College room only:*** $5463. Room and board charges vary according to board plan. ***Payment plan:*** installment. ***Waivers:*** senior citizens and employees or children of employees.

Financial Aid Of all full-time matriculated undergraduates who enrolled in 2016, 904 applied for aid, 815 were judged to have need, 128 had their need fully met. In 2016, 143 non-need-based awards were made. ***Average percent of need met:*** 77. ***Average financial aid package:*** $23,805. ***Average need-based loan:*** $4476. ***Average need-based gift aid:*** $19,220. ***Average non-need-based aid:*** $13,561. ***Average indebtedness upon graduation:*** $34,884.

APPLYING

Standardized Tests *Required:* SAT or ACT (for admission).

Options: electronic application, deferred entrance.

Required: high school transcript. ***Required for some:*** interview. ***Recommended:*** essay or personal statement.

Notification: continuous (freshmen), continuous (transfers).

CONTACT

Ms. Jennifer Bostrom, Director of Admissions, Franklin College, 101 Branigin Boulevard, Franklin, IN 46131-2623. *Phone:* 317-738-8075. *Toll-free phone:* 800-852-0232. *Fax:* 317-738-8075. *E-mail:* admissions@franklincollege.edu.

Goshen College

Goshen, Indiana

http://www.goshen.edu/

- **Independent Mennonite** comprehensive, founded 1894
- **Small-town** 135-acre campus
- **Endowment** $101.0 million
- **Coed** 800 undergraduate students, 93% full-time, 60% women, 40% men
- **Moderately difficult** entrance level, 68% of applicants were admitted

UNDERGRAD STUDENTS

741 full-time, 59 part-time. Students come from 34 states and territories; 25 other countries; 40% are from out of state; 4% Black or African American, non-Hispanic/Latino; 18% Hispanic/Latino; 2% Asian, non-Hispanic/Latino; 0.1% American Indian or Alaska Native, non-Hispanic/Latino; 2% Two or more races, non-Hispanic/Latino; 0.5% Race/ethnicity unknown; 9% international; 9% transferred in; 53% live on campus.

Freshmen:

Admission: 1,004 applied, 687 admitted, 185 enrolled. ***Average high school GPA:*** 3.46. ***Test scores:*** SAT critical reading scores over 500: 51%; SAT math scores over 500: 50%; SAT writing scores over 500: 43%; ACT scores over 18: 92%; SAT critical reading scores over 600: 30%; SAT math scores over 600: 21%; SAT writing scores over 600: 24%; ACT scores over 24: 64%; SAT critical reading scores over 700: 7%; SAT math scores over 700: 7%; SAT writing scores over 700: 7%; ACT scores over 30: 21%.

Retention: 82% of full-time freshmen returned.

FACULTY

Total: 106, 66% full-time, 54% with terminal degrees.

Student/faculty ratio: 10:1.

ACADEMICS

Calendar: semesters. *Degrees:* bachelor's and master's.

Special study options: academic remediation for entering students, accelerated degree program, adult/continuing education programs, advanced placement credit, distance learning, double majors, independent study, internships, off-campus study, part-time degree program, services for LD students, student-designed majors, study abroad, summer session for credit.

Unusual degree programs: 3-2 engineering with Case Western Reserve University, University of Illinois at Urbana–Champaign, University of Notre Dame, Washington University in St. Louis.

Computers: 160 computers/terminals and 2,000 ports are available on campus for general student use. Students can access the following: campus intranet, computer help desk, free student e-mail accounts, online (class) grades, online (class) registration, online (class) schedules. Campuswide network is available. 100% of college-owned or -operated housing units are wired for high-speed Internet access. Wireless service is available via entire campus.

Library: The Harold and Wilma Good Library plus 1 other. *Books:* 106,274 (physical), 157,167 (digital/electronic); *Serial titles:* 2,769 (physical), 30,977 (digital/electronic); *Databases:* 69. Weekly public service hours: 81; students can reserve study rooms.

STUDENT LIFE

Housing options: on-campus residence required through junior year; coed, men-only, women-only, special housing for students with disabilities. Campus housing is university owned. Freshman campus housing is guaranteed.

Activities and organizations: drama/theater group, student-run newspaper, radio and television station, choral group, International Student Club, Latino Student Union, PAX - Peace Club, Goshen Student Women's Organization, Business Club.

Athletics Member NAIA. ***Intercollegiate sports:*** baseball M(s), basketball M(s)/W(s), cross-country running M(s)/W(s), soccer M(s)/W(s), softball W(s), tennis M(s)/W(s), track and field M(s)/W(s), volleyball W(s). ***Intramural sports:*** badminton M/W, baseball M, basketball M/W, racquetball M/W, soccer M/W, softball W, table tennis M/W, tennis M/W, ultimate Frisbee M/W, volleyball M/W.

Campus security: 24-hour emergency response devices and patrols, late-night transport/escort service, controlled dormitory access.

Student services: health clinic, personal/psychological counseling.

COSTS & FINANCIAL AID

Costs (2017–18) ***Comprehensive fee:*** $43,700 includes full-time tuition ($33,200) and room and board ($10,500). Full-time tuition and fees vary according to degree level and program. Part-time tuition: $1380 per credit hour. Part-time tuition and fees vary according to course load, degree level, and program. ***College room only:*** $5675. Room and board charges vary according to board plan and housing facility. ***Payment plan:*** installment. ***Waivers:*** employees or children of employees.

Financial Aid Of all full-time matriculated undergraduates who enrolled in 2015, 575 applied for aid, 518 were judged to have need, 99 had their need fully met. 293 Federal Work-Study jobs (averaging $1101). 48 state and other part-time jobs (averaging $1725). In 2015, 171 non-need-based awards were made. ***Average percent of need met:*** 83. ***Average financial aid package:*** $25,492. ***Average need-based loan:*** $5470. ***Average need-based gift aid:*** $21,112. ***Average non-need-based aid:*** $14,199. ***Average indebtedness upon graduation:*** $25,403.

APPLYING

Standardized Tests *Required:* SAT or ACT (for admission).

Options: electronic application, deferred entrance.

Application fee: $25.

Required: minimum 2.0 GPA. ***Required for some:*** essay or personal statement, high school transcript. ***Recommended:*** minimum 2.8 GPA, 1 letter of recommendation, interview, rank in upper 50% of high school class.

Application deadlines: 8/15 (freshmen), 8/15 (transfers).

Notification: continuous (freshmen), continuous (transfers).

CONTACT

Adela Hufford, Director of Admission, Goshen College, 1700 South Main Street, Goshen, IN 46526-4794. *Phone:* 574-535-7535. *Toll-free phone:* 800-348-7422. *Fax:* 574-535-7609. *E-mail:* ahufford@goshen.edu.

See previous page for display ad and page 1364 for the College Close-Up.

Grace College

Winona Lake, Indiana

http://www.grace.edu/

- **Independent** comprehensive, founded 1948, affiliated with Fellowship of Grace Brethren Churches
- **Small-town** 160-acre campus
- **Endowment** $12.3 million
- **Coed** 1,934 undergraduate students, 79% full-time, 56% women, 44% men
- **Moderately difficult** entrance level, 78% of applicants were admitted

UNDERGRAD STUDENTS

1,521 full-time, 413 part-time. Students come from 33 states and territories; 7 other countries; 26% are from out of state; 6% Black or African American, non-Hispanic/Latino; 5% Hispanic/Latino; 1% Asian, non-Hispanic/Latino; 3% Two or more races, non-Hispanic/Latino; 4% Race/ethnicity unknown; 0.6% international; 3% transferred in; 51% live on campus.

Freshmen:

Admission: 4,204 applied, 3,299 admitted, 398 enrolled. ***Average high school GPA:*** 3.59. ***Test scores:*** SAT critical reading scores over 500: 66%; SAT math scores over 500: 63%; ACT scores over 18: 91%; SAT critical reading scores over 600: 24%; SAT math scores over 600: 22%; ACT scores over 24: 51%; SAT critical reading scores over 700: 3%; SAT math scores over 700: 2%; ACT scores over 30: 11%.

Retention: 80% of full-time freshmen returned.

FACULTY

Total: 184, 27% full-time, 41% with terminal degrees.

Student/faculty ratio: 22:1.

ACADEMICS

Calendar: semesters. *Degrees:* certificates, diplomas, associate, bachelor's, master's, and doctoral.

Special study options: academic remediation for entering students, accelerated degree program, adult/continuing education programs, advanced placement credit, cooperative education, distance learning, double majors, honors programs, independent study, internships, off-campus study, part-time degree program, services for LD students, study abroad, summer session for credit.

Computers: 150 computers/terminals are available on campus for general student use. Students can access the following: campus intranet, computer help desk, free student e-mail accounts, online (class) grades, online (class) registration, online (class) schedules. Campuswide network is available. 100% of college-owned or -operated housing units are wired for high-speed Internet access. Wireless service is available via entire campus.

Library: Morgan Library.

STUDENT LIFE

Housing options: on-campus residence required through senior year; men-only, women-only. Campus housing is university owned. Freshman campus housing is guaranteed.

Activities and organizations: drama/theater group, student-run newspaper, choral group, Grace Ministries in Action, Student Activities Board, Funfest, women's ministries, Breakout.

Athletics Member NAIA, NCCAA. ***Intercollegiate sports:*** baseball M(s), basketball M(s)/W(s), cheerleading M(s)/W(s), cross-country running M(s)/W(s), golf M(s)/W(s), soccer M(s)/W(s), softball W(s), tennis M(s)/W(s), track and field M(s)/W(s), volleyball W(s). ***Intramural sports:*** basketball M/W, rugby M, soccer M/W, volleyball M/W.

Campus security: 24-hour emergency response devices and patrols, student patrols, late-night transport/escort service, controlled dormitory access.

Student services: health clinic, personal/psychological counseling.

COSTS & FINANCIAL AID

Costs (2017–18) ***Comprehensive fee:*** $31,524 includes full-time tuition ($23,120) and room and board ($8404). Part-time tuition: $824 per credit hour. ***College room only:*** $4378. ***Waivers:*** senior citizens and employees or children of employees.

Financial Aid Of all full-time matriculated undergraduates who enrolled in 2009, 1,276 applied for aid, 1,273 were judged to have need. ***Average financial aid package:*** $11,338.

APPLYING

Standardized Tests *Required:* SAT or ACT (for admission).

Options: electronic application, early admission, early action, deferred entrance.

Application fee: $30.

Required: essay or personal statement, high school transcript, minimum 2.3 GPA, 2 letters of recommendation, personal statement of faith. ***Required for some:*** interview.

Application deadlines: 8/1 (freshmen), 8/1 (transfers), 12/1 (early action).

Notification: 8/15 (freshmen), continuous until 8/15 (transfers).

CONTACT
Mrs. Nikki Sproul, Admissions Office, Grace College, 200 Seminary Drive, Winona Lake, IN 46590. *Phone:* 574-372-5100 Ext. 6008. *Toll-free phone:* 800-54-GRACE. *Fax:* 574-372-5120. *E-mail:* enroll@grace.edu.

Hanover College

Hanover, Indiana

http://www.hanover.edu/

- **Independent Presbyterian** 4-year, founded 1827
- **Rural** 630-acre campus with easy access to Louisville
- **Endowment** $136.2 million
- **Coed** 1,090 undergraduate students, 99% full-time, 57% women, 43% men
- **Moderately difficult** entrance level, 57% of applicants were admitted

UNDERGRAD STUDENTS
1,084 full-time, 6 part-time. Students come from 28 states and territories; 26 other countries; 33% are from out of state; 5% Black or African American, non-Hispanic/Latino; 3% Hispanic/Latino; 1% Asian, non-Hispanic/Latino; 0.1% Native Hawaiian or other Pacific Islander, non-Hispanic/Latino; 0.6% American Indian or Alaska Native, non-Hispanic/Latino; 1% Two or more races, non-Hispanic/Latino; 4% Race/ethnicity unknown; 4% international; 1% transferred in; 93% live on campus.

Freshmen:
Admission: 3,696 applied, 2,119 admitted, 308 enrolled. ***Average high school GPA:*** 3.67. ***Test scores:*** SAT critical reading scores over 500: 60%; SAT math scores over 500: 62%; SAT writing scores over 500: 53%; ACT scores over 18: 99%; SAT critical reading scores over 600: 13%; SAT math scores over 600: 19%; SAT writing scores over 600: 9%; ACT scores over 24: 65%; SAT critical reading scores over 700: 2%; ACT scores over 30: 9%.

Retention: 82% of full-time freshmen returned.

FACULTY
Total: 99, 88% full-time, 94% with terminal degrees.

Student/faculty ratio: 12:1.

ACADEMICS
Calendar: 4-4-1. *Degree:* bachelor's.

Special study options: advanced placement credit, cooperative education, distance learning, double majors, independent study, internships, off-campus study, services for LD students, student-designed majors, study abroad, summer session for credit.

Computers: 120 computers/terminals and 1,550 ports are available on campus for general student use. Students can access the following: campus intranet, computer help desk, free student e-mail accounts, online (class) grades, online (class) registration, online (class) schedules. Campuswide network is available. 100% of college-owned or -operated housing units are wired for high-speed Internet access. Wireless service is available via entire campus.

Library: Duggan Library. Students can reserve study rooms.

STUDENT LIFE
Housing options: on-campus residence required through senior year; coed, men-only, women-only. Campus housing is university owned and leased by the school. Freshman campus housing is guaranteed.

Activities and organizations: drama/theater group, student-run newspaper, radio and television station, choral group, marching band, Delight Ministries, Alpha Lambda Delta, Love Out Loud, Art Club, International Club, national fraternities, national sororities.

Athletics Member NCAA. All Division III. ***Intercollegiate sports:*** baseball M, basketball M/W, cross-country running M/W, football M, golf M/W, lacrosse M/W, soccer M/W, softball W, tennis M/W, track and field M/W, volleyball W. ***Intramural sports:*** archery W(c), basketball M/W, football M/W, rugby M(c)/W(c), soccer M/W, softball M/W, ultimate Frisbee M(c), volleyball M/W.

Campus security: 24-hour emergency response devices and patrols, late-night transport/escort service, controlled dormitory access.

Student services: health clinic, personal/psychological counseling.

COSTS & FINANCIAL AID
Costs (2017–18) ***One-time required fee:*** $350. ***Comprehensive fee:*** $47,750 includes full-time tuition ($35,750), mandatory fees ($770), and room and board ($11,230). Full-time tuition and fees vary according to reciprocity agreements. Part-time tuition: $3972 per unit. Part-time tuition and fees vary according to course load and reciprocity agreements. ***College room only:*** $5600. Room and board charges vary according to housing facility. ***Payment plan:*** installment. ***Waivers:*** senior citizens and employees or children of employees.

Financial Aid Of all full-time matriculated undergraduates who enrolled in 2015, 975 applied for aid, 856 were judged to have need, 189 had their need fully met. 384 Federal Work-Study jobs (averaging $457). In 2015, 262 non-need-based awards were made. ***Average percent of need met:*** 79. ***Average financial aid package:*** $28,284. ***Average need-based loan:*** $4290. ***Average need-based gift aid:*** $24,741. ***Average non-need-based aid:*** $19,305. ***Average indebtedness upon graduation:*** $29,745.

APPLYING
Standardized Tests *Required:* SAT or ACT (for admission).

Options: electronic application, early admission, early action, deferred entrance.

Required: essay or personal statement, high school transcript, 1 letter of recommendation. ***Recommended:*** interview.

Application deadlines: rolling (freshmen), rolling (transfers), 12/1 (early action).

Notification: continuous until 9/1 (freshmen), continuous (transfers), 12/20 (early action).

CONTACT
Ms. Victoria Hidalgo, Director of Admission, Hanover College, 517 Ball Drive, Hanover, IN 47243. *Phone:* 812-866-7031. *Toll-free phone:* 800-213-2178. *Fax:* 812-866-7098. *E-mail:* admission@hanover.edu.

Harrison College

Indianapolis, Indiana

http://www.harrison.edu/

CONTACT
Mr. Jason Howanec, Vice President of Enrollment, Harrison College, 500 N. Meridian Street, Indianapolis, IN 46204. *Phone:* 888-544-4422. *Toll-free phone:* 888-544-4422. *E-mail:* admissions@harrison.edu.

Holy Cross College

Notre Dame, Indiana

http://www.hcc-nd.edu/

- **Independent Roman Catholic** 4-year, founded 1966
- **Suburban** 150-acre campus with easy access to Chicago, Indianapolis
- **Coed** 601 undergraduate students, 90% full-time, 44% women, 56% men
- **Moderately difficult** entrance level, 91% of applicants were admitted

UNDERGRAD STUDENTS
541 full-time, 60 part-time. Students come from 32 states and territories; 12 other countries; 50% are from out of state; 10% Black or African American, non-Hispanic/Latino; 9% Hispanic/Latino; 2% Asian, non-Hispanic/Latino; 0.2% Native Hawaiian or other Pacific Islander, non-Hispanic/Latino; 0.7% American Indian or Alaska Native, non-Hispanic/Latino; 3% Two or more races, non-Hispanic/Latino; 5% Race/ethnicity unknown; 4% international; 5% transferred in; 67% live on campus.

Freshmen:
Admission: 638 applied, 578 admitted, 211 enrolled. ***Average high school GPA:*** 3.2. ***Test scores:*** SAT critical reading scores over 500: 42%; SAT math scores over 500: 46%; SAT critical reading scores over 600: 11%; SAT math scores over 600: 5%.

Retention: 65% of full-time freshmen returned.

FACULTY
Total: 73, 32% full-time, 44% with terminal degrees.

Student/faculty ratio: 14:1.

ACADEMICS
Calendar: semesters. *Degrees:* associate and bachelor's.

Special study options: academic remediation for entering students, double majors, honors programs, independent study, internships, part-time degree program, services for LD students, student-designed majors, study abroad, summer session for credit. ***ROTC:*** Army (c), Air Force (c).

Computers: 60 computers/terminals are available on campus for general student use. Students can access the following: campus intranet, computer help desk, free student e-mail accounts, online (class) grades, online (class) registration, online (class) schedules. Campuswide network is available. 100% of college-owned or -operated housing units are wired for high-speed Internet access. Wireless service is available via entire campus.
Library: McKenna Library. *Books:* 21,257 (physical), 10,401 (digital/electronic); *Serial titles:* 74 (physical); *Databases:* 55. Weekly public service hours: 86.

STUDENT LIFE
Housing options: on-campus residence required through sophomore year; men-only, women-only. Campus housing is university owned and leased by the school. Freshman campus housing is guaranteed.

Activities and organizations: drama/theater group, choral group, marching band, Student Government Association, Campus Ministry, Intramural athletics, Commuter Student Organization, SAGE.

Athletics Member NAIA. ***Intercollegiate sports:*** basketball M(s)/W(s), crew M(c)/W(c), equestrian sports M(c)/W(c), golf M(s)/W(s), ice hockey M(c), lacrosse M(c), rowing M(c)/W(c), rugby M(c)/W(c), soccer M(s)/W(s), tennis M(s)/W(s). ***Intramural sports:*** basketball M/W, cheerleading M/W, football M/W, skiing (downhill) M(c)/W(c), softball M/W, table tennis M/W, ultimate Frisbee M/W, volleyball M/W, weight lifting M/W.

Campus security: 24-hour emergency response devices, late-night transport/escort service, controlled dormitory access.

Student services: health clinic, personal/psychological counseling.

COSTS
Costs (2016–17) ***Comprehensive fee:*** $39,360 includes full-time tuition ($27,810), mandatory fees ($1050), and room and board ($10,500). Full-time tuition and fees vary according to course load. Part-time tuition: $927 per credit. Part-time tuition and fees vary according to course load. ***Payment plan:*** installment. ***Waivers:*** employees or children of employees.

APPLYING
Standardized Tests *Required:* SAT or ACT (for admission).

Options: electronic application, deferred entrance.

Required: high school transcript. ***Required for some:*** essay or personal statement. ***Recommended:*** essay or personal statement, 2 letters of recommendation, interview.

Application deadlines: rolling (freshmen), rolling (transfers).
Notification: continuous (freshmen), continuous (transfers).

CONTACT
Holy Cross College, 54515 SR 933 N., PO Box 308, Notre Dame, IN 46556. *Phone:* 574-239-8338. *E-mail:* admissions@hcc-nd.edu.

Huntington University

Huntington, Indiana

http://www.huntington.edu/

- **Independent** comprehensive, founded 1897, affiliated with Church of the United Brethren in Christ
- **Small-town** 170-acre campus with easy access to Fort Wayne
- **Endowment** $22.7 million
- **Coed** 1,053 undergraduate students, 91% full-time, 57% women, % men
- **Moderately difficult** entrance level, 97% of applicants were admitted

UNDERGRAD STUDENTS
961 full-time, 92 part-time. Students come from 31 states and territories; 20 other countries; 35% are from out of state; 2% Black or African American, non-Hispanic/Latino; 3% Hispanic/Latino; 0.5% Asian, non-Hispanic/Latino; 0.1% Native Hawaiian or other Pacific Islander, non-Hispanic/Latino; 0.4% American Indian or Alaska Native, non-Hispanic/Latino; 1% Two or more races, non-Hispanic/Latino; 4% international; 4% transferred in; 76% live on campus.

Freshmen:
Admission: 780 applied, 759 admitted, 226 enrolled. ***Average high school GPA:*** 3.46. ***Test scores:*** SAT critical reading scores over 500: 56%; SAT math scores over 500: 50%; SAT writing scores over 500: 44%; ACT scores over 18: 93%; SAT critical reading scores over 600: 14%; SAT math scores over 600: 14%; SAT writing scores over 600: 11%; ACT scores over 24: 52%; SAT critical reading scores over 700: 3%; SAT math scores over 700: 3%; SAT writing scores over 700: 1%; ACT scores over 30: 8%.

Retention: 79% of full-time freshmen returned.

FACULTY
Total: 106, 52% full-time, 57% with terminal degrees.

Student/faculty ratio: 13:1.

ACADEMICS
Calendar: 4-1-4. *Degrees:* associate, bachelor's, and master's.

Special study options: academic remediation for entering students, accelerated degree program, adult/continuing education programs, advanced placement credit, distance learning, double majors, English as a second language, independent study, internships, off-campus study, part-time degree program, services for LD students, study abroad, summer session for credit.

Unusual degree programs: 3-2 athletic training with Manchester University.

Computers: 209 computers/terminals and 3,167 ports are available on campus for general student use. Students can access the following: campus intranet, computer help desk, free student e-mail accounts, online (class) grades, online (class) registration, online (class) schedules. Campuswide network is available. 100% of college-owned or -operated housing units are wired for high-speed Internet access. Wireless service is available via classrooms, computer centers, computer labs, dorm rooms, learning centers, libraries, student centers.
Library: RichLyn Library.

STUDENT LIFE
Housing options: on-campus residence required through junior year; men-only, women-only, special housing for students with disabilities. Campus housing is university owned. Freshman campus housing is guaranteed.

Activities and organizations: drama/theater group, student-run newspaper, radio and television station, choral group, Film Club, Friesen Center for Volunteer Service, Mu Kappa, Social Work Student Council, Investment Club.

Athletics Member NAIA, NCCAA. ***Intercollegiate sports:*** baseball M(s), basketball M(s)/W(s), bowling M(s)/W(s), cheerleading M/W, cross-country running M(s)/W(s), golf M(s), soccer M(s)/W(s), softball W(s), tennis M(s)/W(s), track and field M(s)/W(s), ultimate Frisbee M(c), volleyball W(s). ***Intramural sports:*** basketball M/W, football M/W, racquetball M/W, soccer M/W, table tennis M/W, volleyball M/W.

Campus security: 24-hour emergency response devices, late-night transport/escort service, campus police on duty from 6 pm to 6 am.

COSTS & FINANCIAL AID
Costs (2017–18) ***Comprehensive fee:*** $33,996 includes full-time tuition ($24,694), mandatory fees ($846), and room and board ($8456). ***College room only:*** $3980.

Financial Aid Of all full-time matriculated undergraduates who enrolled in 2016, 743 applied for aid, 645 were judged to have need, 1 had their need fully met. In 2016, 149 non-need-based awards were made. ***Average percent of need met:*** 82. ***Average financial aid package:*** $22,123. ***Average need-based loan:*** $4538. ***Average need-based gift aid:*** $9657. ***Average non-need-based aid:*** $2511. ***Average indebtedness upon graduation:*** $32,509.

APPLYING
Standardized Tests *Required:* SAT or ACT (for admission).

Options: electronic application, deferred entrance.

Application fee: $20.

Required: essay or personal statement, high school transcript, minimum 2.3 GPA. ***Recommended:*** interview.

Application deadlines: 8/1 (freshmen), rolling (transfers).

Notification: continuous (freshmen), continuous (out-of-state freshmen), continuous (transfers).

CONTACT
Huntington University, 2303 College Avenue, Huntington, IN 46750-1299. *Phone:* 260-356-6000. *Toll-free phone:* 800-642-6493.

Indiana State University

Terre Haute, Indiana

http://www.indstate.edu/

- **State-supported** university, founded 1865
- **Small-town** 435-acre campus with easy access to Indianapolis
- **Endowment** $42.2 million
- **Coed** 11,202 undergraduate students, 84% full-time, 54% women, 46% men
- **Moderately difficult** entrance level, 86% of applicants were admitted

UNDERGRAD STUDENTS
9,364 full-time, 1,838 part-time. Students come from 50 states and territories; 63 other countries; 17% are from out of state; 19% Black or African American, non-Hispanic/Latino; 4% Hispanic/Latino; 1% Asian, non-Hispanic/Latino; 0.3% American Indian or Alaska Native, non-Hispanic/Latino; 4% Two or more races, non-Hispanic/Latino; 0.7% Race/ethnicity unknown; 6% international; 8% transferred in; 36% live on campus.

Freshmen:
Admission: 11,101 applied, 9,534 admitted, 2,447 enrolled. ***Average high school GPA:*** 3.07. ***Test scores:*** SAT critical reading scores over 500: 29%; SAT math scores over 500: 29%; SAT writing scores over 500: 22%; ACT scores over 18: 61%; SAT critical reading scores over 600: 6%; SAT math scores over 600: 5%; SAT writing scores over 600: 3%; ACT scores over 24: 18%; ACT scores over 30: 1%.

Retention: 64% of full-time freshmen returned.

FACULTY
Total: 674, 73% full-time, 63% with terminal degrees.

Student/faculty ratio: 21:1.

ACADEMICS
Calendar: semesters. *Degrees:* certificates, bachelor's, master's, doctoral, post-master's, and postbachelor's certificates.

Special study options: academic remediation for entering students, accelerated degree program, adult/continuing education programs, advanced placement credit, cooperative education, distance learning, double majors, English as a second language, freshman honors college, honors programs, independent study, internships, off-campus study, part-time degree program, services for LD students, study abroad, summer session for credit. ***ROTC:*** Army (b), Air Force (b).

Computers: 922 computers/terminals are available on campus for general student use. Students can access the following: campus intranet, computer help desk, free student e-mail accounts, online (class) grades, online (class) registration, online (class) schedules. Campuswide network is available. 100% of college-owned or -operated housing units are wired for high-speed Internet access. Wireless service is available via entire campus.

Library: Cunningham Memorial Library plus 1 other. *Books:* 1.2 million (physical), 713,272 (digital/electronic); *Serial titles:* 74,724 (digital/electronic); *Databases:* 298. Weekly public service hours: 132; study areas open 24 hours, 5-7 days a week; students can reserve study rooms.

STUDENT LIFE
Housing options: on-campus residence required for freshman year; coed, men-only, women-only, special housing for students with disabilities. Campus housing is university owned. Freshman campus housing is guaranteed.

Activities and organizations: drama/theater group, student-run newspaper, radio station, choral group, marching band, Union Board, Student Government Association, Panhellenic Council (sororities), Interfraternity Council (fraternities), Residence Hall Association, national fraternities, national sororities.

Athletics Member NCAA. All Division I except football (Division I-AA). ***Intercollegiate sports:*** baseball M(s), basketball M(s)/W(s), cross-country running M(s)/W(s), golf W(s), soccer W(s), softball W(s), swimming and diving W(s), track and field M(s)/W(s), volleyball W(s). ***Intramural sports:*** badminton M/W, basketball M/W, bowling M(c)/W(c), rugby M(c)/W(c), sand volleyball M/W, soccer M(c)/W(c), softball M/W, swimming and diving M/W, tennis M(c)/W(c), track and field M/W, ultimate Frisbee M(c)/W(c), volleyball M(c)/W(c), wrestling M(c).

Campus security: 24-hour emergency response devices and patrols, student patrols, late-night transport/escort service.

Student services: health clinic, personal/psychological counseling, women's center.

COSTS & FINANCIAL AID
Costs (2016–17) ***Tuition:*** state resident $8546 full-time, $310 per credit hour part-time; nonresident $18,876 full-time, $669 per credit hour part-time. Full-time tuition and fees vary according to reciprocity agreements. Part-time tuition and fees vary according to course load and reciprocity agreements. ***Required fees:*** $200 full-time, $100 per term part-time. ***Room and board:*** $9696. Room and board charges vary according to board plan, housing facility, and student level. ***Payment plans:*** installment, deferred payment. ***Waivers:*** senior citizens and employees or children of employees.

Financial Aid Of all full-time matriculated undergraduates who enrolled in 2015, 8,312 applied for aid, 7,121 were judged to have need, 1,023 had their need fully met. In 2015, 890 non-need-based awards were made. ***Average percent of need met:*** 82. ***Average financial aid package:*** $10,813. ***Average need-based loan:*** $3898. ***Average need-based gift aid:*** $5792. ***Average non-need-based aid:*** $4153. ***Average indebtedness upon graduation:*** $27,705. ***Financial aid deadline:*** 7/1.

APPLYING
Standardized Tests *Required:* SAT or ACT (for admission).

Options: electronic application, deferred entrance.

Application fee: $25.

Required: high school transcript. ***Required for some:*** interview. ***Recommended:*** minimum 2.5 GPA.

Notification: continuous (freshmen), continuous (transfers).

CONTACT
Mr. Richard Toomey, Assistant Vice President of Enrollment Management, Indiana State University, 318 North Sixth Street, John W. Moore Welcome Center, Terre Haute, IN 47809-9989. *Phone:* 812-237-2121. *Toll-free phone:* 800-468-6478. *Fax:* 812-237-8023. *E-mail:* admissions@indstate.edu.

Indiana Tech

Fort Wayne, Indiana

http://https://www.indianatech.edu/

CONTACT
Mrs. Monica L. Chamberlain, Associate Vice President of Enrollment Management, Indiana Tech, 1600 East Washington Boulevard, Fort Wayne, IN 46803. *Phone:* 260-422-5561 Ext. 2348. *Toll-free phone:* 800-937-2448. *Fax:* 260-422-7696. *E-mail:* admissions@indianatech.edu.

Indiana University Bloomington

Bloomington, Indiana

http://www.iub.edu/

- **State-supported** university, founded 1820, part of Indiana University System
- **Small-town** 1936-acre campus with easy access to Indianapolis
- **Endowment** $1.1 billion
- **Coed** 39,184 undergraduate students, 82% full-time, 51% women, 49% men
- **Moderately difficult** entrance level, 79% of applicants were admitted

UNDERGRAD STUDENTS
32,005 full-time, 7,179 part-time. Students come from 53 states and territories; 122 other countries; 33% are from out of state; 4% Black or African American, non-Hispanic/Latino; 6% Hispanic/Latino; 5% Asian, non-Hispanic/Latino; 0.1% American Indian or Alaska Native, non-Hispanic/Latino; 4% Two or more races, non-Hispanic/Latino; 0.3%

Race/ethnicity unknown; 11% international; 2% transferred in; 35% live on campus.

Freshmen:

Admission: 34,646 applied, 27,272 admitted, 6,971 enrolled. *Average high school GPA:* 3.69. *Test scores:* SAT critical reading scores over 500: 84%; SAT math scores over 500: 89%; SAT writing scores over 500: 81%; ACT scores over 18: 99%; SAT critical reading scores over 600: 38%; SAT math scores over 600: 49%; SAT writing scores over 600: 34%; ACT scores over 24: 82%; SAT critical reading scores over 700: 8%; SAT math scores over 700: 15%; SAT writing scores over 700: 6%; ACT scores over 30: 31%.

Retention: 91% of full-time freshmen returned.

FACULTY

Total: 2,494, 86% full-time, 75% with terminal degrees.

Student/faculty ratio: 17:1.

ACADEMICS

Calendar: semesters plus summer sessions. *Degrees:* certificates, associate, bachelor's, master's, doctoral, and postbachelor's certificates.

Special study options: academic remediation for entering students, accelerated degree program, adult/continuing education programs, advanced placement credit, cooperative education, distance learning, double majors, English as a second language, external degree program, freshman honors college, honors programs, independent study, internships, off-campus study, part-time degree program, services for LD students, student-designed majors, study abroad, summer session for credit. *ROTC:* Army (b), Air Force (b).

Unusual degree programs: 3-2 business administration.

Computers: 2,100 computers/terminals are available on campus for general student use. Students can access the following: campus intranet, computer help desk, free student e-mail accounts, online (class) grades, online (class) registration, online (class) schedules. Campuswide network is available. 95% of college-owned or -operated housing units are wired for high-speed Internet access. Wireless service is available via entire campus.

Library: Indiana University Library plus 18 others. *Books:* 8.2 million (physical), 2.0 million (digital/electronic); *Serial titles:* 365,705 (physical), 33.4 million (digital/electronic); *Databases:* 1,871. Study areas open 24 hours, 5-7 days a week; students can reserve study rooms.

STUDENT LIFE

Housing options: on-campus residence required for freshman year; coed, men-only, women-only, cooperative, special housing for students with disabilities. Campus housing is university owned. Freshman applicants given priority for college housing.

Activities and organizations: drama/theater group, student-run newspaper, radio and television station, choral group, marching band, Union Board, Student Association, Student Foundation, Habitat for Humanity, Student Athletic Board, national fraternities, national sororities.

Athletics Member NCAA. All Division I except football (Division I-A). *Intercollegiate sports:* baseball M(s), basketball M(s)/W(s), crew W(s), cross-country running M(s)/W(s), field hockey W, golf M(s)/W(s), rowing W(s), soccer M(s)/W(s), softball W(s), swimming and diving M(s)/W(s), tennis M(s)/W(s), track and field M(s)/W(s), volleyball W(s), water polo W(s), wrestling M(s). *Intramural sports:* badminton M(c)/W(c), baseball M/W, basketball M/W, crew M(c)/W(c), cross-country running M(c)/W(c), equestrian sports M(c)/W(c), fencing M(c)/W(c), field hockey W(c), golf M/W, gymnastics M(c)/W(c), ice hockey M(c)/W(c), lacrosse M(c)/W, racquetball M/W, rowing M(c)/W(c), rugby M(c)/W(c), sailing M(c)/W(c), soccer M(c)/W(c), softball M/W, swimming and diving M(c)/W(c), table tennis M/W, tennis M(c)/W(c), track and field M/W, ultimate Frisbee M(c)/W(c), volleyball M(c)/W(c), water polo M(c)/W, wrestling M(c).

Campus security: 24-hour emergency response devices and patrols, late-night transport/escort service, safety seminars, lighted pathways, escort service, shuttle bus service.

Student services: health clinic, personal/psychological counseling, women's center, legal services.

COSTS & FINANCIAL AID

Costs (2016–17) *Tuition:* state resident $9087 full-time, $284 per credit hour part-time; nonresident $32,945 full-time, $1030 per credit hour part-time. Full-time tuition and fees vary according to location and program. Part-time tuition and fees vary according to course load, location, and program. *Required fees:* $1301 full-time. *Room and board:* $10,041. Room and board charges vary according to board plan and housing facility. *Payment plans:* installment, deferred payment. *Waivers:* employees or children of employees.

Financial Aid Of all full-time matriculated undergraduates who enrolled in 2015, 18,554 applied for aid, 13,125 were judged to have need, 3,541 had their need fully met. In 2015, 9252 non-need-based awards were made. *Average percent of need met:* 67. *Average financial aid package:* $12,864. *Average need-based loan:* $4302. *Average need-based gift aid:* $10,983. *Average non-need-based aid:* $5776. *Average indebtedness upon graduation:* $28,039.

APPLYING

Standardized Tests *Required:* SAT or ACT (for admission). *Recommended:* SAT Subject Tests (for admission).

Options: electronic application, deferred entrance.

Application fee: $60.

Required: high school transcript. *Recommended:* interview.

Application deadlines: rolling (freshmen), rolling (transfers).

Notification: continuous (freshmen), continuous (transfers).

CONTACT

Ms. Sacha Thieme, Executive Director of Admissions, Indiana University Bloomington, 300 North Jordan Avenue, Bloomington, IN 47405-1106. *Phone:* 812-855-0661. *Fax:* 812-855-5102. *E-mail:* iuadmit@indiana.edu.

Indiana University East

Richmond, Indiana

http://www.iue.edu/

- **State-supported** comprehensive, founded 1971, part of Indiana University System
- **Small-town** 182-acre campus with easy access to Indianapolis
- **Endowment** $4.6 million
- **Coed** 4,287 undergraduate students, 44% full-time, 64% women, 36% men
- **Moderately difficult** entrance level, 60% of applicants were admitted

UNDERGRAD STUDENTS

1,868 full-time, 2,419 part-time. Students come from 43 states and territories; 40 other countries; 24% are from out of state; 4% Black or African American, non-Hispanic/Latino; 3% Hispanic/Latino; 0.9% Asian, non-Hispanic/Latino; 0.3% American Indian or Alaska Native, non-Hispanic/Latino; 3% Two or more races, non-Hispanic/Latino; 1% Race/ethnicity unknown; 0.9% international; 9% transferred in.

Freshmen:

Admission: 1,226 applied, 739 admitted, 357 enrolled. *Average high school GPA:* 3.14. *Test scores:* SAT critical reading scores over 500: 33%; SAT math scores over 500: 33%; SAT writing scores over 500: 27%; ACT scores over 18: 76%; SAT critical reading scores over 600: 5%; SAT math scores over 600: 7%; SAT writing scores over 600: 3%; ACT scores over 24: 23%; SAT critical reading scores over 700: 1%; ACT scores over 30: 1%.

Retention: 67% of full-time freshmen returned.

FACULTY

Total: 296, 36% full-time, 40% with terminal degrees.

Student/faculty ratio: 14:1.

ACADEMICS

Calendar: semesters. *Degrees:* certificates, bachelor's, master's, and postbachelor's certificates.

Special study options: academic remediation for entering students, accelerated degree program, adult/continuing education programs, advanced placement credit, cooperative education, distance learning, double majors, external degree program, honors programs, independent study, internships, off-campus study, part-time degree program, services for LD students, study abroad, summer session for credit.

Computers: 187 computers/terminals are available on campus for general student use. Students can access the following: campus intranet, computer

help desk, free student e-mail accounts, online (class) grades, online (class) registration, online (class) schedules. Campuswide network is available. Wireless service is available via entire campus.
Library: IU East Campus Library. *Books:* 29,252 (physical), 157,849 (digital/electronic); *Serial titles:* 9,444 (physical), 1,234 (digital/electronic); *Databases:* 299. Students can reserve study rooms.

STUDENT LIFE
Housing options: college housing not available.

Activities and organizations: drama/theater group, student-run newspaper, television station, choral group, Student Government Association, Psychology Club, Sociology Club, Humanities Club, Business Club.

Athletics Member NAIA. ***Intercollegiate sports:*** basketball M/W, cross-country running M/W, golf M/W, soccer M/W, tennis M/W, track and field M/W, volleyball W. ***Intramural sports:*** basketball M/W, cheerleading W(c), cross-country running M/W, equestrian sports M(c)/W(c), golf M/W, softball M/W, tennis M/W, track and field M/W, volleyball W.

Campus security: 24-hour emergency response devices, late-night transport/escort service, safety awareness, lighted pathways, 14-hour foot and vehicle patrol.

Student services: personal/psychological counseling.

COSTS & FINANCIAL AID
Costs (2016–17) ***Tuition:*** state resident $6478 full-time, $216 per credit hour part-time; nonresident $18,088 full-time, $603 per credit hour part-time. Full-time tuition and fees vary according to course load, location, program, and reciprocity agreements. Part-time tuition and fees vary according to course load, location, program, and reciprocity agreements. ***Required fees:*** $595 full-time. ***Payment plans:*** installment, deferred payment. ***Waivers:*** employees or children of employees.

Financial Aid Of all full-time matriculated undergraduates who enrolled in 2015, 1,785 applied for aid, 1,565 were judged to have need, 231 had their need fully met. In 2015, 117 non-need-based awards were made. ***Average percent of need met:*** 63. ***Average financial aid package:*** $8844. ***Average need-based loan:*** $3811. ***Average need-based gift aid:*** $6931. ***Average non-need-based aid:*** $1955. ***Average indebtedness upon graduation:*** $27,379.

APPLYING
Standardized Tests *Required:* SAT or ACT (for admission).

Options: electronic application, early admission, deferred entrance.

Application fee: $35.

Required: high school transcript, Core 40 high school curriculum for recent Indiana graduates, minimum of 28 semester hours of college preparatory courses for nonresidents. ***Recommended:*** minimum 2.0 GPA.

Application deadlines: rolling (freshmen), rolling (transfers).

Notification: continuous (freshmen), continuous (transfers).

CONTACT
Ms. Molly Vanderpool, Executive Director, Recruitment & Transitions, Admissions, Indiana University East, 2325 Chester Boulevard, Whitewater Hall 151, Richmond, IN 47374-1289. *Phone:* 765-973-8208. *Toll-free phone:* 800-959-EAST. *Fax:* 765-973-8209. *E-mail:* applynow@iue.edu.

Indiana University Kokomo

Kokomo, Indiana

http://www.iuk.edu/

- **State-supported** comprehensive, founded 1945, part of Indiana University System
- **Small-town** 52-acre campus with easy access to Indianapolis
- **Endowment** $5.6 million
- **Coed** 3,977 undergraduate students, 53% full-time, 66% women, 34% men
- **Minimally difficult** entrance level, 69% of applicants were admitted

UNDERGRAD STUDENTS
2,089 full-time, 1,888 part-time. Students come from 12 states and territories; 27 other countries; 0.7% are from out of state; 4% Black or African American, non-Hispanic/Latino; 5% Hispanic/Latino; 0.8% Asian, non-Hispanic/Latino; 0.1% Native Hawaiian or other Pacific Islander, non-Hispanic/Latino; 0.3% American Indian or Alaska Native, non-Hispanic/Latino; 3% Two or more races, non-Hispanic/Latino; 2% Race/ethnicity unknown; 0.6% international; 7% transferred in.

Freshmen:
Admission: 1,513 applied, 1,046 admitted, 499 enrolled. ***Average high school GPA:*** 3.12. ***Test scores:*** SAT critical reading scores over 500: 36%; SAT math scores over 500: 33%; SAT writing scores over 500: 23%; ACT scores over 18: 80%; SAT critical reading scores over 600: 5%; SAT math scores over 600: 5%; SAT writing scores over 600: 4%; ACT scores over 24: 17%; ACT scores over 30: 1%.

Retention: 63% of full-time freshmen returned.

FACULTY
Total: 234, 53% full-time, 41% with terminal degrees.

Student/faculty ratio: 15:1.

ACADEMICS
Calendar: semesters. *Degrees:* certificates, associate, bachelor's, master's, and postbachelor's certificates.

Special study options: academic remediation for entering students, accelerated degree program, adult/continuing education programs, advanced placement credit, distance learning, double majors, English as a second language, external degree program, freshman honors college, honors programs, independent study, internships, part-time degree program, services for LD students, study abroad, summer session for credit. ***ROTC:*** Army (b).

Computers: 325 computers/terminals are available on campus for general student use. Students can access the following: campus intranet, computer help desk, free student e-mail accounts, online (class) grades, online (class) registration, online (class) schedules. Campuswide network is available. Wireless service is available via entire campus.
Library: IU Kokomo Library. *Books:* 129,040 (physical), 543,407 (digital/electronic); *Serial titles:* 4,210 (physical), 41,148 (digital/electronic); *Databases:* 317. Students can reserve study rooms.

STUDENT LIFE
Housing options: college housing not available.

Activities and organizations: drama/theater group, student-run newspaper, choral group, national fraternities, national sororities.

Athletics Member NAIA. ***Intercollegiate sports:*** baseball M, basketball M/W, cross-country running M/W, golf M/W, tennis W, volleyball W. ***Intramural sports:*** basketball M/W, cheerleading M(c)/W(c), soccer M/W, softball M/W, volleyball M/W.

Campus security: 24-hour patrols, late-night transport/escort service, campus police, lighted pathways.

Student services: personal/psychological counseling.

COSTS & FINANCIAL AID
Costs (2016–17) ***Tuition:*** state resident $6478 full-time, $216 per credit hour part-time; nonresident $18,088 full-time, $603 per credit hour part-time. Full-time tuition and fees vary according to course load, location, and program. Part-time tuition and fees vary according to course load, location, and program. ***Required fees:*** $595 full-time. ***Payment plans:*** installment, deferred payment. ***Waivers:*** employees or children of employees.

Financial Aid Of all full-time matriculated undergraduates who enrolled in 2015, 1,920 applied for aid, 1,571 were judged to have need, 161 had their need fully met. In 2015, 130 non-need-based awards were made. ***Average percent of need met:*** 64. ***Average financial aid package:*** $8568. ***Average need-based loan:*** $3527. ***Average need-based gift aid:*** $7104. ***Average non-need-based aid:*** $1494. ***Average indebtedness upon graduation:*** $25,675. ***Financial aid deadline:*** 6/30.

APPLYING
Standardized Tests *Required:* SAT or ACT (for admission).

Options: electronic application, deferred entrance.

Application fee: $35.

Required: high school transcript.

Notification: continuous (freshmen), continuous (transfers).

CONTACT
Ms. Angie Siders, Director of Admissions, Indiana University Kokomo, Kelley Student Center, Room 230, 2300 South Washington Street, Kokomo, IN 46904-9003. *Phone:* 765-455-9217. *Toll-free phone:* 888-875-4485. *Fax:* 765-455-9537. *E-mail:* iuadmis@iuk.edu.

Indiana University Northwest

Gary, Indiana

http://www.iun.edu/

- **State-supported** comprehensive, founded 1959, part of Indiana University System
- **Urban** 43-acre campus with easy access to Chicago
- **Endowment** $8.8 million
- **Coed** 5,244 undergraduate students, 53% full-time, 66% women, 34% men
- **Minimally difficult** entrance level, 76% of applicants were admitted

UNDERGRAD STUDENTS

2,776 full-time, 2,468 part-time. Students come from 7 states and territories; 28 other countries; 3% are from out of state; 16% Black or African American, non-Hispanic/Latino; 22% Hispanic/Latino; 2% Asian, non-Hispanic/Latino; 0.2% American Indian or Alaska Native, non-Hispanic/Latino; 3% Two or more races, non-Hispanic/Latino; 1% Race/ethnicity unknown; 0.3% international; 5% transferred in.

Freshmen:

Admission: 1,723 applied, 1,306 admitted, 585 enrolled. ***Average high school GPA:*** 2.99. ***Test scores:*** SAT critical reading scores over 500: 30%; SAT math scores over 500: 30%; SAT writing scores over 500: 26%; ACT scores over 18: 76%; SAT critical reading scores over 600: 4%; SAT math scores over 600: 6%; SAT writing scores over 600: 3%; ACT scores over 24: 24%; SAT critical reading scores over 700: 1%; ACT scores over 30: 4%.

Retention: 65% of full-time freshmen returned.

FACULTY

Total: 360, 46% full-time, 47% with terminal degrees.

Student/faculty ratio: 14:1.

ACADEMICS

Calendar: semesters. *Degrees:* certificates, associate, bachelor's, master's, and postbachelor's certificates.

Special study options: academic remediation for entering students, accelerated degree program, adult/continuing education programs, advanced placement credit, cooperative education, distance learning, double majors, external degree program, honors programs, independent study, internships, off-campus study, part-time degree program, services for LD students, student-designed majors, study abroad, summer session for credit. ***ROTC:*** Army (b).

Computers: 605 computers/terminals are available on campus for general student use. Students can access the following: campus intranet, computer help desk, free student e-mail accounts, online (class) grades, online (class) registration, online (class) schedules. Campuswide network is available. Wireless service is available via entire campus.

Library: IUN Library. *Books:* 251,000 (physical), 605,000 (digital/electronic); *Serial titles:* 7,500 (physical), 100 (digital/electronic); *Databases:* 325. Students can reserve study rooms.

STUDENT LIFE

Housing options: college housing not available.

Activities and organizations: drama/theater group, student-run newspaper, radio station, choral group, Student Government Association, Student Ambassadors, Art Club, Modern Languages Club, national fraternities, national sororities.

Athletics Member NAIA. ***Intercollegiate sports:*** basketball M(s)/W(s), cross-country running M/W, golf M/W, volleyball W. ***Intramural sports:*** baseball M(c), basketball M/W, cheerleading M(c)/W(c), cross-country running M(c)/W(c), football M(c)/W(c), ice hockey M(c)/W(c), soccer M(c)/W(c), softball M(c)/W(c), tennis M(c)/W(c), volleyball M/W.

Campus security: 24-hour emergency response devices and patrols, late-night transport/escort service, lighted pathways.

Student services: health clinic, personal/psychological counseling.

COSTS & FINANCIAL AID

Costs (2016–17) ***Tuition:*** state resident $6478 full-time, $216 per credit hour part-time; nonresident $18,088 full-time, $603 per credit hour part-time. Full-time tuition and fees vary according to course load, location, and program. Part-time tuition and fees vary according to course load, location, and program. ***Required fees:*** $595 full-time. ***Payment plans:*** installment, deferred payment. ***Waivers:*** employees or children of employees.

Financial Aid Of all full-time matriculated undergraduates who enrolled in 2015, 2,544 applied for aid, 2,011 were judged to have need, 240 had their need fully met. In 2015, 201 non-need-based awards were made. ***Average percent of need met:*** 65. ***Average financial aid package:*** $8109. ***Average need-based loan:*** $3562. ***Average need-based gift aid:*** $6785. ***Average non-need-based aid:*** $3976. ***Average indebtedness upon graduation:*** $29,701.

APPLYING

Standardized Tests *Required:* SAT or ACT (for admission).

Options: electronic application, deferred entrance.

Application fee: $35.

Required: high school transcript, minimum 2.0 GPA.

Application deadlines: rolling (freshmen), rolling (transfers).

Notification: continuous (freshmen), continuous (transfers).

CONTACT

Office of Admissions, Indiana University Northwest, Hawthorn Hall 100, 3400 Broadway, Gary, IN 46408-1197. *Phone:* 219-980-6991. *Toll-free phone:* 800-968-7486. *Fax:* 219-981-4219. *E-mail:* admit@iun.edu.

Indiana University–Purdue University Fort Wayne

Fort Wayne, Indiana

http://www.ipfw.edu/

CONTACT

Angela Morren, Undergraduate Applications Coordinator, Indiana University–Purdue University Fort Wayne, 2101 East Coliseum Boulevard, Fort Wayne, IN 46805-1499. *Phone:* 260-481-6142. *Toll-free phone:* 800-324-4739. *Fax:* 260-481-6880. *E-mail:* morrena@ipfw.edu.

Indiana University–Purdue University Indianapolis

Indianapolis, Indiana

http://www.iupui.edu/

- **State-supported** university, founded 1969, part of Indiana University System
- **Urban** 534-acre campus with easy access to Indianapolis
- **Endowment** $795.4 million
- **Coed** 21,748 undergraduate students, 80% full-time, 56% women, 44% men
- **Moderately difficult** entrance level, 74% of applicants were admitted

UNDERGRAD STUDENTS

17,389 full-time, 4,359 part-time. Students come from 37 states and territories; 129 other countries; 3% are from out of state; 10% Black or African American, non-Hispanic/Latino; 7% Hispanic/Latino; 4% Asian, non-Hispanic/Latino; 0.1% Native Hawaiian or other Pacific Islander, non-Hispanic/Latino; 0.1% American Indian or Alaska Native, non-Hispanic/Latino; 4% Two or more races, non-Hispanic/Latino; 0.6% Race/ethnicity unknown; 4% international; 6% transferred in; 12% live on campus.

Freshmen:

Admission: 13,301 applied, 9,839 admitted, 3,737 enrolled. ***Average high school GPA:*** 3.45. ***Test scores:*** SAT critical reading scores over 500: 51%; SAT math scores over 500: 55%; SAT writing scores over 500: 42%; ACT scores over 18: 87%; SAT critical reading scores over 600: 15%; SAT math scores over 600: 17%; SAT writing scores over 600: 9%; ACT scores over 24: 40%; SAT critical reading scores over 700: 2%; SAT math scores over 700: 2%; SAT writing scores over 700: 1%; ACT scores over 30: 7%.

Retention: 74% of full-time freshmen returned.

FACULTY

Total: 3,346, 70% full-time, 69% with terminal degrees.

Student/faculty ratio: 17:1.

ACADEMICS

Calendar: semesters. *Degrees:* certificates, associate, bachelor's, master's, doctoral, post-master's, and postbachelor's certificates.

Special study options: academic remediation for entering students, accelerated degree program, adult/continuing education programs, advanced placement credit, cooperative education, distance learning, double majors, English as a second language, external degree program, freshman honors college, honors programs, independent study, internships, off-campus study, part-time degree program, services for LD students, student-designed majors, study abroad, summer session for credit. ***ROTC:*** Army (b), Air Force (c).

Computers: 1,158 computers/terminals are available on campus for general student use. Students can access the following: campus intranet, computer help desk, free student e-mail accounts, online (class) grades, online (class) registration, online (class) schedules. Campuswide network is available. 100% of college-owned or -operated housing units are wired for high-speed Internet access. Wireless service is available via entire campus.

Library: University Library plus 4 others. *Books:* 1.4 million (physical), 700,000 (digital/electronic); *Serial titles:* 43,147 (physical), 1.8 million (digital/electronic); *Databases:* 600. Study areas open 24 hours, 5-7 days a week; students can reserve study rooms.

STUDENT LIFE

Housing options: coed. Campus housing is university owned.

Activities and organizations: drama/theater group, student-run newspaper, national fraternities, national sororities.

Athletics Member NCAA. All Division I. ***Intercollegiate sports:*** basketball M(s)/W(s), cheerleading M/W, cross-country running M(s)/W(s), golf M(s)/W(s), soccer M(s)/W(s), softball W(s), swimming and diving M(s)/W(s), tennis M(s)/W(s), track and field M/W, volleyball W(s). ***Intramural sports:*** baseball M(c)/W(c), basketball M/W, crew M(c)/W(c), cross-country running M/W, equestrian sports M(c)/W(c), fencing M(c)/W(c), football M/W, golf M/W, gymnastics M(c)/W(c), ice hockey M(c)/W(c), rowing M(c)/W(c), rugby M(c)/W(c), soccer M/W, softball M/W, swimming and diving M(c)/W(c), tennis M(c)/W(c), track and field M/W, ultimate Frisbee M/W, volleyball M/W, water polo M/W.

Campus security: 24-hour emergency response devices and patrols, late-night transport/escort service, controlled dormitory access, lighted pathways, self-defense education.

Student services: health clinic, personal/psychological counseling, women's center.

COSTS & FINANCIAL AID

Costs (2016–17) ***Tuition:*** state resident $8141 full-time, $271 per credit hour part-time; nonresident $28,727 full-time, $958 per credit hour part-time. Full-time tuition and fees vary according to course load, location, and program. Part-time tuition and fees vary according to course load, location, and program. ***Required fees:*** $1064 full-time. ***Room and board:*** $8462. Room and board charges vary according to board plan and housing facility. ***Payment plan:*** deferred payment. ***Waivers:*** employees or children of employees.

Financial Aid Of all full-time matriculated undergraduates who enrolled in 2015, 14,147 applied for aid, 11,486 were judged to have need, 1,936 had their need fully met. In 2015, 1727 non-need-based awards were made. ***Average percent of need met:*** 65. ***Average financial aid package:*** $10,391. ***Average need-based loan:*** $4009. ***Average need-based gift aid:*** $8662. ***Average non-need-based aid:*** $4862. ***Average indebtedness upon graduation:*** $28,951.

APPLYING

Standardized Tests *Required:* SAT or ACT (for admission).

Options: electronic application, deferred entrance.

Application fee: $55.

Required: high school transcript. ***Required for some:*** interview. ***Recommended:*** portfolio for art program.

Application deadlines: 5/1 (freshmen), rolling (transfers).

Notification: continuous (freshmen), continuous (transfers).

CONTACT

Director of Admissions, Indiana University–Purdue University Indianapolis, 420 University Boulevard, Campus Center 255, Indianapolis, IN 46202-5143. *Phone:* 317-274-4591. *Fax:* 317-278-1862. *E-mail:* apply@iupui.edu.

Indiana University South Bend

South Bend, Indiana

http://www.iusb.edu/

- **State-supported** comprehensive, founded 1922, part of Indiana University System
- **Suburban** 104-acre campus with easy access to Chicago
- **Endowment** $13.8 million
- **Coed** 6,653 undergraduate students, 57% full-time, 61% women, 39% men
- **Moderately difficult** entrance level, 77% of applicants were admitted

UNDERGRAD STUDENTS

3,815 full-time, 2,838 part-time. Students come from 18 states and territories; 62 other countries; 4% are from out of state; 8% Black or African American, non-Hispanic/Latino; 10% Hispanic/Latino; 1% Asian, non-Hispanic/Latino; 0.1% Native Hawaiian or other Pacific Islander, non-Hispanic/Latino; 0.2% American Indian or Alaska Native, non-Hispanic/Latino; 4% Two or more races, non-Hispanic/Latino; 0.8% Race/ethnicity unknown; 3% international; 6% transferred in; 8% live on campus.

Freshmen:

Admission: 2,451 applied, 1,888 admitted, 894 enrolled. ***Average high school GPA:*** 3.11. ***Test scores:*** SAT critical reading scores over 500: 36%; SAT math scores over 500: 39%; SAT writing scores over 500: 28%; ACT scores over 18: 78%; SAT critical reading scores over 600: 9%; SAT math scores over 600: 9%; SAT writing scores over 600: 5%; ACT scores over 24: 23%; SAT critical reading scores over 700: 1%; SAT math scores over 700: 1%; ACT scores over 30: 1%.

Retention: 64% of full-time freshmen returned.

FACULTY

Total: 443, 59% full-time, 55% with terminal degrees.

Student/faculty ratio: 14:1.

ACADEMICS

Calendar: semesters. *Degrees:* certificates, diplomas, associate, bachelor's, master's, and postbachelor's certificates.

Special study options: accelerated degree program, adult/continuing education programs, advanced placement credit, distance learning, double majors, English as a second language, external degree program, freshman honors college, honors programs, independent study, internships, off-campus study, part-time degree program, services for LD students, study abroad, summer session for credit. ***ROTC:*** Army (c), Navy (c), Air Force (c).

Computers: 775 computers/terminals are available on campus for general student use. Students can access the following: campus intranet, computer help desk, free student e-mail accounts, online (class) grades, online (class) registration, online (class) schedules. Campuswide network is available. 100% of college-owned or -operated housing units are wired for high-speed Internet access. Wireless service is available via entire campus.

Library: Franklin D. Schurz Library. *Books:* 523,612 (physical), 364,427 (digital/electronic); *Serial titles:* 39,990 (physical), 16,293 (digital/electronic); *Databases:* 315. Students can reserve study rooms.

STUDENT LIFE

Housing options: coed. Campus housing is university owned.

Activities and organizations: drama/theater group, student-run newspaper, choral group, national fraternities, national sororities.

Athletics Member NAIA. ***Intercollegiate sports:*** baseball M, basketball M(s)/W(s), cross-country running M/W, golf M, softball W, volleyball W. ***Intramural sports:*** badminton M/W, basketball M/W, bowling M/W, cheerleading W(c), cross-country running M(c)/W(c), equestrian sports M(c)/W(c), football M/W, golf M(c)/W(c), racquetball M/W, soccer M(c)/W(c), softball M/W, table tennis M/W, tennis M/W, volleyball M/W(c).

Campus security: 24-hour emergency response devices and patrols, late-night transport/escort service, safety seminars, lighted pathways.

Student services: health clinic, personal/psychological counseling, women's center.

COSTS & FINANCIAL AID
Costs (2016–17) ***Tuition:*** state resident $6478 full-time, $216 per credit hour part-time; nonresident $18,088 full-time, $603 per credit hour part-time. Full-time tuition and fees vary according to course load, location, and program. Part-time tuition and fees vary according to course load, location, and program. ***Required fees:*** $595 full-time. ***Room only:*** $7222. Room and board charges vary according to housing facility. ***Payment plans:*** installment, deferred payment. ***Waivers:*** employees or children of employees.

Financial Aid Of all full-time matriculated undergraduates who enrolled in 2015, 3,311 applied for aid, 2,849 were judged to have need, 271 had their need fully met. In 2015, 273 non-need-based awards were made. ***Average percent of need met:*** 61. ***Average financial aid package:*** $8524. ***Average need-based loan:*** $3576. ***Average need-based gift aid:*** $6933. ***Average non-need-based aid:*** $1761. ***Average indebtedness upon graduation:*** $27,306.

APPLYING
Standardized Tests *Required:* SAT or ACT (for admission).

Options: electronic application, deferred entrance.

Application fee: $35.

Required: high school transcript, minimum 2.0 GPA. ***Required for some:*** interview.

Application deadlines: rolling (freshmen), rolling (transfers).

Notification: continuous (freshmen), continuous (transfers).

CONTACT
Ms. Constance Peterson-Miller, Director of Admissions, Indiana University South Bend, 1700 Mishawaka Avenue, PO Box 7111, South Bend, IN 46634-7111. *Phone:* 574-520-4839. *Toll-free phone:* 877-GO-2-IUSB. *Fax:* 574-520-4834. *E-mail:* admissions@iusb.edu.

★ Indiana University Southeast

New Albany, Indiana

http://www.ius.edu/

- **State-supported** comprehensive, founded 1941, part of Indiana University System
- **Suburban** 179-acre campus with easy access to Louisville
- **Endowment** $13.1 million
- **Coed** 5,486 undergraduate students, 61% full-time, 60% women, 40% men
- **Minimally difficult** entrance level, 84% of applicants were admitted

UNDERGRAD STUDENTS
3,326 full-time, 2,160 part-time. Students come from 15 states and territories; 35 other countries; 30% are from out of state; 7% Black or African American, non-Hispanic/Latino; 3% Hispanic/Latino; 1% Asian, non-Hispanic/Latino; 0.1% Native Hawaiian or other Pacific Islander, non-Hispanic/Latino; 0.1% American Indian or Alaska Native, non-Hispanic/Latino; 3% Two or more races, non-Hispanic/Latino; 0.5% Race/ethnicity unknown; 0.5% international; 8% transferred in; 7% live on campus.

Freshmen:
Admission: 2,177 applied, 1,829 admitted, 862 enrolled. ***Average high school GPA:*** 3.18. ***Test scores:*** SAT critical reading scores over 500: 38%; SAT math scores over 500: 32%; SAT writing scores over 500: 31%; ACT scores over 18: 73%; SAT critical reading scores over 600: 9%; SAT math scores over 600: 6%; SAT writing scores over 600: 4%; ACT scores over 24: 19%; SAT critical reading scores over 700: 1%; ACT scores over 30: 1%.

Retention: 62% of full-time freshmen returned.

FACULTY
Total: 459, 47% full-time, 52% with terminal degrees.

Student/faculty ratio: 13:1.

ACADEMICS
Calendar: semesters. *Degrees:* certificates, associate, bachelor's, master's, and postbachelor's certificates.

Special study options: academic remediation for entering students, accelerated degree program, adult/continuing education programs, advanced placement credit, distance learning, double majors, English as a second language, external degree program, honors programs, independent study, internships, off-campus study, part-time degree program, services for LD students, student-designed majors, study abroad, summer session for credit. ***ROTC:*** Army (c), Air Force (c).

Computers: 924 computers/terminals are available on campus for general student use. Students can access the following: campus intranet, computer help desk, free student e-mail accounts, online (class) grades, online (class) registration, online (class) schedules. Campuswide network is available. 100% of college-owned or -operated housing units are wired for high-speed Internet access. Wireless service is available via entire campus.

Library: IU Southeast Library. *Books:* 400,000 (physical), 590,000 (digital/electronic); *Serial titles:* 35,780 (physical), 60,000 (digital/electronic); *Databases:* 300. Students can reserve study rooms.

STUDENT LIFE
Housing options: coed. Campus housing is university owned.

Activities and organizations: drama/theater group, student-run newspaper, choral group, national fraternities, national sororities.

Athletics Member NAIA. ***Intercollegiate sports:*** baseball M(s), basketball M(s)/W(s), softball W, tennis M/W, volleyball W(s). ***Intramural sports:*** basketball M/W, football M/W, golf M/W, soccer M/W, softball M/W, ultimate Frisbee M/W, volleyball M/W, weight lifting M.

Campus security: 24-hour emergency response devices and patrols, self-defense education, lighted pathways, police department on campus.

Student services: personal/psychological counseling.

COSTS & FINANCIAL AID
Costs (2016–17) ***Tuition:*** state resident $6478 full-time, $216 per credit hour part-time; nonresident $18,088 full-time, $603 per credit hour part-time. Full-time tuition and fees vary according to course load, location, program, and reciprocity agreements. Part-time tuition and fees vary according to course load, location, program, and reciprocity agreements. ***Required fees:*** $595 full-time. ***Room only:*** $6520. Room and board charges vary according to board plan and housing facility. ***Payment plans:*** installment, deferred payment. ***Waivers:*** employees or children of employees.

Financial Aid Of all full-time matriculated undergraduates who enrolled in 2015, 2,904 applied for aid, 2,358 were judged to have need, 219 had their need fully met. In 2015, 217 non-need-based awards were made. ***Average percent of need met:*** 59. ***Average financial aid package:*** $7993. ***Average need-based loan:*** $3772. ***Average need-based gift aid:*** $6336. ***Average non-need-based aid:*** $1568. ***Average indebtedness upon graduation:*** $22,612.

APPLYING
Standardized Tests *Required:* SAT or ACT (for admission).

Options: electronic application, early admission, deferred entrance.

Application fee: $35.

Required: high school transcript. ***Required for some:*** interview.

Application deadlines: rolling (freshmen), rolling (transfers).

Notification: continuous (freshmen), continuous (transfers).

CONTACT
Ms. Christopher Crews, Director of Recruitment and Admission, Indiana University Southeast, University Center South Room 102, 4201 Grant Line Road, New Albany, IN 47150. *Phone:* 812-941-2212. *Toll-free phone:* 800-852-8835. *Fax:* 812-941-2595. *E-mail:* admissions@ius.edu.

Indiana Wesleyan University

Marion, Indiana

http://www.indwes.edu/

- **Independent Wesleyan** comprehensive, founded 1920
- **Small-town** 300-acre campus with easy access to Indianapolis
- **Coed**
- **Moderately difficult** entrance level

FACULTY
Student/faculty ratio: 14:1.

ACADEMICS
Calendar: semesters. *Degrees:* associate, bachelor's, master's, doctoral, post-master's, and postbachelor's certificates (also offers adult program with significant enrollment not reflected in profile).
Library: Lewis A. Jackson Library. Students can reserve study rooms.

STUDENT LIFE
Housing options: on-campus residence required through junior year; men-only, women-only. Campus housing is university owned. Freshman campus housing is guaranteed.
Activities and organizations: drama/theater group, student-run newspaper, radio and television station, choral group, Student Government Organization, Student Activities Council, University Players, World Christian Fellowship, Sixth Man Club.
Athletics Member NAIA, NCCAA.
Campus security: 24-hour emergency response devices and patrols, late-night transport/escort service, controlled dormitory access.
Student services: health clinic, personal/psychological counseling.

COSTS & FINANCIAL AID
Costs (2016–17) ***Comprehensive fee:*** $33,494 includes full-time tuition ($25,346) and room and board ($8148). Full-time tuition and fees vary according to course load and degree level. Part-time tuition: $538 per credit hour. Part-time tuition and fees vary according to course load and degree level. ***College room only:*** $4074. Room and board charges vary according to board plan. ***Payment plans:*** installment, deferred payment.
Financial Aid Of all full-time matriculated undergraduates who enrolled in 2016, 2,297 applied for aid, 2,003 were judged to have need, 1,087 had their need fully met. In 2016, 277 non-need-based awards were made. ***Average percent of need met:*** 92. ***Average financial aid package:*** $27,709. ***Average need-based loan:*** $4077. ***Average need-based gift aid:*** $17,155. ***Average non-need-based aid:*** $8682. ***Average indebtedness upon graduation:*** $28,907.

APPLYING
Standardized Tests *Required:* SAT or ACT (for admission). *Required for some:* TOEFL for non-English speaking and some non-resident alien students.
Options: electronic application, deferred entrance.
Required: essay or personal statement, high school transcript, minimum 2.5 GPA, 2 letters of recommendation.

CONTACT
Mr. Adam Farmer, Director of Admissions, Indiana Wesleyan University, 4201 South Washington Street, Marion, IN 46953. *Phone:* 866-468-6498 Ext. 2138. *Toll-free phone:* 866-468-6498.
E-mail: admissions@indwes.edu.

International Business College

Fort Wayne, Indiana

http://www.ibcfortwayne.edu/

- **Proprietary** 4-year, founded 1889
- **Suburban** campus
- **Coed**
- 75% of applicants were admitted

ACADEMICS
Calendar: semesters. *Degrees:* diplomas, associate, and bachelor's.

CONTACT
Admissions Office, International Business College, 5699 Coventry Lane, Fort Wayne, IN 46804. *Phone:* 260-459-4500. *Toll-free phone:* 800-589-6363.

Manchester University

North Manchester, Indiana

http://www.manchester.edu/

- **Independent** comprehensive, founded 1889, affiliated with Church of the Brethren
- **Small-town** 125-acre campus
- **Endowment** $55.8 million
- **Coed** 1,272 undergraduate students, 98% full-time, 52% women, 48% men
- **Moderately difficult** entrance level, 71% of applicants were admitted

UNDERGRAD STUDENTS
1,250 full-time, 22 part-time. Students come from 23 states and territories; 19 other countries; 12% are from out of state; 7% Black or African American, non-Hispanic/Latino; 6% Hispanic/Latino; 2% Asian, non-Hispanic/Latino; 0.2% American Indian or Alaska Native, non-Hispanic/Latino; 4% Two or more races, non-Hispanic/Latino; 0.7% Race/ethnicity unknown; 4% international; 2% transferred in; 78% live on campus.

Freshmen:
Admission: 2,431 applied, 1,715 admitted, 389 enrolled. ***Average high school GPA:*** 3.29. ***Test scores:*** SAT critical reading scores over 500: 45%; SAT math scores over 500: 46%; SAT writing scores over 500: 32%; ACT scores over 18: 80%; SAT critical reading scores over 600: 8%; SAT math scores over 600: 12%; SAT writing scores over 600: 5%; ACT scores over 24: 32%; SAT math scores over 700: 1%; ACT scores over 30: 3%.
Retention: 69% of full-time freshmen returned.

FACULTY
Total: 113, 73% full-time, 73% with terminal degrees.
Student/faculty ratio: 14:1.

ACADEMICS
Calendar: 4-1-4. *Degrees:* associate, bachelor's, master's, and doctoral.
Special study options: accelerated degree program, advanced placement credit, distance learning, double majors, honors programs, independent study, internships, off-campus study, part-time degree program, services for LD students, student-designed majors, study abroad, summer session for credit.
Unusual degree programs: 3-2 engineering with Washington University in St. Louis, Purdue University, Ohio State University, Columbia University.
Computers: 226 computers/terminals are available on campus for general student use. Students can access the following: campus intranet, computer help desk, free student e-mail accounts, online (class) grades, online (class) registration, online (class) schedules. Campuswide network is available. 100% of college-owned or -operated housing units are wired for high-speed Internet access. Wireless service is available via classrooms, computer centers, computer labs, dorm rooms, learning centers, libraries, student centers.
Library: Funderburg Library.

STUDENT LIFE
Housing options: on-campus residence required through junior year; coed, special housing for students with disabilities. Campus housing is university owned. Freshman campus housing is guaranteed.
Activities and organizations: drama/theater group, student-run newspaper, radio station, choral group, College of Business Club, Manchester University Athletic Training Club, Fellowship of Christian Athletes, Student Education Association, Pre-Professionals of Science Club.
Athletics Member NCAA. All Division III. ***Intercollegiate sports:*** baseball M, basketball M/W, cheerleading W, cross-country running M/W, football M, golf M/W, soccer M/W, softball W, swimming and diving M/W, tennis M/W, track and field M/W, volleyball W, wrestling M. ***Intramural sports:*** basketball M/W, football M/W, soccer M/W, softball M/W, volleyball M/W.
Campus security: 24-hour emergency response devices and patrols, student patrols, late-night transport/escort service, alarm system, locked residence hall entrances.
Student services: health clinic, personal/psychological counseling.

COSTS & FINANCIAL AID
Costs (2017–18) ***One-time required fee:*** $250. ***Comprehensive fee:*** $41,540 includes full-time tuition ($30,450), mandatory fees ($1210), and room and board ($9880). Part-time tuition: $700 per credit hour. Part-time tuition and fees vary according to course load. ***Required fees:*** $30 per credit hour part-time. ***College room only:*** $5750. Room and board charges vary according to board plan and housing facility. ***Payment plan:*** installment. ***Waivers:*** employees or children of employees.

Financial Aid Of all full-time matriculated undergraduates who enrolled in 2016, 1,131 applied for aid, 1,048 were judged to have need, 266 had their need fully met. In 2016, 172 non-need-based awards were made. ***Average percent of need met:*** 86. ***Average financial aid package:*** $28,495. ***Average need-based loan:*** $4304. ***Average need-based gift aid:*** $22,528. ***Average non-need-based aid:*** $18,192. ***Average indebtedness upon graduation:*** $33,011.

APPLYING
Options: electronic application, deferred entrance.

Application fee: $25.

Required: high school transcript, 1 letter of recommendation, rank in upper 50% of high school class. ***Required for some:*** essay or personal statement, minimum 3.0 GPA. ***Recommended:*** minimum 2.3 GPA.

Application deadlines: rolling (freshmen), rolling (transfers).

Notification: continuous (freshmen), continuous (transfers).

CONTACT
Mr. Adam Hohman, Associate Director of Admissions, Manchester University, 604 East College Avenue, North Manchester, IN 46962-1225. *Phone:* 260-982-5235. *Toll-free phone:* 800-852-3648. *Fax:* 260-982-5239. *E-mail:* arhohman@manchester.edu.

Marian University

Indianapolis, Indiana

http://www.marian.edu/

- **Independent Roman Catholic** comprehensive, founded 1851
- **Suburban** 114-acre campus with easy access to Indianapolis
- **Endowment** $40.1 million
- **Coed** 2,147 undergraduate students, 82% full-time, 61% women, 39% men
- **Moderately difficult** entrance level, 59% of applicants were admitted

UNDERGRAD STUDENTS
1,764 full-time, 383 part-time. Students come from 34 states and territories; 18 other countries; 21% are from out of state; 12% Black or African American, non-Hispanic/Latino; 5% Hispanic/Latino; 2% Asian, non-Hispanic/Latino; 0.1% Native Hawaiian or other Pacific Islander, non-Hispanic/Latino; 0.2% American Indian or Alaska Native, non-Hispanic/Latino; 3% Two or more races, non-Hispanic/Latino; 5% Race/ethnicity unknown; 1% international; 4% transferred in; 37% live on campus.

Freshmen:
Admission: 2,191 applied, 1,303 admitted, 392 enrolled. ***Average high school GPA:*** 3.41. ***Test scores:*** SAT critical reading scores over 500: 62%; SAT math scores over 500: 62%; SAT writing scores over 500: 56%; ACT scores over 18: 90%; SAT critical reading scores over 600: 19%; SAT math scores over 600: 25%; SAT writing scores over 600: 19%; ACT scores over 24: 41%; SAT critical reading scores over 700: 3%; SAT math scores over 700: 3%; SAT writing scores over 700: 3%; ACT scores over 30: 7%.

Retention: 77% of full-time freshmen returned.

FACULTY
Total: 278, 53% full-time, 41% with terminal degrees.

Student/faculty ratio: 13:1.

ACADEMICS
Calendar: semesters. *Degrees:* associate, bachelor's, master's, and doctoral.

Special study options: academic remediation for entering students, accelerated degree program, adult/continuing education programs, advanced placement credit, cooperative education, distance learning, double majors, honors programs, independent study, internships, off-campus study, part-time degree program, services for LD students, study abroad, summer session for credit. ***ROTC:*** Army (c).

Computers: 118 computers/terminals are available on campus for general student use. Students can access the following: computer help desk, free student e-mail accounts, online (class) grades, online (class) registration, online (class) schedules. Campuswide network is available. 100% of college-owned or -operated housing units are wired for high-speed Internet access. Wireless service is available via entire campus.

Library: Mother Theresa Hackelmeier Memorial Library. *Books:* 79,801 (physical); *Serial titles:* 150 (physical). Weekly public service hours: 95.

STUDENT LIFE
Housing options: on-campus residence required through junior year; coed. Campus housing is university owned. Freshman campus housing is guaranteed.

Activities and organizations: drama/theater group, student-run newspaper, choral group, marching band, Student Government Association, College Mentors for Kids, Best Buddies, Knight Nation, Sophia Club.

Athletics Member NAIA. ***Intercollegiate sports:*** baseball M(s), basketball M(s)/W(s), bowling M(s)/W(s), cheerleading M(s)(c)/W(s)(c), cross-country running M(s)/W(s), football M(s), golf M(s)/W(s), lacrosse W(s), soccer M(s)/W(s), softball W(s), tennis M(s)/W(s), track and field M(s)/W(s), volleyball W(s), wrestling M(s). ***Intramural sports:*** basketball M/W, cheerleading M/W, football M/W, ultimate Frisbee M/W, volleyball M/W.

Campus security: 24-hour emergency response devices and patrols, student patrols, late-night transport/escort service, controlled dormitory access.

Student services: health clinic, personal/psychological counseling.

COSTS & FINANCIAL AID
Costs (2017–18) ***Comprehensive fee:*** $43,206 includes full-time tuition ($33,000) and room and board ($10,206). Part-time tuition: $1450 per credit hour. ***College room only:*** $5050. Room and board charges vary according to housing facility. ***Payment plan:*** installment. ***Waivers:*** children of alumni and employees or children of employees.

Financial Aid Of all full-time matriculated undergraduates who enrolled in 2008, 1,192 applied for aid, 1,068 were judged to have need, 231 had their need fully met. 200 Federal Work-Study jobs (averaging $1500). In 2008, 185 non-need-based awards were made. ***Average percent of need met:*** 75. ***Average financial aid package:*** $19,509. ***Average need-based loan:*** $4478. ***Average need-based gift aid:*** $11,188. ***Average non-need-based aid:*** $12,191. ***Average indebtedness upon graduation:*** $23,467.

APPLYING
Standardized Tests *Required:* SAT or ACT (for admission).

Options: electronic application, deferred entrance.

Application fee: $35.

Required: high school transcript, minimum 2.3 GPA, college transcripts. ***Required for some:*** essay or personal statement, 1 letter of recommendation, interview.

Application deadlines: 8/1 (freshmen), 8/1 (transfers).

Notification: continuous (freshmen), continuous (out-of-state freshmen), continuous (transfers).

CONTACT
Ms. Luann Brames, Director of Freshmen Admission, Marian University, 3200 Cold Spring Road, Indianapolis, IN 46222-1997. *Phone:* 317-955-6300. *Toll-free phone:* 800-772-7264. *Fax:* 317-955-6401. *E-mail:* admissions@marian.edu.

Martin University

Indianapolis, Indiana

http://www.martin.edu/

CONTACT
Ms. Brenda Shaheed, Director of Enrollment Management, Martin University, 2171 Avondale Place, PO Box 18567, Indianapolis, IN 46218-3867. *Phone:* 317-543-3237. *Fax:* 317-543-4790.

Mid-America College of Funeral Service

Jeffersonville, Indiana

http://www.mid-america.edu/

CONTACT

Mr. Richard Nelson, Dean of Students, Mid-America College of Funeral Service, 3111 Hamburg Pike, Jeffersonville, IN 47130-9630. *Phone:* 812-288-8878. *Toll-free phone:* 800-221-6158. *Fax:* 812-288-5942. *E-mail:* macfs@mindspring.com.

Oakland City University

Oakland City, Indiana

http://www.oak.edu/

- **Independent General Baptist** comprehensive, founded 1885
- **Rural** 20-acre campus
- **Endowment** $4.9 million
- **Coed** 1,270 undergraduate students, 43% full-time, 57% women, 43% men
- **Minimally difficult** entrance level, 33% of applicants were admitted

UNDERGRAD STUDENTS

540 full-time, 730 part-time. Students come from 18 states and territories; 10 other countries; 20% are from out of state; 7% Black or African American, non-Hispanic/Latino; 3% Hispanic/Latino; 0.2% Asian, non-Hispanic/Latino; 0.4% American Indian or Alaska Native, non-Hispanic/Latino; 1% Two or more races, non-Hispanic/Latino; 13% Race/ethnicity unknown; 4% international; 5% transferred in; 36% live on campus.

Freshmen:

Admission: 628 applied, 208 admitted, 93 enrolled. ***Average high school GPA:*** 3.1. ***Test scores:*** SAT critical reading scores over 500: 32%; SAT math scores over 500: 51%; ACT scores over 18: 76%; SAT math scores over 600: 8%; ACT scores over 24: 31%.

Retention: 64% of full-time freshmen returned.

FACULTY

Total: 149, 26% full-time.

Student/faculty ratio: 12:1.

ACADEMICS

Calendar: semesters. *Degrees:* certificates, associate, bachelor's, master's, and doctoral.

Special study options: academic remediation for entering students, accelerated degree program, adult/continuing education programs, advanced placement credit, distance learning, external degree program, part-time degree program, services for LD students, summer session for credit.

Computers: 200 computers/terminals are available on campus for general student use. Students can access the following: campus intranet, computer help desk, free student e-mail accounts, online (class) grades, online (class) registration, online (class) schedules. Campuswide network is available. Wireless service is available via entire campus.

Library: Barger-Richardson Library. *Books:* 84,412 (physical), 50,255 (digital/electronic); *Databases:* 52.

STUDENT LIFE

Housing options: on-campus residence required for freshman year; men-only, women-only. Campus housing is university owned. Freshman campus housing is guaranteed.

Activities and organizations: drama/theater group, student-run newspaper, choral group, Student Government Association, Good News Players, Art Guild, FOCUS, intramural sports.

Athletics Member NCAA, NCCAA. All NCAA Division II.
Intercollegiate sports: baseball M(s), basketball M(s)/W(s), cheerleading W(s), cross-country running M(s)/W(s), golf M(s)/W(s), soccer M(s)/W(s), softball W(s), tennis M(s)/W(s), volleyball W(s). ***Intramural sports:*** basketball M/W, bowling M/W, football M/W, softball M/W, table tennis M/W, tennis M/W, volleyball M/W.

Campus security: 24-hour patrols, student patrols.

Student services: personal/psychological counseling.

COSTS & FINANCIAL AID

Costs (2017–18) ***Comprehensive fee:*** $33,150 includes full-time tuition ($23,700) and room and board ($9450). Full-time tuition and fees vary according to degree level. Part-time tuition: $790 per credit hour. ***College room only:*** $3200. Room and board charges vary according to board plan and housing facility. ***Payment plan:*** deferred payment. ***Waivers:*** employees or children of employees.

Financial Aid Of all full-time matriculated undergraduates who enrolled in 2015, 462 applied for aid, 462 were judged to have need. ***Average percent of need met:*** 37. ***Average financial aid package:*** $21,000. ***Average need-based gift aid:*** $4189.

APPLYING

Standardized Tests *Required for some:* SAT or ACT (for admission).

Options: electronic application, early admission, deferred entrance.

Application fee: $35.

Required: high school transcript, minimum 2.0 GPA. ***Recommended:*** essay or personal statement, interview.

CONTACT

Miss Jennifer Cates, Assistant Director of Admissions, Oakland City University, 138 North Lucretia Street, Oakland City, IN 47660. *Phone:* 812-749-1220. *Toll-free phone:* 800-737-5125. *E-mail:* jcates@oak.edu.

★ Purdue University

West Lafayette, Indiana

http://www.purdue.edu/

- **State-supported** university, founded 1869, part of Purdue University System
- **Suburban** 2660-acre campus with easy access to Indianapolis
- **Endowment** $2.3 billion
- **Coed** 30,043 undergraduate students, 96% full-time, 42% women, 58% men
- **Moderately difficult** entrance level, 56% of applicants were admitted

UNDERGRAD STUDENTS

28,712 full-time, 1,331 part-time. Students come from 52 states and territories; 101 other countries; 36% are from out of state; 3% Black or African American, non-Hispanic/Latino; 5% Hispanic/Latino; 7% Asian, non-Hispanic/Latino; 0.1% Native Hawaiian or other Pacific Islander, non-Hispanic/Latino; 0.1% American Indian or Alaska Native, non-Hispanic/Latino; 2% Two or more races, non-Hispanic/Latino; 3% Race/ethnicity unknown; 17% international; 10% transferred in; 41% live on campus.

Freshmen:

Admission: 48,774 applied, 27,227 admitted, 7,243 enrolled. ***Average high school GPA:*** 3.74. ***Test scores:*** SAT critical reading scores over 500: 87%; SAT math scores over 500: 92%; SAT writing scores over 500: 84%; ACT scores over 18: 99%; SAT critical reading scores over 600: 44%; SAT math scores over 600: 63%; SAT writing scores over 600: 40%; ACT scores over 24: 81%; SAT critical reading scores over 700: 10%; SAT math scores over 700: 24%; SAT writing scores over 700: 8%; ACT scores over 30: 40%.

Retention: 92% of full-time freshmen returned.

FACULTY

Total: 2,671, 87% full-time, 97% with terminal degrees.

Student/faculty ratio: 12:1.

ACADEMICS

Calendar: semesters. *Degrees:* certificates, associate, bachelor's, master's, doctoral, post-master's, and postbachelor's certificates.

Special study options: accelerated degree program, adult/continuing education programs, cooperative education, distance learning, double majors, English as a second language, honors programs, independent study, part-time degree program, services for LD students, study abroad, summer session for credit. ***ROTC:*** Army (b), Navy (b), Air Force (b).

Unusual degree programs: 3-2 business administration; engineering; forestry; nursing; social work; pharmacy.

Computers: 5,237 computers/terminals and 77,041 ports are available on campus for general student use. Students can access the following: campus intranet, computer help desk, online (class) grades, online (class) registration, online (class) schedules. Campuswide network is available.

100% of college-owned or -operated housing units are wired for high-speed Internet access. Wireless service is available via entire campus.

Library: Purdue University Libraries plus 12 others. *Books:* 1.1 million (physical), 2.3 million (digital/electronic); *Serial titles:* 1,100 (physical), 177,006 (digital/electronic); *Databases:* 450. Weekly public service hours: 168; study areas open 24 hours, 5-7 days a week; students can reserve study rooms.

STUDENT LIFE

Housing options: coed, men-only, women-only, cooperative, special housing for students with disabilities. Campus housing is university owned. Freshman applicants given priority for college housing.

Activities and organizations: drama/theater group, student-run newspaper, radio station, choral group, marching band, Purdue Student Government, Purdue University Dance Marathon, Society of Women Engineers, Purdue student union board, Krannert Graduate Student Association, national fraternities, national sororities.

Athletics Member NCAA. All Division I except football (Division I-A). ***Intercollegiate sports:*** baseball M(s), basketball M(s)/W(s), cross-country running M(s)/W(s), golf M(s)/W(s), soccer W(s), softball W(s), swimming and diving M(s)/W(s), tennis M(s)/W(s), track and field M(s)/W(s), volleyball W(s), wrestling M(s). ***Intramural sports:*** archery M(c)/W(c), badminton M(c)/W(c), baseball M(c), basketball M(c)/W(c), bowling M(c)/W(c), crew M(c)/W(c), cross-country running M(c)/W(c), equestrian sports M(c)/W(c), fencing M(c)/W(c), gymnastics M(c)/W(c), ice hockey M(c), lacrosse M(c)/W(c), racquetball M(c)/W(c), riflery M(c)/W(c), rock climbing M(c)/W(c), rugby M(c)/W(c), sailing M(c)/W(c), soccer M(c)/W(c), squash M(c)/W(c), swimming and diving M(c)/W(c), table tennis M(c)/W(c), tennis M(c)/W(c), track and field M(c)/W(c), ultimate Frisbee M(c)/W(c), volleyball M(c)/W(c), water polo M(c)/W(c).

Campus security: 24-hour emergency response devices and patrols, student patrols, late-night transport/escort service, controlled dormitory access.

Student services: health clinic, personal/psychological counseling, women's center, legal services.

COSTS & FINANCIAL AID

Costs (2016–17) ***Tuition:*** state resident $9208 full-time, $330 per credit hour part-time; nonresident $28,010 full-time, $930 per credit hour part-time. Full-time tuition and fees vary according to course load and program. Part-time tuition and fees vary according to course load. ***Required fees:*** $794 full-time, $18 per credit hour part-time. ***Room and board:*** $10,030; room only: $4860. Room and board charges vary according to board plan and housing facility. ***Payment plan:*** installment. ***Waivers:*** senior citizens and employees or children of employees.

Financial Aid Of all full-time matriculated undergraduates who enrolled in 2016, 16,737 applied for aid, 11,986 were judged to have need, 5,636 had their need fully met. 1,772 Federal Work-Study jobs (averaging $2229). In 2016, 3772 non-need-based awards were made. ***Average percent of need met:*** 85. ***Average financial aid package:*** $13,849. ***Average need-based loan:*** $5117. ***Average need-based gift aid:*** $13,404. ***Average non-need-based aid:*** $5959. ***Average indebtedness upon graduation:*** $27,530.

APPLYING

Standardized Tests *Required:* SAT or ACT (for admission).

Options: electronic application, early admission, early action, deferred entrance.

Application fee: $60.

Required: essay or personal statement, high school transcript.

Application deadlines: rolling (freshmen), rolling (transfers), 11/1 (early action).

Notification: 12/12 (freshmen), 12/12 (early action).

CONTACT

Ms. Pamela T. Horne, Assistant Vice President for Enrollment Management and Dean of Admissions, Purdue University, 475 Stadium Mall Drive, Schleman Hall, West Lafayette, IN 47907-2050. *Phone:* 765-494-1776. *Fax:* 765-494-0544. *E-mail:* admissions@purdue.edu.

Purdue University Northwest

Hammond, Indiana

http://www.pnw.edu/

- **State-supported** comprehensive, founded 2016, part of Purdue University System
- **Urban** 441-acre campus with easy access to Chicago
- **Coed** 14,385 undergraduate students, 46% full-time, 59% women, 41% men
- **Moderately difficult** entrance level, 44% of applicants were admitted

UNDERGRAD STUDENTS

6,620 full-time, 7,765 part-time. Students come from 30 states and territories; 39 other countries; 9% are from out of state; 10% Black or African American, non-Hispanic/Latino; 17% Hispanic/Latino; 2% Asian, non-Hispanic/Latino; 0.1% Native Hawaiian or other Pacific Islander, non-Hispanic/Latino; 0.2% American Indian or Alaska Native, non-Hispanic/Latino; 3% Two or more races, non-Hispanic/Latino; 1% Race/ethnicity unknown; 4% international; 4% transferred in; 5% live on campus.

Freshmen:

Admission: 3,882 applied, 1,713 admitted, 1,301 enrolled. ***Average high school GPA:*** 3.14. ***Test scores:*** SAT critical reading scores over 500: 41%; SAT math scores over 500: 40%; SAT writing scores over 500: 31%; SAT critical reading scores over 600: 7%; SAT math scores over 600: 8%; SAT writing scores over 600: 5%; SAT math scores over 700: 1%. ***Retention:*** 61% of full-time freshmen returned.

FACULTY

Total: 735, 54% full-time, 43% with terminal degrees.

Student/faculty ratio: 19:1.

ACADEMICS

Calendar: semesters. *Degrees:* certificates, associate, bachelor's, master's, doctoral, post-master's, and postbachelor's certificates.

Special study options: academic remediation for entering students, accelerated degree program, adult/continuing education programs, advanced placement credit, cooperative education, distance learning, double majors, English as a second language, freshman honors college, honors programs, independent study, internships, part-time degree program, services for LD students, study abroad, summer session for credit. ***ROTC:*** Army (b).

Computers: 1,700 computers/terminals and 1,700 ports are available on campus for general student use. Students can access the following: campus intranet, computer help desk, free student e-mail accounts, online (class) grades, online (class) registration, online (class) schedules. Campuswide network is available. 100% of college-owned or -operated housing units are wired for high-speed Internet access. Wireless service is available via entire campus.

Library: Purdue University Northwest Libraries plus 2 others. *Books:* 204,012 (physical), 379,047 (digital/electronic); *Serial titles:* 3,736 (physical), 70,787 (digital/electronic); *Databases:* 174. Weekly public service hours: 147.

STUDENT LIFE

Housing options: coed. Campus housing is university owned.

Activities and organizations: drama/theater group, student-run newspaper, choral group, Teachers Network Together, Psychology Club, National Society of Black Engineers, Dean's Leadership Group, Brother 2 Brother, national fraternities, national sororities.

Athletics Member NCAA, NAIA. All NCAA Division II. ***Intercollegiate sports:*** baseball M(s), basketball M(s)/W(s), cross-country running M(s)/W(s), golf M(s)/W(s), soccer M(s)/W(s), softball W(s), tennis M(s)/W(s), volleyball W(s). ***Intramural sports:*** badminton M/W, basketball M/W, bowling M/W, football M/W, golf M/W, racquetball M/W, soccer M/W, softball M/W, table tennis M/W, ultimate Frisbee M/W, volleyball M/W, weight lifting M/W.

Campus security: 24-hour emergency response devices and patrols, student patrols, late-night transport/escort service, controlled dormitory access.

Student services: health clinic, personal/psychological counseling.

FINANCIAL AID

Financial Aid Of all full-time matriculated undergraduates who enrolled in 2014, 4,236 applied for aid, 3,567 were judged to have need, 172 had their need fully met. 105 Federal Work-Study jobs (averaging $2322). In 2014, 215 non-need-based awards were made. ***Average percent of need met:*** 11. ***Average financial aid package:*** $7768. ***Average need-based loan:*** $3388. ***Average need-based gift aid:*** $5782. ***Average non-need-based aid:*** $3124. ***Average indebtedness upon graduation:*** $27,902.

APPLYING

Standardized Tests *Required:* SAT or ACT (for admission).

Options: electronic application.

Application fee: $25.

Required: high school transcript, minimum 2.0 GPA.

Application deadlines: 8/1 (freshmen), 8/1 (transfers).

Notification: continuous (freshmen), continuous (out-of-state freshmen), continuous (transfers).

CONTACT

Purdue University Northwest, 2200 169th Street, Hammond, IN 46323-2094. *Phone:* 219-989-2213. *Toll-free phone:* 800-447-8738.

Rose-Hulman Institute of Technology

Terre Haute, Indiana

http://www.rose-hulman.edu/

- **Independent** comprehensive, founded 1874
- **Suburban** 200-acre campus with easy access to Indianapolis
- **Endowment** $191.6 million
- **Coed, primarily men** 2,202 undergraduate students, 99% full-time, 25% women, 75% men
- **Very difficult** entrance level, 61% of applicants were admitted

UNDERGRAD STUDENTS

2,180 full-time, 22 part-time. Students come from 47 states and territories; 12 other countries; 65% are from out of state; 2% Black or African American, non-Hispanic/Latino; 4% Hispanic/Latino; 4% Asian, non-Hispanic/Latino; 0.1% Native Hawaiian or other Pacific Islander, non-Hispanic/Latino; 0.1% American Indian or Alaska Native, non-Hispanic/Latino; 4% Two or more races, non-Hispanic/Latino; 0.2% Race/ethnicity unknown; 13% international; 0.9% transferred in; 60% live on campus.

Freshmen:

Admission: 4,241 applied, 2,590 admitted, 543 enrolled. ***Average high school GPA:*** 4. ***Test scores:*** SAT critical reading scores over 500: 95%; SAT math scores over 500: 100%; SAT writing scores over 500: 93%; ACT scores over 18: 100%; SAT critical reading scores over 600: 57%; SAT math scores over 600: 91%; SAT writing scores over 600: 57%; ACT scores over 24: 96%; SAT critical reading scores over 700: 15%; SAT math scores over 700: 49%; SAT writing scores over 700: 11%; ACT scores over 30: 54%.

Retention: 94% of full-time freshmen returned.

FACULTY

Total: 196, 94% full-time, 99% with terminal degrees.

Student/faculty ratio: 12:1.

ACADEMICS

Calendar: quarters. *Degrees:* bachelor's and master's.

Special study options: accelerated degree program, adult/continuing education programs, advanced placement credit, cooperative education, distance learning, double majors, English as a second language, independent study, internships, off-campus study, services for LD students, study abroad, summer session for credit. ***ROTC:*** Army (b), Air Force (b).

Computers: 48 computers/terminals and 8,000 ports are available on campus for general student use. Students can access the following: campus intranet, computer help desk, free student e-mail accounts, online (class) grades, online (class) registration, online (class) schedules. Campuswide network is available. 100% of college-owned or -operated housing units are wired for high-speed Internet access. Wireless service is available via classrooms, computer centers, computer labs, dorm rooms, learning centers, libraries, student centers.

Library: John A. Logan Library. *Books:* 25,985 (physical), 283,399 (digital/electronic); *Serial titles:* 46 (physical), 41,278 (digital/electronic); *Databases:* 34. Weekly public service hours: 101; students can reserve study rooms.

STUDENT LIFE

Housing options: on-campus residence required for freshman year; coed, men-only. Campus housing is university owned. Freshman campus housing is guaranteed.

Activities and organizations: drama/theater group, student-run newspaper, radio station, choral group, Residence Hall Association, Student Activities Board, Branam Innovation Center competition teams, Drama Club, Diversity organizations, national fraternities, national sororities.

Athletics Member NCAA. All Division III. ***Intercollegiate sports:*** baseball M, basketball M/W, cross-country running M/W, football M, golf M/W, riflery M/W, soccer M/W, softball W, swimming and diving M/W, tennis M/W, track and field M/W, volleyball W. ***Intramural sports:*** badminton M/W, basketball M/W, bowling M/W, cross-country running M/W, football M/W, golf M/W, lacrosse M(c)/W(c), racquetball M/W, soccer M/W, softball M/W, swimming and diving M/W, table tennis M/W, tennis M/W, track and field M/W, ultimate Frisbee M/W, volleyball M/W.

Campus security: 24-hour emergency response devices and patrols, late-night transport/escort service, controlled dormitory access.

Student services: health clinic, personal/psychological counseling.

COSTS & FINANCIAL AID

Costs (2016–17) ***One-time required fee:*** $2200. ***Comprehensive fee:*** $57,303 includes full-time tuition ($43,122), mandatory fees ($888), and room and board ($13,293). Full-time tuition and fees vary according to course load. Part-time tuition: $1259 per credit hour. Part-time tuition and fees vary according to course load. ***College room only:*** $8151. Room and board charges vary according to board plan. ***Payment plans:*** tuition prepayment, installment. ***Waivers:*** employees or children of employees.

Financial Aid Of all full-time matriculated undergraduates who enrolled in 2016, 1,502 applied for aid, 1,301 were judged to have need, 245 had their need fully met. 307 Federal Work-Study jobs (averaging $1230). 500 state and other part-time jobs (averaging $1238). In 2016, 839 non-need-based awards were made. ***Average percent of need met:*** 73. ***Average financial aid package:*** $29,940. ***Average need-based loan:*** $5366. ***Average need-based gift aid:*** $25,299. ***Average non-need-based aid:*** $11,938. ***Average indebtedness upon graduation:*** $59,113.

APPLYING

Standardized Tests *Required:* SAT or ACT (for admission).

Options: electronic application, early action, deferred entrance.

Application fee: $40.

Required: high school transcript, 1 letter of recommendation, curricular prerequisites. ***Recommended:*** essay or personal statement.

Notification: continuous (freshmen), continuous (transfers).

CONTACT

Mrs. Lisa Norton, Director of Admissions, Rose-Hulman Institute of Technology, 5500 Wabash Avenue, CM 1, Terre Haute, IN 47803-3920. *Phone:* 812-877-8213. *Toll-free phone:* 800-248-7448. *Fax:* 812-877-8941. *E-mail:* admissions@rose-hulman.edu.

Saint Mary-of-the-Woods College

Saint Mary of the Woods, Indiana

http://www.smwc.edu/

- **Independent Roman Catholic** comprehensive, founded 1840
- **Rural** 67-acre campus with easy access to Indianapolis
- **Coed, primarily women** 746 undergraduate students, 55% full-time, 93% women, 7% men
- **Minimally difficult** entrance level, 100% of applicants were admitted

UNDERGRAD STUDENTS

407 full-time, 339 part-time. 80% are from out of state; 4% Black or African American, non-Hispanic/Latino; 1% Hispanic/Latino; 0.4% Asian, non-Hispanic/Latino; 0.1% Native Hawaiian or other Pacific Islander, non-Hispanic/Latino; 1% American Indian or Alaska Native, non-Hispanic/Latino; 20% Race/ethnicity unknown; 0.6% international.

Freshmen:
Admission: 284 applied, 284 admitted, 94 enrolled.
Retention: 82% of full-time freshmen returned.

FACULTY
Total: 167, 28% full-time.
Student/faculty ratio: 8:1.

ACADEMICS
Calendar: semesters. *Degrees:* certificates, associate, bachelor's, and master's (also offers external degree program with significant enrollment not reflected in profile).
Special study options: academic remediation for entering students, accelerated degree program, adult/continuing education programs, advanced placement credit, distance learning, double majors, external degree program, honors programs, independent study, internships, off-campus study, part-time degree program, services for LD students, student-designed majors, study abroad, summer session for credit.
Unusual degree programs: 3-2 business administration.
Computers: Students can access the following: campus intranet, computer help desk, free student e-mail accounts, online (class) grades, online (class) schedules. Campuswide network is available. 100% of college-owned or -operated housing units are wired for high-speed Internet access. Wireless service is available via entire campus.
Library: Rooney Library.

STUDENT LIFE
Housing options: on-campus residence required through senior year; women-only, special housing for students with disabilities. Campus housing is university owned. Freshman campus housing is guaranteed.
Activities and organizations: drama/theater group, student-run newspaper, choral group, Student Activities Committee, Chorale, Student Senate, Woods Newspaper.
Athletics Member USCAA. *Intercollegiate sports:* basketball W(s), cross-country running W(s), equestrian sports W(s), golf W(s), soccer W(s), softball W(s).
Campus security: 24-hour emergency response devices and patrols, late-night transport/escort service, Resident Assistants (RAs) patrol the residence hall 3-4 times per night.
Student services: health clinic, personal/psychological counseling.

COSTS & FINANCIAL AID
Costs (2016–17) ***Comprehensive fee:*** $39,632 includes full-time tuition ($28,932) and room and board ($10,700). Full-time tuition and fees vary according to student level. Part-time tuition: $496 per credit hour. Part-time tuition and fees vary according to course load and student level. No tuition increase for student's term of enrollment. ***College room only:*** $5350. Room and board charges vary according to housing facility. ***Payment plan:*** installment. ***Waivers:*** employees or children of employees.
Financial Aid Of all full-time matriculated undergraduates who enrolled in 2016, 398 applied for aid, 398 were judged to have need. ***Average financial aid package:*** $21,115. ***Average need-based loan:*** $3987. ***Average need-based gift aid:*** $18,631. ***Financial aid deadline:*** 3/10.

APPLYING
Standardized Tests *Required:* SAT or ACT (for admission).
Options: electronic application, early admission, deferred entrance.
Required: high school transcript, minimum 2.0 GPA. ***Required for some:*** essay or personal statement, minimum 1.0 GPA, official transcripts from all previous institutions for transfers; proof of RN license, valid driver's license, and background check for RN-to-BSN program; background check and Praxis II scores for teacher licensure. ***Recommended:*** essay or personal statement.

CONTACT
Ryan McDonald, Director of Campus Admissions, Saint Mary-of-the-Woods College, Rooney Library, 1 St. Mary of the Woods College, St Mary of the Woods, IN 47876. *Phone:* 812-535-5106. *Toll-free phone:* 800-926-SMWC. *Fax:* 812-535-5010. *E-mail:* rmcdonald@smwc.edu.

Saint Mary's College
Notre Dame, Indiana
http://www.saintmarys.edu/

- **Independent Roman Catholic** comprehensive, founded 1844
- **Suburban** 100-acre campus
- **Endowment** $164.9 million
- **Women only** 1,625 undergraduate students, 97% full-time
- **Moderately difficult** entrance level, 82% of applicants were admitted

UNDERGRAD STUDENTS
1,569 full-time, 56 part-time. Students come from 43 states and territories; 10 other countries; 73% are from out of state; 2% Black or African American, non-Hispanic/Latino; 11% Hispanic/Latino; 2% Asian, non-Hispanic/Latino; 0.1% Native Hawaiian or other Pacific Islander, non-Hispanic/Latino; 0.1% American Indian or Alaska Native, non-Hispanic/Latino; 3% Two or more races, non-Hispanic/Latino; 5% Race/ethnicity unknown; 2% international; 2% transferred in; 86% live on campus.

Freshmen:
Admission: 1,771 applied, 1,446 admitted, 427 enrolled. ***Average high school GPA:*** 3.7. ***Test scores:*** SAT critical reading scores over 500: 75%; SAT math scores over 500: 67%; SAT writing scores over 500: 72%; ACT scores over 18: 99%; SAT critical reading scores over 600: 25%; SAT math scores over 600: 19%; SAT writing scores over 600: 25%; ACT scores over 24: 63%; SAT critical reading scores over 700: 3%; SAT math scores over 700: 3%; SAT writing scores over 700: 1%; ACT scores over 30: 11%.
Retention: 86% of full-time freshmen returned.

FACULTY
Total: 210, 67% full-time, 68% with terminal degrees.
Student/faculty ratio: 10:1.

ACADEMICS
Calendar: semesters. *Degrees:* bachelor's, master's, and doctoral.
Special study options: advanced placement credit, distance learning, double majors, English as a second language, independent study, internships, off-campus study, part-time degree program, services for LD students, student-designed majors, study abroad, summer session for credit. ***ROTC:*** Army (c), Navy (c), Air Force (c).
Computers: 291 computers/terminals are available on campus for general student use. Students can access the following: campus intranet, computer help desk, free student e-mail accounts, online (class) grades, online (class) registration, online (class) schedules. Campuswide network is available. 100% of college-owned or -operated housing units are wired for high-speed Internet access. Wireless service is available via classrooms, computer centers, computer labs, dorm rooms, learning centers, libraries, student centers.
Library: Cushwa-Leighton Library. *Books:* 260,077 (physical), 140,170 (digital/electronic); *Serial titles:* 4,136 (physical), 205,506 (digital/electronic); *Databases:* 74. Weekly public service hours: 54; study areas open 24 hours, 5-7 days a week; students can reserve study rooms.

STUDENT LIFE
Housing options: on-campus residence required through junior year; women-only, special housing for students with disabilities. Campus housing is university owned. Freshman campus housing is guaranteed.
Activities and organizations: drama/theater group, student-run newspaper, radio and television station, choral group, marching band, Student Government Association, Dance Marathon, Class Boards, Residence Hall Association, Student Diversity Board.
Athletics Member NCAA. All Division III. ***Intercollegiate sports:*** basketball W, cross-country running W, golf W, lacrosse W, soccer W, softball W, tennis W, volleyball W. ***Intramural sports:*** cheerleading W(c), field hockey W(c), volleyball W(c).
Campus security: 24-hour emergency response devices and patrols, late-night transport/escort service, controlled dormitory access.
Student services: health clinic, personal/psychological counseling, women's center.

COSTS & FINANCIAL AID
Costs (2017–18) ***One-time required fee:*** $150. ***Comprehensive fee:*** $52,900 includes full-time tuition ($39,980), mandatory fees ($820), and

room and board ($12,100). Full-time tuition and fees vary according to course load. Part-time tuition: $1500 per credit hour. Part-time tuition and fees vary according to course load. ***College room only:*** $7500. Room and board charges vary according to board plan and housing facility. ***Payment plan:*** installment. ***Waivers:*** employees or children of employees.

Financial Aid Of all full-time matriculated undergraduates who enrolled in 2016, 1,259 applied for aid, 1,083 were judged to have need, 243 had their need fully met. In 2016, 454 non-need-based awards were made. ***Average percent of need met:*** 84. ***Average financial aid package:*** $33,468. ***Average need-based loan:*** $4687. ***Average need-based gift aid:*** $28,661. ***Average non-need-based aid:*** $14,460. ***Average indebtedness upon graduation:*** $31,036. ***Financial aid deadline:*** 3/1.

APPLYING

Standardized Tests *Required:* SAT or ACT (for admission).

Options: electronic application, early admission, early decision, deferred entrance.

Required: essay or personal statement, high school transcript, 1 letter of recommendation, 16 high school academic units, at least two years of study of the same foreign language. ***Recommended:*** interview.

Application deadlines: 2/15 (freshmen), 4/15 (transfers).

Early decision deadline: 11/15.

Notification: continuous (freshmen), continuous (transfers), 12/15 (early decision).

CONTACT

Sarah Dvorak, Director of Admission, Saint Mary's College, Notre Dame, IN 46556. *Phone:* 574-284-4587. *Toll-free phone:* 800-551-7621. *Fax:* 574-284-4841. *E-mail:* sdvorak@saintmarys.edu.

See page 1496 for the College Close-Up.

Taylor University

Upland, Indiana

http://www.taylor.edu/

- **Independent interdenominational** comprehensive, founded 1846
- **Rural** 950-acre campus with easy access to Indianapolis
- **Endowment** $81.1 million
- **Coed** 2,131 undergraduate students, 86% full-time, 57% women, 43% men
- **Moderately difficult** entrance level, 80% of applicants were admitted

UNDERGRAD STUDENTS

1,826 full-time, 305 part-time. Students come from 43 states and territories; 30 other countries; 59% are from out of state; 3% Black or African American, non-Hispanic/Latino; 4% Hispanic/Latino; 3% Asian, non-Hispanic/Latino; 0.2% Native Hawaiian or other Pacific Islander, non-Hispanic/Latino; 1% American Indian or Alaska Native, non-Hispanic/Latino; 0.4% Two or more races, non-Hispanic/Latino; 6% international; 2% transferred in; 89% live on campus.

Freshmen:

Admission: 1,775 applied, 1,413 admitted, 473 enrolled. ***Average high school GPA:*** 3.7. ***Test scores:*** SAT critical reading scores over 500: 69%; SAT math scores over 500: 70%; SAT writing scores over 500: 69%; ACT scores over 18: 97%; SAT critical reading scores over 600: 33%; SAT math scores over 600: 35%; SAT writing scores over 600: 28%; ACT scores over 24: 67%; SAT critical reading scores over 700: 10%; SAT math scores over 700: 6%; SAT writing scores over 700: 5%; ACT scores over 30: 19%.

Retention: 85% of full-time freshmen returned.

FACULTY

Total: 204, 64% full-time, 70% with terminal degrees.

Student/faculty ratio: 13:1.

ACADEMICS

Calendar: 4-1-4. *Degrees:* diplomas, bachelor's, and master's.

Special study options: academic remediation for entering students, advanced placement credit, cooperative education, distance learning, double majors, English as a second language, honors programs, independent study, internships, off-campus study, part-time degree program, services for LD students, student-designed majors, study abroad, summer session for credit.

Computers: 375 computers/terminals are available on campus for general student use. Students can access the following: campus intranet, computer help desk, free student e-mail accounts, online (class) grades, online (class) registration, online (class) schedules. Campuswide network is available. 100% of college-owned or -operated housing units are wired for high-speed Internet access. Wireless service is available via entire campus.

Library: Zondervan Library. *Books:* 199,651 (physical), 224,500 (digital/electronic); *Serial titles:* 275 (physical), 45,000 (digital/electronic); *Databases:* 78. Weekly public service hours: 96; study areas open 24 hours, 5-7 days a week.

STUDENT LIFE

Housing options: on-campus residence required through junior year; men-only, women-only. Campus housing is university owned and is provided by a third party. Freshman campus housing is guaranteed.

Activities and organizations: drama/theater group, student-run newspaper, radio and television station, choral group, Spring Break Missions, Lighthouse, Alpha Pi Lota, Encounter, Kappa Delta Pi.

Athletics Member NAIA. ***Intercollegiate sports:*** baseball M(s), basketball M(s)/W(s), cross-country running M(s)/W(s), football M(s), golf M(s)/W(s), soccer M(s)/W(s), softball W(s), tennis M(s)/W(s), track and field M(s)/W(s), volleyball W(s). ***Intramural sports:*** badminton M/W, basketball M/W, equestrian sports W(c), lacrosse M(c)/W(c), racquetball M/W, soccer M/W, softball M/W, tennis M/W, ultimate Frisbee M/W, volleyball M/W.

Campus security: 24-hour patrols, student patrols, late-night transport/escort service, controlled dormitory access.

Student services: health clinic, personal/psychological counseling.

COSTS & FINANCIAL AID

Costs (2016–17) ***Comprehensive fee:*** $40,317 includes full-time tuition ($31,232), mandatory fees ($240), and room and board ($8845). Full-time tuition and fees vary according to course load. Part-time tuition: $1100 per credit hour. Part-time tuition and fees vary according to course load. ***Required fees:*** $38 per term part-time. ***College room only:*** $4649. Room and board charges vary according to board plan and housing facility. ***Payment plan:*** installment. ***Waivers:*** senior citizens and employees or children of employees.

Financial Aid Of all full-time matriculated undergraduates who enrolled in 2016, 1,288 applied for aid, 1,057 were judged to have need, 282 had their need fully met. 774 Federal Work-Study jobs (averaging $561). In 2016, 571 non-need-based awards were made. ***Average percent of need met:*** 76. ***Average financial aid package:*** $21,985. ***Average need-based loan:*** $4771. ***Average need-based gift aid:*** $17,757. ***Average non-need-based aid:*** $11,652. ***Average indebtedness upon graduation:*** $29,263. ***Financial aid deadline:*** 3/10.

APPLYING

Standardized Tests *Required:* SAT or ACT (for admission).

Options: electronic application, early action, deferred entrance.

Application fee: $25.

Required: essay or personal statement, high school transcript, 2 letters of recommendation, interview. ***Recommended:*** minimum 2.8 GPA.

Application deadlines: rolling (freshmen), rolling (transfers).

Notification: continuous (freshmen), continuous (transfers).

CONTACT

Morgan Riessen, Visit Coordinator, Taylor University, 236 West Reade Avenue, Upland, IN 46989-1001. *Phone:* 765-998-5560. *Toll-free phone:* 800-882-3456. *Fax:* 765-998-4925. *E-mail:* admissions@taylor.edu.

★ Trine University

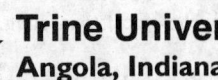

Angola, Indiana

http://www.trine.edu/

- **Independent** comprehensive, founded 1884
- **Small-town** 400-acre campus
- **Endowment** $29.3 million
- **Coed** 3,372 undergraduate students, 51% full-time, 43% women, 57% men
- **Moderately difficult** entrance level, 77% of applicants were admitted

UNDERGRAD STUDENTS
1,729 full-time, 1,643 part-time. Students come from 32 states and territories; 16 other countries; 39% are from out of state; 3% Black or African American, non-Hispanic/Latino; 8% Hispanic/Latino; 2% Asian, non-Hispanic/Latino; 0.1% Native Hawaiian or other Pacific Islander, non-Hispanic/Latino; 0.3% American Indian or Alaska Native, non-Hispanic/Latino; 3% Two or more races, non-Hispanic/Latino; 2% Race/ethnicity unknown; 6% international; 1% transferred in; 69% live on campus.

Freshmen:
Admission: 2,890 applied, 2,217 admitted, 461 enrolled. ***Average high school GPA:*** 3.45. ***Test scores:*** SAT critical reading scores over 500: 58%; SAT math scores over 500: 73%; ACT scores over 18: 91%; SAT critical reading scores over 600: 20%; SAT math scores over 600: 33%; ACT scores over 24: 47%; SAT critical reading scores over 700: 3%; SAT math scores over 700: 4%; ACT scores over 30: 9%.

Retention: 76% of full-time freshmen returned.

FACULTY
Total: 256, 45% full-time.

Student/faculty ratio: 13:1.

ACADEMICS
Calendar: semesters. *Degrees:* associate, bachelor's, master's, and doctoral.

Special study options: academic remediation for entering students, adult/continuing education programs, advanced placement credit, cooperative education, distance learning, double majors, English as a second language, honors programs, internships, part-time degree program, services for LD students, student-designed majors, study abroad, summer session for credit. ***ROTC:*** Air Force (c).

Unusual degree programs: 3-2 engineering.

Computers: 400 computers/terminals and 1,100 ports are available on campus for general student use. Students can access the following: computer help desk, free student e-mail accounts, online (class) grades, online (class) registration, online (class) schedules, online campus billing accounts, course management system. Campuswide network is available. 100% of college-owned or -operated housing units are wired for high-speed Internet access. Wireless service is available via entire campus.

Library: Sponsel Library plus 1 other. *Books:* 23,523 (physical), 225,584 (digital/electronic); *Serial titles:* 19 (physical), 21,141 (digital/electronic); *Databases:* 87.

STUDENT LIFE
Housing options: on-campus residence required through senior year; coed, men-only, women-only. Campus housing is university owned and is provided by a third party. Freshman campus housing is guaranteed.

Activities and organizations: drama/theater group, student-run newspaper, radio station, choral group, marching band, Campus Christian House, Fellowship of Christian Athletes, Multicultural Student Organization, Math Club, Trine Disc Golf Collective, national fraternities, national sororities.

Athletics Member NCAA. All Division III. ***Intercollegiate sports:*** baseball M, basketball M/W, cross-country running M/W, field hockey W, football M, golf M/W, lacrosse M/W, soccer M/W, softball W, tennis M/W, track and field M/W, volleyball W, wrestling M. ***Intramural sports:*** badminton M/W, basketball M/W, football M, golf M/W, racquetball M/W, skiing (downhill) M(c)/W(c), table tennis M(c)/W(c), ultimate Frisbee M(c)/W(c), volleyball M/W.

Campus security: 24-hour emergency response devices and patrols, late-night transport/escort service, controlled dormitory access.

Student services: health clinic, personal/psychological counseling.

COSTS & FINANCIAL AID
Costs (2017–18) ***Comprehensive fee:*** $42,110 includes full-time tuition ($31,080), mandatory fees ($460), and room and board ($10,570). Full-time tuition and fees vary according to degree level, location, and program. Part-time tuition: $970 per credit hour. Part-time tuition and fees vary according to degree level, location, and program. ***Room and board:*** Room and board charges vary according to board plan and housing facility. ***Payment plan:*** installment. ***Waivers:*** senior citizens and employees or children of employees.

Financial Aid Of all full-time matriculated undergraduates who enrolled in 2016, 1,496 applied for aid, 1,355 were judged to have need, 300 had their need fully met. In 2016, 220 non-need-based awards were made. ***Average percent of need met:*** 82. ***Average financial aid package:*** $27,021. ***Average need-based loan:*** $5413. ***Average need-based gift aid:*** $20,794. ***Average non-need-based aid:*** $12,829. ***Average indebtedness upon graduation:*** $38,161.

APPLYING
Standardized Tests *Required:* SAT or ACT (for admission).

Options: electronic application, deferred entrance.

Required: high school transcript, minimum 2.5 GPA. ***Recommended:*** essay or personal statement, 2 letters of recommendation, interview.

Application deadlines: 8/1 (freshmen), 8/1 (transfers).

Notification: 8/15 (freshmen), continuous until 8/15 (transfers).

CONTACT
Mr. Travis Foster, Associate Director of Admission, Trine University, 1 University Avenue, Angola, IN 46703. *Phone:* 260-665-4819. *Toll-free phone:* 800-347-4878. *Fax:* 260-665-4578. *E-mail:* admit@trine.edu.

See page 1534 for the College Close-Up.

University of Evansville

Evansville, Indiana

http://www.evansville.edu/

- **Independent** comprehensive, founded 1854, affiliated with United Methodist Church
- **Urban** 75-acre campus
- **Endowment** $128.8 million
- **Coed** 2,348 undergraduate students, 93% full-time, 55% women, 45% men
- **Moderately difficult** entrance level, 71% of applicants were admitted

UNDERGRAD STUDENTS
2,186 full-time, 162 part-time. Students come from 44 states and territories; 55 other countries; 39% are from out of state; 3% Black or African American, non-Hispanic/Latino; 4% Hispanic/Latino; 2% Asian, non-Hispanic/Latino; 0.1% American Indian or Alaska Native, non-Hispanic/Latino; 2% Two or more races, non-Hispanic/Latino; 8% Race/ethnicity unknown; 15% international; 3% transferred in; 61% live on campus.

Freshmen:
Admission: 4,033 applied, 2,859 admitted, 537 enrolled. ***Average high school GPA:*** 3.65. ***Test scores:*** SAT critical reading scores over 500: 73%; SAT math scores over 500: 77%; SAT writing scores over 500: 66%; ACT scores over 18: 95%; SAT critical reading scores over 600: 29%; SAT math scores over 600: 35%; SAT writing scores over 600: 25%; ACT scores over 24: 70%; SAT critical reading scores over 700: 6%; SAT math scores over 700: 8%; SAT writing scores over 700: 2%; ACT scores over 30: 21%.

Retention: 89% of full-time freshmen returned.

FACULTY
Total: 244, 69% full-time, 71% with terminal degrees.

Student/faculty ratio: 12:1.

ACADEMICS
Calendar: semesters. *Degrees:* associate, bachelor's, master's, and doctoral.

Special study options: accelerated degree program, adult/continuing education programs, advanced placement credit, cooperative education, distance learning, double majors, English as a second language, external degree program, honors programs, independent study, internships, part-time degree program, services for LD students, student-designed majors, study abroad, summer session for credit. ***ROTC:*** Army (c).

Computers: 223 computers/terminals and 3,273 ports are available on campus for general student use. Students can access the following: campus intranet, computer help desk, free student e-mail accounts, online (class) grades, online (class) registration, online (class) schedules. Campuswide network is available. 100% of college-owned or -operated housing units are wired for high-speed Internet access. Wireless service is available via entire campus.

Library: University of Evansville Libraries. *Books:* 236,405 (physical), 48,641 (digital/electronic); *Serial titles:* 55,604 (digital/electronic); *Databases:* 115. Weekly public service hours: 97; students can reserve study rooms.

STUDENT LIFE

Housing options: on-campus residence required through sophomore year; coed, men-only, women-only, special housing for students with disabilities. Campus housing is university owned. Freshman campus housing is guaranteed.

Activities and organizations: drama/theater group, student-run newspaper, radio station, choral group, Resident Students Association, International Club, PT Club, Newman Club, Venturing, national fraternities, national sororities.

Athletics Member NCAA. All Division I. ***Intercollegiate sports:*** baseball M(s), basketball M(s)/W(s), cross-country running M(s)/W(s), golf M(s)/W(s), soccer M(s)/W(s), softball W(s), swimming and diving M(s)/W(s), tennis W(s), volleyball W(s). ***Intramural sports:*** badminton M/W, basketball M/W, cross-country running M/W, racquetball M/W, soccer M/W, tennis M/W, ultimate Frisbee M/W, volleyball M/W.

Campus security: 24-hour emergency response devices and patrols, student patrols, late-night transport/escort service, controlled dormitory access.

Student services: health clinic, personal/psychological counseling.

COSTS & FINANCIAL AID

Costs (2017–18) ***Comprehensive fee:*** $47,556 includes full-time tuition ($34,300), mandatory fees ($1096), and room and board ($12,160). Part-time tuition and fees vary according to course load. ***College room only:*** $6410. Room and board charges vary according to board plan and housing facility. ***Payment plan:*** installment. ***Waivers:*** minority students, children of alumni, adult students, senior citizens, and employees or children of employees.

Financial Aid Of all full-time matriculated undergraduates who enrolled in 2016, 1,550 applied for aid, 1,377 were judged to have need, 387 had their need fully met. 311 Federal Work-Study jobs (averaging $1469). 37 state and other part-time jobs (averaging $1583). In 2016, 546 non-need-based awards were made. ***Average percent of need met:*** 82. ***Average financial aid package:*** $28,569. ***Average need-based loan:*** $4790. ***Average need-based gift aid:*** $26,608. ***Average non-need-based aid:*** $19,026. ***Average indebtedness upon graduation:*** $35,346.

APPLYING

Standardized Tests *Required:* SAT or ACT (for admission).

Options: electronic application, early admission, early action, deferred entrance.

Required: high school transcript. ***Required for some:*** essay or personal statement, interview. ***Recommended:*** minimum 3.0 GPA, 1 letter of recommendation, interview.

Application deadlines: 8/15 (freshmen), 8/15 (transfers), 12/1 (early action).

CONTACT

Kenton Hargis, Director of Admission, University of Evansville, 1800 Lincoln Avenue, Evansville, IN 47722. *Phone:* 812-488-2142. *T oll-free phone:* 800-423-8633 Ext. 2468. *E-mail:* kh88@evansville.edu.

University of Indianapolis

Indianapolis, Indiana

http://www.uindy.edu/

- **Independent** comprehensive, founded 1902, affiliated with United Methodist Church
- **Urban** 65-acre campus with easy access to Indianapolis
- **Coed** 4,346 undergraduate students, 83% full-time, 64% women, 36% men
- **Moderately difficult** entrance level, 86% of applicants were admitted

UNDERGRAD STUDENTS

3,589 full-time, 757 part-time. 10% are from out of state; 9% Black or African American, non-Hispanic/Latino; 5% Hispanic/Latino; 2% Asian, non-Hispanic/Latino; 0.1% Native Hawaiian or other Pacific Islander, non-Hispanic/Latino; 0.2% American Indian or Alaska Native, non-Hispanic/Latino; 3% Two or more races, non-Hispanic/Latino; 6% Race/ethnicity unknown; 8% international; 5% transferred in; 36% live on campus.

Freshmen:

Admission: 7,301 applied, 6,291 admitted, 994 enrolled. ***Average high school GPA:*** 3.5. ***Test scores:*** SAT critical reading scores over 500: 51%; SAT math scores over 500: 53%; SAT writing scores over 500: 43%; ACT scores over 18: 90%; SAT critical reading scores over 600: 12%; SAT math scores over 600: 15%; SAT writing scores over 600: 10%; ACT scores over 24: 43%; SAT critical reading scores over 700: 2%; SAT math scores over 700: 2%; SAT writing scores over 700: 1%; ACT scores over 30: 8%.

Retention: 77% of full-time freshmen returned.

FACULTY

Student/faculty ratio: 12:1.

ACADEMICS

Calendar: semesters. *Degrees:* associate, bachelor's, master's, and doctoral.

Special study options: academic remediation for entering students, accelerated degree program, adult/continuing education programs, advanced placement credit, cooperative education, distance learning, double majors, English as a second language, freshman honors college, honors programs, independent study, internships, off-campus study, part-time degree program, services for LD students, student-designed majors, study abroad, summer session for credit. ***ROTC:*** Army (c).

Unusual degree programs: 3-2 business administration; engineering with Indiana University–Purdue University Indianapolis; physical therapy, occupational therapy.

Computers: 255 computers/terminals are available on campus for general student use. Students can access the following: campus intranet, computer help desk, free student e-mail accounts, online (class) grades, online (class) registration, online (class) schedules. Campuswide network is available. 100% of college-owned or -operated housing units are wired for high-speed Internet access. Wireless service is available via entire campus.

Library: Krannert Memorial Library. Students can reserve study rooms.

STUDENT LIFE

Housing options: coed, women-only. Campus housing is university owned.

Activities and organizations: drama/theater group, student-run newspaper, radio and television station, choral group, Fellowship of Christian Athletes, Intercultural Association, Circle K, Indianapolis Student Government, Residence Hall Association.

Athletics Member NCAA. All Division II. ***Intercollegiate sports:*** baseball M(s), basketball M(s)/W(s), cross-country running M(s)/W(s), football M(s), golf M(s)/W(s), lacrosse M/W, soccer M(s)/W(s), softball W(s), swimming and diving M(s)/W(s), tennis M(s)/W(s), track and field M(s)/W(s), volleyball W(s), wrestling M(s). ***Intramural sports:*** badminton M/W, basketball M/W, cheerleading M/W, football M/W, racquetball M/W, softball M/W, table tennis M/W, tennis M/W, volleyball M/W.

Campus security: 24-hour emergency response devices and patrols, student patrols, late-night transport/escort service, controlled dormitory access, emergency call boxes.

Student services: health clinic, personal/psychological counseling.

COSTS & FINANCIAL AID

Costs (2017–18) ***Comprehensive fee:*** $38,378 includes full-time tuition ($27,860), mandatory fees ($530), and room and board ($9988). Full-time tuition and fees vary according to class time. Part-time tuition and fees vary according to class time and course load. ***Room and board:*** Room and board charges vary according to board plan and housing facility. ***Payment plan:*** installment. ***Waivers:*** senior citizens and employees or children of employees.

Financial Aid Of all full-time matriculated undergraduates who enrolled in 2015, 3,253 applied for aid, 2,856 were judged to have need, 312 had their need fully met. 332 Federal Work-Study jobs (averaging $881). 165 state and other part-time jobs (averaging $7212). In 2015, 579 non-need-based awards were made. ***Average percent of need met:*** 64. ***Average financial aid package:*** $18,471. ***Average need-based loan:*** $4565. ***Average need-based gift aid:*** $8390. ***Average non-need-based aid:*** $10,214. ***Average indebtedness upon graduation:*** $36,304.

APPLYING

Standardized Tests *Required:* SAT or ACT (for admission).

Options: electronic application, deferred entrance.

Application fee: $25.

Required: high school transcript, minimum 2.0 GPA. ***Required for some:*** interview.

Application deadlines: rolling (freshmen), rolling (transfers).

Notification: continuous (freshmen), continuous (transfers).

CONTACT

Mr. Ronald Wilks, Associate Vice President of Admissions, University of Indianapolis, 1400 East Hanna Avenue, Indianapolis, IN 46227-3697. *Phone:* 317-788-3216. *Toll-free phone:* 800-232-8634 Ext. 3216. *Fax:* 317-788-3300. *E-mail:* admissions@uindy.edu.

University of Notre Dame

Notre Dame, Indiana

http://www.nd.edu/

- **Independent Roman Catholic** university, founded 1842
- **Suburban** 1250-acre campus
- **Endowment** $10.6 billion
- **Coed** 8,530 undergraduate students, 100% full-time, 47% women, 53% men
- **Most difficult** entrance level, 19% of applicants were admitted

UNDERGRAD STUDENTS

8,514 full-time, 16 part-time. Students come from 52 states and territories; 68 other countries; 92% are from out of state; 4% Black or African American, non-Hispanic/Latino; 11% Hispanic/Latino; 5% Asian, non-Hispanic/Latino; 0.1% American Indian or Alaska Native, non-Hispanic/Latino; 5% Two or more races, non-Hispanic/Latino; 0.5% Race/ethnicity unknown; 6% international; 2% transferred in; 79% live on campus.

Freshmen:

Admission: 19,505 applied, 3,654 admitted, 2,046 enrolled. ***Test scores:*** SAT critical reading scores over 500: 99%; SAT math scores over 500: 100%; SAT writing scores over 500: 99%; ACT scores over 18: 100%; SAT critical reading scores over 600: 91%; SAT math scores over 600: 96%; SAT writing scores over 600: 90%; ACT scores over 24: 99%; SAT critical reading scores over 700: 62%; SAT math scores over 700: 68%; SAT writing scores over 700: 52%; ACT scores over 30: 90%.

Retention: 98% of full-time freshmen returned.

FACULTY

Total: 1,309, 88% full-time, 88% with terminal degrees.

Student/faculty ratio: 10:1.

ACADEMICS

Calendar: semesters. *Degrees:* bachelor's, master's, and doctoral.

Special study options: advanced placement credit, distance learning, double majors, honors programs, independent study, internships, off-campus study, services for LD students, student-designed majors, study abroad, summer session for credit. ***ROTC:*** Army (b), Navy (b), Air Force (b).

Computers: 232 computers/terminals are available on campus for general student use. Students can access the following: computer help desk, free student e-mail accounts, online (class) grades, online (class) registration, online (class) schedules. Campuswide network is available. Wireless service is available via entire campus.

Library: Hesburgh Library plus 10 others.

STUDENT LIFE

Housing options: on-campus residence required for freshman year; men-only, women-only. Campus housing is university owned. Freshman campus housing is guaranteed.

Activities and organizations: drama/theater group, student-run newspaper, radio station, choral group, marching band, marching band, Circle K, Finance Club, Notre Dame/St. Mary's Right to Life.

Athletics Member NCAA. All Division I except football (Division I-A). ***Intercollegiate sports:*** baseball M(s), basketball M(s)/W(s), crew W(s), cross-country running M(s)/W(s), fencing M(s)/W(s), golf M(s)/W(s), ice hockey M(s), lacrosse M(s)/W(s), soccer M(s)/W(s), softball W(s), swimming and diving M(s)/W(s), tennis M(s)/W(s), track and field M(s)/W(s), volleyball W(s). ***Intramural sports:*** badminton M/W, baseball M, basketball M/W, bowling M(c)/W(c), crew M(c), equestrian sports M(c)/W(c), field hockey W(c), football M/W, golf M/W, gymnastics M(c)/W(c), ice hockey M/W(c), lacrosse M/W, racquetball M/W, rugby M(c)/W(c), sailing M(c)/W(c), skiing (cross-country) M(c)/W(c), skiing (downhill) M(c)/W(c), soccer M/W, softball M/W, squash M(c)/W(c), table tennis M/W, tennis M/W, ultimate Frisbee M/W, volleyball M(c)/W(c), water polo M(c)/W(c), wrestling M(c).

Campus security: 24-hour emergency response devices and patrols, student patrols, late-night transport/escort service, controlled dormitory access, crime prevention and personal safety workshops, full-time trained police investigators, fire sprinklers in all residence halls.

Student services: health clinic, personal/psychological counseling, women's center.

COSTS & FINANCIAL AID

Costs (2016–17) ***Comprehensive fee:*** $64,043 includes full-time tuition ($49,178), mandatory fees ($507), and room and board ($14,358). Part-time tuition: $2049 per credit hour. ***Payment plan:*** installment. ***Waivers:*** employees or children of employees.

Financial Aid Of all full-time matriculated undergraduates who enrolled in 2016, 4,898 applied for aid, 4,112 were judged to have need, 4,077 had their need fully met. 1,210 Federal Work-Study jobs (averaging $2660). 3,376 state and other part-time jobs (averaging $3319). In 2016, 389 non-need-based awards were made. ***Average percent of need met:*** 100. ***Average financial aid package:*** $47,884. ***Average need-based loan:*** $5017. ***Average need-based gift aid:*** $37,390. ***Average non-need-based aid:*** $12,919. ***Average indebtedness upon graduation:*** $28,406.

APPLYING

Standardized Tests *Required:* SAT or ACT (for admission). *Required for some:* SAT Subject Tests (for admission).

Options: electronic application, early action, deferred entrance.

Application fee: $75.

Required: essay or personal statement, high school transcript, 1 letter of recommendation.

Application deadlines: 1/1 (freshmen), 3/15 (transfers), 11/1 (early action).

Notification: 4/10 (freshmen), 12/21 (early action).

CONTACT

Office of Undergraduate Admissions, University of Notre Dame, 220 Main Building, Notre Dame, IN 46556-5612. *Phone:* 574-631-7505. *Fax:* 574-631-8865. *E-mail:* admissions@nd.edu.

University of Saint Francis

Fort Wayne, Indiana

http://www.sf.edu/

- **Independent Roman Catholic** comprehensive, founded 1890
- **Urban** 110-acre campus
- **Endowment** $20.8 million
- **Coed** 1,810 undergraduate students, 81% full-time, 72% women, 28% men
- **Minimally difficult** entrance level, 97% of applicants were admitted

UNDERGRAD STUDENTS

1,475 full-time, 335 part-time. Students come from 17 states and territories; 12 other countries; 9% are from out of state; 7% Black or African American, non-Hispanic/Latino; 8% Hispanic/Latino; 1% Asian, non-Hispanic/Latino; 0.2% Native Hawaiian or other Pacific Islander, non-Hispanic/Latino; 0.2% American Indian or Alaska Native, non-Hispanic/Latino; 2% Two or more races, non-Hispanic/Latino; 0.9% Race/ethnicity unknown; 0.5% international; 12% transferred in; 20% live on campus.

Freshmen:

Admission: 977 applied, 945 admitted, 343 enrolled. ***Average high school GPA:*** 3.34. ***Test scores:*** SAT critical reading scores over 500: 50%; SAT math scores over 500: 49%; SAT writing scores over 500: 44%; ACT scores over 18: 85%; SAT critical reading scores over 600: 10%; SAT math scores over 600: 9%; SAT writing scores over 600: 8%; ACT scores over 24: 30%; SAT math scores over 700: 1%; SAT writing scores over 700: 1%; ACT scores over 30: 1%.

Retention: 71% of full-time freshmen returned.

FACULTY
Total: 283, 43% full-time, 31% with terminal degrees.

Student/faculty ratio: 11:1.

ACADEMICS
Calendar: semesters. *Degrees:* certificates, associate, bachelor's, master's, post-master's, and postbachelor's certificates.

Special study options: academic remediation for entering students, advanced placement credit, cooperative education, distance learning, double majors, honors programs, independent study, internships, off-campus study, part-time degree program, services for LD students, student-designed majors, summer session for credit. ***ROTC:*** Army (c).

Computers: 435 computers/terminals are available on campus for general student use. Students can access the following: campus intranet, computer help desk, free student e-mail accounts, online (class) grades, online (class) registration, online (class) schedules. Campuswide network is available. 100% of college-owned or -operated housing units are wired for high-speed Internet access. Wireless service is available via entire campus.

Library: Lee and Jim Vann Library. *Books:* 71,000 (physical), 152,000 (digital/electronic); *Serial titles:* 805 (physical), 42,445 (digital/electronic); *Databases:* 112. Weekly public service hours: 86; study areas open 24 hours, 5-7 days a week; students can reserve study rooms.

STUDENT LIFE
Housing options: on-campus residence required through sophomore year; coed, special housing for students with disabilities. Campus housing is university owned. Freshman applicants given priority for college housing.

Activities and organizations: drama/theater group, student-run newspaper, choral group, marching band, Student Activities Council, Pre-Professional Healthcare Club, Student Government Organization, Student Nursing Association, Residence Hall Association.

Athletics Member NAIA. ***Intercollegiate sports:*** baseball M(s), basketball M(s)/W(s), cheerleading M(s)/W(s), cross-country running M(s)/W(s), football M(s), golf M(s)/W(s), soccer M(s)/W(s), softball W(s), tennis M(s)/W(s), track and field M(s)/W(s), volleyball W(s). ***Intramural sports:*** basketball M/W, volleyball M/W.

Campus security: 24-hour emergency response devices and patrols, late-night transport/escort service, controlled dormitory access, video surveillance system.

Student services: personal/psychological counseling.

COSTS & FINANCIAL AID
Costs (2017–18) ***One-time required fee:*** $100. ***Tuition:*** $900 per credit hour part-time. Full-time tuition and fees vary according to course load. Part-time tuition and fees vary according to course load. ***Required fees:*** $30 per credit hour part-time, $145 per term part-time. ***Room only:*** Room and board charges vary according to board plan and housing facility. ***Payment plan:*** installment. ***Waivers:*** employees or children of employees.

Financial Aid Of all full-time matriculated undergraduates who enrolled in 2009, 1,477 applied for aid, 1,316 were judged to have need, 258 had their need fully met. 629 Federal Work-Study jobs (averaging $1411). In 2009, 146 non-need-based awards were made. ***Average percent of need met:*** 72. ***Average financial aid package:*** $16,158. ***Average need-based loan:*** $4028. ***Average need-based gift aid:*** $12,247. ***Average non-need-based aid:*** $5446. ***Average indebtedness upon graduation:*** $28,428. ***Financial aid deadline:*** 6/30.

APPLYING
Standardized Tests *Required:* SAT or ACT (for admission).

Options: electronic application, deferred entrance.

Required: high school transcript, minimum 2.3 GPA. ***Required for some:*** essay or personal statement, interview. ***Recommended:*** essay or personal statement.

Application deadlines: rolling (freshmen), rolling (transfers).

Notification: continuous until 8/1 (freshmen), continuous until 8/1 (transfers).

CONTACT
Mrs. Maria Gerber, Director of Undergraduate Admissions, University of Saint Francis, 2701 Spring Street, Fort Wayne, IN 46808. *Phone:* 260-399-7700 Ext. 6308. *Toll-free phone:* 800-729-4732.
E-mail: admis@sf.edu.

★ University of Southern Indiana
Evansville, Indiana
http://www.usi.edu/

- **State-supported** comprehensive, founded 1965, part of Indiana Commission for Higher Education
- **Suburban** 1400-acre campus
- **Coed** 7,956 undergraduate students, 84% full-time, 62% women, 38% men
- **Moderately difficult** entrance level, 92% of applicants were admitted

UNDERGRAD STUDENTS
6,705 full-time, 1,251 part-time. Students come from 33 states and territories; 46 other countries; 12% are from out of state; 4% Black or African American, non-Hispanic/Latino; 3% Hispanic/Latino; 1% Asian, non-Hispanic/Latino; 0.1% Native Hawaiian or other Pacific Islander, non-Hispanic/Latino; 0.2% American Indian or Alaska Native, non-Hispanic/Latino; 2% Two or more races, non-Hispanic/Latino; 2% international; 6% transferred in; 31% live on campus.

Freshmen:
Admission: 4,552 applied, 4,183 admitted, 1,685 enrolled. ***Average high school GPA:*** 3.37. ***Test scores:*** SAT critical reading scores over 500: 49%; SAT math scores over 500: 50%; SAT writing scores over 500: 37%; ACT scores over 18: 87%; SAT critical reading scores over 600: 9%; SAT math scores over 600: 11%; SAT writing scores over 600: 5%; ACT scores over 24: 32%; SAT critical reading scores over 700: 1%; ACT scores over 30: 3%.

Retention: 70% of full-time freshmen returned.

FACULTY
Total: 676, 53% full-time, 49% with terminal degrees.

Student/faculty ratio: 17:1.

ACADEMICS
Calendar: semesters. *Degrees:* certificates, associate, bachelor's, master's, doctoral, post-master's, and postbachelor's certificates.

Special study options: academic remediation for entering students, accelerated degree program, adult/continuing education programs, advanced placement credit, cooperative education, distance learning, double majors, English as a second language, honors programs, independent study, internships, part-time degree program, services for LD students, study abroad, summer session for credit. ***ROTC:*** Army (b).

Computers: 1,165 computers/terminals are available on campus for general student use. Students can access the following: campus intranet, computer help desk, free student e-mail accounts, online (class) grades, online (class) registration, online (class) schedules. Campuswide network is available. 100% of college-owned or -operated housing units are wired for high-speed Internet access. Wireless service is available via entire campus.

Library: David L. Rice Library. *Books:* 222,413 (physical), 215,058 (digital/electronic); *Serial titles:* 127 (physical), 52,315 (digital/electronic); *Databases:* 122. Weekly public service hours: 114; students can reserve study rooms.

STUDENT LIFE
Housing options: coed, special housing for students with disabilities. Campus housing is university owned.

Activities and organizations: drama/theater group, student-run newspaper, radio and television station, choral group, Sororities, Fraternities, Riley Dance Marathon, Activities Programming Board, Student Government Association, national fraternities, national sororities.

Athletics Member NCAA. All Division II. ***Intercollegiate sports:*** baseball M(s), basketball M(s)/W(s), cross-country running M(s)/W(s), golf M(s)/W(s), soccer M(s)/W(s), softball W(s), tennis M(s)/W(s), track and field M(s)/W(s), volleyball W(s). ***Intramural sports:*** badminton M/W, basketball M/W, bowling M/W, cheerleading M(c)/W(c), football M/W, golf M/W, rock climbing M/W, rugby M(c)/W(c), sand volleyball M/W, skiing (downhill) M/W, soccer M/W, softball M/W, table tennis

M/W, tennis M/W, ultimate Frisbee M(c)/W(c), volleyball M/W, wrestling M(c).

Campus security: 24-hour emergency response devices and patrols, student patrols, late-night transport/escort service, controlled dormitory access.

Student services: health clinic, personal/psychological counseling.

COSTS & FINANCIAL AID

Costs (2017–18) ***One-time required fee:*** $500. ***Tuition:*** state resident $7105 full-time, $237 per credit hour part-time; nonresident $17,347 full-time, $578 per credit hour part-time. Full-time tuition and fees vary according to course level, course load, program, and reciprocity agreements. Part-time tuition and fees vary according to course level, course load, program, and reciprocity agreements. ***Required fees:*** $60 full-time, $23 per term part-time. ***Room and board:*** $8896; room only: $4856. Room and board charges vary according to board plan and housing facility. ***Payment plan:*** installment. ***Waivers:*** employees or children of employees.

Financial Aid Of all full-time matriculated undergraduates who enrolled in 2016, 6,108 applied for aid, 4,112 were judged to have need, 154 had their need fully met. 154 Federal Work-Study jobs (averaging $1298). In 2016, 1154 non-need-based awards were made. ***Average percent of need met:*** 74. ***Average financial aid package:*** $9507. ***Average need-based loan:*** $4086. ***Average need-based gift aid:*** $7343. ***Average non-need-based aid:*** $3449. ***Average indebtedness upon graduation:*** $24,762.

APPLYING

Standardized Tests *Required:* SAT or ACT (for admission).

Options: electronic application.

Application fee: $40.

Required: high school transcript. ***Required for some:*** interview. ***Recommended:*** minimum 2.5 GPA.

Notification: continuous (freshmen), continuous (transfers).

CONTACT

Mr. Rashad Smith, Director of Undergraduate Admissions, University of Southern Indiana, 8600 University Boulevard, Evansville, IN 47712-3590. *Phone:* 812-464-1765. *Toll-free phone:* 800-467-1965. *Fax:* 812-465-7154. *E-mail:* enroll@usi.edu.

Valparaiso University

Valparaiso, Indiana

http://www.valpo.edu/

- **Independent** comprehensive, founded 1859, affiliated with Lutheran Church
- **Small-town** 350-acre campus with easy access to Chicago
- **Endowment** $204.7 million
- **Coed** 3,294 undergraduate students, 98% full-time, 54% women, 46% men
- **Moderately difficult** entrance level, 83% of applicants were admitted

UNDERGRAD STUDENTS

3,242 full-time, 52 part-time. Students come from 47 states and territories; 32 other countries; 57% are from out of state; 6% Black or African American, non-Hispanic/Latino; 9% Hispanic/Latino; 2% Asian, non-Hispanic/Latino; 0.2% American Indian or Alaska Native, non-Hispanic/Latino; 3% Two or more races, non-Hispanic/Latino; 3% Race/ethnicity unknown; 5% international; 6% transferred in; 66% live on campus.

Freshmen:

Admission: 7,484 applied, 6,205 admitted, 862 enrolled. ***Average high school GPA:*** 3.71. ***Test scores:*** SAT critical reading scores over 500: 77%; SAT math scores over 500: 72%; SAT writing scores over 500: 65%; ACT scores over 18: 99%; SAT critical reading scores over 600: 26%; SAT math scores over 600: 29%; SAT writing scores over 600: 17%; ACT scores over 24: 73%; SAT critical reading scores over 700: 7%; SAT math scores over 700: 5%; SAT writing scores over 700: 3%; ACT scores over 30: 21%.

Retention: 86% of full-time freshmen returned.

FACULTY

Total: 404, 71% full-time, 75% with terminal degrees.

Student/faculty ratio: 13:1.

ACADEMICS

Calendar: semesters. *Degrees:* certificates, associate, bachelor's, master's, doctoral, post-master's, and postbachelor's certificates.

Special study options: accelerated degree program, adult/continuing education programs, advanced placement credit, cooperative education, distance learning, double majors, English as a second language, freshman honors college, honors programs, independent study, internships, off-campus study, part-time degree program, services for LD students, student-designed majors, study abroad, summer session for credit. ***ROTC:*** Army (c), Air Force (c).

Unusual degree programs: 3-2 physician assistant.

Computers: 500 computers/terminals are available on campus for general student use. Students can access the following: campus intranet, computer help desk, free student e-mail accounts, online (class) grades, online (class) registration, online (class) schedules, Web academic information, degree audit, online course evaluations. Campuswide network is available. 100% of college-owned or -operated housing units are wired for high-speed Internet access. Wireless service is available via classrooms, computer centers, computer labs, dorm rooms, learning centers, libraries, student centers.

Library: Christopher Center for Library and Information Resources plus 1 other. *Books:* 545,491 (physical); *Serial titles:* 2,588 (physical), 79,749 (digital/electronic). Weekly public service hours: 112.

STUDENT LIFE

Housing options: on-campus residence required through junior year; coed, women-only. Campus housing is university owned and leased by the school. Freshman campus housing is guaranteed.

Activities and organizations: drama/theater group, student-run newspaper, radio station, choral group, Student Government, Student volunteer organization, Chapel programs, Union Board, national fraternities, national sororities.

Athletics Member NCAA. All Division I except football (Division I-AA). ***Intercollegiate sports:*** baseball M(s), basketball M(s)/W(s), bowling W(s), cross-country running M(s)/W(s), golf M(s)/W(s), soccer M(s)/W(s), softball W(s), swimming and diving M(s)/W(s), tennis M(s)/W(s), track and field M(s)/W(s), volleyball W(s). ***Intramural sports:*** badminton M/W, basketball M/W, bowling M/W, cheerleading M/W, football M/W, golf M/W, racquetball M/W, soccer M(c)/W(c), softball M/W, table tennis M/W, tennis M(c)/W(c), triathlon M/W, ultimate Frisbee M(c)/W(c), volleyball M/W.

Campus security: 24-hour emergency response devices and patrols, late-night transport/escort service, controlled dormitory access.

Student services: health clinic, personal/psychological counseling, legal services.

COSTS & FINANCIAL AID

Costs (2017–18) ***Comprehensive fee:*** $50,160 includes full-time tuition ($37,550), mandatory fees ($1210), and room and board ($11,400). Full-time tuition and fees vary according to course load and program. Part-time tuition: $1665 per credit hour. Part-time tuition and fees vary according to course load and program. ***Required fees:*** $116 per term part-time. ***College room only:*** $7000. Room and board charges vary according to housing facility and student level. ***Payment plans:*** tuition prepayment, installment. ***Waivers:*** employees or children of employees.

Financial Aid Of all full-time matriculated undergraduates who enrolled in 2015, 2,536 applied for aid, 2,274 were judged to have need, 1,389 had their need fully met. 570 Federal Work-Study jobs (averaging $1440). 884 state and other part-time jobs (averaging $2145). In 2015, 627 non-need-based awards were made. ***Average percent of need met:*** 93. ***Average financial aid package:*** $29,069. ***Average need-based loan:*** $4837. ***Average need-based gift aid:*** $26,100. ***Average non-need-based aid:*** $15,226. ***Average indebtedness upon graduation:*** $37,294.

APPLYING

Standardized Tests *Required:* SAT or ACT (for admission).

Options: electronic application, deferred entrance.

Required: essay or personal statement, high school transcript. ***Required for some:*** interview. ***Recommended:*** 2 letters of recommendation, interview.

Application deadlines: rolling (freshmen), rolling (transfers).

Notification: continuous (freshmen), continuous (transfers).

CONTACT
Mr. Bart Harvey, Director of Freshman Admission and Operations, Valparaiso University, Kretzmann Hall, 1700 Chapel Drive, Valparaiso, IN 46383-6493. *Phone:* 219-464-5011. *Toll-free phone:* 888-GO-VALPO. *Fax:* 219-464-6898. *E-mail:* undergrad.admission@valpo.edu.

Vincennes University

Vincennes, Indiana

http://www.vinu.edu/

- **State-supported** primarily 2-year, founded 1801
- **Small-town** 160-acre campus
- **Coed** 18,897 undergraduate students, 30% full-time, 46% women, 54% men
- **Noncompetitive** entrance level, 79% of applicants were admitted

UNDERGRAD STUDENTS
5,630 full-time, 13,267 part-time. Students come from 40 states and territories; 15 other countries; 19% are from out of state; 10% Black or African American, non-Hispanic/Latino; 8% Hispanic/Latino; 0.7% Asian, non-Hispanic/Latino; 0.3% Native Hawaiian or other Pacific Islander, non-Hispanic/Latino; 0.3% American Indian or Alaska Native, non-Hispanic/Latino; 2% Two or more races, non-Hispanic/Latino; 5% Race/ethnicity unknown; 0.7% international; 0.9% transferred in; 40% live on campus.

Freshmen:
Admission: 5,486 applied, 4,346 admitted, 2,620 enrolled.
Retention: 54% of full-time freshmen returned.

FACULTY
Total: 1,344, 16% full-time.
Student/faculty ratio: 16:1.

ACADEMICS
Calendar: semesters. *Degrees:* certificates, associate, and bachelor's.
Special study options: academic remediation for entering students, accelerated degree program, adult/continuing education programs, advanced placement credit, distance learning, double majors, English as a second language, external degree program, freshman honors college, honors programs, independent study, internships, off-campus study, part-time degree program, services for LD students, student-designed majors, summer session for credit. ***ROTC:*** Army (b), Air Force (c).
Computers: 1,500 computers/terminals are available on campus for general student use. Campuswide network is available.
Library: Shake Learning Resource Center.

STUDENT LIFE
Housing options: on-campus residence required for freshman year; coed, men-only, women-only. Campus housing is university owned. Freshman campus housing is guaranteed.
Activities and organizations: drama/theater group, student-run newspaper, radio and television station, choral group, national fraternities, national sororities.
Athletics Member NJCAA. ***Intercollegiate sports:*** baseball M, basketball M/W, bowling M, cross-country running M/W, golf M, track and field M/W, volleyball W.
Campus security: 24-hour emergency response devices and patrols, student patrols, late-night transport/escort service, controlled dormitory access, surveillance cameras.
Student services: health clinic, personal/psychological counseling.

COSTS
Costs (2016–17) ***Tuition:*** state resident $5122 full-time; nonresident $12,731 full-time. Full-time tuition and fees vary according to course level, course load, location, program, reciprocity agreements, and student level. Part-time tuition and fees vary according to course level, course load, location, program, reciprocity agreements, and student level. ***Required fees:*** $453 full-time. ***Room and board:*** $9332. Room and board charges vary according to board plan, gender, and housing facility. ***Payment plan:*** installment. ***Waivers:*** senior citizens and employees or children of employees.

APPLYING
Options: electronic application, deferred entrance.
Application fee: $20.
Required: high school transcript. ***Required for some:*** interview.
Application deadlines: rolling (freshmen), rolling (transfers).
Notification: continuous until 8/1 (freshmen), continuous (transfers).

CONTACT
Vincennes University, 1002 North First Street, Vincennes, IN 47591. *Phone:* 812-888-4313. *Toll-free phone:* 800-742-9198.

Wabash College

Crawfordsville, Indiana

http://www.wabash.edu/

- **Independent** 4-year, founded 1832
- **Small-town** 60-acre campus with easy access to Indianapolis
- **Endowment** $354.9 million
- **Men only** 842 undergraduate students, 100% full-time
- **Moderately difficult** entrance level, 63% of applicants were admitted

UNDERGRAD STUDENTS
842 full-time. Students come from 31 states and territories; 14 other countries; 23% are from out of state; 6% Black or African American, non-Hispanic/Latino; 8% Hispanic/Latino; 1% Asian, non-Hispanic/Latino; 0.2% American Indian or Alaska Native, non-Hispanic/Latino; 2% Two or more races, non-Hispanic/Latino; 2% Race/ethnicity unknown; 7% international; 0.7% transferred in; 91% live on campus.

Freshmen:
Admission: 1,284 applied, 812 admitted, 215 enrolled. ***Average high school GPA:*** 3.66. ***Test scores:*** SAT critical reading scores over 500: 74%; SAT math scores over 500: 86%; SAT writing scores over 500: 61%; ACT scores over 18: 100%; SAT critical reading scores over 600: 26%; SAT math scores over 600: 42%; SAT writing scores over 600: 23%; ACT scores over 24: 65%; SAT critical reading scores over 700: 3%; SAT math scores over 700: 5%; SAT writing scores over 700: 2%; ACT scores over 30: 18%.
Retention: 92% of full-time freshmen returned.

FACULTY
Total: 105, 82% full-time, 90% with terminal degrees.
Student/faculty ratio: 9:1.

ACADEMICS
Calendar: semesters. *Degree:* bachelor's.
Special study options: advanced placement credit, double majors, independent study, internships, off-campus study, services for LD students, student-designed majors, study abroad.
Unusual degree programs: 3-2 engineering with Purdue University, Columbia University, Washington University in St. Louis.
Computers: 296 computers/terminals and 2,600 ports are available on campus for general student use. Students can access the following: campus intranet, computer help desk, free student e-mail accounts, online (class) grades, online (class) registration, online (class) schedules, online course management, degree audit, expenses. Campuswide network is available. 100% of college-owned or -operated housing units are wired for high-speed Internet access. Wireless service is available via entire campus.
Library: Lilly Library. *Books:* 198,775 (physical), 228,949 (digital/electronic); *Serial titles:* 1,850 (physical), 223,882 (digital/electronic); *Databases:* 82. Weekly public service hours: 112.

STUDENT LIFE
Housing options: on-campus residence required through junior year; men-only. Campus housing is university owned. Freshman campus housing is guaranteed.
Activities and organizations: drama/theater group, student-run newspaper, radio station, choral group, Inter-Fraternity Council, Malcolm X Institute for Black Studies, Sphinx Club, Student Government, College Mentors for Kids, national fraternities.
Athletics Member NCAA. All Division III. ***Intercollegiate sports:*** baseball M, basketball M, cross-country running M, football M, golf M, lacrosse M, rugby M(c), soccer M, swimming and diving M, tennis M, track and field M, ultimate Frisbee M(c), wrestling M. ***Intramural sports:*** badminton M, basketball M, bowling M, cross-country running M,

football M, golf M, racquetball M, soccer M, softball M, swimming and diving M, table tennis M, tennis M, track and field M, volleyball M, weight lifting M, wrestling M.

Campus security: 24-hour emergency response devices and patrols.

Student services: health clinic, personal/psychological counseling.

COSTS & FINANCIAL AID

Costs (2017–18) ***Comprehensive fee:*** $52,100 includes full-time tuition ($41,600), mandatory fees ($650), and room and board ($9850). Part-time tuition: $6933 per course. Part-time tuition and fees vary according to course load. ***Required fees:*** $50 per term part-time. ***College room only:*** $5250. Room and board charges vary according to board plan and housing facility. ***Payment plans:*** tuition prepayment, installment. ***Waivers:*** employees or children of employees.

Financial Aid Of all full-time matriculated undergraduates who enrolled in 2016, 792 applied for aid, 617 were judged to have need, 442 had their need fully met. 57 Federal Work-Study jobs (averaging $2691). 338 state and other part-time jobs (averaging $2872). In 2016, 217 non-need-based awards were made. ***Average percent of need met:*** 92. ***Average financial aid package:*** $34,144. ***Average need-based loan:*** $4913. ***Average need-based gift aid:*** $26,374. ***Average non-need-based aid:*** $19,928. ***Average indebtedness upon graduation:*** $37,495.

APPLYING

Standardized Tests *Required:* SAT or ACT (for admission).

Options: electronic application, early admission, early decision, early action, deferred entrance.

Application fee: $50.

Required: essay or personal statement, high school transcript, 1 letter of recommendation, high school report. ***Required for some:*** interview. ***Recommended:*** interview.

Application deadlines: rolling (freshmen), rolling (transfers), 11/1 (early action).

Early decision deadline: 10/15.

Notification: continuous (freshmen), continuous (transfers), 11/1 (early decision), 12/7 (early action).

CONTACT

Mr. Charles Timmons, Associate Dean for Enrollment, Wabash College, PO Box 362, Crawfordsville, IN 47933-0352. *Phone:* 765-361-6225. *Toll-free phone:* 800-345-5385. *Fax:* 765-361-6437. *E-mail:* admissions@wabash.edu.

IOWA

Allen College

Waterloo, Iowa

http://www.allencollege.edu/

- **Independent** comprehensive, founded 1989
- **Suburban** 20-acre campus
- **Endowment** $6.9 million
- **Coed, primarily women** 360 undergraduate students, 74% full-time, 91% women, 9% men
- **Moderately difficult** entrance level

UNDERGRAD STUDENTS

268 full-time, 92 part-time. Students come from 7 states and territories; 3% are from out of state; 2% Black or African American, non-Hispanic/Latino; 1% Asian, non-Hispanic/Latino; 0.6% Native Hawaiian or other Pacific Islander, non-Hispanic/Latino; 0.3% American Indian or Alaska Native, non-Hispanic/Latino; 0.8% Two or more races, non-Hispanic/Latino; 7% Race/ethnicity unknown; 37% transferred in.

Freshmen:

Admission: 1 applied.

Retention: 96% of full-time freshmen returned.

FACULTY

Total: 54, 78% full-time, 31% with terminal degrees.

Student/faculty ratio: 17:1.

ACADEMICS

Calendar: semesters. *Degrees:* certificates, associate, bachelor's, master's, doctoral, and post-master's certificates (liberal arts and general education courses offered at either University of North Iowa or Wartburg College).

Special study options: accelerated degree program, advanced placement credit, cooperative education, distance learning, honors programs, independent study, internships, off-campus study, part-time degree program. ***ROTC:*** Army (c).

Unusual degree programs: 3-2 nursing with Wartburg College, Loras College, Central College, Simpson College.

Computers: 32 computers/terminals are available on campus for general student use. Students can access the following: campus intranet, computer help desk, free student e-mail accounts, online (class) grades, online (class) schedules. Campuswide network is available. 100% of college-owned or -operated housing units are wired for high-speed Internet access. Wireless service is available via entire campus.

Library: Barrett Library plus 1 other. *Books:* 12,926 (physical), 200 (digital/electronic); *Serial titles:* 218 (physical), 279 (digital/electronic); *Databases:* 38. Weekly public service hours: 50; study areas open 24 hours, 5-7 days a week.

STUDENT LIFE

Housing options: college housing not available.

Activities and organizations: choral group, Allen Student Nurses' Association, Nurses' Christian Fellowship.

Campus security: 24-hour patrols, late-night transport/escort service, controlled dormitory access.

Student services: health clinic, personal/psychological counseling.

COSTS & FINANCIAL AID

Costs (2017–18) ***Tuition:*** $16,876 full-time, $603 per credit hour part-time. Full-time tuition and fees vary according to course load, degree level, and program. Part-time tuition and fees vary according to course load, degree level, and program. ***Required fees:*** $1660 full-time. ***Payment plan:*** deferred payment.

Financial Aid Of all full-time matriculated undergraduates who enrolled in 2014, 272 applied for aid, 244 were judged to have need, 13 had their need fully met. 8 Federal Work-Study jobs (averaging $2750). In 2014, 19 non-need-based awards were made. ***Average percent of need met:*** 45. ***Average financial aid package:*** $10,958. ***Average need-based loan:*** $4911. ***Average need-based gift aid:*** $7209. ***Average non-need-based aid:*** $1175.

APPLYING

Standardized Tests *Required for some:* SAT or ACT (for admission), ATI, TEAS for undergraduate pre-licensure students.

Options: electronic application.

Application fee: $50.

Required for some: essay or personal statement, high school transcript, 1 letter of recommendation, interview.

Application deadlines: 2/1 (freshmen), 2/1 (transfers).

Notification: continuous until 3/1 (freshmen), continuous until 3/1 (transfers).

CONTACT

Jamie Jordan, Administrative Assistant, Student Services, Allen College, Barrett Forum, 1825 Logan Avenue, Waterloo, IA 50703. *Phone:* 319-226-2014. *Fax:* 319-226-2010. *E-mail:* admissions@allencollege.edu.

Briar Cliff University

Sioux City, Iowa

http://www.briarcliff.edu/

- **Independent Roman Catholic** comprehensive, founded 1930
- **Suburban** 75-acre campus
- **Coed** 1,022 undergraduate students, 77% full-time, 56% women, 44% men
- **Moderately difficult** entrance level, 53% of applicants were admitted

UNDERGRAD STUDENTS

792 full-time, 230 part-time. 38% are from out of state; 7% Black or African American, non-Hispanic/Latino; 11% Hispanic/Latino; 1% Asian, non-Hispanic/Latino; 0.5% Native Hawaiian or other Pacific Islander,

non-Hispanic/Latino; 1% American Indian or Alaska Native, non-Hispanic/Latino; 2% Two or more races, non-Hispanic/Latino; 4% international; 12% transferred in; 47% live on campus.

Freshmen:
Admission: 1,741 applied, 919 admitted, 185 enrolled. ***Average high school GPA:*** 3.27. ***Test scores:*** SAT critical reading scores over 500: 29%; SAT math scores over 500: 39%; ACT scores over 18: 90%; SAT critical reading scores over 600: 4%; ACT scores over 24: 24%; ACT scores over 30: 4%.

Retention: 70% of full-time freshmen returned.

FACULTY
Total: 94, 65% full-time, 59% with terminal degrees.

Student/faculty ratio: 14:1.

ACADEMICS
Calendar: 3 10-week terms plus two 5-week summer sessions. *Degrees:* associate, bachelor's, master's, doctoral, post-master's, and postbachelor's certificates.

Special study options: academic remediation for entering students, accelerated degree program, adult/continuing education programs, advanced placement credit, distance learning, double majors, honors programs, independent study, internships, off-campus study, part-time degree program, services for LD students, student-designed majors, study abroad, summer session for credit.

Computers: Students can access the following: campus intranet, computer help desk, free student e-mail accounts, online (class) grades, online (class) schedules. Campuswide network is available. Wireless service is available via classrooms, computer centers, computer labs, libraries, student centers.

Library: Bishop Mueller Library.

STUDENT LIFE
Housing options: on-campus residence required through junior year; coed. Campus housing is university owned. Freshman campus housing is guaranteed.

Activities and organizations: drama/theater group, student-run newspaper, radio station, choral group, Residence Hall Association, Briar Cliff Student Government, Choices, Blue Crew, Catholic Daughters of America.

Athletics Member NAIA. ***Intercollegiate sports:*** baseball M(s), basketball M(s)/W(s), cheerleading W(s), cross-country running M(s)/W(s), football M(s), golf M(s)/W(s), soccer M(s)/W(s), softball W(s), tennis M(s)/W(s), track and field M(s)/W(s), volleyball W(s), wrestling M(s). ***Intramural sports:*** basketball M/W, bowling M/W, football M, golf M/W, softball M/W, table tennis M/W, tennis M/W, volleyball M/W.

Campus security: 24-hour emergency response devices and patrols, student patrols, late-night transport/escort service, controlled dormitory access.

Student services: health clinic, personal/psychological counseling.

COSTS & FINANCIAL AID
Costs (2017–18) ***Comprehensive fee:*** $38,872 includes full-time tuition ($28,650), mandatory fees ($1136), and room and board ($9086). Full-time tuition and fees vary according to class time, course load, degree level, location, and program. Part-time tuition: $956 per credit hour. Part-time tuition and fees vary according to class time, course load, degree level, location, and program. ***College room only:*** $4300. Room and board charges vary according to board plan, housing facility, and location. ***Payment plans:*** installment, deferred payment. ***Waivers:*** employees or children of employees.

Financial Aid Of all full-time matriculated undergraduates who enrolled in 2015, 778 applied for aid, 656 were judged to have need, 156 had their need fully met. In 2015, 133 non-need-based awards were made. ***Average percent of need met:*** 26. ***Average financial aid package:*** $30,582. ***Average need-based loan:*** $4837. ***Average need-based gift aid:*** $14,647. ***Average non-need-based aid:*** $2524. ***Average indebtedness upon graduation:*** $29,484. ***Financial aid deadline:*** 3/15.

APPLYING
Standardized Tests *Required:* SAT or ACT (for admission).

Options: electronic application, early admission, deferred entrance.

Application fee: $20.

Required: high school transcript, minimum 2.0 GPA. ***Required for some:*** essay or personal statement, 3 letters of recommendation, interview.

CONTACT
Mr. Brian Eben, Assistant Vice President for Enrollment Management, Briar Cliff University, 3303 Rebecca Street, Sioux City, IA 51104. *Phone:* 712-279-5200. *Toll-free phone:* 800-662-3303. *Fax:* 712-279-1632. *E-mail:* admissions@briarcliff.edu.

Buena Vista University

Storm Lake, Iowa

http://www.bvu.edu/

- **Independent** comprehensive, founded 1891, affiliated with Presbyterian Church (U.S.A.)
- **Small-town** 60-acre campus
- **Endowment** $127.3 million
- **Coed** 795 undergraduate students, 99% full-time, 51% women, 49% men
- **Moderately difficult** entrance level, 64% of applicants were admitted

UNDERGRAD STUDENTS
784 full-time, 11 part-time. Students come from 27 states and territories; 15 other countries; 21% are from out of state; 3% Black or African American, non-Hispanic/Latino; 7% Hispanic/Latino; 2% Asian, non-Hispanic/Latino; 0.1% Native Hawaiian or other Pacific Islander, non-Hispanic/Latino; 4% Two or more races, non-Hispanic/Latino; 4% Race/ethnicity unknown; 5% international; 4% transferred in; 90% live on campus.

Freshmen:
Admission: 1,256 applied, 800 admitted, 183 enrolled. ***Average high school GPA:*** 3.41. ***Test scores:*** ACT scores over 18: 88%; ACT scores over 24: 39%; ACT scores over 30: 5%.

Retention: 73% of full-time freshmen returned.

FACULTY
Total: 113, 73% full-time, 58% with terminal degrees.

Student/faculty ratio: 9:1.

ACADEMICS
Calendar: 4-1-4. *Degrees:* bachelor's and master's.

Special study options: academic remediation for entering students, adult/continuing education programs, advanced placement credit, distance learning, double majors, English as a second language, external degree program, honors programs, independent study, internships, off-campus study, part-time degree program, services for LD students, student-designed majors, study abroad, summer session for credit. ***ROTC:*** Army (b).

Unusual degree programs: 3-2 engineering with Washington University in St. Louis.

Computers: Students can access the following: campus intranet, computer help desk, free student e-mail accounts, online (class) grades, online (class) registration, online (class) schedules. Campuswide network is available. 100% of college-owned or -operated housing units are wired for high-speed Internet access. Wireless service is available via entire campus.

Library: BVU Library. Weekly public service hours: 94; students can reserve study rooms.

STUDENT LIFE
Housing options: on-campus residence required through senior year; coed, special housing for students with disabilities. Campus housing is university owned. Freshman campus housing is guaranteed.

Activities and organizations: drama/theater group, student-run newspaper, radio and television station, choral group, Student Activities Board, Orientation Team, Esprit De Corps, Student Senate, Student Mobilizing Outreach and Volunteer Efforts.

Athletics Member NCAA. All Division III. ***Intercollegiate sports:*** baseball M, basketball M/W, cross-country running M/W, football M, golf M/W, soccer M/W, softball W, tennis M/W, track and field M/W, volleyball W, wrestling M. ***Intramural sports:*** basketball M/W, racquetball M/W, softball M/W, table tennis M/W, tennis M/W, volleyball M/W.

Campus security: 24-hour emergency response devices, late-night transport/escort service, controlled dormitory access, night security patrols.

Student services: health clinic, personal/psychological counseling.

COSTS & FINANCIAL AID

Costs (2017–18) ***Comprehensive fee:*** $42,344 includes full-time tuition ($32,854) and room and board ($9490). Full-time tuition and fees vary according to location. Part-time tuition: $1105 per credit hour. Part-time tuition and fees vary according to location. ***College room only:*** $4774. Room and board charges vary according to board plan and housing facility. ***Payment plan:*** installment. ***Waivers:*** employees or children of employees.

Financial Aid Of all full-time matriculated undergraduates who enrolled in 2016, 690 applied for aid, 627 were judged to have need, 153 had their need fully met. In 2016, 145 non-need-based awards were made. ***Average percent of need met:*** 84. ***Average financial aid package:*** $28,121. ***Average need-based loan:*** $5316. ***Average need-based gift aid:*** $22,862. ***Average non-need-based aid:*** $18,724.

APPLYING

Standardized Tests *Required:* SAT or ACT (for admission). *Recommended:* ACT (for admission).

Options: electronic application, deferred entrance.

Required: high school transcript. ***Required for some:*** essay or personal statement, interview. ***Recommended:*** minimum 3.0 GPA.

Notification: continuous (freshmen), continuous (transfers).

CONTACT

Michael Fox, Director of Admissions, Buena Vista University, 610 West Fourth Street, Storm Lake, IA 50588. *Phone:* 712-749-2078. *Toll-free phone:* 800-383-9600. *E-mail:* admissions@bvu.edu.

Central College

Pella, Iowa

http://www.central.edu/

- **Independent** 4-year, founded 1853, affiliated with Reformed Church in America
- **Small-town** 169-acre campus with easy access to Des Moines
- **Endowment** $79.9 million
- **Coed**
- **Moderately difficult** entrance level

FACULTY

Student/faculty ratio: 12:1.

ACADEMICS

Calendar: semesters. *Degree:* bachelor's.

Library: Geisler Library plus 2 others. *Books:* 180,617 (physical), 977 (digital/electronic); *Databases:* 26. Students can reserve study rooms.

STUDENT LIFE

Housing options: on-campus residence required through senior year; coed, men-only, women-only, special housing for students with disabilities. Campus housing is university owned. Freshman campus housing is guaranteed.

Activities and organizations: drama/theater group, choral group, Academic Honorary Associations and Health Professions Club, Music Ensembles, Campus Ministries, Student Senate, Students Concerned About the Environment (SCATE).

Athletics Member NCAA. All Division III.

Campus security: 24-hour emergency response devices and patrols, late-night transport/escort service, controlled dormitory access.

Student services: personal/psychological counseling.

COSTS & FINANCIAL AID

Costs (2016–17) ***Comprehensive fee:*** $44,592 includes full-time tuition ($34,612) and room and board ($9980). Part-time tuition: $1442 per credit hour. Part-time tuition and fees vary according to course load. ***College room only:*** $4892. Room and board charges vary according to board plan.

Financial Aid Of all full-time matriculated undergraduates who enrolled in 2015, 1,077 applied for aid, 989 were judged to have need, 153 had their need fully met. 669 Federal Work-Study jobs (averaging $1167). 455 state and other part-time jobs (averaging $1364). In 2015, 216 non-need-based awards were made. ***Average percent of need met:*** 81. ***Average financial aid package:*** $28,501. ***Average need-based loan:*** $3850. ***Average need-based gift aid:*** $23,866. ***Average non-need-based aid:*** $17,970. ***Average indebtedness upon graduation:*** $37,169.

APPLYING

Standardized Tests *Required:* SAT or ACT (for admission).

Options: electronic application, deferred entrance.

Application fee: $25.

Required: high school transcript. ***Required for some:*** essay or personal statement, 3 letters of recommendation, interview. ***Recommended:*** minimum 2.7 GPA.

CONTACT

Chevy Freiburger, Director of Admission, Central College, 812 University, Pella, IA 50112. *Phone:* 641-628-7637. *Toll-free phone:* 877-462-3687. *Fax:* 641-628-5983. *E-mail:* freiburgerc@central.edu.

Clarke University

Dubuque, Iowa

http://www.clarke.edu/

- **Independent Roman Catholic** comprehensive, founded 1843
- **Urban** 55-acre campus
- **Endowment** $31.3 million
- **Coed** 801 undergraduate students, 91% full-time, 66% women, 34% men
- **Moderately difficult** entrance level, 65% of applicants were admitted

UNDERGRAD STUDENTS

732 full-time, 69 part-time. Students come from 29 states and territories; 5 other countries; 54% are from out of state; 7% transferred in; 60% live on campus.

Freshmen:

Admission: 1,172 applied, 760 admitted, 158 enrolled. ***Average high school GPA:*** 3.41. ***Test scores:*** SAT critical reading scores over 500: 55%; SAT math scores over 500: 55%; ACT scores over 18: 94%; SAT critical reading scores over 600: 10%; SAT math scores over 600: 10%; ACT scores over 24: 38%; ACT scores over 30: 2%.

Retention: 71% of full-time freshmen returned.

FACULTY

Total: 96, 98% full-time, 81% with terminal degrees.

Student/faculty ratio: 8:1.

ACADEMICS

Calendar: semesters. *Degrees:* associate, bachelor's, master's, and doctoral.

Special study options: accelerated degree program, adult/continuing education programs, advanced placement credit, cooperative education, distance learning, double majors, honors programs, independent study, internships, off-campus study, part-time degree program, services for LD students, student-designed majors, study abroad, summer session for credit. ***ROTC:*** Army (c).

Computers: 237 computers/terminals are available on campus for general student use. Students can access the following: campus intranet, computer help desk, free student e-mail accounts, online (class) grades, online (class) registration, online (class) schedules. Campuswide network is available. 100% of college-owned or -operated housing units are wired for high-speed Internet access. Wireless service is available via entire campus.

Library: Nicholas J. Schrupp Library. *Books:* 78,500 (physical), 136,800 (digital/electronic); *Serial titles:* 150 (physical), 53,000 (digital/electronic); *Databases:* 60. Weekly public service hours: 90.

STUDENT LIFE

Housing options: on-campus residence required through sophomore year; coed, men-only, women-only. Campus housing is university owned. Freshman campus housing is guaranteed.

Activities and organizations: drama/theater group, choral group, Admissions Student Team, Student Multicultural Organization, Concert Choir, Campus Ministry, Student Government.

Athletics Member NAIA. ***Intercollegiate sports:*** baseball M(s), basketball M(s)/W(s), bowling M(s)/W(s), cheerleading W, cross-country running M(s)/W(s), golf M(s)/W(s), lacrosse M(s)/W(s), soccer

M(s)/W(s), softball W(s), track and field M(s)/W(s), volleyball M(s)/W(s). ***Intramural sports:*** badminton M/W, basketball M/W, bowling M/W, football M/W, golf M/W, skiing (cross-country) M/W, skiing (downhill) M/W, softball M/W, table tennis M/W, tennis M/W, track and field M/W, volleyball M/W, weight lifting M/W.

Campus security: 24-hour emergency response devices and patrols, late-night transport/escort service, controlled dormitory access.

Student services: health clinic, personal/psychological counseling.

COSTS & FINANCIAL AID

Costs (2017–18) ***Comprehensive fee:*** $41,350 includes full-time tuition ($30,950), mandatory fees ($1000), and room and board ($9400). Part-time tuition: $720 per credit hour. ***College room only:*** $4500. Room and board charges vary according to board plan. ***Payment plans:*** installment, deferred payment. ***Waivers:*** employees or children of employees.

Financial Aid Of all full-time matriculated undergraduates who enrolled in 2015, 714 applied for aid, 663 were judged to have need, 154 had their need fully met. 381 Federal Work-Study jobs (averaging $2000). In 2015, 95 non-need-based awards were made. ***Average percent of need met:*** 75. ***Average financial aid package:*** $25,080. ***Average need-based loan:*** $4504. ***Average need-based gift aid:*** $20,152. ***Average non-need-based aid:*** $18,816. ***Average indebtedness upon graduation:*** $39,907.

APPLYING

Standardized Tests *Required:* SAT or ACT (for admission).

Options: electronic application, deferred entrance.

Application fee: $25.

Required: high school transcript, minimum 2.0 GPA.

Application deadlines: rolling (freshmen), rolling (transfers).

Notification: 7/15 (freshmen), continuous until 8/15 (transfers).

CONTACT

Mrs. Alicia Schmitt, Associate Director of Admissions, Clarke University, 1550 Clarke Drive, Dubuque, IA 52001-3198. *Phone:* 563-588-6373. *Toll-free phone:* 800-383-2345. *E-mail:* admissions@clarke.edu.

Coe College

Cedar Rapids, Iowa

http://www.coe.edu/

- **Independent** 4-year, founded 1851, affiliated with Presbyterian Church
- **Urban** 53-acre campus
- **Endowment** $86.1 million
- **Coed** 1,409 undergraduate students, 95% full-time, 57% women, 43% men
- **Moderately difficult** entrance level, 50% of applicants were admitted

UNDERGRAD STUDENTS

1,344 full-time, 65 part-time. Students come from 39 states and territories; 14 other countries; 53% are from out of state; 7% Black or African American, non-Hispanic/Latino; 9% Hispanic/Latino; 2% Asian, non-Hispanic/Latino; 0.2% Native Hawaiian or other Pacific Islander, non-Hispanic/Latino; 0.4% American Indian or Alaska Native, non-Hispanic/Latino; 3% Two or more races, non-Hispanic/Latino; 3% Race/ethnicity unknown; 3% international; 3% transferred in; 86% live on campus.

Freshmen:

Admission: 6,725 applied, 3,359 admitted, 374 enrolled. ***Average high school GPA:*** 3.6. ***Test scores:*** SAT critical reading scores over 500: 80%; SAT math scores over 500: 86%; SAT writing scores over 500: 65%; ACT scores over 18: 99%; SAT critical reading scores over 600: 37%; SAT math scores over 600: 46%; SAT writing scores over 600: 39%; ACT scores over 24: 63%; SAT critical reading scores over 700: 14%; SAT math scores over 700: 14%; SAT writing scores over 700: 4%; ACT scores over 30: 16%.

Retention: 75% of full-time freshmen returned.

FACULTY

Total: 178, 54% full-time, 66% with terminal degrees.

Student/faculty ratio: 11:1.

ACADEMICS

Calendar: 4-4-1. *Degree:* bachelor's.

Special study options: advanced placement credit, double majors, English as a second language, honors programs, independent study, internships, off-campus study, part-time degree program, services for LD students, student-designed majors, study abroad, summer session for credit. ***ROTC:*** Army (b), Air Force (c).

Unusual degree programs: 3-2 engineering; public health with University of Iowa; law with University of Iowa.

Computers: 450 computers/terminals and 2,000 ports are available on campus for general student use. Students can access the following: campus intranet, computer help desk, free student e-mail accounts, online (class) grades, online (class) registration, online (class) schedules. Campuswide network is available. 100% of college-owned or -operated housing units are wired for high-speed Internet access. Wireless service is available via entire campus.

Library: Stewart Memorial Library plus 1 other. *Books:* 238,880 (physical), 272,768 (digital/electronic); *Serial titles:* 761 (physical), 3,639 (digital/electronic); *Databases:* 40. Weekly public service hours: 106.

STUDENT LIFE

Housing options: on-campus residence required through senior year; coed, men-only, women-only, special housing for students with disabilities. Campus housing is university owned. Freshman campus housing is guaranteed.

Activities and organizations: drama/theater group, student-run newspaper, radio station, choral group, Multicultural Fusion, Coe Alliance, Student Senate, Habitat for Humanity, International Club, national fraternities, national sororities.

Athletics Member NCAA. All Division III. ***Intercollegiate sports:*** baseball M, basketball M/W, cross-country running M/W, football M, golf M/W, soccer M/W, softball W, swimming and diving M/W, tennis M/W, track and field M/W, volleyball W, wrestling M. ***Intramural sports:*** lacrosse M/W, rock climbing M/W, soccer M/W, ultimate Frisbee M(c)/W(c), volleyball W.

Campus security: 24-hour emergency response devices and patrols, late-night transport/escort service, controlled dormitory access.

Student services: health clinic, personal/psychological counseling.

COSTS & FINANCIAL AID

Costs (2017–18) ***Comprehensive fee:*** $51,570 includes full-time tuition ($42,090), mandatory fees ($340), and room and board ($9140). Part-time tuition: $5261 per course. Part-time tuition and fees vary according to course load. ***College room only:*** $4350. Room and board charges vary according to board plan and housing facility. ***Payment plan:*** installment. ***Waivers:*** adult students, senior citizens, and employees or children of employees.

Financial Aid Of all full-time matriculated undergraduates who enrolled in 2016, 1,174 applied for aid, 1,096 were judged to have need, 235 had their need fully met. 584 Federal Work-Study jobs (averaging $2565). 215 state and other part-time jobs (averaging $1431). In 2016, 201 non-need-based awards were made. ***Average percent of need met:*** 83. ***Average financial aid package:*** $33,486. ***Average need-based loan:*** $5122. ***Average need-based gift aid:*** $28,610. ***Average non-need-based aid:*** $23,175. ***Average indebtedness upon graduation:*** $35,782.

APPLYING

Standardized Tests *Required:* SAT or ACT (for admission).

Options: electronic application, early admission, early action, deferred entrance.

Application fee: $30.

Required: essay or personal statement, high school transcript, 1 letter of recommendation. ***Recommended:*** minimum 3.0 GPA, interview.

Application deadlines: 3/1 (freshmen), rolling (transfers), 12/10 (early action).

Notification: 3/15 (freshmen), continuous (transfers).

CONTACT

Ms. Julie Staker, Dean of Admission, Coe College, 1220 1st Avenue NE, Cedar Rapids, IA 52402-5070. *Phone:* 319-399-8500. *Toll-free phone:* 877-225-5263. *Fax:* 319-399-8816. *E-mail:* admission@coe.edu.

COLLEGES AT-A-GLANCE

Cornell College

Mount Vernon, Iowa

http://www.cornellcollege.edu/

- **Independent Methodist** 4-year, founded 1853
- **Small-town** 129-acre campus
- **Endowment** $67.0 million
- **Coed** 978 undergraduate students, 100% full-time, 50% women, 50% men
- **Moderately difficult** entrance level, 71% of applicants were admitted

UNDERGRAD STUDENTS
975 full-time, 1 part-time. Students come from 46 states and territories; 21 other countries; 81% are from out of state; 5% Black or African American, non-Hispanic/Latino; 12% Hispanic/Latino; 3% Asian, non-Hispanic/Latino; 0.9% American Indian or Alaska Native, non-Hispanic/Latino; 3% Two or more races, non-Hispanic/Latino; 5% Race/ethnicity unknown; 5% international; 3% transferred in; 92% live on campus.

Freshmen:
Admission: 1,965 applied, 1,394 admitted, 287 enrolled. ***Average high school GPA:*** 3.46. ***Test scores:*** SAT critical reading scores over 500: 71%; SAT math scores over 500: 75%; ACT scores over 18: 99%; SAT critical reading scores over 600: 45%; SAT math scores over 600: 34%; ACT scores over 24: 74%; SAT critical reading scores over 700: 15%; SAT math scores over 700: 8%; ACT scores over 30: 22%.
Retention: 78% of full-time freshmen returned.

FACULTY
Total: 105, 80% full-time, 77% with terminal degrees.
Student/faculty ratio: 10:1.

ACADEMICS
Calendar: 8 3.5 week terms. *Degree:* bachelor's.
Special study options: advanced placement credit, double majors, English as a second language, independent study, internships, off-campus study, services for LD students, student-designed majors, study abroad.
Unusual degree programs: 3-2 engineering with University of Minnesota; forestry with Duke University; architecture with Washington University in St. Louis.
Computers: 259 computers/terminals and 1,200 ports are available on campus for general student use. Students can access the following: campus intranet, computer help desk, free student e-mail accounts, online (class) grades, online (class) registration, online (class) schedules. Campuswide network is available. 100% of college-owned or -operated housing units are wired for high-speed Internet access. Wireless service is available via entire campus.
Library: Cole Library plus 1 other. *Books:* 232,914 (physical); *Serial titles:* 491 (digital/electronic). Weekly public service hours: 70; students can reserve study rooms.

STUDENT LIFE
Housing options: on-campus residence required through senior year; coed, women-only. Campus housing is university owned and leased by the school. Freshman campus housing is guaranteed.
Activities and organizations: drama/theater group, student-run newspaper, radio station, choral group, Student-initiated Living-Learning Community, Chess and Games, Environmental Club, Performing Arts and Activities Council, Alliance.
Athletics Member NCAA. All Division III. ***Intercollegiate sports:*** baseball M, basketball M/W, cross-country running M/W, football M, lacrosse M/W, soccer M/W, softball W, tennis M/W, track and field M/W, ultimate Frisbee M(c)/W(c), volleyball M(c)/W, wrestling M. ***Intramural sports:*** badminton M/W, basketball M/W, bowling M/W, cheerleading M/W, fencing M(c)/W(c), football M/W, golf M/W, ice hockey M/W, lacrosse M(c)/W(c), racquetball M/W, soccer M/W, softball M/W, table tennis M/W, tennis M/W, track and field M/W, ultimate Frisbee M/W, volleyball M/W, weight lifting M/W, wrestling M/W.
Campus security: 24-hour emergency response devices and patrols, late-night transport/escort service, controlled dormitory access.
Student services: health clinic, personal/psychological counseling.

COSTS & FINANCIAL AID
Costs (2017–18) ***Comprehensive fee:*** $48,800 includes full-time tuition ($39,675), mandatory fees ($225), and room and board ($8900). Part-time tuition: $39,375 per year. Part-time tuition and fees vary according to course load. ***College room only:*** $4100. Room and board charges vary according to board plan and housing facility. ***Payment plan:*** installment. ***Waivers:*** employees or children of employees.
Financial Aid Of all full-time matriculated undergraduates who enrolled in 2016, 771 applied for aid, 705 were judged to have need, 110 had their need fully met. 355 Federal Work-Study jobs (averaging $1558). 83 state and other part-time jobs (averaging $919). In 2016, 256 non-need-based awards were made. ***Average percent of need met:*** 78. ***Average financial aid package:*** $31,933. ***Average need-based loan:*** $4502. ***Average need-based gift aid:*** $26,642. ***Average non-need-based aid:*** $19,876. ***Average indebtedness upon graduation:*** $31,975.

APPLYING
Standardized Tests *Recommended:* SAT or ACT (for admission).
Options: electronic application, early admission, early decision, early action, deferred entrance.
Application fee: $30.
Required: essay or personal statement, high school transcript, 1 letter of recommendation.
Application deadlines: 2/1 (freshmen), 3/1 (transfers), 12/1 (early action).
Early decision deadline: 11/1 (for plan 1), 2/1 (for plan 2).
Notification: 3/20 (freshmen), continuous (transfers), 12/15 (early decision plan 1), 3/15 (early decision plan 2), 2/1 (early action).

CONTACT
Ms. Marie Schofer, Director of Admissions, Cornell College, 600 First Street SW, Mount Vernon, IA 52314-1098. *Phone:* 319-895-4159. *Toll-free phone:* 800-747-1112. *Fax:* 319-895-4451. *E-mail:* admission@cornellcollege.edu.

Divine Word College

Epworth, Iowa

http://www.dwci.edu/

CONTACT
Divine Word College, 102 Jacoby Drive SW, Epworth, IA 52045-0380. *Phone:* 563-876-3353. *Toll-free phone:* 800-553-3321.

Dordt College

Sioux Center, Iowa

http://www.dordt.edu/

CONTACT
Mr. Howard Wislon, Vice President for Enrollment, Dordt College, 498 4th Avenue, NE, Sioux Center, IA 51250-1697. *Phone:* 712-722-6080. *Toll-free phone:* 800-343-6738. *Fax:* 712-722-6035. *E-mail:* admissions@dordt.edu.

★ Drake University

Des Moines, Iowa

http://www.drake.edu/

- **Independent** university, founded 1881
- **Urban** 120-acre campus
- **Endowment** $196.5 million
- **Coed** 3,338 undergraduate students, 95% full-time, 56% women, 44% men
- **Moderately difficult** entrance level, 67% of applicants were admitted

UNDERGRAD STUDENTS
3,167 full-time, 171 part-time. Students come from 45 states and territories; 43 other countries; 72% are from out of state; 4% Black or African American, non-Hispanic/Latino; 4% Hispanic/Latino; 3% Asian, non-Hispanic/Latino; 0.1% American Indian or Alaska Native, non-Hispanic/Latino; 2% Two or more races, non-Hispanic/Latino; 0.9% Race/ethnicity unknown; 8% international; 4% transferred in; 70% live on campus.

Freshmen:
Admission: 6,514 applied, 4,356 admitted, 803 enrolled. ***Average high school GPA:*** 3.71. ***Test scores:*** SAT critical reading scores over 500: 82%; SAT math scores over 500: 87%; ACT scores over 18: 99%; SAT critical reading scores over 600: 46%; SAT math scores over 600: 60%; ACT scores over 24: 81%; SAT critical reading scores over 700: 13%; SAT math scores over 700: 18%; ACT scores over 30: 25%.
Retention: 88% of full-time freshmen returned.

FACULTY
Total: 456, 63% full-time, 66% with terminal degrees.
Student/faculty ratio: 13:1.

ACADEMICS
Calendar: semesters. *Degrees:* bachelor's, master's, doctoral, post-master's, and postbachelor's certificates.
Special study options: accelerated degree program, advanced placement credit, cooperative education, distance learning, double majors, English as a second language, honors programs, independent study, internships, off-campus study, part-time degree program, services for LD students, student-designed majors, study abroad, summer session for credit. ***ROTC:*** Army (c), Air Force (c).
Unusual degree programs: 3-2 journalism and law, arts and sciences and law, accounting.
Computers: 1,000 computers/terminals are available on campus for general student use. Students can access the following: campus intranet, computer help desk, free student e-mail accounts, online (class) grades, online (class) registration, online (class) schedules. Campuswide network is available. 100% of college-owned or -operated housing units are wired for high-speed Internet access. Wireless service is available via classrooms, computer centers, computer labs, dorm rooms, libraries, student centers.
Library: Cowles Library plus 1 other. *Books:* 4,389 (physical), 129,239 (digital/electronic); *Serial titles:* 745 (physical), 121,135 (digital/electronic); *Databases:* 344. Weekly public service hours: 108; study areas open 24 hours, 5-7 days a week; students can reserve study rooms.

STUDENT LIFE
Housing options: on-campus residence required through sophomore year; coed, special housing for students with disabilities. Campus housing is university owned and is provided by a third party. Freshman campus housing is guaranteed.
Activities and organizations: drama/theater group, student-run newspaper, radio and television station, choral group, marching band, Student Activities Board, Drake Magazine, Dog Pound Pep Squad, Alpha Phi Omega, Residence Hall Association, national fraternities, national sororities.
Athletics Member NCAA. All Division I except football (Division I-AA). ***Intercollegiate sports:*** basketball M(s)/W(s), cheerleading M(s)/W(s), crew W, cross-country running M(s)/W(s), golf M(s)/W, soccer M(s)/W(s), softball W(s), tennis M(s)/W(s), track and field M(s)/W(s), volleyball W(s). ***Intramural sports:*** badminton M/W, basketball M/W, football M/W, golf M/W, racquetball M/W, soccer M(c)/W, softball M/W, swimming and diving M/W, tennis M/W, volleyball M/W(c).
Campus security: 24-hour emergency response devices and patrols, late-night transport/escort service, controlled dormitory access, 24-hour desk attendants in residence halls.
Student services: health clinic, personal/psychological counseling, legal services.

COSTS & FINANCIAL AID
Costs (2016–17) ***Comprehensive fee:*** $45,056 includes full-time tuition ($35,060), mandatory fees ($146), and room and board ($9850). Full-time tuition and fees vary according to course load, degree level, program, and student level. Part-time tuition: $695 per credit. Part-time tuition and fees vary according to class time, degree level, and program. ***College room only:*** $5300. Room and board charges vary according to board plan and housing facility. ***Payment plan:*** installment. ***Waivers:*** children of alumni, senior citizens, and employees or children of employees.
Financial Aid Of all full-time matriculated undergraduates who enrolled in 2016, 2,200 applied for aid, 1,816 were judged to have need, 490 had their need fully met. 1,478 Federal Work-Study jobs (averaging $1917). In 2016, 1038 non-need-based awards were made. ***Average percent of need met:*** 79. ***Average financial aid package:*** $27,171. ***Average need-based loan:*** $5769. ***Average need-based gift aid:*** $18,979. ***Average non-need-based aid:*** $14,399. ***Average indebtedness upon graduation:*** $33,649.

APPLYING
Standardized Tests *Required:* SAT or ACT (for admission).
Options: electronic application, early admission, deferred entrance.
Application fee: $25.
Required: essay or personal statement, high school transcript. ***Recommended:*** interview.
Application deadlines: 3/1 (freshmen), rolling (transfers).
Notification: continuous (freshmen), continuous (transfers).

CONTACT
Ms. Laura Linn, Director of Admission, Drake University, 2507 University Avenue, Des Moines, IA 50311. *Phone:* 515-271-3181 Ext. 3182. *Toll-free phone:* 800-44-DRAKE Ext. 3181. *Fax:* 515-271-2831. *E-mail:* admission@drake.edu.

Emmaus Bible College
Dubuque, Iowa
http://www.emmaus.edu/

- **Independent nondenominational** 4-year, founded 1941
- **Small-town** 22-acre campus
- **Coed** 265 undergraduate students, 89% full-time, 55% women, 45% men
- **Noncompetitive** entrance level, 36% of applicants were admitted

UNDERGRAD STUDENTS
236 full-time, 29 part-time. Students come from 33 states and territories; 9 other countries; 41% are from out of state; 4% Black or African American, non-Hispanic/Latino; 6% Hispanic/Latino; 4% Asian, non-Hispanic/Latino; 0.4% Native Hawaiian or other Pacific Islander, non-Hispanic/Latino; 0.8% American Indian or Alaska Native, non-Hispanic/Latino; 2% Two or more races, non-Hispanic/Latino; 8% Race/ethnicity unknown; 9% transferred in; 90% live on campus.

Freshmen:
Admission: 432 applied, 154 admitted, 69 enrolled. ***Average high school GPA:*** 3.37.
Retention: 77% of full-time freshmen returned.

FACULTY
Total: 34, 65% full-time, 24% with terminal degrees.
Student/faculty ratio: 9:1.

ACADEMICS
Calendar: semesters. *Degrees:* certificates, associate, and bachelor's.
Special study options: advanced placement credit, distance learning, double majors, independent study, internships, off-campus study, part-time degree program, summer session for credit.
Computers: Students can access the following: campus intranet, computer help desk, free student e-mail accounts, online (class) grades, online (class) registration, online (class) schedules. Campuswide network is available. 100% of college-owned or -operated housing units are wired for high-speed Internet access. Wireless service is available via entire campus.
Library: The Emmaus Bible College Library plus 1 other. Weekly public service hours: 130.

STUDENT LIFE
Housing options: on-campus residence required through senior year; men-only, women-only. Campus housing is university owned. Freshman campus housing is guaranteed.
Activities and organizations: choral group.
Athletics Member NCCAA. ***Intercollegiate sports:*** basketball M/W, soccer M, volleyball W. ***Intramural sports:*** badminton M/W, basketball M/W, golf M/W, racquetball M/W, soccer M/W, softball M/W, table tennis M/W, tennis M/W, ultimate Frisbee M/W, volleyball M/W.
Campus security: 24-hour emergency response devices, student patrols, controlled dormitory access.
Student services: personal/psychological counseling.

COSTS

Costs (2017–18) ***Comprehensive fee:*** $25,620 includes full-time tuition ($17,520) and room and board ($8100). Full-time tuition and fees vary according to course load and reciprocity agreements. Part-time tuition: $730 per credit hour. Part-time tuition and fees vary according to reciprocity agreements. ***Payment plan:*** installment. ***Waivers:*** employees or children of employees.

APPLYING

Standardized Tests *Required:* SAT or ACT (for admission).

Options: electronic application, deferred entrance.

Application fee: $25.

Required: essay or personal statement, high school transcript, minimum 2.0 GPA, 1 letter of recommendation.

Application deadlines: 8/1 (freshmen), 8/1 (transfers).

Notification: continuous (freshmen), continuous (transfers).

CONTACT

Miss Terra Boston, Applications Coordinator, Emmaus Bible College, Emmaus Bible College, Admissions, 2570 Asbury Road, Dubuque, IA 52001. *Phone:* 563-588-8000 Ext. 1320. *Toll-free phone:* 800-397-2425. *Fax:* 563-588-1216. *E-mail:* tboston@emmaus.edu.

Faith Baptist Bible College and Theological Seminary

Ankeny, Iowa

http://www.faith.edu/

- **Independent** comprehensive, founded 1921, affiliated with General Association of Regular Baptist Churches
- **Suburban** 52-acre campus
- **Endowment** $4.0 million
- **Coed** 226 undergraduate students, 86% full-time, 55% women, 45% men
- **Minimally difficult** entrance level, 49% of applicants were admitted

UNDERGRAD STUDENTS

194 full-time, 32 part-time. Students come from 33 states and territories; 4 other countries; 62% are from out of state; 0.4% Black or African American, non-Hispanic/Latino; 0.9% Hispanic/Latino; 1% Asian, non-Hispanic/Latino; 0.9% American Indian or Alaska Native, non-Hispanic/Latino; 2% Two or more races, non-Hispanic/Latino; 5% Race/ethnicity unknown; 0.4% international; 5% transferred in; 99% live on campus.

Freshmen:

Admission: 133 applied, 65 admitted, 74 enrolled. ***Average high school GPA:*** 3.42. ***Test scores:*** SAT critical reading scores over 500: 67%; SAT math scores over 500: 33%; ACT scores over 18: 92%; SAT critical reading scores over 600: 33%; ACT scores over 24: 48%; ACT scores over 30: 8%.

Retention: 73% of full-time freshmen returned.

FACULTY

Total: 30, 57% full-time, 50% with terminal degrees.

Student/faculty ratio: 11:1.

ACADEMICS

Calendar: semesters. *Degrees:* certificates, associate, bachelor's, and master's.

Special study options: academic remediation for entering students, adult/continuing education programs, advanced placement credit, distance learning, double majors, independent study, internships, part-time degree program, study abroad, summer session for credit.

Computers: 45 computers/terminals and 250 ports are available on campus for general student use. Students can access the following: free student e-mail accounts, online (class) grades, online (class) registration, online (class) schedules. Campuswide network is available. 100% of college-owned or -operated housing units are wired for high-speed Internet access. Wireless service is available via entire campus.

Library: John L. Patten Library.

STUDENT LIFE

Housing options: on-campus residence required through senior year; men-only, women-only, special housing for students with disabilities. Campus housing is university owned. Freshman campus housing is guaranteed.

Activities and organizations: drama/theater group, choral group, Student Association, Student Missionary Fellowship, Intramural Sports, Photo Club, Chapel Orchestra.

Athletics Member NCCAA. ***Intercollegiate sports:*** basketball M/W, cross-country running M/W, soccer M/W, track and field M/W, volleyball W. ***Intramural sports:*** basketball M/W, football M, ultimate Frisbee M/W, volleyball M/W.

Campus security: 24-hour emergency response devices and patrols, late-night transport/escort service.

Student services: personal/psychological counseling.

FINANCIAL AID

Financial Aid Of all full-time matriculated undergraduates who enrolled in 2004, 311 applied for aid, 290 were judged to have need, 5 had their need fully met. In 2004, 21 non-need-based awards were made. ***Average percent of need met:*** 48. ***Average financial aid package:*** $7124. ***Average need-based loan:*** $3142. ***Average need-based gift aid:*** $6299. ***Average non-need-based aid:*** $2465. ***Average indebtedness upon graduation:*** $15,006.

APPLYING

Standardized Tests *Required:* SAT or ACT (for admission).

Options: electronic application, deferred entrance.

Application fee: $45.

Required: essay or personal statement, high school transcript, 2 letters of recommendation. ***Required for some:*** interview. ***Recommended:*** minimum 2.0 GPA.

Application deadlines: 8/1 (freshmen), 8/1 (transfers).

Notification: 9/1 (freshmen), continuous until 9/1 (transfers).

CONTACT

Miss Mary Tubbs, Admissions Coordinator, Faith Baptist Bible College and Theological Seminary, 1900 NW 4th Street, Ankeny, IA 50023. *Phone:* 515-964-0601. *Toll-free phone:* 888-FAITH 4U. *Fax:* 515-964-1638. *E-mail:* admissions@faith.edu.

Graceland University

Lamoni, Iowa

http://www.graceland.edu/

- **Independent Community of Christ** comprehensive, founded 1895
- **Small-town** 170-acre campus with easy access to Des Moines
- **Endowment** $47.4 million
- **Coed** 1,446 undergraduate students, 81% full-time, 59% women, 41% men
- **Moderately difficult** entrance level, 48% of applicants were admitted

UNDERGRAD STUDENTS

1,166 full-time, 280 part-time. Students come from 43 states and territories; 9 other countries; 80% are from out of state; 10% Black or African American, non-Hispanic/Latino; 12% Hispanic/Latino; 1% Asian, non-Hispanic/Latino; 1% Native Hawaiian or other Pacific Islander, non-Hispanic/Latino; 0.3% American Indian or Alaska Native, non-Hispanic/Latino; 4% Two or more races, non-Hispanic/Latino; 7% Race/ethnicity unknown; 3% international; 12% transferred in; 70% live on campus.

Freshmen:

Admission: 2,440 applied, 1,181 admitted, 256 enrolled. ***Average high school GPA:*** 3.23. ***Test scores:*** SAT critical reading scores over 500: 27%; SAT math scores over 500: 30%; ACT scores over 18: 81%; SAT critical reading scores over 600: 6%; SAT math scores over 600: 8%; ACT scores over 24: 28%; ACT scores over 30: 3%.

Retention: 66% of full-time freshmen returned.

FACULTY

Total: 172, 45% full-time, 38% with terminal degrees.

Student/faculty ratio: 14:1.

ACADEMICS

Calendar: 4-1-4. *Degrees:* certificates, bachelor's, master's, doctoral, and post-master's certificates.

Special study options: academic remediation for entering students, accelerated degree program, adult/continuing education programs, advanced placement credit, cooperative education, distance learning, double majors, English as a second language, freshman honors college, honors programs, independent study, internships, off-campus study, part-time degree program, services for LD students, student-designed majors, study abroad, summer session for credit.

Computers: Students can access the following: campus intranet, computer help desk, free student e-mail accounts, online (class) grades, online (class) registration, online (class) schedules. Campuswide network is available. 100% of college-owned or -operated housing units are wired for high-speed Internet access. Wireless service is available via classrooms, computer centers, computer labs, dorm rooms, learning centers, libraries, student centers.

Library: F. M. Smith Library. *Books:* 80,000 (physical); *Serial titles:* 153 (physical). Weekly public service hours: 80; students can reserve study rooms.

STUDENT LIFE

Housing options: on-campus residence required through sophomore year; coed, men-only, women-only. Campus housing is university owned. Freshman campus housing is guaranteed.

Activities and organizations: drama/theater group, student-run newspaper, radio station, choral group, marching band, Black Student Union, Latin Club, Enactus, Social Equality Alliance, Communication Club.

Athletics Member NAIA. ***Intercollegiate sports:*** baseball M(s), basketball M(s)/W(s), cheerleading M(s)/W(s), cross-country running M(s)/W(s), football M(s), golf M(s)/W(s), soccer M(s)/W(s), softball W(s), track and field M(s)/W(s), volleyball M(s)/W(s), wrestling M(s). ***Intramural sports:*** basketball M/W, football M/W, golf M/W, racquetball M/W, soccer M/W, softball M/W, swimming and diving M/W, table tennis M/W, ultimate Frisbee M/W, volleyball M/W.

Campus security: 24-hour emergency response devices and patrols, late-night transport/escort service, controlled dormitory access.

Student services: health clinic, personal/psychological counseling.

COSTS & FINANCIAL AID

Costs (2017–18) ***Comprehensive fee:*** $36,590 includes full-time tuition ($27,500), mandatory fees ($610), and room and board ($8480). Full-time tuition and fees vary according to course load, location, and program. Part-time tuition: $800 per semester hour. Part-time tuition and fees vary according to course load, location, and program. ***Required fees:*** $285 per semester part-time. ***College room only:*** $3300. Room and board charges vary according to board plan, housing facility, and location. ***Payment plan:*** installment. ***Waivers:*** senior citizens and employees or children of employees.

Financial Aid Of all full-time matriculated undergraduates who enrolled in 2016, 1,081 applied for aid, 985 were judged to have need, 154 had their need fully met. In 2016, 188 non-need-based awards were made. ***Average percent of need met:*** 72. ***Average financial aid package:*** $22,282. ***Average need-based loan:*** $4581. ***Average need-based gift aid:*** $18,222. ***Average non-need-based aid:*** $12,738. ***Average indebtedness upon graduation:*** $30,676.

APPLYING

Standardized Tests *Required:* SAT or ACT (for admission), TOEFL for all students whose first language is not English (for admission).

Options: electronic application.

Required: high school transcript, 2 of the following: minimum high school GPA of 2.5 or rank in top half of class or minimum of 21 on ACT or 960 on the SAT. ***Required for some:*** essay or personal statement, 2 letters of recommendation, interview.

Application deadlines: rolling (freshmen), rolling (transfers).

Notification: continuous (freshmen), continuous (transfers).

CONTACT

Mr. Kevin Brown, Director of Admissions, Graceland University, 1 University Place, Lamoni, IA 50140. *Phone:* 641-784-5149. *Toll-free phone:* 866-GRACELAND. *Fax:* 641-784-5480.
E-mail: admissions@graceland.edu.

★ Grand View University

Des Moines, Iowa

http://www.grandview.edu/

- **Independent** comprehensive, founded 1896, affiliated with Evangelical Lutheran Church in America
- **Urban** 25-acre campus
- **Endowment** $19.8 million
- **Coed** 1,910 undergraduate students, 86% full-time, 55% women, 45% men
- **Minimally difficult** entrance level, 97% of applicants were admitted

UNDERGRAD STUDENTS

1,643 full-time, 267 part-time. Students come from 39 states and territories; 21 other countries; 7% are from out of state; 8% Black or African American, non-Hispanic/Latino; 4% Hispanic/Latino; 3% Asian, non-Hispanic/Latino; 0.2% Native Hawaiian or other Pacific Islander, non-Hispanic/Latino; 0.4% American Indian or Alaska Native, non-Hispanic/Latino; 4% Two or more races, non-Hispanic/Latino; 78% Race/ethnicity unknown; 2% international; 14% transferred in; 45% live on campus.

Freshmen:

Admission: 886 applied, 856 admitted, 338 enrolled. ***Average high school GPA:*** 3.26. ***Test scores:*** SAT critical reading scores over 500: 29%; SAT math scores over 500: 41%; SAT writing scores over 500: 13%; ACT scores over 18: 76%; SAT math scores over 600: 6%; ACT scores over 24: 21%; ACT scores over 30: 1%.

Retention: 68% of full-time freshmen returned.

FACULTY

Total: 217, 41% full-time, 35% with terminal degrees.

Student/faculty ratio: 13:1.

ACADEMICS

Calendar: semesters. *Degrees:* certificates, bachelor's, master's, and postbachelor's certificates.

Special study options: academic remediation for entering students, accelerated degree program, adult/continuing education programs, advanced placement credit, cooperative education, distance learning, double majors, English as a second language, freshman honors college, honors programs, independent study, internships, off-campus study, part-time degree program, services for LD students, student-designed majors, study abroad, summer session for credit. ***ROTC:*** Army (c), Air Force (c).

Unusual degree programs: 3-2 engineering with Iowa State University.

Computers: 336 computers/terminals are available on campus for general student use. Students can access the following: campus intranet, computer help desk, free student e-mail accounts, online (class) grades, online (class) registration, online (class) schedules. Campuswide network is available. 100% of college-owned or -operated housing units are wired for high-speed Internet access. Wireless service is available via classrooms, computer labs, libraries, student centers.

Library: Grand View University Library plus 1 other. *Books:* 88,250 (physical), 972 (digital/electronic); *Serial titles:* 517 (physical), 34,598 (digital/electronic); *Databases:* 29. Weekly public service hours: 86.

STUDENT LIFE

Housing options: on-campus residence required through junior year; coed. Campus housing is university owned. Freshman applicants given priority for college housing.

Activities and organizations: drama/theater group, student-run newspaper, radio and television station, choral group, Nursing Student Association, Art Club, Science Club, Education Club, Business Club.

Athletics Member NAIA. ***Intercollegiate sports:*** baseball M(s), basketball M(s)/W(s), bowling M(s)/W(s), cheerleading M(s)/W(s), cross-country running M(s)/W(s), football M(s), golf M(s)/W(s), riflery M(s)/W(s), soccer M(s)/W(s), softball W(s), tennis M(s)/W(s), track and field M(s)/W(s), volleyball M(s)/W(s), wrestling M(s). ***Intramural sports:*** basketball M/W, football M/W, soccer M/W, table tennis M/W, ultimate Frisbee M/W, volleyball M/W.

Campus security: 24-hour emergency response devices and patrols, late-night transport/escort service, controlled dormitory access, night security patrols.

Student services: health clinic, personal/psychological counseling.

COSTS & FINANCIAL AID

Costs (2017–18) ***Comprehensive fee:*** $35,350 includes full-time tuition ($25,836), mandatory fees ($680), and room and board ($8834). Full-time tuition and fees vary according to class time and course load. Part-time tuition: $642 per credit hour. Part-time tuition and fees vary according to class time and course load. ***Room and board:*** Room and board charges vary according to board plan and housing facility. ***Payment plan:*** installment. ***Waivers:*** children of alumni, senior citizens, and employees or children of employees.

Financial Aid Of all full-time matriculated undergraduates who enrolled in 2016, 1,499 applied for aid, 1,348 were judged to have need, 361 had their need fully met. 336 Federal Work-Study jobs (averaging $1354). In 2016, 261 non-need-based awards were made. ***Average percent of need met:*** 78. ***Average financial aid package:*** $19,738. ***Average need-based loan:*** $4535. ***Average need-based gift aid:*** $17,665. ***Average non-need-based aid:*** $9015. ***Average indebtedness upon graduation:*** $37,158.

APPLYING

Standardized Tests *Required:* SAT or ACT (for admission).

Options: electronic application.

Required: high school transcript. ***Recommended:*** minimum 2.0 GPA.

Application deadlines: 8/15 (freshmen), 8/15 (transfers).

Notification: 9/15 (freshmen), continuous until 9/15 (transfers).

CONTACT

Mr. Ryan Thompson, Director of Admissions, Grand View University, 1200 Grandview Avenue, Des Moines, IA 50316-1599. *Phone:* 515-263-2810. *Toll-free phone:* 800-444-6083. *Fax:* 515-263-2974. *E-mail:* admissions@grandview.edu.

See below for display ad and page 1366 for the College Close-Up.

Grinnell College

Grinnell, Iowa

http://www.grinnell.edu/

- **Independent** 4-year, founded 1846
- **Small-town** 120-acre campus
- **Endowment** $1.8 billion
- **Coed** 1,699 undergraduate students, 98% full-time, 55% women, 45% men
- **Very difficult** entrance level, 20% of applicants were admitted

UNDERGRAD STUDENTS

1,658 full-time, 41 part-time. Students come from 49 states and territories; 47 other countries; 90% are from out of state; 6% Black or African American, non-Hispanic/Latino; 7% Hispanic/Latino; 8% Asian, non-Hispanic/Latino; 0.1% American Indian or Alaska Native, non-Hispanic/Latino; 5% Two or more races, non-Hispanic/Latino; 5% Race/ethnicity unknown; 18% international; 0.4% transferred in; 82% live on campus.

Freshmen:

Admission: 7,370 applied, 1,488 admitted, 407 enrolled. ***Test scores:*** SAT critical reading scores over 500: 99%; SAT math scores over 500: 100%; ACT scores over 18: 100%; SAT critical reading scores over 600: 90%; SAT math scores over 600: 94%; ACT scores over 24: 100%; SAT critical reading scores over 700: 49%; SAT math scores over 700: 68%; ACT scores over 30: 79%.

Retention: 93% of full-time freshmen returned.

FACULTY

Total: 197, 87% full-time, 93% with terminal degrees.

Student/faculty ratio: 9:1.

ACADEMICS

Calendar: semesters. *Degree:* bachelor's.

Special study options: accelerated degree program, advanced placement credit, double majors, independent study, internships, off-campus study, services for LD students, student-designed majors, study abroad.

Unusual degree programs: 3-2 engineering with Columbia University, California Institute of Technology, Rensselaer Polytechnic Institute, Washington University in St. Louis; architecture with Washington University in St. Louis, law at Columbia University.

Computers: 200 computers/terminals are available on campus for general student use. Students can access the following: campus intranet, computer help desk, free student e-mail accounts, online (class) grades, online (class) registration, online (class) schedules. Campuswide network is available. 100% of college-owned or -operated housing units are wired for high-speed Internet access. Wireless service is available via entire campus.

Library: Burling Library plus 2 others. *Books:* 488,334 (physical), 474,326 (digital/electronic); *Serial titles:* 6,491 (physical), 11,577 (digital/electronic); *Databases:* 346. Weekly public service hours: 109.

STUDENT LIFE

Housing options: on-campus residence required through sophomore year; coed, cooperative, special housing for students with disabilities. Campus housing is university owned. Freshman campus housing is guaranteed.

Activities and organizations: drama/theater group, student-run newspaper, radio station, choral group, Concerned Black Students, International Student Organization, Student Organization of Latinas/Latinos, Campus Democrats, Ultimate Frisbee.

Athletics Member NCAA. All Division III. ***Intercollegiate sports:*** baseball M, basketball M/W, cross-country running M/W, football M, golf M/W, soccer M/W, softball W, swimming and diving M/W, tennis M/W, track and field M/W, volleyball W. ***Intramural sports:*** archery M(c)/W(c), badminton M/W, baseball M(c)/W(c), basketball M/W, equestrian sports M(c)/W(c), fencing M(c)/W(c), rugby M(c)/W(c), sailing M(c)/W(c), soccer M/W, softball M/W, tennis M/W, ultimate Frisbee M(c)/W, volleyball M/W, water polo M/W.

Campus security: 24-hour emergency response devices and patrols, student patrols, late-night transport/escort service, controlled dormitory access.

Student services: health clinic, personal/psychological counseling.

COSTS & FINANCIAL AID

Costs (2017–18) ***Comprehensive fee:*** $62,864 includes full-time tuition ($50,014), mandatory fees ($450), and room and board ($12,400). Part-time tuition: $1563 per credit hour. ***College room only:*** $5856. Room and board charges vary according to board plan and housing facility. ***Payment plan:*** installment. ***Waivers:*** employees or children of employees.

Financial Aid Of all full-time matriculated undergraduates who enrolled in 2016, 1,218 applied for aid, 1,125 were judged to have need, 1,125 had their need fully met. 551 Federal Work-Study jobs (averaging $2032). 575 state and other part-time jobs (averaging $2149). In 2016, 305 non-need-based awards were made. ***Average percent of need met:*** 100. ***Average financial aid package:*** $45,717. ***Average need-based loan:*** $4078. ***Average need-based gift aid:*** $39,444. ***Average non-need-based aid:*** $17,026. ***Average indebtedness upon graduation:*** $18,780. ***Financial aid deadline:*** 1/15.

APPLYING

Standardized Tests *Required:* SAT or ACT (for admission).

Options: electronic application, early admission, early decision, deferred entrance.

Required: essay or personal statement, high school transcript, 3 letters of recommendation. ***Recommended:*** interview.

Application deadlines: 1/15 (freshmen), 4/1 (transfers).

Early decision deadline: 11/15 (for plan 1), 1/1 (for plan 2).

Notification: 4/1 (freshmen), 5/20 (transfers), 12/15 (early decision plan 1), 2/1 (early decision plan 2).

CONTACT

Ms. Sarah Fischer, Director of Admission, Grinnell College, 1103 Park Street, Grinnell, IA 50112. *Phone:* 641-269-3600. *Toll-free phone:* 800-247-0113. *Fax:* 641-269-4800. *E-mail:* askgrin@grinnell.edu.

Hamilton Technical College

Davenport, Iowa

http://www.hamiltontechcollege.edu/

CONTACT

Hamilton Technical College, 1011 East 53rd Street, Davenport, IA 52807-2653. *Phone:* 563-386-3570. *Toll-free phone:* 866-966-4825.

INSTE Bible College

Ankeny, Iowa

http://www.inste.edu/

CONTACT

Admissions, INSTE Bible College, 2302 SW 3rd Street, Ankeny, IA 50023. *Phone:* 515-289-9200. *Fax:* 515-289-9201. *E-mail:* inste@inste.edu.

Iowa State University of Science and Technology

Ames, Iowa

http://www.iastate.edu/

- **State-supported** university, founded 1858
- **Suburban** 1795-acre campus with easy access to Des Moines
- **Endowment** $760.5 million
- **Coed** 30,671 undergraduate students, 94% full-time, 43% women, 57% men
- **Moderately difficult** entrance level, 87% of applicants were admitted

UNDERGRAD STUDENTS

28,872 full-time, 1,799 part-time. Students come from 53 states and territories; 124 other countries; 31% are from out of state; 3% Black or African American, non-Hispanic/Latino; 5% Hispanic/Latino; 3% Asian, non-Hispanic/Latino; 0.1% Native Hawaiian or other Pacific Islander, non-Hispanic/Latino; 0.2% American Indian or Alaska Native, non-Hispanic/Latino; 2% Two or more races, non-Hispanic/Latino; 5% Race/ethnicity unknown; 7% international; 6% transferred in; 33% live on campus.

Freshmen:

Admission: 19,433 applied, 17,002 admitted, 6,325 enrolled. ***Average high school GPA:*** 3.6. ***Test scores:*** SAT critical reading scores over 500: 64%; SAT math scores over 500: 81%; ACT scores over 18: 98%; SAT critical reading scores over 600: 30%; SAT math scores over 600: 49%; ACT scores over 24: 65%; SAT critical reading scores over 700: 9%; SAT math scores over 700: 15%; ACT scores over 30: 16%.

Retention: 88% of full-time freshmen returned.

FACULTY

Total: 1,842, 84% full-time, 87% with terminal degrees.

Student/faculty ratio: 19:1.

ACADEMICS

Calendar: semesters. *Degrees:* bachelor's, master's, doctoral, post-master's, and postbachelor's certificates.

Special study options: academic remediation for entering students, accelerated degree program, adult/continuing education programs, advanced placement credit, cooperative education, distance learning, double majors, English as a second language, external degree program, freshman honors college, honors programs, independent study, internships, off-campus study, part-time degree program, services for LD students, student-designed majors, study abroad, summer session for credit. ***ROTC:*** Army (b), Navy (b), Air Force (b).

Unusual degree programs: 3-2 engineering with William Penn College.

Computers: 2,400 computers/terminals are available on campus for general student use. Students can access the following: campus intranet, computer help desk, free student e-mail accounts, online (class) grades, online (class) registration, online (class) schedules, network services. Campuswide network is available. 100% of college-owned or -operated housing units are wired for high-speed Internet access. Wireless service is available via entire campus.

Library: University Library plus 1 other. *Books:* 2.9 million (physical), 457,967 (digital/electronic); *Serial titles:* 14,057 (physical), 96,398

(digital/electronic); *Databases:* 301. Weekly public service hours: 113; students can reserve study rooms.

STUDENT LIFE

Housing options: coed, men-only, women-only, special housing for students with disabilities. Campus housing is university owned. Freshman applicants given priority for college housing.

Activities and organizations: drama/theater group, student-run newspaper, radio and television station, choral group, marching band, national fraternities, national sororities.

Athletics Member NCAA. All Division I except football (Division I-A). ***Intercollegiate sports:*** basketball M(s)/W(s), cross-country running M(s)/W(s), golf M(s)/W(s), gymnastics W(s), soccer W(s), softball W(s), swimming and diving M(s)/W(s), tennis W(s), track and field M(s)/W(s), volleyball W(s), wrestling M(s). ***Intramural sports:*** archery M(c)/W(c), badminton M(c)/W(c), basketball M/W, bowling M(c)/W(c), cross-country running M/W, equestrian sports M(c)/W(c), fencing M(c)/W(c), football M/W, golf M/W, ice hockey M(c)/W(c), lacrosse M(c)/W(c), racquetball M(c)/W(c), riflery M(c)/W(c), rugby M(c)/W(c), sailing M(c)/W(c), skiing (cross-country) M(c)/W(c), skiing (downhill) M(c)/W(c), soccer M(c)/W(c), softball M/W, squash M/W, swimming and diving M/W, table tennis M(c)/W(c), tennis M/W, volleyball M(c)/W(c), water polo M(c)/W(c), weight lifting M(c)/W(c), wrestling M/W.

Campus security: 24-hour emergency response devices and patrols, late-night transport/escort service, controlled dormitory access, crime prevention programs, threat assessment team, motor vehicle help van.

Student services: health clinic, personal/psychological counseling, women's center, legal services.

COSTS & FINANCIAL AID

Costs (2017–18) ***Tuition:*** state resident $7240 full-time, $296 per credit hour part-time; nonresident $21,076 full-time, $853 per credit hour part-time. Full-time tuition and fees vary according to class time, degree level, program, and student level. Part-time tuition and fees vary according to class time, course load, degree level, program, and student level. ***Required fees:*** $1180 full-time. ***Room and board:*** $8356; room only: $4429. Room and board charges vary according to board plan and housing facility. ***Payment plans:*** installment, deferred payment.

Financial Aid Of all full-time matriculated undergraduates who enrolled in 2015, 21,462 applied for aid, 14,055 were judged to have need, 4,842 had their need fully met. 1,579 Federal Work-Study jobs (averaging $915). 11,344 state and other part-time jobs (averaging $2026). In 2015, 9570 non-need-based awards were made. ***Average percent of need met:*** 79. ***Average financial aid package:*** $11,923. ***Average need-based loan:*** $4429. ***Average need-based gift aid:*** $7125. ***Average non-need-based aid:*** $3164. ***Average indebtedness upon graduation:*** $28,617.

APPLYING

Standardized Tests *Required:* SAT or ACT (for admission).

Options: electronic application, early admission, deferred entrance.

Application fee: $40.

Required: high school transcript, minimum Regent Admission Index (RAI) of245, high school course requirements.

Application deadlines: rolling (freshmen), rolling (transfers).

Notification: continuous (freshmen), continuous (transfers).

CONTACT

Mr. Phillip B. Caffrey, Associate Director for Freshman Admissions, Iowa State University of Science and Technology, 100 Enrollment Services Center, Ames, IA 50011-2010. *Phone:* 515-294-5836. *Toll-free phone:* 800-262-3810. *Fax:* 515-294-2592. *E-mail:* admissions@iastate.edu.

Iowa Wesleyan University

Mount Pleasant, Iowa

http://www.iw.edu/

- **Independent United Methodist** 4-year, founded 1842
- **Small-town** 60-acre campus
- **Endowment** $9.7 million
- **Coed** 473 undergraduate students, 82% full-time, 60% women, 40% men
- **Moderately difficult** entrance level, 41% of applicants were admitted

UNDERGRAD STUDENTS

386 full-time, 87 part-time. Students come from 26 states and territories; 2 other countries; 36% are from out of state; 6% Black or African American, non-Hispanic/Latino; 4% Hispanic/Latino; 1% Asian, non-Hispanic/Latino; 0.2% Native Hawaiian or other Pacific Islander, non-Hispanic/Latino; 0.8% American Indian or Alaska Native, non-Hispanic/Latino; 2% Two or more races, non-Hispanic/Latino; 21% Race/ethnicity unknown; 5% international; 11% transferred in; 68% live on campus.

Freshmen:

Admission: 1,696 applied, 700 admitted, 75 enrolled. ***Average high school GPA:*** 3.02. ***Test scores:*** SAT critical reading scores over 500: 40%; SAT math scores over 500: 80%; SAT writing scores over 500: 80%; ACT scores over 18: 87%; SAT critical reading scores over 600: 20%; SAT math scores over 600: 20%; ACT scores over 24: 27%.

Retention: 58% of full-time freshmen returned.

FACULTY

Total: 84, 43% full-time, 25% with terminal degrees.

Student/faculty ratio: 10:1.

ACADEMICS

Calendar: semesters. *Degree:* bachelor's.

Special study options: academic remediation for entering students, adult/continuing education programs, advanced placement credit, cooperative education, distance learning, double majors, honors programs, independent study, internships, off-campus study, part-time degree program, services for LD students, student-designed majors, study abroad, summer session for credit.

Unusual degree programs: 3-2 medical technology program with St. Luke's Hospital in Cedar Rapids, IA.

Computers: 97 computers/terminals are available on campus for general student use. Students can access the following: campus intranet, computer help desk, free student e-mail accounts, online (class) grades, online (class) schedules. Campuswide network is available. 100% of college-owned or -operated housing units are wired for high-speed Internet access. Wireless service is available via entire campus.

Library: Chadwick Library plus 1 other. *Books:* 93,754 (physical), 3,338 (digital/electronic); *Serial titles:* 2,169 (physical), 4,827 (digital/electronic); *Databases:* 32. Weekly public service hours: 80; students can reserve study rooms.

STUDENT LIFE

Housing options: on-campus residence required through senior year; coed, men-only, women-only. Campus housing is university owned. Freshman campus housing is guaranteed.

Activities and organizations: choral group, Student Union Board, Student Government Association, Behavioral Science Club, Student Nurses Association, Homecoming Committee.

Athletics Member NCAA. All Division III. ***Intercollegiate sports:*** baseball M, basketball M/W, football M, golf M/W, soccer M/W, softball W, volleyball W. ***Intramural sports:*** badminton M/W, basketball M/W, cheerleading M/W, football M/W, soccer M/W, softball M/W, table tennis M/W, tennis M/W, volleyball M/W, weight lifting M/W.

Campus security: late-night transport/escort service, controlled dormitory access, evening patrols by trained security personnel.

Student services: personal/psychological counseling.

COSTS & FINANCIAL AID

Costs (2016–17) ***Comprehensive fee:*** $39,200 includes full-time tuition ($28,146), mandatory fees ($1000), and room and board ($10,054). Part-time tuition: $710 per credit hour. Part-time tuition and fees vary according to class time, course load, and location. ***Required fees:*** $20 per credit hour part-time. ***College room only:*** $3826. Room and board charges vary according to housing facility. ***Payment plans:*** installment, deferred payment. ***Waivers:*** employees or children of employees.

Financial Aid Of all full-time matriculated undergraduates who enrolled in 2015, 381 applied for aid, 381 were judged to have need, 38 had their need fully met. 100 Federal Work-Study jobs (averaging $661). In 2015, 38 non-need-based awards were made. ***Average percent of need met:*** 66. ***Average financial aid package:*** $11,900. ***Average need-based loan:*** $3190. ***Average need-based gift aid:*** $2269. ***Average non-need-based aid:*** $21,500. ***Average indebtedness upon graduation:*** $33,152.

APPLYING
Standardized Tests *Required:* SAT or ACT (for admission).
Options: electronic application, early admission, deferred entrance.
Application fee: $20.
Required: high school transcript, minimum 2.5 GPA, minimum ACT score of 19 or SAT of 890. ***Required for some:*** essay or personal statement, 1 letter of recommendation, interview.
Application deadlines: 8/15 (freshmen), 8/15 (transfers).

CONTACT
Julie Duplessis, Director of Enrollment, Iowa Wesleyan University, 601 N Main Street, Mount Pleasant, IA 52641. *Phone:* 319-385-6208. *Toll-free phone:* 800-582-2383. *Fax:* 319-385-6240.
E-mail: julie.duplessis@iw.edu.

Kaplan University, Cedar Falls
Cedar Falls, Iowa
http://www.kaplanuniversity.edu/

CONTACT
Kaplan University, Cedar Falls, 7009 Nordic Drive, Cedar Falls, IA 50613. *Phone:* 319-277-0220. *Toll-free phone:* 800-987-7734.

Kaplan University, Cedar Rapids
Cedar Rapids, Iowa
http://www.kaplanuniversity.edu/

CONTACT
Kaplan University, Cedar Rapids, 3165 Edgewood Parkway, SW, Cedar Rapids, IA 52404. *Phone:* 319-363-0481. *Toll-free phone:* 800-987-7734.

Kaplan University, Davenport Campus
Davenport, Iowa
http://www.kaplanuniversity.edu/

CONTACT
Kaplan University, Davenport Campus, 1801 East Kimberly Road, Suite 1, Davenport, IA 52807. *Phone:* 563-355-3500. *Toll-free phone:* 800-987-7734.

Kaplan University, Des Moines
Urbandale, Iowa
http://www.kaplanuniversity.edu/

CONTACT
Kaplan University, Des Moines, 4655 121st Street, Urbandale, IA 50323. *Phone:* 515-727-2100. *Toll-free phone:* 800-987-7734.

Kaplan University, Mason City Campus
Mason City, Iowa
http://www.kaplanuniversity.edu/

CONTACT
Kaplan University, Mason City Campus, 2570 4th Street, SW, Mason City, IA 50401. *Phone:* 641-423-2530. *Toll-free phone:* 800-987-7734.

Loras College
Dubuque, Iowa
http://www.loras.edu/

- **Independent Roman Catholic** comprehensive, founded 1839
- **Urban** 64-acre campus
- **Endowment** $31.0 million
- **Coed** 1,463 undergraduate students, 96% full-time, 47% women, 53% men
- **Moderately difficult** entrance level, 92% of applicants were admitted

UNDERGRAD STUDENTS
1,400 full-time, 63 part-time. Students come from 26 states and territories; 9 other countries; 60% are from out of state; 2% Black or African American, non-Hispanic/Latino; 7% Hispanic/Latino; 0.9% Asian, non-Hispanic/Latino; 0.1% Native Hawaiian or other Pacific Islander, non-Hispanic/Latino; 2% Two or more races, non-Hispanic/Latino; 3% Race/ethnicity unknown; 1% international; 5% transferred in; 65% live on campus.

Freshmen:
Admission: 1,269 applied, 1,172 admitted, 328 enrolled. ***Average high school GPA:*** 3.38. ***Test scores:*** SAT critical reading scores over 500: 63%; SAT math scores over 500: 75%; ACT scores over 18: 97%; SAT critical reading scores over 600: 38%; SAT math scores over 600: 25%; ACT scores over 24: 40%; ACT scores over 30: 4%.
Retention: 79% of full-time freshmen returned.

FACULTY
Total: 150, 67% full-time, 78% with terminal degrees.
Student/faculty ratio: 13:1.

ACADEMICS
Calendar: semesters plus January term. *Degrees:* bachelor's, master's, and postbachelor's certificates.
Special study options: academic remediation for entering students, advanced placement credit, cooperative education, distance learning, double majors, honors programs, independent study, internships, off-campus study, part-time degree program, services for LD students, student-designed majors, study abroad, summer session for credit. ***ROTC:*** Army (c).
Unusual degree programs: 3-2 business administration; nursing with Allen College; athletic training.
Computers: 5 computers/terminals and 991 ports are available on campus for general student use. Students can access the following: campus intranet, computer help desk, free student e-mail accounts, online (class) grades, online (class) registration, online (class) schedules. Campuswide network is available. 100% of college-owned or -operated housing units are wired for high-speed Internet access. Wireless service is available via entire campus.
Library: Loras College Library. *Books:* 300,586 (physical), 141,947 (digital/electronic); *Serial titles:* 146 (physical), 52,290 (digital/electronic); *Databases:* 64. Weekly public service hours: 91; students can reserve study rooms.

STUDENT LIFE
Housing options: on-campus residence required through junior year; coed, men-only, women-only. Campus housing is university owned. Freshman campus housing is guaranteed.
Activities and organizations: drama/theater group, student-run newspaper, radio and television station, choral group, Dance Marathon, Campus Activities Board, DuBuddies, Sigma Phi Epsilon, Sport Business Club, national fraternities, national sororities.
Athletics Member NCAA. All Division III. ***Intercollegiate sports:*** baseball M, basketball M/W, cheerleading M(c)/W(c), cross-country running M/W, football M, golf M/W, ice hockey M(c)/W(c), lacrosse W, rugby M(c)/W(c), soccer M/W, softball W, swimming and diving M/W, tennis M/W, track and field M/W, ultimate Frisbee M(c)/W(c), volleyball M/W, wrestling M. ***Intramural sports:*** basketball M/W, racquetball M/W, soccer M/W, softball M/W, volleyball M/W.
Campus security: 24-hour emergency response devices and patrols, late-night transport/escort service, controlled dormitory access, online anonymous reporting system.
Student services: health clinic, personal/psychological counseling.

COSTS & FINANCIAL AID
Costs (2017–18) ***Comprehensive fee:*** $40,726 includes full-time tuition ($31,418), mandatory fees ($1468), and room and board ($7840). Full-time tuition and fees vary according to course load and degree level. Part-time tuition: $610 per credit. ***Required fees:*** $35 per credit part-time. ***College room only:*** $4000. Room and board charges vary according to board plan and housing facility. ***Payment plan:*** installment. ***Waivers:*** employees or children of employees.
Financial Aid Of all full-time matriculated undergraduates who enrolled in 2016, 1,190 applied for aid, 1,026 were judged to have need, 355 had

their need fully met. 507 Federal Work-Study jobs (averaging $2422). In 2016, 373 non-need-based awards were made. ***Average percent of need met:*** 89. ***Average financial aid package:*** $26,390. ***Average need-based loan:*** $5261. ***Average need-based gift aid:*** $20,037. ***Average non-need-based aid:*** $17,841. ***Average indebtedness upon graduation:*** $34,775.

APPLYING

Standardized Tests *Required:* SAT or ACT (for admission).

Options: electronic application, deferred entrance.

Required: high school transcript, minimum 2.5 GPA. ***Required for some:*** essay or personal statement, 1 letter of recommendation, interview. ***Recommended:*** essay or personal statement, 1 letter of recommendation.

Application deadlines: rolling (freshmen), rolling (transfers).

Notification: continuous (freshmen), continuous (transfers).

CONTACT

Loras College, 1450 Alta Vista Street, Dubuque, IA 52001. *Phone:* 800-245-6727. *Toll-free phone:* 800-245-6727. *Fax:* 563-588-7119. *E-mail:* admissions@loras.edu.

★ Luther College
Decorah, Iowa
http://www.luther.edu/

- **Independent** 4-year, founded 1861, affiliated with Evangelical Lutheran Church in America
- **Small-town** 200-acre campus
- **Endowment** $148.9 million
- **Coed** 2,169 undergraduate students, 98% full-time, 55% women, 45% men
- **Moderately difficult** entrance level, 68% of applicants were admitted

UNDERGRAD STUDENTS

2,131 full-time, 38 part-time. Students come from 38 states and territories; 69 other countries; 65% are from out of state; 2% Black or African American, non-Hispanic/Latino; 5% Hispanic/Latino; 2% Asian, non-Hispanic/Latino; 0.3% American Indian or Alaska Native, non-Hispanic/Latino; 2% Two or more races, non-Hispanic/Latino; 0.1% Race/ethnicity unknown; 7% international; 1% transferred in; 89% live on campus.

Freshmen:

Admission: 3,856 applied, 2,608 admitted, 520 enrolled. ***Average high school GPA:*** 3.66. ***Test scores:*** SAT critical reading scores over 500: 53%; SAT math scores over 500: 72%; SAT writing scores over 500: 45%; ACT scores over 18: 92%; SAT critical reading scores over 600: 20%; SAT math scores over 600: 33%; SAT writing scores over 600: 18%; ACT scores over 24: 66%; SAT critical reading scores over 700: 8%; SAT math scores over 700: 21%; SAT writing scores over 700: 8%; ACT scores over 30: 12%.

Retention: 84% of full-time freshmen returned.

FACULTY

Total: 221, 79% full-time, 83% with terminal degrees.

Student/faculty ratio: 11:1.

ACADEMICS

Calendar: 4-1-4. *Degree:* bachelor's.

Special study options: academic remediation for entering students, advanced placement credit, double majors, honors programs, independent study, internships, off-campus study, part-time degree program, services for LD students, student-designed majors, study abroad, summer session for credit.

Unusual degree programs: 3-2 engineering with Washington University in St. Louis; University of Minnesota, Twin Cities Campus.

Computers: 592 computers/terminals are available on campus for general student use. Students can access the following: campus intranet, computer help desk, free student e-mail accounts, online (class) grades, online (class) registration, online (class) schedules. Campuswide network is available. 100% of college-owned or -operated housing units are wired for high-speed Internet access. Wireless service is available via entire campus.

Library: Preus Library. *Books:* 341,855 (physical), 263,345 (digital/electronic); *Databases:* 106. Weekly public service hours: 104; students can reserve study rooms.

STUDENT LIFE
Housing options: on-campus residence required through senior year; coed, special housing for students with disabilities. Campus housing is university owned. Freshman campus housing is guaranteed.

Activities and organizations: drama/theater group, student-run newspaper, radio station, choral group, Alpha Phi Omega, college ministries, recreational sports, Student Activities Council, Diversity groups.

Athletics Member NCAA. All Division III. ***Intercollegiate sports:*** baseball M, basketball M/W, cross-country running M/W, football M, golf M/W, soccer M/W, softball W, swimming and diving M/W, tennis M/W, track and field M/W, ultimate Frisbee M(c)/W(c), volleyball W, wrestling M. ***Intramural sports:*** archery M/W, badminton M/W, basketball M/W, bowling M/W, football M/W, golf M/W, lacrosse W(c), racquetball M/W, rugby M(c)/W(c), soccer M/W, softball M/W, table tennis M/W, tennis M/W, track and field M/W, ultimate Frisbee M(c)/W(c), volleyball M/W.

Campus security: 24-hour emergency response devices and patrols, late-night transport/escort service, controlled dormitory access.

Student services: health clinic, personal/psychological counseling, women's center.

COSTS & FINANCIAL AID
Costs (2017–18) ***Comprehensive fee:*** $49,990 includes full-time tuition ($40,710), mandatory fees ($310), and room and board ($8970). Full-time tuition and fees vary according to course load. Part-time tuition: $1454 per credit hour. Part-time tuition and fees vary according to course load. ***College room only:*** $4170. Room and board charges vary according to board plan and housing facility. ***Payment plan:*** installment. ***Waivers:*** employees or children of employees.

Financial Aid Of all full-time matriculated undergraduates who enrolled in 2016, 1,827 applied for aid, 1,619 were judged to have need, 618 had their need fully met. 832 Federal Work-Study jobs (averaging $2086). 989 state and other part-time jobs (averaging $2051). In 2016, 423 non-need-based awards were made. ***Average percent of need met:*** 88. ***Average financial aid package:*** $33,407. ***Average need-based loan:*** $5815. ***Average need-based gift aid:*** $23,960. ***Average non-need-based aid:*** $19,184. ***Average indebtedness upon graduation:*** $35,642.

APPLYING
Standardized Tests *Required:* SAT or ACT (for admission).

Options: electronic application, deferred entrance.

Required: essay or personal statement, high school transcript, 1 letter of recommendation. ***Recommended:*** interview.

Notification: continuous (freshmen), continuous (transfers).

CONTACT
Mr. Kirk Neubauer, Director of Recruiting Services, Luther College, 700 College Drive, Decorah, IA 52101. *Phone:* 563-387-1287. *Toll-free phone:* 800-458-8437. *Fax:* 563-387-2159. *E-mail:* neubauki@luther.edu.

See previous page for display ad and page 1404 for the College Close-Up.

Maharishi University of Management
Fairfield, Iowa
http://www.mum.edu/

- **Independent** university, founded 1971
- **Small-town** campus
- **Coed** 353 undergraduate students, 63% full-time, 50% women, 50% men
- **Moderately difficult** entrance level, 37% of applicants were admitted

UNDERGRAD STUDENTS
224 full-time, 129 part-time. 79% are from out of state; 7% Black or African American, non-Hispanic/Latino; 8% Hispanic/Latino; 3% Asian, non-Hispanic/Latino; 0.6% Native Hawaiian or other Pacific Islander, non-Hispanic/Latino; 0.6% American Indian or Alaska Native, non-Hispanic/Latino; 3% Two or more races, non-Hispanic/Latino; 38% international; 24% transferred in; 49% live on campus.

Freshmen:
Admission: 84 applied, 31 admitted, 21 enrolled. ***Average high school GPA:*** 3.14.
Retention: 91% of full-time freshmen returned.

FACULTY
Student/faculty ratio: 9:1.

ACADEMICS
Calendar: semesters. *Degrees:* certificates, bachelor's, master's, doctoral, post-master's, and postbachelor's certificates.

Special study options: adult/continuing education programs.

Computers: Students can access the following: campus intranet, computer help desk, free student e-mail accounts, online (class) grades, online (class) schedules. Campuswide network is available. 100% of college-owned or -operated housing units are wired for high-speed Internet access.

Library: Maharishi University of Management Library.

STUDENT LIFE
Housing options: on-campus residence required through senior year; men-only, women-only. Campus housing is university owned. Freshman campus housing is guaranteed.

Athletics ***Intercollegiate sports:*** soccer M(c)/W(c), ultimate Frisbee M(c)/W(c), volleyball M(c)/W(c). ***Intramural sports:*** archery M/W, badminton M/W, basketball M/W, football M/W, gymnastics M/W, rock climbing M/W, sailing M/W, soccer M/W, table tennis M/W, tennis M/W, ultimate Frisbee M/W, volleyball M/W.

Campus security: 24-hour emergency response devices and patrols, late-night transport/escort service, controlled dormitory access.

COSTS & FINANCIAL AID
Costs (2016–17) ***Comprehensive fee:*** $34,930 includes full-time tuition ($27,000), mandatory fees ($530), and room and board ($7400). Part-time tuition: $450 per unit. Part-time tuition and fees vary according to course load. ***Payment plan:*** installment. ***Waivers:*** employees or children of employees.

Financial Aid Of all full-time matriculated undergraduates who enrolled in 2006, 150 applied for aid, 148 were judged to have need, 32 had their need fully met. 120 Federal Work-Study jobs (averaging $1422). 7 state and other part-time jobs (averaging $2729). In 2006, 5 non-need-based awards were made. ***Average percent of need met:*** 89. ***Average financial aid package:*** $23,963. ***Average need-based loan:*** $8281. ***Average need-based gift aid:*** $14,082. ***Average non-need-based aid:*** $9300. ***Average indebtedness upon graduation:*** $22,691.

APPLYING
Standardized Tests *Required for some:* SAT or ACT (for admission).

Options: electronic application, early admission, deferred entrance.

Application fee: $25.

Required: essay or personal statement, high school transcript, minimum 2.5 GPA, 2 letters of recommendation. ***Recommended:*** interview.

CONTACT
Maharishi University of Management, Office of Admissions, Fairfield, IA 52557. *Phone:* 641-472-1110. *Toll-free phone:* 800-369-6480. *Fax:* 641-472-1179. *E-mail:* admissions@mum.edu.

Mercy College of Health Sciences
Des Moines, Iowa
http://www.mchs.edu/

- **Independent** 4-year, founded 1995, affiliated with Roman Catholic Church
- **Urban** 5-acre campus with easy access to Des Moines, IA
- **Coed** 771 undergraduate students, 61% full-time, 87% women, 13% men

UNDERGRAD STUDENTS
472 full-time, 299 part-time. Students come from 5 states and territories; 2% are from out of state; 7% Black or African American, non-Hispanic/Latino; 4% Hispanic/Latino; 3% Asian, non-Hispanic/Latino; 2% Two or more races, non-Hispanic/Latino.

Freshmen:
Test scores: ACT scores over 18: 90%; ACT scores over 24: 28%.
Retention: 100% of full-time freshmen returned.

FACULTY
Total: 92, 47% full-time, 21% with terminal degrees.
Student/faculty ratio: 10:1.

ACADEMICS
Calendar: semesters. *Degrees:* certificates, associate, and bachelor's.

Special study options: academic remediation for entering students, accelerated degree program, adult/continuing education programs, advanced placement credit, distance learning, English as a second language, independent study, off-campus study, part-time degree program, services for LD students, study abroad, summer session for credit.

Computers: 46 computers/terminals are available on campus for general student use. Students can access the following: campus intranet, computer help desk, free student e-mail accounts, online (class) grades, online (class) registration, online (class) schedules. Campuswide network is available. Wireless service is available via classrooms, computer centers, computer labs, libraries.

Library: Mercy College Library plus 1 other. Students can reserve study rooms.

STUDENT LIFE
Housing options: college housing not available.

Activities and organizations: student senate, Campus Ministry, Science Club, Mercy College Association of Nursing Students, Zeta Chi—At Large Chapter.

Campus security: 24-hour emergency response devices and patrols, late-night transport/escort service.

Student services: personal/psychological counseling.

COSTS
Costs (2016–17) ***Tuition:*** $16,920 full-time. Full-time tuition and fees vary according to program. Part-time tuition and fees vary according to course load. ***Payment plan:*** installment.

APPLYING
Standardized Tests *Recommended:* ACT (for admission).

Required: high school transcript, minimum 2.3 GPA.

CONTACT
Heather Gaumer, Director of Admissions, Mercy College of Health Sciences, 921 Sixth Avenue, Des Moines, IA 50309-1200. *Phone:* 515-643-6604. *Toll-free phone:* 800-637-2994. *Fax:* 515-643-6698.
E-mail: hgaumer@mercydesmoines.org.

Morningside College

Sioux City, Iowa

http://www.morningside.edu/

- **Independent** comprehensive, founded 1894, affiliated with United Methodist Church
- **Suburban** 69-acre campus with easy access to Omaha, NE
- **Endowment** $44.9 million
- **Coed** 1,321 undergraduate students, 98% full-time, 54% women, 46% men
- **Moderately difficult** entrance level, 57% of applicants were admitted

UNDERGRAD STUDENTS
1,295 full-time, 26 part-time. Students come from 30 states and territories; 16 other countries; 40% are from out of state; 2% Black or African American, non-Hispanic/Latino; 6% Hispanic/Latino; 1% Asian, non-Hispanic/Latino; 0.2% Native Hawaiian or other Pacific Islander, non-Hispanic/Latino; 0.6% American Indian or Alaska Native, non-Hispanic/Latino; 3% Two or more races, non-Hispanic/Latino; 4% Race/ethnicity unknown; 5% international; 4% transferred in; 60% live on campus.

Freshmen:
Admission: 4,561 applied, 2,597 admitted, 341 enrolled. ***Average high school GPA:*** 3.45. ***Test scores:*** ACT scores over 18: 93%; ACT scores over 24: 41%; ACT scores over 30: 9%.
Retention: 69% of full-time freshmen returned.

FACULTY
Total: 272, 32% full-time, 50% with terminal degrees.
Student/faculty ratio: 13:1.

ACADEMICS
Calendar: semesters. *Degrees:* bachelor's, master's, and postbachelor's certificates.

Special study options: academic remediation for entering students, adult/continuing education programs, advanced placement credit, distance learning, double majors, English as a second language, honors programs, independent study, internships, off-campus study, part-time degree program, services for LD students, student-designed majors, study abroad, summer session for credit. ***ROTC:*** Army (c).

Computers: 150 computers/terminals are available on campus for general student use. Students can access the following: campus intranet, computer help desk, free student e-mail accounts, online (class) grades, online (class) registration, online (class) schedules, academic and financial records. Campuswide network is available. 100% of college-owned or -operated housing units are wired for high-speed Internet access. Wireless service is available via entire campus.

Library: Hickman-Johnson-Furrow Learning Center. *Books:* 47,802 (physical), 285,794 (digital/electronic); *Serial titles:* 170 (physical); *Databases:* 34. Weekly public service hours: 93.

STUDENT LIFE
Housing options: on-campus residence required through junior year; coed. Campus housing is university owned. Freshman campus housing is guaranteed.

Activities and organizations: drama/theater group, student-run newspaper, radio and television station, choral group, marching band, Student Government/Activities Council, Student Ambassadors, Homecoming Committee, national fraternities, national sororities.

Athletics Member NCAA, NAIA. All NCAA Division II. ***Intercollegiate sports:*** baseball M(s), basketball M(s)/W(s), bowling M/W, cross-country running M(s)/W(s), football M(s), golf M(s)/W(s), soccer M(s)/W(s), softball W(s), swimming and diving M(s)/W(s), tennis M(s)/W(s), track and field M(s)/W(s), volleyball W(s), wrestling M(s). ***Intramural sports:*** basketball M/W, bowling M/W, ultimate Frisbee M/W, volleyball M/W.

Campus security: 24-hour emergency response devices and patrols, student patrols, late-night transport/escort service, controlled dormitory access.

Student services: health clinic, personal/psychological counseling, women's center.

COSTS & FINANCIAL AID
Costs (2016–17) ***Comprehensive fee:*** $37,684 includes full-time tuition ($27,620), mandatory fees ($1474), and room and board ($8590). Full-time tuition and fees vary according to program. Part-time tuition: $880 per credit hour. Part-time tuition and fees vary according to course load and program. ***College room only:*** $4390. Room and board charges vary according to housing facility. ***Payment plan:*** installment. ***Waivers:*** children of alumni, senior citizens, and employees or children of employees.

Financial Aid Of all full-time matriculated undergraduates who enrolled in 2016, 1,149 applied for aid, 1,032 were judged to have need, 381 had their need fully met. 526 Federal Work-Study jobs (averaging $1184). 251 state and other part-time jobs (averaging $2027). In 2016, 255 non-need-based awards were made. ***Average percent of need met:*** 78. ***Average financial aid package:*** $23,298. ***Average need-based loan:*** $4684. ***Average need-based gift aid:*** $6471. ***Average non-need-based aid:*** $14,978. ***Average indebtedness upon graduation:*** $36,233.

APPLYING
Standardized Tests *Required:* SAT or ACT (for admission).

Options: electronic application, deferred entrance.

Required: high school transcript, minimum ACT score of 20 or SAT of 1410 and either rank in top half of class or 2.5 GPA.
Recommended: interview.

Application deadlines: rolling (freshmen), rolling (transfers).

Notification: continuous (freshmen), continuous (transfers).

CONTACT
Mrs. Stephanie Peters, Director of Admissions, Morningside College, 1501 Morningside Avenue, Sioux City, IA 51106. *Phone:* 712-274-5111. *Toll-free phone:* 800-831-0806 Ext. 5111. *Fax:* 712-274-5101.
E-mail: mscadm@morningside.edu.

Mount Mercy University

Cedar Rapids, Iowa

http://www.mtmercy.edu/

- **Independent Roman Catholic** comprehensive, founded 1928
- **Suburban** 40-acre campus with easy access to Iowa City
- **Endowment** $24.2 million
- **Coed** 1,580 undergraduate students, 66% full-time, 69% women, 31% men
- **Moderately difficult** entrance level, 62% of applicants were admitted

UNDERGRAD STUDENTS
1,046 full-time, 534 part-time. Students come from 28 states and territories; 38 other countries; 10% are from out of state; 7% Black or African American, non-Hispanic/Latino; 2% Hispanic/Latino; 2% Asian, non-Hispanic/Latino; 0.1% Native Hawaiian or other Pacific Islander, non-Hispanic/Latino; 1% American Indian or Alaska Native, non-Hispanic/Latino; 2% Two or more races, non-Hispanic/Latino; 3% Race/ethnicity unknown; 4% international; 14% transferred in; 40% live on campus.

Freshmen:
Admission: 1,288 applied, 797 admitted, 241 enrolled. ***Average high school GPA:*** 3.4. ***Test scores:*** ACT scores over 18: 85%; ACT scores over 24: 27%; ACT scores over 30: 3%.
Retention: 72% of full-time freshmen returned.

FACULTY
Total: 168, 53% full-time, 46% with terminal degrees.
Student/faculty ratio: 14:1.

ACADEMICS
Calendar: 4-1-4. *Degrees:* bachelor's and master's.
Special study options: academic remediation for entering students, accelerated degree program, adult/continuing education programs, advanced placement credit, double majors, honors programs, independent study, internships, off-campus study, part-time degree program, services for LD students, study abroad, summer session for credit.
Computers: 120 computers/terminals and 200 ports are available on campus for general student use. Students can access the following: campus intranet, computer help desk, free student e-mail accounts, online (class) grades, online (class) registration, online (class) schedules. Campuswide network is available. 100% of college-owned or -operated housing units are wired for high-speed Internet access. Wireless service is available via entire campus.
Library: Busse Library. *Books:* 124,873 (physical), 197,040 (digital/electronic); *Serial titles:* 3,529 (physical). Students can reserve study rooms.

STUDENT LIFE
Housing options: on-campus residence required through sophomore year; coed, men-only, women-only. Campus housing is university owned. Freshman campus housing is guaranteed.
Activities and organizations: drama/theater group, student-run newspaper, choral group, Student Ambassadors, Mount Mercy University Association of Nursing Students, Cheerleaders, Best Buddies, Student Government Association.
Athletics Member NCAA, NAIA. All NCAA Division III. ***Intercollegiate sports:*** baseball M(s), basketball M(s)/W(s), bowling M/W, cheerleading M/W, cross-country running M(s)/W(s), golf M(s)/W(s), soccer M(s)/W(s), softball W(s), track and field M(s)/W(s), volleyball M/W(s). ***Intramural sports:*** baseball M, basketball M/W, bowling M/W, cheerleading W, football M/W, racquetball M/W, tennis M/W, volleyball M/W, weight lifting M/W.
Campus security: 24-hour emergency response devices and patrols, student patrols, late-night transport/escort service, controlled dormitory access, Department of Public Safety operational 24-hours a day, 7 days a week.
Student services: health clinic, personal/psychological counseling.

COSTS & FINANCIAL AID
Costs (2017–18) ***Comprehensive fee:*** $39,748 includes full-time tuition ($30,382), mandatory fees ($200), and room and board ($9166). Full-time tuition and fees vary according to course load and degree level. Part-time tuition: $920 per credit hour. Part-time tuition and fees vary according to course load and degree level. ***Required fees:*** $200 per year part-time. ***Room and board:*** Room and board charges vary according to board plan and housing facility. ***Payment plan:*** installment. ***Waivers:*** employees or children of employees.
Financial Aid Of all full-time matriculated undergraduates who enrolled in 2016, 955 applied for aid, 878 were judged to have need, 176 had their need fully met. 254 Federal Work-Study jobs (averaging $1552). 419 state and other part-time jobs (averaging $915). In 2016, 176 non-need-based awards were made. ***Average percent of need met:*** 74. ***Average financial aid package:*** $23,169. ***Average need-based loan:*** $3852. ***Average need-based gift aid:*** $19,697. ***Average non-need-based aid:*** $13,254. ***Average indebtedness upon graduation:*** $26,603.

APPLYING
Standardized Tests *Required:* SAT or ACT (for admission).
Options: electronic application, deferred entrance.
Required: high school transcript, minimum 2.5 GPA. ***Required for some:*** 1 letter of recommendation.
Application deadlines: 8/15 (freshmen), 8/15 (transfers).
Notification: continuous (freshmen), continuous (transfers).

CONTACT
Dr. Teresa Crumley, Dean of Admission, Mount Mercy University, 1330 Elmhurst Drive, NE, Cedar Rapids, IA 52402. *Phone:* 319-368-6460. *Toll-free phone:* 800-248-4504. *Fax:* 319-363-5270.
E-mail: tcrumley@mtmercy.edu.

Northwestern College

Orange City, Iowa

http://www.nwciowa.edu/

- **Independent** comprehensive, founded 1882, affiliated with Reformed Church in America
- **Small-town** 100-acre campus
- **Endowment** $44.2 million
- **Coed** 1,099 undergraduate students, 95% full-time, 56% women, 44% men
- **Moderately difficult** entrance level, 66% of applicants were admitted

UNDERGRAD STUDENTS
1,045 full-time, 54 part-time. Students come from 31 states and territories; 24 other countries; 40% are from out of state; 2% Black or African American, non-Hispanic/Latino; 5% Hispanic/Latino; 0.8% Asian, non-Hispanic/Latino; 0.1% American Indian or Alaska Native, non-Hispanic/Latino; 2% Two or more races, non-Hispanic/Latino; 5% Race/ethnicity unknown; 4% international; 5% transferred in; 89% live on campus.

Freshmen:
Admission: 2,199 applied, 1,441 admitted, 282 enrolled. ***Average high school GPA:*** 3.58. ***Test scores:*** SAT critical reading scores over 500: 53%; SAT math scores over 500: 68%; SAT writing scores over 500: 44%; ACT scores over 18: 96%; SAT critical reading scores over 600: 18%; SAT math scores over 600: 33%; SAT writing scores over 600: 11%; ACT scores over 24: 56%; SAT critical reading scores over 700: 11%; SAT math scores over 700: 9%; SAT writing scores over 700: 11%; ACT scores over 30: 16%.
Retention: 82% of full-time freshmen returned.

FACULTY
Total: 141, 58% full-time.
Student/faculty ratio: 11:1.

ACADEMICS
Calendar: semesters. *Degrees:* bachelor's, master's, and postbachelor's certificates.
Special study options: academic remediation for entering students, advanced placement credit, cooperative education, distance learning, double majors, English as a second language, honors programs, independent study, internships, off-campus study, services for LD students, student-designed majors, study abroad, summer session for credit.
Unusual degree programs: 3-2 engineering with Washington University in St. Louis.

Computers: 250 computers/terminals are available on campus for general student use. Students can access the following: campus intranet, computer help desk, free student e-mail accounts, online (class) grades, online (class) registration, online (class) schedules, online degree audits. Campuswide network is available. 100% of college-owned or -operated housing units are wired for high-speed Internet access. Wireless service is available via entire campus.

Library: DeWitt Learning Commons plus 1 other. *Books:* 80,887 (physical), 151,137 (digital/electronic); *Serial titles:* 2,286 (physical), 80,593 (digital/electronic); *Databases:* 65. Weekly public service hours: 100; students can reserve study rooms.

STUDENT LIFE

Housing options: on-campus residence required through senior year; men-only, women-only, special housing for students with disabilities. Campus housing is university owned. Freshman campus housing is guaranteed.

Activities and organizations: drama/theater group, student-run newspaper, choral group, Drama Ministries Ensemble, Acappella Choir, Discipleship Groups, Fellowship of Christian Athletes, International Club.

Athletics Member NAIA. ***Intercollegiate sports:*** baseball M(s), basketball M(s)/W(s), cheerleading M(s)/W(s), cross-country running M(s)/W(s), football M(s), golf M(s)/W(s), lacrosse M(c)/W(c), soccer M(s)/W(s), softball W(s), tennis W(s), track and field M(s)/W(s), volleyball W(s), wrestling M(s). ***Intramural sports:*** badminton M/W, basketball M/W, bowling M/W, football M/W, golf M/W, racquetball M/W, soccer M/W, softball M/W, table tennis M/W, tennis M/W, ultimate Frisbee M/W, volleyball M/W.

Campus security: 24-hour emergency response devices, controlled dormitory access.

Student services: health clinic, personal/psychological counseling.

COSTS & FINANCIAL AID

Costs (2017–18) ***Comprehensive fee:*** $39,300 includes full-time tuition ($30,000), mandatory fees ($300), and room and board ($9000). Part-time tuition: $650 per credit hour. Part-time tuition and fees vary according to course load. ***Required fees:*** $75 per term part-time. ***Room and board:*** Room and board charges vary according to board plan and housing facility. ***Payment plans:*** tuition prepayment, installment. ***Waivers:*** employees or children of employees.

Financial Aid Of all full-time matriculated undergraduates who enrolled in 2015, 916 applied for aid, 767 were judged to have need, 453 had their need fully met. 217 Federal Work-Study jobs (averaging $987). 676 state and other part-time jobs (averaging $991). In 2015, 258 non-need-based awards were made. ***Average percent of need met:*** 92. ***Average financial aid package:*** $24,640. ***Average need-based loan:*** $5187. ***Average need-based gift aid:*** $7490. ***Average non-need-based aid:*** $10,699. ***Average indebtedness upon graduation:*** $28,501.

APPLYING

Standardized Tests *Required:* SAT or ACT (for admission).

Options: electronic application, early admission, deferred entrance.

Required: essay or personal statement, high school transcript, minimum 2.0 GPA. ***Recommended:*** minimum 2.5 GPA, 1 letter of recommendation, interview.

Application deadlines: rolling (freshmen), rolling (transfers).

Notification: continuous (freshmen), continuous (transfers).

CONTACT

Mrs. Jackie Davis, Director of Admissions, Northwestern College, 101 7th Street SW, Orange City, IA 51041. *Phone:* 712-737-7114. *Toll-free phone:* 800-747-4757. *Fax:* 712-707-7164. *E-mail:* admissions@nwciowa.edu.

Palmer College of Chiropractic

Davenport, Iowa

http://www.palmer.edu/

CONTACT

Ms. Lisa Gisel, Undergraduate Admissions Representative, Palmer College of Chiropractic, 1000 Brady Street, Davenport, IA 52803-5287. *Phone:* 563-884-5743. *Toll-free phone:* 800-722-3648. *Fax:* 563-884-5226. *E-mail:* lisa.gisel@palmer.edu.

St. Ambrose University

Davenport, Iowa

http://www.sau.edu/

- **Independent Roman Catholic** comprehensive, founded 1882
- **Urban** 118-acre campus
- **Endowment** $127.3 million
- **Coed** 2,398 undergraduate students, 91% full-time, 57% women, 43% men
- **Moderately difficult** entrance level, 64% of applicants were admitted

UNDERGRAD STUDENTS

2,188 full-time, 210 part-time. Students come from 27 states and territories; 18 other countries; 60% are from out of state; 4% Black or African American, non-Hispanic/Latino; 7% Hispanic/Latino; 1% Asian, non-Hispanic/Latino; 0.1% American Indian or Alaska Native, non-Hispanic/Latino; 2% Two or more races, non-Hispanic/Latino; 4% Race/ethnicity unknown; 3% international; 10% transferred in; 64% live on campus.

Freshmen:

Admission: 4,426 applied, 2,814 admitted, 454 enrolled. ***Average high school GPA:*** 3.32. ***Test scores:*** ACT scores over 18: 97%; ACT scores over 24: 38%; ACT scores over 30: 4%.

Retention: 77% of full-time freshmen returned.

FACULTY

Total: 317, 57% full-time, 62% with terminal degrees.

Student/faculty ratio: 9:1.

ACADEMICS

Calendar: 4-1-4. *Degrees:* bachelor's, master's, doctoral, post-master's, and postbachelor's certificates.

Special study options: academic remediation for entering students, accelerated degree program, adult/continuing education programs, advanced placement credit, cooperative education, distance learning, double majors, external degree program, independent study, internships, off-campus study, part-time degree program, services for LD students, student-designed majors, study abroad, summer session for credit.

Unusual degree programs: 3-2 social work; physical therapy, criminal justice.

Computers: 391 computers/terminals and 517 ports are available on campus for general student use. Students can access the following: campus intranet, computer help desk, free student e-mail accounts, online (class) registration, online (class) schedules, online course syllabi, online payments. Campuswide network is available. 100% of college-owned or -operated housing units are wired for high-speed Internet access. Wireless service is available via entire campus.

Library: SAU Library plus 1 other. *Books:* 172,923 (physical), 13,678 (digital/electronic); *Serial titles:* 502 (physical); *Databases:* 85. Weekly public service hours: 95; students can reserve study rooms.

STUDENT LIFE

Housing options: on-campus residence required through sophomore year; coed, women-only, special housing for students with disabilities. Campus housing is university owned. Freshman campus housing is guaranteed.

Activities and organizations: drama/theater group, student-run newspaper, radio and television station, choral group, marching band, Dance Marathon, Habitat for Humanity, Biology Club, Ambrosians for Peace and Justice, SPTO - Student Physical Therapy Organization.

Athletics Member NAIA. ***Intercollegiate sports:*** baseball M(s), basketball M(s)/W(s), bowling M(s)/W(s), cheerleading M(s)/W(s), cross-country running M(s)/W(s), football M(s), golf M(s)/W(s), lacrosse M(s), soccer M(s)/W(s), softball W(s), tennis M(s)/W(s), track and field M(s)/W(s), volleyball M(s)/W(s). ***Intramural sports:*** basketball M/W, bowling M/W, golf M/W, lacrosse W, racquetball M(c)/W(c), rugby M(c), sand volleyball M/W, softball M/W, swimming and diving M/W, volleyball M/W, wrestling M/W.

Campus security: 24-hour emergency response devices and patrols, student patrols, late-night transport/escort service, controlled dormitory access, off-duty officer available three nights/week for 4.5 hours per night, twelve cameras record various public areas on campus.

Student services: health clinic, personal/psychological counseling.

COSTS & FINANCIAL AID
Costs (2017–18) ***Comprehensive fee:*** $40,180 includes full-time tuition ($29,736), mandatory fees ($280), and room and board ($10,164). Full-time tuition and fees vary according to course load and location. Part-time tuition: $915 per credit hour. Part-time tuition and fees vary according to course load and location. ***Required fees:*** $280 per term part-time. ***Room and board:*** Room and board charges vary according to board plan and housing facility. ***Payment plans:*** installment, deferred payment. ***Waivers:*** employees or children of employees.

Financial Aid Of all full-time matriculated undergraduates who enrolled in 2016, 1,877 applied for aid, 1,607 were judged to have need, 380 had their need fully met. In 2016, 447 non-need-based awards were made. ***Average percent of need met:*** 70. ***Average financial aid package:*** $22,153. ***Average need-based loan:*** $4724. ***Average need-based gift aid:*** $16,958. ***Average non-need-based aid:*** $12,731. ***Average indebtedness upon graduation:*** $27,929.

APPLYING
Standardized Tests *Required:* SAT or ACT (for admission). *Recommended:* ACT (for admission).

Options: electronic application, deferred entrance.

Required: high school transcript, minimum 2.5 GPA. ***Required for some:*** interview. ***Recommended:*** interview.

Application deadlines: rolling (freshmen), rolling (transfers).

Notification: 10/1 (freshmen), continuous (transfers).

CONTACT
Ms. Allison Conklin, Associate Director of First Year Admissions, St. Ambrose University, 518 W Locust Street, Davenport, IA 52803. *Phone:* 563-333-6300. *Toll-free phone:* 800-383-2627. *Fax:* 563-333-6297. *E-mail:* conklinallisonj@sau.edu.

St. Luke's College
Sioux City, Iowa
http://stlukescollege.edu/

- **Independent** primarily 2-year, founded 1967, part of UnityPoint Health
- **Rural** 3-acre campus with easy access to Omaha
- **Endowment** $1.0 million
- **Coed** 259 undergraduate students, 46% full-time, 90% women, 10% men
- **Minimally difficult** entrance level, 67% of applicants were admitted

UNDERGRAD STUDENTS
118 full-time, 141 part-time. Students come from 13 states and territories; 1 other country; 35% are from out of state; 2% Black or African American, non-Hispanic/Latino; 9% Hispanic/Latino; 2% Asian, non-Hispanic/Latino; 0.4% American Indian or Alaska Native, non-Hispanic/Latino; 2% Race/ethnicity unknown; 8% transferred in.

Freshmen:
Admission: 15 applied, 10 admitted, 10 enrolled. ***Average high school GPA:*** 3.37.
Retention: 86% of full-time freshmen returned.

FACULTY
Total: 48, 52% full-time, 8% with terminal degrees.

Student/faculty ratio: 5:1.

ACADEMICS
Calendar: semesters. *Degrees:* certificates, associate, and bachelor's.

Special study options: advanced placement credit, distance learning, services for LD students, summer session for credit.

Computers: 9 computers/terminals are available on campus for general student use. Students can access the following: campus intranet, computer help desk, free student e-mail accounts, online (class) grades, online (class) registration, online (class) schedules. Campuswide network is available. Wireless service is available via entire campus.
Library: St. Luke's College. *Books:* 2,705 (physical); *Serial titles:* 63 (physical); *Databases:* 31. Weekly public service hours: 65.

STUDENT LIFE
Housing options: college housing not available.

Campus security: 24-hour emergency response devices and patrols, late-night transport/escort service.

Student services: health clinic, personal/psychological counseling.

COSTS & FINANCIAL AID
Costs (2017–18) ***Tuition:*** $18,900 full-time, $525 per credit part-time. Full-time tuition and fees vary according to course load, degree level, and program. Part-time tuition and fees vary according to course load, degree level, and program. ***Required fees:*** $1560 full-time. ***Payment plans:*** installment, deferred payment. ***Waivers:*** employees or children of employees.

Financial Aid Of all full-time matriculated undergraduates who enrolled in 2016, 78 applied for aid, 78 were judged to have need. 6 Federal Work-Study jobs (averaging $750). 1 state and other part-time job (averaging $500). ***Average percent of need met:*** 80. ***Average financial aid package:*** $14,964. ***Average need-based loan:*** $6000. ***Average need-based gift aid:*** $5123. ***Average indebtedness upon graduation:*** $18,665.

APPLYING
Standardized Tests *Required:* SAT or ACT (for admission).

Options: electronic application.

Application fee: $50.

Required: essay or personal statement, high school transcript, minimum 2.5 GPA, interview.

Notification: continuous (transfers).

CONTACT
Ms. Sherry McCarthy, Admissions Coordinator, St. Luke's College, 2720 Stone Park Boulevard, Sioux City, IA 51104. *Phone:* 712-279-3149. *Toll-free phone:* 800-352-4660 Ext. 3149. *Fax:* 712-233-8017. *E-mail:* sherry.mccarthy@stlukescollege.edu.

Shiloh University
Kalona, Iowa
http://www.shilohuniversity.edu/

- **Independent** comprehensive, founded 2007
- **Small-town** 200-acre campus
- **Coed** 23 undergraduate students, 4% full-time, 43% women, 57% men
- **Noncompetitive** entrance level

UNDERGRAD STUDENTS
1 full-time, 22 part-time. Students come from 4 states and territories; 1 other country; 61% are from out of state; 7% Native Hawaiian or other Pacific Islander, non-Hispanic/Latino; 7% international; 343% transferred in.

FACULTY
Total: 37, 14% full-time, 43% with terminal degrees.

Student/faculty ratio: 1:1.

ACADEMICS
Degrees: certificates, associate, bachelor's, master's, doctoral, and postbachelor's certificates.

Special study options: distance learning, off-campus study, part-time degree program, services for LD students, summer session for credit.
Library: University e-Library. *Databases:* 2.

COSTS
Costs (2017–18) ***Tuition:*** $3600 full-time, $150 per credit hour part-time. Full-time tuition and fees vary according to course load. Part-time tuition and fees vary according to course load. ***Required fees:*** $10 full-time, $10 per year part-time. ***Payment plan:*** installment.

APPLYING
Options: electronic application, early admission, deferred entrance.

Required: essay or personal statement, high school transcript, minimum 2.0 GPA.

Application deadlines: 7/5 (freshmen), 7/5 (transfers).

Notification: 7/19 (freshmen), 7/19 (transfers).

CONTACT
Mr. Andrew R. Thompson, Admissions Coordinator, Shiloh University, 100 Shiloh Drive, Kalona, IA 52247. *Phone:* 319-656-2447. *Fax:* 319-656-2448. *E-mail:* admissions@shilohuniversity.edu.

★ Simpson College

Indianola, Iowa

http://www.simpson.edu/

- **Independent United Methodist** comprehensive, founded 1860
- **Suburban** 85-acre campus with easy access to Des Moines
- **Endowment** $79.8 million
- **Coed** 1,543 undergraduate students, 89% full-time, 56% women, 44% men
- **Moderately difficult** entrance level, 85% of applicants were admitted

UNDERGRAD STUDENTS

1,379 full-time, 164 part-time. Students come from 28 states and territories; 5 other countries; 18% are from out of state; 2% Black or African American, non-Hispanic/Latino; 4% Hispanic/Latino; 1% Asian, non-Hispanic/Latino; 0.2% Native Hawaiian or other Pacific Islander, non-Hispanic/Latino; 0.1% American Indian or Alaska Native, non-Hispanic/Latino; 2% Two or more races, non-Hispanic/Latino; 4% Race/ethnicity unknown; 0.3% international; 5% transferred in; 86% live on campus.

Freshmen:

Admission: 1,265 applied, 1,081 admitted, 348 enrolled. ***Test scores:*** ACT scores over 18: 98%; ACT scores over 24: 57%; ACT scores over 30: 12%.

Retention: 77% of full-time freshmen returned.

FACULTY

Total: 195, 54% full-time, 54% with terminal degrees.

Student/faculty ratio: 11:1.

ACADEMICS

Calendar: 4-4-1. *Degrees:* bachelor's, master's, and postbachelor's certificates.

Special study options: accelerated degree program, adult/continuing education programs, advanced placement credit, cooperative education, double majors, independent study, internships, off-campus study, part-time degree program, services for LD students, student-designed majors, study abroad, summer session for credit.

Unusual degree programs: 3-2 engineering with Washington University in St. Louis, Iowa State University, University of Minnesota; nursing with Allen College.

Computers: 425 computers/terminals are available on campus for general student use. Students can access the following: campus intranet, computer help desk, free student e-mail accounts, online (class) grades, online (class) registration, online (class) schedules. Campuswide network is available. 100% of college-owned or -operated housing units are wired for high-speed Internet access. Wireless service is available via entire campus.

Library: Dunn Library. *Books:* 126,173 (physical), 147,925 (digital/electronic); *Serial titles:* 243 (physical), 242,512 (digital/electronic); *Databases:* 62. Weekly public service hours: 95.

STUDENT LIFE

Housing options: on-campus residence required through junior year; coed, men-only, women-only. Campus housing is university owned. Freshman campus housing is guaranteed.

Activities and organizations: drama/theater group, student-run newspaper, radio station, choral group, Religious Life Community, Campus Activities Board, Student Government Association, Residence Hall Association, intramurals, national fraternities, national sororities.

Athletics Member NCAA. All Division III. ***Intercollegiate sports:*** baseball M, basketball M/W, cheerleading M/W, cross-country running M/W, football M, golf M/W, soccer M/W, softball W, swimming and diving M/W, tennis M/W, track and field M/W, volleyball W, wrestling M. ***Intramural sports:*** badminton M/W, basketball M/W, bowling M/W, football M/W, golf M/W, racquetball M/W, rugby M(c)/W(c), soccer M/W, softball M/W, swimming and diving M/W, table tennis M/W, tennis M/W, ultimate Frisbee M/W, volleyball M/W.

Campus security: 24-hour emergency response devices and patrols, student patrols, late-night transport/escort service, controlled dormitory access, SAFE (Simpson Alert for Emergencies) provides phone calls in case of campus security/weather emergencies.

Student services: health clinic, personal/psychological counseling, women's center.

COSTS & FINANCIAL AID

Costs (2017–18) ***One-time required fee:*** $200. ***Comprehensive fee:*** $45,626 includes full-time tuition ($36,969), mandatory fees ($694), and room and board ($7963). Full-time tuition and fees vary according to class time, course load, degree level, and program. Part-time tuition: $415 per credit hour. Part-time tuition and fees vary according to class time, course load, degree level, and program. ***Required fees:*** $6 per credit hour part-time. ***College room only:*** $3860. Room and board charges vary according to board plan and housing facility. ***Payment plan:*** installment. ***Waivers:*** children of alumni, senior citizens, and employees or children of employees.

Financial Aid Of all full-time matriculated undergraduates who enrolled in 2016, 1,371 applied for aid, 1,126 were judged to have need, 257 had their need fully met. 335 Federal Work-Study jobs (averaging $1158). 451 state and other part-time jobs (averaging $1545). In 2016, 217 non-need-based awards were made. ***Average percent of need met:*** 79. ***Average financial aid package:*** $27,950. ***Average need-based loan:*** $4981. ***Average need-based gift aid:*** $22,580. ***Average non-need-based aid:*** $20,338. ***Average indebtedness upon graduation:*** $37,228.

APPLYING

Standardized Tests *Required:* SAT or ACT (for admission).

Options: electronic application, deferred entrance.

Required: high school transcript, guidance counselor recommendation form. ***Recommended:*** minimum 3.0 GPA, interview.

Application deadlines: 8/15 (freshmen), 8/15 (transfers).

Notification: continuous (freshmen), continuous (transfers).

CONTACT

Deborah Tierney, Vice President for Enrollment, Simpson College, 701 North C Street, Indianola, IA 50125. *Phone:* 515-961-1624. *Toll-free phone:* 800-362-2454. *Fax:* 515-961-1870. *E-mail:* admiss@simpson.edu.

See next page for display ad and page 1506 for the College Close-Up.

University of Dubuque

Dubuque, Iowa

http://www.dbq.edu/

- **Independent Presbyterian** comprehensive, founded 1852
- **Suburban** 77-acre campus
- **Endowment** $94.6 million
- **Coed** 1,924 undergraduate students, 87% full-time, 41% women, 59% men
- **Moderately difficult** entrance level, 76% of applicants were admitted

UNDERGRAD STUDENTS

1,679 full-time, 245 part-time. Students come from 44 states and territories; 26 other countries; 55% are from out of state; 10% Black or African American, non-Hispanic/Latino; 8% Hispanic/Latino; 2% Asian, non-Hispanic/Latino; 0.4% Native Hawaiian or other Pacific Islander, non-Hispanic/Latino; 0.5% American Indian or Alaska Native, non-Hispanic/Latino; 4% Two or more races, non-Hispanic/Latino; 0.6% Race/ethnicity unknown; 6% international; 8% transferred in; 43% live on campus.

Freshmen:

Admission: 1,662 applied, 1,258 admitted, 441 enrolled. ***Average high school GPA:*** 2.95. ***Test scores:*** SAT critical reading scores over 500: 26%; SAT math scores over 500: 20%; ACT scores over 18: 67%; SAT critical reading scores over 600: 8%; SAT math scores over 600: 4%; ACT scores over 24: 17%; SAT math scores over 700: 2%; ACT scores over 30: 1%.

Retention: 65% of full-time freshmen returned.

FACULTY

Total: 377, 25% full-time, 21% with terminal degrees.

Student/faculty ratio: 15:1.

ACADEMICS

Calendar: semesters. *Degrees:* associate, bachelor's, master's, and doctoral.

Special study options: academic remediation for entering students, accelerated degree program, adult/continuing education programs, advanced placement credit, distance learning, double majors, English as a second language, honors programs, independent study, internships, off-campus study, part-time degree program, services for LD students, student-designed majors, study abroad, summer session for credit. ***ROTC:*** Army (b).

Unusual degree programs: 3-2 business administration; communications, theology.

Computers: 196 computers/terminals and 942 ports are available on campus for general student use. Students can access the following: campus intranet, computer help desk, free student e-mail accounts, online (class) grades, online (class) registration, online (class) schedules. Campuswide network is available. 100% of college-owned or -operated housing units are wired for high-speed Internet access. Wireless service is available via entire campus.

Library: Charles C. Myers Library. *Books:* 155,943 (physical), 162,037 (digital/electronic); *Serial titles:* 212 (physical); *Databases:* 103. Weekly public service hours: 109.

STUDENT LIFE

Housing options: on-campus residence required through junior year; coed, special housing for students with disabilities. Campus housing is university owned. Freshman campus housing is guaranteed.

Activities and organizations: drama/theater group, student-run newspaper, choral group, Student Nurse's association, Greek Council, Concert Choir, Teacher Education Student Organization, Accounting Club.

Athletics Member NCAA. All Division III. ***Intercollegiate sports:*** baseball M, basketball M/W, cross-country running M/W, football M, golf M/W, soccer M/W, softball W, tennis M/W, track and field M/W, volleyball W, wrestling M. ***Intramural sports:*** badminton M/W, basketball M/W, bowling M/W, cheerleading M(c)/W(c), football M, golf M/W, racquetball M/W, soccer M/W, softball M/W, table tennis M/W, tennis M/W, ultimate Frisbee M/W, volleyball M/W.

Campus security: 24-hour patrols, late-night transport/escort service, controlled dormitory access.

Student services: health clinic, personal/psychological counseling.

COSTS & FINANCIAL AID

Costs (2016–17) ***One-time required fee:*** $100. ***Comprehensive fee:*** $38,050 includes full-time tuition ($27,400), mandatory fees ($1300), and room and board ($9350). Part-time tuition: $775 per credit hour. ***College room only:*** $4510. Room and board charges vary according to board plan and housing facility. ***Payment plan:*** installment. ***Waivers:*** employees or children of employees.

Financial Aid Of all full-time matriculated undergraduates who enrolled in 2016, 1,462 applied for aid, 1,364 were judged to have need, 232 had their need fully met. 180 Federal Work-Study jobs (averaging $2000). 175 state and other part-time jobs (averaging $2000). In 2016, 171 non-need-based awards were made. ***Average percent of need met:*** 59. ***Average financial aid package:*** $24,370. ***Average need-based loan:*** $7620. ***Average need-based gift aid:*** $17,301. ***Average non-need-based aid:*** $9455. ***Average indebtedness upon graduation:*** $26,674.

APPLYING

Standardized Tests *Required:* SAT or ACT (for admission).

Options: electronic application, deferred entrance.

Application fee: $25.

Required: essay or personal statement, high school transcript, 2 letters of recommendation. ***Recommended:*** interview.

Application deadlines: rolling (freshmen), rolling (transfers).

Notification: continuous (freshmen), continuous (transfers).

CONTACT

Mr. Bob Broshous, Director of Admissions, University of Dubuque, 2000 University Avenue, Dubuque, IA 52001-5099. *Phone:* 563-589-3199. *Toll-free phone:* 800-722-5583. *Fax:* 563-589-3690. *E-mail:* admissns@dbq.edu.

See next page for display ad and page 1554 for the College Close-Up.

The University of Iowa

Iowa City, Iowa

http://www.uiowa.edu/

CONTACT
Debra Miller, Sr. Associate Director, Undergraduate Evaluation, The University of Iowa, 108 Calvin Hall, Iowa City, IA 52242. *Phone:* 319-335-3847. *Toll-free phone:* 800-553-4692. *Fax:* 319-335-1535. *E-mail:* admissions@uiowa.edu.

University of Northern Iowa

Cedar Falls, Iowa

http://www.uni.edu/

- **State-supported** comprehensive, founded 1876, part of Board of Regents, State of Iowa
- **Small-town** 908-acre campus
- **Endowment** $115.0 million
- **Coed** 10,104 undergraduate students, 91% full-time, 57% women, 43% men
- **Moderately difficult** entrance level, 82% of applicants were admitted

UNDERGRAD STUDENTS
9,146 full-time, 958 part-time. Students come from 36 states and territories; 68 other countries; 6% are from out of state; 3% Black or African American, non-Hispanic/Latino; 4% Hispanic/Latino; 1% Asian, non-Hispanic/Latino; 0.1% Native Hawaiian or other Pacific Islander, non-Hispanic/Latino; 0.3% American Indian or Alaska Native, non-Hispanic/Latino; 2% Two or more races, non-Hispanic/Latino; 4% Race/ethnicity unknown; 4% international; 9% transferred in; 41% live on campus.

Freshmen:
Admission: 5,287 applied, 4,346 admitted, 2,000 enrolled. ***Average high school GPA:*** 3.49. ***Test scores:*** ACT scores over 18: 94%; ACT scores over 24: 42%; ACT scores over 30: 6%.

Retention: 86% of full-time freshmen returned.

FACULTY
Total: 755, 76% full-time, 68% with terminal degrees.

Student/faculty ratio: 17:1.

ACADEMICS
Calendar: semesters. *Degrees:* bachelor's, master's, and doctoral.

Special study options: academic remediation for entering students, accelerated degree program, adult/continuing education programs, advanced placement credit, cooperative education, distance learning, double majors, English as a second language, external degree program, honors programs, independent study, internships, off-campus study, part-time degree program, services for LD students, student-designed majors, study abroad, summer session for credit. ***ROTC:*** Army (b).

Unusual degree programs: 3-2 nursing with Allen College, University of Iowa; medical technology with University of Iowa Medical School, cytotechnology with Mayo School of Health-Related Sciences and Mercy College of Health Sciences, chiropractic with Logan College of Chiropractic and Palmer College of Chiropractic.

Computers: 1,900 computers/terminals are available on campus for general student use. Students can access the following: campus intranet, computer help desk, free student e-mail accounts, online (class) grades, online (class) registration, online (class) schedules, student account, degree audit, program of study. Campuswide network is available. 100% of college-owned or -operated housing units are wired for high-speed Internet access. Wireless service is available via entire campus.

Library: Rod Library. *Books:* 783,450 (physical), 372,113 (digital/electronic); *Serial titles:* 6,291 (physical), 16,652 (digital/electronic); *Databases:* 189. Weekly public service hours: 99; students can reserve study rooms.

STUDENT LIFE
Housing options: coed, special housing for students with disabilities. Campus housing is university owned. Freshman campus housing is guaranteed.

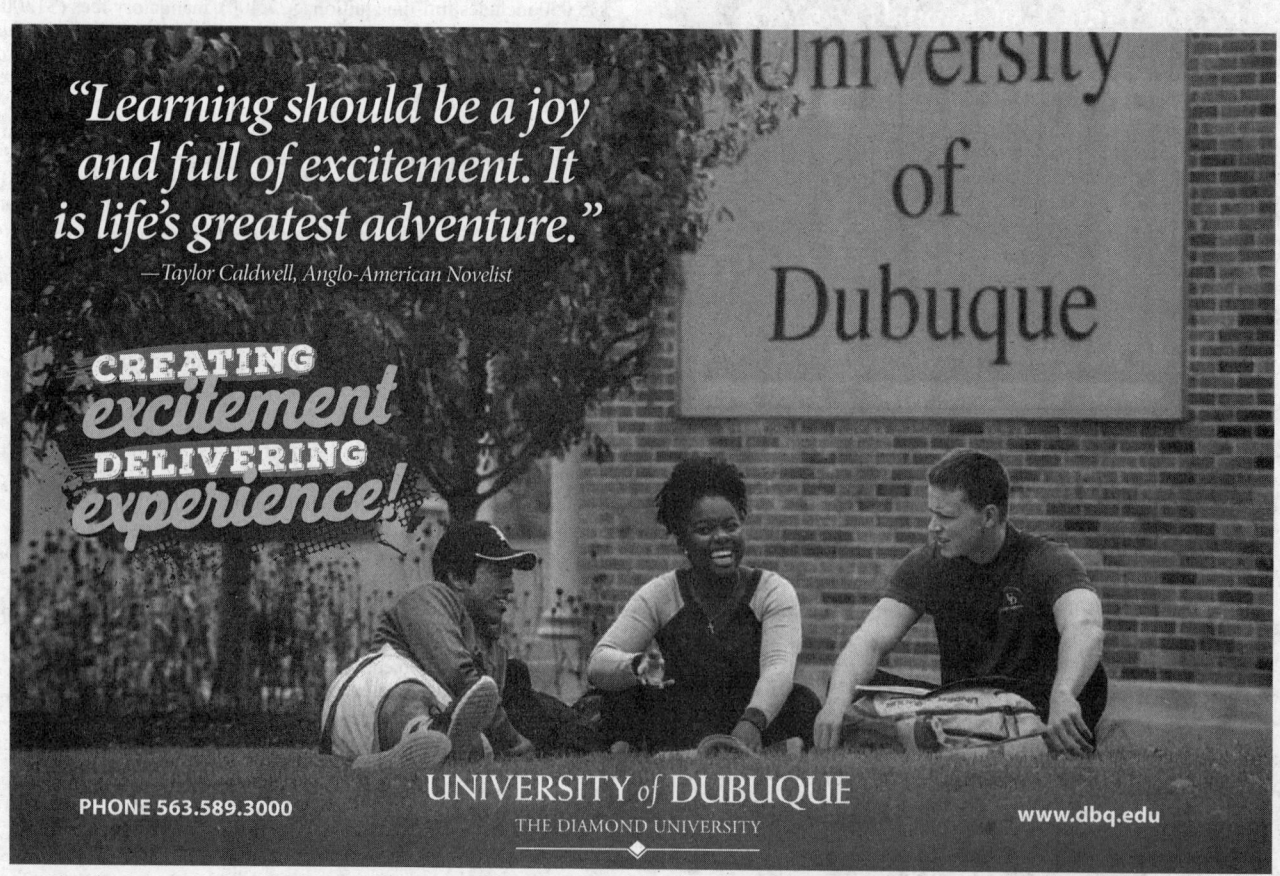

Activities and organizations: drama/theater group, student-run newspaper, radio station, choral group, marching band, Dance Marathon, Colleges Against Cancer/Relay for Life, Accounting Club, Phi Eta Sigma,

Students Today Alumni Tomorrow, national fraternities, national sororities.

Athletics Member NCAA. All Division I except football (Division I-AA). ***Intercollegiate sports:*** basketball M(s)/W(s), cross-country running M(s)/W(s), golf M(s)/W(s), soccer W(s), softball W(s), swimming and diving W(s), tennis W(s), track and field M(s)/W(s), volleyball W(s), wrestling M(s). ***Intramural sports:*** badminton M/W, baseball M(c), basketball M/W, bowling M(c)/W(c), cheerleading M/W, crew M(c)/W(c), cross-country running M(c)/W(c), football M(c), golf M(c)/W(c), ice hockey M(c), racquetball M(c)/W(c), rugby M(c)/W(c), skiing (downhill) M(c)/W(c), soccer M(c)/W(c), softball M(c)/W(c), swimming and diving M(c)/W(c), table tennis M/W, tennis M(c)/W(c), track and field M(c)/W(c), ultimate Frisbee M(c)/W(c), volleyball M/W(c).

Campus security: 24-hour emergency response devices and patrols, student patrols, late-night transport/escort service, controlled dormitory access, automatic external defibrillators, silent witness online, vehicle assistance.

Student services: health clinic, personal/psychological counseling.

COSTS & FINANCIAL AID

Costs (2017–18) ***Tuition:*** state resident $7240 full-time, $302 per credit hour part-time; nonresident $17,782 full-time, $741 per credit hour part-time. Full-time tuition and fees vary according to course load and program. Part-time tuition and fees vary according to course load and program. ***Required fees:*** $1243 full-time. ***Room and board:*** $8781; room only: $4473. Room and board charges vary according to board plan and housing facility. ***Payment plan:*** installment.

Financial Aid Of all full-time matriculated undergraduates who enrolled in 2015, 6,973 applied for aid, 5,431 were judged to have need, 805 had their need fully met. 452 Federal Work-Study jobs (averaging $1507). In 2015, 972 non-need-based awards were made. ***Average percent of need met:*** 65. ***Average financial aid package:*** $8363. ***Average need-based loan:*** $4343. ***Average need-based gift aid:*** $4714. ***Average non-need-based aid:*** $3304. ***Average indebtedness upon graduation:*** $24,325.

APPLYING

Standardized Tests *Required:* SAT or ACT (for admission). *Recommended:* SAT (for admission), ACT (for admission).

Options: electronic application, deferred entrance.

Application fee: $40.

Required: high school transcript, 4 years of English; 3 years each of math, science and social studies; 2 or more years of electives, which may include foreign language and fine arts. ***Required for some:*** interview.

Application deadlines: 8/15 (freshmen), 8/15 (transfers).

Notification: 9/1 (freshmen), 9/1 (transfers).

CONTACT

Amy S. Schipper, Associate Director, University of Northern Iowa, 002 Gilchrist, Cedar Falls, IA 50614. *Phone:* 319-273-2281. *Toll-free phone:* 800-772-2037. *Fax:* 319-273-2885. *E-mail:* admissions@uni.edu.

Upper Iowa University

Fayette, Iowa

http://www.uiu.edu/

- **Independent** comprehensive, founded 1857
- **Rural** 80-acre campus with easy access to Minneapolis-St. Paul, Chicago
- **Endowment** $11.5 million
- **Coed** 3,991 undergraduate students, 56% full-time, 62% women, 38% men
- **Moderately difficult** entrance level, 94% of applicants were admitted

UNDERGRAD STUDENTS

2,236 full-time, 1,755 part-time. Students come from 50 states and territories; 30 other countries; 60% are from out of state; 20% Black or African American, non-Hispanic/Latino; 6% Hispanic/Latino; 1% Asian, non-Hispanic/Latino; 0.2% Native Hawaiian or other Pacific Islander, non-Hispanic/Latino; 0.4% American Indian or Alaska Native, non-Hispanic/Latino; 2% Two or more races, non-Hispanic/Latino; 3% Race/ethnicity unknown; 2% international; 85% transferred in; 56% live on campus.

Freshmen:

Admission: 1,121 applied, 1,056 admitted, 214 enrolled. ***Average high school GPA:*** 3.06. ***Test scores:*** ACT scores over 18: 73%; ACT scores over 24: 25%.

Retention: 60% of full-time freshmen returned.

FACULTY

Total: 529, 14% full-time, 37% with terminal degrees.

Student/faculty ratio: 17:1.

ACADEMICS

Calendar: 6 8-week terms. *Degrees:* certificates, associate, bachelor's, and master's (enrollment figures include extended learning centers and online and distance education programs).

Special study options: academic remediation for entering students, accelerated degree program, adult/continuing education programs, advanced placement credit, cooperative education, distance learning, double majors, English as a second language, external degree program, freshman honors college, honors programs, independent study, internships, off-campus study, part-time degree program, services for LD students, student-designed majors, study abroad, summer session for credit.

Computers: 630 computers/terminals and 630 ports are available on campus for general student use. Students can access the following: campus intranet, computer help desk, free student e-mail accounts, online (class) grades, online (class) registration, online (class) schedules. Campuswide network is available. 100% of college-owned or -operated housing units are wired for high-speed Internet access. Wireless service is available via classrooms, computer centers, computer labs, dorm rooms, learning centers, libraries, student centers.

Library: Henderson Wilder Library. *Books:* 72,854 (physical), 53,173 (digital/electronic); *Serial titles:* 227 (physical).

STUDENT LIFE

Housing options: on-campus residence required through junior year; coed, men-only, women-only. Campus housing is university owned. Freshman campus housing is guaranteed.

Activities and organizations: drama/theater group, student-run newspaper, choral group, Student Athlete Advisory Committee, Peacock Alumni for Student Traditions, UIU Science and Environment Club, Student Government Association, Peacocks for Progress.

Athletics Member NCAA. All Division II. ***Intercollegiate sports:*** baseball M(s), basketball M(s)/W(s), cross-country running W(s), football M(s), golf M(s)/W(s), soccer M(s)/W(s), softball W(s), tennis W(s), track and field W(s), volleyball W(s), wrestling M(s). ***Intramural sports:*** badminton M/W, basketball M/W, bowling M/W, cheerleading M(c)/W(c), football M, golf M/W, soccer M/W, softball M/W, table tennis M/W, ultimate Frisbee M/W, volleyball M/W.

Campus security: late-night transport/escort service, controlled dormitory access.

Student services: health clinic, personal/psychological counseling.

COSTS & FINANCIAL AID

Costs (2017–18) ***Comprehensive fee:*** $37,970 includes full-time tuition ($28,850), mandatory fees ($750), and room and board ($8370). Full-time tuition and fees vary according to degree level, location, and program. ***Room and board:*** Room and board charges vary according to board plan, housing facility, and location. ***Payment plan:*** installment. ***Waivers:*** employees or children of employees.

Financial Aid Of all full-time matriculated undergraduates who enrolled in 2015, 1,831 applied for aid, 1,721 were judged to have need, 145 had their need fully met. 218 Federal Work-Study jobs (averaging $1975). ***Average percent of need met:*** 54. ***Average financial aid package:*** $14,262. ***Average need-based loan:*** $4963. ***Average need-based gift aid:*** $6285. ***Average indebtedness upon graduation:*** $34,123.

APPLYING

Standardized Tests *Required:* SAT or ACT (for admission).

Options: electronic application.

Required: high school transcript, minimum 2.0 GPA. ***Required for some:*** essay or personal statement, interview.

Application deadlines: rolling (freshmen), rolling (transfers).

CONTACT
Ms. Kathy Franken, VP of Enrollment Management, Upper Iowa University, 605 Washington Street, Parker Fox Hall, Fayette, IA 52142. *Phone:* 563-425-5868. *Toll-free phone:* 800-553-4150. *Fax:* 563-4255323. *E-mail:* frankenk@uiu.edu.

Vatterott College

Des Moines, Iowa

http://www.vatterott.edu/

CONTACT
Mr. Dana Smith, Co-Director, Vatterott College, 7000 Fleur Drive, Suite 290, Des Moines, IA 50321. *Phone:* 515-309-9000. *Toll-free phone:* 888-553-6627. *Fax:* 515-309-0366.

Waldorf University

Forest City, Iowa

http://www.waldorf.edu/

- **Independent Lutheran** comprehensive, founded 1903, part of Columbia Southern Education Group
- **Rural** 51-acre campus
- **Coed** 2,058 undergraduate students, 73% full-time, 36% women, 64% men
- **Moderately difficult** entrance level, 67% of applicants were admitted

UNDERGRAD STUDENTS
1,511 full-time, 547 part-time. Students come from 50 states and territories; 24 other countries; 83% are from out of state; 15% Black or African American, non-Hispanic/Latino; 8% Hispanic/Latino; 2% Asian, non-Hispanic/Latino; 0.3% Native Hawaiian or other Pacific Islander, non-Hispanic/Latino; 1% American Indian or Alaska Native, non-Hispanic/Latino; 1% Two or more races, non-Hispanic/Latino; 8% Race/ethnicity unknown; 3% international; 4% transferred in; 70% live on campus.

Freshmen:
Admission: 748 applied, 499 admitted, 154 enrolled. ***Average high school GPA:*** 3.17. ***Test scores:*** SAT critical reading scores over 500: 28%; SAT math scores over 500: 34%; ACT scores over 18: 85%; SAT critical reading scores over 600: 3%; SAT math scores over 600: 3%; ACT scores over 24: 19%; SAT critical reading scores over 700: 3%.

FACULTY
Total: 147, 31% full-time, 45% with terminal degrees.
Student/faculty ratio: 21:1.

ACADEMICS
Calendar: semesters. *Degrees:* certificates, associate, bachelor's, and master's.
Special study options: academic remediation for entering students, adult/continuing education programs, advanced placement credit, cooperative education, distance learning, double majors, freshman honors college, honors programs, independent study, internships, part-time degree program, services for LD students, summer session for credit.
Computers: 621 computers/terminals are available on campus for general student use. Students can access the following: campus intranet, computer help desk, free student e-mail accounts, online (class) grades, online (class) schedules. Campuswide network is available. 100% of college-owned or -operated housing units are wired for high-speed Internet access. Wireless service is available via entire campus.
Library: Luise V. Hanson Library. *Books:* 38,471 (physical), 152,040 (digital/electronic); *Databases:* 45. Weekly public service hours: 97; students can reserve study rooms.

STUDENT LIFE
Housing options: on-campus residence required through junior year; coed, men-only, women-only, cooperative, special housing for students with disabilities. Campus housing is university owned and leased by the school. Freshman campus housing is guaranteed.
Activities and organizations: drama/theater group, student-run newspaper, radio and television station, choral group, Student Activities Team, Education Club, Campus Ministry groups, intramurals, Radio/TV/Newspaper.
Athletics Member NAIA. ***Intercollegiate sports:*** baseball M(s), basketball M(s)/W(s), bowling M(s)/W(s), cheerleading M(s)/W(s), cross-country running M(s)/W(s), football M(s), golf M(s)/W(s), ice hockey M(c), soccer M(s)/W(s), softball W(s), volleyball W(s), wrestling M(s)/W(s). ***Intramural sports:*** basketball M/W, bowling M/W, football M, racquetball M/W, soccer M/W, softball M/W, table tennis M/W, tennis M/W, ultimate Frisbee M/W, volleyball M/W.
Campus security: 24-hour emergency response devices, student patrols, late-night transport/escort service, controlled dormitory access, evening and night patrols by trained security personnel, camera surveillance system.
Student services: health clinic, personal/psychological counseling.

COSTS & FINANCIAL AID
Costs (2016–17) ***Comprehensive fee:*** $28,506 includes full-time tuition ($20,160), mandatory fees ($1100), and room and board ($7246). Full-time tuition and fees vary according to class time, course load, and program. ***Room and board:*** Room and board charges vary according to board plan and housing facility. ***Payment plans:*** installment, deferred payment. ***Waivers:*** employees or children of employees.
Financial Aid Of all full-time matriculated undergraduates who enrolled in 2014, 947 applied for aid, 781 were judged to have need, 85 had their need fully met. In 2014, 115 non-need-based awards were made. ***Average percent of need met:*** 60. ***Average financial aid package:*** $13,082. ***Average need-based loan:*** $4488. ***Average need-based gift aid:*** $9802. ***Average non-need-based aid:*** $6833. ***Average indebtedness upon graduation:*** $33,494.

APPLYING
Standardized Tests *Required:* SAT or ACT (for admission).
Options: electronic application.
Required: high school transcript. ***Required for some:*** 1 letter of recommendation, interview. ***Recommended:*** minimum 2.0 GPA.
Application deadlines: rolling (freshmen), rolling (transfers).
Notification: continuous (freshmen), continuous (transfers).

CONTACT
Scott Pitcher, Director for Admissions, Waldorf University, 106 South 6th Street, Forest City, IA 50436. *Phone:* 641-585-8112. *Toll-free phone:* 800-292-1903. *Fax:* 641-585-8125. *E-mail:* admissions@waldorf.edu.

Wartburg College

Waverly, Iowa

http://www.wartburg.edu/

- **Independent Lutheran** 4-year, founded 1852
- **Small-town** 170-acre campus
- **Endowment** $64.2 million
- **Coed** 1,482 undergraduate students, 97% full-time, 52% women, 48% men
- **Moderately difficult** entrance level, 68% of applicants were admitted

UNDERGRAD STUDENTS
1,434 full-time, 48 part-time. Students come from 28 states and territories; 58 other countries; 29% are from out of state; 5% Black or African American, non-Hispanic/Latino; 4% Hispanic/Latino; 1% Asian, non-Hispanic/Latino; 0.1% Native Hawaiian or other Pacific Islander, non-Hispanic/Latino; 3% Two or more races, non-Hispanic/Latino; 3% Race/ethnicity unknown; 8% international; 2% transferred in; 85% live on campus.

Freshmen:
Admission: 4,028 applied, 2,749 admitted, 445 enrolled. ***Average high school GPA:*** 3.51. ***Test scores:*** SAT critical reading scores over 500: 37%; SAT math scores over 500: 53%; SAT writing scores over 500: 50%; ACT scores over 18: 94%; SAT critical reading scores over 600: 10%; SAT math scores over 600: 13%; SAT writing scores over 600: 10%; ACT scores over 24: 51%; SAT critical reading scores over 700: 3%; SAT math scores over 700: 3%; ACT scores over 30: 10%.
Retention: 80% of full-time freshmen returned.

FACULTY
Total: 159, 60% full-time, 58% with terminal degrees.
Student/faculty ratio: 11:1.

ACADEMICS
Calendar: 4-4-1. *Degree:* bachelor's.

Special study options: academic remediation for entering students, accelerated degree program, advanced placement credit, double majors, honors programs, independent study, internships, off-campus study, part-time degree program, services for LD students, student-designed majors, study abroad, summer session for credit.

Unusual degree programs: 3-2 business administration with Iowa State University; engineering; nursing with Allen College; pre-Seminary with Luther Seminary, clinical laboratory science with Mercy College of Health Sciences, medical laboratory sciences with St. Luke's Hospital, law with U of Iowa, museum studies with Western Illinois University.

Computers: 349 computers/terminals are available on campus for general student use. Students can access the following: campus intranet, computer help desk, free student e-mail accounts, online (class) grades, online (class) registration, online (class) schedules, billing, satellite. Campuswide network is available. 100% of college-owned or -operated housing units are wired for high-speed Internet access. Wireless service is available via entire campus.

Library: Vogel Library. *Books:* 146,576 (physical), 143,263 (digital/electronic); *Serial titles:* 1,237 (physical), 64,393 (digital/electronic); *Databases:* 79. Weekly public service hours: 95.

STUDENT LIFE
Housing options: on-campus residence required through senior year; coed, men-only, women-only, special housing for students with disabilities. Campus housing is university owned. Freshman campus housing is guaranteed.

Activities and organizations: drama/theater group, student-run newspaper, radio and television station, choral group, Entertainment To Knight, Student Senate, Campus Ministry, Symphonic Band, Wartburg Choir.

Athletics Member NCAA. All Division III. ***Intercollegiate sports:*** baseball M, basketball M/W, cross-country running M/W, football M, golf M/W, lacrosse W, soccer M/W, softball W, tennis M/W, track and field M/W, volleyball W, wrestling M. ***Intramural sports:*** badminton M/W, basketball M/W, bowling M/W, cheerleading W, golf M/W, racquetball M/W, rugby W(c), softball M/W, tennis M/W, ultimate Frisbee M/W, volleyball M/W.

Campus security: 24-hour emergency response devices and patrols, late-night transport/escort service, controlled dormitory access.

Student services: health clinic, personal/psychological counseling.

COSTS & FINANCIAL AID
Costs (2017–18) ***Comprehensive fee:*** $49,478 includes full-time tuition ($38,710), mandatory fees ($1020), and room and board ($9748). Part-time tuition: $2030 per course. Part-time tuition and fees vary according to course load. ***Required fees:*** $115 per year part-time. ***College room only:*** $4923. Room and board charges vary according to board plan and housing facility. ***Payment plan:*** installment. ***Waivers:*** employees or children of employees.

Financial Aid Of all full-time matriculated undergraduates who enrolled in 2015, 1,228 applied for aid, 1,076 were judged to have need, 214 had their need fully met. 550 Federal Work-Study jobs (averaging $1002). 656 state and other part-time jobs (averaging $1270). In 2015, 362 non-need-based awards were made. ***Average percent of need met:*** 81. ***Average financial aid package:*** $27,932. ***Average need-based loan:*** $5260. ***Average need-based gift aid:*** $23,267. ***Average non-need-based aid:*** $20,797. ***Average indebtedness upon graduation:*** $39,794.

APPLYING
Standardized Tests *Required:* SAT or ACT (for admission).

Options: electronic application, early action, deferred entrance.

Required: high school transcript, minimum 2.5 GPA. ***Recommended:*** letters of recommendation, secondary school report.

Application deadlines: rolling (freshmen), rolling (transfers), 12/1 (early action).

Notification: continuous (freshmen), continuous (transfers).

CONTACT
Tara Winter, Director of Student Recruitment, Wartburg College, 100 Wartburg Boulevard, PO Box 1003, Waverly, IA 50677-0903. *Phone:* 319-352-8475. *Toll-free phone:* 800-772-2085. *Fax:* 319-352-8579. *E-mail:* admissions@wartburg.edu.

William Penn University
Oskaloosa, Iowa
http://www.wmpenn.edu/

- **Independent** comprehensive, founded 1873, affiliated with Society of Friends
- **Rural** 60-acre campus with easy access to Des Moines
- **Endowment** $4.3 million
- **Coed** 1,449 undergraduate students, 82% full-time, 49% women, 51% men
- **Moderately difficult** entrance level, 59% of applicants were admitted

UNDERGRAD STUDENTS
1,183 full-time, 266 part-time. Students come from 40 states and territories; 26 other countries; 43% are from out of state; 19% Black or African American, non-Hispanic/Latino; 10% Hispanic/Latino; 1% Asian, non-Hispanic/Latino; 0.8% Native Hawaiian or other Pacific Islander, non-Hispanic/Latino; 0.8% American Indian or Alaska Native, non-Hispanic/Latino; 2% Two or more races, non-Hispanic/Latino; 3% Race/ethnicity unknown; 5% international; 12% transferred in; 43% live on campus.

Freshmen:
Admission: 1,096 applied, 643 admitted, 241 enrolled. ***Average high school GPA:*** 2.9. ***Test scores:*** ACT scores over 18: 60%; ACT scores over 24: 7%.

Retention: 55% of full-time freshmen returned.

FACULTY
Total: 177, 25% full-time, 13% with terminal degrees.

Student/faculty ratio: 16:1.

ACADEMICS
Calendar: semesters. *Degrees:* bachelor's and master's.

Special study options: academic remediation for entering students, adult/continuing education programs, advanced placement credit, cooperative education, distance learning, double majors, honors programs, independent study, internships, part-time degree program, services for LD students, study abroad, summer session for credit.

Unusual degree programs: 3-2 engineering with Iowa State University.

Computers: 200 computers/terminals and 665 ports are available on campus for general student use. Students can access the following: computer help desk, free student e-mail accounts, online (class) grades, online (class) schedules. Campuswide network is available. 100% of college-owned or -operated housing units are wired for high-speed Internet access. Wireless service is available via classrooms, computer centers, computer labs, dorm rooms, libraries, student centers.

Library: Wilcox Library plus 1 other. *Books:* 61,570 (physical), 170,000 (digital/electronic); *Serial titles:* 100 (physical), 47,581 (digital/electronic); *Databases:* 38. Weekly public service hours: 92; students can reserve study rooms.

STUDENT LIFE
Housing options: on-campus residence required through sophomore year; coed, men-only, women-only. Campus housing is university owned. Freshman campus housing is guaranteed.

Activities and organizations: drama/theater group, student-run newspaper, radio and television station, choral group, marching band, Greek Council, Belegarth, Education Club, Student Government Association, Computer Club.

Athletics Member NAIA. ***Intercollegiate sports:*** baseball M(s), basketball M(s)/W(s), bowling M(s)/W(s), cheerleading M(s)/W(s), cross-country running M(s)/W(s), football M(s), golf M(s)/W(s), soccer M(s)/W(s), softball W(s), track and field M(s)/W(s), volleyball W(s), wrestling M(s). ***Intramural sports:*** badminton M/W, basketball M/W, golf M/W, rugby M/W, sand volleyball M/W, soccer M/W, ultimate Frisbee M/W, volleyball M/W, weight lifting M/W.

Campus security: 24-hour emergency response devices and patrols, late-night transport/escort service, controlled dormitory access.

Student services: health clinic, personal/psychological counseling.

COSTS & FINANCIAL AID
Costs (2017–18) ***Comprehensive fee:*** $31,952 includes full-time tuition ($24,270), mandatory fees ($730), and room and board ($6952). Full-time tuition and fees vary according to class time, course load, degree level,

location, and program. Part-time tuition: $380 per credit hour. Part-time tuition and fees vary according to class time, course load, degree level, location, and program. ***Required fees:*** $19 per credit hour part-time. ***College room only:*** $3102. Room and board charges vary according to housing facility. ***Payment plan:*** installment. ***Waivers:*** senior citizens and employees or children of employees.

Financial Aid Of all full-time matriculated undergraduates who enrolled in 2005, 808 applied for aid, 768 were judged to have need, 238 had their need fully met. 511 Federal Work-Study jobs (averaging $1287). 1 state and other part-time job (averaging $1103). In 2005, 2 non-need-based awards were made. ***Average percent of need met:*** 82. ***Average financial aid package:*** $17,782. ***Average need-based loan:*** $4600. ***Average need-based gift aid:*** $11,300. ***Average non-need-based aid:*** $4500. ***Average indebtedness upon graduation:*** $22,169.

APPLYING

Standardized Tests *Required:* SAT or ACT (for admission).

Options: electronic application, deferred entrance.

Required: high school transcript, minimum 2.0 GPA. ***Required for some:*** essay or personal statement, letters of recommendation, interview.

Application deadlines: rolling (freshmen), rolling (transfers).

Notification: continuous (freshmen), continuous (transfers).

CONTACT

Ms. Kerra Strong, Vice President for Enrollment Management, William Penn University, 201 Trueblood Avenue, Oskaloosa, IA 52577-1799. *Phone:* 641-673-1012. *Fax:* 641-673-2113. *E-mail:* admissions@wmpenn.edu.

KANSAS

Baker University

Baldwin City, Kansas

http://www.bakeru.edu/

- **Independent United Methodist** comprehensive, founded 1858
- **Small-town** 26-acre campus with easy access to Kansas City
- **Endowment** $35.7 million
- **Coed** 1,144 undergraduate students, 74% full-time, 49% women, 51% men
- **Moderately difficult** entrance level, 78% of applicants were admitted

UNDERGRAD STUDENTS

848 full-time, 296 part-time. Students come from 28 states and territories; 15 other countries; 34% are from out of state; 11% Black or African American, non-Hispanic/Latino; 8% Hispanic/Latino; 0.3% Asian, non-Hispanic/Latino; 0.7% Native Hawaiian or other Pacific Islander, non-Hispanic/Latino; 2% American Indian or Alaska Native, non-Hispanic/Latino; 3% Two or more races, non-Hispanic/Latino; 3% Race/ethnicity unknown; 2% international; 4% transferred in; 80% live on campus.

Freshmen:

Admission: 899 applied, 699 admitted, 238 enrolled. ***Average high school GPA:*** 3.38. ***Test scores:*** ACT scores over 18: 92%; ACT scores over 24: 43%; ACT scores over 30: 6%.

Retention: 80% of full-time freshmen returned.

FACULTY

Total: 90, 63% full-time, 60% with terminal degrees.

Student/faculty ratio: 13:1.

ACADEMICS

Calendar: 4-1-4 semesters for nursing program. *Degrees:* bachelor's, master's, and doctoral (profile includes information primarily for undergraduate residential campus in Baldwin City, KS).

Special study options: advanced placement credit, double majors, honors programs, independent study, internships, services for LD students, student-designed majors, study abroad, summer session for credit. ***ROTC:*** Army (c), Air Force (c).

Unusual degree programs: 3-2 engineering with Washington University in St. Louis, University of Kansas, University of Missouri–Kansas City.

Computers: 140 computers/terminals are available on campus for general student use. Students can access the following: computer help desk, free student e-mail accounts, online (class) grades, online (class) registration, online (class) schedules. Campuswide network is available. 100% of college-owned or -operated housing units are wired for high-speed Internet access. Wireless service is available via entire campus.

Library: Baker University Library. *Books:* 89,076 (physical), 149,796 (digital/electronic); *Serial titles:* 1,564 (physical); *Databases:* 48. Study areas open 24 hours, 5-7 days a week; students can reserve study rooms.

STUDENT LIFE

Housing options: on-campus residence required through senior year; coed, men-only, women-only, special housing for students with disabilities. Campus housing is university owned. Freshman campus housing is guaranteed.

Activities and organizations: drama/theater group, student-run newspaper, radio and television station, choral group, Exercise Science Student Alliance, Baker University Speech Choir, Mungano, Student Senate, Student Activities Council, national fraternities, national sororities.

Athletics Member NAIA. ***Intercollegiate sports:*** baseball M(s), basketball M(s)/W(s), bowling W(s), cheerleading M(s)/W(s), cross-country running M(s)/W(s), football M(s), golf M(s)/W(s), soccer M(s)/W(s), softball W(s), tennis M(s)/W(s), track and field M(s)/W(s), volleyball W(s), wrestling M(s). ***Intramural sports:*** basketball M/W, football M/W, softball M/W, table tennis M/W, volleyball M/W.

Campus security: 24-hour emergency response devices and patrols, controlled dormitory access.

Student services: health clinic, personal/psychological counseling.

COSTS & FINANCIAL AID

Costs (2017–18) ***One-time required fee:*** $80. ***Comprehensive fee:*** $37,190 includes full-time tuition ($28,430), mandatory fees ($450), and room and board ($8310). Full-time tuition and fees vary according to course load, degree level, location, and program. Part-time tuition: $890 per credit hour. Part-time tuition and fees vary according to course load, degree level, location, and program. ***Required fees:*** $200 per year part-time. ***College room only:*** $3910. Room and board charges vary according to board plan and housing facility. ***Payment plan:*** installment. ***Waivers:*** senior citizens and employees or children of employees.

Financial Aid Of all full-time matriculated undergraduates who enrolled in 2008, 839 applied for aid, 713 were judged to have need, 268 had their need fully met. In 2008, 180 non-need-based awards were made. ***Average percent of need met:*** 84. ***Average financial aid package:*** $13,600. ***Average need-based loan:*** $5622. ***Average need-based gift aid:*** $6787. ***Average non-need-based aid:*** $9006. ***Average indebtedness upon graduation:*** $26,869.

APPLYING

Standardized Tests *Required:* SAT or ACT (for admission).

Options: electronic application, deferred entrance.

Required: high school transcript. ***Required for some:*** essay or personal statement, 1 letter of recommendation, interview.

Application deadlines: rolling (freshmen), rolling (transfers).

CONTACT

Mrs. Cheryl McCrary, Director of Enrollment Management, Baker University, PO Box 65, Baldwin City, KS 66006-0065. *Phone:* 785-594-8327. *Toll-free phone:* 800-873-4282. *Fax:* 785-594-8353. *E-mail:* admissions@bakeru.edu.

Barclay College

Haviland, Kansas

http://www.barclaycollege.edu/

- **Independent** comprehensive, founded 1917, affiliated with Society of Friends
- **Rural** 17-acre campus
- **Endowment** $1.4 million
- **Coed** 250 undergraduate students, 80% full-time, 48% women, 52% men
- **Minimally difficult** entrance level, 71% of applicants were admitted

UNDERGRAD STUDENTS

199 full-time, 51 part-time. Students come from 37 states and territories; 5 other countries; 62% are from out of state; 14% Black or African

American, non-Hispanic/Latino; 4% Hispanic/Latino; 0.4% Asian, non-Hispanic/Latino; 0.4% American Indian or Alaska Native, non-Hispanic/Latino; 4% Two or more races, non-Hispanic/Latino; 0.4% Race/ethnicity unknown; 2% international; 11% transferred in; 78% live on campus.

Freshmen:
Admission: 89 applied, 63 admitted, 52 enrolled. ***Test scores:*** SAT critical reading scores over 500: 32%; SAT math scores over 500: 67%; SAT writing scores over 500: 40%; ACT scores over 18: 71%; SAT critical reading scores over 600: 16%; SAT math scores over 600: 32%; ACT scores over 24: 21%; SAT math scores over 700: 16%.
Retention: 61% of full-time freshmen returned.

FACULTY
Total: 42, 60% full-time, 33% with terminal degrees.
Student/faculty ratio: 10:1.

ACADEMICS
Calendar: semesters. *Degrees:* certificates, associate, bachelor's, and master's.
Special study options: academic remediation for entering students, adult/continuing education programs, advanced placement credit, distance learning, double majors, external degree program, independent study, internships, off-campus study, part-time degree program.
Unusual degree programs: 3-2 nursing with Pratt Community College.
Computers: 28 computers/terminals are available on campus for general student use. Students can access the following: campus intranet, computer help desk, free student e-mail accounts, online (class) grades, online (class) registration, online (class) schedules. Campuswide network is available. 100% of college-owned or -operated housing units are wired for high-speed Internet access. Wireless service is available via entire campus.
Library: Worden Memorial Library. *Books:* 44,420 (physical), 23 (digital/electronic); *Serial titles:* 410 (physical), 4 (digital/electronic); *Databases:* 48. Weekly public service hours: 95.

STUDENT LIFE
Housing options: on-campus residence required through senior year; men-only, women-only. Campus housing is university owned. Freshman campus housing is guaranteed.
Activities and organizations: drama/theater group, choral group.
Athletics Member NCCAA. ***Intercollegiate sports:*** basketball M/W, cheerleading M/W, soccer M, tennis M/W, volleyball W. ***Intramural sports:*** basketball M/W, volleyball M/W.
Campus security: student patrols.
Student services: personal/psychological counseling.

COSTS & FINANCIAL AID
Costs (2016–17) ***Comprehensive fee:*** $24,390 includes full-time tuition ($12,500), mandatory fees ($3490), and room and board ($8400). Part-time tuition: $295 per credit hour. Part-time tuition and fees vary according to course load. ***Room and board:*** Room and board charges vary according to board plan and housing facility. ***Payment plan:*** installment. ***Waivers:*** employees or children of employees.
Financial Aid Of all full-time matriculated undergraduates who enrolled in 2014, 159 applied for aid, 159 were judged to have need, 7 had their need fully met. In 2014, 15 non-need-based awards were made. ***Average percent of need met:*** 89. ***Average financial aid package:*** $25,301. ***Average need-based loan:*** $2013. ***Average need-based gift aid:*** $10,854. ***Average non-need-based aid:*** $11,000. ***Average indebtedness upon graduation:*** $7220.

APPLYING
Standardized Tests *Required:* SAT or ACT (for admission).
Options: electronic application, early admission, deferred entrance.
Application fee: $15.
Required: essay or personal statement, high school transcript, minimum 2.3 GPA, 2 letters of recommendation, interview.
Application deadlines: 9/1 (freshmen), 9/1 (transfers).
Notification: continuous (freshmen), continuous (transfers).

CONTACT
Mr. Justin Kendall, Admissions Recruiter, Barclay College, 607 North Kingman, Haviland, KS 67059. *Phone:* 620-862-5252 Ext. 21. *Toll-free phone:* 800-862-0226. *Fax:* 620-862-5242.
E-mail: jkendall@barclaycollege.edu.

Benedictine College

Atchison, Kansas

http://www.benedictine.edu/

- **Independent Roman Catholic** comprehensive, founded 1859
- **Small-town** 225-acre campus with easy access to Kansas City
- **Endowment** $19.4 million
- **Coed** 2,133 undergraduate students, 87% full-time, 55% women, 45% men
- **Minimally difficult** entrance level, 98% of applicants were admitted

UNDERGRAD STUDENTS
1,857 full-time, 276 part-time. Students come from 48 states and territories; 11 other countries; 75% are from out of state; 3% Black or African American, non-Hispanic/Latino; 5% Hispanic/Latino; 1% Asian, non-Hispanic/Latino; 0.4% Native Hawaiian or other Pacific Islander, non-Hispanic/Latino; 0.3% American Indian or Alaska Native, non-Hispanic/Latino; 5% Two or more races, non-Hispanic/Latino; 3% Race/ethnicity unknown; 3% international; 3% transferred in; 81% live on campus.

Freshmen:
Admission: 2,182 applied, 2,132 admitted, 508 enrolled. ***Average high school GPA:*** 3.55. ***Test scores:*** SAT critical reading scores over 500: 85%; SAT math scores over 500: 73%; ACT scores over 18: 95%; SAT critical reading scores over 600: 42%; SAT math scores over 600: 41%; ACT scores over 24: 54%; SAT critical reading scores over 700: 16%; SAT math scores over 700: 2%; ACT scores over 30: 14%.
Retention: 77% of full-time freshmen returned.

FACULTY
Total: 194, 57% full-time, 46% with terminal degrees.
Student/faculty ratio: 14:1.

ACADEMICS
Calendar: semesters. *Degrees:* certificates, diplomas, associate, bachelor's, master's, and postbachelor's certificates.
Special study options: academic remediation for entering students, advanced placement credit, cooperative education, distance learning, double majors, English as a second language, honors programs, independent study, internships, off-campus study, part-time degree program, services for LD students, student-designed majors, study abroad, summer session for credit. ***ROTC:*** Army (c).
Computers: 100 computers/terminals and 1,800 ports are available on campus for general student use. Students can access the following: computer help desk, free student e-mail accounts, online (class) grades, online (class) registration, online (class) schedules. Campuswide network is available. 100% of college-owned or -operated housing units are wired for high-speed Internet access. Wireless service is available via entire campus.
Library: Benedictine College Library. *Books:* 198,277 (physical), 139,987 (digital/electronic); *Serial titles:* 45,794 (physical); *Databases:* 88. Weekly public service hours: 85.

STUDENT LIFE
Housing options: on-campus residence required through senior year; men-only, women-only. Campus housing is university owned. Freshman campus housing is guaranteed.
Activities and organizations: drama/theater group, student-run newspaper, choral group, marching band, Student Government, ENACTUS, Knights of Columbus, Concert Chorale/Chamber Singers, Ravens Respect Life.
Athletics Member NAIA. ***Intercollegiate sports:*** baseball M(s), basketball M(s)/W(s), cheerleading W(s), cross-country running M(s)/W(s), football M(s), lacrosse M/W, soccer M(s)/W(s), softball W(s), track and field M(s)/W(s), volleyball W(s), wrestling M(s). ***Intramural sports:*** basketball M/W, football M/W, golf M/W, lacrosse M/W, racquetball M/W, rugby M/W, soccer M/W, softball M/W, table tennis M/W, ultimate Frisbee M/W, volleyball M/W.

Campus security: 24-hour emergency response devices and patrols, late-night transport/escort service, controlled dormitory access.

Student services: health clinic, personal/psychological counseling.

COSTS & FINANCIAL AID
Costs (2016–17) ***Comprehensive fee:*** $37,010 includes full-time tuition ($26,730), mandatory fees ($750), and room and board ($9530). Full-time tuition and fees vary according to course load and degree level. Part-time tuition: $775 per credit hour. Part-time tuition and fees vary according to course load and degree level. ***Required fees:*** $50 per credit hour part-time. ***College room only:*** $5140. Room and board charges vary according to board plan and housing facility. ***Payment plan:*** installment. ***Waivers:*** senior citizens and employees or children of employees.

Financial Aid Of all full-time matriculated undergraduates who enrolled in 2016, 1,474 applied for aid, 1,232 were judged to have need, 293 had their need fully met. 290 Federal Work-Study jobs (averaging $725). In 2016, 673 non-need-based awards were made. ***Average percent of need met:*** 78. ***Average financial aid package:*** $22,440. ***Average need-based loan:*** $4734. ***Average need-based gift aid:*** $17,185. ***Average non-need-based aid:*** $12,021. ***Average indebtedness upon graduation:*** $29,602.

APPLYING
Standardized Tests *Required:* SAT or ACT (for admission).

Options: electronic application, deferred entrance.

Application fee: $50.

Required: high school transcript, minimum 2.0 GPA, 1 letter of recommendation. ***Required for some:*** interview.

Application deadlines: rolling (freshmen), rolling (transfers).

Notification: continuous (freshmen), continuous (transfers).

CONTACT
Mr. Pete Helgesen, Dean of Enrollment Management, Benedictine College, 1020 North 2nd Street, Atchison, KS 66002-1499. *Phone:* 913-367-5340 Ext. 2476. *Toll-free phone:* 800-467-5340.
E-mail: phelgesen@benedictine.edu.

Bethany College

Lindsborg, Kansas

http://www.bethanylb.edu/

CONTACT
Katie Laier, Dean of Admissions and Financial Aid, Bethany College, 335 East Swensson Avenue, Lindsborg, KS 67456-1895. *Phone:* 785-227-3311 Ext. 8344. *Toll-free phone:* 800-826-2281. *Fax:* 785-227-8993.
E-mail: admissions@bethanylb.edu.

Bethel College

North Newton, Kansas

http://www.bethelks.edu/

- **Independent** 4-year, founded 1887, affiliated with Mennonite Church USA
- **Small-town** 90-acre campus with easy access to Wichita
- **Endowment** $17.2 million
- **Coed** 460 undergraduate students, 96% full-time, 50% women, 50% men
- **Moderately difficult** entrance level, 56% of applicants were admitted

UNDERGRAD STUDENTS
441 full-time, 19 part-time. Students come from 28 states and territories; 1 other country; 36% are from out of state; 14% Black or African American, non-Hispanic/Latino; 6% Hispanic/Latino; 1% Asian, non-Hispanic/Latino; 0.2% Native Hawaiian or other Pacific Islander, non-Hispanic/Latino; 0.9% American Indian or Alaska Native, non-Hispanic/Latino; 3% Two or more races, non-Hispanic/Latino; 3% Race/ethnicity unknown; 13% transferred in; 68% live on campus.

Freshmen:
Admission: 770 applied, 431 admitted, 99 enrolled. ***Average high school GPA:*** 3.49. ***Test scores:*** SAT critical reading scores over 500: 25%; SAT math scores over 500: 50%; ACT scores over 18: 97%; SAT critical reading scores over 600: 13%; SAT math scores over 600: 13%; ACT scores over 24: 36%; SAT critical reading scores over 700: 13%; SAT math scores over 700: 13%; ACT scores over 30: 6%.
Retention: 62% of full-time freshmen returned.

FACULTY
Total: 81, 52% full-time, 37% with terminal degrees.

Student/faculty ratio: 10:1.

ACADEMICS
Calendar: 4-1-4. *Degree:* certificates and bachelor's.

Special study options: adult/continuing education programs, advanced placement credit, cooperative education, double majors, honors programs, independent study, internships, part-time degree program, services for LD students, student-designed majors, study abroad, summer session for credit.

Computers: 62 computers/terminals and 500 ports are available on campus for general student use. Students can access the following: campus intranet, computer help desk, free student e-mail accounts, online (class) grades, online (class) registration, online (class) schedules. Campuswide network is available. 100% of college-owned or -operated housing units are wired for high-speed Internet access. Wireless service is available via entire campus.

Library: Mantz Library plus 1 other. *Books:* 119,391 (physical), 149,966 (digital/electronic); *Serial titles:* 3,157 (physical), 107,370 (digital/electronic); *Databases:* 80. Weekly public service hours: 88; students can reserve study rooms.

STUDENT LIFE
Housing options: on-campus residence required through senior year; coed, special housing for students with disabilities. Campus housing is university owned. Freshman campus housing is guaranteed.

Activities and organizations: drama/theater group, student-run newspaper, radio and television station, choral group, Student Activities Committee, Student Alumni Association, Students for Social Change, Intramurals, KBCU FM 88.1.

Athletics Member NAIA. ***Intercollegiate sports:*** basketball M(s)/W(s), cross-country running M(s)/W(s), football M(s), golf M(s)/W(s), soccer M(s)/W(s), tennis M(s)/W(s), track and field M(s)/W(s), volleyball W(s). ***Intramural sports:*** badminton M/W, basketball M/W, cheerleading M/W, cross-country running M/W, golf M/W, soccer M/W, softball W, tennis M/W, track and field M/W, ultimate Frisbee M/W, volleyball M/W.

Campus security: 24-hour emergency response devices and patrols, controlled dormitory access, SMS Alert System.

Student services: health clinic, personal/psychological counseling.

COSTS & FINANCIAL AID
Costs (2017–18) ***Comprehensive fee:*** $36,990 includes full-time tuition ($27,480), mandatory fees ($240), and room and board ($9270). Part-time tuition: $985 per credit hour. Part-time tuition and fees vary according to course load. ***Required fees:*** $10 per credit hour part-time. ***College room only:*** $4890. Room and board charges vary according to board plan, housing facility, and student level. ***Payment plans:*** installment, deferred payment. ***Waivers:*** minority students, children of alumni, senior citizens, and employees or children of employees.

Financial Aid Of all full-time matriculated undergraduates who enrolled in 2015, 452 applied for aid, 436 were judged to have need, 86 had their need fully met. 150 state and other part-time jobs (averaging $1026). In 2015, 69 non-need-based awards were made. ***Average percent of need met:*** 80. ***Average financial aid package:*** $24,435. ***Average need-based loan:*** $8251. ***Average need-based gift aid:*** $5498. ***Average non-need-based aid:*** $10,892. ***Average indebtedness upon graduation:*** $5633.

APPLYING
Standardized Tests *Recommended:* SAT (for admission), ACT (for admission), SAT or ACT (for admission), SAT Subject Tests (for admission).

Options: electronic application, deferred entrance.

Application fee: $20.

Required: high school transcript, minimum 2.5 GPA. ***Required for some:*** essay or personal statement, 2 letters of recommendation. ***Recommended:*** interview.

Application deadlines: rolling (freshmen), rolling (transfers), rolling (early action).

Early decision deadline: rolling (for plan 1), rolling (for plan 2).

Notification: continuous (freshmen), continuous (transfers), rolling (early decision plan 1), rolling (early decision plan 2), rolling (early action).

CONTACT
Mr. Andy Johnson, Vice President for Admissions, Bethel College, 300 East 27th Street, North Newton, KS 67117-0531. *Phone:* 316-284-5230. *Toll-free phone:* 800-522-1887 Ext. 230. *Fax:* 316-284-5870. *E-mail:* admissions@bethelks.edu.

Central Christian College of Kansas

McPherson, Kansas

http://www.centralchristian.edu/

CONTACT
Central Christian College of Kansas, 1200 South Main, PO Box 1403, McPherson, KS 67460-5799. *Phone:* 620-241-0723 Ext. 380. *Toll-free phone:* 800-835-0078.

Cleveland University–Kansas City

Overland Park, Kansas

http://www.cleveland.edu/

- **Independent** comprehensive, founded 1922
- **Suburban** 34-acre campus with easy access to Kansas City
- **Coed**
- **Noncompetitive** entrance level

FACULTY
Student/faculty ratio: 10:1.

ACADEMICS
Calendar: trimesters. *Degrees:* associate, bachelor's, master's, and doctoral.
Library: Ruth R. Cleveland Memorial Library.

STUDENT LIFE
Housing options: college housing not available.
Campus security: 24-hour patrols.
Student services: health clinic, personal/psychological counseling.

APPLYING
Standardized Tests *Required for some:* SAT or ACT (for admission).
Options: electronic application, deferred entrance.
Application fee: $50.
Required: high school transcript, minimum 2.5 GPA. ***Required for some:*** interview, cumulative college GPA of 2.0 for BS degree transfer students.

CONTACT
Ms. Melissa Denton, Director of Admissions, Cleveland University–Kansas City, 10850 Lowell Avenue, Overland Park, KS 66210. *Phone:* 913-234-0750. *Toll-free phone:* 800-467-2252. *Fax:* 913-234-0906. *E-mail:* kc.admissions@cleveland.edu.

Donnelly College

Kansas City, Kansas

http://www.donnelly.edu/

- **Independent Roman Catholic** primarily 2-year, founded 1949
- **Urban** 4-acre campus
- **Coed** 318 undergraduate students, 74% full-time, 73% women, 27% men
- **Noncompetitive** entrance level, 100% of applicants were admitted

UNDERGRAD STUDENTS
236 full-time, 82 part-time. Students come from 2 states and territories; 24 other countries; 32% are from out of state; 33% Black or African American, non-Hispanic/Latino; 45% Hispanic/Latino; 5% Asian, non-Hispanic/Latino; 0.9% Native Hawaiian or other Pacific Islander, non-Hispanic/Latino; 0.6% American Indian or Alaska Native, non-Hispanic/Latino; 3% Two or more races, non-Hispanic/Latino; 0.3% Race/ethnicity unknown; 2% international; 14% transferred in.

Freshmen:
Admission: 408 applied, 408 admitted, 97 enrolled.
Retention: 55% of full-time freshmen returned.

FACULTY
Total: 49, 45% full-time.
Student/faculty ratio: 10:1.

ACADEMICS
Calendar: semesters. *Degrees:* certificates, associate, and bachelor's.
Special study options: academic remediation for entering students, advanced placement credit, distance learning, English as a second language, external degree program, honors programs, independent study, part-time degree program, services for LD students, summer session for credit.
Computers: 75 computers/terminals and 75 ports are available on campus for general student use. Students can access the following: campus intranet, computer help desk, free student e-mail accounts, online (class) grades, online (class) registration, online (class) schedules. Campuswide network is available. Wireless service is available via entire campus.
Library: Trant Memorial Library plus 1 other.

STUDENT LIFE
Housing options: men-only, women-only. Campus housing is university owned.
Activities and organizations: Organization of Student Leadership, Student Ambassadors, Healthy Student Task Force, Men's Soccer Club, Women's Soccer Club.
Athletics ***Intramural sports:*** basketball M/W, soccer M/W, volleyball M/W.
Campus security: 24-hour emergency response devices.
Student services: personal/psychological counseling.

COSTS
Costs (2016–17) ***Comprehensive fee:*** $13,702 includes full-time tuition ($6720), mandatory fees ($132), and room and board ($6850). Full-time tuition and fees vary according to course level, degree level, and program. Part-time tuition: $278 per credit hour. Part-time tuition and fees vary according to course level. ***Required fees:*** $3 per credit hour part-time, $60 per term part-time. ***College room only:*** $4000. Room and board charges vary according to housing facility. ***Payment plan:*** installment. ***Waivers:*** senior citizens and employees or children of employees.

APPLYING
Options: electronic application, early admission, deferred entrance.
Recommended: high school transcript.
Application deadlines: rolling (freshmen), rolling (transfers).

CONTACT
Ms. Kimkisha Stevenson, Director of Admissions, Donnelly College, 608 North 18th Street, Kansas City, KS 66102. *Phone:* 913-621-8762. *Fax:* 913-621-8719. *E-mail:* admissions@donnelly.edu.

Emporia State University

Emporia, Kansas

http://www.emporia.edu/

- **State-supported** comprehensive, founded 1863, part of Kansas State Board of Regents
- **Small-town** 207-acre campus with easy access to Wichita
- **Endowment** $68.8 million
- **Coed** 3,702 undergraduate students, 93% full-time, 62% women, 38% men
- **Noncompetitive** entrance level, 87% of applicants were admitted

UNDERGRAD STUDENTS
3,431 full-time, 271 part-time. Students come from 20 states and territories; 41 other countries; 10% are from out of state; 6% Black or African American, non-Hispanic/Latino; 7% Hispanic/Latino; 0.9% Asian, non-Hispanic/Latino; 0.1% Native Hawaiian or other Pacific Islander, non-Hispanic/Latino; 0.4% American Indian or Alaska Native, non-Hispanic/Latino; 8% Two or more races, non-Hispanic/Latino; 2% Race/ethnicity unknown; 7% international; 9% transferred in; 27% live on campus.

Freshmen:
Admission: 1,702 applied, 1,488 admitted, 665 enrolled. ***Average high school GPA:*** 3.35. ***Test scores:*** ACT scores over 18: 88%; ACT scores over 24: 34%; ACT scores over 30: 5%.
Retention: 71% of full-time freshmen returned.

FACULTY
Total: 275, 92% full-time, 76% with terminal degrees.
Student/faculty ratio: 18:1.

ACADEMICS
Calendar: semesters. *Degrees:* bachelor's, master's, doctoral, post-master's, and postbachelor's certificates.
Special study options: academic remediation for entering students, accelerated degree program, adult/continuing education programs, advanced placement credit, cooperative education, distance learning, double majors, English as a second language, freshman honors college, honors programs, independent study, internships, off-campus study, part-time degree program, services for LD students, study abroad, summer session for credit.
Unusual degree programs: 3-2 engineering with Kansas State University, University of Kansas, Wichita State University.
Computers: 410 computers/terminals are available on campus for general student use. Students can access the following: campus intranet, computer help desk, free student e-mail accounts, online (class) grades, online (class) registration, online (class) schedules. Campuswide network is available. 100% of college-owned or -operated housing units are wired for high-speed Internet access. Wireless service is available via entire campus.
Library: William Allen White Library plus 1 other. *Books:* 389,595 (physical), 153,016 (digital/electronic); *Serial titles:* 35,153 (physical), 278 (digital/electronic); *Databases:* 97. Weekly public service hours: 79; study areas open 24 hours, 5-7 days a week; students can reserve study rooms.

STUDENT LIFE
Housing options: on-campus residence required for freshman year; coed, men-only, women-only, special housing for students with disabilities. Campus housing is university owned. Freshman campus housing is guaranteed.
Activities and organizations: drama/theater group, student-run newspaper, radio station, choral group, marching band, Phi Eta Sigma, Student Chapter of the American Library Association of ESU, TradPlus Student Organization, Arabic Culture Student Organization, Emporia Kansas Association of Nursing Students, national fraternities, national sororities.
Athletics Member NCAA. All Division II. ***Intercollegiate sports:*** baseball M(s), basketball M(s)/W(s), cheerleading M(s)/W(s), cross-country running M(s)/W(s), football M(s), soccer W(s), softball W(s), tennis M(s)/W(s), track and field M(s)/W(s), volleyball W(s). ***Intramural sports:*** badminton M/W, basketball M/W, fencing M(c)/W(c), football M/W, rugby M(c), soccer M(c)/W(c), softball M/W, table tennis M/W, tennis M/W, volleyball M/W.
Campus security: 24-hour emergency response devices and patrols, student patrols, late-night transport/escort service, controlled dormitory access, 24-hour residence hall monitoring, safety and self-awareness programs.
Student services: health clinic, personal/psychological counseling, women's center, legal services.

COSTS & FINANCIAL AID
Costs (2016–17) ***Tuition:*** state resident $4893 full-time, $163 per credit hour part-time; nonresident $18,106 full-time, $604 per credit hour part-time. Full-time tuition and fees vary according to course load, degree level, and location. Part-time tuition and fees vary according to course load, degree level, and location. ***Required fees:*** $1286 full-time, $79 per credit hour part-time. ***Room and board:*** $8391; room only: $4836. Room and board charges vary according to board plan, housing facility, and location. ***Payment plans:*** installment, deferred payment. ***Waivers:*** senior citizens and employees or children of employees.
Financial Aid Of all full-time matriculated undergraduates who enrolled in 2016, 2,618 applied for aid, 2,108 were judged to have need, 286 had their need fully met. 185 Federal Work-Study jobs (averaging $2180). 16 state and other part-time jobs (averaging $2471). In 2016, 618 non-need-based awards were made. ***Average percent of need met:*** 66. ***Average financial aid package:*** $9163. ***Average need-based loan:*** $6693. ***Average need-based gift aid:*** $5821. ***Average non-need-based aid:*** $2662. ***Average indebtedness upon graduation:*** $20,433.

APPLYING
Standardized Tests *Required:* SAT or ACT (for admission).
Options: electronic application, early admission, deferred entrance.
Application fee: $30.
Required: high school transcript, minimum ACT score of 21, or rank in the top 1/3 and completed QA core classes with cum 2.0 GPA, 22 Math subscore, or completed 4th year of math. ***Recommended:*** minimum 2.0 GPA.
Application deadlines: rolling (freshmen), rolling (transfers).
Notification: continuous (freshmen), continuous (transfers).

CONTACT
Mr. Lyndel Landgren, Associate Director, Emporia State University, 1 Kellogg Circle, Campus Box 4034, Emporia, KS 66801-5087. *Phone:* 620-341-5465. *Toll-free phone:* 877-GOTOESU (in-state); 877-468-6378 (out-of-state). *Fax:* 620-341-5599. *E-mail:* go2esu@emporia.edu.

Fort Hays State University

Hays, Kansas

http://www.fhsu.edu/

- **State-supported** comprehensive, founded 1902
- **Small-town** 200-acre campus
- **Coed**

FACULTY
Student/faculty ratio: 16:1.

ACADEMICS
Calendar: semesters. *Degrees:* certificates, associate, bachelor's, master's, and post-master's certificates.
Library: Forsyth Library.

STUDENT LIFE
Housing options: on-campus residence required for freshman year; coed, men-only, women-only. Campus housing is university owned and leased by the school.
Activities and organizations: drama/theater group, student-run newspaper, radio and television station, choral group, marching band, Students for Life, Honors Society, Panhellenic Council, Residents Hall Association, Catholic Disciples.
Campus security: 24-hour emergency response devices and patrols.
Student services: health clinic.

FINANCIAL AID
Financial Aid Of all full-time matriculated undergraduates who enrolled in 2015, 4,647 applied for aid, 3,901 were judged to have need, 347 had their need fully met. In 2015, 504 non-need-based awards were made. ***Average percent of need met:*** 50. ***Average financial aid package:*** $7361. ***Average need-based loan:*** $3910. ***Average need-based gift aid:*** $4887. ***Average non-need-based aid:*** $1557. ***Average indebtedness upon graduation:*** $26,820.

APPLYING
Standardized Tests *Required for some:* SAT or ACT (for admission).
Required: high school transcript.

CONTACT
Tricia Cline, Director, Admissions, Fort Hays State University, 600 Park Street, Hays, KS 67601-4099. *Phone:* 785-628-4091.
Toll-free phone: 800-628-FHSU. *E-mail:* tcline@fhsu.edu.

Friends University

Wichita, Kansas

http://www.friends.edu/

- **Independent** comprehensive, founded 1898, affiliated with Christian non-denominational
- **Urban** 55-acre campus
- **Endowment** $43.1 million
- **Coed** 1,192 undergraduate students, 77% full-time, 54% women, 46% men
- **Moderately difficult** entrance level, 55% of applicants were admitted

UNDERGRAD STUDENTS
920 full-time, 272 part-time. Students come from 36 states and territories; 18 other countries; 22% are from out of state; 12% Black or African American, non-Hispanic/Latino; 7% Hispanic/Latino; 0.8% Asian, non-Hispanic/Latino; 0.2% Native Hawaiian or other Pacific Islander, non-Hispanic/Latino; 1% American Indian or Alaska Native, non-Hispanic/Latino; 7% Two or more races, non-Hispanic/Latino; 8% Race/ethnicity unknown; 0.2% international; 14% transferred in; 25% live on campus.

Freshmen:
Admission: 749 applied, 412 admitted, 165 enrolled. ***Average high school GPA:*** 3.4. ***Test scores:*** SAT critical reading scores over 500: 20%; SAT math scores over 500: 33%; ACT scores over 18: 89%; SAT critical reading scores over 600: 13%; SAT math scores over 600: 13%; ACT scores over 24: 33%; ACT scores over 30: 5%.
Retention: 63% of full-time freshmen returned.

FACULTY
Total: 274, 22% full-time, 27% with terminal degrees.
Student/faculty ratio: 10:1.

ACADEMICS
Calendar: semesters. *Degrees:* bachelor's and master's.
Special study options: academic remediation for entering students, accelerated degree program, adult/continuing education programs, advanced placement credit, cooperative education, distance learning, double majors, honors programs, independent study, internships, off-campus study, part-time degree program, services for LD students, student-designed majors, study abroad, summer session for credit.
Computers: 360 computers/terminals are available on campus for general student use. Students can access the following: campus intranet, computer help desk, free student e-mail accounts, online (class) grades, online (class) registration, online (class) schedules. Campuswide network is available. 90% of college-owned or -operated housing units are wired for high-speed Internet access. Wireless service is available via entire campus.
Library: Edmund Stanley Library plus 1 other. *Books:* 88,223 (physical), 141,741 (digital/electronic); *Serial titles:* 202 (physical); *Databases:* 102.

STUDENT LIFE
Housing options: coed. Campus housing is university owned.
Activities and organizations: drama/theater group, choral group, Concert Choir, Singing Quakers, Zoo Science Club, Psychology Club, Spanish Club.
Athletics Member NAIA. ***Intercollegiate sports:*** baseball M(s), basketball M(s)/W(s), cheerleading M(s)/W(s), cross-country running M(s)/W(s), football M(s), golf W(s), soccer M(s)/W(s), softball W(s), tennis M(s)/W(s), track and field M(s)/W(s), volleyball W(s). ***Intramural sports:*** basketball M/W, football M/W, racquetball M/W, sand volleyball M/W, soccer M/W, table tennis M/W, tennis M/W, ultimate Frisbee M/W, volleyball M/W.
Campus security: 24-hour patrols, late-night transport/escort service, controlled dormitory access.
Student services: health clinic, personal/psychological counseling.

COSTS & FINANCIAL AID
Costs (2017–18) ***Comprehensive fee:*** $35,205 includes full-time tuition ($27,150), mandatory fees ($315), and room and board ($7740). Full-time tuition and fees vary according to class time, course load, degree level, and location. Part-time tuition: $905 per credit hour. Part-time tuition and fees vary according to class time, course load, degree level, and location. ***College room only:*** $3680. Room and board charges vary according to board plan and housing facility. ***Payment plan:*** installment. ***Waivers:*** senior citizens and employees or children of employees.
Financial Aid Of all full-time matriculated undergraduates who enrolled in 2014, 985 applied for aid, 906 were judged to have need, 207 had their need fully met. 222 Federal Work-Study jobs (averaging $1637). 234 state and other part-time jobs (averaging $1792). In 2014, 79 non-need-based awards were made. ***Average percent of need met:*** 74. ***Average financial aid package:*** $15,845. ***Average need-based loan:*** $4178. ***Average need-based gift aid:*** $8273. ***Average non-need-based aid:*** $5417. ***Average indebtedness upon graduation:*** $19,008.

APPLYING
Standardized Tests *Required for some:* SAT or ACT (for admission). *Recommended:* ACT (for admission), SAT and SAT Subject Tests or ACT (for admission).
Options: electronic application.
Required for some: high school transcript, minimum 2.0 GPA, interview, audition for music, dance and theater programs; portfolio for art program.
Application deadlines: rolling (freshmen), rolling (transfers).
Notification: continuous (freshmen), continuous (transfers).

CONTACT
Mr. Brandon Pierce, Senior Director of Admissions and Financial Aid, Friends University, 2100 West University Avenue, Wichita, KS 67213. *Phone:* 316-295-5100. *Toll-free phone:* 800-794-6945. *Fax:* 316-295-5101. *E-mail:* learn@friends.edu.

Grantham University

Lenexa, Kansas

http://www.grantham.edu/

CONTACT
Mr. Les Hyde, Vice President Admissions, Grantham University, 7200 NW 86th Street, Kansas City, MO 64153. *Phone:* 800-955-2527. *Toll-free phone:* 800-955-2527. *Fax:* 816-595-5757. *E-mail:* admissions@grantham.edu.

Haskell Indian Nations University

Lawrence, Kansas

http://www.haskell.edu/

CONTACT
Ms. Patty Grant, Recruitment Officer, Haskell Indian Nations University, 155 Indian Avenue, #5031, Lawrence, KS 66046-4800. *Phone:* 785-749-8437 Ext. 437.

Hesston College

Hesston, Kansas

http://www.hesston.edu/

- **Independent Mennonite** primarily 2-year, founded 1909
- **Small-town** 50-acre campus with easy access to Wichita
- **Coed**
- **Noncompetitive** entrance level

FACULTY
Student/faculty ratio: 9:1.

ACADEMICS
Calendar: semesters. *Degrees:* associate and bachelor's.
Library: Mary Miller Library.

STUDENT LIFE
Housing options: on-campus residence required through sophomore year; men-only, women-only. Campus housing is university owned. Freshman campus housing is guaranteed.
Activities and organizations: drama/theater group, student-run newspaper, choral group, Peace and Service Club, Intramural Sports, Ministry Assistants.
Athletics Member NJCAA.
Campus security: 24-hour emergency response devices, controlled dormitory access.
Student services: health clinic, personal/psychological counseling, women's center.

COSTS & FINANCIAL AID
Costs (2016–17) ***Comprehensive fee:*** $34,170 includes full-time tuition ($25,382), mandatory fees ($420), and room and board ($8368). Full-time tuition and fees vary according to course load and program. Part-time tuition: $1058 per credit hour. Part-time tuition and fees vary according to course load. ***Required fees:*** $105 per term part-time. ***Payment plans:*** installment, deferred payment.
Financial Aid Of all full-time matriculated undergraduates who enrolled in 2015, 120 Federal Work-Study jobs (averaging $800).

APPLYING

Standardized Tests *Required:* SAT or ACT (for admission).

Options: electronic application, early admission, deferred entrance.

Application fee: $15.

Required: high school transcript, 2 letters of recommendation. ***Required for some:*** interview.

CONTACT

Rachel Swartzendruber-Miller, Vice President of Admissions, Hesston College, Hesston, KS 67062. *Phone:* 620-327-8206. *Toll-free phone:* 800-995-2757. *Fax:* 620-327-8300. *E-mail:* admissions@hesston.edu.

Kansas State University

Manhattan, Kansas

http://www.k-state.edu/

- **State-supported** university, founded 1863, part of Kansas Board of Regents
- **Suburban** 668-acre campus
- **Endowment** $475.6 million
- **Coed** 19,472 undergraduate students, 91% full-time, 48% women, 52% men
- **Minimally difficult** entrance level, 94% of applicants were admitted

UNDERGRAD STUDENTS

17,699 full-time, 1,773 part-time. Students come from 52 states and territories; 80 other countries; 18% are from out of state; 4% Black or African American, non-Hispanic/Latino; 7% Hispanic/Latino; 1% Asian, non-Hispanic/Latino; 0.1% Native Hawaiian or other Pacific Islander, non-Hispanic/Latino; 0.4% American Indian or Alaska Native, non-Hispanic/Latino; 3% Two or more races, non-Hispanic/Latino; 1% Race/ethnicity unknown; 5% international; 7% transferred in.

Freshmen:

Admission: 9,018 applied, 8,511 admitted, 3,581 enrolled. ***Average high school GPA:*** 3.52. ***Test scores:*** ACT scores over 18: 97%; ACT scores over 24: 62%; ACT scores over 30: 17%.

Retention: 85% of full-time freshmen returned.

FACULTY

Total: 1,281, 86% full-time, 80% with terminal degrees.

Student/faculty ratio: 18:1.

ACADEMICS

Calendar: semesters. *Degrees:* certificates, associate, bachelor's, master's, doctoral, and postbachelor's certificates.

Special study options: academic remediation for entering students, accelerated degree program, adult/continuing education programs, advanced placement credit, cooperative education, distance learning, double majors, English as a second language, freshman honors college, honors programs, independent study, internships, off-campus study, part-time degree program, services for LD students, study abroad, summer session for credit. ***ROTC:*** Army (b), Air Force (b).

Unusual degree programs: 3-2 engineering; biology, kinesiology, horticulture, master of public health, biochemistry, mathematics, human nutrition, hospitality management, agricultural economics, political science/master of public administration, accounting/MBA, architectural engineering, industrial engineering, bio/ag engineering.

Computers: Students can access the following: computer help desk, free student e-mail accounts, online (class) grades, online (class) registration, online (class) schedules. Campuswide network is available. Wireless service is available via entire campus.

Library: Hale Library plus 3 others. *Books:* 1.4 million (physical), 1.5 million (digital/electronic); *Serial titles:* 162,581 (physical), 101,651 (digital/electronic); *Databases:* 309. Weekly public service hours: 80; study areas open 24 hours, 5-7 days a week; students can reserve study rooms.

STUDENT LIFE

Housing options: coed, men-only, women-only, cooperative. Campus housing is university owned.

Activities and organizations: drama/theater group, student-run newspaper, radio and television station, choral group, marching band, athletic department groups, marching band, Union Governing Board, theater productions, debate team, national fraternities, national sororities.

Athletics Member NCAA. All Division I except football (Division I-A). ***Intercollegiate sports:*** baseball M(s), basketball M(s)/W(s), crew W(s), cross-country running M(s)/W(s), golf M(s)/W(s), soccer W, tennis W(s), track and field M(s)/W(s), volleyball W(s). ***Intramural sports:*** badminton M/W, basketball M/W, bowling M/W, crew M/W, cross-country running M/W, football M/W, golf M/W, ice hockey M, lacrosse M, racquetball M/W, soccer M/W, softball M/W, table tennis M/W, tennis M/W, track and field M/W, volleyball M/W, water polo M/W, weight lifting M/W, wrestling M.

Campus security: 24-hour emergency response devices and patrols, late-night transport/escort service, controlled dormitory access.

Student services: health clinic, personal/psychological counseling, women's center, legal services.

COSTS & FINANCIAL AID

Costs (2016–17) ***Tuition:*** state resident $9012 full-time; nonresident $23,913 full-time. Full-time tuition and fees vary according to course level, course load, degree level, location, program, and reciprocity agreements. Part-time tuition and fees vary according to course level, course load, degree level, location, program, and reciprocity agreements. ***Required fees:*** $862 full-time. ***Room and board:*** $9150. Room and board charges vary according to board plan, housing facility, and location. ***Payment plans:*** installment, deferred payment. ***Waivers:*** employees or children of employees.

Financial Aid Of all full-time matriculated undergraduates who enrolled in 2015, 12,011 applied for aid, 8,925 were judged to have need, 1,676 had their need fully met. In 2015, 1596 non-need-based awards were made. ***Average percent of need met:*** 78. ***Average financial aid package:*** $12,646. ***Average need-based loan:*** $4501. ***Average need-based gift aid:*** $4329. ***Average non-need-based aid:*** $4250. ***Average indebtedness upon graduation:*** $27,198.

APPLYING

Standardized Tests *Required for some:* SAT or ACT (for admission). *Recommended:* SAT or ACT (for admission).

Options: electronic application, early admission.

Application fee: $30.

Required: high school transcript, minimum 2.0 GPA, minimum ACT composite of 21 or top third of high school graduating class.

Application deadlines: rolling (freshmen), rolling (transfers).

Notification: continuous (freshmen), continuous (transfers).

CONTACT

Ms. Molly McGaughey, Associate Director of Admissions, Kansas State University, 119 Anderson Hall, Manhattan, KS 66506. *Phone:* 785-532-6250. *Toll-free phone:* 800-432-8270. *Fax:* 785-532-6393. *E-mail:* k-state@k-state.edu.

Kansas Wesleyan University

Salina, Kansas

http://www.kwu.edu/

- **Independent United Methodist** comprehensive, founded 1886
- **Small-town** 28-acre campus
- **Endowment** $27.1 million
- **Coed** 693 undergraduate students, 92% full-time, 44% women, 56% men
- **Moderately difficult** entrance level, 55% of applicants were admitted

UNDERGRAD STUDENTS

638 full-time, 55 part-time. Students come from 33 states and territories; 10 other countries; 54% are from out of state; 12% Black or African American, non-Hispanic/Latino; 15% Hispanic/Latino; 0.6% Asian, non-Hispanic/Latino; 0.4% Native Hawaiian or other Pacific Islander, non-Hispanic/Latino; 0.3% American Indian or Alaska Native, non-Hispanic/Latino; 3% Two or more races, non-Hispanic/Latino; 1% Race/ethnicity unknown; 2% international; 15% transferred in; 66% live on campus.

Freshmen:

Admission: 805 applied, 440 admitted, 162 enrolled. ***Average high school GPA:*** 3.33. ***Test scores:*** ACT scores over 18: 93%; ACT scores over 24: 28%; ACT scores over 30: 2%.

Retention: 59% of full-time freshmen returned.

FACULTY
Total: 119, 31% full-time, 26% with terminal degrees.

Student/faculty ratio: 10:1.

ACADEMICS
Calendar: semesters plus summer term. *Degrees:* associate, bachelor's, and master's.

Special study options: academic remediation for entering students, advanced placement credit, distance learning, double majors, honors programs, independent study, internships, off-campus study, part-time degree program, services for LD students, student-designed majors, study abroad, summer session for credit.

Unusual degree programs: 3-2 engineering with Washington University in St. Louis; ecospheric studies with Western Colorado Stat University.

Computers: 195 computers/terminals are available on campus for general student use. Students can access the following: computer help desk, free student e-mail accounts, online (class) grades, online (class) registration, online (class) schedules. Campuswide network is available. 100% of college-owned or -operated housing units are wired for high-speed Internet access. Wireless service is available via entire campus.

Library: Memorial Library. *Books:* 71,409 (physical), 6,730 (digital/electronic); *Serial titles:* 402 (physical); *Databases:* 57. Weekly public service hours: 83; students can reserve study rooms.

STUDENT LIFE
Housing options: on-campus residence required through sophomore year; coed, men-only, women-only. Campus housing is university owned. Freshman campus housing is guaranteed.

Activities and organizations: drama/theater group, student-run newspaper, radio and television station, choral group, marching band, Fellowship of Christian Athletes, Student Government, Wesleyan Chorale, Coyote Gaming Club, Coyote Activities Board.

Athletics Member NAIA. ***Intercollegiate sports:*** baseball M(s), basketball M(s)/W(s), bowling M(s)/W(s), cheerleading M(s)/W(s), cross-country running M(s)/W(s), football M(s), golf M(s)/W(s), soccer M(s)/W(s), softball W(s), tennis M(s)/W(s), track and field M(s)/W(s), volleyball W(s), wrestling M(s). ***Intramural sports:*** basketball M/W, softball M/W, table tennis M/W, volleyball M/W.

Campus security: 24-hour emergency response devices, student patrols, late-night transport/escort service, controlled dormitory access, evening patrols by security.

Student services: personal/psychological counseling.

COSTS & FINANCIAL AID
Costs (2017–18) ***One-time required fee:*** **$300.** ***Comprehensive fee:*** $37,930 includes full-time tuition ($28,980) and room and board ($8950). Part-time tuition: $2600 per term. Part-time tuition and fees vary according to course load. ***Room and board:*** Room and board charges vary according to housing facility. ***Payment plan:*** installment. ***Waivers:*** children of alumni, senior citizens, and employees or children of employees.

Financial Aid Of all full-time matriculated undergraduates who enrolled in 2016, 658 applied for aid, 560 were judged to have need, 103 had their need fully met. 92 Federal Work-Study jobs (averaging $1560). 13 state and other part-time jobs (averaging $1377). In 2016, 81 non-need-based awards were made. ***Average percent of need met:*** 100. ***Average financial aid package:*** $68. ***Average need-based loan:*** $4296. ***Average need-based gift aid:*** $7609. ***Average non-need-based aid:*** $11,422. ***Average indebtedness upon graduation:*** $34,526.

APPLYING
Standardized Tests *Required:* SAT or ACT (for admission).

Options: electronic application, deferred entrance.

Application fee: $20.

Required: high school transcript, minimum 2.5 GPA. ***Required for some:*** essay or personal statement, interview.

Application deadlines: rolling (freshmen), rolling (transfers).

Notification: continuous (freshmen), continuous (transfers).

CONTACT
Kansas Wesleyan University, 100 East Claflin Avenue, Salina, KS 67401-6196. *Phone:* 785-833-4307. *Toll-free phone:* 800-874-1154 Ext. 1285.

Manhattan Christian College
Manhattan, Kansas
http://www.mccks.edu/

CONTACT
Teka Wilson, Admissions Office Manager, Manhattan Christian College, 1415 Anderson Avenue, Manhattan, KS 66502. *Phone:* 877-246-4622 Ext. 212. *Toll-free phone:* 877-246-4622.
E-mail: teka.wilson@mccks.edu.

McPherson College
McPherson, Kansas
http://www.mcpherson.edu/

CONTACT
Mr. Matt Pfannenstiel, Director of Admissions, McPherson College, 1600 East Euclid, McPherson, KS 67460. *Phone:* 800-365-7402.
Toll-free phone: 800-365-7402. *E-mail:* admiss@mcpherson.edu.

MidAmerica Nazarene University
Olathe, Kansas
http://www.mnu.edu/

- **Independent** comprehensive, founded 1966, affiliated with Church of the Nazarene
- **Suburban** 105-acre campus with easy access to Kansas City
- **Endowment** $9.3 million
- **Coed** 1,309 undergraduate students, 76% full-time, 58% women, 42% men
- **Minimally difficult** entrance level, 52% of applicants were admitted

UNDERGRAD STUDENTS
1,001 full-time, 308 part-time. Students come from 40 states and territories; 14 other countries; 42% are from out of state; 14% Black or African American, non-Hispanic/Latino; 2% Hispanic/Latino; 2% Asian, non-Hispanic/Latino; 1% Native Hawaiian or other Pacific Islander, non-Hispanic/Latino; 1% American Indian or Alaska Native, non-Hispanic/Latino; 2% Two or more races, non-Hispanic/Latino; 15% Race/ethnicity unknown; 6% transferred in; 67% live on campus.

Freshmen:
Admission: 1,077 applied, 558 admitted, 169 enrolled. ***Average high school GPA:*** 3.23. ***Test scores:*** ACT scores over 18: 82%; ACT scores over 24: 34%; ACT scores over 30: 5%.

Retention: 68% of full-time freshmen returned.

FACULTY
Total: 179, 45% full-time.

Student/faculty ratio: 17:1.

ACADEMICS
Calendar: semesters. *Degrees:* associate, bachelor's, master's, post-master's, and postbachelor's certificates.

Special study options: academic remediation for entering students, accelerated degree program, adult/continuing education programs, advanced placement credit, cooperative education, distance learning, double majors, English as a second language, freshman honors college, honors programs, independent study, internships, off-campus study, part-time degree program, services for LD students, student-designed majors, study abroad, summer session for credit. ***ROTC:*** Army (c), Air Force (c).

Unusual degree programs: 3-2 nursing.

Computers: 85 computers/terminals and 100 ports are available on campus for general student use. Students can access the following: campus intranet, computer help desk, free student e-mail accounts, online (class) grades, online (class) registration, online (class) schedules. Campuswide network is available. 100% of college-owned or -operated housing units are wired for high-speed Internet access. Wireless service is available via entire campus.

Library: Mabee Library. *Books:* 88,000 (physical), 249,000 (digital/electronic); *Serial titles:* 397 (physical), 25 (digital/electronic); *Databases:* 35. Weekly public service hours: 81; study areas open 24 hours, 5-7 days a week; students can reserve study rooms.

STUDENT LIFE

Housing options: on-campus residence required through senior year; men-only, women-only, special housing for students with disabilities. Campus housing is university owned. Freshman campus housing is guaranteed.

Activities and organizations: drama/theater group, student-run newspaper, radio and television station, choral group, LOL - Loving on Littles, S.M.I.L.E. - Students Ministering in the Lives of Elderly, Center for Grace, Freedom Fire, Students for Social Justice.

Athletics Member NAIA. ***Intercollegiate sports:*** baseball M(s), basketball M(s)/W(s), cheerleading M(s)/W(s), cross-country running M(s)/W(s), football M(s), soccer M(s)/W(s), softball W(s), track and field M(s)/W(s), volleyball W(s). ***Intramural sports:*** basketball M/W, football M/W, soccer M/W, softball M/W, tennis M/W, volleyball M/W, weight lifting M.

Campus security: 24-hour emergency response devices and patrols, student patrols, late-night transport/escort service, controlled dormitory access.

Student services: personal/psychological counseling.

COSTS & FINANCIAL AID

Costs (2017–18) ***Comprehensive fee:*** $37,808 includes full-time tuition ($29,170), mandatory fees ($500), and room and board ($8138). Full-time tuition and fees vary according to course load, degree level, program, and reciprocity agreements. Part-time tuition: $1050 per credit hour. Part-time tuition and fees vary according to course load, degree level, program, and reciprocity agreements. ***Required fees:*** $125 per term part-time. ***Room and board:*** Room and board charges vary according to board plan and housing facility. ***Payment plan:*** installment. ***Waivers:*** senior citizens and employees or children of employees.

Financial Aid Of all full-time matriculated undergraduates who enrolled in 2008, 796 applied for aid, 692 were judged to have need, 97 had their need fully met. In 2008, 187 non-need-based awards were made. ***Average percent of need met:*** 65. ***Average financial aid package:*** $13,686. ***Average need-based loan:*** $5638. ***Average need-based gift aid:*** $8989. ***Average non-need-based aid:*** $4891. ***Average indebtedness upon graduation:*** $28,859.

APPLYING

Standardized Tests *Required for some:* SAT or ACT (for admission). *Recommended:* TOEFL for international applicants.

Options: electronic application, deferred entrance.

Required: high school transcript, minimum 2.0 GPA.

Application deadlines: 8/1 (freshmen), 8/1 (transfers).

Notification: continuous (freshmen), continuous (transfers).

CONTACT

Meghan Westerhold, MidAmerica Nazarene University, 2030 College Avenue, Olathe, IN 66062. *Phone:* 913-971-3783. *Toll-free phone:* 800-800-8887. *E-mail:* mvwesterhold@mnu.edu.

National American University

Overland Park, Kansas

http://www.national.edu/

CONTACT

Admissions Office, National American University, 10310 Mastin Street, Overland Park, KS 66212. *Toll-free phone:* 866-628-1288.

Newman University

Wichita, Kansas

http://www.newmanu.edu/

- **Independent Roman Catholic** comprehensive, founded 1933
- **Urban** 61-acre campus with easy access to Sedgwick County
- **Endowment** $17.8 million
- **Coed** 2,535 undergraduate students, 39% full-time, 62% women, 38% men
- **Minimally difficult** entrance level, 58% of applicants were admitted

UNDERGRAD STUDENTS

1,001 full-time, 1,534 part-time. Students come from 27 states and territories; 36 other countries; 14% are from out of state; 5% Black or African American, non-Hispanic/Latino; 15% Hispanic/Latino; 5% Asian, non-Hispanic/Latino; 0.1% Native Hawaiian or other Pacific Islander, non-Hispanic/Latino; 1% American Indian or Alaska Native, non-Hispanic/Latino; 3% Two or more races, non-Hispanic/Latino; 0.2% Race/ethnicity unknown; 8% international; 6% transferred in; 26% live on campus.

Freshmen:

Admission: 1,331 applied, 769 admitted, 180 enrolled. ***Average high school GPA:*** 3.5. ***Test scores:*** SAT critical reading scores over 500: 25%; SAT math scores over 500: 63%; SAT writing scores over 500: 25%; ACT scores over 18: 91%; SAT critical reading scores over 600: 13%; SAT writing scores over 600: 13%; ACT scores over 24: 43%; ACT scores over 30: 11%.

Retention: 74% of full-time freshmen returned.

FACULTY

Total: 219, 33% full-time.

Student/faculty ratio: 11:1.

ACADEMICS

Calendar: semesters. *Degrees:* associate, bachelor's, and master's.

Special study options: academic remediation for entering students, accelerated degree program, adult/continuing education programs, advanced placement credit, cooperative education, distance learning, double majors, honors programs, independent study, internships, off-campus study, part-time degree program, services for LD students, student-designed majors, study abroad, summer session for credit.

Unusual degree programs: 3-2 occupational therapy with Washington University in St. Louis.

Computers: 90 computers/terminals and 300 ports are available on campus for general student use. Students can access the following: computer help desk, free student e-mail accounts, online (class) grades, online (class) registration, online (class) schedules. Campuswide network is available. 100% of college-owned or -operated housing units are wired for high-speed Internet access. Wireless service is available via entire campus.

Library: Dugan Library. *Books:* 55,967 (physical), 8,120 (digital/electronic); *Serial titles:* 582 (physical), 54,323 (digital/electronic); *Databases:* 70. Weekly public service hours: 87; students can reserve study rooms.

STUDENT LIFE

Housing options: on-campus residence required for freshman year; coed. Campus housing is university owned. Freshman campus housing is guaranteed.

Activities and organizations: drama/theater group, student-run newspaper, choral group, Newman University Medical Professionals Club (NUMPC), National Society of Leadership and Success, Student Athlete Advisory Committee, Swing Dance Club, Hispanic American Leadership Organization (HALO).

Athletics Member NCAA. All Division II. ***Intercollegiate sports:*** baseball M(s), basketball M(s)/W(s), bowling M(s)(c)/W(s)(c), cross-country running M(s)/W(s), golf M(s)/W(s), soccer M(s)/W(s), softball W(s), tennis M(s)/W(s), volleyball W(s), wrestling M(s). ***Intramural sports:*** baseball M, basketball M/W, bowling M/W, football M/W, golf M/W, soccer M/W, softball M/W, table tennis M/W, triathlon M/W, ultimate Frisbee M/W, volleyball M/W, weight lifting M/W.

Campus security: 24-hour emergency response devices and patrols, student patrols, late-night transport/escort service, controlled dormitory access.

Student services: personal/psychological counseling.

COSTS & FINANCIAL AID

Costs (2016–17) ***One-time required fee:*** $160. ***Comprehensive fee:*** $35,014 includes full-time tuition ($26,416), mandatory fees ($1140), and room and board ($7458). Part-time tuition: $881 per credit hour. Part-time tuition and fees vary according to course load. ***Required fees:*** $17 per credit hour part-time, $50 per term part-time. ***College room only:*** $3976. Room and board charges vary according to board plan and housing facility. ***Payment plan:*** installment. ***Waivers:*** employees or children of employees.

Financial Aid Of all full-time matriculated undergraduates who enrolled in 2013, 1,027 applied for aid, 877 were judged to have need, 225 had their need fully met. 59 Federal Work-Study jobs (averaging $2000). 89 state and other part-time jobs (averaging $2000). In 2013, 55 non-need-based awards were made. ***Average percent of need met:*** 67. ***Average financial aid package:*** $19,844. ***Average need-based loan:*** $4051. ***Average need-based gift aid:*** $4844. ***Average non-need-based aid:*** $8927. ***Average indebtedness upon graduation:*** $23,843.

APPLYING
Standardized Tests *Required for some:* SAT or ACT (for admission).
Options: electronic application, early admission, deferred entrance.
Required: high school transcript, minimum 2.0 GPA. ***Recommended:*** interview.
Application deadlines: rolling (freshmen), rolling (transfers).
Notification: continuous (freshmen), continuous (transfers).

CONTACT
Kristen English, Director of Undergraduate Admissions, Newman University, 3100 McCormick Avenue, Wichita, KS 67213. *Phone:* 316-942-4291 Ext. 2146. *Toll-free phone:* 877-NEWMANU. *Fax:* 316-942-4483. *E-mail:* englishk@newmanu.edu.

Ottawa University
Ottawa, Kansas
http://www.ottawa.edu/

CONTACT
Ottawa University, 1001 South Cedar, Ottawa, KS 66067-3399. *Phone:* 785-229-1051. *Toll-free phone:* 800-755-5200.

Pinnacle Career Institute
Lawrence, Kansas
http://www.pcitraining.edu/

CONTACT
Pinnacle Career Institute, 1601 West 23rd Street, Suite 200, Lawrence, KS 66046. *Toll-free phone:* 877-241-3097.

Pittsburg State University
Pittsburg, Kansas
http://www.pittstate.edu/

- **State-supported** comprehensive, founded 1903, part of Kansas State Board of Regents
- **Small-town** 630-acre campus
- **Coed** 6,093 undergraduate students, 90% full-time, 47% women, 53% men
- **Minimally difficult** entrance level, 81% of applicants were admitted

UNDERGRAD STUDENTS
5,455 full-time, 638 part-time. 28% are from out of state; 4% Black or African American, non-Hispanic/Latino; 5% Hispanic/Latino; 0.9% Asian, non-Hispanic/Latino; 0.1% Native Hawaiian or other Pacific Islander, non-Hispanic/Latino; 1% American Indian or Alaska Native, non-Hispanic/Latino; 6% Two or more races, non-Hispanic/Latino; 0.2% Race/ethnicity unknown; 3% international; 8% transferred in.

Freshmen:
Admission: 2,697 applied, 2,194 admitted, 1,059 enrolled. ***Average high school GPA:*** 3.3. ***Test scores:*** ACT scores over 18: 88%; ACT scores over 24: 30%; ACT scores over 30: 4%.
Retention: 75% of full-time freshmen returned.

FACULTY
Total: 408, 77% full-time, 72% with terminal degrees.
Student/faculty ratio: 19:1.

ACADEMICS
Calendar: semesters. *Degrees:* certificates, associate, bachelor's, master's, doctoral, post-master's, and postbachelor's certificates.
Special study options: accelerated degree program, adult/continuing education programs, distance learning, double majors, freshman honors college, honors programs, independent study, internships, off-campus study, part-time degree program, services for LD students, student-designed majors, study abroad, summer session for credit. ***ROTC:*** Army (b).
Computers: Students can access the following: campus intranet, computer help desk, free student e-mail accounts, online (class) grades, online (class) registration, online (class) schedules. Campuswide network is available. 100% of college-owned or -operated housing units are wired for high-speed Internet access. Wireless service is available via entire campus.
Library: Leonard H. Axe Library plus 2 others.

STUDENT LIFE
Housing options: on-campus residence required for freshman year; coed. Campus housing is university owned. Freshman applicants given priority for college housing.
Activities and organizations: drama/theater group, student-run newspaper, radio and television station, choral group, marching band, Student Government Association, student yearbook, student newspaper, Student Activities Council, Students in Free Enterprise (SIFE), national fraternities, national sororities.
Athletics Member NCAA. All Division II. ***Intercollegiate sports:*** baseball M(s), basketball M(s)/W(s), cheerleading M(s)/W(s), cross-country running M(s)/W(s), football M(s), golf M(s), softball W(s), track and field M(s)/W(s), volleyball W(s). ***Intramural sports:*** badminton M/W, basketball M/W, football M/W, lacrosse M(c), racquetball M/W, rugby M(c), soccer M(c)/W(c), softball M/W, table tennis M/W, tennis M/W, ultimate Frisbee M/W, volleyball M/W.
Campus security: 24-hour emergency response devices and patrols, late-night transport/escort service, controlled dormitory access.
Student services: health clinic, personal/psychological counseling, legal services.

FINANCIAL AID
Financial Aid ***Average financial aid package:*** $6926. ***Average need-based loan:*** $4030. ***Average need-based gift aid:*** $4498. ***Average non-need-based aid:*** $2334. ***Average indebtedness upon graduation:*** $24,384.

APPLYING
Standardized Tests *Required:* SAT or ACT (for admission).
Options: electronic application, deferred entrance.
Application fee: $30.
Required: high school transcript. ***Required for some:*** minimum 2.0 GPA.
Application deadlines: rolling (freshmen), rolling (transfers).

CONTACT
Director of Admission, Pittsburg State University, 1701 South Broadway, Pittsburg, KS 66762. *Phone:* 620-235-4251. *Toll-free phone:* 800-854-7488. *Fax:* 620-235-6003. *E-mail:* psuadmit@pittstate.edu.

Rasmussen College Kansas City/Overland Park
Overland Park, Kansas
http://www.rasmussen.edu/

- **Proprietary** 4-year, founded 2013, part of Rasmussen College System
- **Suburban** campus
- **Coed** 169 undergraduate students, 58% full-time, 80% women, 20% men
- **Minimally difficult** entrance level, 76% of applicants were admitted

UNDERGRAD STUDENTS
98 full-time, 71 part-time.

Freshmen:
Admission: 21 applied, 16 admitted, 16 enrolled.

FACULTY
Total: 6, 17% full-time.
Student/faculty ratio: 22:1.

ACADEMICS
Calendar: quarters. *Degrees:* certificates, diplomas, associate, bachelor's, and postbachelor's certificates.
Special study options: academic remediation for entering students, accelerated degree program, adult/continuing education programs,

distance learning, double majors, internships, part-time degree program, summer session for credit.

Computers: Students can access the following: computer help desk, free student e-mail accounts, online (class) grades, online (class) schedules. Campuswide network is available. Wireless service is available via entire campus.

Library: Rasmussen College Library - Kansas City/Overland Park.

STUDENT LIFE

Housing options: college housing not available.

COSTS

Costs (2017–18) ***Tuition:*** $11,055 full-time. Full-time tuition and fees vary according to course level, course load, degree level, location, and program. Part-time tuition and fees vary according to course level, course load, degree level, location, and program. No tuition increase for student's term of enrollment. ***Required fees:*** $1695 full-time. ***Payment plans:*** installment, deferred payment. ***Waivers:*** employees or children of employees.

APPLYING

Standardized Tests *Required:* institutional exam (for admission).

Options: electronic application, early admission, deferred entrance.

Required: high school transcript, minimum 2.0 GPA. ***Required for some:*** interview.

Application deadlines: rolling (freshmen), rolling (transfers).

CONTACT

Ms. Susan Hammerstrom, Director of Admissions, Rasmussen College Kansas City/Overland Park, 11600 College Boulevard, Overland Park, KS 66210. *Phone:* 913-491-7870. *Toll-free phone:* 888-549-6755.
E-mail: susan.hammerstrom@rasmussen.edu.

Rasmussen College Topeka

Topeka, Kansas

http://www.rasmussen.edu/

- **Proprietary** 4-year, founded 2013, part of Rasmussen College System
- **Suburban** campus
- **Coed** 141 undergraduate students, 59% full-time, 70% women, 30% men
- **Minimally difficult** entrance level, 93% of applicants were admitted

UNDERGRAD STUDENTS

83 full-time, 58 part-time.

Freshmen:

Admission: 15 applied, 14 admitted, 14 enrolled.

FACULTY

Total: 46, 7% full-time.

Student/faculty ratio: 22:1.

ACADEMICS

Calendar: quarters. *Degrees:* certificates, diplomas, associate, bachelor's, and postbachelor's certificates.

Special study options: academic remediation for entering students, accelerated degree program, adult/continuing education programs, distance learning, double majors, internships, part-time degree program, summer session for credit.

Computers: Students can access the following: computer help desk, free student e-mail accounts, online (class) grades, online (class) schedules. Campuswide network is available. Wireless service is available via entire campus.

Library: Rasmussen College Library - Topeka.

STUDENT LIFE

Housing options: college housing not available.

COSTS

Costs (2017–18) ***Tuition:*** $11,055 full-time. Full-time tuition and fees vary according to course level, course load, degree level, location, and program. Part-time tuition and fees vary according to course level, course load, degree level, location, and program. No tuition increase for student's term of enrollment. ***Required fees:*** $1695 full-time. ***Payment plans:*** installment, deferred payment. ***Waivers:*** employees or children of employees.

APPLYING

Standardized Tests *Required:* institutional exam (for admission).

Options: electronic application, early admission, deferred entrance.

Required: high school transcript, minimum 2.0 GPA. ***Required for some:*** interview.

Application deadlines: rolling (freshmen), rolling (transfers).

CONTACT

Ms. Susan Hammerstrom, Director of Admissions, Rasmussen College Topeka, 620 SW Governor View, Topeka, KS 66606. *Phone:* 785-228-7320. *Toll-free phone:* 888-549-6755.
E-mail: susan.hammerstrom@rasmussen.edu.

Southwestern College

Winfield, Kansas

http://www.sckans.edu/

- **Independent United Methodist** comprehensive, founded 1885
- **Small-town** 70-acre campus with easy access to Wichita
- **Endowment** $26.8 million
- **Coed** 1,226 undergraduate students, 42% full-time, 40% women, 60% men
- **Minimally difficult** entrance level, 92% of applicants were admitted

UNDERGRAD STUDENTS

513 full-time, 713 part-time. Students come from 42 states and territories; 10 other countries; 59% are from out of state; 11% Black or African American, non-Hispanic/Latino; 8% Hispanic/Latino; 1% Asian, non-Hispanic/Latino; 0.1% Native Hawaiian or other Pacific Islander, non-Hispanic/Latino; 2% American Indian or Alaska Native, non-Hispanic/Latino; 4% Two or more races, non-Hispanic/Latino; 25% Race/ethnicity unknown; 4% international; 18% transferred in; 30% live on campus.

Freshmen:

Admission: 395 applied, 364 admitted, 181 enrolled. ***Average high school GPA:*** 3.22. ***Test scores:*** SAT critical reading scores over 500: 29%; SAT math scores over 500: 37%; ACT scores over 18: 87%; SAT critical reading scores over 600: 5%; SAT math scores over 600: 7%; ACT scores over 24: 21%; SAT critical reading scores over 700: 5%; ACT scores over 30: 3%.

Retention: 60% of full-time freshmen returned.

FACULTY

Total: 180, 23% full-time, 33% with terminal degrees.

Student/faculty ratio: 10:1.

ACADEMICS

Calendar: semesters. *Degrees:* certificates, bachelor's, master's, doctoral, and postbachelor's certificates.

Special study options: academic remediation for entering students, accelerated degree program, adult/continuing education programs, advanced placement credit, distance learning, double majors, English as a second language, honors programs, independent study, internships, off-campus study, part-time degree program, services for LD students, student-designed majors, study abroad, summer session for credit.

Computers: 50 computers/terminals and 150 ports are available on campus for general student use. Students can access the following: campus intranet, computer help desk, free student e-mail accounts, online (class) grades, online (class) registration, online (class) schedules. Campuswide network is available. 100% of college-owned or -operated housing units are wired for high-speed Internet access. Wireless service is available via entire campus.

Library: Harold and Mary Ellen Deets Library. *Books:* 47,687 (physical), 478,000 (digital/electronic); *Serial titles:* 12 (physical), 19 (digital/electronic); *Databases:* 78. Weekly public service hours: 91; students can reserve study rooms.

STUDENT LIFE

Housing options: on-campus residence required through sophomore year; coed, men-only, women-only. Campus housing is university owned. Freshman campus housing is guaranteed.

Activities and organizations: drama/theater group, student-run newspaper, radio and television station, choral group, Discipleship SC, Leadership SC, Acappella Choir, Concert Band, Southwestern Singers.

Athletics Member NAIA. ***Intercollegiate sports:*** baseball M(s), basketball M(s)/W(s), cross-country running M(s)/W(s), football M(s), golf M(s)/W(s), soccer M(s)/W(s), softball W(s), tennis M(s)/W(s), track and field M(s)/W(s), volleyball W(s). ***Intramural sports:*** basketball M/W, swimming and diving M(c)/W(c), ultimate Frisbee M(c)/W(c).

Campus security: 24-hour emergency response devices and patrols, late-night transport/escort service, controlled dormitory access.

Student services: health clinic, personal/psychological counseling.

COSTS & FINANCIAL AID

Costs (2017–18) ***Comprehensive fee:*** $36,270 includes full-time tuition ($28,600), mandatory fees ($150), and room and board ($7520). Full-time tuition and fees vary according to course load, degree level, location, and program. Part-time tuition: $1192 per credit hour. Part-time tuition and fees vary according to course load, degree level, location, and program. ***College room only:*** $3500. Room and board charges vary according to board plan and housing facility. ***Payment plan:*** installment. ***Waivers:*** senior citizens and employees or children of employees.

Financial Aid Of all full-time matriculated undergraduates who enrolled in 2015, 396 applied for aid, 367 were judged to have need, 50 had their need fully met. 164 Federal Work-Study jobs (averaging $1492). 127 state and other part-time jobs (averaging $1472). In 2015, 65 non-need-based awards were made. ***Average percent of need met:*** 74. ***Average financial aid package:*** $21,780. ***Average need-based loan:*** $6170. ***Average need-based gift aid:*** $15,224. ***Average non-need-based aid:*** $7618. ***Average indebtedness upon graduation:*** $38,318.

APPLYING

Standardized Tests *Required:* SAT or ACT (for admission).

Options: electronic application.

Application fee: $25.

Required: high school transcript, minimum 2.5 GPA. ***Required for some:*** 2 letters of recommendation, interview. ***Recommended:*** essay or personal statement.

Application deadlines: 8/1 (freshmen), 8/1 (transfers).

Notification: continuous (freshmen), continuous (out-of-state freshmen), continuous (transfers).

CONTACT

Southwestern College, 100 College Street, Winfield, KS 67156-2499. *Phone:* 620-229-6241. *Toll-free phone:* 800-846-1543.

Sterling College

Sterling, Kansas

http://www.sterling.edu/

- **Independent Presbyterian** 4-year, founded 1887
- **Rural** 46-acre campus
- **Endowment** $16.0 million
- **Coed** 650 undergraduate students, 88% full-time, 50% women, 50% men
- **Minimally difficult** entrance level, 37% of applicants were admitted

UNDERGRAD STUDENTS

574 full-time, 76 part-time. Students come from 36 states and territories; 7 other countries; 53% are from out of state; 11% Black or African American, non-Hispanic/Latino; 12% Hispanic/Latino; 0.9% Asian, non-Hispanic/Latino; 3% American Indian or Alaska Native, non-Hispanic/Latino; 2% international; 9% transferred in; 80% live on campus.

Freshmen:

Admission: 1,033 applied, 386 admitted, 128 enrolled. ***Average high school GPA:*** 3.14. ***Test scores:*** ACT scores over 18: 82%; ACT scores over 24: 21%; ACT scores over 30: 3%.

Retention: 61% of full-time freshmen returned.

ACADEMICS

Calendar: 4-1-4. *Degree:* bachelor's.

Special study options: advanced placement credit, distance learning, double majors, honors programs, independent study, internships, off-campus study, services for LD students, student-designed majors, study abroad, summer session for credit.

Unusual degree programs: 3-2 biology/medical technology with Wichita State University.

Computers: 50 computers/terminals are available on campus for general student use. Students can access the following: campus intranet, computer help desk, free student e-mail accounts, online (class) grades, online (class) registration, online (class) schedules. Campuswide network is available. 100% of college-owned or -operated housing units are wired for high-speed Internet access. Wireless service is available via entire campus.

Library: Mabee Library. *Books:* 50,908 (physical), 80,159 (digital/electronic); *Serial titles:* 74 (physical); *Databases:* 28. Weekly public service hours: 75; students can reserve study rooms.

STUDENT LIFE

Housing options: on-campus residence required through senior year; men-only, women-only. Campus housing is university owned. Freshman campus housing is guaranteed.

Activities and organizations: drama/theater group, student-run newspaper, radio and television station, choral group, Fellowship of Christian Athletes, Student Activities Council, Bible study groups, theatre, Mission teams.

Athletics Member NAIA. ***Intercollegiate sports:*** baseball M(s), basketball M(s)/W(s), cheerleading M(s)/W(s), cross-country running M(s)/W(s), football M(s), golf M(s)/W(s), soccer M(s)/W(s), softball W(s), track and field M(s)/W(s), volleyball W(s). ***Intramural sports:*** basketball M/W, softball M/W, ultimate Frisbee M/W, volleyball M/W.

Campus security: controlled dormitory access, late night security patrol.

Student services: health clinic, personal/psychological counseling.

COSTS & FINANCIAL AID

Costs (2017–18) ***One-time required fee:*** $100. ***Comprehensive fee:*** $33,065 includes full-time tuition ($23,985), mandatory fees ($500), and room and board ($8580). Full-time tuition and fees vary according to course load. Part-time tuition: $448 per credit hour. Part-time tuition and fees vary according to course load. ***Room and board:*** Room and board charges vary according to board plan and housing facility. ***Payment plan:*** installment. ***Waivers:*** senior citizens and employees or children of employees.

Financial Aid Of all full-time matriculated undergraduates who enrolled in 2015, 578 applied for aid, 505 were judged to have need, 115 had their need fully met. 381 Federal Work-Study jobs (averaging $861). In 2015, 69 non-need-based awards were made. ***Average percent of need met:*** 85. ***Average financial aid package:*** $22,294. ***Average need-based loan:*** $5307. ***Average need-based gift aid:*** $11,826. ***Average non-need-based aid:*** $9473. ***Average indebtedness upon graduation:*** $28,221.

APPLYING

Standardized Tests *Required:* SAT or ACT (for admission).

Options: electronic application, deferred entrance.

Application fee: $25.

Required: high school transcript, minimum 2.2 GPA. ***Required for some:*** 2 letters of recommendation. ***Recommended:*** essay or personal statement, interview.

Application deadlines: rolling (freshmen), rolling (transfers).

Notification: continuous (freshmen), continuous (transfers).

CONTACT

Marge Jones, Admissions Office Manager, Sterling College, 125 West Cooper, Sterling, KS 67579. *Phone:* 620-278-4275. *Toll-free phone:* 800-346-1017. *Fax:* 620-278-4416. *E-mail:* admissions@sterling.edu.

Tabor College

Hillsboro, Kansas

http://www.tabor.edu/

- **Independent Mennonite Brethren** comprehensive, founded 1908
- **Small-town** 87-acre campus with easy access to Wichita
- **Endowment** $8.7 million
- **Coed** 670 undergraduate students, 78% full-time, 46% women, 54% men
- **Moderately difficult** entrance level, 56% of applicants were admitted

UNDERGRAD STUDENTS

523 full-time, 147 part-time. Students come from 33 states and territories; 13 other countries; 47% are from out of state; 9% Black or African American, non-Hispanic/Latino; 13% Hispanic/Latino; 0.4% Asian, non-Hispanic/Latino; 0.1% Native Hawaiian or other Pacific Islander, non-

Hispanic/Latino; 0.7% American Indian or Alaska Native, non-Hispanic/Latino; 4% Two or more races, non-Hispanic/Latino; 3% Race/ethnicity unknown; 4% international; 10% transferred in; 72% live on campus.

Freshmen:
Admission: 631 applied, 353 admitted, 136 enrolled. ***Average high school GPA:*** 3.27. ***Test scores:*** SAT critical reading scores over 500: 32%; SAT math scores over 500: 41%; ACT scores over 18: 83%; SAT math scores over 600: 7%; ACT scores over 24: 29%; ACT scores over 30: 3%.
Retention: 59% of full-time freshmen returned.

FACULTY
Total: 109, 34% full-time, 39% with terminal degrees.
Student/faculty ratio: 10:1.

ACADEMICS
Calendar: 4-1-4 (adult and graduate studies programs run by cohort groups). *Degrees:* associate, bachelor's, and master's.
Special study options: academic remediation for entering students, accelerated degree program, adult/continuing education programs, advanced placement credit, cooperative education, distance learning, double majors, honors programs, independent study, internships, off-campus study, part-time degree program, services for LD students, student-designed majors, study abroad.
Computers: 39 computers/terminals are available on campus for general student use. Students can access the following: computer help desk, free student e-mail accounts, online (class) grades, online (class) schedules, online registration for Hillsboro undergraduate students. Campuswide network is available. 100% of college-owned or -operated housing units are wired for high-speed Internet access. Wireless service is available via entire campus.
Library: Tabor College Library. *Books:* 61,171 (physical), 125,000 (digital/electronic); *Serial titles:* 147 (physical), 1,000 (digital/electronic); *Databases:* 22. Weekly public service hours: 85; students can reserve study rooms.

STUDENT LIFE
Housing options: on-campus residence required through senior year; men-only, women-only, special housing for students with disabilities. Campus housing is university owned. Freshman campus housing is guaranteed.
Activities and organizations: drama/theater group, student-run newspaper, choral group, Student Activities Board, CHUMS (Challenging, Helping and Understanding through Mentorship), Intramurals, WUMP (Wichita Urban Ministries Plunge), Multi-Cultural Student Union.
Athletics Member NAIA. ***Intercollegiate sports:*** baseball M(s), basketball M(s)/W(s), cheerleading M(s)/W(s), cross-country running M(s)/W(s), football M(s), soccer M(s)/W(s), softball W(s), swimming and diving M(s)/W(s), tennis M(s)/W(s), track and field M(s)/W(s), volleyball W(s). ***Intramural sports:*** basketball M/W, soccer M/W, softball M/W, volleyball M/W.
Campus security: Emergency Alert System (voluntary individual sign-up).
Student services: personal/psychological counseling.

COSTS & FINANCIAL AID
Costs (2017–18) ***Comprehensive fee:*** $37,378 includes full-time tuition ($26,300), mandatory fees ($920), and room and board ($10,158). Full-time tuition and fees vary according to course load and program. Part-time tuition: $548 per semester hour. Part-time tuition and fees vary according to course load and program. ***Required fees:*** $19 per credit hour part-time. ***College room only:*** $4234. Room and board charges vary according to housing facility and location. ***Payment plan:*** installment. ***Waivers:*** employees or children of employees.
Financial Aid Of all full-time matriculated undergraduates who enrolled in 2014, 542 applied for aid, 448 were judged to have need, 60 had their need fully met. In 2014, 93 non-need-based awards were made. ***Average percent of need met:*** 73. ***Average financial aid package:*** $22,141. ***Average need-based loan:*** $5417. ***Average need-based gift aid:*** $5487. ***Average non-need-based aid:*** $11,390. ***Average indebtedness upon graduation:*** $47,172. ***Financial aid deadline:*** 8/15.

APPLYING
Standardized Tests *Required:* SAT or ACT (for admission).
Options: electronic application.
Application fee: $50.
Required: essay or personal statement, high school transcript, minimum 2.0 GPA, validation of high school graduation date for transfers. ***Recommended:*** interview.
Application deadlines: rolling (freshmen), rolling (transfers).
Notification: continuous (freshmen), continuous (transfers).

CONTACT
Ms. Kelly Dugger, Interim Director of Admissions, Tabor College, 400 South Jefferson, Hillsboro, KS 67063. *Phone:* 620-947-3121 Ext. 1727. *Toll-free phone:* 800-822-6799. *Fax:* 620-947-3789.
E-mail: kellydugger@tabor.edu.

The University of Kansas

Lawrence, Kansas

http://www.ku.edu/

- **State-supported** university, founded 1866, part of Kansas Board of Regents
- **Suburban** 1000-acre campus with easy access to Kansas City
- **Endowment** $2.0 billion
- **Coed** 19,262 undergraduate students, 89% full-time, 51% women, 49% men
- **Moderately difficult** entrance level, 93% of applicants were admitted

UNDERGRAD STUDENTS
17,141 full-time, 2,121 part-time. Students come from 54 states and territories; 76 other countries; 27% are from out of state; 4% Black or African American, non-Hispanic/Latino; 8% Hispanic/Latino; 5% Asian, non-Hispanic/Latino; 0.4% American Indian or Alaska Native, non-Hispanic/Latino; 5% Two or more races, non-Hispanic/Latino; 0.8% Race/ethnicity unknown; 6% international; 6% transferred in; 25% live on campus.

Freshmen:
Admission: 15,015 applied, 13,965 admitted, 4,233 enrolled. ***Average high school GPA:*** 3.6. ***Test scores:*** ACT scores over 18: 99%; ACT scores over 24: 70%; ACT scores over 30: 19%.
Retention: 81% of full-time freshmen returned.

FACULTY
Total: 1,774, 81% full-time, 80% with terminal degrees.
Student/faculty ratio: 16:1.

ACADEMICS
Calendar: semesters. *Degrees:* certificates, bachelor's, master's, doctoral, post-master's, and postbachelor's certificates (University of Kansas is a single institution with academic programs and facilities at two primary locations: Lawrence and Kansas City).
Special study options: academic remediation for entering students, accelerated degree program, advanced placement credit, cooperative education, distance learning, double majors, English as a second language, freshman honors college, honors programs, independent study, internships, part-time degree program, services for LD students, study abroad, summer session for credit. ***ROTC:*** Army (b), Navy (b), Air Force (b).
Computers: 1,500 computers/terminals are available on campus for general student use. Students can access the following: campus intranet, computer help desk, free student e-mail accounts, online (class) grades, online (class) registration, online (class) schedules, online payments. Campuswide network is available. 100% of college-owned or -operated housing units are wired for high-speed Internet access. Wireless service is available via entire campus.
Library: Watson Library plus 11 others. *Books:* 4.7 million (physical), 988,900 (digital/electronic). Weekly public service hours: 168; study areas open 24 hours, 5-7 days a week; students can reserve study rooms.

STUDENT LIFE
Housing options: coed, men-only, women-only, cooperative. Campus housing is university owned.

Activities and organizations: drama/theater group, student-run newspaper, radio and television station, choral group, marching band, Adventure Club, Panhellenic Association, Center for Community Outreach, Pre-Nursing Club, American Red Cross Club, national fraternities, national sororities.

Athletics Member NCAA. All Division I except football (Division I-A). ***Intercollegiate sports:*** baseball M(s), basketball M(s)/W(s), crew W(s), cross-country running M(s)/W(s), golf M(s)/W(s), rugby M(c), soccer W(s), softball W(s), swimming and diving W(s), tennis W(s), track and field M(s)/W(s), volleyball W(s). ***Intramural sports:*** badminton M(c)/W(c), baseball M(c), basketball M/W, crew M(c)/W(c), equestrian sports M(c)/W(c), field hockey M/W, football M/W, golf M/W, ice hockey M(c), lacrosse M(c)/W(c), racquetball M/W, rock climbing M(c)/W(c), rugby M(c)/W(c), sailing M(c)/W(c), sand volleyball M/W, soccer M(c)/W(c), softball W(c), swimming and diving M(c)/W(c), table tennis M/W, tennis M/W, ultimate Frisbee M(c)/W(c), volleyball M(c)/W(c), water polo M(c)/W(c), weight lifting W(c).

Campus security: 24-hour emergency response devices and patrols, late-night transport/escort service, controlled dormitory access, University police department.

Student services: health clinic, personal/psychological counseling, women's center, legal services.

COSTS & FINANCIAL AID

Costs (2016–17) ***Tuition:*** state resident $9579 full-time, $319 per credit hour part-time; nonresident $24,962 full-time, $832 per credit hour part-time. Full-time tuition and fees vary according to program, reciprocity agreements, and student level. Part-time tuition and fees vary according to program, reciprocity agreements, and student level. No tuition increase for student's term of enrollment. ***Required fees:*** $970 full-time, $78 per credit hour part-time. ***Room and board:*** $9586; room only: $5738. Room and board charges vary according to board plan and housing facility. ***Payment plan:*** installment. ***Waivers:*** employees or children of employees.

Financial Aid Of all full-time matriculated undergraduates who enrolled in 2015, 11,075 applied for aid, 8,081 were judged to have need, 2,922 had their need fully met. 652 Federal Work-Study jobs (averaging $2326). 62 state and other part-time jobs (averaging $4447). In 2015, 3198 non-need-based awards were made. ***Average percent of need met:*** 75. ***Average financial aid package:*** $14,746. ***Average need-based loan:*** $4253. ***Average need-based gift aid:*** $6855. ***Average non-need-based aid:*** $5267. ***Average indebtedness upon graduation:*** $27,479.

APPLYING

Standardized Tests *Required:* SAT or ACT (for admission).

Options: electronic application.

Application fee: $40.

Required: high school transcript, minimum 3.0 GPA, Kansas Qualified Admissions Curriculum with minimum 2.0 GPA for state residents and 2.5 for nonresidents and minimum 3.0 overall GPA and ACT score of 24/SAT of 1160 or minimum 3.25 overall GPA and ACT score of 21/SAT of 1060.

Application deadlines: 8/7 (freshmen), 8/7 (transfers).

Notification: continuous (freshmen), continuous (transfers).

CONTACT

Ms. Lisa Pinamonti Kress, Director of Admissions, The University of Kansas, KU Visitor Center, 1502 Iowa Street, Lawrence, KS 66045-7576. *Phone:* 785-864-3911. *Toll-free phone:* 888-686-7323. *Fax:* 785-864-5017. *E-mail:* adm@ku.edu.

University of Saint Mary

Leavenworth, Kansas

http://www.stmary.edu/

- **Independent Roman Catholic** comprehensive, founded 1923
- **Small-town** 240-acre campus with easy access to Kansas City
- **Endowment** $18.0 million
- **Coed** 837 undergraduate students, 77% full-time, 57% women, 43% men
- **Moderately difficult** entrance level, 49% of applicants were admitted

UNDERGRAD STUDENTS

648 full-time, 189 part-time. Students come from 42 states and territories; 49% are from out of state; 9% Black or African American, non-Hispanic/Latino; 20% Hispanic/Latino; 1% Asian, non-Hispanic/Latino; 0.9% Native Hawaiian or other Pacific Islander, non-Hispanic/Latino; 0.4% American Indian or Alaska Native, non-Hispanic/Latino; 4% Two or more races, non-Hispanic/Latino; 5% Race/ethnicity unknown; 1% international; 13% transferred in; 32% live on campus.

Freshmen:
Admission: 888 applied, 439 admitted, 122 enrolled. ***Average high school GPA:*** 3.31. ***Test scores:*** SAT critical reading scores over 500: 43%; SAT math scores over 500: 43%; ACT scores over 18: 98%; SAT critical reading scores over 600: 8%; SAT math scores over 600: 17%; ACT scores over 24: 28%; SAT critical reading scores over 700: 4%; ACT scores over 30: 2%.

Retention: 71% of full-time freshmen returned.

FACULTY

Total: 187, 35% full-time, 55% with terminal degrees.

Student/faculty ratio: 11:1.

ACADEMICS

Calendar: semesters. *Degrees:* associate, bachelor's, master's, and doctoral.

Special study options: academic remediation for entering students, adult/continuing education programs, advanced placement credit, cooperative education, distance learning, double majors, honors programs, independent study, internships, off-campus study, part-time degree program, services for LD students, student-designed majors, study abroad, summer session for credit. ***ROTC:*** Army (c), Air Force (c).

Computers: 30 computers/terminals are available on campus for general student use. Students can access the following: campus intranet, computer help desk, free student e-mail accounts, online (class) grades, online (class) registration, online (class) schedules. Campuswide network is available. 100% of college-owned or -operated housing units are wired for high-speed Internet access. Wireless service is available via entire campus.

Library: De Paul Library plus 1 other. *Books:* 105,000 (physical), 103,000 (digital/electronic); *Serial titles:* 10 (physical), 12,000 (digital/electronic); *Databases:* 59. Weekly public service hours: 68; students can reserve study rooms.

STUDENT LIFE

Housing options: on-campus residence required through sophomore year; coed. Campus housing is university owned. Freshman campus housing is guaranteed.

Activities and organizations: drama/theater group, choral group, Student Government Association, BACCHUS, Theatrical Union, campus ministry, Amnesty International.

Athletics Member NAIA. ***Intercollegiate sports:*** baseball M(s), basketball M(s)/W(s), cheerleading M(s)/W(s), cross-country running M(s)/W(s), football M(s), soccer M(s)/W(s), softball W(s), track and field M(s)/W(s), volleyball W(s), wrestling M(s)/W(s). ***Intramural sports:*** badminton M/W, basketball M/W, bowling M/W, football M, lacrosse M/W, racquetball M/W, soccer M/W, softball W, table tennis M/W, ultimate Frisbee M/W, volleyball M/W, weight lifting M/W.

Campus security: 24-hour patrols, late-night transport/escort service, controlled dormitory access.

Student services: personal/psychological counseling.

COSTS & FINANCIAL AID

Costs (2017–18) ***Comprehensive fee:*** $37,383 includes full-time tuition ($26,940), mandatory fees ($890), and room and board ($9553). Full-time tuition and fees vary according to class time, course load, degree level, location, program, and reciprocity agreements. Part-time tuition: $625 per credit hour. Part-time tuition and fees vary according to class time, course load, degree level, location, program, and reciprocity agreements. ***Required fees:*** $370 per term part-time. ***Room and board:*** Room and board charges vary according to board plan and housing facility. ***Payment plan:*** installment. ***Waivers:*** senior citizens and employees or children of employees.

Financial Aid ***Average percent of need met:*** 82.

APPLYING

Standardized Tests *Required:* SAT or ACT (for admission).

Options: electronic application.

Application fee: $25.

Required: high school transcript, minimum 2.5 GPA. ***Recommended:*** 1 letter of recommendation, interview.

Application deadlines: rolling (freshmen), rolling (transfers).

Notification: continuous (freshmen), continuous (transfers).

CONTACT

Ms. Kristen Owsley, Director of Operations, University of Saint Mary, 4100 South Fourth Street, Leavenworth, KS 66048. *Phone:* 913-758-6303. *Toll-free phone:* 800-752-7043. *Fax:* 913-758-6140. *E-mail:* admiss@stmary.edu.

Washburn University

Topeka, Kansas

http://www.washburn.edu/

- **City-supported** comprehensive, founded 1865
- **Urban** 160-acre campus with easy access to Kansas City
- **Endowment** $172.4 million
- **Coed** 5,793 undergraduate students, 65% full-time, 59% women, 41% men
- **Noncompetitive** entrance level, 99% of applicants were admitted

UNDERGRAD STUDENTS

3,767 full-time, 2,026 part-time. Students come from 38 states and territories; 38 other countries; 7% are from out of state; 5% Black or African American, non-Hispanic/Latino; 7% Hispanic/Latino; 1% Asian, non-Hispanic/Latino; 0.1% Native Hawaiian or other Pacific Islander, non-Hispanic/Latino; 0.5% American Indian or Alaska Native, non-Hispanic/Latino; 4% Two or more races, non-Hispanic/Latino; 16% Race/ethnicity unknown; 4% international; 9% transferred in; 18% live on campus.

Freshmen:

Admission: 1,458 applied, 1,440 admitted, 813 enrolled. ***Average high school GPA:*** 3.4. ***Test scores:*** ACT scores over 18: 85%; ACT scores over 24: 34%; ACT scores over 30: 2%.

Retention: 68% of full-time freshmen returned.

FACULTY

Total: 512, 48% full-time, 59% with terminal degrees.

Student/faculty ratio: 12:1.

ACADEMICS

Calendar: semesters. *Degrees:* certificates, associate, bachelor's, master's, doctoral, post-master's, and postbachelor's certificates.

Special study options: academic remediation for entering students, adult/continuing education programs, advanced placement credit, cooperative education, distance learning, double majors, English as a second language, honors programs, independent study, internships, off-campus study, part-time degree program, services for LD students, student-designed majors, study abroad, summer session for credit. ***ROTC:*** Army (b), Navy (c), Air Force (c).

Unusual degree programs: 3-2 engineering with University of Kansas, Kansas State University.

Computers: 542 computers/terminals are available on campus for general student use. Students can access the following: campus intranet, computer help desk, free student e-mail accounts, online (class) grades, online (class) registration, online (class) schedules. Campuswide network is available. 100% of college-owned or -operated housing units are wired for high-speed Internet access. Wireless service is available via entire campus.

Library: Mabee Library plus 1 other. *Books:* 441,448 (physical), 292,840 (digital/electronic); *Serial titles:* 93,914 (physical); *Databases:* 182. Weekly public service hours: 104; students can reserve study rooms.

STUDENT LIFE

Housing options: coed. Campus housing is university owned.

Activities and organizations: drama/theater group, student-run newspaper, television station, choral group, marching band, national fraternities, national sororities.

Athletics Member NCAA. All Division II. ***Intercollegiate sports:*** baseball M(s), basketball M(s)/W(s), cheerleading M(s)/W(s), football M(s), golf M(s), soccer W(s), softball W(s), tennis M(s)/W(s), volleyball W(s). ***Intramural sports:*** badminton M/W, basketball M/W, crew M(c)/W(c), football M/W, rugby M(c), soccer M/W, softball M/W, table tennis M/W, tennis M/W, triathlon M/W, volleyball M/W.

Campus security: 24-hour emergency response devices and patrols, student patrols, late-night transport/escort service.

Student services: health clinic, personal/psychological counseling, legal services.

COSTS & FINANCIAL AID

Costs (2017–18) ***Tuition:*** state resident $8190 full-time, $273 per credit hour part-time; nonresident $18,510 full-time, $617 per credit hour part-time. Full-time tuition and fees vary according to program. Part-time tuition and fees vary according to program. ***Required fees:*** $110 full-time. ***Room and board:*** $7527; room only: $4287. Room and board charges vary according to board plan and housing facility. ***Payment plan:*** installment. ***Waivers:*** senior citizens and employees or children of employees.

Financial Aid Of all full-time matriculated undergraduates who enrolled in 2016, 3,366 applied for aid, 2,314 were judged to have need, 286 had their need fully met. In 2016, 521 non-need-based awards were made. ***Average percent of need met:*** 37. ***Average financial aid package:*** $9580. ***Average need-based loan:*** $4128. ***Average need-based gift aid:*** $5140. ***Average non-need-based aid:*** $3331. ***Average indebtedness upon graduation:*** $23,552.

APPLYING

Standardized Tests *Required:* ACT (for admission).

Options: electronic application.

Application fee: $20.

Required: high school transcript.

Application deadlines: 8/1 (freshmen), 8/1 (transfers).

Notification: continuous (freshmen), continuous (transfers).

CONTACT

Ms. Kris Klima, Director of Admissions, Washburn University, 1700 SW College, MO 114, Topeka, KS 66621. *Phone:* 785-670-1030. *Toll-free phone:* 800-332-0291. *Fax:* 785-670-1113. *E-mail:* admissions@washburn.edu.

Wichita State University

Wichita, Kansas

http://www.wichita.edu/

- **State-supported** university, founded 1895, part of Kansas Board of Regents
- **Urban** 335-acre campus
- **Endowment** $278.0 million
- **Coed** 11,823 undergraduate students, 73% full-time, 53% women, 47% men
- **Noncompetitive** entrance level, 96% of applicants were admitted

UNDERGRAD STUDENTS

8,687 full-time, 3,136 part-time. Students come from 47 states and territories; 97 other countries; 8% are from out of state; 6% Black or African American, non-Hispanic/Latino; 11% Hispanic/Latino; 7% Asian, non-Hispanic/Latino; 0.1% Native Hawaiian or other Pacific Islander, non-Hispanic/Latino; 0.7% American Indian or Alaska Native, non-Hispanic/Latino; 4% Two or more races, non-Hispanic/Latino; 3% Race/ethnicity unknown; 8% international; 12% transferred in; 10% live on campus.

Freshmen:

Admission: 6,306 applied, 6,067 admitted, 1,476 enrolled. ***Average high school GPA:*** 3.42. ***Test scores:*** SAT critical reading scores over 500: 59%; SAT math scores over 500: 78%; ACT scores over 18: 92%; SAT critical reading scores over 600: 25%; SAT math scores over 600: 31%; ACT scores over 24: 49%; SAT critical reading scores over 700: 7%; SAT math scores over 700: 16%; ACT scores over 30: 9%.

Retention: 72% of full-time freshmen returned.

FACULTY

Total: 793, 66% full-time, 57% with terminal degrees.

Student/faculty ratio: 19:1.

ACADEMICS
Calendar: semesters. *Degrees:* certificates, associate, bachelor's, master's, doctoral, post-master's, and postbachelor's certificates.

Special study options: academic remediation for entering students, accelerated degree program, adult/continuing education programs, advanced placement credit, cooperative education, distance learning, double majors, English as a second language, freshman honors college, honors programs, independent study, internships, off-campus study, part-time degree program, services for LD students, study abroad, summer session for credit.

Computers: 1,500 computers/terminals are available on campus for general student use. Students can access the following: computer help desk, free student e-mail accounts, online (class) grades, online (class) registration, online (class) schedules, learning management system. Campuswide network is available. 100% of college-owned or -operated housing units are wired for high-speed Internet access. Wireless service is available via entire campus.

Library: Ablah Library plus 2 others. *Books:* 1.9 million (physical), 428,856 (digital/electronic); *Serial titles:* 281 (physical), 76,462 (digital/electronic); *Databases:* 250. Weekly public service hours: 92; study areas open 24 hours, 5-7 days a week; students can reserve study rooms.

STUDENT LIFE
Housing options: on-campus residence required for freshman year; coed, special housing for students with disabilities. Campus housing is university owned. Freshman applicants given priority for college housing.

Activities and organizations: drama/theater group, student-run newspaper, radio and television station, choral group, national fraternities, national sororities.

Athletics Member NCAA. All Division I. ***Intercollegiate sports:*** baseball M(s), basketball M(s)/W(s), bowling M(s)/W(s), cheerleading M/W, cross-country running M(s)/W(s), golf M(s)/W(s), softball W(s), tennis M(s)/W(s), track and field M(s)/W(s), volleyball M(c)/W(s), wrestling M(c)/W(c). ***Intramural sports:*** badminton M/W, basketball M/W, bowling M/W, crew M/W, football M, golf M/W, racquetball M/W, soccer M/W, softball M/W, swimming and diving M/W, table tennis M/W, tennis M/W, track and field M/W, volleyball M/W.

Campus security: 24-hour emergency response devices and patrols, student patrols, late-night transport/escort service, controlled dormitory access, bicycle patrols by campus security.

Student services: health clinic, personal/psychological counseling, women's center.

COSTS & FINANCIAL AID
Costs (2016–17) ***Tuition:*** state resident $6385 full-time, $213 per credit hour part-time; nonresident $15,124 full-time, $504 per credit hour part-time. Full-time tuition and fees vary according to course level, course load, degree level, program, and student level. Part-time tuition and fees vary according to course level, course load, degree level, program, and student level. ***Required fees:*** $1510 full-time. ***Room and board:*** $10,980. Room and board charges vary according to board plan and housing facility. ***Payment plan:*** installment. ***Waivers:*** senior citizens and employees or children of employees.

Financial Aid Of all full-time matriculated undergraduates who enrolled in 2015, 7,784 applied for aid, 3,660 were judged to have need, 2,438 had their need fully met. In 2015, 1817 non-need-based awards were made. ***Average percent of need met:*** 63. ***Average financial aid package:*** $5842. ***Average need-based loan:*** $2564. ***Average need-based gift aid:*** $4287. ***Average non-need-based aid:*** $1499. ***Average indebtedness upon graduation:*** $39,122.

APPLYING
Standardized Tests *Required for some:* SAT or ACT (for admission). *Recommended:* SAT or ACT (for admission).

Options: electronic application, deferred entrance.

Application fee: $30.

Required for some: minimum 2.5 GPA, rank in upper one-third of high school class or complete the pre-college curriculum with a minimum 2.0 GPA (2.5 GPA for nonresidents). ***Recommended:*** high school transcript, .

Application deadlines: rolling (freshmen), rolling (transfers).

Notification: continuous (freshmen), continuous (transfers).

CONTACT
Wichita State University, 1845 North Fairmount, Wichita, KS 67260.
Phone: 316-978-3085. *Toll-free phone:* 800-362-2594.

KENTUCKY

Alice Lloyd College

Pippa Passes, Kentucky

http://www.alc.edu/

- **Independent** 4-year, founded 1923
- **Rural** 175-acre campus
- **Endowment** $38.0 million
- **Coed** 599 undergraduate students, 95% full-time, 54% women, 46% men

UNDERGRAD STUDENTS
572 full-time, 27 part-time. Students come from 6 states and territories; 2 other countries; 18% are from out of state; 1% Black or African American, non-Hispanic/Latino; 1% Hispanic/Latino; 0.2% Native Hawaiian or other Pacific Islander, non-Hispanic/Latino; 0.2% American Indian or Alaska Native, non-Hispanic/Latino; 0.3% Two or more races, non-Hispanic/Latino; 2% Race/ethnicity unknown; 0.3% international; 5% transferred in; 69% live on campus.

Freshmen:
Admission: 168 enrolled. ***Average high school GPA:*** 3.59. ***Test scores:*** SAT critical reading scores over 500: 57%; SAT math scores over 500: 72%; SAT writing scores over 500: 72%; ACT scores over 18: 90%; SAT critical reading scores over 600: 14%; ACT scores over 24: 33%; ACT scores over 30: 4%.

Retention: 62% of full-time freshmen returned.

FACULTY
Total: 50, 58% full-time, 44% with terminal degrees.

Student/faculty ratio: 17:1.

ACADEMICS
Calendar: semesters. *Degree:* bachelor's.

Special study options: academic remediation for entering students, advanced placement credit, double majors, independent study, internships, part-time degree program, study abroad.

Unusual degree programs: 3-2 nursing with University of Kentucky, Eastern Kentucky University.

Computers: 124 computers/terminals and 550 ports are available on campus for general student use. Students can access the following: campus intranet, computer help desk, free student e-mail accounts. Campuswide network is available. 100% of college-owned or -operated housing units are wired for high-speed Internet access. Wireless service is available via entire campus.

Library: McGaw Library and Learning Center. *Books:* 72,168 (physical), 141,804 (digital/electronic); *Serial titles:* 57 (physical), 4,212 (digital/electronic); *Databases:* 5,875. Weekly public service hours: 74.

STUDENT LIFE
Housing options: men-only, women-only. Campus housing is university owned.

Activities and organizations: drama/theater group, student-run newspaper, radio and television station, choral group, Voices of Appalachia, Intramurals, Baptist Collegiate Ministries, Allied Health Sciences Club, Alpha Chi National Honor Society.

Athletics Member NAIA, NCCAA. ***Intercollegiate sports:*** baseball M(s), basketball M(s)/W(s), cheerleading W, cross-country running M/W, golf M, softball W, tennis M/W, volleyball W. ***Intramural sports:*** basketball M/W, softball M, volleyball M/W, weight lifting M.

Campus security: 24-hour emergency response devices and patrols, late-night transport/escort service, controlled dormitory access, video cameras.

Student services: health clinic, personal/psychological counseling.

COSTS & FINANCIAL AID
Costs (2017–18) ***Tuition:*** The cost of tuition is covered by a combination of scholarships and other other financial aid. ***Required fees:*** $2050 full-time, $225 per credit hour part-time. ***Room and board:*** $6550; room only:

$3140. ***Payment plan:*** installment. ***Waivers:*** employees or children of employees.

Financial Aid Of all full-time matriculated undergraduates who enrolled in 2016, 572 applied for aid, 526 were judged to have need, 70 had their need fully met. 418 Federal Work-Study jobs (averaging $2320). 168 state and other part-time jobs (averaging $2320). In 2016, 56 non-need-based awards were made. ***Average percent of need met:*** 71. ***Average financial aid package:*** $13,775. ***Average need-based loan:*** $2225. ***Average need-based gift aid:*** $9889. ***Average non-need-based aid:*** $5898. ***Average indebtedness upon graduation:*** $10,714.

APPLYING
Standardized Tests *Required:* SAT or ACT (for admission).

Required: high school transcript, minimum 2.3 GPA, interview. ***Required for some:*** essay or personal statement, 2 letters of recommendation.

CONTACT
Ms. Angie Phipps, Director of Admissions, Alice Lloyd College, 100 Purpose Road, Pippa Passes, KY 41844. *Phone:* 606-368-6134. *Toll-free phone:* 888-280-4252. *Fax:* 606-368-6038. *E-mail:* angiephipps@alc.edu.

American National University
Lexington, Kentucky
http://www.an.edu/

CONTACT
Kim Thomasson, Campus Director, American National University, 2376 Sir Barton Way, Lexington, KY 40509. *Phone:* 859-253-0621. *Toll-free phone:* 888-9-JOBREADY.

American National University
Louisville, Kentucky
http://www.an.edu/

CONTACT
Vincent C. Tinebra, Campus Director, American National University, 4205 Dixie Highway, Louisville, KY 40216. *Phone:* 502-447-7634. *Toll-free phone:* 888-9-JOBREADY.

Asbury University
Wilmore, Kentucky
http://www.asbury.edu/

- **Independent nondenominational** comprehensive, founded 1890
- **Small-town** 400-acre campus with easy access to Lexington
- **Endowment** $47.8 million
- **Coed** 1,624 undergraduate students, 80% full-time, 61% women, 39% men
- **Moderately difficult** entrance level, 70% of applicants were admitted

UNDERGRAD STUDENTS
1,301 full-time, 323 part-time. Students come from 42 states and territories; 30 other countries; 48% are from out of state; 4% Black or African American, non-Hispanic/Latino; 2% Hispanic/Latino; 1% Asian, non-Hispanic/Latino; 0.2% Native Hawaiian or other Pacific Islander, non-Hispanic/Latino; 0.1% American Indian or Alaska Native, non-Hispanic/Latino; 5% Two or more races, non-Hispanic/Latino; 3% Race/ethnicity unknown; 3% international; 3% transferred in; 85% live on campus.

Freshmen:
Admission: 1,285 applied, 895 admitted, 306 enrolled. ***Average high school GPA:*** 3.65. ***Test scores:*** SAT critical reading scores over 500: 82%; SAT math scores over 500: 73%; ACT scores over 18: 96%; SAT critical reading scores over 600: 41%; SAT math scores over 600: 31%; ACT scores over 24: 52%; SAT critical reading scores over 700: 9%; SAT math scores over 700: 6%; ACT scores over 30: 14%.
Retention: 82% of full-time freshmen returned.

FACULTY
Total: 204, 46% full-time, 52% with terminal degrees.
Student/faculty ratio: 12:1.

ACADEMICS
Calendar: semesters. *Degrees:* associate, bachelor's, and master's.
Special study options: adult/continuing education programs, advanced placement credit, distance learning, double majors, off-campus study, services for LD students, study abroad, summer session for credit. ***ROTC:*** Army (c), Air Force (c).
Unusual degree programs: 3-2 engineering with University of Kentucky; nursing with University of Kentucky.
Computers: 250 computers/terminals and 950 ports are available on campus for general student use. Students can access the following: campus intranet, computer help desk, free student e-mail accounts, online (class) grades, online (class) registration, online (class) schedules. Campuswide network is available. 100% of college-owned or -operated housing units are wired for high-speed Internet access. Wireless service is available via classrooms, computer centers, computer labs, dorm rooms, learning centers, libraries, student centers.
Library: Kinlaw Library. *Books:* 157,131 (physical), 168,625 (digital/electronic); *Serial titles:* 442 (physical), 37,780 (digital/electronic); *Databases:* 60. Weekly public service hours: 88; students can reserve study rooms.

STUDENT LIFE
Housing options: on-campus residence required through senior year; men-only, women-only. Campus housing is university owned. Freshman campus housing is guaranteed.
Activities and organizations: drama/theater group, student-run newspaper, radio and television station, choral group, Asbury Student Congress, Spiritual Life Board, Summer Ministry Teams, Asbury Outdoors, WGM Global Cafe.
Athletics Member NAIA, NCCAA. ***Intercollegiate sports:*** baseball M(s), basketball M(s)/W(s), cross-country running M(s)/W(s), golf M(s)/W(s), lacrosse M(s)/W(s), soccer M(s)/W(s), softball W(s), swimming and diving M(s)/W(s), tennis M(s)/W(s), track and field M(s)/W(s), volleyball W(s). ***Intramural sports:*** basketball M/W, football M/W, golf M/W, racquetball M/W, soccer M/W, softball M/W, ultimate Frisbee M/W, volleyball M/W.
Campus security: 24-hour emergency response devices, late-night transport/escort service, controlled dormitory access, late night security personnel.
Student services: health clinic, personal/psychological counseling.

COSTS & FINANCIAL AID
Costs (2017–18) ***Comprehensive fee:*** $36,450 includes full-time tuition ($29,302), mandatory fees ($198), and room and board ($6950). Full-time tuition and fees vary according to course load and program. Part-time tuition: $1127 per credit hour. Part-time tuition and fees vary according to course load and program. ***Room and board:*** Room and board charges vary according to board plan and housing facility. ***Payment plan:*** installment. ***Waivers:*** senior citizens and employees or children of employees.
Financial Aid Of all full-time matriculated undergraduates who enrolled in 2015, 1,127 applied for aid, 1,017 were judged to have need. 326 Federal Work-Study jobs (averaging $1711). ***Average indebtedness upon graduation:*** $30,123.

APPLYING
Standardized Tests *Required:* SAT or ACT (for admission).
Options: electronic application, early admission, deferred entrance.
Required: essay or personal statement, high school transcript, minimum 2.5 GPA, 1 letter of recommendation.
Application deadlines: rolling (freshmen), rolling (transfers).
Notification: continuous (freshmen), continuous (transfers).

CONTACT
Mr. Brandon Combs, Director of Undergraduate Admissions, Asbury University, One Macklem Drive, Wilmore, KY 40390. *Phone:* 800-888-1818. *Toll-free phone:* 800-888-1818. *E-mail:* admissions@asbury.edu.

Beckfield College

Florence, Kentucky

http://www.beckfield.edu/

- **Proprietary** primarily 2-year, founded 1984
- **Suburban** campus
- **Coed**

ACADEMICS

Calendar: quarters. *Degrees:* certificates, diplomas, associate, bachelor's, and postbachelor's certificates.

STUDENT LIFE

Housing options: college housing not available.

APPLYING

Application fee: $150.

CONTACT

Mrs. Leah Boerger, Director of Admissions, Beckfield College, 16 Spiral Drive, Florence, KY 41042. *Phone:* 859-371-9393. *E-mail:* lboerger@beckfield.edu.

Bellarmine University

Louisville, Kentucky

http://www.bellarmine.edu/

- **Independent Roman Catholic** comprehensive, founded 1950
- **Suburban** 175-acre campus with easy access to Louisville
- **Endowment** $50.5 million
- **Coed** 2,650 undergraduate students, 93% full-time, 64% women, 36% men
- **Moderately difficult** entrance level, 82% of applicants were admitted

UNDERGRAD STUDENTS

2,476 full-time, 174 part-time. Students come from 39 states and territories; 17 other countries; 30% are from out of state; 4% Black or African American, non-Hispanic/Latino; 3% Hispanic/Latino; 2% Asian, non-Hispanic/Latino; 0.1% Native Hawaiian or other Pacific Islander, non-Hispanic/Latino; 0.4% American Indian or Alaska Native, non-Hispanic/Latino; 3% Two or more races, non-Hispanic/Latino; 4% Race/ethnicity unknown; 0.9% international; 3% transferred in; 41% live on campus.

Freshmen:
Admission: 6,212 applied, 5,122 admitted, 636 enrolled. ***Average high school GPA:*** 3.46. ***Test scores:*** SAT math scores over 500: 69%; SAT writing scores over 500: 38%; ACT scores over 18: 98%; SAT math scores over 600: 15%; SAT writing scores over 600: 14%; ACT scores over 24: 58%; SAT writing scores over 700: 5%; ACT scores over 30: 11%.
Retention: 80% of full-time freshmen returned.

FACULTY

Total: 435, 40% full-time, 56% with terminal degrees.

Student/faculty ratio: 12:1.

ACADEMICS

Calendar: semesters. *Degrees:* bachelor's, master's, doctoral, and postbachelor's certificates.

Special study options: accelerated degree program, adult/continuing education programs, advanced placement credit, cooperative education, double majors, freshman honors college, honors programs, independent study, internships, part-time degree program, services for LD students, student-designed majors, study abroad, summer session for credit. ***ROTC:*** Army (c), Air Force (c).

Unusual degree programs: 3-2 business administration.

Computers: 440 computers/terminals and 440 ports are available on campus for general student use. Students can access the following: campus intranet, computer help desk, free student e-mail accounts, online (class) grades, online (class) registration, online (class) schedules, mobile app. Campuswide network is available. 100% of college-owned or -operated housing units are wired for high-speed Internet access. Wireless service is available via classrooms, computer centers, computer labs, dorm rooms, learning centers, libraries, student centers.

Library: W. L. Lyons Brown Library. *Books:* 121,125 (physical), 233,857 (digital/electronic); *Serial titles:* 207 (physical), 88,144 (digital/electronic); *Databases:* 145. Weekly public service hours: 140; study areas open 24 hours, 5-7 days a week.

STUDENT LIFE

Housing options: on-campus residence required through junior year; coed, men-only, women-only, special housing for students with disabilities. Campus housing is university owned. Freshman campus housing is guaranteed.

Activities and organizations: drama/theater group, student-run newspaper, radio station, choral group, Student Government, Bellarmine Activities Council, Knights Nation, Fellowship of Christian Athletes, Delta Sigma Pi, national fraternities, national sororities.

Athletics Member NCAA. All Division II except lacrosse (Division I). ***Intercollegiate sports:*** baseball M(s), basketball M(s)/W(s), cheerleading M(s)/W(s), cross-country running M(s)/W(s), field hockey W(s), golf M(s)/W(s), lacrosse M(s), soccer M(s)/W(s), softball W(s), swimming and diving M(s)/W(s), tennis M(s)/W(s), track and field M(s)/W(s), volleyball W(s), wrestling M(s). ***Intramural sports:*** basketball M/W, bowling M(c)/W(c), football M/W, golf M/W, soccer M/W, softball M/W, swimming and diving M/W, table tennis M/W, tennis M/W, ultimate Frisbee M/W, volleyball M/W.

Campus security: 24-hour emergency response devices and patrols, student patrols, late-night transport/escort service, controlled dormitory access, 24-hour locked residence hall entrances, security cameras.

Student services: health clinic, personal/psychological counseling.

COSTS & FINANCIAL AID

Costs (2017–18) ***One-time required fee:*** $400. ***Comprehensive fee:*** $52,532 includes full-time tuition ($38,800), mandatory fees ($1550), and room and board ($12,182). Part-time tuition: $905 per credit hour. ***College room only:*** $7652. Room and board charges vary according to board plan and housing facility. ***Payment plan:*** installment. ***Waivers:*** employees or children of employees.

Financial Aid Of all full-time matriculated undergraduates who enrolled in 2016, 2,192 applied for aid, 1,935 were judged to have need, 408 had their need fully met. In 2016, 483 non-need-based awards were made. ***Average percent of need met:*** 74. ***Average financial aid package:*** $30,651. ***Average need-based loan:*** $4475. ***Average need-based gift aid:*** $23,040. ***Average non-need-based aid:*** $21,948. ***Average indebtedness upon graduation:*** $30,759.

APPLYING

Standardized Tests *Required:* SAT or ACT (for admission).

Options: electronic application, early admission, early action, deferred entrance.

Application fee: $25.

Required: high school transcript, minimum 2.5 GPA, 1 letter of recommendation. ***Required for some:*** essay or personal statement. ***Recommended:*** interview.

Application deadlines: 8/15 (freshmen), rolling (transfers), 11/1 (early action).

Notification: continuous (freshmen), continuous (transfers), 11/15 (early action).

CONTACT

Mr. Timothy A. Sturgeon, Dean of Admission, Bellarmine University, 2001 Newburg Road, Louisville, KY 40205-0671. *Phone:* 502-272-8131. *Toll-free phone:* 800-274-4723 Ext. 8131. *E-mail:* admissions@bellarmine.edu.

Berea College

Berea, Kentucky

http://www.berea.edu/

- **Independent** 4-year, founded 1855
- **Small-town** 140-acre campus
- **Endowment** $1.1 billion
- **Coed** 1,665 undergraduate students, 97% full-time, 56% women, 44% men
- **Moderately difficult** entrance level, 33% of applicants were admitted

UNDERGRAD STUDENTS
1,616 full-time, 49 part-time. Students come from 43 states and territories; 70 other countries; 53% are from out of state; 15% Black or African American, non-Hispanic/Latino; 9% Hispanic/Latino; 2% Asian, non-Hispanic/Latino; 0.2% Native Hawaiian or other Pacific Islander, non-Hispanic/Latino; 0.2% American Indian or Alaska Native, non-Hispanic/Latino; 6% Two or more races, non-Hispanic/Latino; 0.9% Race/ethnicity unknown; 8% international; 3% transferred in; 97% live on campus.

Freshmen:
Admission: 1,744 applied, 572 admitted, 418 enrolled. ***Average high school GPA:*** 3.48. ***Test scores:*** SAT critical reading scores over 500: 71%; SAT math scores over 500: 88%; SAT writing scores over 500: 78%; ACT scores over 18: 100%; SAT critical reading scores over 600: 27%; SAT math scores over 600: 32%; SAT writing scores over 600: 32%; ACT scores over 24: 57%; SAT math scores over 700: 2%; SAT writing scores over 700: 2%; ACT scores over 30: 9%.
Retention: 84% of full-time freshmen returned.

FACULTY
Total: 178, 77% full-time, 86% with terminal degrees.
Student/faculty ratio: 11:1.

ACADEMICS
Calendar: semesters. *Degree:* bachelor's.
Special study options: academic remediation for entering students, advanced placement credit, double majors, English as a second language, honors programs, independent study, internships, off-campus study, services for LD students, student-designed majors, study abroad, summer session for credit.
Unusual degree programs: 3-2 engineering with University of Kentucky.
Computers: 7,000 ports are available on campus for general student use. Students can access the following: campus intranet, computer help desk, free student e-mail accounts, online (class) grades, online (class) registration, online (class) schedules. Campuswide network is available. 100% of college-owned or -operated housing units are wired for high-speed Internet access. Wireless service is available via entire campus.
Library: Hutchins Library plus 1 other. *Books:* 346,053 (physical), 238,420 (digital/electronic); *Serial titles:* 258 (physical), 68,520 (digital/electronic). Weekly public service hours: 94; students can reserve study rooms.

STUDENT LIFE
Housing options: on-campus residence required through senior year; men-only, women-only. Campus housing is university owned. Freshman campus housing is guaranteed.
Activities and organizations: drama/theater group, student-run newspaper, choral group, Campus Activities Board, Cosmopolitan Club, CELTS (Center for Excellence in Learning through Service), Black Cultural Center, African Student Association.
Athletics Member NCAA. All Division III. ***Intercollegiate sports:*** baseball M, basketball M/W, cross-country running M/W, golf M, soccer M/W, softball W, tennis M/W, track and field M/W, volleyball W. ***Intramural sports:*** basketball M/W, football M/W, racquetball M/W, soccer M/W, softball M/W, ultimate Frisbee M/W, volleyball M/W.
Campus security: 24-hour emergency response devices and patrols, late-night transport/escort service, controlled dormitory access, crime prevention programs.
Student services: health clinic, personal/psychological counseling, women's center.

COSTS & FINANCIAL AID
Costs (2016–17) ***Comprehensive fee:*** includes mandatory fees ($570) and room and board ($6472). Financial aid is provided to all students for tuition costs. ***Room and board:*** Room and board charges vary according to board plan.
Financial Aid Of all full-time matriculated undergraduates who enrolled in 2016, 1,612 applied for aid, 1,612 were judged to have need. ***Average percent of need met:*** 93. ***Average financial aid package:*** $32,460. ***Average need-based loan:*** $1147. ***Average need-based gift aid:*** $30,149. ***Average indebtedness upon graduation:*** $7062. ***Financial aid deadline:*** 5/1.

APPLYING
Standardized Tests *Required:* SAT or ACT (for admission).
Options: electronic application.
Required: essay or personal statement, high school transcript, interview. ***Recommended:*** 2 letters of recommendation.
Application deadlines: 4/30 (freshmen), 3/31 (transfers).
Notification: continuous (freshmen), continuous until 4/15 (transfers).

CONTACT
Mr. Luke Hodson, Director of Admissions, Berea College, CPO 2220, Berea, KY 40404. *Phone:* 859-985-3500. *Toll-free phone:* 800-326-5948. *Fax:* 859-985-3512. *E-mail:* admissions@berea.edu.

Brescia University
Owensboro, Kentucky
http://www.brescia.edu/

- **Independent Roman Catholic** comprehensive, founded 1950
- **Urban** 9-acre campus
- **Endowment** $12.4 million
- **Coed** 1,272 undergraduate students, 56% full-time, 71% women, 29% men
- **Moderately difficult** entrance level, 47% of applicants were admitted

UNDERGRAD STUDENTS
710 full-time, 562 part-time. Students come from 48 states and territories; 6 other countries; 56% are from out of state; 11% Black or African American, non-Hispanic/Latino; 5% Hispanic/Latino; 0.5% Asian, non-Hispanic/Latino; 0.1% Native Hawaiian or other Pacific Islander, non-Hispanic/Latino; 0.5% American Indian or Alaska Native, non-Hispanic/Latino; 0.2% Two or more races, non-Hispanic/Latino; 31% Race/ethnicity unknown; 2% international; 10% transferred in; 41% live on campus.

Freshmen:
Admission: 4,438 applied, 2,094 admitted, 129 enrolled. ***Average high school GPA:*** 3.02. ***Test scores:*** SAT math scores over 500: 20%; ACT scores over 18: 87%; ACT scores over 24: 29%; ACT scores over 30: 2%.
Retention: 61% of full-time freshmen returned.

FACULTY
Total: 134, 38% full-time, 60% with terminal degrees.
Student/faculty ratio: 24:1.

ACADEMICS
Calendar: semesters. *Degrees:* certificates, associate, bachelor's, master's, and postbachelor's certificates.
Special study options: academic remediation for entering students, adult/continuing education programs, advanced placement credit, distance learning, double majors, honors programs, independent study, internships, off-campus study, part-time degree program, services for LD students, student-designed majors, study abroad, summer session for credit.
Computers: 90 computers/terminals and 90 ports are available on campus for general student use. Students can access the following: computer help desk, free student e-mail accounts, online (class) grades, online (class) schedules. Campuswide network is available. 100% of college-owned or -operated housing units are wired for high-speed Internet access. Wireless service is available via entire campus.
Library: Fr. Leonard Alvey Library. *Books:* 72,970 (physical), 1,245 (digital/electronic); *Databases:* 75. Students can reserve study rooms.

STUDENT LIFE
Housing options: on-campus residence required through junior year; coed, men-only, women-only. Campus housing is university owned. Freshman applicants given priority for college housing.
Activities and organizations: drama/theater group, student-run newspaper, choral group, Student Government, Alpha Chi, Kentucky Education Association, National Society for Speech Language and Hearing Association, ZEST.
Athletics Member NAIA. ***Intercollegiate sports:*** baseball M(s), basketball M(s)/W(s), cheerleading M(s)/W(s), cross-country running M(s)/W(s), golf M(s)/W(s), soccer M(s)/W(s), softball W(s), track and field M/W(s), volleyball W(s). ***Intramural sports:*** basketball M/W, soccer M/W, table tennis M/W, volleyball M/W.

Campus security: 24-hour emergency response devices, late-night transport/escort service, controlled dormitory access.

Student services: personal/psychological counseling.

COSTS & FINANCIAL AID

Costs (2017–18) ***One-time required fee:*** $200. ***Tuition:*** $20,960 full-time, $590 per credit hour part-time. Full-time tuition and fees vary according to course load and degree level. Part-time tuition and fees vary according to course load and degree level. ***Required fees:*** $890 full-time. ***Room only:*** Room and board charges vary according to board plan and housing facility. ***Payment plan:*** installment. ***Waivers:*** senior citizens and employees or children of employees.

Financial Aid Of all full-time matriculated undergraduates who enrolled in 2015, 925 applied for aid, 899 were judged to have need. 50 Federal Work-Study jobs (averaging $909). 48 state and other part-time jobs (averaging $849). In 2015, 57 non-need-based awards were made. ***Average financial aid package:*** $25,489. ***Average need-based loan:*** $3414. ***Average need-based gift aid:*** $7811. ***Average non-need-based aid:*** $16,191. ***Average indebtedness upon graduation:*** $19,060.

APPLYING

Standardized Tests *Required:* SAT or ACT (for admission). *Required for some:* SAT or ACT (for admission).

Options: electronic application, deferred entrance.

Application fee: $25.

Required: high school transcript. ***Required for some:*** essay or personal statement, 1 letter of recommendation, interview.

Application deadlines: rolling (freshmen), rolling (transfers).

Notification: continuous (freshmen), continuous (transfers).

CONTACT

Brescia University, 717 Frederica Street, Owensboro, KY 42301-3023. *Phone:* 270-686-4241 Ext. 241. *Toll-free phone:* 877-273-7242.

Campbellsville University

Campbellsville, Kentucky

http://www.campbellsville.edu/

- **Independent** comprehensive, founded 1906, affiliated with Kentucky Baptist Convention
- **Small-town** 90-acre campus
- **Endowment** $13.0 million
- **Coed** 3,349 undergraduate students, 60% full-time, 58% women, 42% men
- **Moderately difficult** entrance level, 70% of applicants were admitted

UNDERGRAD STUDENTS

1,998 full-time, 1,351 part-time. Students come from 41 states and territories; 56 other countries; 15% are from out of state; 9% Black or African American, non-Hispanic/Latino; 2% Hispanic/Latino; 1% Asian, non-Hispanic/Latino; 0.1% Native Hawaiian or other Pacific Islander, non-Hispanic/Latino; 0.3% American Indian or Alaska Native, non-Hispanic/Latino; 1% Two or more races, non-Hispanic/Latino; 3% Race/ethnicity unknown; 7% international; 8% transferred in; 46% live on campus.

Freshmen:

Admission: 2,966 applied, 2,072 admitted, 595 enrolled. ***Average high school GPA:*** 3.3. ***Test scores:*** SAT critical reading scores over 500: 35%; SAT math scores over 500: 58%; SAT writing scores over 500: 29%; ACT scores over 18: 85%; SAT critical reading scores over 600: 12%; SAT math scores over 600: 18%; SAT writing scores over 600: 3%; ACT scores over 24: 29%; SAT critical reading scores over 700: 3%; SAT math scores over 700: 5%; ACT scores over 30: 4%.

Retention: 61% of full-time freshmen returned.

FACULTY

Total: 342, 45% full-time, 30% with terminal degrees.

Student/faculty ratio: 15:1.

ACADEMICS

Calendar: semesters. *Degrees:* certificates, associate, bachelor's, master's, post-master's, and postbachelor's certificates.

Special study options: academic remediation for entering students, accelerated degree program, adult/continuing education programs, advanced placement credit, cooperative education, distance learning, double majors, English as a second language, honors programs, independent study, internships, off-campus study, part-time degree program, services for LD students, study abroad, summer session for credit. ***ROTC:*** Army (c).

Computers: 220 computers/terminals are available on campus for general student use. Students can access the following: campus intranet, computer help desk, free student e-mail accounts, online (class) grades, online (class) registration, online (class) schedules. Campuswide network is available. 100% of college-owned or -operated housing units are wired for high-speed Internet access. Wireless service is available via entire campus.

Library: Montgomery Library. *Books:* 172,863 (physical), 236,674 (digital/electronic); *Serial titles:* 126 (physical); *Databases:* 72. Weekly public service hours: 77; students can reserve study rooms.

STUDENT LIFE

Housing options: on-campus residence required through sophomore year; men-only, women-only. Campus housing is university owned. Freshman campus housing is guaranteed.

Activities and organizations: drama/theater group, student-run newspaper, radio and television station, choral group, marching band, Baptist Campus Ministries, Student Government Association, International Student Association, Green Minds, KANS (Nursing Society).

Athletics Member NAIA, NCCAA. ***Intercollegiate sports:*** archery M(s)/W(s), baseball M(s), basketball M(s)/W(s), bowling M(s)/W(s), cheerleading M(s)/W(s), cross-country running M(s)/W(s), football M(s), golf M(s)/W(s), soccer M(s)/W(s), softball W(s), swimming and diving M(s)/W(s), tennis M(s)/W(s), track and field M(s)/W(s), volleyball M(s)/W(s), wrestling M(s)/W(s). ***Intramural sports:*** basketball M/W, bowling M/W, football M/W, racquetball M/W, sand volleyball M/W, soccer M/W, softball M/W, swimming and diving M/W, table tennis M/W, tennis M/W, ultimate Frisbee M/W, volleyball M/W, weight lifting M/W.

Campus security: 24-hour emergency response devices and patrols, student patrols, late-night transport/escort service, controlled dormitory access.

Student services: health clinic, personal/psychological counseling.

COSTS & FINANCIAL AID

Costs (2016–17) ***Comprehensive fee:*** $32,492 includes full-time tuition ($24,096), mandatory fees ($500), and room and board ($7896). Full-time tuition and fees vary according to course load, location, and program. Part-time tuition: $1004 per credit hour. Part-time tuition and fees vary according to class time, course load, location, and program. ***Required fees:*** $250 per year part-time. ***Room and board:*** Room and board charges vary according to housing facility. ***Payment plan:*** installment. ***Waivers:*** adult students, senior citizens, and employees or children of employees.

Financial Aid Of all full-time matriculated undergraduates who enrolled in 2015, 1,589 applied for aid, 1,495 were judged to have need, 230 had their need fully met. 265 Federal Work-Study jobs (averaging $1500). 30 state and other part-time jobs (averaging $1200). In 2015, 124 non-need-based awards were made. ***Average percent of need met:*** 74. ***Average financial aid package:*** $19,624. ***Average need-based loan:*** $3690. ***Average need-based gift aid:*** $16,723. ***Average non-need-based aid:*** $11,286. ***Average indebtedness upon graduation:*** $24,224.

APPLYING

Standardized Tests *Required:* SAT or ACT (for admission).

Options: electronic application, deferred entrance.

Application fee: $20.

Required: high school transcript, minimum 2.0 GPA. ***Recommended:*** essay or personal statement, minimum 3.0 GPA, interview.

Application deadlines: rolling (freshmen), rolling (transfers).

Notification: continuous (freshmen), continuous (transfers).

CONTACT

Mrs. Paula S. Caldwell, Director of Admissions, Campbellsville University, 1 University Drive, UPO 782, Campbellsville, KY 42718-2799. *Phone:* 270-789-5220 Ext. 5007. *Toll-free phone:* 800-264-6014. *Fax:* 270-789-5071. *E-mail:* admissions@campbellsville.edu.

Centre College

Danville, Kentucky

http://www.centre.edu/

- **Independent** 4-year, founded 1819, affiliated with Presbyterian Church (U.S.A.)
- **Small-town** 152-acre campus
- **Endowment** $269.8 million
- **Coed** 1,430 undergraduate students, 100% full-time, 51% women, 49% men
- **Very difficult** entrance level, 74% of applicants were admitted

UNDERGRAD STUDENTS

1,428 full-time, 2 part-time. Students come from 44 states and territories; 16 other countries; 43% are from out of state; 5% Black or African American, non-Hispanic/Latino; 4% Hispanic/Latino; 4% Asian, non-Hispanic/Latino; 0.1% Native Hawaiian or other Pacific Islander, non-Hispanic/Latino; 0.3% American Indian or Alaska Native, non-Hispanic/Latino; 3% Two or more races, non-Hispanic/Latino; 0.6% Race/ethnicity unknown; 7% international; 0.6% transferred in; 98% live on campus.

Freshmen:

Admission: 2,595 applied, 1,927 admitted, 400 enrolled. ***Average high school GPA:*** 3.63. ***Test scores:*** SAT critical reading scores over 500: 86%; SAT math scores over 500: 92%; SAT writing scores over 500: 91%; ACT scores over 18: 100%; SAT critical reading scores over 600: 45%; SAT math scores over 600: 64%; SAT writing scores over 600: 51%; ACT scores over 24: 93%; SAT critical reading scores over 700: 13%; SAT math scores over 700: 24%; SAT writing scores over 700: 12%; ACT scores over 30: 43%.

Retention: 93% of full-time freshmen returned.

FACULTY

Total: 159, 81% full-time, 81% with terminal degrees.

Student/faculty ratio: 10:1.

ACADEMICS

Calendar: 4-1-4. *Degree:* bachelor's.

Special study options: advanced placement credit, cooperative education, double majors, honors programs, independent study, internships, off-campus study, services for LD students, student-designed majors, study abroad. ***ROTC:*** Army (c), Air Force (c).

Unusual degree programs: 3-2 engineering with Washington University in St. Louis, Columbia University, Vanderbilt University, University of Kentucky.

Computers: 425 computers/terminals and 1,500 ports are available on campus for general student use. Students can access the following: campus intranet, computer help desk, free student e-mail accounts, online (class) grades, online (class) registration, online (class) schedules. Campuswide network is available. 100% of college-owned or -operated housing units are wired for high-speed Internet access. Wireless service is available via entire campus.

Library: Doherty Library. *Books:* 234,538 (physical), 33,042 (digital/electronic); *Serial titles:* 536 (physical), 27,570 (digital/electronic); *Databases:* 530. Weekly public service hours: 113; study areas open 24 hours, 5-7 days a week; students can reserve study rooms.

STUDENT LIFE

Housing options: on-campus residence required through senior year; coed, men-only, women-only, special housing for students with disabilities. Campus housing is university owned. Freshman campus housing is guaranteed.

Activities and organizations: drama/theater group, student-run newspaper, radio station, choral group, Student Government Association, Centre Action Reaches Everyone, Student Activities Council, Christian fellowship group, Diversity Student Union, national fraternities, national sororities.

Athletics Member NCAA. All Division III. ***Intercollegiate sports:*** baseball M, basketball M/W, cheerleading W, cross-country running M/W, field hockey W, football M, golf M/W, lacrosse M/W, soccer M/W, softball W, swimming and diving M/W, tennis M/W, track and field M/W, volleyball W. ***Intramural sports:*** basketball M/W, football M/W, golf M/W, soccer M/W, softball M/W, tennis M/W, volleyball M/W.

Campus security: 24-hour emergency response devices and patrols, late-night transport/escort service, controlled dormitory access.

Student services: health clinic, personal/psychological counseling.

COSTS & FINANCIAL AID

Costs (2017–18) ***Comprehensive fee:*** $50,750 includes full-time tuition ($40,500) and room and board ($10,250). Part-time tuition: $1455 per credit hour. ***College room only:*** $5125. Room and board charges vary according to housing facility. ***Payment plan:*** installment. ***Waivers:*** employees or children of employees.

Financial Aid Of all full-time matriculated undergraduates who enrolled in 2016, 1,021 applied for aid, 789 were judged to have need, 255 had their need fully met. 334 Federal Work-Study jobs (averaging $1665). In 2016, 582 non-need-based awards were made. ***Average percent of need met:*** 86. ***Average financial aid package:*** $32,001. ***Average need-based loan:*** $4512. ***Average need-based gift aid:*** $28,880. ***Average non-need-based aid:*** $20,689. ***Average indebtedness upon graduation:*** $26,740. ***Financial aid deadline:*** 1/31.

APPLYING

Standardized Tests *Required:* SAT or ACT (for admission).

Options: electronic application, early admission, early decision, early action, deferred entrance.

Required: essay or personal statement, high school transcript, 1 letter of recommendation. ***Recommended:*** interview.

Application deadlines: 1/15 (freshmen), rolling (transfers), 12/1 (early action).

Early decision deadline: 11/15.

Notification: 3/15 (freshmen), 3/15 (out-of-state freshmen), 12/15 (early decision), 1/15 (early action).

CONTACT

Mr. Bob Nesmith, Dean of Admission and Student Financial Aid, Centre College, 600 West Walnut Street, Danville, KY 40422-1394. *Phone:* 859-238-5350. *Toll-free phone:* 800-423-6236. *Fax:* 859-238-5373. *E-mail:* admission@centre.edu.

Clear Creek Baptist Bible College

Pineville, Kentucky

http://www.ccbbc.edu/

CONTACT

Mr. Billy Howell, Director of Admissions, Clear Creek Baptist Bible College, 300 Clear Creek Road, Pineville, KY 40977. *Phone:* 606-337-3196 Ext. 103. *Fax:* 606-337-1631. *E-mail:* bhowell@ccbbc.edu.

Eastern Kentucky University

Richmond, Kentucky

http://www.eku.edu/

- **State-supported** comprehensive, founded 1906
- **Small-town** 500-acre campus with easy access to Lexington
- **Endowment** $60.2 million
- **Coed**
- **Minimally difficult** entrance level

FACULTY

Student/faculty ratio: 17:1.

ACADEMICS

Calendar: semesters. *Degrees:* certificates, associate, bachelor's, master's, doctoral, post-master's, and postbachelor's certificates.

Library: John Grant Crabbe Library plus 2 others.

STUDENT LIFE

Housing options: on-campus residence required through sophomore year; coed, men-only, women-only. Campus housing is university owned and leased by the school. Freshman campus housing is guaranteed.

Activities and organizations: drama/theater group, student-run newspaper, radio station, choral group, marching band, Honor Society, Regular Society, national fraternities, national sororities.

Athletics Member NCAA. All Division I.

Campus security: 24-hour emergency response devices and patrols, student patrols, late-night transport/escort service, controlled dormitory access.

Student services: health clinic, personal/psychological counseling.

COSTS & FINANCIAL AID

Costs (2016–17) ***Tuition:*** state resident $8568 full-time, $357 per credit hour part-time; nonresident $17,880 full-time, $745 per credit hour part-time. Full-time tuition and fees vary according to degree level and location. Part-time tuition and fees vary according to course load. ***Room and board:*** $8466; room only: $4986. Room and board charges vary according to board plan and housing facility.

Financial Aid Of all full-time matriculated undergraduates who enrolled in 2016, 9,193 applied for aid, 7,883 were judged to have need, 2,694 had their need fully met. 1,200 Federal Work-Study jobs (averaging $2400). 1,200 state and other part-time jobs (averaging $2400). In 2016, 1466 non-need-based awards were made. ***Average percent of need met:*** 80. ***Average financial aid package:*** $10,962. ***Average need-based loan:*** $4042. ***Average need-based gift aid:*** $5857. ***Average non-need-based aid:*** $5596. ***Average indebtedness upon graduation:*** $34,358.

APPLYING

Standardized Tests *Required:* SAT or ACT (for admission). *Required for some:* SAT and SAT Subject Tests or ACT (for admission).

Options: electronic application, deferred entrance.

Application fee: $35.

Required: high school transcript, minimum 2.0 GPA. ***Recommended:*** minimum 2.5 GPA.

CONTACT

Ms. Stephanie Leigh Whaley, Director of Admissions, Eastern Kentucky University, SSB CPO 54, 521 Lancaster Avenue, Richmond, KY 40475-3102. *Phone:* 859-622-2106. *Toll-free phone:* 800-465-9191. *Fax:* 859-622-8024. *E-mail:* admissions@eku.edu.

Galen College of Nursing

Louisville, Kentucky

http://www.galencollege.edu/

CONTACT

Galen College of Nursing, 1031 Zorn Avenue, Suite 400, Louisville, KY 40207. *Toll-free phone:* 877-223-7040.

Georgetown College

Georgetown, Kentucky

http://www.georgetowncollege.edu/

- **Independent** comprehensive, founded 1829, affiliated with Baptist Church
- **Suburban** 104-acre campus with easy access to Cincinnati, OH; Louisville, KY
- **Endowment** $30.9 million
- **Coed** 986 undergraduate students, 93% full-time, 54% women, 46% men
- **Moderately difficult** entrance level, 66% of applicants were admitted

UNDERGRAD STUDENTS

917 full-time, 69 part-time. Students come from 29 states and territories; 8 other countries; 23% are from out of state; 9% Black or African American, non-Hispanic/Latino; 2% Hispanic/Latino; 0.8% Asian, non-Hispanic/Latino; 0.2% American Indian or Alaska Native, non-Hispanic/Latino; 4% Two or more races, non-Hispanic/Latino; 5% Race/ethnicity unknown; 0.8% international; 5% transferred in; 89% live on campus.

Freshmen:

Admission: 2,127 applied, 1,414 admitted, 296 enrolled. ***Average high school GPA:*** 3.5. ***Test scores:*** SAT critical reading scores over 500: 37%; SAT math scores over 500: 36%; ACT scores over 18: 99%; SAT critical reading scores over 600: 1%; SAT math scores over 600: 12%; ACT scores over 24: 49%; ACT scores over 30: 8%.

Retention: 71% of full-time freshmen returned.

FACULTY

Total: 134, 57% full-time, 60% with terminal degrees.

Student/faculty ratio: 11:1.

ACADEMICS

Calendar: semesters. *Degrees:* bachelor's, master's, and post-master's certificates.

Special study options: advanced placement credit, cooperative education, distance learning, double majors, English as a second language, honors programs, independent study, internships, off-campus study, part-time degree program, services for LD students, student-designed majors, study abroad, summer session for credit. ***ROTC:*** Army (c), Air Force (c).

Unusual degree programs: 3-2 engineering with University of Kentucky; nursing with University of Kentucky; diplomacy and international commerce with University of Kentucky.

Computers: 135 computers/terminals and 2,000 ports are available on campus for general student use. Students can access the following: campus intranet, computer help desk, free student e-mail accounts, online (class) grades, online (class) registration, online (class) schedules, library apps for smartphones. Campuswide network is available. 100% of college-owned or -operated housing units are wired for high-speed Internet access. Wireless service is available via entire campus.

Library: Anna Ashcraft Ensor Learning Resource Center. *Books:* 121,081 (physical), 327,868 (digital/electronic); *Serial titles:* 1,108 (physical), 43,132 (digital/electronic); *Databases:* 107. Weekly public service hours: 91.

STUDENT LIFE

Housing options: on-campus residence required through senior year; men-only, women-only. Campus housing is university owned and leased by the school. Freshman campus housing is guaranteed.

Activities and organizations: drama/theater group, student-run newspaper, radio station, choral group, national fraternities, national sororities.

Athletics Member NAIA. ***Intercollegiate sports:*** baseball M(s), basketball M(s)/W(s), cheerleading W(s), cross-country running M(s)/W(s), football M(s), golf M(s)/W(s), lacrosse W(s), soccer M(s)/W(s), softball W(s), tennis M(s)/W(s), track and field M(s)/W(s), volleyball W(s). ***Intramural sports:*** basketball M/W, football M/W, golf M/W, racquetball M/W, soccer M/W, softball M/W, table tennis M/W, tennis M/W, ultimate Frisbee M/W, volleyball M/W.

Campus security: 24-hour patrols, late-night transport/escort service, controlled dormitory access.

Student services: health clinic, personal/psychological counseling.

COSTS & FINANCIAL AID

Costs (2016–17) ***Comprehensive fee:*** $44,700 includes full-time tuition ($35,650) and room and board ($9050). Full-time tuition and fees vary according to course load and degree level. Part-time tuition: $957 per credit hour. Part-time tuition and fees vary according to course load and degree level. ***College room only:*** $4360. Room and board charges vary according to board plan and housing facility. ***Payment plan:*** installment. ***Waivers:*** employees or children of employees.

Financial Aid Of all full-time matriculated undergraduates who enrolled in 2014, 884 applied for aid, 805 were judged to have need, 56 had their need fully met. 545 Federal Work-Study jobs (averaging $916). In 2014, 71 non-need-based awards were made. ***Average percent of need met:*** 86. ***Average financial aid package:*** $29,023. ***Average need-based loan:*** $3018. ***Average need-based gift aid:*** $14,998. ***Average non-need-based aid:*** $13,372. ***Average indebtedness upon graduation:*** $31,267.

APPLYING

Standardized Tests *Required:* SAT or ACT (for admission). *Recommended:* ACT (for admission).

Options: electronic application, deferred entrance.

Required: high school transcript, minimum 2.0 GPA. ***Required for some:*** essay or personal statement, interview.

Application deadlines: rolling (freshmen), rolling (transfers).

Notification: continuous (freshmen), continuous (transfers).

CONTACT

Mr. Jeremiah Tudor, Senior Associate Director of Admissions, Georgetown College, 400 East College Street, Georgetown, KY 40324. *Phone:* 502-863-8727. *Toll-free phone:* 800-788-9985. *Fax:* 502-868-7733. *E-mail:* admissions@georgetowncollege.edu.

Kentucky Christian University
Grayson, Kentucky
http://www.kcu.edu/

CONTACT
Ms. Heather Stacy, Director of Admissions, Kentucky Christian University, 100 Academic Parkway, Grayson, KY 41143. *Phone:* 606-474-3284. *Toll-free phone:* 800-522-3181. *Fax:* 606-474-3155. *E-mail:* sgreer@kcu.edu.

Kentucky Mountain Bible College
Jackson, Kentucky
http://www.kmbc.edu/

- **Independent interdenominational** 4-year, founded 1931
- **Rural** 500-acre campus with easy access to Lexington
- **Coed** 85 undergraduate students, 72% full-time, 38% women, 62% men
- **Minimally difficult** entrance level, 41% of applicants were admitted

UNDERGRAD STUDENTS
61 full-time, 24 part-time. Students come from 14 states and territories; 3 other countries; 56% are from out of state; 4% transferred in; 92% live on campus.

Freshmen:
Admission: 59 applied, 24 admitted, 20 enrolled. ***Average high school GPA:*** 3.37.
Retention: 87% of full-time freshmen returned.

FACULTY
Total: 14, 7% full-time, 7% with terminal degrees.
Student/faculty ratio: 13:1.

ACADEMICS
Calendar: semesters. *Degrees:* associate and bachelor's.
Special study options: academic remediation for entering students, cooperative education, distance learning, independent study, internships, part-time degree program.
Computers: 4 computers/terminals are available on campus for general student use. Students can access the following: campus intranet, free student e-mail accounts, online (class) grades, online (class) registration, online (class) schedules. Campuswide network is available. 100% of college-owned or -operated housing units are wired for high-speed Internet access. Wireless service is available via entire campus.
Library: Gibson Library plus 1 other. *Books:* 31,235 (physical), 52 (digital/electronic); *Serial titles:* 95 (physical). Weekly public service hours: 70.

STUDENT LIFE
Housing options: on-campus residence required through senior year; men-only, women-only. Campus housing is university owned. Freshman campus housing is guaranteed.
Activities and organizations: drama/theater group, student-run newspaper, choral group, Missionary Involvement, Class Organizations.
Athletics ***Intramural sports:*** basketball M, volleyball W.
Campus security: student patrols.
Student services: personal/psychological counseling.

COSTS & FINANCIAL AID
Costs (2016–17) ***One-time required fee:*** $640. ***Comprehensive fee:*** $12,920 includes full-time tuition ($7360), mandatory fees ($710), and room and board ($4850). Full-time tuition and fees vary according to program. Part-time tuition: $230 per credit hour. Part-time tuition and fees vary according to program. ***Required fees:*** $250 per semester part-time. ***College room only:*** $1750. ***Payment plan:*** installment. ***Waivers:*** employees or children of employees.
Financial Aid Of all full-time matriculated undergraduates who enrolled in 2015, 54 applied for aid, 53 were judged to have need, 5 had their need fully met. In 2015, 7 non-need-based awards were made. ***Average percent of need met;*** 66. ***Average financial aid package:*** $9336. ***Average need-based loan:*** $3707. ***Average need-based gift aid:*** $5889. ***Average non-need-based aid:*** $2808. ***Average indebtedness upon graduation:*** $7370.

APPLYING
Standardized Tests *Required:* ACT (for admission).
Application fee: $25.
Required: essay or personal statement, high school transcript, minimum 2.0 GPA, testimony of Christian belief and practice. ***Recommended:*** minimum 2.0 GPA, interview.
Application deadlines: rolling (freshmen), rolling (transfers).
Notification: continuous (freshmen), continuous (transfers).

CONTACT
Mr. David Lorimer, Director of Recruiting, Kentucky Mountain Bible College, PO Box 10, Vancleve, KY 41385. *Phone:* 606-693-5000 Ext. 138. *Toll-free phone:* 800-879-KMBC. *Fax:* 606-693-4884. *E-mail:* dlorimer@kmbc.edu.

Kentucky State University
Frankfort, Kentucky
http://www.kysu.edu/

- **State-related** comprehensive, founded 1886
- **Small-town** 916-acre campus with easy access to Louisville
- **Endowment** $15.1 million
- **Coed** 1,568 undergraduate students, 67% full-time, 61% women, 39% men

UNDERGRAD STUDENTS
1,049 full-time, 519 part-time. Students come from 39 states and territories; 9 other countries; 32% are from out of state; 47% Black or African American, non-Hispanic/Latino; 2% Hispanic/Latino; 0.8% Asian, non-Hispanic/Latino; 0.3% American Indian or Alaska Native, non-Hispanic/Latino; 2% Two or more races, non-Hispanic/Latino; 22% Race/ethnicity unknown; 0.4% international; 8% transferred in; 36% live on campus.

Freshmen:
Admission: 204 enrolled. ***Average high school GPA:*** 3.03. ***Test scores:*** ACT scores over 18: 63%; ACT scores over 24: 12%; ACT scores over 30: 1%.
Retention: 59% of full-time freshmen returned.

FACULTY
Total: 111, 97% full-time, 80% with terminal degrees.
Student/faculty ratio: 12:1.

ACADEMICS
Calendar: semesters. *Degrees:* certificates, associate, bachelor's, master's, and doctoral.
Special study options: academic remediation for entering students, adult/continuing education programs, advanced placement credit, cooperative education, distance learning, double majors, external degree program, freshman honors college, honors programs, independent study, internships, part-time degree program, services for LD students, student-designed majors, study abroad, summer session for credit. ***ROTC:*** Army (c), Air Force (c).
Unusual degree programs: 3-2 engineering with University of Kentucky.
Computers: 142 computers/terminals and 92 ports are available on campus for general student use. Students can access the following: campus intranet, computer help desk, free student e-mail accounts, online (class) grades, online (class) registration, online (class) schedules, student bill-pay, address verification, ability to accept financial aid awards. Campuswide network is available. 100% of college-owned or -operated housing units are wired for high-speed Internet access. Wireless service is available via entire campus.
Library: Paul G. Blazer Library. *Books:* 170,726 (physical), 23,417 (digital/electronic); *Serial titles:* 1,894 (physical), 38,647 (digital/electronic); *Databases:* 56. Weekly public service hours: 101; study areas open 24 hours, 5-7 days a week.

STUDENT LIFE
Housing options: on-campus residence required through sophomore year; coed, men-only, women-only, special housing for students with disabilities. Campus housing is university owned. Freshman campus housing is guaranteed.
Activities and organizations: drama/theater group, student-run newspaper, choral group, marching band, Collegiate100, Alpha Phi Omega, Drive Our Peer's Education DOPE, Student Ambassador's, Alpha Phi Alpha, national fraternities, national sororities.

Athletics Member NCAA. All Division II. ***Intercollegiate sports:*** baseball M(s), basketball M(s)/W(s), cross-country running M(s)/W(s), football M(s), golf M(s), softball W(s), track and field M(s)/W(s), volleyball W(s). ***Intramural sports:*** badminton M/W, basketball M/W, cheerleading W(c), gymnastics M/W, racquetball M/W, volleyball W.

Campus security: 24-hour emergency response devices and patrols, student patrols, late-night transport/escort service, controlled dormitory access.

Student services: health clinic, personal/psychological counseling.

COSTS & FINANCIAL AID

Costs (2016–17) ***Tuition:*** state resident $7406 full-time, $309 per credit hour part-time; nonresident $18,314 full-time, $763 per credit hour part-time. Full-time tuition and fees vary according to course load. Part-time tuition and fees vary according to course load. ***Required fees:*** $390 full-time. ***Room and board:*** $6690; room only: $3340. Room and board charges vary according to board plan and housing facility. ***Payment plan:*** installment. ***Waivers:*** senior citizens and employees or children of employees.

Financial Aid Of all full-time matriculated undergraduates who enrolled in 2016, 1,004 applied for aid, 526 were judged to have need, 14 had their need fully met. 115 Federal Work-Study jobs (averaging $4215). 25 state and other part-time jobs (averaging $469). In 2016, 122 non-need-based awards were made. ***Average percent of need met:*** 83. ***Average financial aid package:*** $11,792. ***Average need-based loan:*** $4078. ***Average need-based gift aid:*** $7697. ***Average non-need-based aid:*** $4822. ***Average indebtedness upon graduation:*** $36,323.

APPLYING

Standardized Tests *Required:* SAT or ACT (for admission).

Required: high school transcript, minimum 2.5 GPA, minimum ACT score of 18.

CONTACT

Admissions Counselor, Kentucky State University, 400 East Main Street, Academic Suite Building 312, Frankfort, KY 40601. *Phone:* 502-597-6813. *Toll-free phone:* 877-367-5978. *Fax:* 502-597-5814. *E-mail:* admissions@kysu.edu.

Kentucky Wesleyan College

Owensboro, Kentucky

http://www.kwc.edu/

- **Independent Methodist** 4-year, founded 1858
- **Suburban** 52-acre campus
- **Endowment** $32.6 million
- **Coed** 709 undergraduate students, 93% full-time, 46% women, 54% men
- **Moderately difficult** entrance level, 61% of applicants were admitted

UNDERGRAD STUDENTS

662 full-time, 47 part-time. Students come from 28 states and territories; 12 other countries; 29% are from out of state; 14% Black or African American, non-Hispanic/Latino; 2% Hispanic/Latino; 0.4% Asian, non-Hispanic/Latino; 0.1% American Indian or Alaska Native, non-Hispanic/Latino; 15% Race/ethnicity unknown; 0.7% international; 7% transferred in; 46% live on campus.

Freshmen:

Admission: 1,087 applied, 660 admitted, 239 enrolled. ***Average high school GPA:*** 3.3.

Retention: 66% of full-time freshmen returned.

FACULTY

Total: 92, 51% full-time.

Student/faculty ratio: 11:1.

ACADEMICS

Calendar: semesters. *Degree:* bachelor's.

Special study options: academic remediation for entering students, accelerated degree program, adult/continuing education programs, advanced placement credit, cooperative education, distance learning, double majors, independent study, internships, off-campus study, part-time degree program, services for LD students, study abroad, summer session for credit. ***ROTC:*** Army (c).

Unusual degree programs: 3-2 engineering with Auburn University, University of Kentucky; nursing with University of Louisville.

Computers: 125 computers/terminals are available on campus for general student use. Students can access the following: campus intranet, computer help desk, free student e-mail accounts, online (class) grades, online (class) registration, online (class) schedules. Campuswide network is available. 100% of college-owned or -operated housing units are wired for high-speed Internet access. Wireless service is available via entire campus.

Library: Library Learning Center.

STUDENT LIFE

Housing options: on-campus residence required through senior year; coed, men-only, women-only, special housing for students with disabilities. Campus housing is university owned. Freshman campus housing is guaranteed.

Activities and organizations: drama/theater group, student-run newspaper, radio station, choral group, Student Government Association, Student Activities Programming Board, Campus Ministries, Pre Professional, St Jude Up 'Til Dawn Executive Board, national fraternities, national sororities.

Athletics Member NCAA. All Division II. ***Intercollegiate sports:*** baseball M(s), basketball M(s)/W(s), bowling W(s), cheerleading M/W, cross-country running M(s)/W(s), football M(s), golf M(s)/W(s), soccer M(s)/W(s), softball W(s), tennis W(s), track and field M(s)/W(s), volleyball W(s). ***Intramural sports:*** basketball M/W, soccer M/W, volleyball M/W.

Campus security: 24-hour emergency response devices, late-night transport/escort service, 12-hour patrols by trained security personnel.

Student services: health clinic, personal/psychological counseling, women's center.

COSTS & FINANCIAL AID

Costs (2017–18) ***Comprehensive fee:*** $33,820 includes full-time tuition ($24,290), mandatory fees ($780), and room and board ($8750). Full-time tuition and fees vary according to course load. Part-time tuition: $700 per credit hour. Part-time tuition and fees vary according to course load. ***Required fees:*** $650 per term part-time. ***Room and board:*** Room and board charges vary according to board plan and housing facility. ***Payment plans:*** installment, deferred payment. ***Waivers:*** children of alumni, senior citizens, and employees or children of employees.

Financial Aid ***Average indebtedness upon graduation:*** $24,150. ***Financial aid deadline:*** 3/15.

APPLYING

Standardized Tests *Required:* SAT or ACT (for admission).

Options: electronic application, early admission, deferred entrance.

Required: high school transcript.

Notification: continuous (freshmen), continuous (transfers).

CONTACT

Kentucky Wesleyan College, 3000 Frederica Street, Owensboro, KY 42301. *Phone:* 270-852-3120. *Toll-free phone:* 800-999-0592 (in-state); 800-990-0592 (out-of-state).

Lindsey Wilson College

Columbia, Kentucky

http://www.lindsey.edu/

- **Independent United Methodist** comprehensive, founded 1903
- **Rural** 225-acre campus
- **Endowment** $20.9 million
- **Coed** 2,143 undergraduate students, 94% full-time, 60% women, 40% men
- **Minimally difficult** entrance level, 72% of applicants were admitted

UNDERGRAD STUDENTS

2,005 full-time, 138 part-time. Students come from 34 states and territories; 35 other countries; 20% are from out of state; 9% Black or African American, non-Hispanic/Latino; 1% Hispanic/Latino; 0.5% Asian, non-Hispanic/Latino; 0.0% Native Hawaiian or other Pacific Islander, non-Hispanic/Latino; 0.4% American Indian or Alaska Native, non-Hispanic/Latino; 2% Two or more races, non-Hispanic/Latino; 20%

Race/ethnicity unknown; 0.0% international; 14% transferred in; 53% live on campus.

Freshmen:
Admission: 2,887 applied, 2,068 admitted, 493 enrolled. ***Average high school GPA:*** 3.27. ***Test scores:*** ACT scores over 18: 83%; ACT scores over 24: 27%; ACT scores over 30: 2%.
Retention: 63% of full-time freshmen returned.

FACULTY
Total: 243, 47% full-time, 37% with terminal degrees.
Student/faculty ratio: 13:1.

ACADEMICS
Calendar: semesters. *Degrees:* associate, bachelor's, master's, and doctoral.
Special study options: academic remediation for entering students, accelerated degree program, adult/continuing education programs, advanced placement credit, cooperative education, double majors, English as a second language, independent study, internships, off-campus study, part-time degree program, services for LD students, student-designed majors, study abroad, summer session for credit.
Computers: 120 computers/terminals are available on campus for general student use. Students can access the following: campus intranet, computer help desk, free student e-mail accounts, online (class) grades, online (class) registration, online (class) schedules. Campuswide network is available. 100% of college-owned or -operated housing units are wired for high-speed Internet access. Wireless service is available via entire campus.
Library: Katie Murrell Library.

STUDENT LIFE
Housing options: on-campus residence required through senior year; men-only, women-only. Campus housing is university owned. Freshman campus housing is guaranteed.
Activities and organizations: drama/theater group, student-run newspaper, choral group, marching band.
Athletics Member NAIA. ***Intercollegiate sports:*** baseball M(s), basketball M(s)/W(s), bowling M(s)/W(s), cheerleading M(s)/W(s), cross-country running M(s)/W(s), football M(s)/W(s), golf M(s)/W(s), soccer M(s)/W(s), softball W(s), swimming and diving M(s)/W(s), tennis M(s)/W(s), track and field M(s)/W(s), volleyball W(s), wrestling M(s). ***Intramural sports:*** basketball M/W, football M/W, softball M/W, table tennis M/W, tennis M/W, volleyball M/W, weight lifting M/W.
Campus security: 24-hour emergency response devices and patrols.
Student services: health clinic, personal/psychological counseling, women's center.

COSTS & FINANCIAL AID
Costs (2017–18) ***Comprehensive fee:*** $33,546 includes full-time tuition ($24,000), mandatory fees ($246), and room and board ($9300). Full-time tuition and fees vary according to class time, degree level, and location. Part-time tuition: $1000 per credit hour. Part-time tuition and fees vary according to class time, degree level, and location. ***Required fees:*** $48 per term part-time. ***College room only:*** $3370. ***Payment plan:*** installment. ***Waivers:*** senior citizens and employees or children of employees.
Financial Aid Of all full-time matriculated undergraduates who enrolled in 2016, 2,059 applied for aid, 1,936 were judged to have need, 424 had their need fully met. 252 Federal Work-Study jobs (averaging $2158). 16 state and other part-time jobs (averaging $2344). ***Average need-based loan:*** $4176. ***Average need-based gift aid:*** $18,556. ***Average indebtedness upon graduation:*** $26,869.

APPLYING
Standardized Tests *Required for some:* SAT or ACT (for admission).
Options: electronic application.
Required: high school transcript. ***Recommended:*** interview.
Application deadlines: rolling (freshmen), rolling (transfers).
Notification: continuous (freshmen), continuous (transfers).

CONTACT
Mrs. Charity Ferguson, Assistant Director of Admissions, Lindsey Wilson College, 210 Lindsey Wilson Street, Columbia, KY 42728-1298. *Phone:* 270-384-8100. *Toll-free phone:* 800-264-0138. *Fax:* 270-384-8591.

Midway University
Midway, Kentucky
http://www.midway.edu/

CONTACT
Midway University, 512 East Stephens Street, Midway, KY 40347-1120. *Phone:* 859-846-5799. *Toll-free phone:* 800-755-0031.

Morehead State University
Morehead, Kentucky
http://www.moreheadstate.edu/

- **State-supported** comprehensive, founded 1922
- **Small-town** 1187-acre campus
- **Endowment** $43.0 million
- **Coed** 9,783 undergraduate students, 63% full-time, 60% women, 40% men
- **Minimally difficult** entrance level, 85% of applicants were admitted

UNDERGRAD STUDENTS
6,209 full-time, 3,574 part-time. Students come from 37 states and territories; 24 other countries; 12% are from out of state; 4% Black or African American, non-Hispanic/Latino; 1% Hispanic/Latino; 0.4% Asian, non-Hispanic/Latino; 0.1% Native Hawaiian or other Pacific Islander, non-Hispanic/Latino; 0.1% American Indian or Alaska Native, non-Hispanic/Latino; 2% Two or more races, non-Hispanic/Latino; 1% Race/ethnicity unknown; 2% international; 5% transferred in; 40% live on campus.

Freshmen:
Admission: 4,888 applied, 4,174 admitted, 1,461 enrolled. ***Test scores:*** SAT critical reading scores over 500: 49%; SAT math scores over 500: 40%; ACT scores over 18: 91%; SAT critical reading scores over 600: 11%; SAT math scores over 600: 11%; ACT scores over 24: 37%; ACT scores over 30: 4%.
Retention: 66% of full-time freshmen returned.

FACULTY
Total: 438, 80% full-time.
Student/faculty ratio: 18:1.

ACADEMICS
Calendar: semesters. *Degrees:* certificates, associate, bachelor's, master's, doctoral, post-master's, and postbachelor's certificates.
Special study options: academic remediation for entering students, accelerated degree program, adult/continuing education programs, advanced placement credit, cooperative education, distance learning, double majors, English as a second language, honors programs, independent study, internships, off-campus study, part-time degree program, services for LD students, student-designed majors, study abroad, summer session for credit. ***ROTC:*** Army (b).
Unusual degree programs: 3-2 engineering with University of Kentucky.
Computers: 1,000 computers/terminals and 1,820 ports are available on campus for general student use. Students can access the following: campus intranet, computer help desk, free student e-mail accounts, online (class) grades, online (class) registration, online (class) schedules. Campuswide network is available. 100% of college-owned or -operated housing units are wired for high-speed Internet access. Wireless service is available via entire campus.
Library: Camden Carroll Library.

STUDENT LIFE
Housing options: on-campus residence required through sophomore year; coed, special housing for students with disabilities. Campus housing is university owned. Freshman applicants given priority for college housing.
Activities and organizations: drama/theater group, student-run newspaper, radio and television station, choral group, marching band, Delta Tau Delta Fraternity, Delta Gamma, Phi Sigma Pi (Honors), Baptist Campus Ministries (BCM), Collegiate Future Farmers of America (FFA), national fraternities, national sororities.
Athletics Member NCAA. All Division I except football (Division I-AA). ***Intercollegiate sports:*** baseball M(s), basketball M(s)/W(s), bowling M(c)/W(c), cheerleading M(s)/W(s), cross-country running M(s)/W(s), equestrian sports M(c)/W(c), golf M(s)/W(s), riflery M(s)/W(s), soccer

W(s), softball W(s), tennis M(s)/W(s), track and field M(s)/W(s), volleyball W(s). ***Intramural sports:*** badminton M/W, basketball M/W, bowling M/W, football M/W, golf M/W, racquetball M/W, soccer M(c), softball M/W, table tennis M/W, tennis M/W, ultimate Frisbee M/W, volleyball M/W.

Campus security: 24-hour emergency response devices and patrols, student patrols, late-night transport/escort service, controlled dormitory access.

Student services: health clinic, personal/psychological counseling.

COSTS & FINANCIAL AID

Costs (2016–17) ***Tuition:*** state resident $8496 full-time, $356 per credit hour part-time; nonresident $12,744 full-time, $534 per credit hour part-time. Full-time tuition and fees vary according to course load, degree level, location, reciprocity agreements, and student level. Part-time tuition and fees vary according to course load, degree level, location, reciprocity agreements, and student level. ***Room and board:*** $8892; room only: $4962. Room and board charges vary according to board plan and housing facility. ***Payment plans:*** installment, deferred payment. ***Waivers:*** minority students, children of alumni, senior citizens, and employees or children of employees.

Financial Aid Of all full-time matriculated undergraduates who enrolled in 2016, 4,964 applied for aid, 4,283 were judged to have need, 812 had their need fully met. 374 Federal Work-Study jobs (averaging $2381). 733 state and other part-time jobs (averaging $2805). In 2016, 818 non-need-based awards were made. ***Average percent of need met:*** 62. ***Average financial aid package:*** $11,197. ***Average need-based loan:*** $3839. ***Average need-based gift aid:*** $5742. ***Average non-need-based aid:*** $6212. ***Average indebtedness upon graduation:*** $28,125.

APPLYING

Standardized Tests *Required:* SAT or ACT (for admission).

Options: electronic application, early admission, deferred entrance.

Application fee: $30.

Required: high school transcript. ***Required for some:*** essay or personal statement, 1 letter of recommendation, interview.

Application deadlines: rolling (freshmen), rolling (out-of-state freshmen), rolling (transfers).

Notification: continuous (freshmen), continuous (out-of-state freshmen), continuous (transfers).

CONTACT

Mr. Jeffrey R. Liles, Assistant Vice President for Enrollment Services, Morehead State University, 100 Admissions Center, Morehead, KY 40351. *Phone:* 606-783-2000. *Toll-free phone:* 800-585-6781. *Fax:* 606-783-5038. *E-mail:* admissions@moreheadstate.edu.

Murray State University

Murray, Kentucky

http://www.murraystate.edu/

- **State-supported** university, founded 1922
- **Small-town** 261-acre campus
- **Endowment** $19.2 million
- **Coed** 8,886 undergraduate students, 79% full-time, 58% women, 42% men
- **Moderately difficult** entrance level, 85% of applicants were admitted

UNDERGRAD STUDENTS

6,980 full-time, 1,906 part-time. Students come from 44 states and territories; 42 other countries; 32% are from out of state; 6% Black or African American, non-Hispanic/Latino; 2% Hispanic/Latino; 1% Asian, non-Hispanic/Latino; 0.1% Native Hawaiian or other Pacific Islander, non-Hispanic/Latino; 0.2% American Indian or Alaska Native, non-Hispanic/Latino; 2% Two or more races, non-Hispanic/Latino; 3% Race/ethnicity unknown; 4% international; 7% transferred in; 33% live on campus.

Freshmen:

Admission: 6,479 applied, 5,530 admitted, 1,502 enrolled. ***Average high school GPA:*** 3.53. ***Test scores:*** SAT critical reading scores over 500: 58%; SAT math scores over 500: 59%; ACT scores over 18: 99%; SAT critical reading scores over 600: 25%; SAT math scores over 600: 13%; ACT scores over 24: 52%; SAT critical reading scores over 700: 4%; SAT math scores over 700: 1%; ACT scores over 30: 9%.

Retention: 74% of full-time freshmen returned.

FACULTY

Total: 686, 65% full-time, 62% with terminal degrees.

Student/faculty ratio: 15:1.

ACADEMICS

Calendar: semesters. *Degrees:* certificates, associate, bachelor's, master's, doctoral, and postbachelor's certificates.

Special study options: academic remediation for entering students, adult/continuing education programs, advanced placement credit, cooperative education, distance learning, double majors, English as a second language, external degree program, freshman honors college, honors programs, independent study, internships, off-campus study, part-time degree program, services for LD students, student-designed majors, study abroad, summer session for credit. ***ROTC:*** Army (b).

Computers: Students can access the following: campus intranet, computer help desk, free student e-mail accounts, online (class) grades, online (class) registration, online (class) schedules, billing accounts, course evaluation forms, receive instant campus alerts, secure on-campus housing, pre-order of food or take-out. Campuswide network is available. 100% of college-owned or -operated housing units are wired for high-speed Internet access. Wireless service is available via entire campus.

Library: Waterfield Library plus 4 others. *Books:* 363,292 (physical), 193,453 (digital/electronic); *Serial titles:* 317 (physical), 639 (digital/electronic); *Databases:* 128. Weekly public service hours: 107; students can reserve study rooms.

STUDENT LIFE

Housing options: on-campus residence required through sophomore year; coed, women-only, special housing for students with disabilities. Campus housing is university owned. Freshman applicants given priority for college housing.

Activities and organizations: drama/theater group, student-run newspaper, television station, choral group, marching band, Racer Band, Student Government Association, National Panhellenic Council, International Student Organization, MSU Student Ambassadors, national fraternities, national sororities.

Athletics Member NCAA. All Division I except football (Division I-AA). ***Intercollegiate sports:*** baseball M(s), basketball M(s)/W(s), cheerleading M(c)/W(c), crew M(c)/W(c), cross-country running M/W(s), equestrian sports M(c)/W(c), golf M(s)/W(s), riflery M(s)/W(s), rowing M(c)/W(c), soccer W(s), softball W(s), tennis W(s), track and field W(s), volleyball W(s). ***Intramural sports:*** archery M(c)/W(c), baseball M(c), basketball M/W, bowling M/W, fencing M(c)/W(c), football M/W, golf M/W, racquetball M(c)/W(c), rugby M(c), soccer M/W, softball M/W, swimming and diving M/W, table tennis M/W, tennis M/W, ultimate Frisbee M/W, volleyball M/W, water polo M/W.

Campus security: 24-hour emergency response devices and patrols, student patrols, late-night transport/escort service, controlled dormitory access, LiveSafe, a mobile safety app.

Student services: health clinic, personal/psychological counseling, women's center.

COSTS & FINANCIAL AID

Costs (2016–17) ***Tuition:*** state resident $8400 full-time, $350 per credit hour part-time; nonresident $22,680 full-time, $945 per credit hour part-time. Full-time tuition and fees vary according to course load. ***Room and board:*** $8588; room only: $5044. Room and board charges vary according to board plan and housing facility. ***Payment plan:*** installment. ***Waivers:*** children of alumni, senior citizens, and employees or children of employees.

Financial Aid Of all full-time matriculated undergraduates who enrolled in 2015, 5,353 applied for aid, 4,415 were judged to have need, 1,159 had their need fully met. 343 Federal Work-Study jobs (averaging $1584). 1,993 state and other part-time jobs (averaging $2122). In 2015, 478 non-need-based awards were made. ***Average percent of need met:*** 31. ***Average financial aid package:*** $12,577. ***Average need-based loan:*** $6265. ***Average need-based gift aid:*** $6089. ***Average non-need-based aid:*** $5056. ***Average indebtedness upon graduation:*** $27,564.

APPLYING

Standardized Tests *Required:* SAT or ACT (for admission). *Recommended:* ACT (for admission).

Options: electronic application, early admission.

Application fee: $40.

Required: high school transcript, minimum 3.0 GPA, minimum ACT composite score of 18 or SAT score of 870, rank in the top half of high school class or minimum 3.0 GPA; high school curriculum criteria.

Application deadlines: 8/15 (freshmen), 8/15 (transfers).

Notification: continuous (freshmen), continuous (transfers).

CONTACT

Ms. Stacy Bell, Assistant Director of Undergraduate Admissions, Murray State University, 102 Curris Center, Murray, KY 42701-0009. *Phone:* 270-809-3741. *Toll-free phone:* 800-272-4678. *Fax:* 270-809-3780. *E-mail:* msu.admissions@murraystate.edu.

Northern Kentucky University

Highland Heights, Kentucky

http://www.nku.edu/

- **State-supported** comprehensive, founded 1968
- **Suburban** 400-acre campus with easy access to Cincinnati
- **Endowment** $94.9 million
- **Coed** 12,389 undergraduate students, 74% full-time, 57% women, 43% men
- 91% of applicants were admitted

UNDERGRAD STUDENTS

9,193 full-time, 3,196 part-time. Students come from 41 states and territories; 56 other countries; 33% are from out of state; 7% Black or African American, non-Hispanic/Latino; 3% Hispanic/Latino; 1% Asian, non-Hispanic/Latino; 0.3% American Indian or Alaska Native, non-Hispanic/Latino; 2% Two or more races, non-Hispanic/Latino; 0.6% Race/ethnicity unknown; 3% international; 6% transferred in; 15% live on campus.

Freshmen:

Admission: 6,059 applied, 5,519 admitted, 2,148 enrolled. ***Average high school GPA:*** 3.43. ***Test scores:*** SAT critical reading scores over 500: 48%; SAT math scores over 500: 53%; SAT writing scores over 500: 49%; ACT scores over 18: 94%; SAT critical reading scores over 600: 21%; SAT math scores over 600: 22%; SAT writing scores over 600: 21%; ACT scores over 24: 47%; SAT critical reading scores over 700: 2%; SAT math scores over 700: 4%; SAT writing scores over 700: 4%; ACT scores over 30: 9%.

Retention: 72% of full-time freshmen returned.

FACULTY

Total: 1,023, 56% full-time, 51% with terminal degrees.

Student/faculty ratio: 19:1.

ACADEMICS

Calendar: semesters. *Degrees:* certificates, bachelor's, master's, doctoral, post-master's, and postbachelor's certificates.

Special study options: academic remediation for entering students, accelerated degree program, adult/continuing education programs, advanced placement credit, cooperative education, distance learning, double majors, English as a second language, honors programs, independent study, internships, off-campus study, part-time degree program, services for LD students, student-designed majors, study abroad, summer session for credit. ***ROTC:*** Army (c), Air Force (c).

Unusual degree programs: 3-2 engineering with University of Louisville, University of Kentucky; law with Mount St. Joseph University.

Computers: 200 computers/terminals and 1,500 ports are available on campus for general student use. Students can access the following: campus intranet, computer help desk, free student e-mail accounts, online (class) grades, online (class) registration, online (class) schedules. Campuswide network is available. 100% of college-owned or -operated housing units are wired for high-speed Internet access. Wireless service is available via entire campus.

Library: W. Frank Steely Library plus 1 other. *Books:* 325,491 (physical), 39,096 (digital/electronic); *Serial titles:* 54,274 (digital/electronic);

Databases: 113. Weekly public service hours: 104; students can reserve study rooms.

STUDENT LIFE
Housing options: on-campus residence required for freshman year; coed, special housing for students with disabilities. Campus housing is university owned. Freshman applicants given priority for college housing.

Activities and organizations: drama/theater group, student-run newspaper, television station, choral group, Sororities, Fraternities, Freshmen Service Leadership Committee, Student Alumni Association, Activities Programming Board, national fraternities, national sororities.

Athletics Member NCAA. All Division I. ***Intercollegiate sports:*** baseball M(s), basketball M(s)/W(s), cheerleading M(s)/W(s), cross-country running M(s)/W(s), golf M(s)/W(s), soccer M(s)/W(s), softball W(s), tennis M(s)/W(s), track and field M(s)/W(s), volleyball W(s). ***Intramural sports:*** badminton M(c)/W(c), basketball M/W, bowling M(c)/W(c), equestrian sports M(c)/W(c), lacrosse M(c)/W(c), rock climbing M(c)/W(c), sand volleyball W, soccer M(c)/W(c), softball W(c), tennis M/W, ultimate Frisbee M(c)/W(c), volleyball W(c), water polo M/W, weight lifting M/W, wrestling M(c).

Campus security: 24-hour emergency response devices and patrols, late-night transport/escort service, controlled dormitory access.

Student services: health clinic, personal/psychological counseling, women's center, legal services.

COSTS & FINANCIAL AID
Costs (2016–17) ***Tuition:*** state resident $9000 full-time, $375 per credit hour part-time; nonresident $18,000 full-time, $750 per credit hour part-time. Full-time tuition and fees vary according to course load and reciprocity agreements. Part-time tuition and fees vary according to course load and reciprocity agreements. ***Required fees:*** $384 full-time, $16 per credit hour part-time. ***Room and board:*** $6549. Room and board charges vary according to board plan and housing facility. ***Payment plan:*** installment. ***Waivers:*** senior citizens and employees or children of employees.

Financial Aid Of all full-time matriculated undergraduates who enrolled in 2015, 7,400 applied for aid, 6,081 were judged to have need, 1,221 had their need fully met. In 2015, 1124 non-need-based awards were made. ***Average percent of need met:*** 64. ***Average financial aid package:*** $10,940. ***Average need-based loan:*** $4475. ***Average need-based gift aid:*** $5687. ***Average non-need-based aid:*** $6162. ***Average indebtedness upon graduation:*** $28,355.

APPLYING
Standardized Tests *Required:* SAT or ACT (for admission).

Options: electronic application, deferred entrance.

Application fee: $40.

Required: high school transcript, minimum 2.0 GPA.

Application deadlines: 8/22 (freshmen), 8/1 (transfers).

Notification: continuous (freshmen), continuous (transfers).

CONTACT
Mrs. Melissa Gorbandt, Office of Admissions, Northern Kentucky University, Lucas Administrative Center, 400 Nunn Drive, Highland Heights, KY 41099. *Phone:* 859-572-5220. *Toll-free phone:* 800-637-9948. *Fax:* 859-572-6665. *E-mail:* admitnku@nku.edu.

See previous page for display ad and page 1446 for the College Close-Up.

Simmons College of Kentucky
Louisville, Kentucky
http://www.simmonscollegeky.edu/

CONTACT
Simmons College of Kentucky, 1018 South 7th Street, Louisville, KY 40203.

The Southern Baptist Theological Seminary
Louisville, Kentucky
http://www.sbts.edu/

CONTACT
Dr. Daniel DeWitt, The Southern Baptist Theological Seminary, 2825 Lexington Road, Louisville, KY 40280-0004. *Phone:* 502-897-4011 Ext. 4617.

Spalding University
Louisville, Kentucky
http://www.spalding.edu/

- **Independent** comprehensive, founded 1814, affiliated with Roman Catholic Church
- **Urban** 24-acre campus with easy access to Louisville
- **Endowment** $16.6 million
- **Coed** 1,316 undergraduate students, 70% full-time, 71% women, 29% men
- **Moderately difficult** entrance level, 51% of applicants were admitted

UNDERGRAD STUDENTS
920 full-time, 396 part-time. Students come from 1 other state; 2 other countries; 20% are from out of state; 17% Black or African American, non-Hispanic/Latino; 3% Hispanic/Latino; 2% Asian, non-Hispanic/Latino; 0.1% Native Hawaiian or other Pacific Islander, non-Hispanic/Latino; 0.1% American Indian or Alaska Native, non-Hispanic/Latino; 3% Two or more races, non-Hispanic/Latino; 15% Race/ethnicity unknown; 0.2% international; 11% transferred in; 5% live on campus.

Freshmen:
Admission: 990 applied, 500 admitted, 168 enrolled. ***Average high school GPA:*** 3.87. ***Test scores:*** SAT math scores over 500: 53%; ACT scores over 18: 80%; SAT math scores over 600: 29%; ACT scores over 24: 25%; ACT scores over 30: 1%.

FACULTY
Total: 170, 58% full-time.
Student/faculty ratio: 12:1.

ACADEMICS
Calendar: other. *Degrees:* associate, bachelor's, master's, doctoral, post-master's, and postbachelor's certificates.

Special study options: academic remediation for entering students, accelerated degree program, adult/continuing education programs, advanced placement credit, cooperative education, distance learning, double majors, independent study, internships, off-campus study, part-time degree program, services for LD students, study abroad, summer session for credit. ***ROTC:*** Army (c), Air Force (c).

Computers: 259 computers/terminals are available on campus for general student use. Students can access the following: computer help desk, free student e-mail accounts, online (class) grades, online (class) registration, online (class) schedules. Campuswide network is available. 100% of college-owned or -operated housing units are wired for high-speed Internet access. Wireless service is available via entire campus.

Library: Spalding Library. *Books:* 70,000 (physical), 425,638 (digital/electronic); *Serial titles:* 102 (physical), 100,000 (digital/electronic); *Databases:* 70. Students can reserve study rooms.

STUDENT LIFE
Housing options: coed, special housing for students with disabilities. Campus housing is university owned.

Activities and organizations: student-run radio station, choral group, Egan Service Learning Program, Student Occupational Therapy Association, Spalding University Nursing Students, Campus Activities Board, Best Buddies.

Athletics Member NCAA. All Division III. ***Intercollegiate sports:*** baseball M, basketball M/W, bowling W, cross-country running M/W, golf M/W, soccer M/W, softball W, track and field M/W, volleyball W.

Campus security: 24-hour emergency response devices and patrols, late-night transport/escort service, controlled dormitory access.

Student services: personal/psychological counseling.

COSTS & FINANCIAL AID
Costs (2016–17) ***Comprehensive fee:*** $31,937 includes full-time tuition ($24,337) and room and board ($7600). Full-time tuition and fees vary according to class time, course load, degree level, and program. Part-time tuition and fees vary according to class time, course load, degree level, and program. ***College room only:*** $4800. Room and board charges vary according to board plan. ***Payment plans:*** installment, deferred payment. ***Waivers:*** children of alumni and employees or children of employees.

Financial Aid ***Average percent of need met:*** 75. ***Average financial aid package:*** $11,500.

APPLYING
Standardized Tests *Required:* SAT or ACT (for admission).

Options: electronic application, early admission, deferred entrance.

Application fee: $20.

Required: high school transcript, minimum 2.5 GPA. ***Required for some:*** essay or personal statement. ***Recommended:*** interview.

Application deadlines: rolling (freshmen), rolling (transfers).

Notification: continuous (freshmen), continuous (transfers).

CONTACT
Mr. Matt Elder, Director, Undergraduate Admissions, Spalding University, 845 South Third Street, Louisville, KY 40203. *Phone:* 502-873-4177. *Toll-free phone:* 800-896-8941. *Fax:* 502-992-2418. *E-mail:* melder@spalding.edu.

Spencerian College

Louisville, Kentucky

http://www.spencerian.edu/

- **Proprietary** primarily 2-year, founded 1892
- **Urban** 10-acre campus
- **Coed** 416 undergraduate students, 56% full-time, 86% women, 14% men
- **Minimally difficult** entrance level

UNDERGRAD STUDENTS
231 full-time, 185 part-time. Students come from 4 states and territories; 19% are from out of state; 19% Black or African American, non-Hispanic/Latino; 2% Hispanic/Latino; 1% Asian, non-Hispanic/Latino; 0.2% American Indian or Alaska Native, non-Hispanic/Latino; 12% Two or more races, non-Hispanic/Latino; 9% Race/ethnicity unknown; 13% transferred in; 1% live on campus.

Freshmen:
Admission: 99 enrolled.

FACULTY
Total: 90, 38% full-time.
Student/faculty ratio: 6:1.

ACADEMICS
Calendar: quarters. *Degrees:* certificates, diplomas, associate, and bachelor's.

Special study options: distance learning, internships, summer session for credit.

Computers: 142 computers/terminals are available on campus for general student use. Students can access the following: free student e-mail accounts, online (class) grades, online (class) schedules. Campuswide network is available.
Library: Spencerian College Learning Resource Center.

STUDENT LIFE
Housing options: coed. Campus housing is university owned.

Campus security: security on campus during school hours.

COSTS
Costs (2017–18) ***Tuition:*** $19,800 full-time. Full-time tuition and fees vary according to class time, degree level, and program. Part-time tuition and fees vary according to class time, degree level, and program. ***Room only:*** Room and board charges vary according to housing facility. ***Waivers:*** children of alumni and employees or children of employees.

APPLYING
Application fee: $50.

Required: high school transcript. ***Required for some:*** essay or personal statement, interview, specific selective admission criteria for some medical programs.

Notification: continuous (freshmen), continuous (transfers).

CONTACT
Spencerian College, 4627 Dixie Highway, Louisville, KY 40216. *Phone:* 502-447-1000 Ext. 7808. *Toll-free phone:* 800-264-1799.

Sullivan College of Technology and Design

Louisville, Kentucky

http://www.sctd.edu/

CONTACT
Ms. Heather Wilson, Director of Admissions, Sullivan College of Technology and Design, 3901 Atkinson Square Drive, Louisville, KY 40218. *Phone:* 502-456-6509 Ext. 8220. *Toll-free phone:* 800-884-6528. *Fax:* 502-456-2341. *E-mail:* hwilson@sctd.edu.

Sullivan University

Louisville, Kentucky

http://www.sullivan.edu/

- **Proprietary** comprehensive, founded 1864, part of The Sullivan University System, Inc.
- **Suburban** 15-acre campus
- **Coed** 2,504 undergraduate students, 65% full-time, 61% women, 39% men
- **Minimally difficult** entrance level, 77% of applicants were admitted

UNDERGRAD STUDENTS
1,624 full-time, 880 part-time. Students come from 46 states and territories; 50 other countries; 21% are from out of state; 18% Black or African American, non-Hispanic/Latino; 1% Asian, non-Hispanic/Latino; 0.3% Native Hawaiian or other Pacific Islander, non-Hispanic/Latino; 0.8% American Indian or Alaska Native, non-Hispanic/Latino; 9% Two or more races, non-Hispanic/Latino; 21% Race/ethnicity unknown; 0.3% international; 9% live on campus.

Freshmen:
Admission: 3,091 applied, 2,393 admitted, 288 enrolled.

FACULTY
Total: 291, 43% full-time.
Student/faculty ratio: 18:1.

ACADEMICS
Calendar: quarters. *Degrees:* certificates, diplomas, associate, bachelor's, master's, doctoral, and postbachelor's certificates.

Special study options: academic remediation for entering students, accelerated degree program, adult/continuing education programs, cooperative education, distance learning, double majors, independent study, internships, part-time degree program, services for LD students, student-designed majors, summer session for credit.

Computers: 93 computers/terminals are available on campus for general student use. Students can access the following: campus intranet, computer help desk, free student e-mail accounts, online (class) grades, online (class) registration, online (class) schedules. Campuswide network is available. 100% of college-owned or -operated housing units are wired for high-speed Internet access. Wireless service is available via entire campus.
Library: Sullivan University Library and Learning Resource Center. *Books:* 31,314 (physical), 66,899 (digital/electronic); *Serial titles:* 51 (physical), 123,192 (digital/electronic); *Databases:* 190. Weekly public service hours: 86.

STUDENT LIFE
Housing options: coed, men-only, women-only, special housing for students with disabilities. Campus housing is university owned. Freshman campus housing is guaranteed.

Activities and organizations: Student Activities Committee, Student Veterans Association, Sullivan Christian Fellowship, Chess Club, Phi Beta Lambda.

Athletics ***Intramural sports:*** basketball M/W, bowling M/W, sand volleyball M/W, soccer M/W, softball M/W, ultimate Frisbee M/W, volleyball M/W, weight lifting M/W.

Campus security: 24-hour patrols, late-night transport/escort service, controlled dormitory access.

Student services: personal/psychological counseling.

FINANCIAL AID

Financial Aid Of all full-time matriculated undergraduates who enrolled in 2002, 6,028 applied for aid, 5,247 were judged to have need. 31 Federal Work-Study jobs (averaging $2065). In 2002, 374 non-need-based awards were made. ***Average non-need-based aid:*** $2000. ***Average indebtedness upon graduation:*** $15,000.

APPLYING

Standardized Tests *Recommended:* SAT or ACT (for admission).

Options: electronic application, deferred entrance.

Application fee: $50.

Required: high school transcript, interview. ***Required for some:*** essay or personal statement, criminal background check and no felony convictions.

Application deadlines: rolling (freshmen), rolling (transfers).

Notification: continuous (freshmen), continuous (transfers).

CONTACT

Ms. Heather Cunningham, Senior Director of Admissions, Sullivan University, 3101 Bardstown Road, Louisville, KY 40205. *Phone:* 502-456-6505. *Toll-free phone:* 800-844-1354. *Fax:* 502-456-0040. *E-mail:* admissions@sullivan.edu.

★ Thomas More College

Crestview Hills, Kentucky

http://www.thomasmore.edu/

- **Independent Roman Catholic** comprehensive, founded 1921
- **Suburban** 100-acre campus with easy access to Cincinnati
- **Endowment** $20.7 million
- **Coed** 1,821 undergraduate students, 75% full-time, 53% women, 47% men
- **Moderately difficult** entrance level, 89% of applicants were admitted

UNDERGRAD STUDENTS

1,369 full-time, 452 part-time. Students come from 25 states and territories; 3 other countries; 47% are from out of state; 7% Black or African American, non-Hispanic/Latino; 3% Hispanic/Latino; 0.7% Asian, non-Hispanic/Latino; 0.3% Native Hawaiian or other Pacific Islander, non-Hispanic/Latino; 0.1% American Indian or Alaska Native, non-Hispanic/Latino; 4% Two or more races, non-Hispanic/Latino; 7% Race/ethnicity unknown; 0.6% international; 4% transferred in; 31% live on campus.

Freshmen:

Admission: 2,401 applied, 2,139 admitted, 414 enrolled. ***Average high school GPA:*** 3.35. ***Test scores:*** SAT critical reading scores over 500: 40%; SAT math scores over 500: 22%; SAT critical reading scores over 600: 6%; SAT math scores over 600: 11%.

Retention: 70% of full-time freshmen returned.

FACULTY

Total: 139, 57% full-time, 50% with terminal degrees.

Student/faculty ratio: 16:1.

ACADEMICS

Calendar: semesters. *Degrees:* certificates, associate, bachelor's, and master's.

Special study options: academic remediation for entering students, accelerated degree program, adult/continuing education programs, advanced placement credit, cooperative education, distance learning, double majors, honors programs, independent study, internships, off-campus study, part-time degree program, services for LD students, student-designed majors, study abroad, summer session for credit. ***ROTC:*** Army (c), Air Force (c).

Unusual degree programs: 3-2 engineering.

Computers: 96 computers/terminals are available on campus for general student use. Students can access the following: campus intranet, computer help desk, free student e-mail accounts, online (class) grades, online (class) registration, online (class) schedules. Campuswide network is available. 100% of college-owned or -operated housing units are wired for high-speed Internet access. Wireless service is available via entire campus.

Library: Thomas More College Library plus 1 other. *Books:* 87,667 (physical), 3,056 (digital/electronic); *Serial titles:* 329 (physical); *Databases:* 65. Weekly public service hours: 76.

STUDENT LIFE

Housing options: on-campus residence required through sophomore year; men-only, women-only, special housing for students with disabilities. Campus housing is university owned. Freshman campus housing is guaranteed.

Activities and organizations: drama/theater group, choral group, marching band, Student Government Association, Student Activities Board, More Ministry, Outdoors Adventure Club, Education Club, national fraternities, national sororities.

Athletics Member NCAA. All Division III. ***Intercollegiate sports:*** baseball M, basketball M/W, bowling M/W, cheerleading W, cross-country running M/W, football M, golf M/W, lacrosse W, rugby M(c)/W(c), soccer M/W, softball W, tennis M/W, track and field M/W, volleyball W, wrestling M. ***Intramural sports:*** basketball M/W, football M/W, volleyball M/W.

Campus security: 24-hour emergency response devices and patrols, late-night transport/escort service, controlled dormitory access.

Student services: health clinic, personal/psychological counseling.

COSTS & FINANCIAL AID

Costs (2016–17) ***One-time required fee:*** $125. ***Comprehensive fee:*** $36,754 includes full-time tuition ($28,050), mandatory fees ($1400), and room and board ($7304). Part-time tuition: $620 per semester hour. ***Required fees:*** $70 per semester hour part-time. ***College room only:*** $2624. Room and board charges vary according to board plan and housing facility. ***Payment plans:*** installment, deferred payment. ***Waivers:*** senior citizens and employees or children of employees.

Financial Aid Of all full-time matriculated undergraduates who enrolled in 2016, 1,177 applied for aid, 1,049 were judged to have need, 264 had their need fully met. 171 Federal Work-Study jobs (averaging $739). 189 state and other part-time jobs (averaging $1031). In 2016, 234 non-need-based awards were made. ***Average percent of need met:*** 73. ***Average financial aid package:*** $20,739. ***Average need-based loan:*** $3748. ***Average need-based gift aid:*** $16,719. ***Average non-need-based aid:*** $15,432. ***Average indebtedness upon graduation:*** $31,235.

APPLYING

Standardized Tests *Required:* SAT or ACT (for admission).

Options: electronic application, deferred entrance.

Application fee: $25.

Required: high school transcript, minimum 2.5 GPA.

Application deadlines: 8/1 (freshmen), 8/1 (transfers).

Notification: continuous (freshmen), continuous (transfers).

CONTACT

Justin Vogel, Director of Admissions, Thomas More College, 333 Thomas More Parkway, Crestview Hills, KY 41017-3495. *Phone:* 859-344-3307. *Toll-free phone:* 800-825-4557. *Fax:* 859-344-3444. *E-mail:* admissions@thomasmore.edu.

Transylvania University

Lexington, Kentucky

http://www.transy.edu/

- **Independent** 4-year, founded 1780, affiliated with Christian Church (Disciples of Christ)
- **Urban** 40-acre campus with easy access to Cincinnati, Louisville
- **Endowment** $167.3 million
- **Coed** 963 undergraduate students, 99% full-time, 58% women, 42% men
- **Very difficult** entrance level, 95% of applicants were admitted

UNDERGRAD STUDENTS

953 full-time, 10 part-time. Students come from 28 states and territories; 7 other countries; 22% are from out of state; 4% Black or African American, non-Hispanic/Latino; 6% Hispanic/Latino; 1% Asian, non-

Hispanic/Latino; 0.1% American Indian or Alaska Native, non-Hispanic/Latino; 3% Two or more races, non-Hispanic/Latino; 2% Race/ethnicity unknown; 4% international; 1% transferred in; 65% live on campus.

Freshmen:
Admission: 1,216 applied, 1,153 admitted, 242 enrolled. ***Average high school GPA:*** 3.69. ***Test scores:*** SAT critical reading scores over 500: 83%; SAT math scores over 500: 66%; ACT scores over 18: 100%; SAT critical reading scores over 600: 35%; SAT math scores over 600: 42%; ACT scores over 24: 86%; SAT critical reading scores over 700: 4%; SAT math scores over 700: 28%; ACT scores over 30: 28%.
Retention: 86% of full-time freshmen returned.

FACULTY
Total: 101, 83% full-time, 90% with terminal degrees.
Student/faculty ratio: 11:1.

ACADEMICS
Calendar: 4-4-1. *Degree:* bachelor's.
Special study options: advanced placement credit, double majors, independent study, internships, off-campus study, part-time degree program, services for LD students, student-designed majors, study abroad, summer session for credit. ***ROTC:*** Army (c), Air Force (c).
Unusual degree programs: 3-2 engineering with University of Kentucky, Vanderbilt University.
Computers: 90 computers/terminals are available on campus for general student use. Students can access the following: campus intranet, computer help desk, free student e-mail accounts, online (class) grades, online (class) registration, online (class) schedules. Campuswide network is available. 100% of college-owned or -operated housing units are wired for high-speed Internet access. Wireless service is available via entire campus.
Library: J. Douglas Gay Jr./Frances Carrick Thomas Library. *Books:* 124,199 (physical), 170,342 (digital/electronic); *Serial titles:* 530 (physical), 23,600 (digital/electronic); *Databases:* 70. Weekly public service hours: 102; students can reserve study rooms.

STUDENT LIFE
Housing options: on-campus residence required through junior year; coed, men-only, women-only, special housing for students with disabilities. Campus housing is university owned. Freshman campus housing is guaranteed.
Activities and organizations: drama/theater group, student-run newspaper, radio station, choral group, Student Government Association, Delta Sigma Phi, Phi Mu, Delta Delta Delta, Chi Omega, national fraternities, national sororities.
Athletics Member NCAA. All Division III. ***Intercollegiate sports:*** baseball M, basketball M/W, cheerleading M/W, cross-country running M/W, equestrian sports M/W, field hockey W, golf M/W, lacrosse M/W, soccer M/W, softball W, swimming and diving M/W, tennis M/W, track and field M/W, volleyball W. ***Intramural sports:*** badminton M/W, basketball M/W, soccer M/W, table tennis M/W, ultimate Frisbee M/W, volleyball M/W.
Campus security: 24-hour emergency response devices and patrols, late-night transport/escort service, controlled dormitory access.
Student services: health clinic, personal/psychological counseling.

COSTS & FINANCIAL AID
Costs (2017–18) ***Comprehensive fee:*** $47,450 includes full-time tuition ($35,770), mandatory fees ($1520), and room and board ($10,160). Part-time tuition: $3980 per course. Part-time tuition and fees vary according to course load. ***College room only:*** $5750. Room and board charges vary according to board plan and housing facility. ***Payment plan:*** installment. ***Waivers:*** employees or children of employees.
Financial Aid Of all full-time matriculated undergraduates who enrolled in 2016, 731 applied for aid, 628 were judged to have need, 145 had their need fully met. 310 Federal Work-Study jobs (averaging $1656). 40 state and other part-time jobs (averaging $5641). In 2016, 315 non-need-based awards were made. ***Average percent of need met:*** 81. ***Average financial aid package:*** $28,085. ***Average need-based loan:*** $4284. ***Average need-based gift aid:*** $24,196. ***Average non-need-based aid:*** $17,513. ***Average indebtedness upon graduation:*** $30,514.

APPLYING
Options: electronic application, early admission, early action, deferred entrance.
Required: essay or personal statement, high school transcript, minimum 2.8 GPA, 2 letters of recommendation. ***Required for some:*** interview. ***Recommended:*** interview.
Application deadlines: 2/1 (freshmen), rolling (transfers), 10/15 (early action).
Notification: 2/15 (freshmen), 12/20 (early action).

CONTACT
Dr. Holly Sheilley, Vice President for Enrollment and Student Life, Transylvania University, 300 North Broadway, Lexington, KY 40508-1797. *Phone:* 859-233-8242. *Toll-free phone:* 800-872-6798. *Fax:* 859-281-3649. *E-mail:* admissions@transy.edu.

Union College
Barbourville, Kentucky
http://www.unionky.edu/

- **Independent United Methodist** comprehensive, founded 1879
- **Small-town** 100-acre campus
- **Coed** 975 undergraduate students, 87% full-time, 49% women, 51% men
- **Moderately difficult** entrance level, 67% of applicants were admitted

UNDERGRAD STUDENTS
853 full-time, 122 part-time. Students come from 37 states and territories; 18 other countries; 29% are from out of state; 15% Black or African American, non-Hispanic/Latino; 3% Hispanic/Latino; 0.3% Asian, non-Hispanic/Latino; 0.1% Native Hawaiian or other Pacific Islander, non-Hispanic/Latino; 0.3% American Indian or Alaska Native, non-Hispanic/Latino; 4% Two or more races, non-Hispanic/Latino; 1% Race/ethnicity unknown; 6% international; 7% transferred in; 47% live on campus.

Freshmen:
Admission: 1,344 applied, 907 admitted, 264 enrolled. ***Average high school GPA:*** 3.15. ***Test scores:*** ACT scores over 18: 78%; ACT scores over 24: 18%; ACT scores over 30: 1%.
Retention: 65% of full-time freshmen returned.

FACULTY
Total: 81, 57% full-time, 70% with terminal degrees.
Student/faculty ratio: 12:1.

ACADEMICS
Calendar: semesters. *Degrees:* bachelor's, master's, post-master's, and postbachelor's certificates.
Special study options: academic remediation for entering students, accelerated degree program, advanced placement credit, double majors, English as a second language, honors programs, independent study, off-campus study, part-time degree program, services for LD students, student-designed majors, study abroad, summer session for credit.
Computers: 290 computers/terminals and 550 ports are available on campus for general student use. Students can access the following: campus intranet, computer help desk, free student e-mail accounts, online (class) grades, online (class) registration, online (class) schedules. Campuswide network is available. 100% of college-owned or -operated housing units are wired for high-speed Internet access. Wireless service is available via classrooms, computer centers, computer labs, dorm rooms, learning centers, libraries, student centers.
Library: Weeks-Townsend Memorial Library plus 1 other.

STUDENT LIFE
Housing options: on-campus residence required through sophomore year; men-only, women-only. Campus housing is university owned. Freshman campus housing is guaranteed.
Activities and organizations: drama/theater group, choral group.
Athletics Member NAIA. ***Intercollegiate sports:*** archery M(s)/W(s), baseball M(s), basketball M(s)/W(s), bowling M(s)/W(s), cheerleading M(s)/W(s), cross-country running M(s)/W(s), football M(s), golf M(s)/W(s), lacrosse M(s), soccer M(s)/W(s), softball W(s), swimming and diving M(s)/W(s), tennis M(s)/W(s), track and field M(s)/W(s), volleyball W(s). ***Intramural sports:*** basketball M/W, football M, soccer M/W,

softball M/W, table tennis M/W, ultimate Frisbee M/W, volleyball M/W, water polo W.

Campus security: 24-hour emergency response devices and patrols, late-night transport/escort service, controlled dormitory access.

Student services: health clinic, personal/psychological counseling.

COSTS & FINANCIAL AID

Costs (2017–18) ***Comprehensive fee:*** $33,480 includes full-time tuition ($24,590), mandatory fees ($1490), and room and board ($7400). Part-time tuition: $345 per credit hour. Part-time tuition and fees vary according to location. ***Required fees:*** $25 per term part-time. ***College room only:*** $3350. Room and board charges vary according to housing facility. ***Payment plan:*** installment. ***Waivers:*** employees or children of employees.

Financial Aid Of all full-time matriculated undergraduates who enrolled in 2015, 632 applied for aid, 593 were judged to have need, 88 had their need fully met. 111 Federal Work-Study jobs (averaging $1500). 9 state and other part-time jobs (averaging $1500). In 2015, 79 non-need-based awards were made. ***Average percent of need met:*** 69. ***Average financial aid package:*** $22,110. ***Average need-based loan:*** $4337. ***Average need-based gift aid:*** $18,228. ***Average non-need-based aid:*** $15,399. ***Average indebtedness upon graduation:*** $32,691.

APPLYING

Standardized Tests *Required:* SAT or ACT (for admission).

Options: electronic application, deferred entrance.

Application fee: $10.

Required: high school transcript, minimum 2.0 GPA. ***Required for some:*** interview.

Application deadlines: rolling (freshmen), rolling (transfers).

Notification: continuous (freshmen), continuous (transfers).

CONTACT

Mr. Craig Grooms, Director: Undergraduate Enrollment, Union College, 310 College Street, Barbourville, KY 40906. *Phone:* 606-546-4151 Ext. 1709. *Toll-free phone:* 800-489-8646. *Fax:* 606-546-1667. *E-mail:* cgrooms@unionky.edu.

University of Kentucky

Lexington, Kentucky

http://www.uky.edu/

- **State-supported** university, founded 1865
- **Urban** 813-acre campus with easy access to Cincinnati, Louisville
- **Endowment** $1.2 billion
- **Coed** 22,621 undergraduate students, 92% full-time, 54% women, 46% men
- **Moderately difficult** entrance level, 91% of applicants were admitted

UNDERGRAD STUDENTS

20,833 full-time, 1,788 part-time. Students come from 52 states and territories; 75 other countries; 31% are from out of state; 8% Black or African American, non-Hispanic/Latino; 4% Hispanic/Latino; 3% Asian, non-Hispanic/Latino; 0.1% Native Hawaiian or other Pacific Islander, non-Hispanic/Latino; 0.2% American Indian or Alaska Native, non-Hispanic/Latino; 4% Two or more races, non-Hispanic/Latino; 3% Race/ethnicity unknown; 3% international; 4% transferred in; 28% live on campus.

Freshmen:

Admission: 20,480 applied, 18,593 admitted, 5,117 enrolled. ***Average high school GPA:*** 3.69. ***Test scores:*** SAT critical reading scores over 500: 76%; SAT math scores over 500: 77%; SAT writing scores over 500: 72%; ACT scores over 18: 99%; SAT critical reading scores over 600: 34%; SAT math scores over 600: 39%; SAT writing scores over 600: 29%; ACT scores over 24: 66%; SAT critical reading scores over 700: 11%; SAT math scores over 700: 12%; SAT writing scores over 700: 7%; ACT scores over 30: 21%.

Retention: 82% of full-time freshmen returned.

FACULTY

Total: 1,746, 79% full-time, 85% with terminal degrees.

Student/faculty ratio: 17:1.

ACADEMICS

Calendar: semesters. *Degrees:* certificates, bachelor's, master's, doctoral, post-master's, and postbachelor's certificates.

Special study options: academic remediation for entering students, accelerated degree program, adult/continuing education programs, advanced placement credit, cooperative education, distance learning, double majors, English as a second language, honors programs, independent study, internships, off-campus study, part-time degree program, services for LD students, student-designed majors, study abroad, summer session for credit. ***ROTC:*** Army (b), Air Force (b).

Unusual degree programs: 3-2 business administration.

Computers: 1,000 computers/terminals are available on campus for general student use. Students can access the following: campus intranet, computer help desk, free student e-mail accounts, online (class) grades, online (class) registration, online (class) schedules. Campuswide network is available. 100% of college-owned or -operated housing units are wired for high-speed Internet access. Wireless service is available via entire campus.

Library: William T. Young Library plus 10 others. *Books:* 1.9 million (physical), 1.7 million (digital/electronic); *Serial titles:* 56,138 (physical), 172,838 (digital/electronic); *Databases:* 410. Weekly public service hours: 144; study areas open 24 hours, 5-7 days a week; students can reserve study rooms.

STUDENT LIFE

Housing options: coed, special housing for students with disabilities. Campus housing is university owned, leased by the school and is provided by a third party. Freshman applicants given priority for college housing.

Activities and organizations: drama/theater group, student-run newspaper, radio and television station, choral group, marching band, Student Activities Board, Student Government Association, Campus Progressive Coalition, Ski and Snowboard Club, Society of Women Engineers, national fraternities, national sororities.

Athletics Member NCAA. All Division I except football (Division I-A). ***Intercollegiate sports:*** baseball M(s), basketball M(s)/W(s), cross-country running M(s)/W(s), golf M(s)/W(s), gymnastics W(s), riflery M(s)/W(s), soccer M(s)/W(s), softball W(s), swimming and diving M(s)/W(s), tennis M(s)/W(s), track and field M(s)/W(s), volleyball W(s). ***Intramural sports:*** archery M/W, badminton M/W, basketball M/W, fencing M/W, football M/W, golf M/W, ice hockey M, lacrosse M, rugby M, soccer M/W, softball M/W, swimming and diving M/W, table tennis M/W, tennis M/W, track and field M/W, volleyball M/W.

Campus security: 24-hour emergency response devices and patrols, late-night transport/escort service, controlled dormitory access.

Student services: health clinic, personal/psychological counseling, women's center, legal services.

COSTS & FINANCIAL AID

Costs (2016–17) ***Tuition:*** state resident $10,172 full-time, $424 per credit hour part-time; nonresident $25,023 full-time, $1042 per credit hour part-time. Full-time tuition and fees vary according to location, program, reciprocity agreements, and student level. Part-time tuition and fees vary according to course load, location, program, reciprocity agreements, and student level. ***Required fees:*** $1311 full-time, $41 per credit hour part-time. ***Room and board:*** $12,184. Room and board charges vary according to board plan and housing facility. ***Payment plan:*** installment. ***Waivers:*** employees or children of employees.

Financial Aid Of all full-time matriculated undergraduates who enrolled in 2013, 13,018 applied for aid, 10,344 were judged to have need, 1,737 had their need fully met. In 2013, 3892 non-need-based awards were made. ***Average percent of need met:*** 60. ***Average financial aid package:*** $10,872. ***Average need-based loan:*** $4403. ***Average need-based gift aid:*** $5457. ***Average non-need-based aid:*** $7487. ***Average indebtedness upon graduation:*** $25,102.

APPLYING

Standardized Tests *Required:* SAT or ACT (for admission).

Options: electronic application, early admission, early action, deferred entrance.

Application fee: $50.

Required: essay or personal statement, high school transcript, minimum 2.0 GPA, 1 letter of recommendation.

Application deadlines: 2/15 (freshmen), rolling (transfers), 12/1 (early action).

Notification: continuous until 5/1 (freshmen), continuous until 5/1 (out-of-state freshmen), continuous (transfers), rolling (early action).

CONTACT
Ms. Michelle R. Nordin, Associate Director of Admissions, University of Kentucky, 100 W.D. Funkhouser Building, Lexington, KY 40506-0054. *Phone:* 859-257-2000. *Toll-free phone:* 866-900-GO-UK. *E-mail:* admissio@uky.edu.

University of Louisville
Louisville, Kentucky
http://www.louisville.edu/

- **State-supported** university, founded 1798
- **Urban** 640-acre campus with easy access to Louisville
- **Endowment** $691.6 million
- **Coed** 15,827 undergraduate students, 79% full-time, 51% women, 49% men
- **Moderately difficult** entrance level, 73% of applicants were admitted

UNDERGRAD STUDENTS
12,434 full-time, 3,393 part-time. Students come from 54 states and territories; 62 other countries; 18% are from out of state; 11% Black or African American, non-Hispanic/Latino; 5% Hispanic/Latino; 4% Asian, non-Hispanic/Latino; 0.1% Native Hawaiian or other Pacific Islander, non-Hispanic/Latino; 0.1% American Indian or Alaska Native, non-Hispanic/Latino; 5% Two or more races, non-Hispanic/Latino; 0.1% Race/ethnicity unknown; 2% international; 6% transferred in; 33% live on campus.

Freshmen:
Admission: 10,165 applied, 7,377 admitted, 2,883 enrolled. ***Average high school GPA:*** 3.6. ***Test scores:*** SAT critical reading scores over 500: 76%; SAT math scores over 500: 76%; ACT scores over 18: 100%; SAT critical reading scores over 600: 32%; SAT math scores over 600: 33%; ACT scores over 24: 64%; SAT critical reading scores over 700: 8%; SAT math scores over 700: 8%; ACT scores over 30: 20%.

Retention: 80% of full-time freshmen returned.

FACULTY
Total: 1,390, 68% full-time, 75% with terminal degrees.

Student/faculty ratio: 15:1.

ACADEMICS
Calendar: semesters. *Degrees:* certificates, associate, bachelor's, master's, doctoral, post-master's, and postbachelor's certificates.

Special study options: academic remediation for entering students, accelerated degree program, adult/continuing education programs, advanced placement credit, cooperative education, distance learning, double majors, English as a second language, honors programs, independent study, internships, off-campus study, part-time degree program, services for LD students, study abroad, summer session for credit. ***ROTC:*** Army (b), Air Force (b).

Unusual degree programs: 3-2 engineering.

Computers: 400 computers/terminals are available on campus for general student use. Students can access the following: computer help desk, free student e-mail accounts, online (class) grades, online (class) registration, online (class) schedules. Campuswide network is available. 100% of college-owned or -operated housing units are wired for high-speed Internet access. Wireless service is available via entire campus.

Library: William F. Ekstrom Library plus 6 others. *Books:* 2.2 million (physical), 156,972 (digital/electronic); *Serial titles:* 2,181 (physical), 51,544 (digital/electronic); *Databases:* 343. Weekly public service hours: 97; study areas open 24 hours, 5-7 days a week; students can reserve study rooms.

STUDENT LIFE
Housing options: on-campus residence required for freshman year; coed, men-only, special housing for students with disabilities. Campus housing is university owned and is provided by a third party. Freshman campus housing is guaranteed.

Activities and organizations: drama/theater group, student-run newspaper, choral group, marching band, Baptist Campus Ministry, Society of Porter Scholars, Association of Black Students, Common Ground, Raise Red Dance Marathon, national fraternities, national sororities.

Athletics Member NCAA. All Division I except football (Division I-A). ***Intercollegiate sports:*** baseball M(s), basketball M(s)/W(s), cheerleading M(s)/W(s), cross-country running M(s)/W(s), field hockey W(s), golf M(s)/W(s), lacrosse W(s), rowing W(s), soccer M(s)/W(s), softball W(s), swimming and diving M(s)/W(s), tennis M(s)/W(s), track and field M(s)/W(s), volleyball W(s). ***Intramural sports:*** badminton M/W, basketball M/W, bowling M/W, cross-country running M/W, equestrian sports W(c), fencing M/W, football M/W, golf M/W, gymnastics W(c), ice hockey M, lacrosse M(c)/W(c), racquetball M/W, rugby M(c), soccer M/W, softball W, swimming and diving M/W, table tennis M/W, tennis M/W, track and field M/W, ultimate Frisbee M/W, volleyball M/W.

Campus security: 24-hour emergency response devices and patrols, late-night transport/escort service, controlled dormitory access, alert notification system.

Student services: health clinic, personal/psychological counseling, women's center.

COSTS & FINANCIAL AID
Costs (2017–18) ***Tuition:*** state resident $11,068 full-time, $462 per credit hour part-time; nonresident $26,090 full-time, $1088 per credit hour part-time. Full-time tuition and fees vary according to reciprocity agreements. Part-time tuition and fees vary according to course load and reciprocity agreements. ***Required fees:*** $196 full-time. ***Room and board:*** $8560; room only: $5776. Room and board charges vary according to board plan and housing facility. ***Payment plan:*** installment. ***Waivers:*** senior citizens and employees or children of employees.

Financial Aid Of all full-time matriculated undergraduates who enrolled in 2016, 9,095 applied for aid, 7,334 were judged to have need, 1,411 had their need fully met. 398 Federal Work-Study jobs (averaging $3356). In 2016, 1873 non-need-based awards were made. ***Average percent of need met:*** 59. ***Average financial aid package:*** $11,864. ***Average need-based loan:*** $4141. ***Average need-based gift aid:*** $9166. ***Average non-need-based aid:*** $8101. ***Average indebtedness upon graduation:*** $23,553.

APPLYING
Standardized Tests *Required:* SAT or ACT (for admission). *Required for some:* TOEFL for students whose primary language is not English.

Options: electronic application, deferred entrance.

Application fee: $50.

Required: high school transcript, minimum 2.5 GPA.

Application deadlines: rolling (freshmen), rolling (transfers).

Notification: continuous (transfers).

CONTACT
Ms. Jenny L. Sawyer, Executive Director of Admissions, University of Louisville, 2301 South Third Street, Houchens Room 150, Louisville, KY 40292-0001. *Phone:* 502-852-6531. *Toll-free phone:* 800-334-8635. *Fax:* 502-852-4776. *E-mail:* admitme@louisville.edu.

University of Pikeville
Pikeville, Kentucky
http://www.upike.edu/

- **Independent** comprehensive, founded 1889, affiliated with Presbyterian Church (U.S.A.)
- **Small-town** 25-acre campus
- **Endowment** $13.8 million
- **Coed** 1,658 undergraduate students, 68% full-time, 53% women, 47% men
- **Noncompetitive** entrance level, 100% of applicants were admitted

UNDERGRAD STUDENTS
1,129 full-time, 529 part-time. Students come from 31 states and territories; 16 other countries; 20% are from out of state; 7% Black or African American, non-Hispanic/Latino; 2% Hispanic/Latino; 0.5% Asian, non-Hispanic/Latino; 0.2% Native Hawaiian or other Pacific Islander, non-Hispanic/Latino; 0.7% American Indian or Alaska Native, non-Hispanic/Latino; 2% international; 6% transferred in; 53% live on campus.

Freshmen:
Admission: 2,437 applied, 2,437 admitted, 329 enrolled. ***Average high school GPA:*** 3.1. ***Test scores:*** SAT critical reading scores over 500: 8%; SAT math scores over 500: 36%; SAT writing scores over 500: 17%; ACT scores over 18: 71%; SAT math scores over 600: 12%; ACT scores over 24: 15%; ACT scores over 30: 2%.
Retention: 57% of full-time freshmen returned.

FACULTY
Total: 113, 58% full-time, 43% with terminal degrees.
Student/faculty ratio: 14:1.

ACADEMICS
Calendar: semesters. *Degrees:* associate, bachelor's, master's, and doctoral.
Special study options: academic remediation for entering students, advanced placement credit, distance learning, double majors, English as a second language, internships, part-time degree program, services for LD students, student-designed majors, study abroad, summer session for credit. ***ROTC:*** Army (c).
Computers: 308 computers/terminals are available on campus for general student use. Students can access the following: computer help desk, free student e-mail accounts, online (class) grades, online (class) schedules. Campuswide network is available. 100% of college-owned or -operated housing units are wired for high-speed Internet access. Wireless service is available via entire campus.
Library: Allara Library plus 2 others. *Books:* 73,924 (physical), 214,499 (digital/electronic); *Serial titles:* 1,437 (physical), 88,386 (digital/electronic); *Databases:* 73. Weekly public service hours: 105; students can reserve study rooms.

STUDENT LIFE
Housing options: coed, men-only, women-only. Campus housing is university owned.
Activities and organizations: drama/theater group, student-run newspaper, television station, choral group, Student Government, Phi Beta Lambda, Lambda Sigma, Concert Choir, Student Nurses at UPIKE.
Athletics Member NAIA. ***Intercollegiate sports:*** baseball M(s), basketball M(s)/W(s), bowling M(s)/W(s), cheerleading M(s)/W(s), cross-country running M(s)/W(s), football M(s), golf M(s)/W(s), soccer M(s)/W(s), softball W(s), tennis M(s)/W(s), track and field M(s)/W(s), volleyball W(s). ***Intramural sports:*** basketball M/W, football M.
Campus security: 24-hour patrols, controlled dormitory access.
Student services: health clinic.

COSTS & FINANCIAL AID
Costs (2017–18) ***Comprehensive fee:*** $27,700 includes full-time tuition ($20,200) and room and board ($7500). Full-time tuition and fees vary according to course load. Part-time tuition: $842 per semester hour. Part-time tuition and fees vary according to course load. ***Room and board:*** Room and board charges vary according to housing facility. ***Payment plan:*** installment. ***Waivers:*** senior citizens and employees or children of employees.
Financial Aid Of all full-time matriculated undergraduates who enrolled in 2016, 1,062 applied for aid, 1,052 were judged to have need, 537 had their need fully met. 210 Federal Work-Study jobs (averaging $1907). ***Average percent of need met:*** 86. ***Average financial aid package:*** $18,612. ***Average need-based loan:*** $4156. ***Average need-based gift aid:*** $18,234. ***Average indebtedness upon graduation:*** $26,013.

APPLYING
Standardized Tests *Required:* SAT or ACT (for admission).
Options: electronic application, deferred entrance.
Required: high school transcript.
Application deadlines: 8/15 (freshmen), 8/15 (transfers).
Notification: continuous (freshmen), continuous (out-of-state freshmen), continuous (transfers).

CONTACT
Mr. John Yancey, Director of Admissions, University of Pikeville, 147 Sycamore Street, Pikeville, KY 41501. *Phone:* 606-218-5251. *Toll-free phone:* 866-232-7700. *Fax:* 606-218-5255. *E-mail:* wewantyou@pc.edu.

University of the Cumberlands
Williamsburg, Kentucky
http://www.ucumberlands.edu/

- **Independent Kentucky Baptist** university, founded 1889
- **Rural** 150-acre campus with easy access to Knoxville
- **Coed** 3,082 undergraduate students, 58% full-time, 56% women, 44% men
- **Moderately difficult** entrance level, 71% of applicants were admitted

UNDERGRAD STUDENTS
1,780 full-time, 1,302 part-time. Students come from 38 states and territories; 26 other countries; 32% are from out of state; 5% Black or African American, non-Hispanic/Latino; 2% Hispanic/Latino; 0.4% Asian, non-Hispanic/Latino; 0.1% Native Hawaiian or other Pacific Islander, non-Hispanic/Latino; 0.4% American Indian or Alaska Native, non-Hispanic/Latino; 2% Two or more races, non-Hispanic/Latino; 9% Race/ethnicity unknown; 4% international; 5% transferred in; 80% live on campus.

Freshmen:
Admission: 2,326 applied, 1,656 admitted, 419 enrolled. ***Average high school GPA:*** 3.47. ***Test scores:*** SAT critical reading scores over 500: 32%; SAT math scores over 500: 43%; ACT scores over 18: 92%; SAT critical reading scores over 600: 2%; SAT math scores over 600: 13%; ACT scores over 24: 35%; SAT math scores over 700: 2%; ACT scores over 30: 8%.
Retention: 65% of full-time freshmen returned.

FACULTY
Total: 378, 43% full-time.
Student/faculty ratio: 15:1.

ACADEMICS
Calendar: semesters. *Degrees:* associate, bachelor's, master's, doctoral, post-master's, and postbachelor's certificates.
Special study options: academic remediation for entering students, accelerated degree program, adult/continuing education programs, advanced placement credit, cooperative education, distance learning, double majors, honors programs, independent study, internships, part-time degree program, student-designed majors, study abroad, summer session for credit.
Unusual degree programs: 3-2 engineering with University of Kentucky; physician assistant.
Computers: 171 computers/terminals and 1,258 ports are available on campus for general student use. Students can access the following: campus intranet, computer help desk, free student e-mail accounts, online (class) grades, online (class) registration, online (class) schedules, online housing requests. Campuswide network is available. 100% of college-owned or -operated housing units are wired for high-speed Internet access. Wireless service is available via entire campus.
Library: Norma Perkins Hagan Memorial Library plus 1 other. *Books:* 127,545 (physical), 325,906 (digital/electronic); *Serial titles:* 428 (physical), 63,756 (digital/electronic); *Databases:* 83. Weekly public service hours: 79.

STUDENT LIFE
Housing options: on-campus residence required through senior year; men-only, women-only. Campus housing is university owned. Freshman campus housing is guaranteed.
Activities and organizations: drama/theater group, student-run newspaper, radio and television station, choral group, marching band, Campus Activity Board, Baptist Campus Ministries, Mountain Outreach, Appalachian Ministries, Student Government Association.
Athletics Member NAIA. ***Intercollegiate sports:*** archery M(s)/W(s), baseball M(s), basketball M(s)/W(s), bowling M(s)/W(s), cheerleading M(s)/W(s), cross-country running M(s)/W(s), football M(s), golf M(s)/W(s), lacrosse M(s)/W(s), soccer M(s)/W(s), softball W(s), swimming and diving M(s)/W(s), tennis M(s)/W(s), track and field M(s)/W(s), volleyball W(s), wrestling M(s)/W(s). ***Intramural sports:*** badminton M/W, baseball M/W, basketball M/W, football M/W, golf M/W, sand volleyball M/W, soccer M/W, softball M/W, table tennis M/W, ultimate Frisbee M/W.
Campus security: 24-hour emergency response devices and patrols, student patrols, late-night transport/escort service.

Student services: health clinic, personal/psychological counseling.

COSTS & FINANCIAL AID

Costs (2017–18) ***Comprehensive fee:*** $32,000 includes full-time tuition ($22,640), mandatory fees ($360), and room and board ($9000). Part-time tuition: $720 per credit hour. Part-time tuition and fees vary according to course load. ***Required fees:*** $90 per term part-time. ***Payment plan:*** installment. ***Waivers:*** senior citizens and employees or children of employees.

Financial Aid Of all full-time matriculated undergraduates who enrolled in 2015, 1,529 applied for aid, 1,447 were judged to have need, 253 had their need fully met. 830 Federal Work-Study jobs (averaging $1939). 11 state and other part-time jobs (averaging $2095). In 2015, 179 non-need-based awards were made. ***Average percent of need met:*** 76. ***Average financial aid package:*** $19,977. ***Average need-based loan:*** $3737. ***Average need-based gift aid:*** $16,231. ***Average non-need-based aid:*** $10,469. ***Average indebtedness upon graduation:*** $25,198.

APPLYING

Standardized Tests *Required:* SAT or ACT (for admission).

Options: electronic application, deferred entrance.

Required: high school transcript, minimum 2.0 GPA.

Application deadlines: 8/31 (freshmen), 8/31 (transfers).

Notification: 8/31 (freshmen), 8/31 (transfers).

CONTACT

Mrs. Erica Harris, Director of Admissions, University of the Cumberlands, 6178 College Station Drive, Williamsburg, KY 40769. *Phone:* 606-539-4241. *Toll-free phone:* 800-343-1609. *Fax:* 606-539-4303. *E-mail:* admiss@ucumberlands.edu.

Western Kentucky University

Bowling Green, Kentucky

http://www.wku.edu/

- **State-supported** comprehensive, founded 1906
- **Suburban** 235-acre campus with easy access to Nashville
- **Endowment** $139.9 million
- **Coed** 17,595 undergraduate students, 75% full-time, 58% women, 42% men
- **Minimally difficult** entrance level, 94% of applicants were admitted

UNDERGRAD STUDENTS

13,160 full-time, 4,435 part-time. Students come from 45 states and territories; 77 other countries; 20% are from out of state; 9% Black or African American, non-Hispanic/Latino; 3% Hispanic/Latino; 2% Asian, non-Hispanic/Latino; 0.1% Native Hawaiian or other Pacific Islander, non-Hispanic/Latino; 0.2% American Indian or Alaska Native, non-Hispanic/Latino; 3% Two or more races, non-Hispanic/Latino; 1% Race/ethnicity unknown; 5% international; 6% transferred in; 33% live on campus.

Freshmen:

Admission: 9,693 applied, 9,113 admitted, 3,192 enrolled. ***Average high school GPA:*** 3.27. ***Test scores:*** SAT critical reading scores over 500: 44%; SAT math scores over 500: 46%; ACT scores over 18: 85%; SAT critical reading scores over 600: 13%; SAT math scores over 600: 12%; ACT scores over 24: 41%; SAT critical reading scores over 700: 4%; SAT math scores over 700: 3%; ACT scores over 30: 9%.

Retention: 73% of full-time freshmen returned.

FACULTY

Total: 1,160, 66% full-time, 59% with terminal degrees.

Student/faculty ratio: 18:1.

ACADEMICS

Calendar: semesters. *Degrees:* certificates, associate, bachelor's, master's, doctoral, post-master's, and postbachelor's certificates.

Special study options: academic remediation for entering students, accelerated degree program, adult/continuing education programs, advanced placement credit, cooperative education, distance learning, double majors, English as a second language, freshman honors college, honors programs, independent study, internships, off-campus study, part-time degree program, services for LD students, student-designed majors, study abroad, summer session for credit. ***ROTC:*** Army (b), Air Force (c).

Unusual degree programs: 3-2 physics, applied sciences, engineering/physics, astronomy, engineering, applied science.

Computers: 364 computers/terminals are available on campus for general student use. Students can access the following: campus intranet, computer help desk, free student e-mail accounts, online (class) grades, online (class) registration, online (class) schedules. Campuswide network is available. 100% of college-owned or -operated housing units are wired for high-speed Internet access. Wireless service is available via entire campus.

Library: Helm-Cravens Library plus 2 others. *Books:* 2.0 million (physical), 8,812 (digital/electronic); *Serial titles:* 1,300 (physical), 44,443 (digital/electronic); *Databases:* 281. Weekly public service hours: 107; students can reserve study rooms.

STUDENT LIFE

Housing options: on-campus residence required through sophomore year; coed, men-only, women-only. Campus housing is university owned. Freshman applicants given priority for college housing.

Activities and organizations: drama/theater group, student-run newspaper, radio and television station, choral group, marching band, Student Government Association, Campus Activities Board, Campus Crusade for Christ, Campus Ministries, Residence Hall Association, national fraternities, national sororities.

Athletics Member NCAA. All Division I except football (Division I-A). ***Intercollegiate sports:*** baseball M(s), basketball M(s)/W(s), cross-country running M(s)/W(s), golf M(s)/W(s), soccer W, softball W(s), tennis M(s)/W(s), track and field M(s)/W(s), volleyball W(s). ***Intramural sports:*** badminton M(c)/W(c), basketball M/W, fencing M(c)/W(c), field hockey M(c)/W(c), football M/W, lacrosse M(c)/W(c), racquetball M/W, rugby M(c)/W(c), soccer M/W, softball M/W, tennis M(c)/W(c), ultimate Frisbee M/W, volleyball M/W, weight lifting M(c)/W(c).

Campus security: 24-hour emergency response devices and patrols, student patrols, late-night transport/escort service, controlled dormitory access.

Student services: health clinic, personal/psychological counseling, women's center, legal services.

COSTS & FINANCIAL AID

Costs (2016–17) ***Tuition:*** state resident $9912 full-time, $413 per credit hour part-time; nonresident $24,792 full-time, $1033 per credit hour part-time. Full-time tuition and fees vary according to program and reciprocity agreements. Part-time tuition and fees vary according to course load, program, and reciprocity agreements. ***Room and board:*** $7713; room only: $4463. Room and board charges vary according to board plan and housing facility. ***Payment plan:*** installment. ***Waivers:*** senior citizens and employees or children of employees.

Financial Aid Of all full-time matriculated undergraduates who enrolled in 2015, 10,141 applied for aid, 8,053 were judged to have need, 2,584 had their need fully met. 583 Federal Work-Study jobs (averaging $2050). 1,825 state and other part-time jobs (averaging $2717). In 2015, 1656 non-need-based awards were made. ***Average percent of need met:*** 33. ***Average financial aid package:*** $14,221. ***Average need-based loan:*** $3847. ***Average need-based gift aid:*** $5165. ***Average non-need-based aid:*** $6745. ***Average indebtedness upon graduation:*** $28,081.

APPLYING

Standardized Tests *Required:* SAT or ACT (for admission).

Options: electronic application.

Application fee: $45.

Required: high school transcript, minimum ACT composite score of 20 or greater, minimum SAT score (math and critical reading) of 940, unweighted high school GPA of 2.50 or higher, or minimum on Composite Admission Index score.

Application deadlines: 8/1 (freshmen), 8/1 (transfers).

Notification: continuous (freshmen), continuous (transfers).

CONTACT

Western Kentucky University, 1906 College Heights Boulevard, Bowling Green, KY 42101. *Phone:* 270-7452551. *Toll-free phone:* 800-495-8463.

LOUISIANA

Centenary College of Louisiana

Shreveport, Louisiana

http://www.centenary.edu/

- **Independent United Methodist** comprehensive, founded 1825
- **Urban** 65-acre campus with easy access to Shreveport
- **Coed** 481 undergraduate students, 98% full-time, 57% women, 43% men
- **Moderately difficult** entrance level, 64% of applicants were admitted

UNDERGRAD STUDENTS

472 full-time, 9 part-time. 45% are from out of state; 16% Black or African American, non-Hispanic/Latino; 7% Hispanic/Latino; 3% Asian, non-Hispanic/Latino; 0.2% Native Hawaiian or other Pacific Islander, non-Hispanic/Latino; 1% American Indian or Alaska Native, non-Hispanic/Latino; 6% Two or more races, non-Hispanic/Latino; 2% international; 3% transferred in; 89% live on campus.

Freshmen:

Admission: 886 applied, 569 admitted, 130 enrolled. ***Average high school GPA:*** 3.52. ***Test scores:*** SAT critical reading scores over 500: 57%; SAT math scores over 500: 64%; ACT scores over 18: 98%; SAT critical reading scores over 600: 20%; SAT math scores over 600: 23%; ACT scores over 24: 60%; SAT critical reading scores over 700: 5%; SAT math scores over 700: 8%; ACT scores over 30: 14%.

Retention: 73% of full-time freshmen returned.

FACULTY

Total: 89, 64% full-time, 72% with terminal degrees.

Student/faculty ratio: 8:1.

ACADEMICS

Calendar: 4-4-1. *Degrees:* bachelor's and master's.

Special study options: advanced placement credit, double majors, honors programs, independent study, internships, off-campus study, part-time degree program, services for LD students, student-designed majors, study abroad, summer session for credit.

Unusual degree programs: 3-2 engineering; psychology.

Computers: Students can access the following: free student e-mail accounts, online (class) grades, online (class) registration, online (class) schedules. Campuswide network is available. Wireless service is available via classrooms, dorm rooms, libraries, student centers.

Library: Magale Library plus 1 other. *Books:* 151,971 (physical), 155,940 (digital/electronic); *Serial titles:* 9,794 (physical), 255,780 (digital/electronic); *Databases:* 323. Weekly public service hours: 82; students can reserve study rooms.

STUDENT LIFE

Housing options: on-campus residence required through senior year; coed. Campus housing is university owned. Freshman campus housing is guaranteed.

Activities and organizations: drama/theater group, student-run newspaper, radio station, choral group, Intramural sports, Residence Life (Centenary Activities Board), Fellowship of Christian Athletes, Christian Leadership Center, Media Group, national fraternities, national sororities.

Athletics Member NCAA. All Division III. ***Intercollegiate sports:*** baseball M, basketball M/W, golf M/W, gymnastics W, lacrosse M(c), soccer M/W, softball W, swimming and diving M/W, tennis M/W, triathlon W, volleyball W. ***Intramural sports:*** basketball M/W, football M/W, soccer M/W, softball M/W, volleyball M/W.

Campus security: 24-hour emergency response devices and patrols, late-night transport/escort service, controlled dormitory access.

Student services: health clinic, personal/psychological counseling.

COSTS & FINANCIAL AID

Costs (2017–18) ***One-time required fee:*** $250. ***Comprehensive fee:*** $49,050 includes full-time tuition ($35,900) and room and board ($13,150). Full-time tuition and fees vary according to course load, degree level, and student level. Part-time tuition: $1455 per credit hour. Part-time tuition and fees vary according to course load, degree level, and student level. ***Room and board:*** Room and board charges vary according to board plan, housing facility, and student level. ***Payment plan:*** installment. ***Waivers:*** employees or children of employees.

Financial Aid Of all full-time matriculated undergraduates who enrolled in 2016, 409 applied for aid, 374 were judged to have need, 80 had their need fully met. 171 Federal Work-Study jobs (averaging $2182). 38 state and other part-time jobs (averaging $1533). In 2016, 82 non-need-based awards were made. ***Average percent of need met:*** 73. ***Average financial aid package:*** $27,996. ***Average need-based loan:*** $4442. ***Average need-based gift aid:*** $24,252. ***Average non-need-based aid:*** $21,080. ***Average indebtedness upon graduation:*** $26,643.

APPLYING

Standardized Tests *Required:* SAT or ACT (for admission).

Options: electronic application, early admission, early action, deferred entrance.

Required: essay or personal statement, high school transcript, minimum 2.0 GPA, 1 letter of recommendation. ***Required for some:*** interview.

Application deadlines: rolling (freshmen), rolling (transfers), 12/15 (early action).

Notification: continuous (freshmen), continuous (transfers).

CONTACT

Ms. Lauren Carlton, Associate Director of Admission - Recruitment, Centenary College of Louisiana, Office of Admission, 2911 Centenary Boulevard, Shreveport, LA 71104. *Phone:* 318-869-5748. *Toll-free phone:* 800-234-4448. *Fax:* 318-869-5005. *E-mail:* lcarlton@centenary.edu.

Dillard University

New Orleans, Louisiana

http://www.dillard.edu/

- **Independent interdenominational** 4-year, founded 1869
- **Urban** 55-acre campus
- **Endowment** $58.4 million
- **Coed**
- **Moderately difficult** entrance level

FACULTY

Student/faculty ratio: 12:1.

ACADEMICS

Calendar: semesters. *Degree:* bachelor's.

Library: Will W. Alexander Library plus 1 other.

STUDENT LIFE

Housing options: on-campus residence required for freshman year; coed, men-only, women-only, special housing for students with disabilities. Campus housing is university owned and leased by the school. Freshman campus housing is guaranteed.

Activities and organizations: drama/theater group, student-run newspaper, radio and television station, choral group, Student Government Association, Student Activities Board, National Pan-Hellenic Council, Collegiate 100, Class Councils, national fraternities, national sororities.

Athletics Member NAIA.

Campus security: 24-hour emergency response devices and patrols, late-night transport/escort service, controlled dormitory access.

Student services: health clinic, personal/psychological counseling, legal services.

COSTS & FINANCIAL AID

Costs (2016–17) ***Comprehensive fee:*** $27,404 includes full-time tuition ($15,790), mandatory fees ($1741), and room and board ($9873).

Financial Aid Of all full-time matriculated undergraduates who enrolled in 2013, 1,129 applied for aid, 1,096 were judged to have need, 55 had their need fully met. 204 Federal Work-Study jobs (averaging $1632). In 2013, 43 non-need-based awards were made. ***Average percent of need met:*** 59. ***Average financial aid package:*** $14,972. ***Average need-based loan:*** $5244. ***Average need-based gift aid:*** $9946. ***Average non-need-based aid:*** $8078. ***Average indebtedness upon graduation:*** $30,095.

APPLYING

Standardized Tests *Required:* SAT or ACT (for admission), minimum SAT score of 870 (math and verbal) or minimum ACT composite score of 18 (for admission).

Options: electronic application, early admission.

Application fee: $35.

Required: high school transcript, minimum 2.5 GPA. ***Required for some:*** essay or personal statement, 2 letters of recommendation.

CONTACT

Ms. Monica White, Director for Recruitment, Admissions and Programming, Dillard University, 2601 Gentilly Boulevard, New Orleans, LA 70122-3097. *Phone:* 504-816-4374. *Toll-free phone:* 800-216-8094. *Fax:* 504-816-4895. *E-mail:* acyprian@dillard.edu.

Grambling State University

Grambling, Louisiana

http://www.gram.edu/

- **State-supported** university, founded 1901, part of University of Louisiana System
- **Small-town** 590-acre campus with easy access to Shreveport
- **Endowment** $7.2 million
- **Coed** 3,883 undergraduate students, 93% full-time, 57% women, 43% men
- **Noncompetitive** entrance level, 45% of applicants were admitted

UNDERGRAD STUDENTS

3,598 full-time, 285 part-time. Students come from 40 states and territories; 25 other countries; 31% are from out of state; 91% Black or African American, non-Hispanic/Latino; 1% Hispanic/Latino; 0.1% Asian, non-Hispanic/Latino; 0.1% Native Hawaiian or other Pacific Islander, non-Hispanic/Latino; 0.2% American Indian or Alaska Native, non-Hispanic/Latino; 2% Two or more races, non-Hispanic/Latino; 0.5% Race/ethnicity unknown; 5% international; 7% transferred in.

Freshmen:

Admission: 6,340 applied, 2,862 admitted, 865 enrolled. ***Average high school GPA:*** 2.81. ***Test scores:*** SAT critical reading scores over 500: 14%; SAT math scores over 500: 20%; SAT writing scores over 500: 10%; ACT scores over 18: 59%; SAT math scores over 600: 1%; ACT scores over 24: 4%.

Retention: 60% of full-time freshmen returned.

FACULTY

Total: 208, 94% full-time, 100% with terminal degrees.

Student/faculty ratio: 20:1.

ACADEMICS

Calendar: semesters. *Degrees:* bachelor's, master's, doctoral, and post-master's certificates.

Special study options: academic remediation for entering students, adult/continuing education programs, advanced placement credit, cooperative education, distance learning, double majors, honors programs, internships, off-campus study, part-time degree program, services for LD students, summer session for credit. ***ROTC:*** Army (b), Air Force (c).

Computers: 500 computers/terminals and 500 ports are available on campus for general student use. Students can access the following: campus intranet, computer help desk, free student e-mail accounts, online (class) grades, online (class) registration, online (class) schedules. Campuswide network is available. Wireless service is available via classrooms, computer centers, computer labs, dorm rooms, learning centers, libraries, student centers.

Library: A. C. Lewis Memorial Library. *Books:* 101,358 (physical), 902 (digital/electronic); *Serial titles:* 802 (physical), 2,326 (digital/electronic); *Databases:* 101. Weekly public service hours: 73; students can reserve study rooms.

STUDENT LIFE

Housing options: on-campus residence required through sophomore year; coed, men-only, women-only, special housing for students with disabilities. Campus housing is university owned and leased by the school. Freshman applicants given priority for college housing.

Activities and organizations: drama/theater group, student-run newspaper, radio and television station, choral group, marching band, Tiger Marching Band, Black Dynasty Modeling Troupe, Academic and Professional Clubs, sororities, fraternities, national fraternities, national sororities.

Athletics Member NCAA. All Division I except football (Division I-AA). ***Intercollegiate sports:*** baseball M(s), basketball M(s)/W(s), bowling W(s), cross-country running M/W, soccer W, softball W(s), tennis W(s), track and field M(s)/W(s), volleyball W(s). ***Intramural sports:*** badminton M/W, basketball M/W, bowling M(c)/W(c), racquetball M(c)/W(c), soccer M(c)/W(c), softball W, table tennis M/W, tennis M(c)/W(c), volleyball M(c)/W(c), weight lifting M/W.

Campus security: 24-hour patrols, student patrols, controlled dormitory access.

Student services: health clinic, personal/psychological counseling.

COSTS & FINANCIAL AID

Costs (2017–18) ***Tuition:*** state resident $5140 full-time, $215 per credit hour part-time; nonresident $14,163 full-time, $591 per credit hour part-time. Full-time tuition and fees vary according to course load, degree level, and student level. Part-time tuition and fees vary according to course load, degree level, and student level. ***Required fees:*** $1116 full-time. ***Room and board:*** $8954; room only: $5480. Room and board charges vary according to housing facility. ***Payment plans:*** installment, deferred payment. ***Waivers:*** children of alumni, senior citizens, and employees or children of employees.

Financial Aid Of all full-time matriculated undergraduates who enrolled in 2016, 3,378 applied for aid, 3,358 were judged to have need. 719 Federal Work-Study jobs (averaging $1127). In 2016, 101 non-need-based awards were made. ***Average financial aid package:*** $3731. ***Average need-based loan:*** $3812. ***Average need-based gift aid:*** $4051. ***Average non-need-based aid:*** $2313. ***Financial aid deadline:*** 6/1.

APPLYING

Standardized Tests *Required:* SAT or ACT (for admission).

Options: electronic application, early admission.

Application fee: $20.

Required: high school transcript, minimum 2.0 GPA, 19 units from Required Core 4 Curriculum including no more than one developmental course; minimum ACT English score of 18 and ACT Math of 19 or SAT Critical Reading of 450 and SAT Math of 460 or COMPASS Writing of 68 and COMPASS Algebra of 40.

Application deadlines: 8/15 (freshmen), 7/15 (transfers).

Notification: 4/1 (freshmen), continuous until 6/15 (transfers).

CONTACT

Chemia Herron, Director of Admissions and Recruitment, Grambling State University, GSU Box 4200, Grambling, LA 71245. *Phone:* 318-274-6100. *Toll-free phone:* 800-569-4714. *Fax:* 318-274-3292. *E-mail:* herronc@gram.edu.

Herzing University

Kenner, Louisiana

http://www.herzing.edu/new-orleans

CONTACT

Herzing University, 2500 Williams Boulevard, Kenner, LA 70062. *Toll-free phone:* 800-596-0724.

Louisiana College

Pineville, Louisiana

http://www.lacollege.edu/

- **Independent Southern Baptist** comprehensive, founded 1906
- **Small-town** 81-acre campus
- **Coed** 909 undergraduate students, 91% full-time, 46% women, 54% men
- **Moderately difficult** entrance level, 72% of applicants were admitted

UNDERGRAD STUDENTS

830 full-time, 79 part-time. Students come from 17 states and territories; 9 other countries; 10% are from out of state; 29% Black or African American, non-Hispanic/Latino; 2% Hispanic/Latino; 0.7% Asian, non-Hispanic/Latino; 0.1% Native Hawaiian or other Pacific Islander, non-Hispanic/Latino; 0.9% American Indian or Alaska Native, non-Hispanic/Latino; 0.8% Two or more races, non-Hispanic/Latino; 0.3% Race/ethnicity unknown; 3% international; 7% transferred in; 55% live on campus.

Freshmen:

Admission: 755 applied, 545 admitted, 248 enrolled. ***Test scores:*** SAT critical reading scores over 500: 38%; SAT math scores over 500: 25%;

ACT scores over 18: 78%; ACT scores over 24: 23%; ACT scores over 30: 2%.

Retention: 50% of full-time freshmen returned.

FACULTY

Total: 95, 69% full-time, 59% with terminal degrees.

Student/faculty ratio: 12:1.

ACADEMICS

Calendar: semesters. *Degrees:* associate, bachelor's, and master's.

Special study options: academic remediation for entering students, accelerated degree program, adult/continuing education programs, advanced placement credit, distance learning, double majors, English as a second language, honors programs, independent study, internships, part-time degree program, services for LD students, student-designed majors, summer session for credit. ***ROTC:*** Army (b).

Unusual degree programs: 3-2 engineering with Louisiana Tech University.

Computers: 323 computers/terminals are available on campus for general student use. Students can access the following: campus intranet, computer help desk, free student e-mail accounts, online (class) grades, online (class) registration, online (class) schedules. Campuswide network is available. 100% of college-owned or -operated housing units are wired for high-speed Internet access. Wireless service is available via entire campus.

Library: Richard W. Norton Memorial Library. *Books:* 124,328 (physical), 281,138 (digital/electronic); *Serial titles:* 369 (physical), 28,876 (digital/electronic); *Databases:* 112. Weekly public service hours: 70.

STUDENT LIFE

Housing options: on-campus residence required through junior year; coed, men-only, women-only. Campus housing is university owned. Freshman campus housing is guaranteed.

Activities and organizations: drama/theater group, student-run newspaper, radio station, choral group, marching band, Baptist Collegiate Ministry, Delta Xi Omega, Student Government Association, Union Board, Lambda Chi Beta.

Athletics Member NCAA. All Division III. ***Intercollegiate sports:*** baseball M, basketball M/W, cheerleading M/W, cross-country running M/W, football M, golf M/W, soccer M/W, softball W, tennis M/W, track and field M/W, volleyball W. ***Intramural sports:*** badminton M/W, basketball M/W, football M/W, soccer M/W, softball M/W, table tennis M/W, ultimate Frisbee M/W, volleyball M/W.

Campus security: 24-hour emergency response devices and patrols, student patrols, late-night transport/escort service, controlled dormitory access.

Student services: health clinic, personal/psychological counseling.

COSTS & FINANCIAL AID

Costs (2017–18) ***Comprehensive fee:*** $19,062 includes full-time tuition ($11,960), mandatory fees ($1878), and room and board ($5224). Full-time tuition and fees vary according to course load and program. Part-time tuition: $460 per credit hour. Part-time tuition and fees vary according to course load and program. ***Room and board:*** Room and board charges vary according to board plan and housing facility. ***Payment plan:*** installment. ***Waivers:*** senior citizens and employees or children of employees.

Financial Aid ***Average indebtedness upon graduation:*** $22,969.

APPLYING

Standardized Tests *Required:* SAT or ACT (for admission).

Options: electronic application.

Application fee: $25.

Required: minimum 2.0 GPA. ***Required for some:*** high school transcript.

Application deadlines: rolling (freshmen), rolling (transfers).

Notification: continuous (freshmen), continuous (transfers).

CONTACT

Dr. Brandon Bannon, Vice President of Enrollment Management, Louisiana College, LC Box 566, Pineville, LA 71359. *Phone:* 318-487-7439. *Toll-free phone:* 800-487-1906. *E-mail:* admissions@lacollege.edu.

Louisiana Culinary Institute

Baton Rouge, Louisiana

http://www.lci.edu/

CONTACT

Louisiana Culinary Institute, 10550 Airline Highway, Baton Rouge, LA 70816. *Toll-free phone:* 877-533-3198.

Louisiana State University and Agricultural & Mechanical College

Baton Rouge, Louisiana

http://www.lsu.edu/

- **State-supported** university, founded 1860, part of Louisiana State University System
- **Urban** 2000-acre campus with easy access to New Orleans
- **Endowment** $416.3 million
- **Coed** 26,156 undergraduate students, 90% full-time, 52% women, 48% men
- **Moderately difficult** entrance level, 76% of applicants were admitted

UNDERGRAD STUDENTS

23,602 full-time, 2,554 part-time. Students come from 51 states and territories; 78 other countries; 17% are from out of state; 12% Black or African American, non-Hispanic/Latino; 6% Hispanic/Latino; 4% Asian, non-Hispanic/Latino; 0.1% Native Hawaiian or other Pacific Islander, non-Hispanic/Latino; 0.3% American Indian or Alaska Native, non-Hispanic/Latino; 2% Two or more races, non-Hispanic/Latino; 0.4% Race/ethnicity unknown; 2% international; 4% transferred in; 24% live on campus.

Freshmen:

Admission: 17,429 applied, 13,300 admitted, 5,624 enrolled. ***Average high school GPA:*** 3.43. ***Test scores:*** SAT critical reading scores over 500: 80%; SAT math scores over 500: 84%; ACT scores over 18: 100%; SAT critical reading scores over 600: 34%; SAT math scores over 600: 39%; ACT scores over 24: 69%; SAT critical reading scores over 700: 8%; SAT math scores over 700: 9%; ACT scores over 30: 15%.

Retention: 85% of full-time freshmen returned.

FACULTY

Total: 1,450, 88% full-time, 85% with terminal degrees.

Student/faculty ratio: 22:1.

ACADEMICS

Calendar: semesters. *Degrees:* certificates, bachelor's, master's, doctoral, post-master's, and postbachelor's certificates.

Special study options: accelerated degree program, adult/continuing education programs, advanced placement credit, cooperative education, distance learning, double majors, English as a second language, freshman honors college, honors programs, independent study, internships, off-campus study, part-time degree program, services for LD students, student-designed majors, study abroad, summer session for credit. ***ROTC:*** Army (b), Navy (c), Air Force (b).

Computers: 1,180 computers/terminals and 8,300 ports are available on campus for general student use. Students can access the following: computer help desk, free student e-mail accounts, online (class) grades, online (class) registration, online (class) schedules, free software for download, storage, discounts on hardware, virtual computer lab. Campuswide network is available. 100% of college-owned or -operated housing units are wired for high-speed Internet access. Wireless service is available via entire campus.

Library: Troy H. Middleton Library plus 4 others. *Books:* 3.0 million (physical), 576,672 (digital/electronic); *Serial titles:* 631,742 (physical), 203,712 (digital/electronic); *Databases:* 358. Study areas open 24 hours, 5-7 days a week; students can reserve study rooms.

STUDENT LIFE

Housing options: coed, men-only, women-only, special housing for students with disabilities. Campus housing is university owned.

Activities and organizations: drama/theater group, student-run newspaper, radio and television station, choral group, marching band, intramural athletics, student political organizations, student professional organizations, religious organizations, cultural organizations, national fraternities, national sororities.

Athletics Member NCAA. All Division I except football (Division I-A). ***Intercollegiate sports:*** baseball M(s), basketball M(s)/W(s), cheerleading M/W, cross-country running M(s)/W(s), golf M(s)/W(s), gymnastics W(s), soccer W(s), softball W(s), swimming and diving M(s)/W(s), tennis M(s)/W(s), track and field M(s)/W(s), volleyball W(s). ***Intramural sports:*** badminton M/W, baseball M(c), basketball M(c)/W, cross-country running M(c)/W(c), equestrian sports W(c), football M/W, golf M/W, ice hockey M(c)/W(c), lacrosse M(c)/W(c), racquetball M/W, rock climbing M/W, rowing M(c)/W(c), rugby M(c)/W(c), sand volleyball M/W, soccer M(c)/W(c), softball M/W, table tennis M(c)/W(c), tennis M(c)/W(c), triathlon M(c)/W(c), ultimate Frisbee M(c)/W(c), volleyball M(c)/W(c), water polo M(c)/W(c), weight lifting M(c)/W(c).

Campus security: 24-hour emergency response devices and patrols, late-night transport/escort service, controlled dormitory access, self-defense education, crime prevention programs.

Student services: health clinic, personal/psychological counseling, women's center, legal services.

COSTS & FINANCIAL AID

Costs (2016–17) ***Tuition:*** state resident $8038 full-time; nonresident $24,715 full-time. Full-time tuition and fees vary according to course load. Part-time tuition and fees vary according to course load. ***Required fees:*** $2776 full-time. ***Room and board:*** $11,540; room only: $7530. Room and board charges vary according to board plan and housing facility. ***Payment plan:*** deferred payment. ***Waivers:*** employees or children of employees.

Financial Aid Of all full-time matriculated undergraduates who enrolled in 2015, 14,289 applied for aid, 10,863 were judged to have need, 2,173 had their need fully met. 786 Federal Work-Study jobs (averaging $2000). 4,918 state and other part-time jobs (averaging $2300). In 2015, 3501 non-need-based awards were made. ***Average percent of need met:*** 66. ***Average financial aid package:*** $16,020. ***Average need-based loan:*** $6725. ***Average need-based gift aid:*** $11,020. ***Average non-need-based aid:*** $4299. ***Average indebtedness upon graduation:*** $24,699.

APPLYING

Standardized Tests *Required:* SAT or ACT (for admission).

Options: electronic application, early admission, deferred entrance.

Application fee: $40.

Required: high school transcript, minimum 3.0 GPA, 22 ACT Composite (1030 Old SAT or 1100 New SAT) with a minimum ACT English subscore of 18 (a New SAT Writing and Language score of 25 or Old SAT Critical Reading score of 450) and a minimum ACT Math subscore of 19 (500 New SAT Math or 460 Old SAT Math).. ***Required for some:*** essay or personal statement.

Application deadlines: 4/15 (freshmen), 4/15 (transfers).

Notification: continuous (freshmen), continuous (transfers).

CONTACT

Mr. Emmett Brown, Assistant Director, Undergraduate Admissions, Louisiana State University and Agricultural & Mechanical College, 1146 Pleasant Hall, Baton Rouge, LA 70803. *Phone:* 225-578-1175. *Fax:* 225-578-4433. *E-mail:* cbrow63@lsu.edu.

Louisiana State University at Alexandria

Alexandria, Louisiana

http://www.lsua.edu/

- **State-supported** 4-year, founded 1960, part of Louisiana State University System
- **Rural** 3114-acre campus
- **Endowment** $15.3 million
- **Coed** 3,277 undergraduate students, 56% full-time, 67% women, 33% men
- **Moderately difficult** entrance level, 31% of applicants were admitted

UNDERGRAD STUDENTS

1,850 full-time, 1,427 part-time. Students come from 27 states and territories; 30 other countries; 4% are from out of state; 17% Black or African American, non-Hispanic/Latino; 2% Hispanic/Latino; 2% Asian, non-Hispanic/Latino; 7% American Indian or Alaska Native, non-Hispanic/Latino; 2% Two or more races, non-Hispanic/Latino; 3% Race/ethnicity unknown; 3% international; 16% transferred in; 9% live on campus.

Freshmen:
Admission: 2,102 applied, 655 admitted, 529 enrolled. ***Average high school GPA:*** 3.16. ***Test scores:*** SAT critical reading scores over 500: 45%; SAT math scores over 500: 61%; ACT scores over 18: 86%; SAT critical reading scores over 600: 15%; SAT math scores over 600: 16%; ACT scores over 24: 19%; SAT critical reading scores over 700: 5%; SAT math scores over 700: 6%.

Retention: 56% of full-time freshmen returned.

FACULTY

Total: 172, 52% full-time, 40% with terminal degrees.

Student/faculty ratio: 18:1.

ACADEMICS

Calendar: semesters. *Degrees:* certificates, associate, and bachelor's.

Special study options: accelerated degree program, adult/continuing education programs, advanced placement credit, cooperative education, distance learning, double majors, honors programs, independent study, internships, part-time degree program, services for LD students, summer session for credit. ***ROTC:*** Army (b).

Computers: 325 computers/terminals are available on campus for general student use. Students can access the following: campus intranet, computer help desk, free student e-mail accounts, online (class) grades, online (class) registration, online (class) schedules. Campuswide network is available. 100% of college-owned or -operated housing units are wired for high-speed Internet access. Wireless service is available via entire campus.

Library: James C. Bolton Library. *Books:* 123,993 (physical), 224,774 (digital/electronic); *Serial titles:* 505 (physical), 501,390 (digital/electronic); *Databases:* 85. Students can reserve study rooms.

STUDENT LIFE

Housing options: on-campus residence required for freshman year; coed, special housing for students with disabilities. Campus housing is university owned. Freshman applicants given priority for college housing.

Activities and organizations: drama/theater group, student-run newspaper, choral group, Student Government Association.

Athletics Member NAIA. ***Intercollegiate sports:*** baseball M, basketball M/W, golf M(c)/W(c), rugby M(c), soccer M/W, softball W, tennis W. ***Intramural sports:*** baseball M, softball W.

Campus security: 24-hour emergency response devices and patrols.

Student services: health clinic, personal/psychological counseling.

COSTS & FINANCIAL AID

Costs (2016–17) ***Tuition:*** state resident $6117 full-time, $204 per credit hour part-time; nonresident $9082 full-time, $303 per credit hour part-time. ***Required fees:*** $4273 full-time, $132 per credit hour part-time, $15 per term part-time. ***Room and board:*** $6810; room only: $3810. Room and board charges vary according to board plan and housing facility. ***Payment plan:*** installment.

Financial Aid Of all full-time matriculated undergraduates who enrolled in 2015, 53 Federal Work-Study jobs (averaging $1226). 76 state and other part-time jobs (averaging $1261).

APPLYING

Standardized Tests *Required:* SAT or ACT (for admission).

Options: electronic application, early admission.

Application fee: $20.

Required: high school transcript. ***Required for some:*** minimum 2.0 GPA.

Application deadlines: rolling (freshmen), rolling (transfers).

Notification: continuous (freshmen), continuous (transfers).

CONTACT

Ms. Shelly Kieffer, Director of Enrollment Management, Louisiana State University at Alexandria, 8100 Highway 71 South, Alexandria, LA 71302-9121. *Phone:* 318-473-6424. *Toll-free phone:* 888-473-6417. *Fax:* 318-473-6418. *E-mail:* admissions@lsua.edu.

Louisiana State University Health Sciences Center

New Orleans, Louisiana

http://www.lsuhsc.edu/

- **State-supported** university, founded 1931, part of Louisiana State University System
- **Urban** 80-acre campus
- **Endowment** $68.5 million
- **Coed** 873 undergraduate students, 75% full-time, 86% women, 14% men

UNDERGRAD STUDENTS
654 full-time, 219 part-time. Students come from 10 states and territories; 4 other countries; 1% are from out of state; 10% Black or African American, non-Hispanic/Latino; 6% Hispanic/Latino; 7% Asian, non-Hispanic/Latino; 0.5% American Indian or Alaska Native, non-Hispanic/Latino; 1% Two or more races, non-Hispanic/Latino; 1% Race/ethnicity unknown; 0.1% international; 10% live on campus.

FACULTY
Total: 893, 81% full-time, 100% with terminal degrees.

ACADEMICS
Calendar: varies by academic program. *Degrees:* associate, bachelor's, master's, doctoral, and post-master's certificates.
Special study options: accelerated degree program, advanced placement credit, cooperative education, distance learning, double majors, independent study, internships, services for LD students, summer session for credit. ***ROTC:*** Army (c), Navy (c), Air Force (c).
Computers: 120 computers/terminals and 1,800 ports are available on campus for general student use. Students can access the following: campus intranet, computer help desk, free student e-mail accounts. Campuswide network is available. 100% of college-owned or -operated housing units are wired for high-speed Internet access. Wireless service is available via classrooms, learning centers, libraries, student centers.
Library: John P. Ische Library plus 1 other.

STUDENT LIFE
Housing options: coed. Campus housing is university owned.
Campus security: 24-hour emergency response devices and patrols, late-night transport/escort service, controlled dormitory access.
Student services: health clinic, personal/psychological counseling.

COSTS
Costs (2017–18) ***Tuition:*** state resident $5612 full-time; nonresident $12,394 full-time. ***Required fees:*** $1311 full-time. ***Room only:*** $5370.

APPLYING
Application fee: $50.
Notification: 8/1 (transfers).

CONTACT
Louisiana State University Health Sciences Center, 433 Bolivar Street, New Orleans, LA 70112-2223. *Phone:* 504-568-4829.

Louisiana State University in Shreveport

Shreveport, Louisiana

http://www.lsus.edu/

- **State-supported** comprehensive, founded 1965, part of Louisiana State University System
- **Urban** 250-acre campus
- **Endowment** $16.7 million
- **Coed**
- **Moderately difficult** entrance level

FACULTY
Student/faculty ratio: 21:1.

ACADEMICS
Calendar: semesters plus 8-week and two 4-week summer terms. *Degrees:* certificates, bachelor's, master's, doctoral, and post-master's certificates.
Library: Noel Memorial Library. *Databases:* 142. Weekly public service hours: 71; students can reserve study rooms.

STUDENT LIFE
Housing options: Campus housing is provided by a third party.
Activities and organizations: drama/theater group, student-run newspaper, national fraternities, national sororities.
Athletics Member NAIA.
Campus security: 24-hour emergency response devices and patrols, student patrols, controlled dormitory access.
Student services: personal/psychological counseling.

COSTS & FINANCIAL AID
Costs (2016–17) ***Tuition:*** state resident $5806 full-time, $236 per credit hour part-time; nonresident $9480 full-time, $784 per credit hour part-time. Full-time tuition and fees vary according to course load. Part-time tuition and fees vary according to course load. ***Required fees:*** $1533 full-time, $62 per credit hour part-time.
Financial Aid Of all full-time matriculated undergraduates who enrolled in 2015, 38 Federal Work-Study jobs (averaging $2804).
Average need-based gift aid: $4174.

APPLYING
Standardized Tests *Required:* SAT or ACT (for admission).
Options: electronic application.
Application fee: $20.
Required: high school transcript, minimum 2.0 GPA.

CONTACT
Louisiana State University in Shreveport, 1 University Place, Shreveport, LA 71115-2399. *Phone:* 318-797-5063. *Toll-free phone:* 800-229-5957.

Louisiana Tech University

Ruston, Louisiana

http://www.latech.edu/

- **State-supported** university, founded 1894, part of University of Louisiana System
- **Small-town** 247-acre campus
- **Coed** 10,682 undergraduate students, 69% full-time, 48% women, 52% men
- **Moderately difficult** entrance level, 64% of applicants were admitted

UNDERGRAD STUDENTS
7,386 full-time, 3,296 part-time. 2% are from out of state; 14% Black or African American, non-Hispanic/Latino; 4% Hispanic/Latino; 1% Asian, non-Hispanic/Latino; 0.1% Native Hawaiian or other Pacific Islander, non-Hispanic/Latino; 0.3% American Indian or Alaska Native, non-Hispanic/Latino; 3% Two or more races, non-Hispanic/Latino; 7% Race/ethnicity unknown; 3% international; 3% transferred in; 15% live on campus.

Freshmen:
Admission: 6,378 applied, 4,072 admitted, 1,962 enrolled. ***Average high school GPA:*** 3.5. ***Test scores:*** ACT scores over 18: 97%; ACT scores over 24: 55%; ACT scores over 30: 12%.
Retention: 81% of full-time freshmen returned.

FACULTY
Total: 437, 81% full-time, 68% with terminal degrees.
Student/faculty ratio: 22:1.

ACADEMICS
Calendar: quarters. *Degrees:* associate, bachelor's, master's, doctoral, post-master's, and postbachelor's certificates.
Special study options: academic remediation for entering students, adult/continuing education programs, advanced placement credit, distance learning, double majors, honors programs, independent study, internships, off-campus study, part-time degree program, study abroad, summer session for credit. ***ROTC:*** Army (c), Air Force (b).
Computers: Campuswide network is available.
Library: Prescott Memorial Library.

STUDENT LIFE
Housing options: on-campus residence required through sophomore year; men-only, women-only, special housing for students with disabilities. Campus housing is university owned and is provided by a third party.

Activities and organizations: drama/theater group, student-run newspaper, radio and television station, choral group, marching band, Student Government Association, Association of Women's Studies, Union Board, national fraternities, national sororities.

Athletics Member NCAA. All Division I except football (Division I-A). ***Intercollegiate sports:*** baseball M(s), basketball M(s)/W(s), cross-country running M(s)/W(s), golf M(s), softball W(s), tennis W(s), track and field M(s)/W(s), volleyball W(s), weight lifting M/W. ***Intramural sports:*** basketball M/W, bowling M/W, cross-country running M/W, football M/W, golf M, racquetball M/W, soccer M, softball M/W, tennis M/W, track and field M/W, volleyball M/W.

Campus security: 24-hour emergency response devices and patrols, student patrols, late-night transport/escort service, controlled dormitory access.

Student services: health clinic, personal/psychological counseling, legal services.

COSTS & FINANCIAL AID

Costs (2016–17) ***Tuition:*** state resident $6401 full-time, $380 per credit hour part-time; nonresident $23,135 full-time, $1077 per credit hour part-time. Full-time tuition and fees vary according to course load, location, and program. Part-time tuition and fees vary according to course load, location, and program. ***Required fees:*** $2716 full-time. ***Room and board:*** $5925. Room and board charges vary according to board plan and housing facility. ***Payment plans:*** installment, deferred payment. ***Waivers:*** children of alumni, senior citizens, and employees or children of employees.

Financial Aid Of all full-time matriculated undergraduates who enrolled in 2015, 5,887 applied for aid, 4,011 were judged to have need, 871 had their need fully met. 297 Federal Work-Study jobs (averaging $1753). 1,172 state and other part-time jobs (averaging $2159). In 2015, 1657 non-need-based awards were made. ***Average percent of need met:*** 81. ***Average financial aid package:*** $11,606. ***Average need-based loan:*** $3506. ***Average need-based gift aid:*** $10,040. ***Average non-need-based aid:*** $4030. ***Average indebtedness upon graduation:*** $23,001.

APPLYING

Standardized Tests *Required:* SAT or ACT (for admission). *Recommended:* ACT (for admission).

Options: early admission.

Application fee: $20.

Required: high school transcript, minimum 2.2 GPA.

CONTACT

Mrs. Jan B. Albritton, Director of Admissions, Louisiana Tech University, PO Box 3168, Ruston, LA 71272. *Phone:* 318-257-3036. *Toll-free phone:* 800-528-3241. *Fax:* 318-257-2499. *E-mail:* bulldog@latech.edu.

Loyola University New Orleans

New Orleans, Louisiana

http://www.loyno.edu/

- **Independent Roman Catholic (Jesuit)** comprehensive, founded 1912
- **Suburban** 22-acre campus with easy access to New Orleans
- **Endowment** $244.0 million
- **Coed** 2,483 undergraduate students, 94% full-time, 61% women, 39% men
- **Moderately difficult** entrance level, 68% of applicants were admitted

UNDERGRAD STUDENTS

2,338 full-time, 145 part-time. Students come from 48 states and territories; 39 other countries; 59% are from out of state; 15% Black or African American, non-Hispanic/Latino; 17% Hispanic/Latino; 3% Asian, non-Hispanic/Latino; 0.4% American Indian or Alaska Native, non-Hispanic/Latino; 5% Two or more races, non-Hispanic/Latino; 5% Race/ethnicity unknown; 3% international; 4% transferred in; 50% live on campus.

Freshmen:

Admission: 5,160 applied, 3,496 admitted, 615 enrolled. ***Average high school GPA:*** 3.58. ***Test scores:*** SAT critical reading scores over 500: 89%; SAT math scores over 500: 72%; ACT scores over 18: 99%; SAT critical reading scores over 600: 42%; SAT math scores over 600: 29%; ACT scores over 24: 69%; SAT critical reading scores over 700: 9%; SAT math scores over 700: 4%; ACT scores over 30: 19%.

Retention: 79% of full-time freshmen returned.

FACULTY

Total: 430, 60% full-time, 78% with terminal degrees.

Student/faculty ratio: 12:1.

ACADEMICS

Calendar: semesters. *Degrees:* bachelor's, master's, doctoral, post-master's, and postbachelor's certificates.

Special study options: accelerated degree program, adult/continuing education programs, advanced placement credit, cooperative education, distance learning, double majors, English as a second language, external degree program, honors programs, independent study, internships, off-campus study, part-time degree program, services for LD students, student-designed majors, study abroad, summer session for credit. ***ROTC:*** Army (c), Navy (c), Air Force (c).

Unusual degree programs: 3-2 engineering.

Computers: 300 computers/terminals and 2,500 ports are available on campus for general student use. Students can access the following: campus intranet, computer help desk, free student e-mail accounts, online (class) grades, online (class) registration, online (class) schedules. Campuswide network is available. 100% of college-owned or -operated housing units are wired for high-speed Internet access. Wireless service is available via entire campus.

Library: Monroe Library plus 1 other. *Books:* 387,652 (physical), 42,637 (digital/electronic); *Serial titles:* 221,718 (physical). Weekly public service hours: 114; students can reserve study rooms.

STUDENT LIFE

Housing options: on-campus residence required through sophomore year; coed, special housing for students with disabilities. Campus housing is university owned. Freshman campus housing is guaranteed.

Activities and organizations: drama/theater group, student-run newspaper, radio station, choral group, University Programming Board, Student Government Association, Black Student Union, Loyola University Community Action Program (LUCAP), Panhellenic Council, national fraternities, national sororities.

Athletics Member NAIA. ***Intercollegiate sports:*** baseball M, basketball M(s)/W(s), cheerleading M(s)/W(s), cross-country running M(s)/W(s), golf M(s)(c)/W(s)(c), swimming and diving M(s)/W(s), table tennis M/W, tennis M(s)/W(s), track and field M(s)/W(s), volleyball W(s). ***Intramural sports:*** basketball M/W, racquetball M/W, soccer M/W, softball M/W, volleyball M/W, weight lifting M/W.

Campus security: 24-hour emergency response devices and patrols, student patrols, late-night transport/escort service, controlled dormitory access, self-defense education, bicycle patrols, closed circuit TV monitors, door alarms, crime prevention programs, card access control.

Student services: health clinic, personal/psychological counseling, women's center.

COSTS & FINANCIAL AID

Costs (2017–18) ***One-time required fee:*** $250. ***Comprehensive fee:*** $52,456 includes full-time tuition ($37,676), mandatory fees ($1566), and room and board ($13,214). Full-time tuition and fees vary according to class time, course load, and degree level. Part-time tuition: $1073 per credit hour. Part-time tuition and fees vary according to class time and degree level. ***Required fees:*** $402 per term part-time. ***College room only:*** $7430. Room and board charges vary according to board plan and housing facility. ***Payment plan:*** installment. ***Waivers:*** senior citizens and employees or children of employees.

Financial Aid Of all full-time matriculated undergraduates who enrolled in 2015, 1,949 applied for aid, 1,731 were judged to have need, 215 had their need fully met. In 2015, 579 non-need-based awards were made. ***Average percent of need met:*** 73. ***Average financial aid package:*** $30,614. ***Average need-based loan:*** $4331. ***Average need-based gift aid:*** $26,814. ***Average non-need-based aid:*** $16,148. ***Average indebtedness upon graduation:*** $25,133.

APPLYING

Standardized Tests *Required:* SAT or ACT (for admission).

Options: electronic application, early admission.

Required: essay or personal statement, high school transcript, 1 letter of recommendation. ***Required for some:*** interview. ***Recommended:*** interview.

Application deadlines: rolling (freshmen), rolling (transfers).

Notification: continuous (freshmen).

CONTACT

Ms. Roberta E. Kaskel, Vice President for Enrollment Management, Loyola University New Orleans, 6363 St. Charles Avenue, Campus Box 18, New Orleans, LA 70118. *Phone:* 504-865-3240. *Toll-free phone:* 800-4-LOYOLA. *Fax:* 504-865-3383. *E-mail:* rekaskel@loyno.edu.

McNeese State University

Lake Charles, Louisiana

http://www.mcneese.edu/

- **State-supported** comprehensive, founded 1939, part of University of Louisiana System
- **Suburban** 766-acre campus
- **Coed** 6,961 undergraduate students, 79% full-time, 60% women, 40% men
- **Moderately difficult** entrance level, 64% of applicants were admitted

UNDERGRAD STUDENTS

5,468 full-time, 1,493 part-time. Students come from 43 states and territories; 65 other countries; 8% are from out of state; 17% Black or African American, non-Hispanic/Latino; 3% Hispanic/Latino; 2% Asian, non-Hispanic/Latino; 0.1% Native Hawaiian or other Pacific Islander, non-Hispanic/Latino; 0.4% American Indian or Alaska Native, non-Hispanic/Latino; 3% Two or more races, non-Hispanic/Latino; 6% international; 5% transferred in.

Freshmen:

Admission: 3,160 applied, 2,013 admitted, 1,244 enrolled. ***Average high school GPA:*** 3.4.

Retention: 66% of full-time freshmen returned.

FACULTY

Total: 440, 56% full-time, 48% with terminal degrees.

Student/faculty ratio: 21:1.

ACADEMICS

Calendar: semesters. *Degrees:* associate, bachelor's, master's, post-master's, and postbachelor's certificates.

Special study options: academic remediation for entering students, accelerated degree program, advanced placement credit, cooperative education, distance learning, double majors, English as a second language, freshman honors college, honors programs, independent study, internships, off-campus study, part-time degree program, services for LD students, study abroad, summer session for credit.

Computers: Students can access the following: computer help desk, free student e-mail accounts, online (class) grades, online (class) registration, online (class) schedules. Campuswide network is available. Wireless service is available via entire campus.

Library: Frazar Memorial Library plus 1 other.

STUDENT LIFE

Housing options: coed. Campus housing is university owned and leased by the school.

Activities and organizations: drama/theater group, student-run newspaper, choral group, marching band, Student Government Association, International Students Association, Resident Student Association, national fraternities, national sororities.

Athletics Member NCAA. All Division I except football (Division I-AA). ***Intercollegiate sports:*** baseball M(s), basketball M(s)/W(s), cross-country running M(s)/W(s), golf M(s)/W(s), soccer W(s), softball W(s), tennis W(s), track and field M(s)/W(s), volleyball W(s). ***Intramural sports:*** badminton M/W, baseball M, basketball M/W, football M/W, golf M/W, racquetball M/W, soccer M/W, softball W, swimming and diving M/W, table tennis M/W, tennis M/W, ultimate Frisbee M/W, volleyball M/W, water polo M/W, weight lifting M/W.

Campus security: 24-hour emergency response devices and patrols, late-night transport/escort service, controlled dormitory access.

Student services: health clinic, personal/psychological counseling, women's center.

COSTS & FINANCIAL AID

Costs (2016–17) ***Tuition:*** $648 per credit hour part-time; state resident $5703 full-time; nonresident $16,778 full-time. Full-time tuition and fees vary according to course load. Part-time tuition and fees vary according to course load. ***Required fees:*** $2335 full-time. ***Room and board:*** $7060; room only: $4000. Room and board charges vary according to board plan and housing facility. ***Payment plan:*** installment. ***Waivers:*** senior citizens and employees or children of employees.

Financial Aid Of all full-time matriculated undergraduates who enrolled in 2014, 4,704 applied for aid, 3,627 were judged to have need, 408 had their need fully met. ***Average percent of need met:*** 61. ***Average financial aid package:*** $9508. ***Average need-based loan:*** $3711. ***Average need-based gift aid:*** $4838.

APPLYING

Standardized Tests *Required:* SAT or ACT (for admission).

Options: electronic application, early admission, deferred entrance.

Application fee: $20.

Required: high school transcript, minimum 2.0 GPA, Louisiana Board of Regents high school Core 4 curriculum, no more than one developmental course, minimum high school GPA of 2.35 and minimum high school core GPA of 2.0 or minimum ACT composite score of 20 (SAT critical reading/math combined score of 940).

Application deadlines: rolling (freshmen), rolling (transfers).

Notification: continuous (freshmen), continuous (transfers).

CONTACT

Ms. Kourtney Istre, Director of Admissions and Recruiting, McNeese State University, Box 91740, Lake Charles, LA 70609. *Phone:* 337-475-5505. *Toll-free phone:* 800-622-3352. *Fax:* 337-475-5978. *E-mail:* kistre@mcneese.edu.

New Orleans Baptist Theological Seminary

New Orleans, Louisiana

http://www.nobts.edu/

CONTACT

Dr. Paul E. Gregoire Jr., Registrar/Director of Admissions, New Orleans Baptist Theological Seminary, 3939 Gentilly Boulevard, New Orleans, LA 70126-4858. *Phone:* 504-282-4455 Ext. 3337. *Toll-free phone:* 800-662-8701.

Nicholls State University

Thibodaux, Louisiana

http://www.nicholls.edu/

CONTACT

Mrs. Becky L. Durocher, Director of Admissions, Nicholls State University, PO Box 2004-NSU, Thibodaux, LA 70310. *Phone:* 985-448-4507. *Toll-free phone:* 877-NICHOLLS. *Fax:* 985-448-4929. *E-mail:* nicholls@nicholls.edu.

Northwestern State University of Louisiana

Natchitoches, Louisiana

http://www.nsula.edu/

- **State-supported** comprehensive, founded 1884, part of University of Louisiana System
- **Small-town** 916-acre campus
- **Endowment** $12.4 million
- **Coed** 8,700 undergraduate students, 60% full-time, 69% women, 31% men
- **Moderately difficult** entrance level, 58% of applicants were admitted

UNDERGRAD STUDENTS

5,224 full-time, 3,476 part-time. Students come from 56 states and territories; 27 other countries; 17% are from out of state; 28% Black or African American, non-Hispanic/Latino; 6% Hispanic/Latino; 0.7% Asian, non-Hispanic/Latino; 0.2% Native Hawaiian or other Pacific Islander, non-Hispanic/Latino; 2% American Indian or Alaska Native, non-Hispanic/Latino; 4% Two or more races, non-Hispanic/Latino; 2% Race/ethnicity unknown; 1% international; 8% transferred in.

Freshmen:
Admission: 4,088 applied, 2,366 admitted, 1,420 enrolled. ***Average high school GPA:*** 3.44. ***Test scores:*** SAT critical reading scores over 500: 38%; SAT math scores over 500: 50%; ACT scores over 18: 89%; SAT critical reading scores over 600: 4%; SAT math scores over 600: 7%; ACT scores over 24: 28%; SAT critical reading scores over 700: 1%; SAT math scores over 700: 1%; ACT scores over 30: 2%.

Retention: 70% of full-time freshmen returned.

FACULTY
Total: 452, 63% full-time, 49% with terminal degrees.

Student/faculty ratio: 19:1.

ACADEMICS
Calendar: semesters. *Degrees:* associate, bachelor's, master's, doctoral, post-master's, and postbachelor's certificates.

Special study options: academic remediation for entering students, adult/continuing education programs, advanced placement credit, cooperative education, distance learning, double majors, freshman honors college, honors programs, independent study, internships, part-time degree program, services for LD students, study abroad, summer session for credit. ***ROTC:*** Army (b), Air Force (c).

Computers: 1,500 computers/terminals and 1,500 ports are available on campus for general student use. Students can access the following: computer help desk, free student e-mail accounts, online (class) grades, online (class) registration, online (class) schedules. Campuswide network is available. 100% of college-owned or -operated housing units are wired for high-speed Internet access. Wireless service is available via classrooms, computer centers, computer labs, dorm rooms, learning centers, libraries, student centers.

Library: Eugene P. Watson Memorial Library plus 1 other. *Books:* 303,592 (physical), 38,166 (digital/electronic).

STUDENT LIFE
Housing options: coed, special housing for students with disabilities. Campus housing is university owned and is provided by a third party. Freshman applicants given priority for college housing.

Activities and organizations: drama/theater group, student-run newspaper, radio and television station, choral group, marching band, Student Activities Board, Student Government Associate, College Panhellenic Council, national fraternities, national sororities.

Athletics Member NCAA. All Division I except football (Division I-AA). ***Intercollegiate sports:*** baseball M(s), basketball M(s)/W(s), cross-country running M(s)/W(s), soccer W(s), softball W(s), tennis W(s), track and field M(s)/W(s), volleyball W(s). ***Intramural sports:*** archery M(c)/W(c), badminton M/W, basketball M/W, bowling M/W, crew M(c)/W(c), fencing M(c)/W(c), football M/W, golf M/W, racquetball M/W, softball M/W, swimming and diving M/W, table tennis M/W, tennis M/W, volleyball M/W.

Campus security: 24-hour emergency response devices and patrols, student patrols, late-night transport/escort service, controlled dormitory access.

Student services: health clinic, personal/psychological counseling.

APPLYING
Standardized Tests *Required:* SAT or ACT (for admission).

Options: electronic application, deferred entrance.

Application fee: $20.

Required: high school transcript, minimum 2.0 GPA, college preparatory curriculum.

Application deadlines: 7/6 (freshmen), 7/6 (transfers).

Notification: continuous (freshmen), continuous (out-of-state freshmen), continuous (transfers).

CONTACT
Ms. Jana Lucky, Director of University Recruiting, Northwestern State University of Louisiana, 175 Sam Sibley Drive, Recruiting Office, Student Services Center, 1st Floor, Natchitoches, LA 71497. *Phone:* 318-357-4503. *Toll-free phone:* 800-327-1903. *Fax:* 318-357-5567. *E-mail:* recruiting@nsula.edu.

Our Lady of the Lake College
Baton Rouge, Louisiana
http://www.ololcollege.edu/

- **Independent Roman Catholic** comprehensive, founded 1990
- **Urban** 5-acre campus with easy access to New Orleans
- **Coed** 1,265 undergraduate students, 43% full-time, 88% women, 12% men
- **Minimally difficult** entrance level, 54% of applicants were admitted

UNDERGRAD STUDENTS
544 full-time, 721 part-time. Students come from 38 states and territories; 12% are from out of state; 18% Black or African American, non-Hispanic/Latino; 10% Hispanic/Latino; 4% Asian, non-Hispanic/Latino; 0.5% Native Hawaiian or other Pacific Islander, non-Hispanic/Latino; 0.6% American Indian or Alaska Native, non-Hispanic/Latino; 8% Race/ethnicity unknown; 8% transferred in.

Freshmen:
Admission: 269 applied, 145 admitted, 84 enrolled.

ACADEMICS
Calendar: semesters. *Degrees:* certificates, associate, bachelor's, master's, doctoral, and postbachelor's certificates.

Special study options: accelerated degree program, advanced placement credit, distance learning, off-campus study, part-time degree program, services for LD students, summer session for credit. ***ROTC:*** Army (c), Air Force (c).

Unusual degree programs: 3-2 biology/physician's assistant.

Computers: 150 computers/terminals are available on campus for general student use. Students can access the following: campus intranet, computer help desk, free student e-mail accounts, online (class) grades, online (class) registration, online (class) schedules. Campuswide network is available. Wireless service is available via entire campus.

Library: Students can reserve study rooms.

STUDENT LIFE
Housing options: college housing not available.

Activities and organizations: Student Government Association, Cultural Arts Association, Christian Fellowship Association, Mathematics/Science Association.

Campus security: 24-hour patrols.

Student services: health clinic, personal/psychological counseling.

COSTS & FINANCIAL AID
Costs (2016–17) ***Tuition:*** $12,033 full-time, $454 per credit hour part-time. ***Required fees:*** $1126 full-time. ***Payment plan:*** installment.

Financial Aid Of all full-time matriculated undergraduates who enrolled in 2008, 684 applied for aid, 546 were judged to have need, 10 had their need fully met. ***Average financial aid package:*** $5175. ***Average need-based loan:*** $3664. ***Average need-based gift aid:*** $2486. ***Average indebtedness upon graduation:*** $12,019.

APPLYING
Standardized Tests *Required:* SAT or ACT (for admission), ACT ASSET (for admission).

Options: electronic application, early admission, deferred entrance.

Application fee: $35.

Required: high school transcript, minimum 2.5 GPA.

Application deadlines: 8/1 (freshmen), rolling (transfers).

Notification: continuous (freshmen).

CONTACT
Mrs. Kim Dudley, Our Lady of the Lake College, LA. *Phone:* 225-768-1718. *E-mail:* admissions@ololcollege.edu.

Saint Joseph Seminary College
Saint Benedict, Louisiana
http://www.sjasc.edu/

CONTACT
Saint Joseph Seminary College, 75376 River Road, St. Benedict, LA 70457. *Phone:* 985-867-2273. *Fax:* 985-327-1085. *E-mail:* registrar@sjasc.edu.

Southeastern Louisiana University

Hammond, Louisiana

http://www.southeastern.edu/

- **State-supported** comprehensive, founded 1925, part of University of Louisiana System
- **Small-town** 375-acre campus with easy access to New Orleans
- **Endowment** $36.6 million
- **Coed** 13,559 undergraduate students, 67% full-time, 62% women, 38% men
- **Moderately difficult** entrance level, 88% of applicants were admitted

UNDERGRAD STUDENTS

9,020 full-time, 4,539 part-time. Students come from 40 states and territories; 51 other countries; 5% are from out of state; 20% Black or African American, non-Hispanic/Latino; 8% Hispanic/Latino; 0.7% Asian, non-Hispanic/Latino; 0.1% Native Hawaiian or other Pacific Islander, non-Hispanic/Latino; 0.2% American Indian or Alaska Native, non-Hispanic/Latino; 6% Two or more races, non-Hispanic/Latino; 0.9% Race/ethnicity unknown; 2% international; 4% transferred in; 21% live on campus.

Freshmen:

Admission: 4,226 applied, 3,722 admitted, 2,618 enrolled. ***Average high school GPA:*** 3.23. ***Test scores:*** ACT scores over 18: 96%; ACT scores over 24: 32%; ACT scores over 30: 2%.

Retention: 63% of full-time freshmen returned.

FACULTY

Total: 573, 82% full-time, 64% with terminal degrees.

Student/faculty ratio: 20:1.

ACADEMICS

Calendar: semesters. *Degrees:* associate, bachelor's, master's, doctoral, post-master's, and postbachelor's certificates.

Special study options: adult/continuing education programs, advanced placement credit, distance learning, double majors, English as a second language, honors programs, independent study, internships, off-campus study, part-time degree program, services for LD students, study abroad, summer session for credit. ***ROTC:*** Army (b).

Computers: 1,031 computers/terminals and 600 ports are available on campus for general student use. Students can access the following: campus intranet, computer help desk, free student e-mail accounts, online (class) grades, online (class) registration, online (class) schedules, campus Webmail, student newspaper, transcripts, bookstore. Campuswide network is available. 100% of college-owned or -operated housing units are wired for high-speed Internet access. Wireless service is available via classrooms, computer centers, computer labs, dorm rooms, learning centers, libraries, student centers.

Library: Linus A. Sims Memorial Library plus 1 other. *Books:* 1.5 million (physical), 233,457 (digital/electronic); *Serial titles:* 1,167 (physical), 362 (digital/electronic). Students can reserve study rooms.

STUDENT LIFE

Housing options: coed, women-only, special housing for students with disabilities. Campus housing is university owned.

Activities and organizations: drama/theater group, student-run newspaper, radio and television station, choral group, marching band, Student Government Association, Gamma Beta Phi, Black Student Union, NAACP, All Greek Organization, national fraternities, national sororities.

Athletics Member NCAA. All Division I except football (Division I-AA). ***Intercollegiate sports:*** baseball M(s), basketball M(s)/W(s), cross-country running M(s)/W(s), golf M(s), soccer W(s), softball W(s), tennis W(s), track and field M(s)/W(s), volleyball W(s). ***Intramural sports:*** baseball M/W, basketball M/W, football M/W, racquetball M/W, rugby M(c), soccer M/W, softball M/W, tennis M/W, volleyball M/W, weight lifting M/W.

Campus security: 24-hour emergency response devices and patrols, student patrols, late-night transport/escort service, controlled dormitory access, video cameras, motorist assistance.

Student services: health clinic, personal/psychological counseling.

COSTS & FINANCIAL AID

Costs (2016–17) ***Tuition:*** state resident $5652 full-time, $324 per credit hour part-time; nonresident $18,130 full-time, $844 per credit hour part-time. Full-time tuition and fees vary according to course load. Part-time tuition and fees vary according to course load. ***Required fees:*** $2121 full-time. ***Room and board:*** $7510; room only: $4800. Room and board charges vary according to board plan and housing facility. ***Payment plan:*** installment. ***Waivers:*** employees or children of employees.

Financial Aid Of all full-time matriculated undergraduates who enrolled in 2015, 7,539 applied for aid, 6,054 were judged to have need, 770 had their need fully met. 151 Federal Work-Study jobs (averaging $2119). 973 state and other part-time jobs (averaging $2268). In 2015, 1260 non-need-based awards were made. ***Average financial aid package:*** $9745. ***Average need-based loan:*** $3701. ***Average need-based gift aid:*** $5178. ***Average non-need-based aid:*** $2443. ***Average indebtedness upon graduation:*** $23,536.

APPLYING

Standardized Tests *Required:* SAT or ACT (for admission).

Options: electronic application, early admission, deferred entrance.

Application fee: $20.

Required: minimum 2.4 GPA, proof of immunization; college transcripts and statement of good standing required for some. ***Required for some:*** high school transcript.

Application deadlines: 8/1 (freshmen), 8/1 (transfers).

CONTACT

Southeastern Louisiana University, 548 Ned McGehee Drive, Hammond, LA 70402. *Phone:* 985-549-5629. *Toll-free phone:* 800-222-7358.

Southern University and Agricultural and Mechanical College

Baton Rouge, Louisiana

http://www.subr.edu/

CONTACT

Ms. Velva Thomas, Director of Admissions, Southern University and Agricultural and Mechanical College, PO Box 9901, Baton Rouge, LA 70813. *Phone:* 225-771-2430. *Fax:* 225-771-2500. *E-mail:* velva_thomas@subr.edu.

Southern University at New Orleans

New Orleans, Louisiana

http://www.suno.edu/

CONTACT

Southern University at New Orleans, 6400 Press Drive, New Orleans, LA 70126-1009. *Phone:* 504-286-5033.

Southwest University

Kenner, Louisiana

http://www.southwest.edu/

CONTACT

Admissions Office, Southwest University, 2200 Veterans Memorial Boulevard, Kenner, LA 70062. *Phone:* 504-468-2900. *Toll-free phone:* 800-433-5923. *Fax:* 504-468-3213. *E-mail:* admissions@southwest.edu.

Tulane University

New Orleans, Louisiana

http://www.tulane.edu/

- **Independent** university, founded 1834
- **Urban** 110-acre campus
- **Endowment** $1.4 billion
- **Coed** 6,821 undergraduate students, 100% full-time, 59% women, 41% men
- **Very difficult** entrance level, 26% of applicants were admitted

UNDERGRAD STUDENTS

6,793 full-time, 28 part-time. Students come from 53 states and territories; 48 other countries; 76% are from out of state; 4% Black or African American, non-Hispanic/Latino; 6% Hispanic/Latino; 4% Asian, non-Hispanic/Latino; 0.1% Native Hawaiian or other Pacific Islander, non-Hispanic/Latino; 0.1% American Indian or Alaska Native, non-

Hispanic/Latino; 4% Two or more races, non-Hispanic/Latino; 2% Race/ethnicity unknown; 3% international; 1% transferred in; 45% live on campus.

Freshmen:
Admission: 32,006 applied, 8,162 admitted, 1,856 enrolled. ***Average high school GPA:*** 3.52. ***Test scores:*** SAT critical reading scores over 500: 97%; SAT writing scores over 500: 97%; ACT scores over 18: 100%; SAT critical reading scores over 600: 87%; SAT writing scores over 600: 91%; ACT scores over 24: 98%; SAT critical reading scores over 700: 31%; SAT writing scores over 700: 36%; ACT scores over 30: 74%.
Retention: 92% of full-time freshmen returned.

FACULTY
Total: 1,176, 60% full-time, 77% with terminal degrees.

Student/faculty ratio: 9:1.

ACADEMICS
Calendar: semesters plus 3 summer sessions. *Degrees:* certificates, bachelor's, master's, doctoral, and postbachelor's certificates.

Special study options: accelerated degree program, adult/continuing education programs, advanced placement credit, cooperative education, distance learning, double majors, English as a second language, freshman honors college, honors programs, independent study, internships, off-campus study, part-time degree program, services for LD students, student-designed majors, study abroad, summer session for credit. ***ROTC:*** Army (b), Navy (b), Air Force (b).

Unusual degree programs: 3-2 business administration; public health tropical medicine, science and engineering.

Computers: 556 computers/terminals are available on campus for general student use. Students can access the following: campus intranet, computer help desk, free student e-mail accounts, online (class) grades, online (class) registration, online (class) schedules. Campuswide network is available. 100% of college-owned or -operated housing units are wired for high-speed Internet access. Wireless service is available via entire campus.

Library: Howard Tilton Memorial Library plus 8 others. *Books:* 4.6 million (physical); *Serial titles:* 107,639 (physical).

STUDENT LIFE
Housing options: on-campus residence required through sophomore year; coed, women-only, special housing for students with disabilities. Campus housing is university owned. Freshman campus housing is guaranteed.

Activities and organizations: drama/theater group, student-run newspaper, radio and television station, choral group, marching band, Community Action Council of Tulane Students (CACTUS), Associated Student Body, Tulane University Campus Programming (TUCP), Association of Club Sports (ACS), National Pan-Hellenic Council, national fraternities, national sororities.

Athletics Member NCAA. All Division I except football (Division I-A). ***Intercollegiate sports:*** baseball M(s), basketball M(s)/W(s), crew M(c)/W(c), cross-country running M(s)/W(s), golf W(s), gymnastics M(c)/W(c), ice hockey M(c)/W(c), lacrosse M(c)/W(c), rugby M(c), sailing M(c)/W(c), soccer M(c)/W(s), swimming and diving M(c)/W(s), tennis M(s)/W(s), track and field M(c)/W(s), volleyball M(c)/W(s), water polo M(c)/W(c). ***Intramural sports:*** baseball M(c), cheerleading M(c)/W(c), crew M(c)/W(c), cross-country running M(c), fencing M(c)/W(c), field hockey M(c)/W(c), gymnastics M(c)/W(c), ice hockey M(c), lacrosse M(c)/W(c), racquetball M(c)/W(c), rock climbing M(c)/W(c), rugby M(c), sailing M(c)/W(c), soccer M(c)/W(c), swimming and diving M(c)/W(c), tennis M(c)/W(c), track and field M(c)/W, ultimate Frisbee M(c)/W(c), volleyball M(c)/W(c), water polo M(c)/W(c).

Campus security: 24-hour emergency response devices and patrols, student patrols, late-night transport/escort service, controlled dormitory access, on and off-campus shuttle service, crime prevention programs, lighted pathways.

Student services: health clinic, personal/psychological counseling, women's center, legal services.

COSTS & FINANCIAL AID
Costs (2016–17) ***Comprehensive fee:*** $64,854 includes full-time tuition ($47,130), mandatory fees ($3880), and room and board ($13,844). ***College room only:*** $7942. Room and board charges vary according to board plan, housing facility, and student level. ***Payment plans:*** tuition prepayment, installment. ***Waivers:*** employees or children of employees.

Financial Aid Of all full-time matriculated undergraduates who enrolled in 2016, 2,942 applied for aid, 2,142 were judged to have need, 1,407 had their need fully met. 1,084 Federal Work-Study jobs (averaging $2892). 114 state and other part-time jobs (averaging $8510). In 2016, 2465 non-need-based awards were made. ***Average percent of need met:*** 96. ***Average financial aid package:*** $45,124. ***Average need-based loan:*** $7753. ***Average need-based gift aid:*** $33,003. ***Average non-need-based aid:*** $25,779. ***Average indebtedness upon graduation:*** $31,642.

APPLYING
Standardized Tests *Required:* SAT or ACT (for admission). *Required for some:* SAT and SAT Subject Tests or ACT (for admission).

Options: electronic application, early action, deferred entrance.

Required: essay or personal statement, high school transcript, 1 letter of recommendation.

Application deadlines: 1/15 (freshmen), 11/15 (early action).

Notification: 4/1 (freshmen), 11/15 (early action).

CONTACT
Satyajit Dattagupta, Vice President for Enrollment Management and Dean of Admissions, Tulane University, Office of Admissions, 210 Gibson Hall, New Orleans, LA 70118. *Phone:* 504-865-5731. *Toll-free phone:* 800-873-9283. *Fax:* 504-862-8715.
E-mail: undergrad.admission@tulane.edu.

University of Holy Cross
New Orleans, Louisiana
http://www.uhcno.edu/

CONTACT
Donna Kennedy, Director of Admissions and Financial Aid, University of Holy Cross, 4123 Woodland Drive, New Orleans, LA 70131-7399. *Phone:* 504-398-2175. *Toll-free phone:* 800-259-7744. *E-mail:* dkennedy@olhcc.edu.

University of Louisiana at Lafayette
Lafayette, Louisiana
http://www.louisiana.edu/

- **State-supported** university, founded 1898, part of University of Louisiana System
- **Urban** 1375-acre campus
- **Endowment** $143.1 million
- **Coed**
- **Moderately difficult** entrance level

FACULTY
Student/faculty ratio: 23:1.

ACADEMICS
Calendar: semesters. *Degrees:* bachelor's, master's, doctoral, post-master's, and postbachelor's certificates.

Library: Edith Garland Dupre Library. *Books:* 1.4 million (physical); *Serial titles:* 20,881 (physical); *Databases:* 149. Students can reserve study rooms.

STUDENT LIFE
Housing options: on-campus residence required for freshman year; coed, men-only, women-only. Campus housing is university owned. Freshman campus housing is guaranteed.

Activities and organizations: drama/theater group, student-run newspaper, radio station, choral group, marching band, Union Program Council, Chi Alpha, Student Government Association, Greek Council, Newman Club, national fraternities, national sororities.

Athletics Member NCAA. All Division I except football (Division I-A).

Campus security: 24-hour emergency response devices and patrols, late-night transport/escort service, controlled dormitory access.

Student services: health clinic, personal/psychological counseling, women's center, legal services.

FINANCIAL AID
Financial Aid Of all full-time matriculated undergraduates who enrolled in 2015, 10,588 applied for aid, 7,498 were judged to have need, 770 had their need fully met. In 2015, 1155 non-need-based awards were made.

Average percent of need met: 54. ***Average financial aid package:*** $9903. ***Average need-based loan:*** $3707. ***Average need-based gift aid:*** $8002. ***Average non-need-based aid:*** $3459.

APPLYING

Standardized Tests *Required:* SAT or ACT (for admission).

Options: electronic application, early admission, deferred entrance.

Application fee: $25.

Required: high school transcript, minimum 2.0 GPA, core requirements.

CONTACT

Mr. Andy Benoit Jr., Assistant Vice President for Enrollment Management and Director of Enrollment Services and Recruitment, University of Louisiana at Lafayette, PO Drawer 41210, Lafayette, LA 70504. *Phone:* 337-482-6473. *Toll-free phone:* 800-752-6553. *Fax:* 337-482-1317. *E-mail:* admissions@louisiana.edu.

University of Louisiana at Monroe

Monroe, Louisiana

http://www.ulm.edu/

- **State-supported** university, founded 1931, part of University of Louisiana System
- **Urban** 238-acre campus
- **Endowment** $50.6 million
- **Coed** 7,276 undergraduate students, 67% full-time, 63% women, 37% men
- **Moderately difficult** entrance level, 94% of applicants were admitted

UNDERGRAD STUDENTS

4,894 full-time, 2,382 part-time. Students come from 37 states and territories; 52 other countries; 7% are from out of state; 25% Black or African American, non-Hispanic/Latino; 2% Hispanic/Latino; 2% Asian, non-Hispanic/Latino; 0.1% Native Hawaiian or other Pacific Islander, non-Hispanic/Latino; 0.3% American Indian or Alaska Native, non-Hispanic/Latino; 2% Two or more races, non-Hispanic/Latino; 2% Race/ethnicity unknown; 2% international; 5% transferred in; 24% live on campus.

Freshmen:

Admission: 3,187 applied, 2,997 admitted, 1,338 enrolled. ***Average high school GPA:*** 3.41. ***Test scores:*** SAT math scores over 500: 76%; SAT writing scores over 500: 50%; ACT scores over 18: 97%; SAT math scores over 600: 50%; SAT writing scores over 600: 13%; ACT scores over 24: 35%; SAT math scores over 700: 13%; SAT writing scores over 700: 1%; ACT scores over 30: 6%.

Retention: 67% of full-time freshmen returned.

FACULTY

Total: 415, 69% full-time.

Student/faculty ratio: 19:1.

ACADEMICS

Calendar: semesters. *Degrees:* associate, bachelor's, master's, doctoral, post-master's, and postbachelor's certificates.

Special study options: academic remediation for entering students, accelerated degree program, adult/continuing education programs, advanced placement credit, cooperative education, distance learning, double majors, English as a second language, external degree program, honors programs, independent study, internships, off-campus study, part-time degree program, services for LD students, study abroad, summer session for credit. ***ROTC:*** Army (c).

Computers: Students can access the following: campus intranet, computer help desk, free student e-mail accounts, online (class) grades, online (class) registration, online (class) schedules. Campuswide network is available. 100% of college-owned or -operated housing units are wired for high-speed Internet access. Wireless service is available via entire campus.

Library: University Library. *Books:* 419,336 (physical), 225,998 (digital/electronic); *Serial titles:* 9,950 (physical); *Databases:* 47. Students can reserve study rooms.

STUDENT LIFE

Housing options: coed, men-only, women-only. Campus housing is university owned and leased by the school. Freshman applicants given priority for college housing.

Activities and organizations: drama/theater group, student-run newspaper, radio and television station, choral group, marching band, Maroon Platoon, Alpha Lambda Delta, Louisiana Pharmacist Alliance, Association for Students in Kinesiology, Pre-Pharmacy Organization/Sound of Today, national fraternities, national sororities.

Athletics Member NCAA. All Division I except football (Division I-A). ***Intercollegiate sports:*** baseball M(s), basketball M(s)/W(s), cross-country running M(s)/W(s), golf M(s)/W(s), sand volleyball W(s), soccer W(s), softball W(s), tennis W(s), track and field M(s)/W(s), volleyball W(s).

Campus security: 24-hour emergency response devices and patrols, student patrols, late-night transport/escort service, controlled dormitory access.

Student services: health clinic, personal/psychological counseling.

COSTS & FINANCIAL AID

Costs (2016–17) ***Tuition:*** state resident $5788 full-time, $364 per credit hour part-time; nonresident $17,888 full-time, $364 per credit hour part-time. Full-time tuition and fees vary according to course load, degree level, and program. Part-time tuition and fees vary according to course load, degree level, and program. ***Required fees:*** $2494 full-time, $305 per credit hour part-time. ***Room and board:*** $7304; room only: $4282. Room and board charges vary according to board plan and housing facility. ***Payment plan:*** installment. ***Waivers:*** senior citizens and employees or children of employees.

Financial Aid Of all full-time matriculated undergraduates who enrolled in 2015, 7,506 applied for aid, 6,891 were judged to have need. 605 Federal Work-Study jobs (averaging $1373). In 2015, 480 non-need-based awards were made. ***Average financial aid package:*** $15,431. ***Average need-based gift aid:*** $5629. ***Average non-need-based aid:*** $11,365.

APPLYING

Standardized Tests *Required:* SAT or ACT (for admission).

Options: electronic application, early admission.

Application fee: $20.

Required: high school transcript, minimum 2.4 GPA.

Application deadlines: rolling (freshmen), rolling (transfers).

Notification: continuous (freshmen), continuous (transfers).

CONTACT

Ms. Mary Peterson, Coordinator of Enrollment Services, University of Louisiana at Monroe, Office of Recruitment and Admissions, University Library, 202, Monroe, LA 71209. *Phone:* 318-342-5397. *Toll-free phone:* 800-372-5127. *Fax:* 318-342-1915. *E-mail:* peterson@ulm.edu.

University of New Orleans

New Orleans, Louisiana

http://www.uno.edu/

- **State-supported** university, founded 1958, part of University of Louisiana System
- **Urban** 345-acre campus
- **Endowment** $20.6 million
- **Coed** 6,442 undergraduate students, 73% full-time, 51% women, 49% men
- **Moderately difficult** entrance level, 60% of applicants were admitted

UNDERGRAD STUDENTS

4,684 full-time, 1,758 part-time. Students come from 45 states and territories; 70 other countries; 5% are from out of state; 16% Black or African American, non-Hispanic/Latino; 12% Hispanic/Latino; 8% Asian, non-Hispanic/Latino; 0.1% Native Hawaiian or other Pacific Islander, non-Hispanic/Latino; 0.4% American Indian or Alaska Native, non-Hispanic/Latino; 4% Two or more races, non-Hispanic/Latino; 1% Race/ethnicity unknown; 4% international; 12% transferred in; 10% live on campus.

Freshmen:

Admission: 3,409 applied, 2,047 admitted, 876 enrolled. ***Average high school GPA:*** 3.15. ***Test scores:*** SAT critical reading scores over 500: 65%; SAT math scores over 500: 69%; ACT scores over 18: 95%; SAT critical reading scores over 600: 27%; SAT math scores over 600: 33%; ACT scores over 24: 31%; SAT critical reading scores over 700: 7%; SAT math scores over 700: 13%; ACT scores over 30: 4%.

Retention: 64% of full-time freshmen returned.

FACULTY
Total: 399, 68% full-time, 65% with terminal degrees.
Student/faculty ratio: 19:1.

ACADEMICS
Calendar: semesters. *Degrees:* bachelor's, master's, doctoral, and post-master's certificates.
Special study options: advanced placement credit, cooperative education, distance learning, double majors, English as a second language, honors programs, independent study, internships, off-campus study, part-time degree program, services for LD students, study abroad, summer session for credit. ***ROTC:*** Army (c), Navy (c), Air Force (c).
Unusual degree programs: 3-2 engineering with Xavier University of Louisiana; Southern University at New Orleans; Loyola University, New Orleans; Dillard University.
Computers: 946 computers/terminals and 1,191 ports are available on campus for general student use. Students can access the following: campus intranet, computer help desk, free student e-mail accounts, online (class) grades, online (class) registration, online (class) schedules, learning management system. Campuswide network is available. 100% of college-owned or -operated housing units are wired for high-speed Internet access. Wireless service is available via entire campus.
Library: Earl K. Long Library. *Books:* 1.0 million (physical), 200,401 (digital/electronic); *Serial titles:* 25,830 (physical), 30,944 (digital/electronic); *Databases:* 129. Weekly public service hours: 85; students can reserve study rooms.

STUDENT LIFE
Housing options: coed, special housing for students with disabilities. Campus housing is university owned and is provided by a third party. Freshman applicants given priority for college housing.
Activities and organizations: drama/theater group, student-run newspaper, choral group, Student Activities Council, Student Government, International Student Organization, Vietnamese American Student Association, Greek Life, national fraternities, national sororities.
Athletics Member NCAA. All Division I. ***Intercollegiate sports:*** baseball M(s), basketball M(s)/W(s), cross-country running M(s)/W(s), golf M(s), tennis M(s)/W(s), track and field M(s)/W(s), volleyball W(s). ***Intramural sports:*** basketball M, football M, racquetball M/W, sailing M(c)/W(c), soccer M, table tennis M(c)/W(c), weight lifting M(c)/W(c), wrestling M(c).
Campus security: 24-hour emergency response devices and patrols, late-night transport/escort service, controlled dormitory access.
Student services: health clinic, personal/psychological counseling, women's center, legal services.

COSTS & FINANCIAL AID
Costs (2016–17) ***Tuition:*** state resident $6090 full-time; nonresident $19,907 full-time. Full-time tuition and fees vary according to course load and program. Part-time tuition and fees vary according to course load and program. ***Required fees:*** $2604 full-time. ***Room and board:*** $9730. Room and board charges vary according to board plan and housing facility. ***Waivers:*** senior citizens and employees or children of employees.
Financial Aid Of all full-time matriculated undergraduates who enrolled in 2016, 3,991 applied for aid, 3,426 were judged to have need, 192 had their need fully met. In 2016, 327 non-need-based awards were made. ***Average percent of need met:*** 58. ***Average financial aid package:*** $10,007. ***Average need-based loan:*** $4221. ***Average need-based gift aid:*** $5427. ***Average non-need-based aid:*** $2374. ***Average indebtedness upon graduation:*** $21,767.

APPLYING
Standardized Tests *Required:* SAT or ACT (for admission).
Options: electronic application, deferred entrance.
Application fee: $20.
Required: high school transcript, core requirements (19 units), minimum ACT math score of 19 (460 SAT), minimum ACT English score of 18 (450 SAT) and minimum ACT composite score of 23 (SAT 1060) or minimum high school core GPA of 2.5.
Application deadlines: rolling (freshmen), rolling (transfers).

CONTACT
Mr. Carlos Gooden, Assistant Director for Recruitment, Enrollment Services, University of New Orleans, Privateer Enrollment Center, University of New Orleans, 105 Earl K. Long Library, New Orleans, LA 70148. *Phone:* 504-280-7464. *Toll-free phone:* 888-514-4275. *Fax:* 504-280-5522. *E-mail:* cagooden@uno.edu.

Xavier University of Louisiana

New Orleans, Louisiana

http://www.xula.edu/

- **Independent Roman Catholic** comprehensive, founded 1925
- **Urban** 23-acre campus
- **Coed** 2,327 undergraduate students, 95% full-time, 73% women, 27% men
- **Moderately difficult** entrance level, 48% of applicants were admitted

UNDERGRAD STUDENTS
2,201 full-time, 126 part-time. 44% are from out of state; 78% Black or African American, non-Hispanic/Latino; 3% Hispanic/Latino; 9% Asian, non-Hispanic/Latino; 0.1% Native Hawaiian or other Pacific Islander, non-Hispanic/Latino; 0.1% American Indian or Alaska Native, non-Hispanic/Latino; 3% Two or more races, non-Hispanic/Latino; 0.7% Race/ethnicity unknown; 2% international; 6% transferred in; 48% live on campus.

Freshmen:
Admission: 6,640 applied, 3,184 admitted, 762 enrolled. ***Average high school GPA:*** 3.4. ***Test scores:*** SAT critical reading scores over 500: 50%; SAT math scores over 500: 45%; SAT writing scores over 500: 35%; ACT scores over 18: 96%; SAT critical reading scores over 600: 13%; SAT math scores over 600: 15%; SAT writing scores over 600: 9%; ACT scores over 24: 51%; SAT critical reading scores over 700: 2%; SAT math scores over 700: 2%; ACT scores over 30: 6%.
Retention: 72% of full-time freshmen returned.

FACULTY
Total: 250, 88% full-time, 94% with terminal degrees.
Student/faculty ratio: 14:1.

ACADEMICS
Calendar: semesters. *Degrees:* bachelor's, master's, and doctoral.
Special study options: academic remediation for entering students, accelerated degree program, adult/continuing education programs, advanced placement credit, cooperative education, distance learning, double majors, freshman honors college, honors programs, independent study, internships, off-campus study, part-time degree program, services for LD students, study abroad, summer session for credit. ***ROTC:*** Army (c), Navy (c), Air Force (c).
Unusual degree programs: 3-2 business administration with Tulane University; engineering with Tulane University, University of Maryland, University of New Orleans, Georgia Institute of Technology, University of Wisconsin–Madison, Morgan State University, Southern University and Agricultural and Mechanical College; biostatistics with Louisiana State University Medical Center.
Computers: Students can access the following: computer help desk, free student e-mail accounts, online (class) grades, online (class) registration, online (class) schedules. Campuswide network is available. 100% of college-owned or -operated housing units are wired for high-speed Internet access. Wireless service is available via entire campus.
Library: Xavier Library.

STUDENT LIFE
Housing options: coed, men-only, women-only, special housing for students with disabilities. Campus housing is university owned. Freshman applicants given priority for college housing.
Activities and organizations: drama/theater group, student-run newspaper, television station, choral group, Mobilization at Xavier, AWARE, NAACP, California Club, Beta Beta Beta (Biology Club), national fraternities, national sororities.
Athletics Member NAIA. ***Intercollegiate sports:*** basketball M(s)/W(s), cross-country running M/W, tennis M(s)/W(s). ***Intramural sports:*** badminton M/W, basketball M/W, football M/W, golf M/W, softball M/W, swimming and diving M/W, table tennis M/W, tennis M/W, track and field M/W, volleyball M/W.
Campus security: 24-hour emergency response devices and patrols, student patrols, bicycle patrols.

Student services: health clinic, personal/psychological counseling.

COSTS & FINANCIAL AID
Costs (2016–17) ***Comprehensive fee:*** $32,198 includes full-time tuition ($20,594), mandatory fees ($2452), and room and board ($9152). Part-time tuition: $858 per credit hour. Part-time tuition and fees vary according to course load. ***Required fees:*** $250 per term part-time. ***Room and board:*** Room and board charges vary according to housing facility. ***Payment plan:*** installment. ***Waivers:*** employees or children of employees.

Financial Aid ***Average indebtedness upon graduation:*** $24,570.

APPLYING
Standardized Tests *Required:* SAT or ACT (for admission).

Options: electronic application, deferred entrance.

Required: high school transcript, minimum 2.0 GPA, 1 letter of recommendation. ***Required for some:*** interview.

Notification: continuous (freshmen).

CONTACT
Mr. Winston Brown, Dean of Admissions, Xavier University of Louisiana, 7325 Palmetto Street, New Orleans, LA 70125. *Phone:* 504-520-7388. *Toll-free phone:* 877-XAVIERU. *Fax:* 504-520-7941. *E-mail:* apply@xula.edu.

MAINE

Bates College
Lewiston, Maine
http://www.bates.edu/

- **Independent** 4-year, founded 1855
- **Small-town** 133-acre campus
- **Endowment** $251.0 million
- **Coed** 1,780 undergraduate students, 100% full-time, 51% women, 49% men
- **Very difficult** entrance level, 23% of applicants were admitted

UNDERGRAD STUDENTS
1,780 full-time. Students come from 43 states and territories; 59 other countries; 91% are from out of state; 6% Black or African American, non-Hispanic/Latino; 9% Hispanic/Latino; 4% Asian, non-Hispanic/Latino; 0.1% American Indian or Alaska Native, non-Hispanic/Latino; 4% Two or more races, non-Hispanic/Latino; 0.2% Race/ethnicity unknown; 7% international; 91% live on campus.

Freshmen:
Admission: 5,356 applied, 1,213 admitted, 498 enrolled. ***Test scores:*** SAT critical reading scores over 500: 94%; SAT math scores over 500: 95%; SAT writing scores over 500: 94%; ACT scores over 18: 99%; SAT critical reading scores over 600: 66%; SAT math scores over 600: 68%; SAT writing scores over 600: 70%; ACT scores over 24: 90%; SAT critical reading scores over 700: 21%; SAT math scores over 700: 26%; SAT writing scores over 700: 23%; ACT scores over 30: 54%.
Retention: 95% of full-time freshmen returned.

FACULTY
Total: 190, 89% full-time, 93% with terminal degrees.

Student/faculty ratio: 10:1.

ACADEMICS
Calendar: 4-4-1. *Degree:* bachelor's.

Special study options: accelerated degree program, advanced placement credit, cooperative education, double majors, honors programs, independent study, internships, off-campus study, services for LD students, student-designed majors, study abroad.

Unusual degree programs: 3-2 engineering with Columbia University, Rensselaer Polytechnic Institute, Case Western Reserve University, Washington University in St. Louis, Dartmouth College.

Computers: 400 computers/terminals and 2,075 ports are available on campus for general student use. Students can access the following: computer help desk, free student e-mail accounts, online (class) grades, online (class) registration, online (class) schedules, course Web pages; course management system; software applications for learning, teaching and research; online course evaluation, transcripts, major declaration, degree audit, financial records. Campuswide network is available. 100% of college-owned or -operated housing units are wired for high-speed Internet access. Wireless service is available via classrooms, computer labs, dorm rooms, learning centers, libraries, student centers.

Library: Ladd Library plus 1 other. *Books:* 602,011 (physical), 725,335 (digital/electronic); *Databases:* 371.

STUDENT LIFE
Housing options: on-campus residence required through senior year; coed, men-only, women-only. Campus housing is university owned. Freshman campus housing is guaranteed.

Activities and organizations: drama/theater group, student-run newspaper, radio station, choral group, Outing Club (outdoor recreation), International Club, Chase Hall Committee (student activities planning), Representative Assembly, WRBC (student radio station).

Athletics Member NCAA. All Division III. ***Intercollegiate sports:*** baseball M, basketball M/W, crew M/W, cross-country running M/W, equestrian sports M(c)/W(c), fencing M(c)/W(c), field hockey W, football M, golf M/W, ice hockey M(c)/W(c), lacrosse M/W, rugby M(c)/W(c), sailing M(c)/W(c), skiing (cross-country) M/W, skiing (downhill) M/W, soccer M/W, softball W, squash M/W, swimming and diving M/W, tennis M/W, track and field M/W, ultimate Frisbee M(c)/W(c), volleyball M(c)/W, water polo M(c)/W(c). ***Intramural sports:*** basketball M/W, bowling M/W, ice hockey M/W, racquetball M/W, soccer M/W, softball M/W, squash M/W, tennis M/W, volleyball M/W.

Campus security: 24-hour emergency response devices and patrols, student patrols, late-night transport/escort service, controlled dormitory access, emergency contact/notification system.

Student services: health clinic, personal/psychological counseling, women's center.

COSTS & FINANCIAL AID
Costs (2016–17) ***Comprehensive fee:*** $64,500 includes full-time tuition ($50,310) and room and board ($14,190). ***Payment plans:*** tuition prepayment, installment. ***Waivers:*** employees or children of employees.

Financial Aid Of all full-time matriculated undergraduates who enrolled in 2016, 849 applied for aid, 774 were judged to have need, 774 had their need fully met. 446 Federal Work-Study jobs (averaging $1750). 309 state and other part-time jobs (averaging $1757). ***Average percent of need met:*** 100. ***Average financial aid package:*** $45,494. ***Average need-based loan:*** $3064. ***Average need-based gift aid:*** $41,478. ***Average indebtedness upon graduation:*** $22,845. ***Financial aid deadline:*** 2/1.

APPLYING
Options: electronic application, early admission, early decision, deferred entrance.

Application fee: $60.

Required: essay or personal statement, high school transcript, 3 letters of recommendation. ***Recommended:*** interview.

Application deadlines: 1/1 (freshmen), 3/1 (transfers).

Early decision deadline: 11/15 (for plan 1), 1/1 (for plan 2).

Notification: 4/1 (freshmen), 4/30 (transfers), 12/20 (early decision plan 1), 2/15 (early decision plan 2).

CONTACT
Leigh Weisenburger, Dean of Admission and Financial Aid, Bates College, 23 Campus Avenue, Lindholm House, Bates College, Lewiston, ME 04240-6028. *Phone:* 855-228-3755. *Toll-free phone:* 855-228-3755. *Fax:* 207-786-6025. *E-mail:* admission@bates.edu.

Bowdoin College
Brunswick, Maine
http://www.bowdoin.edu/

- **Independent** 4-year, founded 1794
- **Small-town** 207-acre campus with easy access to Portland
- **Endowment** $1.3 billion
- **Coed** 1,806 undergraduate students, 100% full-time, 50% women, 50% men
- **Most difficult** entrance level, 15% of applicants were admitted

UNDERGRAD STUDENTS
1,801 full-time, 5 part-time. Students come from 51 states and territories; 32 other countries; 90% are from out of state; 6% Black or African American, non-Hispanic/Latino; 11% Hispanic/Latino; 6% Asian, non-Hispanic/Latino; 0.1% Native Hawaiian or other Pacific Islander, non-Hispanic/Latino; 0.3% American Indian or Alaska Native, non-Hispanic/Latino; 7% Two or more races, non-Hispanic/Latino; 1% Race/ethnicity unknown; 5% international; 0.2% transferred in; 88% live on campus.

Freshmen:
Admission: 6,799 applied, 1,009 admitted, 503 enrolled. ***Test scores:*** SAT critical reading scores over 500: 98%; SAT math scores over 500: 97%; SAT writing scores over 500: 97%; ACT scores over 18: 100%; SAT critical reading scores over 600: 89%; SAT math scores over 600: 87%; SAT writing scores over 600: 90%; ACT scores over 24: 97%; SAT critical reading scores over 700: 59%; SAT math scores over 700: 54%; SAT writing scores over 700: 56%; ACT scores over 30: 80%.

Retention: 94% of full-time freshmen returned.

FACULTY
Total: 234, 83% full-time, 97% with terminal degrees.

Student/faculty ratio: 9:1.

ACADEMICS
Calendar: semesters. *Degree:* bachelor's.

Special study options: accelerated degree program, advanced placement credit, double majors, independent study, off-campus study, services for LD students, student-designed majors, study abroad.

Unusual degree programs: 3-2 engineering with California Institute of Technology, Columbia University, Dartmouth College, University of Maine Orono; law with Columbia University.

Computers: 500 computers/terminals and 600 ports are available on campus for general student use. Students can access the following: campus intranet, computer help desk, free student e-mail accounts, online (class) grades, online (class) registration, online (class) schedules, computer repair; training classes; 24/7 software support; free equipment loaner pool: laptops, video and digital cameras, sound and lighting systems, iPads; movie streaming service; free office software; digital media lab. Campuswide network is available. 100% of college-owned or -operated housing units are wired for high-speed Internet access. Wireless service is available via entire campus.

Library: Hawthorne-Longfellow Library plus 4 others. *Books:* 1.0 million (physical), 591,975 (digital/electronic); *Serial titles:* 7,120 (physical), 74,756 (digital/electronic); *Databases:* 485. Weekly public service hours: 112; students can reserve study rooms.

STUDENT LIFE
Housing options: on-campus residence required through sophomore year; coed, special housing for students with disabilities. Campus housing is university owned. Freshman campus housing is guaranteed.

Activities and organizations: drama/theater group, student-run newspaper, radio station, choral group, Outing Club, Intramural sports, Community Service Volunteer Programs, WBOR 91.1 FM Radio, Bowdoin Orient Student Newspaper.

Athletics Member NCAA. All Division III except men's and women's sailing (Division I), men's and women's skiing (cross-country) (Division I), men's and women's squash (Division I). ***Intercollegiate sports:*** baseball M, basketball M/W, crew M(c)/W(c), cross-country running M/W, equestrian sports M(c)/W(c), fencing M(c)/W(c), field hockey W, football M, golf M/W, ice hockey M/W, lacrosse M/W, rugby M(c)/W, sailing M/W, skiing (cross-country) M/W, soccer M/W, softball W, squash M/W, swimming and diving M/W, tennis M/W, track and field M/W, ultimate Frisbee M(c)/W(c), volleyball M(c)/W, water polo M(c)/W(c). ***Intramural sports:*** badminton M/W, basketball M/W, cheerleading M(c)/W(c), field hockey M/W, ice hockey M/W, lacrosse M(c), skiing (downhill) M(c)/W(c), soccer M/W, softball M/W, tennis M(c)/W(c).

Campus security: 24-hour emergency response devices and patrols, late-night transport/escort service, controlled dormitory access, self-defense education, safe ride service, emergency notification system.

Student services: health clinic, personal/psychological counseling, women's center.

COSTS & FINANCIAL AID
Costs (2016–17) ***Comprehensive fee:*** $63,500 includes full-time tuition ($49,416), mandatory fees ($484), and room and board ($13,600). Part-time tuition: $965 per credit hour. ***College room only:*** $6356. Room and board charges vary according to board plan. ***Payment plans:*** installment, deferred payment. ***Waivers:*** employees or children of employees.

Financial Aid Of all full-time matriculated undergraduates who enrolled in 2016, 887 applied for aid, 806 were judged to have need, 806 had their need fully met. 542 Federal Work-Study jobs (averaging $1899). 257 state and other part-time jobs (averaging $1900). In 2016, 39 non-need-based awards were made. ***Average percent of need met:*** 100. ***Average financial aid package:*** $44,088. ***Average need-based gift aid:*** $42,206. ***Average non-need-based aid:*** $1000. ***Average indebtedness upon graduation:*** $23,120. ***Financial aid deadline:*** 2/15.

APPLYING
Options: electronic application, early admission, early decision, deferred entrance.

Application fee: $65.

Required: essay or personal statement, high school transcript, 3 letters of recommendation. ***Recommended:*** interview.

Application deadlines: 1/1 (freshmen), 3/1 (transfers).

Early decision deadline: 11/15 (for plan 1), 1/1 (for plan 2).

Notification: 3/20 (freshmen), 5/1 (transfers), 12/15 (early decision plan 1), 2/15 (early decision plan 2).

CONTACT
Jacob Daly, Associate Dean of Admissions, Bowdoin College, 5000 College Station, Brunswick, ME 04011-8411. *Phone:* 207-725-3730. *Fax:* 207-725-3101. *E-mail:* admissions@bowdoin.edu.

Colby College
Waterville, Maine
http://www.colby.edu/

- **Independent** 4-year, founded 1813
- **Small-town** 714-acre campus with easy access to Portland, ME
- **Endowment** $711.0 million
- **Coed** 1,857 undergraduate students, 100% full-time, 52% women, 48% men
- **Most difficult** entrance level, 23% of applicants were admitted

UNDERGRAD STUDENTS
1,857 full-time. Students come from 48 states and territories; 74 other countries; 87% are from out of state; 3% Black or African American, non-Hispanic/Latino; 6% Hispanic/Latino; 6% Asian, non-Hispanic/Latino; 0.1% Native Hawaiian or other Pacific Islander, non-Hispanic/Latino; 0.3% American Indian or Alaska Native, non-Hispanic/Latino; 5% Two or more races, non-Hispanic/Latino; 7% Race/ethnicity unknown; 11% international; 0.2% transferred in; 94% live on campus.

Freshmen:
Admission: 7,593 applied, 1,710 admitted, 508 enrolled. ***Test scores:*** SAT critical reading scores over 500: 100%; SAT math scores over 500: 99%; SAT writing scores over 500: 99%; ACT scores over 18: 100%; SAT critical reading scores over 600: 87%; SAT math scores over 600: 92%; SAT writing scores over 600: 88%; ACT scores over 24: 98%; SAT critical reading scores over 700: 34%; SAT math scores over 700: 44%; SAT writing scores over 700: 45%; ACT scores over 30: 62%.

Retention: 93% of full-time freshmen returned.

FACULTY
Total: 211, 91% full-time, 96% with terminal degrees.

Student/faculty ratio: 9:1.

ACADEMICS
Calendar: 4-1-4. *Degree:* bachelor's.

Special study options: advanced placement credit, double majors, honors programs, independent study, internships, off-campus study, services for LD students, student-designed majors, study abroad. ***ROTC:*** Army (c).

Unusual degree programs: 3-2 engineering with Dartmouth College, Columbia University.

Computers: 380 computers/terminals and 7,000 ports are available on campus for general student use. Students can access the following:

campus intranet, computer help desk, free student e-mail accounts, online (class) grades, online (class) registration, online (class) schedules, software license for every student computer, unlimited technology training, video editing lab, high performance natural science research computing, GIS lab. Campuswide network is available. 100% of college-owned or -operated housing units are wired for high-speed Internet access. Wireless service is available via entire campus.

Library: Miller Library plus 3 others. *Books:* 552,347 (physical), 427,718 (digital/electronic); *Serial titles:* 2,800 (physical), 117,717 (digital/electronic); *Databases:* 584. Weekly public service hours: 119; study areas open 24 hours, 5-7 days a week.

STUDENT LIFE

Housing options: on-campus residence required through senior year; coed. Campus housing is university owned. Freshman campus housing is guaranteed.

Activities and organizations: drama/theater group, student-run newspaper, radio station, choral group, Outing Club, volunteer center, WMHB-FM (College Radio Station), Student Government, Powder and Wig (theater).

Athletics Member NCAA. All Division III except men's and women's skiing (cross-country) (Division I), men's and women's skiing (downhill) (Division I). ***Intercollegiate sports:*** baseball M, basketball M/W, crew M/W, cross-country running M/W, fencing M(c)/W(c), field hockey W, football M, golf M/W, ice hockey M/W, lacrosse M/W, rugby M(c)/W(c), sailing M(c)/W(c), skiing (cross-country) M/W, skiing (downhill) M/W, soccer M/W, softball W, squash M/W, swimming and diving M/W, tennis M/W, track and field M/W, ultimate Frisbee M(c)/W(c), volleyball M(c)/W, water polo M(c)/W(c). ***Intramural sports:*** basketball M/W, field hockey M/W, football M/W, soccer M/W, softball M/W, tennis M/W.

Campus security: 24-hour emergency response devices and patrols, student patrols, late-night transport/escort service, controlled dormitory access, campus lighting, student emergency response team, self-defense class, property ID program, party monitors.

Student services: health clinic, personal/psychological counseling, women's center.

COSTS & FINANCIAL AID

Costs (2016–17) ***Comprehensive fee:*** $64,060 includes full-time tuition ($48,820), mandatory fees ($2140), and room and board ($13,100). Part-time tuition: $1880 per credit hour. Part-time tuition and fees vary according to course load. ***Room and board:*** Room and board charges vary according to housing facility. ***Payment plan:*** installment. ***Waivers:*** employees or children of employees.

Financial Aid Of all full-time matriculated undergraduates who enrolled in 2016, 907 applied for aid, 783 were judged to have need, 783 had their need fully met. In 2016, 32 non-need-based awards were made. ***Average percent of need met:*** 100. ***Average financial aid package:*** $45,306. ***Average need-based loan:*** $3689. ***Average need-based gift aid:*** $43,906. ***Average non-need-based aid:*** $11,824. ***Average indebtedness upon graduation:*** $27,953. ***Financial aid deadline:*** 2/1.

APPLYING

Standardized Tests *Required:* SAT, ACT, or 3 SAT Subject Tests (for admission). *Required for some:* SAT (for admission), ACT (for admission), SAT or ACT (for admission), SAT and SAT Subject Tests or ACT (for admission), SAT Subject Tests (for admission).

Options: electronic application, early admission, early decision, deferred entrance.

Required: essay or personal statement, high school transcript, 2 letters of recommendation. ***Recommended:*** interview.

Application deadlines: 1/1 (freshmen), 3/1 (transfers).

Early decision deadline: 11/15 (for plan 1), 1/1 (for plan 2).

Notification: 4/1 (freshmen), 4/1 (out-of-state freshmen), 5/15 (transfers), 12/15 (early decision plan 1), 2/15 (early decision plan 2).

CONTACT

Denise Walden, Associate Director of Admissions, Colby College, 4000 Mayflower Hill, Waterville, ME 04901-8840. *Phone:* 207-859-4800. *Toll-free phone:* 800-723-3032. *Fax:* 207-859-4828. *E-mail:* admissions@colby.edu.

College of the Atlantic

Bar Harbor, Maine

http://www.coa.edu/

- **Independent** comprehensive, founded 1969
- **Small-town** 35-acre campus
- **Endowment** $47.7 million
- **Coed** 338 undergraduate students, 92% full-time, 73% women, 27% men
- **Very difficult** entrance level, 65% of applicants were admitted

UNDERGRAD STUDENTS

312 full-time, 26 part-time. Students come from 36 states and territories; 46 other countries; 75% are from out of state; 0.9% Black or African American, non-Hispanic/Latino; 5% Hispanic/Latino; 3% Asian, non-Hispanic/Latino; 0.3% American Indian or Alaska Native, non-Hispanic/Latino; 1% Two or more races, non-Hispanic/Latino; 3% Race/ethnicity unknown; 21% international; 6% transferred in; 45% live on campus.

Freshmen:

Admission: 485 applied, 314 admitted, 79 enrolled. ***Average high school GPA:*** 3.54. ***Test scores:*** SAT critical reading scores over 500: 94%; SAT math scores over 500: 85%; SAT writing scores over 500: 97%; ACT scores over 18: 100%; SAT critical reading scores over 600: 70%; SAT math scores over 600: 27%; SAT writing scores over 600: 55%; ACT scores over 24: 94%; SAT critical reading scores over 700: 21%; SAT writing scores over 700: 9%; ACT scores over 30: 31%.

Retention: 84% of full-time freshmen returned.

FACULTY

Total: 46, 54% full-time, 74% with terminal degrees.

Student/faculty ratio: 10:1.

ACADEMICS

Calendar: trimesters. *Degrees:* bachelor's and master's.

Special study options: academic remediation for entering students, accelerated degree program, advanced placement credit, cooperative education, independent study, internships, off-campus study, part-time degree program, services for LD students, student-designed majors, study abroad, summer session for credit.

Computers: 45 computers/terminals and 85 ports are available on campus for general student use. Students can access the following: computer help desk, free student e-mail accounts, online (class) grades, online (class) registration, online (class) schedules, online billing, transcript, financial aid, course management system. Campuswide network is available. 100% of college-owned or -operated housing units are wired for high-speed Internet access. Wireless service is available via entire campus.

Library: Thorndike Library. *Books:* 45,700 (physical), 15,500 (digital/electronic); *Serial titles:* 400 (physical), 62,600 (digital/electronic); *Databases:* 76. Weekly public service hours: 101; students can reserve study rooms.

STUDENT LIFE

Housing options: on-campus residence required for freshman year; coed. Campus housing is university owned. Freshman campus housing is guaranteed.

Activities and organizations: drama/theater group, student-run newspaper, choral group, Earth in Brackets [earth], Outing Club, Campus Committee for Sustainability, Spectrum (LGBTQ+), Futbol (soccer) Club.

Athletics ***Intramural sports:*** badminton M/W, basketball M/W, bowling M/W, cross-country running M/W, fencing M/W, ice hockey M/W, rock climbing M/W, sailing M/W, skiing (cross-country) M/W, soccer M/W, softball M/W, table tennis M/W, ultimate Frisbee M/W, volleyball M/W, water polo M/W.

Campus security: 24-hour emergency response devices and patrols, late-night transport/escort service.

Student services: health clinic, personal/psychological counseling.

COSTS & FINANCIAL AID

Costs (2017–18) ***Comprehensive fee:*** $53,289 includes full-time tuition ($42,993), mandatory fees ($549), and room and board ($9747). Full-time tuition and fees vary according to course load and degree level. Part-time tuition: $4777 per credit. Part-time tuition and fees vary according to course load and degree level. ***Required fees:*** $183 per term part-time. ***College room only:*** $6210. Room and board charges vary according to board plan. ***Payment plan:*** installment. ***Waivers:*** employees or children of employees.

Financial Aid Of all full-time matriculated undergraduates who enrolled in 2016, 284 applied for aid, 262 were judged to have need, 114 had their need fully met. 189 Federal Work-Study jobs (averaging $2774). 81 state and other part-time jobs (averaging $2773). In 2016, 38 non-need-based awards were made. ***Average percent of need met:*** 96. ***Average financial aid package:*** $40,946. ***Average need-based loan:*** $4877. ***Average need-based gift aid:*** $35,189. ***Average non-need-based aid:*** $13,444. ***Average indebtedness upon graduation:*** $26,723. ***Financial aid deadline:*** 2/1.

APPLYING

Options: electronic application, early admission, early decision, deferred entrance.

Application fee: $50.

Required: essay or personal statement, high school transcript, 3 letters of recommendation. ***Recommended:*** minimum 3.0 GPA, interview.

Application deadlines: 2/1 (freshmen), 3/15 (transfers).

Early decision deadline: 12/1 (for plan 1), 1/15 (for plan 2).

Notification: 4/1 (freshmen), 4/15 (transfers), 12/15 (early decision plan 1), 1/30 (early decision plan 2).

CONTACT

Ms. Heather Albert-Knopp, Dean of Admission, College of the Atlantic, 105 Eden Street, Bar Harbor, ME 04609-1198. *Phone:* 207-288-5015. *Toll-free phone:* 800-528-0025. *Fax:* 207-288-4126. *E-mail:* inquiry@coa.edu.

Husson University

Bangor, Maine

http://www.husson.edu/

- **Independent** comprehensive, founded 1898
- **Suburban** 208-acre campus
- **Endowment** $15.6 million
- **Coed** 2,834 undergraduate students, 83% full-time, 55% women, 45% men
- **Moderately difficult** entrance level, 80% of applicants were admitted

UNDERGRAD STUDENTS

2,339 full-time, 495 part-time. Students come from 39 states and territories; 26 other countries; 27% are from out of state; 4% Black or African American, non-Hispanic/Latino; 2% Hispanic/Latino; 0.8% Asian, non-Hispanic/Latino; 0.3% Native Hawaiian or other Pacific Islander, non-Hispanic/Latino; 0.5% American Indian or Alaska Native, non-Hispanic/Latino; 2% Two or more races, non-Hispanic/Latino; 2% Race/ethnicity unknown; 3% international; 39% live on campus.

Freshmen:

Admission: 2,460 applied, 1,974 admitted, 626 enrolled. ***Average high school GPA:*** 3.3. ***Test scores:*** SAT critical reading scores over 500: 41%; SAT math scores over 500: 46%; SAT writing scores over 500: 36%; ACT scores over 18: 68%; SAT critical reading scores over 600: 10%; SAT math scores over 600: 8%; SAT writing scores over 600: 5%; ACT scores over 24: 13%; SAT critical reading scores over 700: 1%; SAT math scores over 700: 1%.

Retention: 76% of full-time freshmen returned.

FACULTY

Total: 376, 39% full-time, 41% with terminal degrees.

Student/faculty ratio: 14:1.

ACADEMICS

Calendar: semesters. *Degrees:* certificates, associate, bachelor's, master's, doctoral, post-master's, and postbachelor's certificates.

Special study options: academic remediation for entering students, adult/continuing education programs, advanced placement credit, cooperative education, distance learning, double majors, English as a second language, independent study, internships, off-campus study, part-time degree program, services for LD students, student-designed majors, study abroad, summer session for credit. ***ROTC:*** Army (b), Navy (c).

Unusual degree programs: 3-2 business administration; nursing.

Computers: 131 computers/terminals and 131 ports are available on campus for general student use. Students can access the following: campus intranet, computer help desk, free student e-mail accounts, online (class) grades, online (class) registration, online (class) schedules. Campuswide network is available. 100% of college-owned or -operated housing units are wired for high-speed Internet access. Wireless service is available via entire campus.

Library: Sawyer Library. *Books:* 41,541 (physical), 27,592 (digital/electronic); *Serial titles:* 71 (physical), 39 (digital/electronic); *Databases:* 101. Weekly public service hours: 98; study areas open 24 hours, 5-7 days a week; students can reserve study rooms.

STUDENT LIFE

Housing options: on-campus residence required through sophomore year; coed. Campus housing is university owned. Freshman campus housing is guaranteed.

Activities and organizations: drama/theater group, student-run radio station, choral group, CRU (Campus Crusade), Outdoors Club, International Student Association, Habitat for Humanity, Veteran's Club, national fraternities, national sororities.

Athletics Member NCAA. All Division III. ***Intercollegiate sports:*** baseball M, basketball M/W, cross-country running M/W, field hockey W, football M, golf M/W, lacrosse M/W, soccer M/W, softball W, swimming and diving M/W, tennis W, track and field M/W, volleyball W. ***Intramural sports:*** basketball M/W, cheerleading M(c)/W(c), football M/W, ice hockey M(c), soccer M/W, softball M/W, volleyball M/W, wrestling M(c).

Campus security: 24-hour emergency response devices and patrols, late-night transport/escort service, controlled dormitory access.

Student services: health clinic, personal/psychological counseling.

COSTS & FINANCIAL AID

Costs (2017–18) ***One-time required fee:*** $125. ***Comprehensive fee:*** $27,059 includes full-time tuition ($17,081), mandatory fees ($480), and room and board ($9498). Full-time tuition and fees vary according to class time and location. Part-time tuition: $551 per credit. Part-time tuition and fees vary according to class time, course load, and location. ***Required fees:*** $110 per year part-time. ***College room only:*** $4760. Room and board charges vary according to board plan and housing facility. ***Payment plans:*** tuition prepayment, installment. ***Waivers:*** senior citizens and employees or children of employees.

Financial Aid Of all full-time matriculated undergraduates who enrolled in 2016, 2,208 applied for aid, 1,983 were judged to have need, 391 had their need fully met. 425 Federal Work-Study jobs (averaging $1600). In 2016, 187 non-need-based awards were made. ***Average percent of need met:*** 65. ***Average financial aid package:*** $12,592. ***Average need-based loan:*** $4248. ***Average need-based gift aid:*** $8302. ***Average non-need-based aid:*** $2666. ***Average indebtedness upon graduation:*** $33,412. ***Financial aid deadline:*** 4/15.

APPLYING

Standardized Tests *Required:* SAT or ACT (for admission).

Options: electronic application, deferred entrance.

Application fee: $40.

Required: essay or personal statement, high school transcript, 1 letter of recommendation. ***Recommended:*** minimum 3.0 GPA, interview.

Application deadlines: 8/15 (freshmen), 8/15 (transfers).

Notification: continuous (freshmen), continuous (transfers).

CONTACT

Mr. John Champoli, Director of Undergraduate Admissions, Husson University, 1 College Circle, Bangor, ME 04401-2999. *Phone:* 207-941-7175. *Toll-free phone:* 800-4-HUSSON. *Fax:* 207-941-7935. *E-mail:* champolij@husson.edu.

Kaplan University, Augusta

Augusta, Maine

http://www.kaplanuniversity.edu/

CONTACT

Kaplan University, Augusta, 14 Marketplace Drive, Augusta, ME 04330. *Toll-free phone:* 888-561-4343.

Maine College of Art

Portland, Maine

http://www.meca.edu/

CONTACT

Maine College of Art, 522 Congress Street, Portland, ME 04101. *Phone:* 207-699-5023. *Toll-free phone:* 800-699-1509.

Maine Maritime Academy

Castine, Maine

http://www.mainemaritime.edu/

CONTACT

Maine Maritime Academy, 1 Pleasant Street, Castine, ME 04420. *Phone:* 207-326-2215. *Toll-free phone:* 800-464-6565 (in-state); 800-227-8465 (out-of-state).

Saint Joseph's College of Maine

Standish, Maine

http://www.sjcme.edu/

CONTACT

Kathleen Davis, Vice President for Enrollment Management, Saint Joseph's College of Maine, 278 Whites Bridge Road, Standish, ME 04084-5263. *Phone:* 207-893-7746. *Toll-free phone:* 800-338-7057. *Fax:* 207-893-7862. *E-mail:* admission@sjcme.edu.

Thomas College

Waterville, Maine

http://www.thomas.edu/

- **Independent** comprehensive, founded 1894
- **Small-town** 70-acre campus
- **Endowment** $10.5 million
- **Coed**

FACULTY

Student/faculty ratio: 19:1.

ACADEMICS

Calendar: semesters. *Degrees:* associate, bachelor's, and master's.
Library: Marriner Library. *Books:* 17,925 (physical), 5,600 (digital/electronic); *Serial titles:* 30 (physical), 6 (digital/electronic); *Databases:* 80. Weekly public service hours: 90; study areas open 24 hours, 5-7 days a week; students can reserve study rooms.

STUDENT LIFE

Housing options: coed, men-only, women-only, special housing for students with disabilities. Campus housing is university owned. Freshman campus housing is guaranteed.

Activities and organizations: drama/theater group, Phi Beta Lambda, Music Club, Gaming Club, Otherwise, Education Club, national fraternities.

Athletics Member NCAA, NAIA. All NCAA Division III.

Campus security: 24-hour emergency response devices and patrols, student patrols, controlled dormitory access.

Student services: health clinic, personal/psychological counseling.

COSTS & FINANCIAL AID

Costs (2016–17) ***Comprehensive fee:*** $35,950 includes full-time tuition ($24,468), mandatory fees ($1254), and room and board ($10,228). Part-time tuition: $3059 per course. Part-time tuition and fees vary according to class time. ***College room only:*** $4990. Room and board charges vary according to board plan and housing facility.

Financial Aid Of all full-time matriculated undergraduates who enrolled in 2016, 785 applied for aid, 740 were judged to have need, 74 had their need fully met. 102 Federal Work-Study jobs (averaging $1950). In 2016, 72 non-need-based awards were made. ***Average percent of need met:*** 85. ***Average financial aid package:*** $20,932. ***Average need-based loan:*** $4547. ***Average need-based gift aid:*** $15,927. ***Average non-need-based aid:*** $9240. ***Average indebtedness upon graduation:*** $31,713.

APPLYING

Required: essay or personal statement, high school transcript, 1 letter of recommendation. ***Recommended:*** minimum 2.0 GPA, interview, rank in upper 50% of high school class.

CONTACT

Ms. Angela Stinchfield, Director of Admissions, Thomas College, 180 West River Road, Waterville, ME 04901. *Phone:* 207-859-1101. *Toll-free phone:* 800-339-7001. *Fax:* 207-859-1114. *E-mail:* admiss@thomas.edu.

★ Unity College

Unity, Maine

http://www.unity.edu/

- **Independent** comprehensive, founded 1965
- **Rural** 300-acre campus
- **Endowment** $14.0 million
- **Coed** 709 undergraduate students, 99% full-time, 50% women, 50% men
- **Moderately difficult** entrance level, 91% of applicants were admitted

UNDERGRAD STUDENTS

705 full-time, 4 part-time. Students come from 34 states and territories; 1 other country; 72% are from out of state; 0.7% Black or African American, non-Hispanic/Latino; 2% Hispanic/Latino; 2% Asian, non-Hispanic/Latino; 2% American Indian or Alaska Native, non-Hispanic/Latino; 3% Two or more races, non-Hispanic/Latino; 3% Race/ethnicity unknown; 0.1% international; 8% transferred in; 69% live on campus.

Freshmen:

Admission: 1,011 applied, 920 admitted, 216 enrolled. ***Average high school GPA:*** 3.3. ***Test scores:*** SAT critical reading scores over 500: 58%; SAT math scores over 500: 53%; SAT writing scores over 500: 48%; ACT scores over 18: 86%; SAT critical reading scores over 600: 17%; SAT math scores over 600: 17%; SAT writing scores over 600: 12%; ACT scores over 24: 12%; ACT scores over 30: 9%.

Retention: 72% of full-time freshmen returned.

FACULTY

Total: 65, 66% full-time, 78% with terminal degrees.

Student/faculty ratio: 14:1.

ACADEMICS

Calendar: semesters. *Degrees:* bachelor's and master's.

Special study options: academic remediation for entering students, accelerated degree program, advanced placement credit, cooperative education, double majors, honors programs, independent study, internships, off-campus study, part-time degree program, services for LD students, study abroad, summer session for credit.

Computers: 140 computers/terminals and 150 ports are available on campus for general student use. Students can access the following: campus intranet, computer help desk, free student e-mail accounts, online (class) grades, online (class) registration, online (class) schedules. Campuswide network is available. 100% of college-owned or -operated housing units are wired for high-speed Internet access. Wireless service is available via entire campus.

Library: Dorothy Webb Quimby Library. *Books:* 52,723 (physical), 15,329 (digital/electronic); *Databases:* 72.
Weekly public service hours: 40.

STUDENT LIFE

Housing options: on-campus residence required through sophomore year; coed, men-only, women-only, cooperative, special housing for students with disabilities. Campus housing is university owned. Freshman campus housing is guaranteed.

Activities and organizations: drama/theater group, choral group, Woodsmen Team, Ultimate Frisbee, Outing Club.

Athletics Member USCAA. ***Intercollegiate sports:*** basketball M/W, cross-country running M/W, soccer M/W, volleyball W. ***Intramural sports:*** baseball M, basketball M/W, cross-country running M/W, golf M/W, ice hockey M/W, soccer W, softball M/W, table tennis M/W, tennis M/W, ultimate Frisbee M/W, volleyball M/W, weight lifting M/W.

Campus security: 24-hour emergency response devices and patrols, security cameras in certain areas.

Student services: health clinic, personal/psychological counseling.

A ★ indicates that the school has detailed information with a Premium Profile on Petersons.com.

COSTS & FINANCIAL AID
Costs (2017–18) ***Comprehensive fee:*** $38,750 includes full-time tuition ($27,150), mandatory fees ($1200), and room and board ($10,400). Part-time tuition: $980 per credit. ***Room and board:*** Room and board charges vary according to board plan and housing facility. ***Payment plan:*** installment. ***Waivers:*** employees or children of employees.

Financial Aid Of all full-time matriculated undergraduates who enrolled in 2016, 655 applied for aid, 588 were judged to have need, 69 had their need fully met. 468 Federal Work-Study jobs (averaging $1186). 21 state and other part-time jobs (averaging $1271). In 2016, 105 non-need-based awards were made. ***Average percent of need met:*** 72. ***Average financial aid package:*** $20,247. ***Average need-based loan:*** $6595. ***Average need-based gift aid:*** $13,707. ***Average non-need-based aid:*** $9346.

APPLYING
Standardized Tests *Recommended:* SAT or ACT (for admission).

Options: electronic application, early action, deferred entrance.

Required: essay or personal statement, high school transcript, 2 letters of recommendation. ***Required for some:*** interview. ***Recommended:*** minimum 2.5 GPA, interview.

Application deadlines: 2/15 (freshmen), rolling (out-of-state freshmen), 2/15 (transfers), 12/15 (early action).

Notification: continuous (freshmen), continuous (out-of-state freshmen), continuous (transfers).

CONTACT
Mr. Joe Saltalamachia, Director of Admissions, Unity College, 90 Quaker Hill Road, Unity, ME 04988. *Phone:* 207-509-7205.
E-mail: jsalty@unity.edu.

★ University of Maine
Orono, Maine
http://www.umaine.edu/

- **State-supported** university, founded 1865, part of University of Maine System
- **Small-town** 660-acre campus
- **Coed** 9,323 undergraduate students, 87% full-time, 47% women, 53% men
- **Moderately difficult** entrance level, 90% of applicants were admitted

UNDERGRAD STUDENTS
8,125 full-time, 1,198 part-time. Students come from 53 states and territories; 33 other countries; 30% are from out of state; 2% Black or African American, non-Hispanic/Latino; 3% Hispanic/Latino; 2% Asian, non-Hispanic/Latino; 0.9% American Indian or Alaska Native, non-Hispanic/Latino; 3% Two or more races, non-Hispanic/Latino; 4% Race/ethnicity unknown; 2% international; 4% transferred in; 39% live on campus.

Freshmen:
Admission: 12,952 applied, 11,625 admitted, 2,230 enrolled. ***Average high school GPA:*** 3.23. ***Test scores:*** SAT critical reading scores over 500: 67%; SAT math scores over 500: 68%; SAT writing scores over 500: 60%; ACT scores over 18: 93%; SAT critical reading scores over 600: 22%; SAT math scores over 600: 26%; SAT writing scores over 600: 15%; ACT scores over 24: 49%; SAT critical reading scores over 700: 3%; SAT math scores over 700: 4%; SAT writing scores over 700: 2%; ACT scores over 30: 7%.

Retention: 76% of full-time freshmen returned.

FACULTY
Total: 850, 59% full-time, 59% with terminal degrees.
Student/faculty ratio: 16:1.

ACADEMICS
Calendar: semesters. *Degrees:* bachelor's, master's, doctoral, post-master's, and postbachelor's certificates.

Special study options: accelerated degree program, advanced placement credit, distance learning, double majors, English as a second language, freshman honors college, honors programs, independent study, internships, off-campus study, part-time degree program, services for LD students, student-designed majors, study abroad, summer session for credit. ***ROTC:*** Army (b), Navy (b).

Computers: 600 computers/terminals are available on campus for general student use. Students can access the following: campus intranet, computer help desk, free student e-mail accounts, online (class) grades, online (class) registration, online (class) schedules, online housing and financial aid information. Campuswide network is available. 100% of college-owned or -operated housing units are wired for high-speed Internet access. Wireless service is available via entire campus.

Library: Fogler Library. *Books:* 1.2 million (physical), 850,047 (digital/electronic); *Serial titles:* 420 (physical), 117,230 (digital/electronic); *Databases:* 379. Weekly public service hours: 103; students can reserve study rooms.

STUDENT LIFE

Housing options: on-campus residence required for freshman year; coed, special housing for students with disabilities. Campus housing is university owned. Freshman campus housing is guaranteed.

Activities and organizations: drama/theater group, student-run newspaper, radio station, choral group, marching band, Fraternity and Sorority Life, Alternative Breaks, UMaine Student Government, Campus Activities Board, Wilde Stein, national fraternities, national sororities.

Athletics Member NCAA. All Division I except football (Division I-AA). ***Intercollegiate sports:*** baseball M(s), basketball M(s)/W(s), cheerleading M(c)/W(c), cross-country running M(s)/W(s), field hockey W(s), ice hockey M(s)/W(s), soccer W(s), softball W(s), swimming and diving M/W(s), track and field M(s)/W(s). ***Intramural sports:*** badminton M/W, basketball M/W, crew M(c)/W(c), equestrian sports M(c)/W(c), fencing M(c)/W(c), field hockey M(c)/W(c), football M(c), golf M(c)/W(c), ice hockey M(c)/W(c), lacrosse M(c)/W(c), racquetball M/W, rock climbing M(c)/W(c), rugby M(c)/W(c), skiing (cross-country) M/W, skiing (downhill) M(c)/W(c), soccer M/W, softball M/W, swimming and diving M/W, table tennis M/W, tennis M/W, track and field M/W, ultimate Frisbee M(c)/W(c), volleyball M(c)/W(c), water polo M/W, wrestling M(c).

Campus security: 24-hour emergency response devices and patrols, late-night transport/escort service, controlled dormitory access, area emergency text and email message system.

Student services: health clinic, personal/psychological counseling, women's center, legal services.

COSTS & FINANCIAL AID

Costs (2016–17) ***Tuition:*** state resident $8370 full-time, $279 per credit hour part-time; nonresident $27,240 full-time, $908 per credit hour part-time. Full-time tuition and fees vary according to course load. Part-time tuition and fees vary according to course load. ***Required fees:*** $2258 full-time. ***Room and board:*** $10,164; room only: $5154. Room and board charges vary according to board plan and housing facility. ***Payment plan:*** installment. ***Waivers:*** senior citizens and employees or children of employees.

Financial Aid Of all full-time matriculated undergraduates who enrolled in 2016, 6,789 applied for aid, 5,490 were judged to have need, 945 had their need fully met. 1,038 Federal Work-Study jobs (averaging $2152). In 2016, 1466 non-need-based awards were made. ***Average percent of need met:*** 83. ***Average financial aid package:*** $16,723. ***Average need-based loan:*** $4523. ***Average need-based gift aid:*** $8495. ***Average non-need-based aid:*** $5495. ***Average indebtedness upon graduation:*** $34,923. ***Financial aid deadline:*** 4/15.

APPLYING

Standardized Tests *Required:* SAT or ACT (for admission).

Options: electronic application, early admission, early action, deferred entrance.

Application fee: $40.

Required: essay or personal statement, high school transcript, letters of recommendation. ***Required for some:*** audition for music majors.

Application deadlines: 2/1 (freshmen), rolling (transfers), 12/1 (early action).

Notification: continuous (freshmen), continuous (transfers), 1/15 (early action).

CONTACT

Front Desk, Director of Admissions, University of Maine, 5713 Chadbourne Hall, Orono, ME 04469-5713. *Phone:* 207-581-1561. *Toll-free phone:* 877-486-2364. *Fax:* 207-581-1213. *E-mail:* um-admit@maine.edu.

See previous page for display ad and page 1562 for the College Close-Up.

University of Maine at Augusta

Augusta, Maine

http://www.uma.edu/

- **State-supported** 4-year, founded 1965, part of University of Maine System
- **Small-town** 159-acre campus
- **Endowment** $7.3 million
- **Coed**
- **Noncompetitive** entrance level

FACULTY

Student/faculty ratio: 16:1.

ACADEMICS

Calendar: semesters. *Degrees:* certificates, associate, and bachelor's (also offers some graduate courses and continuing education programs with significant enrollment not reflected in profile).

Library: The Bennett D. Katz Library.

STUDENT LIFE

Housing options: college housing not available.

Activities and organizations: drama/theater group, student-run newspaper, Honors Program Student Association, Arts and Architecture Students of UMA, Student Nurse Association, Student American Dental Hygiene Association, International Student Club.

Athletics Member USCAA.

Campus security: 24-hour emergency response devices, late-night transport/escort service.

Student services: personal/psychological counseling.

COSTS & FINANCIAL AID

Costs (2016–17) ***Tuition:*** state resident $6510 full-time, $217 per credit part-time; nonresident $16,110 full-time, $537 per credit part-time. Full-time tuition and fees vary according to course load, location, program, and reciprocity agreements. Part-time tuition and fees vary according to course load, location, program, and reciprocity agreements. ***Required fees:*** $938 full-time, $31 per credit hour part-time.

Financial Aid Of all full-time matriculated undergraduates who enrolled in 2014, 1,609 applied for aid, 1,526 were judged to have need, 48 had their need fully met. In 2014, 1 non-need-based awards were made. ***Average percent of need met:*** 52. ***Average financial aid package:*** $9172. ***Average need-based loan:*** $7755. ***Average need-based gift aid:*** $5749. ***Average non-need-based aid:*** $1000. ***Average indebtedness upon graduation:*** $30,827.

APPLYING

Options: electronic application, early admission, deferred entrance.

Application fee: $40.

Required for some: high school transcript, interview, music audition. ***Recommended:*** essay or personal statement.

CONTACT

Pamela Proulx-Curry, Interim Dean of Enrollment Services, University of Maine at Augusta, 46 University Drive, Robinson Hall, Augusta, ME 04330. *Phone:* 207-621-3465. *Toll-free phone:* 877-862-1234 Ext. 3185 (in-state); 877-862-1234 (out-of-state). *Fax:* 207-621-3333. *E-mail:* umaadm@maine.edu.

University of Maine at Farmington

Farmington, Maine

http://www.umf.maine.edu/

- **State-supported** comprehensive, founded 1863, part of University of Maine System
- **Small-town** 55-acre campus
- **Endowment** $12.3 million
- **Coed** 1,782 undergraduate students, 93% full-time, 66% women, 34% men

UNDERGRAD STUDENTS

1,662 full-time, 120 part-time. Students come from 26 states and territories; 8 other countries; 16% are from out of state; 2% Black or African American, non-Hispanic/Latino; 2% Hispanic/Latino; 0.8% Asian, non-Hispanic/Latino; 0.1% Native Hawaiian or other Pacific Islander, non-Hispanic/Latino; 0.4% American Indian or Alaska Native, non-Hispanic/Latino; 2% Two or more races, non-Hispanic/Latino; 5% Race/ethnicity unknown; 0.8% international; 6% transferred in; 50% live on campus.

Freshmen:

Admission: 435 enrolled. ***Average high school GPA:*** 3.05. ***Test scores:*** SAT critical reading scores over 500: 58%; SAT math scores over 500: 48%; SAT writing scores over 500: 48%; ACT scores over 18: 85%; SAT critical reading scores over 600: 18%; SAT math scores over 600: 12%; SAT writing scores over 600: 11%; ACT scores over 24: 45%; SAT critical reading scores over 700: 2%; SAT math scores over 700: 2%; SAT writing scores over 700: 1%.

Retention: 74% of full-time freshmen returned.

FACULTY

Total: 188, 62% full-time, 66% with terminal degrees.

Student/faculty ratio: 13:1.

ACADEMICS

Calendar: semesters 3 summer sessions: one of 5 weeks and two of 4 weeks each. *Degrees:* bachelor's, master's, and postbachelor's certificates.

Special study options: academic remediation for entering students, accelerated degree program, advanced placement credit, distance learning, double majors, honors programs, independent study, internships, off-campus study, part-time degree program, services for LD students, student-designed majors, study abroad, summer session for credit.

Unusual degree programs: 3-2 social work with University of Southern Maine.

Computers: 220 computers/terminals and 3,000 ports are available on campus for general student use. Students can access the following: campus intranet, computer help desk, free student e-mail accounts, online (class) grades, online (class) registration, online (class) schedules. Campuswide network is available. 100% of college-owned or -operated housing units are wired for high-speed Internet access. Wireless service is available via entire campus.

Library: Mantor Library plus 1 other. *Books:* 59,750 (physical), 249,038 (digital/electronic); *Serial titles:* 184 (physical), 76,545 (digital/electronic); *Databases:* 135. Weekly public service hours: 88; students can reserve study rooms.

STUDENT LIFE

Housing options: on-campus residence required for freshman year; coed, women-only, cooperative, special housing for students with disabilities. Campus housing is university owned. Freshman campus housing is guaranteed.

Activities and organizations: drama/theater group, student-run newspaper, radio station, choral group, Bust-A-Move Beavers, Commuter Council, Intervarsity Christian Fellowship, Student Senate, Campus Residence Council.

Athletics Member NCAA. All Division III. ***Intercollegiate sports:*** baseball M, basketball M/W, cross-country running M/W, field hockey W, golf M, lacrosse W, skiing (cross-country) M/W, skiing (downhill) M/W, soccer M/W, softball W, tennis M(c)/W(c), track and field M/W. ***Intramural sports:*** basketball M/W, cheerleading M(c)/W(c), equestrian sports M(c)/W(c), football M/W, ice hockey M(c)/W(c), rugby M(c)/W(c), skiing (cross-country) M(c)/W(c), skiing (downhill) M(c)/W(c), soccer M/W, softball M/W, swimming and diving M/W, tennis M/W, ultimate Frisbee M(c)/W(c), volleyball M/W.

Campus security: 24-hour emergency response devices and patrols, student patrols, late-night transport/escort service, controlled dormitory access, safety whistles, security cameras.

Student services: health clinic, personal/psychological counseling.

COSTS & FINANCIAL AID

Costs (2017–18) ***Tuition:*** state resident $8576 full-time, $268 per credit hour part-time; nonresident $18,144 full-time, $567 per credit hour part-time. Full-time tuition and fees vary according to course load and reciprocity agreements. Part-time tuition and fees vary according to course load and reciprocity agreements. ***Required fees:*** $882 full-time. ***Room and board:*** $9334; room only: $5038. Room and board charges vary according to board plan and housing facility. ***Payment plan:*** installment. ***Waivers:*** minority students, children of alumni, senior citizens, and employees or children of employees.

Financial Aid Of all full-time matriculated undergraduates who enrolled in 2014, 1,535 applied for aid, 1,332 were judged to have need, 610 had their need fully met. In 2014, 58 non-need-based awards were made. ***Average percent of need met:*** 83. ***Average financial aid package:*** $13,876. ***Average need-based loan:*** $6910. ***Average need-based gift aid:*** $7079. ***Average non-need-based aid:*** $2789. ***Average indebtedness upon graduation:*** $31,529.

APPLYING

Required: high school transcript, 1 letter of recommendation. ***Required for some:*** essay or personal statement, minimum 2.75 GPA for College of Education transfers, 2.5 for Health and Rehabilitation, 2.0 for all others. ***Recommended:*** essay or personal statement, interview.

CONTACT

Lisa Ellrich, Associate Director of Admissions, University of Maine at Farmington, 246 Main Street, Farmington, ME 04938-1994.
Phone: 207-778-7050. *E-mail:* ellrich@maine.edu.

University of Maine at Fort Kent

Fort Kent, Maine

http://www.umfk.maine.edu/

- **State-supported** 4-year, founded 1878, part of University of Maine System
- **Rural** 52-acre campus
- **Endowment** $3.1 million
- **Coed** 1,559 undergraduate students, 37% full-time, 69% women, 31% men
- **Minimally difficult** entrance level, 89% of applicants were admitted

UNDERGRAD STUDENTS

583 full-time, 976 part-time. Students come from 27 states and territories; 23 other countries; 7% are from out of state; 3% Black or African American, non-Hispanic/Latino; 1% Hispanic/Latino; 0.5% Asian, non-Hispanic/Latino; 0.2% Native Hawaiian or other Pacific Islander, non-Hispanic/Latino; 0.8% American Indian or Alaska Native, non-Hispanic/Latino; 2% Two or more races, non-Hispanic/Latino; 31% Race/ethnicity unknown; 7% international; 13% transferred in; 29% live on campus.

Freshmen:

Admission: 215 applied, 192 admitted, 124 enrolled. ***Average high school GPA:*** 3. ***Test scores:*** SAT critical reading scores over 500: 17%; SAT writing scores over 500: 16%; SAT critical reading scores over 600: 3%; SAT writing scores over 600: 1%; SAT critical reading scores over 700: 1%.

Retention: 70% of full-time freshmen returned.

FACULTY

Total: 87, 38% full-time, 25% with terminal degrees.

Student/faculty ratio: 15:1.

ACADEMICS

Calendar: semesters. *Degrees:* certificates, associate, and bachelor's.

Special study options: academic remediation for entering students, accelerated degree program, advanced placement credit, cooperative education, distance learning, double majors, English as a second language, external degree program, honors programs, independent study, internships, part-time degree program, services for LD students, student-designed majors, summer session for credit.

Computers: 100 computers/terminals are available on campus for general student use. Students can access the following: campus intranet, computer help desk, free student e-mail accounts, online (class) grades, online (class) registration, online (class) schedules. Campuswide network is available. Wireless service is available via entire campus.

Library: Waneta Blake Library. *Books:* 46,000 (physical), 472,000 (digital/electronic); *Serial titles:* 160 (physical); *Databases:* 58,425. Weekly public service hours: 88; students can reserve study rooms.

STUDENT LIFE

Housing options: on-campus residence required for freshman yearCampus housing is university owned. Freshman applicants given priority for college housing.

Activities and organizations: drama/theater group, choral group, Student Nurses Organization, Student Teachers Educational Professional Society, Student Senate, Student Activities Board, Dorm Council, national fraternities, national sororities.

Athletics Member USCAA. ***Intercollegiate sports:*** basketball M/W, soccer M/W, volleyball W. ***Intramural sports:*** basketball M/W, racquetball M/W, soccer M/W, softball M/W, volleyball M/W.

Campus security: controlled dormitory access, night patrols by security personnel 11pm-7am.

Student services: health clinic, personal/psychological counseling.

COSTS & FINANCIAL AID

Costs (2017–18) ***Tuition:*** state resident $6600 full-time, $220 per credit hour part-time; nonresident $10,230 full-time, $330 per credit hour part-time. ***Required fees:*** $975 full-time, $65 per credit hour part-time, $65 per credit hour part-time. ***Room and board:*** $7910; room only: $4250. Room and board charges vary according to board plan and housing facility. ***Payment plan:*** installment. ***Waivers:*** senior citizens and employees or children of employees.

Financial Aid Of all full-time matriculated undergraduates who enrolled in 2016, 501 applied for aid, 428 were judged to have need, 242 had their need fully met. 98 Federal Work-Study jobs (averaging $1583). In 2016, 24 non-need-based awards were made. ***Average percent of need met:*** 82. ***Average financial aid package:*** $11,403. ***Average need-based loan:*** $6479. ***Average need-based gift aid:*** $6036. ***Average non-need-based aid:*** $1516. ***Average indebtedness upon graduation:*** $29,910.

APPLYING

Standardized Tests *Required for some:* SAT (for admission), SAT and SAT Subject Tests or ACT (for admission). *Recommended:* SAT and SAT Subject Tests or ACT (for admission).

Options: electronic application, deferred entrance.

Application fee: $40.

Required: essay or personal statement, high school transcript. ***Required for some:*** interview.

Application deadlines: rolling (freshmen), rolling (out-of-state freshmen), rolling (transfers).

Notification: continuous (freshmen), continuous (out-of-state freshmen), continuous (transfers).

CONTACT

University of Maine at Fort Kent, 23 University Drive, Fort Kent, ME 04743-1292. *Phone:* 207-834-7600. *Toll-free phone:* 888-TRY-UMFK.

University of Maine at Machias

Machias, Maine

http://www.machias.edu/

- **State-supported** 4-year, founded 1909, part of University of Maine System
- **Rural** 42-acre campus
- **Coed**
- **Moderately difficult** entrance level

FACULTY

Student/faculty ratio: 12:1.

ACADEMICS

Calendar: semesters. *Degrees:* certificates, associate, and bachelor's.

Library: Merrill Library.

STUDENT LIFE

Housing options: on-campus residence required through sophomore year; coed, special housing for students with disabilities. Campus housing is university owned.

Athletics Member NAIA.

COSTS & FINANCIAL AID

Costs (2016–17) ***Tuition:*** state resident $6660 full-time, $222 per semester hour part-time; nonresident $18,480 full-time, $616 per semester hour part-time. ***Required fees:*** $820 full-time. ***Room and board:*** $8466; room only: $4140.

Financial Aid Of all full-time matriculated undergraduates who enrolled in 2015, 381 applied for aid, 350 were judged to have need, 221 had their need fully met. In 2015, 5 non-need-based awards were made. ***Average percent of need met:*** 82. ***Average financial aid package:*** $13,982. ***Average need-based loan:*** $6093. ***Average need-based gift aid:*** $8794. ***Average non-need-based aid:*** $1420. ***Average indebtedness upon graduation:*** $23,734.

APPLYING

Standardized Tests *Required:* SAT or ACT (for admission).

Options: electronic application, early admission, early action, deferred entrance.

Application fee: $40.

Required: essay or personal statement, high school transcript, 1 letter of recommendation. ***Required for some:*** minimum 2.0 GPA, interview. ***Recommended:*** minimum 2.5 GPA, 2 letters of recommendation, interview.

CONTACT

Director of Admissions, University of Maine at Machias, 9 O'Brien Avenue, Machias, ME 04654. *Phone:* 207-255-1318. *Toll-free phone:* 888-GOTOUMM (in-state); 888-468-6866 (out-of-state). *Fax:* 207-255-1363. *E-mail:* ummadmissions@maine.edu.

University of Maine at Presque Isle

Presque Isle, Maine

http://www.umpi.edu/

- **State-supported** 4-year, founded 1903, part of University of Maine System
- **Small-town** campus
- **Coed** 1,326 undergraduate students, 55% full-time, 62% women, 38% men
- **Minimally difficult** entrance level, 87% of applicants were admitted

UNDERGRAD STUDENTS

726 full-time, 600 part-time. Students come from 23 states and territories; 7 other countries; 9% are from out of state; 2% Black or African American, non-Hispanic/Latino; 1% Hispanic/Latino; 0.9% Asian, non-Hispanic/Latino; 2% American Indian or Alaska Native, non-Hispanic/Latino; 3% Two or more races, non-Hispanic/Latino; 12% Race/ethnicity unknown; 4% international; 6% transferred in; 29% live on campus.

Freshmen:

Admission: 1,491 applied, 1,293 admitted, 178 enrolled. ***Average high school GPA:*** 3.04. ***Test scores:*** SAT math scores over 500: 28%; SAT writing scores over 500: 24%; ACT scores over 18: 54%; SAT math scores over 600: 6%; SAT writing scores over 600: 4%; ACT scores over 24: 9%; SAT math scores over 700: 1%.

Retention: 62% of full-time freshmen returned.

FACULTY

Total: 102, 41% full-time, 40% with terminal degrees.

Student/faculty ratio: 15:1.

ACADEMICS

Calendar: semesters. *Degrees:* certificates, associate, and bachelor's.

Special study options: academic remediation for entering students, accelerated degree program, adult/continuing education programs, advanced placement credit, cooperative education, distance learning, double majors, honors programs, independent study, internships, off-campus study, part-time degree program, services for LD students, student-designed majors, study abroad, summer session for credit.

Computers: Students can access the following: campus intranet, computer help desk, free student e-mail accounts, online (class) grades, online (class) registration, online (class) schedules. Campuswide network is available. Wireless service is available via entire campus.

Library: Center for Innovative Learning plus 1 other.

STUDENT LIFE

Housing options: coed, special housing for students with disabilities. Campus housing is university owned. Freshman applicants given priority for college housing.

Activities and organizations: student-run newspaper, radio station, national fraternities, national sororities.

Athletics Member NCAA, USCAA. All Division III except men's and women's skiing (cross-country) (Division I). ***Intercollegiate sports:*** baseball M, basketball M/W, cross-country running M/W, golf M, skiing (cross-country) M/W, soccer M/W, softball W, volleyball W. ***Intramural sports:*** basketball M/W, cross-country running M/W, ice hockey M(c)/W(c), skiing (cross-country) M/W, skiing (downhill) M/W, soccer M/W, softball M/W, tennis M, track and field W, volleyball M/W.

Campus security: student patrols, late-night transport/escort service, controlled dormitory access.

Student services: health clinic, personal/psychological counseling.

COSTS & FINANCIAL AID

Costs (2017–18) ***Tuition:*** state resident $6840 full-time, $228 per credit hour part-time; nonresident $10,590 full-time, $353 per credit hour part-time. Full-time tuition and fees vary according to course load. Part-time tuition and fees vary according to course load. ***Required fees:*** $1044 full-time. ***Room and board:*** $8264. Room and board charges vary according to board plan. ***Payment plan:*** installment. ***Waivers:*** senior citizens and employees or children of employees.

Financial Aid Of all full-time matriculated undergraduates who enrolled in 2016, 574 applied for aid, 510 were judged to have need, 298 had their need fully met. In 2016, 26 non-need-based awards were made. ***Average percent of need met:*** 85. ***Average financial aid package:*** $11,665. ***Average need-based loan:*** $4537. ***Average need-based gift aid:*** $6873. ***Average non-need-based aid:*** $2452. ***Average indebtedness upon graduation:*** $22,934.

APPLYING

Options: electronic application, early admission, deferred entrance.

Required: essay or personal statement, high school transcript, 1 letter of recommendation. ***Required for some:*** interview. ***Recommended:*** minimum 2.0 GPA.

Application deadlines: rolling (freshmen), rolling (out-of-state freshmen), rolling (transfers).

CONTACT

Mrs. Erin V. Benson, Director of Admission, University of Maine at Presque Isle, 181 Main Street, Presque Isle, ME 04769. *Phone:* 207-768-9453. *E-mail:* erin.benson@maine.edu.

University of New England

Biddeford, Maine

http://www.une.edu/

- **Independent** comprehensive, founded 1831
- **Small-town** 540-acre campus
- **Endowment** $32.4 million
- **Coed** 4,247 undergraduate students, 56% full-time, 75% women, 25% men
- **Moderately difficult** entrance level, 83% of applicants were admitted

UNDERGRAD STUDENTS

2,374 full-time, 1,873 part-time. Students come from 40 states and territories; 6 other countries; 70% are from out of state; 3% Black or African American, non-Hispanic/Latino; 0.1% Hispanic/Latino; 5% Asian, non-Hispanic/Latino; 0.1% Native Hawaiian or other Pacific Islander, non-Hispanic/Latino; 0.6% American Indian or Alaska Native, non-Hispanic/Latino; 0.8% Two or more races, non-Hispanic/Latino; 25% Race/ethnicity unknown; 0.3% international; 2% transferred in; 65% live on campus.

Freshmen:

Admission: 4,883 applied, 4,056 admitted, 722 enrolled. ***Average high school GPA:*** 3.33. ***Test scores:*** SAT critical reading scores over 500: 60%; SAT math scores over 500: 65%; SAT writing scores over 500: 59%; ACT scores over 18: 95%; SAT critical reading scores over 600: 15%; SAT math scores over 600: 22%; SAT writing scores over 600: 14%; ACT scores over 24: 49%; SAT critical reading scores over 700: 2%; SAT math scores over 700: 2%; SAT writing scores over 700: 1%; ACT scores over 30: 4%.

Retention: 81% of full-time freshmen returned.

FACULTY

Total: 568, 48% full-time, 60% with terminal degrees.

Student/faculty ratio: 13:1.

ACADEMICS

Calendar: semesters. *Degrees:* bachelor's, master's, doctoral, post-master's, and postbachelor's certificates.

Special study options: academic remediation for entering students, accelerated degree program, adult/continuing education programs, advanced placement credit, cooperative education, distance learning, double majors, honors programs, independent study, internships, off-campus study, part-time degree program, services for LD students, study abroad, summer session for credit. ***ROTC:*** Army (c).

Unusual degree programs: 3-2 physician assistant, occupational therapy.

Computers: 91 computers/terminals are available on campus for general student use. Students can access the following: campus intranet, computer help desk, free student e-mail accounts, online (class) grades, online (class) registration, online (class) schedules. Campuswide network is available. 100% of college-owned or -operated housing units are wired for high-speed Internet access. Wireless service is available via entire campus.

Library: Jack S. Ketchum Library plus 1 other. *Books:* 135,000 (physical), 660,000 (digital/electronic); *Serial titles:* 95,000 (digital/electronic); *Databases:* 200. Weekly public service hours: 146; study areas open 24 hours, 5-7 days a week; students can reserve study rooms.

STUDENT LIFE

Housing options: on-campus residence required through junior year; coed, women-only, special housing for students with disabilities. Campus housing is university owned. Freshman campus housing is guaranteed.

Activities and organizations: drama/theater group, student-run newspaper, choral group, Student Government, Outing Club, Campus Programming Board, Earth's Eco, Dance Team.

Athletics Member NCAA. All Division III. ***Intercollegiate sports:*** basketball M/W, cross-country running M/W, field hockey W, football M, golf M, ice hockey M/W, lacrosse M/W, rugby W, soccer M/W, softball W, swimming and diving W, volleyball W. ***Intramural sports:*** baseball M(c), basketball M/W, cheerleading M(c)/W(c), equestrian sports M(c)/W(c), gymnastics M(c)/W(c), ice hockey M(c)/W(c), racquetball M/W, rugby M(c)/W(c), sailing M(c)/W(c), soccer M/W, softball M/W, swimming and diving M(c), table tennis M/W, tennis M(c)/W(c), track and field M(c)/W(c), ultimate Frisbee M/W, volleyball M(c)/W(c), water polo W(c).

Campus security: 24-hour emergency response devices and patrols, late-night transport/escort service, controlled dormitory access.

Student services: health clinic, personal/psychological counseling.

COSTS

Costs (2016–17) ***Comprehensive fee:*** $48,880 includes full-time tuition ($34,380), mandatory fees ($1250), and room and board ($13,250). Full-time tuition and fees vary according to course load and program. Part-time tuition: $1210 per credit hour. Part-time tuition and fees vary according to course load and program. ***Room and board:*** Room and board charges vary according to board plan and housing facility. ***Payment plan:*** installment. ***Waivers:*** children of alumni and employees or children of employees.

APPLYING

Standardized Tests *Required:* SAT or ACT (for admission).

Options: electronic application, early admission, early action, deferred entrance.

Application fee: $40.

Required: essay or personal statement, high school transcript. ***Recommended:*** 1 letter of recommendation.

Application deadlines: 2/15 (freshmen), rolling (transfers).

Notification: continuous (freshmen), continuous (transfers).

CONTACT
Peter Heeley, Senior Associate Director of Undergraduate Admission, University of New England, 11 Hills Beach Road, Biddeford, ME 04005-9526. *Phone:* 800-477-4863. *Toll-free phone:* 800-477-4863. *Fax:* 207-602-5900. *E-mail:* admissions@une.edu.

See this page for display ad and page 1566 for the College Close-Up.

University of Southern Maine

Portland, Maine

http://www.usm.maine.edu/

- **State-supported** comprehensive, founded 1878, part of University of Maine System
- **Urban** 144-acre campus
- **Endowment** $35.9 million
- **Coed** 6,189 undergraduate students, 61% full-time, 58% women, 42% men
- **Moderately difficult** entrance level, 80% of applicants were admitted

UNDERGRAD STUDENTS
3,750 full-time, 2,439 part-time. Students come from 38 states and territories; 16 other countries; 12% are from out of state; 4% Black or African American, non-Hispanic/Latino; 2% Hispanic/Latino; 2% Asian, non-Hispanic/Latino; 0.7% American Indian or Alaska Native, non-Hispanic/Latino; 3% Two or more races, non-Hispanic/Latino; 14% Race/ethnicity unknown; 1% international; 11% transferred in; 23% live on campus.

Freshmen:
Admission: 4,111 applied, 3,299 admitted, 805 enrolled. ***Average high school GPA:*** 3.16. ***Test scores:*** SAT critical reading scores over 500: 50%; SAT math scores over 500: 46%; SAT writing scores over 500: 43%; ACT scores over 18: 84%; SAT critical reading scores over 600: 14%; SAT math scores over 600: 12%; SAT writing scores over 600: 9%; ACT scores over 24: 39%; SAT critical reading scores over 700: 1%; SAT math scores over 700: 1%; SAT writing scores over 700: 1%; ACT scores over 30: 2%.

Retention: 63% of full-time freshmen returned.

FACULTY
Total: 662, 40% full-time, 46% with terminal degrees.

Student/faculty ratio: 14:1.

ACADEMICS
Calendar: semesters. *Degrees:* certificates, bachelor's, master's, doctoral, post-master's, and postbachelor's certificates.

Special study options: academic remediation for entering students, accelerated degree program, adult/continuing education programs, advanced placement credit, cooperative education, distance learning, double majors, English as a second language, honors programs, independent study, internships, off-campus study, part-time degree program, services for LD students, student-designed majors, study abroad, summer session for credit. ***ROTC:*** Army (c), Air Force (c).

Unusual degree programs: 3-2 business administration.

Computers: 219 computers/terminals are available on campus for general student use. Students can access the following: campus intranet, computer help desk, free student e-mail accounts, online (class) grades, online (class) registration, online (class) schedules. Campuswide network is available. 100% of college-owned or -operated housing units are wired for high-speed Internet access. Wireless service is available via entire campus.

Library: Glickman Library plus 3 others.

STUDENT LIFE
Housing options: coed, special housing for students with disabilities. Campus housing is university owned. Freshman applicants given priority for college housing.

Activities and organizations: drama/theater group, student-run newspaper, radio station, choral group, Outing and Ski Clubs, Gorham

Events Board, Commuter Student Group, Circle K, national fraternities, national sororities.

Athletics Member NCAA. All Division III. ***Intercollegiate sports:*** baseball M, basketball M/W, cross-country running M/W, fencing M/W(c), field hockey W, golf M/W, ice hockey M/W, lacrosse M/W, sailing M/W, soccer M/W, softball W, tennis M/W, track and field M/W, volleyball W, wrestling M. ***Intramural sports:*** baseball M, basketball M/W, cheerleading M(c)/W(c), football M/W, ice hockey M/W, lacrosse M(c)/W(c), racquetball M/W, rugby M(c)/W(c), skiing (downhill) M(c)/W(c), soccer M/W, softball M/W, squash M/W, table tennis M/W, tennis M/W, ultimate Frisbee M/W, volleyball M/W, weight lifting M/W.

Campus security: 24-hour emergency response devices and patrols, late-night transport/escort service, controlled dormitory access, security lighting, preventive programs within residence halls.

Student services: health clinic, personal/psychological counseling, women's center, legal services.

COSTS & FINANCIAL AID

Costs (2016–17) ***Tuition:*** state resident $7590 full-time, $253 per credit hour part-time; nonresident $19,950 full-time, $380 per credit hour part-time. Full-time tuition and fees vary according to course load, degree level, and reciprocity agreements. Part-time tuition and fees vary according to course load, degree level, and reciprocity agreements. ***Required fees:*** $1330 full-time, $1330 per year part-time. ***Room and board:*** $9200; room only: $5000. Room and board charges vary according to board plan and housing facility. ***Payment plan:*** installment. ***Waivers:*** employees or children of employees.

Financial Aid Of all full-time matriculated undergraduates who enrolled in 2015, 3,267 applied for aid, 2,788 were judged to have need, 1,646 had their need fully met. In 2015, 152 non-need-based awards were made. ***Average percent of need met:*** 79. ***Average financial aid package:*** $13,894. ***Average need-based loan:*** $6939. ***Average need-based gift aid:*** $7911. ***Average non-need-based aid:*** $3741.

APPLYING

Standardized Tests *Required:* SAT (for admission).

Options: electronic application, early admission, deferred entrance.

Application fee: $40.

Required: essay or personal statement, high school transcript. ***Required for some:*** interview, audition for music majors. ***Recommended:*** 1 letter of recommendation, interview.

Notification: continuous (freshmen), continuous (out-of-state freshmen), continuous (transfers).

CONTACT

Admissions, University of Southern Maine, Portland, ME 04104-9300.
Phone: 207-780-5670. *Toll-free phone:* 800-800-4USM Ext. 5670.
E-mail: admitusm@maine.edu.

MARYLAND

Bais HaMedrash and Mesivta of Baltimore

Baltimore, Maryland

CONTACT

Bais HaMedrash and Mesivta of Baltimore, 6823 Old Pimlico Road, Baltimore, MD 21209.

Bowie State University

Bowie, Maryland

http://www.bowiestate.edu/

- **State-supported** comprehensive, founded 1865, part of University System of Maryland
- **Small-town** 295-acre campus with easy access to Baltimore and Washington, DC
- **Coed** 4,711 undergraduate students, 84% full-time, 62% women, 38% men
- **Minimally difficult** entrance level, 41% of applicants were admitted

UNDERGRAD STUDENTS

3,939 full-time, 772 part-time. Students come from 31 states and territories; 9% are from out of state; 86% Black or African American, non-Hispanic/Latino; 3% Hispanic/Latino; 1% Asian, non-Hispanic/Latino; 0.1% Native Hawaiian or other Pacific Islander, non-Hispanic/Latino; 0.1% American Indian or Alaska Native, non-Hispanic/Latino; 4% Two or more races, non-Hispanic/Latino; 2% Race/ethnicity unknown; 1% international; 35% live on campus.

Freshmen:

Admission: 6,720 applied, 2,775 admitted, 967 enrolled. ***Average high school GPA:*** 2.53. ***Test scores:*** SAT critical reading scores over 500: 23%; SAT math scores over 500: 18%; SAT critical reading scores over 600: 2%; SAT math scores over 600: 1%.

Retention: 70% of full-time freshmen returned.

FACULTY

Total: 414, 52% full-time, 88% with terminal degrees.

Student/faculty ratio: 16:1.

ACADEMICS

Calendar: semesters. *Degrees:* certificates, bachelor's, master's, doctoral, and postbachelor's certificates.

Special study options: academic remediation for entering students, adult/continuing education programs, advanced placement credit, cooperative education, distance learning, double majors, external degree program, honors programs, independent study, internships, off-campus study, part-time degree program, services for LD students, study abroad, summer session for credit. ***ROTC:*** Army (b).

Unusual degree programs: 3-2 engineering with George Washington University, University of Maryland College Park, Howard University.

Computers: 3,950 computers/terminals are available on campus for general student use. Students can access the following: computer help desk, free student e-mail accounts, online (class) grades, online (class) registration. Campuswide network is available. Wireless service is available via entire campus.

Library: Thurgood Marshall Library. Students can reserve study rooms.

STUDENT LIFE

Housing options: coed, men-only, women-only. Campus housing is university owned and is provided by a third party. Freshman applicants given priority for college housing.

Activities and organizations: drama/theater group, student-run newspaper, radio and television station, choral group, marching band, Honda Campus All-Star Challenge, national fraternities, national sororities.

Athletics Member NCAA. All Division II. ***Intercollegiate sports:*** basketball M(s)/W(s), bowling W, cross-country running M(s)/W(s), football M(s), softball W(s), tennis W(s), track and field M(s)/W(s), volleyball W(s).

Campus security: 24-hour emergency response devices and patrols, student patrols, late-night transport/escort service, controlled dormitory access.

Student services: health clinic, personal/psychological counseling.

COSTS & FINANCIAL AID

Costs (2016–17) ***Tuition:*** state resident $5321 full-time, $234 per credit hour part-time; nonresident $15,857 full-time, $667 per credit hour part-time. Part-time tuition and fees vary according to course load. ***Required fees:*** $2558 full-time, $115 per credit hour part-time. ***Room and board:*** $10,970; room only: $6970. Room and board charges vary according to board plan and housing facility. ***Payment plans:*** installment, deferred payment. ***Waivers:*** senior citizens and employees or children of employees.

Financial Aid Of all full-time matriculated undergraduates who enrolled in 2014, 2,750 applied for aid, 2,739 were judged to have need, 887 had their need fully met. 80 Federal Work-Study jobs (averaging $2657). In 2014, 69 non-need-based awards were made. ***Average percent of need met:*** 45. ***Average financial aid package:*** $8911. ***Average need-based loan:*** $4008. ***Average need-based gift aid:*** $7003. ***Average indebtedness upon graduation:*** $29,737.

APPLYING

Standardized Tests *Required:* SAT or ACT (for admission).

Options: electronic application.

Application fee: $40.
Required: high school transcript, minimum 2.5 GPA.
Application deadlines: 4/1 (freshmen), 4/1 (transfers).
Notification: continuous (freshmen), continuous (transfers).

CONTACT
Mrs. Shirley Holt, Assistant Director of Admissions, Bowie State University, Administration Building, 1st Floor. *Phone:* 301-860-3415. *Toll-free phone:* 877-772-6943. *Fax:* 301-860-3438. *E-mail:* sholt@bowiestate.edu.

Capitol Technology University
Laurel, Maryland
http://www.captechu.edu/

CONTACT
Capitol Technology University, 11301 Springfield Road, Laurel, MD 20708-9759. *Phone:* 301-953-3200 Ext. 3033. *Toll-free phone:* 800-950-1992.

Cecil College
North East, Maryland
http://www.cecil.edu/

- **County-supported** primarily 2-year, founded 1968
- **Small-town** 159-acre campus with easy access to Baltimore
- **Coed** 2,612 undergraduate students, 36% full-time, 63% women, 37% men
- **Noncompetitive** entrance level, 100% of applicants were admitted

UNDERGRAD STUDENTS
947 full-time, 1,665 part-time. Students come from 10 states and territories; 21 other countries; 11% are from out of state; 11% Black or African American, non-Hispanic/Latino; 6% Hispanic/Latino; 1% Asian, non-Hispanic/Latino; 0.1% Native Hawaiian or other Pacific Islander, non-Hispanic/Latino; 0.2% American Indian or Alaska Native, non-Hispanic/Latino; 4% Two or more races, non-Hispanic/Latino; 0.5% Race/ethnicity unknown; 0.7% international; 4% transferred in.

Freshmen:
Admission: 247 applied, 247 admitted, 448 enrolled.
Retention: 60% of full-time freshmen returned.

FACULTY
Total: 294, 17% full-time, 5% with terminal degrees.
Student/faculty ratio: 11:1.

ACADEMICS
Calendar: semesters. *Degrees:* certificates, associate, and bachelor's.
Special study options: academic remediation for entering students, accelerated degree program, adult/continuing education programs, advanced placement credit, cooperative education, distance learning, double majors, English as a second language, independent study, internships, off-campus study, part-time degree program, services for LD students, summer session for credit.
Computers: 100 computers/terminals are available on campus for general student use. Students can access the following: computer help desk, free student e-mail accounts, online (class) grades, online (class) registration, online (class) schedules. Campuswide network is available. Wireless service is available via entire campus.
Library: Cecil County Veterans Memorial Library.

STUDENT LIFE
Activities and organizations: drama/theater group, Student Government, Non-Traditional Student Organization, Student Nurses Association, national fraternities.
Athletics Member NJCAA. ***Intercollegiate sports:*** baseball M(s), basketball M(s)/W(s), cheerleading W, lacrosse M(c), soccer M(s)/W(s), softball W(s), tennis W(s), volleyball W(s).
Campus security: 24-hour emergency response devices, late-night transport/escort service, armed patrols from 6:30 am until 7:00 pm.
Student services: personal/psychological counseling, women's center.

COSTS
Costs (2017–18) ***Tuition:*** area resident $3210 full-time, $107 per credit hour part-time; state resident $5910 full-time, $197 per credit hour part-time; nonresident $7260 full-time, $242 per credit hour part-time. ***Required fees:*** $420 full-time. ***Payment plan:*** deferred payment. ***Waivers:*** senior citizens and employees or children of employees.

APPLYING
Options: electronic application, early admission, deferred entrance.
Required: high school transcript.
Application deadlines: rolling (freshmen), rolling (transfers).
Notification: continuous (freshmen), continuous (transfers).

CONTACT
Dr. Diane Lane, Cecil College, One Seahawk Drive, North East, MD 21901-1999. *Phone:* 410-287-1002. *Fax:* 410-287-1001. *E-mail:* dlane@cecil.edu.

Coppin State University
Baltimore, Maryland
http://www.coppin.edu/

CONTACT
Ms. Michelle Gross, Director of Admissions, Coppin State University, 2500 West North Avenue, Baltimore, MD 21216-3698. *Phone:* 410-951-3600. *Toll-free phone:* 800-635-3674. *Fax:* 410-523-7351. *E-mail:* mgross@coppin.edu.

Faith Theological Seminary
Baltimore, Maryland
http://www.faiththeological.org/

CONTACT
Faith Theological Seminary, 529 Walker Avenue, Baltimore, MD 21212. *Phone:* 410-323-6211.

Frostburg State University
Frostburg, Maryland
http://www.frostburg.edu/

- **State-supported** comprehensive, founded 1898, part of University System of Maryland
- **Small-town** 260-acre campus with easy access to Baltimore and Washington, DC
- **Endowment** $22.5 million
- **Coed** 4,884 undergraduate students, 85% full-time, 52% women, 48% men
- **Moderately difficult** entrance level, 63% of applicants were admitted

UNDERGRAD STUDENTS
4,141 full-time, 743 part-time. Students come from 31 states and territories; 41 other countries; 6% are from out of state; 31% Black or African American, non-Hispanic/Latino; 6% Hispanic/Latino; 2% Asian, non-Hispanic/Latino; 0.2% American Indian or Alaska Native, non-Hispanic/Latino; 5% Two or more races, non-Hispanic/Latino; 0.8% Race/ethnicity unknown; 2% international; 11% transferred in; 28% live on campus.

Freshmen:
Admission: 4,228 applied, 2,652 admitted, 830 enrolled. ***Average high school GPA:*** 3.22. ***Test scores:*** ACT scores over 18: 77%; ACT scores over 24: 28%; ACT scores over 30: 3%.
Retention: 77% of full-time freshmen returned.

FACULTY
Total: 387, 67% full-time, 64% with terminal degrees.
Student/faculty ratio: 16:1.

ACADEMICS
Calendar: semesters. *Degrees:* bachelor's, master's, and doctoral.
Special study options: adult/continuing education programs, advanced placement credit, cooperative education, distance learning, double majors, freshman honors college, honors programs, independent study,

internships, off-campus study, part-time degree program, services for LD students, study abroad, summer session for credit.

Unusual degree programs: 3-2 business administration; engineering with University of Maryland, College Park.

Computers: 577 computers/terminals are available on campus for general student use. Students can access the following: campus intranet, computer help desk, free student e-mail accounts, online (class) grades, online (class) registration, online (class) schedules. Campuswide network is available. 100% of college-owned or -operated housing units are wired for high-speed Internet access. Wireless service is available via entire campus.

Library: Lewis J. Ort Library.

STUDENT LIFE

Housing options: coed, men-only, women-only. Campus housing is university owned and is provided by a third party.

Activities and organizations: drama/theater group, student-run newspaper, radio and television station, choral group, marching band, Student Government Association, Black Student Association, Campus Activities Board, Residence Hall Association, University Programming Council, national fraternities, national sororities.

Athletics Member NCAA. All Division III. ***Intercollegiate sports:*** baseball M, basketball M/W, cross-country running M/W, field hockey W, football M, lacrosse M/W, soccer M/W, softball W, swimming and diving M/W, tennis M/W, track and field M/W, volleyball W. ***Intramural sports:*** basketball M/W, football M/W, lacrosse M(c), racquetball M/W, rugby M(c), soccer M/W, softball M/W, tennis M/W, volleyball M(c)/W, wrestling M.

Campus security: 24-hour emergency response devices and patrols, student patrols, late-night transport/escort service, controlled dormitory access, bicycle patrols.

Student services: health clinic, personal/psychological counseling, women's center.

COSTS & FINANCIAL AID

Costs (2016–17) ***Tuition:*** state resident $6340 full-time, $262 per credit part-time; nonresident $18,864 full-time, $530 per credit part-time. Full-time tuition and fees vary according to location. Part-time tuition and fees vary according to course load and location. ***Required fees:*** $2362 full-time, $111 per credit part-time, $25 per term part-time. ***Room and board:*** $8898; room only: $4316. Room and board charges vary according to board plan and housing facility. ***Payment plans:*** installment, deferred payment. ***Waivers:*** senior citizens and employees or children of employees.

Financial Aid Of all full-time matriculated undergraduates who enrolled in 2016, 3,691 applied for aid, 2,830 were judged to have need, 366 had their need fully met. 149 Federal Work-Study jobs (averaging $681). In 2016, 976 non-need-based awards were made. ***Average percent of need met:*** 58. ***Average financial aid package:*** $9743. ***Average need-based loan:*** $4022. ***Average need-based gift aid:*** $7452. ***Average non-need-based aid:*** $3432. ***Average indebtedness upon graduation:*** $25,347.

APPLYING

Standardized Tests *Required:* SAT or ACT (for admission).

Options: electronic application, early admission.

Application fee: $30.

Required: high school transcript, minimum 2.0 GPA. ***Required for some:*** essay or personal statement. ***Recommended:*** interview.

Application deadlines: 2/15 (freshmen), 2/30 (out-of-state freshmen), 6/1 (transfers).

CONTACT

Frostburg State University, 101 Braddock Road, Frostburg, MD 21532-1099. *Phone:* 301-687-4201.

Goucher College

Baltimore, Maryland

http://www.goucher.edu/

- **Independent** comprehensive, founded 1885
- **Suburban** 287-acre campus with easy access to Baltimore and Washington, DC
- **Endowment** $201.5 million
- **Coed** 1,473 undergraduate students, 98% full-time, 68% women, 32% men
- **Moderately difficult** entrance level, 79% of applicants were admitted

UNDERGRAD STUDENTS

1,444 full-time, 29 part-time. Students come from 48 states and territories; 26 other countries; 72% are from out of state; 13% Black or African American, non-Hispanic/Latino; 6% Hispanic/Latino; 4% Asian, non-Hispanic/Latino; 0.3% Native Hawaiian or other Pacific Islander, non-Hispanic/Latino; 6% Two or more races, non-Hispanic/Latino; 5% Race/ethnicity unknown; 3% international; 2% transferred in; 84% live on campus.

Freshmen:

Admission: 3,443 applied, 2,728 admitted, 441 enrolled. ***Average high school GPA:*** 3.14. ***Test scores:*** SAT critical reading scores over 500: 76%; SAT math scores over 500: 78%; SAT writing scores over 500: 73%; ACT scores over 18: 95%; SAT critical reading scores over 600: 42%; SAT math scores over 600: 33%; SAT writing scores over 600: 35%; ACT scores over 24: 60%; SAT critical reading scores over 700: 10%; SAT math scores over 700: 10%; SAT writing scores over 700: 6%; ACT scores over 30: 14%.

Retention: 79% of full-time freshmen returned.

FACULTY

Total: 175, 74% full-time, 79% with terminal degrees.

Student/faculty ratio: 10:1.

ACADEMICS

Calendar: semesters. *Degrees:* bachelor's, master's, and postbachelor's certificates.

Special study options: accelerated degree program, adult/continuing education programs, advanced placement credit, distance learning, double majors, independent study, internships, off-campus study, part-time degree program, services for LD students, student-designed majors, study abroad, summer session for credit. ***ROTC:*** Army (c), Air Force (c).

Unusual degree programs: 3-2 engineering with Johns Hopkins University, Columbia University FU Foundation School of Engineering and Applied Science.

Computers: 130 computers/terminals are available on campus for general student use. Students can access the following: campus intranet, computer help desk, free student e-mail accounts, online (class) grades, online (class) registration, online (class) schedules, transcripts, financial aid information, billing, ePortfolios, academic progress reports, study abroad plans. Campuswide network is available. 100% of college-owned or -operated housing units are wired for high-speed Internet access. Wireless service is available via entire campus.

Library: Goucher College Library plus 1 other. *Books:* 250,000 (physical), 300,000 (digital/electronic); *Serial titles:* 96,000 (digital/electronic); *Databases:* 120. Weekly public service hours: 168; study areas open 24 hours, 5-7 days a week.

STUDENT LIFE

Housing options: on-campus residence required through senior year; coed, men-only, women-only, special housing for students with disabilities. Campus housing is university owned. Freshman applicants given priority for college housing.

Activities and organizations: drama/theater group, student-run newspaper, radio station, choral group, Ultimate Frisbee, Yoga Club, Hip Hop Team, Umoja: The Black Student Union, Model Senate.

Athletics Member NCAA. All Division III. ***Intercollegiate sports:*** basketball M/W, cross-country running M/W, equestrian sports M/W, field hockey W, lacrosse M/W, soccer M/W, swimming and diving M/W, tennis M/W, track and field M/W, volleyball W. ***Intramural sports:*** basketball M/W, fencing M(c)/W(c), soccer M/W, ultimate Frisbee M/W.

Campus security: 24-hour emergency response devices and patrols, late-night transport/escort service, controlled dormitory access, E2 campus alerts.

Student services: health clinic, personal/psychological counseling.

COSTS & FINANCIAL AID
Costs (2017–18) ***Comprehensive fee:*** $56,110 includes full-time tuition ($42,600), mandatory fees ($840), and room and board ($12,670). Part-time tuition: $1420 per credit hour. ***Room and board:*** Room and board charges vary according to board plan and housing facility. ***Payment plans:*** tuition prepayment, installment. ***Waivers:*** employees or children of employees.

Financial Aid Of all full-time matriculated undergraduates who enrolled in 2016, 1,080 applied for aid, 973 were judged to have need, 219 had their need fully met. 365 Federal Work-Study jobs (averaging $1150). In 2016, 427 non-need-based awards were made. ***Average percent of need met:*** 81. ***Average financial aid package:*** $34,502. ***Average need-based loan:*** $3924. ***Average need-based gift aid:*** $30,811. ***Average non-need-based aid:*** $17,200. ***Average indebtedness upon graduation:*** $33,446.

APPLYING
Options: electronic application, early admission, early decision, early action, deferred entrance.

Application fee: $55.

Required: essay or personal statement, a short video, digital application, signed statement of academic integrity, two works from high school career (one of which must be a graded writing assignment) for Goucher Video Application. ***Required for some:*** high school transcript. ***Recommended:*** 3 letters of recommendation, interview.

Application deadlines: 2/1 (freshmen), 4/1 (transfers), 12/1 (early action).

Early decision deadline: 11/15.

Notification: 4/1 (freshmen), 5/1 (transfers), 12/15 (early decision), 2/1 (early action).

CONTACT
Mr. Carlton E. Surbeck, Director of Admissions, Goucher College, 1021 Dulaney Valley Road, Baltimore, MD 21204. *Phone:* 410-337-6100. *Toll-free phone:* 800-468-2437. *Fax:* 410-337-6354.
E-mail: admissions@goucher.edu.

Hood College

Frederick, Maryland

http://www.hood.edu/

- **Independent** comprehensive, founded 1893
- **Suburban** 50-acre campus with easy access to Baltimore and Washington, DC
- **Endowment** $80.9 million
- **Coed** 1,174 undergraduate students, 93% full-time, 61% women, 39% men
- **Moderately difficult** entrance level, 71% of applicants were admitted

UNDERGRAD STUDENTS
1,090 full-time, 84 part-time. Students come from 26 states and territories; 23 other countries; 24% are from out of state; 13% Black or African American, non-Hispanic/Latino; 10% Hispanic/Latino; 3% Asian, non-Hispanic/Latino; 0.2% Native Hawaiian or other Pacific Islander, non-Hispanic/Latino; 5% Two or more races, non-Hispanic/Latino; 5% Race/ethnicity unknown; 2% international; 8% transferred in; 52% live on campus.

Freshmen:
Admission: 1,727 applied, 1,218 admitted, 219 enrolled. ***Average high school GPA:*** 3.52.

Retention: 81% of full-time freshmen returned.

FACULTY
Total: 253, 41% full-time, 62% with terminal degrees.

Student/faculty ratio: 10:1.

ACADEMICS
Calendar: semesters. *Degrees:* certificates, bachelor's, master's, doctoral, and postbachelor's certificates (also offers adult program with significant enrollment not reflected in profile).

Special study options: academic remediation for entering students, advanced placement credit, double majors, honors programs, independent study, internships, off-campus study, part-time degree program, services for LD students, student-designed majors, study abroad, summer session for credit. ***ROTC:*** Army (b).

Unusual degree programs: 3-2 business administration; nursing; social work; communication arts, integrated marketing communications, education.

Computers: 470 computers/terminals are available on campus for general student use. Students can access the following: campus intranet, computer help desk, free student e-mail accounts, online (class) grades, online (class) registration, online (class) schedules. Campuswide network is available. 100% of college-owned or -operated housing units are wired for high-speed Internet access. Wireless service is available via entire campus.

Library: Beneficial-Hodson Library and Information Technology Center plus 1 other. *Books:* 172,311 (physical), 295,531 (digital/electronic); *Serial titles:* 235 (physical), 42,000 (digital/electronic); *Databases:* 96. Students can reserve study rooms.

STUDENT LIFE
Housing options: on-campus residence required through sophomore year; coed. Campus housing is university owned. Freshman campus housing is guaranteed.

Activities and organizations: drama/theater group, student-run newspaper, radio station, choral group, Black Student Union (BSU), Campus Activities Board (CAB), International Club, Queer Student Union (QSU), Enactus.

Athletics Member NCAA. All Division III. ***Intercollegiate sports:*** baseball M, basketball M/W, cross-country running M/W, equestrian sports M(c)/W(c), field hockey W, golf M/W, lacrosse M/W, soccer M/W, softball W, swimming and diving M/W, tennis M/W, track and field M/W, volleyball W. ***Intramural sports:*** cheerleading W(c).

Campus security: 24-hour emergency response devices and patrols, late-night transport/escort service, controlled dormitory access.

Student services: health clinic, personal/psychological counseling.

COSTS & FINANCIAL AID
Costs (2017–18) ***Comprehensive fee:*** $50,540 includes full-time tuition ($37,400), mandatory fees ($560), and room and board ($12,580). Part-time tuition: $1090 per credit hour. ***Required fees:*** $280 per term part-time. ***College room only:*** $6600. Room and board charges vary according to board plan. ***Payment plan:*** installment. ***Waivers:*** senior citizens and employees or children of employees.

Financial Aid Of all full-time matriculated undergraduates who enrolled in 2016, 957 applied for aid, 873 were judged to have need, 175 had their need fully met. 205 Federal Work-Study jobs (averaging $2000). 132 state and other part-time jobs (averaging $2000). In 2016, 188 non-need-based awards were made. ***Average percent of need met:*** 75. ***Average financial aid package:*** $29,186. ***Average need-based loan:*** $4553. ***Average need-based gift aid:*** $25,391. ***Average non-need-based aid:*** $16,993. ***Average indebtedness upon graduation:*** $30,554.

APPLYING
Options: electronic application.

Required: essay or personal statement, high school transcript, minimum 2.0 GPA, 2 letters of recommendation. ***Recommended:*** interview.

Application deadlines: rolling (freshmen), rolling (transfers).

Notification: continuous (freshmen), continuous (transfers).

CONTACT
Ms. Jennifer Decker, Director of Undergraduate Admissions, Hood College, 401 Rosemont Avenue, Frederick, MD 21701. *Phone:* 301-696-3400. *Toll-free phone:* 800-922-1599. *Fax:* 301-696-3819.
E-mail: admission@hood.edu.

Johns Hopkins University

Baltimore, Maryland

http://www.jhu.edu/

- **Independent** university, founded 1876
- **Urban** 140-acre campus with easy access to Baltimore and Washington, DC
- **Endowment** $3.4 billion
- **Coed** 5,386 undergraduate students, 99% full-time, 49% women, 51% men
- 13% of applicants were admitted

UNDERGRAD STUDENTS

5,339 full-time, 47 part-time. Students come from 53 states and territories; 61 other countries; 88% are from out of state; 6% Black or African American, non-Hispanic/Latino; 13% Hispanic/Latino; 23% Asian, non-Hispanic/Latino; 0.1% Native Hawaiian or other Pacific Islander, non-Hispanic/Latino; 0.2% American Indian or Alaska Native, non-Hispanic/Latino; 5% Two or more races, non-Hispanic/Latino; 3% Race/ethnicity unknown; 10% international; 1% transferred in; 52% live on campus.

Freshmen:

Admission: 24,716 applied, 3,251 admitted, 1,299 enrolled. ***Average high school GPA:*** 3.9. ***Test scores:*** SAT critical reading scores over 500: 100%; SAT math scores over 500: 100%; SAT writing scores over 500: 100%; ACT scores over 18: 100%; SAT critical reading scores over 600: 97%; SAT math scores over 600: 99%; SAT writing scores over 600: 96%; ACT scores over 24: 100%; SAT critical reading scores over 700: 69%; SAT math scores over 700: 81%; SAT writing scores over 700: 69%; ACT scores over 30: 97%.

Retention: 97% of full-time freshmen returned.

FACULTY

Total: 751, 94% full-time, 92% with terminal degrees.

Student/faculty ratio: 10:1.

ACADEMICS

Calendar: 4-1-4. *Degrees:* certificates, diplomas, bachelor's, master's, doctoral, post-master's, and postbachelor's certificates.

Special study options: advanced placement credit, double majors, independent study, internships, off-campus study, services for LD students, student-designed majors, study abroad, summer session for credit. ***ROTC:*** Army (b), Air Force (c).

Unusual degree programs: 3-2 engineering; international studies with Johns Hopkins University, biology, classics, German, history, neuroscience, public policy, mathematics, education.

Computers: 200 computers/terminals and 4,000 ports are available on campus for general student use. Students can access the following: campus intranet, computer help desk, free student e-mail accounts, online (class) grades, online (class) registration, online (class) schedules. Campuswide network is available. 100% of college-owned or -operated housing units are wired for high-speed Internet access. Wireless service is available via entire campus.

Library: The Sheridan Libraries plus 2 others. *Books:* 4.1 million (physical). Study areas open 24 hours, 5-7 days a week; students can reserve study rooms.

STUDENT LIFE

Housing options: on-campus residence required through sophomore year; coed, special housing for students with disabilities. Campus housing is university owned. Freshman campus housing is guaranteed.

Activities and organizations: drama/theater group, student-run newspaper, radio station, choral group, Hopkins Organization for Programming (The Hop), Johns Hopkins Model United Nations Conference (JHUMUNC), The Outdoors Club, JHU Tutorial Project, JHU Student Government Association (SGA), national fraternities, national sororities.

Athletics Member NCAA. All Division III except men's and women's lacrosse (Division I). ***Intercollegiate sports:*** baseball M, basketball M/W, cross-country running M/W, fencing M/W, field hockey W, football M, lacrosse M(s)/W(s), soccer M/W, swimming and diving M/W, tennis M/W, track and field M/W, volleyball W, water polo M, wrestling M. ***Intramural sports:*** badminton M(c)/W(c), baseball M(c), basketball M/W, cheerleading W(c), equestrian sports M(c)/W(c), field hockey W(c), football M/W, golf M(c)/W(c), gymnastics M(c)/W(c), ice hockey M(c)/W(c), lacrosse M(c)/W(c), racquetball M(c)/W(c), riflery M(c)/W(c), rock climbing M/W, rugby M(c)/W(c), soccer M/W, softball W(c), squash M(c)/W(c), swimming and diving M(c)/W(c), table tennis M(c)/W(c), tennis M(c)/W(c), track and field M(c)/W(c), triathlon M(c)/W(c), ultimate Frisbee M(c)/W(c), volleyball M(c)/W(c), water polo M(c)/W(c), wrestling M(c).

Campus security: 24-hour emergency response devices and patrols, student patrols, late-night transport/escort service, controlled dormitory access, CCTV monitoring of public areas.

Student services: health clinic, personal/psychological counseling.

COSTS & FINANCIAL AID

Costs (2016–17) ***One-time required fee:*** $500. ***Comprehensive fee:*** $65,386 includes full-time tuition ($50,410) and room and board ($14,976). Part-time tuition: $1680 per credit hour. ***College room only:*** $8652. Room and board charges vary according to board plan and housing facility. ***Payment plan:*** installment. ***Waivers:*** employees or children of employees.

Financial Aid Of all full-time matriculated undergraduates who enrolled in 2015, 3,043 applied for aid, 2,554 were judged to have need, 2,552 had their need fully met. 1,696 Federal Work-Study jobs (averaging $2428). In 2015, 87 non-need-based awards were made. ***Average percent of need met:*** 100. ***Average financial aid package:*** $39,344. ***Average need-based loan:*** $4384. ***Average need-based gift aid:*** $36,687. ***Average non-need-based aid:*** $27,941. ***Average indebtedness upon graduation:*** $24,702. ***Financial aid deadline:*** 3/1.

APPLYING

Standardized Tests *Required:* SAT or ACT (for admission). *Recommended:* SAT and SAT Subject Tests or ACT (for admission).

Options: early decision, deferred entrance.

Application fee: $70.

Required: essay or personal statement, high school transcript, 2 letters of recommendation.

Application deadlines: 1/1 (freshmen), 3/1 (transfers).

Early decision deadline: 11/1.

Notification: 4/1 (freshmen), 5/15 (transfers), 12/15 (early decision).

CONTACT

Kate Estes, Assistant Director of Undergraduate Admissions, Johns Hopkins University, 3400 North Charles Street, Mason Hall, Baltimore, MD 21218-2699. *Phone:* 410-516-8171. *Fax:* 410-516-6025. *E-mail:* gotojhu@jhu.edu.

See previous page for display ad and page 1384 for the College Close-Up.

Kaplan University, Hagerstown Campus

Hagerstown, Maryland

http://www.kaplanuniversity.edu/

CONTACT

Kaplan University, Hagerstown Campus, 18618 Crestwood Drive, Hagerstown, MD 21742. *Phone:* 301-739-2680 Ext. 217. *Toll-free phone:* 800-987-7734.

★ Loyola University Maryland

Baltimore, Maryland

http://www.loyola.edu/

- **Independent Roman Catholic (Jesuit)** university, founded 1852
- **Urban** 89-acre campus with easy access to Washington, DC
- **Endowment** $193.8 million
- **Coed** 4,104 undergraduate students, 99% full-time, 57% women, 43% men
- **Moderately difficult** entrance level, 66% of applicants were admitted

UNDERGRAD STUDENTS

4,050 full-time, 54 part-time. 82% are from out of state; 5% Black or African American, non-Hispanic/Latino; 10% Hispanic/Latino; 4% Asian, non-Hispanic/Latino; 0.1% Native Hawaiian or other Pacific Islander, non-Hispanic/Latino; 0.1% American Indian or Alaska Native, non-Hispanic/Latino; 3% Two or more races, non-Hispanic/Latino; 0.3% Race/ethnicity unknown; 1% international; 1% transferred in; 83% live on campus.

Freshmen:

Admission: 12,727 applied, 8,340 admitted, 1,095 enrolled. ***Average high school GPA:*** 3.42. ***Test scores:*** SAT critical reading scores over 500: 94%; SAT math scores over 500: 95%; SAT writing scores over 500: 94%; ACT scores over 18: 100%; SAT critical reading scores over 600: 51%; SAT math scores over 600: 53%; SAT writing scores over 600: 50%; ACT scores over 24: 91%; SAT critical reading scores over 700: 6%; SAT math scores over 700: 6%; SAT writing scores over 700: 6%; ACT scores over 30: 22%.

Retention: 87% of full-time freshmen returned.

FACULTY

Total: 553, 67% full-time, 59% with terminal degrees.

Student/faculty ratio: 12:1.

ACADEMICS

Calendar: semesters. *Degrees:* bachelor's, master's, doctoral, post-master's, and postbachelor's certificates.

Special study options: accelerated degree program, advanced placement credit, cooperative education, double majors, honors programs, independent study, internships, off-campus study, part-time degree program, services for LD students, study abroad, summer session for credit. ***ROTC:*** Army (b), Air Force (c).

Unusual degree programs: 3-2 nursing with Johns Hopkins University.

Computers: 690 computers/terminals and 50 ports are available on campus for general student use. Students can access the following: campus intranet, computer help desk, free student e-mail accounts, online (class) grades, online (class) registration, online (class) schedules. Campuswide network is available. 100% of college-owned or -operated housing units are wired for high-speed Internet access. Wireless service is available via entire campus.

Library: Loyola/Notre Dame Library plus 1 other.

STUDENT LIFE

Housing options: coed, cooperative. Freshman campus housing is guaranteed.

Activities and organizations: drama/theater group, student-run newspaper, radio and television station, choral group, Student Government Association, Resident Affairs Council (RAC), Relay for Life, Resident Assistants (RA), The Evergreens.

Athletics Member NCAA. All Division I. ***Intercollegiate sports:*** basketball M(s)/W(s), crew M(s)/W(s), cross-country running M(s)/W(s), golf M(s), lacrosse M(s)/W(s), soccer M(s)/W(s), swimming and diving M(s)/W(s), tennis M(s)/W(s), track and field W(s), volleyball W(s). ***Intramural sports:*** badminton M(c)/W(c), baseball M(c), basketball M(c)/W(c), field hockey W(c), ice hockey M(c), lacrosse M(c)/W(c), riflery M(c)/W(c), rugby M(c), sailing M(c)/W(c), soccer M(c)/W(c), softball W(c), swimming and diving M(c)/W(c), tennis M(c)/W(c), ultimate Frisbee M(c)/W(c), volleyball M(c)/W(c), water polo M(c)/W(c).

Campus security: 24-hour emergency response devices and patrols, late-night transport/escort service, controlled dormitory access.

Student services: health clinic, personal/psychological counseling, women's center.

COSTS & FINANCIAL AID

Costs (2016–17) ***Comprehensive fee:*** $60,465 includes full-time tuition ($45,030), mandatory fees ($1565), and room and board ($13,870). Full-time tuition and fees vary according to course load. Part-time tuition: $730 per credit. Part-time tuition and fees vary according to course load. ***Room and board:*** Room and board charges vary according to board plan and housing facility. ***Payment plan:*** installment. ***Waivers:*** employees or children of employees.

Financial Aid Of all full-time matriculated undergraduates who enrolled in 2014, 2,669 applied for aid, 2,290 were judged to have need, 2,072 had their need fully met. In 2014, 611 non-need-based awards were made. ***Average percent of need met:*** 92. ***Average financial aid package:*** $30,520. ***Average need-based loan:*** $5520. ***Average need-based gift aid:*** $22,245. ***Average non-need-based aid:*** $14,960. ***Average indebtedness upon graduation:*** $34,375. ***Financial aid deadline:*** 2/15.

APPLYING

Options: electronic application, early admission, early decision, early action, deferred entrance.

Application fee: $60.

Required: essay or personal statement, high school transcript.

Application deadlines: 1/15 (freshmen), 7/15 (transfers), 11/15 (early action).

Early decision deadline: 11/1.

Notification: 4/1 (freshmen), 4/1 (out-of-state freshmen), continuous (transfers), 1/15 (early action).

CONTACT

Loyola University Maryland, 4501 North Charles Street, Baltimore, MD 21210-2699. *Phone:* 410-617-2000. *Toll-free phone:* 800-221-9107.

See below for display ad and page 1402 for the College Close-Up.

Maple Springs Baptist Bible College and Seminary

Capitol Heights, Maryland

http://www.msbbcs.edu/

CONTACT

Ms. Jeannie Bowman, Assistant Director of Admissions and Records, Maple Springs Baptist Bible College and Seminary, 4130 Belt Road, Capitol Heights, MD 20743. *Phone:* 301-736-3631. *Fax:* 301-735-6507.

Maryland Institute College of Art

Baltimore, Maryland

http://www.mica.edu/

- **Independent** comprehensive, founded 1826
- **Urban** 16-acre campus with easy access to Washington, DC
- **Endowment** $79.0 million
- **Coed** 1,679 undergraduate students, 99% full-time, 74% women, 26% men
- **Very difficult** entrance level, 57% of applicants were admitted

UNDERGRAD STUDENTS

1,654 full-time, 25 part-time. Students come from 45 states and territories; 40 other countries; 77% are from out of state; 6% Black or African American, non-Hispanic/Latino; 4% Hispanic/Latino; 13% Asian, non-Hispanic/Latino; 0.1% Native Hawaiian or other Pacific Islander, non-Hispanic/Latino; 0.1% American Indian or Alaska Native, non-Hispanic/Latino; 10% Two or more races, non-Hispanic/Latino; 4% Race/ethnicity unknown; 18% international; 5% transferred in; 88% live on campus.

Freshmen:

Admission: 3,475 applied, 1,984 admitted, 351 enrolled. ***Average high school GPA:*** 3.3.

Retention: 87% of full-time freshmen returned.

FACULTY

Total: 347, 46% full-time, 76% with terminal degrees.

Student/faculty ratio: 9:1.

ACADEMICS

Calendar: semesters. *Degrees:* bachelor's, master's, and postbachelor's certificates.

Special study options: accelerated degree program, adult/continuing education programs, advanced placement credit, distance learning, double majors, English as a second language, independent study, internships, off-campus study, services for LD students, student-designed majors, study abroad, summer session for credit. ***ROTC:*** Army (c).

Computers: 1,100 computers/terminals and 3,000 ports are available on campus for general student use. Students can access the following: campus intranet, computer help desk, free student e-mail accounts, online (class) grades, online (class) registration, online (class) schedules, campus portal, online gallery space, network storage space, personal websites, online software training tutorials, learning management system. Campuswide network is available. 100% of college-owned or -operated housing units are wired for high-speed Internet access. Wireless service is available via entire campus.

Library: Decker Library. *Books:* 75,000 (physical), 163,918 (digital/electronic); *Serial titles:* 671 (physical), 71 (digital/electronic);

Databases: 47. Weekly public service hours: 70; students can reserve study rooms.

STUDENT LIFE
Housing options: on-campus residence required through sophomore year; coed, special housing for students with disabilities. Campus housing is university owned. Freshman campus housing is guaranteed.

Activities and organizations: drama/theater group, student-run radio station, choral group, Haunted House, Urban Gaming Club, Oy , Korean International Student Association, MICA Design League.

Athletics ***Intramural sports:*** volleyball M(c)/W(c).

Campus security: 24-hour emergency response devices and patrols, student patrols, late-night transport/escort service, controlled dormitory access, self-defense education, 24-hour building security, safety awareness programs, campus patrols by city police.

Student services: health clinic, personal/psychological counseling.

COSTS & FINANCIAL AID
Costs (2016–17) ***One-time required fee:*** $180. ***Comprehensive fee:*** $57,850 includes full-time tuition ($43,760), mandatory fees ($1640), and room and board ($12,450). Part-time tuition: $1820 per credit hour. ***Required fees:*** $820 per term part-time. ***College room only:*** $9350. Room and board charges vary according to board plan and housing facility. ***Payment plan:*** installment. ***Waivers:*** employees or children of employees.

Financial Aid ***Average indebtedness upon graduation:*** $17,472.

APPLYING
Standardized Tests *Required:* SAT or ACT (for admission).

Options: electronic application, early admission, early decision, deferred entrance.

Application fee: $70.

Required: essay or personal statement, high school transcript, 3 letters of recommendation, art portfolio. ***Recommended:*** interview.

Application deadlines: 2/1 (freshmen), 3/1 (transfers).

Early decision deadline: 11/1.

Notification: 2/26 (freshmen), 4/15 (transfers), 12/1 (early decision).

CONTACT
Director of Undergraduate Admission, Maryland Institute College of Art, 1300 Mount Royal Avenue, Baltimore, MD 21217. *Phone:* 410-225-2222. *Fax:* 410-225-2337.

McDaniel College

Westminster, Maryland

http://www.mcdaniel.edu/

- **Independent** comprehensive, founded 1867
- **Suburban** 160-acre campus with easy access to Baltimore and Washington, DC
- **Endowment** $109.3 million
- **Coed** 1,559 undergraduate students, 98% full-time, 51% women, 49% men
- **Moderately difficult** entrance level, 79% of applicants were admitted

UNDERGRAD STUDENTS
1,525 full-time, 34 part-time. Students come from 37 states and territories; 32 other countries; 35% are from out of state; 14% Black or African American, non-Hispanic/Latino; 7% Hispanic/Latino; 4% Asian, non-Hispanic/Latino; 0.1% Native Hawaiian or other Pacific Islander, non-Hispanic/Latino; 0.2% American Indian or Alaska Native, non-Hispanic/Latino; 3% Two or more races, non-Hispanic/Latino; 6% Race/ethnicity unknown; 4% transferred in; 82% live on campus.

Freshmen:
Admission: 2,385 applied, 1,876 admitted, 388 enrolled. ***Average high school GPA:*** 3.5. ***Test scores:*** SAT critical reading scores over 500: 69%; SAT math scores over 500: 73%; ACT scores over 18: 98%; SAT critical reading scores over 600: 26%; SAT math scores over 600: 28%; ACT scores over 24: 55%; SAT critical reading scores over 700: 7%; SAT math scores over 700: 5%; ACT scores over 30: 13%.

Retention: 79% of full-time freshmen returned.

FACULTY
Total: 624, 21% full-time, 40% with terminal degrees.

Student/faculty ratio: 10:1.

ACADEMICS
Calendar: 4-1-4. *Degrees:* bachelor's, master's, and postbachelor's certificates.

Special study options: academic remediation for entering students, adult/continuing education programs, advanced placement credit, distance learning, double majors, honors programs, independent study, internships, off-campus study, part-time degree program, services for LD students, student-designed majors, study abroad, summer session for credit. ***ROTC:*** Army (b).

Unusual degree programs: 3-2 gerontology, human services management, music education, secondary education, secondary education, special education.

Computers: 138 computers/terminals and 1,500 ports are available on campus for general student use. Students can access the following: campus intranet, computer help desk, free student e-mail accounts, online (class) grades, online (class) registration, online (class) schedules, online billing summaries, financial aid letter, tax information. Campuswide network is available. 100% of college-owned or -operated housing units are wired for high-speed Internet access. Wireless service is available via entire campus.

Library: Hoover Library. *Books:* 179,112 (physical), 152,246 (digital/electronic); *Serial titles:* 1,422 (physical), 64,815 (digital/electronic); *Databases:* 79. Study areas open 24 hours, 5-7 days a week; students can reserve study rooms.

STUDENT LIFE
Housing options: on-campus residence required through junior year; coed, special housing for students with disabilities. Campus housing is university owned. Freshman campus housing is guaranteed.

Activities and organizations: drama/theater group, student-run newspaper, radio and television station, choral group, Student Government Association, Black Student Union, International Club, Maryland State Legislature, McDaniel Allies, national fraternities, national sororities.

Athletics Member NCAA. All Division III. ***Intercollegiate sports:*** baseball M, basketball M/W, cross-country running M/W, field hockey W, football M, golf M/W, lacrosse M/W, soccer M/W, softball W, swimming and diving M/W, tennis M/W, track and field M/W, volleyball W, wrestling M. ***Intramural sports:*** basketball M/W, cheerleading M(c)/W(c), football M/W, golf M/W, soccer M/W, softball M/W, ultimate Frisbee M/W, volleyball M/W.

Campus security: 24-hour emergency response devices and patrols, late-night transport/escort service, patrol force containing campus police, all certified to US DOT First Responder standards.

Student services: health clinic, personal/psychological counseling.

COSTS & FINANCIAL AID
Costs (2017–18) ***Comprehensive fee:*** $52,910 includes full-time tuition ($41,800) and room and board ($11,110). Full-time tuition and fees vary according to course load. Part-time tuition: $1306 per credit hour. Part-time tuition and fees vary according to course load and reciprocity agreements. ***College room only:*** $5100. Room and board charges vary according to board plan and housing facility. ***Payment plan:*** installment. ***Waivers:*** employees or children of employees.

Financial Aid Of all full-time matriculated undergraduates who enrolled in 2016, 1,278 applied for aid, 1,167 were judged to have need, 286 had their need fully met. In 2016, 344 non-need-based awards were made. ***Average percent of need met:*** 86. ***Average financial aid package:*** $35,192. ***Average need-based loan:*** $4583. ***Average need-based gift aid:*** $31,289. ***Average non-need-based aid:*** $19,544. ***Average indebtedness upon graduation:*** $35,397.

APPLYING
Standardized Tests *Required:* SAT or ACT (for admission).

Options: electronic application, early admission, early decision, early action, deferred entrance.

Application fee: $50.

Required: essay or personal statement, high school transcript, minimum 2.5 GPA, 2 letters of recommendation. ***Required for some:*** interview. ***Recommended:*** interview.

Application deadlines: 2/1 (freshmen), 6/1 (transfers), 11/15 (early action).

Early decision deadline: 11/1 (for plan 1), 1/15 (for plan 2).

Notification: 3/1 (freshmen), 6/15 (transfers), 12/1 (early decision plan 1), 2/1 (early decision plan 2), 12/15 (early action).

CONTACT

Ms. Florence Hines, Vice President for Enrollment Management and Dean of Admissions, McDaniel College, 2 College Hill, Westminster, MD 21157-4390. *Phone:* 410-857-2230. *Toll-free phone:* 800-638-5005. *Fax:* 410-857-2757. *E-mail:* admissions@mcdaniel.edu.

Morgan State University

Baltimore, Maryland

http://www.morgan.edu/

CONTACT

Ms. Shonda Gray, Acting Director of Admissions and Recruitment, Morgan State University, 1700 East Cold Spring Lane, Baltimore, MD 21251. *Phone:* 443-885-3000. *Toll-free phone:* 800-332-6674. *E-mail:* shantell.saunders@morgan.edu.

Mount St. Mary's University

Emmitsburg, Maryland

http://www.msmary.edu/

- **Independent Roman Catholic** comprehensive, founded 1808
- **Rural** 1400-acre campus with easy access to Baltimore and Washington, DC
- **Endowment** $50.0 million
- **Coed** 1,729 undergraduate students, 94% full-time, 54% women, 46% men
- **Moderately difficult** entrance level, 62% of applicants were admitted

UNDERGRAD STUDENTS

1,629 full-time, 100 part-time. Students come from 38 states and territories; 9 other countries; 45% are from out of state; 13% Black or African American, non-Hispanic/Latino; 10% Hispanic/Latino; 3% Asian, non-Hispanic/Latino; 0.2% Native Hawaiian or other Pacific Islander, non-Hispanic/Latino; 0.3% American Indian or Alaska Native, non-Hispanic/Latino; 4% Two or more races, non-Hispanic/Latino; 1% Race/ethnicity unknown; 0.9% international; 3% transferred in; 80% live on campus.

Freshmen:

Admission: 6,086 applied, 3,745 admitted, 417 enrolled. ***Average high school GPA:*** 3.42. ***Test scores:*** SAT critical reading scores over 500: 64%; SAT math scores over 500: 63%; SAT writing scores over 500: 52%; ACT scores over 18: 92%; SAT critical reading scores over 600: 21%; SAT math scores over 600: 21%; SAT writing scores over 600: 13%; ACT scores over 24: 30%; SAT critical reading scores over 700: 3%; SAT math scores over 700: 2%; SAT writing scores over 700: 1%; ACT scores over 30: 4%.

Retention: 75% of full-time freshmen returned.

FACULTY

Total: 206, 61% full-time, 64% with terminal degrees.

Student/faculty ratio: 12:1.

ACADEMICS

Calendar: semesters. *Degrees:* bachelor's, master's, post-master's, and postbachelor's certificates.

Special study options: academic remediation for entering students, accelerated degree program, adult/continuing education programs, advanced placement credit, double majors, honors programs, independent study, internships, off-campus study, part-time degree program, services for LD students, student-designed majors, study abroad, summer session for credit. ***ROTC:*** Army (c).

Unusual degree programs: 3-2 nursing with University of Maryland, Shenandoah University.

Computers: 80 computers/terminals are available on campus for general student use. Students can access the following: campus intranet, computer help desk, free student e-mail accounts, online (class) grades, online (class) registration, online (class) schedules, tuition payment, course management system. Campuswide network is available. 100% of college-owned or -operated housing units are wired for high-speed Internet access. Wireless service is available via entire campus.

Library: Phillips Library. *Books:* 149,287 (physical), 227,412 (digital/electronic); *Serial titles:* 233 (physical), 26,544 (digital/electronic); *Databases:* 130.

STUDENT LIFE

Housing options: on-campus residence required for freshman year; coed, special housing for students with disabilities. Campus housing is university owned. Freshman campus housing is guaranteed.

Activities and organizations: drama/theater group, student-run newspaper, radio station, choral group, Mount Students for Life, CRUX - Outdoor Adventures, Campus Ministry Student Organization, FOCUS, Mount Chorale.

Athletics Member NCAA. All Division I. ***Intercollegiate sports:*** baseball M(s), basketball M(s)/W(s), cheerleading W(c), cross-country running M(s)/W(s), equestrian sports M(c)/W(c), ice hockey M(c)/W(c), lacrosse M(s)/W(s), rugby M(c)/W(c), soccer W(s), softball W(s), swimming and diving M(s)/W(s), tennis M(s)/W(s), track and field M(s)/W(s). ***Intramural sports:*** basketball M, field hockey M/W, skiing (downhill) M/W, soccer M/W, softball M/W, tennis M/W, ultimate Frisbee M/W, volleyball W.

Campus security: 24-hour emergency response devices and patrols, late-night transport/escort service, controlled dormitory access.

Student services: health clinic, personal/psychological counseling.

COSTS & FINANCIAL AID

Costs (2017–18) ***Comprehensive fee:*** $53,380 includes full-time tuition ($39,200), mandatory fees ($1350), and room and board ($12,830). Full-time tuition and fees vary according to location and program. Part-time tuition: $1275 per credit hour. Part-time tuition and fees vary according to location and program. ***College room only:*** $6500. Room and board charges vary according to housing facility. ***Payment plan:*** installment. ***Waivers:*** employees or children of employees.

Financial Aid Of all full-time matriculated undergraduates who enrolled in 2016, 1,311 applied for aid, 1,154 were judged to have need, 273 had their need fully met. 105 Federal Work-Study jobs (averaging $1862). 665 state and other part-time jobs (averaging $1320). In 2016, 410 non-need-based awards were made. ***Average percent of need met:*** 71. ***Average financial aid package:*** $26,219. ***Average need-based loan:*** $4636. ***Average need-based gift aid:*** $21,936. ***Average non-need-based aid:*** $17,586. ***Average indebtedness upon graduation:*** $33,894. ***Financial aid deadline:*** 3/1.

APPLYING

Standardized Tests *Required:* SAT or ACT (for admission).

Options: electronic application, early action, deferred entrance.

Application fee: $45.

Required: high school transcript, minimum 2.0 GPA, 1 letter of recommendation. ***Recommended:*** essay or personal statement, minimum 3.0 GPA, interview.

Application deadlines: 3/1 (freshmen), 6/1 (transfers), 12/1 (early action).

Notification: continuous (freshmen), continuous (transfers), 12/25 (early action).

CONTACT

Mr. Michael Post, Dean of Admissions and Enrollment Management, Mount St. Mary's University, 16300 Old Emmitsburg Road, Emmitsburg, MD 21727. *Phone:* 301-447-5214. *Toll-free phone:* 800-448-4347. *Fax:* 301-447-5860. *E-mail:* admissions@msmary.edu.

Ner Israel Rabbinical College

Baltimore, Maryland

CONTACT

Ner Israel Rabbinical College, 400 Mount Wilson Lane, Baltimore, MD 21208. *Phone:* 410-484-7200.

Notre Dame of Maryland University

Baltimore, Maryland

http://www.ndm.edu/

CONTACT

Angela Baumler, Director of Admissions (Women's College), Notre Dame of Maryland University, 4701 North Charles Street, Baltimore, MD 21210. *Phone:* -410-532-5330. *Toll-free phone:* 800-435-0200. *E-mail:* abaumler@ndm.edu.

Peabody Conservatory of The Johns Hopkins University

Baltimore, Maryland

http://www.peabody.jhu.edu/

CONTACT

Mr. David Lane, Director of Admissions, Peabody Conservatory of The Johns Hopkins University, Peabody Conservatory Admissions Office, One East Mount Vernon Place, Baltimore, MD 21202-2397. *Phone:* 410-234-4848. *Toll-free phone:* 800-368-2521.

St. John's College

Annapolis, Maryland

http://www.sjc.edu/

- **Independent** comprehensive, founded 1784
- **Small-town** 36-acre campus with easy access to Washington, D.C. and Baltimore, MD
- **Endowment** $152.0 million
- **Coed** 434 undergraduate students, 100% full-time, 45% women, 55% men
- **Moderately difficult** entrance level, 53% of applicants were admitted

UNDERGRAD STUDENTS

432 full-time, 2 part-time. Students come from 41 states and territories; 29 other countries; 78% are from out of state; 1% Black or African American, non-Hispanic/Latino; 5% Hispanic/Latino; 4% Asian, non-Hispanic/Latino; 0.2% American Indian or Alaska Native, non-Hispanic/Latino; 2% Two or more races, non-Hispanic/Latino; 0.5% Race/ethnicity unknown; 18% international; 5% transferred in; 78% live on campus.

Freshmen:

Admission: 612 applied, 326 admitted, 127 enrolled. ***Average high school GPA:*** 3.48. ***Test scores:*** SAT critical reading scores over 500: 96%; SAT math scores over 500: 92%; SAT writing scores over 500: 96%; ACT scores over 18: 100%; SAT critical reading scores over 600: 80%; SAT math scores over 600: 71%; SAT writing scores over 600: 75%; ACT scores over 24: 93%; SAT critical reading scores over 700: 41%; SAT math scores over 700: 28%; SAT writing scores over 700: 26%; ACT scores over 30: 64%.

Retention: 79% of full-time freshmen returned.

FACULTY

Total: 76, 78% full-time, 88% with terminal degrees.

Student/faculty ratio: 7:1.

ACADEMICS

Calendar: semesters. *Degrees:* bachelor's and master's.

Special study options: internships, off-campus study, services for LD students, study abroad.

Computers: 26 computers/terminals are available on campus for general student use. Students can access the following: computer help desk, free student e-mail accounts. Campuswide network is available. 100% of college-owned or -operated housing units are wired for high-speed Internet access. Wireless service is available via entire campus.

Library: Greenfield Library plus 1 other. *Books:* 108,811 (physical), 486 (digital/electronic); *Serial titles:* 127 (physical), 1,439 (digital/electronic); *Databases:* 14. Weekly public service hours: 94; students can reserve study rooms.

STUDENT LIFE

Housing options: on-campus residence required for freshman year; coed, special housing for students with disabilities. Campus housing is university owned. Freshman campus housing is guaranteed.

Activities and organizations: drama/theater group, student-run newspaper, choral group, King William's Players (drama), Reality (social), Delegate Council (student government), Waltz (social), Student Committee on Instruction (advisory).

Athletics Member USCAA. ***Intercollegiate sports:*** crew M(c)/W(c), fencing M(c)/W(c), sailing M(c)/W(c). ***Intramural sports:*** badminton M(c)/W(c), basketball M/W, fencing M(c)/W(c), football M/W, sailing M(c)/W(c), soccer M(c)/W(c), swimming and diving M(c)/W(c), tennis M(c)/W(c), track and field M(c)/W(c), ultimate Frisbee M/W(c), volleyball M/W, weight lifting M(c)/W(c).

Campus security: 24-hour emergency response devices and patrols, late-night transport/escort service, controlled dormitory access, Personal Whistle Safety Program, Operation ID (identification of valuables), LiveSafe App.

Student services: health clinic, personal/psychological counseling.

COSTS & FINANCIAL AID

Costs (2017–18) ***One-time required fee:*** $125. ***Comprehensive fee:*** $63,904 includes full-time tuition ($51,200), mandatory fees ($470), and room and board ($12,234). ***College room only:*** $5984. Room and board charges vary according to board plan and housing facility. ***Payment plans:*** tuition prepayment, installment. ***Waivers:*** employees or children of employees.

Financial Aid Of all full-time matriculated undergraduates who enrolled in 2016, 359 applied for aid, 317 were judged to have need, 80 had their need fully met. 52 Federal Work-Study jobs (averaging $2700). 130 state and other part-time jobs (averaging $2700). In 2016, 106 non-need-based awards were made. ***Average percent of need met:*** 88. ***Average financial aid package:*** $41,636. ***Average need-based loan:*** $4823. ***Average need-based gift aid:*** $36,355. ***Average non-need-based aid:*** $19,112. ***Average indebtedness upon graduation:*** $34,212.

APPLYING

Standardized Tests *Required for some:* SAT or ACT (for admission), SAT/ACT, TOEFL/IELTS or interview for international applicants, SAT/ACT/CLTfor homeschooled students and applicants who have not and will not graduate high school.

Options: electronic application, early admission, early action, deferred entrance.

Required: essay or personal statement, high school transcript, 2 letters of recommendation. ***Required for some:*** outline of curriculum for home-schooled applicants. ***Recommended:*** interview.

Application deadlines: rolling (freshmen), 11/15 (early action).

Notification: continuous (freshmen), 12/15 (early action).

CONTACT

Mr. Benjamin Baum, Director of Admissions, St. John's College, 60 College Avenue, Annapolis, MD 21401. *Phone:* 410-626-2522. *Toll-free phone:* 800-727-9238. *Fax:* 410-269-7916. *E-mail:* annapolis.admissions@sjc.edu.

St. Mary's College of Maryland

St. Mary's City, Maryland

http://www.smcm.edu/

- **State-supported** comprehensive, founded 1840
- **Rural** 361-acre campus
- **Endowment** $31.3 million
- **Coed** 1,643 undergraduate students, 97% full-time, 57% women, 43% men
- **Moderately difficult** entrance level, 80% of applicants were admitted

UNDERGRAD STUDENTS

1,587 full-time, 56 part-time. Students come from 24 states and territories; 9 other countries; 7% are from out of state; 9% Black or African American, non-Hispanic/Latino; 9% Hispanic/Latino; 4% Asian, non-Hispanic/Latino; 0.3% American Indian or Alaska Native, non-Hispanic/Latino; 5% Two or more races, non-Hispanic/Latino; 4% Race/ethnicity unknown; 0.5% international; 7% transferred in; 83% live on campus.

Freshmen:
Admission: 1,767 applied, 1,413 admitted, 334 enrolled. ***Average high school GPA:*** 3.34. ***Test scores:*** SAT critical reading scores over 500: 80%; SAT math scores over 500: 73%; SAT writing scores over 500: 72%; ACT scores over 18: 97%; SAT critical reading scores over 600: 44%; SAT math scores over 600: 31%; SAT writing scores over 600: 27%; ACT scores over 24: 73%; SAT critical reading scores over 700: 10%; SAT math scores over 700: 6%; SAT writing scores over 700: 4%; ACT scores over 30: 23%.

Retention: 87% of full-time freshmen returned.

FACULTY
Total: 195, 72% full-time, 79% with terminal degrees.

Student/faculty ratio: 10:1.

ACADEMICS
Calendar: semesters. *Degrees:* bachelor's and master's.

Special study options: advanced placement credit, cooperative education, double majors, freshman honors college, honors programs, independent study, internships, off-campus study, part-time degree program, services for LD students, student-designed majors, study abroad, summer session for credit.

Computers: 231 computers/terminals and 500 ports are available on campus for general student use. Students can access the following: campus intranet, computer help desk, free student e-mail accounts, online (class) grades, online (class) registration, online (class) schedules, learning management system. Campuswide network is available. 100% of college-owned or -operated housing units are wired for high-speed Internet access. Wireless service is available via entire campus.

Library: Library, Archives, and Media Center. *Books:* 121,122 (physical), 100,678 (digital/electronic); *Serial titles:* 1,192 (physical), 67,806 (digital/electronic); *Databases:* 109. Weekly public service hours: 106; study areas open 24 hours, 5-7 days a week; students can reserve study rooms.

STUDENT LIFE
Housing options: coed, men-only, women-only, special housing for students with disabilities. Campus housing is university owned. Freshman campus housing is guaranteed.

Activities and organizations: drama/theater group, student-run newspaper, radio station, choral group, Dance Club, Humans vs. Zombies, InterVarsity Christian Fellowship, Habitat for Humanity, History Club.

Athletics Member NCAA. All Division III. ***Intercollegiate sports:*** baseball M, basketball M/W, crew M(c)/W(c), cross-country running M/W, equestrian sports M(c)/W(c), fencing M(c)/W(c), field hockey W, lacrosse M/W, rock climbing M(c)/W(c), rowing M/W, rugby M(c)/W(c), sailing M/W, soccer M/W, softball W(c), swimming and diving M/W, tennis M/W, ultimate Frisbee M(c)/W(c), volleyball W. ***Intramural sports:*** badminton M/W, basketball M/W, soccer M/W, volleyball M/W.

Campus security: 24-hour emergency response devices and patrols, late-night transport/escort service, controlled dormitory access.

Student services: health clinic, personal/psychological counseling.

COSTS & FINANCIAL AID
Costs (2016–17) ***Tuition:*** state resident $11,418 full-time, $200 per credit hour part-time; nonresident $26,566 full-time, $200 per credit hour part-time. Full-time tuition and fees vary according to course load. Part-time tuition and fees vary according to course load. ***Required fees:*** $2774 full-time. ***Room and board:*** $12,442; room only: $7184. Room and board charges vary according to board plan and housing facility. ***Payment plan:*** installment. ***Waivers:*** senior citizens and employees or children of employees.

Financial Aid Of all full-time matriculated undergraduates who enrolled in 2015, 1,202 applied for aid, 826 were judged to have need, 36 had their need fully met. 229 Federal Work-Study jobs (averaging $960). In 2015, 397 non-need-based awards were made. ***Average percent of need met:*** 67. ***Average financial aid package:*** $12,632. ***Average need-based loan:*** $4107. ***Average need-based gift aid:*** $9707. ***Average non-need-based aid:*** $3717. ***Average indebtedness upon graduation:*** $24,213.

APPLYING
Standardized Tests *Required:* SAT or ACT (for admission).

Options: electronic application, early action, deferred entrance.

Application fee: $50.

Required: essay or personal statement, high school transcript, 2 letters of recommendation, Common Application. ***Recommended:*** interview.

Application deadlines: 2/15 (freshmen), 4/1 (transfers), 11/15 (early action).

Notification: continuous until 4/1 (freshmen), continuous until 5/1 (transfers), 12/20 (early action).

CONTACT
Mr. David Boisvert, Interim Vice President for Enrollment, St. Mary's College of Maryland, 47645 College Drive, St. Mary's City, MD 20686-3001. *Phone:* 240-895-5000. *Toll-free phone:* 800-492-7181. *Fax:* 240-895-5001. *E-mail:* admissions@smcm.edu.

Salisbury University

Salisbury, Maryland

http://www.salisbury.edu/

- **State-supported** comprehensive, founded 1925, part of University System of Maryland
- **Small-town** 184-acre campus
- **Endowment** $60.4 million
- **Coed** 7,861 undergraduate students, 92% full-time, 57% women, 43% men
- **Moderately difficult** entrance level, 66% of applicants were admitted

UNDERGRAD STUDENTS
7,250 full-time, 611 part-time. Students come from 31 states and territories; 38 other countries; 14% are from out of state; 14% Black or African American, non-Hispanic/Latino; 4% Hispanic/Latino; 3% Asian, non-Hispanic/Latino; 0.2% Native Hawaiian or other Pacific Islander, non-Hispanic/Latino; 0.6% American Indian or Alaska Native, non-Hispanic/Latino; 3% Two or more races, non-Hispanic/Latino; 3% Race/ethnicity unknown; 2% international; 11% transferred in; 40% live on campus.

Freshmen:
Admission: 8,307 applied, 5,477 admitted, 1,329 enrolled. ***Average high school GPA:*** 3.67. ***Test scores:*** SAT critical reading scores over 500: 95%; SAT math scores over 500: 95%; SAT writing scores over 500: 91%; ACT scores over 18: 96%; SAT critical reading scores over 600: 34%; SAT math scores over 600: 40%; SAT writing scores over 600: 28%; ACT scores over 24: 39%; SAT critical reading scores over 700: 3%; SAT math scores over 700: 2%; SAT writing scores over 700: 2%; ACT scores over 30: 4%.

Retention: 84% of full-time freshmen returned.

FACULTY
Total: 637, 65% full-time, 58% with terminal degrees.

Student/faculty ratio: 16:1.

ACADEMICS
Calendar: 4-1-4. *Degrees:* bachelor's, master's, doctoral, and postbachelor's certificates.

Special study options: accelerated degree program, advanced placement credit, cooperative education, distance learning, double majors, English as a second language, freshman honors college, honors programs, independent study, internships, off-campus study, part-time degree program, services for LD students, student-designed majors, study abroad, summer session for credit. ***ROTC:*** Army (b), Air Force (c).

Unusual degree programs: 3-2 engineering with University of Maryland, College Park; Old Dominion University; Widener University; social work with University of Maryland Eastern Shore; biology and environmental marine science with University of Maryland Eastern Shore.

Computers: 750 computers/terminals and 3,552 ports are available on campus for general student use. Students can access the following: campus intranet, computer help desk, free student e-mail accounts, online (class) grades, online (class) registration, online (class) schedules, university accounts, student Web hosting. Campuswide network is available. 100% of college-owned or -operated housing units are wired for high-speed Internet access. Wireless service is available via entire campus.

Library: SU Libraries plus 1 other. *Books:* 205,155 (physical), 225 (digital/electronic); *Serial titles:* 722 (physical), 146 (digital/electronic); *Databases:* 106. Weekly public service hours: 111; study areas open 24 hours, 5-7 days a week; students can reserve study rooms.

STUDENT LIFE
Housing options: on-campus residence required through sophomore year; coed, special housing for students with disabilities. Campus housing is university owned. Freshman applicants given priority for college housing.

Activities and organizations: drama/theater group, student-run newspaper, radio and television station, choral group, Student Government Association, Radio (WXSU) / SU TV / The Flyer Newspaper, Student Organization for Activity Planning (SOAP), Campus Crusade for Christ, Union of African American Students, national fraternities, national sororities.

Athletics Member NCAA. All Division III. ***Intercollegiate sports:*** baseball M, basketball M/W, cross-country running M/W, field hockey W, football M, lacrosse M/W, soccer M/W, softball W, swimming and diving W, tennis M/W, track and field M/W, volleyball W. ***Intramural sports:*** basketball W, cheerleading M(c)/W(c), equestrian sports M(c)/W(c), field hockey M(c)/W(c), golf M(c)/W(c), gymnastics M(c)/W(c), ice hockey M(c), lacrosse M(c)/W(c), racquetball M/W, rock climbing M(c)/W(c), rugby M(c)/W(c), sailing M(c)/W(c), sand volleyball M, soccer M/W(c), softball M/W, ultimate Frisbee M(c)/W(c), volleyball M(c)/W, weight lifting M(c)/W(c).

Campus security: 24-hour emergency response devices and patrols, student patrols, late-night transport/escort service, controlled dormitory access, video surveillance system, shuttle buses, emergency notification system, self-defense education.

Student services: health clinic, personal/psychological counseling.

COSTS & FINANCIAL AID
Costs (2016–17) ***Tuition:*** state resident $6846 full-time, $281 per credit hour part-time; nonresident $15,258 full-time, $631 per credit hour part-time. ***Required fees:*** $2518 full-time, $84 per credit hour part-time. ***Room and board:*** $11,350; room only: $6550. Room and board charges vary according to board plan and housing facility. ***Payment plan:*** installment. ***Waivers:*** senior citizens and employees or children of employees.

Financial Aid Of all full-time matriculated undergraduates who enrolled in 2015, 5,263 applied for aid, 3,813 were judged to have need, 448 had their need fully met. 73 Federal Work-Study jobs (averaging $1779). In 2015, 872 non-need-based awards were made. ***Average percent of need met:*** 48. ***Average financial aid package:*** $8246. ***Average need-based loan:*** $4252. ***Average need-based gift aid:*** $6043. ***Average non-need-based aid:*** $2569. ***Average indebtedness upon graduation:*** $26,940.

APPLYING
Standardized Tests *Required for some:* SAT (for admission), ACT (for admission), SAT or ACT (for admission).

Options: electronic application, early admission, early decision, early action, deferred entrance.

Application fee: $50.

Required: essay or personal statement, minimum 2.0 GPA. ***Required for some:*** high school transcript.

Application deadlines: 1/15 (freshmen), rolling (transfers), 12/1 (early action).

Early decision deadline: 11/15.

Notification: 3/15 (freshmen), continuous (transfers), 12/15 (early decision), 1/15 (early action).

CONTACT
Ms. Elizabeth Skoglund, Director of Admissions, Salisbury University, Salisbury University - Admissions House, 1101 Camden Avenue, Salisbury, MD 21801. *Phone:* 410-543-6161. *Toll-free phone:* 888-543-0148. *Fax:* 410-546-6016. *E-mail:* admissions@salisbury.edu.

★ Stevenson University

Stevenson, Maryland

http://www.stevenson.edu/

- **Independent** comprehensive, founded 1952
- **Suburban** 163-acre campus with easy access to Baltimore
- **Endowment** $79.1 million
- **Coed**
- **Moderately difficult** entrance level

UNDERGRAD STUDENTS
Students come from 1 other country.

ACADEMICS
Calendar: semesters. *Degrees:* bachelor's and master's.

Special study options: academic remediation for entering students, accelerated degree program, adult/continuing education programs, advanced placement credit, cooperative education, distance learning, independent study, internships, off-campus study, part-time degree program, services for LD students, student-designed majors, study abroad, summer session for credit. ***ROTC:*** Army (c), Air Force (c).

Computers: 300 computers/terminals and 1,000 ports are available on campus for general student use. Students can access the following: campus intranet, computer help desk, free student e-mail accounts, online (class) grades, online (class) registration, online (class) schedules. Campuswide network is available. 100% of college-owned or -operated housing units are wired for high-speed Internet access. Wireless service is available via entire campus.

Library: Stevenson University Learning Resource Center-Greenspring Campus plus 1 other. Students can reserve study rooms.

STUDENT LIFE
Housing options: coed. Campus housing is university owned. Freshman applicants given priority for college housing.

Activities and organizations: drama/theater group, student-run newspaper, radio station, choral group, marching band, Relay for Life, Mustang Activities Programming, Black Student Union, American Chemical Society, Phi Sigma Sigma.

Athletics Member NCAA. All Division III. ***Intercollegiate sports:*** baseball M, basketball M/W, cheerleading M/W, cross-country running M/W, field hockey W, football M, golf M/W, ice hockey W, lacrosse M/W, soccer M/W, softball W, tennis M/W, track and field M/W, volleyball M/W. ***Intramural sports:*** badminton M/W, baseball M, basketball M/W, fencing M(c)/W(c), field hockey W, football M/W, skiing (downhill) M/W, softball W, table tennis M/W, tennis M/W, volleyball M.

Campus security: 24-hour emergency response devices and patrols, late-night transport/escort service, controlled dormitory access, patrols by trained security personnel during campus hours.

Student services: health clinic, personal/psychological counseling.

COSTS & FINANCIAL AID
Costs (2017–18) ***One-time required fee:*** $780. ***Tuition:*** $30,884 full-time. ***Room only:*** $8718. Room and board charges vary according to board plan. ***Payment plan:*** installment. ***Waivers:*** employees or children of employees.

Financial Aid Of all full-time matriculated undergraduates who enrolled in 2016, 2,691 applied for aid, 2,425 were judged to have need, 359 had their need fully met. 157 Federal Work-Study jobs (averaging $1655). In 2016, 551 non-need-based awards were made. ***Average percent of need met:*** 59. ***Average financial aid package:*** $21,222. ***Average need-based loan:*** $4256. ***Average need-based gift aid:*** $18,721. ***Average non-need-based aid:*** $12,969. ***Average indebtedness upon graduation:*** $34,324.

APPLYING
Standardized Tests *Required:* SAT or ACT (for admission).

Options: electronic application, deferred entrance.

Application fee: $40.

Required: essay or personal statement, high school transcript, 2 letters of recommendation. ***Recommended:*** interview.

Application deadlines: rolling (freshmen), rolling (transfers).

Notification: continuous (freshmen), continuous (transfers).

CONTACT
Mr. Mark Hergan, Vice President, Enrollment Management, Stevenson University, 1525 Greenspring Valley Road, Stevenson, MD 21153. *Phone:* 410-486-7001. *Toll-free phone:* 877-468-6852 (in-state); 877-468-3852 (out-of-state). *Fax:* 410-352-4440. *E-mail:* admissions@stevenson.edu.

See next page for display ad and page 1526 for the College Close-Up.

Stratford University

Baltimore, Maryland

http://www.stratford.edu/

- **Proprietary** comprehensive, founded 1972
- **Urban** 6-acre campus with easy access to Baltimore and Washington, DC
- **Coed** 318 undergraduate students, 9% full-time, 60% women, 40% men
- **Minimally difficult** entrance level

UNDERGRAD STUDENTS
30 full-time, 288 part-time. 78% Black or African American, non-Hispanic/Latino; 2% Hispanic/Latino; 1% Asian, non-Hispanic/Latino; 0.3% American Indian or Alaska Native, non-Hispanic/Latino; 0.3% Two or more races, non-Hispanic/Latino.

Freshmen:
Admission: 22 enrolled.

FACULTY
Total: 41, 37% full-time.

ACADEMICS
Calendar: quarters. *Degrees:* associate, bachelor's, and master's.
Special study options: academic remediation for entering students, accelerated degree program, adult/continuing education programs, cooperative education, independent study, internships, off-campus study, part-time degree program, services for LD students, summer session for credit.
Computers: Students can access the following: campus intranet, computer help desk, free student e-mail accounts, online (class) grades, online (class) registration, online (class) schedules. Campuswide network is available. Wireless service is available via entire campus.
Library: Learning Resource Center.

COSTS
Costs (2016–17) ***One-time required fee:*** $100. ***Tuition:*** $14,985 full-time, $1665 per course part-time. Full-time tuition and fees vary according to course level, course load, degree level, and program. Part-time tuition and fees vary according to course level, course load, degree level, and program. ***Payment plan:*** installment. ***Waivers:*** employees or children of employees.

APPLYING
Options: electronic application.
Application fee: $50.
Required: high school transcript, interview. ***Required for some:*** 1 letter of recommendation. ***Recommended:*** essay or personal statement.
Application deadlines: rolling (freshmen), rolling (transfers).
Notification: continuous (freshmen), continuous (transfers).

CONTACT
Admissions, Stratford University, 210 South Central Avenue, Baltimore, MD 21202. *Phone:* 410-752-4710. *Toll-free phone:* 800-624-9926 (in-state); 800-624-9926 Ext. 120 (out-of-state). *E-mail:* baadmissions@stratford.edu.

Strayer University–Anne Arundel Campus

Millersville, Maryland

http://www.strayer.edu/maryland/anne-arundel/

CONTACT
Strayer University–Anne Arundel Campus, 1520 Jabez Run, Millersville, MD 21108.

Strayer University–Owings Mills Campus

Owings Mills, Maryland

http://www.strayer.edu/maryland/owings-mills/

CONTACT
Strayer University–Owings Mills Campus, 500 Redland Court, Suite 100, Owings Mills, MD 21117.

Strayer University–Prince George's Campus

Suitland, Maryland

http://www.strayer.edu/maryland/prince-georges/

CONTACT

Strayer University–Prince George's Campus, 4710 Auth Place, First Floor, Suitland, MD 20746.

Strayer University–Rockville Campus

Rockville, Maryland

http://www.strayer.edu/maryland/rockville/

CONTACT

Strayer University–Rockville Campus, 4 Research Place, Suite 100, Rockville, MD 20850.

Strayer University–White Marsh Campus

Nottingham, Maryland

http://www.strayer.edu/maryland/white-marsh/

CONTACT

Strayer University–White Marsh Campus, 9920 Franklin Square Drive, Suite 200, Nottingham, MD 21236.

Towson University

Towson, Maryland

http://www.towson.edu/

- **State-supported** university, founded 1866, part of University System of Maryland
- **Suburban** 329-acre campus with easy access to Baltimore and Washington, DC
- **Endowment** $68.7 million
- **Coed** 19,198 undergraduate students, 88% full-time, 60% women, 40% men
- **Moderately difficult** entrance level, 74% of applicants were admitted

UNDERGRAD STUDENTS

16,893 full-time, 2,305 part-time. Students come from 45 states and territories; 71 other countries; 14% are from out of state; 19% Black or African American, non-Hispanic/Latino; 7% Hispanic/Latino; 6% Asian, non-Hispanic/Latino; 0.1% Native Hawaiian or other Pacific Islander, non-Hispanic/Latino; 0.2% American Indian or Alaska Native, non-Hispanic/Latino; 5% Two or more races, non-Hispanic/Latino; 2% Race/ethnicity unknown; 2% international; 12% transferred in; 26% live on campus.

Freshmen:

Admission: 11,897 applied, 8,773 admitted, 2,755 enrolled. ***Average high school GPA:*** 3.59. ***Test scores:*** SAT critical reading scores over 500: 71%; SAT math scores over 500: 72%; SAT writing scores over 500: 70%; ACT scores over 18: 97%; SAT critical reading scores over 600: 18%; SAT math scores over 600: 20%; SAT writing scores over 600: 15%; ACT scores over 24: 41%; SAT critical reading scores over 700: 2%; SAT math scores over 700: 2%; SAT writing scores over 700: 1%; ACT scores over 30: 4%.

Retention: 85% of full-time freshmen returned.

FACULTY

Total: 1,660, 55% full-time, 57% with terminal degrees.

Student/faculty ratio: 17:1.

ACADEMICS

Calendar: semesters. *Degrees:* bachelor's, master's, doctoral, post-master's, and postbachelor's certificates.

Special study options: academic remediation for entering students, adult/continuing education programs, advanced placement credit, cooperative education, distance learning, double majors, English as a second language, freshman honors college, honors programs, independent study, internships, off-campus study, part-time degree program, services for LD students, student-designed majors, study abroad, summer session for credit. ***ROTC:*** Army (c), Air Force (c).

Unusual degree programs: 3-2 engineering with University of Maryland, College Park; law with University of Baltimore.

Computers: 2,500 computers/terminals and 8,445 ports are available on campus for general student use. Students can access the following: computer help desk, free student e-mail accounts, online (class) grades, online (class) registration, online (class) schedules. Campuswide network is available. 100% of college-owned or -operated housing units are wired for high-speed Internet access. Wireless service is available via entire campus.

Library: Cook Library. *Books:* 400,658 (physical), 264,958 (digital/electronic); *Serial titles:* 525 (physical), 48,289 (digital/electronic); *Databases:* 192. Weekly public service hours: 109; study areas open 24 hours, 5-7 days a week; students can reserve study rooms.

STUDENT LIFE

Housing options: coed, special housing for students with disabilities. Campus housing is university owned and is provided by a third party. Freshman campus housing is guaranteed.

Activities and organizations: drama/theater group, student-run newspaper, radio and television station, choral group, marching band, University Residence Government, Latin American Student Organization, Black Student Union, Hillel, African Diaspora Club, national fraternities, national sororities.

Athletics Member NCAA. All Division I except football (Division I-A). ***Intercollegiate sports:*** baseball M(s), basketball M(s)/W(s), cross-country running W(s), field hockey W(s), golf M(s)/W(s), gymnastics W(s), lacrosse M(s)/W(s), soccer W(s), softball W(s), swimming and diving M(s)/W(s), tennis W(s), track and field W(s), ultimate Frisbee M/W, volleyball M/W(s). ***Intramural sports:*** badminton M/W, basketball M/W, cheerleading M(c)/W(c), cross-country running M(c)/W(c), equestrian sports M(c)/W(c), field hockey W(c), football M/W, golf M(c), gymnastics W(c), ice hockey M(c)/W(c), lacrosse M(c)/W(c), riflery M(c)/W(c), rugby M(c)/W(c), skiing (downhill) M(c)/W(c), soccer M/W, softball M/W, swimming and diving M(c)/W(c), tennis M(c)/W(c), track and field M(c)/W(c), ultimate Frisbee M(c)/W(c), volleyball M/W, water polo M(c)/W(c), wrestling M(c).

Campus security: 24-hour emergency response devices and patrols, late-night transport/escort service, controlled dormitory access.

Student services: health clinic, personal/psychological counseling, women's center.

COSTS & FINANCIAL AID

Costs (2016–17) ***Tuition:*** state resident $6560 full-time, $283 per credit hour part-time; nonresident $18,228 full-time, $768 per credit hour part-time. Full-time tuition and fees vary according to course load and location. Part-time tuition and fees vary according to course load and location. ***Required fees:*** $2848 full-time, $124 per credit hour part-time. ***Room and board:*** $11,754; room only: $6748. Room and board charges vary according to board plan and housing facility. ***Payment plan:*** installment. ***Waivers:*** senior citizens and employees or children of employees.

Financial Aid Of all full-time matriculated undergraduates who enrolled in 2016, 11,997 applied for aid, 9,220 were judged to have need, 878 had their need fully met. 603 Federal Work-Study jobs (averaging $1752). In 2016, 1082 non-need-based awards were made. ***Average percent of need met:*** 58. ***Average financial aid package:*** $10,201. ***Average need-based loan:*** $4096. ***Average need-based gift aid:*** $8715. ***Average non-need-based aid:*** $5362. ***Average indebtedness upon graduation:*** $25,483.

APPLYING

Standardized Tests *Required:* SAT or ACT (for admission).

Options: electronic application, early admission, deferred entrance.

Application fee: $45.

Required: essay or personal statement, high school transcript. ***Required for some:*** interview. ***Recommended:*** minimum 3.0 GPA, 2 letters of recommendation, resumé or activity list.

Application deadlines: 1/17 (freshmen), 1/17 (transfers).

Notification: continuous (freshmen), continuous (transfers).

CONTACT
Mr. David Fedorchak, Director of University Admissions, Towson University, 8000 York Road, Towson, MD 21252. *Phone:* 410-704-2113. *Fax:* 410-704-3030. *E-mail:* admissions@towson.edu.

United States Naval Academy

Annapolis, Maryland

http://www.usna.edu/

- **Federally supported** 4-year, founded 1845
- **Small-town** 338-acre campus with easy access to Baltimore and Washington, DC
- **Endowment** $223.3 million
- **Coed**
- **Very difficult** entrance level

FACULTY
Student/faculty ratio: 8:1.

ACADEMICS
Calendar: semesters. *Degree:* bachelor's.
Library: Nimitz Library. *Books:* 580,342 (physical), 425,564 (digital/electronic); *Serial titles:* 4,594 (physical), 71,757 (digital/electronic); *Databases:* 170. Weekly public service hours: 100.

STUDENT LIFE
Housing options: on-campus residence required through senior year; coed. Campus housing is university owned. Freshman campus housing is guaranteed.

Activities and organizations: drama/theater group, student-run radio station, choral group, marching band, Mountaineering Club, Semper Fi, Black Studies Club, Midshipmen Action Club, Martial Arts Club.

Athletics Member NCAA. All Division I except football (Division I-A).

Campus security: 24-hour emergency response devices and patrols, campus gate security.

Student services: health clinic, personal/psychological counseling, women's center, legal services.

COSTS
Costs (2016–17) ***Comprehensive fee:*** The Navy pays for the tuition, room and board, medical and dental care of Naval Academy midshipmen.

APPLYING
Standardized Tests *Required:* SAT or ACT (for admission).

Options: electronic application, early action.

Required: essay or personal statement, high school transcript, 2 letters of recommendation, interview, age 17-22, medical exam, authorized nomination, candidate fitness test.

CONTACT
Capt. Ann Kubera, Director of Admissions, United States Naval Academy, 52 King George Street, Annapolis, MD 21402. *Phone:* 410-293-4361. *Toll-free phone:* 888-249-7707. *Fax:* 410-293-4348. *E-mail:* webmail@usna.edu.

University of Baltimore

Baltimore, Maryland

http://www.ubalt.edu/

CONTACT
David Waggoner, Associate Vice President of Admission, University of Baltimore, 1420 North Charles Street, Baltimore, MD 21201.
Phone: 410-837-4777. *Fax:* 410-837-4793.
E-mail: admission@ubalt.edu.

University of Maryland, Baltimore County

Baltimore, Maryland

http://www.umbc.edu/

- **State-supported** university, founded 1963, part of University System of Maryland
- **Suburban** 530-acre campus with easy access to Washington, DC
- **Endowment** $83.0 million
- **Coed** 11,142 undergraduate students, 85% full-time, 45% women, 55% men
- **Moderately difficult** entrance level, 57% of applicants were admitted

UNDERGRAD STUDENTS
9,484 full-time, 1,658 part-time. Students come from 46 states and territories; 83 other countries; 5% are from out of state; 17% Black or African American, non-Hispanic/Latino; 7% Hispanic/Latino; 21% Asian, non-Hispanic/Latino; 0.1% Native Hawaiian or other Pacific Islander, non-Hispanic/Latino; 0.2% American Indian or Alaska Native, non-Hispanic/Latino; 4% Two or more races, non-Hispanic/Latino; 4% Race/ethnicity unknown; 4% international; 11% transferred in; 35% live on campus.

Freshmen:
Admission: 10,812 applied, 6,144 admitted, 1,538 enrolled. ***Average high school GPA:*** 3.75. ***Test scores:*** SAT critical reading scores over 500: 92%; SAT math scores over 500: 96%; SAT writing scores over 500: 88%; ACT scores over 18: 97%; SAT critical reading scores over 600: 49%; SAT math scores over 600: 63%; SAT writing scores over 600: 41%; ACT scores over 24: 79%; SAT critical reading scores over 700: 12%; SAT math scores over 700: 15%; SAT writing scores over 700: 8%; ACT scores over 30: 24%.

Retention: 87% of full-time freshmen returned.

FACULTY
Total: 811, 66% full-time, 69% with terminal degrees.
Student/faculty ratio: 19:1.

ACADEMICS
Calendar: 4-1-4. *Degrees:* bachelor's, master's, doctoral, and postbachelor's certificates.

Special study options: academic remediation for entering students, adult/continuing education programs, advanced placement credit, cooperative education, distance learning, double majors, English as a second language, external degree program, freshman honors college, honors programs, independent study, internships, off-campus study, part-time degree program, services for LD students, student-designed majors, study abroad, summer session for credit. ***ROTC:*** Army (c), Navy (b), Air Force (c).

Computers: 1,065 computers/terminals and 4,000 ports are available on campus for general student use. Students can access the following: campus intranet, computer help desk, free student e-mail accounts, online (class) grades, online (class) registration, online (class) schedules, billing, housing, parking, degree audit and advising. Campuswide network is available. 100% of college-owned or -operated housing units are wired for high-speed Internet access. Wireless service is available via entire campus.

Library: Albin O. Kuhn Library and Gallery. *Books:* 727,421 (physical), 171,487 (digital/electronic); *Serial titles:* 27,505 (physical), 14,296 (digital/electronic); *Databases:* 388. Weekly public service hours: 94; study areas open 24 hours, 5-7 days a week; students can reserve study rooms.

STUDENT LIFE
Housing options: coed, special housing for students with disabilities. Campus housing is university owned and is provided by a third party. Freshman campus housing is guaranteed.

Activities and organizations: drama/theater group, student-run newspaper, radio station, choral group, Student Government Association, Student Events Board, Retriever Weekly, Resident Student Association, WMBC, Campus Radio, national fraternities, national sororities.

Athletics Member NCAA. All Division I except field hockey (Division II). ***Intercollegiate sports:*** baseball M(s), basketball M(s)/W(s), crew M(c)/W(c), cross-country running M(s)/W(s), fencing M(c)/W(c), field hockey W, ice hockey M(c), lacrosse M(s)/W(s), rugby M(c)/W(c), sailing M(c)/W(c), skiing (downhill) M(c)/W(c), soccer M(s)/W(s), softball W(s), swimming and diving M(s)/W(s), track and field M(s)/W(s), ultimate Frisbee M(c)/W(c), volleyball M(c)/W(s), wrestling M(c). ***Intramural sports:*** basketball M/W, football M/W, lacrosse M(c)/W(c), soccer M(c)/W(c), softball M/W, tennis M(c)/W(c), volleyball M/W(c).

Campus security: 24-hour emergency response devices and patrols, late-night transport/escort service.

Student services: health clinic, personal/psychological counseling, women's center, legal services.

COSTS & FINANCIAL AID

Costs (2016–17) ***One-time required fee:*** $125. ***Tuition:*** state resident $8204 full-time, $341 per credit hour part-time; nonresident $21,432 full-time, $890 per credit hour part-time. Full-time tuition and fees vary according to location and program. Part-time tuition and fees vary according to location and program. ***Required fees:*** $3060 full-time, $134 per credit hour part-time. ***Room and board:*** $11,218; room only: $6796. Room and board charges vary according to board plan and housing facility. ***Payment plan:*** installment. ***Waivers:*** senior citizens and employees or children of employees.

Financial Aid Of all full-time matriculated undergraduates who enrolled in 2016, 6,316 applied for aid, 5,065 were judged to have need, 476 had their need fully met. 191 Federal Work-Study jobs (averaging $1934). 119 state and other part-time jobs (averaging $10,431). In 2016, 1362 non-need-based awards were made. ***Average percent of need met:*** 54. ***Average financial aid package:*** $10,023. ***Average need-based loan:*** $4334. ***Average need-based gift aid:*** $8058. ***Average non-need-based aid:*** $8666. ***Average indebtedness upon graduation:*** $25,505.

APPLYING

Standardized Tests *Required:* SAT (for admission), ACT (for admission), SAT or ACT (for admission).

Options: electronic application, early admission, early action, deferred entrance.

Application fee: $50.

Required: essay or personal statement, high school transcript. ***Recommended:*** minimum 3.0 GPA, 2 letters of recommendation.

Application deadlines: 2/1 (freshmen), 12/15 (transfers), 11/1 (early action).

Notification: continuous (freshmen), continuous (transfers), 12/15 (early action).

CONTACT

Mr. Dale Bittinger, Director of Admissions, University of Maryland, Baltimore County, 1000 Hilltop Circle, Baltimore, MD 21250. *Phone:* 410-455-2291. *Toll-free phone:* 800-UMBC-4U2 (in-state); 800-862-2402 (out-of-state). *Fax:* 410-455-1094. *E-mail:* admissions@umbc.edu.

University of Maryland, College Park

College Park, Maryland

http://www.maryland.edu/

- **State-supported** university, founded 1856, part of University System of Maryland
- **Suburban** 1335-acre campus with easy access to Baltimore and Washington, DC
- **Endowment** $448.5 million
- **Coed** 28,472 undergraduate students, 93% full-time, 47% women, 53% men
- **Moderately difficult** entrance level, 48% of applicants were admitted

UNDERGRAD STUDENTS

26,350 full-time, 2,122 part-time. Students come from 49 states and territories; 58 other countries; 21% are from out of state; 13% Black or African American, non-Hispanic/Latino; 10% Hispanic/Latino; 16% Asian, non-Hispanic/Latino; 0.1% Native Hawaiian or other Pacific Islander, non-Hispanic/Latino; 0.1% American Indian or Alaska Native, non-Hispanic/Latino; 4% Two or more races, non-Hispanic/Latino; 1% Race/ethnicity unknown; 4% international; 8% transferred in; 40% live on campus.

Freshmen:

Admission: 30,272 applied, 14,568 admitted, 4,551 enrolled. ***Average high school GPA:*** 4.2. ***Test scores:*** SAT critical reading scores over 500: 95%; SAT math scores over 500: 96%; ACT scores over 18: 99%; SAT critical reading scores over 600: 73%; SAT math scores over 600: 81%; ACT scores over 24: 93%; SAT critical reading scores over 700: 24%; SAT math scores over 700: 39%; ACT scores over 30: 58%.

Retention: 95% of full-time freshmen returned.

FACULTY

Total: 2,575, 70% full-time, 80% with terminal degrees.

Student/faculty ratio: 17:1.

ACADEMICS

Calendar: semesters. *Degrees:* certificates, bachelor's, master's, doctoral, post-master's, and postbachelor's certificates.

Special study options: academic remediation for entering students, accelerated degree program, adult/continuing education programs, advanced placement credit, cooperative education, distance learning, double majors, English as a second language, external degree program, honors programs, independent study, internships, off-campus study, part-time degree program, services for LD students, student-designed majors, study abroad, summer session for credit. ***ROTC:*** Army (b), Navy (c), Air Force (b).

Computers: 3,890 computers/terminals are available on campus for general student use. Students can access the following: campus intranet, computer help desk, free student e-mail accounts, online (class) grades, online (class) registration, online (class) schedules, student account information, financial aid summary. Campuswide network is available. 100% of college-owned or -operated housing units are wired for high-speed Internet access. Wireless service is available via entire campus.

Library: McKeldin Library plus 6 others. *Books:* 2.2 million (physical), 1.3 million (digital/electronic); *Serial titles:* 17,759 (physical), 137,842 (digital/electronic); *Databases:* 973. Weekly public service hours: 140; study areas open 24 hours, 5-7 days a week; students can reserve study rooms.

STUDENT LIFE

Housing options: coed, women-only, cooperative, special housing for students with disabilities. Campus housing is university owned and is provided by a third party. Freshman campus housing is guaranteed.

Activities and organizations: drama/theater group, student-run newspaper, radio and television station, choral group, marching band, Student Government Association, Residence Hall Association, Black Student Union, Asian-American Student Union/Jewish Student Union, Commuter Students Association, national fraternities, national sororities.

Athletics Member NCAA. All Division I. ***Intercollegiate sports:*** baseball M(s), basketball M(s)/W(s), cross-country running W(s), field hockey W(s), football M(s), golf M(s)/W(s), gymnastics W(s), lacrosse M(s)/W(s), soccer M(s)/W(s), softball W(s), swimming and diving M/W, tennis M/W, track and field M/W(s), volleyball W(s), water polo W(s), wrestling M(s). ***Intramural sports:*** badminton M(c)/W(c), baseball M(c), basketball M(c)/W(c), crew M(c)/W(c), cross-country running M(c)/W(c), equestrian sports M(c)/W(c), fencing M(c)/W(c), field hockey W(c), football M/W, golf M(c)/W(c), ice hockey M(c)/W(c), lacrosse M(c)/W(c), racquetball M(c)/W(c), rock climbing M(c)/W(c), rugby M(c)/W(c), sailing M(c)/W(c), soccer M(c)/W(c), softball W(c), squash M(c)/W(c), swimming and diving M(c)/W(c), table tennis M(c)/W(c), tennis M(c)/W(c), ultimate Frisbee M/W, volleyball M(c)/W(c), water polo M(c)/W(c), wrestling M(c).

Campus security: 24-hour emergency response devices and patrols, student patrols, late-night transport/escort service, controlled dormitory access, campus police, video camera surveillance.

Student services: health clinic, personal/psychological counseling, women's center, legal services.

COSTS & FINANCIAL AID

Costs (2016–17) ***Tuition:*** state resident $8315 full-time, $346 per credit hour part-time; nonresident $30,179 full-time, $1258 per credit hour part-time. Full-time tuition and fees vary according to location, program, and student level. Part-time tuition and fees vary according to course load, location, program, and student level. ***Required fees:*** $1866 full-time, $433 per term part-time. ***Room and board:*** $11,758; room only: $6944. Room and board charges vary according to board plan and housing facility.

Payment plans: installment, deferred payment. ***Waivers:*** employees or children of employees.

Financial Aid Of all full-time matriculated undergraduates who enrolled in 2015, 15,359 applied for aid, 10,711 were judged to have need, 1,649 had their need fully met. In 2015, 3381 non-need-based awards were made. ***Average percent of need met:*** 66. ***Average financial aid package:*** $12,001. ***Average need-based loan:*** $4511. ***Average need-based gift aid:*** $9444. ***Average non-need-based aid:*** $6671. ***Average indebtedness upon graduation:*** $27,559.

APPLYING

Standardized Tests *Required:* SAT or ACT (for admission).

Options: electronic application, early admission, early action, deferred entrance.

Application fee: $65.

Required: essay or personal statement, high school transcript. ***Required for some:*** resumé of activities, audition for music applicants, drawing requirement for architecture. ***Recommended:*** 2 letters of recommendation.

Application deadlines: 1/20 (freshmen), 6/1 (transfers), 11/1 (early action).

Notification: 4/1 (freshmen), continuous (transfers), 1/31 (early action).

CONTACT

Ms. Barbara Gill, Associate Vice President, Enrollment Management, University of Maryland, College Park, College Park, MD 20742.
Phone: 301-314-8385. *Toll-free phone:* 800-422-5867.
Fax: 301-314-9693.

University of Maryland Eastern Shore

Princess Anne, Maryland

http://www.umes.edu/

CONTACT

University of Maryland Eastern Shore, Princess Anne, MD 21853-1299.
Phone: 410-651-6410.

University of Maryland University College

Adelphi, Maryland

http://www.umuc.edu/

- **State-supported** comprehensive, founded 1947, part of University System of Maryland
- **Suburban** campus with easy access to Washington, DC
- **Coed** 44,219 undergraduate students, 22% full-time, 44% women, 56% men
- **Noncompetitive** entrance level, 100% of applicants were admitted

UNDERGRAD STUDENTS

9,530 full-time, 34,689 part-time. Students come from 52 states and territories; 53 other countries; 60% are from out of state; 26% Black or African American, non-Hispanic/Latino; 13% Hispanic/Latino; 5% Asian, non-Hispanic/Latino; 0.8% Native Hawaiian or other Pacific Islander, non-Hispanic/Latino; 0.5% American Indian or Alaska Native, non-Hispanic/Latino; 4% Two or more races, non-Hispanic/Latino; 8% Race/ethnicity unknown; 1% international; 21% transferred in.

Freshmen:

Admission: 1,981 applied, 1,981 admitted, 990 enrolled.

FACULTY

Total: 3,504, 6% full-time, 56% with terminal degrees.

Student/faculty ratio: 20:1.

ACADEMICS

Calendar: semesters. *Degrees:* certificates, associate, bachelor's, master's, doctoral, and postbachelor's certificates (offers primarily part-time evening and weekend degree programs at more than 30 off-campus locations in Maryland and the Washington, DC area, and more than 180 military communities in Europe and Asia with military enrollment not reflected in this profile; associate of arts program available to military students only).

Special study options: academic remediation for entering students, accelerated degree program, advanced placement credit, cooperative education, distance learning, double majors, external degree program, independent study, internships, off-campus study, part-time degree program, services for LD students, summer session for credit.

Computers: 448 computers/terminals are available on campus for general student use. Students can access the following: campus intranet, computer help desk, free student e-mail accounts, online (class) grades, online (class) registration, online (class) schedules. Campuswide network is available. Wireless service is available via entire campus.

Library: Information and Library Services plus 1 other. *Books:* 1,234 (physical), 110,012 (digital/electronic).

STUDENT LIFE

Housing options: college housing not available.

Campus security: 24-hour emergency response devices and patrols, late-night transport/escort service.

COSTS & FINANCIAL AID

Costs (2017–18) ***Tuition:*** state resident $6816 full-time, $284 per credit hour part-time; nonresident $11,976 full-time, $499 per credit hour part-time. ***Required fees:*** $360 full-time. ***Payment plan:*** installment. ***Waivers:*** senior citizens and employees or children of employees.

Financial Aid Of all full-time matriculated undergraduates who enrolled in 2015, 5,675 applied for aid, 5,375 were judged to have need, 44 had their need fully met. ***Average percent of need met:*** 30. ***Average financial aid package:*** $7217. ***Average need-based loan:*** $4254. ***Average need-based gift aid:*** $4711.

APPLYING

Options: electronic application, deferred entrance.

Application fee: $50.

Required: high school transcript.

Application deadlines: rolling (freshmen), rolling (transfers).

Notification: continuous (freshmen), continuous (transfers).

CONTACT

University of Maryland University College, 3501 University Boulevard East, Adelphi, MD 20783. *Phone:* 800-888-UMUC (8682). *Toll-free phone:* 800-888-8682. *E-mail:* enroll@umuc.edu.

Washington Adventist University

Takoma Park, Maryland

http://www.wau.edu/

CONTACT

Elaine Oliver, Associate Vice President, Enrollment Services, Washington Adventist University, 7600 Flower Avenue, Takoma Park, MD 20912.
Phone: 301-891-4502. *Toll-free phone:* 800-835-4212.
Fax: 301-971-4230. *E-mail:* enroll@cuc.edu.

Washington College

Chestertown, Maryland

http://www.washcoll.edu/

- **Independent** 4-year, founded 1782
- **Small-town** 140-acre campus with easy access to Baltimore and Washington, DC
- **Endowment** $198.4 million
- **Coed** 1,479 undergraduate students, 99% full-time, 56% women, 44% men
- **Moderately difficult** entrance level, 49% of applicants were admitted

UNDERGRAD STUDENTS

1,458 full-time, 21 part-time. Students come from 39 states and territories; 30 other countries; 53% are from out of state; 7% Black or African American, non-Hispanic/Latino; 5% Hispanic/Latino; 3% Asian, non-Hispanic/Latino; 0.1% Native Hawaiian or other Pacific Islander, non-Hispanic/Latino; 0.6% American Indian or Alaska Native, non-Hispanic/Latino; 1% Two or more races, non-Hispanic/Latino; 5% Race/ethnicity unknown; 11% international; 2% transferred in; 85% live on campus.

Freshmen:
Admission: 6,720 applied, 3,295 admitted, 410 enrolled. ***Average high school GPA:*** 3.63. ***Test scores:*** SAT critical reading scores over 500: 81%; SAT math scores over 500: 77%; ACT scores over 18: 99%; SAT critical reading scores over 600: 39%; SAT math scores over 600: 36%; ACT scores over 24: 71%; SAT critical reading scores over 700: 9%; SAT math scores over 700: 5%; ACT scores over 30: 12%.

Retention: 86% of full-time freshmen returned.

FACULTY
Total: 182, 59% full-time, 72% with terminal degrees.

Student/faculty ratio: 11:1.

ACADEMICS
Calendar: semesters. *Degree:* bachelor's.

Special study options: accelerated degree program, double majors, English as a second language, honors programs, independent study, internships, off-campus study, part-time degree program, services for LD students, student-designed majors, study abroad, summer session for credit.

Unusual degree programs: 3-2 engineering with Columbia University; nursing with University of Maryland; pharmacy with University of Maryland.

Computers: 100 computers/terminals and 1,450 ports are available on campus for general student use. Students can access the following: campus intranet, computer help desk, free student e-mail accounts, online (class) grades, online (class) registration, online (class) schedules. Campuswide network is available. 100% of college-owned or -operated housing units are wired for high-speed Internet access. Wireless service is available via entire campus.

Library: Clifton M. Miller Library.

STUDENT LIFE
Housing options: on-campus residence required through sophomore year; coed, men-only, women-only, special housing for students with disabilities. Campus housing is university owned. Freshman campus housing is guaranteed.

Activities and organizations: drama/theater group, student-run newspaper, radio station, choral group, Writers Union, Student Government Association, Hands Out, Omicron Delta Kappa, Dale Adams Society, national fraternities, national sororities.

Athletics Member NCAA. All Division III. ***Intercollegiate sports:*** baseball M, basketball M/W, cheerleading W(c), crew M/W, equestrian sports M(c)/W(c), field hockey W, ice hockey M(c), lacrosse M/W, rugby M(c)/W(c), sailing M/W, soccer M/W, softball W, swimming and diving M/W, tennis M/W, volleyball W, water polo M(c)/W(c). ***Intramural sports:*** badminton M/W, basketball M/W, football M/W, lacrosse M(c), racquetball M/W, rugby M/W, sailing M/W, soccer M/W, squash M/W, table tennis M/W, tennis M/W, ultimate Frisbee M/W, volleyball M/W.

Campus security: 24-hour emergency response devices and patrols, student patrols, late-night transport/escort service, controlled dormitory access, LiveSafe mobile app.

Student services: health clinic, personal/psychological counseling.

COSTS & FINANCIAL AID
Costs (2017–18) ***Comprehensive fee:*** $55,740 includes full-time tuition ($43,702), mandatory fees ($998), and room and board ($11,040). Part-time tuition: $1785 per credit hour. Part-time tuition and fees vary according to course load. No tuition increase for student's term of enrollment. ***College room only:*** $5608. Room and board charges vary according to board plan, housing facility, and location. ***Payment plans:*** tuition prepayment, installment. ***Waivers:*** employees or children of employees.

Financial Aid Of all full-time matriculated undergraduates who enrolled in 2015, 946 applied for aid, 825 were judged to have need, 263 had their need fully met. 117 Federal Work-Study jobs (averaging $1200). In 2015, 440 non-need-based awards were made. ***Average percent of need met:*** 86. ***Average financial aid package:*** $31,250. ***Average need-based loan:*** $4472. ***Average need-based gift aid:*** $27,166. ***Average non-need-based aid:*** $16,766. ***Average indebtedness upon graduation:*** $36,991.

APPLYING
Standardized Tests *Required:* SAT or ACT (for admission).

Options: electronic application, early admission, early decision, early action, deferred entrance.

Required: essay or personal statement, high school transcript, 1 letter of recommendation. ***Required for some:*** interview. ***Recommended:*** interview.

Application deadlines: 2/15 (freshmen), rolling (transfers), 12/1 (early action).

Early decision deadline: 11/15 (for plan 1), 12/15 (for plan 2).

Notification: continuous (freshmen), continuous (transfers), 12/15 (early decision plan 1), 1/15 (early decision plan 2), 1/15 (early action).

CONTACT
Mr. Bradly Booke, Assistant Vice President of Admissions and Financial Aid, Washington College, 300 Washington Avenue, Chestertown, MD 21620. *Phone:* 410-778-7700. *Toll-free phone:* 800-422-1782. *Fax:* 410-778-7287. *E-mail:* wc_admissions@washcoll.edu.

Yeshiva College of the Nation's Capital

Silver Spring, Maryland

http://www.yeshiva.edu/

CONTACT
Yeshiva College of the Nation's Capital, 1216 Arcola Avenue, Silver Spring, MD 20902.

MASSACHUSETTS

American International College

Springfield, Massachusetts

http://www.aic.edu/

- **Independent** comprehensive, founded 1885
- **Urban** 58-acre campus
- **Endowment** $15.0 million
- **Coed** 1,424 undergraduate students, 95% full-time, 60% women, 40% men
- **Minimally difficult** entrance level, 69% of applicants were admitted

UNDERGRAD STUDENTS
1,347 full-time, 77 part-time. Students come from 38 states and territories; 20 other countries; 60% are from out of state; 25% Black or African American, non-Hispanic/Latino; 16% Hispanic/Latino; 1% Asian, non-Hispanic/Latino; 0.6% Native Hawaiian or other Pacific Islander, non-Hispanic/Latino; 0.4% American Indian or Alaska Native, non-Hispanic/Latino; 2% Two or more races, non-Hispanic/Latino; 13% Race/ethnicity unknown; 4% international; 9% transferred in; 52% live on campus.

Freshmen:
Admission: 1,906 applied, 1,321 admitted, 322 enrolled. ***Average high school GPA:*** 2.85. ***Test scores:*** SAT critical reading scores over 500: 22%; SAT math scores over 500: 26%; SAT writing scores over 500: 17%; ACT scores over 18: 68%; SAT critical reading scores over 600: 3%; SAT math scores over 600: 4%; SAT writing scores over 600: 2%; ACT scores over 24: 11%; ACT scores over 30: 1%.

Retention: 69% of full-time freshmen returned.

FACULTY
Total: 255, 28% full-time, 47% with terminal degrees.

Student/faculty ratio: 17:1.

ACADEMICS
Calendar: semesters. *Degrees:* associate, bachelor's, master's, doctoral, post-master's, and postbachelor's certificates.

Special study options: academic remediation for entering students, accelerated degree program, adult/continuing education programs, advanced placement credit, distance learning, double majors, honors programs, independent study, internships, off-campus study, part-time degree program, services for LD students, study abroad, summer session for credit. ***ROTC:*** Army (c), Air Force (c).

Unusual degree programs: 3-2 business administration; education.

Computers: 230 computers/terminals and 100 ports are available on campus for general student use. Students can access the following: campus intranet, computer help desk, free student e-mail accounts, online (class) grades, online (class) registration, online (class) schedules. Campuswide network is available. 100% of college-owned or -operated housing units are wired for high-speed Internet access. Wireless service is available via entire campus.

Library: James J. Shea Sr. Library. *Books:* 56,511 (physical), 179,160 (digital/electronic); *Serial titles:* 183 (physical), 962 (digital/electronic); *Databases:* 64. Weekly public service hours: 100; students can reserve study rooms.

STUDENT LIFE

Housing options: on-campus residence required for freshman year; coed, women-only. Campus housing is university owned. Freshman campus housing is guaranteed.

Activities and organizations: drama/theater group, student-run newspaper, choral group, Student Activities Committee, Best Buddies Program, PRIDE (Persons Ready in Defense of Ebony), Student Government, School newspaper.

Athletics Member NCAA. All Division II except ice hockey (Division I), rugby (Division I). ***Intercollegiate sports:*** baseball M(s), basketball M(s)/W(s), cross-country running M(s)/W(s), field hockey W(s), football M(s), golf M(s)/W(s), ice hockey M(s), lacrosse M(s)/W(s), rugby M(s)(c)/W(s), soccer M(s)/W(s), softball W(s), tennis W(s), track and field M(s)/W(s), volleyball W(s), wrestling M(s). ***Intramural sports:*** basketball M/W, cheerleading M(c)/W(c), softball M/W, volleyball M/W.

Campus security: 24-hour emergency response devices and patrols, late-night transport/escort service, controlled dormitory access.

Student services: health clinic, personal/psychological counseling.

COSTS & FINANCIAL AID

Costs (2017–18) ***Comprehensive fee:*** $48,020 includes full-time tuition ($34,470) and room and board ($13,550). Full-time tuition and fees vary according to course load and program. Part-time tuition: $710 per credit hour. Part-time tuition and fees vary according to course load. ***Required fees:*** $30 per term part-time. ***College room only:*** $6930. Room and board charges vary according to board plan and housing facility. ***Payment plan:*** installment. ***Waivers:*** employees or children of employees.

Financial Aid Of all full-time matriculated undergraduates who enrolled in 2013, 1,394 applied for aid, 1,333 were judged to have need, 159 had their need fully met. 466 Federal Work-Study jobs (averaging $640). 161 state and other part-time jobs (averaging $1190). ***Average percent of need met:*** 70. ***Average financial aid package:*** $23,969. ***Average need-based loan:*** $4133. ***Average need-based gift aid:*** $19,916. ***Average indebtedness upon graduation:*** $35,587.

APPLYING

Standardized Tests *Required:* SAT or ACT (for admission).

Options: electronic application, deferred entrance.

Required: high school transcript. ***Required for some:*** interview. ***Recommended:*** essay or personal statement, 1 letter of recommendation.

Application deadlines: rolling (freshmen), rolling (transfers).

Notification: continuous (freshmen), continuous (transfers).

CONTACT

Mr. Jonathan Scully, Director of Undergraduate Admissions, American International College, 1000 State Street, Springfield, MA 01109-3189. *Phone:* 413-205-3270. *Toll-free phone:* 800-242-3142. *Fax:* 413-205-3051. *E-mail:* jonathan.scully@aic.edu.

Amherst College

Amherst, Massachusetts

http://www.amherst.edu/

- **Independent** 4-year, founded 1821
- **Small-town** 1020-acre campus
- **Coed** 1,849 undergraduate students, 100% full-time, 50% women, 50% men
- **Most difficult** entrance level, 14% of applicants were admitted

UNDERGRAD STUDENTS

1,849 full-time. Students come from 54 other countries; 87% are from out of state; 12% Black or African American, non-Hispanic/Latino; 14% Hispanic/Latino; 14% Asian, non-Hispanic/Latino; 0.4% American Indian or Alaska Native, non-Hispanic/Latino; 5% Two or more races, non-Hispanic/Latino; 3% Race/ethnicity unknown; 9% international; 0.9% transferred in; 98% live on campus.

Freshmen:

Admission: 8,406 applied, 1,161 admitted, 471 enrolled. ***Test scores:*** SAT critical reading scores over 500: 100%; SAT math scores over 500: 100%; SAT writing scores over 500: 100%; ACT scores over 18: 100%; SAT critical reading scores over 600: 99%; SAT math scores over 600: 99%; SAT writing scores over 600: 97%; ACT scores over 24: 100%; SAT critical reading scores over 700: 68%; SAT math scores over 700: 67%; SAT writing scores over 700: 70%; ACT scores over 30: 89%.

Retention: 96% of full-time freshmen returned.

FACULTY

Total: 291, 72% full-time, 84% with terminal degrees.

Student/faculty ratio: 8:1.

ACADEMICS

Calendar: semesters. *Degree:* bachelor's.

Special study options: double majors, independent study, off-campus study, services for LD students, student-designed majors, study abroad. ***ROTC:*** Army (c), Air Force (c).

Unusual degree programs: 3-2 engineering with Dartmouth College.

Computers: Students can access the following: campus intranet, computer help desk, free student e-mail accounts, online (class) grades, online (class) registration, online (class) schedules. Campuswide network is available. 100% of college-owned or -operated housing units are wired for high-speed Internet access. Wireless service is available via entire campus.

Library: Robert Frost Library plus 5 others.

STUDENT LIFE

Housing options: on-campus residence required for freshman year; coed, cooperative, special housing for students with disabilities. Campus housing is university owned. Freshman campus housing is guaranteed.

Activities and organizations: drama/theater group, student-run newspaper, radio station, choral group, Association of Amherst Students, Black Students Union, Student Publications (e.g., Amherst Student, Indicator), A Capella Groups (e.g., Zumbye's, Bluestockings), Amherst Dance.

Athletics Member NCAA. All Division III. ***Intercollegiate sports:*** baseball M, basketball M/W, cheerleading W(c), crew M(c)/W(c), cross-country running M/W, equestrian sports M(c)/W(c), fencing M(c)/W(c), field hockey W, football M, golf M/W, ice hockey M/W, lacrosse M/W, rugby M(c)/W(c), sailing M(c)/W(c), skiing (downhill) M(c)/W(c), soccer M/W, softball W, squash M/W, swimming and diving M/W, tennis M/W, track and field M/W, ultimate Frisbee M(c)/W(c), volleyball M(c)/W, water polo M(c)/W(c), wrestling M(c)/W(c). ***Intramural sports:*** badminton M/W, basketball M/W, golf M/W, ice hockey M/W, rock climbing M/W, soccer M/W, softball M/W, squash M/W, table tennis M/W, tennis M/W, track and field M/W, volleyball M/W.

Campus security: 24-hour emergency response devices and patrols, student patrols, late-night transport/escort service, controlled dormitory access.

Student services: health clinic, personal/psychological counseling, women's center.

COSTS & FINANCIAL AID

Costs (2016–17) ***Comprehensive fee:*** $66,186 includes full-time tuition ($51,620), mandatory fees ($856), and room and board ($13,710). ***College room only:*** $7430. ***Payment plan:*** installment.

Financial Aid Of all full-time matriculated undergraduates who enrolled in 2016, 1,237 applied for aid, 1,066 were judged to have need, 1,066 had their need fully met. 834 Federal Work-Study jobs (averaging $1482). 230 state and other part-time jobs (averaging $2256). ***Average percent of need met:*** 100. ***Average financial aid package:*** $51,775. ***Average need-based loan:*** $478. ***Average need-based gift aid:*** $50,380. ***Average indebtedness upon graduation:*** $18,662.

APPLYING
Standardized Tests *Required:* SAT or ACT (for admission).
Options: electronic application, early admission, early decision, deferred entrance.
Application fee: $60.
Required: essay or personal statement, high school transcript, 3 letters of recommendation, Amherst College Supplement.
Application deadlines: 1/1 (freshmen), 3/1 (transfers).
Early decision deadline: 11/15.
Notification: 4/1 (freshmen), 5/15 (transfers), 12/15 (early decision).

CONTACT
Katharine L. Fretwell, Dean of Admission and Financial Aid, Amherst College, PO Box 5000, Amherst, MA 01002-5000. *Phone:* 413-542-2328. *Fax:* 413-542-2040. *E-mail:* admission@amherst.edu.

★ Anna Maria College
Paxton, Massachusetts
http://www.annamaria.edu/

- **Independent Roman Catholic** comprehensive, founded 1946
- **Rural** 192-acre campus with easy access to Boston
- **Endowment** $4.3 million
- **Coed**
- **Minimally difficult** entrance level

FACULTY
Student/faculty ratio: 11:1.

ACADEMICS
Calendar: semesters. *Degrees:* certificates, bachelor's, master's, doctoral, post-master's, and postbachelor's certificates.
Library: Mondor-Eagen Library. *Books:* 59,659 (physical), 132,939 (digital/electronic); *Databases:* 98.

STUDENT LIFE
Housing options: coed, special housing for students with disabilities. Campus housing is university owned. Freshman campus housing is guaranteed.
Activities and organizations: drama/theater group, choral group, marching band, Habitat for Humanity, Social Action Group, Chorus Club, Alana, Programming Board - AMCAB.
Athletics Member NCAA. All Division III.
Campus security: 24-hour emergency response devices and patrols, late-night transport/escort service, controlled dormitory access.
Student services: health clinic, personal/psychological counseling.

COSTS & FINANCIAL AID
Costs (2016–17) ***Comprehensive fee:*** $49,620 includes full-time tuition ($33,840), mandatory fees ($2270), and room and board ($13,510). Full-time tuition and fees vary according to course load, degree level, and program. Part-time tuition: $1410 per credit. Part-time tuition and fees vary according to course load, degree level, and program. ***Room and board:*** Room and board charges vary according to board plan and housing facility.
Financial Aid Of all full-time matriculated undergraduates who enrolled in 2014, 721 applied for aid, 678 were judged to have need, 107 had their need fully met. In 2014, 37 non-need-based awards were made. ***Average percent of need met:*** 66. ***Average financial aid package:*** $25,076. ***Average need-based loan:*** $4489. ***Average need-based gift aid:*** $8963. ***Average non-need-based aid:*** $9947.

APPLYING
Options: electronic application, deferred entrance.
Application fee: $25.
Required: high school transcript, minimum 2.0 GPA. ***Required for some:*** essay or personal statement, audition for music programs, portfolio for art programs. ***Recommended:*** 1 letter of recommendation, interview.

CONTACT
Mr. Peter Miller, Dean of Admissions and Financial Aid, Anna Maria College, 50 Sunset Lane, Paxton, MA 01612. *Phone:* 508-849-3586. *Fax:* 508-849-3362. *E-mail:* admissions@annamaria.edu.

See previous page for display ad and page 1282 for the College Close-Up.

★ Assumption College

Worcester, Massachusetts

http://www.assumption.edu/

- **Independent Roman Catholic** comprehensive, founded 1904
- **Suburban** 180-acre campus with easy access to Boston
- **Endowment** $101.1 million
- **Coed** 1,987 undergraduate students, 99% full-time, 59% women, 41% men
- **Moderately difficult** entrance level, 76% of applicants were admitted

UNDERGRAD STUDENTS
1,975 full-time, 12 part-time. Students come from 27 states and territories; 20 other countries; 35% are from out of state; 6% Black or African American, non-Hispanic/Latino; 7% Hispanic/Latino; 2% Asian, non-Hispanic/Latino; 0.1% Native Hawaiian or other Pacific Islander, non-Hispanic/Latino; 0.1% American Indian or Alaska Native, non-Hispanic/Latino; 2% Two or more races, non-Hispanic/Latino; 6% Race/ethnicity unknown; 2% international; 2% transferred in; 87% live on campus.

Freshmen:
Admission: 4,769 applied, 3,614 admitted, 570 enrolled. ***Average high school GPA:*** 3.38. ***Test scores:*** SAT critical reading scores over 500: 81%; SAT math scores over 500: 81%; ACT scores over 18: 98%; SAT critical reading scores over 600: 25%; SAT math scores over 600: 30%; ACT scores over 24: 78%; SAT critical reading scores over 700: 2%; SAT math scores over 700: 2%; ACT scores over 30: 5%.

Retention: 83% of full-time freshmen returned.

FACULTY
Total: 224, 64% full-time, 79% with terminal degrees.

Student/faculty ratio: 12:1.

ACADEMICS
Calendar: semesters. *Degrees:* bachelor's, master's, post-master's, and postbachelor's certificates.

Special study options: advanced placement credit, double majors, honors programs, independent study, internships, off-campus study, part-time degree program, services for LD students, student-designed majors, study abroad, summer session for credit. ***ROTC:*** Army (c), Air Force (c).

Unusual degree programs: 3-2 business administration; engineering with University of Notre Dame; forestry with Duke University; nursing with Massachusetts College of Pharmacy and Health Sciences; special education, rehabilitation counseling, school counseling; law with Duquesne U School of Law, Western NE College School of Law, Vermont Law School; optometry with New England College of Optometry; osteopathic medicine with Des Moines U; environmental science management with Duke U.

Computers: 361 computers/terminals and 1,900 ports are available on campus for general student use. Students can access the following: campus intranet, computer help desk, free student e-mail accounts, online (class) grades, online (class) registration, online (class) schedules. Campuswide network is available. 100% of college-owned or -operated housing units are wired for high-speed Internet access. Wireless service is available via entire campus.

Library: Emmanuel d'Alzon Library. *Books:* 219,895 (physical), 8,579 (digital/electronic); *Serial titles:* 396 (physical), 318 (digital/electronic); *Databases:* 98. Weekly public service hours: 106; students can reserve study rooms.

STUDENT LIFE
Housing options: coed, women-only, special housing for students with disabilities. Campus housing is university owned. Freshman campus housing is guaranteed.

Activities and organizations: drama/theater group, student-run newspaper, television station, choral group, Volunteer center, Campus Activities Board, Student Government, Campus Ministry, intramural sports.

Athletics Member NCAA. All Division II. ***Intercollegiate sports:*** baseball M, basketball M(s)/W(s), cheerleading M(c)/W(c), cross-country running M/W, field hockey W, football M, golf M, ice hockey M, lacrosse M/W, rowing W, soccer M/W, softball W, swimming and diving W, tennis M/W, track and field M/W, volleyball M(c)/W. ***Intramural sports:*** badminton M/W, basketball M/W, equestrian sports M(c)/W(c), football M/W, golf M/W, ice hockey M/W, racquetball M/W, soccer M/W, softball M/W, swimming and diving M/W, table tennis M/W, tennis M/W, volleyball M/W.

Campus security: 24-hour emergency response devices and patrols, student patrols, late-night transport/escort service, controlled dormitory access, front gate security, well-lit pathways.

Student services: health clinic, personal/psychological counseling.

COSTS & FINANCIAL AID

Costs (2016–17) ***Comprehensive fee:*** $47,920 includes full-time tuition ($35,510), mandatory fees ($750), and room and board ($11,660). Full-time tuition and fees vary according to course load and reciprocity agreements. Part-time tuition: $1184 per credit hour. Part-time tuition and fees vary according to course load. No tuition increase for student's term of enrollment. ***College room only:*** $7356. Room and board charges vary according to housing facility. ***Waivers:*** employees or children of employees.

Financial Aid Of all full-time matriculated undergraduates who enrolled in 2016, 1,623 applied for aid, 1,461 were judged to have need, 382 had their need fully met. 309 Federal Work-Study jobs (averaging $1341). In 2016, 416 non-need-based awards were made. ***Average percent of need met:*** 76. ***Average financial aid package:*** $26,539. ***Average need-based loan:*** $4674. ***Average need-based gift aid:*** $21,546. ***Average non-need-based aid:*** $15,079. ***Financial aid deadline:*** 2/15.

APPLYING

Options: electronic application, early action, deferred entrance.

Application fee: $50.

Required: essay or personal statement, high school transcript, 1 letter of recommendation. ***Recommended:*** interview.

Application deadlines: 2/15 (freshmen), 7/1 (transfers), 11/1 (early action).

Notification: continuous (freshmen), continuous (transfers), 12/15 (early action).

CONTACT

Ms. Kathleen Murphy, Dean of Enrollment, Assumption College, 500 Salisbury Street, Worcester, MA 01609-1296. *Phone:* 508-767-7110. *Toll-free phone:* 866-477-7776. *Fax:* 508-799-4412. *E-mail:* admiss@assumption.edu.

See previous page for display ad and page 1286 for the College Close-Up.

★ Babson College

Wellesley, Massachusetts

http://www.babson.edu/

- **Independent** comprehensive, founded 1919
- **Suburban** 370-acre campus with easy access to Boston
- **Endowment** $348.6 million
- **Coed**
- **Very difficult** entrance level

FACULTY

Student/faculty ratio: 14:1.

ACADEMICS

Calendar: semesters. *Degrees:* bachelor's, master's, and post-master's certificates.

Library: Horn Library plus 1 other.

STUDENT LIFE

Housing options: on-campus residence required for freshman year; coed, men-only, special housing for students with disabilities. Campus housing is university owned. Freshman campus housing is guaranteed.

Activities and organizations: drama/theater group, student-run newspaper, radio station, choral group, national fraternities, national sororities.

Athletics Member NCAA. All Division III.

Campus security: 24-hour emergency response devices and patrols, late-night transport/escort service, controlled dormitory access.

Student services: health clinic, personal/psychological counseling, women's center.

FINANCIAL AID
Financial Aid Of all full-time matriculated undergraduates who enrolled in 2016, 1,072 applied for aid, 957 were judged to have need, 504 had their need fully met. In 2016, 152 non-need-based awards were made. ***Average percent of need met:*** 97. ***Average financial aid package:*** $40,358. ***Average need-based loan:*** $5041. ***Average need-based gift aid:*** $37,388. ***Average non-need-based aid:*** $17,687. ***Average indebtedness upon graduation:*** $36,556. ***Financial aid deadline:*** 2/1.

APPLYING
Standardized Tests *Required:* SAT or ACT (for admission). *Recommended:* TOEFL or IELTS for non-native English speakers.

Options: electronic application, early decision, early action, deferred entrance.

Application fee: $75.

Required: essay or personal statement, high school transcript, 2 letters of recommendation. ***Recommended:*** interview.

CONTACT
Mrs. Adrienne Ramsey, Associate Director of Undergraduate Admission, Babson College, Lunder Undergraduate Admission Center, Babson Park, MA 02457-0310. *Phone:* 781-239-5522. *Toll-free phone:* 800-488-3696. *Fax:* 781-239-4135. *E-mail:* ugradadmission@babson.edu.

See previous page for display ad and page 1288 for the College Close-Up.

Bard College at Simon's Rock
Great Barrington, Massachusetts
http://www.simons-rock.edu/

- **Independent** 4-year, founded 1964
- **Small-town** 210-acre campus with easy access to Boston, New York City
- **Coed**
- **Moderately difficult** entrance level

FACULTY
Student/faculty ratio: 6:1.

ACADEMICS
Calendar: semesters. *Degrees:* associate and bachelor's.
Library: Alumni Library. *Books:* 68,511 (physical), 3,850 (digital/electronic); *Serial titles:* 120 (physical), 41,033 (digital/electronic); *Databases:* 22. Weekly public service hours: 106.

STUDENT LIFE
Housing options: on-campus residence required through senior year; coed, men-only, women-only. Campus housing is university owned. Freshman campus housing is guaranteed.

Activities and organizations: drama/theater group, student-run newspaper, choral group, Black Student Union, QueerSA, Student Action Service Learning, U.S.O. (Untitled Student Organization), Boffing.

Campus security: 24-hour emergency response devices and patrols, controlled dormitory access, security escorts, late night transport.

Student services: health clinic, personal/psychological counseling, women's center.

COSTS & FINANCIAL AID
Costs (2016–17) ***Comprehensive fee:*** $65,795 includes full-time tuition ($50,600), mandatory fees ($1135), and room and board ($14,060). Full-time tuition and fees vary according to course load. Part-time tuition: $2110 per credit hour. Part-time tuition and fees vary according to course load.

Financial Aid Of all full-time matriculated undergraduates who enrolled in 2011, 271 applied for aid, 245 were judged to have need, 38 had their need fully met. 156 Federal Work-Study jobs (averaging $1000). In 2011, 73 non-need-based awards were made. ***Average percent of need met:*** 77. ***Average financial aid package:*** $34,687. ***Average need-based loan:*** $4721. ***Average need-based gift aid:*** $17,845. ***Average non-need-based aid:*** $16,504. ***Average indebtedness upon graduation:*** $30,000.

APPLYING
Options: electronic application.

Application fee: $50.

Required: essay or personal statement, high school transcript, 3 letters of recommendation, interview, school report, parent supplement.

CONTACT
Chandra Joos deKoven, Director of Admissions, Bard College at Simon's Rock, 84 Alford Road, Great Barrington, MA 01230-9702. *Phone:* 800-235-7186. *Toll-free phone:* 800-235-7186. *Fax:* 413-541-0081. *E-mail:* admit@simons-rock.edu.

See previous page for display ad and page 1292 for the College Close-Up.

Bay Path University
Longmeadow, Massachusetts
http://www.baypath.edu/

- **Independent** comprehensive, founded 1897
- **Suburban** 48-acre campus with easy access to Hartford, CT and Boston, MA
- **Endowment** $41.5 million
- **Undergraduate: women only; graduate: coed** 1,893 undergraduate students, 75% full-time, 100% women
- **Moderately difficult** entrance level, 60% of applicants were admitted

UNDERGRAD STUDENTS
1,415 full-time, 478 part-time. Students come from 8 states and territories; 5 other countries; 42% are from out of state; 13% Black or African American, non-Hispanic/Latino; 19% Hispanic/Latino; 2% Asian, non-Hispanic/Latino; 0.2% Native Hawaiian or other Pacific Islander, non-Hispanic/Latino; 0.2% American Indian or Alaska Native, non-Hispanic/Latino; 3% Two or more races, non-Hispanic/Latino; 5% Race/ethnicity unknown; 0.6% international; 5% transferred in; 45% live on campus.

Freshmen:
Admission: 1,542 applied, 924 admitted, 153 enrolled. ***Average high school GPA:*** 3.32.
Retention: 72% of full-time freshmen returned.

FACULTY
Total: 480, 13% full-time, 36% with terminal degrees.
Student/faculty ratio: 11:1.

ACADEMICS
Calendar: semesters. *Degrees:* certificates, associate, bachelor's, master's, doctoral, post-master's, and postbachelor's certificates.
Special study options: academic remediation for entering students, accelerated degree program, adult/continuing education programs, advanced placement credit, cooperative education, distance learning, double majors, English as a second language, external degree program, honors programs, independent study, internships, off-campus study, part-time degree program, services for LD students, student-designed majors, study abroad, summer session for credit. ***ROTC:*** Army (c), Air Force (c).
Unusual degree programs: 3-2 business administration; occupational therapy.
Computers: 235 computers/terminals are available on campus for general student use. Students can access the following: campus intranet, computer help desk, free student e-mail accounts, online (class) grades, online (class) registration, online (class) schedules. Campuswide network is available. 100% of college-owned or -operated housing units are wired for high-speed Internet access. Wireless service is available via entire campus.
Library: Hatch Library. *Books:* 52,565 (physical), 408,000 (digital/electronic); *Serial titles:* 80 (physical), 55,000 (digital/electronic); *Databases:* 110. Weekly public service hours: 86; students can reserve study rooms.

STUDENT LIFE
Housing options: women-only. Campus housing is university owned. Freshman campus housing is guaranteed.
Activities and organizations: drama/theater group, choral group, Habitat for Humanity, Tactical Team, Wellness Wildcats, Women of Culture, Alliance Club.
Athletics Member NCAA. All Division III. ***Intercollegiate sports:*** basketball W, cross-country running W, field hockey W, lacrosse W, soccer W, softball W, tennis W, volleyball W. ***Intramural sports:*** swimming and diving W(c), track and field W(c).
Campus security: 24-hour emergency response devices and patrols, late-night transport/escort service, controlled dormitory access.
Student services: health clinic, personal/psychological counseling.

COSTS & FINANCIAL AID
Costs (2017–18) ***Comprehensive fee:*** $45,349 includes full-time tuition ($32,739) and room and board ($12,610). Part-time tuition: $500 per credit hour. Part-time tuition and fees vary according to course load. ***Room and board:*** Room and board charges vary according to board plan. ***Payment plan:*** installment. ***Waivers:*** employees or children of employees.
Financial Aid Of all full-time matriculated undergraduates who enrolled in 2016, 624 applied for aid, 589 were judged to have need, 46 had their need fully met. 113 Federal Work-Study jobs (averaging $2500). 72 state and other part-time jobs (averaging $2500). In 2016, 63 non-need-based awards were made. ***Average percent of need met:*** 72. ***Average financial aid package:*** $26,392. ***Average need-based loan:*** $4886. ***Average need-based gift aid:*** $21,203. ***Average non-need-based aid:*** $14,176. ***Average indebtedness upon graduation:*** $29,954.

APPLYING
Options: electronic application, deferred entrance.
Required for some: essay or personal statement, high school transcript, interview. ***Recommended:*** minimum 2.0 GPA, interview.
Application deadlines: 8/1 (freshmen), rolling (transfers).
Notification: continuous (transfers).

CONTACT
Dawn Bryden, Dean of Traditional Undergraduate Enrollment and Admissions, Bay Path University, 588 Longmeadow Street, Longmeadow, MA 01106-2292. *Phone:* 413-565-1235. *Toll-free phone:* 800-782-7284 Ext. 1331. *E-mail:* dbryden@baypath.edu.

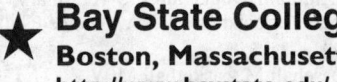

★ Bay State College
Boston, Massachusetts
http://www.baystate.edu/

CONTACT
Kimberly Odusami, Director of Admissions, Bay State College, 122 Commonwealth Avenue, Boston, MA 02116. *Phone:* 617-217-9186. *Toll-free phone:* 800-81-LEARN. *E-mail:* admissions@baystate.edu.

See next page for display ad and page 1296 for the College Close-Up.

Becker College
Worcester, Massachusetts
http://www.becker.edu/

- **Independent** comprehensive, founded 1784
- **Urban** 100-acre campus with easy access to Boston, MA; Providence, RI; Hartford, CT
- **Coed** 2,178 undergraduate students, 72% full-time, 61% women, 39% men
- **Moderately difficult** entrance level, 65% of applicants were admitted

UNDERGRAD STUDENTS
1,565 full-time, 613 part-time. Students come from 32 states and territories; 24 other countries; 47% are from out of state; 8% Black or African American, non-Hispanic/Latino; 9% Hispanic/Latino; 2% Asian, non-Hispanic/Latino; 0.2% Native Hawaiian or other Pacific Islander, non-Hispanic/Latino; 0.5% American Indian or Alaska Native, non-Hispanic/Latino; 3% Two or more races, non-Hispanic/Latino; 7% Race/ethnicity unknown; 0.7% international; 6% transferred in; 44% live on campus.

Freshmen:
Admission: 4,458 applied, 2,913 admitted, 421 enrolled. ***Average high school GPA:*** 3.18. ***Test scores:*** SAT critical reading scores over 500: 57%; SAT math scores over 500: 59%; SAT writing scores over 500: 47%; ACT scores over 18: 94%; SAT critical reading scores over 600: 17%; SAT math scores over 600: 14%; SAT writing scores over 600: 11%; ACT scores over 24: 46%; SAT critical reading scores over 700: 2%; SAT math scores over 700: 2%; SAT writing scores over 700: 1%; ACT scores over 30: 5%.
Retention: 68% of full-time freshmen returned.

FACULTY
Total: 235, 19% full-time, 38% with terminal degrees.
Student/faculty ratio: 17:1.

ACADEMICS
Calendar: semesters. *Degrees:* certificates, associate, bachelor's, and master's (also includes Leicester, MA small town campus).

Special study options: academic remediation for entering students, accelerated degree program, adult/continuing education programs, advanced placement credit, cooperative education, distance learning, double majors, independent study, internships, off-campus study, part-time degree program, services for LD students, study abroad, summer session for credit. ***ROTC:*** Army (c), Air Force (c).

Unusual degree programs: business administration; nursing; mental health counseling.

Computers: 404 computers/terminals and 1,005 ports are available on campus for general student use. Students can access the following: campus intranet, computer help desk, free student e-mail accounts, online (class) grades, online (class) registration, online (class) schedules. Campuswide network is available. 100% of college-owned or -operated housing units are wired for high-speed Internet access. Wireless service is available via entire campus.

Library: Ruska Library plus 1 other. *Books:* 33,803 (physical), 3,526 (digital/electronic); *Serial titles:* 15 (physical), 87 (digital/electronic); *Databases:* 56. Weekly public service hours: 119; students can reserve study rooms.

STUDENT LIFE
Housing options: coed, special housing for students with disabilities. Campus housing is university owned and leased by the school.

Activities and organizations: drama/theater group, choral group, Campus Activities Board (CAB), Animal Health Club/Pre-Veterinary Club, International Game Developers Association (IGDA), Dance Club, Marine Wildlife Conversation Club.

Athletics *Intercollegiate sports:* baseball M, basketball M/W, cheerleading M(c)/W(c), equestrian sports M/W, field hockey W, football M, golf M, ice hockey M/W, lacrosse M/W, soccer M/W, softball W, tennis M/W, volleyball W.

Campus security: 24-hour emergency response devices and patrols, late-night transport/escort service, controlled dormitory access.

Student services: health clinic, personal/psychological counseling.

COSTS & FINANCIAL AID
Costs (2017–18) ***One-time required fee:*** $100. ***Comprehensive fee:*** $51,550 includes full-time tuition ($34,650), mandatory fees ($3600), and room and board ($13,300). Full-time tuition and fees vary according to class time, course load, program, and student level. Part-time tuition: $1444 per credit. Part-time tuition and fees vary according to class time, course load, program, and student level. ***Room and board:*** Room and board charges vary according to housing facility. ***Payment plan:*** installment. ***Waivers:*** employees or children of employees.

Financial Aid Of all full-time matriculated undergraduates who enrolled in 2015, 1,439 applied for aid, 1,334 were judged to have need, 139 had their need fully met. In 2015, 220 non-need-based awards were made. ***Average percent of need met:*** 63. ***Average financial aid package:*** $21,722. ***Average need-based loan:*** $4326. ***Average need-based gift aid:*** $8410. ***Average non-need-based aid:*** $11,610.

APPLYING
Standardized Tests *Required:* SAT or ACT (for admission).

Options: electronic application, early admission, early decision, early action.

Required: high school transcript, minimum 2.0 GPA, 1 letter of recommendation. ***Recommended:*** essay or personal statement, interview.

Application deadlines: rolling (freshmen), rolling (transfers), 11/15 (early action).

Early decision deadline: 11/15.

Notification: continuous (freshmen), continuous (transfers), 12/15 (early decision), 12/15 (early action).

CONTACT
Mr. Michael Perron, Dean of Admissions, Becker College, 61 Sever Street, Worcester, MA 01609. *Phone:* 508-373-9400. *Toll-free phone:* 877-5BECKER. *Fax:* 508-890-1500. *E-mail:* admissions@becker.edu.

Benjamin Franklin Institute of Technology

Boston, Massachusetts

http://www.bfit.edu/

CONTACT
Ms. Brittainy Johnson, Associate Director of Admissions, Benjamin Franklin Institute of Technology, Boston, MA 02116. *Phone:* 617-423-4630 Ext. 122. *Toll-free phone:* 877-400-BFIT. *Fax:* 617-482-3706. *E-mail:* bjohnson@bfit.edu.

★ Bentley University

Waltham, Massachusetts

http://www.bentley.edu/

- **Independent** comprehensive, founded 1917
- **Suburban** 163-acre campus with easy access to Boston
- **Endowment** $250.6 million
- **Coed** 4,222 undergraduate students, 98% full-time, 41% women, 59% men
- **Very difficult** entrance level, 46% of applicants were admitted

UNDERGRAD STUDENTS
4,140 full-time, 82 part-time. Students come from 43 states and territories; 74 other countries; 57% are from out of state; 3% Black or African American, non-Hispanic/Latino; 8% Hispanic/Latino; 8% Asian, non-Hispanic/Latino; 0.1% Native Hawaiian or other Pacific Islander, non-Hispanic/Latino; 2% Two or more races, non-Hispanic/Latino; 4% Race/ethnicity unknown; 14% international; 2% transferred in; 80% live on campus.

Freshmen:
Admission: 8,281 applied, 3,836 admitted, 1,041 enrolled. ***Test scores:*** SAT critical reading scores over 500: 91%; SAT math scores over 500: 97%; SAT writing scores over 500: 93%; ACT scores over 18: 100%; SAT critical reading scores over 600: 47%; SAT math scores over 600: 78%; SAT writing scores over 600: 54%; ACT scores over 24: 94%; SAT critical reading scores over 700: 6%; SAT math scores over 700: 24%; SAT writing scores over 700: 6%; ACT scores over 30: 30%.
Retention: 94% of full-time freshmen returned.

FACULTY
Total: 461, 62% full-time, 74% with terminal degrees.
Student/faculty ratio: 12:1.

ACADEMICS
Calendar: semesters. *Degrees:* bachelor's, master's, doctoral, post-master's, and postbachelor's certificates.
Special study options: accelerated degree program, adult/continuing education programs, advanced placement credit, distance learning, double majors, English as a second language, honors programs, independent study, internships, off-campus study, part-time degree program, services for LD students, study abroad, summer session for credit. ***ROTC:*** Army (c), Air Force (c).
Computers: 4,490 computers/terminals and 10,752 ports are available on campus for general student use. Students can access the following: campus intranet, computer help desk, free student e-mail accounts, online (class) grades, online (class) registration, online (class) schedules, learning management system, student employment, free software. Campuswide network is available. 100% of college-owned or -operated housing units are wired for high-speed Internet access. Wireless service is available via entire campus.
Library: Bentley Library. *Books:* 183,873 (physical), 202,640 (digital/electronic); *Serial titles:* 1,650 (physical), 80,549 (digital/electronic); *Databases:* 87. Weekly public service hours: 110; students can reserve study rooms.

STUDENT LIFE
Housing options: coed, special housing for students with disabilities. Campus housing is university owned. Freshman campus housing is guaranteed.
Activities and organizations: drama/theater group, student-run newspaper, radio and television station, choral group, South Asian Student Association, Campus Activities Board, Delta Sigma Pi, Bentley Investment Group, National Association of Black Accountants, national fraternities, national sororities.
Athletics Member NCAA. All Division II except ice hockey (Division I). ***Intercollegiate sports:*** baseball M, basketball M(s)/W(s), cross-country running M/W, field hockey W, football M, golf M, ice hockey M(s), lacrosse M/W, soccer M/W, softball W, swimming and diving M/W, tennis M/W, track and field M/W, volleyball W. ***Intramural sports:*** basketball M/W, cheerleading W(c), equestrian sports W(c), football M, golf M(c)/W(c), racquetball M(c)/W(c), rugby M(c)/W(c), sailing M(c)/W(c), soccer M/W, softball M/W, triathlon M(c)/W(c), ultimate Frisbee M/W, volleyball M/W, water polo M(c), wrestling M(c).
Campus security: 24-hour emergency response devices and patrols, late-night transport/escort service, controlled dormitory access, security cameras; Community Policing Team; self-defense classes; CPR and first-aid training; anonymous crime reporting; fire drills.
Student services: health clinic, personal/psychological counseling, women's center.

COSTS & FINANCIAL AID
Costs (2016–17) ***Comprehensive fee:*** $60,890 includes full-time tuition ($44,210), mandatory fees ($1550), and room and board ($15,130). Part-time tuition: $2250 per course. Part-time tuition and fees vary according to class time and course load. ***Required fees:*** $25 per term part-time. ***College room only:*** $9180. Room and board charges vary according to board plan and housing facility. ***Payment plan:*** installment. ***Waivers:*** employees or children of employees.
Financial Aid Of all full-time matriculated undergraduates who enrolled in 2015, 2,387 applied for aid, 1,764 were judged to have need, 731 had their need fully met. 761 Federal Work-Study jobs (averaging $1794). 900 state and other part-time jobs (averaging $1077). In 2015, 853 non-need-based awards were made. ***Average percent of need met:*** 93. ***Average financial aid package:*** $35,525. ***Average need-based loan:*** $5106. ***Average need-based gift aid:*** $30,600. ***Average non-need-based aid:*** $18,705. ***Average indebtedness upon graduation:*** $31,046. ***Financial aid deadline:*** 1/7.

APPLYING
Standardized Tests *Required:* SAT or ACT (for admission), TOEFL (or IELTS) is required for non-native English speakers unless the student receives at least 577 (paper-based) or 90 (Internet-based) on the writing section of the SAT (for admission).
Options: electronic application, early admission, early decision, deferred entrance.
Application fee: $50.
Required: essay or personal statement, high school transcript, 2 letters of recommendation. ***Required for some:*** TOEFL or IELTS required of non-native English speakers. SAT or ACT with writing test (required of all). . ***Recommended:*** interview.
Application deadlines: 1/7 (freshmen), 4/15 (transfers).
Early decision deadline: 11/15.
Notification: 3/31 (freshmen), continuous (transfers), 12/22 (early decision).

CONTACT
Office of Undergraduate Admissions, Bentley University, 175 Forest Street, Waltham, MA 02452. *Phone:* 781-891-2244. *Toll-free phone:* 800-523-2354. *Fax:* 781-891-3414. *E-mail:* ugadmission@bentley.edu.

See page 1298 for the College Close-Up.

★ Berklee College of Music

Boston, Massachusetts

http://www.berklee.edu/

- **Independent** comprehensive, founded 1945
- **Urban** campus
- **Coed**
- **Moderately difficult** entrance level

FACULTY
Student/faculty ratio: 11:1.

ACADEMICS
Calendar: semesters. *Degrees:* diplomas, bachelor's, and master's.
Library: The Stan Getz Media Center and Library.

STUDENT LIFE
Housing options: coed, special housing for students with disabilities. Campus housing is university owned. Freshman applicants given priority for college housing.
Activities and organizations: drama/theater group, student-run newspaper, radio station, choral group.
Campus security: 24-hour patrols.

COSTS & FINANCIAL AID
Costs (2016–17) ***Comprehensive fee:*** $59,398 includes full-time tuition ($40,220), mandatory fees ($1178), and room and board ($18,000). Part-time tuition: $1461 per credit. ***Payment plans:*** tuition prepayment, deferred payment.
Financial Aid Of all full-time matriculated undergraduates who enrolled in 2016, 2,120 applied for aid, 1,847 were judged to have need, 210 had their need fully met. In 2016, 1372 non-need-based awards were made. ***Average percent of need met:*** 38. ***Average financial aid package:*** $18,827. ***Average need-based loan:*** $4548. ***Average need-based gift aid:*** $1892. ***Average non-need-based aid:*** $18,776. ***Average indebtedness upon graduation:*** $48,331.

APPLYING
Options: electronic application, early action, deferred entrance.
Application fee: $150.
Required: essay or personal statement, high school transcript, 2 letters of recommendation, interview, 2 years of formal music study and audition.

CONTACT
Mr. Damien Bracken, Director of Admissions, Berklee College of Music, 1140 Boylston Street, Boston, MA 02215-3693. *Phone:* 617-747-2222. *Toll-free phone:* 800-BERKLEE. *Fax:* 617-747-2047. *E-mail:* admissions@berklee.edu.

See page 1300 for the College Close-Up.

Boston Architectural College
Boston, Massachusetts
http://www.the-bac.edu/

- **Independent** comprehensive, founded 1889
- **Urban** 1-acre campus with easy access to Boston
- **Endowment** $10.1 million
- **Coed** 472 undergraduate students, 75% full-time, 42% women, 58% men
- **Noncompetitive** entrance level, 16% of applicants were admitted

UNDERGRAD STUDENTS
354 full-time, 118 part-time. 6% Black or African American, non-Hispanic/Latino; 17% Hispanic/Latino; 9% Asian, non-Hispanic/Latino; 0.3% Native Hawaiian or other Pacific Islander, non-Hispanic/Latino; 0.3% American Indian or Alaska Native, non-Hispanic/Latino; 4% Two or more races, non-Hispanic/Latino; 8% Race/ethnicity unknown; 5% international.

Freshmen:
Admission: 152 applied, 24 admitted, 24 enrolled.
Retention: 75% of full-time freshmen returned.

FACULTY
Total: 301, 6% full-time, 72% with terminal degrees.
Student/faculty ratio: 6:1.

ACADEMICS
Calendar: semesters. *Degrees:* certificates, bachelor's, and master's.
Special study options: adult/continuing education programs, advanced placement credit, distance learning, independent study, internships, off-campus study, services for LD students, summer session for credit.
Computers: 84 computers/terminals are available on campus for general student use. Students can access the following: campus intranet, computer help desk, free student e-mail accounts, online (class) grades, online (class) registration, online (class) schedules. Campuswide network is available. Wireless service is available via entire campus.
Library: Shaw and Stone Library. *Books:* 42,224 (physical), 117,108 (digital/electronic); *Serial titles:* 613 (physical), 313,728 (digital/electronic); *Databases:* 73. Weekly public service hours: 71.

STUDENT LIFE
Housing options: college housing not available.
Activities and organizations: Student Government Association, Student American Society of Landscape Architects, BAC Interior Design Society (IIDA and ASID), National Organization of Minority Architecture Students (NOMAS), American Institute of Architectural Students.
Campus security: 24-hour emergency response devices and patrols, late-night transport/escort service, electronically operated building access, closed-circuit TV systems.
Student services: personal/psychological counseling, legal services.

COSTS & FINANCIAL AID
Costs (2017–18) ***Tuition:*** $20,016 full-time, $1668 per credit hour part-time. Full-time tuition and fees vary according to course load, degree level, and program. Part-time tuition and fees vary according to course load, degree level, and program. ***Required fees:*** $650 full-time, $175 per term part-time. ***Payment plan:*** installment. ***Waivers:*** employees or children of employees.
Financial Aid Of all full-time matriculated undergraduates who enrolled in 2016, 93 applied for aid, 88 were judged to have need, 2 had their need fully met. 20 Federal Work-Study jobs (averaging $2875). In 2016, 7 non-need-based awards were made. ***Average percent of need met:*** 35. ***Average financial aid package:*** $11,288. ***Average need-based loan:*** $5589. ***Average need-based gift aid:*** $6793. ***Average non-need-based aid:*** $3189.

APPLYING
Options: electronic application.
Required: essay or personal statement, high school transcript, resumé and creative exercise. ***Recommended:*** interview.

CONTACT
Ms. Meredith Spinnato, Admission Office, Boston Architectural College, 320 Newbury Street, Boston, MA 02115-2795. *Phone:* 617-585-0123. *Fax:* 617-585-0121. *E-mail:* admissions@the-bac.edu.

Boston Baptist College
Boston, Massachusetts
http://www.boston.edu/

CONTACT
Mrs. Kim Melton, Director of Admissions, Boston Baptist College, 950 Metropolitan Avenue, Boston, MA 02136. *Phone:* 617-364-3510 Ext. 233. *Toll-free phone:* 888-235-2014. *Fax:* 617-399-8220. *E-mail:* kmelton@boston.edu.

Boston College
Chestnut Hill, Massachusetts
http://www.bc.edu/

- **Independent Roman Catholic (Jesuit)** university, founded 1863
- **Suburban** 338-acre campus with easy access to Boston
- **Endowment** $2.2 billion
- **Coed** 9,309 undergraduate students, 100% full-time, 54% women, 46% men
- **Very difficult** entrance level, 31% of applicants were admitted

UNDERGRAD STUDENTS
9,309 full-time. Students come from 53 states and territories; 68 other countries; 75% are from out of state; 4% Black or African American, non-Hispanic/Latino; 10% Hispanic/Latino; 10% Asian, non-Hispanic/Latino; 0.1% American Indian or Alaska Native, non-Hispanic/Latino; 3% Two or more races, non-Hispanic/Latino; 4% Race/ethnicity unknown; 7% international; 2% transferred in; 82% live on campus.

Freshmen:
Admission: 28,956 applied, 9,017 admitted, 2,316 enrolled. ***Test scores:*** SAT critical reading scores over 500: 98%; SAT math scores over 500: 99%; SAT writing scores over 500: 98%; ACT scores over 18: 100%; SAT critical reading scores over 600: 84%; SAT math scores over 600: 89%; SAT writing scores over 600: 85%; ACT scores over 24: 98%; SAT critical reading scores over 700: 34%; SAT math scores over 700: 45%; SAT writing scores over 700: 44%; ACT scores over 30: 82%.
Retention: 95% of full-time freshmen returned.

FACULTY
Total: 1,603, 50% full-time, 96% with terminal degrees.

Student/faculty ratio: 12:1.

ACADEMICS
Calendar: semesters. *Degrees:* certificates, bachelor's, master's, doctoral, and post-master's certificates (also offers continuing education program with significant enrollment not reflected in profile).

Special study options: accelerated degree program, advanced placement credit, double majors, honors programs, independent study, internships, off-campus study, part-time degree program, services for LD students, student-designed majors, study abroad, summer session for credit. ***ROTC:*** Army (c), Navy (c), Air Force (c).

Computers: 1,000 computers/terminals are available on campus for general student use. Students can access the following: campus intranet, computer help desk, free student e-mail accounts, online (class) grades, online (class) registration, online (class) schedules. Campuswide network is available. 100% of college-owned or -operated housing units are wired for high-speed Internet access. Wireless service is available via entire campus.

Library: O'Neill Library plus 8 others. *Books:* 3.2 million (physical), 817,757 (digital/electronic); *Serial titles:* 3,937 (physical), 41,900 (digital/electronic). Study areas open 24 hours, 5-7 days a week; students can reserve study rooms.

STUDENT LIFE
Housing options: coed, women-only. Campus housing is university owned. Freshman campus housing is guaranteed.

Activities and organizations: drama/theater group, student-run newspaper, radio and television station, choral group, marching band, UGBC and individual School Senates, Asian Caucus, Appalachia Volunteers, Dance Marathon, 4Boston.

Athletics Member NCAA. All Division I except football (Division I-A). ***Intercollegiate sports:*** baseball M(s), basketball M(s)/W(s), cheerleading M(c)/W(c), crew W(s), cross-country running M(s)/W(s), fencing M/W, field hockey W(s), golf M(s)/W(s), ice hockey M(s)/W(s), lacrosse W(s), sailing M/W, skiing (downhill) M/W, soccer M(s)/W(s), softball W(s), swimming and diving M(s)/W(s), tennis M(s)/W(s), track and field M(s)/W(s), volleyball W(s). ***Intramural sports:*** badminton M/W, basketball M(c)/W(c), crew M(c), cross-country running M(c)/W(c), equestrian sports M(c)/W(c), field hockey W(c), golf M(c)/W(c), ice hockey M/W, lacrosse M(c)/W(c), racquetball M/W, rugby M(c)/W(c), soccer M(c)/W(c), softball M/W, squash M/W, tennis M/W, track and field M(c)/W(c), ultimate Frisbee M(c)/W(c), volleyball M(c)/W, water polo M(c)/W(c).

Campus security: 24-hour emergency response devices and patrols, late-night transport/escort service, controlled dormitory access, emergency text alerts, self defense training, student EMT program.

Student services: health clinic, personal/psychological counseling, women's center.

COSTS & FINANCIAL AID
Costs (2016–17) ***One-time required fee:*** $530. ***Comprehensive fee:*** $65,114 includes full-time tuition ($50,480), mandatory fees ($816), and room and board ($13,818). ***College room only:*** $8610. Room and board charges vary according to housing facility. ***Payment plan:*** installment. ***Waivers:*** employees or children of employees.

Financial Aid Of all full-time matriculated undergraduates who enrolled in 2015, 4,136 applied for aid, 3,720 were judged to have need, 3,720 had their need fully met. In 2015, 196 non-need-based awards were made. ***Average percent of need met:*** 100. ***Average financial aid package:*** $39,942. ***Average need-based loan:*** $4035. ***Average need-based gift aid:*** $36,755. ***Average non-need-based aid:*** $19,645. ***Average indebtedness upon graduation:*** $20,849.

APPLYING
Standardized Tests *Required:* SAT or ACT (for admission).

Options: electronic application, early admission, early action, deferred entrance.

Application fee: $75.

Required: essay or personal statement, high school transcript, 2 letters of recommendation.

Application deadlines: 1/1 (freshmen), 3/15 (transfers), 11/1 (early action).

Notification: 4/15 (freshmen), 6/1 (transfers), 12/25 (early action).

CONTACT
Office of Undergraduate Admissions, Boston College, 140 Commonwealth Avenue, Devlin 208, Chestnut Hill, MA 02467-3809. *Phone:* 617-552-3100. *Toll-free phone:* 800-360-2522. *Fax:* 617-552-0798.

See page 1304 for the College Close-Up.

Boston University

Boston, Massachusetts

http://www.bu.edu/

- **Independent** university, founded 1839
- **Urban** 134-acre campus with easy access to Boston
- **Endowment** $1.7 billion
- **Coed** 17,944 undergraduate students, 93% full-time, 61% women, 39% men
- **Very difficult** entrance level, 29% of applicants were admitted

UNDERGRAD STUDENTS
16,627 full-time, 1,317 part-time. Students come from 54 states and territories; 106 other countries; 80% are from out of state; 4% Black or African American, non-Hispanic/Latino; 10% Hispanic/Latino; 14% Asian, non-Hispanic/Latino; 0.1% Native Hawaiian or other Pacific Islander, non-Hispanic/Latino; 0.1% American Indian or Alaska Native, non-Hispanic/Latino; 3% Two or more races, non-Hispanic/Latino; 7% Race/ethnicity unknown; 21% international; 3% transferred in; 75% live on campus.

Freshmen:
Admission: 57,441 applied, 16,907 admitted, 3,552 enrolled. ***Average high school GPA:*** 3.62. ***Test scores:*** SAT critical reading scores over 500: 98%; SAT math scores over 500: 100%; SAT writing scores over 500: 99%; ACT scores over 18: 100%; SAT critical reading scores over 600: 71%; SAT math scores over 600: 89%; SAT writing scores over 600: 83%; ACT scores over 24: 99%; SAT critical reading scores over 700: 22%; SAT math scores over 700: 42%; SAT writing scores over 700: 27%; ACT scores over 30: 59%.

Retention: 93% of full-time freshmen returned.

FACULTY
Total: 2,626, 68% full-time.

Student/faculty ratio: 12:1.

ACADEMICS
Calendar: semesters. *Degrees:* certificates, bachelor's, master's, doctoral, post-master's, and postbachelor's certificates.

Special study options: accelerated degree program, adult/continuing education programs, advanced placement credit, cooperative education, distance learning, double majors, English as a second language, freshman honors college, honors programs, independent study, internships, off-campus study, part-time degree program, services for LD students, student-designed majors, study abroad, summer session for credit. ***ROTC:*** Army (b), Navy (b), Air Force (b).

Computers: 250 computers/terminals and 1,650 ports are available on campus for general student use. Students can access the following: campus intranet, computer help desk, free student e-mail accounts, online (class) grades, online (class) registration, online (class) schedules, research and educational networks. Campuswide network is available. 100% of college-owned or -operated housing units are wired for high-speed Internet access. Wireless service is available via classrooms, computer labs, dorm rooms, libraries, student centers.

Library: Mugar Memorial Library plus 20 others. *Books:* 2.6 million (physical), 1.5 million (digital/electronic); *Databases:* 578. Weekly public service hours: 123; students can reserve study rooms.

STUDENT LIFE
Housing options: on-campus residence required for freshman year; coed, women-only, cooperative, special housing for students with disabilities. Campus housing is university owned. Freshman campus housing is guaranteed.

Activities and organizations: drama/theater group, student-run newspaper, radio and television station, choral group, marching band, performing and Acappella groups, cultural organizations, service organizations, Student Government, residence hall associations, national fraternities, national sororities.

Athletics Member NCAA. All Division I. ***Intercollegiate sports:*** badminton M(c)/W(c), baseball M(c), basketball M(s)/W(s), cheerleading M(c)/W(c), crew M(s)/W(s), cross-country running M(s)/W(s), equestrian sports M(c)/W(c), fencing M(c)/W(c), field hockey W(s), golf M(c)/W(s), gymnastics M(c)/W(c), ice hockey M(s)/W(s), lacrosse M(s)/W(s), rowing M(s)/W(s), rugby M(c)/W(c), sailing M(c)/W(c), skiing (downhill) M(c)/W(c), soccer M(s)/W(s), softball W(s), squash M(c)/W(c), swimming and diving M(s)/W(s), table tennis M(c)/W(c), tennis M/W(s), track and field M(s)/W(s), triathlon M(c)/W(c), ultimate Frisbee M(c)/W(c), volleyball M(c)/W(c), water polo M(c)/W(c). ***Intramural sports:*** basketball M/W, football M/W, ice hockey M(c)/W(c), rowing M(c)/W(c), soccer M(c)/W(c), softball M/W, volleyball M/W.

Campus security: 24-hour emergency response devices and patrols, late-night transport/escort service, controlled dormitory access, security personnel at residence hall entrances, self-defense education, well-lit sidewalks, Emergency Alert System, Blue Light System.

Student services: health clinic, personal/psychological counseling, women's center.

COSTS & FINANCIAL AID

Costs (2017–18) ***Comprehensive fee:*** $65,110 includes full-time tuition ($49,176), mandatory fees ($1064), and room and board ($14,870). Full-time tuition and fees vary according to class time and course load. Part-time tuition: $1537 per credit hour. Part-time tuition and fees vary according to class time, course level, and course load. ***Required fees:*** $60 per term part-time. ***College room only:*** $9810. Room and board charges vary according to board plan, housing facility, and location. ***Payment plans:*** tuition prepayment, installment. ***Waivers:*** employees or children of employees.

Financial Aid Of all full-time matriculated undergraduates who enrolled in 2016, 6,587 applied for aid, 5,895 were judged to have need, 1,212 had their need fully met. 2,880 Federal Work-Study jobs (averaging $2277). In 2016, 1277 non-need-based awards were made. ***Average percent of need met:*** 85. ***Average financial aid package:*** $40,232. ***Average need-based loan:*** $4694. ***Average need-based gift aid:*** $33,521. ***Average non-need-based aid:*** $19,975. ***Average indebtedness upon graduation:*** $41,098. ***Financial aid deadline:*** 2/1.

APPLYING

Standardized Tests *Required:* SAT or ACT (for admission). *Required for some:* SAT Subject Tests (for admission).

Options: electronic application, early admission, early decision, deferred entrance.

Application fee: $80.

Required: essay or personal statement, high school transcript, 2 letters of recommendation. ***Required for some:*** interview, audition, portfolio.

Application deadlines: 1/2 (freshmen), 3/1 (transfers).

Early decision deadline: 11/1 (for plan 1), 1/2 (for plan 2).

Notification: 4/1 (freshmen), continuous until 6/1 (transfers), 12/15 (early decision plan 1), 2/15 (early decision plan 2).

CONTACT

Ms. Kelly A. Walter, Associate Vice President and Executive Director of Admissions, Boston University, 233 Bay State Road, Boston, MA 02215. *Phone:* 617-353-2300. *Fax:* 617-353-9695. *E-mail:* admissions@bu.edu.

See page 1306 for the College Close-Up.

Brandeis University
Waltham, Massachusetts
http://www.brandeis.edu/

- **Independent** university, founded 1948
- **Suburban** 235-acre campus with easy access to Boston
- **Endowment** $866.8 million
- **Coed** 3,608 undergraduate students, 100% full-time, 58% women, 42% men
- **Most difficult** entrance level, 33% of applicants were admitted

UNDERGRAD STUDENTS

3,591 full-time, 17 part-time. Students come from 47 states and territories; 58 other countries; 72% are from out of state; 5% Black or African American, non-Hispanic/Latino; 8% Hispanic/Latino; 13% Asian, non-Hispanic/Latino; 0.1% Native Hawaiian or other Pacific Islander, non-Hispanic/Latino; 0.1% American Indian or Alaska Native, non-Hispanic/Latino; 3% Two or more races, non-Hispanic/Latino; 4% Race/ethnicity unknown; 21% international; 1% transferred in; 78% live on campus.

Freshmen:

Admission: 11,351 applied, 3,796 admitted, 841 enrolled. ***Average high school GPA:*** 3.88. ***Test scores:*** SAT critical reading scores over 500: 98%; SAT math scores over 500: 99%; SAT writing scores over 500: 99%; ACT scores over 18: 100%; SAT critical reading scores over 600: 82%; SAT math scores over 600: 94%; SAT writing scores over 600: 93%; ACT scores over 24: 99%; SAT critical reading scores over 700: 31%; SAT math scores over 700: 58%; SAT writing scores over 700: 43%; ACT scores over 30: 74%.

Retention: 94% of full-time freshmen returned.

FACULTY

Total: 524, 69% full-time, 84% with terminal degrees.

Student/faculty ratio: 10:1.

ACADEMICS

Calendar: semesters. *Degrees:* bachelor's, master's, and doctoral.

Special study options: advanced placement credit, double majors, English as a second language, independent study, internships, off-campus study, services for LD students, student-designed majors, study abroad, summer session for credit. ***ROTC:*** Army (c), Air Force (c).

Unusual degree programs: 3-2 engineering with Columbia University.

Computers: 130 computers/terminals are available on campus for general student use. Students can access the following: computer help desk, free student e-mail accounts, online (class) grades, online (class) registration, online (class) schedules, educational software. Campuswide network is available. 100% of college-owned or -operated housing units are wired for high-speed Internet access. Wireless service is available via entire campus.

Library: Goldfarb Library plus 1 other. *Books:* 984,446 (physical), 1.2 million (digital/electronic); *Serial titles:* 10,862 (physical), 35,968 (digital/electronic); *Databases:* 285. Students can reserve study rooms.

STUDENT LIFE

Housing options: on-campus residence required for freshman year; coed, men-only, women-only, special housing for students with disabilities. Campus housing is university owned. Freshman campus housing is guaranteed.

Activities and organizations: drama/theater group, student-run newspaper, radio and television station, choral group, Waltham Group, Undergraduate Theater Collective, Student Union, Student Events (Programming Board), BEMCo - student EMTs.

Athletics Member NCAA. All Division III. ***Intercollegiate sports:*** baseball M, basketball M/W, cross-country running M/W, fencing M/W, soccer M/W, softball W, swimming and diving M/W, tennis M/W, track and field M/W, volleyball W. ***Intramural sports:*** archery M(c)/W(c), cheerleading M(c)/W(c), crew M(c)/W(c), equestrian sports M(c)/W(c), field hockey M(c)/W(c), gymnastics M(c)/W(c), lacrosse W(c), rugby M(c)/W(c), sailing M(c)/W(c), skiing (downhill) M(c)/W(c), squash M/W, table tennis M/W, ultimate Frisbee M(c)/W(c), volleyball M.

Campus security: 24-hour emergency response devices and patrols, late-night transport/escort service, controlled dormitory access.

Student services: health clinic, personal/psychological counseling.

COSTS & FINANCIAL AID

Costs (2016–17) ***Comprehensive fee:*** $65,925 includes full-time tuition ($49,586), mandatory fees ($1959), and room and board ($14,380). Full-time tuition and fees vary according to student level. Part-time tuition: $1549 per credit. Part-time tuition and fees vary according to course load. ***Required fees:*** $1959 per year part-time. ***College room only:*** $8060. Room and board charges vary according to board plan and housing facility. ***Payment plan:*** installment. ***Waivers:*** employees or children of employees.

Financial Aid Of all full-time matriculated undergraduates who enrolled in 2015, 2,010 applied for aid, 1,808 were judged to have need, 1,226 had their need fully met. 291 Federal Work-Study jobs (averaging $2707). 16 state and other part-time jobs (averaging $2874). In 2015, 282 non-need-based awards were made. ***Average percent of need met:*** 96. ***Average***

financial aid package: $41,876. *Average need-based loan:* $4983. *Average need-based gift aid:* $37,351. *Average non-need-based aid:* $15,200. *Average indebtedness upon graduation:* $32,922. *Financial aid deadline:* 1/1.

APPLYING

Standardized Tests *Required:* SAT or ACT (for admission).

Options: electronic application, early admission, early decision, deferred entrance.

Application fee: $80.

Required: essay or personal statement, high school transcript, 1 letter of recommendation. *Recommended:* interview.

Application deadlines: 1/1 (freshmen), 4/1 (transfers).

Early decision deadline: 11/1 (for plan 1), 1/1 (for plan 2).

Notification: 4/1 (freshmen), 5/25 (transfers), 12/15 (early decision plan 1), 2/1 (early decision plan 2).

CONTACT

Jennifer Walker, Dean of Admissions, Brandeis University, 415 South Street, PO Box 549110, Waltham, MA 02454-9110. *Phone:* 781-736-3500. *Toll-free phone:* 800-622-0622. *Fax:* 781-736-3536. *E-mail:* admissions@brandeis.edu.

Bridgewater State University

Bridgewater, Massachusetts

http://www.bridgew.edu/

- **State-supported** comprehensive, founded 1840, part of Massachusetts Department of Higher Education
- **Suburban** 278-acre campus with easy access to Boston
- **Endowment** $36.7 million
- **Coed** 9,562 undergraduate students, 82% full-time, 59% women, 41% men
- **Moderately difficult** entrance level, 81% of applicants were admitted

UNDERGRAD STUDENTS

7,826 full-time, 1,736 part-time. Students come from 28 states and territories; 27 other countries; 4% are from out of state; 10% Black or African American, non-Hispanic/Latino; 7% Hispanic/Latino; 2% Asian, non-Hispanic/Latino; 0.1% Native Hawaiian or other Pacific Islander, non-Hispanic/Latino; 0.2% American Indian or Alaska Native, non-Hispanic/Latino; 4% Two or more races, non-Hispanic/Latino; 2% Race/ethnicity unknown; 0.6% international; 12% transferred in; 42% live on campus.

Freshmen:

Admission: 6,007 applied, 4,863 admitted, 1,420 enrolled. *Average high school GPA:* 3.13. *Test scores:* SAT critical reading scores over 500: 48%; SAT math scores over 500: 51%; ACT scores over 18: 86%; SAT critical reading scores over 600: 10%; SAT math scores over 600: 10%; ACT scores over 24: 28%; SAT critical reading scores over 700: 1%; SAT math scores over 700: 1%; ACT scores over 30: 2%.

Retention: 80% of full-time freshmen returned.

FACULTY

Total: 767, 47% full-time, 62% with terminal degrees.

Student/faculty ratio: 19:1.

ACADEMICS

Calendar: semesters. *Degrees:* bachelor's, master's, post-master's, and postbachelor's certificates.

Special study options: academic remediation for entering students, accelerated degree program, adult/continuing education programs, advanced placement credit, distance learning, double majors, English as a second language, honors programs, independent study, internships, off-campus study, part-time degree program, services for LD students, study abroad, summer session for credit. *ROTC:* Army (c), Air Force (c).

Computers: 780 computers/terminals and 20 ports are available on campus for general student use. Students can access the following: campus intranet, computer help desk, free student e-mail accounts, online (class) grades, online (class) registration, online (class) schedules, student account information, application software. Campuswide network is available. 100% of college-owned or -operated housing units are wired for high-speed Internet access. Wireless service is available via entire campus.

Library: Clement C. Maxwell Library. *Books:* 327,542 (physical); *Serial titles:* 47,544 (digital/electronic); *Databases:* 84. Weekly public service hours: 93.

STUDENT LIFE

Housing options: coed, special housing for students with disabilities. Campus housing is university owned. Freshman applicants given priority for college housing.

Activities and organizations: drama/theater group, student-run newspaper, radio station, choral group, Dance Company, African American Society (Afro-Am), Program Committee, Panhellenic Association, Inter-Fraternity Council, national fraternities, national sororities.

Athletics Member NCAA. All Division III. *Intercollegiate sports:* baseball M, basketball M/W, cross-country running M/W, field hockey W, football M, lacrosse W, soccer M/W, softball W, swimming and diving M/W, tennis M/W, track and field M/W, volleyball W, wrestling M. *Intramural sports:* badminton M/W, basketball M/W, cheerleading W(c), equestrian sports W(c), football M/W, ice hockey M(c), lacrosse M(c), rugby W(c), soccer M/W, softball M/W, ultimate Frisbee M(c)/W(c), volleyball M/W.

Campus security: 24-hour emergency response devices and patrols, late-night transport/escort service, controlled dormitory access.

Student services: health clinic, personal/psychological counseling.

COSTS & FINANCIAL AID

Costs (2017–18) *Tuition:* state resident $910 full-time, $38 per credit hour part-time; nonresident $7050 full-time, $294 per credit hour part-time. Full-time tuition and fees vary according to course load. *Required fees:* $8960 full-time, $373 per credit hour part-time. *Room and board:* $12,750; room only: $8400. Room and board charges vary according to board plan and housing facility. *Payment plan:* installment. *Waivers:* senior citizens and employees or children of employees.

Financial Aid Of all full-time matriculated undergraduates who enrolled in 2015, 7,161 applied for aid, 5,528 were judged to have need, 427 had their need fully met. 406 Federal Work-Study jobs (averaging $1371). In 2015, 29 non-need-based awards were made. *Average financial aid package:* $8186. *Average need-based loan:* $4143. *Average need-based gift aid:* $5420. *Average non-need-based aid:* $5883. *Average indebtedness upon graduation:* $27,104.

APPLYING

Standardized Tests *Recommended:* SAT or ACT (for admission).

Options: electronic application, early action, deferred entrance.

Application fee: $50.

Required: high school transcript, minimum 2.0 GPA. *Recommended:* essay or personal statement, letters of recommendation.

Application deadlines: 2/15 (freshmen), 2/15 (transfers), 11/15 (early action).

Notification: continuous until 4/15 (freshmen), continuous until 4/15 (out-of-state freshmen), continuous until 4/15 (transfers), 12/15 (early action).

CONTACT

Mr. Gregg Meyer, Dean of University Admissions, Bridgewater State University, Gates House, 40 Cedar Street, Bridgewater, MA 02325. *Phone:* 508-531-1237. *Fax:* 508-531-1746. *E-mail:* admission@bridgew.edu.

Cambridge College

Cambridge, Massachusetts

http://www.cambridgecollege.edu/

CONTACT

Denise Haile, Director of Admissions, Cambridge College, 1000 Massachusetts Avenue, Cambridge, MA 02138-5304. *Phone:* 800-877-4725. *Toll-free phone:* 800-877-4723. *Fax:* 617-349-3561. *E-mail:* denise.haile@cambridgecollege.edu.

Clark University

Worcester, Massachusetts

http://www.clarku.edu/

- **Independent** university, founded 1887
- **Urban** 50-acre campus with easy access to Boston
- **Endowment** $404.9 million
- **Coed** 2,397 undergraduate students, 97% full-time, 60% women, 40% men
- **Moderately difficult** entrance level, 55% of applicants were admitted

UNDERGRAD STUDENTS
2,320 full-time, 77 part-time. Students come from 42 states and territories; 64 other countries; 63% are from out of state; 4% Black or African American, non-Hispanic/Latino; 7% Hispanic/Latino; 7% Asian, non-Hispanic/Latino; 0.1% Native Hawaiian or other Pacific Islander, non-Hispanic/Latino; 0.2% American Indian or Alaska Native, non-Hispanic/Latino; 2% Two or more races, non-Hispanic/Latino; 8% Race/ethnicity unknown; 15% international; 1% transferred in; 70% live on campus.

Freshmen:
Admission: 8,045 applied, 4,430 admitted, 671 enrolled. ***Average high school GPA:*** 3.66. ***Test scores:*** SAT critical reading scores over 500: 94%; SAT math scores over 500: 96%; SAT writing scores over 500: 92%; ACT scores over 18: 99%; SAT critical reading scores over 600: 63%; SAT math scores over 600: 63%; SAT writing scores over 600: 63%; ACT scores over 24: 87%; SAT critical reading scores over 700: 16%; SAT math scores over 700: 17%; SAT writing scores over 700: 15%; ACT scores over 30: 32%.
Retention: 87% of full-time freshmen returned.

FACULTY
Total: 312, 65% full-time.
Student/faculty ratio: 10:1.

ACADEMICS
Calendar: semesters. *Degrees:* bachelor's, master's, doctoral, and post-master's certificates.
Special study options: accelerated degree program, adult/continuing education programs, advanced placement credit, distance learning, double majors, English as a second language, honors programs, independent study, internships, off-campus study, part-time degree program, services for LD students, student-designed majors, study abroad, summer session for credit. ***ROTC:*** Army (c), Air Force (c).
Unusual degree programs: 3-2 business administration; engineering with Columbia University, Washington University in St. Louis, Worcester Polytechnic Institute; environmental studies, international development, community planning, biology, biochemistry, chemistry, physics, economics, history, communications, public administration, geographic information systems.
Computers: 322 computers/terminals and 4,000 ports are available on campus for general student use. Students can access the following: campus intranet, computer help desk, free student e-mail accounts, online (class) grades, online (class) registration, online (class) schedules, online course support. Campuswide network is available. 100% of college-owned or -operated housing units are wired for high-speed Internet access. Wireless service is available via entire campus.
Library: Robert Hutchings Goddard Library plus 8 others. *Books:* 661,744 (physical), 46,250 (digital/electronic); *Serial titles:* 2,443 (physical), 105,990 (digital/electronic); *Databases:* 82. Weekly public service hours: 151; students can reserve study rooms.

STUDENT LIFE
Housing options: on-campus residence required through sophomore year; coed, women-only, special housing for students with disabilities. Campus housing is university owned. Freshman campus housing is guaranteed.
Activities and organizations: drama/theater group, student-run newspaper, radio and television station, choral group, marching band, International Students Association, Science Fiction People of Clark, Outing Club, Hillel, Clark Musical Theater.
Athletics Member NCAA, NAIA. All NCAA Division III. ***Intercollegiate sports:*** baseball M, basketball M/W, crew M/W, cross-country running M/W, field hockey W, lacrosse M, soccer M/W, softball W, swimming and diving M/W, tennis M/W, volleyball W. ***Intramural sports:*** basketball M/W, equestrian sports W(c), ice hockey M(c), lacrosse W(c), racquetball M/W, soccer M(c)/W, softball M/W, tennis M(c)/W(c), ultimate Frisbee M(c)/W(c), volleyball M(c)/W(c), water polo M/W.
Campus security: 24-hour emergency response devices and patrols, student patrols, late-night transport/escort service, controlled dormitory access.
Student services: health clinic, personal/psychological counseling, women's center.

COSTS & FINANCIAL AID
Costs (2016–17) ***Comprehensive fee:*** $51,600 includes full-time tuition ($42,800), mandatory fees ($350), and room and board ($8450). Part-time tuition: $1338 per credit. ***College room only:*** $4900. Room and board charges vary according to board plan and housing facility. ***Payment plans:*** tuition prepayment, installment. ***Waivers:*** employees or children of employees.
Financial Aid Of all full-time matriculated undergraduates who enrolled in 2016, 1,700 applied for aid, 1,425 were judged to have need, 580 had their need fully met. In 2016, 723 non-need-based awards were made. ***Average percent of need met:*** 82. ***Average financial aid package:*** $36,022. ***Average need-based loan:*** $5298. ***Average need-based gift aid:*** $25,648. ***Average non-need-based aid:*** $18,160. ***Average indebtedness upon graduation:*** $26,870. ***Financial aid deadline:*** 2/1.

APPLYING
Options: electronic application, early admission, early decision, early action, deferred entrance.
Application fee: $60.
Required: essay or personal statement, high school transcript, 2 letters of recommendation. ***Recommended:*** interview.
Application deadlines: 1/15 (freshmen), 5/1 (transfers), 11/1 (early action).
Early decision deadline: 11/1.
Notification: 4/1 (freshmen), 6/1 (transfers), 12/15 (early decision), 12/15 (early action).

CONTACT
Mr. Donald Honeman, Dean of Admissions, Clark University, Admissions House, 950 Main Street, Worcester, MA 01610. *Phone:* 508-793-7431. *Toll-free phone:* 800-GO-CLARK. *Fax:* 508-793-8821. *E-mail:* admissions@clarku.edu.

College of the Holy Cross

Worcester, Massachusetts

http://www.holycross.edu/

- **Independent Roman Catholic (Jesuit)** 4-year, founded 1843
- **Suburban** 174-acre campus with easy access to Boston
- **Endowment** $681.0 million
- **Coed** 2,941 undergraduate students, 99% full-time, 51% women, 49% men
- **Very difficult** entrance level, 38% of applicants were admitted

UNDERGRAD STUDENTS
2,910 full-time, 31 part-time. Students come from 50 states and territories; 18 other countries; 60% are from out of state; 4% Black or African American, non-Hispanic/Latino; 10% Hispanic/Latino; 5% Asian, non-Hispanic/Latino; 0.1% Native Hawaiian or other Pacific Islander, non-Hispanic/Latino; 0.1% American Indian or Alaska Native, non-Hispanic/Latino; 3% Two or more races, non-Hispanic/Latino; 5% Race/ethnicity unknown; 3% international; 0.5% transferred in; 89% live on campus.

Freshmen:
Admission: 6,693 applied, 2,574 admitted, 764 enrolled. ***Test scores:*** SAT critical reading scores over 500: 98%; SAT math scores over 500: 99%; SAT writing scores over 500: 99%; ACT scores over 18: 100%; SAT critical reading scores over 600: 77%; SAT math scores over 600: 85%; SAT writing scores over 600: 78%; ACT scores over 24: 97%; SAT critical reading scores over 700: 19%; SAT math scores over 700: 24%; SAT writing scores over 700: 26%; ACT scores over 30: 50%.
Retention: 96% of full-time freshmen returned.

FACULTY
Total: 315, 89% full-time, 89% with terminal degrees.

Student/faculty ratio: 10:1.

ACADEMICS

Calendar: semesters. *Degree:* bachelor's.

Special study options: accelerated degree program, advanced placement credit, double majors, honors programs, independent study, internships, off-campus study, services for LD students, student-designed majors, study abroad, summer session for credit. ***ROTC:*** Army (c), Navy (b), Air Force (c).

Unusual degree programs: 3-2 engineering with Columbia University.

Computers: 485 computers/terminals are available on campus for general student use. Students can access the following: computer help desk, free student e-mail accounts, online (class) grades, online (class) registration. Campuswide network is available. 100% of college-owned or -operated housing units are wired for high-speed Internet access. Wireless service is available via entire campus.

Library: Dinand Library plus 4 others. *Books:* 646,531 (physical), 166,984 (digital/electronic); *Serial titles:* 637 (physical), 9,772 (digital/electronic); *Databases:* 219. Study areas open 24 hours, 5-7 days a week; students can reserve study rooms.

STUDENT LIFE

Housing options: on-campus residence required through sophomore year; coed, special housing for students with disabilities. Campus housing is university owned. Freshman campus housing is guaranteed.

Activities and organizations: drama/theater group, student-run newspaper, radio station, choral group, marching band, SPUD (community service organization), choral and music groups, Campus Activities Board, Student Government Association, Purple Key Society.

Athletics Member NCAA. All Division I except football (Division I-AA). ***Intercollegiate sports:*** baseball M, basketball M(s)/W(s), crew M/W(s), cross-country running M/W(s), field hockey W(s), golf M/W, ice hockey M(s)/W, lacrosse M(s)/W(s), soccer M(s)/W(s), softball W(s), swimming and diving M/W(s), tennis M/W, track and field M/W(s), volleyball W(s). ***Intramural sports:*** baseball M(c), basketball M(c)/W(c), equestrian sports M(c)/W(c), field hockey W(c), football M/W, golf M(c)/W(c), ice hockey M(c), lacrosse M(c)/W(c), rugby M(c)/W(c), sailing M(c)/W(c), skiing (downhill) M(c)/W(c), soccer M(c)/W(c), softball M/W, swimming and diving M(c)/W(c), tennis M(c)/W(c), ultimate Frisbee M(c)/W(c), volleyball M(c)/W(c), water polo M/W.

Campus security: 24-hour emergency response devices and patrols, late-night transport/escort service, controlled dormitory access.

Student services: health clinic, personal/psychological counseling.

COSTS & FINANCIAL AID

Costs (2017–18) ***Comprehensive fee:*** $64,320 includes full-time tuition ($49,980), mandatory fees ($650), and room and board ($13,690). ***College room only:*** $7390. Room and board charges vary according to board plan and housing facility. ***Payment plan:*** installment. ***Waivers:*** employees or children of employees.

Financial Aid Of all full-time matriculated undergraduates who enrolled in 2016, 1,823 applied for aid, 1,452 were judged to have need, 1,452 had their need fully met. In 2016, 25 non-need-based awards were made. ***Average percent of need met:*** 100. ***Average financial aid package:*** $39,079. ***Average need-based loan:*** $5363. ***Average need-based gift aid:*** $35,521. ***Average non-need-based aid:*** $40,213. ***Average indebtedness upon graduation:*** $25,446. ***Financial aid deadline:*** 1/15.

APPLYING

Options: electronic application, early admission, early decision, deferred entrance.

Application fee: $60.

Required: high school transcript, 2 letters of recommendation. ***Recommended:*** interview.

Application deadlines: 1/15 (freshmen), 3/1 (transfers).

Early decision deadline: 12/15.

Notification: 4/1 (freshmen), continuous (transfers), 1/15 (early decision).

CONTACT

College of the Holy Cross, 1 College Street, Worcester, MA 01610-2395. *Phone:* 508-793-2443. *Toll-free phone:* 800-442-2421.

Curry College

Milton, Massachusetts

http://www.curry.edu/

- **Independent** comprehensive, founded 1879
- **Suburban** 131-acre campus with easy access to Boston
- **Endowment** $95.9 million
- **Coed** 2,688 undergraduate students, 79% full-time, 59% women, 41% men
- **Moderately difficult** entrance level, 89% of applicants were admitted

UNDERGRAD STUDENTS

2,111 full-time, 577 part-time. Students come from 31 states and territories; 23 other countries; 33% are from out of state; 10% Black or African American, non-Hispanic/Latino; 6% Hispanic/Latino; 2% Asian, non-Hispanic/Latino; 0.3% Native Hawaiian or other Pacific Islander, non-Hispanic/Latino; 0.1% American Indian or Alaska Native, non-Hispanic/Latino; 2% Two or more races, non-Hispanic/Latino; 9% Race/ethnicity unknown; 2% international; 2% transferred in; 87% live on campus.

Freshmen:

Admission: 6,143 applied, 5,442 admitted, 678 enrolled. ***Average high school GPA:*** 2.8. ***Test scores:*** SAT critical reading scores over 500: 36%; SAT math scores over 500: 38%; SAT writing scores over 500: 32%; ACT scores over 18: 79%; SAT critical reading scores over 600: 4%; SAT math scores over 600: 6%; SAT writing scores over 600: 3%; ACT scores over 24: 21%; ACT scores over 30: 2%.

Retention: 71% of full-time freshmen returned.

FACULTY

Total: 474, 25% full-time, 42% with terminal degrees.

Student/faculty ratio: 11:1.

ACADEMICS

Calendar: semesters. *Degrees:* bachelor's, master's, and post-master's certificates.

Special study options: academic remediation for entering students, accelerated degree program, adult/continuing education programs, advanced placement credit, double majors, English as a second language, honors programs, independent study, internships, off-campus study, part-time degree program, services for LD students, student-designed majors, study abroad, summer session for credit. ***ROTC:*** Army (c).

Unusual degree programs: 3-2 education.

Computers: 245 computers/terminals and 2,500 ports are available on campus for general student use. Students can access the following: campus intranet, computer help desk, free student e-mail accounts, online (class) grades, online (class) registration, online (class) schedules. Campuswide network is available. 100% of college-owned or -operated housing units are wired for high-speed Internet access. Wireless service is available via entire campus.

Library: Levin Library plus 1 other. *Books:* 71,678 (physical), 231,354 (digital/electronic); *Serial titles:* 65 (physical), 51,102 (digital/electronic); *Databases:* 98. Weekly public service hours: 98; students can reserve study rooms.

STUDENT LIFE

Housing options: coed, men-only, women-only. Campus housing is university owned.

Activities and organizations: drama/theater group, student-run newspaper, radio and television station, choral group, Student radio station, Student government, Student Program Board, Curry Cares: Community Service, Theatre.

Athletics Member NCAA. All Division III. ***Intercollegiate sports:*** baseball M, basketball M/W, cross-country running W, equestrian sports M(c)/W(c), football M, ice hockey M/W(c), lacrosse M/W, rugby M(c), soccer M/W, softball W, tennis M/W, volleyball W. ***Intramural sports:*** badminton M/W, basketball M/W, bowling M/W, cheerleading M(c)/W(c), field hockey W, skiing (downhill) M/W, soccer M/W, softball M/W, tennis M/W, ultimate Frisbee M/W, volleyball M/W.

Campus security: 24-hour emergency response devices and patrols, late-night transport/escort service, controlled dormitory access, campus safety office.

Student services: health clinic, personal/psychological counseling.

COSTS & FINANCIAL AID
Costs (2017–18) ***One-time required fee:*** $340. ***Comprehensive fee:*** $54,011 includes full-time tuition ($36,780), mandatory fees ($1816), and room and board ($15,415). Full-time tuition and fees vary according to class time, course load, location, and program. Part-time tuition: $1226 per credit. Part-time tuition and fees vary according to class time, course load, location, and program. ***Room and board:*** Room and board charges vary according to board plan and housing facility. ***Payment plan:*** installment. ***Waivers:*** children of alumni and employees or children of employees.

Financial Aid Of all full-time matriculated undergraduates who enrolled in 2016, 1,586 applied for aid, 1,584 were judged to have need, 200 had their need fully met. 932 Federal Work-Study jobs (averaging $2320). In 2016, 439 non-need-based awards were made. ***Average percent of need met:*** 72. ***Average financial aid package:*** $27,281. ***Average need-based loan:*** $4347. ***Average need-based gift aid:*** $22,927. ***Average non-need-based aid:*** $13,962. ***Average indebtedness upon graduation:*** $42,191.

APPLYING
Standardized Tests *Required for some:* SAT or ACT (for admission), TOEFL for international applicants whose native language is not English.

Options: electronic application, early admission, early action, deferred entrance.

Application fee: $50.

Required: essay or personal statement, high school transcript, minimum 2.0 GPA, 1 letter of recommendation, Common Application Supplement and Program for Advancement of Learning (PAL), Cognitive and Achievement Testing for PAL. ***Required for some:*** interview.

Application deadlines: 4/1 (freshmen), 7/1 (transfers), 12/1 (early action).

Notification: continuous (freshmen), continuous (transfers), 12/15 (early action).

CONTACT
Ms. Jane P. Fidler, VP of Admission and Dean of Undergraduate Admission, Curry College, 1071 Blue Hill Avenue, Milton, MA 02186. *Phone:* 617-333-2210. *Toll-free phone:* 800-669-0686. *Fax:* 617-333-2114. *E-mail:* curryadm@curry.edu.

Dean College
Franklin, Massachusetts
http://www.dean.edu/

- **Independent** 4-year, founded 1865
- **Small-town** 100-acre campus with easy access to Boston, MA and Providence, RI
- **Endowment** $38.9 million
- **Coed** 1,339 undergraduate students, 85% full-time, 53% women, 47% men
- **Minimally difficult** entrance level, 67% of applicants were admitted

UNDERGRAD STUDENTS
1,132 full-time, 207 part-time. Students come from 37 states and territories; 12 other countries; 46% are from out of state; 15% Black or African American, non-Hispanic/Latino; 8% Hispanic/Latino; 0.7% Asian, non-Hispanic/Latino; 0.3% Native Hawaiian or other Pacific Islander, non-Hispanic/Latino; 0.3% American Indian or Alaska Native, non-Hispanic/Latino; 5% Two or more races, non-Hispanic/Latino; 16% Race/ethnicity unknown; 6% international; 4% transferred in; 89% live on campus.

Freshmen:
Admission: 3,824 applied, 2,570 admitted, 436 enrolled. ***Average high school GPA:*** 2.44. ***Test scores:*** SAT critical reading scores over 500: 23%; SAT math scores over 500: 23%; ACT scores over 18: 10%; SAT critical reading scores over 600: 6%; SAT math scores over 600: 5%; ACT scores over 24: 1%; SAT critical reading scores over 700: 1%. ***Retention:*** 74% of full-time freshmen returned.

FACULTY
Total: 166, 19% full-time, 17% with terminal degrees.

Student/faculty ratio: 17:1.

ACADEMICS
Calendar: semesters. *Degrees:* certificates, associate, and bachelor's.

Special study options: adult/continuing education programs, advanced placement credit, cooperative education, distance learning, double majors, English as a second language, honors programs, independent study,

internships, off-campus study, part-time degree program, services for LD students, student-designed majors, study abroad, summer session for credit.

Computers: 40 computers/terminals are available on campus for general student use. Students can access the following: campus intranet, computer help desk, free student e-mail accounts, online (class) grades, online (class) registration, online (class) schedules. Campuswide network is available. 100% of college-owned or -operated housing units are wired for high-speed Internet access. Wireless service is available via entire campus.

Library: E. Ross Anderson Library.

STUDENT LIFE

Housing options: coed, women-only, special housing for students with disabilities. Campus housing is university owned. Freshman campus housing is guaranteed.

Activities and organizations: student-run radio and television station, National Society of Leadership and Success, Student Activities Committee, Residence Hall Association, International Student Association, Phi Theta Kappa.

Athletics Member NCAA, USCAA. All Division III. ***Intercollegiate sports:*** baseball M, basketball M/W, football M, golf M, lacrosse M/W, soccer M/W, volleyball M/W.

Campus security: 24-hour emergency response devices and patrols, student patrols, late-night transport/escort service, controlled dormitory access.

Student services: health clinic, personal/psychological counseling.

COSTS

Costs (2016–17) ***Comprehensive fee:*** $52,692 includes full-time tuition ($36,660), mandatory fees ($300), and room and board ($15,732). Full-time tuition and fees vary according to class time, course load, and program. Part-time tuition: $335 per credit. Part-time tuition and fees vary according to class time, course load, and program. ***Required fees:*** $25 per term part-time. ***College room only:*** $9936. Room and board charges vary according to housing facility. ***Payment plan:*** installment. ***Waivers:*** employees or children of employees.

APPLYING

Standardized Tests *Recommended:* SAT or ACT (for admission).

Options: electronic application, early admission, early action, deferred entrance.

Required: high school transcript. ***Required for some:*** audition for performing arts majors. ***Recommended:*** essay or personal statement, minimum 2.0 GPA, 1 letter of recommendation, interview.

Application deadlines: rolling (freshmen), 12/1 (early action).

Notification: continuous (freshmen), 1/15 (early action).

CONTACT

Iris P. Godes, Associate Vice President of Enrollment Services /Dean of Admissions, Dean College, 99 Main Street, Franklin, MA 02038. *Phone:* 508-541-1547. *Toll-free phone:* 877-TRY-DEAN. *Fax:* 508-541-8726. *E-mail:* igodes@dean.edu.

See previous page for display ad and page 1332 for the College Close-Up.

Eastern Nazarene College

Quincy, Massachusetts

http://www.enc.edu/

- **Independent** comprehensive, founded 1918, affiliated with Church of the Nazarene
- **Urban** 17-acre campus with easy access to Boston
- **Endowment** $12.9 million
- **Coed** 862 undergraduate students, 99% full-time, 57% women, 43% men
- **Moderately difficult** entrance level, 63% of applicants were admitted

UNDERGRAD STUDENTS

850 full-time, 12 part-time. Students come from 32 states and territories; 24 other countries; 35% are from out of state; 15% Black or African American, non-Hispanic/Latino; 11% Hispanic/Latino; 4% Asian, non-Hispanic/Latino; 0.1% Native Hawaiian or other Pacific Islander, non-Hispanic/Latino; 0.1% American Indian or Alaska Native, non-Hispanic/Latino; 5% Two or more races, non-Hispanic/Latino; 11% Race/ethnicity unknown; 1% international; 10% transferred in; 50% live on campus.

Freshmen:

Admission: 989 applied, 620 admitted, 172 enrolled. ***Average high school GPA:*** 3. ***Test scores:*** SAT critical reading scores over 500: 46%; SAT math scores over 500: 48%; ACT scores over 18: 81%; SAT critical reading scores over 600: 17%; SAT math scores over 600: 19%; ACT scores over 24: 34%; SAT critical reading scores over 700: 3%; SAT math scores over 700: 4%; ACT scores over 30: 14%.

Retention: 69% of full-time freshmen returned.

ACADEMICS

Calendar: semesters. *Degrees:* certificates, associate, bachelor's, and master's.

Special study options: academic remediation for entering students, accelerated degree program, adult/continuing education programs, advanced placement credit, cooperative education, double majors, honors programs, independent study, internships, off-campus study, part-time degree program, services for LD students, study abroad, summer session for credit.

Unusual degree programs: engineering with Boston University; nursing with Boston College; Massachusetts College of Pharmacy.

Computers: 200 ports are available on campus for general student use. Students can access the following: computer help desk, free student e-mail accounts, online (class) grades, online (class) registration, online (class) schedules. Campuswide network is available. 100% of college-owned or -operated housing units are wired for high-speed Internet access. Wireless service is available via entire campus.

Library: Nease Library. *Books:* 113,825 (physical), 314,187 (digital/electronic); *Serial titles:* 748 (physical), 295,387 (digital/electronic); *Databases:* 90. Weekly public service hours: 95; study areas open 24 hours, 5-7 days a week; students can reserve study rooms.

STUDENT LIFE

Housing options: on-campus residence required through senior year; men-only, women-only, special housing for students with disabilities. Campus housing is university owned. Freshman campus housing is guaranteed.

Activities and organizations: drama/theater group, student-run newspaper, choral group, Gospel Choir, Acappella Choir, Germantown Tutoring, ALANA, Spirit Team.

Athletics Member NCAA. All Division III. ***Intercollegiate sports:*** baseball M, basketball M/W, cross-country running M/W, golf M, soccer M/W, softball W, tennis M/W, track and field M/W, volleyball M/W. ***Intramural sports:*** basketball M/W, soccer M/W, swimming and diving M(c)/W(c), ultimate Frisbee M.

Campus security: 24-hour emergency response devices and patrols, student patrols, late-night transport/escort service, controlled dormitory access.

Student services: health clinic, personal/psychological counseling.

COSTS & FINANCIAL AID

Costs (2017–18) ***Comprehensive fee:*** $41,114 includes full-time tuition ($31,158), mandatory fees ($622), and room and board ($9334). Full-time tuition and fees vary according to class time, course load, degree level, location, program, and reciprocity agreements. Part-time tuition: $1298 per credit hour. Part-time tuition and fees vary according to class time, degree level, location, program, and reciprocity agreements. ***Room and board:*** Room and board charges vary according to board plan and housing facility. ***Payment plan:*** installment. ***Waivers:*** employees or children of employees.

Financial Aid Of all full-time matriculated undergraduates who enrolled in 2014, 761 applied for aid, 395 were judged to have need, 128 had their need fully met. 40 Federal Work-Study jobs (averaging $2500). In 2014, 67 non-need-based awards were made. ***Average percent of need met:*** 80. ***Average financial aid package:*** $29,431. ***Average need-based loan:*** $8837. ***Average need-based gift aid:*** $17,673. ***Average non-need-based aid:*** $13,644. ***Average indebtedness upon graduation:*** $25,251.

APPLYING

Standardized Tests *Required:* SAT or ACT (for admission).

Options: electronic application, early admission, deferred entrance.

Required: high school transcript, minimum 2.0 GPA, 1 letter of recommendation. ***Recommended:*** essay or personal statement, minimum 3.0 GPA, 2 letters of recommendation, interview.

Application deadlines: rolling (freshmen), rolling (out-of-state freshmen), rolling (transfers).

Notification: continuous (freshmen), continuous (out-of-state freshmen), continuous (transfers).

CONTACT

Ms. Ashley Rudeen, Assistant Director of Admission / International DSO, Eastern Nazarene College, 23 East Elm Avenue, Quincy, MA 02170. *Phone:* 617-745-3861. *Toll-free phone:* 800-88-ENC88. *Fax:* 617-745-3992. *E-mail:* ashley.rudeen@enc.edu.

Elms College

Chicopee, Massachusetts

http://www.elms.edu/

- **Independent Roman Catholic** comprehensive, founded 1928
- **Suburban** 32-acre campus
- **Coed** 1,188 undergraduate students, 80% full-time, 75% women, 25% men
- **Moderately difficult** entrance level, 76% of applicants were admitted

UNDERGRAD STUDENTS

954 full-time, 234 part-time. Students come from 20 states and territories; 25 other countries; 22% are from out of state; 8% Black or African American, non-Hispanic/Latino; 12% Hispanic/Latino; 2% Asian, non-Hispanic/Latino; 0.3% American Indian or Alaska Native, non-Hispanic/Latino; 21% Race/ethnicity unknown; 0.7% international; 4% transferred in; 31% live on campus.

Freshmen:

Admission: 684 applied, 523 admitted, 164 enrolled. ***Average high school GPA:*** 3.34.

Retention: 81% of full-time freshmen returned.

FACULTY

Total: 227, 28% full-time.

Student/faculty ratio: 10:1.

ACADEMICS

Calendar: semesters. *Degrees:* associate, bachelor's, master's, doctoral, post-master's, and postbachelor's certificates.

Special study options: academic remediation for entering students, accelerated degree program, adult/continuing education programs, advanced placement credit, double majors, English as a second language, honors programs, internships, off-campus study, part-time degree program, student-designed majors, study abroad, summer session for credit. ***ROTC:*** Army (c), Air Force (c).

Computers: Campuswide network is available.

Library: Alumnae Library.

STUDENT LIFE

Housing options: coed, women-only. Campus housing is university owned. Freshman campus housing is guaranteed.

Activities and organizations: drama/theater group, student-run newspaper, choral group.

Athletics Member NCAA. All Division III. ***Intercollegiate sports:*** baseball M, basketball M/W, cross-country running M/W, field hockey W, golf M, lacrosse W, soccer M/W, softball W, swimming and diving M/W, track and field M/W, volleyball M/W. ***Intramural sports:*** basketball M/W, bowling M/W, cross-country running M/W, field hockey W, golf W, lacrosse M/W, racquetball M/W, skiing (cross-country) M/W, soccer M/W, softball M/W, swimming and diving M/W, volleyball M/W, water polo M/W, weight lifting M/W.

Campus security: 24-hour emergency response devices and patrols, late-night transport/escort service, controlled dormitory access.

Student services: health clinic, personal/psychological counseling.

COSTS & FINANCIAL AID

Costs (2016–17) ***Comprehensive fee:*** $45,648 includes full-time tuition ($31,846), mandatory fees ($1566), and room and board ($12,236). Part-time tuition: $646 per credit hour. Part-time tuition and fees vary according to location and program. ***Room and board:*** Room and board charges vary according to board plan. ***Payment plan:*** installment. ***Waivers:*** senior citizens and employees or children of employees.

Financial Aid Of all full-time matriculated undergraduates who enrolled in 2016, 895 applied for aid, 855 were judged to have need, 80 had their need fully met. 138 Federal Work-Study jobs (averaging $1192). In 2016, 74 non-need-based awards were made. ***Average percent of need met:*** 62. ***Average financial aid package:*** $22,505. ***Average need-based loan:*** $4768. ***Average need-based gift aid:*** $18,629. ***Average non-need-based aid:*** $15,004. ***Average indebtedness upon graduation:*** $37,052.

APPLYING

Standardized Tests *Required:* SAT or ACT (for admission).

Options: early admission, deferred entrance.

Application fee: $30.

Required: essay or personal statement, high school transcript, 2 letters of recommendation. ***Recommended:*** interview.

Application deadlines: rolling (freshmen), rolling (transfers).

Notification: continuous (freshmen), continuous (transfers).

CONTACT

Mr. Joseph Wagner, Director of Admissions, Elms College, Chicopee, MA 01013-2839. *Phone:* 413-592-3189 Ext. 350. *Toll-free phone:* 800-255-ELMS. *Fax:* 413-594-2781. *E-mail:* admissions@elms.edu.

Emerson College

Boston, Massachusetts

http://www.emerson.edu/

- **Independent** comprehensive, founded 1880
- **Urban** campus with easy access to Boston, MA
- **Endowment** $149.2 million
- **Coed** 3,790 undergraduate students, 98% full-time, 60% women, 40% men
- **Very difficult** entrance level, 48% of applicants were admitted

UNDERGRAD STUDENTS

3,733 full-time, 57 part-time. Students come from 53 states and territories; 47 other countries; 68% are from out of state; 3% Black or African American, non-Hispanic/Latino; 11% Hispanic/Latino; 4% Asian, non-Hispanic/Latino; 0.1% Native Hawaiian or other Pacific Islander, non-Hispanic/Latino; 0.1% American Indian or Alaska Native, non-Hispanic/Latino; 4% Two or more races, non-Hispanic/Latino; 2% Race/ethnicity unknown; 8% international; 4% transferred in; 57% live on campus.

Freshmen:

Admission: 9,149 applied, 4,397 admitted, 881 enrolled. ***Average high school GPA:*** 3.68. ***Test scores:*** SAT critical reading scores over 500: 94%; SAT math scores over 500: 91%; SAT writing scores over 500: 94%; ACT scores over 18: 99%; SAT critical reading scores over 600: 62%; SAT math scores over 600: 49%; SAT writing scores over 600: 60%; ACT scores over 24: 90%; SAT critical reading scores over 700: 14%; SAT math scores over 700: 9%; SAT writing scores over 700: 13%; ACT scores over 30: 24%.

Retention: 87% of full-time freshmen returned.

FACULTY

Total: 479, 42% full-time, 56% with terminal degrees.

Student/faculty ratio: 13:1.

ACADEMICS

Calendar: semesters. *Degrees:* certificates, bachelor's, master's, and doctoral.

Special study options: adult/continuing education programs, advanced placement credit, double majors, honors programs, independent study, internships, off-campus study, part-time degree program, services for LD students, student-designed majors, study abroad, summer session for credit.

Computers: 480 computers/terminals and 1,900 ports are available on campus for general student use. Students can access the following: computer help desk, free student e-mail accounts, online (class) grades, online (class) registration, online (class) schedules. Campuswide network is available. 100% of college-owned or -operated housing units are wired for high-speed Internet access. Wireless service is available via entire campus.

Library: Iwasaki Library plus 1 other. *Books:* 336,669 (physical), 2,484 (digital/electronic); *Serial titles:* 67,760 (digital/electronic); *Databases:* 125. Weekly public service hours: 93; students can reserve study rooms.

STUDENT LIFE

Housing options: on-campus residence required through sophomore year; coed. Campus housing is university owned. Freshman campus housing is guaranteed.

Activities and organizations: drama/theater group, student-run newspaper, radio and television station, choral group, EIV (Emerson Independent Video), National Broadcasting Society (student chapter), SPEC (Screenwriting), Emertainment Monthly (entertainment news), Emerson International (international student group), national fraternities, national sororities.

Athletics Member NCAA. All Division III. ***Intercollegiate sports:*** baseball M, basketball M/W, cross-country running M/W, golf M(c)/W(c), lacrosse M/W, soccer M/W, softball W, tennis M/W, track and field W, volleyball M/W. ***Intramural sports:*** basketball M/W, soccer M/W, volleyball M/W.

Campus security: 24-hour emergency response devices and patrols, late-night transport/escort service, controlled dormitory access.

Student services: health clinic, personal/psychological counseling.

COSTS & FINANCIAL AID

Costs (2017–18) ***Comprehensive fee:*** $59,228 includes full-time tuition ($42,144), mandatory fees ($764), and room and board ($16,320). Full-time tuition and fees vary according to student level. Part-time tuition: $1317 per credit hour. Part-time tuition and fees vary according to student level. ***Room and board:*** Room and board charges vary according to board plan. ***Payment plan:*** installment. ***Waivers:*** employees or children of employees.

Financial Aid Of all full-time matriculated undergraduates who enrolled in 2016, 2,410 applied for aid, 2,038 were judged to have need, 137 had their need fully met. 383 Federal Work-Study jobs (averaging $1980). 85 state and other part-time jobs (averaging $12,943). In 2016, 361 non-need-based awards were made. ***Average percent of need met:*** 52. ***Average financial aid package:*** $21,848. ***Average need-based loan:*** $4788. ***Average need-based gift aid:*** $18,820. ***Average non-need-based aid:*** $15,402. ***Average indebtedness upon graduation:*** $23,225.

APPLYING

Standardized Tests *Required:* SAT or ACT (for admission).

Options: electronic application, early admission, early action, deferred entrance.

Application fee: $65.

Required: essay or personal statement, high school transcript, 1 letter of recommendation. ***Required for some:*** interview.

Application deadlines: 1/15 (freshmen), 3/15 (transfers), 11/1 (early action).

Notification: continuous until 4/1 (freshmen), continuous until 4/1 (out-of-state freshmen), 5/1 (transfers), 12/15 (early action).

CONTACT

Emerson College, 120 Boylston Street, Boston, MA 02116-4624. *Phone:* 617-824-8600.

See previous page for display ad and page 1346 for the College Close-Up.

Emmanuel College

Boston, Massachusetts

http://www.emmanuel.edu/

- **Independent Roman Catholic** comprehensive, founded 1919
- **Urban** 17-acre campus
- **Endowment** $125.7 million
- **Coed** 2,012 undergraduate students, 91% full-time, 74% women, 26% men
- 71% of applicants were admitted

UNDERGRAD STUDENTS

1,834 full-time, 178 part-time. Students come from 33 states and territories; 52 other countries; 44% are from out of state; 5% Black or African American, non-Hispanic/Latino; 10% Hispanic/Latino; 4% Asian, non-Hispanic/Latino; 0.1% Native Hawaiian or other Pacific Islander, non-Hispanic/Latino; 0.2% American Indian or Alaska Native, non-Hispanic/Latino; 3% Two or more races, non-Hispanic/Latino; 4% Race/ethnicity unknown; 2% international; 1% transferred in; 70% live on campus.

Freshmen:
Admission: 6,223 applied, 4,443 admitted, 596 enrolled. ***Average high school GPA:*** 3.67. ***Test scores:*** SAT critical reading scores over 500: 83%; SAT math scores over 500: 83%; SAT writing scores over 500: 78%; ACT scores over 18: 99%; SAT critical reading scores over 600: 30%; SAT math scores over 600: 27%; SAT writing scores over 600: 28%; ACT scores over 24: 68%; SAT critical reading scores over 700: 6%; SAT math scores over 700: 2%; SAT writing scores over 700: 2%; ACT scores over 30: 4%.

Retention: 80% of full-time freshmen returned.

FACULTY

Total: 198, 47% full-time, 67% with terminal degrees.

Student/faculty ratio: 13:1.

ACADEMICS

Calendar: semesters. *Degrees:* bachelor's, master's, post-master's, and postbachelor's certificates.

Special study options: advanced placement credit, distance learning, double majors, honors programs, independent study, internships, off-campus study, part-time degree program, services for LD students, student-designed majors, study abroad, summer session for credit. ***ROTC:*** Army (c).

Computers: 284 computers/terminals are available on campus for general student use. Students can access the following: campus intranet, computer help desk, free student e-mail accounts, online (class) grades, online (class) registration, online (class) schedules. Campuswide network is available. 100% of college-owned or -operated housing units are wired for high-speed Internet access. Wireless service is available via entire campus.

Library: Cardinal Cushing Library. *Books:* 93,952 (physical), 216,096 (digital/electronic); *Serial titles:* 228 (physical), 5,592 (digital/electronic); *Databases:* 68. Weekly public service hours: 106; students can reserve study rooms.

STUDENT LIFE

Housing options: coed, special housing for students with disabilities. Campus housing is university owned and leased by the school. Freshman campus housing is guaranteed.

Activities and organizations: drama/theater group, student-run newspaper, radio station, choral group, Student Government Association, Model United Nations, Black Student Union, Habitat for Humanity, Emmanuel College Dance Marathon.

Athletics Member NCAA. All Division III. ***Intercollegiate sports:*** basketball M/W, cross-country running M/W, golf M, lacrosse M/W, soccer M/W, softball W, track and field M/W, volleyball M/W. ***Intramural sports:*** baseball M(c), field hockey W(c), ultimate Frisbee M(c)/W(c).

Campus security: 24-hour emergency response devices and patrols, late-night transport/escort service, controlled dormitory access.

Student services: health clinic, personal/psychological counseling.

COSTS & FINANCIAL AID

Costs (2017–18) ***One-time required fee:*** $300. ***Comprehensive fee:*** $53,472 includes full-time tuition ($38,584), mandatory fees ($260), and room and board ($14,628). Part-time tuition: $1206 per credit hour. ***Room and board:*** Room and board charges vary according to board plan and housing facility. ***Waivers:*** employees or children of employees.

Financial Aid Of all full-time matriculated undergraduates who enrolled in 2016, 1,611 applied for aid, 1,481 were judged to have need, 561 had their need fully met. 516 Federal Work-Study jobs (averaging $2047). In 2016, 341 non-need-based awards were made. ***Average percent of need met:*** 73. ***Average financial aid package:*** $26,986. ***Average need-based loan:*** $4709. ***Average need-based gift aid:*** $22,528. ***Average non-need-based aid:*** $14,794. ***Average indebtedness upon graduation:*** $36,818.

APPLYING

Options: early admission, early action, deferred entrance.

Application fee: $60.

Required: essay or personal statement, high school transcript, 2 letters of recommendation. ***Recommended:*** interview.

Application deadlines: 2/15 (freshmen), 4/1 (transfers), 11/1 (early action).

Notification: continuous until 1/15 (freshmen), 5/1 (transfers), 12/15 (early action).

CONTACT
Ms. Sandra Robbins, Dean for Enrollment, Emmanuel College, Admission Office, 400 The Fenway, Boston, MA 02115. *Phone:* 617-735-9715. *Fax:* 617-735-9801. *E-mail:* enroll@emmanuel.edu.

See previous page for display ad and page 1348 for the College Close-Up.

Endicott College

Beverly, Massachusetts

http://www.endicott.edu/

- **Independent** comprehensive, founded 1939
- **Suburban** 235-acre campus with easy access to Boston
- **Endowment** $67.2 million
- **Coed** 3,268 undergraduate students, 89% full-time, 60% women, 40% men
- **Moderately difficult** entrance level, 79% of applicants were admitted

UNDERGRAD STUDENTS
2,897 full-time, 371 part-time. Students come from 38 states and territories; 34 other countries; 52% are from out of state; 2% Black or African American, non-Hispanic/Latino; 5% Hispanic/Latino; 1% Asian, non-Hispanic/Latino; 0.1% Native Hawaiian or other Pacific Islander, non-Hispanic/Latino; 0.2% American Indian or Alaska Native, non-Hispanic/Latino; 1% Two or more races, non-Hispanic/Latino; 9% Race/ethnicity unknown; 2% international; 4% transferred in; 91% live on campus.

Freshmen:
Admission: 3,619 applied, 2,850 admitted, 726 enrolled. ***Average high school GPA:*** 3.3. ***Test scores:*** SAT critical reading scores over 500: 72%; SAT math scores over 500: 78%; SAT writing scores over 500: 70%; ACT scores over 18: 94%; SAT critical reading scores over 600: 15%; SAT math scores over 600: 21%; SAT writing scores over 600: 15%; ACT scores over 24: 46%; SAT critical reading scores over 700: 1%; SAT math scores over 700: 1%; SAT writing scores over 700: 1%; ACT scores over 30: 4%.

Retention: 86% of full-time freshmen returned.

FACULTY
Total: 480, 21% full-time, 40% with terminal degrees.

Student/faculty ratio: 13:1.

ACADEMICS
Calendar: semesters. *Degrees:* certificates, associate, bachelor's, master's, doctoral, and postbachelor's certificates.

Special study options: accelerated degree program, adult/continuing education programs, advanced placement credit, cooperative education, distance learning, double majors, English as a second language, honors programs, independent study, internships, off-campus study, part-time degree program, services for LD students, student-designed majors, study abroad, summer session for credit. ***ROTC:*** Army (c).

Computers: 285 computers/terminals are available on campus for general student use. Students can access the following: campus intranet, computer help desk, free student e-mail accounts, online (class) grades, online (class) registration, online (class) schedules. Campuswide network is available. 100% of college-owned or -operated housing units are wired for high-speed Internet access. Wireless service is available via entire campus.

Library: Diane M. Halle Library. *Books:* 103,315 (physical), 157,531 (digital/electronic); *Serial titles:* 64 (physical), 86,483 (digital/electronic); *Databases:* 173. Weekly public service hours: 97; students can reserve study rooms.

STUDENT LIFE
Housing options: coed, women-only, special housing for students with disabilities. Campus housing is university owned. Freshman campus housing is guaranteed.

Activities and organizations: drama/theater group, student-run newspaper, radio and television station, choral group.

Athletics Member NCAA. All Division III. ***Intercollegiate sports:*** baseball M, basketball M/W, cheerleading W(c), crew M(c)/W(c), cross-country running M/W, equestrian sports M/W, field hockey W, football M, golf M, ice hockey M/W, lacrosse M/W, rowing M(c)/W(c), rugby M(c)/W(c), soccer M/W, softball W, tennis M/W, volleyball M/W. ***Intramural sports:*** basketball M/W, football M/W, ice hockey M/W, soccer M/W, softball M/W, volleyball M/W.

Campus security: 24-hour emergency response devices and patrols, student patrols, late-night transport/escort service, controlled dormitory access, crime prevention programs, rape awareness defense, property identification, security cameras, front gate.

Student services: health clinic, personal/psychological counseling.

COSTS & FINANCIAL AID
Costs (2016–17) ***Comprehensive fee:*** $45,812 includes full-time tuition ($30,612), mandatory fees ($700), and room and board ($14,500). Full-time tuition and fees vary according to location and program. Part-time tuition: $940 per credit hour. Part-time tuition and fees vary according to location and program. ***College room only:*** $9996. Room and board charges vary according to housing facility. ***Payment plans:*** tuition prepayment, installment. ***Waivers:*** employees or children of employees.

Financial Aid Of all full-time matriculated undergraduates who enrolled in 2016, 2,458 applied for aid, 1,762 were judged to have need, 207 had their need fully met. 709 Federal Work-Study jobs (averaging $200). In 2016, 665 non-need-based awards were made. ***Average percent of need met:*** 64. ***Average financial aid package:*** $21,634. ***Average need-based loan:*** $4550. ***Average need-based gift aid:*** $10,875. ***Average non-need-based aid:*** $8972. ***Average indebtedness upon graduation:*** $41,901.

APPLYING
Standardized Tests *Required for some:* SAT or ACT (for admission).

Options: electronic application.

Application fee: $50.

Required: essay or personal statement, high school transcript, minimum 2.5 GPA, 1 letter of recommendation. ***Required for some:*** interview. ***Recommended:*** interview.

Application deadlines: 2/15 (freshmen), 3/15 (transfers).

Notification: continuous (freshmen), continuous (transfers).

CONTACT
Mr. Thomas J. Redman, Vice President of Admission and Financial Aid, Endicott College, 376 Hale Street, Beverly, MA 01915. *Phone:* 978-921-1000. *Toll-free phone:* 800-325-1114. *Fax:* 978-232-2520. *E-mail:* admissio@endicott.edu.

Fisher College

Boston, Massachusetts

http://www.fisher.edu/

- **Independent** comprehensive, founded 1903
- **Urban** 1-acre campus with easy access to Boston
- **Endowment** $30.0 million
- **Coed** 1,996 undergraduate students, 59% full-time, 74% women, 26% men

UNDERGRAD STUDENTS
1,171 full-time, 825 part-time. Students come from 34 states and territories; 43 other countries; 22% are from out of state; 11% Black or African American, non-Hispanic/Latino; 8% Hispanic/Latino; 0.9% Asian, non-Hispanic/Latino; 0.1% Native Hawaiian or other Pacific Islander, non-Hispanic/Latino; 0.1% American Indian or Alaska Native, non-Hispanic/Latino; 2% Two or more races, non-Hispanic/Latino; 43% Race/ethnicity unknown; 7% international; 6% transferred in; 16% live on campus.

Freshmen:
Admission: 282 enrolled. ***Average high school GPA:*** 2.23. ***Test scores:*** SAT critical reading scores over 500: 15%; SAT math scores over 500: 10%; ACT scores over 18: 54%; SAT critical reading scores over 600: 2%; SAT math scores over 600: 2%; ACT scores over 24: 8%; SAT math scores over 700: 1%.

Retention: 62% of full-time freshmen returned.

FACULTY
Total: 188, 18% full-time, 12% with terminal degrees.

Student/faculty ratio: 17:1.

ACADEMICS
Calendar: semesters. *Degrees:* certificates, associate, bachelor's, and master's.

Special study options: academic remediation for entering students, accelerated degree program, adult/continuing education programs, advanced placement credit, distance learning, English as a second language, honors programs, independent study, internships, off-campus study, part-time degree program, services for LD students, study abroad, summer session for credit. ***ROTC:*** Army (c).

Computers: 208 computers/terminals are available on campus for general student use. Students can access the following: campus intranet, computer help desk, free student e-mail accounts, online (class) grades, online (class) registration, online (class) schedules. Campuswide network is available. 100% of college-owned or -operated housing units are wired for high-speed Internet access. Wireless service is available via entire campus.

Library: Fisher College Library. *Books:* 22,541 (physical), 8,035 (digital/electronic); *Serial titles:* 40 (physical); *Databases:* 81. Weekly public service hours: 68; study areas open 24 hours, 5-7 days a week; students can reserve study rooms.

STUDENT LIFE

Housing options: coed, women-only. Campus housing is university owned and leased by the school.

Activities and organizations: drama/theater group, choral group, National Society of Leadership and Success (NSLS), Psychology Club, Criminal Justice Club, Fashion Club, Multi-Cultural Club.

Athletics Member NAIA. ***Intercollegiate sports:*** baseball M, basketball M/W, soccer M/W, softball W.

Campus security: 24-hour emergency response devices and patrols, controlled dormitory access.

Student services: health clinic, personal/psychological counseling, women's center.

COSTS & FINANCIAL AID

Costs (2017–18) ***Comprehensive fee:*** $46,267 includes full-time tuition ($29,504), mandatory fees ($995), and room and board ($15,768). Part-time tuition: $983 per course. Part-time tuition and fees vary according to course load. ***Required fees:*** $995 per term part-time. ***Room and board:*** Room and board charges vary according to housing facility. ***Payment plan:*** installment. ***Waivers:*** employees or children of employees.

Financial Aid Of all full-time matriculated undergraduates who enrolled in 2015, 1,097 applied for aid, 816 were judged to have need. 58 Federal Work-Study jobs (averaging $1406). In 2015, 76 non-need-based awards were made. ***Average financial aid package:*** $20,048. ***Average need-based loan:*** $4005. ***Average need-based gift aid:*** $13,530. ***Average non-need-based aid:*** $6423. ***Average indebtedness upon graduation:*** $12,724. ***Financial aid deadline:*** 3/15.

APPLYING

Standardized Tests *Required for some:* SAT or ACT (for admission).

Required: high school transcript. ***Required for some:*** essay or personal statement, interview. ***Recommended:*** minimum 2.0 GPA.

CONTACT

Mr. Robert Melaragni, Vice President of Enrollment Management, Fisher College, Boston, MA 02116. *Phone:* 617-236-8818. *Fax:* 617-236-5473. *E-mail:* admissions@fisher.edu.

★ Fitchburg State University

Fitchburg, Massachusetts

http://www.fitchburgstate.edu/

- **State-supported** comprehensive, founded 1894, part of Massachusetts Public Higher Education System
- **Suburban** 78-acre campus with easy access to Boston
- **Endowment** $13.6 million
- **Coed** 4,162 undergraduate students, 82% full-time, 53% women, 47% men
- **Moderately difficult** entrance level, 75% of applicants were admitted

UNDERGRAD STUDENTS

3,428 full-time, 734 part-time. Students come from 28 states and territories; 5 other countries; 8% are from out of state; 9% Black or African American, non-Hispanic/Latino; 11% Hispanic/Latino; 2% Asian, non-Hispanic/Latino; 0.1% American Indian or Alaska Native, non-Hispanic/Latino; 3% Two or more races, non-Hispanic/Latino; 2% Race/ethnicity unknown; 0.5% international; 9% transferred in; 57% live on campus.

Freshmen:

Admission: 3,566 applied, 2,662 admitted, 763 enrolled. ***Average high school GPA:*** 3.1. ***Test scores:*** SAT critical reading scores over 500: 50%; SAT math scores over 500: 50%; SAT writing scores over 500: 40%; ACT scores over 18: 86%; SAT critical reading scores over 600: 12%; SAT math scores over 600: 11%; SAT writing scores over 600: 7%; ACT scores over 24: 71%; SAT critical reading scores over 700: 1%; SAT math scores over 700: 1%; SAT writing scores over 700: 1%; ACT scores over 30: 6%.

Retention: 75% of full-time freshmen returned.

FACULTY

Total: 326, 62% full-time.

Student/faculty ratio: 14:1.

ACADEMICS

Calendar: semesters. *Degrees:* certificates, bachelor's, master's, post-master's, and postbachelor's certificates.

Special study options: academic remediation for entering students, accelerated degree program, adult/continuing education programs, advanced placement credit, distance learning, double majors, honors programs, independent study, internships, off-campus study, part-time degree program, services for LD students, student-designed majors, study abroad, summer session for credit. ***ROTC:*** Army (b).

Computers: 500 computers/terminals are available on campus for general student use. Students can access the following: computer help desk, free student e-mail accounts, online (class) grades, online (class) registration, online (class) schedules. Campuswide network is available. 100% of college-owned or -operated housing units are wired for high-speed Internet access. Wireless service is available via entire campus.

Library: Amelia V. Galucci-Cirio Library. *Books:* 222,517 (physical); *Databases:* 150. Weekly public service hours: 77.

STUDENT LIFE

Housing options: coed, special housing for students with disabilities. Campus housing is university owned. Freshman applicants given priority for college housing.

Activities and organizations: drama/theater group, student-run newspaper, radio station, choral group, Student Government Association, Dance Club, Activities Board, Greek Council, MASSPIRG, national fraternities, national sororities.

Athletics Member NCAA. All Division III. ***Intercollegiate sports:*** baseball M, basketball M/W, cross-country running M/W, field hockey W, football M, ice hockey M, lacrosse W, soccer M/W, softball W, track and field M/W. ***Intramural sports:*** basketball M/W, football M/W, racquetball M/W, soccer M/W, softball M/W, swimming and diving M/W, table tennis M/W, ultimate Frisbee M/W, volleyball M/W, water polo M/W.

Campus security: 24-hour emergency response devices and patrols, student patrols, late-night transport/escort service, controlled dormitory access.

Student services: health clinic, personal/psychological counseling.

COSTS & FINANCIAL AID

Costs (2016–17) ***Tuition:*** state resident $970 full-time, $40 per credit hour part-time; nonresident $7050 full-time, $294 per credit hour part-time. Full-time tuition and fees vary according to class time and reciprocity agreements. Part-time tuition and fees vary according to class time and reciprocity agreements. ***Required fees:*** $9165 full-time, $382 per credit hour part-time. ***Room and board:*** $9210. Room and board charges vary according to board plan and housing facility. ***Payment plan:*** installment. ***Waivers:*** senior citizens and employees or children of employees.

Financial Aid Of all full-time matriculated undergraduates who enrolled in 2015, 3,003 applied for aid, 2,259 were judged to have need. 197 Federal Work-Study jobs (averaging $1713). In 2015, 142 non-need-based awards were made. ***Average percent of need met:*** 76. ***Average financial aid package:*** $10,238. ***Average need-based loan:*** $4726. ***Average need-based gift aid:*** $6126. ***Average non-need-based aid:*** $1196. ***Average indebtedness upon graduation:*** $26,684.

APPLYING

Standardized Tests *Required:* SAT or ACT (for admission).

Options: electronic application, deferred entrance.

Application fee: $50.

Required: essay or personal statement, high school transcript, minimum 2.0 GPA, 16 core courses.

Application deadlines: rolling (freshmen), rolling (transfers).

Notification: continuous (freshmen), continuous (transfers).

CONTACT
Sean Ganas, Director of Admissions, Fitchburg State University, 160 Pearl Street, Fitchburg, MA 01420-2697. *Phone:* 978-665-3140. *Toll-free phone:* 800-705-9692. *Fax:* 978-665-4540.
E-mail: admissions@fitchburgstate.edu.

Framingham State University

Framingham, Massachusetts

http://www.framingham.edu/

- **State-supported** comprehensive, founded 1839, part of Massachusetts Public Higher Education System
- **Suburban** 77-acre campus with easy access to Boston
- **Endowment** $34.5 million
- **Coed** 4,337 undergraduate students, 85% full-time, 61% women, 39% men
- **Moderately difficult** entrance level, 65% of applicants were admitted

UNDERGRAD STUDENTS
3,701 full-time, 636 part-time. Students come from 23 states and territories; 21 other countries; 6% are from out of state; 10% Black or African American, non-Hispanic/Latino; 12% Hispanic/Latino; 3% Asian, non-Hispanic/Latino; 0.2% American Indian or Alaska Native, non-Hispanic/Latino; 4% Two or more races, non-Hispanic/Latino; 3% Race/ethnicity unknown; 0.4% international; 9% transferred in; 46% live on campus.

Freshmen:
Admission: 6,204 applied, 4,021 admitted, 749 enrolled. ***Test scores:*** SAT critical reading scores over 500: 45%; SAT math scores over 500: 52%; SAT writing scores over 500: 59%; ACT scores over 18: 88%; SAT critical reading scores over 600: 10%; SAT math scores over 600: 10%; SAT writing scores over 600: 13%; ACT scores over 24: 42%; SAT critical reading scores over 700: 1%; ACT scores over 30: 2%.
Retention: 74% of full-time freshmen returned.

FACULTY
Total: 330, 60% full-time.

Student/faculty ratio: 14:1.

ACADEMICS
Calendar: semesters. *Degrees:* bachelor's, master's, and postbachelor's certificates.

Special study options: advanced placement credit, cooperative education, distance learning, double majors, English as a second language, honors programs, independent study, internships, off-campus study, part-time degree program, services for LD students, student-designed majors, study abroad, summer session for credit.

Computers: 216 computers/terminals and 3,500 ports are available on campus for general student use. Students can access the following: free student e-mail accounts, online (class) grades, online (class) registration, online (class) schedules. Campuswide network is available. 100% of college-owned or -operated housing units are wired for high-speed Internet access. Wireless service is available via entire campus.

Library: Henry Whittemore Library. *Books:* 162,259 (physical), 28,774 (digital/electronic); *Serial titles:* 120 (physical); *Databases:* 72. Weekly public service hours: 97.

STUDENT LIFE
Housing options: coed, women-only, special housing for students with disabilities. Campus housing is university owned. Freshman applicants given priority for college housing.

Activities and organizations: drama/theater group, student-run newspaper, radio station, choral group, Dance Club, Student Union Activities Board, Gatepost (student newspaper), Student Government Association, Hilltop Players (theater group).

Athletics Member NCAA. All Division III. ***Intercollegiate sports:*** baseball M, basketball M/W, cross-country running M/W, field hockey W, football M, ice hockey M, lacrosse W, soccer M/W, softball W, volleyball W. ***Intramural sports:*** basketball M/W, cheerleading W(c), football M/W, golf M/W, lacrosse M(c), rugby M(c)/W(c), soccer M/W, volleyball M/W, weight lifting M/W.

Campus security: 24-hour emergency response devices and patrols, student patrols, late-night transport/escort service, controlled dormitory access.

Student services: health clinic, personal/psychological counseling, legal services.

COSTS & FINANCIAL AID
Costs (2017–18) ***Tuition:*** state resident $970 full-time; nonresident $7050 full-time. Full-time tuition and fees vary according to class time and degree level. Part-time tuition and fees vary according to class time, course load, and degree level. ***Required fees:*** $8370 full-time. ***Room and board:*** $11,250; room only: $7690. Room and board charges vary according to board plan and housing facility. ***Payment plans:*** tuition prepayment, installment. ***Waivers:*** senior citizens and employees or children of employees.

Financial Aid Of all full-time matriculated undergraduates who enrolled in 2015, 3,063 applied for aid, 2,413 were judged to have need, 888 had their need fully met. In 2015, 233 non-need-based awards were made. ***Average percent of need met:*** 60. ***Average financial aid package:*** $9900. ***Average need-based loan:*** $5300. ***Average need-based gift aid:*** $4400. ***Average non-need-based aid:*** $2200. ***Average indebtedness upon graduation:*** $29,493.

APPLYING
Standardized Tests *Required:* SAT or ACT (for admission).

Options: electronic application, early action, deferred entrance.

Application fee: $50.

Required: high school transcript, minimum 2.0 GPA, minimum of 16 college preparatory courses in specified areas. ***Recommended:*** minimum 3.0 GPA.

Application deadlines: 2/15 (freshmen), 11/15 (early action).

Notification: continuous (freshmen), continuous (transfers), 12/15 (early action).

CONTACT
Ms. Shayna Eddy, Associate Dean of Admissions, Framingham State University, 100 State Street, PO Box 9101, Framingham, MA 01701-9101. *Phone:* 508-626-4500. *Fax:* 508-626-4017.
E-mail: admissions@framingham.edu.

Franklin W. Olin College of Engineering

Needham, Massachusetts

http://www.olin.edu/

- **Independent** 4-year, founded 2002
- **Suburban** 75-acre campus with easy access to Boston
- **Endowment** $352.8 million
- **Coed** 378 undergraduate students, 90% full-time, 49% women, 51% men
- **Most difficult** entrance level, 10% of applicants were admitted

UNDERGRAD STUDENTS
340 full-time, 38 part-time. Students come from 40 states and territories; 12 other countries; 86% are from out of state; 0.8% Black or African American, non-Hispanic/Latino; 5% Hispanic/Latino; 12% Asian, non-Hispanic/Latino; 0.3% American Indian or Alaska Native, non-Hispanic/Latino; 6% Two or more races, non-Hispanic/Latino; 15% Race/ethnicity unknown; 12% international; 2% transferred in; 100% live on campus.

Freshmen:
Admission: 1,296 applied, 132 admitted, 79 enrolled. ***Average high school GPA:*** 3.9. ***Test scores:*** SAT critical reading scores over 500: 100%; SAT math scores over 500: 100%; SAT writing scores over 500: 100%; ACT scores over 18: 100%; SAT critical reading scores over 600: 96%; SAT math scores over 600: 100%; SAT writing scores over 600: 96%; ACT scores over 24: 100%; SAT critical reading scores over 700:

74%; SAT math scores over 700: 88%; SAT writing scores over 700: 59%; ACT scores over 30: 98%.

Retention: 99% of full-time freshmen returned.

FACULTY

Total: 61, 70% full-time, 85% with terminal degrees.

Student/faculty ratio: 7:1.

ACADEMICS

Calendar: semesters. *Degree:* bachelor's.

Special study options: independent study, internships, off-campus study, services for LD students, student-designed majors, study abroad.

Computers: 2,364 ports are available on campus for general student use. Students can access the following: campus intranet, computer help desk, free student e-mail accounts, online (class) grades, online (class) registration, online (class) schedules. Campuswide network is available. 100% of college-owned or -operated housing units are wired for high-speed Internet access. Wireless service is available via entire campus.

Library: Franklin W. Olin Library. *Books:* 18,330 (physical), 419,195 (digital/electronic); *Databases:* 168. Study areas open 24 hours, 5-7 days a week; students can reserve study rooms.

STUDENT LIFE

Housing options: on-campus residence required through senior year; coed, special housing for students with disabilities. Campus housing is university owned. Freshman campus housing is guaranteed.

Activities and organizations: drama/theater group, student-run newspaper, choral group, Council of Olin Representatives, Stay Late and Create, Support, Encourage and Recognize Volunteerism (SERV), Mini Baja, Olin Fire Arts Club.

Athletics ***Intercollegiate sports:*** soccer M(c)/W(c), ultimate Frisbee M(c)/W(c). ***Intramural sports:*** basketball M/W, softball M/W, volleyball M/W.

Campus security: 24-hour emergency response devices and patrols, controlled dormitory access.

Student services: health clinic, personal/psychological counseling.

COSTS & FINANCIAL AID

Costs (2017–18) ***One-time required fee:*** $2656. ***Comprehensive fee:*** $65,580 includes full-time tuition ($48,600), mandatory fees ($680), and room and board ($16,300). Part-time tuition: $1520 per credit hour. ***Payment plan:*** installment.

Financial Aid Of all full-time matriculated undergraduates who enrolled in 2016, 184 applied for aid, 155 were judged to have need, 151 had their need fully met. In 2016, 188 non-need-based awards were made. ***Average percent of need met:*** 99. ***Average financial aid package:*** $44,286. ***Average need-based loan:*** $3193. ***Average need-based gift aid:*** $42,535. ***Average non-need-based aid:*** $24,044. ***Average indebtedness upon graduation:*** $18,704. ***Financial aid deadline:*** 2/15.

APPLYING

Standardized Tests *Required:* SAT or ACT (for admission).

Options: electronic application, deferred entrance.

Application fee: $85.

Required: essay or personal statement, high school transcript, 3 letters of recommendation, interview.

Notification: 3/24 (freshmen).

CONTACT

Franklin W. Olin College of Engineering, 1000 Olin Way, Needham, MA 02492-1200. *Phone:* 781-292-2222. *Fax:* 781-292-2210. *E-mail:* apply@olin.edu.

Gordon College

Wenham, Massachusetts

http://www.gordon.edu/

- **Independent nondenominational** comprehensive, founded 1889
- **Suburban** 485-acre campus with easy access to Boston
- **Endowment** $44.2 million
- **Coed** 1,657 undergraduate students, 95% full-time, 63% women, 37% men
- **Moderately difficult** entrance level, 92% of applicants were admitted

UNDERGRAD STUDENTS

1,574 full-time, 83 part-time. Students come from 44 states and territories; 55 other countries; 65% are from out of state; 5% Black or African American, non-Hispanic/Latino; 7% Hispanic/Latino; 5% Asian, non-Hispanic/Latino; 0.1% Native Hawaiian or other Pacific Islander, non-Hispanic/Latino; 0.2% American Indian or Alaska Native, non-Hispanic/Latino; 4% Two or more races, non-Hispanic/Latino; 0.7% Race/ethnicity unknown; 9% international; 3% transferred in; 86% live on campus.

Freshmen:

Admission: 2,714 applied, 2,496 admitted, 425 enrolled. ***Average high school GPA:*** 3.56. ***Test scores:*** SAT critical reading scores over 500: 71%; SAT math scores over 500: 70%; SAT writing scores over 500: 69%; ACT scores over 18: 97%; SAT critical reading scores over 600: 33%; SAT math scores over 600: 32%; SAT writing scores over 600: 31%; ACT scores over 24: 67%; SAT critical reading scores over 700: 8%; SAT math scores over 700: 6%; SAT writing scores over 700: 3%; ACT scores over 30: 22%.

Retention: 86% of full-time freshmen returned.

FACULTY

Total: 219, 41% full-time, 35% with terminal degrees.

Student/faculty ratio: 12:1.

ACADEMICS

Calendar: semesters. *Degrees:* bachelor's and master's.

Special study options: advanced placement credit, cooperative education, double majors, honors programs, independent study, internships, off-campus study, part-time degree program, services for LD students, student-designed majors, study abroad, summer session for credit. ***ROTC:*** Army (c).

Unusual degree programs: 3-2 engineering with University of Southern California.

Computers: 100 computers/terminals and 10 ports are available on campus for general student use. Students can access the following: campus intranet, computer help desk, free student e-mail accounts, online (class) grades, online (class) registration, online (class) schedules. Campuswide network is available. 100% of college-owned or -operated housing units are wired for high-speed Internet access. Wireless service is available via entire campus.

Library: Jenks Learning Resource Center. *Books:* 132,914 (physical); *Serial titles:* 1,540 (physical). Weekly public service hours: 103; students can reserve study rooms.

STUDENT LIFE

Housing options: coed, men-only, women-only, special housing for students with disabilities. Campus housing is university owned. Freshman campus housing is guaranteed.

Activities and organizations: drama/theater group, student-run newspaper, radio station, choral group, Student Government Association, Student ministries and volunteer programs, Diverse music ensembles, Intramural sports, Short-term missions.

Athletics Member NCAA. All Division III. ***Intercollegiate sports:*** baseball M, basketball M/W, cross-country running M/W, field hockey W, lacrosse M/W, soccer M/W, softball W, swimming and diving M/W, tennis M/W, track and field M/W, volleyball W. ***Intramural sports:*** badminton M/W, basketball M/W, football M/W, racquetball M/W, rowing M(c)/W(c), soccer M/W, triathlon M/W, volleyball M/W, water polo M/W.

Campus security: 24-hour emergency response devices and patrols, late-night transport/escort service, controlled dormitory access, gated entrance.

Student services: health clinic, personal/psychological counseling.

COSTS & FINANCIAL AID

Costs (2017–18) ***Comprehensive fee:*** $47,740 includes full-time tuition ($35,180), mandatory fees ($1560), and room and board ($11,000). Full-time tuition and fees vary according to course load and program. Part-time tuition: $879 per credit. Part-time tuition and fees vary according to course load and program. ***College room only:*** $7000. Room and board charges vary according to board plan and housing facility. ***Payment plan:*** installment. ***Waivers:*** employees or children of employees.

Financial Aid Of all full-time matriculated undergraduates who enrolled in 2015, 1,283 applied for aid, 1,103 were judged to have need, 169 had their need fully met. 477 Federal Work-Study jobs (averaging $510). In

2015, 504 non-need-based awards were made. ***Average percent of need met:*** 70. ***Average financial aid package:*** $23,819. ***Average need-based loan:*** $4805. ***Average need-based gift aid:*** $18,906. ***Average non-need-based aid:*** $14,330. ***Average indebtedness upon graduation:*** $35,169.

APPLYING

Standardized Tests *Required:* SAT or ACT (for admission).

Options: electronic application, early admission, early action, deferred entrance.

Application fee: $50.

Required: essay or personal statement, high school transcript, 1 letter of recommendation, interview, pastoral recommendation and statement of Christian faith. ***Recommended:*** minimum 3.0 GPA.

Application deadlines: 8/1 (freshmen), rolling (out-of-state freshmen), rolling (transfers), 11/15 (early action).

Notification: continuous until 8/15 (freshmen), continuous until 8/15 (out-of-state freshmen), continuous (transfers), 12/1 (early action).

CONTACT

Miss June Bodoni, Associate Vice President for Enrollment, Gordon College, 255 Grapevine Road, Wenham, MA 01984. *Phone:* 978-867-4218. *Toll-free phone:* 866-464-6736. *Fax:* 978-867-4682. *E-mail:* admissions@gordon.edu.

Hampshire College

Amherst, Massachusetts

http://www.hampshire.edu/

- **Independent** 4-year, founded 1965
- **Small-town** 800-acre campus
- **Endowment** $39.6 million
- **Coed** 1,321 undergraduate students, 100% full-time, 62% women, 38% men
- **Moderately difficult** entrance level, 64% of applicants were admitted

UNDERGRAD STUDENTS

1,321 full-time. 79% are from out of state; 5% Black or African American, non-Hispanic/Latino; 10% Hispanic/Latino; 2% Asian, non-Hispanic/Latino; 0.1% Native Hawaiian or other Pacific Islander, non-Hispanic/Latino; 0.2% American Indian or Alaska Native, non-Hispanic/Latino; 7% Two or more races, non-Hispanic/Latino; 4% Race/ethnicity unknown; 5% international; 4% transferred in; 82% live on campus.

Freshmen:

Admission: 2,347 applied, 1,511 admitted, 327 enrolled.

Retention: 79% of full-time freshmen returned.

FACULTY

Total: 165, 75% full-time.

Student/faculty ratio: 10:1.

ACADEMICS

Calendar: 4-1-4. *Degree:* bachelor's.

Special study options: advanced placement credit, independent study, internships, off-campus study, services for LD students, student-designed majors, study abroad. ***ROTC:*** Army (c).

Computers: 205 computers/terminals are available on campus for general student use. Students can access the following: campus intranet, computer help desk, free student e-mail accounts, online (class) grades, online (class) registration, online (class) schedules. Campuswide network is available. 100% of college-owned or -operated housing units are wired for high-speed Internet access. Wireless service is available via entire campus.

Library: Harold F. Johnson Library. *Books:* 123,827 (physical), 151,197 (digital/electronic); *Serial titles:* 34,444 (digital/electronic); *Databases:* 136. Weekly public service hours: 102; study areas open 24 hours, 5-7 days a week; students can reserve study rooms.

STUDENT LIFE

Housing options: on-campus residence required through senior year; coed, men-only, women-only, special housing for students with disabilities. Campus housing is university owned. Freshman campus housing is guaranteed.

Activities and organizations: drama/theater group, student-run newspaper, radio station, choral group, Red Scare Frisbee, Queer Community Alliance, Excalibur (fantasy/role playing), Sports Coop, Circus Folks Unite.

Athletics Member USCAA. ***Intercollegiate sports:*** basketball M(c)/W(c), cross-country running M/W, equestrian sports M(c)/W(c), fencing M/W, soccer M/W, ultimate Frisbee M/W. ***Intramural sports:*** basketball M/W, equestrian sports M(c)/W(c), rock climbing M(c)/W(c), soccer M/W, table tennis M(c)/W(c), ultimate Frisbee M/W.

Campus security: 24-hour emergency response devices and patrols.

Student services: health clinic, personal/psychological counseling, women's center.

COSTS & FINANCIAL AID

Costs (2017–18) ***Comprehensive fee:*** $63,636 includes full-time tuition ($50,030) and room and board ($13,606). ***College room only:*** $8520. Room and board charges vary according to board plan. ***Payment plan:*** installment. ***Waivers:*** employees or children of employees.

Financial Aid Of all full-time matriculated undergraduates who enrolled in 2015, 1,040 applied for aid, 899 were judged to have need, 159 had their need fully met. In 2015, 375 non-need-based awards were made. ***Average percent of need met:*** 88. ***Average financial aid package:*** $37,881. ***Average need-based loan:*** $3947. ***Average need-based gift aid:*** $33,045. ***Average non-need-based aid:*** $11,010. ***Average indebtedness upon graduation:*** $25,393.

APPLYING

Options: electronic application, early admission, early decision, early action, deferred entrance.

Required: essay or personal statement, high school transcript, 1 letter of recommendation. ***Recommended:*** interview.

Application deadlines: 1/15 (freshmen), 3/15 (transfers), 12/1 (early action).

Early decision deadline: 11/15 (for plan 1), 1/1 (for plan 2).

Notification: 4/1 (freshmen), 4/15 (transfers), 12/15 (early decision plan 1), 2/1 (early decision plan 2), 2/1 (early action).

CONTACT

Hampshire College, 893 West Street, Amherst, MA 01002. *Phone:* 413-559-5471. *Toll-free phone:* 877-937-4267. *E-mail:* admissions@hampshire.edu.

Harvard University

Cambridge, Massachusetts

http://www.harvard.edu/

- **Independent** university, founded 1636
- **Urban** 380-acre campus with easy access to Boston
- **Endowment** $35.7 billion
- **Coed** 6,712 undergraduate students, 100% full-time, 47% women, 53% men
- **Most difficult** entrance level, 5% of applicants were admitted

UNDERGRAD STUDENTS

6,712 full-time. Students come from 54 states and territories; 107 other countries; 84% are from out of state; 7% Black or African American, non-Hispanic/Latino; 11% Hispanic/Latino; 20% Asian, non-Hispanic/Latino; 0.3% American Indian or Alaska Native, non-Hispanic/Latino; 7% Two or more races, non-Hispanic/Latino; 2% Race/ethnicity unknown; 12% international; 0.2% transferred in; 98% live on campus.

Freshmen:

Admission: 39,041 applied, 2,110 admitted, 1,661 enrolled. ***Average high school GPA:*** 4.17. ***Test scores:*** SAT critical reading scores over 500: 100%; SAT math scores over 500: 100%; SAT writing scores over 500: 100%; SAT critical reading scores over 600: 98%; SAT math scores over 600: 99%; SAT writing scores over 600: 98%; ACT scores over 24: 100%; SAT critical reading scores over 700: 81%; SAT math scores over 700: 84%; SAT writing scores over 700: 81%; ACT scores over 30: 93%.

Retention: 97% of full-time freshmen returned.

FACULTY

Total: 1,175, 83% full-time, 86% with terminal degrees.

Student/faculty ratio: 7:1.

ACADEMICS
Calendar: semesters. *Degrees:* bachelor's, master's, and doctoral.

Special study options: accelerated degree program, advanced placement credit, double majors, honors programs, independent study, internships, off-campus study, services for LD students, student-designed majors, study abroad, summer session for credit. ***ROTC:*** Army (b), Navy (b), Air Force (b).

Computers: 605 computers/terminals are available on campus for general student use. Students can access the following: computer help desk, free student e-mail accounts, online (class) grades, online (class) registration, online (class) schedules. Campuswide network is available. 100% of college-owned or -operated housing units are wired for high-speed Internet access. Wireless service is available via entire campus.
Library: Widener Library plus 73 others.

STUDENT LIFE
Housing options: on-campus residence required for freshman year; coed, cooperative, special housing for students with disabilities. Campus housing is university owned. Freshman campus housing is guaranteed.

Activities and organizations: drama/theater group, student-run newspaper, radio and television station, choral group, marching band, Phillips Brooks House Association, Asian-American Association, International Relations Council, Harvard Crimson (newspaper), Harvard/Radcliffe Chorus.

Athletics Member NCAA. All Division I except football (Division I-AA). ***Intercollegiate sports:*** baseball M, basketball M/W, crew M/W, cross-country running M/W, fencing M/W, field hockey W, golf M/W, ice hockey M/W, lacrosse M/W, rugby W, sailing M/W, skiing (cross-country) M/W, skiing (downhill) M/W, soccer M/W, softball W, squash M/W, swimming and diving M/W, tennis M/W, track and field M/W, volleyball M/W, water polo M/W, wrestling M. ***Intramural sports:*** archery M(c)/W(c), badminton M(c)/W(c), baseball M(c), basketball M/W, cheerleading M(c)/W(c), cross-country running M/W, fencing M/W, field hockey W(c), golf M(c)/W(c), ice hockey M/W, lacrosse M(c)/W(c), riflery M(c)/W(c), rugby M(c), skiing (cross-country) M(c)/W(c), skiing (downhill) M(c)/W(c), soccer M/W, squash M/W, swimming and diving M/W, table tennis M/W, tennis M/W, ultimate Frisbee M/W, volleyball M/W, water polo M(c)/W(c), weight lifting M(c)/W(c), wrestling M(c)/W(c).

Campus security: 24-hour emergency response devices and patrols, late-night transport/escort service, controlled dormitory access, required and optional safety courses.

Student services: health clinic, personal/psychological counseling, women's center.

COSTS & FINANCIAL AID
Costs (2016–17) ***Comprehensive fee:*** $63,025 includes full-time tuition ($43,280), mandatory fees ($3794), and room and board ($15,951). ***College room only:*** $9894. ***Payment plans:*** tuition prepayment, installment.

Financial Aid Of all full-time matriculated undergraduates who enrolled in 2015, 3,985 applied for aid, 3,695 were judged to have need, 3,695 had their need fully met. 2,997 state and other part-time jobs (averaging $2896). In 2015, 17 non-need-based awards were made. ***Average percent of need met:*** 100. ***Average financial aid package:*** $51,308. ***Average need-based loan:*** $2901. ***Average need-based gift aid:*** $48,598. ***Average non-need-based aid:*** $23,954. ***Average indebtedness upon graduation:*** $16,702.

APPLYING
Standardized Tests *Required:* SAT or ACT (for admission), SAT Subject Tests (for admission).

Options: electronic application, early action, deferred entrance.

Application fee: $75.

Required: essay or personal statement, high school transcript. ***Recommended:*** 2 letters of recommendation, interview.

Application deadlines: 1/1 (freshmen), 3/1 (transfers).

Notification: 4/1 (freshmen), 6/15 (transfers).

CONTACT
Harvard University, Cambridge, MA 02138. *Phone:* 617-495-1551.

Hellenic College
Brookline, Massachusetts
http://www.hchc.edu/

- **Independent Greek Orthodox** comprehensive, founded 1937
- **Suburban** 52-acre campus with easy access to Boston
- **Endowment** $24.4 million
- **Coed**
- **Minimally difficult** entrance level

FACULTY
Student/faculty ratio: 9:1.

ACADEMICS
Calendar: semesters. *Degrees:* bachelor's and master's (also offers graduate degree programs through Holy Cross Greek Orthodox School of Theology).
Library: Archbishop Iakovos Library. *Books:* 63,725 (physical), 246 (digital/electronic); *Serial titles:* 414 (physical); *Databases:* 80. Weekly public service hours: 76; students can reserve study rooms.

STUDENT LIFE
Housing options: on-campus residence required through senior year; coed, men-only, women-only. Campus housing is university owned. Freshman campus housing is guaranteed.

Activities and organizations: student-run newspaper, choral group, Campus Activities Board, Student Government Association, Intramural sports.

Campus security: 24-hour patrols, controlled dormitory access.

Student services: personal/psychological counseling.

COSTS & FINANCIAL AID
Costs (2016–17) ***Tuition:*** $21,940 full-time, $950 per credit hour part-time. ***Required fees:*** $550 full-time, $450 per year part-time. ***Room only:*** Room and board charges vary according to board plan and housing facility.

Financial Aid Of all full-time matriculated undergraduates who enrolled in 2015, 12 Federal Work-Study jobs (averaging $2500).

APPLYING
Standardized Tests *Required:* SAT or ACT (for admission), TOEFL for international students (for admission).

Options: electronic application, early action, deferred entrance.

Application fee: $50.

Required: essay or personal statement, high school transcript, minimum 2.0 GPA, interview.

CONTACT
Mr. Gregory Floor, Director of Admissions, Hellenic College, 50 Goddard Avenue, Brookline, MA 02445-7496. *Phone:* 617-850-1285. *Toll-free phone:* 866-424-2338. *Fax:* 617-850-1460.
E-mail: admissions@hchc.edu.

Hult International Business School
Cambridge, Massachusetts
http://www.hult.edu/

CONTACT
Hult International Business School, 1 Education Street, Cambridge, MA 02141.

Lasell College
Newton, Massachusetts
http://www.lasell.edu/

- **Independent** comprehensive, founded 1851
- **Suburban** 53-acre campus with easy access to Boston
- **Endowment** $36.2 million
- **Coed** 1,788 undergraduate students, 98% full-time, 65% women, 35% men
- **Moderately difficult** entrance level, 76% of applicants were admitted

UNDERGRAD STUDENTS
1,747 full-time, 41 part-time. Students come from 27 states and territories; 26 other countries; 42% are from out of state; 5% Black or African

American, non-Hispanic/Latino; 9% Hispanic/Latino; 2% Asian, non-Hispanic/Latino; 0.1% Native Hawaiian or other Pacific Islander, non-Hispanic/Latino; 0.1% American Indian or Alaska Native, non-Hispanic/Latino; 2% Two or more races, non-Hispanic/Latino; 5% Race/ethnicity unknown; 6% international; 4% transferred in; 75% live on campus.

Freshmen:
Admission: 3,221 applied, 2,450 admitted, 439 enrolled. ***Average high school GPA:*** 3. ***Test scores:*** SAT critical reading scores over 500: 41%; SAT math scores over 500: 38%; SAT writing scores over 500: 39%; ACT scores over 18: 87%; SAT critical reading scores over 600: 6%; SAT math scores over 600: 5%; SAT writing scores over 600: 4%; ACT scores over 24: 20%; ACT scores over 30: 3%.

Retention: 80% of full-time freshmen returned.

FACULTY
Total: 268, 35% full-time, 47% with terminal degrees.

Student/faculty ratio: 13:1.

ACADEMICS
Calendar: semesters. *Degrees:* bachelor's and master's.

Special study options: accelerated degree program, advanced placement credit, cooperative education, distance learning, double majors, English as a second language, honors programs, independent study, internships, off-campus study, part-time degree program, services for LD students, student-designed majors, study abroad, summer session for credit.

Unusual degree programs: 3-2 business administration with Lasell College; communication, sport management.

Computers: 219 computers/terminals are available on campus for general student use. Students can access the following: campus intranet, computer help desk, free student e-mail accounts, online (class) grades, online (class) registration, online (class) schedules, online tutoring. Campuswide network is available. 100% of college-owned or -operated housing units are wired for high-speed Internet access. Wireless service is available via entire campus.
Library: Brennan Library. Study areas open 24 hours, 5-7 days a week.

STUDENT LIFE
Housing options: coed, women-only, special housing for students with disabilities. Campus housing is university owned. Freshman campus housing is guaranteed.

Activities and organizations: drama/theater group, student-run newspaper, radio station, choral group, 19851 Chronicle, Campus Activities Board, Hope for Humanity, Lasell College Drama Club, Lasell College Radio (Marathon Monday).

Athletics Member NCAA. All Division III. ***Intercollegiate sports:*** baseball M, basketball M/W, cross-country running M/W, field hockey W, lacrosse M/W, soccer M/W, softball W, track and field M/W, volleyball M/W. ***Intramural sports:*** basketball M/W, cheerleading M(c)/W(c), crew M(c)/W(c), golf M(c)/W(c), rugby M(c)/W(c), skiing (downhill) M(c)/W(c), tennis M(c)/W(c), ultimate Frisbee M(c).

Campus security: 24-hour emergency response devices and patrols, late-night transport/escort service, controlled dormitory access.

Student services: health clinic, personal/psychological counseling.

COSTS & FINANCIAL AID
Costs (2017–18) ***Comprehensive fee:*** $49,400 includes full-time tuition ($33,300), mandatory fees ($1300), and room and board ($14,800). Part-time tuition: $1075 per credit hour. Part-time tuition and fees vary according to course load. ***Required fees:*** $325 per term part-time. ***Room and board:*** Room and board charges vary according to housing facility. ***Payment plan:*** installment. ***Waivers:*** children of alumni and employees or children of employees.

Financial Aid Of all full-time matriculated undergraduates who enrolled in 2016, 1,455 applied for aid, 1,352 were judged to have need, 225 had their need fully met. 1,120 Federal Work-Study jobs (averaging $1800). In 2016, 264 non-need-based awards were made. ***Average percent of need met:*** 74. ***Average financial aid package:*** $26,531. ***Average need-based loan:*** $4133. ***Average need-based gift aid:*** $22,074. ***Average non-need-based aid:*** $12,019. ***Average indebtedness upon graduation:*** $41,100.

APPLYING
Options: electronic application, early action, deferred entrance.

Application fee: $40.

Required: essay or personal statement, high school transcript, 2 letters of recommendation, college preparatory program. ***Recommended:*** interview.

Application deadlines: 9/1 (freshmen), rolling (transfers), 11/15 (early action).

Notification: continuous until 12/15 (freshmen), continuous (transfers), 12/1 (early action).

CONTACT
Dean James Tweed, Dean of Undergraduate Admission, Lasell College, 1844 Commonwealth Avenue, Newton, MA 02466. *Phone:* 617-243-2225. *Toll-free phone:* 888-LASELL-4. *Fax:* 617-243-2380.
E-mail: info@lasell.edu.

Lesley University

Cambridge, Massachusetts

http://www.lesley.edu/

- **Independent** comprehensive, founded 1909
- **Urban** campus with easy access to Boston
- **Coed, primarily women** 1,521 undergraduate students, 90% full-time, 75% women, 25% men
- 69% of applicants were admitted

UNDERGRAD STUDENTS
1,365 full-time, 156 part-time. 57% are from out of state; 4% Black or African American, non-Hispanic/Latino; 10% Hispanic/Latino; 4% Asian, non-Hispanic/Latino; 0.1% Native Hawaiian or other Pacific Islander, non-Hispanic/Latino; 0.1% American Indian or Alaska Native, non-Hispanic/Latino; 4% Two or more races, non-Hispanic/Latino; 5% Race/ethnicity unknown; 2% international; 8% transferred in; 60% live on campus.

Freshmen:
Admission: 3,115 applied, 2,135 admitted, 379 enrolled. ***Average high school GPA:*** 3.31. ***Test scores:*** SAT critical reading scores over 500: 73%; SAT math scores over 500: 63%; SAT writing scores over 500: 72%; ACT scores over 18: 95%; SAT critical reading scores over 600: 25%; SAT math scores over 600: 17%; SAT writing scores over 600: 28%; ACT scores over 24: 59%; SAT critical reading scores over 700: 3%; SAT math scores over 700: 1%; SAT writing scores over 700: 4%; ACT scores over 30: 5%.

Retention: 78% of full-time freshmen returned.

FACULTY
Total: 243, 33% full-time, 42% with terminal degrees.

Student/faculty ratio: 9:1.

ACADEMICS
Calendar: semesters. *Degrees:* certificates, associate, bachelor's, master's, doctoral, post-master's, and postbachelor's certificates.

Special study options: academic remediation for entering students, accelerated degree program, adult/continuing education programs, advanced placement credit, distance learning, double majors, external degree program, freshman honors college, honors programs, independent study, internships, off-campus study, part-time degree program, services for LD students, student-designed majors, study abroad, summer session for credit.

Computers: Students can access the following: free student e-mail accounts, online (class) registration. Campuswide network is available. Wireless service is available via classrooms, student centers.
Library: Sherrill Library.

STUDENT LIFE
Housing options: coed, women-only. Campus housing is university owned and leased by the school. Freshman applicants given priority for college housing.

Activities and organizations: drama/theater group, student-run newspaper, choral group.

Athletics Member NCAA. All Division III except baseball (Division II). ***Intercollegiate sports:*** baseball M, basketball M/W, cross-country running M/W, soccer M/W, softball W, volleyball M/W. ***Intramural sports:*** swimming and diving M/W, tennis M.

Campus security: 24-hour emergency response devices and patrols, late-night transport/escort service, controlled dormitory access.

Student services: health clinic, personal/psychological counseling.

COSTS & FINANCIAL AID

Costs (2017–18) ***Comprehensive fee:*** $42,050 includes full-time tuition ($26,300) and room and board ($15,750). Full-time tuition and fees vary according to class time, course level, course load, degree level, location, program, and reciprocity agreements. Part-time tuition: $877 per credit hour. ***College room only:*** $9750. Room and board charges vary according to board plan. ***Payment plan:*** installment. ***Waivers:*** employees or children of employees.

Financial Aid Of all full-time matriculated undergraduates who enrolled in 2015, 1,217 applied for aid, 1,047 were judged to have need, 76 had their need fully met. In 2015, 396 non-need-based awards were made. ***Average percent of need met:*** 70. ***Average financial aid package:*** $16,470. ***Average need-based gift aid:*** $8278. ***Average non-need-based aid:*** $8278. ***Average indebtedness upon graduation:*** $23,000.

APPLYING

Standardized Tests *Required:* SAT or ACT (for admission).

Options: electronic application, early action, deferred entrance.

Required: essay or personal statement, high school transcript. ***Recommended:*** interview.

Application deadlines: rolling (freshmen), rolling (transfers), 12/1 (early action).

Notification: continuous (freshmen), continuous (transfers), 12/23 (early action).

CONTACT

Lesley University, 29 Everett Street, Cambridge, MA 02138-2790. *Phone:* 617-349-8800. *Toll-free phone:* 800-999-1959 Ext. 8800.

★ Massachusetts College of Art and Design

Boston, Massachusetts

http://www.massart.edu/

- **State-supported** comprehensive, founded 1873, part of Massachusetts Public Higher Education System
- **Urban** 5-acre campus
- **Endowment** $15.4 million
- **Coed** 1,835 undergraduate students, 85% full-time, 71% women, 29% men
- **Moderately difficult** entrance level, 71% of applicants were admitted

UNDERGRAD STUDENTS

1,560 full-time, 275 part-time. Students come from 32 states and territories; 45 other countries; 30% are from out of state; 4% Black or African American, non-Hispanic/Latino; 10% Hispanic/Latino; 8% Asian, non-Hispanic/Latino; 0.1% Native Hawaiian or other Pacific Islander, non-Hispanic/Latino; 0.3% American Indian or Alaska Native, non-Hispanic/Latino; 1% Two or more races, non-Hispanic/Latino; 6% Race/ethnicity unknown; 5% international; 5% transferred in; 39% live on campus.

Freshmen:

Admission: 1,531 applied, 1,085 admitted, 374 enrolled. ***Average high school GPA:*** 3.45.

Retention: 90% of full-time freshmen returned.

FACULTY

Total: 274, 43% full-time.

Student/faculty ratio: 8:1.

ACADEMICS

Calendar: semesters. *Degrees:* certificates, bachelor's, master's, and postbachelor's certificates.

Special study options: double majors, independent study, internships, off-campus study, part-time degree program, student-designed majors, study abroad, summer session for credit.

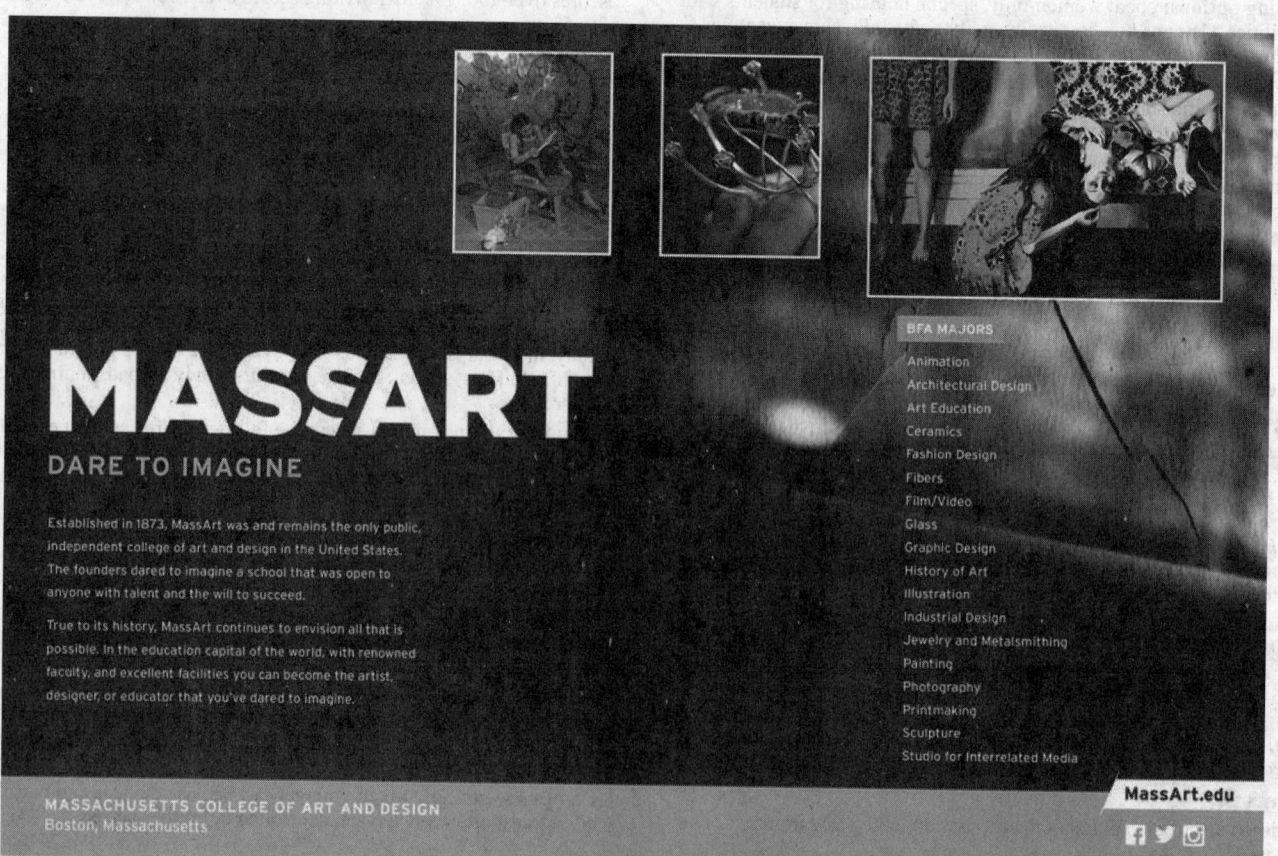

Computers: 370 computers/terminals are available on campus for general student use. Students can access the following: campus intranet, computer help desk, free student e-mail accounts, online (class) grades, online (class) registration, online (class) schedules. Campuswide network is available. 100% of college-owned or -operated housing units are wired for high-speed Internet access. Wireless service is available via entire campus.

Library: Morton R. Godine Library. *Books:* 106,885 (physical), 173,498 (digital/electronic); *Databases:* 75.

STUDENT LIFE

Housing options: coed. Campus housing is university owned. Freshman campus housing is guaranteed.

Activities and organizations: drama/theater group, student-run newspaper, radio and television station, choral group, International Students' Club, Design Research Unit, Spectrum, film society, Event Works.

Athletics ***Intramural sports:*** basketball M/W, cross-country running M/W, soccer M/W, softball M/W, table tennis M/W, tennis M/W, volleyball M/W.

Campus security: 24-hour emergency response devices and patrols, late-night transport/escort service, controlled dormitory access, security lighting, self-defense workshops.

Student services: health clinic, personal/psychological counseling, women's center.

COSTS & FINANCIAL AID

Costs (2016–17) ***Tuition:*** state resident $12,200 full-time; nonresident $32,800 full-time. Part-time tuition and fees vary according to course load. ***Room and board:*** $13,100. Room and board charges vary according to board plan and housing facility. ***Payment plan:*** installment. ***Waivers:*** senior citizens and employees or children of employees.

Financial Aid Of all full-time matriculated undergraduates who enrolled in 2015, 1,080 applied for aid, 800 were judged to have need. 154 Federal Work-Study jobs (averaging $1258). In 2015, 204 non-need-based awards were made. ***Average financial aid package:*** $10,741. ***Average need-based loan:*** $4277. ***Average need-based gift aid:*** $9310. ***Average non-need-based aid:*** $6373. ***Average indebtedness upon graduation:*** $26,792.

APPLYING

Options: electronic application, early action, deferred entrance.

Application fee: $70.

Required: essay or personal statement, high school transcript, 2 letters of recommendation, portfolio of 15-20 pieces of artwork completed in the last 2 years. ***Recommended:*** minimum 3.0 GPA.

Application deadlines: 2/1 (freshmen), 2/1 (transfers), 12/1 (early action).

Notification: 1/5 (early action).

CONTACT

Lauren Wilshusen, Massachusetts College of Art and Design, 621 Huntington Avenue, Boston, MA 02115. *Phone:* 617-879-7222. *Fax:* 617-879-7250. *E-mail:* admissions@massart.edu.

See previous page for display ad and page 1416 for the College Close-Up.

Massachusetts College of Liberal Arts

North Adams, Massachusetts

http://www.mcla.edu/

- **State-supported** comprehensive, founded 1894, part of Massachusetts State University System
- **Small-town** 105-acre campus with easy access to Albany-Schenectady-Troy New York Metro Area
- **Coed** 1,444 undergraduate students, 87% full-time, 63% women, 37% men
- **Moderately difficult** entrance level, 77% of applicants were admitted

UNDERGRAD STUDENTS

1,255 full-time, 189 part-time. Students come from 19 states and territories; 2 other countries; 26% are from out of state; 9% Black or African American, non-Hispanic/Latino; 7% Hispanic/Latino; 2% Asian, non-Hispanic/Latino; 0.5% American Indian or Alaska Native, non-Hispanic/Latino; 3% Two or more races, non-Hispanic/Latino; 2% Race/ethnicity unknown; 0.6% international; 9% transferred in; 60% live on campus.

Freshmen:

Admission: 2,013 applied, 1,552 admitted, 327 enrolled. ***Average high school GPA:*** 3.2. ***Test scores:*** SAT critical reading scores over 500: 59%; SAT math scores over 500: 53%; SAT writing scores over 500: 49%; ACT scores over 18: 95%; SAT critical reading scores over 600: 23%; SAT math scores over 600: 12%; SAT writing scores over 600: 13%; ACT scores over 24: 60%; SAT critical reading scores over 700: 2%; SAT math scores over 700: 1%; SAT writing scores over 700: 1%; ACT scores over 30: 7%.

Retention: 79% of full-time freshmen returned.

FACULTY

Total: 166, 55% full-time.

Student/faculty ratio: 12:1.

ACADEMICS

Calendar: semesters. *Degrees:* certificates, bachelor's, master's, post-master's, and postbachelor's certificates.

Special study options: academic remediation for entering students, accelerated degree program, adult/continuing education programs, advanced placement credit, cooperative education, distance learning, double majors, honors programs, independent study, internships, off-campus study, part-time degree program, services for LD students, student-designed majors, study abroad, summer session for credit.

Unusual degree programs: 3-2 engineering with University of Massachusetts Amherst; podiatric medicine with the New York School of Podiatric Medicine.

Computers: 140 computers/terminals are available on campus for general student use. Students can access the following: campus intranet, computer help desk, free student e-mail accounts, online (class) grades, online (class) registration, online (class) schedules. Campuswide network is available. 100% of college-owned or -operated housing units are wired for high-speed Internet access. Wireless service is available via entire campus.

Library: Eugene L. Freel Library. *Books:* 151,000 (physical), 180,000 (digital/electronic); *Serial titles:* 4,600 (physical), 30,000 (digital/electronic); *Databases:* 80.

STUDENT LIFE

Housing options: on-campus residence required through junior year; coed, special housing for students with disabilities. Campus housing is university owned. Freshman campus housing is guaranteed.

Activities and organizations: drama/theater group, student-run newspaper, radio and television station, choral group, Student Activities Council, Student Government Association, The Beacon (Student Newspaper), Harlequin-Musical Theatre Company, Dance Company, national fraternities, national sororities.

Athletics Member NCAA. All Division III. ***Intercollegiate sports:*** baseball M, basketball M/W, cross-country running M/W, golf M, lacrosse W, soccer M/W, softball W, tennis M/W, volleyball M/W. ***Intramural sports:*** basketball M/W, cheerleading W(c), equestrian sports M/W, football M/W, golf M/W, lacrosse M(c), racquetball M/W, rugby M(c)/W(c), skiing (cross-country) M/W, skiing (downhill) M/W, soccer M/W, softball M/W, squash M/W, swimming and diving M/W, tennis M/W, ultimate Frisbee M/W, volleyball M/W.

Campus security: 24-hour emergency response devices and patrols, late-night transport/escort service, controlled dormitory access.

Student services: health clinic, personal/psychological counseling, women's center.

COSTS & FINANCIAL AID

Costs (2016–17) ***Tuition:*** state resident $1030 full-time, $43 per credit part-time; nonresident $9975 full-time, $416 per credit part-time. Full-time tuition and fees vary according to reciprocity agreements. Part-time tuition and fees vary according to course load and reciprocity agreements. ***Required fees:*** $9020 full-time, $300 per credit part-time. ***Room and board:*** $10,078. Room and board charges vary according to board plan and housing facility. ***Payment plan:*** installment. ***Waivers:*** senior citizens and employees or children of employees.

Financial Aid Of all full-time matriculated undergraduates who enrolled in 2016, 1,154 applied for aid, 949 were judged to have need, 719 had their need fully met. In 2016, 90 non-need-based awards were made. ***Average percent of need met:*** 80. ***Average financial aid package:*** $15,633. ***Average need-based loan:*** $4138. ***Average need-based gift aid:*** $6517. ***Average non-need-based aid:*** $3212. ***Average indebtedness upon graduation:*** $29,933.

APPLYING

Standardized Tests *Required:* SAT or ACT (for admission).

Options: electronic application, early admission, early action, deferred entrance.

Required: essay or personal statement, high school transcript, minimum 3.0 GPA, 1 letter of recommendation. ***Required for some:*** interview, sliding scale applies (GPA and SAT) if below 3.0.

Application deadlines: rolling (freshmen), rolling (transfers), 12/1 (early action).

Notification: continuous (freshmen), continuous (transfers), 12/15 (early action).

CONTACT

Massachusetts College of Liberal Arts, 375 Church Street, North Adams, MA 01247-4100. *Phone:* 413-662-5410. *Toll-free phone:* 800-989-MCLA.

Massachusetts Institute of Technology

Cambridge, Massachusetts

http://www.mit.edu/

- **Independent** university, founded 1861
- **Urban** 168-acre campus with easy access to Boston
- **Endowment** $13.2 billion
- **Coed** 4,524 undergraduate students, 99% full-time, 46% women, 54% men
- **Most difficult** entrance level, 8% of applicants were admitted

UNDERGRAD STUDENTS

4,476 full-time, 48 part-time. Students come from 55 states and territories; 108 other countries; 90% are from out of state; 6% Black or African American, non-Hispanic/Latino; 15% Hispanic/Latino; 26% Asian, non-Hispanic/Latino; 0.1% American Indian or Alaska Native, non-Hispanic/Latino; 7% Two or more races, non-Hispanic/Latino; 2% Race/ethnicity unknown; 10% international; 0.5% transferred in; 94% live on campus.

Freshmen:

Admission: 19,020 applied, 1,511 admitted, 1,110 enrolled. ***Test scores:*** SAT critical reading scores over 500: 100%; SAT math scores over 500: 100%; SAT writing scores over 500: 100%; ACT scores over 18: 100%; SAT critical reading scores over 600: 97%; SAT math scores over 600: 100%; SAT writing scores over 600: 97%; ACT scores over 24: 100%; SAT critical reading scores over 700: 77%; SAT math scores over 700: 97%; SAT writing scores over 700: 74%; ACT scores over 30: 98%.

Retention: 98% of full-time freshmen returned.

FACULTY

Total: 1,538, 82% full-time, 88% with terminal degrees.

Student/faculty ratio: 3:1.

ACADEMICS

Calendar: 4-1-4. *Degrees:* bachelor's, master's, and doctoral.

Special study options: advanced placement credit, cooperative education, double majors, English as a second language, independent study, internships, off-campus study, services for LD students, study abroad. ***ROTC:*** Army (b), Navy (b), Air Force (b).

Computers: 1,050 computers/terminals and 50,000 ports are available on campus for general student use. Students can access the following: campus intranet, computer help desk, free student e-mail accounts, online (class) grades, online (class) registration, online (class) schedules. Campuswide network is available. 100% of college-owned or -operated housing units are wired for high-speed Internet access. Wireless service is available via entire campus.

Library: MIT Libraries plus 5 others. *Books:* 1.7 million (physical), 698,043 (digital/electronic); *Serial titles:* 51,946 (physical), 55,502 (digital/electronic); *Databases:* 351. Weekly public service hours: 95; study areas open 24 hours, 5-7 days a week; students can reserve study rooms.

STUDENT LIFE

Housing options: on-campus residence required for freshman year; coed, women-only, cooperative, special housing for students with disabilities. Campus housing is university owned. Freshman campus housing is guaranteed.

Activities and organizations: drama/theater group, student-run newspaper, radio and television station, choral group, marching band, Educational Studies Program, Dance Troupe, Science Fiction Society, The Tech (student newspaper), Anime Club, national fraternities, national sororities.

Athletics Member NCAA. All Division III except men's and women's crew (Division I), men's and women's rowing (Division I). ***Intercollegiate sports:*** baseball M, basketball M/W, crew M/W, cross-country running M/W, fencing M/W, field hockey W, football M, lacrosse M/W, riflery M/W, rowing M/W, sailing M/W, soccer M/W, softball W, squash M, swimming and diving M/W, tennis M/W, track and field M/W, volleyball M/W, water polo M. ***Intramural sports:*** archery M(c)/W(c), badminton M/W, basketball M/W, cheerleading M(c)/W(c), crew M(c)/W(c), golf M(c)/W(c), gymnastics M(c)/W(c), ice hockey M/W, rowing M(c)/W(c), rugby M(c)/W(c), soccer M/W, softball M/W, table tennis M/W, tennis M/W, triathlon M(c)/W(c), ultimate Frisbee M/W, volleyball M/W, water polo M/W, wrestling M(c).

Campus security: 24-hour emergency response devices and patrols, late-night transport/escort service, controlled dormitory access.

Student services: health clinic, personal/psychological counseling.

COSTS & FINANCIAL AID

Costs (2017–18) ***Comprehensive fee:*** $64,612 includes full-time tuition ($49,580), mandatory fees ($312), and room and board ($14,720). Part-time tuition and fees vary according to course load. ***College room only:*** $9420. Room and board charges vary according to board plan and housing facility. ***Payment plan:*** installment. ***Waivers:*** employees or children of employees.

Financial Aid Of all full-time matriculated undergraduates who enrolled in 2015, 2,967 applied for aid, 2,564 were judged to have need, 2,564 had their need fully met. 734 Federal Work-Study jobs (averaging $2417). 1,093 state and other part-time jobs (averaging $2712). ***Average percent of need met:*** 100. ***Average financial aid package:*** $44,056. ***Average need-based loan:*** $2679. ***Average need-based gift aid:*** $41,767. ***Average indebtedness upon graduation:*** $24,954. ***Financial aid deadline:*** 2/15.

APPLYING

Standardized Tests *Required:* SAT or ACT (for admission), SAT Subject Tests (for admission).

Options: electronic application, early action, deferred entrance.

Application fee: $75.

Required: essay or personal statement, high school transcript, 2 letters of recommendation. ***Recommended:*** interview.

Application deadlines: 1/1 (freshmen), 2/15 (transfers), 11/1 (early action).

Notification: 3/20 (freshmen), 5/1 (transfers), 12/20 (early action).

CONTACT

Admissions Counselors, Massachusetts Institute of Technology, 77 Massachusetts Avenue, Building 3-108, Cambridge, MA 02139-4307. *Phone:* 617-253-3400. *Fax:* 617-258-8304. *E-mail:* admissions@mit.edu.

Massachusetts Maritime Academy

Buzzards Bay, Massachusetts

http://www.maritime.edu/

- **State-supported** comprehensive, founded 1891, part of Massachusetts State University System
- **Small-town** 54-acre campus with easy access to Boston, Providence
- **Endowment** $13.8 million
- **Coed, primarily men** 1,677 undergraduate students, 96% full-time, 13% women, 87% men
- **Moderately difficult** entrance level, 80% of applicants were admitted

UNDERGRAD STUDENTS
1,605 full-time, 72 part-time. 21% are from out of state; 1% Black or African American, non-Hispanic/Latino; 4% Hispanic/Latino; 1% Asian, non-Hispanic/Latino; 0.2% American Indian or Alaska Native, non-Hispanic/Latino; 3% Two or more races, non-Hispanic/Latino; 4% Race/ethnicity unknown; 0.6% international; 3% transferred in; 95% live on campus.

Freshmen:
Admission: 825 applied, 664 admitted, 402 enrolled. ***Average high school GPA:*** 3.11. ***Test scores:*** SAT critical reading scores over 500: 53%; SAT math scores over 500: 75%; SAT writing scores over 500: 46%; ACT scores over 18: 90%; SAT critical reading scores over 600: 12%; SAT math scores over 600: 23%; SAT writing scores over 600: 5%; ACT scores over 24: 36%; SAT math scores over 700: 1%.

Retention: 87% of full-time freshmen returned.

FACULTY
Total: 129, 64% full-time, 45% with terminal degrees.
Student/faculty ratio: 17:1.

ACADEMICS
Calendar: 4-1-4 plus sea term. *Degrees:* bachelor's and master's.
Special study options: academic remediation for entering students, advanced placement credit, cooperative education, distance learning, double majors, internships, off-campus study, part-time degree program, services for LD students, study abroad, summer session for credit. ***ROTC:*** Army (c), Navy (b).
Computers: 130 computers/terminals and 1,800 ports are available on campus for general student use. Students can access the following: computer help desk, free student e-mail accounts, online (class) grades, online (class) registration, online (class) schedules, course-supported e-learning. Campuswide network is available. 100% of college-owned or -operated housing units are wired for high-speed Internet access. Wireless service is available via entire campus.
Library: American Bureau of Shipping Information Commons plus 1 other. *Books:* 35,434 (physical), 185,500 (digital/electronic); *Serial titles:* 83 (physical), 52,750 (digital/electronic); *Databases:* 122. Weekly public service hours: 81.

STUDENT LIFE
Housing options: on-campus residence required through senior year; coed. Campus housing is university owned. Freshman campus housing is guaranteed.
Activities and organizations: drama/theater group, marching band, Student Government, Intramurals, Regimental Leadership, Band/Honor Guard, NCAA Division 3 Athletics.
Athletics Member NCAA. All Division III. ***Intercollegiate sports:*** baseball M, crew M/W, cross-country running M/W, football M, lacrosse M/W, sailing M/W, soccer M/W, softball W, track and field M/W, volleyball W. ***Intramural sports:*** baseball M(c)/W(c), basketball M/W, golf M(c)/W(c), ice hockey M(c)/W(c), lacrosse M(c)/W(c), rugby M(c)/W(c), soccer M/W, swimming and diving M(c)/W(c), water polo M/W, weight lifting M(c)/W(c).
Campus security: 24-hour emergency response devices and patrols, late-night transport/escort service, controlled dormitory access.
Student services: health clinic, personal/psychological counseling, women's center.

COSTS & FINANCIAL AID
Costs (2016–17) ***Tuition:*** state resident $1632 full-time, $322 per credit part-time; nonresident $18,228 full-time, $1014 per credit part-time. ***Required fees:*** $6372 full-time. ***Room and board:*** $11,978; room only: $7134. ***Payment plan:*** installment.
Financial Aid Of all full-time matriculated undergraduates who enrolled in 2016, 1,260 applied for aid, 898 were judged to have need, 292 had their need fully met. 190 Federal Work-Study jobs (averaging $1467). In 2016, 105 non-need-based awards were made. ***Average percent of need met:*** 72. ***Average financial aid package:*** $12,188. ***Average need-based loan:*** $4087. ***Average need-based gift aid:*** $10,061. ***Average non-need-based aid:*** $3131. ***Average indebtedness upon graduation:*** $37,414.

APPLYING
Standardized Tests *Required:* SAT or ACT (for admission).
Options: electronic application, early action.
Application fee: $50.
Required: essay or personal statement, high school transcript, minimum 2.0 GPA, 2 letters of recommendation, minimum college GPA 2.5 if transferring 12-23 credits, minimum college GPA 2.0 for more than 24 transferable credits. ***Recommended:*** interview.
Application deadlines: rolling (freshmen), rolling (out-of-state freshmen), rolling (transfers), 11/1 (early action).
Notification: continuous (freshmen), continuous (out-of-state freshmen), continuous (transfers), 12/31 (early action).

CONTACT
Mr. Joshua Tefft, Director of Admissions, Massachusetts Maritime Academy, 101 Academy Drive, Flanagan Hall, Buzzards Bay, MA 02532.
Phone: 508-830-6687. *Toll-free phone:* 800-544-3411.
E-mail: jtefft@maritime.edu.

MCPHS University

Boston, Massachusetts

http://www.mcphs.edu/

- **Independent** university, founded 1823
- **Urban** 3-acre campus
- **Endowment** $514.0 million
- **Coed** 3,843 undergraduate students, 93% full-time, 71% women, 29% men
- 84% of applicants were admitted

UNDERGRAD STUDENTS
3,591 full-time, 252 part-time. Students come from 49 states and territories; 62 other countries; 38% are from out of state; 7% Black or African American, non-Hispanic/Latino; 6% Hispanic/Latino; 23% Asian, non-Hispanic/Latino; 0.1% Native Hawaiian or other Pacific Islander, non-Hispanic/Latino; 0.2% American Indian or Alaska Native, non-Hispanic/Latino; 2% Two or more races, non-Hispanic/Latino; 8% Race/ethnicity unknown; 13% international; 6% transferred in; 19% live on campus.

Freshmen:
Admission: 5,531 applied, 4,672 admitted, 798 enrolled. ***Average high school GPA:*** 3.51. ***Test scores:*** SAT critical reading scores over 500: 59%; SAT math scores over 500: 72%; SAT writing scores over 500: 64%; SAT critical reading scores over 600: 16%; SAT math scores over 600: 32%; SAT writing scores over 600: 19%; SAT critical reading scores over 700: 1%; SAT math scores over 700: 8%; SAT writing scores over 700: 2%.
Retention: 85% of full-time freshmen returned.

FACULTY
Total: 737, 42% full-time.

ACADEMICS
Calendar: semesters. *Degrees:* certificates, bachelor's, master's, doctoral, post-master's, and postbachelor's certificates.
Special study options: accelerated degree program, adult/continuing education programs, advanced placement credit, cooperative education, distance learning, double majors, independent study, internships, off-campus study, part-time degree program, services for LD students, study abroad, summer session for credit.
Computers: 507 computers/terminals are available on campus for general student use. Students can access the following: computer help desk, free student e-mail accounts, online (class) grades, online (class) registration, online (class) schedules. Campuswide network is available. 100% of college-owned or -operated housing units are wired for high-speed Internet access. Wireless service is available via entire campus.
Library: Henrietta DeBenedictis Library plus 2 others.

STUDENT LIFE
Housing options: coed, special housing for students with disabilities. Campus housing is university owned, leased by the school and is provided by a third party. Freshman campus housing is guaranteed.
Activities and organizations: drama/theater group, student-run newspaper, choral group, Residence Hall Council, Vietnamese Student Association, Student Government Association, Campus Activities Board, Student Indian Organization, national fraternities.

Athletics ***Intramural sports:*** basketball M/W, bowling M/W, cross-country running M/W, field hockey M/W, football M/W, racquetball M/W, soccer M/W, softball M/W, tennis M/W, ultimate Frisbee M/W, volleyball M/W.

Campus security: 24-hour emergency response devices and patrols, late-night transport/escort service, controlled dormitory access, electronically operated academic area entrances, security guards at entrance.

Student services: health clinic, personal/psychological counseling.

COSTS & FINANCIAL AID

Costs (2017–18) ***Comprehensive fee:*** $47,504 includes full-time tuition ($30,600), mandatory fees ($1070), and room and board ($15,834). Full-time tuition and fees vary according to course load, degree level, location, program, and student level. Part-time tuition: $1125 per credit. ***Required fees:*** $253 per term part-time. ***College room only:*** $12,600. Room and board charges vary according to board plan, housing facility, and location. ***Payment plan:*** installment. ***Waivers:*** employees or children of employees.

Financial Aid Of all full-time matriculated undergraduates who enrolled in 2016, 2,722 applied for aid, 2,535 were judged to have need, 962 had their need fully met. In 2016, 767 non-need-based awards were made. ***Average percent of need met:*** 23. ***Average financial aid package:*** $8724. ***Average need-based loan:*** $2952. ***Average need-based gift aid:*** $6408. ***Average non-need-based aid:*** $6116.

APPLYING

Standardized Tests *Required:* SAT or ACT (for admission).

Options: electronic application, early action, deferred entrance.

Required: essay or personal statement, 2 letters of recommendation. ***Required for some:*** high school transcript, interview.

Application deadlines: rolling (freshmen), 2/1 (transfers), 11/15 (early action).

Notification: continuous until 2/15 (freshmen), continuous (transfers), 12/19 (early action).

CONTACT

Giselle Colon, Visit Concierge, MCPHS University, 179 Longwood Avenue, Boston, MA 02115. *Phone:* 617-732-2744. *Fax:* 617-732-2118. *E-mail:* admissions@mcphs.edu.

Merrimack College

North Andover, Massachusetts

http://www.merrimack.edu/

- **Independent Roman Catholic** comprehensive, founded 1947
- **Suburban** 220-acre campus with easy access to Boston
- **Endowment** $49.9 million
- **Coed** 3,448 undergraduate students, 96% full-time, 52% women, 48% men
- **Moderately difficult** entrance level, 82% of applicants were admitted

UNDERGRAD STUDENTS

3,313 full-time, 135 part-time. Students come from 34 states and territories; 30 other countries; 30% are from out of state; 3% Black or African American, non-Hispanic/Latino; 6% Hispanic/Latino; 1% Asian, non-Hispanic/Latino; 0.1% Native Hawaiian or other Pacific Islander, non-Hispanic/Latino; 0.1% American Indian or Alaska Native, non-Hispanic/Latino; 2% Two or more races, non-Hispanic/Latino; 8% Race/ethnicity unknown; 3% international; 2% transferred in; 75% live on campus.

Freshmen:

Admission: 8,214 applied, 6,728 admitted, 1,005 enrolled. ***Average high school GPA:*** 3.1.

Retention: 82% of full-time freshmen returned.

FACULTY

Total: 415, 42% full-time.

Student/faculty ratio: 14:1.

ACADEMICS

Calendar: semesters. *Degrees:* bachelor's, master's, and post-master's certificates.

Special study options: academic remediation for entering students, accelerated degree program, adult/continuing education programs, advanced placement credit, cooperative education, double majors, honors programs, independent study, internships, off-campus study, part-time degree program, services for LD students, student-designed majors, study abroad, summer session for credit. ***ROTC:*** Air Force (c).

Computers: Students can access the following: campus intranet, computer help desk, free student e-mail accounts, online (class) grades, online (class) registration, online (class) schedules. Campuswide network is available. 100% of college-owned or -operated housing units are wired for high-speed Internet access. Wireless service is available via entire campus.

Library: McQuade Library.

STUDENT LIFE

Housing options: coed, special housing for students with disabilities. Campus housing is university owned and leased by the school. Freshman campus housing is guaranteed.

Activities and organizations: drama/theater group, student-run newspaper, radio and television station, choral group, Merrimack Programming Board, Best Buddies, Greek Life, Onstagers, Live 2 Give, national fraternities, national sororities.

Athletics Member NCAA. All Division II except men's and women's ice hockey (Division I). ***Intercollegiate sports:*** baseball M(s), basketball M(s)/W(s), crew W(s), cross-country running M(s)/W(s), field hockey W(s), football M(s), golf W(s), ice hockey M(s)/W(s), lacrosse M(s)/W(s), soccer M(s)/W(s), softball W(s), swimming and diving W(s), tennis M(s)/W(s), track and field M(s)/W(s), volleyball W(s). ***Intramural sports:*** badminton M/W, baseball M(c), basketball M/W, cheerleading W(c), cross-country running M(c)/W(c), golf M(c), ice hockey M(c)/W(c), lacrosse M(c), rugby M(c)/W(c), soccer M(c)/W, softball W(c), ultimate Frisbee M(c)/W(c), volleyball W(c).

Campus security: 24-hour emergency response devices and patrols, student patrols, late-night transport/escort service, controlled dormitory access, staffed dorm entrances.

Student services: health clinic, personal/psychological counseling.

COSTS & FINANCIAL AID

Costs (2016–17) ***Comprehensive fee:*** $53,170 includes full-time tuition ($36,625), mandatory fees ($2200), and room and board ($14,345). Full-time tuition and fees vary according to degree level. Part-time tuition: $1310 per credit. Part-time tuition and fees vary according to class time, course load, and degree level. ***Room and board:*** Room and board charges vary according to board plan and housing facility. ***Payment plan:*** installment. ***Waivers:*** senior citizens and employees or children of employees.

Financial Aid Of all full-time matriculated undergraduates who enrolled in 2016, 2,656 applied for aid, 2,366 were judged to have need, 303 had their need fully met. In 2016, 709 non-need-based awards were made. ***Average percent of need met:*** 65. ***Average financial aid package:*** $23,143. ***Average need-based loan:*** $4527. ***Average need-based gift aid:*** $19,409. ***Average non-need-based aid:*** $12,017.

APPLYING

Options: electronic application, early admission, early decision, early action, deferred entrance.

Required: essay or personal statement, high school transcript, 1 letter of recommendation, first quarter senior grades. ***Required for some:*** interview. ***Recommended:*** interview.

Application deadlines: 2/15 (freshmen), 8/15 (transfers), 1/15 (early action).

Early decision deadline: 11/15.

Notification: continuous until 3/15 (freshmen), continuous (transfers), 12/15 (early decision), 2/15 (early action).

CONTACT

Admissions Office, Merrimack College, 510 Turnpike St, North Andover, MA 01845. *Phone:* 978-837-5100. *Fax:* 978-837-5133. *E-mail:* admission@merrimack.edu.

Montserrat College of Art

Beverly, Massachusetts

http://www.montserrat.edu/

CONTACT

Mr. Jeffrey Newell, Director of Admissions, Montserrat College of Art, 23 Essex Street, Beverly, MA 01915. *Phone:* 978-921-4242 Ext. 1152. *Toll-free phone:* 800-836-0487. *Fax:* 978-921-4241.
E-mail: jeffrey.newell@montserrat.edu.

Mount Holyoke College

South Hadley, Massachusetts

http://www.mtholyoke.edu/

- **Independent** comprehensive, founded 1837
- **Small-town** 800-acre campus with easy access to Springfield
- **Endowment** $667.6 million
- **Women only** 2,202 undergraduate students, 98% full-time
- **Very difficult** entrance level, 52% of applicants were admitted

UNDERGRAD STUDENTS

2,162 full-time, 40 part-time. Students come from 46 states and territories; 57 other countries; 75% are from out of state; 5% Black or African American, non-Hispanic/Latino; 8% Hispanic/Latino; 11% Asian, non-Hispanic/Latino; 0.1% American Indian or Alaska Native, non-Hispanic/Latino; 3% Two or more races, non-Hispanic/Latino; 0.9% Race/ethnicity unknown; 27% international; 2% transferred in; 95% live on campus.

Freshmen:
Admission: 3,543 applied, 1,849 admitted, 569 enrolled. ***Average high school GPA:*** 3.79. ***Test scores:*** SAT critical reading scores over 500: 98%; SAT math scores over 500: 99%; SAT writing scores over 500: 99%; ACT scores over 18: 100%; SAT critical reading scores over 600: 81%; SAT math scores over 600: 81%; SAT writing scores over 600: 87%; ACT scores over 24: 98%; SAT critical reading scores over 700: 33%; SAT math scores over 700: 42%; SAT writing scores over 700: 34%; ACT scores over 30: 59%.
Retention: 91% of full-time freshmen returned.

FACULTY

Total: 238, 84% full-time, 95% with terminal degrees.
Student/faculty ratio: 10:1.

ACADEMICS

Calendar: semesters. *Degrees:* bachelor's, master's, and postbachelor's certificates.

Special study options: adult/continuing education programs, advanced placement credit, distance learning, double majors, independent study, internships, off-campus study, part-time degree program, services for LD students, student-designed majors, study abroad, summer session for credit. ***ROTC:*** Army (c), Air Force (c).

Unusual degree programs: 3-2 engineering with Dartmouth College, University of Massachusetts, California Institute of Technology.

Computers: 364 computers/terminals and 3,000 ports are available on campus for general student use. Students can access the following: campus intranet, computer help desk, free student e-mail accounts, online (class) grades, online (class) registration, online (class) schedules, personal Web pages. Campuswide network is available. 100% of college-owned or -operated housing units are wired for high-speed Internet access. Wireless service is available via classrooms, computer centers, computer labs, dorm rooms, learning centers, libraries, student centers.

Library: Williston Memorial Library plus 2 others. *Books:* 662,010 (physical), 853,290 (digital/electronic); *Serial titles:* 603 (physical), 8,098 (digital/electronic); *Databases:* 227. Weekly public service hours: 115; students can reserve study rooms.

STUDENT LIFE

Housing options: on-campus residence required through senior year; women-only, special housing for students with disabilities. Campus housing is university owned. Freshman campus housing is guaranteed.

Activities and organizations: drama/theater group, student-run newspaper, radio station, choral group, Student Government Association, C.A.U.S.E. (Creating Awareness and Unity for Social Equality), MHC Outing Club, Mount Holyoke Symphony Orchestra, Mount Holyoke News.

Athletics Member NCAA. All Division III. ***Intercollegiate sports:*** basketball W, crew W, cross-country running W, equestrian sports W, field hockey W, golf W, lacrosse W, soccer W, squash W, swimming and diving W, tennis W, track and field W, volleyball W. ***Intramural sports:*** equestrian sports W(c), fencing W(c), ice hockey W(c), rugby W(c), ultimate Frisbee W(c).

Campus security: 24-hour emergency response devices and patrols, student patrols, late-night transport/escort service, controlled dormitory access, police officers on-campus.

Student services: health clinic, personal/psychological counseling.

COSTS & FINANCIAL AID

Costs (2016–17) ***Comprehensive fee:*** $59,306 includes full-time tuition ($45,680), mandatory fees ($186), and room and board ($13,440). Part-time tuition: $1430 per credit hour. ***College room only:*** $6560. ***Payment plan:*** installment. ***Waivers:*** employees or children of employees.

Financial Aid Of all full-time matriculated undergraduates who enrolled in 2016, 1,620 applied for aid, 1,152 were judged to have need, 1,152 had their need fully met. 773 Federal Work-Study jobs (averaging $2115). 346 state and other part-time jobs (averaging $2167). In 2016, 391 non-need-based awards were made. ***Average percent of need met:*** 100. ***Average financial aid package:*** $37,763. ***Average need-based loan:*** $4371. ***Average need-based gift aid:*** $32,773. ***Average non-need-based aid:*** $24,244. ***Average indebtedness upon graduation:*** $23,872. ***Financial aid deadline:*** 3/1.

APPLYING

Options: electronic application, early admission, early decision, deferred entrance.

Application fee: $60.

Required: essay or personal statement, high school transcript, 2 letters of recommendation. ***Recommended:*** interview.

Application deadlines: 1/15 (freshmen), 5/15 (transfers).

Early decision deadline: 11/15 (for plan 1), 1/1 (for plan 2).

Notification: 4/1 (freshmen), continuous (transfers), 1/1 (early decision plan 1), 2/1 (early decision plan 2).

CONTACT

Ms. Gail Berson, Vice President of Enrollment and Dean of Admission, Mount Holyoke College, Office of Admission, Mount Holyoke College, South Hadley, MA 01075. *Phone:* 413-538-2023. *Fax:* 413-538-2409.
E-mail: admission@mtholyoke.edu.

Mount Ida College

Newton, Massachusetts

http://www.mountida.edu/

- **Independent** comprehensive, founded 1899
- **Suburban** 72-acre campus with easy access to Boston
- **Coed** 1,320 undergraduate students, 94% full-time, 67% women, 33% men
- **Moderately difficult** entrance level, 63% of applicants were admitted

UNDERGRAD STUDENTS

1,241 full-time, 79 part-time. Students come from 29 states and territories; 22 other countries; 41% are from out of state; 8% transferred in; 63% live on campus.

Freshmen:
Admission: 2,319 applied, 1,467 admitted, 433 enrolled. ***Average high school GPA:*** 2.6. ***Test scores:*** SAT critical reading scores over 500: 19%; SAT math scores over 500: 22%; SAT writing scores over 500: 17%; ACT scores over 18: 54%; SAT critical reading scores over 600: 4%; SAT math scores over 600: 3%; SAT writing scores over 600: 2%; ACT scores over 24: 11%.
Retention: 59% of full-time freshmen returned.

FACULTY

Total: 181, 35% full-time, 44% with terminal degrees.
Student/faculty ratio: 13:1.

ACADEMICS
Calendar: semesters. *Degrees:* certificates, associate, bachelor's, and master's.

Special study options: academic remediation for entering students, advanced placement credit, cooperative education, distance learning, double majors, English as a second language, honors programs, independent study, internships, part-time degree program, services for LD students, study abroad, summer session for credit.

Unusual degree programs: 3-2 business administration.

Computers: 82 computers/terminals are available on campus for general student use. Students can access the following: computer help desk, free student e-mail accounts, online (class) grades, online (class) schedules. Campuswide network is available. 100% of college-owned or -operated housing units are wired for high-speed Internet access. Wireless service is available via computer labs, dorm rooms, student centers.
Library: Wadsworth Learning Resource Center plus 1 other. Students can reserve study rooms.

STUDENT LIFE
Housing options: coed, women-only, special housing for students with disabilities. Campus housing is university owned and is provided by a third party. Freshman campus housing is guaranteed.

Activities and organizations: drama/theater group, student-run newspaper, radio station, choral group, Student Government Association, Campus Activities Team, Balfour Peer Leaders, Black Student Achievement Coalition, Alpha Chi.

Athletics Member NCAA. All Division III. ***Intercollegiate sports:*** basketball M/W, cheerleading M/W, cross-country running M/W, equestrian sports M/W, field hockey W, football M, lacrosse M/W, soccer M/W, softball W, tennis W, volleyball M/W. ***Intramural sports:*** basketball M/W, soccer M/W, ultimate Frisbee M/W, volleyball M/W.

Campus security: 24-hour emergency response devices and patrols, student patrols, late-night transport/escort service, controlled dormitory access, secured campus entrance.

Student services: health clinic, personal/psychological counseling.

COSTS & FINANCIAL AID
Costs (2017–18) ***Comprehensive fee:*** $49,400 includes full-time tuition ($34,200), mandatory fees ($1520), and room and board ($13,680). Full-time tuition and fees vary according to program. Part-time tuition: $1075 per credit. Part-time tuition and fees vary according to program. ***Room and board:*** Room and board charges vary according to board plan. ***Payment plan:*** installment.

Financial Aid Of all full-time matriculated undergraduates who enrolled in 2015, 1,071 applied for aid, 1,011 were judged to have need, 101 had their need fully met. 158 Federal Work-Study jobs (averaging $1439). 21 state and other part-time jobs (averaging $1902). In 2015, 230 non-need-based awards were made. ***Average percent of need met:*** 64. ***Average financial aid package:*** $24,176. ***Average need-based loan:*** $4078. ***Average need-based gift aid:*** $19,682. ***Average non-need-based aid:*** $8930. ***Average indebtedness upon graduation:*** $44,963.

APPLYING
Standardized Tests *Required for some:* SAT or ACT (for admission). *Recommended:* SAT or ACT (for admission).

Options: electronic application, deferred entrance.

Required: high school transcript, 1 letter of recommendation. ***Required for some:*** interview. ***Recommended:*** essay or personal statement, minimum 2.0 GPA.

Application deadlines: rolling (freshmen), rolling (transfers).

Notification: continuous (freshmen), continuous (transfers).

CONTACT
Mrs. Melissa Hagerstrom, Director of Admissions, Mount Ida College, 777 Dedham Street, Newton, MA 02459-3310. *Phone:* 617-928-4734. *Fax:* 617-928-4507. *E-mail:* admissions@mountida.edu.

Newbury College

Brookline, Massachusetts

http://www.newbury.edu/

- **Independent** 4-year, founded 1962
- **Suburban** 10-acre campus with easy access to Boston
- **Endowment** $2.1 million
- **Coed**
- **Minimally difficult** entrance level

FACULTY
Student/faculty ratio: 14:1.

ACADEMICS
Calendar: semesters. *Degrees:* certificates, associate, and bachelor's.
Library: Newbury College Library plus 1 other. Weekly public service hours: 73.

STUDENT LIFE
Housing options: coed. Campus housing is university owned and leased by the school. Freshman applicants given priority for college housing.

Activities and organizations: drama/theater group, student-run radio and television station, choral group, Campus Activities Board, Innkeeper's Club, Games Club, Commuter Council, Quidditch Club.

Athletics Member NCAA. All Division III.

Campus security: 24-hour emergency response devices and patrols, late-night transport/escort service.

Student services: personal/psychological counseling.

COSTS & FINANCIAL AID
Costs (2016–17) ***Comprehensive fee:*** $47,710 includes full-time tuition ($31,990), mandatory fees ($1520), and room and board ($14,200). Full-time tuition and fees vary according to class time, course load, location, and program. Part-time tuition: $1070 per credit. Part-time tuition and fees vary according to class time, course load, location, and program. ***Required fees:*** $700 per year part-time. ***Room and board:*** Room and board charges vary according to board plan and housing facility.

Financial Aid Of all full-time matriculated undergraduates who enrolled in 2012, 837 applied for aid, 792 were judged to have need, 3 had their need fully met. 208 Federal Work-Study jobs (averaging $1582). In 2012, 27 non-need-based awards were made. ***Average percent of need met:*** 47. ***Average financial aid package:*** $13,034. ***Average need-based loan:*** $4180. ***Average need-based gift aid:*** $11,702. ***Average non-need-based aid:*** $9778. ***Average indebtedness upon graduation:*** $30,802.

APPLYING
Options: electronic application.

Required: essay or personal statement, high school transcript, 2 letters of recommendation.

CONTACT
Mr. Salvadore Liberto, Vice President of Enrollment Management, Newbury College, 129 Fisher Avenue, Brookline, MA 02445-5796. *Phone:* 617-730-7066. *Toll-free phone:* 800-NEWBURY. *Fax:* 617-731-9618. *E-mail:* salvadore.liberto@newbury.edu.

New England College of Business and Finance

Boston, Massachusetts

http://necb.edu/

CONTACT
New England College of Business and Finance, 10 High Street, Suite 204, Boston, MA 02111-2645. *Phone:* 617-951-2350 Ext. 6912. *Toll-free phone:* 800-997-1673.

New England Conservatory of Music

Boston, Massachusetts

http://necmusic.edu/

- **Independent** comprehensive, founded 1867
- **Urban** 2-acre campus
- **Endowment** $120.3 million
- **Coed**
- **Very difficult** entrance level

FACULTY
Student/faculty ratio: 5:1.

ACADEMICS
Calendar: semesters. *Degrees:* certificates, diplomas, bachelor's, master's, doctoral, post-master's, and postbachelor's certificates.
Library: Spaulding Library plus 3 others. *Books:* 103,097 (physical), 248,432 (digital/electronic); *Serial titles:* 161 (physical), 98 (digital/electronic); *Databases:* 109. Weekly public service hours: 85.

STUDENT LIFE
Housing options: on-campus residence required for freshman year; coed. Campus housing is university owned. Freshman campus housing is guaranteed.

Activities and organizations: drama/theater group, student-run newspaper, choral group, The Penguin (newspaper).

Campus security: 24-hour patrols, late-night transport/escort service.

Student services: health clinic, personal/psychological counseling.

COSTS & FINANCIAL AID
Costs (2016–17) ***Comprehensive fee:*** $58,655 includes full-time tuition ($44,300), mandatory fees ($455), and room and board ($13,900). Part-time tuition: $1420 per credit. ***Required fees:*** $455 per year part-time. ***Room and board:*** Room and board charges vary according to board plan.

Financial Aid Of all full-time matriculated undergraduates who enrolled in 2015, 221 applied for aid, 170 were judged to have need, 34 had their need fully met. 212 Federal Work-Study jobs (averaging $367,255). In 2015, 182 non-need-based awards were made. ***Average percent of need met:*** 67. ***Average financial aid package:*** $28,008. ***Average need-based loan:*** $6891. ***Average need-based gift aid:*** $21,634. ***Average non-need-based aid:*** $15,027. ***Average indebtedness upon graduation:*** $31,039.

APPLYING
Options: electronic application, deferred entrance.

Application fee: $115.

Required: essay or personal statement, high school transcript, minimum 2.8 GPA, 2 letters of recommendation, audition recording, repertoire list.

CONTACT
New England Conservatory of Music, 290 Huntington Avenue, Boston, MA 02115-5000. *Phone:* 617-585-1103.

Nichols College

Dudley, Massachusetts

http://www.nichols.edu/

- **Independent** comprehensive, founded 1815
- **Small-town** 250-acre campus with easy access to Boston
- **Endowment** $11.3 million
- **Coed** 1,272 undergraduate students, 91% full-time, 40% women, 60% men

UNDERGRAD STUDENTS
1,163 full-time, 109 part-time. Students come from 28 states and territories; 13 other countries; 2% are from out of state; 8% Black or African American, non-Hispanic/Latino; 7% Hispanic/Latino; 1% Asian, non-Hispanic/Latino; 3% Two or more races, non-Hispanic/Latino; 2% international; 2% transferred in; 80% live on campus.

Freshmen:
Admission: 353 enrolled. ***Average high school GPA:*** 2.87. ***Test scores:*** SAT critical reading scores over 500: 33%; SAT math scores over 500: 41%; SAT writing scores over 500: 30%; ACT scores over 18: 69%; SAT critical reading scores over 600: 8%; SAT math scores over 600: 10%; SAT writing scores over 600: 4%; ACT scores over 24: 24%.
Retention: 71% of full-time freshmen returned.

FACULTY
Total: 98, 51% full-time, 33% with terminal degrees.
Student/faculty ratio: 17:1.

ACADEMICS
Calendar: semesters. *Degrees:* certificates, associate, bachelor's, master's, and post-master's certificates.
Special study options: accelerated degree program, adult/continuing education programs, advanced placement credit, cooperative education, double majors, honors programs, independent study, internships, off-campus study, part-time degree program, services for LD students, study abroad, summer session for credit.
Unusual degree programs: 3-2 business administration; accounting, criminal justice.
Computers: 127 computers/terminals are available on campus for general student use. Students can access the following: campus intranet, computer help desk, free student e-mail accounts, online (class) grades, online (class) registration, online (class) schedules. Campuswide network is available. 100% of college-owned or -operated housing units are wired for high-speed Internet access. Wireless service is available via entire campus.
Library: Conant Library. *Books:* 29,670 (physical), 135,329 (digital/electronic); *Databases:* 43. Study areas open 24 hours, 5-7 days a week; students can reserve study rooms.

STUDENT LIFE
Housing options: coed, men-only, women-only, special housing for students with disabilities. Campus housing is university owned. Freshman campus housing is guaranteed.
Activities and organizations: drama/theater group, student-run radio station, Campus Activities Board, Institute for Women's Leadership, Student Government Association, Student Athletic Advisory Council, Student Alumni Association.
Athletics Member NCAA. All Division III. ***Intercollegiate sports:*** baseball M, basketball M/W, cheerleading M(c)/W(c), cross-country running M/W, field hockey W, football M, golf M, ice hockey M/W, lacrosse M/W, racquetball M(c)/W(c), rugby M(c)/W(c), soccer M/W, softball W, tennis M/W, track and field M/W, volleyball W. ***Intramural sports:*** basketball M/W, cheerleading M/W, football M/W, ice hockey M(c)/W(c), racquetball M(c)/W(c), skiing (downhill) M(c)/W(c), soccer M/W, volleyball M(c)/W(c).
Campus security: 24-hour emergency response devices and patrols, student patrols, late-night transport/escort service, controlled dormitory access.
Student services: health clinic, personal/psychological counseling, women's center.

COSTS & FINANCIAL AID
Costs (2017–18) ***Comprehensive fee:*** $47,800 includes full-time tuition ($33,600), mandatory fees ($400), and room and board ($13,800). Part-time tuition: $1120 per credit. Part-time tuition and fees vary according to course load. ***Required fees:*** $200 per term part-time. ***Room and board:*** Room and board charges vary according to board plan and housing facility. ***Payment plan:*** installment. ***Waivers:*** employees or children of employees.
Financial Aid Of all full-time matriculated undergraduates who enrolled in 2016, 1,047 applied for aid, 954 were judged to have need, 203 had their need fully met. 638 Federal Work-Study jobs (averaging $2310). In 2016, 215 non-need-based awards were made. ***Average percent of need met:*** 84. ***Average financial aid package:*** $28,590. ***Average need-based loan:*** $4214. ***Average need-based gift aid:*** $20,349. ***Average non-need-based aid:*** $15,404. ***Average indebtedness upon graduation:*** $35,392.

APPLYING
Standardized Tests *Required for some:* SAT or ACT (for admission).
Required: essay or personal statement, high school transcript, 1 letter of recommendation. ***Required for some:*** interview. ***Recommended:*** 2 letters of recommendation.

CONTACT
Mr. Paul Brower, Assistant Dean for Enrollment, Nichols College, 129 Center Road, Dudley, MA 01571. *Phone:* 508-213-2371. *Toll-free phone:* 800-470-3379. *E-mail:* paul.brower@nichols.edu.

★ Northeastern University
Boston, Massachusetts
http://www.northeastern.edu/

- **Independent** university, founded 1898
- **Urban** 73-acre campus
- **Coed** 17,923 undergraduate students, 100% full-time, 51% women, 49% men
- **Very difficult** entrance level, 29% of applicants were admitted

UNDERGRAD STUDENTS
17,894 full-time, 29 part-time. Students come from 122 other countries; 72% are from out of state; 4% Black or African American, non-Hispanic/Latino; 7% Hispanic/Latino; 13% Asian, non-Hispanic/Latino; 0.1% American Indian or Alaska Native, non-Hispanic/Latino; 4% Two or more races, non-Hispanic/Latino; 5% Race/ethnicity unknown; 20% international; 3% transferred in; 45% live on campus.

Freshmen:
Admission: 51,063 applied, 14,747 admitted, 2,676 enrolled. *Test scores:* SAT critical reading scores over 500: 99%; SAT math scores over 500: 99%; SAT writing scores over 500: 98%; ACT scores over 18: 99%; SAT critical reading scores over 600: 91%; SAT math scores over 600: 93%; SAT writing scores over 600: 87%; ACT scores over 24: 98%; SAT critical reading scores over 700: 54%; SAT math scores over 700: 64%; SAT writing scores over 700: 44%; ACT scores over 30: 92%.

Retention: 97% of full-time freshmen returned.

FACULTY
Total: 1,667, 76% full-time, 83% with terminal degrees.
Student/faculty ratio: 14:1.

ACADEMICS
Calendar: semesters. *Degrees:* bachelor's, master's, doctoral, and post-master's certificates.

Special study options: accelerated degree program, cooperative education, double majors, honors programs, independent study, internships, off-campus study, services for LD students, student-designed majors, study abroad, summer session for credit. ***ROTC:*** Army (b), Navy (c), Air Force (c).

Computers: Students can access the following: campus intranet, computer help desk, free student e-mail accounts, online (class) grades, online (class) registration, online (class) schedules. Campuswide network is available. 100% of college-owned or -operated housing units are wired for high-speed Internet access. Wireless service is available via entire campus.

Library: Snell Library plus 3 others. *Books:* 829,604 (physical), 548,629 (digital/electronic); *Databases:* 292. Study areas open 24 hours, 5-7 days a week; students can reserve study rooms.

STUDENT LIFE
Housing options: on-campus residence required through sophomore year; coed. Campus housing is university owned and leased by the school. Freshman campus housing is guaranteed.

Activities and organizations: drama/theater group, student-run newspaper, radio and television station, choral group, Student Government Association, Council for University Programs, Resident Student Association, Society of Collegiate Scholars, No Limits Dance Crew, national fraternities, national sororities.

Athletics Member NCAA. All Division I. ***Intercollegiate sports:*** baseball M(s), basketball M(s)/W(s), cheerleading M(c)/W(c), crew M(s)/W(s), cross-country running M(s)/W(s), field hockey W(s), golf M(c)/W(c), ice hockey M(s)/W(s), lacrosse M(c)/W(c), riflery M(c)/W(c), rowing W, rugby M(c)/W(c), sailing M(c)/W(c), soccer M(s)/W(s), softball M(c)/W(c), squash M(c)/W(c), swimming and diving W(s), table tennis M(c)/W(c), tennis M(c)/W(c), track and field M(s)/W(s), ultimate Frisbee M(c)/W(c), volleyball W(s), water polo M(c)/W(c), weight lifting M(c)/W(c), wrestling M(c). ***Intramural sports:*** basketball M/W, field hockey W(c), ice hockey M/W, lacrosse M/W, racquetball M/W, skiing (cross-country) M(c)/W(c), skiing (downhill) M(c)/W(c), soccer M/W, softball M/W, swimming and diving M(c)/W(c), tennis M/W, track and field M(c)/W(c), volleyball M(c)/W(c), water polo M/W.

Campus security: 24-hour emergency response devices and patrols, student patrols, late-night transport/escort service, controlled dormitory access, Public safety website.

Student services: health clinic, personal/psychological counseling.

COSTS & FINANCIAL AID
Costs (2016–17) ***Comprehensive fee:*** $63,253 includes full-time tuition ($46,720), mandatory fees ($933), and room and board ($15,600). ***College room only:*** $8400. Room and board charges vary according to board plan and housing facility. ***Payment plan:*** installment. ***Waivers:*** employees or children of employees.

Financial Aid Of all full-time matriculated undergraduates who enrolled in 2015, 8,793 applied for aid, 6,586 were judged to have need, 2,411 had their need fully met. In 2015, 4402 non-need-based awards were made. ***Average percent of need met:*** 85. ***Average financial aid package:*** $29,567. ***Average need-based loan:*** $4815. ***Average need-based gift aid:*** $25,281. ***Average non-need-based aid:*** $15,331.

APPLYING
Standardized Tests *Required:* SAT or ACT (for admission).

Options: electronic application, early decision, early action, deferred entrance.

Application fee: $75.

Application deadlines: 1/1 (freshmen), 4/1 (transfers), 11/1 (early action).

Early decision deadline: 11/1.

Notification: continuous until 4/1 (freshmen), continuous (transfers), 12/15 (early decision), 12/31 (early action).

CONTACT
Northeastern University, 360 Huntington Avenue, Boston, MA 02115. *Phone:* 617-373-2200. *E-mail:* admissions@neu.edu.

See page 1442 for the College Close-Up.

Northpoint Bible College
Haverhill, Massachusetts
http://northpoint.edu/

CONTACT
Helen Brouillette, Admissions Director, Northpoint Bible College, 320 South Main Street, Haverhill, MA 01835. *Phone:* 800-356-4014. *Toll-free phone:* 800-356-4014. *E-mail:* admissions@zbc.edu.

Pine Manor College
Chestnut Hill, Massachusetts
http://www.pmc.edu/

- **Independent** comprehensive, founded 1911
- **Suburban** 50-acre campus
- **Endowment** $11.0 million
- **Coed** 447 undergraduate students, 98% full-time, 57% women, 43% men
- **Moderately difficult** entrance level, 69% of applicants were admitted

UNDERGRAD STUDENTS
438 full-time, 9 part-time. Students come from 20 states and territories; 11 other countries; 48% are from out of state; 25% Black or African American, non-Hispanic/Latino; 15% Hispanic/Latino; 2% Asian, non-Hispanic/Latino; 0.7% American Indian or Alaska Native, non-Hispanic/Latino; 6% Two or more races, non-Hispanic/Latino; 10% Race/ethnicity unknown; 36% international; 4% transferred in.

Freshmen:
Admission: 784 applied, 542 admitted, 97 enrolled.

Retention: 46% of full-time freshmen returned.

FACULTY
Total: 21, 167% with terminal degrees.
Student/faculty ratio: 15:1.

ACADEMICS
Calendar: semesters. *Degrees:* associate, bachelor's, and master's.

Special study options: academic remediation for entering students, adult/continuing education programs, advanced placement credit, double majors, English as a second language, external degree program, honors programs, independent study, internships, off-campus study, part-time degree program, services for LD students, student-designed majors, study abroad, summer session for credit.

Computers: 85 computers/terminals are available on campus for general student use. Students can access the following: campus intranet, computer help desk, free student e-mail accounts, online (class) grades, online (class) schedules. Campuswide network is available. Wireless service is available via entire campus.
Library: Annenberg Library plus 1 other. Weekly public service hours: 73; students can reserve study rooms.

STUDENT LIFE
Housing options: coed. Campus housing is university owned.
Activities and organizations: drama/theater group, student-run newspaper, radio station, choral group, African American, Latina, Asian, Native American and All (ALANA), Community Service Committee, International Student Club, The Model UN, Student Government Association (SGA).
Athletics Member NCAA. All Division III. ***Intercollegiate sports:*** basketball M/W, cross-country running M/W, soccer M/W, softball W, volleyball W.
Campus security: 24-hour emergency response devices and patrols, student patrols, late-night transport/escort service, controlled dormitory access.
Student services: health clinic, personal/psychological counseling, women's center.

COSTS & FINANCIAL AID
Costs (2016–17) ***Comprehensive fee:*** $42,060 includes full-time tuition ($27,860), mandatory fees ($920), and room and board ($13,280). Full-time tuition and fees vary according to course load. Part-time tuition: $760 per credit hour. Part-time tuition and fees vary according to course load. ***Required fees:*** $560 per year part-time. ***Room and board:*** Room and board charges vary according to housing facility. ***Payment plan:*** installment. ***Waivers:*** children of alumni and employees or children of employees.
Financial Aid Of all full-time matriculated undergraduates who enrolled in 2015, 267 applied for aid, 267 were judged to have need, 8 had their need fully met. In 2015, 33 non-need-based awards were made. ***Average percent of need met:*** 71. ***Average financial aid package:*** $23,834. ***Average need-based loan:*** $3927. ***Average need-based gift aid:*** $18,291. ***Average non-need-based aid:*** $12,923. ***Average indebtedness upon graduation:*** $32,975.

APPLYING
Standardized Tests *Recommended:* SAT or ACT (for admission).
Options: electronic application, deferred entrance.
Application fee: $25.
Required: essay or personal statement, high school transcript, letters of recommendation. ***Recommended:*** minimum 2.0 GPA, interview.
Application deadlines: rolling (freshmen), rolling (transfers).
Notification: continuous (freshmen), continuous (transfers).

CONTACT
Pine Manor College, 400 Heath Street, Chestnut Hill, MA 02467.
Phone: 617-731-7107. *Toll-free phone:* 800-762-1357.

Regis College
Weston, Massachusetts
http://www.regiscollege.edu/

- **Independent Roman Catholic** comprehensive, founded 1927
- **Small-town** 131-acre campus with easy access to Boston
- **Endowment** $33.7 million
- **Coed** 1,235 undergraduate students, 78% full-time, 79% women, 21% men
- **Moderately difficult** entrance level, 84% of applicants were admitted

UNDERGRAD STUDENTS
958 full-time, 277 part-time. Students come from 22 states and territories; 10 other countries; 19% are from out of state; 19% Black or African American, non-Hispanic/Latino; 11% Hispanic/Latino; 4% Asian, non-Hispanic/Latino; 0.1% Native Hawaiian or other Pacific Islander, non-Hispanic/Latino; 0.2% American Indian or Alaska Native, non-Hispanic/Latino; 1% Two or more races, non-Hispanic/Latino; 12% Race/ethnicity unknown; 2% international; 2% transferred in; 60% live on campus.

Freshmen:
Admission: 2,023 applied, 1,704 admitted, 267 enrolled. ***Average high school GPA:*** 3.06. ***Test scores:*** SAT critical reading scores over 500: 36%; SAT math scores over 500: 45%; SAT writing scores over 500: 36%; ACT scores over 18: 76%; SAT critical reading scores over 600: 4%; SAT math scores over 600: 8%; SAT writing scores over 600: 4%; ACT scores over 24: 43%; ACT scores over 30: 5%.

Retention: 82% of full-time freshmen returned.

FACULTY
Total: 210, 46% full-time, 51% with terminal degrees.
Student/faculty ratio: 11:1.

ACADEMICS
Calendar: semesters. *Degrees:* associate, bachelor's, master's, doctoral, and post-master's certificates.

Special study options: academic remediation for entering students, accelerated degree program, adult/continuing education programs, advanced placement credit, double majors, English as a second language, honors programs, independent study, internships, off-campus study, part-time degree program, services for LD students, student-designed majors, study abroad, summer session for credit. ***ROTC:*** Army (c).

Computers: 196 computers/terminals are available on campus for general student use. Students can access the following: campus intranet, computer help desk, free student e-mail accounts, online (class) grades, online (class) registration, online (class) schedules, online bills, financial aid award letters and check-in requirements. Campuswide network is available. 100% of college-owned or -operated housing units are wired for high-speed Internet access. Wireless service is available via computer labs, dorm rooms, learning centers, libraries, student centers.
Library: Regis College Library. *Books:* 108,313 (physical), 421,975 (digital/electronic); *Serial titles:* 126 (physical), 153 (digital/electronic); *Databases:* 58. Weekly public service hours: 108.

STUDENT LIFE
Housing options: coed, women-only. Campus housing is university owned. Freshman campus housing is guaranteed.

Activities and organizations: drama/theater group, student-run newspaper, radio station, choral group, Campus Ministry, SGA-Student Government Association, Asian American Student Organization, Dynasty Step Squad, Black Student Organization.

Athletics Member NCAA. All Division III. ***Intercollegiate sports:*** basketball M/W, field hockey W, lacrosse M/W, soccer M/W, softball W, swimming and diving M/W, tennis M/W, track and field M/W, volleyball M/W.

Campus security: 24-hour emergency response devices and patrols, late-night transport/escort service, controlled dormitory access.

Student services: health clinic, personal/psychological counseling.

COSTS & FINANCIAL AID
Costs (2017–18) ***Comprehensive fee:*** $51,920 includes full-time tuition ($37,540) and room and board ($14,380). ***Payment plan:*** installment. ***Waivers:*** employees or children of employees.

Financial Aid ***Average indebtedness upon graduation:*** $24,178.

APPLYING
Standardized Tests *Required for some:* SAT or ACT (for admission).

Options: electronic application, early admission, early action, deferred entrance.

Application fee: $50.

Required: essay or personal statement, high school transcript, minimum 2.0 GPA, 2 letters of recommendation. ***Required for some:*** interview. ***Recommended:*** minimum 3.0 GPA, interview, rank in upper 50% of high school class.

Application deadlines: rolling (freshmen), rolling (transfers), 12/1 (early action).

Notification: 12/23 (early action).

CONTACT
Mr. Zakaree Marcus Harris, Director of Admission, Regis College, 235 Wellesley Street, Weston, MA 02493. *Phone:* 781-768-7100. *Toll-free phone:* 866-438-7344. *Fax:* 781-768-7071.
E-mail: admission@regiscollege.edu.

See previous page for display ad and page 1470 for the College Close-Up.

Salem State University

Salem, Massachusetts

http://www.salemstate.edu/

CONTACT
Dr. Mary Dunn, Assistant Dean for Undergraduate Admissions, Salem State University, 352 Lafayette Street, Salem, MA 01970. *Phone:* 978-542-6202. *Fax:* 978-542-6893. *E-mail:* admissions@salemstate.edu.

Simmons College

Boston, Massachusetts

http://www.simmons.edu/

- **Independent** university, founded 1899
- **Urban** 12-acre campus with easy access to Boston
- **Endowment** $175.8 million
- **Undergraduate: women only; graduate: coed** 1,802 undergraduate students, 88% full-time, 99% women, 1% men
- **Moderately difficult** entrance level, 64% of applicants were admitted

UNDERGRAD STUDENTS
1,594 full-time, 208 part-time. Students come from 41 states and territories; 52 other countries; 40% are from out of state; 7% Black or African American, non-Hispanic/Latino; 7% Hispanic/Latino; 9% Asian, non-Hispanic/Latino; 0.1% Native Hawaiian or other Pacific Islander, non-Hispanic/Latino; 0.2% American Indian or Alaska Native, non-Hispanic/Latino; 4% Two or more races, non-Hispanic/Latino; 3% Race/ethnicity unknown; 4% international; 2% transferred in; 60% live on campus.

Freshmen:
Admission: 3,362 applied, 2,139 admitted, 452 enrolled. ***Average high school GPA:*** 3.37. ***Test scores:*** SAT critical reading scores over 500: 91%; SAT math scores over 500: 88%; SAT writing scores over 500: 87%; ACT scores over 18: 100%; SAT critical reading scores over 600: 50%; SAT math scores over 600: 34%; SAT writing scores over 600: 42%; ACT scores over 24: 81%; SAT critical reading scores over 700: 10%; SAT math scores over 700: 3%; SAT writing scores over 700: 7%; ACT scores over 30: 20%.

Retention: 83% of full-time freshmen returned.

FACULTY
Total: 1,594, 14% full-time.
Student/faculty ratio: 10:1.

ACADEMICS
Calendar: semesters. *Degrees:* certificates, bachelor's, master's, doctoral, post-master's, and postbachelor's certificates.

Special study options: accelerated degree program, adult/continuing education programs, advanced placement credit, distance learning, double majors, external degree program, honors programs, independent study, internships, off-campus study, part-time degree program, services for LD students, student-designed majors, study abroad, summer session for credit. ***ROTC:*** Army (c).

Unusual degree programs: 3-2 business administration; nursing; social work.

Computers: 350 computers/terminals are available on campus for general student use. Students can access the following: campus intranet, computer help desk, free student e-mail accounts, online (class) grades, online (class) registration, online (class) schedules. Campuswide network is available. 100% of college-owned or -operated housing units are wired for high-speed Internet access. Wireless service is available via entire campus.
Library: Beatley Library. *Books:* 253,094 (physical), 33,326 (digital/electronic); *Serial titles:* 25,707 (physical), 291,590 (digital/electronic); *Databases:* 96. Weekly public service hours: 105; students can reserve study rooms.

STUDENT LIFE
Housing options: on-campus residence required for freshman year; coed, women-only. Campus housing is university owned. Freshman applicants given priority for college housing.

Activities and organizations: drama/theater group, student-run newspaper, radio station, choral group, Simmons College Dance

Company, Student Government Association, Simmons Student Nursing Association, Sexuality Women and Gender (SWAG), Class Councils (2017, 2018, 2019, 2020).

Athletics Member NCAA. All Division III. ***Intercollegiate sports:*** basketball W, crew W, cross-country running W, field hockey W, lacrosse W, soccer W, softball W, swimming and diving W, tennis W, volleyball W. ***Intramural sports:*** basketball M/W, rugby W(c), soccer M/W, softball M/W, tennis M/W, volleyball M/W.

Campus security: 24-hour emergency response devices and patrols, late-night transport/escort service, controlled dormitory access.

Student services: health clinic, personal/psychological counseling, women's center.

COSTS & FINANCIAL AID

Costs (2017–18) ***Comprehensive fee:*** $54,410 includes full-time tuition ($38,500), mandatory fees ($1110), and room and board ($14,800). Full-time tuition and fees vary according to course load and program. Part-time tuition: $1200 per credit hour. Part-time tuition and fees vary according to course load and program. ***Required fees:*** $260 per term part-time. ***Room and board:*** Room and board charges vary according to board plan and location. ***Payment plan:*** installment. ***Waivers:*** employees or children of employees.

Financial Aid Of all full-time matriculated undergraduates who enrolled in 2016, 1,349 applied for aid, 1,230 were judged to have need, 161 had their need fully met. 841 Federal Work-Study jobs (averaging $2345). In 2016, 312 non-need-based awards were made. ***Average percent of need met:*** 75. ***Average financial aid package:*** $30,318. ***Average need-based loan:*** $4096. ***Average need-based gift aid:*** $26,528. ***Average non-need-based aid:*** $17,279.

APPLYING

Standardized Tests *Required:* SAT or ACT (for admission).

Options: electronic application, early action, deferred entrance.

Application fee: $55.

Required: essay or personal statement, high school transcript, 2 letters of recommendation. ***Recommended:*** minimum 3.0 GPA, interview.

Application deadlines: 2/1 (freshmen), 4/1 (transfers), 12/1 (early action).

Notification: continuous until 3/15 (freshmen), 3/15 (out-of-state freshmen), 1/15 (early action).

CONTACT

Ellen Johnson, Director of Undergraduate Admission, Simmons College, 300 The Fenway, Boston, MA 02115. *Phone:* 617-521-2515. *Toll-free phone:* 800-345-8468. *Fax:* 617-521-3190.

Smith College

Northampton, Massachusetts

http://www.smith.edu/

- **Independent** comprehensive, founded 1871
- **Small-town** 147-acre campus with easy access to Hartford
- **Undergraduate: women only; graduate: coed** 2,478 undergraduate students, 99% full-time, 100% women, 0% men
- **Very difficult** entrance level, 38% of applicants were admitted

UNDERGRAD STUDENTS

2,460 full-time, 18 part-time. 82% are from out of state; 5% Black or African American, non-Hispanic/Latino; 10% Hispanic/Latino; 12% Asian, non-Hispanic/Latino; 0.1% Native Hawaiian or other Pacific Islander, non-Hispanic/Latino; 0.2% American Indian or Alaska Native, non-Hispanic/Latino; 5% Two or more races, non-Hispanic/Latino; 8% Race/ethnicity unknown; 14% international; 2% transferred in; 95% live on campus.

Freshmen:

Admission: 5,006 applied, 1,897 admitted, 609 enrolled. ***Average high school GPA:*** 3.94. ***Test scores:*** SAT critical reading scores over 500: 99%; SAT math scores over 500: 98%; SAT writing scores over 500: 98%; ACT scores over 18: 100%; SAT critical reading scores over 600: 82%; SAT math scores over 600: 83%; SAT writing scores over 600: 89%; ACT scores over 24: 94%; SAT critical reading scores over 700: 40%; SAT math scores over 700: 37%; SAT writing scores over 700: 41%; ACT scores over 30: 49%.

Retention: 90% of full-time freshmen returned.

ACADEMICS

Calendar: semesters. *Degrees:* bachelor's, master's, doctoral, post-master's, and postbachelor's certificates.

Special study options: accelerated degree program, adult/continuing education programs, double majors, honors programs, independent study, internships, part-time degree program, student-designed majors, study abroad. ***ROTC:*** Army (c), Air Force (c).

Computers: Students can access the following: campus intranet, computer help desk, free student e-mail accounts, online (class) grades, online (class) registration, online (class) schedules. Campuswide network is available. 100% of college-owned or -operated housing units are wired for high-speed Internet access. Wireless service is available via classrooms, computer centers, computer labs, dorm rooms, learning centers, libraries, student centers.

Library: Neilson Library.

STUDENT LIFE

Housing options: on-campus residence required through senior year; women-only, cooperative. Campus housing is university owned. Freshman campus housing is guaranteed.

Activities and organizations: drama/theater group, student-run newspaper, radio and television station, choral group.

Athletics Member NCAA. All Division III. ***Intercollegiate sports:*** basketball W, crew W, cross-country running W, equestrian sports W, field hockey W, lacrosse W, soccer W, softball W, squash W, swimming and diving W, tennis W, track and field W, volleyball W. ***Intramural sports:*** badminton W(c), cheerleading W(c), crew W, equestrian sports W(c), fencing W(c), golf W(c), ice hockey W(c), rock climbing W, rugby W(c), soccer W, squash W, ultimate Frisbee W(c).

Campus security: 24-hour emergency response devices and patrols, late-night transport/escort service, self-defense workshops, emergency telephones, programs in crime and sexual assault prevention.

COSTS & FINANCIAL AID

Costs (2017–18) ***Comprehensive fee:*** $66,774 includes full-time tuition ($49,760), mandatory fees ($284), and room and board ($16,730). Part-time tuition: $1560 per credit hour. ***Payment plans:*** tuition prepayment, installment. ***Waivers:*** employees or children of employees.

Financial Aid Of all full-time matriculated undergraduates who enrolled in 2015, 1,687 applied for aid, 1,487 were judged to have need, 1,487 had their need fully met. In 2015, 106 non-need-based awards were made. ***Average percent of need met:*** 100. ***Average financial aid package:*** $45,628. ***Average need-based loan:*** $4474. ***Average need-based gift aid:*** $38,040. ***Average non-need-based aid:*** $14,178. ***Average indebtedness upon graduation:*** $20,514. ***Financial aid deadline:*** 2/15.

APPLYING

Standardized Tests *Required for some:* SAT or ACT (for admission).

Options: electronic application, early admission, early decision, deferred entrance.

Required: essay or personal statement, high school transcript, 3 letters of recommendation. ***Recommended:*** interview.

Early decision deadline: 11/15 (for plan 1), 1/1 (for plan 2).

Notification: 12/15 (early decision plan 1), 1/31 (early decision plan 2).

CONTACT

Ms. Debra Shaver, Dean of Admissions, Smith College, 7 College Lane, Northampton, MA 01063. *Phone:* 413-585-2500. *Toll-free phone:* 800-383-3232. *Fax:* 413-585-2527. *E-mail:* admission@smith.edu.

★ Springfield College

Springfield, Massachusetts

http://www.springfield.edu/

- **Independent** comprehensive, founded 1885
- **Suburban** 150-acre campus
- **Coed**
- **Moderately difficult** entrance level

ACADEMICS

Calendar: semesters. *Degrees:* bachelor's, master's, doctoral, and postbachelor's certificates.

Library: Babson Library.

STUDENT LIFE
Housing options: on-campus residence required through junior year; coed, men-only, special housing for students with disabilities. Campus housing is university owned. Freshman campus housing is guaranteed.
Activities and organizations: drama/theater group, student-run newspaper, radio and television station, choral group.
Athletics Member NCAA. All Division III.
Student services: health clinic, personal/psychological counseling.

FINANCIAL AID
Financial Aid Of all full-time matriculated undergraduates who enrolled in 2015, 1,861 applied for aid, 1,690 were judged to have need, 147 had their need fully met. In 2015, 240 non-need-based awards were made. ***Average percent of need met:*** 74. ***Average financial aid package:*** $26,129. ***Average need-based loan:*** $4445. ***Average need-based gift aid:*** $20,688. ***Average non-need-based aid:*** $10,342. ***Average indebtedness upon graduation:*** $40,062.

APPLYING
Standardized Tests *Required:* SAT or ACT (for admission).
Options: electronic application, early decision, deferred entrance.
Application fee: $50.
Required: high school transcript, 1 letter of recommendation. ***Required for some:*** portfolio. ***Recommended:*** interview.

CONTACT
Richard K. Veres, Director of Undergraduate Admissions, Springfield College, 263 Alden Street, Springfield, MA 01109. *Phone:* 413-748-3136. *Toll-free phone:* 800-343-1257. *Fax:* 413-748-3694.
E-mail: admissions@spfldcol.edu.

See page 1518 for the College Close-Up.

★ Stonehill College
Easton, Massachusetts
http://www.stonehill.edu/

- **Independent Roman Catholic** 4-year, founded 1948
- **Suburban** 384-acre campus with easy access to Boston
- **Endowment** $1.8 billion
- **Coed** 2,481 undergraduate students, 99% full-time, 60% women, 40% men
- **Very difficult** entrance level, 73% of applicants were admitted

UNDERGRAD STUDENTS
2,455 full-time, 26 part-time. Students come from 30 states and territories; 15 other countries; 40% are from out of state; 5% Black or African American, non-Hispanic/Latino; 5% Hispanic/Latino; 2% Asian, non-Hispanic/Latino; 2% Two or more races, non-Hispanic/Latino; 2% Race/ethnicity unknown; 0.9% international; 1% transferred in; 90% live on campus.

Freshmen:
Admission: 6,362 applied, 4,639 admitted, 734 enrolled. ***Average high school GPA:*** 3.31. ***Test scores:*** SAT critical reading scores over 500: 75%; SAT math scores over 500: 78%; SAT writing scores over 500: 76%; ACT scores over 18: 98%; SAT critical reading scores over 600: 28%; SAT math scores over 600: 29%; SAT writing scores over 600: 28%; ACT scores over 24: 64%; SAT critical reading scores over 700: 4%; SAT math scores over 700: 2%; SAT writing scores over 700: 2%; ACT scores over 30: 14%.
Retention: 92% of full-time freshmen returned.

FACULTY
Total: 282, 58% full-time, 63% with terminal degrees.
Student/faculty ratio: 12:1.

ACADEMICS
Calendar: semesters. *Degree:* bachelor's.
Special study options: advanced placement credit, double majors, honors programs, independent study, internships, off-campus study, part-time degree program, services for LD students, student-designed majors, study abroad, summer session for credit. ***ROTC:*** Army (b).
Unusual degree programs: 3-2 engineering with University of Notre Dame; political science with Catholic University.
Computers: 458 computers/terminals and 300 ports are available on campus for general student use. Students can access the following: campus intranet, computer help desk, free student e-mail accounts, online (class) grades, online (class) registration, online (class) schedules, Learning Management System, online degree evaluation/planning, add funds to ID, use at off campus locations, housing contracts and room lottery, financial aid awards, time sheets and payments for campus jobs, ebill. Campuswide network is available. 100% of college-owned or -operated housing units are wired for high-speed Internet access. Wireless service is available via entire campus.
Library: MacPhaidin Library plus 2 others. *Books:* 257,031 (physical), 304,867 (digital/electronic); *Serial titles:* 13,841 (physical), 80,308 (digital/electronic); *Databases:* 48. Weekly public service hours: 106; students can reserve study rooms.

STUDENT LIFE
Housing options: coed, women-only, special housing for students with disabilities. Campus housing is university owned.
Activities and organizations: drama/theater group, student-run newspaper, radio station, choral group, Into the Streets, Recreation/Intramural Sports Teams, Dance Club, Student Government Association, Education Society.
Athletics Member NCAA. All Division II. ***Intercollegiate sports:*** baseball M(s), basketball M(s)/W(s), bowling M(c)/W(c), cheerleading M(c)/W(c), cross-country running M(s)/W(s), equestrian sports W, field hockey W(s), football M(s), golf M(c), ice hockey M/W(c), lacrosse M(c)/W(s), rugby M(c)/W(c), soccer M(s)/W(s), softball W(s), table tennis M(c)/W(c), tennis M(s)/W(s), track and field M(s)/W(s), ultimate Frisbee M(c)/W(c), volleyball M(c)/W(s). ***Intramural sports:*** basketball M/W, field hockey M/W, soccer M/W, softball M/W, table tennis M/W, tennis M/W, volleyball M/W(c).
Campus security: 24-hour emergency response devices and patrols, late-night transport/escort service, controlled dormitory access, restricted access on weekends.
Student services: health clinic, personal/psychological counseling.

COSTS & FINANCIAL AID
Costs (2016–17) ***Comprehensive fee:*** $55,130 includes full-time tuition ($39,900) and room and board ($15,230). Part-time tuition: $1330 per credit. Part-time tuition and fees vary according to course load. ***Room and board:*** Room and board charges vary according to board plan. ***Payment plans:*** tuition prepayment, installment. ***Waivers:*** employees or children of employees.
Financial Aid Of all full-time matriculated undergraduates who enrolled in 2016, 1,891 applied for aid, 1,610 were judged to have need, 732 had their need fully met. In 2016, 680 non-need-based awards were made. ***Average percent of need met:*** 91. ***Average financial aid package:*** $30,606. ***Average need-based loan:*** $4660. ***Average need-based gift aid:*** $25,017. ***Average non-need-based aid:*** $17,418. ***Average indebtedness upon graduation:*** $35,462.

APPLYING
Options: electronic application, early decision, early action, deferred entrance.
Application fee: $60.
Required: essay or personal statement, high school transcript, 2 letters of recommendation. ***Recommended:*** interview.
Application deadlines: 1/15 (freshmen), 4/1 (transfers), 11/1 (early action).
Early decision deadline: 12/1.
Notification: 3/15 (freshmen), continuous until 5/31 (transfers), 12/31 (early decision), 12/31 (early action).

CONTACT
Stonehill College, 320 Washington Street, Easton, MA 02357-5610. *Phone:* 508-565-1373. *Fax:* 508-565-1545.
E-mail: admission@stonehill.edu.

See page 1530 for the College Close-Up.

Suffolk University

Boston, Massachusetts

http://www.suffolk.edu/

- **Independent** comprehensive, founded 1906
- **Urban** 2-acre campus with easy access to Boston, MA
- **Endowment** $181.6 million
- **Coed** 5,290 undergraduate students, 95% full-time, 55% women, 45% men
- **Moderately difficult** entrance level, 84% of applicants were admitted

UNDERGRAD STUDENTS

5,004 full-time, 286 part-time. Students come from 44 states and territories; 100 other countries; 32% are from out of state; 6% Black or African American, non-Hispanic/Latino; 11% Hispanic/Latino; 8% Asian, non-Hispanic/Latino; 0.1% Native Hawaiian or other Pacific Islander, non-Hispanic/Latino; 0.1% American Indian or Alaska Native, non-Hispanic/Latino; 2% Two or more races, non-Hispanic/Latino; 6% Race/ethnicity unknown; 22% international; 6% transferred in; 25% live on campus.

Freshmen:

Admission: 8,624 applied, 7,271 admitted, 1,205 enrolled. ***Average high school GPA:*** 3.2. ***Test scores:*** SAT critical reading scores over 500: 55%; SAT math scores over 500: 59%; SAT writing scores over 500: 55%; ACT scores over 18: 90%; SAT critical reading scores over 600: 15%; SAT math scores over 600: 15%; SAT writing scores over 600: 12%; ACT scores over 24: 44%; SAT critical reading scores over 700: 2%; SAT math scores over 700: 1%; SAT writing scores over 700: 1%; ACT scores over 30: 5%.

Retention: 76% of full-time freshmen returned.

FACULTY

Total: 684, 50% full-time, 63% with terminal degrees.

Student/faculty ratio: 13:1.

ACADEMICS

Calendar: semesters. *Degrees:* certificates, diplomas, associate, bachelor's, master's, doctoral, post-master's, and postbachelor's certificates (doctoral degree in law).

Special study options: academic remediation for entering students, accelerated degree program, adult/continuing education programs, advanced placement credit, cooperative education, distance learning, double majors, English as a second language, honors programs, independent study, internships, off-campus study, part-time degree program, services for LD students, study abroad, summer session for credit. ***ROTC:*** Army (c).

Computers: 539 computers/terminals and 8,000 ports are available on campus for general student use. Students can access the following: campus intranet, computer help desk, free student e-mail accounts, online (class) grades, online (class) registration, online (class) schedules. Campuswide network is available. 100% of college-owned or -operated housing units are wired for high-speed Internet access. Wireless service is available via entire campus.

Library: Mildred Sawyer Library plus 3 others. *Books:* 159,014 (physical), 212,904 (digital/electronic); *Serial titles:* 302 (physical), 35,386 (digital/electronic); *Databases:* 1,904. Weekly public service hours: 16; students can reserve study rooms.

STUDENT LIFE

Housing options: coed. Campus housing is university owned. Freshman applicants given priority for college housing.

Activities and organizations: drama/theater group, student-run newspaper, radio and television station, choral group, Student Government Association, Program Committee, Suffolk Free Radio, Black Student Union, Journey Leadership Program, national fraternities, national sororities.

Athletics Member NCAA. All Division III. ***Intercollegiate sports:*** baseball M, basketball M/W, cross-country running M/W, golf M, ice hockey M, soccer M, softball W, tennis M/W, volleyball W. ***Intramural sports:*** basketball M/W, soccer M/W, softball M/W, volleyball M/W.

Campus security: 24-hour emergency response devices, late-night transport/escort service, controlled dormitory access.

Student services: health clinic, personal/psychological counseling, women's center.

COSTS & FINANCIAL AID

Costs (2017–18) ***One-time required fee:*** $220. ***Comprehensive fee:*** $53,842 includes full-time tuition ($37,128), mandatory fees ($138), and room and board ($16,576). Full-time tuition and fees vary according to course level and reciprocity agreements. Part-time tuition: $1092 per credit hour. Part-time tuition and fees vary according to course level, course load, and reciprocity agreements. ***Required fees:*** $17 per term part-time. ***College room only:*** $13,928. Room and board charges vary according to board plan and housing facility. ***Payment plans:*** installment, deferred payment. ***Waivers:*** children of alumni, senior citizens, and employees or children of employees.

Financial Aid Of all full-time matriculated undergraduates who enrolled in 2016, 3,100 applied for aid, 2,858 were judged to have need, 698 had their need fully met. 925 Federal Work-Study jobs (averaging $2396). 565 state and other part-time jobs (averaging $3643). In 2016, 1324 non-need-based awards were made. ***Average percent of need met:*** 76. ***Average financial aid package:*** $31,105. ***Average need-based loan:*** $5266. ***Average need-based gift aid:*** $13,578. ***Average non-need-based aid:*** $13,834. ***Average indebtedness upon graduation:*** $39,091. ***Financial aid deadline:*** 3/1.

APPLYING

Standardized Tests *Required:* SAT or ACT (for admission).

Options: electronic application, early action, deferred entrance.

Application fee: $50.

Required: essay or personal statement, high school transcript, 2 letters of recommendation. ***Required for some:*** interview.

Application deadlines: 2/1 (freshmen), 6/30 (transfers), 11/15 (early action).

Notification: continuous until 3/20 (freshmen), continuous (transfers), 12/15 (early action).

CONTACT

Ms. Donna Grand Pre, Assistant Vice President/Director Undergraduate Admissions, Suffolk University, 8 Ashburton Place, Boston, MA 02108. *Phone:* 617-573-8460. *Toll-free phone:* 800-6-SUFFOLK. *Fax:* 617-742-4291. *E-mail:* admission@suffolk.edu.

Tufts University

Medford, Massachusetts

http://www.tufts.edu/

- **Independent** university, founded 1852
- **Suburban** 150-acre campus with easy access to Boston
- **Endowment** $1.6 billion
- **Coed** 5,508 undergraduate students, 99% full-time, 50% women, 50% men
- **Most difficult** entrance level, 14% of applicants were admitted

UNDERGRAD STUDENTS

5,435 full-time, 73 part-time. Students come from 52 states and territories; 82 other countries; 74% are from out of state; 4% Black or African American, non-Hispanic/Latino; 7% Hispanic/Latino; 12% Asian, non-Hispanic/Latino; 5% Two or more races, non-Hispanic/Latino; 6% Race/ethnicity unknown; 10% international; 0.3% transferred in; 62% live on campus.

Freshmen:

Admission: 20,223 applied, 2,889 admitted, 1,336 enrolled. ***Test scores:*** SAT critical reading scores over 500: 100%; SAT math scores over 500: 100%; SAT writing scores over 500: 100%; ACT scores over 18: 100%; SAT critical reading scores over 600: 96%; SAT math scores over 600: 99%; SAT writing scores over 600: 97%; ACT scores over 24: 100%; SAT critical reading scores over 700: 64%; SAT math scores over 700: 73%; SAT writing scores over 700: 66%; ACT scores over 30: 88%.

Retention: 96% of full-time freshmen returned.

FACULTY

Total: 1,053, 64% full-time, 81% with terminal degrees.

Student/faculty ratio: 8:1.

ACADEMICS

Calendar: semesters. *Degrees:* certificates, bachelor's, master's, doctoral, post-master's, and postbachelor's certificates.

Special study options: academic remediation for entering students, adult/continuing education programs, advanced placement credit, cooperative education, double majors, independent study, internships, off-campus study, services for LD students, student-designed majors, study abroad, summer session for credit. ***ROTC:*** Army (c), Navy (c), Air Force (c).

Unusual degree programs: 3-2 New England Conservatory of Music, School of the Museum of Fine Arts.

Computers: 1,039 computers/terminals are available on campus for general student use. Students can access the following: campus intranet, computer help desk, free student e-mail accounts, online (class) grades, online (class) registration, online (class) schedules, Cloud storage for all students, staff, and faculty. Campuswide network is available. 100% of college-owned or -operated housing units are wired for high-speed Internet access. Wireless service is available via entire campus.

Library: Tisch Library plus 3 others. *Books:* 1.3 million (physical), 432,877 (digital/electronic); *Serial titles:* 1,012 (physical); *Databases:* 83,216. Weekly public service hours: 110; students can reserve study rooms.

STUDENT LIFE

Housing options: on-campus residence required through sophomore year; coed, women-only, special housing for students with disabilities. Campus housing is university owned. Freshman campus housing is guaranteed.

Activities and organizations: drama/theater group, student-run newspaper, radio and television station, choral group, Leonard Carmichael Society (community service), Tufts Dance Collective, intramural sports, Tufts Daily (newspaper), Tufts Mountain Club, national fraternities, national sororities.

Athletics Member NCAA. All Division III. ***Intercollegiate sports:*** baseball M, basketball M/W, crew M/W, cross-country running M/W, equestrian sports M(c)/W(c), fencing W, field hockey W, football M, golf M, ice hockey M, lacrosse M/W, rugby M(c)/W(c), sailing M/W, soccer M/W, softball W, squash M/W, swimming and diving M/W, tennis M/W, track and field M/W, ultimate Frisbee M(c)/W(c), volleyball M(c)/W, water polo M(c)/W(c). ***Intramural sports:*** badminton M/W, baseball M(c), basketball M/W, cheerleading W, fencing M(c), field hockey W(c), football M(c)/W(c), ice hockey M(c), lacrosse M(c)/W(c), racquetball M/W, rock climbing M(c)/W(c), skiing (downhill) M/W, soccer M/W, softball M/W(c), table tennis M(c)/W(c), tennis M/W, volleyball M/W.

Campus security: 24-hour emergency response devices and patrols, late-night transport/escort service, controlled dormitory access, security lighting, call boxes to campus police.

Student services: health clinic, personal/psychological counseling, women's center, legal services.

COSTS & FINANCIAL AID

Costs (2016–17) ***Comprehensive fee:*** $65,996 includes full-time tuition ($51,304), mandatory fees ($1126), and room and board ($13,566). ***College room only:*** $7392. Room and board charges vary according to board plan. ***Payment plans:*** tuition prepayment, installment. ***Waivers:*** employees or children of employees.

Financial Aid Of all full-time matriculated undergraduates who enrolled in 2016, 2,187 applied for aid, 1,935 were judged to have need, 1,911 had their need fully met. 1,432 Federal Work-Study jobs (averaging $1894). 160 state and other part-time jobs (averaging $1902). In 2016, 72 non-need-based awards were made. ***Average percent of need met:*** 100. ***Average financial aid package:*** $43,325. ***Average need-based loan:*** $3122. ***Average need-based gift aid:*** $41,366. ***Average non-need-based aid:*** $500. ***Average indebtedness upon graduation:*** $24,267. ***Financial aid deadline:*** 2/1.

APPLYING

Standardized Tests *Required:* SAT and SAT Subject Tests or ACT (for admission). *Required for some:* art portfolio in lieu of Subject Tests for applicants to the School of Museum of Fine Arts.

Options: electronic application, early admission, early decision, deferred entrance.

Application fee: $75.

Required: essay or personal statement, high school transcript, 2 letters of recommendation, Common Application or Coalition Application or QuestBridge Application, the Tufts Supplement. ***Recommended:*** interview.

Application deadlines: 1/1 (freshmen), 3/15 (transfers).

Early decision deadline: 11/1 (for plan 1), 1/1 (for plan 2).

Notification: 4/1 (freshmen), continuous until 5/15 (transfers), 12/15 (early decision plan 1), 2/15 (early decision plan 2).

CONTACT

Office of Undergraduate Admissions, Tufts University, Bendetson Hall, Medford, MA 02155. *Phone:* 617-627-3170. *Fax:* 617-627-3860. *E-mail:* undergraduate.admissions@tufts.edu.

University of Massachusetts Amherst

Amherst, Massachusetts

http://www.umass.edu/

- **State-supported** university, founded 1863, part of University of Massachusetts
- **Small-town** 1463-acre campus with easy access to Springfield, MA and Hartford, CT
- **Endowment** $287.2 million
- **Coed**
- **Moderately difficult** entrance level

UNDERGRAD STUDENTS

Students come from 49 states and territories; 74 other countries.

ACADEMICS

Calendar: semesters. *Degrees:* certificates, associate, bachelor's, master's, doctoral, and postbachelor's certificates.

Special study options: accelerated degree program, adult/continuing education programs, advanced placement credit, cooperative education, distance learning, double majors, English as a second language, freshman honors college, honors programs, independent study, internships, off-campus study, part-time degree program, services for LD students, student-designed majors, study abroad, summer session for credit. ***ROTC:*** Army (b), Air Force (b).

Computers: 472 computers/terminals and 406 ports are available on campus for general student use. Students can access the following: computer help desk, free student e-mail accounts, online (class) grades, online (class) registration, online (class) schedules, online housing assignments, bill payment, Learning Management System, file storage, Web hosting, blogs. Campuswide network is available. 100% of college-owned or -operated housing units are wired for high-speed Internet access. Wireless service is available via entire campus.

Library: W. E. B. Du Bois Library plus 1 other. *Books:* 2.7 million (physical), 1.7 million (digital/electronic); *Serial titles:* 115,786 (digital/electronic); *Databases:* 287. Weekly public service hours: 142; study areas open 24 hours, 5-7 days a week; students can reserve study rooms.

STUDENT LIFE

Housing options: on-campus residence required for freshman year; coed, men-only, women-only, special housing for students with disabilities. Campus housing is university owned. Freshman campus housing is guaranteed.

Activities and organizations: drama/theater group, student-run newspaper, radio and television station, choral group, marching band, Minutemen Marching Band, Ski Club, Outing Club, University Programming Council, Student Government Association, national fraternities, national sororities.

Athletics Member NCAA. All Division I except football (Division I-A). ***Intercollegiate sports:*** baseball M(s), basketball M(s)/W(s), crew W(s), cross-country running M(s)/W(s), field hockey W(s), ice hockey M(s), lacrosse M(s)/W(s), soccer M(s)/W(s), softball W(s), swimming and diving M(s)/W(s), tennis W(s), track and field M(s)/W(s). ***Intramural sports:*** badminton M/W, baseball M(c), basketball M/W, cheerleading M/W, equestrian sports M(c)/W(c), fencing M(c)/W(c), field hockey W(c), football M/W, golf M(c)/W(c), gymnastics W(c), ice hockey M/W(c), lacrosse M(c)/W(c), racquetball M/W, rugby M(c)/W(c), sailing M(c)/W(c), skiing (downhill) M(c)/W(c), soccer M/W, softball W(c), swimming and diving M(c)/W(c), table tennis M/W, tennis M/W, triathlon M(c)/W(c), ultimate Frisbee M(c)/W(c), volleyball M/W, water polo M(c)/W(c), wrestling M(c)/W(c).

Campus security: 24-hour emergency response devices and patrols, student patrols, late-night transport/escort service, controlled dormitory access.

Student services: health clinic, personal/psychological counseling, women's center, legal services.

COSTS & FINANCIAL AID

Costs (2016–17) ***One-time required fee:*** $185. ***Tuition:*** state resident $14,590 full-time, $5110 per term part-time; nonresident $31,823 full-time, $11,236 per term part-time. Full-time tuition and fees vary according to class time, location, program, reciprocity agreements, and student level. Part-time tuition and fees vary according to class time, course load, location, program, reciprocity agreements, and student level. ***Required fees:*** $381 full-time, $191 per term part-time. ***Room and board:*** $11,897; room only: $6659. Room and board charges vary according to board plan and housing facility. ***Payment plan:*** installment. ***Waivers:*** senior citizens and employees or children of employees.

Financial Aid Of all full-time matriculated undergraduates who enrolled in 2015, 16,792 applied for aid, 11,901 were judged to have need, 1,675 had their need fully met. 2,026 Federal Work-Study jobs (averaging $1248). In 2015, 2889 non-need-based awards were made. ***Average percent of need met:*** 85. ***Average financial aid package:*** $16,749. ***Average need-based loan:*** $4555. ***Average need-based gift aid:*** $10,249. ***Average non-need-based aid:*** $5132. ***Average indebtedness upon graduation:*** $31,397.

APPLYING

Standardized Tests *Required:* SAT or ACT (for admission).

Options: electronic application, early action, deferred entrance.

Required: essay or personal statement, high school transcript, 1 letter of recommendation.

Application deadlines: 1/15 (freshmen), 4/15 (transfers), 11/1 (early action).

Notification: continuous (freshmen), continuous (out-of-state freshmen), continuous (transfers), 12/15 (early action).

CONTACT

Mr. Dale Hendricks, Director of Undergraduate Admissions, University of Massachusetts Amherst, 255 Whitmore, Amherst, MA 01003. *Phone:* 413-545-0222. *Fax:* 413-545-4312. *E-mail:* mail@admissions.umass.edu.

University of Massachusetts Boston

Boston, Massachusetts

http://www.umb.edu/

- **State-supported** university, founded 1964, part of University of Massachusetts
- **Urban** 120-acre campus
- **Endowment** $74.4 million
- **Coed** 12,847 undergraduate students, 72% full-time, 53% women, 47% men
- **Moderately difficult** entrance level, 69% of applicants were admitted

UNDERGRAD STUDENTS

9,283 full-time, 3,564 part-time. Students come from 38 states and territories; 143 other countries; 5% are from out of state; 16% Black or African American, non-Hispanic/Latino; 14% Hispanic/Latino; 12% Asian, non-Hispanic/Latino; 0.2% American Indian or Alaska Native, non-Hispanic/Latino; 3% Two or more races, non-Hispanic/Latino; 8% Race/ethnicity unknown; 12% international; 12% transferred in.

Freshmen:

Admission: 9,886 applied, 6,774 admitted, 1,651 enrolled. ***Average high school GPA:*** 3.25. ***Test scores:*** SAT critical reading scores over 500: 64%; SAT math scores over 500: 73%; ACT scores over 18: 97%; SAT critical reading scores over 600: 20%; SAT math scores over 600: 26%; ACT scores over 24: 49%; SAT critical reading scores over 700: 3%; SAT math scores over 700: 2%; ACT scores over 30: 6%.

Retention: 80% of full-time freshmen returned.

FACULTY

Total: 1,243, 57% full-time, 70% with terminal degrees.

Student/faculty ratio: 16:1.

ACADEMICS

Calendar: semesters. *Degrees:* certificates, bachelor's, master's, doctoral, post-master's, and postbachelor's certificates.

Special study options: academic remediation for entering students, accelerated degree program, adult/continuing education programs, advanced placement credit, cooperative education, distance learning, double majors, English as a second language, freshman honors college, honors programs, independent study, internships, off-campus study, part-time degree program, services for LD students, student-designed majors, study abroad, summer session for credit. ***ROTC:*** Army (c), Navy (c), Air Force (c).

Computers: 350 computers/terminals are available on campus for general student use. Students can access the following: computer help desk, free student e-mail accounts, online (class) grades, online (class) registration, online (class) schedules. Campuswide network is available. Wireless service is available via entire campus.

Library: Joseph P. Healey Library. *Books:* 459,163 (physical), 547,086 (digital/electronic); *Databases:* 124.

STUDENT LIFE

Housing options: college housing not available.

Activities and organizations: drama/theater group, student-run newspaper, radio station, choral group, Student Arts and Events Council, Haitian Student Association, Golden Key Honor Society, Campus Kitchens, Mass Media.

Athletics Member NCAA. All Division III. ***Intercollegiate sports:*** baseball M, basketball M/W, cross-country running M/W, ice hockey M/W, lacrosse M, soccer M/W, softball W, tennis M/W, track and field M/W, volleyball W. ***Intramural sports:*** basketball M/W, bowling M/W, football M/W, golf M/W, racquetball M/W, soccer M/W, softball M/W, volleyball M/W.

Campus security: 24-hour emergency response devices and patrols, late-night transport/escort service, crime prevention program, bicycle patrols.

Student services: health clinic, personal/psychological counseling, women's center.

COSTS & FINANCIAL AID

Costs (2016–17) ***Tuition:*** state resident $13,435 full-time, $546 per credit hour part-time; nonresident $32,023 full-time, $1321 per credit hour part-time. Full-time tuition and fees vary according to program. Part-time tuition and fees vary according to program. ***Required fees:*** $14 per credit hour part-time.

Financial Aid Of all full-time matriculated undergraduates who enrolled in 2015, 6,734 applied for aid, 6,048 were judged to have need, 2,354 had their need fully met. In 2015, 310 non-need-based awards were made. ***Average percent of need met:*** 89. ***Average financial aid package:*** $15,856. ***Average need-based loan:*** $7025. ***Average need-based gift aid:*** $9448. ***Average non-need-based aid:*** $5955. ***Average indebtedness upon graduation:*** $28,368.

APPLYING

Standardized Tests *Required for some:* SAT or ACT (for admission).

Options: electronic application, early admission, early action, deferred entrance.

Application fee: $60.

Required: high school transcript, minimum 2.5 GPA. ***Required for some:*** essay or personal statement, minimum 2.8 GPA, interview. ***Recommended:*** essay or personal statement.

Application deadlines: 3/1 (freshmen), 12/1 (early action).

Notification: continuous (freshmen).

CONTACT

Mr. Corey Ford, Director of Undergraduate Admissions, University of Massachusetts Boston, 100 Morrissey Boulevard, Boston, MA 02125-3393. *Phone:* 617-287-6100. *Fax:* 617-287-5999. *E-mail:* enrollment.info@umb.edu.

University of Massachusetts Dartmouth

North Dartmouth, Massachusetts

http://www.umassd.edu/

- **State-supported** university, founded 1895, part of University of Massachusetts
- **Suburban** 710-acre campus with easy access to Boston, Providence
- **Endowment** $48.0 million
- **Coed** 6,999 undergraduate students, 86% full-time, 49% women, 51% men
- **Moderately difficult** entrance level, 76% of applicants were admitted

UNDERGRAD STUDENTS

6,011 full-time, 988 part-time. Students come from 37 states and territories; 34 other countries; 6% are from out of state; 15% Black or African American, non-Hispanic/Latino; 9% Hispanic/Latino; 4% Asian, non-Hispanic/Latino; 0.2% American Indian or Alaska Native, non-Hispanic/Latino; 4% Two or more races, non-Hispanic/Latino; 5% Race/ethnicity unknown; 2% international; 7% transferred in; 55% live on campus.

Freshmen:

Admission: 8,211 applied, 6,242 admitted, 1,367 enrolled. ***Average high school GPA:*** 3.21. ***Test scores:*** SAT critical reading scores over 500: 54%; SAT math scores over 500: 62%; ACT scores over 18: 90%; SAT critical reading scores over 600: 14%; SAT math scores over 600: 17%; ACT scores over 24: 41%; SAT critical reading scores over 700: 2%; SAT math scores over 700: 2%; ACT scores over 30: 5%.

Retention: 73% of full-time freshmen returned.

FACULTY

Total: 673, 59% full-time, 66% with terminal degrees.

Student/faculty ratio: 16:1.

ACADEMICS

Calendar: semesters. *Degrees:* certificates, bachelor's, master's, doctoral, post-master's, and postbachelor's certificates.

Special study options: academic remediation for entering students, accelerated degree program, advanced placement credit, cooperative education, distance learning, double majors, English as a second language, honors programs, independent study, internships, off-campus study, part-time degree program, services for LD students, student-designed majors, study abroad, summer session for credit. ***ROTC:*** Army (c).

Unusual degree programs: 3-2 engineering; nursing; liberal arts, English, political science.

Computers: 368 computers/terminals and 5,000 ports are available on campus for general student use. Students can access the following: campus intranet, computer help desk, free student e-mail accounts, online (class) grades, online (class) registration, online (class) schedules. Campuswide network is available. 100% of college-owned or -operated housing units are wired for high-speed Internet access. Wireless service is available via classrooms, computer centers, computer labs, learning centers, libraries, student centers.

Library: Claire T. Carney Library plus 1 other. *Books:* 239,929 (physical), 84,639 (digital/electronic); *Serial titles:* 1,436 (physical), 87,444 (digital/electronic); *Databases:* 133. Students can reserve study rooms.

STUDENT LIFE

Housing options: coed, special housing for students with disabilities. Campus housing is university owned.

Activities and organizations: drama/theater group, student-run newspaper, radio station, choral group, Outdoor Club, Ski and Snowboard Club, 20 Cent Fiction, Relay for Life, American Red Cross, national fraternities, national sororities.

Athletics Member NCAA. All Division III. ***Intercollegiate sports:*** baseball M, basketball M/W, cross-country running M/W, equestrian sports W, field hockey W, football M, golf M, ice hockey M, lacrosse M/W, sailing W, soccer M/W, softball W, swimming and diving M/W, tennis M/W, track and field M/W, volleyball W. ***Intramural sports:*** badminton M/W, basketball M/W, rugby M/W, sand volleyball M/W, skiing (downhill) M/W, soccer M/W, softball M/W, tennis M/W, ultimate Frisbee M/W, water polo M.

Campus security: 24-hour emergency response devices and patrols, student patrols, late-night transport/escort service, controlled dormitory access.

Student services: health clinic, personal/psychological counseling, women's center.

COSTS & FINANCIAL AID

Costs (2016–17) ***One-time required fee:*** $100. ***Tuition:*** state resident $12,783 full-time, $533 per credit part-time; nonresident $27,068 full-time, $1128 per credit part-time. Full-time tuition and fees vary according to class time, program, and reciprocity agreements. Part-time tuition and fees vary according to class time, course load, program, and reciprocity agreements. ***Required fees:*** $405 full-time, $26 per credit part-time. ***Room and board:*** $12,470; room only: $4519. Room and board charges vary according to board plan and housing facility. ***Payment plan:*** installment. ***Waivers:*** senior citizens and employees or children of employees.

Financial Aid Of all full-time matriculated undergraduates who enrolled in 2016, 5,028 applied for aid, 4,245 were judged to have need, 1,931 had their need fully met. 933 Federal Work-Study jobs (averaging $1300). In 2016, 409 non-need-based awards were made. ***Average percent of need met:*** 87. ***Average financial aid package:*** $17,213. ***Average need-based loan:*** $8333. ***Average need-based gift aid:*** $10,181. ***Average non-need-based aid:*** $4596. ***Average indebtedness upon graduation:*** $32,099.

APPLYING

Standardized Tests *Required:* SAT or ACT (for admission).

Options: electronic application, early admission, early action, deferred entrance.

Application fee: $60.

Required: high school transcript, minimum 3.0 GPA. ***Recommended:*** essay or personal statement, 1 letter of recommendation.

Application deadlines: rolling (freshmen), rolling (transfers), 11/15 (early action).

Notification: continuous (freshmen), continuous (transfers), 12/15 (early action).

CONTACT

University of Massachusetts Dartmouth, 285 Old Westport Road, North Dartmouth, MA 02747-2300. *Phone:* 508-999-8605. *Fax:* 508-999-8755. *E-mail:* admissions@umassd.edu.

★ University of Massachusetts Lowell

Lowell, Massachusetts

http://www.uml.edu/

- **State-supported** university, founded 1894, part of University of Massachusetts
- **Urban** 100-acre campus with easy access to Boston
- **Endowment** $81.0 million
- **Coed** 13,639 undergraduate students, 73% full-time, 38% women, 62% men
- **Moderately difficult** entrance level, 60% of applicants were admitted

UNDERGRAD STUDENTS

10,019 full-time, 3,620 part-time. Students come from 36 states and territories; 68 other countries; 10% are from out of state; 6% Black or African American, non-Hispanic/Latino; 11% Hispanic/Latino; 9% Asian, non-Hispanic/Latino; 0.1% American Indian or Alaska Native, non-Hispanic/Latino; 3% Two or more races, non-Hispanic/Latino; 4% Race/ethnicity unknown; 4% international; 8% transferred in; 37% live on campus.

Freshmen:

Admission: 11,231 applied, 6,771 admitted, 1,685 enrolled. ***Average high school GPA:*** 3.58. ***Test scores:*** SAT critical reading scores over 500: 86%; SAT math scores over 500: 94%; SAT writing scores over 500: 75%; ACT scores over 18: 99%; SAT critical reading scores over 600: 35%; SAT math scores over 600: 52%; SAT writing scores over 600: 24%; ACT scores over 24: 76%; SAT critical reading scores over 700: 6%; SAT math scores over 700: 9%; SAT writing scores over 700: 2%; ACT scores over 30: 17%.

Retention: 85% of full-time freshmen returned.

FACULTY

Total: 1,112, 52% full-time, 70% with terminal degrees.

Student/faculty ratio: 17:1.

ACADEMICS

Calendar: semesters. *Degrees:* certificates, associate, bachelor's, master's, doctoral, post-master's, and postbachelor's certificates.

Special study options: accelerated degree program, adult/continuing education programs, advanced placement credit, cooperative education, distance learning, double majors, honors programs, independent study, internships, off-campus study, part-time degree program, services for LD students, study abroad, summer session for credit. ***ROTC:*** Army (b), Air Force (b).

Computers: 2,145 computers/terminals and 4,100 ports are available on campus for general student use. Students can access the following: campus intranet, computer help desk, free student e-mail accounts, online (class) grades, online (class) registration, online (class) schedules. Campuswide network is available. 100% of college-owned or -operated housing units are wired for high-speed Internet access. Wireless service is available via entire campus.

Library: O'Leary Library and Learning Commons plus 2 others. *Books:* 224,000 (physical), 192,600 (digital/electronic); *Serial titles:* 5,383 (physical), 125,533 (digital/electronic); *Databases:* 135. Weekly public service hours: 118; students can reserve study rooms.

STUDENT LIFE

Housing options: coed. Campus housing is university owned and leased by the school.

Activities and organizations: drama/theater group, student-run newspaper, radio station, choral group, marching band, Student Government Association, Recreational Sports Clubs, Association of Students of African Origin, WUML (radio station), Campus Activities Programming Association, national fraternities, national sororities.

Athletics Member NCAA. All Division I. ***Intercollegiate sports:*** baseball M(s), basketball M(s)/W(s), cross-country running M(s)/W(s), field hockey W(s), ice hockey M(s), lacrosse M(s)/W(s), soccer M(s)/W(s), softball W(s), track and field M(s)/W(s), volleyball W(s). ***Intramural sports:*** badminton M/W, baseball M(c), basketball M/W, cheerleading M(c)/W(c), crew M(c)/W(c), cross-country running M/W, field hockey W(c), football M/W, golf M(c)/W(c), ice hockey M/W, lacrosse M(c)/W(c), racquetball M/W, rock climbing M/W, rowing M(c)/W(c), rugby M(c)/W(c), skiing (cross-country) M/W, skiing (downhill) M/W, soccer M/W, softball M/W, squash M/W, swimming and diving M(c)/W(c), table tennis M/W, tennis M(c)/W(c), track and field M(c)/W(c), ultimate Frisbee M/W, volleyball M/W, weight lifting M/W.

Campus security: 24-hour emergency response devices and patrols, controlled dormitory access, police and security patrols.

Student services: health clinic, personal/psychological counseling.

COSTS & FINANCIAL AID

Costs (2016–17) ***Tuition:*** state resident $13,932 full-time, $581 per credit hour part-time; nonresident $30,500 full-time, $1271 per credit hour part-time. Part-time tuition and fees vary according to course load. ***Required fees:*** $375 full-time, $16 per credit hour part-time. ***Room and board:*** $12,073; room only: $7975. Room and board charges vary according to board plan and housing facility. ***Payment plan:*** installment. ***Waivers:*** senior citizens and employees or children of employees.

Financial Aid Of all full-time matriculated undergraduates who enrolled in 2015, 7,326 applied for aid, 5,758 were judged to have need, 2,881 had their need fully met. In 2015, 837 non-need-based awards were made. ***Average percent of need met:*** 89. ***Average financial aid package:*** $15,497. ***Average need-based loan:*** $4379. ***Average need-based gift aid:*** $8630. ***Average non-need-based aid:*** $4617. ***Average indebtedness upon graduation:*** $30,915.

APPLYING

Standardized Tests *Required:* SAT or ACT (for admission). *Required for some:* short answer questions for No Test option.

Options: electronic application, early action, deferred entrance.

Application fee: $60.

Required: essay or personal statement, high school transcript, minimum 3.0 GPA, 1 letter of recommendation. ***Required for some:*** audition for

music students, art portfolio for art majors, three additional short answer questions for No Test option.

Application deadlines: 2/1 (freshmen), 8/15 (transfers), 11/1 (early action).

Notification: 3/10 (freshmen), continuous (transfers), 12/10 (early action).

CONTACT

Admissions Office, University of Massachusetts Lowell, University Crossing, Suite 420, 220 Pawtucket Street, Lowell, MA 01854-2874. *Phone:* 978-934-3931. *Fax:* 978-934-3086. *E-mail:* admissions@uml.edu.

See previous page for display ad and page 1564 for the College Close-Up.

Wellesley College

Wellesley, Massachusetts

http://www.wellesley.edu/

- **Independent** 4-year, founded 1870
- **Suburban** 500-acre campus with easy access to Boston
- **Endowment** $1.9 billion
- **Women only**
- **Most difficult** entrance level

FACULTY

Student/faculty ratio: 7:1.

ACADEMICS

Calendar: semesters. *Degrees:* bachelor's (double bachelor's degree with Massachusetts Institute of Technology).

Library: Margaret Clapp Library plus 5 others. *Books:* 717,924 (physical), 770,553 (digital/electronic); *Serial titles:* 319,932 (physical), 94,450 (digital/electronic). Students can reserve study rooms.

STUDENT LIFE

Housing options: women-only, cooperative. Campus housing is university owned. Freshman campus housing is guaranteed.

Activities and organizations: drama/theater group, student-run newspaper, radio and television station, choral group, Student Government, community service organizations, cultural clubs, societies, theater groups.

Athletics Member NCAA. All Division III.

Campus security: 24-hour emergency response devices and patrols, late-night transport/escort service, controlled dormitory access.

Student services: health clinic, personal/psychological counseling, women's center.

COSTS & FINANCIAL AID

Costs (2016–17) ***Comprehensive fee:*** $63,916 includes full-time tuition ($48,510), mandatory fees ($292), and room and board ($15,114). Part-time tuition: $6064 per course. Part-time tuition and fees vary according to course load. ***Required fees:*** $37 per course part-time. ***College room only:*** $7672. ***Payment plans:*** tuition prepayment, installment.

Financial Aid Of all full-time matriculated undergraduates who enrolled in 2015, 1,623 applied for aid, 1,379 were judged to have need, 1,379 had their need fully met. ***Average percent of need met:*** 100. ***Average financial aid package:*** $44,218. ***Average need-based loan:*** $3471. ***Average need-based gift aid:*** $46,012. ***Average indebtedness upon graduation:*** $12,455.

APPLYING

Standardized Tests *Required:* SAT and SAT Subject Tests or ACT (for admission).

Options: electronic application, early admission, early decision, deferred entrance.

Required: essay or personal statement, high school transcript, 3 letters of recommendation, first senior marking period grades and mid-year report. ***Required for some:*** interview. ***Recommended:*** interview.

CONTACT

Director of Admission, Wellesley College, 106 Central Street, Wellesley, MA 02481. *Phone:* 781-283-2270. *Fax:* 781-283-3678. *E-mail:* admission@wellesley.edu.

★ Wentworth Institute of Technology

Boston, Massachusetts

http://www.wit.edu/

- **Independent** comprehensive, founded 1904
- **Urban** 31-acre campus with easy access to Boston, MA
- **Endowment** $91.5 million
- **Coed** 3,974 undergraduate students, 98% full-time, 20% women, 80% men
- **Moderately difficult** entrance level, 71% of applicants were admitted

UNDERGRAD STUDENTS

3,889 full-time, 85 part-time. Students come from 24 states and territories; 24 other countries; 35% are from out of state; 4% Black or African American, non-Hispanic/Latino; 3% Hispanic/Latino; 8% Asian, non-Hispanic/Latino; 0.2% American Indian or Alaska Native, non-Hispanic/Latino; 6% Two or more races, non-Hispanic/Latino; 9% Race/ethnicity unknown; 9% international; 3% transferred in; 52% live on campus.

Freshmen:

Admission: 7,556 applied, 5,333 admitted, 961 enrolled. ***Average high school GPA:*** 3.06. ***Test scores:*** SAT critical reading scores over 500: 68%; SAT math scores over 500: 88%; ACT scores over 18: 96%; SAT critical reading scores over 600: 22%; SAT math scores over 600: 41%; ACT scores over 24: 61%; SAT critical reading scores over 700: 2%; SAT math scores over 700: 6%; ACT scores over 30: 15%.

Retention: 84% of full-time freshmen returned.

FACULTY

Total: 379, 41% full-time, 24% with terminal degrees.

Student/faculty ratio: 17:1.

ACADEMICS

Calendar: semesters for freshmen and sophomores, trimesters for juniors and seniors. *Degrees:* certificates, associate, bachelor's, and master's.

Special study options: academic remediation for entering students, advanced placement credit, cooperative education, internships, off-campus study, part-time degree program, services for LD students, study abroad, summer session for credit. ***ROTC:*** Army (c), Air Force (c).

Computers: 320 computers/terminals and 200 ports are available on campus for general student use. Students can access the following: campus intranet, computer help desk, free student e-mail accounts, online (class) grades, online (class) registration, online (class) schedules. Campuswide network is available. 100% of college-owned or -operated housing units are wired for high-speed Internet access. Wireless service is available via entire campus.

Library: Wentworth Alumni Library plus 1 other. *Books:* 51,085 (physical), 229,005 (digital/electronic); *Serial titles:* 211 (physical), 27,903 (digital/electronic); *Databases:* 77.
Weekly public service hours: 95.

STUDENT LIFE

Housing options: on-campus residence required through sophomore year; coed. Campus housing is university owned. Freshman campus housing is guaranteed.

Activities and organizations: student-run radio station, Intramural Sports, Wentworth Events Board, Multicultural Student Association, Phi Sigma Pi, Major Particular Professional Student Associations.

Athletics Member NCAA. All Division III. ***Intercollegiate sports:*** baseball M, basketball M/W, crew M, cross-country running M, golf M, ice hockey M, lacrosse M/W, rugby M(c)/W(c), soccer M/W, softball W, tennis M/W, ultimate Frisbee M(c)/W(c), volleyball M/W.

Campus security: 24-hour emergency response devices and patrols, student patrols, late-night transport/escort service, controlled dormitory access.

Student services: health clinic, personal/psychological counseling, women's center.

COSTS & FINANCIAL AID

Costs (2017–18) ***Comprehensive fee:*** $44,410 includes full-time tuition ($31,840) and room and board ($12,570). Part-time tuition: $995 per credit hour. Part-time tuition and fees vary according to course load.

Room and board: Room and board charges vary according to board plan and housing facility. ***Payment plan:*** installment. ***Waivers:*** employees or children of employees.

Financial Aid Of all full-time matriculated undergraduates who enrolled in 2016, 2,998 applied for aid, 2,703 were judged to have need, 184 had their need fully met. 692 Federal Work-Study jobs (averaging $820). In 2016, 936 non-need-based awards were made. ***Average financial aid package:*** $9764. ***Average need-based loan:*** $2309. ***Average need-based gift aid:*** $3019. ***Average non-need-based aid:*** $9846. ***Average indebtedness upon graduation:*** $23.0 million.

APPLYING

Standardized Tests *Required:* SAT or ACT (for admission).

Options: electronic application, deferred entrance.

Application fee: $50.

Required: essay or personal statement, high school transcript, 1 letter of recommendation. ***Recommended:*** minimum 2.0 GPA, interview.

Application deadlines: 2/15 (freshmen), rolling (out-of-state freshmen), 5/1 (transfers).

Notification: continuous (freshmen), continuous (transfers).

CONTACT

Ms. Amy Dufour, Senior Associate Director of Admissions, Wentworth Institute of Technology, 550 Huntington Avenue, Boston, MA 02115. *Phone:* 617-989-4116. *Toll-free phone:* 800-556-0610. *Fax:* 617-989-4010. *E-mail:* dufoura@wit.edu.

See below for display ad and page 1592 for the College Close-Up.

Western New England University

Springfield, Massachusetts

http://www.wne.edu/

- **Independent** comprehensive, founded 1919
- **Suburban** 215-acre campus
- **Endowment** $66.3 million
- **Coed** 2,724 undergraduate students, 95% full-time, 38% women, 62% men
- **Moderately difficult** entrance level, 80% of applicants were admitted

UNDERGRAD STUDENTS

2,580 full-time, 144 part-time. Students come from 31 states and territories; 18 other countries; 48% are from out of state; 6% Black or African American, non-Hispanic/Latino; 8% Hispanic/Latino; 3% Asian, non-Hispanic/Latino; 0.1% Native Hawaiian or other Pacific Islander, non-Hispanic/Latino; 0.2% American Indian or Alaska Native, non-Hispanic/Latino; 2% Two or more races, non-Hispanic/Latino; 4% Race/ethnicity unknown; 3% international; 4% transferred in; 62% live on campus.

Freshmen:

Admission: 6,399 applied, 5,094 admitted, 723 enrolled. ***Average high school GPA:*** 3.38. ***Test scores:*** SAT critical reading scores over 500: 70%; SAT math scores over 500: 81%; ACT scores over 18: 98%; SAT critical reading scores over 600: 20%; SAT math scores over 600: 32%; ACT scores over 24: 61%; SAT critical reading scores over 700: 2%; SAT math scores over 700: 3%; ACT scores over 30: 10%.

Retention: 76% of full-time freshmen returned.

FACULTY

Total: 377, 63% full-time.

Student/faculty ratio: 12:1.

ACADEMICS

Calendar: semesters. *Degrees:* certificates, associate, bachelor's, master's, doctoral, and postbachelor's certificates.

Special study options: accelerated degree program, adult/continuing education programs, advanced placement credit, distance learning, double majors, English as a second language, honors programs, independent study, internships, off-campus study, part-time degree program, services for LD students, student-designed majors, study abroad, summer session for credit. ***ROTC:*** Army (b), Air Force (c).

Unusual degree programs: 3-2 business administration; engineering.

Computers: 530 computers/terminals are available on campus for general student use. Students can access the following: campus intranet, computer help desk, free student e-mail accounts, online (class) grades, online (class) registration, online (class) schedules. Campuswide network is available. 100% of college-owned or -operated housing units are wired for high-speed Internet access. Wireless service is available via entire campus.

Library: D'Amour Library plus 1 other. *Books:* 107,000 (physical), 26,728 (digital/electronic); *Serial titles:* 46 (physical), 98,700 (digital/electronic); *Databases:* 122. Weekly public service hours: 97; study areas open 24 hours, 5-7 days a week.

STUDENT LIFE

Housing options: coed, special housing for students with disabilities. Campus housing is university owned. Freshman campus housing is guaranteed.

Activities and organizations: drama/theater group, student-run newspaper, radio and television station, choral group, Student Senate, Residence Hall Association, Campus Activities Board, student radio station, The Westerner (student newspaper).

Athletics Member NCAA. All Division III. ***Intercollegiate sports:*** baseball M, basketball M/W, cross-country running M/W, field hockey W, football M, golf M, ice hockey M, lacrosse M/W, soccer M/W, softball W, swimming and diving W, tennis M/W, volleyball W, wrestling M. ***Intramural sports:*** basketball M/W, bowling M(c)/W(c), football M/W, rock climbing M/W, rugby M(c), soccer M/W, softball M/W, table tennis M/W, ultimate Frisbee M/W, volleyball M/W, water polo M/W.

Campus security: 24-hour emergency response devices and patrols, student patrols, late-night transport/escort service, controlled dormitory access, security cameras.

Student services: health clinic, personal/psychological counseling.

COSTS & FINANCIAL AID

Costs (2016–17) ***Comprehensive fee:*** $48,088 includes full-time tuition ($32,524), mandatory fees ($2350), and room and board ($13,214). Full-time tuition and fees vary according to course load and program. Part-time tuition: $613 per credit hour. Part-time tuition and fees vary according to course load and program. ***Room and board:*** Room and board charges vary according to board plan and housing facility. ***Payment plans:*** tuition prepayment, installment. ***Waivers:*** senior citizens and employees or children of employees.

Financial Aid Of all full-time matriculated undergraduates who enrolled in 2016, 2,201 applied for aid, 2,013 were judged to have need, 274 had their need fully met. 1,075 Federal Work-Study jobs (averaging $1983). In 2016, 401 non-need-based awards were made. ***Average percent of need met:*** 74. ***Average financial aid package:*** $25,735. ***Average need-based loan:*** $4663. ***Average need-based gift aid:*** $20,616. ***Average non-need-based aid:*** $13,110. ***Average indebtedness upon graduation:*** $44,013.

APPLYING

Standardized Tests *Required for some:* SAT or ACT (for admission).

Options: electronic application, early admission, deferred entrance.

Application fee: $40.

Required: high school transcript, 1 letter of recommendation. ***Recommended:*** essay or personal statement, interview.

Application deadlines: rolling (freshmen), rolling (transfers).

Notification: continuous (freshmen), continuous (transfers).

CONTACT

Mr. Bryan Gross, Vice President for Enrollment Management, Western New England University, 1215 Wilbraham Road, Springfield, MA 01119. *Phone:* 413-782-1321. *Toll-free phone:* 800-325-1122 Ext. 1321. *Fax:* 413-782-1777. *E-mail:* learn@wne.edu.

Westfield State University
Westfield, Massachusetts
http://www.westfield.ma.edu/

- **State-supported** comprehensive, founded 1838, part of Massachusetts Public Higher Education System
- **Suburban** 256-acre campus
- **Endowment** $5.0 million
- **Coed** 5,610 undergraduate students, 89% full-time, 54% women, 46% men
- **Moderately difficult** entrance level, 78% of applicants were admitted

UNDERGRAD STUDENTS

4,982 full-time, 628 part-time. Students come from 22 states and territories; 15 other countries; 7% are from out of state; 5% Black or African American, non-Hispanic/Latino; 9% Hispanic/Latino; 2% Asian, non-Hispanic/Latino; 0.1% Native Hawaiian or other Pacific Islander, non-Hispanic/Latino; 0.1% American Indian or Alaska Native, non-Hispanic/Latino; 5% Two or more races, non-Hispanic/Latino; 3% Race/ethnicity unknown; 0.4% international; 8% transferred in; 54% live on campus.

Freshmen:

Admission: 4,740 applied, 3,695 admitted, 1,068 enrolled. ***Average high school GPA:*** 3.11. ***Test scores:*** SAT critical reading scores over 500: 47%; SAT math scores over 500: 52%; SAT writing scores over 500: 43%; ACT scores over 18: 88%; SAT critical reading scores over 600: 9%; SAT math scores over 600: 10%; SAT writing scores over 600: 5%; ACT scores over 24: 28%; SAT critical reading scores over 700: 1%; SAT math scores over 700: 1%; ACT scores over 30: 2%.

Retention: 77% of full-time freshmen returned.

FACULTY

Total: 476, 49% full-time, 59% with terminal degrees.

Student/faculty ratio: 17:1.

ACADEMICS

Calendar: semesters. *Degrees:* bachelor's, master's, post-master's, and postbachelor's certificates.

Special study options: adult/continuing education programs, advanced placement credit, distance learning, double majors, honors programs, independent study, internships, off-campus study, part-time degree program, services for LD students, student-designed majors, study abroad, summer session for credit. ***ROTC:*** Army (c), Air Force (c).

Computers: 727 computers/terminals are available on campus for general student use. Students can access the following: computer help desk, free student e-mail accounts, online (class) grades, online (class) registration, online (class) schedules, online transcripts and billing information, Web portal. Campuswide network is available. 100% of college-owned or -operated housing units are wired for high-speed Internet access. Wireless service is available via entire campus.

Library: Governor Joseph B. Ely Library. *Books:* 139,363 (physical), 156,760 (digital/electronic); *Serial titles:* 612 (physical), 26,637 (digital/electronic); *Databases:* 90. Weekly public service hours: 92; students can reserve study rooms.

STUDENT LIFE

Housing options: coed, special housing for students with disabilities. Campus housing is university owned. Freshman applicants given priority for college housing.

Activities and organizations: drama/theater group, student-run newspaper, radio and television station, choral group, Student National Education Association, Student Government Association, Campus Activities Board, The Dance Company, Multicultural Student Association.

Athletics Member NCAA. All Division III. ***Intercollegiate sports:*** baseball M, basketball M/W, cross-country running M/W, field hockey W, football M, golf M/W, ice hockey M, lacrosse W, soccer M/W, softball W, swimming and diving W, track and field M/W, volleyball W. ***Intramural sports:*** basketball M, equestrian sports M(c)/W(c), football M, ice hockey M(c)/W(c), lacrosse M(c), rugby M(c)/W(c), skiing (downhill) M(c)/W(c), soccer M/W, softball M, ultimate Frisbee M(c)/W(c), volleyball M(c)/W.

Campus security: 24-hour emergency response devices and patrols, student patrols, late-night transport/escort service, controlled dormitory access.

Student services: health clinic, personal/psychological counseling, legal services.

COSTS & FINANCIAL AID
Costs (2016–17) ***Tuition:*** state resident $970 full-time, $297 per credit hour part-time; nonresident $7050 full-time, $297 per credit hour part-time. Full-time tuition and fees vary according to program and reciprocity agreements. Part-time tuition and fees vary according to course load. ***Required fees:*** $8305 full-time, $75 per term part-time. ***Room and board:*** $10,396. Room and board charges vary according to board plan and housing facility. ***Payment plan:*** installment. ***Waivers:*** senior citizens and employees or children of employees.

Financial Aid Of all full-time matriculated undergraduates who enrolled in 2015, 4,076 applied for aid, 3,181 were judged to have need, 334 had their need fully met. 333 state and other part-time jobs (averaging $1461). In 2015, 81 non-need-based awards were made. ***Average percent of need met:*** 62. ***Average financial aid package:*** $8386. ***Average need-based loan:*** $4026. ***Average need-based gift aid:*** $5693. ***Average non-need-based aid:*** $3904. ***Average indebtedness upon graduation:*** $29,602.

APPLYING
Standardized Tests *Required:* SAT or ACT (for admission).

Options: electronic application, deferred entrance.

Application fee: $50.

Required: high school transcript, minimum 2.0 GPA. ***Required for some:*** interview, audition for music majors, portfolio for art majors, essay and interview for nursing majors, sliding scale minimum high school GPA using SAT/ACT scores for GPAs between 2.0 and 3.0.

Application deadlines: 3/1 (freshmen), 3/1 (transfers).

Notification: continuous until 3/15 (freshmen), continuous until 3/15 (transfers).

CONTACT
Dr. Kelly Hart, Director of Admissions, Westfield State University, 333 Western Avenue, Westfield, MA 01002. *Phone:* 413-572-5218. *Fax:* 413-572-0520. *E-mail:* admission@westfield.ma.edu.

Wheaton College

Norton, Massachusetts

http://www.wheatoncollege.edu/

- **Independent** 4-year, founded 1834
- **Suburban** 478-acre campus with easy access to Boston, MA
- **Endowment** $184.8 million
- **Coed** 1,651 undergraduate students, 99% full-time, 62% women, 38% men
- **Very difficult** entrance level, 62% of applicants were admitted

UNDERGRAD STUDENTS
1,638 full-time, 13 part-time. Students come from 34 states and territories; 76 other countries; 60% are from out of state; 6% Black or African American, non-Hispanic/Latino; 7% Hispanic/Latino; 5% Asian, non-Hispanic/Latino; 0.1% Native Hawaiian or other Pacific Islander, non-Hispanic/Latino; 0.1% American Indian or Alaska Native, non-Hispanic/Latino; 3% Two or more races, non-Hispanic/Latino; 2% Race/ethnicity unknown; 12% international; 0.8% transferred in; 97% live on campus.

Freshmen:
Admission: 4,478 applied, 2,779 admitted, 528 enrolled. ***Average high school GPA:*** 3.5. ***Test scores:*** SAT critical reading scores over 500: 86%; SAT math scores over 500: 89%; SAT writing scores over 500: 84%; ACT scores over 18: 99%; SAT critical reading scores over 600: 38%; SAT math scores over 600: 42%; SAT writing scores over 600: 40%; ACT scores over 24: 83%; SAT critical reading scores over 700: 9%; SAT math scores over 700: 7%; SAT writing scores over 700: 6%; ACT scores over 30: 26%.

Retention: 86% of full-time freshmen returned.

FACULTY
Total: 191, 72% full-time, 74% with terminal degrees.

Student/faculty ratio: 10:1.

ACADEMICS
Calendar: semesters. *Degree:* bachelor's.

Special study options: accelerated degree program, advanced placement credit, cooperative education, double majors, English as a second language, honors programs, independent study, internships, off-campus study, services for LD students, student-designed majors, study abroad, summer session for credit. ***ROTC:*** Army (c).

Unusual degree programs: engineering with Dartmouth College; theology with Andover Newton Theological School, optometry with New England School of Optometry, integrated marketing communication studies with Emerson College, Clark University.

Computers: 196 computers/terminals are available on campus for general student use. Students can access the following: campus intranet, computer help desk, free student e-mail accounts, online (class) grades, online (class) registration, online (class) schedules, assistive technology, online software training, media equipment loan program. Campuswide network is available. 100% of college-owned or -operated housing units are wired for high-speed Internet access. Wireless service is available via entire campus.

Library: Madeleine Clark Wallace Library. *Books:* 343,772 (physical), 158,465 (digital/electronic); *Serial titles:* 2,897 (physical), 80,798 (digital/electronic); *Databases:* 92. Weekly public service hours: 114; students can reserve study rooms.

STUDENT LIFE
Housing options: coed, men-only, women-only, special housing for students with disabilities. Campus housing is university owned. Freshman campus housing is guaranteed.

Activities and organizations: drama/theater group, student-run newspaper, radio station, choral group, Student Government Association, Performance Groups (a capella, dance and improv), Black Student Association (BSA), Programming Council (PC), Feminist Association of Wheaton (FAW).

Athletics Member NCAA. All Division III. ***Intercollegiate sports:*** baseball M, basketball M/W, cross-country running M/W, field hockey W, lacrosse M/W, soccer M/W, softball W, swimming and diving M/W, tennis M/W, track and field M/W, volleyball W. ***Intramural sports:*** archery M(c)/W(c), cheerleading M(c)/W(c), equestrian sports M(c)/W(c), fencing M(c)/W(c), ice hockey M(c)/W(c), rugby M(c)/W(c), soccer M(c)/W(c), tennis M(c)/W(c), ultimate Frisbee M(c)/W(c).

Campus security: 24-hour emergency response devices and patrols, student patrols, late-night transport/escort service, controlled dormitory access.

Student services: health clinic, personal/psychological counseling, women's center.

COSTS & FINANCIAL AID
Costs (2017–18) ***One-time required fee:*** $50. ***Comprehensive fee:*** $63,818 includes full-time tuition ($50,520), mandatory fees ($330), and room and board ($12,968). Part-time tuition: $6315 per course. ***College room only:*** $6918. ***Payment plan:*** installment. ***Waivers:*** employees or children of employees.

Financial Aid Of all full-time matriculated undergraduates who enrolled in 2016, 1,211 applied for aid, 1,045 were judged to have need, 502 had their need fully met. 656 Federal Work-Study jobs (averaging $1648). 332 state and other part-time jobs (averaging $1606). In 2016, 457 non-need-based awards were made. ***Average percent of need met:*** 92. ***Average financial aid package:*** $37,725. ***Average need-based loan:*** $4142. ***Average need-based gift aid:*** $30,737. ***Average non-need-based aid:*** $15,097. ***Average indebtedness upon graduation:*** $33,040. ***Financial aid deadline:*** 2/1.

APPLYING
Options: electronic application, early admission, early decision, early action, deferred entrance.

Application fee: $60.

Required: essay or personal statement, high school transcript, 2 letters of recommendation. ***Recommended:*** interview.

Application deadlines: 1/1 (freshmen), 5/1 (transfers), 11/1 (early action).

Early decision deadline: 11/1 (for plan 1), 1/1 (for plan 2).

Notification: 4/1 (freshmen), 5/15 (transfers), 12/15 (early decision plan 1), 2/15 (early decision plan 2), 1/15 (early action).

CONTACT
Grant M. Gosselin, Vice President for Enrollment & Dean of Admission and Student Aid, Wheaton College, 26 East Main Street, Norton, MA 02766. *Phone:* 508-286-8251. *Toll-free phone:* 800-394-6003. *Fax:* 508-286-8271. *E-mail:* admission@wheatoncollege.edu.

Wheelock College

Boston, Massachusetts

http://www.wheelock.edu/

- **Independent** comprehensive, founded 1888
- **Urban** 6-acre campus with easy access to Boston
- **Coed, primarily women** 726 undergraduate students, 98% full-time, 82% women, 18% men
- **Minimally difficult** entrance level, 84% of applicants were admitted

UNDERGRAD STUDENTS
713 full-time, 13 part-time. Students come from 28 states and territories; 10 other countries; 37% are from out of state; 15% Black or African American, non-Hispanic/Latino; 12% Hispanic/Latino; 4% Asian, non-Hispanic/Latino; 0.1% Native Hawaiian or other Pacific Islander, non-Hispanic/Latino; 0.1% American Indian or Alaska Native, non-Hispanic/Latino; 4% Two or more races, non-Hispanic/Latino; 5% Race/ethnicity unknown; 2% international; 3% transferred in; 60% live on campus.

Freshmen:
Admission: 1,305 applied, 1,095 admitted, 158 enrolled.
Retention: 68% of full-time freshmen returned.

FACULTY
Total: 155, 45% full-time, 53% with terminal degrees.
Student/faculty ratio: 9:1.

ACADEMICS
Calendar: semesters. *Degrees:* bachelor's, master's, and postbachelor's certificates.
Special study options: advanced placement credit, distance learning, double majors, honors programs, independent study, internships, off-campus study, part-time degree program, services for LD students, study abroad, summer session for credit.
Computers: 100 computers/terminals and 1,100 ports are available on campus for general student use. Students can access the following: campus intranet, computer help desk, free student e-mail accounts, online (class) grades, online (class) registration, online (class) schedules. Campuswide network is available. Wireless service is available via classrooms, computer labs, dorm rooms, learning centers, libraries, student centers.
Library: Wheelock College Library plus 1 other. *Books:* 83,435 (physical), 205,717 (digital/electronic); *Databases:* 58. Students can reserve study rooms.

STUDENT LIFE
Housing options: coed, women-only, special housing for students with disabilities. Campus housing is university owned. Freshman campus housing is guaranteed.
Activities and organizations: drama/theater group, student-run newspaper, choral group.
Athletics Member NCAA. All Division III. ***Intercollegiate sports:*** basketball M/W, cross-country running M/W, field hockey W, lacrosse M/W, soccer M/W, softball W, tennis M. ***Intramural sports:*** basketball M/W, racquetball M/W, soccer M, softball M/W, squash M/W, table tennis M/W, ultimate Frisbee M/W, volleyball M/W, water polo M/W.
Campus security: 24-hour patrols, late-night transport/escort service, controlled dormitory access.
Student services: personal/psychological counseling.

COSTS & FINANCIAL AID
Costs (2017–18) ***Comprehensive fee:*** $51,175 includes full-time tuition ($34,950), mandatory fees ($1250), and room and board ($14,975). Part-time tuition: $1090 per credit hour. ***Payment plan:*** installment. ***Waivers:*** employees or children of employees.
Financial Aid Of all full-time matriculated undergraduates who enrolled in 2015, 702 applied for aid, 656 were judged to have need, 82 had their need fully met. In 2015, 121 non-need-based awards were made. ***Average percent of need met:*** 64. ***Average financial aid package:*** $24,314. ***Average need-based loan:*** $4435. ***Average need-based gift aid:*** $20,021. ***Average non-need-based aid:*** $13,681. ***Average indebtedness upon graduation:*** $46,690.

APPLYING
Options: electronic application, early admission, early action, deferred entrance.
Required: essay or personal statement, high school transcript, minimum 2.0 GPA, 1 letter of recommendation. ***Recommended:*** interview.
Application deadlines: 5/1 (freshmen), 6/1 (transfers), 12/1 (early action).
Notification: continuous (freshmen), continuous (transfers), 12/20 (early action).

CONTACT
Cory Meyers, Assistant Vice President for Admissions, Wheelock College, 200 Riverway, Boston, MA 02215. *Phone:* 617-879-2037. *Toll-free phone:* 800-734-5212. *Fax:* 617-879-2449. *E-mail:* admissions@wheelock.edu.

Williams College

Williamstown, Massachusetts

http://www.williams.edu/

- **Independent** comprehensive, founded 1793
- **Small-town** 450-acre campus with easy access to Albany NY
- **Endowment** $2.3 billion
- **Coed** 2,076 undergraduate students, 98% full-time, 49% women, 51% men
- **Most difficult** entrance level, 18% of applicants were admitted

UNDERGRAD STUDENTS
2,043 full-time, 33 part-time. Students come from 50 states and territories; 57 other countries; 88% are from out of state; 7% Black or African American, non-Hispanic/Latino; 12% Hispanic/Latino; 13% Asian, non-Hispanic/Latino; 0.1% American Indian or Alaska Native, non-Hispanic/Latino; 6% Two or more races, non-Hispanic/Latino; 8% international; 0.3% transferred in; 93% live on campus.

Freshmen:
Admission: 6,985 applied, 1,230 admitted, 553 enrolled. ***Test scores:*** SAT critical reading scores over 500: 99%; SAT math scores over 500: 100%; SAT writing scores over 500: 99%; ACT scores over 18: 99%; SAT critical reading scores over 600: 94%; SAT math scores over 600: 93%; SAT writing scores over 600: 93%; ACT scores over 24: 99%; SAT critical reading scores over 700: 64%; SAT math scores over 700: 61%; SAT writing scores over 700: 65%; ACT scores over 30: 88%.
Retention: 97% of full-time freshmen returned.

FACULTY
Total: 349, 80% full-time, 93% with terminal degrees.
Student/faculty ratio: 7:1.

ACADEMICS
Calendar: 4-1-4. *Degrees:* bachelor's and master's.
Special study options: double majors, independent study, internships, off-campus study, services for LD students, student-designed majors, study abroad. ***ROTC:*** Air Force (c).
Unusual degree programs: 3-2 engineering with Columbia University.
Computers: 500 computers/terminals are available on campus for general student use. Students can access the following: computer help desk, free student e-mail accounts, online (class) grades, online (class) registration. Campuswide network is available. 100% of college-owned or -operated housing units are wired for high-speed Internet access. Wireless service is available via entire campus.
Library: Sawyer Library plus 2 others. Weekly public service hours: 118; study areas open 24 hours, 5-7 days a week; students can reserve study rooms.

STUDENT LIFE
Housing options: on-campus residence required for freshman year; coed, cooperative, special housing for students with disabilities. Campus housing is university owned.

Activities and organizations: drama/theater group, student-run newspaper, radio station, choral group, marching band.

Athletics Member NCAA. All Division III except men's and women's skiing (cross-country) (Division I), men's and women's skiing (downhill) (Division I). ***Intercollegiate sports:*** baseball M, basketball M/W, crew M/W, cross-country running M/W, equestrian sports M(c)/W(c), field hockey W, football M, golf M/W(c), ice hockey M/W, lacrosse M/W, rugby M(c)/W(c), sailing M(c)/W(c), skiing (cross-country) M/W, skiing (downhill) M/W, soccer M/W, softball W, squash M/W, swimming and diving M/W, tennis M/W, track and field M/W, ultimate Frisbee M(c)/W(c), volleyball M(c)/W, water polo M(c)/W(c), wrestling M. ***Intramural sports:*** badminton M/W, baseball M(c), basketball M/W, fencing M(c)/W(c), gymnastics M(c)/W(c), ice hockey M/W, skiing (cross-country) M/W, skiing (downhill) M/W, soccer M/W, softball M/W, ultimate Frisbee M(c)/W(c), volleyball M/W, water polo M/W.

Campus security: 24-hour emergency response devices and patrols, student patrols, late-night transport/escort service, controlled dormitory access.

Student services: health clinic, personal/psychological counseling.

COSTS & FINANCIAL AID

Costs (2016–17) ***Comprehensive fee:*** $65,480 includes full-time tuition ($51,490), mandatory fees ($300), and room and board ($13,690). ***College room only:*** $6930. Room and board charges vary according to board plan. ***Payment plan:*** installment.

Financial Aid Of all full-time matriculated undergraduates who enrolled in 2016, 1,164 applied for aid, 1,014 were judged to have need, 1,014 had their need fully met. ***Average percent of need met:*** 100. ***Average financial aid package:*** $51,890. ***Average need-based loan:*** $2852. ***Average need-based gift aid:*** $48,885. ***Average indebtedness upon graduation:*** $15,496. ***Financial aid deadline:*** 1/15.

APPLYING

Standardized Tests *Required:* SAT or ACT (for admission).

Options: electronic application, early admission, early decision, deferred entrance.

Application fee: $65.

Required: essay or personal statement, high school transcript, 2 letters of recommendation.

Application deadlines: 1/1 (freshmen), 4/1 (transfers).

Early decision deadline: 11/15.

Notification: 4/7 (freshmen), 5/15 (transfers), 12/15 (early decision).

CONTACT

Mr. Richard L. Nesbitt, Director of Admission, Williams College, 995 Main Street, Williamstown, MA 01267. *Phone:* 413-597-2211. *Fax:* 413-597-4052. *E-mail:* admission@williams.edu.

Worcester Polytechnic Institute

Worcester, Massachusetts

http://www.wpi.edu/

- **Independent** university, founded 1865
- **Suburban** 80-acre campus with easy access to Boston
- **Endowment** $466.3 million
- **Coed** 4,432 undergraduate students, 96% full-time, 34% women, 66% men
- **Very difficult** entrance level, 48% of applicants were admitted

UNDERGRAD STUDENTS

4,275 full-time, 157 part-time. Students come from 49 states and territories; 69 other countries; 57% are from out of state; 3% Black or African American, non-Hispanic/Latino; 9% Hispanic/Latino; 4% Asian, non-Hispanic/Latino; 0.4% American Indian or Alaska Native, non-Hispanic/Latino; 3% Two or more races, non-Hispanic/Latino; 7% Race/ethnicity unknown; 11% international; 0.6% transferred in; 57% live on campus.

Freshmen:

Admission: 10,468 applied, 5,071 admitted, 1,120 enrolled. ***Average high school GPA:*** 3.84. ***Test scores:*** SAT critical reading scores over 500: 95%; SAT math scores over 500: 100%; SAT writing scores over 500: 94%; ACT scores over 18: 100%; SAT critical reading scores over 600: 65%; SAT math scores over 600: 91%; SAT writing scores over 600: 61%; ACT scores over 24: 97%; SAT critical reading scores over 700: 17%; SAT math scores over 700: 39%; SAT writing scores over 700: 12%; ACT scores over 30: 56%.

Retention: 95% of full-time freshmen returned.

FACULTY

Total: 534, 69% full-time, 79% with terminal degrees.

Student/faculty ratio: 13:1.

ACADEMICS

Calendar: 4 7-week terms. *Degrees:* bachelor's, master's, doctoral, and post-master's certificates.

Special study options: accelerated degree program, advanced placement credit, cooperative education, distance learning, double majors, English as a second language, independent study, internships, off-campus study, part-time degree program, services for LD students, student-designed majors, study abroad, summer session for credit. ***ROTC:*** Army (b), Navy (c), Air Force (b).

Computers: 860 computers/terminals and 800 ports are available on campus for general student use. Students can access the following: campus intranet, computer help desk, free student e-mail accounts, online (class) grades, online (class) registration, online (class) schedules, online course content. Campuswide network is available. 100% of college-owned or -operated housing units are wired for high-speed Internet access. Wireless service is available via entire campus.

Library: George C. Gordon Library. *Books:* 249,084 (physical), 1.1 million (digital/electronic); *Serial titles:* 5,533 (physical), 76,238 (digital/electronic); *Databases:* 380. Weekly public service hours: 107; students can reserve study rooms.

STUDENT LIFE

Housing options: coed, special housing for students with disabilities. Campus housing is university owned. Freshman campus housing is guaranteed.

Activities and organizations: drama/theater group, student-run newspaper, radio station, choral group, Student Government Association, Social Committee (Student Events Programming Board), Music Association (all music-performing groups), Intramural and club sports, International Student Council, national fraternities, national sororities.

Athletics Member NCAA. All Division III. ***Intercollegiate sports:*** baseball M, basketball M/W, crew M/W, cross-country running M/W, field hockey W, football M, soccer M/W, softball W, swimming and diving M/W, track and field M/W, volleyball W, wrestling M. ***Intramural sports:*** badminton M(c)/W(c), basketball M/W, cheerleading M(c)/W(c), fencing M(c)/W(c), golf M(c)/W(c), ice hockey M(c)/W(c), lacrosse M(c)/W(c), racquetball M(c)/W(c), rugby M(c)/W(c), sailing M(c)/W(c), skiing (cross-country) M(c)/W(c), skiing (downhill) M(c)/W(c), soccer M/W, squash M(c)/W(c), table tennis M(c)/W(c), tennis M(c)/W(c), ultimate Frisbee M(c)/W(c), volleyball M/W, water polo M(c)/W(c), wrestling M(c)/W(c).

Campus security: 24-hour emergency response devices and patrols, student patrols, late-night transport/escort service, controlled dormitory access.

Student services: health clinic, personal/psychological counseling.

COSTS & FINANCIAL AID

Costs (2016–17) ***One-time required fee:*** $200. ***Comprehensive fee:*** $60,730 includes full-time tuition ($46,364), mandatory fees ($630), and room and board ($13,736). Part-time tuition: $1288 per credit hour. Part-time tuition and fees vary according to course load. ***College room only:*** $7846. Room and board charges vary according to board plan and housing facility. ***Payment plans:*** tuition prepayment, installment, deferred payment. ***Waivers:*** employees or children of employees.

Financial Aid Of all full-time matriculated undergraduates who enrolled in 2015, 3,015 applied for aid, 2,607 were judged to have need, 1,153 had their need fully met. 574 Federal Work-Study jobs (averaging $973). In 2015, 1400 non-need-based awards were made. ***Average percent of need met:*** 83. ***Average financial aid package:*** $35,932. ***Average need-based loan:*** $2584. ***Average need-based gift aid:*** $22,934. ***Average non-need-based aid:*** $16,002. ***Financial aid deadline:*** 2/1.

APPLYING

Standardized Tests *Required for some:* IELTS or TOEFL.

Options: electronic application, early admission, early action, deferred entrance.

Application fee: $65.

Required: essay or personal statement, high school transcript, 2 letters of recommendation. ***Required for some:*** interview.

Application deadlines: 2/1 (freshmen), 4/15 (transfers), 11/1 (early action).

Notification: 4/1 (freshmen), continuous (transfers), 12/20 (early action).

CONTACT

Mrs. Jennifer A. Cluett, Director of Undergraduate Admissions, Worcester Polytechnic Institute, 100 Institute Road, Worcester, MA 01609-2280. *Phone:* 508-831-5286. *Fax:* 508-831-5875. *E-mail:* admissions@wpi.edu.

See below for display ad and page 1607 for the College Close-Up.

Worcester State University

Worcester, Massachusetts

http://www.worcester.edu/

- **State-supported** comprehensive, founded 1874, part of Massachusetts Public Higher Education System
- **Urban** 58-acre campus with easy access to Boston
- **Endowment** $12.9 million
- **Coed** 5,381 undergraduate students, 75% full-time, 60% women, 40% men
- **Moderately difficult** entrance level, 71% of applicants were admitted

UNDERGRAD STUDENTS

4,033 full-time, 1,348 part-time. Students come from 25 states and territories; 27 other countries; 5% are from out of state; 8% Black or African American, non-Hispanic/Latino; 10% Hispanic/Latino; 4% Asian, non-Hispanic/Latino; 0.4% American Indian or Alaska Native, non-Hispanic/Latino; 3% Two or more races, non-Hispanic/Latino; 7% Race/ethnicity unknown; 1% international; 10% transferred in; 30% live on campus.

Freshmen:

Admission: 3,876 applied, 2,735 admitted, 789 enrolled. ***Average high school GPA:*** 3.24. ***Test scores:*** SAT critical reading scores over 500: 50%; SAT math scores over 500: 44%; ACT scores over 18: 95%; SAT critical reading scores over 600: 8%; SAT math scores over 600: 4%; ACT scores over 24: 47%; ACT scores over 30: 3%.

Retention: 80% of full-time freshmen returned.

FACULTY

Total: 388, 53% full-time, 51% with terminal degrees.

Student/faculty ratio: 18:1.

ACADEMICS

Calendar: semesters. *Degrees:* bachelor's, master's, post-master's, and postbachelor's certificates.

Special study options: academic remediation for entering students, accelerated degree program, adult/continuing education programs, advanced placement credit, distance learning, double majors, English as a second language, honors programs, independent study, internships, off-campus study, part-time degree program, services for LD students, study abroad, summer session for credit. ***ROTC:*** Army (c), Navy (c), Air Force (c).

Computers: 500 computers/terminals and 1,700 ports are available on campus for general student use. Students can access the following: campus intranet, computer help desk, free student e-mail accounts, online (class) grades, online (class) registration, online (class) schedules. Campuswide network is available. 100% of college-owned or -operated housing units are wired for high-speed Internet access. Wireless service is available via entire campus.

Library: Worcester State University Library. *Books:* 144,910 (physical), 140,521 (digital/electronic); *Serial titles:* 129 (physical), 56,397 (digital/electronic); *Databases:* 133. Weekly public service hours: 100.

STUDENT LIFE

Housing options: coed, men-only, women-only, special housing for students with disabilities. Campus housing is university owned.

Activities and organizations: drama/theater group, student-run newspaper, radio and television station, choral group, Senate, SEC (Student Events Committee), TWA (Third World Alliance), WSCW (radio station), Dance Company/Club.

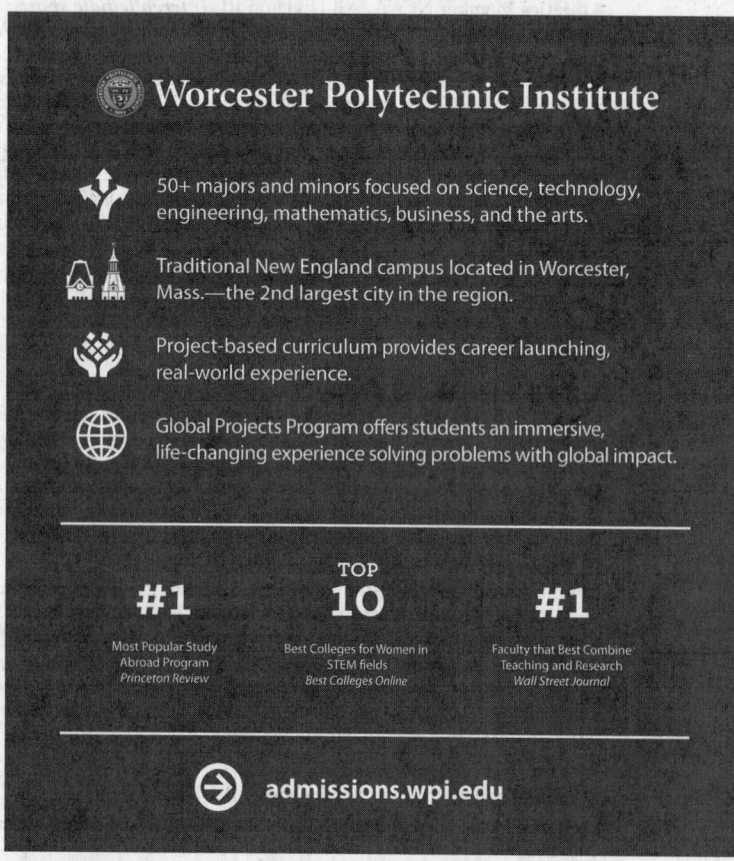

Athletics Member NCAA. All Division III. ***Intercollegiate sports:*** baseball M, basketball M/W, cross-country running M/W, field hockey W, football M, golf M, ice hockey M, lacrosse W, soccer M/W, softball W, tennis W, track and field M/W, volleyball W. ***Intramural sports:*** basketball M/W, football M, lacrosse W, soccer M/W, softball W, ultimate Frisbee M/W.

Campus security: 24-hour emergency response devices and patrols, late-night transport/escort service, controlled dormitory access, well-lit campus, limited access to campus at night.

Student services: health clinic, personal/psychological counseling.

COSTS & FINANCIAL AID

Costs (2016–17) ***Tuition:*** state resident $970 full-time, $40 per credit hour part-time; nonresident $7050 full-time, $294 per credit hour part-time. Full-time tuition and fees vary according to class time, course load, degree level, and reciprocity agreements. Part-time tuition and fees vary according to class time, course load, and reciprocity agreements. ***Required fees:*** $8232 full-time, $329 per credit hour part-time. ***Room and board:*** $11,775; room only: $8135. Room and board charges vary according to board plan and housing facility. ***Payment plan:*** installment. ***Waivers:*** senior citizens and employees or children of employees.

Financial Aid Of all full-time matriculated undergraduates who enrolled in 2015, 3,523 applied for aid, 2,578 were judged to have need, 1,012 had their need fully met. 200 Federal Work-Study jobs (averaging $1500). In 2015, 120 non-need-based awards were made. ***Average percent of need met:*** 80. ***Average financial aid package:*** $11,975. ***Average need-based loan:*** $3188. ***Average need-based gift aid:*** $4864. ***Average non-need-based aid:*** $2593. ***Average indebtedness upon graduation:*** $28,940. ***Financial aid deadline:*** 5/1.

APPLYING

Standardized Tests *Required:* SAT or ACT (for admission).

Options: electronic application, early action, deferred entrance.

Application fee: $50.

Required: high school transcript, minimum 2.0 GPA. ***Required for some:*** essay or personal statement.

Application deadlines: 5/1 (freshmen), rolling (transfers), 11/15 (early action).

Notification: 1/2 (freshmen), continuous (transfers), 12/15 (early action).

CONTACT

Ms. Sabine Dupoux, Admissions Receptionist, Worcester State University, 486 Chandler Street, Administration Building, Worcester, MA 01602-2597. *Phone:* 508-929-8040. *Fax:* 508-929-8183.
E-mail: admissions@worcester.edu.

MICHIGAN

Adrian College

Adrian, Michigan

http://www.adrian.edu/

CONTACT

Mr. Frank Hribar, Vice President for Enrollment, Adrian College, 110 S. Madison Street, Adrian, MI 49221. *Phone:* 800-877-2246. *Toll-free phone:* 800-877-2246. *Fax:* 517-264-3331.
E-mail: admissions@adrian.edu.

Albion College

Albion, Michigan

http://www.albion.edu/

- **Independent Methodist** 4-year, founded 1835
- **Small-town** 574-acre campus with easy access to Detroit
- **Endowment** $173.4 million
- **Coed** 1,418 undergraduate students, 98% full-time, 52% women, 48% men
- **Moderately difficult** entrance level, 72% of applicants were admitted

UNDERGRAD STUDENTS

1,393 full-time, 25 part-time. Students come from 28 states and territories; 19 other countries; 17% are from out of state; 9% Black or African American, non-Hispanic/Latino; 7% Hispanic/Latino; 3% Asian, non-Hispanic/Latino; 0.1% Native Hawaiian or other Pacific Islander, non-Hispanic/Latino; 0.3% American Indian or Alaska Native, non-Hispanic/Latino; 3% Two or more races, non-Hispanic/Latino; 6% Race/ethnicity unknown; 2% international; 2% transferred in; 94% live on campus.

Freshmen:

Admission: 3,338 applied, 2,412 admitted, 394 enrolled. ***Average high school GPA:*** 3.37. ***Test scores:*** ACT scores over 18: 94%; ACT scores over 24: 48%; ACT scores over 30: 7%.

Retention: 82% of full-time freshmen returned.

FACULTY

Total: 149, 70% full-time, 79% with terminal degrees.

Student/faculty ratio: 12:1.

ACADEMICS

Calendar: semesters. *Degree:* bachelor's.

Special study options: advanced placement credit, distance learning, double majors, honors programs, independent study, internships, off-campus study, part-time degree program, services for LD students, student-designed majors, study abroad, summer session for credit.

Unusual degree programs: 3-2 engineering with Columbia University, University of Michigan, Case Western Reserve University, Michigan Technological University; forestry with Duke University; nursing with Oakland University.

Computers: 185 computers/terminals and 2,000 ports are available on campus for general student use. Students can access the following: computer help desk, free student e-mail accounts, online (class) grades, online (class) registration, online (class) schedules, online student account and financial aid. Campuswide network is available. 100% of college-owned or -operated housing units are wired for high-speed Internet access. Wireless service is available via classrooms, computer centers, computer labs, dorm rooms, learning centers, libraries, student centers.

Library: Stockwell Mudd Libraries. *Books:* 346,622 (physical), 291,052 (digital/electronic); *Serial titles:* 779 (physical), 76,739 (digital/electronic); *Databases:* 205. Weekly public service hours: 110.

STUDENT LIFE

Housing options: on-campus residence required through senior year; coed, men-only, women-only, cooperative, special housing for students with disabilities. Campus housing is university owned. Freshman campus housing is guaranteed.

Activities and organizations: drama/theater group, student-run newspaper, radio station, choral group, marching band, Greek Life (Fraternities and Sororities), Student Senate (Student Government), Umbrella (Diversity Groups), Union Board (Programming Board), Spiritual Life (Religious Centered groups), national fraternities, national sororities.

Athletics Member NCAA. All Division III. ***Intercollegiate sports:*** baseball M, basketball M/W, cross-country running M/W, equestrian sports M/W, football M, golf M/W, lacrosse M/W, soccer M/W, softball W, swimming and diving M/W, tennis M/W, track and field M/W, volleyball W. ***Intramural sports:*** basketball M/W, cheerleading M(c)/W(c), equestrian sports M(c)/W(c), ice hockey M(c)/W(c), racquetball M/W, rugby M/W, sailing M(c)/W(c), soccer M/W, softball M/W, swimming and diving M/W, tennis M/W, ultimate Frisbee M/W, volleyball M/W, water polo M(c)/W(c).

Campus security: 24-hour emergency response devices and patrols, late-night transport/escort service, controlled dormitory access.

Student services: health clinic, personal/psychological counseling, women's center.

COSTS & FINANCIAL AID

Costs (2016–17) ***One-time required fee:*** $185. ***Comprehensive fee:*** $52,650 includes full-time tuition ($40,570), mandatory fees ($470), and room and board ($11,610). Full-time tuition and fees vary according to course load. Part-time tuition: $1720 per semester hour. Part-time tuition and fees vary according to course load. ***College room only:*** $5680. Room and board charges vary according to board plan and housing facility.

Payment plans: installment, deferred payment. ***Waivers:*** employees or children of employees.

Financial Aid Of all full-time matriculated undergraduates who enrolled in 2016, 1,143 applied for aid, 1,048 were judged to have need, 203 had their need fully met. 269 Federal Work-Study jobs (averaging $1334). 120 state and other part-time jobs (averaging $1581). In 2016, 341 non-need-based awards were made. ***Average percent of need met:*** 86. ***Average financial aid package:*** $35,866. ***Average need-based loan:*** $4953. ***Average need-based gift aid:*** $31,104. ***Average non-need-based aid:*** $21,079. ***Average indebtedness upon graduation:*** $38,356.

APPLYING

Standardized Tests *Required:* SAT or ACT (for admission).

Options: electronic application, early decision, deferred entrance.

Required: high school transcript, 1 letter of recommendation. ***Recommended:*** essay or personal statement, interview.

Application deadlines: rolling (freshmen), rolling (transfers).

Early decision deadline: 12/1.

Notification: continuous (freshmen), continuous (transfers), 12/15 (early decision).

CONTACT

Shar Sanders, Admissions Assistant, Albion College, 611 E. Porter Street, Albion, MI 49224. *Phone:* 517-629-0466. *Toll-free phone:* 800-858-6770. *Fax:* 517-629-0569. *E-mail:* ssanders@albion.edu.

Alma College

Alma, Michigan

http://www.alma.edu/

- **Independent Presbyterian** 4-year, founded 1886
- **Small-town** 128-acre campus with easy access to Lansing
- **Endowment** $109.9 million
- **Coed** 1,451 undergraduate students, 95% full-time, 58% women, 42% men
- **Moderately difficult** entrance level, 68% of applicants were admitted

UNDERGRAD STUDENTS

1,379 full-time, 72 part-time. Students come from 30 states and territories; 8 other countries; 8% are from out of state; 4% Black or African American, non-Hispanic/Latino; 5% Hispanic/Latino; 1% Asian, non-Hispanic/Latino; 0.1% Native Hawaiian or other Pacific Islander, non-Hispanic/Latino; 0.3% American Indian or Alaska Native, non-Hispanic/Latino; 2% Two or more races, non-Hispanic/Latino; 8% Race/ethnicity unknown; 2% international; 3% transferred in; 91% live on campus.

Freshmen:

Admission: 4,695 applied, 3,184 admitted, 447 enrolled. ***Average high school GPA:*** 3.5. ***Test scores:*** SAT critical reading scores over 500: 46%; SAT math scores over 500: 65%; SAT writing scores over 500: 39%; ACT scores over 18: 98%; SAT critical reading scores over 600: 23%; SAT math scores over 600: 27%; SAT writing scores over 600: 28%; ACT scores over 24: 52%; SAT critical reading scores over 700: 8%; SAT math scores over 700: 4%; SAT writing scores over 700: 6%; ACT scores over 30: 6%.

Retention: 80% of full-time freshmen returned.

FACULTY

Total: 163, 61% full-time, 64% with terminal degrees.

Student/faculty ratio: 12:1.

ACADEMICS

Calendar: 4-4-1. *Degree:* bachelor's.

Special study options: cooperative education, double majors, honors programs, independent study, internships, off-campus study, services for LD students, student-designed majors, study abroad. ***ROTC:*** Army (c).

Unusual degree programs: 3-2 engineering with University of Michigan, Kettering University.

Computers: 410 computers/terminals are available on campus for general student use. Students can access the following: campus intranet, computer help desk, free student e-mail accounts, online (class) grades, online (class) registration, online (class) schedules. Campuswide network is available. 100% of college-owned or -operated housing units are wired for high-speed Internet access. Wireless service is available via entire campus.

Library: Kerhl Building-Monteith Library. *Books:* 245,133 (physical), 130,789 (digital/electronic); *Serial titles:* 1,000 (physical). Weekly public service hours: 100; students can reserve study rooms.

STUDENT LIFE

Housing options: on-campus residence required through senior year; coed, special housing for students with disabilities. Campus housing is university owned. Freshman campus housing is guaranteed.

Activities and organizations: drama/theater group, student-run newspaper, radio station, choral group, marching band, Alma Ambassadors, Alma College Union Board, New Life Campus Ministries, Student Congress, Alpha Phi Omega, national fraternities, national sororities.

Athletics Member NCAA. All Division III. ***Intercollegiate sports:*** baseball M, basketball M/W, bowling W, cheerleading M/W, cross-country running M/W, football M, golf M/W, lacrosse M/W, soccer M/W, softball W, swimming and diving M/W, tennis M/W, track and field M/W, volleyball W, wrestling M. ***Intramural sports:*** basketball M/W, equestrian sports W(c), sand volleyball M/W, soccer M/W, softball M/W, table tennis M/W, volleyball M/W.

Campus security: 24-hour emergency response devices, late-night transport/escort service, controlled dormitory access.

Student services: health clinic, personal/psychological counseling.

COSTS & FINANCIAL AID

Costs (2016–17) ***Comprehensive fee:*** $47,548 includes full-time tuition ($36,890), mandatory fees ($420), and room and board ($10,238). Full-time tuition and fees vary according to student level. Part-time tuition: $1150 per credit hour. Part-time tuition and fees vary according to course load and student level. ***College room only:*** $5119. Room and board charges vary according to board plan and housing facility. ***Payment plans:*** installment, deferred payment. ***Waivers:*** employees or children of employees.

Financial Aid Of all full-time matriculated undergraduates who enrolled in 2016, 1,268 applied for aid, 1,161 were judged to have need, 143 had their need fully met. 592 Federal Work-Study jobs (averaging $1500). In 2016, 106 non-need-based awards were made. ***Average percent of need met:*** 68. ***Average financial aid package:*** $26,369. ***Average need-based loan:*** $4571. ***Average need-based gift aid:*** $25,234. ***Average non-need-based aid:*** $19,008. ***Average indebtedness upon graduation:*** $36,046.

APPLYING

Standardized Tests *Required:* SAT or ACT (for admission).

Options: electronic application.

Application fee: $25.

Required: essay or personal statement, high school transcript. ***Required for some:*** interview.

Application deadlines: rolling (freshmen), rolling (transfers).

Notification: continuous (freshmen), continuous (transfers).

CONTACT

Craig Aimar, Director of Admissions, Alma College, 614 W. Superior Street, Alma, MI 48801-1599. *Phone:* 800-321-2562. *Toll-free phone:* 800-321-ALMA. *E-mail:* admissions@alma.edu.

Andrews University

Berrien Springs, Michigan

http://www.andrews.edu/

- **Independent Seventh-day Adventist** university, founded 1874
- **Small-town** 1650-acre campus
- **Endowment** $52.3 million
- **Coed** 1,688 undergraduate students, 81% full-time, 54% women, 46% men
- **Moderately difficult** entrance level, 40% of applicants were admitted

UNDERGRAD STUDENTS

1,373 full-time, 315 part-time. Students come from 51 states and territories; 63 other countries; 64% are from out of state; 19% Black or African American, non-Hispanic/Latino; 15% Hispanic/Latino; 15% Asian, non-Hispanic/Latino; 0.2% Native Hawaiian or other Pacific Islander, non-Hispanic/Latino; 0.3% American Indian or Alaska Native, non-Hispanic/Latino; 4% Two or more races, non-Hispanic/Latino; 3% Race/ethnicity unknown; 17% international; 9% transferred in; 60% live on campus.

Freshmen:
Admission: 2,417 applied, 977 admitted, 304 enrolled. ***Average high school GPA:*** 3.5. ***Test scores:*** SAT critical reading scores over 500: 68%; SAT math scores over 500: 62%; SAT writing scores over 500: 63%; ACT scores over 18: 94%; SAT critical reading scores over 600: 42%; SAT math scores over 600: 32%; SAT writing scores over 600: 32%; ACT scores over 24: 54%; SAT critical reading scores over 700: 16%; SAT math scores over 700: 12%; SAT writing scores over 700: 9%; ACT scores over 30: 22%.

Retention: 87% of full-time freshmen returned.

FACULTY
Total: 306, 75% full-time, 61% with terminal degrees.

Student/faculty ratio: 11:1.

ACADEMICS
Calendar: semesters. *Degrees:* associate, bachelor's, master's, doctoral, post-master's, and postbachelor's certificates.

Special study options: academic remediation for entering students, accelerated degree program, adult/continuing education programs, advanced placement credit, cooperative education, distance learning, double majors, English as a second language, freshman honors college, honors programs, internships, off-campus study, part-time degree program, student-designed majors, study abroad, summer session for credit.

Unusual degree programs: 3-2 physical therapy and architecture.

Computers: 100 computers/terminals are available on campus for general student use. Students can access the following: campus intranet, computer help desk, free student e-mail accounts, online (class) grades, online (class) registration, online (class) schedules, degree audit. Campuswide network is available. 99% of college-owned or -operated housing units are wired for high-speed Internet access. Wireless service is available via entire campus.

Library: James White Library plus 2 others. *Books:* 895,090 (physical), 449,347 (digital/electronic); *Serial titles:* 908,572 (physical), 502,424 (digital/electronic); *Databases:* 185.

STUDENT LIFE
Housing options: on-campus residence required through senior year; men-only, women-only. Campus housing is university owned. Freshman campus housing is guaranteed.

Activities and organizations: drama/theater group, student-run newspaper, radio station, choral group.

Athletics ***Intramural sports:*** basketball M/W, football M/W, golf M/W, gymnastics M/W, racquetball M/W, soccer M/W, softball M/W, volleyball M/W, water polo M/W.

Campus security: 24-hour emergency response devices and patrols, controlled dormitory access.

Student services: health clinic, personal/psychological counseling.

COSTS & FINANCIAL AID
Costs (2016–17) ***Comprehensive fee:*** $36,426 includes full-time tuition ($26,790), mandatory fees ($894), and room and board ($8742). Full-time tuition and fees vary according to course load. Part-time tuition: $1116 per credit hour. Part-time tuition and fees vary according to course load. ***College room only:*** $4642. Room and board charges vary according to board plan. ***Payment plan:*** installment. ***Waivers:*** senior citizens and employees or children of employees.

Financial Aid Of all full-time matriculated undergraduates who enrolled in 2016, 927 applied for aid, 853 were judged to have need, 155 had their need fully met. 571 Federal Work-Study jobs (averaging $920). In 2016, 506 non-need-based awards were made. ***Average percent of need met:*** 86. ***Average financial aid package:*** $29,204. ***Average need-based loan:*** $4620. ***Average need-based gift aid:*** $6824. ***Average non-need-based aid:*** $11,445. ***Average indebtedness upon graduation:*** $36,708.

APPLYING
Standardized Tests *Required:* SAT or ACT (for admission).

Options: electronic application, deferred entrance.

Application fee: $30.

Required: high school transcript, minimum 2.3 GPA, 2 letters of recommendation.

Application deadlines: rolling (freshmen), rolling (transfers).

Notification: continuous (freshmen), continuous (transfers).

CONTACT
Elivette Diaz, Undergraduate Admissions Coordinator, Andrews University, Berrien Springs, MI 49104. *Phone:* 800-253-2874. *Toll-free phone:* 800-253-2874. *Fax:* 269-471-3228. *E-mail:* enroll@andrews.edu.

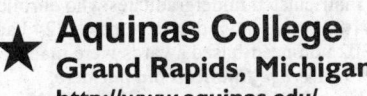

★ Aquinas College
Grand Rapids, Michigan
http://www.aquinas.edu/

- **Independent Roman Catholic** comprehensive, founded 1886
- **Suburban** 107-acre campus with easy access to Grand Rapids
- **Coed** 1,692 undergraduate students, 91% full-time, 60% women, 40% men
- **Moderately difficult** entrance level, 72% of applicants were admitted

UNDERGRAD STUDENTS
1,537 full-time, 155 part-time. Students come from 28 states and territories; 8 other countries; 3% Black or African American, non-Hispanic/Latino; 6% Hispanic/Latino; 1% Asian, non-Hispanic/Latino; 0.4% American Indian or Alaska Native, non-Hispanic/Latino; 3% Two or more races, non-Hispanic/Latino; 3% Race/ethnicity unknown; 0.9% international; 3% transferred in.

Freshmen:
Admission: 2,635 applied, 1,908 admitted, 370 enrolled. ***Average high school GPA:*** 3.48. ***Test scores:*** ACT scores over 18: 98%; ACT scores over 24: 53%; ACT scores over 30: 7%.

FACULTY
Total: 223, 39% full-time, 42% with terminal degrees.

Student/faculty ratio: 13:1.

ACADEMICS
Calendar: semesters. *Degrees:* associate, bachelor's, and master's.

Special study options: academic remediation for entering students, adult/continuing education programs, advanced placement credit, cooperative education, distance learning, double majors, external degree program, honors programs, independent study, internships, off-campus study, part-time degree program, services for LD students, student-designed majors, study abroad, summer session for credit.

Computers: 210 computers/terminals are available on campus for general student use. Students can access the following: campus intranet, computer help desk, free student e-mail accounts, online (class) grades, online (class) registration, online (class) schedules. Campuswide network is available. 100% of college-owned or -operated housing units are wired for high-speed Internet access. Wireless service is available via entire campus.

Library: Grace Hauenstein Library plus 1 other.

STUDENT LIFE
Housing options: on-campus residence required through junior year; coed. Campus housing is university owned. Freshman campus housing is guaranteed.

Activities and organizations: drama/theater group, student-run newspaper, radio station, choral group, Community Senate Programming Board, The Saint (newspaper), Insignis Honors Group, Community Action Volunteers of Aquinas (CAVA), RHC.

Athletics Member NAIA. ***Intercollegiate sports:*** baseball M, basketball M/W, bowling M/W, cheerleading W, cross-country running M/W, golf M/W, ice hockey M/W, lacrosse M/W, soccer M/W, softball W, tennis M/W, track and field M/W, volleyball W. ***Intramural sports:*** basketball M/W, football M/W, golf M, skiing (cross-country) M/W, skiing (downhill) M/W, soccer M/W, softball M/W, tennis M/W, volleyball M/W.

Campus security: 24-hour emergency response devices and patrols, student patrols, late-night transport/escort service, controlled dormitory access.

Student services: health clinic, personal/psychological counseling, women's center.

COSTS & FINANCIAL AID

Costs (2017–18) ***Comprehensive fee:*** $40,314 includes full-time tuition ($30,746), mandatory fees ($498), and room and board ($9070). Full-time tuition and fees vary according to course load. Part-time tuition: $498 per credit hour. Part-time tuition and fees vary according to course load. ***Required fees:*** $60 per term part-time. ***College room only:*** $4254. Room and board charges vary according to board plan and housing facility. ***Payment plans:*** installment, deferred payment. ***Waivers:*** employees or children of employees.

Financial Aid Of all full-time matriculated undergraduates who enrolled in 2016, 1,313 applied for aid, 1,081 were judged to have need, 224 had their need fully met. In 2016, 302 non-need-based awards were made. ***Average percent of need met:*** 79. ***Average financial aid package:*** $22,824. ***Average need-based loan:*** $2850. ***Average need-based gift aid:*** $19,974. ***Average non-need-based aid:*** $13,789. ***Average indebtedness upon graduation:*** $30,503.

APPLYING

Standardized Tests *Required:* SAT or ACT (for admission).

Options: electronic application, deferred entrance.

Required: high school transcript, minimum 2.0 GPA. ***Required for some:*** essay or personal statement, interview.

Application deadlines: rolling (freshmen), rolling (transfers).

CONTACT

Ms. Rebecca Roberts, Admissions Office Applications Specialist, Aquinas College, 1607 Robinson Road, SE, Grand Rapids, MI 49506-1799. *Phone:* 616-632-2900. *Toll-free phone:* 800-678-9593. *Fax:* 616-732-4469. *E-mail:* admissions@aquinas.edu.

See below for display ad and page 1284 for the College Close-Up.

The Art Institute of Michigan

Novi, Michigan

http://www.artinstitutes.edu/detroit/

CONTACT

The Art Institute of Michigan, 28125 Cabot Drive, Suite 120, Novi, MI 48377. *Phone:* 248-675-3800. *Toll-free phone:* 800-479-0087.

Baker College

Flint, Michigan

http://www.baker.edu/

- **Independent** comprehensive, founded 1911, part of The Baker College System
- **Suburban** campus with easy access to Detroit
- **Coed**
- **Minimally difficult** entrance level

FACULTY

Student/faculty ratio: 13:1.

ACADEMICS

Calendar: quarters. *Degrees:* certificates, diplomas, associate, bachelor's, master's, doctoral, and postbachelor's certificates.

Library: Marianne Jewell Library.

STUDENT LIFE

Housing options: on-campus residence required for freshman year; coed. Campus housing is university owned.

Activities and organizations: Occupational Therapy Club, Interior Design Society, Medical Assistants Student Organization, Physical Therapist Assistant Club, Cyber Defense Team.

Campus security: 24-hour emergency response devices, late-night transport/escort service, video monitoring of high traffic areas.

Student services: personal/psychological counseling.

COSTS

Costs (2016–17) ***Tuition:*** $9000 full-time, $4500 per year part-time. Full-time tuition and fees vary according to program. Part-time tuition and fees vary according to program. ***Room only:*** $3000.

APPLYING

Standardized Tests *Recommended:* SAT or ACT (for admission).

Options: electronic application, early admission, deferred entrance.

Application fee: $20.

Required: high school transcript.

CONTACT
Mr. Mark Heaton, System Marketing/Admission, Baker College, 1050 West Bristol Road, Flint, MI 48507-5508. *Phone:* 810-766-4280. *Toll-free phone:* 800-964-4299. *Fax:* 810-766-4279. *E-mail:* mark.heaton@baker.edu.

Calvin College
Grand Rapids, Michigan
http://www.calvin.edu/

- **Independent Christian Reformed** comprehensive, founded 1876
- **Suburban** 400-acre campus with easy access to Grand Rapids
- **Endowment** $131.5 million
- **Coed** 3,807 undergraduate students, 95% full-time, 54% women, 46% men
- **Moderately difficult** entrance level, 75% of applicants were admitted

UNDERGRAD STUDENTS
3,602 full-time, 205 part-time. Students come from 48 states and territories; 60 other countries; 43% are from out of state; 3% Black or African American, non-Hispanic/Latino; 4% Hispanic/Latino; 4% Asian, non-Hispanic/Latino; 0.1% American Indian or Alaska Native, non-Hispanic/Latino; 4% Two or more races, non-Hispanic/Latino; 2% Race/ethnicity unknown; 11% international; 2% transferred in; 60% live on campus.

Freshmen:
Admission: 3,981 applied, 2,970 admitted, 925 enrolled. ***Average high school GPA:*** 3.7. ***Test scores:*** SAT critical reading scores over 500: 82%; SAT math scores over 500: 88%; ACT scores over 18: 99%; SAT critical reading scores over 600: 45%; SAT math scores over 600: 51%; ACT scores over 24: 74%; SAT critical reading scores over 700: 11%; SAT math scores over 700: 13%; ACT scores over 30: 25%.
Retention: 85% of full-time freshmen returned.

FACULTY
Total: 356, 71% full-time, 72% with terminal degrees.
Student/faculty ratio: 13:1.

ACADEMICS
Calendar: 4-1-4. *Degrees:* bachelor's and master's.
Special study options: academic remediation for entering students, accelerated degree program, advanced placement credit, distance learning, double majors, honors programs, independent study, internships, off-campus study, part-time degree program, services for LD students, student-designed majors, study abroad, summer session for credit.
ROTC: Army (c).
Unusual degree programs: 3-2 occupational therapy with Washington University in St. Louis.
Computers: 1,025 computers/terminals and 2,656 ports are available on campus for general student use. Students can access the following: campus intranet, computer help desk, free student e-mail accounts, online (class) grades, online (class) registration, online (class) schedules. Campuswide network is available. 100% of college-owned or -operated housing units are wired for high-speed Internet access. Wireless service is available via classrooms, computer centers, computer labs, dorm rooms, learning centers, libraries, student centers.
Library: Hekman Library. *Books:* 714,950 (physical), 346,117 (digital/electronic); *Serial titles:* 5,893 (physical), 34,583 (digital/electronic); *Databases:* 137. Weekly public service hours: 90.

STUDENT LIFE
Housing options: on-campus residence required through sophomore year; men-only, women-only. Campus housing is university owned. Freshman campus housing is guaranteed.
Activities and organizations: drama/theater group, student-run newspaper, choral group, Dance Guild, Pre-Health Professionals, Calvin Outdoor Recreation, National Student Speech, Language, and Hearing Association, African Students Association.
Athletics Member NCAA. All Division III. ***Intercollegiate sports:*** baseball M, basketball M/W, cross-country running M/W, equestrian sports M(c)/W(c), golf M/W, ice hockey M(c), lacrosse M/W, rugby M(c)/W(c), soccer M/W, softball W, swimming and diving M/W, tennis M/W, track and field M/W, ultimate Frisbee M(c)/W(c), volleyball M(c)/W. ***Intramural sports:*** badminton M/W, basketball M/W, cross-country running M/W, football M/W, golf M/W, racquetball M/W, rock climbing M/W, sand volleyball M/W, soccer M/W, softball M/W, swimming and diving M/W, table tennis M/W, tennis M/W, track and field M/W, volleyball M/W, water polo M/W.
Campus security: 24-hour emergency response devices and patrols, student patrols, late-night transport/escort service, controlled dormitory access, crime prevention programs, crime alert bulletins.
Student services: health clinic, personal/psychological counseling.

COSTS & FINANCIAL AID
Costs (2016–17) ***Comprehensive fee:*** $41,570 includes full-time tuition ($31,730) and room and board ($9840). Full-time tuition and fees vary according to degree level, program, and student level. Part-time tuition: $760 per credit hour. Part-time tuition and fees vary according to course load, degree level, and student level. ***Room and board:*** Room and board charges vary according to board plan and housing facility. ***Payment plans:*** tuition prepayment, installment. ***Waivers:*** employees or children of employees.
Financial Aid Of all full-time matriculated undergraduates who enrolled in 2015, 3,402 applied for aid, 2,337 were judged to have need, 411 had their need fully met. 1,079 Federal Work-Study jobs (averaging $1550). 1,032 state and other part-time jobs (averaging $1413). In 2015, 1167 non-need-based awards were made. ***Average percent of need met:*** 73. ***Average financial aid package:*** $22,838. ***Average need-based loan:*** $6494. ***Average need-based gift aid:*** $16,111. ***Average non-need-based aid:*** $8421. ***Average indebtedness upon graduation:*** $30,998.

APPLYING
Standardized Tests *Required:* SAT or ACT (for admission).
Options: electronic application, deferred entrance.
Application fee: $35.
Required: essay or personal statement, high school transcript, minimum 2.5 GPA, 1 letter of recommendation. ***Recommended:*** interview.
Application deadlines: 8/15 (freshmen), rolling (transfers).
Notification: continuous (freshmen).

CONTACT
Dr. Ben Arendt, Director of Admissions, Calvin College, 3201 Burton Street, SE, Grand Rapids, MI 49546. *Phone:* 616-526-6106. *Toll-free phone:* 800-688-0122. *Fax:* 616-526-6777.
E-mail: admissions@calvin.edu.

Central Michigan University
Mount Pleasant, Michigan
http://www.cmich.edu/

- **State-supported** university, founded 1892
- **Small-town** 854-acre campus
- **Endowment** $130.7 million
- **Coed** 19,923 undergraduate students, 86% full-time, 57% women, 43% men
- **Moderately difficult** entrance level, 72% of applicants were admitted

UNDERGRAD STUDENTS
17,202 full-time, 2,721 part-time. Students come from 52 states and territories; 44 other countries; 5% are from out of state; 9% Black or African American, non-Hispanic/Latino; 4% Hispanic/Latino; 1% Asian, non-Hispanic/Latino; 0.1% Native Hawaiian or other Pacific Islander, non-Hispanic/Latino; 0.8% American Indian or Alaska Native, non-Hispanic/Latino; 4% Two or more races, non-Hispanic/Latino; 2% Race/ethnicity unknown; 2% international; 7% transferred in; 37% live on campus.

Freshmen:
Admission: 18,875 applied, 13,594 admitted, 3,519 enrolled. ***Average high school GPA:*** 3.38. ***Test scores:*** SAT critical reading scores over 500: 56%; SAT math scores over 500: 52%; SAT writing scores over 500: 65%; ACT scores over 18: 95%; SAT critical reading scores over 600: 17%; SAT math scores over 600: 19%; SAT writing scores over 600: 10%; ACT scores over 24: 42%; SAT critical reading scores over 700: 4%; SAT math scores over 700: 1%; SAT writing scores over 700: 1%; ACT scores over 30: 5%.
Retention: 77% of full-time freshmen returned.

FACULTY

Total: 1,162, 52% full-time, 68% with terminal degrees.

Student/faculty ratio: 22:1.

ACADEMICS

Calendar: semesters. *Degrees:* bachelor's, master's, doctoral, post-master's, and postbachelor's certificates.

Special study options: academic remediation for entering students, accelerated degree program, advanced placement credit, distance learning, double majors, English as a second language, honors programs, independent study, internships, off-campus study, part-time degree program, services for LD students, student-designed majors, study abroad, summer session for credit. ***ROTC:*** Army (b), Air Force (c).

Unusual degree programs: 3-2 business administration; engineering; apparel product development and merchandising technology, computer science, economics, experimental psychology, higher education administration, history, geographic information science, administration, Spanish, mathematics, political science, human development and family studies.

Computers: 490 computers/terminals and 26,902 ports are available on campus for general student use. Students can access the following: campus intranet, computer help desk, free student e-mail accounts, online (class) grades, online (class) registration, online (class) schedules, learning management system. Campuswide network is available. 100% of college-owned or -operated housing units are wired for high-speed Internet access. Wireless service is available via entire campus.

Library: Charles V. Park Library plus 1 other. *Books:* 734,063 (physical), 423,429 (digital/electronic); *Serial titles:* 6,091 (physical), 72,302 (digital/electronic); *Databases:* 287. Weekly public service hours: 125; students can reserve study rooms.

STUDENT LIFE

Housing options: on-campus residence required through sophomore year; coed, special housing for students with disabilities. Campus housing is university owned. Freshman campus housing is guaranteed.

Activities and organizations: drama/theater group, student-run newspaper, radio and television station, choral group, marching band, national fraternities, national sororities.

Athletics Member NCAA. All Division I except football (Division I-A). ***Intercollegiate sports:*** baseball M(s), basketball M(s)/W(s), cross-country running M(s)/W(s), field hockey W(s), golf W(s), gymnastics W(s), lacrosse W(s), soccer W(s), softball W(s), track and field M(s)/W(s), volleyball W(s), wrestling M(s). ***Intramural sports:*** baseball M(c), basketball M/W, bowling M/W, cross-country running M(c)/W(c), equestrian sports M(c)/W(c), football M/W, golf M(c)/W(c), gymnastics M(c)/W(c), ice hockey M(c)/W(c), lacrosse M(c)/W(c), racquetball M/W, rugby M(c)/W(c), sand volleyball M/W, skiing (downhill) M(c)/W(c), soccer M/W, softball M/W, swimming and diving M(c)/W(c), table tennis M/W, tennis M/W, track and field M(c)/W(c), triathlon M(c)/W(c), ultimate Frisbee M(c)/W(c), volleyball M/W, water polo M(c)/W(c), weight lifting M(c)/W(c), wrestling M/W.

Campus security: 24-hour emergency response devices and patrols, late-night transport/escort service.

Student services: health clinic, personal/psychological counseling, women's center.

COSTS & FINANCIAL AID

Costs (2016–17) ***Tuition:*** state resident $12,150 full-time, $405 per credit hour part-time; nonresident $23,670 full-time, $789 per credit hour part-time. Full-time tuition and fees vary according to location. Part-time tuition and fees vary according to location. ***Room and board:*** $9406; room only: $4703. Room and board charges vary according to board plan and housing facility. ***Payment plan:*** installment. ***Waivers:*** children of alumni, senior citizens, and employees or children of employees.

Financial Aid Of all full-time matriculated undergraduates who enrolled in 2015, 13,178 applied for aid, 10,329 were judged to have need, 5,016 had their need fully met. 974 Federal Work-Study jobs (averaging $1776). 4,900 state and other part-time jobs (averaging $2448). In 2015, 2110 non-need-based awards were made. ***Average percent of need met:*** 79. ***Average financial aid package:*** $13,708. ***Average need-based loan:*** $7824. ***Average need-based gift aid:*** $6661. ***Average non-need-based aid:*** $4908. ***Average indebtedness upon graduation:*** $33,480.

APPLYING

Standardized Tests *Required:* SAT or ACT (for admission).

Options: electronic application, early admission, early action, deferred entrance.

Application fee: $35.

Required: high school transcript. ***Required for some:*** essay or personal statement, interview.

Application deadlines: 7/1 (freshmen), rolling (transfers).

Notification: continuous (freshmen), continuous (transfers).

CONTACT

Central Michigan University, Warriner Hall 102, Mt Pleasant, MI 48859. *Phone:* 989-774-3076. *Toll-free phone:* 888-292-5366. *Fax:* 989-774-7267. *E-mail:* cmuadmit@cmich.edu.

Chamberlain College of Nursing

Troy, Michigan

http://www.chamberlain.edu/

- **Proprietary** 4-year
- **Coed**

FACULTY

Student/faculty ratio: 14:1.

ACADEMICS

Degree: bachelor's.

STUDENT LIFE

Housing options: college housing not available.

COSTS

Costs (2016–17) ***Tuition:*** $18,900 full-time, $675 per credit hour part-time. ***Required fees:*** $600 full-time.

APPLYING

Standardized Tests *Required:* SAT or ACT (for admission).

Options: deferred entrance.

Application fee: $95.

CONTACT

Chamberlain College of Nursing, 200 Kirts Boulevard, Troy, MI 48084. *Toll-free phone:* 877-751-5783.

Cleary University

Howell, Michigan

http://www.cleary.edu/

- **Independent** comprehensive, founded 1883
- **Suburban** 32-acre campus with easy access to Detroit, Ann Arbor
- **Endowment** $998,704
- **Coed**
- **Moderately difficult** entrance level

FACULTY

Student/faculty ratio: 15:1.

ACADEMICS

Calendar: semesters. *Degrees:* certificates, associate, bachelor's, and master's.

Library: Cleary Online Library.

STUDENT LIFE

Housing options: on-campus residence required for freshman year; coed. Campus housing is university owned. Freshman applicants given priority for college housing.

Activities and organizations: Cleary Professional Accounting Associates, Human Resourcesand Organizational Leadership Association, Event and Meeting Planning Student Association, Veterans Club, Accounting/Fraud Examiners Club.

Athletics Member USCAA.

Campus security: 24-hour emergency response devices, access to facilities limited to authorized persons.

Student services: personal/psychological counseling.

COSTS & FINANCIAL AID

Costs (2016–17) ***Comprehensive fee:*** $27,200 includes full-time tuition ($17,500), mandatory fees ($100), and room and board ($9600). Part-time tuition: $625 per credit hour. ***College room only:*** $7200.

Financial Aid Of all full-time matriculated undergraduates who enrolled in 2015, 11 Federal Work-Study jobs (averaging $3209).

APPLYING

Standardized Tests *Required:* SAT or ACT (for admission). *Required for some:* SAT Subject Tests (for admission).

Options: electronic application, early admission, deferred entrance.

Application fee: $35.

Required: high school transcript, minimum 2.5 GPA. ***Required for some:*** essay or personal statement, minimum ACT score of 19 for freshmen, minimum high school GPA of 2.0 for non-traditional and transfer students. ***Recommended:*** interview.

CONTACT

Eric Brown, Director of Admissions, Cleary University, 3750 Cleary Drive, Howell, MI 48843. *Phone:* 800-686-1883. *Toll-free phone:* 800-686-1883. *Fax:* 517-338-5075. *E-mail:* admissions@cleary.edu.

★ College for Creative Studies

Detroit, Michigan

http://www.collegeforcreativestudies.edu/

CONTACT

Office of Admissions, College for Creative Studies, 201 East Kirby, Detroit, MI 48202-4034. *Phone:* 800-952-2787. *Toll-free phone:* 800-952-ARTS. *Fax:* 313-872-2739. *E-mail:* admissions@collegeforcreativestudies.edu.

See below for display ad and page 1320 for the College Close-Up.

Compass College of Cinematic Arts

Grand Rapids, Michigan

http://www.compass.edu/

CONTACT

Compass College of Cinematic Arts, 41 Sheldon Boulevard SE, Grand Rapids, MI 49503.

Concordia University Ann Arbor

Ann Arbor, Michigan

http://www.cuaa.edu/

CONTACT

Mr. Ben Limback, Director of Admissions, Concordia University Ann Arbor, 4090 Geddes Road, Ann Arbor, MI 48105-2797. *Phone:* 734-995-7311. *Toll-free phone:* 877-995-7520 (in-state); 877-955-7520 (out-of-state). *Fax:* 734-995-4610. *E-mail:* admissions@cuaa.edu.

Cornerstone University

Grand Rapids, Michigan

http://www.cornerstone.edu/

- **Independent nondenominational** comprehensive, founded 1941
- **Suburban** 132-acre campus with easy access to Grand Rapids
- **Endowment** $8.4 million
- **Coed** 1,856 undergraduate students, 73% full-time, 61% women, 39% men
- **Minimally difficult** entrance level, 63% of applicants were admitted

UNDERGRAD STUDENTS

1,363 full-time, 493 part-time. Students come from 27 states and territories; 28 other countries; 25% are from out of state; 13% Black or African American, non-Hispanic/Latino; 4% Hispanic/Latino; 1% Asian, non-Hispanic/Latino; 0.2% Native Hawaiian or other Pacific Islander, non-Hispanic/Latino; 0.5% American Indian or Alaska Native, non-Hispanic/Latino; 0.6% Two or more races, non-Hispanic/Latino; 3% international; 7% transferred in; 61% live on campus.

Freshmen:
Admission: 2,892 applied, 1,834 admitted, 283 enrolled. ***Average high school GPA:*** 3.46. ***Test scores:*** SAT critical reading scores over 500: 74%; SAT math scores over 500: 53%; SAT writing scores over 500: 58%; ACT scores over 18: 92%; SAT critical reading scores over 600: 37%; SAT math scores over 600: 32%; SAT writing scores over 600: 21%; ACT scores over 24: 42%; SAT critical reading scores over 700: 11%; SAT writing scores over 700: 5%; ACT scores over 30: 6%.
Retention: 82% of full-time freshmen returned.

FACULTY
Total: 417, 16% full-time, 37% with terminal degrees.
Student/faculty ratio: 21:1.

ACADEMICS
Calendar: semesters. *Degrees:* diplomas, associate, bachelor's, master's, and doctoral.
Special study options: academic remediation for entering students, accelerated degree program, adult/continuing education programs, advanced placement credit, distance learning, double majors, English as a second language, honors programs, independent study, internships, off-campus study, part-time degree program, services for LD students, student-designed majors, study abroad, summer session for credit. ***ROTC:*** Army (c).
Computers: 43 computers/terminals are available on campus for general student use. Students can access the following: campus intranet, computer help desk, free student e-mail accounts, online (class) grades, online (class) registration, online (class) schedules. Campuswide network is available. 100% of college-owned or -operated housing units are wired for high-speed Internet access. Wireless service is available via entire campus.
Library: Miller Library. *Books:* 102,008 (physical), 298,380 (digital/electronic); *Serial titles:* 541 (physical), 44,211 (digital/electronic); *Databases:* 176. Weekly public service hours: 88; students can reserve study rooms.

STUDENT LIFE
Housing options: on-campus residence required through junior year; men-only, women-only, special housing for students with disabilities. Campus housing is university owned. Freshman campus housing is guaranteed.
Activities and organizations: drama/theater group, student-run newspaper, choral group, Student Government, Student Education Association, Intramural Sports, Student Activities Council, International Justice Mission.
Athletics Member NAIA. ***Intercollegiate sports:*** baseball M(s), basketball M(s)/W(s), bowling M(s)/W(s), cheerleading W(s), cross-country running M(s)/W(s), golf M(s)/W(s), soccer M(s)/W(s), softball W(s), track and field M(s)/W(s), volleyball W(s). ***Intramural sports:*** basketball M/W, football M, soccer M/W, softball M/W, volleyball M/W.
Campus security: 24-hour emergency response devices and patrols, student patrols, late-night transport/escort service, controlled dormitory access.
Student services: health clinic, personal/psychological counseling.

COSTS & FINANCIAL AID
Costs (2017–18) ***Comprehensive fee:*** $36,550 includes full-time tuition ($27,150), mandatory fees ($370), and room and board ($9030). Full-time tuition and fees vary according to course load and reciprocity agreements. Part-time tuition: $1030 per credit hour. Part-time tuition and fees vary according to course load. ***Room and board:*** Room and board charges vary according to board plan and housing facility. ***Payment plan:*** installment. ***Waivers:*** employees or children of employees.
Financial Aid Of all full-time matriculated undergraduates who enrolled in 2016, 972 applied for aid, 889 were judged to have need, 145 had their need fully met. 167 Federal Work-Study jobs (averaging $1365). In 2016, 218 non-need-based awards were made. ***Average percent of need met:*** 69. ***Average financial aid package:*** $20,891. ***Average need-based loan:*** $4633. ***Average need-based gift aid:*** $16,455. ***Average non-need-based aid:*** $10,983. ***Average indebtedness upon graduation:*** $32,191.

APPLYING
Standardized Tests *Required:* SAT or ACT (for admission).
Options: electronic application.
Required: essay or personal statement, high school transcript, minimum 2.5 GPA, 1 letter of recommendation, pastoral letter.
Application deadlines: rolling (freshmen), rolling (transfers).
Notification: continuous (freshmen), continuous (transfers).

CONTACT
Mrs. Lisa Link, Office of Admissions, Cornerstone University, 1001 East Beltline Avenue, NE, Grand Rapids, MI 49525. *Phone:* 616-222-1426. *Toll-free phone:* 800-787-9778. *Fax:* 616-222-1418.
E-mail: admissions@cornerstone.edu.

Davenport University
Grand Rapids, Michigan
http://www.davenport.edu/

- **Independent** comprehensive, founded 1866
- **Suburban** 77-acre campus with easy access to Grand Rapids
- **Coed** 5,950 undergraduate students, 40% full-time, 57% women, 43% men
- **Noncompetitive** entrance level

UNDERGRAD STUDENTS
2,378 full-time, 3,572 part-time. Students come from 52 states and territories; 29 other countries; 8% are from out of state; 13% Black or African American, non-Hispanic/Latino; 3% Hispanic/Latino; 2% Asian, non-Hispanic/Latino; 0.2% Native Hawaiian or other Pacific Islander, non-Hispanic/Latino; 0.7% American Indian or Alaska Native, non-Hispanic/Latino; 3% Two or more races, non-Hispanic/Latino; 9% Race/ethnicity unknown; 2% international; 14% transferred in; 6% live on campus.

Freshmen:
Admission: 644 enrolled. ***Average high school GPA:*** 3.09.
Retention: 74% of full-time freshmen returned.

FACULTY
Total: 832, 16% full-time, 27% with terminal degrees.
Student/faculty ratio: 12:1.

ACADEMICS
Calendar: semesters. *Degrees:* certificates, diplomas, associate, bachelor's, master's, post-master's, and postbachelor's certificates.
Special study options: academic remediation for entering students, accelerated degree program, adult/continuing education programs, advanced placement credit, cooperative education, distance learning, English as a second language, independent study, internships, part-time degree program, services for LD students, study abroad, summer session for credit. ***ROTC:*** Army (c).
Computers: 3,098 computers/terminals and 315 ports are available on campus for general student use. Students can access the following: campus intranet, computer help desk, free student e-mail accounts, online (class) grades, online (class) registration, online (class) schedules. Campuswide network is available. 100% of college-owned or -operated housing units are wired for high-speed Internet access. Wireless service is available via entire campus.
Library: Margaret D. Sneden Library Information Commons plus 3 others. Students can reserve study rooms.

STUDENT LIFE
Housing options: coed. Campus housing is university owned. Freshman applicants given priority for college housing.
Activities and organizations: marching band, Business Professionals of America, Delta Epsilon Chi, Student Government, Health Occupations Students of America, Connect.
Athletics Member NAIA. ***Intercollegiate sports:*** baseball M(s), basketball M(s)/W(s), bowling M(s)/W(s), cheerleading W(s), cross-country running M(s)/W(s), football M(s), golf M(s)/W(s), ice hockey M(s)/W(s), lacrosse M(s)/W(s), rugby M(s)/W(s), soccer M(s)/W(s), softball W(s), tennis M(s)/W(s), track and field M(s)/W(s), volleyball W(s).
Campus security: 24-hour emergency response devices and patrols, late-night transport/escort service, controlled dormitory access.
Student services: personal/psychological counseling.

COSTS
Costs (2016–17) ***Comprehensive fee:*** $26,522 includes full-time tuition ($15,936), mandatory fees ($684), and room and board ($9902). Full-time tuition and fees vary according to location and program. Part-time tuition: $664 per credit hour. Part-time tuition and fees vary according to location and program. ***Required fees:*** $380 per term part-time. ***College room only:*** $6510. Room and board charges vary according to board plan and housing facility. ***Payment plan:*** installment. ***Waivers:*** employees or children of employees.

APPLYING
Standardized Tests *Recommended:* SAT (for admission), ACT (for admission).
Options: electronic application, deferred entrance.
Application fee: $25.
Required: high school transcript. ***Recommended:*** interview.
Application deadlines: rolling (freshmen), rolling (transfers).
Notification: continuous (freshmen), continuous (transfers).

CONTACT
Ms. Amy Lucas, Interim Executive Director of Admissions, Davenport University, 6191 Kraft Avenue SE, Grand Rapids, MI 49512. *Phone:* 616-451-3511. *Toll-free phone:* 800-686-1600 (in-state); 866-686-1600 (out-of-state). *Fax:* 616-732-1145. *E-mail:* amy.lucas@davenport.edu.

Eastern Michigan University

Ypsilanti, Michigan

http://www.emich.edu/

- **State-supported** comprehensive, founded 1849
- **Suburban** 460-acre campus with easy access to Detroit
- **Endowment** $67.2 million
- **Coed** 17,541 undergraduate students, 73% full-time, 59% women, 41% men
- **Moderately difficult** entrance level, 73% of applicants were admitted

UNDERGRAD STUDENTS
12,846 full-time, 4,695 part-time. 10% are from out of state; 19% Black or African American, non-Hispanic/Latino; 5% Hispanic/Latino; 3% Asian, non-Hispanic/Latino; 0.1% Native Hawaiian or other Pacific Islander, non-Hispanic/Latino; 0.3% American Indian or Alaska Native, non-Hispanic/Latino; 4% Two or more races, non-Hispanic/Latino; 2% Race/ethnicity unknown; 2% international; 10% transferred in; 22% live on campus.

Freshmen:
Admission: 14,736 applied, 10,769 admitted, 2,808 enrolled. ***Average high school GPA:*** 3.3. ***Test scores:*** SAT critical reading scores over 500: 55%; SAT math scores over 500: 56%; SAT writing scores over 500: 51%; ACT scores over 18: 87%; SAT critical reading scores over 600: 14%; SAT math scores over 600: 16%; SAT writing scores over 600: 11%; ACT scores over 24: 33%; ACT scores over 30: 3%.
Retention: 74% of full-time freshmen returned.

FACULTY
Total: 1,356, 56% full-time, 55% with terminal degrees.
Student/faculty ratio: 17:1.

ACADEMICS
Calendar: semesters. *Degrees:* bachelor's, master's, doctoral, post-master's, and postbachelor's certificates.
Special study options: academic remediation for entering students, accelerated degree program, advanced placement credit, cooperative education, distance learning, double majors, English as a second language, external degree program, honors programs, independent study, internships, part-time degree program, services for LD students, student-designed majors, study abroad, summer session for credit. ***ROTC:*** Army (b), Navy (c), Air Force (c).
Unusual degree programs: 3-2 accounting, occupational therapy.
Computers: 1,600 computers/terminals and 200 ports are available on campus for general student use. Students can access the following: campus intranet, computer help desk, free student e-mail accounts, online (class) grades, online (class) registration, online (class) schedules. Campuswide network is available. 100% of college-owned or -operated housing units are wired for high-speed Internet access. Wireless service is available via entire campus.
Library: Bruce T. Halle Library.

STUDENT LIFE
Housing options: on-campus residence required through sophomore year; coed, special housing for students with disabilities. Campus housing is university owned.
Activities and organizations: drama/theater group, student-run newspaper, radio and television station, choral group, marching band, International Student Association, Golden Key International Honor Society, Psychology Club, Indian Student Association, GREEN (Gathering Resources to Educate about our Environment and Nature), national fraternities, national sororities.
Athletics Member NCAA. All Division I except football (Division I-A). ***Intercollegiate sports:*** baseball M(s), basketball M(s)/W(s), crew W(s), cross-country running M(s)/W(s), golf M(s)/W(s), gymnastics W(s), soccer W(s), softball W(s), swimming and diving M(s)/W(s), tennis W(s), track and field M(s)/W(s), volleyball W(s), wrestling M(s). ***Intramural sports:*** badminton M/W, basketball M/W, bowling M/W, cross-country running M/W, golf M/W, racquetball M/W, rock climbing M/W, soccer M/W, softball M/W, swimming and diving M/W, table tennis M/W, track and field M/W, ultimate Frisbee M/W, volleyball M/W, weight lifting M/W.
Campus security: 24-hour emergency response devices and patrols, student patrols, late-night transport/escort service, controlled dormitory access, bicycle patrols, local police in dormitories, self-defense education, lighted pathways, bike lock lease program.
Student services: health clinic, personal/psychological counseling, women's center, legal services.

COSTS & FINANCIAL AID
Costs (2017–18) ***One-time required fee:*** $323. ***Tuition:*** state resident $12,120 full-time, $323 per credit hour part-time; nonresident $27,711 full-time, $873 per credit hour part-time. Full-time tuition and fees vary according to course level and reciprocity agreements. Part-time tuition and fees vary according to course level and reciprocity agreements. ***Required fees:*** $1529 full-time, $47 per credit hour part-time, $50 per credit hour part-time. ***Room and board:*** Room and board charges vary according to board plan, housing facility, and location. ***Payment plan:*** installment. ***Waivers:*** employees or children of employees.
Financial Aid Of all full-time matriculated undergraduates who enrolled in 2015, 10,796 applied for aid, 8,978 were judged to have need, 365 had their need fully met. 615 Federal Work-Study jobs (averaging $1626). In 2015, 2264 non-need-based awards were made. ***Average percent of need met:*** 47. ***Average financial aid package:*** $8785. ***Average need-based loan:*** $6756. ***Average need-based gift aid:*** $5423. ***Average non-need-based aid:*** $5427. ***Average indebtedness upon graduation:*** $30,588.

APPLYING
Standardized Tests *Required:* SAT or ACT (for admission).
Options: electronic application, deferred entrance.
Application fee: $35.
Required: high school transcript, minimum 2.0 GPA. ***Required for some:*** 1 letter of recommendation, interview.
Application deadlines: rolling (freshmen), rolling (transfers).
Notification: continuous (freshmen), continuous (transfers).

CONTACT
Eastern Michigan University, Ypsilanti, MI 48197. *Phone:* 734-487-3060. *Toll-free phone:* 800-GO TO EMU.

Ferris State University

Big Rapids, Michigan

http://www.ferris.edu/

- **State-supported** comprehensive, founded 1884
- **Small-town** 935-acre campus with easy access to Grand Rapids
- **Endowment** $65.2 million
- **Coed** 12,866 undergraduate students, 68% full-time, 53% women, 47% men
- **Minimally difficult** entrance level, 78% of applicants were admitted

UNDERGRAD STUDENTS
8,785 full-time, 4,081 part-time. Students come from 44 states and territories; 43 other countries; 7% are from out of state; 7% Black or African American, non-Hispanic/Latino; 5% Hispanic/Latino; 2% Asian, non-Hispanic/Latino; 0.1% Native Hawaiian or other Pacific Islander, non-Hispanic/Latino; 0.6% American Indian or Alaska Native, non-Hispanic/Latino; 3% Two or more races, non-Hispanic/Latino; 1% Race/ethnicity unknown; 0.8% international; 10% transferred in; 26% live on campus.

Freshmen:
Admission: 10,883 applied, 8,455 admitted, 1,824 enrolled. ***Average high school GPA:*** 3.26. ***Test scores:*** ACT scores over 18: 86%; ACT scores over 24: 32%; ACT scores over 30: 6%.
Retention: 75% of full-time freshmen returned.

FACULTY
Total: 952, 62% full-time.
Student/faculty ratio: 16:1.

ACADEMICS
Calendar: semesters. *Degrees:* certificates, associate, bachelor's, master's, doctoral, and postbachelor's certificates.
Special study options: academic remediation for entering students, accelerated degree program, adult/continuing education programs, advanced placement credit, cooperative education, distance learning, double majors, English as a second language, external degree program, freshman honors college, honors programs, independent study, internships, off-campus study, part-time degree program, services for LD students, student-designed majors, study abroad, summer session for credit. ***ROTC:*** Army (c).
Computers: 1,940 computers/terminals are available on campus for general student use. Students can access the following: computer help desk, free student e-mail accounts, online (class) grades, online (class) registration, online (class) schedules. Campuswide network is available. 100% of college-owned or -operated housing units are wired for high-speed Internet access. Wireless service is available via entire campus.
Library: Ferris Library for Information, Technology and Education. *Books:* 233,023 (physical), 221,325 (digital/electronic); *Serial titles:* 2,107 (physical), 80,766 (digital/electronic); *Databases:* 197. Weekly public service hours: 96; study areas open 24 hours, 5-7 days a week.

STUDENT LIFE
Housing options: on-campus residence required for freshman year; coed, special housing for students with disabilities. Campus housing is university owned. Freshman campus housing is guaranteed.
Activities and organizations: drama/theater group, student-run newspaper, radio and television station, choral group, Pre-Pharm D, Honors Peer Mentoring, American Marketing Association, Music Industry Management Association, Social Work Association, national fraternities, national sororities.
Athletics Member NCAA. All Division II. ***Intercollegiate sports:*** basketball M(s)/W(s), cross-country running M(s)/W(s), football M(s), golf M(s)/W(s), ice hockey M(s), soccer W(s), softball W(s), tennis M(s)/W(s), track and field M(s)/W(s), volleyball W(s). ***Intramural sports:*** badminton M/W, baseball M(c), basketball M/W, bowling M/W, cheerleading M(c)/W(c), equestrian sports M(c)/W(c), football M/W, golf M(c)/W(c), ice hockey M/W, lacrosse M(c)/W(c), rugby M(c)/W(c), skiing (downhill) M(c)/W(c), soccer M/W, softball M/W, table tennis M/W, tennis M(c)/W(c), ultimate Frisbee M/W, volleyball M/W, water polo M/W, weight lifting M/W, wrestling M(c)/W(c).
Campus security: 24-hour emergency response devices, student patrols, late-night transport/escort service, controlled dormitory access.
Student services: health clinic, personal/psychological counseling.

COSTS & FINANCIAL AID
Costs (2016–17) ***Tuition:*** state resident $11,760 full-time, $392 per credit hour part-time; nonresident $17,640 full-time, $588 per credit hour part-time. Full-time tuition and fees vary according to location, program, and student level. Part-time tuition and fees vary according to location and student level. ***Room and board:*** $9651. Room and board charges vary according to board plan and housing facility. ***Payment plan:*** installment. ***Waivers:*** employees or children of employees.
Financial Aid Of all full-time matriculated undergraduates who enrolled in 2016, 8,411 applied for aid, 6,456 were judged to have need, 982 had their need fully met. 410 Federal Work-Study jobs (averaging $2391). 218 state and other part-time jobs (averaging $2031). In 2016, 1267 non-need-based awards were made. ***Average percent of need met:*** 66. ***Average financial aid package:*** $11,350. ***Average need-based loan:*** $4600. ***Average need-based gift aid:*** $4890. ***Average non-need-based aid:*** $4420. ***Average indebtedness upon graduation:*** $35,710.

APPLYING
Standardized Tests *Required for some:* SAT or ACT (for admission).
Options: electronic application.
Required: high school transcript, minimum 2.5 GPA.
Application deadlines: 8/1 (freshmen), 7/1 (transfers).
Notification: continuous (freshmen), continuous (transfers).

CONTACT
Mr. Jason Daday, Associate Director of Admissions, Ferris State University, 1201 South State Street, CSS 201, Big Rapids, MI 49307-2742. *Phone:* 231-591-3106. *Toll-free phone:* 800-433-7747. *Fax:* 231-591-2242. *E-mail:* dadayja@ferris.edu.

Finlandia University
Hancock, Michigan
http://www.finlandia.edu/

CONTACT
Martin Kinard, Finlandia University, 601 Quincy Street, Hancock, MI 49930. *Phone:* 906-487-7352. *Toll-free phone:* 877-202-5491. *Fax:* 906-487-7383. *E-mail:* admissions@finlandia.edu.

Grace Bible College
Grand Rapids, Michigan
http://www.gbcol.edu/

CONTACT
Mr. Kevin Gilliam, Director of Enrollment, Grace Bible College, 1101 Aldon Street, SW, PO Box 910, Grand Rapids, MI 49509. *Phone:* 616-538-2330 Ext. 239. *Toll-free phone:* 800-968-1887. *Fax:* 616-538-0599. *E-mail:* gbc@gbcol.edu.

Grand Valley State University
Allendale, Michigan
http://www.gvsu.edu/

- **State-supported** comprehensive, founded 1960
- **Small-town** 1391-acre campus with easy access to Grand Rapids
- **Endowment** $102.4 million
- **Coed** 22,209 undergraduate students, 89% full-time, 58% women, 42% men
- **Moderately difficult** entrance level, 82% of applicants were admitted

UNDERGRAD STUDENTS
19,668 full-time, 2,541 part-time. Students come from 42 states and territories; 68 other countries; 6% are from out of state; 5% Black or African American, non-Hispanic/Latino; 5% Hispanic/Latino; 2% Asian, non-Hispanic/Latino; 0.3% American Indian or Alaska Native, non-Hispanic/Latino; 3% Two or more races, non-Hispanic/Latino; 0.3% Race/ethnicity unknown; 1% international; 7% transferred in; 28% live on campus.

Freshmen:
Admission: 17,104 applied, 13,972 admitted, 4,306 enrolled. ***Average high school GPA:*** 3.5. ***Test scores:*** ACT scores over 18: 98%; ACT scores over 24: 50%; ACT scores over 30: 7%.
Retention: 84% of full-time freshmen returned.

FACULTY
Total: 1,761, 66% full-time, 55% with terminal degrees.
Student/faculty ratio: 17:1.

ACADEMICS
Calendar: semesters. *Degrees:* certificates, bachelor's, master's, doctoral, post-master's, and postbachelor's certificates.
Special study options: academic remediation for entering students, accelerated degree program, adult/continuing education programs,

advanced placement credit, cooperative education, distance learning, double majors, English as a second language, freshman honors college, honors programs, independent study, internships, part-time degree program, services for LD students, study abroad, summer session for credit.

Computers: 2,600 computers/terminals are available on campus for general student use. Students can access the following: campus intranet, computer help desk, free student e-mail accounts, online (class) grades, online (class) registration, online (class) schedules, transcript, degree audit, credit card payments. Campuswide network is available. 100% of college-owned or -operated housing units are wired for high-speed Internet access. Wireless service is available via entire campus.

Library: Mary Idema Pew Library Learning and Information Commons plus 5 others. *Books:* 567,197 (physical), 1.0 million (digital/electronic). Students can reserve study rooms.

STUDENT LIFE

Housing options: coed. Campus housing is university owned. Freshman campus housing is guaranteed.

Activities and organizations: drama/theater group, student-run newspaper, radio and television station, choral group, marching band, Habitat for Humanity, Alternative Breaks, Hospitality and tourism Management Club, Dance Troupe, Colleges Against Cancer, national fraternities, national sororities.

Athletics Member NCAA. All Division II. ***Intercollegiate sports:*** baseball M(s), basketball M(s)/W(s), cheerleading M(c)/W(c), crew M(c)/W(c), cross-country running M(s)/W(s), football M(s), golf M(s)/W(s), ice hockey M/W, lacrosse M(c)/W, rowing M/W, rugby M(c)/W(c), sailing M(c)/W(c), skiing (downhill) M(c)/W(c), soccer M(c)/W(s), softball W(s), swimming and diving M(s)/W(s), tennis M(s)/W(s), track and field M(s)/W(s), volleyball M(c)/W(s), water polo M(c)/W(c), wrestling M(c). ***Intramural sports:*** archery M/W, basketball M/W, bowling M/W, cheerleading M/W, crew M/W, cross-country running M/W, fencing M/W, field hockey M/W, football M, golf M/W, gymnastics M/W, lacrosse M/W, racquetball M/W, skiing (cross-country) M/W, skiing (downhill) M/W, soccer M/W, softball M/W, squash M/W, swimming and diving M/W, tennis M/W, volleyball M/W, water polo M/W, weight lifting M/W, wrestling M.

Campus security: 24-hour emergency response devices and patrols, student patrols, late-night transport/escort service, controlled dormitory access.

Student services: health clinic, personal/psychological counseling, women's center.

COSTS & FINANCIAL AID

Costs (2016–17) ***Tuition:*** state resident $11,520 full-time, $506 per credit hour part-time; nonresident $16,392 full-time, $709 per credit hour part-time. Full-time tuition and fees vary according to course level, course load, program, and student level. Part-time tuition and fees vary according to course level, course load, program, and student level. ***Room and board:*** $8400. Room and board charges vary according to board plan and housing facility. ***Payment plans:*** installment, deferred payment. ***Waivers:*** employees or children of employees.

Financial Aid Of all full-time matriculated undergraduates who enrolled in 2016, 15,826 applied for aid, 11,301 were judged to have need, 2,001 had their need fully met. 1,302 Federal Work-Study jobs (averaging $2526). In 2016, 3352 non-need-based awards were made. ***Average percent of need met:*** 69. ***Average financial aid package:*** $9698. ***Average need-based loan:*** $4055. ***Average need-based gift aid:*** $6699. ***Average non-need-based aid:*** $3256. ***Average indebtedness upon graduation:*** $29,675.

APPLYING

Standardized Tests *Required:* SAT or ACT (for admission).

Options: electronic application.

Application fee: $30.

Required: high school transcript. ***Required for some:*** essay or personal statement, interview.

Application deadlines: 5/1 (freshmen), 7/24 (transfers).

Notification: 5/1 (freshmen), continuous (transfers).

CONTACT

Ms. Jodi Chycinski, Director of Admissions, Grand Valley State University, 1 Campus Drive, Allendale, MI 49401. *Phone:* 616-331-2025. *Toll-free phone:* 800-748-0246. *Fax:* 616-331-2000. *E-mail:* go2gvsu@gvsu.edu.

Great Lakes Christian College

Lansing, Michigan

http://www.glcc.edu/

CONTACT

Mrs. Judy Carter, Admissions Office Manager, Great Lakes Christian College, 6211 West Willow Highway, Lansing, MI 48917-1299. *Phone:* 517-321-0242 Ext. 221. *Toll-free phone:* 800-YES-GLCC. *Fax:* 517-321-5902. *E-mail:* jcarter@glcc.edu.

Hillsdale College

Hillsdale, Michigan

http://www.hillsdale.edu/

- **Independent** comprehensive, founded 1844
- **Small-town** 400-acre campus
- **Endowment** $458.6 million
- **Coed** 1,486 undergraduate students, 97% full-time, 50% women, 50% men
- **Very difficult** entrance level, 45% of applicants were admitted

UNDERGRAD STUDENTS

1,440 full-time, 46 part-time. Students come from 48 states and territories; 13 other countries; 65% are from out of state; 100% Race/ethnicity unknown; 0.8% transferred in; 69% live on campus.

Freshmen:

Admission: 1,934 applied, 874 admitted, 364 enrolled. ***Average high school GPA:*** 3.77. ***Test scores:*** SAT critical reading scores over 500: 98%; SAT math scores over 500: 95%; SAT writing scores over 500: 100%; ACT scores over 18: 100%; SAT critical reading scores over 600: 87%; SAT math scores over 600: 70%; SAT writing scores over 600: 80%; ACT scores over 24: 99%; SAT critical reading scores over 700: 45%; SAT math scores over 700: 24%; SAT writing scores over 700: 34%; ACT scores over 30: 59%.

Retention: 94% of full-time freshmen returned.

FACULTY

Total: 173, 73% full-time, 88% with terminal degrees.

Student/faculty ratio: 10:1.

ACADEMICS

Calendar: semesters. *Degrees:* bachelor's, master's, and doctoral.

Special study options: advanced placement credit, double majors, honors programs, independent study, internships, off-campus study, part-time degree program, student-designed majors, study abroad, summer session for credit.

Unusual degree programs: 3-2 engineering.

Computers: 181 computers/terminals and 1,228 ports are available on campus for general student use. Students can access the following: campus intranet, computer help desk, free student e-mail accounts, online (class) grades, online (class) registration, online (class) schedules. Campuswide network is available. 95% of college-owned or -operated housing units are wired for high-speed Internet access. Wireless service is available via entire campus.

Library: Michael Alex Mossey Library. *Books:* 268,001 (physical), 1.6 million (digital/electronic); *Serial titles:* 570 (physical), 86,771 (digital/electronic); *Databases:* 235. Weekly public service hours: 108.

STUDENT LIFE

Housing options: on-campus residence required through sophomore year; men-only, women-only, cooperative. Campus housing is university owned. Freshman campus housing is guaranteed.

Activities and organizations: drama/theater group, student-run newspaper, radio station, choral group, College Republicans, InterVarsity, Students for Life, American Chemical Society, PRAXIS - Political Economy Club, national fraternities, national sororities.

Athletics Member NCAA. All Division II. ***Intercollegiate sports:*** baseball M(s), basketball M(s)/W(s), cheerleading W(c), crew M(c)/W(c), cross-country running M(s)/W(s), equestrian sports M(c)/W(c), football M(s), golf M(s), riflery M(s)/W(s), rugby M(c), soccer M(c)/W(c), softball W(s), swimming and diving M(c)/W(s), tennis M(s)/W(s), track and field M(s)/W(s), volleyball M(c)/W(s). ***Intramural sports:*** basketball M/W, cheerleading W(c), football M/W, golf M, racquetball M/W, rugby M(c), soccer M/W, swimming and diving M(c), table tennis M/W, volleyball M/W.

Campus security: 24-hour emergency response devices and patrols, student patrols, late-night transport/escort service, controlled dormitory access.

Student services: health clinic, personal/psychological counseling.

COSTS & FINANCIAL AID

Costs (2016–17) ***One-time required fee:*** $300. ***Comprehensive fee:*** $35,722 includes full-time tuition ($24,670), mandatory fees ($852), and room and board ($10,200). Full-time tuition and fees vary according to degree level. Part-time tuition: $985 per credit hour. Part-time tuition and fees vary according to degree level. ***Required fees:*** $85 per credit hour part-time, $852 per year part-time. ***College room only:*** $5040. Room and board charges vary according to board plan. ***Payment plan:*** installment. ***Waivers:*** children of alumni and employees or children of employees.

Financial Aid Of all full-time matriculated undergraduates who enrolled in 2016, 817 applied for aid, 779 were judged to have need, 320 had their need fully met. In 2016, 677 non-need-based awards were made. ***Average percent of need met:*** 65. ***Average financial aid package:*** $15,776. ***Average need-based loan:*** $5701. ***Average need-based gift aid:*** $7275. ***Average non-need-based aid:*** $13,159. ***Average indebtedness upon graduation:*** $26,941.

APPLYING

Standardized Tests *Required:* SAT or ACT (for admission). *Recommended:* SAT Subject Tests (for admission).

Options: electronic application, early admission, early decision.

Application fee: $35.

Required: essay or personal statement, high school transcript, 2 letters of recommendation. ***Recommended:*** minimum 3.5 GPA, interview, campus visit, college prep courses.

Application deadlines: 4/1 (freshmen), 4/1 (transfers).

Early decision deadline: 11/1.

Notification: continuous (freshmen), continuous (transfers), 12/1 (early decision).

CONTACT

Mr. Douglas Banbury, Vice President Admissions, Hillsdale College, 33 East College Street, Hillsdale, MI 49242-1298. *Phone:* 517-607-2327. *Fax:* 517-607-2223. *E-mail:* admissions@hillsdale.edu.

See below for display ad and page 1376 for the College Close-Up.

Hope College

Holland, Michigan

http://www.hope.edu/

- **Independent** 4-year, founded 1866, affiliated with Reformed Church in America
- **Suburban** 91-acre campus with easy access to Grand Rapids
- **Endowment** $18.6 billion
- **Coed** 3,234 undergraduate students, 94% full-time, 61% women, 39% men
- **Moderately difficult** entrance level, 84% of applicants were admitted

UNDERGRAD STUDENTS

3,039 full-time, 195 part-time. Students come from 40 states and territories; 29 other countries; 30% are from out of state; 3% Black or African American, non-Hispanic/Latino; 9% Hispanic/Latino; 2% Asian, non-Hispanic/Latino; 2% Two or more races, non-Hispanic/Latino; 0.3% Race/ethnicity unknown; 2% international; 2% transferred in; 88% live on campus.

Freshmen:

Admission: 3,899 applied, 3,291 admitted, 727 enrolled. ***Average high school GPA:*** 3.7. ***Test scores:*** SAT critical reading scores over 500: 75%; SAT math scores over 500: 77%; ACT scores over 18: 99%; SAT critical reading scores over 600: 42%; SAT math scores over 600: 46%; ACT scores over 24: 71%; SAT critical reading scores over 700: 7%; SAT math scores over 700: 9%; ACT scores over 30: 21%.

Retention: 91% of full-time freshmen returned.

FACULTY
Total: 357, 66% full-time.

Student/faculty ratio: 11:1.

ACADEMICS
Calendar: semesters. *Degree:* bachelor's.

Special study options: advanced placement credit, double majors, English as a second language, external degree program, independent study, internships, off-campus study, part-time degree program, services for LD students, student-designed majors, study abroad, summer session for credit. ***ROTC:*** Army (c).

Computers: 300 computers/terminals and 5,000 ports are available on campus for general student use. Students can access the following: campus intranet, computer help desk, free student e-mail accounts, online (class) grades, online (class) registration, online (class) schedules. Campuswide network is available. 100% of college-owned or -operated housing units are wired for high-speed Internet access. Wireless service is available via entire campus.

Library: Van Wylen Library plus 2 others. *Books:* 235,059 (physical), 414,858 (digital/electronic); *Serial titles:* 6,511 (physical), 69,156 (digital/electronic); *Databases:* 203. Weekly public service hours: 96.

STUDENT LIFE
Housing options: on-campus residence required through junior year; coed, men-only, women-only, special housing for students with disabilities. Campus housing is university owned and leased by the school. Freshman campus housing is guaranteed.

Activities and organizations: drama/theater group, student-run newspaper, radio station, choral group, Social Activities Committee, Greek Life, Dance Marathon, Hockey Club, Relay for Life, national fraternities, national sororities.

Athletics Member NCAA. All Division III. ***Intercollegiate sports:*** baseball M, basketball M/W, cheerleading M/W, cross-country running M/W, football M, golf M/W, ice hockey M(c), lacrosse M/W, sailing M(c)/W(c), soccer M/W, softball W, swimming and diving M/W, tennis M/W, track and field M/W, volleyball W. ***Intramural sports:*** badminton M/W, basketball M/W, football M/W, ice hockey M(c), rugby M(c), sailing M(c)/W(c), soccer M/W, softball M/W, tennis M/W, ultimate Frisbee M/W, volleyball M/W, water polo M/W.

Campus security: 24-hour emergency response devices and patrols, late-night transport/escort service, controlled dormitory access.

Student services: health clinic, personal/psychological counseling.

COSTS & FINANCIAL AID
Costs (2016–17) ***Comprehensive fee:*** $41,250 includes full-time tuition ($31,380), mandatory fees ($180), and room and board ($9690). Part-time tuition: $1207 per semester hour. Part-time tuition and fees vary according to course load and program. ***College room only:*** $4450. Room and board charges vary according to board plan. ***Payment plan:*** installment. ***Waivers:*** employees or children of employees.

Financial Aid Of all full-time matriculated undergraduates who enrolled in 2016, 2,084 applied for aid, 1,706 were judged to have need, 417 had their need fully met. 145 Federal Work-Study jobs (averaging $2111). 567 state and other part-time jobs (averaging $1152). In 2016, 875 non-need-based awards were made. ***Average percent of need met:*** 80. ***Average financial aid package:*** $25,792. ***Average need-based loan:*** $5134. ***Average need-based gift aid:*** $19,244. ***Average non-need-based aid:*** $8527. ***Average indebtedness upon graduation:*** $33,969.

APPLYING
Standardized Tests *Required:* SAT or ACT (for admission).

Options: electronic application, early admission, deferred entrance.

Application fee: $35.

Required: essay or personal statement, high school transcript. ***Required for some:*** 1 letter of recommendation. ***Recommended:*** interview.

Application deadlines: rolling (freshmen), rolling (transfers).

Notification: continuous (freshmen), continuous (transfers).

CONTACT
Admissions Office, Hope College, 69 East 10th Street, PO Box 9000, Holland, MI 49422-9000. *Phone:* 616-395-7850. *Toll-free phone:* 800-968-7850. *E-mail:* admissions@hope.edu.

Kalamazoo College

Kalamazoo, Michigan

http://www.kzoo.edu/

- **Independent** 4-year, founded 1833, affiliated with American Baptist Churches in the U.S.A.
- **Urban** 60-acre campus with easy access to Grand Rapids
- **Endowment** $206.8 million
- **Coed** 1,443 undergraduate students, 100% full-time, 56% women, 44% men
- **Very difficult** entrance level, 66% of applicants were admitted

UNDERGRAD STUDENTS
1,437 full-time, 6 part-time. Students come from 43 states and territories; 30 other countries; 33% are from out of state; 6% Black or African American, non-Hispanic/Latino; 10% Hispanic/Latino; 7% Asian, non-Hispanic/Latino; 0.1% Native Hawaiian or other Pacific Islander, non-Hispanic/Latino; 0.1% American Indian or Alaska Native, non-Hispanic/Latino; 5% Two or more races, non-Hispanic/Latino; 5% Race/ethnicity unknown; 9% international; 1% transferred in; 65% live on campus.

Freshmen:
Admission: 3,626 applied, 2,381 admitted, 347 enrolled. ***Average high school GPA:*** 3.73. ***Test scores:*** SAT critical reading scores over 500: 86%; SAT math scores over 500: 90%; SAT writing scores over 500: 84%; ACT scores over 18: 99%; SAT critical reading scores over 600: 52%; SAT math scores over 600: 64%; SAT writing scores over 600: 60%; ACT scores over 24: 89%; SAT critical reading scores over 700: 14%; SAT math scores over 700: 22%; SAT writing scores over 700: 16%; ACT scores over 30: 36%.

Retention: 88% of full-time freshmen returned.

FACULTY
Total: 125, 84% full-time, 85% with terminal degrees.

Student/faculty ratio: 13:1.

ACADEMICS
Calendar: quarters. *Degree:* bachelor's.

Special study options: advanced placement credit, double majors, independent study, internships, off-campus study, services for LD students, student-designed majors, study abroad. ***ROTC:*** Army (c).

Unusual degree programs: 3-2 engineering with University of Michigan, Washington University in St. Louis.

Computers: 250 computers/terminals are available on campus for general student use. Students can access the following: campus intranet, computer help desk, free student e-mail accounts, online (class) grades, online (class) registration, online (class) schedules, residential computer consultant. Campuswide network is available. 100% of college-owned or -operated housing units are wired for high-speed Internet access. Wireless service is available via entire campus.

Library: Upjohn Library Commons. Weekly public service hours: 114; students can reserve study rooms.

STUDENT LIFE
Housing options: on-campus residence required through junior year; coed, special housing for students with disabilities. Campus housing is university owned. Freshman campus housing is guaranteed.

Activities and organizations: drama/theater group, student-run newspaper, radio station, choral group, Cirque du K, Acappella groups, Food Recovery Network, Women of Color, Swing Club.

Athletics Member NCAA. All Division III. ***Intercollegiate sports:*** baseball M, basketball M/W, cross-country running M/W, football M, golf M/W, lacrosse M/W, soccer M/W, softball W, swimming and diving M/W, tennis M/W, volleyball W. ***Intramural sports:*** badminton M/W, basketball M/W, cheerleading M(c)/W(c), lacrosse M(c)/W(c), racquetball M/W, soccer M/W, softball M/W, table tennis M/W, tennis M/W, ultimate Frisbee M(c)/W(c), volleyball M/W.

Campus security: 24-hour emergency response devices and patrols, late-night transport/escort service, controlled dormitory access.

Student services: health clinic, personal/psychological counseling.

COSTS & FINANCIAL AID
Costs (2017–18) ***Comprehensive fee:*** $56,082 includes full-time tuition ($46,350), mandatory fees ($342), and room and board ($9390). Full-time

tuition and fees vary according to course load. Part-time tuition and fees vary according to course load. ***College room only:*** $4680. Room and board charges vary according to board plan and housing facility. ***Payment plan:*** installment. ***Waivers:*** employees or children of employees.

Financial Aid Of all full-time matriculated undergraduates who enrolled in 2016, 1,083 applied for aid, 970 were judged to have need, 394 had their need fully met. In 2016, 399 non-need-based awards were made. ***Average percent of need met:*** 92. ***Average financial aid package:*** $37,979. ***Average need-based loan:*** $6214. ***Average need-based gift aid:*** $29,998. ***Average non-need-based aid:*** $19,558. ***Average indebtedness upon graduation:*** $27,653.

APPLYING

Options: electronic application, early decision, early action, deferred entrance.

Required: essay or personal statement, high school transcript, 2 letters of recommendation. ***Recommended:*** minimum 3.0 GPA, interview.

Application deadlines: 1/15 (freshmen), 5/1 (transfers), 11/1 (early action).

Early decision deadline: 11/1 (for plan 1), 2/15 (for plan 2).

Notification: 4/1 (freshmen), 5/15 (transfers), 12/1 (early decision plan 1), 3/1 (early decision plan 2), 12/20 (early action).

CONTACT

Kathy Gustafson, Records Associate, Kalamazoo College, Mandelle Hall, 1200 Academy Street, Kalamazoo, MI 49006-3295. *Phone:* 269-337-5759. *Toll-free phone:* 800-253-3602. *Fax:* 269-337-7390. *E-mail:* admission.records@kzoo.edu.

★ Kettering University
Flint, Michigan
http://www.kettering.edu/

- **Independent** comprehensive, founded 1919
- **Urban** 85-acre campus with easy access to Detroit
- **Endowment** $81.3 million
- **Coed** 1,741 undergraduate students, 92% full-time, 18% women, 82% men
- **Very difficult** entrance level, 72% of applicants were admitted

UNDERGRAD STUDENTS

1,608 full-time, 133 part-time. Students come from 39 states and territories; 18 other countries; 18% are from out of state; 4% Black or African American, non-Hispanic/Latino; 3% Hispanic/Latino; 3% Asian, non-Hispanic/Latino; 0.1% Native Hawaiian or other Pacific Islander, non-Hispanic/Latino; 0.2% American Indian or Alaska Native, non-Hispanic/Latino; 3% Two or more races, non-Hispanic/Latino; 6% Race/ethnicity unknown; 7% international; 2% transferred in; 34% live on campus.

Freshmen:

Admission: 1,587 applied, 1,137 admitted, 364 enrolled. ***Average high school GPA:*** 3.65. ***Test scores:*** SAT critical reading scores over 500: 85%; SAT math scores over 500: 100%; ACT scores over 18: 100%; SAT critical reading scores over 600: 42%; SAT math scores over 600: 73%; ACT scores over 24: 87%; SAT critical reading scores over 700: 4%; SAT math scores over 700: 11%; ACT scores over 30: 23%.

Retention: 92% of full-time freshmen returned.

FACULTY

Total: 134, 89% full-time, 75% with terminal degrees.

Student/faculty ratio: 13:1.

ACADEMICS

Calendar: semesters (11 weeks of full-time study plus 12 weeks of paid co-op experience per semester). *Degrees:* bachelor's and master's.

Special study options: advanced placement credit, cooperative education, distance learning, double majors, external degree program, independent

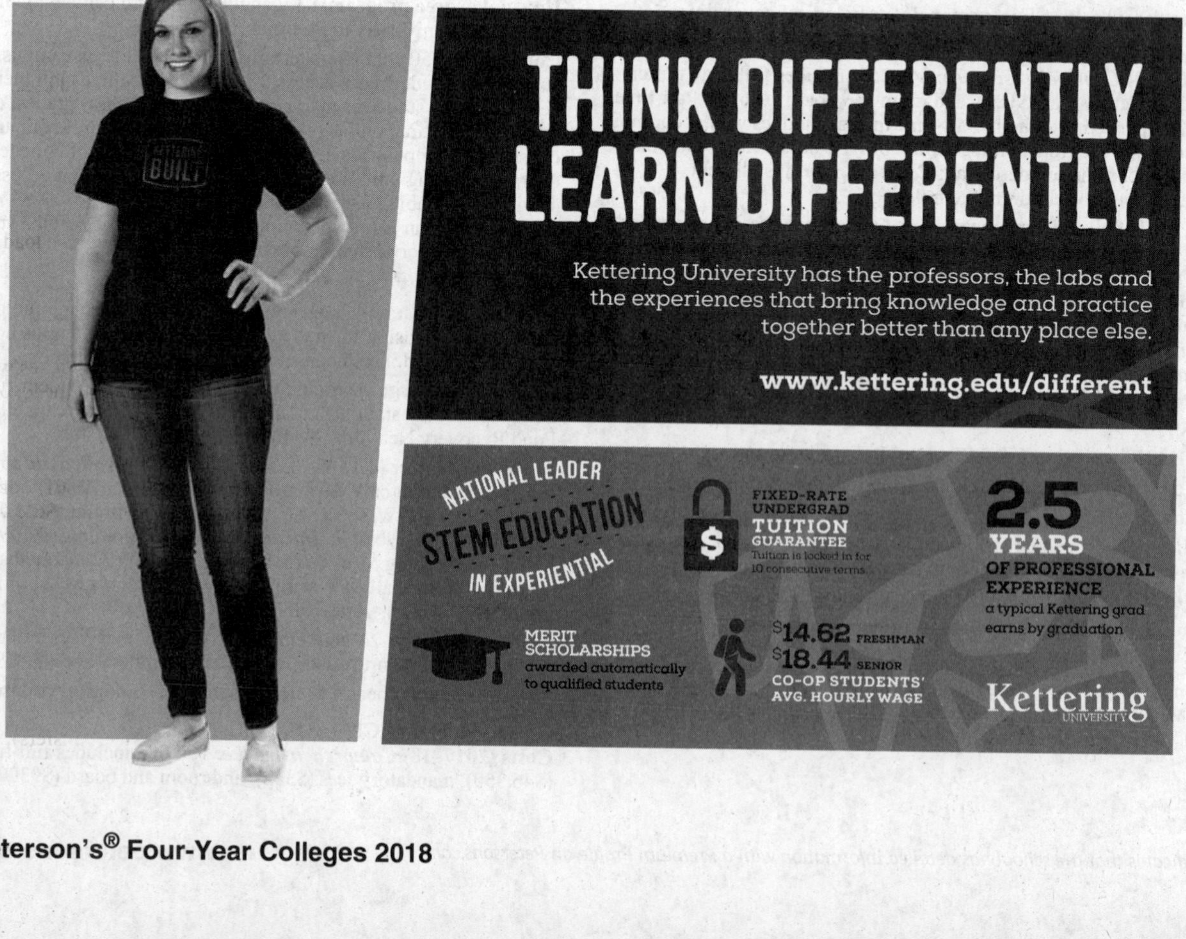

study, internships, services for LD students, study abroad, summer session for credit.

Computers: 450 computers/terminals and 800 ports are available on campus for general student use. Students can access the following: campus intranet, computer help desk, free student e-mail accounts, online (class) grades, online (class) registration, online (class) schedules. Campuswide network is available. 100% of college-owned or -operated housing units are wired for high-speed Internet access. Wireless service is available via entire campus.

Library: Kettering University Library.

STUDENT LIFE

Housing options: on-campus residence required for freshman year; coed. Campus housing is university owned and is provided by a third party. Freshman campus housing is guaranteed.

Activities and organizations: student-run newspaper, radio station, choral group, Student Government, Dance Club, Firebirds, Outdoors Club, International Club, national fraternities, national sororities.

Athletics ***Intramural sports:*** baseball M(c)/W(c), basketball M/W, bowling M/W, football M/W, golf M(c)/W(c), ice hockey M(c)/W(c), lacrosse M(c)/W(c), racquetball M/W, riflery M(c)/W(c), soccer M/W, softball M/W, squash M/W, table tennis M(c)/W(c), tennis M/W, ultimate Frisbee M(c)/W(c), volleyball M/W, water polo M/W.

Campus security: 24-hour emergency response devices and patrols, late-night transport/escort service, controlled dormitory access, security card access to all campus buildings 24/7 except the campus center main entrance which is secure 11pm-7am.

Student services: health clinic, personal/psychological counseling, women's center.

COSTS & FINANCIAL AID

Costs (2016–17) ***Comprehensive fee:*** $47,570 includes full-time tuition ($39,790) and room and board ($7780). No tuition increase for student's term of enrollment. ***Payment plan:*** installment. ***Waivers:*** employees or children of employees.

Financial Aid Of all full-time matriculated undergraduates who enrolled in 2015, 1,747 applied for aid, 1,306 were judged to have need, 129 had their need fully met. In 2015, 446 non-need-based awards were made. ***Average percent of need met:*** 63. ***Average financial aid package:*** $21,047. ***Average need-based loan:*** $4336. ***Average need-based gift aid:*** $16,951. ***Average non-need-based aid:*** $13,804.

APPLYING

Standardized Tests *Required:* SAT or ACT (for admission).

Options: electronic application, deferred entrance.

Required: high school transcript. ***Required for some:*** essay or personal statement. ***Recommended:*** minimum 3.0 GPA, interview.

Application deadlines: rolling (freshmen), rolling (out-of-state freshmen), rolling (transfers).

Notification: continuous (freshmen), continuous (out-of-state freshmen), continuous (transfers).

CONTACT

Mr. Kip Darcy, Vice President of Marketing, Communications and Enrollment, Kettering University, 1700 University Avenue, Flint, MI 48504-6214. *Phone:* 810-762-9511. *Toll-free phone:* 800-955-4464 Ext. 7865 (in-state); 800-955-4464 (out-of-state). *Fax:* 810-762-9837. *E-mail:* kdarcy@kettering.edu.

See previous page for display ad and page 1386 for the College Close-Up.

Kuyper College

Grand Rapids, Michigan

http://www.kuyper.edu/

- **Independent Christian** 4-year, founded 1939
- **Suburban** 34-acre campus with easy access to Grand Rapids
- **Endowment** $7.4 million
- **Coed** 208 undergraduate students, 81% full-time, 62% women, 38% men
- **Moderately difficult** entrance level, 73% of applicants were admitted

UNDERGRAD STUDENTS

168 full-time, 40 part-time. Students come from 14 states and territories; 6 other countries; 8% are from out of state; 3% Black or African American, non-Hispanic/Latino; 0.5% Hispanic/Latino; 3% Asian, non-Hispanic/Latino; 0.5% American Indian or Alaska Native, non-Hispanic/Latino; 4% Two or more races, non-Hispanic/Latino; 3% Race/ethnicity unknown; 3% international; 7% transferred in; 42% live on campus.

Freshmen:

Admission: 154 applied, 113 admitted, 38 enrolled. ***Average high school GPA:*** 3.3. ***Test scores:*** ACT scores over 18: 79%; ACT scores over 24: 21%; ACT scores over 30: 3%.

Retention: 63% of full-time freshmen returned.

FACULTY

Total: 41, 32% full-time, 29% with terminal degrees.

Student/faculty ratio: 12:1.

ACADEMICS

Calendar: semesters. *Degrees:* certificates, associate, bachelor's, and postbachelor's certificates.

Special study options: academic remediation for entering students, advanced placement credit, cooperative education, double majors, independent study, internships, off-campus study, part-time degree program, services for LD students, student-designed majors, study abroad, summer session for credit. ***ROTC:*** Army (c).

Computers: 70 computers/terminals and 70 ports are available on campus for general student use. Students can access the following: campus intranet, computer help desk, free student e-mail accounts, online (class) grades, online (class) registration, online (class) schedules. Campuswide network is available. 100% of college-owned or -operated housing units are wired for high-speed Internet access. Wireless service is available via entire campus.

Library: Zondervan Library plus 1 other. *Books:* 78,702 (physical), 14,199 (digital/electronic); *Databases:* 101. Weekly public service hours: 72; students can reserve study rooms.

STUDENT LIFE

Housing options: on-campus residence required through sophomore year; coed. Campus housing is university owned. Freshman campus housing is guaranteed.

Activities and organizations: drama/theater group, choral group, intramurals, Student Activities Club, Helping and Nurturing During Service, Yearbook, Roots.

Athletics ***Intramural sports:*** basketball M/W, soccer M/W, softball M/W, table tennis M/W, ultimate Frisbee M/W, volleyball M/W.

Campus security: 24-hour emergency response devices, student patrols, late-night transport/escort service, controlled dormitory access.

Student services: health clinic, personal/psychological counseling.

COSTS & FINANCIAL AID

Costs (2016–17) ***One-time required fee:*** $554. ***Comprehensive fee:*** $27,102 includes full-time tuition ($19,718), mandatory fees ($584), and room and board ($6800). Full-time tuition and fees vary according to course load and reciprocity agreements. Part-time tuition: $945 per credit hour. Part-time tuition and fees vary according to course load and reciprocity agreements. ***Required fees:*** $295 per year part-time. ***Room and board:*** Room and board charges vary according to board plan, housing facility, and student level. ***Payment plans:*** installment, deferred payment. ***Waivers:*** employees or children of employees.

Financial Aid Of all full-time matriculated undergraduates who enrolled in 2016, 156 applied for aid, 140 were judged to have need, 6 had their need fully met. 19 Federal Work-Study jobs (averaging $1737). 100 state and other part-time jobs (averaging $3226). In 2016, 25 non-need-based awards were made. ***Average percent of need met:*** 69. ***Average financial aid package:*** $15,300. ***Average need-based loan:*** $4661. ***Average need-based gift aid:*** $11,984. ***Average non-need-based aid:*** $6574. ***Average indebtedness upon graduation:*** $25,906.

APPLYING

Standardized Tests *Required:* SAT or ACT (for admission).

Options: electronic application, deferred entrance.

Required: essay or personal statement, high school transcript, minimum 2.5 GPA. ***Recommended:*** interview.

Application deadlines: rolling (freshmen), rolling (transfers).

Notification: continuous (freshmen), continuous (transfers).

CONTACT
Admissions Office, Kuyper College, 3333 East Beltline Avenue, NE, Grand Rapids, MI 49525. *Phone:* 616-222-3000 Ext. 632. *Fax:* 616-222-3045. *E-mail:* admissions@kuyper.edu.

Lake Superior State University

Sault Sainte Marie, Michigan

http://www.lssu.edu/

CONTACT
Lake Superior State University, 650 West Easterday Avenue, Sault Sainte Marie, MI 49783. *Phone:* 906-635-2231. *Toll-free phone:* 888-800-LSSU Ext. 2231.

★ Lawrence Technological University

Southfield, Michigan

http://www.ltu.edu/

- **Independent** university, founded 1932
- **Suburban** 107-acre campus with easy access to Detroit
- **Endowment** $67.7 million
- **Coed** 2,164 undergraduate students, 79% full-time, 28% women, 72% men
- **Moderately difficult** entrance level, 69% of applicants were admitted

UNDERGRAD STUDENTS
1,711 full-time, 453 part-time. Students come from 33 states and territories; 52 other countries; 6% are from out of state; 7% Black or African American, non-Hispanic/Latino; 4% Hispanic/Latino; 3% Asian, non-Hispanic/Latino; 0.3% American Indian or Alaska Native, non-Hispanic/Latino; 2% Two or more races, non-Hispanic/Latino; 2% Race/ethnicity unknown; 16% international; 7% transferred in; 35% live on campus.

Freshmen:
Admission: 2,318 applied, 1,607 admitted, 375 enrolled. ***Average high school GPA:*** 3.5. ***Test scores:*** SAT critical reading scores over 500: 70%; SAT math scores over 500: 85%; SAT writing scores over 500: 72%; ACT scores over 18: 89%; SAT critical reading scores over 600: 30%; SAT math scores over 600: 61%; SAT writing scores over 600: 19%; ACT scores over 24: 57%; SAT critical reading scores over 700: 3%; SAT math scores over 700: 3%; ACT scores over 30: 20%.
Retention: 80% of full-time freshmen returned.

FACULTY
Total: 383, 32% full-time, 43% with terminal degrees.
Student/faculty ratio: 11:1.

ACADEMICS
Calendar: semesters. *Degrees:* certificates, associate, bachelor's, master's, doctoral, and postbachelor's certificates.
Special study options: academic remediation for entering students, accelerated degree program, adult/continuing education programs, advanced placement credit, cooperative education, distance learning, double majors, English as a second language, honors programs, independent study, internships, off-campus study, part-time degree program, services for LD students, study abroad, summer session for credit. ***ROTC:*** Air Force (c).
Computers: 72 computers/terminals and 3,618 ports are available on campus for general student use. Students can access the following: campus intranet, computer help desk, free student e-mail accounts, online (class) grades, online (class) registration, online (class) schedules, degree audit, learning management system, learning management system, personal websites, document collection, placement. Campuswide network is available. 100% of college-owned or -operated housing units are wired for high-speed Internet access. Wireless service is available via entire campus.
Library: Lawrence Technological University Library plus 1 other. *Books:* 64,982 (physical), 267,794 (digital/electronic); *Serial titles:* 1,829 (physical), 43,887 (digital/electronic); *Databases:* 171. Weekly public service hours: 73.

STUDENT LIFE
Housing options: coed, special housing for students with disabilities. Campus housing is university owned and is provided by a third party. Freshman applicants given priority for college housing.
Activities and organizations: drama/theater group, student-run newspaper, American Institute of Architecture Students, American Society of Mechanical Engineers, Sigma Phi Epsilon, American Society of Civil Engineers, Student Government, national fraternities, national sororities.
Athletics Member NAIA. ***Intercollegiate sports:*** basketball M(s)/W(s), bowling M(s)/W(s), cross-country running M(s)/W(s), golf M(s)/W(s), ice hockey M, lacrosse M(s)/W(s), soccer M(s)/W(s), tennis M(s)/W(s), volleyball W(s). ***Intramural sports:*** badminton M/W, basketball M/W, football M/W, ice hockey M(c), racquetball M/W, skiing (downhill) M/W, soccer M/W, softball M/W, table tennis M/W, tennis M/W, ultimate Frisbee M(c), volleyball M/W.
Campus security: 24-hour emergency response devices and patrols, late-night transport/escort service, controlled dormitory access.
Student services: personal/psychological counseling.

COSTS & FINANCIAL AID
Costs (2016–17) ***Comprehensive fee:*** $41,247 includes full-time tuition ($30,420), mandatory fees ($720), and room and board ($10,107). Full-time tuition and fees vary according to course level, degree level, location, program, and student level. Part-time tuition: $1014 per credit hour. Part-time tuition and fees vary according to course level, degree level, location, program, and student level. ***Required fees:*** $360 per term part-time. ***College room only:*** $5907. Room and board charges vary according to board plan and housing facility. ***Payment plan:*** installment. ***Waivers:*** employees or children of employees.
Financial Aid Of all full-time matriculated undergraduates who enrolled in 2015, 1,323 applied for aid, 987 were judged to have need, 163 had their need fully met. 101 Federal Work-Study jobs (averaging $1213). In 2015, 285 non-need-based awards were made. ***Average percent of need met:*** 69. ***Average financial aid package:*** $24,577. ***Average need-based loan:*** $7299. ***Average need-based gift aid:*** $14,835. ***Average non-need-based aid:*** $14,871. ***Average indebtedness upon graduation:*** $40,976.

APPLYING
Standardized Tests *Required:* SAT or ACT (for admission).
Options: electronic application, deferred entrance.
Application fee: $30.
Required: high school transcript, minimum 2.5 GPA. ***Required for some:*** essay or personal statement, minimum 2.8 GPA, 1 letter of recommendation, interview.
Application deadlines: 8/15 (freshmen), 8/15 (transfers).
Notification: continuous until 8/26 (freshmen), continuous until 8/26 (transfers).

CONTACT
Jane Rohrback, Director of Admissions, Lawrence Technological University, 21000 West Ten Mile Road, Southfield, MI 48075. *Phone:* 248-204-3160. *Toll-free phone:* 800-225-5588. *Fax:* 248-204-2228. *E-mail:* admissions@ltu.edu.

Madonna University

Livonia, Michigan

http://www.madonna.edu/

- **Independent Roman Catholic** comprehensive, founded 1947
- **Suburban** 85-acre campus with easy access to Detroit
- **Endowment** $35.6 million
- **Coed** 2,629 undergraduate students, 51% full-time, 68% women, 32% men
- **Moderately difficult** entrance level, 60% of applicants were admitted

UNDERGRAD STUDENTS
1,353 full-time, 1,276 part-time. Students come from 9 states and territories; 40 other countries; 1% are from out of state; 12% Black or African American, non-Hispanic/Latino; 4% Hispanic/Latino; 1% Asian, non-Hispanic/Latino; 0.2% Native Hawaiian or other Pacific Islander, non-Hispanic/Latino; 2% Two or more races, non-Hispanic/Latino; 6% Race/ethnicity unknown; 15% international; 9% transferred in; 11% live on campus.

Freshmen:
Admission: 972 applied, 582 admitted, 219 enrolled. ***Average high school GPA:*** 3.1. ***Test scores:*** ACT scores over 18: 77%; ACT scores over 24: 24%; ACT scores over 30: 1%.

Retention: 82% of full-time freshmen returned.

FACULTY
Total: 271, 37% full-time, 41% with terminal degrees.

Student/faculty ratio: 11:1.

ACADEMICS
Calendar: semesters. *Degrees:* certificates, diplomas, associate, bachelor's, master's, doctoral, post-master's, and postbachelor's certificates.

Special study options: accelerated degree program, adult/continuing education programs, advanced placement credit, cooperative education, distance learning, double majors, English as a second language, independent study, internships, off-campus study, part-time degree program, services for LD students, student-designed majors, study abroad, summer session for credit. ***ROTC:*** Army (c).

Computers: 258 computers/terminals and 258 ports are available on campus for general student use. Students can access the following: campus intranet, computer help desk, free student e-mail accounts, online (class) grades, online (class) registration, online (class) schedules, online payments, online statements, online unofficial transcripts. Campuswide network is available. 100% of college-owned or -operated housing units are wired for high-speed Internet access. Wireless service is available via classrooms, computer labs, dorm rooms, learning centers, libraries, student centers.

Library: Madonna University Library. *Books:* 71,692 (physical), 166,462 (digital/electronic); *Serial titles:* 349 (physical), 59,430 (digital/electronic); *Databases:* 138. Weekly public service hours: 97; students can reserve study rooms.

STUDENT LIFE
Housing options: men-only, women-only. Campus housing is university owned. Freshman campus housing is guaranteed.

Activities and organizations: drama/theater group, student-run newspaper, radio and television station, choral group, Campus Ministry, Red Cross Club, Madonna University Nursing Student Association, Broadcast and Film Club, Society of Future Teachers.

Athletics Member NAIA. ***Intercollegiate sports:*** baseball M(s), basketball M(s)/W(s), bowling M(s)/W(s), cross-country running M(s)/W(s), golf M(s)/W(s), lacrosse M(s)/W(s), soccer M(s)/W(s), softball W(s), track and field M(s)/W(s), volleyball W(s).

Campus security: 24-hour emergency response devices and patrols, late-night transport/escort service, controlled dormitory access.

Student services: personal/psychological counseling.

COSTS & FINANCIAL AID
Costs (2017–18) ***Comprehensive fee:*** $30,450 includes full-time tuition ($20,700) and room and board ($9750). Full-time tuition and fees vary according to course load. Part-time tuition: $690 per credit hour. Part-time tuition and fees vary according to course load. ***College room only:*** $4800. Room and board charges vary according to board plan. ***Payment plan:*** deferred payment. ***Waivers:*** senior citizens and employees or children of employees.

Financial Aid Of all full-time matriculated undergraduates who enrolled in 2007, 862 applied for aid, 698 were judged to have need, 122 had their need fully met. In 2007, 172 non-need-based awards were made. ***Average percent of need met:*** 56. ***Average financial aid package:*** $7396. ***Average need-based loan:*** $3862. ***Average need-based gift aid:*** $4508. ***Average non-need-based aid:*** $2427.

APPLYING
Standardized Tests *Required:* SAT or ACT (for admission).

Options: electronic application, early decision, deferred entrance.

Application fee: $25.

Required: high school transcript. ***Required for some:*** essay or personal statement.

Application deadlines: rolling (freshmen), rolling (transfers).

Early decision deadline: 12/1.

Notification: continuous (freshmen), continuous (transfers), 1/15 (early decision).

CONTACT
Mr. Mark A. Schroeder, Director of Undergraduate Admissions, Madonna University, 36600 Schoolcraft Road, Livonia, MI 48150-1173. *Phone:* 734-432-5339. *Toll-free phone:* 800-852-4951. *Fax:* 734-432-5424. *E-mail:* mschroeder@madonna.edu.

Manthano Christian College

Westland, Michigan

http://www.manthanochristian.org/

CONTACT
Manthano Christian College, 6420 N. Newburgh, Westland, MI 48185-1919.

Marygrove College

Detroit, Michigan

http://www.marygrove.edu/

CONTACT
Mr. John Ambrose, Director of Undergraduate Admissions, Marygrove College, Admissions Office, Detroit, MI 48221-2599. *Phone:* 313-927-1236. *Toll-free phone:* 866-313-1297. *Fax:* 313-927-1345. *E-mail:* info@marygrove.edu.

Michigan State University

East Lansing, Michigan

http://www.msu.edu/

- **State-supported** university, founded 1855
- **Suburban** 5192-acre campus with easy access to Detroit
- **Endowment** $2.6 billion
- **Coed** 39,090 undergraduate students, 91% full-time, 51% women, 49% men
- **Moderately difficult** entrance level, 66% of applicants were admitted

UNDERGRAD STUDENTS
35,447 full-time, 3,643 part-time. Students come from 55 states and territories; 105 other countries; 14% are from out of state; 7% Black or African American, non-Hispanic/Latino; 4% Hispanic/Latino; 5% Asian, non-Hispanic/Latino; 0.1% Native Hawaiian or other Pacific Islander, non-Hispanic/Latino; 0.2% American Indian or Alaska Native, non-Hispanic/Latino; 3% Two or more races, non-Hispanic/Latino; 0.8% Race/ethnicity unknown; 12% international; 4% transferred in; 39% live on campus.

Freshmen:
Admission: 37,480 applied, 24,641 admitted, 8,190 enrolled. ***Average high school GPA:*** 3.7. ***Test scores:*** SAT critical reading scores over 500: 60%; SAT math scores over 500: 87%; SAT writing scores over 500: 63%; ACT scores over 18: 98%; SAT critical reading scores over 600: 24%; SAT math scores over 600: 54%; SAT writing scores over 600: 21%; ACT scores over 24: 77%; SAT critical reading scores over 700: 6%; SAT math scores over 700: 17%; SAT writing scores over 700: 3%; ACT scores over 30: 19%.

Retention: 92% of full-time freshmen returned.

FACULTY
Total: 2,938, 86% full-time, 85% with terminal degrees.

Student/faculty ratio: 17:1.

ACADEMICS
Calendar: semesters. *Degrees:* certificates, bachelor's, master's, doctoral, and post-master's certificates.

Special study options: academic remediation for entering students, accelerated degree program, adult/continuing education programs, advanced placement credit, cooperative education, distance learning, double majors, English as a second language, freshman honors college, honors programs, independent study, internships, off-campus study, part-time degree program, services for LD students, student-designed majors, study abroad, summer session for credit. ***ROTC:*** Army (b), Air Force (b).

Unusual degree programs: 3-2 engineering.

Computers: Students can access the following: campus intranet, computer help desk, free student e-mail accounts, online (class) grades, online (class) registration, online (class) schedules. Campuswide network is available. 100% of college-owned or -operated housing units are wired for high-speed Internet access. Wireless service is available via classrooms, computer centers, computer labs, dorm rooms, learning centers, libraries, student centers.
Library: Main Library plus 4 others.

STUDENT LIFE
Housing options: on-campus residence required for freshman year; coed, women-only, cooperative, special housing for students with disabilities. Campus housing is university owned. Freshman campus housing is guaranteed.

Activities and organizations: drama/theater group, student-run newspaper, radio and television station, choral group, marching band, national fraternities, national sororities.

Athletics Member NCAA. All Division I except football (Division I-A). ***Intercollegiate sports:*** baseball M(s), basketball M(s)/W(s), cheerleading M/W, crew M(c)/W(s), cross-country running M(s)/W(s), equestrian sports M(c)/W(c), fencing M(c)/W(c), field hockey W(s), golf M(s)/W(s), gymnastics W(s), ice hockey M(s)/W(c), lacrosse M(c)/W(c), rowing M(c)/W(s), rugby M(c)/W(c), sailing M(c)/W(c), soccer M(s)/W(s), softball W(s), swimming and diving M(s)/W(s), table tennis M(c)/W(c), tennis M(s)/W(s), track and field M(s)/W(s), volleyball M(c)/W(s), water polo M(c)/W(c), wrestling M(s). ***Intramural sports:*** baseball M(c), basketball M/W, cheerleading W(c), crew M(c)/W(c), football M/W, ice hockey M/W, racquetball M/W, riflery M/W, rowing M(c)/W(c), rugby M(c)/W(c), sand volleyball M/W, soccer M(c)/W(c), softball M/W, squash M/W, table tennis M/W, tennis M/W, ultimate Frisbee M(c)/W(c), volleyball M/W, water polo M/W.

Campus security: 24-hour emergency response devices and patrols, late-night transport/escort service, controlled dormitory access, self-defense workshops.

Student services: health clinic, personal/psychological counseling, women's center, legal services.

COSTS & FINANCIAL AID
Costs (2016–17) ***Tuition:*** state resident $14,063 full-time, $469 per credit hour part-time; nonresident $37,890 full-time, $1263 per credit hour part-time. Full-time tuition and fees vary according to course load, program, and student level. Part-time tuition and fees vary according to course load, program, and student level. ***Room and board:*** $9734; room only: $4020. Room and board charges vary according to board plan and housing facility. ***Payment plan:*** deferred payment. ***Waivers:*** employees or children of employees.

Financial Aid Of all full-time matriculated undergraduates who enrolled in 2016, 21,594 applied for aid, 16,641 were judged to have need, 2,285 had their need fully met. 1,690 Federal Work-Study jobs (averaging $1825). In 2016, 3042 non-need-based awards were made. ***Average percent of need met:*** 60. ***Average financial aid package:*** $13,202. ***Average need-based loan:*** $4003. ***Average need-based gift aid:*** $10,183. ***Average non-need-based aid:*** $9960.

APPLYING
Standardized Tests *Required:* SAT or ACT (for admission).

Options: electronic application, deferred entrance.

Application fee: $65.

Required: essay or personal statement, high school transcript.

Application deadlines: rolling (freshmen), rolling (transfers).

Notification: continuous (freshmen), continuous (transfers).

CONTACT
James Cotter, Director of Admissions, Michigan State University, 250 Administration Building, East Lansing, MI 48824. *Phone:* 517-355-8332. *Fax:* 517-353-1647. *E-mail:* admis@msu.edu.

Michigan Technological University
Houghton, Michigan
http://www.mtu.edu/

- **State-supported** university, founded 1885
- **Small-town** 925-acre campus
- **Endowment** $97.6 million
- **Coed** 5,829 undergraduate students, 94% full-time, 27% women, 73% men
- **Moderately difficult** entrance level, 76% of applicants were admitted

UNDERGRAD STUDENTS
5,460 full-time, 369 part-time. Students come from 43 states and territories; 34 other countries; 23% are from out of state; 0.9% Black or African American, non-Hispanic/Latino; 2% Hispanic/Latino; 1% Asian, non-Hispanic/Latino; 0.1% Native Hawaiian or other Pacific Islander, non-Hispanic/Latino; 0.3% American Indian or Alaska Native, non-Hispanic/Latino; 3% Two or more races, non-Hispanic/Latino; 2% Race/ethnicity unknown; 3% international; 3% transferred in; 47% live on campus.

Freshmen:
Admission: 5,589 applied, 4,272 admitted, 1,381 enrolled. ***Average high school GPA:*** 3.7. ***Test scores:*** SAT critical reading scores over 500: 78%; SAT math scores over 500: 92%; SAT writing scores over 500: 67%; ACT scores over 18: 100%; SAT critical reading scores over 600: 43%; SAT math scores over 600: 63%; SAT writing scores over 600: 30%; ACT scores over 24: 84%; SAT critical reading scores over 700: 18%; SAT math scores over 700: 17%; SAT writing scores over 700: 1%; ACT scores over 30: 27%.
Retention: 83% of full-time freshmen returned.

FACULTY
Total: 453, 90% full-time, 85% with terminal degrees.
Student/faculty ratio: 12:1.

ACADEMICS
Calendar: semesters. *Degrees:* certificates, associate, bachelor's, master's, doctoral, and postbachelor's certificates.

Special study options: accelerated degree program, advanced placement credit, cooperative education, distance learning, double majors, English as a second language, honors programs, independent study, internships, off-campus study, part-time degree program, services for LD students, study abroad, summer session for credit. ***ROTC:*** Army (b), Air Force (b).

Unusual degree programs: 3-2 engineering with Adrian College, Albion College, Augsburg College, Northland College, Olivet College, University of Wisconsin–Superior; forestry with Northland College, University of Wisconsin–Superior.

Computers: 1,079 computers/terminals and 6,082 ports are available on campus for general student use. Students can access the following: campus intranet, computer help desk, free student e-mail accounts, online (class) grades, online (class) registration, online (class) schedules. Campuswide network is available. 100% of college-owned or -operated housing units are wired for high-speed Internet access. Wireless service is available via entire campus.
Library: J. R. Van Pelt and John and Ruanne Opie Library. *Books:* 478,976 (physical), 133,000 (digital/electronic); *Databases:* 152. Weekly public service hours: 119; study areas open 24 hours, 5-7 days a week; students can reserve study rooms.

STUDENT LIFE
Housing options: on-campus residence required for freshman year; coed, special housing for students with disabilities. Campus housing is university owned. Freshman campus housing is guaranteed.

Activities and organizations: drama/theater group, student-run newspaper, radio station, choral group, Indian Students Associate, Society of Women Engineers, Huskies Pep Band, WMTU, Fishing Club, national fraternities, national sororities.

Athletics Member NCAA. All Division II except ice hockey (Division I). ***Intercollegiate sports:*** archery M(c)/W(c), badminton M(c)/W(c), baseball M(c), basketball M(s)/W(s), cheerleading M(c)/W(c), crew M(c)/W(c), cross-country running M(s)/W(s), fencing M(c)/W(c), football M(s), golf M(c)/W(c), gymnastics M(c)/W(c), ice hockey M(s)/W(c), lacrosse M(c)/W(c), racquetball M(c)/W(c), riflery M(c)/W(c), rugby M(c)/W(c), sailing M(c)/W(c), skiing (cross-country)

M(s)/W(s), skiing (downhill) M(c)/W(c), soccer M(c)/W(s), softball W(c), tennis M(s)/W(s), track and field M(s)/W(s), ultimate Frisbee M(c)/W(c), volleyball M(c)/W(s), water polo M(c)/W(c). ***Intramural sports:*** badminton M/W, basketball M/W, bowling M/W, golf M/W, ice hockey M/W, racquetball M/W, riflery M/W, sand volleyball M/W, soccer M/W, softball M/W, swimming and diving M/W, table tennis M/W, tennis M/W, ultimate Frisbee M/W, volleyball M/W, water polo M/W.

Campus security: 24-hour emergency response devices and patrols, late-night transport/escort service, controlled dormitory access.

Student services: health clinic, personal/psychological counseling, women's center.

COSTS & FINANCIAL AID

Costs (2016–17) ***Tuition:*** state resident $14,334 full-time, $542 per credit hour part-time; nonresident $30,668 full-time, $1136 per credit hour part-time. Full-time tuition and fees vary according to program and student level. Part-time tuition and fees vary according to course load, program, and student level. ***Required fees:*** $300 full-time, $150 per term part-time. ***Room and board:*** $10,105; room only: $5610. Room and board charges vary according to board plan and housing facility. ***Payment plans:*** installment, deferred payment. ***Waivers:*** children of alumni, senior citizens, and employees or children of employees.

Financial Aid Of all full-time matriculated undergraduates who enrolled in 2016, 4,317 applied for aid, 3,465 were judged to have need, 621 had their need fully met. 227 Federal Work-Study jobs (averaging $1477). In 2016, 1430 non-need-based awards were made. ***Average percent of need met:*** 73. ***Average financial aid package:*** $14,423. ***Average need-based loan:*** $4693. ***Average need-based gift aid:*** $7785. ***Average non-need-based aid:*** $5468. ***Average indebtedness upon graduation:*** $34,942.

APPLYING

Standardized Tests *Required:* SAT or ACT (for admission).

Options: electronic application, deferred entrance.

Required: high school transcript. ***Required for some:*** essay or personal statement, examples of creative work for some majors in Visual and Performing Arts Department. ***Recommended:*** minimum 2.8 GPA.

Application deadlines: rolling (freshmen), rolling (transfers).

Notification: continuous (freshmen), continuous (transfers).

CONTACT

Ms. Allison Carter, Director of Admissions, Michigan Technological University, 1400 Townsend Drive, Houghton, MI 49931-1295. *Phone:* 906-487-2335. *Toll-free phone:* 888-MTU-1885. *Fax:* 906-487-2125. *E-mail:* mtu4u@mtu.edu.

Northern Michigan University

Marquette, Michigan

http://www.nmu.edu/

CONTACT

Ms. Gerri Daniels, Director of Admissions, Northern Michigan University, 1401 Presque Isle Avenue, Marquette, MI 49855. *Phone:* 906-227-2650. *Toll-free phone:* 800-682-9797. *Fax:* 906-227-1747. *E-mail:* admiss@nmu.edu.

Northwestern Michigan College

Traverse City, Michigan

http://www.nmc.edu/

CONTACT

Catheryn Claerhout, Director of Admissions, Northwestern Michigan College, 1701 E. Front Street, Traverse City, MI 49686. *Phone:* 231-995-1034. *Toll-free phone:* 800-748-0566. *E-mail:* c.claerhout@nmc.edu.

Northwood University, Michigan Campus

Midland, Michigan

http://www.northwood.edu/

- **Independent** comprehensive, founded 1959
- **Small-town** 434-acre campus
- **Endowment** $31.1 million
- **Coed** 1,442 undergraduate students, 97% full-time, 36% women, 64% men
- **Moderately difficult** entrance level, 72% of applicants were admitted

UNDERGRAD STUDENTS

1,394 full-time, 48 part-time. Students come from 29 states and territories; 22 other countries; 13% are from out of state; 5% Black or African American, non-Hispanic/Latino; 3% Hispanic/Latino; 0.5% Asian, non-Hispanic/Latino; 0.4% Native Hawaiian or other Pacific Islander, non-Hispanic/Latino; 0.1% American Indian or Alaska Native, non-Hispanic/Latino; 2% Two or more races, non-Hispanic/Latino; 9% Race/ethnicity unknown; 7% international; 12% transferred in; 39% live on campus.

Freshmen:

Admission: 2,265 applied, 1,636 admitted, 321 enrolled. ***Average high school GPA:*** 3.23. ***Test scores:*** ACT scores over 18: 90%; ACT scores over 24: 36%; ACT scores over 30: 1%.

Retention: 78% of full-time freshmen returned.

FACULTY

Total: 155, 30% full-time, 31% with terminal degrees.

Student/faculty ratio: 20:1.

ACADEMICS

Calendar: semesters. *Degrees:* associate, bachelor's, and master's.

Special study options: academic remediation for entering students, accelerated degree program, adult/continuing education programs, advanced placement credit, cooperative education, distance learning, double majors, English as a second language, external degree program, honors programs, internships, off-campus study, part-time degree program, services for LD students, study abroad, summer session for credit.

Computers: 215 computers/terminals are available on campus for general student use. Students can access the following: campus intranet, computer help desk, free student e-mail accounts, online (class) grades, online (class) registration, online (class) schedules. Campuswide network is available. 100% of college-owned or -operated housing units are wired for high-speed Internet access. Wireless service is available via entire campus.

Library: Strosacker Library. *Books:* 29,908 (physical); *Databases:* 50. Weekly public service hours: 89; students can reserve study rooms.

STUDENT LIFE

Housing options: on-campus residence required for freshman year; coed, men-only, women-only, special housing for students with disabilities. Campus housing is university owned. Freshman campus housing is guaranteed.

Activities and organizations: drama/theater group, student-run newspaper, Student Senate, intramural sports/club sports, campus art, Northwood University International Auto Show (NUTAS), national fraternities, national sororities.

Athletics Member NCAA. All Division II. ***Intercollegiate sports:*** baseball M(s), basketball M(s)/W(s), cheerleading M(s)/W(s), cross-country running M(s)/W(s), football M(s), golf M(s)/W(s), soccer M(s)/W(s), softball W(s), tennis M(s)/W(s), track and field M(s)/W(s), volleyball W(s). ***Intramural sports:*** badminton M/W, baseball M(c), basketball M/W, football M, ice hockey M(c), lacrosse M(c), soccer M(c)/W, softball M/W, table tennis M/W, tennis M/W, ultimate Frisbee M/W, volleyball M/W.

Campus security: 24-hour emergency response devices and patrols, late-night transport/escort service, controlled dormitory access.

Student services: health clinic, personal/psychological counseling.

COSTS & FINANCIAL AID
Costs (2017–18) ***Comprehensive fee:*** $36,250 includes full-time tuition ($24,770), mandatory fees ($1310), and room and board ($10,170). Full-time tuition and fees vary according to course load. Part-time tuition: $953 per semester hour. Part-time tuition and fees vary according to course load. ***Room and board:*** Room and board charges vary according to board plan. ***Payment plan:*** installment. ***Waivers:*** employees or children of employees.

Financial Aid Of all full-time matriculated undergraduates who enrolled in 2013, 1,115 applied for aid, 996 were judged to have need, 219 had their need fully met. 99 Federal Work-Study jobs (averaging $1577). In 2013, 247 non-need-based awards were made. ***Average percent of need met:*** 62. ***Average financial aid package:*** $18,737. ***Average need-based loan:*** $4323. ***Average need-based gift aid:*** $5159. ***Average non-need-based aid:*** $8057. ***Average indebtedness upon graduation:*** $30,857.

APPLYING
Standardized Tests *Required:* SAT or ACT (for admission).

Options: electronic application, early admission, deferred entrance.

Application fee: $30.

Required: essay or personal statement, high school transcript, minimum 2.0 GPA. ***Recommended:*** 1 letter of recommendation, interview.

Application deadlines: 8/1 (freshmen), rolling (transfers).

Notification: continuous (freshmen), continuous (out-of-state freshmen), continuous (transfers).

CONTACT
Miss Heidi Schall, Director of Admission, Northwood University, Michigan Campus, 4000 Whiting Drive, Midland, MI 48640. *Phone:* 989-837-4342. *Toll-free phone:* 800-457-7878. *Fax:* 989-837-4490. *E-mail:* miadmit@northwood.edu.

Oakland University

Rochester, Michigan

http://www.oakland.edu/

- **State-supported** university, founded 1957
- **Suburban** 1444-acre campus with easy access to Detroit
- **Endowment** $79.0 million
- **Coed**
- **Moderately difficult** entrance level

FACULTY
Student/faculty ratio: 21:1.

ACADEMICS
Calendar: semesters. *Degrees:* bachelor's, master's, doctoral, post-master's, and postbachelor's certificates.
Library: Kresge Library plus 1 other. *Books:* 579,176 (physical), 344,635 (digital/electronic); *Serial titles:* 395 (physical), 26,313 (digital/electronic); *Databases:* 289. Weekly public service hours: 168; study areas open 24 hours, 5-7 days a week; students can reserve study rooms.

STUDENT LIFE
Housing options: coed, cooperative, special housing for students with disabilities. Campus housing is university owned. Freshman applicants given priority for college housing.

Activities and organizations: drama/theater group, student-run newspaper, radio and television station, choral group, Beta Alpha Psi, OASIS, AMA, InterVarsity Christian Fellowship, Alternative Spring Break and Global Brigades, Greek Life (Sororities and Fraternities), Grizz Gang, Club Sports (Recreational), national fraternities, national sororities.

Athletics Member NCAA. All Division I.

Campus security: 24-hour emergency response devices and patrols, student patrols, late-night transport/escort service, controlled dormitory access, state certified police officers, security lighting, extensive camera system, self-defense/alcohol abuse classes.

Student services: health clinic, personal/psychological counseling.

COSTS & FINANCIAL AID
Costs (2016–17) ***Tuition:*** state resident $11,970 full-time, $399 per credit hour part-time; nonresident $23,873 full-time, $796 per credit hour part-time. Full-time tuition and fees vary according to program and student level. Part-time tuition and fees vary according to program and student level. ***Room and board:*** $9620. Room and board charges vary according to housing facility. ***Payment plans:*** installment, deferred payment.

Financial Aid Of all full-time matriculated undergraduates who enrolled in 2014, 9,637 applied for aid, 8,060 were judged to have need, 705 had their need fully met. 217 Federal Work-Study jobs (averaging $2089). In 2014, 1648 non-need-based awards were made. ***Average percent of need met:*** 72. ***Average financial aid package:*** $13,190. ***Average need-based loan:*** $4151. ***Average need-based gift aid:*** $5232. ***Average non-need-based aid:*** $4524. ***Average indebtedness upon graduation:*** $28,778.

APPLYING
Standardized Tests *Required:* SAT or ACT (for admission).

Options: electronic application, deferred entrance.

Required: high school transcript, minimum 2.5 GPA. ***Required for some:*** interview, audition for music, theatre, and dance.

CONTACT
Ms. Dawn M. Aubry, Director of Admissions, Oakland University, Rochester, MI 48309-4401. *Phone:* 248-370-3228. *Toll-free phone:* 800-OAK-UNIV. *Fax:* 248-370-4462. *E-mail:* ouinfo@oakland.edu.

Olivet College

Olivet, Michigan

http://www.olivetcollege.edu/

CONTACT
Olivet College, 320 South Main Street, Olivet, MI 49076-9701. *Phone:* 800-456-7189. *Toll-free phone:* 800-456-7189.

Rochester College

Rochester Hills, Michigan

http://www.rc.edu/

CONTACT
Mr. Larry Norman, Dean of Admissions, Rochester College, 800 West Avon Road, Rochester Hills, MI 48307-2764. *Phone:* 248-218-2190. *Toll-free phone:* 800-521-6010. *Fax:* 248-218-2035. *E-mail:* admissions@rc.edu.

Sacred Heart Major Seminary

Detroit, Michigan

http://www.shms.edu/

CONTACT
Fr. Michael Byrnes, Vice Rector, Sacred Heart Major Seminary, 2701 Chicago Boulevard, Detroit, MI 48206. *Phone:* 313-883-8552. *Fax:* 313-868-6400.

Saginaw Valley State University

University Center, Michigan

http://www.svsu.edu/

- **State-supported** comprehensive, founded 1963
- **Small-town** 782-acre campus
- **Endowment** $63.2 million
- **Coed** 8,397 undergraduate students, 83% full-time, 58% women, 42% men
- **Moderately difficult** entrance level, 76% of applicants were admitted

UNDERGRAD STUDENTS
6,988 full-time, 1,409 part-time. Students come from 27 states and territories; 45 other countries; 2% are from out of state; 9% Black or African American, non-Hispanic/Latino; 4% Hispanic/Latino; 0.7% Asian, non-Hispanic/Latino; 0.2% American Indian or Alaska Native, non-Hispanic/Latino; 2% Two or more races, non-Hispanic/Latino; 6% Race/ethnicity unknown; 8% international; 6% transferred in; 30% live on campus.

Freshmen:
Admission: 6,700 applied, 5,083 admitted, 1,353 enrolled. ***Average high school GPA:*** 3.39. ***Test scores:*** ACT scores over 18: 93%; ACT scores over 24: 38%; ACT scores over 30: 5%.
Retention: 67% of full-time freshmen returned.

FACULTY
Total: 294, 100% full-time, 86% with terminal degrees.
Student/faculty ratio: 17:1.

ACADEMICS
Calendar: semesters plus summer session. *Degrees:* bachelor's, master's, doctoral, and post-master's certificates.
Special study options: academic remediation for entering students, accelerated degree program, adult/continuing education programs, advanced placement credit, cooperative education, distance learning, double majors, English as a second language, honors programs, independent study, internships, part-time degree program, services for LD students, student-designed majors, study abroad, summer session for credit.
Computers: 424 computers/terminals are available on campus for general student use. Students can access the following: computer help desk, free student e-mail accounts, online (class) grades, online (class) registration, online (class) schedules. Campuswide network is available. 100% of college-owned or -operated housing units are wired for high-speed Internet access. Wireless service is available via entire campus.
Library: Zahnow Library. *Books:* 217,900 (physical), 107,479 (digital/electronic); *Serial titles:* 127 (physical), 50,164 (digital/electronic); *Databases:* 63. Weekly public service hours: 95.

STUDENT LIFE
Housing options: coed, special housing for students with disabilities. Campus housing is university owned. Freshman applicants given priority for college housing.
Activities and organizations: drama/theater group, student-run newspaper, radio station, choral group, marching band, His House Christian Fellowship, Criminal Justice Society, Delta Sigma Pi, Alpha Phi Omega, International Students Club, national fraternities, national sororities.
Athletics Member NCAA. All Division II. ***Intercollegiate sports:*** baseball M(s), basketball M(s)/W(s), bowling M(c)/W(c), cheerleading M(c)/W(c), cross-country running M(s)/W(s), equestrian sports M(c)/W(c), football M(s), golf M(s), gymnastics M(c)/W(c), ice hockey M(c)/W(c), lacrosse M(c)/W(c), rugby M(c)/W(c), soccer M(s)/W(s), softball W(s), swimming and diving M(s)/W(s), tennis M(c)/W(s), track and field M(s)/W(s), volleyball W(s), wrestling M(c). ***Intramural sports:*** badminton M/W, basketball M/W, football M/W, golf M/W, ice hockey M/W, racquetball M/W, soccer M/W, softball M/W, table tennis M/W, tennis M/W, volleyball M/W, water polo M/W.
Campus security: 24-hour emergency response devices and patrols, student patrols, late-night transport/escort service, controlled dormitory access, Sexual Assault Prevention Program.
Student services: health clinic, personal/psychological counseling.

COSTS & FINANCIAL AID
Costs (2016–17) ***Tuition:*** state resident $8907 full-time, $297 per credit hour part-time; nonresident $21,509 full-time, $717 per credit hour part-time. Full-time tuition and fees vary according to course level, degree level, location, and program. Part-time tuition and fees vary according to course level, degree level, location, and program. ***Required fees:*** $438 full-time, $15 per credit hour part-time. ***Room and board:*** $7950; room only: $4300. Room and board charges vary according to board plan and housing facility. ***Payment plan:*** installment. ***Waivers:*** employees or children of employees.
Financial Aid Of all full-time matriculated undergraduates who enrolled in 2016, 5,287 applied for aid, 4,460 were judged to have need. In 2016, 954 non-need-based awards were made. ***Average need-based gift aid:*** $5960. ***Average non-need-based aid:*** $5737. ***Average indebtedness upon graduation:*** $31,695.

APPLYING
Standardized Tests *Required:* SAT or ACT (for admission).
Options: electronic application, deferred entrance.
Application fee: $30.
Required: high school transcript, minimum 2.5 GPA.
Application deadlines: rolling (freshmen), rolling (transfers).
Notification: continuous (freshmen), continuous (transfers).

CONTACT
Jennifer Pahl, Director of Admissions, Saginaw Valley State University, 7400 Bay Road, University Center, MI 48710-0001. *Phone:* 989-964-4200. *Toll-free phone:* 800-968-9500. *Fax:* 989-790-0180.
E-mail: admissions@svsu.edu.

Schoolcraft College

Livonia, Michigan

http://www.schoolcraft.edu/

- **District-supported** primarily 2-year, founded 1961, part of Michigan Department of Education
- **Suburban** campus with easy access to Detroit
- **Coed** 11,339 undergraduate students, 28% full-time, 54% women, 46% men
- **Noncompetitive** entrance level

UNDERGRAD STUDENTS
3,134 full-time, 8,205 part-time. 14% Black or African American, non-Hispanic/Latino; 4% Hispanic/Latino; 4% Asian, non-Hispanic/Latino; 0.1% Native Hawaiian or other Pacific Islander, non-Hispanic/Latino; 0.7% American Indian or Alaska Native, non-Hispanic/Latino; 3% Two or more races, non-Hispanic/Latino; 7% Race/ethnicity unknown; 1% international; 24% transferred in.

Freshmen:
Admission: 2,118 enrolled.
Retention: 62% of full-time freshmen returned.

FACULTY
Total: 524, 19% full-time.
Student/faculty ratio: 24:1.

ACADEMICS
Calendar: semesters. *Degrees:* certificates, associate, and bachelor's.
Special study options: academic remediation for entering students, accelerated degree program, adult/continuing education programs, advanced placement credit, distance learning, English as a second language, honors programs, independent study, internships, part-time degree program, services for LD students, study abroad, summer session for credit.
Computers: Students can access the following: campus intranet, computer help desk, free student e-mail accounts, online (class) grades, online (class) registration, online (class) schedules. Campuswide network is available. Wireless service is available via entire campus.
Library: Bradner Library. Students can reserve study rooms.

STUDENT LIFE
Housing options: college housing not available.
Activities and organizations: drama/theater group, student-run newspaper, choral group, Phi Theta Kappa, The Schoolcraft Connection Newspaper, Student Activities Board, Project Playhem Gaming Club, Otaku Anime Japanese Animation Club.
Athletics Member NJCAA. ***Intercollegiate sports:*** baseball M, basketball M(s)/W(s), bowling M/W, cross-country running M/W, golf M, soccer M(s)/W(s), softball W, volleyball W(s).
Campus security: 24-hour emergency response devices and patrols, late-night transport/escort service.
Student services: personal/psychological counseling, women's center.

COSTS & FINANCIAL AID
Costs (2016–17) ***Tuition:*** area resident $3060 full-time, $102 per credit hour part-time; state resident $4440 full-time, $148 per credit hour part-time; nonresident $6540 full-time, $218 per credit hour part-time. ***Required fees:*** $776 full-time, $23 per credit hour part-time, $43 per term part-time. ***Payment plans:*** installment, deferred payment. ***Waivers:*** senior citizens and employees or children of employees.
Financial Aid Of all full-time matriculated undergraduates who enrolled in 2015, 42 Federal Work-Study jobs (averaging $1722).

APPLYING
Options: electronic application, early admission, deferred entrance.
Required for some: high school transcript. ***Recommended:*** high school transcript.
Application deadlines: rolling (freshmen), rolling (transfers).

CONTACT
Ms. Lisa Bushaw, Director of Admissions, Schoolcraft College, 18600 Haggerty Road, Livonia, MI 48152-2696. *Phone:* 734-462-4683. *E-mail:* admissions@schoolcraft.edu.

Siena Heights University

Adrian, Michigan

http://www.sienaheights.edu/

CONTACT
Ms. Trudy Mohre, Director of Admissions, Siena Heights University, 1247 East Siena Heights Drive, Adrian, MI 49221. *Phone:* 517-264-7185. *Toll-free phone:* 800-521-0009. *E-mail:* tmohre@sienaheights.edu.

South University

Novi, Michigan

http://www.southuniversity.edu/novi.aspx

CONTACT
South University, 41555 Twelve Mile Road, Novi, MI 48377. *Phone:* 248-675-0200. *Toll-free phone:* 877-693-2085.

Spring Arbor University

Spring Arbor, Michigan

http://www.arbor.edu/

- **Independent Free Methodist** comprehensive, founded 1873
- **Rural** 100-acre campus
- **Endowment** $13.3 million
- **Coed**
- **Moderately difficult** entrance level

FACULTY
Student/faculty ratio: 13:1.

ACADEMICS
Calendar: 4-1-4. *Degrees:* associate, bachelor's, master's, and postbachelor's certificates.
Library: Hugh A. White Library. *Books:* 95,739 (physical), 142,749 (digital/electronic); *Databases:* 49. Students can reserve study rooms.

STUDENT LIFE
Housing options: on-campus residence required through senior year; men-only, women-only, special housing for students with disabilities. Campus housing is university owned. Freshman campus housing is guaranteed.
Activities and organizations: drama/theater group, student-run newspaper, radio and television station, choral group, Inter-faith Shelter Ministries, Band of Brothers, Action Jackson, Circle of Sisters, Heartside Homeless.
Athletics Member NAIA, NCCAA.
Campus security: 24-hour emergency response devices and patrols, student patrols, late-night transport/escort service, controlled dormitory access.
Student services: health clinic, personal/psychological counseling.

COSTS & FINANCIAL AID
Costs (2016–17) ***Comprehensive fee:*** $36,000 includes full-time tuition ($26,130), mandatory fees ($600), and room and board ($9270). Full-time tuition and fees vary according to course load, degree level, and program. Part-time tuition: $635 per credit hour. Part-time tuition and fees vary according to course load, degree level, program, and reciprocity agreements. ***Required fees:*** $285 per term part-time. ***College room only:*** $4320. Room and board charges vary according to board plan and housing facility.
Financial Aid Of all full-time matriculated undergraduates who enrolled in 2015, 1,130 applied for aid, 1,028 were judged to have need, 222 had their need fully met. ***Average percent of need met:*** 79. ***Average financial aid package:*** $22,330. ***Average need-based loan:*** $4729. ***Average need-based gift aid:*** $14,747. ***Average indebtedness upon graduation:*** $32,973.

APPLYING
Standardized Tests *Required:* SAT or ACT (for admission). *Recommended:* ACT (for admission).
Options: electronic application, early admission, deferred entrance.
Application fee: $30.
Required: high school transcript. ***Required for some:*** essay or personal statement, interview. ***Recommended:*** minimum 2.6 GPA, guidance counselor's form, minimum ACT score of 20 or SAT score of 930.

CONTACT
Office of Admissions, Spring Arbor University, 106 East Main Street, Spring Arbor, MI 49283-9799. *Phone:* 517-750-1200 Ext. 1468. *Toll-free phone:* 800-968-0011. *Fax:* 517-750-6620. *E-mail:* admissions@arbor.edu.

University of Detroit Mercy

Detroit, Michigan

http://www.udmercy.edu/

- **Independent Roman Catholic (Jesuit)** university, founded 1877
- **Urban** 70-acre campus with easy access to Detroit, MI
- **Endowment** $41.2 million
- **Coed** 2,672 undergraduate students, 78% full-time, 64% women, 36% men
- **Moderately difficult** entrance level, 73% of applicants were admitted

UNDERGRAD STUDENTS
2,081 full-time, 591 part-time. Students come from 29 states and territories; 23 other countries; 5% are from out of state; 15% Black or African American, non-Hispanic/Latino; 4% Hispanic/Latino; 5% Asian, non-Hispanic/Latino; 0.3% American Indian or Alaska Native, non-Hispanic/Latino; 3% Two or more races, non-Hispanic/Latino; 4% Race/ethnicity unknown; 5% international; 6% transferred in; 30% live on campus.

Freshmen:
Admission: 4,450 applied, 3,269 admitted, 516 enrolled. ***Average high school GPA:*** 3.51. ***Test scores:*** SAT critical reading scores over 500: 61%; SAT math scores over 500: 68%; SAT writing scores over 500: 49%; ACT scores over 18: 98%; SAT critical reading scores over 600: 29%; SAT math scores over 600: 36%; SAT writing scores over 600: 28%; ACT scores over 24: 53%; SAT math scores over 700: 7%; SAT writing scores over 700: 7%; ACT scores over 30: 8%.
Retention: 85% of full-time freshmen returned.

FACULTY
Total: 724, 44% full-time, 77% with terminal degrees.
Student/faculty ratio: 11:1.

ACADEMICS
Calendar: semesters. *Degrees:* certificates, diplomas, bachelor's, master's, doctoral, post-master's, and postbachelor's certificates.
Special study options: academic remediation for entering students, accelerated degree program, advanced placement credit, cooperative education, distance learning, double majors, English as a second language, honors programs, independent study, internships, off-campus study, part-time degree program, services for LD students, study abroad, summer session for credit.
Computers: 157 computers/terminals are available on campus for general student use. Students can access the following: campus intranet, computer help desk, free student e-mail accounts, online (class) grades, online (class) registration, online (class) schedules. Campuswide network is available. 100% of college-owned or -operated housing units are wired for high-speed Internet access. Wireless service is available via entire campus.
Library: McNichols Campus Library. *Books:* 468,257 (physical), 175,312 (digital/electronic); *Serial titles:* 107,735 (digital/electronic); *Databases:* 84. Weekly public service hours: 80.

STUDENT LIFE
Housing options: coed. Campus housing is university owned. Freshman campus housing is guaranteed.
Activities and organizations: drama/theater group, student-run newspaper, radio station, choral group, Alpha Phi Omega, Biology Club,

Chemistry Club, Pre-Dentistry Club, Greek Organizations - NPC, NIC, and NPHC, national fraternities, national sororities.

Athletics Member NCAA. All Division I. ***Intercollegiate sports:*** basketball M(s)/W(s), cross-country running M(s)/W(s), fencing M(s)/W(s), golf M(s)/W(s), lacrosse M(s)/W(s), soccer M(s)/W(s), softball W(s), tennis M(s)/W(s), track and field M(s)/W(s). ***Intramural sports:*** basketball M/W, cheerleading M/W, field hockey M/W, table tennis M/W, volleyball M/W.

Campus security: 24-hour emergency response devices and patrols, student patrols, late-night transport/escort service.

Student services: health clinic, personal/psychological counseling.

COSTS & FINANCIAL AID

Costs (2017–18) ***Comprehensive fee:*** $50,610 includes full-time tuition ($41,158) and room and board ($9452). Full-time tuition and fees vary according to program. Part-time tuition: $1049 per credit hour. Part-time tuition and fees vary according to location and program. ***Room and board:*** Room and board charges vary according to board plan and housing facility. ***Payment plans:*** installment, deferred payment. ***Waivers:*** children of alumni, senior citizens, and employees or children of employees.

Financial Aid Of all full-time matriculated undergraduates who enrolled in 2016, 1,822 applied for aid, 1,494 were judged to have need, 136 had their need fully met. 397 Federal Work-Study jobs (averaging $2500). In 2016, 625 non-need-based awards were made. ***Average percent of need met:*** 76. ***Average financial aid package:*** $33,808. ***Average need-based loan:*** $5766. ***Average need-based gift aid:*** $26,032. ***Average non-need-based aid:*** $20,196. ***Average indebtedness upon graduation:*** $33,631.

APPLYING

Standardized Tests *Required:* SAT or ACT (for admission).

Options: electronic application, deferred entrance.

Required: essay or personal statement, high school transcript, minimum 2.5 GPA. ***Required for some:*** interview. ***Recommended:*** 1 letter of recommendation, interview.

Application deadlines: rolling (freshmen), rolling (transfers).

Notification: continuous (freshmen), continuous (transfers).

CONTACT

Office of Admissions, University of Detroit Mercy, 4001 West McNichols Road, Detroit, MI 48221-3038. *Phone:* 313-993-1245. *Toll-free phone:* 800-635-5020. *Fax:* 313-993-3326. *E-mail:* admissions@udmercy.edu.

University of Michigan

Ann Arbor, Michigan

http://www.umich.edu/

- **State-supported** university, founded 1817
- **Urban** 3207-acre campus with easy access to Detroit
- **Endowment** $9.6 billion
- **Coed** 28,983 undergraduate students, 97% full-time, 50% women, 50% men
- **Very difficult** entrance level, 29% of applicants were admitted

UNDERGRAD STUDENTS

27,969 full-time, 1,014 part-time. Students come from 56 states and territories; 87 other countries; 40% are from out of state; 4% Black or African American, non-Hispanic/Latino; 5% Hispanic/Latino; 14% Asian, non-Hispanic/Latino; 0.2% American Indian or Alaska Native, non-Hispanic/Latino; 4% Two or more races, non-Hispanic/Latino; 5% Race/ethnicity unknown; 7% international; 4% transferred in; 32% live on campus.

Freshmen:

Admission: 55,504 applied, 15,871 admitted, 6,689 enrolled. ***Average high school GPA:*** 3.84. ***Test scores:*** SAT critical reading scores over 500: 98%; SAT math scores over 500: 98%; SAT writing scores over 500: 98%; ACT scores over 18: 99%; SAT critical reading scores over 600: 88%; SAT math scores over 600: 93%; SAT writing scores over 600: 89%; ACT scores over 24: 97%; SAT critical reading scores over 700: 43%; SAT math scores over 700: 64%; SAT writing scores over 700: 51%; ACT scores over 30: 74%.

Retention: 97% of full-time freshmen returned.

FACULTY

Total: 3,434, 81% full-time, 85% with terminal degrees.

Student/faculty ratio: 15:1.

ACADEMICS

Calendar: trimesters. *Degrees:* bachelor's, master's, doctoral, post-master's, and postbachelor's certificates.

Special study options: accelerated degree program, adult/continuing education programs, advanced placement credit, cooperative education, distance learning, double majors, English as a second language, external degree program, honors programs, independent study, internships, off-campus study, part-time degree program, services for LD students, student-designed majors, study abroad, summer session for credit. ***ROTC:*** Army (b), Navy (b), Air Force (b).

Unusual degree programs: 3-2 business administration; engineering.

Computers: 3,940 computers/terminals are available on campus for general student use. Students can access the following: campus intranet, computer help desk, free student e-mail accounts, online (class) grades, online (class) registration, online (class) schedules, file storage, personal Web pages, printing. Campuswide network is available. 100% of college-owned or -operated housing units are wired for high-speed Internet access. Wireless service is available via entire campus.

Library: Shapiro Undergraduate Library plus 9 others. *Books:* 9.0 million (physical), 3.3 million (digital/electronic); *Serial titles:* 464,460 (physical), 163,830 (digital/electronic); *Databases:* 10,078. Weekly public service hours: 168; study areas open 24 hours, 5-7 days a week; students can reserve study rooms.

STUDENT LIFE

Housing options: coed, women-only, cooperative. Campus housing is university owned. Freshman campus housing is guaranteed.

Activities and organizations: drama/theater group, student-run newspaper, radio and television station, choral group, marching band, Hillel Society, K-Grams (Kids' Program), M-Powered Entrepreneurial Club, Dance Marathon, Alternative Spring Break, national fraternities, national sororities.

Athletics Member NCAA. All Division I except football (Division I-AA). ***Intercollegiate sports:*** baseball M(s), basketball M(s)/W(s), cheerleading M(s)(c)/W(s)(c), crew M(c)/W(s), cross-country running M(s)/W(s), fencing M(c)/W(c), field hockey W(s), golf M(s)/W(s), gymnastics M(s)/W(s), ice hockey M(s), lacrosse M(s)/W(s), riflery M(c)/W(c), rowing M(c), rugby M(c)/W(c), sailing M(c)/W(c), soccer M(s)/W(s), softball W(s), swimming and diving M(s)/W(s), table tennis M(c)/W(c), tennis M(s)/W(s), track and field M(s)/W(s), triathlon M(c), ultimate Frisbee M(c)/W(c), volleyball M(c)/W(s), water polo M(c)/W(s), wrestling M(s). ***Intramural sports:*** badminton M/W, baseball M(c), basketball M/W, cross-country running M(c)/W(c), field hockey M/W, gymnastics W(c), ice hockey M(c)/W(c), lacrosse W(c), racquetball M/W, soccer M(c)/W(c), softball W(c), squash M/W, swimming and diving M/W(c), table tennis M/W, tennis M(c)/W(c), track and field M/W, ultimate Frisbee M/W, volleyball M/W(c), water polo W(c), wrestling M(c).

Campus security: 24-hour emergency response devices and patrols, student patrols, late-night transport/escort service, controlled dormitory access, Safewalk (no-cost night-time escorts), SafeRide (no-cost night-time ride service).

Student services: health clinic, personal/psychological counseling, women's center, legal services.

COSTS & FINANCIAL AID

Costs (2016–17) ***Tuition:*** state resident $14,074 full-time, $556 per credit hour part-time; nonresident $45,082 full-time, $1848 per credit hour part-time. Full-time tuition and fees vary according to course load, degree level, program, and student level. Part-time tuition and fees vary according to course load, degree level, program, and student level. ***Required fees:*** $328 full-time, $164 per term part-time. ***Room and board:*** $10,872. Room and board charges vary according to board plan and housing facility. ***Payment plan:*** installment.

Financial Aid Of all full-time matriculated undergraduates who enrolled in 2015, 14,276 applied for aid, 10,405 were judged to have need, 8,277 had their need fully met. 2,451 Federal Work-Study jobs (averaging $1550). In 2015, 4196 non-need-based awards were made. ***Average percent of need met:*** 87. ***Average financial aid package:*** $24,323. ***Average need-based loan:*** $5401. ***Average need-based gift aid:*** $17,673. ***Average non-need-based aid:*** $7442. ***Average indebtedness upon graduation:*** $25,712. ***Financial aid deadline:*** 4/30.

APPLYING

Standardized Tests *Required:* SAT or ACT (for admission). *Required for some:* SAT Subject Tests (for admission).

Options: electronic application, early action, deferred entrance.

Application fee: $75.

Required: essay or personal statement, high school transcript, 1 letter of recommendation. ***Required for some:*** interview, audition for School of Music, Theatre and Dance; portfolio for School of Art and Design.

Application deadlines: 2/1 (freshmen), 2/1 (transfers), 11/1 (early action).

Notification: continuous (freshmen), continuous (transfers), 12/24 (early action).

CONTACT

University of Michigan, Ann Arbor, MI 48109. *Phone:* 734-764-7433.

University of Michigan–Dearborn

Dearborn, Michigan

http://www.umdearborn.edu/

- **State-supported** comprehensive, founded 1959, part of University of Michigan System
- **Suburban** 210-acre campus with easy access to Detroit
- **Endowment** $46.9 million
- **Coed** 7,141 undergraduate students, 70% full-time, 48% women, 52% men
- **Moderately difficult** entrance level, 65% of applicants were admitted

UNDERGRAD STUDENTS

4,985 full-time, 2,156 part-time. Students come from 34 states and territories; 44 other countries; 4% are from out of state; 9% Black or African American, non-Hispanic/Latino; 6% Hispanic/Latino; 8% Asian, non-Hispanic/Latino; 0.1% Native Hawaiian or other Pacific Islander, non-Hispanic/Latino; 0.4% American Indian or Alaska Native, non-Hispanic/Latino; 3% Two or more races, non-Hispanic/Latino; 3% Race/ethnicity unknown; 2% international; 11% transferred in.

Freshmen:

Admission: 5,328 applied, 3,448 admitted, 1,074 enrolled. ***Average high school GPA:*** 3.55. ***Test scores:*** ACT scores over 18: 100%; ACT scores over 24: 61%; ACT scores over 30: 13%.

Retention: 82% of full-time freshmen returned.

FACULTY

Total: 561, 57% full-time, 66% with terminal degrees.

Student/faculty ratio: 17:1.

ACADEMICS

Calendar: semesters. *Degrees:* certificates, bachelor's, master's, doctoral, and postbachelor's certificates.

Special study options: academic remediation for entering students, accelerated degree program, adult/continuing education programs, advanced placement credit, cooperative education, distance learning, double majors, English as a second language, honors programs, independent study, internships, off-campus study, part-time degree program, services for LD students, student-designed majors, study abroad, summer session for credit. ***ROTC:*** Army (b), Navy (c), Air Force (c).

Computers: 975 computers/terminals are available on campus for general student use. Students can access the following: campus intranet, computer help desk, free student e-mail accounts, online (class) grades, online (class) registration, online (class) schedules, tuition and application payments accepted online. Campuswide network is available. Wireless service is available via entire campus.

Library: Mardigian Library. *Books:* 308,824 (physical), 569,242 (digital/electronic); *Serial titles:* 390 (physical), 80,875 (digital/electronic). Weekly public service hours: 48; students can reserve study rooms.

STUDENT LIFE

Housing options: college housing not available.

Activities and organizations: drama/theater group, student-run newspaper, radio station, national fraternities, national sororities.

Athletics Member NAIA. ***Intercollegiate sports:*** basketball M(s)/W(s), bowling M(c)/W(c), cheerleading W(c), cross-country running M(s)/W(s), ice hockey M(c), lacrosse M(s), soccer M(s)/W(c), softball W(s), tennis M(c)/W(c), volleyball W(s), wrestling M(c)/W(c). ***Intramural sports:*** basketball M/W, soccer M/W, volleyball M/W.

Campus security: 24-hour emergency response devices and patrols, late-night transport/escort service.

Student services: personal/psychological counseling, women's center.

COSTS & FINANCIAL AID

Costs (2016–17) ***Tuition:*** state resident $11,310 full-time, $447 per credit hour part-time; nonresident $23,550 full-time, $937 per credit hour part-time. Full-time tuition and fees vary according to course level, course load, degree level, program, and student level. Part-time tuition and fees vary according to course level, course load, degree level, program, and student level. ***Required fees:*** $722 full-time, $293 per term part-time. ***Payment plan:*** installment. ***Waivers:*** senior citizens and employees or children of employees.

Financial Aid Of all full-time matriculated undergraduates who enrolled in 2015, 3,784 applied for aid, 3,198 were judged to have need, 190 had their need fully met. 187 Federal Work-Study jobs (averaging $1963). 709 state and other part-time jobs (averaging $3209). In 2015, 649 non-need-based awards were made. ***Average percent of need met:*** 55. ***Average financial aid package:*** $10,087. ***Average need-based loan:*** $4424. ***Average need-based gift aid:*** $5776. ***Average non-need-based aid:*** $6018. ***Average indebtedness upon graduation:*** $26,192.

APPLYING

Standardized Tests *Required:* SAT or ACT (for admission), SAT and SAT Subject Tests or ACT (for admission).

Options: electronic application, deferred entrance.

Application fee: $30.

Required: high school transcript. ***Recommended:*** minimum 2.5 GPA.

Application deadlines: rolling (freshmen), rolling (transfers).

Notification: continuous (freshmen), continuous (transfers).

CONTACT

Ms. Deb Peffer, Director of Admissions and Orientation, University of Michigan–Dearborn, 4901 Evergreen Road, Room 1145 UC, Dearborn, MI 48128-1491. *Phone:* 313-593-5100. *Fax:* 313-436-9167. *E-mail:* admissions@umd.umich.edu.

University of Michigan–Flint

Flint, Michigan

http://www.umflint.edu/

- **State-supported** comprehensive, founded 1956, part of University of Michigan System
- **Urban** 75-acre campus with easy access to Detroit, Lansing
- **Endowment** $96.0 million
- **Coed** 6,585 undergraduate students, 58% full-time, 61% women, 39% men
- **Moderately difficult** entrance level, 65% of applicants were admitted

UNDERGRAD STUDENTS

3,844 full-time, 2,741 part-time. Students come from 32 states and territories; 34 other countries; 2% are from out of state; 14% Black or African American, non-Hispanic/Latino; 4% Hispanic/Latino; 2% Asian, non-Hispanic/Latino; 0.1% Native Hawaiian or other Pacific Islander, non-Hispanic/Latino; 0.8% American Indian or Alaska Native, non-Hispanic/Latino; 3% Two or more races, non-Hispanic/Latino; 3% Race/ethnicity unknown; 5% international; 11% transferred in; 6% live on campus.

Freshmen:

Admission: 4,033 applied, 2,627 admitted, 640 enrolled. ***Average high school GPA:*** 3.36. ***Test scores:*** SAT critical reading scores over 500: 70%; SAT math scores over 500: 70%; SAT writing scores over 500: 40%; ACT scores over 18: 85%; SAT critical reading scores over 600: 10%; SAT math scores over 600: 30%; SAT writing scores over 600: 20%; ACT scores over 24: 44%; SAT critical reading scores over 700: 10%; ACT scores over 30: 7%.

Retention: 68% of full-time freshmen returned.

FACULTY

Total: 570, 55% full-time, 56% with terminal degrees.

Student/faculty ratio: 14:1.

ACADEMICS

Calendar: semesters. *Degrees:* bachelor's, master's, doctoral, post-master's, and postbachelor's certificates.

Special study options: academic remediation for entering students, accelerated degree program, adult/continuing education programs, advanced placement credit, cooperative education, distance learning, double majors, English as a second language, honors programs, independent study, internships, off-campus study, part-time degree program, services for LD students, student-designed majors, study abroad, summer session for credit. ***ROTC:*** Army (c), Navy (c), Air Force (c).

Unusual degree programs: 3-2 engineering with University of Michigan (Ann Arbor).

Computers: 517 computers/terminals are available on campus for general student use. Students can access the following: campus intranet, computer help desk, free student e-mail accounts, online (class) grades, online (class) registration, online (class) schedules. Campuswide network is available. 100% of college-owned or -operated housing units are wired for high-speed Internet access. Wireless service is available via entire campus.

Library: Frances Willson Thompson Library plus 1 other. *Books:* 262,791 (physical), 746,088 (digital/electronic); *Serial titles:* 1,862 (physical), 146,663 (digital/electronic); *Databases:* 1,227. Weekly public service hours: 96; students can reserve study rooms.

STUDENT LIFE

Housing options: coed. Campus housing is university owned.

Activities and organizations: drama/theater group, student-run newspaper, choral group, Fraternity and Sorority Life, National Society for Leadership and Success, Black Student Union, Campus Activities Board, Community Engagement, national fraternities, national sororities.

Athletics ***Intramural sports:*** badminton M/W, basketball M/W, cheerleading W(c), football M(c), golf M(c)/W(c), ice hockey M(c)/W(c), lacrosse M(c), soccer M/W, ultimate Frisbee M(c)/W(c), volleyball M/W.

Campus security: 24-hour emergency response devices and patrols, student patrols, late-night transport/escort service, controlled dormitory access.

Student services: personal/psychological counseling, women's center.

COSTS & FINANCIAL AID

Costs (2016–17) ***Tuition:*** state resident $10,452 full-time, $413 per credit hour part-time; nonresident $20,370 full-time, $823 per credit hour part-time. Full-time tuition and fees vary according to course level, course load, degree level, program, and student level. Part-time tuition and fees vary according to course level, course load, degree level, program, and student level. ***Required fees:*** $432 full-time, $167 per term part-time. ***Room and board:*** $8178; room only: $5178. Room and board charges vary according to housing facility. ***Payment plan:*** installment. ***Waivers:*** senior citizens.

Financial Aid Of all full-time matriculated undergraduates who enrolled in 2015, 3,189 applied for aid, 2,853 were judged to have need, 72 had their need fully met. 189 Federal Work-Study jobs (averaging $2341). In 2015, 87 non-need-based awards were made. ***Average percent of need met:*** 69. ***Average financial aid package:*** $12,767. ***Average need-based loan:*** $4157. ***Average need-based gift aid:*** $5824. ***Average non-need-based aid:*** $4114. ***Average indebtedness upon graduation:*** $27,358.

APPLYING

Standardized Tests *Required:* SAT or ACT (for admission).

Options: electronic application, deferred entrance.

Application fee: $30.

Required: high school transcript, minimum 2.7 GPA.

Application deadlines: 8/18 (freshmen), 8/18 (transfers).

Notification: continuous (freshmen), continuous (transfers).

CONTACT

Mr. Jon Davidson, Admissions Director, University of Michigan–Flint, 303 East Kearsley Street, 245 University Pavilion, Flint, MI 48502. *Phone:* 810-762-3300. *Toll-free phone:* 800-942-5636. *Fax:* 810-762-3272. *E-mail:* admissions@umflint.edu.

University of Phoenix–Detroit Campus

Southfield, Michigan

http://www.phoenix.edu/

CONTACT

University of Phoenix–Detroit Campus, 26261 Evergreen Road, Southfield, MI 48076. *Toll-free phone:* 866-766-0766.

Walsh College of Accountancy and Business Administration

Troy, Michigan

http://www.walshcollege.edu/

- **Independent** upper-level, founded 1922
- **Suburban** 29-acre campus with easy access to Detroit
- **Endowment** $7.1 million
- **Coed** 935 undergraduate students, 8% full-time, 49% women, 51% men
- **Noncompetitive** entrance level

UNDERGRAD STUDENTS

73 full-time, 862 part-time. Students come from 5 states and territories; 35 other countries; 0.6% are from out of state; 5% Black or African American, non-Hispanic/Latino; 2% Hispanic/Latino; 4% Asian, non-Hispanic/Latino; 0.2% Native Hawaiian or other Pacific Islander, non-Hispanic/Latino; 0.3% American Indian or Alaska Native, non-Hispanic/Latino; 2% Two or more races, non-Hispanic/Latino; 2% Race/ethnicity unknown; 2% international; 98% transferred in.

FACULTY

Total: 182, 13% full-time.

ACADEMICS

Calendar: 4 11-week semesters. *Degrees:* bachelor's, master's, and postbachelor's certificates.

Special study options: academic remediation for entering students, adult/continuing education programs, advanced placement credit, distance learning, double majors, independent study, internships, off-campus study, part-time degree program, services for LD students, summer session for credit.

Computers: 400 computers/terminals are available on campus for general student use. Students can access the following: campus intranet, computer help desk, free student e-mail accounts, online (class) grades, online (class) registration, online (class) schedules. Campuswide network is available. Wireless service is available via entire campus.

Library: Vollbrecht Library plus 1 other. *Books:* 23,586 (physical), 2,695 (digital/electronic); *Serial titles:* 515 (physical), 23,818 (digital/electronic); *Databases:* 72. Weekly public service hours: 113.

STUDENT LIFE

Housing options: college housing not available.

Activities and organizations: Delta Mu Delta, Accounting and Taxation Student Organization, International Student Organization, MBA Association, Walsh College Marketing Association.

Campus security: 24-hour emergency response devices.

COSTS

Costs (2016–17) ***Tuition:*** $16,215 full-time, $8295 per year part-time. Full-time tuition and fees vary according to course level and degree level. Part-time tuition and fees vary according to course level and degree level. ***Required fees:*** $375 full-time, $375 per year part-time. ***Payment plan:*** deferred payment. ***Waivers:*** employees or children of employees.

APPLYING

Options: electronic application, deferred entrance.

Application fee: $35.

Notification: continuous (transfers).

CONTACT

Walsh College of Accountancy and Business Administration, 3838 Livernois Road, Troy, MI 48083. *Phone:* 248-823-1610. *Toll-free phone:* 800-925-7401.

★ Wayne State University
Detroit, Michigan
http://www.wayne.edu/

- **State-supported** university, founded 1868
- **Urban** 195-acre campus with easy access to Detroit
- **Endowment** $313.6 million
- **Coed** 17,280 undergraduate students, 70% full-time, 56% women, 44% men
- **Moderately difficult** entrance level, 81% of applicants were admitted

UNDERGRAD STUDENTS
12,041 full-time, 5,239 part-time. Students come from 35 states and territories; 45 other countries; 1% are from out of state; 17% Black or African American, non-Hispanic/Latino; 5% Hispanic/Latino; 9% Asian, non-Hispanic/Latino; 0.1% Native Hawaiian or other Pacific Islander, non-Hispanic/Latino; 0.3% American Indian or Alaska Native, non-Hispanic/Latino; 4% Two or more races, non-Hispanic/Latino; 4% Race/ethnicity unknown; 2% international; 11% transferred in; 13% live on campus.

Freshmen:
Admission: 11,093 applied, 9,036 admitted, 2,588 enrolled. ***Average high school GPA:*** 3.37. ***Test scores:*** ACT scores over 18: 92%; ACT scores over 24: 49%; ACT scores over 30: 11%.
Retention: 82% of full-time freshmen returned.

FACULTY
Total: 1,778, 57% full-time.
Student/faculty ratio: 16:1.

ACADEMICS
Calendar: semesters. *Degrees:* certificates, bachelor's, master's, doctoral, post-master's, and postbachelor's certificates.
Special study options: academic remediation for entering students, accelerated degree program, advanced placement credit, cooperative education, distance learning, double majors, English as a second language, freshman honors college, honors programs, independent study, internships, off-campus study, part-time degree program, services for LD students, study abroad, summer session for credit. ***ROTC:*** Army (b), Air Force (c).
Unusual degree programs: 3-2 engineering.
Computers: Students can access the following: computer help desk, free student e-mail accounts, online (class) grades, online (class) registration, online (class) schedules. Campuswide network is available. 100% of college-owned or -operated housing units are wired for high-speed Internet access. Wireless service is available via entire campus.
Library: David Adamany Undergraduate Library plus 5 others. *Books:* 2.0 million (physical), 1.0 million (digital/electronic); *Serial titles:* 63,572 (physical), 105,564 (digital/electronic); *Databases:* 750. Weekly public service hours: 138; study areas open 24 hours, 5-7 days a week.

STUDENT LIFE
Housing options: coed, special housing for students with disabilities. Campus housing is university owned. Freshman applicants given priority for college housing.
Activities and organizations: drama/theater group, student-run newspaper, radio station, choral group, marching band, national fraternities, national sororities.
Athletics Member NCAA. All Division II. ***Intercollegiate sports:*** baseball M(s), basketball M(s)/W(s), cheerleading M(s)/W(s), cross-country running M(s)/W(s), fencing M(s)/W(s), football M(s), golf M(s)/W(s), lacrosse M(c), soccer M(c)/W(c), softball W(s), swimming and diving M(s)/W(s), tennis M(s)/W(s), track and field W(s), volleyball W(s). ***Intramural sports:*** badminton M/W, basketball M/W(c), football M/W, rock climbing M/W, soccer M/W, softball M/W, table tennis M/W, tennis M/W, ultimate Frisbee M/W, volleyball M/W(c).
Campus security: 24-hour emergency response devices and patrols, late-night transport/escort service, controlled dormitory access, VIN etching, bike patrol, safety and defense classes, K-9 unit, victim assistance, confidential tip line.
Student services: health clinic, personal/psychological counseling, legal services.

FINANCIAL AID
Financial Aid Of all full-time matriculated undergraduates who enrolled in 2014, 9,727 applied for aid, 8,919 were judged to have need, 487 had

their need fully met. 380 Federal Work-Study jobs (averaging $3808). In 2014, 1567 non-need-based awards were made. ***Average percent of need met:*** 48. ***Average financial aid package:*** $10,386. ***Average need-based loan:*** $4235. ***Average need-based gift aid:*** $6515. ***Average non-need-based aid:*** $5114. ***Average indebtedness upon graduation:*** $24,516.

APPLYING

Standardized Tests *Required:* SAT or ACT (for admission).

Options: electronic application, deferred entrance.

Application fee: $25.

Required: high school transcript.

Application deadlines: 8/1 (freshmen), 8/15 (transfers).

Notification: continuous (freshmen), continuous (transfers).

CONTACT

Ms. Ericka M. Jackson, Director of Undergraduate Admissions, Wayne State University, 42 West Warren, Office of Undergraduate Admissions, Detroit 48202. *Phone:* 313-577-2100. *Toll-free phone:* 877-WSU-INFO. *E-mail:* admissions@wayne.edu.

See previous page for display ad and page 1588 for the College Close-Up.

Western Michigan University

Kalamazoo, Michigan

http://www.wmich.edu/

- **State-supported** university, founded 1903
- **Urban** 1289-acre campus
- **Endowment** $345.5 million
- **Coed** 18,313 undergraduate students, 82% full-time, 50% women, 50% men
- **Moderately difficult** entrance level, 82% of applicants were admitted

UNDERGRAD STUDENTS

15,048 full-time, 3,265 part-time. Students come from 41 states and territories; 63 other countries; 8% are from out of state; 13% Black or African American, non-Hispanic/Latino; 6% Hispanic/Latino; 2% Asian, non-Hispanic/Latino; 0.1% Native Hawaiian or other Pacific Islander, non-Hispanic/Latino; 0.4% American Indian or Alaska Native, non-Hispanic/Latino; 4% Two or more races, non-Hispanic/Latino; 0.8% Race/ethnicity unknown; 4% international; 9% transferred in; 27% live on campus.

Freshmen:

Admission: 13,613 applied, 11,205 admitted, 2,930 enrolled. ***Average high school GPA:*** 3.33. ***Test scores:*** ACT scores over 18: 86%; ACT scores over 24: 36%; ACT scores over 30: 5%.

Retention: 79% of full-time freshmen returned.

FACULTY

Total: 1,446, 65% full-time, 50% with terminal degrees.

Student/faculty ratio: 17:1.

ACADEMICS

Calendar: semesters. *Degrees:* certificates, bachelor's, master's, doctoral, post-master's, and postbachelor's certificates.

Special study options: academic remediation for entering students, accelerated degree program, adult/continuing education programs, advanced placement credit, cooperative education, distance learning, double majors, English as a second language, freshman honors college, honors programs, independent study, internships, off-campus study, part-time degree program, services for LD students, student-designed majors, study abroad, summer session for credit. ***ROTC:*** Army (b).

Computers: 2,330 computers/terminals and 100 ports are available on campus for general student use. Students can access the following: computer help desk, free student e-mail accounts, online (class) grades, online (class) registration, online (class) schedules. Campuswide network is available. 100% of college-owned or -operated housing units are wired for high-speed Internet access. Wireless service is available via entire campus.

Library: Waldo Library plus 4 others. *Books:* 2.1 million (physical), 674,471 (digital/electronic); *Serial titles:* 1,365 (physical), 184,666 (digital/electronic); *Databases:* 490. Weekly public service hours: 106; students can reserve study rooms.

STUDENT LIFE

Housing options: coed, men-only, women-only, special housing for students with disabilities. Campus housing is university owned. Freshman campus housing is guaranteed.

Activities and organizations: drama/theater group, student-run newspaper, radio station, choral group, marching band, Campus Activities Board, Western Student Association, Young Black Male Support Network, Drive Safe Kalamazoo, Alternative Spring Break, national fraternities, national sororities.

Athletics Member NCAA. All Division I except football (Division I-A). ***Intercollegiate sports:*** baseball M(s), basketball M(s)/W(s), cross-country running W(s), equestrian sports W(c), golf M(c)/W(s), gymnastics W(s), ice hockey M(s), lacrosse M(c)/W(c), rock climbing M(c)/W(c), rugby M(c)/W(c), sailing M(c)/W(c), skiing (downhill) M(c)/W(c), soccer M(s)/W(s), softball W(s), swimming and diving M(c)/W(c), tennis M(s)/W(s), track and field W(s), ultimate Frisbee M(c), volleyball M(c)/W(s), water polo M(c)/W(c). ***Intramural sports:*** badminton M/W, basketball M/W, golf M/W, ice hockey M, racquetball M/W, rock climbing M/W, sand volleyball M/W, soccer M/W, softball M/W, table tennis M/W, tennis M/W, ultimate Frisbee M/W, volleyball M/W.

Campus security: 24-hour emergency response devices and patrols, student patrols, late-night transport/escort service, controlled dormitory access, residence hall security system, engravers for identification of items, free bicycle registration.

Student services: health clinic, personal/psychological counseling, women's center.

COSTS & FINANCIAL AID

Costs (2016–17) ***One-time required fee:*** $300. ***Tuition:*** state resident $10,570 full-time, $384 per credit hour part-time; nonresident $25,928 full-time, $943 per credit hour part-time. Full-time tuition and fees vary according to course load, location, program, reciprocity agreements, and student level. Part-time tuition and fees vary according to course load, location, program, reciprocity agreements, and student level. ***Required fees:*** $923 full-time, $259 per term part-time. ***Room and board:*** $9561; room only: $4931. Room and board charges vary according to board plan and housing facility. ***Payment plan:*** installment. ***Waivers:*** senior citizens and employees or children of employees.

Financial Aid Of all full-time matriculated undergraduates who enrolled in 2015, 13,633 applied for aid, 10,646 were judged to have need, 2,274 had their need fully met. In 2015, 1422 non-need-based awards were made. ***Average percent of need met:*** 75. ***Average financial aid package:*** $13,577. ***Average need-based loan:*** $4471. ***Average need-based gift aid:*** $5616. ***Average non-need-based aid:*** $5760. ***Average indebtedness upon graduation:*** $35,454.

APPLYING

Standardized Tests *Required:* SAT or ACT (for admission).

Options: electronic application.

Application fee: $40.

Required: high school transcript. ***Required for some:*** interview.

Application deadlines: rolling (freshmen), rolling (transfers).

Notification: continuous (freshmen), continuous (transfers).

CONTACT

Western Michigan University, 1903 West Michigan Avenue, Kalamazoo, MI 49008. *Phone:* 269-387-2000. *E-mail:* ask-wmu@wmich.edu.

Yeshiva Beth Yehuda–Yeshiva Gedolah of Greater Detroit

Oak Park, Michigan

CONTACT

Rabbi P. Rushnawitz, Director, Yeshiva Beth Yehuda–Yeshiva Gedolah of Greater Detroit, 24600 Greenfield, Oak Park, MI 48237-1544.

MINNESOTA

Academy College

Bloomington, Minnesota

http://www.academycollege.edu/

- **Proprietary** 4-year, founded 1936
- **Urban** campus
- **Coed** 116 undergraduate students, 49% full-time, 19% women, 81% men
- **Noncompetitive** entrance level

UNDERGRAD STUDENTS

57 full-time, 59 part-time. Students come from 4 states and territories; 5% are from out of state; 12% Black or African American, non-Hispanic/Latino; 3% Hispanic/Latino; 9% Asian, non-Hispanic/Latino; 0.9% American Indian or Alaska Native, non-Hispanic/Latino; 2% Two or more races, non-Hispanic/Latino; 9% Race/ethnicity unknown; 5% transferred in.

Freshmen:

Admission: 2 enrolled.

Retention: 100% of full-time freshmen returned.

FACULTY

Student/faculty ratio: 8:1.

ACADEMICS

Calendar: quarters. *Degrees:* associate and bachelor's.

Special study options: academic remediation for entering students, accelerated degree program, adult/continuing education programs, advanced placement credit, cooperative education, distance learning, internships, part-time degree program, summer session for credit.

Computers: 25 computers/terminals are available on campus for general student use. Students can access the following: online (class) registration. Campuswide network is available. Wireless service is available via entire campus.

Library: Learning Resource Center plus 1 other.

STUDENT LIFE

Housing options: college housing not available.

COSTS & FINANCIAL AID

Costs (2017–18) ***One-time required fee:*** $280. ***Tuition:*** $17,009 full-time, $450 per credit hour part-time. Full-time tuition and fees vary according to course load and program. Part-time tuition and fees vary according to course load and program. ***Required fees:*** $120 full-time, $40 per term part-time. ***Payment plan:*** installment.

Financial Aid Of all full-time matriculated undergraduates who enrolled in 2015, 25 applied for aid, 25 were judged to have need. ***Average indebtedness upon graduation:*** $14,476.

APPLYING

Options: electronic application, early admission, deferred entrance.

Application fee: $40.

Required: high school transcript, interview.

Notification: continuous (freshmen), continuous (transfers).

CONTACT

Ms. Ashley LaLiberte, Education Specialist, Academy College, 1600 W 82nd Street, Suite 100, Bloomington, MN 55431. *Phone:* 952-851-0066. *Toll-free phone:* 800-292-9149. *Fax:* 952-851-0094. *E-mail:* admissions@academycollege.edu.

Argosy University, Twin Cities

Eagan, Minnesota

http://www.argosy.edu/locations/twin-cities/

CONTACT

Argosy University, Twin Cities, 1515 Central Parkway, Eagan, MN 55121. *Phone:* 651-846-2882. *Toll-free phone:* 888-844-2004.

Augsburg College

Minneapolis, Minnesota

http://www.augsburg.edu/

- **Independent Lutheran** comprehensive, founded 1869
- **Urban** 23-acre campus with easy access to Minneapolis-St. Paul
- **Endowment** $39.9 million
- **Coed** 2,536 undergraduate students, 80% full-time, 53% women, 47% men
- **Moderately difficult** entrance level, 59% of applicants were admitted

UNDERGRAD STUDENTS

2,032 full-time, 504 part-time. Students come from 39 states and territories; 53 other countries; 18% are from out of state; 11% Black or African American, non-Hispanic/Latino; 8% Hispanic/Latino; 7% Asian, non-Hispanic/Latino; 0.1% Native Hawaiian or other Pacific Islander, non-Hispanic/Latino; 2% American Indian or Alaska Native, non-Hispanic/Latino; 2% Two or more races, non-Hispanic/Latino; 16% Race/ethnicity unknown; 2% international; 11% transferred in; 37% live on campus.

Freshmen:

Admission: 2,925 applied, 1,731 admitted, 478 enrolled. ***Average high school GPA:*** 3.15. ***Test scores:*** SAT critical reading scores over 500: 53%; SAT math scores over 500: 47%; SAT writing scores over 500: 67%; ACT scores over 18: 87%; SAT critical reading scores over 600: 33%; SAT math scores over 600: 20%; SAT writing scores over 600: 13%; ACT scores over 24: 33%; SAT critical reading scores over 700: 13%; SAT math scores over 700: 7%; ACT scores over 30: 4%.

Retention: 79% of full-time freshmen returned.

FACULTY

Total: 383, 45% full-time, 66% with terminal degrees.

Student/faculty ratio: 12:1.

ACADEMICS

Calendar: semesters for undergraduate programs; trimesters for graduate programs and weekend college. *Degrees:* certificates, bachelor's, master's, doctoral, and postbachelor's certificates.

Special study options: academic remediation for entering students, adult/continuing education programs, advanced placement credit, cooperative education, double majors, English as a second language, freshman honors college, honors programs, independent study, internships, off-campus study, part-time degree program, services for LD students, student-designed majors, study abroad, summer session for credit. *ROTC:* Army (c), Navy (c), Air Force (c).

Unusual degree programs: 3-2 engineering with Michigan Technological University.

Computers: 250 computers/terminals are available on campus for general student use. Students can access the following: campus intranet, computer help desk, free student e-mail accounts, online (class) grades, online (class) registration, online (class) schedules. Campuswide network is available. 100% of college-owned or -operated housing units are wired for high-speed Internet access. Wireless service is available via entire campus.

Library: James G. Lindell Library. *Books:* 177,161 (physical), 52,445 (digital/electronic); *Serial titles:* 993 (physical); *Databases:* 120. Weekly public service hours: 94; students can reserve study rooms.

STUDENT LIFE

Housing options: coed, men-only, women-only, special housing for students with disabilities. Campus housing is university owned. Freshman applicants given priority for college housing.

Activities and organizations: drama/theater group, student-run newspaper, radio station, choral group, Pan-Afrikan Student Union, Augsburg Business Organization, Queer Pride Alliance, Students for Racial Justice, Augsburg Asian Student Association.

Athletics Member NCAA. All Division III. ***Intercollegiate sports:*** baseball M, basketball M/W, cross-country running M/W, football M, golf M/W, ice hockey M/W, lacrosse W, soccer M/W, softball W, swimming and diving W, track and field M/W, volleyball W, wrestling M. ***Intramural sports:*** basketball M/W, football M, skiing (cross-country) M(c)/W(c), skiing (downhill) M(c)/W(c), softball M/W, volleyball M/W, wrestling M.

Campus security: 24-hour emergency response devices and patrols, student patrols, late-night transport/escort service, controlled dormitory access.

Student services: health clinic, personal/psychological counseling, women's center.

COSTS & FINANCIAL AID

Costs (2017–18) ***Comprehensive fee:*** $47,554 includes full-time tuition ($36,950), mandatory fees ($665), and room and board ($9939). Full-time tuition and fees vary according to class time and location. Part-time tuition: $1155 per credit hour. Part-time tuition and fees vary according to class time and location. ***College room only:*** $5154. Room and board charges vary according to board plan and housing facility. ***Payment plan:*** installment. ***Waivers:*** employees or children of employees.

Financial Aid Of all full-time matriculated undergraduates who enrolled in 2012, 2,326 applied for aid, 2,141 were judged to have need, 309 had their need fully met. 174 Federal Work-Study jobs (averaging $1938). 825 state and other part-time jobs (averaging $2892). In 2012, 351 non-need-based awards were made. ***Average percent of need met:*** 65. ***Average financial aid package:*** $21,349. ***Average need-based loan:*** $5706. ***Average need-based gift aid:*** $16,603. ***Average non-need-based aid:*** $10,489. ***Average indebtedness upon graduation:*** $27,081. ***Financial aid deadline:*** 8/15.

APPLYING

Standardized Tests *Required:* SAT or ACT (for admission).

Options: electronic application, deferred entrance.

Required: essay or personal statement, high school transcript, 1 letter of recommendation, letter of recommendation from an academic teacher. ***Recommended:*** minimum 2.8 GPA, interview.

Application deadlines: 8/1 (freshmen), 8/1 (transfers).

Notification: continuous (freshmen), continuous (transfers).

CONTACT

Ms. Keri VanOverschelde, Admissions Operations Program Director, Augsburg College, 2211 Riverside Avenue, Minneapolis, MN 55454-1351. *Phone:* 612-330-1001. *Toll-free phone:* 800-788-5678. *E-mail:* vanovers@augsburg.edu.

Bemidji State University

Bemidji, Minnesota

http://www.bemidjistate.edu/

- **State-supported** comprehensive, founded 1919, part of Minnesota State Colleges and Universities System
- **Small-town** 89-acre campus
- **Coed** 4,739 undergraduate students, 72% full-time, 57% women, 43% men
- **Moderately difficult** entrance level, 94% of applicants were admitted

UNDERGRAD STUDENTS

3,410 full-time, 1,329 part-time. 10% are from out of state; 2% Black or African American, non-Hispanic/Latino; 2% Hispanic/Latino; 1% Asian, non-Hispanic/Latino; 3% American Indian or Alaska Native, non-Hispanic/Latino; 3% Two or more races, non-Hispanic/Latino; 2% Race/ethnicity unknown; 2% international; 6% transferred in; 28% live on campus.

Freshmen:

Admission: 2,566 applied, 2,407 admitted, 748 enrolled. ***Average high school GPA:*** 3.11. ***Test scores:*** ACT scores over 18: 89%; ACT scores over 24: 25%; ACT scores over 30: 2%.

Retention: 66% of full-time freshmen returned.

FACULTY

Total: 267, 65% full-time, 50% with terminal degrees.

Student/faculty ratio: 19:1.

ACADEMICS

Calendar: semesters. *Degrees:* certificates, associate, bachelor's, master's, and postbachelor's certificates.

Special study options: adult/continuing education programs, part-time degree program.

Computers: Students can access the following: computer help desk, free student e-mail accounts, online (class) grades, online (class) registration, online (class) schedules. Wireless service is available via entire campus.

Library: A. C. Clark Library.

STUDENT LIFE

Housing options: coed, special housing for students with disabilities. Campus housing is university owned. Freshman applicants given priority for college housing.

Athletics Member NCAA. All Division II except men's and women's ice hockey (Division I). ***Intercollegiate sports:*** baseball M(s), basketball M(s)/W(s), cross-country running W(s), football M(s), golf M(s)/W(s), ice hockey M(s)/W(s), soccer W(s), softball W(s), tennis W(s), track and field W(s), volleyball W(s). ***Intramural sports:*** basketball M/W, football M, ice hockey M/W, soccer M/W, softball M/W, volleyball M/W.

Campus security: 24-hour emergency response devices and patrols, late-night transport/escort service, controlled dormitory access.

COSTS & FINANCIAL AID

Costs (2016–17) ***Tuition:*** state resident $7360 full-time, $257 per credit part-time; nonresident $7360 full-time, $257 per credit part-time. Full-time tuition and fees vary according to course load, location, program, and reciprocity agreements. Part-time tuition and fees vary according to course load, location, program, and reciprocity agreements. ***Required fees:*** $1034 full-time, $18 per credit part-time. ***Room and board:*** $7924. Room and board charges vary according to board plan and housing facility. ***Payment plan:*** installment. ***Waivers:*** senior citizens and employees or children of employees.

Financial Aid Of all full-time matriculated undergraduates who enrolled in 2015, 2,765 applied for aid, 2,039 were judged to have need, 334 had their need fully met. 278 Federal Work-Study jobs (averaging $1624). 218 state and other part-time jobs (averaging $1737). In 2015, 664 non-need-based awards were made. ***Average percent of need met:*** 61. ***Average financial aid package:*** $9028. ***Average need-based loan:*** $4060. ***Average need-based gift aid:*** $5474. ***Average non-need-based aid:*** $10,488.

APPLYING

Standardized Tests *Required:* SAT or ACT (for admission).

Options: electronic application, early action, deferred entrance.

Application fee: $20.

Required: high school transcript. ***Required for some:*** essay or personal statement, interview.

CONTACT

Bemidji State University, 1500 Birchmont Drive, NE, Bemidji, MN 56601-2699. *Phone:* 218-755-2602. *Toll-free phone:* 800-475-2001.

Bethany Global University

Bloomington, Minnesota

http://www.bethanygu.edu/

CONTACT

Bethany Global University, 6820 Auto Club Road, Suite C, Bloomington, MN 55438. *Toll-free phone:* 800-323-3417.

Bethany Lutheran College

Mankato, Minnesota

http://www.blc.edu/

- **Independent Lutheran** 4-year, founded 1927
- **Small-town** 50-acre campus with easy access to Minneapolis-St. Paul
- **Endowment** $39.9 million
- **Coed** 587 undergraduate students, 88% full-time, 57% women, 43% men
- **Moderately difficult** entrance level, 80% of applicants were admitted

UNDERGRAD STUDENTS

514 full-time, 73 part-time. Students come from 24 states and territories; 11 other countries; 23% are from out of state; 2% Black or African American, non-Hispanic/Latino; 4% Hispanic/Latino; 0.2% Asian, non-Hispanic/Latino; 0.2% Native Hawaiian or other Pacific Islander, non-Hispanic/Latino; 0.3% American Indian or Alaska Native, non-Hispanic/Latino; 2% Two or more races, non-Hispanic/Latino; 2% Race/ethnicity unknown; 6% international; 5% transferred in; 69% live on campus.

Freshmen:
Admission: 328 applied, 264 admitted, 138 enrolled. ***Average high school GPA:*** 3.39. ***Test scores:*** ACT scores over 18: 95%; ACT scores over 24: 47%; ACT scores over 30: 7%.

Retention: 82% of full-time freshmen returned.

FACULTY
Total: 63, 70% full-time, 35% with terminal degrees.

Student/faculty ratio: 10:1.

ACADEMICS
Calendar: semesters. *Degree:* bachelor's.

Special study options: academic remediation for entering students, advanced placement credit, cooperative education, distance learning, double majors, English as a second language, independent study, internships, services for LD students, student-designed majors, study abroad, summer session for credit. ***ROTC:*** Army (c).

Unusual degree programs: engineering with University of Minnesota, Twin Cities Campus.

Computers: 100 computers/terminals and 400 ports are available on campus for general student use. Students can access the following: computer help desk, free student e-mail accounts, online (class) grades, online (class) registration, online (class) schedules. Campuswide network is available. 100% of college-owned or -operated housing units are wired for high-speed Internet access. Wireless service is available via entire campus.

Library: Memorial Library plus 1 other. *Books:* 63,879 (physical), 4,600 (digital/electronic); *Serial titles:* 382 (physical), 205 (digital/electronic); *Databases:* 50. Weekly public service hours: 83.

STUDENT LIFE
Housing options: on-campus residence required through sophomore year; men-only, women-only. Campus housing is university owned. Freshman campus housing is guaranteed.

Activities and organizations: drama/theater group, student-run newspaper, television station, choral group, Bethany Activities Committee, Student Senate, Scholastic Leadership Society, PAMA (Promoting Awareness, spurring Motivation, and encouraging Action), Bethany Society of Royal Scientists.

Athletics Member NCAA. All Division III. ***Intercollegiate sports:*** baseball M, basketball M/W, cross-country running M/W, equestrian sports M(c)/W(c), golf M/W, soccer M/W, softball W, tennis M/W, track and field M/W, volleyball W. ***Intramural sports:*** basketball M/W, football M/W, racquetball M/W, table tennis M/W, tennis M/W, ultimate Frisbee M/W, volleyball M/W.

Campus security: 24-hour emergency response devices and patrols, late-night transport/escort service, controlled dormitory access.

Student services: health clinic, personal/psychological counseling.

COSTS & FINANCIAL AID
Costs (2016–17) ***One-time required fee:*** $130. ***Comprehensive fee:*** $33,850 includes full-time tuition ($25,440), mandatory fees ($450), and room and board ($7960). Part-time tuition: $1080 per credit hour. Part-time tuition and fees vary according to course load. ***Required fees:*** $225 per term part-time. ***Room and board:*** Room and board charges vary according to board plan, housing facility, and student level. ***Payment plan:*** installment. ***Waivers:*** senior citizens and employees or children of employees.

Financial Aid Of all full-time matriculated undergraduates who enrolled in 2015, 422 applied for aid, 389 were judged to have need, 62 had their need fully met. 26 Federal Work-Study jobs (averaging $1705). 276 state and other part-time jobs (averaging $1028). In 2015, 66 non-need-based awards were made. ***Average percent of need met:*** 84. ***Average financial aid package:*** $20,972. ***Average need-based loan:*** $5046. ***Average need-based gift aid:*** $16,242. ***Average non-need-based aid:*** $7783. ***Average indebtedness upon graduation:*** $32,310.

APPLYING
Standardized Tests *Required:* SAT or ACT (for admission).

Options: electronic application.

Required: essay or personal statement, high school transcript, minimum 2.4 GPA. ***Required for some:*** interview. ***Recommended:*** minimum 3.2 GPA, interview.

Notification: continuous (transfers).

CONTACT
Mr. Daniel Tomhave, Vice President of Admissions and Enrollment Management, Bethany Lutheran College, 700 Luther Drive, Mankato, MN 56001. *Phone:* 507-344-7000 Ext. 451. *Toll-free phone:* 800-944-3066. *Fax:* 507-344-7376. *E-mail:* dtomhave@blc.edu.

★ Bethel University
St. Paul, Minnesota
http://www.bethel.edu/

- **Independent** comprehensive, founded 1871, affiliated with Baptist General Conference
- **Suburban** 289-acre campus with easy access to Minneapolis-St. Paul
- **Endowment** $42.0 million
- **Coed** 2,965 undergraduate students, 83% full-time, 62% women, 38% men
- **Moderately difficult** entrance level, 82% of applicants were admitted

UNDERGRAD STUDENTS
2,454 full-time, 511 part-time. Students come from 34 states and territories; 14 other countries; 20% are from out of state; 4% Black or African American, non-Hispanic/Latino; 5% Hispanic/Latino; 3% Asian, non-Hispanic/Latino; 0.2% Native Hawaiian or other Pacific Islander, non-Hispanic/Latino; 0.2% American Indian or Alaska Native, non-Hispanic/Latino; 3% Two or more races, non-Hispanic/Latino; 13% Race/ethnicity unknown; 0.3% international; 4% transferred in; 68% live on campus.

Freshmen:
Admission: 1,798 applied, 1,481 admitted, 565 enrolled. ***Average high school GPA:*** 3.5. ***Test scores:*** ACT scores over 18: 96%; ACT scores over 24: 58%; ACT scores over 30: 12%.

Retention: 88% of full-time freshmen returned.

FACULTY
Total: 290, 63% full-time, 58% with terminal degrees.

Student/faculty ratio: 11:1.

ACADEMICS
Calendar: 4-1-4. *Degrees:* associate, bachelor's, master's, doctoral, post-master's, and postbachelor's certificates.

Special study options: academic remediation for entering students, adult/continuing education programs, advanced placement credit, distance learning, double majors, honors programs, independent study, internships, off-campus study, part-time degree program, services for LD students, student-designed majors, study abroad, summer session for credit. ***ROTC:*** Army (c), Air Force (c).

Unusual degree programs: 3-2 engineering with University of Minnesota.

Computers: 203 computers/terminals are available on campus for general student use. Students can access the following: campus intranet, computer help desk, free student e-mail accounts, online (class) grades, online (class) registration, online (class) schedules. Campuswide network is available. 100% of college-owned or -operated housing units are wired for high-speed Internet access. Wireless service is available via classrooms, computer centers, computer labs, dorm rooms, learning centers, libraries, student centers.

Library: Bethel University Library plus 1 other. *Books:* 141,904 (physical), 153,597 (digital/electronic); *Serial titles:* 890 (physical), 31,538 (digital/electronic); *Databases:* 93. Weekly public service hours: 96; students can reserve study rooms.

STUDENT LIFE
Housing options: on-campus residence required through sophomore year; special housing for students with disabilities. Campus housing is university owned. Freshman campus housing is guaranteed.

Activities and organizations: drama/theater group, student-run newspaper, radio station, choral group, Bethel Student Government, Bethel Business and Economics Association, Bethel Rec Sports, Welcome Week.

Athletics Member NCAA. All Division III. ***Intercollegiate sports:*** baseball M, basketball M/W, cross-country running M/W, football M, golf M/W, ice hockey M/W, soccer M/W, softball W, tennis M/W, track and field M/W, volleyball M(c)/W. ***Intramural sports:*** basketball M/W, football M, lacrosse M(c)/W(c), rugby M(c), volleyball M(c)/W.

Campus security: 24-hour emergency response devices and patrols, student patrols, late-night transport/escort service, controlled dormitory access, video surveillance for residence halls, academic buildings, and parking lots.

Student services: health clinic, personal/psychological counseling.

COSTS & FINANCIAL AID

Costs (2017–18) ***Comprehensive fee:*** $46,550 includes full-time tuition ($36,060), mandatory fees ($150), and room and board ($10,340). Part-time tuition: $1510 per credit. Part-time tuition and fees vary according to course load. ***College room only:*** $5830. Room and board charges vary according to board plan. ***Payment plans:*** tuition prepayment, installment. ***Waivers:*** employees or children of employees.

Financial Aid Of all full-time matriculated undergraduates who enrolled in 2016, 2,005 applied for aid, 1,711 were judged to have need, 348 had their need fully met. 1,278 Federal Work-Study jobs (averaging $2781). In 2016, 623 non-need-based awards were made. ***Average percent of need met:*** 81. ***Average financial aid package:*** $27,371. ***Average need-based loan:*** $3971. ***Average need-based gift aid:*** $21,019. ***Average non-need-based aid:*** $12,232. ***Average indebtedness upon graduation:*** $36,132.

APPLYING

Standardized Tests *Required:* SAT or ACT (for admission).

Options: electronic application, early admission.

Required: essay or personal statement, high school transcript, rank in upper 50% of high school class. ***Required for some:*** 2 letters of recommendation. ***Recommended:*** minimum 2.5 GPA, interview.

Application deadlines: rolling (freshmen), rolling (transfers).

Notification: continuous (freshmen), continuous (transfers).

CONTACT

Office of Admissions, Bethel University, 3900 Bethel Drive, St. Paul, MN 55112. *Phone:* 651-638-6242. *Toll-free phone:* 800-255-8706 Ext. 6242. *Fax:* 651-635-1490. *E-mail:* undergrad-admissions@bethel.edu.

Capella University

Minneapolis, Minnesota

http://www.capella.edu/

CONTACT

Enrollment Services, Capella University, 225 South Sixth Street, Capella Tower, 9th Floor, Minneapolis, MN 55402. *Phone:* 866-2837921. *Toll-free phone:* 866-283-7921. *Fax:* 612-977-5060. *E-mail:* info@capella.edu.

Carleton College

Northfield, Minnesota

http://www.carleton.edu/

- **Independent** 4-year, founded 1866
- **Small-town** 955-acre campus with easy access to Minneapolis-St. Paul
- **Endowment** $738.1 million
- **Coed** 2,105 undergraduate students, 99% full-time, 51% women, 49% men
- **Very difficult** entrance level, 23% of applicants were admitted

UNDERGRAD STUDENTS

2,087 full-time, 18 part-time. Students come from 50 states and territories; 38 other countries; 83% are from out of state; 4% Black or African American, non-Hispanic/Latino; 7% Hispanic/Latino; 9% Asian, non-Hispanic/Latino; 0.1% Native Hawaiian or other Pacific Islander, non-Hispanic/Latino; 0.1% American Indian or Alaska Native, non-Hispanic/Latino; 6% Two or more races, non-Hispanic/Latino; 2% Race/ethnicity unknown; 10% international; 100% live on campus.

Freshmen:

Admission: 6,485 applied, 1,467 admitted. ***Test scores:*** SAT critical reading scores over 500: 99%; SAT math scores over 500: 100%; SAT writing scores over 500: 100%; ACT scores over 18: 100%; SAT critical reading scores over 600: 93%; SAT math scores over 600: 92%; SAT writing scores over 600: 88%; ACT scores over 24: 99%; SAT critical reading scores over 700: 64%; SAT math scores over 700: 60%; SAT writing scores over 700: 51%; ACT scores over 30: 77%.

Retention: 96% of full-time freshmen returned.

FACULTY

Total: 269, 78% full-time, 91% with terminal degrees.

Student/faculty ratio: 9:1.

ACADEMICS

Calendar: 3 courses for each of three terms. *Degree:* bachelor's.

Special study options: accelerated degree program, advanced placement credit, double majors, independent study, internships, off-campus study, services for LD students, student-designed majors, study abroad.

Unusual degree programs: 3-2 engineering with Columbia University.

Computers: 250 computers/terminals and 220 ports are available on campus for general student use. Students can access the following: campus intranet, computer help desk, free student e-mail accounts, online (class) grades, online (class) registration, online (class) schedules. Campuswide network is available. 100% of college-owned or -operated housing units are wired for high-speed Internet access. Wireless service is available via classrooms, computer centers, computer labs, dorm rooms, learning centers, libraries, student centers.

Library: Laurence McKinley Gould Library plus 1 other. *Books:* 499,801 (physical), 640,539 (digital/electronic); *Serial titles:* 82,879 (digital/electronic); *Databases:* 31,508. Weekly public service hours: 118.

STUDENT LIFE

Housing options: on-campus residence required through senior year; coed, special housing for students with disabilities. Campus housing is university owned. Freshman campus housing is guaranteed.

Activities and organizations: drama/theater group, student-run newspaper, radio station, choral group, CANOE (Carleton Association of Nature and Outdoor Enthusiasts), Farm Club, Ebony II, WHIMS (Women in Math and Science), Amnesty International.

Athletics Member NCAA. All Division III. ***Intercollegiate sports:*** badminton M(c)/W(c), baseball M, basketball M/W, cross-country running M/W, equestrian sports M(c)/W(c), fencing M(c)/W(c), field hockey W(c), football M, golf M/W, ice hockey M(c)/W(c), lacrosse M(c)/W(c), rugby M(c)/W(c), sailing M(c)/W(c), skiing (cross-country) M(c)/W(c), skiing (downhill) M(c)/W(c), soccer M/W, softball W, swimming and diving M/W, table tennis M(c)/W(c), tennis M/W, track and field M/W, ultimate Frisbee M(c)/W(c), volleyball M(c)/W, water polo M(c)/W(c). ***Intramural sports:*** badminton M/W, basketball M/W, soccer M/W, softball M/W, table tennis M/W, tennis M/W, ultimate Frisbee M/W, volleyball M/W.

Campus security: 24-hour emergency response devices and patrols, student patrols, late-night transport/escort service, controlled dormitory access, Emergency Notification Service (cell phone text and email alerts).

Student services: health clinic, personal/psychological counseling, women's center.

COSTS & FINANCIAL AID

Costs (2016–17) ***Comprehensive fee:*** $64,071 includes full-time tuition ($50,580), mandatory fees ($294), and room and board ($13,197). ***College room only:*** $6864. Room and board charges vary according to board plan. ***Payment plan:*** installment. ***Waivers:*** employees or children of employees.

Financial Aid Of all full-time matriculated undergraduates who enrolled in 2015, 1,757 applied for aid, 1,147 were judged to have need, 1,147 had their need fully met. 377 Federal Work-Study jobs (averaging $2556). 1,327 state and other part-time jobs (averaging $2530). In 2015, 105 non-need-based awards were made. ***Average percent of need met:*** 100. ***Average financial aid package:*** $45,763. ***Average need-based loan:*** $5201. ***Average need-based gift aid:*** $38,382. ***Average non-need-based aid:*** $4584. ***Average indebtedness upon graduation:*** $20,063. ***Financial aid deadline:*** 1/15.

APPLYING

Standardized Tests *Required:* SAT or ACT (for admission). *Recommended:* SAT Subject Tests (for admission).

Options: electronic application, early admission, early decision, deferred entrance.

Application fee: $30.

Required: essay or personal statement, high school transcript, 2 letters of recommendation, Common Application Supplement. ***Recommended:*** interview.

Application deadlines: 1/15 (freshmen), 3/31 (transfers).

Early decision deadline: 11/15 (for plan 1), 1/15 (for plan 2).

Notification: 3/31 (freshmen), 5/15 (transfers), 12/15 (early decision plan 1), 2/15 (early decision plan 2).

CONTACT
Carleton College, One North College Street, Northfield, MN 55057-4001. *Phone:* 507-222-4190. *Toll-free phone:* 800-995-2275.

College of Saint Benedict

Saint Joseph, Minnesota

http://www.csbsju.edu/

- **Independent Roman Catholic** 4-year, founded 1913
- **Small-town** 300-acre campus with easy access to Minneapolis-St. Paul
- **Endowment** $63.6 million
- **Women only** 1,958 undergraduate students, 99% full-time
- **Moderately difficult** entrance level, 88% of applicants were admitted

UNDERGRAD STUDENTS
1,939 full-time, 19 part-time. Students come from 34 states and territories; 16 other countries; 16% are from out of state; 3% Black or African American, non-Hispanic/Latino; 7% Hispanic/Latino; 6% Asian, non-Hispanic/Latino; 0.2% Native Hawaiian or other Pacific Islander, non-Hispanic/Latino; 0.8% American Indian or Alaska Native, non-Hispanic/Latino; 0.6% Two or more races, non-Hispanic/Latino; 4% international; 0.9% transferred in; 89% live on campus.

Freshmen:
Admission: 1,859 applied, 1,631 admitted, 503 enrolled. ***Average high school GPA:*** 3.67. ***Test scores:*** SAT critical reading scores over 500: 62%; SAT math scores over 500: 49%; SAT writing scores over 500: 59%; ACT scores over 18: 99%; SAT critical reading scores over 600: 21%; SAT math scores over 600: 10%; SAT writing scores over 600: 8%; ACT scores over 24: 64%; SAT critical reading scores over 700: 3%; SAT writing scores over 700: 5%; ACT scores over 30: 18%.
Retention: 83% of full-time freshmen returned.

FACULTY
Total: 168, 85% full-time, 79% with terminal degrees.
Student/faculty ratio: 12:1.

ACADEMICS
Calendar: semesters. *Degrees:* bachelor's (coordinate with Saint John's University for men).
Special study options: advanced placement credit, double majors, English as a second language, honors programs, independent study, internships, off-campus study, services for LD students, student-designed majors, study abroad. ***ROTC:*** Army (c).
Computers: 243 computers/terminals and 4,600 ports are available on campus for general student use. Students can access the following: campus intranet, computer help desk, free student e-mail accounts, online (class) grades, online (class) registration, online (class) schedules, online student accounts. 100% of college-owned or -operated housing units are wired for high-speed Internet access. Wireless service is available via entire campus.
Library: Clemens Library plus 2 others. *Books:* 698,393 (physical), 57,768 (digital/electronic); *Serial titles:* 918 (physical), 57,926 (digital/electronic); *Databases:* 242. Weekly public service hours: 104; students can reserve study rooms.

STUDENT LIFE
Housing options: on-campus residence required through senior year; women-only, special housing for students with disabilities. Campus housing is university owned. Freshman campus housing is guaranteed.
Activities and organizations: drama/theater group, student-run newspaper, radio and television station, choral group, Joint Events Council, Global Health Affairs Club, Magis Ministries, PRiSM, Archipelago Association.
Athletics Member NCAA. All Division III. ***Intercollegiate sports:*** basketball W, crew W(c), cross-country running W, golf W, ice hockey W, lacrosse W(c), rugby W(c), skiing (cross-country) W(c), soccer W, softball W, swimming and diving W, tennis W, track and field W, ultimate Frisbee W(c), volleyball W. ***Intramural sports:*** badminton W, basketball W, football W, racquetball W, soccer W, softball W, tennis W, volleyball W.
Campus security: 24-hour emergency response devices and patrols, student patrols, late-night transport/escort service, controlled dormitory access, well-lit pathways.
Student services: health clinic, personal/psychological counseling, women's center.

COSTS & FINANCIAL AID
Costs (2016–17) ***Comprehensive fee:*** $52,806 includes full-time tuition ($41,245), mandatory fees ($1026), and room and board ($10,535). Part-time tuition: $1719 per credit hour. Part-time tuition and fees vary according to course load. ***College room only:*** $5098. Room and board charges vary according to board plan and housing facility. ***Payment plan:*** installment. ***Waivers:*** employees or children of employees.
Financial Aid Of all full-time matriculated undergraduates who enrolled in 2016, 1,617 applied for aid, 1,436 were judged to have need, 495 had their need fully met. 344 Federal Work-Study jobs (averaging $2751). 1,202 state and other part-time jobs (averaging $2891). In 2016, 432 non-need-based awards were made. ***Average percent of need met:*** 90. ***Average financial aid package:*** $35,174. ***Average need-based loan:*** $5208. ***Average need-based gift aid:*** $28,598. ***Average non-need-based aid:*** $17,814. ***Average indebtedness upon graduation:*** $39,536.

APPLYING
Standardized Tests *Required:* SAT or ACT (for admission).
Options: electronic application, early action, deferred entrance.
Required: high school transcript, college preparatory program. *Recommended:* minimum 3.0 GPA.
Application deadlines: rolling (transfers), 11/15 (early action).
Notification: continuous (transfers), 12/15 (early action).

CONTACT
Ms. Karen Backes, Dean of Admissions, College of Saint Benedict, 37 South College Avenue, St. Joseph, MN 56374. *Phone:* 320-363-5055. *Toll-free phone:* 800-544-1489. *Fax:* 320-363-5650. *E-mail:* admissions@csbsju.edu.

The College of St. Scholastica

Duluth, Minnesota

http://www.css.edu/

- **Independent** comprehensive, founded 1912, affiliated with Roman Catholic Church
- **Suburban** 186-acre campus
- **Endowment** $69.4 million
- **Coed** 2,841 undergraduate students, 79% full-time, 72% women, 28% men
- **Moderately difficult** entrance level, 64% of applicants were admitted

UNDERGRAD STUDENTS
2,255 full-time, 586 part-time. Students come from 50 states and territories; 32 other countries; 15% are from out of state; 3% Black or African American, non-Hispanic/Latino; 4% Hispanic/Latino; 2% Asian, non-Hispanic/Latino; 0.1% Native Hawaiian or other Pacific Islander, non-Hispanic/Latino; 1% American Indian or Alaska Native, non-Hispanic/Latino; 3% Two or more races, non-Hispanic/Latino; 0.6% Race/ethnicity unknown; 3% international; 17% transferred in; 51% live on campus.

Freshmen:
Admission: 3,232 applied, 2,059 admitted, 451 enrolled. ***Average high school GPA:*** 3.5. ***Test scores:*** SAT critical reading scores over 500: 53%; SAT math scores over 500: 42%; SAT writing scores over 500: 42%; ACT scores over 18: 94%; SAT critical reading scores over 600: 11%; SAT math scores over 600: 11%; ACT scores over 24: 48%; ACT scores over 30: 6%.
Retention: 81% of full-time freshmen returned.

FACULTY
Total: 376, 51% full-time, 48% with terminal degrees.
Student/faculty ratio: 15:1.

ACADEMICS
Calendar: semesters. *Degrees:* certificates, bachelor's, master's, doctoral, post-master's, and postbachelor's certificates.

Special study options: accelerated degree program, adult/continuing education programs, advanced placement credit, distance learning, double majors, honors programs, independent study, internships, off-campus study, part-time degree program, services for LD students, student-designed majors, study abroad, summer session for credit.
ROTC: Air Force (c).

Unusual degree programs: 3-2 occupational therapy.

Computers: 614 computers/terminals are available on campus for general student use. Students can access the following: campus intranet, computer help desk, free student e-mail accounts, online (class) grades, online (class) registration, online (class) schedules, student account information, transcripts. Campuswide network is available. 100% of college-owned or -operated housing units are wired for high-speed Internet access. Wireless service is available via classrooms, computer centers, computer labs, dorm rooms, learning centers, libraries, student centers.
Library: College of St. Scholastica Library. *Books:* 110,444 (physical), 9,561 (digital/electronic); *Databases:* 124.

STUDENT LIFE
Housing options: on-campus residence required through sophomore year; coed, special housing for students with disabilities. Campus housing is university owned. Freshman applicants given priority for college housing.

Activities and organizations: drama/theater group, student-run newspaper, television station, choral group, Campus Activity Board, Inter-Varsity, Habitat for Humanity, SHIMA, Volunteers Involved Through Action.

Athletics Member NCAA. All Division III. ***Intercollegiate sports:*** baseball M, basketball M/W, cross-country running M/W, football M, golf M/W, ice hockey M/W, skiing (cross-country) M/W, soccer M/W, softball W, tennis M/W, track and field M/W, volleyball W. ***Intramural sports:*** basketball M/W, football M/W, soccer M/W, tennis M/W, volleyball M/W.

Campus security: 24-hour emergency response devices and patrols, late-night transport/escort service, controlled dormitory access, student door monitor at night.

Student services: health clinic, personal/psychological counseling.

COSTS & FINANCIAL AID
Costs (2016–17) ***Comprehensive fee:*** $44,640 includes full-time tuition ($34,764), mandatory fees ($562), and room and board ($9314). Full-time tuition and fees vary according to class time and program. Part-time tuition: $1088 per credit. Part-time tuition and fees vary according to class time, course load, and program. ***College room only:*** $5150. Room and board charges vary according to board plan and housing facility. ***Payment plan:*** installment. ***Waivers:*** senior citizens and employees or children of employees.

Financial Aid Of all full-time matriculated undergraduates who enrolled in 2016, 1,929 applied for aid, 1,764 were judged to have need, 366 had their need fully met. In 2016, 142 non-need-based awards were made. ***Average percent of need met:*** 71. ***Average financial aid package:*** $24,815. ***Average need-based loan:*** $4717. ***Average need-based gift aid:*** $7593. ***Average non-need-based aid:*** $17,321. ***Average indebtedness upon graduation:*** $40,774.

APPLYING
Standardized Tests *Required:* SAT or ACT (for admission).

Options: electronic application, deferred entrance.

Required: high school transcript. ***Required for some:*** minimum 2.0 GPA, interview. ***Recommended:*** interview.

Application deadlines: rolling (freshmen), rolling (transfers).

Notification: continuous (freshmen), continuous (transfers).

CONTACT
Mr. Eric Berg, Vice President for Enrollment Management, The College of St. Scholastica, 1200 Kenwood Avenue, Duluth, MN 55811-4199.
Phone: 218-723-6053. *Toll-free phone:* 800-249-6412.
E-mail: admissions@css.edu.

Concordia College

Moorhead, Minnesota

http://www.concordiacollege.edu/

- **Independent** comprehensive, founded 1891, affiliated with Evangelical Lutheran Church in America
- **Suburban** 113-acre campus
- **Endowment** $111.3 million
- **Coed** 2,114 undergraduate students, 98% full-time, 59% women, 41% men
- **Moderately difficult** entrance level, 65% of applicants were admitted

UNDERGRAD STUDENTS
2,066 full-time, 48 part-time. Students come from 38 states and territories; 26 other countries; 30% are from out of state; 2% Black or African American, non-Hispanic/Latino; 2% Hispanic/Latino; 1% Asian, non-Hispanic/Latino; 0.8% American Indian or Alaska Native, non-Hispanic/Latino; 2% Two or more races, non-Hispanic/Latino; 5% Race/ethnicity unknown; 4% international; 2% transferred in; 62% live on campus.

Freshmen:
Admission: 3,741 applied, 2,435 admitted, 545 enrolled. ***Average high school GPA:*** 3.54. ***Test scores:*** ACT scores over 18: 98%; ACT scores over 24: 61%; ACT scores over 30: 13%.
Retention: 84% of full-time freshmen returned.

FACULTY
Total: 246, 68% full-time, 65% with terminal degrees.
Student/faculty ratio: 11:1.

ACADEMICS
Calendar: semesters. *Degrees:* bachelor's and master's.
Special study options: accelerated degree program, advanced placement credit, cooperative education, distance learning, double majors, honors programs, independent study, internships, off-campus study, part-time degree program, services for LD students, student-designed majors, study abroad, summer session for credit. ***ROTC:*** Army (c), Air Force (c).

Computers: 570 computers/terminals and 87 ports are available on campus for general student use. Students can access the following: campus intranet, computer help desk, free student e-mail accounts, online (class) grades, online (class) registration, online (class) schedules, online degree audit. Campuswide network is available. 100% of college-owned or -operated housing units are wired for high-speed Internet access. Wireless service is available via entire campus.
Library: Carl B. Ylvisaker Library. *Books:* 347,087 (physical), 134,773 (digital/electronic); *Databases:* 148. Weekly public service hours: 93; students can reserve study rooms.

STUDENT LIFE
Housing options: on-campus residence required through sophomore year; coed. Campus housing is university owned. Freshman campus housing is guaranteed.
Activities and organizations: drama/theater group, student-run newspaper, radio and television station, choral group, Campus Entertainment Commission, Habitat for Humanity, Dance Marathon, Student Government Association, Campus Ministry Commission.
Athletics Member NCAA. All Division III. ***Intercollegiate sports:*** baseball M, basketball M/W, cheerleading M(c)/W(c), cross-country running M/W, football M, golf M/W, ice hockey M/W, soccer M/W, softball W, swimming and diving W, tennis M/W, track and field M/W, volleyball M(c)/W, wrestling M. ***Intramural sports:*** basketball M/W, bowling M/W, football M, ice hockey M(c)/W(c), lacrosse M(c)/W(c), rugby W(c), skiing (cross-country) M(c)/W(c), skiing (downhill) M(c)/W(c), swimming and diving M(c)/W(c), tennis M(c)/W(c), ultimate Frisbee M(c)/W(c), volleyball M/W.
Campus security: 24-hour emergency response devices and patrols, controlled dormitory access, well-lighted campus; outdoor campus emergency phones.
Student services: health clinic, personal/psychological counseling, women's center.

COSTS & FINANCIAL AID
Costs (2016–17) ***Comprehensive fee:*** $44,688 includes full-time tuition ($36,650), mandatory fees ($228), and room and board ($7810). Full-time

tuition and fees vary according to course load and degree level. Part-time tuition: $1380 per credit. Part-time tuition and fees vary according to course load and degree level. ***Required fees:*** $114 per term part-time. ***College room only:*** $3360. Room and board charges vary according to board plan and housing facility. ***Payment plan:*** installment. ***Waivers:*** employees or children of employees.

Financial Aid Of all full-time matriculated undergraduates who enrolled in 2015, 1,788 applied for aid, 1,539 were judged to have need, 328 had their need fully met. In 2015, 542 non-need-based awards were made. ***Average percent of need met:*** 90. ***Average financial aid package:*** $28,457. ***Average need-based loan:*** $5463. ***Average need-based gift aid:*** $20,861. ***Average non-need-based aid:*** $14,568.

APPLYING

Standardized Tests *Required:* SAT or ACT (for admission).

Options: electronic application, early admission, deferred entrance.

Application fee: $20.

Required: high school transcript, 2 letters of recommendation.

Application deadlines: rolling (freshmen), rolling (transfers).

Notification: continuous (freshmen), continuous (transfers).

CONTACT

Ms. Carola Thorson, Executive Director of Admissions and Scholarships, Concordia College, 901 8th Street South, Moorhead, MN 56562. *Phone:* 218-299-3004. *Toll-free phone:* 800-699-9897. *Fax:* 218-299-4720. *E-mail:* cthorson@cord.edu.

Concordia University, St. Paul

St. Paul, Minnesota

http://www.csp.edu/

- **Independent** comprehensive, founded 1893, affiliated with Lutheran Church–Missouri Synod
- **Urban** 37-acre campus with easy access to Minneapolis-St. Paul
- **Endowment** $47.2 million
- **Coed** 2,659 undergraduate students, 52% full-time, 60% women, 40% men
- **Minimally difficult** entrance level, 56% of applicants were admitted

UNDERGRAD STUDENTS

1,393 full-time, 1,266 part-time. Students come from 26 states and territories; 7 other countries; 24% are from out of state; 12% Black or African American, non-Hispanic/Latino; 4% Hispanic/Latino; 8% Asian, non-Hispanic/Latino; 0.2% Native Hawaiian or other Pacific Islander, non-Hispanic/Latino; 0.5% American Indian or Alaska Native, non-Hispanic/Latino; 4% Two or more races, non-Hispanic/Latino; 2% Race/ethnicity unknown; 5% international; 17% transferred in; 21% live on campus.

Freshmen:

Admission: 1,704 applied, 949 admitted, 248 enrolled. ***Average high school GPA:*** 3.17. ***Test scores:*** ACT scores over 18: 83%; ACT scores over 24: 27%; ACT scores over 30: 2%.

Retention: 72% of full-time freshmen returned.

FACULTY

Total: 446, 23% full-time, 32% with terminal degrees.

Student/faculty ratio: 17:1.

ACADEMICS

Calendar: semesters. *Degrees:* certificates, associate, bachelor's, master's, doctoral, post-master's, and postbachelor's certificates.

Special study options: academic remediation for entering students, accelerated degree program, adult/continuing education programs, advanced placement credit, distance learning, double majors, honors programs, independent study, internships, off-campus study, part-time degree program, services for LD students, student-designed majors, study abroad, summer session for credit. ***ROTC:*** Army (c), Air Force (c).

Computers: 10 computers/terminals and 150 ports are available on campus for general student use. Students can access the following: campus intranet, computer help desk, free student e-mail accounts, online (class) grades, online (class) registration, online (class) schedules. Campuswide network is available. 100% of college-owned or -operated housing units are wired for high-speed Internet access. Wireless service is available via entire campus.

Library: Library Technology Center. *Books:* 113,983 (physical), 170,320 (digital/electronic); *Serial titles:* 726 (physical), 119,903 (digital/electronic); *Databases:* 60. Weekly public service hours: 74; students can reserve study rooms.

STUDENT LIFE

Housing options: on-campus residence required for freshman year; coed, men-only, women-only, special housing for students with disabilities. Campus housing is university owned. Freshman campus housing is guaranteed.

Activities and organizations: drama/theater group, student-run newspaper, choral group, Southeast Asian Student Organization, United Minds of Joint Action.

Athletics Member NCAA. All Division II. ***Intercollegiate sports:*** baseball M(s), basketball M(s)/W(s), cross-country running M(s)/W(s), football M(s), golf M(s)/W(s), lacrosse W(s), soccer W(s), softball W(s), track and field M(s)/W(s), volleyball W(s). ***Intramural sports:*** basketball M/W, football M/W, soccer M/W, volleyball M/W.

Campus security: 24-hour emergency response devices and patrols, student patrols, late-night transport/escort service, controlled dormitory access.

Student services: personal/psychological counseling.

COSTS & FINANCIAL AID

Costs (2017–18) ***Comprehensive fee:*** $30,500 includes full-time tuition ($21,750) and room and board ($8750). Full-time tuition and fees vary according to degree level and program. Part-time tuition: $600 per credit. Part-time tuition and fees vary according to course load, degree level, and program. ***Room and board:*** Room and board charges vary according to board plan and housing facility. ***Payment plan:*** installment. ***Waivers:*** employees or children of employees.

Financial Aid Of all full-time matriculated undergraduates who enrolled in 2016, 1,113 applied for aid, 947 were judged to have need, 100 had their need fully met. 110 Federal Work-Study jobs (averaging $2358). 282 state and other part-time jobs (averaging $2335). In 2016, 151 non-need-based awards were made. ***Average percent of need met:*** 59. ***Average financial aid package:*** $14,088. ***Average need-based loan:*** $4493. ***Average need-based gift aid:*** $9941. ***Average non-need-based aid:*** $4806. ***Average indebtedness upon graduation:*** $33,183.

APPLYING

Standardized Tests *Required:* SAT or ACT (for admission).

Options: electronic application, early admission, deferred entrance.

Application fee: $30.

Required: high school transcript, 2 letters of recommendation. ***Required for some:*** essay or personal statement. ***Recommended:*** minimum 2.0 GPA.

Application deadlines: 8/1 (freshmen), 8/1 (transfers).

Notification: continuous (freshmen), continuous (transfers).

CONTACT

Ms. Briana Eicheldinger, Director of Traditional Admission, Concordia University, St. Paul, 1282 Concordia Avenue, St. Paul, MN 55104-5494. *Phone:* 651-641-8230. *Toll-free phone:* 800-333-4705. *Fax:* 651-603-6320. *E-mail:* admission@csp.edu.

Crossroads College

Rochester, Minnesota

http://www.crossroadscollege.edu/

CONTACT

Mr. Todd Looney, Director of Admissions, Crossroads College, 920 Mayowood Road, SW, Rochester, MN 55902-2382. *Phone:* 507-288-4563. *Toll-free phone:* 800-456-7651. *Fax:* 507-288-9046. *E-mail:* admissions@crossroadscollege.edu.

Crown College

St. Bonifacius, Minnesota

http://www.crown.edu/

CONTACT
Mr. Bret Hyder, Assistant Director of Admissions, Crown College, 8700 College View Drive, St. Bonifacius, MN 55375-9001. *Phone:* 952-446-4142. *Toll-free phone:* 800-68-CROWN. *Fax:* 952-446-4149.
E-mail: admissions@crown.edu.

Duluth Business University

Duluth, Minnesota

http://www.dbumn.edu/

- **Proprietary** primarily 2-year, founded 1891
- **Small-town** 2-acre campus
- **Coed, primarily women** 111 undergraduate students, 59% full-time, 95% women, 5% men

UNDERGRAD STUDENTS
65 full-time, 46 part-time. Students come from 6 states and territories; 21% are from out of state; 2% Black or African American, non-Hispanic/Latino; 0.9% Hispanic/Latino; 4% American Indian or Alaska Native, non-Hispanic/Latino.

Freshmen:
Admission: 12 enrolled.

ACADEMICS
Calendar: quarters. *Degrees:* diplomas, associate, and bachelor's.
Special study options: part-time degree program.
Computers: Wireless service is available via entire campus.

STUDENT LIFE
Housing options: college housing not available.

APPLYING
Standardized Tests *Required:* ACT (for admission).
Application fee: $35.
Required: high school transcript, interview.

CONTACT
Mrs. Teri Linder, Admissions Representative, Duluth Business University, 4724 Mike Colalillo Drive, Duluth, MN 55807. *Phone:* 218-722-4000.
Toll-free phone: 800-777-8406. *Fax:* 218-628-2127.
E-mail: teri@dbumn.edu.

Dunwoody College of Technology

Minneapolis, Minnesota

http://www.dunwoody.edu/

- **Independent** primarily 2-year, founded 1914
- **Urban** 12-acre campus with easy access to Minneapolis-St. Paul
- **Endowment** $25.0 million
- **Coed, primarily men** 1,264 undergraduate students, 84% full-time, 16% women, 84% men
- **Minimally difficult** entrance level, 65% of applicants were admitted

UNDERGRAD STUDENTS
1,062 full-time, 202 part-time. 3% are from out of state; 5% Black or African American, non-Hispanic/Latino; 3% Hispanic/Latino; 7% Asian, non-Hispanic/Latino; 0.2% Native Hawaiian or other Pacific Islander, non-Hispanic/Latino; 0.2% American Indian or Alaska Native, non-Hispanic/Latino; 4% Two or more races, non-Hispanic/Latino; 4% Race/ethnicity unknown; 20% transferred in.

Freshmen:
Admission: 1,168 applied, 763 admitted, 209 enrolled. ***Average high school GPA:*** 2.62.
Retention: 50% of full-time freshmen returned.

FACULTY
Total: 142, 61% full-time, 13% with terminal degrees.
Student/faculty ratio: 11:1.

ACADEMICS
Calendar: semesters. *Degrees:* certificates, associate, and bachelor's.
Special study options: academic remediation for entering students, adult/continuing education programs, cooperative education, distance learning, independent study, internships, study abroad, summer session for credit.
Computers: 300 computers/terminals and 1,000 ports are available on campus for general student use. Students can access the following: campus intranet, computer help desk, free student e-mail accounts, online (class) grades, online (class) registration, online (class) schedules. Campuswide network is available. Wireless service is available via entire campus.
Library: Learning Resource Center plus 1 other. *Books:* 2,500 (physical), 162,865 (digital/electronic); *Serial titles:* 131 (physical); *Databases:* 24. Weekly public service hours: 55.

STUDENT LIFE
Housing options: college housing not available.
Activities and organizations: Phi Theta Kappa, Historic Green, Dunwoody Motorsports Club, Architectural Institute of America Student Chapter, Professional Association for Design.
Campus security: 24-hour emergency response devices, late-night transport/escort service.
Student services: women's center.

COSTS & FINANCIAL AID
Costs (2017–18) ***Tuition:*** $18,826 full-time, $654 per credit part-time. Full-time tuition and fees vary according to course load, degree level, and program. Part-time tuition and fees vary according to course load, degree level, and program. ***Required fees:*** $1652 full-time, $1458 per term part-time. ***Payment plan:*** installment. ***Waivers:*** employees or children of employees.
Financial Aid Of all full-time matriculated undergraduates who enrolled in 2015, 859 applied for aid, 769 were judged to have need, 34 had their need fully met. 26 Federal Work-Study jobs (averaging $2376). 29 state and other part-time jobs (averaging $3546). In 2015, 46 non-need-based awards were made. ***Average percent of need met:*** 33. ***Average financial aid package:*** $8555. ***Average need-based loan:*** $3599. ***Average need-based gift aid:*** $6254. ***Average non-need-based aid:*** $2119.

APPLYING
Standardized Tests *Required for some:* ACT (for admission).
Options: electronic application.
Application fee: $50.
Required: essay or personal statement, high school transcript. ***Required for some:*** minimum 3.0 GPA, letters of recommendation, resumé. *Recommended:* minimum 2.5 GPA, interview.
Application deadlines: rolling (freshmen), rolling (transfers).
Notification: continuous (freshmen), continuous (transfers).

CONTACT
Kelly OBrien, Director of Admissions, Dunwoody College of Technology, 818 Dunwoody Boulevard, Minneapolis, MN 55403. *Phone:* 612-381-3302. *Toll-free phone:* 800-292-4625. *Fax:* 612-677-3131.
E-mail: kobrien@dunwoody.edu.

Globe University–Minneapolis

Minneapolis, Minnesota

http://www.globeuniversity.edu/

CONTACT
Globe University–Minneapolis, 80 South 8th Street, Suite 51, Minneapolis, MN 55402.

Globe University–Woodbury

Woodbury, Minnesota

http://www.globeuniversity.edu/

CONTACT
Globe University–Woodbury, 8089 Globe Drive, Woodbury, MN 55125.
Toll-free phone: 800-231-0660.

Gustavus Adolphus College

St. Peter, Minnesota

http://www.gustavus.edu/

- **Independent** 4-year, founded 1862, affiliated with Evangelical Lutheran Church in America
- **Small-town** 340-acre campus with easy access to Minneapolis-St. Paul
- **Coed**
- **Very difficult** entrance level

FACULTY
Student/faculty ratio: 11:1.

ACADEMICS
Calendar: 4-1-4. *Degree:* bachelor's.
Library: Folke Bernadotte Memorial Library.

STUDENT LIFE
Housing options: on-campus residence required through senior year; coed, special housing for students with disabilities. Campus housing is university owned. Freshman campus housing is guaranteed.

Activities and organizations: drama/theater group, student-run newspaper, radio and television station, choral group, Proclaim, Big Partner/Little Partner, Study Buddies, I am...We are, Pound Pals, national fraternities, national sororities.

Athletics Member NCAA. All Division III.

Campus security: 24-hour emergency response devices and patrols, late-night transport/escort service, controlled dormitory access.

Student services: health clinic, personal/psychological counseling, women's center.

COSTS & FINANCIAL AID
Costs (2016–17) ***One-time required fee:*** $480. ***Comprehensive fee:*** $51,950 includes full-time tuition ($42,360), mandatory fees ($190), and room and board ($9400). Part-time tuition: $7290 per course. ***College room only:*** $5990. Room and board charges vary according to board plan and housing facility. ***Payment plans:*** tuition prepayment, installment.

Financial Aid Of all full-time matriculated undergraduates who enrolled in 2015, 1,847 applied for aid, 1,652 were judged to have need, 522 had their need fully met. In 2015, 671 non-need-based awards were made. ***Average percent of need met:*** 90. ***Average financial aid package:*** $34,694. ***Average need-based loan:*** $3489. ***Average need-based gift aid:*** $29,745. ***Average non-need-based aid:*** $20,598. ***Average indebtedness upon graduation:*** $34,773. ***Financial aid deadline:*** 4/15.

APPLYING
Options: electronic application, early admission, early action, deferred entrance.

Required: essay or personal statement, high school transcript, 1 letter of recommendation. ***Recommended:*** interview.

CONTACT
Dr. Tom M. Crady, Vice President for Enrollment Management, Gustavus Adolphus College, 800 West College Avenue, St. Peter, MN 56082-1498. *Phone:* 507-933-7676. *Toll-free phone:* 800-GUSTAVU(S). *Fax:* 507-933-7474. *E-mail:* admission@gac.edu.

Hamline University

St. Paul, Minnesota

http://www.hamline.edu/

- **Independent** comprehensive, founded 1854, affiliated with United Methodist Church
- **Urban** 60-acre campus with easy access to Minneapolis-St. Paul
- **Coed** 2,184 undergraduate students, 96% full-time, 60% women, 40% men
- **Moderately difficult** entrance level, 70% of applicants were admitted

UNDERGRAD STUDENTS
2,090 full-time, 94 part-time. Students come from 40 states and territories; 35 other countries; 20% are from out of state; 6% Black or African American, non-Hispanic/Latino; 8% Hispanic/Latino; 6% Asian, non-Hispanic/Latino; 0.3% American Indian or Alaska Native, non-Hispanic/Latino; 6% Two or more races, non-Hispanic/Latino; 2% Race/ethnicity unknown; 2% international; 6% transferred in; 39% live on campus.

Freshmen:
Admission: 4,252 applied, 2,989 admitted, 548 enrolled. ***Average high school GPA:*** 3.46. ***Test scores:*** SAT critical reading scores over 500: 68%; SAT math scores over 500: 73%; SAT writing scores over 500: 51%; ACT scores over 18: 97%; SAT critical reading scores over 600: 27%; SAT math scores over 600: 30%; SAT writing scores over 600: 14%; ACT scores over 24: 53%; SAT critical reading scores over 700: 8%; SAT math scores over 700: 3%; ACT scores over 30: 8%.
Retention: 79% of full-time freshmen returned.

FACULTY
Total: 333, 46% full-time, 59% with terminal degrees.
Student/faculty ratio: 12:1.

ACADEMICS
Calendar: 4-1-4. *Degrees:* certificates, bachelor's, master's, doctoral, post-master's, and postbachelor's certificates.

Special study options: advanced placement credit, distance learning, double majors, English as a second language, honors programs, independent study, internships, off-campus study, part-time degree program, services for LD students, student-designed majors, study abroad, summer session for credit. ***ROTC:*** Army (c), Air Force (c).

Unusual degree programs: 3-2 engineering with University of Minnesota, Washington University in St. Louis.

Computers: 300 computers/terminals are available on campus for general student use. Students can access the following: campus intranet, computer help desk, free student e-mail accounts, online (class) grades, online (class) registration, online (class) schedules. Campuswide network is available. 99% of college-owned or -operated housing units are wired for high-speed Internet access. Wireless service is available via entire campus.

Library: Bush Library.

STUDENT LIFE
Housing options: coed, special housing for students with disabilities. Campus housing is university owned. Freshman campus housing is guaranteed.

Activities and organizations: drama/theater group, student-run newspaper, radio and television station, choral group, International Student Association, Chemistry Club, Hand in Hand, Hamline Book Club, Hamline Student Athlete Advisory Committee, national fraternities, national sororities.

Athletics Member NCAA. All Division III. ***Intercollegiate sports:*** baseball M, basketball M/W, cheerleading W(c), cross-country running M/W, football M, gymnastics W, ice hockey M/W, lacrosse W, soccer M/W, softball W, swimming and diving M/W, tennis M/W, track and field M/W, volleyball W. ***Intramural sports:*** basketball M(c)/W(c), football M(c)/W(c), golf M(c)/W(c), lacrosse M(c)/W(c), rock climbing M(c)/W(c), soccer M(c)/W(c), ultimate Frisbee M(c)/W(c), volleyball M(c)/W(c).

Campus security: 24-hour emergency response devices and patrols, student patrols, late-night transport/escort service, controlled dormitory access, security cameras on campus and in residence halls, security officers are trained as first responders.

Student services: health clinic, personal/psychological counseling, women's center.

COSTS & FINANCIAL AID
Costs (2017–18) ***Comprehensive fee:*** $50,488 includes full-time tuition ($39,206), mandatory fees ($1126), and room and board ($10,156). Part-time tuition: $1225 per credit hour. Part-time tuition and fees vary according to course load. ***Required fees:*** $767 per year part-time. ***College room only:*** $5076. Room and board charges vary according to board plan and housing facility. ***Payment plan:*** installment. ***Waivers:*** employees or children of employees.

Financial Aid Of all full-time matriculated undergraduates who enrolled in 2016, 1,861 applied for aid, 1,728 were judged to have need, 297 had their need fully met. 323 Federal Work-Study jobs (averaging $2261). 1,009 state and other part-time jobs (averaging $2589). In 2016, 309 non-need-based awards were made. ***Average percent of need met:*** 79. ***Average financial aid package:*** $29,877. ***Average need-based loan:*** $4748. ***Average need-based gift aid:*** $23,426. ***Average non-need-based aid:*** $16,630. ***Average indebtedness upon graduation:*** $34,935.

APPLYING
Standardized Tests *Required:* SAT or ACT (for admission).

Options: electronic application, early admission, early decision, early action, deferred entrance.

Required: high school transcript. ***Recommended:*** essay or personal statement, 1 letter of recommendation, interview.

Application deadlines: rolling (freshmen), rolling (transfers), 12/1 (early action).

Early decision deadline: 11/1.

Notification: continuous (freshmen), continuous (transfers), 11/15 (early decision).

CONTACT
Admissions Office, Hamline University, 1536 Hewitt Avenue, St. Paul, MN 55104-1284. *Phone:* 651-523-2207. *Toll-free phone:* 800-753-9753. *E-mail:* admission@hamline.edu.

Herzing University

Minneapolis, Minnesota

http://www.herzing.edu/minneapolis

CONTACT
Ms. Shelly Larson, Director of Admissions, Herzing University, 5700 West Broadway, Minneapolis, MN 55428. *Phone:* 763-231-3155. *Toll-free phone:* 800-596-0724. *Fax:* 763-535-9205. *E-mail:* info@mpls.herzing.edu.

Macalester College

St. Paul, Minnesota

http://www.macalester.edu/

- **Independent** 4-year, founded 1874
- **Urban** 53-acre campus
- **Endowment** $700.2 million
- **Coed** 2,146 undergraduate students, 98% full-time, 60% women, 40% men
- **Very difficult** entrance level, 37% of applicants were admitted

UNDERGRAD STUDENTS
2,108 full-time, 38 part-time. Students come from 52 states and territories; 66 other countries; 83% are from out of state; 3% Black or African American, non-Hispanic/Latino; 6% Hispanic/Latino; 7% Asian, non-Hispanic/Latino; 0.1% Native Hawaiian or other Pacific Islander, non-Hispanic/Latino; 0.2% American Indian or Alaska Native, non-Hispanic/Latino; 5% Two or more races, non-Hispanic/Latino; 0.1% Race/ethnicity unknown; 15% international; 0.7% transferred in; 72% live on campus.

Freshmen:
Admission: 5,946 applied, 2,206 admitted, 506 enrolled. ***Test scores:*** SAT critical reading scores over 500: 99%; SAT math scores over 500: 99%; SAT writing scores over 500: 98%; ACT scores over 18: 100%; SAT critical reading scores over 600: 84%; SAT math scores over 600: 87%; SAT writing scores over 600: 89%; ACT scores over 24: 97%; SAT critical reading scores over 700: 48%; SAT math scores over 700: 45%; SAT writing scores over 700: 44%; ACT scores over 30: 68%.

Retention: 93% of full-time freshmen returned.

FACULTY
Total: 246, 74% full-time, 82% with terminal degrees.

Student/faculty ratio: 10:1.

ACADEMICS
Calendar: semesters. *Degree:* bachelor's.

Special study options: advanced placement credit, double majors, honors programs, independent study, internships, off-campus study, part-time degree program, services for LD students, student-designed majors, study abroad, summer session for credit. ***ROTC:*** Army (c), Navy (c), Air Force (c).

Unusual degree programs: 3-2 architecture with Washington University in St. Louis.

Computers: 550 computers/terminals and 2,600 ports are available on campus for general student use. Students can access the following: campus intranet, computer help desk, free student e-mail accounts, online (class) grades, online (class) registration, online (class) schedules, wireless networking, free printing, specialized tools. Campuswide network is available. 100% of college-owned or -operated housing units are wired for high-speed Internet access. Wireless service is available via entire campus.

Library: DeWitt Wallace Library. *Books:* 348,727 (physical), 51,212 (digital/electronic); *Serial titles:* 3,221 (physical), 12,151 (digital/electronic); *Databases:* 200. Weekly public service hours: 109; study areas open 24 hours, 5-7 days a week; students can reserve study rooms.

STUDENT LIFE
Housing options: on-campus residence required through sophomore year; coed, men-only, women-only, cooperative. Campus housing is university owned. Freshman campus housing is guaranteed.

Activities and organizations: drama/theater group, student-run newspaper, radio station, choral group, Program Board, Queer Union, The Mac Weekly, Adelante , Outing Club.

Athletics Member NCAA. All Division III. ***Intercollegiate sports:*** baseball M, basketball M/W, crew M(c)/W(c), cross-country running M/W, football M, golf M/W, ice hockey M(c)/W(c), lacrosse W(c), rugby M(c)/W(c), skiing (cross-country) M(c)/W(c), soccer M/W, softball W, swimming and diving M/W, tennis M/W, track and field M/W, ultimate Frisbee M(c)/W(c), volleyball M(c)/W, water polo M(c)/W. ***Intramural sports:*** basketball M/W, racquetball M/W, soccer M/W, softball M/W, table tennis M/W, ultimate Frisbee M/W.

Campus security: 24-hour emergency response devices and patrols, late-night transport/escort service, controlled dormitory access, Rave Alert Notification System (texting/email).

Student services: health clinic, personal/psychological counseling.

COSTS & FINANCIAL AID
Costs (2017–18) ***Comprehensive fee:*** $64,136 includes full-time tuition ($52,234), mandatory fees ($230), and room and board ($11,672). Full-time tuition and fees vary according to course load. Part-time tuition: $1632 per credit. Part-time tuition and fees vary according to course load. ***College room only:*** $6238. Room and board charges vary according to board plan and housing facility. ***Payment plan:*** installment. ***Waivers:*** employees or children of employees.

Financial Aid Of all full-time matriculated undergraduates who enrolled in 2016, 1,587 applied for aid, 1,432 were judged to have need, 1,432 had their need fully met. In 2016, 258 non-need-based awards were made. ***Average percent of need met:*** 100. ***Average financial aid package:*** $43,969. ***Average need-based loan:*** $5065. ***Average need-based gift aid:*** $37,392. ***Average non-need-based aid:*** $13,752. ***Average indebtedness upon graduation:*** $23,875.

APPLYING
Standardized Tests *Required:* SAT or ACT (for admission).

Options: electronic application, early admission, early decision, deferred entrance.

Application fee: $40.

Required: essay or personal statement, high school transcript, 2 letters of recommendation. ***Recommended:*** interview.

Application deadlines: 1/15 (freshmen), 4/15 (transfers).

Early decision deadline: 11/15 (for plan 1), 1/1 (for plan 2).

Notification: 3/30 (freshmen), 5/15 (transfers), 12/15 (early decision plan 1), 2/7 (early decision plan 2).

CONTACT
Mr. Lorne T. Robinson, Dean of Admissions and Financial Aid, Macalester College, 1600 Grand Avenue, St. Paul, MN 55105-1899. *Phone:* 651-696-6357. *Toll-free phone:* 800-231-7974. *Fax:* 651-696-6724. *E-mail:* admissions@macalester.edu.

Martin Luther College

New Ulm, Minnesota

http://www.mlc-wels.edu/

- **Independent** comprehensive, founded 1995, affiliated with Wisconsin Evangelical Lutheran Synod
- **Small-town** 50-acre campus
- **Coed** 827 undergraduate students, 85% full-time, 51% women, 49% men
- **Moderately difficult** entrance level, 78% of applicants were admitted

UNDERGRAD STUDENTS
705 full-time, 122 part-time. 79% are from out of state; 1% Black or African American, non-Hispanic/Latino; 0.9% Hispanic/Latino; 0.7% Asian, non-Hispanic/Latino; 0.1% American Indian or Alaska Native, non-Hispanic/Latino; 1% Two or more races, non-Hispanic/Latino; 3% international; 3% transferred in; 92% live on campus.

Freshmen:
Admission: 262 applied, 204 admitted, 172 enrolled. ***Average high school GPA:*** 3.5. ***Test scores:*** ACT scores over 18: 98%; ACT scores over 24: 59%; ACT scores over 30: 12%.
Retention: 83% of full-time freshmen returned.

FACULTY
Total: 73, 68% full-time, 38% with terminal degrees.
Student/faculty ratio: 12:1.

ACADEMICS
Calendar: semesters. *Degrees:* certificates, diplomas, bachelor's, and master's.
Special study options: advanced placement credit, distance learning, double majors, summer session for credit.
Computers: Campuswide network is available.
Library: Martin Luther College Library.

STUDENT LIFE
Housing options: on-campus residence required through junior year; men-only, women-only, special housing for students with disabilities. Campus housing is university owned.
Activities and organizations: drama/theater group, choral group.
Athletics Member NCAA, NAIA. All NCAA Division III. ***Intercollegiate sports:*** baseball M, basketball M/W, cross-country running M/W, football M, golf M, soccer M/W, softball W, tennis M/W, track and field M/W, volleyball W. ***Intramural sports:*** badminton M/W, basketball M/W, bowling M/W, football M, soccer M/W, softball M/W, tennis M/W, volleyball M/W.
Student services: health clinic, personal/psychological counseling.

COSTS & FINANCIAL AID
Costs (2017–18) ***Comprehensive fee:*** $20,470 includes full-time tuition ($14,680) and room and board ($5790). ***Room and board:*** Room and board charges vary according to housing facility. ***Payment plan:*** installment.
Financial Aid Of all full-time matriculated undergraduates who enrolled in 2015, 571 applied for aid, 499 were judged to have need, 63 had their need fully met. In 2015, 99 non-need-based awards were made. ***Average percent of need met:*** 70. ***Average financial aid package:*** $11,797. ***Average need-based loan:*** $4554. ***Average need-based gift aid:*** $7554. ***Average non-need-based aid:*** $2746. ***Average indebtedness upon graduation:*** $22,582. ***Financial aid deadline:*** 4/15.

APPLYING
Standardized Tests *Required:* ACT (for admission).
Options: deferred entrance.
Required: high school transcript, minimum 2.0 GPA.

CONTACT
Prof. Mark A. Stein, Director of Admissions, Martin Luther College, 1995 Luther Court, New Ulm, MN 56073. *Phone:* 507-354-8221 Ext. 280. *Toll-free phone:* 877-MLC-1995. *E-mail:* brutlaro@mlc-wels.edu.

McNally Smith College of Music

Saint Paul, Minnesota

http://www.mcnallysmith.edu/

CONTACT
Mrs. Katie Marshall, Admissions Representative, McNally Smith College of Music, 19 Exchange Street East, St. Paul, MN 55101. *Phone:* 651-361-3451. *Toll-free phone:* 800-594-9500. *Fax:* 651-291-0366. *E-mail:* katie.marshall@mcnallysmith.edu.

Metropolitan State University

St. Paul, Minnesota

http://www.metrostate.edu/

CONTACT
Mr. Daryl Johnson, Director, Metropolitan State University, 700 East 7th Street, St. Paul, MN 55106. *Phone:* 651-793-1227. *Fax:* 651-793-1546. *E-mail:* daryl.johnson@metrostate.edu.

Minneapolis College of Art and Design

Minneapolis, Minnesota

http://www.mcad.edu/

- **Independent** comprehensive, founded 1886
- **Urban** campus
- **Coed** 668 undergraduate students, 98% full-time, 66% women, 34% men
- **Moderately difficult** entrance level

UNDERGRAD STUDENTS
653 full-time, 15 part-time. 35% are from out of state; 4% Black or African American, non-Hispanic/Latino; 6% Hispanic/Latino; 8% Asian, non-Hispanic/Latino; 1% American Indian or Alaska Native, non-Hispanic/Latino; 3% Two or more races, non-Hispanic/Latino; 18% Race/ethnicity unknown; 7% transferred in.

Freshmen:
Admission: 145 enrolled.
Retention: 81% of full-time freshmen returned.

ACADEMICS
Calendar: semesters. *Degrees:* bachelor's, master's, and postbachelor's certificates.
Special study options: adult/continuing education programs, advanced placement credit, cooperative education, distance learning, independent study, internships, off-campus study, part-time degree program, services for LD students, study abroad, summer session for credit.
Computers: Students can access the following: campus intranet, computer help desk, free student e-mail accounts, online (class) grades. Campuswide network is available. Wireless service is available via entire campus.

STUDENT LIFE
Housing options: coed. Campus housing is university owned, leased by the school and is provided by a third party. Freshman applicants given priority for college housing.
Activities and organizations: student-run radio station.
Athletics ***Intramural sports:*** basketball M(c), soccer M(c)/W(c), softball M(c)/W(c).
Campus security: 24-hour emergency response devices and patrols, late-night transport/escort service, controlled dormitory access.
Student services: personal/psychological counseling.

COSTS & FINANCIAL AID
Costs (2017–18) ***Tuition:*** $37,362 full-time, $1557 per credit hour part-time. Part-time tuition and fees vary according to course load. ***Required fees:*** $450 full-time, $225 per term part-time. ***Room only:*** $5450. Room and board charges vary according to housing facility. ***Payment plan:*** installment. ***Waivers:*** children of alumni and employees or children of employees.
Financial Aid Of all full-time matriculated undergraduates who enrolled in 2014, 546 applied for aid, 490 were judged to have need, 54 had their need fully met. In 2014, 112 non-need-based awards were made. ***Average***

percent of need met: 68. *Average financial aid package:* $22,825. *Average need-based loan:* $4747. *Average need-based gift aid:* $17,718. *Average non-need-based aid:* $11,165. *Average indebtedness upon graduation:* $33,400. *Financial aid deadline:* 4/1.

APPLYING
Standardized Tests *Required for some:* SAT or ACT (for admission).
Options: electronic application, early action.
Required: essay or personal statement, high school transcript. *Recommended:* interview.
Application deadlines: 5/1 (freshmen), 5/1 (transfers), 12/1 (early action).
Notification: continuous (freshmen), continuous (out-of-state freshmen), continuous (transfers), 12/15 (early action).

CONTACT
Minneapolis College of Art and Design, 2501 Stevens Avenue, Minneapolis, MN 55404-4347. *Phone:* 612-874-3764. *Toll-free phone:* 800-874-6223.

Minnesota State University Mankato
Mankato, Minnesota
http://www.mnsu.edu/

- **State-supported** university, founded 1868, part of Minnesota State Colleges and Universities System
- **Small-town** 303-acre campus with easy access to Minneapolis-St. Paul
- **Coed** 13,459 undergraduate students, 85% full-time, 52% women, 48% men

UNDERGRAD STUDENTS
11,412 full-time, 2,047 part-time. Students come from 91 other countries; 12% are from out of state; 5% Black or African American, non-Hispanic/Latino; 3% Hispanic/Latino; 3% Asian, non-Hispanic/Latino; 0.2% American Indian or Alaska Native, non-Hispanic/Latino; 2% Two or more races, non-Hispanic/Latino; 3% Race/ethnicity unknown; 5% international; 8% transferred in; 25% live on campus.

Freshmen:
Admission: 2,456 enrolled. *Average high school GPA:* 3.21. *Test scores:* ACT scores over 18: 91%; ACT scores over 24: 30%; ACT scores over 30: 2%.
Retention: 81% of full-time freshmen returned.

FACULTY
Total: 754, 58% full-time.
Student/faculty ratio: 20:1.

ACADEMICS
Calendar: semesters. *Degrees:* certificates, associate, bachelor's, master's, doctoral, and post-master's certificates.
Special study options: academic remediation for entering students, accelerated degree program, adult/continuing education programs, advanced placement credit, cooperative education, distance learning, double majors, English as a second language, external degree program, honors programs, independent study, internships, off-campus study, part-time degree program, services for LD students, student-designed majors, study abroad, summer session for credit. *ROTC:* Army (b).
Computers: 900 computers/terminals are available on campus for general student use. Students can access the following: campus intranet, computer help desk, free student e-mail accounts, online (class) grades, online (class) registration, online (class) schedules. Campuswide network is available. Wireless service is available via entire campus.
Library: Memorial Library.

STUDENT LIFE
Housing options: coed. Campus housing is university owned and leased by the school. Freshman applicants given priority for college housing.
Activities and organizations: drama/theater group, student-run newspaper, radio station, choral group, marching band, national fraternities, national sororities.
Athletics Member NCAA. All Division II except men's and women's ice hockey (Division I). *Intercollegiate sports:* baseball M(s), basketball M(s)/W(s), bowling W, cheerleading M/W, cross-country running M(s)/W(s), football M(s), golf M(s)/W(s), ice hockey M(s)/W(s), soccer W(s), softball W(s), swimming and diving W(s), tennis M(s)/W(s), track and field M(s)/W(s), volleyball W(s), wrestling M(s). *Intramural sports:* archery M/W, basketball M/W, bowling M/W, fencing M/W, football M/W, golf M/W, ice hockey M/W, lacrosse M/W, racquetball M/W, rock climbing M/W, rugby M(c)/W(c), sailing M/W, skiing (downhill) M/W, soccer M/W, softball M/W, swimming and diving W, table tennis M/W, tennis M/W, track and field M/W, volleyball M/W, wrestling M.
Campus security: 24-hour emergency response devices and patrols, student patrols, late-night transport/escort service, controlled dormitory access, Night Owl security program in residence halls, closed circuit cameras in parking lots.
Student services: health clinic, personal/psychological counseling, women's center, legal services.

COSTS & FINANCIAL AID
Costs (2016–17) *Tuition:* $408 per credit hour part-time; state resident $7858 full-time, $272 per credit hour part-time; nonresident $15,602 full-time, $584 per credit hour part-time. Full-time tuition and fees vary according to course load, location, program, and reciprocity agreements. Part-time tuition and fees vary according to course load, location, program, and reciprocity agreements. *Required fees:* $954 full-time, $40 per credit hour part-time. *Room and board:* $8716; room only: $5314. Room and board charges vary according to board plan and housing facility. *Payment plan:* installment. *Waivers:* senior citizens and employees or children of employees.
Financial Aid Of all full-time matriculated undergraduates who enrolled in 2016, 8,380 applied for aid, 5,903 were judged to have need, 1,246 had their need fully met. 373 Federal Work-Study jobs (averaging $4316). 483 state and other part-time jobs (averaging $4093). In 2016, 777 non-need-based awards were made. *Average percent of need met:* 74. *Average financial aid package:* $9396. *Average need-based loan:* $4294. *Average need-based gift aid:* $5508. *Average non-need-based aid:* $4907. *Average indebtedness upon graduation:* $31,453.

APPLYING
Standardized Tests *Required:* SAT or ACT (for admission).
Required: high school transcript. *Required for some:* essay or personal statement, 1 letter of recommendation, personal statement, letter and senior grades.

CONTACT
Office of Admissions, Minnesota State University Mankato, 122 Taylor Center, Mankato, MN 56001. *Phone:* 507-389-1822.
Toll-free phone: 800-722-0544. *Fax:* 507-389-1511.
E-mail: admissions@mnsu.edu.

Minnesota State University Moorhead
Moorhead, Minnesota
http://www.mnstate.edu/

- **State-supported** comprehensive, founded 1885, part of Minnesota State Colleges and Universities System
- **Urban** 119-acre campus
- **Endowment** $17.5 million
- **Coed** 5,245 undergraduate students, 82% full-time, 60% women, 40% men
- **Moderately difficult** entrance level, 82% of applicants were admitted

UNDERGRAD STUDENTS
4,324 full-time, 921 part-time. 33% are from out of state; 3% Black or African American, non-Hispanic/Latino; 3% Hispanic/Latino; 1% Asian, non-Hispanic/Latino; 0.1% Native Hawaiian or other Pacific Islander, non-Hispanic/Latino; 0.7% American Indian or Alaska Native, non-Hispanic/Latino; 3% Two or more races, non-Hispanic/Latino; 5% Race/ethnicity unknown; 8% international; 10% transferred in; 25% live on campus.

Freshmen:
Admission: 2,610 applied, 2,143 admitted, 729 enrolled.
Retention: 73% of full-time freshmen returned.

FACULTY
Total: 367, 62% full-time.
Student/faculty ratio: 17:1.

ACADEMICS
Calendar: semesters. *Degrees:* certificates, associate, bachelor's, master's, post-master's, and postbachelor's certificates.
Special study options: academic remediation for entering students, adult/continuing education programs, advanced placement credit, distance learning, double majors, English as a second language, honors programs, independent study, internships, off-campus study, part-time degree program, services for LD students, student-designed majors, study abroad, summer session for credit. ***ROTC:*** Army (c), Air Force (c).
Computers: 2,200 computers/terminals are available on campus for general student use. Students can access the following: computer help desk, free student e-mail accounts, online (class) grades, online (class) registration, online (class) schedules. Campuswide network is available. 100% of college-owned or -operated housing units are wired for high-speed Internet access. Wireless service is available via entire campus.
Library: Livingston Lord Library plus 1 other. *Books:* 561,220 (physical), 15,357 (digital/electronic); *Databases:* 558. Students can reserve study rooms.

STUDENT LIFE
Housing options: coed, men-only, women-only, special housing for students with disabilities. Campus housing is university owned.
Activities and organizations: drama/theater group, student-run newspaper, radio and television station, choral group, Chi Alpha, International Students Organization, Student Orientation Counselor and Friends, Education Minnesota Student Program, Student Senate, national fraternities, national sororities.
Athletics Member NCAA. All Division II. ***Intercollegiate sports:*** basketball M(s)/W(s), cheerleading M/W, cross-country running M(s)/W(s), football M(s), golf W(s), soccer W(s), softball W(s), swimming and diving W(s), tennis W(s), track and field M(s)/W(s), volleyball W(s), wrestling M(s). ***Intramural sports:*** badminton M/W, basketball M/W, football M/W, golf W, ice hockey M/W, soccer M(c)/W(c), softball M/W, tennis M/W, ultimate Frisbee M/W, volleyball M/W.
Campus security: 24-hour emergency response devices and patrols, student patrols, late-night transport/escort service, controlled dormitory access.
Student services: health clinic, personal/psychological counseling, women's center.

COSTS & FINANCIAL AID
Costs (2017–18) ***Tuition:*** state resident $7136 full-time, $230 per credit hour part-time; nonresident $14,272 full-time, $461 per credit hour part-time. Full-time tuition and fees vary according to course load. Part-time tuition and fees vary according to reciprocity agreements. ***Required fees:*** $40 per credit part-time, $490 per term part-time. ***Room and board:*** $8076; room only: $5072. ***Waivers:*** employees or children of employees.
Financial Aid Of all full-time matriculated undergraduates who enrolled in 2016, 3,303 applied for aid, 2,512 were judged to have need. 181 Federal Work-Study jobs (averaging $2260). 246 state and other part-time jobs (averaging $2391). ***Average financial aid package:*** $3208. ***Average need-based loan:*** $3935. ***Average need-based gift aid:*** $2637. ***Average indebtedness upon graduation:*** $34,697.

APPLYING
Standardized Tests *Required:* SAT or ACT (for admission).
Options: electronic application, early admission, deferred entrance.
Application fee: $20.
Required: high school transcript.
Application deadlines: 8/1 (freshmen), 8/1 (transfers).

CONTACT
Admissions Office, Minnesota State University Moorhead, Owens Hall, Moorhead, MN 56563-0002. *Phone:* 218-477-2161. *Toll-free phone:* 800-593-7246. *Fax:* 218-477-4374. *E-mail:* admissionsoffice@mnstate.edu.

National American University
Bloomington, Minnesota
http://www.national.edu/

CONTACT
Ms. Jennifer Michaelson, Admissions Assistant, National American University, 321 Kansas City Street, Rapid City, SD 57201. *Phone:* 605-394-4827. *Toll-free phone:* 866-628-6387. *E-mail:* jmichaelson@national.edu.

National American University
Brooklyn Center, Minnesota
http://www.national.edu/

CONTACT
Admissions Office, National American University, 6200 Shingle Creek Parkway, Suite 130, Brooklyn Center, MN 55430. *Toll-free phone:* 866-628-6387.

National American University
Burnsville, Minnesota
http://www.national.edu/

CONTACT
National American University, 513 West Travelers Trail, Burnsville, MN 55337. *Toll-free phone:* 866-628-6387.

National American University
Roseville, Minnesota
http://www.national.edu/

CONTACT
Mr. Steve Grunlan, Director of Admissions, National American University, 1550 West Highway 36, Roseville, MN 55113. *Phone:* 651-644-1265. *Toll-free phone:* 866-628-6387.

North Central University
Minneapolis, Minnesota
http://www.northcentral.edu/

CONTACT
Ms. Sigi Shawa, Assistant Director, North Central University, 910 Elliot Avenue, Minneapolis, MN 55404-1322. *Phone:* 612-343-4460. *Toll-free phone:* 800-289-6222. *Fax:* 612-343-4146. *E-mail:* admissions@northcentral.edu.

Oak Hills Christian College
Bemidji, Minnesota
http://www.oakhills.edu/

CONTACT
Shelly Fast, Assistant Director of Admissions, Oak Hills Christian College, 1600 Oak Hills Road SW, Bemidji, MN 56601. *Phone:* 218-751-8670 Ext. 1285. *Toll-free phone:* 888-751-8670 Ext. 1285. *Fax:* 218-751-8825. *E-mail:* admissions@oakhills.edu.

Rasmussen College Blaine
Blaine, Minnesota
http://www.rasmussen.edu/

- **Proprietary** 4-year, part of Rasmussen College System
- **Suburban** campus with easy access to Minneapolis-St. Paul
- **Coed** 393 undergraduate students, 58% full-time, 73% women, 27% men
- **Minimally difficult** entrance level, 93% of applicants were admitted

UNDERGRAD STUDENTS
228 full-time, 165 part-time.

Freshmen:
Admission: 28 applied, 26 admitted, 27 enrolled.

FACULTY
Total: 34, 24% full-time.

Student/faculty ratio: 22:1.

ACADEMICS
Calendar: quarters. *Degrees:* certificates, diplomas, associate, and bachelor's.

Special study options: academic remediation for entering students, accelerated degree program, adult/continuing education programs, distance learning, double majors, internships, part-time degree program, summer session for credit.

Computers: 81 computers/terminals are available on campus for general student use. Students can access the following: computer help desk, free student e-mail accounts, online (class) grades, online (class) schedules. Campuswide network is available. Wireless service is available via entire campus.
Library: Rasmussen College Library - Blaine.

STUDENT LIFE
Housing options: college housing not available.

COSTS
Costs (2017–18) ***Tuition:*** $11,055 full-time. Full-time tuition and fees vary according to course level, course load, degree level, location, and program. Part-time tuition and fees vary according to course level, course load, degree level, location, and program. No tuition increase for student's term of enrollment. ***Required fees:*** $1695 full-time. ***Payment plans:*** installment, deferred payment. ***Waivers:*** employees or children of employees.

APPLYING
Standardized Tests *Required:* institutional exam (for admission).

Options: electronic application, early admission, deferred entrance.

Required: high school transcript, minimum 2.0 GPA. ***Required for some:*** interview.

Application deadlines: rolling (freshmen), rolling (transfers).

CONTACT
Ms. Susan Hammerstrom, Director of Admissions, Rasmussen College Blaine, 3629 95th Avenue NE, Blaine, MN 55014.
Phone: 763-795-4720. *Toll-free phone:* 888-549-6755.
E-mail: susan.hammerstrom@rasmussen.edu.

Rasmussen College Bloomington

Bloomington, Minnesota

http://www.rasmussen.edu/

- **Proprietary** 4-year, founded 1904, part of Rasmussen College System
- **Suburban** campus with easy access to Minneapolis-St. Paul
- **Coed** 429 undergraduate students, 51% full-time, 67% women, 33% men
- **Minimally difficult** entrance level, 94% of applicants were admitted

UNDERGRAD STUDENTS
218 full-time, 211 part-time.

Freshmen:
Admission: 35 applied, 33 admitted, 33 enrolled.

FACULTY
Total: 74, 18% full-time.

Student/faculty ratio: 22:1.

ACADEMICS
Calendar: quarters. *Degrees:* certificates, diplomas, associate, bachelor's, and postbachelor's certificates.

Special study options: academic remediation for entering students, accelerated degree program, adult/continuing education programs, distance learning, double majors, internships, part-time degree program, summer session for credit.

Computers: 68 computers/terminals are available on campus for general student use. Students can access the following: computer help desk, free student e-mail accounts, online (class) grades, online (class) schedules. Campuswide network is available. Wireless service is available via entire campus.
Library: Rasmussen College Library - Bloomington.

STUDENT LIFE
Housing options: college housing not available.

COSTS & FINANCIAL AID
Costs (2017–18) ***Tuition:*** $11,055 full-time. Full-time tuition and fees vary according to course level, course load, degree level, location, and program. Part-time tuition and fees vary according to course level, course load, degree level, location, and program. No tuition increase for student's term of enrollment. ***Required fees:*** $1695 full-time. ***Payment plans:*** installment, deferred payment. ***Waivers:*** employees or children of employees.

Financial Aid Of all full-time matriculated undergraduates who enrolled in 2015, 3 state and other part-time jobs (averaging $4338).

APPLYING
Standardized Tests *Required:* institutional exam (for admission).

Options: electronic application, early admission, deferred entrance.

Required: high school transcript, minimum 2.0 GPA. ***Required for some:*** interview.

Application deadlines: rolling (freshmen), rolling (transfers).

CONTACT
Susan Hammerstrom, Director of Admissions, Rasmussen College Bloomington, 4400 West 78th Street, Bloomington, MN 55435.
Phone: 952-545-2000. *Toll-free phone:* 888-549-6755.

Rasmussen College Brooklyn Park

Brooklyn Park, Minnesota

http://www.rasmussen.edu/

- **Proprietary** 4-year, part of Rasmussen College System
- **Suburban** campus with easy access to Minneapolis-St. Paul
- **Coed** 542 undergraduate students, 47% full-time, 73% women, 27% men
- **Minimally difficult** entrance level, 72% of applicants were admitted

UNDERGRAD STUDENTS
253 full-time, 289 part-time.

Freshmen:
Admission: 25 applied, 18 admitted, 19 enrolled.

FACULTY
Total: 53, 23% full-time.

Student/faculty ratio: 22:1.

ACADEMICS
Calendar: quarters. *Degrees:* certificates, diplomas, associate, and bachelor's.

Special study options: academic remediation for entering students, accelerated degree program, adult/continuing education programs, distance learning, double majors, internships, part-time degree program, summer session for credit.

Computers: 80 computers/terminals are available on campus for general student use. Students can access the following: computer help desk, free student e-mail accounts, online (class) grades, online (class) schedules. Campuswide network is available. Wireless service is available via entire campus.
Library: Rasmussen College Library - Brooklyn Park.

STUDENT LIFE
Housing options: college housing not available.

COSTS
Costs (2017–18) ***Tuition:*** $11,055 full-time. Full-time tuition and fees vary according to course level, course load, degree level, location, and program. Part-time tuition and fees vary according to course level, course load, degree level, location, and program. No tuition increase for student's term of enrollment. ***Required fees:*** $1695 full-time. ***Payment plans:*** installment, deferred payment. ***Waivers:*** employees or children of employees.

APPLYING
Standardized Tests *Required:* institutional exam (for admission).

Options: electronic application, early admission, deferred entrance.

Required: high school transcript, minimum 2.0 GPA. ***Required for some:*** interview.

Application deadlines: rolling (freshmen), rolling (transfers).

CONTACT

Ms. Susan Hammerstrom, Director of Admissions, Rasmussen College Brooklyn Park, 8301 93rd Avenue North, Brooklyn Park, MN 55445. *Phone:* 763-493-4500. *Toll-free phone:* 888-549-6755. *E-mail:* susan.hammerstrom@rasmussen.edu.

Rasmussen College Eagan

Eagan, Minnesota

http://www.rasmussen.edu/

- **Proprietary** 4-year, founded 1904, part of Rasmussen College System
- **Suburban** campus with easy access to Minneapolis-St. Paul
- **Coed** 501 undergraduate students, 51% full-time, 65% women, 35% men
- **Minimally difficult** entrance level, 88% of applicants were admitted

UNDERGRAD STUDENTS

254 full-time, 247 part-time.

Freshmen:

Admission: 41 applied, 36 admitted, 36 enrolled.

FACULTY

Total: 83, 13% full-time.

Student/faculty ratio: 22:1.

ACADEMICS

Calendar: quarters. *Degrees:* certificates, diplomas, associate, bachelor's, and postbachelor's certificates.

Special study options: academic remediation for entering students, accelerated degree program, adult/continuing education programs, distance learning, double majors, internships, part-time degree program, summer session for credit.

Computers: 93 computers/terminals are available on campus for general student use. Students can access the following: computer help desk, free student e-mail accounts, online (class) grades, online (class) schedules. Campuswide network is available. Wireless service is available via entire campus.

Library: Rasmussen College Library - Eagan.

STUDENT LIFE

Housing options: college housing not available.

COSTS

Costs (2017–18) ***Tuition:*** $11,055 full-time. Full-time tuition and fees vary according to course level, course load, degree level, location, and program. Part-time tuition and fees vary according to course level, course load, degree level, location, and program. No tuition increase for student's term of enrollment. ***Required fees:*** $1695 full-time. ***Payment plans:*** installment, deferred payment. ***Waivers:*** employees or children of employees.

APPLYING

Standardized Tests *Required:* institutional exam (for admission).

Options: electronic application, early admission, deferred entrance.

Required: high school transcript, minimum 2.0 GPA. ***Required for some:*** interview.

Application deadlines: rolling (freshmen), rolling (transfers).

CONTACT

Susan Hammerstrom, Director of Admissions, Rasmussen College Eagan, 3500 Federal Drive, Eagan, MN 55122. *Phone:* 651-687-9000. *Toll-free phone:* 888-549-6755. *E-mail:* susan.hammerstrom@rasmussen.edu.

Rasmussen College Lake Elmo/Woodbury

Lake Elmo, Minnesota

http://www.rasmussen.edu/

- **Proprietary** 4-year, part of Rasmussen College System
- **Suburban** campus with easy access to Minneapolis-St. Paul
- **Coed** 2,169 undergraduate students, 12% full-time, 85% women, 15% men
- **Minimally difficult** entrance level, 75% of applicants were admitted

UNDERGRAD STUDENTS

269 full-time, 1,900 part-time.

Freshmen:

Admission: 32 applied, 24 admitted, 141 enrolled.

FACULTY

Total: 23, 26% full-time.

Student/faculty ratio: 22:1.

ACADEMICS

Calendar: quarters. *Degrees:* certificates, diplomas, associate, and bachelor's.

Special study options: academic remediation for entering students, accelerated degree program, adult/continuing education programs, distance learning, double majors, internships, part-time degree program, summer session for credit.

Computers: 85 computers/terminals are available on campus for general student use. Students can access the following: computer help desk, free student e-mail accounts, online (class) grades, online (class) schedules. Campuswide network is available. Wireless service is available via entire campus.

Library: Rasmussen College Library - Lake Elmo.

STUDENT LIFE

Housing options: college housing not available.

COSTS

Costs (2017–18) ***Tuition:*** $11,055 full-time. Full-time tuition and fees vary according to course level, course load, degree level, location, and program. Part-time tuition and fees vary according to course level, course load, degree level, location, and program. No tuition increase for student's term of enrollment. ***Required fees:*** $1695 full-time. ***Payment plans:*** installment, deferred payment. ***Waivers:*** employees or children of employees.

APPLYING

Standardized Tests *Required:* institutional exam (for admission).

Options: electronic application, early admission, deferred entrance.

Required: high school transcript, minimum 2.0 GPA. ***Required for some:*** interview.

Application deadlines: rolling (freshmen), rolling (transfers).

CONTACT

Ms. Susan Hammerstrom, Director of Admissions, Rasmussen College Lake Elmo/Woodbury, 8565 Eagle Point Circle, Lake Elmo, MN 55042. *Phone:* 651-259-6600. *Toll-free phone:* 888-549-6755. *E-mail:* susan.hammerstrom@rasmussen.edu.

Rasmussen College Mankato

Mankato, Minnesota

http://www.rasmussen.edu/

- **Proprietary** 4-year, founded 1904, part of Rasmussen College System
- **Suburban** campus with easy access to Minneapolis-St. Paul
- **Coed** 382 undergraduate students, 55% full-time, 79% women, 21% men
- **Minimally difficult** entrance level, 88% of applicants were admitted

UNDERGRAD STUDENTS

210 full-time, 172 part-time.

Freshmen:

Admission: 17 applied, 15 admitted, 15 enrolled.

FACULTY

Total: 62, 29% full-time.

Student/faculty ratio: 22:1.

ACADEMICS

Calendar: quarters. *Degrees:* certificates, diplomas, associate, bachelor's, and postbachelor's certificates.

Special study options: academic remediation for entering students, accelerated degree program, adult/continuing education programs, distance learning, double majors, internships, part-time degree program, summer session for credit.

Computers: 116 computers/terminals are available on campus for general student use. Students can access the following: computer help desk, free

student e-mail accounts, online (class) grades, online (class) schedules. Campuswide network is available. Wireless service is available via entire campus.
Library: Rasmussen College Library - Mankato.

STUDENT LIFE
Housing options: college housing not available.

COSTS & FINANCIAL AID
Costs (2017–18) ***Tuition:*** $11,055 full-time. Full-time tuition and fees vary according to course level, course load, degree level, location, and program. Part-time tuition and fees vary according to course level, course load, degree level, location, and program. No tuition increase for student's term of enrollment. ***Required fees:*** $1695 full-time. ***Payment plans:*** installment, deferred payment. ***Waivers:*** employees or children of employees.

Financial Aid Of all full-time matriculated undergraduates who enrolled in 2015, 15 Federal Work-Study jobs (averaging $4000). 13 state and other part-time jobs (averaging $4000).

APPLYING
Standardized Tests *Required:* institutional exam (for admission).

Options: electronic application, early admission, deferred entrance.

Required: high school transcript, minimum 2.0 GPA. ***Required for some:*** interview.

Application deadlines: rolling (freshmen), rolling (transfers).

CONTACT
Susan Hammerstrom, Director of Admissions, Rasmussen College Mankato, 130 Saint Andrews Drive, Mankato, MN 56001.
Phone: 507-625-6556. *Toll-free phone:* 888-549-6755.
E-mail: susan.hammerstrom@rasmussen.edu.

Rasmussen College Moorhead

Moorhead, Minnesota

http://www.rasmussen.edu/

- **Proprietary** 4-year, part of Rasmussen College System
- **Suburban** campus
- **Coed** 190 undergraduate students, 60% full-time, 77% women, 23% men
- **Minimally difficult** entrance level, 100% of applicants were admitted

UNDERGRAD STUDENTS
114 full-time, 76 part-time.

Freshmen:
Admission: 10 applied, 10 admitted, 10 enrolled.

FACULTY
Total: 55, 15% full-time.

Student/faculty ratio: 22:1.

ACADEMICS
Calendar: quarters. *Degrees:* certificates, diplomas, associate, and bachelor's.

Special study options: academic remediation for entering students, accelerated degree program, adult/continuing education programs, distance learning, double majors, internships, part-time degree program, summer session for credit.

Computers: 31 computers/terminals are available on campus for general student use. Students can access the following: computer help desk, free student e-mail accounts, online (class) grades, online (class) schedules. Campuswide network is available. Wireless service is available via entire campus.
Library: Rasmussen College Library - Moorhead.

STUDENT LIFE
Housing options: college housing not available.

COSTS
Costs (2017–18) ***Tuition:*** $11,055 full-time. Full-time tuition and fees vary according to course level, course load, degree level, location, and program. Part-time tuition and fees vary according to course level, course load, degree level, location, and program. No tuition increase for student's term of enrollment. ***Required fees:*** $1695 full-time. ***Payment plans:*** installment, deferred payment. ***Waivers:*** employees or children of employees.

APPLYING
Standardized Tests *Required:* institutional exam (for admission).

Options: electronic application, early admission, deferred entrance.

Required: high school transcript, minimum 2.0 GPA. ***Required for some:*** interview.

Application deadlines: rolling (freshmen), rolling (transfers).

CONTACT
Ms. Susan Hammerstrom, Director of Admissions, Rasmussen College Moorhead, 1250 29th Avenue South, Moorhead, MN 56560. *Phone:* 218-304-6200. *Toll-free phone:* 888-549-6755.
E-mail: susan.hammerstrom@rasmussen.edu.

Rasmussen College St. Cloud

St. Cloud, Minnesota

http://www.rasmussen.edu/

- **Proprietary** 4-year, founded 1904, part of Rasmussen College System
- **Suburban** campus
- **Coed** 542 undergraduate students, 57% full-time, 79% women, 21% men
- **Minimally difficult** entrance level, 93% of applicants were admitted

UNDERGRAD STUDENTS
310 full-time, 232 part-time.

Freshmen:
Admission: 40 applied, 37 admitted, 37 enrolled.

FACULTY
Total: 62, 26% full-time.

Student/faculty ratio: 22:1.

ACADEMICS
Calendar: quarters. *Degrees:* certificates, diplomas, associate, bachelor's, and postbachelor's certificates.

Special study options: academic remediation for entering students, accelerated degree program, adult/continuing education programs, distance learning, double majors, internships, part-time degree program, summer session for credit.

Computers: 91 computers/terminals are available on campus for general student use. Students can access the following: computer help desk, free student e-mail accounts, online (class) grades, online (class) schedules. Campuswide network is available. Wireless service is available via entire campus.
Library: Rasmussen College Library - St. Cloud.

STUDENT LIFE
Housing options: college housing not available.

COSTS & FINANCIAL AID
Costs (2017–18) ***Tuition:*** $11,055 full-time. Full-time tuition and fees vary according to course level, course load, degree level, location, and program. Part-time tuition and fees vary according to course level, course load, degree level, location, and program. No tuition increase for student's term of enrollment. ***Required fees:*** $1695 full-time. ***Payment plans:*** installment, deferred payment. ***Waivers:*** employees or children of employees.

Financial Aid Of all full-time matriculated undergraduates who enrolled in 2015, 34 Federal Work-Study jobs (averaging $866). 51 state and other part-time jobs (averaging $700).

APPLYING
Standardized Tests *Required:* institutional exam (for admission).

Options: electronic application, early admission, deferred entrance.

Required: high school transcript, minimum 2.0 GPA. ***Required for some:*** interview.

Application deadlines: rolling (freshmen), rolling (transfers).

CONTACT
Susan Hammerstrom, Director of Admissions, Rasmussen College St. Cloud, 226 Park Avenue South, St. Cloud, MN 56301. *Phone:* 320-251-5600. *Toll-free phone:* 888-549-6755.
E-mail: susan.hammerstrom@rasmussen.edu.

Rochester Community and Technical College

Rochester, Minnesota

http://www.rctc.edu/

CONTACT
Mr. Troy Tynsky, Director of Admissions, Rochester Community and Technical College, 851 30th Avenue, SE, Rochester, MN 55904-4999. *Phone:* 507-280-3509.

St. Catherine University

St. Paul, Minnesota

http://www.stkate.edu/

- **Independent Roman Catholic** comprehensive, founded 1905
- **Urban** 110-acre campus with easy access to Minneapolis-St. Paul
- **Undergraduate: women only; graduate: coed** 3,320 undergraduate students, 64% full-time, 97% women, 3% men
- **Moderately difficult** entrance level, 67% of applicants were admitted

UNDERGRAD STUDENTS
2,128 full-time, 1,192 part-time. 11% are from out of state; 9% Black or African American, non-Hispanic/Latino; 7% Hispanic/Latino; 12% Asian, non-Hispanic/Latino; 0.2% Native Hawaiian or other Pacific Islander, non-Hispanic/Latino; 0.5% American Indian or Alaska Native, non-Hispanic/Latino; 3% Two or more races, non-Hispanic/Latino; 4% Race/ethnicity unknown; 1% international; 17% transferred in; 41% live on campus.

Freshmen:
Admission: 2,999 applied, 2,021 admitted, 431 enrolled. ***Average high school GPA:*** 3.61. ***Test scores:*** SAT critical reading scores over 500: 80%; SAT math scores over 500: 73%; ACT scores over 18: 95%; SAT critical reading scores over 600: 33%; SAT math scores over 600: 13%; ACT scores over 24: 43%; ACT scores over 30: 5%.

Retention: 86% of full-time freshmen returned.

FACULTY
Total: 525, 56% full-time, 66% with terminal degrees.

Student/faculty ratio: 10:1.

ACADEMICS
Calendar: 4-1-4. *Degrees:* certificates, associate, bachelor's, master's, doctoral, and postbachelor's certificates.

Special study options: adult/continuing education programs, distance learning, double majors, honors programs, independent study, internships, part-time degree program, student-designed majors, study abroad. ***ROTC:*** Army (c), Air Force (c).

Computers: Students can access the following: campus intranet, computer help desk, free student e-mail accounts, online (class) grades, online (class) registration, online (class) schedules, transcript. Campuswide network is available. Wireless service is available via entire campus.

Library: St. Catherine Library.

STUDENT LIFE
Housing options: women-only. Campus housing is university owned. Freshman campus housing is guaranteed.

Activities and organizations: drama/theater group, student-run newspaper, radio station, choral group.

Athletics Member NCAA. All Division III. ***Intercollegiate sports:*** basketball W, cross-country running W, ice hockey W, soccer W, softball W, swimming and diving W, tennis W, track and field W, volleyball W. ***Intramural sports:*** basketball W, cheerleading W, cross-country running W, football W, golf W, lacrosse W, racquetball W, soccer W, softball W, swimming and diving W, tennis W, track and field W, volleyball W.

Campus security: 24-hour emergency response devices and patrols, student patrols, late-night transport/escort service, controlled dormitory access.

COSTS & FINANCIAL AID
Costs (2016–17) ***Comprehensive fee:*** $46,009 includes full-time tuition ($36,240), mandatory fees ($759), and room and board ($9010). Full-time tuition and fees vary according to class time and degree level. Part-time tuition: $1208 per credit hour. Part-time tuition and fees vary according to class time and degree level. ***College room only:*** $5300. Room and board charges vary according to board plan and housing facility. ***Payment plan:*** installment. ***Waivers:*** senior citizens and employees or children of employees.

Financial Aid Of all full-time matriculated undergraduates who enrolled in 2015, 1,800 applied for aid, 1,520 were judged to have need, 440 had their need fully met. In 2015, 272 non-need-based awards were made. ***Average percent of need met:*** 89. ***Average financial aid package:*** $34,000. ***Average need-based loan:*** $5300. ***Average need-based gift aid:*** $9300. ***Average non-need-based aid:*** $16,000. ***Average indebtedness upon graduation:*** $39,150.

APPLYING
Standardized Tests *Required:* SAT or ACT (for admission).

Options: deferred entrance.

Required: high school transcript, 1 letter of recommendation. ***Required for some:*** essay or personal statement, interview. ***Recommended:*** interview.

CONTACT
Ms. Cory Piper-Hauswirth, Associate Director of Admission and Financial Aid, St. Catherine University, 2004 Randolph Avenue, St. Paul, MN 55105. *Phone:* 651-690-6047. *Toll-free phone:* 800-945-4599. *E-mail:* stkate@stkate.edu.

St. Cloud State University

St. Cloud, Minnesota

http://www.stcloudstate.edu/

- **State-supported** comprehensive, founded 1869, part of Minnesota State Colleges and Universities System
- **Suburban** 100-acre campus with easy access to Minneapolis-St. Paul
- **Endowment** $23.1 million
- **Coed** 14,641 undergraduate students, 67% full-time, 52% women, 48% men
- **Moderately difficult** entrance level, 82% of applicants were admitted

UNDERGRAD STUDENTS
9,860 full-time, 4,781 part-time. Students come from 47 states and territories; 70 other countries; 8% are from out of state; 6% Black or African American, non-Hispanic/Latino; 3% Hispanic/Latino; 4% Asian, non-Hispanic/Latino; 0.1% Native Hawaiian or other Pacific Islander, non-Hispanic/Latino; 0.4% American Indian or Alaska Native, non-Hispanic/Latino; 3% Two or more races, non-Hispanic/Latino; 1% Race/ethnicity unknown; 5% international; 7% transferred in; 19% live on campus.

Freshmen:
Admission: 5,965 applied, 4,905 admitted, 1,703 enrolled. ***Average high school GPA:*** 3.12. ***Test scores:*** ACT scores over 18: 81%; ACT scores over 24: 25%; ACT scores over 30: 2%.

Retention: 71% of full-time freshmen returned.

FACULTY
Total: 880, 62% full-time, 58% with terminal degrees.

Student/faculty ratio: 19:1.

ACADEMICS
Calendar: semesters. *Degrees:* certificates, diplomas, associate, bachelor's, master's, doctoral, post-master's, and postbachelor's certificates.

Special study options: academic remediation for entering students, accelerated degree program, adult/continuing education programs, advanced placement credit, cooperative education, distance learning, double majors, English as a second language, honors programs, independent study, internships, off-campus study, part-time degree program, services for LD students, student-designed majors, study abroad, summer session for credit. ***ROTC:*** Army (b).

Unusual degree programs: 3-2 economics.

Computers: 1,355 computers/terminals and 350 ports are available on campus for general student use. Students can access the following: campus intranet, computer help desk, free student e-mail accounts, online (class) grades, online (class) registration, online (class) schedules. Campuswide network is available. 100% of college-owned or -operated

housing units are wired for high-speed Internet access. Wireless service is available via entire campus.
Library: James W. Miller Learning Resources Center.

STUDENT LIFE
Housing options: coed, men-only, women-only, special housing for students with disabilities. Campus housing is university owned. Freshman applicants given priority for college housing.

Activities and organizations: drama/theater group, student-run newspaper, radio and television station, choral group, Nepalese Student Association, Residence Hall Association, International Student Association, American Marketing Association, KVSC - Campus Radio Station, national fraternities, national sororities.

Athletics Member NCAA. All Division II except men's and women's ice hockey (Division I). ***Intercollegiate sports:*** baseball M(s), basketball M(s)/W(s), bowling M(c)/W(c), cheerleading M(c)/W(c), crew M(c)/W(c), cross-country running M(s)/W(s), equestrian sports M(c)/W(c), football M(s), golf M(s)/W(s), ice hockey M(s)/W(s), rock climbing M(c)/W(c), skiing (cross-country) M(c)/W(s), skiing (downhill) M(c)/W(c), soccer M(c)/W(s), softball W(s), swimming and diving M(s)/W(s), tennis M(s)/W(s), track and field M(s)/W(s), ultimate Frisbee M(c)/W(c), volleyball M(c)/W(s), wrestling M(s). ***Intramural sports:*** archery M(c)/W(c), badminton M/W, basketball M/W, bowling M/W, crew M/W, equestrian sports M(c)/W(c), field hockey M/W, football M/W, golf M/W, ice hockey M(c), lacrosse M(c)/W(c), racquetball M/W, rock climbing M/W, rugby M(c)/W(c), skiing (downhill) M(c)/W(c), soccer M/W, softball M/W, squash M/W, tennis M/W, ultimate Frisbee M(c)/W(c), volleyball M/W, wrestling M.

Campus security: 24-hour emergency response devices and patrols, student patrols, late-night transport/escort service.

Student services: health clinic, personal/psychological counseling, women's center, legal services.

COSTS & FINANCIAL AID
Costs (2016–17) ***Tuition:*** state resident $7393 full-time, $228 per credit hour part-time; nonresident $15,311 full-time, $491 per credit hour part-time. Full-time tuition and fees vary according to course load, location, and reciprocity agreements. Part-time tuition and fees vary according to course load, location, and reciprocity agreements. ***Required fees:*** $517 full-time, $38 per credit hour part-time. ***Room and board:*** $8230; room only: $5110. Room and board charges vary according to board plan and housing facility. ***Payment plan:*** installment. ***Waivers:*** senior citizens and employees or children of employees.

Financial Aid Of all full-time matriculated undergraduates who enrolled in 2015, 6,811 applied for aid, 5,313 were judged to have need, 675 had their need fully met. In 2015, 1496 non-need-based awards were made. ***Average percent of need met:*** 62. ***Average financial aid package:*** $9708. ***Average need-based loan:*** $4094. ***Average need-based gift aid:*** $5639. ***Average non-need-based aid:*** $9998. ***Average indebtedness upon graduation:*** $31,305.

APPLYING
Standardized Tests *Required:* SAT or ACT (for admission).

Options: electronic application, deferred entrance.

Application fee: $20.

Required: high school transcript.

Application deadlines: 8/1 (freshmen), 8/1 (transfers).

Notification: continuous (freshmen), continuous (out-of-state freshmen), continuous (transfers).

CONTACT
Mr. Richard Shearer, Director of Admissions, St. Cloud State University, 720 4th Avenue South, AS 115, St. Cloud, MN 56301-4498. *Phone:* 320-308-4046. *Toll-free phone:* 877-654-7278. *Fax:* 320-308-2243. *E-mail:* scsu4u@stcloudstate.edu.

Saint John's University
Collegeville, Minnesota
http://www.csbsju.edu/

- **Independent Roman Catholic** comprehensive, founded 1857
- **Rural** 2500-acre campus with easy access to Minneapolis-St. Paul
- **Endowment** $159.3 million
- **Undergraduate: men only; graduate: coed** 1,754 undergraduate students, 99% full-time, 100% men
- **Moderately difficult** entrance level, 88% of applicants were admitted

UNDERGRAD STUDENTS
1,737 full-time, 17 part-time. Students come from 39 states and territories; 15 other countries; 20% are from out of state; 5% Black or African American, non-Hispanic/Latino; 8% Hispanic/Latino; 3% Asian, non-Hispanic/Latino; 0.3% Native Hawaiian or other Pacific Islander, non-Hispanic/Latino; 0.5% American Indian or Alaska Native, non-Hispanic/Latino; 0.4% Two or more races, non-Hispanic/Latino; 4% international; 1% transferred in; 90% live on campus.

Freshmen:
Admission: 1,457 applied, 1,279 admitted, 461 enrolled. ***Average high school GPA:*** 3.45. ***Test scores:*** SAT critical reading scores over 500: 67%; SAT math scores over 500: 65%; SAT writing scores over 500: 41%; ACT scores over 18: 98%; SAT critical reading scores over 600: 14%; SAT math scores over 600: 24%; SAT writing scores over 600: 10%; ACT scores over 24: 64%; SAT critical reading scores over 700: 2%; SAT writing scores over 700: 2%; ACT scores over 30: 17%.
Retention: 89% of full-time freshmen returned.

FACULTY
Total: 154, 86% full-time, 81% with terminal degrees.
Student/faculty ratio: 12:1.

ACADEMICS
Calendar: semesters. *Degrees:* bachelor's and master's (coordinate with College of Saint Benedict for women).

Special study options: advanced placement credit, double majors, English as a second language, honors programs, independent study, internships, off-campus study, services for LD students, student-designed majors, study abroad. ***ROTC:*** Army (b).

Computers: 243 computers/terminals and 4,600 ports are available on campus for general student use. Students can access the following: campus intranet, computer help desk, free student e-mail accounts, online (class) grades, online (class) registration, online (class) schedules, online student accounts. Campuswide network is available. 100% of college-owned or -operated housing units are wired for high-speed Internet access. Wireless service is available via entire campus.
Library: Alcuin Library plus 2 others. *Books:* 698,393 (physical), 57,768 (digital/electronic); *Serial titles:* 918 (physical), 57,926 (digital/electronic); *Databases:* 242. Weekly public service hours: 104; students can reserve study rooms.

STUDENT LIFE
Housing options: on-campus residence required through senior year; men-only, special housing for students with disabilities. Campus housing is university owned. Freshman campus housing is guaranteed.

Activities and organizations: drama/theater group, student-run newspaper, radio and television station, choral group, Joint Events Council, Global Health Affairs, Magis Ministries, PRiSM, Archipelago Association.

Athletics Member NCAA. All Division III. ***Intercollegiate sports:*** baseball M, basketball M, crew M(c), cross-country running M, football M, golf M, ice hockey M, lacrosse M(c), riflery M(c), rugby M(c), skiing (cross-country) M(c), soccer M, swimming and diving M, tennis M, track and field M, ultimate Frisbee M(c), volleyball M(c), water polo M(c), wrestling M. ***Intramural sports:*** basketball M, football M, racquetball M, soccer M, softball M, ultimate Frisbee M, volleyball M.

Campus security: 24-hour emergency response devices and patrols, student patrols, late-night transport/escort service, controlled dormitory access, well-lit pathways, 911 center on campus.

Student services: health clinic, personal/psychological counseling.

COSTS & FINANCIAL AID
Costs (2016–17) ***Comprehensive fee:*** $51,624 includes full-time tuition ($41,016), mandatory fees ($716), and room and board ($9892). Part-time tuition: $1709 per credit. Part-time tuition and fees vary according to course load. ***College room only:*** $4946. Room and board charges vary according to board plan and housing facility. ***Payment plan:*** installment. ***Waivers:*** employees or children of employees.

Financial Aid Of all full-time matriculated undergraduates who enrolled in 2016, 1,379 applied for aid, 1,188 were judged to have need, 438 had their need fully met. 205 Federal Work-Study jobs (averaging $3345). 721 state and other part-time jobs (averaging $3345). In 2016, 438 non-need-based awards were made. ***Average percent of need met:*** 90. ***Average financial aid package:*** $32,178. ***Average need-based loan:*** $3245. ***Average need-based gift aid:*** $28,255. ***Average non-need-based aid:*** $16,453. ***Average indebtedness upon graduation:*** $40,272.

APPLYING
Standardized Tests *Required:* SAT or ACT (for admission).

Options: electronic application, early action, deferred entrance.

Required: high school transcript, college preparatory program. ***Recommended:*** minimum 3.0 GPA.

Application deadlines: rolling (transfers), 11/15 (early action).

Notification: continuous (transfers), 12/15 (early action).

CONTACT
Mr. Matt Beirne, Director of Admission, Saint John's University, 2850 Abbey Plaza, Collegeville, MN 56321-7155. *Phone:* 320-363-5055. *Toll-free phone:* 800-544-1489. *Fax:* 320-363-5650. *E-mail:* admissions@csbsju.edu.

Saint Mary's University of Minnesota
Winona, Minnesota
http://www.smumn.edu/

- **Independent Roman Catholic** comprehensive, founded 1912
- **Small-town** 350-acre campus
- **Coed** 1,590 undergraduate students, 73% full-time, 54% women, 46% men
- **Moderately difficult** entrance level, 79% of applicants were admitted

UNDERGRAD STUDENTS
1,168 full-time, 422 part-time. Students come from 31 states and territories; 16 other countries; 29% are from out of state; 6% Black or African American, non-Hispanic/Latino; 5% Hispanic/Latino; 2% Asian, non-Hispanic/Latino; 0.1% Native Hawaiian or other Pacific Islander, non-Hispanic/Latino; 0.5% American Indian or Alaska Native, non-Hispanic/Latino; 1% Two or more races, non-Hispanic/Latino; 24% Race/ethnicity unknown; 3% international; 11% transferred in; 93% live on campus.

Freshmen:
Admission: 1,686 applied, 1,336 admitted, 283 enrolled. ***Average high school GPA:*** 3.34. ***Test scores:*** SAT critical reading scores over 500: 52%; SAT math scores over 500: 52%; SAT writing scores over 500: 41%; ACT scores over 18: 92%; SAT critical reading scores over 600: 10%; SAT math scores over 600: 19%; SAT writing scores over 600: 12%; ACT scores over 24: 42%; SAT critical reading scores over 700: 5%; SAT math scores over 700: 5%; SAT writing scores over 700: 6%; ACT scores over 30: 5%.
Retention: 70% of full-time freshmen returned.

FACULTY
Total: 473, 21% full-time, 53% with terminal degrees.

Student/faculty ratio: 20:1.

ACADEMICS
Calendar: semesters. *Degrees:* certificates, diplomas, bachelor's, master's, doctoral, post-master's, and postbachelor's certificates.

Special study options: academic remediation for entering students, accelerated degree program, adult/continuing education programs, advanced placement credit, cooperative education, distance learning, double majors, English as a second language, honors programs, independent study, internships, off-campus study, part-time degree program, services for LD students, student-designed majors, study abroad, summer session for credit. ***ROTC:*** Army (c).

Computers: 200 computers/terminals and 50 ports are available on campus for general student use. Students can access the following: campus intranet, computer help desk, free student e-mail accounts, online (class) grades, online (class) registration, online (class) schedules. Campuswide network is available. 100% of college-owned or -operated housing units are wired for high-speed Internet access. Wireless service is available via computer centers, computer labs, dorm rooms, libraries, student centers.

Library: Fitzgerald Library plus 1 other. *Books:* 210,639 (physical), 10,144 (digital/electronic); *Serial titles:* 169 (physical), 82,154 (digital/electronic); *Databases:* 77. Weekly public service hours: 97; students can reserve study rooms.

STUDENT LIFE
Housing options: on-campus residence required through sophomore year; coed, men-only, women-only, special housing for students with disabilities. Campus housing is university owned. Freshman campus housing is guaranteed.

Activities and organizations: drama/theater group, student-run newspaper, radio station, choral group, Student Activity Committee, PR Business Club, Serving Others United in Love (Soul) - Mission Trips, Colleges Against Cancer, Club Hockey, national fraternities, national sororities.

Athletics Member NCAA. All Division III. ***Intercollegiate sports:*** baseball M, basketball M/W, cross-country running M/W, golf M/W, ice hockey M/W, soccer M/W, softball W, swimming and diving M/W, tennis M/W, track and field M/W, volleyball W. ***Intramural sports:*** basketball M/W, cheerleading W(c), fencing M(c)/W(c), field hockey M/W, football M/W, ice hockey M, lacrosse M(c)/W(c), rugby M(c), skiing (downhill) M(c)/W(c), soccer M/W, softball M/W, tennis M/W, ultimate Frisbee M/W, volleyball M/W, water polo M(c)/W(c).

Campus security: 24-hour emergency response devices and patrols, late-night transport/escort service, controlled dormitory access.

Student services: health clinic, personal/psychological counseling.

COSTS & FINANCIAL AID
Costs (2017–18) ***Comprehensive fee:*** $42,440 includes full-time tuition ($33,020), mandatory fees ($540), and room and board ($8880). Full-time tuition and fees vary according to course load and location. Part-time tuition: $1110 per credit. Part-time tuition and fees vary according to course load and location. ***College room only:*** $5000. Room and board charges vary according to board plan and housing facility. ***Payment plan:*** installment. ***Waivers:*** employees or children of employees.

Financial Aid Of all full-time matriculated undergraduates who enrolled in 2016, 925 applied for aid, 827 were judged to have need, 187 had their need fully met. 130 Federal Work-Study jobs (averaging $1932). 228 state and other part-time jobs (averaging $3784). In 2016, 263 non-need-based awards were made. ***Average percent of need met:*** 76. ***Average financial aid package:*** $25,847. ***Average need-based loan:*** $4747. ***Average need-based gift aid:*** $20,523. ***Average non-need-based aid:*** $17,903. ***Average indebtedness upon graduation:*** $39,196.

APPLYING
Standardized Tests *Required:* SAT or ACT (for admission).

Options: electronic application, early admission, deferred entrance.

Application fee: $25.

Required: essay or personal statement, high school transcript, minimum 2.5 GPA. ***Required for some:*** interview. ***Recommended:*** 2 letters of recommendation.

Application deadlines: 5/1 (freshmen), rolling (transfers).

Notification: continuous (freshmen), continuous (transfers).

CONTACT
Mr. Mark Kormann, Assistant Vice President, Admission, Saint Mary's University of Minnesota, 700 Terrace Heights, Winona, MN 55987. *Phone:* 507-457-1750. *Toll-free phone:* 800-635-5987. *Fax:* 507-457-1722. *E-mail:* mkormann@smumn.edu.

St. Olaf College

Northfield, Minnesota

http://www.stolaf.edu/

- **Independent Lutheran** 4-year, founded 1874
- **Small-town** 300-acre campus with easy access to Minneapolis-St. Paul
- **Endowment** $447.7 million
- **Coed** 3,040 undergraduate students, 98% full-time, 56% women, 44% men
- **Very difficult** entrance level, 45% of applicants were admitted

UNDERGRAD STUDENTS

2,990 full-time, 50 part-time. Students come from 49 states and territories; 78 other countries; 55% are from out of state; 2% Black or African American, non-Hispanic/Latino; 6% Hispanic/Latino; 6% Asian, non-Hispanic/Latino; 0.1% American Indian or Alaska Native, non-Hispanic/Latino; 3% Two or more races, non-Hispanic/Latino; 1% Race/ethnicity unknown; 8% international; 0.8% transferred in; 93% live on campus.

Freshmen:

Admission: 6,041 applied, 2,704 admitted, 824 enrolled. ***Average high school GPA:*** 3.63. ***Test scores:*** SAT critical reading scores over 500: 87%; SAT math scores over 500: 90%; ACT scores over 18: 100%; SAT critical reading scores over 600: 62%; SAT math scores over 600: 65%; ACT scores over 24: 89%; SAT critical reading scores over 700: 29%; SAT math scores over 700: 27%; ACT scores over 30: 42%.

Retention: 92% of full-time freshmen returned.

FACULTY

Total: 332, 64% full-time, 80% with terminal degrees.

Student/faculty ratio: 12:1.

ACADEMICS

Calendar: 4-1-4. *Degree:* bachelor's.

Special study options: advanced placement credit, double majors, English as a second language, independent study, internships, off-campus study, part-time degree program, services for LD students, student-designed majors, study abroad, summer session for credit.

Unusual degree programs: 3-2 engineering with Washington University in St. Louis.

Computers: 824 computers/terminals and 3,300 ports are available on campus for general student use. Students can access the following: campus intranet, computer help desk, free student e-mail accounts, online (class) grades, online (class) registration, online (class) schedules. Campuswide network is available. 100% of college-owned or -operated housing units are wired for high-speed Internet access. Wireless service is available via entire campus.

Library: Rolvaag Memorial Library plus 2 others. *Books:* 708,768 (physical), 503,398 (digital/electronic); *Databases:* 317.

STUDENT LIFE

Housing options: on-campus residence required through senior year; coed, special housing for students with disabilities. Campus housing is university owned. Freshman campus housing is guaranteed.

Activities and organizations: drama/theater group, student-run newspaper, radio station, choral group, Student Government Association, Ultimate Frisbee Teams, Ole Spring Relief, Alpha Phi Omega, SARN: Sexual Assault Resource Network.

Athletics Member NCAA. All Division III. ***Intercollegiate sports:*** baseball M, basketball M/W, cross-country running M/W, football M, golf M/W, ice hockey M/W, skiing (cross-country) M/W, skiing (downhill) M/W, soccer M/W, softball W, swimming and diving M/W, tennis M/W, track and field M/W, volleyball W, wrestling M. ***Intramural sports:*** badminton M(c)/W(c), basketball M/W, bowling M/W, equestrian sports M(c)/W(c), fencing M(c)/W(c), football M/W, ice hockey M(c), lacrosse M(c)/W(c), rowing M(c)/W(c), rugby M(c)/W(c), sand volleyball M/W, soccer M/W, softball M/W, table tennis M/W, tennis M/W, triathlon M/W, ultimate Frisbee M/W, volleyball M(c)/W, water polo M/W.

Campus security: 24-hour emergency response devices and patrols, late-night transport/escort service, controlled dormitory access, lighted pathways and sidewalks, first-year only dorms.

Student services: health clinic, personal/psychological counseling.

COSTS & FINANCIAL AID

Costs (2017–18) ***Comprehensive fee:*** $56,430 includes full-time tuition ($46,000) and room and board ($10,430). Part-time tuition: $5750 per course. Part-time tuition and fees vary according to course load. ***College room only:*** $5000. Room and board charges vary according to board plan. ***Payment plan:*** installment. ***Waivers:*** senior citizens and employees or children of employees.

Financial Aid Of all full-time matriculated undergraduates who enrolled in 2016, 2,078 applied for aid, 1,916 were judged to have need, 1,707 had their need fully met. 440 Federal Work-Study jobs (averaging $2161). 1,662 state and other part-time jobs (averaging $1976). In 2016, 691 non-need-based awards were made. ***Average percent of need met:*** 98. ***Average financial aid package:*** $37,224. ***Average need-based loan:*** $3548. ***Average need-based gift aid:*** $30,463. ***Average non-need-based aid:*** $14,942. ***Average indebtedness upon graduation:*** $27,945. ***Financial aid deadline:*** 3/1.

APPLYING

Standardized Tests *Required:* SAT or ACT (for admission).

Options: electronic application, early decision, deferred entrance.

Required: essay or personal statement, high school transcript, 1 letter of recommendation. ***Recommended:*** 2 letters of recommendation, interview.

Application deadlines: 1/15 (freshmen), 4/1 (transfers).

Early decision deadline: 11/15 (for plan 1), 1/8 (for plan 2).

Notification: 3/20 (freshmen), 5/1 (transfers), 12/15 (early decision plan 1), 2/1 (early decision plan 2).

CONTACT

Dave Wagner, Director of Admissions, St. Olaf College, 1520 St. Olaf Avenue, Northfield, MN 55057. *Phone:* 507-786-3025. *Toll-free phone:* 800-800-3025. *Fax:* 507-786-3832. *E-mail:* admissions@stolaf.edu.

Southwest Minnesota State University

Marshall, Minnesota

http://www.smsu.edu/

CONTACT

Mr. Andrew Hlubeck, Director of Admissions, Southwest Minnesota State University, 1501 State Street, Marshall, MN 56258. *Phone:* 507-537-6286. *Toll-free phone:* 800-642-0684. *Fax:* 507-537-7145. *E-mail:* andrew.hlubek@smsu.edu.

University of Minnesota, Crookston

Crookston, Minnesota

http://www.umcrookston.edu/

- **State-supported** 4-year, founded 1966, part of University of Minnesota System
- **Rural** 237-acre campus
- **Endowment** $15.2 million
- **Coed** 2,823 undergraduate students, 45% full-time, 53% women, 47% men
- **Minimally difficult** entrance level, 78% of applicants were admitted

UNDERGRAD STUDENTS

1,281 full-time, 1,542 part-time. Students come from 45 states and territories; 17 other countries; 30% are from out of state; 7% Black or African American, non-Hispanic/Latino; 4% Hispanic/Latino; 2% Asian, non-Hispanic/Latino; 0.2% Native Hawaiian or other Pacific Islander, non-Hispanic/Latino; 0.4% American Indian or Alaska Native, non-Hispanic/Latino; 2% Two or more races, non-Hispanic/Latino; 2% Race/ethnicity unknown; 5% international; 9% transferred in; 39% live on campus.

Freshmen:

Admission: 1,073 applied, 839 admitted, 239 enrolled. ***Average high school GPA:*** 3.21. ***Test scores:*** SAT critical reading scores over 500: 45%; SAT math scores over 500: 56%; SAT writing scores over 500: 28%; ACT scores over 18: 90%; SAT critical reading scores over 600: 17%; SAT math scores over 600: 6%; SAT writing scores over 600: 6%; ACT scores over 24: 32%; SAT critical reading scores over 700: 6%; ACT scores over 30: 4%.

Retention: 65% of full-time freshmen returned.

FACULTY
Total: 116, 61% full-time, 34% with terminal degrees.
Student/faculty ratio: 16:1.

ACADEMICS
Calendar: semesters. *Degree:* bachelor's.

Special study options: academic remediation for entering students, advanced placement credit, cooperative education, distance learning, double majors, English as a second language, honors programs, independent study, internships, off-campus study, part-time degree program, services for LD students, student-designed majors, study abroad, summer session for credit. ***ROTC:*** Air Force (c).

Computers: 25 computers/terminals are available on campus for general student use. Students can access the following: campus intranet, computer help desk, free student e-mail accounts, online (class) grades, online (class) registration, online (class) schedules, personal Web pages. Campuswide network is available. 100% of college-owned or -operated housing units are wired for high-speed Internet access. Wireless service is available via entire campus.

Library: UMC Library. *Books:* 47,423 (physical), 336,375 (digital/electronic); *Serial titles:* 412 (physical), 8,500 (digital/electronic); *Databases:* 152. Weekly public service hours: 76.

STUDENT LIFE
Housing options: coed, special housing for students with disabilities. Campus housing is university owned. Freshman applicants given priority for college housing.

Activities and organizations: drama/theater group, choral group, National Society for Leadership and Success, Archery Club, Crookston Futbol Club, Choir, Student Athletic Advisory Council, national fraternities.

Athletics Member NCAA. All Division II. ***Intercollegiate sports:*** baseball M(s), basketball M(s)/W(s), equestrian sports W(s), football M(s), golf M(s)/W(s), soccer W(s), softball W(s), tennis W(s), volleyball W(s). ***Intramural sports:*** basketball M/W, football M/W, golf M/W, ice hockey M(c), racquetball M/W, soccer M(c)/W, softball M/W, table tennis M/W, tennis M/W, volleyball M/W.

Campus security: 24-hour emergency response devices, student patrols, controlled dormitory access.

Student services: health clinic, personal/psychological counseling, women's center.

COSTS & FINANCIAL AID
Costs (2016–17) ***Tuition:*** state resident $10,180 full-time, $392 per credit part-time; nonresident $10,180 full-time, $392 per credit part-time. ***Required fees:*** $1520 full-time, $760 per term part-time. ***Room and board:*** $7658; room only: $3572. Room and board charges vary according to board plan and housing facility. ***Payment plan:*** installment. ***Waivers:*** senior citizens.

Financial Aid Of all full-time matriculated undergraduates who enrolled in 2016, 911 applied for aid, 747 were judged to have need, 118 had their need fully met. In 2016, 80 non-need-based awards were made. ***Average percent of need met:*** 73. ***Average financial aid package:*** $11,692. ***Average need-based loan:*** $4098. ***Average need-based gift aid:*** $8642. ***Average non-need-based aid:*** $2534. ***Average indebtedness upon graduation:*** $30,018.

APPLYING
Standardized Tests *Required:* SAT or ACT (for admission). *Recommended:* ACT (for admission).

Options: electronic application, deferred entrance.

Application fee: $30.

Required: high school transcript, minimum 2.0 GPA, minimum ACT composite score of 21 or SAT of 980.

Application deadlines: rolling (freshmen), rolling (out-of-state freshmen), rolling (transfers).

Notification: continuous (freshmen), continuous (out-of-state freshmen), continuous (transfers).

CONTACT
Carola Thorson, Director of Admissions, University of Minnesota, Crookston, 2900 University Avenue, Crookston, MN 56716-5001. *Phone:* 218-281-8568. *Toll-free phone:* 800-862-6466. *E-mail:* cthorson@umn.edu.

University of Minnesota, Duluth

Duluth, Minnesota

http://www.d.umn.edu/

- **State-supported** comprehensive, founded 1947, part of University of Minnesota System
- **Suburban** 250-acre campus
- **Endowment** $154.5 million
- **Coed** 9,967 undergraduate students, 88% full-time, 47% women, 53% men
- **Moderately difficult** entrance level, 77% of applicants were admitted

UNDERGRAD STUDENTS
8,755 full-time, 1,212 part-time. Students come from 39 states and territories; 38 other countries; 12% are from out of state; 2% Black or African American, non-Hispanic/Latino; 3% Hispanic/Latino; 3% Asian, non-Hispanic/Latino; 0.1% Native Hawaiian or other Pacific Islander, non-Hispanic/Latino; 0.6% American Indian or Alaska Native, non-Hispanic/Latino; 3% Two or more races, non-Hispanic/Latino; 0.8% Race/ethnicity unknown; 2% international; 5% transferred in; 32% live on campus.

Freshmen:
Admission: 7,973 applied, 6,105 admitted, 2,138 enrolled. ***Average high school GPA:*** 3.48. ***Test scores:*** SAT critical reading scores over 500: 63%; SAT math scores over 500: 81%; SAT writing scores over 500: 53%; ACT scores over 18: 98%; SAT critical reading scores over 600: 25%; SAT math scores over 600: 38%; SAT writing scores over 600: 13%; ACT scores over 24: 54%; SAT math scores over 700: 9%; SAT writing scores over 700: 3%; ACT scores over 30: 7%.

Retention: 78% of full-time freshmen returned.

FACULTY
Total: 618, 82% full-time, 65% with terminal degrees.
Student/faculty ratio: 18:1.

ACADEMICS
Calendar: semesters. *Degrees:* certificates, bachelor's, master's, doctoral, and postbachelor's certificates.

Special study options: academic remediation for entering students, accelerated degree program, adult/continuing education programs, advanced placement credit, cooperative education, distance learning, double majors, English as a second language, honors programs, independent study, internships, off-campus study, part-time degree program, services for LD students, student-designed majors, study abroad, summer session for credit. ***ROTC:*** Air Force (b).

Computers: 471 computers/terminals are available on campus for general student use. Students can access the following: campus intranet, computer help desk, free student e-mail accounts, online (class) grades, online (class) registration, online (class) schedules. Campuswide network is available. 100% of college-owned or -operated housing units are wired for high-speed Internet access. Wireless service is available via entire campus.

Library: Kathryn A. Martin Library. *Books:* 311,405 (physical), 626,042 (digital/electronic); *Serial titles:* 11,861 (physical), 159,288 (digital/electronic); *Databases:* 164. Weekly public service hours: 94; students can reserve study rooms.

STUDENT LIFE
Housing options: coed, men-only, women-only, special housing for students with disabilities. Campus housing is university owned. Freshman applicants given priority for college housing.

Activities and organizations: drama/theater group, student-run newspaper, radio station, choral group, marching band, Newman Catholic Campus Ministries, Phi Sigma Sigma, International Club, Psychology Club, Rod & Gun Club, national fraternities, national sororities.

Athletics Member NCAA. All Division II except men's and women's ice hockey (Division I). ***Intercollegiate sports:*** badminton M(c)/W(c), baseball M(s), basketball M(s)/W(s), cheerleading W(c), cross-country running M(s)/W(s), football M(s), ice hockey M(s)/W(s), lacrosse M(c)/W(c), rugby M(c)/W(c), skiing (downhill) M(c)/W(c), soccer M(c)/W(s), softball W(s), tennis W(s), track and field M/W, volleyball

M(c)/W(s), water polo W. ***Intramural sports:*** badminton M/W, basketball M/W, bowling M/W, football M/W, ice hockey M/W, rock climbing M(c)/W(c), soccer M/W, softball M/W, tennis W, volleyball M/W.

Campus security: 24-hour emergency response devices and patrols, late-night transport/escort service.

Student services: health clinic, personal/psychological counseling, women's center.

COSTS & FINANCIAL AID

Costs (2016–17) ***Tuition:*** state resident $11,896 full-time, $458 per credit part-time; nonresident $16,242 full-time, $625 per credit part-time. Full-time tuition and fees vary according to course load, program, and reciprocity agreements. Part-time tuition and fees vary according to course load, program, and reciprocity agreements. ***Required fees:*** $1186 full-time. ***Room and board:*** Room and board charges vary according to board plan and housing facility. ***Payment plan:*** installment. ***Waivers:*** children of alumni and employees or children of employees.

Financial Aid Of all full-time matriculated undergraduates who enrolled in 2015, 6,844 applied for aid, 4,913 were judged to have need, 1,328 had their need fully met. 365 Federal Work-Study jobs (averaging $1380). 894 state and other part-time jobs (averaging $1067). In 2015, 1198 non-need-based awards were made. ***Average percent of need met:*** 71. ***Average financial aid package:*** $12,275. ***Average need-based loan:*** $6087. ***Average need-based gift aid:*** $8124. ***Average non-need-based aid:*** $2473. ***Average indebtedness upon graduation:*** $30,579.

APPLYING

Standardized Tests *Required:* SAT or ACT (for admission).

Options: electronic application.

Application fee: $40.

Required: high school transcript. ***Required for some:*** interview. ***Recommended:*** essay or personal statement.

Application deadlines: 6/15 (freshmen), 6/15 (transfers).

Notification: continuous until 9/15 (freshmen), continuous (transfers).

CONTACT

Office of Admissions, University of Minnesota, Duluth, 25 Solon Campus Center, 1117 University Drive, Duluth, MN 55812-3000. *Phone:* 218-726-7171. *Toll-free phone:* 800-232-1339. *Fax:* 218-726-7040. *E-mail:* umdadmis@d.umn.edu.

University of Minnesota, Morris

Morris, Minnesota

http://www.morris.umn.edu/

- **State-supported** 4-year, founded 1959, part of University of Minnesota System
- **Rural** 130-acre campus
- **Endowment** $11.2 million
- **Coed** 1,771 undergraduate students, 93% full-time, 56% women, 44% men
- **Moderately difficult** entrance level, 58% of applicants were admitted

UNDERGRAD STUDENTS

1,646 full-time, 125 part-time. Students come from 32 states and territories; 24 other countries; 13% are from out of state; 2% Black or African American, non-Hispanic/Latino; 4% Hispanic/Latino; 3% Asian, non-Hispanic/Latino; 6% American Indian or Alaska Native, non-Hispanic/Latino; 12% Two or more races, non-Hispanic/Latino; 0.8% Race/ethnicity unknown; 11% international; 6% transferred in; 60% live on campus.

Freshmen:

Admission: 3,414 applied, 1,982 admitted, 376 enrolled. ***Average high school GPA:*** 3.55. ***Test scores:*** SAT critical reading scores over 500: 68%; SAT math scores over 500: 84%; SAT writing scores over 500: 72%; ACT scores over 18: 97%; SAT critical reading scores over 600: 24%; SAT math scores over 600: 44%; SAT writing scores over 600: 28%; ACT scores over 24: 64%; SAT critical reading scores over 700: 12%; SAT math scores over 700: 20%; SAT writing scores over 700: 4%; ACT scores over 30: 15%.

Retention: 78% of full-time freshmen returned.

FACULTY

Total: 168, 70% full-time, 77% with terminal degrees.

Student/faculty ratio: 12:1.

ACADEMICS

Calendar: semesters. *Degree:* bachelor's.

Special study options: advanced placement credit, distance learning, double majors, English as a second language, freshman honors college, honors programs, independent study, internships, off-campus study, part-time degree program, services for LD students, student-designed majors, study abroad, summer session for credit.

Unusual degree programs: 3-2 engineering with University of Minnesota, Twin Cities Campus.

Computers: 350 computers/terminals and 548 ports are available on campus for general student use. Students can access the following: campus intranet, computer help desk, free student e-mail accounts, online (class) grades, online (class) registration, online (class) schedules. Campuswide network is available. 100% of college-owned or -operated housing units are wired for high-speed Internet access. Wireless service is available via classrooms, computer labs, dorm rooms, learning centers, libraries, student centers.

Library: Rodney A. Briggs Library plus 1 other. *Books:* 223,472 (physical), 60,000 (digital/electronic); *Serial titles:* 152 (physical), 82,000 (digital/electronic); *Databases:* 142. Weekly public service hours: 99.

STUDENT LIFE

Housing options: coed, special housing for students with disabilities. Campus housing is university owned. Freshman campus housing is guaranteed.

Activities and organizations: drama/theater group, student-run newspaper, radio station, choral group, Student Radio Station, Inter-Varsity Christian Fellowship, Jazz Ensemble/Concert Choir, Big Friend, Little Friend, Student Newspaper.

Athletics Member NCAA. All Division III. ***Intercollegiate sports:*** baseball M, basketball M/W, cross-country running M/W, football M, golf M/W, soccer M/W, softball W, swimming and diving W, tennis M/W, track and field M/W, volleyball W. ***Intramural sports:*** baseball M/W, basketball M/W, bowling M/W, cheerleading M(c)/W(c), equestrian sports M(c)/W(c), fencing M(c)/W(c), football M/W, racquetball M(c)/W(c), rugby M(c)/W(c), skiing (cross-country) M/W, soccer M(c)/W(c), softball M/W, swimming and diving M(c)/W(c), table tennis M/W, triathlon M(c)/W(c), ultimate Frisbee M(c)/W(c), volleyball M/W, weight lifting M(c)/W(c).

Campus security: 24-hour emergency response devices and patrols, late-night transport/escort service, controlled dormitory access.

Student services: health clinic, personal/psychological counseling, women's center, legal services.

COSTS & FINANCIAL AID

Costs (2016–17) ***Tuition:*** state resident $11,896 full-time, $458 per credit hour part-time; nonresident $13,896 full-time, $534 per credit hour part-time. Full-time tuition and fees vary according to reciprocity agreements. Part-time tuition and fees vary according to course load and reciprocity agreements. ***Required fees:*** $950 full-time. ***Room and board:*** $7914; room only: $3752. Room and board charges vary according to board plan and housing facility. ***Payment plan:*** installment. ***Waivers:*** senior citizens.

Financial Aid Of all full-time matriculated undergraduates who enrolled in 2016, 1,256 applied for aid, 1,019 were judged to have need, 257 had their need fully met. 307 Federal Work-Study jobs (averaging $1317). 96 state and other part-time jobs (averaging $1515). In 2016, 188 non-need-based awards were made. ***Average percent of need met:*** 75. ***Average financial aid package:*** $12,633. ***Average need-based loan:*** $3730. ***Average need-based gift aid:*** $10,095. ***Average non-need-based aid:*** $4187. ***Average indebtedness upon graduation:*** $25,732.

APPLYING

Standardized Tests *Required:* SAT or ACT (for admission).

Options: electronic application, deferred entrance.

Application fee: $35.

Required: high school transcript. ***Required for some:*** essay or personal statement, 1 letter of recommendation, interview.

Application deadlines: 3/15 (freshmen), 5/1 (transfers).

Notification: continuous (freshmen), continuous (transfers).

CONTACT
University of Minnesota, Morris, 600 East 4th Street, Morris, MN 56267-2134. *Phone:* 320-539-6035. *Toll-free phone:* 888-866-3382. *Fax:* 320-589-6051. *E-mail:* admissions@morris.umn.edu.

University of Minnesota Rochester

Rochester, Minnesota

http://www.r.umn.edu/

CONTACT
University of Minnesota Rochester, 111 South Broadway, Suite 300, Rochester, MN 55904.

University of Minnesota, Twin Cities Campus

Minneapolis, Minnesota

http://www.umn.edu/tc/

- **State-supported** university, founded 1851, part of University of Minnesota System
- **Urban** 2000-acre campus with easy access to Minneapolis-St. Paul
- **Coed** 34,871 undergraduate students, 85% full-time, 52% women, 48% men
- **Moderately difficult** entrance level, 44% of applicants were admitted

UNDERGRAD STUDENTS
29,567 full-time, 5,304 part-time. Students come from 51 states and territories; 103 other countries; 27% are from out of state; 4% Black or African American, non-Hispanic/Latino; 4% Hispanic/Latino; 9% Asian, non-Hispanic/Latino; 0.1% Native Hawaiian or other Pacific Islander, non-Hispanic/Latino; 0.3% American Indian or Alaska Native, non-Hispanic/Latino; 4% Two or more races, non-Hispanic/Latino; 0.6% Race/ethnicity unknown; 9% international; 7% transferred in; 22% live on campus.

Freshmen:
Admission: 49,129 applied, 21,820 admitted, 5,880 enrolled. ***Test scores:*** SAT critical reading scores over 500: 92%; SAT math scores over 500: 96%; SAT writing scores over 500: 96%; ACT scores over 18: 100%; SAT critical reading scores over 600: 63%; SAT math scores over 600: 82%; SAT writing scores over 600: 70%; ACT scores over 24: 91%; SAT critical reading scores over 700: 27%; SAT math scores over 700: 48%; SAT writing scores over 700: 23%; ACT scores over 30: 38%.
Retention: 93% of full-time freshmen returned.

FACULTY
Total: 3,676, 70% full-time, 69% with terminal degrees.
Student/faculty ratio: 17:1.

ACADEMICS
Calendar: semesters. *Degrees:* certificates, diplomas, bachelor's, master's, doctoral, post-master's, and postbachelor's certificates.
Special study options: academic remediation for entering students, accelerated degree program, adult/continuing education programs, advanced placement credit, cooperative education, distance learning, double majors, English as a second language, external degree program, freshman honors college, honors programs, independent study, internships, off-campus study, part-time degree program, services for LD students, student-designed majors, study abroad, summer session for credit. ***ROTC:*** Army (b), Navy (b), Air Force (b).
Computers: Students can access the following: computer help desk, free student e-mail accounts, online (class) grades, online (class) registration, online (class) schedules. Campuswide network is available.
Library: Wilson Library plus 17 others. *Books:* 3.5 million (physical), 1.0 million (digital/electronic); *Serial titles:* 150,445 (physical), 211,166 (digital/electronic); *Databases:* 891.

STUDENT LIFE
Housing options: coed, cooperative, special housing for students with disabilities. Campus housing is university owned. Freshman campus housing is guaranteed.
Activities and organizations: drama/theater group, student-run newspaper, radio and television station, choral group, marching band, Student Government, national fraternities, national sororities.
Athletics Member NCAA. All Division I except football (Division I-A). ***Intercollegiate sports:*** baseball M(s), basketball M(s)/W(s), cross-country running M(s)/W(s), golf M(s)/W(s), gymnastics M(s)/W(s), ice hockey M(s)/W(s), soccer W(s), softball W(s), swimming and diving M(s)/W(s), tennis M(s)/W(s), track and field M(s)/W(s), volleyball W(s), wrestling M(s). ***Intramural sports:*** baseball M/W, basketball M/W, bowling M/W, crew M/W, football M/W, golf M/W, ice hockey M/W, rugby M/W, skiing (cross-country) M/W, skiing (downhill) M/W, soccer M/W, softball M/W, tennis M/W, volleyball M/W, water polo M/W, wrestling M/W.
Campus security: 24-hour emergency response devices and patrols, student patrols, late-night transport/escort service, controlled dormitory access, safety/security orientation, security lighting.
Student services: health clinic, personal/psychological counseling, women's center, legal services.

COSTS & FINANCIAL AID
Costs (2016–17) ***Tuition:*** state resident $12,546 full-time, $483 per credit hour part-time; nonresident $22,210 full-time, $854 per credit hour part-time. Full-time tuition and fees vary according to program and reciprocity agreements. Part-time tuition and fees vary according to course load, program, and reciprocity agreements. ***Required fees:*** $1596 full-time. ***Room and board:*** $9377; room only: $5270. Room and board charges vary according to board plan, housing facility, and location. ***Payment plan:*** installment. ***Waivers:*** senior citizens.
Financial Aid Of all full-time matriculated undergraduates who enrolled in 2016, 19,218 applied for aid, 13,864 were judged to have need, 3,273 had their need fully met. In 2016, 2198 non-need-based awards were made. ***Average percent of need met:*** 73. ***Average financial aid package:*** $13,153. ***Average need-based loan:*** $4575. ***Average need-based gift aid:*** $10,140. ***Average non-need-based aid:*** $4836. ***Average indebtedness upon graduation:*** $26,644.

APPLYING
Standardized Tests *Required:* SAT or ACT (for admission).
Options: electronic application, early admission, deferred entrance.
Application fee: $55.
Required: high school transcript. ***Recommended:*** minimum 2.0 GPA.
Application deadlines: rolling (freshmen), rolling (transfers).
Notification: continuous (freshmen), continuous (transfers).

CONTACT
Rachelle Hernandez, Director of Admissions, University of Minnesota, Twin Cities Campus, 240 Williamson, Minneapolis, MN 55455-0213. *Phone:* 612-625-2008. *Toll-free phone:* 800-752-1000. *Fax:* 612-626-1693. *E-mail:* admissions@tc.umn.edu.

University of Northwestern–St. Paul

St. Paul, Minnesota

http://www.unwsp.edu/

CONTACT
Admissions, University of Northwestern–St. Paul, Officer of Admissions, 3003 Snelling Avenue North, 212 Nazareth Hall, St. Paul, MN 55113-1598. *Phone:* 651-631-5111. *Toll-free phone:* 800-827-6827. *Fax:* 651-631-5680. *E-mail:* admissions@unwsp.edu.

University of St. Thomas

St. Paul, Minnesota

http://www.stthomas.edu/

- **Independent Roman Catholic** university, founded 1885
- **Urban** 78-acre campus with easy access to Minneapolis-St. Paul
- **Endowment** $368.5 million
- **Coed** 6,111 undergraduate students, 96% full-time, 46% women, 54% men
- **Moderately difficult** entrance level, 83% of applicants were admitted

UNDERGRAD STUDENTS
5,849 full-time, 262 part-time. Students come from 43 states and territories; 66 other countries; 21% are from out of state; 3% Black or African American, non-Hispanic/Latino; 4% Hispanic/Latino; 4% Asian, non-Hispanic/Latino; 0.1% American Indian or Alaska Native, non-Hispanic/Latino; 3% Two or more races, non-Hispanic/Latino; 1%

Race/ethnicity unknown; 3% international; 3% transferred in; 40% live on campus.

Freshmen:
Admission: 6,221 applied, 5,142 admitted, 1,349 enrolled. ***Average high school GPA:*** 3.61. ***Test scores:*** SAT critical reading scores over 500: 80%; SAT math scores over 500: 94%; ACT scores over 18: 100%; SAT critical reading scores over 600: 46%; SAT math scores over 600: 54%; ACT scores over 24: 81%; SAT critical reading scores over 700: 14%; SAT math scores over 700: 12%; ACT scores over 30: 19%.
Retention: 85% of full-time freshmen returned.

FACULTY
Total: 928, 47% full-time, 50% with terminal degrees.
Student/faculty ratio: 14:1.

ACADEMICS
Calendar: 4-1-4. *Degrees:* certificates, bachelor's, master's, doctoral, post-master's, and postbachelor's certificates.
Special study options: accelerated degree program, advanced placement credit, cooperative education, distance learning, double majors, English as a second language, honors programs, independent study, internships, off-campus study, part-time degree program, services for LD students, student-designed majors, study abroad, summer session for credit. ***ROTC:*** Army (c), Navy (c), Air Force (b).
Unusual degree programs: 3-2 engineering with University of Notre Dame; University of Minnesota, Twin Cities Campus.
Computers: Students can access the following: campus intranet, computer help desk, free student e-mail accounts, online (class) grades, online (class) registration, online (class) schedules. Campuswide network is available. Wireless service is available via entire campus.
Library: O'Shaughnessy-Frey Library plus 7 others. *Books:* 502,033 (physical), 251,462 (digital/electronic); *Serial titles:* 16,463 (physical), 118,059 (digital/electronic); *Databases:* 406. Students can reserve study rooms.

STUDENT LIFE
Housing options: coed, men-only, women-only, cooperative, special housing for students with disabilities. Campus housing is university owned. Freshman applicants given priority for college housing.
Activities and organizations: drama/theater group, student-run newspaper, radio and television station, choral group.
Athletics Member NCAA. All Division III. ***Intercollegiate sports:*** baseball M, basketball M/W, cross-country running M/W, football M, golf M/W, ice hockey M/W, lacrosse M(c)/W(c), soccer M/W, softball W, swimming and diving M/W, tennis M/W, volleyball W. ***Intramural sports:*** badminton M/W, basketball M/W, crew M(c)/W(c), golf M/W, racquetball M/W, sailing M(c)/W, skiing (downhill) M(c)/W(c), soccer M/W, table tennis M/W, tennis M/W, track and field M(c)/W(c), volleyball M/W.
Campus security: 24-hour emergency response devices and patrols, late-night transport/escort service, controlled dormitory access.
Student services: health clinic, personal/psychological counseling, women's center, legal services.

COSTS & FINANCIAL AID
Costs (2017–18) ***Comprehensive fee:*** $51,187 includes full-time tuition ($40,224), mandatory fees ($909), and room and board ($10,054). Part-time tuition: $1257 per credit. ***College room only:*** $6304. Room and board charges vary according to board plan and housing facility. ***Payment plans:*** installment, deferred payment. ***Waivers:*** senior citizens and employees or children of employees.
Financial Aid Of all full-time matriculated undergraduates who enrolled in 2016, 3,965 applied for aid, 3,269 were judged to have need, 610 had their need fully met. 860 Federal Work-Study jobs (averaging $2971). 1,117 state and other part-time jobs (averaging $3044). In 2016, 636 non-need-based awards were made. ***Average percent of need met:*** 84. ***Average financial aid package:*** $26,846. ***Average need-based loan:*** $8992. ***Average need-based gift aid:*** $20,378. ***Average non-need-based aid:*** $17,372. ***Average indebtedness upon graduation:*** $40,307.

APPLYING
Standardized Tests *Required:* SAT or ACT (for admission).
Options: electronic application, early action, deferred entrance.
Required: essay or personal statement, high school transcript. ***Recommended:*** interview.
Application deadlines: rolling (freshmen), rolling (transfers), 11/1 (early action).
Notification: continuous (freshmen), continuous (transfers), 12/15 (early action).

CONTACT
University of St. Thomas, 2115 Summit Avenue, St. Paul, MN 55105-1096. *Toll-free phone:* 800-328-6819. *E-mail:* admissions@stthomas.edu.

Walden University
Minneapolis, Minnesota
http://www.waldenu.edu/

- **Proprietary** university, founded 1970, part of Laureate International Universities
- **Coed**
- 98% of applicants were admitted

ACADEMICS
Calendar: quarter/semester depending on program. *Degrees:* certificates, bachelor's, master's, doctoral, post-master's, and postbachelor's certificates.
Library: Walden University Library. *Books:* 206,177 (digital/electronic); *Serial titles:* 69,602 (digital/electronic); *Databases:* 106. Weekly public service hours: 69.

STUDENT LIFE
Student services: personal/psychological counseling, legal services.

FINANCIAL AID
Financial Aid Of all full-time matriculated undergraduates who enrolled in 2009, 908 applied for aid, 878 were judged to have need, 7 had their need fully met. In 2009, 17 non-need-based awards were made. ***Average percent of need met:*** 26. ***Average financial aid package:*** $6301. ***Average need-based loan:*** $3755. ***Average need-based gift aid:*** $3222. ***Average non-need-based aid:*** $1225.

APPLYING
Options: electronic application, deferred entrance.
Required: high school transcript.

CONTACT
Walden University, 100 Washington South, Suite 900, Minneapolis, MN 55401. *Toll-free phone:* 866-492-5336.

Winona State University
Winona, Minnesota
http://www.winona.edu/

- **State-supported** comprehensive, founded 1858, part of Minnesota State Colleges and Universities System
- **Small-town** 125-acre campus with easy access to Minneapolis-St.Paul
- **Endowment** $22.6 million
- **Coed** 7,656 undergraduate students, 87% full-time, 63% women, 37% men
- **Moderately difficult** entrance level, 60% of applicants were admitted

UNDERGRAD STUDENTS
6,697 full-time, 959 part-time. Students come from 40 states and territories; 52 other countries; 29% are from out of state; 3% Black or African American, non-Hispanic/Latino; 3% Hispanic/Latino; 2% Asian, non-Hispanic/Latino; 0.1% Native Hawaiian or other Pacific Islander, non-Hispanic/Latino; 0.2% American Indian or Alaska Native, non-Hispanic/Latino; 2% Two or more races, non-Hispanic/Latino; 0.8% Race/ethnicity unknown; 3% international; 7% transferred in; 29% live on campus.

Freshmen:
Admission: 7,476 applied, 4,467 admitted, 1,586 enrolled. ***Average high school GPA:*** 3.35. ***Test scores:*** ACT scores over 18: 97%; ACT scores over 24: 37%; ACT scores over 30: 3%.
Retention: 77% of full-time freshmen returned.

FACULTY
Total: 525, 65% full-time, 55% with terminal degrees.

Student/faculty ratio: 18:1.

ACADEMICS

Calendar: semesters. *Degrees:* associate, bachelor's, master's, doctoral, post-master's, and postbachelor's certificates.

Special study options: academic remediation for entering students, adult/continuing education programs, advanced placement credit, distance learning, double majors, English as a second language, independent study, internships, off-campus study, part-time degree program, services for LD students, student-designed majors, study abroad, summer session for credit. ***ROTC:*** Army (c).

Computers: 50 computers/terminals and 19,500 ports are available on campus for general student use. Students can access the following: campus intranet, computer help desk, free student e-mail accounts, online (class) grades, online (class) registration, online (class) schedules. Campuswide network is available. 100% of college-owned or -operated housing units are wired for high-speed Internet access. Wireless service is available via entire campus.

Library: Darrel W. Krueger Library. *Books:* 344,659 (physical), 50,000 (digital/electronic); *Serial titles:* 2,097 (physical), 34,000 (digital/electronic); *Databases:* 100. Weekly public service hours: 99; students can reserve study rooms.

STUDENT LIFE

Housing options: coed, men-only, women-only, special housing for students with disabilities. Campus housing is university owned and leased by the school. Freshman campus housing is guaranteed.

Activities and organizations: drama/theater group, student-run newspaper, radio station, choral group, University Program Activities Committee, Student Senate, Residence Hall Association, Inter Varsity, national fraternities, national sororities.

Athletics Member NCAA. All Division II except gymnastics (Division III). ***Intercollegiate sports:*** baseball M(s), basketball M(s)/W(s), cross-country running M(s)/W(s), football M(s), golf M(s)/W(s), gymnastics W, soccer W(s), softball W(s), tennis W(s), track and field W(s), volleyball W(s). ***Intramural sports:*** badminton M(c)/W(c), baseball M(c)/W(c), basketball M/W, bowling M(c)/W(c), cheerleading M(c)/W(c), cross-country running M(c)/W(c), fencing M(c)/W(c), ice hockey M(c)/W(c), lacrosse M(c)/W(c), rugby M(c)/W(c), skiing (cross-country) M(c)/W(c), skiing (downhill) M(c)/W(c), soccer M/W, softball M/W, swimming and diving M(c)/W(c), table tennis M(c)/W(c), tennis M(c)/W(c), ultimate Frisbee M(c)/W(c), volleyball M/W, wrestling M(c)/W(c).

Campus security: 24-hour emergency response devices and patrols, student patrols, late-night transport/escort service, controlled dormitory access, security cameras.

Student services: health clinic, personal/psychological counseling.

COSTS & FINANCIAL AID

Costs (2016–17) ***Tuition:*** state resident $7103 full-time, $235 per credit hour part-time; nonresident $12,800 full-time, $426 per credit hour part-time. Full-time tuition and fees vary according to location, program, and reciprocity agreements. Part-time tuition and fees vary according to course load, location, program, and reciprocity agreements. ***Required fees:*** $1972 full-time, $38 per credit hour part-time, $485 per term part-time. ***Room and board:*** $8460. Room and board charges vary according to board plan, housing facility, and location. ***Payment plan:*** installment. ***Waivers:*** employees or children of employees.

Financial Aid Of all full-time matriculated undergraduates who enrolled in 2015, 5,622 applied for aid, 4,117 were judged to have need, 447 had their need fully met. 160 Federal Work-Study jobs (averaging $2226). 353 state and other part-time jobs (averaging $2364). In 2015, 911 non-need-based awards were made. ***Average percent of need met:*** 51. ***Average financial aid package:*** $7785. ***Average need-based loan:*** $3959. ***Average need-based gift aid:*** $5432. ***Average non-need-based aid:*** $3270. ***Average indebtedness upon graduation:*** $35,221.

APPLYING

Standardized Tests *Required:* SAT or ACT (for admission).

Options: electronic application, deferred entrance.

Application fee: $20.

Required: high school transcript, 16 high school preparation requirements and either minimum composite ACT of 21 with top two-thirds of high school class rank or minimum cumulative GPA of 2.75 or, minimum composite ACT of 18 with either top half of high school class rank or minimum cumulative high school GPA of 3.0.

Application deadlines: 7/1 (freshmen), 7/1 (transfers).

Notification: continuous (freshmen), continuous (out-of-state freshmen), continuous (transfers).

CONTACT

Carl Stange, Director of Admissions, Winona State University, 175 West Mark Street, Winona, MN 55987. *Phone:* 507-457-5100. *Toll-free phone:* 800-DIAL WSU. *Fax:* 507-457-5620. *E-mail:* admissions@winona.edu.

MISSISSIPPI

Alcorn State University

Lorman, Mississippi

http://www.alcorn.edu/

- **State-supported** comprehensive, founded 1871, part of Mississippi Institutions of Higher Learning
- **Rural** 1756-acre campus
- **Endowment** $15.9 million
- **Coed** 2,825 undergraduate students, 92% full-time, 64% women, 36% men
- **Moderately difficult** entrance level, 78% of applicants were admitted

UNDERGRAD STUDENTS

2,589 full-time, 236 part-time. Students come from 33 states and territories; 23 other countries; 24% are from out of state; 92% Black or African American, non-Hispanic/Latino; 0.9% Hispanic/Latino; 0.1% Asian, non-Hispanic/Latino; 0.3% Native Hawaiian or other Pacific Islander, non-Hispanic/Latino; 0.1% American Indian or Alaska Native, non-Hispanic/Latino; 2% Two or more races, non-Hispanic/Latino; 2% international; 7% transferred in; 64% live on campus.

Freshmen:

Admission: 2,078 applied, 1,630 admitted, 536 enrolled. ***Average high school GPA:*** 3.19. ***Test scores:*** SAT critical reading scores over 500: 34%; SAT math scores over 500: 32%; SAT critical reading scores over 600: 8%; SAT math scores over 600: 4%; SAT math scores over 700: 2%. ***Retention:*** 72% of full-time freshmen returned.

FACULTY

Total: 217, 72% full-time, 67% with terminal degrees.

Student/faculty ratio: 17:1.

ACADEMICS

Calendar: semesters. *Degrees:* associate, bachelor's, master's, and post-master's certificates.

Special study options: academic remediation for entering students, accelerated degree program, adult/continuing education programs, advanced placement credit, cooperative education, distance learning, double majors, honors programs, independent study, internships, off-campus study, part-time degree program, study abroad, summer session for credit. ***ROTC:*** Army (b).

Computers: 500 computers/terminals and 2,500 ports are available on campus for general student use. Students can access the following: campus intranet, computer help desk, free student e-mail accounts, online (class) grades, online (class) registration, online (class) schedules, online payment; online transcript request. Campuswide network is available. 100% of college-owned or -operated housing units are wired for high-speed Internet access. Wireless service is available via classrooms, computer centers, computer labs, dorm rooms, learning centers, libraries, student centers.

Library: John Dewey Boyd Library plus 1 other. *Books:* 412,321 (physical), 44,114 (digital/electronic); *Serial titles:* 312 (physical), 117,823 (digital/electronic); *Databases:* 75. Weekly public service hours: 88; study areas open 24 hours, 5-7 days a week; students can reserve study rooms.

STUDENT LIFE

Housing options: men-only, women-only. Campus housing is university owned. Freshman campus housing is guaranteed.

Activities and organizations: drama/theater group, student-run newspaper, radio and television station, choral group, marching band, marching band, Gospel Choir, inter-faith choir, national fraternities, national sororities.

Athletics Member NCAA. All Division I. ***Intercollegiate sports:*** baseball M(s), basketball M(s)/W(s), cross-country running M(s)/W(s), football M(s), golf M(s)/W(s), soccer W(s), softball W(s), tennis M(s)/W(s), track and field M(s)/W(s), volleyball W(s). ***Intramural sports:*** basketball M/W, football M.

Campus security: 24-hour emergency response devices and patrols, late-night transport/escort service, controlled dormitory access.

Student services: health clinic, personal/psychological counseling.

COSTS & FINANCIAL AID

Costs (2016–17) ***Tuition:*** state resident $6552 full-time, $546 per credit hour part-time; nonresident $6552 full-time, $546 per credit hour part-time. Full-time tuition and fees vary according to course load. Part-time tuition and fees vary according to course load. ***Room and board:*** $9356; room only: $6384. Room and board charges vary according to board plan and housing facility. ***Payment plan:*** installment. ***Waivers:*** employees or children of employees.

Financial Aid Of all full-time matriculated undergraduates who enrolled in 2016, 1,337 applied for aid, 1,284 were judged to have need, 129 had their need fully met. 281 Federal Work-Study jobs (averaging $1111). In 2016, 721 non-need-based awards were made. ***Average percent of need met:*** 49. ***Average financial aid package:*** $15,032. ***Average need-based loan:*** $3892. ***Average need-based gift aid:*** $5902. ***Average non-need-based aid:*** $8158. ***Average indebtedness upon graduation:*** $35,077.

APPLYING

Standardized Tests *Required:* SAT or ACT (for admission).

Options: electronic application, deferred entrance.

Required: high school transcript, minimum 2.0 GPA.

Application deadlines: rolling (freshmen), rolling (transfers).

Notification: continuous (freshmen), continuous (transfers).

CONTACT

Mrs. Kantangelia Tenner, Director of Admissions, Alcorn State University, 1000 ASU Drive, #300, Alcorn State, MS 39096-7500. *Phone:* 601-877-6147. *Toll-free phone:* 800-222-6790. *Fax:* 601-877-6347. *E-mail:* ksampson@alcorn.edu.

Belhaven University

Jackson, Mississippi

http://www.belhaven.edu/

- **Independent Presbyterian** comprehensive, founded 1883
- **Urban** 46-acre campus
- **Endowment** $5.6 million
- **Coed** 2,715 undergraduate students, 49% full-time, 65% women, 35% men
- **Moderately difficult** entrance level, 43% of applicants were admitted

UNDERGRAD STUDENTS

1,331 full-time, 1,384 part-time. Students come from 47 states and territories; 25 other countries; 28% are from out of state; 49% Black or African American, non-Hispanic/Latino; 5% Hispanic/Latino; 0.9% Asian, non-Hispanic/Latino; 0.1% Native Hawaiian or other Pacific Islander, non-Hispanic/Latino; 0.5% American Indian or Alaska Native, non-Hispanic/Latino; 2% Two or more races, non-Hispanic/Latino; 7% Race/ethnicity unknown; 2% international; 18% transferred in; 25% live on campus.

Freshmen:

Admission: 2,474 applied, 1,053 admitted, 237 enrolled. ***Average high school GPA:*** 3.4. ***Test scores:*** SAT critical reading scores over 500: 63%; SAT math scores over 500: 45%; ACT scores over 18: 98%; SAT critical reading scores over 600: 29%; SAT math scores over 600: 25%; ACT scores over 24: 24%; SAT critical reading scores over 700: 5%; SAT math scores over 700: 5%; ACT scores over 30: 5%.

Retention: 66% of full-time freshmen returned.

FACULTY

Total: 468, 22% full-time, 19% with terminal degrees.

Student/faculty ratio: 11:1.

ACADEMICS

Calendar: semesters. *Degrees:* certificates, associate, bachelor's, and master's.

Special study options: academic remediation for entering students, accelerated degree program, adult/continuing education programs, advanced placement credit, distance learning, double majors, English as a second language, honors programs, independent study, internships, off-campus study, part-time degree program, student-designed majors, study abroad, summer session for credit. ***ROTC:*** Army (c), Air Force (c).

Unusual degree programs: 3-2 engineering with Mississippi State University.

Computers: 36 computers/terminals are available on campus for general student use. Students can access the following: campus intranet, computer help desk, free student e-mail accounts, online (class) grades, online (class) registration, online (class) schedules. Campuswide network is available. 100% of college-owned or -operated housing units are wired for high-speed Internet access. Wireless service is available via classrooms, computer labs, dorm rooms, libraries, student centers.

Library: Warren A. Hood Library plus 1 other. *Books:* 45,076 (physical), 50,445 (digital/electronic); *Serial titles:* 160 (physical), 40,370 (digital/electronic); *Databases:* 46. Weekly public service hours: 104.

STUDENT LIFE

Housing options: on-campus residence required through sophomore year; men-only, women-only. Campus housing is university owned. Freshman campus housing is guaranteed.

Activities and organizations: drama/theater group, student-run newspaper, choral group, marching band, Belhaven Activities Team, intramurals, Reformed University Fellowship, Quartertone, Sports Medicine: Exercise Science Club.

Athletics Member NCAA. All Division III. ***Intercollegiate sports:*** baseball M(s), basketball M(s)/W(s), cross-country running M(s)/W(s), football M(s), golf M(s)/W(s), soccer M(s)/W(s), softball W(s), tennis M(s)/W(s), volleyball W(s). ***Intramural sports:*** basketball M/W, football M/W, soccer M/W, softball M/W, volleyball M/W.

Campus security: 24-hour emergency response devices and patrols, late-night transport/escort service, controlled dormitory access.

Student services: health clinic, personal/psychological counseling.

COSTS & FINANCIAL AID

Costs (2017–18) ***Comprehensive fee:*** $32,250 includes full-time tuition ($23,900), mandatory fees ($350), and room and board ($8000). Part-time tuition: $425 per credit hour. Part-time tuition and fees vary according to course load. ***Room and board:*** Room and board charges vary according to housing facility. ***Payment plan:*** installment. ***Waivers:*** employees or children of employees.

Financial Aid Of all full-time matriculated undergraduates who enrolled in 2015, 1,136 applied for aid, 1,057 were judged to have need, 59 had their need fully met. 215 Federal Work-Study jobs (averaging $1500). 42 state and other part-time jobs (averaging $2000). In 2015, 279 non-need-based awards were made. ***Average percent of need met:*** 59. ***Average financial aid package:*** $15,764. ***Average need-based loan:*** $4298. ***Average need-based gift aid:*** $12,671. ***Average non-need-based aid:*** $14,171. ***Average indebtedness upon graduation:*** $29,738.

APPLYING

Standardized Tests *Required:* SAT or ACT (for admission).

Options: electronic application, early admission, deferred entrance.

Application fee: $25.

Required: high school transcript, minimum 2.0 GPA, 1 letter of recommendation. ***Required for some:*** essay or personal statement, interview.

Application deadlines: rolling (freshmen), rolling (transfers).

Notification: continuous (freshmen), continuous (transfers).

CONTACT

Ms. Suzanne T. Sullivan, Assistant Vice President for Traditional and Online Admissions, Belhaven University, 1500 Peachtree Street, Jackson, MS 39202. *Phone:* 601-968-5940. *Toll-free phone:* 800-960-5940. *Fax:* 601-968-8946. *E-mail:* admission@belhaven.edu.

Blue Mountain College
Blue Mountain, Mississippi
http://www.bmc.edu/

- **Independent Southern Baptist** comprehensive, founded 1873
- **Rural** 190-acre campus with easy access to Memphis
- **Endowment** $13.2 million
- **Coed** 457 undergraduate students, 87% full-time, 57% women, 43% men
- **Moderately difficult** entrance level, 38% of applicants were admitted

UNDERGRAD STUDENTS
397 full-time, 60 part-time. Students come from 16 states and territories; 6 other countries; 20% are from out of state; 10% Black or African American, non-Hispanic/Latino; 2% Hispanic/Latino; 0.2% Asian, non-Hispanic/Latino; 0.2% American Indian or Alaska Native, non-Hispanic/Latino; 0.9% Two or more races, non-Hispanic/Latino; 2% international; 18% transferred in; 54% live on campus.

Freshmen:
Admission: 326 applied, 125 admitted, 56 enrolled. ***Average high school GPA:*** 3.47. ***Test scores:*** ACT scores over 18: 84%; ACT scores over 24: 29%; ACT scores over 30: 5%.

Retention: 69% of full-time freshmen returned.

FACULTY
Total: 50, 66% full-time, 66% with terminal degrees.
Student/faculty ratio: 11:1.

ACADEMICS
Calendar: semesters. *Degrees:* bachelor's and master's.

Special study options: academic remediation for entering students, accelerated degree program, adult/continuing education programs, advanced placement credit, distance learning, double majors, honors programs, internships, part-time degree program, services for LD students, summer session for credit.

Unusual degree programs: 3-2 nursing with Baptist College of Health Sciences, Union University; medical studies with Baptist College of Health Sciences.

Computers: 52 computers/terminals are available on campus for general student use. Students can access the following: computer help desk, free student e-mail accounts, online (class) grades, online (class) registration, online (class) schedules. Campuswide network is available. 100% of college-owned or -operated housing units are wired for high-speed Internet access. Wireless service is available via classrooms, computer centers, computer labs, dorm rooms, learning centers, libraries, student centers.

Library: Guyton Library plus 1 other. *Books:* 43,019 (physical), 35,899 (digital/electronic); *Serial titles:* 148 (physical); *Databases:* 22. Weekly public service hours: 69.

STUDENT LIFE
Housing options: men-only, women-only. Campus housing is university owned.

Activities and organizations: drama/theater group, choral group, Baptist Student Union, Student Body Association, Intramural Association, Ministerial Association, Mississippi Association of Educators/Student Program.

Athletics Member NAIA. ***Intercollegiate sports:*** baseball M(s), basketball M(s)/W(s), cross-country running M(s)/W(s), golf M(s), softball W(s). ***Intramural sports:*** basketball M/W, football M, soccer M, softball M/W, swimming and diving W, table tennis W, tennis W, track and field M/W, ultimate Frisbee M, volleyball M/W.

Campus security: 24-hour emergency response devices and patrols, controlled dormitory access.

COSTS & FINANCIAL AID
Costs (2016–17) ***Comprehensive fee:*** $16,976 includes full-time tuition ($9518), mandatory fees ($1694), and room and board ($5764). Full-time tuition and fees vary according to course load, degree level, and program. Part-time tuition: $317 per semester hour. Part-time tuition and fees vary according to course load, degree level, and program. ***Required fees:*** $511 per term part-time. ***Room and board:*** Room and board charges vary according to gender, housing facility, and location. ***Payment plans:*** installment, deferred payment. ***Waivers:*** employees or children of employees.

Financial Aid Of all full-time matriculated undergraduates who enrolled in 2016, 487 applied for aid, 411 were judged to have need, 86 had their need fully met. 46 Federal Work-Study jobs (averaging $841). 55 state and other part-time jobs (averaging $868). In 2016, 41 non-need-based awards were made. ***Average percent of need met:*** 78. ***Average financial aid package:*** $8869. ***Average need-based loan:*** $3676. ***Average need-based gift aid:*** $8869. ***Average non-need-based aid:*** $4835. ***Average indebtedness upon graduation:*** $19,695.

APPLYING
Standardized Tests *Required:* SAT or ACT (for admission).

Options: electronic application, deferred entrance.

Application fee: $10.

Required for some: high school transcript. ***Recommended:*** minimum 2.0 GPA.

Application deadlines: rolling (freshmen), rolling (out-of-state freshmen), rolling (transfers).

Notification: continuous (freshmen), continuous (out-of-state freshmen), continuous (transfers).

CONTACT
Mr. Lynn Gibson, Vice President for Enrollment Services, Blue Mountain College, PO Box 160, Blue Mountain, MS 38610-0160. *Phone:* 662-685-4771 Ext. 176. *Toll-free phone:* 800-235-0136. *Fax:* 662-685-4776. *E-mail:* lgibson@bmc.edu.

Delta State University
Cleveland, Mississippi
http://www.deltastate.edu/

CONTACT
Mr. Chris Gaines, Director of Recruiting, Delta State University, 1003 West Sunflower Road, Kent Wyatt Hall, Office of Admissions, Cleveland, MS 38733. *Phone:* 662-846-4020. *Toll-free phone:* 800-468-6378. *E-mail:* admissions@deltastate.edu.

Jackson State University
Jackson, Mississippi
http://www.jsums.edu/

- **State-supported** university, founded 1877, part of Mississippi Institutions of Higher Learning
- **Urban** 250-acre campus
- **Endowment** $38.9 million
- **Coed** 7,492 undergraduate students, 87% full-time, 63% women, 37% men
- **Minimally difficult** entrance level, 69% of applicants were admitted

UNDERGRAD STUDENTS
6,507 full-time, 985 part-time. Students come from 42 states and territories; 47 other countries; 24% are from out of state; 92% Black or African American, non-Hispanic/Latino; 0.6% Hispanic/Latino; 0.3% Asian, non-Hispanic/Latino; 0.3% American Indian or Alaska Native, non-Hispanic/Latino; 1% Two or more races, non-Hispanic/Latino; 2% international; 10% transferred in; 36% live on campus.

Freshmen:
Admission: 8,516 applied, 5,857 admitted, 1,292 enrolled. ***Average high school GPA:*** 2.9. ***Test scores:*** ACT scores over 18: 63%; ACT scores over 24: 12%.

Retention: 71% of full-time freshmen returned.

FACULTY
Total: 612, 61% full-time, 65% with terminal degrees.
Student/faculty ratio: 18:1.

ACADEMICS
Calendar: semesters. *Degrees:* bachelor's, master's, doctoral, and post-master's certificates.

Special study options: academic remediation for entering students, accelerated degree program, adult/continuing education programs, advanced placement credit, cooperative education, distance learning, double majors, English as a second language, honors programs, independent study, internships, off-campus study, part-time degree program, services for LD students, study abroad, summer session for credit. ***ROTC:*** Army (b), Air Force (b).

Computers: 1,224 computers/terminals are available on campus for general student use. Students can access the following: computer help desk, free student e-mail accounts, online (class) grades, online (class) registration, online (class) schedules. Campuswide network is available. 100% of college-owned or -operated housing units are wired for high-speed Internet access. Wireless service is available via entire campus.

Library: H. T. Sampson Library plus 4 others. *Books:* 300,587 (physical), 339,368 (digital/electronic); *Serial titles:* 292,055 (digital/electronic); *Databases:* 68.

STUDENT LIFE

Housing options: men-only, women-only, special housing for students with disabilities. Campus housing is university owned and leased by the school. Freshman applicants given priority for college housing.

Activities and organizations: drama/theater group, student-run newspaper, choral group, marching band, Student Government Association, Sonic Boom of the South, MADDRAMA, Interfaith, NAACP, national fraternities, national sororities.

Athletics Member NCAA. All Division I except football (Division I-AA). ***Intercollegiate sports:*** baseball M(s), basketball M(s)/W(s), bowling W(s), cheerleading M/W, cross-country running M(s)/W(s), golf M(s)/W(s), soccer W(s), softball W(s), tennis M(s)/W(s), track and field M(s)/W(s), volleyball W(s). ***Intramural sports:*** basketball M/W, football M/W, softball M/W, volleyball M/W.

Campus security: 24-hour emergency response devices and patrols, controlled dormitory access.

Student services: health clinic, personal/psychological counseling.

COSTS & FINANCIAL AID

Costs (2016–17) ***Tuition:*** state resident $7141 full-time, $298 per credit hour part-time; nonresident $17,494 full-time, $432 per credit hour part-time. Full-time tuition and fees vary according to course level, course load, degree level, location, program, and student level. Part-time tuition and fees vary according to course level, degree level, location, program, and student level. ***Required fees:*** $120 full-time. ***Room and board:*** $8708; room only: $5258. Room and board charges vary according to housing facility. ***Payment plan:*** installment. ***Waivers:*** children of alumni and employees or children of employees.

Financial Aid Of all full-time matriculated undergraduates who enrolled in 2016, 6,143 applied for aid, 5,574 were judged to have need, 244 had their need fully met. 1,184 state and other part-time jobs (averaging $2341). In 2016, 77 non-need-based awards were made. ***Average percent of need met:*** 53. ***Average financial aid package:*** $12,324. ***Average need-based loan:*** $4163. ***Average need-based gift aid:*** $7543. ***Average non-need-based aid:*** $12,373. ***Average indebtedness upon graduation:*** $28,311.

APPLYING

Standardized Tests *Required:* SAT or ACT (for admission).

Options: electronic application.

Required: high school transcript, immunization record, minimum ACT Composite score of 16.

Application deadlines: 9/5 (freshmen), rolling (transfers), rolling (early action).

Notification: continuous (freshmen), continuous (transfers).

CONTACT

Ms. Latoysha Smith, Interim Director of Undergraduate Recruitment, Jackson State University, PO Box 18389, 1400 John R. Lynch Street, Jackson, MS 39217. *Phone:* 601-979-2914. *Toll-free phone:* 800-848-6817. *Fax:* 601-979-0360. *E-mail:* laytoysha.smith@jsums.edu.

Millsaps College

Jackson, Mississippi

http://www.millsaps.edu/

- **Independent United Methodist** comprehensive, founded 1890
- **Urban** 100-acre campus
- **Endowment** $100.7 million
- **Coed** 809 undergraduate students, 98% full-time, 49% women, 51% men
- **Moderately difficult** entrance level, 59% of applicants were admitted

UNDERGRAD STUDENTS

795 full-time, 14 part-time. Students come from 22 states and territories; 24 other countries; 59% are from out of state; 14% Black or African American, non-Hispanic/Latino; 4% Hispanic/Latino; 4% Asian, non-Hispanic/Latino; 0.9% American Indian or Alaska Native, non-Hispanic/Latino; 0.1% Two or more races, non-Hispanic/Latino; 3% Race/ethnicity unknown; 4% international; 2% transferred in; 90% live on campus.

Freshmen:

Admission: 4,269 applied, 2,525 admitted, 259 enrolled. ***Average high school GPA:*** 3.6. ***Test scores:*** ACT scores over 18: 100%; ACT scores over 24: 65%; SAT critical reading scores over 700: 100%; SAT math scores over 700: 100%; ACT scores over 30: 14%.

Retention: 81% of full-time freshmen returned.

FACULTY

Total: 109, 79% full-time, 87% with terminal degrees.

Student/faculty ratio: 9:1.

ACADEMICS

Calendar: semesters. *Degrees:* bachelor's and master's.

Special study options: accelerated degree program, advanced placement credit, double majors, honors programs, independent study, internships, off-campus study, part-time degree program, services for LD students, student-designed majors, study abroad, summer session for credit. ***ROTC:*** Army (c), Air Force (c).

Unusual degree programs: 3-2 engineering with Auburn University, Columbia University, Vanderbilt University; nursing with University of Mississippi Medical Center, Vanderbilt University.

Computers: 150 computers/terminals are available on campus for general student use. Students can access the following: campus intranet, computer help desk, free student e-mail accounts, online (class) grades, online (class) registration, online (class) schedules, online transcripts. Campuswide network is available. 100% of college-owned or -operated housing units are wired for high-speed Internet access. Wireless service is available via entire campus.

Library: Millsaps-Wilson Library.

STUDENT LIFE

Housing options: on-campus residence required through sophomore year; coed, men-only, women-only, special housing for students with disabilities. Campus housing is university owned. Freshman campus housing is guaranteed.

Activities and organizations: drama/theater group, student-run newspaper, choral group, Campus Ministry Team, Student Body Association, SAPS (Campus Programming Board), Inter-fraternity/Panhellenic Councils, intramural sports, national fraternities, national sororities.

Athletics Member NCAA. All Division III. ***Intercollegiate sports:*** baseball M, basketball M/W, cross-country running M/W, football M, golf M/W, lacrosse M/W, soccer M/W, softball W, tennis M/W, track and field M/W, volleyball W. ***Intramural sports:*** basketball M/W, cheerleading W(c), fencing M(c)/W(c), football M/W, lacrosse W(c), soccer M/W, softball M/W, swimming and diving M(c)/W(c), ultimate Frisbee M(c)/W(c), volleyball M/W.

Campus security: 24-hour emergency response devices and patrols, student patrols, late-night transport/escort service, controlled dormitory access, self-defense education, lighted pathways.

Student services: health clinic, personal/psychological counseling.

COSTS & FINANCIAL AID

Costs (2017–18) ***Comprehensive fee:*** $52,780 includes full-time tuition ($36,830), mandatory fees ($2550), and room and board ($13,400). Part-time tuition: $1120 per semester hour. ***Required fees:*** $36 per semester hour part-time. ***College room only:*** $7500. Room and board charges vary according to board plan and housing facility. ***Waivers:*** employees or children of employees.

Financial Aid Of all full-time matriculated undergraduates who enrolled in 2015, 561 applied for aid, 496 were judged to have need, 120 had their need fully met. In 2015, 286 non-need-based awards were made. ***Average percent of need met:*** 79. ***Average financial aid package:*** $33,569. ***Average need-based loan:*** $4809. ***Average need-based gift aid:*** $26,997.

Average non-need-based aid: $22,981. ***Average indebtedness upon graduation:*** $31,419.

APPLYING

Standardized Tests *Required:* SAT or ACT (for admission).

Options: electronic application, early admission, early action, deferred entrance.

Required: essay or personal statement, high school transcript, minimum 2.5 GPA, 1 letter of recommendation, secondary school report. ***Required for some:*** interview.

Application deadlines: 2/1 (freshmen), rolling (out-of-state freshmen), 7/1 (transfers), 11/15 (early action).

Notification: continuous until 3/15 (freshmen), continuous until 3/15 (out-of-state freshmen), continuous until 3/15 (transfers), 1/15 (early action).

CONTACT

Dr. Robert Alexander, Millsaps College, 1701 North State Street, Jackson, MS 39210-0001. *Phone:* 601-974-1050. *Toll-free phone:* 800-352-1050. *Fax:* 601-974-1059. *E-mail:* admissions@millsaps.edu.

Mississippi College

Clinton, Mississippi

http://www.mc.edu/

- **Independent Southern Baptist** comprehensive, founded 1826, part of Mississippi Baptist Convention
- **Suburban** 140-acre campus with easy access to Jackson
- **Endowment** $72.5 million
- **Coed**
- **Moderately difficult** entrance level

FACULTY

Student/faculty ratio: 15:1.

ACADEMICS

Calendar: semesters. *Degrees:* bachelor's, master's, doctoral, post-master's, and postbachelor's certificates.

Library: Leland Speed Library plus 1 other. *Books:* 252,127 (physical), 1,634 (digital/electronic); *Serial titles:* 9,071 (physical), 21 (digital/electronic); *Databases:* 55.

STUDENT LIFE

Housing options: on-campus residence required through junior year; men-only, women-only, special housing for students with disabilities. Campus housing is university owned. Freshman applicants given priority for college housing.

Activities and organizations: drama/theater group, student-run newspaper, radio station, choral group, marching band, Baptist Student Union, Nenamoosha Social Tribe, Laguna Social Tribe, Civitan Service Club, Shawreth Service Club.

Athletics Member NCAA. All Division II.

Campus security: 24-hour emergency response devices and patrols, late-night transport/escort service, controlled dormitory access.

Student services: health clinic, personal/psychological counseling.

COSTS & FINANCIAL AID

Costs (2016–17) ***Comprehensive fee:*** $25,930 includes full-time tuition ($15,800), mandatory fees ($940), and room and board ($9190). Part-time tuition: $495 per credit. ***Required fees:*** $490 per term part-time. ***Room and board:*** Room and board charges vary according to housing facility.

Financial Aid Of all full-time matriculated undergraduates who enrolled in 2015, 2,048 applied for aid, 1,402 were judged to have need, 181 had their need fully met. 193 Federal Work-Study jobs (averaging $825). In 2015, 969 non-need-based awards were made. ***Average percent of need met:*** 67. ***Average financial aid package:*** $15,035. ***Average need-based loan:*** $7014. ***Average need-based gift aid:*** $10,676. ***Average non-need-based aid:*** $7746. ***Average indebtedness upon graduation:*** $29,189.

APPLYING

Standardized Tests *Required:* SAT or ACT (for admission).

Options: electronic application, early admission, deferred entrance.

Application fee: $25.

Required: high school transcript. ***Required for some:*** 2 letters of recommendation. ***Recommended:*** minimum 2.0 GPA, interview.

CONTACT

Mr. William Kyle Brantley, Director of Admissions, Mississippi College, Box 4026, 200 South Capitol Street, Clinton, MS 39058-0001. *Phone:* 601-925-7634. *Toll-free phone:* 800-738-1236. *Fax:* 601-925-3950. *E-mail:* enrollment-services@mc.edu.

Mississippi State University

Mississippi State, Mississippi

http://www.msstate.edu/

- **State-supported** university, founded 1878, part of Mississippi Institutions of Higher Learning
- **Small-town** 4200-acre campus
- **Endowment** $444.5 million
- **Coed** 18,090 undergraduate students, 92% full-time, 50% women, 50% men
- **Moderately difficult** entrance level, 71% of applicants were admitted

UNDERGRAD STUDENTS

16,695 full-time, 1,395 part-time. Students come from 52 states and territories; 56 other countries; 30% are from out of state; 21% Black or African American, non-Hispanic/Latino; 3% Hispanic/Latino; 0.1% Asian, non-Hispanic/Latino; 0.1% Native Hawaiian or other Pacific Islander, non-Hispanic/Latino; 0.4% American Indian or Alaska Native, non-Hispanic/Latino; 2% Two or more races, non-Hispanic/Latino; 0.4% Race/ethnicity unknown; 1% international; 10% transferred in; 28% live on campus.

Freshmen:

Admission: 13,930 applied, 9,866 admitted, 3,624 enrolled. ***Average high school GPA:*** 3.41. ***Test scores:*** ACT scores over 18: 95%; ACT scores over 24: 54%; ACT scores over 30: 15%.

Retention: 80% of full-time freshmen returned.

FACULTY

Total: 1,067, 86% full-time, 75% with terminal degrees.

Student/faculty ratio: 20:1.

ACADEMICS

Calendar: semesters. *Degrees:* associate, bachelor's, master's, doctoral, and post-master's certificates.

Special study options: academic remediation for entering students, accelerated degree program, adult/continuing education programs, advanced placement credit, cooperative education, distance learning, double majors, English as a second language, freshman honors college, honors programs, independent study, internships, off-campus study, part-time degree program, services for LD students, student-designed majors, study abroad, summer session for credit. ***ROTC:*** Army (b), Air Force (b).

Computers: 1,000 computers/terminals and 1,000 ports are available on campus for general student use. Students can access the following: campus intranet, computer help desk, free student e-mail accounts, online (class) grades, online (class) registration, online (class) schedules. Campuswide network is available. 100% of college-owned or -operated housing units are wired for high-speed Internet access. Wireless service is available via entire campus.

Library: Mitchell Memorial Library plus 2 others. *Books:* 2.5 million (physical), 52,173 (digital/electronic); *Serial titles:* 4,400 (physical), 114,771 (digital/electronic); *Databases:* 102. Weekly public service hours: 110; students can reserve study rooms.

STUDENT LIFE

Housing options: on-campus residence required for freshman year; coed, men-only, women-only, special housing for students with disabilities. Campus housing is university owned. Freshman applicants given priority for college housing.

Activities and organizations: drama/theater group, student-run newspaper, radio and television station, choral group, marching band, Student Association, Black Student Alliance, Residence Hall Association, Fashion Board, Campus Activities Board, national fraternities, national sororities.

Athletics Member NCAA. All Division I except football (Division I-A). ***Intercollegiate sports:*** baseball M(s), basketball M(s)/W(s), cheerleading M(s)/W(s), cross-country running M/W(s), golf M(s)/W(s), soccer W(s), softball W(s), tennis M(s)/W(s), track and field M(s)/W(s), volleyball W(s). ***Intramural sports:*** archery M(c)/W(c), badminton M(c)/W(c), basketball M/W, bowling M/W, cross-country running W(c), equestrian sports M/W, fencing M(c)/W(c), football M/W, golf M/W, ice hockey M(c)/W(c), lacrosse M(c)/W(c), racquetball M/W, riflery M/W, rugby M(c), soccer M(c)/W(c), softball M(c)/W(c), swimming and diving M(c)/W(c), table tennis M(c)/W(c), tennis M(c)/W(c), ultimate Frisbee M/W, volleyball M(c)/W(c), water polo M/W, weight lifting M/W.

Campus security: 24-hour emergency response devices and patrols, late-night transport/escort service, controlled dormitory access, bicycle patrols, crime prevention program, RAD program, general law enforcement services.

Student services: health clinic, personal/psychological counseling.

COSTS & FINANCIAL AID

Costs (2016–17) ***One-time required fee:*** $55. ***Tuition:*** state resident $7780 full-time, $324 per credit hour part-time; nonresident $20,900 full-time, $871 per credit hour part-time. Full-time tuition and fees vary according to degree level and location. Part-time tuition and fees vary according to course load, degree level, and location. ***Room and board:*** $9418; room only: $5848. Room and board charges vary according to board plan, housing facility, and student level. ***Payment plans:*** tuition prepayment, installment. ***Waivers:*** children of alumni, senior citizens, and employees or children of employees.

Financial Aid Of all full-time matriculated undergraduates who enrolled in 2015, 11,640 applied for aid, 10,017 were judged to have need, 2,295 had their need fully met. 832 Federal Work-Study jobs (averaging $3126). In 2015, 3403 non-need-based awards were made. ***Average percent of need met:*** 59. ***Average financial aid package:*** $14,105. ***Average need-based loan:*** $3896. ***Average need-based gift aid:*** $6000. ***Average non-need-based aid:*** $4553. ***Average indebtedness upon graduation:*** $30,659.

APPLYING

Standardized Tests *Required:* SAT or ACT (for admission).

Options: electronic application, early decision.

Application fee: $40.

Required: high school transcript, minimum 2.0 GPA.

Application deadlines: 8/1 (freshmen), 8/1 (transfers).

Notification: continuous (freshmen), continuous (transfers).

CONTACT

Ms. Lori Ball, Director of Undergraduate Admissions, Mississippi State University, PO Box 6334, Mississippi State, MS 39762. *Phone:* 662-325-2224. *Fax:* 662-325-1MSU. *E-mail:* admit@msstate.edu.

Mississippi University for Women

Columbus, Mississippi

http://www.muw.edu/

- **State-supported** comprehensive, founded 1884, part of Mississippi Institutions of Higher Learning
- **Small-town** 110-acre campus
- **Endowment** $50.3 million
- **Coed**
- **Moderately difficult** entrance level

FACULTY

Student/faculty ratio: 14:1.

ACADEMICS

Calendar: semesters. *Degrees:* associate, bachelor's, master's, doctoral, and post-master's certificates.

Library: John Clayton Fant Memorial Library plus 2 others. *Books:* 197,660 (physical); *Serial titles:* 4,889 (physical), 1,560 (digital/electronic); *Databases:* 74. Weekly public service hours: 76; students can reserve study rooms.

STUDENT LIFE

Housing options: men-only, women-only, special housing for students with disabilities. Campus housing is university owned. Freshman campus housing is guaranteed.

Activities and organizations: drama/theater group, student-run newspaper, radio station, choral group, Student Government Association, Wesley Foundation, International Student Association, Baptist Student Union, International Justice Mission, national fraternities, national sororities.

Campus security: 24-hour emergency response devices and patrols, late-night transport/escort service, controlled dormitory access, tornado and voice-over sirens, voice mail and text messaging emergency notification system.

Student services: health clinic, personal/psychological counseling, women's center.

COSTS & FINANCIAL AID

Costs (2016–17) ***Tuition:*** state resident $5965 full-time, $253 per credit hour part-time; nonresident $16,534 full-time, $693 per credit hour part-time. Part-time tuition and fees vary according to course load. ***Required fees:*** $100 full-time. ***Room and board:*** $6808. Room and board charges vary according to housing facility.

Financial Aid Of all full-time matriculated undergraduates who enrolled in 2014, 1,783 applied for aid, 1,640 were judged to have need, 472 had their need fully met. 75 Federal Work-Study jobs (averaging $2042). 247 state and other part-time jobs (averaging $1739). In 2014, 292 non-need-based awards were made. ***Average percent of need met:*** 50. ***Average financial aid package:*** $8948. ***Average need-based loan:*** $5223. ***Average need-based gift aid:*** $5487. ***Average non-need-based aid:*** $5548. ***Average indebtedness upon graduation:*** $31,851.

APPLYING

Standardized Tests *Required for some:* SAT or ACT (for admission). *Recommended:* SAT or ACT (for admission).

Options: electronic application, early admission.

Required: high school transcript. ***Required for some:*** minimum 2.0 GPA, rank in upper 50% of high school class.

CONTACT

Mississippi University for Women, 1100 College Street, MUW-1600, Columbus, MS 39701-9998. *Phone:* 662-329-7106. *Toll-free phone:* 877-GO 2 THE W.

Mississippi Valley State University

Itta Bena, Mississippi

http://www.mvsu.edu/

- **State-supported** comprehensive, founded 1946, part of Mississippi Institutions of Higher Learning
- **Small-town** 450-acre campus
- **Endowment** $1.6 million
- **Coed** 2,011 undergraduate students, 87% full-time, 60% women, 40% men
- **Minimally difficult** entrance level, 84% of applicants were admitted

UNDERGRAD STUDENTS

1,744 full-time, 267 part-time. Students come from 33 states and territories; 11 other countries; 25% are from out of state; 91% Black or African American, non-Hispanic/Latino; 1% Hispanic/Latino; 0.2% Asian, non-Hispanic/Latino; 0.2% Native Hawaiian or other Pacific Islander, non-Hispanic/Latino; 0.0% American Indian or Alaska Native, non-Hispanic/Latino; 0.5% Two or more races, non-Hispanic/Latino; 4% Race/ethnicity unknown; 10% transferred in; 46% live on campus.

Freshmen:

Admission: 2,605 applied, 2,200 admitted, 393 enrolled. ***Average high school GPA:*** 2.86. ***Test scores:*** ACT scores over 18: 40%; ACT scores over 24: 7%.

Retention: 60% of full-time freshmen returned.

FACULTY

Total: 172, 70% full-time, 53% with terminal degrees.

Student/faculty ratio: 15:1.

ACADEMICS

Calendar: semesters. *Degrees:* bachelor's and master's.

Special study options: academic remediation for entering students, cooperative education, distance learning, double majors, freshman honors college, honors programs, internships, part-time degree program, summer session for credit. ***ROTC:*** Army (b).

Computers: 285 computers/terminals are available on campus for general student use. Students can access the following: computer help desk, free student e-mail accounts, online (class) registration. Campuswide network

is available. 100% of college-owned or -operated housing units are wired for high-speed Internet access.
Library: James Herbert White Library. *Books:* 127,541 (physical), 53,358 (digital/electronic); *Databases:* 62. Weekly public service hours: 84; students can reserve study rooms.

STUDENT LIFE
Housing options: men-only, women-only. Campus housing is university owned.
Activities and organizations: drama/theater group, student-run newspaper, radio and television station, choral group, marching band, Student Government Association, Baptist Student Union, Black Student Fellowship, National Education Association, national fraternities, national sororities.
Athletics Member NCAA. All Division I except football (Division I-AA). ***Intercollegiate sports:*** baseball M(s), basketball M(s)/W(s), bowling W, cross-country running M(s)/W(s), golf M(s)/W(s), softball W(s), tennis M(s)/W(s), track and field M(s)/W(s). ***Intramural sports:*** baseball M, basketball M/W, cross-country running M/W, football M, golf M/W, softball M/W, tennis M/W, track and field M/W.
Campus security: 24-hour emergency response devices and patrols, controlled dormitory access.
Student services: health clinic, personal/psychological counseling.

COSTS
Costs (2017–18) ***Tuition:*** state resident $6096 full-time, $254 per credit hour part-time; nonresident $6096 full-time, $254 per credit hour part-time. ***Required fees:*** $20 full-time. ***Room and board:*** $7394; room only: $4055. ***Payment plan:*** installment. ***Waivers:*** children of alumni and employees or children of employees.

APPLYING
Standardized Tests *Required:* SAT or ACT (for admission).
Options: deferred entrance.
Required: high school transcript. ***Required for some:*** 2.5 letters of recommendation. ***Recommended:*** interview.
Application deadlines: rolling (freshmen), rolling (transfers).
Notification: continuous (freshmen), continuous (transfers).

CONTACT
Mississippi Valley State University, 14000 Highway 82 West, Itta Bena, MS 38941-1400. *Phone:* 662-254-3345. *Toll-free phone:* 800-844-6885.

Rust College
Holly Springs, Mississippi
http://www.rustcollege.edu/

- **Independent United Methodist** 4-year, founded 1866
- **Small-town** 126-acre campus with easy access to Memphis
- **Endowment** $34.3 million
- **Coed** 1,004 undergraduate students, 87% full-time, 60% women, 40% men
- **Minimally difficult** entrance level, 7% of applicants were admitted

UNDERGRAD STUDENTS
873 full-time, 131 part-time. Students come from 22 states and territories; 6 other countries; 58% are from out of state; 95% Black or African American, non-Hispanic/Latino; 0.1% Asian, non-Hispanic/Latino; 2% Race/ethnicity unknown; 2% international; 7% transferred in; 76% live on campus.

Freshmen:
Admission: 5,337 applied, 360 admitted, 360 enrolled. ***Average high school GPA:*** 2.66.
Retention: 59% of full-time freshmen returned.

FACULTY
Total: 51, 94% full-time, 53% with terminal degrees.
Student/faculty ratio: 20:1.

ACADEMICS
Calendar: semesters. *Degrees:* associate and bachelor's.
Special study options: academic remediation for entering students, accelerated degree program, adult/continuing education programs, advanced placement credit, double majors, honors programs, independent study, internships, part-time degree program, study abroad, summer session for credit.
Computers: 339 computers/terminals are available on campus for general student use. Students can access the following: campus intranet, computer help desk, free student e-mail accounts, online (class) grades. Campuswide network is available. 100% of college-owned or -operated housing units are wired for high-speed Internet access. Wireless service is available via computer centers, computer labs, dorm rooms, libraries.
Library: Leontyne Price Library. *Books:* 126,854 (physical), 400 (digital/electronic); *Serial titles:* 261 (physical), 18 (digital/electronic); *Databases:* 4. Weekly public service hours: 10; study areas open 24 hours, 5-7 days a week; students can reserve study rooms.

STUDENT LIFE
Housing options: on-campus residence required for freshman year; men-only, women-only. Campus housing is university owned. Freshman campus housing is guaranteed.
Activities and organizations: drama/theater group, student-run radio and television station, choral group, marching band, National Sororities, National Fraternities, Choral Group, Television Station, Radio Station, national fraternities, national sororities.
Athletics Member NCAA. All Division III. ***Intercollegiate sports:*** baseball M, basketball M/W, cheerleading M/W, cross-country running M/W, softball W, tennis M/W, track and field M/W, volleyball M/W. ***Intramural sports:*** badminton M/W, basketball M/W, swimming and diving M/W, table tennis M/W, tennis M/W, volleyball M/W.
Campus security: 24-hour emergency response devices and patrols, controlled dormitory access.
Student services: health clinic, women's center.

COSTS & FINANCIAL AID
Costs (2016–17) ***Comprehensive fee:*** $13,600 includes full-time tuition ($9500) and room and board ($4100). Full-time tuition and fees vary according to course load. Part-time tuition: $404 per credit hour. Part-time tuition and fees vary according to course load. ***College room only:*** $1870. ***Payment plan:*** installment. ***Waivers:*** senior citizens and employees or children of employees.
Financial Aid Of all full-time matriculated undergraduates who enrolled in 2004, 806 applied for aid, 806 were judged to have need, 481 had their need fully met. 492 Federal Work-Study jobs (averaging $714). 189 state and other part-time jobs (averaging $546). In 2004, 112 non-need-based awards were made. ***Average percent of need met:*** 60. ***Average financial aid package:*** $5067. ***Average need-based loan:*** $2158. ***Average need-based gift aid:*** $4281. ***Average non-need-based aid:*** $2795. ***Average indebtedness upon graduation:*** $9314.

APPLYING
Standardized Tests *Required:* ACT (for admission).
Application fee: $10.
Required: high school transcript, minimum 2.5 GPA, 2 letters of recommendation.
Application deadlines: rolling (freshmen), rolling (transfers).
Notification: continuous (freshmen), continuous (transfers).

CONTACT
Mr. Braque Talley, Dean of Enrollment, Rust College, 150 Rust Avenue, Holly Springs, MS 38635-2328. *Phone:* 601-252-8000 Ext. 4059. *Toll-free phone:* 888-886-8492 Ext. 4065. *Fax:* 662-252-8895. *E-mail:* btalley@rustcollege.edu.

Southeastern Baptist College
Laurel, Mississippi
http://www.southeasternbaptist.edu/

CONTACT
Mrs. Emma Bond, Director of Admissions, Southeastern Baptist College, 4229 Highway 15 North, Laurel, MS 39440-1096. *Phone:* 601-426-6346.

Strayer University–Jackson Campus

Jackson, Mississippi

http://www.strayer.edu/mississippi/jackson/

CONTACT

Strayer University–Jackson Campus, 460 Briarwood Drive, Suite 200, Jackson, MS 39206.

Tougaloo College

Tougaloo, Mississippi

http://www.tougaloo.edu/

CONTACT

Dr. Juno Jacobs, Director of Admissions, Tougaloo College, 500 West County Line Road, Tougaloo, MS 39174. *Phone:* 601-977-7765. *Toll-free phone:* 888-42GALOO. *Fax:* 601-977-4501. *E-mail:* jjacobs@tougaloo.edu.

University of Mississippi

Oxford, Mississippi

http://www.olemiss.edu/

- **State-supported** university, founded 1844, part of Mississippi Institutions of Higher Learning
- **Small-town** 3902-acre campus with easy access to Memphis
- **Endowment** $606.4 million
- **Coed**
- **Moderately difficult** entrance level

ACADEMICS

Calendar: semesters. *Degrees:* bachelor's, master's, doctoral, post-master's, and postbachelor's certificates.

Library: J. D. Williams Library plus 1 other. *Books:* 3.3 million (physical), 814,143 (digital/electronic); *Serial titles:* 39,667 (physical), 135,210 (digital/electronic); *Databases:* 389. Weekly public service hours: 109.

STUDENT LIFE

Housing options: on-campus residence required for freshman year; men-only, women-only. Campus housing is university owned, leased by the school and is provided by a third party. Freshman campus housing is guaranteed.

Activities and organizations: drama/theater group, student-run newspaper, radio and television station, choral group, marching band, Associated Student Body, Gospel Choir, sport clubs, Black Student Union, Student Programming Board, national fraternities, national sororities.

Athletics Member NCAA. All Division I except football (Division I-A).

Campus security: 24-hour emergency response devices and patrols, late-night transport/escort service, controlled dormitory access, crime prevention programs.

Student services: health clinic, personal/psychological counseling, women's center.

COSTS & FINANCIAL AID

Costs (2016–17) ***Tuition:*** state resident $7644 full-time, $319 per credit hour part-time; nonresident $21,912 full-time, $913 per credit hour part-time. Full-time tuition and fees vary according to course load and program. Part-time tuition and fees vary according to course load and program. ***Required fees:*** $100 full-time, $4 per credit hour part-time. ***Room and board:*** $10,002. Room and board charges vary according to board plan and housing facility.

Financial Aid Of all full-time matriculated undergraduates who enrolled in 2015, 10,859 applied for aid, 8,327 were judged to have need, 1,035 had their need fully met. 397 Federal Work-Study jobs (averaging $1378). In 2015, 4181 non-need-based awards were made. ***Average percent of need met:*** 73. ***Average financial aid package:*** $10,202. ***Average need-based loan:*** $4579. ***Average need-based gift aid:*** $8561. ***Average non-need-based aid:*** $8057. ***Average indebtedness upon graduation:*** $28,162.

APPLYING

Standardized Tests *Required:* SAT or ACT (for admission).

Options: electronic application, deferred entrance.

Required: high school transcript, minimum 2.0 GPA.

CONTACT

Ms. Martina Brewer, Associate Director of Admissions, University of Mississippi, 128 Martindale Student Services Center, University, MS 38677. *Phone:* 662-915-7226. *Toll-free phone:* 800-653-6477. *Fax:* 662-915-5869. *E-mail:* admissions@olemiss.edu.

University of Mississippi Medical Center

Jackson, Mississippi

http://www.umc.edu/

CONTACT

Ms. Barbara Westerfield, Director of Student Records and Registrar, University of Mississippi Medical Center, 2500 North State Street, Jackson, MS 39216-4505. *Phone:* 601-984-1080. *Fax:* 601-984-1079.

University of Southern Mississippi

Hattiesburg, Mississippi

http://www.usm.edu/

- **State-supported** university, founded 1910, part of Mississippi Institutions of Higher Learning
- **Suburban** 1090-acre campus
- **Endowment** $82.7 million
- **Coed** 11,779 undergraduate students, 87% full-time, 63% women, 37% men
- **Moderately difficult** entrance level, 46% of applicants were admitted

UNDERGRAD STUDENTS

10,246 full-time, 1,533 part-time. Students come from 54 states and territories; 74 other countries; 16% are from out of state; 29% Black or African American, non-Hispanic/Latino; 3% Hispanic/Latino; 1% Asian, non-Hispanic/Latino; 0.1% Native Hawaiian or other Pacific Islander, non-Hispanic/Latino; 0.4% American Indian or Alaska Native, non-Hispanic/Latino; 2% Two or more races, non-Hispanic/Latino; 0.7% Race/ethnicity unknown; 2% international; 15% transferred in; 25% live on campus.

Freshmen:

Admission: 6,607 applied, 3,019 admitted, 1,558 enrolled. ***Average high school GPA:*** 3.33. ***Test scores:*** SAT critical reading scores over 500: 41%; SAT math scores over 500: 78%; ACT scores over 18: 91%; SAT critical reading scores over 600: 14%; SAT math scores over 600: 47%; ACT scores over 24: 44%; SAT critical reading scores over 700: 1%; SAT math scores over 700: 12%; ACT scores over 30: 9%.

Retention: 74% of full-time freshmen returned.

FACULTY

Total: 903, 76% full-time, 70% with terminal degrees.

Student/faculty ratio: 17:1.

ACADEMICS

Calendar: semesters. *Degrees:* certificates, bachelor's, master's, doctoral, post-master's, and postbachelor's certificates.

Special study options: academic remediation for entering students, accelerated degree program, adult/continuing education programs, advanced placement credit, cooperative education, distance learning, double majors, English as a second language, honors programs, independent study, internships, off-campus study, part-time degree program, services for LD students, study abroad, summer session for credit. ***ROTC:*** Army (c), Air Force (b).

Computers: 436 computers/terminals are available on campus for general student use. Students can access the following: campus intranet, computer help desk, free student e-mail accounts, online (class) grades, online (class) registration, online (class) schedules. Campuswide network is available. 100% of college-owned or -operated housing units are wired for high-speed Internet access. Wireless service is available via entire campus.

Library: Cook Memorial Library plus 4 others. *Books:* 1.4 million (physical), 331,932 (digital/electronic); *Serial titles:* 27,243 (physical), 118,798 (digital/electronic); *Databases:* 200. Weekly public service hours: 117; students can reserve study rooms.

STUDENT LIFE
Housing options: men-only, women-only, special housing for students with disabilities. Campus housing is university owned. Freshman applicants given priority for college housing.
Activities and organizations: drama/theater group, student-run newspaper, radio station, choral group, marching band, national fraternities, national sororities.
Athletics Member NCAA. All Division I. ***Intercollegiate sports:*** baseball M(s), basketball M(s)/W(s), cheerleading M/W, cross-country running W(s), football M(s), golf M(s)/W(s), soccer W(s), softball W(s), tennis M(s)/W(s), track and field M(s)/W(s), volleyball W(s). ***Intramural sports:*** badminton M/W, basketball M/W, bowling M/W, racquetball M/W, rugby M, soccer M/W, softball W, tennis M/W, track and field M/W, ultimate Frisbee M/W, volleyball M/W.
Campus security: 24-hour emergency response devices and patrols, late-night transport/escort service, controlled dormitory access.
Student services: health clinic, personal/psychological counseling, women's center, legal services.

COSTS & FINANCIAL AID
Costs (2017–18) ***Tuition:*** state resident $7854 full-time, $306 per credit hour part-time; nonresident $9854 full-time, $676 per credit hour part-time. Part-time tuition and fees vary according to course load and degree level. ***Required fees:*** $5 per credit hour part-time, $55 per semester part-time. ***Room and board:*** $9012; room only: $5222. Room and board charges vary according to board plan and housing facility. ***Payment plan:*** installment. ***Waivers:*** children of alumni, senior citizens, and employees or children of employees.
Financial Aid Of all full-time matriculated undergraduates who enrolled in 2015, 8,663 applied for aid, 7,628 were judged to have need, 1,810 had their need fully met. In 2015, 634 non-need-based awards were made. ***Average percent of need met:*** 69. ***Average financial aid package:*** $13,604. ***Average need-based loan:*** $4714. ***Average need-based gift aid:*** $4671. ***Average non-need-based aid:*** $5425. ***Average indebtedness upon graduation:*** $28,700.

APPLYING
Standardized Tests *Required:* SAT or ACT (for admission).
Options: electronic application, early admission.
Application fee: $40.
Required: minimum 2.0 GPA. ***Required for some:*** high school transcript, statement of good standing from prior institutions, college transcripts.
Application deadlines: 6/30 (freshmen), 8/19 (transfers).

CONTACT
University of Southern Mississippi, 118 College Drive, Hattiesburg, MS 39406-0001. *Phone:* 601-266-5000.

William Carey University
Hattiesburg, Mississippi
http://www.wmcarey.edu/

CONTACT
Mr. William N. Curry, Dean of Enrollment Management, William Carey University, 498 Tuscan Avenue, Hattiesburg, MS 39401-5499. *Phone:* 601-318-6051. *Toll-free phone:* 800-962-5991. *Fax:* 601-318-6154. *E-mail:* admissions@wmcarey.edu.

MISSOURI

American Business & Technology University
Saint Joseph, Missouri
http://www.abtu.edu/

CONTACT
Richard Lingle, Lead Admission Coordinator, American Business & Technology University, 2300 Frederick Avenue, Saint Joseph, MO 64506. *Phone:* 800-908-9329 Ext. 13. *Toll-free phone:* 800-908-9329. *E-mail:* ricahrd@acot.edu.

The Art Institute of St. Louis
St. Charles, Missouri
http://www.artinstitutes.edu/st-louis/

CONTACT
The Art Institute of St. Louis, 1520 South Fifth Street, St. Charles, MO 63303. *Phone:* 636-688-3012.

Avila University
Kansas City, Missouri
http://www.avila.edu/

- **Independent Roman Catholic** comprehensive, founded 1916
- **Suburban** 50-acre campus
- **Coed** 1,320 undergraduate students, 85% full-time, 59% women, 41% men
- **Minimally difficult** entrance level, 56% of applicants were admitted

UNDERGRAD STUDENTS
1,122 full-time, 198 part-time. Students come from 30 states and territories; 25 other countries; 34% are from out of state; 20% Black or African American, non-Hispanic/Latino; 9% Hispanic/Latino; 2% Asian, non-Hispanic/Latino; 0.2% Native Hawaiian or other Pacific Islander, non-Hispanic/Latino; 0.6% American Indian or Alaska Native, non-Hispanic/Latino; 4% Two or more races, non-Hispanic/Latino; 9% international; 9% transferred in; 29% live on campus.

Freshmen:
Admission: 1,382 applied, 778 admitted, 203 enrolled. ***Average high school GPA:*** 3.24. ***Test scores:*** SAT critical reading scores over 500: 29%; ACT scores over 18: 96%; SAT critical reading scores over 600: 4%; ACT scores over 24: 25%; ACT scores over 30: 2%.
Retention: 62% of full-time freshmen returned.

FACULTY
Total: 238, 31% full-time, 49% with terminal degrees.
Student/faculty ratio: 13:1.

ACADEMICS
Calendar: semesters. *Degrees:* bachelor's, master's, and postbachelor's certificates.
Special study options: academic remediation for entering students, accelerated degree program, adult/continuing education programs, advanced placement credit, cooperative education, distance learning, double majors, English as a second language, independent study, internships, off-campus study, part-time degree program, services for LD students, study abroad, summer session for credit. ***ROTC:*** Army (c).
Unusual degree programs: 3-2 occupational therapy, physical therapy, law with Rockhurst University, University of Missouri–Kansas City.
Computers: 141 computers/terminals and 225 ports are available on campus for general student use. Students can access the following: campus intranet, computer help desk, free student e-mail accounts, online (class) grades, online (class) registration, online (class) schedules, laptop checkout through library. Campuswide network is available. 100% of college-owned or -operated housing units are wired for high-speed Internet access. Wireless service is available via entire campus.
Library: Hooley-Bundshu Library plus 1 other. *Books:* 39,963 (physical), 309,288 (digital/electronic); *Serial titles:* 205 (physical), 389,497 (digital/electronic); *Databases:* 72. Weekly public service hours: 91; students can reserve study rooms.

STUDENT LIFE
Housing options: on-campus residence required through sophomore year; coed, men-only, women-only. Campus housing is university owned. Freshman campus housing is guaranteed.
Activities and organizations: drama/theater group, student-run newspaper, choral group, Avila Ambassadors, Avila Student Nurses Association, Campus Ministries, Saudi Arabian Student Association, Avila University Theatre Company.
Athletics Member NAIA. ***Intercollegiate sports:*** baseball M(s), basketball M(s)/W(s), cheerleading W(s), cross-country running

M(s)/W(s), football M(s), golf M(s)/W(s), soccer M(s)/W(s), softball W(s), track and field M(s)/W(s), volleyball W(s). ***Intramural sports:*** bowling M/W, table tennis M/W.

Campus security: 24-hour emergency response devices and patrols, student patrols, late-night transport/escort service, controlled dormitory access.

Student services: health clinic, personal/psychological counseling.

COSTS & FINANCIAL AID

Costs (2016–17) ***Comprehensive fee:*** $35,480 includes full-time tuition ($26,230), mandatory fees ($1750), and room and board ($7500). Full-time tuition and fees vary according to course load and program. Part-time tuition: $758 per credit. Part-time tuition and fees vary according to course load and program. No tuition increase for student's term of enrollment. ***College room only:*** $3300. Room and board charges vary according to board plan and housing facility. ***Payment plans:*** installment, deferred payment. ***Waivers:*** children of alumni, senior citizens, and employees or children of employees.

Financial Aid Of all full-time matriculated undergraduates who enrolled in 2008, 1,927 applied for aid, 1,852 were judged to have need, 1,846 had their need fully met. 161 Federal Work-Study jobs (averaging $903). 55 state and other part-time jobs (averaging $885). In 2008, 60 non-need-based awards were made. ***Average percent of need met:*** 35. ***Average financial aid package:*** $12,976. ***Average need-based loan:*** $5465. ***Average need-based gift aid:*** $7854. ***Average non-need-based aid:*** $9152. ***Average indebtedness upon graduation:*** $16,508.

APPLYING

Standardized Tests *Required:* SAT or ACT (for admission).

Options: electronic application, early admission.

Required: high school transcript, minimum 2.5 GPA, secondary school report. ***Required for some:*** essay or personal statement. ***Recommended:*** interview.

Application deadlines: 8/15 (freshmen), 8/15 (transfers).

Notification: 8/15 (freshmen), 8/15 (transfers).

CONTACT

Josh Parisse, Director of Undergraduate Admissions, Avila University, 11901 Wornall Road, Kansas City, MO 64145. *Phone:* 816-501-2400. *Toll-free phone:* 800-GO-AVILA. *Fax:* 816-501-2453. *E-mail:* josh.parisse@avila.edu.

Baptist Bible College

Springfield, Missouri

http://www.gobbc.edu/

CONTACT

Mr. Terry Allcorn, Director of Admissions, Baptist Bible College, 628 East Kearney Street, Springfield, MO 65803-3498. *Phone:* 417-268-6000. *Toll-free phone:* 800-228-5754. *Fax:* 417-268-6694.

Bryan University

Springfield, Missouri

http://www.bryanu.edu/

CONTACT

Bryan University, 4255 South Nature Center Way, Springfield, MO 65804. *Toll-free phone:* 855-566-0650.

Calvary University

Kansas City, Missouri

http://www.calvary.edu/

- **Independent nondenominational** comprehensive, founded 1932
- **Suburban** 55-acre campus with easy access to Kansas City
- **Endowment** $727,074
- **Coed** 231 undergraduate students, 60% full-time, 48% women, 52% men
- **Noncompetitive** entrance level, 98% of applicants were admitted

UNDERGRAD STUDENTS

138 full-time, 93 part-time. Students come from 18 states and territories; 1 other country; 49% are from out of state; 10% Black or African American, non-Hispanic/Latino; 1% Hispanic/Latino; 3% Asian, non-Hispanic/Latino; 0.4% Native Hawaiian or other Pacific Islander, non-Hispanic/Latino; 1% American Indian or Alaska Native, non-Hispanic/Latino; 5% Two or more races, non-Hispanic/Latino; 0.4% Race/ethnicity unknown; 12% transferred in; 41% live on campus.

Freshmen:

Admission: 44 applied, 43 admitted, 32 enrolled. ***Average high school GPA:*** 3.53. ***Test scores:*** ACT scores over 18: 95%; ACT scores over 24: 45%; ACT scores over 30: 15%.

Retention: 53% of full-time freshmen returned.

FACULTY

Total: 44, 25% full-time, 36% with terminal degrees.

Student/faculty ratio: 7:1.

ACADEMICS

Calendar: semesters. *Degrees:* certificates, associate, bachelor's, and master's.

Special study options: accelerated degree program, adult/continuing education programs, advanced placement credit, cooperative education, distance learning, double majors, independent study, internships, off-campus study, part-time degree program, services for LD students, student-designed majors, summer session for credit. ***ROTC:*** Army (c).

Computers: 32 computers/terminals are available on campus for general student use. Students can access the following: computer help desk, free student e-mail accounts, online (class) grades, online (class) registration, online (class) schedules. Campuswide network is available. 100% of college-owned or -operated housing units are wired for high-speed Internet access. Wireless service is available via classrooms, computer centers, computer labs, dorm rooms, learning centers, libraries, student centers.

Library: Hilda Kroeker Library. *Books:* 41,841 (physical), 420 (digital/electronic); *Serial titles:* 268 (physical); *Databases:* 4.

STUDENT LIFE

Housing options: men-only, women-only. Campus housing is university owned. Freshman campus housing is guaranteed.

Activities and organizations: drama/theater group, choral group, Missions Encounter, Masterworks (Fine Arts).

Athletics Member NCCAA. ***Intercollegiate sports:*** basketball M/W, soccer M, volleyball W.

Campus security: 24-hour emergency response devices and patrols, late-night transport/escort service, controlled dormitory access, night patrols by trained security personnel, monitored closed circuit cameras.

Student services: personal/psychological counseling.

COSTS & FINANCIAL AID

Costs (2017–18) ***One-time required fee:*** $100. ***Comprehensive fee:*** $14,688 includes full-time tuition ($8760), mandatory fees ($438), and room and board ($5490). Full-time tuition and fees vary according to location and program. Part-time tuition: $365 per credit hour. Part-time tuition and fees vary according to location and program. ***College room only:*** $2600. Room and board charges vary according to board plan and housing facility. ***Payment plan:*** installment. ***Waivers:*** employees or children of employees.

Financial Aid Of all full-time matriculated undergraduates who enrolled in 2016, 101 applied for aid, 95 were judged to have need, 7 had their need fully met. 8 Federal Work-Study jobs (averaging $1687). In 2016, 4 non-need-based awards were made. ***Average percent of need met:*** 66. ***Average financial aid package:*** $12,774. ***Average need-based loan:*** $4265. ***Average need-based gift aid:*** $5694. ***Average non-need-based aid:*** $2543. ***Average indebtedness upon graduation:*** $19,246.

APPLYING

Standardized Tests *Required:* SAT or ACT (for admission).

Options: electronic application.

Required: essay or personal statement, minimum 2.0 GPA, 2 letters of recommendation. ***Required for some:*** high school transcript. ***Recommended:*** interview.

Application deadlines: rolling (freshmen), rolling (transfers), rolling (early action).

Notification: continuous (freshmen), continuous (transfers).

CONTACT
Ms. Ann Rogers, Admissions Secretary, Calvary University, 15800 Calvary Road, Kansas City, MO 64147-1341. *Phone:* 816-322-0110 Ext. 1323. *Toll-free phone:* 800-326-3960. *Fax:* 816-331-4474. *E-mail:* ann.rogers@cavalry.edu.

Central Christian College of the Bible

Moberly, Missouri

http://www.cccb.edu/

CONTACT
Mr. Aaron Merritt, Director of Admissions, Central Christian College of the Bible, 911 Urbandale Drive East, Moberly, MO 65270-1997. *Phone:* 660-263-3900. *Toll-free phone:* 888-263-3900. *Fax:* 660-263-3936. *E-mail:* admissions@cccb.edu.

Central Methodist University

Fayette, Missouri

http://www.centralmethodist.edu/

- **Independent Methodist** comprehensive, founded 1854
- **Small-town** 80-acre campus
- **Coed** 1,094 undergraduate students, 98% full-time, 52% women, 48% men
- **Moderately difficult** entrance level, 58% of applicants were admitted

UNDERGRAD STUDENTS
1,072 full-time, 22 part-time. 13% are from out of state; 8% Black or African American, non-Hispanic/Latino; 3% Hispanic/Latino; 0.4% Asian, non-Hispanic/Latino; 0.4% American Indian or Alaska Native, non-Hispanic/Latino; 3% Two or more races, non-Hispanic/Latino; 3% Race/ethnicity unknown; 4% international; 10% transferred in; 61% live on campus.

Freshmen:
Admission: 1,430 applied, 827 admitted, 286 enrolled. ***Average high school GPA:*** 3.45. ***Test scores:*** SAT critical reading scores over 500: 32%; SAT math scores over 500: 55%; SAT writing scores over 500: 23%; ACT scores over 18: 96%; SAT critical reading scores over 600: 5%; SAT math scores over 600: 9%; SAT writing scores over 600: 5%; ACT scores over 24: 32%; SAT critical reading scores over 700: 5%; ACT scores over 30: 5%.

Retention: 65% of full-time freshmen returned.

FACULTY
Total: 113, 57% full-time, 45% with terminal degrees.

Student/faculty ratio: 13:1.

ACADEMICS
Calendar: semesters. *Degrees:* associate, bachelor's, and master's.

Special study options: academic remediation for entering students, advanced placement credit, cooperative education, double majors, honors programs, independent study, internships, part-time degree program, services for LD students, student-designed majors, study abroad, summer session for credit. ***ROTC:*** Army (c), Air Force (c).

Unusual degree programs: 3-2 engineering with Missouri University of Science and Technology.

Computers: Students can access the following: computer help desk, free student e-mail accounts, online (class) grades, online (class) registration, online (class) schedules. Campuswide network is available. 100% of college-owned or -operated housing units are wired for high-speed Internet access. Wireless service is available via entire campus.
Library: Smiley Library.

STUDENT LIFE
Housing options: on-campus residence required through senior year; coed, men-only, women-only. Campus housing is university owned. Freshman applicants given priority for college housing.

Activities and organizations: drama/theater group, student-run newspaper, radio and television station, choral group, marching band, Student Government Association, Enactus, Alpha Phi Omega, Beta Beta Beta, Campus Ministries, national fraternities, national sororities.

Athletics Member NAIA. ***Intercollegiate sports:*** baseball M(s), basketball M(s)/W(s), cross-country running M(s)/W(s), football M(s), soccer M(s)/W(s), softball W(s), track and field M(s)/W(s), volleyball W(s). ***Intramural sports:*** basketball M/W, football M/W, racquetball M/W, soccer M/W, softball M/W, tennis M/W, track and field M/W, volleyball M/W, water polo M/W.

Campus security: 24-hour emergency response devices, late-night transport/escort service, controlled dormitory access.

Student services: health clinic, personal/psychological counseling.

COSTS & FINANCIAL AID
Costs (2017–18) ***Comprehensive fee:*** $31,500 includes full-time tuition ($23,000), mandatory fees ($770), and room and board ($7730). Full-time tuition and fees vary according to program and reciprocity agreements. Part-time tuition: $210 per credit hour. Part-time tuition and fees vary according to course load and program. ***College room only:*** $3780. Room and board charges vary according to board plan and housing facility. ***Payment plan:*** installment. ***Waivers:*** children of alumni and employees or children of employees.

Financial Aid Of all full-time matriculated undergraduates who enrolled in 2016, 925 applied for aid, 847 were judged to have need, 175 had their need fully met. In 2016, 150 non-need-based awards were made. ***Average percent of need met:*** 75. ***Average financial aid package:*** $19,890. ***Average need-based loan:*** $4336. ***Average need-based gift aid:*** $5384. ***Average non-need-based aid:*** $11,840. ***Average indebtedness upon graduation:*** $27,308.

APPLYING
Standardized Tests *Required:* SAT or ACT (for admission).

Options: electronic application, deferred entrance.

Required: high school transcript, minimum 2.5 GPA. ***Required for some:*** 2 letters of recommendation.

Application deadlines: rolling (freshmen), rolling (out-of-state freshmen), rolling (transfers).

Notification: continuous (freshmen), continuous (out-of-state freshmen), continuous (transfers).

CONTACT
Mr. Adam Jenkins, Director of Admissions, Central Methodist University, 411 Central Methodist Square, Fayette, MO 65248. *Phone:* 660-248-6247. *Toll-free phone:* 888-CMU-1854 (in-state); 877-CMU-1854 (out-of-state). *Fax:* 660-248-1872. *E-mail:* admissions@centralmethodist.edu.

Chamberlain College of Nursing

St. Louis, Missouri

http://www.chamberlain.edu/

- **Proprietary** 4-year, founded 1889, part of DeVry University
- **Urban** campus
- **Coed**
- **Moderately difficult** entrance level

FACULTY
Student/faculty ratio: 12:1.

ACADEMICS
Calendar: semesters. *Degree:* bachelor's.

STUDENT LIFE
Housing options: college housing not available.

Campus security: 24-hour patrols, late-night transport/escort service, controlled dormitory access.

COSTS
Costs (2016–17) ***Tuition:*** $18,900 full-time.

APPLYING
Standardized Tests *Required:* SAT or ACT (for admission).

Options: deferred entrance.

Application fee: $95.

Required: essay or personal statement, high school transcript. ***Required for some:*** interview.

CONTACT
Admissions, Chamberlain College of Nursing, 11830 Westline Industrial Drive, Suite 106, St. Louis, MO 63146. *Phone:* 314-991-6200. *Toll-free phone:* 877-751-5783.

City Vision University

Kansas City, Missouri

http://www.cityvision.edu/

- **Independent Christian** comprehensive
- **Coed** 96 undergraduate students, 25% full-time, 58% women, 42% men
- **Noncompetitive** entrance level, 100% of applicants were admitted

UNDERGRAD STUDENTS
24 full-time, 72 part-time. Students come from 31 states and territories; 3 other countries; 94% are from out of state; 16% transferred in.

Freshmen:
Admission: 1 applied, 1 admitted, 5 enrolled.

FACULTY
Total: 21, 57% with terminal degrees.
Student/faculty ratio: 5:1.

ACADEMICS
Calendar: 5 terms that are 8 week long course offerings. *Degrees:* associate, bachelor's, and master's.

Special study options: adult/continuing education programs, distance learning, double majors, independent study, internships, part-time degree program, services for LD students, summer session for credit.

Computers: Students can access the following: computer help desk, free student e-mail accounts, online (class) grades, online (class) registration, online (class) schedules.
Library: http://www.cityvision.edu/library.

COSTS & FINANCIAL AID
Costs (2017–18) ***Tuition:*** $7000 full-time, $3500 per year part-time. Full-time tuition and fees vary according to course load and degree level. Part-time tuition and fees vary according to course load and degree level. ***Payment plan:*** installment. ***Waivers:*** employees or children of employees.

Financial Aid Of all full-time matriculated undergraduates who enrolled in 2014, 60 applied for aid, 60 were judged to have need, 40 had their need fully met. In 2014, 9 non-need-based awards were made. ***Average percent of need met:*** 100. ***Average financial aid package:*** $3806. ***Average need-based loan:*** $4054. ***Average need-based gift aid:*** $2548. ***Average non-need-based aid:*** $850.

APPLYING
Options: electronic application.
Required: high school transcript.
Application deadlines: rolling (freshmen), rolling (transfers).
Notification: continuous (freshmen), continuous (transfers).

CONTACT
Mrs. Nancy Young, Director of Admissions, City Vision University, 3101 Troost Avenue, Suite 200, Kansas City, MO 64109-1845. *Phone:* 816-960-2008 Ext. 3. *Fax:* 816-256-8471. *E-mail:* newstudents@cityvision.edu.

College of the Ozarks

Point Lookout, Missouri

http://www.cofo.edu/

- **Independent Presbyterian** 4-year, founded 1906
- **Small-town** 1000-acre campus
- **Endowment** $416.2 million
- **Coed** 1,512 undergraduate students, 99% full-time, 55% women, 45% men
- **Moderately difficult** entrance level, 14% of applicants were admitted

UNDERGRAD STUDENTS
1,499 full-time, 13 part-time. Students come from 27 states and territories; 18 other countries; 22% are from out of state; 0.8% Black or African American, non-Hispanic/Latino; 2% Hispanic/Latino; 0.8% Asian, non-Hispanic/Latino; 0.1% Native Hawaiian or other Pacific Islander, non-Hispanic/Latino; 0.3% American Indian or Alaska Native, non-Hispanic/Latino; 2% Two or more races, non-Hispanic/Latino; 0.1% Race/ethnicity unknown; 1% international; 2% transferred in; 90% live on campus.

Freshmen:
Admission: 2,896 applied, 413 admitted, 385 enrolled. ***Average high school GPA:*** 3.66. ***Test scores:*** SAT critical reading scores over 500: 86%; SAT math scores over 500: 79%; SAT writing scores over 500: 72%; ACT scores over 18: 99%; SAT critical reading scores over 600: 50%; SAT math scores over 600: 28%; SAT writing scores over 600: 28%; ACT scores over 24: 45%; SAT critical reading scores over 700: 7%; SAT math scores over 700: 7%; SAT writing scores over 700: 7%; ACT scores over 30: 4%.
Retention: 75% of full-time freshmen returned.

FACULTY
Total: 142, 63% full-time, 42% with terminal degrees.
Student/faculty ratio: 14:1.

ACADEMICS
Calendar: semesters. *Degree:* bachelor's.

Special study options: academic remediation for entering students, advanced placement credit, double majors, independent study, internships, off-campus study, services for LD students, student-designed majors. ***ROTC:*** Army (b).

Unusual degree programs: 3-2 medical technology with Cox Medical Center Springfield, MO.

Computers: 294 computers/terminals and 1,531 ports are available on campus for general student use. Students can access the following: campus intranet, computer help desk, free student e-mail accounts, online (class) grades, online (class) registration, online (class) schedules. Campuswide network is available. 100% of college-owned or -operated housing units are wired for high-speed Internet access. Wireless service is available via classrooms, dorm rooms, libraries, student centers.
Library: Lyons Memorial Library plus 2 others. *Books:* 99,500 (physical), 350,000 (digital/electronic); *Serial titles:* 350 (physical), 52,500 (digital/electronic); *Databases:* 45. Weekly public service hours: 77.

STUDENT LIFE
Housing options: on-campus residence required through senior year; men-only, women-only. Campus housing is university owned.
Activities and organizations: drama/theater group, student-run newspaper, radio station, choral group, Young Americans for Freedom, Student Senate, Baptist Student Union, ROTC, Business Undergraduate Society.

Athletics Member NCAA, NAIA. All NCAA Division II. ***Intercollegiate sports:*** baseball M(s), basketball M(s)/W(s), cheerleading M/W, cross-country running M/W, track and field M/W, volleyball W(s). ***Intramural sports:*** basketball M/W, football M/W, racquetball M/W, soccer M/W, softball M/W, table tennis M/W, tennis M/W, ultimate Frisbee M/W, volleyball M/W.

Campus security: 24-hour emergency response devices and patrols, student patrols, late-night transport/escort service, controlled dormitory access, front gate closed 6 p.m. to 5 a.m., security checks cars for proper credentials for entry.

Student services: health clinic, personal/psychological counseling.

COSTS & FINANCIAL AID
Costs (2016–17) ***Comprehensive fee:*** includes mandatory fees ($430) and room and board ($6800). Part-time tuition: $310 per credit hour. Part-time tuition and fees vary according to course load. Each student participates in the on-campus work program for 15 hours per week and two forty-hour work weeks. Earnings from participation in the work program, plus any federal and/or state aid for which students qualify, plus a College of the Ozarks Cost of Education Scholarship combine to meet each student's full tuition charge. ***College room only:*** $3400. ***Payment plan:*** installment.

Financial Aid Of all full-time matriculated undergraduates who enrolled in 2015, 1,354 applied for aid, 1,287 were judged to have need, 412 had their need fully met. In 2015, 114 non-need-based awards were made. ***Average percent of need met:*** 83. ***Average financial aid package:*** $20,163. ***Average need-based gift aid:*** $15,488. ***Average non-need-based aid:*** $14,956. ***Average indebtedness upon graduation:*** $5339.

APPLYING
Standardized Tests *Required:* SAT or ACT (for admission).
Options: electronic application.

Required: high school transcript, 2 letters of recommendation, interview, medical history, financial statement. ***Recommended:*** minimum 3.0 GPA.

Application deadlines: 12/31 (freshmen), 12/31 (transfers).

Notification: continuous (freshmen), continuous (transfers).

CONTACT
Mrs. Kim Williams, Admissions Secretary, College of the Ozarks, PO Box 17, Point Lookout, MO 65726. *Phone:* 417-690-2636. *Toll-free phone:* 800-222-0525. *Fax:* 417-335-2618. *E-mail:* admiss4@cofo.edu.

Columbia College

Columbia, Missouri

http://www.ccis.edu/

- **Independent** comprehensive, founded 1851, affiliated with Christian Church (Disciples of Christ)
- **Urban** 33-acre campus with easy access to St. Louis and Kansas City
- **Endowment** $149.1 million
- **Coed** 936 undergraduate students, 86% full-time, 59% women, 41% men
- **Minimally difficult** entrance level, 51% of applicants were admitted

UNDERGRAD STUDENTS
804 full-time, 132 part-time. Students come from 24 states and territories; 33 other countries; 12% are from out of state; 3% Black or African American, non-Hispanic/Latino; 2% Hispanic/Latino; 1% Asian, non-Hispanic/Latino; 0.7% American Indian or Alaska Native, non-Hispanic/Latino; 5% Two or more races, non-Hispanic/Latino; 4% Race/ethnicity unknown; 9% international; 16% transferred in; 40% live on campus.

Freshmen:
Admission: 1,580 applied, 801 admitted, 204 enrolled. ***Average high school GPA:*** 3.49. ***Test scores:*** SAT critical reading scores over 500: 54%; SAT math scores over 500: 78%; ACT scores over 18: 97%; SAT critical reading scores over 600: 23%; SAT math scores over 600: 16%; ACT scores over 24: 45%; SAT critical reading scores over 700: 15%; SAT math scores over 700: 8%; ACT scores over 30: 6%.

Retention: 73% of full-time freshmen returned.

FACULTY
Total: 127, 54% full-time, 51% with terminal degrees.

Student/faculty ratio: 12:1.

ACADEMICS
Calendar: semesters. *Degrees:* associate, bachelor's, and master's (offers continuing education program with significant enrollment not reflected in profile).

Special study options: adult/continuing education programs, advanced placement credit, cooperative education, distance learning, double majors, English as a second language, honors programs, independent study, internships, off-campus study, part-time degree program, services for LD students, student-designed majors, study abroad, summer session for credit. ***ROTC:*** Army (c), Navy (c), Air Force (c).

Unusual degree programs: 3-2 education.

Computers: 134 computers/terminals and 1,000 ports are available on campus for general student use. Students can access the following: campus intranet, computer help desk, free student e-mail accounts, online (class) grades, online (class) registration, online (class) schedules. Campuswide network is available. 100% of college-owned or -operated housing units are wired for high-speed Internet access. Wireless service is available via entire campus.

Library: J. W. and Lois Stafford Library. *Books:* 61,486 (physical), 128,017 (digital/electronic); *Serial titles:* 133 (physical), 107,640 (digital/electronic); *Databases:* 60. Weekly public service hours: 94; students can reserve study rooms.

STUDENT LIFE
Housing options: on-campus residence required through sophomore year; coed, women-only, special housing for students with disabilities. Campus housing is university owned. Freshman campus housing is guaranteed.

Activities and organizations: drama/theater group, choral group, International Club, Science Club, Royal Ping-Pong Club, A Cappella Society, Commited and Serving Together.

Athletics Member NAIA. ***Intercollegiate sports:*** baseball M(s), basketball M(s)/W(s), cross-country running M(s)/W(s), golf M(s)/W(s), soccer M(s)/W(s), softball W(s), volleyball W(s). ***Intramural sports:*** basketball M/W, football M/W, soccer M/W, softball M/W, volleyball M/W.

Campus security: 24-hour emergency response devices and patrols, late-night transport/escort service, controlled dormitory access, building monitor patrols off-campus site.

Student services: health clinic, personal/psychological counseling.

COSTS & FINANCIAL AID
Costs (2017–18) ***Comprehensive fee:*** $29,568 includes full-time tuition ($21,936) and room and board ($7632). Full-time tuition and fees vary according to class time, course load, degree level, program, reciprocity agreements, and student level. Part-time tuition: $471 per credit hour. Part-time tuition and fees vary according to class time, course load, degree level, location, and reciprocity agreements. No tuition increase for student's term of enrollment. ***College room only:*** $4855. Room and board charges vary according to board plan and housing facility. ***Payment plans:*** installment, deferred payment. ***Waivers:*** children of alumni, senior citizens, and employees or children of employees.

Financial Aid Of all full-time matriculated undergraduates who enrolled in 2015, 493 applied for aid, 446 were judged to have need, 89 had their need fully met. 154 Federal Work-Study jobs (averaging $2313). 70 state and other part-time jobs (averaging $1650). In 2015, 92 non-need-based awards were made. ***Average percent of need met:*** 65. ***Average financial aid package:*** $17,042. ***Average need-based loan:*** $3516. ***Average need-based gift aid:*** $5314. ***Average non-need-based aid:*** $10,178. ***Average indebtedness upon graduation:*** $21,934.

APPLYING
Standardized Tests *Required:* SAT or ACT (for admission).

Options: electronic application, deferred entrance.

Application fee: $35.

Required: high school transcript, minimum 2.5 GPA. ***Required for some:*** essay or personal statement, interview.

Notification: continuous (freshmen), continuous (out-of-state freshmen), continuous (transfers).

CONTACT
Admissions Office, Columbia College, 1001 Rogers Street, Columbia, MO 65216. *Phone:* 573-875-7352. *Toll-free phone:* 800-231-2391. *Fax:* 573-875-7506. *E-mail:* admissions@ccis.edu.

Conception Seminary College

Conception, Missouri

http://www.conception.edu/

- **Independent Roman Catholic** 4-year, founded 1886
- **Rural** 30-acre campus
- **Men only**
- **Noncompetitive** entrance level

FACULTY
Student/faculty ratio: 4:1.

ACADEMICS
Calendar: semesters. *Degrees:* bachelor's and postbachelor's certificates.

Library: Conception Seminary College Library.

STUDENT LIFE
Housing options: on-campus residence required through senior year; men-only. Campus housing is university owned.

Activities and organizations: drama/theater group, student-run newspaper, choral group.

Campus security: 24-hour emergency response devices.

Student services: health clinic, personal/psychological counseling.

COSTS & FINANCIAL AID
Costs (2016–17) ***Comprehensive fee:*** $33,022 includes full-time tuition ($20,506), mandatory fees ($200), and room and board ($12,316). Part-time tuition: $200 per credit hour. ***College room only:*** $5152.

Financial Aid Of all full-time matriculated undergraduates who enrolled in 2014, 76 applied for aid, 44 were judged to have need, 34 had their need fully met. 23 Federal Work-Study jobs (averaging $679). 35 state and other part-time jobs (averaging $1040). In 2014, 37 non-need-based awards were made. ***Average percent of need met:*** 98. ***Average financial***

aid package: $30,517. ***Average need-based loan:*** $4276. ***Average need-based gift aid:*** $5517. ***Average non-need-based aid:*** $1187. ***Average indebtedness upon graduation:*** $27,258.

APPLYING

Standardized Tests *Required:* SAT or ACT (for admission).

Options: early admission, deferred entrance.

Required: essay or personal statement, high school transcript, minimum 2.0 GPA, 2 letters of recommendation, church certificate, medical history.

CONTACT

Br. Luke Kral OSB, Director of Recruitment and Admissions, Conception Seminary College, PO Box 502, Conception, MO 64433-0502. *Phone:* 660-944-2886. *Fax:* 660-944-2829. *E-mail:* vocations@conception.edu.

Cottey College

Nevada, Missouri

http://www.cottey.edu/

- **Independent** primarily 2-year, founded 1884
- **Small-town** 51-acre campus
- **Endowment** $108.8 million
- **Women only**
- 74% of applicants were admitted

FACULTY

Student/faculty ratio: 10:1.

ACADEMICS

Calendar: semesters. *Degrees:* associate and bachelor's.

Library: Blanche Skiff Ross Memorial Library plus 1 other.

STUDENT LIFE

Housing options: women-only. Campus housing is university owned.

Activities and organizations: drama/theater group, choral group, International Friendship Circle, Cottey Intramural Association, Ozarks Explorers Club, Inter-Varsity Club, Golden Keys.

Athletics Member NJCAA.

Campus security: 24-hour emergency response devices and patrols, late-night transport/escort service, controlled dormitory access.

Student services: health clinic, personal/psychological counseling.

COSTS & FINANCIAL AID

Costs (2016–17) ***Comprehensive fee:*** $27,200 includes full-time tuition ($19,300), mandatory fees ($900), and room and board ($7000). Part-time tuition: $125 per credit hour. Part-time tuition and fees vary according to course load and program. ***Required fees:*** $21 per credit hour part-time, $63 per term part-time. ***College room only:*** $4000. Room and board charges vary according to housing facility.

Financial Aid Of all full-time matriculated undergraduates who enrolled in 2015, 255 applied for aid, 238 were judged to have need, 79 had their need fully met. 21 Federal Work-Study jobs (averaging $2099). 159 state and other part-time jobs (averaging $2056). In 2015, 73 non-need-based awards were made. ***Average percent of need met:*** 86. ***Average financial aid package:*** $20,584. ***Average need-based loan:*** $3087. ***Average need-based gift aid:*** $17,312. ***Average non-need-based aid:*** $14,919. ***Average indebtedness upon graduation:*** $26,427.

APPLYING

Standardized Tests *Required:* SAT or ACT (for admission). *Required for some:* TOEFL, IELTS.

Options: early decision, early action.

Required: essay or personal statement, high school transcript, 1 letter of recommendation. ***Recommended:*** minimum 2.6 GPA, interview.

CONTACT

Enrollment Office, Cottey College, 1000 West Austin Boulevard, Nevada, MO 64772. *Phone:* 417-667-8181. *Toll-free phone:* 888-526-8839. *Fax:* 417-667-8103. *E-mail:* enrollmgt@cottey.edu.

Cox College

Springfield, Missouri

http://www.coxcollege.edu/

- **Independent** comprehensive, founded 1907
- **Urban** campus
- **Coed, primarily women** 778 undergraduate students, 48% full-time, 87% women, 13% men
- 59% of applicants were admitted

UNDERGRAD STUDENTS

373 full-time, 405 part-time. 6% are from out of state; 2% Black or African American, non-Hispanic/Latino; 2% Hispanic/Latino; 2% Asian, non-Hispanic/Latino; 0.5% American Indian or Alaska Native, non-Hispanic/Latino; 1% Two or more races, non-Hispanic/Latino; 5% Race/ethnicity unknown; 11% transferred in.

Freshmen:

Admission: 27 applied, 16 admitted.

Retention: 100% of full-time freshmen returned.

FACULTY

Total: 190, 54% full-time.

Student/faculty ratio: 9:1.

ACADEMICS

Calendar: semesters. *Degrees:* certificates, associate, bachelor's, master's, post-master's, and postbachelor's certificates.

Special study options: academic remediation for entering students, accelerated degree program, distance learning, part-time degree program, summer session for credit.

Computers: 75 computers/terminals are available on campus for general student use. Students can access the following: campus intranet, computer help desk, free student e-mail accounts, online (class) grades, online (class) registration, online (class) schedules. Campuswide network is available. Wireless service is available via entire campus.

Library: The Cox Health Systems Libraries plus 2 others. Weekly public service hours: 60.

STUDENT LIFE

Housing options: college housing not available.

Campus security: 24-hour emergency response devices and patrols, late-night transport/escort service, controlled dormitory access.

Student services: personal/psychological counseling.

COSTS & FINANCIAL AID

Costs (2016–17) ***One-time required fee:*** $225. ***Tuition:*** $8800 full-time, $400 per credit hour part-time. Full-time tuition and fees vary according to course load, degree level, and program. Part-time tuition and fees vary according to course load, degree level, and program. ***Required fees:*** $1470 full-time. ***Payment plans:*** installment, deferred payment.

Financial Aid Of all full-time matriculated undergraduates who enrolled in 2015, 271 applied for aid, 249 were judged to have need. 21 Federal Work-Study jobs (averaging $1807). ***Average financial aid package:*** $2626. ***Average need-based loan:*** $3718. ***Average need-based gift aid:*** $4585.

APPLYING

Standardized Tests *Recommended:* SAT or ACT (for admission).

Options: electronic application, early decision.

Application fee: $50.

Required: high school transcript, minimum 2.5 GPA.

Application deadlines: 1/15 (freshmen), 8/1 (transfers).

Early decision deadline: 11/1.

Notification: 3/1 (freshmen), continuous (transfers), 12/1 (early decision).

CONTACT

Cox College, 1423 North Jefferson, Springfield, MO 65802. *Phone:* 417-269-3083. *Toll-free phone:* 866-898-5355.

Culver-Stockton College
Canton, Missouri
http://www.culver.edu/

- **Independent** comprehensive, founded 1853, affiliated with Christian Church (Disciples of Christ)
- **Rural** 143-acre campus
- **Endowment** $20.0 million
- **Coed** 1,058 undergraduate students, 89% full-time, 51% women, 49% men
- **Moderately difficult** entrance level, 58% of applicants were admitted

UNDERGRAD STUDENTS
944 full-time, 114 part-time. Students come from 34 states and territories; 13 other countries; 48% are from out of state; 11% Black or African American, non-Hispanic/Latino; 5% Hispanic/Latino; 0.6% Asian, non-Hispanic/Latino; 0.4% Native Hawaiian or other Pacific Islander, non-Hispanic/Latino; 0.2% American Indian or Alaska Native, non-Hispanic/Latino; 2% Two or more races, non-Hispanic/Latino; 6% international; 7% transferred in; 73% live on campus.

Freshmen:
Admission: 3,305 applied, 1,921 admitted, 269 enrolled. ***Average high school GPA:*** 3.24. ***Test scores:*** SAT critical reading scores over 500: 18%; ACT scores over 18: 87%; ACT scores over 24: 18%; ACT scores over 30: 1%.
Retention: 64% of full-time freshmen returned.

FACULTY
Total: 93, 55% full-time, 43% with terminal degrees.
Student/faculty ratio: 15:1.

ACADEMICS
Calendar: semesters. *Degrees:* bachelor's and master's.
Special study options: academic remediation for entering students, accelerated degree program, adult/continuing education programs, advanced placement credit, distance learning, double majors, honors programs, independent study, internships, part-time degree program, services for LD students, student-designed majors, study abroad, summer session for credit.
Unusual degree programs: 3-2 occupational therapy with Washington University in St. Louis.
Computers: 125 computers/terminals and 50 ports are available on campus for general student use. Students can access the following: campus intranet, computer help desk, free student e-mail accounts, online (class) grades, online (class) registration, online (class) schedules. Campuswide network is available. 100% of college-owned or -operated housing units are wired for high-speed Internet access. Wireless service is available via entire campus.
Library: Carl Johann Memorial Library plus 1 other. *Books:* 107,398 (physical), 165,339 (digital/electronic); *Serial titles:* 100 (physical), 29,497 (digital/electronic); *Databases:* 32. Weekly public service hours: 87; students can reserve study rooms.

STUDENT LIFE
Housing options: on-campus residence required through senior year; coed, men-only, women-only. Campus housing is university owned. Freshman campus housing is guaranteed.
Activities and organizations: drama/theater group, student-run newspaper, radio and television station, choral group, Up 'til Dawn (benefiting St. Jude's Hospital), Interfraternity Council/Panhellenic Council, Student Government Association, ENACTUS, Campus Programming Council, national fraternities, national sororities.
Athletics Member NAIA. ***Intercollegiate sports:*** baseball M(s), basketball M(s)/W(s), bowling M(s)/W(s), cheerleading M(s)/W(s), cross-country running M(s)/W(s), football M(s), golf M(s)/W(s), soccer M(s)/W(s), softball W(s), track and field M(s)/W(s), volleyball M(s)/W(s). ***Intramural sports:*** baseball M/W, basketball M/W, football M/W, soccer M/W, softball M/W, volleyball M/W.
Campus security: 24-hour emergency response devices and patrols, late-night transport/escort service, controlled dormitory access, lighted pathways/sidewalks, self defense education.
Student services: personal/psychological counseling.

COSTS & FINANCIAL AID
Costs (2017–18) ***One-time required fee:*** $210. ***Comprehensive fee:*** $34,350 includes full-time tuition ($25,615), mandatory fees ($425), and room and board ($8310). Part-time tuition: $590 per credit hour. ***Required fees:*** $18 per credit hour part-time. ***College room only:*** $3720. Room and board charges vary according to board plan and housing facility. ***Payment plan:*** installment. ***Waivers:*** senior citizens and employees or children of employees.
Financial Aid Of all full-time matriculated undergraduates who enrolled in 2016, 824 applied for aid, 757 were judged to have need, 121 had their need fully met. 80 Federal Work-Study jobs (averaging $1096). 396 state and other part-time jobs (averaging $1014). In 2016, 152 non-need-based awards were made. ***Average percent of need met:*** 73. ***Average financial aid package:*** $19,954. ***Average need-based loan:*** $4145. ***Average need-based gift aid:*** $16,376. ***Average non-need-based aid:*** $9710. ***Average indebtedness upon graduation:*** $28,605. ***Financial aid deadline:*** 6/1.

APPLYING
Standardized Tests *Required:* SAT or ACT (for admission).
Options: electronic application, deferred entrance.
Required: high school transcript, minimum 2.0 GPA. ***Recommended:*** essay or personal statement, 1 letter of recommendation, interview.
Application deadlines: rolling (freshmen), rolling (transfers).
Notification: continuous (freshmen), continuous (transfers).

CONTACT
Misty McBee, Executive Director of Admission & Marketing, Culver-Stockton College, One College Hill, Canton, MO 63435-1299. *Phone:* 573-288-6331. *Toll-free phone:* 800-537-1883. *Fax:* 573-288-6618. *E-mail:* admission@culver.edu.

DeVry University–Kansas City Campus
Kansas City, Missouri
http://www.devry.edu/

- **Proprietary** comprehensive, founded 1931, part of DeVry University
- **Urban** campus
- **Coed**
- **Minimally difficult** entrance level

FACULTY
Student/faculty ratio: 15:1.

ACADEMICS
Calendar: semesters. *Degrees:* associate, bachelor's, master's, and postbachelor's certificates.

COSTS & FINANCIAL AID
Costs (2016–17) ***Tuition:*** $17,052 full-time, $609 per credit hour part-time. ***Required fees:*** $460 full-time.
Financial Aid Of all full-time matriculated undergraduates who enrolled in 2007, 294 applied for aid, 281 were judged to have need, 12 had their need fully met. In 2007, 30 non-need-based awards were made. ***Average percent of need met:*** 40. ***Average financial aid package:*** $11,948. ***Average need-based loan:*** $8396. ***Average need-based gift aid:*** $5419. ***Average non-need-based aid:*** $13,609. ***Average indebtedness upon graduation:*** $8969.

APPLYING
Options: deferred entrance.
Application fee: $30.

CONTACT
Admissions Office, DeVry University–Kansas City Campus, 11224 Holmes Road, Kansas City, MO 64131. *Phone:* 816-943-7300. *Toll-free phone:* 866-338-7934.

Drury University

Springfield, Missouri

http://www.drury.edu/

- **Independent** comprehensive, founded 1873
- **Urban** 80-acre campus
- **Endowment** $88.8 million
- **Coed** 1,370 undergraduate students, 98% full-time, 54% women, 46% men
- **Moderately difficult** entrance level, 70% of applicants were admitted

UNDERGRAD STUDENTS

1,342 full-time, 28 part-time. Students come from 27 states and territories; 53 other countries; 15% are from out of state; 3% Black or African American, non-Hispanic/Latino; 3% Hispanic/Latino; 1% Asian, non-Hispanic/Latino; 0.1% Native Hawaiian or other Pacific Islander, non-Hispanic/Latino; 0.4% American Indian or Alaska Native, non-Hispanic/Latino; 3% Two or more races, non-Hispanic/Latino; 10% international; 8% transferred in; 65% live on campus.

Freshmen:

Admission: 1,563 applied, 1,088 admitted, 393 enrolled. ***Average high school GPA:*** 3.66. ***Test scores:*** ACT scores over 18: 99%; ACT scores over 24: 60%; ACT scores over 30: 14%.

Retention: 79% of full-time freshmen returned.

FACULTY

Total: 144, 76% full-time, 92% with terminal degrees.

Student/faculty ratio: 12:1.

ACADEMICS

Calendar: semesters. *Degrees:* bachelor's and master's (also offers evening program with significant enrollment not reflected in profile).

Special study options: academic remediation for entering students, accelerated degree program, adult/continuing education programs, advanced placement credit, cooperative education, distance learning, double majors, English as a second language, freshman honors college, honors programs, independent study, internships, off-campus study, part-time degree program, services for LD students, student-designed majors, study abroad, summer session for credit. ***ROTC:*** Army (c).

Unusual degree programs: 3-2 engineering with Washington University in St. Louis; international management with American Graduate School of International Management, occupational therapy with Washington University in St. Louis.

Computers: 385 computers/terminals are available on campus for general student use. Students can access the following: campus intranet, computer help desk, free student e-mail accounts, online (class) grades, online (class) registration, online (class) schedules, digital imaging lab, online bill payment/student information. Campuswide network is available. 100% of college-owned or -operated housing units are wired for high-speed Internet access. Wireless service is available via entire campus.

Library: F. W. Olin Library plus 1 other. *Books:* 149,706 (physical), 185,811 (digital/electronic); *Serial titles:* 751 (physical), 38 (digital/electronic); *Databases:* 44. Weekly public service hours: 92; students can reserve study rooms.

STUDENT LIFE

Housing options: on-campus residence required through junior year; coed, men-only, women-only. Campus housing is university owned and leased by the school. Freshman campus housing is guaranteed.

Activities and organizations: drama/theater group, student-run newspaper, radio and television station, choral group, Drury Volunteer Corps (DVC), International Student Association, Fanthers, Drury Allies, Commuter Student Association, national fraternities, national sororities.

Athletics Member NCAA. All Division II. ***Intercollegiate sports:*** baseball M(s), basketball M(s)/W(s), cheerleading M(s)/W(s), cross-country running M(s)/W(s), golf M(s)/W(s), soccer M(s)/W(s), softball W(s), swimming and diving M(s)/W(s), tennis M(s)/W(s), track and field M(s)/W(s), volleyball W(s), wrestling M. ***Intramural sports:*** basketball M/W, bowling M(c)/W(c), football M/W, ice hockey M(c), soccer M/W, softball M/W, triathlon M/W, ultimate Frisbee M(c)/W(c), volleyball M/W.

Campus security: 24-hour emergency response devices and patrols, student patrols, late-night transport/escort service, controlled dormitory access, security cameras in parking areas, police substation on campus, well-lit campus.

Student services: health clinic, personal/psychological counseling.

COSTS & FINANCIAL AID

Costs (2017–18) ***One-time required fee:*** $150. ***Comprehensive fee:*** $35,041 includes full-time tuition ($25,850), mandatory fees ($1155), and room and board ($8036). Full-time tuition and fees vary according to class time. Part-time tuition and fees vary according to class time. ***Room and board:*** Room and board charges vary according to board plan and housing facility. ***Payment plans:*** installment, deferred payment. ***Waivers:*** minority students, children of alumni, and employees or children of employees.

Financial Aid Of all full-time matriculated undergraduates who enrolled in 2015, 929 applied for aid, 805 were judged to have need, 147 had their need fully met. 111 Federal Work-Study jobs (averaging $2892). 280 state and other part-time jobs (averaging $2405). In 2015, 399 non-need-based awards were made. ***Average percent of need met:*** 71. ***Average financial aid package:*** $19,616. ***Average need-based loan:*** $4524. ***Average need-based gift aid:*** $15,600. ***Average non-need-based aid:*** $8552. ***Average indebtedness upon graduation:*** $31,011.

APPLYING

Standardized Tests *Required:* SAT or ACT (for admission).

Options: electronic application, deferred entrance.

Required: essay or personal statement, high school transcript, minimum 2.7 GPA, 1 letter of recommendation. ***Recommended:*** interview.

Application deadlines: rolling (freshmen), rolling (transfers).

Notification: continuous (freshmen), continuous (transfers).

CONTACT

Mr. Kevin Kropf, Dean of Enrollment, Drury University, 900 North Benton Avenue, Springfield, MO 65802. *Phone:* 417-873-7205. *Toll-free phone:* 800-922-2274. *Fax:* 417-866-3873. *E-mail:* druryad@drury.edu.

Evangel University

Springfield, Missouri

http://www.evangel.edu/

- **Independent** comprehensive, founded 1955, affiliated with Assemblies of God
- **Urban** 80-acre campus
- **Coed** 1,724 undergraduate students, 90% full-time, 55% women, 45% men
- **Moderately difficult** entrance level, 61% of applicants were admitted

UNDERGRAD STUDENTS

1,559 full-time, 165 part-time. 50% are from out of state; 4% Black or African American, non-Hispanic/Latino; 4% Hispanic/Latino; 2% Asian, non-Hispanic/Latino; 0.1% Native Hawaiian or other Pacific Islander, non-Hispanic/Latino; 1% American Indian or Alaska Native, non-Hispanic/Latino; 3% Two or more races, non-Hispanic/Latino; 8% Race/ethnicity unknown; 0.7% international; 6% transferred in; 68% live on campus.

Freshmen:

Admission: 1,483 applied, 912 admitted, 362 enrolled.

Retention: 71% of full-time freshmen returned.

ACADEMICS

Calendar: semesters. *Degrees:* associate, bachelor's, master's, and doctoral.

ROTC: Army (c).

Computers: Students can access the following: computer help desk, free student e-mail accounts, online (class) grades, online (class) registration, online (class) schedules, online payment. Campuswide network is available. Wireless service is available via classrooms, computer labs, learning centers, libraries, student centers.

Library: Claude Kendrick Library.

STUDENT LIFE

Housing options: on-campus residence required through senior year; coed, men-only, women-only. Campus housing is university owned.

Activities and organizations: drama/theater group, student-run newspaper, radio and television station, choral group, marching band,

Activities Board, student government, CrossWalk Student Ministries, Honor Societies, Music Ensembles.

Athletics Member NAIA. ***Intercollegiate sports:*** baseball M(s), basketball M(s)/W(s), cross-country running M(s)/W(s), football M(s), golf M(s)/W(s), softball W(s), tennis M(s)/W(s), track and field M(s)/W(s), volleyball W(s). ***Intramural sports:*** baseball M, basketball M/W, football M, golf M/W, soccer M/W, softball W, tennis M/W, volleyball W.

Campus security: 24-hour emergency response devices and patrols, student patrols, late-night transport/escort service, controlled dormitory access.

Student services: health clinic, personal/psychological counseling.

COSTS & FINANCIAL AID

Costs (2017–18) ***Comprehensive fee:*** $30,825 includes full-time tuition ($21,500), mandatory fees ($1207), and room and board ($8118). Full-time tuition and fees vary according to course load. Part-time tuition: $717 per credit hour. Part-time tuition and fees vary according to course load. ***College room only:*** $4210. Room and board charges vary according to board plan. ***Payment plan:*** installment. ***Waivers:*** employees or children of employees.

Financial Aid Of all full-time matriculated undergraduates who enrolled in 2015, 1,489 applied for aid, 1,297 were judged to have need, 134 had their need fully met. 978 Federal Work-Study jobs (averaging $1469). In 2015, 192 non-need-based awards were made. ***Average percent of need met:*** 68. ***Average financial aid package:*** $16,755. ***Average need-based loan:*** $4427. ***Average need-based gift aid:*** $12,159. ***Average non-need-based aid:*** $6771. ***Average indebtedness upon graduation:*** $32,032.

APPLYING

Standardized Tests *Required:* SAT or ACT (for admission).

Options: electronic application, deferred entrance.

Required: essay or personal statement, high school transcript, interview. ***Recommended:*** minimum 2.0 GPA.

CONTACT

Evangel University, 1111 North Glenstone, Springfield, MO 65802. *Phone:* 417-865-2811 Ext. 7205. *Toll-free phone:* 800-382-6435. *Fax:* 417-865-9599. *E-mail:* admissions@evangel.edu.

Fontbonne University

St. Louis, Missouri

http://www.fontbonne.edu/

- **Independent Roman Catholic** comprehensive, founded 1917
- **Suburban** 13-acre campus with easy access to St. Louis
- **Endowment** $19.2 million
- **Coed**
- **Moderately difficult** entrance level

FACULTY

Student/faculty ratio: 11:1.

ACADEMICS

Calendar: semesters. *Degrees:* certificates, bachelor's, master's, post-master's, and postbachelor's certificates.

Library: The Jack C. Taylor Library at Fontbonne University plus 1 other. *Books:* 87,793 (physical), 210,611 (digital/electronic); *Databases:* 38.

STUDENT LIFE

Housing options: coed, men-only, women-only, special housing for students with disabilities. Campus housing is university owned. Freshman campus housing is guaranteed.

Activities and organizations: drama/theater group, student-run newspaper, choral group, Future Teachers Association, Students for the Enhancement of Black Awareness, Fontbonne Athletic Association, Fontbonne in Service and Humility, Student Government Association.

Athletics Member NCAA, NAIA. All NCAA Division III.

Campus security: 24-hour patrols, late-night transport/escort service, controlled dormitory access.

Student services: health clinic, personal/psychological counseling.

COSTS & FINANCIAL AID

Costs (2016–17) ***Comprehensive fee:*** $33,717 includes full-time tuition ($24,250), mandatory fees ($360), and room and board ($9107). Full-time tuition and fees vary according to course load and program. Part-time tuition: $648 per credit. Part-time tuition and fees vary according to course load and program. ***Required fees:*** $18 per credit hour part-time. ***Room and board:*** Room and board charges vary according to board plan and housing facility.

Financial Aid Of all full-time matriculated undergraduates who enrolled in 2015, 116 Federal Work-Study jobs (averaging $1546). 76 state and other part-time jobs (averaging $1623). ***Average indebtedness upon graduation:*** $24,281.

APPLYING

Standardized Tests *Required:* SAT or ACT (for admission).

Options: electronic application, deferred entrance.

Application fee: $25.

Required: high school transcript, minimum 2.5 GPA. ***Required for some:*** essay or personal statement. ***Recommended:*** 2 letters of recommendation, interview.

CONTACT

Mr. Michelle Palumbo, Associate Vice President of Undergraduate Admissions, Fontbonne University, 6800 Wydown Boulevard, St. Louis, MO 63105. *Phone:* 314-889-1400. *Toll-free phone:* 800-205-5862. *Fax:* 314-889-1451. *E-mail:* fbyou@fontbonne.edu.

Global University

Springfield, Missouri

http://www.globaluniversity.edu/

- **Independent** comprehensive, founded 1948, affiliated with Assemblies of God
- **Small-town** campus
- **Coed** 4,176 undergraduate students, 9% full-time, 34% women, 66% men
- **Noncompetitive** entrance level

UNDERGRAD STUDENTS

381 full-time, 3,795 part-time. Students come from 50 states and territories; 127 other countries; 98% are from out of state.

FACULTY

Total: 633, 13% full-time, 46% with terminal degrees.

Student/faculty ratio: 11:1.

ACADEMICS

Calendar: continuous. *Degrees:* certificates, diplomas, associate, bachelor's, master's, doctoral, and postbachelor's certificates (offers only external degree programs).

Special study options: adult/continuing education programs, advanced placement credit, distance learning, double majors, external degree program, independent study, off-campus study, part-time degree program.

Computers: Students can access the following: free student e-mail accounts.

Library: Global University Library.

STUDENT LIFE

Campus security: 24-hour emergency response devices.

APPLYING

Application fee: $50.

Required: high school transcript. ***Required for some:*** 1 letter of recommendation. ***Recommended:*** essay or personal statement.

Application deadlines: rolling (freshmen), rolling (transfers).

CONTACT

Rev. Todd Waggoner, Enrollment and International Student Services Director, Global University, 1211 South Glenstone Avenue, Springfield, MO 65804. *Phone:* 417-862-9533 Ext. 2335. *Toll-free phone:* 800-443-1083. *Fax:* 417-863-9621. *E-mail:* twaggoner@globaluniversity.edu.

Goldfarb School of Nursing at Barnes-Jewish College

St. Louis, Missouri

http://www.barnesjewishcollege.edu/

- **Independent** comprehensive, founded 1902
- **Urban** 2-acre campus with easy access to St. Louis, Missouri
- **Endowment** $24.8 million
- **Coed, primarily women** 616 undergraduate students, 89% full-time, 88% women, 12% men
- **Moderately difficult** entrance level

UNDERGRAD STUDENTS
547 full-time, 69 part-time. Students come from 13 states and territories; 11 other countries; 30% are from out of state; 6% Black or African American, non-Hispanic/Latino; 2% Hispanic/Latino; 2% Asian, non-Hispanic/Latino; 0.2% Native Hawaiian or other Pacific Islander, non-Hispanic/Latino; 0.5% American Indian or Alaska Native, non-Hispanic/Latino; 2% Two or more races, non-Hispanic/Latino; 7% Race/ethnicity unknown; 100% transferred in.

FACULTY
Total: 53, 79% full-time, 43% with terminal degrees.

Student/faculty ratio: 13:1.

ACADEMICS
Calendar: trimesters. *Degrees:* bachelor's, master's, doctoral, and post-master's certificates.

Special study options: accelerated degree program, advanced placement credit, independent study, off-campus study, services for LD students, summer session for credit.

Computers: 160 computers/terminals are available on campus for general student use. Students can access the following: campus intranet, computer help desk, free student e-mail accounts, software, research databases. Campuswide network is available. Wireless service is available via entire campus.

Library: Goldfarb School of Nursing Library plus 2 others. *Books:* 1,100 (physical), 20,000 (digital/electronic); *Serial titles:* 40 (digital/electronic); *Databases:* 11.

STUDENT LIFE
Housing options: college housing not available.

Activities and organizations: student-run newspaper, Student Nurses Association.

Campus security: 24-hour patrols, late-night transport/escort service.

Student services: health clinic, personal/psychological counseling.

COSTS
Costs (2017–18) ***Tuition:*** $19,058 full-time, $733 per credit hour part-time. Full-time tuition and fees vary according to course load and degree level. Part-time tuition and fees vary according to course load and degree level. ***Required fees:*** $1130 full-time, $615 per term part-time. ***Payment plan:*** installment.

APPLYING
Options: deferred entrance.

Application fee: $50.

Notification: continuous (transfers).

CONTACT
Goldfarb School of Nursing at Barnes-Jewish College, 4483 Duncan Avenue, St. Louis, MO 63110. *Phone:* 314-362-9155. *Toll-free phone:* 800-832-9009.

Graceland University

Independence, Missouri

http://www.graceland.edu/

CONTACT
Admissions, Graceland University, 1401 West Truman Road, Independence, MO 64050-3434. *Phone:* 816-833-0524. *Toll-free phone:* 866-GRACELAND. *E-mail:* gic@graceland.edu.

Hannibal-LaGrange University

Hannibal, Missouri

http://www.hlg.edu/

- **Independent Southern Baptist** comprehensive, founded 1858
- **Small-town** 110-acre campus
- **Endowment** $8.4 million
- **Coed** 1,303 undergraduate students, 99% full-time, 62% women, 37% men
- **Minimally difficult** entrance level

UNDERGRAD STUDENTS
1,291 full-time. Students come from 27 states and territories; 25 other countries; 26% are from out of state; 5% Black or African American, non-Hispanic/Latino; 2% Hispanic/Latino; 0.8% Asian, non-Hispanic/Latino; 0.2% Native Hawaiian or other Pacific Islander, non-Hispanic/Latino; 0.5% American Indian or Alaska Native, non-Hispanic/Latino; 2% Two or more races, non-Hispanic/Latino; 0.2% Race/ethnicity unknown; 6% international.

FACULTY
Total: 138, 45% full-time.

ACADEMICS
Calendar: semesters. *Degrees:* certificates, associate, bachelor's, and master's.

Special study options: academic remediation for entering students, accelerated degree program, adult/continuing education programs, advanced placement credit, distance learning, double majors, English as a second language, honors programs, independent study, internships, off-campus study, part-time degree program, services for LD students, student-designed majors, study abroad, summer session for credit.

Computers: 258 computers/terminals are available on campus for general student use. Students can access the following: free student e-mail accounts, online (class) grades, online (class) registration, online (class) schedules. Campuswide network is available. 100% of college-owned or -operated housing units are wired for high-speed Internet access. Wireless service is available via classrooms, computer centers, computer labs, dorm rooms, learning centers, libraries, student centers.

Library: Roland Library plus 1 other. *Books:* 113,238 (physical), 11,053 (digital/electronic); *Databases:* 77. Students can reserve study rooms.

STUDENT LIFE
Housing options: on-campus residence required through junior year; men-only, women-only. Campus housing is university owned. Freshman applicants given priority for college housing.

Activities and organizations: drama/theater group, student-run newspaper, choral group, Phi Beta Lambda, Student Nursing Association, Student Teachers Organization, Phi Beta Delta, Alpha Tau Beta.

Athletics Member NAIA. ***Intercollegiate sports:*** baseball M(s), basketball M(s)/W(s), cheerleading M(s)/W(s), cross-country running M(s)/W(s), golf M(s)/W(s), soccer M(s)/W(s), softball W(s), track and field M(s)/W(s), volleyball W(s), wrestling M(s). ***Intramural sports:*** basketball M/W, bowling M/W, racquetball M/W, table tennis M/W, ultimate Frisbee M/W, volleyball M/W.

Campus security: 24-hour emergency response devices and patrols, student patrols, late-night transport/escort service, controlled dormitory access, camera surveillance, alert system.

COSTS & FINANCIAL AID
Costs (2017–18) ***Comprehensive fee:*** $29,818 includes full-time tuition ($20,610), mandatory fees ($1100), and room and board ($8108). Full-time tuition and fees vary according to course load, degree level, location, program, and student level. Part-time tuition and fees vary according to course load, degree level, location, program, and student level. ***Room and board:*** Room and board charges vary according to housing facility. ***Payment plan:*** installment. ***Waivers:*** employees or children of employees.

Financial Aid Of all full-time matriculated undergraduates who enrolled in 2015, 80 Federal Work-Study jobs (averaging $750).

APPLYING
Standardized Tests *Required:* SAT or ACT (for admission).

Options: electronic application, early admission, deferred entrance.

Application fee: $25.

Required: high school transcript, minimum 2.0 GPA.

Application deadlines: rolling (freshmen), 8/10 (out-of-state freshmen), rolling (transfers).

Notification: continuous until 9/10 (freshmen), 9/10 (out-of-state freshmen), continuous (transfers).

CONTACT

Dr. Ray Carty, Vice President for Enrollment Management, Hannibal-LaGrange University, 2800 Palmyra Road, Hannibal, MO 63401-1999. *Phone:* 573-629-3094. *Toll-free phone:* 800-HLG-1119. *E-mail:* admissions@hlg.edu.

Harris-Stowe State University

St. Louis, Missouri

http://www.hssu.edu/

- **State-supported** 4-year, founded 1857, part of Missouri Coordinating Board for Higher Education
- **Urban** 22-acre campus
- **Endowment** $1.2 million
- **Coed** 1,390 undergraduate students, 75% full-time, 67% women, 33% men
- **Noncompetitive** entrance level, 51% of applicants were admitted

UNDERGRAD STUDENTS

1,036 full-time, 354 part-time. Students come from 20 states and territories; 14 other countries; 17% are from out of state; 82% Black or African American, non-Hispanic/Latino; 2% Hispanic/Latino; 0.3% Asian, non-Hispanic/Latino; 0.2% American Indian or Alaska Native, non-Hispanic/Latino; 3% Two or more races, non-Hispanic/Latino; 6% Race/ethnicity unknown; 0.4% international; 12% transferred in; 26% live on campus.

Freshmen:

Admission: 2,573 applied, 1,321 admitted, 279 enrolled. ***Average high school GPA:*** 2.69. ***Test scores:*** SAT critical reading scores over 500: 7%; SAT math scores over 500: 16%; ACT scores over 18: 33%; SAT math scores over 600: 3%; ACT scores over 24: 1%; SAT math scores over 700: 1%.

Retention: 47% of full-time freshmen returned.

FACULTY

Total: 174, 24% full-time.

Student/faculty ratio: 13:1.

ACADEMICS

Calendar: semesters. *Degree:* certificates and bachelor's.

Special study options: academic remediation for entering students, accelerated degree program, advanced placement credit, cooperative education, distance learning, honors programs, internships, off-campus study, part-time degree program, services for LD students, student-designed majors, study abroad, summer session for credit. ***ROTC:*** Army (c), Air Force (c).

Unusual degree programs: 3-2 engineering with Saint Louis University.

Computers: 272 computers/terminals and 272 ports are available on campus for general student use. Students can access the following: computer help desk, free student e-mail accounts, online (class) grades, online (class) registration, online (class) schedules. Campuswide network is available. 100% of college-owned or -operated housing units are wired for high-speed Internet access. Wireless service is available via entire campus.

Library: AT&T Library and Technology Center plus 1 other. *Books:* 75,467 (physical); *Serial titles:* 100 (physical).

STUDENT LIFE

Housing options: coed. Campus housing is university owned. Freshman applicants given priority for college housing.

Activities and organizations: drama/theater group, choral group, Drama Club, Concert chorale, Student Government Association, Multicultural Council, Student Ambassadors, national fraternities, national sororities.

Athletics Member NAIA. ***Intercollegiate sports:*** baseball M(s), basketball M(s)/W(s), cheerleading M(s)/W(s), soccer M(s)/W(s), softball W(s), volleyball W(s). ***Intramural sports:*** basketball M/W, sand volleyball M/W.

Campus security: 24-hour emergency response devices and patrols, late-night transport/escort service, controlled dormitory access.

Student services: health clinic, personal/psychological counseling.

COSTS & FINANCIAL AID

Costs (2017–18) ***Tuition:*** state resident $4776 full-time, $199 per credit hour part-time; nonresident $9409 full-time, $392 per credit hour part-time. Full-time tuition and fees vary according to course load. ***Required fees:*** $444 full-time. ***Room only:*** $6500. Room and board charges vary according to housing facility. ***Payment plan:*** installment. ***Waivers:*** employees or children of employees.

Financial Aid Of all full-time matriculated undergraduates who enrolled in 2008, 990 applied for aid, 890 were judged to have need, 200 had their need fully met. 86 Federal Work-Study jobs (averaging $2000). 80 state and other part-time jobs (averaging $2000). ***Average percent of need met:*** 90. ***Average financial aid package:*** $9500. ***Average need-based loan:*** $5000. ***Average need-based gift aid:*** $4500. ***Average non-need-based aid:*** $3000. ***Average indebtedness upon graduation:*** $16,000.

APPLYING

Standardized Tests *Recommended:* SAT or ACT (for admission).

Options: electronic application, early admission, deferred entrance.

Application fee: $20.

Required: high school transcript.

Application deadlines: 7/31 (freshmen), rolling (transfers).

Notification: continuous (freshmen), continuous (transfers).

CONTACT

Dr. Chauvette McElmurry-Green, Registrar, Harris-Stowe State University, 3026 Laclede Avenue, St. Louis, MO 63103. *Phone:* 314-340-3300. *Fax:* 314-340-3555. *E-mail:* admissions@hssu.edu.

Hickey College

St. Louis, Missouri

http://www.hickeycollege.edu/

- **Private** 4-year, founded 1933
- **Suburban** campus with easy access to St. Louis
- **Coed**
- 71% of applicants were admitted

ACADEMICS

Calendar: semesters. *Degrees:* diplomas, associate, and bachelor's.

CONTACT

Admissions Office, Hickey College, 2700 North Lindbergh Boulevard, St. Louis, MO 63114. *Phone:* 314-434-2212. *Toll-free phone:* 800-777-1544.

Kansas City Art Institute

Kansas City, Missouri

http://www.kcai.edu/

- **Independent** 4-year, founded 1885
- **Urban** 18-acre campus with easy access to Kansas City, MO
- **Endowment** $56.8 million
- **Coed** 635 undergraduate students, 99% full-time, 74% women, 26% men
- **Moderately difficult** entrance level, 65% of applicants were admitted

UNDERGRAD STUDENTS

627 full-time, 8 part-time. Students come from 36 states and territories; 7 other countries; 63% are from out of state; 6% Black or African American, non-Hispanic/Latino; 7% Hispanic/Latino; 3% Asian, non-Hispanic/Latino; 0.6% American Indian or Alaska Native, non-Hispanic/Latino; 11% Two or more races, non-Hispanic/Latino; 9% Race/ethnicity unknown; 1% international; 9% transferred in; 35% live on campus.

Freshmen:

Admission: 778 applied, 508 admitted, 163 enrolled. ***Average high school GPA:*** 3.29. ***Test scores:*** SAT critical reading scores over 500: 73%; SAT math scores over 500: 58%; SAT writing scores over 500: 60%; ACT scores over 18: 92%; SAT critical reading scores over 600: 34%; SAT math scores over 600: 15%; SAT writing scores over 600: 13%; ACT scores over 24: 44%; SAT critical reading scores over 700: 6%; ACT scores over 30: 10%.

Retention: 81% of full-time freshmen returned.

FACULTY
Total: 111, 46% full-time, 60% with terminal degrees.
Student/faculty ratio: 9:1.

ACADEMICS
Calendar: semesters. *Degree:* certificates, diplomas, and bachelor's.
Special study options: double majors, independent study, internships, off-campus study, part-time degree program, services for LD students, study abroad, summer session for credit.
Computers: 150 computers/terminals and 1,000 ports are available on campus for general student use. Students can access the following: campus intranet, computer help desk, free student e-mail accounts, online (class) grades, online (class) registration, online (class) schedules. Campuswide network is available. 100% of college-owned or -operated housing units are wired for high-speed Internet access. Wireless service is available via entire campus.
Library: Jannes Library. *Books:* 29,732 (physical), 188,154 (digital/electronic); *Serial titles:* 214 (physical), 8 (digital/electronic); *Databases:* 14. Weekly public service hours: 84; students can reserve study rooms.

STUDENT LIFE
Housing options: on-campus residence required for freshman year; coed, men-only, women-only. Campus housing is university owned. Freshman applicants given priority for college housing.
Activities and organizations: student-run radio station, ArtPlay, Black Artist Culture and Community, Quiltbag app (LGBTQIA), Student Activists for Equality (SAFE), Night Owls - soccer team.
Campus security: 24-hour emergency response devices and patrols, late-night transport/escort service, controlled dormitory access.
Student services: personal/psychological counseling.

COSTS & FINANCIAL AID
Costs (2017–18) ***Comprehensive fee:*** $47,950 includes full-time tuition ($37,400), mandatory fees ($150), and room and board ($10,400). Full-time tuition and fees vary according to program. Part-time tuition: $1510 per credit hour. Part-time tuition and fees vary according to program. ***Payment plan:*** installment. ***Waivers:*** employees or children of employees.
Financial Aid Of all full-time matriculated undergraduates who enrolled in 2016, 587 applied for aid, 542 were judged to have need, 65 had their need fully met. 109 Federal Work-Study jobs (averaging $1037). 193 state and other part-time jobs (averaging $1216). In 2016, 87 non-need-based awards were made. ***Average percent of need met:*** 62. ***Average financial aid package:*** $25,758. ***Average need-based loan:*** $4606. ***Average need-based gift aid:*** $21,321. ***Average non-need-based aid:*** $17,330. ***Average indebtedness upon graduation:*** $25,000.

APPLYING
Standardized Tests *Required:* SAT or ACT (for admission). *Required for some:* TOEFL.
Options: electronic application, early admission, deferred entrance.
Application fee: $45.
Required: essay or personal statement, high school transcript, 1 letter of recommendation, portfolio. ***Recommended:*** minimum 2.5 GPA, interview.
Application deadlines: 8/1 (freshmen), 8/1 (transfers).
Notification: 8/15 (freshmen), 8/15 (transfers).

CONTACT
Mr. Gerald Valet, Director of Admission Technology, Kansas City Art Institute, 4415 Warwick Boulevard, Kansas City, MO 64111-1874.
Phone: 816-474-5224. *Toll-free phone:* 800-522-5224.
Fax: 816-802-3309. *E-mail:* admiss@kcai.edu.

Lincoln University
Jefferson City, Missouri
http://www.lincolnu.edu/

- **State-supported** comprehensive, founded 1866
- **Small-town** 174-acre campus
- **Coed** 2,618 undergraduate students, 71% full-time, 57% women, 43% men
- **Noncompetitive** entrance level, 52% of applicants were admitted

UNDERGRAD STUDENTS
1,851 full-time, 767 part-time. Students come from 30 states and territories; 8 other countries; 24% are from out of state; 43% Black or African American, non-Hispanic/Latino; 2% Hispanic/Latino; 0.8% Asian, non-Hispanic/Latino; 0.1% Native Hawaiian or other Pacific Islander, non-Hispanic/Latino; 0.6% American Indian or Alaska Native, non-Hispanic/Latino; 3% Two or more races, non-Hispanic/Latino; 4% Race/ethnicity unknown; 2% international; 7% transferred in; 43% live on campus.

Freshmen:
Admission: 5,077 applied, 2,631 admitted, 460 enrolled. ***Average high school GPA:*** 2.79. ***Test scores:*** ACT scores over 18: 44%; ACT scores over 24: 7%.
Retention: 47% of full-time freshmen returned.

FACULTY
Total: 184, 69% full-time, 51% with terminal degrees.
Student/faculty ratio: 15:1.

ACADEMICS
Calendar: semesters. *Degrees:* associate, bachelor's, master's, and postbachelor's certificates.
Special study options: academic remediation for entering students, accelerated degree program, adult/continuing education programs, advanced placement credit, cooperative education, distance learning, double majors, freshman honors college, honors programs, independent study, internships, off-campus study, part-time degree program, services for LD students, study abroad, summer session for credit. ***ROTC:*** Army (b).
Computers: 365 computers/terminals and 1,100 ports are available on campus for general student use. Students can access the following: campus intranet, computer help desk, free student e-mail accounts, online (class) grades, online (class) registration, online (class) schedules. Campuswide network is available. 100% of college-owned or -operated housing units are wired for high-speed Internet access. Wireless service is available via entire campus.
Library: Inman E. Page Library. *Books:* 99,126 (physical), 197,476 (digital/electronic); *Serial titles:* 1,194 (physical), 19,000 (digital/electronic); *Databases:* 39. Weekly public service hours: 90.

STUDENT LIFE
Housing options: on-campus residence required through sophomore year; coed. Campus housing is university owned.
Activities and organizations: student-run newspaper, choral group, marching band, Student Government Association (SGA), Lincoln University Band, Alpha Kappa Mu, Army ROTC, International Students Association, national fraternities, national sororities.
Athletics Member NCAA. All Division II. ***Intercollegiate sports:*** basketball M(s)/W(s), bowling W(s), cheerleading W(s), cross-country running W(s), football M(s), golf M(s)/W(s), softball W(s), track and field M(s)/W(s). ***Intramural sports:*** basketball M/W, bowling M/W, volleyball M/W, weight lifting M/W.
Campus security: 24-hour emergency response devices and patrols, student patrols, late-night transport/escort service, controlled dormitory access, security-related training upon request, Operation ID-ent, timely warnings, text message safety alerts, Webpage with helpful tips.
Student services: health clinic, personal/psychological counseling, women's center.

COSTS & FINANCIAL AID
Costs (2016–17) ***Tuition:*** state resident $6150 full-time, $205 per credit hour part-time; nonresident $12,540 full-time, $418 per credit hour part-time. Full-time tuition and fees vary according to course load, location, and reciprocity agreements. Part-time tuition and fees vary according to course load, location, and reciprocity agreements. ***Required fees:*** $892 full-time, $7 per credit hour part-time, $345 per term part-time. ***Room and board:*** $6560; room only: $3400. Room and board charges vary according to board plan and housing facility. ***Payment plans:*** installment, deferred payment. ***Waivers:*** senior citizens and employees or children of employees.
Financial Aid Of all full-time matriculated undergraduates who enrolled in 2016, 1,692 applied for aid, 1,497 were judged to have need, 72 had their need fully met. 178 Federal Work-Study jobs (averaging $602). 49 state and other part-time jobs (averaging $1456). In 2016, 2 non-need-

based awards were made. ***Average percent of need met:*** 62. ***Average financial aid package:*** $11,908. ***Average need-based loan:*** $4092. ***Average need-based gift aid:*** $6014. ***Average non-need-based aid:*** $5288. ***Average indebtedness upon graduation:*** $32,691.

APPLYING

Standardized Tests *Required:* SAT or ACT (for admission).

Options: electronic application, deferred entrance.

Required: high school transcript. ***Required for some:*** minimum 2.0 GPA.

Notification: continuous (freshmen), continuous (transfers).

CONTACT

DeRecco Lynch, Director of Admissions, Lincoln University, Office of Admissions, 820 Chestnut Street, B-7 Young Hall, Jefferson City, MO 65101. *Phone:* 573-681-5599. *Fax:* 573-681-5889. *E-mail:* enroll@lincolnu.edu.

Lindenwood University

St. Charles, Missouri

http://www.lindenwood.edu/

- **Independent Presbyterian** comprehensive, founded 1827
- **Suburban** 550-acre campus with easy access to St. Louis
- **Endowment** $139.3 million
- **Coed** 7,549 undergraduate students, 90% full-time, 54% women, 46% men
- **Moderately difficult** entrance level, 55% of applicants were admitted

UNDERGRAD STUDENTS

6,794 full-time, 755 part-time. Students come from 48 states and territories; 89 other countries; 37% are from out of state; 13% Black or African American, non-Hispanic/Latino; 3% Hispanic/Latino; 0.6% Asian, non-Hispanic/Latino; 0.5% Native Hawaiian or other Pacific Islander, non-Hispanic/Latino; 0.3% American Indian or Alaska Native, non-Hispanic/Latino; 3% Two or more races, non-Hispanic/Latino; 14% Race/ethnicity unknown; 12% international; 10% transferred in; 55% live on campus.

Freshmen:

Admission: 4,039 applied, 2,209 admitted, 1,008 enrolled. ***Average high school GPA:*** 3.31. ***Test scores:*** SAT critical reading scores over 500: 47%; SAT math scores over 500: 63%; SAT writing scores over 500: 33%; ACT scores over 18: 98%; SAT critical reading scores over 600: 10%; SAT math scores over 600: 17%; SAT writing scores over 600: 5%; ACT scores over 24: 37%; SAT critical reading scores over 700: 1%; SAT math scores over 700: 1%; ACT scores over 30: 7%.

Retention: 70% of full-time freshmen returned.

FACULTY

Total: 1,424, 21% full-time, 38% with terminal degrees.

Student/faculty ratio: 10:1.

ACADEMICS

Calendar: 4-1-4 for daytime programs; quarters and trimesters for evening programs. *Degrees:* bachelor's, master's, doctoral, post-master's, and postbachelor's certificates.

Special study options: academic remediation for entering students, accelerated degree program, adult/continuing education programs, advanced placement credit, distance learning, double majors, English as a second language, external degree program, freshman honors college, honors programs, independent study, internships, off-campus study, part-time degree program, services for LD students, student-designed majors, study abroad, summer session for credit. ***ROTC:*** Army (c), Air Force (c).

Unusual degree programs: 3-2 engineering with University of Missouri–Columbia, University of Missouri–St. Louis, Washington University in St. Louis; nursing with Goldfarb School of Nursing.

Computers: 286 computers/terminals are available on campus for general student use. Students can access the following: campus intranet, computer help desk, free student e-mail accounts, online (class) grades, online (class) registration, online (class) schedules. Campuswide network is available. 100% of college-owned or -operated housing units are wired for high-speed Internet access. Wireless service is available via classrooms, computer centers, computer labs, dorm rooms, learning centers, libraries, student centers.

Library: Butler Library plus 1 other. *Books:* 93,916 (physical), 200,752 (digital/electronic); *Serial titles:* 272 (physical), 139 (digital/electronic); *Databases:* 96. Study areas open 24 hours, 5-7 days a week.

STUDENT LIFE

Housing options: men-only, women-only. Campus housing is university owned and leased by the school. Freshman applicants given priority for college housing.

Activities and organizations: drama/theater group, student-run newspaper, radio and television station, choral group, marching band, Kappa Delta Pi, Accounting and Finance Club, Black Student Union, Gay Straight Alliance, Psychology Interest Club, national fraternities, national sororities.

Athletics Member NCAA, NAIA, USCAA. All NCAA Division II. ***Intercollegiate sports:*** baseball M(s), basketball M(s)/W(s), bowling M(s)/W(s), cheerleading M(s)/W(s), cross-country running M(s)/W(s), field hockey W(s), football M(s), golf M(s)/W(s), gymnastics W(s), ice hockey M(s)/W(s), lacrosse M(s)/W(s), riflery M(s)/W(s), rugby M(s)/W(s), soccer M(s)/W(s), softball W(s), swimming and diving M(s)/W(s), table tennis M(s)/W(s), tennis M(s)/W(s), track and field M(s)/W(s), volleyball M(s)/W(s), water polo M(s)/W(s), weight lifting M(s)/W(s), wrestling M(s)/W(s). ***Intramural sports:*** basketball M/W, sand volleyball M/W, soccer M/W, softball M/W, volleyball M/W.

Campus security: 24-hour emergency response devices and patrols, late-night transport/escort service, controlled dormitory access, surveillance cameras throughout the campus and facilities.

Student services: health clinic, personal/psychological counseling.

COSTS & FINANCIAL AID

Costs (2016–17) ***Comprehensive fee:*** $25,132 includes full-time tuition ($15,672), mandatory fees ($660), and room and board ($8800). Full-time tuition and fees vary according to class time. Part-time tuition: $453 per credit hour. Part-time tuition and fees vary according to course load. ***Required fees:*** $255 per term part-time. ***Room and board:*** Room and board charges vary according to board plan. ***Payment plans:*** installment, deferred payment. ***Waivers:*** senior citizens and employees or children of employees.

Financial Aid Of all full-time matriculated undergraduates who enrolled in 2016, 4,603 applied for aid, 3,782 were judged to have need, 748 had their need fully met. 311 Federal Work-Study jobs (averaging $2358). In 2016, 2087 non-need-based awards were made. ***Average percent of need met:*** 76. ***Average financial aid package:*** $9635. ***Average need-based loan:*** $4023. ***Average need-based gift aid:*** $5986. ***Average non-need-based aid:*** $5628. ***Average indebtedness upon graduation:*** $31,488.

APPLYING

Standardized Tests *Required for some:* SAT or ACT (for admission).

Options: electronic application.

Application fee: $30.

Required: minimum 2.5 GPA, personal resumé indicating community service, youth leadership, clubs, organizations, and non-academic experience. ***Required for some:*** essay or personal statement, high school transcript. ***Recommended:*** 3 letters of recommendation, interview.

Application deadlines: rolling (freshmen), rolling (transfers).

Notification: continuous (freshmen), continuous (transfers).

CONTACT

Mrs. Comela Mathis, Director of Day Admissions, Lindenwood University, 209 South Kings Highway, St. Charles, MO 63301. *Phone:* 636-949-4665. *Fax:* 636-949-4989. *E-mail:* cmathis@lindenwood.edu.

Logan University

Chesterfield, Missouri

http://www.logan.edu/

- **Independent** upper-level, founded 1935
- **Suburban** 112-acre campus with easy access to St. Louis
- **Endowment** $15.6 million
- **Coed** 131 undergraduate students, 39% full-time, 56% women, 44% men

UNDERGRAD STUDENTS

51 full-time, 80 part-time. Students come from 18 states and territories; 1 other country; 58% are from out of state; 2% Black or African American, non-Hispanic/Latino; 0.8% Hispanic/Latino; 2% Asian, non-

Hispanic/Latino; 0.8% Native Hawaiian or other Pacific Islander, non-Hispanic/Latino; 0.8% American Indian or Alaska Native, non-Hispanic/Latino; 3% Two or more races, non-Hispanic/Latino; 65% Race/ethnicity unknown; 0.8% international; 24% transferred in.

FACULTY
Total: 114, 43% full-time, 73% with terminal degrees.

Student/faculty ratio: 9:1.

ACADEMICS
Calendar: trimesters. *Degrees:* bachelor's, master's, and doctoral.

Special study options: accelerated degree program, adult/continuing education programs, advanced placement credit, cooperative education, distance learning, external degree program, independent study, part-time degree program, services for LD students, summer session for credit.

Computers: 100 computers/terminals are available on campus for general student use. Students can access the following: computer help desk, free student e-mail accounts, online (class) grades, online (class) registration, online (class) schedules, student portal, learning management system, online storage, specialty health care software, high-speed printing. Campuswide network is available. Wireless service is available via entire campus.

Library: Learning Resources Center. *Books:* 12,651 (physical), 3,044 (digital/electronic); *Serial titles:* 23 (physical), 20,360 (digital/electronic); *Databases:* 87. Weekly public service hours: 84.

STUDENT LIFE
Activities and organizations: Chi Rho sigma, Family Wellness, Student American Black Chiropractors Association, Activator, Rehab2Performance, national fraternities, national sororities.

Athletics ***Intercollegiate sports:*** basketball M(c)/W(c), golf M(c), soccer M(c), tennis M(c). ***Intramural sports:*** basketball M/W, football M, ice hockey M, softball M/W, volleyball M/W.

Campus security: 24-hour patrols, late-night transport/escort service.

Student services: health clinic, personal/psychological counseling.

COSTS & FINANCIAL AID
Costs (2016–17) ***Tuition:*** $6600 full-time, $275 per credit hour part-time. Full-time tuition and fees vary according to course load, degree level, and program. Part-time tuition and fees vary according to course load, degree level, and program. ***Required fees:*** $160 full-time, $80 per term part-time. ***Waivers:*** employees or children of employees.

Financial Aid Of all full-time matriculated undergraduates who enrolled in 2016, 45 applied for aid, 44 were judged to have need, 2 had their need fully met. 7 Federal Work-Study jobs (averaging $2603). ***Average percent of need met:*** 28. ***Average financial aid package:*** $10,203. ***Average need-based loan:*** $7216. ***Average need-based gift aid:*** $4616.

APPLYING
Options: electronic application.

Application fee: $25.

Required: minimum cumulative 2.0 GPA for transfer students.

CONTACT
Mrs. Natach Douglas, Director of Admissions, Logan University, 1851 Schoettler Road, Chesterfield, MO 63017. *Phone:* 636-227-2100 Ext. 1718. *Toll-free phone:* 800-533-9210. *Fax:* 636-207-2425. *E-mail:* admissions@logan.edu.

Maryville University of Saint Louis

St. Louis, Missouri

http://www.maryville.edu/

- **Independent** comprehensive, founded 1872
- **Suburban** 130-acre campus with easy access to St. Louis
- **Endowment** $47.8 million
- **Coed** 2,967 undergraduate students, 72% full-time, 67% women, 33% men
- **Moderately difficult** entrance level, 93% of applicants were admitted

UNDERGRAD STUDENTS
2,147 full-time, 820 part-time. Students come from 50 states and territories; 36 other countries; 24% are from out of state; 8% Black or African American, non-Hispanic/Latino; 4% Hispanic/Latino; 3% Asian, non-Hispanic/Latino; 0.1% Native Hawaiian or other Pacific Islander, non-Hispanic/Latino; 0.4% American Indian or Alaska Native, non-Hispanic/Latino; 2% Two or more races, non-Hispanic/Latino; 5% Race/ethnicity unknown; 5% international; 12% transferred in; 25% live on campus.

Freshmen:
Admission: 1,846 applied, 1,713 admitted, 554 enrolled. ***Average high school GPA:*** 3.6. ***Test scores:*** ACT scores over 18: 94%; ACT scores over 24: 63%; ACT scores over 30: 10%.

Retention: 86% of full-time freshmen returned.

FACULTY
Total: 623, 23% full-time, 47% with terminal degrees.

Student/faculty ratio: 13:1.

ACADEMICS
Calendar: semesters. *Degrees:* bachelor's, master's, doctoral, post-master's, and postbachelor's certificates.

Special study options: accelerated degree program, adult/continuing education programs, advanced placement credit, cooperative education, distance learning, double majors, English as a second language, honors programs, independent study, internships, off-campus study, part-time degree program, services for LD students, study abroad, summer session for credit. ***ROTC:*** Army (c).

Unusual degree programs: 3-2 business administration; engineering with Washington University in St. Louis; social work with Saint Louis University; education.

Computers: 575 computers/terminals are available on campus for general student use. Students can access the following: campus intranet, computer help desk, free student e-mail accounts, online (class) grades, online (class) registration, online (class) schedules, specialized software, university catalog. Campuswide network is available. 100% of college-owned or -operated housing units are wired for high-speed Internet access. Wireless service is available via entire campus.

Library: Maryville University Library. *Books:* 60,082 (physical), 224,165 (digital/electronic); *Serial titles:* 94,642 (digital/electronic); *Databases:* 122. Weekly public service hours: 101; study areas open 24 hours, 5-7 days a week.

STUDENT LIFE
Housing options: coed. Campus housing is university owned.

Activities and organizations: drama/theater group, student-run newspaper, choral group, Campus Activities Board, Physical Therapy Club, Student Nurses Association, Community Service Club, Green Maryville Student Association.

Athletics Member NCAA. All Division II. ***Intercollegiate sports:*** baseball M(s), basketball M(s)/W(s), bowling W(s), cross-country running M(s)/W(s), golf M(s)/W(s), lacrosse M(s), soccer M(s)/W(s), softball W(s), swimming and diving M(s)/W(s), tennis W(s), track and field M(s)/W(s), volleyball W(s), wrestling M(s). ***Intramural sports:*** basketball M/W, cheerleading M/W, lacrosse M/W, rugby M, soccer M/W, softball W, table tennis M/W, ultimate Frisbee M/W, volleyball M/W.

Campus security: 24-hour emergency response devices and patrols, late-night transport/escort service, controlled dormitory access, video security system in residence halls, self-defense and education programs.

Student services: health clinic, personal/psychological counseling.

COSTS & FINANCIAL AID
Costs (2017–18) ***Comprehensive fee:*** $38,046 includes full-time tuition ($25,558), mandatory fees ($2400), and room and board ($10,088). Full-time tuition and fees vary according to course load, degree level, and program. Part-time tuition: $766 per credit hour. Part-time tuition and fees vary according to class time, degree level, and program. ***Required fees:*** $450 per term part-time. ***Room and board:*** Room and board charges vary according to board plan and housing facility. ***Payment plans:*** installment, deferred payment. ***Waivers:*** senior citizens and employees or children of employees.

Financial Aid Of all full-time matriculated undergraduates who enrolled in 2016, 1,609 applied for aid, 1,457 were judged to have need, 169 had their need fully met. 350 Federal Work-Study jobs (averaging $959). 334 state and other part-time jobs (averaging $316). In 2016, 578 non-need-based awards were made. ***Average percent of need met:*** 52. ***Average financial aid package:*** $19,215. ***Average need-based loan:*** $3964.

Average need-based gift aid: $15,556. ***Average non-need-based aid:*** $17,414. ***Average indebtedness upon graduation:*** $19,266.

APPLYING

Standardized Tests *Required for some:* SAT or ACT (for admission).

Options: electronic application, deferred entrance.

Required: high school transcript, minimum 2.5 GPA. ***Required for some:*** essay or personal statement, interview, audition, portfolio.

Application deadlines: 8/15 (freshmen), rolling (transfers).

Notification: continuous (freshmen), continuous (out-of-state freshmen), continuous (transfers).

CONTACT

Ms. Shani Lenore-Jenkins, Associate Vice President of Enrollment, Maryville University of Saint Louis, 650 Maryville University Drive, St. Louis, MO 63141-7299. *Phone:* 314-529-9350. *Toll-free phone:* 800-627-9855. *Fax:* 314-529-9927. *E-mail:* admissions@maryville.edu.

Metro Business College

Cape Girardeau, Missouri

http://www.metrobusinesscollege.edu/

CONTACT

Ms. Kyla Evans, Admissions Director, Metro Business College, 1732 North Kingshighway, Cape Girardeau, MO 63701. *Phone:* 573-334-9181. *Toll-free phone:* 888-206-4545. *Fax:* 573-334-0617.

Midwest University

Wentzville, Missouri

http://www.midwest.edu/

CONTACT

Jeoung H. Ham, Registrar/Director of Admissions, Midwest University, 851 Parr Road, Wentzville, MO 63385. *Phone:* 636-327-4645. *Fax:* 636-327-4715. *E-mail:* usa@midwest.edu.

Missouri Baptist University

St. Louis, Missouri

http://www.mobap.edu/

- **Independent Southern Baptist** comprehensive, founded 1964
- **Suburban** 65-acre campus with easy access to St. Louis
- **Endowment** $4.5 million
- **Coed** 4,631 undergraduate students, 31% full-time, 61% women, 39% men
- **Moderately difficult** entrance level, 51% of applicants were admitted

UNDERGRAD STUDENTS

1,439 full-time, 3,192 part-time. Students come from 35 states and territories; 21 other countries; 29% are from out of state; 13% Black or African American, non-Hispanic/Latino; 1% Hispanic/Latino; 0.5% Asian, non-Hispanic/Latino; 0.2% Native Hawaiian or other Pacific Islander, non-Hispanic/Latino; 0.8% American Indian or Alaska Native, non-Hispanic/Latino; 3% Two or more races, non-Hispanic/Latino; 12% Race/ethnicity unknown; 2% international; 9% transferred in; 33% live on campus.

Freshmen:

Admission: 1,005 applied, 516 admitted, 287 enrolled. ***Average high school GPA:*** 3.2.

Retention: 60% of full-time freshmen returned.

FACULTY

Total: 294, 24% full-time, 27% with terminal degrees.

Student/faculty ratio: 20:1.

ACADEMICS

Calendar: semesters. *Degrees:* certificates, associate, bachelor's, master's, doctoral, post-master's, and postbachelor's certificates.

Special study options: academic remediation for entering students, accelerated degree program, adult/continuing education programs, advanced placement credit, distance learning, double majors, honors programs, independent study, internships, off-campus study, part-time degree program, services for LD students, student-designed majors, study abroad, summer session for credit. ***ROTC:*** Army (c).

Computers: 100 computers/terminals are available on campus for general student use. Students can access the following: campus intranet, computer help desk, free student e-mail accounts, online (class) grades, online (class) registration, online (class) schedules. Campuswide network is available. 100% of college-owned or -operated housing units are wired for high-speed Internet access. Wireless service is available via entire campus.

Library: Jung-Kellogg Library. *Books:* 54,795 (physical), 6,626 (digital/electronic); *Serial titles:* 433 (physical), 117 (digital/electronic); *Databases:* 44. Weekly public service hours: 70.

STUDENT LIFE

Housing options: men-only, women-only, special housing for students with disabilities. Campus housing is university owned. Freshman applicants given priority for college housing.

Activities and organizations: drama/theater group, student-run radio station, choral group, Enactus: Students in Free Enterprise, Amp Ministries, Student Missouri State Teacher's Association, Gamma Delta Sigma, Ministerial Alliance, national fraternities, national sororities.

Athletics Member NAIA. ***Intercollegiate sports:*** baseball M(s), basketball M(s)/W(s), bowling M(s)(c)/W(s)(c), cheerleading M(s)/W(s), cross-country running M(s)/W(s), football M(s), golf M(s)/W(s), lacrosse M(s)(c)/W(s)(c), soccer M(s)/W(s), softball W(s), tennis M(s)/W(s), track and field M(s)/W(s), volleyball M(s)/W(s), wrestling M(s)/W(s). ***Intramural sports:*** basketball M/W, bowling M/W, football M/W, soccer M/W, softball M/W, volleyball M/W.

Campus security: 24-hour emergency response devices and patrols, late-night transport/escort service, controlled dormitory access, self-defense classes.

Student services: health clinic, personal/psychological counseling.

COSTS & FINANCIAL AID

Costs (2017–18) ***Comprehensive fee:*** $36,400 includes full-time tuition ($24,764), mandatory fees ($1256), and room and board ($10,380). Full-time tuition and fees vary according to course load and location. Part-time tuition: $857 per credit hour. Part-time tuition and fees vary according to course load and location. ***Required fees:*** $27 per credit hour part-time. ***Room and board:*** Room and board charges vary according to board plan and housing facility. ***Payment plan:*** installment. ***Waivers:*** children of alumni, senior citizens, and employees or children of employees.

Financial Aid Of all full-time matriculated undergraduates who enrolled in 2016, 1,254 applied for aid, 1,117 were judged to have need, 264 had their need fully met. 553 Federal Work-Study jobs (averaging $1711). In 2016, 36 non-need-based awards were made. ***Average financial aid package:*** $18,734. ***Average need-based loan:*** $4546. ***Average need-based gift aid:*** $5288. ***Average non-need-based aid:*** $10,573. ***Average indebtedness upon graduation:*** $26,015.

APPLYING

Standardized Tests *Required:* SAT or ACT (for admission).

Options: electronic application.

Application fee: $35.

Required: high school transcript, minimum 2.0 GPA, 1 letter of recommendation.

Application deadlines: rolling (freshmen), rolling (transfers).

Notification: continuous (freshmen), continuous (transfers).

CONTACT

Mrs. Cynthia Sutton, Director of Admissions, Missouri Baptist University, One College Park Drive, St. Louis, MO 63141-8660. *Phone:* 877-434-1115. *Toll-free phone:* 877-434-1115 Ext. 2290. *Fax:* 314-434-7596. *E-mail:* admissions@mobap.edu.

Missouri Southern State University

Joplin, Missouri

http://www.mssu.edu/

- **State-supported** comprehensive, founded 1937
- **Small-town** 365-acre campus
- **Coed**
- **Moderately difficult** entrance level

FACULTY
Student/faculty ratio: 18:1.

ACADEMICS
Calendar: semesters. *Degrees:* certificates, associate, bachelor's, and master's.
Library: George A. Spiva Library. *Books:* 262,310 (physical), 362,170 (digital/electronic); *Serial titles:* 6,081 (physical); *Databases:* 221.

STUDENT LIFE
Housing options: on-campus residence required for freshman year; coed, men-only, women-only. Campus housing is university owned. Freshman campus housing is guaranteed.

Activities and organizations: drama/theater group, student-run newspaper, radio and television station, choral group, marching band, national fraternities, national sororities.

Athletics Member NCAA. All Division II.

Campus security: 24-hour emergency response devices and patrols, late-night transport/escort service, controlled dormitory access, security at campus events, emergency vehicle assistance, safety awareness information to students.

Student services: health clinic, personal/psychological counseling.

COSTS & FINANCIAL AID
Costs (2016–17) ***Tuition:*** state resident $5311 full-time, $177 per credit hour part-time; nonresident $10,717 full-time, $357 per credit hour part-time. ***Required fees:*** $566 full-time, $168 per term part-time. ***Room and board:*** $6627.

Financial Aid Of all full-time matriculated undergraduates who enrolled in 2014, 2,960 applied for aid, 1,839 were judged to have need, 442 had their need fully met. 61 Federal Work-Study jobs (averaging $2807). 223 state and other part-time jobs (averaging $3848). In 2014, 224 non-need-based awards were made. ***Average percent of need met:*** 70. ***Average financial aid package:*** $8485. ***Average need-based loan:*** $3806. ***Average need-based gift aid:*** $4635. ***Average non-need-based aid:*** $2553. ***Average indebtedness upon graduation:*** $20,638.

APPLYING
Standardized Tests *Required:* SAT or ACT (for admission), SAT and SAT Subject Tests or ACT (for admission). *Recommended:* ACT (for admission).

Options: electronic application, deferred entrance.

Application fee: $25.

Required: high school transcript, minimum 2.3 GPA, class rank of at least 50%, minimum recommended ACT score of at 21. ***Required for some:*** 2 letters of recommendation.

CONTACT
Mr. Derek Skaggs, Director of Enrollment Services, Missouri Southern State University, 3950 East Newman Road, Hearnes 106B, Joplin, MO 64801-1595. *Phone:* 417-625-9537. *Toll-free phone:* 866-818-MSSU. *Fax:* 417-659-4429. *E-mail:* admissions@mssu.edu.

Missouri State University

Springfield, Missouri

http://www.missouristate.edu/

- **State-supported** comprehensive, founded 1905
- **Suburban** 225-acre campus
- **Coed** 18,980 undergraduate students, 77% full-time, 58% women, 42% men
- **Moderately difficult** entrance level, 16% of applicants were admitted

UNDERGRAD STUDENTS
14,540 full-time, 4,440 part-time. 13% are from out of state; 5% Black or African American, non-Hispanic/Latino; 3% Hispanic/Latino; 1% Asian, non-Hispanic/Latino; 0.1% Native Hawaiian or other Pacific Islander, non-Hispanic/Latino; 0.5% American Indian or Alaska Native, non-Hispanic/Latino; 3% Two or more races, non-Hispanic/Latino; 1% Race/ethnicity unknown; 5% international; 9% transferred in; 24% live on campus.

Freshmen:
Admission: 7,445 applied, 1,196 admitted, 3,244 enrolled. ***Average high school GPA:*** 3.63. ***Test scores:*** SAT critical reading scores over 500: 67%; SAT math scores over 500: 72%; ACT scores over 18: 97%; SAT critical reading scores over 600: 27%; SAT math scores over 600: 29%; ACT scores over 24: 51%; SAT critical reading scores over 700: 5%; SAT math scores over 700: 3%; ACT scores over 30: 8%.

Retention: 78% of full-time freshmen returned.

FACULTY
Total: 1,142, 64% full-time, 58% with terminal degrees.
Student/faculty ratio: 21:1.

ACADEMICS
Calendar: semesters. *Degrees:* certificates, bachelor's, master's, doctoral, post-master's, and postbachelor's certificates.

Special study options: accelerated degree program, advanced placement credit, cooperative education, distance learning, double majors, English as a second language, freshman honors college, honors programs, independent study, internships, off-campus study, part-time degree program, services for LD students, student-designed majors, study abroad, summer session for credit. ***ROTC:*** Army (b).

Computers: Students can access the following: campus intranet, computer help desk, free student e-mail accounts, online (class) grades, online (class) registration, online (class) schedules. Campuswide network is available. 100% of college-owned or -operated housing units are wired for high-speed Internet access. Wireless service is available via classrooms, computer centers, computer labs, learning centers, libraries, student centers.
Library: Meyer Library.

STUDENT LIFE
Housing options: on-campus residence required for freshman year; coed, special housing for students with disabilities. Campus housing is university owned. Freshman campus housing is guaranteed.

Activities and organizations: drama/theater group, student-run newspaper, radio and television station, choral group, marching band, Residence Hall Association, Campus Ministries, Fraternity and Sorority Life, Student Government Association, Student Activities Council, national fraternities, national sororities.

Athletics Member NCAA. All Division I except football (Division I-AA). ***Intercollegiate sports:*** baseball M(s), basketball M(s)/W(s), bowling M(c)/W(c), cross-country running W(s), equestrian sports M(c)/W(c), field hockey W(s), golf M(s)/W(s), ice hockey M(c), lacrosse M(c), racquetball M(c)/W(c), soccer M(s)/W(s), softball W(s), swimming and diving M(s)/W(s), track and field W(s), ultimate Frisbee M(c)/W(c), volleyball M(c)/W(s), wrestling M(c). ***Intramural sports:*** basketball M/W, bowling M/W, football M/W, golf M/W, racquetball M/W, soccer M/W, softball M/W, table tennis M/W, tennis M/W, track and field W, ultimate Frisbee M/W, volleyball M/W, weight lifting M/W.

Campus security: 24-hour emergency response devices and patrols, late-night transport/escort service, controlled dormitory access, on-campus police substation.

Student services: health clinic, personal/psychological counseling, legal services.

COSTS & FINANCIAL AID
Costs (2016–17) ***Tuition:*** state resident $6150 full-time, $258 per credit hour part-time; nonresident $13,020 full-time, $518 per credit hour part-time. Full-time tuition and fees vary according to course level, course load, and program. Part-time tuition and fees vary according to course level, course load, and program. ***Required fees:*** $910 full-time. ***Room and board:*** $8288. Room and board charges vary according to board plan, housing facility, and location. ***Payment plan:*** deferred payment. ***Waivers:*** children of alumni, senior citizens, and employees or children of employees.

Financial Aid Of all full-time matriculated undergraduates who enrolled in 2016, 11,741 applied for aid, 9,025 were judged to have need, 1,317 had their need fully met. In 2016, 1746 non-need-based awards were made. ***Average percent of need met:*** 60. ***Average financial aid package:*** $9171. ***Average need-based loan:*** $4198. ***Average need-based gift aid:*** $6017. ***Average non-need-based aid:*** $3332. ***Average indebtedness upon graduation:*** $24,734.

APPLYING
Standardized Tests *Required:* SAT or ACT (for admission).
Options: electronic application.

Application fee: $35.

Required: high school transcript. ***Required for some:*** essay or personal statement, interview.

CONTACT

Mr. Andrew Wright, Director of Admissions, Missouri State University, 901 South National Avenue, Springfield, MO 65897. *Phone:* 417-836-5517. *Toll-free phone:* 800-492-7900. *Fax:* 417-836-5137.
E-mail: info@missouristate.edu.

Missouri University of Science and Technology

Rolla, Missouri

http://www.mst.edu/

- **State-supported** university, founded 1870, part of University of Missouri System
- **Small-town** 284-acre campus
- **Coed** 6,909 undergraduate students, 90% full-time, 23% women, 77% men
- **Very difficult** entrance level, 79% of applicants were admitted

UNDERGRAD STUDENTS

6,215 full-time, 694 part-time. 17% are from out of state; 3% Black or African American, non-Hispanic/Latino; 3% Hispanic/Latino; 3% Asian, non-Hispanic/Latino; 0.4% American Indian or Alaska Native, non-Hispanic/Latino; 3% Two or more races, non-Hispanic/Latino; 3% Race/ethnicity unknown; 4% international; 33% live on campus.

Freshmen:

Admission: 4,166 applied, 3,305 admitted. ***Average high school GPA:*** 3.61. ***Test scores:*** SAT critical reading scores over 500: 95%; SAT math scores over 500: 95%; SAT writing scores over 500: 75%; ACT scores over 18: 97%; SAT critical reading scores over 600: 63%; SAT math scores over 600: 76%; SAT writing scores over 600: 41%; ACT scores over 24: 88%; SAT critical reading scores over 700: 18%; SAT math scores over 700: 26%; SAT writing scores over 700: 10%; ACT scores over 30: 38%.

FACULTY

Total: 491, 76% full-time, 81% with terminal degrees.

Student/faculty ratio: 19:1.

ACADEMICS

Calendar: semesters. *Degrees:* bachelor's, master's, doctoral, and postbachelor's certificates.

Special study options: accelerated degree program, adult/continuing education programs, advanced placement credit, cooperative education, distance learning, double majors, English as a second language, freshman honors college, honors programs, independent study, internships, off-campus study, part-time degree program, services for LD students, study abroad, summer session for credit. ***ROTC:*** Army (b), Air Force (b).

Computers: 969 computers/terminals and 5,720 ports are available on campus for general student use. Students can access the following: campus intranet, computer help desk, free student e-mail accounts, online (class) grades, online (class) registration, online (class) schedules. Campuswide network is available. 100% of college-owned or -operated housing units are wired for high-speed Internet access. Wireless service is available via entire campus.

Library: Curtis Laws Wilson Library. *Books:* 295,079 (physical), 348,067 (digital/electronic); *Serial titles:* 14,178 (physical), 79,586 (digital/electronic); *Databases:* 180. Weekly public service hours: 112; students can reserve study rooms.

STUDENT LIFE

Housing options: on-campus residence required through sophomore year; coed, cooperative, special housing for students with disabilities. Campus housing is university owned and leased by the school. Freshman campus housing is guaranteed.

Activities and organizations: drama/theater group, student-run newspaper, radio station, choral group, marching band, Academic Organizations, Honor Society, Special Interest Group, Greek Organizations, Recreational and Sports Club, national fraternities, national sororities.

Athletics Member NCAA. All Division II. ***Intercollegiate sports:*** baseball M(s), basketball M(s)/W(s), cross-country running M(s)/W(s), football M(s), soccer M(s)/W(s), softball W(s), swimming and diving M(s), track and field M(s)/W(s), volleyball W(s). ***Intramural sports:*** badminton M/W, basketball M/W, bowling M/W, football M/W, golf M/W, racquetball M/W, soccer M/W, softball M/W, swimming and diving M/W, table tennis M/W, tennis M/W, track and field M/W, ultimate Frisbee M/W, volleyball M/W, water polo M/W, weight lifting M/W.

Campus security: 24-hour emergency response devices and patrols, student patrols, late-night transport/escort service, controlled dormitory access, crime prevention programs.

Student services: health clinic, personal/psychological counseling, women's center.

COSTS & FINANCIAL AID

Costs (2017–18) ***Tuition:*** state resident $8286 full-time, $276 per credit hour part-time; nonresident $25,554 full-time, $842 per credit hour part-time. Full-time tuition and fees vary according to course load, degree level, program, and student level. Part-time tuition and fees vary according to course load, degree level, program, and student level. ***Required fees:*** $1351 full-time, $49 per credit hour part-time. ***Room and board:*** $9780. Room and board charges vary according to board plan, housing facility, and location. ***Payment plan:*** installment. ***Waivers:*** employees or children of employees.

Financial Aid Of all full-time matriculated undergraduates who enrolled in 2015, 3,545 applied for aid, 3,375 were judged to have need, 980 had their need fully met. 156 Federal Work-Study jobs (averaging $1675). 17 state and other part-time jobs (averaging $639). In 2015, 703 non-need-based awards were made. ***Average percent of need met:*** 35. ***Average financial aid package:*** $14,980. ***Average need-based loan:*** $7472. ***Average need-based gift aid:*** $7931. ***Average non-need-based aid:*** $5583. ***Average indebtedness upon graduation:*** $28,259.

APPLYING

Standardized Tests *Required:* SAT or ACT (for admission). *Recommended:* ACT (for admission).

Options: electronic application, deferred entrance.

Application fee: $50.

Required: high school transcript. ***Required for some:*** essay or personal statement, interview.

Application deadlines: 7/1 (freshmen), rolling (out-of-state freshmen), 8/20 (transfers).

Notification: continuous until 10/1 (freshmen), continuous until 10/1 (out-of-state freshmen), continuous (transfers).

CONTACT

Ms. Lynn Stichnote, Admissions Office, Missouri University of Science and Technology, 300 West 13th Street, 106 Parker Hall, Rolla, MO 65409. *Phone:* 573-341-4075. *Toll-free phone:* 800-522-0938. *Fax:* 573-341-4082. *E-mail:* admissions@mst.edu.

Missouri Valley College

Marshall, Missouri

http://www.moval.edu/

- **Independent** comprehensive, founded 1889, affiliated with Presbyterian Church
- **Small-town** 140-acre campus with easy access to Kansas City
- **Endowment** $5.7 million
- **Coed** 1,785 undergraduate students, 74% full-time, 44% women, 56% men
- **Minimally difficult** entrance level, 46% of applicants were admitted

UNDERGRAD STUDENTS

1,329 full-time, 456 part-time. Students come from 43 states and territories; 42 other countries; 28% are from out of state; 15% Black or African American, non-Hispanic/Latino; 8% Hispanic/Latino; 0.8% Asian, non-Hispanic/Latino; 0.7% Native Hawaiian or other Pacific Islander, non-Hispanic/Latino; 0.4% American Indian or Alaska Native, non-Hispanic/Latino; 4% Two or more races, non-Hispanic/Latino; 3% Race/ethnicity unknown; 12% international; 9% transferred in; 73% live on campus.

Freshmen:
Admission: 3,265 applied, 1,518 admitted, 451 enrolled. ***Average high school GPA:*** 2.9. ***Test scores:*** SAT critical reading scores over 500: 29%; ACT scores over 18: 68%; SAT critical reading scores over 600: 3%; ACT scores over 24: 9%; ACT scores over 30: 1%.
Retention: 43% of full-time freshmen returned.

FACULTY
Total: 171, 50% full-time.
Student/faculty ratio: 16:1.

ACADEMICS
Calendar: semesters plus 2 summer sessions. *Degrees:* associate, bachelor's, and master's.
Special study options: academic remediation for entering students, adult/continuing education programs, advanced placement credit, cooperative education, distance learning, double majors, English as a second language, honors programs, independent study, internships, part-time degree program, services for LD students, student-designed majors, study abroad, summer session for credit. ***ROTC:*** Army (b).
Computers: 300 computers/terminals are available on campus for general student use. Students can access the following: campus intranet, computer help desk, free student e-mail accounts, online (class) grades, online (class) registration, online (class) schedules. Campuswide network is available. 100% of college-owned or -operated housing units are wired for high-speed Internet access. Wireless service is available via entire campus.
Library: Murrell Memorial Library plus 1 other. *Books:* 77,222 (physical), 281,938 (digital/electronic); *Databases:* 37.

STUDENT LIFE
Housing options: coed, men-only, women-only. Campus housing is university owned. Freshman campus housing is guaranteed.
Activities and organizations: drama/theater group, student-run newspaper, radio and television station, choral group, Tau Kappa Epsilon, Alpha Sigma Alpha, Theta Phi Alpha, Alpha Sigma Phi, Phi Beta Sigma, national fraternities, national sororities.
Athletics Member NAIA. ***Intercollegiate sports:*** baseball M(s), basketball M(s)/W(s), cheerleading M(s)/W(s), cross-country running M(s)/W(s), football M(s), golf M(s)/W(s), lacrosse M(s)/W(s), soccer M(s)/W(s), softball W(s), tennis M(s)/W(s), track and field M(s)/W(s), volleyball M(s)/W(s), wrestling M(s)/W(s). ***Intramural sports:*** badminton M/W, baseball M, basketball M/W, bowling M/W, football M/W, soccer M/W, softball M/W, table tennis M/W, tennis M/W, volleyball M/W.
Campus security: 24-hour emergency response devices, student patrols, late-night transport/escort service, evening to 4 am patrol by trained security personnel.
Student services: health clinic, personal/psychological counseling.

COSTS & FINANCIAL AID
Costs (2016–17) ***Comprehensive fee:*** $28,150 includes full-time tuition ($18,500), mandatory fees ($1250), and room and board ($8400). Full-time tuition and fees vary according to program. Part-time tuition: $350 per credit hour. Part-time tuition and fees vary according to program. ***Required fees:*** $625 per term part-time. ***College room only:*** $4450. Room and board charges vary according to board plan, gender, housing facility, location, and student level. ***Payment plans:*** tuition prepayment, installment, deferred payment.
Financial Aid Of all full-time matriculated undergraduates who enrolled in 2014, 1,150 applied for aid, 1,127 were judged to have need, 452 had their need fully met. 119 Federal Work-Study jobs (averaging $1860). 450 state and other part-time jobs (averaging $1860). In 2014, 452 non-need-based awards were made. ***Average percent of need met:*** 85. ***Average financial aid package:*** $12,850. ***Average need-based loan:*** $3750. ***Average need-based gift aid:*** $12,850. ***Average non-need-based aid:*** $12,850. ***Average indebtedness upon graduation:*** $25,200.

APPLYING
Standardized Tests *Required:* SAT or ACT (for admission).
Options: electronic application, early admission, deferred entrance.
Required: high school transcript. ***Required for some:*** essay or personal statement, 3 letters of recommendation, interview. ***Recommended:*** minimum 2.0 GPA, interview.
Application deadlines: rolling (freshmen), rolling (transfers).
Notification: continuous (freshmen), continuous (transfers).

CONTACT
Ms. Jessica Green, Admissions and Student Visit Coordinator, Missouri Valley College, 500 East College, Marshall, MO 65340-3197. *Phone:* 660-831-4114. *Fax:* 660-831-4233. *E-mail:* admissions@moval.edu.

Missouri Western State University

St. Joseph, Missouri

http://www.missouriwestern.edu/

- **State-supported** comprehensive, founded 1915
- **Suburban** 744-acre campus with easy access to Kansas City
- **Coed** 5,120 undergraduate students, 67% full-time, 59% women, 41% men
- **Noncompetitive** entrance level, 75% of applicants were admitted

UNDERGRAD STUDENTS
3,439 full-time, 1,681 part-time. Students come from 34 states and territories; 32 other countries; 12% are from out of state; 10% Black or African American, non-Hispanic/Latino; 1% Hispanic/Latino; 2% Asian, non-Hispanic/Latino; 0.2% Native Hawaiian or other Pacific Islander, non-Hispanic/Latino; 0.5% American Indian or Alaska Native, non-Hispanic/Latino; 3% Two or more races, non-Hispanic/Latino; 3% Race/ethnicity unknown; 1% international; 7% transferred in; 21% live on campus.

Freshmen:
Admission: 3,669 applied, 2,734 admitted, 844 enrolled. ***Average high school GPA:*** 3.31. ***Test scores:*** ACT scores over 18: 80%; ACT scores over 24: 22%; ACT scores over 30: 1%.
Retention: 66% of full-time freshmen returned.

FACULTY
Total: 360, 59% full-time, 54% with terminal degrees.
Student/faculty ratio: 16:1.

ACADEMICS
Calendar: semesters. *Degrees:* certificates, associate, bachelor's, master's, and postbachelor's certificates.
Special study options: academic remediation for entering students, accelerated degree program, adult/continuing education programs, advanced placement credit, distance learning, double majors, English as a second language, freshman honors college, honors programs, independent study, internships, off-campus study, part-time degree program, services for LD students, student-designed majors, study abroad, summer session for credit. ***ROTC:*** Army (b).
Computers: Students can access the following: campus intranet, computer help desk, free student e-mail accounts, online (class) grades, online (class) registration, online (class) schedules, personal online storage. Campuswide network is available. 100% of college-owned or -operated housing units are wired for high-speed Internet access. Wireless service is available via entire campus.
Library: Missouri Western State University Library. *Books:* 229,238 (physical), 431,211 (digital/electronic); *Serial titles:* 13,079 (physical), 6,056 (digital/electronic); *Databases:* 68.

STUDENT LIFE
Housing options: on-campus residence required for freshman year; coed, special housing for students with disabilities. Campus housing is university owned.
Activities and organizations: drama/theater group, student-run newspaper, television station, choral group, marching band, national fraternities, national sororities.
Athletics Member NCAA. All Division II. ***Intercollegiate sports:*** baseball M(s), basketball M(s)/W(s), cheerleading W, cross-country running M(s)/W(s), football M(s), golf M(s)/W(s), soccer W(s), softball W(s), tennis W(s), track and field M(s)/W(s), volleyball W(s). ***Intramural sports:*** badminton M/W, basketball M/W, football M/W, sand volleyball M/W, soccer M/W, table tennis M/W, tennis M/W, volleyball M/W.
Campus security: 24-hour emergency response devices and patrols, student patrols, late-night transport/escort service, controlled dormitory access.

Student services: health clinic, personal/psychological counseling, women's center.

COSTS & FINANCIAL AID

Costs (2016–17) ***Tuition:*** state resident $5934 full-time, $198 per credit hour part-time; nonresident $12,362 full-time, $412 per credit hour part-time. Full-time tuition and fees vary according to course load, location, and program. Part-time tuition and fees vary according to course load, location, and program. ***Required fees:*** $718 full-time, $99 per credit hour part-time. ***Room and board:*** $7834; room only: $4508. Room and board charges vary according to board plan and housing facility. ***Payment plan:*** installment. ***Waivers:*** senior citizens and employees or children of employees.

Financial Aid Of all full-time matriculated undergraduates who enrolled in 2016, 311 Federal Work-Study jobs (averaging $1495). 665 state and other part-time jobs (averaging $1912).

APPLYING

Standardized Tests *Required:* SAT or ACT (for admission).

Options: electronic application, early admission.

Required: high school transcript.

Application deadlines: 5/1 (freshmen), 6/1 (transfers).

Notification: continuous (freshmen), continuous (transfers).

CONTACT

Mrs. Jamie Sweiger, Assistant Director of Admissions, Missouri Western State University, 4525 Downs Drive, St. Joseph, MO 64507-2294. *Phone:* 816-271-4183. *Toll-free phone:* 800-662-7041. *E-mail:* admission@missouriwestern.edu.

National American University

Kansas City, Missouri

http://www.national.edu/

CONTACT

Admissions Office, National American University, 7490 Northwest 87th Street, Kansas City, MO 64153. *Phone:* 816-412-5500. *Toll-free phone:* 866-628-1288. *E-mail:* zradmissions@national.edu.

National American University

Lee's Summit, Missouri

http://www.national.edu/

CONTACT

National American University, 401 NW Murray Road, Lee's Summit, MO 64081. *Toll-free phone:* 866-628-1288.

Northwest Missouri State University

Maryville, Missouri

http://www.nwmissouri.edu/

- **State-supported** comprehensive, founded 1905, part of Missouri Coordinating Board for Higher Education
- **Small-town** 370-acre campus with easy access to Kansas City
- **Endowment** $22.2 million
- **Coed** 5,628 undergraduate students, 87% full-time, 57% women, 43% men
- **Moderately difficult** entrance level, 74% of applicants were admitted

UNDERGRAD STUDENTS

4,918 full-time, 710 part-time. Students come from 36 states and territories; 31 other countries; 30% are from out of state; 6% Black or African American, non-Hispanic/Latino; 4% Hispanic/Latino; 0.7% Asian, non-Hispanic/Latino; 0.1% Native Hawaiian or other Pacific Islander, non-Hispanic/Latino; 0.3% American Indian or Alaska Native, non-Hispanic/Latino; 3% Two or more races, non-Hispanic/Latino; 2% Race/ethnicity unknown; 4% international; 5% transferred in; 37% live on campus.

Freshmen:

Admission: 5,382 applied, 3,986 admitted, 1,405 enrolled. ***Average high school GPA:*** 3.38. ***Test scores:*** ACT scores over 18: 92%; ACT scores over 24: 39%; ACT scores over 30: 4%.

Retention: 71% of full-time freshmen returned.

FACULTY

Total: 314, 83% full-time, 59% with terminal degrees.

Student/faculty ratio: 21:1.

ACADEMICS

Calendar: trimesters. *Degrees:* certificates, bachelor's, master's, post-master's, and postbachelor's certificates.

Special study options: academic remediation for entering students, advanced placement credit, distance learning, double majors, English as a second language, honors programs, independent study, internships, off-campus study, part-time degree program, services for LD students, study abroad, summer session for credit. ***ROTC:*** Army (c).

Computers: 6,500 computers/terminals and 6,000 ports are available on campus for general student use. Students can access the following: campus intranet, computer help desk, free student e-mail accounts, online (class) grades, online (class) registration, online (class) schedules, online courses with library and databases. Campuswide network is available. 100% of college-owned or -operated housing units are wired for high-speed Internet access. Wireless service is available via classrooms, computer centers, computer labs, dorm rooms, learning centers, libraries, student centers.

Library: Owens Library. *Books:* 240,370 (physical), 240,370 (digital/electronic); *Serial titles:* 33,868 (digital/electronic). Students can reserve study rooms.

STUDENT LIFE

Housing options: on-campus residence required for freshman year; coed, special housing for students with disabilities. Campus housing is university owned. Freshman campus housing is guaranteed.

Activities and organizations: drama/theater group, student-run newspaper, radio and television station, choral group, marching band, Indian Student Association, ACM, National Society of Leadership and Success, Student Senate, Resident Hall Association (RHA), national fraternities, national sororities.

Athletics Member NCAA. All Division II. ***Intercollegiate sports:*** baseball M(s), basketball M(s)/W(s), cheerleading M(s)/W(s), cross-country running M(s)/W(s), football M(s), golf W(s), soccer W(s), softball W(s), tennis M(s)/W(s), track and field M(s)/W(s), volleyball W(s). ***Intramural sports:*** badminton M/W, basketball M/W, cross-country running M/W, football M/W, golf M/W, racquetball M/W, sand volleyball M/W, skiing (cross-country) M/W, soccer M(c)/W(c), softball W, swimming and diving M/W, table tennis M/W, tennis M/W, track and field M/W, volleyball M/W, wrestling M(c).

Campus security: 24-hour emergency response devices and patrols, student patrols, late-night transport/escort service, controlled dormitory access, security personnel are all police officers.

Student services: health clinic, personal/psychological counseling, women's center.

COSTS & FINANCIAL AID

Costs (2016–17) ***Tuition:*** state resident $5418 full-time, $181 per credit hour part-time; nonresident $11,739 full-time, $391 per credit hour part-time. Full-time tuition and fees vary according to course load, location, and reciprocity agreements. Part-time tuition and fees vary according to course load and location. ***Required fees:*** $3761 full-time, $125 per credit hour part-time. ***Room and board:*** $9612; room only: $6138. Room and board charges vary according to board plan and housing facility. ***Payment plans:*** installment, deferred payment. ***Waivers:*** senior citizens and employees or children of employees.

Financial Aid Of all full-time matriculated undergraduates who enrolled in 2015, 4,147 applied for aid, 3,312 were judged to have need, 1,272 had their need fully met. 388 Federal Work-Study jobs (averaging $1263). 1,058 state and other part-time jobs (averaging $1772). In 2015, 435 non-need-based awards were made. ***Average percent of need met:*** 57. ***Average financial aid package:*** $9731. ***Average need-based loan:*** $3917. ***Average need-based gift aid:*** $6243. ***Average non-need-based aid:*** $2808. ***Average indebtedness upon graduation:*** $28,332.

APPLYING

Standardized Tests *Required:* SAT or ACT (for admission).

Options: electronic application, deferred entrance.

Required: high school transcript, minimum 2.0 GPA. ***Required for some:*** interview.

Application deadlines: rolling (freshmen), rolling (transfers).
Notification: continuous (freshmen), continuous (transfers).

CONTACT
Mrs. Tammi Grow, Associate Director of Admissions, Northwest Missouri State University, 800 University Drive, Maryville, MO 64468-6001. *Phone:* 660-562-1146. *Toll-free phone:* 800-633-1175. *Fax:* 660-562-1146. *E-mail:* admissions@nwmissouri.edu.

Ozark Christian College

Joplin, Missouri

http://www.occ.edu/

CONTACT
Mr. Troy B. Nelson, Executive Director of Admissions, Ozark Christian College, 1111 North Main Street, Joplin, MO 64801-4804.
Phone: 417-624-2518. *Toll-free phone:* 800-299-4622.
Fax: 417-624-0090.
E-mail: occadmin@occ.edu.

Park University

Parkville, Missouri

http://www.park.edu/

CONTACT
Mr. Eric Blair, Director of Undergraduate Admissions, Park University, 8700 NW River Park Drive, Campus Box 1, Parkville, MO 64152. *Phone:* 816-584-6858. *Toll-free phone:* 800-745-7275. *Fax:* 816-741-4462. *E-mail:* admissions@mail.park.edu.

Ranken Technical College

St. Louis, Missouri

http://www.ranken.edu/

- **Independent** primarily 2-year, founded 1907
- **Urban** 10-acre campus
- **Coed, primarily men**
- **Moderately difficult** entrance level

ACADEMICS
Calendar: semesters. *Degrees:* certificates, associate, and bachelor's.
Library: Ashley Gray, Jr. Learning Center.

STUDENT LIFE
Housing options: men-only, women-only. Campus housing is provided by a third party.
Activities and organizations: student-run newspaper.
Campus security: 24-hour emergency response devices and patrols.
Student services: personal/psychological counseling, women's center.

FINANCIAL AID
Financial Aid Of all full-time matriculated undergraduates who enrolled in 2015, 30 Federal Work-Study jobs (averaging $2000).

APPLYING
Options: electronic application.
Application fee: $25.
Required: essay or personal statement, high school transcript, interview.

CONTACT
Ranken Technical College, 4431 Finney Avenue, St. Louis, MO 63113. *Phone:* 314-371-0233 Ext. 4811. *Toll-free phone:* 866-4-RANKEN.

Research College of Nursing

Kansas City, Missouri

http://www.researchcollege.edu/

- **Independent** comprehensive, founded 1980, part of Rockhurst University
- **Urban** 66-acre campus with easy access to Kansas City
- **Coed, primarily women** 340 undergraduate students, 100% full-time, 90% women, 10% men
- **Moderately difficult** entrance level, 73% of applicants were admitted

UNDERGRAD STUDENTS
339 full-time, 1 part-time. Students come from 7 states and territories; 5% Black or African American, non-Hispanic/Latino; 3% Hispanic/Latino; 3% Asian, non-Hispanic/Latino; 0.3% Native Hawaiian or other Pacific Islander, non-Hispanic/Latino; 0.3% American Indian or Alaska Native, non-Hispanic/Latino; 0.6% Two or more races, non-Hispanic/Latino; 15% Race/ethnicity unknown; 2% transferred in.

Freshmen:
Admission: 339 applied, 249 admitted, 78 enrolled. ***Average high school GPA:*** 3.53. ***Test scores:*** ACT scores over 18: 100%; ACT scores over 24: 56%; ACT scores over 30: 4%.

FACULTY
Total: 29, 90% full-time, 14% with terminal degrees.
Student/faculty ratio: 7:1.

ACADEMICS
Calendar: semesters. *Degrees:* bachelor's, master's, and post-master's certificates (bachelor's degree offered jointly with Rockhurst College).
Special study options: accelerated degree program, advanced placement credit, double majors, honors programs, independent study, services for LD students, study abroad, summer session for credit. ***ROTC:*** Army (c).
Computers: 125 computers/terminals are available on campus for general student use. Students can access the following: online (class) registration. Campuswide network is available.
Library: Greenlease Library.

STUDENT LIFE
Housing options: coed, men-only, women-only. Campus housing is university owned. Freshman campus housing is guaranteed.
Activities and organizations: drama/theater group, student-run newspaper, radio station, choral group, national fraternities, national sororities.
Athletics Member NCAA. All Division II. ***Intercollegiate sports:*** baseball M(s), basketball M(s)/W(s), golf M(s)/W(s), soccer M(s)/W(s), softball W(s), tennis M(s)/W(s), volleyball W(s). ***Intramural sports:*** badminton M/W, basketball M/W, cross-country running M/W, field hockey M/W, golf M/W, lacrosse M/W, racquetball M/W, rugby M/W, soccer M/W, softball M/W, table tennis M/W, tennis M/W, volleyball M/W, weight lifting M.
Campus security: 24-hour emergency response devices and patrols, late-night transport/escort service, controlled dormitory access.
Student services: health clinic, personal/psychological counseling.

COSTS
Costs (2016–17) ***Comprehensive fee:*** $45,050 includes full-time tuition ($34,880), mandatory fees ($820), and room and board ($9350). Part-time tuition: $1164 per credit hour. Part-time tuition and fees vary according to class time. ***College room only:*** $5850. Room and board charges vary according to board plan, housing facility, and location. ***Payment plans:*** installment, deferred payment. ***Waivers:*** senior citizens and employees or children of employees.

APPLYING
Standardized Tests *Required:* SAT or ACT (for admission).
Options: electronic application, deferred entrance.
Required: high school transcript, 1 letter of recommendation. ***Recommended:*** minimum 2.8 GPA, interview.
Application deadlines: 6/30 (freshmen), 2/15 (transfers).
Notification: 8/15 (freshmen), 6/20 (out-of-state freshmen), 3/15 (transfers).

CONTACT
Mr. Kyle Johnson, Director of Admission, Research College of Nursing, 1100 Rockhurst Road, Kansas City, MO 64110. *Phone:* 816-501-4000. *E-mail:* kyle.johnson@rockhurst.edu.

Rockhurst University
Kansas City, Missouri
http://www.rockhurst.edu/

- **Independent Roman Catholic (Jesuit)** comprehensive, founded 1910
- **Urban** 35-acre campus
- **Endowment** $34.8 million
- **Coed** 2,042 undergraduate students, 69% full-time, 61% women, 39% men
- **Moderately difficult** entrance level, 74% of applicants were admitted

UNDERGRAD STUDENTS
1,409 full-time, 633 part-time. Students come from 34 states and territories; 19 other countries; 43% are from out of state; 4% Black or African American, non-Hispanic/Latino; 8% Hispanic/Latino; 3% Asian, non-Hispanic/Latino; 0.1% Native Hawaiian or other Pacific Islander, non-Hispanic/Latino; 0.3% American Indian or Alaska Native, non-Hispanic/Latino; 4% Two or more races, non-Hispanic/Latino; 7% Race/ethnicity unknown; 1% international; 3% transferred in; 53% live on campus.

Freshmen:
Admission: 3,038 applied, 2,250 admitted, 403 enrolled. ***Average high school GPA:*** 3.68. ***Test scores:*** SAT critical reading scores over 500: 87%; SAT math scores over 500: 50%; ACT scores over 18: 98%; SAT critical reading scores over 600: 25%; SAT math scores over 600: 19%; ACT scores over 24: 67%; ACT scores over 30: 14%.

Retention: 83% of full-time freshmen returned.

FACULTY
Total: 238, 53% full-time, 61% with terminal degrees.

Student/faculty ratio: 11:1.

ACADEMICS
Calendar: semesters. *Degrees:* certificates, bachelor's, master's, doctoral, and postbachelor's certificates.

Special study options: academic remediation for entering students, accelerated degree program, advanced placement credit, cooperative education, distance learning, double majors, freshman honors college, honors programs, independent study, internships, off-campus study, part-time degree program, services for LD students, study abroad, summer session for credit. ***ROTC:*** Army (c).

Computers: 270 computers/terminals are available on campus for general student use. Students can access the following: campus intranet, computer help desk, free student e-mail accounts, online (class) grades, online (class) registration, online (class) schedules, campus portal and mobile application. Campuswide network is available. 100% of college-owned or -operated housing units are wired for high-speed Internet access. Wireless service is available via entire campus.

Library: Greenlease Library. *Books:* 112,979 (physical), 180,624 (digital/electronic); *Serial titles:* 798 (physical), 103,252 (digital/electronic); *Databases:* 110. Weekly public service hours: 85.

STUDENT LIFE
Housing options: on-campus residence required through sophomore year; coed, men-only, women-only, special housing for students with disabilities. Campus housing is university owned. Freshman campus housing is guaranteed.

Activities and organizations: drama/theater group, student-run newspaper, choral group, Student Activities Board, Student Senate, Voices for Justice, Panhellenic Sororities, IFC Fraternities, national fraternities, national sororities.

Athletics Member NCAA. All Division II. ***Intercollegiate sports:*** baseball M(s), basketball M(s)/W(s), cross-country running W(s), golf M(s)/W(s), lacrosse M(s)/W(s), soccer M(s)/W(s), softball W(s), tennis M(s)/W(s), volleyball W(s). ***Intramural sports:*** basketball M/W, bowling M/W, cheerleading M(c)/W(c), ultimate Frisbee M(c)/W(c).

Campus security: 24-hour emergency response devices and patrols, late-night transport/escort service, controlled dormitory access, closed-circuit TV monitors.

Student services: health clinic, personal/psychological counseling.

COSTS & FINANCIAL AID
Costs (2016–17) ***Comprehensive fee:*** $45,350 includes full-time tuition ($34,880), mandatory fees ($790), and room and board ($9680). Full-time tuition and fees vary according to class time and course load. Part-time tuition: $582 per semester hour. Part-time tuition and fees vary according to class time and course load. ***Required fees:*** $25 per credit hour part-time. ***College room only:*** $5880. Room and board charges vary according to board plan and housing facility. ***Payment plans:*** installment, deferred payment. ***Waivers:*** senior citizens and employees or children of employees.

Financial Aid Of all full-time matriculated undergraduates who enrolled in 2015, 1,431 applied for aid, 1,026 were judged to have need, 264 had their need fully met. In 2015, 396 non-need-based awards were made. ***Average percent of need met:*** 87. ***Average financial aid package:*** $29,123. ***Average need-based loan:*** $4521. ***Average need-based gift aid:*** $21,074. ***Average non-need-based aid:*** $19,287. ***Average indebtedness upon graduation:*** $23,753.

APPLYING
Standardized Tests *Required:* SAT or ACT (for admission).

Options: electronic application, deferred entrance.

Application fee: $25.

Required: high school transcript, minimum 2.0 GPA, 1 letter of recommendation. ***Required for some:*** essay or personal statement, interview.

Application deadlines: 6/30 (freshmen), rolling (transfers).

Notification: continuous (freshmen), continuous (transfers).

CONTACT
Kyle Johnson, Director of Freshman Admissions, Rockhurst University, 1100 Rockhurst Road, Kansas City, MO 64110-2561. *Phone:* 816-501-4100. *Toll-free phone:* 800-842-6776. *Fax:* 816-501-4142. *E-mail:* admission@rockhurst.edu.

Saint Louis Christian College
Florissant, Missouri
http://www.stlchristian.edu/

- **Independent Christian** 4-year, founded 1956
- **Suburban** 30-acre campus with easy access to St. Louis
- **Endowment** $1.1 million
- **Coed** 113 undergraduate students, 83% full-time, 42% women, 58% men
- **Minimally difficult** entrance level, 27% of applicants were admitted

UNDERGRAD STUDENTS
94 full-time, 19 part-time. Students come from 9 states and territories; 2 other countries; 34% are from out of state; 37% Black or African American, non-Hispanic/Latino; 3% Two or more races, non-Hispanic/Latino; 2% international; 12% transferred in; 68% live on campus.

Freshmen:
Admission: 51 applied, 14 admitted, 14 enrolled. ***Average high school GPA:*** 2.52.

Retention: 55% of full-time freshmen returned.

FACULTY
Total: 26, 23% full-time, 8% with terminal degrees.

Student/faculty ratio: 9:1.

ACADEMICS
Calendar: semesters. *Degrees:* associate and bachelor's.

Special study options: academic remediation for entering students, accelerated degree program, adult/continuing education programs, advanced placement credit, double majors, independent study, internships, part-time degree program, services for LD students, study abroad, summer session for credit.

Computers: 10 computers/terminals are available on campus for general student use. Students can access the following: computer help desk, free student e-mail accounts, online (class) grades, online (class) registration, online (class) schedules. Campuswide network is available. 100% of college-owned or -operated housing units are wired for high-speed Internet access. Wireless service is available via entire campus.

Library: St. Louis Christian College Library. *Books:* 30,076 (physical); *Serial titles:* 332 (physical).

STUDENT LIFE
Housing options: men-only, women-only. Campus housing is university owned.
Activities and organizations: drama/theater group, choral group, World Christians Unlimited, Drama Club, pep band.
Athletics Member NCCAA. ***Intercollegiate sports:*** baseball M, basketball M/W, cross-country running W, volleyball W. ***Intramural sports:*** basketball M/W, ultimate Frisbee M/W, volleyball M/W.
Campus security: 24-hour emergency response devices and patrols, controlled dormitory access, night security.
Student services: personal/psychological counseling.

COSTS & FINANCIAL AID
Costs (2016–17) ***Comprehensive fee:*** $15,845 includes full-time tuition ($10,850), mandatory fees ($195), and room and board ($4800). ***Room and board:*** Room and board charges vary according to housing facility. ***Payment plan:*** installment. ***Waivers:*** employees or children of employees.
Financial Aid Of all full-time matriculated undergraduates who enrolled in 2014, 122 applied for aid, 113 were judged to have need, 4 had their need fully met. In 2014, 4 non-need-based awards were made. ***Average percent of need met:*** 59. ***Average financial aid package:*** $7966. ***Average need-based loan:*** $3797. ***Average need-based gift aid:*** $4828. ***Average non-need-based aid:*** $3257. ***Average indebtedness upon graduation:*** $32,975.

APPLYING
Standardized Tests *Required:* SAT or ACT (for admission).
Options: electronic application.
Application fee: $30.
Required: essay or personal statement, high school transcript, 2 letters of recommendation, minimum ACT score of 18 or SAT of 940. ***Required for some:*** interview. ***Recommended:*** minimum 2.0 GPA.
Application deadlines: 8/7 (freshmen), 8/7 (transfers).
Notification: continuous (freshmen), continuous (transfers).

CONTACT
Bob Farrar, Admissions Director, Saint Louis Christian College, 1360 Grandview Drive, Florissant, MO 63033. *Phone:* 314-837-6777 Ext. 1314. *Toll-free phone:* 800-887-SLCC. *E-mail:* bfarrar@stlchristian.edu.

St. Louis College of Health Careers
Fenton, Missouri
http://www.slchc.com/

CONTACT
St. Louis College of Health Careers, 1297 North Highway Drive, Fenton, MO 63026.

★ St. Louis College of Pharmacy
St. Louis, Missouri
http://www.stlcop.edu/

- **Independent** comprehensive, founded 1864
- **Urban** 9-acre campus with easy access to St. Louis
- **Endowment** $138.9 million
- **Coed** 539 undergraduate students, 98% full-time, 62% women, 38% men
- **Moderately difficult** entrance level, 71% of applicants were admitted

UNDERGRAD STUDENTS
528 full-time, 11 part-time. Students come from 23 states and territories; 11 other countries; 49% are from out of state; 7% Black or African American, non-Hispanic/Latino; 1% Hispanic/Latino; 20% Asian, non-Hispanic/Latino; 0.2% Native Hawaiian or other Pacific Islander, non-Hispanic/Latino; 0.2% American Indian or Alaska Native, non-Hispanic/Latino; 2% Two or more races, non-Hispanic/Latino; 6% Race/ethnicity unknown; 5% international; 11% transferred in; 57% live on campus.

Freshmen:
Admission: 322 applied, 230 admitted, 120 enrolled. ***Average high school GPA:*** 3.65. ***Test scores:*** ACT scores over 18: 100%; ACT scores over 24: 82%; ACT scores over 30: 18%.
Retention: 90% of full-time freshmen returned.

FACULTY
Total: 161, 69% full-time, 85% with terminal degrees.
Student/faculty ratio: 10:1.

ACADEMICS
Calendar: semesters. *Degree:* bachelor's and doctoral.
Special study options: academic remediation for entering students, advanced placement credit, independent study, internships, services for LD students, study abroad, summer session for credit. ***ROTC:*** Army (c), Navy (c), Air Force (c).
Computers: 1,390 computers/terminals and 3,760 ports are available on campus for general student use. Students can access the following: campus intranet, computer help desk, free student e-mail accounts, online (class) grades, online (class) registration, online (class) schedules. Campuswide network is available. 100% of college-owned or -operated housing units are wired for high-speed Internet access. Wireless service is available via entire campus.
Library: O. J. Cloughly Alumni Library. *Books:* 56,675 (physical), 175,165 (digital/electronic); *Serial titles:* 63 (physical), 217 (digital/electronic); *Databases:* 64. Weekly public service hours: 101; study areas open 24 hours, 5-7 days a week; students can reserve study rooms.

STUDENT LIFE
Housing options: on-campus residence required through sophomore year; coed, special housing for students with disabilities. Campus housing is university owned. Freshman applicants given priority for college housing.
Activities and organizations: drama/theater group, student-run newspaper, choral group, Outdoor Club, Student Body Union, International Student Organization, Student Pharmacists Association, Student Organization for Drug and Alcohol Awareness, national fraternities, national sororities.
Athletics Member NAIA. ***Intercollegiate sports:*** basketball M(s)/W(s), cross-country running W(s), soccer M(s)/W(s), softball W(s), tennis M(s)/W(s), track and field M(s)/W(s), volleyball W(s). ***Intramural sports:*** basketball M/W, cheerleading W(c), football M/W, golf M(c)/W(c), rugby M(c), soccer M/W, tennis M(c)/W(c), volleyball M(c)/W.
Campus security: 24-hour emergency response devices and patrols, late-night transport/escort service, controlled dormitory access.
Student services: personal/psychological counseling.

COSTS & FINANCIAL AID
Costs (2016–17) ***Comprehensive fee:*** $38,711 includes full-time tuition ($27,400), mandatory fees ($1220), and room and board ($10,091). Full-time tuition and fees vary according to student level. Part-time tuition: $914 per credit hour. ***Required fees:*** $1220 per year part-time. ***College room only:*** $5880. Room and board charges vary according to board plan and housing facility. ***Payment plan:*** deferred payment. ***Waivers:*** employees or children of employees.
Financial Aid Of all full-time matriculated undergraduates who enrolled in 2015, 587 applied for aid, 537 were judged to have need, 47 had their need fully met. 138 Federal Work-Study jobs (averaging $854). In 2015, 125 non-need-based awards were made. ***Average percent of need met:*** 48. ***Average financial aid package:*** $16,526. ***Average need-based loan:*** $5789. ***Average need-based gift aid:*** $12,168. ***Average non-need-based aid:*** $9403. ***Average indebtedness upon graduation:*** $112,161.

APPLYING
Standardized Tests *Required:* SAT or ACT (for admission).
Options: electronic application, early admission, early decision, deferred entrance.
Application fee: $55.
Required: essay or personal statement, high school transcript, minimum 3.0 GPA, 3 letters of recommendation, letter of reference from science teacher. ***Required for some:*** interview.
Application deadlines: 3/1 (freshmen), 3/1 (transfers).
Early decision deadline: 12/15.

A ★ indicates that the school has detailed information with a Premium Profile on Petersons.com.

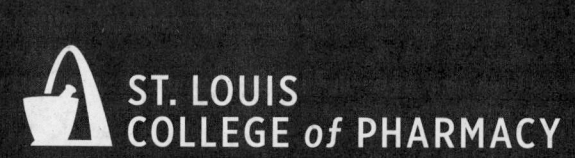

Notification: 4/1 (freshmen), 5/1 (transfers), 1/15 (early decision).

CONTACT

Mrs. Connie Horrall, Administrative Assistant, St. Louis College of Pharmacy, 4588 Parkview Place, St. Louis, MO 63110-1088. *Phone:* 314-446-8328. *Toll-free phone:* 800-278-5267. *Fax:* 314-446-8310. *E-mail:* connie.horrall@stlcop.edu.

See this page for display ad and page 1494 for the College Close-Up.

Saint Louis University

St. Louis, Missouri

http://www.slu.edu/

- **Independent Roman Catholic (Jesuit)** university, founded 1818
- **Urban** 286-acre campus
- **Endowment** $1.1 billion
- **Coed** 7,454 undergraduate students, 91% full-time, 59% women, 41% men
- 65% of applicants were admitted

UNDERGRAD STUDENTS

6,747 full-time, 707 part-time. Students come from 50 states and territories; 59 other countries; 65% are from out of state; 6% Black or African American, non-Hispanic/Latino; 5% Hispanic/Latino; 9% Asian, non-Hispanic/Latino; 0.1% American Indian or Alaska Native, non-Hispanic/Latino; 4% Two or more races, non-Hispanic/Latino; 1% Race/ethnicity unknown; 6% international; 5% transferred in; 46% live on campus.

Freshmen:

Admission: 12,737 applied, 8,258 admitted, 1,559 enrolled. ***Average high school GPA:*** 3.89. ***Test scores:*** SAT critical reading scores over 500: 86%; SAT math scores over 500: 95%; ACT scores over 18: 100%; SAT critical reading scores over 600: 54%; SAT math scores over 600: 65%; ACT scores over 24: 91%; SAT critical reading scores over 700: 10%; SAT math scores over 700: 17%; ACT scores over 30: 37%.

Retention: 92% of full-time freshmen returned.

FACULTY

Total: 1,221, 60% full-time, 62% with terminal degrees.

Student/faculty ratio: 9:1.

ACADEMICS

Calendar: semesters. *Degrees:* certificates, bachelor's, master's, doctoral, post-master's, and postbachelor's certificates.

Special study options: academic remediation for entering students, accelerated degree program, adult/continuing education programs, advanced placement credit, cooperative education, distance learning, double majors, English as a second language, honors programs, independent study, internships, off-campus study, part-time degree program, services for LD students, student-designed majors, study abroad, summer session for credit. ***ROTC:*** Army (c), Air Force (b).

Unusual degree programs: 3-2 engineering with Washington University in St. Louis.

Computers: 1,091 computers/terminals and 5,610 ports are available on campus for general student use. Students can access the following: campus intranet, computer help desk, free student e-mail accounts, online (class) grades, online (class) registration, online (class) schedules. Campuswide network is available. 100% of college-owned or -operated housing units are wired for high-speed Internet access. Wireless service is available via entire campus.

Library: Pius XII Memorial Library plus 2 others. *Books:* 1.9 million (physical), 13,083 (digital/electronic); *Serial titles:* 686 (physical), 11,948 (digital/electronic); *Databases:* 477. Weekly public service hours: 141; study areas open 24 hours, 5-7 days a week; students can reserve study rooms.

STUDENT LIFE

Housing options: on-campus residence required through sophomore year; coed, men-only, women-only, special housing for students with disabilities. Campus housing is university owned and leased by the school. Freshman campus housing is guaranteed.

Activities and organizations: drama/theater group, student-run newspaper, radio and television station, choral group, Alpha Phi Omega,

Alpha Epsilon Delta, Habitat for Humanity, Interfraternity Council, Panhellenic Council, national fraternities, national sororities.

Athletics Member NCAA. All Division I. ***Intercollegiate sports:*** badminton M(c)/W(c), baseball M(s), basketball M(s)/W(s), bowling M(c)/W(c), crew M(c)/W(c), cross-country running M(s)/W(s), equestrian sports M(c)/W(c), fencing M(c)/W(c), field hockey W(s), golf M(c)/W(c), ice hockey M(c), lacrosse M(c)/W(c), racquetball M(c)/W(c), rugby M(c), soccer M(s)/W(s), softball W(s), swimming and diving M(s)/W(s), table tennis M(c)/W(c), tennis M(s)/W(s), track and field M(s)/W(s), ultimate Frisbee M(c)/W(c), volleyball M(c)/W(s), water polo M(c)/W(c). ***Intramural sports:*** badminton M/W, basketball M/W, bowling M/W, football M/W, golf M/W, racquetball M/W, sand volleyball M/W, soccer M/W, softball M/W, squash M/W, table tennis M/W, triathlon M/W, ultimate Frisbee M/W, volleyball M/W.

Campus security: 24-hour emergency response devices and patrols, late-night transport/escort service, controlled dormitory access, prevention awareness program, bike patrol, self-defense classes, shuttles, video cameras, limited dorm access.

Student services: health clinic, personal/psychological counseling, women's center.

COSTS & FINANCIAL AID

Costs (2016–17) ***Comprehensive fee:*** $51,366 includes full-time tuition ($40,100), mandatory fees ($626), and room and board ($10,640). Full-time tuition and fees vary according to course level, course load, degree level, location, program, and reciprocity agreements. Part-time tuition: $1400 per credit hour. Part-time tuition and fees vary according to course level, course load, degree level, location, program, and reciprocity agreements. ***Required fees:*** $198 per term part-time. ***College room only:*** $5974. Room and board charges vary according to board plan, housing facility, and location. ***Payment plan:*** installment. ***Waivers:*** children of alumni and employees or children of employees.

Financial Aid Of all full-time matriculated undergraduates who enrolled in 2015, 4,768 applied for aid, 4,105 were judged to have need, 929 had their need fully met. 623 Federal Work-Study jobs (averaging $1794). 203 state and other part-time jobs (averaging $1771). In 2015, 2446 non-need-based awards were made. ***Average percent of need met:*** 72. ***Average financial aid package:*** $26,841. ***Average need-based loan:*** $4793. ***Average need-based gift aid:*** $22,446. ***Average non-need-based aid:*** $16,283. ***Average indebtedness upon graduation:*** $33,299.

APPLYING

Standardized Tests *Required:* SAT or ACT (for admission).

Options: electronic application, early admission, deferred entrance.

Required: essay or personal statement, high school transcript, minimum 2.5 GPA. ***Recommended:*** 2 letters of recommendation, interview, secondary school report form, health examination.

Application deadlines: 8/20 (freshmen), 8/20 (transfers).

Notification: continuous until 11/1 (freshmen), continuous until 2/1 (transfers).

CONTACT

Jean M. Gilman-Cox, Assistant Vice President, Office of Admission, Saint Louis University, One North Grand Boulevard, DuBourg Hall, Room 119, St. Louis, MO 63103. *Phone:* 314-977-2500. *Toll-free phone:* 800-758-3678. *Fax:* 314-977-7136. *E-mail:* admission@slu.edu.

Saint Luke's College of Health Sciences

Kansas City, Missouri

http://www.saintlukescollege.edu/

CONTACT

Mrs. Jennifer Wright, Student Services Associate, Saint Luke's College of Health Sciences, 624 Westport Road, Kansas City, MO 64111. *Phone:* 816-932-8629. *Fax:* 816-932-9064.

Southeast Missouri State University

Cape Girardeau, Missouri

http://www.semo.edu/

- **State-supported** comprehensive, founded 1873, part of Missouri Coordinating Board for Higher Education
- **Small-town** 400-acre campus
- **Endowment** $64.9 million
- **Coed** 10,693 undergraduate students, 74% full-time, 57% women, 43% men
- **Moderately difficult** entrance level, 83% of applicants were admitted

UNDERGRAD STUDENTS

7,896 full-time, 2,797 part-time. 19% are from out of state; 10% Black or African American, non-Hispanic/Latino; 2% Hispanic/Latino; 1% Asian, non-Hispanic/Latino; 0.4% American Indian or Alaska Native, non-Hispanic/Latino; 0.7% Two or more races, non-Hispanic/Latino; 0.8% Race/ethnicity unknown; 7% international; 5% transferred in; 31% live on campus.

Freshmen:

Admission: 5,184 applied, 4,293 admitted, 1,858 enrolled. ***Average high school GPA:*** 3.43. ***Test scores:*** SAT critical reading scores over 500: 55%; SAT math scores over 500: 60%; ACT scores over 18: 95%; SAT critical reading scores over 600: 18%; SAT math scores over 600: 23%; ACT scores over 24: 37%; SAT critical reading scores over 700: 8%; SAT math scores over 700: 5%; ACT scores over 30: 5%.

Retention: 74% of full-time freshmen returned.

FACULTY

Total: 581, 69% full-time, 59% with terminal degrees.

Student/faculty ratio: 21:1.

ACADEMICS

Calendar: semesters. *Degrees:* certificates, associate, bachelor's, master's, post-master's, and postbachelor's certificates.

Special study options: academic remediation for entering students, accelerated degree program, adult/continuing education programs, advanced placement credit, distance learning, double majors, English as a second language, honors programs, independent study, internships, off-campus study, part-time degree program, services for LD students, student-designed majors, study abroad, summer session for credit. ***ROTC:*** Air Force (b).

Computers: 1,550 computers/terminals are available on campus for general student use. Students can access the following: campus intranet, computer help desk, free student e-mail accounts, online (class) grades, online (class) registration, online (class) schedules. Campuswide network is available. 100% of college-owned or -operated housing units are wired for high-speed Internet access. Wireless service is available via classrooms, computer centers, computer labs, dorm rooms, learning centers, libraries, student centers.

Library: Kent Library. *Books:* 488,369 (physical), 180,596 (digital/electronic); *Serial titles:* 11,646 (physical), 66,947 (digital/electronic); *Databases:* 135. Weekly public service hours: 92.

STUDENT LIFE

Housing options: on-campus residence required through sophomore year; coed, special housing for students with disabilities. Campus housing is university owned. Freshman campus housing is guaranteed.

Activities and organizations: drama/theater group, student-run newspaper, radio and television station, choral group, marching band, Student Government, Student Activities Council, Greek Life, Residence Hall Association, International Students Association, national fraternities, national sororities.

Athletics Member NCAA. All Division I. ***Intercollegiate sports:*** baseball M(s), basketball M(s)/W(s), cheerleading M(s)/W(s), cross-country running M(s)/W(s), football M(s), gymnastics W(s), soccer W(s), softball W(s), tennis W(s), track and field M(s)/W(s), volleyball W(s). ***Intramural sports:*** basketball M/W, bowling M/W, equestrian sports M(c)/W(c), fencing M/W, football M/W, golf M/W, racquetball M/W, riflery M/W, rock climbing M/W, rugby M/W, soccer M/W, softball M/W, swimming and diving M/W, table tennis M/W, tennis M/W, ultimate Frisbee M/W, volleyball M/W, weight lifting M/W.

Campus security: 24-hour emergency response devices and patrols, late-night transport/escort service, controlled dormitory access.

Student services: health clinic, personal/psychological counseling.

COSTS & FINANCIAL AID

Costs (2016–17) ***Tuition:*** state resident $5979 full-time, $199 per credit hour part-time; nonresident $11,364 full-time, $379 per credit hour part-time. Full-time tuition and fees vary according to course load and location. Part-time tuition and fees vary according to course load and location. ***Required fees:*** $1011 full-time, $34 per credit hour part-time. ***Room and board:*** $8508. Room and board charges vary according to board plan and housing facility. ***Payment plans:*** installment, deferred payment. ***Waivers:*** senior citizens and employees or children of employees.

Financial Aid Of all full-time matriculated undergraduates who enrolled in 2015, 6,073 applied for aid, 4,787 were judged to have need, 621 had their need fully met. 217 Federal Work-Study jobs (averaging $1583). 1,565 state and other part-time jobs (averaging $2172). In 2015, 1425 non-need-based awards were made. ***Average percent of need met:*** 58. ***Average financial aid package:*** $8995. ***Average need-based loan:*** $4154. ***Average need-based gift aid:*** $5990. ***Average non-need-based aid:*** $3934. ***Average indebtedness upon graduation:*** $27,991.

APPLYING

Standardized Tests *Required:* SAT or ACT (for admission).

Options: electronic application, deferred entrance.

Application fee: $30.

Required: high school transcript, minimum 2.0 GPA.

Application deadlines: 7/1 (freshmen), rolling (out-of-state freshmen), 7/1 (transfers).

Notification: 9/1 (freshmen), continuous until 9/1 (transfers).

CONTACT

Southeast Missouri State University, One University Plaza, Cape Girardeau, MO 63701-4799. *Phone:* 573-651-2590.

Southwest Baptist University

Bolivar, Missouri

http://www.sbuniv.edu/

- **Independent Southern Baptist** comprehensive, founded 1878
- **Small-town** 152-acre campus
- **Endowment** $23.5 million
- **Coed** 2,881 undergraduate students
- **Moderately difficult** entrance level, 62% of applicants were admitted

UNDERGRAD STUDENTS

63% live on campus.

Freshmen:

Admission: 1,604 applied, 992 admitted. ***Average high school GPA:*** 3.57. ***Test scores:*** ACT scores over 18: 87%; ACT scores over 24: 39%; ACT scores over 30: 5%.

Retention: 70% of full-time freshmen returned.

FACULTY

Total: 301, 49% full-time.

Student/faculty ratio: 16:1.

ACADEMICS

Calendar: 4-1-4. *Degrees:* associate, bachelor's, master's, doctoral, and post-master's certificates.

Special study options: academic remediation for entering students, advanced placement credit, cooperative education, distance learning, double majors, honors programs, independent study, internships, off-campus study, part-time degree program, services for LD students, student-designed majors, study abroad, summer session for credit. ***ROTC:*** Army (c).

Computers: 345 computers/terminals are available on campus for general student use. Students can access the following: campus intranet, computer help desk, free student e-mail accounts, online (class) grades, online (class) registration, online (class) schedules. Campuswide network is available. 100% of college-owned or -operated housing units are wired for high-speed Internet access. Wireless service is available via entire campus.

Library: Harriett K. Hutchens Library.

STUDENT LIFE

Housing options: on-campus residence required through junior year; men-only, women-only, special housing for students with disabilities. Campus housing is university owned. Freshman campus housing is guaranteed.

Activities and organizations: drama/theater group, student-run newspaper, choral group, Enactus, Student Government Association, Fellowship of Christian Athletes, Student Missouri State Teachers Association, PSY CHI.

Athletics Member NCAA. All Division II. ***Intercollegiate sports:*** baseball M(s), basketball M(s)/W(s), cheerleading M/W, cross-country running M(s)/W(s), football M(s), golf M(s), soccer M/W(s), softball W(s), tennis M(s)/W(s), track and field M(s)/W(s), volleyball W(s). ***Intramural sports:*** basketball M/W, football M/W, soccer M/W, softball M/W, table tennis M/W, volleyball M/W.

Campus security: 24-hour emergency response devices and patrols, controlled dormitory access.

Student services: health clinic, personal/psychological counseling.

COSTS & FINANCIAL AID

Costs (2016–17) ***Comprehensive fee:*** $29,900 includes full-time tuition ($21,600), mandatory fees ($840), and room and board ($7460). Full-time tuition and fees vary according to course load and location. Part-time tuition: $840 per credit hour. Part-time tuition and fees vary according to course load and location. ***Required fees:*** $180 per term part-time. ***College room only:*** $3400. Room and board charges vary according to board plan and housing facility. ***Payment plan:*** installment. ***Waivers:*** employees or children of employees.

Financial Aid Of all full-time matriculated undergraduates who enrolled in 2016, 1,592 applied for aid, 1,466 were judged to have need, 234 had their need fully met. 341 Federal Work-Study jobs (averaging $1842). In 2016, 94 non-need-based awards were made. ***Average percent of need met:*** 67. ***Average financial aid package:*** $17,297. ***Average need-based loan:*** $3982. ***Average need-based gift aid:*** $5295. ***Average non-need-based aid:*** $7267. ***Average indebtedness upon graduation:*** $26,615.

APPLYING

Standardized Tests *Required:* SAT or ACT (for admission).

Options: electronic application.

Application fee: $30.

Required: high school transcript, minimum 2.5 GPA. ***Required for some:*** 3 letters of recommendation. ***Recommended:*** essay or personal statement, interview.

Application deadlines: rolling (freshmen), rolling (transfers).

Notification: continuous (freshmen), continuous (transfers).

CONTACT

Becky Van Stavern, Director of Admissions, Southwest Baptist University, 1600 University Avenue, Bolivar, MO 65613-2597. *Phone:* 417-328-1815. *Toll-free phone:* 800-526-5859. *Fax:* 417-328-1808. *E-mail:* bvanstavern@sbuniv.edu.

Stephens College

Columbia, Missouri

http://www.stephens.edu/

- **Independent** comprehensive, founded 1833
- **Urban** 48-acre campus
- **Endowment** $46.8 million
- **Undergraduate: women only; graduate: coed** 706 undergraduate students, 84% full-time, 99% women, 1% men
- **Moderately difficult** entrance level, 54% of applicants were admitted

UNDERGRAD STUDENTS

595 full-time, 111 part-time. Students come from 36 states and territories; 2 other countries; 43% are from out of state; 15% Black or African American, non-Hispanic/Latino; 5% Hispanic/Latino; 1% Asian, non-Hispanic/Latino; 0.6% Native Hawaiian or other Pacific Islander, non-Hispanic/Latino; 1% American Indian or Alaska Native, non-Hispanic/Latino; 6% Two or more races, non-Hispanic/Latino; 1% Race/ethnicity unknown; 0.3% international; 8% transferred in; 71% live on campus.

Freshmen:
Admission: 1,153 applied, 618 admitted, 191 enrolled. ***Average high school GPA:*** 3.27. ***Test scores:*** ACT scores over 18: 100%; ACT scores over 24: 83%.

Retention: 72% of full-time freshmen returned.

FACULTY
Total: 117, 46% full-time, 38% with terminal degrees.

Student/faculty ratio: 8:1.

ACADEMICS
Calendar: semesters. *Degrees:* certificates, associate, bachelor's, master's, post-master's, and postbachelor's certificates.

Special study options: academic remediation for entering students, accelerated degree program, adult/continuing education programs, advanced placement credit, cooperative education, distance learning, double majors, external degree program, freshman honors college, honors programs, independent study, internships, off-campus study, part-time degree program, services for LD students, student-designed majors, study abroad, summer session for credit. ***ROTC:*** Army (c), Navy (c), Air Force (c).

Computers: 130 computers/terminals are available on campus for general student use. Students can access the following: campus intranet, computer help desk, free student e-mail accounts, online (class) grades, online (class) registration, online (class) schedules. Campuswide network is available. Wireless service is available via entire campus.
Library: Hugh Stephens Library.

STUDENT LIFE
Housing options: on-campus residence required through senior year; women-only. Campus housing is university owned and is provided by a third party. Freshman campus housing is guaranteed.

Activities and organizations: drama/theater group, student-run newspaper, television station, choral group, Innovative Fashion Association, Warehouse Theatre, Student Government Association, American Marketing Association (AMA), national sororities.

Athletics Member NAIA. ***Intercollegiate sports:*** basketball W(s), cross-country running W(s), golf W(s), soccer W(s), softball W(s), tennis W(s), volleyball W(s). ***Intramural sports:*** equestrian sports W(c).

Campus security: 24-hour emergency response devices and patrols, student patrols, late-night transport/escort service, controlled dormitory access.

Student services: health clinic, personal/psychological counseling.

FINANCIAL AID
Financial Aid *Average indebtedness upon graduation:* $26,824.

APPLYING
Standardized Tests *Required:* SAT or ACT (for admission).

Options: electronic application, deferred entrance.

Application fee: $25.

Required: essay or personal statement, high school transcript, minimum 2.0 GPA. ***Required for some:*** 1 letter of recommendation, audition for dance, audition recommended for theater. ***Recommended:*** minimum 2.5 GPA, interview.

Notification: continuous until 9/15 (freshmen), continuous until 9/15 (transfers).

CONTACT
Tiffany Goalder, Director of Undergraduate Admissions, Stephens College, 1200 East Broadway, Box 2121, Columbia, MO 65215-0002.
Phone: 573-876-7239. *Toll-free phone:* 800-876-7207.
Fax: 573-876-7237. *E-mail:* apply@stephens.edu.

Stevens–The Institute of Business & Arts

St. Louis, Missouri

http://www.siba.edu/

CONTACT
Mr. John Willmon, Director of Admissions, Stevens–The Institute of Business & Arts, 1521 Washington Avenue, St. Louis, MO 63103.
Phone: 314-421-0949 Ext. 1119. *Toll-free phone:* 800-871-0949.
Fax: 314-421-0304. *E-mail:* admission@siba.edu.

Truman State University

Kirksville, Missouri

http://www.truman.edu/

- **State-supported** comprehensive, founded 1867
- **Small-town** 140-acre campus
- **Endowment** $40.8 million
- **Coed** 6,039 undergraduate students, 86% full-time, 59% women, 41% men
- **Moderately difficult** entrance level, 68% of applicants were admitted

UNDERGRAD STUDENTS
5,187 full-time, 852 part-time. Students come from 42 states and territories; 50 other countries; 19% are from out of state; 3% Black or African American, non-Hispanic/Latino; 3% Hispanic/Latino; 2% Asian, non-Hispanic/Latino; 0.1% Native Hawaiian or other Pacific Islander, non-Hispanic/Latino; 0.2% American Indian or Alaska Native, non-Hispanic/Latino; 3% Two or more races, non-Hispanic/Latino; 2% Race/ethnicity unknown; 7% international; 3% transferred in; 46% live on campus.

Freshmen:
Admission: 5,178 applied, 3,505 admitted, 1,263 enrolled. ***Average high school GPA:*** 3.79. ***Test scores:*** SAT critical reading scores over 500: 90%; SAT math scores over 500: 84%; ACT scores over 18: 100%; SAT critical reading scores over 600: 51%; SAT math scores over 600: 49%; ACT scores over 24: 82%; SAT critical reading scores over 700: 18%; SAT math scores over 700: 16%; ACT scores over 30: 28%.

Retention: 87% of full-time freshmen returned.

FACULTY
Total: 398, 83% full-time, 76% with terminal degrees.
Student/faculty ratio: 16:1.

ACADEMICS
Calendar: semesters. *Degrees:* bachelor's and master's.

Special study options: accelerated degree program, advanced placement credit, cooperative education, double majors, honors programs, independent study, internships, off-campus study, part-time degree program, services for LD students, student-designed majors, study abroad, summer session for credit. ***ROTC:*** Army (b).

Unusual degree programs: 3-2 engineering with Missouri University of Science and Technology; University of Missouri, Columbia; chiropractic with Logan University.

Computers: 1,056 computers/terminals and 3,690 ports are available on campus for general student use. Students can access the following: campus intranet, computer help desk, free student e-mail accounts, online (class) grades, online (class) registration, online (class) schedules. Campuswide network is available. 100% of college-owned or -operated housing units are wired for high-speed Internet access. Wireless service is available via entire campus.
Library: Pickler Memorial Library. *Books:* 495,359 (physical), 325,994 (digital/electronic); *Serial titles:* 601 (physical), 2,584 (digital/electronic); *Databases:* 107. Students can reserve study rooms.

STUDENT LIFE
Housing options: on-campus residence required for freshman year; coed, special housing for students with disabilities. Campus housing is university owned. Freshman campus housing is guaranteed.

Activities and organizations: drama/theater group, student-run newspaper, radio and television station, choral group, marching band, American Medical Student Association, Nursing Students Association, Alpha Phi Omega (co-ed service fraternity), Beta Beta Beta (biology honors), Alpha Sigma Gamma (service sorority), national fraternities, national sororities.

Athletics Member NCAA. All Division II. ***Intercollegiate sports:*** baseball M(s), basketball M(s)/W(s), bowling M(c)/W(c), cheerleading M(c)/W(c), cross-country running M(s)/W(s), equestrian sports M(c)/W(c), football M(s), golf W(s), lacrosse W(c), riflery M(c)/W(c), rock climbing M(c)/W(c), rugby M(c)/W(c), soccer M(s)/W(s), softball W(s), swimming and diving M/W(s), tennis M(s)/W(s), track and field M(s)/W(s), ultimate Frisbee M(c)/W(c), volleyball M(c)/W(s), weight lifting M(c)/W(c), wrestling M(s). ***Intramural sports:*** badminton M/W, basketball M/W, cross-country running M/W, football M/W, skiing (cross-country) M(c)/W(c), skiing (downhill) M(c)/W(c), soccer M/W, softball M/W, swimming and diving M/W, table tennis M/W, tennis M/W, track and field M/W, ultimate Frisbee M/W, volleyball M/W.

Campus security: 24-hour emergency response devices and patrols, student patrols, late-night transport/escort service, controlled dormitory access, patrols by commissioned officers, perimeter access system, dual 911 call center for campus/community, emergency text messaging system.

Student services: health clinic, personal/psychological counseling, women's center.

COSTS & FINANCIAL AID

Costs (2016–17) ***One-time required fee:*** $325. ***Tuition:*** state resident $7152 full-time, $298 per credit hour part-time; nonresident $13,636 full-time, $568 per credit hour part-time. Full-time tuition and fees vary according to course load, degree level, and program. Part-time tuition and fees vary according to course load, degree level, and program. ***Required fees:*** $304 full-time, $304 per year part-time. ***Room and board:*** $8558; room only: $5730. Room and board charges vary according to housing facility. ***Payment plan:*** installment. ***Waivers:*** children of alumni, senior citizens, and employees or children of employees.

Financial Aid Of all full-time matriculated undergraduates who enrolled in 2015, 3,732 applied for aid, 2,659 were judged to have need, 914 had their need fully met. 423 Federal Work-Study jobs (averaging $1619). 1,437 state and other part-time jobs (averaging $1148). In 2015, 1905 non-need-based awards were made. ***Average percent of need met:*** 84. ***Average financial aid package:*** $12,437. ***Average need-based loan:*** $4479. ***Average need-based gift aid:*** $7636. ***Average non-need-based aid:*** $5812. ***Average indebtedness upon graduation:*** $24,811.

APPLYING

Options: electronic application, deferred entrance.

Required: essay or personal statement, high school transcript. ***Recommended:*** minimum 3.0 GPA, interview, activities list/resumé.

Application deadlines: rolling (freshmen), rolling (transfers).

Notification: continuous until 9/1 (freshmen), continuous (transfers).

CONTACT

Melody Chambers, Director of Admissions, Truman State University, Ruth Towne Museum and Visitors Center, 100 East Normal Avenue, Kirksville, MO 63501-4221. *Phone:* 660-785-4114. *Toll-free phone:* 800-892-7792. *Fax:* 660-785-7456. *E-mail:* mchamber@truman.edu.

See below for display ad and page 1536 for the College Close-Up.

University of Central Missouri

Warrensburg, Missouri

http://www.ucmo.edu/

- **State-supported** comprehensive, founded 1871
- **Small-town** 1561-acre campus with easy access to Kansas City
- **Coed** 9,786 undergraduate students, 80% full-time, 56% women, 44% men
- **Moderately difficult** entrance level, 98% of applicants were admitted

UNDERGRAD STUDENTS

7,858 full-time, 1,928 part-time. Students come from 46 states and territories; 42 other countries; 11% are from out of state; 10% Black or African American, non-Hispanic/Latino; 4% Hispanic/Latino; 0.9% Asian, non-Hispanic/Latino; 0.2% Native Hawaiian or other Pacific Islander, non-Hispanic/Latino; 0.3% American Indian or Alaska Native, non-Hispanic/Latino; 4% Two or more races, non-Hispanic/Latino; 2% Race/ethnicity unknown; 2% international; 9% transferred in; 34% live on campus.

Freshmen:

Admission: 3,941 applied, 3,866 admitted, 1,605 enrolled. ***Average high school GPA:*** 3.39. ***Test scores:*** ACT scores over 18: 93%; ACT scores over 24: 33%; ACT scores over 30: 3%.

Retention: 71% of full-time freshmen returned.

FACULTY

Total: 714, 73% full-time, 56% with terminal degrees.

Student/faculty ratio: 19:1.

ACADEMICS
Calendar: semesters. *Degrees:* certificates, bachelor's, master's, post-master's, and postbachelor's certificates.
Special study options: academic remediation for entering students, accelerated degree program, adult/continuing education programs, advanced placement credit, distance learning, double majors, English as a second language, honors programs, internships, off-campus study, part-time degree program, services for LD students, student-designed majors, study abroad, summer session for credit. ***ROTC:*** Army (b), Air Force (c).
Unusual degree programs: 3-2 engineering with University of Missouri–Columbia, Missouri University of Science and Technology, University of Missouri–Kansas City; law, medicine.
Computers: 6,395 computers/terminals and 19,008 ports are available on campus for general student use. Students can access the following: campus intranet, computer help desk, free student e-mail accounts, online (class) grades, online (class) registration, online (class) schedules. Campuswide network is available. 100% of college-owned or -operated housing units are wired for high-speed Internet access. Wireless service is available via classrooms, computer centers, computer labs, dorm rooms, learning centers, libraries, student centers.
Library: James C. Kirkpatrick Library plus 1 other. *Books:* 656,005 (physical), 254,201 (digital/electronic); *Serial titles:* 2,121 (physical), 88,133 (digital/electronic); *Databases:* 105. Weekly public service hours: 96; students can reserve study rooms.

STUDENT LIFE
Housing options: on-campus residence required through sophomore year; coed, women-only, special housing for students with disabilities. Campus housing is university owned. Freshman campus housing is guaranteed.
Activities and organizations: drama/theater group, student-run newspaper, radio and television station, choral group, marching band, Roaring Red (Student Booster Club), Greek Organization, Campus Christian House, BSU (Baptist Student Union), International Student Organization, national fraternities, national sororities.
Athletics Member NCAA. All Division II. ***Intercollegiate sports:*** baseball M(s), basketball M(s)/W(s), bowling M(s)(c)/W(s)(c), cheerleading M/W, cross-country running M(s)/W(s), football M(s), golf M(s)/W(s), rugby M(c)/W(c), soccer M(c)/W(s), softball W(s), track and field M(s)/W(s), volleyball M(c)/W(s), wrestling M(s). ***Intramural sports:*** archery M/W, badminton M/W, basketball M/W, bowling M/W, cheerleading M/W, fencing M/W, football M/W, golf M/W, racquetball M/W, riflery M/W, rock climbing M/W, sand volleyball M/W, soccer M/W, softball M/W, swimming and diving M/W, table tennis M/W, tennis M/W, track and field M/W, ultimate Frisbee M(c)/W(c), volleyball M/W.
Campus security: 24-hour emergency response devices and patrols, student patrols, late-night transport/escort service, controlled dormitory access, canine patrol.
Student services: health clinic, personal/psychological counseling, women's center.

COSTS & FINANCIAL AID
Costs (2016–17) ***Tuition:*** state resident $6446 full-time, $215 per credit hour part-time; nonresident $12,891 full-time, $430 per credit hour part-time. Full-time tuition and fees vary according to course load and location. Part-time tuition and fees vary according to location. ***Required fees:*** $876 full-time, $29 per credit hour part-time. ***Room and board:*** $8318; room only: $5288. Room and board charges vary according to board plan, housing facility, and student level. ***Payment plans:*** installment, deferred payment. ***Waivers:*** employees or children of employees.
Financial Aid Of all full-time matriculated undergraduates who enrolled in 2015, 6,670 applied for aid, 5,026 were judged to have need, 352 had their need fully met. 134 Federal Work-Study jobs (averaging $1482). 1,358 state and other part-time jobs (averaging $2165). In 2015, 1568 non-need-based awards were made. ***Average percent of need met:*** 62. ***Average financial aid package:*** $8562. ***Average need-based gift aid:*** $4284. ***Average non-need-based aid:*** $3338. ***Average indebtedness upon graduation:*** $28,673.

APPLYING
Standardized Tests *Required:* SAT or ACT (for admission).
Options: electronic application, deferred entrance.
Application fee: $30.
Required: high school transcript, rank in upper two-thirds of high school class.
Application deadlines: rolling (freshmen), rolling (transfers).
Notification: continuous (freshmen), continuous (transfers).

CONTACT
Mr. J. D. Gragg, Director of Admissions, University of Central Missouri, 1400 Ward Edwards, Warrensburg, MO 64093. *Phone:* 660-543-4290. *Toll-free phone:* 800-729-8266. *Fax:* 660-543-8517.
E-mail: admit@ucmo.edu.

University of Missouri
Columbia, Missouri
http://www.missouri.edu/

- **State-supported** university, founded 1839, part of University of Missouri System
- **Suburban** 1262-acre campus
- **Endowment** $852.3 million
- **Coed**
- **Moderately difficult** entrance level

FACULTY
Student/faculty ratio: 20:1.

ACADEMICS
Calendar: semesters. *Degrees:* bachelor's, master's, doctoral, and post-master's certificates.
Library: Ellis Library plus 10 others. *Books:* 4.7 million (physical), 1.4 million (digital/electronic). Students can reserve study rooms.

STUDENT LIFE
Housing options: on-campus residence required for freshman year; coed, men-only, women-only, special housing for students with disabilities. Campus housing is university owned. Freshman campus housing is guaranteed.
Activities and organizations: drama/theater group, student-run newspaper, radio and television station, choral group, marching band, Academic organizations, Greek organizations, Religious/Spiritual organizations, Sports clubs, Student Governance, national fraternities, national sororities.
Athletics Member NCAA. All Division I except football (Division I-A).
Campus security: 24-hour emergency response devices and patrols, late-night transport/escort service, controlled dormitory access.
Student services: health clinic, personal/psychological counseling, women's center, legal services.

COSTS & FINANCIAL AID
Costs (2016–17) ***Tuition:*** state resident $8286 full-time, $276 per credit hour part-time; nonresident $24,660 full-time, $822 per credit hour part-time. Full-time tuition and fees vary according to course load, program, and reciprocity agreements. Part-time tuition and fees vary according to course load, program, and reciprocity agreements. ***Required fees:*** $1232 full-time. ***Room and board:*** $10,298; room only: $7263. Room and board charges vary according to board plan and housing facility.
Financial Aid Of all full-time matriculated undergraduates who enrolled in 2015, 17,326 applied for aid, 12,389 were judged to have need, 1,657 had their need fully met. In 2015, 4991 non-need-based awards were made. ***Average percent of need met:*** 76. ***Average financial aid package:*** $15,239. ***Average need-based loan:*** $4454. ***Average need-based gift aid:*** $9460. ***Average non-need-based aid:*** $5531. ***Average indebtedness upon graduation:*** $26,060.

APPLYING
Standardized Tests *Required:* SAT or ACT (for admission). *Recommended:* ACT (for admission).
Options: electronic application, deferred entrance.
Application fee: $55.
Required: high school transcript, specific high school curriculum.

CONTACT
Mr. Charles May, Director of Admissions, University of Missouri, 230 Jesse Hall, Columbia, MO 65211. *Phone:* 573-882-7786. *Toll-free phone:* 800-225-6075. *Fax:* 573-882-7887. *E-mail:* mu4u@missouri.edu.

University of Missouri–Kansas City

Kansas City, Missouri

http://www.umkc.edu/

- **State-supported** university, founded 1929, part of University of Missouri System
- **Urban** 191-acre campus with easy access to Kansas City
- **Endowment** $305.8 million
- **Coed** 11,708 undergraduate students, 57% full-time, 58% women, 42% men
- **Moderately difficult** entrance level, 62% of applicants were admitted

UNDERGRAD STUDENTS
6,669 full-time, 5,039 part-time. Students come from 39 states and territories; 55 other countries; 24% are from out of state; 12% Black or African American, non-Hispanic/Latino; 8% Hispanic/Latino; 6% Asian, non-Hispanic/Latino; 0.2% Native Hawaiian or other Pacific Islander, non-Hispanic/Latino; 0.4% American Indian or Alaska Native, non-Hispanic/Latino; 4% Two or more races, non-Hispanic/Latino; 4% Race/ethnicity unknown; 4% international; 11% transferred in; 25% live on campus.

Freshmen:
Admission: 5,138 applied, 3,179 admitted, 1,212 enrolled. ***Average high school GPA:*** 3.38. ***Test scores:*** SAT math scores over 500: 72%; ACT scores over 18: 95%; SAT math scores over 600: 35%; ACT scores over 24: 56%; SAT math scores over 700: 16%; ACT scores over 30: 16%.
Retention: 75% of full-time freshmen returned.

FACULTY
Total: 1,207, 62% full-time, 68% with terminal degrees.
Student/faculty ratio: 14:1.

ACADEMICS
Calendar: semesters. *Degrees:* bachelor's, master's, doctoral, and post-master's certificates.
Special study options: accelerated degree program, adult/continuing education programs, advanced placement credit, cooperative education, distance learning, double majors, English as a second language, freshman honors college, honors programs, independent study, internships, off-campus study, part-time degree program, services for LD students, student-designed majors, study abroad, summer session for credit. ***ROTC:*** Army (b), Air Force (c).
Computers: 400 computers/terminals are available on campus for general student use. Students can access the following: campus intranet, computer help desk, free student e-mail accounts, online (class) grades, online (class) registration, online (class) schedules. Campuswide network is available. 100% of college-owned or -operated housing units are wired for high-speed Internet access. Wireless service is available via classrooms, computer labs, dorm rooms, libraries, student centers.
Library: Miller-Nichols Library plus 3 others. Students can reserve study rooms.

STUDENT LIFE
Housing options: coed, special housing for students with disabilities. Campus housing is university owned.
Activities and organizations: drama/theater group, student-run newspaper, radio station, choral group, Union Programming Board, International Student Council, Alpha Phi Omega, Omicron Delta Kappa, Greek Organizations, national fraternities, national sororities.
Athletics Member NCAA. All Division I. ***Intercollegiate sports:*** basketball M(s)/W(s), cross-country running M(s)/W(s), golf M(s)/W(s), soccer M(s)/W(s), softball W(s), tennis M(s)/W(s), track and field M(s)/W(s), volleyball W(s). ***Intramural sports:*** badminton M/W, basketball M/W, football M/W, racquetball M/W, soccer M/W, softball M/W, swimming and diving M/W, table tennis M/W, volleyball M/W.
Campus security: 24-hour emergency response devices and patrols, late-night transport/escort service, controlled dormitory access.
Student services: health clinic, personal/psychological counseling, women's center, legal services.

COSTS & FINANCIAL AID
Costs (2017–18) ***Tuition:*** state resident $8169 full-time, $272 per credit hour part-time; nonresident $23,362 full-time, $832 per credit hour part-time. Full-time tuition and fees vary according to course load and program. Part-time tuition and fees vary according to course load and program. ***Required fees:*** $1394 full-time, $100 per credit hour part-time. ***Room and board:*** Room and board charges vary according to board plan and housing facility. ***Payment plan:*** installment. ***Waivers:*** employees or children of employees.
Financial Aid Of all full-time matriculated undergraduates who enrolled in 2016, 5,942 applied for aid, 4,998 were judged to have need, 413 had their need fully met. 632 Federal Work-Study jobs (averaging $4144). In 2016, 1022 non-need-based awards were made. ***Average percent of need met:*** 54. ***Average financial aid package:*** $9810. ***Average need-based loan:*** $7966. ***Average need-based gift aid:*** $7152. ***Average non-need-based aid:*** $5397. ***Average indebtedness upon graduation:*** $25,912.

APPLYING
Standardized Tests *Required:* SAT or ACT (for admission).
Options: electronic application, deferred entrance.
Application fee: $45.
Required: high school transcript. ***Required for some:*** essay or personal statement, interview.
Application deadlines: rolling (freshmen), rolling (transfers).
Notification: continuous (freshmen), continuous (transfers).

CONTACT
Ms. Tamera Byland, Director of Admissions, University of Missouri–Kansas City, Office of Admissions, 5100 Rockhill Road, Kansas City, MO 64110-2499. *Phone:* 816-235-1111. *Toll-free phone:* 800-775-8652. *Fax:* 816-235-5544. *E-mail:* admit@umkc.edu.

University of Missouri–St. Louis

St. Louis, Missouri

http://www.umsl.edu/

- **State-supported** university, founded 1963, part of University of Missouri System
- **Suburban** 350-acre campus with easy access to St. Louis
- **Endowment** $76.6 million
- **Coed** 13,923 undergraduate students, 39% full-time, 57% women, 43% men
- **Moderately difficult** entrance level, 71% of applicants were admitted

UNDERGRAD STUDENTS
5,434 full-time, 8,489 part-time. Students come from 40 states and territories; 42 other countries; 11% are from out of state; 18% Black or African American, non-Hispanic/Latino; 3% Hispanic/Latino; 5% Asian, non-Hispanic/Latino; 0.2% Native Hawaiian or other Pacific Islander, non-Hispanic/Latino; 0.4% American Indian or Alaska Native, non-Hispanic/Latino; 3% Two or more races, non-Hispanic/Latino; 4% Race/ethnicity unknown; 3% international; 10% transferred in; 9% live on campus.

Freshmen:
Admission: 1,947 applied, 1,375 admitted, 441 enrolled.
Retention: 78% of full-time freshmen returned.

FACULTY
Total: 843, 52% full-time, 57% with terminal degrees.
Student/faculty ratio: 18:1.

ACADEMICS
Calendar: semesters. *Degrees:* bachelor's, master's, doctoral, post-master's, and postbachelor's certificates.
Special study options: accelerated degree program, adult/continuing education programs, advanced placement credit, cooperative education, distance learning, double majors, English as a second language, freshman honors college, honors programs, independent study, internships, off-campus study, part-time degree program, services for LD students, student-designed majors, study abroad, summer session for credit. ***ROTC:*** Army (b), Air Force (c).
Unusual degree programs: 3-2 engineering with Washington University in St. Louis; economics, history, philosophy, political science, sociology.
Computers: 1,280 computers/terminals and 1,280 ports are available on campus for general student use. Students can access the following: campus intranet, computer help desk, free student e-mail accounts, online (class) grades, online (class) registration, online (class) schedules.

Campuswide network is available. 90% of college-owned or -operated housing units are wired for high-speed Internet access. Wireless service is available via classrooms, computer centers, computer labs, dorm rooms, learning centers, libraries, student centers.

Library: Thomas Jefferson Library plus 1 other. *Books:* 1.3 million (physical), 206,207 (digital/electronic); *Serial titles:* 1,041 (physical), 1,232 (digital/electronic); *Databases:* 205. Weekly public service hours: 82; students can reserve study rooms.

STUDENT LIFE

Housing options: coed, men-only, women-only, special housing for students with disabilities. Campus housing is university owned and is provided by a third party.

Activities and organizations: drama/theater group, student-run newspaper, radio station, choral group, Student Government Association, Associated Black Collegians, Pierre laclede Honors College Student Association, Residence Hall Association, UMSL Radio Station, national fraternities, national sororities.

Athletics Member NCAA. All Division II. ***Intercollegiate sports:*** baseball M(s), basketball M(s)/W(s), cheerleading W, golf M(s)/W(s), ice hockey M(c), soccer M(s)/W(s), softball W(s), swimming and diving M(s)/W(s), table tennis M(c)/W(c), tennis M(s)/W(s), volleyball W(s). ***Intramural sports:*** badminton M/W, basketball M/W, bowling M/W, football M/W, golf M/W, racquetball M/W, rock climbing M/W, sand volleyball M/W, skiing (downhill) M/W, soccer M/W, softball M/W, table tennis M/W, tennis M/W, ultimate Frisbee M/W, volleyball M/W, weight lifting M/W.

Campus security: 24-hour emergency response devices and patrols, late-night transport/escort service, controlled dormitory access.

Student services: health clinic, personal/psychological counseling, women's center.

COSTS & FINANCIAL AID

Costs (2016–17) ***Tuition:*** state resident $336 per credit hour part-time; nonresident $876 per credit hour part-time. Full-time tuition and fees vary according to course level, course load, location, program, and reciprocity agreements. Part-time tuition and fees vary according to course level, course load, location, program, and reciprocity agreements. ***Room and board:*** Room and board charges vary according to board plan and housing facility. ***Payment plan:*** installment. ***Waivers:*** senior citizens and employees or children of employees.

Financial Aid Of all full-time matriculated undergraduates who enrolled in 2016, 4,272 applied for aid, 3,696 were judged to have need, 685 had their need fully met. 50 Federal Work-Study jobs (averaging $4275). In 2016, 377 non-need-based awards were made. ***Average percent of need met:*** 66. ***Average financial aid package:*** $11,633. ***Average need-based loan:*** $4416. ***Average need-based gift aid:*** $8162. ***Average non-need-based aid:*** $5561. ***Average indebtedness upon graduation:*** $24,186.

APPLYING

Options: electronic application.

Application fee: $35.

Required: high school transcript, minimum 2.0 GPA, CBHE core requirements. ***Required for some:*** essay or personal statement, 2 letters of recommendation, interview.

Application deadlines: rolling (freshmen), rolling (transfers).

Notification: continuous (freshmen), continuous (transfers).

CONTACT

Mr. Andrew L. Griffin, Dean of Admissions, University of Missouri–St. Louis, 351 Millennium Student Center, One University Boulevard, St. Louis, MO 63121-4400. *Phone:* 314-516-6941. *Toll-free phone:* 888-GO2-UMSL (in-state); 888-GO2-USML (out-of-state). *Fax:* 314-516-5310. *E-mail:* askdrew@umsl.edu.

Vatterott College

Berkeley, Missouri

http://www.vatterott.edu/

CONTACT

Ann Farajallah, Director of Admissions, Vatterott College, 8580 Evans Avenue, Berkeley, MO 63134. *Phone:* 314-264-1020. *Toll-free phone:* 888-553-6627.

Vatterott College

Sunset Hills, Missouri

http://www.vatterott.edu/

CONTACT

Director of Admission, Vatterott College, 12900 Maurer Industrial Drive, Sunset Hills, MO 63127. *Phone:* 314-843-4200. *Toll-free phone:* 888-553-6627. *Fax:* 314-843-1709.

Washington University in St. Louis

St. Louis, Missouri

http://www.wustl.edu/

- **Independent** university, founded 1853
- **Suburban** 169-acre campus with easy access to St. Louis
- **Endowment** $6.5 billion
- **Coed** 7,540 undergraduate students, 92% full-time, 53% women, 47% men
- **Most difficult** entrance level, 17% of applicants were admitted

UNDERGRAD STUDENTS

6,915 full-time, 625 part-time. Students come from 54 states and territories; 48 other countries; 92% are from out of state; 7% Black or African American, non-Hispanic/Latino; 8% Hispanic/Latino; 18% Asian, non-Hispanic/Latino; 0.1% American Indian or Alaska Native, non-Hispanic/Latino; 4% Two or more races, non-Hispanic/Latino; 2% Race/ethnicity unknown; 8% international; 1% transferred in; 77% live on campus.

Freshmen:

Admission: 29,197 applied, 4,827 admitted, 1,776 enrolled. ***Test scores:*** SAT critical reading scores over 500: 100%; SAT math scores over 500: 100%; SAT writing scores over 500: 100%; ACT scores over 18: 100%; SAT critical reading scores over 600: 99%; SAT math scores over 600: 98%; SAT writing scores over 600: 98%; ACT scores over 24: 100%; SAT critical reading scores over 700: 72%; SAT math scores over 700: 80%; SAT writing scores over 700: 72%; ACT scores over 30: 93%.

Retention: 96% of full-time freshmen returned.

FACULTY

Total: 1,230, 76% full-time.

Student/faculty ratio: 8:1.

ACADEMICS

Calendar: semesters. *Degrees:* certificates, bachelor's, master's, doctoral, post-master's, and postbachelor's certificates.

Special study options: accelerated degree program, adult/continuing education programs, advanced placement credit, cooperative education, double majors, English as a second language, independent study, internships, off-campus study, part-time degree program, services for LD students, student-designed majors, study abroad, summer session for credit. ***ROTC:*** Army (b), Air Force (c).

Unusual degree programs: 3-2 business administration; engineering; social work; art, occupational therapy, physical therapy.

Computers: 2,500 computers/terminals and 3,500 ports are available on campus for general student use. Students can access the following: campus intranet, computer help desk, free student e-mail accounts, online (class) grades, online (class) registration, online (class) schedules. Campuswide network is available. 95% of college-owned or -operated housing units are wired for high-speed Internet access. Wireless service is available via classrooms, computer centers, computer labs, dorm rooms, learning centers, libraries, student centers.

Library: John M. Olin Library plus 12 others. *Books:* 2.5 million (physical), 1.8 million (digital/electronic); *Serial titles:* 892 (physical), 139,649 (digital/electronic); *Databases:* 554. Weekly public service hours: 118; study areas open 24 hours, 5-7 days a week; students can reserve study rooms.

STUDENT LIFE

Housing options: on-campus residence required for freshman year; coed, men-only, women-only, cooperative. Campus housing is university owned. Freshman campus housing is guaranteed.

Activities and organizations: drama/theater group, student-run newspaper, radio and television station, choral group, national fraternities, national sororities.

Athletics Member NCAA. All Division III. ***Intercollegiate sports:*** baseball M, basketball M/W, crew M(c)/W(c), cross-country running M/W, equestrian sports M(c)/W(c), fencing M(c)/W(c), field hockey W(c), football M, golf M(c)/W, gymnastics M(c)/W(c), ice hockey M(c), lacrosse M(c)/W(c), rugby M(c)/W(c), sailing M(c)/W(c), soccer M/W, softball W, swimming and diving M/W, table tennis M(c)/W(c), tennis M/W, track and field M/W, ultimate Frisbee M(c)/W(c), volleyball M(c)/W, water polo M(c)/W(c), wrestling M(c). ***Intramural sports:*** archery M/W, badminton M/W, basketball M/W, bowling M/W, cross-country running M/W, football M/W, golf M/W, racquetball M/W, soccer M(c)/W(c), softball M/W, squash M/W, swimming and diving M/W, table tennis M/W, tennis M/W, track and field M/W, ultimate Frisbee M/W, volleyball M/W, water polo M/W.

Campus security: 24-hour emergency response devices and patrols, student patrols, late-night transport/escort service, controlled dormitory access.

Student services: health clinic, personal/psychological counseling, women's center.

COSTS & FINANCIAL AID

Costs (2017–18) ***Comprehensive fee:*** $67,539 includes full-time tuition ($50,650), mandatory fees ($883), and room and board ($16,006). ***College room only:*** $10,982. Room and board charges vary according to board plan and housing facility. ***Payment plans:*** tuition prepayment, installment. ***Waivers:*** employees or children of employees.

Financial Aid Of all full-time matriculated undergraduates who enrolled in 2016, 3,102 applied for aid, 2,865 were judged to have need, 2,842 had their need fully met. 1,211 Federal Work-Study jobs (averaging $2259). In 2016, 640 non-need-based awards were made. ***Average percent of need met:*** 100. ***Average financial aid package:*** $43,722. ***Average need-based loan:*** $4901. ***Average need-based gift aid:*** $40,509. ***Average non-need-based aid:*** $6111. ***Average indebtedness upon graduation:*** $23,577. ***Financial aid deadline:*** 2/1.

APPLYING

Standardized Tests *Required:* SAT or ACT (for admission).

Options: electronic application, early admission, early decision, deferred entrance.

Application fee: $75.

Required: essay or personal statement, high school transcript, 2 letters of recommendation. ***Required for some:*** portfolio for the College of Art and College of Architecture. ***Recommended:*** minimum 3.5 GPA.

Application deadlines: 1/15 (freshmen), 3/15 (transfers).

Early decision deadline: 11/15.

Notification: 4/1 (freshmen), 5/15 (transfers), 12/15 (early decision).

CONTACT

Ms. Julie Shimabukuro, Director of Admissions, Washington University in St. Louis, Campus Box 1089, One Brookings Drive, St. Louis, MO 63130-4899. *Phone:* 314-935-6000. *Toll-free phone:* 800-638-0700. *Fax:* 314-935-4290. *E-mail:* admissions@wustl.edu.

Webster University

St. Louis, Missouri

http://www.webster.edu/

- **Independent** comprehensive, founded 1915
- **Suburban** 47-acre campus with easy access to St. Louis
- **Endowment** $123.4 million
- **Coed** 2,621 undergraduate students, 85% full-time, 54% women, 46% men
- **Moderately difficult** entrance level, 47% of applicants were admitted

UNDERGRAD STUDENTS

2,231 full-time, 390 part-time. Students come from 40 states and territories; 56 other countries; 28% are from out of state; 12% Black or African American, non-Hispanic/Latino; 6% Hispanic/Latino; 2% Asian, non-Hispanic/Latino; 0.1% Native Hawaiian or other Pacific Islander, non-Hispanic/Latino; 0.2% American Indian or Alaska Native, non-Hispanic/Latino; 4% Two or more races, non-Hispanic/Latino; 7% Race/ethnicity unknown; 4% international; 12% transferred in; 31% live on campus.

Freshmen:
Admission: 2,630 applied, 1,225 admitted, 443 enrolled. ***Average high school GPA:*** 3.48. ***Test scores:*** ACT scores over 18: 93%; ACT scores over 24: 54%; ACT scores over 30: 10%.

Retention: 75% of full-time freshmen returned.

FACULTY

Total: 622, 32% full-time, 53% with terminal degrees.

Student/faculty ratio: 9:1.

ACADEMICS

Calendar: semesters. *Degrees:* certificates, bachelor's, master's, doctoral, post-master's, and postbachelor's certificates.

Special study options: accelerated degree program, adult/continuing education programs, advanced placement credit, cooperative education, distance learning, double majors, English as a second language, independent study, internships, off-campus study, part-time degree program, services for LD students, student-designed majors, study abroad, summer session for credit. ***ROTC:*** Army (c), Air Force (c).

Unusual degree programs: 3-2 engineering with Washington University in St. Louis; occupational therapy with Washington University in St. Louis.

Computers: 714 computers/terminals and 340 ports are available on campus for general student use. Students can access the following: campus intranet, computer help desk, free student e-mail accounts, online (class) grades, online (class) registration, online (class) schedules. Campuswide network is available. 100% of college-owned or -operated housing units are wired for high-speed Internet access. Wireless service is available via entire campus.

Library: Emerson Library. *Books:* 260,133 (physical), 70,612 (digital/electronic); *Serial titles:* 1,167 (physical), 180 (digital/electronic); *Databases:* 165. Weekly public service hours: 91; study areas open 24 hours, 5-7 days a week; students can reserve study rooms.

STUDENT LIFE

Housing options: on-campus residence required through sophomore year; coed, special housing for students with disabilities. Campus housing is university owned and leased by the school. Freshman applicants given priority for college housing.

Activities and organizations: drama/theater group, student-run newspaper, radio and television station, choral group, Student Government Association, Association for African American Collegians, International Student Association, Commuter Council, Residential Housing Association, national sororities.

Athletics Member NCAA. All Division III. ***Intercollegiate sports:*** baseball M, basketball M/W, cross-country running M/W, golf M, soccer M/W, softball W, tennis M/W, track and field M/W, volleyball W. ***Intramural sports:*** basketball M/W, bowling M/W, cheerleading M(c)/W(c), football M/W, soccer M(c)/W(c), swimming and diving M(c)/W(c), volleyball M/W.

Campus security: 24-hour emergency response devices and patrols, student patrols, late-night transport/escort service, controlled dormitory access.

Student services: health clinic, personal/psychological counseling.

COSTS & FINANCIAL AID

Costs (2016–17) ***One-time required fee:*** $125. ***Comprehensive fee:*** $37,490 includes full-time tuition ($26,100), mandatory fees ($200), and room and board ($11,190). Full-time tuition and fees vary according to program. Part-time tuition: $670 per credit hour. ***College room only:*** $6050. Room and board charges vary according to board plan and housing facility. ***Payment plan:*** deferred payment. ***Waivers:*** employees or children of employees.

Financial Aid Of all full-time matriculated undergraduates who enrolled in 2016, 1,925 applied for aid, 1,613 were judged to have need, 201 had their need fully met. 1,214 Federal Work-Study jobs (averaging $2760). In 2016, 284 non-need-based awards were made. ***Average percent of need met:*** 61. ***Average financial aid package:*** $25,521. ***Average need-based loan:*** $4275. ***Average need-based gift aid:*** $8762. ***Average non-need-based aid:*** $8870. ***Average indebtedness upon graduation:*** $28,479.

APPLYING
Standardized Tests *Required:* SAT or ACT (for admission).

Options: electronic application, early admission, deferred entrance.

Application fee: $35.

Required: essay or personal statement, high school transcript, minimum 2.5 GPA, 1 letter of recommendation. ***Required for some:*** interview, audition, portfolio review, and/or interview. ***Recommended:*** minimum 3.0 GPA.

Application deadlines: 8/1 (freshmen), 8/1 (transfers).

Notification: continuous (freshmen), continuous (out-of-state freshmen), continuous (transfers).

CONTACT
Mr. John Massena, Director of Undergraduate Admissions, Webster University, 470 East Lockwood Avenue, St. Louis, MO 63119-3194. *Phone:* 314-968-7114. *Toll-free phone:* 800-753-6765. *E-mail:* johnmassena24@webster.edu.

Westminster College

Fulton, Missouri

http://www.westminster-mo.edu/

- **Independent** 4-year, founded 1851, affiliated with Presbyterian Church
- **Small-town** 80-acre campus
- **Endowment** $56.6 million
- **Coed**
- **Moderately difficult** entrance level

FACULTY
Student/faculty ratio: 14:1.

ACADEMICS
Calendar: semesters. *Degree:* bachelor's.

Library: Reeves Memorial Library plus 1 other. *Books:* 104,327 (physical), 156,300 (digital/electronic); *Databases:* 58. Students can reserve study rooms.

STUDENT LIFE
Housing options: on-campus residence required through junior year; coed, men-only, women-only. Campus housing is university owned. Freshman campus housing is guaranteed.

Activities and organizations: drama/theater group, student-run newspaper, choral group, Student Government Association, Environmentally Concerned Students, International Student Club, Habitat for Humanity, Little Brother/Little Sister, national fraternities, national sororities.

Athletics Member NCAA. All Division III.

Campus security: 24-hour emergency response devices and patrols, late-night transport/escort service, controlled dormitory access, well-lit campus.

Student services: health clinic, personal/psychological counseling, women's center.

COSTS & FINANCIAL AID
Costs (2016–17) ***Comprehensive fee:*** $34,020 includes full-time tuition ($23,200), mandatory fees ($1340), and room and board ($9480). Full-time tuition and fees vary according to reciprocity agreements. Part-time tuition: $800 per credit hour. ***College room only:*** $5120. Room and board charges vary according to board plan and housing facility.

Financial Aid Of all full-time matriculated undergraduates who enrolled in 2015, 721 applied for aid, 595 were judged to have need, 304 had their need fully met. 483 Federal Work-Study jobs (averaging $1370). 169 state and other part-time jobs (averaging $2168). In 2015, 314 non-need-based awards were made. ***Average percent of need met:*** 92. ***Average financial aid package:*** $21,714. ***Average need-based loan:*** $4145. ***Average need-based gift aid:*** $16,989. ***Average non-need-based aid:*** $12,574. ***Average indebtedness upon graduation:*** $29,573.

APPLYING
Standardized Tests *Required:* SAT or ACT (for admission).

Options: electronic application, early admission, deferred entrance.

Required: high school transcript, 1 letter of recommendation. ***Required for some:*** interview. ***Recommended:*** essay or personal statement, minimum 2.5 GPA.

CONTACT
Robert Andrews, Vice President and Dean of Enrollment Management, Westminster College, 501 Westminster Avenue, Fulton, MO 65251-1299. *Phone:* 573-592-5251. *Toll-free phone:* 800-475-3361. *Fax:* 573-592-5255. *E-mail:* admissions@westminster-mo.edu.

William Jewell College

Liberty, Missouri

http://www.jewell.edu/

- **Independent** comprehensive, founded 1849
- **Suburban** 200-acre campus with easy access to Kansas City
- **Endowment** $59.9 million
- **Coed** 992 undergraduate students, 98% full-time, 58% women, 42% men
- **Moderately difficult** entrance level, 51% of applicants were admitted

UNDERGRAD STUDENTS
977 full-time, 15 part-time. Students come from 31 states and territories; 23 other countries; 39% are from out of state; 4% Black or African American, non-Hispanic/Latino; 4% Hispanic/Latino; 1% Asian, non-Hispanic/Latino; 0.1% Native Hawaiian or other Pacific Islander, non-Hispanic/Latino; 0.1% American Indian or Alaska Native, non-Hispanic/Latino; 4% Two or more races, non-Hispanic/Latino; 3% Race/ethnicity unknown; 5% international; 4% transferred in; 87% live on campus.

Freshmen:
Admission: 2,081 applied, 1,063 admitted, 241 enrolled. ***Average high school GPA:*** 3.73. ***Test scores:*** SAT critical reading scores over 500: 72%; SAT math scores over 500: 82%; ACT scores over 18: 98%; SAT critical reading scores over 600: 28%; SAT math scores over 600: 23%; ACT scores over 24: 62%; SAT critical reading scores over 700: 14%; SAT math scores over 700: 5%; ACT scores over 30: 19%.

Retention: 79% of full-time freshmen returned.

FACULTY
Total: 134, 60% full-time, 56% with terminal degrees.
Student/faculty ratio: 10:1.

ACADEMICS
Calendar: semesters. *Degrees:* bachelor's, master's, and postbachelor's certificates (also offers evening program with significant enrollment not reflected in profile).

Special study options: accelerated degree program, advanced placement credit, cooperative education, distance learning, double majors, English as a second language, honors programs, independent study, internships, off-campus study, services for LD students, student-designed majors, study abroad, summer session for credit. ***ROTC:*** Army (c).

Unusual degree programs: 3-2 engineering with Washington University in St. Louis, University of Kansas, Vanderbilt University, Columbia University, Missouri University of Science and Technology; forestry with Duke University; occupational therapy with Washington University in St. Louis.

Computers: 25 computers/terminals and 900 ports are available on campus for general student use. Students can access the following: campus intranet, computer help desk, free student e-mail accounts, online (class) grades, online (class) registration, online (class) schedules, all students provided with an iPad and support service. Campuswide network is available. 100% of college-owned or -operated housing units are wired for high-speed Internet access. Wireless service is available via entire campus.

Library: Charles F. Curry Library. *Books:* 112,204 (physical), 637,803 (digital/electronic); *Serial titles:* 47 (physical), 115,287 (digital/electronic); *Databases:* 39. Weekly public service hours: 90; study areas open 24 hours, 5-7 days a week; students can reserve study rooms.

STUDENT LIFE
Housing options: on-campus residence required through senior year; coed, men-only, women-only, special housing for students with disabilities. Campus housing is university owned. Freshman campus housing is guaranteed.

Activities and organizations: drama/theater group, student-run newspaper, choral group, College Union Activities, Intramurals, Mosaic, Student Senate, Black Student Association, national fraternities, national sororities.

Athletics Member NCAA. All Division II. ***Intercollegiate sports:*** baseball M(s), basketball M(s)/W(s), cheerleading M(s)/W(s), cross-country running M(s)/W(s), football M(s), golf M(s)/W(s), soccer M(s)/W(s), softball W(s), swimming and diving M(s)/W(s), tennis M(s)/W(s), track and field M(s)/W(s), volleyball W(s). ***Intramural sports:*** racquetball M/W, sand volleyball M/W, soccer M/W, softball M/W, tennis M/W, ultimate Frisbee M/W, volleyball M/W.

Campus security: 24-hour emergency response devices and patrols, late-night transport/escort service, controlled dormitory access.

Student services: health clinic, personal/psychological counseling.

COSTS & FINANCIAL AID

Costs (2017–18) ***Comprehensive fee:*** $43,260 includes full-time tuition ($32,850), mandatory fees ($770), and room and board ($9640). Full-time tuition and fees vary according to program. Part-time tuition: $960 per credit hour. ***Room and board:*** Room and board charges vary according to board plan and housing facility. ***Payment plan:*** installment. ***Waivers:*** employees or children of employees.

Financial Aid Of all full-time matriculated undergraduates who enrolled in 2016, 776 applied for aid, 676 were judged to have need, 182 had their need fully met. 408 Federal Work-Study jobs (averaging $2341). 150 state and other part-time jobs (averaging $437). In 2016, 296 non-need-based awards were made. ***Average percent of need met:*** 82. ***Average financial aid package:*** $28,073. ***Average need-based loan:*** $4712. ***Average need-based gift aid:*** $21,406. ***Average non-need-based aid:*** $17,584. ***Average indebtedness upon graduation:*** $31,183.

APPLYING

Standardized Tests *Recommended:* SAT or ACT (for admission).

Options: electronic application, deferred entrance.

Required: high school transcript. ***Required for some:*** essay or personal statement, interview.

Application deadlines: rolling (freshmen), rolling (transfers).

Notification: 9/15 (freshmen), continuous (transfers).

CONTACT

Dr. Cory Scheer, Dean of Admission, William Jewell College, 500 College Hill, Liberty, MO 64068. *Phone:* 816-415-7872. *Toll-free phone:* 888-2JEWELL. *Fax:* 816-415-5040. *E-mail:* scheerc@william.jewell.edu.

William Woods University

Fulton, Missouri

http://www.williamwoods.edu/

- **Independent** comprehensive, founded 1870, affiliated with Christian Church (Disciples of Christ)
- **Small-town** 200-acre campus with easy access to St. Louis, Kansas City
- **Endowment** $18.5 million
- **Coed** 973 undergraduate students, 86% full-time, 73% women, 26% men
- **Moderately difficult** entrance level, 70% of applicants were admitted

UNDERGRAD STUDENTS

834 full-time, 137 part-time. Students come from 39 states and territories; 15 other countries; 39% are from out of state; 4% Black or African American, non-Hispanic/Latino; 5% Hispanic/Latino; 0.6% Asian, non-Hispanic/Latino; 0.1% Native Hawaiian or other Pacific Islander, non-Hispanic/Latino; 0.5% American Indian or Alaska Native, non-Hispanic/Latino; 2% Two or more races, non-Hispanic/Latino; 3% Race/ethnicity unknown; 4% international; 8% transferred in; 63% live on campus.

Freshmen:

Admission: 895 applied, 628 admitted, 198 enrolled. ***Average high school GPA:*** 3.4. ***Test scores:*** SAT critical reading scores over 500: 47%; SAT math scores over 500: 53%; ACT scores over 18: 90%; SAT critical reading scores over 600: 21%; SAT math scores over 600: 16%; ACT scores over 24: 32%; ACT scores over 30: 10%.

Retention: 75% of full-time freshmen returned.

FACULTY

Total: 236, 24% full-time, 43% with terminal degrees.

Student/faculty ratio: 11:1.

ACADEMICS

Calendar: semesters. *Degrees:* associate, bachelor's, master's, doctoral, and post-master's certificates.

Special study options: academic remediation for entering students, accelerated degree program, advanced placement credit, distance learning, double majors, honors programs, independent study, internships, off-campus study, part-time degree program, services for LD students, student-designed majors, study abroad, summer session for credit. ***ROTC:*** Army (c), Navy (c), Air Force (c).

Unusual degree programs: 3-2 business administration.

Computers: 152 computers/terminals and 1,339 ports are available on campus for general student use. Students can access the following: campus intranet, computer help desk, free student e-mail accounts, online (class) grades, online (class) registration, online (class) schedules. Campuswide network is available. 100% of college-owned or -operated housing units are wired for high-speed Internet access. Wireless service is available via entire campus.

Library: Dulany Library. *Books:* 88,695 (physical), 179,344 (digital/electronic); *Serial titles:* 1,194 (physical), 98,990 (digital/electronic); *Databases:* 50. Weekly public service hours: 91; students can reserve study rooms.

STUDENT LIFE

Housing options: on-campus residence required through senior year; coed, men-only, women-only. Campus housing is university owned. Freshman campus housing is guaranteed.

Activities and organizations: drama/theater group, student-run radio station, choral group, Campus Crusade for Christ, Students of Social Work, Active Minds, International Justice Mission, Kindness Connection, national fraternities, national sororities.

Athletics Member NAIA. ***Intercollegiate sports:*** baseball M(s), basketball M(s)/W(s), cheerleading W(s), cross-country running M(s)/W(s), golf M(s)/W(s), soccer M(s)/W(s), softball W(s), tennis M(s)/W(s), track and field M(s)/W(s), volleyball W(s). ***Intramural sports:*** basketball M/W, equestrian sports M/W, tennis M/W.

Campus security: 24-hour emergency response devices and patrols, late-night transport/escort service, controlled dormitory access.

Student services: health clinic, personal/psychological counseling.

COSTS & FINANCIAL AID

Costs (2017–18) ***Comprehensive fee:*** $32,660 includes full-time tuition ($22,450), mandatory fees ($810), and room and board ($9400). Full-time tuition and fees vary according to degree level and program. Part-time tuition: $400 per credit hour. Part-time tuition and fees vary according to course load, degree level, and program. ***Required fees:*** $50 per term part-time. ***College room only:*** $4900. Room and board charges vary according to board plan and housing facility. ***Payment plan:*** installment. ***Waivers:*** children of alumni, senior citizens, and employees or children of employees.

Financial Aid Of all full-time matriculated undergraduates who enrolled in 2016, 794 applied for aid, 682 were judged to have need, 170 had their need fully met. 186 Federal Work-Study jobs (averaging $1625). 57 state and other part-time jobs (averaging $1989). In 2016, 260 non-need-based awards were made. ***Average percent of need met:*** 72. ***Average financial aid package:*** $17,620. ***Average need-based loan:*** $5159. ***Average need-based gift aid:*** $13,141. ***Average non-need-based aid:*** $9191. ***Average indebtedness upon graduation:*** $27,729.

APPLYING

Standardized Tests *Required:* SAT or ACT (for admission).

Options: electronic application, deferred entrance.

Required: high school transcript, minimum 2.5 GPA, 16 hours college preparatory units.

Application deadlines: 8/15 (freshmen), rolling (transfers).

Notification: continuous (freshmen), continuous (transfers).

CONTACT

Mrs. Ashley Sundin, Office Manager, William Woods University, One University Avenue, Fulton, MO 65251. *Phone:* 573-592-4400. *Toll-free phone:* 800-995-3159 Ext. 4221. *Fax:* 573-592-1146. *E-mail:* ashley.sundin@williamwoods.edu.

MONTANA

Carroll College

Helena, Montana

http://www.carroll.edu/

- **Independent Roman Catholic** 4-year, founded 1909
- **Small-town** 61-acre campus
- **Endowment** $36.0 million
- **Coed** 1,373 undergraduate students, 96% full-time, 59% women, 41% men
- **Moderately difficult** entrance level, 71% of applicants were admitted

UNDERGRAD STUDENTS

1,324 full-time, 49 part-time. Students come from 35 states and territories; 14 other countries; 5% are from out of state; 0.4% Black or African American, non-Hispanic/Latino; 6% Hispanic/Latino; 1% Asian, non-Hispanic/Latino; 0.1% Native Hawaiian or other Pacific Islander, non-Hispanic/Latino; 0.9% American Indian or Alaska Native, non-Hispanic/Latino; 3% Two or more races, non-Hispanic/Latino; 9% Race/ethnicity unknown; 2% international; 3% transferred in; 57% live on campus.

Freshmen:

Admission: 3,005 applied, 2,148 admitted, 339 enrolled. ***Average high school GPA:*** 3.6. ***Test scores:*** SAT critical reading scores over 500: 72%; SAT math scores over 500: 76%; SAT writing scores over 500: 73%; ACT scores over 18: 97%; SAT critical reading scores over 600: 31%; SAT math scores over 600: 30%; SAT writing scores over 600: 24%; ACT scores over 24: 63%; SAT critical reading scores over 700: 4%; SAT math scores over 700: 6%; SAT writing scores over 700: 5%; ACT scores over 30: 11%.

Retention: 79% of full-time freshmen returned.

FACULTY

Total: 163, 56% full-time.

Student/faculty ratio: 12:1.

ACADEMICS

Calendar: semesters. *Degrees:* associate and bachelor's.

Special study options: accelerated degree program, adult/continuing education programs, advanced placement credit, cooperative education, double majors, English as a second language, freshman honors college, honors programs, independent study, internships, part-time degree program, student-designed majors, study abroad, summer session for credit. ***ROTC:*** Army (b).

Unusual degree programs: 3-2 engineering with Columbia University, University of Southern California, University of Notre Dame, Montana State University, Gonzaga University, Montana College of Mineral Science and Technology, University of Minnesota.

Computers: Students can access the following: campus intranet, computer help desk, free student e-mail accounts, online (class) grades, online (class) registration, online (class) schedules, online book order. Campuswide network is available. 100% of college-owned or -operated housing units are wired for high-speed Internet access. Wireless service is available via entire campus.

Library: Corette Library plus 1 other. *Books:* 76,993 (physical), 230,000 (digital/electronic); *Databases:* 79. Study areas open 24 hours, 5-7 days a week; students can reserve study rooms.

STUDENT LIFE

Housing options: on-campus residence required through sophomore year; coed. Campus housing is university owned. Freshman campus housing is guaranteed.

Activities and organizations: drama/theater group, student-run newspaper, radio station, choral group, Student Government, Carroll Outreach Team, Carroll Adventure and Mountaineering Program, Up 'Til Dawn, Engineers Without Borders.

Athletics Member NAIA. ***Intercollegiate sports:*** basketball M(s)/W(s), cheerleading M(s)/W(s), cross-country running M(s)/W(s), football M(s), golf M(s)/W(s), soccer M(s)/W(s), softball W(s), track and field M(s)/W(s), volleyball W(s). ***Intramural sports:*** ice hockey M(c).

Campus security: 24-hour emergency response devices, late-night transport/escort service, controlled dormitory access.

Student services: health clinic, personal/psychological counseling.

COSTS & FINANCIAL AID

Costs (2017–18) ***Comprehensive fee:*** $44,304 includes full-time tuition ($33,500), mandatory fees ($980), and room and board ($9824). Full-time tuition and fees vary according to program. Part-time tuition: $1395 per credit hour. Part-time tuition and fees vary according to program. ***Room and board:*** Room and board charges vary according to board plan. ***Payment plan:*** installment. ***Waivers:*** senior citizens and employees or children of employees.

Financial Aid Of all full-time matriculated undergraduates who enrolled in 2015, 1,063 applied for aid, 927 were judged to have need, 178 had their need fully met. 209 Federal Work-Study jobs (averaging $1175). In 2015, 442 non-need-based awards were made. ***Average percent of need met:*** 75. ***Average financial aid package:*** $22,667. ***Average need-based loan:*** $4079. ***Average need-based gift aid:*** $17,608. ***Average non-need-based aid:*** $12,983. ***Average indebtedness upon graduation:*** $32,768.

APPLYING

Standardized Tests *Required:* SAT or ACT (for admission). *Required for some:* SAT Subject Tests (for admission).

Options: electronic application, deferred entrance.

Application fee: $35.

Required: essay or personal statement, high school transcript. ***Required for some:*** interview. ***Recommended:*** interview.

Application deadlines: 2/15 (freshmen), 6/15 (transfers).

Notification: continuous (freshmen), continuous (out-of-state freshmen), continuous (transfers).

CONTACT

Director of Admission, Carroll College, 1601 North Benton Avenue, Helena, MT 59625-0002. *Phone:* 406-447-4384.
Toll-free phone: 800-992-3648. *E-mail:* admission@carroll.edu.

Montana Bible College

Bozeman, Montana

http://www.montanabiblecollege.edu/

- **Independent Christian** 4-year
- **Urban** campus
- **Coed**

ACADEMICS

Calendar: semesters. *Degree:* certificates and bachelor's.

APPLYING

Standardized Tests *Required:* SAT or ACT (for admission).

CONTACT

Montana Bible College, 3625 South 19th Avenue, Bozeman, MT 59718.
Toll-free phone: 888-462-2463.

Montana State University

Bozeman, Montana

http://www.montana.edu/

- **State-supported** university, founded 1893, part of Montana University System
- **Small-town** 1850-acre campus
- **Endowment** $126.5 million
- **Coed** 13,707 undergraduate students
- **Moderately difficult** entrance level

UNDERGRAD STUDENTS

Students come from 52 states and territories; 59 other countries; 48% are from out of state; 0.6% Black or African American, non-Hispanic/Latino; 4% Hispanic/Latino; 0.9% Asian, non-Hispanic/Latino; 0.2% Native Hawaiian or other Pacific Islander, non-Hispanic/Latino; 2% American Indian or Alaska Native, non-Hispanic/Latino; 3% Two or more races, non-Hispanic/Latino; 1% Race/ethnicity unknown; 3% international; 25% live on campus.

Freshmen:

Average high school GPA: 3.36. ***Test scores:*** SAT critical reading scores over 500: 78%; SAT math scores over 500: 80%; ACT scores over 18: 95%; SAT critical reading scores over 600: 38%; SAT math scores over

600: 42%; ACT scores over 24: 58%; SAT critical reading scores over 700: 7%; SAT math scores over 700: 7%; ACT scores over 30: 15%.

Retention: 77% of full-time freshmen returned.

FACULTY

Total: 984, 59% full-time, 56% with terminal degrees.

Student/faculty ratio: 19:1.

ACADEMICS

Calendar: semesters. *Degrees:* certificates, associate, bachelor's, master's, doctoral, post-master's, and postbachelor's certificates.

Special study options: academic remediation for entering students, adult/continuing education programs, advanced placement credit, distance learning, double majors, English as a second language, freshman honors college, honors programs, independent study, internships, off-campus study, part-time degree program, services for LD students, student-designed majors, study abroad, summer session for credit. ***ROTC:*** Army (b), Air Force (b).

Computers: 1,000 computers/terminals are available on campus for general student use. Students can access the following: computer help desk, free student e-mail accounts, online (class) grades, online (class) registration, online (class) schedules. Campuswide network is available. 100% of college-owned or -operated housing units are wired for high-speed Internet access. Wireless service is available via entire campus.

Library: Renne Library plus 2 others. Students can reserve study rooms.

STUDENT LIFE

Housing options: on-campus residence required for freshman year; coed, men-only, women-only, special housing for students with disabilities. Campus housing is university owned. Freshman campus housing is guaranteed.

Activities and organizations: drama/theater group, student-run newspaper, radio and television station, choral group, marching band, Spurs, Inter-Varsity Christian Fellowship, Campus Crusade for Christ, Fangs, Mortar Board, national fraternities, national sororities.

Athletics Member NCAA. All Division I except football (Division I-AA). ***Intercollegiate sports:*** basketball M(s)/W(s), cheerleading M(s)/W(s), cross-country running M(s)/W(s), golf W(s), skiing (cross-country) M(s)/W(s), skiing (downhill) M(s)/W(s), tennis M(s)/W(s), track and field M(s)/W(s), volleyball W(s). ***Intramural sports:*** archery W, badminton M/W, baseball M, basketball M/W, bowling M/W, cross-country running M/W, fencing M/W, football M, golf M/W, gymnastics M/W, racquetball M/W, rugby M/W, skiing (cross-country) M/W, skiing (downhill) M/W, soccer M/W, softball M/W, swimming and diving M/W, table tennis M/W, tennis M/W, track and field M/W, ultimate Frisbee M/W, volleyball M/W, water polo M/W, weight lifting M/W, wrestling M.

Campus security: 24-hour emergency response devices and patrols, student patrols, late-night transport/escort service, 24-hour residence hall monitoring.

Student services: health clinic, personal/psychological counseling, women's center, legal services.

COSTS & FINANCIAL AID

Costs (2017–18) ***Tuition:*** state resident $222 per credit hour part-time; nonresident $889 per credit hour part-time. Full-time tuition and fees vary according to course load, degree level, location, and program. Part-time tuition and fees vary according to course load, degree level, location, and program. ***Room and board:*** Room and board charges vary according to board plan and housing facility. ***Payment plans:*** installment, deferred payment. ***Waivers:*** minority students, senior citizens, and employees or children of employees.

Financial Aid Of all full-time matriculated undergraduates who enrolled in 2015, 7,337 applied for aid, 5,273 were judged to have need, 1,599 had their need fully met. In 2015, 1100 non-need-based awards were made. ***Average percent of need met:*** 74. ***Average financial aid package:*** $11,297. ***Average need-based loan:*** $7293. ***Average need-based gift aid:*** $4878. ***Average non-need-based aid:*** $1849. ***Average indebtedness upon graduation:*** $28,463.

APPLYING

Standardized Tests *Required:* SAT or ACT (for admission).

Options: electronic application, early admission, deferred entrance.

Application fee: $30.

Required: high school transcript, minimum 2.5 GPA.

Application deadlines: rolling (freshmen), rolling (out-of-state freshmen), rolling (transfers).

Notification: continuous (freshmen), continuous (out-of-state freshmen), continuous (transfers).

CONTACT

Ms. Ronda Russell, Director of Admissions, Montana State University, PO Box 172190, Bozeman, MT 59717-2190. *Phone:* 406-994-2452. *Toll-free phone:* 888-MSU-CATS. *Fax:* 406-994-1923. *E-mail:* admissions@montana.edu.

Montana State University Billings

Billings, Montana

http://www.msubillings.edu/

- **State-supported** comprehensive, founded 1927, part of Montana University System
- **Urban** 92-acre campus
- **Endowment** $21.9 million
- **Coed** 3,972 undergraduate students
- **Minimally difficult** entrance level, 100% of applicants were admitted

UNDERGRAD STUDENTS

Students come from 36 states and territories; 23 other countries; 9% are from out of state; 1% Black or African American, non-Hispanic/Latino; 5% Hispanic/Latino; 0.9% Asian, non-Hispanic/Latino; 0.3% Native Hawaiian or other Pacific Islander, non-Hispanic/Latino; 4% American Indian or Alaska Native, non-Hispanic/Latino; 3% Two or more races, non-Hispanic/Latino; 1% Race/ethnicity unknown; 2% international; 12% live on campus.

Freshmen:

Admission: 1,478 applied, 1,476 admitted. ***Average high school GPA:*** 3.13. ***Test scores:*** SAT critical reading scores over 500: 41%; SAT math scores over 500: 35%; ACT scores over 18: 76%; SAT critical reading scores over 600: 10%; SAT math scores over 600: 14%; ACT scores over 24: 17%; ACT scores over 30: 1%.

Retention: 55% of full-time freshmen returned.

FACULTY

Total: 325, 54% full-time, 42% with terminal degrees.

Student/faculty ratio: 17:1.

ACADEMICS

Calendar: semesters. *Degrees:* certificates, associate, bachelor's, and master's.

Special study options: academic remediation for entering students, accelerated degree program, adult/continuing education programs, advanced placement credit, cooperative education, distance learning, double majors, English as a second language, external degree program, honors programs, independent study, internships, off-campus study, part-time degree program, services for LD students, study abroad, summer session for credit. ***ROTC:*** Army (b).

Computers: 1,500 computers/terminals and 1,500 ports are available on campus for general student use. Students can access the following: campus intranet, computer help desk, free student e-mail accounts, online (class) grades, online (class) registration, online (class) schedules, online degree programs. Campuswide network is available. 95% of college-owned or -operated housing units are wired for high-speed Internet access. Wireless service is available via classrooms, computer labs, dorm rooms, libraries, student centers.

Library: Montana State University Billings Library plus 2 others. *Books:* 138,650 (physical), 351,351 (digital/electronic); *Serial titles:* 1,368 (physical), 669,204 (digital/electronic); *Databases:* 170. Weekly public service hours: 82; students can reserve study rooms.

STUDENT LIFE

Housing options: on-campus residence required for freshman year; coed, women-only, special housing for students with disabilities. Campus housing is university owned. Freshman applicants given priority for college housing.

Activities and organizations: drama/theater group, student-run newspaper, radio station, choral group, Art Student League, Band Club, Inter-Varsity Christian Fellowship, Residence Hall Association, Student Council for Exceptional Children.

Athletics Member NCAA. All Division II. ***Intercollegiate sports:*** baseball M, basketball M(s)/W(s), cross-country running M(s)/W(s), golf M/W, soccer M(s)/W(s), softball W, volleyball W(s). ***Intramural sports:*** baseball M/W, basketball M/W, bowling M/W, cheerleading M/W, cross-country running M/W, football M/W, golf M/W, racquetball M/W, skiing (cross-country) M/W, soccer M/W, softball M/W, swimming and diving M/W, table tennis M/W, track and field M/W, volleyball M/W.

Campus security: 24-hour emergency response devices and patrols, late-night transport/escort service, controlled dormitory access.

Student services: health clinic, personal/psychological counseling, women's center, legal services.

COSTS & FINANCIAL AID

Costs (2017–18) ***Tuition:*** state resident $4397 full-time, $183 per credit hour part-time; nonresident $16,662 full-time, $694 per credit hour part-time. Full-time tuition and fees vary according to course load and location. Part-time tuition and fees vary according to course load and location. ***Required fees:*** $1429 full-time. ***Room and board:*** $7510. Room and board charges vary according to board plan and housing facility. ***Payment plan:*** installment. ***Waivers:*** senior citizens and employees or children of employees.

Financial Aid Of all full-time matriculated undergraduates who enrolled in 2015, 1,570 applied for aid, 1,570 were judged to have need, 440 had their need fully met. In 2015, 172 non-need-based awards were made. ***Average percent of need met:*** 72. ***Average financial aid package:*** $6981. ***Average need-based loan:*** $6241. ***Average need-based gift aid:*** $4513. ***Average non-need-based aid:*** $2671. ***Average indebtedness upon graduation:*** $28,337.

APPLYING

Standardized Tests *Required for some:* SAT or ACT (for admission).

Options: electronic application.

Application fee: $30.

Required: high school transcript.

Application deadlines: rolling (freshmen), rolling (transfers).

Notification: continuous (freshmen), continuous (transfers).

CONTACT

Ms. Tammi Watson, Associate Director of Admissions, Montana State University Billings, 1500 University Drive, Billings, MT 59101. *Phone:* 406-657-2158. *Toll-free phone:* 800-565-6782. *Fax:* 406-657-2302. *E-mail:* tammi.watson@msubillings.edu.

Montana State University–Northern

Havre, Montana

http://www.msun.edu/

- **State-supported** comprehensive, founded 1929, part of Montana University System
- **Small-town** 10-acre campus
- **Coed** 1,208 undergraduate students, 76% full-time, 50% women, 50% men
- **Moderately difficult** entrance level, 64% of applicants were admitted

UNDERGRAD STUDENTS

923 full-time, 285 part-time. 89% are from out of state; 0.9% Black or African American, non-Hispanic/Latino; 2% Hispanic/Latino; 1% Asian, non-Hispanic/Latino; 13% American Indian or Alaska Native, non-Hispanic/Latino; 6% Race/ethnicity unknown; 1% international; 15% transferred in; 22% live on campus.

Freshmen:

Admission: 378 applied, 242 admitted, 228 enrolled. ***Average high school GPA:*** 2.79.

Retention: 58% of full-time freshmen returned.

FACULTY

Total: 96, 65% full-time, 23% with terminal degrees.

Student/faculty ratio: 15:1.

ACADEMICS

Calendar: semesters. *Degrees:* certificates, diplomas, associate, bachelor's, and master's.

Special study options: adult/continuing education programs, part-time degree program.

Computers: Students can access the following: online (class) registration. Campuswide network is available. Wireless service is available via entire campus.

Library: Vande Bogart Libraries.

STUDENT LIFE

Housing options: on-campus residence required for freshman year; coed. Campus housing is university owned.

Athletics Member NAIA. ***Intercollegiate sports:*** basketball M(s)/W(s), football M(s), golf W(s), volleyball W(s), wrestling M(s). ***Intramural sports:*** basketball M/W, bowling M/W, football M/W, golf M/W, gymnastics M/W, racquetball M/W, skiing (cross-country) M/W, skiing (downhill) M/W, soccer M/W, softball M/W, swimming and diving M/W, table tennis M/W, tennis M/W, track and field M/W, volleyball M/W, water polo M/W, weight lifting M/W.

COSTS & FINANCIAL AID

Costs (2017–18) ***Tuition:*** state resident $5480 full-time; nonresident $17,312 full-time. ***Room and board:*** $7500. ***Payment plan:*** deferred payment.

Financial Aid Of all full-time matriculated undergraduates who enrolled in 2012, 772 applied for aid, 686 were judged to have need, 21 had their need fully met. 61 Federal Work-Study jobs (averaging $1382). 25 state and other part-time jobs (averaging $1644). In 2012, 7 non-need-based awards were made. ***Average percent of need met:*** 60. ***Average financial aid package:*** $10,291. ***Average need-based loan:*** $3522. ***Average need-based gift aid:*** $4826. ***Average non-need-based aid:*** $715. ***Average indebtedness upon graduation:*** $21,365.

APPLYING

Options: early admission, deferred entrance.

Application fee: $30.

Required: high school transcript. ***Required for some:*** minimum 2.0 GPA.

Application deadlines: rolling (freshmen), rolling (transfers).

Notification: continuous (freshmen), continuous (transfers).

CONTACT

Montana State University–Northern, PO Box 7751, Havre, MT 59501-7751. *Phone:* 406-265-3704. *Toll-free phone:* 800-662-6132.

Montana Tech of The University of Montana

Butte, Montana

http://www.mtech.edu/

- **State-supported** comprehensive, founded 1895, part of Montana University System
- **Small-town** 56-acre campus
- **Endowment** $32.9 million
- **Coed** 2,594 undergraduate students, 80% full-time, 37% women, 63% men
- **Moderately difficult** entrance level, 89% of applicants were admitted

UNDERGRAD STUDENTS

2,076 full-time, 518 part-time. Students come from 36 states and territories; 14 other countries; 16% are from out of state; 1% Black or African American, non-Hispanic/Latino; 2% Hispanic/Latino; 0.7% Asian, non-Hispanic/Latino; 2% American Indian or Alaska Native, non-Hispanic/Latino; 0.3% Two or more races, non-Hispanic/Latino; 6% Race/ethnicity unknown; 11% international; 7% transferred in; 10% live on campus.

Freshmen:

Admission: 894 applied, 795 admitted, 346 enrolled. ***Average high school GPA:*** 3.53. ***Test scores:*** SAT critical reading scores over 500: 76%; SAT math scores over 500: 88%; SAT writing scores over 500: 55%; ACT scores over 18: 98%; SAT critical reading scores over 600: 18%; SAT math scores over 600: 39%; SAT writing scores over 600: 6%; ACT scores over 24: 55%; SAT math scores over 700: 3%; ACT scores over 30: 5%.

Retention: 76% of full-time freshmen returned.

FACULTY

Total: 228, 65% full-time, 41% with terminal degrees.

Student/faculty ratio: 15:1.

ACADEMICS
Calendar: semesters. *Degrees:* certificates, diplomas, associate, bachelor's, master's, doctoral, and postbachelor's certificates.

Special study options: academic remediation for entering students, adult/continuing education programs, advanced placement credit, cooperative education, distance learning, double majors, external degree program, honors programs, independent study, internships, part-time degree program, services for LD students, student-designed majors, summer session for credit.

Unusual degree programs: engineering.

Computers: 660 computers/terminals are available on campus for general student use. Students can access the following: campus intranet, computer help desk, free student e-mail accounts, online (class) grades, online (class) registration, online (class) schedules. Campuswide network is available. 100% of college-owned or -operated housing units are wired for high-speed Internet access. Wireless service is available via entire campus.

Library: Montana Tech Library. *Books:* 80,864 (physical), 91,830 (digital/electronic); *Serial titles:* 1,859 (physical), 67,191 (digital/electronic); *Databases:* 148. Weekly public service hours: 80; students can reserve study rooms.

STUDENT LIFE
Housing options: on-campus residence required for freshman year; coed, special housing for students with disabilities. Campus housing is university owned. Freshman campus housing is guaranteed.

Activities and organizations: student-run newspaper, radio station, choral group, Circle K, Ski/Snowboard Club, BSU, Hockey Club, Dance Club.

Athletics Member NAIA. ***Intercollegiate sports:*** basketball M(s)/W(s), football M(s), golf M(s)/W(s), volleyball W(s). ***Intramural sports:*** basketball M/W, cheerleading M(c)/W(c), football M/W, ice hockey M(c)/W(c), racquetball M/W, rugby M(c)/W(c), skiing (cross-country) M(c)/W(c), skiing (downhill) M(c)/W(c), softball M/W, volleyball M/W.

Campus security: 24-hour patrols, controlled dormitory access.

Student services: health clinic, personal/psychological counseling.

COSTS & FINANCIAL AID
Costs (2016–17) ***Tuition:*** state resident $5177 full-time, $216 per credit part-time; nonresident $19,303 full-time, $801 per credit part-time. Full-time tuition and fees vary according to course load, degree level, location, program, and student level. Part-time tuition and fees vary according to course load, degree level, location, program, and student level. ***Required fees:*** $1704 full-time, $69 per credit part-time. ***Room and board:*** $8932; room only: $3978. Room and board charges vary according to board plan. ***Payment plan:*** installment. ***Waivers:*** minority students, senior citizens, and employees or children of employees.

Financial Aid Of all full-time matriculated undergraduates who enrolled in 2015, 1,515 applied for aid, 1,182 were judged to have need, 156 had their need fully met. In 2015, 300 non-need-based awards were made. ***Average percent of need met:*** 63. ***Average financial aid package:*** $11,159. ***Average need-based loan:*** $3826. ***Average need-based gift aid:*** $5646. ***Average non-need-based aid:*** $4085. ***Average indebtedness upon graduation:*** $27,193.

APPLYING
Standardized Tests *Required:* SAT or ACT (for admission).

Options: electronic application, deferred entrance.

Application fee: $30.

Required: high school transcript, proof of immunization. ***Required for some:*** minimum 2.5 GPA.

Application deadlines: rolling (freshmen), rolling (transfers).

Notification: continuous (freshmen), continuous (transfers).

CONTACT
Stephanie Crowe, Montana Tech of The University of Montana, 1300 West Park Street, Butte, MT 59701-8997. *Phone:* 406-496-4568. *Toll-free phone:* 800-445-TECH. *Fax:* 406-496-4705. *E-mail:* scrowe@mtech.edu.

Rocky Mountain College
Billings, Montana
http://www.rocky.edu/

- **Independent interdenominational** comprehensive, founded 1878
- **Suburban** 60-acre campus
- **Endowment** $26.5 million
- **Coed** 908 undergraduate students, 94% full-time, 50% women, 50% men
- **Moderately difficult** entrance level, 62% of applicants were admitted

UNDERGRAD STUDENTS
857 full-time, 51 part-time. Students come from 41 states and territories; 14 other countries; 47% are from out of state; 2% Black or African American, non-Hispanic/Latino; 6% Hispanic/Latino; 0.8% Asian, non-Hispanic/Latino; 1% Native Hawaiian or other Pacific Islander, non-Hispanic/Latino; 2% American Indian or Alaska Native, non-Hispanic/Latino; 4% Two or more races, non-Hispanic/Latino; 3% Race/ethnicity unknown; 4% international; 7% transferred in; 45% live on campus.

Freshmen:

Admission: 1,545 applied, 959 admitted, 217 enrolled. ***Average high school GPA:*** 3.31. ***Test scores:*** SAT critical reading scores over 500: 52%; SAT math scores over 500: 50%; SAT writing scores over 500: 33%; ACT scores over 18: 89%; SAT critical reading scores over 600: 11%; SAT math scores over 600: 12%; SAT writing scores over 600: 4%; ACT scores over 24: 29%; SAT math scores over 700: 1%; SAT writing scores over 700: 2%; ACT scores over 30: 5%.

Retention: 69% of full-time freshmen returned.

FACULTY
Total: 125, 54% full-time, 56% with terminal degrees.

Student/faculty ratio: 11:1.

ACADEMICS
Calendar: semesters. *Degrees:* associate, bachelor's, and master's.

Special study options: academic remediation for entering students, accelerated degree program, adult/continuing education programs, advanced placement credit, double majors, English as a second language, honors programs, independent study, internships, off-campus study, part-time degree program, services for LD students, student-designed majors, study abroad, summer session for credit. ***ROTC:*** Army (c).

Unusual degree programs: 3-2 athletic training with Montana State University Billings, accountancy.

Computers: 113 computers/terminals are available on campus for general student use. Students can access the following: campus intranet, computer help desk, free student e-mail accounts, online (class) grades, online (class) registration, online (class) schedules. Campuswide network is available. 100% of college-owned or -operated housing units are wired for high-speed Internet access. Wireless service is available via entire campus.

Library: Paul M. Adams Memorial Library. *Books:* 46,317 (physical), 4,156 (digital/electronic); *Serial titles:* 402 (physical), 50,020 (digital/electronic); *Databases:* 64. Weekly public service hours: 89.

STUDENT LIFE
Housing options: on-campus residence required through sophomore year; coed, special housing for students with disabilities. Campus housing is university owned. Freshman campus housing is guaranteed.

Activities and organizations: drama/theater group, student-run newspaper, radio station, choral group, Outdoor Recreation, Enactus, Flight Team/Club, Residence Hall Association, InterVarsity Christian Fellowship.

Athletics Member NAIA. ***Intercollegiate sports:*** basketball M(s)/W(s), cheerleading M(s)/W(s), cross-country running M(s)/W(s), equestrian sports M(c)/W(c), football M(s), golf M(s)/W(s), skiing (downhill) M(s)/W(s), soccer M(s)/W(s), track and field M(s)/W(s), volleyball W(s). ***Intramural sports:*** basketball M/W, fencing M(c)/W(c), football M/W, golf M/W, ice hockey M(c)/W(c), racquetball M/W, rock climbing M/W, skiing (downhill) M/W, soccer M/W, softball M/W, swimming and diving M/W, table tennis M/W, ultimate Frisbee M/W, volleyball M/W, weight lifting M(c)/W(c).

Campus security: 24-hour emergency response devices, student patrols, late-night transport/escort service, controlled dormitory access, security cameras.

Student services: health clinic, personal/psychological counseling.

COSTS & FINANCIAL AID

Costs (2017–18) ***Comprehensive fee:*** $35,776 includes full-time tuition ($27,036), mandatory fees ($530), and room and board ($8210). Full-time tuition and fees vary according to course load, degree level, and program. Part-time tuition: $1127 per credit. Part-time tuition and fees vary according to course load, degree level, and program. ***Required fees:*** $160 per term part-time. ***College room only:*** $3898. Room and board charges vary according to board plan and housing facility. ***Payment plan:*** installment. ***Waivers:*** employees or children of employees.

Financial Aid Of all full-time matriculated undergraduates who enrolled in 2016, 712 applied for aid, 633 were judged to have need, 122 had their need fully met. 298 Federal Work-Study jobs (averaging $466). 170 state and other part-time jobs (averaging $771). In 2016, 53 non-need-based awards were made. ***Average percent of need met:*** 76. ***Average financial aid package:*** $23,133. ***Average need-based loan:*** $4273. ***Average need-based gift aid:*** $18,115. ***Average non-need-based aid:*** $11,271. ***Average indebtedness upon graduation:*** $30,035.

APPLYING

Standardized Tests *Required:* SAT or ACT (for admission).

Options: electronic application, deferred entrance.

Application fee: $35.

Required: high school transcript, minimum 2.5 GPA. ***Required for some:*** essay or personal statement, 2 letters of recommendation, interview.

Application deadlines: rolling (freshmen), rolling (transfers).

Notification: continuous (freshmen), continuous (transfers).

CONTACT

Austin Mapston, Dean for Enrollment Services, Rocky Mountain College, 1511 Poly Drive, Billings, MT 59102. *Phone:* 406-657-1026. *Toll-free phone:* 800-877-6259. *Fax:* 406-259-9751. *E-mail:* admissions@rocky.edu.

Salish Kootenai College

Pablo, Montana

http://www.skc.edu/

CONTACT

Ms. Jackie Moran, Admissions Officer, Salish Kootenai College, PO Box 70, Pablo, MT 59855-0117. *Phone:* 406-275-4866. *Fax:* 406-275-4810. *E-mail:* jackie_moran@skc.edu.

University of Great Falls

Great Falls, Montana

http://www.ugf.edu/

- **Independent Roman Catholic** comprehensive, founded 1932
- **Urban** 40-acre campus
- **Coed** 1,052 undergraduate students, 58% full-time, 67% women, 33% men
- **Noncompetitive** entrance level, 84% of applicants were admitted

UNDERGRAD STUDENTS

610 full-time, 442 part-time. 62% are from out of state; 3% Black or African American, non-Hispanic/Latino; 7% Hispanic/Latino; 3% Asian, non-Hispanic/Latino; 1% Native Hawaiian or other Pacific Islander, non-Hispanic/Latino; 2% American Indian or Alaska Native, non-Hispanic/Latino; 0.3% Two or more races, non-Hispanic/Latino; 8% Race/ethnicity unknown; 15% transferred in; 38% live on campus.

Freshmen:

Admission: 828 applied, 693 admitted, 168 enrolled. ***Average high school GPA:*** 3.28. ***Test scores:*** SAT critical reading scores over 500: 43%; SAT math scores over 500: 37%; SAT writing scores over 500: 32%; ACT scores over 18: 77%; SAT critical reading scores over 600: 5%; SAT math scores over 600: 9%; SAT writing scores over 600: 8%; ACT scores over 24: 20%; ACT scores over 30: 2%.

Retention: 65% of full-time freshmen returned.

FACULTY

Total: 116, 38% full-time, 43% with terminal degrees.

Student/faculty ratio: 14:1.

ACADEMICS

Calendar: semesters. *Degrees:* certificates, associate, bachelor's, and master's.

Special study options: adult/continuing education programs, part-time degree program.

Computers: Students can access the following: campus intranet, computer help desk, free student e-mail accounts, online (class) grades, online (class) registration, online (class) schedules. Campuswide network is available. Wireless service is available via classrooms, computer centers, computer labs, dorm rooms, learning centers, libraries, student centers.

Library: University of Great Falls Library.

STUDENT LIFE

Housing options: on-campus residence required through sophomore year; coed. Campus housing is university owned and leased by the school. Freshman campus housing is guaranteed.

Athletics Member NAIA. ***Intercollegiate sports:*** basketball M(s)/W(s), cheerleading M(s)/W(s), cross-country running M/W, equestrian sports M(s)/W(s), golf M(s)/W(s), soccer M(s)/W(s), softball W, track and field M(s)/W(s), volleyball W(s), wrestling M(s). ***Intramural sports:*** basketball M/W, equestrian sports M/W(c), football M/W, golf M/W, skiing (downhill) M/W, soccer M/W, softball W, table tennis M/W, track and field M/W, ultimate Frisbee M/W, volleyball M/W, wrestling M.

Campus security: 24-hour emergency response devices and patrols, late-night transport/escort service, controlled dormitory access.

COSTS & FINANCIAL AID

Costs (2017–18) ***Comprehensive fee:*** $33,550 includes full-time tuition ($24,400), mandatory fees ($650), and room and board ($8500). Part-time tuition: $789 per credit hour. ***College room only:*** $4800.

Financial Aid Of all full-time matriculated undergraduates who enrolled in 2016, 415 applied for aid, 360 were judged to have need, 6 had their need fully met. In 2016, 59 non-need-based awards were made. ***Average percent of need met:*** 70. ***Average financial aid package:*** $20,083. ***Average need-based loan:*** $3829. ***Average need-based gift aid:*** $10,788. ***Average non-need-based aid:*** $7724. ***Average indebtedness upon graduation:*** $30,118.

APPLYING

Standardized Tests *Required:* SAT or ACT (for admission). *Recommended:* SAT and SAT Subject Tests or ACT (for admission), SAT Subject Tests (for admission).

Options: electronic application, early admission, deferred entrance.

Application fee: $35.

Required: high school transcript. ***Recommended:*** essay or personal statement, interview.

Notification: continuous (freshmen), continuous (transfers).

CONTACT

Kelly Braun, Assistant Director of Admissions, University of Great Falls, 1301 20th Street South, Great Falls, MT 59405. *Phone:* 406-791-5202 Ext. 5211. *Toll-free phone:* 800-856-9544. *Fax:* 406-791-5209. *E-mail:* enroll@ugf.edu.

University of Montana

Missoula, Montana

http://www.umt.edu/

- **State-supported** university, founded 1893, part of Montana University System
- **Urban** 220-acre campus
- **Endowment** $166.4 million
- **Coed**
- **Moderately difficult** entrance level

FACULTY

Student/faculty ratio: 17:1.

ACADEMICS

Calendar: semesters. *Degrees:* certificates, associate, bachelor's, master's, doctoral, post-master's, and postbachelor's certificates.

Library: Maureen and Mike Mansfield Library plus 2 others. *Books:* 1.3 million (physical), 111,080 (digital/electronic); *Databases:* 224. Students can reserve study rooms.

STUDENT LIFE

Housing options: on-campus residence required for freshman year; coed, men-only, women-only, special housing for students with disabilities. Campus housing is university owned. Freshman campus housing is guaranteed.

Activities and organizations: drama/theater group, student-run newspaper, radio station, choral group, marching band, national fraternities, national sororities.

Athletics Member NCAA. All Division I except football (Division I-AA).

Campus security: 24-hour emergency response devices and patrols, student patrols, late-night transport/escort service, controlled dormitory access.

Student services: health clinic, personal/psychological counseling, women's center, legal services.

COSTS & FINANCIAL AID

Costs (2016–17) ***Tuition:*** state resident $4604 full-time, $192 per credit hour part-time; nonresident $22,720 full-time, $947 per credit hour part-time. Full-time tuition and fees vary according to degree level, location, program, reciprocity agreements, and student level. Part-time tuition and fees vary according to course load, degree level, location, and student level. ***Required fees:*** $1842 full-time. ***Room and board:*** $8826. Room and board charges vary according to board plan and housing facility.

Financial Aid Of all full-time matriculated undergraduates who enrolled in 2015, 6,325 applied for aid, 5,164 were judged to have need, 536 had their need fully met. 1,667 Federal Work-Study jobs (averaging $2886). 31 state and other part-time jobs (averaging $2776). In 2015, 611 non-need-based awards were made. ***Average percent of need met:*** 81. ***Average financial aid package:*** $13,619. ***Average need-based loan:*** $4340. ***Average need-based gift aid:*** $4707. ***Average non-need-based aid:*** $3305. ***Average indebtedness upon graduation:*** $23,927.

APPLYING

Standardized Tests *Required:* SAT or ACT (for admission).

Options: electronic application, early admission, deferred entrance.

Application fee: $36.

Required: high school transcript, minimum 2.5 GPA.

CONTACT

University of Montana, Missoula, MT 59812-0002.
Phone: 406-243-6266. *Toll-free phone:* 800-462-8636.
Fax: 406-243-5711.
E-mail: admiss@umontana.edu.

The University of Montana Western

Dillon, Montana

http://www.umwestern.edu/

- **State-supported** 4-year, founded 1893, part of Montana University System
- **Small-town** 30-acre campus
- **Endowment** $4.3 million
- **Coed** 1,505 undergraduate students, 82% full-time, 61% women, 39% men
- **Minimally difficult** entrance level, 73% of applicants were admitted

UNDERGRAD STUDENTS

1,232 full-time, 273 part-time. Students come from 33 states and territories; 1 other country; 24% are from out of state; 1% Black or African American, non-Hispanic/Latino; 4% Hispanic/Latino; 0.7% Asian, non-Hispanic/Latino; 0.3% Native Hawaiian or other Pacific Islander, non-Hispanic/Latino; 3% American Indian or Alaska Native, non-Hispanic/Latino; 2% Two or more races, non-Hispanic/Latino; 3% Race/ethnicity unknown; 11% transferred in; 27% live on campus.

Freshmen:

Admission: 785 applied, 574 admitted, 336 enrolled. ***Average high school GPA:*** 3.08. ***Test scores:*** SAT critical reading scores over 500: 39%; SAT math scores over 500: 33%; ACT scores over 18: 69%; SAT critical reading scores over 600: 10%; SAT math scores over 600: 3%; ACT scores over 24: 14%; SAT critical reading scores over 700: 2%; ACT scores over 30: 1%.

Retention: 68% of full-time freshmen returned.

FACULTY

Total: 90, 69% full-time, 70% with terminal degrees.

Student/faculty ratio: 17:1.

ACADEMICS

Calendar: semesters. *Degrees:* certificates, associate, and bachelor's.

Special study options: academic remediation for entering students, advanced placement credit, cooperative education, distance learning, double majors, honors programs, independent study, internships, off-campus study, part-time degree program, services for LD students, study abroad, summer session for credit.

Computers: 247 computers/terminals and 240 ports are available on campus for general student use. Students can access the following: campus intranet, computer help desk, free student e-mail accounts, online (class) grades, online (class) registration, online (class) schedules. Campuswide network is available. 100% of college-owned or -operated housing units are wired for high-speed Internet access. Wireless service is available via entire campus.

Library: Lucy Carson Memorial Library. *Books:* 90,019 (physical), 583,775 (digital/electronic); *Serial titles:* 109 (physical); *Databases:* 117. Weekly public service hours: 85; students can reserve study rooms.

STUDENT LIFE

Housing options: on-campus residence required for freshman year; coed, men-only, women-only, special housing for students with disabilities. Campus housing is university owned. Freshman campus housing is guaranteed.

Activities and organizations: drama/theater group, student-run radio station, choral group, Biology Club, Rodeo Club, YoungLife Club, Education Club, Social Club.

Athletics Member NAIA. ***Intercollegiate sports:*** basketball M(s)/W(s), cheerleading M(s)/W(s), cross-country running M(s)/W(s), football M(s), track and field M(s)/W(s), volleyball W(s). ***Intramural sports:*** badminton M/W, basketball M/W, equestrian sports M(c)/W(c), golf M/W, rock climbing M(c)/W(c), skiing (downhill) M(c)/W(c), track and field M/W, volleyball M/W, wrestling M(c)/W(c).

Campus security: 24-hour emergency response devices and patrols, student patrols, late-night transport/escort service.

Student services: health clinic, personal/psychological counseling.

COSTS & FINANCIAL AID

Costs (2016–17) ***Tuition:*** state resident $3699 full-time, $153 per credit hour part-time; nonresident $16,497 full-time, $829 per credit hour part-time. Full-time tuition and fees vary according to course load, location, program, reciprocity agreements, and student level. Part-time tuition and fees vary according to course load, location, program, reciprocity agreements, and student level. ***Required fees:*** $1194 full-time. ***Room and board:*** $7482; room only: $2752. Room and board charges vary according to housing facility. ***Payment plans:*** installment, deferred payment. ***Waivers:*** minority students, senior citizens, and employees or children of employees.

Financial Aid Of all full-time matriculated undergraduates who enrolled in 2016, 1,117 applied for aid, 922 were judged to have need, 1 had their need fully met. 107 Federal Work-Study jobs (averaging $2000). 24 state and other part-time jobs (averaging $2000). In 2016, 16 non-need-based awards were made. ***Average percent of need met:*** 16. ***Average financial aid package:*** $3423. ***Average need-based loan:*** $3954. ***Average need-based gift aid:*** $3514. ***Average non-need-based aid:*** $1261. ***Average indebtedness upon graduation:*** $29,779.

APPLYING

Standardized Tests *Required:* SAT or ACT (for admission).

Options: electronic application, deferred entrance.

Application fee: $30.

Required: high school transcript, MMR immunization record.

Application deadlines: rolling (freshmen), rolling (out-of-state freshmen), rolling (transfers).

Notification: continuous (freshmen), continuous (out-of-state freshmen), continuous (transfers).

CONTACT

Mrs. Janet Jones, Admissions Evaluator, The University of Montana Western, 710 South Atlantic, Dillon, MT 59725. *Phone:* 406-683-7331. *Toll-free phone:* 877-683-7331. *E-mail:* janet.jones@umwestern.edu.

NEBRASKA

Bellevue University

Bellevue, Nebraska

http://www.bellevue.edu/

CONTACT
Nick Baker, Director of Undergraduate Enrollment, Bellevue University, 1000 Galvin Road South, Bellevue, NE 68005-3098. *Phone:* 402-557-7250. *Toll-free phone:* 800-756-7920. *E-mail:* nick.baker@bellevue.edu.

Bryan College of Health Sciences

Lincoln, Nebraska

http://www.bryanhealth.com/CollegeofHealthSciences

CONTACT
Bryan College of Health Sciences, 5035 Everett Street, Lincoln, NE 68506-1398.

Chadron State College

Chadron, Nebraska

http://www.csc.edu/

CONTACT
Ms. Tena Cook, Director of Admissions, Chadron State College, 1000 Main Street, Chadron, NE 69337-2690. *Phone:* 308-432-6263. *Toll-free phone:* 800-242-3766. *Fax:* 308-432-6229. *E-mail:* inquire@csc.edu.

Clarkson College

Omaha, Nebraska

http://www.clarksoncollege.edu/

CONTACT
Clarkson College, 101 South 42nd Street, Omaha, NE 68131-2739. *Phone:* 402-552-3100. *Toll-free phone:* 800-647-5500.

College of Saint Mary

Omaha, Nebraska

http://www.csm.edu/

- **Independent Roman Catholic** comprehensive, founded 1923
- **Urban** 25-acre campus
- **Endowment** $14.8 million
- **Women only** 760 undergraduate students, 94% full-time
- **Minimally difficult** entrance level, 53% of applicants were admitted

UNDERGRAD STUDENTS
717 full-time, 43 part-time. Students come from 23 states and territories; 6 other countries; 23% are from out of state; 8% Black or African American, non-Hispanic/Latino; 13% Hispanic/Latino; 2% Asian, non-Hispanic/Latino; 0.3% Native Hawaiian or other Pacific Islander, non-Hispanic/Latino; 1% American Indian or Alaska Native, non-Hispanic/Latino; 2% Two or more races, non-Hispanic/Latino; 0.1% Race/ethnicity unknown; 0.7% international; 19% transferred in; 27% live on campus.

Freshmen:
Admission: 333 applied, 176 admitted, 103 enrolled. ***Average high school GPA:*** 3.4. ***Test scores:*** ACT scores over 18: 91%; ACT scores over 24: 37%; ACT scores over 30: 7%.
Retention: 70% of full-time freshmen returned.

FACULTY
Total: 164, 38% full-time, 41% with terminal degrees.
Student/faculty ratio: 6:1.

ACADEMICS
Calendar: semesters. *Degrees:* certificates, associate, bachelor's, master's, doctoral, and postbachelor's certificates.
Special study options: academic remediation for entering students, accelerated degree program, advanced placement credit, distance learning, double majors, honors programs, independent study, internships, part-time degree program, services for LD students, study abroad, summer session for credit. ***ROTC:*** Army (c), Air Force (c).
Computers: 190 computers/terminals and 320 ports are available on campus for general student use. Students can access the following: campus intranet, computer help desk, free student e-mail accounts, online (class) grades, online (class) registration, online (class) schedules. Campuswide network is available. 100% of college-owned or -operated housing units are wired for high-speed Internet access. Wireless service is available via entire campus.
Library: College of Saint Mary Library. *Books:* 62,939 (physical), 25,800 (digital/electronic); *Serial titles:* 50 (physical), 54 (digital/electronic); *Databases:* 27. Weekly public service hours: 83; students can reserve study rooms.

STUDENT LIFE
Housing options: on-campus residence required through sophomore year; women-only. Campus housing is university owned. Freshman campus housing is guaranteed.
Activities and organizations: drama/theater group, choral group, Residence Hall Council, Campus Activities Board, Student Education Association of Nebraska, Student Occupational Therapy Club, Student Nurses Association.
Athletics Member NAIA. ***Intercollegiate sports:*** basketball W(s), cross-country running W(s), golf W(s), soccer W(s), softball W(s), swimming and diving W(s), tennis W(s), volleyball W(s).
Campus security: 24-hour emergency response devices and patrols, late-night transport/escort service, controlled dormitory access, surveillance cameras at residence hall entrances; CSM Alert Text Message System.
Student services: health clinic, personal/psychological counseling.

COSTS & FINANCIAL AID
Costs (2017–18) ***Comprehensive fee:*** $27,500 includes full-time tuition ($19,950) and room and board ($7550). Full-time tuition and fees vary according to program. Part-time tuition: $985 per credit. Part-time tuition and fees vary according to course load and program. ***Payment plans:*** installment, deferred payment. ***Waivers:*** senior citizens and employees or children of employees.
Financial Aid Of all full-time matriculated undergraduates who enrolled in 2016, 640 applied for aid, 579 were judged to have need, 65 had their need fully met. 173 Federal Work-Study jobs (averaging $2918). 12 state and other part-time jobs (averaging $5063). In 2016, 117 non-need-based awards were made. ***Average percent of need met:*** 66. ***Average financial aid package:*** $21,185. ***Average need-based loan:*** $5820. ***Average need-based gift aid:*** $15,036. ***Average non-need-based aid:*** $16,024. ***Average indebtedness upon graduation:*** $33,658.

APPLYING
Standardized Tests *Required:* SAT or ACT (for admission). *Required for some:* ACT (for admission).
Options: electronic application.
Application fee: $30.
Required: high school transcript, minimum 2.0 GPA. ***Required for some:*** essay or personal statement, 3 letters of recommendation, interview.
Application deadlines: rolling (freshmen), rolling (transfers).
Notification: continuous (freshmen), continuous (transfers).

CONTACT
Enrollment Services, College of Saint Mary, 7000 Mercy Road, Omaha, NE 68106. *Phone:* 402-399-2355. *Toll-free phone:* 800-926-5534. *Fax:* 402-399-2412. *E-mail:* enroll@csm.edu.

Concordia University, Nebraska

Seward, Nebraska

http://www.cune.edu/

- **Independent** comprehensive, founded 1894, affiliated with Lutheran Church–Missouri Synod
- **Small-town** 120-acre campus with easy access to Omaha
- **Endowment** $45.7 million
- **Coed** 1,794 undergraduate students, 67% full-time, 53% women, 47% men
- **Moderately difficult** entrance level, 73% of applicants were admitted

UNDERGRAD STUDENTS
1,205 full-time, 589 part-time. Students come from 40 states and territories; 10 other countries; 54% are from out of state; 4% Black or African American, non-Hispanic/Latino; 6% Hispanic/Latino; 1% Asian, non-Hispanic/Latino; 0.2% Native Hawaiian or other Pacific Islander, non-Hispanic/Latino; 0.2% American Indian or Alaska Native, non-Hispanic/Latino; 0.1% Two or more races, non-Hispanic/Latino; 10% Race/ethnicity unknown; 2% international; 3% transferred in; 71% live on campus.

Freshmen:
Admission: 1,396 applied, 1,023 admitted, 323 enrolled. ***Average high school GPA:*** 3.49. ***Test scores:*** SAT critical reading scores over 500: 43%; SAT math scores over 500: 55%; ACT scores over 18: 92%; SAT critical reading scores over 600: 17%; SAT math scores over 600: 17%; ACT scores over 24: 44%; SAT critical reading scores over 700: 3%; SAT math scores over 700: 3%; ACT scores over 30: 10%.
Retention: 74% of full-time freshmen returned.

FACULTY
Total: 225, 28% full-time, 51% with terminal degrees.
Student/faculty ratio: 13:1.

ACADEMICS
Calendar: 4-4-1. *Degrees:* bachelor's and master's.
Special study options: academic remediation for entering students, accelerated degree program, adult/continuing education programs, advanced placement credit, distance learning, double majors, independent study, internships, off-campus study, part-time degree program, services for LD students, study abroad, summer session for credit. ***ROTC:*** Army (c), Air Force (c).
Computers: 220 computers/terminals and 1,508 ports are available on campus for general student use. Students can access the following: campus intranet, computer help desk, free student e-mail accounts, online (class) grades, online (class) registration, online (class) schedules, academic plans, human resource data. Campuswide network is available. 100% of college-owned or -operated housing units are wired for high-speed Internet access. Wireless service is available via entire campus.
Library: Link Library plus 1 other. *Books:* 129,751 (physical), 38,421 (digital/electronic); *Serial titles:* 626 (physical), 85 (digital/electronic); *Databases:* 22. Weekly public service hours: 89.

STUDENT LIFE
Housing options: on-campus residence required through junior year; men-only, women-only, special housing for students with disabilities. Campus housing is university owned. Freshman campus housing is guaranteed.
Activities and organizations: drama/theater group, student-run newspaper, choral group, Student Activities Council, Musical Groups, Curtain/Drama Club, Student Senate, Concordia Youth Ministry.
Athletics Member NAIA. ***Intercollegiate sports:*** baseball M(s), basketball M(s)/W(s), cheerleading W(s), cross-country running M(s)/W(s), football M(s), golf M(s)/W(s), riflery M(s)(c)/W(s)(c), soccer M(s)/W(s), softball W(s), tennis M(s)/W(s), track and field M(s)/W(s), volleyball W(s), wrestling M(s). ***Intramural sports:*** badminton M/W, basketball M/W, bowling M/W, cross-country running M/W, soccer M/W, softball M/W, table tennis M/W, tennis M/W, ultimate Frisbee M/W, volleyball M/W.
Campus security: 24-hour emergency response devices and patrols, controlled dormitory access.
Student services: health clinic, personal/psychological counseling.

COSTS & FINANCIAL AID
Costs (2017–18) ***Comprehensive fee:*** $39,100 includes full-time tuition ($30,400), mandatory fees ($600), and room and board ($8100). Part-time tuition: $890 per credit hour. ***College room only:*** $3400. Room and board charges vary according to board plan and housing facility. ***Payment plan:*** installment. ***Waivers:*** employees or children of employees.
Financial Aid Of all full-time matriculated undergraduates who enrolled in 2016, 1,023 applied for aid, 903 were judged to have need, 260 had their need fully met. 80 Federal Work-Study jobs (averaging $1400). In 2016, 124 non-need-based awards were made. ***Average percent of need met:*** 81. ***Average financial aid package:*** $23,520. ***Average need-based loan:*** $4658. ***Average need-based gift aid:*** $18,466. ***Average non-need-based aid:*** $14,690. ***Average indebtedness upon graduation:*** $26,328.

APPLYING
Standardized Tests *Required:* SAT or ACT (for admission).
Options: electronic application, deferred entrance.
Required: high school transcript. ***Required for some:*** essay or personal statement, 2 letters of recommendation.
Application deadlines: 8/1 (freshmen), 8/1 (transfers).
Notification: continuous (freshmen), continuous (transfers).

CONTACT
Mr. Aaron W. Roberts, Director of Undergraduate Recruitment, Concordia University, Nebraska, 800 North Columbia Avenue, Seward, NE 68434-1556. *Phone:* 800-535-5494 Ext. 7233. *Toll-free phone:* 800-535-5494. *Fax:* 402-643-4073. *E-mail:* admiss@cune.edu.

Creative Center
Omaha, Nebraska
http://www.creativecenter.edu/

- **Proprietary** 4-year, founded 1993
- **Urban** 2-acre campus with easy access to Omaha
- **Coed** 60 undergraduate students, 97% full-time, 68% women, 32% men

UNDERGRAD STUDENTS
58 full-time, 2 part-time.

Freshmen:
Admission: 22 enrolled.
Retention: 100% of full-time freshmen returned.

FACULTY
Total: 12, 17% full-time.
Student/faculty ratio: 12:1.

ACADEMICS
Calendar: semesters. *Degrees:* associate and bachelor's.
Special study options: accelerated degree program, part-time degree program, services for LD students.
Computers: 8 computers/terminals are available on campus for general student use. Students can access the following: campus intranet, computer help desk. Campuswide network is available. Wireless service is available via entire campus.
Library: Student Library plus 1 other.

STUDENT LIFE
Housing options: college housing not available.

COSTS
Costs (2017–18) ***One-time required fee:*** $2800. ***Tuition:*** $25,600 full-time, $2560 per course part-time. Full-time tuition and fees vary according to course load, degree level, program, and student level. Part-time tuition and fees vary according to course load, degree level, program, and student level. ***Required fees:*** $2055 full-time, $200 per course part-time.

APPLYING
Required: essay or personal statement, high school transcript, 1 letter of recommendation, interview, portfolio. ***Recommended:*** minimum 2.0 GPA.

CONTACT
Mr. Richard Caldwell, Director of Admissions, Creative Center, 10850 Emmet Street, Omaha, NE 68164. *Phone:* 402-898-1000 Ext. 216. *Toll-free phone:* 888-898-1789. *Fax:* 402-898-1301. *E-mail:* rich_c@creativecenter.edu.

Creighton University
Omaha, Nebraska
http://www.creighton.edu/

- **Independent Roman Catholic (Jesuit)** university, founded 1878
- **Urban** 139-acre campus with easy access to Omaha
- **Endowment** $448.5 million
- **Coed** 4,203 undergraduate students, 95% full-time, 57% women, 43% men
- **Moderately difficult** entrance level, 71% of applicants were admitted

UNDERGRAD STUDENTS
3,981 full-time, 222 part-time. Students come from 46 states and territories; 34 other countries; 76% are from out of state; 2% Black or African American, non-Hispanic/Latino; 8% Hispanic/Latino; 9% Asian, non-Hispanic/Latino; 0.4% Native Hawaiian or other Pacific Islander, non-Hispanic/Latino; 0.4% American Indian or Alaska Native, non-Hispanic/Latino; 4% Two or more races, non-Hispanic/Latino; 2% Race/ethnicity unknown; 3% international; 1% transferred in; 58% live on campus.

Freshmen:
Admission: 10,352 applied, 7,315 admitted, 1,033 enrolled. ***Average high school GPA:*** 3.76. ***Test scores:*** SAT critical reading scores over 500: 81%; SAT math scores over 500: 90%; SAT writing scores over 500: 80%; ACT scores over 18: 100%; SAT critical reading scores over 600: 39%; SAT math scores over 600: 47%; SAT writing scores over 600: 32%; ACT scores over 24: 83%; SAT critical reading scores over 700: 7%; SAT math scores over 700: 11%; SAT writing scores over 700: 5%; ACT scores over 30: 27%.

Retention: 89% of full-time freshmen returned.

FACULTY
Total: 887, 64% full-time, 81% with terminal degrees.

Student/faculty ratio: 11:1.

ACADEMICS
Calendar: semesters. *Degrees:* certificates, associate, bachelor's, master's, doctoral, post-master's, and postbachelor's certificates.

Special study options: accelerated degree program, adult/continuing education programs, advanced placement credit, distance learning, double majors, English as a second language, honors programs, independent study, internships, off-campus study, part-time degree program, services for LD students, study abroad, summer session for credit. ***ROTC:*** Army (b), Air Force (c).

Computers: 404 computers/terminals are available on campus for general student use. Students can access the following: campus intranet, computer help desk, free student e-mail accounts, online (class) grades, online (class) registration, online (class) schedules, financial aid information. Campuswide network is available. 100% of college-owned or -operated housing units are wired for high-speed Internet access. Wireless service is available via entire campus.

Library: Reinert Alumni Memorial Library plus 2 others. Study areas open 24 hours, 5-7 days a week.

STUDENT LIFE
Housing options: on-campus residence required through sophomore year; coed, special housing for students with disabilities. Campus housing is university owned. Freshman campus housing is guaranteed.

Activities and organizations: drama/theater group, student-run newspaper, radio station, choral group, Birdcage, Hui O Hawaii, Pre-Med Society, Partners Against Cancer, American Pharmacists Association Academy of Student Pharmacist, national fraternities, national sororities.

Athletics Member NCAA. All Division I. ***Intercollegiate sports:*** baseball M(s), basketball M(s)/W(s), crew W(s), cross-country running M(s)/W(s), golf M(s)/W(s), soccer M(s)/W(s), softball W(s), tennis M(s)/W(s), volleyball W(s). ***Intramural sports:*** badminton M(c)/W(c), basketball M/W, crew M(c), football M/W, golf M/W, ice hockey M(c), lacrosse M(c)/W(c), racquetball M/W, rugby M(c), skiing (downhill) M(c)/W(c), soccer M/W, softball M/W, table tennis M/W, tennis M/W, ultimate Frisbee M/W, volleyball M/W.

Campus security: 24-hour emergency response devices and patrols, student patrols, late-night transport/escort service, controlled dormitory access, shuttle buses, lighted pathway/sidewalks, self-defense education, crime prevention officer, violence intervention and prevention center.

Student services: health clinic, personal/psychological counseling, women's center.

COSTS & FINANCIAL AID
Costs (2017–18) ***Comprehensive fee:*** $49,452 includes full-time tuition ($37,086), mandatory fees ($1664), and room and board ($10,702). Full-time tuition and fees vary according to program. Part-time tuition: $1160 per credit hour. Part-time tuition and fees vary according to course load and program. ***Required fees:*** $163 per term part-time. ***Room and board:*** Room and board charges vary according to housing facility. ***Payment plan:*** installment. ***Waivers:*** adult students, senior citizens, and employees or children of employees.

Financial Aid Of all full-time matriculated undergraduates who enrolled in 2016, 2,626 applied for aid, 2,155 were judged to have need, 551 had their need fully met. 807 Federal Work-Study jobs (averaging $2179). In 2016, 1543 non-need-based awards were made. ***Average percent of need met:*** 79. ***Average financial aid package:*** $27,537. ***Average need-based loan:*** $6062. ***Average need-based gift aid:*** $21,068. ***Average non-need-based aid:*** $15,136. ***Average indebtedness upon graduation:*** $35,921.

APPLYING
Standardized Tests *Required:* SAT or ACT (for admission).

Options: electronic application, early action, deferred entrance.

Application fee: $40.

Required: essay or personal statement, high school transcript, 1 letter of recommendation. ***Recommended:*** minimum 3.0 GPA.

Application deadlines: 2/15 (freshmen), 8/1 (transfers), 11/1 (early action).

Notification: continuous (freshmen), continuous (transfers), rolling (early action).

CONTACT
Ms. Sarah Richardson, Director of Admissions and Scholarships, Creighton University, 2500 California Plaza, Omaha, NE 68178-0001. *Phone:* 402-280-2703. *Toll-free phone:* 800-282-5835. *Fax:* 402-280-2685. *E-mail:* admissions@creighton.edu.

Doane University

Crete, Nebraska

http://www.doane.edu/

- **Independent** comprehensive, founded 1872, affiliated with United Church of Christ
- **Small-town** 300-acre campus with easy access to Omaha
- **Endowment** $112.9 million
- **Coed** 1,047 undergraduate students, 99% full-time, 49% women, 51% men

UNDERGRAD STUDENTS
1,038 full-time, 9 part-time. Students come from 26 states and territories; 8 other countries; 23% are from out of state; 3% Black or African American, non-Hispanic/Latino; 8% Hispanic/Latino; 1% Asian, non-Hispanic/Latino; 0.2% Native Hawaiian or other Pacific Islander, non-Hispanic/Latino; 0.2% American Indian or Alaska Native, non-Hispanic/Latino; 3% Two or more races, non-Hispanic/Latino; 1% Race/ethnicity unknown; 2% international; 6% transferred in; 82% live on campus.

Freshmen:
Admission: 303 enrolled. ***Average high school GPA:*** 3.55. ***Test scores:*** ACT scores over 18: 97%; ACT scores over 24: 45%; ACT scores over 30: 5%.

Retention: 71% of full-time freshmen returned.

FACULTY
Total: 133, 63% full-time, 81% with terminal degrees.

Student/faculty ratio: 11:1.

ACADEMICS
Calendar: 4-1-4. *Degrees:* bachelor's, master's, doctoral, and post-master's certificates (non-traditional undergraduate programs and graduate programs offered at Lincoln campus).

Special study options: advanced placement credit, cooperative education, double majors, English as a second language, honors programs, independent study, internships, off-campus study, student-designed majors, study abroad, summer session for credit. ***ROTC:*** Army (c), Air Force (c).

Unusual degree programs: 3-2 engineering with Columbia University, Washington University in St. Louis; forestry with Duke University; environmental studies with Duke University.

Computers: 250 computers/terminals and 1,000 ports are available on campus for general student use. Students can access the following: campus intranet, computer help desk, free student e-mail accounts, online (class) grades, online (class) registration, online (class) schedules.

Campuswide network is available. 100% of college-owned or -operated housing units are wired for high-speed Internet access. Wireless service is available via entire campus.
Library: Perkins Library plus 1 other. Study areas open 24 hours, 5-7 days a week; students can reserve study rooms.

STUDENT LIFE
Housing options: on-campus residence required through senior year; coed, women-only. Campus housing is university owned. Freshman campus housing is guaranteed.

Activities and organizations: drama/theater group, student-run newspaper, radio and television station, choral group, marching band, Student Activities Council, Hansen Leadership Program, band/choir, Doane Ambassadors, Doane Art League.

Athletics Member NAIA. ***Intercollegiate sports:*** baseball M(s), basketball M(s)/W(s), cross-country running M(s)/W(s), football M(s), golf M(s)/W(s), soccer M(s)/W(s), softball W(s), tennis M/W, track and field M(s)/W(s), volleyball W(s). ***Intramural sports:*** baseball M(c)/W(c), basketball M/W, bowling M/W, football M/W, golf M/W, ice hockey M, racquetball M(c)/W(c), softball M/W, swimming and diving M/W, table tennis M(c)/W(c), tennis M/W, volleyball M/W, water polo M/W.

Campus security: 24-hour emergency response devices and patrols, student patrols, late-night transport/escort service, controlled dormitory access, evening patrols by trained security personnel.

Student services: health clinic, personal/psychological counseling.

COSTS & FINANCIAL AID
Costs (2016–17) ***Comprehensive fee:*** $39,184 includes full-time tuition ($29,720), mandatory fees ($714), and room and board ($8750). Full-time tuition and fees vary according to location. Part-time tuition: $990 per credit hour. Part-time tuition and fees vary according to course load and location. ***Room and board:*** Room and board charges vary according to board plan, housing facility, and location. ***Payment plan:*** installment. ***Waivers:*** senior citizens and employees or children of employees.

Financial Aid Of all full-time matriculated undergraduates who enrolled in 2016, 890 applied for aid, 793 were judged to have need, 255 had their need fully met. In 2016, 86 non-need-based awards were made. ***Average percent of need met:*** 87. ***Average financial aid package:*** $23,742. ***Average need-based loan:*** $4499. ***Average need-based gift aid:*** $19,722. ***Average non-need-based aid:*** $14,600. ***Average indebtedness upon graduation:*** $30,720.

APPLYING
Standardized Tests *Required:* SAT or ACT (for admission).
Required: high school transcript, 2 letters of recommendation. ***Required for some:*** interview. ***Recommended:*** minimum 2.0 GPA.

CONTACT
Mr. Kyle McMurray, Director of Admission, Doane University, 1014 Boswell Avenue, Crete, NE 68333. *Phone:* 402-826-8222. *Toll-free phone:* 800-333-6263. *E-mail:* kyle.mcmurray@doane.edu.

Grace University
Omaha, Nebraska
http://www.graceuniversity.edu/

CONTACT
Angela Wayman, Director of Admissions, Grace University, 1311 South Ninth Street, Omaha, NE 68108. *Phone:* 402-449-2831. *Toll-free phone:* 800-383-1422. *Fax:* 402-341-9587. *E-mail:* admissions@graceuniversity.com.

Hastings College
Hastings, Nebraska
http://www.hastings.edu/

- **Independent Presbyterian** comprehensive, founded 1882
- **Small-town** 109-acre campus
- **Endowment** $87.2 million
- **Coed**
- **Moderately difficult** entrance level

FACULTY
Student/faculty ratio: 13:1.

ACADEMICS
Calendar: 4-1-4. *Degrees:* bachelor's and master's.
Library: Perkins Library. *Books:* 108,388 (physical), 126,378 (digital/electronic); *Serial titles:* 6,962 (physical), 21,582 (digital/electronic); *Databases:* 56. Weekly public service hours: 93; students can reserve study rooms.

STUDENT LIFE
Housing options: on-campus residence required through junior year; coed, men-only, women-only. Campus housing is university owned. Freshman campus housing is guaranteed.

Activities and organizations: drama/theater group, student-run newspaper, radio and television station, choral group, marching band, Student Association, Student Alumni Ambassadors, Fellowship of Christian Athletes, Phi Mu Alpha Sinfonia, Hastings College Singers.

Athletics Member NAIA.

Campus security: 24-hour emergency response devices, student patrols, late-night transport/escort service, controlled dormitory access, security cameras at entrances and in parking lots.

Student services: health clinic, personal/psychological counseling.

FINANCIAL AID
Financial Aid Of all full-time matriculated undergraduates who enrolled in 2015, 869 applied for aid, 778 were judged to have need, 185 had their need fully met. 62 Federal Work-Study jobs (averaging $1736). In 2015, 283 non-need-based awards were made. ***Average percent of need met:*** 79. ***Average financial aid package:*** $22,923. ***Average need-based loan:*** $4719. ***Average need-based gift aid:*** $19,011. ***Average non-need-based aid:*** $14,776. ***Average indebtedness upon graduation:*** $27,784. ***Financial aid deadline:*** 9/1.

APPLYING
Standardized Tests *Required:* SAT or ACT (for admission).
Options: electronic application.
Required: high school transcript, minimum 2.0 GPA, counselor's recommendation. ***Required for some:*** essay or personal statement, 2 letters of recommendation, interview.

CONTACT
Mr. Chris Schukei, Director of Admissions, Hastings College, 710 North Turner Avenue, Hastings, NE 68901-7621. *Phone:* 402-461-7341. *Toll-free phone:* 800-532-7642. *Fax:* 402-461-7490. *E-mail:* cschukei@hastings.edu.

Kaplan University, Lincoln
Lincoln, Nebraska
http://www.kaplanuniversity.edu/

CONTACT
Kaplan University, Lincoln, 1821 K Street, Lincoln, NE 68508. *Phone:* 402-474-5315. *Toll-free phone:* 800-987-7734.

Kaplan University, Omaha
Omaha, Nebraska
http://www.kaplanuniversity.edu/

CONTACT
Kaplan University, Omaha, 5425 North 103rd Street, Omaha, NE 68134. *Phone:* 402-572-8500. *Toll-free phone:* 800-987-7734.

Midland University
Fremont, Nebraska
http://www.midlandu.edu/

CONTACT
Danielle Oliver, Associate Director of Admissions, Midland University, Fremont, NE 68025-4200. *Phone:* 402-941-6501. *Toll-free phone:* 800-642-8382 Ext. 6501. *E-mail:* oliver@midlandu.edu.

National American University

Bellevue, Nebraska

http://www.national.edu/

CONTACT

National American University, 3604 Summit Plaza Drive, Bellevue, NE 68123.

Nebraska Christian College

Papillion, Nebraska

http://www.nechristian.edu/

- **Independent** 4-year, founded 1944, affiliated with Christian Churches and Churches of Christ
- **Small-town** 85-acre campus with easy access to Omaha, NE
- **Endowment** $1.3 million
- **Coed**

FACULTY

Student/faculty ratio: 5:1.

ACADEMICS

Calendar: semesters. *Degrees:* certificates, associate, and bachelor's. **Library:** Swedberg Library. *Books:* 30,000 (physical), 140,000 (digital/electronic); *Serial titles:* 54 (physical), 3,760 (digital/electronic); *Databases:* 8. Weekly public service hours: 69.

STUDENT LIFE

Housing options: on-campus residence required through junior year; men-only, women-only, special housing for students with disabilities. Campus housing is university owned. Freshman campus housing is guaranteed.

Activities and organizations: choral group, Global Gospel Group, Running Club, Minority Students Organization, Spiritual Life Group, Writing Club.

Athletics Member NCCAA.

Campus security: student patrols, controlled dormitory access.

COSTS & FINANCIAL AID

Costs (2016–17) ***Comprehensive fee:*** $24,500 includes full-time tuition ($16,200), mandatory fees ($300), and room and board ($8000). Full-time tuition and fees vary according to course load. Part-time tuition: $700 per credit hour. Part-time tuition and fees vary according to course load. ***Room and board:*** Room and board charges vary according to board plan and housing facility. ***Payment plans:*** installment, deferred payment.

Financial Aid Of all full-time matriculated undergraduates who enrolled in 2014, 119 applied for aid.

APPLYING

Standardized Tests *Required:* ACT (for admission).

Required: essay or personal statement, high school transcript, 2 letters of recommendation. ***Required for some:*** interview, minimum ACT score of 18 for recent high school graduates.

CONTACT

Mr. D. J. Perkey, Associate Director of Admissions, Nebraska Christian College, 12550 S. 114th Street, Papillion, NE 68046. *Phone:* 402-935-9439. *E-mail:* dj.parkey@nechristian.edu.

Nebraska Methodist College

Omaha, Nebraska

http://www.methodistcollege.edu/

- **Independent** comprehensive, founded 1891, affiliated with United Methodist Church
- **Urban** 8-acre campus
- **Coed** 865 undergraduate students, 56% full-time, 89% women, 11% men
- **Moderately difficult** entrance level, 35% of applicants were admitted

UNDERGRAD STUDENTS

485 full-time, 380 part-time. Students come from 15 states and territories; 3 other countries; 10% are from out of state; 4% Black or African American, non-Hispanic/Latino; 4% Hispanic/Latino; 2% Asian, non-Hispanic/Latino; 0.1% American Indian or Alaska Native, non-Hispanic/Latino; 2% Two or more races, non-Hispanic/Latino; 2% Race/ethnicity unknown; 0.4% international; 25% transferred in; 9% live on campus.

Freshmen:

Admission: 240 applied, 85 admitted, 44 enrolled. ***Average high school GPA:*** 3.51. ***Test scores:*** ACT scores over 18: 100%; ACT scores over 24: 32%; ACT scores over 30: 2%.

Retention: 69% of full-time freshmen returned.

FACULTY

Total: 111, 55% full-time, 19% with terminal degrees.

Student/faculty ratio: 12:1.

ACADEMICS

Calendar: semesters. *Degrees:* certificates, associate, bachelor's, master's, doctoral, post-master's, and postbachelor's certificates.

Special study options: academic remediation for entering students, accelerated degree program, adult/continuing education programs, advanced placement credit, cooperative education, distance learning, external degree program, independent study, services for LD students, summer session for credit. ***ROTC:*** Air Force (c).

Computers: 50 computers/terminals and 25 ports are available on campus for general student use. Students can access the following: campus intranet, computer help desk, free student e-mail accounts, online (class) grades, online (class) registration, online (class) schedules. Campuswide network is available. 100% of college-owned or -operated housing units are wired for high-speed Internet access. Wireless service is available via entire campus.

Library: John Moritz Library. *Books:* 1,957 (physical), 19 (digital/electronic); *Serial titles:* 285 (physical), 10,559 (digital/electronic); *Databases:* 24. Weekly public service hours: 65.

STUDENT LIFE

Housing options: coed. Campus housing is university owned.

Activities and organizations: Student Nurses Association, Methodist Allied Health Student Association, Student Government, Student Ambassadors, Residence Hall Council.

Campus security: 24-hour emergency response devices and patrols, late-night transport/escort service, controlled dormitory access.

Student services: health clinic, personal/psychological counseling.

COSTS & FINANCIAL AID

Costs (2017–18) ***Tuition:*** $15,768 full-time, $584 per credit hour part-time. Full-time tuition and fees vary according to course load, degree level, and program. Part-time tuition and fees vary according to course load, degree level, and program. ***Required fees:*** $320 full-time, $160 per term part-time. ***Room only:*** $6318. ***Payment plan:*** installment. ***Waivers:*** employees or children of employees.

Financial Aid Of all full-time matriculated undergraduates who enrolled in 2016, 430 applied for aid, 377 were judged to have need, 11 had their need fully met. 27 Federal Work-Study jobs (averaging $1500). In 2016, 69 non-need-based awards were made. ***Average percent of need met:*** 32. ***Average financial aid package:*** $9043. ***Average need-based loan:*** $4342. ***Average need-based gift aid:*** $6101. ***Average non-need-based aid:*** $3980. ***Average indebtedness upon graduation:*** $28,461.

APPLYING

Standardized Tests *Required:* SAT or ACT (for admission).

Options: electronic application, deferred entrance.

Application fee: $25.

Required: essay or personal statement, high school transcript, minimum 2.5 GPA.

Application deadlines: rolling (freshmen), rolling (transfers).

CONTACT

Ms. Megan Maryott, Director of Enrollment Services, Nebraska Methodist College, 720 North 87th Street, Omaha, NE 68114. *Phone:* 402-354-7111. *Toll-free phone:* 800-335-5510. *Fax:* 402-354-7020. *E-mail:* megan.maryott@methodistcollege.edu.

Nebraska Wesleyan University

Lincoln, Nebraska

http://www.nebrwesleyan.edu/

- **Independent United Methodist** comprehensive, founded 1887
- **Suburban** 50-acre campus with easy access to Omaha
- **Endowment** $50.9 million
- **Coed** 1,816 undergraduate students, 87% full-time, 58% women, 42% men
- **Moderately difficult** entrance level, 74% of applicants were admitted

UNDERGRAD STUDENTS
1,586 full-time, 230 part-time. Students come from 24 states and territories; 19 other countries; 14% are from out of state; 3% Black or African American, non-Hispanic/Latino; 6% Hispanic/Latino; 2% Asian, non-Hispanic/Latino; 0.1% Native Hawaiian or other Pacific Islander, non-Hispanic/Latino; 0.2% American Indian or Alaska Native, non-Hispanic/Latino; 2% Two or more races, non-Hispanic/Latino; 2% Race/ethnicity unknown; 2% international; 6% transferred in.

Freshmen:
Admission: 1,803 applied, 1,341 admitted, 420 enrolled. ***Average high school GPA:*** 3.63. ***Test scores:*** SAT critical reading scores over 500: 70%; SAT math scores over 500: 70%; ACT scores over 18: 98%; SAT critical reading scores over 600: 20%; SAT math scores over 600: 40%; ACT scores over 24: 54%; SAT math scores over 700: 20%; ACT scores over 30: 9%.

Retention: 78% of full-time freshmen returned.

FACULTY
Total: 111.

Student/faculty ratio: 12:1.

ACADEMICS
Calendar: semesters. *Degrees:* certificates, bachelor's, master's, post-master's, and postbachelor's certificates.

Special study options: accelerated degree program, adult/continuing education programs, advanced placement credit, double majors, independent study, internships, off-campus study, part-time degree program, services for LD students, student-designed majors, study abroad, summer session for credit. ***ROTC:*** Army (c), Navy (c), Air Force (c).

Unusual degree programs: 3-2 engineering with Washington University in St. Louis, Columbia University, University of Nebraska–Lincoln.

Computers: 360 computers/terminals are available on campus for general student use. Students can access the following: computer help desk, free student e-mail accounts, online (class) grades, online (class) registration, online (class) schedules. Campuswide network is available. 100% of college-owned or -operated housing units are wired for high-speed Internet access. Wireless service is available via entire campus.

Library: Cochrane Woods Library. *Books:* 316,222 (physical), 185,022 (digital/electronic); *Serial titles:* 1,711 (physical), 16,353 (digital/electronic); *Databases:* 69. Weekly public service hours: 91; students can reserve study rooms.

STUDENT LIFE
Housing options: on-campus residence required through junior year; coed, women-only. Campus housing is university owned. Freshman campus housing is guaranteed.

Activities and organizations: drama/theater group, student-run newspaper, radio station, choral group, marching band, national fraternities, national sororities.

Athletics Member NCAA. All Division III. ***Intercollegiate sports:*** baseball M, basketball M/W, cheerleading W, cross-country running M/W, football M, golf M/W, soccer M/W, softball W, swimming and diving M/W, tennis M/W, track and field M/W, volleyball W, wrestling M. ***Intramural sports:*** basketball M/W, football M/W, racquetball M/W, sand volleyball M/W, soccer M/W, softball M/W, tennis M/W, ultimate Frisbee M/W, volleyball M/W, weight lifting M/W.

Campus security: 24-hour emergency response devices and patrols, late-night transport/escort service, controlled dormitory access.

Student services: health clinic, personal/psychological counseling, women's center.

FINANCIAL AID
Financial Aid Of all full-time matriculated undergraduates who enrolled in 2012, 1,172 applied for aid, 1,008 were judged to have need, 178 had their need fully met. In 2012, 415 non-need-based awards were made. ***Average percent of need met:*** 69. ***Average financial aid package:*** $17,992. ***Average need-based loan:*** $4729. ***Average need-based gift aid:*** $13,077. ***Average non-need-based aid:*** $8867. ***Average indebtedness upon graduation:*** $28,077.

APPLYING
Standardized Tests *Required:* SAT or ACT (for admission).

Options: electronic application, early decision, deferred entrance.

Required: high school transcript. ***Required for some:*** essay or personal statement.

Application deadlines: 8/15 (freshmen), 8/15 (transfers).

Early decision deadline: 12/1.

Notification: continuous (freshmen), continuous (transfers).

CONTACT
Mr. Gordie Coffin, Director of Admissions, Nebraska Wesleyan University, 5000 Saint Paul Avenue, Lincoln, NE 68504. *Phone:* 402-465-2218. *Toll-free phone:* 800-541-3818. *Fax:* 402-465-2177. *E-mail:* admissions@nebrwesleyan.edu.

Peru State College

Peru, Nebraska

http://www.peru.edu/

- **State-supported** comprehensive, founded 1867, part of Nebraska State College System
- **Rural** 104-acre campus
- **Coed**
- **Noncompetitive** entrance level

FACULTY
Student/faculty ratio: 24:1.

ACADEMICS
Calendar: semesters. *Degrees:* bachelor's and master's.
Library: Peru State College Library.

STUDENT LIFE
Housing options: on-campus residence required through sophomore year; coed, men-only, women-only. Campus housing is university owned. Freshman campus housing is guaranteed.

Activities and organizations: drama/theater group, student-run newspaper, choral group, marching band, Campus Activities Board, Black Student Union, Peru Student Education Association (PSEA), Phi Beta Lambda (PBL), Pilot Club.

Athletics Member NAIA.

Campus security: 24-hour emergency response devices and patrols, late-night transport/escort service.

Student services: health clinic.

APPLYING
Standardized Tests *Required for some:* SAT or ACT (for admission).

Options: electronic application.

Required: high school transcript.

CONTACT
Ms. Micki Willis, Vice President for Enrollment Management and Student Affairs, Peru State College, PO Box 10, Peru, NE 68421. *Phone:* 402-872-2221. *Toll-free phone:* 800-742-4412 (in-state); 800-741-4412 (out-of-state). *Fax:* 402-872-2296. *E-mail:* mwillis@peru.edu.

St. Gregory the Great Seminary

Seward, Nebraska

http://www.stgregoryseminary.edu/

CONTACT
Rev. Peter M. Mitchell, Dean of Men, St. Gregory the Great Seminary, 800 Fletcher Road, Seward, NE 68434. *Phone:* 402-643-4052. *Fax:* 402-643-6964. *E-mail:* sggs@stgregoryseminary.edu.

Union College

Lincoln, Nebraska

http://www.ucollege.edu/

- **Independent Seventh-day Adventist** comprehensive, founded 1891
- **Suburban** 26-acre campus with easy access to Omaha
- **Coed** 805 undergraduate students, 87% full-time, 59% women, 41% men
- **Moderately difficult** entrance level, 64% of applicants were admitted

UNDERGRAD STUDENTS

698 full-time, 107 part-time. Students come from 47 states and territories; 32 other countries; 83% are from out of state; 7% Black or African American, non-Hispanic/Latino; 21% Hispanic/Latino; 4% Asian, non-Hispanic/Latino; 1% Native Hawaiian or other Pacific Islander, non-Hispanic/Latino; 0.1% American Indian or Alaska Native, non-Hispanic/Latino; 5% Two or more races, non-Hispanic/Latino; 0.8% Race/ethnicity unknown; 9% international; 9% transferred in; 63% live on campus.

Freshmen:

Admission: 1,811 applied, 1,150 admitted, 156 enrolled. ***Average high school GPA:*** 3.34. ***Test scores:*** SAT math scores over 500: 45%; SAT writing scores over 500: 40%; ACT scores over 18: 78%; SAT math scores over 600: 25%; SAT writing scores over 600: 25%; ACT scores over 24: 36%; SAT math scores over 700: 5%; SAT writing scores over 700: 5%; ACT scores over 30: 11%.

Retention: 81% of full-time freshmen returned.

FACULTY

Total: 125, 49% full-time, 24% with terminal degrees.

Student/faculty ratio: 11:1.

ACADEMICS

Calendar: semesters. *Degrees:* associate, bachelor's, and master's.

Special study options: accelerated degree program, adult/continuing education programs, advanced placement credit, cooperative education, double majors, honors programs, independent study, internships, off-campus study, part-time degree program, services for LD students, student-designed majors, study abroad, summer session for credit.

Computers: Students can access the following: free student e-mail accounts, online (class) grades, online (class) registration, online (class) schedules. Campuswide network is available. 100% of college-owned or -operated housing units are wired for high-speed Internet access. Wireless service is available via entire campus.

Library: Ella Johnson Crandall Library. Students can reserve study rooms.

STUDENT LIFE

Housing options: on-campus residence required through junior year; men-only, women-only, special housing for students with disabilities. Campus housing is university owned. Freshman campus housing is guaranteed.

Activities and organizations: drama/theater group, student-run newspaper, choral group, Business and Computer Science Club, Math and Science Club, Nursing Club, Amnesty International, International Club.

Athletics ***Intercollegiate sports:*** basketball M/W, golf M, volleyball W. ***Intramural sports:*** basketball M/W, football M/W, gymnastics M(c)/W(c), soccer M(c), softball M/W, volleyball M/W.

Campus security: 24-hour emergency response devices, student patrols, late-night transport/escort service.

Student services: health clinic, personal/psychological counseling.

COSTS & FINANCIAL AID

Costs (2017–18) ***Comprehensive fee:*** $29,996 includes full-time tuition ($21,970), mandatory fees ($1100), and room and board ($6926). Full-time tuition and fees vary according to course load, degree level, and program. Part-time tuition: $916 per credit hour. Part-time tuition and fees vary according to program. ***College room only:*** $3980. Room and board charges vary according to board plan and housing facility. ***Payment plan:*** installment. ***Waivers:*** employees or children of employees.

Financial Aid Of all full-time matriculated undergraduates who enrolled in 2015, 584 applied for aid, 511 were judged to have need, 72 had their need fully met. In 2015, 193 non-need-based awards were made. ***Average percent of need met:*** 65. ***Average financial aid package:*** $15,934. ***Average need-based loan:*** $5022. ***Average need-based gift aid:*** $11,662. ***Average non-need-based aid:*** $6267. ***Average indebtedness upon graduation:*** $34,186.

APPLYING

Standardized Tests *Required:* SAT or ACT (for admission).

Options: electronic application.

Required: high school transcript, minimum 2.5 GPA, 3 letters of recommendation. ***Required for some:*** essay or personal statement, interview.

CONTACT

Addison Hudgins, Assistant Director of Admissions, Union College, 3800 South 48th Street, Lincoln, NE 68506. *Phone:* 402-486-2969 Ext. 2052. *Toll-free phone:* 800-228-4600. *Fax:* 402-486-2895. *E-mail:* enroll@ucollege.edu.

University of Nebraska at Kearney

Kearney, Nebraska

http://www.unk.edu/

- **State-supported** comprehensive, founded 1903, part of University of Nebraska System
- **Small-town** 235-acre campus
- **Coed** 5,108 undergraduate students, 87% full-time, 58% women, 42% men
- **Moderately difficult** entrance level, 85% of applicants were admitted

UNDERGRAD STUDENTS

4,432 full-time, 676 part-time. Students come from 47 states and territories; 59 other countries; 8% are from out of state; 2% Black or African American, non-Hispanic/Latino; 11% Hispanic/Latino; 0.9% Asian, non-Hispanic/Latino; 0.1% Native Hawaiian or other Pacific Islander, non-Hispanic/Latino; 0.2% American Indian or Alaska Native, non-Hispanic/Latino; 2% Two or more races, non-Hispanic/Latino; 0.5% Race/ethnicity unknown; 5% international; 6% transferred in; 90% live on campus.

Freshmen:

Admission: 2,511 applied, 2,144 admitted, 938 enrolled. ***Average high school GPA:*** 3.47. ***Test scores:*** ACT scores over 18: 92%; ACT scores over 24: 39%; ACT scores over 30: 6%.

Retention: 80% of full-time freshmen returned.

FACULTY

Total: 453, 74% full-time, 59% with terminal degrees.

Student/faculty ratio: 14:1.

ACADEMICS

Calendar: semesters. *Degrees:* bachelor's, master's, and post-master's certificates.

Special study options: distance learning, double majors, honors programs, independent study, internships, part-time degree program, services for LD students, study abroad. ***ROTC:*** Army (b).

Computers: 600 computers/terminals and 8,500 ports are available on campus for general student use. Students can access the following: computer help desk, free student e-mail accounts, online (class) grades, online (class) registration, online (class) schedules, online degree audit, online personal information update, online bill viewing and payment, online financial aid awards and acceptance. Campuswide network is available. 92% of college-owned or -operated housing units are wired for high-speed Internet access. Wireless service is available via entire campus.

Library: Calvin T. Ryan Library.

STUDENT LIFE

Housing options: on-campus residence required for freshman year; coed. Campus housing is university owned. Freshman campus housing is guaranteed.

Activities and organizations: drama/theater group, student-run newspaper, radio and television station, marching band, national fraternities, national sororities.

Athletics Member NCAA. All Division II. ***Intercollegiate sports:*** baseball M(s), basketball M(s)/W(s), cross-country running M(s)/W(s), football M(s), golf M(s)/W(s), soccer W(s), softball W(s), swimming and diving W(s), tennis M(s)/W(s), track and field M(s)/W(s), volleyball

W(s), wrestling M(s). ***Intramural sports:*** badminton M/W, basketball M/W, cross-country running M/W, football M/W, golf M/W, racquetball M/W, soccer M/W, softball M/W, tennis M/W, volleyball M/W, water polo M/W, wrestling M/W.

Campus security: 24-hour emergency response devices and patrols, late-night transport/escort service.

Student services: health clinic, personal/psychological counseling.

COSTS & FINANCIAL AID

Costs (2016–17) ***Tuition:*** state resident $5460 full-time, $182 per credit hour part-time; nonresident $11,888 full-time, $396 per credit hour part-time. Full-time tuition and fees vary according to course level, course load, degree level, location, and program. Part-time tuition and fees vary according to course level, course load, degree level, location, and program. ***Required fees:*** $1493 full-time. ***Room and board:*** $9594; room only: $4914. Room and board charges vary according to board plan and housing facility. ***Payment plan:*** installment. ***Waivers:*** employees or children of employees.

Financial Aid Of all full-time matriculated undergraduates who enrolled in 2015, 3,391 applied for aid, 2,805 were judged to have need, 604 had their need fully met. In 2015, 775 non-need-based awards were made. ***Average percent of need met:*** 67. ***Average financial aid package:*** $10,368. ***Average need-based loan:*** $4029. ***Average need-based gift aid:*** $7801. ***Average non-need-based aid:*** $4791. ***Average indebtedness upon graduation:*** $23,879.

APPLYING

Standardized Tests *Required:* SAT or ACT (for admission).

Options: electronic application.

Application fee: $45.

Required: high school transcript, rank in upper 50% of high school class.

Application deadlines: 9/1 (freshmen), rolling (transfers).

Notification: continuous (freshmen), continuous (transfers).

CONTACT

Mr. Dusty Newton, Director of Admissions, University of Nebraska at Kearney, 905 West 25th Street, Kearney, NE 68849-0001. *Phone:* 308-865-8702. *Toll-free phone:* 800-532-7639. *Fax:* 308-865-8987. *E-mail:* admissionsug@unk.edu.

University of Nebraska at Omaha

Omaha, Nebraska

http://www.unomaha.edu/

CONTACT

University of Nebraska at Omaha, 6001 Dodge Street, Omaha, NE 68182. *Phone:* 402-554-3520. *Toll-free phone:* 800-858-8648.

University of Nebraska–Lincoln

Lincoln, Nebraska

http://www.unl.edu/

- **State-supported** university, founded 1869, part of University of Nebraska System
- **Urban** 622-acre campus with easy access to Omaha
- **Endowment** $1.5 billion
- **Coed**
- **Moderately difficult** entrance level

FACULTY

Student/faculty ratio: 22:1.

ACADEMICS

Calendar: semesters. *Degrees:* bachelor's, master's, doctoral, post-master's, and postbachelor's certificates.

Library: Love Memorial Library plus 7 others. *Books:* 3.0 million (physical), 797,644 (digital/electronic); *Serial titles:* 96,500 (physical).

STUDENT LIFE

Housing options: on-campus residence required for freshman year; coed, women-only, cooperative, special housing for students with disabilities. Campus housing is university owned. Freshman campus housing is guaranteed.

Activities and organizations: drama/theater group, student-run newspaper, radio station, choral group, marching band, Student Alumni Association, University Ambassadors, University Program Council, Golden Key Honor Society, ASUN (Association of Students of the University of Nebraska, student body government), national fraternities, national sororities.

Athletics Member NCAA. All Division I except football (Division I-A).

Campus security: 24-hour emergency response devices and patrols, controlled dormitory access.

Student services: health clinic, personal/psychological counseling, women's center, legal services.

COSTS & FINANCIAL AID

Costs (2016–17) ***Tuition:*** state resident $6758 full-time, $225 per credit hour part-time; nonresident $21,278 full-time, $709 per credit hour part-time. Full-time tuition and fees vary according to course load, program, and reciprocity agreements. Part-time tuition and fees vary according to course load, program, and reciprocity agreements. ***Required fees:*** $1780 full-time, $17 per credit hour part-time, $380 per term part-time. ***Room and board:*** $10,670. Room and board charges vary according to board plan and housing facility.

Financial Aid Of all full-time matriculated undergraduates who enrolled in 2014, 11,109 applied for aid, 8,349 were judged to have need, 1,622 had their need fully met. 1,469 Federal Work-Study jobs (averaging $2579). In 2014, 1160 non-need-based awards were made. ***Average percent of need met:*** 78. ***Average financial aid package:*** $13,071. ***Average need-based loan:*** $4441. ***Average need-based gift aid:*** $7325. ***Average non-need-based aid:*** $6486. ***Average indebtedness upon graduation:*** $23,307.

APPLYING

Standardized Tests *Required:* SAT or ACT (for admission). *Recommended:* ACT (for admission).

Options: electronic application.

Application fee: $45.

Required: high school transcript. ***Required for some:*** minimum ACT score of 20 or SAT reading and math of 950 or rank in upper 50% of high school class.

CONTACT

Ms. Amber Williams, Associate Dean - Enrollment Management, University of Nebraska–Lincoln, 1410 Q Street, Lincoln, NE 68588-0417. *Phone:* 402-472-2023. *Toll-free phone:* 800-742-8800. *Fax:* 402-472-0670. *E-mail:* admissions@unl.edu.

University of Nebraska Medical Center

Omaha, Nebraska

http://www.unmc.edu/

CONTACT

University of Nebraska Medical Center, Nebraska Medical Center, Omaha, NE 68198. *Toll-free phone:* 800-626-8431 Ext. 6468.

Wayne State College

Wayne, Nebraska

http://www.wsc.edu/

- **State-supported** comprehensive, founded 1910, part of Nebraska State College System
- **Small-town** 128-acre campus
- **Endowment** $19.0 million
- **Coed** 2,837 undergraduate students, 87% full-time, 57% women, 43% men
- **Noncompetitive** entrance level, 100% of applicants were admitted

UNDERGRAD STUDENTS

2,455 full-time, 382 part-time. Students come from 24 states and territories; 20 other countries; 15% are from out of state; 3% Black or African American, non-Hispanic/Latino; 8% Hispanic/Latino; 0.6% Asian, non-Hispanic/Latino; 1% American Indian or Alaska Native, non-Hispanic/Latino; 2% Two or more races, non-Hispanic/Latino; 2%

Race/ethnicity unknown; 0.5% international; 7% transferred in; 38% live on campus.

Freshmen:
Admission: 1,764 applied, 1,764 admitted, 579 enrolled. ***Average high school GPA:*** 3.22.
Retention: 67% of full-time freshmen returned.

FACULTY
Total: 228, 53% full-time, 48% with terminal degrees.
Student/faculty ratio: 18:1.

ACADEMICS
Calendar: semesters. *Degrees:* bachelor's, master's, and post-master's certificates.
Special study options: adult/continuing education programs, advanced placement credit, cooperative education, distance learning, double majors, honors programs, independent study, internships, off-campus study, part-time degree program, services for LD students, student-designed majors, study abroad, summer session for credit. ***ROTC:*** Army (b).
Computers: 365 computers/terminals are available on campus for general student use. Students can access the following: campus intranet, computer help desk, free student e-mail accounts, online (class) grades, online (class) registration, online (class) schedules. Campuswide network is available. 100% of college-owned or -operated housing units are wired for high-speed Internet access. Wireless service is available via classrooms, computer centers, computer labs, learning centers, libraries, student centers.
Library: U. S. Conn Library. *Books:* 193,749 (physical), 267,267 (digital/electronic); *Databases:* 51.

STUDENT LIFE
Housing options: on-campus residence required for freshman year; coed. Campus housing is university owned. Freshman campus housing is guaranteed.
Activities and organizations: drama/theater group, student-run newspaper, radio and television station, choral group, marching band, national fraternities, national sororities.
Athletics Member NCAA. All Division II. ***Intercollegiate sports:*** baseball M(s), basketball M(s)/W(s), cheerleading M(c)/W(c), cross-country running M(s)/W(s), football M(s), rugby M(c)/W(c), soccer M(c)/W(s), softball W(s), track and field M(s)/W(s), volleyball W(s), wrestling M(c). ***Intramural sports:*** archery M/W, badminton M/W, basketball M/W, bowling M/W, football M/W, golf M/W, racquetball M/W, softball M/W, swimming and diving M/W, table tennis M/W, tennis M/W, track and field M/W, volleyball M/W, weight lifting M/W, wrestling M.
Campus security: 24-hour emergency response devices and patrols, student patrols, late-night transport/escort service, controlled dormitory access.
Student services: health clinic, personal/psychological counseling.

COSTS & FINANCIAL AID
Costs (2016–17) ***Tuition:*** state resident $4800 full-time, $160 per credit hour part-time; nonresident $9600 full-time, $320 per credit hour part-time. Full-time tuition and fees vary according to course level and course load. Part-time tuition and fees vary according to course level and course load. ***Required fees:*** $1627 full-time, $63 per credit hour part-time. ***Room and board:*** $7110; room only: $3470. Room and board charges vary according to board plan and housing facility. ***Payment plan:*** installment. ***Waivers:*** employees or children of employees.
Financial Aid Of all full-time matriculated undergraduates who enrolled in 2016, 2,229 applied for aid, 1,715 were judged to have need, 758 had their need fully met. In 2016, 153 non-need-based awards were made. ***Average percent of need met:*** 56. ***Average financial aid package:*** $9181. ***Average need-based loan:*** $3875. ***Average need-based gift aid:*** $4241. ***Average non-need-based aid:*** $2838.

APPLYING
Options: electronic application, deferred entrance.
Required: high school transcript.
Application deadlines: rolling (freshmen), rolling (transfers).
Notification: continuous (freshmen), continuous (transfers).

CONTACT
Mr. Kevin Halle, Director of Admissions, Wayne State College, 1111 Main Street, Wayne, NE 68787. *Phone:* 402-375-7234. *Toll-free phone:* 866-WSC-CATS. *Fax:* 402-375-7204. *E-mail:* admit1@wsc.edu.

York College

York, Nebraska
http://www.york.edu/

CONTACT
Ms. Janae Parsons, York College, 1125 East 8th Street, York, NE 68467-2699. *Phone:* 402-363-5627. *Toll-free phone:* 800-950-9675. *Fax:* 402-363-5623. *E-mail:* enroll@york.edu.

NEVADA

The Art Institute of Las Vegas

Henderson, Nevada
http://www.artinstitutes.edu/lasvegas/

CONTACT
The Art Institute of Las Vegas, 2350 Corporate Circle Drive, Henderson, NV 89074. *Phone:* 702-369-9944. *Toll-free phone:* 800-833-2678.

Chamberlain College of Nursing

Las Vegas, Nevada
http://www.chamberlain.edu/

- **Proprietary** 4-year
- **Coed**

FACULTY
Student/faculty ratio: 24:1.

ACADEMICS
Degree: bachelor's.

STUDENT LIFE
Housing options: college housing not available.

COSTS
Costs (2016–17) ***Tuition:*** $18,900 full-time, $675 per credit hour part-time. ***Required fees:*** $600 full-time.

APPLYING
Standardized Tests *Required:* SAT or ACT (for admission).
Options: deferred entrance.
Application fee: $95.

CONTACT
Chamberlain College of Nursing, 9901 Covington Cross Drive, Las Vegas, NV 89144. *Toll-free phone:* 877-751-5783.

College of Southern Nevada

Las Vegas, Nevada
http://www.csn.edu/

CONTACT
Admissions and Records, College of Southern Nevada, 6375 West Charleston Boulevard, Las Vegas, NV 89146. *Phone:* 702-651-4060.

DeVry University–Henderson Campus

Henderson, Nevada
http://www.devry.edu/

CONTACT
Admissions Office, DeVry University–Henderson Campus, 2490 Paseo Verde Parkway, Suite 150, Henderson, NV 89074-7120. *Phone:* 702-933-9700. *Toll-free phone:* 866-338-7934.

Great Basin College

Elko, Nevada

http://www.gbcnv.edu/

- **State-supported** primarily 2-year, founded 1967, part of Nevada System of Higher Education
- **Small-town** 45-acre campus
- **Endowment** $6.7 million
- **Coed** 3,362 undergraduate students, 27% full-time, 65% women, 35% men
- **Noncompetitive** entrance level, 61% of applicants were admitted

UNDERGRAD STUDENTS

903 full-time, 2,459 part-time. Students come from 28 states and territories; 26 other countries; 6% are from out of state; 2% Black or African American, non-Hispanic/Latino; 19% Hispanic/Latino; 2% Asian, non-Hispanic/Latino; 0.6% Native Hawaiian or other Pacific Islander, non-Hispanic/Latino; 3% American Indian or Alaska Native, non-Hispanic/Latino; 3% Two or more races, non-Hispanic/Latino; 6% Race/ethnicity unknown; 7% transferred in; 4% live on campus.

Freshmen:

Admission: 804 applied, 490 admitted, 411 enrolled.

Retention: 65% of full-time freshmen returned.

ACADEMICS

Calendar: semesters. *Degrees:* certificates, associate, bachelor's, and postbachelor's certificates.

Special study options: academic remediation for entering students, accelerated degree program, adult/continuing education programs, cooperative education, distance learning, double majors, English as a second language, external degree program, independent study, off-campus study, part-time degree program, services for LD students, summer session for credit.

Computers: 95 computers/terminals are available on campus for general student use. Students can access the following: computer help desk, free student e-mail accounts, online (class) grades, online (class) registration, online (class) schedules. Campuswide network is available. 100% of college-owned or -operated housing units are wired for high-speed Internet access. Wireless service is available via classrooms, computer centers, computer labs, learning centers, libraries, student centers.

Library: Learning Resource Center. *Books:* 94,193 (physical), 250,157 (digital/electronic); *Serial titles:* 2,946 (physical), 230,872 (digital/electronic); *Databases:* 80. Weekly public service hours: 46; students can reserve study rooms.

STUDENT LIFE

Housing options: coed, special housing for students with disabilities. Campus housing is university owned.

Campus security: late-night transport/escort service, evening patrols by trained security personnel.

Student services: personal/psychological counseling.

COSTS & FINANCIAL AID

Costs (2017–18) ***Tuition:*** state resident $2850 full-time, $1330 per year part-time; nonresident $9628 full-time, $2383 per year part-time. ***Required fees:*** $165 full-time, $6 per unit part-time. ***Room only:*** $3150. Room and board charges vary according to housing facility. ***Payment plan:*** installment. ***Waivers:*** employees or children of employees.

Financial Aid Of all full-time matriculated undergraduates who enrolled in 2016, 425 applied for aid, 383 were judged to have need, 17 had their need fully met. In 2016, 90 non-need-based awards were made. ***Average financial aid package:*** $2220. ***Average need-based loan:*** $3201. ***Average need-based gift aid:*** $2885. ***Average non-need-based aid:*** $992.

APPLYING

Options: electronic application, early admission, deferred entrance.

Application fee: $10.

Application deadlines: rolling (freshmen), rolling (transfers).

Notification: continuous (freshmen), continuous (transfers).

CONTACT

Ms. Jan King, Director of Admissions and Registrar, Great Basin College, 1500 College Parkway, Elko, NV 89801. *Phone:* 775-753-2102. *E-mail:* jan.king@gbcnv.edu.

Nevada State College

Henderson, Nevada

http://www.nsc.edu/

- **State-supported** 4-year, founded 2002, part of Nevada System of Higher Education
- **Suburban** 520-acre campus with easy access to Las Vegas
- **Endowment** $1.0 million
- **Coed** 3,747 undergraduate students, 39% full-time, 75% women, 25% men
- **Minimally difficult** entrance level, 76% of applicants were admitted

UNDERGRAD STUDENTS

1,460 full-time, 2,287 part-time. 2% are from out of state; 9% Black or African American, non-Hispanic/Latino; 27% Hispanic/Latino; 12% Asian, non-Hispanic/Latino; 2% Native Hawaiian or other Pacific Islander, non-Hispanic/Latino; 0.6% American Indian or Alaska Native, non-Hispanic/Latino; 5% Two or more races, non-Hispanic/Latino; 8% Race/ethnicity unknown; 10% transferred in.

Freshmen:

Admission: 924 applied, 703 admitted, 282 enrolled. ***Average high school GPA:*** 2.75.

Retention: 72% of full-time freshmen returned.

FACULTY

Total: 267, 27% full-time.

Student/faculty ratio: 18:1.

ACADEMICS

Calendar: semesters. *Degree:* bachelor's.

Special study options: academic remediation for entering students, accelerated degree program, adult/continuing education programs, advanced placement credit, cooperative education, distance learning, double majors, independent study, internships, part-time degree program, services for LD students, student-designed majors, study abroad, summer session for credit. ***ROTC:*** Army (c).

Computers: 140 computers/terminals are available on campus for general student use. Students can access the following: computer help desk, free student e-mail accounts, online (class) grades, online (class) registration, online (class) schedules. Campuswide network is available. Wireless service is available via entire campus.

Library: Nevada State College Library plus 1 other. *Books:* 15,768 (physical), 206,855 (digital/electronic); *Serial titles:* 53,083 (digital/electronic); *Databases:* 98. Students can reserve study rooms.

STUDENT LIFE

Housing options: college housing not available.

Activities and organizations: student-run newspaper, Nevada State Student Alliance (Student Government), Pre-Professional Club, American Sign Language Club, Student Nurses Association, Circle K International.

Campus security: private contracted security patrols.

Student services: health clinic, personal/psychological counseling.

COSTS

Costs (2017–18) ***Tuition:*** state resident $4830 full-time, $161 per credit part-time; nonresident $11,113 full-time, $322 per credit part-time. Full-time tuition and fees vary according to program. Part-time tuition and fees vary according to program. ***Payment plans:*** installment, deferred payment. ***Waivers:*** children of alumni and employees or children of employees.

APPLYING

Options: electronic application.

Application fee: $30.

Required: high school transcript, minimum 2.0 GPA.

Application deadlines: rolling (freshmen), rolling (transfers).

Notification: continuous (freshmen), continuous (transfers).

CONTACT

Adelfa Sullivan, Registrar, Nevada State College, Office of Admissions and Records, 1300 Nevada State Drive, Henderson, NV 89002. *Phone:* 702-992-2115. *Fax:* 702-992-2111. *E-mail:* admissions@nsc.edu.

Pima Medical Institute

Las Vegas, Nevada

http://www.pmi.edu/

CONTACT
Admissions Office, Pima Medical Institute, 3333 East Flamingo Road, Las Vegas, NV 89121. *Phone:* 702-458-9650 Ext. 202. *Toll-free phone:* 800-477-PIMA.

Sierra Nevada College

Incline Village, Nevada

http://www.sierranevada.edu/

- **Independent** comprehensive, founded 1969
- **Small-town** 20-acre campus with easy access to Reno
- **Endowment** $4.3 million
- **Coed** 479 undergraduate students, 97% full-time, 42% women, 58% men
- **Moderately difficult** entrance level, 51% of applicants were admitted

UNDERGRAD STUDENTS
464 full-time, 15 part-time. Students come from 19 states and territories; 7 other countries; 85% are from out of state; 3% Black or African American, non-Hispanic/Latino; 4% Hispanic/Latino; 4% Asian, non-Hispanic/Latino; 2% Native Hawaiian or other Pacific Islander, non-Hispanic/Latino; 3% American Indian or Alaska Native, non-Hispanic/Latino; 8% Race/ethnicity unknown; 1% international; 16% transferred in; 40% live on campus.

Freshmen:
Admission: 851 applied, 438 admitted, 94 enrolled. *Average high school GPA:* 3.14. *Test scores:* ACT scores over 18: 76%; ACT scores over 24: 16%; ACT scores over 30: 2%.
Retention: 63% of full-time freshmen returned.

FACULTY
Total: 155, 31% full-time, 40% with terminal degrees.
Student/faculty ratio: 10:1.

ACADEMICS
Calendar: semesters. *Degrees:* certificates, diplomas, bachelor's, and master's.
Special study options: academic remediation for entering students, accelerated degree program, adult/continuing education programs, advanced placement credit, cooperative education, distance learning, double majors, English as a second language, honors programs, independent study, internships, part-time degree program, services for LD students, student-designed majors, study abroad, summer session for credit.
Unusual degree programs: 3-2 education.
Computers: 50 computers/terminals are available on campus for general student use. Students can access the following: campus intranet, computer help desk, free student e-mail accounts, online (class) grades, online (class) schedules. Campuswide network is available. 100% of college-owned or -operated housing units are wired for high-speed Internet access. Wireless service is available via entire campus.
Library: Prim Library. *Books:* 27,716 (physical), 7,520 (digital/electronic); *Serial titles:* 1,106 (physical); *Databases:* 35. Weekly public service hours: 40.

STUDENT LIFE
Housing options: on-campus residence required through sophomore year; coed, special housing for students with disabilities. Campus housing is university owned. Freshman campus housing is guaranteed.
Activities and organizations: student-run newspaper, choral group, Film Club, International Club, Sustainability Club, Rock Climbing Club, First Generation Club.
Athletics Member NAIA. *Intercollegiate sports:* cross-country running M(s)/W(s), golf M(s)/W(s), lacrosse M(s)/W(s), rock climbing M/W, skiing (downhill) M(s)/W(s), soccer M(s)/W(s). *Intramural sports:* rock climbing M/W, skiing (downhill) M/W, soccer M/W, softball M/W, volleyball M/W.
Campus security: 24-hour emergency response devices and patrols, student patrols, controlled dormitory access.
Student services: personal/psychological counseling.

COSTS
Costs (2017–18) ***Comprehensive fee:*** $45,403 includes full-time tuition ($31,685), mandatory fees ($954), and room and board ($12,764). Full-time tuition and fees vary according to course load, degree level, program, and reciprocity agreements. Part-time tuition: $1348 per credit hour. Part-time tuition and fees vary according to course load, degree level, program, and reciprocity agreements. ***College room only:*** $6382. Room and board charges vary according to board plan. ***Payment plan:*** installment. ***Waivers:*** employees or children of employees.

APPLYING
Standardized Tests *Required:* SAT or ACT (for admission).
Options: electronic application, deferred entrance.
Required: high school transcript, minimum 2.6 GPA. ***Required for some:*** 1 letter of recommendation. ***Recommended:*** essay or personal statement, interview.
Application deadlines: rolling (freshmen), rolling (transfers).

CONTACT
Ms. Julie Hernandez, Sierra Nevada College, 999 Tahoe Boulevard, Incline Village, NV 89451. *Phone:* 866-412-4636. *Fax:* 775-831-6223. *E-mail:* admissions@sierranevada.edu.

Truckee Meadows Community College

Reno, Nevada

http://www.tmcc.edu/

- **State-supported** primarily 2-year, founded 1971, part of Nevada System of Higher Education
- **Suburban** 63-acre campus
- **Endowment** $9.4 million
- **Coed** 10,873 undergraduate students, 26% full-time, 54% women, 46% men
- **Noncompetitive** entrance level, 100% of applicants were admitted

UNDERGRAD STUDENTS
2,843 full-time, 8,030 part-time. Students come from 24 states and territories; 19 other countries; 7% are from out of state; 2% Black or African American, non-Hispanic/Latino; 27% Hispanic/Latino; 6% Asian, non-Hispanic/Latino; 0.1% Native Hawaiian or other Pacific Islander, non-Hispanic/Latino; 1% American Indian or Alaska Native, non-Hispanic/Latino; 4% Two or more races, non-Hispanic/Latino; 2% Race/ethnicity unknown; 0.4% international; 6% transferred in.

Freshmen:
Admission: 2,012 applied, 2,012 admitted, 1,485 enrolled.
Retention: 63% of full-time freshmen returned.

FACULTY
Total: 530, 29% full-time.
Student/faculty ratio: 21:1.

ACADEMICS
Calendar: semesters. *Degrees:* certificates, associate, and bachelor's.
Special study options: academic remediation for entering students, accelerated degree program, adult/continuing education programs, advanced placement credit, cooperative education, distance learning, double majors, English as a second language, independent study, internships, part-time degree program, services for LD students, summer session for credit. ***ROTC:*** Army (c).
Computers: Students can access the following: computer help desk, free student e-mail accounts, online (class) grades, online (class) registration, online (class) schedules. Campuswide network is available. Wireless service is available via entire campus.
Library: Elizabeth Sturm Library.

STUDENT LIFE
Housing options: college housing not available.
Activities and organizations: drama/theater group, student-run newspaper, Entrepreneurship Club, International Club, Phi Theta Kappa, Student Government Association, Student Media and Broadcasting Club.

Campus security: 24-hour emergency response devices and patrols, late-night transport/escort service.

Student services: personal/psychological counseling.

COSTS & FINANCIAL AID

Costs (2016–17) ***Tuition:*** state resident $3030 full-time, $92 per credit hour part-time; nonresident $9675 full-time, $192 per credit hour part-time. Full-time tuition and fees vary according to course load, degree level, and program. Part-time tuition and fees vary according to course load, degree level, and program. ***Required fees:*** $165 full-time, $9 per credit hour part-time. ***Payment plan:*** installment. ***Waivers:*** employees or children of employees.

Financial Aid Of all full-time matriculated undergraduates who enrolled in 2015, 126 Federal Work-Study jobs (averaging $5000). 368 state and other part-time jobs (averaging $5000).

APPLYING

Options: electronic application, early admission, early decision.

Application fee: $10.

Application deadlines: rolling (freshmen), rolling (out-of-state freshmen), rolling (transfers).

Notification: continuous (freshmen), continuous (out-of-state freshmen), continuous (transfers).

CONTACT

Truckee Meadows Community College, 7000 Dandini Boulevard, Reno, NV 89512-3901. *Phone:* 775-673-7240.

University of Nevada, Las Vegas

Las Vegas, Nevada

http://www.unlv.edu/

- **State-supported** university, founded 1957
- **Urban** 332-acre campus with easy access to Las Vegas
- **Endowment** $49.7 million
- **Coed** 24,714 undergraduate students, 74% full-time, 56% women, 44% men
- **Moderately difficult** entrance level, 83% of applicants were admitted

UNDERGRAD STUDENTS

18,322 full-time, 6,392 part-time. Students come from 54 states and territories; 11% are from out of state; 8% Black or African American, non-Hispanic/Latino; 28% Hispanic/Latino; 16% Asian, non-Hispanic/Latino; 1% Native Hawaiian or other Pacific Islander, non-Hispanic/Latino; 0.2% American Indian or Alaska Native, non-Hispanic/Latino; 10% Two or more races, non-Hispanic/Latino; 0.6% Race/ethnicity unknown; 4% international; 10% transferred in; 7% live on campus.

Freshmen:

Admission: 8,533 applied, 7,064 admitted, 3,859 enrolled. ***Average high school GPA:*** 3.31. ***Test scores:*** SAT critical reading scores over 500: 54%; SAT math scores over 500: 57%; SAT writing scores over 500: 46%; ACT scores over 18: 82%; SAT critical reading scores over 600: 15%; SAT math scores over 600: 18%; SAT writing scores over 600: 9%; ACT scores over 24: 29%; SAT critical reading scores over 700: 2%; SAT math scores over 700: 3%; SAT writing scores over 700: 1%; ACT scores over 30: 3%.

Retention: 77% of full-time freshmen returned.

ACADEMICS

Calendar: semesters. *Degrees:* certificates, bachelor's, master's, doctoral, post-master's, and postbachelor's certificates.

Special study options: academic remediation for entering students, adult/continuing education programs, advanced placement credit, cooperative education, distance learning, double majors, English as a second language, honors programs, independent study, internships, part-time degree program, services for LD students, study abroad, summer session for credit. ***ROTC:*** Army (b), Air Force (b).

Computers: 2,100 computers/terminals and 8,000 ports are available on campus for general student use. Students can access the following: campus intranet, computer help desk, free student e-mail accounts, online (class) grades, online (class) registration, online (class) schedules. Campuswide network is available. 100% of college-owned or -operated housing units are wired for high-speed Internet access. Wireless service is available via entire campus.

Library: Lied Library. *Books:* 939,652 (physical), 1.3 million (digital/electronic); *Serial titles:* 20,453 (physical), 59,248 (digital/electronic); *Databases:* 320. Weekly public service hours: 101; students can reserve study rooms.

STUDENT LIFE

Housing options: coed, special housing for students with disabilities. Campus housing is university owned. Freshman applicants given priority for college housing.

Activities and organizations: drama/theater group, student-run newspaper, radio and television station, choral group, marching band, National Society of Leadership and Success, National Society of Minorities in Hospitality, Residential Hall Association, Social sororities and fraternities, `Ewalu Club, national fraternities, national sororities.

Athletics Member NCAA. All Division I except football (Division I-A). ***Intercollegiate sports:*** baseball M(s), basketball M(s)/W(s), cheerleading M(s)/W(s), cross-country running W(s), golf M(s), soccer M(s)/W(s), softball W(s), swimming and diving M(s)/W(s), tennis M(s)/W(s), track and field W(s), volleyball W(s). ***Intramural sports:*** badminton M/W, basketball M/W, bowling M/W, football M/W, golf M/W, racquetball M/W, soccer M/W, softball M/W, swimming and diving M/W, tennis M/W, volleyball M/W.

Campus security: 24-hour emergency response devices and patrols, late-night transport/escort service, controlled dormitory access.

Student services: health clinic, personal/psychological counseling, women's center, legal services.

COSTS & FINANCIAL AID

Costs (2017–18) ***One-time required fee:*** $120. ***Tuition:*** state resident $6764 full-time, $216 per credit hour part-time; nonresident $20,952 full-time. Full-time tuition and fees vary according to course level, program, and reciprocity agreements. Part-time tuition and fees vary according to course level, program, and reciprocity agreements. ***Required fees:*** $546 full-time, $10 per credit hour part-time, $273 per term part-time. ***Room and board:*** $10,806; room only: $5880. Room and board charges vary according to board plan and housing facility. ***Payment plan:*** deferred payment. ***Waivers:*** employees or children of employees.

Financial Aid Of all full-time matriculated undergraduates who enrolled in 2015, 13,264 applied for aid, 11,243 were judged to have need, 1,495 had their need fully met. In 2015, 1225 non-need-based awards were made. ***Average percent of need met:*** 69. ***Average financial aid package:*** $11,291. ***Average need-based loan:*** $3915. ***Average need-based gift aid:*** $5986. ***Average non-need-based aid:*** $4231. ***Average indebtedness upon graduation:*** $24,890.

APPLYING

Standardized Tests *Required:* SAT or ACT (for admission).

Options: electronic application, early admission, deferred entrance.

Application fee: $60.

Required: high school transcript, minimum 3.0 GPA.

Application deadlines: 7/1 (freshmen), 7/1 (transfers).

Notification: continuous (freshmen), continuous (transfers).

CONTACT

Director of Admissions, University of Nevada, Las Vegas, 4505 Maryland Parkway, Box 451021, Las Vegas, NV 89154-1021.
Phone: 702-774-8658. *Fax:* 702-774-8008.
E-mail: admissions@unlv.edu.

University of Nevada, Reno

Reno, Nevada

http://www.unr.edu/

- **State-supported** university, founded 1874, part of Nevada System of Higher Education
- **Urban** 200-acre campus
- **Endowment** $302.7 million
- **Coed** 18,191 undergraduate students, 85% full-time, 53% women, 47% men
- **Moderately difficult** entrance level, 83% of applicants were admitted

UNDERGRAD STUDENTS

15,408 full-time, 2,783 part-time. Students come from 45 states and territories; 65 other countries; 30% are from out of state; 32% Black or

African American, non-Hispanic/Latino; 192% Hispanic/Latino; 7% Asian, non-Hispanic/Latino; 71% Native Hawaiian or other Pacific Islander, non-Hispanic/Latino; 7% American Indian or Alaska Native, non-Hispanic/Latino; 6% Two or more races, non-Hispanic/Latino; 16% Race/ethnicity unknown; 15% international; 7% transferred in; 22% live on campus.

Freshmen:
Admission: 9,644 applied, 7,986 admitted, 3,353 enrolled. ***Average high school GPA:*** 3.38. ***Test scores:*** SAT critical reading scores over 500: 71%; SAT math scores over 500: 73%; SAT writing scores over 500: 61%; ACT scores over 18: 93%; SAT critical reading scores over 600: 25%; SAT math scores over 600: 29%; SAT writing scores over 600: 18%; ACT scores over 24: 46%; SAT critical reading scores over 700: 3%; SAT math scores over 700: 3%; SAT writing scores over 700: 2%; ACT scores over 30: 7%.
Retention: 81% of full-time freshmen returned.

FACULTY
Total: 1,231, 56% full-time, 65% with terminal degrees.
Student/faculty ratio: 21:1.

ACADEMICS
Calendar: semesters. *Degrees:* certificates, bachelor's, master's, doctoral, post-master's, and postbachelor's certificates.
Special study options: academic remediation for entering students, adult/continuing education programs, advanced placement credit, distance learning, double majors, English as a second language, honors programs, independent study, internships, off-campus study, part-time degree program, services for LD students, study abroad, summer session for credit. ***ROTC:*** Army (b).
Unusual degree programs: 3-2 biotechnology.
Computers: Students can access the following: computer help desk, free student e-mail accounts, online (class) grades, online (class) registration, online (class) schedules. Campuswide network is available. 100% of college-owned or -operated housing units are wired for high-speed Internet access. Wireless service is available via entire campus.
Library: Mathewson-IGT Knowledge Center plus 2 others. *Books:* 1.4 million (physical), 588,940 (digital/electronic). Students can reserve study rooms.

STUDENT LIFE
Housing options: coed, men-only, women-only, special housing for students with disabilities. Campus housing is university owned. Freshman applicants given priority for college housing.
Activities and organizations: drama/theater group, student-run newspaper, radio station, choral group, marching band, Intervarsity Christian Fellowship, Student Ambassadors, Young Democrats, Asian American Association, Blue Crew, national fraternities, national sororities.
Athletics Member NCAA. All Division I except football (Division I-A). ***Intercollegiate sports:*** baseball M(s), basketball M(s)/W(s), cheerleading M(c)/W(c), cross-country running W(s), golf M(s)/W(s), riflery M(s)/W(s), soccer W(s), softball W(s), swimming and diving W(s), tennis M(s)/W(s), track and field W(s), volleyball W(s). ***Intramural sports:*** basketball M/W, bowling M/W, cross-country running M/W, equestrian sports M/W, football M, golf M/W, racquetball M/W, rock climbing M/W, rugby M/W, skiing (cross-country) M/W, skiing (downhill) M/W, soccer M/W, softball M/W, swimming and diving M/W, table tennis M/W, tennis M/W, track and field M/W, ultimate Frisbee M/W, volleyball M/W, water polo M/W.
Campus security: 24-hour emergency response devices and patrols, late-night transport/escort service, controlled dormitory access.
Student services: health clinic, personal/psychological counseling, women's center, legal services.

COSTS & FINANCIAL AID
Costs (2017–18) ***Tuition:*** state resident $6735 full-time, $225 per credit part-time; nonresident $20,923 full-time, $462 per credit hour part-time. Full-time tuition and fees vary according to course level, course load, degree level, and program. Part-time tuition and fees vary according to course level, course load, degree level, and program. ***Required fees:*** $642 full-time, $282 per term part-time. ***Room and board:*** $10,868; room only: $6100. Room and board charges vary according to board plan and housing facility. ***Payment plan:*** installment. ***Waivers:*** senior citizens and employees or children of employees.
Financial Aid Of all full-time matriculated undergraduates who enrolled in 2015, 10,201 applied for aid, 7,911 were judged to have need, 729 had their need fully met. In 2015, 1968 non-need-based awards were made. ***Average percent of need met:*** 61. ***Average financial aid package:*** $8756. ***Average need-based loan:*** $4095. ***Average need-based gift aid:*** $5080. ***Average non-need-based aid:*** $2250. ***Average indebtedness upon graduation:*** $23,110.

APPLYING
Standardized Tests *Required:* SAT or ACT (for admission).
Options: electronic application, early admission, deferred entrance.
Application fee: $60.
Required: high school transcript, minimum 3.0 GPA.
Application deadlines: 5/1 (freshmen), 7/1 (transfers).
Notification: continuous (freshmen), continuous (out-of-state freshmen), continuous (transfers).

CONTACT
Dr. Steve Maples, Director of Undergraduate Admissions, University of Nevada, Reno, Mail Stop 120, Reno, NV 89557. *Phone:* 775-784-4700. *Toll-free phone:* 866-263-8232. *Fax:* 775-784-4283.
E-mail: asknevada@unr.edu.

University of Phoenix–Las Vegas Campus

Las Vegas, Nevada

http://www.phoenix.edu/

CONTACT
Marc Booker, Sr. Director, Office of Admissions and Evaluation, University of Phoenix–Las Vegas Campus, 4305 South Riverpoint Parkway, Mail Stop CF-L101, Phoenix, AZ 85040. *Phone:* 602-557-4609. *Toll-free phone:* 866-766-0766. *Fax:* 480-643-1156.

Western Nevada College

Carson City, Nevada

http://www.wnc.edu/

- **State-supported** primarily 2-year, founded 1971, part of Nevada System of Higher Education
- **Small-town** 200-acre campus
- **Endowment** $250,000
- **Coed** 3,567 undergraduate students, 35% full-time, 55% women, 45% men
- **Noncompetitive** entrance level, 81% of applicants were admitted

UNDERGRAD STUDENTS
1,231 full-time, 2,336 part-time. Students come from 6 states and territories; 21 other countries; 3% are from out of state; 2% Black or African American, non-Hispanic/Latino; 22% Hispanic/Latino; 2% Asian, non-Hispanic/Latino; 0.8% Native Hawaiian or other Pacific Islander, non-Hispanic/Latino; 2% American Indian or Alaska Native, non-Hispanic/Latino; 3% Two or more races, non-Hispanic/Latino; 4% Race/ethnicity unknown; 0.3% international; 6% transferred in.

Freshmen:
Admission: 804 applied, 652 admitted, 652 enrolled.
Retention: 55% of full-time freshmen returned.

FACULTY
Total: 241, 22% full-time.
Student/faculty ratio: 18:1.

ACADEMICS
Calendar: semesters. *Degrees:* certificates, associate, and bachelor's.
Special study options: academic remediation for entering students, adult/continuing education programs, advanced placement credit, cooperative education, distance learning, double majors, English as a second language, honors programs, independent study, internships, part-time degree program, services for LD students, summer session for credit.

Computers: 669 computers/terminals and 25 ports are available on campus for general student use. Students can access the following: computer help desk, online (class) grades, online (class) registration, online (class) schedules. Campuswide network is available. Wireless service is available via entire campus.

Library: Western Nevada College Library and Media Services plus 1 other. *Books:* 35,923 (physical), 4,544 (digital/electronic); *Serial titles:* 2,725 (physical); *Databases:* 33. Weekly public service hours: 61; students can reserve study rooms.

STUDENT LIFE

Housing options: college housing not available.

Activities and organizations: drama/theater group, choral group, Associated Students of Western Nevada, Soccer Club, Veterans Club, National Student Nurses Association, American Sign Language Club.

Athletics ***Intramural sports:*** soccer M(c)/W(c).

Campus security: late-night transport/escort service.

Student services: personal/psychological counseling.

COSTS & FINANCIAL AID

Costs (2017–18) ***Tuition:*** state resident $3015 full-time, $1407 per credit part-time; nonresident $9793 full-time, $2460 per credit part-time. Full-time tuition and fees vary according to degree level. Part-time tuition and fees vary according to degree level. ***Payment plans:*** tuition prepayment, installment. ***Waivers:*** employees or children of employees.

Financial Aid Of all full-time matriculated undergraduates who enrolled in 2016, 445 applied for aid, 413 were judged to have need, 8 had their need fully met. In 2016, 52 non-need-based awards were made. ***Average financial aid package:*** $2308. ***Average need-based loan:*** $2450. ***Average need-based gift aid:*** $2607. ***Average non-need-based aid:*** $627.

APPLYING

Options: electronic application, early admission.

Application fee: $15.

Required for some: high school transcript. ***Recommended:*** high school transcript.

Application deadlines: rolling (freshmen), rolling (transfers).

CONTACT

Admissions and Records, Western Nevada College, 2201 West College Parkway, Carson City, NV 89703. *Phone:* 775-445-2377. *Fax:* 775-445-3147. *E-mail:* wncc_aro@wncc.edu.

NEW HAMPSHIRE

Colby-Sawyer College

New London, New Hampshire

http://www.colby-sawyer.edu/

- **Independent** 4-year, founded 1837
- **Small-town** 200-acre campus
- **Endowment** $36.0 million
- **Coed** 1,090 undergraduate students, 93% full-time, 70% women, 30% men
- **Moderately difficult** entrance level, 87% of applicants were admitted

UNDERGRAD STUDENTS

1,011 full-time, 79 part-time. Students come from 29 states and territories; 25 other countries; 72% are from out of state; 6% Black or African American, non-Hispanic/Latino; 3% Hispanic/Latino; 2% Asian, non-Hispanic/Latino; 1% American Indian or Alaska Native, non-Hispanic/Latino; 0.2% Two or more races, non-Hispanic/Latino; 10% Race/ethnicity unknown; 8% international; 3% transferred in; 87% live on campus.

Freshmen:

Admission: 1,989 applied, 1,731 admitted, 252 enrolled. ***Average high school GPA:*** 3.3.

Retention: 78% of full-time freshmen returned.

FACULTY

Total: 101, 66% full-time, 57% with terminal degrees.

Student/faculty ratio: 14:1.

ACADEMICS

Calendar: semesters. *Degrees:* certificates, associate, and bachelor's.

Special study options: accelerated degree program, advanced placement credit, distance learning, double majors, honors programs, independent study, internships, off-campus study, part-time degree program, services for LD students, student-designed majors, study abroad. ***ROTC:*** Army (c).

Unusual degree programs: 3-2 Vermont Law School.

Computers: 180 computers/terminals and 1,200 ports are available on campus for general student use. Students can access the following: campus intranet, computer help desk, free student e-mail accounts, online (class) grades, online (class) registration, online (class) schedules, online bill payment, SmartCard (for use on campus and with selected local vendors), learning management systems, tutoring, reference librarians via chat, e-databases/e-journals, disk storage space. Campuswide network is available. 100% of college-owned or -operated housing units are wired for high-speed Internet access. Wireless service is available via entire campus.

Library: Susan Colgate Cleveland Library Learning Center. *Books:* 83,409 (physical), 144,473 (digital/electronic); *Serial titles:* 486 (physical); *Databases:* 119. Weekly public service hours: 100; students can reserve study rooms.

STUDENT LIFE

Housing options: on-campus residence required through sophomore year; coed, women-only. Campus housing is university owned and leased by the school. Freshman campus housing is guaranteed.

Activities and organizations: drama/theater group, student-run newspaper, choral group, Campus Activities Board, Student Government Association, Dance Club, Colby-Sawyer Players (Theater), Student Nurses Association.

Athletics Member NCAA. All Division III. ***Intercollegiate sports:*** baseball M, basketball M/W, cross-country running M/W, equestrian sports M/W, field hockey W, golf M(c)/W(c), ice hockey M(c)/W(c), lacrosse W, rugby M(c)/W(c), skiing (downhill) M/W, soccer M/W, softball W(c), swimming and diving M/W, tennis M/W, track and field M/W, volleyball W. ***Intramural sports:*** basketball M/W, cheerleading W(c), football M/W, golf M/W, lacrosse M(c), racquetball M/W, volleyball M/W.

Campus security: 24-hour emergency response devices and patrols, late-night transport/escort service, controlled dormitory access, awareness seminars.

Student services: health clinic, personal/psychological counseling.

COSTS & FINANCIAL AID

Costs (2017–18) ***Comprehensive fee:*** $54,836 includes full-time tuition ($40,386), mandatory fees ($800), and room and board ($13,650). Part-time tuition: $1346 per credit. Part-time tuition and fees vary according to course load. ***Room and board:*** Room and board charges vary according to board plan and housing facility. ***Payment plan:*** installment. ***Waivers:*** employees or children of employees.

Financial Aid ***Financial aid deadline:*** 3/1.

APPLYING

Options: electronic application, early admission, early action, deferred entrance.

Application fee: $45.

Required: essay or personal statement, high school transcript, minimum 2.5 GPA, college preparatory courses: 4 years of English, 3 years of math, 3 years of lab science, 3 years of social science and 2 years of the same language. ***Recommended:*** 1 letter of recommendation, interview.

Application deadlines: 4/1 (freshmen), 8/1 (transfers), 12/1 (early action).

Notification: continuous until 1/1 (freshmen), continuous until 1/1 (transfers).

CONTACT

Ms. Jaimee Hofstetter, Director of Enrollment Operations, Colby-Sawyer College, 541 Main Street, New London, NH 03257-4648. *Phone:* 603-526-3887. *Toll-free phone:* 800-272-1015. *Fax:* 603-526-3452. *E-mail:* admissions@colby-sawyer.edu.

Dartmouth College

Hanover, New Hampshire

http://www.dartmouth.edu/

- **Independent** university, founded 1769
- **Small-town** 269-acre campus
- **Endowment** $4.5 billion
- **Coed** 4,310 undergraduate students, 99% full-time, 50% women, 50% men
- **Most difficult** entrance level, 11% of applicants were admitted

UNDERGRAD STUDENTS

4,270 full-time, 40 part-time. Students come from 52 states and territories; 71 other countries; 98% are from out of state; 7% Black or African American, non-Hispanic/Latino; 9% Hispanic/Latino; 15% Asian, non-Hispanic/Latino; 0.3% Native Hawaiian or other Pacific Islander, non-Hispanic/Latino; 2% American Indian or Alaska Native, non-Hispanic/Latino; 5% Two or more races, non-Hispanic/Latino; 3% Race/ethnicity unknown; 9% international; 0.4% transferred in; 98% live on campus.

Freshmen:

Admission: 20,675 applied, 2,190 admitted, 1,116 enrolled. ***Test scores:*** SAT critical reading scores over 500: 99%; SAT math scores over 500: 100%; SAT writing scores over 500: 100%; SAT critical reading scores over 600: 91%; SAT math scores over 600: 95%; SAT writing scores over 600: 93%; SAT critical reading scores over 700: 66%; SAT math scores over 700: 68%; SAT writing scores over 700: 70%.

Retention: 97% of full-time freshmen returned.

FACULTY

Total: 757, 78% full-time, 91% with terminal degrees.

Student/faculty ratio: 7:1.

ACADEMICS

Calendar: quarters. *Degrees:* bachelor's, master's, and doctoral.

Special study options: advanced placement credit, double majors, honors programs, independent study, internships, off-campus study, services for LD students, student-designed majors, study abroad, summer session for credit. ***ROTC:*** Army (c).

Unusual degree programs: 3-2 engineering.

Computers: 200 computers/terminals are available on campus for general student use. Students can access the following: campus intranet, computer help desk, free student e-mail accounts, online (class) grades, online (class) registration, online (class) schedules. Campuswide network is available. 100% of college-owned or -operated housing units are wired for high-speed Internet access. Wireless service is available via entire campus.

Library: Baker-Berry Library plus 9 others. *Books:* 2.6 million (physical); *Serial titles:* 72,726 (physical). Study areas open 24 hours, 5-7 days a week; students can reserve study rooms.

STUDENT LIFE

Housing options: on-campus residence required for freshman year; coed, cooperative. Campus housing is university owned. Freshman campus housing is guaranteed.

Activities and organizations: drama/theater group, student-run newspaper, radio and television station, choral group, marching band, Dartmouth Student Assembly, Dartmouth Outing Club, Collis After Dark, Green Key Society, GLOS - Greek Letter Organizations and Societies, national fraternities, national sororities.

Athletics Member NCAA. All Division I except football (Division I-AA). ***Intercollegiate sports:*** badminton M(c)/W(c), baseball M, basketball M/W, cheerleading M(c)/W(c), crew M/W, cross-country running M/W, equestrian sports M/W, fencing M(c)/W(c), field hockey W, golf M/W, gymnastics M(c)/W(c), ice hockey M/W, lacrosse M/W, rowing M/W, rugby M(c)/W(c), sailing M/W, skiing (cross-country) M/W, skiing (downhill) M/W, soccer M/W, softball W, squash M/W, swimming and diving M/W, table tennis M(c)/W(c), tennis M/W, track and field M/W, ultimate Frisbee M(c)/W(c), volleyball M(c)/W, water polo M(c)/W(c), wrestling M(c). ***Intramural sports:*** baseball M, basketball M/W, cross-country running M/W, football M/W, golf M/W, ice hockey M/W, lacrosse M/W, rugby M/W, skiing (cross-country) M/W, skiing (downhill) M/W, soccer M/W, softball M/W, squash M/W, swimming and diving M/W, table tennis M/W, tennis M/W, track and field M/W, volleyball M/W, water polo M/W, weight lifting M/W, wrestling M.

Campus security: 24-hour emergency response devices and patrols, student patrols, late-night transport/escort service, controlled dormitory access.

Student services: health clinic, personal/psychological counseling, women's center.

COSTS & FINANCIAL AID

Costs (2016–17) ***One-time required fee:*** $405. ***Comprehensive fee:*** $66,174 includes full-time tuition ($49,998), mandatory fees ($1440), and room and board ($14,736). ***College room only:*** $8886. Room and board charges vary according to board plan. ***Payment plans:*** tuition prepayment, installment.

Financial Aid Of all full-time matriculated undergraduates who enrolled in 2016, 2,458 applied for aid, 2,179 were judged to have need, 2,179 had their need fully met. 1,232 Federal Work-Study jobs (averaging $2196). 567 state and other part-time jobs (averaging $2480). ***Average percent of need met:*** 100. ***Average financial aid package:*** $49,141. ***Average need-based loan:*** $4579. ***Average need-based gift aid:*** $46,770. ***Average indebtedness upon graduation:*** $17,849. ***Financial aid deadline:*** 2/1.

APPLYING

Standardized Tests *Required:* SAT or ACT (for admission). *Recommended:* SAT Subject Tests (for admission).

Options: electronic application, early admission, early decision, deferred entrance.

Application fee: $80.

Required: essay or personal statement, high school transcript, 2 letters of recommendation, peer evaluation. ***Recommended:*** interview.

Application deadlines: 1/1 (freshmen), 3/1 (transfers).

Early decision deadline: 11/1.

Notification: 4/10 (freshmen), 5/15 (transfers), 12/15 (early decision).

CONTACT

Paul Sunde, Interim Dean of Admissions and Financial Aid, Dartmouth College, 6016 McNutt Hall, Hanover, NH 03755. *Phone:* 603-646-2875. *E-mail:* admissions.reply@dartmouth.edu.

Franklin Pierce University

Rindge, New Hampshire

http://www.franklinpierce.edu/

- **Independent** university, founded 1962
- **Rural** 1000-acre campus
- **Endowment** $5.0 million
- **Coed** 1,752 undergraduate students, 90% full-time, 55% women, 45% men
- **Minimally difficult** entrance level, 81% of applicants were admitted

UNDERGRAD STUDENTS

1,582 full-time, 170 part-time. Students come from 27 states and territories; 15 other countries; 81% are from out of state; 7% Black or African American, non-Hispanic/Latino; 7% Hispanic/Latino; 1% Asian, non-Hispanic/Latino; 0.1% Native Hawaiian or other Pacific Islander, non-Hispanic/Latino; 0.4% American Indian or Alaska Native, non-Hispanic/Latino; 1% Two or more races, non-Hispanic/Latino; 7% Race/ethnicity unknown; 3% international; 2% transferred in; 92% live on campus.

Freshmen:

Admission: 6,506 applied, 5,295 admitted, 653 enrolled. ***Average high school GPA:*** 2.77.

Retention: 62% of full-time freshmen returned.

FACULTY

Total: 303, 31% full-time.

Student/faculty ratio: 13:1.

ACADEMICS

Calendar: differs by branch and program. *Degrees:* certificates, associate, bachelor's, master's, doctoral, and postbachelor's certificates (profile does not reflect significant enrollment at 6 continuing education sites; master's degree is only offered at these sites).

Special study options: academic remediation for entering students, accelerated degree program, adult/continuing education programs, advanced placement credit, distance learning, double majors, English as a second language, external degree program, freshman honors college, honors programs, independent study, internships, off-campus study, part-time degree program, services for LD students, student-designed majors, study abroad, summer session for credit. ***ROTC:*** Army (c), Air Force (c).

Computers: 100 computers/terminals are available on campus for general student use. Students can access the following: campus intranet, computer help desk, free student e-mail accounts, online (class) grades, online (class) registration, online (class) schedules. Campuswide network is available. 100% of college-owned or -operated housing units are wired for high-speed Internet access. Wireless service is available via classrooms, computer labs, libraries, student centers.

Library: Frank S. DiPietro Library plus 1 other. *Books:* 115,797 (physical), 191,482 (digital/electronic); *Serial titles:* 112 (physical), 65,000 (digital/electronic); *Databases:* 64. Weekly public service hours: 95.

STUDENT LIFE

Housing options: on-campus residence required for freshman year; coed. Campus housing is university owned. Freshman campus housing is guaranteed.

Activities and organizations: drama/theater group, student-run newspaper, radio and television station, choral group, Outing Club, WFPR Radio, Student Senate, Law Club, Business Club.

Athletics Member NCAA. All Division II. ***Intercollegiate sports:*** baseball M(s), basketball M(s)/W(s), crew M/W, cross-country running M/W, field hockey W(s), golf M, ice hockey M, lacrosse M/W, soccer M(s)/W(s), softball W(s), tennis M(s)/W(s), volleyball W(s). ***Intramural sports:*** baseball M, basketball M/W, cheerleading W(c), cross-country running M/W, fencing M(c)/W(c), field hockey W, football M, golf M, ice hockey M, lacrosse M/W, rugby M/W, soccer M/W, softball W, tennis M/W, volleyball M/W.

Campus security: 24-hour emergency response devices and patrols, student patrols, late-night transport/escort service, controlled dormitory access.

Student services: health clinic, personal/psychological counseling.

COSTS & FINANCIAL AID

Costs (2017–18) ***Tuition:*** Full-time tuition and fees vary according to course load, degree level, location, and program. Part-time tuition and fees vary according to course load, degree level, location, and program. ***Room and board:*** Room and board charges vary according to board plan, housing facility, and student level. ***Payment plan:*** installment. ***Waivers:*** senior citizens and employees or children of employees.

Financial Aid Of all full-time matriculated undergraduates who enrolled in 2015, 1,209 applied for aid, 1,098 were judged to have need, 203 had their need fully met. 388 Federal Work-Study jobs (averaging $1500). In 2015, 245 non-need-based awards were made. ***Average percent of need met:*** 67. ***Average financial aid package:*** $23,948. ***Average need-based loan:*** $5365. ***Average need-based gift aid:*** $19,707. ***Average non-need-based aid:*** $14,295. ***Average indebtedness upon graduation:*** $36,614.

APPLYING

Standardized Tests *Required for some:* SAT or ACT (for admission).

Options: electronic application, early admission, deferred entrance.

Application fee: $40.

Required: essay or personal statement, high school transcript, 1 letter of recommendation. ***Required for some:*** minimum 2.0 GPA. ***Recommended:*** minimum 2.2 GPA, interview.

Application deadlines: rolling (freshmen), rolling (transfers).

Notification: continuous (freshmen), continuous (transfers).

CONTACT

Office of Admissions, Franklin Pierce University, 40 University Drive, Rindge, NH 03461. *Phone:* 603-899-4050. *Toll-free phone:* 800-437-0048. *Fax:* 603-899-4394. *E-mail:* admissions@franklinpierce.edu.

Granite State College

Concord, New Hampshire

http://www.granite.edu/

- **State and locally supported** comprehensive, founded 1972, part of University System of New Hampshire
- **Suburban** campus
- **Endowment** $5.7 million
- **Coed** 1,851 undergraduate students, 50% full-time, 71% women, 29% men
- **Noncompetitive** entrance level, 100% of applicants were admitted

UNDERGRAD STUDENTS

933 full-time, 918 part-time. Students come from 44 states and territories; 4 other countries; 19% are from out of state; 3% Black or African American, non-Hispanic/Latino; 4% Hispanic/Latino; 1% Asian, non-Hispanic/Latino; 0.1% Native Hawaiian or other Pacific Islander, non-Hispanic/Latino; 0.4% American Indian or Alaska Native, non-Hispanic/Latino; 2% Two or more races, non-Hispanic/Latino; 7% Race/ethnicity unknown; 0.1% international; 31% transferred in.

Freshmen:

Admission: 289 applied, 289 admitted, 75 enrolled.

Retention: 74% of full-time freshmen returned.

FACULTY

Total: 200, 3% full-time.

Student/faculty ratio: 13:1.

ACADEMICS

Calendar: trimesters. *Degrees:* associate, bachelor's, master's, and postbachelor's certificates (offers primarily part-time degree programs; courses offered at 50 locations in New Hampshire).

Special study options: academic remediation for entering students, accelerated degree program, adult/continuing education programs, advanced placement credit, cooperative education, distance learning, double majors, independent study, internships, off-campus study, part-time degree program, services for LD students, student-designed majors, summer session for credit. ***ROTC:*** Army (c), Air Force (c).

Computers: 146 computers/terminals are available on campus for general student use. Students can access the following: campus intranet, computer help desk, free student e-mail accounts, online (class) grades, online (class) registration, online (class) schedules. Campuswide network is available. Wireless service is available via classrooms, computer centers, computer labs, learning centers.

Library: GSC Library and Research Commons. *Books:* 200,000 (digital/electronic); *Serial titles:* 23,000 (digital/electronic); *Databases:* 20. Weekly public service hours: 126.

STUDENT LIFE

Activities and organizations: Alumni Learner Association, Green Team.

Campus security: UNH Alert system provides emergency notifications via text and voice messages.

Student services: personal/psychological counseling.

COSTS

Costs (2016–17) ***Tuition:*** state resident $7200 full-time, $300 per credit part-time; nonresident $8040 full-time, $335 per credit part-time. ***Required fees:*** $225 full-time, $75 per term part-time. ***Payment plan:*** installment. ***Waivers:*** senior citizens and employees or children of employees.

APPLYING

Options: electronic application.

Required for some: high school transcript, Associate degree for some BS programs.

Application deadlines: rolling (freshmen), rolling (transfers).

Notification: continuous (freshmen), continuous (transfers).

CONTACT

Ms. Cortney Henry, Associate Registrar, Granite State College, 25 Hall Street, Concord, NH 03301. *Phone:* 603-228-3000. *Toll-free phone:* 888-228-3000. *Fax:* 603-513-1386. *E-mail:* gsc.admissions@granite.edu.

Keene State College

Keene, New Hampshire

http://www.keene.edu/

- **State-supported** comprehensive, founded 1909, part of University System of New Hampshire
- **Small-town** 150-acre campus
- **Coed** 4,165 undergraduate students, 96% full-time, 55% women, 45% men
- **Moderately difficult** entrance level, 83% of applicants were admitted

UNDERGRAD STUDENTS

4,004 full-time, 161 part-time. Students come from 26 states and territories; 6 other countries; 57% are from out of state; 1% Black or African American, non-Hispanic/Latino; 4% Hispanic/Latino; 1% Asian, non-Hispanic/Latino; 0.1% Native Hawaiian or other Pacific Islander, non-Hispanic/Latino; 0.2% American Indian or Alaska Native, non-Hispanic/Latino; 2% Two or more races, non-Hispanic/Latino; 5% Race/ethnicity unknown; 0.1% international; 4% transferred in; 53% live on campus.

Freshmen:

Admission: 5,466 applied, 4,511 admitted, 1,049 enrolled. ***Average high school GPA:*** 3. ***Test scores:*** SAT critical reading scores over 500: 44%; SAT math scores over 500: 45%; SAT writing scores over 500: 39%; ACT scores over 18: 79%; SAT critical reading scores over 600: 10%; SAT math scores over 600: 8%; SAT writing scores over 600: 6%; ACT scores over 24: 27%; SAT critical reading scores over 700: 1%; SAT math scores over 700: 1%; ACT scores over 30: 4%.

Retention: 75% of full-time freshmen returned.

ACADEMICS

Calendar: semesters. *Degrees:* certificates, bachelor's, master's, post-master's, and postbachelor's certificates.

Special study options: accelerated degree program, advanced placement credit, cooperative education, distance learning, double majors, freshman honors college, honors programs, independent study, internships, off-campus study, part-time degree program, services for LD students, student-designed majors, study abroad, summer session for credit. ***ROTC:*** Army (c), Air Force (c).

Unusual degree programs: 3-2 engineering with Clarkson University.

Computers: 600 computers/terminals are available on campus for general student use. Students can access the following: campus intranet, computer help desk, free student e-mail accounts, online (class) grades, online (class) registration, online (class) schedules. Campuswide network is available. 100% of college-owned or -operated housing units are wired for high-speed Internet access. Wireless service is available via entire campus.

Library: Mason Library. *Books:* 259,538 (physical), 275,694 (digital/electronic); *Serial titles:* 245 (physical), 68,825 (digital/electronic); *Databases:* 92. Weekly public service hours: 102; students can reserve study rooms.

STUDENT LIFE

Housing options: on-campus residence required through sophomore year; coed, women-only. Campus housing is university owned. Freshman campus housing is guaranteed.

Activities and organizations: drama/theater group, student-run newspaper, radio and television station, choral group, Social Activities Council, Ski and Snowboard Club, Student Government, Campus Ecology, The Equinox student newspaper, national fraternities, national sororities.

Athletics Member NCAA. All Division III. ***Intercollegiate sports:*** baseball M, basketball M/W, cheerleading W, cross-country running M/W, field hockey W, ice hockey M(c)/W(c), lacrosse M/W, rugby M(c)/W(c), soccer M/W, softball W, swimming and diving M/W, track and field M/W, ultimate Frisbee M(c)/W(c), volleyball W. ***Intramural sports:*** badminton M/W, basketball M/W, bowling M/W, fencing M(c)/W(c), racquetball M/W, soccer M/W, softball M/W, table tennis M/W, tennis M/W, volleyball M/W, water polo M/W, weight lifting M(c)/W(c).

Campus security: 24-hour emergency response devices and patrols, late-night transport/escort service, controlled dormitory access.

Student services: health clinic, personal/psychological counseling, women's center.

COSTS & FINANCIAL AID

Costs (2016–17) ***Tuition:*** state resident $10,968 full-time, $458 per credit hour part-time; nonresident $19,352 full-time, $806 per credit hour part-time. Part-time tuition and fees vary according to course load. ***Required fees:*** $2645 full-time, $106 per credit hour part-time. ***Room and board:*** $10,390. Room and board charges vary according to board plan and housing facility. ***Payment plan:*** installment. ***Waivers:*** senior citizens and employees or children of employees.

Financial Aid Of all full-time matriculated undergraduates who enrolled in 2015, 3,420 applied for aid, 2,684 were judged to have need, 293 had their need fully met. 1,375 Federal Work-Study jobs (averaging $2304). 661 state and other part-time jobs (averaging $1318). In 2015, 589 non-need-based awards were made. ***Average percent of need met:*** 65. ***Average financial aid package:*** $12,285. ***Average need-based loan:*** $4334. ***Average need-based gift aid:*** $7227. ***Average non-need-based aid:*** $3548. ***Average indebtedness upon graduation:*** $41,016. ***Financial aid deadline:*** 3/1.

APPLYING

Standardized Tests *Required:* SAT or ACT (for admission).

Options: electronic application, deferred entrance.

Application fee: $50.

Required: essay or personal statement, high school transcript, 1 letter of recommendation.

Application deadlines: 4/1 (freshmen), rolling (transfers).

Notification: continuous (freshmen), continuous (transfers).

CONTACT

Ms. Peggy Richmond, Director of Admissions, Keene State College, 229 Main Street, Keene, NH 03435-2604. *Phone:* 603-358-2273. *Toll-free phone:* 800-KSC-1909. *Fax:* 603-358-2767.
E-mail: mrichmon@keene.edu.

New England College

Henniker, New Hampshire

http://www.nec.edu/

- **Independent** comprehensive, founded 1946
- **Small-town** 225-acre campus with easy access to Boston
- **Endowment** $11.9 million
- **Coed** 1,756 undergraduate students, 99% full-time, 59% women, 41% men
- **Minimally difficult** entrance level, 99% of applicants were admitted

UNDERGRAD STUDENTS

1,730 full-time, 26 part-time. Students come from 51 states and territories; 19 other countries; 82% are from out of state; 24% Black or African American, non-Hispanic/Latino; 8% Hispanic/Latino; 1% Asian, non-Hispanic/Latino; 0.1% Native Hawaiian or other Pacific Islander, non-Hispanic/Latino; 0.7% American Indian or Alaska Native, non-Hispanic/Latino; 2% Two or more races, non-Hispanic/Latino; 7% Race/ethnicity unknown; 4% international; 8% transferred in; 36% live on campus.

Freshmen:

Admission: 4,204 applied, 4,163 admitted, 353 enrolled.
Average high school GPA: 2.57.

Retention: 60% of full-time freshmen returned.

FACULTY

Total: 267, 16% full-time, 49% with terminal degrees.

Student/faculty ratio: 16:1.

ACADEMICS

Calendar: semesters for residential undergraduates; 7-week terms for online undergraduate and graduate programs. *Degrees:* associate, bachelor's, master's, and doctoral.

Special study options: academic remediation for entering students, accelerated degree program, adult/continuing education programs, advanced placement credit, distance learning, double majors, English as a second language, external degree program, freshman honors college, honors programs, independent study, internships, off-campus study, part-time degree program, services for LD students, student-designed majors, study abroad, summer session for credit. ***ROTC:*** Army (c), Air Force (c).

Unusual degree programs: business administration; nursing with Massachusetts College of Pharmacy and Health Sciences; education, political science, law with New York Law School.

Computers: 200 computers/terminals and 350 ports are available on campus for general student use. Students can access the following: campus intranet, computer help desk, free student e-mail accounts, online (class) grades, online (class) registration, online (class) schedules, financial aid, billing, advising, degree audit. Campuswide network is available. 100% of college-owned or -operated housing units are wired for high-speed Internet access. Wireless service is available via entire campus.

Library: Danforth Library. *Books:* 98,000 (physical), 152,000 (digital/electronic); *Serial titles:* 101 (physical), 100,000 (digital/electronic); *Databases:* 22. Weekly public service hours: 126; study areas open 24 hours, 5-7 days a week; students can reserve study rooms.

STUDENT LIFE

Housing options: on-campus residence required through junior year; coed. Campus housing is university owned. Freshman campus housing is guaranteed.

Activities and organizations: drama/theater group, student-run newspaper, radio station, Student Senate, Campus Activities Board, Role Playing Association, International Student Association, Political Science Club, national fraternities, national sororities.

Athletics Member NCAA. All Division III. ***Intercollegiate sports:*** baseball M, basketball M/W, cross-country running M/W, field hockey W, ice hockey M/W, lacrosse M/W, rugby M(c)/W(c), skiing (downhill) M/W, soccer M/W, softball W, volleyball W, wrestling M. ***Intramural sports:*** basketball M/W, cheerleading W, golf M/W, ice hockey M/W, lacrosse M/W, soccer M/W, softball W, table tennis M/W, tennis M/W, ultimate Frisbee M/W, volleyball M/W.

Campus security: 24-hour emergency response devices and patrols, student patrols, late-night transport/escort service, controlled dormitory access, emergency text system.

Student services: health clinic, personal/psychological counseling, women's center.

COSTS & FINANCIAL AID

Costs (2017–18) ***Comprehensive fee:*** $50,828 includes full-time tuition ($35,858), mandatory fees ($1096), and room and board ($13,874). Full-time tuition and fees vary according to class time, course load, location, program, and reciprocity agreements. Part-time tuition: $439 per credit hour. Part-time tuition and fees vary according to class time, course load, location, and program. ***College room only:*** $6274. Room and board charges vary according to board plan and housing facility. ***Payment plan:*** installment. ***Waivers:*** children of alumni, adult students, senior citizens, and employees or children of employees.

Financial Aid Of all full-time matriculated undergraduates who enrolled in 2016, 1,511 applied for aid, 1,457 were judged to have need, 147 had their need fully met. 357 Federal Work-Study jobs (averaging $1913). 39 state and other part-time jobs (averaging $1121). In 2016, 119 non-need-based awards were made. ***Average percent of need met:*** 74. ***Average financial aid package:*** $21,673. ***Average need-based loan:*** $2824. ***Average need-based gift aid:*** $17,062. ***Average non-need-based aid:*** $19,073. ***Average indebtedness upon graduation:*** $35,230.

APPLYING

Options: electronic application, deferred entrance.

Application fee: $35.

Required: essay or personal statement, high school transcript, 2 letters of recommendation. ***Recommended:*** interview.

Application deadlines: 9/5 (freshmen), 9/5 (transfers).

Notification: continuous (freshmen), continuous (transfers).

CONTACT

Kay Reynolds, Associate Director of Undergraduate Admissions, New England College, 102 Bridge Street, Henniker, NH 03242. *Phone:* 603-428-2341. *Toll-free phone:* 800-521-7642. *Fax:* 603-428 3155. *E-mail:* klucier@nec.edu.

New Hampshire Institute of Art

Manchester, New Hampshire

http://www.nhia.edu/

- **Independent** comprehensive, founded 1898
- **Urban** campus with easy access to Boston
- **Endowment** $22.8 million
- **Coed** 342 undergraduate students, 92% full-time, 67% women, 33% men
- **Moderately difficult** entrance level, 97% of applicants were admitted

UNDERGRAD STUDENTS

316 full-time, 26 part-time. Students come from 14 states and territories; 48% are from out of state; 1% Black or African American, non-Hispanic/Latino; 9% Hispanic/Latino; 1% Asian, non-Hispanic/Latino; 0.6% Native Hawaiian or other Pacific Islander, non-Hispanic/Latino; 0.6% American Indian or Alaska Native, non-Hispanic/Latino; 2% Two or more races, non-Hispanic/Latino; 25% Race/ethnicity unknown; 4% transferred in; 52% live on campus.

Freshmen:

Admission: 320 applied, 310 admitted, 66 enrolled. ***Average high school GPA:*** 2.97.

Retention: 73% of full-time freshmen returned.

FACULTY

Total: 73, 25% full-time.

Student/faculty ratio: 10:1.

ACADEMICS

Calendar: semesters. *Degrees:* certificates, bachelor's, and master's.

Special study options: accelerated degree program, adult/continuing education programs, advanced placement credit, cooperative education, independent study, internships, part-time degree program, services for LD students, study abroad, summer session for credit.

Computers: 100 computers/terminals and 32 ports are available on campus for general student use. Students can access the following: computer help desk, free student e-mail accounts, online (class) grades, online (class) registration, online (class) schedules. Campuswide network is available. 100% of college-owned or -operated housing units are wired for high-speed Internet access. Wireless service is available via entire campus.

Library: Teti Library. *Books:* 17,000 (physical), 144,463 (digital/electronic); *Serial titles:* 80 (physical), 7,800 (digital/electronic); *Databases:* 30. Weekly public service hours: 63.

STUDENT LIFE

Housing options: on-campus residence required through sophomore year; coed. Campus housing is university owned and leased by the school. Freshman applicants given priority for college housing.

Activities and organizations: student-run newspaper, radio station, Student Leadership Council, Comic/Arts Club, Neo-Victorian Club, Design Ink, Gay/Straight Alliance.

Campus security: late-night transport/escort service, controlled dormitory access.

Student services: health clinic, personal/psychological counseling.

COSTS

Costs (2017–18) ***Comprehensive fee:*** $38,040 includes full-time tuition ($24,490), mandatory fees ($2390), and room and board ($11,160). Full-time tuition and fees vary according to degree level. Part-time tuition: $3285 per course. Part-time tuition and fees vary according to course load and degree level. ***Required fees:*** $95 per credit hour part-time, $100 per term part-time. ***Room and board:*** Room and board charges vary according to board plan. ***Payment plan:*** installment. ***Waivers:*** employees or children of employees.

APPLYING

Standardized Tests *Required for some:* SAT or ACT (for admission).

Options: electronic application, early action, deferred entrance.

Application fee: $25.

Required: essay or personal statement, high school transcript, slideroom portfolio. ***Recommended:*** minimum 2.5 GPA, 2 letters of recommendation.

Application deadlines: rolling (freshmen), rolling (out-of-state freshmen), rolling (transfers), 12/15 (early action).

Notification: continuous (freshmen), continuous (out-of-state freshmen), continuous (transfers), 1/15 (early action).

CONTACT
Mrs. Laura Stevenson, Director of Student Recruitment, New Hampshire Institute of Art, 148 Concord Street, Manchester, NH 03104-4158. *Phone:* 603-836-2148. *Toll-free phone:* 866-241-4918.
E-mail: admissions@nhia.edu.

Northeast Catholic College

Warner, New Hampshire

http://www.magdalen.edu/

CONTACT
Admissions Director, Northeast Catholic College, 511 Kearsarge Mountain Road, Warner, NH 03278. *Phone:* 603-456-2656. *Toll-free phone:* 877-498-1723. *Fax:* 603-456-2660.
E-mail: admissions@magdalen.edu.

Plymouth State University

Plymouth, New Hampshire

http://www.plymouth.edu/

- **State-supported** comprehensive, founded 1871, part of University System of New Hampshire
- **Small-town** 170-acre campus with easy access to Manchester
- **Endowment** $19.3 million
- **Coed** 4,125 undergraduate students, 95% full-time, 50% women, 50% men
- **Moderately difficult** entrance level, 79% of applicants were admitted

UNDERGRAD STUDENTS
3,935 full-time, 190 part-time. Students come from 44 states and territories; 18 other countries; 45% are from out of state; 2% Black or African American, non-Hispanic/Latino; 1% Hispanic/Latino; 2% Asian, non-Hispanic/Latino; 0.1% Native Hawaiian or other Pacific Islander, non-Hispanic/Latino; 0.5% American Indian or Alaska Native, non-Hispanic/Latino; 2% Two or more races, non-Hispanic/Latino; 8% Race/ethnicity unknown; 2% international; 5% transferred in; 56% live on campus.

Freshmen:
Admission: 6,864 applied, 5,407 admitted, 1,144 enrolled.
Average high school GPA: 2.95.
Retention: 70% of full-time freshmen returned.

FACULTY
Total: 426, 44% full-time, 51% with terminal degrees.
Student/faculty ratio: 17:1.

ACADEMICS
Calendar: semesters. *Degrees:* certificates, bachelor's, master's, doctoral, post-master's, and postbachelor's certificates.
Special study options: adult/continuing education programs, advanced placement credit, distance learning, double majors, honors programs, independent study, internships, off-campus study, part-time degree program, services for LD students, student-designed majors, study abroad, summer session for credit. ***ROTC:*** Army (c), Air Force (c).
Computers: 600 computers/terminals are available on campus for general student use. Students can access the following: campus intranet, computer help desk, free student e-mail accounts, online (class) grades, online (class) registration, online (class) schedules, degree audit, academic history, account status. Campuswide network is available. 100% of college-owned or -operated housing units are wired for high-speed Internet access. Wireless service is available via entire campus.
Library: Lamson Learning Commons. *Books:* 344,605 (physical), 155,000 (digital/electronic); *Serial titles:* 790 (physical), 1,500 (digital/electronic); *Databases:* 87. Weekly public service hours: 94.

STUDENT LIFE
Housing options: on-campus residence required through sophomore year; coed, cooperative, special housing for students with disabilities. Campus housing is university owned. Freshman campus housing is guaranteed.
Activities and organizations: drama/theater group, student-run newspaper, radio station, choral group, Pre Medical Professional Society, Student Nurse Association, Marketing Association of Plymouth State, Gaming Club, Programing Activities in a Campus Environment, national sororities.
Athletics Member NCAA. All Division III. ***Intercollegiate sports:*** baseball M, basketball M/W, cross-country running M/W, field hockey W, football M, ice hockey M/W, lacrosse M/W, skiing (downhill) M/W, soccer M/W, softball W, swimming and diving W, tennis W, track and field M/W, volleyball W, wrestling M. ***Intramural sports:*** basketball M/W, cheerleading M(c)/W(c), football M/W, golf M/W, rock climbing M(c)/W(c), rugby M(c)/W(c), sailing M(c)/W(c), skiing (downhill) M(c)/W(c), soccer M/W, softball M/W, table tennis M/W, tennis M(c)/W(c), ultimate Frisbee M(c)/W(c), volleyball M/W, weight lifting M/W.
Campus security: 24-hour emergency response devices and patrols, late-night transport/escort service, controlled dormitory access, shuttle bus service, crime prevention programs, self-defense education.
Student services: health clinic, personal/psychological counseling, women's center.

COSTS & FINANCIAL AID
Costs (2016–17) ***Tuition:*** state resident $11,020 full-time, $459 per credit hour part-time; nonresident $19,280 full-time, $803 per credit hour part-time. Full-time tuition and fees vary according to reciprocity agreements. Part-time tuition and fees vary according to reciprocity agreements. ***Required fees:*** $2452 full-time, $102 per credit hour part-time. ***Room and board:*** $11,008; room only: $6850. Room and board charges vary according to board plan, housing facility, and student level. ***Payment plan:*** installment. ***Waivers:*** senior citizens and employees or children of employees.
Financial Aid Of all full-time matriculated undergraduates who enrolled in 2015, 3,338 applied for aid, 2,644 were judged to have need, 445 had their need fully met. 1,960 Federal Work-Study jobs (averaging $2257). In 2015, 770 non-need-based awards were made. ***Average percent of need met:*** 60. ***Average financial aid package:*** $11,792. ***Average need-based loan:*** $4101. ***Average need-based gift aid:*** $5229. ***Average non-need-based aid:*** $3788. ***Average indebtedness upon graduation:*** $37,801.

APPLYING
Options: electronic application, deferred entrance.
Application fee: $50.
Required: essay or personal statement, 1 letter of recommendation. ***Required for some:*** high school transcript, interview. ***Recommended:*** minimum 2.5 GPA.
Application deadlines: 4/1 (freshmen), 4/1 (transfers).
Notification: continuous until 11/1 (freshmen), continuous until 11/1 (transfers).

CONTACT
Mr. Tony Trodella, Director of Undergraduate Recruitment, Plymouth State University, Plymouth, NH 03264-1595. *Phone:* 603-535-2237. *Toll-free phone:* 800-842-6900. *Fax:* 603-535-2714.
E-mail: admissions@plymouth.edu.

★ Rivier University

Nashua, New Hampshire

http://www.rivier.edu/

CONTACT
Karen Schedin, Vice President for Enrollment Management, Rivier University, 420 South Main Street, Nashua, NH 03060. *Phone:* 603-897-8507. *Toll-free phone:* 800-44RIVIER. *Fax:* 603-891-1799.
E-mail: rivadmit@rivier.edu.

See next page for display ad and page 1480 for the College Close-Up.

Saint Anselm College
Manchester, New Hampshire
http://www.anselm.edu/

- **Independent Roman Catholic** 4-year, founded 1889
- **Suburban** 380-acre campus with easy access to Boston
- **Endowment** $130.0 million
- **Coed** 1,930 undergraduate students, 97% full-time, 61% women, 39% men
- **Moderately difficult** entrance level, 76% of applicants were admitted

UNDERGRAD STUDENTS
1,876 full-time, 54 part-time. Students come from 35 states and territories; 6 other countries; 77% are from out of state; 2% Black or African American, non-Hispanic/Latino; 3% Hispanic/Latino; 0.9% Asian, non-Hispanic/Latino; 0.1% American Indian or Alaska Native, non-Hispanic/Latino; 2% Two or more races, non-Hispanic/Latino; 4% Race/ethnicity unknown; 0.5% international; 0.6% transferred in; 92% live on campus.

Freshmen:
Admission: 3,826 applied, 2,904 admitted, 518 enrolled. ***Average high school GPA:*** 3.26. ***Test scores:*** SAT critical reading scores over 500: 83%; SAT math scores over 500: 88%; SAT writing scores over 500: 83%; ACT scores over 18: 96%; SAT critical reading scores over 600: 33%; SAT math scores over 600: 32%; SAT writing scores over 600: 26%; ACT scores over 24: 73%; SAT critical reading scores over 700: 4%; SAT math scores over 700: 4%; SAT writing scores over 700: 3%; ACT scores over 30: 8%.
Retention: 85% of full-time freshmen returned.

FACULTY
Total: 220, 69% full-time, 75% with terminal degrees.
Student/faculty ratio: 11:1.

ACADEMICS
Calendar: semesters. *Degree:* bachelor's.
Special study options: accelerated degree program, advanced placement credit, double majors, honors programs, independent study, internships, off-campus study, part-time degree program, services for LD students, study abroad, summer session for credit. ***ROTC:*** Army (c).
Unusual degree programs: 3-2 engineering with University of Massachusetts Lowell, The Catholic University of America, University of Notre Dame, Manhattan College; pharmacy, optometry, physical therapy, physician assistant with Massachusetts College of Pharmacy and Health Sciences.
Computers: 400 computers/terminals are available on campus for general student use. Students can access the following: campus intranet, computer help desk, free student e-mail accounts, online (class) registration, online (class) schedules. Campuswide network is available. 100% of college-owned or -operated housing units are wired for high-speed Internet access. Wireless service is available via classrooms, computer centers, computer labs, dorm rooms, learning centers, libraries, student centers.
Library: Geisel Library plus 2 others. Students can reserve study rooms.

STUDENT LIFE
Housing options: coed, men-only, women-only, special housing for students with disabilities. Campus housing is university owned. Freshman campus housing is guaranteed.
Activities and organizations: drama/theater group, student-run newspaper, choral group, Meelia Center for Community Engagement, Anselmian Abbey Players, Club Sports, Service and Solidarity Mission Trips, Saint Anselm College Crier (School Newspaper).
Athletics Member NCAA. All Division II. ***Intercollegiate sports:*** baseball M, basketball M/W, cross-country running M/W, field hockey W, football M, golf M, ice hockey M/W, lacrosse M/W, skiing (downhill) M/W, soccer M/W, softball W, tennis M/W, volleyball W. ***Intramural sports:*** basketball M/W, football M/W, ice hockey M/W, racquetball M(c)/W(c), soccer M/W, softball M/W, table tennis M(c)/W(c), tennis M/W, track and field M(c)/W(c), ultimate Frisbee M/W, volleyball M/W.
Campus security: 24-hour emergency response devices and patrols, student patrols, late-night transport/escort service, controlled dormitory access.
Student services: health clinic, personal/psychological counseling.

COSTS & FINANCIAL AID

Costs (2017–18) ***Comprehensive fee:*** $54,136 includes full-time tuition ($38,960), mandatory fees ($1030), and room and board ($14,146). Full-time tuition and fees vary according to program. ***College room only:*** $8676. Room and board charges vary according to housing facility. ***Payment plan:*** installment. ***Waivers:*** employees or children of employees.

Financial Aid Of all full-time matriculated undergraduates who enrolled in 2016, 1,564 applied for aid, 1,309 were judged to have need, 368 had their need fully met. 1,030 Federal Work-Study jobs (averaging $1474). 8 state and other part-time jobs (averaging $1938). In 2016, 484 non-need-based awards were made. ***Average percent of need met:*** 81. ***Average financial aid package:*** $26,687. ***Average need-based loan:*** $3970. ***Average need-based gift aid:*** $22,330. ***Average non-need-based aid:*** $14,323. ***Average indebtedness upon graduation:*** $35,601. ***Financial aid deadline:*** 2/15.

APPLYING

Standardized Tests *Required for some:* SAT or ACT (for admission).

Options: electronic application, early admission, early decision, early action, deferred entrance.

Application fee: $50.

Required: essay or personal statement, high school transcript, 2 letters of recommendation. ***Required for some:*** interview. ***Recommended:*** interview.

Application deadlines: 2/1 (freshmen), rolling (transfers), 11/15 (early action).

Early decision deadline: 12/1.

Notification: 3/15 (freshmen), continuous (transfers), 12/31 (early decision), 1/15 (early action).

CONTACT

Saint Anselm College, 100 Saint Anselm Drive, Manchester, NH 03102. *Phone:* 603-641-7500. *Toll-free phone:* 888-4ANSELM. *Fax:* 603-641-7550. *E-mail:* admission@anselm.edu.

See page 1486 for the College Close-Up.

Southern New Hampshire University

Manchester, New Hampshire

http://www.snhu.edu/

- **Independent** university, founded 1932
- **Suburban** 317-acre campus with easy access to Boston
- **Coed** 3,020 undergraduate students, 97% full-time, 53% women, 47% men
- **Moderately difficult** entrance level, 93% of applicants were admitted

UNDERGRAD STUDENTS

2,935 full-time, 85 part-time. Students come from 29 states and territories; 35 other countries; 53% are from out of state; 3% Black or African American, non-Hispanic/Latino; 4% Hispanic/Latino; 2% Asian, non-Hispanic/Latino; 0.1% Native Hawaiian or other Pacific Islander, non-Hispanic/Latino; 0.4% American Indian or Alaska Native, non-Hispanic/Latino; 2% Two or more races, non-Hispanic/Latino; 5% Race/ethnicity unknown; 7% international; 8% transferred in; 62% live on campus.

Freshmen:

Admission: 4,207 applied, 3,907 admitted, 768 enrolled. ***Average high school GPA:*** 3.06. ***Test scores:*** SAT critical reading scores over 500: 48%; SAT math scores over 500: 50%; SAT writing scores over 500: 43%; ACT scores over 18: 90%; SAT critical reading scores over 600: 10%; SAT math scores over 600: 12%; SAT writing scores over 600: 9%; ACT scores over 24: 37%; SAT critical reading scores over 700: 1%; ACT scores over 30: 2%.

Retention: 72% of full-time freshmen returned.

FACULTY

Total: 445, 30% full-time, 32% with terminal degrees.

Student/faculty ratio: 13:1.

ACADEMICS

Calendar: semesters. *Degrees:* certificates, associate, bachelor's, master's, doctoral, post-master's, and postbachelor's certificates.

Special study options: academic remediation for entering students, accelerated degree program, adult/continuing education programs, advanced placement credit, cooperative education, distance learning, double majors, English as a second language, honors programs, independent study, internships, off-campus study, part-time degree program, services for LD students, study abroad, summer session for credit. ***ROTC:*** Army (c), Air Force (c).

Computers: Students can access the following: campus intranet, computer help desk, free student e-mail accounts, online (class) grades, online (class) registration, online (class) schedules. Campuswide network is available. 100% of college-owned or -operated housing units are wired for high-speed Internet access. Wireless service is available via entire campus.

Library: Shapiro Library and Learning Commons. Students can reserve study rooms.

STUDENT LIFE

Housing options: coed, special housing for students with disabilities. Campus housing is university owned.

Activities and organizations: drama/theater group, student-run newspaper, radio and television station, choral group, Coordinators of Activities and Programming Events (CAPE), Psychology Club, Economics/Finance Association, Gaming Club, Outing Club, national fraternities, national sororities.

Athletics Member NCAA. All Division II. ***Intercollegiate sports:*** baseball M(s), basketball M(s)/W(s), cheerleading M/W, cross-country running M(s)/W(s), field hockey W(s), golf M(s)/W(s), ice hockey M, lacrosse M(s)/W(s), soccer M(s)/W(s), softball W(s), tennis M(s)/W(s), track and field W(s), volleyball W(s). ***Intramural sports:*** badminton M/W, baseball M(c), basketball M/W, crew M(c)/W(c), football M/W, ice hockey M(c), racquetball M/W, soccer M/W, softball M/W, table tennis M/W, tennis M/W, ultimate Frisbee M/W, volleyball M/W.

Campus security: 24-hour emergency response devices and patrols, student patrols, late-night transport/escort service, controlled dormitory access.

Student services: health clinic, women's center.

COSTS & FINANCIAL AID

Costs (2017–18) ***Comprehensive fee:*** $43,198 includes full-time tuition ($30,756), mandatory fees ($380), and room and board ($12,062). Full-time tuition and fees vary according to course load. Part-time tuition: $1282 per credit hour. ***College room only:*** $8583. Room and board charges vary according to board plan and housing facility. ***Payment plans:*** installment, deferred payment. ***Waivers:*** senior citizens and employees or children of employees.

Financial Aid Of all full-time matriculated undergraduates who enrolled in 2016, 2,294 applied for aid, 2,090 were judged to have need, 348 had their need fully met. 1,258 Federal Work-Study jobs (averaging $3033). In 2016, 583 non-need-based awards were made. ***Average percent of need met:*** 66. ***Average financial aid package:*** $23,425. ***Average need-based loan:*** $4330. ***Average need-based gift aid:*** $6558. ***Average non-need-based aid:*** $13,342. ***Average indebtedness upon graduation:*** $41,028. ***Financial aid deadline:*** 6/30.

APPLYING

Options: electronic application, early action, deferred entrance.

Application fee: $40.

Required: essay or personal statement, high school transcript, minimum 2.0 GPA, 1 letter of recommendation. ***Recommended:*** interview.

Application deadlines: rolling (freshmen), rolling (transfers), 11/15 (early action).

Notification: continuous (freshmen), continuous (transfers), 12/15 (early action).

CONTACT

Mr. Tim Whittum, Director of Freshman Admission, Southern New Hampshire University, 2500 North River Road, Manchester, NH 03106-1045. *Phone:* 603-645-9611. *Toll-free phone:* 888-327-7648. *Fax:* 603-645-9693. *E-mail:* t.whittum@snhu.edu.

See page 1514 for the College Close-Up.

Thomas More College of Liberal Arts

Merrimack, New Hampshire

http://www.thomasmorecollege.edu/

CONTACT

Teddy Sifert, Director of Admissions, Thomas More College of Liberal Arts, 6 Manchester Street, Merrimack, NH 03054-4818. *Toll-free phone:* 800-880-8308. *Fax:* 603-880-9280.
E-mail: admissions@thomasmorecollege.edu.

University of New Hampshire

Durham, New Hampshire

http://www.unh.edu/

- **State-supported** university, founded 1866, part of University System of New Hampshire
- **Small-town** 2600-acre campus with easy access to Boston
- **Endowment** $330.1 million
- **Coed** 12,871 undergraduate students, 97% full-time, 54% women, 46% men
- **Moderately difficult** entrance level, 76% of applicants were admitted

UNDERGRAD STUDENTS

12,467 full-time, 404 part-time. Students come from 43 states and territories; 37 other countries; 52% are from out of state; 1% Black or African American, non-Hispanic/Latino; 3% Hispanic/Latino; 2% Asian, non-Hispanic/Latino; 0.2% American Indian or Alaska Native, non-Hispanic/Latino; 2% Two or more races, non-Hispanic/Latino; 6% Race/ethnicity unknown; 3% international; 5% transferred in; 55% live on campus.

Freshmen:

Admission: 20,203 applied, 15,326 admitted, 2,881 enrolled. ***Average high school GPA:*** 3.46. ***Test scores:*** SAT critical reading scores over 500: 72%; SAT math scores over 500: 79%; SAT writing scores over 500: 71%; ACT scores over 18: 98%; SAT critical reading scores over 600: 24%; SAT math scores over 600: 31%; SAT writing scores over 600: 22%; ACT scores over 24: 64%; SAT critical reading scores over 700: 3%; SAT math scores over 700: 3%; SAT writing scores over 700: 2%; ACT scores over 30: 11%.

Retention: 86% of full-time freshmen returned.

FACULTY

Total: 1,045, 62% full-time, 67% with terminal degrees.

Student/faculty ratio: 18:1.

ACADEMICS

Calendar: semesters. *Degrees:* associate, bachelor's, master's, doctoral, post-master's, and postbachelor's certificates.

Special study options: accelerated degree program, advanced placement credit, cooperative education, distance learning, double majors, English as a second language, honors programs, independent study, internships, off-campus study, part-time degree program, services for LD students, student-designed majors, study abroad, summer session for credit. ***ROTC:*** Army (b), Air Force (b).

Unusual degree programs: 3-2 business administration; social work; accounting, biochemistry, occupational therapy, education, kineseology.

Computers: 360 computers/terminals and 7,500 ports are available on campus for general student use. Students can access the following: campus intranet, computer help desk, free student e-mail accounts, online (class) grades, online (class) registration, online (class) schedules. Campuswide network is available. 100% of college-owned or -operated housing units are wired for high-speed Internet access. Wireless service is available via entire campus.

Library: Dimond Library plus 4 others. *Books:* 1.2 million (physical), 765,290 (digital/electronic); *Serial titles:* 4,607 (physical), 78,291 (digital/electronic); *Databases:* 471. Weekly public service hours: 117; students can reserve study rooms.

STUDENT LIFE

Housing options: coed, special housing for students with disabilities. Campus housing is university owned. Freshman campus housing is guaranteed.

Activities and organizations: drama/theater group, student-run newspaper, radio station, choral group, marching band, Campus Activity Board, The Outing Club, Resident Hall Association, Alpha Phi Omega,

Memorial Union Student Organization, national fraternities, national sororities.

Athletics Member NCAA. All Division I except football (Division I-AA). ***Intercollegiate sports:*** archery M(c)/W(c), badminton M(c)/W(c), baseball M(c), basketball M(s)/W(s), crew M(c)/W(c), cross-country running M(s)/W(s), fencing M(c)/W(c), field hockey W(s), golf M(c)/W(c), gymnastics W(s), ice hockey M(s)/W(s), lacrosse M(c)/W(s), riflery M(c)/W(c), rock climbing M(c)/W(c), rugby M(c)/W(c), sailing M(c)/W(c), skiing (cross-country) M(s)/W(s), skiing (downhill) M(s)/W(s), soccer M(s)/W(s), softball W(c), swimming and diving W(s), tennis M(c)/W(c), track and field M(s)/W(s), ultimate Frisbee M(c)/W(c), volleyball M(c)/W(s), wrestling M(c)/W(c). ***Intramural sports:*** basketball M/W, football M/W, ice hockey M/W, racquetball M/W, sand volleyball M/W, soccer M/W, softball M/W, table tennis M/W, tennis M/W, ultimate Frisbee M/W, volleyball M/W, water polo M/W.

Campus security: 24-hour emergency response devices and patrols, student patrols, late-night transport/escort service, controlled dormitory access, lighted pathways and sidewalks.

Student services: health clinic, personal/psychological counseling, women's center.

COSTS & FINANCIAL AID

Costs (2016–17) ***Tuition:*** state resident $14,410 full-time, $600 per credit hour part-time; nonresident $28,210 full-time, $1175 per credit hour part-time. Full-time tuition and fees vary according to program. Part-time tuition and fees vary according to course load and program. ***Required fees:*** $3214 full-time, $1607 per year part-time. ***Room and board:*** $10,938; room only: $6820. Room and board charges vary according to board plan and housing facility. ***Payment plan:*** installment. ***Waivers:*** employees or children of employees.

Financial Aid Of all full-time matriculated undergraduates who enrolled in 2015, 9,991 applied for aid, 8,222 were judged to have need, 1,247 had their need fully met. 5,807 Federal Work-Study jobs (averaging $2491). 4,016 state and other part-time jobs (averaging $1683). In 2015, 1940 non-need-based awards were made. ***Average percent of need met:*** 76. ***Average financial aid package:*** $23,451. ***Average need-based loan:*** $3296. ***Average need-based gift aid:*** $5985. ***Average non-need-based aid:*** $6885. ***Average indebtedness upon graduation:*** $38,799.

APPLYING

Standardized Tests *Required:* SAT or ACT (for admission).

Options: electronic application, early action, deferred entrance.

Application fee: $50.

Required: high school transcript, 1 letter of recommendation, Common Application, SAT or ACT scores, audition for some majors in music and theater, portfolio for art studio majors.
Recommended: minimum 3.0 GPA.

Application deadlines: 2/1 (freshmen), 4/1 (transfers), 11/15 (early action).

Notification: continuous until 12/1 (freshmen), continuous until 4/15 (transfers), 12/1 (early action).

CONTACT

Admissions Office, University of New Hampshire, 3 Garrison Avenue, Durham, NH 03824. *Phone:* 603-862-1360. *Fax:* 603-862-0077. *E-mail:* admissions@unh.edu.

See previous page for display ad and page 1568 for the College Close-Up.

University of New Hampshire at Manchester

Manchester, New Hampshire

http://manchester.unh.edu/

- **State-supported** comprehensive, founded 1967, part of University of New Hampshire
- **Urban** campus with easy access to Boston
- **Coed** 741 undergraduate students, 75% full-time, 51% women, 49% men
- **Moderately difficult** entrance level, 73% of applicants were admitted

UNDERGRAD STUDENTS

555 full-time, 186 part-time. 2% Black or African American, non-Hispanic/Latino; 4% Hispanic/Latino; 3% Asian, non-Hispanic/Latino; 0.1% American Indian or Alaska Native, non-Hispanic/Latino; 2% Two or more races, non-Hispanic/Latino; 14% Race/ethnicity unknown; 0.1% international.

Freshmen:

Admission: 205 applied, 150 admitted, 57 enrolled. ***Test scores:*** SAT critical reading scores over 500: 59%; SAT math scores over 500: 59%; SAT writing scores over 500: 50%; SAT critical reading scores over 600: 13%; SAT math scores over 600: 15%; SAT writing scores over 600: 9%; SAT critical reading scores over 700: 2%.

Retention: 76% of full-time freshmen returned.

FACULTY

Total: 112, 36% full-time.

Student/faculty ratio: 11:1.

ACADEMICS

Calendar: semesters. *Degrees:* associate, bachelor's, and master's.

Special study options: academic remediation for entering students, adult/continuing education programs, advanced placement credit, cooperative education, double majors, English as a second language, independent study, internships, off-campus study, part-time degree program, services for LD students, student-designed majors, study abroad, summer session for credit. ***ROTC:*** Army (c), Air Force (c).

Unusual degree programs: 3-2 pharmacy, physician assistant with Massachusetts College of Pharmacy and Health Sciences.

Computers: 108 computers/terminals are available on campus for general student use. Students can access the following: computer help desk, free student e-mail accounts, online (class) grades, online (class) registration, online (class) schedules. Campuswide network is available. Wireless service is available via entire campus.

Library: UNH Manchester Library plus 1 other. *Books:* 30,000 (physical). Students can reserve study rooms.

STUDENT LIFE

Housing options: Campus housing is provided by a third party.

Activities and organizations: drama/theater group, choral group.

Campus security: 24-hour emergency response devices, late-night transport/escort service.

COSTS & FINANCIAL AID

Costs (2017–18) ***Tuition:*** state resident $14,430 full-time, $437 per credit hour part-time; nonresident $28,990 full-time, $481 per credit hour part-time. Full-time tuition and fees vary according to course load and program. Part-time tuition and fees vary according to course load and program. ***Required fees:*** $430 full-time. ***Room and board:*** Room and board charges vary according to housing facility. ***Payment plan:*** installment. ***Waivers:*** employees or children of employees.

Financial Aid Of all full-time matriculated undergraduates who enrolled in 2015, 543 applied for aid, 450 were judged to have need, 43 had their need fully met. 197 Federal Work-Study jobs (averaging $2477). In 2015, 36 non-need-based awards were made. ***Average percent of need met:*** 58. ***Average financial aid package:*** $13,154. ***Average need-based loan:*** $3855. ***Average need-based gift aid:*** $1492. ***Average non-need-based aid:*** $2233. ***Average indebtedness upon graduation:*** $39,034.

APPLYING

Standardized Tests *Required:* SAT or ACT (for admission).

Options: electronic application, deferred entrance.

Application fee: $60.

Required: essay or personal statement, high school transcript, 1 letter of recommendation. ***Recommended:*** interview.

Application deadlines: 4/1 (freshmen), 4/1 (transfers).

Notification: continuous (freshmen), continuous (transfers).

CONTACT

Ms. Lukasiak, University of New Hampshire at Manchester, NH 03101. *Phone:* 603-641-4150.

NEW JERSEY

Bais Medrash Toras Chesed

Lakewood, New Jersey

CONTACT

Bais Medrash Toras Chesed, 910 Monmouth Avenue, Lakewood, NJ 08701.

Berkeley College–Woodland Park Campus

Woodland Park, New Jersey

http://www.berkeleycollege.edu/

- **Proprietary** comprehensive, founded 1931
- **Suburban** 25-acre campus with easy access to New York City
- **Coed** 3,813 undergraduate students, 84% full-time, 73% women, 27% men
- **Minimally difficult** entrance level, 99% of applicants were admitted

UNDERGRAD STUDENTS

3,189 full-time, 624 part-time. 3% are from out of state; 21% Black or African American, non-Hispanic/Latino; 34% Hispanic/Latino; 2% Asian, non-Hispanic/Latino; 0.3% Native Hawaiian or other Pacific Islander, non-Hispanic/Latino; 0.2% American Indian or Alaska Native, non-Hispanic/Latino; 26% Race/ethnicity unknown; 0.5% international; 18% transferred in.

Freshmen:

Admission: 2,508 applied, 2,471 admitted, 642 enrolled.
Retention: 63% of full-time freshmen returned.

FACULTY

Total: 412, 33% full-time.

Student/faculty ratio: 15:1.

ACADEMICS

Calendar: quarters. *Degrees:* certificates, associate, bachelor's, and master's.

Special study options: academic remediation for entering students, accelerated degree program, adult/continuing education programs, advanced placement credit, cooperative education, distance learning, honors programs, independent study, internships, off-campus study, part-time degree program, summer session for credit. ***ROTC:*** Army (c).

Computers: 955 computers/terminals are available on campus for general student use. Students can access the following: computer help desk, free student e-mail accounts, online (class) grades, online (class) registration, online (class) schedules. Campuswide network is available. Wireless service is available via entire campus.

Library: Walter A. Brower Library. *Books:* 61,728 (physical), 140,720 (digital/electronic); *Databases:* 77. Students can reserve study rooms.

STUDENT LIFE

Activities and organizations: student-run newspaper.

Athletics Member USCAA. ***Intercollegiate sports:*** cross-country running M/W, soccer M.

Campus security: 24-hour emergency response devices.

Student services: personal/psychological counseling.

COSTS

Costs (2017–18) ***One-time required fee:*** $100. ***Tuition:*** $23,600 full-time, $825 per credit hour part-time. Full-time tuition and fees vary according to course load. Part-time tuition and fees vary according to course load. No tuition increase for student's term of enrollment. ***Required fees:*** $1700 full-time, $425 per term part-time. ***Payment plan:*** installment. ***Waivers:*** employees or children of employees.

APPLYING

Options: electronic application, deferred entrance.

Application fee: $50.

Required: high school transcript. ***Recommended:*** interview.

Application deadlines: rolling (freshmen), rolling (out-of-state freshmen), rolling (transfers).

Notification: continuous (freshmen), continuous (out-of-state freshmen), continuous (transfers).

CONTACT

Carol J Covino, Associate Vice President, High School Admissions, Berkeley College–Woodland Park Campus, 44 Rifle Camp Road, Woodland Park, NJ 07424. *Phone:* 973-278-5400. *Toll-free phone:* 800-446-5400. *E-mail:* info@berkeleycollege.edu.

Beth Medrash Govoha

Lakewood, New Jersey

- **Independent Jewish** comprehensive, founded 1943
- **Small-town** campus with easy access to New York City, Philadelphia
- **Men only**
- **Moderately difficult** entrance level

ACADEMICS

Calendar: semesters. *Degrees:* diplomas, bachelor's, and master's.

APPLYING

Application fee: $125.

CONTACT

Beth Medrash Govoha, 617 Sixth Street, Lakewood, NJ 08701-2797. *Phone:* 732-367-1060 Ext. 4224.

Bloomfield College

Bloomfield, New Jersey

http://www.bloomfield.edu/

- **Independent** comprehensive, founded 1868, affiliated with Presbyterian Church (U.S.A.)
- **Suburban** 12-acre campus with easy access to New York City
- **Endowment** $13.1 million
- **Coed** 1,978 undergraduate students, 89% full-time, 64% women, 36% men
- **Moderately difficult** entrance level, 60% of applicants were admitted

UNDERGRAD STUDENTS

1,752 full-time, 226 part-time. Students come from 21 states and territories; 12 other countries; 5% are from out of state; 50% Black or African American, non-Hispanic/Latino; 26% Hispanic/Latino; 3% Asian, non-Hispanic/Latino; 0.5% Native Hawaiian or other Pacific Islander, non-Hispanic/Latino; 0.4% American Indian or Alaska Native, non-Hispanic/Latino; 0.8% Two or more races, non-Hispanic/Latino; 5% Race/ethnicity unknown; 4% international; 10% transferred in; 32% live on campus.

Freshmen:

Admission: 3,027 applied, 1,807 admitted, 436 enrolled. ***Average high school GPA:*** 2.68. ***Test scores:*** SAT critical reading scores over 500: 12%; SAT math scores over 500: 20%; ACT scores over 18: 42%; SAT critical reading scores over 600: 2%; SAT math scores over 600: 2%; ACT scores over 24: 5%.

Retention: 70% of full-time freshmen returned.

FACULTY

Total: 219, 33% full-time, 32% with terminal degrees.

Student/faculty ratio: 15:1.

ACADEMICS

Calendar: semesters. *Degrees:* certificates, bachelor's, master's, and postbachelor's certificates.

Special study options: academic remediation for entering students, accelerated degree program, advanced placement credit, distance learning, double majors, English as a second language, freshman honors college, honors programs, independent study, internships, part-time degree program, services for LD students, student-designed majors, study abroad, summer session for credit. ***ROTC:*** Army (c).

Computers: 400 computers/terminals are available on campus for general student use. Students can access the following: campus intranet, computer help desk, free student e-mail accounts, online (class) grades, online (class) registration, online (class) schedules. Campuswide network is available. 100% of college-owned or -operated housing units are wired for high-speed Internet access. Wireless service is available via classrooms,

computer centers, computer labs, dorm rooms, learning centers, libraries, student centers.
Library: Bloomfield College Library plus 1 other. *Books:* 64,000 (physical), 127,000 (digital/electronic); *Serial titles:* 360 (physical), 50,000 (digital/electronic); *Databases:* 41.
Weekly public service hours: 100.

STUDENT LIFE
Housing options: coed. Campus housing is university owned.

Activities and organizations: drama/theater group, student-run radio station, First Ladies, Green Hearts Environmental Club, Black Student Union, Team Infinite, Christian Fellowship, national fraternities, national sororities.

Athletics Member NCAA. All Division II. ***Intercollegiate sports:*** baseball M(s), basketball M(s)/W(s), cross-country running M(s)/W(s), soccer M(s)/W(s), softball W(s), tennis M(s), volleyball W(s). ***Intramural sports:*** basketball M/W, volleyball M/W.

Campus security: 24-hour emergency response devices and patrols, late-night transport/escort service, controlled dormitory access, security cameras in high-traffic areas, controlled access to dormitories.

Student services: health clinic, personal/psychological counseling.

COSTS & FINANCIAL AID
Costs (2017–18) ***Comprehensive fee:*** $41,000 includes full-time tuition ($29,300) and room and board ($11,700). Full-time tuition and fees vary according to degree level. Part-time tuition: $3670 per course. Part-time tuition and fees vary according to course load and degree level. ***College room only:*** $5850. Room and board charges vary according to housing facility. ***Payment plans:*** installment, deferred payment. ***Waivers:*** senior citizens and employees or children of employees.

Financial Aid Of all full-time matriculated undergraduates who enrolled in 2015, 1,714 applied for aid, 1,600 were judged to have need, 279 had their need fully met. 647 Federal Work-Study jobs (averaging $2028). In 2015, 85 non-need-based awards were made. ***Average percent of need met:*** 76. ***Average financial aid package:*** $25,767. ***Average need-based gift aid:*** $16,761. ***Average non-need-based aid:*** $10,375. ***Average indebtedness upon graduation:*** $46,574. ***Financial aid deadline:*** 6/1.

APPLYING
Standardized Tests *Required:* SAT or ACT (for admission).

Options: electronic application, early action, deferred entrance.

Application fee: $40.

Required: essay or personal statement, high school transcript, minimum 2.5 GPA, 2 letters of recommendation, graded essay/term paper or personal essay. ***Recommended:*** interview.

Application deadlines: 8/1 (freshmen), rolling (out-of-state freshmen), 8/1 (transfers), 12/1 (early action).

Notification: continuous until 10/1 (freshmen), continuous until 10/1 (out-of-state freshmen), continuous until 10/1 (transfers), 12/23 (early action).

CONTACT
Ms. Nicole Cibelli, Director of Admissions, Bloomfield College, Office of Enrollment Management and Admission, Bloomfield, NJ 07003-9981. *Phone:* 973-748-9000 Ext. 1390. *Toll-free phone:* 800-848-4555 Ext. 230. *Fax:* 973-748-0916. *E-mail:* nicole_cibelli@bloomfield.edu.

Caldwell University

Caldwell, New Jersey

http://www.caldwell.edu/

- **Independent Roman Catholic** comprehensive, founded 1939
- **Suburban** 70-acre campus with easy access to New York City
- **Coed** 1,633 undergraduate students, 89% full-time, 70% women, 30% men
- **Moderately difficult** entrance level, 85% of applicants were admitted

UNDERGRAD STUDENTS
1,446 full-time, 187 part-time. Students come from 4 states and territories; 5 other countries; 3% are from out of state; 14% Black or African American, non-Hispanic/Latino; 17% Hispanic/Latino; 3% Asian, non-Hispanic/Latino; 0.2% Native Hawaiian or other Pacific Islander, non-Hispanic/Latino; 2% Two or more races, non-Hispanic/Latino; 18% Race/ethnicity unknown; 8% international; 5% transferred in; 35% live on campus.

Freshmen:
Admission: 2,831 applied, 2,418 admitted, 400 enrolled. ***Average high school GPA:*** 3.49. ***Test scores:*** SAT critical reading scores over 500: 35%; SAT math scores over 500: 49%; SAT writing scores over 500: 34%; ACT scores over 18: 76%; SAT critical reading scores over 600: 5%; SAT math scores over 600: 15%; SAT writing scores over 600: 8%; ACT scores over 24: 23%; SAT critical reading scores over 700: 1%; SAT math scores over 700: 6%; ACT scores over 30: 2%.

Retention: 71% of full-time freshmen returned.

FACULTY
Total: 269, 31% full-time.

Student/faculty ratio: 12:1.

ACADEMICS
Calendar: semesters. *Degrees:* bachelor's, master's, doctoral, post-master's, and postbachelor's certificates.

Special study options: academic remediation for entering students, accelerated degree program, adult/continuing education programs, advanced placement credit, cooperative education, distance learning, double majors, English as a second language, external degree program, honors programs, independent study, internships, off-campus study, part-time degree program, services for LD students, student-designed majors, study abroad, summer session for credit. ***ROTC:*** Army (c).

Unusual degree programs: 3-2 social work with Rutgers University; biology or psychology/occupational therapy with Columbia University, biology/athletic training with Seton Hall University, psychology/counseling psychology, psychology/applied behavior analysis, education/curriculum and instruction.

Computers: 286 computers/terminals and 796 ports are available on campus for general student use. Students can access the following: campus intranet, computer help desk, free student e-mail accounts, online (class) grades, online (class) registration, online (class) schedules. Campuswide network is available. 100% of college-owned or -operated housing units are wired for high-speed Internet access. Wireless service is available via entire campus.
Library: Jennings Library plus 1 other. *Books:* 143,827 (physical), 147,084 (digital/electronic); *Databases:* 64. Students can reserve study rooms.

STUDENT LIFE
Housing options: coed. Campus housing is university owned. Freshman applicants given priority for college housing.

Activities and organizations: drama/theater group, student-run newspaper, choral group, Black Student Union, Latino American Student Organization, Autism Awareness Club, Martial Arts Club, Marketing Club, national fraternities, national sororities.

Athletics Member NCAA. All Division II. ***Intercollegiate sports:*** baseball M(s), basketball M(s)/W(s), bowling W(s), cross-country running M(s)/W(s), football M(c), lacrosse W(s), soccer M(s)/W(s), softball W(s), tennis M(s)/W(s), track and field M(s)/W(s), volleyball W(s). ***Intramural sports:*** basketball M/W, football M/W, soccer M/W, tennis M/W, ultimate Frisbee M/W, volleyball M/W.

Campus security: 24-hour emergency response devices and patrols, late-night transport/escort service, controlled dormitory access, campus is patrolled 24/7 by trained security officers.

Student services: health clinic, personal/psychological counseling.

COSTS & FINANCIAL AID
Costs (2016–17) ***Comprehensive fee:*** $44,200 includes full-time tuition ($31,150), mandatory fees ($1650), and room and board ($11,400). Full-time tuition and fees vary according to course load, location, and program. Part-time tuition: $865 per credit. Part-time tuition and fees vary according to course load, location, and program. ***Required fees:*** $200 per term part-time. ***Room and board:*** Room and board charges vary according to housing facility. ***Payment plan:*** installment. ***Waivers:*** children of alumni, adult students, senior citizens, and employees or children of employees.

Financial Aid Of all full-time matriculated undergraduates who enrolled in 2015, 1,124 applied for aid, 1,053 were judged to have need, 122 had their need fully met. 103 Federal Work-Study jobs (averaging $1500). 200

state and other part-time jobs (averaging $2500). In 2015, 236 non-need-based awards were made. ***Average percent of need met:*** 74. ***Average financial aid package:*** $24,199. ***Average need-based loan:*** $3854. ***Average need-based gift aid:*** $21,263. ***Average non-need-based aid:*** $17,610. ***Average indebtedness upon graduation:*** $24,612.

APPLYING
Standardized Tests *Required:* SAT or ACT (for admission).

Options: electronic application, early admission, early action, deferred entrance.

Application fee: $50.

Required: essay or personal statement, high school transcript, 2 letters of recommendation. ***Required for some:*** interview. ***Recommended:*** minimum 3.0 GPA, interview.

Application deadlines: rolling (freshmen), rolling (transfers), 12/1 (early action).

Notification: continuous (freshmen), continuous (transfers), 12/31 (early action).

CONTACT
Mr. Stephen Quinn, Assistant Vice President, Enrollment Management, Caldwell University, 120 Bloomfield Avenue, Caldwell, NJ 07006. *Phone:* 973-618-3320. *Fax:* 973-618-3600. *E-mail:* squinn@caldwell.edu.

Centenary University

Hackettstown, New Jersey

http://www.centenaryuniversity.edu/

- **Independent** comprehensive, founded 1867, affiliated with United Methodist Church
- **Suburban** 105-acre campus with easy access to New York City
- **Endowment** $10.7 million
- **Coed** 1,518 undergraduate students, 95% full-time, 62% women, 38% men
- **Moderately difficult** entrance level, 88% of applicants were admitted

UNDERGRAD STUDENTS
1,444 full-time, 74 part-time. 10% Black or African American, non-Hispanic/Latino; 12% Hispanic/Latino; 2% Asian, non-Hispanic/Latino; 0.2% American Indian or Alaska Native, non-Hispanic/Latino; 18% Race/ethnicity unknown; 3% international.

Freshmen:
Admission: 1,160 applied, 1,018 admitted, 283 enrolled. ***Test scores:*** ACT scores over 30: 7%.

Retention: 87% of full-time freshmen returned.

FACULTY
Total: 82.

ACADEMICS
Calendar: semesters. *Degrees:* certificates, associate, bachelor's, master's, doctoral, and postbachelor's certificates.

Special study options: accelerated degree program, adult/continuing education programs, advanced placement credit, distance learning, double majors, English as a second language, independent study, internships, off-campus study, part-time degree program, services for LD students, student-designed majors, study abroad, summer session for credit.

Computers: Students can access the following: campus intranet, computer help desk, free student e-mail accounts, online (class) grades, online (class) registration, online (class) schedules. Campuswide network is available. Wireless service is available via entire campus.

Library: Taylor Memorial Library. *Books:* 45,025 (physical), 114 (digital/electronic); *Serial titles:* 2,710 (physical), 1,896 (digital/electronic); *Databases:* 85. Weekly public service hours: 82.

STUDENT LIFE
Housing options: coed, women-only. Campus housing is university owned. Freshman applicants given priority for college housing.

Activities and organizations: drama/theater group, student-run newspaper, First Year Leaders, Student Government, ENACTUS, Honor Societies, Fraternities and Sororities, national fraternities, national sororities.

Athletics Member NCAA. All Division III. ***Intercollegiate sports:*** baseball M, basketball M/W, cross-country running M/W, equestrian sports M(c)/W(c), golf M, lacrosse M/W, soccer M/W, softball W, volleyball W, wrestling M.

Campus security: 24-hour emergency response devices and patrols, late-night transport/escort service, controlled dormitory access.

Student services: health clinic, personal/psychological counseling.

COSTS & FINANCIAL AID
Costs (2017–18) ***Comprehensive fee:*** $43,690 includes full-time tuition ($31,156), mandatory fees ($1424), and room and board ($11,110). Full-time tuition and fees vary according to program. Part-time tuition: $600 per credit hour. Part-time tuition and fees vary according to program. ***Required fees:*** $11 per credit hour part-time, $18 per term part-time. ***Room and board:*** Room and board charges vary according to board plan. ***Payment plan:*** installment.

Financial Aid Of all full-time matriculated undergraduates who enrolled in 2010, 1,219 applied for aid, 1,094 were judged to have need, 121 had their need fully met. In 2010, 303 non-need-based awards were made. ***Average percent of need met:*** 72. ***Average financial aid package:*** $19,967. ***Average need-based loan:*** $5414. ***Average need-based gift aid:*** $15,457. ***Average non-need-based aid:*** $9157. ***Average indebtedness upon graduation:*** $25,019.

APPLYING
Standardized Tests *Required:* SAT or ACT (for admission).

Options: electronic application, deferred entrance.

Application fee: $30.

Required: essay or personal statement, high school transcript. ***Required for some:*** interview. ***Recommended:*** interview.

Application deadlines: rolling (freshmen), rolling (transfers).

Notification: continuous (freshmen), continuous (transfers).

CONTACT
Jenna Yount, Director of Admissions, Centenary University, 400 Jefferson Street, Hackettstown, NJ 07840. *Phone:* 908-852-1400 Ext. 2082. *Toll-free phone:* 800-236-8679. *E-mail:* yountj@centenaryuniversity.edu.

Chamberlain College of Nursing

North Brunswick, New Jersey

http://www.chamberlain.edu/

- **Proprietary** 4-year
- **Coed**

FACULTY
Student/faculty ratio: 30:1.

ACADEMICS
Degree: bachelor's.

STUDENT LIFE
Housing options: college housing not available.

COSTS
Costs (2016–17) ***Tuition:*** $18,900 full-time, $675 per credit hour part-time. ***Required fees:*** $600 full-time.

APPLYING
Standardized Tests *Required:* SAT or ACT (for admission).

Options: deferred entrance.

Application fee: $95.

CONTACT
Chamberlain College of Nursing, 630 U.S. Highway 1, North Brunswick, NJ 08902. *Toll-free phone:* 877-751-5783.

The College of New Jersey

Ewing, New Jersey

http://www.tcnj.edu/

- **State-supported** comprehensive, founded 1855
- **Suburban** 255-acre campus with easy access to Philadelphia
- **Coed** 6,787 undergraduate students, 96% full-time, 58% women, 42% men
- **Very difficult** entrance level, 49% of applicants were admitted

UNDERGRAD STUDENTS
6,496 full-time, 291 part-time. Students come from 24 states and territories; 4 other countries; 6% are from out of state; 6% Black or African American, non-Hispanic/Latino; 13% Hispanic/Latino; 11% Asian, non-Hispanic/Latino; 0.2% Native Hawaiian or other Pacific Islander, non-Hispanic/Latino; 0.2% American Indian or Alaska Native, non-Hispanic/Latino; 0.4% Two or more races, non-Hispanic/Latino; 4% Race/ethnicity unknown; 0.2% international; 4% transferred in; 58% live on campus.

Freshmen:
Admission: 11,825 applied, 5,778 admitted, 1,457 enrolled. ***Test scores:*** SAT critical reading scores over 500: 92%; SAT math scores over 500: 96%; SAT writing scores over 500: 91%; ACT scores over 18: 100%; SAT critical reading scores over 600: 46%; SAT math scores over 600: 61%; SAT writing scores over 600: 48%; ACT scores over 24: 89%; SAT critical reading scores over 700: 10%; SAT math scores over 700: 14%; SAT writing scores over 700: 11%; ACT scores over 30: 26%.

Retention: 94% of full-time freshmen returned.

FACULTY
Total: 848, 42% full-time, 56% with terminal degrees.
Student/faculty ratio: 13:1.

ACADEMICS
Calendar: semesters. *Degrees:* bachelor's, master's, post-master's, and postbachelor's certificates.

Special study options: academic remediation for entering students, accelerated degree program, advanced placement credit, double majors, English as a second language, honors programs, independent study, internships, off-campus study, part-time degree program, services for LD students, student-designed majors, study abroad, summer session for credit. ***ROTC:*** Army (c), Air Force (c).

Unusual degree programs: 3-2 education of the deaf and hard of hearing, elementary education, special education and urban education.

Computers: 631 computers/terminals are available on campus for general student use. Students can access the following: campus intranet, computer help desk, free student e-mail accounts, online (class) grades, online (class) registration, online (class) schedules. Campuswide network is available. 100% of college-owned or -operated housing units are wired for high-speed Internet access. Wireless service is available via classrooms, computer labs, learning centers, libraries, student centers.

Library: The College of New Jersey Library. *Books:* 694,461 (physical), 6,455 (digital/electronic); *Serial titles:* 44,898 (physical), 8,859 (digital/electronic); *Databases:* 114. Weekly public service hours: 98; students can reserve study rooms.

STUDENT LIFE
Housing options: on-campus residence required for freshman year; coed, special housing for students with disabilities. Campus housing is university owned. Freshman campus housing is guaranteed.

Activities and organizations: drama/theater group, student-run newspaper, radio and television station, choral group, Student Government Association, College Union Board, Inter-Greek Council, The Signal, national fraternities, national sororities.

Athletics Member NCAA. All Division III. ***Intercollegiate sports:*** baseball M, basketball M/W, cross-country running M/W, field hockey W, football M, lacrosse W, soccer M/W, softball W, swimming and diving M/W, tennis M/W, track and field M/W, wrestling M. ***Intramural sports:*** baseball M(c), basketball M(c)/W, bowling M(c)/W(c), cheerleading M(c)/W(c), crew M(c)/W(c), fencing M(c)/W(c), field hockey M/W, football M/W, golf M(c)/W(c), ice hockey M(c), lacrosse M(c)/W(c), racquetball M/W, rugby M(c)/W(c), skiing (cross-country) M(c)/W(c), skiing (downhill) M(c)/W(c), soccer M(c)/W(c), softball M/W(c), swimming and diving M(c)/W(c), table tennis M(c)/W(c), tennis M(c)/W(c), ultimate Frisbee M(c)/W(c), volleyball M(c)/W(c), water polo M(c)/W(c).

Campus security: 24-hour emergency response devices and patrols, student patrols, late-night transport/escort service, controlled dormitory access.

Student services: health clinic, personal/psychological counseling, women's center, legal services.

COSTS & FINANCIAL AID
Costs (2017–18) ***Tuition:*** state resident $11,124 full-time, $394 per credit hour part-time; nonresident $22,301 full-time, $789 per credit hour part-

time. Part-time tuition and fees vary according to course load. ***Required fees:*** $4670 full-time, $187 per credit hour part-time. ***Room and board:*** $12,881; room only: $8794. Room and board charges vary according to board plan. ***Payment plan:*** installment. ***Waivers:*** senior citizens and employees or children of employees.

Financial Aid Of all full-time matriculated undergraduates who enrolled in 2016, 4,588 applied for aid, 3,318 were judged to have need, 344 had their need fully met. In 2016, 496 non-need-based awards were made. ***Average percent of need met:*** 43. ***Average financial aid package:*** $10,955. ***Average need-based loan:*** $4564. ***Average need-based gift aid:*** $11,951. ***Average non-need-based aid:*** $5018. ***Average indebtedness upon graduation:*** $35,798. ***Financial aid deadline:*** 10/1.

APPLYING

Standardized Tests *Required:* SAT or ACT (for admission).

Options: electronic application, early decision, deferred entrance.

Application fee: $75.

Required: essay or personal statement, high school transcript. ***Required for some:*** interview, art portfolio or music audition. ***Recommended:*** minimum 2.5 GPA, 3 letters of recommendation.

Application deadlines: 2/1 (freshmen), 2/15 (transfers).

Early decision deadline: 11/1 (for plan 1), 1/1 (for plan 2).

Notification: continuous until 4/1 (freshmen), continuous until 4/1 (transfers), 12/1 (early decision plan 1), 2/1 (early decision plan 2).

CONTACT

Ms. Grecia Montero, Director of Admissions, The College of New Jersey, PO Box 7718, Ewing, NJ 08628. *Phone:* 609-771-2131. *Fax:* 609-637-5174. *E-mail:* admiss@tcnj.edu.

See previous page for display ad and page 1322 for the College Close-Up.

★ College of Saint Elizabeth

Morristown, New Jersey

http://www.cse.edu/

- **Independent Roman Catholic** comprehensive, founded 1899
- **Suburban** 200-acre campus with easy access to New York City
- **Endowment** $19.5 million
- **Coed, primarily women** 763 undergraduate students, 75% full-time, 85% women, 15% men
- **Moderately difficult** entrance level, 66% of applicants were admitted

UNDERGRAD STUDENTS

573 full-time, 190 part-time. Students come from 14 states and territories; 8 other countries; 5% are from out of state; 33% Black or African American, non-Hispanic/Latino; 22% Hispanic/Latino; 3% Asian, non-Hispanic/Latino; 0.3% Native Hawaiian or other Pacific Islander, non-Hispanic/Latino; 0.3% American Indian or Alaska Native, non-Hispanic/Latino; 2% Two or more races, non-Hispanic/Latino; 9% Race/ethnicity unknown; 3% international; 4% transferred in; 47% live on campus.

Freshmen:

Admission: 1,626 applied, 1,075 admitted, 167 enrolled. ***Average high school GPA:*** 2.82. ***Test scores:*** ACT scores over 18: 73%; ACT scores over 24: 13%.

Retention: 71% of full-time freshmen returned.

FACULTY

Total: 164, 30% full-time.

Student/faculty ratio: 10:1.

ACADEMICS

Calendar: semesters. *Degrees:* certificates, bachelor's, master's, doctoral, and postbachelor's certificates (also offers coed adult undergraduate degree program and coed graduate programs).

Special study options: academic remediation for entering students, accelerated degree program, adult/continuing education programs, advanced placement credit, distance learning, double majors, English as a second language, external degree program, honors programs, independent study, internships, off-campus study, part-time degree program, services for LD students, student-designed majors, study abroad, summer session for credit.

Unusual degree programs: 3-2 nursing; biology/medical technology, podiatric medicine or pharmacy.

Computers: 127 computers/terminals and 668 ports are available on campus for general student use. Students can access the following: campus intranet, computer help desk, free student e-mail accounts, online (class) grades, online (class) registration, online (class) schedules. Campuswide network is available. 100% of college-owned or -operated housing units are wired for high-speed Internet access. Wireless service is available via entire campus.

Library: Mahoney Library plus 1 other.

STUDENT LIFE

Housing options: coed. Campus housing is university owned. Freshman campus housing is guaranteed.

Activities and organizations: drama/theater group, choral group, Student Government Association, Students Take Action Committee, International/Intercultural Club, College Activities Board, Campus Ministry.

Athletics Member NCAA. All Division III. ***Intercollegiate sports:*** basketball M/W, cross-country running M/W, soccer M/W, softball W, tennis M/W, volleyball M/W.

Campus security: 24-hour emergency response devices and patrols, late-night transport/escort service, controlled dormitory access.

Student services: health clinic, personal/psychological counseling.

COSTS & FINANCIAL AID

Costs (2017–18) ***Comprehensive fee:*** $45,021 includes full-time tuition ($30,326), mandatory fees ($1951), and room and board ($12,744). Part-time tuition: $843 per credit hour. Part-time tuition and fees vary according to course load and location. ***Room and board:*** Room and board charges vary according to board plan. ***Payment plan:*** installment. ***Waivers:*** children of alumni, senior citizens, and employees or children of employees.

Financial Aid Of all full-time matriculated undergraduates who enrolled in 2014, 487 applied for aid, 487 were judged to have need, 484 had their need fully met. In 2014, 379 non-need-based awards were made. ***Average percent of need met:*** 94. ***Average financial aid package:*** $19,406. ***Average need-based loan:*** $4617. ***Average need-based gift aid:*** $17,140. ***Average non-need-based aid:*** $14,507.

APPLYING

Standardized Tests *Required:* SAT or ACT (for admission).

Options: electronic application, deferred entrance.

Application fee: $35.

Required: essay or personal statement, high school transcript, minimum 2.0 GPA, 2 letters of recommendation. ***Recommended:*** interview.

Application deadlines: rolling (freshmen), rolling (transfers).

Notification: continuous (freshmen), continuous (transfers).

CONTACT

Adrianna Arroyo, Director of Undergraduate Admissions, College of Saint Elizabeth, 2 Convent Road, Morristown, NJ 07960-6989. *Phone:* 973-290-4700. *Toll-free phone:* 800-210-7900. *Fax:* 973-290-4710. *E-mail:* apply@cse.edu.

DeVry University–North Brunswick Campus

North Brunswick, New Jersey

http://www.devry.edu/

- **Proprietary** comprehensive, founded 1969, part of DeVry University
- **Urban** campus
- **Coed**
- **Minimally difficult** entrance level

FACULTY

Student/faculty ratio: 14:1.

ACADEMICS

Calendar: semesters. *Degrees:* associate, bachelor's, and master's.

Library: Learning Resource Center.

STUDENT LIFE

Housing options: college housing not available.

COSTS
Costs (2016–17) ***Tuition:*** $17,052 full-time, $609 per credit hour part-time. ***Required fees:*** $460 full-time.

APPLYING
Options: deferred entrance.

Application fee: $30.

Required: high school transcript, interview.

CONTACT
DeVry University–North Brunswick Campus, 630 US Highway 1, North Brunswick, NJ 08902. *Phone:* 732-729-3532.
Toll-free phone: 866-338-7934.

Drew University

Madison, New Jersey

http://www.drew.edu/

- **Independent** university, founded 1867, affiliated with United Methodist Church
- **Suburban** 186-acre campus with easy access to New York City
- **Coed** 1,521 undergraduate students, 97% full-time, 59% women, 41% men
- **Moderately difficult** entrance level, 57% of applicants were admitted

UNDERGRAD STUDENTS
1,476 full-time, 45 part-time. Students come from 43 states and territories; 49 other countries; 33% are from out of state; 9% Black or African American, non-Hispanic/Latino; 11% Hispanic/Latino; 6% Asian, non-Hispanic/Latino; 0.1% Native Hawaiian or other Pacific Islander, non-Hispanic/Latino; 5% Two or more races, non-Hispanic/Latino; 7% Race/ethnicity unknown; 8% international; 5% transferred in; 78% live on campus.

Freshmen:
Admission: 3,494 applied, 1,997 admitted, 350 enrolled. ***Average high school GPA:*** 3.44. ***Test scores:*** SAT critical reading scores over 500: 84%; SAT math scores over 500: 83%; SAT writing scores over 500: 79%; ACT scores over 18: 98%; SAT critical reading scores over 600: 45%; SAT math scores over 600: 33%; SAT writing scores over 600: 35%; ACT scores over 24: 73%; SAT critical reading scores over 700: 10%; SAT math scores over 700: 6%; SAT writing scores over 700: 5%; ACT scores over 30: 16%.
Retention: 87% of full-time freshmen returned.

FACULTY
Total: 251, 60% full-time.

Student/faculty ratio: 10:1.

ACADEMICS
Calendar: semesters. *Degrees:* bachelor's, master's, doctoral, post-master's, and postbachelor's certificates.

Special study options: accelerated degree program, adult/continuing education programs, advanced placement credit, double majors, English as a second language, freshman honors college, honors programs, independent study, internships, off-campus study, part-time degree program, services for LD students, student-designed majors, study abroad, summer session for credit. ***ROTC:*** Army (c).

Unusual degree programs: 3-2 engineering with Columbia University, Stevens Institute of Technology; forestry with Duke University; nursing with Drexel University; management with Wake Forest University, environmental management with Duke University, teaching.

Computers: Students can access the following: campus intranet, computer help desk, free student e-mail accounts, online (class) grades, online (class) registration, online (class) schedules. Campuswide network is available. 100% of college-owned or -operated housing units are wired for high-speed Internet access. Wireless service is available via entire campus.

Library: Rose Memorial Library plus 1 other. *Books:* 610,346 (physical), 133,970 (digital/electronic); *Databases:* 370. Weekly public service hours: 83.

STUDENT LIFE
Housing options: coed, special housing for students with disabilities. Campus housing is university owned. Freshman campus housing is guaranteed.

Activities and organizations: drama/theater group, student-run newspaper, radio station, choral group, Pre_Health Society, Drew University Dramatic Society, Drew Organization of Anime, University Program Board, Drew Democrats.

Athletics Member NCAA. All Division III. ***Intercollegiate sports:*** baseball M, basketball M/W, cross-country running M/W, equestrian sports W, fencing M/W, field hockey W, golf M/W, lacrosse M/W, rugby M(c)/W(c), soccer M/W, softball W, swimming and diving M/W, tennis M/W, track and field M/W. ***Intramural sports:*** badminton M/W, basketball M/W, football M, racquetball M/W, soccer M/W, squash M/W, table tennis M/W, volleyball M/W.

Campus security: 24-hour emergency response devices and patrols, late-night transport/escort service, controlled dormitory access.

Student services: health clinic, personal/psychological counseling.

COSTS & FINANCIAL AID
Costs (2016–17) ***Comprehensive fee:*** $61,048 includes full-time tuition ($46,920), mandatory fees ($832), and room and board ($13,296). Part-time tuition: $1955 per credit. Part-time tuition and fees vary according to course load. ***College room only:*** $8396. Room and board charges vary according to board plan and housing facility. ***Payment plans:*** tuition prepayment, installment, deferred payment. ***Waivers:*** employees or children of employees.

Financial Aid Of all full-time matriculated undergraduates who enrolled in 2016, 1,058 applied for aid, 997 were judged to have need, 161 had their need fully met. 710 Federal Work-Study jobs (averaging $2000). In 2016, 385 non-need-based awards were made. ***Average percent of need met:*** 84. ***Average financial aid package:*** $42,435. ***Average need-based loan:*** $4541. ***Average need-based gift aid:*** $36,371. ***Average non-need-based aid:*** $21,987. ***Average indebtedness upon graduation:*** $24,964.

APPLYING
Options: electronic application, early admission, early decision, deferred entrance.

Application fee: $40.

Required: essay or personal statement, high school transcript, 2 letters of recommendation. ***Recommended:*** interview.

Application deadlines: 2/1 (freshmen), 12/15 (transfers).

Early decision deadline: 11/15 (for plan 1), 1/15 (for plan 2).

Notification: 3/18 (freshmen), continuous (transfers), 12/15 (early decision plan 1), 2/15 (early decision plan 2).

CONTACT
Drew University, 36 Madison Avenue, Madison, NJ 07940-1493.
Phone: 973-408-DREW.

Eastern International College

Belleville, New Jersey

http://www.eicollege.edu/

CONTACT
Eastern International College, 251 Washington Avenue, Belleville, NJ 07109.

Eastern International College

Jersey City, New Jersey

http://www.eicollege.edu/

CONTACT
Eastern International College, 684 Newark Avenue, Jersey City, NJ 07306.

Eastwick College

Ramsey, New Jersey

http://www.eastwickcollege.edu/

CONTACT
Eastwick College, 10 South Franklin Turnpike, Ramsey, NJ 07446.

Fairleigh Dickinson University, College at Florham

Madison, New Jersey

http://www.fdu.edu/

- **Independent** comprehensive, founded 1942
- **Suburban** 178-acre campus with easy access to New York City
- **Coed** 2,402 undergraduate students, 93% full-time, 54% women, 46% men
- **Moderately difficult** entrance level, 81% of applicants were admitted

UNDERGRAD STUDENTS

2,236 full-time, 166 part-time. 16% are from out of state; 11% Black or African American, non-Hispanic/Latino; 15% Hispanic/Latino; 4% Asian, non-Hispanic/Latino; 0.2% Native Hawaiian or other Pacific Islander, non-Hispanic/Latino; 0.6% American Indian or Alaska Native, non-Hispanic/Latino; 2% Two or more races, non-Hispanic/Latino; 7% Race/ethnicity unknown; 0.6% international; 4% transferred in; 62% live on campus.

Freshmen:
Admission: 3,828 applied, 3,091 admitted, 703 enrolled. ***Average high school GPA:*** 3.07. ***Test scores:*** SAT critical reading scores over 500: 53%; SAT math scores over 500: 62%; SAT writing scores over 500: 54%; SAT critical reading scores over 600: 16%; SAT math scores over 600: 20%; SAT writing scores over 600: 15%; SAT critical reading scores over 700: 1%; SAT math scores over 700: 2%; SAT writing scores over 700: 3%.
Retention: 82% of full-time freshmen returned.

ACADEMICS

Calendar: semesters. *Degrees:* bachelor's, master's, doctoral, post-master's, and postbachelor's certificates.
Special study options: academic remediation for entering students, accelerated degree program, adult/continuing education programs, advanced placement credit, cooperative education, distance learning, double majors, honors programs, independent study, internships, off-campus study, part-time degree program, services for LD students, student-designed majors, study abroad, summer session for credit. ***ROTC:*** Army (c), Air Force (c).
Computers: Students can access the following: computer help desk, free student e-mail accounts, online (class) grades, online (class) registration, online (class) schedules. Campuswide network is available. 100% of college-owned or -operated housing units are wired for high-speed Internet access. Wireless service is available via entire campus.
Library: College of Florham Library.

STUDENT LIFE

Housing options: coed, special housing for students with disabilities. Campus housing is university owned. Freshman applicants given priority for college housing.
Activities and organizations: drama/theater group, student-run newspaper, choral group, College Panhellenic Council, Association of Black Collegians, Latin American Student Organization, Florham Programming Committee, InterFraternity Council, national fraternities, national sororities.
Athletics Member NCAA. All Division III. ***Intercollegiate sports:*** baseball M, basketball M/W, cross-country running M/W, field hockey W, football M, golf M/W, lacrosse M/W, soccer M/W, softball W, swimming and diving M/W, tennis M/W, volleyball W. ***Intramural sports:*** basketball M/W, football M/W, soccer M/W, softball M/W, volleyball M/W, weight lifting M/W.
Campus security: 24-hour emergency response devices and patrols, late-night transport/escort service, controlled dormitory access, trained law enforcement personnel on staff.
Student services: health clinic, personal/psychological counseling.

FINANCIAL AID

Financial Aid Of all full-time matriculated undergraduates who enrolled in 2007, 1,788 applied for aid, 1,568 were judged to have need. In 2007, 213 non-need-based awards were made. ***Average financial aid package:*** $17,400. ***Average need-based loan:*** $4001. ***Average need-based gift aid:*** $9956. ***Average non-need-based aid:*** $6501.

APPLYING

Standardized Tests *Required:* SAT or ACT (for admission).
Options: electronic application.
Application fee: $40.
Required: high school transcript, 2 letters of recommendation.

CONTACT

Fairleigh Dickinson University, College at Florham, 285 Madison Avenue, Madison, NJ 07940-1099. *Toll-free phone:* 800-338-8803.

Fairleigh Dickinson University, Metropolitan Campus

Teaneck, New Jersey

http://www.fdu.edu/

- **Independent** comprehensive, founded 1942
- **Suburban** 88-acre campus with easy access to New York City
- **Coed** 6,048 undergraduate students, 44% full-time, 58% women, 42% men
- **Moderately difficult** entrance level, 80% of applicants were admitted

UNDERGRAD STUDENTS

2,691 full-time, 3,357 part-time. 14% are from out of state; 14% Black or African American, non-Hispanic/Latino; 35% Hispanic/Latino; 5% Asian, non-Hispanic/Latino; 0.2% Native Hawaiian or other Pacific Islander, non-Hispanic/Latino; 0.1% American Indian or Alaska Native, non-Hispanic/Latino; 1% Two or more races, non-Hispanic/Latino; 12% Race/ethnicity unknown; 8% international; 6% transferred in; 19% live on campus.

Freshmen:
Admission: 4,258 applied, 3,411 admitted, 650 enrolled. ***Average high school GPA:*** 3.08. ***Test scores:*** SAT critical reading scores over 500: 44%; SAT math scores over 500: 52%; SAT writing scores over 500: 38%; SAT critical reading scores over 600: 8%; SAT math scores over 600: 11%; SAT writing scores over 600: 9%; SAT critical reading scores over 700: 1%; SAT math scores over 700: 1%; SAT writing scores over 700: 1%.
Retention: 67% of full-time freshmen returned.

ACADEMICS

Calendar: semesters. *Degrees:* certificates, associate, bachelor's, master's, doctoral, post-master's, and postbachelor's certificates.
Special study options: academic remediation for entering students, accelerated degree program, adult/continuing education programs, advanced placement credit, cooperative education, distance learning, double majors, English as a second language, honors programs, independent study, internships, off-campus study, part-time degree program, services for LD students, student-designed majors, study abroad, summer session for credit. ***ROTC:*** Army (c), Air Force (c).
Computers: Students can access the following: computer help desk, free student e-mail accounts, online (class) grades, online (class) registration, online (class) schedules. Campuswide network is available. 100% of college-owned or -operated housing units are wired for high-speed Internet access. Wireless service is available via entire campus.
Library: Giovatto Library.

STUDENT LIFE

Housing options: coed, men-only, women-only. Campus housing is university owned.
Activities and organizations: drama/theater group, student-run newspaper, radio station, choral group, Student Programming Board, Student Government Association, Greek Life, Residence Hall Association, Spectrum (LGBT), national fraternities, national sororities.
Athletics Member NCAA. All Division I. ***Intercollegiate sports:*** baseball M(s), basketball M(s)/W(s), bowling W(s), cross-country running M(s)/W(s), fencing W(s), golf M(s)/W(s), soccer M(s)/W(s), softball W(s), tennis M(s)/W(s), track and field M(s)/W(s), volleyball W(s). ***Intramural sports:*** badminton M/W, basketball M/W, football M/W, rugby M(c)/W(c), soccer M/W, table tennis M/W, tennis M/W, volleyball M/W.
Campus security: 24-hour emergency response devices and patrols, late-night transport/escort service, controlled dormitory access, trained law enforcement personnel on staff.

Student services: health clinic, personal/psychological counseling, women's center.

FINANCIAL AID
Financial Aid Of all full-time matriculated undergraduates who enrolled in 2007, 1,671 applied for aid, 1,549 were judged to have need. In 2007, 117 non-need-based awards were made. ***Average financial aid package:*** $18,283. ***Average need-based loan:*** $3808. ***Average need-based gift aid:*** $8702. ***Average non-need-based aid:*** $6403.

APPLYING
Standardized Tests *Required:* SAT or ACT (for admission).

Options: electronic application, early admission.

Application fee: $40.

Required: high school transcript, 2 letters of recommendation. ***Required for some:*** interview.

CONTACT
Fairleigh Dickinson University, Metropolitan Campus, 1000 River Road, Teaneck, NJ 07666-1914. *Toll-free phone:* 800-338-8803.

Felician University

Lodi, New Jersey

http://www.felician.edu/

- **Independent Roman Catholic** comprehensive, founded 1942
- **Small-town** 37-acre campus with easy access to New York City
- **Endowment** $6.2 million
- **Coed** 1,648 undergraduate students, 87% full-time, 72% women, 28% men
- **Moderately difficult** entrance level, 79% of applicants were admitted

UNDERGRAD STUDENTS
1,433 full-time, 215 part-time. Students come from 12 states and territories; 8 other countries; 10% are from out of state; 23% Black or African American, non-Hispanic/Latino; 30% Hispanic/Latino; 5% Asian, non-Hispanic/Latino; 0.4% Native Hawaiian or other Pacific Islander, non-Hispanic/Latino; 0.5% American Indian or Alaska Native, non-Hispanic/Latino; 0.6% Two or more races, non-Hispanic/Latino; 9% Race/ethnicity unknown; 2% international; 12% transferred in; 30% live on campus.

Freshmen:
Admission: 2,173 applied, 1,707 admitted, 316 enrolled. ***Average high school GPA:*** 3. ***Test scores:*** SAT critical reading scores over 500: 25%; SAT math scores over 500: 30%; SAT writing scores over 500: 21%; SAT critical reading scores over 600: 2%; SAT math scores over 600: 3%; SAT writing scores over 600: 2%.

Retention: 84% of full-time freshmen returned.

FACULTY
Total: 232, 38% full-time, 40% with terminal degrees.

Student/faculty ratio: 13:1.

ACADEMICS
Calendar: semesters. *Degrees:* certificates, associate, bachelor's, master's, doctoral, post-master's, and postbachelor's certificates.

Special study options: academic remediation for entering students, accelerated degree program, adult/continuing education programs, advanced placement credit, cooperative education, distance learning, double majors, English as a second language, external degree program, honors programs, independent study, internships, off-campus study, part-time degree program, services for LD students, student-designed majors, study abroad, summer session for credit. ***ROTC:*** Army (c), Air Force (c).

Unusual degree programs: business administration; psychology/counseling.

Computers: 170 computers/terminals and 50 ports are available on campus for general student use. Students can access the following: computer help desk, free student e-mail accounts, online (class) grades, online (class) registration, online (class) schedules. Campuswide network is available. 100% of college-owned or -operated housing units are wired for high-speed Internet access. Wireless service is available via entire campus.

Library: Felician University Library plus 1 other. *Books:* 70,383 (physical), 193,005 (digital/electronic); *Serial titles:* 186 (physical), 33,942 (digital/electronic); *Databases:* 45. Weekly public service hours: 133; students can reserve study rooms.

STUDENT LIFE
Housing options: coed, men-only, women-only, special housing for students with disabilities. Campus housing is university owned. Freshman applicants given priority for college housing.

Activities and organizations: drama/theater group, student-run radio station, choral group, Student Nurses Association, Zeta Alpha Zeta teaching sorority, Campus Activity Board, Students in Free Enterprise (SIFE), Student Government Association.

Athletics Member NCAA, NAIA. All NCAA Division II. ***Intercollegiate sports:*** baseball M(s), basketball M(s)/W(s), bowling W(s), cross-country running M(s)/W(s), golf M(s), soccer M(s)/W(s), softball W(s), volleyball W(s). ***Intramural sports:*** cheerleading W(c), soccer M/W, softball W, volleyball M/W, weight lifting M/W.

Campus security: 24-hour patrols, student patrols, late-night transport/escort service.

Student services: health clinic, personal/psychological counseling.

COSTS & FINANCIAL AID
Costs (2017–18) ***Comprehensive fee:*** $46,280 includes full-time tuition ($31,290), mandatory fees ($2360), and room and board ($12,630). Full-time tuition and fees vary according to program. Part-time tuition: $1035 per credit hour. Part-time tuition and fees vary according to course load and program. ***Required fees:*** $465 per term part-time. ***Room and board:*** Room and board charges vary according to housing facility. ***Payment plan:*** installment. ***Waivers:*** employees or children of employees.

Financial Aid Of all full-time matriculated undergraduates who enrolled in 2015, 1,283 applied for aid, 1,239 were judged to have need, 70 had their need fully met. 63 Federal Work-Study jobs (averaging $2583). In 2015, 81 non-need-based awards were made. ***Average percent of need met:*** 64. ***Average financial aid package:*** $25,736. ***Average need-based loan:*** $4246. ***Average need-based gift aid:*** $13,755. ***Average non-need-based aid:*** $14,498. ***Average indebtedness upon graduation:*** $32,032.

APPLYING
Standardized Tests *Required:* SAT or ACT (for admission). *Required for some:* ACT (for admission), SAT Subject Tests (for admission). *Recommended:* SAT and SAT Subject Tests or ACT (for admission).

Options: early action, deferred entrance.

Application fee: $30.

Required: essay or personal statement, high school transcript, minimum 2.0 GPA, letters of recommendation. ***Required for some:*** interview.

Application deadlines: 5/1 (freshmen), 2/15 (out-of-state freshmen), rolling (transfers), 11/15 (early action).

Notification: continuous (freshmen), continuous (out-of-state freshmen), continuous (transfers), 1/16 (early action).

CONTACT
Colleen Fuller, Director, Undergraduate Admissions, Felician University, 262 South Main Street, Lodi, NJ 07644-2117. *Phone:* 201-355-1444. *E-mail:* fullerc@felician.edu.

★ Georgian Court University

Lakewood, New Jersey

http://www.georgian.edu/

- **Independent Roman Catholic** comprehensive, founded 1908
- **Suburban** 156-acre campus with easy access to New York City, Philadelphia
- **Endowment** $49.0 million
- **Coed** 1,591 undergraduate students, 83% full-time, 72% women, 28% men
- **Moderately difficult** entrance level, 78% of applicants were admitted

UNDERGRAD STUDENTS
1,319 full-time, 272 part-time. Students come from 21 states and territories; 12 other countries; 6% are from out of state; 11% Black or African American, non-Hispanic/Latino; 10% Hispanic/Latino; 3% Asian, non-Hispanic/Latino; 0.2% Native Hawaiian or other Pacific Islander, non-Hispanic/Latino; 0.4% American Indian or Alaska Native, non-Hispanic/Latino; 2% Two or more races, non-Hispanic/Latino; 17%

Race/ethnicity unknown; 1% international; 13% transferred in; 30% live on campus.

Freshmen:
Admission: 526 applied, 410 admitted, 221 enrolled. ***Average high school GPA:*** 3.27. ***Test scores:*** SAT critical reading scores over 500: 31%; SAT math scores over 500: 43%; SAT writing scores over 500: 29%; ACT scores over 18: 56%; SAT critical reading scores over 600: 5%; SAT math scores over 600: 6%; SAT writing scores over 600: 3%; ACT scores over 24: 20%; SAT critical reading scores over 700: 1%; SAT math scores over 700: 1%; SAT writing scores over 700: 1%; ACT scores over 30: 4%.
Retention: 85% of full-time freshmen returned.

FACULTY
Total: 260, 33% full-time, 50% with terminal degrees.
Student/faculty ratio: 12:1.

ACADEMICS
Calendar: semesters. *Degrees:* certificates, bachelor's, master's, post-master's, and postbachelor's certificates.
Special study options: academic remediation for entering students, accelerated degree program, adult/continuing education programs, advanced placement credit, distance learning, double majors, English as a second language, honors programs, independent study, internships, off-campus study, part-time degree program, services for LD students, student-designed majors, study abroad, summer session for credit.
Computers: 221 computers/terminals and 300 ports are available on campus for general student use. Students can access the following: campus intranet, computer help desk, free student e-mail accounts, online (class) grades, online (class) registration, online (class) schedules. Campuswide network is available. 100% of college-owned or -operated housing units are wired for high-speed Internet access. Wireless service is available via entire campus.
Library: The Sister Mary Joseph Cunningham Library. *Books:* 129,114 (physical), 85,957 (digital/electronic); *Serial titles:* 2,709 (physical), 31,176 (digital/electronic); *Databases:* 119. Weekly public service hours: 85; students can reserve study rooms.

STUDENT LIFE
Housing options: coed. Campus housing is university owned. Freshman campus housing is guaranteed.
Activities and organizations: student-run newspaper, Basketball Club, Black Student Union, Math Club, Dance Theatre Club, History Club.
Athletics Member NCAA. All Division II. ***Intercollegiate sports:*** basketball M(s)/W(s), cross-country running M(s)/W(s), lacrosse M(s)/W(s), soccer M(s)/W(s), softball W(s), track and field M(s)/W(s), volleyball W(s).
Campus security: 24-hour emergency response devices and patrols, late-night transport/escort service, controlled dormitory access.
Student services: health clinic, personal/psychological counseling.

COSTS & FINANCIAL AID
Costs (2016–17) ***Comprehensive fee:*** $42,426 includes full-time tuition ($30,158), mandatory fees ($1460), and room and board ($10,808). Full-time tuition and fees vary according to location, program, and reciprocity agreements. Part-time tuition: $690 per credit hour. Part-time tuition and fees vary according to location, program, and reciprocity agreements. ***Required fees:*** $365 per term part-time. ***Payment plan:*** installment. ***Waivers:*** children of alumni, senior citizens, and employees or children of employees.
Financial Aid Of all full-time matriculated undergraduates who enrolled in 2016, 1,193 applied for aid, 1,135 were judged to have need, 242 had their need fully met. In 2016, 143 non-need-based awards were made. ***Average percent of need met:*** 74. ***Average financial aid package:*** $28,364. ***Average need-based loan:*** $7548. ***Average need-based gift aid:*** $18,406. ***Average non-need-based aid:*** $13,890. ***Average indebtedness upon graduation:*** $40,267. ***Financial aid deadline:*** 7/1.

APPLYING
Standardized Tests *Required:* SAT or ACT (for admission).
Options: electronic application, early action, deferred entrance.
Application fee: $40.
Required: high school transcript, minimum 2.5 GPA. ***Recommended:*** essay or personal statement, letters of recommendation, interview.

Application deadlines: 8/1 (freshmen), 8/1 (transfers), 12/1 (early action).

Notification: continuous (transfers).

CONTACT

Stephen Lambert, Director of Undergraduate Admissions, Georgian Court University, 900 Lakewood Avenue, Lakewood, NJ 08701-2697. *Phone:* 732-987-2745. *Toll-free phone:* 800-458-8422. *Fax:* 732-987-2000. *E-mail:* admissions@georgian.edu.

See previous page for display ad and page 1360 for the College Close-Up.

Kean University

Union, New Jersey

http://www.kean.edu/

- **State-supported** university, founded 1855, part of New Jersey State College System
- **Suburban** 185-acre campus with easy access to New York City
- **Coed** 11,812 undergraduate students, 78% full-time, 61% women, 39% men
- **Moderately difficult** entrance level, 74% of applicants were admitted

UNDERGRAD STUDENTS

9,239 full-time, 2,573 part-time. Students come from 18 states and territories; 45 other countries; 2% are from out of state; 19% Black or African American, non-Hispanic/Latino; 27% Hispanic/Latino; 5% Asian, non-Hispanic/Latino; 0.2% Native Hawaiian or other Pacific Islander, non-Hispanic/Latino; 0.2% American Indian or Alaska Native, non-Hispanic/Latino; 2% Two or more races, non-Hispanic/Latino; 8% Race/ethnicity unknown; 2% international; 12% transferred in; 15% live on campus.

Freshmen:

Admission: 8,785 applied, 6,536 admitted, 1,526 enrolled. ***Average high school GPA:*** 3.1. ***Test scores:*** SAT critical reading scores over 500: 25%; SAT math scores over 500: 34%; ACT scores over 18: 72%; SAT critical reading scores over 600: 3%; SAT math scores over 600: 5%; ACT scores over 24: 14%; ACT scores over 30: 1%.

Retention: 73% of full-time freshmen returned.

FACULTY

Total: 1,436, 23% full-time.

Student/faculty ratio: 16:1.

ACADEMICS

Calendar: semesters. *Degrees:* bachelor's, master's, doctoral, and post-master's certificates.

Special study options: academic remediation for entering students, accelerated degree program, adult/continuing education programs, advanced placement credit, cooperative education, distance learning, double majors, English as a second language, external degree program, honors programs, independent study, internships, off-campus study, part-time degree program, services for LD students, study abroad, summer session for credit. ***ROTC:*** Army (c), Air Force (c).

Computers: 1,700 computers/terminals and 2,000 ports are available on campus for general student use. Students can access the following: free student e-mail accounts, online (class) grades, online (class) registration, online (class) schedules. Campuswide network is available. 100% of college-owned or -operated housing units are wired for high-speed Internet access. Wireless service is available via entire campus.

Library: Nancy Thompson Library. *Books:* 201,146 (physical), 10,966 (digital/electronic); *Serial titles:* 56,478 (digital/electronic); *Databases:* 246. Weekly public service hours: 102.

STUDENT LIFE

Housing options: coed, special housing for students with disabilities. Campus housing is university owned. Freshman applicants given priority for college housing.

Activities and organizations: drama/theater group, student-run newspaper, radio station, choral group, Kean University Council for Exceptional Children, American Sign Language Club, Speech, Language and Hearing Student Association, PSY Organization, Outdoor Adventure and Recreation Club, national fraternities, national sororities.

Athletics Member NCAA. All Division III. ***Intercollegiate sports:*** baseball M, basketball M/W, field hockey W, football M, lacrosse M/W, soccer M/W, softball W, tennis W, volleyball M/W. ***Intramural sports:*** basketball M/W, sand volleyball M/W, soccer M/W, softball M/W, tennis M/W, ultimate Frisbee M/W, volleyball M/W, weight lifting M/W.

Campus security: 24-hour emergency response devices and patrols, student patrols, late-night transport/escort service, controlled dormitory access.

Student services: health clinic, personal/psychological counseling.

COSTS & FINANCIAL AID

Costs (2016–17) ***Tuition:*** state resident $7754 full-time, $302 per credit part-time; nonresident $14,521 full-time, $513 per credit part-time. Part-time tuition and fees vary according to course load. ***Required fees:*** $4116 full-time, $151 per credit part-time. ***Room and board:*** $12,780. Room and board charges vary according to board plan, housing facility, and student level. ***Payment plan:*** installment. ***Waivers:*** senior citizens and employees or children of employees.

Financial Aid Of all full-time matriculated undergraduates who enrolled in 2016, 7,574 applied for aid, 6,544 were judged to have need, 57 had their need fully met. 252 Federal Work-Study jobs (averaging $2455). In 2016, 102 non-need-based awards were made. ***Average percent of need met:*** 82. ***Average financial aid package:*** $10,497. ***Average need-based loan:*** $4450. ***Average need-based gift aid:*** $8204. ***Average non-need-based aid:*** $3814. ***Average indebtedness upon graduation:*** $33,693.

APPLYING

Standardized Tests *Required:* SAT or ACT (for admission).

Options: electronic application, early action, deferred entrance.

Application fee: $75.

Required: high school transcript. ***Required for some:*** interview. ***Recommended:*** essay or personal statement, 2 letters of recommendation.

Application deadlines: 8/15 (freshmen), 8/1 (transfers), 12/1 (early action).

Notification: continuous until 11/1 (freshmen), continuous (transfers), 1/1 (early action).

CONTACT

Ms. Jennifer Kanellis, Director of Admissions, Kean University, 1000 Morris Avenue, Union, NJ 07083. *Phone:* 908-737-7100. *Fax:* 908-737-7105. *E-mail:* admitme@kean.edu.

Mesivta Keser Torah

Lakewood, New Jersey

CONTACT

Mesivta Keser Torah, 613 Madison Avenue, Lakewood, NJ 08701.

★ Monmouth University

West Long Branch, New Jersey

http://www.monmouth.edu/

- **Independent** comprehensive, founded 1933
- **Suburban** 159-acre campus with easy access to New York City, Philadelphia
- **Endowment** $80.3 million
- **Coed** 4,693 undergraduate students, 95% full-time, 58% women, 42% men
- **Moderately difficult** entrance level, 78% of applicants were admitted

UNDERGRAD STUDENTS

4,450 full-time, 243 part-time. Students come from 31 states and territories; 23 other countries; 14% are from out of state; 5% Black or African American, non-Hispanic/Latino; 11% Hispanic/Latino; 3% Asian, non-Hispanic/Latino; 0.1% American Indian or Alaska Native, non-Hispanic/Latino; 2% Two or more races, non-Hispanic/Latino; 3% Race/ethnicity unknown; 0.7% international; 6% transferred in; 46% live on campus.

Freshmen:

Admission: 8,486 applied, 6,651 admitted, 1,128 enrolled. ***Average high school GPA:*** 3.31. ***Test scores:*** SAT critical reading scores over 500: 58%; SAT math scores over 500: 66%; SAT writing scores over 500: 62%; ACT scores over 18: 97%; SAT critical reading scores over 600: 10%; SAT math scores over 600: 15%; SAT writing scores over 600: 14%; ACT scores over 24: 36%; SAT critical reading scores over 700: 1%; SAT math

scores over 700: 2%; SAT writing scores over 700: 1%; ACT scores over 30: 3%.

Retention: 83% of full-time freshmen returned.

FACULTY

Total: 638, 45% full-time, 50% with terminal degrees.

Student/faculty ratio: 14:1.

ACADEMICS

Calendar: semesters. *Degrees:* certificates, bachelor's, master's, doctoral, post-master's, and postbachelor's certificates.

Special study options: academic remediation for entering students, accelerated degree program, advanced placement credit, cooperative education, distance learning, double majors, honors programs, independent study, internships, part-time degree program, services for LD students, student-designed majors, study abroad, summer session for credit. ***ROTC:*** Army (c), Air Force (c).

Computers: 1,000 computers/terminals are available on campus for general student use. Students can access the following: campus intranet, computer help desk, free student e-mail accounts, online (class) grades, online (class) registration, online (class) schedules. Campuswide network is available. 100% of college-owned or -operated housing units are wired for high-speed Internet access. Wireless service is available via classrooms, computer centers, computer labs, dorm rooms, learning centers, libraries, student centers.

Library: Monmouth University Library. *Books:* 285,496 (physical), 31,870 (digital/electronic); *Serial titles:* 1,200 (physical), 71,277 (digital/electronic); *Databases:* 163. Weekly public service hours: 111; students can reserve study rooms.

STUDENT LIFE

Housing options: coed. Campus housing is university owned and leased by the school. Freshman campus housing is guaranteed.

Activities and organizations: drama/theater group, student-run newspaper, radio and television station, choral group, radio station WMCX 88.9 FM, Student Government Association, student newspaper (Outlook), Student Activities Board, Shadows (yearbook), national fraternities, national sororities.

Athletics Member NCAA. All Division I except football (Division I-AA). ***Intercollegiate sports:*** baseball M(s), basketball M(s)/W(s), bowling W(s), cheerleading M(c)/W(c), cross-country running M(s)/W(s), field hockey W(s), golf M(s)/W(s), ice hockey M(c), lacrosse M(s)/W(s), sailing M(c)/W(c), soccer M(s)/W(s), softball W(s), tennis M(s)/W(s), track and field M(s)/W(s). ***Intramural sports:*** baseball M(c), basketball M/W, football M/W, lacrosse M(c)/W(c), soccer M/W, softball M/W, volleyball M/W.

Campus security: 24-hour emergency response devices and patrols, late-night transport/escort service, controlled dormitory access.

Student services: health clinic, personal/psychological counseling, women's center, legal services.

COSTS & FINANCIAL AID

Costs (2017–18) ***One-time required fee:*** $200. ***Comprehensive fee:*** $50,284 includes full-time tuition ($36,032), mandatory fees ($700), and room and board ($13,552). Part-time tuition: $1043 per credit hour. Part-time tuition and fees vary according to course load. ***Required fees:*** $175 per term part-time. ***College room only:*** $7784. Room and board charges vary according to board plan and housing facility. ***Payment plan:*** installment. ***Waivers:*** senior citizens and employees or children of employees.

Financial Aid Of all full-time matriculated undergraduates who enrolled in 2016, 3,680 applied for aid, 3,221 were judged to have need, 450 had their need fully met. 1,032 Federal Work-Study jobs (averaging $2040). In 2016, 1162 non-need-based awards were made. ***Average percent of need met:*** 64. ***Average financial aid package:*** $24,121. ***Average need-based loan:*** $4656. ***Average need-based gift aid:*** $12,285. ***Average non-need-based aid:*** $9131. ***Average indebtedness upon graduation:*** $29,483.

APPLYING

Standardized Tests *Required:* SAT or ACT (for admission).

Options: electronic application, early action, deferred entrance.

Application fee: $50.

Required: essay or personal statement, high school transcript, 1 letter of recommendation. ***Required for some:*** interview. ***Recommended:*** resumé of activities including community involvement and leadership positions.

Application deadlines: 3/1 (freshmen), 7/15 (transfers), 12/1 (early action).

Notification: 4/1 (freshmen), continuous (transfers), 1/15 (early action).

CONTACT

Ms. Victoria Bobik, Director of Undergraduate Admission, Monmouth University, 400 Cedar Avenue, West Long Branch, NJ 07764-1898. *Phone:* 732-571-3456. *Toll-free phone:* 800-543-9671. *Fax:* 732-263-5166. *E-mail:* admission@monmouth.edu.

See previous page for display ad and page 1426 for the College Close-Up.

Montclair State University

Montclair, New Jersey

http://www.montclair.edu/

- **State-supported** university, founded 1908
- **Suburban** 250-acre campus with easy access to New York City
- **Endowment** $59.5 million
- **Coed** 16,810 undergraduate students, 89% full-time, 61% women, 39% men
- **Moderately difficult** entrance level, 70% of applicants were admitted

UNDERGRAD STUDENTS

14,968 full-time, 1,842 part-time. 3% are from out of state; 12% Black or African American, non-Hispanic/Latino; 26% Hispanic/Latino; 6% Asian, non-Hispanic/Latino; 0.2% Native Hawaiian or other Pacific Islander, non-Hispanic/Latino; 0.1% American Indian or Alaska Native, non-Hispanic/Latino; 3% Two or more races, non-Hispanic/Latino; 9% Race/ethnicity unknown; 2% international; 9% transferred in; 32% live on campus.

Freshmen:

Admission: 11,990 applied, 8,401 admitted, 2,984 enrolled. ***Average high school GPA:*** 3.2. ***Test scores:*** SAT critical reading scores over 500: 42%; SAT math scores over 500: 49%; SAT writing scores over 500: 44%; SAT critical reading scores over 600: 8%; SAT math scores over 600: 10%; SAT writing scores over 600: 8%.

Retention: 83% of full-time freshmen returned.

FACULTY

Total: 1,846, 34% full-time, 33% with terminal degrees.

Student/faculty ratio: 17:1.

ACADEMICS

Calendar: semesters. *Degrees:* certificates, bachelor's, master's, doctoral, and postbachelor's certificates.

Special study options: academic remediation for entering students, accelerated degree program, adult/continuing education programs, advanced placement credit, cooperative education, double majors, English as a second language, freshman honors college, honors programs, independent study, internships, off-campus study, part-time degree program, services for LD students, study abroad, summer session for credit.

Unusual degree programs: teaching, music, aquatic and coastal science, chemistry, mathematics, statistics.

Computers: 1,850 computers/terminals and 27,000 ports are available on campus for general student use. Students can access the following: campus intranet, computer help desk, free student e-mail accounts, online (class) grades, online (class) registration, online (class) schedules, online storage, online course delivery, online computing lab, student online portal. Campuswide network is available. 100% of college-owned or -operated housing units are wired for high-speed Internet access. Wireless service is available via entire campus.

Library: Sprague Library. *Books:* 441,470 (physical), 145,833 (digital/electronic); *Serial titles:* 9,751 (physical), 40,969 (digital/electronic); *Databases:* 165. Weekly public service hours: 93; students can reserve study rooms.

STUDENT LIFE

Housing options: coed. Campus housing is university owned and is provided by a third party. Freshman campus housing is guaranteed.

Activities and organizations: drama/theater group, student-run newspaper, radio and television station, choral group, Latin American Student Organization, Campus Recreation, MSU Players, Unified Asian American Student Organization, SLAM (Student Life At Montclair), national fraternities, national sororities.

Athletics Member NCAA. All Division III. ***Intercollegiate sports:*** baseball M, basketball M/W, field hockey W, football M, lacrosse M/W, soccer M/W, softball W, swimming and diving M/W, track and field M/W, volleyball W. ***Intramural sports:*** baseball M(c), basketball M/W, cheerleading W(c), field hockey M(c)/W(c), ice hockey M(c)/W(c), lacrosse M(c), racquetball M/W, rugby M(c)/W(c), soccer M/W, softball M/W, table tennis M/W, tennis M/W, track and field M(c)/W(c), volleyball M/W, water polo M/W, wrestling M(c)/W(c).

Campus security: 24-hour emergency response devices and patrols, late-night transport/escort service, controlled dormitory access, video surveillance, student escorts.

Student services: health clinic, personal/psychological counseling, women's center.

COSTS & FINANCIAL AID

Costs (2016–17) ***Tuition:*** state resident $8768 full-time, $292 per credit part-time; nonresident $16,659 full-time, $555 per credit part-time. ***Required fees:*** $3348 full-time, $112 per credit part-time. ***Room and board:*** $14,094. Room and board charges vary according to board plan and housing facility. ***Payment plan:*** installment. ***Waivers:*** senior citizens and employees or children of employees.

Financial Aid Of all full-time matriculated undergraduates who enrolled in 2015, 11,805 applied for aid, 10,185 were judged to have need, 316 had their need fully met. 475 Federal Work-Study jobs (averaging $1275). In 2015, 673 non-need-based awards were made. ***Average percent of need met:*** 67. ***Average financial aid package:*** $9734. ***Average need-based loan:*** $4399. ***Average need-based gift aid:*** $8862. ***Average non-need-based aid:*** $5571. ***Average indebtedness upon graduation:*** $28,070.

APPLYING

Options: electronic application, deferred entrance.

Application fee: $65.

Required: essay or personal statement, high school transcript. ***Required for some:*** interview.

Application deadlines: 3/1 (freshmen), 6/15 (transfers).

Notification: continuous (freshmen), continuous (transfers).

CONTACT

Jeff Indiveri-Gant, Director of Admissions, Montclair State University, One Normal Avenue, Montclair, NJ 07043-1624. *Phone:* 973-655-3316. *Fax:* 973-655-7700. *E-mail:* undergraduate.admissions@montclair.edu.

New Jersey City University

Jersey City, New Jersey

http://www.njcu.edu/

- **State-supported** comprehensive, founded 1927
- **Urban** 51-acre campus with easy access to New York City
- **Endowment** $7.3 million
- **Coed** 6,317 undergraduate students, 76% full-time, 60% women, 40% men
- **Moderately difficult** entrance level, 87% of applicants were admitted

UNDERGRAD STUDENTS

4,826 full-time, 1,491 part-time. Students come from 18 states and territories; 18 other countries; 1% are from out of state; 21% Black or African American, non-Hispanic/Latino; 35% Hispanic/Latino; 7% Asian, non-Hispanic/Latino; 0.8% Native Hawaiian or other Pacific Islander, non-Hispanic/Latino; 0.3% American Indian or Alaska Native, non-Hispanic/Latino; 2% Two or more races, non-Hispanic/Latino; 7% Race/ethnicity unknown; 3% international; 15% transferred in; 4% live on campus.

Freshmen:

Admission: 2,789 applied, 2,419 admitted, 819 enrolled. ***Average high school GPA:*** 2.9. ***Test scores:*** SAT critical reading scores over 500: 17%; SAT math scores over 500: 27%; SAT critical reading scores over 600: 3%; SAT math scores over 600: 6%; SAT math scores over 700: 1%.

Retention: 74% of full-time freshmen returned.

FACULTY
Total: 809, 31% full-time.

Student/faculty ratio: 14:1.

ACADEMICS
Calendar: semesters. *Degrees:* certificates, bachelor's, master's, doctoral, post-master's, and postbachelor's certificates.

Special study options: academic remediation for entering students, accelerated degree program, adult/continuing education programs, advanced placement credit, cooperative education, distance learning, double majors, English as a second language, honors programs, independent study, internships, off-campus study, part-time degree program, services for LD students, study abroad, summer session for credit. ***ROTC:*** Army (c), Air Force (c).

Computers: 844 computers/terminals are available on campus for general student use. Students can access the following: free student e-mail accounts, online (class) grades, online (class) registration, online (class) schedules. Campuswide network is available. 100% of college-owned or -operated housing units are wired for high-speed Internet access. Wireless service is available via classrooms, computer centers, computer labs, dorm rooms, learning centers, libraries, student centers.

Library: Congressman Frank J. Guarini Library. *Books:* 300,000 (physical), 150,000 (digital/electronic); *Serial titles:* 150 (physical), 32,000 (digital/electronic); *Databases:* 152. Weekly public service hours: 82.

STUDENT LIFE
Housing options: coed, special housing for students with disabilities. Campus housing is university owned.

Activities and organizations: drama/theater group, student-run newspaper, radio station, choral group, national fraternities, national sororities.

Athletics Member NCAA. All Division III. ***Intercollegiate sports:*** baseball M, basketball M/W, bowling W, cross-country running M/W, golf M, soccer M/W, softball W, volleyball M/W. ***Intramural sports:*** basketball M/W, bowling M/W, cheerleading M/W, cross-country running M/W, football M/W, golf M, racquetball M/W, soccer M/W, softball M/W, swimming and diving M/W, table tennis M/W, tennis W, track and field M/W, volleyball M/W.

Campus security: 24-hour emergency response devices and patrols, late-night transport/escort service.

Student services: health clinic, personal/psychological counseling, women's center, legal services.

COSTS & FINANCIAL AID
Costs (2017–18) ***Tuition:*** state resident $8115 full-time, $270 per credit hour part-time; nonresident $17,142 full-time, $571 per credit hour part-time. Part-time tuition and fees vary according to course load. ***Required fees:*** $3316 full-time. ***Room and board:*** $12,446. Room and board charges vary according to board plan and housing facility. ***Payment plan:*** deferred payment. ***Waivers:*** senior citizens and employees or children of employees.

Financial Aid Of all full-time matriculated undergraduates who enrolled in 2014, 4,299 applied for aid, 4,026 were judged to have need, 134 had their need fully met. In 2014, 76 non-need-based awards were made. ***Average percent of need met:*** 58. ***Average financial aid package:*** $10,141. ***Average need-based loan:*** $4129. ***Average need-based gift aid:*** $8080. ***Average non-need-based aid:*** $7197. ***Average indebtedness upon graduation:*** $23,416.

APPLYING
Standardized Tests *Required:* SAT (for admission).

Options: electronic application, deferred entrance.

Application fee: $50.

Required: essay or personal statement, high school transcript, minimum 2.8 GPA. ***Required for some:*** interview. ***Recommended:*** 1 letter of recommendation.

Application deadlines: 7/15 (freshmen), rolling (transfers).

Notification: continuous (freshmen).

CONTACT
Mr. Jose Balda, Director of Admissions, New Jersey City University, 2039 Kennedy Boulevard, Jersey City, NJ 07305. *Phone:* 201-200-3234. *Toll-free phone:* 888-441-NJCU. *E-mail:* admissions@nicu.edu.

★ New Jersey Institute of Technology

Newark, New Jersey

http://www.njit.edu/

- **State-supported** university, founded 1881
- **Urban** 48-acre campus with easy access to New York City
- **Endowment** $99.2 million
- **Coed**
- **Moderately difficult** entrance level

FACULTY
Student/faculty ratio: 17:1.

ACADEMICS
Calendar: semesters. *Degrees:* bachelor's, master's, doctoral, and postbachelor's certificates.

Library: Van Houten Library plus 1 other. *Books:* 170,618 (physical), 27,759 (digital/electronic); *Serial titles:* 59 (physical), 33,674 (digital/electronic); *Databases:* 33. Weekly public service hours: 105; students can reserve study rooms.

STUDENT LIFE
Housing options: coed. Campus housing is university owned.

Activities and organizations: drama/theater group, student-run newspaper, radio station, Student Senate, Student Activities Council, Vector, Institute of Industrial Engineers, WJTB Geek Radio, national fraternities, national sororities.

Athletics Member NCAA. All Division I.

Campus security: 24-hour emergency response devices and patrols, late-night transport/escort service, controlled dormitory access, bicycle patrols.

Student services: health clinic, personal/psychological counseling, women's center.

COSTS & FINANCIAL AID
Costs (2016–17) ***Tuition:*** state resident $13,602 full-time, $517 per credit part-time; nonresident $28,206 full-time, $1206 per credit part-time. Full-time tuition and fees vary according to course load and degree level. Part-time tuition and fees vary according to course load and degree level. ***Required fees:*** $2828 full-time, $166 per credit part-time. ***Room and board:*** $13,400; room only: $9026. Room and board charges vary according to board plan and housing facility. ***Payment plans:*** installment, deferred payment.

Financial Aid Of all full-time matriculated undergraduates who enrolled in 2015, 4,929 applied for aid, 4,411 were judged to have need, 369 had their need fully met. 278 Federal Work-Study jobs (averaging $1405). 1,260 state and other part-time jobs (averaging $1247). In 2015, 561 non-need-based awards were made. ***Average percent of need met:*** 52. ***Average financial aid package:*** $13,200. ***Average need-based loan:*** $4420. ***Average need-based gift aid:*** $12,789. ***Average non-need-based aid:*** $14,346. ***Average indebtedness upon graduation:*** $40,967. ***Financial aid deadline:*** 5/15.

APPLYING
Standardized Tests *Required:* SAT or ACT (for admission).

Options: electronic application, early admission, deferred entrance.

Application fee: $75.

Required: high school transcript. ***Required for some:*** essay or personal statement, interview. ***Recommended:*** 1 letter of recommendation.

CONTACT
Mr. Stephen M. Eck, Director of University Admissions, New Jersey Institute of Technology, University Heights, Newark, NJ 07102. *Phone:* 973-596-3306. *Toll-free phone:* 800-925-NJIT. *Fax:* 973-596-3461. *E-mail:* admissions@njit.edu.

Pillar College
Newark, New Jersey
http://www.pillar.edu/

CONTACT
Ms. Linda Aarni, Senior Admissions Counselor, Pillar College, 60 Park Place, Suite 701, Newark, NJ 07102. *Phone:* 973-803-5000. *Toll-free phone:* 800-234-9305. *Fax:* 732-356-4846. *E-mail:* info@pillar.edu.

★ Princeton University
Princeton, New Jersey
http://www.princeton.edu/

- **Independent** university, founded 1746
- **Suburban** 600-acre campus with easy access to New York City, Philadelphia
- **Endowment** $21.7 billion
- **Coed** 5,400 undergraduate students, 97% full-time, 48% women, 52% men
- **Most difficult** entrance level, 7% of applicants were admitted

UNDERGRAD STUDENTS
5,251 full-time, 149 part-time. Students come from 53 states and territories; 99 other countries; 83% are from out of state; 8% Black or African American, non-Hispanic/Latino; 10% Hispanic/Latino; 21% Asian, non-Hispanic/Latino; 0.2% Native Hawaiian or other Pacific Islander, non-Hispanic/Latino; 0.1% American Indian or Alaska Native, non-Hispanic/Latino; 4% Two or more races, non-Hispanic/Latino; 2% Race/ethnicity unknown; 12% international; 98% live on campus.

Freshmen:
Admission: 29,303 applied, 1,911 admitted, 1,305 enrolled. ***Average high school GPA:*** 3.89. ***Test scores:*** SAT critical reading scores over 500: 100%; SAT math scores over 500: 100%; SAT writing scores over 500: 100%; ACT scores over 18: 100%; SAT critical reading scores over 600: 97%; SAT math scores over 600: 98%; SAT writing scores over 600: 98%; ACT scores over 24: 100%; SAT critical reading scores over 700: 73%; SAT math scores over 700: 81%; SAT writing scores over 700: 76%; ACT scores over 30: 92%.
Retention: 97% of full-time freshmen returned.

FACULTY
Total: 1,172, 79% full-time, 85% with terminal degrees.
Student/faculty ratio: 5:1.

ACADEMICS
Calendar: semesters. *Degrees:* bachelor's, master's, and doctoral.
Special study options: advanced placement credit, independent study, off-campus study, services for LD students, student-designed majors, study abroad. ***ROTC:*** Army (b), Navy (c), Air Force (c).
Computers: 500 computers/terminals and 17,000 ports are available on campus for general student use. Students can access the following: campus intranet, computer help desk, free student e-mail accounts, online (class) grades, online (class) registration, online (class) schedules, academic applications and courseware, printing, network file space, website hosting, media lab, broadcast center. Campuswide network is available. 100% of college-owned or -operated housing units are wired for high-speed Internet access. Wireless service is available via entire campus.
Library: Harvey S. Firestone Memorial Library plus 9 others. *Books:* 8.3 million (physical), 2.0 million (digital/electronic); *Serial titles:* 213,082 (physical), 175,619 (digital/electronic); *Databases:* 1,849. Weekly public service hours: 105.

STUDENT LIFE
Housing options: on-campus residence required through sophomore year; coed, men-only, women-only, special housing for students with disabilities. Campus housing is university owned. Freshman campus housing is guaranteed.
Activities and organizations: drama/theater group, student-run newspaper, radio and television station, choral group, marching band.
Athletics Member NCAA. All Division I except football (Division I-AA). ***Intercollegiate sports:*** baseball M, basketball M/W, crew M/W, cross-country running M/W, fencing M/W, field hockey W, golf M/W, ice hockey M/W, lacrosse M/W, soccer M/W, softball W, squash M/W, swimming and diving M/W, tennis M/W, track and field M/W, volleyball M/W, water polo M/W, wrestling M. ***Intramural sports:*** badminton M(c)/W(c), baseball M(c), basketball M(c)/W(c), cheerleading M(c)/W(c), cross-country running M(c)/W(c), equestrian sports M(c)/W(c), fencing M(c)/W(c), field hockey W(c), ice hockey M(c)/W(c), lacrosse M(c)/W(c), rugby M(c)/W(c), sailing M(c)/W(c), skiing (downhill) M(c)/W(c), soccer M(c)/W(c), softball W(c), squash M(c)/W(c), swimming and diving M(c)/W(c), table tennis M(c)/W(c), tennis M(c)/W(c), ultimate Frisbee M(c)/W(c), volleyball M(c)/W(c).
Campus security: 24-hour emergency response devices and patrols, student patrols, late-night transport/escort service, controlled dormitory access.
Student services: health clinic, personal/psychological counseling, women's center, legal services.

COSTS & FINANCIAL AID
Costs (2017–18) ***Comprehensive fee:*** $60,090 includes full-time tuition ($45,320) and room and board ($14,770). ***College room only:*** $8335. Room and board charges vary according to board plan. ***Payment plans:*** installment, deferred payment. ***Waivers:*** employees or children of employees.
Financial Aid Of all full-time matriculated undergraduates who enrolled in 2016, 3,433 applied for aid, 3,126 were judged to have need, 3,126 had their need fully met. ***Average percent of need met:*** 100. ***Average financial aid package:*** $49,502. ***Average need-based gift aid:*** $47,497. ***Average indebtedness upon graduation:*** $8908.

APPLYING
Standardized Tests *Required:* SAT or ACT (for admission). *Recommended:* SAT Subject Tests (for admission).
Options: electronic application, early action, deferred entrance.
Application fee: $65.
Required: essay or personal statement, high school transcript, 3 letters of recommendation. ***Recommended:*** interview.
Application deadlines: 1/1 (freshmen), 11/1 (early action).
Notification: 4/1 (freshmen), 12/15 (early action).

CONTACT
Ms. Janet Rapelye, Dean of Admission, Princeton University, PO Box 430, Princeton, NJ 08542-0430. *Phone:* 609-258-3060. *Fax:* 609-258-6743. *E-mail:* uaoffice@princeton.edu.

Rabbi Jacob Joseph School
Edison, New Jersey

CONTACT
Rabbi Jacob Joseph School, One Plainfield Ave, Edison, NJ 08817.

Rabbinical College of America
Morristown, New Jersey
http://www.rca.edu/

CONTACT
Shoshana Solomon, Registrar, Rabbinical College of America, 226 Sussex Avenue, PO Box 1996, Morristown, NJ 07962-1996. *Phone:* 973-267-9404. *E-mail:* rca079@aol.com.

Ramapo College of New Jersey
Mahwah, New Jersey
http://www.ramapo.edu/

- **State-supported** comprehensive, founded 1969, part of New Jersey State College System
- **Suburban** 300-acre campus with easy access to New York City
- **Coed** 5,661 undergraduate students, 88% full-time, 55% women, 45% men
- **Moderately difficult** entrance level, 53% of applicants were admitted

UNDERGRAD STUDENTS
4,992 full-time, 669 part-time. 5% are from out of state; 5% Black or African American, non-Hispanic/Latino; 13% Hispanic/Latino; 7% Asian, non-Hispanic/Latino; 0.3% Native Hawaiian or other Pacific Islander,

non-Hispanic/Latino; 0.4% American Indian or Alaska Native, non-Hispanic/Latino; 1% Two or more races, non-Hispanic/Latino; 7% Race/ethnicity unknown; 1% international; 10% transferred in; 49% live on campus.

Freshmen:
Admission: 7,106 applied, 3,783 admitted, 918 enrolled. ***Average high school GPA:*** 3.26. ***Test scores:*** SAT critical reading scores over 500: 73%; SAT math scores over 500: 79%; SAT writing scores over 500: 70%; SAT critical reading scores over 600: 22%; SAT math scores over 600: 29%; SAT writing scores over 600: 23%; SAT critical reading scores over 700: 3%; SAT math scores over 700: 4%; SAT writing scores over 700: 3%.

Retention: 86% of full-time freshmen returned.

FACULTY
Total: 495, 43% full-time, 39% with terminal degrees.

Student/faculty ratio: 17:1.

ACADEMICS
Calendar: semesters. *Degrees:* certificates, bachelor's, master's, post-master's, and postbachelor's certificates.

Special study options: academic remediation for entering students, accelerated degree program, adult/continuing education programs, advanced placement credit, cooperative education, distance learning, double majors, external degree program, freshman honors college, honors programs, independent study, internships, off-campus study, part-time degree program, services for LD students, student-designed majors, study abroad, summer session for credit. ***ROTC:*** Army (c), Air Force (c).

Unusual degree programs: 3-2 biology, chemistry with Rutgers, The State University of New Jersey; dentistry with New York University; optometry with SUNY State College of Optometry.

Computers: Students can access the following: campus intranet, computer help desk, free student e-mail accounts, online (class) grades, online (class) registration, online (class) schedules. Campuswide network is available. 100% of college-owned or -operated housing units are wired for high-speed Internet access. Wireless service is available via classrooms, computer centers, computer labs, learning centers, libraries, student centers.

Library: George T. Potter Library.

STUDENT LIFE
Housing options: coed. Campus housing is university owned. Freshman campus housing is guaranteed.

Activities and organizations: drama/theater group, student-run newspaper, radio and television station, choral group, NORML, 1 Step, Biology & Biochemistry Club, Campus Crusade for Christ, Culture Club, national fraternities, national sororities.

Athletics Member NCAA. All Division III. ***Intercollegiate sports:*** baseball M, basketball M/W, cross-country running M/W, field hockey W, lacrosse W, soccer M/W, softball W, swimming and diving M/W, tennis M/W, track and field M/W, volleyball M/W. ***Intramural sports:*** basketball M/W, bowling M/W, football M/W, rock climbing M/W, soccer M/W, softball M/W, table tennis M/W, ultimate Frisbee M/W, volleyball M/W.

Campus security: 24-hour emergency response devices and patrols, late-night transport/escort service, controlled dormitory access, surveillance cameras, patrols by trained security personnel.

Student services: health clinic, personal/psychological counseling, women's center.

COSTS & FINANCIAL AID
Costs (2016–17) ***Tuition:*** state resident $8998 full-time, $281 per credit hour part-time; nonresident $17,998 full-time, $562 per credit hour part-time. Full-time tuition and fees vary according to reciprocity agreements. Part-time tuition and fees vary according to reciprocity agreements. ***Required fees:*** $4872 full-time, $152 per credit hour part-time. ***Room and board:*** $12,030; room only: $8340. Room and board charges vary according to board plan and housing facility. ***Payment plan:*** installment. ***Waivers:*** senior citizens and employees or children of employees.

Financial Aid Of all full-time matriculated undergraduates who enrolled in 2015, 3,912 applied for aid, 2,766 were judged to have need, 370 had their need fully met. 171 Federal Work-Study jobs (averaging $2347). 926 state and other part-time jobs (averaging $1845). In 2015, 425 non-need-based awards were made. ***Average percent of need met:*** 65. ***Average financial aid package:*** $17,215. ***Average need-based loan:*** $4295. ***Average need-based gift aid:*** $9545. ***Average non-need-based aid:*** $11,002. ***Average indebtedness upon graduation:*** $33,300.

APPLYING
Standardized Tests *Required:* SAT or ACT (for admission).

Options: electronic application, early admission, early decision, deferred entrance.

Application fee: $60.

Required: essay or personal statement, high school transcript. ***Recommended:*** minimum 3.0 GPA.

CONTACT
Michael DiBartolomeo, Associate Director for Freshmen Admissions, Ramapo College of New Jersey, Office of Admissions, 505 Ramapo Valley Road, Mahwah, NJ 07430-1680. *Phone:* 201-684-7300. *Toll-free phone:* 800-9RAMAPO. *Fax:* 201-684-7964. *E-mail:* admissions@ramapo.edu.

Rider University
Lawrenceville, New Jersey
http://www.rider.edu/

- **Independent** comprehensive, founded 1865
- **Suburban** 280-acre campus with easy access to New York City, Philadelphia
- **Endowment** $58.3 million
- **Coed**
- **Moderately difficult** entrance level

FACULTY
Student/faculty ratio: 12:1.

ACADEMICS
Calendar: semesters. *Degrees:* certificates, associate, bachelor's, master's, post-master's, and postbachelor's certificates.

Library: Franklin F. Moore Library plus 1 other.

STUDENT LIFE
Housing options: coed, women-only, special housing for students with disabilities. Campus housing is university owned. Freshman applicants given priority for college housing.

Activities and organizations: drama/theater group, student-run newspaper, radio and television station, choral group, Student Government Association, Greek Council, Association of Commuter Students, Black Student Union, Residence Hall Association, national fraternities, national sororities.

Athletics Member NCAA. All Division I.

Campus security: 24-hour emergency response devices and patrols, student patrols, late-night transport/escort service, controlled dormitory access.

Student services: health clinic, personal/psychological counseling.

COSTS & FINANCIAL AID
Costs (2016–17) ***Comprehensive fee:*** $54,050 includes full-time tuition ($39,080), mandatory fees ($740), and room and board ($14,230). Full-time tuition and fees vary according to program. Part-time tuition: $1140 per credit hour. ***Required fees:*** $17 per credit part-time, $50 per course part-time. ***College room only:*** $9270. Room and board charges vary according to board plan and housing facility.

Financial Aid Of all full-time matriculated undergraduates who enrolled in 2016, 2,976 applied for aid, 2,709 were judged to have need, 412 had their need fully met. In 2016, 701 non-need-based awards were made. ***Average percent of need met:*** 73. ***Average financial aid package:*** $28,684. ***Average need-based loan:*** $3785. ***Average need-based gift aid:*** $24,578. ***Average non-need-based aid:*** $16,998. ***Average indebtedness upon graduation:*** $36,032.

APPLYING
Standardized Tests *Required:* SAT or ACT (for admission).

Options: electronic application, early admission, early action, deferred entrance.

Application fee: $50.

Required: essay or personal statement, high school transcript, 2 letters of recommendation. ***Required for some:*** interview.

CONTACT

Mr. William Larrousse, Director of Admissions, Rider University, 2083 Lawrenceville Road, Lawrenceville, NJ 08648. *Phone:* 609-896-5177. *Toll-free phone:* 800-257-9026. *Fax:* 609-895-6645. *E-mail:* wlarrousse@rider.edu.

See below for display ad and page 1476 for the College Close-Up.

Rowan University

Glassboro, New Jersey

http://www.rowan.edu/

- **State-supported** comprehensive, founded 1923, part of New Jersey State College System
- **Suburban** 921-acre campus with easy access to Philadelphia
- **Endowment** $173.2 million
- **Coed** 14,363 undergraduate students, 89% full-time, 46% women, 54% men
- **Moderately difficult** entrance level, 58% of applicants were admitted

UNDERGRAD STUDENTS

12,740 full-time, 1,623 part-time. Students come from 28 states and territories; 22 other countries; 5% are from out of state; 10% Black or African American, non-Hispanic/Latino; 9% Hispanic/Latino; 5% Asian, non-Hispanic/Latino; 0.1% Native Hawaiian or other Pacific Islander, non-Hispanic/Latino; 0.2% American Indian or Alaska Native, non-Hispanic/Latino; 3% Two or more races, non-Hispanic/Latino; 5% Race/ethnicity unknown; 0.9% international; 13% transferred in; 38% live on campus.

Freshmen:

Admission: 13,382 applied, 7,721 admitted, 2,199 enrolled. ***Average high school GPA:*** 3.46. ***Test scores:*** SAT critical reading scores over 500: 59%; SAT math scores over 500: 69%; SAT writing scores over 500: 55%; SAT critical reading scores over 600: 19%; SAT math scores over 600: 28%; SAT writing scores over 600: 13%; SAT critical reading scores over 700: 2%; SAT math scores over 700: 4%; SAT writing scores over 700: 1%.

Retention: 85% of full-time freshmen returned.

FACULTY

Total: 1,565, 29% full-time, 37% with terminal degrees.

Student/faculty ratio: 17:1.

ACADEMICS

Calendar: semesters. *Degrees:* certificates, bachelor's, master's, doctoral, post-master's, and postbachelor's certificates.

Special study options: academic remediation for entering students, accelerated degree program, adult/continuing education programs, advanced placement credit, cooperative education, distance learning, double majors, English as a second language, freshman honors college, honors programs, independent study, internships, off-campus study, part-time degree program, services for LD students, study abroad, summer session for credit. ***ROTC:*** Army (c).

Unusual degree programs: 3-2 mathematics and computer science.

Computers: 900 computers/terminals and 2,500 ports are available on campus for general student use. Students can access the following: campus intranet, computer help desk, free student e-mail accounts, online (class) grades, online (class) registration, online (class) schedules. Campuswide network is available. 100% of college-owned or -operated housing units are wired for high-speed Internet access. Wireless service is available via entire campus.

Library: Keith and Shirley Campbell Library plus 4 others. *Books:* 328,891 (physical), 249,282 (digital/electronic); *Databases:* 739. Students can reserve study rooms.

STUDENT LIFE

Housing options: on-campus residence required through sophomore year; coed, special housing for students with disabilities. Campus housing is university owned and leased by the school. Freshman campus housing is guaranteed.

Activities and organizations: drama/theater group, student-run newspaper, radio and television station, choral group, Kappa Delta Pi, Public Relations Student Society of America, Student University Programmes, Rowan Television Network, Elementary Education Club, national fraternities, national sororities.

Athletics Member NCAA. All Division III. ***Intercollegiate sports:*** baseball M, basketball M/W, cross-country running M/W, field hockey W,

football M, ice hockey M/W, lacrosse M/W, rugby M/W, soccer M/W, softball W, swimming and diving M/W, track and field M/W, volleyball W. ***Intramural sports:*** basketball M/W, cheerleading M/W(c), field hockey W(c), football M/W, golf M/W, racquetball M/W, rock climbing M(c)/W, skiing (downhill) M(c)/W(c), soccer M/W, softball M/W, table tennis M/W, tennis M(c)/W(c), ultimate Frisbee M(c)/W(c), volleyball M/W, water polo M/W, weight lifting M/W, wrestling M(c).

Campus security: 24-hour emergency response devices and patrols, student patrols, late-night transport/escort service, controlled dormitory access, EMS service including 2 ambulances, security and campus police trained as police officers in NJ.

Student services: health clinic, personal/psychological counseling, legal services.

COSTS & FINANCIAL AID

Costs (2017–18) ***Tuition:*** state resident $9434 full-time, $362 per credit hour part-time; nonresident $17,704 full-time, $682 per credit hour part-time. Full-time tuition and fees vary according to course load, degree level, location, and program. Part-time tuition and fees vary according to course load, degree level, location, and program. ***Required fees:*** $3674 full-time, $157 per credit hour part-time. ***Room and board:*** $11,688; room only: $7608. Room and board charges vary according to board plan and housing facility. ***Payment plans:*** installment, deferred payment. ***Waivers:*** employees or children of employees.

Financial Aid Of all full-time matriculated undergraduates who enrolled in 2014, 8,499 applied for aid, 6,668 were judged to have need, 794 had their need fully met. 412 Federal Work-Study jobs (averaging $1212). In 2014, 988 non-need-based awards were made. ***Average percent of need met:*** 68. ***Average financial aid package:*** $8759. ***Average need-based loan:*** $4246. ***Average need-based gift aid:*** $8318. ***Average non-need-based aid:*** $8159. ***Average indebtedness upon graduation:*** $31,652.

APPLYING

Standardized Tests *Required:* SAT or ACT (for admission).

Options: electronic application, early admission, deferred entrance.

Application fee: $65.

Required: high school transcript, minimum 2.0 GPA. ***Required for some:*** interview.

Application deadlines: 3/1 (freshmen), 3/1 (transfers).

Notification: continuous (freshmen), continuous (transfers).

CONTACT

Mr. Albert Betts, Director of Admissions, Rowan University, 201 Mullica Hill Road, Glassboro, NJ 08028. *Phone:* 856-256-4200. *Toll-free phone:* 800-447-1165 (in-state); 800-447-1165N (out-of-state). *Fax:* 856-256-4430. *E-mail:* admissions@rowan.edu.

Rutgers University–Camden

Camden, New Jersey

http://www.camden.rutgers.edu/

- **State-supported** university, founded 1927
- **Urban** 32-acre campus with easy access to Philadelphia
- **Coed** 5,021 undergraduate students, 81% full-time, 59% women, 41% men
- **Moderately difficult** entrance level, 57% of applicants were admitted

UNDERGRAD STUDENTS

4,056 full-time, 965 part-time. Students come from 19 states and territories; 18 other countries; 2% are from out of state; 17% Black or African American, non-Hispanic/Latino; 14% Hispanic/Latino; 9% Asian, non-Hispanic/Latino; 0.2% Native Hawaiian or other Pacific Islander, non-Hispanic/Latino; 0.1% American Indian or Alaska Native, non-Hispanic/Latino; 4% Two or more races, non-Hispanic/Latino; 2% Race/ethnicity unknown; 1% international; 16% transferred in; 13% live on campus.

Freshmen:

Admission: 8,725 applied, 5,016 admitted, 675 enrolled. ***Test scores:*** SAT critical reading scores over 500: 48%; SAT math scores over 500: 56%; SAT writing scores over 500: 44%; SAT critical reading scores over 600: 11%; SAT math scores over 600: 17%; SAT writing scores over 600: 8%; SAT critical reading scores over 700: 1%; SAT math scores over 700: 3%; SAT writing scores over 700: 1%.

Retention: 89% of full-time freshmen returned.

FACULTY

Total: 685, 46% full-time, 99% with terminal degrees.

Student/faculty ratio: 10:1.

ACADEMICS

Calendar: semesters. *Degrees:* bachelor's, master's, and doctoral.

Special study options: academic remediation for entering students, accelerated degree program, advanced placement credit, cooperative education, distance learning, double majors, English as a second language, freshman honors college, honors programs, independent study, internships, part-time degree program, services for LD students, student-designed majors, study abroad, summer session for credit. ***ROTC:*** Army (c), Air Force (c).

Unusual degree programs: 3-2 business administration; engineering; nursing; medical technology, African-American studies, general science, childhood studies, English, history, liberal studies, psychology, biology, chemistry, mathematics.

Computers: 184 computers/terminals are available on campus for general student use. Students can access the following: campus intranet, computer help desk, free student e-mail accounts, online (class) grades, online (class) registration, online (class) schedules. Campuswide network is available. 100% of college-owned or -operated housing units are wired for high-speed Internet access. Wireless service is available via classrooms, computer centers, computer labs, dorm rooms, learning centers, libraries, student centers.

Library: Paul Robeson Library plus 2 others. Students can reserve study rooms.

STUDENT LIFE

Housing options: coed, special housing for students with disabilities. Campus housing is university owned.

Activities and organizations: drama/theater group, student-run radio station.

Athletics Member NCAA. All Division III. ***Intercollegiate sports:*** baseball M, basketball M/W, crew M/W, cross-country running W, golf M, lacrosse W, soccer M/W, softball W, track and field M/W, volleyball W. ***Intramural sports:*** baseball M, basketball M/W, cheerleading W, crew M, golf M, ice hockey M, lacrosse M, racquetball M, soccer M, tennis M, track and field M, ultimate Frisbee M/W, volleyball M/W.

Campus security: 24-hour emergency response devices and patrols, student patrols, late-night transport/escort service, controlled dormitory access.

COSTS & FINANCIAL AID

Costs (2016–17) ***Tuition:*** state resident $11,408 full-time, $367 per credit hour part-time; nonresident $26,551 full-time, $862 per credit hour part-time. Part-time tuition and fees vary according to course load. ***Required fees:*** $2830 full-time. ***Room and board:*** $11,908; room only: $8298. Room and board charges vary according to board plan and housing facility. ***Payment plan:*** installment. ***Waivers:*** employees or children of employees.

Financial Aid Of all full-time matriculated undergraduates who enrolled in 2015, 3,748 applied for aid, 3,467 were judged to have need, 43 had their need fully met. 198 Federal Work-Study jobs (averaging $2195). 584 state and other part-time jobs (averaging $2810). In 2015, 49 non-need-based awards were made. ***Average percent of need met:*** 47. ***Average financial aid package:*** $11,704. ***Average need-based loan:*** $4463. ***Average need-based gift aid:*** $9207. ***Average non-need-based aid:*** $3956. ***Average indebtedness upon graduation:*** $29,624.

APPLYING

Standardized Tests *Required:* SAT or ACT (for admission).

Options: electronic application.

Application fee: $70.

Required: high school transcript.

Application deadlines: 12/1 (freshmen), 1/15 (transfers).

Notification: 2/28 (freshmen), 5/15 (transfers).

CONTACT

Rutgers University–Camden, 406 Penn Street, Camden, NJ 08102-1401. *Phone:* 856-225-6104.

Rutgers University–Newark

Newark, New Jersey

http://www.newark.rutgers.edu/

- **State-supported** university, founded 1892
- **Urban** 106-acre campus
- **Coed** 8,170 undergraduate students, 82% full-time, 54% women, 46% men
- **Moderately difficult** entrance level, 62% of applicants were admitted

UNDERGRAD STUDENTS

6,680 full-time, 1,490 part-time. Students come from 27 states and territories; 40 other countries; 2% are from out of state; 19% Black or African American, non-Hispanic/Latino; 28% Hispanic/Latino; 20% Asian, non-Hispanic/Latino; 0.3% Native Hawaiian or other Pacific Islander, non-Hispanic/Latino; 3% Two or more races, non-Hispanic/Latino; 2% Race/ethnicity unknown; 5% international; 13% transferred in; 21% live on campus.

Freshmen:

Admission: 4,693 applied, 2,921 admitted, 1,344 enrolled. ***Test scores:*** SAT critical reading scores over 500: 42%; SAT math scores over 500: 63%; SAT writing scores over 500: 47%; SAT critical reading scores over 600: 8%; SAT math scores over 600: 18%; SAT writing scores over 600: 10%; SAT critical reading scores over 700: 1%; SAT math scores over 700: 2%; SAT writing scores over 700: 1%.

Retention: 84% of full-time freshmen returned.

FACULTY

Total: 982, 55% full-time, 99% with terminal degrees.

Student/faculty ratio: 10:1.

ACADEMICS

Calendar: semesters. *Degrees:* associate, bachelor's, master's, and doctoral.

Special study options: academic remediation for entering students, accelerated degree program, adult/continuing education programs, advanced placement credit, cooperative education, distance learning, double majors, English as a second language, freshman honors college, honors programs, independent study, internships, off-campus study, part-time degree program, services for LD students, student-designed majors, study abroad, summer session for credit. ***ROTC:*** Army (b), Navy (b), Air Force (b).

Unusual degree programs: 3-2 business administration; engineering; nursing.

Computers: 708 computers/terminals are available on campus for general student use. Students can access the following: computer help desk, free student e-mail accounts, online (class) grades, online (class) schedules. Campuswide network is available. Wireless service is available via classrooms, computer centers, computer labs, dorm rooms, learning centers, libraries, student centers.

Library: John Cotton Dana Library plus 3 others. *Books:* 300,000 (physical), 30,000 (digital/electronic). Weekly public service hours: 93; students can reserve study rooms.

STUDENT LIFE

Housing options: coed. Campus housing is university owned.

Activities and organizations: drama/theater group, student-run newspaper, radio station, choral group.

Athletics Member NCAA. All Division III except volleyball (Division I). ***Intercollegiate sports:*** baseball M, basketball M/W, cross-country running M/W, soccer M/W, softball W, tennis M/W, track and field M, volleyball M/W. ***Intramural sports:*** baseball M/W, basketball M/W, cross-country running M/W, racquetball M/W, rock climbing M/W, soccer M/W, swimming and diving M/W, tennis M/W, volleyball M/W, weight lifting M/W.

Campus security: 24-hour emergency response devices and patrols, student patrols, late-night transport/escort service, controlled dormitory access.

COSTS & FINANCIAL AID

Costs (2016–17) ***Tuition:*** state resident $11,408 full-time, $367 per credit hour part-time; nonresident $27,059 full-time, $878 per credit hour part-time. Part-time tuition and fees vary according to course load. ***Required fees:*** $2421 full-time. ***Room and board:*** $13,459; room only: $8095. Room and board charges vary according to board plan and housing facility. ***Payment plan:*** installment. ***Waivers:*** employees or children of employees.

Financial Aid Of all full-time matriculated undergraduates who enrolled in 2015, 5,400 applied for aid, 5,132 were judged to have need, 52 had their need fully met. 610 Federal Work-Study jobs (averaging $1917). 868 state and other part-time jobs (averaging $2228). In 2015, 38 non-need-based awards were made. ***Average percent of need met:*** 50. ***Average financial aid package:*** $13,082. ***Average need-based loan:*** $4518. ***Average need-based gift aid:*** $10,557. ***Average non-need-based aid:*** $9427. ***Average indebtedness upon graduation:*** $27,881.

APPLYING

Standardized Tests *Required:* SAT or ACT (for admission).

Options: electronic application.

Application fee: $65.

Required: high school transcript.

Application deadlines: 12/1 (freshmen), 1/15 (transfers).

Notification: 2/28 (freshmen), 5/15 (transfers).

CONTACT

Rutgers University–Newark, 249 University Avenue, Newark, NJ 07102. *Phone:* 973-353-5205 Ext. 0012. *Fax:* 973-353-1440. *E-mail:* newarkadmissions@ugadm.rutgers.edu.

Rutgers University–New Brunswick

Piscataway, New Jersey

http://newbrunswick.rutgers.edu/

- **State-supported** university, founded 1766
- **Urban** 2688-acre campus with easy access to New York City
- **Coed** 36,168 undergraduate students, 94% full-time, 50% women, 50% men
- **Moderately difficult** entrance level, 57% of applicants were admitted

UNDERGRAD STUDENTS

34,020 full-time, 2,148 part-time. Students come from 48 states and territories; 72 other countries; 6% are from out of state; 8% Black or African American, non-Hispanic/Latino; 13% Hispanic/Latino; 26% Asian, non-Hispanic/Latino; 0.3% Native Hawaiian or other Pacific Islander, non-Hispanic/Latino; 0.1% American Indian or Alaska Native, non-Hispanic/Latino; 3% Two or more races, non-Hispanic/Latino; 2% Race/ethnicity unknown; 8% international; 8% transferred in; 43% live on campus.

Freshmen:

Admission: 36,677 applied, 20,884 admitted, 6,466 enrolled. ***Test scores:*** SAT critical reading scores over 500: 85%; SAT math scores over 500: 94%; SAT writing scores over 500: 92%; SAT critical reading scores over 600: 45%; SAT math scores over 600: 69%; SAT writing scores over 600: 52%; SAT critical reading scores over 700: 12%; SAT math scores over 700: 27%; SAT writing scores over 700: 16%.

Retention: 93% of full-time freshmen returned.

FACULTY

Total: 3,700, 52% full-time, 99% with terminal degrees.

Student/faculty ratio: 14:1.

ACADEMICS

Calendar: semesters. *Degrees:* associate, bachelor's, master's, doctoral, post-master's, and postbachelor's certificates.

Special study options: academic remediation for entering students, accelerated degree program, advanced placement credit, cooperative education, distance learning, double majors, English as a second language, honors programs, independent study, internships, part-time degree program, student-designed majors, study abroad. ***ROTC:*** Army (b), Navy (b), Air Force (b).

Unusual degree programs: 3-2 business administration; engineering; nursing; social work; medicine with Rutgers University, New Jersey Medical School and Robert Wood Johnson Medical School.

Computers: 1,450 computers/terminals are available on campus for general student use. Students can access the following: campus intranet, computer help desk, free student e-mail accounts, online (class) grades,

online (class) registration, online (class) schedules. Campuswide network is available. Wireless service is available via entire campus.
Library: Archibald S. Alexander Library plus 11 others.

STUDENT LIFE
Housing options: coed, men-only, women-only, cooperative. Campus housing is university owned.
Activities and organizations: drama/theater group, student-run newspaper, radio and television station, choral group, marching band, national fraternities, national sororities.
Athletics Member NCAA. All Division I except football (Division I-A). ***Intercollegiate sports:*** baseball M, basketball M/W, crew M/W, cross-country running M/W, fencing M/W, golf M/W, gymnastics W, lacrosse M/W, soccer M/W, softball W, swimming and diving W, tennis M/W, track and field M/W, volleyball W, wrestling M. ***Intramural sports:*** badminton M/W, baseball M(c), basketball M/W, bowling M/W, cross-country running M/W, equestrian sports M(c)/W(c), field hockey W(c), football M, golf M/W, ice hockey M(c), lacrosse M/W, racquetball M/W, rugby M(c)/W(c), sailing M(c)/W(c), skiing (cross-country) M(c)/W(c), skiing (downhill) M(c)/W(c), soccer M/W, softball M/W, squash M(c)/W(c), swimming and diving M/W, table tennis M(c)/W(c), tennis M/W, track and field M/W, volleyball M/W, water polo M/W, wrestling M.
Campus security: 24-hour emergency response devices and patrols, student patrols, late-night transport/escort service, controlled dormitory access.
Student services: health clinic, personal/psychological counseling, women's center.

COSTS & FINANCIAL AID
Costs (2016–17) ***Tuition:*** state resident $11,408 full-time, $367 per credit hour part-time; nonresident $27,059 full-time, $878 per credit hour part-time. Part-time tuition and fees vary according to course load. ***Required fees:*** $2964 full-time. ***Room and board:*** $12,260; room only: $7490. Room and board charges vary according to board plan and housing facility. ***Payment plan:*** installment. ***Waivers:*** employees or children of employees.
Financial Aid Of all full-time matriculated undergraduates who enrolled in 2015, 21,739 applied for aid, 18,728 were judged to have need, 673 had their need fully met. 2,495 Federal Work-Study jobs (averaging $2111). 7,712 state and other part-time jobs (averaging $1998). In 2015, 731 non-need-based awards were made. ***Average percent of need met:*** 48. ***Average financial aid package:*** $13,444. ***Average need-based loan:*** $4581. ***Average need-based gift aid:*** $10,883. ***Average non-need-based aid:*** $9759. ***Average indebtedness upon graduation:*** $25,974.

APPLYING
Standardized Tests *Required:* SAT or ACT (for admission).
Options: electronic application.
Application fee: $65.
Required: high school transcript. ***Required for some:*** interview. ***Recommended:*** essay or personal statement.
Application deadlines: 12/1 (freshmen), 1/15 (transfers).
Notification: 2/28 (freshmen), 5/15 (transfers).

CONTACT
Rutgers University–New Brunswick, 65 Davidson Road, Room 202, Piscataway, NJ 08854-8097. *Phone:* 848-445-4636.

Saint Peter's University
Jersey City, New Jersey
http://www.saintpeters.edu/

- **Independent Roman Catholic (Jesuit)** comprehensive, founded 1872
- **Urban** 15-acre campus with easy access to New York City
- **Endowment** $34.1 million
- **Coed** 2,525 undergraduate students, 87% full-time, 62% women, 38% men
- **Moderately difficult** entrance level, 67% of applicants were admitted

UNDERGRAD STUDENTS
2,208 full-time, 317 part-time. Students come from 27 states and territories; 66 other countries; 11% are from out of state; 25% Black or African American, non-Hispanic/Latino; 37% Hispanic/Latino; 7% Asian, non-Hispanic/Latino; 0.6% Native Hawaiian or other Pacific Islander, non-Hispanic/Latino; 0.5% American Indian or Alaska Native, non-Hispanic/Latino; 2% Two or more races, non-Hispanic/Latino; 8% Race/ethnicity unknown; 2% international; 6% transferred in; 31% live on campus.

Freshmen:
Admission: 4,528 applied, 3,048 admitted, 568 enrolled. ***Average high school GPA:*** 3.15. ***Test scores:*** SAT critical reading scores over 500: 27%; SAT math scores over 500: 33%; SAT writing scores over 500: 24%; ACT scores over 18: 58%; SAT critical reading scores over 600: 5%; SAT math scores over 600: 7%; SAT writing scores over 600: 5%; ACT scores over 24: 9%; SAT math scores over 700: 1%; SAT writing scores over 700: 1%; ACT scores over 30: 2%.
Retention: 82% of full-time freshmen returned.

FACULTY
Total: 314, 36% full-time.
Student/faculty ratio: 13:1.

ACADEMICS
Calendar: semesters. *Degrees:* certificates, associate, bachelor's, master's, doctoral, post-master's, and postbachelor's certificates.
Special study options: academic remediation for entering students, accelerated degree program, adult/continuing education programs, advanced placement credit, cooperative education, distance learning, double majors, English as a second language, honors programs, independent study, internships, off-campus study, part-time degree program, services for LD students, student-designed majors, study abroad, summer session for credit. ***ROTC:*** Army (c), Air Force (c).
Unusual degree programs: 3-2 pharmacy, clinical and laboratory sciences with with Rutgers, The State University of New Jersey; physician's assistant, physical therapy with Seton Hall University.
Computers: 415 computers/terminals and 415 ports are available on campus for general student use. Students can access the following: computer help desk, free student e-mail accounts, online (class) grades, online (class) registration, online (class) schedules. Campuswide network is available. Wireless service is available via entire campus.
Library: Theresa and Edward O'Toole Library plus 2 others.

STUDENT LIFE
Housing options: coed, special housing for students with disabilities. Campus housing is university owned. Freshman campus housing is guaranteed.
Activities and organizations: drama/theater group, student-run newspaper, radio station, choral group, Caribbean Culture Club, Black Action Committee, Asian American Student Union, Indian and Pakistani Culture Club, Latin American Student Organization.
Athletics Member NCAA. All Division I. ***Intercollegiate sports:*** baseball M(s), basketball M(s)/W(s), bowling M/W, cross-country running M(s)/W(s), golf M(s), soccer M(s)/W(s), softball W(s), swimming and diving M(s)/W(s), tennis M(s)/W(s), track and field M(s)/W(s), volleyball W(s). ***Intramural sports:*** badminton M/W, basketball M/W, bowling M/W, football M/W, golf M/W, racquetball M/W, soccer M/W, softball M/W, squash M/W, swimming and diving M/W, table tennis M/W, tennis M/W, track and field M/W, volleyball M/W, water polo M/W, weight lifting M/W.
Campus security: 24-hour emergency response devices and patrols, late-night transport/escort service, controlled dormitory access, ID checks at residence halls and library.
Student services: health clinic, personal/psychological counseling.

FINANCIAL AID
Financial Aid Of all full-time matriculated undergraduates who enrolled in 2016, 2,357 applied for aid, 2,169 were judged to have need, 341 had their need fully met. In 2016, 188 non-need-based awards were made. ***Average percent of need met:*** 80. ***Average financial aid package:*** $31,003. ***Average need-based loan:*** $4200. ***Average need-based gift aid:*** $27,665. ***Average non-need-based aid:*** $18,761. ***Average indebtedness upon graduation:*** $29,724.

APPLYING
Standardized Tests *Required for some:* SAT or ACT (for admission).
Options: early action, deferred entrance.

Required: essay or personal statement, high school transcript, minimum 2.0 GPA, 2 letters of recommendation. ***Required for some:*** interview. ***Recommended:*** interview.

Application deadlines: 8/31 (freshmen), rolling (transfers), 12/1 (early action).

Notification: continuous (freshmen), 1/31 (early action).

CONTACT

Miss Kacey Tillotson, Director of Undergraduate Admissions, Saint Peter's University, Office of Admission - Lee House, Jersey City 07306. *Phone:* 201-761-7100. *Toll-free phone:* 888-SPC-9933. *E-mail:* ktillotson@saintpeters.edu.

★ Seton Hall University

South Orange, New Jersey

http://www.shu.edu/

CONTACT

Mary Clare Cullum, Director of Undergraduate Admissions, Seton Hall University, Enrollment Management Office, 400 South Orange Avenue, South Orange, NJ 07079-2697. *Phone:* 973-275-2589. *Toll-free phone:* 800-THE HALL. *Fax:* 973-275-2321. *E-mail:* maryclare.cullum@shu.edu.

See below for display ad and page 1504 for the College Close-Up.

Stevens Institute of Technology

Hoboken, New Jersey

http://www.stevens.edu/

- **Independent** university, founded 1870
- **Urban** 55-acre campus with easy access to New York City
- **Endowment** $166.0 million
- **Coed** 3,115 undergraduate students, 100% full-time, 30% women, 70% men
- **Very difficult** entrance level, 39% of applicants were admitted

UNDERGRAD STUDENTS

3,108 full-time, 7 part-time. Students come from 37 states and territories; 38 other countries; 38% are from out of state; 2% Black or African American, non-Hispanic/Latino; 10% Hispanic/Latino; 11% Asian, non-Hispanic/Latino; 0.1% American Indian or Alaska Native, non-Hispanic/Latino; 6% Race/ethnicity unknown; 5% international; 0.7% transferred in; 68% live on campus.

Freshmen:

Admission: 7,409 applied, 2,898 admitted, 737 enrolled. ***Average high school GPA:*** 3.8. ***Test scores:*** SAT critical reading scores over 500: 97%; SAT math scores over 500: 100%; SAT writing scores over 500: 97%; ACT scores over 18: 100%; SAT critical reading scores over 600: 74%; SAT math scores over 600: 95%; SAT writing scores over 600: 68%; ACT scores over 24: 99%; SAT critical reading scores over 700: 22%; SAT math scores over 700: 52%; SAT writing scores over 700: 19%; ACT scores over 30: 60%.

Retention: 95% of full-time freshmen returned.

FACULTY

Total: 421, 62% full-time, 74% with terminal degrees.

Student/faculty ratio: 10:1.

ACADEMICS

Calendar: semesters. *Degrees:* bachelor's, master's, doctoral, and postbachelor's certificates.

Special study options: accelerated degree program, advanced placement credit, cooperative education, distance learning, double majors, honors programs, independent study, internships, off-campus study, services for LD students, study abroad, summer session for credit. ***ROTC:*** Army (c), Air Force (c).

Computers: 500 computers/terminals and 3,800 ports are available on campus for general student use. Students can access the following: campus intranet, computer help desk, free student e-mail accounts, online (class) grades, online (class) registration, online (class) schedules, online account information, debit dining program, laundry status. Campuswide network is available. 100% of college-owned or -operated housing units are wired for high-speed Internet access. Wireless service is available via entire campus.

Library: Samuel C. Williams Library. Students can reserve study rooms.

STUDENT LIFE

Housing options: on-campus residence required for freshman year; coed, women-only. Campus housing is university owned and leased by the school. Freshman campus housing is guaranteed.

Activities and organizations: drama/theater group, student-run newspaper, radio and television station, choral group, Alpha Phi Omega Service Fraternity, Ethnic Student Council, Entertainment Committee, Student Government Association, Society of Women Engineers, national fraternities, national sororities.

Athletics Member NCAA. All Division III. ***Intercollegiate sports:*** baseball M, basketball M/W, cross-country running M/W, equestrian sports W, fencing M/W, field hockey W, golf M, lacrosse M/W, soccer M/W, softball W, swimming and diving M/W, tennis M/W, track and field M/W, volleyball M/W, wrestling M. ***Intramural sports:*** archery M/W, badminton M/W, baseball M, basketball M/W, bowling M(c)/W(c), cheerleading W(c), crew M, football M/W, ice hockey M(c), racquetball M/W, sailing M(c)/W(c), skiing (cross-country) M(c)/W(c), skiing (downhill) M(c)/W(c), soccer M/W, softball M, squash M/W, table tennis M/W, tennis M/W, ultimate Frisbee M/W, volleyball M/W, weight lifting M(c)/W(c).

Campus security: 24-hour emergency response devices and patrols, late-night transport/escort service, controlled dormitory access.

Student services: health clinic, personal/psychological counseling, women's center.

COSTS & FINANCIAL AID

Costs (2017–18) ***Comprehensive fee:*** $64,954 includes full-time tuition ($48,784), mandatory fees ($1770), and room and board ($14,400). Full-time tuition and fees vary according to course load. Part-time tuition: $1626 per credit. Part-time tuition and fees vary according to course load. ***Required fees:*** $885 per term part-time. ***College room only:*** $8000. Room and board charges vary according to board plan and housing facility. ***Payment plan:*** installment. ***Waivers:*** employees or children of employees.

Financial Aid Of all full-time matriculated undergraduates who enrolled in 2015, 1,653 applied for aid, 1,380 were judged to have need, 276 had their need fully met. In 2015, 734 non-need-based awards were made. ***Average percent of need met:*** 73. ***Average financial aid package:*** $29,633. ***Average need-based loan:*** $4971. ***Average need-based gift aid:*** $12,955. ***Average non-need-based aid:*** $17,730.

APPLYING

Standardized Tests *Required for some:* SAT or ACT (for admission), SAT and SAT Subject Tests or ACT (for admission).

Options: electronic application, early admission, early decision, deferred entrance.

Application fee: $65.

Required: essay or personal statement, high school transcript, 2 letters of recommendation. ***Required for some:*** digital portfolio required for music and technology or visual arts and technology. ***Recommended:*** interview.

Application deadlines: 2/1 (freshmen), 6/1 (transfers).

Early decision deadline: 11/15 (for plan 1), 1/15 (for plan 2).

Notification: 4/1 (freshmen), continuous until 6/30 (transfers), 12/15 (early decision plan 1), 2/15 (early decision plan 2).

CONTACT

Jackie Williams, Dean of Undergraduate Admissions, Stevens Institute of Technology, Castle Point on Hudson, Hoboken, NJ 07030. *Phone:* 201-216-5207. *Toll-free phone:* 800-458-5323.
E-mail: Jackie.Williams@stevens.edu.

★ Stockton University

Galloway, New Jersey

http://www.stockton.edu/

- **State-supported** comprehensive, founded 1969, part of New Jersey State College System
- **Suburban** 2000-acre campus with easy access to Philadelphia
- **Endowment** $19.7 million
- **Coed** 7,808 undergraduate students, 94% full-time, 59% women, 41% men
- **Very difficult** entrance level, 64% of applicants were admitted

UNDERGRAD STUDENTS

7,378 full-time, 430 part-time. Students come from 14 states and territories; 12 other countries; 1% are from out of state; 7% Black or African American, non-Hispanic/Latino; 11% Hispanic/Latino; 5% Asian, non-Hispanic/Latino; 0.2% Native Hawaiian or other Pacific Islander, non-Hispanic/Latino; 0.1% American Indian or Alaska Native, non-Hispanic/Latino; 3% Two or more races, non-Hispanic/Latino; 1% Race/ethnicity unknown; 0.3% international; 13% transferred in; 38% live on campus.

Freshmen:

Admission: 5,483 applied, 3,532 admitted, 1,159 enrolled. ***Test scores:*** SAT critical reading scores over 500: 65%; SAT math scores over 500: 75%; SAT writing scores over 500: 61%; ACT scores over 18: 90%; SAT critical reading scores over 600: 17%; SAT math scores over 600: 26%; SAT writing scores over 600: 16%; ACT scores over 24: 36%; SAT critical reading scores over 700: 2%; SAT math scores over 700: 2%; SAT writing scores over 700: 2%; ACT scores over 30: 3%.

Retention: 87% of full-time freshmen returned.

FACULTY

Total: 676, 47% full-time, 64% with terminal degrees.

Student/faculty ratio: 17:1.

ACADEMICS

Calendar: semesters. *Degrees:* bachelor's, master's, doctoral, and postbachelor's certificates.

Special study options: academic remediation for entering students, accelerated degree program, adult/continuing education programs, advanced placement credit, distance learning, double majors, English as a second language, honors programs, independent study, internships, off-campus study, part-time degree program, services for LD students, student-designed majors, study abroad, summer session for credit. ***ROTC:*** Army (c).

Unusual degree programs: 3-2 business administration; engineering with New Jersey Institute of Technology; Rutgers, The State University of New Jersey; Rowan University; criminal justice/public health with Rutgers University, medical technology with University of Delaware.

Computers: 1,198 computers/terminals and 2,400 ports are available on campus for general student use. Students can access the following: campus intranet, computer help desk, free student e-mail accounts, online (class) grades, online (class) registration, online (class) schedules. Campuswide network is available. 100% of college-owned or -operated housing units are wired for high-speed Internet access. Wireless service is available via entire campus.

Library: Richard E. Bjork Library. *Books:* 228,380 (physical), 135,000 (digital/electronic); *Serial titles:* 127 (physical), 73,336 (digital/electronic). Weekly public service hours: 95.

STUDENT LIFE

Housing options: coed, special housing for students with disabilities. Campus housing is university owned. Freshman campus housing is guaranteed.

Activities and organizations: drama/theater group, student-run newspaper, radio and television station, choral group, Multi-Cultural Connection, Stockton Entertainment Team, Los Latinos Unidos, Unified Black Student Society, Stockton Action Volunteers for the Environment, national fraternities, national sororities.

Athletics Member NCAA. All Division III. ***Intercollegiate sports:*** baseball M, basketball M/W, cheerleading M/W, crew W, cross-country running M/W, field hockey W, lacrosse M, soccer M/W, softball W, tennis W, track and field M/W, volleyball W. ***Intramural sports:*** basketball M/W, bowling M(c)/W(c), crew M(c), fencing M(c)/W(c), golf M(c)/W(c), ice hockey M(c), lacrosse W, soccer M/W, softball M/W, table tennis M/W, ultimate Frisbee M(c)/W(c), volleyball M(c)/W(c).

Campus security: 24-hour emergency response devices and patrols, late-night transport/escort service, controlled dormitory access, on-campus sworn/commissioned police force.

Student services: health clinic, personal/psychological counseling, women's center.

COSTS & FINANCIAL AID

Costs (2016–17) ***Tuition:*** state resident $8435 full-time, $324 per credit part-time; nonresident $15,209 full-time, $585 per credit part-time. Part-time tuition and fees vary according to course load. ***Required fees:*** $4642 full-time, $179 per credit part-time, $100 per term part-time. ***Room and board:*** $11,942; room only: $7912. Room and board charges vary according to board plan and housing facility. ***Payment plans:*** installment, deferred payment. ***Waivers:*** senior citizens and employees or children of employees.

Financial Aid Of all full-time matriculated undergraduates who enrolled in 2016, 6,391 applied for aid, 5,299 were judged to have need, 1,469 had their need fully met. 230 Federal Work-Study jobs (averaging $1908). 872 state and other part-time jobs (averaging $1375). In 2016, 534 non-need-based awards were made. ***Average percent of need met:*** 67. ***Average financial aid package:*** $16,344. ***Average need-based loan:*** $4575. ***Average need-based gift aid:*** $8710. ***Average non-need-based aid:*** $5319. ***Average indebtedness upon graduation:*** $33,201.

APPLYING

Standardized Tests *Required:* SAT or ACT (for admission).

Options: electronic application, early admission.

Application fee: $50.

Required: high school transcript, minimum 2.0 GPA. ***Recommended:*** essay or personal statement, minimum 3.0 GPA, 3 letters of recommendation.

Application deadlines: 5/1 (freshmen), 6/1 (transfers).

Notification: 5/15 (freshmen), continuous until 6/15 (transfers).

CONTACT

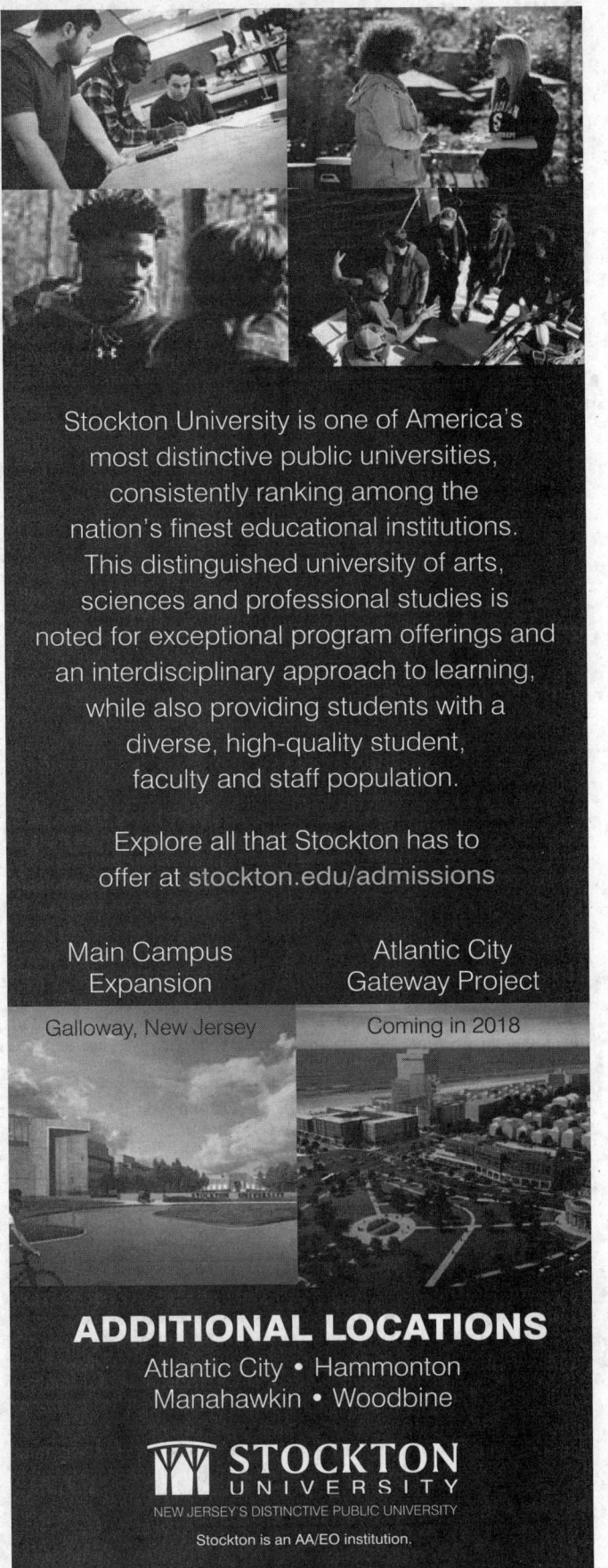

Stockton University, 101 Vera King Farris Drive, Galloway, NJ 08205-9441. *Phone:* 609-652-4261.

See this page for display ad and page 1528 for the College Close-Up.

Strayer University–Cherry Hill Campus

Cherry Hill, New Jersey

http://www.strayer.edu/new-jersey/cherry-hill/

CONTACT

Strayer University–Cherry Hill Campus, 2201 Route 38, Suite 100, Cherry Hill, NJ 08002.

Strayer University–Lawrenceville Campus

Lawrenceville, New Jersey

http://www.strayer.edu/new-jersey/lawrenceville/

CONTACT

Strayer University–Lawrenceville Campus, 3150 Brunswick Pike, Suite 100, Lawrenceville, NJ 08648.

Strayer University–Piscataway Campus

Piscataway, New Jersey

http://www.strayer.edu/new-jersey/piscataway/

CONTACT

Strayer University–Piscataway Campus, 242 Old New Brunswick Road, Suite 220, Piscataway, NJ 08854.

Strayer University–Willingboro Campus

Willingboro, New Jersey

http://www.strayer.edu/new-jersey/willingboro/

CONTACT

Strayer University–Willingboro Campus, 300 Willingboro Parkway, Willingboro Town Center, Suite 125, Willingboro, NJ 08046.

Talmudical Academy of New Jersey
Adelphia, New Jersey

CONTACT
Director of Admissions, Talmudical Academy of New Jersey, 868 Route 524, Adelphia, NJ 07710. *Phone:* 201-431-1600.

Thomas Edison State University
Trenton, New Jersey
http://www.tesu.edu/

- **State-supported** comprehensive, founded 1972
- **Urban** 2-acre campus with easy access to Philadelphia
- **Coed** 16,506 undergraduate students, 1% full-time, 44% women, 56% men
- **Noncompetitive** entrance level

UNDERGRAD STUDENTS
91 full-time, 16,415 part-time. 15% Black or African American, non-Hispanic/Latino; 9% Hispanic/Latino; 4% Asian, non-Hispanic/Latino; 0.5% Native Hawaiian or other Pacific Islander, non-Hispanic/Latino; 0.6% American Indian or Alaska Native, non-Hispanic/Latino; 2% Two or more races, non-Hispanic/Latino; 16% Race/ethnicity unknown; 1% international.

ACADEMICS
Calendar: continuous. *Degrees:* certificates, associate, bachelor's, master's, doctoral, and postbachelor's certificates (offers only distance learning degree programs).

Special study options: accelerated degree program, adult/continuing education programs, advanced placement credit, distance learning, double majors, external degree program, independent study, part-time degree program, services for LD students, student-designed majors, summer session for credit.

Computers: Students can access the following: online (class) grades, online (class) registration, online (class) schedules, undergraduate and Nursing students are able to schedule appointments online with their advisors. Campuswide network is available. Wireless service is available via entire campus.

STUDENT LIFE
Housing options: college housing not available.

Campus security: 24-hour emergency response devices and patrols, late-night transport/escort service, security officer from 7 am to 11 pm, local police patrol.

COSTS
Costs (2016–17) ***Tuition:*** state resident $6350 full-time, $385 per credit hour part-time; nonresident $9352 full-time, $499 per credit hour part-time. ***Payment plan:*** installment. ***Waivers:*** employees or children of employees.

APPLYING
Options: electronic application.

Application fee: $75.

Required: must be 21 or older and a high school graduate.

Application deadlines: rolling (freshmen), rolling (transfers).

CONTACT
Ms. Juliette Punchello, Director, Office of Admissions and Enrollment Services, Thomas Edison State University, 111 West State Street, Trenton, NJ 08608. *Phone:* 888-442-8372. *Toll-free phone:* 888-442-8372. *Fax:* 609-984-8447. *E-mail:* admissions@tesu.edu.

University of Phoenix–Jersey City Campus
Jersey City, New Jersey
http://www.phoenix.edu/

CONTACT
University of Phoenix–Jersey City Campus, 100 Town Square Place, Jersey City, NJ 07310. *Toll-free phone:* 866-766-0766.

William Paterson University of New Jersey
Wayne, New Jersey
http://www.wpunj.edu/

- **State-supported** comprehensive, founded 1855
- **Suburban** 370-acre campus with easy access to New York City
- **Coed** 9,103 undergraduate students, 82% full-time, 54% women, 45% men
- **Moderately difficult** entrance level, 76% of applicants were admitted

UNDERGRAD STUDENTS
7,494 full-time, 1,594 part-time. Students come from 30 states and territories; 44 other countries; 2% are from out of state; 16% Black or African American, non-Hispanic/Latino; 29% Hispanic/Latino; 7% Asian, non-Hispanic/Latino; 0.1% American Indian or Alaska Native, non-Hispanic/Latino; 3% Two or more races, non-Hispanic/Latino; 3% Race/ethnicity unknown; 0.9% international; 12% transferred in; 24% live on campus.

Freshmen:
Admission: 10,787 applied, 8,160 admitted, 1,376 enrolled. ***Average high school GPA:*** 3.15. ***Test scores:*** SAT critical reading scores over 500: 45%; SAT math scores over 500: 50%; SAT writing scores over 500: 34%; SAT critical reading scores over 600: 10%; SAT math scores over 600: 11%; SAT writing scores over 600: 5%; SAT critical reading scores over 700: 2%; SAT math scores over 700: 1%; SAT writing scores over 700: 1%.

Retention: 75% of full-time freshmen returned.

FACULTY
Total: 1,075, 38% full-time, 48% with terminal degrees.

Student/faculty ratio: 14:1.

ACADEMICS
Calendar: semesters. *Degrees:* bachelor's, master's, doctoral, post-master's, and postbachelor's certificates.

Special study options: academic remediation for entering students, accelerated degree program, adult/continuing education programs, advanced placement credit, distance learning, double majors, English as a second language, freshman honors college, honors programs, independent study, internships, off-campus study, part-time degree program, services for LD students, study abroad, summer session for credit.

Computers: 1,271 computers/terminals and 3,000 ports are available on campus for general student use. Students can access the following: campus intranet, computer help desk, free student e-mail accounts, online (class) grades, online (class) registration, online (class) schedules. Campuswide network is available. 100% of college-owned or -operated housing units are wired for high-speed Internet access. Wireless service is available via entire campus.

Library: David and Lorraine Cheng Library. *Books:* 369,216 (physical), 116,597 (digital/electronic); *Serial titles:* 3,772 (physical), 164,249 (digital/electronic); *Databases:* 126. Weekly public service hours: 102; students can reserve study rooms.

STUDENT LIFE
Housing options: coed, special housing for students with disabilities. Campus housing is university owned. Freshman campus housing is guaranteed.

Activities and organizations: drama/theater group, student-run newspaper, radio and television station, choral group, Student Activities Programming Board (SAPB), Students for Awareness Black Leadership and Equality (SABLE), Student Government Association (SGA), The B.A.B.Y. Dolls (Community Service org.), Pioneer Players (drama), national fraternities, national sororities.

Athletics Member NCAA. All Division III. ***Intercollegiate sports:*** baseball M, basketball M/W, field hockey W, football M, golf M, soccer M/W, softball W, swimming and diving M/W, tennis W, volleyball W. ***Intramural sports:*** basketball M/W, bowling M(c), cheerleading M(c)/W(c), equestrian sports M(c)/W(c), field hockey W, ice hockey M(c), racquetball M/W, rugby M(c), soccer W, softball M/W, volleyball M/W.

Campus security: 24-hour emergency response devices and patrols, student patrols, late-night transport/escort service, controlled dormitory access.

Student services: health clinic, personal/psychological counseling, women's center, legal services.

COSTS & FINANCIAL AID

Costs (2016–17) ***Tuition:*** state resident $9976 full-time, $319 per credit part-time; nonresident $17,868 full-time, $579 per credit part-time. Full-time tuition and fees vary according to course load and location. Part-time tuition and fees vary according to course load and location. ***Required fees:*** $2598 full-time, $84 per credit part-time. ***Room and board:*** $11,103; room only: $6973. Room and board charges vary according to board plan and housing facility. ***Payment plan:*** installment. ***Waivers:*** senior citizens and employees or children of employees.

Financial Aid Of all full-time matriculated undergraduates who enrolled in 2016, 6,676 applied for aid, 5,531 were judged to have need, 1,472 had their need fully met. 199 Federal Work-Study jobs (averaging $1832). In 2016, 545 non-need-based awards were made. ***Average financial aid package:*** $10,524. ***Average need-based loan:*** $4377. ***Average need-based gift aid:*** $8185. ***Average non-need-based aid:*** $5273. ***Average indebtedness upon graduation:*** $32,949.

APPLYING

Standardized Tests *Required:* SAT or ACT (for admission).

Options: electronic application.

Application fee: $50.

Required: high school transcript, minimum 2.0 GPA. ***Required for some:*** essay or personal statement, 1 letter of recommendation, interview, portfolio for art, audition for music.

Application deadlines: 6/1 (freshmen), 8/1 (transfers).

Notification: continuous (freshmen), continuous (transfers).

CONTACT

Mr. Anthony Leckey, Senior Associate Director of Admissions, William Paterson University of New Jersey, Undergraduate Admissions, 300 Pompton Road, Wayne, NJ 07470. *Phone:* 973-720-2900. *Toll-free phone:* 877-WPU-EXCEL. *Fax:* 973-720-2910. *E-mail:* leckeya@wpunj.edu.

Yeshiva Gedolah Zichron Leyma

Linden, New Jersey

CONTACT

Yeshiva Gedolah Zichron Leyma, 1000 Orchard Terrace, Linden, NJ 07036.

Yeshivas Be'er Yitzchok

Elizabeth, New Jersey

http://www.elizabethkollel.org/

CONTACT

Yeshivas Be'er Yitzchok, 1391 North Avenue, Elizabeth, NJ 07208.

Yeshiva Toras Chaim

Lakewood, New Jersey

CONTACT

Yeshiva Toras Chaim, 999 Ridge Avenue, Lakewood, NJ 08701.

NEW MEXICO

Brookline College

Albuquerque, New Mexico

http://brooklinecollege.edu/

CONTACT

Mr. Andrew Webb, Campus Director, Brookline College, 4201 Central Avenue NW, Suite J, Albuquerque, NM 87105. *Phone:* 505-880-2877. *Toll-free phone:* 888-660-2428. *Fax:* 505-352-0199. *E-mail:* awebb@brooklinecollege.edu.

Eastern New Mexico University

Portales, New Mexico

http://www.enmu.edu/

CONTACT

Mr. Cody Spitz, Director, Enrollment Services, Eastern New Mexico University, Station #7 ENMU, Portales, NM 88130. *Phone:* 575-562-2178. *Toll-free phone:* 800-367-3668. *Fax:* 575-562-2118. *E-mail:* cody.spitz@enmu.edu.

EC-Council University

Albuquerque, New Mexico

http://www.eccu.edu/

CONTACT

EC-Council University, 101 C Sun Avenue NE, Albuquerque, NM 87109.

Institute of American Indian Arts

Santa Fe, New Mexico

http://www.iaia.edu/

- **Federally supported** comprehensive, founded 1962
- **Suburban** 140-acre campus with easy access to Albuquerque
- **Coed** 463 undergraduate students

UNDERGRAD STUDENTS

0.8% Black or African American, non-Hispanic/Latino; 5% Hispanic/Latino; 0.4% Native Hawaiian or other Pacific Islander, non-Hispanic/Latino; 83% American Indian or Alaska Native, non-Hispanic/Latino; 0.4% Two or more races, non-Hispanic/Latino; 3% Race/ethnicity unknown; 2% international.

FACULTY

Student/faculty ratio: 7:1.

ACADEMICS

Calendar: semesters. *Degrees:* certificates, associate, bachelor's, and master's.

Special study options: academic remediation for entering students, advanced placement credit, distance learning, double majors, independent study, internships, off-campus study, services for LD students, study abroad, summer session for credit.

Computers: 50 computers/terminals are available on campus for general student use. Students can access the following: campus intranet, computer help desk, free student e-mail accounts, online (class) grades, online (class) registration, online (class) schedules. Campuswide network is available. 100% of college-owned or -operated housing units are wired for high-speed Internet access. Wireless service is available via entire campus.

Library: Fogelson Library plus 1 other. Students can reserve study rooms.

STUDENT LIFE

Housing options: on-campus residence required for freshman year; coed. Campus housing is university owned. Freshman campus housing is guaranteed.

Activities and organizations: drama/theater group, student-run newspaper, television station.

Athletics ***Intramural sports:*** archery M/W.

Campus security: 24-hour patrols, late-night transport/escort service, controlled dormitory access.

Student services: health clinic, personal/psychological counseling.

COSTS & FINANCIAL AID

Costs (2017–18) ***Tuition:*** state resident $4700 full-time, $196 per semester hour part-time; nonresident $4700 full-time, $196 per semester hour part-time. ***Required fees:*** $260 full-time, $130 per term part-time. ***Room and board:*** $9100; room only: $3910. Room and board charges vary according to board plan and housing facility. ***Payment plan:*** installment. ***Waivers:*** employees or children of employees.

Financial Aid Of all full-time matriculated undergraduates who enrolled in 2011, 263 applied for aid, 261 were judged to have need, 201 had their need fully met. 2 Federal Work-Study jobs (averaging $2300). 3 state and other part-time jobs (averaging $2300). In 2011, 58 non-need-based awards were made. ***Average percent of need met:*** 71. ***Average financial aid package:*** $5005. ***Average need-based gift aid:*** $2500. ***Average non-need-based aid:*** $2500.

APPLYING
Standardized Tests *Required:* ACCUPLACER, ACT Compass, ACT ASSET (for admission). *Recommended:* SAT or ACT (for admission).

Required: high school transcript. ***Required for some:*** essay or personal statement, interview. ***Recommended:*** interview.

CONTACT
Ms. Mary Curley, Director, Admissions and Recruitment, Institute of American Indian Arts, 83 Avan Nu Po Road, Santa Fe, NM 87508. *Phone:* 505-424-2307. *Fax:* 505-424-0909. *E-mail:* mary.curley@iaia.edu.

National American University

Albuquerque, New Mexico

http://www.national.edu/

CONTACT
Admissions Office, National American University, 10131 Coors Boulevard NW, Suite I-01, Albuquerque, NM 87114. *Toll-free phone:* 800-895-9904.

National American University

Albuquerque, New Mexico

http://www.national.edu/

CONTACT
National American University, 4775 Indian School Road NE, Suite 200, Albuquerque, NM 87110. *Phone:* 505-265-7517. *Toll-free phone:* 800-895-9904.

National College of Midwifery

Taos, New Mexico

http://www.midwiferycollege.org/

CONTACT
Ms. Beth Enson, Dean of Students, National College of Midwifery, 1041 Reed Street, Suite C, Taos, NM 87571. *Phone:* 505-758-8914. *E-mail:* info@midwiferycollege.org.

Navajo Technical University

Crownpoint, New Mexico

http://www.navajotech.edu/

CONTACT
Director of Admission, Navajo Technical University, PO Box 849, Crownpoint, NM 87313. *Phone:* 505-786-4100.

New Mexico Highlands University

Las Vegas, New Mexico

http://www.nmhu.edu/

- **State-supported** comprehensive, founded 1893
- **Small-town** campus
- **Coed** 2,233 undergraduate students, 66% full-time, 62% women, 38% men
- **Minimally difficult** entrance level, 100% of applicants were admitted

UNDERGRAD STUDENTS
1,474 full-time, 759 part-time. 19% are from out of state; 6% Black or African American, non-Hispanic/Latino; 56% Hispanic/Latino; 0.7% Asian, non-Hispanic/Latino; 0.6% Native Hawaiian or other Pacific Islander, non-Hispanic/Latino; 8% American Indian or Alaska Native, non-Hispanic/Latino; 1% Two or more races, non-Hispanic/Latino; 1% Race/ethnicity unknown; 6% international; 18% transferred in; 21% live on campus.

Freshmen:
Admission: 993 applied, 993 admitted, 298 enrolled. ***Average high school GPA:*** 2.95. ***Test scores:*** SAT critical reading scores over 500: 21%; SAT math scores over 500: 15%; SAT writing scores over 500: 15%; ACT scores over 18: 52%; SAT critical reading scores over 600: 5%; SAT math scores over 600: 2%; SAT writing scores over 600: 3%; ACT scores over 24: 7%.

FACULTY
Total: 282, 49% full-time, 39% with terminal degrees.

Student/faculty ratio: 14:1.

ACADEMICS
Calendar: semesters. *Degrees:* bachelor's, master's, post-master's, and postbachelor's certificates.

Special study options: academic remediation for entering students, accelerated degree program, advanced placement credit, cooperative education, distance learning, double majors, honors programs, independent study, internships, off-campus study, part-time degree program, services for LD students, summer session for credit.

Computers: Students can access the following: online (class) registration. Campuswide network is available.

Library: Thomas C. Donnelly Library.

STUDENT LIFE
Housing options: coed, special housing for students with disabilities. Campus housing is university owned.

Activities and organizations: drama/theater group, student-run radio station, choral group, marching band, Vatos Rugby, Fire Escape Club, MeChA, NMHU Cheerleaders, NMHU Student Ambassadors, national fraternities, national sororities.

Athletics Member NCAA. All Division II. ***Intercollegiate sports:*** baseball M(s), basketball M(s)/W(s), cross-country running M(s)/W(s), football M(s), soccer W(s), softball W(s), track and field M/W, volleyball W(s). ***Intramural sports:*** badminton M/W, basketball M/W, football M, golf M/W, racquetball M/W, rugby M, skiing (cross-country) M/W, skiing (downhill) M/W, softball W, swimming and diving M/W, table tennis M/W, tennis M/W, volleyball M/W, weight lifting M/W.

Campus security: 24-hour emergency response devices and patrols, late-night transport/escort service, controlled dormitory access.

Student services: health clinic, personal/psychological counseling, women's center.

COSTS & FINANCIAL AID
Costs (2017–18) ***Tuition:*** state resident $3952 full-time, $165 per credit hour part-time; nonresident $7052 full-time, $294 per credit hour part-time. Full-time tuition and fees vary according to course load and location. Part-time tuition and fees vary according to course load and location. ***Required fees:*** $1598 full-time. ***Room and board:*** $7235; room only: $3635. Room and board charges vary according to board plan and housing facility. ***Payment plan:*** installment. ***Waivers:*** senior citizens and employees or children of employees.

Financial Aid Of all full-time matriculated undergraduates who enrolled in 2015, 1,299 applied for aid, 1,136 were judged to have need, 96 had their need fully met. In 2015, 506 non-need-based awards were made. ***Average percent of need met:*** 19. ***Average financial aid package:*** $1811. ***Average need-based loan:*** $2531. ***Average need-based gift aid:*** $1945. ***Average non-need-based aid:*** $2229. ***Average indebtedness upon graduation:*** $17,312.

APPLYING
Options: electronic application, early admission, deferred entrance.

Required: high school transcript, minimum 2.0 GPA. ***Required for some:*** 2 letters of recommendation, interview.

CONTACT
Ms. Fidel Trujillo, Vice President for Student Affairs, New Mexico Highlands University, Box 9000, Las Vegas, NM 87701. *Phone:* 505-454-3566. *Toll-free phone:* 800-338-6648. *E-mail:* judycordova@nmhu.edu.

New Mexico Institute of Mining and Technology

Socorro, New Mexico

http://www.nmt.edu/

- **State-supported** university, founded 1889
- **Small-town** 320-acre campus with easy access to Albuquerque
- **Endowment** $41.2 million
- **Coed** 1,569 undergraduate students, 88% full-time, 30% women, 70% men
- **Moderately difficult** entrance level, 23% of applicants were admitted

UNDERGRAD STUDENTS

1,388 full-time, 181 part-time. Students come from 31 states and territories; 7 other countries; 13% are from out of state; 2% Black or African American, non-Hispanic/Latino; 31% Hispanic/Latino; 3% Asian, non-Hispanic/Latino; 0.1% Native Hawaiian or other Pacific Islander, non-Hispanic/Latino; 3% American Indian or Alaska Native, non-Hispanic/Latino; 5% Two or more races, non-Hispanic/Latino; 2% Race/ethnicity unknown; 3% international; 5% transferred in; 50% live on campus.

Freshmen:

Admission: 1,663 applied, 390 admitted, 302 enrolled. ***Average high school GPA:*** 3.68. ***Test scores:*** SAT critical reading scores over 500: 89%; SAT math scores over 500: 91%; ACT scores over 18: 100%; SAT critical reading scores over 600: 64%; SAT math scores over 600: 62%; ACT scores over 24: 74%; SAT critical reading scores over 700: 18%; SAT math scores over 700: 14%; ACT scores over 30: 24%.

Retention: 77% of full-time freshmen returned.

FACULTY

Total: 183, 75% full-time.

Student/faculty ratio: 11:1.

ACADEMICS

Calendar: semesters. *Degrees:* associate, bachelor's, master's, and doctoral.

Special study options: accelerated degree program, advanced placement credit, cooperative education, distance learning, double majors, independent study, internships, services for LD students, student-designed majors, summer session for credit.

Unusual degree programs: 3-2 earth science, biology, math, physics.

Computers: 225 computers/terminals are available on campus for general student use. Students can access the following: computer help desk, free student e-mail accounts, online (class) registration, online (class) schedules. Campuswide network is available. Wireless service is available via computer centers, learning centers, student centers.

Library: The Skeen Library. Students can reserve study rooms.

STUDENT LIFE

Housing options: coed, men-only, women-only. Campus housing is university owned.

Activities and organizations: drama/theater group, student-run newspaper, radio station, choral group.

Athletics ***Intercollegiate sports:*** golf M(c)/W(c), rugby M(c)/W(c), soccer M(c)/W(c). ***Intramural sports:*** badminton M/W, basketball M/W, soccer M/W, softball M/W, volleyball M/W.

Campus security: 24-hour emergency response devices and patrols, late-night transport/escort service.

Student services: health clinic, personal/psychological counseling.

COSTS & FINANCIAL AID

Costs (2016–17) ***Tuition:*** state resident $5841 full-time, $243 per credit hour part-time; nonresident $18,991 full-time, $791 per credit hour part-time. Full-time tuition and fees vary according to reciprocity agreements. Part-time tuition and fees vary according to course load. ***Required fees:*** $1050 full-time, $65 per credit hour part-time, $216 per term part-time. ***Room and board:*** $7942. Room and board charges vary according to board plan and housing facility. ***Waivers:*** senior citizens and employees or children of employees.

Financial Aid Of all full-time matriculated undergraduates who enrolled in 2015, 1,264 applied for aid, 724 were judged to have need, 177 had their need fully met. 255 Federal Work-Study jobs (averaging $2500). 51 state and other part-time jobs (averaging $1539). In 2015, 499 non-need-based awards were made. ***Average percent of need met:*** 82. ***Average financial aid package:*** $12,676. ***Average need-based loan:*** $4161. ***Average need-based gift aid:*** $5495. ***Average non-need-based aid:*** $6385. ***Average indebtedness upon graduation:*** $20,611.

APPLYING

Standardized Tests *Required:* SAT or ACT (for admission). *Recommended:* ACT (for admission).

Options: electronic application, deferred entrance.

Application fee: $15.

Required: high school transcript, minimum 2.5 GPA. ***Required for some:*** 2 letters of recommendation. ***Recommended:*** interview.

Application deadlines: 8/1 (freshmen), 8/1 (transfers).

Notification: continuous (freshmen), continuous (transfers).

CONTACT

Mr. Anthony Ortiz, Director of Admissions, New Mexico Institute of Mining and Technology, 801 Leroy Place, Socorro, NM 87801. *Phone:* 575-835-5424. *Toll-free phone:* 800-428-TECH. *Fax:* 575-835-5989. *E-mail:* admission@nmt.edu.

New Mexico State University

Las Cruces, New Mexico

http://www.nmsu.edu/

- **State-supported** university, founded 1888, part of New Mexico State University System
- **Suburban** 900-acre campus with easy access to El Paso, TX
- **Endowment** $214.8 million
- **Coed** 12,027 undergraduate students, 82% full-time, 54% women, 46% men
- **Moderately difficult** entrance level, 60% of applicants were admitted

UNDERGRAD STUDENTS

9,874 full-time, 2,153 part-time. Students come from 52 states and territories; 60 other countries; 25% are from out of state; 3% Black or African American, non-Hispanic/Latino; 56% Hispanic/Latino; 1% Asian, non-Hispanic/Latino; 0.2% Native Hawaiian or other Pacific Islander, non-Hispanic/Latino; 2% American Indian or Alaska Native, non-Hispanic/Latino; 2% Two or more races, non-Hispanic/Latino; 2% Race/ethnicity unknown; 5% international; 5% transferred in; 18% live on campus.

Freshmen:

Admission: 7,618 applied, 4,541 admitted, 1,842 enrolled. ***Average high school GPA:*** 3.49. ***Test scores:*** SAT critical reading scores over 500: 37%; SAT math scores over 500: 41%; SAT writing scores over 500: 30%; ACT scores over 18: 79%; SAT critical reading scores over 600: 9%; SAT math scores over 600: 12%; SAT writing scores over 600: 5%; ACT scores over 24: 27%; SAT critical reading scores over 700: 1%; ACT scores over 30: 3%.

Retention: 72% of full-time freshmen returned.

FACULTY

Total: 988, 66% full-time, 71% with terminal degrees.

Student/faculty ratio: 16:1.

ACADEMICS

Calendar: semesters. *Degrees:* master's, doctoral, post-master's, and postbachelor's certificates.

Special study options: academic remediation for entering students, accelerated degree program, advanced placement credit, cooperative education, distance learning, double majors, English as a second language, freshman honors college, honors programs, independent study, internships, off-campus study, part-time degree program, services for LD students, student-designed majors, study abroad, summer session for credit. ***ROTC:*** Army (b), Air Force (b).

Unusual degree programs: 3-2 engineering; pharmacy with University of New Mexico, accountancy and physics.

Computers: 354 computers/terminals and 600 ports are available on campus for general student use. Students can access the following: campus intranet, computer help desk, free student e-mail accounts, online (class) grades, online (class) registration, online (class) schedules, antivirus software; student portal online with file share/storage space, student employee clock-in, payments system, hardware rentals, short-term tablet checkout, software discounts. Campuswide network is available. 100% of college-owned or -operated housing units are wired for high-speed Internet access. Wireless service is available via entire campus. **Library:** New Mexico State University Library - Zuhl plus 1 other. *Books:* 1.5 million (physical), 159,632 (digital/electronic); *Serial titles:* 474 (physical), 1,055 (digital/electronic); *Databases:* 401. Weekly public service hours: 112; students can reserve study rooms.

STUDENT LIFE

Housing options: on-campus residence required for freshman year; coed. Campus housing is university owned. Freshman campus housing is guaranteed.

Activities and organizations: drama/theater group, student-run newspaper, radio and television station, choral group, marching band, Aggie Startup Club, Sigma Gamma Tau, Beta Alpha Psi, Arts and Science Council, national fraternities, national sororities.

Athletics Member NCAA. All Division I except football (Division I-A). ***Intercollegiate sports:*** baseball M(s), basketball M(s)/W(s), cross-country running M(s)/W(s), equestrian sports W(s), golf M(s)/W(s), soccer W(s), softball W(s), swimming and diving W(s), tennis M(s)/W(s), track and field W(s), volleyball W(s). ***Intramural sports:*** badminton M(c)/W(c), basketball M/W, cheerleading M/W, fencing M(c)/W(c), football M/W, golf M/W, racquetball M/W, rugby M(c)/W(c), soccer M(c)/W(c), softball M/W, table tennis M/W, tennis M(c)/W(c), ultimate Frisbee M(c)/W(c), volleyball M(c)/W(c), water polo M/W, weight lifting M(c)/W(c).

Campus security: 24-hour emergency response devices and patrols, late-night transport/escort service.

Student services: health clinic, personal/psychological counseling, legal services.

COSTS & FINANCIAL AID

Costs (2016–17) ***One-time required fee:*** $40. ***Tuition:*** state resident $4956 full-time, $207 per credit hour part-time; nonresident $18,514 full-time, $771 per credit hour part-time. Full-time tuition and fees vary according to course load and reciprocity agreements. ***Required fees:*** $1138 full-time, $47 per credit hour part-time. ***Room and board:*** $7988; room only: $4296. Room and board charges vary according to board plan and housing facility. ***Payment plans:*** installment, deferred payment. ***Waivers:*** senior citizens and employees or children of employees.

Financial Aid Of all full-time matriculated undergraduates who enrolled in 2015, 7,483 applied for aid, 6,534 were judged to have need, 576 had their need fully met. 308 Federal Work-Study jobs (averaging $2652). 337 state and other part-time jobs (averaging $5609). In 2015, 1201 non-need-based awards were made. ***Average percent of need met:*** 65. ***Average financial aid package:*** $11,817. ***Average need-based loan:*** $3557. ***Average need-based gift aid:*** $9998. ***Average non-need-based aid:*** $2571. ***Average indebtedness upon graduation:*** $21,402. ***Financial aid deadline:*** 6/30.

APPLYING

Standardized Tests *Required:* SAT or ACT (for admission).

Options: electronic application.

Application fee: $20.

Required: high school transcript, minimum 2.0 GPA, minimum cumulative high school GPA of 2.5, ACT composite score of 21 (SAT of 990), or 2.0 high school GPA and 20 ACT composite (950 SAT); minimum high school participation includes 4 units of English, 3 of math, 3 of science beyond general science, and 1 foreign language/fine art.

Application deadlines: rolling (freshmen), rolling (transfers).

Notification: continuous (freshmen), continuous (transfers).

CONTACT

Delia DeLeon, Director of Admissions, New Mexico State University, Box 30001, MSC 3A, Las Cruces, NM 88003-8001. *Phone:* 575-646-3121. *Toll-free phone:* 800-662-6678. *Fax:* 575-646-6330. *E-mail:* admssions@nmsu.edu.

Northern New Mexico College

Española, New Mexico

http://www.nnmc.edu/

CONTACT

Mr. Mike L. Costello, Registrar, Northern New Mexico College, 921 Paseo de Oñate, Española, NM 87532. *Phone:* 505-747-2193. *Fax:* 505-747-2191. *E-mail:* dms@nnmc.edu.

Pima Medical Institute

Albuquerque, New Mexico

http://www.pmi.edu/

CONTACT

Admissions Office, Pima Medical Institute, 4400 Cutler Avenue NE, Albuquerque, NM 87110. *Phone:* 505-881-1234. *Toll-free phone:* 800-477-PIMA. *Fax:* 505-881-5329.

St. John's College

Santa Fe, New Mexico

http://www.sjc.edu/

- **Independent** comprehensive, founded 1964
- **Small-town** 250-acre campus with easy access to Albuquerque, NM
- **Endowment** $152.0 million
- **Coed** 326 undergraduate students, 98% full-time, 44% women, 56% men
- **Moderately difficult** entrance level, 63% of applicants were admitted

UNDERGRAD STUDENTS

320 full-time, 6 part-time. Students come from 43 states and territories; 24 other countries; 89% are from out of state; 0.9% Black or African American, non-Hispanic/Latino; 9% Hispanic/Latino; 3% Asian, non-Hispanic/Latino; 0.3% Native Hawaiian or other Pacific Islander, non-Hispanic/Latino; 3% Two or more races, non-Hispanic/Latino; 0.9% Race/ethnicity unknown; 25% international; 7% transferred in; 93% live on campus.

Freshmen:

Admission: 298 applied, 187 admitted, 67 enrolled. ***Average high school GPA:*** 3.48. ***Test scores:*** SAT critical reading scores over 500: 100%; SAT math scores over 500: 96%; SAT writing scores over 500: 100%; ACT scores over 18: 95%; SAT critical reading scores over 600: 82%; SAT math scores over 600: 74%; SAT writing scores over 600: 81%; ACT scores over 24: 81%; SAT critical reading scores over 700: 52%; SAT math scores over 700: 33%; SAT writing scores over 700: 33%; ACT scores over 30: 45%.

Retention: 83% of full-time freshmen returned.

FACULTY

Total: 54, 74% full-time, 91% with terminal degrees.

Student/faculty ratio: 6:1.

ACADEMICS

Calendar: semesters. *Degrees:* bachelor's and master's.

Special study options: English as a second language, internships, off-campus study, services for LD students, study abroad, summer session for credit.

Computers: 16 computers/terminals and 425 ports are available on campus for general student use. Students can access the following: campus intranet, computer help desk, free student e-mail accounts. Campuswide network is available. 100% of college-owned or -operated housing units are wired for high-speed Internet access. Wireless service is available via entire campus.

Library: Meem Library. *Books:* 70,098 (physical), 297,314 (digital/electronic); *Serial titles:* 74 (physical); *Databases:* 9. Weekly public service hours: 82; study areas open 24 hours, 5-7 days a week.

STUDENT LIFE

Housing options: on-campus residence required through senior year; coed, men-only, women-only, special housing for students with disabilities. Campus housing is university owned. Freshman campus housing is guaranteed.

Activities and organizations: drama/theater group, student-run newspaper, choral group, Social Dance, Student Government/Student

Committee on Instruction, Iron Bookworm Workout, intramural sports, PiYo .

Athletics ***Intercollegiate sports:*** fencing M/W. ***Intramural sports:*** archery M(c)/W(c), badminton M/W, basketball M/W, cross-country running M/W, fencing M/W, ice hockey M/W, racquetball M/W, rock climbing M/W, skiing (cross-country) M/W, skiing (downhill) M/W, soccer M/W, softball M/W, squash M/W, swimming and diving M/W, table tennis M/W, tennis M/W, ultimate Frisbee M/W, volleyball M/W, weight lifting M/W.

Campus security: 24-hour emergency response devices and patrols, late-night transport/escort service, controlled dormitory access.

Student services: health clinic, personal/psychological counseling.

COSTS & FINANCIAL AID

Costs (2017–18) ***Comprehensive fee:*** $63,806 includes full-time tuition ($51,200), mandatory fees ($1120), and room and board ($11,486). Part-time tuition: $1506 per credit. ***Room and board:*** Room and board charges vary according to board plan and housing facility. ***Payment plan:*** installment. ***Waivers:*** employees or children of employees.

Financial Aid Of all full-time matriculated undergraduates who enrolled in 2016, 294 applied for aid, 288 were judged to have need, 162 had their need fully met. 74 Federal Work-Study jobs (averaging $2720). 120 state and other part-time jobs (averaging $3040). In 2016, 38 non-need-based awards were made. ***Average percent of need met:*** 88. ***Average financial aid package:*** $40,988. ***Average need-based loan:*** $7280. ***Average need-based gift aid:*** $32,455. ***Average non-need-based aid:*** $16,250. ***Average indebtedness upon graduation:*** $27,790.

APPLYING

Standardized Tests *Required for some:* SAT or ACT (for admission), SAT/ACT, TOEFL/IELTS or interview for international applicants, SAT/ACT/CLT for homeschooled students and applicants who have not and will not graduate high school.

Options: electronic application, early admission, early action, deferred entrance.

Required: essay or personal statement, high school transcript, 2 letters of recommendation. ***Required for some:*** outline of curriculum for home-schooled applicants. ***Recommended:*** interview.

Application deadlines: rolling (freshmen), rolling (transfers), 11/15 (early action).

Notification: continuous (freshmen), continuous (transfers), 12/15 (early action).

CONTACT

Yvette Sobky Shaffer, Director of Admissions, St. John's College, 1160 Camino Cruz Blanca, Santa Fe, NM 87505. *Phone:* 505-984-6060. *Toll-free phone:* 800-331-5232. *Fax:* 505-984-6162. *E-mail:* santafe.admissions@sjc.edu.

University of New Mexico

Albuquerque, New Mexico

http://www.unm.edu/

- **State-supported** university, founded 1889
- **Urban** 769-acre campus with easy access to Albuquerque
- **Endowment** $400.8 million
- **Coed**
- **Moderately difficult** entrance level

FACULTY

Student/faculty ratio: 17:1.

ACADEMICS

Calendar: semesters. *Degrees:* certificates, associate, bachelor's, master's, doctoral, and post-master's certificates.

Library: College of University Libraries and Learning Sciences plus 7 others. Students can reserve study rooms.

STUDENT LIFE

Housing options: coed, special housing for students with disabilities. Campus housing is university owned and is provided by a third party.

Activities and organizations: drama/theater group, student-run newspaper, radio and television station, choral group, marching band, Associated Students of UNM, Graduate and Professional Students Association, Golden Key National Honor Society, national fraternities, national sororities.

Athletics Member NCAA. All Division I except football (Division I-A).

Campus security: 24-hour emergency response devices and patrols, student patrols, late-night transport/escort service, controlled dormitory access.

Student services: health clinic, personal/psychological counseling, women's center.

APPLYING

Standardized Tests *Required:* SAT or ACT (for admission).

Options: electronic application, early admission, deferred entrance.

Application fee: $20.

Required: high school transcript, minimum 2.5 GPA. ***Required for some:*** essay or personal statement, interview.

CONTACT

Mr. Matthew Hulett, Director of Admissions and Recruitment Services, University of New Mexico, Office of Admissions, PO Box 4895, Albuquerque, NM 87196-4895. *Phone:* 505-277-8900. *Toll-free phone:* 800-CALL-UNM. *Fax:* 505-277-6686. *E-mail:* apply@unm.edu.

University of Phoenix–New Mexico Campus

Albuquerque, New Mexico

http://www.phoenix.edu/

CONTACT

Marc Booker, Sr. Director, Office of Admissions and Evaluation, University of Phoenix–New Mexico Campus, 4035 South Riverpoint Parkway, Mail Stop CF-L101, Phoenix, AZ 85040. *Phone:* 602-557-4609. *Toll-free phone:* 866-766-0766. *Fax:* 480-643-1156.

University of the Southwest

Hobbs, New Mexico

http://www.usw.edu/

- **Independent Christian** comprehensive, founded 1962
- **Small-town** 162-acre campus
- **Endowment** $5.6 million
- **Coed** 450 undergraduate students, 67% full-time, 45% women, 55% men
- **Moderately difficult** entrance level, 66% of applicants were admitted

UNDERGRAD STUDENTS

301 full-time, 149 part-time. Students come from 440 states and territories; 10 other countries; 48% are from out of state; 14% Black or African American, non-Hispanic/Latino; 47% Hispanic/Latino; 0.2% Asian, non-Hispanic/Latino; 0.4% Native Hawaiian or other Pacific Islander, non-Hispanic/Latino; 0.4% American Indian or Alaska Native, non-Hispanic/Latino; 26% Race/ethnicity unknown; 20% transferred in; 55% live on campus.

Freshmen:

Admission: 263 applied, 173 admitted, 100 enrolled. ***Average high school GPA:*** 2.63.

Retention: 56% of full-time freshmen returned.

FACULTY

Total: 78, 45% full-time, 40% with terminal degrees.

Student/faculty ratio: 17:1.

ACADEMICS

Calendar: semesters. *Degrees:* bachelor's and master's.

Special study options: academic remediation for entering students, advanced placement credit, distance learning, double majors, honors programs, internships, part-time degree program, services for LD students, summer session for credit.

Computers: 65 computers/terminals are available on campus for general student use. Students can access the following: campus intranet, computer help desk, free student e-mail accounts, online (class) grades, online (class) registration, online (class) schedules. Campuswide network is available. 100% of college-owned or -operated housing units are wired for

high-speed Internet access. Wireless service is available via entire campus.
Library: Scarborough Memorial Library.

STUDENT LIFE
Housing options: on-campus residence required through sophomore year; coed. Campus housing is university owned. Freshman applicants given priority for college housing.
Activities and organizations: Student Government Association (SGA), Students in Free Enterprise (SIFE), Southwest Association of Future Educators, Fellowship of Christian Athletes, BEST.
Athletics Member NAIA. ***Intercollegiate sports:*** baseball M(s), basketball M(s)/W(s), cross-country running M(s)/W(s), golf M(s)/W(s), soccer M(s)/W(s), softball W(s), tennis M(s)/W(s), track and field M(s)/W(s), volleyball W(s). ***Intramural sports:*** badminton M/W, basketball M/W, soccer M/W, table tennis M/W, volleyball M/W.
Campus security: student patrols, controlled dormitory access, night security.
Student services: personal/psychological counseling.

COSTS & FINANCIAL AID
Costs (2016–17) ***Comprehensive fee:*** $20,708 includes full-time tuition ($13,248), mandatory fees ($150), and room and board ($7310). Full-time tuition and fees vary according to course load. Part-time tuition: $552 per credit hour. Part-time tuition and fees vary according to course load. ***College room only:*** $4300. Room and board charges vary according to board plan and housing facility. ***Payment plan:*** installment. ***Waivers:*** employees or children of employees.
Financial Aid Of all full-time matriculated undergraduates who enrolled in 2015, 278 applied for aid, 251 were judged to have need. 30 Federal Work-Study jobs (averaging $750). 7 state and other part-time jobs (averaging $750).

APPLYING
Standardized Tests *Required:* minimum ACT score of 18 or SAT of 940, top 50% of graduating class (for admission).
Options: electronic application, early admission.
Required: high school transcript, minimum 2.0 GPA. ***Required for some:*** essay or personal statement.
Application deadlines: rolling (freshmen), rolling (transfers).
Notification: continuous (freshmen), continuous (transfers).

CONTACT
Lissete Terrazas, Director of Admissions, University of the Southwest, 6610 North Lovington Highway, Hobbs, NM 88240. *Phone:* 575-492-2122. *Toll-free phone:* 800-530-4400. *Fax:* 575-392-6006.
E-mail: lterrazas@usw.edu.

Western New Mexico University
Silver City, New Mexico
http://www.wnmu.edu/

CONTACT
Mr. Matthew Lara, Director of Admissions, Western New Mexico University, PO Box 680, Silver City, NM 88062-0680. *Phone:* 505-538-6106. *Toll-free phone:* 800-872-WNMU. *Fax:* 505-538-6127.
E-mail: tresslerd@wnmu.edu.

NEW YORK

Adelphi University
Garden City, New York
http://www.adelphi.edu/

- **Independent** university, founded 1896
- **Suburban** 75-acre campus with easy access to New York City
- **Endowment** $159.4 million
- **Coed** 5,205 undergraduate students, 91% full-time, 69% women, 31% men
- **Moderately difficult** entrance level, 70% of applicants were admitted

UNDERGRAD STUDENTS
4,742 full-time, 463 part-time. Students come from 36 states and territories; 41 other countries; 7% are from out of state; 9% Black or African American, non-Hispanic/Latino; 16% Hispanic/Latino; 10% Asian, non-Hispanic/Latino; 0.1% American Indian or Alaska Native, non-Hispanic/Latino; 2% Two or more races, non-Hispanic/Latino; 6% Race/ethnicity unknown; 4% international; 11% transferred in; 22% live on campus.

Freshmen:
Admission: 11,863 applied, 8,339 admitted, 1,226 enrolled. ***Average high school GPA:*** 3.55. ***Test scores:*** SAT critical reading scores over 500: 76%; SAT math scores over 500: 81%; SAT writing scores over 500: 76%; ACT scores over 18: 99%; SAT critical reading scores over 600: 27%; SAT math scores over 600: 31%; SAT writing scores over 600: 27%; ACT scores over 24: 63%; SAT critical reading scores over 700: 4%; SAT math scores over 700: 6%; SAT writing scores over 700: 4%; ACT scores over 30: 16%.
Retention: 83% of full-time freshmen returned.

FACULTY
Total: 1,024, 31% full-time, 38% with terminal degrees.
Student/faculty ratio: 12:1.

ACADEMICS
Calendar: semesters. *Degrees:* certificates, associate, bachelor's, master's, doctoral, post-master's, and postbachelor's certificates.
Special study options: accelerated degree program, advanced placement credit, cooperative education, distance learning, double majors, English as a second language, freshman honors college, honors programs, independent study, internships, part-time degree program, services for LD students, student-designed majors, study abroad, summer session for credit. ***ROTC:*** Army (c), Air Force (c).
Unusual degree programs: 3-2 engineering with Columbia University; physical therapy: New York Medical Coll, New York Institute of Tech; dentistry: NYU Coll of Dentistry; medicine: Philadelphia Coll of Osteopathic Medicine, Lake Erie Coll of Osteopathic Medicine; optometry: SUNY State Coll of Optometry; podiatry: NYCPM.
Computers: 880 computers/terminals are available on campus for general student use. Students can access the following: computer help desk, free student e-mail accounts, online (class) grades, online (class) registration, online (class) schedules, payment, drop/add classes, check application status. Campuswide network is available. 90% of college-owned or -operated housing units are wired for high-speed Internet access. Wireless service is available via entire campus.
Library: Swirbul Library. *Books:* 578,732 (physical), 29,258 (digital/electronic); *Serial titles:* 660 (physical); *Databases:* 240. Students can reserve study rooms.

STUDENT LIFE
Housing options: coed, special housing for students with disabilities. Campus housing is university owned. Freshman applicants given priority for college housing.
Activities and organizations: drama/theater group, student-run newspaper, radio station, choral group, Student Activities Board, C. A. L. I. B. E. R. (Cause to Achieve Leadership, Intelligence, Brotherhood, Excellence, and Respect), Commuter Student Organization, Christian Fellowship, Circle K International, national fraternities, national sororities.
Athletics Member NCAA. All Division II. ***Intercollegiate sports:*** baseball M(s), basketball M(s)/W(s), bowling W(s), cross-country running M(s)/W(s), field hockey W(s), golf M(s)/W(s), lacrosse M(s)/W(s), soccer M(s)/W(s), softball W(s), swimming and diving M(s)/W(s), tennis M(s)/W(s), track and field M(s)/W(s), volleyball W(s). ***Intramural sports:*** badminton M/W, baseball M(c)/W(c), basketball M/W, cheerleading W, equestrian sports M(c)/W(c), fencing M(c)/W(c), soccer M/W, ultimate Frisbee M(c)/W(c), volleyball M/W.
Campus security: 24-hour emergency response devices and patrols, late-night transport/escort service, controlled dormitory access.
Student services: health clinic, personal/psychological counseling.

COSTS & FINANCIAL AID
Costs (2016–17) ***Comprehensive fee:*** $49,792 includes full-time tuition ($34,000), mandatory fees ($1740), and room and board ($14,052). Full-time tuition and fees vary according to course level, course load, location,

program, and student level. Part-time tuition: $1040 per credit hour. Part-time tuition and fees vary according to course level, course load, location, program, and student level. ***Required fees:*** $463 per term part-time. ***Room and board:*** Room and board charges vary according to board plan and housing facility. ***Payment plans:*** tuition prepayment, installment, deferred payment. ***Waivers:*** children of alumni, senior citizens, and employees or children of employees.

Financial Aid Of all full-time matriculated undergraduates who enrolled in 2016, 3,807 applied for aid, 3,210 were judged to have need, 445 had their need fully met. 378 Federal Work-Study jobs (averaging $1719). 1,163 state and other part-time jobs (averaging $2102). In 2016, 962 non-need-based awards were made. ***Average percent of need met:*** 45. ***Average financial aid package:*** $21,500. ***Average need-based loan:*** $4344. ***Average need-based gift aid:*** $15,855. ***Average non-need-based aid:*** $15,467. ***Average indebtedness upon graduation:*** $32,558.

APPLYING

Standardized Tests *Required for some:* SAT or ACT (for admission).

Options: electronic application, early action, deferred entrance.

Application fee: $40.

Required: essay or personal statement, high school transcript. ***Required for some:*** 2 letters of recommendation, interview, auditions/portfolios for performing and fine arts. ***Recommended:*** minimum 3.4 GPA.

Application deadlines: rolling (freshmen), rolling (transfers), 12/1 (early action).

Notification: continuous (freshmen), continuous (transfers), 12/31 (early action).

CONTACT

Ms. Stephanie Espina, Director of Freshman Admissions, Adelphi University, Nexus Building, Room 110, 1 South Ave., PO Box 701, Garden City, NY 11530-0701. *Phone:* 516-877-3056. *Toll-free phone:* 800-ADELPHI. *Fax:* 516-877-3039. *E-mail:* admissions@adelphi.edu.

Albany College of Pharmacy and Health Sciences

Albany, New York

http://www.acphs.edu/

CONTACT

Mr. Matthew Stever, Director of Admissions, Albany College of Pharmacy and Health Sciences, 106 New Scotland Avenue, Albany, NY 12208. *Phone:* 518-694-7221. *Toll-free phone:* 888-203-8010. *Fax:* 518-694-7322. *E-mail:* admissions@acphs.edu.

Alfred University

Alfred, New York

http://www.alfred.edu/

- **Independent** university, founded 1836
- **Rural** 232-acre campus with easy access to Rochester
- **Endowment** $105.8 million
- **Coed** 1,815 undergraduate students, 95% full-time, 48% women, 52% men
- **Moderately difficult** entrance level, 63% of applicants were admitted

UNDERGRAD STUDENTS

1,719 full-time, 96 part-time. Students come from 41 states and territories; 16 other countries; 18% are from out of state; 10% Black or African American, non-Hispanic/Latino; 8% Hispanic/Latino; 2% Asian, non-Hispanic/Latino; 0.4% American Indian or Alaska Native, non-Hispanic/Latino; 3% Two or more races, non-Hispanic/Latino; 10% Race/ethnicity unknown; 2% international; 6% transferred in; 75% live on campus.

Freshmen:

Admission: 3,897 applied, 2,446 admitted, 417 enrolled. ***Average high school GPA:*** 3. ***Test scores:*** SAT critical reading scores over 500: 56%; SAT math scores over 500: 60%; SAT writing scores over 500: 39%; ACT scores over 18: 91%; SAT critical reading scores over 600: 15%; SAT math scores over 600: 20%; SAT writing scores over 600: 7%; ACT scores over 24: 44%; SAT critical reading scores over 700: 2%; SAT math scores over 700: 2%; SAT writing scores over 700: 1%; ACT scores over 30: 10%.

Retention: 76% of full-time freshmen returned.

FACULTY

Total: 193, 79% full-time, 83% with terminal degrees.

Student/faculty ratio: 11:1.

ACADEMICS

Calendar: semesters. *Degrees:* bachelor's, master's, doctoral, and post-master's certificates.

Special study options: advanced placement credit, cooperative education, double majors, honors programs, independent study, internships, off-campus study, part-time degree program, services for LD students, student-designed majors, study abroad, summer session for credit. ***ROTC:*** Army (c).

Computers: Students can access the following: computer help desk, free student e-mail accounts, online (class) grades, online (class) registration, online (class) schedules, online bill pay. Campuswide network is available. 100% of college-owned or -operated housing units are wired for high-speed Internet access. Wireless service is available via entire campus.

Library: Herrick Memorial Library plus 1 other. *Books:* 217,226 (physical), 530,999 (digital/electronic); *Serial titles:* 243 (physical), 114,188 (digital/electronic); *Databases:* 279. Study areas open 24 hours, 5-7 days a week; students can reserve study rooms.

STUDENT LIFE

Housing options: on-campus residence required through junior year; coed, cooperative. Campus housing is university owned. Freshman campus housing is guaranteed.

Activities and organizations: drama/theater group, student-run newspaper, radio station, choral group, Student Senate, Habitat for Humanity, Drawn to Diversity, Student Activities Board.

Athletics Member NCAA. All Division III. ***Intercollegiate sports:*** basketball M/W, cross-country running M/W, equestrian sports M/W, football M, lacrosse M/W, skiing (downhill) M/W, soccer M/W, softball W, swimming and diving M/W, tennis M/W, track and field M/W, volleyball W. ***Intramural sports:*** baseball M(c), basketball M/W, cheerleading W(c), football M/W, golf M/W, ice hockey M(c), lacrosse M/W, racquetball M/W, rugby M(c)/W(c), skiing (cross-country) M/W, soccer M/W, softball M/W, squash M/W, tennis M/W, ultimate Frisbee M(c)/W(c), volleyball M/W.

Campus security: 24-hour emergency response devices, student patrols, late-night transport/escort service, controlled dormitory access, key-only access to dormitories.

Student services: health clinic, personal/psychological counseling, women's center.

COSTS & FINANCIAL AID

Costs (2017–18) ***Comprehensive fee:*** $44,536 includes full-time tuition ($31,274), mandatory fees ($990), and room and board ($12,272). Full-time tuition and fees vary according to program. Part-time tuition: $998 per credit hour. ***Required fees:*** $84 per term part-time. ***College room only:*** $6216. Room and board charges vary according to board plan and housing facility. ***Payment plan:*** installment. ***Waivers:*** employees or children of employees.

Financial Aid Of all full-time matriculated undergraduates who enrolled in 2016, 1,528 applied for aid, 1,385 were judged to have need, 250 had their need fully met. 1,003 Federal Work-Study jobs (averaging $1663). In 2016, 130 non-need-based awards were made. ***Average percent of need met:*** 84. ***Average financial aid package:*** $26,882. ***Average need-based loan:*** $5978. ***Average need-based gift aid:*** $20,478. ***Average non-need-based aid:*** $11,406. ***Average indebtedness upon graduation:*** $37,437. ***Financial aid deadline:*** 3/15.

APPLYING

Standardized Tests *Required:* SAT or ACT (for admission).

Options: electronic application, early admission, early decision, deferred entrance.

Application fee: $50.

Required: essay or personal statement, high school transcript, 1 letter of recommendation. ***Required for some:*** interview, portfolio for applicants to the School of Art and Design. ***Recommended:*** interview.

Application deadlines: 8/1 (freshmen), 8/1 (transfers).

Early decision deadline: 12/1.

Notification: continuous (freshmen), continuous (transfers), 12/15 (early decision).

CONTACT

Mr. William J. Sliwa, Interim Director of Admissions, Alfred University, Alumni Hall, Alfred, NY 14802-1205. *Phone:* 607-871-2115. *Toll-free phone:* 800-541-9229. *Fax:* 607-871-2198. *E-mail:* admissions@alfred.edu.

Bard College

Annandale-on-Hudson, New York

http://www.bard.edu/

- **Independent** comprehensive, founded 1860
- **Rural** 1000-acre campus
- **Coed** 2,023 undergraduate students, 96% full-time, 55% women, 45% men
- **Moderately difficult** entrance level, 32% of applicants were admitted

UNDERGRAD STUDENTS

1,946 full-time, 77 part-time. Students come from 47 states and territories; 57 other countries; 66% are from out of state; 8% Black or African American, non-Hispanic/Latino; 1% Hispanic/Latino; 5% Asian, non-Hispanic/Latino; 0.8% American Indian or Alaska Native, non-Hispanic/Latino; 12% Race/ethnicity unknown; 11% international; 3% transferred in; 73% live on campus.

Freshmen:

Admission: 7,044 applied, 2,266 admitted, 447 enrolled.

Retention: 85% of full-time freshmen returned.

FACULTY

Total: 273, 56% full-time, 89% with terminal degrees.

Student/faculty ratio: 10:1.

ACADEMICS

Calendar: semesters. *Degrees:* bachelor's, master's, and doctoral.

Special study options: adult/continuing education programs, advanced placement credit, double majors, independent study, internships, off-campus study, part-time degree program, services for LD students, student-designed majors, study abroad.

Unusual degree programs: 3-2 business administration; engineering with Columbia University, Washington University in St. Louis, Dartmouth College; forestry with Duke University; social work; teaching.

Computers: 425 computers/terminals are available on campus for general student use. Students can access the following: campus intranet, computer help desk, free student e-mail accounts, online (class) grades, online (class) registration, online (class) schedules. Campuswide network is available. 100% of college-owned or -operated housing units are wired for high-speed Internet access. Wireless service is available via classrooms, computer centers, computer labs, dorm rooms, learning centers, libraries, student centers.

Library: Stevenson Library plus 3 others. *Books:* 434,580 (physical), 434,580 (digital/electronic); *Serial titles:* 36,900 (physical), 36,900 (digital/electronic).

STUDENT LIFE

Housing options: on-campus residence required through sophomore year; coed, women-only, cooperative. Campus housing is university owned. Freshman campus housing is guaranteed.

Activities and organizations: drama/theater group, student-run newspaper, radio station, choral group, Student government, Debate Team, Queer-Straight Alliance, International Student Organization / Black Student Organization, Free Press (student newspaper).

Athletics Member NCAA, NAIA. All NCAA Division III. ***Intercollegiate sports:*** baseball M, basketball M/W, cross-country running M/W, lacrosse M/W, soccer M/W, squash M, swimming and diving M/W, tennis M/W, track and field M/W, volleyball M/W. ***Intramural sports:*** badminton M/W, basketball M/W, bowling M/W, equestrian sports M(c)/W(c), fencing M(c)/W(c), golf M/W, rugby M(c)/W(c), softball M/W, squash M/W, table tennis M/W, tennis M/W, ultimate Frisbee M(c)/W(c), volleyball M/W.

Campus security: 24-hour emergency response devices and patrols, student patrols, late-night transport/escort service, controlled dormitory access.

Student services: health clinic, personal/psychological counseling, legal services.

COSTS & FINANCIAL AID

Costs (2017–18) ***One-time required fee:*** $1635. ***Comprehensive fee:*** $67,981 includes full-time tuition ($52,226), mandatory fees ($689), and room and board ($15,066). Full-time tuition and fees vary according to degree level and location. Part-time tuition: $1635 per credit hour. Part-time tuition and fees vary according to degree level and location. ***Room and board:*** Room and board charges vary according to location. ***Payment plans:*** tuition prepayment, installment. ***Waivers:*** employees or children of employees.

Financial Aid Of all full-time matriculated undergraduates who enrolled in 2016, 1,362 applied for aid, 1,300 were judged to have need, 338 had their need fully met. 890 Federal Work-Study jobs (averaging $1606). In 2016, 47 non-need-based awards were made. ***Average percent of need met:*** 87. ***Average financial aid package:*** $44,760. ***Average need-based loan:*** $6630. ***Average need-based gift aid:*** $39,616. ***Average non-need-based aid:*** $22,045. ***Average indebtedness upon graduation:*** $27,816. ***Financial aid deadline:*** 2/15.

APPLYING

Options: electronic application, early admission, early decision, early action, deferred entrance.

Application fee: $50.

Required: essay or personal statement, high school transcript, minimum 3.0 GPA, 3 letters of recommendation.

Application deadlines: 1/1 (freshmen), 3/1 (transfers), 11/1 (early action).

Early decision deadline: 11/1.

Notification: 4/1 (freshmen), 5/15 (transfers), 1/1 (early action).

CONTACT

Ms. Mary Inga Backlund, Director of Admissions, Bard College, PO Box 5000 / 30 Campus Road, Annandale-on-Hudson, NY 12504-5000. *Phone:* 845-758-7472. *Fax:* 845-758-5208. *E-mail:* admission@bard.edu.

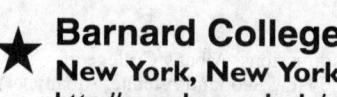

★ Barnard College

New York, New York

http://www.barnard.edu/

- **Independent** 4-year, founded 1889
- **Urban** 4-acre campus
- **Women only** 2,548 undergraduate students, 99% full-time
- **Most difficult** entrance level, 20% of applicants were admitted

UNDERGRAD STUDENTS

2,510 full-time, 38 part-time. Students come from 54 states and territories; 51 other countries; 74% are from out of state; 7% Black or African American, non-Hispanic/Latino; 12% Hispanic/Latino; 14% Asian, non-Hispanic/Latino; 0.1% American Indian or Alaska Native, non-Hispanic/Latino; 6% Two or more races, non-Hispanic/Latino; 0.2% Race/ethnicity unknown; 8% international; 2% transferred in; 91% live on campus.

Freshmen:

Admission: 6,655 applied, 1,306 admitted, 635 enrolled. ***Average high school GPA:*** 3.9. ***Test scores:*** SAT critical reading scores over 500: 98%; SAT math scores over 500: 98%; SAT writing scores over 500: 97%; ACT scores over 18: 100%; SAT critical reading scores over 600: 86%; SAT math scores over 600: 82%; SAT writing scores over 600: 89%; ACT scores over 24: 98%; SAT critical reading scores over 700: 46%; SAT math scores over 700: 35%; SAT writing scores over 700: 51%; ACT scores over 30: 64%.

Retention: 95% of full-time freshmen returned.

FACULTY

Total: 349, 61% full-time, 85% with terminal degrees.

Student/faculty ratio: 10:1.

ACADEMICS

Calendar: semesters. *Degree:* bachelor's.

Special study options: accelerated degree program, advanced placement credit, double majors, independent study, internships, off-campus study, services for LD students, student-designed majors, study abroad. ***ROTC:*** Army (c), Navy (c), Air Force (c).

Unusual degree programs: 3-2 engineering with Columbia University, The Fu Foundation School of Engineering and Applied Science; international affairs, public administration with Columbia University; music with The Juilliard School; religion with Jewish Theological Seminary; music with Manhattan School of Music; law; dentistry.

Computers: 165 computers/terminals are available on campus for general student use. Students can access the following: campus intranet, computer help desk, free student e-mail accounts, online (class) grades, online (class) registration, online (class) schedules. Campuswide network is available. 100% of college-owned or -operated housing units are wired for high-speed Internet access. Wireless service is available via entire campus.

Library: Lefrak Center plus 20 others. Study areas open 24 hours, 5-7 days a week.

STUDENT LIFE

Housing options: women-only, special housing for students with disabilities. Campus housing is university owned and leased by the school. Freshman campus housing is guaranteed.

Activities and organizations: drama/theater group, student-run newspaper, radio and television station, choral group, marching band, Community Impact (community service), Student Government Association, Take Back the Night, Student Activities Council, Musical Theater Society, national sororities.

Athletics Member NCAA. All Division I. ***Intercollegiate sports:*** archery W, basketball W, crew W, cross-country running W, equestrian sports W(c), fencing W, field hockey W, golf W, ice hockey W(c), lacrosse W, rugby W(c), sailing W(c), skiing (downhill) W(c), soccer W, softball W, squash W, swimming and diving W, tennis W, track and field W, volleyball W, water polo W(c). ***Intramural sports:*** archery W, badminton W, basketball W, equestrian sports W, ice hockey W, rugby W, sailing W, soccer W, squash W, table tennis W, tennis W, volleyball W, water polo W.

Campus security: 24-hour emergency response devices and patrols, late-night transport/escort service, controlled dormitory access, gated campus with permanent security posts.

Student services: health clinic, personal/psychological counseling, women's center.

COSTS & FINANCIAL AID

Costs (2016–17) ***Comprehensive fee:*** $65,992 includes full-time tuition ($48,614), mandatory fees ($1780), and room and board ($15,598). Part-time tuition: $1620 per credit hour. ***College room only:*** $9230. Room and board charges vary according to board plan and housing facility. ***Payment plans:*** tuition prepayment, installment, deferred payment. ***Waivers:*** employees or children of employees.

Financial Aid Of all full-time matriculated undergraduates who enrolled in 2016, 1,155 applied for aid, 1,010 were judged to have need, 998 had their need fully met. 189 Federal Work-Study jobs (averaging $2270). 716 state and other part-time jobs (averaging $2100). ***Average percent of need met:*** 100. ***Average financial aid package:*** $49,012. ***Average need-based loan:*** $4557. ***Average need-based gift aid:*** $43,183. ***Average indebtedness upon graduation:*** $22,015. ***Financial aid deadline:*** 2/1.

APPLYING

Standardized Tests *Required:* SAT or ACT (for admission).

Options: electronic application, early admission, early decision, deferred entrance.

Application fee: $75.

Required: essay or personal statement, high school transcript, 3 letters of recommendation, Common Application with Barnard Supplement. ***Recommended:*** interview.

Application deadlines: 1/1 (freshmen), 3/15 (transfers).

Early decision deadline: 11/1.

Notification: 4/1 (freshmen), 5/15 (transfers), 12/15 (early decision).

CONTACT

Ms. Jennifer Gill Fondiller, Dean of Enrollment Management, Barnard College, Barnard College, 3009 Broadway, New York, NY 10027. *Phone:* 212-854-2014. *Fax:* 212-2808797. *E-mail:* admissions@barnard.edu.

See page 1294 for the College Close-Up.

Baruch College of the City University of New York

New York, New York

http://www.baruch.cuny.edu/

- **State and locally supported** comprehensive, founded 1919, part of City University of New York System
- **Urban** 4-acre campus
- **Coed** 15,210 undergraduate students, 74% full-time, 49% women, 51% men
- **Very difficult** entrance level, 31% of applicants were admitted

UNDERGRAD STUDENTS

11,288 full-time, 3,922 part-time. Students come from 35 states and territories; 174 other countries; 3% are from out of state; 9% Black or African American, non-Hispanic/Latino; 25% Hispanic/Latino; 32% Asian, non-Hispanic/Latino; 0.2% Native Hawaiian or other Pacific Islander, non-Hispanic/Latino; 0.2% American Indian or Alaska Native, non-Hispanic/Latino; 1% Two or more races, non-Hispanic/Latino; 11% international; 15% transferred in; 2% live on campus.

Freshmen:

Admission: 20,789 applied, 6,377 admitted, 1,404 enrolled. ***Average high school GPA:*** 3.3. ***Test scores:*** SAT critical reading scores over 500: 82%; SAT math scores over 500: 95%; SAT critical reading scores over 600: 42%; SAT math scores over 600: 67%; SAT critical reading scores over 700: 8%; SAT math scores over 700: 20%.

Retention: 91% of full-time freshmen returned.

FACULTY

Total: 1,215, 41% full-time, 61% with terminal degrees.

Student/faculty ratio: 17:1.

ACADEMICS

Calendar: semesters. *Degrees:* bachelor's, master's, and post-master's certificates.

Special study options: accelerated degree program, adult/continuing education programs, advanced placement credit, distance learning, double majors, English as a second language, freshman honors college, honors programs, independent study, internships, part-time degree program, services for LD students, student-designed majors, study abroad, summer session for credit. ***ROTC:*** Army (c).

Computers: 1,300 computers/terminals are available on campus for general student use. Students can access the following: campus intranet, computer help desk, free student e-mail accounts, online (class) grades, online (class) registration, online (class) schedules. Campuswide network is available. 100% of college-owned or -operated housing units are wired for high-speed Internet access. Wireless service is available via classrooms, computer centers, computer labs, learning centers, libraries, student centers.

Library: The William and Anita Newman Library. *Books:* 626,753 (physical), 2.1 million (digital/electronic); *Serial titles:* 89,951 (physical), 52,020 (digital/electronic). Students can reserve study rooms.

STUDENT LIFE

Housing options: coed. Campus housing is provided by a third party.

Activities and organizations: drama/theater group, student-run newspaper, radio station, choral group, Accounting Society, Caribbean Students Association, Association of Latino Professionals in Finance and Accounting, Golden Key International Honor Society, Helpline, national fraternities, national sororities.

Athletics Member NCAA. All Division III. ***Intercollegiate sports:*** baseball M, basketball M/W, cheerleading M/W, cross-country running M/W, soccer M, softball W, swimming and diving M/W, tennis M/W, volleyball M/W. ***Intramural sports:*** archery M(c)/W(c), badminton M/W, basketball M/W, cross-country running M/W, racquetball M/W, swimming and diving M/W, table tennis M/W, volleyball M/W.

Campus security: 24-hour emergency response devices and patrols, late-night transport/escort service, controlled access by ID card.

Student services: health clinic, personal/psychological counseling, legal services.

COSTS & FINANCIAL AID

Costs (2016–17) ***Tuition:*** state resident $6330 full-time, $275 per credit hour part-time; nonresident $16,800 full-time, $560 per credit hour part-time. Full-time tuition and fees vary according to course load. Part-time tuition and fees vary according to course load. ***Required fees:*** $531 full-time. ***Room and board:*** Room and board charges vary according to housing facility. ***Payment plans:*** installment, deferred payment. ***Waivers:*** senior citizens and employees or children of employees.

Financial Aid Of all full-time matriculated undergraduates who enrolled in 2016, 8,334 applied for aid, 7,500 were judged to have need, 847 had their need fully met. 299 Federal Work-Study jobs (averaging $2459). 69 state and other part-time jobs (averaging $1818). In 2016, 1148 non-need-based awards were made. ***Average percent of need met:*** 21. ***Average financial aid package:*** $5572. ***Average need-based loan:*** $4921. ***Average need-based gift aid:*** $5120. ***Average non-need-based aid:*** $4875. ***Average indebtedness upon graduation:*** $5642.

APPLYING

Standardized Tests *Required:* SAT or ACT (for admission).

Options: electronic application, early admission, early decision, deferred entrance.

Application fee: $65.

Required: high school transcript, minimum 2.5 GPA, 16 academic units. ***Required for some:*** interview.

Application deadlines: 2/1 (freshmen), 2/1 (transfers).

Notification: 5/15 (freshmen), continuous until 5/1 (transfers).

CONTACT

Baruch College of the City University of New York, 1 Bernard Baruch Way, New York, NY 10010-5585. *Phone:* 646-312-1383.

Be'er Yaakov Talmudic Seminary

Spring Valley, New York

CONTACT

Be'er Yaakov Talmudic Seminary, 12 Jefferson Avenue, Spring Valley, NY 10977.

Beis Medrash Heichal Dovid

Far Rockaway, New York

CONTACT

Beis Medrash Heichal Dovid, 257 Beach 17th Street, Far Rockaway, NY 11691.

Berkeley College–New York City Campus

New York, New York

http://www.berkeleycollege.edu/

- **Proprietary** 4-year, founded 1936
- **Urban** campus with easy access to New York City
- **Coed** 3,968 undergraduate students, 88% full-time, 64% women, 36% men
- **Minimally difficult** entrance level

UNDERGRAD STUDENTS

3,472 full-time, 496 part-time. Students come from 38 other countries; 10% are from out of state; 25% Black or African American, non-Hispanic/Latino; 21% Hispanic/Latino; 3% Asian, non-Hispanic/Latino; 0.3% Native Hawaiian or other Pacific Islander, non-Hispanic/Latino; 0.5% American Indian or Alaska Native, non-Hispanic/Latino; 27% Race/ethnicity unknown; 16% international; 17% transferred in.

Freshmen:

Admission: 382 enrolled.

Retention: 59% of full-time freshmen returned.

FACULTY

Student/faculty ratio: 23:1.

ACADEMICS

Calendar: quarters. *Degrees:* certificates, associate, and bachelor's.

Special study options: academic remediation for entering students, accelerated degree program, adult/continuing education programs, advanced placement credit, cooperative education, distance learning, English as a second language, honors programs, independent study, internships, off-campus study, part-time degree program, student-designed majors, study abroad, summer session for credit.

Computers: 500 computers/terminals are available on campus for general student use. Students can access the following: computer help desk, free student e-mail accounts, online (class) grades, online (class) registration, online (class) schedules. Campuswide network is available. Wireless service is available via entire campus.

STUDENT LIFE

Housing options: college housing not available.

Activities and organizations: student-run newspaper.

Athletics Member USCAA. ***Intercollegiate sports:*** basketball M/W, cross-country running M/W, soccer M/W, track and field M/W.

Campus security: 24-hour emergency response devices.

Student services: personal/psychological counseling.

COSTS

Costs (2017–18) ***One-time required fee:*** $100. ***Tuition:*** $23,600 full-time, $810 per credit part-time. Full-time tuition and fees vary according to course load. Part-time tuition and fees vary according to course load. No tuition increase for student's term of enrollment. ***Required fees:*** $1700 full-time, $425 per term part-time. ***Payment plan:*** installment. ***Waivers:*** employees or children of employees.

APPLYING

Options: electronic application, deferred entrance.

Application fee: $50.

Required: high school transcript. ***Recommended:*** interview.

Application deadlines: rolling (freshmen), rolling (out-of-state freshmen), rolling (transfers).

Notification: continuous (freshmen), continuous (out-of-state freshmen), continuous (transfers).

CONTACT

Michelle Gomez, Director, High School Admissions, Berkeley College–New York City Campus, 3 East 43 Street, New York, NY 1007. *Phone:* 212-986-4343. *Toll-free phone:* 800-446-5400. *E-mail:* info@berkeleycollege.edu.

Berkeley College–White Plains Campus

White Plains, New York

http://www.berkeleycollege.edu/

- **Proprietary** 4-year, founded 1945
- **Suburban** campus with easy access to New York City
- **Coed** 467 undergraduate students, 92% full-time, 65% women, 35% men
- **Minimally difficult** entrance level

UNDERGRAD STUDENTS

428 full-time, 39 part-time. Students come from 8 other countries; 22% are from out of state; 29% Black or African American, non-Hispanic/Latino; 23% Hispanic/Latino; 2% Asian, non-Hispanic/Latino; 0.2% American Indian or Alaska Native, non-Hispanic/Latino; 24% Race/ethnicity unknown; 7% international; 20% transferred in.

Freshmen:

Admission: 104 enrolled.

Retention: 59% of full-time freshmen returned.

FACULTY

Student/faculty ratio: 23:1.

ACADEMICS

Calendar: quarters. *Degrees:* associate and bachelor's.

Special study options: academic remediation for entering students, accelerated degree program, adult/continuing education programs, advanced placement credit, cooperative education, distance learning, honors programs, independent study, internships, off-campus study, part-time degree program, study abroad, summer session for credit.

Computers: 158 computers/terminals are available on campus for general student use. Campuswide network is available. Wireless service is available via entire campus.

STUDENT LIFE
Housing options: coed. Campus housing is university owned.

Activities and organizations: student-run newspaper.

Athletics Member USCAA. ***Intercollegiate sports:*** basketball M/W, cross-country running M/W, soccer M/W, tennis M/W.

Campus security: 24-hour emergency response devices, controlled dormitory access, monitored entrance with front desk security guard.

Student services: personal/psychological counseling.

COSTS
Costs (2017–18) ***One-time required fee:*** $100. ***Tuition:*** $23,600 full-time, $825 per credit hour part-time. Full-time tuition and fees vary according to course load. Part-time tuition and fees vary according to course load. No tuition increase for student's term of enrollment. ***Required fees:*** $1700 full-time, $425 per term part-time. ***Room only:*** $9000. ***Payment plan:*** installment. ***Waivers:*** employees or children of employees.

APPLYING
Options: electronic application, deferred entrance.

Application fee: $50.

Required: high school transcript. ***Recommended:*** interview.

Application deadlines: rolling (freshmen), rolling (out-of-state freshmen), rolling (transfers).

Notification: continuous (freshmen), continuous (out-of-state freshmen), continuous (transfers).

CONTACT
Lynn Ovimeleh, Director of High School Admissions, Berkeley College–White Plains Campus, 99 Church Street, White Plains, NY 10601. *Phone:* 914-694-1122. *Toll-free phone:* 800-446-5400.
E-mail: info@berkeleycollege.edu.

Beth HaMedrash Shaarei Yosher Institute
Brooklyn, New York

CONTACT
Director of Admissions, Beth HaMedrash Shaarei Yosher Institute, 4102-10 Sixteenth Avenue, Brooklyn, NY 11204. *Phone:* 718-854-2290.

Beth Hatalmud Rabbinical College
Brooklyn, New York

CONTACT
Rabbi Osina, Director of Admissions, Beth Hatalmud Rabbinical College, 2127 Eighty-second Street, Brooklyn, NY 11214. *Phone:* 718-259-2525.

Binghamton University, State University of New York
Binghamton, New York
http://www.binghamton.edu/

- **State-supported** university, founded 1946, part of State University of New York System
- **Suburban** 930-acre campus
- **Endowment** $93.4 million
- **Coed** 13,632 undergraduate students, 97% full-time, 49% women, 51% men
- **Very difficult** entrance level, 41% of applicants were admitted

UNDERGRAD STUDENTS
13,185 full-time, 447 part-time. Students come from 48 states and territories; 103 other countries; 8% are from out of state; 5% Black or African American, non-Hispanic/Latino; 11% Hispanic/Latino; 14% Asian, non-Hispanic/Latino; 0.1% Native Hawaiian or other Pacific Islander, non-Hispanic/Latino; 0.1% American Indian or Alaska Native, non-Hispanic/Latino; 2% Two or more races, non-Hispanic/Latino; 2% Race/ethnicity unknown; 9% international; 8% transferred in; 52% live on campus.

Freshmen:
Admission: 32,139 applied, 13,056 admitted, 2,708 enrolled. ***Average high school GPA:*** 3.7. ***Test scores:*** SAT critical reading scores over 500: 96%; SAT math scores over 500: 99%; SAT writing scores over 500: 97%; ACT scores over 18: 100%; SAT critical reading scores over 600: 79%; SAT math scores over 600: 87%; SAT writing scores over 600: 80%; ACT scores over 24: 97%; SAT critical reading scores over 700: 21%; SAT math scores over 700: 30%; SAT writing scores over 700: 22%; ACT scores over 30: 47%.
Retention: 92% of full-time freshmen returned.

FACULTY
Total: 1,020, 71% full-time, 80% with terminal degrees.
Student/faculty ratio: 19:1.

ACADEMICS
Calendar: semesters. *Degrees:* bachelor's, master's, doctoral, and post-master's certificates.

Special study options: accelerated degree program, adult/continuing education programs, advanced placement credit, distance learning, double majors, English as a second language, honors programs, independent study, internships, off-campus study, part-time degree program, services for LD students, student-designed majors, study abroad, summer session for credit. ***ROTC:*** Army (c), Air Force (c).

Unusual degree programs: 3-2 business administration; engineering; anthropology; art history; Asian/AsianAmerican studies; biology; chemistry; computer science; economics; education; French; geography; geology; Italian; math; material science; philosophy, politics & law; physics; political science; public administration; sociology; Spanish; systems science; theatre.

Computers: 1,190 computers/terminals and 30,000 ports are available on campus for general student use. Students can access the following: campus intranet, computer help desk, free student e-mail accounts, online (class) registration, online (class) schedules, course management system, personal Web space, wiki, virtual desktop. Campuswide network is available. 100% of college-owned or -operated housing units are wired for high-speed Internet access. Wireless service is available via entire campus.

Library: Glenn G. Bartle Library plus 4 others. *Books:* 2.3 million (physical), 1.1 million (digital/electronic); *Serial titles:* 683 (physical), 125,064 (digital/electronic); *Databases:* 358. Weekly public service hours: 136; study areas open 24 hours, 5-7 days a week; students can reserve study rooms.

STUDENT LIFE
Housing options: on-campus residence required for freshman year; coed, special housing for students with disabilities. Campus housing is university owned. Freshman campus housing is guaranteed.

Activities and organizations: drama/theater group, student-run newspaper, radio and television station, choral group, Finance Society, Student Volunteer Center, Habitat for Humanity, Pre-Medical Association, Sno-Cats Ski and Snowboard Club, national fraternities, national sororities.

Athletics Member NCAA. All Division I. ***Intercollegiate sports:*** baseball M(s), basketball M(s)/W(s), cross-country running M(s)/W(s), golf M(s), lacrosse M(s)/W(s), soccer M(s)/W(s), softball W(s), swimming and diving M(s)/W(s), tennis M(s)/W(s), track and field M(s)/W(s), volleyball W(s), wrestling M(s). ***Intramural sports:*** badminton M(c)/W(c), baseball M(c), basketball M/W, bowling M/W, cheerleading M/W, crew M(c)/W(c), cross-country running M(c)/W(c), equestrian sports M(c)/W(c), fencing M(c)/W(c), field hockey M(c)/W(c), golf M(c)/W(c), gymnastics M(c)/W(c), ice hockey M(c)/W(c), lacrosse M(c)/W(c), racquetball M/W, rugby M(c)/W(c), skiing (downhill) M(c)/W(c), soccer M/W, softball M/W, swimming and diving M(c)/W(c), table tennis

M(c)/W(c), tennis M/W, ultimate Frisbee M(c)/W(c), volleyball M/W, water polo M(c)/W(c).

Campus security: 24-hour emergency response devices and patrols, student patrols, late-night transport/escort service, controlled dormitory access, only main gate open to traffic 12-5 am, emergency text system,self-defense workshops.

Student services: health clinic, personal/psychological counseling, women's center, legal services.

COSTS & FINANCIAL AID

Costs (2016–17) ***Tuition:*** state resident $6470 full-time, $270 per credit hour part-time; nonresident $21,550 full-time, $898 per credit hour part-time. Full-time tuition and fees vary according to program. Part-time tuition and fees vary according to course load and program. ***Required fees:*** $2801 full-time, $114 per credit hour part-time, $30 per term part-time. ***Room and board:*** $13,590; room only: $8804. Room and board charges vary according to board plan and housing facility. ***Payment plan:*** installment.

Financial Aid Of all full-time matriculated undergraduates who enrolled in 2016, 8,696 applied for aid, 6,271 were judged to have need, 950 had their need fully met. 296 Federal Work-Study jobs (averaging $1444). In 2016, 423 non-need-based awards were made. ***Average percent of need met:*** 72. ***Average financial aid package:*** $12,986. ***Average need-based loan:*** $5010. ***Average need-based gift aid:*** $8667. ***Average non-need-based aid:*** $7250. ***Average indebtedness upon graduation:*** $25,718.

APPLYING

Standardized Tests *Required:* SAT or ACT (for admission).

Options: electronic application, early admission, early action, deferred entrance.

Application fee: $50.

Required: essay or personal statement, high school transcript, 1 letter of recommendation. ***Required for some:*** portfolio, audition.

Application deadlines: rolling (freshmen), rolling (transfers), 11/1 (early action).

Notification: 4/1 (freshmen), continuous (transfers), 1/15 (early action).

CONTACT

Randall Edouard, Assistant Vice Provost and Director of Admissions and Enrollment, Binghamton University, State University of New York, PO Box 6001, Binghamton, NY 13902-6001. *Phone:* 607-777-2171. *Fax:* 607-777-4445. *E-mail:* admit@binghamton.edu.

Boricua College

New York, New York

http://www.boricuacollege.edu/

CONTACT

Mrs. Miriam Pfeffer, Director of Student Services, Boricua College, 186 North 6th Street, Brooklyn, NY 11211. *Phone:* 718-782-2200. *Fax:* 718-782-2025. *E-mail:* mpfeffer@boricuacollege.edu.

★ Brooklyn College of the City University of New York

Brooklyn, New York

http://www.brooklyn.cuny.edu/

- **State and locally supported** comprehensive, founded 1930, part of City University of New York System
- **Urban** 35-acre campus with easy access to Manhattan
- **Coed** 14,406 undergraduate students, 71% full-time, 59% women, 41% men
- **Moderately difficult** entrance level, 37% of applicants were admitted

UNDERGRAD STUDENTS

10,198 full-time, 4,208 part-time. Students come from 30 states and territories; 143 other countries; 2% are from out of state; 21% Black or African American, non-Hispanic/Latino; 23% Hispanic/Latino; 19% Asian, non-Hispanic/Latino; 0.2% Native Hawaiian or other Pacific Islander, non-Hispanic/Latino; 0.2% American Indian or Alaska Native, non-Hispanic/Latino; 2% Two or more races, non-Hispanic/Latino; 3% international; 15% transferred in.

Freshmen:

Admission: 20,608 applied, 7,726 admitted, 1,330 enrolled. ***Average high school GPA:*** 3.31. ***Test scores:*** SAT critical reading scores over 500: 63%; SAT math scores over 500: 76%; SAT critical reading scores over 600: 19%; SAT math scores over 600: 31%; SAT critical reading scores over 700: 5%; SAT math scores over 700: 6%.

Retention: 82% of full-time freshmen returned.

FACULTY

Total: 1,286, 42% full-time, 63% with terminal degrees.

Student/faculty ratio: 17:1.

ACADEMICS

Calendar: semesters. *Degrees:* certificates, bachelor's, master's, post-master's, and postbachelor's certificates.

Special study options: adult/continuing education programs, advanced placement credit, distance learning, double majors, English as a second language, freshman honors college, honors programs, independent study, internships, off-campus study, part-time degree program, services for LD students, study abroad, summer session for credit.

Computers: 1,000 computers/terminals are available on campus for general student use. Students can access the following: computer help desk, free student e-mail accounts, online (class) registration, online (class) schedules. Campuswide network is available. Wireless service is available via entire campus.

Library: Brooklyn College Library plus 1 other. Students can reserve study rooms.

STUDENT LIFE

Housing options: college housing not available.

Activities and organizations: drama/theater group, student-run newspaper, radio and television station, choral group, Academic Club Association, Kingsman and Excelsior Newspaper, NY Public Interest Group (NYPIRG), Student Government CIAS, SGS, and GSO, Student Forensics, national fraternities, national sororities.

Athletics Member NCAA. All Division III. ***Intercollegiate sports:*** basketball M/W, cross-country running M/W, soccer M/W, softball W, swimming and diving M/W, tennis M/W, volleyball M/W. ***Intramural sports:*** basketball M/W, football M/W, soccer M/W, tennis M/W, volleyball M/W.

Campus security: 24-hour emergency response devices and patrols, late-night transport/escort service.

Student services: health clinic, personal/psychological counseling, women's center.

COSTS & FINANCIAL AID

Costs (2016–17) ***Tuition:*** state resident $3165 full-time, $275 per credit part-time; nonresident $6330 full-time, $560 per credit part-time. Full-time tuition and fees vary according to course load. Part-time tuition and fees vary according to course load. ***Required fees:*** $505 full-time, $139 per credit part-time. ***Room and board:*** $4210. Room and board charges vary according to housing facility. ***Payment plan:*** installment.

Financial Aid Of all full-time matriculated undergraduates who enrolled in 2015, 9,770 applied for aid, 9,156 were judged to have need, 6,501 had their need fully met. 407 Federal Work-Study jobs (averaging $2613). In 2015, 310 non-need-based awards were made. ***Average percent of need met:*** 89. ***Average financial aid package:*** $7500. ***Average need-based loan:*** $3000. ***Average need-based gift aid:*** $3400. ***Average non-need-based aid:*** $2500. ***Average indebtedness upon graduation:*** $15,235. ***Financial aid deadline:*** 5/1.

APPLYING

Standardized Tests *Required:* SAT or ACT (for admission).

Application fee: $65.

Required: high school transcript, minimum 3.1 GPA, combined SAT or ACT scores of 1000.

Application deadlines: 2/1 (freshmen), 2/1 (transfers).

Notification: continuous (freshmen), continuous (transfers).

CONTACT

Office of Admissions, Brooklyn College of the City University of New York, 2900 Bedford Avenue, West Quad Building, Room 222, Brooklyn, NY 11210-2889. *Phone:* 718-951-5001. *Fax:* 718-951-4506. *E-mail:* adminqry@brooklyn.cuny.edu.

Bryant & Stratton College–Amherst Campus

Clarence, New York

http://www.bryantstratton.edu/

CONTACT

Mr. Brian K. Dioguardi, Director of Admissions, Bryant & Stratton College–Amherst Campus, Audubon Business Center, 40 Hazelwood Drive, Amherst, NY 14228. *Phone:* 716-691-0012. *Fax:* 716-691-0012. *E-mail:* bkdioguardi@bryantstratton.edu.

Bryant & Stratton College–Buffalo Campus

Buffalo, New York

http://www.bryantstratton.edu/

CONTACT

Mr. Philip J. Struebel, Director of Admissions, Bryant & Stratton College–Buffalo Campus, 465 Main Street, Suite 400, Buffalo, NY 14203. *Phone:* 716-884-9120. *Fax:* 716-884-0091. *E-mail:* pjstruebel@bryantstratton.edu.

Bryant & Stratton College–Orchard Park Campus

Orchard Park, New York

http://www.bryantstratton.edu/

CONTACT

Bryant & Stratton College–Orchard Park Campus, 200 Redtail Road, Orchard Park, NY 14127. *Phone:* 716-677-9500.

Buffalo State College, State University of New York

Buffalo, New York

http://www.buffalostate.edu/

- **State-supported** comprehensive, founded 1867, part of State University of New York System
- **Urban** 115-acre campus
- **Endowment** $36.0 million
- **Coed** 8,482 undergraduate students, 90% full-time, 56% women, 44% men
- **Moderately difficult** entrance level, 64% of applicants were admitted

UNDERGRAD STUDENTS

7,598 full-time, 884 part-time. Students come from 29 states and territories; 79 other countries; 1% are from out of state; 31% Black or African American, non-Hispanic/Latino; 13% Hispanic/Latino; 3% Asian, non-Hispanic/Latino; 0.1% Native Hawaiian or other Pacific Islander, non-Hispanic/Latino; 0.5% American Indian or Alaska Native, non-Hispanic/Latino; 4% Two or more races, non-Hispanic/Latino; 0.1% Race/ethnicity unknown; 1% international; 10% transferred in; 32% live on campus.

Freshmen:

Admission: 13,726 applied, 8,793 admitted, 1,628 enrolled. ***Average high school GPA:*** 3.1. ***Test scores:*** SAT critical reading scores over 500: 23%; SAT math scores over 500: 23%; SAT writing scores over 500: 16%; SAT critical reading scores over 600: 3%; SAT math scores over 600: 4%; SAT writing scores over 600: 2%.

Retention: 68% of full-time freshmen returned.

FACULTY

Total: 829, 46% full-time, 51% with terminal degrees.

Student/faculty ratio: 16:1.

ACADEMICS

Calendar: semesters. *Degrees:* bachelor's, master's, and post-master's certificates.

Special study options: academic remediation for entering students, adult/continuing education programs, advanced placement credit, cooperative education, distance learning, double majors, English as a second language, freshman honors college, honors programs, independent study, internships, off-campus study, part-time degree program, services for LD students, study abroad, summer session for credit. ***ROTC:*** Army (c).

Unusual degree programs: 3-2 engineering with Binghamton University, State University of New York; Clarkson University; University at Buffalo, the State University of New York.

Computers: 1,700 computers/terminals are available on campus for general student use. Students can access the following: computer help desk, free student e-mail accounts, online (class) registration, online (class) schedules. Campuswide network is available. 100% of college-owned or -operated housing units are wired for high-speed Internet access. Wireless service is available via entire campus.

Library: E. H. Butler Library plus 1 other.

STUDENT LIFE

Housing options: on-campus residence required through sophomore year; coed. Campus housing is university owned. Freshman campus housing is guaranteed.

Activities and organizations: drama/theater group, student-run newspaper, radio station, choral group, United Student Government, African-American Student Organization, Caribbean Student Organization, The Record, WBNY radio, national fraternities, national sororities.

Athletics Member NCAA. All Division III. ***Intercollegiate sports:*** baseball M(c), basketball M/W, bowling M(c)/W(c), cheerleading W(c), cross-country running M/W, fencing M(c), football M, ice hockey M/W, lacrosse M(c)/W, rugby M(c)/W(c), skiing (cross-country) M(c)/W(c), skiing (downhill) M(c)/W(c), soccer M/W, softball W, swimming and diving M/W, tennis W, track and field M/W, volleyball M(c)/W. ***Intramural sports:*** basketball M, football M, racquetball M/W, softball M/W, volleyball M/W, water polo M(c)/W(c).

Campus security: 24-hour emergency response devices and patrols, student patrols, late-night transport/escort service, controlled dormitory access.

Student services: health clinic, personal/psychological counseling, women's center, legal services.

COSTS & FINANCIAL AID

Costs (2016–17) ***Tuition:*** state resident $6770 full-time, $270 per credit hour part-time; nonresident $16,320 full-time, $680 per credit hour part-time. Part-time tuition and fees vary according to course load. ***Required fees:*** $1199 full-time, $51 per credit hour part-time. ***Room and board:*** $12,614; room only: $7414. Room and board charges vary according to board plan, housing facility, and student level. ***Payment plan:*** installment. ***Waivers:*** employees or children of employees.

Financial Aid Of all full-time matriculated undergraduates who enrolled in 2015, 5,942 applied for aid, 5,939 were judged to have need, 2,526 had their need fully met. 251 Federal Work-Study jobs (averaging $3155). In 2015, 921 non-need-based awards were made. ***Average percent of need met:*** 48. ***Average financial aid package:*** $13,977. ***Average need-based loan:*** $4472. ***Average need-based gift aid:*** $7766. ***Average non-need-based aid:*** $2582. ***Average indebtedness upon graduation:*** $25,861.

APPLYING

Standardized Tests *Required:* SAT or ACT (for admission), SAT and SAT Subject Tests or ACT (for admission). *Recommended:* SAT (for admission).

Options: electronic application, early admission, deferred entrance.

Application fee: $50.

Required: high school transcript, minimum 3.0 GPA. ***Required for some:*** essay or personal statement, interview.

Application deadlines: rolling (freshmen), rolling (transfers).

Notification: continuous (freshmen), continuous (transfers).

CONTACT

Ms. Carmella Thompson, Director of Admissions, Buffalo State College, State University of New York, 110 Moot Hall, Buffalo, NY 14222. *Phone:* 716-878-4017. *Fax:* 716-878-6100. *E-mail:* admissions@buffalostate.edu.

Canisius College
Buffalo, New York
http://www.canisius.edu/

- **Independent Roman Catholic (Jesuit)** comprehensive, founded 1870
- **Urban** 72-acre campus
- **Endowment** $104.3 million
- **Coed** 2,595 undergraduate students, 95% full-time, 52% women, 48% men
- **Moderately difficult** entrance level, 78% of applicants were admitted

UNDERGRAD STUDENTS
2,474 full-time, 121 part-time. Students come from 36 states and territories; 19 other countries; 10% are from out of state; 8% Black or African American, non-Hispanic/Latino; 7% Hispanic/Latino; 2% Asian, non-Hispanic/Latino; 0.2% Native Hawaiian or other Pacific Islander, non-Hispanic/Latino; 0.3% American Indian or Alaska Native, non-Hispanic/Latino; 2% Two or more races, non-Hispanic/Latino; 4% Race/ethnicity unknown; 4% international; 5% transferred in; 46% live on campus.

Freshmen:
Admission: 4,620 applied, 3,597 admitted, 600 enrolled. ***Average high school GPA:*** 3.6. ***Test scores:*** SAT critical reading scores over 500: 67%; SAT math scores over 500: 73%; ACT scores over 18: 98%; SAT critical reading scores over 600: 22%; SAT math scores over 600: 28%; ACT scores over 24: 61%; SAT critical reading scores over 700: 2%; SAT math scores over 700: 4%; ACT scores over 30: 11%.

Retention: 83% of full-time freshmen returned.

FACULTY
Total: 405, 45% full-time, 61% with terminal degrees.

Student/faculty ratio: 11:1.

ACADEMICS
Calendar: semesters. *Degrees:* associate, bachelor's, master's, post-master's, and postbachelor's certificates.

Special study options: academic remediation for entering students, adult/continuing education programs, advanced placement credit, cooperative education, distance learning, double majors, English as a second language, honors programs, independent study, internships, off-campus study, part-time degree program, services for LD students, study abroad, summer session for credit. ***ROTC:*** Army (b).

Unusual degree programs: 3-2 business administration; engineering with University at Buffalo, the State University of New York.

Computers: 700 computers/terminals are available on campus for general student use. Students can access the following: computer help desk, free student e-mail accounts, online (class) grades, online (class) registration, online (class) schedules, online accounts. Campuswide network is available. 100% of college-owned or -operated housing units are wired for high-speed Internet access. Wireless service is available via entire campus.

Library: Andrew L. Bouwhuis Library plus 1 other. *Books:* 300,786 (physical), 96,476 (digital/electronic); *Serial titles:* 1,140 (physical), 66,335 (digital/electronic); *Databases:* 110. Weekly public service hours: 110; students can reserve study rooms.

STUDENT LIFE
Housing options: on-campus residence required through sophomore year; coed, special housing for students with disabilities. Campus housing is university owned. Freshman applicants given priority for college housing.

Activities and organizations: drama/theater group, student-run newspaper, radio and television station, choral group, Campus Programming Board, Undergraduate Student Association, Afro-American Society, Residence Hall Association, Student Association, national fraternities, national sororities.

Athletics Member NCAA. All Division I. ***Intercollegiate sports:*** baseball M(s), basketball M(s)/W(s), cross-country running M(s)/W(s), equestrian sports W(c), golf M(s), ice hockey M(s), lacrosse M(s)/W(s), rugby M(c)/W(c), soccer M(s)/W(s), softball W(s), swimming and diving M(s)/W(s), volleyball M(c)/W(s). ***Intramural sports:*** basketball M/W, bowling M(c)/W(c), cheerleading M(c)/W(c), crew M(c)/W(c), fencing M(c)/W(c), field hockey W(c), ice hockey M(c)/W(c), lacrosse M(c), racquetball M/W, riflery M(c)/W(c), skiing (downhill) M(c)/W(c), soccer M/W, softball M/W, tennis M/W, track and field M(c)/W(c), ultimate Frisbee M(c)/W(c), volleyball M/W, wrestling M(c).

Campus security: 24-hour emergency response devices and patrols, late-night transport/escort service, controlled dormitory access, crime prevention programs, closed-circuit television monitors, emergency call boxes across campus.

Student services: health clinic, personal/psychological counseling.

COSTS & FINANCIAL AID
Costs (2017–18) ***Comprehensive fee:*** $49,672 includes full-time tuition ($34,966), mandatory fees ($1488), and room and board ($13,218). Part-time tuition: $999 per credit hour. ***College room only:*** $7764. Room and board charges vary according to board plan and housing facility. ***Payment plans:*** installment, deferred payment. ***Waivers:*** employees or children of employees.

Financial Aid Of all full-time matriculated undergraduates who enrolled in 2016, 2,072 applied for aid, 1,894 were judged to have need, 440 had their need fully met. 379 Federal Work-Study jobs (averaging $1793). In 2016, 495 non-need-based awards were made. ***Average percent of need met:*** 80. ***Average financial aid package:*** $30,597. ***Average need-based loan:*** $4789. ***Average need-based gift aid:*** $23,879. ***Average non-need-based aid:*** $17,387. ***Average indebtedness upon graduation:*** $33,973.

APPLYING
Standardized Tests *Required:* SAT or ACT (for admission).

Options: electronic application, early admission, deferred entrance.

Application fee: $40.

Required: high school transcript, minimum 2.0 GPA. ***Required for some:*** interview. ***Recommended:*** essay or personal statement, 1 letter of recommendation, interview.

Application deadlines: 5/1 (freshmen), rolling (transfers).

Notification: continuous (freshmen), continuous (transfers).

CONTACT
Mr. Justin P. Rogers, Director of Admissions, Canisius College, 2001 Main Street, Buffalo, NY 14208-1098. *Phone:* 716-888-2200. *Toll-free phone:* 800-843-1517. *Fax:* 716-888-3230. *E-mail:* admissions@canisius.edu.

Cazenovia College
Cazenovia, New York
http://www.cazenovia.edu/

- **Independent** 4-year, founded 1824
- **Small-town** 40-acre campus with easy access to Syracuse
- **Coed** 1,042 undergraduate students, 82% full-time, 72% women, 28% men
- **Minimally difficult** entrance level, 90% of applicants were admitted

UNDERGRAD STUDENTS
858 full-time, 184 part-time. Students come from 27 states and territories; 4 other countries; 12% are from out of state; 8% Black or African American, non-Hispanic/Latino; 6% Hispanic/Latino; 0.7% Asian, non-Hispanic/Latino; 0.7% American Indian or Alaska Native, non-Hispanic/Latino; 2% Two or more races, non-Hispanic/Latino; 15% Race/ethnicity unknown; 0.6% international; 3% transferred in; 81% live on campus.

Freshmen:
Admission: 1,730 applied, 1,555 admitted, 209 enrolled. ***Average high school GPA:*** 3.3.

Retention: 73% of full-time freshmen returned.

FACULTY
Total: 132, 43% full-time.

Student/faculty ratio: 12:1.

ACADEMICS
Calendar: semesters. *Degrees:* certificates, associate, and bachelor's.

Special study options: academic remediation for entering students, accelerated degree program, adult/continuing education programs, advanced placement credit, distance learning, double majors, freshman honors college, honors programs, independent study, internships, off-campus study, part-time degree program, services for LD students, study abroad, summer session for credit. ***ROTC:*** Army (c), Air Force (c).

Computers: Students can access the following: campus intranet, computer help desk, free student e-mail accounts, online (class) grades, online (class) schedules. Campuswide network is available. 100% of college-owned or -operated housing units are wired for high-speed Internet access. Wireless service is available via classrooms, computer centers, computer labs, dorm rooms, learning centers, libraries, student centers.

Library: Witheral Library. Students can reserve study rooms.

STUDENT LIFE

Housing options: on-campus residence required through junior year; coed, men-only, women-only, special housing for students with disabilities. Campus housing is university owned and leased by the school. Freshman campus housing is guaranteed.

Activities and organizations: drama/theater group, student-run newspaper, radio station, choral group, Activities Board, Multicultural Student Group, performing arts, student radio station, yearbook.

Athletics Member NCAA. All Division III. ***Intercollegiate sports:*** baseball M, basketball M/W, cross-country running M/W, equestrian sports M/W, lacrosse M/W, soccer M/W, softball W, swimming and diving M/W, volleyball W. ***Intramural sports:*** baseball M, basketball M/W, bowling M/W, cheerleading M(c)/W(c), crew M(c)/W(c), equestrian sports M/W, field hockey W(c), football M/W, skiing (downhill) M/W, soccer M/W, softball M/W, tennis M(c)/W(c), ultimate Frisbee M/W, volleyball M/W, weight lifting M/W.

Campus security: 24-hour emergency response devices and patrols, late-night transport/escort service, controlled dormitory access.

Student services: health clinic, personal/psychological counseling.

COSTS & FINANCIAL AID

Costs (2017–18) ***Comprehensive fee:*** $47,866 includes full-time tuition ($33,068), mandatory fees ($588), and room and board ($14,210). Full-time tuition and fees vary according to class time, course load, and program. Part-time tuition: $700 per credit hour. Part-time tuition and fees vary according to class time and course load. ***College room only:*** $7620. Room and board charges vary according to board plan and housing facility. ***Payment plan:*** installment. ***Waivers:*** employees or children of employees.

Financial Aid Of all full-time matriculated undergraduates who enrolled in 2015, 899 applied for aid, 858 were judged to have need, 157 had their need fully met. In 2015, 80 non-need-based awards were made. ***Average percent of need met:*** 80. ***Average financial aid package:*** $31,152. ***Average need-based loan:*** $4119. ***Average need-based gift aid:*** $27,096. ***Average non-need-based aid:*** $18,424. ***Average indebtedness upon graduation:*** $33,631.

APPLYING

Standardized Tests *Recommended:* SAT or ACT (for admission).

Options: electronic application, deferred entrance.

Required: high school transcript, 1 letter of recommendation. ***Recommended:*** essay or personal statement, minimum 2.0 GPA, interview, portfolio for art and design students.

Application deadlines: rolling (freshmen), rolling (transfers).

CONTACT

Office of Admission and Enrollment Services, Cazenovia College, 3 Sullivan Street, Cazenovia, NY 13035. *Phone:* 315-655-7208. *Toll-free phone:* 800-654-3210. *Fax:* 315-655-4860. *E-mail:* admission@cazenovia.edu.

Central Yeshiva Tomchei Tmimim-Lubavitch

Brooklyn, New York

CONTACT

Director of Admissions, Central Yeshiva Tomchei Tmimim-Lubavitch, 841-853 Ocean Parkway, Brooklyn, NY 11230. *Phone:* 718-859-7600.

City College of the City University of New York

New York, New York

http://www.ccny.cuny.edu/

- **State and locally supported** comprehensive, founded 1847, part of City University of New York System
- **Urban** 35-acre campus with easy access to New York City
- **Coed** 13,508 undergraduate students
- **Moderately difficult** entrance level, 40% of applicants were admitted

UNDERGRAD STUDENTS

Students come from 140 other countries; 4% are from out of state; 16% Black or African American, non-Hispanic/Latino; 37% Hispanic/Latino; 25% Asian, non-Hispanic/Latino; 0.3% Native Hawaiian or other Pacific Islander, non-Hispanic/Latino; 0.2% American Indian or Alaska Native, non-Hispanic/Latino; 2% Two or more races, non-Hispanic/Latino; 6% international; 1% live on campus.

Freshmen:

Admission: 24,735 applied, 9,794 admitted. ***Average high school GPA:*** 3.37. ***Test scores:*** SAT critical reading scores over 500: 57%; SAT math scores over 500: 83%; SAT critical reading scores over 600: 22%; SAT math scores over 600: 40%; SAT critical reading scores over 700: 7%; SAT math scores over 700: 11%.

Retention: 92% of full-time freshmen returned.

FACULTY

Total: 1,399, 37% full-time, 37% with terminal degrees.

Student/faculty ratio: 15:1.

ACADEMICS

Calendar: semesters. *Degrees:* bachelor's, master's, doctoral, and post-master's certificates.

Special study options: accelerated degree program, adult/continuing education programs, advanced placement credit, English as a second language, freshman honors college, honors programs, independent study, internships, off-campus study, part-time degree program, services for LD students, student-designed majors, study abroad, summer session for credit. ***ROTC:*** Army (b).

Computers: 3,000 computers/terminals are available on campus for general student use. Students can access the following: campus intranet, computer help desk, free student e-mail accounts, online (class) grades, online (class) registration, online (class) schedules. Campuswide network is available. 100% of college-owned or -operated housing units are wired for high-speed Internet access. Wireless service is available via entire campus.

Library: Morris Raphael Cohen Library plus 8 others.

STUDENT LIFE

Housing options: coed. Campus housing is provided by a third party.

Activities and organizations: drama/theater group, student-run newspaper, radio station, choral group, Latin American Engineering Student Assoc./Society of Hispanic Professional Engineers, National Society of Black Engineers, Bangladesh Student Association, Salsa-Mambo, InterVarsity Christian Fellowship, national fraternities.

Athletics Member NCAA. All Division III. ***Intercollegiate sports:*** baseball M, basketball M/W, cross-country running M/W, fencing W, lacrosse M, soccer M/W, softball W, tennis M/W, track and field M/W, volleyball W. ***Intramural sports:*** basketball M/W, fencing W, soccer M, softball W, tennis M/W, track and field M/W, volleyball W.

Campus security: 24-hour patrols, late-night transport/escort service, controlled dormitory access.

Student services: health clinic, personal/psychological counseling.

COSTS & FINANCIAL AID

Costs (2016–17) ***Tuition:*** state resident $6330 full-time; nonresident $16,800 full-time. Full-time tuition and fees vary according to course load and program. Part-time tuition and fees vary according to course load and program. ***Required fees:*** $410 full-time. ***Room and board:*** Room and board charges vary according to housing facility. ***Payment plan:*** deferred payment. ***Waivers:*** senior citizens.

Financial Aid Of all full-time matriculated undergraduates who enrolled in 2016, 8,263 applied for aid, 7,958 were judged to have need, 6,915 had their need fully met. In 2016, 780 non-need-based awards were made. ***Average percent of need met:*** 84. ***Average financial aid package:*** $9597. ***Average need-based loan:*** $4347. ***Average need-based gift aid:*** $8552. ***Average non-need-based aid:*** $4413. ***Average indebtedness upon graduation:*** $16,942.

APPLYING

Standardized Tests *Required:* SAT or ACT (for admission).

Options: early admission, deferred entrance.

Application fee: $65.

Required: high school transcript. ***Required for some:*** essay or personal statement, letters of recommendation, creative challenge for architecture, supplemental application for engineering.

Application deadlines: 2/1 (freshmen), 2/1 (transfers).

Notification: continuous until 2/1 (freshmen), continuous until 3/1 (transfers).

CONTACT

City College of the City University of New York, 160 Convent Avenue, New York, NY 10031-9198. *Phone:* 212-650-6977.

Clarkson University

Potsdam, New York

http://www.clarkson.edu/

- **Independent** university, founded 1896
- **Small-town** 640-acre campus
- **Endowment** $177.1 million
- **Coed** 3,268 undergraduate students, 98% full-time, 30% women, 70% men
- **Very difficult** entrance level, 68% of applicants were admitted

UNDERGRAD STUDENTS

3,203 full-time, 65 part-time. Students come from 43 states and territories; 31 other countries; 27% are from out of state; 2% Black or African American, non-Hispanic/Latino; 5% Hispanic/Latino; 3% Asian, non-Hispanic/Latino; 0.3% American Indian or Alaska Native, non-Hispanic/Latino; 3% Two or more races, non-Hispanic/Latino; 2% Race/ethnicity unknown; 2% international; 3% transferred in; 82% live on campus.

Freshmen:

Admission: 7,066 applied, 4,820 admitted, 797 enrolled. ***Average high school GPA:*** 3.6. ***Test scores:*** SAT critical reading scores over 500: 83%; SAT math scores over 500: 94%; SAT writing scores over 500: 70%; ACT scores over 18: 100%; SAT critical reading scores over 600: 38%; SAT math scores over 600: 60%; SAT writing scores over 600: 23%; ACT scores over 24: 82%; SAT critical reading scores over 700: 5%; SAT math scores over 700: 13%; SAT writing scores over 700: 3%; ACT scores over 30: 24%.

Retention: 89% of full-time freshmen returned.

FACULTY

Total: 363, 69% full-time, 78% with terminal degrees.

Student/faculty ratio: 14:1.

ACADEMICS

Calendar: semesters. *Degrees:* bachelor's, master's, doctoral, and postbachelor's certificates.

Special study options: accelerated degree program, advanced placement credit, cooperative education, distance learning, double majors, English as a second language, honors programs, independent study, internships, off-campus study, part-time degree program, services for LD students, student-designed majors, study abroad, summer session for credit. ***ROTC:*** Army (b), Air Force (b).

Unusual degree programs: 3-2 engineering.

Computers: 350 computers/terminals and 6,000 ports are available on campus for general student use. Students can access the following: campus intranet, computer help desk, free student e-mail accounts, online (class) grades, online (class) registration, online (class) schedules. Campuswide network is available. 100% of college-owned or -operated housing units are wired for high-speed Internet access. Wireless service is available via entire campus.

Library: Harriet Call Burnap Memorial Library plus 1 other. *Books:* 111,436 (physical), 188,698 (digital/electronic); *Serial titles:* 1,975 (physical), 54,563 (digital/electronic); *Databases:* 76. Weekly public service hours: 97; students can reserve study rooms.

STUDENT LIFE

Housing options: on-campus residence required through senior year; coed, men-only, women-only, special housing for students with disabilities. Campus housing is university owned. Freshman campus housing is guaranteed.

Activities and organizations: drama/theater group, student-run newspaper, radio and television station, choral group, Outing Club, Ski Club, Society of Women Engineers, Pep Band, E&M Society, national fraternities, national sororities.

Athletics Member NCAA. All Division III except men's and women's ice hockey (Division I). ***Intercollegiate sports:*** baseball M, basketball M/W, cross-country running M/W, golf M, ice hockey M(s)/W(s), lacrosse M/W, skiing (cross-country) M/W, skiing (downhill) M/W, soccer M/W, softball W, swimming and diving M/W, volleyball W. ***Intramural sports:*** baseball M(c), basketball M/W, bowling M(c)/W(c), crew M(c)/W(c), football M/W, golf M(c), ice hockey M/W, lacrosse M(c)/W(c), racquetball M(c)/W(c), rowing M(c)/W(c), rugby M(c)/W(c), skiing (cross-country) M(c)/W(c), skiing (downhill) M(c)/W(c), soccer M/W, softball M/W, tennis M(c)/W(c), ultimate Frisbee M(c)/W(c), volleyball M/W, wrestling M(c).

Campus security: 24-hour emergency response devices and patrols, controlled dormitory access.

Student services: health clinic, personal/psychological counseling, legal services.

COSTS & FINANCIAL AID

Costs (2016–17) ***Comprehensive fee:*** $60,392 includes full-time tuition ($45,132), mandatory fees ($1000), and room and board ($14,260). Full-time tuition and fees vary according to course load. Part-time tuition: $1505 per credit hour. Part-time tuition and fees vary according to course load. ***College room only:*** $7554. Room and board charges vary according to board plan and housing facility. ***Payment plan:*** installment. ***Waivers:*** employees or children of employees.

Financial Aid Of all full-time matriculated undergraduates who enrolled in 2016, 2,769 applied for aid, 2,535 were judged to have need, 527 had their need fully met. 1,616 Federal Work-Study jobs (averaging $1600). 65 state and other part-time jobs (averaging $10,907). In 2016, 558 non-need-based awards were made. ***Average percent of need met:*** 90. ***Average financial aid package:*** $41,810. ***Average need-based loan:*** $5193. ***Average need-based gift aid:*** $30,647. ***Average non-need-based aid:*** $22,172. ***Average indebtedness upon graduation:*** $23,500. ***Financial aid deadline:*** 3/1.

APPLYING

Standardized Tests *Required:* SAT or ACT (for admission). *Recommended:* SAT Subject Tests (for admission).

Options: electronic application, early admission, early decision, deferred entrance.

Application fee: $50.

Required: essay or personal statement, high school transcript, 2 letters of recommendation. ***Recommended:*** interview.

Early decision deadline: 12/1.

Notification: continuous (freshmen), continuous (transfers), 1/1 (early decision).

CONTACT

Mr. Brian T. Grant, Vice President for Enrollment and Student Advancement, Clarkson University, 8 Clarkson Avenue, Box 5605, CU Box 5605, Potsdam, NY 13699. *Phone:* 315-268-6480. *Toll-free phone:* 800-527-6577. *Fax:* 315-268-7647. *E-mail:* admission@clarkson.edu.

Colgate University

Hamilton, New York

http://www.colgate.edu/

- **Independent** comprehensive, founded 1819
- **Rural** 575-acre campus with easy access to Syracuse, Utica
- **Endowment** $883.8 million
- **Coed** 2,853 undergraduate students, 99% full-time, 55% women, 45% men
- **Most difficult** entrance level, 27% of applicants were admitted

UNDERGRAD STUDENTS

2,834 full-time, 19 part-time. Students come from 48 states and territories; 72 other countries; 73% are from out of state; 4% Black or African American, non-Hispanic/Latino; 9% Hispanic/Latino; 4% Asian, non-Hispanic/Latino; 0.1% American Indian or Alaska Native, non-Hispanic/Latino; 3% Two or more races, non-Hispanic/Latino; 4% Race/ethnicity unknown; 9% international; 0.5% transferred in; 96% live on campus.

Freshmen:

Admission: 8,724 applied, 2,387 admitted, 773 enrolled. ***Average high school GPA:*** 3.69. ***Test scores:*** SAT critical reading scores over 500: 98%; SAT math scores over 500: 100%; ACT scores over 18: 100%; SAT critical reading scores over 600: 81%; SAT math scores over 600: 90%; ACT scores over 24: 98%; SAT critical reading scores over 700: 34%; SAT math scores over 700: 39%; ACT scores over 30: 75%.

Retention: 95% of full-time freshmen returned.

FACULTY

Total: 352, 84% full-time, 93% with terminal degrees.

Student/faculty ratio: 9:1.

ACADEMICS

Calendar: semesters. *Degrees:* bachelor's and master's.

Special study options: advanced placement credit, double majors, honors programs, independent study, internships, off-campus study, services for LD students, student-designed majors, study abroad. ***ROTC:*** Army (c).

Unusual degree programs: 3-2 engineering with Columbia University, Rensselaer Polytechnic Institute, Washington University in St. Louis.

Computers: 300 computers/terminals and 25,000 ports are available on campus for general student use. Students can access the following: campus intranet, computer help desk, free student e-mail accounts, online (class) registration, online (class) schedules, software applications. Campuswide network is available. 100% of college-owned or -operated housing units are wired for high-speed Internet access. Wireless service is available via entire campus.

Library: Case Library and Geyer Center for Information Technology plus 1 other. *Books:* 813,245 (physical), 569,245 (digital/electronic); *Serial titles:* 5,948 (digital/electronic); *Databases:* 479. Students can reserve study rooms.

STUDENT LIFE

Housing options: on-campus residence required through junior year; coed, cooperative, special housing for students with disabilities. Campus housing is university owned. Freshman campus housing is guaranteed.

Activities and organizations: drama/theater group, student-run newspaper, radio and television station, choral group, COVE (40+ community service groups), Student Government Association, cultural/ethnic interest groups, Student communications/publications (including WCRU radio station), Club sports/Outdoor Education, national fraternities, national sororities.

Athletics Member NCAA. All Division I except football (Division I-AA). ***Intercollegiate sports:*** badminton M(c)/W(c), baseball M(c), basketball M(s)/W(s), cheerleading M(c)/W(c), crew M/W, cross-country running M/W, equestrian sports M(c)/W(c), fencing M(c)/W(c), field hockey W(s), golf M/W(c), ice hockey M(s)/W(s), lacrosse M(s)/W(s), rugby M(c)/W(c), sailing M(c)/W(c), skiing (downhill) M(c)/W(c), soccer M(s)/W(s), softball W(s), squash M(c)/W(c), swimming and diving M/W, table tennis M(c)/W(c), tennis M/W, track and field M/W, volleyball M(c)/W(s), water polo M(c)/W(c). ***Intramural sports:*** basketball M/W, bowling M/W, cross-country running M(c)/W(c), football M/W, golf M(c)/W(c), ice hockey M/W, lacrosse M(c)/W(c), racquetball M/W, riflery M/W, rock climbing M/W, skiing (cross-country) M/W, soccer M/W, softball M/W, squash M/W, tennis M/W, triathlon M/W, ultimate Frisbee M/W, volleyball M/W.

Campus security: 24-hour emergency response devices and patrols, student patrols, late-night transport/escort service, controlled dormitory access.

Student services: health clinic, personal/psychological counseling, women's center, legal services.

COSTS & FINANCIAL AID

Costs (2016–17) ***One-time required fee:*** $50. ***Comprehensive fee:*** $65,030 includes full-time tuition ($51,635), mandatory fees ($320), and room and board ($13,075). Full-time tuition and fees vary according to course load. Part-time tuition and fees vary according to course load. ***College room only:*** $6310. Room and board charges vary according to board plan and housing facility. ***Payment plans:*** tuition prepayment, installment, deferred payment. ***Waivers:*** employees or children of employees.

Financial Aid Of all full-time matriculated undergraduates who enrolled in 2016, 1,134 applied for aid, 1,054 were judged to have need, 1,052 had their need fully met. 572 Federal Work-Study jobs (averaging $2272). 295 state and other part-time jobs (averaging $2091). ***Average percent of need met:*** 100. ***Average financial aid package:*** $49,912. ***Average need-based loan:*** $3660. ***Average need-based gift aid:*** $45,724. ***Average indebtedness upon graduation:*** $21,427. ***Financial aid deadline:*** 1/15.

APPLYING

Standardized Tests *Required:* SAT or ACT (for admission).

Options: electronic application, early decision, deferred entrance.

Application fee: $60.

Required: essay or personal statement, high school transcript, 3 letters of recommendation, Colgate supplement.

Application deadlines: 1/15 (freshmen), 3/15 (transfers).

Early decision deadline: 11/15 (for plan 1), 1/15 (for plan 2).

Notification: 4/1 (freshmen), 4/1 (out-of-state freshmen), 5/1 (transfers), 12/15 (early decision plan 1), rolling (early decision plan 2).

CONTACT

Mr. Gary L. Ross, Vice President and Dean of Admission and Financial Aid, Colgate University, Colgate Office of Admission, 13 Oak Drive, Hamilton, NY 13346-1383. *Phone:* 315-228-7401. *Fax:* 315-228-7544. *E-mail:* admission@colgate.edu.

The College at Brockport, State University of New York

Brockport, New York

http://www.brockport.edu/

- **State-supported** comprehensive, founded 1867, part of State University of New York System
- **Small-town** 464-acre campus with easy access to Rochester
- **Endowment** $9.6 million
- **Coed** 7,128 undergraduate students, 89% full-time, 56% women, 44% men
- **Moderately difficult** entrance level, 55% of applicants were admitted

UNDERGRAD STUDENTS

6,375 full-time, 753 part-time. Students come from 31 states and territories; 15 other countries; 2% are from out of state; 11% Black or African American, non-Hispanic/Latino; 7% Hispanic/Latino; 2% Asian, non-Hispanic/Latino; 0.2% American Indian or Alaska Native, non-Hispanic/Latino; 2% Two or more races, non-Hispanic/Latino; 6% Race/ethnicity unknown; 1% international; 13% transferred in; 27% live on campus.

Freshmen:

Admission: 9,211 applied, 5,096 admitted, 1,205 enrolled. ***Average high school GPA:*** 2.93. ***Test scores:*** SAT critical reading scores over 500: 51%; SAT math scores over 500: 62%; ACT scores over 18: 93%; SAT critical reading scores over 600: 12%; SAT math scores over 600: 16%; ACT scores over 24: 43%; SAT critical reading scores over 700: 2%; SAT math scores over 700: 1%; ACT scores over 30: 5%.

Retention: 82% of full-time freshmen returned.

FACULTY
Total: 633, 55% full-time, 48% with terminal degrees.

Student/faculty ratio: 17:1.

ACADEMICS
Calendar: semesters. *Degrees:* bachelor's, master's, post-master's, and postbachelor's certificates.

Special study options: accelerated degree program, advanced placement credit, cooperative education, distance learning, double majors, English as a second language, freshman honors college, honors programs, independent study, internships, off-campus study, part-time degree program, services for LD students, student-designed majors, study abroad, summer session for credit. ***ROTC:*** Army (b), Navy (c), Air Force (c).

Unusual degree programs: 3-2 biology, environmental science, environmental science and biology, pharmacy, history, mathematics, political science, sociology/public administration, psychology.

Computers: 1,000 computers/terminals are available on campus for general student use. Students can access the following: campus intranet, computer help desk, free student e-mail accounts, online (class) grades, online (class) registration, online (class) schedules. Campuswide network is available. 100% of college-owned or -operated housing units are wired for high-speed Internet access. Wireless service is available via entire campus.

Library: Drake Memorial Library. *Books:* 500,461 (physical), 185,000 (digital/electronic); *Serial titles:* 4,747 (physical), 113,396 (digital/electronic); *Databases:* 270. Weekly public service hours: 93; students can reserve study rooms.

STUDENT LIFE
Housing options: on-campus residence required through sophomore year; coed, special housing for students with disabilities. Campus housing is university owned. Freshman campus housing is guaranteed.

Activities and organizations: drama/theater group, student-run newspaper, radio and television station, choral group, Habitat for Humanity, Brockport Pre-Professional Health Club, Brockport Psychology Club, Student Nursing Organization, Caribbean Student Association, national fraternities, national sororities.

Athletics Member NCAA. All Division III. ***Intercollegiate sports:*** baseball M, basketball M/W, cross-country running M/W, field hockey W, football M, gymnastics W, ice hockey M, lacrosse M/W, soccer M/W, softball W, swimming and diving M/W, tennis W, track and field M/W, volleyball W, wrestling M. ***Intramural sports:*** baseball M(c), basketball M/W, bowling M/W, cheerleading M(c)/W(c), equestrian sports M(c)/W(c), field hockey W(c), football M, golf M(c)/W(c), gymnastics M(c)/W(c), ice hockey M(c)/W(c), lacrosse M(c)/W(c), rugby M(c)/W(c), soccer M/W, softball W, table tennis M/W, tennis M(c)/W, track and field M/W, ultimate Frisbee M/W, volleyball M/W, weight lifting M(c), wrestling M.

Campus security: 24-hour emergency response devices and patrols, student patrols, late-night transport/escort service, controlled dormitory access, Emergency Notification System, Community Policing Program.

Student services: health clinic, personal/psychological counseling, women's center.

COSTS & FINANCIAL AID
Costs (2016–17) ***Tuition:*** state resident $6470 full-time, $270 per credit part-time; nonresident $16,320 full-time, $680 per credit part-time. Part-time tuition and fees vary according to course load. ***Required fees:*** $1458 full-time, $60 per credit hour part-time. ***Room and board:*** $12,418; room only: $7682. Room and board charges vary according to board plan and housing facility. ***Payment plans:*** installment, deferred payment. ***Waivers:*** employees or children of employees.

Financial Aid Of all full-time matriculated undergraduates who enrolled in 2015, 4,691 applied for aid, 3,832 were judged to have need, 638 had their need fully met. 488 Federal Work-Study jobs (averaging $2166). 750 state and other part-time jobs (averaging $2223). In 2015, 121 non-need-based awards were made. ***Average percent of need met:*** 72. ***Average financial aid package:*** $10,736. ***Average need-based loan:*** $4879. ***Average need-based gift aid:*** $6685. ***Average non-need-based aid:*** $5181. ***Average indebtedness upon graduation:*** $29,748.

APPLYING
Standardized Tests *Required:* SAT or ACT (for admission). *Recommended:* SAT (for admission), ACT (for admission).

Options: electronic application, deferred entrance.

Application fee: $50.

Required: high school transcript, minimum 2.5 GPA, 1 letter of recommendation. ***Required for some:*** essay or personal statement, interview. ***Recommended:*** essay or personal statement, minimum 3.0 GPA.

Application deadlines: rolling (freshmen), rolling (out-of-state freshmen), 8/1 (transfers).

Notification: continuous (freshmen), continuous (out-of-state freshmen), continuous (transfers).

CONTACT
The College at Brockport, State University of New York, 350 New Campus Drive, Brockport, NY 14420-2997. *Phone:* 585-395-2772.

College of Mount Saint Vincent
Riverdale, New York
http://www.mountsaintvincent.edu/

- **Independent** comprehensive, founded 1911
- **Suburban** 70-acre campus with easy access to New York City
- **Coed** 1,649 undergraduate students, 90% full-time, 72% women, 28% men
- **Moderately difficult** entrance level, 91% of applicants were admitted

UNDERGRAD STUDENTS
1,489 full-time, 160 part-time. 12% are from out of state; 17% Black or African American, non-Hispanic/Latino; 34% Hispanic/Latino; 10% Asian, non-Hispanic/Latino; 0.1% Native Hawaiian or other Pacific Islander, non-Hispanic/Latino; 0.2% American Indian or Alaska Native, non-Hispanic/Latino; 6% Two or more races, non-Hispanic/Latino; 5% Race/ethnicity unknown; 1% international; 2% transferred in; 48% live on campus.

Freshmen:
Admission: 2,416 applied, 2,202 admitted, 386 enrolled. ***Test scores:*** SAT critical reading scores over 500: 30%; SAT math scores over 500: 28%; ACT scores over 18: 75%; SAT critical reading scores over 600: 5%; SAT math scores over 600: 4%; ACT scores over 24: 21%.
Retention: 67% of full-time freshmen returned.

FACULTY
Total: 80.

Student/faculty ratio: 12:1.

ACADEMICS
Calendar: semesters. *Degrees:* associate, bachelor's, master's, and post-master's certificates.

Special study options: academic remediation for entering students, accelerated degree program, adult/continuing education programs, advanced placement credit, double majors, honors programs, independent study, internships, part-time degree program, services for LD students, study abroad, summer session for credit. ***ROTC:*** Air Force (c).

Unusual degree programs: 3-2 occupational therapy with Columbia University, physical therapy with New York Medical College.

Computers: Students can access the following: campus intranet, computer help desk, free student e-mail accounts, online (class) grades, online (class) registration, online (class) schedules. Campuswide network is available. Wireless service is available via classrooms, computer centers, computer labs, dorm rooms, libraries, student centers.

Library: Elizabeth Seton Library.

STUDENT LIFE
Housing options: coed, special housing for students with disabilities. Campus housing is university owned. Freshman campus housing is guaranteed.

Activities and organizations: drama/theater group, student-run newspaper, radio and television station, choral group, Casa Latina, Players, Dance Club, Student Nurse Association.

Athletics Member NCAA. All Division III. ***Intercollegiate sports:*** baseball M, basketball M/W, cheerleading W, cross-country running M/W, lacrosse M/W, soccer M/W, softball W, swimming and diving M/W, tennis M/W, track and field M/W, volleyball M/W, wrestling M. ***Intramural sports:*** basketball M.

Campus security: 24-hour emergency response devices and patrols, late-night transport/escort service, controlled dormitory access, emergency call boxes.

Student services: health clinic, personal/psychological counseling.

COSTS & FINANCIAL AID

Costs (2017–18) ***Comprehensive fee:*** $46,040 includes full-time tuition ($35,620), mandatory fees ($920), and room and board ($9500). Full-time tuition and fees vary according to student level. Part-time tuition: $1020 per credit hour. ***Payment plan:*** installment. ***Waivers:*** employees or children of employees.

Financial Aid Of all full-time matriculated undergraduates who enrolled in 2013, 1,362 applied for aid, 1,250 were judged to have need, 169 had their need fully met. In 2013, 112 non-need-based awards were made. ***Average percent of need met:*** 68. ***Average financial aid package:*** $19,829. ***Average need-based loan:*** $4333. ***Average need-based gift aid:*** $10,243. ***Average non-need-based aid:*** $12,904.

APPLYING

Standardized Tests *Required:* SAT or ACT (for admission).

Options: electronic application, early admission, early action, deferred entrance.

Application fee: $35.

Required: essay or personal statement, high school transcript, minimum 2.0 GPA. ***Required for some:*** interview. ***Recommended:*** 2 letters of recommendation, interview.

CONTACT

Jackie Williams, Director of Admissions, College of Mount Saint Vincent, 6301 Riverdale Avenue, Riverdale, NY 10471-1093. *Phone:* 718-405-3223. *Toll-free phone:* 800-665-CMSV. *Fax:* 718-549-7945. *E-mail:* jackie.williams@mountsaintvincent.edu.

The College of New Rochelle

New Rochelle, New York

http://www.cnr.edu/

- **Independent** comprehensive, founded 1904
- **Suburban** 20-acre campus with easy access to New York City
- **Endowment** $30.4 million
- **Coed, primarily women**
- **Moderately difficult** entrance level

FACULTY

Student/faculty ratio: 10:1.

ACADEMICS

Calendar: semesters. *Degrees:* bachelor's, master's, post-master's, and postbachelor's certificates (also offers a non-traditional adult program with significant enrollment not reflected in profile).

Library: Gill Library. *Books:* 90,490 (physical), 116,155 (digital/electronic); *Databases:* 96.

STUDENT LIFE

Housing options: coed, men-only, women-only, special housing for students with disabilities. Campus housing is university owned. Freshman campus housing is guaranteed.

Activities and organizations: drama/theater group, student-run newspaper, choral group, Music Ensembles, CNR Model United Nations, Student Nurses Association, Campus Ministry, Student Government.

Athletics Member NCAA. All Division III.

Campus security: 24-hour emergency response devices and patrols, late-night transport/escort service, controlled dormitory access, 24-hour monitored security cameras at residence hall entrances.

Student services: health clinic, personal/psychological counseling, women's center.

COSTS & FINANCIAL AID

Costs (2016–17) ***Comprehensive fee:*** $48,168 includes full-time tuition ($33,748), mandatory fees ($1212), and room and board ($13,208). Full-time tuition and fees vary according to course load, degree level, location, and program. Part-time tuition: $1125 per credit. Part-time tuition and fees vary according to course load, degree level, location, and program. ***Required fees:*** $350 per term part-time. ***Room and board:*** Room and board charges vary according to housing facility.

Financial Aid Of all full-time matriculated undergraduates who enrolled in 2015, 564 applied for aid, 526 were judged to have need, 11 had their need fully met. 400 Federal Work-Study jobs (averaging $2598). In 2015, 34 non-need-based awards were made. ***Average percent of need met:*** 57. ***Average financial aid package:*** $22,905. ***Average need-based loan:*** $5172. ***Average need-based gift aid:*** $9705. ***Average non-need-based aid:*** $13,685. ***Average indebtedness upon graduation:*** $35,430.

APPLYING

Standardized Tests *Required:* SAT or ACT (for admission).

Options: electronic application, early admission, early decision, deferred entrance.

Application fee: $35.

Required: high school transcript. ***Recommended:*** essay or personal statement, 1 letter of recommendation, interview.

CONTACT

Michael DiPiazza, Director of Undergraduate Admissions, The College of New Rochelle, 29 Castle Place, New Rochelle, NY 10805-2339. *Phone:* 914-654-5452. *Toll-free phone:* 800-933-5923. *Fax:* 914-654-5464. *E-mail:* mdipiazza@cnr.edu.

The College of Saint Rose

Albany, New York

http://www.strose.edu/

- **Independent** comprehensive, founded 1920
- **Urban** 49-acre campus
- **Endowment** $39.3 million
- **Coed** 2,602 undergraduate students, 96% full-time, 67% women, 33% men
- **Moderately difficult** entrance level, 84% of applicants were admitted

UNDERGRAD STUDENTS

2,510 full-time, 92 part-time. Students come from 30 states and territories; 33 other countries; 12% are from out of state; 13% Black or African American, non-Hispanic/Latino; 7% Hispanic/Latino; 3% Asian, non-Hispanic/Latino; 0.2% Native Hawaiian or other Pacific Islander, non-Hispanic/Latino; 0.2% American Indian or Alaska Native, non-Hispanic/Latino; 8% Two or more races, non-Hispanic/Latino; 4% Race/ethnicity unknown; 2% international; 7% transferred in; 49% live on campus.

Freshmen:

Admission: 6,780 applied, 5,663 admitted, 641 enrolled. ***Average high school GPA:*** 3.39. ***Test scores:*** SAT critical reading scores over 500: 62%; SAT math scores over 500: 57%; ACT scores over 18: 93%; SAT critical reading scores over 600: 19%; SAT math scores over 600: 15%; ACT scores over 24: 49%; SAT critical reading scores over 700: 2%; SAT math scores over 700: 2%; ACT scores over 30: 11%.

Retention: 77% of full-time freshmen returned.

FACULTY

Total: 344, 54% full-time, 73% with terminal degrees.

Student/faculty ratio: 14:1.

ACADEMICS

Calendar: semesters. *Degrees:* certificates, bachelor's, master's, post-master's, and postbachelor's certificates.

Special study options: academic remediation for entering students, accelerated degree program, advanced placement credit, double majors, English as a second language, independent study, internships, off-campus study, part-time degree program, services for LD students, student-designed majors, study abroad, summer session for credit. ***ROTC:*** Army (c), Navy (c), Air Force (c).

Unusual degree programs: 3-2 engineering with Rensselaer Polytechnic Institute; clinical laboratory science and biology/cytotechnology with Albany College of Pharmacy.

Computers: 755 computers/terminals and 4,642 ports are available on campus for general student use. Students can access the following: computer help desk, free student e-mail accounts, online (class) grades, online (class) registration, online (class) schedules. Campuswide network is available. 100% of college-owned or -operated housing units are wired for high-speed Internet access. Wireless service is available via entire campus.

Library: Neil Hellman Library plus 2 others. *Books:* 241,000 (physical), 116,500 (digital/electronic); *Serial titles:* 1,200 (physical), 10 (digital/electronic); *Databases:* 104. Students can reserve study rooms.

STUDENT LIFE

Housing options: on-campus residence required for freshman year; coed, men-only, women-only, special housing for students with disabilities. Campus housing is university owned and leased by the school. Freshman campus housing is guaranteed.

Activities and organizations: drama/theater group, student-run newspaper, radio and television station, choral group, Student Association, Student Events Board, Spectrum-ALANA Student Union, Colleges Against Cancer, Music and Entertainment Industry Student Association.

Athletics Member NCAA. All Division II. ***Intercollegiate sports:*** baseball M(s), basketball M(s)/W(s), cross-country running M(s)/W(s), golf M(s)/W(s), lacrosse M(s), soccer M(s)/W(s), softball W(s), swimming and diving M(s)/W(s), tennis W(s), track and field M(s)/W(s), volleyball W(s). ***Intramural sports:*** basketball M/W, cheerleading M(c)/W(c), soccer M/W, ultimate Frisbee M/W, volleyball M/W.

Campus security: 24-hour emergency response devices and patrols, late-night transport/escort service, controlled dormitory access.

Student services: health clinic, personal/psychological counseling.

COSTS & FINANCIAL AID

Costs (2017–18) ***One-time required fee:*** $469. ***Comprehensive fee:*** $43,968 includes full-time tuition ($30,546), mandatory fees ($1066), and room and board ($12,356). Full-time tuition and fees vary according to course load. Part-time tuition: $1016 per credit hour. Part-time tuition and fees vary according to course load. ***Required fees:*** $37 per credit hour part-time, $128 per term part-time. ***College room only:*** $6214. Room and board charges vary according to board plan and housing facility. ***Payment plan:*** installment. ***Waivers:*** employees or children of employees.

Financial Aid Of all full-time matriculated undergraduates who enrolled in 2015, 2,326 applied for aid, 2,142 were judged to have need, 352 had their need fully met. In 2015, 244 non-need-based awards were made. ***Average percent of need met:*** 77. ***Average financial aid package:*** $20,353. ***Average need-based loan:*** $4370. ***Average need-based gift aid:*** $8532. ***Average non-need-based aid:*** $11,356. ***Average indebtedness upon graduation:*** $31,413. ***Financial aid deadline:*** 4/1.

APPLYING

Standardized Tests *Required for some:* SAT or ACT (for admission).

Options: electronic application, early admission, early action, deferred entrance.

Required: high school transcript, 1 letter of recommendation. ***Required for some:*** interview. ***Recommended:*** essay or personal statement, minimum 2.5 GPA.

Application deadlines: 5/1 (freshmen), 8/1 (transfers), 12/1 (early action).

Notification: continuous (freshmen), continuous (transfers), 12/15 (early action).

CONTACT

Ms. Kathleen Lesko, Assistant Vice President of Undergraduate Admissions, The College of Saint Rose, 1001 Madison Avenue, Albany, NY 12203. *Phone:* 518-454-5154. *Toll-free phone:* 800-637-8556. *Fax:* 518-454-2013. *E-mail:* admit@strose.edu.

★ College of Staten Island of the City University of New York

Staten Island, New York

http://www.csi.cuny.edu/

- **State and locally supported** comprehensive, founded 1955, part of City University of New York System
- **Urban** 204-acre campus with easy access to New York City
- **Endowment** $5.6 million
- **Coed** 12,806 undergraduate students, 76% full-time, 56% women, 44% men

UNDERGRAD STUDENTS

9,693 full-time, 3,113 part-time. Students come from 17 states and territories; 114 other countries; 0.6% are from out of state; 15% Black or African American, non-Hispanic/Latino; 17% Hispanic/Latino; 12% Asian, non-Hispanic/Latino; 0.2% American Indian or Alaska Native, non-Hispanic/Latino; 1% Race/ethnicity unknown; 3% international; 2% transferred in; 3% live on campus.

Freshmen:

Admission: 2,569 enrolled. ***Average high school GPA:*** 3.06. ***Test scores:*** SAT critical reading scores over 500: 45%; SAT math scores over 500: 59%; SAT writing scores over 500: 42%; SAT critical reading scores over 600: 12%; SAT math scores over 600: 16%; SAT writing scores over 600: 6%; SAT critical reading scores over 700: 1%; SAT math scores over 700: 2%; SAT writing scores over 700: 1%.

Retention: 81% of full-time freshmen returned.

FACULTY

Total: 1,094, 31% full-time, 40% with terminal degrees.

Student/faculty ratio: 18:1.

ACADEMICS

Calendar: semesters. *Degrees:* certificates, associate, bachelor's, master's, doctoral, post-master's, and postbachelor's certificates.

Special study options: academic remediation for entering students, adult/continuing education programs, double majors, English as a second language, honors programs, independent study, internships, services for LD students, student-designed majors, study abroad, summer session for credit.

Computers: 1,400 ports are available on campus for general student use. Students can access the following: computer help desk, free student e-mail accounts, online (class) grades, online (class) registration, online (class) schedules. Campuswide network is available. 100% of college-owned or -operated housing units are wired for high-speed Internet access. Wireless service is available via entire campus.

Library: College of Staten Island Library. *Books:* 261,252 (physical), 457,488 (digital/electronic); *Serial titles:* 65,800 (physical); *Databases:* 167. Weekly public service hours: 112; students can reserve study rooms.

STUDENT LIFE

Housing options: coed, special housing for students with disabilities. Campus housing is university owned.

Activities and organizations: drama/theater group, student-run newspaper, radio station, choral group, International Students Club, Campus Activities Board, United African Students in the USA, American Sign Language Club, Muslim Student Association.

Athletics Member NCAA. All Division III. ***Intercollegiate sports:*** baseball M, basketball M/W, cheerleading M(c)/W(c), cross-country running M/W, soccer M/W, softball W, swimming and diving M/W, tennis M/W, track and field M/W, volleyball M/W. ***Intramural sports:*** badminton M/W, basketball M/W, racquetball M/W, soccer M/W, swimming and diving M/W, table tennis M/W, tennis M/W, track and field M/W, ultimate Frisbee M/W, volleyball M/W.

Campus security: 24-hour emergency response devices and patrols, student patrols, late-night transport/escort service, controlled dormitory access, radar-controlled traffic monitoring, vehicle and bicycle patrols.

Student services: health clinic, personal/psychological counseling, women's center.

COSTS & FINANCIAL AID

Costs (2016–17) ***Tuition:*** state resident $6330 full-time, $275 per credit hour part-time; nonresident $16,800 full-time, $560 per credit hour part-time. ***Required fees:*** $559 full-time, $181 per term part-time. ***Room only:*** $13,627. Room and board charges vary according to board plan and housing facility. ***Payment plan:*** installment. ***Waivers:*** senior citizens and employees or children of employees.

Financial Aid Of all full-time matriculated undergraduates who enrolled in 2016, 7,704 applied for aid, 6,956 were judged to have need, 361 had their need fully met. In 2016, 240 non-need-based awards were made. ***Average percent of need met:*** 39. ***Average financial aid package:*** $8225. ***Average need-based loan:*** $8970. ***Average need-based gift aid:*** $7674. ***Average non-need-based aid:*** $3124.

APPLYING

Standardized Tests *Required:* SAT or ACT (for admission).

Required: high school transcript. ***Required for some:*** essay or personal statement, interview.

CONTACT
College of Staten Island of the City University of New York, 2800 Victory Boulevard, 2A-103, Staten Island, NY 10314. *Phone:* 718-982-2010. *Fax:* 718-982-2500. *E-mail:* admissions@csi.cuny.edu.

See this page for display ad and page 1324 for the College Close-Up.

The College of Westchester

White Plains, New York

http://www.cw.edu/

- **Proprietary** primarily 2-year, founded 1915
- **Suburban** campus with easy access to New York City
- **Coed** 1,021 undergraduate students, 79% full-time, 65% women, 35% men
- **Minimally difficult** entrance level, 94% of applicants were admitted

UNDERGRAD STUDENTS
808 full-time, 213 part-time. Students come from 5 states and territories; 3% are from out of state; 36% Black or African American, non-Hispanic/Latino; 46% Hispanic/Latino; 2% Asian, non-Hispanic/Latino; 0.2% American Indian or Alaska Native, non-Hispanic/Latino; 1% Two or more races, non-Hispanic/Latino; 4% Race/ethnicity unknown; 11% transferred in.

Freshmen:
Admission: 735 applied, 690 admitted, 192 enrolled.
Retention: 70% of full-time freshmen returned.

FACULTY
Total: 69, 46% full-time.
Student/faculty ratio: 18:1.

ACADEMICS
Calendar: semesters. *Degrees:* certificates, associate, and bachelor's.
Special study options: academic remediation for entering students, accelerated degree program, adult/continuing education programs, cooperative education, distance learning, double majors, honors programs, internships, part-time degree program, summer session for credit.
Computers: 282 computers/terminals are available on campus for general student use. Students can access the following: campus intranet, computer help desk, free student e-mail accounts, online (class) grades, online (class) schedules. Campuswide network is available.
Library: Dr. William R. Papallo Library.

STUDENT LIFE
Housing options: college housing not available.
Activities and organizations: student-run newspaper.
Student services: personal/psychological counseling.

COSTS
Costs (2017–18) ***Tuition:*** $20,115 full-time, $745 per credit part-time. ***Required fees:*** $1000 full-time, $100 per course part-time. ***Payment plan:*** installment. ***Waivers:*** employees or children of employees.

APPLYING
Standardized Tests *Recommended:* SAT (for admission).
Options: electronic application, deferred entrance.
Application fee: $40.
Required: high school transcript, interview. ***Required for some:*** essay or personal statement.
Application deadlines: rolling (freshmen), rolling (transfers).

CONTACT
Mr. Matt Curtis, Vice President, Enrollment Management, The College of Westchester, 325 Central Avenue, PO Box 710, White Plains, NY 10602. *Phone:* 914-948-4442 Ext. 313. *Toll-free phone:* 855-403-7722. *Fax:* 914-948-5441. *E-mail:* admissions@cw.edu.

Columbia University

New York, New York

http://www.columbia.edu/

- **Independent** university, founded 1754
- **Urban** 36-acre campus
- **Endowment** $9.0 billion
- **Coed** 6,158 undergraduate students, 100% full-time, 48% women, 52% men
- **Most difficult** entrance level, 6% of applicants were admitted

UNDERGRAD STUDENTS
6,158 full-time. Students come from 52 states and territories; 87 other countries; 76% are from out of state; 11% Black or African American, non-Hispanic/Latino; 12% Hispanic/Latino; 23% Asian, non-Hispanic/Latino; 2% American Indian or Alaska Native, non-Hispanic/Latino; 3% Race/ethnicity unknown; 15% international; 3% transferred in; 93% live on campus.

Freshmen:
Admission: 36,292 applied, 2,279 admitted, 1,420 enrolled. ***Test scores:*** SAT critical reading scores over 500: 100%; SAT math scores over 500: 100%; SAT writing scores over 500: 100%; SAT critical reading scores over 600: 98%; SAT math scores over 600: 100%; SAT writing scores over 600: 98%; ACT scores over 24: 100%; SAT critical reading scores over 700: 80%; SAT math scores over 700: 84%; SAT writing scores over 700: 79%; ACT scores over 30: 92%.

Retention: 99% of full-time freshmen returned.

FACULTY
Student/faculty ratio: 6:1.

ACADEMICS
Calendar: semesters. *Degrees:* bachelor's, master's, and doctoral.

Special study options: accelerated degree program, advanced placement credit, double majors, English as a second language, independent study, internships, off-campus study, services for LD students, student-designed majors, study abroad, summer session for credit. ***ROTC:*** Army (c), Navy (b), Air Force (c).

Unusual degree programs: 3-2 engineering.

Computers: 460 computers/terminals are available on campus for general student use. Students can access the following: campus intranet, computer help desk, free student e-mail accounts, online (class) grades, online (class) registration, online (class) schedules. Campuswide network is available. Wireless service is available via entire campus.

Library: Butler plus 20 others. *Books:* 11.2 million (physical), 2.4 million (digital/electronic); *Databases:* 1,646. Weekly public service hours: 86; study areas open 24 hours, 5-7 days a week; students can reserve study rooms.

STUDENT LIFE
Housing options: on-campus residence required for freshman year; coed, men-only, women-only, cooperative, special housing for students with disabilities. Campus housing is university owned. Freshman campus housing is guaranteed.

Activities and organizations: drama/theater group, student-run newspaper, radio and television station, choral group, marching band, community service, cultural organizations, performing arts, athletics, publications, national fraternities, national sororities.

Athletics Member NCAA. All Division I except football (Division I-AA). ***Intercollegiate sports:*** archery M(c)/W, badminton M(c)/W(c), baseball M, basketball M/W, crew M/W, cross-country running M/W, fencing M/W, field hockey W, golf M, ice hockey W(c), lacrosse M(c)/W, racquetball M(c)/W(c), riflery M(c)/W(c), rugby M(c)/W(c), skiing (cross-country) M(c)/W(c), skiing (downhill) M(c)/W(c), soccer M(c)/W(c), softball W, squash M(c)/W(c), swimming and diving M/W, table tennis M(c)/W(c), tennis M(c)/W(c), track and field M/W, ultimate Frisbee M(c)/W(c), volleyball M(c)/W(c), water polo M(c)/W(c), wrestling M. ***Intramural sports:*** archery W(c), badminton M/W, basketball M(c)/W(c), cross-country running M(c)/W(c), field hockey W, lacrosse W(c), racquetball M/W, soccer M/W, softball M/W, squash M/W, swimming and diving M/W, tennis M/W, volleyball M/W, water polo W.

Campus security: 24-hour emergency response devices and patrols, late-night transport/escort service, controlled dormitory access.

Student services: health clinic, personal/psychological counseling, women's center.

COSTS & FINANCIAL AID
Costs (2016–17) ***Comprehensive fee:*** $68,300 includes full-time tuition ($52,478), mandatory fees ($2578), and room and board ($13,244). ***Room and board:*** Room and board charges vary according to board plan and housing facility. ***Payment plans:*** tuition prepayment, installment. ***Waivers:*** employees or children of employees.

Financial Aid Of all full-time matriculated undergraduates who enrolled in 2016, 3,290 applied for aid, 2,993 were judged to have need, 2,911 had their need fully met. ***Average percent of need met:*** 99. ***Average financial aid package:*** $55,521. ***Average need-based loan:*** $3451. ***Average need-based gift aid:*** $50,733.

APPLYING
Standardized Tests *Required:* SAT or ACT (for admission).

Options: electronic application, early admission, early decision, deferred entrance.

Application fee: $85.

Required: essay or personal statement, high school transcript, 3 letters of recommendation.

Application deadlines: 1/1 (freshmen), 3/1 (transfers).

Early decision deadline: 11/1.

Notification: 4/1 (freshmen), 5/15 (transfers), 12/15 (early decision).

CONTACT
Columbia University, 116th Street and Broadway, New York, NY 10027.
Phone: 212-854-1222.

See previous page for display ad and page 1326 for the College Close-Up.

Columbia University, School of General Studies

New York, New York

http://www.gs.columbia.edu/

- **Independent** 4-year, founded 1754, part of Columbia University
- **Urban** 36-acre campus with easy access to New York City
- **Endowment** $9.0 billion
- **Coed** 2,068 undergraduate students, 73% full-time, 41% women, 59% men
- **Most difficult** entrance level, 35% of applicants were admitted

UNDERGRAD STUDENTS
1,504 full-time, 564 part-time. 57% are from out of state; 5% Black or African American, non-Hispanic/Latino; 10% Hispanic/Latino; 9% Asian, non-Hispanic/Latino; 0.2% Native Hawaiian or other Pacific Islander, non-Hispanic/Latino; 0.3% American Indian or Alaska Native, non-Hispanic/Latino; 0.2% Two or more races, non-Hispanic/Latino; 5% Race/ethnicity unknown; 21% international; 23% transferred in; 28% live on campus.

Freshmen:
Admission: 696 applied, 241 admitted, 147 enrolled. ***Average high school GPA:*** 3.83. ***Test scores:*** SAT critical reading scores over 500: 99%; SAT math scores over 500: 96%; SAT writing scores over 500: 97%; ACT scores over 18: 100%; SAT critical reading scores over 600: 86%; SAT math scores over 600: 75%; SAT writing scores over 600: 83%; ACT scores over 24: 100%; SAT critical reading scores over 700: 54%; SAT math scores over 700: 46%; SAT writing scores over 700: 53%; ACT scores over 30: 88%.

ACADEMICS
Calendar: semesters. *Degrees:* bachelor's and postbachelor's certificates.

Special study options: accelerated degree program, adult/continuing education programs, advanced placement credit, double majors, independent study, internships, off-campus study, part-time degree program, services for LD students, student-designed majors, study abroad, summer session for credit. ***ROTC:*** Army (c), Navy (b), Air Force (c).

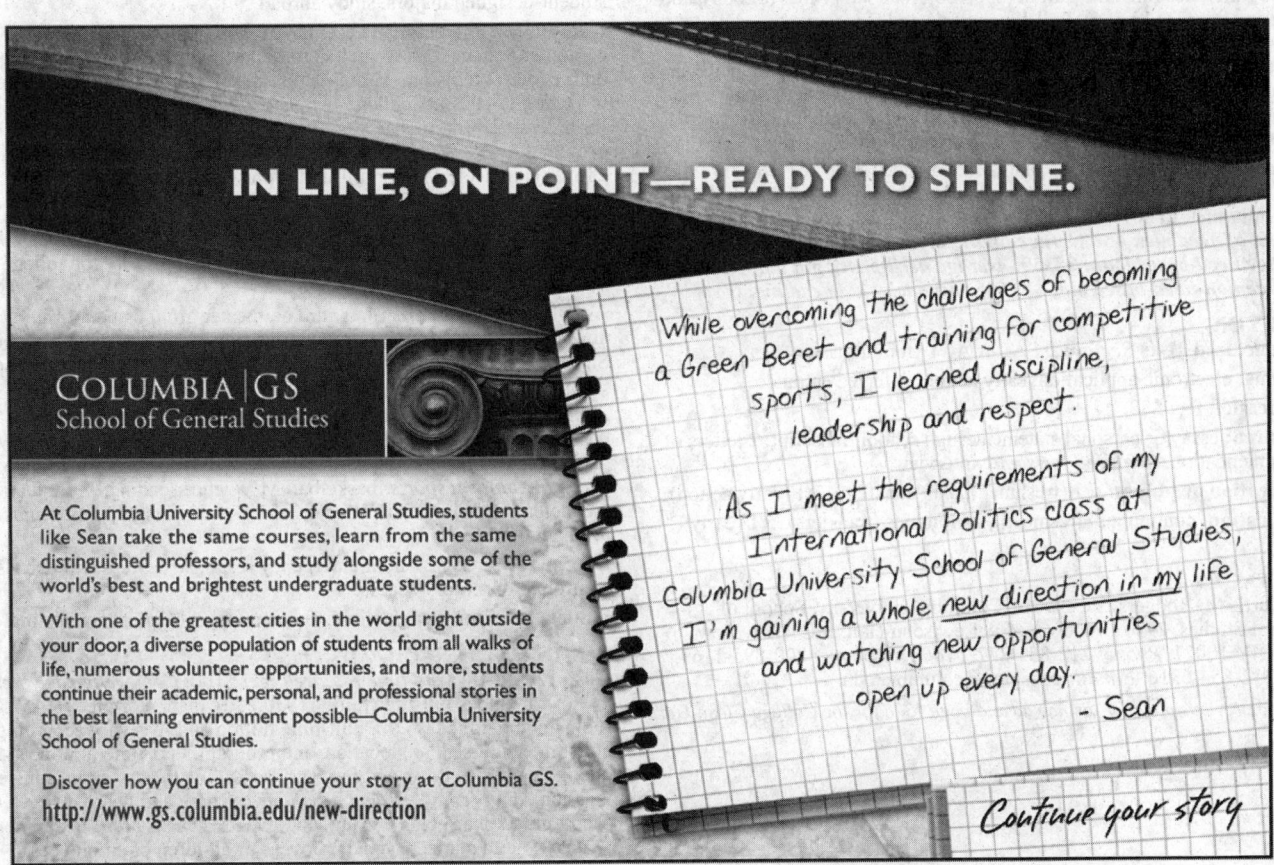

Unusual degree programs: 3-2 business administration; engineering; social work; international affairs, public policy, public health, law, dental medicine, occupational therapy.

Computers: Students can access the following: campus intranet, computer help desk, free student e-mail accounts, online (class) grades, online (class) registration, online (class) schedules. Campuswide network is available. 100% of college-owned or -operated housing units are wired for high-speed Internet access. Wireless service is available via entire campus.

Library: Butler Library plus 20 others.

STUDENT LIFE

Housing options: coed, cooperative, special housing for students with disabilities. Campus housing is university owned, leased by the school and is provided by a third party.

Activities and organizations: drama/theater group, student-run newspaper, radio and television station, choral group, marching band, General Studies Student Council, national fraternities, national sororities.

Athletics Member NCAA. All Division I except football (Division I-AA). ***Intercollegiate sports:*** archery W, badminton M(c)/W(c), baseball M, basketball M/W, crew M/W, cross-country running M/W, equestrian sports M(c)/W(c), fencing M/W, field hockey W, golf M/W, ice hockey M(c)/W(c), lacrosse M(c)/W, racquetball M(c)/W(c), rugby M(c)/W(c), sailing M(c)/W(c), skiing (downhill) M(c)/W(c), soccer M/W, softball W, squash M/W, swimming and diving M/W, table tennis M(c)/W(c), tennis M/W, track and field M/W, ultimate Frisbee M(c)/W(c), volleyball W, water polo M(c)/W(c), wrestling M. ***Intramural sports:*** archery M(c)/W(c), badminton M(c)/W(c), basketball M/W, bowling M(c)/W(c), equestrian sports M/W, football M/W, racquetball M/W, rock climbing M(c)/W(c), soccer M/W, table tennis M/W, volleyball M/W, weight lifting M/W.

Campus security: 24-hour emergency response devices and patrols, late-night transport/escort service.

Student services: health clinic, personal/psychological counseling, women's center.

COSTS & FINANCIAL AID

Costs (2016–17) ***One-time required fee:*** $105. ***Comprehensive fee:*** $67,031 includes full-time tuition ($50,760), mandatory fees ($2685), and room and board ($13,586). Full-time tuition and fees vary according to course load and program. Part-time tuition: $1692 per credit hour. Part-time tuition and fees vary according to course load and program. ***College room only:*** $8320. Room and board charges vary according to board plan and housing facility. ***Payment plans:*** tuition prepayment, installment. ***Waivers:*** employees or children of employees.

Financial Aid Of all full-time matriculated undergraduates who enrolled in 2015, 950 applied for aid, 874 were judged to have need, 29 had their need fully met. In 2015, 65 non-need-based awards were made. ***Average percent of need met:*** 45. ***Average financial aid package:*** $30,819. ***Average need-based loan:*** $8359. ***Average need-based gift aid:*** $22,797. ***Average non-need-based aid:*** $12,545. ***Financial aid deadline:*** 6/1.

APPLYING

Standardized Tests *Required:* SAT or ACT (for admission).

Options: electronic application, early action, deferred entrance.

Application fee: $80.

Required: essay or personal statement, high school transcript, 2 letters of recommendation. ***Required for some:*** interview.

Application deadlines: 6/1 (freshmen), 6/1 (transfers), 3/1 (early action).

Notification: continuous (freshmen), continuous (transfers), 5/1 (early action).

CONTACT

Mr. Curtis M. Rodgers, Vice Dean, Columbia University, School of General Studies, 2970 Broadway, 408 Lewisohn Hall, MC 4101, New York, NY 10027. *Phone:* 212-854-2772. *Toll-free phone:* 800-895-1169. *Fax:* 212-854-6316. *E-mail:* gsdegree@columbia.edu.

See previous page for display ad and page 1328 for the College Close-Up.

Concordia College–New York

Bronxville, New York

http://www.concordia-ny.edu/

- **Independent Lutheran** comprehensive, founded 1881, part of Concordia University System
- **Suburban** 33-acre campus with easy access to New York City
- **Endowment** $6.4 million
- **Coed** 1,185 undergraduate students, 88% full-time, 68% women, 32% men
- **Moderately difficult** entrance level, 71% of applicants were admitted

UNDERGRAD STUDENTS

1,037 full-time, 148 part-time. Students come from 14 states and territories; 31 other countries; 18% Black or African American, non-Hispanic/Latino; 23% Hispanic/Latino; 4% Asian, non-Hispanic/Latino; 0.1% Native Hawaiian or other Pacific Islander, non-Hispanic/Latino; 0.3% American Indian or Alaska Native, non-Hispanic/Latino; 2% Two or more races, non-Hispanic/Latino; 5% Race/ethnicity unknown; 12% international; 60% live on campus.

Freshmen:

Admission: 974 applied, 692 admitted. ***Average high school GPA:*** 3.25. ***Test scores:*** SAT critical reading scores over 500: 20%; SAT critical reading scores over 600: 4%; SAT critical reading scores over 700: 1%.

Retention: 107% of full-time freshmen returned.

FACULTY

Total: 148, 35% full-time.

Student/faculty ratio: 14:1.

ACADEMICS

Calendar: semesters. *Degrees:* certificates, diplomas, associate, bachelor's, and master's.

Special study options: academic remediation for entering students, accelerated degree program, adult/continuing education programs, cooperative education, distance learning, double majors, English as a second language, honors programs, independent study, internships, off-campus study, part-time degree program, services for LD students, student-designed majors, study abroad.

Computers: Students can access the following: campus intranet, computer help desk, free student e-mail accounts, online (class) grades, online (class) registration, online (class) schedules. Campuswide network is available. 100% of college-owned or -operated housing units are wired for high-speed Internet access. Wireless service is available via entire campus.

Library: Scheele Memorial Library plus 1 other.

STUDENT LIFE

Housing options: men-only, women-only, cooperative. Campus housing is university owned. Freshman applicants given priority for college housing.

Activities and organizations: drama/theater group, student-run newspaper, choral group, Campus Christian Ministries, Choral Groups, Student Government Association, International and Afro/Latin American Club, Yearbook and newspaper.

Athletics Member NCAA. All Division II. ***Intercollegiate sports:*** baseball M(s), basketball M(s)/W(s), cross-country running M(s)/W(s), golf M, soccer M(s)/W(s), softball W(s), tennis M(s)/W(s), volleyball W(s). ***Intramural sports:*** basketball M/W, cheerleading W, football M/W, racquetball M/W, softball W, squash M/W, table tennis M/W, tennis M/W, ultimate Frisbee M/W.

Campus security: 24-hour emergency response devices and patrols, controlled dormitory access.

Student services: health clinic, personal/psychological counseling.

COSTS & FINANCIAL AID

Costs (2017–18) ***One-time required fee:*** $100. ***Comprehensive fee:*** $43,651 includes full-time tuition ($30,250), mandatory fees ($1525), and room and board ($11,876). Full-time tuition and fees vary according to class time, course load, location, and program. Part-time tuition: $815 per credit. Part-time tuition and fees vary according to class time, course load, location, and program. ***Room and board:*** Room and board charges vary according to board plan and student level. ***Payment plan:*** installment. ***Waivers:*** adult students and employees or children of employees.

Financial Aid Of all full-time matriculated undergraduates who enrolled in 2008, 533 applied for aid, 448 were judged to have need, 89 had their need fully met. In 2008, 100 non-need-based awards were made. ***Average percent of need met:*** 71. ***Average financial aid package:*** $22,309. ***Average need-based loan:*** $4133. ***Average need-based gift aid:*** $11,129. ***Average non-need-based aid:*** $6170. ***Average indebtedness upon graduation:*** $24,153.

APPLYING

Standardized Tests *Required for some:* SAT or ACT (for admission), TOEFL or IELTS for students for whom English is not their first language.

Options: electronic application, early admission, early action, deferred entrance.

Application fee: $50.

Required: essay or personal statement, high school transcript, 2 letters of recommendation. ***Required for some:*** interview. ***Recommended:*** minimum 2.8 GPA.

Application deadlines: 3/15 (freshmen), 7/15 (transfers), 11/15 (early action).

Notification: continuous (freshmen), continuous until 8/15 (transfers), 12/15 (early action).

CONTACT

Mr. Brian M. Sondey, Director of First Year Admission, Concordia College–New York, 171 White Plains Road, Bronxville, NY 10708. *Phone:* 914-337-9300 Ext. 2124. *Toll-free phone:* 800-YES-COLLEGE. *Fax:* 914-395-4636. *E-mail:* brian.sondey@concordia-ny.edu.

Cooper Union for the Advancement of Science and Art

New York, New York

http://www.cooper.edu/

- **Independent** comprehensive, founded 1859
- **Urban** campus with easy access to New York City
- **Endowment** $771.1 million
- **Coed** 876 undergraduate students, 99% full-time, 34% women, 66% men

UNDERGRAD STUDENTS

863 full-time, 13 part-time. Students come from 35 states and territories; 25 other countries; 51% are from out of state; 3% Black or African American, non-Hispanic/Latino; 9% Hispanic/Latino; 19% Asian, non-Hispanic/Latino; 9% Two or more races, non-Hispanic/Latino; 10% Race/ethnicity unknown; 20% international; 0.9% transferred in; 20% live on campus.

Freshmen:

Admission: 222 enrolled. ***Average high school GPA:*** 3.5. ***Test scores:*** SAT critical reading scores over 500: 93%; SAT math scores over 500: 88%; SAT writing scores over 500: 92%; ACT scores over 18: 100%; SAT critical reading scores over 600: 78%; SAT math scores over 600: 79%; SAT writing scores over 600: 73%; ACT scores over 24: 98%; SAT critical reading scores over 700: 35%; SAT math scores over 700: 63%; SAT writing scores over 700: 32%; ACT scores over 30: 78%.

Retention: 95% of full-time freshmen returned.

FACULTY

Total: 214, 27% full-time, 51% with terminal degrees.

Student/faculty ratio: 8:1.

ACADEMICS

Calendar: semesters. *Degrees:* certificates, bachelor's, and master's (also offers master's program primarily made up of currently-enrolled students).

Special study options: accelerated degree program, advanced placement credit, independent study, internships, off-campus study, services for LD students, student-designed majors, study abroad, summer session for credit. ***ROTC:*** Army (c).

Computers: 100 computers/terminals are available on campus for general student use. Students can access the following: computer help desk, free student e-mail accounts, online (class) grades, online (class) registration, online (class) schedules. Campuswide network is available. 100% of college-owned or -operated housing units are wired for high-speed Internet access. Wireless service is available via entire campus.

Library: Cooper Union Library. *Books:* 97,656 (physical), 15,649 (digital/electronic); *Serial titles:* 73 (physical), 41,326 (digital/electronic); *Databases:* 51. Weekly public service hours: 69.

STUDENT LIFE

Housing options: coed. Campus housing is university owned. Freshman applicants given priority for college housing.

Activities and organizations: drama/theater group, student-run newspaper, choral group, South Asian Society, Pro Musica, Chinese Student Association, Drama Society, Outdoors Club; Intervarsity Christian Fellowship, national fraternities, national sororities.

Athletics ***Intercollegiate sports:*** basketball M/W, cross-country running M/W, soccer M/W, tennis M/W, volleyball M/W. ***Intramural sports:*** badminton M(c)/W(c), basketball M/W, bowling M/W, fencing M(c)/W(c), golf M/W, skiing (downhill) M/W, soccer M(c)/W(c), swimming and diving M/W, table tennis M/W, tennis M/W, ultimate Frisbee M(c)/W(c), volleyball M/W.

Campus security: 24-hour emergency response devices and patrols, controlled dormitory access, security guards.

Student services: personal/psychological counseling.

COSTS & FINANCIAL AID

Costs (2017–18) ***Comprehensive fee:*** $61,370 includes full-time tuition ($43,250), mandatory fees ($1850), and room and board ($16,270). Full-time tuition and fees vary according to degree level. Part-time tuition: $1250 per credit hour. Part-time tuition and fees vary according to degree level. ***Required fees:*** $925 per term part-time. ***College room only:*** $12,270. Room and board charges vary according to housing facility. ***Payment plan:*** installment. ***Waivers:*** employees or children of employees.

Financial Aid Of all full-time matriculated undergraduates who enrolled in 2015, 429 applied for aid, 359 were judged to have need, 359 had their need fully met. 75 Federal Work-Study jobs (averaging $520). 489 state and other part-time jobs (averaging $1340). In 2015, 551 non-need-based awards were made. ***Average percent of need met:*** 89. ***Average financial aid package:*** $38,979. ***Average need-based loan:*** $4077. ***Average need-based gift aid:*** $14,250. ***Average non-need-based aid:*** $32,488. ***Average indebtedness upon graduation:*** $6579. ***Financial aid deadline:*** 5/1.

APPLYING

Standardized Tests *Required:* SAT or ACT (for admission), studio test for architecture, home test for art (for admission). *Required for some:* SAT Subject Tests (for admission).

Required: essay or personal statement, high school transcript. ***Required for some:*** minimum 3.5 GPA, 3 letters of recommendation, interview, portfolio for art, studio test for architecture. ***Recommended:*** minimum 3.0 GPA, 2 letters of recommendation.

CONTACT

Mr. John Falls, Associate Dean of Admissions, Cooper Union for the Advancement of Science and Art, 30 Cooper Square, New York, NY 10003. *Phone:* 212-353-4192. *Fax:* 212-353-4342. *E-mail:* admissions@cooper.edu.

Cornell University

Ithaca, New York

http://www.cornell.edu/

- **Independent** university, founded 1865, part of State University of New York System
- **Small-town** 745-acre campus with easy access to Syracuse
- **Endowment** $5.8 billion
- **Coed** 14,566 undergraduate students, 100% full-time, 52% women, 48% men
- **Most difficult** entrance level, 14% of applicants were admitted

UNDERGRAD STUDENTS

14,566 full-time. Students come from 56 states and territories; 93 other countries; 66% are from out of state; 6% Black or African American, non-Hispanic/Latino; 13% Hispanic/Latino; 18% Asian, non-Hispanic/Latino; 0.1% Native Hawaiian or other Pacific Islander, non-Hispanic/Latino; 0.4% American Indian or Alaska Native, non-Hispanic/Latino; 5% Two or more races, non-Hispanic/Latino; 8% Race/ethnicity unknown; 10% international; 4% transferred in; 54% live on campus.

Freshmen:
Admission: 44,965 applied, 6,337 admitted, 3,315 enrolled. ***Test scores:*** SAT critical reading scores over 500: 100%; SAT math scores over 500: 100%; ACT scores over 18: 100%; SAT critical reading scores over 600: 92%; SAT math scores over 600: 95%; ACT scores over 24: 99%; SAT critical reading scores over 700: 55%; SAT math scores over 700: 70%; ACT scores over 30: 85%.
Retention: 97% of full-time freshmen returned.

FACULTY
Total: 2,136, 84% full-time, 88% with terminal degrees.
Student/faculty ratio: 9:1.

ACADEMICS
Calendar: semesters. *Degrees:* bachelor's, master's, and doctoral.
Special study options: academic remediation for entering students, accelerated degree program, advanced placement credit, cooperative education, distance learning, double majors, English as a second language, honors programs, independent study, internships, off-campus study, services for LD students, student-designed majors, study abroad, summer session for credit. ***ROTC:*** Army (b), Navy (b), Air Force (b).
Computers: 2,650 computers/terminals and 2,500 ports are available on campus for general student use. Students can access the following: campus intranet, computer help desk, free student e-mail accounts, online (class) grades, online (class) registration. Campuswide network is available. 100% of college-owned or -operated housing units are wired for high-speed Internet access. Wireless service is available via entire campus.
Library: Main Library plus 17 others. *Books:* 8.0 million (physical), 1.5 million (digital/electronic); *Serial titles:* 234,422 (physical), 150,277 (digital/electronic); *Databases:* 4,058. Weekly public service hours: 146; study areas open 24 hours, 5-7 days a week; students can reserve study rooms.

STUDENT LIFE
Housing options: coed, women-only, cooperative, special housing for students with disabilities. Campus housing is university owned. Freshman campus housing is guaranteed.
Activities and organizations: drama/theater group, student-run newspaper, radio and television station, choral group, marching band, Student Assembly, Class Councils, Cornell Concert Commission, Interfraternity Council, Panhellenic Association, national fraternities, national sororities.
Athletics Member NCAA. All Division I. ***Intercollegiate sports:*** baseball M, basketball M/W, crew M/W, cross-country running M/W, equestrian sports W, fencing W, field hockey W, football M, golf M, gymnastics W, ice hockey M/W, lacrosse M/W, sailing W, soccer M/W, softball W, squash M/W, swimming and diving M/W, tennis M/W, track and field M/W, ultimate Frisbee M(c)/W(c), volleyball M(c)/W, water polo M(c)/W(c), wrestling M. ***Intramural sports:*** archery M(c)/W(c), badminton M/W, baseball M(c), basketball M/W, bowling M/W, cheerleading W(c), cross-country running M(c)/W(c), equestrian sports M(c)/W(c), fencing M(c)/W(c), field hockey W(c), football M(c)/W(c), golf M/W, gymnastics M(c)/W(c), ice hockey M(c)/W(c), lacrosse W(c), rugby M(c)/W(c), sailing M(c)/W(c), sand volleyball M(c)/W(c), skiing (cross-country) M(c)/W(c), skiing (downhill) M(c)/W(c), soccer M/W, softball M/W, squash M/W, table tennis M/W, tennis M/W, ultimate Frisbee M/W, volleyball M/W, water polo M/W, wrestling M(c)/W(c).
Campus security: 24-hour emergency response devices and patrols, late-night transport/escort service, controlled dormitory access, indoor/outdoor emergency phones, lighted pathways/sidewalks, shuttle buses, safety escorts, weekly safety messages to the community.
Student services: health clinic, personal/psychological counseling, women's center.

COSTS & FINANCIAL AID
Costs (2016–17) ***Comprehensive fee:*** $64,903 includes full-time tuition ($50,712), mandatory fees ($241), and room and board ($13,950). Full-time tuition and fees vary according to degree level. ***College room only:*** $8274. Room and board charges vary according to board plan and housing facility. ***Payment plan:*** installment. ***Waivers:*** employees or children of employees.
Financial Aid Of all full-time matriculated undergraduates who enrolled in 2016, 7,469 applied for aid, 6,538 were judged to have need, 6,538 had their need fully met. 4,970 Federal Work-Study jobs (averaging $2321). 925 state and other part-time jobs (averaging $2235). ***Average percent of need met:*** 100. ***Average financial aid package:*** $46,339. ***Average need-based loan:*** $5037. ***Average need-based gift aid:*** $39,595. ***Average indebtedness upon graduation:*** $23,389. ***Financial aid deadline:*** 2/15.

APPLYING
Standardized Tests *Required:* SAT or ACT (for admission). *Required for some:* SAT Subject Tests (for admission).
Options: electronic application, early decision, deferred entrance.
Application fee: $80.
Required: essay or personal statement, high school transcript, 2 letters of recommendation. ***Required for some:*** interview.
Application deadlines: 1/2 (freshmen), 3/15 (transfers).
Early decision deadline: 11/1.
Notification: 3/31 (freshmen), 6/15 (transfers), 12/15 (early decision).

CONTACT
Director of Undergraduate Admissions, Cornell University, 144 East Avenue, Ithaca, NY 14853. *Phone:* 607-255-5241. *Fax:* 607-255-0659. *E-mail:* admissions@cornell.edu.

The Culinary Institute of America
Hyde Park, New York
http://www.ciachef.edu/

- **Independent** 4-year, founded 1946
- **Suburban** 170-acre campus
- **Endowment** $109.7 million
- **Coed** 2,774 undergraduate students, 100% full-time, 51% women, 49% men
- **Moderately difficult** entrance level, 94% of applicants were admitted

UNDERGRAD STUDENTS
2,774 full-time. Students come from 53 states and territories; 37 other countries; 68% are from out of state; 6% Black or African American, non-Hispanic/Latino; 16% Hispanic/Latino; 7% Asian, non-Hispanic/Latino; 0.4% Native Hawaiian or other Pacific Islander, non-Hispanic/Latino; 0.5% American Indian or Alaska Native, non-Hispanic/Latino; 4% Two or more races, non-Hispanic/Latino; 3% Race/ethnicity unknown; 12% international; 11% transferred in; 61% live on campus.

Freshmen:
Admission: 1,045 applied, 985 admitted, 512 enrolled. ***Average high school GPA:*** 3.1. ***Test scores:*** SAT critical reading scores over 500: 57%; SAT math scores over 500: 54%; SAT writing scores over 500: 45%; ACT scores over 18: 74%; SAT critical reading scores over 600: 13%; SAT math scores over 600: 10%; SAT writing scores over 600: 8%; ACT scores over 24: 22%; SAT math scores over 700: 1%; ACT scores over 30: 3%.

ACADEMICS
Calendar: semesters plus 18 or 21 week externship program. *Degrees:* certificates, associate, bachelor's, and postbachelor's certificates.
Special study options: academic remediation for entering students, double majors, English as a second language, internships, off-campus study, services for LD students.
Computers: 227 computers/terminals are available on campus for general student use. Students can access the following: campus intranet, computer help desk, free student e-mail accounts, online (class) grades, online (class) registration, online (class) schedules, online course guides. Campuswide network is available. 100% of college-owned or -operated housing units are wired for high-speed Internet access. Wireless service is available via entire campus.
Library: Conrad N. Hilton Library. *Books:* 70,500 (physical), 541 (digital/electronic); *Serial titles:* 193 (physical), 10 (digital/electronic); *Databases:* 64. Weekly public service hours: 92; students can reserve study rooms.

STUDENT LIFE
Housing options: coed, special housing for students with disabilities. Campus housing is university owned and is provided by a third party. Freshman campus housing is guaranteed.
Activities and organizations: student-run newspaper, choral group, Korean Association of the Culinary Institute of America, Black Culinary

Society, Culinary Christian Fellowship, Eta Sigma Delta Honor Society, Table Top Gaming Club.

Athletics ***Intercollegiate sports:*** basketball M/W, cross-country running M/W, soccer M/W, tennis M/W, volleyball M(c)/W. ***Intramural sports:*** basketball M/W, football M/W, soccer M/W, softball M/W, tennis M/W, volleyball M/W, weight lifting M/W.

Campus security: 24-hour emergency response devices and patrols, late-night transport/escort service, controlled dormitory access.

Student services: health clinic, personal/psychological counseling.

COSTS & FINANCIAL AID

Costs (2017–18) ***Comprehensive fee:*** $42,486 includes full-time tuition ($29,380), mandatory fees ($2236), and room and board ($10,870). Full-time tuition and fees vary according to location. ***College room only:*** $7320. Room and board charges vary according to board plan, housing facility, and location. ***Payment plan:*** installment. ***Waivers:*** employees or children of employees.

Financial Aid Of all full-time matriculated undergraduates who enrolled in 2016, 1,924 applied for aid, 1,787 were judged to have need, 122 had their need fully met. 1,045 Federal Work-Study jobs (averaging $2238). In 2016, 132 non-need-based awards were made. ***Average percent of need met:*** 71. ***Average financial aid package:*** $16,541. ***Average need-based loan:*** $3825. ***Average need-based gift aid:*** $12,031. ***Average non-need-based aid:*** $6359. ***Average indebtedness upon graduation:*** $51,200.

APPLYING

Options: electronic application, deferred entrance.

Application fee: $50.

Required: essay or personal statement, high school transcript, 1 letter of recommendation. ***Required for some:*** Affidavit of Support.

Notification: continuous (transfers).

CONTACT

Ms. Rachel Birchwood, Director of Admissions, The Culinary Institute of America, 1946 Campus Drive, Hyde Park, NY 12538. *Phone:* 845-451-1459. *Toll-free phone:* 800-CULINARY. *Fax:* 845-451-1068. *E-mail:* admissions@culinary.edu.

★ Daemen College

Amherst, New York

http://www.daemen.edu/

- **Independent** comprehensive, founded 1947
- **Suburban** 35-acre campus with easy access to Buffalo
- **Endowment** $12.5 million
- **Coed** 1,993 undergraduate students, 81% full-time, 71% women, 29% men
- **Moderately difficult** entrance level, 52% of applicants were admitted

UNDERGRAD STUDENTS

1,621 full-time, 372 part-time. Students come from 9 other countries; 11% Black or African American, non-Hispanic/Latino; 7% Hispanic/Latino; 2% Asian, non-Hispanic/Latino; 0.1% Native Hawaiian or other Pacific Islander, non-Hispanic/Latino; 0.4% American Indian or Alaska Native, non-Hispanic/Latino; 1% Two or more races, non-Hispanic/Latino; 2% Race/ethnicity unknown; 1% international; 14% transferred in; 38% live on campus.

Freshmen:

Admission: 3,219 applied, 1,673 admitted, 392 enrolled. ***Average high school GPA:*** 3.63. ***Test scores:*** SAT critical reading scores over 500: 59%; SAT math scores over 500: 65%; SAT writing scores over 500: 45%; ACT scores over 18: 96%; SAT critical reading scores over 600: 16%; SAT math scores over 600: 22%; SAT writing scores over 600: 11%; ACT scores over 24: 61%; SAT critical reading scores over 700: 1%; ACT scores over 30: 6%.

Retention: 79% of full-time freshmen returned.

FACULTY

Total: 308, 46% full-time, 65% with terminal degrees.

Student/faculty ratio: 12:1.

ACADEMICS

Calendar: semesters. *Degrees:* certificates, bachelor's, master's, doctoral, post-master's, and postbachelor's certificates.

Special study options: academic remediation for entering students, accelerated degree program, adult/continuing education programs, advanced placement credit, distance learning, double majors, honors programs, independent study, internships, off-campus study, part-time degree program, services for LD students, student-designed majors, study abroad, summer session for credit. ***ROTC:*** Army (c).

Unusual degree programs: 3-2 business administration; athletic training, physician assistant, professional accountancy, public health.

Computers: 163 computers/terminals are available on campus for general student use. Students can access the following: campus intranet, computer help desk, free student e-mail accounts, online (class) grades, online (class) registration, online (class) schedules. Campuswide network is available. 100% of college-owned or -operated housing units are wired for high-speed Internet access. Wireless service is available via classrooms, computer labs, dorm rooms, learning centers, libraries, student centers.

Library: Research and Information Commons. *Books:* 85,205 (physical), 138,085 (digital/electronic); *Serial titles:* 488 (physical); *Databases:* 38. Weekly public service hours: 117; students can reserve study rooms.

STUDENT LIFE

Housing options: on-campus residence required for freshman year; coed, special housing for students with disabilities. Campus housing is university owned. Freshman campus housing is guaranteed.

Activities and organizations: drama/theater group, student-run newspaper, choral group, Anime Club, Music Club, Best Buddies, CRU, Piano Club.

Athletics Member NCAA. All Division II. ***Intercollegiate sports:*** basketball M(s)/W(s), bowling W(s), cross-country running M(s)/W(s), golf M(s), soccer M(s)/W(s), tennis M(s)/W(s), track and field M(s)/W(s), volleyball W(s). ***Intramural sports:*** baseball M(c), basketball M/W, cheerleading M(c)/W(c), football M, ice hockey M(c), lacrosse W(c), sand volleyball M/W, ultimate Frisbee M/W, volleyball M(c)/W(c).

Campus security: 24-hour emergency response devices and patrols, late-night transport/escort service, controlled dormitory access, 24-hour security cameras.

Student services: personal/psychological counseling.

COSTS

Costs (2016–17) ***Comprehensive fee:*** $39,365 includes full-time tuition ($26,400), mandatory fees ($540), and room and board ($12,425). Full-time tuition and fees vary according to location and reciprocity agreements. Part-time tuition: $880 per credit hour. Part-time tuition and fees vary according to course load, location, and reciprocity agreements. ***Required fees:*** $7 per credit hour part-time, $80 per term part-time. ***Room and board:*** Room and board charges vary according to board plan and housing facility. ***Payment plans:*** installment, deferred payment. ***Waivers:*** senior citizens and employees or children of employees.

APPLYING

Standardized Tests *Required for some:* SAT/ACT or high school course grades, show rigor of courses and teacher recommendations.

Options: electronic application, early admission, deferred entrance.

Application fee: $25.

Required: essay or personal statement, high school transcript, minimum 1.0 GPA, 2 letters of recommendation. ***Required for some:*** 3 letters of recommendation, interview, class rank, writing sample.

Application deadlines: rolling (freshmen), rolling (transfers).

Notification: continuous (freshmen), continuous (transfers).

CONTACT

Mr. David Johnson, Associate Director Undergraduate Admissions, Daemen College, 4380 Main Street, Amherst, NY 14226-3592. *Phone:* 716-839-8225. *Toll-free phone:* 800-462-7652. *Fax:* 716-839-8229. *E-mail:* admissions@daemen.edu.

See next page for display ad and page 1330 for the College Close-Up.

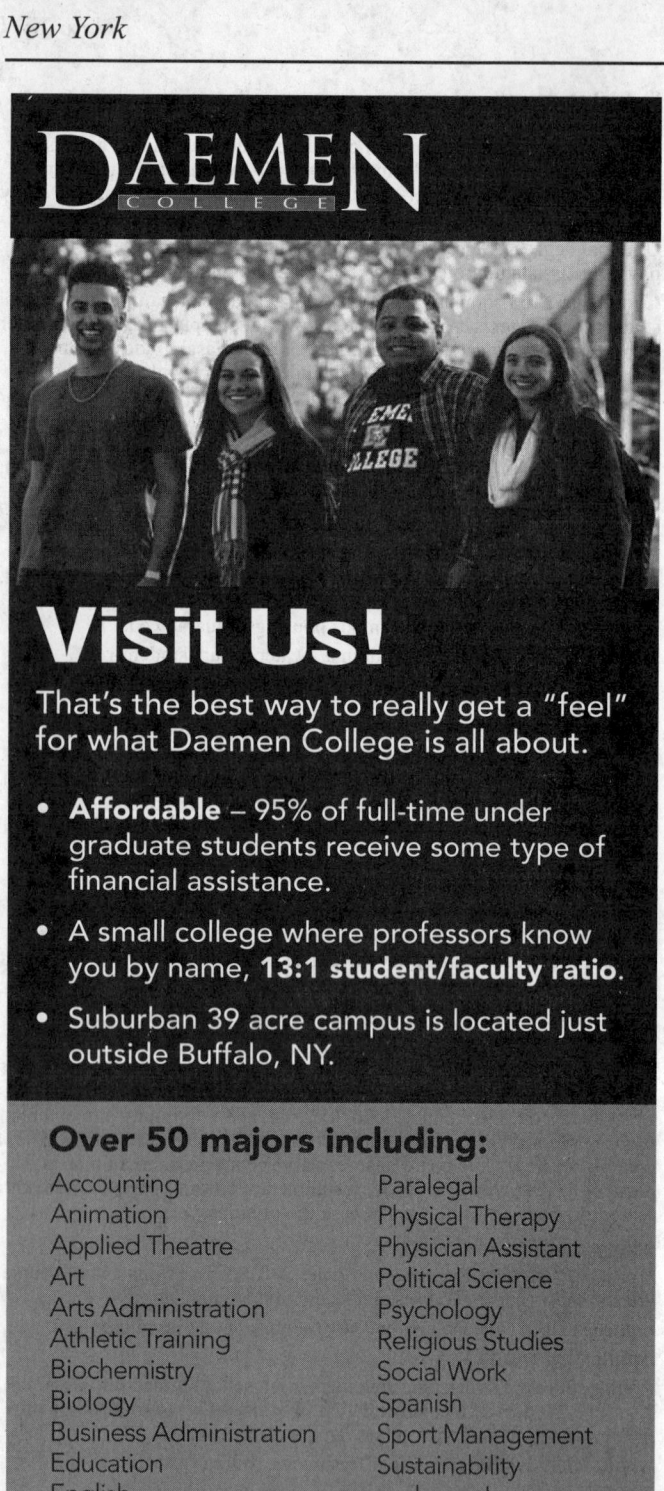

Davis College

Johnson City, New York

http://www.davisny.edu/

- **Independent nondenominational** 4-year, founded 1900
- **Suburban** 22-acre campus with easy access to Syracuse
- **Coed** 216 undergraduate students, 76% full-time, 48% women, 52% men
- **Minimally difficult** entrance level, 52% of applicants were admitted

UNDERGRAD STUDENTS

165 full-time, 51 part-time. Students come from 5 other countries; 60% are from out of state; 20% transferred in; 61% live on campus.

Freshmen:

Admission: 120 applied, 62 admitted, 42 enrolled. ***Average high school GPA:*** 3.18.

Retention: 85% of full-time freshmen returned.

FACULTY

Total: 31, 45% full-time, 52% with terminal degrees.

Student/faculty ratio: 14:1.

ACADEMICS

Calendar: semesters. *Degrees:* certificates, diplomas, associate, and bachelor's.

Special study options: academic remediation for entering students, adult/continuing education programs, advanced placement credit, cooperative education, English as a second language, independent study, internships, part-time degree program, services for LD students, summer session for credit.

Computers: 12 computers/terminals and 20 ports are available on campus for general student use. Students can access the following: campus intranet, computer help desk, free student e-mail accounts, online (class) grades, online (class) registration, online (class) schedules. Campuswide network is available. 100% of college-owned or -operated housing units are wired for high-speed Internet access. Wireless service is available via entire campus.

Library: Alice E. Chatlos Library. Students can reserve study rooms.

STUDENT LIFE

Housing options: on-campus residence required for freshman year; men-only, women-only. Campus housing is university owned. Freshman campus housing is guaranteed.

Activities and organizations: drama/theater group, student-run newspaper, choral group, Student Missionary Fellowship, Student Wives Fellowship, Student Life Committee, Married Couples Fellowship.

Athletics Member NCCAA, USCAA. ***Intercollegiate sports:*** basketball M/W, cross-country running M/W, soccer M, volleyball W. ***Intramural sports:*** soccer M/W, volleyball M/W.

Campus security: 24-hour emergency response devices and patrols, student patrols, late-night transport/escort service, controlled dormitory access.

Student services: health clinic, personal/psychological counseling.

COSTS & FINANCIAL AID

Costs (2017–18) ***One-time required fee:*** $150. ***Comprehensive fee:*** $24,000 includes full-time tuition ($15,000), mandatory fees ($1300), and room and board ($7700). Full-time tuition and fees vary according to course load and location. Part-time tuition: $500 per credit hour. Part-time tuition and fees vary according to course load and location. ***Required fees:*** $650 per year part-time. ***Room and board:*** Room and board charges vary according to board plan and housing facility. ***Payment plan:*** installment. ***Waivers:*** employees or children of employees.

Financial Aid Of all full-time matriculated undergraduates who enrolled in 2015, 178 applied for aid, 175 were judged to have need, 111 had their need fully met. 14 Federal Work-Study jobs (averaging $790). In 2015, 10 non-need-based awards were made. ***Average percent of need met:*** 75. ***Average financial aid package:*** $9475. ***Average need-based gift aid:*** $3000. ***Average non-need-based aid:*** $750. ***Average indebtedness upon graduation:*** $5360.

APPLYING

Standardized Tests *Recommended:* SAT or ACT (for admission).

Options: electronic application, deferred entrance.

Application fee: $45.

Required: essay or personal statement, high school transcript, 1 letter of recommendation. ***Recommended:*** minimum 2.0 GPA, interview.

Application deadlines: rolling (freshmen), rolling (transfers).

Notification: continuous (freshmen), continuous (transfers).

CONTACT

Ms. Hannah Hempstead, Assistant Director of Admissions for Communication, Davis College, 400 Riverside Drive, Johnson City, NY 13790. *Phone:* 607-729-1581 Ext. 341. *Toll-free phone:* 877-949-3248. *Fax:* 607-770-6886. *E-mail:* hhempstead@davisny.edu.

DeVry College of New York–Midtown Manhattan Campus

New York, New York

http://www.devry.edu/

- **Proprietary** comprehensive, founded 1998, part of DeVry University
- **Urban** campus
- **Coed**
- **Minimally difficult** entrance level

FACULTY

Student/faculty ratio: 26:1.

ACADEMICS

Calendar: semesters. *Degrees:* associate, bachelor's, master's, and postbachelor's certificates.

Library: Learning Resource Center.

STUDENT LIFE

Housing options: college housing not available.

COSTS & FINANCIAL AID

Costs (2016–17) ***Tuition:*** $17,052 full-time, $609 per credit hour part-time. ***Required fees:*** $460 full-time.

Financial Aid Of all full-time matriculated undergraduates who enrolled in 2007, 387 applied for aid, 371 were judged to have need, 8 had their need fully met. In 2007, 19 non-need-based awards were made. ***Average percent of need met:*** 5. ***Average financial aid package:*** $15,942. ***Average need-based loan:*** $8712. ***Average need-based gift aid:*** $7343. ***Average non-need-based aid:*** $11,806. ***Average indebtedness upon graduation:*** $29,136.

APPLYING

Application fee: $30.

Required: high school transcript, interview.

CONTACT

DeVry College of New York–Midtown Manhattan Campus, 180 Madison Avenue, Suite 900, New York, NY 10016. *Phone:* 212-312-4300. *Toll-free phone:* 866-338-7934.

Dominican College

Orangeburg, New York

http://www.dc.edu/

- **Independent** comprehensive, founded 1952
- **Suburban** 70-acre campus with easy access to New York City
- **Endowment** $4.5 million
- **Coed** 1,478 undergraduate students, 90% full-time, 67% women, 33% men
- **Noncompetitive** entrance level, 75% of applicants were admitted

UNDERGRAD STUDENTS

1,330 full-time, 148 part-time. Students come from 28 states and territories; 12 other countries; 22% are from out of state; 16% Black or African American, non-Hispanic/Latino; 30% Hispanic/Latino; 6% Asian, non-Hispanic/Latino; 0.7% Native Hawaiian or other Pacific Islander, non-Hispanic/Latino; 3% Two or more races, non-Hispanic/Latino; 8% Race/ethnicity unknown; 1% international; 10% transferred in; 49% live on campus.

Freshmen:

Admission: 1,751 applied, 1,321 admitted, 253 enrolled. ***Average high school GPA:*** 3.03.

Retention: 69% of full-time freshmen returned.

FACULTY

Total: 235, 32% full-time, 36% with terminal degrees.

Student/faculty ratio: 13:1.

ACADEMICS

Calendar: semesters. *Degrees:* certificates, diplomas, associate, bachelor's, master's, doctoral, and postbachelor's certificates.

Special study options: academic remediation for entering students, accelerated degree program, adult/continuing education programs, advanced placement credit, cooperative education, distance learning, double majors, honors programs, independent study, internships, off-campus study, part-time degree program, services for LD students, study abroad, summer session for credit.

Unusual degree programs: 3-2 engineering with Manhattan College; occupational therapy.

Computers: 150 computers/terminals are available on campus for general student use. Students can access the following: campus intranet, computer help desk, free student e-mail accounts, online (class) registration, online (class) schedules, Web portal, learning management system. Campuswide network is available. 100% of college-owned or -operated housing units are wired for high-speed Internet access. Wireless service is available via entire campus.

Library: Sullivan Library plus 1 other. *Books:* 81,325 (physical), 118,178 (digital/electronic); *Serial titles:* 612 (physical), 74,172 (digital/electronic); *Databases:* 82. Weekly public service hours: 89; students can reserve study rooms.

STUDENT LIFE

Housing options: coed. Campus housing is university owned. Freshman campus housing is guaranteed.

Activities and organizations: drama/theater group, student-run radio station, choral group, Student Government Association, Business Club, Aquin Players Drama Society, Anime Magna and Videogame Club, Student Nursing Association.

Athletics Member NCAA. All Division II. ***Intercollegiate sports:*** baseball M(s), basketball M(s)/W(s), cross-country running M(s)/W(s), golf M(s), lacrosse M(s)/W(s), soccer M(s)/W(s), softball W(s), track and field M(s)/W(s), volleyball W(s). ***Intramural sports:*** basketball M/W, ultimate Frisbee M(c)/W(c), volleyball M/W.

Campus security: 24-hour emergency response devices and patrols, student patrols, late-night transport/escort service, controlled dormitory access.

Student services: health clinic, personal/psychological counseling.

COSTS & FINANCIAL AID

Costs (2017–18) ***Comprehensive fee:*** $41,118 includes full-time tuition ($27,588), mandatory fees ($860), and room and board ($12,670). Full-time tuition and fees vary according to degree level. Part-time tuition: $834 per credit hour. Part-time tuition and fees vary according to degree level and program. ***Required fees:*** $200 per term part-time. ***Room and board:*** Room and board charges vary according to board plan and housing facility. ***Payment plans:*** installment, deferred payment. ***Waivers:*** senior citizens and employees or children of employees.

Financial Aid Of all full-time matriculated undergraduates who enrolled in 2016, 1,202 applied for aid, 1,082 were judged to have need, 133 had their need fully met. 305 Federal Work-Study jobs (averaging $213,664). In 2016, 189 non-need-based awards were made. ***Average percent of need met:*** 66. ***Average financial aid package:*** $21,434. ***Average need-based loan:*** $5165. ***Average need-based gift aid:*** $17,255. ***Average non-need-based aid:*** $9422. ***Average indebtedness upon graduation:*** $31,976.

APPLYING

Standardized Tests *Required:* SAT or ACT (for admission).

Options: electronic application, deferred entrance.

Application fee: $35.

Required: high school transcript. ***Required for some:*** essay or personal statement, interview. ***Recommended:*** interview.

Application deadlines: rolling (freshmen), rolling (transfers).

Notification: continuous (freshmen), continuous (transfers).

CONTACT

Mr. Robert Tyrrell, Assistant Director of Freshman Admissions, Dominican College, 470 Western Highway, Orangeburg, NY 10962-1210.

Phone: 845-359-7906. *Toll-free phone:* 866-432-4636. *Fax:* 845-365-3150. *E-mail:* rob.tyrrell@dc.edu.

D'Youville College

Buffalo, New York

http://www.dyc.edu/

- **Independent** comprehensive, founded 1908
- **Urban** 11-acre campus
- **Coed**
- **Moderately difficult** entrance level

FACULTY

Student/faculty ratio: 10:1.

ACADEMICS

Calendar: semesters plus summer session. *Degrees:* bachelor's, master's, doctoral, post-master's, and postbachelor's certificates.
Library: Montante Family Library.

STUDENT LIFE

Housing options: coed, men-only, women-only, special housing for students with disabilities. Campus housing is university owned. Freshman campus housing is guaranteed.

Activities and organizations: drama/theater group, student-run newspaper, choral group, Student Association, Occupational Therapy Student Association, Physical Therapy Student Association, Student Nurses Association, Black Student Union.

Athletics Member NCAA. All Division III.

Campus security: 24-hour emergency response devices and patrols, late-night transport/escort service, controlled dormitory access.

Student services: health clinic, personal/psychological counseling.

COSTS & FINANCIAL AID

Costs (2016–17) ***Comprehensive fee:*** $36,780 includes full-time tuition ($24,740), mandatory fees ($470), and room and board ($11,570). Full-time tuition and fees vary according to course load, degree level, and program. Part-time tuition: $770 per credit hour. Part-time tuition and fees vary according to course load, degree level, and program. No tuition increase for student's term of enrollment. ***Required fees:*** $3 per credit hour part-time, $55 per credit hour part-time. ***Room and board:*** Room and board charges vary according to board plan and housing facility. ***Payment plans:*** installment, deferred payment.

Financial Aid Of all full-time matriculated undergraduates who enrolled in 2015, 828 applied for aid, 743 were judged to have need, 185 had their need fully met. In 2015, 117 non-need-based awards were made. ***Average percent of need met:*** 71. ***Average financial aid package:*** $19,088. ***Average need-based loan:*** $4369. ***Average need-based gift aid:*** $15,255. ***Average non-need-based aid:*** $9231. ***Average indebtedness upon graduation:*** $33,169.

APPLYING

Standardized Tests *Required:* SAT or ACT (for admission).

Options: electronic application, deferred entrance.

Required: high school transcript, minimum 2.0 GPA. ***Required for some:*** essay or personal statement, minimum 3.0 GPA, interview.

CONTACT

D'Youville College, 320 Porter Avenue, Buffalo, NY 14201-1084. *Phone:* 716-829-7600. *Toll-free phone:* 800-777-3921.

Elmira College

Elmira, New York

http://www.elmira.edu/

- **Independent** comprehensive, founded 1855
- **Small-town** 55-acre campus
- **Endowment** $41.2 million
- **Coed** 1,288 undergraduate students, 87% full-time, 70% women, 30% men
- **Moderately difficult** entrance level, 76% of applicants were admitted

UNDERGRAD STUDENTS

1,123 full-time, 165 part-time. Students come from 35 states and territories; 15 other countries; 37% are from out of state; 4% Black or African American, non-Hispanic/Latino; 3% Hispanic/Latino; 2% Asian, non-Hispanic/Latino; 0.4% American Indian or Alaska Native, non-Hispanic/Latino; 2% Two or more races, non-Hispanic/Latino; 4% Race/ethnicity unknown; 5% international; 6% transferred in; 88% live on campus.

Freshmen:

Admission: 2,387 applied, 1,818 admitted, 258 enrolled. ***Average high school GPA:*** 3.28. ***Test scores:*** SAT critical reading scores over 500: 56%; SAT math scores over 500: 56%; ACT scores over 18: 93%; SAT critical reading scores over 600: 14%; SAT math scores over 600: 21%; ACT scores over 24: 56%; SAT math scores over 700: 1%; ACT scores over 30: 9%.

Retention: 79% of full-time freshmen returned.

FACULTY

Total: 170, 39% full-time, 58% with terminal degrees.

Student/faculty ratio: 12:1.

ACADEMICS

Calendar: 4-4-1. *Degrees:* associate, bachelor's, master's, and postbachelor's certificates.

Special study options: accelerated degree program, adult/continuing education programs, advanced placement credit, distance learning, double majors, English as a second language, honors programs, independent study, internships, off-campus study, part-time degree program, services for LD students, student-designed majors, study abroad, summer session for credit. ***ROTC:*** Army (b), Air Force (c).

Unusual degree programs: 3-2 chemistry/chemical engineering with Clarkson University.

Computers: 327 computers/terminals and 186 ports are available on campus for general student use. Students can access the following: campus intranet, computer help desk, free student e-mail accounts, online (class) grades, online (class) registration, online (class) schedules. Campuswide network is available. 100% of college-owned or -operated housing units are wired for high-speed Internet access. Wireless service is available via entire campus.

Library: Gannett-Tripp Library. *Books:* 147,895 (physical), 147,101 (digital/electronic); *Serial titles:* 1,099 (physical), 21,828 (digital/electronic); *Databases:* 94. Weekly public service hours: 110.

STUDENT LIFE

Housing options: on-campus residence required through senior year; coed, women-only, cooperative, special housing for students with disabilities. Campus housing is university owned. Freshman campus housing is guaranteed.

Activities and organizations: drama/theater group, student-run newspaper, radio station, choral group, SAB (Student Activities Board), Enactus, Colleges Against Cancer (Relay for Life), Orchesis, Habitat for Humanity.

Athletics Member NCAA. All Division III. ***Intercollegiate sports:*** baseball M, basketball M/W, cheerleading W, cross-country running M/W, field hockey W, golf M/W, ice hockey M/W, lacrosse M/W, soccer M/W, softball W, tennis M/W, volleyball M/W. ***Intramural sports:*** badminton M/W, basketball M/W, bowling M/W, equestrian sports M/W, football M/W, ice hockey M/W, lacrosse M/W, racquetball M/W, soccer M/W, softball M/W, ultimate Frisbee M/W, volleyball M/W.

Campus security: 24-hour patrols, late-night transport/escort service, controlled dormitory access, 24-hour locked residence hall entrances.

Student services: health clinic, personal/psychological counseling.

COSTS & FINANCIAL AID

Costs (2016–17) ***Comprehensive fee:*** $53,900 includes full-time tuition ($41,900) and room and board ($12,000). Full-time tuition and fees vary according to degree level. Part-time tuition: $1200 per credit. Part-time tuition and fees vary according to course load and degree level. ***College room only:*** $6400. Room and board charges vary according to board plan and housing facility. ***Payment plans:*** tuition prepayment, installment. ***Waivers:*** employees or children of employees.

Financial Aid Of all full-time matriculated undergraduates who enrolled in 2016, 835 applied for aid, 790 were judged to have need, 152 had their need fully met. 144 Federal Work-Study jobs (averaging $1200). 164 state and other part-time jobs (averaging $1000). In 2016, 154 non-need-based awards were made. ***Average percent of need met:*** 76. ***Average financial***

aid package: $30,976. *Average need-based loan:* $4798. *Average need-based gift aid:* $26,785. *Average non-need-based aid:* $22,662. *Average indebtedness upon graduation:* $27,757.

APPLYING
Standardized Tests *Required for some:* SAT or ACT (for admission).

Options: electronic application, early decision, deferred entrance.

Required: essay or personal statement, high school transcript, minimum 2.0 GPA, 1 letter of recommendation. ***Required for some:*** interview. ***Recommended:*** interview.

Application deadlines: rolling (freshmen), rolling (transfers).

Notification: continuous until 11/15 (freshmen), continuous (transfers).

CONTACT
Mr. Brett Moore, Dean of Admissions, Elmira College, 1 Park Place, Elmira, NY 14901. *Phone:* 607-735-1724. *Toll-free phone:* 800-935-6472. *Fax:* 607-735-1718. *E-mail:* admissions@elmira.edu.

Eugene Lang College of Liberal Arts

New York, New York

http://www.newschool.edu/lang

- **Independent** 4-year, founded 1978, part of The New School
- **Urban** campus with easy access to New York City
- **Endowment** $300.1 million
- **Coed** 1,663 undergraduate students, 96% full-time, 76% women, 24% men

UNDERGRAD STUDENTS
1,596 full-time, 67 part-time. Students come from 56 states and territories; 53 other countries; 73% are from out of state; 8% Black or African American, non-Hispanic/Latino; 17% Hispanic/Latino; 6% Asian, non-Hispanic/Latino; 0.2% Native Hawaiian or other Pacific Islander, non-Hispanic/Latino; 6% Two or more races, non-Hispanic/Latino; 7% Race/ethnicity unknown; 8% international; 7% transferred in; 34% live on campus.

Freshmen:
Admission: 494 enrolled. *Average high school GPA:* 3.38. *Test scores:* SAT critical reading scores over 500: 89%; SAT math scores over 500: 74%; SAT writing scores over 500: 89%; ACT scores over 18: 99%; SAT critical reading scores over 600: 57%; SAT math scores over 600: 32%; SAT writing scores over 600: 51%; ACT scores over 24: 79%; SAT critical reading scores over 700: 15%; SAT math scores over 700: 3%; SAT writing scores over 700: 9%; ACT scores over 30: 17%.

Retention: 75% of full-time freshmen returned.

FACULTY
Total: 203, 47% full-time, 37% with terminal degrees.

Student/faculty ratio: 10:1.

ACADEMICS
Calendar: semesters. *Degree:* bachelor's.

Special study options: academic remediation for entering students, accelerated degree program, advanced placement credit, cooperative education, distance learning, double majors, English as a second language, independent study, internships, off-campus study, part-time degree program, services for LD students, student-designed majors, study abroad, summer session for credit.

Unusual degree programs: psychology.

Computers: 420 computers/terminals are available on campus for general student use. Students can access the following: campus intranet, computer help desk, free student e-mail accounts, online (class) grades, online (class) registration, online (class) schedules. Campuswide network is available. 100% of college-owned or -operated housing units are wired for high-speed Internet access. Wireless service is available via entire campus.

Library: New School Libraries & Archives plus 3 others. *Books:* 215,240 (physical), 718,102 (digital/electronic); *Serial titles:* 712 (physical), 90,364 (digital/electronic); *Databases:* 529. Weekly public service hours: 137; study areas open 24 hours, 5-7 days a week; students can reserve study rooms.

STUDENT LIFE
Housing options: coed, special housing for students with disabilities. Campus housing is university owned and leased by the school. Freshman applicants given priority for college housing.

Activities and organizations: drama/theater group, student-run newspaper, radio station, choral group.

Athletics ***Intramural sports:*** basketball M/W, cross-country running M/W, soccer M/W, tennis M/W.

Campus security: 24-hour emergency response devices, controlled dormitory access, 24-hour desk attendants in residence halls.

Student services: health clinic, personal/psychological counseling.

FINANCIAL AID
Financial Aid Of all full-time matriculated undergraduates who enrolled in 2014, 918 applied for aid, 828 were judged to have need, 115 had their need fully met. In 2014, 409 non-need-based awards were made. *Average percent of need met:* 72. *Average financial aid package:* $28,623. *Average need-based loan:* $7007. *Average need-based gift aid:* $18,428. *Average non-need-based aid:* $8824. *Average indebtedness upon graduation:* $26,583. *Financial aid deadline:* 3/1.

APPLYING
Standardized Tests *Required for some:* TOEFL, IELTS and PTE for some applicants whose first language is not English.

Required: essay or personal statement, high school transcript, 1 letter of recommendation, online application, 2 supplemental essays, counselor evaluation or teacher evaluation, academic paper (grade preferred). ***Recommended:*** minimum 3.0 GPA, interview.

CONTACT
Mr. Candice MacLusky, Director of Admissions for Lang, Eugene Lang College of Liberal Arts, 72 Fifth Avenue at 13th Street, New York, NY 10011. *Phone:* 212-229-5155 Ext. 4024. *Toll-free phone:* 800-292-3040. *E-mail:* macluskc@newschool.edu.

Excelsior College

Albany, New York

http://www.excelsior.edu/

- **Independent** comprehensive, founded 1970
- **Suburban** campus with easy access to Albany, NY
- **Coed** 35,161 undergraduate students, 53% women, 47% men

UNDERGRAD STUDENTS
35,161 part-time. Students come from 55 states and territories; 37 other countries; 85% are from out of state; 21% Black or African American, non-Hispanic/Latino; 10% Hispanic/Latino; 3% Asian, non-Hispanic/Latino; 0.5% Native Hawaiian or other Pacific Islander, non-Hispanic/Latino; 0.6% American Indian or Alaska Native, non-Hispanic/Latino; 3% Two or more races, non-Hispanic/Latino; 2% Race/ethnicity unknown; 0.7% international; 5% transferred in.

FACULTY
Total: 1,280, 44% with terminal degrees.

Student/faculty ratio: 10:1.

ACADEMICS
Calendar: continuous. *Degrees:* certificates, associate, bachelor's, master's, post-master's, and postbachelor's certificates (offers only external degree programs).

Special study options: adult/continuing education programs, distance learning, external degree program, independent study, part-time degree program, services for LD students, student-designed majors.

Unusual degree programs: 3-2 business administration; nursing; nuclear engineering technology, health care management, business, information technology/business administration; nursing; information technology/cybersecurity.

Computers: Students can access the following: computer help desk, online (class) grades, online (class) registration, online (class) schedules. Campuswide network is available.

Library: Excelsior College Library.

STUDENT LIFE
Housing options: college housing not available.

COSTS
Costs (2016–17) ***Tuition:*** $510 per credit part-time. Part-time tuition and fees vary according to reciprocity agreements. ***Payment plan:*** installment. ***Waivers:*** employees or children of employees.

APPLYING
Options: electronic application.
Application fee: $50.
Required for some: college transcripts.
Application deadlines: rolling (freshmen), rolling (transfers).
Notification: continuous (freshmen), continuous (transfers).

CONTACT
Admissions, Excelsior College, 7 Columbia Circle, Albany, NY 12203-5159. *Phone:* 518-464-8500. *Toll-free phone:* 888-647-2388. *Fax:* 518-464-8777. *E-mail:* admissions@excelsior.edu.

Farmingdale State College
Farmingdale, New York
http://www.farmingdale.edu/

- **State-supported** comprehensive, founded 1912, part of State University of New York System
- **Suburban** 380-acre campus with easy access to New York City
- **Endowment** $5.2 million
- **Coed** 9,235 undergraduate students, 75% full-time, 44% women, 56% men
- **Moderately difficult** entrance level, 58% of applicants were admitted

UNDERGRAD STUDENTS
6,942 full-time, 2,293 part-time. Students come from 12 states and territories; 68 other countries; 0.3% are from out of state; 10% Black or African American, non-Hispanic/Latino; 18% Hispanic/Latino; 8% Asian, non-Hispanic/Latino; 0.4% Native Hawaiian or other Pacific Islander, non-Hispanic/Latino; 0.2% American Indian or Alaska Native, non-Hispanic/Latino; 2% Two or more races, non-Hispanic/Latino; 0.4% Race/ethnicity unknown; 2% international; 13% transferred in; 6% live on campus.

Freshmen:
Admission: 6,169 applied, 3,580 admitted, 1,281 enrolled. ***Average high school GPA:*** 3.2. ***Test scores:*** SAT critical reading scores over 500: 36%; SAT math scores over 500: 50%; ACT scores over 18: 89%; SAT critical reading scores over 600: 5%; SAT math scores over 600: 8%; ACT scores over 24: 24%; ACT scores over 30: 2%.
Retention: 81% of full-time freshmen returned.

FACULTY
Total: 714, 31% full-time.
Student/faculty ratio: 20:1.

ACADEMICS
Calendar: semesters. *Degrees:* certificates, associate, bachelor's, and master's.
Special study options: academic remediation for entering students, advanced placement credit, cooperative education, distance learning, double majors, independent study, internships, part-time degree program, services for LD students, study abroad, summer session for credit. ***ROTC:*** Army (c), Navy (c), Air Force (b).
Computers: 367 computers/terminals are available on campus for general student use. Students can access the following: computer help desk, free student e-mail accounts, online (class) registration, online (class) schedules. Campuswide network is available. 100% of college-owned or -operated housing units are wired for high-speed Internet access. Wireless service is available via entire campus.
Library: Greenley Library. *Books:* 104,155 (physical), 100,000 (digital/electronic); *Databases:* 102. Weekly public service hours: 80.

STUDENT LIFE
Housing options: coed. Campus housing is university owned.
Activities and organizations: drama/theater group, student-run newspaper, radio station, Campus Activities Board, Farmingdale Student Government, Ram Nation Radio, Rambler Newspaper, national fraternities, national sororities.
Athletics Member NCAA. All Division III. ***Intercollegiate sports:*** baseball M, basketball M/W, cross-country running M/W, golf M, ice hockey M(c), lacrosse M/W, soccer M/W, softball W, tennis M/W, track and field M/W, volleyball W. ***Intramural sports:*** badminton M/W, basketball M/W, football M, sand volleyball M/W, soccer M/W, softball M/W, ultimate Frisbee M/W, volleyball M/W.
Campus security: 24-hour emergency response devices and patrols, controlled dormitory access.
Student services: health clinic, personal/psychological counseling.

COSTS & FINANCIAL AID
Costs (2016–17) ***Tuition:*** state resident $6470 full-time, $270 per credit part-time; nonresident $16,320 full-time, $680 per credit part-time. Full-time tuition and fees vary according to program. Part-time tuition and fees vary according to course load and program. ***Required fees:*** $1390 full-time, $56 per credit part-time, $10 per term part-time. ***Room and board:*** $12,764; room only: $7774. Room and board charges vary according to housing facility. ***Payment plan:*** installment. ***Waivers:*** employees or children of employees.
Financial Aid Of all full-time matriculated undergraduates who enrolled in 2015, 4,444 applied for aid, 3,365 were judged to have need.

APPLYING
Standardized Tests *Required:* SAT or ACT (for admission).
Options: electronic application, early admission, deferred entrance.
Application fee: $50.
Required: high school transcript, minimum 3.0 GPA. ***Required for some:*** interview.
Application deadlines: 6/1 (freshmen), 6/30 (transfers).
Notification: continuous (freshmen), continuous (out-of-state freshmen), continuous (transfers).

CONTACT
Farmingdale State College, 2350 Broadhollow Road, Farmingdale, NY 11735. *Phone:* 631-420-2200.

★ Fashion Institute of Technology
New York, New York
http://www.fitnyc.edu/

- **State and locally supported** comprehensive, founded 1944, part of State University of New York System
- **Urban** 5-acre campus with easy access to New York City
- **Coed, primarily women** 9,096 undergraduate students, 81% full-time, 85% women, 15% men
- **Moderately difficult** entrance level, 40% of applicants were admitted

UNDERGRAD STUDENTS
7,395 full-time, 1,701 part-time. 32% are from out of state; 9% Black or African American, non-Hispanic/Latino; 18% Hispanic/Latino; 11% Asian, non-Hispanic/Latino; 0.2% Native Hawaiian or other Pacific Islander, non-Hispanic/Latino; 0.2% American Indian or Alaska Native, non-Hispanic/Latino; 3% Two or more races, non-Hispanic/Latino; 0.8% Race/ethnicity unknown; 12% international; 8% transferred in; 21% live on campus.

Freshmen:
Admission: 4,632 applied, 1,872 admitted, 1,273 enrolled. ***Average high school GPA:*** 3.6.
Retention: 89% of full-time freshmen returned.

FACULTY
Total: 931, 25% full-time.
Student/faculty ratio: 17:1.

ACADEMICS
Calendar: semesters. *Degrees:* certificates, associate, bachelor's, and master's.
Special study options: academic remediation for entering students, advanced placement credit, distance learning, English as a second language, honors programs, independent study, internships, part-time degree program, services for LD students, study abroad, summer session for credit.
Computers: Campuswide network is available.

Library: Gladys Marcus Library.

STUDENT LIFE
Housing options: coed, women-only, special housing for students with disabilities. Campus housing is university owned. Freshman applicants given priority for college housing.

Activities and organizations: drama/theater group, student-run newspaper, radio and television station, choral group.

Athletics Member NJCAA. ***Intercollegiate sports:*** cross-country running M/W, soccer W, swimming and diving M/W, table tennis M/W, tennis M/W, track and field M/W, volleyball W.

Campus security: 24-hour emergency response devices and patrols, late-night transport/escort service, controlled dormitory access.

Student services: health clinic, personal/psychological counseling.

COSTS & FINANCIAL AID
Costs (2016–17) ***Tuition:*** state resident $6470 full-time, $270 per credit hour part-time; nonresident $19,592 full-time, $816 per credit hour part-time. Full-time tuition and fees vary according to degree level. Part-time tuition and fees vary according to degree level. ***Required fees:*** $745 full-time. ***Room and board:*** $13,386; room only: $8910. Room and board charges vary according to board plan and housing facility. ***Waivers:*** employees or children of employees.

Financial Aid Of all full-time matriculated undergraduates who enrolled in 2015, 4,591 applied for aid, 3,763 were judged to have need, 1,664 had their need fully met. In 2015, 230 non-need-based awards were made. ***Average percent of need met:*** 67. ***Average financial aid package:*** $11,804. ***Average need-based loan:*** $3135. ***Average need-based gift aid:*** $6078. ***Average non-need-based aid:*** $773. ***Average indebtedness upon graduation:*** $24,850.

APPLYING
Options: electronic application.

Application fee: $50.

Required: essay or personal statement, high school transcript. ***Required for some:*** portfolio for art and design programs.

Application deadlines: 1/1 (freshmen), 1/1 (transfers).

Notification: 4/1 (freshmen), 4/1 (transfers).

CONTACT
Ms. Magda Francois, Director of Admissions and Strategic Recruitment, Fashion Institute of Technology, Seventh Avenue at 27th Street, New York, NY 10001-5992. *E-mail:* fitinfo@fitnyc.edu.

See below for display ad and page 1354 for the College Close-Up.

Five Towns College
Dix Hills, New York
http://www.ftc.edu/

- **Independent** comprehensive, founded 1972
- **Suburban** 35-acre campus with easy access to New York City
- **Coed**
- **Moderately difficult** entrance level

FACULTY
Student/faculty ratio: 15:1.

ACADEMICS
Calendar: semesters. *Degrees:* associate, bachelor's, master's, and doctoral.
Library: Five Towns College Library plus 1 other.

STUDENT LIFE
Housing options: coed. Campus housing is university owned.

Activities and organizations: drama/theater group, student-run newspaper, radio station, choral group, Film Video Club, Audio Club, Music Business Club, Jazz Club, yearbook.

Campus security: 24-hour emergency response devices and patrols, late-night transport/escort service, controlled dormitory access.

Student services: personal/psychological counseling.

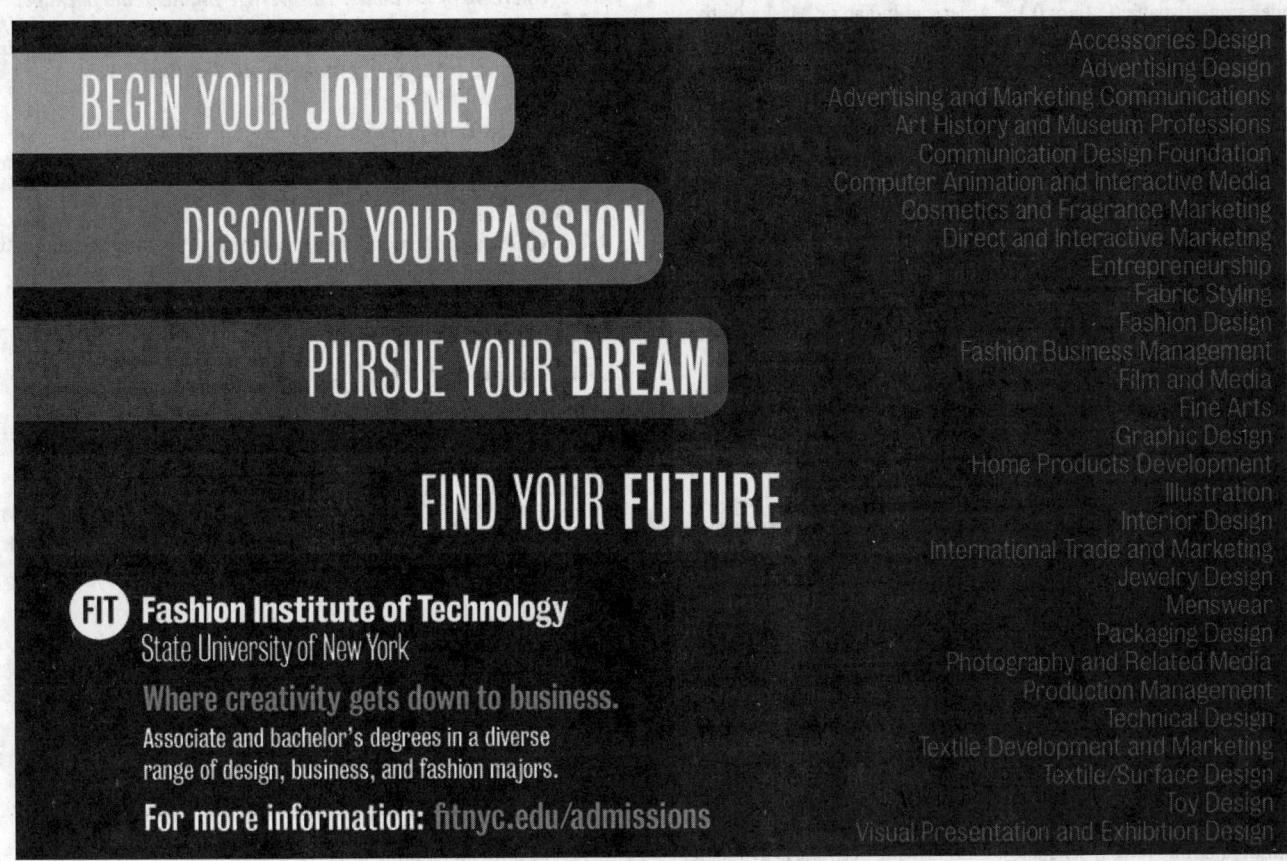

COSTS & FINANCIAL AID
Costs (2016–17) ***Comprehensive fee:*** $33,970 includes full-time tuition ($21,000), mandatory fees ($700), and room and board ($12,270). Full-time tuition and fees vary according to course level, course load, degree level, program, and student level. Part-time tuition: $875 per credit. Part-time tuition and fees vary according to course level, course load, degree

level, program, and student level. ***Room and board:*** Room and board charges vary according to board plan.

Financial Aid Of all full-time matriculated undergraduates who enrolled in 2014, 538 applied for aid, 538 were judged to have need, 120 had their need fully met. In 2014, 43 non-need-based awards were made. ***Average percent of need met:*** 65. ***Average financial aid package:*** $14,821. ***Average need-based loan:*** $4130. ***Average need-based gift aid:*** $2904. ***Average non-need-based aid:*** $3965. ***Average indebtedness upon graduation:*** $35,340.

APPLYING

Standardized Tests *Recommended:* SAT or ACT (for admission).

Options: electronic application, early decision, deferred entrance.

Application fee: $35.

Required: essay or personal statement, minimum 2.3 GPA, 1 letter of recommendation, immunization records; audition for music or theatre. ***Required for some:*** interview.

CONTACT

Ms. Cynthia Catalano, Admissions, Five Towns College, 305 North Service Road, Dix Hills, NY 11746-6055. *Phone:* 631-424-7000 Ext. 2107. *Fax:* 631-656-2107. *E-mail:* cynthia.catalano@ftc.edu.

★ Fordham University

New York, New York

http://www.fordham.edu/

- **Independent Roman Catholic (Jesuit)** university, founded 1841
- **Urban** 93-acre campus with easy access to New York City
- **Endowment** $675.1 million
- **Coed** 9,258 undergraduate students, 95% full-time, 57% women, 43% men
- **Very difficult** entrance level, 48% of applicants were admitted

UNDERGRAD STUDENTS

8,763 full-time, 495 part-time. Students come from 48 states and territories; 73 other countries; 57% are from out of state; 4% Black or African American, non-Hispanic/Latino; 14% Hispanic/Latino; 10% Asian, non-Hispanic/Latino; 0.1% Native Hawaiian or other Pacific Islander, non-Hispanic/Latino; 0.1% American Indian or Alaska Native, non-Hispanic/Latino; 3% Two or more races, non-Hispanic/Latino; 2% Race/ethnicity unknown; 8% international; 4% transferred in; 55% live on campus.

Freshmen:

Admission: 42,811 applied, 20,366 admitted, 2,199 enrolled. ***Average high school GPA:*** 3.64. ***Test scores:*** SAT critical reading scores over 500: 95%; SAT math scores over 500: 96%; SAT writing scores over 500: 95%; ACT scores over 18: 99%; SAT critical reading scores over 600: 65%; SAT math scores over 600: 71%; SAT writing scores over 600: 73%; ACT scores over 24: 89%; SAT critical reading scores over 700: 16%; SAT math scores over 700: 20%; SAT writing scores over 700: 19%; ACT scores over 30: 30%.

Retention: 91% of full-time freshmen returned.

FACULTY

Total: 1,598, 46% full-time, 66% with terminal degrees.

Student/faculty ratio: 14:1.

ACADEMICS

Calendar: semesters. *Degrees:* bachelor's, master's, doctoral, post-master's, and postbachelor's certificates (branch locations at Rose Hill and Lincoln Center).

Special study options: accelerated degree program, adult/continuing education programs, advanced placement credit, double majors, English as a second language, honors programs, independent study, internships, off-campus study, part-time degree program, services for LD students, student-designed majors, study abroad, summer session for credit. ***ROTC:*** Army (b), Navy (c), Air Force (c).

Unusual degree programs: 3-2 engineering with Columbia University, Case Western Reserve University.

Computers: 1,400 computers/terminals are available on campus for general student use. Students can access the following: computer help desk, free student e-mail accounts, online (class) grades, online (class) registration, online (class) schedules. Campuswide network is available. 100% of college-owned or -operated housing units are wired for high-speed Internet access. Wireless service is available via entire campus.

Library: Walsh Library plus 3 others. *Books:* 2.3 million (physical), 600,000 (digital/electronic); *Serial titles:* 9,200 (physical), 76,000 (digital/electronic); *Databases:* 275. Weekly public service hours: 108; study areas open 24 hours, 5-7 days a week.

STUDENT LIFE

Housing options: coed, special housing for students with disabilities. Campus housing is university owned and leased by the school.

Activities and organizations: drama/theater group, student-run newspaper, radio and television station, choral group, marching band, United Student Government, Commuting Student Association, Residence Hall Association, Ambassador Program (Admission Department Student Tour Guides), Campus Activities Board.

Athletics Member NCAA. All Division I except football (Division I-AA). ***Intercollegiate sports:*** baseball M(s), basketball M(s)/W(s), cheerleading W, crew W(s), cross-country running M(s)/W(s), golf M(s), ice hockey M(c), sailing M(c)/W(c), soccer M(s)/W(s), softball W(s), squash M(s), swimming and diving M(s)/W(s), tennis M(s)/W(s), track and field M(s)/W(s), volleyball W(s), water polo M(s). ***Intramural sports:*** baseball M(c), basketball M(c)/W(c), crew M(c), lacrosse M(c)/W(c), rugby M(c)/W(c), soccer M/W, ultimate Frisbee M(c)/W(c).

Campus security: 24-hour emergency response devices and patrols, student patrols, late-night transport/escort service, controlled dormitory access, security at each campus entrance and at residence halls.

Student services: health clinic, personal/psychological counseling.

COSTS & FINANCIAL AID

Costs (2016–17) ***Comprehensive fee:*** $65,918 includes full-time tuition ($47,850), mandatory fees ($1223), and room and board ($16,845). Part-time tuition and fees vary according to class time and course load. ***Room and board:*** Room and board charges vary according to board plan, housing facility, and location. ***Payment plan:*** installment. ***Waivers:*** employees or children of employees.

Financial Aid Of all full-time matriculated undergraduates who enrolled in 2015, 6,960 applied for aid, 5,201 were judged to have need, 1,488 had their need fully met. In 2015, 1739 non-need-based awards were made. ***Average percent of need met:*** 78. ***Average financial aid package:*** $33,566. ***Average need-based loan:*** $6396. ***Average need-based gift aid:*** $25,493. ***Average non-need-based aid:*** $15,724. ***Average indebtedness upon graduation:*** $25,069. ***Financial aid deadline:*** 2/1.

APPLYING

Standardized Tests *Required:* SAT or ACT (for admission).

Options: electronic application, early admission, early decision, early action, deferred entrance.

Application fee: $70.

Required: essay or personal statement, high school transcript, 1 letter of recommendation, Common Application or Fordham Application. ***Recommended:*** 1 letter of recommendation.

Application deadlines: 1/1 (freshmen), 6/1 (transfers), 11/1 (early action).

Early decision deadline: 11/1.

Notification: 4/1 (freshmen), continuous (transfers), 12/20 (early decision), 12/20 (early action).

CONTACT

Dr. Patricia Peek, Director of Undergraduate Admission, Fordham University, Office of Undergraduate Admission, Duane Library, 441 East Fordham Road, Bronx, NY 10458. *Phone:* 718-817-3706. *Toll-free phone:* 800-FORDHAM. *Fax:* 718-367-9404. *E-mail:* peek@fordham.edu.

Hamilton College

Clinton, New York

http://www.hamilton.edu/

- **Independent** 4-year, founded 1812
- **Small-town** 1300-acre campus
- **Endowment** $817.2 million
- **Coed** 1,879 undergraduate students, 99% full-time, 52% women, 48% men
- **Very difficult** entrance level, 26% of applicants were admitted

UNDERGRAD STUDENTS
1,868 full-time, 11 part-time. Students come from 49 states and territories; 47 other countries; 71% are from out of state; 4% Black or African American, non-Hispanic/Latino; 8% Hispanic/Latino; 7% Asian, non-Hispanic/Latino; 0.1% American Indian or Alaska Native, non-Hispanic/Latino; 3% Two or more races, non-Hispanic/Latino; 7% Race/ethnicity unknown; 7% international; 1% transferred in; 100% live on campus.

Freshmen:
Admission: 5,230 applied, 1,364 admitted, 472 enrolled. ***Test scores:*** SAT critical reading scores over 500: 100%; SAT math scores over 500: 100%; SAT writing scores over 500: 100%; ACT scores over 18: 100%; SAT critical reading scores over 600: 90%; SAT math scores over 600: 90%; SAT writing scores over 600: 91%; ACT scores over 24: 100%; SAT critical reading scores over 700: 52%; SAT math scores over 700: 48%; SAT writing scores over 700: 52%; ACT scores over 30: 90%.

Retention: 94% of full-time freshmen returned.

FACULTY
Total: 224, 83% full-time, 92% with terminal degrees.

Student/faculty ratio: 9:1.

ACADEMICS
Calendar: semesters. *Degree:* bachelor's.

Special study options: accelerated degree program, adult/continuing education programs, advanced placement credit, double majors, English as a second language, independent study, internships, off-campus study, part-time degree program, services for LD students, student-designed majors, study abroad. ***ROTC:*** Army (c), Air Force (c).

Unusual degree programs: 3-2 engineering with Columbia University, Dartmouth College, Rensselaer Polytechnic Institute, Washington University in St. Louis.

Computers: 804 computers/terminals and 10,519 ports are available on campus for general student use. Students can access the following: campus intranet, computer help desk, free student e-mail accounts, online (class) grades, online (class) registration, online (class) schedules. Campuswide network is available. 100% of college-owned or -operated housing units are wired for high-speed Internet access. Wireless service is available via entire campus.

Library: Burke Library plus 1 other. *Books:* 482,004 (physical), 414,932 (digital/electronic); *Serial titles:* 3,424 (physical), 127,978 (digital/electronic); *Databases:* 182. Weekly public service hours: 114; study areas open 24 hours, 5-7 days a week; students can reserve study rooms.

STUDENT LIFE
Housing options: on-campus residence required through senior year; coed, cooperative, special housing for students with disabilities. Campus housing is university owned. Freshman campus housing is guaranteed.

Activities and organizations: drama/theater group, student-run newspaper, radio and television station, choral group, WHCL (Hamilton College Radio), Habitat for Humanity, GNAR Club, Powder Club, Spanish Club, national fraternities.

Athletics Member NCAA. All Division III. ***Intercollegiate sports:*** baseball M, basketball M/W, crew M/W, cross-country running M/W, equestrian sports M(c)/W(c), fencing M(c)/W(c), field hockey W, football M, golf M/W, ice hockey M/W, lacrosse M/W, rugby M(c)/W(c), sailing M(c)/W(c), skiing (cross-country) M(c)/W(c), skiing (downhill) M(c)/W(c), soccer M/W, softball W, squash M/W, swimming and diving M/W, tennis M/W, track and field M/W, ultimate Frisbee M(c)/W(c), volleyball M(c)/W, water polo M(c). ***Intramural sports:*** badminton M/W, basketball M/W, football M/W, golf M/W, ice hockey M/W, racquetball M/W, skiing (cross-country) M/W, soccer M/W, softball M/W, squash M/W, tennis M/W, volleyball M/W, water polo M/W.

Campus security: 24-hour emergency response devices and patrols, late-night transport/escort service, controlled dormitory access, student safety program.

Student services: health clinic, personal/psychological counseling.

COSTS & FINANCIAL AID
Costs (2016–17) ***Comprehensive fee:*** $64,250 includes full-time tuition ($50,730), mandatory fees ($510), and room and board ($13,010). Part-time tuition: $6341 per course. ***College room only:*** $7110. Room and board charges vary according to board plan. ***Payment plan:*** installment. ***Waivers:*** employees or children of employees.

Financial Aid Of all full-time matriculated undergraduates who enrolled in 2016, 938 applied for aid, 892 were judged to have need, 892 had their need fully met. 563 Federal Work-Study jobs (averaging $1837). 52 state and other part-time jobs (averaging $1942). ***Average percent of need met:*** 100. ***Average financial aid package:*** $47,003. ***Average need-based loan:*** $4292. ***Average need-based gift aid:*** $41,825. ***Average indebtedness upon graduation:*** $21,491. ***Financial aid deadline:*** 2/15.

APPLYING
Standardized Tests *Required:* (for admission).

Options: electronic application, early decision, deferred entrance.

Application fee: $50.

Required: essay or personal statement, high school transcript, 1 letter of recommendation. ***Recommended:*** interview.

Application deadlines: 1/1 (freshmen), 4/1 (transfers).

Early decision deadline: 11/15 (for plan 1), 1/1 (for plan 2).

Notification: 4/1 (freshmen), 5/15 (transfers), 12/15 (early decision plan 1), 2/15 (early decision plan 2).

CONTACT
Ms. Monica Inzer, Vice President and Dean of Admission and Financial Aid, Hamilton College, 198 College Hill Road, Clinton, NY 13323. *Phone:* 800-843-2655. *Toll-free phone:* 800-843-2655. *Fax:* 315-859-4457. *E-mail:* admission@hamilton.edu.

Hartwick College

Oneonta, New York

http://www.hartwick.edu/

- **Independent** 4-year, founded 1797
- **Small-town** 425-acre campus with easy access to Capital District, NY
- **Endowment** $67.5 million
- **Coed** 1,396 undergraduate students, 98% full-time, 60% women, 40% men
- **Moderately difficult** entrance level, 94% of applicants were admitted

UNDERGRAD STUDENTS
1,362 full-time, 34 part-time. Students come from 33 states and territories; 33 other countries; 20% are from out of state; 9% Black or African American, non-Hispanic/Latino; 8% Hispanic/Latino; 2% Asian, non-Hispanic/Latino; 0.1% Native Hawaiian or other Pacific Islander, non-Hispanic/Latino; 0.2% American Indian or Alaska Native, non-Hispanic/Latino; 2% Two or more races, non-Hispanic/Latino; 11% Race/ethnicity unknown; 3% international; 3% transferred in; 77% live on campus.

Freshmen:
Admission: 3,085 applied, 2,889 admitted, 402 enrolled. ***Test scores:*** SAT critical reading scores over 500: 50%; SAT math scores over 500: 56%; ACT scores over 18: 91%; SAT critical reading scores over 600: 13%; SAT math scores over 600: 15%; ACT scores over 24: 47%; SAT critical reading scores over 700: 2%; SAT math scores over 700: 1%; ACT scores over 30: 6%.

Retention: 75% of full-time freshmen returned.

FACULTY
Total: 183, 60% full-time, 63% with terminal degrees.

Student/faculty ratio: 10:1.

ACADEMICS
Calendar: 4-1-4. *Degree:* bachelor's.

Special study options: accelerated degree program, advanced placement credit, distance learning, double majors, honors programs, independent study, internships, off-campus study, part-time degree program, services for LD students, student-designed majors, study abroad, summer session for credit.

Unusual degree programs: 3-2 engineering with Clarkson University, Columbia University.

Computers: 80 computers/terminals are available on campus for general student use. Students can access the following: computer help desk, free student e-mail accounts, online (class) grades, online (class) registration, online (class) schedules. Campuswide network is available. 100% of college-owned or -operated housing units are wired for high-speed Internet access. Wireless service is available via entire campus.

Library: Stevens-German Library. *Books:* 208,822 (physical), 4,560 (digital/electronic); *Serial titles:* 1,392 (physical), 38,755 (digital/electronic); *Databases:* 59. Weekly public service hours: 96; students can reserve study rooms.

STUDENT LIFE

Housing options: on-campus residence required through junior year; coed. Campus housing is university owned. Freshman campus housing is guaranteed.

Activities and organizations: drama/theater group, student-run newspaper, radio station, choral group, Student Union, student radio station, Student Senate, Hilltops campus newspaper, Cardboard Alley Players (theater), national fraternities, national sororities.

Athletics Member NCAA. All Division III except soccer (Division I), water polo (Division I). ***Intercollegiate sports:*** basketball M/W, cheerleading W(c), cross-country running M/W, equestrian sports W, field hockey W, football M, lacrosse M/W, soccer M(s)/W, swimming and diving M/W, tennis M/W, volleyball W, water polo M(c)/W(s). ***Intramural sports:*** basketball M/W, football M, riflery M(c)/W(c), rugby M(c), skiing (downhill) M(c)/W(c), soccer M/W, softball W(c), volleyball M/W, water polo M/W.

Campus security: 24-hour emergency response devices and patrols, late-night transport/escort service, controlled dormitory access.

Student services: health clinic, personal/psychological counseling, legal services.

COSTS & FINANCIAL AID

Costs (2017–18) ***One-time required fee:*** $400. ***Comprehensive fee:*** $56,227 includes full-time tuition ($43,312), mandatory fees ($822), and room and board ($12,093). Full-time tuition and fees vary according to course load. Part-time tuition: $1390 per credit hour. Part-time tuition and fees vary according to course load. ***College room only:*** $6268. Room and board charges vary according to board plan and housing facility. ***Payment plan:*** installment. ***Waivers:*** employees or children of employees.

Financial Aid Of all full-time matriculated undergraduates who enrolled in 2016, 1,198 applied for aid, 1,141 were judged to have need, 161 had their need fully met. 890 Federal Work-Study jobs (averaging $2000). In 2016, 206 non-need-based awards were made. ***Average percent of need met:*** 79. ***Average financial aid package:*** $33,725. ***Average need-based loan:*** $4965. ***Average need-based gift aid:*** $27,125. ***Average non-need-based aid:*** $22,312. ***Average indebtedness upon graduation:*** $27,653.

APPLYING

Standardized Tests *Required for some:* SAT or ACT (for admission).

Options: electronic application, early admission, early decision, deferred entrance.

Required: high school transcript. ***Required for some:*** audition for music program, portfolio for art majors. ***Recommended:*** minimum 2.5 GPA.

Application deadlines: rolling (freshmen), 8/1 (transfers).

Early decision deadline: 11/1.

Notification: continuous (freshmen), continuous until 8/15 (transfers), 12/1 (early decision plan 1), rolling (early decision plan 2).

CONTACT

Ms. Lisa Starkey-Wood, Director of Admissions, Hartwick College, PO Box 4022, Oneonta, NY 13820-4022. *Phone:* 607-431-4150. *Toll-free phone:* 888-HARTWICK. *Fax:* 607-431-4102. *E-mail:* admissions@hartwick.edu.

Helene Fuld College of Nursing

New York, New York

http://www.helenefuld.edu/

- **Independent** primarily 2-year, founded 1945
- **Urban** campus
- **Coed, primarily women**
- **Moderately difficult** entrance level

FACULTY

Student/faculty ratio: 11:1.

ACADEMICS

Calendar: quarters semester for BS program. *Degrees:* associate and bachelor's (program only open to licensed practical nurses).

Library: Peggy Wines Memorial Library plus 1 other.

STUDENT LIFE

Campus security: security guard during hours of operation.

Student services: personal/psychological counseling.

COSTS

Costs (2016–17) ***Tuition:*** $341 per quarter hour part-time. Full-time tuition and fees vary according to course load, degree level, and program. Part-time tuition and fees vary according to course load, degree level, and program.

APPLYING

Standardized Tests *Required:* Nelson Denny Reading Test (for admission).

Options: deferred entrance.

Application fee: $110.

Required: essay or personal statement, high school transcript, 2 letters of recommendation, must be Licensed Practical Nurse. ***Required for some:*** interview.

CONTACT

Helene Fuld College of Nursing, 24 East 120th Street, New York, NY 10035. *Phone:* 212-616-7271.

Hilbert College

Hamburg, New York

http://www.hilbert.edu/

- **Independent Roman Catholic** comprehensive, founded 1957
- **Suburban** 40-acre campus with easy access to Buffalo
- **Endowment** $6.4 million
- **Coed** 809 undergraduate students, 91% full-time, 56% women, 44% men
- **Minimally difficult** entrance level, 81% of applicants were admitted

UNDERGRAD STUDENTS

740 full-time, 69 part-time. Students come from 22 states and territories; 2 other countries; 5% are from out of state; 7% Black or African American, non-Hispanic/Latino; 4% Hispanic/Latino; 0.2% Asian, non-Hispanic/Latino; 0.2% Native Hawaiian or other Pacific Islander, non-Hispanic/Latino; 1% American Indian or Alaska Native, non-Hispanic/Latino; 7% Two or more races, non-Hispanic/Latino; 6% Race/ethnicity unknown; 0.5% international; 11% transferred in; 29% live on campus.

Freshmen:

Admission: 968 applied, 785 admitted, 148 enrolled. ***Test scores:*** SAT critical reading scores over 500: 31%; SAT math scores over 500: 47%; SAT writing scores over 500: 16%; ACT scores over 18: 84%; SAT critical reading scores over 600: 4%; SAT math scores over 600: 3%; SAT writing scores over 600: 2%; ACT scores over 24: 15%.

Retention: 72% of full-time freshmen returned.

FACULTY

Total: 134, 32% full-time, 40% with terminal degrees.

Student/faculty ratio: 12:1.

ACADEMICS

Calendar: semesters. *Degrees:* associate, bachelor's, and master's.

Special study options: academic remediation for entering students, accelerated degree program, adult/continuing education programs, advanced placement credit, cooperative education, distance learning, honors programs, independent study, internships, services for LD students, study abroad, summer session for credit. ***ROTC:*** Army (c).

Computers: 146 computers/terminals are available on campus for general student use. Students can access the following: campus intranet, computer help desk, free student e-mail accounts, online (class) grades, online (class) registration, online (class) schedules. Campuswide network is available. 100% of college-owned or -operated housing units are wired for high-speed Internet access. Wireless service is available via entire campus.

Library: McGrath Library. *Books:* 35,000 (physical), 1,484 (digital/electronic); *Serial titles:* 132 (physical), 83,818

(digital/electronic); *Databases:* 86. Weekly public service hours: 78; students can reserve study rooms.

STUDENT LIFE

Housing options: coed. Campus housing is university owned and leased by the school. Freshman applicants given priority for college housing.

Activities and organizations: drama/theater group, student-run newspaper, radio station, Student Government Association, Student Business and Accounting Association, SADD, Students in Free Enterprise (SIFE), Criminal Justice Association.

Athletics Member NCAA. All Division III. ***Intercollegiate sports:*** baseball M, basketball M/W, cross-country running M/W, golf M, lacrosse M/W, soccer M/W, softball W, volleyball M/W. ***Intramural sports:*** baseball M, basketball M/W, bowling M/W, cheerleading W, football M/W, golf M, ice hockey M(c), lacrosse W(c), skiing (downhill) M(c)/W(c), soccer M/W, softball W, table tennis M/W, ultimate Frisbee M/W, volleyball M/W.

Campus security: 24-hour emergency response devices and patrols, student patrols, late-night transport/escort service, controlled dormitory access.

Student services: health clinic, personal/psychological counseling.

COSTS & FINANCIAL AID

Costs (2017–18) ***Comprehensive fee:*** $31,350 includes full-time tuition ($21,750), mandatory fees ($600), and room and board ($9000). Part-time tuition: $545 per credit hour. ***Required fees:*** $13 per credit hour part-time, $55 per term part-time. ***Room and board:*** Room and board charges vary according to board plan and housing facility. ***Payment plan:*** installment. ***Waivers:*** minority students, children of alumni, adult students, senior citizens, and employees or children of employees.

Financial Aid Of all full-time matriculated undergraduates who enrolled in 2016, 710 applied for aid, 650 were judged to have need, 145 had their need fully met. 80 Federal Work-Study jobs (averaging $1860). In 2016, 68 non-need-based awards were made. ***Average percent of need met:*** 70. ***Average financial aid package:*** $15,037. ***Average need-based loan:*** $5171. ***Average need-based gift aid:*** $10,857. ***Average non-need-based aid:*** $6091. ***Average indebtedness upon graduation:*** $19,233.

APPLYING

Standardized Tests *Recommended:* SAT or ACT (for admission).

Options: electronic application, deferred entrance.

Application fee: $25.

Required: high school transcript. ***Required for some:*** interview. ***Recommended:*** essay or personal statement, interview.

Application deadlines: rolling (freshmen), rolling (out-of-state freshmen), rolling (transfers).

Notification: continuous (freshmen), continuous (out-of-state freshmen), continuous (transfers).

CONTACT

Mr. Jacob Yale, Director, Admissions, Hilbert College, 5200 South Park Avenue, Hamburg, NY 14075-1597. *Phone:* 716-649-7900 Ext. 244. *Toll-free phone:* 800-649-8003. *Fax:* 716-649-1152.
E-mail: jyale@hilbert.edu.

Hobart and William Smith Colleges

Geneva, New York

http://www.hws.edu/

- **Independent** comprehensive, founded 1822
- **Small-town** 200-acre campus with easy access to Rochester, Syracuse
- **Endowment** $188.3 million
- **Coed** 2,262 undergraduate students, 99% full-time, 50% women, 50% men
- **Very difficult** entrance level, 60% of applicants were admitted

UNDERGRAD STUDENTS

2,246 full-time, 16 part-time. Students come from 40 states and territories; 26 other countries; 60% are from out of state; 6% Black or African American, non-Hispanic/Latino; 5% Hispanic/Latino; 3% Asian, non-Hispanic/Latino; 0.1% Native Hawaiian or other Pacific Islander, non-Hispanic/Latino; 0.4% American Indian or Alaska Native, non-Hispanic/Latino; 7% Race/ethnicity unknown; 7% international; 0.5% transferred in; 90% live on campus.

Freshmen:
Admission: 4,614 applied, 2,788 admitted, 581 enrolled. ***Average high school GPA:*** 3.47. ***Test scores:*** SAT critical reading scores over 500: 97%; SAT math scores over 500: 97%; SAT writing scores over 500: 96%; SAT critical reading scores over 600: 70%; SAT math scores over 600: 70%; SAT writing scores over 600: 61%; SAT critical reading scores over 700: 13%; SAT math scores over 700: 15%; SAT writing scores over 700: 11%.

Retention: 85% of full-time freshmen returned.

FACULTY

Total: 237, 93% full-time, 97% with terminal degrees.

Student/faculty ratio: 10:1.

ACADEMICS

Calendar: semesters. *Degrees:* bachelor's, master's, and postbachelor's certificates.

Special study options: accelerated degree program, adult/continuing education programs, advanced placement credit, double majors, English as a second language, honors programs, independent study, internships, off-campus study, services for LD students, student-designed majors, study abroad. ***ROTC:*** Army (c), Air Force (c).

Unusual degree programs: 3-2 business administration with Clarkson University, Rochester Institute of Technology; engineering with Columbia University, Rensselaer Polytechnic Institute, Dartmouth College; architecture with Washington University in St. Louis.

Computers: 247 computers/terminals and 10,215 ports are available on campus for general student use. Students can access the following: campus intranet, computer help desk, free student e-mail accounts, online (class) grades, online (class) registration, online (class) schedules. Campuswide network is available. 100% of college-owned or -operated housing units are wired for high-speed Internet access. Wireless service is available via entire campus.

Library: Warren Hunting Smith Library plus 1 other. *Books:* 387,217 (physical), 274,574 (digital/electronic); *Serial titles:* 1,853 (physical), 54,085 (digital/electronic); *Databases:* 122. Weekly public service hours: 114; study areas open 24 hours, 5-7 days a week; students can reserve study rooms.

STUDENT LIFE

Housing options: on-campus residence required through junior year; coed, men-only, women-only, cooperative. Campus housing is university owned. Freshman campus housing is guaranteed.

Activities and organizations: drama/theater group, student-run newspaper, radio station, choral group, Student Life and Leadership, student government, campus publications, Service Network, sports clubs, national fraternities, national sororities.

Athletics Member NCAA. All Division III except lacrosse (Division I). ***Intercollegiate sports:*** basketball M/W, crew M/W, cross-country running M/W, equestrian sports M(c)/W(c), field hockey W, football M, golf M/W, ice hockey M/W, lacrosse M/W, rock climbing M(c)/W(c), rugby M(c)/W(c), sailing M/W, skiing (downhill) M(c)/W(c), soccer M/W, squash M/W, swimming and diving W, tennis M/W, ultimate Frisbee M(c)/W(c). ***Intramural sports:*** badminton M/W, baseball M, basketball M/W, fencing M/W, football M, golf M/W, ice hockey M/W, lacrosse M/W, racquetball M/W, skiing (cross-country) M/W, skiing (downhill) M/W, soccer M/W, softball M/W, squash M/W, swimming and diving M/W, table tennis M/W, tennis M/W, track and field M/W, ultimate Frisbee M/W, volleyball M/W, water polo M/W, weight lifting M/W.

Campus security: 24-hour emergency response devices and patrols, late-night transport/escort service, controlled dormitory access.

Student services: health clinic, personal/psychological counseling, women's center.

COSTS & FINANCIAL AID

Costs (2017–18) ***Comprehensive fee:*** $67,050 includes full-time tuition ($52,345), mandatory fees ($1180), and room and board ($13,525). ***Room and board:*** Room and board charges vary according to board plan. ***Payment plans:*** tuition prepayment, installment. ***Waivers:*** employees or children of employees.

Financial Aid Of all full-time matriculated undergraduates who enrolled in 2015, 1,493 applied for aid, 1,274 were judged to have need, 871 had their need fully met. 834 Federal Work-Study jobs (averaging $1836). 490 state and other part-time jobs (averaging $1865). In 2015, 664 non-need-

based awards were made. ***Average percent of need met:*** 79. ***Average financial aid package:*** $35,123. ***Average need-based loan:*** $3906. ***Average need-based gift aid:*** $31,175. ***Average non-need-based aid:*** $14,853. ***Average indebtedness upon graduation:*** $35,935. ***Financial aid deadline:*** 2/1.

APPLYING

Standardized Tests *Required for some:* SAT or ACT (for admission).

Options: electronic application, early admission, early decision, deferred entrance.

Required: essay or personal statement, high school transcript, 1 letter of recommendation. ***Recommended:*** interview.

Application deadlines: 2/1 (freshmen), 7/1 (transfers).

Early decision deadline: 11/15 (for plan 1), 1/1 (for plan 2).

Notification: 4/1 (freshmen), continuous (transfers), 12/15 (early decision plan 1), 2/1 (early decision plan 2).

CONTACT

Hobart and William Smith Colleges, 300 Pulteney Street, Geneva, NY 14456. *Phone:* 315-781-3622. *Toll-free phone:* 800-852-2256.

★ Hofstra University
Hempstead, New York
http://www.hofstra.edu/

- **Independent** university, founded 1935
- **Suburban** 244-acre campus with easy access to New York City
- **Endowment** $418.0 million
- **Coed** 6,899 undergraduate students, 94% full-time, 54% women, 46% men
- **Moderately difficult** entrance level, 62% of applicants were admitted

UNDERGRAD STUDENTS

6,497 full-time, 402 part-time. Students come from 45 states and territories; 64 other countries; 37% are from out of state; 8% Black or African American, non-Hispanic/Latino; 14% Hispanic/Latino; 10% Asian, non-Hispanic/Latino; 0.8% Native Hawaiian or other Pacific Islander, non-Hispanic/Latino; 0.3% American Indian or Alaska Native, non-Hispanic/Latino; 2% Two or more races, non-Hispanic/Latino; 3% Race/ethnicity unknown; 5% international; 5% transferred in; 46% live on campus.

Freshmen:

Admission: 28,617 applied, 17,806 admitted, 1,647 enrolled. ***Average high school GPA:*** 3.61. ***Test scores:*** SAT critical reading scores over 500: 88%; SAT math scores over 500: 91%; ACT scores over 18: 99%; SAT critical reading scores over 600: 40%; SAT math scores over 600: 45%; ACT scores over 24: 82%; SAT critical reading scores over 700: 6%; SAT math scores over 700: 7%; ACT scores over 30: 18%.

Retention: 82% of full-time freshmen returned.

FACULTY

Total: 1,181, 41% full-time, 63% with terminal degrees.

Student/faculty ratio: 14:1.

ACADEMICS

Calendar: semesters. *Degrees:* certificates, bachelor's, master's, doctoral, post-master's, and postbachelor's certificates.

Special study options: accelerated degree program, advanced placement credit, cooperative education, distance learning, double majors, English as a second language, external degree program, freshman honors college, honors programs, independent study, internships, off-campus study, part-time degree program, services for LD students, student-designed majors, study abroad, summer session for credit. ***ROTC:*** Army (b).

Unusual degree programs: 3-2 business administration; physician assistant studies, computer science, law.

Computers: 1,536 computers/terminals and 1,900 ports are available on campus for general student use. Students can access the following: campus intranet, computer help desk, free student e-mail accounts, online (class) grades, online (class) registration, online (class) schedules, emergency alert system, software tutoring, repair and rebuild after virus service, course management system, e-portfolio, card services balance update, printing services, support for specific technology-enhanced assignments. 100% of college-owned or -operated housing units are wired for high-speed Internet access. Wireless service is available via entire campus.

Library: Axinn Library plus 2 others. *Books:* 953,971 (physical), 175,393 (digital/electronic); *Serial titles:* 1,848 (physical), 14,521 (digital/electronic); *Databases:* 241. Weekly public service hours: 102; study areas open 24 hours, 5-7 days a week; students can reserve study rooms.

STUDENT LIFE

Housing options: coed, special housing for students with disabilities. Campus housing is university owned. Freshman applicants given priority for college housing.

Activities and organizations: drama/theater group, student-run newspaper, radio and television station, choral group, Hofstra Habitat for Humanity, Hofstra vs. Zombies, APHOS: Associatin of Pre-Health Oriented Students, HEAT: Hofstra Entertainment Access Television, HAMA: Hofstra American Marketing Association, national fraternities, national sororities.

Athletics Member NCAA. All Division I. ***Intercollegiate sports:*** baseball M(s), basketball M(s)/W(s), cross-country running M(s)/W(s), field hockey W(s), golf M(s)/W(s), lacrosse M(s)/W(s), soccer M(s)/W(s), softball W(s), tennis M(s)/W(s), volleyball W(s), wrestling M(s). ***Intramural sports:*** baseball M(c), basketball M/W, bowling M(c)/W(c), cheerleading M(c)/W(c), crew M(c)/W(c), cross-country running M(c)/W(c), equestrian sports M(c)/W(c), field hockey W(c), golf M(c)/W(c), ice hockey M(c), lacrosse M(c)/W(c), rock climbing M(c)/W(c), rugby M(c)/W(c), skiing (downhill) M(c)/W(c), soccer M(c)/W(c), softball M/W, table tennis M(c)/W(c), tennis M(c)/W(c), ultimate Frisbee M(c)/W(c), volleyball M(c)/W(c), weight lifting M(c)/W(c).

Campus security: 24-hour emergency response devices and patrols, student patrols, late-night transport/escort service, controlled dormitory access, security cameras monitoring residence hall entrances 24/7, bike patrol, motorist assistance program.

Student services: health clinic, personal/psychological counseling.

COSTS & FINANCIAL AID

Costs (2016–17) ***Comprehensive fee:*** $56,620 includes full-time tuition ($41,100), mandatory fees ($1060), and room and board ($14,460). Full-time tuition and fees vary according to course load. Part-time tuition: $1380 per credit hour. Part-time tuition and fees vary according to course load. No tuition increase for student's term of enrollment. ***Required fees:*** $155 per term part-time. ***College room only:*** $9700. Room and board charges vary according to board plan and housing facility. ***Payment plan:*** installment. ***Waivers:*** employees or children of employees.

Financial Aid Of all full-time matriculated undergraduates who enrolled in 2015, 4,978 applied for aid, 4,189 were judged to have need, 999 had their need fully met. 1,595 Federal Work-Study jobs (averaging $3005). 1,454 state and other part-time jobs (averaging $3088). In 2015, 1462 non-need-based awards were made. ***Average percent of need met:*** 64. ***Average financial aid package:*** $27,000. ***Average need-based loan:*** $5000. ***Average need-based gift aid:*** $18,000. ***Average non-need-based aid:*** $16,000.

APPLYING

Standardized Tests *Required for some:* TOEFL for international students.

Options: electronic application, early admission, early action, deferred entrance.

Application fee: $70.

Required: essay or personal statement, high school transcript, 2 letters of recommendation. ***Required for some:*** interview.

Application deadlines: rolling (freshmen), 12/15 (early action).

Notification: 2/1 (freshmen), continuous (transfers), 1/15 (early action).

CONTACT

Sunil A. Samuel, Assistant Vice President of Admissions, Hofstra University, 100 Hofstra University, Hempstead, NY 11549. *Phone:* 516-463-6700. *Toll-free phone:* 800-HOFSTRA. *Fax:* 516-463-5100. *E-mail:* admission@hofstra.edu.

See previous page for display ad and page 1378 for the College Close-Up.

Holy Trinity Orthodox Seminary

Jordanville, New York

http://www.hts.edu/

- **Independent Russian Orthodox** 4-year, founded 1948
- **Rural** 900-acre campus
- **Men only** 58 undergraduate students, 43% full-time
- **Noncompetitive** entrance level

UNDERGRAD STUDENTS

25 full-time, 33 part-time.

Freshmen:
Admission: 4 enrolled.

FACULTY

Total: 16, 25% with terminal degrees.

Student/faculty ratio: 2:1.

ACADEMICS

Calendar: semesters. *Degree:* certificates and bachelor's.

Special study options: accelerated degree program, English as a second language, external degree program, independent study.

Computers: 2 computers/terminals are available on campus for general student use. Students can access the following: free student e-mail accounts, online (class) grades, online (class) schedules. Campuswide network is available. Wireless service is available via classrooms, dorm rooms, libraries.

Library: Holy Trinity Orthodox Seminary Library. *Books:* 40,000 (physical).

STUDENT LIFE

Activities and organizations: student-run newspaper, choral group, Student Union.

Campus security: 24-hour emergency response devices.

Student services: health clinic, personal/psychological counseling.

COSTS

Costs (2017–18) ***Comprehensive fee:*** $11,650 includes full-time tuition ($7250), mandatory fees ($300), and room and board ($4100). Part-time tuition and fees vary according to program. ***College room only:*** $4100. ***Payment plan:*** installment. ***Waivers:*** employees or children of employees.

APPLYING

Options: electronic application, deferred entrance.

Application fee: $40.

Required: essay or personal statement, high school transcript, minimum 2.0 GPA, 1 letter of recommendation, interview, Orthodoxy/Orthodox baptism, entrance exam, recommendation from spiritual father or parish priest.

Application deadlines: 6/1 (freshmen), 6/1 (transfers).

CONTACT

Rev. Fr. Ephraim Willmarth, Assistant Dean and Director of Admissions, Holy Trinity Orthodox Seminary, PO Box 36, Jordanville, NY 13361. *Phone:* 315-858-0945. *Fax:* 315-858-0945. *E-mail:* ejwillmarth@hts.edu.

Houghton College

Houghton, New York

http://www.houghton.edu/

- **Independent Wesleyan** comprehensive, founded 1883
- **Rural** 1300-acre campus with easy access to Buffalo, Rochester
- **Endowment** $42.5 million
- **Coed** 1,053 undergraduate students, 94% full-time, 64% women, 36% men
- **Moderately difficult** entrance level, 94% of applicants were admitted

UNDERGRAD STUDENTS

990 full-time, 63 part-time. Students come from 32 states and territories; 38 other countries; 68% are from out of state; 3% Black or African American, non-Hispanic/Latino; 2% Hispanic/Latino; 2% Asian, non-Hispanic/Latino; 0.1% Native Hawaiian or other Pacific Islander, non-Hispanic/Latino; 0.2% American Indian or Alaska Native, non-Hispanic/Latino; 4% Two or more races, non-Hispanic/Latino; 0.6%

Race/ethnicity unknown; 11% international; 5% transferred in; 81% live on campus.

Freshmen:
Admission: 737 applied, 696 admitted, 267 enrolled. ***Average high school GPA:*** 3.52. ***Test scores:*** SAT critical reading scores over 500: 75%; SAT math scores over 500: 74%; SAT writing scores over 500: 70%; ACT scores over 18: 91%; SAT critical reading scores over 600: 38%; SAT math scores over 600: 33%; SAT writing scores over 600: 28%; ACT scores over 24: 60%; SAT critical reading scores over 700: 9%; SAT math scores over 700: 2%; SAT writing scores over 700: 6%; ACT scores over 30: 16%.
Retention: 84% of full-time freshmen returned.

FACULTY
Total: 131, 56% full-time, 66% with terminal degrees.
Student/faculty ratio: 11:1.

ACADEMICS
Calendar: semesters. *Degrees:* associate, bachelor's, and master's.
Special study options: accelerated degree program, adult/continuing education programs, advanced placement credit, cooperative education, distance learning, double majors, English as a second language, freshman honors college, honors programs, independent study, internships, off-campus study, services for LD students, student-designed majors, study abroad, summer session for credit. ***ROTC:*** Army (c).
Unusual degree programs: 3-2 engineering with Clarkson University.
Computers: 30 computers/terminals and 820 ports are available on campus for general student use. Students can access the following: campus intranet, computer help desk, free student e-mail accounts, online (class) grades, online (class) registration, online (class) schedules. Campuswide network is available. 100% of college-owned or -operated housing units are wired for high-speed Internet access. Wireless service is available via entire campus.
Library: Willard J. Houghton Library plus 1 other. *Books:* 203,165 (physical), 227,475 (digital/electronic); *Serial titles:* 59,807 (physical); *Databases:* 99. Weekly public service hours: 82; students can reserve study rooms.

STUDENT LIFE
Housing options: on-campus residence required through senior year; men-only, women-only. Campus housing is university owned. Freshman campus housing is guaranteed.
Activities and organizations: drama/theater group, student-run newspaper, choral group, Global Christian Fellowship, Student Government Association, Mercy Seat, Allegany County Outreach, Kairos (formerly Intercultural Student Association).
Athletics Member NCAA, NCCAA. All NCAA Division III.
Intercollegiate sports: baseball M, basketball M/W, cross-country running M/W, field hockey W, lacrosse M/W, soccer M/W, softball W, tennis M/W, track and field M/W, volleyball W. ***Intramural sports:*** baseball M, basketball M/W, equestrian sports M(c)/W(c), football M, racquetball M/W, rock climbing M(c)/W(c), skiing (cross-country) M(c)/W(c), skiing (downhill) M(c)/W(c), soccer M/W, swimming and diving M(c)/W(c), table tennis M/W, ultimate Frisbee M(c)/W(c), volleyball M/W, water polo M/W.
Campus security: 24-hour emergency response devices and patrols, late-night transport/escort service, controlled dormitory access, emergency phone number rings directly to cell phone carried by officer on duty 24/7, automatic fire alarms throughout campus.
Student services: health clinic, personal/psychological counseling.

COSTS & FINANCIAL AID
Costs (2017–18) ***Comprehensive fee:*** $40,258 includes full-time tuition ($31,040), mandatory fees ($200), and room and board ($9018). Full-time tuition and fees vary according to course load and location. Part-time tuition: $1267 per semester hour. Part-time tuition and fees vary according to course load and location. ***Room and board:*** Room and board charges vary according to board plan and housing facility. ***Payment plan:*** installment. ***Waivers:*** senior citizens and employees or children of employees.
Financial Aid Of all full-time matriculated undergraduates who enrolled in 2015, 857 applied for aid, 802 were judged to have need, 242 had their need fully met. 503 Federal Work-Study jobs (averaging $1966). 42 state and other part-time jobs (averaging $2100). In 2015, 149 non-need-based awards were made. ***Average percent of need met:*** 78. ***Average financial aid package:*** $23,990. ***Average need-based loan:*** $4766. ***Average need-based gift aid:*** $11,351. ***Average non-need-based aid:*** $13,386. ***Average indebtedness upon graduation:*** $30,494.

APPLYING
Standardized Tests *Required:* SAT or ACT (for admission).
Options: electronic application, deferred entrance.
Application fee: $40.
Required: high school transcript, 1 letter of recommendation. ***Required for some:*** essay or personal statement. ***Recommended:*** essay or personal statement, minimum 3.0 GPA, interview.
Application deadlines: rolling (freshmen), rolling (out-of-state freshmen), rolling (transfers).
Notification: continuous (freshmen), continuous (out-of-state freshmen), continuous (transfers).

CONTACT
Mr. Ryan Spear, Associate Director of Admission Operations, Houghton College, PO Box 128, Houghton, NY 14744. *Phone:* 585-567-9353. *Toll-free phone:* 800-777-2556. *Fax:* 585-567-9522.
E-mail: admission@houghton.edu.

Hunter College of the City University of New York

New York, New York

http://www.hunter.cuny.edu/

- **State and locally supported** comprehensive, founded 1870, part of City University of New York System
- **Urban** campus
- **Endowment** $63.1 million
- **Coed** 16,723 undergraduate students, 73% full-time, 64% women, 36% men
- **Moderately difficult** entrance level, 39% of applicants were admitted

UNDERGRAD STUDENTS
12,223 full-time, 4,500 part-time. Students come from 41 states and territories; 153 other countries; 3% are from out of state; 13% Black or African American, non-Hispanic/Latino; 21% Hispanic/Latino; 29% Asian, non-Hispanic/Latino; 0.1% American Indian or Alaska Native, non-Hispanic/Latino; 6% international; 11% transferred in; 1% live on campus.

Freshmen:
Admission: 28,510 applied, 10,984 admitted, 2,208 enrolled. ***Average high school GPA:*** 3.27. ***Test scores:*** SAT critical reading scores over 500: 88%; SAT math scores over 500: 95%; SAT critical reading scores over 600: 32%; SAT math scores over 600: 45%; SAT critical reading scores over 700: 9%; SAT math scores over 700: 10%.
Retention: 85% of full-time freshmen returned.

FACULTY
Total: 2,246, 30% full-time, 51% with terminal degrees.
Student/faculty ratio: 14:1.

ACADEMICS
Calendar: semesters. *Degrees:* bachelor's, master's, doctoral, post-master's, and postbachelor's certificates.
Special study options: advanced placement credit, distance learning, double majors, English as a second language, freshman honors college, honors programs, independent study, internships, off-campus study, part-time degree program, services for LD students, student-designed majors, study abroad, summer session for credit.
Unusual degree programs: 3-2 anthropology, economics, English, history, mathematics, music, physics, sociology.
Computers: 600 computers/terminals are available on campus for general student use. Students can access the following: computer help desk, free student e-mail accounts, online (class) registration, online (class) schedules. Campuswide network is available. Wireless service is available via entire campus.
Library: Hunter College Library plus 1 other.

STUDENT LIFE

Housing options: coed.

Activities and organizations: drama/theater group, student-run newspaper, radio and television station, choral group.

Athletics Member NCAA. All Division III. ***Intercollegiate sports:*** basketball M/W, cross-country running M/W, fencing M/W, gymnastics W, soccer M, swimming and diving W, tennis M/W, track and field M/W, volleyball M/W, wrestling M. ***Intramural sports:*** basketball M/W, cross-country running M/W, gymnastics M/W, racquetball M/W, rugby M, soccer M/W, swimming and diving M/W, tennis M/W, volleyball M/W.

Campus security: 24-hour emergency response devices and patrols.

Student services: personal/psychological counseling, women's center.

COSTS & FINANCIAL AID

Costs (2017–18) ***Tuition:*** state resident $6330 full-time, $275 per credit hour part-time; nonresident $16,800 full-time, $560 per credit hour part-time. Full-time tuition and fees vary according to course load, degree level, and program. Part-time tuition and fees vary according to course load, degree level, and program. ***Required fees:*** $450 full-time, $133 per term part-time. ***Room only:*** $4857. Room and board charges vary according to housing facility and location. ***Payment plan:*** installment.

Financial Aid Of all full-time matriculated undergraduates who enrolled in 2013, 11,095 applied for aid, 9,732 were judged to have need, 1,260 had their need fully met. In 2013, 540 non-need-based awards were made. ***Average percent of need met:*** 72. ***Average financial aid package:*** $7641. ***Average need-based loan:*** $3003. ***Average need-based gift aid:*** $6547. ***Average non-need-based aid:*** $3152. ***Average indebtedness upon graduation:*** $13,000.

APPLYING

Standardized Tests *Required:* SAT or ACT (for admission).

Options: early admission.

Application fee: $65.

Required: high school transcript.

Application deadlines: 3/15 (freshmen), 3/15 (transfers).

Notification: continuous (freshmen), continuous (transfers).

CONTACT

Ms. Lori Janowski, Associate Director of Undergraduate Admissions, Hunter College of the City University of New York, 695 Park Avenue, New York, NY 10065-5085. *Phone:* 212-772-4490. *Fax:* 212-650-3472. *E-mail:* lori.janowski@hunter.cuny.edu.

Iona College

New Rochelle, New York

http://www.iona.edu/

- **Independent** comprehensive, founded 1940, affiliated with Roman Catholic Church
- **Suburban** 35-acre campus with easy access to New York City
- **Endowment** $116.4 million
- **Coed** 3,329 undergraduate students, 92% full-time, 52% women, 48% men
- **Moderately difficult** entrance level, 91% of applicants were admitted

UNDERGRAD STUDENTS

3,069 full-time, 260 part-time. Students come from 38 states and territories; 43 other countries; 24% are from out of state; 9% Black or African American, non-Hispanic/Latino; 22% Hispanic/Latino; 2% Asian, non-Hispanic/Latino; 0.2% Native Hawaiian or other Pacific Islander, non-Hispanic/Latino; 0.2% American Indian or Alaska Native, non-Hispanic/Latino; 2% Two or more races, non-Hispanic/Latino; 5% Race/ethnicity unknown; 3% international; 3% transferred in; 45% live on campus.

Freshmen:

Admission: 10,896 applied, 9,965 admitted, 935 enrolled. ***Average high school GPA:*** 3. ***Test scores:*** SAT critical reading scores over 500: 51%; SAT math scores over 500: 50%; ACT scores over 18: 94%; SAT critical reading scores over 600: 11%; SAT math scores over 600: 13%; ACT scores over 24: 44%; SAT critical reading scores over 700: 1%; SAT math scores over 700: 1%; ACT scores over 30: 4%.

Retention: 77% of full-time freshmen returned.

FACULTY

Total: 355, 49% full-time, 44% with terminal degrees.

Student/faculty ratio: 15:1.

ACADEMICS

Calendar: semesters. *Degrees:* certificates, bachelor's, master's, post-master's, and postbachelor's certificates.

Special study options: accelerated degree program, adult/continuing education programs, advanced placement credit, distance learning, double majors, English as a second language, honors programs, independent study, internships, part-time degree program, services for LD students, study abroad, summer session for credit. ***ROTC:*** Army (c), Air Force (c).

Unusual degree programs: 3-2 business administration.

Computers: 10,000 ports are available on campus for general student use. Students can access the following: campus intranet, computer help desk, free student e-mail accounts, online (class) grades, online (class) registration, online (class) schedules, bill payment. Campuswide network is available. 100% of college-owned or -operated housing units are wired for high-speed Internet access. Wireless service is available via entire campus.

Library: Ryan Library plus 1 other. *Books:* 269,396 (physical), 324,744 (digital/electronic); *Serial titles:* 112 (physical), 369 (digital/electronic); *Databases:* 150. Weekly public service hours: 101; students can reserve study rooms.

STUDENT LIFE

Housing options: coed, special housing for students with disabilities. Campus housing is university owned and leased by the school. Freshman campus housing is guaranteed.

Activities and organizations: drama/theater group, student-run newspaper, radio and television station, choral group, Student Government Association, Gaels Activities Board, Council for Greek Governance, Student Leader Alliance for Multiculturism, The Ionian - Student Newspaper, national fraternities, national sororities.

Athletics Member NCAA. All Division I. ***Intercollegiate sports:*** baseball M(s), basketball M(s)/W(s), cross-country running M(s)/W(s), golf M(s), lacrosse W(s), rowing M/W, soccer M(s)/W(s), softball W(s), swimming and diving M(s)/W(s), track and field M(s)/W(s), volleyball W(s), water polo M/W(s). ***Intramural sports:*** basketball M/W, cheerleading M(c)/W(c), football M/W, rugby M(c), soccer M/W, table tennis M/W, volleyball M/W.

Campus security: 24-hour emergency response devices and patrols, controlled dormitory access.

Student services: health clinic, personal/psychological counseling.

COSTS & FINANCIAL AID

Costs (2017–18) ***Comprehensive fee:*** $52,514 includes full-time tuition ($35,482), mandatory fees ($2200), and room and board ($14,832). Part-time tuition: $1176 per credit hour. Part-time tuition and fees vary according to course load. ***Required fees:*** $540 per term part-time. ***Room and board:*** Room and board charges vary according to board plan. ***Payment plan:*** installment. ***Waivers:*** children of alumni and employees or children of employees.

Financial Aid Of all full-time matriculated undergraduates who enrolled in 2016, 3,004 applied for aid, 2,567 were judged to have need, 517 had their need fully met. 352 Federal Work-Study jobs (averaging $1482). In 2016, 430 non-need-based awards were made. ***Average percent of need met:*** 16. ***Average financial aid package:*** $25,451. ***Average need-based loan:*** $3629. ***Average need-based gift aid:*** $5626. ***Average non-need-based aid:*** $17,647. ***Average indebtedness upon graduation:*** $34,199. ***Financial aid deadline:*** 4/15.

APPLYING

Standardized Tests *Required:* SAT or ACT (for admission).

Options: electronic application, early action, deferred entrance.

Application fee: $50.

Required: high school transcript. ***Required for some:*** interview. ***Recommended:*** essay or personal statement, 2 letters of recommendation.

Application deadlines: 2/15 (freshmen), 8/15 (transfers), 12/1 (early action).

Notification: continuous (freshmen), continuous (transfers), 12/19 (early action).

CONTACT
Mr. Alick Letang, Assistant Vice President for Enrollment Management, Iona College, Admissions, 715 North Avenue, New Rochelle, NY 10801. *Phone:* 914-633-2439. *Toll-free phone:* 800-231-IONA. *Fax:* 914-633-2778. *E-mail:* admissions@iona.edu.

Ithaca College
Ithaca, New York
http://www.ithaca.edu/

- **Independent** comprehensive, founded 1892
- **Small-town** 669-acre campus with easy access to Syracuse
- **Endowment** $270.0 million
- **Coed** 6,221 undergraduate students, 98% full-time, 58% women, 42% men
- **Moderately difficult** entrance level, 70% of applicants were admitted

UNDERGRAD STUDENTS
6,103 full-time, 118 part-time. Students come from 51 states and territories; 53 other countries; 54% are from out of state; 6% Black or African American, non-Hispanic/Latino; 8% Hispanic/Latino; 4% Asian, non-Hispanic/Latino; 0.1% American Indian or Alaska Native, non-Hispanic/Latino; 3% Two or more races, non-Hispanic/Latino; 5% Race/ethnicity unknown; 2% international; 2% transferred in; 71% live on campus.

Freshmen:
Admission: 14,380 applied, 10,054 admitted, 1,634 enrolled.
Retention: 85% of full-time freshmen returned.

FACULTY
Total: 788, 65% full-time, 74% with terminal degrees.
Student/faculty ratio: 11:1.

ACADEMICS
Calendar: semesters. *Degrees:* certificates, bachelor's, master's, and doctoral.
Special study options: accelerated degree program, adult/continuing education programs, advanced placement credit, distance learning, double majors, freshman honors college, honors programs, independent study, internships, off-campus study, part-time degree program, services for LD students, student-designed majors, study abroad, summer session for credit. ***ROTC:*** Army (c), Air Force (c).
Unusual degree programs: 3-2 engineering with Cornell University, Rensselaer Polytechnic Institute, Clarkson University, State University of New York at Binghamton.
Computers: 640 computers/terminals and 20 ports are available on campus for general student use. Students can access the following: campus intranet, computer help desk, free student e-mail accounts, online (class) grades, online (class) registration, online (class) schedules. Campuswide network is available. 100% of college-owned or -operated housing units are wired for high-speed Internet access. Wireless service is available via entire campus.
Library: Ithaca College Library. *Books:* 311,396 (physical), 151,885 (digital/electronic); *Databases:* 151. Weekly public service hours: 148; study areas open 24 hours, 5-7 days a week.

STUDENT LIFE
Housing options: on-campus residence required through junior year; coed, women-only, special housing for students with disabilities. Campus housing is university owned. Freshman campus housing is guaranteed.
Activities and organizations: drama/theater group, student-run newspaper, radio and television station, choral group, Student Governance Council, Colleges Against Cancer, Brothers 4 Brothers, International Club, Asian American Alliance, national fraternities.
Athletics Member NCAA. All Division III. ***Intercollegiate sports:*** baseball M, basketball M/W, crew M/W, cross-country running M/W, field hockey W, football M, golf W, gymnastics W, lacrosse M/W, soccer M/W, softball W, swimming and diving M/W, tennis M/W, track and field M/W, volleyball W, wrestling M. ***Intramural sports:*** basketball M/W, equestrian sports M(c)/W(c), fencing M(c)/W(c), football M, golf M/W, ice hockey M(c), lacrosse M(c)/W(c), rugby M(c)/W(c), skiing (downhill) M(c)/W(c), soccer M/W, softball M/W, squash M(c)/W(c), table tennis M(c)/W(c), tennis M/W, ultimate Frisbee M(c)/W(c), volleyball M/W.
Campus security: 24-hour emergency response devices and patrols, student patrols, late-night transport/escort service, controlled dormitory access.
Student services: health clinic, personal/psychological counseling.

COSTS & FINANCIAL AID
Costs (2017–18) ***Tuition:*** $42,884 full-time, $1429 per credit hour part-time. ***Room only:*** Room and board charges vary according to board plan and housing facility. ***Payment plan:*** installment. ***Waivers:*** children of alumni and employees or children of employees.
Financial Aid Of all full-time matriculated undergraduates who enrolled in 2016, 4,757 applied for aid, 4,114 were judged to have need, 1,688 had their need fully met. 2,936 Federal Work-Study jobs (averaging $2352). 1,802 state and other part-time jobs (averaging $2402). In 2016, 1521 non-need-based awards were made. ***Average percent of need met:*** 85. ***Average financial aid package:*** $35,707. ***Average need-based loan:*** $6569. ***Average need-based gift aid:*** $25,787. ***Average non-need-based aid:*** $14,882. ***Average indebtedness upon graduation:*** $40,595.

APPLYING
Options: electronic application, early admission, early decision, early action, deferred entrance.
Application fee: $60.
Required: essay or personal statement, high school transcript, 1 letter of recommendation. ***Required for some:*** audition for some programs. ***Recommended:*** minimum 3.0 GPA.
Application deadlines: 2/1 (freshmen), 3/1 (transfers), 12/1 (early action).
Early decision deadline: 11/1.
Notification: 4/15 (freshmen), continuous (transfers), 12/15 (early decision), 2/1 (early action).

CONTACT
Nicole Eversley Bradwell, Director of Admission, Ithaca College, 953 Danby Road, Ithaca, NY 14850-7002. *Phone:* 607-274-3124. *Toll-free phone:* 800-429-4274. *Fax:* 607-274-1900.
E-mail: admission@ithaca.edu.

Jamestown Business College
Jamestown, New York
http://www.jbc.edu/

- **Proprietary** primarily 2-year, founded 1886
- **Small-town** 1-acre campus
- **Coed**
- **Minimally difficult** entrance level

FACULTY
Student/faculty ratio: 23:1.

ACADEMICS
Calendar: quarters. *Degrees:* certificates, associate, and bachelor's.
Library: James Prendergast Library.

STUDENT LIFE
Housing options: college housing not available.
Campus security: 24-hour emergency response devices.

COSTS & FINANCIAL AID
Costs (2016–17) ***One-time required fee:*** $25. ***Tuition:*** $11,700 full-time, $325 per credit hour part-time. Full-time tuition and fees vary according to course load. Part-time tuition and fees vary according to course load. ***Required fees:*** $900 full-time, $150 per term part-time.
Financial Aid Of all full-time matriculated undergraduates who enrolled in 2014, 316 applied for aid, 316 were judged to have need.

APPLYING
Application fee: $25.
Required: essay or personal statement, high school transcript, interview.

CONTACT
Mrs. Brenda Salemme, Director of Admissions and Placement, Jamestown Business College, 7 Fairmount Avenue, Box 429, Jamestown, NY 14702-0429. *Phone:* 716-664-5100. *Fax:* 716-664-3144.
E-mail: brendasalemme@jamestownbusinesscollege.edu.

The Jewish Theological Seminary

New York, New York

http://www.jtsa.edu/

CONTACT
Mr. Sergio Lineberge, List College Admissions Coordinator, The Jewish Theological Seminary, 3080 Broadway, New York, NY 10027. *Phone:* 212-678-8820. *E-mail:* lcadmissions@jtsa.edu.

John Jay College of Criminal Justice of the City University of New York

New York, New York

http://www.jjay.cuny.edu/

- **State and locally supported** comprehensive, founded 1964, part of City University of New York
- **Urban** campus with easy access to New York City
- **Coed** 12,674 undergraduate students, 78% full-time, 56% women, 44% men
- **Moderately difficult** entrance level, 34% of applicants were admitted

UNDERGRAD STUDENTS
9,831 full-time, 2,843 part-time. Students come from 21 states and territories; 38 other countries; 4% are from out of state; 19% Black or African American, non-Hispanic/Latino; 43% Hispanic/Latino; 0.3% Asian, non-Hispanic/Latino; 12% Native Hawaiian or other Pacific Islander, non-Hispanic/Latino; 23% American Indian or Alaska Native, non-Hispanic/Latino; 3% international; 14% transferred in.

Freshmen:
Admission: 13,899 applied, 4,692 admitted, 1,523 enrolled. ***Average high school GPA:*** 2.84. ***Test scores:*** SAT critical reading scores over 500: 38%; SAT math scores over 500: 45%; SAT critical reading scores over 600: 7%; SAT math scores over 600: 9%; SAT critical reading scores over 700: 1%; SAT math scores over 700: 1%.

Retention: 77% of full-time freshmen returned.

ACADEMICS
Calendar: semesters. *Degrees:* certificates, bachelor's, and master's.

Special study options: academic remediation for entering students, advanced placement credit, cooperative education, distance learning, double majors, English as a second language, honors programs, independent study, internships, off-campus study, part-time degree program, services for LD students, student-designed majors, study abroad, summer session for credit.

Unusual degree programs: 3-2 social work; public management, law enforcement.

Computers: 1,980 computers/terminals are available on campus for general student use. Students can access the following: campus intranet, computer help desk, free student e-mail accounts, online (class) grades, online (class) registration, online (class) schedules. Campuswide network is available. Wireless service is available via classrooms, computer centers, computer labs, learning centers, libraries, student centers.

Library: Lloyd George Sealy Library. *Books:* 182,059 (physical), 631,447 (digital/electronic); *Serial titles:* 7,124 (physical), 101,219 (digital/electronic); *Databases:* 178. Weekly public service hours: 77; study areas open 24 hours, 5-7 days a week; students can reserve study rooms.

STUDENT LIFE
Housing options: college housing not available.

Activities and organizations: drama/theater group, student-run newspaper, radio station, choral group, Auxiliary University Program, Student Athlete Advisory Community Club, Environmental Club, Law Society, Artists United.

Athletics Member NCAA. All Division III. ***Intercollegiate sports:*** baseball M, basketball M/W, cheerleading M/W, cross-country running M/W, riflery M/W, soccer M/W, softball W, swimming and diving W, tennis M/W, volleyball M/W. ***Intramural sports:*** basketball M/W, cheerleading M/W, riflery M/W, soccer M/W, swimming and diving M/W.

Campus security: 24-hour emergency response devices and patrols, controlled dormitory access.

Student services: health clinic, personal/psychological counseling, women's center, legal services.

FINANCIAL AID
Financial Aid Of all full-time matriculated undergraduates who enrolled in 2015, 9,810 applied for aid, 9,451 were judged to have need. ***Average percent of need met:*** 85. ***Average financial aid package:*** $8437. ***Average need-based loan:*** $3825. ***Average need-based gift aid:*** $2639.

APPLYING
Standardized Tests *Required:* SAT or ACT (for admission).

Options: deferred entrance.

Application fee: $65.

Required: high school transcript, minimum 2.0 GPA, minimum SAT score of 1100.

Application deadlines: 5/31 (freshmen), 5/31 (transfers).

Notification: continuous until 2/15 (freshmen), continuous until 2/15 (transfers).

CONTACT
Mr. Vincent Papandrea, Director, John Jay College of Criminal Justice of the City University of New York, 524 West 59th Street, L.64.14NB, New York, NY 10019. *Phone:* 212-237-8864. *Toll-free phone:* 877-JOHNJAY. *E-mail:* vpapandrea@jjay.cuny.edu.

The Juilliard School

New York, New York

http://www.juilliard.edu/

- **Independent** comprehensive, founded 1905
- **Urban** campus
- **Coed** 580 undergraduate students, 86% full-time, 49% women, 51% men
- **Most difficult** entrance level, 7% of applicants were admitted

UNDERGRAD STUDENTS
498 full-time, 82 part-time. 89% are from out of state; 4% Black or African American, non-Hispanic/Latino; 7% Hispanic/Latino; 14% Asian, non-Hispanic/Latino; 0.2% American Indian or Alaska Native, non-Hispanic/Latino; 5% Two or more races, non-Hispanic/Latino; 6% Race/ethnicity unknown; 24% international; 3% transferred in.

Freshmen:
Admission: 2,533 applied, 166 admitted, 114 enrolled.

FACULTY
Total: 337, 40% full-time.

Student/faculty ratio: 4:1.

ACADEMICS
Calendar: semesters. *Degrees:* diplomas, bachelor's, master's, doctoral, post-master's, and postbachelor's certificates.

Special study options: adult/continuing education programs.

Computers: Campuswide network is available. Wireless service is available via entire campus.

Library: Lila Acheson Wallace Library.

STUDENT LIFE
Housing options: on-campus residence required for freshman year; coed. Campus housing is university owned. Freshman campus housing is guaranteed.

Activities and organizations: drama/theater group, student-run newspaper.

Campus security: 24-hour emergency response devices and patrols, controlled dormitory access, electronically operated main building entrances.

Student services: health clinic, personal/psychological counseling.

COSTS & FINANCIAL AID
Costs (2016–17) ***Comprehensive fee:*** $57,040 includes full-time tuition ($41,310), mandatory fees ($350), and room and board ($15,380). ***Payment plan:*** installment. ***Waivers:*** employees or children of employees.

Financial Aid Of all full-time matriculated undergraduates who enrolled in 2016, 433 applied for aid, 369 were judged to have need, 89 had their need fully met. 168 Federal Work-Study jobs (averaging $1970). 202 state and other part-time jobs (averaging $1988). In 2016, 51 non-need-based awards were made. ***Average percent of need met:*** 74. ***Average financial aid package:*** $32,644. ***Average need-based loan:*** $5046. ***Average need-based gift aid:*** $27,980. ***Average non-need-based aid:*** $20,950. ***Average indebtedness upon graduation:*** $32,493. ***Financial aid deadline:*** 3/1.

APPLYING

Standardized Tests *Required for some:* SAT or ACT (for admission).

Options: electronic application.

Application fee: $110.

Required: essay or personal statement, high school transcript, audition.

Application deadlines: 12/1 (freshmen), 12/1 (transfers).

Notification: 4/1 (freshmen), 4/1 (transfers).

CONTACT

Ms. Kathy Tesar, Associate Dean for Enrollment Management, The Juilliard School, 60 Lincoln Center Plaza, New York, NY 10023-6588. *Phone:* 212-799-5000 Ext. 223. *Fax:* 212-724-0263. *E-mail:* admissions@juilliard.edu.

Kehilath Yakov Rabbinical Seminary

Ossining, New York

http://kehilathyakov.com/

CONTACT

Admissions Officer, Kehilath Yakov Rabbinical Seminary, 340 Illington Road, Ossining, NY 10562. *Phone:* 718-963-1212.

Keuka College

Keuka Park, New York

http://www.keuka.edu/

- **Independent** comprehensive, founded 1890, affiliated with American Baptist Churches in the U.S.A.
- **Rural** 173-acre campus with easy access to Rochester
- **Endowment** $13.3 million
- **Coed** 1,730 undergraduate students, 78% full-time, 75% women, 25% men
- **Moderately difficult** entrance level, 94% of applicants were admitted

UNDERGRAD STUDENTS

1,351 full-time, 379 part-time. Students come from 3 states and territories; 12 other countries; 0.1% are from out of state; 9% Black or African American, non-Hispanic/Latino; 5% Hispanic/Latino; 0.6% Asian, non-Hispanic/Latino; 0.1% Native Hawaiian or other Pacific Islander, non-Hispanic/Latino; 0.5% American Indian or Alaska Native, non-Hispanic/Latino; 2% Two or more races, non-Hispanic/Latino; 6% Race/ethnicity unknown; 3% international; 3% transferred in; 46% live on campus.

Freshmen:

Admission: 1,996 applied, 1,871 admitted, 365 enrolled.
Retention: 70% of full-time freshmen returned.

FACULTY

Total: 439, 20% full-time, 24% with terminal degrees.

Student/faculty ratio: 11:1.

ACADEMICS

Calendar: 4-1-4. *Degrees:* bachelor's and master's.

Special study options: academic remediation for entering students, accelerated degree program, adult/continuing education programs, advanced placement credit, cooperative education, distance learning, double majors, English as a second language, independent study, internships, off-campus study, part-time degree program, services for LD students, student-designed majors, study abroad, summer session for credit.

Unusual degree programs: occupational therapy.

Computers: 185 computers/terminals and 3,357 ports are available on campus for general student use. Students can access the following: campus intranet, computer help desk, free student e-mail accounts, online (class) grades, online (class) registration, online (class) schedules, phone app for cancellations. Campuswide network is available. 100% of college-owned or -operated housing units are wired for high-speed Internet access. Wireless service is available via entire campus.

Library: Lightner Library plus 1 other. *Books:* 79,009 (physical), 1,083 (digital/electronic); *Serial titles:* 687 (physical), 112 (digital/electronic); *Databases:* 89. Weekly public service hours: 96.

STUDENT LIFE

Housing options: on-campus residence required through senior year; coed, women-only, cooperative, special housing for students with disabilities. Campus housing is university owned. Freshman campus housing is guaranteed.

Activities and organizations: drama/theater group, student-run newspaper, choral group, Sigma Alpha Pi Honor Society, SOTA, ASL Club, Art Club, KC Chemistry Club.

Athletics Member NCAA. All Division III. ***Intercollegiate sports:*** baseball M, basketball M/W, cross-country running M/W, field hockey W, golf M/W, lacrosse M/W, soccer M/W, softball W, volleyball M/W. ***Intramural sports:*** badminton M/W, basketball M/W, bowling M/W, cheerleading M(c)/W(c), equestrian sports M(c)/W(c), football M/W, soccer M/W, volleyball M/W.

Campus security: 24-hour emergency response devices and patrols, late-night transport/escort service.

Student services: health clinic, personal/psychological counseling, women's center.

COSTS & FINANCIAL AID

Costs (2017–18) ***One-time required fee:*** $225. ***Comprehensive fee:*** $42,398 includes full-time tuition ($29,926), mandatory fees ($1020), and room and board ($11,452). Full-time tuition and fees vary according to course load, degree level, program, and reciprocity agreements. Part-time tuition: $999 per credit hour. Part-time tuition and fees vary according to course load, degree level, program, and reciprocity agreements. ***College room only:*** $5520. Room and board charges vary according to board plan and housing facility. ***Payment plan:*** installment. ***Waivers:*** employees or children of employees.

Financial Aid Of all full-time matriculated undergraduates who enrolled in 2015, 1,206 applied for aid, 1,126 were judged to have need, 99 had their need fully met. In 2015, 43 non-need-based awards were made. ***Average financial aid package:*** $20,979. ***Average need-based loan:*** $4288. ***Average need-based gift aid:*** $8769. ***Average non-need-based aid:*** $11,602.

APPLYING

Options: electronic application, early admission, deferred entrance.

Required: high school transcript. ***Required for some:*** interview. ***Recommended:*** minimum 2.8 GPA, 1 letter of recommendation, interview.

Application deadlines: rolling (freshmen), rolling (transfers).

CONTACT

Mrs. Megan Perkins (Ryan), Keuka College, 141 Central Avenue, Keuka Park, NY 14478. *Phone:* 315-279-5254. *Toll-free phone:* 800-33-KEUKA. *Fax:* 315-279-5386. *E-mail:* admissions@keuka.edu.

The King's College

New York, New York

http://www.tkc.edu/

- **Independent nondenominational** 4-year, founded 1939
- **Urban** campus with easy access to New York City
- **Endowment** $488,024
- **Coed** 534 undergraduate students, 97% full-time, 64% women, 36% men
- **Moderately difficult** entrance level, 41% of applicants were admitted

UNDERGRAD STUDENTS

520 full-time, 14 part-time. Students come from 45 states and territories; 10 other countries; 93% are from out of state; 6% Black or African American, non-Hispanic/Latino; 8% Hispanic/Latino; 4% Asian, non-Hispanic/Latino; 0.6% Native Hawaiian or other Pacific Islander, non-Hispanic/Latino; 0.4% American Indian or Alaska Native, non-Hispanic/Latino; 1% Two or more races, non-Hispanic/Latino; 14% Race/ethnicity unknown; 3% international; 8% transferred in.

Freshmen:

Admission: 2,672 applied, 1,092 admitted, 161 enrolled. ***Average high school GPA:*** 3.77. ***Test scores:*** SAT critical reading scores over 500: 90%; SAT math scores over 500: 72%; SAT writing scores over 500: 76%;

ACT scores over 18: 100%; SAT critical reading scores over 600: 49%; SAT math scores over 600: 31%; SAT writing scores over 600: 38%; ACT scores over 24: 84%; SAT critical reading scores over 700: 15%; SAT math scores over 700: 4%; SAT writing scores over 700: 11%; ACT scores over 30: 19%.

Retention: 69% of full-time freshmen returned.

FACULTY

Total: 60, 43% full-time, 73% with terminal degrees.

Student/faculty ratio: 14:1.

ACADEMICS

Calendar: semesters. *Degree:* bachelor's.

Special study options: advanced placement credit, distance learning, double majors, independent study, internships, services for LD students, study abroad, summer session for credit. ***ROTC:*** Army (c).

Computers: Students can access the following: computer help desk, free student e-mail accounts, online (class) grades, online (class) registration, online (class) schedules. Campuswide network is available. 100% of college-owned or -operated housing units are wired for high-speed Internet access. Wireless service is available via entire campus.

Library: Battles Library.

STUDENT LIFE

Housing options: men-only, women-only. Campus housing is university owned and leased by the school. Freshman campus housing is guaranteed.

Activities and organizations: drama/theater group, student-run newspaper, choral group, The King's Players, King's Debate Society, Refuge, Empire State Tribune, The Kings of Swing.

Athletics Member NCCAA, USCAA. ***Intercollegiate sports:*** baseball M, basketball M/W, golf M/W, soccer M/W, volleyball W. ***Intramural sports:*** basketball M(c)/W(c), cheerleading W(c), fencing M(c)/W(c), football M(c), rugby M(c), ultimate Frisbee M(c)/W(c).

Campus security: 24-hour emergency response devices, 24-hour security/doormen, fire sprinklers, fire/evacuation emergency plan.

COSTS & FINANCIAL AID

Costs (2016–17) ***Tuition:*** $34,320 full-time, $1410 per credit part-time. Full-time tuition and fees vary according to course load. Part-time tuition and fees vary according to course load. ***Required fees:*** $400 full-time, $200 per term part-time. ***Room only:*** $13,650. Room and board charges vary according to location. ***Payment plans:*** installment, deferred payment. ***Waivers:*** employees or children of employees.

Financial Aid Of all full-time matriculated undergraduates who enrolled in 2015, 394 applied for aid, 349 were judged to have need, 48 had their need fully met. In 2015, 131 non-need-based awards were made. ***Average percent of need met:*** 68. ***Average financial aid package:*** $26,187. ***Average need-based loan:*** $4204. ***Average need-based gift aid:*** $21,913. ***Average non-need-based aid:*** $16,036. ***Average indebtedness upon graduation:*** $32,934.

APPLYING

Standardized Tests *Required:* SAT, ACT or CLT (for admission).

Options: electronic application, early action, deferred entrance.

Application fee: $30.

Required: high school transcript. ***Recommended:*** minimum 3.0 GPA, interview.

Application deadlines: rolling (freshmen), rolling (transfers).

Notification: continuous (freshmen), continuous (transfers).

CONTACT

Mr. Luke Smith, Director of Admissions, The King's College, 56 Broadway, New York, NY 10004. *Phone:* 212-659-3615. *Toll-free phone:* 888-969-7200 Ext. 3610. *Fax:* 212-659-3611. *E-mail:* lsmith@tkc.edu.

Lehman College of the City University of New York

Bronx, New York

http://www.lehman.cuny.edu/

- **State and locally supported** comprehensive, founded 1931, part of City University of New York System
- **Urban** 37-acre campus with easy access to New York City
- **Endowment** $7.1 million
- **Coed** 11,477 undergraduate students, 59% full-time, 67% women, 33% men
- **Moderately difficult** entrance level, 32% of applicants were admitted

UNDERGRAD STUDENTS

6,729 full-time, 4,748 part-time. Students come from 15 states and territories; 99 other countries; 1% are from out of state; 31% Black or African American, non-Hispanic/Latino; 52% Hispanic/Latino; 7% Asian, non-Hispanic/Latino; 0.2% American Indian or Alaska Native, non-Hispanic/Latino; 3% international; 18% transferred in.

Freshmen:

Admission: 14,318 applied, 4,651 admitted, 690 enrolled. ***Test scores:*** SAT critical reading scores over 500: 34%; SAT math scores over 500: 37%; SAT writing scores over 500: 26%; SAT critical reading scores over 600: 6%; SAT math scores over 600: 6%; SAT writing scores over 600: 4%; SAT critical reading scores over 700: 1%.

Retention: 86% of full-time freshmen returned.

FACULTY

Total: 912, 40% full-time, 42% with terminal degrees.

Student/faculty ratio: 13:1.

ACADEMICS

Calendar: semesters. *Degrees:* certificates, bachelor's, master's, and post-master's certificates.

Special study options: adult/continuing education programs, advanced placement credit, cooperative education, distance learning, double majors, English as a second language, freshman honors college, honors programs, independent study, internships, off-campus study, part-time degree program, services for LD students, student-designed majors, study abroad, summer session for credit. ***ROTC:*** Army (c).

Unusual degree programs: 3-2 mathematics.

Computers: 800 computers/terminals are available on campus for general student use. Students can access the following: campus intranet, computer help desk, free student e-mail accounts, online (class) grades, online (class) registration, online (class) schedules. Campuswide network is available. Wireless service is available via entire campus.

Library: Leonard Lief Library plus 1 other. *Books:* 693,922 (physical); *Serial titles:* 668,565 (physical). Weekly public service hours: 40; students can reserve study rooms.

STUDENT LIFE

Housing options: Campus housing is university owned.

Activities and organizations: drama/theater group, student-run newspaper, radio and television station, choral group, Club Mac, African Students Association, Dominican Student Association, The Sociology Club, Club Live.

Athletics Member NCAA. All Division III. ***Intercollegiate sports:*** baseball M, basketball M/W, cross-country running M/W, racquetball M/W, soccer M/W, softball M/W, swimming and diving M/W, table tennis M/W, tennis M/W, track and field M/W, volleyball M/W, water polo M, wrestling M. ***Intramural sports:*** badminton M/W, baseball M/W, basketball M/W, cross-country running M/W, racquetball M/W, soccer M, softball M/W, swimming and diving M/W, tennis M/W, volleyball M/W, wrestling M.

Campus security: 24-hour emergency response devices and patrols, student patrols, late-night transport/escort service.

Student services: health clinic, personal/psychological counseling, women's center.

COSTS & FINANCIAL AID

Costs (2017–18) ***Tuition:*** state resident $6330 full-time; nonresident $13,440 full-time. ***Required fees:*** $680 full-time.

Financial Aid Of all full-time matriculated undergraduates who enrolled in 2016, 6,168 applied for aid, 6,168 were judged to have need, 5,565 had their need fully met. 1,115 Federal Work-Study jobs (averaging $1485). In 2016, 2465 non-need-based awards were made. ***Average percent of need met:*** 90. ***Average financial aid package:*** $7344. ***Average need-based loan:*** $2083. ***Average need-based gift aid:*** $7169. ***Average non-need-based aid:*** $1450. ***Average indebtedness upon graduation:*** $8525.

APPLYING

Standardized Tests *Required:* SAT or ACT (for admission).

Options: deferred entrance.

Application fee: $65.

Required: high school transcript, minimum 3.0 GPA. ***Required for some:*** essay or personal statement, interview.

Application deadlines: rolling (freshmen), rolling (transfers).

Notification: continuous (freshmen), continuous (transfers).

CONTACT

Ms. Laurie Austin, Director of Admissions, Lehman College of the City University of New York, 250 Bedford Park Boulevard West, Bronx, NY 10468. *Phone:* 718-960-8706. *Toll-free phone:* 877-LEHMAN1. *Fax:* 718-960-8712. *E-mail:* enroll@lehman.cuny.edu.

★ Le Moyne College

Syracuse, New York

http://www.lemoyne.edu/

- **Independent Roman Catholic (Jesuit)** comprehensive, founded 1946
- **Suburban** 161-acre campus
- **Endowment** $158.1 million
- **Coed** 2,897 undergraduate students, 87% full-time, 61% women, 39% men
- **Moderately difficult** entrance level, 65% of applicants were admitted

UNDERGRAD STUDENTS

2,534 full-time, 363 part-time. Students come from 27 states and territories; 45 other countries; 5% are from out of state; 6% Black or African American, non-Hispanic/Latino; 5% Hispanic/Latino; 2% Asian, non-Hispanic/Latino; 0.1% Native Hawaiian or other Pacific Islander, non-Hispanic/Latino; 0.3% American Indian or Alaska Native, non-Hispanic/Latino; 2% Two or more races, non-Hispanic/Latino; 4% Race/ethnicity unknown; 1% international; 6% transferred in; 57% live on campus.

Freshmen:

Admission: 6,832 applied, 4,462 admitted, 631 enrolled. ***Average high school GPA:*** 3.45. ***Test scores:*** SAT critical reading scores over 500: 73%; SAT math scores over 500: 81%; ACT scores over 18: 99%; SAT critical reading scores over 600: 27%; SAT math scores over 600: 30%; ACT scores over 24: 59%; SAT critical reading scores over 700: 5%; SAT math scores over 700: 4%; ACT scores over 30: 11%.

Retention: 86% of full-time freshmen returned.

FACULTY

Total: 350, 49% full-time, 63% with terminal degrees.

Student/faculty ratio: 13:1.

ACADEMICS

Calendar: semesters. *Degrees:* bachelor's, master's, post-master's, and postbachelor's certificates.

Special study options: academic remediation for entering students, accelerated degree program, adult/continuing education programs, advanced placement credit, distance learning, double majors, honors programs, independent study, internships, off-campus study, part-time degree program, services for LD students, study abroad, summer session for credit. ***ROTC:*** Army (c), Air Force (c).

Unusual degree programs: 3-2 engineering with Syracuse University.

Computers: 330 computers/terminals and 330 ports are available on campus for general student use. Students can access the following: campus intranet, computer help desk, free student e-mail accounts, online (class) grades, online (class) registration, online (class) schedules, ECHO (campus-wide portal), some virtual access from off campus. Campuswide network is available. 100% of college-owned or -operated housing units are wired for high-speed Internet access. Wireless service is available via entire campus.

Library: Noreen Reale Falcone Library. *Books:* 259,932 (physical), 31,050 (digital/electronic); *Serial titles:* 1,991 (physical), 1,143 (digital/electronic); *Databases:* 260. Weekly public service hours: 109; study areas open 24 hours, 5-7 days a week; students can reserve study rooms.

STUDENT LIFE

Housing options: on-campus residence required through senior year; coed, special housing for students with disabilities. Campus housing is university owned. Freshman campus housing is guaranteed.

Activities and organizations: drama/theater group, student-run newspaper, radio and television station, choral group, Student Programming Board, Outing Club, Performing Arts Groups, Cultural Groups, New Student Orientation Committee.

Athletics Member NCAA. All Division II. ***Intercollegiate sports:*** baseball M(s), basketball M(s)/W(s), cross-country running M(s)/W(s), golf M(s)/W(s), lacrosse M(s)/W(s), soccer M(s)/W(s), softball W(s), swimming and diving M(s)/W(s), tennis M(s)/W(s), track and field M(s)/W(s), volleyball W(s). ***Intramural sports:*** basketball M/W, bowling M(c)/W(c), cheerleading M(c)/W(c), crew M(c)/W(c), equestrian sports M(c)/W(c), fencing M(c)/W(c), field hockey W(c), football M/W, ice hockey M(c), lacrosse M(c)/W(c), racquetball M/W, rugby M(c)/W(c), sailing M(c)/W(c), soccer M/W, softball M/W, ultimate Frisbee M(c)/W(c), volleyball M/W.

Campus security: 24-hour emergency response devices and patrols, late-night transport/escort service, controlled dormitory access, lighted pathways, closed-circuit security cameras, and emergency code blue phones.

Student services: health clinic, personal/psychological counseling.

COSTS & FINANCIAL AID

Costs (2016–17) ***Comprehensive fee:*** $46,000 includes full-time tuition ($32,040), mandatory fees ($990), and room and board ($12,970). Part-time tuition: $672 per credit hour. Part-time tuition and fees vary according to class time and course load. ***College room only:*** $8120. Room and board charges vary according to board plan and housing facility. ***Payment plans:*** installment, deferred payment. ***Waivers:*** employees or children of employees.

Financial Aid Of all full-time matriculated undergraduates who enrolled in 2015, 2,247 applied for aid, 2,041 were judged to have need, 482 had their need fully met. 294 Federal Work-Study jobs (averaging $1091). 464 state and other part-time jobs (averaging $1800). In 2015, 331 non-need-based awards were made. ***Average percent of need met:*** 77. ***Average financial aid package:*** $25,276. ***Average need-based loan:*** $4676. ***Average need-based gift aid:*** $20,514. ***Average non-need-based aid:*** $13,829. ***Average indebtedness upon graduation:*** $37,337.

APPLYING

Standardized Tests *Required for some:* SAT or ACT (for admission).

Options: electronic application, early admission, early action, deferred entrance.

Application fee: $35.

Required: essay or personal statement, high school transcript, 3 letters of recommendation. ***Recommended:*** interview.

Application deadlines: 2/1 (freshmen), 8/1 (transfers), 11/15 (early action).

Notification: continuous until 1/1 (freshmen), continuous (transfers), 12/15 (early action).

CONTACT

Mrs. Mary M. Chandler, Sr. Director of Admission, Le Moyne College, 1419 Salt Springs Road, Syracuse, NY 13214-1301. *Phone:* 315-445-4300. *Toll-free phone:* 800-333-4733. *Fax:* 315-445-4711. *E-mail:* admission@lemoyne.edu.

See next page for display ad and page 1394 for the College Close-Up.

★ LIM College
New York, New York
http://www.limcollege.edu/

- **Proprietary** comprehensive, founded 1939
- **Urban** campus with easy access to New York City
- **Coed, primarily women** 1,515 undergraduate students, 94% full-time, 93% women, 7% men

UNDERGRAD STUDENTS
1,428 full-time, 87 part-time. Students come from 44 states and territories; 26 other countries; 61% are from out of state; 15% Black or African American, non-Hispanic/Latino; 12% Hispanic/Latino; 6% Asian, non-Hispanic/Latino; 0.5% Native Hawaiian or other Pacific Islander, non-Hispanic/Latino; 0.7% American Indian or Alaska Native, non-Hispanic/Latino; 1% Two or more races, non-Hispanic/Latino; 5% Race/ethnicity unknown; 4% international; 11% transferred in; 27% live on campus.

Freshmen:
Admission: 269 enrolled. ***Average high school GPA:*** 3. ***Test scores:*** ACT scores over 18: 81%; ACT scores over 24: 28%; ACT scores over 30: 3%.
Retention: 73% of full-time freshmen returned.

FACULTY
Total: 196, 16% full-time.
Student/faculty ratio: 8:1.

ACADEMICS
Calendar: semesters. *Degrees:* certificates, associate, bachelor's, and master's.
Special study options: academic remediation for entering students, accelerated degree program, advanced placement credit, cooperative education, distance learning, honors programs, internships, off-campus study, part-time degree program, services for LD students, study abroad, summer session for credit.
Computers: 352 computers/terminals are available on campus for general student use. Students can access the following: campus intranet, computer help desk, free student e-mail accounts, online (class) grades, online (class) registration, online (class) schedules. Campuswide network is available. 100% of college-owned or -operated housing units are wired for high-speed Internet access. Wireless service is available via entire campus.
Library: Adrian G. Marcuse Library. *Books:* 15,000 (physical), 700 (digital/electronic); *Serial titles:* 172 (physical); *Databases:* 55. Students can reserve study rooms.

STUDENT LIFE
Housing options: coed. Campus housing is leased by the school.
Activities and organizations: Fashion Styling Club, The Writers Circle, Student Life Activities Board, Dance Team, Black Retail Action Group.
Campus security: controlled dormitory access.
Student services: personal/psychological counseling.

COSTS & FINANCIAL AID
Costs (2017–18) ***Comprehensive fee:*** $46,700 includes full-time tuition ($25,575), mandatory fees ($775), and room and board ($20,350). Part-time tuition: $850 per credit. ***Required fees:*** $388 per term part-time. ***College room only:*** $16,350. Room and board charges vary according to housing facility. ***Payment plan:*** installment. ***Waivers:*** employees or children of employees.
Financial Aid Of all full-time matriculated undergraduates who enrolled in 2014, 1,364 applied for aid, 950 were judged to have need, 20 had their need fully met. In 2014, 174 non-need-based awards were made. ***Average percent of need met:*** 41. ***Average financial aid package:*** $10,162. ***Average need-based loan:*** $4230. ***Average need-based gift aid:*** $7840. ***Average non-need-based aid:*** $4249. ***Average indebtedness upon graduation:*** $37,328. ***Financial aid deadline:*** 11/15.

APPLYING
Standardized Tests *Required:* SAT or ACT (for admission).
Required: essay or personal statement, high school transcript, 2 letters of recommendation. ***Required for some:*** interview. ***Recommended:*** minimum 2.5 GPA.

CONTACT
Mr. Anthony Urmey, Assistant Director of Admissions, LIM College, 12 East 53rd Street, New York, NY 10022. *Phone:* 212-3100608 Ext. 238. *Toll-free phone:* 800-677-1323. *E-mail:* admissions@limcollege.edu.

Long Island University–LIU Brooklyn
Brooklyn, New York
http://www.liu.edu/

- **Independent** university, founded 1926
- **Urban** 11-acre campus with easy access to New York City
- **Endowment** $56.3 million
- **Coed**
- **Moderately difficult** entrance level

FACULTY
Student/faculty ratio: 15:1.

ACADEMICS
Calendar: semesters. *Degrees:* associate, bachelor's, master's, doctoral, post-master's, and postbachelor's certificates.
Library: Salena Library. *Books:* 217,633 (physical), 170,074 (digital/electronic); *Serial titles:* 327,932 (physical), 94,194 (digital/electronic); *Databases:* 396.

STUDENT LIFE
Housing options: coed. Campus housing is university owned and leased by the school. Freshman campus housing is guaranteed.
Activities and organizations: drama/theater group, student-run newspaper, radio and television station, choral group, The Student Government Association, The American Pharmacists Association - Academy of Student Pharmacists, Hillel Jewish Students Organization, Student Activities Board, Indo American Pharmaceutical Association, national fraternities, national sororities.
Athletics Member NCAA. All Division I.
Campus security: 24-hour emergency response devices and patrols, controlled dormitory access, lighted pathways/sidewalks.
Student services: personal/psychological counseling.

COSTS & FINANCIAL AID
Costs (2016–17) ***Comprehensive fee:*** $49,682 includes full-time tuition ($34,352), mandatory fees ($1904), and room and board ($13,426). Full-time tuition and fees vary according to program. Part-time tuition: $1072 per credit. Part-time tuition and fees vary according to program. ***Required fees:*** $451 per term part-time. ***Room and board:*** Room and board charges vary according to board plan and housing facility.
Financial Aid Of all full-time matriculated undergraduates who enrolled in 2016, 3,578 applied for aid, 3,421 were judged to have need, 153 had their need fully met. 437 Federal Work-Study jobs (averaging $2168). In 2016, 142 non-need-based awards were made. ***Average percent of need met:*** 50. ***Average financial aid package:*** $20,506. ***Average need-based loan:*** $4561. ***Average need-based gift aid:*** $11,883. ***Average non-need-based aid:*** $12,577. ***Average indebtedness upon graduation:*** $43,243.

APPLYING
Standardized Tests *Recommended:* SAT or ACT (for admission).
Options: electronic application, early action, deferred entrance.
Application fee: $50.
Required: essay or personal statement, high school transcript. ***Recommended:*** interview.

CONTACT
Mr. Richard Sunday, Dean of Admissions, Long Island University–LIU Brooklyn, 1 University Plaza, Brooklyn, NY 11201. *Phone:* 718-488-1011. *Toll-free phone:* 800-LIU-PLAN. *Fax:* 718-780-6110. *E-mail:* bkln-admissions@liu.edu.

Long Island University–LIU Post
Brookville, New York
http://www.liu.edu/

- **Independent** comprehensive, founded 1954
- **Suburban** 308-acre campus with easy access to New York City
- **Endowment** $63.2 million
- **Coed**
- **Moderately difficult** entrance level

FACULTY
Student/faculty ratio: 12:1.

ACADEMICS
Calendar: semesters. *Degrees:* associate, bachelor's, master's, doctoral, post-master's, and postbachelor's certificates.
Library: B. Davis Schwartz Memorial Library. *Books:* 1.6 million (physical), 170,023 (digital/electronic); *Serial titles:* 459,188 (physical), 94,194 (digital/electronic); *Databases:* 383.

STUDENT LIFE
Housing options: coed, special housing for students with disabilities. Campus housing is university owned. Freshman campus housing is guaranteed.
Activities and organizations: drama/theater group, student-run newspaper, radio and television station, choral group, Student Government Association, Association for Campus Programming, Student Dance Association, Commuter Student Association, Inter Fraternal Sorority Council, national fraternities, national sororities.
Athletics Member NCAA. All Division II.
Campus security: 24-hour emergency response devices and patrols, late-night transport/escort service, controlled dormitory access, lighted pathways/sidewalks.
Student services: health clinic, personal/psychological counseling.

COSTS & FINANCIAL AID
Costs (2016–17) ***Comprehensive fee:*** $49,682 includes full-time tuition ($34,352), mandatory fees ($1904), and room and board ($13,426). Full-time tuition and fees vary according to program. Part-time tuition: $1072 per credit. Part-time tuition and fees vary according to program. ***Required fees:*** $451 per term part-time. ***Room and board:*** Room and board charges vary according to board plan and housing facility.
Financial Aid Of all full-time matriculated undergraduates who enrolled in 2016, 2,490 applied for aid, 2,142 were judged to have need, 270 had their need fully met. 489 Federal Work-Study jobs (averaging $2029). In 2016, 353 non-need-based awards were made. ***Average percent of need met:*** 55. ***Average financial aid package:*** $21,316. ***Average need-based loan:*** $4751. ***Average need-based gift aid:*** $9647. ***Average non-need-based aid:*** $13,089. ***Average indebtedness upon graduation:*** $35,102.

APPLYING
Standardized Tests *Required:* SAT or ACT (for admission).
Options: electronic application, early action, deferred entrance.
Application fee: $50.
Required: essay or personal statement, high school transcript, 1 letter of recommendation. ***Recommended:*** interview.

CONTACT
Ms. Marcelle Hicks, Director of Freshman Admissions, Long Island University–LIU Post, 720 Northern Boulevard, Brookville, NY 11548-1300. *Phone:* 516-299-2900. *Toll-free phone:* 800-LIU-PLAN. *Fax:* 516-299-2137. *E-mail:* post-enroll@liu.edu.

Machzikei Hadath Rabbinical College
Brooklyn, New York

CONTACT
Rabbi Abraham M. Lezerowitz, Director of Admissions, Machzikei Hadath Rabbinical College, 5407 Sixteenth Avenue, Brooklyn, NY 11204-1805. *Phone:* 718-854-8777.

★ Manhattan College
Riverdale, New York
http://www.manhattan.edu/

- **Independent** comprehensive, founded 1853, affiliated with Roman Catholic Church
- **Urban** 31-acre campus with easy access to New York City
- **Endowment** $74.9 million
- **Coed** 3,637 undergraduate students, 95% full-time, 45% women, 55% men
- **Moderately difficult** entrance level, 67% of applicants were admitted

UNDERGRAD STUDENTS
3,444 full-time, 193 part-time. 31% are from out of state; 5% Black or African American, non-Hispanic/Latino; 21% Hispanic/Latino; 5% Asian, non-Hispanic/Latino; 0.2% American Indian or Alaska Native, non-Hispanic/Latino; 2% Two or more races, non-Hispanic/Latino; 7% Race/ethnicity unknown; 3% international; 5% transferred in; 67% live on campus.

Freshmen:
Admission: 8,313 applied, 5,557 admitted, 816 enrolled. ***Average high school GPA:*** 3.4. ***Test scores:*** SAT critical reading scores over 500: 71%; SAT math scores over 500: 82%; SAT writing scores over 500: 71%; ACT scores over 18: 100%; SAT critical reading scores over 600: 24%; SAT math scores over 600: 36%; SAT writing scores over 600: 21%; ACT scores over 24: 65%; SAT critical reading scores over 700: 3%; SAT math scores over 700: 4%; SAT writing scores over 700: 2%; ACT scores over 30: 16%.
Retention: 89% of full-time freshmen returned.

FACULTY
Total: 436, 55% full-time, 75% with terminal degrees.
Student/faculty ratio: 13:1.

ACADEMICS
Calendar: semesters. *Degrees:* bachelor's, master's, and post-master's certificates.
Special study options: accelerated degree program, adult/continuing education programs, advanced placement credit, cooperative education, distance learning, double majors, English as a second language, honors programs, independent study, internships, off-campus study, part-time degree program, services for LD students, student-designed majors, study abroad, summer session for credit. ***ROTC:*** Army (c), Air Force (b).
Unusual degree programs: 3-2 business administration; engineering; education.
Computers: 450 computers/terminals and 3,000 ports are available on campus for general student use. Students can access the following: campus intranet, computer help desk, free student e-mail accounts, online (class) grades, online (class) registration, online (class) schedules, course management system, degree audit/planning tool, campus card access. Campuswide network is available. 100% of college-owned or -operated housing units are wired for high-speed Internet access. Wireless service is available via entire campus.
Library: Mary Alice and Tom O'Malley Library. *Books:* 259,987 (physical), 191,706 (digital/electronic); *Serial titles:* 379 (physical), 186,500 (digital/electronic). Weekly public service hours: 168; study areas open 24 hours, 5-7 days a week.

STUDENT LIFE
Housing options: men-only, women-only, special housing for students with disabilities. Campus housing is university owned. Freshman campus housing is guaranteed.
Activities and organizations: drama/theater group, student-run newspaper, choral group, Society of Hispanic Professional Engineers, Singers, Student Government, Social Life Commission, Manhattan College Players (Theater/Drama group), national fraternities, national sororities.
Athletics Member NCAA. All Division I. ***Intercollegiate sports:*** baseball M(s), basketball M(s)/W(s), cheerleading W, crew M(c)/W, cross-country running M(s)/W(s), golf M(s), lacrosse M(s)/W(s), rugby M(c), soccer M(s)/W(s), softball W(s), swimming and diving M(s)/W(s), track and field M(s)/W(s), volleyball W(s). ***Intramural sports:*** baseball M, basketball M/W, cheerleading M/W, cross-country running M/W, football M/W, soccer M/W, softball M/W, swimming and diving W, track and field M/W, volleyball M/W.

Campus security: 24-hour emergency response devices and patrols, late-night transport/escort service, controlled dormitory access.

Student services: health clinic, personal/psychological counseling.

COSTS & FINANCIAL AID

Costs (2016–17) ***Comprehensive fee:*** $55,649 includes full-time tuition ($36,900), mandatory fees ($3739), and room and board ($15,010). Full-time tuition and fees vary according to course load, program, and student level. Part-time tuition: $945 per credit. Part-time tuition and fees vary according to course load. ***Room and board:*** Room and board charges vary according to board plan. ***Payment plans:*** installment, deferred payment. ***Waivers:*** employees or children of employees.

Financial Aid Of all full-time matriculated undergraduates who enrolled in 2015, 3,080 applied for aid, 3,080 were judged to have need, 373 had their need fully met. In 2015, 812 non-need-based awards were made. ***Average percent of need met:*** 70. ***Average financial aid package:*** $23,453. ***Average need-based gift aid:*** $15,542. ***Average non-need-based aid:*** $4877. ***Average indebtedness upon graduation:*** $39,443.

APPLYING

Standardized Tests *Required:* SAT (for admission), ACT (for admission), SAT or ACT (for admission).

Options: electronic application, early admission, early decision, deferred entrance.

Application fee: $60.

Required: essay or personal statement, high school transcript, minimum 2.5 GPA, 1 letter of recommendation. ***Required for some:*** interview. ***Recommended:*** minimum 3.0 GPA, interview.

Application deadlines: 4/15 (freshmen), 7/1 (transfers).

Early decision deadline: 11/15.

Notification: continuous until 4/15 (freshmen), continuous until 8/15 (transfers), 12/1 (early decision).

CONTACT

Dr. William Bisset, Vice President for Enrollment Management, Manhattan College, 4513 Manhattan College Parkway, Riverdale, NY 10471. *Phone:* 718-862-7200. *Toll-free phone:* 800-622-9235. *Fax:* 718-862-8019. *E-mail:* admit@manhattan.edu.

See previous page for display ad and page 1408 for the College Close-Up.

Manhattan School of Music

New York, New York

http://www.msmnyc.edu/

CONTACT

Ms. Amy Anderson, Dean of Enrollment Management, Manhattan School of Music, 120 Claremont Avenue, New York, NY 10027-4698. *Phone:* 917-493-4501. *Fax:* 212-749-3025. *E-mail:* aanderson@msmnyc.edu.

Manhattanville College

Purchase, New York

http://www.mville.edu/

- **Independent** comprehensive, founded 1841
- **Suburban** 100-acre campus with easy access to New York City
- **Endowment** $27.7 million
- **Coed** 1,794 undergraduate students, 95% full-time, 64% women, 36% men
- **Moderately difficult** entrance level, 77% of applicants were admitted

UNDERGRAD STUDENTS

1,701 full-time, 93 part-time. Students come from 37 states and territories; 49 other countries; 29% are from out of state; 8% Black or African American, non-Hispanic/Latino; 18% Hispanic/Latino; 2% Asian, non-Hispanic/Latino; 0.3% Native Hawaiian or other Pacific Islander, non-Hispanic/Latino; 0.3% American Indian or Alaska Native, non-Hispanic/Latino; 2% Two or more races, non-Hispanic/Latino; 18% Race/ethnicity unknown; 8% international; 4% transferred in; 60% live on campus.

Freshmen:

Admission: 4,132 applied, 3,198 admitted, 483 enrolled. ***Average high school GPA:*** 3.16. ***Test scores:*** SAT critical reading scores over 500: 65%; SAT math scores over 500: 67%; SAT writing scores over 500: 64%;

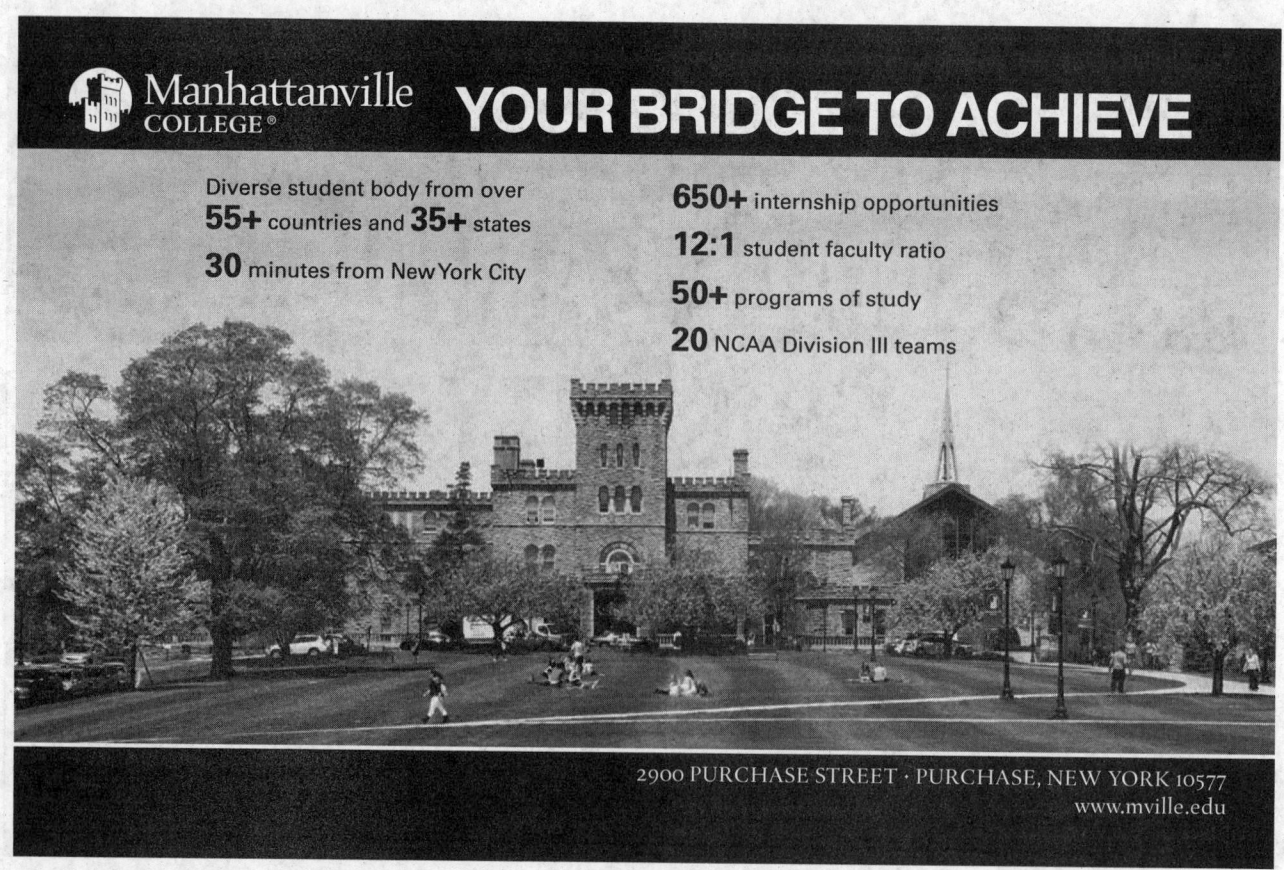

ACT scores over 18: 100%; SAT critical reading scores over 600: 19%; SAT math scores over 600: 16%; SAT writing scores over 600: 20%; ACT scores over 24: 49%; SAT critical reading scores over 700: 2%; SAT math scores over 700: 2%; SAT writing scores over 700: 4%; ACT scores over 30: 8%.

Retention: 76% of full-time freshmen returned.

FACULTY

Total: 379, 30% full-time, 46% with terminal degrees.

Student/faculty ratio: 11:1.

ACADEMICS

Calendar: semesters. *Degrees:* bachelor's, master's, doctoral, and post-master's certificates.

Special study options: academic remediation for entering students, accelerated degree program, adult/continuing education programs, advanced placement credit, double majors, English as a second language, honors programs, independent study, internships, off-campus study, part-time degree program, services for LD students, student-designed majors, study abroad, summer session for credit.

Unusual degree programs: 3-2 business administration; education.

Computers: 150 computers/terminals are available on campus for general student use. Students can access the following: campus intranet, computer help desk, free student e-mail accounts, online (class) grades, online (class) registration, online (class) schedules, mobile apps. Campuswide network is available. 100% of college-owned or -operated housing units are wired for high-speed Internet access. Wireless service is available via entire campus.

Library: Manhattanville College Library. *Books:* 229,036 (physical), 152,619 (digital/electronic); *Serial titles:* 949 (physical), 58,002 (digital/electronic); *Databases:* 117. Weekly public service hours: 139; study areas open 24 hours, 5-7 days a week.

STUDENT LIFE

Housing options: coed, special housing for students with disabilities. Campus housing is university owned. Freshman campus housing is guaranteed.

Activities and organizations: drama/theater group, student-run newspaper, radio station, choral group, Women's Rugby, Manhattanville Dance Ensemble, Pride, Broadway at Manhattanville, Latin American Student Organization.

Athletics Member NCAA. All Division III. ***Intercollegiate sports:*** baseball M, basketball M/W, cross-country running M/W, field hockey W, golf M/W, ice hockey M/W, lacrosse M/W, soccer M/W, softball W, track and field M/W, volleyball W.

Campus security: 24-hour emergency response devices and patrols, late-night transport/escort service, controlled dormitory access.

Student services: health clinic, personal/psychological counseling.

COSTS & FINANCIAL AID

Costs (2017–18) ***Comprehensive fee:*** $52,430 includes full-time tuition ($36,460), mandatory fees ($1450), and room and board ($14,520). Full-time tuition and fees vary according to course load. Part-time tuition: $825 per credit. Part-time tuition and fees vary according to course load and program. ***Required fees:*** $60 per term part-time. ***College room only:*** $8680. Room and board charges vary according to board plan. ***Payment plans:*** installment, deferred payment. ***Waivers:*** children of alumni and employees or children of employees.

Financial Aid Of all full-time matriculated undergraduates who enrolled in 2016, 1,415 applied for aid, 1,172 were judged to have need, 189 had their need fully met. 507 Federal Work-Study jobs (averaging $1530). In 2016, 384 non-need-based awards were made. ***Average percent of need met:*** 75. ***Average financial aid package:*** $27,769. ***Average need-based loan:*** $4549. ***Average need-based gift aid:*** $5609. ***Average non-need-based aid:*** $18,604. ***Average indebtedness upon graduation:*** $32,212.

APPLYING

Standardized Tests *Required for some:* SAT and SAT Subject Tests or ACT (for admission). *Recommended:* SAT (for admission), ACT (for admission), SAT or ACT (for admission).

Options: electronic application, early action, deferred entrance.

Application fee: $50.

Required: essay or personal statement, high school transcript, minimum 2.5 GPA, 2 letters of recommendation. ***Recommended:*** interview.

Application deadlines: 3/1 (freshmen), 3/1 (transfers), 12/1 (early action).

Notification: continuous (freshmen), continuous (transfers), 12/20 (early action).

CONTACT

Mr. Joseph Cosentino, Director of Admissions, Manhattanville College, 2900 Purchase Street, Purchase, NY 10577. *Phone:* 914-323-5125. *Toll-free phone:* 800-328-4553. *Fax:* 914-694-1732.
E-mail: joseph.Cosentino@mville.edu.

See previous page for display ad and page 1410 for the College Close-Up.

Maria College

Albany, New York

http://www.mariacollege.edu/

- **Independent** 4-year, founded 1958
- **Urban** 9-acre campus
- **Coed** 779 undergraduate students, 31% full-time, 87% women, 13% men
- **Minimally difficult** entrance level, 46% of applicants were admitted

UNDERGRAD STUDENTS

245 full-time, 534 part-time. Students come from 9 states and territories; 1 other country; 3% are from out of state; 10% Black or African American, non-Hispanic/Latino; 4% Hispanic/Latino; 4% Asian, non-Hispanic/Latino; 0.1% Native Hawaiian or other Pacific Islander, non-Hispanic/Latino; 1% Two or more races, non-Hispanic/Latino; 26% Race/ethnicity unknown; 18% transferred in.

Freshmen:

Admission: 306 applied, 141 admitted, 48 enrolled. ***Test scores:*** SAT critical reading scores over 500: 26%; SAT math scores over 500: 26%; SAT writing scores over 500: 26%; ACT scores over 18: 83%; SAT math scores over 600: 5%; ACT scores over 24: 33%.

Retention: 65% of full-time freshmen returned.

FACULTY

Total: 76, 45% full-time, 14% with terminal degrees.

Student/faculty ratio: 9:1.

ACADEMICS

Calendar: semesters. *Degrees:* certificates, associate, and bachelor's.

Special study options: adult/continuing education programs, advanced placement credit, distance learning, independent study, off-campus study, part-time degree program, services for LD students, summer session for credit. ***ROTC:*** Air Force (c).

Computers: 70 computers/terminals are available on campus for general student use. Students can access the following: campus intranet, computer help desk, free student e-mail accounts, online (class) grades, online (class) registration, online (class) schedules. Campuswide network is available. Wireless service is available via entire campus.

Library: Maria College Library. *Books:* 19,779 (physical), 160,512 (digital/electronic); *Serial titles:* 55 (physical), 230,969 (digital/electronic); *Databases:* 27. Weekly public service hours: 131.

STUDENT LIFE

Housing options: college housing not available.

Campus security: late-night transport/escort service, 4 pm-10 pm security guard coverage in campus buildings.

Student services: personal/psychological counseling.

COSTS & FINANCIAL AID

Costs (2016–17) ***Comprehensive fee:*** $21,710 includes full-time tuition ($13,800), mandatory fees ($410), and room and board ($7500). Full-time tuition and fees vary according to course load, program, and reciprocity agreements. Part-time tuition: $595 per credit hour. Part-time tuition and fees vary according to course load, program, and reciprocity agreements. ***Payment plan:*** installment. ***Waivers:*** employees or children of employees.

Financial Aid Of all full-time matriculated undergraduates who enrolled in 2016, 242 applied for aid, 201 were judged to have need, 5 had their need fully met. 36 Federal Work-Study jobs (averaging $1198). In 2016, 1 non-need-based awards were made. ***Average percent of need met:*** 43. ***Average financial aid package:*** $7789. ***Average need-based loan:*** $3472. ***Average need-based gift aid:*** $6531. ***Average non-need-based aid:*** $6900.

APPLYING
Standardized Tests *Required for some:* SAT or ACT (for admission), TEAS for AAS in nursing and practical nursing certificate programs. *Recommended:* SAT or ACT (for admission).
Options: electronic application, early admission, early decision, deferred entrance.
Application fee: $35.
Required: high school transcript. ***Recommended:*** essay or personal statement, minimum 2.5 GPA, 1 letter of recommendation, interview.
Application deadlines: 3/1 (freshmen), 8/23 (transfers).
Early decision deadline: 12/1.
Notification: continuous (freshmen), continuous (transfers), 1/15 (early decision).

CONTACT
Mr. John Ramoska, Director of Admissions, Maria College, 700 New Scotland Ave, Albany, NY 12065. *Phone:* 518-861-2519. *Fax:* 518-453-1366. *E-mail:* admissions@mariacollege.edu.

Marist College
Poughkeepsie, New York
http://www.marist.edu/

- **Independent** comprehensive, founded 1929
- **Suburban** 210-acre campus with easy access to Albany, New York City
- **Endowment** $216.4 million
- **Coed** 5,616 undergraduate students, 88% full-time, 59% women, 41% men
- **Very difficult** entrance level, 41% of applicants were admitted

UNDERGRAD STUDENTS
4,966 full-time, 650 part-time. Students come from 47 states and territories; 52 other countries; 48% are from out of state; 4% Black or African American, non-Hispanic/Latino; 10% Hispanic/Latino; 3% Asian, non-Hispanic/Latino; 0.1% Native Hawaiian or other Pacific Islander, non-Hispanic/Latino; 0.1% American Indian or Alaska Native, non-Hispanic/Latino; 2% Two or more races, non-Hispanic/Latino; 1% Race/ethnicity unknown; 2% international; 3% transferred in; 61% live on campus.

Freshmen:
Admission: 11,087 applied, 4,545 admitted, 1,225 enrolled. ***Average high school GPA:*** 3.3. ***Test scores:*** SAT critical reading scores over 500: 86%; SAT math scores over 500: 89%; SAT writing scores over 500: 85%; ACT scores over 18: 99%; SAT critical reading scores over 600: 40%; SAT math scores over 600: 47%; SAT writing scores over 600: 41%; ACT scores over 24: 78%; SAT critical reading scores over 700: 7%; SAT math scores over 700: 5%; SAT writing scores over 700: 7%; ACT scores over 30: 18%.
Retention: 90% of full-time freshmen returned.

FACULTY
Total: 618, 38% full-time, 42% with terminal degrees.
Student/faculty ratio: 16:1.

ACADEMICS
Calendar: semesters. *Degrees:* certificates, bachelor's, master's, and postbachelor's certificates.
Special study options: academic remediation for entering students, accelerated degree program, adult/continuing education programs, advanced placement credit, cooperative education, distance learning, double majors, English as a second language, honors programs, independent study, internships, off-campus study, part-time degree program, services for LD students, study abroad, summer session for credit. ***ROTC:*** Army (b).
Computers: 896 computers/terminals and 650 ports are available on campus for general student use. Students can access the following: campus intranet, computer help desk, free student e-mail accounts, online (class) grades, online (class) registration, online (class) schedules, billing/payments, transcripts, degree audit, financial aid application/award review, student account summary, campus OneCard account, parking registration, cap and gown orders. 100% of college-owned or -operated housing units are wired for high-speed Internet access. Wireless service is available via entire campus.
Library: James A. Cannavino Library. *Books:* 199,563 (physical), 246,335 (digital/electronic); *Serial titles:* 79 (physical), 82,956 (digital/electronic); *Databases:* 112. Weekly public service hours: 113; students can reserve study rooms.

STUDENT LIFE
Housing options: coed, special housing for students with disabilities. Campus housing is university owned and is provided by a third party. Freshman campus housing is guaranteed.
Activities and organizations: drama/theater group, student-run newspaper, radio and television station, choral group, marching band, Marist Singers, Dance Club, Student Government, Theater Club, Community Service and Campus Ministry, national fraternities, national sororities.
Athletics Member NCAA. All Division I except football (Division I-AA). ***Intercollegiate sports:*** baseball M(s), basketball M(s)/W(s), bowling M(c)/W(c), cheerleading M(c)/W(c), crew M/W(s), cross-country running M(s)/W(s), equestrian sports M(c)/W(c), fencing M(c)/W(c), ice hockey M(c), lacrosse M(s)/W(s), rugby M(c)/W(c), skiing (downhill) M(c)/W(c), soccer M(s)/W(s), softball W(s), swimming and diving M(s)/W(s), tennis M(s)/W(s), track and field M(s)/W(s), volleyball M(c)/W(s), water polo W(s). ***Intramural sports:*** basketball M/W, field hockey W, football M(c)/W(c), golf M(c)/W(c), soccer M/W, softball M/W, ultimate Frisbee M(c)/W(c), volleyball M/W.
Campus security: 24-hour emergency response devices and patrols, student patrols, late-night transport/escort service, controlled dormitory access, night residence hall monitors.
Student services: health clinic, personal/psychological counseling.

COSTS & FINANCIAL AID
Costs (2016–17) ***One-time required fee:*** $100. ***Comprehensive fee:*** $51,273 includes full-time tuition ($34,550), mandatory fees ($560), and room and board ($16,163). Full-time tuition and fees vary according to course load and location. Part-time tuition: $650 per credit. Part-time tuition and fees vary according to course load. ***Required fees:*** $40 per term part-time. ***Room and board:*** Room and board charges vary according to board plan, housing facility, and location. ***Payment plan:*** installment. ***Waivers:*** adult students and employees or children of employees.
Financial Aid Of all full-time matriculated undergraduates who enrolled in 2016, 3,461 applied for aid, 2,761 were judged to have need, 460 had their need fully met. 1,414 Federal Work-Study jobs (averaging $2598). 576 state and other part-time jobs (averaging $2004). In 2016, 1405 non-need-based awards were made. ***Average percent of need met:*** 62. ***Average financial aid package:*** $20,750. ***Average need-based loan:*** $5065. ***Average need-based gift aid:*** $17,371. ***Average non-need-based aid:*** $8440. ***Average indebtedness upon graduation:*** $39,584. ***Financial aid deadline:*** 5/1.

APPLYING
Options: electronic application, early admission, early decision, early action, deferred entrance.
Application fee: $50.
Required: essay or personal statement, high school transcript, 2 letters of recommendation.
Application deadlines: 2/1 (freshmen), 6/1 (transfers), 11/15 (early action).
Early decision deadline: 11/15 (for plan 1), 2/1 (for plan 2).
Notification: continuous until 4/1 (freshmen), continuous (transfers), 12/15 (early decision plan 1), 2/15 (early decision plan 2), 1/15 (early action).

CONTACT
Mr. Kent Rinehart, Dean of Undergraduate Admissions, Marist College, 3399 North Road, Poughkeepsie, NY 12601. *Phone:* 845-575-3226. *Toll-free phone:* 800-436-5483. *Fax:* 845-575-3215. *E-mail:* admission@marist.edu.

Marymount Manhattan College

New York, New York

http://www.mmm.edu/

- **Independent** 4-year, founded 1936
- **Urban** campus
- **Endowment** $18.1 million
- **Coed** 2,069 undergraduate students, 89% full-time, 77% women, 23% men
- **Moderately difficult** entrance level, 78% of applicants were admitted

UNDERGRAD STUDENTS
1,841 full-time, 228 part-time. Students come from 49 states and territories; 44 other countries; 60% are from out of state; 10% Black or African American, non-Hispanic/Latino; 16% Hispanic/Latino; 4% Asian, non-Hispanic/Latino; 1% American Indian or Alaska Native, non-Hispanic/Latino; 1% Two or more races, non-Hispanic/Latino; 6% Race/ethnicity unknown; 5% international; 6% transferred in; 36% live on campus.

Freshmen:
Admission: 5,265 applied, 4,118 admitted, 552 enrolled. ***Average high school GPA:*** 3.41. ***Test scores:*** SAT critical reading scores over 500: 68%; SAT math scores over 500: 54%; SAT writing scores over 500: 65%; ACT scores over 18: 98%; SAT critical reading scores over 600: 25%; SAT math scores over 600: 16%; SAT writing scores over 600: 22%; ACT scores over 24: 62%; SAT critical reading scores over 700: 2%; SAT math scores over 700: 2%; SAT writing scores over 700: 2%; ACT scores over 30: 13%.
Retention: 73% of full-time freshmen returned.

FACULTY
Total: 342, 27% full-time.
Student/faculty ratio: 11:1.

ACADEMICS
Calendar: semesters plus summer and January mini-semesters. *Degrees:* associate and bachelor's.
Special study options: academic remediation for entering students, accelerated degree program, adult/continuing education programs, advanced placement credit, distance learning, double majors, honors programs, independent study, internships, off-campus study, part-time degree program, services for LD students, student-designed majors, study abroad, summer session for credit.
Computers: 120 computers/terminals are available on campus for general student use. Students can access the following: campus intranet, computer help desk, free student e-mail accounts, online (class) grades, online (class) registration, online (class) schedules, online payments, direct deposits. Campuswide network is available. 100% of college-owned or -operated housing units are wired for high-speed Internet access. Wireless service is available via entire campus.
Library: Thomas J. Shanahan Library. *Books:* 48,966 (physical), 108,552 (digital/electronic); *Serial titles:* 213 (physical), 40,105 (digital/electronic); *Databases:* 52. Weekly public service hours: 80.

STUDENT LIFE
Housing options: coed, men-only, women-only. Campus housing is university owned and leased by the school. Freshman applicants given priority for college housing.
Activities and organizations: drama/theater group, student-run newspaper, radio station, choral group, Student Government Association (SGA), Black and Latino Student Association (BLSA), The Monitor-Student Newspaper, Musical Theater Association (MTA), Christian Fellowship.
Campus security: 24-hour emergency response devices and patrols, student patrols, 24-hour security in residence halls.
Student services: health clinic, personal/psychological counseling.

COSTS & FINANCIAL AID
Costs (2017–18) ***Comprehensive fee:*** $48,350 includes full-time tuition ($30,458), mandatory fees ($1492), and room and board ($16,400). Full-time tuition and fees vary according to course load and program. Part-time tuition: $1018 per credit hour. Part-time tuition and fees vary according to course load and program. ***Required fees:*** $684 per term part-time. ***College room only:*** $14,400. Room and board charges vary according to board plan. ***Payment plan:*** installment. ***Waivers:*** senior citizens and employees or children of employees.
Financial Aid Of all full-time matriculated undergraduates who enrolled in 2015, 1,330 applied for aid, 1,146 were judged to have need, 86 had their need fully met. 139 Federal Work-Study jobs (averaging $3181). In 2015, 160 non-need-based awards were made. ***Average percent of need met:*** 51. ***Average financial aid package:*** $17,046. ***Average need-based loan:*** $4219. ***Average need-based gift aid:*** $13,396. ***Average non-need-based aid:*** $8889. ***Average indebtedness upon graduation:*** $31,606.

APPLYING
Standardized Tests *Required:* SAT or ACT (for admission).
Options: electronic application, deferred entrance.
Application fee: $60.
Required: essay or personal statement, high school transcript, 2 letters of recommendation. ***Required for some:*** interview.
Application deadlines: rolling (freshmen), rolling (transfers).
Notification: continuous (freshmen), continuous (transfers).

CONTACT
Jim Rogers, Dean of Admissions, Marymount Manhattan College, 221 East 71st Street, New York, NY 10021. *Phone:* 212-517-0430. *Toll-free phone:* 800-627-9668. *E-mail:* jrogers@mmm.edu.

Medaille College

Buffalo, New York

http://www.medaille.edu/

CONTACT
Christopher LaRusso, Vice President for Enrollment Management and Undergraduate Admissions, Medaille College, Office of Admissions, Buffalo, NY 14214. *Phone:* 716-880-2200. *Toll-free phone:* 800-292-1582. *Fax:* 716-880-2007. *E-mail:* admissionsug@medaille.edu.

Medgar Evers College of the City University of New York

Brooklyn, New York

http://www.mec.cuny.edu/

- **State and locally supported** 4-year, founded 1969, part of City University of New York System
- **Urban** 8-acre campus
- **Endowment** $515,142
- **Coed** 6,819 undergraduate students, 70% full-time, 72% women, 28% men
- **Noncompetitive** entrance level, 98% of applicants were admitted

UNDERGRAD STUDENTS
4,760 full-time, 2,059 part-time. Students come from 7 states and territories; 77 other countries; 1% are from out of state; 62% Black or African American, non-Hispanic/Latino; 13% Hispanic/Latino; 2% Asian, non-Hispanic/Latino; 0.3% American Indian or Alaska Native, non-Hispanic/Latino; 20% Race/ethnicity unknown; 0.7% international.

Freshmen:
Admission: 10,105 applied, 9,864 admitted. ***Test scores:*** SAT critical reading scores over 500: 7%; SAT math scores over 500: 6%; SAT writing scores over 500: 5%; SAT math scores over 600: 1%.

FACULTY
Total: 528, 34% full-time, 41% with terminal degrees.
Student/faculty ratio: 18:1.

ACADEMICS
Calendar: semesters. *Degrees:* certificates, associate, and bachelor's.
Special study options: academic remediation for entering students, adult/continuing education programs, advanced placement credit, cooperative education, double majors, English as a second language, external degree program, honors programs, independent study, internships, off-campus study, part-time degree program, services for LD students, study abroad, summer session for credit.
Computers: 120 computers/terminals are available on campus for general student use. Students can access the following: free student e-mail

accounts, online (class) grades, online (class) registration, online (class) schedules. Campuswide network is available. Wireless service is available via entire campus.
Library: Charles Evans Inniss Memorial Library plus 1 other.

STUDENT LIFE
Housing options: college housing not available.
Activities and organizations: drama/theater group, student-run newspaper, radio and television station, choral group, American Marketing Association, Drama Students Association, Rising Stars, Medgar Evers College Society of Public Administrators, National Society of Black Accountants.
Athletics Member NCAA. All Division III. ***Intercollegiate sports:*** basketball M/W, cross-country running M/W, soccer M/W, tennis W, track and field M/W, volleyball M/W. ***Intramural sports:*** basketball M/W, tennis W.
Campus security: 24-hour patrols.
Student services: women's center, legal services.

COSTS
Costs (2016–17) ***Tuition:*** state resident $6330 full-time, $275 per credit part-time; nonresident $16,800 full-time, $560 per credit part-time. Full-time tuition and fees vary according to course load. Part-time tuition and fees vary according to course load. ***Required fees:*** $320 full-time, $101 per term part-time. ***Payment plans:*** installment, deferred payment.

APPLYING
Standardized Tests *Recommended:* SAT and SAT Subject Tests or ACT (for admission).
Options: electronic application, deferred entrance.
Application fee: $65.
Required: high school transcript.
Application deadlines: rolling (freshmen), rolling (transfers).
Notification: continuous (freshmen), continuous (transfers).

CONTACT
Dr. Shannon Clarke-Anderson, Director of Admissions, Medgar Evers College of the City University of New York, 1650 Bedford Avenue, Brooklyn, NY 11225. *Phone:* 718-270-5143. *Fax:* 718-270-6411. *E-mail:* shannon@mec.cuny.edu.

★ Mercy College
Dobbs Ferry, New York
http://www.mercy.edu/

- **Independent** comprehensive, founded 1951
- **Suburban** 66-acre campus with easy access to New York City
- **Endowment** $192.5 million
- **Coed** 7,157 undergraduate students, 72% full-time, 67% women, 33% men
- **Moderately difficult** entrance level, 78% of applicants were admitted

UNDERGRAD STUDENTS
5,182 full-time, 1,975 part-time. Students come from 36 states and territories; 48 other countries; 9% are from out of state; 24% Black or African American, non-Hispanic/Latino; 38% Hispanic/Latino; 4% Asian, non-Hispanic/Latino; 0.3% Native Hawaiian or other Pacific Islander, non-Hispanic/Latino; 0.3% American Indian or Alaska Native, non-Hispanic/Latino; 1% Two or more races, non-Hispanic/Latino; 6% Race/ethnicity unknown; 2% international; 11% transferred in; 12% live on campus.

Freshmen:
Admission: 6,617 applied, 5,140 admitted, 948 enrolled. ***Average high school GPA:*** 3.38.
Retention: 72% of full-time freshmen returned.

FACULTY
Total: 928, 23% full-time, 19% with terminal degrees.
Student/faculty ratio: 17:1.

ACADEMICS
Calendar: semesters. *Degrees:* certificates, associate, bachelor's, master's, doctoral, post-master's, and postbachelor's certificates.
Special study options: accelerated degree program, adult/continuing education programs, advanced placement credit, cooperative education, distance learning, double majors, freshman honors college, honors programs, independent study, internships, off-campus study, part-time degree program, services for LD students, study abroad, summer session for credit. ***ROTC:*** Army (c), Air Force (c).
Unusual degree programs: 3-2 business administration; education, cybersecurity.
Computers: 972 computers/terminals and 300 ports are available on campus for general student use. Students can access the following: campus intranet, computer help desk, free student e-mail accounts, online (class) grades, online (class) registration, online (class) schedules. Campuswide network is available. 100% of college-owned or -operated housing units are wired for high-speed Internet access. Wireless service is available via entire campus.
Library: Mercy College Library plus 3 others. *Books:* 85,689 (digital/electronic); *Serial titles:* 21,126 (digital/electronic). Students can reserve study rooms.

STUDENT LIFE
Housing options: coed, special housing for students with disabilities. Campus housing is university owned and leased by the school. Freshman applicants given priority for college housing.
Activities and organizations: student-run newspaper, choral group, Model United Nations, Honors Club and 17 National Honor Societies, Mercy Gives Back, Maverick Society, ROTARACT Club for Community Volunteer Service.
Athletics Member NCAA. All Division II. ***Intercollegiate sports:*** baseball M(s), basketball M(s)/W(s), field hockey W(s), lacrosse M(s)/W(s), soccer M(s)/W(s), softball W(s), volleyball W(s). ***Intramural sports:*** baseball M, basketball M/W, softball W.
Campus security: 24-hour emergency response devices and patrols, late-night transport/escort service, controlled dormitory access.
Student services: health clinic, personal/psychological counseling.

COSTS & FINANCIAL AID
Costs (2016–17) ***Comprehensive fee:*** $31,892 includes full-time tuition ($17,772), mandatory fees ($620), and room and board ($13,500). Full-time tuition and fees vary according to course load. Part-time tuition: $748 per credit. Part-time tuition and fees vary according to course load. ***Required fees:*** $155 per term part-time. ***College room only:*** $9150. Room and board charges vary according to board plan. ***Payment plans:*** installment, deferred payment. ***Waivers:*** senior citizens and employees or children of employees.
Financial Aid Of all full-time matriculated undergraduates who enrolled in 2015, 4,821 applied for aid, 4,556 were judged to have need, 126 had their need fully met. In 2015, 120 non-need-based awards were made. ***Average percent of need met:*** 51. ***Average financial aid package:*** $13,223. ***Average need-based loan:*** $4076. ***Average need-based gift aid:*** $9597. ***Average non-need-based aid:*** $4139. ***Average indebtedness upon graduation:*** $29,197.

APPLYING
Options: electronic application, early action, deferred entrance.
Application fee: $40.
Required: high school transcript, minimum 2.5 GPA, 1 letter of recommendation. ***Required for some:*** essay or personal statement, interview. ***Recommended:*** interview.
Application deadlines: rolling (freshmen), rolling (transfers), 12/1 (early action).
Notification: continuous (freshmen), continuous (transfers), 1/2 (early action).

CONTACT
Mrs. Tara Fay-Reilly, Senior Director of Admissions, Mercy College, 555 Broadway, Dobbs Ferry, NY 10522-1189. *Phone:* 877-637-2946. *Toll-free phone:* 877-637-2946 (in-state); 877-MERCY-GO (out-of-state). *Fax:* 914-674-7382. *E-mail:* admissions@mercy.edu.

Mesivta of Eastern Parkway–Yeshiva Zichron Meilech

Brooklyn, New York

- **Independent Jewish** comprehensive, founded 1947
- **Urban** 1-acre campus with easy access to New York City
- **Men only**
- **Moderately difficult** entrance level

ACADEMICS
Calendar: semesters. *Degrees:* bachelor's and master's.

APPLYING
Required: high school transcript, 1 letter of recommendation, interview, Orthodox Jewish commitment.

CONTACT
Mesivta of Eastern Parkway–Yeshiva Zichron Meilech, 510 Dahill Road, Brooklyn, NY 11218-5559. *Phone:* 718-438-1002.

Mesivta Torah Vodaath Rabbinical Seminary

Brooklyn, New York

http://www.torahvodaath.org/

CONTACT
Rabbi Issac Braun, Administrator, Mesivta Torah Vodaath Rabbinical Seminary, 425 East Ninth Street, Brooklyn, NY 11218-5299. *Phone:* 718-941-8000.

Mesivtha Tifereth Jerusalem of America

New York, New York

CONTACT
Rabbi Fishellis, Director of Admissions, Mesivtha Tifereth Jerusalem of America, 145 East Broadway, New York, NY 10002-6301. *Phone:* 212-964-2830.

Metropolitan College of New York

New York, New York

http://www.metropolitan.edu/

- **Independent** comprehensive, founded 1964
- **Urban** campus
- **Coed** 697 undergraduate students, 89% full-time, 74% women, 26% men
- **Moderately difficult** entrance level, 40% of applicants were admitted

UNDERGRAD STUDENTS
621 full-time, 76 part-time. Students come from 11 states and territories; 4% are from out of state; 58% Black or African American, non-Hispanic/Latino; 24% Hispanic/Latino; 3% Asian, non-Hispanic/Latino; 0.4% Native Hawaiian or other Pacific Islander, non-Hispanic/Latino; 0.3% American Indian or Alaska Native, non-Hispanic/Latino; 2% Two or more races, non-Hispanic/Latino; 7% Race/ethnicity unknown; 3% international; 18% transferred in.

Freshmen:
Admission: 257 applied, 104 admitted, 75 enrolled.
Retention: 34% of full-time freshmen returned.

FACULTY
Student/faculty ratio: 9:1.

ACADEMICS
Calendar: 3 15-week semesters. *Degrees:* certificates, associate, bachelor's, and master's.

Special study options: academic remediation for entering students, accelerated degree program, adult/continuing education programs, cooperative education, distance learning, English as a second language, honors programs, independent study, internships, part-time degree program, services for LD students, study abroad, summer session for credit.

Computers: 120 computers/terminals are available on campus for general student use. Students can access the following: free student e-mail accounts, online (class) grades, online (class) registration, online (class) schedules. Campuswide network is available. Wireless service is available via entire campus.

Library: Main Library plus 1 other. *Books:* 26,191 (physical), 156,497 (digital/electronic); *Serial titles:* 29,206 (digital/electronic); *Databases:* 91. Weekly public service hours: 72.

STUDENT LIFE
Housing options: college housing not available.

Activities and organizations: student-run newspaper, Student Government, Student Newsletter, Networking Club, Yearbook Committee.

Campus security: 24-hour patrols.

Student services: personal/psychological counseling.

COSTS & FINANCIAL AID
Costs (2017–18) ***Tuition:*** $18,330 full-time, $766 per credit part-time. Full-time tuition and fees vary according to degree level and program. Part-time tuition and fees vary according to degree level and program. No tuition increase for student's term of enrollment. ***Required fees:*** $850 full-time. ***Payment plans:*** installment, deferred payment. ***Waivers:*** employees or children of employees.

Financial Aid Of all full-time matriculated undergraduates who enrolled in 2016, 588 applied for aid, 585 were judged to have need, 2 had their need fully met. In 2016, 14 non-need-based awards were made. ***Average percent of need met:*** 44. ***Average financial aid package:*** $16,577. ***Average need-based loan:*** $5264. ***Average need-based gift aid:*** $11,596. ***Average non-need-based aid:*** $2430. ***Average indebtedness upon graduation:*** $49,357.

APPLYING
Standardized Tests *Required for some:* ACCUPLACER. *Recommended:* SAT or ACT (for admission).

Options: electronic application, deferred entrance.

Application fee: $30.

Required: high school transcript, 2 letters of recommendation, interview. ***Recommended:*** essay or personal statement, minimum 3.0 GPA.

Application deadlines: 9/9 (freshmen), rolling (transfers).

Notification: continuous (freshmen), continuous (transfers).

CONTACT
Metropolitan College of New York, 60 West Street, New York, NY 10006. *Phone:* 212-343-1234 Ext. 2700. *Toll-free phone:* 800-33-THINK Ext. 5001. *Fax:* 212-343-8470.

Mirrer Yeshiva

Brooklyn, New York

CONTACT
Director of Admissions, Mirrer Yeshiva, 1795 Ocean Parkway, Brooklyn, NY 11223-2010. *Phone:* 718-645-0536.

★ Molloy College

Rockville Centre, New York

http://www.molloy.edu/

- **Independent** comprehensive, founded 1955
- **Suburban** 30-acre campus with easy access to New York City
- **Endowment** $33.4 million
- **Coed** 3,598 undergraduate students, 81% full-time, 75% women, 25% men
- **Moderately difficult** entrance level, 77% of applicants were admitted

UNDERGRAD STUDENTS
2,906 full-time, 692 part-time. Students come from 27 states and territories; 12 other countries; 3% are from out of state; 12% Black or African American, non-Hispanic/Latino; 16% Hispanic/Latino; 7% Asian, non-Hispanic/Latino; 0.3% Native Hawaiian or other Pacific Islander, non-Hispanic/Latino; 0.5% American Indian or Alaska Native, non-Hispanic/Latino; 1% Two or more races, non-Hispanic/Latino; 2% Race/ethnicity unknown; 0.4% international; 11% transferred in; 8% live on campus.

A ★ indicates that the school has detailed information with a Premium Profile on Petersons.com.

Freshmen:
Admission: 4,030 applied, 3,100 admitted, 565 enrolled. ***Average high school GPA:*** 3. ***Test scores:*** SAT critical reading scores over 500: 73%; SAT math scores over 500: 73%; SAT writing scores over 500: 64%; ACT scores over 18: 100%; SAT critical reading scores over 600: 17%; SAT math scores over 600: 23%; SAT writing scores over 600: 15%; ACT scores over 24: 52%; SAT critical reading scores over 700: 2%; SAT math scores over 700: 1%; SAT writing scores over 700: 2%; ACT scores over 30: 6%.

Retention: 85% of full-time freshmen returned.

FACULTY
Total: 723, 26% full-time, 34% with terminal degrees.

Student/faculty ratio: 10:1.

ACADEMICS
Calendar: 4-1-4. *Degrees:* associate, bachelor's, master's, doctoral, and post-master's certificates.

Special study options: academic remediation for entering students, accelerated degree program, adult/continuing education programs, advanced placement credit, distance learning, double majors, English as a second language, honors programs, independent study, internships, part-time degree program, services for LD students, student-designed majors, study abroad, summer session for credit. ***ROTC:*** Army (c), Navy (c).

Computers: 784 computers/terminals are available on campus for general student use. Students can access the following: computer help desk, free student e-mail accounts, online (class) grades, online (class) registration, online (class) schedules. Campuswide network is available. 100% of college-owned or -operated housing units are wired for high-speed Internet access. Wireless service is available via entire campus.

Library: James Edward Tobin Library plus 1 other. *Books:* 45,477 (physical), 247,157 (digital/electronic); *Serial titles:* 55 (physical), 59,417 (digital/electronic); *Databases:* 180.

STUDENT LIFE
Housing options: coed. Campus housing is university owned. Freshman applicants given priority for college housing.

Activities and organizations: drama/theater group, student-run newspaper, choral group, Molloy Nursing Student Association, Molloy Performing Arts Club, Men's Rugby, National Student Speech Language Hearing Association, Molloy Student Government.

Athletics Member NCAA. All Division II. ***Intercollegiate sports:*** baseball M(s), basketball M(s)/W(s), bowling W(s), cross-country running M(s)/W(s), field hockey W(s), lacrosse M(s)/W(s), rugby W(s), soccer M(s)/W(s), softball W(s), tennis W(s), track and field M(s)/W(s), volleyball W(s). ***Intramural sports:*** cheerleading M(c)/W(c), equestrian sports W(c), rugby M(c), ultimate Frisbee M(c)/W(c).

Campus security: 24-hour emergency response devices and patrols, late-night transport/escort service, controlled dormitory access.

Student services: health clinic, women's center.

COSTS & FINANCIAL AID
Costs (2016–17) ***Comprehensive fee:*** $43,350 includes full-time tuition ($28,000), mandatory fees ($1100), and room and board ($14,250). Full-time tuition and fees vary according to degree level. Part-time tuition: $925 per credit hour. Part-time tuition and fees vary according to degree level. ***Room and board:*** Room and board charges vary according to board plan. ***Payment plans:*** installment, deferred payment. ***Waivers:*** senior citizens and employees or children of employees.

Financial Aid Of all full-time matriculated undergraduates who enrolled in 2015, 2,561 applied for aid, 2,267 were judged to have need, 193 had their need fully met. 204 Federal Work-Study jobs (averaging $1389). In 2015, 229 non-need-based awards were made. ***Average percent of need met:*** 47. ***Average financial aid package:*** $15,825. ***Average need-based loan:*** $4183. ***Average need-based gift aid:*** $12,044. ***Average non-need-based aid:*** $9280. ***Average indebtedness upon graduation:*** $33,826. ***Financial aid deadline:*** 5/1.

APPLYING
Standardized Tests *Required:* SAT or ACT (for admission).

Options: electronic application, early action, deferred entrance.

Application fee: $40.

Required for some: essay or personal statement, high school transcript, 1 letter of recommendation. ***Recommended:*** interview.

Application deadlines: rolling (freshmen), rolling (transfers), 12/1 (early action).

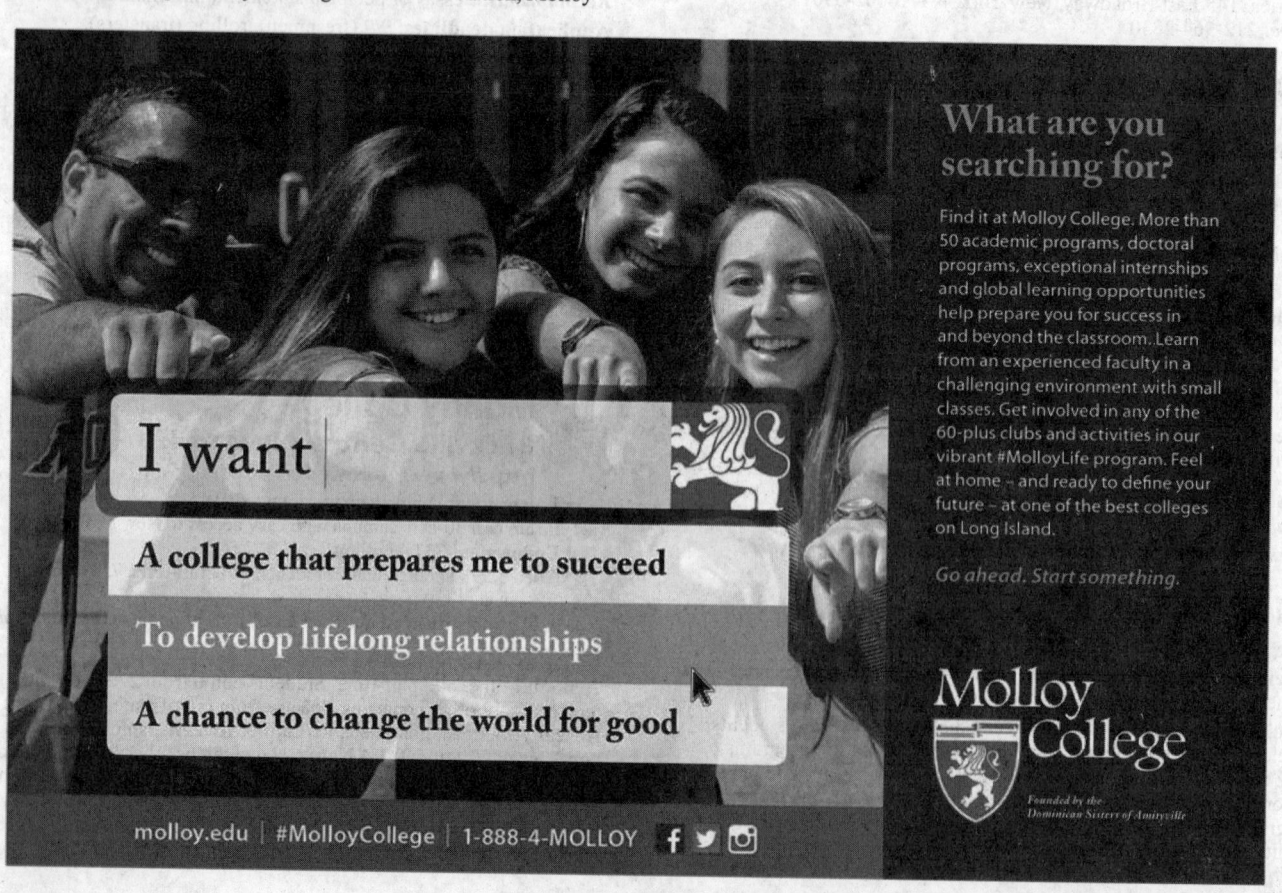

Notification: continuous (freshmen), continuous (transfers), 12/15 (early action).

CONTACT
Ms. Marguerite Lane, Dean of Admissions, Molloy College, 1000 Hempstead Avenue, PO Box 5002, Rockville Centre, NY 11571-5002.
Phone: 516-323-4000. *Toll-free phone:* 888-4MOLLOY.
E-mail: admissions@molloy.edu.

See previous page for display ad and page 1424 for the College Close-Up.

Monroe College

Bronx, New York

http://www.monroecollege.edu/

- **Proprietary** comprehensive, founded 1933
- **Urban** campus
- **Coed**
- **Moderately difficult** entrance level

FACULTY
Student/faculty ratio: 18:1.

ACADEMICS
Calendar: semesters. *Degrees:* certificates, associate, bachelor's, and master's.
Library: Main Library plus 1 other. *Books:* 44,109 (physical), 2,466 (digital/electronic); *Serial titles:* 739 (physical), 8 (digital/electronic); *Databases:* 73.

STUDENT LIFE
Housing options: coed. Campus housing is university owned and leased by the school. Freshman applicants given priority for college housing.
Activities and organizations: drama/theater group, marching band, Students in Free Enterprise (SIFE), Creative Campus Club, Multicultural Student Association, Criminal Justice Club, Poetry is Truth.
Athletics Member NJCAA.
Campus security: 24-hour patrols, late-night transport/escort service.
Student services: health clinic, personal/psychological counseling.

COSTS & FINANCIAL AID
Costs (2016–17) ***Comprehensive fee:*** $24,230 includes full-time tuition ($13,560), mandatory fees ($900), and room and board ($9770). Part-time tuition: $565 per credit hour. ***Required fees:*** $225 per term part-time. ***Room and board:*** Room and board charges vary according to board plan and housing facility. ***Payment plans:*** tuition prepayment, installment.
Financial Aid Of all full-time matriculated undergraduates who enrolled in 2015, 4,573 applied for aid, 4,548 were judged to have need, 1,719 had their need fully met. 173 Federal Work-Study jobs (averaging $4335). In 2015, 14 non-need-based awards were made. ***Average percent of need met:*** 78. ***Average financial aid package:*** $12,530. ***Average need-based loan:*** $5451. ***Average need-based gift aid:*** $9296. ***Average non-need-based aid:*** $4913. ***Average indebtedness upon graduation:*** $28,134.

APPLYING
Standardized Tests *Required for some:* SAT or ACT (for admission).
Options: electronic application, early admission, early decision, early action, deferred entrance.
Application fee: $35.
Required: essay or personal statement, high school transcript, interview. ***Required for some:*** 2 letters of recommendation.

CONTACT
Monroe College, 2501 Jerome Avenue, Bronx, NY 10468.
Phone: 718-933-6700. *Toll-free phone:* 800-55MONROE.

Morrisville State College

Morrisville, New York

http://www.morrisville.edu/

- **State-supported** 4-year, founded 1908, part of State University of New York System
- **Rural** 185-acre campus with easy access to Syracuse
- **Coed** 3,003 undergraduate students, 87% full-time, 50% women, 50% men
- **Moderately difficult** entrance level, 77% of applicants were admitted

UNDERGRAD STUDENTS
2,624 full-time, 379 part-time. Students come from 22 states and territories; 11 other countries; 6% are from out of state; 17% Black or African American, non-Hispanic/Latino; 8% Hispanic/Latino; 1% Asian, non-Hispanic/Latino; 0.4% American Indian or Alaska Native, non-Hispanic/Latino; 2% Two or more races, non-Hispanic/Latino; 2% Race/ethnicity unknown; 2% international; 7% transferred in; 53% live on campus.

Freshmen:
Admission: 4,031 applied, 3,118 admitted, 912 enrolled. ***Average high school GPA:*** 2.6. ***Test scores:*** SAT critical reading scores over 500: 25%; SAT math scores over 500: 28%; SAT writing scores over 500: 15%; ACT scores over 18: 74%; SAT critical reading scores over 600: 4%; SAT math scores over 600: 4%; SAT writing scores over 600: 3%; ACT scores over 24: 16%.
Retention: 65% of full-time freshmen returned.

FACULTY
Total: 253, 55% full-time, 25% with terminal degrees.
Student/faculty ratio: 11:1.

ACADEMICS
Calendar: semesters. *Degrees:* certificates, associate, and bachelor's.
Special study options: academic remediation for entering students, advanced placement credit, cooperative education, distance learning, double majors, independent study, internships, off-campus study, part-time degree program, services for LD students, student-designed majors, study abroad, summer session for credit. ***ROTC:*** Army (c), Air Force (c).
Computers: 100 computers/terminals and 1,985 ports are available on campus for general student use. Students can access the following: campus intranet, computer help desk, free student e-mail accounts, online (class) grades, online (class) registration, online (class) schedules. Campuswide network is available. 100% of college-owned or -operated housing units are wired for high-speed Internet access. Wireless service is available via entire campus.
Library: Morrisville State Library (Butcher Library) plus 1 other. Students can reserve study rooms.

STUDENT LIFE
Housing options: on-campus residence required through sophomore year; coed, special housing for students with disabilities. Campus housing is university owned. Freshman campus housing is guaranteed.
Activities and organizations: drama/theater group, student-run newspaper, radio station, Campus Activities Board, Conservation Tri Society, CASU, CollegiateFFA, Automotive Club.
Athletics Member NCAA. All Division III. ***Intercollegiate sports:*** basketball M/W, cross-country running M/W, equestrian sports M/W, field hockey W, football M, golf M, ice hockey M/W, lacrosse M/W, soccer M/W, softball W, volleyball W. ***Intramural sports:*** badminton M/W, baseball M/W, basketball M/W, equestrian sports M/W, ice hockey M/W, soccer M/W, softball M/W, table tennis M/W, tennis M/W, ultimate Frisbee M/W, volleyball M/W.
Campus security: 24-hour emergency response devices and patrols, student patrols, late-night transport/escort service, controlled dormitory access.
Student services: health clinic, personal/psychological counseling.

COSTS & FINANCIAL AID
Costs (2017–18) ***Tuition:*** state resident $6470 full-time, $270 per credit hour part-time; nonresident $11,300 full-time, $458 per credit hour part-time. Full-time tuition and fees vary according to course level, degree level, location, and program. Part-time tuition and fees vary according to class time, course level, course load, degree level, location, and program. ***Required fees:*** $1553 full-time, $66 per credit hour part-time. ***Room and board:*** $13,837; room only: $8448. Room and board charges vary according to board plan, housing facility, and location. ***Payment plans:*** installment, deferred payment. ***Waivers:*** minority students, children of alumni, senior citizens, and employees or children of employees.
Financial Aid Of all full-time matriculated undergraduates who enrolled in 2014, 2,369 applied for aid, 2,162 were judged to have need, 19 had their need fully met. In 2014, 209 non-need-based awards were made. ***Average percent of need met:*** 50. ***Average financial aid package:*** $10,033. ***Average need-based loan:*** $3987. ***Average need-based gift aid:***

$7017. ***Average non-need-based aid:*** $1753. ***Average indebtedness upon graduation:*** $30,054.

APPLYING

Standardized Tests *Required for some:* SAT or ACT (for admission). *Recommended:* SAT or ACT (for admission).

Options: electronic application, deferred entrance.

Application fee: $50.

Required: essay or personal statement, high school transcript. ***Required for some:*** minimum 2.5 GPA, letters of recommendation. ***Recommended:*** minimum 2.0 GPA, letters of recommendation, interview.

Application deadlines: 8/15 (freshmen), 8/15 (transfers).

Notification: continuous (freshmen), continuous (transfers).

CONTACT

Ms. Melissa Ward, Assistant Director of Enrollment Marketing, Morrisville State College, PO Box 901, Morrisville, NY 13408. *Phone:* 315-684-6046. *Toll-free phone:* 800-258-0111. *Fax:* 315-684-6427.

Mount Saint Mary College

Newburgh, New York

http://www.msmc.edu/

- **Independent** comprehensive, founded 1960
- **Suburban** 86-acre campus with easy access to New York City
- **Endowment** $65.0 million
- **Coed** 2,128 undergraduate students, 82% full-time, 72% women, 28% men
- **Moderately difficult** entrance level, 90% of applicants were admitted

UNDERGRAD STUDENTS

1,750 full-time, 378 part-time. Students come from 14 states and territories; 11% are from out of state; 8% Black or African American, non-Hispanic/Latino; 16% Hispanic/Latino; 2% Asian, non-Hispanic/Latino; 0.1% Native Hawaiian or other Pacific Islander, non-Hispanic/Latino; 0.3% American Indian or Alaska Native, non-Hispanic/Latino; 2% Two or more races, non-Hispanic/Latino; 8% Race/ethnicity unknown; 0.5% international; 10% transferred in; 47% live on campus.

Freshmen:

Admission: 3,747 applied, 3,368 admitted, 387 enrolled. ***Average high school GPA:*** 3.2. ***Test scores:*** SAT critical reading scores over 500: 43%; SAT math scores over 500: 50%; SAT writing scores over 500: 45%; ACT scores over 18: 92%; SAT critical reading scores over 600: 7%; SAT math scores over 600: 10%; SAT writing scores over 600: 5%; ACT scores over 24: 27%; ACT scores over 30: 1%.

Retention: 77% of full-time freshmen returned.

FACULTY

Total: 279, 32% full-time, 38% with terminal degrees.

Student/faculty ratio: 13:1.

ACADEMICS

Calendar: semesters. *Degrees:* certificates, bachelor's, master's, and post-master's certificates.

Special study options: academic remediation for entering students, accelerated degree program, adult/continuing education programs, advanced placement credit, cooperative education, distance learning, double majors, freshman honors college, honors programs, independent study, internships, off-campus study, part-time degree program, services for LD students, student-designed majors, study abroad, summer session for credit. ***ROTC:*** Army (c).

Unusual degree programs: 3-2 business administration; social work with Fordham University; publishing, counseling with Pace University.

Computers: 470 computers/terminals are available on campus for general student use. Students can access the following: campus intranet, computer help desk, free student e-mail accounts, online (class) grades, online (class) registration, online (class) schedules. Campuswide network is available. 100% of college-owned or -operated housing units are wired for high-speed Internet access. Wireless service is available via entire campus.

Library: Kaplan Family Library and Learning Center. *Books:* 86,692 (physical), 11,600 (digital/electronic); *Serial titles:* 208 (physical), 61,954 (digital/electronic); *Databases:* 85. Students can reserve study rooms.

STUDENT LIFE

Housing options: on-campus residence required through junior year; coed, men-only, women-only, special housing for students with disabilities. Campus housing is university owned. Freshman campus housing is guaranteed.

Activities and organizations: drama/theater group, student-run newspaper, radio station, choral group, Nursing Student Union, Colleges Against Cancer, Big Brothers/Big Sisters, Dance Team, Habitat for Humanity.

Athletics Member NCAA. All Division III. ***Intercollegiate sports:*** baseball M, basketball M/W, cheerleading W, cross-country running M/W, golf M, lacrosse M/W, soccer M/W, softball W, swimming and diving M/W, tennis M/W, track and field M/W, volleyball W. ***Intramural sports:*** basketball M/W, bowling M/W, football M, soccer M/W, softball M/W, swimming and diving M/W, table tennis M/W, volleyball M/W.

Campus security: 24-hour emergency response devices and patrols, student patrols, late-night transport/escort service, controlled dormitory access, monitored surveillance cameras in all residence halls.

Student services: health clinic, personal/psychological counseling.

COSTS & FINANCIAL AID

Costs (2017–18) ***Comprehensive fee:*** $44,448 includes full-time tuition ($28,890), mandatory fees ($1030), and room and board ($14,528). Full-time tuition and fees vary according to class time, course load, location, and program. Part-time tuition: $963 per credit. Part-time tuition and fees vary according to class time, course load, location, and program. ***Required fees:*** $82 per term part-time. ***College room only:*** $8416. Room and board charges vary according to board plan and housing facility. ***Payment plan:*** installment. ***Waivers:*** employees or children of employees.

Financial Aid Of all full-time matriculated undergraduates who enrolled in 2016, 1,594 applied for aid, 1,409 were judged to have need, 218 had their need fully met. 394 Federal Work-Study jobs (averaging $1449). In 2016, 270 non-need-based awards were made. ***Average percent of need met:*** 62. ***Average financial aid package:*** $19,472. ***Average need-based loan:*** $4354. ***Average need-based gift aid:*** $15,486. ***Average non-need-based aid:*** $10,356. ***Average indebtedness upon graduation:*** $26,773. ***Financial aid deadline:*** 3/1.

APPLYING

Standardized Tests *Required:* SAT or ACT (for admission).

Options: electronic application, early admission, deferred entrance.

Application fee: $45.

Required: essay or personal statement, high school transcript. ***Required for some:*** 2 letters of recommendation, interview. ***Recommended:*** minimum 3.0 GPA, 2 letters of recommendation.

Notification: continuous (freshmen).

CONTACT

Ms. Nancy Scaffidi-Clark, Director of Admissions, Mount Saint Mary College, 330 Powell Avenue, Newburgh, NY 12550. *Phone:* 845-569-3254. *Toll-free phone:* 888-937-6762. *Fax:* 845-562-6762. *E-mail:* admissions@msmc.edu.

Nazareth College of Rochester

Rochester, New York

http://www.naz.edu/

- **Independent** comprehensive, founded 1924
- **Suburban** 150-acre campus
- **Endowment** $59.6 million
- **Coed** 2,159 undergraduate students, 95% full-time, 72% women, 28% men
- **Moderately difficult** entrance level, 72% of applicants were admitted

UNDERGRAD STUDENTS

2,045 full-time, 114 part-time. Students come from 29 states and territories; 33 other countries; 13% are from out of state; 6% Black or African American, non-Hispanic/Latino; 5% Hispanic/Latino; 3% Asian, non-Hispanic/Latino; 2% Two or more races, non-Hispanic/Latino; 4% Race/ethnicity unknown; 2% international; 7% transferred in; 62% live on campus.

Freshmen:
Admission: 4,118 applied, 2,969 admitted, 517 enrolled. ***Test scores:*** SAT critical reading scores over 500: 74%; SAT math scores over 500: 73%; SAT writing scores over 500: 60%; ACT scores over 18: 99%; SAT critical reading scores over 600: 25%; SAT math scores over 600: 26%; SAT writing scores over 600: 20%; ACT scores over 24: 65%; SAT critical reading scores over 700: 3%; SAT math scores over 700: 1%; SAT writing scores over 700: 2%; ACT scores over 30: 9%.
Retention: 85% of full-time freshmen returned.

FACULTY
Total: 493, 37% full-time, 46% with terminal degrees.
Student/faculty ratio: 9:1.

ACADEMICS
Calendar: semesters. *Degrees:* bachelor's, master's, doctoral, post-master's, and postbachelor's certificates.
Special study options: academic remediation for entering students, adult/continuing education programs, advanced placement credit, cooperative education, double majors, English as a second language, honors programs, independent study, internships, off-campus study, part-time degree program, services for LD students, study abroad, summer session for credit. ***ROTC:*** Army (c), Air Force (c).
Computers: 240 computers/terminals are available on campus for general student use. Students can access the following: computer help desk, free student e-mail accounts, online (class) grades, online (class) registration, online (class) schedules. Campuswide network is available. 100% of college-owned or -operated housing units are wired for high-speed Internet access. Wireless service is available via entire campus.
Library: Lorette Wilmot Library. *Books:* 45,000 (physical), 137,000 (digital/electronic); *Databases:* 137,000. Students can reserve study rooms.

STUDENT LIFE
Housing options: on-campus residence required through sophomore year; coed, special housing for students with disabilities. Campus housing is university owned. Freshman campus housing is guaranteed.
Activities and organizations: drama/theater group, student-run newspaper, radio station, choral group, Campus Activities Board, Center for Spirituality, Physical Therapy Club, Diversity Council, Intramurals.
Athletics Member NCAA. All Division III. ***Intercollegiate sports:*** basketball M/W, cross-country running M/W, equestrian sports M/W, field hockey W, golf M/W, ice hockey M, lacrosse M/W, soccer M/W, softball W, swimming and diving M/W, tennis M/W, track and field M/W, volleyball M/W. ***Intramural sports:*** basketball M/W, racquetball M/W, rowing M/W, skiing (downhill) M/W, soccer M/W, ultimate Frisbee M/W, volleyball M/W.
Campus security: 24-hour emergency response devices and patrols, late-night transport/escort service, controlled dormitory access, alarm system, security beeper, lighted pathways, alert system.
Student services: health clinic, personal/psychological counseling, women's center.

COSTS & FINANCIAL AID
Costs (2017–18) ***Comprehensive fee:*** $45,574 includes full-time tuition ($31,024), mandatory fees ($1400), and room and board ($13,150). Full-time tuition and fees vary according to course load, program, and reciprocity agreements. Part-time tuition: $740 per credit hour. ***Required fees:*** $80 per term part-time. ***Room and board:*** Room and board charges vary according to board plan and housing facility. ***Payment plans:*** installment, deferred payment. ***Waivers:*** minority students, children of alumni, and employees or children of employees.
Financial Aid Of all full-time matriculated undergraduates who enrolled in 2016, 1,852 applied for aid, 1,667 were judged to have need, 527 had their need fully met. 1,054 Federal Work-Study jobs (averaging $2070). In 2016, 360 non-need-based awards were made. ***Average percent of need met:*** 80. ***Average financial aid package:*** $26,668. ***Average need-based loan:*** $4493. ***Average need-based gift aid:*** $16,818. ***Average non-need-based aid:*** $16,510. ***Average indebtedness upon graduation:*** $40,567.

APPLYING
Standardized Tests *Required for some:* SAT or ACT (for admission).
Options: electronic application, early admission, early decision, deferred entrance.
Application fee: $45.
Required: essay or personal statement, high school transcript, 1 letter of recommendation. ***Required for some:*** audition/portfolio review. ***Recommended:*** interview.
Application deadlines: 2/1 (freshmen), rolling (transfers).
Early decision deadline: 11/15 (for plan 1), 1/10 (for plan 2).
Notification: continuous until 3/1 (freshmen), continuous (transfers), 12/15 (early decision plan 1), 1/25 (early decision plan 2).

CONTACT
Mr. Ian Mortimer, Vice President for Enrollment Management, Nazareth College of Rochester, 4245 East Avenue, Rochester, NY 14618-3790. *Phone:* 585-389-2830. *Toll-free phone:* 800-462-3944. *Fax:* 585-389-2826. *E-mail:* admissions@naz.edu.

The New School College of Performing Arts

New York, New York

http://www.newschool.edu/performing-arts/

- **Independent** comprehensive, part of The New School
- **Urban** campus with easy access to New York City
- **Endowment** $346.9 million
- **Coed** 564 undergraduate students, 97% full-time, 43% women, 57% men
- **Moderately difficult** entrance level, 43% of applicants were admitted

UNDERGRAD STUDENTS
547 full-time, 17 part-time. Students come from 43 states and territories; 39 other countries; 78% are from out of state; 6% Black or African American, non-Hispanic/Latino; 11% Hispanic/Latino; 4% Asian, non-Hispanic/Latino; 0.2% Native Hawaiian or other Pacific Islander, non-Hispanic/Latino; 0.4% American Indian or Alaska Native, non-Hispanic/Latino; 4% Two or more races, non-Hispanic/Latino; 4% Race/ethnicity unknown; 29% international; 6% transferred in; 29% live on campus.

Freshmen:
Admission: 1,384 applied, 593 admitted, 144 enrolled. ***Average high school GPA:*** 3.28. ***Test scores:*** SAT critical reading scores over 500: 87%; SAT math scores over 500: 73%; SAT writing scores over 500: 84%; ACT scores over 18: 90%; SAT critical reading scores over 600: 51%; SAT math scores over 600: 46%; SAT writing scores over 600: 51%; ACT scores over 24: 80%; SAT critical reading scores over 700: 5%; SAT writing scores over 700: 5%; ACT scores over 30: 40%.
Retention: 84% of full-time freshmen returned.

FACULTY
Total: 211, 9% full-time, 0.9% with terminal degrees.
Student/faculty ratio: 5:1.

ACADEMICS
Calendar: semesters. *Degrees:* diplomas, bachelor's, and master's.
Special study options: accelerated degree program, distance learning, double majors, English as a second language, independent study, internships, off-campus study, part-time degree program, services for LD students, student-designed majors, study abroad, summer session for credit.
Computers: 400 computers/terminals are available on campus for general student use. Students can access the following: campus intranet, computer help desk, free student e-mail accounts, online (class) grades, online (class) registration, online (class) schedules. Campuswide network is available. 100% of college-owned or -operated housing units are wired for high-speed Internet access. Wireless service is available via entire campus.
Library: New School Libraries & Archives plus 3 others. *Books:* 215,240 (physical), 718,102 (digital/electronic); *Serial titles:* 712 (physical), 90,364 (digital/electronic); *Databases:* 529. Weekly public service hours: 137; study areas open 24 hours, 5-7 days a week; students can reserve study rooms.

STUDENT LIFE
Housing options: coed, special housing for students with disabilities. Campus housing is university owned and leased by the school. Freshman applicants given priority for college housing.

Activities and organizations: drama/theater group, student-run newspaper, radio station, choral group.

Athletics ***Intramural sports:*** basketball M/W, cross-country running M/W, soccer M/W, tennis M/W.

Campus security: 24-hour emergency response devices, controlled dormitory access, 24-hour desk attendants in residence halls.

Student services: health clinic, personal/psychological counseling.

FINANCIAL AID

Financial Aid Of all full-time matriculated undergraduates who enrolled in 2014, 242 applied for aid, 222 were judged to have need, 33 had their need fully met. In 2014, 155 non-need-based awards were made. ***Average percent of need met:*** 66. ***Average financial aid package:*** $19,614. ***Average need-based loan:*** $6865. ***Average need-based gift aid:*** $10,301. ***Average non-need-based aid:*** $16,158. ***Average indebtedness upon graduation:*** $20,736. ***Financial aid deadline:*** 3/1.

APPLYING

Options: electronic application, early admission, early action, deferred entrance.

Application fee: $50.

Required: essay or personal statement, high school transcript, 1 letter of recommendation. ***Required for some:*** interview, prescreening, live audition/interview. ***Recommended:*** minimum 3.0 GPA.

Application deadlines: rolling (freshmen), rolling (out-of-state freshmen), rolling (transfers), 11/1 (early action).

Notification: continuous until 4/1 (freshmen), continuous until 4/1 (out-of-state freshmen), continuous until 4/1 (transfers), 12/20 (early action).

CONTACT

Ms. Georgia Schmitt, Director of Performing Arts Admission, The New School College of Performing Arts, 72 Fifth Avenue, New York, NY 10003. *Phone:* 212-580-0210 Ext. 4805. *Toll-free phone:* 800-292-3040. *E-mail:* didierg@newschool.edu.

The New School for Public Engagement

New York, New York

http://www.newschool.edu/public-engagement/

- **Independent** comprehensive, founded 1919, part of The New School
- **Urban** campus with easy access to New York City
- **Endowment** $346.9 million
- **Coed** 486 undergraduate students, 51% full-time, 66% women, 34% men

UNDERGRAD STUDENTS

246 full-time, 240 part-time. Students come from 33 states and territories; 17 other countries; 48% are from out of state; 9% Black or African American, non-Hispanic/Latino; 17% Hispanic/Latino; 3% Asian, non-Hispanic/Latino; 0.2% Native Hawaiian or other Pacific Islander, non-Hispanic/Latino; 0.4% American Indian or Alaska Native, non-Hispanic/Latino; 4% Two or more races, non-Hispanic/Latino; 5% Race/ethnicity unknown; 10% international; 27% transferred in; 3% live on campus.

Freshmen:

Admission: 15 enrolled.

FACULTY

Total: 284, 31% full-time, 20% with terminal degrees.

Student/faculty ratio: 6:1.

ACADEMICS

Calendar: semesters. *Degrees:* certificates, bachelor's, master's, doctoral, post-master's, and postbachelor's certificates.

Special study options: accelerated degree program, adult/continuing education programs, distance learning, double majors, English as a second language, independent study, internships, off-campus study, part-time degree program, services for LD students, student-designed majors, study abroad, summer session for credit.

Unusual degree programs: psychology.

Computers: 400 computers/terminals are available on campus for general student use. Students can access the following: campus intranet, computer help desk, free student e-mail accounts, online (class) grades, online (class) registration, online (class) schedules. Campuswide network is available. 100% of college-owned or -operated housing units are wired for high-speed Internet access. Wireless service is available via entire campus.

Library: New School Libraries & Archives plus 3 others. *Books:* 215,240 (physical), 718,102 (digital/electronic); *Serial titles:* 712 (physical), 90,364 (digital/electronic); *Databases:* 529. Weekly public service hours: 137; study areas open 24 hours, 5-7 days a week; students can reserve study rooms.

STUDENT LIFE

Housing options: coed, special housing for students with disabilities. Campus housing is university owned and leased by the school. Freshman applicants given priority for college housing.

Activities and organizations: drama/theater group, student-run newspaper, radio station, choral group.

Athletics ***Intramural sports:*** basketball M/W, cross-country running M/W, soccer M/W, tennis M/W.

Campus security: 24-hour emergency response devices, controlled dormitory access, trained security personnel in central buildings and 24-hour desk attendants in residence halls.

Student services: health clinic, personal/psychological counseling.

COSTS & FINANCIAL AID

Costs (2016–17) ***Tuition:*** Part-time tuition and fees vary according to course load. ***Room and board:*** $18,930; room only: $15,660. Room and board charges vary according to housing facility and location. ***Payment plan:*** installment. ***Waivers:*** employees or children of employees.

Financial Aid Of all full-time matriculated undergraduates who enrolled in 2014, 141 applied for aid, 133 were judged to have need, 8 had their need fully met. In 2014, 29 non-need-based awards were made. ***Average percent of need met:*** 57. ***Average financial aid package:*** $17,178. ***Average need-based loan:*** $9141. ***Average need-based gift aid:*** $12,341. ***Average non-need-based aid:*** $2519. ***Average indebtedness upon graduation:*** $46,625. ***Financial aid deadline:*** 3/1.

APPLYING

Required: essay or personal statement, high school transcript. ***Recommended:*** 1 letter of recommendation, interview.

CONTACT

Ms. Elizabeth Puleio, Associate Director of Admission, The New School for Public Engagement, 72 Fifth Avenue, New York, NY 10011. *Phone:* 212-229-5150 Ext. 3789. *Toll-free phone:* 800-292-3040. *E-mail:* puleioe@newschool.edu.

New York City College of Technology of the City University of New York

Brooklyn, New York

http://www.citytech.cuny.edu/

- **State and locally supported** 4-year, founded 1946, part of City University of New York System
- **Urban** campus with easy access to New York City
- **Endowment** $16.8 million
- **Coed** 17,424 undergraduate students, 62% full-time, 44% women, 56% men
- **Noncompetitive** entrance level, 38% of applicants were admitted

UNDERGRAD STUDENTS

10,821 full-time, 6,603 part-time. Students come from 14 states and territories; 84 other countries; 3% are from out of state; 30% Black or African American, non-Hispanic/Latino; 32% Hispanic/Latino; 20% Asian, non-Hispanic/Latino; 0.4% Native Hawaiian or other Pacific Islander, non-Hispanic/Latino; 0.4% American Indian or Alaska Native, non-Hispanic/Latino; 1% Two or more races, non-Hispanic/Latino; 5% international; 8% transferred in.

Freshmen:

Admission: 14,338 applied, 5,387 admitted, 3,405 enrolled. ***Test scores:*** SAT critical reading scores over 500: 11%; SAT math scores over 500: 24%; SAT writing scores over 500: 9%; SAT critical reading scores over 600: 1%; SAT math scores over 600: 5%; SAT writing scores over 600: 1%.

Retention: 77% of full-time freshmen returned.

FACULTY
Total: 1,427, 31% full-time, 35% with terminal degrees.

Student/faculty ratio: 17:1.

ACADEMICS
Calendar: semesters. *Degrees:* certificates, associate, and bachelor's.

Special study options: academic remediation for entering students, accelerated degree program, adult/continuing education programs, advanced placement credit, distance learning, English as a second language, freshman honors college, honors programs, independent study, internships, off-campus study, part-time degree program, services for LD students, student-designed majors, study abroad, summer session for credit.

Computers: 689 computers/terminals are available on campus for general student use. Students can access the following: campus intranet, computer help desk, free student e-mail accounts, online (class) grades, online (class) registration, online (class) schedules. Campuswide network is available. Wireless service is available via entire campus.

Library: Ursula C. Schwerin Library. *Books:* 142,886 (physical), 471,528 (digital/electronic); *Serial titles:* 2,525 (physical), 103,757 (digital/electronic); *Databases:* 133. Weekly public service hours: 75; students can reserve study rooms.

STUDENT LIFE
Housing options: college housing not available.

Activities and organizations: drama/theater group, student-run newspaper, International Business Organization (IBO), NYCCT - Mock Trial Club, Chess Club, Women in Islam, ASCE-Student Chapter of American Society of Civil Engineering.

Campus security: 24-hour emergency response devices and patrols.

Student services: health clinic, personal/psychological counseling, women's center.

COSTS & FINANCIAL AID
Costs (2016–17) ***Tuition:*** state resident $6330 full-time, $275 per credit part-time; nonresident $16,800 full-time, $560 per credit part-time. Full-time tuition and fees vary according to course load and program. Part-time tuition and fees vary according to course load and program. ***Required fees:*** $339 full-time, $78 per term part-time. ***Payment plan:*** installment. ***Waivers:*** senior citizens and employees or children of employees.

Financial Aid Of all full-time matriculated undergraduates who enrolled in 2012, 8,718 applied for aid, 8,272 were judged to have need, 350 had their need fully met. In 2012, 128 non-need-based awards were made. ***Average percent of need met:*** 57. ***Average financial aid package:*** $8867. ***Average need-based loan:*** $4267. ***Average need-based gift aid:*** $8356. ***Average non-need-based aid:*** $233.

APPLYING
Standardized Tests *Required for some:* SAT or ACT (for admission).

Options: electronic application, deferred entrance.

Application fee: $65.

Required: high school transcript.

Application deadlines: 2/1 (freshmen), 2/1 (transfers).

Notification: continuous until 2/1 (freshmen), 4/1 (transfers).

CONTACT
Alexis Chaconis, Director of Admissions, New York City College of Technology of the City University of New York, 300 Jay Street, Brooklyn, NY 11201-2983. *Phone:* 718-260-5500.
E-mail: achaconis@citytech.cuny.edu.

New York College of Health Professions
Syosset, New York
http://www.nycollege.edu/

CONTACT
Ms. Mary Rodas, Associate Director of Admissions, New York College of Health Professions, 6801 Jericho Turnpike, Syosset, NY 11791-4413. *Toll-free phone:* 800-922-7337 Ext. 351. *E-mail:* rdodas@nycollege.edu.

New York Institute of Technology
Old Westbury, New York
http://www.nyit.edu/

- **Independent** university, founded 1955
- **Suburban** 215-acre campus with easy access to New York City
- **Endowment** $103.4 million
- **Coed** 3,609 undergraduate students, 89% full-time, 36% women, 64% men
- **Moderately difficult** entrance level, 73% of applicants were admitted

UNDERGRAD STUDENTS
3,213 full-time, 396 part-time. Students come from 37 states and territories; 62 other countries; 13% are from out of state; 8% Black or African American, non-Hispanic/Latino; 15% Hispanic/Latino; 16% Asian, non-Hispanic/Latino; 0.4% Native Hawaiian or other Pacific Islander, non-Hispanic/Latino; 0.2% American Indian or Alaska Native, non-Hispanic/Latino; 3% Two or more races, non-Hispanic/Latino; 20% Race/ethnicity unknown; 15% international; 8% transferred in; 15% live on campus.

Freshmen:
Admission: 10,135 applied, 7,366 admitted, 713 enrolled. ***Average high school GPA:*** 3.4. ***Test scores:*** SAT critical reading scores over 500: 58%; SAT math scores over 500: 74%; ACT scores over 18: 97%; SAT critical reading scores over 600: 16%; SAT math scores over 600: 28%; ACT scores over 24: 59%; SAT critical reading scores over 700: 2%; SAT math scores over 700: 6%; ACT scores over 30: 11%.
Retention: 74% of full-time freshmen returned.

FACULTY
Total: 869, 35% full-time, 31% with terminal degrees.

Student/faculty ratio: 14:1.

ACADEMICS
Calendar: semesters. *Degrees:* certificates, associate, bachelor's, master's, doctoral, post-master's, and postbachelor's certificates.

Special study options: academic remediation for entering students, accelerated degree program, adult/continuing education programs, advanced placement credit, cooperative education, distance learning, double majors, English as a second language, honors programs, internships, off-campus study, part-time degree program, services for LD students, study abroad, summer session for credit. ***ROTC:*** Army (c), Air Force (c).

Unusual degree programs: 3-2 life sciences/osteopathic medicine, occupational therapy, physical therapy, physician assistant studies.

Computers: 1,250 computers/terminals are available on campus for general student use. Students can access the following: computer help desk, free student e-mail accounts, online (class) grades, online (class) registration, online (class) schedules. Campuswide network is available. 100% of college-owned or -operated housing units are wired for high-speed Internet access. Wireless service is available via entire campus.

Library: George and Gertrude Wisser Memorial Library plus 3 others. *Books:* 177,496 (physical), 64,280 (digital/electronic); *Serial titles:* 424 (physical), 80,477 (digital/electronic); *Databases:* 200. Weekly public service hours: 78; students can reserve study rooms.

STUDENT LIFE
Housing options: coed. Campus housing is university owned and leased by the school. Freshman campus housing is guaranteed.

Activities and organizations: student-run newspaper, television station, choral group, national fraternities, national sororities.

Athletics Member NCAA. All Division II except baseball (Division I). ***Intercollegiate sports:*** baseball M(s), basketball M(s)/W(s), cross-country running M(s)/W(s), lacrosse M(s)/W(s), soccer M(s)/W(s), softball W(s), tennis M(s)/W(s), volleyball W(s). ***Intramural sports:*** basketball M/W, cheerleading M(c)/W(c), soccer M/W, softball W, tennis M/W, volleyball W.

Campus security: 24-hour emergency response devices and patrols, late-night transport/escort service, controlled dormitory access.

Student services: health clinic, personal/psychological counseling.

COSTS & FINANCIAL AID
Costs (2016–17) ***Comprehensive fee:*** $48,730 includes full-time tuition ($33,920), mandatory fees ($1240), and room and board ($13,570). Full-

time tuition and fees vary according to program. Part-time tuition: $1150 per credit. Part-time tuition and fees vary according to course load and program. ***Required fees:*** $515 per term part-time. ***College room only:*** $8790. Room and board charges vary according to location. ***Payment plan:*** installment. ***Waivers:*** senior citizens and employees or children of employees.

Financial Aid Of all full-time matriculated undergraduates who enrolled in 2014, 2,763 applied for aid, 2,483 were judged to have need. In 2014, 508 non-need-based awards were made. ***Average financial aid package:*** $19,693. ***Average need-based loan:*** $4280. ***Average need-based gift aid:*** $7152. ***Average non-need-based aid:*** $11,493.

APPLYING

Standardized Tests *Required:* SAT or ACT (for admission).

Options: electronic application, deferred entrance.

Application fee: $50.

Required: essay or personal statement, high school transcript, 2 letters of recommendation. ***Required for some:*** interview. ***Recommended:*** minimum 2.7 GPA.

Application deadlines: rolling (freshmen), rolling (transfers).

Notification: continuous (freshmen), continuous (transfers).

CONTACT

Ms. Cheryl Bradley, Senior Advisor, Undergraduate Admissions, New York Institute of Technology, Old Westbury, NY. *Phone:* 516-686-1017. *Toll-free phone:* 800-345-NYIT. *E-mail:* admissions@nyit.edu.

New York School of Interior Design

New York, New York

http://www.nysid.edu/

- **Independent** comprehensive, founded 1916
- **Urban** 1-acre campus
- **Endowment** $3.1 million
- **Coed, primarily women**
- **Moderately difficult** entrance level

FACULTY

Student/faculty ratio: 8:1.

ACADEMICS

Calendar: semesters. *Degrees:* certificates, associate, bachelor's, and master's.

STUDENT LIFE

Housing options: coed. Campus housing is leased by the school and is provided by a third party.

Activities and organizations: American Society of Interior Designers, Contract Club, Student Council.

Campus security: security during school hours.

COSTS & FINANCIAL AID

Costs (2016–17) ***Tuition:*** $30,195 full-time, $915 per credit part-time. Full-time tuition and fees vary according to course load. Part-time tuition and fees vary according to course load. ***Required fees:*** $750 full-time. ***Room only:*** $16,000.

Financial Aid Of all full-time matriculated undergraduates who enrolled in 2016, 65 applied for aid, 57 were judged to have need. 14 Federal Work-Study jobs (averaging $3019). In 2016, 15 non-need-based awards were made. ***Average percent of need met:*** 25. ***Average financial aid package:*** $12,753. ***Average need-based loan:*** $4372. ***Average need-based gift aid:*** $10,346. ***Average non-need-based aid:*** $8633. ***Average indebtedness upon graduation:*** $26,458.

APPLYING

Standardized Tests *Required for some:* SAT or ACT (for admission).

Options: electronic application, deferred entrance.

Application fee: $60.

Required: essay or personal statement, high school transcript, minimum 2.8 GPA, 2 letters of recommendation, portfolio.

CONTACT

Jaspreet Bains, Admissions Associate, New York School of Interior Design, 170 East 70th Street, New York, NY 10021-5110. *Phone:* 212-472-1500 Ext. 212. *Toll-free phone:* 800-336-9743 Ext. 205. *Fax:* 212-472-1867. *E-mail:* admissions@nysid.edu.

New York University

New York, New York

http://www.nyu.edu/

CONTACT

Kristy Materasso, Undergraduate Admissions Processing Center, New York University, 665 Broadway, 11th Floor, New York, NY 10011. *Phone:* 212-998-4500. *Fax:* 212-995-4902. *E-mail:* admissions@nyu.edu.

★ Niagara University

Niagara Falls, New York

http://www.niagara.edu/

- **Independent** comprehensive, founded 1856, affiliated with Roman Catholic Church
- **Suburban** 160-acre campus with easy access to Buffalo, NY and Toronto, Ontario (Canada)
- **Endowment** $87.3 million
- **Coed** 3,136 undergraduate students, 94% full-time, 62% women, 38% men
- **Moderately difficult** entrance level, 83% of applicants were admitted

UNDERGRAD STUDENTS

2,950 full-time, 186 part-time. Students come from 35 states and territories; 36 other countries; 9% are from out of state; 5% Black or African American, non-Hispanic/Latino; 4% Hispanic/Latino; 1% Asian, non-Hispanic/Latino; 0.7% American Indian or Alaska Native, non-Hispanic/Latino; 2% Two or more races, non-Hispanic/Latino; 2% Race/ethnicity unknown; 12% international; 6% transferred in; 41% live on campus.

Freshmen:

Admission: 3,359 applied, 2,784 admitted, 625 enrolled. ***Average high school GPA:*** 3.38. ***Test scores:*** SAT critical reading scores over 500: 57%; SAT math scores over 500: 63%; ACT scores over 18: 94%; SAT critical reading scores over 600: 12%; SAT math scores over 600: 16%; ACT scores over 24: 40%; SAT critical reading scores over 700: 1%; SAT math scores over 700: 1%; ACT scores over 30: 4%.

Retention: 81% of full-time freshmen returned.

FACULTY

Total: 407, 41% full-time, 57% with terminal degrees.

Student/faculty ratio: 12:1.

ACADEMICS

Calendar: semesters. *Degrees:* certificates, associate, bachelor's, master's, doctoral, post-master's, and postbachelor's certificates.

Special study options: academic remediation for entering students, accelerated degree program, advanced placement credit, cooperative education, distance learning, double majors, English as a second language, independent study, internships, off-campus study, part-time degree program, services for LD students, student-designed majors, study abroad, summer session for credit. ***ROTC:*** Army (b).

Computers: 81 computers/terminals are available on campus for general student use. Students can access the following: campus intranet, computer help desk, free student e-mail accounts, online (class) grades, online (class) registration, online (class) schedules. Campuswide network is available. 100% of college-owned or -operated housing units are wired for high-speed Internet access. Wireless service is available via entire campus.

Library: Our Lady of Angels Library. *Books:* 171,911 (physical), 322,812 (digital/electronic); *Serial titles:* 160 (physical), 31,384 (digital/electronic); *Databases:* 85. Weekly public service hours: 106; study areas open 24 hours, 5-7 days a week; students can reserve study rooms.

STUDENT LIFE

Housing options: on-campus residence required through sophomore year; coed. Campus housing is university owned. Freshman campus housing is guaranteed.

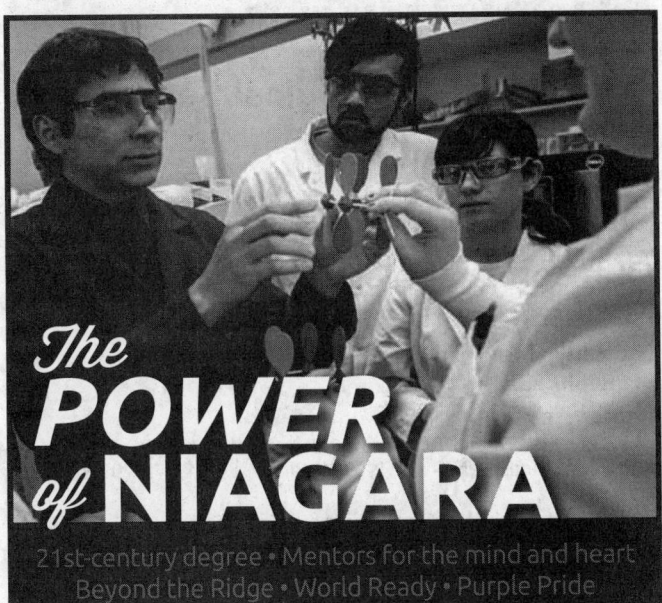

Activities and organizations: drama/theater group, student-run newspaper, radio and television station, Beta Alpha Psi, American Sign Language, Biology Club, Circle K, Sports Management Association, national fraternities, national sororities.

Athletics Member NCAA. All Division I. ***Intercollegiate sports:*** baseball M(s), basketball M(s)/W(s), cross-country running M(s)/W(s), golf M(s)/W(s), ice hockey M(s), lacrosse W(s), soccer M(s)/W(s), softball W(s), swimming and diving M(s)/W(s), tennis M(s)/W(s), track and field W(s), volleyball W(s). ***Intramural sports:*** badminton M(c)/W(c), baseball M(c), basketball M(c)/W(c), bowling M(c)/W(c), field hockey M(c)/W(c), golf M(c), ice hockey M(c)/W(c), lacrosse M(c)/W(c), racquetball M(c)/W(c), rugby M(c)/W(c), soccer M(c)/W(c), softball M/W(c), tennis M/W, volleyball M(c)/W(c), weight lifting M(c)/W(c), wrestling M(c).

Campus security: 24-hour emergency response devices and patrols, late-night transport/escort service, controlled dormitory access, 24-hour escort service, Emergency Notification System, self-defense education.

Student services: health clinic, personal/psychological counseling.

COSTS & FINANCIAL AID

Costs (2016–17) ***Comprehensive fee:*** $43,650 includes full-time tuition ($29,500), mandatory fees ($1450), and room and board ($12,700). Full-time tuition and fees vary according to program. Part-time tuition: $985 per credit hour. Part-time tuition and fees vary according to program. ***Room and board:*** Room and board charges vary according to housing facility. ***Payment plans:*** installment, deferred payment. ***Waivers:*** employees or children of employees.

Financial Aid Of all full-time matriculated undergraduates who enrolled in 2016, 2,302 applied for aid, 2,109 were judged to have need, 1,111 had their need fully met. 424 Federal Work-Study jobs (averaging $3380). 46 state and other part-time jobs (averaging $5335). In 2016, 492 non-need-based awards were made. ***Average percent of need met:*** 83. ***Average financial aid package:*** $25,326. ***Average need-based loan:*** $4984. ***Average need-based gift aid:*** $20,970. ***Average non-need-based aid:*** $14,868. ***Average indebtedness upon graduation:*** $32,251.

APPLYING

Standardized Tests *Required:* SAT or ACT (for admission).

Options: electronic application, early admission, early action, deferred entrance.

Required: high school transcript. ***Recommended:*** minimum 3.0 GPA, 3 letters of recommendation, interview.

Application deadlines: 8/1 (freshmen), 8/15 (transfers).

Notification: continuous (freshmen), continuous (transfers).

CONTACT

Mr. Mark Wojnowski, Director of Undergraduate Admissions, Niagara University, 5795 Lewiston Road, Gacioch Center, Niagara University, NY 14109. *Phone:* 716-286-8700. *Toll-free phone:* 800-462-2111. *Fax:* 716-286-8733. *E-mail:* admissions@niagara.edu.

See this page for display ad and page 1440 for the College Close-Up.

Nyack College

Nyack, New York

http://www.nyack.edu/

- **Independent** comprehensive, founded 1882, affiliated with The Christian and Missionary Alliance
- **Suburban** 125-acre campus with easy access to New York City
- **Coed** 1,545 undergraduate students, 84% full-time, 61% women, 39% men
- **Minimally difficult** entrance level, 99% of applicants were admitted

UNDERGRAD STUDENTS

1,300 full-time, 245 part-time. 30% are from out of state; 30% Black or African American, non-Hispanic/Latino; 31% Hispanic/Latino; 8% Asian, non-Hispanic/Latino; 0.3% Native Hawaiian or other Pacific Islander, non-Hispanic/Latino; 0.5% American Indian or Alaska Native, non-Hispanic/Latino; 2% Two or more races, non-Hispanic/Latino; 2% Race/ethnicity unknown; 6% international; 12% transferred in; 72% live on campus.

Freshmen:

Admission: 489 applied, 482 admitted, 239 enrolled. ***Average high school GPA:*** 2.81. ***Test scores:*** SAT critical reading scores over 500: 30%; SAT math scores over 500: 31%; ACT scores over 18: 54%; SAT critical reading scores over 600: 6%; SAT math scores over 600: 9%; ACT scores over 24: 18%; SAT critical reading scores over 700: 1%; SAT math scores over 700: 1%.

Retention: 68% of full-time freshmen returned.

FACULTY

Total: 284, 35% full-time, 45% with terminal degrees.

Student/faculty ratio: 12:1.

ACADEMICS

Calendar: semesters. *Degrees:* associate, bachelor's, master's, and doctoral.

Special study options: academic remediation for entering students, adult/continuing education programs, advanced placement credit, distance learning, double majors, honors programs, independent study, internships, off-campus study, part-time degree program, services for LD students, student-designed majors, study abroad, summer session for credit.

Unusual degree programs: 3-2 childhood special education.

Computers: Students can access the following: campus intranet, computer help desk, free student e-mail accounts, online (class) grades, online (class) registration, online (class) schedules. Campuswide network is available. 95% of college-owned or -operated housing units are wired for high-speed Internet access. Wireless service is available via classrooms, computer labs, dorm rooms, libraries, student centers.

Library: Bailey Library plus 3 others.

STUDENT LIFE

Housing options: on-campus residence required through sophomore year; men-only, women-only. Campus housing is university owned. Freshman campus housing is guaranteed.

Activities and organizations: drama/theater group, student-run newspaper, radio station, choral group, Student leadership, Choral groups, Lost & Found, Small group ministries, Intramurals.

Athletics Member NCAA. All Division II. ***Intercollegiate sports:*** baseball M(s), basketball M(s)/W(s), cross-country running M(s)/W(s), golf M(s), lacrosse W(s), soccer M(s)/W(s), softball W(s), volleyball W(s). ***Intramural sports:*** baseball M, basketball M/W, skiing (downhill) M/W, soccer M/W, softball W, ultimate Frisbee M/W, volleyball M/W.

Campus security: 24-hour emergency response devices and patrols.

Student services: health clinic, personal/psychological counseling.

COSTS & FINANCIAL AID

Costs (2017–18) ***Comprehensive fee:*** $34,800 includes full-time tuition ($25,000), mandatory fees ($350), and room and board ($9450). Part-time tuition: $1040 per credit hour. Part-time tuition and fees vary according to course load. ***Room and board:*** Room and board charges vary according to board plan and housing facility. ***Payment plan:*** installment. ***Waivers:*** employees or children of employees.

Financial Aid Of all full-time matriculated undergraduates who enrolled in 2014, 1,257 applied for aid, 1,172 were judged to have need, 107 had their need fully met. 184 Federal Work-Study jobs (averaging $1125). 73 state and other part-time jobs (averaging $1875). In 2014, 207 non-need-based awards were made. ***Average percent of need met:*** 64. ***Average financial aid package:*** $20,230. ***Average need-based loan:*** $4028. ***Average need-based gift aid:*** $9923. ***Average non-need-based aid:*** $10,808. ***Average indebtedness upon graduation:*** $34,670.

APPLYING

Standardized Tests *Required for some:* SAT or ACT (for admission), SAT and SAT Subject Tests or ACT (for admission).

Options: electronic application, early action, deferred entrance.

Application fee: $25.

Required: essay or personal statement, high school transcript, minimum 2.0 GPA, 1 letter of recommendation, signed statement of faith and community life form. ***Required for some:*** interview.

Application deadlines: rolling (freshmen), rolling (out-of-state freshmen), rolling (transfers).

Notification: continuous (freshmen), continuous (out-of-state freshmen), continuous (transfers).

CONTACT

Mr. Dan Bailey, Director of Admissions, Nyack College, 1 South Boulevard, Nyack, NY 10960-3698. *Phone:* 845-675-4401. *Toll-free phone:* 800-33-NYACK. *Fax:* 845-358-3047. *E-mail:* admissions@nyack.edu.

Ohr Hameir Theological Seminary

Cortlandt Manor, New York

CONTACT

Director of Admissions, Ohr Hameir Theological Seminary, 141 Furnace Woods Road, Cortlandt Manor, NY 10567. *Phone:* 914-736-1500.

Ohr Somayach/Joseph Tanenbaum Educational Center

Monsey, New York

http://ohr.edu/

CONTACT

Ohr Somayach/Joseph Tanenbaum Educational Center, PO Box 334, 244 Route 306, Monsey, NY 10952-0334. *Phone:* 845-425-1370 Ext. 22.

★ Pace University

New York, New York

http://www.pace.edu/nyc

- **Independent** university, founded 1906
- **Urban** campus with easy access to New York City
- **Endowment** $152.2 million
- **Coed** 6,284 undergraduate students, 88% full-time, 62% women, 38% men
- **Moderately difficult** entrance level, 87% of applicants were admitted

UNDERGRAD STUDENTS

5,505 full-time, 779 part-time. Students come from 49 states and territories; 96 other countries; 48% are from out of state; 10% Black or African American, non-Hispanic/Latino; 13% Hispanic/Latino; 9% Asian, non-Hispanic/Latino; 0.1% Native Hawaiian or other Pacific Islander, non-Hispanic/Latino; 0.2% American Indian or Alaska Native, non-Hispanic/Latino; 4% Two or more races, non-Hispanic/Latino; 2% Race/ethnicity unknown; 14% international; 6% transferred in; 37% live on campus.

Freshmen:

Admission: 14,545 applied, 12,638 admitted, 1,460 enrolled. ***Average high school GPA:*** 3.3. ***Test scores:*** SAT critical reading scores over 500: 64%; SAT math scores over 500: 65%; ACT scores over 18: 98%; SAT critical reading scores over 600: 22%; SAT math scores over 600: 22%; ACT scores over 24: 56%; SAT critical reading scores over 700: 3%; SAT math scores over 700: 2%; ACT scores over 30: 10%.

Retention: 75% of full-time freshmen returned.

FACULTY

Total: 834, 37% full-time, 48% with terminal degrees.

Student/faculty ratio: 16:1.

ACADEMICS

Calendar: semesters. *Degrees:* certificates, associate, bachelor's, master's, doctoral, post-master's, and postbachelor's certificates.

Special study options: accelerated degree program, adult/continuing education programs, advanced placement credit, cooperative education, distance learning, double majors, English as a second language, freshman honors college, honors programs, independent study, internships, part-time degree program, services for LD students, study abroad, summer session for credit. ***ROTC:*** Army (c), Air Force (c).

Unusual degree programs: 3-2 business administration; engineering with Manhattan College, Rensselaer Polytechnic Institute; occupational Therapy with Columbia University, optometry with SUNY College of Optometry, physical therapy with New York Medical College, podiatry with the New York College of Podiatric Medicine.

Computers: 156 computers/terminals are available on campus for general student use. Students can access the following: computer help desk, free student e-mail accounts, online (class) grades, online (class) registration, online (class) schedules, administrative functions (tuition, student records, financial aid, health insurance waiver). Campuswide network is available.

100% of college-owned or -operated housing units are wired for high-speed Internet access. Wireless service is available via entire campus.
Library: Henry Birnbaum Library. *Books:* 176,661 (physical), 193,680 (digital/electronic); *Serial titles:* 75 (physical), 143,640 (digital/electronic); *Databases:* 208. Weekly public service hours: 93; students can reserve study rooms.

STUDENT LIFE
Housing options: coed, special housing for students with disabilities. Campus housing is university owned and leased by the school. Freshman campus housing is guaranteed.
Activities and organizations: drama/theater group, student-run newspaper, radio and television station, choral group, Pace Board of Programming and Entertainment, Black Student Union, National Society of Leadership and Success, Stand-up Productions, Pace Advertising Club, national fraternities, national sororities.
Athletics Member NCAA. All Division II. ***Intercollegiate sports:*** baseball M(s), basketball M(s)/W(s), cross-country running M(s)/W(s), field hockey W(s), football M(s), lacrosse M(s)/W(s), soccer W(s), softball W(s), swimming and diving M(s)/W(s), volleyball W(s). ***Intramural sports:*** badminton M/W, basketball M/W, soccer M/W, ultimate Frisbee M/W, volleyball M/W.
Campus security: 24-hour emergency response devices and patrols, late-night transport/escort service, controlled dormitory access.
Student services: health clinic, personal/psychological counseling.

COSTS & FINANCIAL AID
Costs (2016–17) ***Comprehensive fee:*** $61,142 includes full-time tuition ($41,120), mandatory fees ($1602), and room and board ($18,420). Full-time tuition and fees vary according to location. Part-time tuition: $1180 per credit hour. Part-time tuition and fees vary according to course load and location. ***Room and board:*** Room and board charges vary according to board plan, housing facility, location, and student level. ***Payment plan:*** installment. ***Waivers:*** senior citizens and employees or children of employees.
Financial Aid Of all full-time matriculated undergraduates who enrolled in 2014, 5,656 applied for aid, 5,240 were judged to have need, 583 had their need fully met. 1,123 Federal Work-Study jobs (averaging $2241). In 2014, 1533 non-need-based awards were made. ***Average percent of need met:*** 70. ***Average financial aid package:*** $29,194. ***Average need-based loan:*** $4582. ***Average need-based gift aid:*** $24,743. ***Average non-need-based aid:*** $15,903. ***Average indebtedness upon graduation:*** $35,442.

APPLYING
Standardized Tests *Required for some:* SAT or ACT (for admission).
Options: electronic application, early action, deferred entrance.
Application fee: $50.
Required: essay or personal statement, high school transcript, 2 letters of recommendation. ***Recommended:*** interview.
Application deadlines: 2/15 (freshmen), rolling (transfers), 12/1 (early action).
Notification: continuous (freshmen), continuous (transfers), 1/1 (early action).

CONTACT
Mr. Todd Heilman, Dean of Admissions, Pace University, One Pace Plaza, 163 William Street, New York, NY 10038. *Phone:* 212-346-1794. *Toll-free phone:* 800-874-7223. *Fax:* 212-346-1821.
E-mail: theilman@pace.edu.

Pace University, Pleasantville Campus

Pleasantville, New York

http://www.pace.edu/westchester

- **Independent** university
- **Suburban** campus with easy access to New York City
- **Endowment** $152.2 million
- **Coed** 2,630 undergraduate students, 83% full-time, 59% women, 41% men
- **Moderately difficult** entrance level, 77% of applicants were admitted

UNDERGRAD STUDENTS
2,186 full-time, 444 part-time. Students come from 49 states and territories; 22 other countries; 28% are from out of state; 13% Black or African American, non-Hispanic/Latino; 17% Hispanic/Latino; 6% Asian, non-Hispanic/Latino; 0.2% American Indian or Alaska Native, non-Hispanic/Latino; 3% Two or more races, non-Hispanic/Latino; 3% Race/ethnicity unknown; 1% international; 7% transferred in; 52% live on campus.

Freshmen:
Admission: 3,917 applied, 3,028 admitted, 571 enrolled. ***Average high school GPA:*** 3.3. ***Test scores:*** SAT critical reading scores over 500: 59%; SAT math scores over 500: 63%; ACT scores over 18: 99%; SAT critical reading scores over 600: 11%; SAT math scores over 600: 16%; ACT scores over 24: 41%; SAT math scores over 700: 1%; ACT scores over 30: 3%.
Retention: 81% of full-time freshmen returned.

FACULTY
Total: 440, 37% full-time, 40% with terminal degrees.
Student/faculty ratio: 11:1.

ACADEMICS
Calendar: semesters. *Degrees:* certificates, diplomas, associate, bachelor's, master's, doctoral, post-master's, and postbachelor's certificates.
Special study options: accelerated degree program, adult/continuing education programs, advanced placement credit, cooperative education, distance learning, double majors, English as a second language, freshman honors college, honors programs, independent study, internships, part-time degree program, services for LD students, study abroad, summer session for credit. ***ROTC:*** Army (c), Air Force (c).
Unusual degree programs: 3-2 business administration; engineering with Manhattan College, Rensselaer Polytechnic Institute; occupational therapy with Columbia University, optometry with SUNY College of Optometry, physical therapy with New York Medical College, podiatry with the New York College of Podiatric Medicine.
Computers: 127 computers/terminals are available on campus for general student use. Students can access the following: computer help desk, online (class) grades, online (class) registration, online (class) schedules, administrative functions (tuition, student records, financial aid, health insurance waiver). Campuswide network is available. 100% of college-owned or -operated housing units are wired for high-speed Internet access. Wireless service is available via entire campus.
Library: Edward and Doris Mortola Library. *Books:* 176,661 (physical), 665,273 (digital/electronic). Weekly public service hours: 113; students can reserve study rooms.

STUDENT LIFE
Housing options: coed. Campus housing is university owned. Freshman campus housing is guaranteed.
Activities and organizations: drama/theater group, student-run newspaper, radio and television station, choral group, Lubin Business Association, National Student Nurses Association, Future Leaders in Healthcare, Black Student Union, Accounting Society, national fraternities, national sororities.
Athletics Member NCAA. All Division II. ***Intercollegiate sports:*** baseball M(s), basketball M(s)/W(s), cross-country running M(s)/W(s), field hockey W(s), football M(s), lacrosse M(s)/W(s), soccer W(s), softball W(s), swimming and diving M(s)/W(s), volleyball W(s). ***Intramural sports:*** badminton M/W, basketball M/W, soccer M/W, softball M/W, tennis M/W, ultimate Frisbee M/W, volleyball M/W.
Campus security: 24-hour emergency response devices and patrols, late-night transport/escort service, controlled dormitory access.
Student services: health clinic, personal/psychological counseling.

COSTS
Costs (2016–17) ***Comprehensive fee:*** $58,388 includes full-time tuition ($41,120), mandatory fees ($1652), and room and board ($15,616). Full-time tuition and fees vary according to location. Part-time tuition: $1180 per credit hour. Part-time tuition and fees vary according to course load and location. ***Room and board:*** Room and board charges vary according to board plan, housing facility, location, and student level. ***Payment plan:*** installment. ***Waivers:*** senior citizens and employees or children of employees.

APPLYING

Standardized Tests *Required for some:* SAT or ACT (for admission).

Options: electronic application, early action, deferred entrance.

Application fee: $50.

Required: essay or personal statement, high school transcript, 2 letters of recommendation. ***Recommended:*** interview.

Application deadlines: 2/15 (freshmen), rolling (transfers), 12/1 (early action).

Notification: continuous (freshmen), continuous (transfers), 1/1 (early action).

CONTACT

Mr. Todd Heilman, Dean of Admission, Pace University, Pleasantville Campus, 861 Bedford Road, Pleasantville, NY 10570. *Phone:* 212-346-1794. *Toll-free phone:* 800-874-PACE. *Fax:* 212-346-1821. *E-mail:* theilman@pace.edu.

Parsons School of Design

New York, New York

http://www.newschool.edu/parsons/

- **Independent** comprehensive, founded 1896, part of The New School
- **Urban** campus with easy access to New York City
- **Endowment** $300.1 million
- **Coed** 4,301 undergraduate students, 88% full-time, 78% women, 22% men

UNDERGRAD STUDENTS

3,795 full-time, 506 part-time. Students come from 56 states and territories; 90 other countries; 73% are from out of state; 4% Black or African American, non-Hispanic/Latino; 10% Hispanic/Latino; 12% Asian, non-Hispanic/Latino; 0.1% Native Hawaiian or other Pacific Islander, non-Hispanic/Latino; 0.1% American Indian or Alaska Native, non-Hispanic/Latino; 3% Two or more races, non-Hispanic/Latino; 3% Race/ethnicity unknown; 45% international; 8% transferred in; 25% live on campus.

Freshmen:

Admission: 953 enrolled. ***Average high school GPA:*** 3.33. ***Test scores:*** SAT critical reading scores over 500: 79%; SAT math scores over 500: 80%; SAT writing scores over 500: 84%; ACT scores over 18: 97%; SAT critical reading scores over 600: 36%; SAT math scores over 600: 53%; SAT writing scores over 600: 44%; ACT scores over 24: 69%; SAT critical reading scores over 700: 4%; SAT math scores over 700: 18%; SAT writing scores over 700: 6%; ACT scores over 30: 10%.
Retention: 85% of full-time freshmen returned.

FACULTY

Total: 1,306, 12% full-time, 8% with terminal degrees.

Student/faculty ratio: 11:1.

ACADEMICS

Calendar: semesters. *Degrees:* associate, bachelor's, master's, and postbachelor's certificates.

Special study options: advanced placement credit, cooperative education, distance learning, English as a second language, independent study, internships, off-campus study, services for LD students, student-designed majors, study abroad, summer session for credit.

Computers: 400 computers/terminals are available on campus for general student use. Students can access the following: campus intranet, computer help desk, free student e-mail accounts, online (class) grades, online (class) registration, online (class) schedules. Campuswide network is available. 100% of college-owned or -operated housing units are wired for high-speed Internet access. Wireless service is available via entire campus.

Library: New School Libraries & Archives plus 3 others. *Books:* 215,240 (physical), 718,102 (digital/electronic); *Serial titles:* 712 (physical), 90,364 (digital/electronic); *Databases:* 529. Weekly public service hours: 137; study areas open 24 hours, 5-7 days a week; students can reserve study rooms.

STUDENT LIFE

Housing options: coed, special housing for students with disabilities. Campus housing is university owned and leased by the school. Freshman applicants given priority for college housing.

Activities and organizations: drama/theater group, student-run newspaper, radio station, choral group.

Athletics ***Intramural sports:*** basketball M/W, cross-country running M/W, soccer M/W, tennis M/W.

Campus security: 24-hour emergency response devices, controlled dormitory access, 24-hour security desk personnel.

Student services: health clinic, personal/psychological counseling.

FINANCIAL AID

Financial Aid Of all full-time matriculated undergraduates who enrolled in 2014, 1,612 applied for aid, 1,454 were judged to have need, 206 had their need fully met. In 2014, 1909 non-need-based awards were made. ***Average percent of need met:*** 67. ***Average financial aid package:*** $24,817. ***Average need-based loan:*** $7214. ***Average need-based gift aid:*** $17,130. ***Average non-need-based aid:*** $6119. ***Average indebtedness upon graduation:*** $30,659. ***Financial aid deadline:*** 3/1.

APPLYING

Standardized Tests *Required for some:* TOEFL/IELTS /PTE for students whose native language is not English.

Required: essay or personal statement, high school transcript, 1 letter of recommendation, online application, Parso's Challenge portfolio, artist statement. ***Recommended:*** minimum 3.0 GPA, interview.

CONTACT

Ms. Erin Stine, Director of Admissions for Parsons School of Design, Parsons School of Design, 72 Fifth Avenue at 13th Street, New York, NY 10011. *Phone:* 212-229-5600. *Toll-free phone:* 800-292-3040. *E-mail:* stinee@newschool.edu.

★ Paul Smith's College

Paul Smiths, New York

http://www.paulsmiths.edu/

CONTACT

Admissions Office, Paul Smith's College, Routes 86 and 30, PO Box 265, Paul Smiths, NY 12970. *Phone:* 518-327-6227. *Toll-free phone:* 800-421-2605. *Fax:* 518-327-6016. *E-mail:* admissions@paulsmiths.edu.

Phillips Beth Israel School of Nursing

New York, New York

http://www.pbisn.edu/

- **Independent** primarily 2-year, founded 1904
- **Urban** campus
- **Endowment** $750,000
- **Coed**
- **Moderately difficult** entrance level

FACULTY

Student/faculty ratio: 8:1.

ACADEMICS

Calendar: semesters. *Degrees:* associate and bachelor's.

Library: Phillips Health Science Library. *Books:* 400 (physical), 25 (digital/electronic); *Databases:* 10.

STUDENT LIFE

Housing options: college housing not available.

Activities and organizations: student-run newspaper, choral group, Student Government Organization, National Student Nurses Association.

Campus security: 24-hour emergency response devices.

Student services: health clinic, personal/psychological counseling.

COSTS & FINANCIAL AID

Costs (2016–17) ***Tuition:*** $18,950 full-time, $575 per credit part-time. Full-time tuition and fees vary according to degree level. Part-time tuition and fees vary according to degree level. ***Required fees:*** $2775 full-time.

Financial Aid ***Financial aid deadline:*** 6/1.

APPLYING

Standardized Tests *Recommended:* SAT (for admission).

Options: deferred entrance.

Application fee: $50.

Required: essay or personal statement, high school transcript, minimum 2.5 GPA, 2 letters of recommendation, interview.

CONTACT

Mrs. Bernice Pass-Stern, Assistant Dean, Phillips Beth Israel School of Nursing, 776 Sixth Avenue, 4th Floor, New York, NY 10010-6354. *Phone:* 212-614-6176. *Fax:* 212-614-6109. *E-mail:* bstern@chpnet.org.

Plaza College

Forest Hills, New York

http://www.plazacollege.edu/

CONTACT

Dean Vanessa Lopez, Dean of Admissions, Plaza College, 118-33 Queens Boulevard, Forest Hills, NY 11375. *Phone:* 718-779-1430. *E-mail:* info@plazacollege.edu.

★ Pratt Institute

Brooklyn, New York

http://www.pratt.edu/

- **Independent** comprehensive, founded 1887
- **Urban** 25-acre campus
- **Coed** 3,226 undergraduate students, 96% full-time, 69% women, 31% men
- **Very difficult** entrance level, 66% of applicants were admitted

UNDERGRAD STUDENTS

3,103 full-time, 123 part-time. 71% are from out of state; 4% Black or African American, non-Hispanic/Latino; 10% Hispanic/Latino; 15% Asian, non-Hispanic/Latino; 0.2% Native Hawaiian or other Pacific Islander, non-Hispanic/Latino; 0.3% American Indian or Alaska Native, non-Hispanic/Latino; 2% Two or more races, non-Hispanic/Latino; 2% Race/ethnicity unknown; 26% international; 4% transferred in; 54% live on campus.

Freshmen:

Admission: 4,819 applied, 3,186 admitted, 705 enrolled. ***Average high school GPA:*** 3.63. ***Test scores:*** SAT critical reading scores over 500: 85%; SAT math scores over 500: 85%; SAT writing scores over 500: 86%; ACT scores over 18: 100%; SAT critical reading scores over 600: 41%; SAT math scores over 600: 52%; SAT writing scores over 600: 44%; ACT scores over 24: 74%; SAT critical reading scores over 700: 6%; SAT math scores over 700: 15%; SAT writing scores over 700: 6%; ACT scores over 30: 16%.

Retention: 85% of full-time freshmen returned.

FACULTY

Total: 1,113, 14% full-time, 10% with terminal degrees.

Student/faculty ratio: 9:1.

ACADEMICS

Calendar: semesters plus optional May term and summer session. *Degrees:* associate, bachelor's, master's, and post-master's certificates.

Special study options: part-time degree program. ***ROTC:*** Army (c).

Computers: Students can access the following: online (class) registration. Campuswide network is available.

Library: Pratt Institute Library.

STUDENT LIFE

Housing options: coed, special housing for students with disabilities. Campus housing is university owned. Freshman campus housing is guaranteed.

Athletics Member NCAA. All Division III. ***Intercollegiate sports:*** basketball M, cross-country running M/W, soccer M/W, tennis M/W, track and field M/W, volleyball W. ***Intramural sports:*** badminton M/W, basketball M, field hockey M, football M, golf M, lacrosse M/W, volleyball M, weight lifting M/W.

Campus security: 24-hour emergency response devices and patrols, late-night transport/escort service.

COSTS & FINANCIAL AID

Costs (2017–18) ***Comprehensive fee:*** $62,058 includes full-time tuition ($47,986), mandatory fees ($2052), and room and board ($12,020). Full-time tuition and fees vary according to program. Part-time tuition: $1548 per credit hour. Part-time tuition and fees vary according to program. ***College room only:*** $8400. Room and board charges vary according to board plan and housing facility.

Financial Aid Of all full-time matriculated undergraduates who enrolled in 2015, 2,498 applied for aid, 2,459 were judged to have need. In 2015, 785 non-need-based awards were made. ***Average percent of need met:*** 42. ***Average financial aid package:*** $22,733. ***Average need-based gift aid:*** $11,623. ***Average non-need-based aid:*** $14,000. ***Financial aid deadline:*** 3/1.

APPLYING

Standardized Tests *Required:* SAT or ACT (for admission). *Required for some:* SAT Subject Tests (for admission).

Options: electronic application, early action, deferred entrance.

Application fee: $50.

Required: essay or personal statement, high school transcript, 1 letter of recommendation. ***Required for some:*** portfolio. ***Recommended:*** minimum 3.0 GPA.

CONTACT

Ms. Olga Burger, Visit Coordinator, Pratt Institute, 200 Willoughby Avenue, DeKalb Hall, Brooklyn, NY 11205. *Phone:* 718-636-3779. *Toll-free phone:* 800-331-0834. *Fax:* 718-636-3670. *E-mail:* visit@pratt.edu.

See page 1464 for the College Close-Up.

Purchase College, State University of New York

Purchase, New York

http://www.purchase.edu/

- **State-supported** comprehensive, founded 1967, part of State University of New York System
- **Small-town** 500-acre campus with easy access to New York City
- **Coed** 4,121 undergraduate students, 91% full-time, 57% women, 43% men
- **Moderately difficult** entrance level, 44% of applicants were admitted

UNDERGRAD STUDENTS

3,755 full-time, 366 part-time. Students come from 42 states and territories; 30 other countries; 15% are from out of state; 11% Black or African American, non-Hispanic/Latino; 19% Hispanic/Latino; 4% Asian, non-Hispanic/Latino; 0.2% Native Hawaiian or other Pacific Islander, non-Hispanic/Latino; 0.3% American Indian or Alaska Native, non-Hispanic/Latino; 5% Two or more races, non-Hispanic/Latino; 6% Race/ethnicity unknown; 2% international; 10% transferred in; 67% live on campus.

Freshmen:

Admission: 6,762 applied, 2,942 admitted, 732 enrolled. ***Average high school GPA:*** 3.24. ***Test scores:*** SAT critical reading scores over 500: 76%; SAT math scores over 500: 62%; ACT scores over 18: 94%; SAT critical reading scores over 600: 32%; SAT math scores over 600: 16%; ACT scores over 24: 54%; SAT critical reading scores over 700: 6%; SAT math scores over 700: 2%; ACT scores over 30: 12%.

Retention: 81% of full-time freshmen returned.

FACULTY

Total: 461, 36% full-time, 31% with terminal degrees.

Student/faculty ratio: 14:1.

ACADEMICS

Calendar: semesters. *Degrees:* certificates, bachelor's, master's, and post-master's certificates.

Special study options: academic remediation for entering students, adult/continuing education programs, advanced placement credit, double majors, English as a second language, independent study, internships, off-campus study, part-time degree program, services for LD students, student-designed majors, study abroad, summer session for credit.

Computers: 600 computers/terminals and 3,500 ports are available on campus for general student use. Students can access the following: campus intranet, computer help desk, free student e-mail accounts, online (class) grades, online (class) registration, online (class) schedules. Campuswide network is available. 100% of college-owned or -operated housing units are wired for high-speed Internet access. Wireless service is

available via classrooms, computer centers, computer labs, learning centers, libraries, student centers.
Library: Purchase College Library.

STUDENT LIFE
Housing options: coed. Campus housing is university owned. Freshman applicants given priority for college housing.

Activities and organizations: drama/theater group, student-run newspaper, radio and television station, choral group, Student Union, WPUR radio station, Latinos Unidos, Gay/Lesbian/Bisexual/Transgender Union, Organization of African People in America.

Athletics Member NCAA. All Division III. ***Intercollegiate sports:*** baseball M, basketball M/W, cross-country running M/W, golf M, lacrosse M/W, soccer M/W, softball W, swimming and diving M/W, tennis M/W, volleyball M/W. ***Intramural sports:*** badminton M/W, basketball M/W, bowling M/W, cross-country running M/W, fencing M/W, football M/W, golf M/W, racquetball M/W, skiing (cross-country) M/W, skiing (downhill) M/W, soccer M/W, softball M/W, squash M/W, swimming and diving M/W, table tennis M/W, tennis M/W, volleyball M/W, water polo M/W, weight lifting M/W.

Campus security: 24-hour emergency response devices and patrols, late-night transport/escort service, controlled dormitory access, 24-hour patrols by police officers.

Student services: health clinic, personal/psychological counseling, women's center, legal services.

COSTS & FINANCIAL AID
Costs (2017–18) ***One-time required fee:*** $210. ***Tuition:*** state resident $6470 full-time, $270 per credit part-time; nonresident $16,320 full-time, $680 per credit part-time. Full-time tuition and fees vary according to program. Part-time tuition and fees vary according to course load and program. ***Required fees:*** $1828 full-time, $75 per credit part-time. ***Room and board:*** $12,952; room only: $8442. Room and board charges vary according to board plan and housing facility. ***Payment plan:*** installment. ***Waivers:*** employees or children of employees.

Financial Aid Of all full-time matriculated undergraduates who enrolled in 2016, 2,879 applied for aid, 2,214 were judged to have need, 14 had their need fully met. In 2016, 418 non-need-based awards were made. ***Average percent of need met:*** 49. ***Average financial aid package:*** $10,029. ***Average need-based loan:*** $4453. ***Average need-based gift aid:*** $9724. ***Average non-need-based aid:*** $2174. ***Average indebtedness upon graduation:*** $31,188.

APPLYING
Standardized Tests *Required:* SAT or ACT (for admission). *Recommended:* SAT (for admission).

Options: electronic application, early admission, early action, deferred entrance.

Application fee: $50.

Required: high school transcript, minimum 3.0 GPA. ***Required for some:*** essay or personal statement, 1 letter of recommendation, interview, audition, portfolio.

Application deadlines: 7/15 (freshmen), rolling (transfers), 11/15 (early action).

Notification: continuous until 5/1 (freshmen), continuous (transfers), 12/15 (early action).

CONTACT
Stephanie McCaine, Director of Admissions, Purchase College, State University of New York, 735 Anderson Hill Road, Purchase, NY 10577-1400. *Phone:* 914-251-6300. *Fax:* 914-251-6314. *E-mail:* admission@purchase.edu.

Queens College of the City University of New York

Queens, New York

http://www.qc.cuny.edu/

- **State and locally supported** comprehensive, founded 1937, part of City University of New York
- **Urban** 80-acre campus with easy access to New York City
- **Endowment** $50.4 million
- **Coed** 16,326 undergraduate students, 72% full-time, 55% women, 45% men
- **Very difficult** entrance level, 41% of applicants were admitted

UNDERGRAD STUDENTS
11,693 full-time, 4,633 part-time. Students come from 28 states and territories; 144 other countries; 2% are from out of state; 10% Black or African American, non-Hispanic/Latino; 20% Hispanic/Latino; 31% Asian, non-Hispanic/Latino; 0.3% American Indian or Alaska Native, non-Hispanic/Latino; 5% international; 16% transferred in; 2% live on campus.

Freshmen:
Admission: 18,142 applied, 7,499 admitted, 1,481 enrolled. ***Average high school GPA:*** 3.5. ***Test scores:*** SAT critical reading scores over 500: 63%; SAT math scores over 500: 87%; SAT writing scores over 500: 51%; SAT critical reading scores over 600: 17%; SAT math scores over 600: 33%; SAT writing scores over 600: 11%; SAT critical reading scores over 700: 3%; SAT math scores over 700: 7%; SAT writing scores over 700: 2%.
Retention: 84% of full-time freshmen returned.

FACULTY
Total: 1,560, 39% full-time, 49% with terminal degrees.
Student/faculty ratio: 14:1.

ACADEMICS
Calendar: semesters. *Degrees:* bachelor's, master's, post-master's, and postbachelor's certificates.

Special study options: accelerated degree program, adult/continuing education programs, advanced placement credit, cooperative education, double majors, English as a second language, honors programs, independent study, internships, off-campus study, part-time degree program, services for LD students, study abroad, summer session for credit. ***ROTC:*** Army (c), Air Force (c).

Unusual degree programs: biology, chemistry, computer science, history, music, philosophy, physics, political science, and urban studies, accounting, physics/photonics.

Computers: 2,448 computers/terminals are available on campus for general student use. Students can access the following: campus intranet, computer help desk, free student e-mail accounts, online (class) grades, online (class) registration, online (class) schedules. Campuswide network is available. 100% of college-owned or -operated housing units are wired for high-speed Internet access. Wireless service is available via entire campus.

Library: The Benjamin S. Rosenthal Library plus 1 other. *Books:* 1.1 million (physical), 341,721 (digital/electronic); *Serial titles:* 303 (physical), 123,332 (digital/electronic); *Databases:* 274. Weekly public service hours: 90; students can reserve study rooms.

STUDENT LIFE
Housing options: coed. Campus housing is university owned.

Activities and organizations: drama/theater group, student-run newspaper, radio station, choral group, Science Fiction and Animation, Chabad of QC, La Tertulia, PRISM: The Sexuality and Gender Alliance of QC, Muslim Students Association, national fraternities, national sororities.

Athletics Member NCAA. All Division II. ***Intercollegiate sports:*** baseball M(s), basketball M(s)/W(s), cross-country running M(s)/W(s), fencing W(s), lacrosse W(s), soccer M(s)/W(s), softball W(s), swimming and diving M(s)/W(s), tennis M(s)/W(s), track and field M(s)/W(s), volleyball W(s). ***Intramural sports:*** badminton M(c)/W(c), basketball M/W, cross-country running M(c)/W(c), football M/W, soccer M/W, swimming and diving M(c)/W(c), tennis M(c)/W(c), track and field M/W, ultimate Frisbee M(c)/W(c), volleyball M/W.

Campus security: 24-hour emergency response devices and patrols, controlled dormitory access.

Student services: health clinic, personal/psychological counseling.

COSTS & FINANCIAL AID

Costs (2017–18) ***Tuition:*** state resident $6330 full-time, $275 per credit part-time; nonresident $16,800 full-time, $560 per credit part-time. Full-time tuition and fees vary according to course load. Part-time tuition and fees vary according to course load. ***Required fees:*** $608 full-time, $209 per term part-time. ***Room and board:*** $14,370; room only: $12,020. Room and board charges vary according to board plan and housing facility. ***Payment plan:*** installment. ***Waivers:*** senior citizens and employees or children of employees.

Financial Aid Of all full-time matriculated undergraduates who enrolled in 2015, 8,000 applied for aid, 7,000 were judged to have need, 6,056 had their need fully met. 1,881 Federal Work-Study jobs (averaging $2000). In 2015, 209 non-need-based awards were made. ***Average percent of need met:*** 95. ***Average financial aid package:*** $6808. ***Average need-based loan:*** $5267. ***Average need-based gift aid:*** $4379. ***Average non-need-based aid:*** $7800. ***Average indebtedness upon graduation:*** $5204.

APPLYING

Standardized Tests *Required:* SAT or ACT (for admission). *Required for some:* SAT Subject Tests (for admission). *Recommended:* SAT Subject Tests (for admission).

Options: electronic application, deferred entrance.

Application fee: $65.

Required: high school transcript, minimum 3.0 GPA. ***Required for some:*** essay or personal statement.

Application deadlines: 2/1 (freshmen), 2/1 (transfers).

Notification: 2/1 (freshmen), continuous (transfers).

CONTACT

Ms. Chelsea Lavington, Director of Undergraduate Admissions, Queens College of the City University of New York, 65-30 Kissena Boulevard, Queens, NY 11367. *Phone:* 718-997-5600. *Fax:* 718-997-5617.

Rabbinical Academy Mesivta Rabbi Chaim Berlin

Brooklyn, New York

CONTACT

Executive Administrator, Rabbinical Academy Mesivta Rabbi Chaim Berlin, 1605 Coney Island Avenue, Brooklyn, NY 11230-4715. *Phone:* 718-377-0777. *Fax:* 718-338-5578.

Rabbinical College Beth Shraga

Monsey, New York

CONTACT

Rabbi Sydney Schiff, Director of Admissions, Rabbinical College Beth Shraga, 28 Saddle River Road, Monsey, NY 10952-3035.

Rabbinical College Bobover Yeshiva B'nei Zion

Brooklyn, New York

CONTACT

Director of Admissions, Rabbinical College Bobover Yeshiva B'nei Zion, 1577 Forty-eighth Street, Brooklyn, NY 11219. *Phone:* 718-438-2018.

Rabbinical College Ch'san Sofer

Brooklyn, New York

CONTACT

Director of Admissions, Rabbinical College Ch'san Sofer, 1876 Fiftieth Street, Brooklyn, NY 11204. *Phone:* 718-236-1171.

Rabbinical College of Long Island

Long Beach, New York

CONTACT

Director of Admissions, Rabbinical College of Long Island, 205 West Beech Street, Long Beach, NY 11561-3305. *Phone:* 516-431-7414.

Rabbinical College of Ohr Shimon Yisroel

Brooklyn, New York

CONTACT

Rabbinical College of Ohr Shimon Yisroel, 215-217 Hewes Street, Brooklyn, NY 11211.

Rabbinical Seminary of America

Flushing, New York

CONTACT

Rabbi Abraham Semmel, Director of Admissions, Rabbinical Seminary of America, 76-01 147th Street, Flushing, NY 11367. *Phone:* 718-268-4700.

Rensselaer Polytechnic Institute

Troy, New York

http://www.rpi.edu/

- **Independent** university, founded 1824
- **Suburban** 284-acre campus with easy access to Albany, NY
- **Endowment** $673.7 million
- **Coed** 6,265 undergraduate students, 100% full-time, 32% women, 68% men
- **Very difficult** entrance level, 44% of applicants were admitted

UNDERGRAD STUDENTS

6,246 full-time, 19 part-time. Students come from 48 states and territories; 41 other countries; 66% are from out of state; 3% Black or African American, non-Hispanic/Latino; 9% Hispanic/Latino; 11% Asian, non-Hispanic/Latino; 0.1% American Indian or Alaska Native, non-Hispanic/Latino; 7% Two or more races, non-Hispanic/Latino; 2% Race/ethnicity unknown; 11% international; 2% transferred in; 57% live on campus.

Freshmen:

Admission: 18,524 applied, 8,215 admitted, 1,691 enrolled. ***Average high school GPA:*** 3.88. ***Test scores:*** SAT critical reading scores over 500: 98%; SAT math scores over 500: 100%; ACT scores over 18: 100%; SAT critical reading scores over 600: 81%; SAT math scores over 600: 95%; ACT scores over 24: 96%; SAT critical reading scores over 700: 32%; SAT math scores over 700: 62%; ACT scores over 30: 57%.

Retention: 93% of full-time freshmen returned.

FACULTY

Total: 478, 85% full-time, 90% with terminal degrees.

ACADEMICS

Calendar: semesters. *Degrees:* bachelor's, master's, and doctoral.

Special study options: accelerated degree program, adult/continuing education programs, advanced placement credit, cooperative education, double majors, English as a second language, honors programs, independent study, internships, off-campus study, part-time degree program, services for LD students, student-designed majors, study abroad, summer session for credit. ***ROTC:*** Army (b), Navy (b), Air Force (b).

Unusual degree programs: 3-2 engineering.

Computers: Students can access the following: campus intranet, computer help desk, free student e-mail accounts, online (class) grades, online (class) registration, online (class) schedules, billing, downloadable software, webpages. Campuswide network is available. 100% of college-owned or -operated housing units are wired for high-speed Internet access. Wireless service is available via entire campus.

Library: Folsom Library plus 2 others. Students can reserve study rooms.

STUDENT LIFE
Housing options: on-campus residence required through sophomore year; coed, special housing for students with disabilities. Campus housing is university owned. Freshman campus housing is guaranteed.

Activities and organizations: drama/theater group, student-run newspaper, radio and television station, choral group, Red Army Spirit Club, Outing Club, Indian Student Association, Chinese American Student Association, pep band, national fraternities, national sororities.

Athletics Member NCAA. All Division III except men's and women's ice hockey (Division I). ***Intercollegiate sports:*** archery M(c)/W(c), badminton M(c)/W(c), baseball M/W(c), basketball M/W, crew M(c)/W(c), cross-country running M/W, equestrian sports M(c)/W(c), fencing M(c)/W(c), field hockey W, football M, golf M, ice hockey M(s)/W(s), lacrosse M/W, racquetball M(c)/W(c), riflery M(c)/W(c), rugby M(c)/W(c), sailing M(c)/W(c), skiing (cross-country) M(c)/W(c), soccer M/W, softball W, squash M(c)/W(c), swimming and diving M/W, table tennis M(c)/W(c), tennis M/W, track and field M/W, ultimate Frisbee M(c)/W(c), volleyball M(c)/W(c), water polo M(c)/W(c), weight lifting M(c)/W(c). ***Intramural sports:*** basketball M/W, bowling M(c)/W(c), cheerleading W, ice hockey M/W, lacrosse M(c), racquetball M/W, rock climbing M(c)/W(c), skiing (downhill) M/W, soccer M/W, softball M/W, swimming and diving M(c)/W(c), table tennis M/W, tennis M(c)/W(c), ultimate Frisbee M/W, volleyball M/W, wrestling M.

Campus security: 24-hour emergency response devices and patrols, late-night transport/escort service, controlled dormitory access, campus foot patrols at night.

Student services: health clinic, personal/psychological counseling, women's center, legal services.

COSTS & FINANCIAL AID
Costs (2017–18) ***Comprehensive fee:*** $67,265 includes full-time tuition ($51,000), mandatory fees ($1305), and room and board ($14,960). Part-time tuition: $1595 per credit hour. ***College room only:*** $8480. Room and board charges vary according to board plan and location. ***Payment plan:*** installment. ***Waivers:*** employees or children of employees.

Financial Aid Of all full-time matriculated undergraduates who enrolled in 2016, 4,239 applied for aid, 3,760 were judged to have need, 725 had their need fully met. 795 Federal Work-Study jobs (averaging $1983). In 2016, 1631 non-need-based awards were made. ***Average percent of need met:*** 80. ***Average financial aid package:*** $38,742. ***Average need-based loan:*** $5398. ***Average need-based gift aid:*** $33,119. ***Average non-need-based aid:*** $17,920.

APPLYING
Standardized Tests *Required:* SAT or ACT (for admission). *Required for some:* SAT and SAT Subject Tests or ACT (for admission).

Options: electronic application, early admission, early decision, deferred entrance.

Application fee: $70.

Required for some: essay or personal statement, high school transcript, interview, portfolio for electronic arts. ***Recommended:*** minimum 3.0 GPA, 1 letter of recommendation.

Early decision deadline: 11/1 (for plan 1), 12/15 (for plan 2).

Notification: 3/12 (freshmen), continuous (transfers), 12/10 (early decision plan 1), 1/14 (early decision plan 2).

CONTACT
Ms. Karen Long, Director, Undergrad Admissions, Rensselaer Polytechnic Institute, 110 8th Street, Troy, NY 12180. *Phone:* 518-276-6216. *Fax:* 518-276-4072. *E-mail:* admissions@rpi.edu.

Roberts Wesleyan College

Rochester, New York

http://www.roberts.edu/

- **Independent** comprehensive, founded 1866, affiliated with Free Methodist Church of North America
- **Suburban** 188-acre campus with easy access to Rochester
- **Endowment** $24.2 million
- **Coed** 1,316 undergraduate students, 92% full-time, 69% women, 31% men
- **Moderately difficult** entrance level, 65% of applicants were admitted

UNDERGRAD STUDENTS
1,207 full-time, 109 part-time. Students come from 24 states and territories; 29 other countries; 15% are from out of state; 10% Black or African American, non-Hispanic/Latino; 5% Hispanic/Latino; 2% Asian, non-Hispanic/Latino; 0.1% American Indian or Alaska Native, non-Hispanic/Latino; 4% Two or more races, non-Hispanic/Latino; 2% Race/ethnicity unknown; 4% international; 7% transferred in; 65% live on campus.

Freshmen:
Admission: 1,270 applied, 822 admitted, 227 enrolled. ***Average high school GPA:*** 3.51. ***Test scores:*** SAT critical reading scores over 500: 65%; SAT math scores over 500: 69%; SAT writing scores over 500: 51%; ACT scores over 18: 96%; SAT critical reading scores over 600: 17%; SAT math scores over 600: 23%; SAT writing scores over 600: 16%; ACT scores over 24: 47%; SAT critical reading scores over 700: 5%; SAT math scores over 700: 2%; SAT writing scores over 700: 2%; ACT scores over 30: 14%.

Retention: 76% of full-time freshmen returned.

FACULTY
Total: 259, 37% full-time, 35% with terminal degrees.

Student/faculty ratio: 11:1.

ACADEMICS
Calendar: semesters. *Degrees:* bachelor's and master's.

Special study options: academic remediation for entering students, accelerated degree program, adult/continuing education programs, advanced placement credit, cooperative education, distance learning, double majors, English as a second language, honors programs, independent study, internships, off-campus study, services for LD students, student-designed majors, study abroad, summer session for credit. ***ROTC:*** Army (c), Air Force (c).

Unusual degree programs: 3-2 engineering with Clarkson University, Rensselaer Polytechnic Institute, Rochester Institute of Technology.

Computers: 140 computers/terminals are available on campus for general student use. Students can access the following: campus intranet, computer help desk, free student e-mail accounts, online (class) grades, online (class) registration, online (class) schedules. Campuswide network is available. 100% of college-owned or -operated housing units are wired for high-speed Internet access. Wireless service is available via entire campus.

Library: B. Thomas Golisano Library. *Books:* 128,708 (physical), 6,200 (digital/electronic); *Databases:* 105. Study areas open 24 hours, 5-7 days a week; students can reserve study rooms.

STUDENT LIFE
Housing options: on-campus residence required through senior year; men-only, women-only. Campus housing is university owned. Freshman campus housing is guaranteed.

Activities and organizations: drama/theater group, student-run newspaper, choral group, Intramurals, Foot of the Cross, Fellowship of Christian Athletes, Nursing Club, Drama Club.

Athletics Member NCAA, NCCAA. All NCAA Division II. ***Intercollegiate sports:*** basketball M(s)/W(s), bowling W(s), cheerleading M(c)/W(c), cross-country running M(s)/W(s), golf M(s), lacrosse M(s)/W(s), soccer M(s)/W(s), swimming and diving M(s)/W(s), tennis M(s)/W(s), track and field M(s)/W(s), volleyball W(s). ***Intramural sports:*** basketball M/W, field hockey M/W, football M/W, racquetball M/W, skiing (downhill) M/W, soccer M/W, softball M/W, swimming and diving M/W, table tennis M/W, tennis M/W, ultimate Frisbee M/W, volleyball M/W, water polo M/W.

Campus security: 24-hour emergency response devices and patrols, student patrols, late-night transport/escort service, controlled dormitory access, 24-hour Resident Life staff on-call.

Student services: health clinic, personal/psychological counseling.

COSTS & FINANCIAL AID
Costs (2017–18) ***Comprehensive fee:*** $41,116 includes full-time tuition ($29,600), mandatory fees ($1086), and room and board ($10,430). Part-time tuition and fees vary according to course load. ***College room only:*** $6548. Room and board charges vary according to board plan and housing facility. ***Payment plan:*** installment. ***Waivers:*** senior citizens and employees or children of employees.

Financial Aid Of all full-time matriculated undergraduates who enrolled in 2016, 1,082 applied for aid, 1,023 were judged to have need, 129 had their need fully met. 646 Federal Work-Study jobs (averaging $447). 41 state and other part-time jobs (averaging $1878). In 2016, 175 non-need-based awards were made. ***Average percent of need met:*** 70. ***Average financial aid package:*** $21,746. ***Average need-based loan:*** $5387. ***Average need-based gift aid:*** $16,755. ***Average non-need-based aid:*** $10,221. ***Average indebtedness upon graduation:*** $34,679.

APPLYING

Standardized Tests *Required:* SAT or ACT (for admission).

Options: electronic application, deferred entrance.

Required: essay or personal statement, high school transcript. ***Recommended:*** minimum 2.7 GPA, interview.

Application deadlines: rolling (freshmen), rolling (transfers).

Notification: continuous (freshmen), continuous (transfers).

CONTACT

Mr. J. P. Anderson, Associate Vice President of Undergraduate Admissions, Roberts Wesleyan College, 2301 Westside Drive, Rochester, NY 14624-1997. *Phone:* 585-594-6400. *Toll-free phone:* 800-777-4RWC. *Fax:* 585-594-6371. *E-mail:* admissions@roberts.edu.

Rochester Institute of Technology

Rochester, New York

http://www.rit.edu/

- **Independent** comprehensive, founded 1829
- **Suburban** 1300-acre campus with easy access to Rochester
- **Endowment** $750.9 million
- **Coed** 13,384 undergraduate students, 92% full-time, 33% women, 67% men
- **Moderately difficult** entrance level, 55% of applicants were admitted

UNDERGRAD STUDENTS

12,253 full-time, 1,131 part-time. Students come from 52 states and territories; 97 other countries; 46% are from out of state; 5% Black or African American, non-Hispanic/Latino; 7% Hispanic/Latino; 8% Asian, non-Hispanic/Latino; 0.2% American Indian or Alaska Native, non-Hispanic/Latino; 3% Two or more races, non-Hispanic/Latino; 77% Race/ethnicity unknown; 6% international; 52% live on campus.

Freshmen:

Admission: 19,824 applied, 10,889 admitted. ***Average high school GPA:*** 3.7. ***Test scores:*** SAT critical reading scores over 500: 92%; SAT math scores over 500: 97%; SAT writing scores over 500: 84%; ACT scores over 18: 100%; SAT critical reading scores over 600: 54%; SAT math scores over 600: 71%; SAT writing scores over 600: 39%; ACT scores over 24: 93%; SAT critical reading scores over 700: 12%; SAT math scores over 700: 20%; SAT writing scores over 700: 4%; ACT scores over 30: 43%.

Retention: 87% of full-time freshmen returned.

FACULTY

Total: 1,464, 70% full-time, 50% with terminal degrees.

Student/faculty ratio: 13:1.

ACADEMICS

Calendar: semesters. *Degrees:* certificates, associate, bachelor's, master's, doctoral, and postbachelor's certificates.

Special study options: accelerated degree program, adult/continuing education programs, advanced placement credit, cooperative education, distance learning, double majors, English as a second language, honors programs, independent study, internships, off-campus study, part-time degree program, services for LD students, student-designed majors, study abroad, summer session for credit. ***ROTC:*** Army (b), Navy (c), Air Force (b).

Computers: 2,500 computers/terminals and 20,000 ports are available on campus for general student use. Students can access the following: campus intranet, computer help desk, free student e-mail accounts, online (class) grades, online (class) registration, student account information. Campuswide network is available. 100% of college-owned or -operated housing units are wired for high-speed Internet access. Wireless service is available via entire campus.

Library: Wallace Memorial Library. *Books:* 429,176 (physical), 240,712 (digital/electronic); *Serial titles:* 58,293 (digital/electronic); *Databases:* 113. Weekly public service hours: 147; study areas open 24 hours, 5-7 days a week; students can reserve study rooms.

STUDENT LIFE
Housing options: on-campus residence required for freshman year; coed, men-only, women-only, special housing for students with disabilities. Campus housing is university owned. Freshman campus housing is guaranteed.

Activities and organizations: drama/theater group, student-run newspaper, radio station, choral group, national fraternities, national sororities.

Athletics Member NCAA. All Division III except men's and women's ice hockey (Division I). ***Intercollegiate sports:*** baseball M, basketball M/W, bowling M(c)/W(c), cheerleading M(c)/W(c), crew M/W, cross-country running M/W, equestrian sports M(c)/W(c), fencing M(c)/W(c), field hockey W(c), ice hockey M/W, lacrosse M/W, skiing (downhill) M(c)/W(c), soccer M/W, softball W, swimming and diving M/W, tennis M/W, track and field M/W, ultimate Frisbee M(c)/W(c), volleyball M(c)/W, water polo M(c)/W(c), wrestling M. ***Intramural sports:*** badminton M/W, basketball M/W, bowling M/W, football M, golf M/W, ice hockey M/W, lacrosse M(c), racquetball M/W, rock climbing M(c)/W(c), soccer M/W, softball M/W, table tennis M/W, tennis M/W, volleyball M/W.

Campus security: 24-hour emergency response devices and patrols, student patrols, late-night transport/escort service, controlled dormitory access.

Student services: health clinic, personal/psychological counseling, women's center, legal services.

COSTS & FINANCIAL AID
Costs (2016–17) ***Comprehensive fee:*** $50,842 includes full-time tuition ($38,024), mandatory fees ($544), and room and board ($12,274). Full-time tuition and fees vary according to course load. Part-time tuition: $1408 per credit hour. Part-time tuition and fees vary according to class time and course load. ***Required fees:*** $69 per term part-time. ***College room only:*** $7162. Room and board charges vary according to board plan and housing facility. ***Payment plans:*** tuition prepayment, installment, deferred payment. ***Waivers:*** employees or children of employees.

Financial Aid Of all full-time matriculated undergraduates who enrolled in 2015, 10,265 applied for aid, 9,220 were judged to have need, 7,440 had their need fully met. In 2015, 2192 non-need-based awards were made. ***Average percent of need met:*** 86. ***Average financial aid package:*** $24,700. ***Average need-based loan:*** $6500. ***Average need-based gift aid:*** $20,000. ***Average non-need-based aid:*** $10,800. ***Average indebtedness upon graduation:*** $38,198.

APPLYING
Standardized Tests *Required:* SAT or ACT (for admission).

Options: electronic application, early admission, early decision, deferred entrance.

Application fee: $60.

Required: essay or personal statement, high school transcript. ***Required for some:*** portfolio of original artwork for School of Art, Design and Crafts; interview for BS/MS physician assistant program. ***Recommended:*** minimum 3.4 GPA, 1 letter of recommendation, interview.

Early decision deadline: 11/15.

Notification: continuous until 2/15 (freshmen), continuous (transfers), 12/15 (early decision).

CONTACT
Dr. Daniel Shelley, Associate Vice President, Rochester Institute of Technology, 60 Lomb Memorial Drive, Rochester, NY 14623-5604. *Phone:* 585-475-6631. *Fax:* 585-475-7424. *E-mail:* admissions@rit.edu.

See previous page for display ad and page 1484 for the College Close-Up.

The Sage Colleges
Troy, New York
http://www.sage.edu/

- **Independent** comprehensive
- **Urban** 23-acre campus
- **Endowment** $32.3 million
- **Coed** 1,473 undergraduate students, 87% full-time, 80% women, 20% men
- **Moderately difficult** entrance level, 58% of applicants were admitted

UNDERGRAD STUDENTS
1,278 full-time, 195 part-time. Students come from 21 states and territories; 1 other country; 8% are from out of state; 13% Black or African American, non-Hispanic/Latino; 8% Hispanic/Latino; 4% Asian, non-Hispanic/Latino; 0.1% Native Hawaiian or other Pacific Islander, non-Hispanic/Latino; 0.1% American Indian or Alaska Native, non-Hispanic/Latino; 3% Two or more races, non-Hispanic/Latino; 7% Race/ethnicity unknown; 0.2% international; 12% transferred in; 55% live on campus.

Freshmen:
Admission: 2,117 applied, 1,220 admitted, 206 enrolled. ***Average high school GPA:*** 3.3. ***Test scores:*** SAT critical reading scores over 500: 39%; SAT math scores over 500: 42%; ACT scores over 18: 93%; SAT critical reading scores over 600: 15%; SAT math scores over 600: 8%; ACT scores over 24: 26%.

Retention: 78% of full-time freshmen returned.

FACULTY
Total: 313, 44% full-time, 56% with terminal degrees.
Student/faculty ratio: 11:1.

ACADEMICS
Calendar: semesters. *Degrees:* certificates, bachelor's, master's, doctoral, post-master's, and postbachelor's certificates.

Special study options: academic remediation for entering students, accelerated degree program, adult/continuing education programs, advanced placement credit, cooperative education, distance learning, double majors, honors programs, independent study, internships, off-campus study, part-time degree program, services for LD students, student-designed majors, study abroad, summer session for credit. ***ROTC:*** Army (c), Air Force (c).

Unusual degree programs: 3-2 business administration with Sage Graduate School; engineering with Rensselaer Polytechnic Institute; nursing with Sage Graduate School; occupational therapy and physical therapy with Sage Graduate School, clinical biology with Albany College of Pharmacy.

Computers: 452 computers/terminals are available on campus for general student use. Students can access the following: campus intranet, computer help desk, free student e-mail accounts, online (class) grades, online (class) registration, online (class) schedules. Campuswide network is available. 100% of college-owned or -operated housing units are wired for high-speed Internet access. Wireless service is available via classrooms, computer labs, learning centers, libraries, student centers.

Library: James Wheelock Clark Library plus 1 other. *Books:* 184,209 (physical), 160,067 (digital/electronic); *Serial titles:* 245 (physical), 63,276 (digital/electronic); *Databases:* 105. Weekly public service hours: 91; students can reserve study rooms.

STUDENT LIFE
Housing options: coed, women-only. Campus housing is university owned and leased by the school. Freshman campus housing is guaranteed.

Activities and organizations: drama/theater group, student-run newspaper, choral group, Dance Ensamble, SALANA (African American, Latino, Asian, Native American), BLSA (Black Latino), ASIC (Interior Design), AIGA (Graphic Design).

Athletics Member NCAA. All Division III. ***Intercollegiate sports:*** basketball M/W, cross-country running M/W, golf M, lacrosse W, soccer M/W, softball W, tennis M/W, track and field M/W, volleyball M/W. ***Intramural sports:*** badminton M/W, cheerleading W(c), crew W(c), football M/W, ice hockey M(c)/W(c), lacrosse W(c), skiing (downhill) M(c)/W(c), ultimate Frisbee M(c)/W(c).

Campus security: 24-hour emergency response devices and patrols, late-night transport/escort service, controlled dormitory access.

Student services: health clinic, personal/psychological counseling, women's center.

COSTS & FINANCIAL AID
Costs (2016–17) ***Comprehensive fee:*** $41,213 includes full-time tuition ($27,405), mandatory fees ($1400), and room and board ($12,408). Part-time tuition: $914 per credit hour. ***College room only:*** $6430. Room and board charges vary according to board plan. ***Payment plan:*** installment. ***Waivers:*** employees or children of employees.

Financial Aid Of all full-time matriculated undergraduates who enrolled in 2016, 1,243 applied for aid, 1,167 were judged to have need. In 2016, 76 non-need-based awards were made. ***Average need-based loan:*** $4573. ***Average need-based gift aid:*** $13,925. ***Average non-need-based aid:*** $11,274. ***Average indebtedness upon graduation:*** $31,699.

APPLYING

Standardized Tests *Required for some:* SAT or ACT (for admission).

Options: electronic application, early admission, early action, deferred entrance.

Application fee: $30.

Required: essay or personal statement, high school transcript, minimum 2.5 GPA, 2 letters of recommendation. ***Required for some:*** portfolio for art and design programs. ***Recommended:*** interview.

Application deadlines: rolling (freshmen), rolling (transfers).

Notification: continuous (freshmen), continuous (transfers).

CONTACT

Mr. Thomas Breen, Senior Director of Undergraduate Admission, TSC, The Sage Colleges, 140 New Scotland Avenue, Albany, NY 12208. *Phone:* 518-292-1926. *Fax:* 518-292-1912. *E-mail:* breent@sage.edu.

St. Bonaventure University

St. Bonaventure, New York

http://www.sbu.edu/

- **Independent** comprehensive, founded 1858, affiliated with Roman Catholic Church
- **Small-town** 500-acre campus
- **Coed** 1,660 undergraduate students, 96% full-time, 49% women, 51% men
- **Moderately difficult** entrance level, 66% of applicants were admitted

UNDERGRAD STUDENTS

1,592 full-time, 68 part-time. Students come from 37 states and territories; 16 other countries; 28% are from out of state; 6% Black or African American, non-Hispanic/Latino; 8% Hispanic/Latino; 4% Asian, non-Hispanic/Latino; 0.1% Native Hawaiian or other Pacific Islander, non-Hispanic/Latino; 0.3% American Indian or Alaska Native, non-Hispanic/Latino; 3% Two or more races, non-Hispanic/Latino; 8% Race/ethnicity unknown; 3% international; 3% transferred in; 80% live on campus.

Freshmen:

Admission: 2,871 applied, 1,892 admitted, 433 enrolled. ***Average high school GPA:*** 3.4. ***Test scores:*** SAT critical reading scores over 500: 60%; SAT math scores over 500: 66%; SAT writing scores over 500: 53%; ACT scores over 18: 95%; SAT critical reading scores over 600: 19%; SAT math scores over 600: 23%; SAT writing scores over 600: 15%; ACT scores over 24: 47%; SAT critical reading scores over 700: 2%; SAT math scores over 700: 3%; SAT writing scores over 700: 2%; ACT scores over 30: 12%.

Retention: 82% of full-time freshmen returned.

FACULTY

Total: 239, 53% full-time, 53% with terminal degrees.

Student/faculty ratio: 11:1.

ACADEMICS

Calendar: semesters. *Degrees:* associate, bachelor's, master's, post-master's, and postbachelor's certificates.

Special study options: accelerated degree program, advanced placement credit, distance learning, double majors, honors programs, independent study, internships, off-campus study, part-time degree program, services for LD students, student-designed majors, study abroad, summer session for credit. ***ROTC:*** Army (b).

Unusual degree programs: 3-2 business administration.

Computers: 300 computers/terminals and 2,500 ports are available on campus for general student use. Students can access the following: campus intranet, computer help desk, free student e-mail accounts, online (class) grades, online (class) registration, online (class) schedules. Campuswide network is available. 100% of college-owned or -operated housing units are wired for high-speed Internet access. Wireless service is available via entire campus.

Library: Friedsam Memorial Library. *Books:* 369,279 (physical), 1.6 million (digital/electronic); *Serial titles:* 253 (physical), 269,989 (digital/electronic); *Databases:* 64. Weekly public service hours: 109; students can reserve study rooms.

STUDENT LIFE

Housing options: on-campus residence required through junior year; coed, special housing for students with disabilities. Campus housing is university owned. Freshman campus housing is guaranteed.

Activities and organizations: drama/theater group, student-run newspaper, radio and television station, choral group, Student Government Association, Bona Responds, BV newspaper, Students for the Mountain, Student Ambassadors.

Athletics Member NCAA. All Division I. ***Intercollegiate sports:*** baseball M(s), basketball M(s)/W(s), cross-country running M(s)/W(s), field hockey W(c), golf M(s), gymnastics W(c), ice hockey M(c), lacrosse M(c)/W(s), rugby M(c)/W(c), soccer M(s)/W(s), softball W(s), swimming and diving M(s)/W(s), tennis M(s)/W(s), track and field M/W. ***Intramural sports:*** baseball M(c), basketball M(c)/W(c), field hockey W, football M/W, golf M/W, ice hockey M(c)/W(c), lacrosse M(c)/W(c), rugby M(c)/W(c), skiing (downhill) M/W, soccer M(c)/W(c), softball M/W(c), tennis M/W, ultimate Frisbee M/W, volleyball M(c)/W(c).

Campus security: 24-hour emergency response devices and patrols, late-night transport/escort service, controlled dormitory access.

Student services: health clinic, personal/psychological counseling.

COSTS & FINANCIAL AID

Costs (2016–17) ***One-time required fee:*** $100. ***Comprehensive fee:*** $43,804 includes full-time tuition ($31,366), mandatory fees ($965), and room and board ($11,473). Part-time tuition and fees vary according to course load. ***Required fees:*** $934 per credit hour part-time. ***College room only:*** $6048. Room and board charges vary according to board plan and housing facility. ***Waivers:*** senior citizens and employees or children of employees.

Financial Aid Of all full-time matriculated undergraduates who enrolled in 2015, 1,402 applied for aid, 1,216 were judged to have need, 272 had their need fully met. 305 Federal Work-Study jobs (averaging $898). 362 state and other part-time jobs (averaging $904). In 2015, 418 non-need-based awards were made. ***Average percent of need met:*** 87. ***Average financial aid package:*** $24,764. ***Average need-based loan:*** $4598. ***Average need-based gift aid:*** $20,750. ***Average non-need-based aid:*** $12,440. ***Average indebtedness upon graduation:*** $36,649.

APPLYING

Standardized Tests *Required:* SAT or ACT (for admission). *Required for some:* SAT and SAT Subject Tests or ACT (for admission).

Options: electronic application, deferred entrance.

Required: high school transcript, 1 letter of recommendation. ***Required for some:*** essay or personal statement. ***Recommended:*** essay or personal statement, minimum 3.0 GPA, 3 letters of recommendation, interview.

Application deadlines: 7/1 (freshmen), 8/15 (transfers).

Notification: continuous until 10/15 (freshmen), continuous until 10/1 (transfers).

CONTACT

Mr. Bernard Valento, Vice President for Enrollment, St. Bonaventure University, 3261 West State Road, St. Bonaventure, NY 14778. *Phone:* 716-375-2400. *Toll-free phone:* 800-462-5050. *Fax:* 716-375-4005. *E-mail:* bvalento@sbu.edu.

St. Francis College

Brooklyn Heights, New York

http://www.sfc.edu/

- **Independent Roman Catholic** comprehensive, founded 1884
- **Urban** 1-acre campus with easy access to New York City
- **Endowment** $74.7 million
- **Coed**

FACULTY

Student/faculty ratio: 17:1.

ACADEMICS

Calendar: semesters. *Degrees:* associate, bachelor's, master's, and postbachelor's certificates.

Library: McCardle Student Library.

STUDENT LIFE

Housing options: cooperative. Campus housing is provided by a third party.

Activities and organizations: drama/theater group, student-run newspaper, radio station, choral group, Latin American Society, Fine Arts Society, Power Lifting Club, Games Club, Haitian American Students Alliance, national fraternities, national sororities.

Athletics Member NCAA. All Division I.

Campus security: ID checks, crime awareness workshops, pamphlets, posters, films, emergency notification system.

Student services: personal/psychological counseling.

FINANCIAL AID

Financial Aid Of all full-time matriculated undergraduates who enrolled in 2014, 1,917 applied for aid, 1,765 were judged to have need, 189 had their need fully met. 125 Federal Work-Study jobs (averaging $2000). In 2014, 482 non-need-based awards were made. ***Average percent of need met:*** 61. ***Average financial aid package:*** $14,255. ***Average need-based loan:*** $4170. ***Average need-based gift aid:*** $10,675. ***Average non-need-based aid:*** $9300. ***Average indebtedness upon graduation:*** $23,835.

APPLYING

Standardized Tests *Required:* SAT (for admission).

Required: essay or personal statement, high school transcript, minimum 2.0 GPA, 1 letter of recommendation. ***Recommended:*** interview.

CONTACT

Mrs. Lisa Randazzo, Associate Director of Admissions, St. Francis College, 180 Remsen Street, Brooklyn Heights, NY 11201-4398. *Phone:* 718-489-5336. *Fax:* 718-802-0453. *E-mail:* lrandazzo@sfc.edu.

St. John Fisher College

Rochester, New York

http://www.sjfc.edu/

- **Independent** comprehensive, founded 1948, affiliated with Roman Catholic Church
- **Suburban** 154-acre campus
- **Endowment** $73.8 million
- **Coed** 2,786 undergraduate students, 94% full-time, 60% women, 40% men
- **Moderately difficult** entrance level, 65% of applicants were admitted

UNDERGRAD STUDENTS

2,607 full-time, 179 part-time. Students come from 18 states and territories; 2 other countries; 3% are from out of state; 4% Black or African American, non-Hispanic/Latino; 4% Hispanic/Latino; 4% Asian, non-Hispanic/Latino; 0.1% Native Hawaiian or other Pacific Islander, non-Hispanic/Latino; 0.3% American Indian or Alaska Native, non-Hispanic/Latino; 2% Two or more races, non-Hispanic/Latino; 2% Race/ethnicity unknown; 0.1% international; 7% transferred in; 50% live on campus.

Freshmen:

Admission: 4,551 applied, 2,937 admitted, 576 enrolled. ***Average high school GPA:*** 3.5. ***Test scores:*** SAT critical reading scores over 500: 66%; SAT math scores over 500: 75%; SAT writing scores over 500: 52%; ACT scores over 18: 97%; SAT critical reading scores over 600: 15%; SAT math scores over 600: 21%; SAT writing scores over 600: 10%; ACT scores over 24: 51%; SAT critical reading scores over 700: 1%; SAT math scores over 700: 1%; SAT writing scores over 700: 1%; ACT scores over 30: 7%.

Retention: 84% of full-time freshmen returned.

FACULTY

Total: 451, 53% full-time, 47% with terminal degrees.

Student/faculty ratio: 11:1.

ACADEMICS

Calendar: semesters. *Degrees:* certificates, bachelor's, master's, doctoral, post-master's, and postbachelor's certificates.

Special study options: accelerated degree program, adult/continuing education programs, advanced placement credit, distance learning, double majors, honors programs, independent study, internships, off-campus study, part-time degree program, services for LD students, student-designed majors, study abroad, summer session for credit. ***ROTC:*** Army (c), Navy (c), Air Force (c).

Unusual degree programs: 3-2 engineering with Columbia University, Rensselaer Polytechnic Institute, University of Rochester.

Computers: 550 computers/terminals and 1,875 ports are available on campus for general student use. Students can access the following: campus intranet, computer help desk, free student e-mail accounts, online (class) grades, online (class) registration, online (class) schedules. Campuswide network is available. 100% of college-owned or -operated housing units are wired for high-speed Internet access. Wireless service is available via entire campus.

Library: Charles J. Lavery Library plus 1 other. *Books:* 162,694 (physical), 137,162 (digital/electronic); *Databases:* 197. Students can reserve study rooms.

STUDENT LIFE

Housing options: coed, women-only, special housing for students with disabilities. Campus housing is university owned. Freshman campus housing is guaranteed.

Activities and organizations: drama/theater group, student-run newspaper, television station, choral group, Student Government, Student Activities Board, Commuter Council, Resident Student Association, Teddi Dance for Love.

Athletics Member NCAA. All Division III. ***Intercollegiate sports:*** baseball M, basketball M/W, crew W, cross-country running M/W, field hockey W, football M, golf M/W, lacrosse M/W, soccer M/W, softball W, tennis M/W, track and field M/W, volleyball M/W. ***Intramural sports:*** basketball M/W, cheerleading W(c), crew M(c), equestrian sports M(c)/W(c), ice hockey M(c)/W(c), rugby M(c)/W(c), soccer M/W, volleyball M.

Campus security: 24-hour emergency response devices and patrols, late-night transport/escort service, controlled dormitory access.

Student services: health clinic, personal/psychological counseling.

COSTS & FINANCIAL AID

Costs (2017–18) ***Comprehensive fee:*** $45,270 includes full-time tuition ($32,540), mandatory fees ($580), and room and board ($12,150). Full-time tuition and fees vary according to program. Part-time tuition: $885 per credit hour. Part-time tuition and fees vary according to course load and program. ***Required fees:*** $10 per credit hour part-time. ***College room only:*** $7780. Room and board charges vary according to board plan. ***Payment plans:*** installment, deferred payment. ***Waivers:*** employees or children of employees.

Financial Aid Of all full-time matriculated undergraduates who enrolled in 2016, 2,331 applied for aid, 2,118 were judged to have need, 779 had their need fully met. 1,238 Federal Work-Study jobs (averaging $1283). In 2016, 480 non-need-based awards were made. ***Average percent of need met:*** 70. ***Average financial aid package:*** $22,202. ***Average need-based loan:*** $4925. ***Average need-based gift aid:*** $17,370. ***Average non-need-based aid:*** $11,112. ***Average indebtedness upon graduation:*** $35,925.

APPLYING

Standardized Tests *Required:* SAT or ACT (for admission).

Options: electronic application, early decision, deferred entrance.

Required: essay or personal statement, high school transcript, minimum 3.0 GPA, 1 letter of recommendation. ***Recommended:*** interview.

Application deadlines: rolling (freshmen), rolling (transfers).

Early decision deadline: 12/1.

Notification: continuous until 12/1 (freshmen), continuous until 9/1 (transfers), 12/15 (early decision).

CONTACT

Mrs. Stacy A. Ledermann, Director of Freshmen Admissions, St. John Fisher College, 3690 East Avenue, Rochester, NY 14618. *Phone:* 585-385-8064. *Toll-free phone:* 800-444-4640. *Fax:* 585-385-8386. *E-mail:* admissions@sjfc.edu.

St. John's University
Queens, New York
http://www.stjohns.edu/

- **Independent** university, founded 1870, affiliated with Roman Catholic Church
- **Urban** 105-acre campus with easy access to New York City
- **Endowment** $685.9 million
- **Coed** 16,210 undergraduate students, 68% full-time, 57% women, 43% men
- **Moderately difficult** entrance level, 65% of applicants were admitted

UNDERGRAD STUDENTS
11,051 full-time, 5,159 part-time. Students come from 47 states and territories; 85 other countries; 29% are from out of state; 14% Black or African American, non-Hispanic/Latino; 13% Hispanic/Latino; 14% Asian, non-Hispanic/Latino; 0.3% Native Hawaiian or other Pacific Islander, non-Hispanic/Latino; 0.2% American Indian or Alaska Native, non-Hispanic/Latino; 4% Two or more races, non-Hispanic/Latino; 9% Race/ethnicity unknown; 4% international; 2% transferred in; 29% live on campus.

Freshmen:
Admission: 36,105 applied, 23,431 admitted, 3,253 enrolled. ***Average high school GPA:*** 3.49. ***Test scores:*** SAT critical reading scores over 500: 68%; SAT math scores over 500: 70%; ACT scores over 18: 99%; SAT critical reading scores over 600: 20%; SAT math scores over 600: 27%; ACT scores over 24: 58%; SAT critical reading scores over 700: 3%; SAT math scores over 700: 5%; ACT scores over 30: 13%.
Retention: 80% of full-time freshmen returned.

FACULTY
Total: 1,432, 43% full-time, 55% with terminal degrees.
Student/faculty ratio: 17:1.

ACADEMICS
Calendar: semesters. *Degrees:* certificates, bachelor's, master's, doctoral, post-master's, and postbachelor's certificates.
Special study options: accelerated degree program, adult/continuing education programs, advanced placement credit, distance learning, double majors, English as a second language, honors programs, independent study, internships, off-campus study, part-time degree program, services for LD students, study abroad, summer session for credit. ***ROTC:*** Army (b).
Unusual degree programs: 3-2 engineering with Manhattan College.
Computers: 12,124 computers/terminals and 400 ports are available on campus for general student use. Students can access the following: campus intranet, computer help desk, free student e-mail accounts, online (class) grades, online (class) registration, online (class) schedules. Campuswide network is available. 100% of college-owned or -operated housing units are wired for high-speed Internet access. Wireless service is available via entire campus.
Library: St. John's University Library plus 4 others. *Books:* 815,686 (physical), 603,068 (digital/electronic); *Serial titles:* 7,633 (physical), 95,025 (digital/electronic); *Databases:* 232. Study areas open 24 hours, 5-7 days a week; students can reserve study rooms.

STUDENT LIFE
Housing options: coed. Campus housing is university owned and leased by the school. Freshman applicants given priority for college housing.
Activities and organizations: drama/theater group, student-run newspaper, radio and television station, choral group, Student Government, Incorporated, Haraya (Pan-African Students Coalition), Student Programming Board, American Pharmaceutical Association, Muslim Student Organization, national fraternities, national sororities.
Athletics Member NCAA. All Division I. ***Intercollegiate sports:*** baseball M(s), basketball M(s)/W(s), cross-country running W(s), fencing M(s)/W(s), golf M(s)/W(s), lacrosse M(s), soccer M(s)/W(s), softball W(s), tennis M(s)/W(s), track and field W(s), volleyball W(s). ***Intramural sports:*** badminton M/W, basketball M/W, bowling M(c)/W(c), cheerleading M/W, cross-country running M(c)/W(c), fencing M/W, football M/W, soccer M/W, softball M/W, table tennis M/W, tennis M(c)/W(c), track and field M(c)/W(c), ultimate Frisbee M(c)/W(c), volleyball M/W.
Campus security: 24-hour emergency response devices and patrols, late-night transport/escort service, controlled dormitory access, Emergency Notification System.
Student services: health clinic, personal/psychological counseling.

COSTS & FINANCIAL AID
Costs (2016–17) ***One-time required fee:*** $250. ***Comprehensive fee:*** $55,850 includes full-time tuition ($38,630), mandatory fees ($830), and room and board ($16,390). Full-time tuition and fees vary according to course load, location, program, and student level. Part-time tuition: $1288 per credit. Part-time tuition and fees vary according to course load, location, program, and student level. ***Required fees:*** $313 per term part-time. ***College room only:*** $10,510. Room and board charges vary according to board plan, housing facility, and location. ***Payment plan:*** installment. ***Waivers:*** adult students, senior citizens, and employees or children of employees.
Financial Aid Of all full-time matriculated undergraduates who enrolled in 2015, 9,419 applied for aid, 8,721 were judged to have need, 1,104 had their need fully met. 816 Federal Work-Study jobs (averaging $2309). In 2015, 634 non-need-based awards were made. ***Average percent of need met:*** 64. ***Average financial aid package:*** $26,295. ***Average need-based loan:*** $4602. ***Average need-based gift aid:*** $9951. ***Average non-need-based aid:*** $17,343. ***Average indebtedness upon graduation:*** $34,234.

APPLYING
Standardized Tests *Required:* SAT or ACT (for admission).
Options: electronic application, early admission, deferred entrance.
Application fee: $50.
Required: high school transcript. ***Required for some:*** essay or personal statement, 2 letters of recommendation, interview. ***Recommended:*** essay or personal statement, minimum 3.0 GPA.
Application deadlines: rolling (freshmen), rolling (out-of-state freshmen), rolling (transfers).
Notification: continuous (freshmen), continuous (out-of-state freshmen), continuous (transfers).

CONTACT
Ms. Samantha R. Wright, Director of Admissions, St. John's University, 8000 Utopia Parkway, Queens, NY 11439. *Phone:* 718-990-2000. *Toll-free phone:* 888-9STJOHNS. *Fax:* 718-990-2096.
E-mail: admission@stjohns.edu.

St. Joseph's College, Long Island Campus
Patchogue, New York
http://www.sjcny.edu/

- **Independent** comprehensive, founded 1916
- **Suburban** 56-acre campus with easy access to New York City
- **Endowment** $20.7 million
- **Coed** 3,075 undergraduate students, 84% full-time, 65% women, 35% men
- **Moderately difficult** entrance level, 72% of applicants were admitted

UNDERGRAD STUDENTS
2,591 full-time, 484 part-time. Students come from 16 states and territories; 9 other countries; 1% are from out of state; 5% Black or African American, non-Hispanic/Latino; 11% Hispanic/Latino; 2% Asian, non-Hispanic/Latino; 0.1% Native Hawaiian or other Pacific Islander, non-Hispanic/Latino; 0.3% American Indian or Alaska Native, non-Hispanic/Latino; 2% Two or more races, non-Hispanic/Latino; 12% Race/ethnicity unknown; 19% transferred in.

Freshmen:
Admission: 1,770 applied, 1,272 admitted, 431 enrolled. ***Average high school GPA:*** 3.6. ***Test scores:*** SAT critical reading scores over 500: 63%; SAT math scores over 500: 68%; SAT writing scores over 500: 52%; ACT scores over 18: 94%; SAT critical reading scores over 600: 13%; SAT math scores over 600: 20%; SAT writing scores over 600: 9%; ACT scores over 24: 46%; SAT critical reading scores over 700: 1%; SAT math scores over 700: 2%; SAT writing scores over 700: 1%; ACT scores over 30: 3%.
Retention: 87% of full-time freshmen returned.

FACULTY
Total: 393, 27% full-time, 38% with terminal degrees.
Student/faculty ratio: 15:1.

ACADEMICS
Calendar: 4-1-4. *Degrees:* certificates, bachelor's, master's, and postbachelor's certificates.
Special study options: accelerated degree program, adult/continuing education programs, advanced placement credit, distance learning, double majors, honors programs, independent study, internships, off-campus study, part-time degree program, services for LD students, study abroad, summer session for credit.
Computers: 265 computers/terminals are available on campus for general student use. Students can access the following: campus intranet, computer help desk, free student e-mail accounts, online (class) grades, online (class) registration, online (class) schedules, learning management system, course evaluations, print management, virtual application labs, office software, student suggestion box. Campuswide network is available. 100% of college-owned or -operated housing units are wired for high-speed Internet access. Wireless service is available via entire campus.
Library: Callahan Library plus 1 other. *Books:* 95,674 (physical), 121,688 (digital/electronic); *Serial titles:* 224 (physical), 60,197 (digital/electronic); *Databases:* 116. Weekly public service hours: 80; students can reserve study rooms.

STUDENT LIFE
Housing options: college housing not available.
Activities and organizations: drama/theater group, student-run newspaper, radio station, choral group, STARS (Students Taking an Active Role in Society), All Greek Life (Alpha Phi Delta and Delta Kappa Epsilon Fraternities), Drama Society, Project Sunshine, SJC Sharps, national fraternities, national sororities.
Athletics Member NCAA. All Division III. ***Intercollegiate sports:*** baseball M, basketball M/W, cross-country running M/W, equestrian sports W(c), golf M, lacrosse M/W, soccer M/W, softball W, swimming and diving W, tennis M/W, track and field M/W, volleyball M/W.
Campus security: 24-hour emergency response devices and patrols, late-night transport/escort service, Emergency Notification System via cell phones, lighted pathways/sidewalks.
Student services: personal/psychological counseling.

COSTS & FINANCIAL AID
Costs (2017–18) ***Tuition:*** $25,930 full-time, $840 per credit part-time. Full-time tuition and fees vary according to course load, location, and program. Part-time tuition and fees vary according to course load, location, and program. ***Payment plan:*** installment. ***Waivers:*** employees or children of employees.
Financial Aid Of all full-time matriculated undergraduates who enrolled in 2015, 2,251 applied for aid, 1,793 were judged to have need, 601 had their need fully met. 105 Federal Work-Study jobs (averaging $2951). 81 state and other part-time jobs (averaging $2884). In 2015, 388 non-need-based awards were made. ***Average percent of need met:*** 63. ***Average financial aid package:*** $13,213. ***Average need-based loan:*** $4285. ***Average need-based gift aid:*** $10,945. ***Average non-need-based aid:*** $8984. ***Average indebtedness upon graduation:*** $27,364.

APPLYING
Standardized Tests *Required:* SAT or ACT (for admission).
Options: electronic application, deferred entrance.
Application fee: $25.
Required: essay or personal statement, high school transcript, minimum 3.0 GPA, 2 letters of recommendation. ***Required for some:*** RN for RN-BSN program. ***Recommended:*** interview.
Application deadlines: rolling (freshmen), rolling (transfers).
Notification: continuous until 11/1 (freshmen), continuous until 11/1 (transfers).

CONTACT
Ms. Gigi Lamens, Vice President for Enrollment Management, St. Joseph's College, Long Island Campus, 155 West Roe Boulevard, Patchogue, NY 11772. *Phone:* 631-687-4500. *E-mail:* glamens@sjcny.edu.

St. Joseph's College, New York
Brooklyn, New York
http://www.sjcny.edu/

- **Independent** comprehensive, founded 1916
- **Urban** 5-acre campus
- **Endowment** $6.2 million
- **Coed** 965 undergraduate students, 82% full-time, 67% women, 33% men
- **Moderately difficult** entrance level, 62% of applicants were admitted

UNDERGRAD STUDENTS
789 full-time, 176 part-time. Students come from 24 states and territories; 34 other countries; 4% are from out of state; 24% Black or African American, non-Hispanic/Latino; 20% Hispanic/Latino; 7% Asian, non-Hispanic/Latino; 0.3% Native Hawaiian or other Pacific Islander, non-Hispanic/Latino; 0.1% American Indian or Alaska Native, non-Hispanic/Latino; 2% Two or more races, non-Hispanic/Latino; 9% Race/ethnicity unknown; 12% transferred in; 5% live on campus.

Freshmen:
Admission: 1,903 applied, 1,181 admitted, 198 enrolled. ***Average high school GPA:*** 3.3. ***Test scores:*** SAT critical reading scores over 500: 33%; SAT math scores over 500: 35%; SAT writing scores over 500: 34%; SAT critical reading scores over 600: 5%; SAT math scores over 600: 7%; SAT writing scores over 600: 6%; SAT critical reading scores over 700: 1%; SAT math scores over 700: 1%; SAT writing scores over 700: 1%.
Retention: 81% of full-time freshmen returned.

FACULTY
Total: 157, 37% full-time, 40% with terminal degrees.
Student/faculty ratio: 11:1.

ACADEMICS
Calendar: semesters. *Degrees:* certificates, bachelor's, master's, and postbachelor's certificates.
Special study options: accelerated degree program, adult/continuing education programs, advanced placement credit, distance learning, double majors, English as a second language, honors programs, independent study, internships, off-campus study, part-time degree program, services for LD students, study abroad, summer session for credit.
Computers: 238 computers/terminals are available on campus for general student use. Students can access the following: campus intranet, computer help desk, free student e-mail accounts, online (class) grades, online (class) registration, online (class) schedules, learning management system, course evaluations, print management, virtual application labs, office software, student suggestion box. Campuswide network is available. 100% of college-owned or -operated housing units are wired for high-speed Internet access. Wireless service is available via entire campus.
Library: McEntegart Hall Library plus 1 other. *Books:* 81,405 (physical), 121,688 (digital/electronic); *Serial titles:* 35 (physical), 60,197 (digital/electronic); *Databases:* 116. Weekly public service hours: 83; students can reserve study rooms.

STUDENT LIFE
Housing options: coed. Campus housing is leased by the school.
Activities and organizations: drama/theater group, student-run newspaper, Campus Activities Board (C.A.B.), Student Senate, Greek Organizations (Alpha Gamma Delta, Alpha Phi Delta, Beta Upsilon Delta), Chapel Players Drama Club, The Spirit Publishing Co., national fraternities, national sororities.
Athletics Member NCAA. All Division III. ***Intercollegiate sports:*** baseball M, basketball M/W, cross-country running M/W, soccer M/W, softball W, swimming and diving M/W, tennis M/W, volleyball M/W. ***Intramural sports:*** basketball W.
Campus security: 24-hour emergency response devices and patrols, late-night transport/escort service, controlled dormitory access, Emergency Notification System via cell phones, lighted pathways/sidewalks.
Student services: health clinic, personal/psychological counseling.

COSTS & FINANCIAL AID
Costs (2017–18) ***Tuition:*** $25,930 full-time, $840 per credit part-time. Full-time tuition and fees vary according to course load and program. Part-time tuition and fees vary according to course load and program. ***Payment plan:*** installment. ***Waivers:*** employees or children of employees.

Financial Aid Of all full-time matriculated undergraduates who enrolled in 2015, 722 applied for aid, 605 were judged to have need, 135 had their need fully met. 93 Federal Work-Study jobs (averaging $2244). 17 state and other part-time jobs (averaging $2401). In 2015, 104 non-need-based awards were made. ***Average percent of need met:*** 65. ***Average financial aid package:*** $16,186. ***Average need-based loan:*** $3747. ***Average need-based gift aid:*** $14,636. ***Average non-need-based aid:*** $10,377. ***Average indebtedness upon graduation:*** $23,124.

APPLYING

Standardized Tests *Required:* SAT or ACT (for admission).

Options: electronic application, early admission, deferred entrance.

Application fee: $25.

Required: essay or personal statement, high school transcript, minimum 2.7 GPA, 1 letter of recommendation. ***Required for some:*** RN license for the RN to BSN Program. ***Recommended:*** interview.

Application deadlines: 8/31 (freshmen), rolling (transfers).

Notification: continuous until 11/1 (freshmen), continuous (transfers).

CONTACT

Ms. Christine Murphy, Vice President for Enrollment Management, St. Joseph's College, New York, 245 Clinton Avenue, Brooklyn, NY 11205. *Phone:* 718-940-5820. *E-mail:* cmurphy@sjcny.edu.

★ St. Lawrence University

Canton, New York

http://www.stlawu.edu/

- **Independent** comprehensive, founded 1856
- **Small-town** 1100-acre campus
- **Endowment** $282.1 million
- **Coed**
- **Moderately difficult** entrance level

FACULTY

Student/faculty ratio: 11:1.

ACADEMICS

Calendar: semesters. *Degrees:* bachelor's, master's, and post-master's certificates.

Library: Owen D. Young Library plus 2 others. *Books:* 1.0 million (physical), 154,251 (digital/electronic); *Serial titles:* 594,400 (physical), 115,421 (digital/electronic); *Databases:* 169. Students can reserve study rooms.

STUDENT LIFE

Housing options: on-campus residence required through senior year; coed, women-only, cooperative. Campus housing is university owned. Freshman campus housing is guaranteed.

Activities and organizations: drama/theater group, student-run newspaper, radio station, choral group, The Thelomathesian Society (student government), Outing Club, Environmental Action Organization, Association for Campus Entertainment, La Sociedad Hispana, national fraternities, national sororities.

Athletics Member NCAA. All Division III except equestrian sports (Division II), men's and women's ice hockey (Division I).

Campus security: 24-hour emergency response devices and patrols, student patrols, late-night transport/escort service, controlled dormitory access.

Student services: health clinic, personal/psychological counseling.

COSTS & FINANCIAL AID

Costs (2016–17) ***Comprehensive fee:*** $64,390 includes full-time tuition ($50,830), mandatory fees ($370), and room and board ($13,190). Part-time tuition: $1765 per credit hour. ***College room only:*** $7104. Room and board charges vary according to board plan. ***Payment plans:*** tuition prepayment, installment.

Financial Aid Of all full-time matriculated undergraduates who enrolled in 2016, 1,719 applied for aid, 1,435 were judged to have need, 402 had their need fully met. 811 Federal Work-Study jobs (averaging $1579). 318 state and other part-time jobs (averaging $1608). In 2016, 785 non-need-based awards were made. ***Average percent of need met:*** 84. ***Average financial aid package:*** $41,517. ***Average need-based loan:*** $4625. ***Average need-based gift aid:*** $34,115. ***Average non-need-based aid:*** $19,174. ***Average indebtedness upon graduation:*** $37,919. ***Financial aid deadline:*** 2/1.

APPLYING

Options: electronic application, early admission, early decision, deferred entrance.

Application fee: $60.

Required: essay or personal statement, high school transcript, 2 letters of recommendation. ***Recommended:*** interview.

CONTACT

Jeremy Freeman, Director of Admissions, St. Lawrence University, 23 Romoda Drive, Canton, NY 13617-1455. *Phone:* 315-229-5261. *Toll-free phone:* 800-285-1856. *Fax:* 315-229-5818. *E-mail:* jfreeman@stlawu.edu.

See next page for display ad and page 1492 for the College Close-Up.

★ St. Thomas Aquinas College

Sparkill, New York

http://www.stac.edu/

- **Independent** comprehensive, founded 1952
- **Suburban** 46-acre campus with easy access to New York City
- **Endowment** $30.6 million
- **Coed** 1,721 undergraduate students, 66% full-time, 56% women, 44% men
- **Moderately difficult** entrance level, 79% of applicants were admitted

UNDERGRAD STUDENTS

1,130 full-time, 591 part-time. Students come from 17 states and territories; 14 other countries; 20% are from out of state; 8% Black or African American, non-Hispanic/Latino; 20% Hispanic/Latino; 3% Asian, non-Hispanic/Latino; 0.2% Native Hawaiian or other Pacific Islander, non-Hispanic/Latino; 0.1% American Indian or Alaska Native, non-Hispanic/Latino; 2% Two or more races, non-Hispanic/Latino; 6% Race/ethnicity unknown; 2% international; 5% transferred in.

Freshmen:

Admission: 1,953 applied, 1,546 admitted, 256 enrolled. ***Average high school GPA:*** 3. ***Test scores:*** SAT critical reading scores over 500: 36%; SAT math scores over 500: 38%; ACT scores over 18: 65%; SAT critical reading scores over 600: 8%; SAT math scores over 600: 9%; ACT scores over 24: 14%; SAT critical reading scores over 700: 1%; SAT math scores over 700: 1%; ACT scores over 30: 2%.

Retention: 74% of full-time freshmen returned.

FACULTY

Total: 162, 38% full-time, 44% with terminal degrees.

Student/faculty ratio: 13:1.

ACADEMICS

Calendar: semesters. *Degrees:* associate, bachelor's, master's, post-master's, and postbachelor's certificates.

Special study options: academic remediation for entering students, accelerated degree program, adult/continuing education programs, advanced placement credit, double majors, freshman honors college, honors programs, independent study, internships, off-campus study, part-time degree program, services for LD students, study abroad, summer session for credit. ***ROTC:*** Air Force (c).

Unusual degree programs: 3-2 engineering with George Washington University, Manhattan College; social work with New York University School of Social Work; physical therapy with New York Medical College.

Computers: 200 computers/terminals are available on campus for general student use. Students can access the following: campus intranet, computer help desk, free student e-mail accounts, online (class) grades, online (class) registration, online (class) schedules. Campuswide network is available. 100% of college-owned or -operated housing units are wired for high-speed Internet access. Wireless service is available via entire campus.

Library: Lougheed Library plus 1 other. *Books:* 50,000 (physical); *Serial titles:* 110 (physical), 75,000 (digital/electronic); *Databases:* 68. Weekly public service hours: 83; students can reserve study rooms.

STUDENT LIFE

Housing options: men-only, women-only, special housing for students with disabilities. Campus housing is university owned. Freshman campus housing is guaranteed.

Activities and organizations: drama/theater group, student-run newspaper, radio station, choral group, Spartan Volunteers, Campus Activities Board, WSTK campus radio, Bowling Club, Laetare Players, national fraternities.

Athletics Member NCAA, NAIA. All NCAA Division II. ***Intercollegiate sports:*** baseball M(s), basketball M(s)/W(s), cross-country running M(s)/W(s), golf M/W, lacrosse W, soccer M(s)/W(s), softball W(s), tennis M/W, volleyball W(s). ***Intramural sports:*** basketball M/W, volleyball M/W.

Campus security: 24-hour emergency response devices and patrols, student patrols, late-night transport/escort service, controlled dormitory access.

Student services: health clinic, personal/psychological counseling.

COSTS & FINANCIAL AID

Costs (2016–17) ***Comprehensive fee:*** $42,190 includes full-time tuition ($28,800), mandatory fees ($1000), and room and board ($12,390). Part-time tuition: $920 per credit. ***Required fees:*** $200 per term part-time. ***College room only:*** $6690. Room and board charges vary according to board plan and housing facility. ***Payment plan:*** installment. ***Waivers:*** employees or children of employees.

Financial Aid Of all full-time matriculated undergraduates who enrolled in 2016, 1,093 applied for aid, 850 were judged to have need, 133 had their need fully met. 124 Federal Work-Study jobs (averaging $1284). In 2016, 222 non-need-based awards were made. ***Average percent of need met:*** 38. ***Average financial aid package:*** $17,100. ***Average need-based loan:*** $4800. ***Average need-based gift aid:*** $10,815. ***Average non-need-based aid:*** $12,375. ***Average indebtedness upon graduation:*** $28,750.

APPLYING

Standardized Tests *Required:* SAT or ACT (for admission).

Options: electronic application, deferred entrance.

Application fee: $30.

Required: high school transcript, minimum 2.0 GPA. ***Required for some:*** 3 letters of recommendation. ***Recommended:*** essay or personal statement, 2 letters of recommendation, interview.

Application deadlines: rolling (freshmen), rolling (transfers).

Notification: continuous (transfers).

CONTACT

Mr. Samantha Bazile, Director of Admissions, St. Thomas Aquinas College, 125 Route 340, Sparkill, NY 10976. *Phone:* 845-398-4104. *Fax:* 845-398-4114. *E-mail:* sbazile@stac.edu.

See page 1500 for the College Close-Up.

Sarah Lawrence College

Bronxville, New York

http://www.sarahlawrence.edu/

- **Independent** comprehensive, founded 1926
- **Suburban** 44-acre campus with easy access to New York City
- **Endowment** $90.0 million
- **Coed** 1,438 undergraduate students, 98% full-time, 72% women, 28% men
- **Very difficult** entrance level, 50% of applicants were admitted

UNDERGRAD STUDENTS

1,411 full-time, 27 part-time. Students come from 51 states and territories; 44 other countries; 78% are from out of state; 4% Black or African American, non-Hispanic/Latino; 9% Hispanic/Latino; 5% Asian, non-Hispanic/Latino; 0.1% Native Hawaiian or other Pacific Islander, non-Hispanic/Latino; 0.1% American Indian or Alaska Native, non-Hispanic/Latino; 7% Two or more races, non-Hispanic/Latino; 9% Race/ethnicity unknown; 14% international; 3% transferred in; 84% live on campus.

Freshmen:

Admission: 3,183 applied, 1,589 admitted, 377 enrolled. ***Average high school GPA:*** 3.62. ***Test scores:*** SAT critical reading scores over 500: 97%; SAT math scores over 500: 94%; SAT writing scores over 500: 98%;

ACT scores over 18: 98%; SAT critical reading scores over 600: 86%; SAT math scores over 600: 60%; SAT writing scores over 600: 81%; ACT scores over 24: 96%; SAT critical reading scores over 700: 29%; SAT math scores over 700: 13%; SAT writing scores over 700: 22%; ACT scores over 30: 40%.
Retention: 89% of full-time freshmen returned.

FACULTY
Total: 300, 36% full-time, 69% with terminal degrees.

Student/faculty ratio: 10:1.

ACADEMICS
Calendar: semesters. *Degrees:* bachelor's and master's.

Special study options: accelerated degree program, advanced placement credit, double majors, independent study, internships, off-campus study, services for LD students, student-designed majors, study abroad, summer session for credit. ***ROTC:*** Air Force (c).

Unusual degree programs: 3-2 engineering with Columbia University; art of teaching, child development, women's history, health advocacy.

Computers: 143 computers/terminals are available on campus for general student use. Students can access the following: campus intranet, computer help desk, free student e-mail accounts, online (class) grades, online (class) schedules. Campuswide network is available. 100% of college-owned or -operated housing units are wired for high-speed Internet access. Wireless service is available via entire campus.

Library: Esther Rauschenbush Library plus 2 others. *Books:* 332,623 (physical), 310,800 (digital/electronic); *Serial titles:* 4,113 (physical), 31,083 (digital/electronic); *Databases:* 110. Weekly public service hours: 109; study areas open 24 hours, 5-7 days a week; students can reserve study rooms.

STUDENT LIFE
Housing options: on-campus residence required for freshman year; coed, men-only, women-only, cooperative, special housing for students with disabilities. Campus housing is university owned. Freshman campus housing is guaranteed.

Activities and organizations: drama/theater group, student-run newspaper, radio station, choral group, Sarah Lawrence Activities Council, Hillel, Queer Voice Coalition, SLC Phoenix Newspaper, The Rocky Horror Picture Show Shadow Cast Production.

Athletics Member NCAA. All Division III. ***Intercollegiate sports:*** basketball M/W, crew W, cross-country running M/W, equestrian sports M/W, soccer M/W, softball W, swimming and diving M/W, tennis M/W, volleyball M/W. ***Intramural sports:*** basketball M/W, soccer M/W, squash M/W, table tennis M/W, ultimate Frisbee M/W, volleyball M/W.

Campus security: 24-hour emergency response devices and patrols, late-night transport/escort service, controlled dormitory access.

Student services: health clinic, personal/psychological counseling.

COSTS & FINANCIAL AID
Costs (2016–17) ***Comprehensive fee:*** $67,186 includes full-time tuition ($51,196), mandatory fees ($1154), and room and board ($14,836). Full-time tuition and fees vary according to course load. Part-time tuition: $1707 per credit hour. Part-time tuition and fees vary according to course load. ***Required fees:*** $276 per term part-time. ***College room only:*** $9640. Room and board charges vary according to board plan. ***Payment plan:*** installment. ***Waivers:*** employees or children of employees.

Financial Aid Of all full-time matriculated undergraduates who enrolled in 2016, 958 applied for aid, 822 were judged to have need, 134 had their need fully met. 604 Federal Work-Study jobs (averaging $1663). 43 state and other part-time jobs (averaging $1724). In 2016, 286 non-need-based awards were made. ***Average percent of need met:*** 76. ***Average financial aid package:*** $37,319. ***Average need-based loan:*** $2690. ***Average need-based gift aid:*** $34,799. ***Average non-need-based aid:*** $15,178. ***Average indebtedness upon graduation:*** $19,772. ***Financial aid deadline:*** 2/1.

APPLYING
Options: electronic application, early admission, early decision, deferred entrance.

Application fee: $60.

Required: essay or personal statement, high school transcript, 2 letters of recommendation, counselor recommendation, school report. ***Recommended:*** minimum 3.0 GPA, interview.

Application deadlines: 1/15 (freshmen), 3/1 (transfers).

Early decision deadline: 11/1 (for plan 1), 1/1 (for plan 2).

Notification: 4/1 (freshmen), 6/1 (transfers), 12/15 (early decision plan 1), 2/15 (early decision plan 2).

CONTACT
Ms. Jennifer Gayles, Director of Admission and Multicultural Recruitment, Sarah Lawrence College, 1 Mead Way, Bronxville, NY 10708-5999. *Phone:* 914-395-2510. *Toll-free phone:* 800-888-2858. *Fax:* 914-395-2515. *E-mail:* slcadmit@sarahlawrence.edu.

★ School of Visual Arts

New York, New York

http://www.sva.edu/

- **Proprietary** comprehensive, founded 1947
- **Urban** 1-acre campus
- **Coed**
- **Moderately difficult** entrance level

FACULTY
Student/faculty ratio: 8:1.

ACADEMICS
Calendar: semesters. *Degrees:* bachelor's and master's.
Library: School of Visual Arts Library.

STUDENT LIFE
Housing options: coed, women-only. Campus housing is university owned, leased by the school and is provided by a third party. Freshman applicants given priority for college housing.

Activities and organizations: student-run newspaper, radio station.

Campus security: 24-hour patrols.

Student services: health clinic, personal/psychological counseling.

COSTS & FINANCIAL AID
Costs (2016–17) ***Comprehensive fee:*** $54,800 includes full-time tuition ($36,500) and room and board ($18,300). Part-time tuition: $1270 per credit hour. ***College room only:*** $15,400.

Financial Aid Of all full-time matriculated undergraduates who enrolled in 2016, 1,581 applied for aid, 1,477 were judged to have need, 16 had their need fully met. In 2016, 272 non-need-based awards were made. ***Average financial aid package:*** $17,121. ***Average need-based loan:*** $4253. ***Average need-based gift aid:*** $13,772. ***Average non-need-based aid:*** $12,192. ***Average indebtedness upon graduation:*** $46,328. ***Financial aid deadline:*** 3/1.

APPLYING
Standardized Tests *Required:* SAT or ACT (for admission).

Options: electronic application, deferred entrance.

Application fee: $50.

Required: essay or personal statement, high school transcript, minimum 2.5 GPA, portfolio. ***Recommended:*** interview.

CONTACT
Admissions Office, School of Visual Arts, 209 East 23rd Street, New York, NY 10010. *Phone:* 212-592-2100. *Toll-free phone:* 800-436-4204. *Fax:* 212-592-2116. *E-mail:* admissions@sva.edu.

Sh'or Yoshuv Rabbinical College

Lawrence, New York

http://www.shoryoshuv.org/

CONTACT
Rabbi Moshe Rubin, Registrar, Sh'or Yoshuv Rabbinical College, 1 Cedarlawn Avenue, Lawrence, NY 11559-1714. *Phone:* 516-239-9002 Ext. 124. *Fax:* 516-977-1282. *E-mail:* mrubin@shoryoshuv.org.

Siena College
Loudonville, New York
http://www.siena.edu/

- **Independent Roman Catholic** comprehensive, founded 1937
- **Suburban** 175-acre campus with easy access to Albany, NY
- **Endowment** $121.5 million
- **Coed** 3,186 undergraduate students, 96% full-time, 52% women, 48% men
- **Moderately difficult** entrance level, 73% of applicants were admitted

UNDERGRAD STUDENTS
3,061 full-time, 125 part-time. Students come from 34 states and territories; 15 other countries; 18% are from out of state; 4% Black or African American, non-Hispanic/Latino; 8% Hispanic/Latino; 4% Asian, non-Hispanic/Latino; 0.1% Native Hawaiian or other Pacific Islander, non-Hispanic/Latino; 0.1% American Indian or Alaska Native, non-Hispanic/Latino; 2% Two or more races, non-Hispanic/Latino; 1% Race/ethnicity unknown; 2% international; 5% transferred in; 77% live on campus.

Freshmen:
Admission: 8,037 applied, 5,835 admitted, 764 enrolled. ***Average high school GPA:*** 3.52. ***Test scores:*** SAT critical reading scores over 500: 68%; SAT math scores over 500: 76%; SAT writing scores over 500: 61%; ACT scores over 18: 96%; SAT critical reading scores over 600: 24%; SAT math scores over 600: 32%; SAT writing scores over 600: 17%; ACT scores over 24: 63%; SAT critical reading scores over 700: 3%; SAT math scores over 700: 6%; SAT writing scores over 700: 2%; ACT scores over 30: 13%.

Retention: 87% of full-time freshmen returned.

FACULTY
Total: 332, 65% full-time, 72% with terminal degrees.

Student/faculty ratio: 12:1.

ACADEMICS
Calendar: semesters. *Degrees:* certificates, bachelor's, and master's.

Special study options: advanced placement credit, cooperative education, double majors, English as a second language, honors programs, independent study, internships, off-campus study, part-time degree program, services for LD students, student-designed majors, study abroad, summer session for credit. ***ROTC:*** Army (b), Air Force (c).

Unusual degree programs: 3-2 engineering with Binghamton University, Catholic University, Clarkson University, Manhattan College, Rensselaer Polytechnic Institute, Western New England College, Union Graduate College.

Computers: 402 computers/terminals and 5,341 ports are available on campus for general student use. Students can access the following: campus intranet, computer help desk, free student e-mail accounts, online (class) grades, online (class) registration, online (class) schedules. Campuswide network is available. 100% of college-owned or -operated housing units are wired for high-speed Internet access. Wireless service is available via entire campus.

Library: J. Spencer and Patricia Standish Library. *Books:* 333,182 (physical), 303,315 (digital/electronic); *Serial titles:* 30,000 (digital/electronic); *Databases:* 157. Weekly public service hours: 102; students can reserve study rooms.

STUDENT LIFE
Housing options: on-campus residence required through senior year; coed, special housing for students with disabilities. Campus housing is university owned. Freshman applicants given priority for college housing.

Activities and organizations: drama/theater group, student-run newspaper, radio and television station, choral group, Outing Club, Best Buddies, Make-a-Wish Wishmakers on Campus, Fitness Club, Psychology Club.

Athletics Member NCAA. All Division I. ***Intercollegiate sports:*** baseball M(s), basketball M(s)/W(s), cross-country running M(s)/W(s), field hockey W(s), golf M(s)/W(s), lacrosse M(s)/W(s), soccer M(s)/W(s), softball W(s), swimming and diving W(s), tennis M(s)/W(s), track and field M/W, volleyball W(s), water polo W(s). ***Intramural sports:*** basketball M/W, cheerleading W(c), equestrian sports W(c), football M/W, ice hockey M, rugby M(c)/W(c), soccer M/W, softball M/W, squash M(c), tennis M(c)/W(c), track and field M(c)/W(c), ultimate Frisbee M(c), volleyball M/W.

Campus security: 24-hour emergency response devices and patrols, late-night transport/escort service, controlled dormitory access.

Student services: health clinic, personal/psychological counseling, women's center.

COSTS & FINANCIAL AID
Costs (2017–18) ***Comprehensive fee:*** $50,285 includes full-time tuition ($35,435), mandatory fees ($300), and room and board ($14,550). Full-time tuition and fees vary according to course load. Part-time tuition: $675 per credit. Part-time tuition and fees vary according to course load. ***Required fees:*** $100 per term part-time. ***College room only:*** $8580. Room and board charges vary according to board plan and housing facility. ***Payment plan:*** installment. ***Waivers:*** employees or children of employees.

Financial Aid Of all full-time matriculated undergraduates who enrolled in 2015, 2,481 applied for aid, 2,179 were judged to have need, 630 had their need fully met. In 2015, 533 non-need-based awards were made. ***Average percent of need met:*** 82. ***Average financial aid package:*** $28,167. ***Average need-based loan:*** $4346. ***Average need-based gift aid:*** $21,101. ***Average non-need-based aid:*** $10,554. ***Average indebtedness upon graduation:*** $35,874. ***Financial aid deadline:*** 5/1.

APPLYING
Standardized Tests *Required for some:* SAT or ACT (for admission).

Options: electronic application, early admission, early decision, early action, deferred entrance.

Application fee: $50.

Required: essay or personal statement, high school transcript, 1 letter of recommendation. ***Required for some:*** interview. ***Recommended:*** interview.

Application deadlines: 2/15 (freshmen), 8/15 (transfers), 12/1 (early action).

Early decision deadline: 12/1.

Notification: 3/15 (freshmen), continuous (transfers), 1/1 (early decision), 1/7 (early action).

CONTACT
Ms. Katie Szalda, Director of Admissions, Siena College, 515 Loudon Road, Loudonville, NY 12211-1462. *Phone:* 518-782-6767. *Toll-free phone:* 888-AT-SIENA. *Fax:* 518-783-2436.
E-mail: admissions@siena.edu.

★ Skidmore College
Saratoga Springs, New York
http://www.skidmore.edu/

- **Independent** 4-year, founded 1903
- **Small-town** 890-acre campus with easy access to Albany, NY
- **Endowment** $326.9 million
- **Coed** 2,680 undergraduate students, 99% full-time, 60% women, 40% men
- **Very difficult** entrance level, 29% of applicants were admitted

UNDERGRAD STUDENTS
2,643 full-time, 37 part-time. Students come from 44 states and territories; 59 other countries; 67% are from out of state; 4% Black or African American, non-Hispanic/Latino; 9% Hispanic/Latino; 5% Asian, non-Hispanic/Latino; 4% Two or more races, non-Hispanic/Latino; 3% Race/ethnicity unknown; 10% international; 1% transferred in; 89% live on campus.

Freshmen:
Admission: 9,181 applied, 2,670 admitted, 714 enrolled. ***Test scores:*** SAT critical reading scores over 500: 93%; SAT math scores over 500: 94%; SAT writing scores over 500: 93%; ACT scores over 18: 100%; SAT critical reading scores over 600: 63%; SAT math scores over 600: 59%; SAT writing scores over 600: 67%; ACT scores over 24: 91%; SAT critical reading scores over 700: 16%; SAT math scores over 700: 13%; SAT writing scores over 700: 13%; ACT scores over 30: 35%.

Retention: 91% of full-time freshmen returned.

FACULTY
Total: 382, 73% full-time, 71% with terminal degrees.

Student/faculty ratio: 8:1.

ACADEMICS

Calendar: semesters plus optional 6-week internship period. *Degree:* bachelor's.

Special study options: accelerated degree program, advanced placement credit, distance learning, double majors, honors programs, independent study, internships, off-campus study, services for LD students, student-designed majors, study abroad, summer session for credit. ***ROTC:*** Army (c), Air Force (c).

Unusual degree programs: 3-2 business administration with Clarkson University, Rochester Institute of Technology, Syracuse University; engineering with Dartmouth College, Clarkson University, Rensselaer Polytechnic Institute; nursing with New York University; finance or accounting with Syracuse University, physical or occupational therapy with Sage Graduate School, accounting with Wake Forest.

Computers: 600 computers/terminals are available on campus for general student use. Students can access the following: campus intranet, computer help desk, free student e-mail accounts, online (class) grades, online (class) registration, online (class) schedules. Campuswide network is available. 100% of college-owned or -operated housing units are wired for high-speed Internet access. Wireless service is available via classrooms, computer centers, computer labs, dorm rooms, learning centers, libraries, student centers.

Library: Scribner Library. *Books:* 411,106 (physical), 107,851 (digital/electronic); *Serial titles:* 2,202 (physical); *Databases:* 337. Weekly public service hours: 109; students can reserve study rooms.

STUDENT LIFE

Housing options: on-campus residence required through sophomore year; coed, women-only, special housing for students with disabilities. Campus housing is university owned. Freshman campus housing is guaranteed.

Activities and organizations: drama/theater group, student-run newspaper, radio and television station, choral group, Student Government Association, Student radio station (WSPN), Benefaction (Student Volunteer), Outing Club, UJIMA.

Athletics Member NCAA. All Division III. ***Intercollegiate sports:*** baseball M, basketball M/W, crew M/W, equestrian sports W, field hockey W, golf M, ice hockey M, lacrosse M/W, soccer M/W, softball W, swimming and diving M/W, tennis M/W, volleyball W. ***Intramural sports:*** basketball M/W, football M/W, racquetball M/W, soccer M/W, tennis M/W, volleyball M/W.

Campus security: 24-hour emergency response devices and patrols, late-night transport/escort service, controlled dormitory access, well-lit campus.

Student services: health clinic, personal/psychological counseling.

COSTS & FINANCIAL AID

Costs (2016–17) ***One-time required fee:*** $150. ***Comprehensive fee:*** $64,214 includes full-time tuition ($49,716), mandatory fees ($968), and room and board ($13,530). Full-time tuition and fees vary according to course load. Part-time tuition: $1657 per credit. Part-time tuition and fees vary according to course load. ***Required fees:*** $25 per term part-time. ***College room only:*** $7998. Room and board charges vary according to board plan and housing facility. ***Payment plans:*** tuition prepayment, installment. ***Waivers:*** senior citizens and employees or children of employees.

Financial Aid Of all full-time matriculated undergraduates who enrolled in 2016, 1,365 applied for aid, 1,070 were judged to have need, 998 had their need fully met. In 2016, 11 non-need-based awards were made. ***Average percent of need met:*** 94. ***Average financial aid package:*** $45,900. ***Average need-based loan:*** $4200. ***Average need-based gift aid:*** $40,300. ***Average non-need-based aid:*** $12,800. ***Average indebtedness upon graduation:*** $25,001. ***Financial aid deadline:*** 2/1.

APPLYING

Standardized Tests *Required for some:* SAT or ACT (for admission).

Options: electronic application, early admission, early decision, deferred entrance.

Application fee: $65.

Required: essay or personal statement, high school transcript, 2 letters of recommendation. ***Recommended:*** interview.

Application deadlines: 1/15 (freshmen), 4/1 (transfers).

Early decision deadline: 11/15 (for plan 1), 1/15 (for plan 2).

Notification: 4/1 (freshmen), 12/15 (early decision plan 1), 2/15 (early decision plan 2).

CONTACT

Ms. Mary Lou Bates, Dean of Admissions and Financial Aid, Skidmore College, 815 North Broadway, Saratoga Springs, NY 12866-1632. *Phone:* 518-580-5570. *Toll-free phone:* 800-867-6007. *Fax:* 518-580-5584. *E-mail:* admissions@skidmore.edu.

See previous page for display ad and page 1508 for the College Close-Up.

State University of New York at Fredonia

Fredonia, New York

http://www.fredonia.edu/

- **State-supported** comprehensive, founded 1826, part of State University of New York System
- **Small-town** 249-acre campus with easy access to Buffalo
- **Endowment** $30.4 million
- **Coed** 4,386 undergraduate students, 97% full-time, 57% women, 43% men
- **Moderately difficult** entrance level, 62% of applicants were admitted

UNDERGRAD STUDENTS

4,261 full-time, 125 part-time. Students come from 25 states and territories; 17 other countries; 3% are from out of state; 7% Black or African American, non-Hispanic/Latino; 7% Hispanic/Latino; 2% Asian, non-Hispanic/Latino; 0.6% American Indian or Alaska Native, non-Hispanic/Latino; 3% Two or more races, non-Hispanic/Latino; 2% Race/ethnicity unknown; 2% international; 7% transferred in; 53% live on campus.

Freshmen:

Admission: 5,381 applied, 3,355 admitted, 935 enrolled. ***Average high school GPA:*** 3.27. ***Test scores:*** SAT critical reading scores over 500: 55%; SAT math scores over 500: 56%; ACT scores over 18: 96%; SAT critical reading scores over 600: 15%; SAT math scores over 600: 13%; ACT scores over 24: 51%; SAT critical reading scores over 700: 2%; SAT math scores over 700: 1%; ACT scores over 30: 10%.

Retention: 79% of full-time freshmen returned.

FACULTY

Total: 441, 58% full-time, 56% with terminal degrees.

Student/faculty ratio: 14:1.

ACADEMICS

Calendar: semesters. *Degrees:* bachelor's, master's, and post-master's certificates.

Special study options: accelerated degree program, adult/continuing education programs, advanced placement credit, distance learning, double majors, English as a second language, honors programs, independent study, internships, off-campus study, part-time degree program, services for LD students, student-designed majors, study abroad, summer session for credit.

Unusual degree programs: 3-2 engineering with Clarkson University, State University of New York at Buffalo, Case Western Reserve, Columbia University, Louisiana Technical University, New York State College of Ceramics at Alfred, Ohio State University.

Computers: 500 computers/terminals are available on campus for general student use. Students can access the following: campus intranet, computer help desk, free student e-mail accounts, online (class) grades, online (class) registration, online (class) schedules. Campuswide network is available. 100% of college-owned or -operated housing units are wired for high-speed Internet access. Wireless service is available via entire campus.

Library: Daniel A. Reed Library. *Books:* 18.0 million (physical); *Serial titles:* 48,000 (physical). Weekly public service hours: 68; students can reserve study rooms.

STUDENT LIFE

Housing options: on-campus residence required through sophomore year; coed, men-only, women-only, special housing for students with disabilities. Campus housing is university owned. Freshman campus housing is guaranteed.

Activities and organizations: drama/theater group, student-run newspaper, radio and television station, choral group, Student Association, Undergraduate Alumni Council, Communication Club, ethnic organizations, spectrum entertainment board, national fraternities, national sororities.

Athletics Member NCAA. All Division III. ***Intercollegiate sports:*** baseball M, basketball M/W, cheerleading M/W, cross-country running M/W, field hockey M(c)/W(c), ice hockey M, lacrosse M(c)/W, rugby M(c)/W(c), soccer M/W, softball W, swimming and diving M/W, tennis W, track and field M/W, volleyball W. ***Intramural sports:*** basketball M/W, fencing M(c)/W(c), ice hockey M(c), racquetball M/W, rock climbing M/W, sand volleyball M/W, skiing (downhill) M/W, soccer M/W, softball M/W, squash M/W, tennis M/W, ultimate Frisbee M/W, volleyball M/W, water polo M/W.

Campus security: 24-hour emergency response devices and patrols, late-night transport/escort service, controlled dormitory access.

Student services: health clinic, personal/psychological counseling, legal services.

COSTS & FINANCIAL AID

Costs (2017–18) ***Tuition:*** state resident $6470 full-time, $270 per credit hour part-time; nonresident $16,320 full-time, $680 per credit hour part-time. ***Required fees:*** $1619 full-time, $67 per credit hour part-time, $67 per credit hour part-time. ***Room and board:*** $12,730; room only: $7600. Room and board charges vary according to board plan and housing facility. ***Payment plan:*** installment.

Financial Aid Of all full-time matriculated undergraduates who enrolled in 2016, 3,658 applied for aid, 2,999 were judged to have need, 426 had their need fully met. 201 Federal Work-Study jobs (averaging $1778). In 2016, 362 non-need-based awards were made. ***Average percent of need met:*** 60. ***Average financial aid package:*** $10,936. ***Average need-based loan:*** $5276. ***Average need-based gift aid:*** $5682. ***Average non-need-based aid:*** $3117. ***Average indebtedness upon graduation:*** $32,083.

APPLYING

Standardized Tests *Required:* SAT or ACT (for admission).

Options: electronic application, early admission, deferred entrance.

Application fee: $50.

Required: essay or personal statement, high school transcript, 1 letter of recommendation. ***Required for some:*** interview, audition for music, dance and theater programs: portfolio for visual arts and technical theatre programs.

Application deadlines: rolling (freshmen), rolling (transfers).

Notification: continuous (freshmen), continuous (transfers).

CONTACT

Mr. Cory M. Bezek, Office of Admissions, State University of New York at Fredonia, 178 Central Avenue, Fredonia, NY 14063. *Phone:* 716-673-3251. *Toll-free phone:* 800-252-1212. *Fax:* 716-673-3249. *E-mail:* admissions@fredonia.edu.

State University of New York at New Paltz

New Paltz, New York

http://www.newpaltz.edu/

- **State-supported** comprehensive, founded 1828, part of State University of New York System
- **Small-town** 216-acre campus
- **Endowment** $18.5 million
- **Coed** 6,717 undergraduate students, 92% full-time, 62% women, 38% men
- **Very difficult** entrance level, 43% of applicants were admitted

UNDERGRAD STUDENTS

6,198 full-time, 519 part-time. Students come from 25 states and territories; 43 other countries; 3% are from out of state; 6% Black or African American, non-Hispanic/Latino; 18% Hispanic/Latino; 6% Asian, non-Hispanic/Latino; 0.1% Native Hawaiian or other Pacific Islander, non-Hispanic/Latino; 0.1% American Indian or Alaska Native, non-Hispanic/Latino; 2% Two or more races, non-Hispanic/Latino; 3%

Race/ethnicity unknown; 2% international; 11% transferred in; 47% live on campus.

Freshmen:

Admission: 14,042 applied, 6,030 admitted, 1,092 enrolled. ***Average high school GPA:*** 3.6. ***Test scores:*** SAT critical reading scores over 500: 78%; SAT math scores over 500: 81%; SAT writing scores over 500: 77%; ACT scores over 18: 97%; SAT critical reading scores over 600: 27%; SAT math scores over 600: 26%; SAT writing scores over 600: 23%; ACT scores over 24: 68%; SAT critical reading scores over 700: 3%; SAT math scores over 700: 2%; SAT writing scores over 700: 2%; ACT scores over 30: 10%.

Retention: 87% of full-time freshmen returned.

FACULTY

Total: 674, 55% full-time, 60% with terminal degrees.

Student/faculty ratio: 15:1.

ACADEMICS

Calendar: semesters. *Degrees:* bachelor's, master's, post-master's, and postbachelor's certificates.

Special study options: academic remediation for entering students, advanced placement credit, cooperative education, distance learning, double majors, English as a second language, external degree program, honors programs, independent study, internships, off-campus study, part-time degree program, services for LD students, student-designed majors, study abroad, summer session for credit.

Unusual degree programs: 3-2 business administration; engineering.

Computers: 800 computers/terminals are available on campus for general student use. Students can access the following: campus intranet, computer help desk, free student e-mail accounts, online (class) grades, online (class) registration, online (class) schedules. Campuswide network is available. 100% of college-owned or -operated housing units are wired for high-speed Internet access. Wireless service is available via entire campus.

Library: Sojourner Truth Library. *Books:* 447,549 (physical), 125,825 (digital/electronic); *Serial titles:* 240 (physical), 83,500 (digital/electronic); *Databases:* 95. Weekly public service hours: 103; students can reserve study rooms.

STUDENT LIFE

Housing options: on-campus residence required for freshman year; coed, special housing for students with disabilities. Campus housing is university owned. Freshman campus housing is guaranteed.

Activities and organizations: drama/theater group, student-run newspaper, radio and television station, choral group, Student Association, Residence Hall Student Association, Outing Club, The Oracle Newspaper, United Greek Association, national fraternities, national sororities.

Athletics Member NCAA. All Division III. ***Intercollegiate sports:*** baseball M, basketball M/W, cross-country running M/W, field hockey W, lacrosse W, soccer M/W, swimming and diving M/W, tennis W, volleyball M/W. ***Intramural sports:*** basketball M/W, cheerleading M(c)/W(c), equestrian sports M(c)/W(c), lacrosse M(c)/W(c), racquetball M/W, rugby M(c)/W(c), soccer M/W, swimming and diving M(c)/W(c), table tennis M(c)/W(c), tennis M/W, track and field M(c)/W(c), ultimate Frisbee M(c)/W(c), volleyball M/W, water polo M/W, wrestling M(c).

Campus security: 24-hour emergency response devices and patrols, late-night transport/escort service, controlled dormitory access, safety seminars, RAD Women's Self Defense.

Student services: health clinic, personal/psychological counseling, legal services.

COSTS & FINANCIAL AID

Costs (2016–17) ***Tuition:*** state resident $6470 full-time, $270 per credit hour part-time; nonresident $16,320 full-time, $680 per credit hour part-time. ***Required fees:*** $1284 full-time, $37 per credit hour part-time, $200 per term part-time. ***Room and board:*** $12,000; room only: $8040. Room and board charges vary according to board plan. ***Payment plan:*** installment.

Financial Aid Of all full-time matriculated undergraduates who enrolled in 2016, 4,748 applied for aid, 3,531 were judged to have need, 250 had their need fully met. In 2016, 44 non-need-based awards were made. ***Average percent of need met:*** 56. ***Average financial aid package:*** $11,074. ***Average need-based loan:*** $4293. ***Average need-based gift aid:*** $5016. ***Average non-need-based aid:*** $2504. ***Average indebtedness upon graduation:*** $26,283.

APPLYING

Standardized Tests *Required:* SAT or ACT (for admission).

Options: electronic application, early admission, early action.

Application fee: $50.

Required: essay or personal statement, high school transcript, 1 letter of recommendation. ***Required for some:*** portfolio for art program, audition for music and theater programs.

Application deadlines: 5/1 (freshmen), 5/1 (transfers), 11/15 (early action).

Notification: continuous (freshmen), continuous (transfers), 1/1 (early action).

CONTACT

Ms. Kimberly A. Strano, Director of Freshman Admissions, State University of New York at New Paltz, 1 Hawk Drive, New Paltz, NY 12561-2499. *Phone:* 845-257-3200. *Toll-free phone:* 877-MY-NP-411. *Fax:* 845-257-3209. *E-mail:* admissions@newpaltz.edu.

★ State University of New York at Oswego

Oswego, New York

http://www.oswego.edu/

- **State-supported** comprehensive, founded 1861, part of State University of New York System
- **Small-town** 696-acre campus with easy access to Syracuse
- **Endowment** $28.8 million
- **Coed** 7,150 undergraduate students, 96% full-time, 50% women, 50% men
- **Moderately difficult** entrance level, 54% of applicants were admitted

UNDERGRAD STUDENTS

6,868 full-time, 282 part-time. Students come from 31 states and territories; 30 other countries; 3% are from out of state; 8% Black or African American, non-Hispanic/Latino; 11% Hispanic/Latino; 3% Asian, non-Hispanic/Latino; 0.1% Native Hawaiian or other Pacific Islander, non-Hispanic/Latino; 0.2% American Indian or Alaska Native, non-Hispanic/Latino; 3% Two or more races, non-Hispanic/Latino; 0.2% Race/ethnicity unknown; 2% international; 10% transferred in; 60% live on campus.

Freshmen:

Admission: 10,715 applied, 5,824 admitted, 1,441 enrolled. ***Average high school GPA:*** 3.5. ***Test scores:*** SAT critical reading scores over 500: 75%; SAT math scores over 500: 80%; ACT scores over 18: 100%; SAT critical reading scores over 600: 20%; SAT math scores over 600: 21%; ACT scores over 24: 49%; SAT critical reading scores over 700: 1%; SAT math scores over 700: 2%; ACT scores over 30: 4%.

Retention: 81% of full-time freshmen returned.

FACULTY

Total: 589, 60% full-time, 61% with terminal degrees.

Student/faculty ratio: 17:1.

ACADEMICS

Calendar: semesters. *Degrees:* bachelor's, master's, post-master's, and postbachelor's certificates.

Special study options: accelerated degree program, adult/continuing education programs, advanced placement credit, cooperative education, distance learning, double majors, English as a second language, freshman honors college, honors programs, independent study, internships, off-campus study, part-time degree program, services for LD students, study abroad, summer session for credit. ***ROTC:*** Army (c), Air Force (c).

Unusual degree programs: 3-2 engineering with Clarkson University, Case Western Reserve University, State University of New York at Binghamton.

Computers: 1,250 computers/terminals are available on campus for general student use. Students can access the following: campus intranet, computer help desk, free student e-mail accounts, online (class) grades, online (class) registration, online (class) schedules. Campuswide network is available. 100% of college-owned or -operated housing units are wired for high-speed Internet access. Wireless service is available via entire campus.

Library: Penfield Library. *Books:* 440,144 (physical), 145,720 (digital/electronic); *Serial titles:* 1,936 (physical), 60,428 (digital/electronic); *Databases:* 132. Weekly public service hours: 96; study areas open 24 hours, 5-7 days a week; students can reserve study rooms.

STUDENT LIFE

Housing options: on-campus residence required through sophomore year; coed, special housing for students with disabilities. Campus housing is university owned. Freshman campus housing is guaranteed.

Activities and organizations: drama/theater group, student-run newspaper, radio and television station, choral group, club/intramural sports, student radio/television stations (WNYO and WTOP), Outdoor Club, Dance Organization (Del Sarte), Accounting Society, national fraternities, national sororities.

Athletics Member NCAA. All Division III. ***Intercollegiate sports:*** baseball M, basketball M/W, crew M(c)/W(c), cross-country running M/W, field hockey W, golf M, ice hockey M/W, lacrosse M/W, soccer M/W, softball W, swimming and diving M/W, tennis M/W, track and field M/W, volleyball W, wrestling M. ***Intramural sports:*** badminton M/W, basketball M/W, cheerleading W(c), equestrian sports M(c)/W(c), fencing M(c)/W(c), field hockey W(c), football M/W, golf M/W, gymnastics M(c)/W(c), ice hockey M(c)/W(c), lacrosse M(c), racquetball M/W, rock climbing M(c)/W(c), rugby M(c)/W(c), skiing (cross-country) M(c)/W(c), skiing (downhill) M(c)/W(c), soccer M/W, softball M/W, swimming and diving M/W, table tennis M/W, tennis M/W, ultimate Frisbee M(c)/W(c), volleyball M(c)/W, water polo M/W.

Campus security: 24-hour emergency response devices and patrols, controlled dormitory access, Oswego Guardian.

Student services: health clinic, personal/psychological counseling, women's center, legal services.

COSTS & FINANCIAL AID

Costs (2016–17) ***Tuition:*** state resident $6470 full-time, $270 per credit hour part-time; nonresident $16,320 full-time, $680 per credit hour part-time. Part-time tuition and fees vary according to course load. ***Required fees:*** $1491 full-time, $47 per credit hour part-time. ***Room and board:*** $13,390; room only: $8390. Room and board charges vary according to board plan and housing facility. ***Payment plan:*** installment.

Financial Aid Of all full-time matriculated undergraduates who enrolled in 2016, 5,670 applied for aid, 4,522 were judged to have need, 406 had their need fully met. 457 Federal Work-Study jobs (averaging $1250). 1,612 state and other part-time jobs (averaging $2047). In 2016, 796 non-need-based awards were made. ***Average percent of need met:*** 80. ***Average financial aid package:*** $11,290. ***Average need-based loan:*** $4602. ***Average need-based gift aid:*** $7538. ***Average non-need-based aid:*** $2529. ***Average indebtedness upon graduation:*** $28,676.

APPLYING

Standardized Tests *Required:* SAT or ACT (for admission).

Options: electronic application, early admission, early action, deferred entrance.

Application fee: $50.

Required: essay or personal statement, high school transcript, 1 letter of recommendation. ***Recommended:*** minimum 2.7 GPA, interview.

Application deadlines: rolling (freshmen), rolling (transfers), 11/5 (early action).

Notification: 1/15 (freshmen), 1/15 (transfers), 12/15 (early action).

CONTACT

Mr. Daniel Griffin, Director of Admissions, State University of New York at Oswego, 7060 State Route 104, Oswego, NY 13126. *Phone:* 315-312-2250. *Fax:* 315-312-3260. *E-mail:* admiss@oswego.edu.

See below for display ad and page 1520 for the College Close-Up.

State University of New York at Plattsburgh

Plattsburgh, New York

http://www.plattsburgh.edu/

- **State-supported** comprehensive, founded 1889, part of State University of New York System
- **Small-town** 265-acre campus with easy access to Montreal
- **Endowment** $18.6 million
- **Coed** 5,377 undergraduate students, 92% full-time, 56% women, 44% men
- **Moderately difficult** entrance level, 50% of applicants were admitted

UNDERGRAD STUDENTS

4,960 full-time, 417 part-time. Students come from 27 states and territories; 65 other countries; 6% are from out of state; 7% Black or African American, non-Hispanic/Latino; 10% Hispanic/Latino; 3% Asian, non-Hispanic/Latino; 0.2% Native Hawaiian or other Pacific Islander, non-Hispanic/Latino; 0.4% American Indian or Alaska Native, non-Hispanic/Latino; 2% Two or more races, non-Hispanic/Latino; 4% Race/ethnicity unknown; 6% international; 10% transferred in; 46% live on campus.

Freshmen:

Admission: 8,261 applied, 4,105 admitted, 963 enrolled. ***Average high school GPA:*** 3.2. ***Test scores:*** SAT critical reading scores over 500: 67%; SAT math scores over 500: 71%; ACT scores over 18: 98%; SAT critical reading scores over 600: 17%; SAT math scores over 600: 20%; ACT scores over 24: 40%; SAT critical reading scores over 700: 1%; SAT math scores over 700: 1%; ACT scores over 30: 2%.

Retention: 83% of full-time freshmen returned.

FACULTY

Total: 455, 62% full-time, 60% with terminal degrees.

Student/faculty ratio: 16:1.

ACADEMICS

Calendar: semesters plus 2 5-week summer sessions and 1 winter session. *Degrees:* certificates, bachelor's, master's, and post-master's certificates.

Special study options: academic remediation for entering students, accelerated degree program, adult/continuing education programs, advanced placement credit, cooperative education, distance learning, double majors, English as a second language, honors programs, independent study, internships, off-campus study, part-time degree program, services for LD students, student-designed majors, study abroad, summer session for credit.

Computers: 450 computers/terminals are available on campus for general student use. Students can access the following: campus intranet, computer help desk, free student e-mail accounts, online (class) grades, online (class) registration, online (class) schedules. Campuswide network is available. 100% of college-owned or -operated housing units are wired for high-speed Internet access. Wireless service is available via entire campus.

Library: Feinberg Library. *Books:* 297,997 (physical), 183,957 (digital/electronic); *Serial titles:* 177 (physical), 538 (digital/electronic); *Databases:* 111. Weekly public service hours: 100; students can reserve study rooms.

STUDENT LIFE

Housing options: on-campus residence required through sophomore year; coed, special housing for students with disabilities. Campus housing is university owned. Freshman campus housing is guaranteed.

Activities and organizations: drama/theater group, student-run newspaper, radio and television station, choral group, Student Association, Honor Societies, Student Media Organizations, service/leadership organizations, intramural and recreational sports, national fraternities, national sororities.

Athletics Member NCAA. All Division III. ***Intercollegiate sports:*** baseball M, basketball M/W, cross-country running M/W, ice hockey M/W, lacrosse M, soccer M/W, softball W, tennis W, track and field M/W, volleyball W. ***Intramural sports:*** basketball M/W, cheerleading M(c)/W(c), field hockey M/W, football M, ice hockey M(c)/W(c), racquetball M/W, rock climbing M(c)/W(c), rugby M(c)/W(c), sand volleyball M/W, soccer M/W, softball M/W, tennis M/W, ultimate Frisbee M/W, volleyball M/W.

Campus security: 24-hour emergency response devices and patrols, late-night transport/escort service, controlled dormitory access.

Student services: health clinic, personal/psychological counseling, women's center, legal services.

COSTS & FINANCIAL AID

Costs (2016–17) ***Tuition:*** state resident $6470 full-time, $270 per contact hour part-time; nonresident $16,320 full-time, $680 per contact hour part-time. Full-time tuition and fees vary according to course load and location. Part-time tuition and fees vary according to course load and location. ***Required fees:*** $1436 full-time, $61 per contact hour part-time. ***Room and board:*** $12,150; room only: $7750. Room and board charges vary according to board plan and housing facility. ***Payment plans:*** installment, deferred payment.

Financial Aid Of all full-time matriculated undergraduates who enrolled in 2015, 3,976 applied for aid, 3,170 were judged to have need, 540 had their need fully met. 385 Federal Work-Study jobs (averaging $2556). In 2015, 668 non-need-based awards were made. ***Average percent of need met:*** 76. ***Average financial aid package:*** $13,278. ***Average need-based loan:*** $7806. ***Average need-based gift aid:*** $7606. ***Average non-need-based aid:*** $4235. ***Average indebtedness upon graduation:*** $28,779.

APPLYING

Standardized Tests *Required:* SAT or ACT (for admission).

Options: electronic application, early admission, deferred entrance.

Application fee: $50.

Required: essay or personal statement, high school transcript, minimum 2.5 GPA, 1 letter of recommendation. ***Required for some:*** minimum 3.4 GPA. ***Recommended:*** minimum 3.0 GPA, interview.

Application deadlines: rolling (freshmen), rolling (transfers).

Notification: continuous (freshmen), continuous (transfers).

CONTACT

Mrs. Carrie Woodward, Assistant Director for Freshman Admissions, State University of New York at Plattsburgh, 101 Broad Street, Plattsburgh, NY 12901. *Phone:* 888-673-0012. *Toll-free phone:* 888-673-0012. *Fax:* 518-564-2045. *E-mail:* carrie.woodward@plattsburgh.edu.

State University of New York College at Cortland

Cortland, New York

http://www.cortland.edu/

- **State-supported** comprehensive, founded 1868, part of State University of New York System
- **Small-town** 191-acre campus with easy access to Syracuse
- **Coed** 6,283 undergraduate students, 98% full-time, 56% women, 44% men
- **Moderately difficult** entrance level, 51% of applicants were admitted

UNDERGRAD STUDENTS

6,179 full-time, 104 part-time. 4% are from out of state; 6% Black or African American, non-Hispanic/Latino; 11% Hispanic/Latino; 1% Asian, non-Hispanic/Latino; 0.1% Native Hawaiian or other Pacific Islander, non-Hispanic/Latino; 0.1% American Indian or Alaska Native, non-Hispanic/Latino; 2% Two or more races, non-Hispanic/Latino; 5% Race/ethnicity unknown; 0.5% international; 11% transferred in.

Freshmen:

Admission: 11,060 applied, 5,623 admitted, 1,214 enrolled. ***Test scores:*** SAT critical reading scores over 500: 59%; SAT math scores over 500: 70%; ACT scores over 18: 97%; SAT critical reading scores over 600: 8%; SAT math scores over 600: 12%; ACT scores over 24: 46%; ACT scores over 30: 3%.

Retention: 78% of full-time freshmen returned.

FACULTY

Total: 623, 47% full-time, 47% with terminal degrees.

Student/faculty ratio: 17:1.

ACADEMICS

Calendar: semesters. *Degrees:* bachelor's, master's, post-master's, and postbachelor's certificates.

Special study options: adult/continuing education programs, off-campus study. ***ROTC:*** Army (c), Air Force (c).

Unusual degree programs: 3-2 engineering with University at Buffalo, the State University of New York; Stony Brook University, State University of New York; Alfred University; Clarkson University; Binghamton University, State University of New York; Case Western Reserve University; forestry with Duke University, State University of New York College of Environmental Science and Forestry.

Computers: Campuswide network is available.

Library: Memorial Library.

STUDENT LIFE

Housing options: coed, cooperative, special housing for students with disabilities. Campus housing is university owned.

Activities and organizations: drama/theater group, student-run newspaper, radio and television station, choral group.

Athletics Member NCAA. All Division III. ***Intercollegiate sports:*** baseball M, basketball M/W, cross-country running M/W, field hockey W, football M/W(c), golf W, gymnastics W, ice hockey M/W(c), lacrosse M/W, racquetball M(c)/W(c), rugby M(c)/W(c), soccer M/W, softball W, swimming and diving M/W, tennis W, track and field M/W, volleyball M(c)/W, wrestling M. ***Intramural sports:*** archery M/W, badminton M/W, baseball M, basketball M/W, bowling M/W, cross-country running M/W, fencing M/W, field hockey W, football M/W, golf M/W, gymnastics W, ice hockey M, lacrosse M/W, racquetball M/W, rugby M/W, skiing (cross-country) M/W, skiing (downhill) M/W, soccer M/W, softball M/W, squash M/W, swimming and diving M/W, table tennis M/W, tennis M/W, track and field M/W, volleyball M/W, weight lifting M/W, wrestling M.

Campus security: 24-hour emergency response devices and patrols, late-night transport/escort service.

COSTS & FINANCIAL AID

Costs (2016–17) ***Tuition:*** state resident $6470 full-time, $270 per credit hour part-time; nonresident $16,320 full-time, $680 per credit hour part-time. Full-time tuition and fees vary according to course load and degree level. Part-time tuition and fees vary according to course load and degree level. ***Required fees:*** $1636 full-time. ***Room and board:*** $12,600; room only: $7820. Room and board charges vary according to board plan and housing facility. ***Payment plan:*** installment. ***Waivers:*** employees or children of employees.

Financial Aid Of all full-time matriculated undergraduates who enrolled in 2015, 4,859 applied for aid, 3,737 were judged to have need, 344 had their need fully met. In 2015, 264 non-need-based awards were made. ***Average percent of need met:*** 66. ***Average financial aid package:*** $14,563. ***Average need-based loan:*** $4222. ***Average need-based gift aid:*** $5865. ***Average non-need-based aid:*** $3533. ***Average indebtedness upon graduation:*** $29,674.

APPLYING

Standardized Tests *Required for some:* SAT or ACT (for admission).

Options: electronic application, early admission, early action, deferred entrance.

Application fee: $50.

Required: essay or personal statement, high school transcript, minimum 2.3 GPA, 1 letter of recommendation. ***Recommended:*** minimum 3.0 GPA, 3 letters of recommendation, interview.

CONTACT

Director of Admission, State University of New York College at Cortland, PO Box 2000, Cortland, NY 13045. *Phone:* 607-753-4711. *Fax:* 607-753-5998. *E-mail:* admissions@cortland.edu.

State University of New York College at Geneseo

Geneseo, New York

http://www.geneseo.edu/

- **State-supported** comprehensive, founded 1871, part of State University of New York
- **Small-town** 220-acre campus with easy access to Rochester
- **Endowment** $30.2 million
- **Coed** 5,431 undergraduate students, 98% full-time, 59% women, 41% men
- **Moderately difficult** entrance level, 67% of applicants were admitted

UNDERGRAD STUDENTS

5,316 full-time, 115 part-time. Students come from 25 states and territories; 22 other countries; 2% are from out of state; 3% Black or African American, non-Hispanic/Latino; 7% Hispanic/Latino; 6% Asian, non-Hispanic/Latino; 0.2% American Indian or Alaska Native, non-Hispanic/Latino; 3% Two or more races, non-Hispanic/Latino; 3% Race/ethnicity unknown; 3% international; 5% transferred in; 54% live on campus.

Freshmen:

Admission: 8,892 applied, 5,944 admitted, 1,238 enrolled. ***Average high school GPA:*** 3.67. ***Test scores:*** SAT critical reading scores over 500: 89%; SAT math scores over 500: 91%; ACT scores over 18: 99%; SAT critical reading scores over 600: 51%; SAT math scores over 600: 57%; ACT scores over 24: 85%; SAT critical reading scores over 700: 13%; SAT math scores over 700: 9%; ACT scores over 30: 22%.

Retention: 87% of full-time freshmen returned.

FACULTY

Total: 361, 70% full-time, 71% with terminal degrees.

Student/faculty ratio: 19:1.

ACADEMICS

Calendar: semesters. *Degrees:* bachelor's and master's.

Special study options: advanced placement credit, distance learning, double majors, English as a second language, honors programs, independent study, internships, off-campus study, part-time degree program, services for LD students, study abroad, summer session for credit. ***ROTC:*** Army (c), Air Force (c).

Unusual degree programs: 3-2 business administration with Alfred University; Binghamton University, State University of New York; Clarkson University; Rochester Institute of Technology; Union College; engineering with Case Western Reserve; Clarkson University; Columbia University; University at Buffalo, State University of New York; optometry with SUNY College of Optometry, dentistry with SUNY at Buffalo, physical therapy with SUNY Upstate Medical University, osteopathy with New York Institute of Technology College of Osteopathic Medicine.

Computers: 351 computers/terminals and 3,000 ports are available on campus for general student use. Students can access the following: campus intranet, computer help desk, free student e-mail accounts, online (class) grades, online (class) registration, online (class) schedules. Campuswide network is available. 100% of college-owned or -operated housing units are wired for high-speed Internet access. Wireless service is available via entire campus.

Library: Milne Library plus 1 other. *Books:* 335,648 (physical), 147,389 (digital/electronic); *Serial titles:* 1,420 (physical), 224,286 (digital/electronic); *Databases:* 420. Weekly public service hours: 109; students can reserve study rooms.

STUDENT LIFE

Housing options: on-campus residence required through sophomore year; coed, special housing for students with disabilities. Campus housing is university owned. Freshman campus housing is guaranteed.

Activities and organizations: drama/theater group, student-run newspaper, radio and television station, choral group, Inter-Varsity Christian Fellowship, Alpha Phi Omega, Newman Catholic Community, Orchesis, Habitat for Humanity, national fraternities, national sororities.

Athletics Member NCAA. All Division III. ***Intercollegiate sports:*** baseball M(c), basketball M/W, cheerleading M(c)/W(c), crew M(c)/W(c), cross-country running M/W, equestrian sports W, fencing

M(c)/W(c), field hockey W, ice hockey M/W(c), lacrosse M/W, rugby M(c)/W(c), skiing (downhill) M(c)/W(c), soccer M/W, softball W, swimming and diving M/W, tennis M(c)/W, track and field M/W, ultimate Frisbee M(c)/W(c), volleyball M(c)/W, water polo M(c). ***Intramural sports:*** badminton M/W, basketball M/W, racquetball M/W, table tennis M/W.

Campus security: 24-hour emergency response devices and patrols, student patrols, late-night transport/escort service, controlled dormitory access.

Student services: health clinic, personal/psychological counseling, legal services.

COSTS & FINANCIAL AID

Costs (2016–17) ***Tuition:*** state resident $6470 full-time, $270 per credit hour part-time; nonresident $16,320 full-time, $680 per credit hour part-time. Part-time tuition and fees vary according to course load. ***Required fees:*** $1706 full-time, $71 per credit hour part-time. ***Room and board:*** $12,264; room only: $7660. Room and board charges vary according to board plan and housing facility. ***Payment plans:*** installment, deferred payment.

Financial Aid Of all full-time matriculated undergraduates who enrolled in 2016, 3,947 applied for aid, 2,546 were judged to have need, 263 had their need fully met. In 2016, 368 non-need-based awards were made. ***Average percent of need met:*** 41. ***Average financial aid package:*** $9487. ***Average need-based loan:*** $3624. ***Average need-based gift aid:*** $2242. ***Average non-need-based aid:*** $2774. ***Average indebtedness upon graduation:*** $24,784.

APPLYING

Standardized Tests *Required:* SAT or ACT (for admission).

Options: electronic application, early admission, early decision, deferred entrance.

Application fee: $50.

Required: high school transcript. ***Recommended:*** essay or personal statement, 1 letter of recommendation.

Application deadlines: 1/1 (freshmen), rolling (transfers).

Early decision deadline: 11/15.

Notification: 3/1 (freshmen), 12/15 (early decision).

CONTACT

Mr. Kevin J. Reed, Assistant Director of Admissions, State University of New York College at Geneseo, Doty Hall 200, Geneseo, NY 14454-1401. *Phone:* 585-245-5571. *Toll-free phone:* 866-245-5211. *Fax:* 585-245-5550. *E-mail:* admissions@geneseo.edu.

State University of New York College at Old Westbury

Old Westbury, New York

http://www.oldwestbury.edu/

- **State-supported** comprehensive, founded 1965, part of State University of New York System
- **Suburban** 604-acre campus with easy access to New York City
- **Coed** 4,242 undergraduate students, 86% full-time, 59% women, 41% men
- **Moderately difficult** entrance level, 69% of applicants were admitted

UNDERGRAD STUDENTS

3,632 full-time, 610 part-time. Students come from 14 states and territories; 11 other countries; 1% are from out of state; 27% Black or African American, non-Hispanic/Latino; 24% Hispanic/Latino; 11% Asian, non-Hispanic/Latino; 0.3% Native Hawaiian or other Pacific Islander, non-Hispanic/Latino; 0.3% American Indian or Alaska Native, non-Hispanic/Latino; 3% Two or more races, non-Hispanic/Latino; 2% Race/ethnicity unknown; 0.1% international; 20% transferred in; 19% live on campus.

Freshmen:

Admission: 3,545 applied, 2,432 admitted, 501 enrolled. ***Average high school GPA:*** 3.1. ***Test scores:*** SAT critical reading scores over 500: 40%; SAT math scores over 500: 45%; SAT writing scores over 500: 34%; SAT critical reading scores over 600: 8%; SAT math scores over 600: 8%; SAT writing scores over 600: 5%; SAT critical reading scores over 700: 1%; SAT math scores over 700: 1%; SAT writing scores over 700: 1%.

Retention: 81% of full-time freshmen returned.

FACULTY

Total: 351, 47% full-time, 57% with terminal degrees.

Student/faculty ratio: 16:1.

ACADEMICS

Calendar: semesters. *Degrees:* certificates, bachelor's, master's, and post-master's certificates.

Special study options: academic remediation for entering students, advanced placement credit, distance learning, double majors, freshman honors college, honors programs, independent study, internships, off-campus study, part-time degree program, services for LD students, study abroad, summer session for credit. ***ROTC:*** Army (c), Air Force (c).

Unusual degree programs: 3-2 engineering with Stony Brook University, State University of New York; biological sciences/osteopathic medicine with New York College of Osteopathic Medicine.

Computers: 480 computers/terminals and 700 ports are available on campus for general student use. Students can access the following: campus intranet, free student e-mail accounts, online (class) grades, online (class) registration, financial aid, billing information. Campuswide network is available. 100% of college-owned or -operated housing units are wired for high-speed Internet access. Wireless service is available via entire campus.

Library: SUNY College at Old Westbury Library plus 1 other. *Books:* 156,872 (physical), 144,263 (digital/electronic); *Databases:* 138. Weekly public service hours: 99.

STUDENT LIFE

Housing options: coed. Campus housing is university owned. Freshman campus housing is guaranteed.

Activities and organizations: drama/theater group, student-run newspaper, radio station, choral group, Student Government Association, Alianza Latina, PRIDE, Step Tunes, Anime Magna Games Club, national fraternities, national sororities.

Athletics Member NCAA. All Division III. ***Intercollegiate sports:*** baseball M, basketball M/W, cross-country running M/W, golf M, lacrosse W, soccer M/W, softball W, swimming and diving M/W, volleyball W. ***Intramural sports:*** badminton M/W, basketball M/W, cheerleading M(c)/W(c), equestrian sports M(c)/W(c), football M/W, racquetball M/W, soccer M/W, softball W, squash M/W, ultimate Frisbee M/W, weight lifting M/W.

Campus security: 24-hour emergency response devices and patrols, student patrols, late-night transport/escort service, controlled dormitory access.

Student services: health clinic, personal/psychological counseling, women's center.

COSTS & FINANCIAL AID

Costs (2016–17) ***Tuition:*** state resident $6470 full-time, $270 per credit part-time; nonresident $16,320 full-time, $680 per credit part-time. Part-time tuition and fees vary according to course load. ***Required fees:*** $1213 full-time, $24 per credit part-time, $163 per term part-time. ***Room and board:*** $111,130; room only: $7300. Room and board charges vary according to housing facility. ***Payment plan:*** installment. ***Waivers:*** senior citizens.

Financial Aid Of all full-time matriculated undergraduates who enrolled in 2015, 2,853 applied for aid, 2,509 were judged to have need, 182 had their need fully met. 245 Federal Work-Study jobs (averaging $975). In 2015, 26 non-need-based awards were made. ***Average percent of need met:*** 60. ***Average financial aid package:*** $10,395. ***Average need-based loan:*** $3960. ***Average need-based gift aid:*** $6876. ***Average non-need-based aid:*** $5636.

APPLYING

Standardized Tests *Required:* SAT or ACT (for admission).

Options: electronic application, early admission, early decision, deferred entrance.

Application fee: $50.

Required: essay or personal statement, high school transcript, 2 letters of recommendation. ***Required for some:*** interview.

Application deadlines: rolling (freshmen), 12/15 (transfers).

Early decision deadline: 11/1.

Notification: continuous (freshmen), continuous (transfers), 12/15 (early decision).

CONTACT

State University of New York College at Old Westbury, PO Box 307, Old Westbury, NY 11568. *Phone:* 516-876-3073. *Fax:* 516-876-3307. *E-mail:* enroll@oldwestbury.edu.

State University of New York College at Oneonta

Oneonta, New York

http://www.oneonta.edu/

CONTACT

Ms. Karen Brown, Director of Admissions, State University of New York College at Oneonta, Alumni Hall 116, Oneonta, NY 13820-4015. *Phone:* 607-436-2524. *Toll-free phone:* 800-SUNY-123. *Fax:* 607-436-3074. *E-mail:* admissions@oneonta.edu.

State University of New York College at Potsdam

Potsdam, New York

http://www.potsdam.edu/

- **State-supported** comprehensive, founded 1816, part of State University of New York System
- **Small-town** 240-acre campus
- **Endowment** $27.2 million
- **Coed** 3,416 undergraduate students, 97% full-time, 58% women, 42% men
- **Moderately difficult** entrance level, 72% of applicants were admitted

UNDERGRAD STUDENTS

3,321 full-time, 95 part-time. Students come from 29 states and territories; 9 other countries; 4% are from out of state; 11% Black or African American, non-Hispanic/Latino; 14% Hispanic/Latino; 2% Asian, non-Hispanic/Latino; 0.1% Native Hawaiian or other Pacific Islander, non-Hispanic/Latino; 2% American Indian or Alaska Native, non-Hispanic/Latino; 3% Two or more races, non-Hispanic/Latino; 5% Race/ethnicity unknown; 0.7% international; 7% transferred in; 61% live on campus.

Freshmen:
Admission: 5,454 applied, 3,915 admitted, 788 enrolled.
Retention: 75% of full-time freshmen returned.

FACULTY

Total: 372, 70% full-time, 67% with terminal degrees.
Student/faculty ratio: 11:1.

ACADEMICS

Calendar: semesters. *Degrees:* bachelor's, master's, and post-master's certificates.

Special study options: advanced placement credit, distance learning, double majors, honors programs, independent study, internships, off-campus study, part-time degree program, services for LD students, student-designed majors, study abroad, summer session for credit. ***ROTC:*** Army (c), Air Force (c).

Unusual degree programs: 3-2 engineering with Clarkson University; physics, computer science, chemistry, mathematics with Clarkson University.

Computers: 608 computers/terminals and 80 ports are available on campus for general student use. Students can access the following: campus intranet, computer help desk, free student e-mail accounts, online (class) grades, online (class) registration, online (class) schedules, online access to financial aid status, unofficial transcripts, billing, meal plan and housing sign-up. Campuswide network is available. 100% of college-owned or -operated housing units are wired for high-speed Internet access. Wireless service is available via classrooms, computer centers, computer labs, dorm rooms, learning centers, libraries, student centers.

Library: F. W. Crumb Memorial Library plus 1 other. *Books:* 437,300 (physical), 18,665 (digital/electronic); *Serial titles:* 59,000 (physical). Weekly public service hours: 119; study areas open 24 hours, 5-7 days a week; students can reserve study rooms.

STUDENT LIFE

Housing options: on-campus residence required through sophomore year; coed, special housing for students with disabilities. Campus housing is university owned. Freshman campus housing is guaranteed.

Activities and organizations: drama/theater group, student-run newspaper, radio station, choral group, Student Government Association, Crane Student Association, Black Student Alliance, WAIH Radio, Emerging Leaders, national fraternities, national sororities.

Athletics Member NCAA. All Division III. ***Intercollegiate sports:*** basketball M/W, cross-country running M/W, golf M, ice hockey M/W, lacrosse M/W, soccer M/W, swimming and diving M/W, track and field M/W, volleyball W. ***Intramural sports:*** basketball M/W, bowling M(c)/W(c), cheerleading M(c)/W(c), ice hockey M(c)/W(c), racquetball M/W, rugby M(c)/W(c), skiing (downhill) M(c)/W(c), soccer M/W, softball M/W, track and field M(c)/W(c), triathlon M/W, ultimate Frisbee M(c)/W(c), volleyball M/W.

Campus security: 24-hour emergency response devices and patrols, late-night transport/escort service, controlled dormitory access, foot and bike patrol, educational programs, campus rescue squad, portable jump start packets, vehicle lock outs and parking management.

Student services: health clinic, personal/psychological counseling, women's center, legal services.

COSTS & FINANCIAL AID

Costs (2016–17) ***Tuition:*** state resident $6470 full-time, $270 per credit hour part-time; nonresident $16,320 full-time, $680 per credit hour part-time. ***Required fees:*** $1514 full-time, $81 per credit hour part-time. ***Room and board:*** $12,420; room only: $7120. Room and board charges vary according to board plan and housing facility. ***Payment plan:*** installment. ***Waivers:*** employees or children of employees.

Financial Aid Of all full-time matriculated undergraduates who enrolled in 2016, 3,063 applied for aid, 2,460 were judged to have need, 220 had their need fully met. 206 Federal Work-Study jobs (averaging $1123). In 2016, 279 non-need-based awards were made. ***Average percent of need met:*** 95. ***Average financial aid package:*** $16,045. ***Average need-based loan:*** $4571. ***Average need-based gift aid:*** $8044. ***Average non-need-based aid:*** $3129. ***Average indebtedness upon graduation:*** $28,582. ***Financial aid deadline:*** 5/1.

APPLYING

Options: electronic application, early admission, deferred entrance.
Application fee: $50.
Required: high school transcript, minimum 2.5 GPA, 1 letter of recommendation. ***Required for some:*** essay or personal statement, minimum 2.0 GPA, interview, DVD audition for music.
Application deadlines: rolling (freshmen), rolling (transfers).
Notification: continuous (freshmen), continuous (transfers).

CONTACT

Mr. Thomas Nesbitt, Director of Admissions, State University of New York College at Potsdam, 44 Pierrepont Avenue, Potsdam, NY 13676. *Phone:* 315-267-2180. *Toll-free phone:* 877-POTSDAM. *Fax:* 315-267-2163. *E-mail:* admissions@potsdam.edu.

State University of New York College of Agriculture and Technology at Cobleskill

Cobleskill, New York

http://www.cobleskill.edu/

- **State-supported** 4-year, founded 1916, part of State University of New York System
- **Small-town** 950-acre campus with easy access to Albany, NY
- **Endowment** $2.5 million
- **Coed** 2,304 undergraduate students, 95% full-time, 53% women, 47% men
- **Minimally difficult** entrance level, 78% of applicants were admitted

UNDERGRAD STUDENTS
2,197 full-time, 107 part-time. Students come from 12 states and territories; 8 other countries; 7% are from out of state; 13% Black or African American, non-Hispanic/Latino; 5% Hispanic/Latino; 2% Asian, non-Hispanic/Latino; 0.1% Native Hawaiian or other Pacific Islander, non-Hispanic/Latino; 0.5% American Indian or Alaska Native, non-Hispanic/Latino; 8% Two or more races, non-Hispanic/Latino; 0.3% Race/ethnicity unknown; 1% international; 9% transferred in; 59% live on campus.

Freshmen:
Admission: 2,897 applied, 2,265 admitted, 656 enrolled. ***Average high school GPA:*** 2.75. ***Test scores:*** SAT critical reading scores over 500: 53%; SAT math scores over 500: 54%; ACT scores over 18: 93%; SAT critical reading scores over 600: 9%; SAT math scores over 600: 8%; ACT scores over 24: 26%; SAT critical reading scores over 700: 1%; ACT scores over 30: 2%.
Retention: 70% of full-time freshmen returned.

FACULTY
Total: 178, 59% full-time, 30% with terminal degrees.
Student/faculty ratio: 17:1.

ACADEMICS
Calendar: semesters. *Degrees:* certificates, associate, and bachelor's.
Special study options: academic remediation for entering students, adult/continuing education programs, advanced placement credit, cooperative education, distance learning, honors programs, independent study, internships, off-campus study, part-time degree program, services for LD students, study abroad, summer session for credit.
Computers: 504 computers/terminals and 455 ports are available on campus for general student use. Students can access the following: campus intranet, computer help desk, free student e-mail accounts, online (class) grades, online (class) registration, online (class) schedules. Campuswide network is available. 100% of college-owned or -operated housing units are wired for high-speed Internet access. Wireless service is available via entire campus.
Library: Jared van Wagenen Library. *Books:* 53,260 (physical), 54,322 (digital/electronic); *Serial titles:* 200 (physical), 91,655 (digital/electronic); *Databases:* 60. Weekly public service hours: 76; students can reserve study rooms.

STUDENT LIFE
Housing options: on-campus residence required through sophomore year; coed, men-only, women-only, special housing for students with disabilities. Campus housing is university owned.
Activities and organizations: drama/theater group, student-run newspaper, choral group, Dairy Cattle Club, Wildlife Society, Canine Club, Woodsmen's Club, American Fisheries Society.
Athletics Member NCAA. All Division III. ***Intercollegiate sports:*** basketball M/W, cheerleading M/W, cross-country running M/W, equestrian sports M/W, golf M/W, lacrosse M, soccer M/W, softball W, swimming and diving M/W, tennis W, track and field M/W, volleyball W. ***Intramural sports:*** baseball M(c), bowling M/W, football M/W, soccer M/W, softball M/W.
Campus security: 24-hour emergency response devices and patrols, student patrols, late-night transport/escort service, controlled dormitory access, bicycle patrols, horse-mounted patrols.
Student services: health clinic, personal/psychological counseling.

COSTS & FINANCIAL AID
Costs (2016–17) ***Tuition:*** state resident $6470 full-time, $270 per credit hour part-time; nonresident $16,320 full-time, $680 per credit hour part-time. Full-time tuition and fees vary according to degree level and program. Part-time tuition and fees vary according to degree level and program. ***Required fees:*** $1459 full-time, $58 per credit hour part-time. ***Room and board:*** $13,018; room only: $7800. Room and board charges vary according to board plan and housing facility. ***Payment plans:*** installment, deferred payment. ***Waivers:*** senior citizens and employees or children of employees.
Financial Aid Of all full-time matriculated undergraduates who enrolled in 2015, 2,176 applied for aid, 1,991 were judged to have need, 22 had their need fully met. 136 Federal Work-Study jobs (averaging $622). 460 state and other part-time jobs (averaging $1404). In 2015, 54 non-need-based awards were made. ***Average percent of need met:*** 64. ***Average financial aid package:*** $7513. ***Average need-based loan:*** $225. ***Average need-based gift aid:*** $4432. ***Average non-need-based aid:*** $2453. ***Average indebtedness upon graduation:*** $26,520.

APPLYING
Standardized Tests *Required for some:* SAT or ACT (for admission).
Options: electronic application, early admission, deferred entrance.
Application fee: $50.
Required: high school transcript. ***Required for some:*** essay or personal statement, minimum 2.0 GPA, 3 letters of recommendation, interview. ***Recommended:*** minimum 1.8 GPA.
Application deadlines: rolling (freshmen), rolling (transfers).
Notification: continuous (freshmen), continuous (transfers).

CONTACT
Lisa Starr-DeCarlo, Office Assistant 1, State University of New York College of Agriculture and Technology at Cobleskill, 213 Knapp Hall, Cobleskill, NY 12043. *Phone:* 518-255-5525. *Toll-free phone:* 800-295-8988. *Fax:* 518-255-6769. *E-mail:* admissions@cobleskill.edu.

★ State University of New York College of Environmental Science and Forestry

Syracuse, New York

http://www.esf.edu/

- **State-supported** university, founded 1911, part of State University of New York System
- **Urban** 17-acre campus with easy access to Syracuse
- **Endowment** $27.6 million
- **Coed** 2,271 undergraduate students, 75% full-time, 48% women, 52% men
- **Very difficult** entrance level, 54% of applicants were admitted

UNDERGRAD STUDENTS
1,711 full-time, 560 part-time. Students come from 27 states and territories; 8 other countries; 15% are from out of state; 2% Black or African American, non-Hispanic/Latino; 6% Hispanic/Latino; 4% Asian, non-Hispanic/Latino; 0.1% American Indian or Alaska Native, non-Hispanic/Latino; 3% Two or more races, non-Hispanic/Latino; 5% Race/ethnicity unknown; 2% international; 11% transferred in; 35% live on campus.

Freshmen:
Admission: 1,651 applied, 895 admitted, 327 enrolled. ***Average high school GPA:*** 3.75. ***Test scores:*** SAT critical reading scores over 500: 91%; SAT math scores over 500: 96%; ACT scores over 18: 100%; SAT critical reading scores over 600: 48%; SAT math scores over 600: 53%; ACT scores over 24: 81%; SAT critical reading scores over 700: 7%; SAT math scores over 700: 8%; ACT scores over 30: 17%.
Retention: 83% of full-time freshmen returned.

FACULTY
Total: 159, 73% full-time, 70% with terminal degrees.
Student/faculty ratio: 13:1.

ACADEMICS
Calendar: semesters. *Degrees:* associate, bachelor's, master's, doctoral, and postbachelor's certificates.
Special study options: accelerated degree program, advanced placement credit, cooperative education, distance learning, double majors, English as a second language, freshman honors college, honors programs, independent study, internships, off-campus study, part-time degree program, services for LD students, study abroad, summer session for credit. ***ROTC:*** Army (c), Air Force (c).
Computers: 350 computers/terminals and 2,250 ports are available on campus for general student use. Students can access the following: campus intranet, computer help desk, free student e-mail accounts, online (class) grades, online (class) registration, online (class) schedules. Campuswide network is available. 100% of college-owned or -operated housing units are wired for high-speed Internet access. Wireless service is available via classrooms, computer centers, computer labs, dorm rooms, libraries, student centers.

Library: F. Franklin Moon Library plus 1 other. *Books:* 137,535 (physical), 348,596 (digital/electronic); *Serial titles:* 1,741 (physical), 241,084 (digital/electronic); *Databases:* 171. Weekly public service hours: 97.

STUDENT LIFE

Housing options: on-campus residence required for freshman year; coed, special housing for students with disabilities. Campus housing is university owned and is provided by a third party. Freshman campus housing is guaranteed.

Activities and organizations: drama/theater group, student-run newspaper, choral group, marching band, Bob Marshall/Outing Club, Forestry Club, Student Environmental Action Coalition, Student Green Campus Initiative, Alpha Phi Omega (Service).

Athletics Member USCAA. ***Intercollegiate sports:*** basketball M, cross-country running M/W, golf M/W, soccer M/W, track and field M/W. ***Intramural sports:*** archery M/W, badminton M/W, baseball M, basketball M/W, bowling M/W, cheerleading M/W, crew M/W, cross-country running M/W, equestrian sports M/W, fencing M/W, field hockey W, football M, gymnastics M/W, ice hockey M/W, lacrosse M/W, racquetball M/W, riflery M, rugby M/W, sailing M/W, skiing (downhill) M/W, soccer M/W, softball M/W, squash M/W, swimming and diving M/W, table tennis M/W, tennis M/W, track and field M/W, ultimate Frisbee M/W, volleyball M/W.

Campus security: 24-hour emergency response devices and patrols, late-night transport/escort service, controlled dormitory access.

Student services: health clinic, personal/psychological counseling, women's center, legal services.

COSTS & FINANCIAL AID

Costs (2016–17) ***Tuition:*** state resident $6470 full-time, $270 per credit hour part-time; nonresident $16,320 full-time, $680 per credit hour part-time. Full-time tuition and fees vary according to location. Part-time tuition and fees vary according to course load and location. ***Required fees:*** $1633 full-time. ***Room and board:*** $15,040; room only: $8060. Room and board charges vary according to board plan, housing facility, and location. ***Payment plans:*** installment, deferred payment.

Financial Aid Of all full-time matriculated undergraduates who enrolled in 2015, 1,412 applied for aid, 1,071 were judged to have need, 755 had their need fully met. 170 Federal Work-Study jobs (averaging $1788). 333 state and other part-time jobs (averaging $1063). In 2015, 251 non-need-based awards were made. ***Average percent of need met:*** 87. ***Average financial aid package:*** $15,400. ***Average need-based loan:*** $4400. ***Average need-based gift aid:*** $4700. ***Average non-need-based aid:*** $3075. ***Average indebtedness upon graduation:*** $24,269.

APPLYING

Standardized Tests *Required:* SAT or ACT (for admission).

Options: electronic application, early admission, early decision, deferred entrance.

Application fee: $50.

Required: essay or personal statement, high school transcript, minimum 3.0 GPA, supplemental application. ***Recommended:*** 1 letter of recommendation, interview.

Application deadlines: 2/1 (freshmen), 3/1 (transfers).

Early decision deadline: 12/1.

Notification: continuous (freshmen), continuous (out-of-state freshmen), continuous (transfers), rolling (early decision).

CONTACT

Ms. Susan Sanford, Director of Admissions, State University of New York College of Environmental Science and Forestry, Office of Undergraduate Admissions, Gateway Center 1 Forestry Drive, Syracuse, NY 13210-2779. *Phone:* 315-470-6600. *Fax:* 315-470-6933. *E-mail:* esfinfo@esf.edu.

See page 1522 for the College Close-Up.

State University of New York College of Technology at Alfred

Alfred, New York

http://www.alfredstate.edu/

- **State-supported** primarily 2-year, founded 1908, part of State University of New York System
- **Rural** 1084-acre campus with easy access to Rochester, Buffalo
- **Endowment** $4.5 million
- **Coed** 3,699 undergraduate students, 91% full-time, 38% women, 62% men
- **Moderately difficult** entrance level, 57% of applicants were admitted

UNDERGRAD STUDENTS

3,378 full-time, 321 part-time. Students come from 35 states and territories; 9 other countries; 4% are from out of state; 10% Black or African American, non-Hispanic/Latino; 7% Hispanic/Latino; 1% Asian, non-Hispanic/Latino; 0.1% Native Hawaiian or other Pacific Islander, non-Hispanic/Latino; 0.2% American Indian or Alaska Native, non-Hispanic/Latino; 2% Two or more races, non-Hispanic/Latino; 1% Race/ethnicity unknown; 2% international; 9% transferred in; 64% live on campus.

Freshmen:

Admission: 4,912 applied, 2,790 admitted, 1,058 enrolled. ***Average high school GPA:*** 3.04. ***Test scores:*** SAT critical reading scores over 500: 36%; SAT math scores over 500: 47%; SAT critical reading scores over 600: 8%; SAT math scores over 600: 12%; SAT critical reading scores over 700: 1%; SAT math scores over 700: 1%.

Retention: 88% of full-time freshmen returned.

FACULTY

Total: 226, 77% full-time, 28% with terminal degrees.

Student/faculty ratio: 18:1.

ACADEMICS

Calendar: semesters. *Degrees:* certificates, associate, and bachelor's.

Special study options: academic remediation for entering students, accelerated degree program, adult/continuing education programs, advanced placement credit, cooperative education, distance learning, double majors, English as a second language, honors programs, independent study, internships, off-campus study, part-time degree program, services for LD students, student-designed majors, study abroad, summer session for credit. ***ROTC:*** Army (c).

Computers: 108 computers/terminals are available on campus for general student use. Students can access the following: campus intranet, computer help desk, free student e-mail accounts, online (class) grades, online (class) registration, online (class) schedules. Campuswide network is available. 100% of college-owned or -operated housing units are wired for high-speed Internet access. Wireless service is available via entire campus.

Library: Walter C. Hinkle Memorial Library plus 1 other. *Books:* 54,671 (physical), 49,782 (digital/electronic); *Serial titles:* 253 (physical), 164,768 (digital/electronic); *Databases:* 193. Weekly public service hours: 88.

STUDENT LIFE

Housing options: coed, men-only, women-only, special housing for students with disabilities. Campus housing is university owned. Freshman campus housing is guaranteed.

Activities and organizations: drama/theater group, student-run newspaper, radio station, choral group, Outdoor Recreation Club, Caribbean Student Association, Alfred Programming Board, Pioneer Woodsmen, Disaster Relief Team.

Athletics Member NCAA, USCAA. All Division III. ***Intercollegiate sports:*** baseball M, basketball M/W, cross-country running M/W, football M, lacrosse M, soccer M/W, softball W, swimming and diving M/W, track and field M/W, volleyball W, wrestling M. ***Intramural sports:*** basketball M/W, equestrian sports M(c)/W(c), football M, golf M/W, ice hockey M(c), rock climbing M/W, soccer M/W, softball M/W, swimming and diving M/W, tennis M/W, ultimate Frisbee M/W, volleyball M/W.

Campus security: 24-hour emergency response devices and patrols, late-night transport/escort service, controlled dormitory access, residence hall entrance guards.

Student services: health clinic, personal/psychological counseling.

COSTS & FINANCIAL AID

Costs (2016–17) ***One-time required fee:*** $110. ***Tuition:*** state resident $6470 full-time, $270 per credit part-time; nonresident $9740 full-time, $406 per credit part-time. Full-time tuition and fees vary according to course load and degree level. Part-time tuition and fees vary according to course load and degree level. ***Required fees:*** $1605 full-time, $66 per credit part-time, $10 per credit part-time. ***Room and board:*** $11,820; room only: $7280. Room and board charges vary according to board plan and housing facility. ***Payment plan:*** installment. ***Waivers:*** employees or children of employees.

Financial Aid Of all full-time matriculated undergraduates who enrolled in 2015, 3,095 applied for aid, 2,712 were judged to have need, 330 had their need fully met. In 2015, 184 non-need-based awards were made. ***Average percent of need met:*** 57. ***Average financial aid package:*** $11,156. ***Average need-based loan:*** $3939. ***Average need-based gift aid:*** $6852. ***Average non-need-based aid:*** $5680. ***Average indebtedness upon graduation:*** $30,796.

APPLYING

Standardized Tests *Required for some:* SAT or ACT (for admission). *Recommended:* SAT or ACT (for admission).

Options: electronic application.

Application fee: $50.

Required: high school transcript, minimum 2.0 GPA, Common Application with essay on supplemental application. ***Recommended:*** essay or personal statement, interview.

Application deadlines: rolling (freshmen), rolling (transfers).

Notification: continuous (freshmen), continuous (transfers).

CONTACT

Mrs. Goodrich Deborah, Associate Vice President for Enrollment Management, State University of New York College of Technology at Alfred, Huntington Administration Building, 10 Upper College Drive, Alfred, NY 14802. *Phone:* 607-587-3945. *Toll-free phone:* 800-4-ALFRED. *Fax:* 607-587-4299. *E-mail:* admissions@alfredstate.edu.

State University of New York College of Technology at Canton

Canton, New York

http://www.canton.edu/

- **State-supported** 4-year, founded 1906, part of State University of New York System
- **Small-town** 555-acre campus
- **Endowment** $10.8 million
- **Coed** 3,241 undergraduate students, 83% full-time, 57% women, 43% men
- **Minimally difficult** entrance level, 83% of applicants were admitted

UNDERGRAD STUDENTS

2,676 full-time, 565 part-time. Students come from 31 states and territories; 19 other countries; 3% are from out of state; 14% Black or African American, non-Hispanic/Latino; 11% Hispanic/Latino; 1% Asian, non-Hispanic/Latino; 0.2% Native Hawaiian or other Pacific Islander, non-Hispanic/Latino; 2% American Indian or Alaska Native, non-Hispanic/Latino; 2% Two or more races, non-Hispanic/Latino; 2% Race/ethnicity unknown; 2% international; 11% transferred in; 44% live on campus.

Freshmen:

Admission: 3,017 applied, 2,490 admitted, 699 enrolled. ***Average high school GPA:*** 2.9. ***Test scores:*** SAT critical reading scores over 500: 29%; SAT math scores over 500: 33%; SAT writing scores over 500: 17%; ACT scores over 18: 73%; SAT critical reading scores over 600: 4%; SAT math scores over 600: 5%; SAT writing scores over 600: 3%; ACT scores over 24: 13%; ACT scores over 30: 1%.

Retention: 71% of full-time freshmen returned.

FACULTY

Total: 235, 54% full-time, 34% with terminal degrees.

Student/faculty ratio: 18:1.

ACADEMICS

Calendar: semesters. *Degrees:* certificates, associate, and bachelor's.

Special study options: academic remediation for entering students, advanced placement credit, cooperative education, distance learning, honors programs, independent study, internships, off-campus study, services for LD students, study abroad, summer session for credit. ***ROTC:*** Army (c), Air Force (c).

Computers: 833 computers/terminals are available on campus for general student use. Students can access the following: campus intranet, computer help desk, free student e-mail accounts, online (class) grades, online (class) registration, online (class) schedules, online bill payment. Campuswide network is available. 100% of college-owned or -operated housing units are wired for high-speed Internet access. Wireless service is available via classrooms, computer centers, computer labs, learning centers, libraries, student centers.

Library: Southworth Library. *Books:* 32,088 (physical), 154,715 (digital/electronic); *Serial titles:* 51 (physical), 11 (digital/electronic); *Databases:* 96. Weekly public service hours: 125.

STUDENT LIFE

Housing options: on-campus residence required through sophomore year; coed, special housing for students with disabilities. Campus housing is university owned. Freshman applicants given priority for college housing.

Activities and organizations: drama/theater group, choral group, Student Government Alliance, College Activities Board, Greek Council, Caribbean United, Brother to Brother.

Athletics Member NCAA, USCAA. All Division III. ***Intercollegiate sports:*** baseball M, basketball M/W, cross-country running M/W, golf M/W, ice hockey M/W, lacrosse M/W, soccer M/W, softball W, volleyball W. ***Intramural sports:*** basketball M/W, cheerleading M(c)/W(c), football M/W, ice hockey M(c), soccer M/W, softball M/W, ultimate Frisbee M(c)/W(c), volleyball M/W.

Campus security: 24-hour emergency response devices and patrols, late-night transport/escort service, controlled dormitory access.

Student services: health clinic, personal/psychological counseling.

COSTS & FINANCIAL AID

Costs (2016–17) ***One-time required fee:*** $100. ***Tuition:*** state resident $6470 full-time, $270 per credit hour part-time; nonresident $16,320 full-time, $680 per credit hour part-time. Full-time tuition and fees vary according to degree level. Part-time tuition and fees vary according to degree level. ***Required fees:*** $1411 full-time, $57 per credit hour part-time, $5 per term part-time. ***Room and board:*** $12,150; room only: $7100. Room and board charges vary according to board plan and housing facility. ***Payment plans:*** installment, deferred payment. ***Waivers:*** employees or children of employees.

Financial Aid Of all full-time matriculated undergraduates who enrolled in 2015, 2,454 applied for aid, 2,233 were judged to have need, 388 had their need fully met. 178 Federal Work-Study jobs (averaging $1123). 13 state and other part-time jobs (averaging $1206). In 2015, 20 non-need-based awards were made. ***Average percent of need met:*** 18. ***Average financial aid package:*** $10,876. ***Average need-based loan:*** $3958. ***Average need-based gift aid:*** $8015. ***Average non-need-based aid:*** $2350. ***Average indebtedness upon graduation:*** $31,665.

APPLYING

Standardized Tests *Required for some:* SAT or ACT (for admission).

Options: electronic application, deferred entrance.

Application fee: $50.

Required: high school transcript. ***Required for some:*** essay or personal statement, interview. ***Recommended:*** minimum 2.0 GPA.

Application deadlines: 8/30 (freshmen), rolling (out-of-state freshmen), 8/30 (transfers).

Notification: continuous (freshmen), continuous (out-of-state freshmen), continuous (transfers).

CONTACT

Melissa Evans, Director of Admissions, State University of New York College of Technology at Canton, 34 Cornell Drive, Canton, NY 13617. *Phone:* 315-386-7123. *Toll-free phone:* 800-388-7123. *Fax:* 315-386-7929. *E-mail:* admissions@canton.edu.

State University of New York College of Technology at Delhi

Delhi, New York

http://www.delhi.edu/

- **State-supported** comprehensive, founded 1913, part of State University of New York System
- **Rural** 405-acre campus
- **Endowment** $4.1 million
- **Coed**
- **Moderately difficult** entrance level

FACULTY

Student/faculty ratio: 14:1.

ACADEMICS

Calendar: semesters. *Degrees:* certificates, associate, bachelor's, and master's.

Library: Resnick Library plus 1 other. *Books:* 51,725 (physical), 1,415 (digital/electronic); *Serial titles:* 113 (physical), 300,000 (digital/electronic); *Databases:* 64. Weekly public service hours: 93; students can reserve study rooms.

STUDENT LIFE

Housing options: on-campus residence required through sophomore year; coed, women-only. Campus housing is university owned and is provided by a third party.

Activities and organizations: drama/theater group, student-run newspaper, radio and television station, Latin American Student Organization, Hotel Sales Management Association, student radio station, Phi Theta Kappa, Student Programming Board, national fraternities.

Athletics Member NAIA, NJCAA.

Campus security: 24-hour emergency response devices and patrols, late-night transport/escort service, controlled dormitory access.

Student services: health clinic, personal/psychological counseling.

COSTS & FINANCIAL AID

Costs (2016–17) ***Tuition:*** state resident $6470 full-time, $270 per credit hour part-time; nonresident $10,840 full-time, $452 per credit hour part-time. Full-time tuition and fees vary according to degree level and location. Part-time tuition and fees vary according to course load, degree level, and location. ***Required fees:*** $1625 full-time, $56 per credit hour part-time, $5 per term part-time. ***Room and board:*** $11,680; room only: $6700. Room and board charges vary according to board plan and housing facility.

Financial Aid Of all full-time matriculated undergraduates who enrolled in 2015, 72 Federal Work-Study jobs (averaging $1188). ***Average indebtedness upon graduation:*** $28,367.

APPLYING

Standardized Tests *Recommended:* SAT or ACT (for admission).

Options: electronic application, deferred entrance.

Application fee: $50.

Required: high school transcript. ***Required for some:*** minimum 2.0 GPA, associate degree for some bachelor programs, RN license for BSN program. ***Recommended:*** interview.

CONTACT

State University of New York College of Technology at Delhi, 2 Main Sreet - Stop 2, Delhi, NY 13753. *Phone:* 607-746-4550. *Toll-free phone:* 800-96-DELHI. *Fax:* 607-746-4104. *E-mail:* enroll@delhi.edu.

State University of New York Downstate Medical Center

Brooklyn, New York

http://www.downstate.edu/

CONTACT

Admissions Office, State University of New York Downstate Medical Center, 450 Clarkson Avenue, Brooklyn, NY 11203-2446. *Phone:* 718-270-2446. *Fax:* 718-270-7592. *E-mail:* admissions@downstate.edu.

State University of New York Empire State College

Saratoga Springs, New York

http://www.esc.edu/

- **State-supported** comprehensive, founded 1971, part of State University of New York System
- **Small-town** campus
- **Endowment** $17.0 million
- **Coed** 10,191 undergraduate students, 38% full-time, 62% women, 38% men
- **Noncompetitive** entrance level, 76% of applicants were admitted

UNDERGRAD STUDENTS

3,841 full-time, 6,350 part-time. 5% are from out of state; 15% Black or African American, non-Hispanic/Latino; 13% Hispanic/Latino; 2% Asian, non-Hispanic/Latino; 0.2% Native Hawaiian or other Pacific Islander, non-Hispanic/Latino; 0.5% American Indian or Alaska Native, non-Hispanic/Latino; 2% Two or more races, non-Hispanic/Latino; 6% Race/ethnicity unknown; 1% international; 12% transferred in.

Freshmen:

Admission: 904 applied, 690 admitted, 351 enrolled.

FACULTY

Total: 1,018, 18% full-time.

Student/faculty ratio: 14:1.

ACADEMICS

Calendar: trimesters. *Degrees:* certificates, associate, bachelor's, master's, and postbachelor's certificates (branch locations at 7 regional centers with 35 auxiliary units).

Special study options: accelerated degree program, adult/continuing education programs, advanced placement credit, distance learning, double majors, external degree program, independent study, off-campus study, part-time degree program, services for LD students, student-designed majors, summer session for credit.

Computers: 300 computers/terminals are available on campus for general student use. Students can access the following: computer help desk, free student e-mail accounts, online (class) grades, online (class) registration, online (class) schedules. Campuswide network is available.

Library:*Books:* 229,000 (digital/electronic); *Databases:* 94.

STUDENT LIFE

Housing options: college housing not available.

COSTS

Costs (2017–18) ***Tuition:*** state resident $6470 full-time, $270 per credit hour part-time; nonresident $16,320 full-time, $680 per credit hour part-time. ***Required fees:*** $515 full-time.

APPLYING

Options: electronic application, deferred entrance.

Application fee: $50.

Required: essay or personal statement, high school transcript.

CONTACT

Ms. Jennifer D'Agostino, Senior Director of Admissions, State University of New York Empire State College, Two Union Avenue, Saratoga Springs, NY 12866. *Phone:* 518-587-2100. *Toll-free phone:* 800-847-3000. *E-mail:* admissions@esc.edu.

State University of New York Maritime College

Throggs Neck, New York

http://www.sunymaritime.edu/

- **State-supported** comprehensive, founded 1874, part of State University of New York System
- **Urban** 55-acre campus with easy access to New York City
- **Endowment** $6.2 million
- **Coed** 1,635 undergraduate students, 97% full-time, 12% women, 88% men
- **Very difficult** entrance level, 58% of applicants were admitted

UNDERGRAD STUDENTS
1,590 full-time, 45 part-time. Students come from 29 states and territories; 15 other countries; 24% are from out of state; 4% Black or African American, non-Hispanic/Latino; 13% Hispanic/Latino; 5% Asian, non-Hispanic/Latino; 0.1% American Indian or Alaska Native, non-Hispanic/Latino; 2% Two or more races, non-Hispanic/Latino; 4% Race/ethnicity unknown; 2% international; 5% transferred in; 83% live on campus.

Freshmen:
Admission: 1,449 applied, 841 admitted, 309 enrolled. ***Average high school GPA:*** 3.4. ***Test scores:*** SAT critical reading scores over 500: 78%; SAT math scores over 500: 91%; SAT writing scores over 500: 64%; ACT scores over 18: 98%; SAT critical reading scores over 600: 24%; SAT math scores over 600: 42%; SAT writing scores over 600: 17%; ACT scores over 24: 63%; SAT critical reading scores over 700: 2%; SAT math scores over 700: 5%; SAT writing scores over 700: 1%; ACT scores over 30: 9%.
Retention: 85% of full-time freshmen returned.

FACULTY
Total: 149, 62% full-time, 35% with terminal degrees.

Student/faculty ratio: 16:1.

ACADEMICS
Calendar: semesters plus 2-month summer sea term. *Degrees:* associate, bachelor's, and master's.

Special study options: academic remediation for entering students, advanced placement credit, distance learning, double majors, independent study, internships, off-campus study, part-time degree program, services for LD students, study abroad, summer session for credit. ***ROTC:*** Army (c), Navy (b).

Computers: 160 computers/terminals and 650 ports are available on campus for general student use. Students can access the following: computer help desk, free student e-mail accounts, online (class) grades, online (class) registration, online (class) schedules. Campuswide network is available. 100% of college-owned or -operated housing units are wired for high-speed Internet access. Wireless service is available via classrooms, computer centers, computer labs, dorm rooms, learning centers, libraries, student centers.

Library: Stephen B. Luce Library. *Books:* 60,000 (physical), 40,000 (digital/electronic); *Serial titles:* 290 (physical), 3,217 (digital/electronic); *Databases:* 65. Weekly public service hours: 111; students can reserve study rooms.

STUDENT LIFE
Housing options: on-campus residence required through senior year; coed. Campus housing is university owned.

Activities and organizations: choral group, marching band, Student Government, Maritime Activities and Programs, The Cultural Club, Campus Crusade for Christ, The Maritime Divers Association.

Athletics Member NCAA. All Division III. ***Intercollegiate sports:*** baseball M, basketball M, crew M/W, cross-country running M/W, football M, ice hockey M(c), lacrosse M/W, riflery M(c)/W(c), sailing M/W, soccer M/W, swimming and diving M/W, volleyball W. ***Intramural sports:*** basketball M/W, football M/W, soccer M/W, softball M/W, volleyball M/W, water polo M/W.

Campus security: 24-hour emergency response devices and patrols, student patrols, late-night transport/escort service, controlled dormitory access.

Student services: health clinic, personal/psychological counseling.

COSTS & FINANCIAL AID
Costs (2016–17) ***Tuition:*** state resident $6470 full-time, $270 per credit hour part-time; nonresident $16,320 full-time, $680 per credit hour part-time. Full-time tuition and fees vary according to course load. Part-time tuition and fees vary according to course load. ***Required fees:*** $1364 full-time. ***Room and board:*** $11,948; room only: $7714. Room and board charges vary according to board plan and housing facility. ***Payment plan:*** installment.

Financial Aid Of all full-time matriculated undergraduates who enrolled in 2015, 1,261 applied for aid, 894 were judged to have need, 122 had their need fully met. 101 Federal Work-Study jobs (averaging $352). 235 state and other part-time jobs (averaging $1600). In 2015, 94 non-need-based awards were made. ***Average percent of need met:*** 20. ***Average financial aid package:*** $4446. ***Average need-based loan:*** $2160. ***Average need-based gift aid:*** $3553. ***Average non-need-based aid:*** $1399. ***Average indebtedness upon graduation:*** $3790.

APPLYING
Standardized Tests *Required:* SAT or ACT (for admission).

Options: electronic application, early decision, deferred entrance.

Application fee: $50.

Required: essay or personal statement. ***Recommended:*** high school transcript, interview.

Application deadlines: 1/31 (freshmen), rolling (transfers).

Early decision deadline: 11/1.

Notification: 3/1 (freshmen), continuous (transfers), 12/15 (early decision).

CONTACT
Mr. Rohan Howell, Dean of Admissions, State University of New York Maritime College, 6 Pennyfield Avenue, Throggs Neck, NY 10465. *Phone:* 718-409-2220. *Fax:* 718-409-7465. *E-mail:* rhowell@sunymaritime.edu.

State University of New York Polytechnic Institute

Utica, New York

http://www.sunypoly.edu/

- **State-supported** comprehensive, founded 1966, part of State University of New York System
- **Suburban** 850-acre campus
- **Endowment** $5.3 million
- **Coed** 2,082 undergraduate students, 84% full-time, 36% women, 64% men
- **Moderately difficult** entrance level, 60% of applicants were admitted

UNDERGRAD STUDENTS
1,742 full-time, 340 part-time. Students come from 11 states and territories; 15 other countries; 1% are from out of state; 7% Black or African American, non-Hispanic/Latino; 7% Hispanic/Latino; 4% Asian, non-Hispanic/Latino; 0.1% Native Hawaiian or other Pacific Islander, non-Hispanic/Latino; 0.1% American Indian or Alaska Native, non-Hispanic/Latino; 2% Two or more races, non-Hispanic/Latino; 0.2% Race/ethnicity unknown; 1% international; 16% transferred in; 38% live on campus.

Freshmen:
Admission: 2,319 applied, 1,402 admitted, 347 enrolled. ***Average high school GPA:*** 3.5. ***Test scores:*** SAT critical reading scores over 500: 67%; SAT math scores over 500: 83%; ACT scores over 18: 100%; SAT critical reading scores over 600: 24%; SAT math scores over 600: 36%; ACT scores over 24: 68%; SAT critical reading scores over 700: 4%; SAT math scores over 700: 8%; ACT scores over 30: 13%.
Retention: 74% of full-time freshmen returned.

FACULTY
Total: 244, 51% full-time, 56% with terminal degrees.

Student/faculty ratio: 17:1.

ACADEMICS
Calendar: semesters. *Degrees:* bachelor's, master's, doctoral, post-master's, and postbachelor's certificates.

Special study options: accelerated degree program, advanced placement credit, cooperative education, distance learning, double majors, English as a second language, independent study, internships, off-campus study, part-time degree program, services for LD students, study abroad, summer session for credit. ***ROTC:*** Army (c), Air Force (c).

Computers: 380 computers/terminals and 144 ports are available on campus for general student use. Students can access the following: campus intranet, computer help desk, free student e-mail accounts, online (class) grades, online (class) registration, online (class) schedules. Campuswide network is available. 100% of college-owned or -operated housing units are wired for high-speed Internet access. Wireless service is available via entire campus.

Library: Peter J. Cayan Library. *Books:* 141,702 (physical), 133,949 (digital/electronic); *Serial titles:* 2,526 (physical), 24,750 (digital/electronic); *Databases:* 62. Weekly public service hours: 80.

STUDENT LIFE

Housing options: on-campus residence required through sophomore year; coed, special housing for students with disabilities. Campus housing is university owned and leased by the school. Freshman campus housing is guaranteed.

Activities and organizations: student-run newspaper, radio and television station, International Student Association, SUNY Tech Gamers Club, Black and Latino American Student Union, Magic the Gathering, BAJA SAE (Society of Automotive Engineers).

Athletics Member NCAA. All Division III. ***Intercollegiate sports:*** baseball M, basketball M/W, cross-country running M/W, lacrosse M/W, soccer M/W, softball W, volleyball M/W. ***Intramural sports:*** badminton M/W, basketball M/W, bowling M/W, cross-country running M/W, football M, racquetball M/W, soccer M/W, softball M/W, volleyball M/W.

Campus security: 24-hour emergency response devices and patrols, student patrols, late-night transport/escort service, controlled dormitory access, closed-circuit TV monitors, 24-hour police department.

Student services: health clinic, personal/psychological counseling, legal services.

COSTS & FINANCIAL AID

Costs (2017–18) ***Tuition:*** state resident $6470 full-time, $270 per credit hour part-time; nonresident $16,320 full-time, $680 per credit hour part-time. Full-time tuition and fees vary according to course load and location. Part-time tuition and fees vary according to course load and location. ***Required fees:*** $1420 full-time, $54 per credit hour part-time. ***Room and board:*** $12,068. Room and board charges vary according to board plan and location. ***Payment plan:*** installment.

Financial Aid Of all full-time matriculated undergraduates who enrolled in 2016, 1,402 applied for aid, 1,138 were judged to have need, 1,126 had their need fully met. 126 Federal Work-Study jobs (averaging $1500). In 2016, 236 non-need-based awards were made. ***Average percent of need met:*** 99. ***Average financial aid package:*** $10,449. ***Average need-based loan:*** $4309. ***Average need-based gift aid:*** $7506. ***Average non-need-based aid:*** $4137.

APPLYING

Standardized Tests *Required:* SAT or ACT (for admission). *Recommended:* SAT Subject Tests (for admission).

Options: electronic application, early admission, early action, deferred entrance.

Application fee: $50.

Required: essay or personal statement, high school transcript, minimum 3.0 GPA, 2 letters of recommendation. ***Recommended:*** interview.

Application deadlines: rolling (freshmen), rolling (out-of-state freshmen), 8/1 (transfers), 11/15 (early action).

Notification: continuous until 1/15 (freshmen), continuous until 1/15 (out-of-state freshmen), continuous until 12/1 (transfers), 12/15 (early action).

CONTACT

Ms. Gina Liscio, Director of Admissions, State University of New York Polytechnic Institute, 100 Seymour Road, Utica, NY 13502. *Phone:* 315-792-7500. *Toll-free phone:* 866-278-6948. *Fax:* 315-792-7837. *E-mail:* admissions@sunyit.edu.

State University of New York Upstate Medical University

Syracuse, New York

http://www.upstate.edu/

CONTACT

Mrs. Donna L. Vavonese, Associate Director of Admissions, State University of New York Upstate Medical University, Weiskotten Hall, 766 Irving Avenue, Syracuse, NY 13210. *Phone:* 315-464-4570. *Toll-free phone:* 800-736-2171. *Fax:* 315-464-8867. *E-mail:* admiss@upstate.edu.

Stony Brook University, State University of New York

Stony Brook, New York

http://www.stonybrook.edu/

- **State-supported** university, founded 1957, part of State University of New York System
- **Suburban** 1450-acre campus with easy access to New York City
- **Endowment** $219.7 million
- **Coed** 17,026 undergraduate students, 93% full-time, 46% women, 54% men
- **Very difficult** entrance level, 41% of applicants were admitted

UNDERGRAD STUDENTS

15,858 full-time, 1,168 part-time. Students come from 47 states and territories; 128 other countries; 7% are from out of state; 7% Black or African American, non-Hispanic/Latino; 12% Hispanic/Latino; 24% Asian, non-Hispanic/Latino; 0.1% Native Hawaiian or other Pacific Islander, non-Hispanic/Latino; 0.1% American Indian or Alaska Native, non-Hispanic/Latino; 2% Two or more races, non-Hispanic/Latino; 6% Race/ethnicity unknown; 14% international; 9% transferred in; 51% live on campus.

Freshmen:

Admission: 34,999 applied, 14,233 admitted, 2,934 enrolled. ***Average high school GPA:*** 3.81. ***Test scores:*** SAT critical reading scores over 500: 86%; SAT math scores over 500: 95%; SAT writing scores over 500: 87%; ACT scores over 18: 100%; SAT critical reading scores over 600: 55%; SAT math scores over 600: 77%; SAT writing scores over 600: 51%; ACT scores over 24: 90%; SAT critical reading scores over 700: 14%; SAT math scores over 700: 32%; SAT writing scores over 700: 13%; ACT scores over 30: 36%.

Retention: 89% of full-time freshmen returned.

FACULTY

Total: 1,568, 69% full-time, 75% with terminal degrees.

Student/faculty ratio: 17:1.

ACADEMICS

Calendar: semesters. *Degrees:* bachelor's, master's, doctoral, post-master's, and postbachelor's certificates.

Special study options: academic remediation for entering students, adult/continuing education programs, advanced placement credit, cooperative education, distance learning, double majors, English as a second language, freshman honors college, honors programs, independent study, internships, off-campus study, part-time degree program, services for LD students, student-designed majors, study abroad, summer session for credit. ***ROTC:*** Army (b), Air Force (c).

Unusual degree programs: 3-2 business administration; engineering; nursing; education.

Computers: 1,670 computers/terminals are available on campus for general student use. Students can access the following: campus intranet, computer help desk, free student e-mail accounts, online (class) grades, online (class) registration, online (class) schedules. Campuswide network is available. 100% of college-owned or -operated housing units are wired for high-speed Internet access. Wireless service is available via entire campus.

Library: Frank Melville, Jr. Memorial Library plus 7 others. *Books:* 901,520 (physical), 347,609 (digital/electronic); *Serial titles:* 1,283 (physical), 161,834 (digital/electronic); *Databases:* 661. Weekly public service hours: 128; study areas open 24 hours, 5-7 days a week; students can reserve study rooms.

STUDENT LIFE

Housing options: coed. Campus housing is university owned. Freshman campus housing is guaranteed.

Activities and organizations: drama/theater group, student-run newspaper, radio and television station, choral group, marching band, Community Service Organization, Residence Hall Association, Commuter Student Association, Asian Students Alliance, Chinese Association at Stony Brook, national fraternities, national sororities.

Athletics Member NCAA. All Division I. ***Intercollegiate sports:*** baseball M(s), basketball M(s)/W(s), cross-country running M(s)/W(s), football M(s), lacrosse M(s)/W(s), soccer M(s)/W(s), softball W(s), swimming and diving W(s), tennis M/W(s), track and field M(s)/W(s), volleyball W(s). ***Intramural sports:*** archery M(c)/W(c), badminton M(c)/W(c), baseball W(c), basketball M/W, bowling M(c)/W(c), cheerleading W, crew M(c), equestrian sports M(c)/W(c), fencing M(c)/W(c), field hockey W(c), golf M(c)/W(c), ice hockey M(c), lacrosse M(c)/W(c), racquetball M/W, rugby M(c)/W(c), sailing M(c)/W(c), soccer M/W, softball W, squash W, table tennis M(c)/W(c), tennis M(c)/W(c), ultimate Frisbee M(c)/W(c), volleyball M/W, wrestling M(c).

Campus security: 24-hour emergency response devices and patrols, late-night transport/escort service, controlled dormitory access.

Student services: health clinic, personal/psychological counseling, women's center, legal services.

COSTS & FINANCIAL AID

Costs (2016–17) ***Tuition:*** state resident $6470 full-time, $270 per credit hour part-time; nonresident $23,710 full-time, $988 per credit hour part-time. Full-time tuition and fees vary according to course load and program. Part-time tuition and fees vary according to course load and program. ***Required fees:*** $2529 full-time, $125 per credit hour part-time. ***Room and board:*** $12,882; room only: $8082. Room and board charges vary according to board plan, housing facility, and location. ***Payment plan:*** installment.

Financial Aid Of all full-time matriculated undergraduates who enrolled in 2015, 10,506 applied for aid, 8,581 were judged to have need, 1,375 had their need fully met. 391 Federal Work-Study jobs (averaging $1967). 2,594 state and other part-time jobs (averaging $3523). In 2015, 1503 non-need-based awards were made. ***Average percent of need met:*** 66. ***Average financial aid package:*** $12,521. ***Average need-based loan:*** $4554. ***Average need-based gift aid:*** $8227. ***Average non-need-based aid:*** $5073. ***Average indebtedness upon graduation:*** $24,656.

APPLYING

Standardized Tests *Required:* SAT or ACT (for admission).

Options: electronic application, deferred entrance.

Application fee: $50.

Required: essay or personal statement, high school transcript, 1 letter of recommendation. ***Required for some:*** interview, audition. ***Recommended:*** minimum 3.5 GPA.

Application deadlines: 1/15 (freshmen), 3/1 (transfers).

Notification: 4/1 (freshmen), continuous until 4/1 (transfers).

CONTACT

Ms. Judith Burke-Berhanan, Dean of Undergraduate Admissions, Stony Brook University, State University of New York, Admissions Office, 118 Administration Building, Stony Brook, NY 11794-1901. *Phone:* 631-632-6868. *Fax:* 631-632-9898. *E-mail:* enroll@stonybrook.edu.

Swedish Institute, College of Health Sciences

New York, New York

http://www.swedishinstitute.edu/

CONTACT

Admissions Advisor, Swedish Institute, College of Health Sciences, 226 West 26th Street, New York, NY 10001. *Phone:* 212-914-5900 Ext. 125. *E-mail:* admissions@swedishinstitute.edu.

Syracuse University

Syracuse, New York

http://www.syr.edu/

- **Independent** university, founded 1870
- **Urban** 950-acre campus with easy access to Syracuse
- **Endowment** $1.2 billion
- **Coed** 15,218 undergraduate students, 96% full-time, 54% women, 46% men
- **Very difficult** entrance level, 52% of applicants were admitted

UNDERGRAD STUDENTS

14,607 full-time, 611 part-time. Students come from 50 states and territories; 84 other countries; 59% are from out of state; 8% Black or African American, non-Hispanic/Latino; 10% Hispanic/Latino; 7% Asian, non-Hispanic/Latino; 0.1% Native Hawaiian or other Pacific Islander, non-Hispanic/Latino; 0.6% American Indian or Alaska Native, non-Hispanic/Latino; 3% Two or more races, non-Hispanic/Latino; 3% Race/ethnicity unknown; 12% international; 2% transferred in; 75% live on campus.

Freshmen:

Admission: 30,923 applied, 16,179 admitted, 3,712 enrolled. ***Average high school GPA:*** 3.6. ***Test scores:*** SAT critical reading scores over 500: 87%; SAT math scores over 500: 93%; SAT writing scores over 500: 90%; ACT scores over 18: 100%; SAT critical reading scores over 600: 44%; SAT math scores over 600: 60%; SAT writing scores over 600: 44%; ACT scores over 24: 84%; SAT critical reading scores over 700: 7%; SAT math scores over 700: 14%; SAT writing scores over 700: 7%; ACT scores over 30: 23%.

Retention: 91% of full-time freshmen returned.

FACULTY

Total: 1,678, 65% full-time, 65% with terminal degrees.

Student/faculty ratio: 15:1.

ACADEMICS

Calendar: semesters. *Degrees:* certificates, bachelor's, master's, doctoral, post-master's, and postbachelor's certificates.

Special study options: accelerated degree program, adult/continuing education programs, advanced placement credit, cooperative education, distance learning, double majors, English as a second language, freshman honors college, honors programs, independent study, internships, off-campus study, part-time degree program, services for LD students, student-designed majors, study abroad, summer session for credit. ***ROTC:*** Army (b), Air Force (b).

Computers: 3,500 computers/terminals and 678 ports are available on campus for general student use. Students can access the following: campus intranet, computer help desk, free student e-mail accounts, online (class) grades, online (class) registration, online (class) schedules, web conferencing, learning management system, blogging service, personal Websites, "View My Advising Report" digital asset management system, office software, online video training. Campuswide network is available. 100% of college-owned or -operated housing units are wired for high-speed Internet access. Wireless service is available via classrooms, computer centers, computer labs, dorm rooms, learning centers, libraries, student centers.

Library: E. S. Bird Library plus 3 others. *Books:* 3.5 million (physical), 348,958 (digital/electronic); *Serial titles:* 35,735 (physical), 143,341 (digital/electronic); *Databases:* 1,154. Weekly public service hours: 146; study areas open 24 hours, 5-7 days a week; students can reserve study rooms.

STUDENT LIFE

Housing options: on-campus residence required through sophomore year; coed, special housing for students with disabilities. Campus housing is university owned. Freshman campus housing is guaranteed.

Activities and organizations: drama/theater group, student-run newspaper, radio and television station, choral group, marching band, First Year Players, Ottothon, Otto, Goon Squad, University Union, national fraternities, national sororities.

Athletics Member NCAA. All Division I except football (Division I-A). ***Intercollegiate sports:*** badminton M(c)/W(c), baseball M(c), basketball M(s)/W(s), bowling M(c)/W(c), cheerleading M/W, crew M(s)/W(s), cross-country running M(s)/W(s), equestrian sports M(c)/W(c), fencing M(c)/W(c), field hockey W(s), gymnastics M(c)/W(c), ice hockey M(c)/W(s), lacrosse M(s)/W(s), rugby M(c)/W(c), sailing M(c)/W(c), skiing (downhill) M(c)/W(c), soccer M(s)/W(s), softball W(s), tennis M(c)/W(s), track and field M(s)/W(s), volleyball M(c)/W(s), water polo M(c)/W(c), wrestling M(c). ***Intramural sports:*** basketball M/W, field hockey W(c), golf M(c)/W(c), ice hockey M/W, lacrosse M(c)/W(c), racquetball M/W, soccer M/W, softball M/W, swimming and diving M(c)/W(c), table tennis M(c)/W(c), tennis M/W, ultimate Frisbee M(c)/W(c), volleyball M/W.

Campus security: 24-hour emergency response devices and patrols, student patrols, late-night transport/escort service, controlled dormitory access, crisis alert notification system, off-campus patrols in student rental neighborhoods.

Student services: health clinic, personal/psychological counseling, women's center, legal services.

COSTS & FINANCIAL AID

Costs (2016–17) ***Comprehensive fee:*** $60,239 includes full-time tuition ($43,440), mandatory fees ($1582), and room and board ($15,217). Full-time tuition and fees vary according to course load. Part-time tuition: $1891 per credit hour. Part-time tuition and fees vary according to course load. ***College room only:*** $8067. Room and board charges vary according to board plan and housing facility. ***Payment plans:*** tuition prepayment, installment. ***Waivers:*** employees or children of employees.

Financial Aid Of all full-time matriculated undergraduates who enrolled in 2016, 9,053 applied for aid, 7,491 were judged to have need, 3,154 had their need fully met. 6,149 Federal Work-Study jobs (averaging $2554). In 2016, 2052 non-need-based awards were made. ***Average percent of need met:*** 93. ***Average financial aid package:*** $37,600. ***Average need-based loan:*** $5400. ***Average need-based gift aid:*** $29,432. ***Average non-need-based aid:*** $12,835. ***Average indebtedness upon graduation:*** $37,753. ***Financial aid deadline:*** 2/1.

APPLYING

Standardized Tests *Required:* SAT or ACT (for admission).

Options: electronic application, early admission, early decision, deferred entrance.

Application fee: $75.

Required: essay or personal statement, high school transcript, 2 letters of recommendation, senior year grade report, secondary school counselor evaluation.

Application deadlines: 1/1 (freshmen), 7/1 (transfers).

Early decision deadline: 11/15.

Notification: continuous (transfers).

CONTACT

Office of Admissions, Syracuse University, 100 Crouse-Hinds Hall, 900 South Crouse Avenue, Syracuse, NY 13244-2130. *Phone:* 315-443-3611. *Fax:* 315-443-4226. *E-mail:* orange@syr.edu.

Talmudical Institute of Upstate New York

Rochester, New York

http://www.tiuny.org/

CONTACT

Rabbi Menachem Davidowitz, Director of Admissions, Talmudical Institute of Upstate New York, 769 Park Avenue, Rochester, NY 14607-3046. *Phone:* 716-473-2810. *E-mail:* yeshiva@tiuny.org.

Talmudical Seminary of Bobov

Brooklyn, New York

CONTACT

Talmudical Seminary of Bobov, 5120 New Utrecht Avenue, Brooklyn, NY 11219.

Talmudical Seminary Oholei Torah

Brooklyn, New York

CONTACT

Rabbi Yisroel Friedman, Director of Academic Affairs, Talmudical Seminary Oholei Torah, 667 Eastern Parkway, Brooklyn, NY 11213-3310. *Phone:* 718-363-2034. *E-mail:* info@oholeitorah.com.

Torah Temimah Talmudical Seminary

Brooklyn, New York

CONTACT

Principal, Torah Temimah Talmudical Seminary, 507 Ocean Parkway, Brooklyn, NY 11218-5913. *Phone:* 718-853-8500.

Touro College

New York, New York

http://www.touro.edu/

- **Independent** comprehensive, founded 1971
- **Urban** campus
- **Coed**
- **Moderately difficult** entrance level

ACADEMICS

Calendar: semesters. *Degrees:* certificates, associate, bachelor's, master's, doctoral, post-master's, and postbachelor's certificates.

Library: Touro College Library plus 14 others.

STUDENT LIFE

Housing options: men-only, women-only. Campus housing is university owned.

Activities and organizations: student-run newspaper.

Campus security: 24-hour emergency response devices and patrols.

Student services: personal/psychological counseling.

COSTS & FINANCIAL AID

Costs (2016–17) ***Comprehensive fee:*** $28,950 includes full-time tuition ($16,380), mandatory fees ($600), and room and board ($11,970). Part-time tuition: $680 per credit hour. ***College room only:*** $8320.

Financial Aid Of all full-time matriculated undergraduates who enrolled in 2016, 3,846 applied for aid, 3,131 were judged to have need, 284 had their need fully met. In 2016, 693 non-need-based awards were made. ***Average percent of need met:*** 70. ***Average financial aid package:*** $14,499. ***Average need-based loan:*** $2174. ***Average need-based gift aid:*** $12,711. ***Average non-need-based aid:*** $1940. ***Financial aid deadline:*** 8/15.

APPLYING

Standardized Tests *Recommended:* SAT or ACT (for admission).

Options: early admission, deferred entrance.

Application fee: $50.

Required: high school transcript. ***Required for some:*** minimum 3.0 GPA, 2 letters of recommendation, interview. ***Recommended:*** essay or personal statement, 1 letter of recommendation.

CONTACT

Mr. David Luk, Associate Director of Admissions, Touro College, 27-33 West 23rd Street, New York, NY 10010. *Phone:* 212-463-0400 Ext. 5644. *Fax:* 212-627-9542. *E-mail:* david.luk@touro.edu.

Trocaire College

Buffalo, New York

http://www.trocaire.edu/

- **Independent** primarily 2-year, founded 1958
- **Urban** 1-acre campus
- **Endowment** $7.3 million
- **Coed, primarily women**
- **Minimally difficult** entrance level

FACULTY

Student/faculty ratio: 11:1.

ACADEMICS

Calendar: semesters. *Degrees:* certificates, associate, and bachelor's.

Library: The Rachel R. Savarino Library plus 1 other. *Books:* 10,822 (physical), 1,308 (digital/electronic); *Databases:* 90.

STUDENT LIFE

Housing options: college housing not available.

Activities and organizations: student-run newspaper, Student Governance Association, TroGreen, Diversity Club.

Campus security: 24-hour emergency response devices and patrols, late-night transport/escort service.

Student services: personal/psychological counseling.

APPLYING

Standardized Tests *Required:* ACCUPLACER (for admission).

Options: electronic application, deferred entrance.

Required: high school transcript. ***Required for some:*** essay or personal statement, 1 letter of recommendation. ***Recommended:*** minimum 1.9 GPA, interview.

CONTACT
Trocaire College, 360 Choate Avenue, Buffalo, NY 14220-2094.
Phone: 716-826-2558.

Union College

Schenectady, New York

http://www.union.edu/

- **Independent** 4-year, founded 1795
- **Urban** 100-acre campus
- **Endowment** $441.0 million
- **Coed** 2,269 undergraduate students, 98% full-time, 46% women, 54% men
- **Very difficult** entrance level, 38% of applicants were admitted

UNDERGRAD STUDENTS
2,226 full-time, 43 part-time. Students come from 41 states and territories; 35 other countries; 66% are from out of state; 4% Black or African American, non-Hispanic/Latino; 7% Hispanic/Latino; 6% Asian, non-Hispanic/Latino; 2% Two or more races, non-Hispanic/Latino; 7% international; 1% transferred in; 89% live on campus.

Freshmen:
Admission: 5,996 applied, 2,297 admitted, 568 enrolled. ***Average high school GPA:*** 3.43. ***Test scores:*** SAT critical reading scores over 500: 96%; SAT math scores over 500: 99%; SAT writing scores over 500: 96%; ACT scores over 18: 99%; SAT critical reading scores over 600: 71%; SAT math scores over 600: 87%; SAT writing scores over 600: 75%; ACT scores over 24: 96%; SAT critical reading scores over 700: 16%; SAT math scores over 700: 34%; SAT writing scores over 700: 17%; ACT scores over 30: 58%.

Retention: 93% of full-time freshmen returned.

FACULTY
Total: 234, 89% full-time, 92% with terminal degrees.

Student/faculty ratio: 10:1.

ACADEMICS
Calendar: trimesters. *Degree:* bachelor's.

Special study options: accelerated degree program, advanced placement credit, double majors, honors programs, independent study, internships, off-campus study, student-designed majors, study abroad, summer session for credit. ***ROTC:*** Army (c), Navy (c), Air Force (c).

Computers: 554 computers/terminals and 3,032 ports are available on campus for general student use. Students can access the following: campus intranet, computer help desk, free student e-mail accounts, online (class) grades, online (class) registration, online (class) schedules, digital studio and learning commons. Campuswide network is available. 100% of college-owned or -operated housing units are wired for high-speed Internet access. Wireless service is available via classrooms, computer centers, computer labs, dorm rooms, learning centers, libraries, student centers.

Library: Schaffer Library.

STUDENT LIFE
Housing options: on-campus residence required through senior year; coed. Campus housing is university owned. Freshman campus housing is guaranteed.

Activities and organizations: drama/theater group, student-run newspaper, radio and television station, choral group, U-Program (Programming Board), speaker's forum, student newspaper, Concert Committee, ski club, national fraternities, national sororities.

Athletics Member NCAA. All Division III except men's and women's ice hockey (Division I). ***Intercollegiate sports:*** baseball M, basketball M/W, cheerleading M(c)/W(c), crew M/W, cross-country running M/W, equestrian sports W, field hockey W, football M, golf W, ice hockey M/W, lacrosse M/W, rugby M(c)/W(c), soccer M/W, softball W, swimming and diving M/W, tennis M/W, track and field M/W, ultimate Frisbee M(c)/W(c), volleyball W. ***Intramural sports:*** badminton M(c)/W(c), basketball M/W, bowling M(c)/W(c), equestrian sports M(c)/W(c), fencing M(c)/W(c), football M/W, golf M(c)/W(c), ice hockey M(c)/W(c), lacrosse M(c)/W, racquetball M/W, rock climbing M(c)/W(c), skiing (downhill) M(c)/W(c), soccer M/W, softball M/W, squash M/W, tennis M/W, volleyball M/W, water polo M/W.

Campus security: 24-hour emergency response devices and patrols, late-night transport/escort service, controlled dormitory access, awareness programs, bicycle patrol, shuttle service.

Student services: health clinic, personal/psychological counseling, women's center.

COSTS & FINANCIAL AID
Costs (2017–18) ***Comprehensive fee:*** $66,609 includes full-time tuition ($53,019), mandatory fees ($471), and room and board ($13,119). ***College room only:*** $7194. ***Payment plan:*** installment. ***Waivers:*** senior citizens and employees or children of employees.

Financial Aid Of all full-time matriculated undergraduates who enrolled in 2016, 1,195 applied for aid, 1,099 were judged to have need, 1,099 had their need fully met. In 2016, 640 non-need-based awards were made. ***Average percent of need met:*** 100. ***Average financial aid package:*** $42,155. ***Average need-based loan:*** $4940. ***Average need-based gift aid:*** $36,748. ***Average non-need-based aid:*** $10,544. ***Average indebtedness upon graduation:*** $33,045. ***Financial aid deadline:*** 1/15.

APPLYING
Standardized Tests *Required for some:* SAT I and two SAT II tests or ACT for leadership in medicine program, SAT or ACT for law and public policy program.

Options: electronic application, early admission, early decision, deferred entrance.

Required: essay or personal statement, high school transcript, 2 letters of recommendation. ***Recommended:*** interview.

Application deadlines: 1/15 (freshmen), 4/15 (transfers).

Early decision deadline: 11/15 (for plan 1), 1/15 (for plan 2).

Notification: 4/1 (freshmen), continuous (transfers), 12/15 (early decision plan 1), 2/1 (early decision plan 2).

CONTACT
Union College, Grant Hall, 807 Union Street, Schenectady, NY 12308.
Phone: 518-388-6112. *Toll-free phone:* 888-843-6688. *Fax:* 518-388-6986. *E-mail:* admissions@union.edu.

United States Merchant Marine Academy

Kings Point, New York

http://www.usmma.edu/

- **Federally supported** comprehensive, founded 1943
- **Suburban** 82-acre campus with easy access to New York City
- **Coed** 904 undergraduate students, 100% full-time, 19% women, 81% men
- **Very difficult** entrance level, 15% of applicants were admitted

UNDERGRAD STUDENTS
904 full-time. Students come from 49 states and territories; 3 other countries; 88% are from out of state; 3% Black or African American, non-Hispanic/Latino; 11% Hispanic/Latino; 8% Asian, non-Hispanic/Latino; 0.2% Native Hawaiian or other Pacific Islander, non-Hispanic/Latino; 2% American Indian or Alaska Native, non-Hispanic/Latino; 2% Race/ethnicity unknown; 0.7% international; 2% transferred in; 100% live on campus.

Freshmen:
Admission: 1,872 applied, 279 admitted, 254 enrolled. ***Average high school GPA:*** 3.6. ***Test scores:*** ACT scores over 18: 100%; ACT scores over 24: 98%; ACT scores over 30: 24%.

Retention: 94% of full-time freshmen returned.

FACULTY
Total: 132, 86% full-time.

Student/faculty ratio: 8:1.

ACADEMICS
Calendar: trimesters. *Degrees:* bachelor's and master's.

Special study options: academic remediation for entering students, advanced placement credit, distance learning, honors programs, independent study, internships, off-campus study.

Computers: Students can access the following: campus intranet, computer help desk, free student e-mail accounts, engineering and economics software. Campuswide network is available.

Library: Schuyler Otis Bland Memorial Library.

STUDENT LIFE

Housing options: on-campus residence required through senior year; coed. Campus housing is university owned. Freshman campus housing is guaranteed.

Activities and organizations: drama/theater group, student-run newspaper, choral group, marching band, Regimental Band, CFC, Neuman Club, Honor Guard.

Athletics Member NCAA. All Division III. ***Intercollegiate sports:*** baseball M, basketball M/W, crew M/W, cross-country running M/W, football M, lacrosse M/W, sailing M/W, soccer M, swimming and diving M/W, tennis M, track and field M/W, volleyball W, wrestling M. ***Intramural sports:*** basketball M/W, golf M(c), ice hockey M(c), racquetball M/W, riflery M(c)/W(c), rugby M(c), soccer W(c), ultimate Frisbee M(c), volleyball M(c), water polo M(c), weight lifting M(c)/W(c).

Campus security: 24-hour emergency response devices and patrols, controlled dormitory access.

Student services: health clinic, personal/psychological counseling.

COSTS

Costs (2017–18) ***Tuition:*** state resident $0 full-time; nonresident $0 full-time. ***Required fees:*** $1167 full-time.

APPLYING

Standardized Tests *Required:* SAT or ACT (for admission).

Options: electronic application.

Required: essay or personal statement, high school transcript, 3 letters of recommendation. ***Recommended:*** interview.

Application deadlines: 3/1 (freshmen), 3/1 (transfers).

Notification: continuous until 4/1 (freshmen), continuous until 4/1 (transfers).

CONTACT

Lt. Cdr. Keith L. Watson, Assistant Director of Admissions and Financial Aid, United States Merchant Marine Academy, 300 Steamboat Road, Kings Point, NY 11024-1699. *Phone:* 516-726-5642. *Toll-free phone:* 866-546-4778. *Fax:* 516-773-5390. *E-mail:* admissions@usmma.edu.

See page 1538 for the College Close-Up.

United States Military Academy

West Point, New York

http://www.usma.edu/

- **Federally supported** 4-year, founded 1802
- **Small-town** 16,080-acre campus with easy access to New York City
- **Endowment** $321.5 million
- **Coed, primarily men** 4,389 undergraduate students, 100% full-time, 20% women, 80% men

UNDERGRAD STUDENTS

4,389 full-time. Students come from 61 states and territories; 30 other countries; 94% are from out of state; 11% Black or African American, non-Hispanic/Latino; 12% Hispanic/Latino; 6% Asian, non-Hispanic/Latino; 0.6% Native Hawaiian or other Pacific Islander, non-Hispanic/Latino; 1% American Indian or Alaska Native, non-Hispanic/Latino; 4% Two or more races, non-Hispanic/Latino; 1% Race/ethnicity unknown; 1% international; 100% live on campus.

Freshmen:

Admission: 1,260 enrolled. ***Test scores:*** SAT critical reading scores over 500: 97%; SAT math scores over 500: 99%; SAT writing scores over 500: 93%; ACT scores over 18: 100%; SAT critical reading scores over 600: 68%; SAT math scores over 600: 76%; SAT writing scores over 600: 55%; ACT scores over 24: 91%; SAT critical reading scores over 700: 19%; SAT math scores over 700: 27%; SAT writing scores over 700: 14%; ACT scores over 30: 42%.

Retention: 94% of full-time freshmen returned.

FACULTY

Total: 630, 100% full-time, 50% with terminal degrees.

Student/faculty ratio: 7:1.

ACADEMICS

Calendar: semesters. *Degree:* bachelor's.

Special study options: academic remediation for entering students, advanced placement credit, double majors, honors programs, independent study, off-campus study, student-designed majors, study abroad.

Computers: Students can access the following: computer help desk, free student e-mail accounts, online (class) grades, online (class) registration, online (class) schedules, all cadets will receive a laptop, printer, PDA, and portable memory device; learning management system access. Campuswide network is available. 100% of college-owned or -operated housing units are wired for high-speed Internet access. Wireless service is available via classrooms, dorm rooms, learning centers, libraries, student centers.

Library: United States Military Academy Library at West Point. *Books:* 449,413 (physical), 999,080 (digital/electronic); *Serial titles:* 104 (physical), 110,650 (digital/electronic); *Databases:* 262. Weekly public service hours: 100.

STUDENT LIFE

Housing options: on-campus residence required through senior year; coed. Campus housing is university owned. Freshman campus housing is guaranteed.

Activities and organizations: drama/theater group, student-run radio station, choral group, Spirit Clubs, Big Brother/Big Sister, Cadet Fine Arts Forum, Film Forum, Philosophy Forum.

Athletics Member NCAA. All Division I except football (Division I-A). ***Intercollegiate sports:*** baseball M, basketball M/W, cheerleading M/W, crew M(c)/W(c), cross-country running M/W, equestrian sports M(c)/W(c), fencing M(c)/W(c), golf M, gymnastics M, ice hockey M, lacrosse M/W, riflery M/W, rugby M/W, soccer M/W, softball W, swimming and diving M/W, tennis M/W, track and field M/W, volleyball M(c)/W, water polo M(c), wrestling M. ***Intramural sports:*** basketball M/W, bowling M(c), racquetball M(c)/W(c), sailing M(c)/W(c), skiing (downhill) M(c)/W(c), soccer M/W, swimming and diving M/W, ultimate Frisbee M/W, wrestling M/W.

Campus security: 24-hour emergency response devices and patrols, late-night transport/escort service, controlled dormitory access.

Student services: health clinic, personal/psychological counseling, legal services.

COSTS

Costs (2017–18) ***Comprehensive fee:*** Cadets receive a full scholarship and an annual salary. There is no tuition charge, but there is a requirement for an initial deposit. Room, board, and medical and dental care are provided by the US Government. A portion of the cadet pay is deposited to a "Cadet Account" to help pay for uniforms, books, a laptop computer, and incidentals. The only cost is a one-time deposit upon admission to defray the initial issue of uniforms, books, supplies, and equipment. If needed, loans of $100 to $2,000 are available for the deposit. Upon graduation, cadets incur a 5-year Active Duty service obligation and 3 years of reserve duty in the US Army.

APPLYING

Standardized Tests *Required:* SAT or ACT (for admission).

Required: essay or personal statement, high school transcript, 4 letters of recommendation, nominations from an approved source, Department of Defense qualifying medical examination, must be at least 17 but not yet 23 years of age by July 1 of year of entry, and be an unmarried U.S. citizen (foreign nationals with approval) with no parental obligations. ***Recommended:*** interview.

CONTACT

United States Military Academy, 600 Thayer Road, West Point, NY 10996. *Phone:* 845-938-4041. *E-mail:* admissions@usma.edu.

United Talmudical Seminary
Brooklyn, New York

CONTACT
Director of Admissions, United Talmudical Seminary, 191 Rodney Street, Brooklyn, NY 11211. *Phone:* 718-963-9770.

University at Albany, State University of New York
Albany, New York
http://www.albany.edu/

- **State-supported** university, founded 1844, part of State University of New York System
- **Suburban** 560-acre campus
- **Endowment** $59.8 million
- **Coed** 12,908 undergraduate students, 95% full-time, 49% women, 51% men
- **Very difficult** entrance level, 56% of applicants were admitted

UNDERGRAD STUDENTS
12,223 full-time, 685 part-time. Students come from 30 states and territories; 26 other countries; 6% are from out of state; 16% Black or African American, non-Hispanic/Latino; 15% Hispanic/Latino; 8% Asian, non-Hispanic/Latino; 0.1% Native Hawaiian or other Pacific Islander, non-Hispanic/Latino; 0.2% American Indian or Alaska Native, non-Hispanic/Latino; 3% Two or more races, non-Hispanic/Latino; 3% Race/ethnicity unknown; 6% international; 10% transferred in; 58% live on campus.

Freshmen:
Admission: 22,337 applied, 12,608 admitted, 2,590 enrolled. ***Average high school GPA:*** 3.2. ***Test scores:*** SAT critical reading scores over 500: 72%; SAT math scores over 500: 81%; ACT scores over 18: 99%; SAT critical reading scores over 600: 17%; SAT math scores over 600: 24%; ACT scores over 24: 55%; SAT critical reading scores over 700: 1%; SAT math scores over 700: 2%; ACT scores over 30: 7%.

Retention: 83% of full-time freshmen returned.

FACULTY
Total: 1,188, 58% full-time, 73% with terminal degrees.

Student/faculty ratio: 18:1.

ACADEMICS
Calendar: semesters. *Degrees:* bachelor's, master's, doctoral, post-master's, and postbachelor's certificates.

Special study options: accelerated degree program, advanced placement credit, distance learning, double majors, English as a second language, freshman honors college, honors programs, independent study, internships, off-campus study, part-time degree program, services for LD students, student-designed majors, study abroad, summer session for credit. ***ROTC:*** Army (b), Air Force (c).

Unusual degree programs: 3-2 business administration; engineering with Rensselaer Polytechnic Institute, State University of New York at Binghamton, State University of New York at New Paltz, Clarkson University.

Computers: 500 computers/terminals are available on campus for general student use. Students can access the following: campus intranet, computer help desk, free student e-mail accounts, online (class) grades, online (class) registration, online (class) schedules. Campuswide network is available. 100% of college-owned or -operated housing units are wired for high-speed Internet access. Wireless service is available via classrooms, computer centers, computer labs, dorm rooms, libraries, student centers.

Library: University Library plus 2 others. *Books:* 2.3 million (physical), 342,263 (digital/electronic); *Serial titles:* 97,614 (digital/electronic). Weekly public service hours: 113; students can reserve study rooms.

STUDENT LIFE
Housing options: on-campus residence required through sophomore year; coed. Campus housing is university owned. Freshman campus housing is guaranteed.

Activities and organizations: drama/theater group, student-run newspaper, radio and television station, choral group, intramural athletics, cultural organizations, political organizations, community service, honor societies, national fraternities, national sororities.

Athletics Member NCAA. All Division I. ***Intercollegiate sports:*** baseball M(s), basketball M(s)/W(s), crew M/W, cross-country running M(s)/W(s), field hockey W(s), football M(s), golf W(s), lacrosse M(s)/W(s), rock climbing M/W, soccer M(s)/W(s), softball W(s), tennis W(s), track and field M(s)/W(s), volleyball W(s). ***Intramural sports:*** badminton M/W, baseball M, basketball M/W, equestrian sports W, fencing M/W, football M/W, ice hockey M, lacrosse M/W, racquetball M/W, rugby M/W, skiing (cross-country) M/W, skiing (downhill) M/W, soccer M/W, softball W, tennis M/W, track and field M/W, ultimate Frisbee M/W, volleyball M/W, wrestling M.

Campus security: 24-hour emergency response devices and patrols, late-night transport/escort service, controlled dormitory access, Five Quad Ambulance Service, on-campus car battery assistance.

Student services: health clinic, personal/psychological counseling, legal services.

COSTS & FINANCIAL AID
Costs (2017–18) ***Tuition:*** state resident $6470 full-time, $270 per credit hour part-time; nonresident $21,550 full-time, $898 per credit hour part-time. Part-time tuition and fees vary according to course load. ***Required fees:*** $2753 full-time, $74 per credit hour part-time, $216 per term part-time. ***Room and board:*** $12,942; room only: $8042. Room and board charges vary according to board plan and housing facility.

Financial Aid Of all full-time matriculated undergraduates who enrolled in 2015, 9,631 applied for aid, 7,836 were judged to have need, 447 had their need fully met. 667 Federal Work-Study jobs (averaging $1312). In 2015, 628 non-need-based awards were made. ***Average percent of need met:*** 60. ***Average financial aid package:*** $10,933. ***Average need-based loan:*** $4585. ***Average need-based gift aid:*** $7679. ***Average non-need-based aid:*** $3882. ***Average indebtedness upon graduation:*** $25,727.

APPLYING
Standardized Tests *Required:* SAT or ACT (for admission).

Options: electronic application, early admission, early action, deferred entrance.

Application fee: $50.

Required: essay or personal statement, high school transcript, 1 letter of recommendation. ***Required for some:*** portfolio, audition.

Application deadlines: 3/16 (freshmen), 7/16 (transfers), 11/15 (early action).

Notification: continuous (freshmen), continuous (transfers), 11/15 (early action).

CONTACT
University at Albany, State University of New York, Office of Undergraduate Admissions, 1400 Washington Avenue, Albany, NY 12222. *Phone:* 518-442-5435. *Fax:* 518-442-5383. *E-mail:* ugadmissions@albany.edu.

University at Buffalo, the State University of New York
Buffalo, New York
http://www.buffalo.edu/

- **State-supported** university, founded 1846, part of State University of New York System
- **Suburban** 1350-acre campus
- **Endowment** $619.3 million
- **Coed** 20,411 undergraduate students, 92% full-time, 43% women, 57% men
- **Moderately difficult** entrance level, 59% of applicants were admitted

UNDERGRAD STUDENTS
18,876 full-time, 1,535 part-time. Students come from 40 states and territories; 87 other countries; 3% are from out of state; 7% Black or African American, non-Hispanic/Latino; 7% Hispanic/Latino; 14% Asian, non-Hispanic/Latino; 0.1% Native Hawaiian or other Pacific Islander, non-Hispanic/Latino; 0.3% American Indian or Alaska Native, non-Hispanic/Latino; 2% Two or more races, non-Hispanic/Latino; 5% Race/ethnicity unknown; 16% international; 9% transferred in; 38% live on campus.

Freshmen:
Admission: 26,001 applied, 15,440 admitted, 4,103 enrolled. ***Average high school GPA:*** 3.6. ***Test scores:*** SAT critical reading scores over 500: 82%; SAT math scores over 500: 94%; ACT scores over 18: 99%; SAT critical reading scores over 600: 33%; SAT math scores over 600: 56%; ACT scores over 24: 79%; SAT critical reading scores over 700: 5%; SAT math scores over 700: 11%; ACT scores over 30: 20%.
Retention: 86% of full-time freshmen returned.

FACULTY
Total: 1,809, 69% full-time, 89% with terminal degrees.
Student/faculty ratio: 13:1.

ACADEMICS
Calendar: semesters. *Degrees:* certificates, bachelor's, master's, doctoral, and post-master's certificates.
Special study options: academic remediation for entering students, accelerated degree program, advanced placement credit, cooperative education, distance learning, double majors, English as a second language, freshman honors college, honors programs, independent study, internships, off-campus study, part-time degree program, services for LD students, student-designed majors, study abroad, summer session for credit. ***ROTC:*** Army (c).
Unusual degree programs: 3-2 business administration; engineering; nursing; social work; law.
Computers: 3,061 computers/terminals are available on campus for general student use. Students can access the following: campus intranet, computer help desk, free student e-mail accounts, online (class) grades, online (class) registration, online (class) schedules. Campuswide network is available. 100% of college-owned or -operated housing units are wired for high-speed Internet access. Wireless service is available via entire campus.
Library: Lockwood Memorial Library plus 11 others. *Books:* 3.4 million (physical), 766,305 (digital/electronic); *Serial titles:* 3,828 (physical), 158,728 (digital/electronic); *Databases:* 376. Weekly public service hours: 168; study areas open 24 hours, 5-7 days a week; students can reserve study rooms.

STUDENT LIFE
Housing options: coed, special housing for students with disabilities. Campus housing is university owned. Freshman campus housing is guaranteed.
Activities and organizations: drama/theater group, student-run newspaper, radio and television station, choral group, marching band, national fraternities, national sororities.
Athletics Member NCAA. All Division I. ***Intercollegiate sports:*** baseball M(s), basketball M(s)/W(s), crew W(s), cross-country running M(s)/W(s), football M(s), soccer M(s)/W(s), softball W(s), swimming and diving M(s)/W(s), tennis M(s)/W(s), track and field M(s)/W(s), volleyball W(s), wrestling M(s). ***Intramural sports:*** baseball M(c), basketball M/W(c), crew M(c)/W(c), cross-country running M(c)/W(c), equestrian sports M(c)/W(c), fencing M(c)/W(c), field hockey M(c)/W(c), golf M(c)/W(c), gymnastics M(c)/W(c), ice hockey M(c)/W(c), lacrosse M(c)/W(c), rugby M(c)/W(c), sailing M(c)/W(c), skiing (downhill) M(c)/W(c), soccer M(c)/W(c), swimming and diving M(c)/W(c), table tennis M(c)/W(c), tennis M(c)/W(c), track and field M(c)/W(c), ultimate Frisbee M(c)/W(c), volleyball M(c)/W(c), water polo M(c)/W(c), wrestling M(c).
Campus security: 24-hour emergency response devices and patrols, student patrols, late-night transport/escort service, controlled dormitory access, self-defense and awareness programs, security cameras.
Student services: health clinic, personal/psychological counseling, women's center, legal services.

COSTS & FINANCIAL AID
Costs (2016–17) ***Tuition:*** state resident $6470 full-time, $270 per credit hour part-time; nonresident $23,710 full-time, $988 per credit hour part-time. Part-time tuition and fees vary according to course load. ***Required fees:*** $3104 full-time, $258 per credit hour part-time. ***Room and board:*** $13,548; room only: $7798. Room and board charges vary according to board plan and housing facility. ***Payment plan:*** installment. ***Waivers:*** minority students.
Financial Aid Of all full-time matriculated undergraduates who enrolled in 2015, 13,712 applied for aid, 10,619 were judged to have need, 10,007 had their need fully met. 1,059 Federal Work-Study jobs (averaging $1075). 978 state and other part-time jobs (averaging $14,795). In 2015, 607 non-need-based awards were made. ***Average percent of need met:*** 50. ***Average financial aid package:*** $9246. ***Average need-based loan:*** $4361. ***Average need-based gift aid:*** $7162. ***Average non-need-based aid:*** $4361. ***Average indebtedness upon graduation:*** $26,046.

APPLYING
Standardized Tests *Required:* SAT or ACT (for admission).
Options: electronic application, early admission, early action.
Application fee: $50.
Required: essay or personal statement, high school transcript, 1 letter of recommendation. ***Required for some:*** portfolio for architecture; audition for dance, music theatre, theatre and music.
Notification: continuous (freshmen), continuous (transfers), 1/15 (early action).

CONTACT
Mr. Jose Aviles, Director of Admissions, University at Buffalo, the State University of New York, 12 Capen Hall, North Campus, Buffalo, NY 14260-1660. *Phone:* 716-645-6900. *Toll-free phone:* 888-UB-ADMIT. *E-mail:* ub-admissions@buffalo.edu.

University of Rochester
Rochester, New York
http://www.rochester.edu/

- **Independent** university, founded 1850
- **Suburban** 655-acre campus
- **Endowment** $2.1 billion
- **Coed** 6,345 undergraduate students, 97% full-time, 50% women, 50% men
- **Very difficult** entrance level, 35% of applicants were admitted

UNDERGRAD STUDENTS
6,130 full-time, 215 part-time. Students come from 52 states and territories; 110 other countries; 57% are from out of state; 5% Black or African American, non-Hispanic/Latino; 7% Hispanic/Latino; 11% Asian, non-Hispanic/Latino; 0.1% Native Hawaiian or other Pacific Islander, non-Hispanic/Latino; 0.2% American Indian or Alaska Native, non-Hispanic/Latino; 3% Two or more races, non-Hispanic/Latino; 7% Race/ethnicity unknown; 21% international; 2% transferred in; 90% live on campus.

Freshmen:
Admission: 17,484 applied, 6,167 admitted, 1,461 enrolled. ***Average high school GPA:*** 3.8.
Retention: 96% of full-time freshmen returned.

FACULTY
Student/faculty ratio: 10:1.

ACADEMICS
Calendar: semesters plus optional summer term. *Degrees:* bachelor's, master's, doctoral, post-master's, and postbachelor's certificates.
Special study options: accelerated degree program, advanced placement credit, cooperative education, double majors, English as a second language, honors programs, independent study, internships, off-campus study, part-time degree program, services for LD students, student-designed majors, study abroad, summer session for credit. ***ROTC:*** Army (c), Navy (b), Air Force (c).
Unusual degree programs: 3-2 business administration; nursing; business, computer science, engineering, neuroscience, physics, physics and astronomy, public health.
Computers: 700 computers/terminals and 4,000 ports are available on campus for general student use. Students can access the following: computer help desk, free student e-mail accounts, online (class) grades, online (class) registration, online (class) schedules. Campuswide network is available. 100% of college-owned or -operated housing units are wired for high-speed Internet access. Wireless service is available via entire campus.
Library: Rush Rhees Library plus 7 others. Study areas open 24 hours, 5-7 days a week; students can reserve study rooms.

STUDENT LIFE
Housing options: on-campus residence required through sophomore year; coed. Campus housing is university owned and leased by the school. Freshman campus housing is guaranteed.

Activities and organizations: drama/theater group, student-run newspaper, radio and television station, choral group, marching band, Campus Activities Board, Black Students' Union, Grassroots (environmental group), Women's Caucus, American Sign Language Club, national fraternities, national sororities.

Athletics Member NCAA. All Division III except squash (Division I). ***Intercollegiate sports:*** archery M(c)/W(c), badminton M(c)/W(c), baseball M, basketball M/W, bowling M(c)/W(c), cheerleading M(c)/W(c), crew M(c)/W, cross-country running M/W, equestrian sports M(c)/W(c), fencing M(c)/W(c), field hockey W, football M, golf M, ice hockey M(c)/W(c), lacrosse M(c)/W, rugby M(c)/W(c), sailing M(c)/W(c), skiing (downhill) M(c)/W(c), soccer M/W, softball W, squash M(s), swimming and diving M/W, tennis M/W, track and field M/W, ultimate Frisbee M(c)/W(c), volleyball M(c)/W, water polo M(c)/W(c). ***Intramural sports:*** basketball M/W, football M/W, soccer M/W, tennis M(c)/W(c), ultimate Frisbee M/W, volleyball M/W.

Campus security: 24-hour emergency response devices and patrols, student patrols, late-night transport/escort service, controlled dormitory access.

Student services: health clinic, personal/psychological counseling, women's center, legal services.

COSTS & FINANCIAL AID
Costs (2017–18) ***Comprehensive fee:*** $67,236 includes full-time tuition ($50,984), mandatory fees ($914), and room and board ($15,338). Part-time tuition: $1593 per credit hour. Part-time tuition and fees vary according to course load. ***Room and board:*** Room and board charges vary according to board plan and housing facility. ***Payment plan:*** installment. ***Waivers:*** employees or children of employees.

Financial Aid Of all full-time matriculated undergraduates who enrolled in 2016, 3,701 applied for aid, 3,075 were judged to have need, 2,760 had their need fully met. In 2016, 1856 non-need-based awards were made. ***Average percent of need met:*** 93. ***Average financial aid package:*** $44,425. ***Average need-based loan:*** $5246. ***Average need-based gift aid:*** $39,246. ***Average non-need-based aid:*** $13,597. ***Average indebtedness upon graduation:*** $30,742.

APPLYING
Standardized Tests *Required for some:* SAT and SAT Subject Tests or ACT (for admission). *Recommended:* SAT or ACT (for admission), SAT Subject Tests (for admission).

Options: electronic application, early decision, deferred entrance.

Application fee: $50.

Required: essay or personal statement, high school transcript. ***Required for some:*** audition for Eastman School of Music. ***Recommended:*** 2 letters of recommendation, interview.

Application deadlines: 1/5 (freshmen), 3/15 (transfers).

Early decision deadline: 11/1.

Notification: 4/1 (freshmen), 4/1 (out-of-state freshmen), 3/1 (transfers), 12/15 (early decision).

CONTACT
Office of Admissions, University of Rochester, PO Box 270251, 300 Wilson Boulevard, Rochester, NY 14627-0251. *Phone:* 585-275-3221. *Toll-free phone:* 888-822-2256. *Fax:* 585-461-4595. *E-mail:* admit@admissions.rochester.edu.

U.T.A. Mesivta of Kiryas Joel
Monroe, New York

CONTACT
U.T.A. Mesivta of Kiryas Joel, 9 Nickelsburg Road, Unit 312, Monroe, NY 10950.

Utica College
Utica, New York
http://www.utica.edu/

- **Independent** comprehensive, founded 1946
- **Suburban** 128-acre campus
- **Endowment** $22.8 million
- **Coed** 3,550 undergraduate students, 78% full-time, 61% women, 39% men
- **Moderately difficult** entrance level, 82% of applicants were admitted

UNDERGRAD STUDENTS
2,758 full-time, 792 part-time. Students come from 48 states and territories; 28 other countries; 19% are from out of state; 12% Black or African American, non-Hispanic/Latino; 10% Hispanic/Latino; 3% Asian, non-Hispanic/Latino; 0.1% Native Hawaiian or other Pacific Islander, non-Hispanic/Latino; 0.5% American Indian or Alaska Native, non-Hispanic/Latino; 2% Two or more races, non-Hispanic/Latino; 3% Race/ethnicity unknown; 1% international; 6% transferred in; 34% live on campus.

Freshmen:
Admission: 5,419 applied, 4,441 admitted, 685 enrolled. ***Average high school GPA:*** 3.1. ***Test scores:*** SAT critical reading scores over 500: 55%; SAT math scores over 500: 57%; SAT writing scores over 500: 41%; ACT scores over 18: 95%; SAT critical reading scores over 600: 11%; SAT math scores over 600: 15%; SAT writing scores over 600: 6%; ACT scores over 24: 39%; SAT critical reading scores over 700: 1%; SAT math scores over 700: 1%; SAT writing scores over 700: 1%; ACT scores over 30: 1%.

Retention: 75% of full-time freshmen returned.

FACULTY
Total: 469, 31% full-time, 36% with terminal degrees.

Student/faculty ratio: 12:1.

ACADEMICS
Calendar: semesters. *Degrees:* certificates, bachelor's, master's, doctoral, and postbachelor's certificates.

Special study options: academic remediation for entering students, accelerated degree program, adult/continuing education programs, advanced placement credit, cooperative education, distance learning, double majors, English as a second language, honors programs, independent study, internships, off-campus study, part-time degree program, services for LD students, study abroad, summer session for credit. ***ROTC:*** Army (b), Air Force (c).

Unusual degree programs: 3-2 engineering with Syracuse University.

Computers: 430 computers/terminals are available on campus for general student use. Students can access the following: computer help desk, free student e-mail accounts, online (class) grades, online (class) registration, online (class) schedules. Campuswide network is available. 100% of college-owned or -operated housing units are wired for high-speed Internet access. Wireless service is available via entire campus.
Library: Frank E. Gannett Memorial Library. *Books:* 307,523 (physical); *Serial titles:* 267,023 (physical). Students can reserve study rooms.

STUDENT LIFE
Housing options: on-campus residence required through sophomore year; coed, special housing for students with disabilities. Campus housing is university owned. Freshman campus housing is guaranteed.

Activities and organizations: drama/theater group, student-run newspaper, radio station, choral group, Physical Therapy Society, Student Nurses Association, Kappa Delta Pi, Student Senate, Utica College Honor Association, national fraternities, national sororities.

Athletics Member NCAA. All Division III. ***Intercollegiate sports:*** baseball M, basketball M/W, cross-country running M/W, field hockey W, football M, golf M/W, ice hockey M/W, lacrosse M/W, soccer M/W, softball W, swimming and diving M/W, tennis M/W, track and field M/W, volleyball W, water polo W. ***Intramural sports:*** basketball M/W, bowling M/W, cheerleading M(c)/W(c), fencing M(c)/W(c), racquetball M/W, soccer M/W, softball M/W, tennis M/W, volleyball M/W, water polo M/W.

Campus security: 24-hour emergency response devices and patrols, late-night transport/escort service, controlled dormitory access.

Student services: health clinic, personal/psychological counseling, women's center.

COSTS & FINANCIAL AID

Costs (2016–17) ***Comprehensive fee:*** $30,430 includes full-time tuition ($19,446), mandatory fees ($550), and room and board ($10,434). Full-time tuition and fees vary according to course load, degree level, and location. Part-time tuition: $648 per credit hour. Part-time tuition and fees vary according to course load, degree level, and location. ***Required fees:*** $50 per term part-time. ***Room and board:*** Room and board charges vary according to board plan. ***Waivers:*** employees or children of employees.

Financial Aid Of all full-time matriculated undergraduates who enrolled in 2016, 2,506 applied for aid, 2,261 were judged to have need, 160 had their need fully met. In 2016, 257 non-need-based awards were made. ***Average percent of need met:*** 51. ***Average financial aid package:*** $13,588. ***Average need-based loan:*** $4399. ***Average need-based gift aid:*** $4745. ***Average non-need-based aid:*** $5450. ***Average indebtedness upon graduation:*** $33,336.

APPLYING

Standardized Tests *Required for some:* SAT or ACT (for admission).

Options: electronic application, early decision, early action, deferred entrance.

Application fee: $40.

Required: essay or personal statement, high school transcript, minimum 2.0 GPA, 1 letter of recommendation. ***Required for some:*** minimum 3.0 GPA. ***Recommended:*** interview.

Application deadlines: rolling (freshmen), rolling (transfers).

Notification: 9/1 (freshmen), continuous (transfers).

CONTACT

Utica College, 1600 Burrstone Road, Utica, NY 13502-4892.
Phone: 315-792-3006. *Toll-free phone:* 800-782-8884.

See below for display ad and page 1582 for the College Close-Up.

Vassar College

Poughkeepsie, New York

http://www.vassar.edu/

- **Independent** 4-year, founded 1861
- **Suburban** 1000-acre campus with easy access to New York City
- **Endowment** $948.6 million
- **Coed** 2,424 undergraduate students, 99% full-time, 57% women, 43% men
- **Very difficult** entrance level, 27% of applicants were admitted

UNDERGRAD STUDENTS

2,405 full-time, 19 part-time. Students come from 54 states and territories; 52 other countries; 75% are from out of state; 4% Black or African American, non-Hispanic/Latino; 11% Hispanic/Latino; 12% Asian, non-Hispanic/Latino; 6% Two or more races, non-Hispanic/Latino; 0.4% Race/ethnicity unknown; 8% international; 0.3% transferred in; 96% live on campus.

Freshmen:

Admission: 7,284 applied, 1,964 admitted, 659 enrolled. ***Test scores:*** SAT critical reading scores over 500: 99%; SAT math scores over 500: 100%; SAT writing scores over 500: 99%; ACT scores over 18: 100%; SAT critical reading scores over 600: 97%; SAT math scores over 600: 97%; SAT writing scores over 600: 94%; ACT scores over 24: 100%; SAT critical reading scores over 700: 64%; SAT math scores over 700: 55%; SAT writing scores over 700: 56%; ACT scores over 30: 86%.

Retention: 97% of full-time freshmen returned.

FACULTY

Total: 334, 83% full-time, 83% with terminal degrees.

Student/faculty ratio: 8:1.

ACADEMICS

Calendar: semesters. *Degrees:* bachelor's and master's.

Special study options: advanced placement credit, cooperative education, double majors, independent study, internships, off-campus study, part-time degree program, services for LD students, student-designed majors, study abroad.

Unusual degree programs: 3-2 engineering with Dartmouth College.

Computers: 145 computers/terminals and 5,113 ports are available on campus for general student use. Students can access the following: campus intranet, computer help desk, free student e-mail accounts, online (class) grades, online (class) registration, online (class) schedules, Ethernet. Campuswide network is available. 100% of college-owned or -operated housing units are wired for high-speed Internet access. Wireless service is available via entire campus.

Library: Vassar College Library plus 2 others. *Books:* 1.1 million (physical), 517,970 (digital/electronic); *Serial titles:* 18,037 (physical), 89,234 (digital/electronic); *Databases:* 592. Weekly public service hours: 145; study areas open 24 hours, 5-7 days a week; students can reserve study rooms.

STUDENT LIFE

Housing options: on-campus residence required through senior year; coed, women-only, cooperative, special housing for students with disabilities. Campus housing is university owned. Freshman campus housing is guaranteed.

Activities and organizations: drama/theater group, student-run newspaper, radio station, choral group, Student Association, WVKR radio station, VICE (programming social events), Vassar Greens, Ultimate Frisbee.

Athletics Member NCAA. All Division III. ***Intercollegiate sports:*** baseball M, basketball M/W, crew M(c)/W(c), cross-country running M/W, fencing M/W, field hockey W, golf W, lacrosse M/W, rugby M(c)/W(c), soccer M/W, squash M(c)/W(c), swimming and diving M/W, tennis M/W, track and field M/W, volleyball M/W. ***Intramural sports:*** badminton M(c)/W(c), equestrian sports M(c)/W(c), sailing M(c)/W(c), skiing (cross-country) M(c)/W(c), skiing (downhill) M(c)/W(c), ultimate Frisbee M(c)/W(c).

Campus security: 24-hour emergency response devices and patrols, student patrols, late-night transport/escort service, controlled dormitory access.

Student services: health clinic, personal/psychological counseling, women's center.

COSTS & FINANCIAL AID

Costs (2016–17) ***One-time required fee:*** $80. ***Comprehensive fee:*** $65,490 includes full-time tuition ($52,320), mandatory fees ($770), and room and board ($12,400). Part-time tuition: $6230 per unit. ***College room only:*** $6730. Room and board charges vary according to board plan and housing facility. ***Payment plan:*** installment. ***Waivers:*** employees or children of employees.

Financial Aid Of all full-time matriculated undergraduates who enrolled in 2016, 1,743 applied for aid, 1,559 were judged to have need, 1,559 had their need fully met. 1,057 Federal Work-Study jobs (averaging $2521). 345 state and other part-time jobs (averaging $2471). ***Average percent of need met:*** 100. ***Average financial aid package:*** $50,820. ***Average need-based loan:*** $3779. ***Average need-based gift aid:*** $47,176. ***Average indebtedness upon graduation:*** $18,462. ***Financial aid deadline:*** 2/1.

APPLYING

Standardized Tests *Required:* SAT or ACT (for admission).

Options: electronic application, early decision, deferred entrance.

Application fee: $70.

Required: essay or personal statement, high school transcript, 2 letters of recommendation.

Application deadlines: 1/1 (freshmen), 3/15 (transfers).

Early decision deadline: 11/15.

Notification: 4/1 (freshmen), 5/10 (transfers), 12/15 (early decision).

CONTACT

Dean Art D. Rodriguez, Dean of Admission and Financial Aid, Vassar College, 124 Raymond Avenue, Poughkeepsie, NY 12604. *Phone:* 845-437-7300. *Toll-free phone:* 800-827-7270. *Fax:* 845-437-7063. *E-mail:* admissions@vassar.edu.

Vaughn College of Aeronautics and Technology

Flushing, New York

http://www.vaughn.edu/

- **Independent** comprehensive, founded 1932
- **Urban** 6-acre campus with easy access to New York City
- **Endowment** $22.5 million
- **Coed, primarily men** 1,540 undergraduate students, 83% full-time, 13% women, 87% men
- **Moderately difficult** entrance level, 69% of applicants were admitted

UNDERGRAD STUDENTS

1,275 full-time, 265 part-time. Students come from 24 states and territories; 22 other countries; 11% are from out of state; 17% Black or African American, non-Hispanic/Latino; 33% Hispanic/Latino; 10% Asian, non-Hispanic/Latino; 1% Native Hawaiian or other Pacific Islander, non-Hispanic/Latino; 0.2% American Indian or Alaska Native, non-Hispanic/Latino; 2% Two or more races, non-Hispanic/Latino; 17% Race/ethnicity unknown; 6% international; 11% transferred in; 10% live on campus.

Freshmen:

Admission: 800 applied, 553 admitted, 278 enrolled. ***Test scores:*** SAT critical reading scores over 500: 60%; SAT math scores over 500: 74%; ACT scores over 18: 100%; SAT critical reading scores over 600: 15%; SAT math scores over 600: 31%; ACT scores over 24: 73%; SAT critical reading scores over 700: 1%; SAT math scores over 700: 7%; ACT scores over 30: 18%.

Retention: 79% of full-time freshmen returned.

FACULTY

Total: 205, 20% full-time, 18% with terminal degrees.

Student/faculty ratio: 14:1.

ACADEMICS

Calendar: semesters. *Degrees:* certificates, associate, bachelor's, and master's.

Special study options: academic remediation for entering students, advanced placement credit, distance learning, double majors, English as a second language, internships, part-time degree program, services for LD students, summer session for credit. ***ROTC:*** Army (c), Air Force (c).

Computers: 60 computers/terminals are available on campus for general student use. Students can access the following: campus intranet, computer help desk, free student e-mail accounts, online (class) grades, online (class) registration, online (class) schedules, Vaughn Student Portal. Campuswide network is available. 100% of college-owned or -operated housing units are wired for high-speed Internet access. Wireless service is available via entire campus.

Library: Library and Learning Commons.

STUDENT LIFE

Housing options: coed, special housing for students with disabilities. Campus housing is university owned. Freshman applicants given priority for college housing.

Activities and organizations: Unmanned Aerial Vehicle Club, Women in Aviation-International, Veterans Organization, Robotics Club, Hispanic Society of Aeronautical Engineers.

Athletics Member USCAA. ***Intercollegiate sports:*** basketball M/W, cross-country running M/W, soccer M, tennis M/W. ***Intramural sports:*** basketball M/W, cross-country running M/W, soccer M, tennis M/W.

Campus security: 24-hour emergency response devices and patrols, controlled dormitory access.

Student services: personal/psychological counseling.

COSTS & FINANCIAL AID

Costs (2017–18) ***One-time required fee:*** $160. ***Comprehensive fee:*** $39,062 includes full-time tuition ($23,877), mandatory fees ($1000), and room and board ($14,185). Full-time tuition and fees vary according to course load, degree level, and program. Part-time tuition: $800 per credit hour. Part-time tuition and fees vary according to course load, degree level, and program. ***Required fees:*** $400 per term part-time. ***College room only:*** $10,983. Room and board charges vary according to board plan. ***Payment plan:*** installment. ***Waivers:*** employees or children of employees.

Financial Aid Of all full-time matriculated undergraduates who enrolled in 2008, 704 applied for aid, 704 were judged to have need, 476 had their need fully met. 25 Federal Work-Study jobs (averaging $3000). In 2008, 145 non-need-based awards were made. ***Average percent of need met:*** 82. ***Average financial aid package:*** $18,030. ***Average need-based loan:*** $1770. ***Average need-based gift aid:*** $2950. ***Average non-need-based aid:*** $2000. ***Average indebtedness upon graduation:*** $17,125.

APPLYING

Standardized Tests *Required for some:* SAT or ACT (for admission).

Options: electronic application.

Application fee: $40.

Required: high school transcript. ***Recommended:*** essay or personal statement, 2 letters of recommendation, interview.

Application deadlines: rolling (freshmen), rolling (out-of-state freshmen), rolling (transfers).

Notification: continuous (freshmen), continuous (out-of-state freshmen), continuous (transfers).

CONTACT

Mr. David Sookdeo, Acting Director of Admissions, Vaughn College of Aeronautics and Technology, 8601 23rd Avenue, Flushing, NY 11369. *Phone:* 718-429.6600 Ext. 192. *Toll-free phone:* 866-6VAUGHN. *Fax:* 718-779.2231. *E-mail:* david.sookdeo@vaughn.edu.

Villa Maria College

Buffalo, New York

http://www.villa.edu/

- **Independent** 4-year, founded 1960, affiliated with Roman Catholic Church
- **Suburban** 9-acre campus with easy access to Buffalo-Niagara
- **Endowment** $1.9 million
- **Coed** 589 undergraduate students, 80% full-time, 62% women, 38% men

UNDERGRAD STUDENTS

470 full-time, 119 part-time. Students come from 11 states and territories; 2 other countries; 3% are from out of state; 32% Black or African American, non-Hispanic/Latino; 7% Hispanic/Latino; 1% Asian, non-Hispanic/Latino; 0.5% American Indian or Alaska Native, non-Hispanic/Latino; 6% Two or more races, non-Hispanic/Latino; 0.2% Race/ethnicity unknown; 0.3% international; 12% transferred in.

Freshmen:

Admission: 148 enrolled. ***Average high school GPA:*** 2.55.

Retention: 66% of full-time freshmen returned.

FACULTY

Total: 95, 35% full-time, 12% with terminal degrees.

Student/faculty ratio: 10:1.

ACADEMICS

Calendar: semesters. *Degrees:* certificates, associate, and bachelor's.

Special study options: advanced placement credit, cooperative education, distance learning, honors programs, independent study, internships, off-campus study, part-time degree program, services for LD students.

Computers: 275 computers/terminals are available on campus for general student use. Students can access the following: computer help desk, free student e-mail accounts, online (class) grades, online (class) registration, online (class) schedules. Campuswide network is available.

Library: Villa Maria College Library. *Books:* 18,001 (physical), 132,960 (digital/electronic); *Serial titles:* 87 (physical); *Databases:* 44.

STUDENT LIFE

Housing options: college housing not available.

Activities and organizations: choral group.

Athletics Member USCAA. ***Intercollegiate sports:*** basketball M/W, bowling W, cross-country running M/W, golf M, soccer M/W, swimming and diving M/W.

Campus security: 24-hour emergency response devices, late-night transport/escort service, security guard during hours of operation.

Student services: health clinic, personal/psychological counseling.

COSTS & FINANCIAL AID

Costs (2016–17) ***Tuition:*** $20,030 full-time, $670 per credit hour part-time. Full-time tuition and fees vary according to program and reciprocity agreements. Part-time tuition and fees vary according to course load, program, and reciprocity agreements. ***Required fees:*** $740 full-time, $260 per year part-time. ***Payment plan:*** installment. ***Waivers:*** employees or children of employees.

Financial Aid ***Average indebtedness upon graduation:*** $22,658.

APPLYING

Required: high school transcript, interview. ***Required for some:*** essay, portfolio, interview for BFA programs and associate level interior design assistant; interview for animation program; interview and audition for music programs. ***Recommended:*** essay or personal statement.

CONTACT

Mr. Brian Emerson, Vice President for Enrollment and Student Services, Villa Maria College, 240 Pine Ridge Road, Buffalo, NY 14225. *Phone:* 716-896-0700 Ext. 1838. *Fax:* 716-896-0705. *E-mail:* admissions@villa.edu.

Wagner College

Staten Island, New York

http://www.wagner.edu/

- **Independent** comprehensive, founded 1883
- **Urban** 105-acre campus with easy access to New York City
- **Endowment** $77.3 million
- **Coed** 1,807 undergraduate students, 98% full-time, 64% women, 36% men

UNDERGRAD STUDENTS

1,768 full-time, 39 part-time. Students come from 41 states and territories; 43 other countries; 54% are from out of state; 8% Black or African American, non-Hispanic/Latino; 11% Hispanic/Latino; 3% Asian, non-Hispanic/Latino; 0.1% Native Hawaiian or other Pacific Islander, non-Hispanic/Latino; 0.1% American Indian or Alaska Native, non-Hispanic/Latino; 3% Two or more races, non-Hispanic/Latino; 5% Race/ethnicity unknown; 4% international; 7% transferred in; 71% live on campus.

Freshmen:

Admission: 442 enrolled. ***Average high school GPA:*** 3.6. ***Test scores:*** SAT critical reading scores over 500: 74%; SAT math scores over 500: 77%; SAT writing scores over 500: 72%; ACT scores over 18: 98%; SAT critical reading scores over 600: 30%; SAT math scores over 600: 27%; SAT writing scores over 600: 32%; ACT scores over 24: 59%; SAT critical reading scores over 700: 5%; SAT math scores over 700: 1%; SAT writing scores over 700: 3%; ACT scores over 30: 6%.

Retention: 85% of full-time freshmen returned.

FACULTY

Total: 265, 42% full-time, 45% with terminal degrees.

Student/faculty ratio: 13:1.

ACADEMICS

Calendar: semesters. *Degrees:* bachelor's, master's, doctoral, and post-master's certificates.

Special study options: accelerated degree program, adult/continuing education programs, advanced placement credit, cooperative education, double majors, honors programs, independent study, internships, off-campus study, part-time degree program, services for LD students, student-designed majors, study abroad, summer session for credit. ***ROTC:*** Army (c).

Unusual degree programs: 3-2 business administration; microbiology.

Computers: 230 computers/terminals are available on campus for general student use. Students can access the following: campus intranet, computer help desk, free student e-mail accounts, online (class) grades, online (class) registration, online (class) schedules. Campuswide network is available. 100% of college-owned or -operated housing units are wired for high-speed Internet access. Wireless service is available via entire campus.

Library: August Horrmann Library. *Books:* 70,465 (physical), 180,000 (digital/electronic); *Serial titles:* 79,532 (physical); *Databases:* 61. Weekly public service hours: 120; students can reserve study rooms.

STUDENT LIFE
Housing options: coed. Campus housing is university owned and leased by the school. Freshman campus housing is guaranteed.
Activities and organizations: drama/theater group, student-run newspaper, radio station, choral group, marching band, Student Government Association, Student Activities Board, Wagner College Theatre, Wagner College Choir, student newspaper, national fraternities, national sororities.
Athletics Member NCAA. All Division I except football (Division I-AA). ***Intercollegiate sports:*** baseball M(s), basketball M(s)/W(s), cheerleading W(c), cross-country running M(s)/W(s), fencing W(s), golf M(s)/W(s), ice hockey M(c), lacrosse M(s)/W(s), soccer W(s), softball W(s), swimming and diving W(s), tennis M(s)/W(s), track and field M(s)/W(s), water polo M(s)/W(s). ***Intramural sports:*** basketball M/W, bowling M/W, football M, rugby M(c), soccer M/W, softball M/W.
Campus security: 24-hour emergency response devices and patrols, late-night transport/escort service, controlled dormitory access.
Student services: health clinic, personal/psychological counseling.

COSTS & FINANCIAL AID
Costs (2016–17) ***Comprehensive fee:*** $57,240 includes full-time tuition ($43,500), mandatory fees ($480), and room and board ($13,260). Full-time tuition and fees vary according to program. Part-time tuition: $5438 per unit. ***Payment plan:*** installment. ***Waivers:*** employees or children of employees.
Financial Aid Of all full-time matriculated undergraduates who enrolled in 2015, 1,289 applied for aid, 1,128 were judged to have need, 267 had their need fully met. In 2015, 386 non-need-based awards were made. ***Average percent of need met:*** 73. ***Average financial aid package:*** $29,073. ***Average need-based loan:*** $4958. ***Average need-based gift aid:*** $22,422. ***Average non-need-based aid:*** $16,348.

APPLYING
Standardized Tests *Required for some:* SAT or ACT (for admission).
Required: essay or personal statement, high school transcript, minimum 2.5 GPA, 2 letters of recommendation. ***Required for some:*** interview. ***Recommended:*** minimum 3.0 GPA, interview.

CONTACT
Mr. James Gibbons, Director of Admissions, Wagner College, One Campus Road, Pape Admissions Building, Staten Island, NY 10301. *Phone:* 718-390-3180. *Toll-free phone:* 800-221-1010. *Fax:* 718-390-3105. *E-mail:* jgibbons@wagner.edu.

Webb Institute
Glen Cove, New York
http://www.webb.edu/

- **Independent** 4-year, founded 1889
- **Suburban** 26-acre campus with easy access to New York City
- **Endowment** $70.9 million
- **Coed** 92 undergraduate students, 100% full-time, 17% women, 83% men
- **Most difficult** entrance level, 29% of applicants were admitted

UNDERGRAD STUDENTS
92 full-time. Students come from 27 states and territories; 2 other countries; 79% are from out of state; 12% Asian, non-Hispanic/Latino; 9% Two or more races, non-Hispanic/Latino; 2% Race/ethnicity unknown; 100% live on campus.

Freshmen:
Admission: 116 applied, 34 admitted, 28 enrolled. ***Average high school GPA:*** 4. ***Test scores:*** SAT critical reading scores over 500: 100%; SAT math scores over 500: 100%; SAT writing scores over 500: 100%; SAT critical reading scores over 600: 100%; SAT math scores over 600: 100%; SAT writing scores over 600: 85%; SAT critical reading scores over 700: 65%; SAT math scores over 700: 83%; SAT writing scores over 700: 35%; ACT scores over 30: 100%.
Retention: 81% of full-time freshmen returned.

FACULTY
Total: 14, 64% full-time, 71% with terminal degrees.
Student/faculty ratio: 9:1.

ACADEMICS
Calendar: semesters. *Degree:* bachelor's.

Special study options: double majors, independent study, internships, services for LD students, study abroad.

Computers: 25 computers/terminals are available on campus for general student use. Students can access the following: campus intranet, computer help desk, free student e-mail accounts, online (class) grades. Campuswide network is available. 100% of college-owned or -operated housing units are wired for high-speed Internet access. Wireless service is available via entire campus.

Library: Livingston Library. *Books:* 44,800 (physical), 4,190 (digital/electronic); *Serial titles:* 817 (physical), 43,658 (digital/electronic); *Databases:* 62. Weekly public service hours: 35; study areas open 24 hours, 5-7 days a week.

STUDENT LIFE

Housing options: on-campus residence required through senior year; coed, men-only, women-only. Campus housing is university owned. Freshman campus housing is guaranteed.

Activities and organizations: choral group, Student Organization, Society of Naval Architects and Marine Engineers, American Society of Naval Engineers, Society of Women Engineers, Marine Technology Society.

Athletics ***Intercollegiate sports:*** basketball M/W, cross-country running M(c)/W(c), sailing M/W, soccer M/W, tennis M/W, volleyball M/W. ***Intramural sports:*** crew M/W, cross-country running M/W, ultimate Frisbee M/W.

Campus security: 24-hour emergency response devices and patrols, controlled dormitory access.

Student services: personal/psychological counseling.

COSTS & FINANCIAL AID

Costs (2017–18) ***One-time required fee:*** $3050. ***Comprehensive fee:*** $63,525 includes full-time tuition ($48,350), mandatory fees ($425), and room and board ($14,750). Webb provides scholarships that will fully cover the tuition expenses of U.S. citizens and permanent residents. One-time required fee is for a laptop charged in the first year only.

Financial Aid Of all full-time matriculated undergraduates who enrolled in 2014, 37 applied for aid, 37 were judged to have need. In 2014, 51 non-need-based awards were made. ***Average percent of need met:*** 78. ***Average financial aid package:*** $48,000. ***Average need-based loan:*** $4200. ***Average need-based gift aid:*** $2000. ***Average non-need-based aid:*** $44,750. ***Average indebtedness upon graduation:*** $10,000.

APPLYING

Standardized Tests *Required:* SAT or ACT (for admission), SAT Subject Tests (for admission).

Options: electronic application, early decision.

Application fee: $60.

Required: essay or personal statement, high school transcript, minimum 3.5 GPA, 2 letters of recommendation, interview, proof of U.S. citizenship or permanent residency status.

Application deadlines: 2/1 (freshmen), 2/1 (transfers).

Early decision deadline: 10/15.

Notification: 4/30 (freshmen), 4/30 (transfers), 12/15 (early decision).

CONTACT

Lauren Carballo, Director of Admissions & Student Services, Webb Institute, 298 Crescent Beach Road, Glen Cove, NY 11542. *Phone:* 516-671-8355. *Fax:* 516-674-9838. *E-mail:* admissions@webb.edu.

See previous page for display ad and page 1590 for the College Close-Up.

Wells College

Aurora, New York

http://www.wells.edu/

- **Independent** 4-year, founded 1868
- **Rural** 365-acre campus with easy access to Syracuse
- **Endowment** $23.5 million
- **Coed** 515 undergraduate students, 99% full-time, 66% women, 34% men
- **Moderately difficult** entrance level, 58% of applicants were admitted

UNDERGRAD STUDENTS

509 full-time, 6 part-time. 23% are from out of state; 12% Black or African American, non-Hispanic/Latino; 12% Hispanic/Latino; 0.8% Asian, non-Hispanic/Latino; 0.4% American Indian or Alaska Native, non-Hispanic/Latino; 3% Two or more races, non-Hispanic/Latino; 9% Race/ethnicity unknown; 4% international; 3% transferred in; 94% live on campus.

Freshmen:

Admission: 2,222 applied, 1,295 admitted, 132 enrolled. ***Average high school GPA:*** 3.33. ***Test scores:*** SAT critical reading scores over 500: 53%; SAT math scores over 500: 54%; SAT writing scores over 500: 61%; ACT scores over 18: 85%; SAT critical reading scores over 600: 14%; SAT math scores over 600: 15%; SAT writing scores over 600: 18%; ACT scores over 24: 41%; SAT writing scores over 700: 1%; ACT scores over 30: 4%.

Retention: 78% of full-time freshmen returned.

FACULTY

Total: 60, 63% full-time, 68% with terminal degrees.

Student/faculty ratio: 10:1.

ACADEMICS

Calendar: semesters. *Degree:* bachelor's.

Special study options: accelerated degree program, adult/continuing education programs, advanced placement credit, double majors, English as a second language, independent study, internships, off-campus study, part-time degree program, services for LD students, student-designed majors, study abroad.

Unusual degree programs: 3-2 business administration with Clarkson University; engineering with Columbia University, Clarkson University, Cornell University; education with University of Rochester.

Computers: 96 computers/terminals and 1,224 ports are available on campus for general student use. Students can access the following: campus intranet, computer help desk, free student e-mail accounts, online (class) grades, online (class) registration, online (class) schedules. Campuswide network is available. 100% of college-owned or -operated housing units are wired for high-speed Internet access. Wireless service is available via classrooms, dorm rooms, learning centers, libraries, student centers.

Library: Louis Jefferson Long Library. Students can reserve study rooms.

STUDENT LIFE

Housing options: on-campus residence required through junior year; coed, women-only. Campus housing is university owned. Freshman campus housing is guaranteed.

Activities and organizations: drama/theater group, choral group, Umoja, Prodigy, Red Cross Club, Campus Greens, Programing Board.

Athletics Member NCAA. All Division III. ***Intercollegiate sports:*** baseball M, basketball M/W, cross-country running M/W, field hockey W, lacrosse M/W, soccer M/W, softball W, swimming and diving M/W, tennis W, volleyball M/W. ***Intramural sports:*** rugby M(c)/W(c).

Campus security: 24-hour emergency response devices and patrols, late-night transport/escort service, controlled dormitory access.

Student services: health clinic, personal/psychological counseling, women's center.

COSTS & FINANCIAL AID

Costs (2017–18) ***Comprehensive fee:*** $53,330 includes full-time tuition ($38,100), mandatory fees ($1500), and room and board ($13,730). Part-time tuition: $1600 per credit hour. Part-time tuition and fees vary according to course load. ***Required fees:*** $200 per term part-time. ***College room only:*** $6865. Room and board charges vary according to housing facility. ***Payment plan:*** installment. ***Waivers:*** senior citizens and employees or children of employees.

Financial Aid Of all full-time matriculated undergraduates who enrolled in 2015, 551 applied for aid, 531 were judged to have need, 95 had their need fully met. 58 Federal Work-Study jobs (averaging $1850). 235 state and other part-time jobs (averaging $1850). In 2015, 32 non-need-based awards were made. ***Average percent of need met:*** 84. ***Average financial aid package:*** $34,570. ***Average need-based loan:*** $3649. ***Average need-based gift aid:*** $29,867. ***Average non-need-based aid:*** $20,606. ***Average indebtedness upon graduation:*** $34,735.

APPLYING

Options: electronic application, early admission, early decision, early action, deferred entrance.

Application fee: $40.

Required: essay or personal statement, high school transcript, 2 letters of recommendation. ***Recommended:*** minimum 3.0 GPA, interview.

Application deadlines: 3/1 (freshmen), rolling (transfers), 12/15 (early action).

Early decision deadline: 12/15.

Notification: 4/1 (freshmen), continuous (transfers), 1/15 (early decision), 2/1 (early action).

CONTACT

Ms. Kishan Zuber, Vice President for Enrollment Services, Wells College, 170 Main Street, Aurora, NY 13026. *Phone:* 315-364-3358. *Toll-free phone:* 800-952-9355. *Fax:* 315-364-3227. *E-mail:* admissions@wells.edu.

Yeshiva and Kolel Bais Medrash Elyon

Monsey, New York

CONTACT

Yeshiva and Kolel Bais Medrash Elyon, 73 Main Street, Monsey, NY 10952.

Yeshiva and Kollel Harbotzas Torah

Brooklyn, New York

CONTACT

Yeshiva and Kollel Harbotzas Torah, 1049 East 15th Street, Brooklyn, NY 11230.

Yeshiva Derech Chaim

Brooklyn, New York

- **Independent Jewish** comprehensive, founded 1975
- **Men only**
- 100% of applicants were admitted

ACADEMICS

Calendar: semesters. *Degrees:* bachelor's and master's.

CONTACT

Yeshiva Derech Chaim, 1573 39th Street, Brooklyn, NY 11218.

Yeshiva D'Monsey Rabbinical College

Monsey, New York

CONTACT

Yeshiva D'Monsey Rabbinical College, 2 Roman Boulevard, Monsey, NY 10952.

Yeshiva Gedolah Imrei Yosef D'Spinka

Brooklyn, New York

CONTACT

Yeshiva Gedolah Imrei Yosef D'Spinka, 1466 56th Street, Brooklyn, NY 11219.

Yeshiva Karlin Stolin Rabbinical Institute

Brooklyn, New York

CONTACT

Director of Admissions, Yeshiva Karlin Stolin Rabbinical Institute, 1818 Fifty-fourth Street, Brooklyn, NY 11204. *Phone:* 718-232-7800 Ext. 26.

Yeshiva of Far Rockaway Derech Ayson Rabbinical Seminary

Far Rockaway, New York

http://www.yofr.org/

CONTACT

Yeshiva of Far Rockaway Derech Ayson Rabbinical Seminary, 802 Hicksville Road, Far Rockaway, NY 11691.

Yeshiva of Machzikai Hadas

Brooklyn, New York

CONTACT

Yeshiva of Machzikai Hadas, 1321 43rd Street, Brooklyn, NY 11219.

Yeshiva of Nitra Rabbinical College

Mount Kisco, New York

CONTACT

Administrator, Yeshiva of Nitra Rabbinical College, Pines Bridge Road, Mount Kisco, NY 10549. *Phone:* 718-384-5460. *Fax:* 718-387-9400.

Yeshiva of the Telshe Alumni

Riverdale, New York

CONTACT

Yeshiva of the Telshe Alumni, 4904 Independence Avenue, Riverdale, NY 10471.

Yeshiva Shaarei Torah of Rockland

Suffern, New York

CONTACT

Yeshiva Shaarei Torah of Rockland, 91 West Carlton Road, Suffern, NY 10901.

Yeshiva Shaar Hatorah Talmudic Research Institute

Kew Gardens, New York

CONTACT

Assistant Dean, Yeshiva Shaar Hatorah Talmudic Research Institute, 117-06 84th Avenue, Kew Gardens, NY 11418-1469. *Phone:* 718-846-1940.

Yeshivas Novominsk

Brooklyn, New York

CONTACT

Yeshivas Novominsk, 1569 47th Street, Brooklyn, NY 11219.

Yeshivath Viznitz

Monsey, New York

CONTACT

Registrar, Yeshivath Viznitz, 25 Phyllis Terrace, Monsey, NY 10952. *Phone:* 914-356-1010.

Yeshivath Zichron Moshe

South Fallsburg, New York

CONTACT

Rabbi Abba Gorelick, Dean, Yeshivath Zichron Moshe, Laurel Park Road, South Fallsburg, NY 12779. *Phone:* 914-434-5240.

Yeshivat Mikdash Melech

Brooklyn, New York

CONTACT
Rabbi S. Beyda, Director of Admissions, Yeshivat Mikdash Melech, 1326 Ocean Parkway, Brooklyn, NY 11230-5601. *Phone:* 718-339-1090. *E-mail:* mikdashmelech@verizon.net.

Yeshiva University

New York, New York

http://www.yu.edu/

- **Independent** university, founded 1886
- **Urban** campus
- **Endowment** $894.5 million
- **Coed**
- **Moderately difficult** entrance level

FACULTY
Student/faculty ratio: 7:1.

ACADEMICS
Calendar: semesters. *Degrees:* bachelor's, master's, doctoral, post-master's, and postbachelor's certificates (Yeshiva College and Stern College for Women are coordinate undergraduate colleges of arts and sciences for men and women, respectively. Sy Syms School of Business offers programs at both campuses).
Library: Mendel Gottesman Library. *Books:* 1.1 million (physical), 24,407 (digital/electronic); *Serial titles:* 9,933 (physical); *Databases:* 401.

STUDENT LIFE
Housing options: men-only, women-only. Campus housing is university owned and leased by the school.

Activities and organizations: drama/theater group, student-run newspaper, radio station, choral group.

Athletics Member NCAA. All Division III.

Campus security: 24-hour emergency response devices and patrols, late-night transport/escort service.

Student services: health clinic, personal/psychological counseling.

COSTS & FINANCIAL AID
Costs (2016–17) ***Comprehensive fee:*** $52,805 includes full-time tuition ($39,070), mandatory fees ($1600), and room and board ($12,135). Part-time tuition: $1390 per credit hour. ***College room only:*** $8635. Room and board charges vary according to board plan and housing facility.

Financial Aid ***Average indebtedness upon graduation:*** $24,101.

APPLYING
Standardized Tests *Required:* SAT or ACT (for admission).

Options: electronic application, early admission, early decision, deferred entrance.

Application fee: $65.

Required: essay or personal statement, high school transcript, 2 letters of recommendation, interview.

CONTACT
Yeshiva University, 500 West 185th Street, New York, NY 10033-3201. *Phone:* 212-960-5277.

York College of the City University of New York

Jamaica, New York

http://www.york.cuny.edu/

- **State and locally supported** comprehensive, founded 1967, part of City University of New York System
- **Urban** 50-acre campus with easy access to New York City
- **Endowment** $890,940
- **Coed** 8,258 undergraduate students, 61% full-time, 65% women, 35% men
- **Moderately difficult** entrance level, 61% of applicants were admitted

UNDERGRAD STUDENTS
5,066 full-time, 3,192 part-time. Students come from 4 states and territories; 131 other countries; 1% are from out of state; 40% Black or African American, non-Hispanic/Latino; 22% Hispanic/Latino; 26% Asian, non-Hispanic/Latino; 0.9% American Indian or Alaska Native, non-Hispanic/Latino; 4% international; 10% transferred in.

Freshmen:
Admission: 13,726 applied, 8,334 admitted, 971 enrolled. ***Test scores:*** SAT critical reading scores over 500: 13%; SAT math scores over 500: 21%; SAT writing scores over 500: 11%; SAT critical reading scores over 600: 1%; SAT math scores over 600: 2%; SAT writing scores over 600: 1%.
Retention: 73% of full-time freshmen returned.

FACULTY
Student/faculty ratio: 23:1.

ACADEMICS
Calendar: semesters. *Degrees:* bachelor's and master's.

Special study options: adult/continuing education programs, advanced placement credit, cooperative education, double majors, English as a second language, honors programs, independent study, internships, off-campus study, part-time degree program, services for LD students, study abroad, summer session for credit. ***ROTC:*** Army (b).

Unusual degree programs: 3-2 occupational therapy.

Computers: 650 computers/terminals and 844 ports are available on campus for general student use. Students can access the following: computer help desk, free student e-mail accounts, online (class) registration, online (class) schedules. Campuswide network is available. Wireless service is available via entire campus.

Library: Main Library plus 1 other. *Books:* 150,914 (physical), 473,723 (digital/electronic).

STUDENT LIFE
Housing options: college housing not available.

Activities and organizations: drama/theater group, student-run newspaper, television station, choral group, Haitian Students Association, Caribbean Students Association, Haitian Cultural Association, Latin Caucus, Muslim Student Association.

Athletics Member NCAA. All Division III. ***Intercollegiate sports:*** baseball M/W, basketball M/W, cross-country running M/W, soccer M, softball W, swimming and diving M/W, tennis M, track and field M/W, volleyball M/W. ***Intramural sports:*** basketball M/W, cross-country running M/W, soccer M, softball W, swimming and diving M/W, table tennis M/W, tennis M, track and field M/W, volleyball M/W.

Campus security: 24-hour emergency response devices and patrols, late-night transport/escort service.

Student services: health clinic, personal/psychological counseling, women's center.

COSTS & FINANCIAL AID
Costs (2016–17) ***Tuition:*** state resident $6330 full-time, $275 per credit hour part-time; nonresident $16,800 full-time, $560 per credit hour part-time. Full-time tuition and fees vary according to degree level and student level. Part-time tuition and fees vary according to degree level and student level. ***Required fees:*** $417 full-time, $126 per term part-time. ***Payment plan:*** installment. ***Waivers:*** senior citizens and employees or children of employees.

Financial Aid Of all full-time matriculated undergraduates who enrolled in 2016, 4,269 applied for aid, 4,269 were judged to have need, 79 had their need fully met. In 2016, 61 non-need-based awards were made. ***Average percent of need met:*** 60. ***Average financial aid package:*** $7738. ***Average need-based loan:*** $3931. ***Average need-based gift aid:*** $8254. ***Average non-need-based aid:*** $4914. ***Average indebtedness upon graduation:*** $3828. ***Financial aid deadline:*** 6/30.

APPLYING
Standardized Tests *Required:* SAT (for admission), SAT or ACT (for admission).

Options: electronic application, early admission, deferred entrance.

Application fee: $65.

Required: high school transcript, minimum 2.8 GPA. ***Required for some:*** minimum 2.5 GPA. ***Recommended:*** minimum 3.0 GPA.

Application deadlines: rolling (freshmen), rolling (transfers).

Notification: continuous (freshmen), continuous (transfers).

CONTACT

Dr. La Toro Yates, Director of Admissions, York College of the City University of New York, 94-20 Guy R. Brewer Boulevard, Jamaica, NY 11451. *Phone:* 718-262-2165. *Fax:* 718-262-2601. *E-mail:* lyates@york.cuny.edu.

NORTH CAROLINA

Apex School of Theology

Durham, North Carolina

http://www.apexsot.edu/

CONTACT

Dr. Henry D. Wells Jr., Registrar, Apex School of Theology, 2945 South Miami Boulevard, Suite 114, Durham, NC 27703. *Phone:* 919-572-1625. *Fax:* 919-572-1762. *E-mail:* registrar@apexsot.edu.

Appalachian State University

Boone, North Carolina

http://www.appstate.edu/

- **State-supported** comprehensive, founded 1899, part of University of North Carolina System
- **Small-town** 415-acre campus
- **Endowment** $96.4 million
- **Coed** 16,595 undergraduate students, 94% full-time, 55% women, 45% men
- **Moderately difficult** entrance level, 68% of applicants were admitted

UNDERGRAD STUDENTS

15,542 full-time, 1,053 part-time. Students come from 42 states and territories; 70 other countries; 8% are from out of state; 4% Black or African American, non-Hispanic/Latino; 5% Hispanic/Latino; 2% Asian, non-Hispanic/Latino; 0.1% Native Hawaiian or other Pacific Islander, non-Hispanic/Latino; 0.3% American Indian or Alaska Native, non-Hispanic/Latino; 3% Two or more races, non-Hispanic/Latino; 1% Race/ethnicity unknown; 0.9% international; 10% transferred in; 34% live on campus.

Freshmen:

Admission: 13,202 applied, 9,020 admitted, 3,125 enrolled. ***Average high school GPA:*** 4.17. ***Test scores:*** SAT critical reading scores over 500: 82%; SAT math scores over 500: 85%; SAT writing scores over 500: 73%; ACT scores over 18: 99%; SAT critical reading scores over 600: 35%; SAT math scores over 600: 37%; SAT writing scores over 600: 24%; ACT scores over 24: 70%; SAT critical reading scores over 700: 5%; SAT math scores over 700: 3%; SAT writing scores over 700: 2%; ACT scores over 30: 10%.

Retention: 87% of full-time freshmen returned.

FACULTY

Total: 1,349, 71% full-time, 94% with terminal degrees.

Student/faculty ratio: 16:1.

ACADEMICS

Calendar: semesters. *Degrees:* bachelor's, master's, doctoral, post-master's, and postbachelor's certificates.

Special study options: academic remediation for entering students, adult/continuing education programs, advanced placement credit, distance learning, double majors, English as a second language, honors programs, independent study, internships, off-campus study, part-time degree program, services for LD students, student-designed majors, study abroad, summer session for credit. ***ROTC:*** Army (b).

Unusual degree programs: 3-2 engineering with Auburn University, Clemson University, North Carolina State University.

Computers: 2,280 computers/terminals are available on campus for general student use. Students can access the following: campus intranet, computer help desk, free student e-mail accounts, online (class) grades, online (class) registration, online (class) schedules. Campuswide network is available. 100% of college-owned or -operated housing units are wired for high-speed Internet access. Wireless service is available via entire campus.

Library: Carol Grotnes Belk Library plus 1 other. *Books:* 673,768 (physical), 1.2 million (digital/electronic); *Serial titles:* 14,328 (physical), 117,771 (digital/electronic); *Databases:* 464. Weekly public service hours: 137; students can reserve study rooms.

STUDENT LIFE

Housing options: on-campus residence required for freshman year; coed, women-only, special housing for students with disabilities. Campus housing is university owned. Freshman campus housing is guaranteed.

Activities and organizations: drama/theater group, student-run newspaper, radio and television station, choral group, marching band, Health Professions Club, Appalachian Educators, Gamma Beta Phi, National Society of Collegiate Scholars, App Sits Meditation Club, national fraternities, national sororities.

Athletics Member NCAA, NAIA. All NCAA Division I except football (Division I-AA). ***Intercollegiate sports:*** archery M(c)/W(c), baseball M(s), basketball M(s)/W(s), cross-country running M(s)/W(s), equestrian sports W(c), fencing M(c)/W(c), field hockey W(s), golf M(s)/W(s), ice hockey M(c)/W(c), lacrosse M(c)/W(c), rock climbing M(c)/W(c), rugby M(c)/W(c), skiing (downhill) M(c)/W(c), soccer M(s)/W(s), softball W(s), swimming and diving M(c)/W(c), tennis M(s)/W(s), track and field M(s)/W(s), ultimate Frisbee M(c)/W(c), volleyball W(s), wrestling M(s). ***Intramural sports:*** badminton M/W, basketball M/W, bowling M/W, cross-country running M/W, football M/W, golf M/W, racquetball M/W, soccer M/W, softball M/W, table tennis M/W, tennis M/W, ultimate Frisbee M/W, volleyball M/W.

Campus security: 24-hour emergency response devices and patrols, late-night transport/escort service, controlled dormitory access, Campus Alert System.

Student services: health clinic, personal/psychological counseling, women's center, legal services.

COSTS & FINANCIAL AID

Costs (2016–17) ***Tuition:*** state resident $4159 full-time, $141 per credit hour part-time; nonresident $18,675 full-time, $631 per credit hour part-time. Part-time tuition and fees vary according to course load. ***Required fees:*** $2977 full-time, $19 per credit hour part-time. ***Room and board:*** $8100; room only: $4340. Room and board charges vary according to board plan and housing facility. ***Payment plan:*** installment. ***Waivers:*** employees or children of employees.

Financial Aid Of all full-time matriculated undergraduates who enrolled in 2015, 10,616 applied for aid, 7,870 were judged to have need, 1,285 had their need fully met. 297 Federal Work-Study jobs (averaging $1619). In 2015, 527 non-need-based awards were made. ***Average percent of need met:*** 71. ***Average financial aid package:*** $9759. ***Average need-based loan:*** $4201. ***Average need-based gift aid:*** $8238. ***Average non-need-based aid:*** $2806. ***Average indebtedness upon graduation:*** $22,696.

APPLYING

Standardized Tests *Required:* SAT or ACT (for admission).

Options: electronic application, deferred entrance.

Application fee: $55.

Required: high school transcript.

Application deadlines: 3/15 (freshmen), rolling (transfers).

Notification: continuous until 1/25 (freshmen), continuous (transfers).

CONTACT

Mr. Alexis Pope, Director of Admissions, Appalachian State University, ASU Box 32004, Boone, NC 28608. *Phone:* 828-262-2120. *Fax:* 828-262-3296. *E-mail:* admissions@appstate.edu.

The Art Institute of Charlotte, a branch of Miami International University of Art & Design

Charlotte, North Carolina

http://www.artinstitutes.edu/charlotte/

CONTACT

The Art Institute of Charlotte, a branch of Miami International University of Art & Design, Three LakePointe Plaza, 2110 Water Ridge Parkway, Charlotte, NC 28217. *Phone:* 704-357-8020. *Toll-free phone:* 800-872-4417.

The Art Institute of Raleigh-Durham, a branch of Miami International University of Art & Design

Durham, North Carolina

http://www.artinstitutes.edu/raleigh-durham

CONTACT

The Art Institute of Raleigh-Durham, a branch of Miami International University of Art & Design, 410 Blackwell Street, Suite 200, Durham, NC 27701. *Phone:* 919-317-3050. *Toll-free phone:* 888-245-9593.

Barton College

Wilson, North Carolina

http://www.barton.edu/

- **Independent** comprehensive, founded 1902, affiliated with Christian Church (Disciples of Christ)
- **Small-town** 76-acre campus with easy access to Raleigh-Durham
- **Endowment** $25.9 million
- **Coed** 988 undergraduate students, 91% full-time, 70% women, 30% men
- **Minimally difficult** entrance level, 41% of applicants were admitted

UNDERGRAD STUDENTS

903 full-time, 85 part-time. Students come from 29 states and territories; 17 other countries; 16% are from out of state; 22% Black or African American, non-Hispanic/Latino; 7% Hispanic/Latino; 1% Asian, non-Hispanic/Latino; 0.2% Native Hawaiian or other Pacific Islander, non-Hispanic/Latino; 0.6% American Indian or Alaska Native, non-Hispanic/Latino; 4% Two or more races, non-Hispanic/Latino; 7% Race/ethnicity unknown; 4% international; 8% transferred in; 46% live on campus.

Freshmen:

Admission: 2,828 applied, 1,156 admitted, 241 enrolled. ***Average high school GPA:*** 3.14. ***Test scores:*** SAT math scores over 500: 39%; ACT scores over 18: 76%; SAT math scores over 600: 8%; ACT scores over 24: 22%; SAT math scores over 700: 1%; ACT scores over 30: 1%.

Retention: 72% of full-time freshmen returned.

FACULTY

Total: 115, 61% full-time, 57% with terminal degrees.

Student/faculty ratio: 11:1.

ACADEMICS

Calendar: 4-1-4. *Degrees:* bachelor's and master's.

Special study options: academic remediation for entering students, accelerated degree program, adult/continuing education programs, advanced placement credit, double majors, honors programs, independent study, internships, part-time degree program, services for LD students, student-designed majors, study abroad, summer session for credit.

Unusual degree programs: 3-2 business administration.

Computers: 155 computers/terminals and 380 ports are available on campus for general student use. Students can access the following: campus intranet, computer help desk, free student e-mail accounts, online (class) grades, online (class) registration, online (class) schedules, student picture directory. Campuswide network is available. 100% of college-owned or -operated housing units are wired for high-speed Internet access. Wireless service is available via classrooms, computer centers, computer labs, learning centers, libraries, student centers.

Library: Willis N. Hackney Library. *Books:* 123,892 (physical), 326,162 (digital/electronic); *Serial titles:* 197 (physical), 28,661 (digital/electronic); *Databases:* 163. Weekly public service hours: 96; students can reserve study rooms.

STUDENT LIFE

Housing options: on-campus residence required through sophomore year; coed, women-only. Campus housing is university owned and leased by the school. Freshman campus housing is guaranteed.

Activities and organizations: drama/theater group, student-run newspaper, radio and television station, choral group, Student Ambassador Program, Barton College Association of Nursing, Barton College Orientation Team, Barton College Catholic Campus Ministries, Minority Student Association, national fraternities, national sororities.

Athletics Member NCAA. All Division II. ***Intercollegiate sports:*** baseball M(s), basketball M(s)/W(s), cross-country running M(s)/W(s), golf M(s)/W(s), lacrosse W(s), soccer M(s)/W(s), softball W(s), swimming and diving M(s)/W(s), tennis M(s)/W(s), track and field M(s)/W(s), volleyball M(s)/W(s). ***Intramural sports:*** basketball M/W, football M/W, soccer M/W, softball M/W, volleyball M/W.

Campus security: 24-hour emergency response devices and patrols, late-night transport/escort service, controlled dormitory access, city police substation on campus.

Student services: health clinic, personal/psychological counseling, women's center.

COSTS & FINANCIAL AID

Costs (2017–18) ***Comprehensive fee:*** $39,854 includes full-time tuition ($27,536), mandatory fees ($2462), and room and board ($9856). Full-time tuition and fees vary according to class time, course load, and program. Part-time tuition: $507 per credit hour. Part-time tuition and fees vary according to class time, course load, and program. ***Required fees:*** $75 per credit hour part-time. ***College room only:*** $4256. Room and board charges vary according to board plan and housing facility. ***Payment plan:*** installment. ***Waivers:*** adult students and employees or children of employees.

Financial Aid Of all full-time matriculated undergraduates who enrolled in 2013, 981 applied for aid, 938 were judged to have need, 109 had their need fully met. In 2013, 80 non-need-based awards were made. ***Average percent of need met:*** 59. ***Average financial aid package:*** $17,377. ***Average need-based loan:*** $4201. ***Average need-based gift aid:*** $14,158. ***Average non-need-based aid:*** $8498.

APPLYING

Standardized Tests *Required:* SAT or ACT (for admission).

Options: electronic application.

Required: high school transcript, minimum 2.0 GPA. ***Required for some:*** essay or personal statement, letters of recommendation, interview.

Application deadlines: rolling (freshmen), rolling (transfers).

Notification: continuous (freshmen), continuous (transfers).

CONTACT

Barton College, PO Box 5000, Wilson, NC 27893-7000. *Phone:* 800-345-4973. *Toll-free phone:* 800-345-4973.

Belmont Abbey College

Belmont, North Carolina

http://www.belmontabbeycollege.edu/

- **Independent Roman Catholic** 4-year, founded 1876
- **Small-town** 650-acre campus with easy access to Charlotte
- **Coed** 1,495 undergraduate students, 93% full-time, 54% women, 46% men
- **Moderately difficult** entrance level, 68% of applicants were admitted

UNDERGRAD STUDENTS

1,385 full-time, 110 part-time. Students come from 39 states and territories; 21 other countries; 31% are from out of state; 22% Black or African American, non-Hispanic/Latino; 1% Hispanic/Latino; 1% Asian, non-Hispanic/Latino; 0.1% Native Hawaiian or other Pacific Islander, non-Hispanic/Latino; 0.3% American Indian or Alaska Native, non-Hispanic/Latino; 0.3% Two or more races, non-Hispanic/Latino; 28% Race/ethnicity unknown; 2% international; 9% transferred in; 52% live on campus.

Freshmen:
Admission: 1,967 applied, 1,335 admitted, 307 enrolled. ***Average high school GPA:*** 3.16. ***Test scores:*** SAT critical reading scores over 500: 55%; SAT math scores over 500: 59%; ACT scores over 18: 86%; SAT critical reading scores over 600: 15%; SAT math scores over 600: 16%; ACT scores over 24: 36%; SAT critical reading scores over 700: 2%; SAT math scores over 700: 2%; ACT scores over 30: 2%.

Retention: 60% of full-time freshmen returned.

FACULTY
Total: 135, 56% full-time, 44% with terminal degrees.

Student/faculty ratio: 15:1.

ACADEMICS
Calendar: semesters. *Degree:* bachelor's.

Special study options: accelerated degree program, adult/continuing education programs, advanced placement credit, cooperative education, double majors, external degree program, freshman honors college, honors programs, independent study, internships, off-campus study, part-time degree program, services for LD students, study abroad, summer session for credit. ***ROTC:*** Army (c), Air Force (c).

Computers: 92 computers/terminals are available on campus for general student use. Students can access the following: computer help desk, free student e-mail accounts, online (class) grades, online (class) schedules. Campuswide network is available. 100% of college-owned or -operated housing units are wired for high-speed Internet access. Wireless service is available via classrooms, computer labs, dorm rooms, libraries, student centers.

Library: Abbot Vincent Taylor Library plus 1 other.

STUDENT LIFE
Housing options: men-only, women-only. Campus housing is university owned. Freshman campus housing is guaranteed.

Activities and organizations: drama/theater group, student-run newspaper, choral group, Crusaders for Life, Improv Troupe, Abbey Volunteers, International Club, Green Team, national fraternities, national sororities.

Athletics Member NCAA. All Division II. ***Intercollegiate sports:*** baseball M(s), basketball M(s)/W(s), cheerleading W, cross-country running M(s)/W(s), golf M(s)/W(s), lacrosse M(s)/W(s), soccer M(s)/W(s), softball W(s), tennis M(s)/W(s), track and field M(s)/W(s), volleyball M(s)/W(s), wrestling M(s). ***Intramural sports:*** bowling M/W, cheerleading W, cross-country running M/W, football M/W, soccer M/W, ultimate Frisbee M/W.

Campus security: 24-hour emergency response devices and patrols.

Student services: health clinic, personal/psychological counseling.

COSTS & FINANCIAL AID
Costs (2016–17) ***Comprehensive fee:*** $28,594 includes full-time tuition ($18,500) and room and board ($10,094). Full-time tuition and fees vary according to course load and reciprocity agreements. Part-time tuition: $617 per credit hour. Part-time tuition and fees vary according to course load and reciprocity agreements. No tuition increase for student's term of enrollment. ***College room only:*** $5828. Room and board charges vary according to board plan and housing facility. ***Payment plans:*** installment, deferred payment. ***Waivers:*** employees or children of employees.

Financial Aid Of all full-time matriculated undergraduates who enrolled in 2015, 1,143 applied for aid, 997 were judged to have need, 93 had their need fully met. 72 Federal Work-Study jobs (averaging $2000). In 2015, 274 non-need-based awards were made. ***Average percent of need met:*** 51. ***Average financial aid package:*** $11,710. ***Average need-based loan:*** $4214. ***Average need-based gift aid:*** $8048. ***Average non-need-based aid:*** $5290. ***Average indebtedness upon graduation:*** $28,477.

APPLYING
Standardized Tests *Required for some:* SAT or ACT (for admission).

Options: electronic application, deferred entrance.

Application fee: $35.

Required: high school transcript, minimum 2.3 GPA. ***Required for some:*** essay or personal statement, letters of recommendation. ***Recommended:*** interview.

Application deadlines: 8/1 (freshmen), 8/15 (transfers).

Notification: continuous (freshmen), continuous (transfers).

CONTACT
Ms. Nicole Focareto, Executive Director of Admissions, Belmont Abbey College, 100 Belmont-Mt. Holly Road, Belmont, NC 28012. *Phone:* 704-461-6214. *Toll-free phone:* 888-BAC-0110. *Fax:* 704-461-6220. *E-mail:* nicolefocareto@bac.edu.

Bennett College

Greensboro, North Carolina

http://www.bennett.edu/

- **Independent United Methodist** 4-year, founded 1873
- **Urban** 55-acre campus
- **Endowment** $12.0 million
- **Women only** 583 undergraduate students, 86% full-time
- **Minimally difficult** entrance level, 95% of applicants were admitted

UNDERGRAD STUDENTS
502 full-time, 81 part-time. Students come from 27 states and territories; 1 other country; 55% are from out of state; 82% Black or African American, non-Hispanic/Latino; 3% Hispanic/Latino; 0.2% Asian, non-Hispanic/Latino; 0.2% Native Hawaiian or other Pacific Islander, non-Hispanic/Latino; 0.3% American Indian or Alaska Native, non-Hispanic/Latino; 2% Two or more races, non-Hispanic/Latino; 11% Race/ethnicity unknown; 1% transferred in; 64% live on campus.

Freshmen:
Admission: 1,474 applied, 1,398 admitted, 158 enrolled.

Retention: 54% of full-time freshmen returned.

FACULTY
Total: 61, 77% full-time, 61% with terminal degrees.

Student/faculty ratio: 10:1.

ACADEMICS
Calendar: semesters. *Degree:* bachelor's.

Special study options: academic remediation for entering students, advanced placement credit, double majors, honors programs, independent study, internships, off-campus study, services for LD students, student-designed majors, study abroad, summer session for credit. ***ROTC:*** Army (c), Air Force (c).

Unusual degree programs: engineering with North Carolina Agricultural and Technical State University.

Computers: 203 computers/terminals are available on campus for general student use. Students can access the following: campus intranet, computer help desk, free student e-mail accounts, online (class) grades, online (class) registration. Campuswide network is available. 100% of college-owned or -operated housing units are wired for high-speed Internet access. Wireless service is available via entire campus.

Library: Holgate Library. *Books:* 34,358 (physical), 184,548 (digital/electronic); *Serial titles:* 10 (physical); *Databases:* 78. Weekly public service hours: 83.

STUDENT LIFE
Housing options: on-campus residence required through sophomore year; women-only. Campus housing is university owned. Freshman campus housing is guaranteed.

Activities and organizations: drama/theater group, choral group, Student Government Association, Pre-Alumnae Council, Senior Class, Junior Class, Sophomore Class, national sororities.

Campus security: 24-hour emergency response devices and patrols, late-night transport/escort service, controlled dormitory access, alerts and educational programs.

Student services: health clinic, personal/psychological counseling.

COSTS & FINANCIAL AID
Costs (2016–17) ***One-time required fee:*** $225. ***Comprehensive fee:*** $26,627 includes full-time tuition ($15,964), mandatory fees ($2549), and room and board ($8114). Full-time tuition and fees vary according to course load. Part-time tuition: $665 per credit hour. Part-time tuition and fees vary according to course load. ***Required fees:*** $1067 per term part-time. ***College room only:*** $4040. Room and board charges vary according to board plan. ***Payment plan:*** installment. ***Waivers:*** employees or children of employees.

Financial Aid Of all full-time matriculated undergraduates who enrolled in 2011, 664 applied for aid, 643 were judged to have need, 22 had their

need fully met. In 2011, 7 non-need-based awards were made. ***Average percent of need met:*** 47. ***Average financial aid package:*** $13,092. ***Average need-based loan:*** $4170. ***Average need-based gift aid:*** $9402. ***Average non-need-based aid:*** $4714. ***Financial aid deadline:*** 3/15.

APPLYING
Standardized Tests *Recommended:* SAT or ACT (for admission).

Options: electronic application, deferred entrance.

Application fee: $35.

Required: essay or personal statement, high school transcript, minimum 2.0 GPA, 2 letters of recommendation. ***Required for some:*** interview. ***Recommended:*** interview.

Application deadlines: rolling (freshmen), rolling (out-of-state freshmen), rolling (transfers).

CONTACT
Ms. Jocelyn Biggs, Director of Admissions, Bennett College, 900 East Washington Street, Enrollment Management Center, Greensboro, NC 27401. *Phone:* 336-517-1818. *Toll-free phone:* 800-413-5323. *E-mail:* jbiggs@bennett.edu.

Brevard College
Brevard, North Carolina
http://www.brevard.edu/

CONTACT
Mr. David Volrath, Admissions, Brevard College, One Brevard College Drive, Brevard, NC 28712. *Phone:* 828-884-8367. *Toll-free phone:* 800-527-9090. *Fax:* 828-884-3790. *E-mail:* admissions@brevard.edu.

Cabarrus College of Health Sciences
Concord, North Carolina
http://www.cabarruscollege.edu/

- **Independent** comprehensive, founded 1942
- **Suburban** 5-acre campus with easy access to Charlotte
- **Endowment** $2.0 million
- **Coed, primarily women** 443 undergraduate students, 32% full-time, 88% women, 12% men
- **Moderately difficult** entrance level, 100% of applicants were admitted

UNDERGRAD STUDENTS
142 full-time, 301 part-time. Students come from 5 states and territories; 3% are from out of state; 11% Black or African American, non-Hispanic/Latino; 4% Hispanic/Latino; 1% Asian, non-Hispanic/Latino; 0.5% Native Hawaiian or other Pacific Islander, non-Hispanic/Latino; 0.2% American Indian or Alaska Native, non-Hispanic/Latino; 2% Two or more races, non-Hispanic/Latino; 30% transferred in.

Freshmen:
Admission: 28 applied, 28 admitted, 23 enrolled.

ACADEMICS
Calendar: semesters. *Degrees:* certificates, diplomas, associate, bachelor's, and master's.

Special study options: academic remediation for entering students, accelerated degree program, advanced placement credit, cooperative education, distance learning, independent study, part-time degree program, services for LD students.

Computers: 17 computers/terminals are available on campus for general student use. Students can access the following: free student e-mail accounts, online (class) grades, online (class) registration, online (class) schedules, degree audits. Campuswide network is available. Wireless service is available via entire campus.

Library: Cabarrus College Information Resource Center plus 1 other. Study areas open 24 hours, 5-7 days a week.

STUDENT LIFE
Housing options: college housing not available.

Activities and organizations: Rotaract Service Club, Cabarrus College Association of Nursing Students, Student Government Association, Honor Society, Christian Student Union.

Campus security: 24-hour emergency response devices and patrols.

Student services: health clinic, personal/psychological counseling.

COSTS
Costs (2016–17) ***Tuition:*** $11,948 full-time, $384 per credit hour part-time. Full-time tuition and fees vary according to course load. Part-time tuition and fees vary according to course load. ***Required fees:*** $320 full-time, $125 per term part-time. ***Payment plan:*** installment.

APPLYING
Standardized Tests *Required:* SAT or ACT (for admission).

Options: electronic application.

Application fee: $50.

Required: essay or personal statement, high school transcript, minimum 2.0 GPA, 2 letters of recommendation. ***Required for some:*** interview. ***Recommended:*** minimum 3.0 GPA.

Application deadlines: 2/1 (freshmen), 2/1 (transfers).

Notification: 3/15 (freshmen), 3/15 (transfers).

CONTACT
McKenzie Allen, Admissions Representative, Cabarrus College of Health Sciences, 401 Medical Park Drive, Concord, NC 28025-2077. *Phone:* 704-403-2589. *Fax:* 704-403-2077. *E-mail:* mckenzie.allen@cabarruscollege.edu.

Campbell University
Buies Creek, North Carolina
http://www.campbell.edu/

CONTACT
Ms. Peggy Mason, Director of Admissions, Campbell University, PO Box 546, 450 Leslie Campbell Avenue, Buies Creek, NC 27506. *Phone:* 910-893-1290. *Toll-free phone:* 800-334-4111. *Fax:* 910-893-1288. *E-mail:* adm@mailcenter.campbell.edu.

Carolina Christian College
Winston-Salem, North Carolina
http://www.carolina.edu/

- **Independent nondenominational** comprehensive, founded 1949
- **Small-town** 2-acre campus
- **Endowment** $250,000
- **Coed** 36 undergraduate students, 100% full-time, 50% women, 50% men
- **Noncompetitive** entrance level, 100% of applicants were admitted

UNDERGRAD STUDENTS
36 full-time. Students come from 1 other state; 89% Black or African American, non-Hispanic/Latino; 3% Hispanic/Latino; 3% Asian, non-Hispanic/Latino.

Freshmen:
Admission: 2 applied, 2 admitted, 2 enrolled. ***Average high school GPA:*** 2.6.
Retention: 90% of full-time freshmen returned.

FACULTY
Total: 12, 17% full-time, 8% with terminal degrees.

ACADEMICS
Calendar: semesters. *Degrees:* associate, bachelor's, and master's.

Special study options: accelerated degree program, adult/continuing education programs, external degree program, part-time degree program.

Computers: 8 computers/terminals and 8 ports are available on campus for general student use. Wireless service is available via entire campus.

Library: Aubrey Payne.

STUDENT LIFE
Housing options: college housing not available.

Campus security: 24-hour emergency response devices.

Student services: personal/psychological counseling.

COSTS & FINANCIAL AID
Costs (2017–18) ***One-time required fee:*** $75. ***Tuition:*** $11,000 full-time, $2750 per term part-time. ***Required fees:*** $1200 full-time, $600 per term part-time. ***Payment plan:*** installment. ***Waivers:*** employees or children of employees.

Financial Aid Of all full-time matriculated undergraduates who enrolled in 2016, 15 applied for aid, 15 were judged to have need, 11 had their need fully met. ***Average percent of need met:*** 90. ***Average financial aid package:*** $9500. ***Average need-based loan:*** $2000. ***Average need-based gift aid:*** $5775. ***Average indebtedness upon graduation:*** $9500.

APPLYING

Options: electronic application.

Application fee: $50.

Required: essay or personal statement, high school transcript, 2 letters of recommendation, interview.

Application deadlines: rolling (freshmen), rolling (out-of-state freshmen), rolling (transfers).

Notification: continuous (freshmen), continuous (out-of-state freshmen), continuous (transfers).

CONTACT

Carolina Christian College, 4209 Indiana Avenue, PO Box 777, Winston-Salem, NC 27102-0777. *Phone:* 336-744-0900 Ext. 106.

Carolina College of Biblical Studies

Fayetteville, North Carolina

http://carolinabiblecollege.org/

CONTACT

Carolina College of Biblical Studies, 817 South McPherson Church Road, Fayetteville, NC 28303.

Catawba College

Salisbury, North Carolina

http://www.catawba.edu/

- **Independent** comprehensive, founded 1851, affiliated with United Church of Christ
- **Small-town** 276-acre campus with easy access to Charlotte, NC
- **Endowment** $56.7 million
- **Coed** 1,297 undergraduate students, 96% full-time, 54% women, 46% men
- **Moderately difficult** entrance level, 47% of applicants were admitted

UNDERGRAD STUDENTS

1,243 full-time, 54 part-time. Students come from 35 states and territories; 19 other countries; 21% are from out of state; 19% Black or African American, non-Hispanic/Latino; 7% Hispanic/Latino; 1% Asian, non-Hispanic/Latino; 0.1% Native Hawaiian or other Pacific Islander, non-Hispanic/Latino; 0.4% American Indian or Alaska Native, non-Hispanic/Latino; 3% Two or more races, non-Hispanic/Latino; 0.2% Race/ethnicity unknown; 2% international; 3% transferred in; 60% live on campus.

Freshmen:

Admission: 2,528 applied, 1,190 admitted, 329 enrolled. ***Average high school GPA:*** 3.71.

Retention: 72% of full-time freshmen returned.

FACULTY

Total: 145, 55% full-time, 51% with terminal degrees.

Student/faculty ratio: 13:1.

ACADEMICS

Calendar: semesters. *Degrees:* bachelor's and master's.

Special study options: advanced placement credit, double majors, honors programs, independent study, internships, part-time degree program, services for LD students, student-designed majors, study abroad, summer session for credit. ***ROTC:*** Army (c), Air Force (c).

Computers: 173 computers/terminals are available on campus for general student use. Students can access the following: campus intranet, computer help desk, free student e-mail accounts, online (class) grades, online (class) registration, online (class) schedules. Campuswide network is available. 100% of college-owned or -operated housing units are wired for high-speed Internet access. Wireless service is available via entire campus.

Library: Corriher-Linn-Black Memorial Library plus 1 other. *Books:* 151,650 (physical), 184,548 (digital/electronic); *Serial titles:* 95 (physical), 32,589 (digital/electronic); *Databases:* 102. Weekly public service hours: 83; students can reserve study rooms.

STUDENT LIFE

Housing options: on-campus residence required through senior year; coed, men-only, women-only. Campus housing is university owned. Freshman campus housing is guaranteed.

Activities and organizations: drama/theater group, student-run newspaper, radio station, choral group, marching band, Volunteer Catawba, Catawba Ambassadors (admissions guides), Blue Masque (drama), Fellowship of Christian Athletes, Wigwam Productions (student activities board).

Athletics Member NCAA. All Division II. ***Intercollegiate sports:*** baseball M(s), basketball M(s)/W(s), cheerleading M(c)/W(c), cross-country running M(s)/W(s), football M(s), golf M(s)/W(s), lacrosse M(s)/W(s), soccer M(s)/W(s), softball W(s), swimming and diving M(s)/W(s), tennis M(s)/W(s), track and field M/W, volleyball W(s). ***Intramural sports:*** badminton M/W, basketball M/W, bowling M/W, football M, racquetball M/W, soccer M/W, softball M, table tennis M/W, tennis M/W, ultimate Frisbee M/W, volleyball M/W.

Campus security: 24-hour emergency response devices and patrols, late-night transport/escort service, controlled dormitory access.

Student services: health clinic, personal/psychological counseling.

COSTS & FINANCIAL AID

Costs (2017–18) ***Comprehensive fee:*** $40,408 includes full-time tuition ($29,920) and room and board ($10,488). Full-time tuition and fees vary according to class time, course load, and degree level. Part-time tuition: $785 per credit hour. Part-time tuition and fees vary according to class time, course load, and degree level. ***College room only:*** $6188. ***Payment plan:*** installment. ***Waivers:*** employees or children of employees.

Financial Aid Of all full-time matriculated undergraduates who enrolled in 2015, 1,075 applied for aid, 984 were judged to have need, 226 had their need fully met. 111 Federal Work-Study jobs (averaging $1510). 153 state and other part-time jobs (averaging $1437). In 2015, 171 non-need-based awards were made. ***Average percent of need met:*** 75. ***Average financial aid package:*** $23,873. ***Average need-based loan:*** $4520. ***Average need-based gift aid:*** $6855. ***Average non-need-based aid:*** $14,318. ***Average indebtedness upon graduation:*** $30,490.

APPLYING

Options: electronic application, early admission, deferred entrance.

Required: essay or personal statement, high school transcript, minimum 2.0 GPA, 2 letters of recommendation. ***Recommended:*** interview.

Application deadlines: rolling (freshmen), rolling (transfers).

Notification: continuous (freshmen), continuous (transfers).

CONTACT

Catawba College, 2300 West Innes Street, Salisbury, NC 28144-2488. *Phone:* 704-645-4584. *Toll-free phone:* 800-CATAWBA.

Charlotte Christian College and Theological Seminary

Charlotte, North Carolina

http://www.charlottechristian.edu/

CONTACT

Charlotte Christian College and Theological Seminary, 3117 Whiting Avenue, Charlotte, NC 28205. *Phone:* 704-334-6882 Ext. 08.

Chowan University

Murfreesboro, North Carolina

http://www.chowan.edu/

- **Independent Baptist** comprehensive, founded 1848
- **Small-town** 300-acre campus with easy access to Norfolk
- **Endowment** $24.3 million
- **Coed** 1,525 undergraduate students, 96% full-time, 54% women, 46% men
- **Minimally difficult** entrance level, 57% of applicants were admitted

COLLEGES AT-A-GLANCE

UNDERGRAD STUDENTS
1,468 full-time, 57 part-time. Students come from 28 states and territories; 23 other countries; 41% are from out of state; 70% Black or African American, non-Hispanic/Latino; 4% Hispanic/Latino; 0.2% Asian, non-Hispanic/Latino; 0.3% Native Hawaiian or other Pacific Islander, non-Hispanic/Latino; 0.6% American Indian or Alaska Native, non-Hispanic/Latino; 5% Two or more races, non-Hispanic/Latino; 4% Race/ethnicity unknown; 3% international; 5% transferred in; 84% live on campus.

Freshmen:
Admission: 4,364 applied, 2,486 admitted, 494 enrolled. ***Average high school GPA:*** 2.72. ***Test scores:*** ACT scores over 18: 23%; ACT scores over 24: 3%.

Retention: 48% of full-time freshmen returned.

FACULTY
Total: 135, 50% full-time, 43% with terminal degrees.

Student/faculty ratio: 16:1.

ACADEMICS
Calendar: semesters. *Degrees:* associate, bachelor's, and master's.

Special study options: academic remediation for entering students, advanced placement credit, cooperative education, double majors, freshman honors college, honors programs, independent study, internships, part-time degree program, services for LD students, student-designed majors, study abroad, summer session for credit.

Computers: 215 computers/terminals and 13 ports are available on campus for general student use. Students can access the following: campus intranet, computer help desk, free student e-mail accounts, online (class) grades, online (class) registration, online (class) schedules. Campuswide network is available. 100% of college-owned or -operated housing units are wired for high-speed Internet access. Wireless service is available via entire campus.

Library: Whitaker Library plus 1 other. *Books:* 159,944 (physical), 446,651 (digital/electronic); *Serial titles:* 1,309 (physical), 55,437 (digital/electronic); *Databases:* 135. Weekly public service hours: 84; students can reserve study rooms.

STUDENT LIFE
Housing options: on-campus residence required through sophomore year; men-only, women-only. Campus housing is university owned. Freshman campus housing is guaranteed.

Activities and organizations: drama/theater group, student-run newspaper, choral group, national fraternities, national sororities.

Athletics Member NCAA, NCCAA. All NCAA Division II.
Intercollegiate sports: baseball M(s), basketball M(s)/W(s), bowling W(s), cheerleading M/W, cross-country running M(s)/W(s), football M(s), golf M(s)/W(s), lacrosse M(s)/W(s), soccer M(s)/W(s), softball W(s), swimming and diving W(s), tennis M(s)/W(s), volleyball W(s).
Intramural sports: basketball M/W, football M/W, racquetball M/W, soccer M/W, softball M/W, table tennis M/W, tennis M/W, volleyball M/W.

Campus security: 24-hour emergency response devices and patrols, late-night transport/escort service, controlled dormitory access.

Student services: health clinic, personal/psychological counseling.

COSTS & FINANCIAL AID
Costs (2017–18) ***Tuition:*** $22,480 full-time, $400 per credit hour part-time. ***Room only:*** Room and board charges vary according to board plan. ***Waivers:*** employees or children of employees.

Financial Aid Of all full-time matriculated undergraduates who enrolled in 2016, 1,404 applied for aid, 1,369 were judged to have need, 140 had their need fully met. 315 Federal Work-Study jobs (averaging $1441). 173 state and other part-time jobs (averaging $1977). In 2016, 100 non-need-based awards were made. ***Average percent of need met:*** 66. ***Average financial aid package:*** $21,012. ***Average need-based loan:*** $4048. ***Average need-based gift aid:*** $16,719. ***Average non-need-based aid:*** $7512. ***Average indebtedness upon graduation:*** $41,845.

APPLYING
Standardized Tests *Required:* SAT or ACT (for admission).

Options: electronic application.

Application fee: $20.

Required: high school transcript. ***Required for some:*** essay or personal statement, interview. ***Recommended:*** minimum 2.0 GPA, 2 letters of recommendation.

Application deadlines: rolling (freshmen), rolling (transfers).
Notification: continuous (freshmen), continuous (transfers).

CONTACT
Mr. Scott Parker Esq., Director of Admissions Information, Chowan University, One University Place, Murfreesboro, NC 27855. *Phone:* 252-398-6314. *Toll-free phone:* 888-4-CHOWAN. *Fax:* 252-398-1190. *E-mail:* parkes@chowan.edu.

Davidson College

Davidson, North Carolina

http://www.davidson.edu/

- **Independent Presbyterian** 4-year, founded 1837
- **Small-town** 665-acre campus with easy access to Charlotte
- **Endowment** $662.0 million
- **Coed** 1,796 undergraduate students, 100% full-time, 49% women, 51% men
- **Very difficult** entrance level, 20% of applicants were admitted

UNDERGRAD STUDENTS
1,796 full-time. Students come from 49 states and territories; 49 other countries; 77% are from out of state; 7% Black or African American, non-Hispanic/Latino; 7% Hispanic/Latino; 5% Asian, non-Hispanic/Latino; 0.7% American Indian or Alaska Native, non-Hispanic/Latino; 4% Two or more races, non-Hispanic/Latino; 2% Race/ethnicity unknown; 7% international; 0.7% transferred in; 95% live on campus.

Freshmen:
Admission: 5,618 applied, 1,130 admitted, 514 enrolled. ***Average high school GPA:*** 3.9. ***Test scores:*** SAT critical reading scores over 500: 99%; SAT math scores over 500: 100%; SAT writing scores over 500: 97%; ACT scores over 18: 100%; SAT critical reading scores over 600: 86%; SAT math scores over 600: 88%; SAT writing scores over 600: 84%; ACT scores over 24: 99%; SAT critical reading scores over 700: 40%; SAT math scores over 700: 38%; SAT writing scores over 700: 40%; ACT scores over 30: 64%.

Retention: 94% of full-time freshmen returned.

FACULTY
Total: 189, 98% full-time, 97% with terminal degrees.

Student/faculty ratio: 10:1.

ACADEMICS
Calendar: semesters. *Degree:* bachelor's.

Special study options: advanced placement credit, double majors, independent study, internships, off-campus study, services for LD students, student-designed majors, study abroad. ***ROTC:*** Army (b), Air Force (c).

Unusual degree programs: 3-2 engineering with Columbia University, Washington University in St. Louis.

Computers: 180 computers/terminals are available on campus for general student use. Students can access the following: campus intranet, computer help desk, free student e-mail accounts, online (class) grades, online (class) registration, online (class) schedules. Campuswide network is available. 100% of college-owned or -operated housing units are wired for high-speed Internet access. Wireless service is available via entire campus.

Library: E. H. Little Library plus 1 other. Study areas open 24 hours, 5-7 days a week; students can reserve study rooms.

STUDENT LIFE
Housing options: on-campus residence required through senior year; coed, cooperative. Campus housing is university owned. Freshman campus housing is guaranteed.

Activities and organizations: drama/theater group, student-run newspaper, radio station, choral group, Inter-Varsity Christian Fellowship, Dean Rusk Program Student Advisory Council, music organizations, Community Service Council, Student Government Association, national fraternities, national sororities.

Athletics Member NCAA. All Division I except football (Division I-AA).
Intercollegiate sports: baseball M(s), basketball M(s)/W(s), crew

M(c)/W(c), cross-country running M(s)/W(s), fencing M(c)/W(c), field hockey W(s), golf M(s), lacrosse W(s), rugby M(c), sailing M(c)/W(c), soccer M(s)/W(s), swimming and diving M(s)/W(s), tennis M(s)/W(s), track and field M(s)/W(s), ultimate Frisbee M(c)/W(c), volleyball W(s), weight lifting M(c)/W(c), wrestling M(s). ***Intramural sports:*** basketball M/W, equestrian sports W(c), field hockey M(c)/W(c), football M/W, lacrosse M(c)/W(c), soccer M(c)/W(c), softball M/W, swimming and diving M(c)/W(c), tennis M(c)/W(c), volleyball M/W(c), water polo M(c).

Campus security: 24-hour emergency response devices and patrols, late-night transport/escort service, controlled dormitory access.

Student services: health clinic, personal/psychological counseling, women's center.

COSTS & FINANCIAL AID

Costs (2017–18) ***Comprehensive fee:*** $64,398 includes full-time tuition ($49,949), mandatory fees ($495), and room and board ($13,954). ***College room only:*** $7102. Room and board charges vary according to board plan. ***Payment plan:*** installment. ***Waivers:*** employees or children of employees.

Financial Aid Of all full-time matriculated undergraduates who enrolled in 2016, 1,025 applied for aid, 879 were judged to have need, 877 had their need fully met. In 2016, 131 non-need-based awards were made. ***Average percent of need met:*** 100. ***Average financial aid package:*** $45,001. ***Average need-based loan:*** $3525. ***Average need-based gift aid:*** $41,998. ***Average non-need-based aid:*** $25,572. ***Average indebtedness upon graduation:*** $20,431. ***Financial aid deadline:*** 2/15.

APPLYING

Standardized Tests *Required:* SAT or ACT (for admission). *Recommended:* SAT and SAT Subject Tests or ACT (for admission).

Options: electronic application, early admission, early decision, deferred entrance.

Application fee: $50.

Required: essay or personal statement, high school transcript, 3 letters of recommendation. ***Recommended:*** interview.

Application deadlines: 1/2 (freshmen), 3/15 (transfers).

Early decision deadline: 11/15 (for plan 1), 1/2 (for plan 2).

Notification: 4/1 (freshmen), 5/15 (transfers), 12/15 (early decision plan 1), 2/1 (early decision plan 2).

CONTACT

Mr. Christopher J. Gruber, Vice President and Dean of Admission and Financial Aid, Davidson College, Box 7156, Davidson, NC 28035-7156. *Phone:* 704-894-2230. *Toll-free phone:* 800-768-0380. *Fax:* 704-894-2016. *E-mail:* admission@davidson.edu.

DeVry University–Charlotte Campus

Charlotte, North Carolina

http://www.devry.edu/

CONTACT

Admissions Office, DeVry University–Charlotte Campus, 2015 Ayrsley Town Boulevard, Suite 109, Charlotte, NC 28273-4068. *Phone:* 704-362-2345. *Toll-free phone:* 866-338-7934.

Duke University

Durham, North Carolina

http://www.duke.edu/

- **Independent** university, founded 1838, affiliated with United Methodist Church
- **Suburban** 8500-acre campus
- **Coed**
- **Most difficult** entrance level

FACULTY

Student/faculty ratio: 6:1.

ACADEMICS

Calendar: semesters. *Degrees:* bachelor's, master's, doctoral, post-master's, and postbachelor's certificates.

Library: Perkins Library.

STUDENT LIFE

Housing options: on-campus residence required through junior year; coed, men-only, women-only. Campus housing is university owned. Freshman campus housing is guaranteed.

Activities and organizations: drama/theater group, student-run newspaper, radio and television station, choral group, marching band, national fraternities, national sororities.

Athletics Member NCAA. All Division I except football (Division I-A).

Campus security: 24-hour emergency response devices and patrols, late-night transport/escort service, controlled dormitory access.

Student services: health clinic, personal/psychological counseling, women's center, legal services.

COSTS & FINANCIAL AID

Costs (2016–17) ***Comprehensive fee:*** $65,703 includes full-time tuition ($49,575), mandatory fees ($1690), and room and board ($14,438). Part-time tuition: $1489 per credit hour. ***College room only:*** $8286.

Financial Aid Of all full-time matriculated undergraduates who enrolled in 2016, 3,191 applied for aid, 2,773 were judged to have need, 2,773 had their need fully met. 1,739 Federal Work-Study jobs (averaging $1972). 896 state and other part-time jobs (averaging $2030). In 2016, 186 non-need-based awards were made. ***Average percent of need met:*** 100. ***Average financial aid package:*** $50,312. ***Average need-based loan:*** $3953. ***Average need-based gift aid:*** $47,133. ***Average non-need-based aid:*** $63,649. ***Average indebtedness upon graduation:*** $22,256. ***Financial aid deadline:*** 2/1.

APPLYING

Standardized Tests *Required:* SAT and SAT Subject Tests or ACT (for admission).

Options: electronic application, early decision, deferred entrance.

Application fee: $85.

Required: essay or personal statement, high school transcript. ***Required for some:*** audition tape for dance, drama, or music; slides of work for art. ***Recommended:*** interview.

CONTACT

Mr. Christoph Guttentag, Director of Admissions, Duke University, Durham, NC 27708-0586. *Phone:* 919-684-3214. *E-mail:* askduke@admiss.duke.edu.

East Carolina University

Greenville, North Carolina

http://www.ecu.edu/

- **State-supported** university, founded 1907, part of University of North Carolina System
- **Urban** 1402-acre campus
- **Endowment** $170.0 million
- **Coed** 22,969 undergraduate students, 86% full-time, 56% women, 44% men
- **Moderately difficult** entrance level, 70% of applicants were admitted

UNDERGRAD STUDENTS

19,754 full-time, 3,215 part-time. Students come from 44 states and territories; 41 other countries; 12% are from out of state; 16% Black or African American, non-Hispanic/Latino; 6% Hispanic/Latino; 3% Asian, non-Hispanic/Latino; 0.1% Native Hawaiian or other Pacific Islander, non-Hispanic/Latino; 0.7% American Indian or Alaska Native, non-Hispanic/Latino; 3% Two or more races, non-Hispanic/Latino; 3% Race/ethnicity unknown; 0.7% international; 8% transferred in; 26% live on campus.

Freshmen:

Admission: 17,135 applied, 12,049 admitted, 4,320 enrolled. ***Average high school GPA:*** 3.76. ***Test scores:*** SAT critical reading scores over 500: 63%; SAT math scores over 500: 73%; SAT writing scores over 500: 48%; ACT scores over 18: 99%; SAT critical reading scores over 600: 11%; SAT math scores over 600: 16%; SAT writing scores over 600: 8%; ACT scores over 24: 31%; SAT critical reading scores over 700: 1%; SAT math scores over 700: 1%; SAT writing scores over 700: 1%; ACT scores over 30: 3%.

Retention: 83% of full-time freshmen returned.

FACULTY
Total: 1,466, 80% full-time, 75% with terminal degrees.
Student/faculty ratio: 18:1.

ACADEMICS
Calendar: semesters. *Degrees:* bachelor's, master's, doctoral, post-master's, and postbachelor's certificates.
Special study options: accelerated degree program, adult/continuing education programs, advanced placement credit, cooperative education, distance learning, double majors, English as a second language, freshman honors college, honors programs, independent study, internships, off-campus study, part-time degree program, services for LD students, student-designed majors, study abroad, summer session for credit. ***ROTC:*** Army (b), Air Force (b).
Unusual degree programs: 3-2 business administration.
Computers: 2,375 computers/terminals and 2,375 ports are available on campus for general student use. Students can access the following: campus intranet, computer help desk, free student e-mail accounts, online (class) grades, online (class) registration, online (class) schedules. Campuswide network is available. 100% of college-owned or -operated housing units are wired for high-speed Internet access. Wireless service is available via entire campus.
Library: Joyner Library plus 1 other. *Books:* 1.3 million (physical), 1.6 million (digital/electronic); *Serial titles:* 8,391 (physical), 89,781 (digital/electronic); *Databases:* 428. Weekly public service hours: 142; study areas open 24 hours, 5-7 days a week; students can reserve study rooms.

STUDENT LIFE
Housing options: on-campus residence required for freshman year; coed, women-only, special housing for students with disabilities. Campus housing is university owned. Freshman campus housing is guaranteed.
Activities and organizations: drama/theater group, student-run newspaper, radio and television station, choral group, marching band, Student Government Association, Student Activities Board, Residence Hall Association, Student Pirate Club, Black Student Union, national fraternities, national sororities.
Athletics Member NCAA. All Division I except football (Division I-A). ***Intercollegiate sports:*** baseball M(s), basketball M(s)/W(s), cross-country running M(s)/W(s), golf M(s)/W(s), soccer W(s), softball W(s), swimming and diving M(s)/W(s), tennis M(s)/W(s), track and field M(s)/W(s), volleyball W(s). ***Intramural sports:*** badminton M(c)/W(c), baseball M(c), basketball M/W, bowling M/W, cheerleading W(c), equestrian sports M(c)/W(c), fencing M(c)/W(c), field hockey W(c), football M/W, golf M(c)/W(c), ice hockey M(c), lacrosse M(c)/W(c), racquetball M/W, rock climbing M(c)/W(c), rugby M(c)/W(c), sailing M(c)/W(c), skiing (downhill) M(c)/W(c), soccer M/W, softball M/W, swimming and diving M(c)/W(c), table tennis M/W, tennis M/W, ultimate Frisbee M/W, volleyball M/W, water polo M(c)/W(c), weight lifting M(c)/W(c), wrestling M(c)/W(c).
Campus security: 24-hour emergency response devices and patrols, student patrols, late-night transport/escort service, controlled dormitory access, Operation ID, Staff and Faculty Eyes, ECU Alert, self-defense classes, ECU CARES.
Student services: health clinic, personal/psychological counseling, legal services.

COSTS & FINANCIAL AID
Costs (2017–18) ***Tuition:*** state resident $4365 full-time, $181 per credit hour part-time; nonresident $20,323 full-time, $846 per credit hour part-time. Full-time tuition and fees vary according to location. Part-time tuition and fees vary according to course load and location. ***Required fees:*** $2581 full-time. ***Room and board:*** $9835; room only: $5423. Room and board charges vary according to board plan and housing facility. ***Payment plans:*** installment, deferred payment. ***Waivers:*** employees or children of employees.
Financial Aid Of all full-time matriculated undergraduates who enrolled in 2016, 14,848 applied for aid, 11,928 were judged to have need, 1,116 had their need fully met. 414 Federal Work-Study jobs (averaging $3829). 5,369 state and other part-time jobs (averaging $2922). In 2016, 277 non-need-based awards were made. ***Average percent of need met:*** 63. ***Average financial aid package:*** $10,549. ***Average need-based loan:*** $6717. ***Average need-based gift aid:*** $7748. ***Average non-need-based aid:*** $4375. ***Average indebtedness upon graduation:*** $29,391.

APPLYING
Standardized Tests *Required:* SAT or ACT (for admission).
Options: electronic application, deferred entrance.
Application fee: $70.
Required: high school transcript, minimum 2.5 GPA.
Application deadlines: 3/1 (freshmen), 5/1 (transfers).
Notification: continuous (freshmen), continuous (out-of-state freshmen), continuous (transfers).

CONTACT
Undergraduate Admission, East Carolina University, Whichard Building 106, East Fifth Street, Greenville, NC 27858-4353. *Phone:* 252-328-6640. *E-mail:* admis@ecu.edu.

Elizabeth City State University

Elizabeth City, North Carolina

http://www.ecsu.edu/

- **State-supported** comprehensive, founded 1891, part of University of North Carolina System
- **Small-town** 200-acre campus with easy access to Norfolk
- **Endowment** $6.0 million
- **Coed** 1,310 undergraduate students, 91% full-time, 56% women, 44% men
- **Moderately difficult** entrance level, 54% of applicants were admitted

UNDERGRAD STUDENTS
1,197 full-time, 113 part-time. Students come from 2 other countries; 8% are from out of state; 72% Black or African American, non-Hispanic/Latino; 3% Hispanic/Latino; 0.2% Asian, non-Hispanic/Latino; 0.1% Native Hawaiian or other Pacific Islander, non-Hispanic/Latino; 0.5% American Indian or Alaska Native, non-Hispanic/Latino; 1% Two or more races, non-Hispanic/Latino; 6% Race/ethnicity unknown; 0.2% international; 6% transferred in; 58% live on campus.

Freshmen:
Admission: 1,550 applied, 840 admitted, 203 enrolled. ***Average high school GPA:*** 3.19. ***Test scores:*** SAT critical reading scores over 500: 16%; SAT math scores over 500: 19%; SAT writing scores over 500: 6%; ACT scores over 18: 42%; SAT critical reading scores over 600: 2%; SAT math scores over 600: 2%; SAT writing scores over 600: 1%; ACT scores over 24: 5%.
Retention: 67% of full-time freshmen returned.

FACULTY
Student/faculty ratio: 14:1.

ACADEMICS
Calendar: semesters. *Degrees:* bachelor's and master's.
Special study options: academic remediation for entering students, adult/continuing education programs, advanced placement credit, cooperative education, distance learning, double majors, honors programs, independent study, internships, off-campus study, part-time degree program, services for LD students, study abroad, summer session for credit. ***ROTC:*** Army (b).
Computers: Students can access the following: campus intranet, computer help desk, free student e-mail accounts, online (class) registration, online (class) schedules. Campuswide network is available. Wireless service is available via entire campus.
Library: G. R. Little Library plus 1 other. *Books:* 231,406 (physical), 184,579 (digital/electronic); *Serial titles:* 1,923 (physical), 22,828 (digital/electronic); *Databases:* 101. Weekly public service hours: 82.

STUDENT LIFE
Housing options: coed, men-only, women-only. Campus housing is university owned and leased by the school. Freshman campus housing is guaranteed.
Activities and organizations: drama/theater group, student-run newspaper, choral group, marching band, Vans (Vikings Assisting New Students), Student Activities Committee, Vike Nu' Fashion Troupe, Pep Squad, Essence of Praise, national fraternities, national sororities.
Athletics Member NCAA. All Division II. ***Intercollegiate sports:*** baseball M(s), basketball M(s)/W(s), bowling W(s), cheerleading W,

cross-country running M/W, football M(s), golf M(s), softball W(s), tennis W(s), volleyball W(s).

Campus security: 24-hour emergency response devices and patrols, controlled dormitory access.

Student services: health clinic, personal/psychological counseling.

COSTS & FINANCIAL AID

Costs (2016–17) ***Tuition:*** state resident $2800 full-time, $350 per credit hour part-time; nonresident $15,771 full-time, $1971 per credit hour part-time. Full-time tuition and fees vary according to degree level. Part-time tuition and fees vary according to degree level. ***Required fees:*** $2088 full-time, $272 per term part-time. ***Room and board:*** $7479; room only: $4480. Room and board charges vary according to housing facility. ***Payment plan:*** installment.

Financial Aid Of all full-time matriculated undergraduates who enrolled in 2014, 1,498 applied for aid, 1,498 were judged to have need, 228 had their need fully met. In 2014, 23 non-need-based awards were made. ***Average percent of need met:*** 68. ***Average financial aid package:*** $10,839. ***Average need-based loan:*** $2481. ***Average need-based gift aid:*** $8108. ***Average non-need-based aid:*** $6802. ***Average indebtedness upon graduation:*** $21,608. ***Financial aid deadline:*** 6/1.

APPLYING

Standardized Tests *Required:* SAT or ACT (for admission).

Options: electronic application, deferred entrance.

Application fee: $30.

Required: high school transcript, minimum 2.3 GPA.

CONTACT

Mr. Darius Eure, Assistant Director, Admissions and Recruitment, Elizabeth City State University, 131 Marion D. Thorpe Administration Building Box 901, 1704 Weeksville Road, Elizabeth City, NC 27909. *Phone:* 252-335-8530. *Toll-free phone:* 800-347-3278. *Fax:* 252-335-3537. *E-mail:* ddeure@ecsu.edu.

Elon University

Elon, North Carolina

http://www.elon.edu/

- **Independent** comprehensive, founded 1889, affiliated with United Church of Christ
- **Suburban** 636-acre campus with easy access to Raleigh
- **Endowment** $202.9 million
- **Coed** 6,008 undergraduate students, 97% full-time, 59% women, 41% men
- **Moderately difficult** entrance level, 60% of applicants were admitted

UNDERGRAD STUDENTS

5,839 full-time, 169 part-time. Students come from 52 states and territories; 50 other countries; 78% are from out of state; 5% Black or African American, non-Hispanic/Latino; 6% Hispanic/Latino; 2% Asian, non-Hispanic/Latino; 0.1% American Indian or Alaska Native, non-Hispanic/Latino; 3% Two or more races, non-Hispanic/Latino; 0.4% Race/ethnicity unknown; 2% international; 1% transferred in; 63% live on campus.

Freshmen:

Admission: 10,098 applied, 6,103 admitted, 1,553 enrolled. ***Average high school GPA:*** 4.03. ***Test scores:*** SAT critical reading scores over 500: 93%; SAT math scores over 500: 93%; SAT writing scores over 500: 92%; ACT scores over 18: 100%; SAT critical reading scores over 600: 49%; SAT math scores over 600: 54%; SAT writing scores over 600: 52%; ACT scores over 24: 88%; SAT critical reading scores over 700: 8%; SAT math scores over 700: 7%; SAT writing scores over 700: 9%; ACT scores over 30: 23%.

Retention: 91% of full-time freshmen returned.

FACULTY

Total: 586, 73% full-time, 78% with terminal degrees.

Student/faculty ratio: 12:1.

ACADEMICS

Calendar: semesters 3-week winter term. *Degrees:* bachelor's, master's, and doctoral.

Special study options: accelerated degree program, advanced placement credit, distance learning, double majors, English as a second language, honors programs, independent study, internships, off-campus study, part-time degree program, services for LD students, student-designed majors, study abroad, summer session for credit. ***ROTC:*** Army (b), Air Force (c).

Unusual degree programs: 3-2 engineering with East Carolina University, North Carolina State University, Georgia Tech, Penn State, Virginia Tech, University of Notre Dame, Columbia University, Washington University in St. Louis, North Carolina A&T State University, University of South Carolina.

Computers: 1,200 computers/terminals and 10,000 ports are available on campus for general student use. Students can access the following: computer help desk, free student e-mail accounts, online (class) grades, online (class) registration, online (class) schedules. Campuswide network is available. 100% of college-owned or -operated housing units are wired for high-speed Internet access. Wireless service is available via entire campus.

Library: Carol Grotnes Belk. *Books:* 388,971 (physical), 420,335 (digital/electronic); *Serial titles:* 269 (physical), 60,830 (digital/electronic); *Databases:* 179. Weekly public service hours: 143; study areas open 24 hours, 5-7 days a week; students can reserve study rooms.

STUDENT LIFE

Housing options: on-campus residence required through sophomore year; coed, men-only, women-only. Campus housing is university owned and leased by the school. Freshman campus housing is guaranteed.

Activities and organizations: drama/theater group, student-run newspaper, radio and television station, choral group, marching band, Elon Volunteers, Student Media, Intramural Athletics, Religious Life, Habitat for Humanity, national fraternities, national sororities.

Athletics Member NCAA. All Division I except football (Division I-AA). ***Intercollegiate sports:*** baseball M(s), basketball M(s)/W(s), cheerleading M/W, cross-country running M(s)/W(s), equestrian sports M(c)/W(c), field hockey W(c), golf M(s)/W(s), ice hockey M(c), lacrosse M(c)/W(s), rock climbing M(c), rugby M(c)/W(c), soccer M(s)/W(s), softball W(s), swimming and diving M(c)/W(c), tennis M(s)/W(s), track and field W(s), triathlon M(c)/W(c), ultimate Frisbee M(c)/W(c), volleyball M(s)(c)/W(s). ***Intramural sports:*** basketball M/W, bowling M/W, fencing M/W, football M/W, golf M/W, lacrosse M/W, racquetball M/W, sand volleyball M/W, soccer M/W, softball M/W, squash M/W, table tennis M/W, ultimate Frisbee M/W, volleyball M/W.

Campus security: 24-hour emergency response devices and patrols, late-night transport/escort service, controlled dormitory access, Student Transport Service (Safe Rides).

Student services: health clinic, personal/psychological counseling, women's center.

COSTS & FINANCIAL AID

Costs (2016–17) ***Comprehensive fee:*** $44,599 includes full-time tuition ($32,685), mandatory fees ($419), and room and board ($11,495). Part-time tuition and fees vary according to course load. ***College room only:*** $5728. Room and board charges vary according to board plan and housing facility. ***Payment plan:*** installment. ***Waivers:*** employees or children of employees.

Financial Aid Of all full-time matriculated undergraduates who enrolled in 2016, 2,583 applied for aid, 1,846 were judged to have need, 304 had their need fully met. 1,239 Federal Work-Study jobs (averaging $2397). In 2016, 1255 non-need-based awards were made. ***Average percent of need met:*** 61. ***Average financial aid package:*** $19,000. ***Average need-based loan:*** $4527. ***Average need-based gift aid:*** $15,052. ***Average non-need-based aid:*** $7381. ***Average indebtedness upon graduation:*** $30,170.

APPLYING

Standardized Tests *Required:* SAT or ACT (for admission).

Options: electronic application, early admission, early decision, early action, deferred entrance.

Application fee: $50.

Required: high school transcript, counselor evaluation form. ***Required for some:*** interview. ***Recommended:*** essay or personal statement.

Application deadlines: 1/10 (freshmen), rolling (transfers), 11/10 (early action).

Early decision deadline: 11/1.

Notification: 3/15 (freshmen), continuous (transfers), 12/1 (early decision), 12/20 (early action).

CONTACT
Ms. Melinda Wood, Senior Associate Dean of Admissions, Elon University, 2700 Campus Box, Elon, NC 27244. *Phone:* 336-278-3566. *Toll-free phone:* 800-334-8448. *Fax:* 336-278-7699. *E-mail:* admissions@elon.edu.

Fayetteville State University

Fayetteville, North Carolina

http://www.uncfsu.edu/

- **State-supported** comprehensive, founded 1867, part of University of North Carolina System
- **Urban** 156-acre campus with easy access to Raleigh
- **Endowment** $19.2 million
- **Coed** 5,543 undergraduate students, 75% full-time, 68% women, 32% men
- **Minimally difficult** entrance level, 57% of applicants were admitted

UNDERGRAD STUDENTS
4,141 full-time, 1,402 part-time. Students come from 50 states and territories; 25 other countries; 3% are from out of state; 64% Black or African American, non-Hispanic/Latino; 7% Hispanic/Latino; 2% Asian, non-Hispanic/Latino; 0.3% Native Hawaiian or other Pacific Islander, non-Hispanic/Latino; 3% American Indian or Alaska Native, non-Hispanic/Latino; 0.3% Two or more races, non-Hispanic/Latino; 5% Race/ethnicity unknown; 0.3% international; 14% transferred in; 28% live on campus.

Freshmen:
Admission: 4,594 applied, 2,620 admitted, 646 enrolled. ***Average high school GPA:*** 3.29.

Retention: 68% of full-time freshmen returned.

FACULTY
Total: 359, 71% full-time, 68% with terminal degrees.

Student/faculty ratio: 18:1.

ACADEMICS
Calendar: semesters. *Degrees:* bachelor's, master's, and doctoral.

Special study options: academic remediation for entering students, accelerated degree program, adult/continuing education programs, advanced placement credit, cooperative education, distance learning, double majors, honors programs, independent study, internships, part-time degree program, services for LD students, study abroad, summer session for credit. ***ROTC:*** Army (c), Air Force (b).

Unusual degree programs: 3-2 engineering with North Carolina State University.

Computers: 600 computers/terminals and 2,400 ports are available on campus for general student use. Students can access the following: campus intranet, computer help desk, free student e-mail accounts, online (class) grades, online (class) registration, online (class) schedules. Campuswide network is available. 100% of college-owned or -operated housing units are wired for high-speed Internet access. Wireless service is available via classrooms, computer centers, computer labs, learning centers, libraries, student centers.

Library: Charles W. Chestnut Library. *Books:* 214,552 (physical), 180,637 (digital/electronic); *Serial titles:* 298 (physical), 31,619 (digital/electronic); *Databases:* 382. Weekly public service hours: 97; students can reserve study rooms.

STUDENT LIFE
Housing options: coed, men-only, women-only, special housing for students with disabilities. Campus housing is university owned. Freshman applicants given priority for college housing.

Activities and organizations: drama/theater group, student-run newspaper, radio station, choral group, marching band, Student Government Association, Student Activities Council, Pan-Hellenic Council, Residence Hall Association, Illusions and Black Millennium Modeling Clubs, national fraternities, national sororities.

Athletics Member NCAA. All Division II. ***Intercollegiate sports:*** basketball M(s)/W(s), bowling W, cross-country running M(s)/W(s), football M(s), golf M(s)/W, softball W(s), tennis M/W(s), track and field M/W(s), volleyball W(s). ***Intramural sports:*** baseball M, basketball M/W, bowling M/W, football M, golf M/W, gymnastics M/W, swimming and diving M/W, tennis M, volleyball M/W.

Campus security: 24-hour emergency response devices and patrols, late-night transport/escort service, controlled dormitory access.

Student services: health clinic, personal/psychological counseling.

COSTS & FINANCIAL AID
Costs (2016–17) ***Tuition:*** state resident $2923 full-time; nonresident $14,531 full-time. Full-time tuition and fees vary according to course level, course load, degree level, location, and program. Part-time tuition and fees vary according to course level, course load, degree level, location, and program. ***Required fees:*** $2532 full-time. ***Room and board:*** $7149; room only: $3779. Room and board charges vary according to board plan and housing facility. ***Payment plan:*** installment. ***Waivers:*** senior citizens and employees or children of employees.

Financial Aid Of all full-time matriculated undergraduates who enrolled in 2014, 3,562 applied for aid, 3,380 were judged to have need, 373 had their need fully met. In 2014, 2 non-need-based awards were made. ***Average percent of need met:*** 70. ***Average financial aid package:*** $10,632. ***Average need-based loan:*** $4232. ***Average need-based gift aid:*** $7083. ***Average non-need-based aid:*** $750. ***Average indebtedness upon graduation:*** $25,215. ***Financial aid deadline:*** 3/1.

APPLYING
Standardized Tests *Required:* SAT or ACT (for admission).

Options: electronic application, early admission, early decision, early action, deferred entrance.

Application fee: $40.

Required: high school transcript, minimum 2.5 GPA. ***Recommended:*** essay or personal statement.

Application deadlines: 6/30 (freshmen), 6/30 (transfers).

Notification: continuous (freshmen), continuous (transfers).

CONTACT
Fayetteville State University, 1200 Murchison Road, Fayetteville, NC 28301-4298. *Phone:* 910-672-1371. *Toll-free phone:* 800-222-2594. *Fax:* 910-672-1414.

Gardner-Webb University

Boiling Springs, North Carolina

http://www.gardner-webb.edu/

- **Independent Baptist** university, founded 1905
- **Small-town** 250-acre campus with easy access to Charlotte
- **Endowment** $51.1 million
- **Coed** 2,343 undergraduate students, 82% full-time, 64% women, 36% men
- **Moderately difficult** entrance level, 10% of applicants were admitted

UNDERGRAD STUDENTS
1,912 full-time, 431 part-time. Students come from 42 states and territories; 9 other countries; 3% are from out of state; 15% Black or African American, non-Hispanic/Latino; 3% Hispanic/Latino; 1% Asian, non-Hispanic/Latino; 0.7% American Indian or Alaska Native, non-Hispanic/Latino; 0.3% Two or more races, non-Hispanic/Latino; 13% Race/ethnicity unknown; 0.9% international; 51% live on campus.

Freshmen:
Admission: 4,310 applied, 444 admitted, 444 enrolled. ***Average high school GPA:*** 3.74. ***Test scores:*** SAT critical reading scores over 500: 51%; SAT math scores over 500: 51%; SAT writing scores over 500: 43%; ACT scores over 18: 82%; SAT critical reading scores over 600: 13%; SAT math scores over 600: 14%; SAT writing scores over 600: 10%; ACT scores over 24: 36%; SAT critical reading scores over 700: 2%; SAT math scores over 700: 2%; SAT writing scores over 700: 2%; ACT scores over 30: 5%.

Retention: 66% of full-time freshmen returned.

FACULTY
Total: 300, 55% full-time.

Student/faculty ratio: 13:1.

ACADEMICS
Calendar: semesters. *Degrees:* certificates, associate, bachelor's, master's, and doctoral.

Special study options: academic remediation for entering students, accelerated degree program, adult/continuing education programs, advanced placement credit, cooperative education, distance learning, double majors, English as a second language, honors programs, independent study, internships, off-campus study, part-time degree program, services for LD students, study abroad, summer session for credit. ***ROTC:*** Army (b), Air Force (c).

Unusual degree programs: 3-2 music/business.

Computers: 121 computers/terminals are available on campus for general student use. Students can access the following: campus intranet, free student e-mail accounts, online (class) grades, online (class) registration, online (class) schedules. Campuswide network is available. 100% of college-owned or -operated housing units are wired for high-speed Internet access. Wireless service is available via entire campus.
Library: Dover Memorial Library plus 1 other.

STUDENT LIFE
Housing options: on-campus residence required through junior year; men-only, women-only, special housing for students with disabilities. Campus housing is university owned. Freshman campus housing is guaranteed.

Activities and organizations: drama/theater group, student-run newspaper, radio station, choral group, marching band, Campus Ministries United, Student Government Association, Dawg Pound, Honors Student Association, International Club.

Athletics Member NCAA. All Division I except football (Division I-AA). ***Intercollegiate sports:*** baseball M(s), basketball M(s)/W(s), cheerleading M(s)/W(s), cross-country running M(s)/W(s), golf M(s)/W(s), soccer M(s)/W(s), softball W(s), swimming and diving M(s)/W(s), tennis M(s)/W(s), track and field M(s)/W(s), volleyball W(s), wrestling M(s). ***Intramural sports:*** badminton M/W, baseball M/W, basketball M/W, football M/W, racquetball M/W, soccer M/W, softball M/W, swimming and diving M/W, table tennis M/W, tennis M/W, ultimate Frisbee M/W, volleyball M/W.

Campus security: 24-hour emergency response devices and patrols, student patrols, late-night transport/escort service, controlled dormitory access.

Student services: personal/psychological counseling.

COSTS & FINANCIAL AID
Costs (2016–17) ***Comprehensive fee:*** $39,390 includes full-time tuition ($29,420), mandatory fees ($190), and room and board ($9780). Part-time tuition: $468 per credit hour. ***College room only:*** $4950. Room and board charges vary according to board plan and housing facility. ***Payment plan:*** installment. ***Waivers:*** employees or children of employees.

Financial Aid Of all full-time matriculated undergraduates who enrolled in 2016, 1,308 applied for aid, 1,183 were judged to have need, 242 had their need fully met. 274 Federal Work-Study jobs (averaging $1397). 32 state and other part-time jobs (averaging $1517). In 2016, 320 non-need-based awards were made. ***Average percent of need met:*** 75. ***Average financial aid package:*** $24,191. ***Average need-based loan:*** $4367. ***Average need-based gift aid:*** $7571. ***Average non-need-based aid:*** $11,818. ***Average indebtedness upon graduation:*** $31,901.

APPLYING
Standardized Tests *Required:* SAT or ACT (for admission).

Options: electronic application.

Application fee: $40.

Required: high school transcript, minimum 2.5 GPA. ***Required for some:*** 2 letters of recommendation, interview. ***Recommended:*** essay or personal statement, 2 letters of recommendation.

Application deadlines: rolling (freshmen), rolling (transfers).

Notification: continuous (freshmen), continuous (transfers).

CONTACT
Associate Vice President of Undergraduate Admissions, Gardner-Webb University, PO Box 817, 110 South Main Street, Boiling Springs, NC 28017. *Phone:* 704-406-4491. *Toll-free phone:* 800-253-6472. *Fax:* 704-406-4488. *E-mail:* admissions@gardner-webb.edu.

Grace College of Divinity
Fayetteville, North Carolina
http://www.gcdivinity.org/

CONTACT
Grace College of Divinity, 5117 Cliffdale Road, Fayetteville, NC 28314.

Greensboro College
Greensboro, North Carolina
http://www.greensboro.edu/

- **Independent United Methodist** comprehensive, founded 1838
- **Urban** 75-acre campus with easy access to Charlotte
- **Endowment** $20.5 million
- **Coed**
- **Minimally difficult** entrance level

FACULTY
Student/faculty ratio: 13:1.

ACADEMICS
Calendar: semesters. *Degrees:* certificates, bachelor's, master's, and postbachelor's certificates.
Library: James Addison Jones Library.

STUDENT LIFE
Housing options: on-campus residence required through sophomore year; coed, men-only, women-only. Campus housing is university owned. Freshman campus housing is guaranteed.

Activities and organizations: drama/theater group, student-run newspaper, choral group, marching band, Pheta VI, Alpha Z Delta, Student Athletic Advisor Counsel, Pride Productions, United African American Society, national fraternities, national sororities.

Athletics Member NCAA. All Division III.

Campus security: 24-hour patrols, late-night transport/escort service, controlled dormitory access.

Student services: health clinic, personal/psychological counseling.

COSTS & FINANCIAL AID
Costs (2016–17) ***Comprehensive fee:*** $38,400 includes full-time tuition ($27,350), mandatory fees ($650), and room and board ($10,400). Full-time tuition and fees vary according to degree level and program. Part-time tuition: $750 per credit hour. Part-time tuition and fees vary according to course load, degree level, and program. ***College room only:*** $5200. Room and board charges vary according to housing facility.

Financial Aid Of all full-time matriculated undergraduates who enrolled in 2015, 692 applied for aid, 673 were judged to have need, 54 had their need fully met. 131 Federal Work-Study jobs (averaging $717). In 2015, 24 non-need-based awards were made. ***Average percent of need met:*** 82. ***Average financial aid package:*** $20,493. ***Average need-based loan:*** $7623. ***Average need-based gift aid:*** $8148. ***Average non-need-based aid:*** $10,703. ***Average indebtedness upon graduation:*** $43,509.

APPLYING
Standardized Tests *Required:* SAT or ACT (for admission).

Options: electronic application, early admission, early action, deferred entrance.

Application fee: $35.

Required: high school transcript. ***Required for some:*** 2 letters of recommendation, interview. ***Recommended:*** essay or personal statement, interview.

CONTACT
Ms. Colleen Murphy, Vice President for Enrollment Management and Marketing, Greensboro College, 815 West Market Street, Greensboro, NC 27401-1875. *Phone:* 336-272-7102. *Toll-free phone:* 800-346-8226. *Fax:* 336-378-0154. *E-mail:* admissions@greensborocollege.edu.

Guilford College

Greensboro, North Carolina

http://www.guilford.edu/

- **Independent** 4-year, founded 1837, affiliated with Society of Friends
- **Suburban** 351-acre campus
- **Endowment** $81.7 million
- **Coed** 1,809 undergraduate students, 86% full-time, 52% women, 48% men
- **Moderately difficult** entrance level, 77% of applicants were admitted

UNDERGRAD STUDENTS

1,560 full-time, 249 part-time. Students come from 39 states and territories; 17 other countries; 32% are from out of state; 24% Black or African American, non-Hispanic/Latino; 7% Hispanic/Latino; 5% Asian, non-Hispanic/Latino; 0.1% Native Hawaiian or other Pacific Islander, non-Hispanic/Latino; 0.6% American Indian or Alaska Native, non-Hispanic/Latino; 4% Two or more races, non-Hispanic/Latino; 1% Race/ethnicity unknown; 2% international; 53% live on campus.

Freshmen:

Admission: 2,620 applied, 2,010 admitted, 428 enrolled. ***Average high school GPA:*** 3.18. ***Test scores:*** SAT critical reading scores over 500: 53%; SAT math scores over 500: 50%; SAT writing scores over 500: 45%; ACT scores over 18: 84%; SAT critical reading scores over 600: 22%; SAT math scores over 600: 16%; SAT writing scores over 600: 17%; ACT scores over 24: 41%; SAT critical reading scores over 700: 4%; SAT math scores over 700: 1%; SAT writing scores over 700: 4%; ACT scores over 30: 7%.

Retention: 74% of full-time freshmen returned.

FACULTY

Total: 193, 55% full-time.

Student/faculty ratio: 12:1.

ACADEMICS

Calendar: 4-1-4. *Degrees:* bachelor's and postbachelor's certificates.

Special study options: academic remediation for entering students, accelerated degree program, adult/continuing education programs, advanced placement credit, cooperative education, double majors, English as a second language, honors programs, independent study, internships, off-campus study, part-time degree program, services for LD students, student-designed majors, study abroad, summer session for credit. ***ROTC:*** Army (c), Air Force (c).

Unusual degree programs: 3-2 engineering; law with Elon University.

Computers: 275 computers/terminals are available on campus for general student use. Students can access the following: campus intranet, computer help desk, free student e-mail accounts, online (class) grades, online (class) registration, online (class) schedules, network storage. Campuswide network is available. 100% of college-owned or -operated housing units are wired for high-speed Internet access. Wireless service is available via entire campus.

Library: Hege Library. *Books:* 180,763 (physical), 292,515 (digital/electronic); *Serial titles:* 6,901 (physical), 28,504 (digital/electronic); *Databases:* 166. Weekly public service hours: 93; students can reserve study rooms.

STUDENT LIFE

Housing options: on-campus residence required through junior year; coed, women-only, cooperative, special housing for students with disabilities. Campus housing is university owned. Freshman campus housing is guaranteed.

Activities and organizations: drama/theater group, student-run newspaper, radio station, choral group, Student Government, Student Radio Station, Student Newspaper, Project Community, African-American Cultural Society.

Athletics Member NCAA. All Division III. ***Intercollegiate sports:*** baseball M, basketball M/W, cross-country running M/W, football M, golf M, lacrosse M/W, soccer M/W, softball W, swimming and diving W, tennis M/W, track and field M/W, volleyball W. ***Intramural sports:*** archery M(c)/W(c), badminton M(c)/W(c), basketball M(c), bowling M(c)/W(c), cheerleading M(c)/W(c), fencing M(c)/W(c), football M(c), rugby M(c)/W(c), soccer M(c)/W(c), table tennis M(c)/W(c), tennis M(c)/W(c), ultimate Frisbee M(c)/W(c), volleyball M(c)/W(c).

Campus security: 24-hour emergency response devices and patrols, student patrols, late-night transport/escort service, controlled dormitory access.

Student services: health clinic, personal/psychological counseling, women's center.

COSTS & FINANCIAL AID

Costs (2017–18) ***Comprehensive fee:*** $44,437 includes full-time tuition ($33,710), mandatory fees ($505), and room and board ($10,222). Full-time tuition and fees vary according to program. Part-time tuition: $1032 per credit hour. Part-time tuition and fees vary according to course load and program. ***Required fees:*** $205 per term part-time. ***College room only:*** $5000. Room and board charges vary according to board plan and housing facility. ***Payment plan:*** installment. ***Waivers:*** employees or children of employees.

Financial Aid Of all full-time matriculated undergraduates who enrolled in 2015, 1,183 applied for aid, 1,080 were judged to have need, 8 had their need fully met. In 2015, 105 non-need-based awards were made. ***Average percent of need met:*** 67. ***Average financial aid package:*** $22,816. ***Average need-based loan:*** $3819. ***Average need-based gift aid:*** $5023. ***Average non-need-based aid:*** $8653. ***Average indebtedness upon graduation:*** $20,682.

APPLYING

Standardized Tests *Recommended:* SAT or ACT (for admission).

Options: electronic application, early admission, early decision, early action, deferred entrance.

Required: essay or personal statement, high school transcript, minimum 2.0 GPA. ***Recommended:*** minimum 3.0 GPA, 1 letter of recommendation, interview.

Application deadlines: rolling (freshmen), rolling (transfers), 12/1 (early action).

Early decision deadline: 11/1.

Notification: continuous (freshmen), continuous (transfers), 11/15 (early decision), 12/15 (early action).

CONTACT

Ms. Erin Kelly, Director of Admission, Guilford College, 5800 West Friendly Avenue, Greensboro, NC 27410. *Phone:* 336-316-200. *Toll-free phone:* 800-992-7759. *Fax:* 336-316-2954. *E-mail:* admission@guilford.edu.

Heritage Bible College

Dunn, North Carolina

http://www.heritagebiblecollege.edu/

- **Independent Pentecostal Free Will Baptist** 4-year, founded 1971
- **Small-town** 82-acre campus with easy access to Raleigh-Durham
- **Endowment** $53,446
- **Coed** 69 undergraduate students, 49% full-time, 46% women, 54% men
- **Minimally difficult** entrance level, 100% of applicants were admitted

UNDERGRAD STUDENTS

34 full-time, 35 part-time. Students come from 7 states and territories; 13% are from out of state; 23% Black or African American, non-Hispanic/Latino; 1% Native Hawaiian or other Pacific Islander, non-Hispanic/Latino; 13% transferred in; 13% live on campus.

Freshmen:

Admission: 10 applied, 10 admitted, 10 enrolled. ***Average high school GPA:*** 2.85.

Retention: 52% of full-time freshmen returned.

FACULTY

Total: 18, 22% full-time, 33% with terminal degrees.

ACADEMICS

Calendar: semesters. *Degrees:* associate and bachelor's.

Special study options: academic remediation for entering students, adult/continuing education programs, distance learning, double majors, external degree program, internships, off-campus study, part-time degree program, summer session for credit.

Computers: 25 computers/terminals are available on campus for general student use. Students can access the following: free student e-mail accounts, online (class) grades, online (class) registration, online (class)

schedules. Campuswide network is available. 100% of college-owned or -operated housing units are wired for high-speed Internet access. Wireless service is available via entire campus.
Library: Alphin Ellis Learning Center plus 1 other. Students can reserve study rooms.

STUDENT LIFE
Housing options: coed. Campus housing is university owned.

Activities and organizations: choral group.

FINANCIAL AID
Financial Aid Of all full-time matriculated undergraduates who enrolled in 2015, 33 applied for aid, 33 were judged to have need, 3 had their need fully met. 3 Federal Work-Study jobs. ***Average percent of need met:*** 54. ***Average financial aid package:*** $2739. ***Average need-based loan:*** $1712. ***Average need-based gift aid:*** $200. ***Average indebtedness upon graduation:*** $15,000. ***Financial aid deadline:*** 7/1.

APPLYING
Options: electronic application.

Application fee: $35.

Required: essay or personal statement, high school transcript, medical history required for all, immunization record required for some. ***Required for some:*** interview.

Application deadlines: rolling (freshmen), rolling (transfers).

CONTACT
Ms. Iris Prince, Admissions Director, Heritage Bible College, PO Box 1628, Dunn, NC 28335-1628. *Phone:* 910-892-3178 Ext. 239. *Toll-free phone:* 800-297-6351. *Fax:* 910-891-1660.
E-mail: iprince@heritagebiblecollege.edu.

High Point University
High Point, North Carolina
http://www.highpoint.edu/

- **Independent United Methodist** comprehensive, founded 1924
- **Suburban** 380-acre campus with easy access to Charlotte
- **Endowment** $49.8 million
- **Coed** 4,546 undergraduate students, 99% full-time, 60% women, 40% men
- **Moderately difficult** entrance level, 79% of applicants were admitted

UNDERGRAD STUDENTS
4,508 full-time, 38 part-time. Students come from 47 states and territories; 35 other countries; 79% are from out of state; 5% Black or African American, non-Hispanic/Latino; 5% Hispanic/Latino; 2% Asian, non-Hispanic/Latino; 0.2% American Indian or Alaska Native, non-Hispanic/Latino; 6% Two or more races, non-Hispanic/Latino; 1% Race/ethnicity unknown; 2% international; 1% transferred in; 94% live on campus.

Freshmen:
Admission: 9,683 applied, 7,657 admitted, 1,382 enrolled. ***Average high school GPA:*** 3.27. ***Test scores:*** SAT critical reading scores over 500: 72%; SAT math scores over 500: 77%; SAT writing scores over 500: 68%; ACT scores over 18: 96%; SAT critical reading scores over 600: 22%; SAT math scores over 600: 26%; SAT writing scores over 600: 20%; ACT scores over 24: 49%; SAT critical reading scores over 700: 1%; SAT math scores over 700: 2%; SAT writing scores over 700: 2%; ACT scores over 30: 6%.
Retention: 82% of full-time freshmen returned.

FACULTY
Total: 437, 69% full-time, 63% with terminal degrees.

Student/faculty ratio: 15:1.

ACADEMICS
Calendar: semesters. *Degrees:* bachelor's, master's, doctoral, and postbachelor's certificates.

Special study options: academic remediation for entering students, accelerated degree program, advanced placement credit, cooperative education, double majors, English as a second language, honors programs, independent study, internships, off-campus study, services for LD students, student-designed majors, study abroad, summer session for credit. ***ROTC:*** Army (c), Air Force (c).

Unusual degree programs: 3-2 elementary education, strategic communication.

Computers: 749 computers/terminals are available on campus for general student use. Students can access the following: campus intranet, computer help desk, free student e-mail accounts, online (class) grades, online (class) registration, online (class) schedules. Campuswide network is available. 100% of college-owned or -operated housing units are wired for high-speed Internet access. Wireless service is available via entire campus.

Library: Smith Library plus 1 other. *Books:* 180,000 (physical), 401,000 (digital/electronic); *Serial titles:* 100 (physical), 32,000 (digital/electronic); *Databases:* 190. Study areas open 24 hours, 5-7 days a week; students can reserve study rooms.

STUDENT LIFE

Housing options: on-campus residence required through junior year; coed, men-only, women-only, cooperative, special housing for students with disabilities. Campus housing is university owned. Freshman campus housing is guaranteed.

Activities and organizations: drama/theater group, student-run newspaper, radio station, choral group, Big Brothers Big Sisters, College Republicans, Purple Reign, Entrepreneurship Club, Volunteer Center, national fraternities, national sororities.

Athletics Member NCAA. All Division I. ***Intercollegiate sports:*** baseball M(s), basketball M(s)/W(s), cheerleading W(c), cross-country running M(s)/W(s), golf M(s)/W(s), lacrosse M(s)/W(s), soccer M(s)/W(s), track and field M(s)/W(s), volleyball W(s). ***Intramural sports:*** badminton M/W, basketball M/W, bowling M/W, cross-country running M(c)/W(c), equestrian sports M(c)/W(c), field hockey W(c), football M/W, golf M(c)/W(c), ice hockey M(c), lacrosse M(c)/W(c), racquetball M/W, rowing M(c)/W(c), soccer M/W, softball M/W, swimming and diving M(c)/W(c), tennis M/W, ultimate Frisbee M/W, volleyball M/W, water polo M/W.

Campus security: 24-hour emergency response devices and patrols, student patrols, late-night transport/escort service, controlled dormitory access.

Student services: health clinic, personal/psychological counseling.

COSTS & FINANCIAL AID

Costs (2017–18) ***Comprehensive fee:*** $47,355 includes full-time tuition ($29,800), mandatory fees ($4205), and room and board ($13,350). Full-time tuition and fees vary according to course load and reciprocity agreements. Part-time tuition: $955 per credit hour. Part-time tuition and fees vary according to course load and reciprocity agreements. ***Required fees:*** $200 per term part-time. ***Room and board:*** Room and board charges vary according to board plan and housing facility. ***Payment plan:*** installment. ***Waivers:*** employees or children of employees.

Financial Aid Of all full-time matriculated undergraduates who enrolled in 2015, 2,342 applied for aid, 1,781 were judged to have need, 302 had their need fully met. 281 Federal Work-Study jobs (averaging $1500). In 2015, 380 non-need-based awards were made. ***Average percent of need met:*** 57. ***Average financial aid package:*** $17,929. ***Average need-based loan:*** $4239. ***Average need-based gift aid:*** $5126. ***Average non-need-based aid:*** $7245. ***Average indebtedness upon graduation:*** $35,897.

APPLYING

Standardized Tests *Required:* SAT or ACT (for admission).

Options: electronic application, early decision, early action, deferred entrance.

Application fee: $50.

Required: essay or personal statement, high school transcript, minimum 2.0 GPA. ***Recommended:*** minimum 3.0 GPA, 2 letters of recommendation, interview.

Application deadlines: 3/15 (freshmen), 7/1 (transfers), 11/4 (early action).

Early decision deadline: 11/1 (for plan 1), 2/1 (for plan 2).

Notification: continuous (freshmen), continuous (transfers), 11/28 (early decision plan 1), rolling (early decision plan 2), 12/16 (early action).

CONTACT

Dr. Kerr Ramsay, Associate Vice President of Admissions, High Point University, Office of Undergraduate Admissions, One University Parkway, High Point, NC 27268. *Phone:* 336-841-9176. *Toll-free phone:* 800-345-6993. *Fax:* 336-888-6382. *E-mail:* kramsay@highpoint.edu.

See previous page for display ad and page 1374 for the College Close-Up.

Johnson & Wales University

Charlotte, North Carolina

http://www.jwu.edu/charlotte/

CONTACT

Joseph Campos, Director of Admissions, Johnson & Wales University, 801 West Trade Street, Charlotte, NC 28202. *Phone:* 980-598-1100. *Toll-free phone:* 866-598-2427. *Fax:* 980-598-1111. *E-mail:* clt@admissions.jwu.edu.

Johnson C. Smith University

Charlotte, North Carolina

http://www.jcsu.edu/

- **Independent** comprehensive, founded 1867
- **Urban** 100-acre campus with easy access to Atlanta
- **Endowment** $61.9 million
- **Coed** 1,326 undergraduate students, 97% full-time, 61% women, 39% men
- **Moderately difficult** entrance level, 45% of applicants were admitted

UNDERGRAD STUDENTS

1,284 full-time, 42 part-time. Students come from 30 states and territories; 12 other countries; 41% are from out of state; 84% Black or African American, non-Hispanic/Latino; 4% Hispanic/Latino; 0.2% Asian, non-Hispanic/Latino; 0.1% Native Hawaiian or other Pacific Islander, non-Hispanic/Latino; 0.2% American Indian or Alaska Native, non-Hispanic/Latino; 2% Two or more races, non-Hispanic/Latino; 6% Race/ethnicity unknown; 2% international; 7% transferred in; 66% live on campus.

Freshmen:

Admission: 5,841 applied, 2,646 admitted, 302 enrolled. ***Average high school GPA:*** 2.84. ***Test scores:*** SAT critical reading scores over 500: 8%; SAT math scores over 500: 13%; ACT scores over 18: 37%; SAT critical reading scores over 600: 2%; SAT math scores over 600: 2%; ACT scores over 24: 2%.

Retention: 65% of full-time freshmen returned.

FACULTY

Total: 181, 51% full-time, 62% with terminal degrees.

Student/faculty ratio: 11:1.

ACADEMICS

Calendar: semesters. *Degrees:* bachelor's and master's.

Special study options: accelerated degree program, adult/continuing education programs, advanced placement credit, cooperative education, distance learning, double majors, English as a second language, independent study, internships, part-time degree program, services for LD students, student-designed majors, study abroad, summer session for credit.

Computers: 125 computers/terminals are available on campus for general student use. Students can access the following: campus intranet, computer help desk, free student e-mail accounts, online (class) grades, online (class) registration, online (class) schedules. Campuswide network is available. 100% of college-owned or -operated housing units are wired for high-speed Internet access. Wireless service is available via entire campus.

Library: James B. Duke Library. *Books:* 114,150 (physical), 184,548 (digital/electronic); *Serial titles:* 257 (physical); *Databases:* 78. Weekly public service hours: 79; study areas open 24 hours, 5-7 days a week; students can reserve study rooms.

STUDENT LIFE

Housing options: coed, men-only, women-only. Campus housing is university owned and leased by the school. Freshman campus housing is guaranteed.

Activities and organizations: drama/theater group, choral group, marching band, National Association for the Advancement of Colored People, Association of Non Traditional Students in Higher Education, The Black Ink Monks, Anime Club, Raw Attractions Entertainment, national fraternities, national sororities.

Athletics Member NCAA. All Division II. ***Intercollegiate sports:*** basketball M(s)/W(s), bowling W(s), cheerleading W(c), cross-country running M(s)/W(s), football M(s), golf M(s), softball W(s), tennis M(s)/W(s), track and field M(s)/W(s), volleyball W(s).

Campus security: 24-hour emergency response devices and patrols, late-night transport/escort service, controlled dormitory access.

Student services: health clinic, personal/psychological counseling.

COSTS & FINANCIAL AID

Costs (2017–18) ***Comprehensive fee:*** $25,336 includes full-time tuition ($18,236) and room and board ($7100). Full-time tuition and fees vary according to course load. Part-time tuition: $418 per credit hour. Part-time tuition and fees vary according to course load. ***College room only:*** $4086. Room and board charges vary according to board plan and housing facility. ***Payment plan:*** installment. ***Waivers:*** employees or children of employees.

Financial Aid Of all full-time matriculated undergraduates who enrolled in 2016, 1,222 applied for aid, 1,177 were judged to have need, 65 had their need fully met. 195 Federal Work-Study jobs (averaging $2521). In 2016, 75 non-need-based awards were made. ***Average percent of need met:*** 57. ***Average financial aid package:*** $15,853. ***Average need-based loan:*** $4036. ***Average need-based gift aid:*** $12,023. ***Average non-need-based aid:*** $14,345. ***Average indebtedness upon graduation:*** $38,732. ***Financial aid deadline:*** 4/1.

APPLYING

Standardized Tests *Required:* SAT or ACT (for admission).

Options: electronic application, deferred entrance.

Application fee: $25.

Required: high school transcript. ***Recommended:*** essay or personal statement, 1 letter of recommendation.

Notification: continuous (freshmen), continuous (transfers).

CONTACT

Mr. James Burrell, Director of Admissions, Johnson C. Smith University, 100 Beatties Ford Road, Charlotte, NC 28216. *Phone:* 704-378-1181. *Toll-free phone:* 800-782-7303. *Fax:* 704-378-1242. *E-mail:* jburrell@jcsu.edu.

John Wesley University

High Point, North Carolina

http://www.johnwesley.edu/

- **Independent interdenominational** comprehensive, founded 1932
- **Urban** 24-acre campus
- **Coed** 126 undergraduate students, 87% full-time, 52% women, 48% men
- **Moderately difficult** entrance level, 20% of applicants were admitted

UNDERGRAD STUDENTS

110 full-time, 16 part-time. Students come from 11 states and territories; 4 other countries; 15% are from out of state; 25% Black or African American, non-Hispanic/Latino; 11% Hispanic/Latino; 0.8% Asian, non-Hispanic/Latino; 5% American Indian or Alaska Native, non-Hispanic/Latino; 6% Two or more races, non-Hispanic/Latino; 0.8% Race/ethnicity unknown; 4% international; 8% transferred in; 47% live on campus.

Freshmen:

Admission: 165 applied, 33 admitted, 33 enrolled. ***Average high school GPA:*** 3.

Retention: 38% of full-time freshmen returned.

FACULTY

Total: 19, 21% full-time, 79% with terminal degrees.

Student/faculty ratio: 15:1.

ACADEMICS

Calendar: semesters. *Degrees:* certificates, associate, bachelor's, master's, and doctoral.

Special study options: academic remediation for entering students, adult/continuing education programs, advanced placement credit, distance learning, double majors, independent study, internships, off-campus study, part-time degree program, summer session for credit.

Computers: 7 computers/terminals and 7 ports are available on campus for general student use. Students can access the following: free student e-mail accounts, online (class) grades, online (class) registration, online (class) schedules. 100% of college-owned or -operated housing units are wired for high-speed Internet access. Wireless service is available via entire campus.

Library: Temple Library. *Books:* 3,885 (physical), 26 (digital/electronic); *Serial titles:* 38 (physical), 164 (digital/electronic); *Databases:* 4.

STUDENT LIFE

Housing options: men-only, women-only. Campus housing is university owned.

Activities and organizations: choral group, Student Government, Choir, Praise Band, Ambassadors Club, Men and Womens Leadership.

Athletics Member NCCAA. ***Intercollegiate sports:*** soccer M(s)/W(s), softball W(s), volleyball W(s).

Campus security: 24-hour emergency response devices, full-time retired Police Officer on campus.

COSTS & FINANCIAL AID

Costs (2016–17) ***Tuition:*** $10,500 full-time, $5250 per year part-time. Full-time tuition and fees vary according to program. Part-time tuition and fees vary according to program. ***Required fees:*** $730 full-time, $730 per year part-time. ***Room only:*** $9280. ***Payment plan:*** installment. ***Waivers:*** employees or children of employees.

Financial Aid Of all full-time matriculated undergraduates who enrolled in 2011, 3 Federal Work-Study jobs (averaging $2500).

APPLYING

Standardized Tests *Required:* SAT or ACT (for admission). *Required for some:* ACCUPLACER.

Options: electronic application, early admission, deferred entrance.

Application fee: $20.

Required: essay or personal statement, high school transcript, 2 letters of recommendation. ***Recommended:*** minimum 2.0 GPA, interview.

Application deadlines: 8/1 (freshmen), 8/1 (transfers).

Notification: continuous (freshmen), continuous (out-of-state freshmen), continuous (transfers).

CONTACT

Rosalie Seitz, Admissions, John Wesley University, 1215 Eastchester Drive, High Point, NC 27265-3197. *Phone:* 336-821-2474. *Toll-free phone:* 855-528-7358.

Lees-McRae College

Banner Elk, North Carolina

http://www.lmc.edu/

- **Independent** 4-year, founded 1900, affiliated with Presbyterian Church (U.S.A.)
- **Rural** 460-acre campus
- **Endowment** $12.2 million
- **Coed** 991 undergraduate students, 99% full-time, 66% women, 34% men
- **Minimally difficult** entrance level, 63% of applicants were admitted

UNDERGRAD STUDENTS

978 full-time, 13 part-time. Students come from 34 states and territories; 10 other countries; 23% are from out of state; 6% Black or African American, non-Hispanic/Latino; 4% Hispanic/Latino; 31% Asian, non-Hispanic/Latino; 0.2% Native Hawaiian or other Pacific Islander, non-Hispanic/Latino; 0.7% American Indian or Alaska Native, non-Hispanic/Latino; 1% Two or more races, non-Hispanic/Latino; 12% Race/ethnicity unknown; 2% international; 14% transferred in; 58% live on campus.

Freshmen:
Admission: 1,531 applied, 965 admitted, 187 enrolled. ***Average high school GPA:*** 3.48. ***Test scores:*** SAT critical reading scores over 500: 46%; SAT math scores over 500: 51%; SAT writing scores over 500: 36%; ACT scores over 18: 80%; SAT critical reading scores over 600: 17%; SAT math scores over 600: 14%; SAT writing scores over 600: 9%; ACT scores over 24: 24%; SAT critical reading scores over 700: 2%; SAT writing scores over 700: 1%; ACT scores over 30: 1%.
Retention: 58% of full-time freshmen returned.

FACULTY
Total: 135, 36% full-time, 36% with terminal degrees.
Student/faculty ratio: 13:1.

ACADEMICS
Calendar: semesters. *Degree:* bachelor's.
Special study options: academic remediation for entering students, accelerated degree program, adult/continuing education programs, advanced placement credit, cooperative education, double majors, honors programs, independent study, internships, off-campus study, part-time degree program, services for LD students, study abroad, summer session for credit.
Computers: Students can access the following: computer help desk, free student e-mail accounts, online (class) grades, online (class) registration, online (class) schedules. Campuswide network is available. 100% of college-owned or -operated housing units are wired for high-speed Internet access. Wireless service is available via entire campus.
Library: Dotti M. Shelton Learning Commons. *Books:* 70,132 (physical), 173,083 (digital/electronic); *Serial titles:* 225 (physical), 146,361 (digital/electronic); *Databases:* 143. Students can reserve study rooms.

STUDENT LIFE
Housing options: coed, men-only, women-only, special housing for students with disabilities. Campus housing is university owned. Freshman campus housing is guaranteed.
Activities and organizations: drama/theater group, choral group.
Athletics Member NCAA. All Division II. ***Intercollegiate sports:*** basketball M(s)/W(s), cross-country running M(s)/W(s), lacrosse M(s)/W(s), soccer M(s)/W(s), softball W(s), tennis M(s)/W(s), track and field M(s)/W(s), volleyball M(s)/W(s).
Campus security: 24-hour emergency response devices and patrols, controlled dormitory access.
Student services: health clinic, personal/psychological counseling.

COSTS & FINANCIAL AID
Costs (2017–18) ***Comprehensive fee:*** $36,956 includes full-time tuition ($24,878), mandatory fees ($1320), and room and board ($10,758). Full-time tuition and fees vary according to course load, location, and reciprocity agreements. Part-time tuition: $710 per credit hour. Part-time tuition and fees vary according to course load, location, and reciprocity agreements. No tuition increase for student's term of enrollment. ***College room only:*** $5142. Room and board charges vary according to housing facility. ***Payment plan:*** installment. ***Waivers:*** employees or children of employees.
Financial Aid Of all full-time matriculated undergraduates who enrolled in 2016, 836 applied for aid, 787 were judged to have need, 9 had their need fully met. In 2016, 90 non-need-based awards were made. ***Average percent of need met:*** 70. ***Average financial aid package:*** $24,611. ***Average need-based loan:*** $5492. ***Average need-based gift aid:*** $9137. ***Average non-need-based aid:*** $12,371.

APPLYING
Standardized Tests *Required for some:* SAT or ACT (for admission), SAT or ACT scores for prospective intercollegiate athletes and honors program students.
Options: electronic application, early action.
Application fee: $35.
Required: high school transcript, minimum 2.0 GPA. ***Required for some:*** essay or personal statement, interview.
Application deadlines: rolling (freshmen), rolling (transfers).
Notification: continuous (freshmen), continuous (transfers).

CONTACT
Mrs. Candace Silver, Director of Admissions, Lees-McRae College, PO Box 128, Banner Elk, NC 28604. *Phone:* 800-280-4562. *Toll-free phone:* 800-280-4562. *Fax:* 828-898-8707. *E-mail:* admissions@lmc.edu.

Lenoir-Rhyne University

Hickory, North Carolina

http://www.lr.edu/

- **Independent Lutheran** comprehensive, founded 1891
- **Small-town** 100-acre campus with easy access to Charlotte
- **Endowment** $94.6 million
- **Coed** 1,710 undergraduate students, 85% full-time, 60% women, 40% men
- **Moderately difficult** entrance level, 70% of applicants were admitted

UNDERGRAD STUDENTS
1,453 full-time, 257 part-time. Students come from 27 states and territories; 20 other countries; 17% are from out of state; 12% Black or African American, non-Hispanic/Latino; 6% Hispanic/Latino; 2% Asian, non-Hispanic/Latino; 0.1% Native Hawaiian or other Pacific Islander, non-Hispanic/Latino; 0.5% American Indian or Alaska Native, non-Hispanic/Latino; 3% Two or more races, non-Hispanic/Latino; 9% Race/ethnicity unknown; 2% international; 6% transferred in; 51% live on campus.

Freshmen:
Admission: 6,300 applied, 4,417 admitted, 491 enrolled. ***Average high school GPA:*** 3.26. ***Test scores:*** SAT critical reading scores over 500: 43%; SAT math scores over 500: 50%; SAT critical reading scores over 600: 10%; SAT math scores over 600: 12%; SAT critical reading scores over 700: 1%; SAT math scores over 700: 1%.
Retention: 72% of full-time freshmen returned.

FACULTY
Total: 269, 47% full-time, 61% with terminal degrees.
Student/faculty ratio: 13:1.

ACADEMICS
Calendar: semesters. *Degrees:* bachelor's and master's.
Special study options: academic remediation for entering students, accelerated degree program, adult/continuing education programs, advanced placement credit, distance learning, double majors, freshman honors college, honors programs, independent study, internships, off-campus study, part-time degree program, services for LD students, study abroad, summer session for credit.
Unusual degree programs: 3-2 engineering with North Carolina Agricultural and Technical State University, North Carolina State University, University of North Carolina at Charlotte, Clemson University; forestry with Duke University.
Computers: 150 computers/terminals and 150 ports are available on campus for general student use. Students can access the following: campus intranet, computer help desk, free student e-mail accounts, online (class) grades, online (class) registration, online (class) schedules. Campuswide network is available. 100% of college-owned or -operated housing units are wired for high-speed Internet access. Wireless service is available via entire campus.
Library: Carl Rudisill Library. *Books:* 124,059 (physical), 487,733 (digital/electronic); *Serial titles:* 56 (physical), 29,949 (digital/electronic); *Databases:* 134. Weekly public service hours: 89.

STUDENT LIFE
Housing options: on-campus residence required through junior year; coed. Campus housing is university owned. Freshman campus housing is guaranteed.
Activities and organizations: drama/theater group, student-run newspaper, radio station, choral group, marching band, Circle K, CAB, Nu Generation, Greek Organizations, Sign Troupe, national sororities.
Athletics Member NCAA. All Division II. ***Intercollegiate sports:*** baseball M(s), basketball M(s)/W(s), cheerleading M(s)/W(s), cross-country running M(s)/W(s), football M(s), golf M(s)/W(s), lacrosse M(s)/W(s), soccer M(s)/W(s), softball W(s), swimming and diving M(s)/W(s), tennis M(s)/W(s), track and field M(s)/W(s), volleyball W(s). ***Intramural sports:*** basketball M/W, sand volleyball M/W, soccer M/W, softball M/W, volleyball M/W.

Campus security: 24-hour emergency response devices and patrols, late-night transport/escort service, controlled dormitory access.

Student services: health clinic, personal/psychological counseling.

COSTS & FINANCIAL AID
Costs (2017–18) ***Comprehensive fee:*** $47,500 includes full-time tuition ($35,350) and room and board ($12,150). Part-time tuition: $1460 per credit. ***Room and board:*** Room and board charges vary according to board plan. ***Waivers:*** senior citizens and employees or children of employees.

Financial Aid Of all full-time matriculated undergraduates who enrolled in 2014, 1,246 applied for aid, 1,172 were judged to have need, 158 had their need fully met. In 2014, 155 non-need-based awards were made. ***Average percent of need met:*** 69. ***Average financial aid package:*** $25,657. ***Average need-based loan:*** $4452. ***Average need-based gift aid:*** $20,973. ***Average non-need-based aid:*** $13,463. ***Average indebtedness upon graduation:*** $28,622.

APPLYING
Standardized Tests *Required:* SAT or ACT (for admission).

Options: electronic application, early admission, early action, deferred entrance.

Application fee: $35.

Required: high school transcript, minimum 2.5 GPA. ***Recommended:*** essay or personal statement, letters of recommendation.

Application deadlines: rolling (freshmen), rolling (transfers), 11/7 (early action).

Notification: continuous (freshmen), continuous (transfers), 11/21 (early action).

CONTACT
Lenoir-Rhyne University, 625 7th Avenue NE, Hickory, NC 28601. *Phone:* 828-328-7392. *Toll-free phone:* 800-277-5721.

Living Arts College

Raleigh, North Carolina

http://www.living-arts-college.edu/

- **Proprietary** primarily 2-year, founded 1992
- **Suburban** campus with easy access to Raleigh
- **Coed**
- **Moderately difficult** entrance level

FACULTY
Student/faculty ratio: 10:1.

ACADEMICS
Calendar: quarters. *Degree:* certificates, diplomas, and bachelor's.

STUDENT LIFE
Housing options: Campus housing is university owned. Freshman applicants given priority for college housing.

Activities and organizations: MODIV (student council), Student Ambassadors, Firebreathers Animation Studio, NVTHS (National Vocational Technical Honor Society).

Campus security: controlled dormitory access.

APPLYING
Standardized Tests *Required:* Wonderlic aptitude test (for admission).

Options: electronic application, early admission, early decision, early action, deferred entrance.

Application fee: $25.

Required: essay or personal statement, high school transcript, interview. ***Required for some:*** portfolio.

CONTACT
Julie Wenta, Director of Admissions, Living Arts College, 3000 Wakefield Crossing Drive, Raleigh, NC 27614. *Phone:* 919-488-5902. *Toll-free phone:* 800-288-7442. *Fax:* 919-488-8490. *E-mail:* jwenta@living-arts-college.edu.

Livingstone College

Salisbury, North Carolina

http://www.livingstone.edu/

CONTACT
Mr. Tony Baldwin, Livingstone College, 701 West Monroe Street, Salisbury, NC 28144. *Phone:* 704-216-6001. *Toll-free phone:* 800-835-3435. *Fax:* 704-216-6215. *E-mail:* admissions@livingstone.edu.

Mars Hill University

Mars Hill, North Carolina

http://www.mhu.edu/

- **Independent Baptist** comprehensive, founded 1856
- **Small-town** 194-acre campus
- **Endowment** $42.0 million
- **Coed**
- **Moderately difficult** entrance level

FACULTY
Student/faculty ratio: 12:1.

ACADEMICS
Calendar: semesters. *Degrees:* bachelor's and master's.
Library: Renfro Library plus 1 other. *Books:* 88,868 (physical), 139,088 (digital/electronic); *Databases:* 133.

STUDENT LIFE
Housing options: on-campus residence required through sophomore year; men-only, women-only. Campus housing is university owned. Freshman campus housing is guaranteed.

Activities and organizations: drama/theater group, choral group, marching band, Student Government Association, Fellowship of Christian Athletes, Christian Student Movement, Fraternity/Sorority, Athletic Trainers Association, national fraternities, national sororities.

Athletics Member NCAA. All Division II.

Campus security: 24-hour emergency response devices and patrols, late-night transport/escort service, controlled dormitory access.

Student services: health clinic, personal/psychological counseling.

COSTS & FINANCIAL AID
Costs (2016–17) ***Comprehensive fee:*** $41,104 includes full-time tuition ($28,236), mandatory fees ($3568), and room and board ($9300). Part-time tuition: $1003 per credit hour. Part-time tuition and fees vary according to course load. ***Required fees:*** $151 per credit hour part-time. ***Room and board:*** Room and board charges vary according to housing facility.

Financial Aid Of all full-time matriculated undergraduates who enrolled in 2010, 2,256 applied for aid, 1,007 were judged to have need, 164 had their need fully met. 252 Federal Work-Study jobs (averaging $1354). In 2010, 141 non-need-based awards were made. ***Average percent of need met:*** 73. ***Average financial aid package:*** $17,195. ***Average need-based loan:*** $3988. ***Average need-based gift aid:*** $13,790. ***Average non-need-based aid:*** $8631. ***Average indebtedness upon graduation:*** $27,775.

APPLYING
Standardized Tests *Required:* SAT or ACT (for admission).

Options: electronic application, early admission, deferred entrance.

Application fee: $25.

Required: high school transcript, minimum 2.0 GPA. ***Required for some:*** interview. ***Recommended:*** essay or personal statement, minimum 3.0 GPA.

CONTACT
Kristie Vance, Director of Admissions, Mars Hill University, PO Box 370, Mars Hill, NC 28754. *Phone:* 828-689-1201. *Toll-free phone:* 866-648-4968. *Fax:* 828-689-1473. *E-mail:* admissions@mhu.edu.

★ Meredith College

Raleigh, North Carolina

http://www.meredith.edu/

- **Independent** comprehensive, founded 1891
- **Urban** 225-acre campus
- **Undergraduate: women only; graduate: coed** 1,685 undergraduate students, 96% full-time, 100% women, 0% men
- **Moderately difficult** entrance level, 61% of applicants were admitted

UNDERGRAD STUDENTS
1,616 full-time, 69 part-time. Students come from 27 states and territories; 37 other countries; 7% are from out of state; 8% Black or African American, non-Hispanic/Latino; 0.2% Hispanic/Latino; 3% Asian, non-Hispanic/Latino; 0.1% Native Hawaiian or other Pacific Islander, non-Hispanic/Latino; 0.8% American Indian or Alaska Native, non-Hispanic/Latino; 4% Two or more races, non-Hispanic/Latino; 5% Race/ethnicity unknown; 5% international; 5% transferred in; 54% live on campus.

Freshmen:
Admission: 1,923 applied, 1,169 admitted, 423 enrolled. ***Average high school GPA:*** 3.34. ***Test scores:*** SAT critical reading scores over 500: 59%; SAT math scores over 500: 57%; SAT critical reading scores over 600: 15%; SAT math scores over 600: 12%; SAT critical reading scores over 700: 2%.

Retention: 78% of full-time freshmen returned.

FACULTY
Total: 211, 63% full-time, 65% with terminal degrees.

Student/faculty ratio: 12:1.

ACADEMICS
Calendar: semesters. *Degrees:* bachelor's, master's, and postbachelor's certificates.

Special study options: academic remediation for entering students, accelerated degree program, advanced placement credit, cooperative education, double majors, honors programs, independent study, internships, off-campus study, part-time degree program, services for LD students, student-designed majors, study abroad, summer session for credit. ***ROTC:*** Army (c), Air Force (c).

Unusual degree programs: 3-2 engineering with North Carolina State University.

Computers: 140 computers/terminals are available on campus for general student use. Students can access the following: free student e-mail accounts, online (class) registration. Campuswide network is available. 100% of college-owned or -operated housing units are wired for high-speed Internet access. Wireless service is available via classrooms, computer centers, computer labs, dorm rooms, learning centers, libraries, student centers.
Library: Carlyle Campbell Library.

STUDENT LIFE
Housing options: on-campus residence required through sophomore year; women-only. Campus housing is university owned. Freshman campus housing is guaranteed.

Activities and organizations: drama/theater group, student-run newspaper, choral group, Student Government Association, Entertainment Association, Recreation Association, Class Organizations, choral groups.

Athletics Member NCAA. All Division III. ***Intercollegiate sports:*** basketball W, cross-country running W, lacrosse W, soccer W, softball W, tennis W, track and field W, volleyball W.

Campus security: 24-hour emergency response devices and patrols, late-night transport/escort service, controlled dormitory access.

Student services: health clinic, personal/psychological counseling.

COSTS & FINANCIAL AID
Costs (2016–17) ***Comprehensive fee:*** $45,297 includes full-time tuition ($34,807), mandatory fees ($100), and room and board ($10,390). Full-time tuition and fees vary according to course load. Part-time tuition: $864 per credit hour. Part-time tuition and fees vary according to course load. ***Required fees:*** $100 per year part-time. ***Room and board:*** Room and board charges vary according to board plan and housing facility. ***Waivers:*** employees or children of employees.

Financial Aid Of all full-time matriculated undergraduates who enrolled in 2015, 1,347 applied for aid, 1,204 were judged to have need, 195 had their need fully met. In 2015, 131 non-need-based awards were made. ***Average percent of need met:*** 72. ***Average financial aid package:*** $24,977. ***Average need-based loan:*** $4348. ***Average need-based gift aid:*** $20,935. ***Average non-need-based aid:*** $13,427. ***Average indebtedness upon graduation:*** $33,993.

APPLYING
Standardized Tests *Required:* SAT or ACT (for admission).

Options: electronic application, early admission, early decision, deferred entrance.

Application fee: $40.

Required: high school transcript, minimum 2.0 GPA, 2 letters of recommendation. ***Required for some:*** essay or personal statement, interview. ***Recommended:*** essay or personal statement.

Application deadlines: 2/15 (freshmen), 2/15 (transfers).

Early decision deadline: 10/15.

Notification: continuous (freshmen), continuous (transfers), 11/1 (early decision).

CONTACT
Shery Boyles, Director of Admissions, Meredith College, 3800 Hillsborough Street, Raleigh, NC 27807-5298. *Phone:* 919-760-8026. *Toll-free phone:* 800-MEREDITH. *Fax:* 919-760-2298. *E-mail:* admissions@meredith.edu.

Methodist University

Fayetteville, North Carolina

http://www.methodist.edu/

CONTACT
Mr. Jamie Legg, Director of Admissions, Methodist University, 5400 Ramset Street, Fayetteville, NC 28311-1496. *Phone:* 910-630-7027. *Toll-free phone:* 800-488-7110 Ext. 7027. *Fax:* 910-630-7285. *E-mail:* admissions@methodist.edu.

Mid-Atlantic Christian University

Elizabeth City, North Carolina

http://www.macuniversity.edu/

- **Independent Christian** 4-year, founded 1948
- **Small-town** 19-acre campus with easy access to Norfolk
- **Endowment** $3.1 million
- **Coed** 186 undergraduate students, 85% full-time, 55% women, 45% men
- **Minimally difficult** entrance level, 50% of applicants were admitted

UNDERGRAD STUDENTS
158 full-time, 28 part-time. Students come from 16 states and territories; 3 other countries; 34% are from out of state; 24% Black or African American, non-Hispanic/Latino; 4% Hispanic/Latino; 2% Asian, non-Hispanic/Latino; 0.5% American Indian or Alaska Native, non-Hispanic/Latino; 3% Two or more races, non-Hispanic/Latino; 0.5% international; 10% transferred in; 66% live on campus.

Freshmen:
Admission: 212 applied, 106 admitted, 50 enrolled. ***Average high school GPA:*** 3.06. ***Test scores:*** SAT critical reading scores over 500: 37%; SAT math scores over 500: 41%; SAT writing scores over 500: 18%; SAT critical reading scores over 600: 14%; SAT math scores over 600: 9%; SAT writing scores over 600: 9%.

Retention: 57% of full-time freshmen returned.

FACULTY
Total: 35, 29% full-time, 46% with terminal degrees.

Student/faculty ratio: 11:1.

ACADEMICS
Calendar: semesters. *Degrees:* certificates, associate, bachelor's, and postbachelor's certificates.

Special study options: academic remediation for entering students, adult/continuing education programs, advanced placement credit, distance learning, double majors, internships, part-time degree program, summer session for credit. ***ROTC:*** Army (c).

Computers: 24 computers/terminals are available on campus for general student use. Students can access the following: free student e-mail accounts, online (class) grades, online (class) registration, online (class) schedules. Campuswide network is available. 100% of college-owned or -operated housing units are wired for high-speed Internet access. Wireless service is available via entire campus.

Library: Watson-Griffith Library. *Books:* 33,941 (physical), 1,572 (digital/electronic). Students can reserve study rooms.

STUDENT LIFE

Housing options: on-campus residence required through senior year; men-only, women-only. Campus housing is university owned. Freshman campus housing is guaranteed.

Activities and organizations: national sororities.

Athletics Member USCAA. ***Intercollegiate sports:*** basketball M/W, golf M, soccer M, volleyball W. ***Intramural sports:*** basketball M/W, softball M/W, table tennis M/W, tennis M/W, volleyball M/W.

Campus security: 24-hour emergency response devices, controlled dormitory access.

Student services: personal/psychological counseling.

COSTS & FINANCIAL AID

Costs (2016–17) ***Comprehensive fee:*** $21,800 includes full-time tuition ($13,600) and room and board ($8200). Full-time tuition and fees vary according to program. Part-time tuition: $425 per credit. Part-time tuition and fees vary according to program. ***Room and board:*** Room and board charges vary according to housing facility. ***Payment plan:*** deferred payment. ***Waivers:*** children of alumni, senior citizens, and employees or children of employees.

Financial Aid Of all full-time matriculated undergraduates who enrolled in 2015, 170 applied for aid, 156 were judged to have need, 10 had their need fully met. In 2015, 17 non-need-based awards were made. ***Average percent of need met:*** 55. ***Average financial aid package:*** $11,333. ***Average need-based loan:*** $3758. ***Average need-based gift aid:*** $6671. ***Average non-need-based aid:*** $3478. ***Average indebtedness upon graduation:*** $26,414. ***Financial aid deadline:*** 3/1.

APPLYING

Standardized Tests *Required for some:* SAT or ACT (for admission).

Options: electronic application, early admission, deferred entrance.

Application fee: $50.

Required: essay or personal statement, high school transcript, minimum 2.0 GPA, 1 letter of recommendation, reference from church or character reference. ***Required for some:*** interview.

Application deadlines: 8/1 (freshmen), 8/1 (transfers).

Notification: continuous (freshmen), continuous (transfers).

CONTACT

Mr. Marty Riley, Mid-Atlantic Christian University, 715 North Poindexter Street, Elizabeth City, NC 27909-4054. *Phone:* 252-334-2025. *Toll-free phone:* 866-996-MACU. *Fax:* 252-334-2064. *E-mail:* marty.riley@macuniversity.edu.

Montreat College

Montreat, North Carolina

http://www.montreat.edu/

- **Independent** comprehensive, founded 1916, affiliated with Presbyterian Church (U.S.A.)
- **Small-town** 112-acre campus
- **Coed**
- **Moderately difficult** entrance level

FACULTY

Student/faculty ratio: 12:1.

ACADEMICS

Calendar: semesters. *Degrees:* certificates, associate, bachelor's, and master's.

Library: L. Nelson Bell Library.

STUDENT LIFE

Housing options: on-campus residence required through sophomore year; men-only, women-only. Campus housing is university owned. Freshman campus housing is guaranteed.

Activities and organizations: drama/theater group, student-run newspaper, choral group.

Athletics Member NAIA.

Campus security: 24-hour emergency response devices and patrols, controlled dormitory access.

Student services: health clinic, personal/psychological counseling.

COSTS & FINANCIAL AID

Costs (2016–17) ***Comprehensive fee:*** $33,310 includes full-time tuition ($24,740), mandatory fees ($200), and room and board ($8370). Full-time tuition and fees vary according to course load and degree level. Part-time tuition: $640 per semester hour. Part-time tuition and fees vary according to course load and degree level. ***College room only:*** $4196. Room and board charges vary according to board plan and housing facility.

Financial Aid Of all full-time matriculated undergraduates who enrolled in 2015, 439 applied for aid, 402 were judged to have need, 65 had their need fully met. In 2015, 67 non-need-based awards were made. ***Average percent of need met:*** 68. ***Average financial aid package:*** $19,762. ***Average need-based loan:*** $4135. ***Average need-based gift aid:*** $15,916. ***Average non-need-based aid:*** $10,845. ***Average indebtedness upon graduation:*** $24,512.

APPLYING

Standardized Tests *Required:* SAT or ACT (for admission).

Options: early admission, deferred entrance.

Required: essay or personal statement, high school transcript, minimum 2.8 GPA. ***Required for some:*** 1 letter of recommendation, interview.

CONTACT

Miss Mandi Pike, Senior Admissions Specialist, Montreat College, PO Box 1267, Montreat, NC 28757. *Phone:* 828-669-8012 Ext. 3789. *Toll-free phone:* 800-622-6968. *Fax:* 828-669-0120. *E-mail:* admissions@montreat.edu.

North Carolina Agricultural and Technical State University

Greensboro, North Carolina

http://www.ncat.edu/

CONTACT

Ms. Cheryl Pollard-Burns, Director of Admissions, North Carolina Agricultural and Technical State University, North Carolina Agricultural & Technical State University (Webb Hall), 1601 East Market Street, Greensboro, NC 27411. *Phone:* 336-334-7946. *Toll-free phone:* 800-443-8964. *Fax:* 336-334-7478. *E-mail:* uadmit@ncat.edu.

North Carolina Central University

Durham, North Carolina

http://www.nccu.edu/

- **State-supported** comprehensive, founded 1910, part of University of North Carolina System
- **Urban** 115-acre campus with easy access to Raleigh
- **Endowment** $22.9 million
- **Coed** 6,285 undergraduate students, 85% full-time, 66% women, 34% men
- **Minimally difficult** entrance level, 67% of applicants were admitted

UNDERGRAD STUDENTS

5,343 full-time, 942 part-time. Students come from 34 states and territories; 24 other countries; 9% are from out of state; 77% Black or African American, non-Hispanic/Latino; 5% Hispanic/Latino; 0.9% Asian, non-Hispanic/Latino; 0.4% American Indian or Alaska Native, non-Hispanic/Latino; 4% Two or more races, non-Hispanic/Latino; 3% Race/ethnicity unknown; 2% international; 9% transferred in; 40% live on campus.

Freshmen:

Admission: 8,614 applied, 5,745 admitted, 1,151 enrolled. ***Average high school GPA:*** 3.2. ***Test scores:*** SAT critical reading scores over 500: 14%; SAT math scores over 500: 18%; SAT writing scores over 500: 11%; ACT scores over 18: 49%; SAT critical reading scores over 600: 2%; SAT math scores over 600: 2%; SAT writing scores over 600: 1%; ACT scores over

24: 8%; SAT critical reading scores over 700: 1%; SAT math scores over 700: 1%; ACT scores over 30: 1%.

Retention: 81% of full-time freshmen returned.

FACULTY

Total: 578, 67% full-time, 60% with terminal degrees.

Student/faculty ratio: 16:1.

ACADEMICS

Calendar: semesters. *Degrees:* bachelor's, master's, and doctoral.

Special study options: academic remediation for entering students, accelerated degree program, adult/continuing education programs, advanced placement credit, cooperative education, distance learning, double majors, English as a second language, external degree program, honors programs, independent study, internships, off-campus study, part-time degree program, services for LD students, study abroad, summer session for credit. ***ROTC:*** Army (b), Air Force (b).

Computers: 1,262 computers/terminals and 3,700 ports are available on campus for general student use. Students can access the following: campus intranet, computer help desk, free student e-mail accounts, online (class) grades, online (class) registration, online (class) schedules. Campuswide network is available. 100% of college-owned or -operated housing units are wired for high-speed Internet access. Wireless service is available via entire campus.

Library: Shepherd Library plus 2 others. Study areas open 24 hours, 5-7 days a week.

STUDENT LIFE

Housing options: coed. Campus housing is university owned and leased by the school. Freshman applicants given priority for college housing.

Activities and organizations: drama/theater group, student-run newspaper, choral group, marching band, national fraternities, national sororities.

Athletics Member NCAA, NAIA. All NCAA Division I. ***Intercollegiate sports:*** baseball M(s), basketball M(s)/W(s), bowling W(s), cross-country running M(s)/W(s), football M(s), golf M(s), softball W(s), tennis M(s)/W(s), track and field M(s)/W(s), volleyball W(s). ***Intramural sports:*** basketball M/W, football M, golf M, soccer M, volleyball W.

Campus security: 24-hour emergency response devices and patrols, student patrols, late-night transport/escort service, controlled dormitory access.

Student services: health clinic, personal/psychological counseling, women's center.

COSTS & FINANCIAL AID

Costs (2016–17) ***Tuition:*** state resident $3655 full-time, $457 per credit hour part-time; nonresident $16,113 full-time, $2014 per credit hour part-time. Part-time tuition and fees vary according to course load. ***Required fees:*** $2477 full-time, $510 per credit hour part-time. ***Room and board:*** $8271. Room and board charges vary according to board plan, housing facility, and location. ***Payment plan:*** installment. ***Waivers:*** employees or children of employees.

Financial Aid Of all full-time matriculated undergraduates who enrolled in 2014, 4,987 applied for aid, 4,684 were judged to have need, 222 had their need fully met. In 2014, 45 non-need-based awards were made. ***Average percent of need met:*** 58. ***Average financial aid package:*** $11,745. ***Average need-based loan:*** $4225. ***Average need-based gift aid:*** $7918. ***Average non-need-based aid:*** $13,302. ***Average indebtedness upon graduation:*** $35,017.

APPLYING

Standardized Tests *Required:* SAT or ACT (for admission).

Options: electronic application, deferred entrance.

Application fee: $40.

Required: high school transcript, minimum 2.5 GPA, University of North Carolina System minimum course requirements.

Application deadlines: 8/1 (freshmen), 8/1 (transfers).

Notification: continuous until 10/15 (freshmen), continuous until 10/15 (transfers).

CONTACT

Dr. Nicole Gibbs, Undergraduate Director of Admissions, North Carolina Central University, 1801 Fayetteville Street, McDougald House, Durham, NC 27707. *Phone:* 919-530-6298. *Toll-free phone:* 877-667-7533. *Fax:* 919-530-6326. *E-mail:* admissions@nccu.edu.

North Carolina State University

Raleigh, North Carolina

http://www.ncsu.edu/

- **State-supported** university, founded 1887, part of University of North Carolina System
- **Urban** 2100-acre campus with easy access to Raleigh-Durham
- **Endowment** $998.6 million
- **Coed** 23,847 undergraduate students, 88% full-time, 45% women, 55% men
- **Very difficult** entrance level, 46% of applicants were admitted

UNDERGRAD STUDENTS

20,934 full-time, 2,913 part-time. Students come from 52 states and territories; 107 other countries; 10% are from out of state; 6% Black or African American, non-Hispanic/Latino; 5% Hispanic/Latino; 6% Asian, non-Hispanic/Latino; 0.1% Native Hawaiian or other Pacific Islander, non-Hispanic/Latino; 0.4% American Indian or Alaska Native, non-Hispanic/Latino; 4% Two or more races, non-Hispanic/Latino; 3% Race/ethnicity unknown; 5% international; 5% transferred in; 41% live on campus.

Freshmen:

Admission: 25,929 applied, 12,034 admitted, 4,388 enrolled. ***Average high school GPA:*** 3.72. ***Test scores:*** SAT critical reading scores over 500: 96%; SAT math scores over 500: 99%; SAT writing scores over 500: 92%; ACT scores over 18: 100%; SAT critical reading scores over 600: 63%; SAT math scores over 600: 78%; SAT writing scores over 600: 45%; ACT scores over 24: 97%; SAT critical reading scores over 700: 14%; SAT math scores over 700: 22%; SAT writing scores over 700: 7%; ACT scores over 30: 42%.

Retention: 94% of full-time freshmen returned.

FACULTY

Total: 2,631, 86% full-time, 82% with terminal degrees.

Student/faculty ratio: 13:1.

ACADEMICS

Calendar: semesters. *Degrees:* associate, bachelor's, master's, doctoral, post-master's, and postbachelor's certificates.

Special study options: academic remediation for entering students, accelerated degree program, adult/continuing education programs, advanced placement credit, cooperative education, distance learning, double majors, English as a second language, honors programs, independent study, internships, off-campus study, part-time degree program, services for LD students, student-designed majors, study abroad, summer session for credit. ***ROTC:*** Army (b), Navy (b), Air Force (b).

Unusual degree programs: business administration; engineering; nursing with North Carolina Central University; agriculture, life sciences, physical sciences, communication, computer science, economics, foreign languages, history, mathematics, education, statistics, textiles.

Computers: 3,125 computers/terminals are available on campus for general student use. Students can access the following: campus intranet, computer help desk, free student e-mail accounts, online (class) grades, online (class) registration, online (class) schedules, online course materials, homework submission, testing/quizzes, financial aid/cashier's office account balances, blogging service, Web space, unlimited cloud storage, on site hardware and virus removal support. Campuswide network is available. 100% of college-owned or -operated housing units are wired for high-speed Internet access. Wireless service is available via entire campus.

Library: D. H. Hill Library plus 5 others. *Books:* 2.6 million (physical), 1.0 million (digital/electronic); *Serial titles:* 47,015 (physical), 56,658 (digital/electronic); *Databases:* 590. Weekly public service hours: 146; study areas open 24 hours, 5-7 days a week; students can reserve study rooms.

STUDENT LIFE

Housing options: on-campus residence required for freshman year; coed, men-only, women-only, special housing for students with disabilities. Campus housing is university owned. Freshman campus housing is guaranteed.

Activities and organizations: drama/theater group, student-run newspaper, radio and television station, choral group, marching band, Academic, Cultural, Leadership, Service and Philanthropy, Support and Outreach, national fraternities, national sororities.

Athletics Member NCAA. All Division I. ***Intercollegiate sports:*** baseball M(s), basketball M(s)/W(s), bowling M(c)/W(c), cheerleading M(s)/W(s), crew M(c)/W(c), cross-country running M(s)/W(s), equestrian sports M(c)/W(c), fencing M(c)/W(c), field hockey M(c)/W(c), football M(s), golf M(s)/W(s), gymnastics M(c)/W(s), ice hockey M(c), lacrosse M(c)/W(c), racquetball M(c)/W(c), riflery M(s)/W(s), rugby M(c)/W(c), sailing M(c)/W(c), skiing (downhill) M(c)/W(c), soccer M(s)/W(s), softball W(s), swimming and diving M(s)/W(s), table tennis M(c)/W(c), tennis M(s)/W(s), track and field M(s)/W(s), ultimate Frisbee M(c)/W(c), volleyball M(c)/W(s), water polo M(c)/W(c), wrestling M(s). ***Intramural sports:*** badminton M/W, basketball M/W, bowling M/W, football M/W, golf M/W, racquetball M/W, soccer M/W, softball M/W, swimming and diving M/W, table tennis M/W, tennis M/W, track and field M/W, ultimate Frisbee M/W, volleyball M/W.

Campus security: 24-hour emergency response devices and patrols, late-night transport/escort service, controlled dormitory access, mounted police.

Student services: health clinic, personal/psychological counseling, women's center, legal services.

COSTS & FINANCIAL AID

Costs (2017–18) ***Tuition:*** state resident $6535 full-time; nonresident $24,883 full-time. Full-time tuition and fees vary according to degree level, location, program, and reciprocity agreements. Part-time tuition and fees vary according to course load, degree level, location, program, and reciprocity agreements. No tuition increase for student's term of enrollment. ***Required fees:*** $2523 full-time. ***Room and board:*** $10,854; room only: $6618. Room and board charges vary according to board plan and housing facility. ***Payment plan:*** installment. ***Waivers:*** employees or children of employees.

Financial Aid Of all full-time matriculated undergraduates who enrolled in 2016, 13,940 applied for aid, 10,122 were judged to have need, 2,285 had their need fully met. 876 Federal Work-Study jobs (averaging $1645). 5,385 state and other part-time jobs (averaging $1910). In 2016, 1074 non-need-based awards were made. ***Average percent of need met:*** 77. ***Average financial aid package:*** $13,082. ***Average need-based loan:*** $3944. ***Average need-based gift aid:*** $10,004. ***Average non-need-based aid:*** $5995. ***Average indebtedness upon graduation:*** $21,507.

APPLYING

Standardized Tests *Required:* SAT or ACT (for admission).

Options: electronic application, early action, deferred entrance.

Application fee: $85.

Required: high school transcript. ***Required for some:*** interview. ***Recommended:*** essay or personal statement.

Application deadlines: 1/15 (freshmen), 2/15 (transfers), 10/15 (early action).

Notification: 3/30 (freshmen), 4/15 (transfers), 1/30 (early action).

CONTACT

Mr. Thomas Griffin, Director of Undergraduate Admissions, North Carolina State University, Box 7103, Raleigh, NC 27695. *Phone:* 919-515-2434. *Fax:* 919-515-5039. *E-mail:* undergrad-admissions@ncsu.edu.

North Carolina Wesleyan College

Rocky Mount, North Carolina

http://www.ncwc.edu/

- **Independent** 4-year, founded 1956, affiliated with United Methodist Church
- **Suburban** 200-acre campus
- **Endowment** $10.1 million
- **Coed** 2,092 undergraduate students, 85% full-time, 59% women, 41% men
- **Moderately difficult** entrance level, 62% of applicants were admitted

UNDERGRAD STUDENTS

1,787 full-time, 305 part-time. Students come from 23 states and territories; 34 other countries; 28% are from out of state; 44% Black or African American, non-Hispanic/Latino; 2% Hispanic/Latino; 0.8% Asian, non-Hispanic/Latino; 0.1% Native Hawaiian or other Pacific Islander, non-Hispanic/Latino; 1% American Indian or Alaska Native, non-Hispanic/Latino; 2% Two or more races, non-Hispanic/Latino; 13% Race/ethnicity unknown; 4% international; 3% transferred in; 59% live on campus.

Freshmen:

Admission: 4,038 applied, 2,486 admitted, 327 enrolled. ***Average high school GPA:*** 3.25. ***Test scores:*** SAT critical reading scores over 500: 26%; SAT math scores over 500: 34%; ACT scores over 18: 58%; SAT critical reading scores over 600: 3%; SAT math scores over 600: 11%; ACT scores over 24: 22%; SAT critical reading scores over 700: 1%; SAT math scores over 700: 1%; ACT scores over 30: 1%.

Retention: 54% of full-time freshmen returned.

FACULTY

Total: 277, 20% full-time.

Student/faculty ratio: 15:1.

ACADEMICS

Calendar: semesters. *Degrees:* bachelor's (also offers adult part-time degree program with significant enrollment not reflected in profile).

Special study options: academic remediation for entering students, accelerated degree program, adult/continuing education programs, advanced placement credit, cooperative education, distance learning, double majors, honors programs, independent study, internships, part-time degree program, services for LD students, summer session for credit. ***ROTC:*** Army (c).

Computers: 223 computers/terminals are available on campus for general student use. Students can access the following: campus intranet, computer help desk, free student e-mail accounts, online (class) grades, online (class) schedules. Campuswide network is available. Wireless service is available via entire campus.

Library: Elizabeth Braswell Pearsall Library. *Books:* 78,800 (physical), 44,751 (digital/electronic); *Serial titles:* 4,326 (physical), 4,329 (digital/electronic); *Databases:* 86. Students can reserve study rooms.

STUDENT LIFE

Housing options: on-campus residence required through sophomore year; coed, men-only, women-only, special housing for students with disabilities. Campus housing is university owned. Freshman campus housing is guaranteed.

Activities and organizations: drama/theater group, student-run newspaper, choral group, marching band, Refuge Campus Ministry, NCWC Cheerleaders, Voices of Triumph, Campus Crusade for Christ, Visions of Beauty, national fraternities, national sororities.

Athletics Member NCAA. All Division III. ***Intercollegiate sports:*** baseball M, basketball M/W, cheerleading M/W, cross-country running W, football M, golf M, lacrosse W, soccer M/W, softball W, tennis M/W, volleyball W. ***Intramural sports:*** basketball M/W, football M/W, lacrosse M/W, softball M/W, table tennis M/W, tennis M/W, volleyball M/W.

Campus security: 24-hour emergency response devices and patrols, late-night transport/escort service, controlled dormitory access.

Student services: health clinic, personal/psychological counseling.

COSTS & FINANCIAL AID

Costs (2017–18) ***Comprehensive fee:*** $40,200 includes full-time tuition ($29,750), mandatory fees ($400), and room and board ($10,050). Full-time tuition and fees vary according to location. Part-time tuition: $500 per semester hour. Part-time tuition and fees vary according to course load and location. ***College room only:*** $4650. Room and board charges vary according to housing facility. ***Payment plan:*** installment. ***Waivers:*** employees or children of employees.

Financial Aid Of all full-time matriculated undergraduates who enrolled in 2008, 956 applied for aid, 788 were judged to have need, 360 had their need fully met. 323 Federal Work-Study jobs (averaging $1438). 67 state and other part-time jobs (averaging $565). In 2008, 46 non-need-based awards were made. ***Average percent of need met:*** 70. ***Average financial aid package:*** $12,524. ***Average need-based loan:*** $3898. ***Average need-based gift aid:*** $6696. ***Average non-need-based aid:*** $7876. ***Average indebtedness upon graduation:*** $7269.

APPLYING

Standardized Tests *Required:* SAT or ACT (for admission).

Options: electronic application.

Required: high school transcript. ***Required for some:*** essay or personal statement, interview. ***Recommended:*** minimum 2.0 GPA, 2 letters of recommendation, interview.

Application deadlines: rolling (freshmen), 7/15 (transfers).

Notification: continuous (freshmen), continuous (transfers).

CONTACT

Mr. Ben Lilley, Assistant Director of Admissions, North Carolina Wesleyan College, 3400 North Wesleyan Boulevard, Rocky Mount, NC 27804. *Phone:* 252-985-5113. *Toll-free phone:* 800-488-6292. *Fax:* 252-985-5295. *E-mail:* blilley@ncwc.edu.

Pfeiffer University

Misenheimer, North Carolina

http://www.pfeiffer.edu/

CONTACT

Ms. Diane Martin, Associate Director of Admissions, Pfeiffer University, PO Box 960, Highway 52 North, Misenheimer, NC 28109. *Phone:* 704-463-3052. *Toll-free phone:* 800-338-2060. *Fax:* 704-463-1363. *E-mail:* admiss@pfeiffer.edu.

Piedmont International University

Winston-Salem, North Carolina

http://www.piedmontu.edu/

- **Independent Baptist** comprehensive, founded 1947
- **Urban** 12-acre campus
- **Coed** 197 undergraduate students, 76% full-time, 42% women, 58% men
- **Noncompetitive** entrance level, 49% of applicants were admitted

UNDERGRAD STUDENTS

149 full-time, 48 part-time. Students come from 17 states and territories; 2 other countries; 30% are from out of state; 11% Black or African American, non-Hispanic/Latino; 2% Hispanic/Latino; 0.5% Native Hawaiian or other Pacific Islander, non-Hispanic/Latino; 0.5% Race/ethnicity unknown; 1% international; 10% transferred in; 12% live on campus.

Freshmen:

Admission: 85 applied, 42 admitted, 33 enrolled. ***Average high school GPA:*** 3. ***Test scores:*** SAT critical reading scores over 500: 36%; SAT math scores over 500: 30%; SAT critical reading scores over 600: 13%; SAT math scores over 600: 1%; SAT critical reading scores over 700: 1%.

Retention: 58% of full-time freshmen returned.

FACULTY

Student/faculty ratio: 10:1.

ACADEMICS

Calendar: semesters. *Degrees:* certificates, associate, bachelor's, master's, and doctoral.

Special study options: academic remediation for entering students, adult/continuing education programs, advanced placement credit, distance learning, double majors, internships, part-time degree program, study abroad, summer session for credit.

Computers: 20 computers/terminals are available on campus for general student use. Students can access the following: campus intranet, computer help desk, free student e-mail accounts, online (class) grades, online (class) registration, online (class) schedules. Campuswide network is available. Wireless service is available via entire campus.

Library: George Manuel Memorial Library.

STUDENT LIFE

Housing options: on-campus residence required through sophomore year; men-only, women-only. Campus housing is university owned.

Activities and organizations: drama/theater group, choral group.

Athletics Member NCCAA. ***Intercollegiate sports:*** basketball M, volleyball W. ***Intramural sports:*** soccer M/W, table tennis M/W.

Campus security: 24-hour emergency response devices, student patrols, late-night transport/escort service, controlled dormitory access, security guards on duty from dusk until dawn.

COSTS & FINANCIAL AID

Costs (2017–18) ***Comprehensive fee:*** $17,285 includes full-time tuition ($9300), mandatory fees ($800), and room and board ($7185). Full-time tuition and fees vary according to program. Part-time tuition: $325 per credit hour. Part-time tuition and fees vary according to program. ***Required fees:*** $60 per course part-time, $100 per term part-time. ***Room and board:*** Room and board charges vary according to board plan. ***Payment plan:*** installment. ***Waivers:*** employees or children of employees.

Financial Aid Of all full-time matriculated undergraduates who enrolled in 2016, 174 applied for aid, 161 were judged to have need, 6 had their need fully met. In 2016, 12 non-need-based awards were made. ***Average percent of need met:*** 42. ***Average financial aid package:*** $9317. ***Average need-based loan:*** $4283. ***Average need-based gift aid:*** $6843. ***Average non-need-based aid:*** $4605. ***Average indebtedness upon graduation:*** $19,784.

APPLYING

Standardized Tests *Required:* SAT or ACT (for admission).

Options: electronic application.

Application fee: $55.

Required: essay or personal statement, high school transcript, 2 letters of recommendation, medical history, proof of immunization. ***Recommended:*** minimum 2.0 GPA, interview.

Application deadlines: rolling (freshmen), rolling (transfers).

Notification: continuous (transfers).

CONTACT

Mr. Joe Edgerton, Undergraduate Admissions Counselor, Piedmont International University, 420 South Broad Street, Winston-Salem, NC 27101. *Phone:* 336-714-7933. *Toll-free phone:* 800-937-5097. *Fax:* 336-725-5522. *E-mail:* stevensons@piedmontU.edu.

Queens University of Charlotte

Charlotte, North Carolina

http://www.queens.edu/

- **Independent Presbyterian** comprehensive, founded 1857
- **Urban** 95-acre campus with easy access to Charlotte, NC
- **Endowment** $91.2 million
- **Coed**
- **Moderately difficult** entrance level

FACULTY

Student/faculty ratio: 9:1.

ACADEMICS

Calendar: semesters. *Degrees:* bachelor's, master's, and postbachelor's certificates.

Library: Everett Library. *Books:* 41,620 (physical), 228,153 (digital/electronic); *Serial titles:* 106 (physical), 19,724 (digital/electronic); *Databases:* 81. Weekly public service hours: 93; students can reserve study rooms.

STUDENT LIFE

Housing options: on-campus residence required through junior year; coed, special housing for students with disabilities. Campus housing is university owned. Freshman campus housing is guaranteed.

Activities and organizations: drama/theater group, student-run newspaper, radio station, choral group, Senate, College Union Board, Royal Ambassadors, Students for Black Awareness, International Club, national fraternities, national sororities.

Athletics Member NCAA. All Division II.

Campus security: 24-hour emergency response devices and patrols, late-night transport/escort service, controlled dormitory access, Emergency Alert System.

Student services: health clinic, personal/psychological counseling.

COSTS & FINANCIAL AID

Costs (2016–17) ***Comprehensive fee:*** $44,046 includes full-time tuition ($31,360), mandatory fees ($1200), and room and board ($11,486). Full-time tuition and fees vary according to course load, program, and student level. Part-time tuition and fees vary according to course load and program. ***Room and board:*** Room and board charges vary according to board plan and housing facility.

Financial Aid Of all full-time matriculated undergraduates who enrolled in 2015, 1,012 applied for aid, 875 were judged to have need, 177 had their need fully met. In 2015, 394 non-need-based awards were made. ***Average percent of need met:*** 66. ***Average financial aid package:*** $21,349. ***Average need-based loan:*** $4267. ***Average need-based gift aid:*** $17,769. ***Average non-need-based aid:*** $12,303.

APPLYING
Standardized Tests *Required:* SAT or ACT (for admission).

Options: electronic application, early action, deferred entrance.

Required: essay or personal statement, high school transcript, 1 letter of recommendation. ***Required for some:*** interview.

CONTACT
Evan Sprinkle, Senior Assistant Director, Queens University of Charlotte, 1900 Selwyn Avenue, Harris Welcome Center - MSC 1428, Charlotte, NC 28274. *Phone:* 704-337-2212. *Toll-free phone:* 800-849-0202. *Fax:* 704-337-2403. *E-mail:* admissions@queens.edu.

St. Andrews University
Laurinburg, North Carolina
http://www.sa.edu/

- **Independent Presbyterian** comprehensive, founded 1958
- **Small-town** 600-acre campus
- **Coed** 688 undergraduate students, 94% full-time, 29% women, 71% men
- **Moderately difficult** entrance level, 53% of applicants were admitted

UNDERGRAD STUDENTS
649 full-time, 39 part-time. 10% are from out of state; 23% Black or African American, non-Hispanic/Latino; 12% Hispanic/Latino; 0.1% Asian, non-Hispanic/Latino; 0.1% Native Hawaiian or other Pacific Islander, non-Hispanic/Latino; 0.4% American Indian or Alaska Native, non-Hispanic/Latino; 0.9% Two or more races, non-Hispanic/Latino; 2% Race/ethnicity unknown; 25% international; 10% transferred in.

Freshmen:
Admission: 739 applied, 389 admitted, 182 enrolled. ***Average high school GPA:*** 2.83. ***Test scores:*** SAT critical reading scores over 500: 23%; SAT math scores over 500: 36%; ACT scores over 18: 73%; SAT critical reading scores over 600: 4%; SAT math scores over 600: 13%; ACT scores over 24: 7%; SAT math scores over 700: 1%.

Retention: 57% of full-time freshmen returned.

FACULTY
Total: 47, 45% full-time, 47% with terminal degrees.

Student/faculty ratio: 24:1.

ACADEMICS
Calendar: semesters. *Degrees:* diplomas, bachelor's, and master's.

Special study options: adult/continuing education programs, part-time degree program.

Unusual degree programs: 3-2 engineering with North Carolina State University, St. Andrews University.

Computers: Students can access the following: campus intranet, computer help desk, free student e-mail accounts. Campuswide network is available. Wireless service is available via classrooms, libraries, student centers.

Library: DeTamble Library.

STUDENT LIFE
Housing options: on-campus residence required through senior year; coed, men-only, women-only. Campus housing is university owned.

Athletics Member NCAA, NAIA. All NCAA Division II. ***Intercollegiate sports:*** baseball M(s), basketball M(s)/W(s), cross-country running M(s)/W(s), equestrian sports M(s)/W(s), golf M(s)/W(s), lacrosse M(s)/W(s), soccer M(s)/W(s), softball W(s), wrestling M. ***Intramural sports:*** basketball M/W, football M/W, rugby M(c)/W(c), softball M/W, table tennis M/W, volleyball M/W.

Campus security: 24-hour emergency response devices and patrols, late-night transport/escort service.

COSTS & FINANCIAL AID
Costs (2016–17) ***Comprehensive fee:*** $35,270 includes full-time tuition ($24,874) and room and board ($10,396). Full-time tuition and fees vary according to course load and location. Part-time tuition: $280 per credit hour. Part-time tuition and fees vary according to location. ***Room and board:*** Room and board charges vary according to housing facility. ***Payment plan:*** installment. ***Waivers:*** adult students, senior citizens, and employees or children of employees.

Financial Aid Of all full-time matriculated undergraduates who enrolled in 2014, 461 applied for aid, 420 were judged to have need, 40 had their need fully met. In 2014, 98 non-need-based awards were made. ***Average percent of need met:*** 68. ***Average financial aid package:*** $20,974. ***Average need-based loan:*** $4649. ***Average need-based gift aid:*** $17,250. ***Average non-need-based aid:*** $9371. ***Average indebtedness upon graduation:*** $24,221.

APPLYING
Standardized Tests *Required:* SAT or ACT (for admission).

Options: electronic application, deferred entrance.

Application fee: $35.

Required: high school transcript. ***Required for some:*** essay or personal statement, interview. ***Recommended:*** minimum 2.0 GPA.

CONTACT
Erin Balduf, Director of Admissions, St. Andrews University, 1700 Dogwood Mile, Laurinburg, NC 28352. *Phone:* 910-277-5555. *Toll-free phone:* 800-763-0198. *Fax:* 910-277-5087. *E-mail:* admission@sapc.edu.

Saint Augustine's University
Raleigh, North Carolina
http://www.st-aug.edu/

- **Independent Episcopal** 4-year, founded 1867
- **Urban** 122-acre campus
- **Coed** 944 undergraduate students, 97% full-time, 46% women, 54% men
- **Moderately difficult** entrance level, 71% of applicants were admitted

UNDERGRAD STUDENTS
920 full-time, 24 part-time. Students come from 13 states and territories; 3 other countries; 338% are from out of state; 89% Black or African American, non-Hispanic/Latino; 1% Hispanic/Latino; 0.1% Asian, non-Hispanic/Latino; 0.6% American Indian or Alaska Native, non-Hispanic/Latino; 6% Race/ethnicity unknown; 1% international; 8% transferred in; 76% live on campus.

Freshmen:
Admission: 4,040 applied, 2,853 admitted, 347 enrolled.
Retention: 55% of full-time freshmen returned.

FACULTY
Total: 96, 61% full-time, 44% with terminal degrees.

Student/faculty ratio: 13:1.

ACADEMICS
Calendar: semesters. *Degree:* bachelor's.

Special study options: accelerated degree program, adult/continuing education programs, advanced placement credit, cooperative education, double majors, freshman honors college, honors programs, independent study, internships, off-campus study, part-time degree program, services for LD students, study abroad, summer session for credit. ***ROTC:*** Army (b), Air Force (c).

Computers: 183 computers/terminals and 1,670 ports are available on campus for general student use. Students can access the following: campus intranet, computer help desk, free student e-mail accounts, online (class) grades, online (class) registration, online (class) schedules. Campuswide network is available. 100% of college-owned or -operated housing units are wired for high-speed Internet access. Wireless service is available via entire campus.

Library: Prezell R. Robinson Library. Students can reserve study rooms.

STUDENT LIFE
Housing options: on-campus residence required through sophomore year; men-only, women-only. Campus housing is university owned and leased by the school. Freshman campus housing is guaranteed.

Activities and organizations: drama/theater group, student-run newspaper, radio and television station, choral group, marching band, Campus Activity Board, Christian Fellowship Organization, Collegiate 100 Black Men of America, Student Government Association/Student

Leaders, Falcon Fanatic Pep Squad, national fraternities, national sororities.

Athletics Member NCAA. All Division II. ***Intercollegiate sports:*** baseball M(s), basketball M(s)/W(s), bowling W(s), cheerleading W(s), cross-country running M(s)/W(s), football M(s), golf M(s), softball W(s), track and field M(s)/W(s), volleyball W(s).

Campus security: 24-hour emergency response devices and patrols, RAVE: Emergency Notification System.

Student services: health clinic, personal/psychological counseling, women's center.

COSTS & FINANCIAL AID

Costs (2017–18) ***Comprehensive fee:*** $25,582 includes full-time tuition ($12,890), mandatory fees ($5000), and room and board ($7692). Full-time tuition and fees vary according to course load. Part-time tuition: $537 per credit hour. Part-time tuition and fees vary according to course load. ***Required fees:*** $208 per credit hour part-time. ***College room only:*** $3182. Room and board charges vary according to housing facility. ***Payment plan:*** deferred payment. ***Waivers:*** children of alumni and employees or children of employees.

Financial Aid ***Average indebtedness upon graduation:*** $19,500.

APPLYING

Standardized Tests *Required:* SAT or ACT (for admission).

Options: electronic application, deferred entrance.

Application fee: $50.

Required: high school transcript, minimum 2.0 GPA, 2 letters of recommendation, medical history, background check. ***Required for some:*** essay or personal statement, interview. ***Recommended:*** minimum 2.5 GPA.

Application deadlines: rolling (freshmen), rolling (transfers).

Notification: continuous (freshmen), continuous (transfers).

CONTACT

Mr. Chris J. Withers, Director of Admissions, Saint Augustine's University, 1315 Oakwood Avenue, Raleigh, NC 27610-2298. *Phone:* 919-516-4012. *Toll-free phone:* 800-948-1126. *Fax:* 919-516-5804. *E-mail:* jesousa@st-aug.edu.

Salem College

Winston-Salem, North Carolina

http://www.salem.edu/

- **Independent Moravian** comprehensive, founded 1772
- **Urban** 69-acre campus with easy access to Charlotte
- **Coed, primarily women**
- **Moderately difficult** entrance level

FACULTY

Student/faculty ratio: 10:1.

ACADEMICS

Calendar: 4-1-4. *Degrees:* certificates, bachelor's, and master's (only students age 23 or over are eligible to enroll part-time).

Library: Dale H. Gramley Library plus 2 others. *Books:* 119,591 (physical), 110,764 (digital/electronic); *Databases:* 123.

STUDENT LIFE

Housing options: on-campus residence required through senior year; women-only. Campus housing is university owned. Freshman campus housing is guaranteed.

Activities and organizations: drama/theater group, student-run newspaper, choral group, marching band.

Athletics Member NCAA. All Division III.

Campus security: 24-hour emergency response devices and patrols, late-night transport/escort service, controlled dormitory access.

Student services: health clinic, personal/psychological counseling.

COSTS

Costs (2016–17) ***Comprehensive fee:*** $38,906 includes full-time tuition ($27,040), mandatory fees ($366), and room and board ($11,500). Part-time tuition: $390 per semester hour. ***Required fees:*** $150 per year part-time. ***College room only:*** $5900. Room and board charges vary according to housing facility.

APPLYING

Standardized Tests *Required:* SAT or ACT (for admission).

Options: electronic application, early admission, deferred entrance.

Application fee: $30.

Required: essay or personal statement, high school transcript. ***Recommended:*** interview.

CONTACT

Dean Katherine Knapp Watts, Dean of Admissions and Financial Aid, Salem College, Single Sisters House, 601 South Church Street, Winston-Salem, NC 27101. *Phone:* 336-721-2621. *Toll-free phone:* 800-327-2536. *Fax:* 336-917-5572. *E-mail:* admissions@salem.edu.

Shaw University

Raleigh, North Carolina

http://www.shawu.edu/

- **Independent Baptist** comprehensive, founded 1865
- **Urban** 30-acre campus
- **Coed** 1,713 undergraduate students, 94% full-time, 57% women, 43% men
- **Minimally difficult** entrance level, 49% of applicants were admitted

UNDERGRAD STUDENTS

1,604 full-time, 109 part-time. Students come from 34 states and territories; 15 other countries; 32% are from out of state; 66% Black or African American, non-Hispanic/Latino; 0.3% Hispanic/Latino; 0.2% Asian, non-Hispanic/Latino; 0.3% Native Hawaiian or other Pacific Islander, non-Hispanic/Latino; 0.2% American Indian or Alaska Native, non-Hispanic/Latino; 2% Two or more races, non-Hispanic/Latino; 28% Race/ethnicity unknown; 2% international; 4% transferred in; 58% live on campus.

Freshmen:

Admission: 9,605 applied, 4,692 admitted, 640 enrolled. ***Average high school GPA:*** 2.53.

Retention: 49% of full-time freshmen returned.

FACULTY

Total: 137, 61% full-time.

Student/faculty ratio: 19:1.

ACADEMICS

Calendar: semesters. *Degrees:* certificates, bachelor's, and master's.

Special study options: academic remediation for entering students, accelerated degree program, adult/continuing education programs, advanced placement credit, distance learning, double majors, honors programs, independent study, internships, off-campus study, part-time degree program, services for LD students, student-designed majors, study abroad, summer session for credit. ***ROTC:*** Army (c), Air Force (c).

Computers: Students can access the following: computer help desk, free student e-mail accounts, online (class) grades, online (class) registration, online (class) schedules. Campuswide network is available. Wireless service is available via classrooms, computer centers, computer labs, learning centers, libraries, student centers.

Library: James E. Cheek Learning Resources Center.

STUDENT LIFE

Housing options: on-campus residence required for freshman year; men-only, women-only. Campus housing is university owned. Freshman applicants given priority for college housing.

Activities and organizations: drama/theater group, student-run newspaper, radio station, choral group, marching band, Student Government Association, choir, University band, Shaw Players, academic clubs, national fraternities, national sororities.

Athletics Member NCAA. All Division II. ***Intercollegiate sports:*** basketball M(s)/W(s), bowling W(s), cross-country running M(s)/W(s), football M(s), softball W(s), tennis M(s)/W(s), track and field M(s)/W(s), volleyball W(s). ***Intramural sports:*** basketball M/W, football M, tennis M/W, volleyball M/W.

Campus security: 24-hour emergency response devices and patrols, late-night transport/escort service, 24-hour electronic surveillance cameras.

Student services: health clinic, personal/psychological counseling.

COSTS & FINANCIAL AID
Costs (2016–17) ***Comprehensive fee:*** $24,638 includes full-time tuition ($11,808), mandatory fees ($4672), and room and board ($8158). Part-time tuition: $492 per credit hour. ***College room only:*** $3842. ***Payment plans:*** installment, deferred payment. ***Waivers:*** employees or children of employees.

Financial Aid Of all full-time matriculated undergraduates who enrolled in 2005, 2,197 applied for aid, 2,068 were judged to have need, 201 had their need fully met. 347 Federal Work-Study jobs (averaging $1120). In 2005, 117 non-need-based awards were made. ***Average percent of need met:*** 63. ***Average financial aid package:*** $8992. ***Average need-based loan:*** $3394. ***Average need-based gift aid:*** $5898. ***Average non-need-based aid:*** $9333. ***Average indebtedness upon graduation:*** $15,982. ***Financial aid deadline:*** 6/1.

APPLYING
Standardized Tests *Required:* SAT or ACT (for admission).

Options: electronic application, early admission, deferred entrance.

Application fee: $25.

Required: high school transcript, minimum 2.0 GPA.

Application deadlines: 7/30 (freshmen), 7/30 (transfers).

Notification: continuous (freshmen), continuous (transfers).

CONTACT
Ms. Stacey Sowell, Director of Admissions and Recruitment, Shaw University, 118 East South Street, Raleigh, NC 27601-2399. *Phone:* 919-546-8275/8276. *Toll-free phone:* 800-214-6683. *Fax:* 919-546-8271. *E-mail:* ssowell@shawu.edu.

Southeastern Baptist Theological Seminary

Wake Forest, North Carolina

http://www.sebts.edu/

- **Independent Southern Baptist** comprehensive, founded 1950
- **Suburban** 300-acre campus with easy access to Raleigh
- **Coed** 414 undergraduate students, 57% full-time, 33% women, 67% men
- **Noncompetitive** entrance level, 76% of applicants were admitted

UNDERGRAD STUDENTS
236 full-time, 178 part-time. Students come from 52 states and territories; 30 other countries; 66% are from out of state; 5% Black or African American, non-Hispanic/Latino; 3% Hispanic/Latino; 3% Asian, non-Hispanic/Latino; 0.2% American Indian or Alaska Native, non-Hispanic/Latino; 3% Race/ethnicity unknown; 0.2% international; 9% transferred in.

Freshmen:
Admission: 46 applied, 35 admitted, 37 enrolled.
Retention: 79% of full-time freshmen returned.

FACULTY
Total: 119, 54% full-time, 71% with terminal degrees.
Student/faculty ratio: 15:1.

ACADEMICS
Calendar: semesters. *Degrees:* certificates, associate, bachelor's, master's, and doctoral.

Special study options: academic remediation for entering students, adult/continuing education programs, distance learning, double majors, independent study, internships, off-campus study, part-time degree program, summer session for credit.

Computers: 55 computers/terminals and 1,100 ports are available on campus for general student use. Students can access the following: campus intranet, free student e-mail accounts, online (class) grades, online (class) registration, online (class) schedules. Campuswide network is available. Wireless service is available via classrooms, libraries, student centers.

Library: The Library at Southeastern plus 1 other. *Books:* 195,926 (physical), 135,058 (digital/electronic); *Databases:* 5. Weekly public service hours: 71; students can reserve study rooms.

STUDENT LIFE
Housing options: on-campus residence required for freshman year; men-only, women-only. Campus housing is university owned and leased by the school. Freshman applicants given priority for college housing.

Activities and organizations: drama/theater group, choral group.

Athletics ***Intramural sports:*** basketball M/W, football M/W, golf M/W, racquetball M/W, table tennis M/W, ultimate Frisbee M/W, volleyball M/W.

Campus security: 24-hour emergency response devices and patrols, late-night transport/escort service.

Student services: health clinic, personal/psychological counseling, women's center.

COSTS
Costs (2016–17) ***Tuition:*** $9960 full-time, $332 per credit hour part-time. Full-time tuition and fees vary according to degree level, location, and program. Part-time tuition and fees vary according to degree level, location, and program. ***Required fees:*** $568 full-time, $540 per term part-time. ***Room only:*** $2196. Room and board charges vary according to housing facility. ***Payment plan:*** installment.

APPLYING
Standardized Tests *Required:* SAT or ACT (for admission).

Options: electronic application.

Application fee: $40.

Required: essay or personal statement, high school transcript, minimum 2.0 GPA, 3 letters of recommendation.

Application deadlines: 7/20 (freshmen), 7/20 (transfers).

Notification: continuous until 8/20 (freshmen), continuous until 8/20 (transfers).

CONTACT
Mr. Sean Robinson, Admissions Counselor, Southeastern Baptist Theological Seminary, PO Box 1889, Wake Forest, NC 27588-1889. *Phone:* 919-761-2281. *Toll-free phone:* 800-284-6317.

South University

High Point, North Carolina

http://www.southuniversity.edu/high-point.aspx

CONTACT
South University, 3975 Premier Drive, High Point, NC 27265. *Phone:* 336-812-7200. *Toll-free phone:* 855-268-2187.

Strayer University–Greensboro Campus

Greensboro, North Carolina

http://www.strayer.edu/north-carolina/greensboro/

CONTACT
Strayer University–Greensboro Campus, 4900 Koger Boulevard, Suite 400, Greensboro, NC 27407.

Strayer University–Huntersville Campus

Huntersville, North Carolina

http://www.strayer.edu/north-carolina/huntersville/

CONTACT
Strayer University–Huntersville Campus, 13620 Reese Boulevard, Suite 130, Huntersville, NC 28078.

Strayer University–North Charlotte Campus

Concord, North Carolina

http://www.strayer.edu/north-carolina/north-charlotte/

CONTACT
Strayer University–North Charlotte Campus, 7870 Commons Park Circle NW, Concord, NC 28027.

Strayer University–North Raleigh Campus

Raleigh, North Carolina

http://www.strayer.edu/north-carolina/north-raleigh/

CONTACT
Strayer University–North Raleigh Campus, 8701 Wadford Drive, Raleigh, NC 27616.

Strayer University–RTP Campus

Morrisville, North Carolina

http://www.strayer.edu/north-carolina/rtp/

CONTACT
Strayer University–RTP Campus, 4 Copley Parkway, Morrisville, NC 27560.

Strayer University–South Charlotte Campus

Charlotte, North Carolina

http://www.strayer.edu/north-carolina/south-charlotte/

CONTACT
Strayer University–South Charlotte Campus, 9101 Kings Parade Boulevard, Suite 200, Charlotte, NC 28273.

Strayer University–South Raleigh Campus

Raleigh, North Carolina

http://www.strayer.edu/north-carolina/south-raleigh/

CONTACT
Strayer University–South Raleigh Campus, 3421 Olympia Drive, Raleigh, NC 27603.

University of Mount Olive

Mount Olive, North Carolina

http://www.umo.edu/

CONTACT
University of Mount Olive, 634 Henderson Street, Mount Olive, NC 28365. *Phone:* 919-658-2502 Ext. 3009. *Toll-free phone:* 800-653-0854.

University of North Carolina at Asheville

Asheville, North Carolina

http://www.unca.edu/

- **State-supported** comprehensive, founded 1927, part of University of North Carolina System
- **Urban** 365-acre campus
- **Endowment** $40.5 million
- **Coed** 3,806 undergraduate students, 85% full-time, 58% women, 42% men
- **Moderately difficult** entrance level, 78% of applicants were admitted

UNDERGRAD STUDENTS
3,227 full-time, 579 part-time. Students come from 39 states and territories; 20 other countries; 11% are from out of state; 4% Black or African American, non-Hispanic/Latino; 6% Hispanic/Latino; 2% Asian, non-Hispanic/Latino; 0.7% American Indian or Alaska Native, non-Hispanic/Latino; 4% Two or more races, non-Hispanic/Latino; 4% Race/ethnicity unknown; 1% international; 8% transferred in; 38% live on campus.

Freshmen:
Admission: 3,433 applied, 2,676 admitted, 666 enrolled. ***Average high school GPA:*** 3.48. ***Test scores:*** SAT critical reading scores over 500: 84%; SAT math scores over 500: 81%; SAT writing scores over 500: 71%; ACT scores over 18: 100%; SAT critical reading scores over 600: 42%; SAT math scores over 600: 32%; SAT writing scores over 600: 24%; ACT scores over 24: 68%; SAT critical reading scores over 700: 8%; SAT math scores over 700: 3%; SAT writing scores over 700: 4%; ACT scores over 30: 14%.
Retention: 78% of full-time freshmen returned.

FACULTY
Total: 333, 67% full-time, 73% with terminal degrees.
Student/faculty ratio: 13:1.

ACADEMICS
Calendar: semesters. *Degrees:* bachelor's, master's, and postbachelor's certificates.
Special study options: adult/continuing education programs, advanced placement credit, cooperative education, distance learning, double majors, honors programs, independent study, internships, off-campus study, part-time degree program, services for LD students, student-designed majors, study abroad, summer session for credit.
Computers: 477 computers/terminals are available on campus for general student use. Students can access the following: campus intranet, computer help desk, free student e-mail accounts, online (class) grades, online (class) registration, online (class) schedules. Campuswide network is available. 100% of college-owned or -operated housing units are wired for high-speed Internet access. Wireless service is available via classrooms, computer centers, computer labs, dorm rooms, learning centers, libraries, student centers.
Library: D. Hiden Ramsey Library. *Books:* 282,040 (physical), 539,250 (digital/electronic); *Serial titles:* 187 (physical), 48,748 (digital/electronic); *Databases:* 138. Students can reserve study rooms.

STUDENT LIFE
Housing options: on-campus residence required for freshman year; coed, special housing for students with disabilities. Campus housing is university owned. Freshman campus housing is guaranteed.
Activities and organizations: drama/theater group, student-run newspaper, radio station, choral group, Student Government Association, Alliance, Black Student Association, Gaming Club, Bulldog Nation, national fraternities, national sororities.
Athletics Member NCAA. All Division I. ***Intercollegiate sports:*** archery M(c)/W(c), baseball M(s), basketball M(s)/W(s), cross-country running M(s)/W(s), equestrian sports M(c)/W(c), fencing M(c)/W(c), golf W(s), rugby M(c)/W(c), soccer M(s)/W(s), swimming and diving W(s), tennis M(s)/W(s), track and field M(s)/W(s), volleyball W(s). ***Intramural sports:*** badminton M/W, basketball M/W, football M(c)/W(c), racquetball M/W, soccer M/W, ultimate Frisbee M(c)/W(c), volleyball M/W, water polo M/W.
Campus security: 24-hour emergency response devices and patrols, late-night transport/escort service, controlled dormitory access.
Student services: health clinic, personal/psychological counseling.

COSTS & FINANCIAL AID
Costs (2016–17) ***One-time required fee:*** $150. ***Tuition:*** state resident $4041 full-time, $168 per credit hour part-time; nonresident $20,436 full-time, $852 per credit hour part-time. Full-time tuition and fees vary according to course load and degree level. Part-time tuition and fees vary according to course load and degree level. ***Required fees:*** $2936 full-time, $122 per credit hour part-time. ***Room and board:*** $8746; room only: $4890. Room and board charges vary according to board plan and housing facility. ***Payment plans:*** installment, deferred payment. ***Waivers:*** employees or children of employees.

Financial Aid Of all full-time matriculated undergraduates who enrolled in 2015, 2,529 applied for aid, 1,842 were judged to have need, 496 had their need fully met. 53 Federal Work-Study jobs (averaging $2700). 1,892 state and other part-time jobs (averaging $1135). In 2015, 226 non-need-based awards were made. ***Average percent of need met:*** 76. ***Average financial aid package:*** $11,998. ***Average need-based loan:*** $4445. ***Average need-based gift aid:*** $6778. ***Average non-need-based aid:*** $2434. ***Average indebtedness upon graduation:*** $22,026.

APPLYING

Standardized Tests *Required:* SAT or ACT (for admission).

Options: electronic application, early action, deferred entrance.

Application fee: $75.

Required: essay or personal statement, high school transcript, 1 letter of recommendation, minimum course requirement.

Application deadlines: 2/15 (freshmen), 4/15 (transfers), 11/15 (early action).

Notification: continuous until 12/15 (freshmen), continuous (transfers), 12/15 (early action).

CONTACT

Pat McClellan, Associate Provost for Admissions and Financial Aid, University of North Carolina at Asheville, Brown Hall, CPO # 1320, Asheville, NC 28804-8510. *Phone:* 828-251-6481. *Toll-free phone:* 800-531-9842. *Fax:* 828-251-6482. *E-mail:* admissions@unca.edu.

The University of North Carolina at Chapel Hill

Chapel Hill, North Carolina

http://www.unc.edu/

- **State-supported** university, founded 1789, part of University of North Carolina System
- **Suburban** 729-acre campus with easy access to Raleigh-Durham
- **Endowment** $2.6 billion
- **Coed** 18,523 undergraduate students, 96% full-time, 58% women, 42% men
- **Very difficult** entrance level, 27% of applicants were admitted

UNDERGRAD STUDENTS

17,869 full-time, 654 part-time. Students come from 53 states and territories; 93 other countries; 17% are from out of state; 8% Black or African American, non-Hispanic/Latino; 8% Hispanic/Latino; 10% Asian, non-Hispanic/Latino; 0.1% Native Hawaiian or other Pacific Islander, non-Hispanic/Latino; 0.5% American Indian or Alaska Native, non-Hispanic/Latino; 4% Two or more races, non-Hispanic/Latino; 4% Race/ethnicity unknown; 3% international; 4% transferred in; 51% live on campus.

Freshmen:

Admission: 34,889 applied, 9,400 admitted, 4,228 enrolled. ***Average high school GPA:*** 4.66. ***Test scores:*** SAT critical reading scores over 500: 97%; SAT math scores over 500: 98%; SAT writing scores over 500: 94%; ACT scores over 18: 100%; SAT critical reading scores over 600: 75%; SAT math scores over 600: 78%; SAT writing scores over 600: 68%; ACT scores over 24: 93%; SAT critical reading scores over 700: 26%; SAT math scores over 700: 30%; SAT writing scores over 700: 23%; ACT scores over 30: 53%.

Retention: 97% of full-time freshmen returned.

FACULTY

Total: 2,129, 78% full-time, 79% with terminal degrees.

Student/faculty ratio: 13:1.

ACADEMICS

Calendar: semesters. *Degrees:* certificates, bachelor's, master's, doctoral, post-master's, and postbachelor's certificates.

Special study options: advanced placement credit, distance learning, double majors, honors programs, independent study, internships, off-campus study, part-time degree program, services for LD students, student-designed majors, study abroad, summer session for credit. ***ROTC:*** Army (b), Navy (b), Air Force (b).

Computers: 867 computers/terminals and 9,999 ports are available on campus for general student use. Students can access the following: computer help desk, free student e-mail accounts, online (class) grades, online (class) registration, online (class) schedules. Campuswide network is available. 100% of college-owned or -operated housing units are wired for high-speed Internet access. Wireless service is available via entire campus.

Library: Davis Library plus 12 others. *Books:* 7.6 million (physical), 1.6 million (digital/electronic); *Serial titles:* 161,097 (digital/electronic); *Databases:* 1,282. Weekly public service hours: 109; study areas open 24 hours, 5-7 days a week; students can reserve study rooms.

STUDENT LIFE

Housing options: on-campus residence required for freshman year; coed, men-only, women-only, special housing for students with disabilities. Campus housing is university owned. Freshman campus housing is guaranteed.

Activities and organizations: drama/theater group, student-run newspaper, radio and television station, choral group, marching band, Residence Hall Association, Carolina Fever, Campus Y, UNC-CH Habitat for Humanity, Carolina for the Kids Foundation (Dance Marathon), national fraternities, national sororities.

Athletics Member NCAA. All Division I except football (Division I-A). ***Intercollegiate sports:*** badminton M(c)/W(c), baseball M(s), basketball M(s)/W(s), cheerleading W(c), crew M(c)/W(s), cross-country running M(s)/W(s), equestrian sports M(c)/W(c), fencing M(s)/W(s), field hockey M(c)/W(s), golf M(s)/W(s), gymnastics M(c)/W(s), ice hockey M(c), lacrosse M(s)/W(s), racquetball M(c)/W(c), rugby M(c)/W(c), sailing M(c)/W(c), skiing (downhill) M(c)/W(c), soccer M(s)/W(s), softball W(s), swimming and diving M(s)/W(s), tennis M(s)/W(s), track and field M(s)/W(s), triathlon M(c)/W(c), ultimate Frisbee M(c)/W(c), volleyball M(c)/W(s), water polo M(c)/W(c), wrestling M(s). ***Intramural sports:*** badminton M/W, baseball M(c), basketball M(c)/W(c), crew W(c), cross-country running M(c)/W(c), field hockey W(c), football M(c), golf M(c)/W(c), gymnastics W(c), lacrosse W(c), racquetball M/W, soccer M(c)/W(c), softball M/W(c), swimming and diving M(c)/W(c), table tennis M/W, tennis M(c)/W(c), track and field M(c)/W(c), triathlon M/W, ultimate Frisbee M/W, volleyball M/W(c), water polo M/W.

Campus security: 24-hour emergency response devices and patrols, late-night transport/escort service, controlled dormitory access, crime prevention initiatives, campus-wide emergency alert system, cell phone/GPS security options.

Student services: health clinic, personal/psychological counseling, women's center, legal services.

COSTS & FINANCIAL AID

Costs (2017–18) ***Tuition:*** state resident $7019 full-time; nonresident $32,602 full-time. Full-time tuition and fees vary according to program. Part-time tuition and fees vary according to course load and program. ***Required fees:*** $1986 full-time. ***Room and board:*** $11,556; room only: $6482. Room and board charges vary according to board plan, housing facility, and location. ***Payment plan:*** installment. ***Waivers:*** employees or children of employees.

Financial Aid Of all full-time matriculated undergraduates who enrolled in 2015, 10,311 applied for aid, 8,134 were judged to have need, 6,482 had their need fully met. 1,991 Federal Work-Study jobs (averaging $1631). In 2015, 768 non-need-based awards were made. ***Average percent of need met:*** 100. ***Average financial aid package:*** $19,310. ***Average need-based loan:*** $5246. ***Average need-based gift aid:*** $17,260. ***Average non-need-based aid:*** $7679. ***Average indebtedness upon graduation:*** $20,852.

APPLYING

Standardized Tests *Required:* SAT or ACT (for admission).

Options: electronic application, early action, deferred entrance.

Application fee: $80.

Required: essay or personal statement, high school transcript, 1 letter of recommendation, counselor's statement.

Application deadlines: 1/15 (freshmen), 2/15 (transfers), 10/15 (early action).

Notification: 3/31 (freshmen), 4/15 (transfers), 1/31 (early action).

CONTACT

The University of North Carolina at Chapel Hill, Chapel Hill, NC 27599. *Phone:* 919-966-3932.

The University of North Carolina at Charlotte

Charlotte, North Carolina

http://www.uncc.edu/

- **State-supported** university, founded 1946, part of University of North Carolina System
- **Suburban** 1000-acre campus with easy access to Charlotte
- **Endowment** $73.2 million
- **Coed** 23,404 undergraduate students, 87% full-time, 47% women, 53% men
- **Moderately difficult** entrance level, 62% of applicants were admitted

UNDERGRAD STUDENTS

20,263 full-time, 3,141 part-time. Students come from 45 states and territories; 52 other countries; 5% are from out of state; 16% Black or African American, non-Hispanic/Latino; 9% Hispanic/Latino; 6% Asian, non-Hispanic/Latino; 0.1% Native Hawaiian or other Pacific Islander, non-Hispanic/Latino; 0.3% American Indian or Alaska Native, non-Hispanic/Latino; 4% Two or more races, non-Hispanic/Latino; 3% Race/ethnicity unknown; 2% international; 13% transferred in; 23% live on campus.

Freshmen:

Admission: 17,475 applied, 10,868 admitted, 3,453 enrolled. ***Average high school GPA:*** 3.97. ***Test scores:*** SAT critical reading scores over 500: 83%; SAT math scores over 500: 88%; SAT writing scores over 500: 70%; ACT scores over 18: 99%; SAT critical reading scores over 600: 24%; SAT math scores over 600: 34%; SAT writing scores over 600: 14%; ACT scores over 24: 49%; SAT critical reading scores over 700: 2%; SAT math scores over 700: 3%; SAT writing scores over 700: 1%; ACT scores over 30: 6%.

Retention: 82% of full-time freshmen returned.

FACULTY

Total: 1,692, 68% full-time, 67% with terminal degrees.

Student/faculty ratio: 19:1.

ACADEMICS

Calendar: semesters. *Degrees:* bachelor's, master's, doctoral, post-master's, and postbachelor's certificates.

Special study options: accelerated degree program, adult/continuing education programs, advanced placement credit, cooperative education, distance learning, double majors, English as a second language, freshman honors college, honors programs, independent study, internships, off-campus study, part-time degree program, services for LD students, study abroad, summer session for credit. ***ROTC:*** Army (b), Air Force (b).

Computers: 1,600 computers/terminals are available on campus for general student use. Students can access the following: computer help desk, free student e-mail accounts, online (class) grades, online (class) registration, online (class) schedules. Campuswide network is available. 100% of college-owned or -operated housing units are wired for high-speed Internet access. Wireless service is available via entire campus.

Library: J. Murrey Atkins Library plus 1 other. *Books:* 1.5 million (physical), 527,672 (digital/electronic); *Serial titles:* 29,969 (physical), 83,784 (digital/electronic); *Databases:* 672. Study areas open 24 hours, 5-7 days a week; students can reserve study rooms.

STUDENT LIFE

Housing options: coed, special housing for students with disabilities. Campus housing is university owned.

Activities and organizations: drama/theater group, student-run newspaper, radio station, choral group, marching band, Triveni (Indian Students Association), eSports Club, Kinesiology Student Organization, National Society of Collegiate Scholars, Black Student Union, national fraternities, national sororities.

Athletics Member NCAA. All Division I. ***Intercollegiate sports:*** baseball M(s), basketball M(s)/W(s), cheerleading M(s)/W(s), cross-country running M(s)/W(s), football M(s), golf M(s)/W(s), soccer M(s)/W(s), softball W(s), tennis M(s)/W(s), track and field M(s)/W(s), volleyball W(s). ***Intramural sports:*** archery M(c)/W(c), badminton M/W, baseball M(c), basketball M/W, bowling M/W, equestrian sports M(c)/W(c), fencing M(c)/W(c), football M/W, golf M(c), ice hockey M(c), lacrosse M(c)/W(c), rock climbing M/W, rugby M(c)/W(c), sailing M(c)/W(c), soccer M/W, softball M/W, table tennis M/W, ultimate Frisbee M(c)/W(c), volleyball M/W, water polo M/W, weight lifting M(c)/W(c), wrestling M(c)/W(c).

Campus security: 24-hour emergency response devices and patrols, late-night transport/escort service, controlled dormitory access.

Student services: health clinic, personal/psychological counseling.

COSTS & FINANCIAL AID

Costs (2016–17) ***Tuition:*** state resident $3737 full-time; nonresident $16,908 full-time. Full-time tuition and fees vary according to course load and program. Part-time tuition and fees vary according to course load and program. ***Required fees:*** $3026 full-time. ***Room and board:*** $10,470; room only: $5910. Room and board charges vary according to board plan and housing facility. ***Payment plan:*** installment. ***Waivers:*** employees or children of employees.

Financial Aid Of all full-time matriculated undergraduates who enrolled in 2016, 16,491 applied for aid, 13,462 were judged to have need, 1,897 had their need fully met. 920 Federal Work-Study jobs (averaging $2399). In 2016, 283 non-need-based awards were made. ***Average percent of need met:*** 62. ***Average financial aid package:*** $10,154. ***Average need-based loan:*** $4326. ***Average need-based gift aid:*** $6539. ***Average non-need-based aid:*** $7148. ***Average indebtedness upon graduation:*** $27,453.

APPLYING

Standardized Tests *Required:* SAT or ACT (for admission).

Options: electronic application, early action.

Application fee: $60.

Required: high school transcript, minimum 2.0 GPA.

Application deadlines: 6/1 (freshmen), 6/1 (transfers), 11/1 (early action).

Notification: continuous (freshmen), continuous (out-of-state freshmen), continuous (transfers), 1/30 (early action).

CONTACT

Ms. Claire Kirby, Director of Admissions, The University of North Carolina at Charlotte, 9201 University City Boulevard, 1st Floor, Cato Hall, Charlotte, NC 28223-0001. *Phone:* 704-687-5507. *Fax:* 704-687-6483. *E-mail:* admissions@uncc.edu.

The University of North Carolina at Greensboro

Greensboro, North Carolina

http://www.uncg.edu/

- **State-supported** university, founded 1891, part of University of North Carolina System
- **Urban** 210-acre campus
- **Endowment** $235.6 million
- **Coed** 16,281 undergraduate students, 87% full-time, 66% women, 34% men
- **Moderately difficult** entrance level, 74% of applicants were admitted

UNDERGRAD STUDENTS

14,116 full-time, 2,165 part-time. Students come from 46 states and territories; 42 other countries; 6% are from out of state; 28% Black or African American, non-Hispanic/Latino; 8% Hispanic/Latino; 5% Asian, non-Hispanic/Latino; 0.1% Native Hawaiian or other Pacific Islander, non-Hispanic/Latino; 0.4% American Indian or Alaska Native, non-Hispanic/Latino; 5% Two or more races, non-Hispanic/Latino; 1% Race/ethnicity unknown; 2% international; 12% transferred in; 33% live on campus.

Freshmen:

Admission: 9,035 applied, 6,680 admitted, 2,644 enrolled. ***Average high school GPA:*** 3.81. ***Test scores:*** SAT critical reading scores over 500: 64%; SAT math scores over 500: 44%; SAT writing scores over 500: 47%; ACT scores over 18: 100%; SAT critical reading scores over 600: 16%; SAT math scores over 600: 10%; SAT writing scores over 600: 9%; ACT scores over 24: 41%; SAT critical reading scores over 700: 2%; SAT writing scores over 700: 1%; ACT scores over 30: 4%.

Retention: 76% of full-time freshmen returned.

FACULTY

Total: 1,037, 75% full-time, 70% with terminal degrees.

Student/faculty ratio: 18:1.

ACADEMICS

Calendar: semesters. *Degrees:* bachelor's, master's, doctoral, post-master's, and postbachelor's certificates.

Special study options: academic remediation for entering students, accelerated degree program, adult/continuing education programs, advanced placement credit, distance learning, double majors, English as a second language, freshman honors college, honors programs, independent study, internships, off-campus study, part-time degree program, services for LD students, student-designed majors, study abroad, summer session for credit. ***ROTC:*** Army (c), Air Force (c).

Unusual degree programs: 3-2 accounting, biology/chemistry, chemistry, computer science, economics/public affairs, kinesiology/athletic training, political science/public affairs.

Computers: 474 computers/terminals are available on campus for general student use. Students can access the following: computer help desk, free student e-mail accounts, online (class) grades, online (class) registration, online (class) schedules, wireless printing services, cloud storage services. Campuswide network is available. 100% of college-owned or -operated housing units are wired for high-speed Internet access. Wireless service is available via entire campus.

Library: Walter Clinton Jackson Library plus 4 others. *Books:* 1.3 million (physical), 808,985 (digital/electronic); *Serial titles:* 103,752 (digital/electronic); *Databases:* 640. Weekly public service hours: 136; study areas open 24 hours, 5-7 days a week; students can reserve study rooms.

STUDENT LIFE

Housing options: coed, special housing for students with disabilities. Campus housing is university owned. Freshman campus housing is guaranteed.

Activities and organizations: drama/theater group, student-run newspaper, radio station, choral group, Alpha Psi Omega Honorary (theatre), Spartan Friends Network, Gaming and E-Sports UNCG, Chinese Culture and Language Association, Dental Club, national fraternities, national sororities.

Athletics Member NCAA. All Division I. ***Intercollegiate sports:*** baseball M(s), basketball M(s)/W(s), cross-country running M(s)/W(s), golf M(s)/W(s), soccer M(s)/W(s), softball W(s), tennis M(s)/W(s), track and field M(s)/W(s), volleyball W(s). ***Intramural sports:*** badminton M/W, basketball M/W, cross-country running M(c)/W(c), equestrian sports M(c)/W(c), fencing M(c)/W(c), field hockey M/W, football M(c)/W(c), lacrosse M(c)/W(c), racquetball M/W, rock climbing M/W, rugby M(c)/W(c), sand volleyball M/W, soccer M/W, softball M(c)/W(c), swimming and diving M(c)/W(c), table tennis M/W, tennis M(c)/W(c), ultimate Frisbee M/W, volleyball M(c)/W(c), water polo M/W.

Campus security: 24-hour emergency response devices and patrols, student patrols, late-night transport/escort service, controlled dormitory access.

Student services: health clinic, personal/psychological counseling.

COSTS & FINANCIAL AID

Costs (2016–17) ***Tuition:*** state resident $4336 full-time, $542 per credit hour part-time; nonresident $19,198 full-time, $2400 per credit hour part-time. Part-time tuition and fees vary according to course load. ***Required fees:*** $2706 full-time, $100 per credit hour part-time. ***Room and board:*** $8580; room only: $5084. Room and board charges vary according to board plan and housing facility. ***Payment plan:*** installment. ***Waivers:*** employees or children of employees.

Financial Aid Of all full-time matriculated undergraduates who enrolled in 2016, 11,682 applied for aid, 11,538 were judged to have need, 2,104 had their need fully met. In 2016, 287 non-need-based awards were made. ***Average percent of need met:*** 74. ***Average financial aid package:*** $11,315. ***Average need-based loan:*** $4213. ***Average need-based gift aid:*** $5907. ***Average non-need-based aid:*** $3804. ***Average indebtedness upon graduation:*** $27,073.

APPLYING

Standardized Tests *Required:* SAT or ACT (for admission).

Options: electronic application.

Application fee: $55.

Required: high school transcript, minimum 2.3 GPA.

Application deadlines: 3/1 (freshmen), 7/15 (transfers).

Notification: continuous until 9/15 (freshmen), continuous (transfers).

CONTACT

The University of North Carolina at Greensboro, Armfield-Preyer Admissions and Visitor Center, 1400 Spring Garden Street, Greensboro, NC 27412. *Phone:* 336-334-5243. *Fax:* 336-334-5051. *E-mail:* admissions@uncg.edu.

The University of North Carolina at Pembroke

Pembroke, North Carolina

http://www.uncp.edu/

- **State-supported** comprehensive, founded 1887, part of University of North Carolina System
- **Rural** 264-acre campus
- **Endowment** $20.4 million
- **Coed** 5,514 undergraduate students, 82% full-time, 61% women, 39% men
- **Moderately difficult** entrance level, 74% of applicants were admitted

UNDERGRAD STUDENTS

4,510 full-time, 1,004 part-time. Students come from 25 states and territories; 21 other countries; 3% are from out of state; 36% Black or African American, non-Hispanic/Latino; 5% Hispanic/Latino; 2% Asian, non-Hispanic/Latino; 0.1% Native Hawaiian or other Pacific Islander, non-Hispanic/Latino; 15% American Indian or Alaska Native, non-Hispanic/Latino; 3% Two or more races, non-Hispanic/Latino; 2% Race/ethnicity unknown; 0.7% international; 10% transferred in; 37% live on campus.

Freshmen:

Admission: 4,544 applied, 3,345 admitted, 1,091 enrolled. ***Average high school GPA:*** 3.45. ***Test scores:*** SAT critical reading scores over 500: 29%; SAT math scores over 500: 23%; SAT writing scores over 500: 13%; ACT scores over 18: 75%; SAT critical reading scores over 600: 5%; SAT math scores over 600: 4%; SAT writing scores over 600: 1%; ACT scores over 24: 11%; SAT math scores over 700: 1%; ACT scores over 30: 1%. ***Retention:*** 67% of full-time freshmen returned.

FACULTY

Total: 392, 77% full-time, 65% with terminal degrees.

Student/faculty ratio: 16:1.

ACADEMICS

Calendar: semesters. *Degrees:* bachelor's and master's.

Special study options: academic remediation for entering students, accelerated degree program, adult/continuing education programs, advanced placement credit, cooperative education, distance learning, double majors, English as a second language, honors programs, internships, off-campus study, part-time degree program, services for LD students, study abroad, summer session for credit. ***ROTC:*** Army (b), Air Force (b).

Computers: 501 computers/terminals are available on campus for general student use. Students can access the following: campus intranet, computer help desk, free student e-mail accounts, online (class) grades, online (class) registration, online (class) schedules, commuter/off campus connection to network, discounted computer software/hardware. Campuswide network is available. 100% of college-owned or -operated housing units are wired for high-speed Internet access. Wireless service is available via classrooms, computer centers, computer labs, dorm rooms, learning centers, libraries, student centers.

Library: Livermore Library. *Books:* 499,000 (physical), 235,000 (digital/electronic); *Serial titles:* 53,000 (physical), 53,000 (digital/electronic). Weekly public service hours: 92; students can reserve study rooms.

STUDENT LIFE

Housing options: on-campus residence required for freshman year; coed, men-only, women-only. Campus housing is university owned and is provided by a third party. Freshman applicants given priority for college housing.

Activities and organizations: drama/theater group, student-run newspaper, radio and television station, choral group, marching band, Health Careers Club, Spectrum, Graduate Student Organization, Phi

Alpha, National Association for the Advancement of Colored People, national fraternities, national sororities.

Athletics Member NCAA. All Division II. ***Intercollegiate sports:*** baseball M(s), basketball M(s)/W(s), cheerleading M/W, cross-country running M(s)/W(s), football M(s), golf W(s), soccer M(s)/W(s), softball W(s), swimming and diving W, track and field M(s)/W(s), volleyball W(s), wrestling M(s). ***Intramural sports:*** basketball M/W, bowling M/W, cheerleading M/W, football M, golf M, racquetball M/W, rugby M, sand volleyball M/W, soccer M, softball M/W, swimming and diving M/W, tennis M/W, ultimate Frisbee M/W, volleyball M/W, weight lifting M/W, wrestling M.

Campus security: 24-hour emergency response devices and patrols, late-night transport/escort service, controlled dormitory access.

Student services: health clinic, personal/psychological counseling.

COSTS & FINANCIAL AID

Costs (2016–17) ***Tuition:*** state resident $3531 full-time; nonresident $14,475 full-time. Full-time tuition and fees vary according to course load, location, and program. Part-time tuition and fees vary according to course load, location, and program. ***Required fees:*** $2285 full-time. ***Room and board:*** $8572; room only: $4890. Room and board charges vary according to board plan, housing facility, and location. ***Payment plan:*** installment. ***Waivers:*** employees or children of employees.

Financial Aid Of all full-time matriculated undergraduates who enrolled in 2016, 4,067 applied for aid, 3,644 were judged to have need, 227 had their need fully met. 89 Federal Work-Study jobs (averaging $1839). In 2016, 35 non-need-based awards were made. ***Average percent of need met:*** 64. ***Average financial aid package:*** $10,204. ***Average need-based loan:*** $4214. ***Average need-based gift aid:*** $6932. ***Average non-need-based aid:*** $2005. ***Average indebtedness upon graduation:*** $25,263.

APPLYING

Standardized Tests *Required:* SAT or ACT (for admission). *Required for some:* TOEFL.

Options: electronic application, deferred entrance.

Application fee: $45.

Required: high school transcript. ***Required for some:*** 1 letter of recommendation, interview. ***Recommended:*** essay or personal statement, minimum 2.0 GPA.

Application deadlines: rolling (freshmen), rolling (transfers).

Notification: continuous (freshmen), continuous (transfers).

CONTACT

The University of North Carolina at Pembroke, One University Drive, PO Box 1510, Pembroke, NC 28372-1510. *Phone:* 910-521-6262. *Toll-free phone:* 800-949-UNCP.

University of North Carolina School of the Arts

Winston-Salem, North Carolina

http://www.uncsa.edu/

- **State-supported** comprehensive, founded 1963, part of University of North Carolina system
- **Urban** 74-acre campus
- **Endowment** $51.0 million
- **Coed** 907 undergraduate students, 97% full-time, 50% women, 50% men

UNDERGRAD STUDENTS

883 full-time, 24 part-time. Students come from 46 states and territories; 10 other countries; 49% are from out of state; 9% Black or African American, non-Hispanic/Latino; 7% Hispanic/Latino; 2% Asian, non-Hispanic/Latino; 0.1% Native Hawaiian or other Pacific Islander, non-Hispanic/Latino; 0.7% American Indian or Alaska Native, non-Hispanic/Latino; 4% Two or more races, non-Hispanic/Latino; 2% Race/ethnicity unknown; 2% international; 7% transferred in; 61% live on campus.

Freshmen:

Admission: 213 enrolled. ***Average high school GPA:*** 3.7. ***Test scores:*** SAT critical reading scores over 500: 86%; SAT math scores over 500: 74%; SAT writing scores over 500: 78%; ACT scores over 18: 94%; SAT critical reading scores over 600: 48%; SAT math scores over 600: 29%; SAT writing scores over 600: 38%; ACT scores over 24: 62%; SAT critical reading scores over 700: 9%; SAT math scores over 700: 4%; SAT writing scores over 700: 8%; ACT scores over 30: 13%.

Retention: 85% of full-time freshmen returned.

FACULTY

Total: 187, 76% full-time, 43% with terminal degrees.

Student/faculty ratio: 7:1.

ACADEMICS

Calendar: semesters. *Degrees:* certificates, bachelor's, master's, and post-master's certificates.

Special study options: advanced placement credit, English as a second language, independent study, internships, services for LD students, summer session for credit.

Computers: 86 computers/terminals and 1,000 ports are available on campus for general student use. Students can access the following: computer help desk, free student e-mail accounts, online (class) grades, online (class) registration, online (class) schedules. Campuswide network is available. 100% of college-owned or -operated housing units are wired for high-speed Internet access. Wireless service is available via entire campus.

Library: UNCSA Library. *Books:* 125,840 (physical), 44,708 (digital/electronic); *Serial titles:* 422 (physical), 17,788 (digital/electronic); *Databases:* 150. Weekly public service hours: 90; students can reserve study rooms.

STUDENT LIFE

Housing options: on-campus residence required through sophomore year; coed. Campus housing is university owned. Freshman campus housing is guaranteed.

Activities and organizations: drama/theater group, student-run newspaper, choral group, A.R.T.S. Club (awareness on social issues through artistic expression), The Artist Underground, Art & Soul, UNCSA Artists of Color.

Campus security: 24-hour emergency response devices and patrols, late-night transport/escort service, controlled dormitory access.

Student services: health clinic, personal/psychological counseling.

COSTS & FINANCIAL AID

Costs (2017–18) ***Tuition:*** state resident $6370 full-time, $265 per credit hour part-time; nonresident $22,240 full-time, $927 per credit hour part-time. No tuition increase for student's term of enrollment. ***Required fees:*** $2841 full-time, $118 per credit hour part-time. ***Room and board:*** $8977; room only: $4475. Room and board charges vary according to board plan and housing facility. ***Waivers:*** employees or children of employees.

Financial Aid Of all full-time matriculated undergraduates who enrolled in 2016, 672 applied for aid, 546 were judged to have need, 53 had their need fully met. 146 Federal Work-Study jobs (averaging $800). In 2016, 37 non-need-based awards were made. ***Average percent of need met:*** 63. ***Average financial aid package:*** $13,596. ***Average need-based loan:*** $4538. ***Average need-based gift aid:*** $8575. ***Average non-need-based aid:*** $2070. ***Average indebtedness upon graduation:*** $28,551.

APPLYING

Standardized Tests *Required:* SAT or ACT (for admission).

Required: essay or personal statement, high school transcript, minimum 2.5 GPA, 2 letters of recommendation, audition. ***Required for some:*** interview.

CONTACT

University of North Carolina School of the Arts, 1533 South Main Street, PO Box 12189, Winston-Salem, NC 27127-2738. *Phone:* 336-770-3290.

★ The University of North Carolina Wilmington

Wilmington, North Carolina

http://www.uncw.edu/

- **State-supported** comprehensive, founded 1947, part of University of North Carolina System
- **Urban** 661-acre campus
- **Endowment** $85.3 million
- **Coed** 13,914 undergraduate students, 86% full-time, 62% women, 38% men
- **Moderately difficult** entrance level, 72% of applicants were admitted

UNDERGRAD STUDENTS

12,023 full-time, 1,891 part-time. Students come from 52 states and territories; 51 other countries; 13% are from out of state; 5% Black or African American, non-Hispanic/Latino; 7% Hispanic/Latino; 2% Asian, non-Hispanic/Latino; 0.1% Native Hawaiian or other Pacific Islander, non-Hispanic/Latino; 0.5% American Indian or Alaska Native, non-Hispanic/Latino; 4% Two or more races, non-Hispanic/Latino; 3% Race/ethnicity unknown; 0.9% international; 14% transferred in; 30% live on campus.

Freshmen:

Admission: 10,436 applied, 7,487 admitted, 2,223 enrolled. ***Average high school GPA:*** 4.13. ***Test scores:*** SAT critical reading scores over 500: 97%; SAT math scores over 500: 97%; SAT writing scores over 500: 87%; ACT scores over 18: 100%; SAT critical reading scores over 600: 48%; SAT math scores over 600: 50%; SAT writing scores over 600: 30%; ACT scores over 24: 58%; SAT critical reading scores over 700: 6%; SAT math scores over 700: 3%; SAT writing scores over 700: 1%; ACT scores over 30: 6%.

Retention: 85% of full-time freshmen returned.

FACULTY

Total: 1,041, 59% full-time, 69% with terminal degrees.

Student/faculty ratio: 18:1.

ACADEMICS

Calendar: semesters. *Degrees:* bachelor's, master's, doctoral, post-master's, and postbachelor's certificates.

Special study options: academic remediation for entering students, accelerated degree program, advanced placement credit, cooperative education, distance learning, double majors, English as a second language, honors programs, independent study, internships, off-campus study, services for LD students, study abroad, summer session for credit.

Unusual degree programs: 3-2 English, mathematics, Spanish.

Computers: 1,361 computers/terminals and 6,024 ports are available on campus for general student use. Students can access the following: campus intranet, computer help desk, free student e-mail accounts, online (class) grades, online (class) registration, online (class) schedules. Campuswide network is available. 100% of college-owned or -operated housing units are wired for high-speed Internet access. Wireless service is available via entire campus.

Library: William Madison Randall Library. *Books:* 932,549 (physical), 79,711 (digital/electronic); *Serial titles:* 5,256 (physical), 44,165 (digital/electronic); *Databases:* 215. Weekly public service hours: 97; study areas open 24 hours, 5-7 days a week; students can reserve study rooms.

STUDENT LIFE

Housing options: on-campus residence required for freshman year; coed, special housing for students with disabilities. Campus housing is university owned and is provided by a third party. Freshman applicants given priority for college housing.

Activities and organizations: drama/theater group, student-run newspaper, radio and television station, choral group, Student Government Association, Association of Campus Entertainment, Residence Hall Association, Sports Club Council, Graduate Student Association, national fraternities, national sororities.

Athletics Member NCAA. All Division I. ***Intercollegiate sports:*** baseball M(s), basketball M(s)/W(s), cheerleading M/W, cross-country running M(s)/W(s), golf M(s)/W(s), soccer M(s)/W(s), softball W(s), swimming and diving M(s)/W(s), tennis M(s)/W(s), track and field M(s)/W(s), volleyball W(s). ***Intramural sports:*** badminton M/W, baseball M(c), basketball M/W, crew M(c)/W(c), equestrian sports W(c), field hockey W(c), football M/W, golf M(c)/W(c), gymnastics M(c)/W(c), ice hockey M(c), lacrosse M(c)/W(c), racquetball M/W, rugby M(c)/W(c), sailing M(c)/W(c), sand volleyball M/W, soccer M/W, softball M(c)/W(c), swimming and diving M(c)/W(c), tennis M/W, triathlon M(c)/W(c), ultimate Frisbee M(c)/W(c), volleyball M/W, water polo M/W.

Campus security: 24-hour emergency response devices and patrols, late-night transport/escort service, controlled dormitory access.

Student services: health clinic, personal/psychological counseling, women's center.

COSTS & FINANCIAL AID

Costs (2016–17) ***Tuition:*** state resident $4356 full-time, $159 per credit hour part-time; nonresident $18,324 full-time, $668 per credit hour part-time. Full-time tuition and fees vary according to course load and location. Part-time tuition and fees vary according to course load and location. ***Required fees:*** $2596 full-time, $76 per credit hour part-time. ***Room and board:*** $9489; room only: $5879. Room and board charges vary according to board plan and housing facility. ***Payment plan:*** installment. ***Waivers:*** employees or children of employees.

Financial Aid Of all full-time matriculated undergraduates who enrolled in 2015, 8,234 applied for aid, 6,501 were judged to have need, 1,088 had their need fully met. In 2015, 134 non-need-based awards were made. ***Average percent of need met:*** 60. ***Average financial aid package:*** $8932. ***Average need-based loan:*** $4309. ***Average need-based gift aid:*** $5095. ***Average non-need-based aid:*** $3584. ***Average indebtedness upon graduation:*** $25,112.

APPLYING

Standardized Tests *Required:* SAT or ACT (for admission).

Options: electronic application, early admission, early action, deferred entrance.

Application fee: $75.

Required: essay or personal statement, high school transcript, 1 letter of recommendation.

Application deadlines: 2/1 (freshmen), 3/1 (transfers), 11/1 (early action).

Notification: 4/1 (freshmen), continuous (transfers), 1/20 (early action).

CONTACT

UNCW Office of Admissions, The University of North Carolina Wilmington, 601 South College Road, Wilmington, NC 28403-3297. *Phone:* 910-962-3243. *Fax:* 910-962-3038. *E-mail:* admissions@uncw.edu.

See page 1572 for the College Close-Up.

University of Phoenix–Charlotte Campus

Charlotte, North Carolina

http://www.phoenix.edu/

CONTACT

Marc Booker, Sr. Director, Office of Admissions and Evaluation, University of Phoenix–Charlotte Campus, 4035 South Riverpoint Parkway, Mail Stop CF-L101, Phoenix, AZ 85040. *Phone:* 602-557-4609. *Toll-free phone:* 866-766-0766. *Fax:* 480-643-1156.

Wake Forest University

Winston-Salem, North Carolina

http://www.wfu.edu/

- **Independent** university, founded 1834
- **Suburban** 340-acre campus
- **Coed** 4,955 undergraduate students, 99% full-time, 53% women, 47% men
- **Very difficult** entrance level, 30% of applicants were admitted

UNDERGRAD STUDENTS

4,900 full-time, 55 part-time. 77% are from out of state; 7% Black or African American, non-Hispanic/Latino; 7% Hispanic/Latino; 4% Asian, non-Hispanic/Latino; 0.1% Native Hawaiian or other Pacific Islander, non-Hispanic/Latino; 0.2% American Indian or Alaska Native, non-

Hispanic/Latino; 3% Two or more races, non-Hispanic/Latino; 0.1% Race/ethnicity unknown; 9% international; 0.5% transferred in; 76% live on campus.

Freshmen:
Admission: 14,006 applied, 4,249 admitted, 1,306 enrolled. ***Test scores:*** SAT critical reading scores over 500: 94%; SAT math scores over 500: 98%; SAT writing scores over 500: 95%; ACT scores over 18: 99%; SAT critical reading scores over 600: 79%; SAT math scores over 600: 86%; SAT writing scores over 600: 83%; ACT scores over 24: 93%; SAT critical reading scores over 700: 26%; SAT math scores over 700: 43%; SAT writing scores over 700: 32%; ACT scores over 30: 59%.

Retention: 95% of full-time freshmen returned.

FACULTY
Total: 835, 68% full-time.

Student/faculty ratio: 10:1.

ACADEMICS
Calendar: semesters. *Degrees:* bachelor's, master's, doctoral, and postbachelor's certificates.

Special study options: advanced placement credit, distance learning, double majors, honors programs, independent study, internships, part-time degree program, services for LD students, study abroad, summer session for credit. ***ROTC:*** Army (b).

Unusual degree programs: 3-2 engineering.

Computers: Students can access the following: campus intranet, computer help desk, free student e-mail accounts, online (class) grades, online (class) registration, online (class) schedules, financial information online, drop-add, transcript requests. Campuswide network is available. Wireless service is available via entire campus.

Library: Z. Smith Reynolds Library.

STUDENT LIFE
Housing options: on-campus residence required through sophomore year; coed. Campus housing is university owned. Freshman campus housing is guaranteed.

Activities and organizations: drama/theater group, student-run newspaper, radio and television station, choral group, marching band, national fraternities, national sororities.

Athletics Member NCAA. All Division I except football (Division I-A). ***Intercollegiate sports:*** baseball M(s), basketball M(s)/W(s), cross-country running M(s)/W(s), field hockey W(s), golf M(s)/W(s), soccer M(s)/W(s), tennis M(s)/W(s), track and field M(s)/W(s), volleyball W(s). ***Intramural sports:*** archery M(c)/W(c), baseball M(c), basketball M/W, bowling M/W, cheerleading M(c)/W(c), crew M(c)/W(c), cross-country running M(c)/W(c), equestrian sports M(c)/W(c), fencing M(c)/W(c), field hockey W(c), football M, golf M(c)/W(c), ice hockey M(c)/W(c), lacrosse M(c)/W(c), racquetball M/W, rugby M(c)/W(c), skiing (cross-country) M(c)/W(c), skiing (downhill) M(c)/W(c), soccer M(c)/W(c), softball M/W(c), swimming and diving M/W, table tennis M/W, tennis M/W, ultimate Frisbee M/W, volleyball M/W, water polo M(c)/W(c), wrestling M(c).

Campus security: 24-hour emergency response devices and patrols, late-night transport/escort service, controlled dormitory access.

Student services: health clinic, personal/psychological counseling.

COSTS & FINANCIAL AID
Costs (2017–18) ***Comprehensive fee:*** $66,754 includes full-time tuition ($50,524), mandatory fees ($876), and room and board ($15,354). Part-time tuition: $2090 per credit hour. ***College room only:*** $9012.

Financial Aid Of all full-time matriculated undergraduates who enrolled in 2016, 1,844 applied for aid, 1,506 were judged to have need, 1,506 had their need fully met. In 2016, 428 non-need-based awards were made. ***Average percent of need met:*** 100. ***Average financial aid package:*** $47,228. ***Average need-based loan:*** $9603. ***Average need-based gift aid:*** $43,165. ***Average non-need-based aid:*** $12,582. ***Average indebtedness upon graduation:*** $33,797. ***Financial aid deadline:*** 1/1.

APPLYING
Options: electronic application, early admission, early decision.

Application fee: $50.

Required: essay or personal statement, high school transcript, 1 letter of recommendation. ***Recommended:*** interview.

Early decision deadline: 11/15.

Notification: continuous (freshmen).

CONTACT
Wake Forest University, 1834 Wake Forest Road, PO Box 7373 Reynolda Station, Winston-Salem, NC 27106. *Phone:* 336-758-5201.

Warren Wilson College
Swannanoa, North Carolina
http://www.warren-wilson.edu/

- **Independent** comprehensive, founded 1894, affiliated with Presbyterian Church (U.S.A.)
- **Suburban** 1135-acre campus
- **Coed**
- **Moderately difficult** entrance level

FACULTY
Student/faculty ratio: 10:1.

ACADEMICS
Calendar: semesters. *Degrees:* bachelor's and master's.

Library: Pew Learning Center and Ellison Library.

STUDENT LIFE
Housing options: on-campus residence required for freshman year; coed, men-only, women-only, cooperative. Campus housing is university owned. Freshman campus housing is guaranteed.

Activities and organizations: drama/theater group, student-run newspaper, choral group, Food Not Bombs, Club Sports: Paddling, Cycling, Cyclocross, Timbersports, Multicultural Student Organizations: Engage, WHOLA, Peace, Social and Environmental Justice Groups, Student Religious Groups: Christian, Jewish, Buddhist, Quaker, Pagan, and Unitarian Universalist.

Athletics Member USCAA.

Campus security: 24-hour emergency response devices and patrols, student patrols, late-night transport/escort service, controlled dormitory access.

Student services: health clinic, personal/psychological counseling.

COSTS & FINANCIAL AID
Costs (2016–17) ***Comprehensive fee:*** $44,220 includes full-time tuition ($33,260), mandatory fees ($710), and room and board ($10,250). Full-time tuition and fees vary according to course load. Part-time tuition: $1386 per credit hour. Part-time tuition and fees vary according to course load. ***Required fees:*** $100 per term part-time. ***Room and board:*** Room and board charges vary according to board plan.

Financial Aid Of all full-time matriculated undergraduates who enrolled in 2014, 669 applied for aid, 618 were judged to have need, 183 had their need fully met. In 2014, 128 non-need-based awards were made. ***Average percent of need met:*** 84. ***Average financial aid package:*** $33,715. ***Average need-based loan:*** $4414. ***Average need-based gift aid:*** $20,860. ***Average non-need-based aid:*** $9105. ***Average indebtedness upon graduation:*** $20,768.

APPLYING
Options: electronic application, early admission, early decision, early action, deferred entrance.

Required: essay or personal statement, high school transcript, Common Application, Common Application School Report Form. ***Recommended:*** minimum 2.5 GPA, 2 letters of recommendation, interview.

CONTACT
Monique Cote, Campus Visit Coordinator, Warren Wilson College, PO Box 9000, Asheville, NC 28815-9000. *Phone:* 828-771-2073. *Toll-free phone:* 800-934-3536. *Fax:* 828-298-1440. *E-mail:* admit@warren-wilson.edu.

Western Carolina University
Cullowhee, North Carolina
http://www.wcu.edu/

- **State-supported** comprehensive, founded 1889, part of University of North Carolina System
- **Rural** 682-acre campus
- **Coed** 8,787 undergraduate students, 84% full-time, 54% women, 46% men
- **Moderately difficult** entrance level, 43% of applicants were admitted

UNDERGRAD STUDENTS
7,373 full-time, 1,414 part-time. 7% are from out of state; 6% Black or African American, non-Hispanic/Latino; 5% Hispanic/Latino; 1% Asian, non-Hispanic/Latino; 0.1% Native Hawaiian or other Pacific Islander, non-Hispanic/Latino; 0.8% American Indian or Alaska Native, non-Hispanic/Latino; 3% Two or more races, non-Hispanic/Latino; 1% Race/ethnicity unknown; 2% international; 9% transferred in; 42% live on campus.

Freshmen:
Admission: 15,397 applied, 6,637 admitted, 1,756 enrolled. ***Average high school GPA:*** 3.75. ***Test scores:*** SAT critical reading scores over 500: 60%; SAT math scores over 500: 66%; SAT writing scores over 500: 41%; ACT scores over 18: 96%; SAT critical reading scores over 600: 14%; SAT math scores over 600: 14%; SAT writing scores over 600: 9%; ACT scores over 24: 34%; SAT critical reading scores over 700: 1%; SAT math scores over 700: 1%; SAT writing scores over 700: 1%; ACT scores over 30: 2%.

Retention: 78% of full-time freshmen returned.

FACULTY
Total: 676, 73% full-time, 65% with terminal degrees.

Student/faculty ratio: 16:1.

ACADEMICS
Calendar: semesters. *Degrees:* bachelor's, master's, doctoral, post-master's, and postbachelor's certificates.

Special study options: advanced placement credit, cooperative education, distance learning, double majors, English as a second language, honors programs, independent study, internships, part-time degree program, services for LD students, student-designed majors, study abroad, summer session for credit.

Computers: Students can access the following: campus intranet, computer help desk, free student e-mail accounts, online (class) grades, online (class) registration, online (class) schedules. Campuswide network is available. 100% of college-owned or -operated housing units are wired for high-speed Internet access. Wireless service is available via entire campus.

Library: Hunter Library.

STUDENT LIFE
Housing options: on-campus residence required for freshman year; coed, men-only, women-only, special housing for students with disabilities. Campus housing is university owned, leased by the school and is provided by a third party. Freshman campus housing is guaranteed.

Activities and organizations: drama/theater group, student-run newspaper, radio and television station, choral group, marching band, national fraternities, national sororities.

Athletics Member NCAA. All Division I except football (Division I-AA). ***Intercollegiate sports:*** baseball M(s), basketball M(s)/W(s), cheerleading M/W, cross-country running M(s)/W(s), equestrian sports M(c)/W(c), fencing M(c)/W(c), golf M(s)/W(s), rock climbing M(c)/W(c), rugby M(c), soccer W(s), softball W(s), swimming and diving M(c)/W(c), tennis M(c)/W(s), track and field M(s)/W(s), ultimate Frisbee M(c)/W(c), volleyball W(s), wrestling M(c). ***Intramural sports:*** badminton M/W, basketball M/W, bowling M/W, cross-country running M/W, racquetball M/W, soccer M/W, softball M/W, swimming and diving M/W, table tennis M/W, tennis M/W, ultimate Frisbee M/W, volleyball M/W, water polo M/W, weight lifting M/W, wrestling M/W.

Campus security: 24-hour emergency response devices and patrols, late-night transport/escort service, controlled dormitory access.

Student services: health clinic, personal/psychological counseling, women's center.

COSTS & FINANCIAL AID
Costs (2016–17) ***Tuition:*** state resident $3893 full-time; nonresident $14,286 full-time. Full-time tuition and fees vary according to degree level. Part-time tuition and fees vary according to course load and degree level. ***Required fees:*** $3134 full-time. ***Room and board:*** $8864; room only: $4438. Room and board charges vary according to board plan and housing facility.

Financial Aid Of all full-time matriculated undergraduates who enrolled in 2015, 6,614 applied for aid, 5,394 were judged to have need, 3,608 had their need fully met. In 2015, 406 non-need-based awards were made. ***Average percent of need met:*** 87. ***Average financial aid package:*** $18,861. ***Average need-based loan:*** $8447. ***Average need-based gift aid:*** $10,922. ***Average non-need-based aid:*** $4648. ***Average indebtedness upon graduation:*** $20,201.

APPLYING
Standardized Tests *Required:* SAT or ACT (for admission).

Options: electronic application, early admission, early action.

Application fee: $55.

Required: high school transcript.

CONTACT
Office of Undergraduate Admission, Western Carolina University, 102 Camp Building, Cullowhee, NC 28723. *Phone:* 828-227-7317. *Toll-free phone:* 877-WCU4YOU. *E-mail:* admiss@email.wcu.edu.

William Peace University
Raleigh, North Carolina
http://www.peace.edu/

- **Independent** 4-year, founded 1857, affiliated with Presbyterian Church (U.S.A.)
- **Urban** 21-acre campus with easy access to Raleigh-Cary
- **Endowment** $36.3 million
- **Coed** 1,038 undergraduate students, 85% full-time, 62% women, 38% men
- **Moderately difficult** entrance level, 50% of applicants were admitted

UNDERGRAD STUDENTS
886 full-time, 152 part-time. Students come from 26 states and territories; 4 other countries; 7% are from out of state; 36% Black or African American, non-Hispanic/Latino; 5% Hispanic/Latino; 2% Asian, non-Hispanic/Latino; 0.4% Native Hawaiian or other Pacific Islander, non-Hispanic/Latino; 1% American Indian or Alaska Native, non-Hispanic/Latino; 2% Two or more races, non-Hispanic/Latino; 8% Race/ethnicity unknown; 11% transferred in; 66% live on campus.

Freshmen:
Admission: 1,829 applied, 918 admitted, 231 enrolled. ***Average high school GPA:*** 3.22. ***Test scores:*** SAT critical reading scores over 500: 26%; SAT math scores over 500: 24%; ACT scores over 18: 59%; SAT critical reading scores over 600: 4%; SAT math scores over 600: 3%; ACT scores over 24: 10%; ACT scores over 30: 1%.

Retention: 59% of full-time freshmen returned.

FACULTY
Total: 129, 20% full-time, 48% with terminal degrees.

Student/faculty ratio: 15:1.

ACADEMICS
Calendar: semesters. *Degree:* bachelor's.

Special study options: academic remediation for entering students, accelerated degree program, adult/continuing education programs, advanced placement credit, cooperative education, distance learning, double majors, honors programs, independent study, internships, off-campus study, part-time degree program, services for LD students, study abroad, summer session for credit. ***ROTC:*** Army (c), Navy (c), Air Force (c).

Computers: 92 computers/terminals are available on campus for general student use. Students can access the following: campus intranet, computer help desk, free student e-mail accounts, online (class) grades, online (class) registration, online (class) schedules. Campuswide network is available. 100% of college-owned or -operated housing units are wired for high-speed Internet access. Wireless service is available via entire campus.

Library: Lucy Cooper Finch Library. Students can reserve study rooms.

STUDENT LIFE

Housing options: on-campus residence required through sophomore year; coed, women-only. Campus housing is university owned, leased by the school and is provided by a third party. Freshman applicants given priority for college housing.

Activities and organizations: drama/theater group, student-run newspaper, choral group, Campus Activities Board, Phi Beta Lamda, Gamma Sigma Sigma, Ambassadors for Christ, Class Councils.

Athletics Member NCAA. All Division III. ***Intercollegiate sports:*** baseball M, basketball M/W, cross-country running M/W, golf M, soccer M/W, softball W, tennis M/W, volleyball W. ***Intramural sports:*** basketball M/W, cheerleading M(c)/W(c), football M/W, lacrosse M/W, soccer M/W, tennis M/W, ultimate Frisbee M(c)/W(c), volleyball M/W.

Campus security: 24-hour emergency response devices and patrols, late-night transport/escort service, controlled dormitory access.

Student services: health clinic, personal/psychological counseling.

COSTS & FINANCIAL AID

Costs (2017–18) ***Comprehensive fee:*** $39,500 includes full-time tuition ($28,500), mandatory fees ($200), and room and board ($10,800). Full-time tuition and fees vary according to class time and course load. Part-time tuition: $950 per credit hour. Part-time tuition and fees vary according to class time and course load. ***College room only:*** $7200. Room and board charges vary according to board plan. ***Payment plan:*** installment. ***Waivers:*** employees or children of employees.

Financial Aid Of all full-time matriculated undergraduates who enrolled in 2016, 828 applied for aid, 758 were judged to have need, 8 had their need fully met. 93 Federal Work-Study jobs (averaging $2000). In 2016, 60 non-need-based awards were made. ***Average percent of need met:*** 64. ***Average financial aid package:*** $18,464. ***Average need-based loan:*** $4095. ***Average need-based gift aid:*** $8612. ***Average non-need-based aid:*** $3171. ***Average indebtedness upon graduation:*** $20,921.

APPLYING

Standardized Tests *Required:* SAT or ACT (for admission).

Options: electronic application, early admission, deferred entrance.

Application fee: $35.

Required: high school transcript, minimum 2.0 GPA. ***Required for some:*** essay or personal statement, Dean's evaluation for transfers. ***Recommended:*** interview.

Application deadlines: rolling (freshmen), rolling (out-of-state freshmen), rolling (transfers).

Notification: continuous (freshmen), continuous (out-of-state freshmen), continuous (transfers).

CONTACT

Office of Admissions, William Peace University, 15 East Peace Street, Raleigh, NC 27604. *Phone:* 919-508-2214. *Fax:* 919-508-2326. *E-mail:* admission@peace.edu.

Wingate University

Wingate, North Carolina

http://www.wingate.edu/

- **Independent Baptist** comprehensive, founded 1896
- **Small-town** 400-acre campus with easy access to Charlotte
- **Coed** 2,084 undergraduate students, 98% full-time, 60% women, 40% men
- **Moderately difficult** entrance level, 70% of applicants were admitted

UNDERGRAD STUDENTS

2,044 full-time, 40 part-time. Students come from 36 states and territories; 45 other countries; 24% are from out of state; 15% Black or African American, non-Hispanic/Latino; 4% Hispanic/Latino; 2% Asian, non-Hispanic/Latino; 0.5% American Indian or Alaska Native, non-Hispanic/Latino; 7% Two or more races, non-Hispanic/Latino; 5% Race/ethnicity unknown; 4% international; 4% transferred in; 75% live on campus.

Freshmen:

Admission: 7,581 applied, 5,273 admitted, 625 enrolled. ***Average high school GPA:*** 3.43. ***Test scores:*** SAT critical reading scores over 500: 59%; SAT math scores over 500: 62%; ACT scores over 18: 94%; SAT critical reading scores over 600: 14%; SAT math scores over 600: 18%; ACT scores over 24: 37%; SAT critical reading scores over 700: 1%; SAT math scores over 700: 1%; ACT scores over 30: 6%.

Retention: 77% of full-time freshmen returned.

FACULTY

Total: 307, 59% full-time, 66% with terminal degrees.

Student/faculty ratio: 14:1.

ACADEMICS

Calendar: semesters. *Degrees:* bachelor's, master's, doctoral, and post-master's certificates.

Special study options: adult/continuing education programs, advanced placement credit, double majors, honors programs, independent study, internships, off-campus study, part-time degree program, services for LD students, study abroad, summer session for credit. ***ROTC:*** Army (c), Air Force (c).

Computers: 80 computers/terminals are available on campus for general student use. Students can access the following: campus intranet, computer help desk, free student e-mail accounts, online (class) grades, online (class) registration, online (class) schedules. Campuswide network is available. 100% of college-owned or -operated housing units are wired for high-speed Internet access. Wireless service is available via entire campus.

Library: Ethel K. Smith Library. *Books:* 96,673 (physical); *Databases:* 110. Students can reserve study rooms.

STUDENT LIFE

Housing options: on-campus residence required through senior year; coed, men-only, women-only, cooperative, special housing for students with disabilities. Campus housing is university owned. Freshman campus housing is guaranteed.

Activities and organizations: drama/theater group, student-run newspaper, television station, choral group, University and Community Assistance Network (UCAN), Bulldog Activities Resource Committee, Fellowship of Christian Athletes, Student Bulldog Club, Student Government Association, national fraternities, national sororities.

Athletics Member NCAA. All Division II. ***Intercollegiate sports:*** baseball M(s), basketball M(s)/W(s), cross-country running M(s)/W(s), football M(s), golf M(s)/W(s), lacrosse M(s)/W(s), soccer M(s)/W(s), softball W(s), swimming and diving M(s)/W(s), tennis M(s)/W(s), track and field M(s)/W(s), volleyball W(s). ***Intramural sports:*** basketball M/W, bowling M/W, cross-country running M/W, football M/W, golf M/W, racquetball M/W, swimming and diving M/W, table tennis M/W, tennis M/W, track and field M/W, ultimate Frisbee M/W, volleyball M/W, water polo M/W, weight lifting M/W.

Campus security: 24-hour emergency response devices and patrols, late-night transport/escort service, controlled dormitory access.

Student services: health clinic, personal/psychological counseling.

COSTS & FINANCIAL AID

Costs (2017–18) ***Comprehensive fee:*** $41,900 includes full-time tuition ($31,120) and room and board ($10,780). Part-time tuition: $1035 per credit hour. Part-time tuition and fees vary according to course load. ***Payment plan:*** installment. ***Waivers:*** employees or children of employees.

Financial Aid Of all full-time matriculated undergraduates who enrolled in 2015, 1,731 applied for aid, 1,594 were judged to have need, 397 had their need fully met. In 2015, 406 non-need-based awards were made. ***Average percent of need met:*** 75. ***Average financial aid package:*** $24,280. ***Average need-based loan:*** $3914. ***Average need-based gift aid:*** $20,912. ***Average non-need-based aid:*** $15,467. ***Average indebtedness upon graduation:*** $31,997.

APPLYING

Standardized Tests *Required:* SAT or ACT (for admission).

Options: electronic application, deferred entrance.

Required: high school transcript, minimum 2.7 GPA. ***Required for some:*** essay or personal statement. ***Recommended:*** interview.

Application deadlines: rolling (freshmen), rolling (transfers).

Notification: continuous (freshmen), continuous (transfers).

CONTACT
Mr. Gabe Hollingsworth, Director of Admissions, Wingate University, PO Box 159, Wingate, NC 28174. *Phone:* 704-233-8000. *Toll-free phone:* 800-755-5550. *Fax:* 704-233-8110. *E-mail:* admit@wingate.edu.

Winston-Salem State University

Winston-Salem, North Carolina

http://www.wssu.edu/

CONTACT
Ms. Tomikia LeGrande, Assistant Vice Chancellor for Enrollment Services, Winston-Salem State University, 601 Martin Luther King, Jr. Drive, Thompson Center, Winston-Salem, NC 27110. *Phone:* 336-750-2070. *Toll-free phone:* 800-257-4052. *Fax:* 336-750-2079. *E-mail:* legrandet@wssu.edu.

NORTH DAKOTA

Bismarck State College

Bismarck, North Dakota

http://www.bismarckstate.edu/

- **State-supported** primarily 2-year, founded 1939, part of North Dakota University System
- **Urban** 120-acre campus
- **Endowment** $16.3 million
- **Coed** 3,976 undergraduate students, 56% full-time, 43% women, 57% men
- **Noncompetitive** entrance level, 100% of applicants were admitted

UNDERGRAD STUDENTS
2,241 full-time, 1,735 part-time. Students come from 49 states and territories; 8 other countries; 22% are from out of state; 3% Black or African American, non-Hispanic/Latino; 3% Hispanic/Latino; 0.6% Asian, non-Hispanic/Latino; 0.2% Native Hawaiian or other Pacific Islander, non-Hispanic/Latino; 2% American Indian or Alaska Native, non-Hispanic/Latino; 3% Two or more races, non-Hispanic/Latino; 2% Race/ethnicity unknown; 0.3% international; 7% transferred in; 14% live on campus.

Freshmen:
Admission: 1,068 applied, 1,068 admitted, 878 enrolled. ***Average high school GPA:*** 3.03. ***Test scores:*** ACT scores over 18: 72%; ACT scores over 24: 13%.
Retention: 74% of full-time freshmen returned.

FACULTY
Total: 348, 35% full-time, 11% with terminal degrees.
Student/faculty ratio: 14:1.

ACADEMICS
Calendar: semesters. *Degrees:* certificates, diplomas, associate, and bachelor's.
Special study options: academic remediation for entering students, adult/continuing education programs, advanced placement credit, cooperative education, distance learning, double majors, independent study, internships, part-time degree program, services for LD students, study abroad, summer session for credit.
Computers: 745 computers/terminals are available on campus for general student use. Students can access the following: computer help desk, free student e-mail accounts, online (class) grades, online (class) registration, online (class) schedules, office software, writing software. Campuswide network is available. Wireless service is available via entire campus.
Library: Bismarck State College Library. *Books:* 61,059 (physical), 16,804 (digital/electronic); *Serial titles:* 121 (physical), 114 (digital/electronic); *Databases:* 88. Weekly public service hours: 67; students can reserve study rooms.

STUDENT LIFE
Housing options: coed, men-only, women-only, special housing for students with disabilities. Campus housing is university owned.
Activities and organizations: drama/theater group, student-run newspaper, radio station, choral group, Intramural Sports, Campus Crusade, Student Government Association, Concert/Chamber Choir, Drama Club.
Athletics Member NJCAA. ***Intercollegiate sports:*** baseball M(s), basketball M(s)/W(s), golf M/W, softball W(s), volleyball W(s). ***Intramural sports:*** basketball M/W, football M/W, volleyball M/W.
Campus security: late-night transport/escort service, controlled dormitory access.
Student services: personal/psychological counseling.

COSTS & FINANCIAL AID
Costs (2016–17) ***Tuition:*** state resident $2916 full-time, $121 per credit hour part-time; nonresident $7785 full-time, $324 per credit hour part-time. Full-time tuition and fees vary according to course level, course load, degree level, location, program, and reciprocity agreements. Part-time tuition and fees vary according to course level, course load, degree level, location, program, and reciprocity agreements. ***Required fees:*** $743 full-time, $31 per credit hour part-time. ***Room and board:*** $7400; room only: $2600. Room and board charges vary according to board plan and housing facility. ***Waivers:*** minority students and employees or children of employees.
Financial Aid Of all full-time matriculated undergraduates who enrolled in 2013, 1,731 applied for aid, 1,133 were judged to have need, 429 had their need fully met. In 2013, 236 non-need-based awards were made. ***Average percent of need met:*** 49. ***Average financial aid package:*** $11,129. ***Average need-based loan:*** $4646. ***Average need-based gift aid:*** $4241. ***Average non-need-based aid:*** $709.

APPLYING
Standardized Tests *Recommended:* ACT (for admission).
Options: electronic application, early admission, deferred entrance.
Application fee: $35.
Required: high school transcript. ***Required for some:*** interview.
Application deadlines: rolling (freshmen), rolling (transfers).
Notification: continuous (freshmen), continuous (transfers).

CONTACT
Karen Erickson, Director of Admissions and Enrollment Services, Bismarck State College, PO Box 5587, Bismarck, ND 58506. *Phone:* 701-224-5424. *Toll-free phone:* 800-445-5073. *Fax:* 701-224-5643. *E-mail:* karen.erickson@bismarckstate.edu.

Dickinson State University

Dickinson, North Dakota

http://www.dickinsonstate.edu/

- **State-supported** 4-year, founded 1918, part of North Dakota University System
- **Small-town** 132-acre campus
- **Endowment** $10.9 million
- **Coed** 1,381 undergraduate students, 66% full-time, 59% women, 41% men
- **Minimally difficult** entrance level, 92% of applicants were admitted

UNDERGRAD STUDENTS
912 full-time, 469 part-time. Students come from 40 states and territories; 22 other countries; 28% are from out of state; 4% Black or African American, non-Hispanic/Latino; 6% Hispanic/Latino; 0.6% Asian, non-Hispanic/Latino; 0.5% Native Hawaiian or other Pacific Islander, non-Hispanic/Latino; 1% American Indian or Alaska Native, non-Hispanic/Latino; 3% Two or more races, non-Hispanic/Latino; 2% Race/ethnicity unknown; 6% international; 13% transferred in; 21% live on campus.

Freshmen:
Admission: 362 applied, 332 admitted, 190 enrolled. ***Test scores:*** ACT scores over 18: 88%; ACT scores over 24: 18%.
Retention: 54% of full-time freshmen returned.

FACULTY
Total: 142, 56% full-time, 34% with terminal degrees.
Student/faculty ratio: 11:1.

ACADEMICS
Calendar: semesters. *Degrees:* certificates, associate, and bachelor's.

Special study options: academic remediation for entering students, adult/continuing education programs, advanced placement credit, cooperative education, distance learning, double majors, honors programs, independent study, internships, off-campus study, part-time degree program, services for LD students, study abroad, summer session for credit.

Computers: 216 computers/terminals and 216 ports are available on campus for general student use. Students can access the following: campus intranet, computer help desk, free student e-mail accounts, online (class) grades, online (class) registration, online (class) schedules. Campuswide network is available. 100% of college-owned or -operated housing units are wired for high-speed Internet access. Wireless service is available via entire campus.

Library: Stoxen Library plus 1 other. *Books:* 80,760 (physical), 25,192 (digital/electronic); *Serial titles:* 269 (physical), 200 (digital/electronic); *Databases:* 115. Weekly public service hours: 73.

STUDENT LIFE
Housing options: on-campus residence required through sophomore year; coed. Campus housing is university owned. Freshman campus housing is guaranteed.

Activities and organizations: drama/theater group, student-run newspaper, choral group, Rodeo Club, Blue Hawk Brigade, chorale, Business Club, Navigators, national fraternities.

Athletics Member NAIA. ***Intercollegiate sports:*** badminton M/W, baseball M(s), basketball M(s)/W(s), cheerleading M/W, cross-country running M(s)/W(s), football M(s), golf M(s)/W(s), softball W(s), track and field M(s)/W(s), volleyball W(s), wrestling M(s). ***Intramural sports:*** badminton M/W, basketball M/W, football M/W, soccer M/W, softball W, squash M/W, table tennis M/W, tennis M/W, volleyball M/W, water polo M/W.

Campus security: 24-hour emergency response devices and patrols, late-night transport/escort service, controlled dormitory access, security phone app, Automated Mass Notification System.

Student services: health clinic, personal/psychological counseling.

COSTS & FINANCIAL AID
Costs (2017–18) ***Tuition:*** state resident $5139 full-time, $2569 per year part-time; nonresident $7709 full-time, $3854 per year part-time. Full-time tuition and fees vary according to course load, degree level, program, reciprocity agreements, and student level. Part-time tuition and fees vary according to course load, degree level, program, reciprocity agreements, and student level. ***Required fees:*** $1209 full-time, $50 per term part-time, $302 per term part-time. ***Room and board:*** $6750; room only: $2650. Room and board charges vary according to board plan and housing facility. ***Payment plan:*** installment. ***Waivers:*** employees or children of employees.

Financial Aid Of all full-time matriculated undergraduates who enrolled in 2014, 737 applied for aid, 530 were judged to have need, 167 had their need fully met. 69 Federal Work-Study jobs (averaging $3264). In 2014, 66 non-need-based awards were made. ***Average percent of need met:*** 48. ***Average financial aid package:*** $10,341. ***Average need-based loan:*** $5546. ***Average need-based gift aid:*** $5505. ***Average non-need-based aid:*** $1621. ***Average indebtedness upon graduation:*** $24,418.

APPLYING
Standardized Tests *Required:* SAT or ACT (for admission).

Options: electronic application, early admission, deferred entrance.

Application fee: $35.

Required: high school transcript, medical history, proof of measles-rubella shot.

Application deadlines: rolling (freshmen), rolling (transfers).

Notification: continuous (freshmen), continuous (transfers).

CONTACT
Ms. Heidi Kippenhan, Assistant Dean, Enrollment Management, Dickinson State University, Dickinson, ND 58601. *Phone:* 701-483-2566. *Toll-free phone:* 800-279-4295.
E-mail: heidi.kippenhan@dickinsonstate.edu.

Mayville State University

Mayville, North Dakota

http://www.mayvillestate.edu/

- **State-supported** 4-year, founded 1889, part of North Dakota University System
- **Rural** 60-acre campus
- **Coed**
- **Noncompetitive** entrance level

FACULTY
Student/faculty ratio: 13:1.

ACADEMICS
Calendar: semesters. *Degrees:* associate and bachelor's.
Library: Byrnes-Quanbeck Library plus 1 other.

STUDENT LIFE
Housing options: on-campus residence required through sophomore year; coed, men-only, women-only. Campus housing is university owned and is provided by a third party. Freshman campus housing is guaranteed.

Activities and organizations: drama/theater group, student-run newspaper, radio station, choral group, Student Activities Council, Student Education Association, Health and Physical Education Club, Campus Crusade, Student Ambassadors.

Athletics Member NAIA.

Campus security: controlled dormitory access.

Student services: health clinic, personal/psychological counseling.

COSTS & FINANCIAL AID
Costs (2016–17) ***One-time required fee:*** $35. ***Tuition:*** state resident $5053 full-time, $211 per credit hour part-time; nonresident $7580 full-time, $316 per credit hour part-time. Full-time tuition and fees vary according to course load, location, and reciprocity agreements. Part-time tuition and fees vary according to course load, location, and reciprocity agreements. ***Required fees:*** $1201 full-time, $50 per credit hour part-time. ***Room and board:*** $7107; room only: $3300. Room and board charges vary according to board plan and housing facility.

Financial Aid Of all full-time matriculated undergraduates who enrolled in 2015, 548 applied for aid, 420 were judged to have need, 133 had their need fully met. In 2015, 87 non-need-based awards were made. ***Average percent of need met:*** 79. ***Average financial aid package:*** $11,360. ***Average need-based loan:*** $5858. ***Average need-based gift aid:*** $5306. ***Average non-need-based aid:*** $1293. ***Average indebtedness upon graduation:*** $32,424.

APPLYING
Standardized Tests *Required:* SAT or ACT (for admission).

Options: electronic application, deferred entrance.

Application fee: $35.

Required: high school transcript, minimum 2.0 GPA.

CONTACT
Jim Morowski, Director of Freshmen Enrollment Services, Mayville State University, 330 3rd Street, NE, Mayville, ND 58257-1299. *Phone:* 701-788-4842. *Toll-free phone:* 800-437-4104. *Fax:* 701-788-4748.
E-mail: james.morowski@mayvillestate.edu.

Minot State University

Minot, North Dakota

http://www.minotstateu.edu/

- **State-supported** comprehensive, founded 1913, part of North Dakota University System
- **Small-town** 103-acre campus
- **Coed** 3,064 undergraduate students, 66% full-time, 61% women, 39% men
- **Moderately difficult** entrance level, 57% of applicants were admitted

UNDERGRAD STUDENTS
2,021 full-time, 1,043 part-time. 17% are from out of state; 6% Black or African American, non-Hispanic/Latino; 6% Hispanic/Latino; 2% Asian, non-Hispanic/Latino; 0.5% Native Hawaiian or other Pacific Islander, non-Hispanic/Latino; 1% American Indian or Alaska Native, non-Hispanic/Latino; 4% Two or more races, non-Hispanic/Latino; 2%

Race/ethnicity unknown; 13% international; 10% transferred in; 21% live on campus.

Freshmen:
Admission: 840 applied, 477 admitted, 341 enrolled. ***Average high school GPA:*** 3.36.
Retention: 75% of full-time freshmen returned.

FACULTY
Total: 279, 60% full-time, 35% with terminal degrees.
Student/faculty ratio: 12:1.

ACADEMICS
Calendar: semesters. *Degrees:* certificates, associate, bachelor's, master's, and postbachelor's certificates.
Special study options: academic remediation for entering students, accelerated degree program, advanced placement credit, cooperative education, distance learning, double majors, English as a second language, honors programs, independent study, internships, part-time degree program, services for LD students, student-designed majors, study abroad, summer session for credit.
Computers: Students can access the following: campus intranet, computer help desk, free student e-mail accounts, online (class) grades, online (class) registration, online (class) schedules. Campuswide network is available. Wireless service is available via entire campus.
Library: Gordon B. Olson Library.

STUDENT LIFE
Housing options: on-campus residence required for freshman year; coed, men-only, women-only, special housing for students with disabilities. Campus housing is university owned. Freshman campus housing is guaranteed.
Activities and organizations: drama/theater group, student-run newspaper, radio and television station, choral group, marching band, Residence Hall Association, Student Government Association, Beavers on Business, Student Social Work Organization, National Student Speech and Hearing Association.
Athletics Member NCAA, NAIA, NCCAA. All NCAA Division II. ***Intercollegiate sports:*** baseball M(s), basketball M(s)/W(s), cheerleading W, cross-country running M(s)/W(s), football M(s), golf M/W, ice hockey M(c), soccer W, softball W(s), track and field M(s)/W(s), volleyball W(s), wrestling M. ***Intramural sports:*** basketball M/W, racquetball M/W, softball M/W, volleyball M/W.
Campus security: controlled dormitory access, patrols by trained security personnel.
Student services: health clinic, personal/psychological counseling, women's center.

COSTS & FINANCIAL AID
Costs (2016–17) ***Tuition:*** state resident $5193 full-time, $216 per credit hour part-time; nonresident $5193 full-time, $216 per credit hour part-time. Full-time tuition and fees vary according to class time, course load, degree level, location, program, and reciprocity agreements. Part-time tuition and fees vary according to class time, course load, degree level, location, program, and reciprocity agreements. ***Required fees:*** $1375 full-time, $57 per credit hour part-time. ***Room and board:*** Room and board charges vary according to board plan and housing facility. ***Payment plan:*** installment. ***Waivers:*** minority students, children of alumni, senior citizens, and employees or children of employees.
Financial Aid Of all full-time matriculated undergraduates who enrolled in 2015, 1,322 applied for aid, 902 were judged to have need, 321 had their need fully met. 92 Federal Work-Study jobs (averaging $1581). In 2015, 316 non-need-based awards were made. ***Average percent of need met:*** 68. ***Average financial aid package:*** $10,048. ***Average need-based loan:*** $5778. ***Average need-based gift aid:*** $5106. ***Average non-need-based aid:*** $1348. ***Average indebtedness upon graduation:*** $25,110.

APPLYING
Standardized Tests *Required:* SAT or ACT (for admission).
Options: electronic application, deferred entrance.
Application fee: $35.
Required: high school transcript. ***Required for some:*** minimum 2.5 GPA.

CONTACT
Mr. Kevin Harmon, Vice President of Enrollment Management, Minot State University, 500 University Avenue West, Minot, ND 58707-0002. *Phone:* 701-858-3126. *Toll-free phone:* 800-777-0750 Ext. 3350. *Fax:* 701-858-3825. *E-mail:* askmsu@minotstateu.edu.

North Dakota State University

Fargo, North Dakota

http://www.ndsu.edu/

- **State-supported** university, founded 1890, part of North Dakota University System
- **Urban** 2100-acre campus
- **Endowment** $509,719
- **Coed** 12,010 undergraduate students, 89% full-time, 46% women, 54% men
- **Moderately difficult** entrance level, 93% of applicants were admitted

UNDERGRAD STUDENTS
10,680 full-time, 1,330 part-time. Students come from 45 states and territories; 51 other countries; 57% are from out of state; 3% Black or African American, non-Hispanic/Latino; 2% Hispanic/Latino; 1% Asian, non-Hispanic/Latino; 0.1% Native Hawaiian or other Pacific Islander, non-Hispanic/Latino; 0.7% American Indian or Alaska Native, non-Hispanic/Latino; 3% Two or more races, non-Hispanic/Latino; 1% Race/ethnicity unknown; 2% international; 6% transferred in; 32% live on campus.

Freshmen:
Admission: 5,128 applied, 4,759 admitted, 2,503 enrolled. ***Average high school GPA:*** 3.43. ***Test scores:*** SAT critical reading scores over 500: 74%; SAT math scores over 500: 77%; SAT writing scores over 500: 66%; ACT scores over 18: 98%; SAT critical reading scores over 600: 38%; SAT math scores over 600: 51%; SAT writing scores over 600: 28%; ACT scores over 24: 52%; SAT critical reading scores over 700: 6%; SAT math scores over 700: 15%; SAT writing scores over 700: 2%; ACT scores over 30: 8%.
Retention: 80% of full-time freshmen returned.

FACULTY
Total: 817, 86% full-time, 79% with terminal degrees.
Student/faculty ratio: 17:1.

ACADEMICS
Calendar: semesters. *Degrees:* certificates, bachelor's, master's, doctoral, post-master's, and postbachelor's certificates.
Special study options: accelerated degree program, advanced placement credit, cooperative education, distance learning, double majors, honors programs, independent study, internships, off-campus study, part-time degree program, services for LD students, student-designed majors, study abroad, summer session for credit. ***ROTC:*** Army (b), Air Force (b).
Computers: 601 computers/terminals are available on campus for general student use. Students can access the following: campus intranet, computer help desk, free student e-mail accounts, online (class) grades, online (class) registration, online (class) schedules, online course content (e.g., learning management system, lecture capture video recordings). Campuswide network is available. 100% of college-owned or -operated housing units are wired for high-speed Internet access. Wireless service is available via entire campus.
Library: North Dakota State University Library plus 4 others. Students can reserve study rooms.

STUDENT LIFE
Housing options: on-campus residence required for freshman year; coed, men-only, women-only, special housing for students with disabilities. Campus housing is university owned. Freshman campus housing is guaranteed.
Activities and organizations: drama/theater group, student-run newspaper, radio and television station, choral group, marching band, Saddle and Sirloin, Students Today, Leaders Forever, Chi Alpha Christian Organization, fraternities/sororities, CRU, national fraternities, national sororities.
Athletics Member NCAA. All Division I. ***Intercollegiate sports:*** badminton M(c)/W(c), baseball M(s), basketball M(s)/W(s), bowling M(c)/W(c), cross-country running M(s)/W(s), equestrian sports W(c),

football M(s), golf M/W(s), ice hockey M(c)/W(c), lacrosse M(c)/W(c), riflery M(c)/W(c), rugby M(c)/W(c), soccer M(c)/W(s), softball W(s), track and field M(s)/W(s), volleyball M(c)/W(s), wrestling M(s). *Intramural sports:* baseball M, basketball M/W, football M/W, rock climbing M/W, soccer M/W, softball M/W, tennis M(c)/W(c), ultimate Frisbee M/W, volleyball M/W.

Campus security: 24-hour emergency response devices and patrols, late-night transport/escort service, controlled dormitory access, Pathlight app.

Student services: health clinic, personal/psychological counseling.

COSTS & FINANCIAL AID
Costs (2016–17) ***One-time required fee:*** $120. ***Tuition:*** state resident $6924 full-time, $305 per credit hour part-time; nonresident $18,488 full-time, $814 per credit hour part-time. Full-time tuition and fees vary according to course load, program, and reciprocity agreements. Part-time tuition and fees vary according to course load, program, and reciprocity agreements. ***Required fees:*** $1283 full-time, $53 per credit hour part-time. ***Room and board:*** $7918; room only: $3648. Room and board charges vary according to board plan and housing facility. ***Waivers:*** minority students, children of alumni, senior citizens, and employees or children of employees.

Financial Aid Of all full-time matriculated undergraduates who enrolled in 2007, 7,109 applied for aid, 4,917 were judged to have need, 980 had their need fully met. In 2007, 1763 non-need-based awards were made. ***Average percent of need met:*** 3. ***Average financial aid package:*** $7030. ***Average need-based loan:*** $4378. ***Average need-based gift aid:*** $3419. ***Average non-need-based aid:*** $1533.

APPLYING
Standardized Tests *Required:* SAT or ACT (for admission).

Options: electronic application.

Application fee: $35.

Required: high school transcript, minimum 2.8 GPA.

Application deadlines: 8/1 (freshmen), 8/1 (transfers).

Notification: continuous (freshmen), continuous (transfers).

CONTACT
Ms. Merideth Sherlin, Director of Admission, North Dakota State University, NDSU Department 2832, PO Box 6050, Fargo, ND 58108-6050. *Phone:* 701-231-8643. *Toll-free phone:* 800-488-6378. *Fax:* 701-231-8802. *E-mail:* ndsu.admission@ndsu.edu.

Rasmussen College Fargo

Fargo, North Dakota

http://www.rasmussen.edu/

- **Proprietary** 4-year, founded 1902, part of Rasmussen College System
- **Suburban** campus
- **Coed** 346 undergraduate students, 59% full-time, 67% women, 33% men
- **Minimally difficult** entrance level, 90% of applicants were admitted

UNDERGRAD STUDENTS
205 full-time, 141 part-time.

Freshmen:
Admission: 20 applied, 18 admitted, 19 enrolled.

FACULTY
Total: 8, 50% full-time.

Student/faculty ratio: 22:1.

ACADEMICS
Calendar: quarters. *Degrees:* certificates, diplomas, associate, and bachelor's.

Special study options: academic remediation for entering students, accelerated degree program, adult/continuing education programs, distance learning, double majors, internships, part-time degree program, summer session for credit.

Computers: 87 computers/terminals are available on campus for general student use. Students can access the following: computer help desk, free student e-mail accounts, online (class) grades, online (class) schedules. Campuswide network is available. Wireless service is available via entire campus.

Library: Rasmussen College Library - Fargo.

STUDENT LIFE
Housing options: college housing not available.

COSTS
Costs (2017–18) ***Tuition:*** $11,055 full-time. Full-time tuition and fees vary according to course level, course load, degree level, location, and program. Part-time tuition and fees vary according to course level, course load, degree level, location, and program. No tuition increase for student's term of enrollment. ***Required fees:*** $1695 full-time. ***Payment plans:*** installment, deferred payment. ***Waivers:*** employees or children of employees.

APPLYING
Standardized Tests *Required:* institutional exam (for admission).

Options: electronic application, early admission, deferred entrance.

Required: high school transcript, minimum 2.0 GPA. ***Required for some:*** interview.

Application deadlines: rolling (freshmen), rolling (transfers).

CONTACT
Susan Hammerstrom, Director of Admissions, Rasmussen College Fargo, 4012 19th Avenue South, Fargo, ND 58103. *Phone:* 701-277-3889. *Toll-free phone:* 888-549-6755. *E-mail:* susan.hammerstrom@rasmussen.edu.

Sitting Bull College

Fort Yates, North Dakota

http://www.sittingbull.edu/

CONTACT
Ms. Melody Silk, Director of Registration and Admissions, Sitting Bull College, 1341 92nd Street, Fort Yates, ND 58538-9701. *Phone:* 701-854-3864. *Fax:* 701-854-3403. *E-mail:* melodys@sbcl.edu.

Trinity Bible College

Ellendale, North Dakota

http://www.trinitybiblecollege.edu/

- **Independent Assemblies of God** comprehensive, founded 1948
- **Rural** 28-acre campus
- **Coed**
- **Noncompetitive** entrance level

ACADEMICS
Calendar: semesters. *Degrees:* associate, bachelor's, and master's.

Library: Graham Library.

STUDENT LIFE
Housing options: on-campus residence required through junior year; men-only, women-only. Campus housing is university owned. Freshman campus housing is guaranteed.

Activities and organizations: drama/theater group, student-run radio station, choral group.

Athletics Member NCCAA.

Campus security: 24-hour emergency response devices, student patrols, late-night transport/escort service.

Student services: personal/psychological counseling.

COSTS & FINANCIAL AID
Costs (2016–17) ***Comprehensive fee:*** $21,876 includes full-time tuition ($13,962), mandatory fees ($1950), and room and board ($5964). Full-time tuition and fees vary according to course load. Part-time tuition: $469 per credit hour. Part-time tuition and fees vary according to course load. ***Required fees:*** $500 per term part-time. ***College room only:*** $2766. Room and board charges vary according to board plan, housing facility, and student level.

Financial Aid ***Financial aid deadline:*** 9/1.

APPLYING
Standardized Tests *Required:* SAT or ACT (for admission).

Options: electronic application, deferred entrance.

Application fee: $25.

Required: essay or personal statement, high school transcript, minimum 2.0 GPA, 2 letters of recommendation, health form, evidence of Christian conversion, background check. ***Required for some:*** interview.

CONTACT
Trinity Bible College, 50 Sixth Avenue South, Ellendale, ND 58436.
Phone: 701-349-5399. *Toll-free phone:* 800-523-1603.
E-mail: admissions@trinitybiblecollege.edu.

University of Jamestown
Jamestown, North Dakota
http://www.uj.edu/

- **Independent Presbyterian** comprehensive, founded 1883
- **Small-town** 110-acre campus
- **Endowment** $33.1 million
- **Coed** 955 undergraduate students, 96% full-time, 50% women, 50% men
- **Minimally difficult** entrance level, 57% of applicants were admitted

UNDERGRAD STUDENTS
914 full-time, 41 part-time. Students come from 36 states and territories; 22 other countries; 50% are from out of state; 5% Black or African American, non-Hispanic/Latino; 7% Hispanic/Latino; 1% Asian, non-Hispanic/Latino; 1% Native Hawaiian or other Pacific Islander, non-Hispanic/Latino; 1% American Indian or Alaska Native, non-Hispanic/Latino; 0.2% Race/ethnicity unknown; 10% international; 6% transferred in; 80% live on campus.

Freshmen:
Admission: 1,560 applied, 894 admitted, 262 enrolled. ***Average high school GPA:*** 3.37. ***Test scores:*** SAT critical reading scores over 500: 38%; SAT math scores over 500: 56%; ACT scores over 18: 96%; SAT critical reading scores over 600: 12%; SAT math scores over 600: 10%; ACT scores over 24: 35%; ACT scores over 30: 5%.

Retention: 77% of full-time freshmen returned.

FACULTY
Total: 116, 63% full-time, 38% with terminal degrees.

Student/faculty ratio: 13:1.

ACADEMICS
Calendar: semesters. *Degrees:* bachelor's, master's, and doctoral.

Special study options: advanced placement credit, cooperative education, double majors, honors programs, independent study, internships, part-time degree program, services for LD students, student-designed majors, study abroad, summer session for credit.

Unusual degree programs: 3-2 engineering with North Dakota State University, University of North Dakota, South Dakota State University, Washington University in St. Louis.

Computers: 200 computers/terminals and 570 ports are available on campus for general student use. Students can access the following: campus intranet, computer help desk, free student e-mail accounts, online (class) grades, online (class) registration, online (class) schedules. Campuswide network is available. 100% of college-owned or -operated housing units are wired for high-speed Internet access. Wireless service is available via entire campus.
Library: Raugust Library. *Books:* 103,488 (physical), 15,176 (digital/electronic); *Serial titles:* 82 (physical), 62,342 (digital/electronic); *Databases:* 83. Weekly public service hours: 89; students can reserve study rooms.

STUDENT LIFE
Housing options: on-campus residence required through junior year; coed, special housing for students with disabilities. Campus housing is university owned and leased by the school. Freshman campus housing is guaranteed.
Activities and organizations: drama/theater group, student-run newspaper, choral group, Ignition, Student Senate, Relay for Life, Hibitat for Humanity, Fellowship of Christian Athletes.

Athletics Member NAIA. ***Intercollegiate sports:*** baseball M(s), basketball M(s)/W(s), cross-country running M(s)/W(s), football M(s), golf M(s)/W(s), ice hockey M(c), soccer M(s)/W(s), softball W(s), track and field M(s)/W(s), volleyball W(s), wrestling M(s)/W(s). ***Intramural sports:*** basketball M/W, football M/W, volleyball M/W.

Campus security: 24-hour emergency response devices, late-night transport/escort service, controlled dormitory access, campus security cameras.

Student services: personal/psychological counseling.

COSTS & FINANCIAL AID
Costs (2017–18) ***Comprehensive fee:*** $28,508 includes full-time tuition ($20,578), mandatory fees ($580), and room and board ($7350). Full-time tuition and fees vary according to course load, degree level, and program. Part-time tuition: $435 per semester hour. Part-time tuition and fees vary according to course load, degree level, and program. ***College room only:*** $3466. Room and board charges vary according to housing facility. ***Payment plan:*** installment. ***Waivers:*** employees or children of employees.

Financial Aid Of all full-time matriculated undergraduates who enrolled in 2015, 691 applied for aid, 555 were judged to have need, 140 had their need fully met. 221 Federal Work-Study jobs (averaging $841). 76 state and other part-time jobs (averaging $526). In 2015, 281 non-need-based awards were made. ***Average percent of need met:*** 75. ***Average financial aid package:*** $15,775. ***Average need-based loan:*** $4174. ***Average need-based gift aid:*** $12,412. ***Average non-need-based aid:*** $8540. ***Average indebtedness upon graduation:*** $25,368.

APPLYING
Standardized Tests *Required:* SAT or ACT (for admission).

Options: electronic application, deferred entrance.

Required: high school transcript, minimum 2.5 GPA. ***Required for some:*** interview.

Application deadlines: rolling (freshmen), rolling (transfers).

CONTACT
Mr. Mike Heitkamp, VP of Enrollment Management, University of Jamestown, 6081 College Lane, Jamestown, ND 58401. *Phone:* 701-252-3467 Ext. 5512. *Toll-free phone:* 800-336-2554. *Fax:* 701-253-4318.
E-mail: admissions@uj.edu.

University of Mary
Bismarck, North Dakota
http://www.umary.edu/

- **Independent Roman Catholic** comprehensive, founded 1959
- **Rural** 107-acre campus
- **Endowment** $44.2 million
- **Coed**
- **Minimally difficult** entrance level

FACULTY
Student/faculty ratio: 13:1.

ACADEMICS
Calendar: semesters. *Degrees:* bachelor's, master's, and doctoral.
Library: University of Mary Library.

STUDENT LIFE
Housing options: on-campus residence required through sophomore year; coed, men-only, women-only. Campus housing is university owned. Freshman campus housing is guaranteed.
Activities and organizations: drama/theater group, student-run newspaper, choral group, Collegians for Life, Nursing Students Association, Student Occupational Therapy, UMPHERD, Pre-PT Club.

Athletics Member NCAA. All Division II.

Campus security: 24-hour emergency response devices and patrols, late-night transport/escort service, controlled dormitory access.

Student services: health clinic, personal/psychological counseling.

COSTS
Costs (2016–17) ***Comprehensive fee:*** $23,923 includes full-time tuition ($15,990), mandatory fees ($1555), and room and board ($6378). Full-time tuition and fees vary according to course load, degree level, program, and student level. Part-time tuition: $535 per credit hour. Part-time tuition and fees vary according to course load, degree level, program, and student level. ***Required fees:*** $27 per credit hour part-time. ***College room only:*** $2966. Room and board charges vary according to board plan and housing facility.

APPLYING
Standardized Tests *Required:* SAT or ACT (for admission).

Options: electronic application, early admission, deferred entrance.

Application fee: $25.

Required: high school transcript, minimum 2.0 GPA in College Prep curriculum. ***Required for some:*** essay or personal statement, interview. ***Recommended:*** minimum 2.5 GPA, 2 letters of recommendation.

CONTACT

Mr. Curtis Ray DeGraw, University of Mary, 7500 University Drive, Bismarck, ND 58504-9652. *Phone:* 701-355-8191. *Toll-free phone:* 800-288-6279. *Fax:* 701-255-7687. *E-mail:* mcheitkamp@umary.edu.

University of North Dakota

Grand Forks, North Dakota

http://www.und.edu/

- **State-supported** university, founded 1883, part of North Dakota University System
- **Urban** 521-acre campus
- **Endowment** $22.1 million
- **Coed** 11,255 undergraduate students, 78% full-time, 43% women, 57% men
- **Minimally difficult** entrance level, 84% of applicants were admitted

UNDERGRAD STUDENTS

8,827 full-time, 2,428 part-time. Students come from 60 states and territories; 68 other countries; 60% are from out of state; 2% Black or African American, non-Hispanic/Latino; 3% Hispanic/Latino; 2% Asian, non-Hispanic/Latino; 0.1% Native Hawaiian or other Pacific Islander, non-Hispanic/Latino; 1% American Indian or Alaska Native, non-Hispanic/Latino; 3% Two or more races, non-Hispanic/Latino; 2% Race/ethnicity unknown; 6% international; 7% transferred in; 27% live on campus.

Freshmen:

Admission: 5,144 applied, 4,305 admitted, 1,928 enrolled. ***Average high school GPA:*** 3.4. ***Test scores:*** ACT scores over 18: 97%; ACT scores over 24: 48%; ACT scores over 30: 6%.

Retention: 80% of full-time freshmen returned.

FACULTY

Total: 753, 93% full-time, 72% with terminal degrees.

Student/faculty ratio: 19:1.

ACADEMICS

Calendar: semesters. *Degrees:* certificates, bachelor's, master's, doctoral, post-master's, and postbachelor's certificates.

Special study options: accelerated degree program, adult/continuing education programs, advanced placement credit, cooperative education, distance learning, double majors, English as a second language, external degree program, honors programs, independent study, internships, off-campus study, part-time degree program, services for LD students, student-designed majors, study abroad, summer session for credit. ***ROTC:*** Army (b), Air Force (b).

Unusual degree programs: 3-2 engineering; applied economics, counseling, chemistry, public administration.

Computers: 1,000 computers/terminals and 400 ports are available on campus for general student use. Students can access the following: campus intranet, computer help desk, free student e-mail accounts, online (class) grades, online (class) registration, online (class) schedules. Campuswide network is available. 100% of college-owned or -operated housing units are wired for high-speed Internet access. Wireless service is available via classrooms, computer centers, computer labs, dorm rooms, learning centers, libraries, student centers.

Library: Chester Fritz Library plus 2 others. *Books:* 571,458 (physical), 146,797 (digital/electronic); *Serial titles:* 26,062 (physical), 62,508 (digital/electronic); *Databases:* 90. Weekly public service hours: 99.

STUDENT LIFE

Housing options: coed, men-only, women-only, special housing for students with disabilities. Campus housing is university owned.

Activities and organizations: drama/theater group, student-run newspaper, radio and television station, choral group, marching band, NODAK NATION, Cru, Physical Therapy Club, Nursing Student Association, Sororities/Fraternities, national fraternities, national sororities.

Athletics Member NCAA. All Division I. ***Intercollegiate sports:*** basketball M(s)/W(s), cross-country running M(s)/W(s), football M(s), golf M(s)/W(s), ice hockey M(s)/W(s), soccer W(s), softball W(s), swimming and diving M(s)/W(s), tennis W(s), track and field M(s)/W(s), volleyball W(s). ***Intramural sports:*** basketball M/W, ice hockey M/W, soccer M/W, softball M/W, ultimate Frisbee M/W, volleyball M/W.

Campus security: 24-hour emergency response devices and patrols, student patrols, late-night transport/escort service, controlled dormitory access.

Student services: health clinic, personal/psychological counseling, women's center, legal services.

COSTS & FINANCIAL AID

Costs (2016–17) ***Tuition:*** state resident $6679 full-time, $278 per credit hour part-time; nonresident $17,833 full-time, $743 per credit hour part-time. Full-time tuition and fees vary according to degree level, program, and reciprocity agreements. Part-time tuition and fees vary according to course load, degree level, program, and reciprocity agreements. ***Required fees:*** $1458 full-time. ***Room and board:*** $7630. Room and board charges vary according to board plan and housing facility. ***Payment plan:*** deferred payment. ***Waivers:*** minority students, adult students, senior citizens, and employees or children of employees.

Financial Aid Of all full-time matriculated undergraduates who enrolled in 2010, 6,878 applied for aid, 5,256 were judged to have need, 5,108 had their need fully met. In 2010, 2719 non-need-based awards were made. ***Average percent of need met:*** 39. ***Average financial aid package:*** $9651. ***Average need-based loan:*** $5349. ***Average need-based gift aid:*** $4076. ***Average non-need-based aid:*** $1602. ***Average indebtedness upon graduation:*** $31,764.

APPLYING

Standardized Tests *Required:* SAT or ACT (for admission).

Options: electronic application, deferred entrance.

Application fee: $35.

Required: high school transcript. ***Recommended:*** minimum 2.5 GPA.

Notification: continuous (transfers).

CONTACT

Jason Trainer, Director of Admissions, University of North Dakota, Gorecki Alumni Center, 3501 University Avenue, Stop 8357, Grand Forks, ND 58202. *Phone:* 701-777-3000. *Toll-free phone:* 800-CALL-UND. *Fax:* 701-777-2721. *E-mail:* und.admissions@und.edu.

Valley City State University

Valley City, North Dakota

http://www.vcsu.edu/

- **State-supported** comprehensive, founded 1890, part of North Dakota University System
- **Small-town** 55-acre campus
- **Coed** 1,295 undergraduate students, 62% full-time, 58% women, 42% men
- **Noncompetitive** entrance level, 98% of applicants were admitted

UNDERGRAD STUDENTS

798 full-time, 497 part-time. Students come from 42 states and territories; 11 other countries; 36% are from out of state; 3% Black or African American, non-Hispanic/Latino; 5% Hispanic/Latino; 0.7% Asian, non-Hispanic/Latino; 0.1% Native Hawaiian or other Pacific Islander, non-Hispanic/Latino; 1% American Indian or Alaska Native, non-Hispanic/Latino; 3% Two or more races, non-Hispanic/Latino; 2% Race/ethnicity unknown; 2% international; 9% transferred in; 35% live on campus.

Freshmen:

Admission: 372 applied, 365 admitted, 186 enrolled. ***Average high school GPA:*** 3.12. ***Test scores:*** SAT critical reading scores over 500: 78%; SAT math scores over 500: 11%; ACT scores over 18: 83%; SAT critical reading scores over 600; 22%; ACT scores over 24: 25%; ACT scores over 30: 3%.

Retention: 71% of full-time freshmen returned.

ACADEMICS

Calendar: semesters. *Degrees:* bachelor's and master's.

Special study options: academic remediation for entering students, cooperative education, distance learning, double majors, internships, off-campus study, part-time degree program, services for LD students, student-designed majors, study abroad, summer session for credit.

Computers: 995 computers/terminals are available on campus for general student use. Students can access the following: campus intranet, computer help desk, free student e-mail accounts, online (class) grades, online (class) registration, online (class) schedules. Campuswide network is available. 100% of college-owned or -operated housing units are wired for high-speed Internet access. Wireless service is available via entire campus.

Library: Allen Memorial Library. *Books:* 77,407 (physical), 37,791 (digital/electronic); *Serial titles:* 1,202 (physical), 1,440 (digital/electronic); *Databases:* 91. Students can reserve study rooms.

STUDENT LIFE

Housing options: on-campus residence required for freshman year; coed, men-only, women-only. Campus housing is university owned. Freshman campus housing is guaranteed.

Activities and organizations: drama/theater group, choral group, departmental clubs, Fellowship of Christian Athletes, intramural sports, VCAB, Viking Ambassadors.

Athletics Member NAIA. ***Intercollegiate sports:*** baseball M(s), basketball M(s)/W(s), cross-country running M(s)/W(s), football M(s), golf M(s)/W(s), softball W(s), tennis M(c)/W(c), track and field M(s)/W(s), volleyball W(s). ***Intramural sports:*** basketball M/W, bowling M/W, cross-country running M/W, football M/W, golf M/W, ice hockey M/W, racquetball M/W, skiing (cross-country) M/W, soccer M/W, softball M/W, tennis M/W, track and field M/W, volleyball M/W.

Campus security: controlled dormitory access, security cameras throughout campus.

Student services: health clinic, personal/psychological counseling.

COSTS & FINANCIAL AID

Costs (2016–17) ***Tuition:*** state resident $5282 full-time, $176 per semester hour part-time; nonresident $14,103 full-time, $470 per semester hour part-time. Full-time tuition and fees vary according to course load, location, program, and reciprocity agreements. Part-time tuition and fees vary according to course load, location, program, and reciprocity agreements. ***Required fees:*** $1913 full-time, $80 per semester hour part-time. ***Room and board:*** $6072; room only: $3575. Room and board charges vary according to board plan and housing facility. ***Payment plan:*** installment. ***Waivers:*** employees or children of employees.

Financial Aid Of all full-time matriculated undergraduates who enrolled in 2016, 591 applied for aid, 421 were judged to have need, 226 had their need fully met. 52 Federal Work-Study jobs (averaging $2118). In 2016, 138 non-need-based awards were made. ***Average percent of need met:*** 86. ***Average financial aid package:*** $12,486. ***Average need-based loan:*** $5831. ***Average need-based gift aid:*** $5937. ***Average non-need-based aid:*** $2224. ***Average indebtedness upon graduation:*** $24,281.

APPLYING

Standardized Tests *Required for some:* SAT or ACT (for admission).

Options: electronic application, early admission, deferred entrance.

Application fee: $35.

Required: high school transcript.

Application deadlines: rolling (freshmen), rolling (transfers).

Notification: continuous (freshmen), continuous (transfers).

CONTACT

Ms. Kaleen Peterson, Admission Counselor, Valley City State University, 101 College Street Southwest, Valley City, ND 58072. *Phone:* 701-845-7115. *Toll-free phone:* 800-532-8641 Ext. 7101. *Fax:* 701-845-7299. *E-mail:* kaleen.peterson@vcsu.edu.

OHIO

AIC College of Design

Cincinnati, Ohio

http://www.aic-arts.edu/

CONTACT

Megan Orsburn, Admissions Assistant, AIC College of Design, 1171 E. Kemper Road, Cincinnati, OH 45246. *Phone:* 513-751-1206.

Allegheny Wesleyan College

Salem, Ohio

http://www.awc.edu/

CONTACT

Admissions Office, Allegheny Wesleyan College, 2161 Woodsdale Road, Salem, OH 44460. *Phone:* 330-337-6403. *Toll-free phone:* 800-292-3153. *E-mail:* college@awc.edu.

Antioch College

Yellow Springs, Ohio

http://www.antiochcollege.edu/

- **Independent** 4-year, founded 2011
- **Rural** 1100-acre campus with easy access to Columbus
- **Endowment** $44.4 million
- **Coed** 217 undergraduate students, 100% full-time, 60% women, 40% men
- **Very difficult** entrance level, 73% of applicants were admitted

UNDERGRAD STUDENTS

217 full-time. Students come from 38 states and territories; 70% are from out of state; 8% Black or African American, non-Hispanic/Latino; 9% Hispanic/Latino; 4% Asian, non-Hispanic/Latino; 0.5% Native Hawaiian or other Pacific Islander, non-Hispanic/Latino; 2% American Indian or Alaska Native, non-Hispanic/Latino; 8% Two or more races, non-Hispanic/Latino; 5% Race/ethnicity unknown; 7% transferred in; 65% live on campus.

Freshmen:

Admission: 94 applied, 69 admitted, 32 enrolled. ***Average high school GPA:*** 2.9.

Retention: 59% of full-time freshmen returned.

FACULTY

Total: 39, 87% full-time, 72% with terminal degrees.

Student/faculty ratio: 6:1.

ACADEMICS

Calendar: quarters. *Degree:* bachelor's.

Special study options: academic remediation for entering students, advanced placement credit, cooperative education, independent study, off-campus study, services for LD students, student-designed majors, summer session for credit.

Computers: Students can access the following: campus intranet, computer help desk, free student e-mail accounts, online (class) grades, online (class) registration, online (class) schedules. Campuswide network is available. 100% of college-owned or -operated housing units are wired for high-speed Internet access. Wireless service is available via entire campus.

Library: Olive Kettering Library plus 1 other. *Books:* 335,000 (physical), 120,000 (digital/electronic); *Serial titles:* 147 (physical), 100,000 (digital/electronic); *Databases:* 156. Weekly public service hours: 72.

STUDENT LIFE

Housing options: on-campus residence required through sophomore year; coed. Campus housing is university owned.

Activities and organizations: drama/theater group, student-run newspaper, choral group, People of Color Group, Abilities Group, Queer Center, To Shin Do, Feminism Group.

Campus security: 24-hour emergency response devices and patrols, controlled dormitory access.

Student services: health clinic, personal/psychological counseling, women's center.

COSTS

Costs (2016–17) ***Comprehensive fee:*** $46,932 includes full-time tuition ($34,568), mandatory fees ($1000), and room and board ($11,364). Full-time tuition and fees vary according to reciprocity agreements. Part-time tuition: $500 per credit hour. Part-time tuition and fees vary according to reciprocity agreements. ***College room only:*** $6933. ***Payment plans:*** installment, deferred payment. ***Waivers:*** employees or children of employees.

APPLYING

Options: electronic application, early admission, early decision, deferred entrance.

Required: essay or personal statement, 2 letters of recommendation, interview. ***Recommended:*** high school transcript.

Notification: 4/1 (freshmen).

CONTACT

Mr. Shane Creepingbear, Associate Director of Admission, Antioch College, South Hall, Antioch College, Yellow Springs, OH 45387. *Phone:* 937-284-0830. *E-mail:* screepingbear@antiochcollege.edu.

Antioch University Midwest

Yellow Springs, Ohio

http://midwest.antioch.edu/

- **Independent** upper-level, founded 1988, part of Antioch University
- **Small-town** 100-acre campus with easy access to Dayton
- **Coed** 38 undergraduate students
- **Noncompetitive** entrance level

UNDERGRAD STUDENTS

Students come from 8 states and territories; 1 other country; 1% are from out of state; 13% Black or African American, non-Hispanic/Latino; 34% Race/ethnicity unknown.

ACADEMICS

Calendar: semesters. *Degrees:* certificates, bachelor's, master's, post-master's, and postbachelor's certificates.

Special study options: accelerated degree program, adult/continuing education programs, advanced placement credit, cooperative education, distance learning, double majors, independent study, internships, off-campus study, part-time degree program, services for LD students, student-designed majors, summer session for credit.

Computers: 10 computers/terminals are available on campus for general student use. Students can access the following: campus intranet, computer help desk, free student e-mail accounts, online (class) grades, online (class) registration, online (class) schedules, online bill pay and view/acceptance of financial aid award letter, narrative evaluations. Campuswide network is available. Wireless service is available via entire campus.

Library: Midwest Library.

STUDENT LIFE

Housing options: college housing not available.

Campus security: 24-hour emergency response devices.

Student services: personal/psychological counseling.

COSTS

Costs (2016–17) ***Tuition:*** $18,972 full-time, $527 per credit part-time. ***Required fees:*** $400 full-time, $200 per term part-time. ***Payment plan:*** installment. ***Waivers:*** employees or children of employees.

APPLYING

Options: electronic application, deferred entrance.

Application fee: $45.

CONTACT

Antioch University Midwest, 900 Dayton Street, Yellow Springs, OH 45387-1609. *Phone:* 937-769-1823.

Art Academy of Cincinnati

Cincinnati, Ohio

http://www.artacademy.edu/

CONTACT

Mr. John J. Wadell, Director of Admissions, Art Academy of Cincinnati, 1212 Jackson Street, Cincinnati, OH 45202-7106. *Phone:* 513-562-8744. *Toll-free phone:* 800-323-5692. *Fax:* 513-562-8778. *E-mail:* admissions@artacademy.edu.

Ashland University

Ashland, Ohio

http://www.ashland.edu/

- **Independent** comprehensive, founded 1878, affiliated with Brethren Church
- **Small-town** 135-acre campus with easy access to Cleveland, Akron
- **Endowment** $36.8 million
- **Coed** 4,536 undergraduate students, 75% full-time, 47% women, 53% men
- **Moderately difficult** entrance level, 67% of applicants were admitted

UNDERGRAD STUDENTS

3,414 full-time, 1,122 part-time. Students come from 31 states and territories; 19 other countries; 7% are from out of state; 13% Black or African American, non-Hispanic/Latino; 3% Hispanic/Latino; 0.6% Asian, non-Hispanic/Latino; 0.1% Native Hawaiian or other Pacific Islander, non-Hispanic/Latino; 0.5% American Indian or Alaska Native, non-Hispanic/Latino; 2% Two or more races, non-Hispanic/Latino; 3% Race/ethnicity unknown; 2% international; 4% transferred in; 44% live on campus.

Freshmen:

Admission: 3,443 applied, 2,315 admitted, 623 enrolled. ***Average high school GPA:*** 3.42. ***Test scores:*** SAT critical reading scores over 500: 61%; SAT math scores over 500: 59%; ACT scores over 18: 97%; SAT critical reading scores over 600: 24%; SAT math scores over 600: 20%; ACT scores over 24: 35%; SAT critical reading scores over 700: 2%; SAT math scores over 700: 2%; ACT scores over 30: 4%.

Retention: 80% of full-time freshmen returned.

FACULTY

Total: 392, 44% full-time, 50% with terminal degrees.

Student/faculty ratio: 12:1.

ACADEMICS

Calendar: semesters. *Degrees:* associate, bachelor's, master's, and doctoral.

Special study options: academic remediation for entering students, accelerated degree program, adult/continuing education programs, advanced placement credit, cooperative education, distance learning, double majors, English as a second language, external degree program, honors programs, independent study, internships, off-campus study, part-time degree program, services for LD students, student-designed majors, study abroad, summer session for credit. ***ROTC:*** Army (c), Air Force (c).

Unusual degree programs: 3-2 business administration.

Computers: 760 computers/terminals are available on campus for general student use. Students can access the following: campus intranet, computer help desk, free student e-mail accounts, online (class) grades, online (class) registration, online (class) schedules. Campuswide network is available. 100% of college-owned or -operated housing units are wired for high-speed Internet access. Wireless service is available via classrooms, computer centers, computer labs, learning centers, libraries, student centers.

Library: Ashland University Library plus 2 others. *Books:* 223,607 (physical), 255,789 (digital/electronic); *Serial titles:* 1,070 (physical), 114,001 (digital/electronic); *Databases:* 200. Weekly public service hours: 102; students can reserve study rooms.

STUDENT LIFE

Housing options: on-campus residence required through junior year; coed, men-only, women-only. Campus housing is university owned. Freshman campus housing is guaranteed.

Activities and organizations: drama/theater group, student-run newspaper, radio and television station, choral group, marching band, Campus Activity Board, Fellowship of Christian Athletes, The Well Campus Ministry, intramurals, Sororities, national fraternities, national sororities.

Athletics Member NCAA. All Division II. ***Intercollegiate sports:*** baseball M(s), basketball M(s)/W(s), cross-country running M(s)/W(s), football M(s), golf M(s)/W(s), soccer M(s)/W(s), softball W(s), swimming and diving M(s)/W(s), tennis W(s), track and field M(s)/W(s), volleyball W(s), wrestling M(s). ***Intramural sports:*** badminton M/W, baseball M(c), basketball M/W, bowling M/W, cross-country running M/W, field hockey M/W, football M, golf M/W, lacrosse M(c)/W(c), racquetball M/W, rock climbing M/W, rugby M(c)/W(c), skiing (downhill) M(c)/W(c), soccer M/W, softball M(c)/W(c), swimming and diving M/W, table tennis M/W, tennis M/W, track and field M/W, ultimate Frisbee M/W, volleyball M(c)/W(c), weight lifting M(c)/W(c), wrestling M.

Campus security: 24-hour emergency response devices and patrols, student patrols, late-night transport/escort service, controlled dormitory access.

Student services: health clinic, personal/psychological counseling.

COSTS & FINANCIAL AID

Costs (2017–18) ***Comprehensive fee:*** $30,430 includes full-time tuition ($19,740), mandatory fees ($944), and room and board ($9746). Full-time tuition and fees vary according to location and program. Part-time tuition: $899 per credit hour. Part-time tuition and fees vary according to course load, location, and program. ***Required fees:*** $23 per credit hour part-time. ***College room only:*** $5250. Room and board charges vary according to board plan, housing facility, and location. ***Payment plan:*** installment. ***Waivers:*** children of alumni, senior citizens, and employees or children of employees.

Financial Aid Of all full-time matriculated undergraduates who enrolled in 2014, 2,191 applied for aid, 1,924 were judged to have need. 1,380 Federal Work-Study jobs (averaging $2589). In 2014, 264 non-need-based awards were made. ***Average financial aid package:*** $17,689. ***Average need-based loan:*** $4836. ***Average need-based gift aid:*** $10,445. ***Average non-need-based aid:*** $5248. ***Average indebtedness upon graduation:*** $36,779.

APPLYING

Standardized Tests *Required:* SAT or ACT (for admission).

Options: electronic application, deferred entrance.

Required: high school transcript, minimum 2.5 GPA, minimum 18 ACT or 860 SAT (critical reading and math).

Application deadlines: rolling (freshmen), rolling (transfers).

Notification: continuous (freshmen), continuous (transfers).

CONTACT

Mr. W.C. Vance, Director of Admission, Ashland University, 401 College Avenue, Ashland, OH 44805. *Phone:* 419-289-5052. *Toll-free phone:* 800-882-1548. *Fax:* 419-289-5999. *E-mail:* enrollme@ashland.edu.

Aultman College of Nursing and Health Sciences

Canton, Ohio

http://www.aultmancollege.edu/

- **Independent** 4-year
- **Urban** 5-acre campus with easy access to Cleveland
- **Endowment** $1.4 million
- **Coed** 391 undergraduate students, 27% full-time, 89% women, 11% men
- **Moderately difficult** entrance level, 74% of applicants were admitted

UNDERGRAD STUDENTS

106 full-time, 285 part-time. Students come from 1 other state; 3% Black or African American, non-Hispanic/Latino; 1% Hispanic/Latino; 0.8% Asian, non-Hispanic/Latino; 1% American Indian or Alaska Native, non-Hispanic/Latino; 1% Two or more races, non-Hispanic/Latino; 4% Race/ethnicity unknown; 22% transferred in.

Freshmen:

Admission: 47 applied, 35 admitted, 24 enrolled.
Average high school GPA: 3.28.

FACULTY

Total: 64, 19% full-time, 17% with terminal degrees.

Student/faculty ratio: 7:1.

ACADEMICS

Calendar: semesters. *Degrees:* associate and bachelor's.

Special study options: academic remediation for entering students, advanced placement credit, cooperative education, distance learning, internships, part-time degree program, services for LD students.

Computers: 73 computers/terminals are available on campus for general student use. Students can access the following: campus intranet, computer help desk, free student e-mail accounts, online (class) grades, online (class) registration, online (class) schedules. Campuswide network is available. Wireless service is available via entire campus.

Library: Aultman Health Sciences Library plus 1 other. *Books:* 2,334 (physical), 112,445 (digital/electronic); *Serial titles:* 127 (physical); *Databases:* 100. Study areas open 24 hours, 5-7 days a week.

STUDENT LIFE

Housing options: college housing not available.

Activities and organizations: Aultman College Student Nurse Association, Radiography Club, Aultman College Campus Ministry, Aultman College Veterans Association, Men in Nursing Association.

Campus security: 24-hour emergency response devices and patrols, late-night transport/escort service.

Student services: health clinic.

COSTS

Costs (2017–18) ***Tuition:*** $17,000 full-time. Full-time tuition and fees vary according to course load, degree level, and program. Part-time tuition and fees vary according to course load, degree level, and program. ***Required fees:*** $600 full-time. ***Payment plan:*** installment. ***Waivers:*** employees or children of employees.

APPLYING

Standardized Tests *Required for some:* SAT or ACT (for admission).

Options: electronic application.

Application fee: $45.

Required: high school transcript, minimum 3.0 GPA.

Notification: continuous until 10/1 (freshmen).

CONTACT

Ms. Julie Peterson, Enrollment Specialist, Aultman College of Nursing and Health Sciences, 2600 6th Street SW, Canton, OH 44710. *Phone:* 330-363-6773. *Fax:* 330-5806654.
E-mail: julie.peterson@aultmancollege.edu.

★ Baldwin Wallace University

Berea, Ohio

http://www.bw.edu/

- **Independent Methodist** comprehensive, founded 1845
- **Suburban** 150-acre campus with easy access to Cleveland
- **Endowment** $149.0 million
- **Coed** 3,305 undergraduate students, 93% full-time, 55% women, 45% men
- **Moderately difficult** entrance level, 60% of applicants were admitted

UNDERGRAD STUDENTS

3,058 full-time, 247 part-time. Students come from 40 states and territories; 24 other countries; 22% are from out of state; 10% Black or African American, non-Hispanic/Latino; 5% Hispanic/Latino; 2% Asian, non-Hispanic/Latino; 0.1% Native Hawaiian or other Pacific Islander, non-Hispanic/Latino; 0.1% American Indian or Alaska Native, non-Hispanic/Latino; 5% Two or more races, non-Hispanic/Latino; 0.2% Race/ethnicity unknown; 0.8% international; 5% transferred in; 62% live on campus.

Freshmen:

Admission: 4,515 applied, 2,697 admitted, 706 enrolled. ***Average high school GPA:*** 3.47. ***Test scores:*** SAT critical reading scores over 500: 69%; SAT math scores over 500: 69%; SAT writing scores over 500: 57%; ACT scores over 18: 92%; SAT critical reading scores over 600: 25%; SAT math scores over 600: 22%; SAT writing scores over 600: 16%; ACT scores over 24: 54%; SAT critical reading scores over 700: 5%; SAT math

scores over 700: 3%; SAT writing scores over 700: 3%; ACT scores over 30: 8%.

Retention: 80% of full-time freshmen returned.

FACULTY

Total: 469, 44% full-time, 40% with terminal degrees.

Student/faculty ratio: 12:1.

ACADEMICS

Calendar: semesters. *Degrees:* certificates, bachelor's, and master's.

Special study options: academic remediation for entering students, accelerated degree program, adult/continuing education programs, advanced placement credit, distance learning, double majors, English as a second language, honors programs, independent study, internships, off-campus study, part-time degree program, services for LD students, student-designed majors, study abroad, summer session for credit. ***ROTC:*** Army (c), Air Force (c).

Unusual degree programs: 3-2 engineering with Case Western Reserve University and Columbia University; social work with Case Western Reserve University; accounting, computer information systems, computer science, or human resources/business administration.

Computers: 500 computers/terminals and 100 ports are available on campus for general student use. Students can access the following: campus intranet, computer help desk, free student e-mail accounts, online (class) grades, online (class) registration, online (class) schedules. Campuswide network is available. 100% of college-owned or -operated housing units are wired for high-speed Internet access. Wireless service is available via entire campus.

Library: Ritter Library plus 2 others. *Books:* 106,767 (physical), 408,078 (digital/electronic); *Serial titles:* 174 (physical), 71,231 (digital/electronic); *Databases:* 265. Weekly public service hours: 90; study areas open 24 hours, 5-7 days a week; students can reserve study rooms.

STUDENT LIFE

Housing options: on-campus residence required through sophomore year; coed, special housing for students with disabilities. Campus housing is university owned. Freshman applicants given priority for college housing.

Activities and organizations: drama/theater group, student-run newspaper, radio and television station, choral group, marching band, BW Dodgeball Club, Games and Multimedia Entertainment (G.A.M.E. Guild), Habitat for Humanity, Ohio Collegiate Music Educators Association (OCMEA), Sociology, Criminal Justice and Forensic Science Club, national fraternities, national sororities.

Athletics Member NCAA, NCCAA. All NCAA Division III.

Intercollegiate sports: baseball M, basketball M/W, cross-country running M/W, football M, golf M/W, lacrosse M/W, soccer M/W, softball W, swimming and diving M/W, tennis M/W, track and field M/W, volleyball W, wrestling M. ***Intramural sports:*** archery M(c)/W(c), badminton M/W, basketball M/W, cheerleading W(c), crew M(c)/W(c), football M, golf M/W, racquetball M/W, riflery M(c)/W(c), rowing M(c)/W(c), rugby M(c)/W(c), skiing (cross-country) M(c)/W(c), skiing (downhill) M(c)/W(c), soccer M/W, softball M/W, table tennis M/W, tennis M/W, ultimate Frisbee M/W, volleyball M/W, wrestling M.

Campus security: 24-hour emergency response devices and patrols, student patrols, late-night transport/escort service, controlled dormitory access, emergency text messaging.

Student services: health clinic, personal/psychological counseling.

COSTS & FINANCIAL AID

Costs (2017–18) ***Comprehensive fee:*** $40,810 includes full-time tuition ($31,668) and room and board ($9142). Full-time tuition and fees vary according to class time, course level, course load, degree level, program, and reciprocity agreements. Part-time tuition: $984 per credit hour. Part-time tuition and fees vary according to class time, course level, course load, degree level, program, and reciprocity agreements. ***College room only:*** $5280. Room and board charges vary according to housing facility. ***Payment plans:*** installment, deferred payment. ***Waivers:*** children of alumni and employees or children of employees.

Financial Aid Of all full-time matriculated undergraduates who enrolled in 2016, 2,557 applied for aid, 2,221 were judged to have need, 956 had their need fully met. 919 Federal Work-Study jobs (averaging $1449). 527 state and other part-time jobs (averaging $1446). In 2016, 335 non-need-based awards were made. ***Average percent of need met:*** 86. ***Average financial aid package:*** $23,841. ***Average need-based loan:*** $4678.

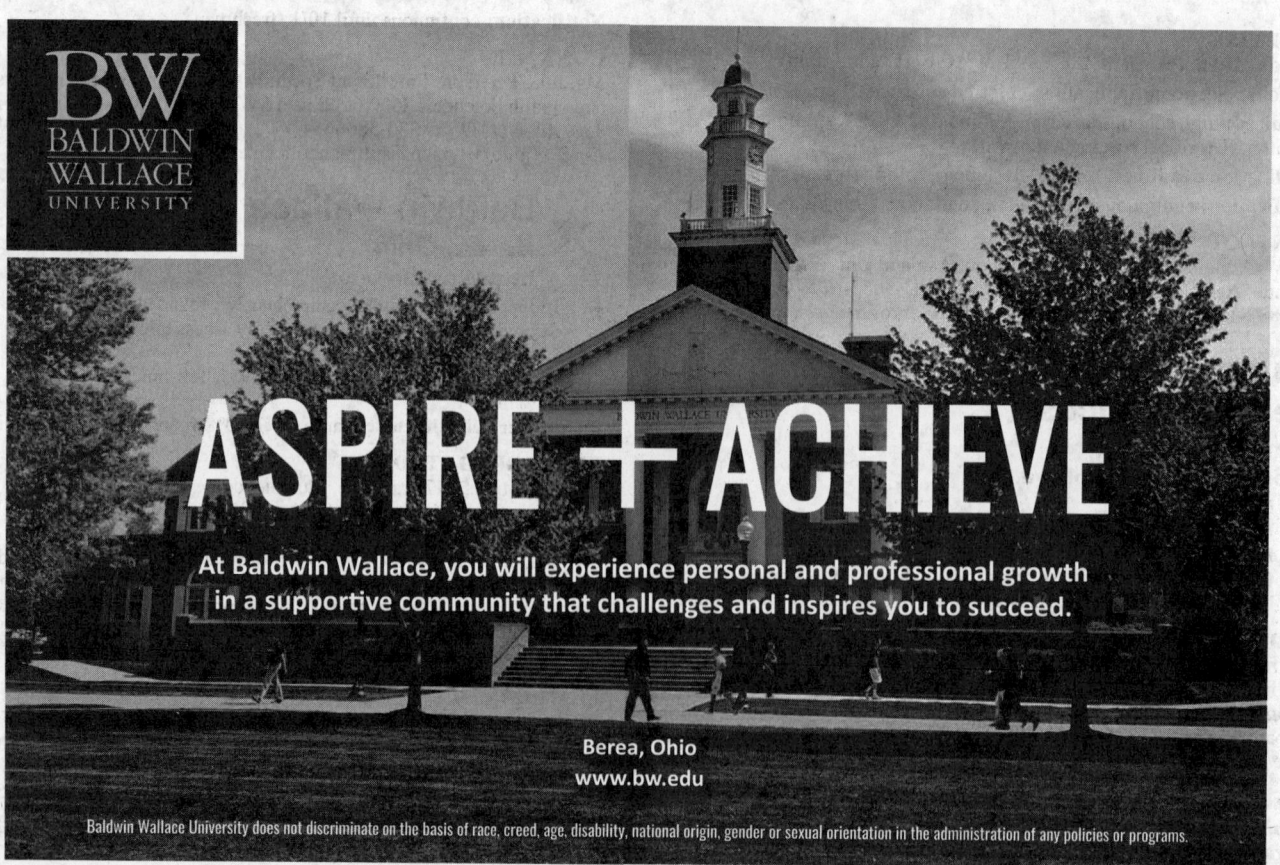

Average need-based gift aid: $19,305. ***Average non-need-based aid:*** $13,832. ***Average indebtedness upon graduation:*** $34,423.

APPLYING

Standardized Tests *Required for some:* SAT or ACT (for admission).

Options: electronic application, deferred entrance.

Application fee: $25.

Required: essay or personal statement, high school transcript. ***Required for some:*** minimum 3.0 cum GPA and recently graded paper in lieu of ACT or SAT scores for Test Optional applicants. ***Recommended:*** minimum 3.0 GPA, 1 letter of recommendation, interview.

Application deadlines: 5/1 (freshmen), 8/1 (transfers).

Notification: continuous (freshmen), continuous (out-of-state freshmen), continuous (transfers).

CONTACT

Joyce J Cendroski, Director of First Year RCMT & Admission, Baldwin Wallace University, Durst Welcome Center, 115 Tressel Street, Berea, OH 44017. *Phone:* 440-826-2222. *Toll-free phone:* 877-BW-APPLY. *Fax:* 440-826-3830. *E-mail:* admission@bw.edu.

See previous page for display ad and page 1290 for the College Close-Up.

Bluffton University

Bluffton, Ohio

http://www.bluffton.edu/

- **Independent Mennonite** comprehensive, founded 1899
- **Small-town** 65-acre campus with easy access to Dayton
- **Endowment** $22.6 million
- **Coed** 865 undergraduate students, 84% full-time, 50% women, 50% men
- **Moderately difficult** entrance level, 50% of applicants were admitted

UNDERGRAD STUDENTS

728 full-time, 137 part-time. Students come from 23 states and territories; 6 other countries; 12% are from out of state; 6% Black or African American, non-Hispanic/Latino; 4% Hispanic/Latino; 0.5% Asian, non-Hispanic/Latino; 4% Two or more races, non-Hispanic/Latino; 2% Race/ethnicity unknown; 0.9% international; 6% transferred in; 87% live on campus.

Freshmen:

Admission: 1,480 applied, 733 admitted, 208 enrolled. ***Average high school GPA:*** 3.2. ***Test scores:*** ACT scores over 18: 83%; ACT scores over 24: 26%; ACT scores over 30: 2%.

Retention: 67% of full-time freshmen returned.

FACULTY

Total: 103, 56% full-time, 53% with terminal degrees.

Student/faculty ratio: 12:1.

ACADEMICS

Calendar: semesters. *Degrees:* bachelor's, master's, and postbachelor's certificates.

Special study options: academic remediation for entering students, accelerated degree program, adult/continuing education programs, advanced placement credit, distance learning, double majors, English as a second language, honors programs, independent study, internships, off-campus study, part-time degree program, services for LD students, student-designed majors, study abroad, summer session for credit.

Computers: 170 computers/terminals and 1,300 ports are available on campus for general student use. Students can access the following: campus intranet, computer help desk, free student e-mail accounts, online (class) grades, online (class) registration, online (class) schedules. Campuswide network is available. 100% of college-owned or -operated housing units are wired for high-speed Internet access. Wireless service is available via classrooms, computer centers, computer labs, dorm rooms, libraries, student centers.

Library: Musselman Library plus 1 other. *Books:* 73,858 (physical), 282,112 (digital/electronic); *Serial titles:* 1,086 (physical), 44,747 (digital/electronic); *Databases:* 261. Weekly public service hours: 81; students can reserve study rooms.

STUDENT LIFE

Housing options: on-campus residence required through senior year; coed, men-only, women-only. Campus housing is university owned. Freshman campus housing is guaranteed.

Activities and organizations: drama/theater group, student-run newspaper, radio station, choral group, Intramurals, Music Groups/Chorale, Campus Ministries, Multicultural Student Organization, SERVE.

Athletics Member NCAA. All Division III. ***Intercollegiate sports:*** baseball M, basketball M/W, cross-country running M/W, football M, golf M/W, soccer M/W, softball W, track and field M/W, volleyball W. ***Intramural sports:*** basketball M/W, bowling M/W, football M/W, golf M/W, softball M/W, tennis M/W, ultimate Frisbee M, volleyball M/W.

Campus security: 24-hour emergency response devices, controlled dormitory access, night security guards.

Student services: health clinic, personal/psychological counseling.

COSTS & FINANCIAL AID

Costs (2017–18) ***Comprehensive fee:*** $42,156 includes full-time tuition ($31,222), mandatory fees ($450), and room and board ($10,484). Part-time tuition: $1301 per credit hour. ***Required fees:*** $113 per term part-time. ***College room only:*** $5160. Room and board charges vary according to board plan and housing facility. ***Payment plan:*** installment. ***Waivers:*** employees or children of employees.

Financial Aid Of all full-time matriculated undergraduates who enrolled in 2016, 666 applied for aid, 627 were judged to have need, 87 had their need fully met. 520 Federal Work-Study jobs (averaging $2247). 194 state and other part-time jobs (averaging $2303). In 2016, 88 non-need-based awards were made. ***Average percent of need met:*** 77. ***Average financial aid package:*** $26,316. ***Average need-based loan:*** $4880. ***Average need-based gift aid:*** $20,842. ***Average non-need-based aid:*** $14,816. ***Average indebtedness upon graduation:*** $38,701. ***Financial aid deadline:*** 10/1.

APPLYING

Standardized Tests *Required:* SAT or ACT (for admission).

Options: electronic application, deferred entrance.

Required: high school transcript, minimum 2.3 GPA, 1 letter of recommendation, rank in upper 50% of high school class or minimum ACT score of 19. ***Required for some:*** essay or personal statement. ***Recommended:*** interview.

Application deadlines: rolling (freshmen), rolling (transfers).

Notification: continuous (freshmen), continuous (transfers).

CONTACT

Mrs. Robin Hopkins, Director of Undergraduate Admissions, Bluffton University, 1 University Drive, Bluffton, OH 45817. *Phone:* 419-358-336141. *Toll-free phone:* 800-488-3257. *Fax:* 419-358-3081. *E-mail:* admissions@bluffton.edu.

Bowling Green State University

Bowling Green, Ohio

http://www.bgsu.edu/

- **State-supported** university, founded 1910
- **Small-town** 1338-acre campus with easy access to Toledo
- **Endowment** $146.7 million
- **Coed** 14,852 undergraduate students, 89% full-time, 56% women, 44% men
- **Moderately difficult** entrance level, 74% of applicants were admitted

UNDERGRAD STUDENTS

13,184 full-time, 1,668 part-time. Students come from 51 states and territories; 57 other countries; 12% are from out of state; 9% Black or African American, non-Hispanic/Latino; 4% Hispanic/Latino; 0.8% Asian, non-Hispanic/Latino; 0.1% Native Hawaiian or other Pacific Islander, non-Hispanic/Latino; 0.2% American Indian or Alaska Native, non-Hispanic/Latino; 3% Two or more races, non-Hispanic/Latino; 3% Race/ethnicity unknown; 3% international; 4% transferred in; 44% live on campus.

Freshmen:

Admission: 14,891 applied, 10,957 admitted, 3,545 enrolled. ***Average high school GPA:*** 3.35. ***Test scores:*** SAT critical reading scores over 500: 57%; SAT math scores over 500: 62%; SAT writing scores over 500: 49%;

ACT scores over 18: 94%; SAT critical reading scores over 600: 20%; SAT math scores over 600: 21%; SAT writing scores over 600: 13%; ACT scores over 24: 37%; SAT critical reading scores over 700: 2%; SAT math scores over 700: 1%; SAT writing scores over 700: 2%; ACT scores over 30: 4%.

Retention: 76% of full-time freshmen returned.

FACULTY

Total: 1,094, 65% full-time, 60% with terminal degrees.

Student/faculty ratio: 19:1.

ACADEMICS

Calendar: semesters. *Degrees:* bachelor's, master's, doctoral, post-master's, and postbachelor's certificates.

Special study options: academic remediation for entering students, accelerated degree program, adult/continuing education programs, advanced placement credit, cooperative education, distance learning, double majors, English as a second language, freshman honors college, independent study, internships, off-campus study, part-time degree program, services for LD students, student-designed majors, study abroad, summer session for credit. ***ROTC:*** Army (b), Air Force (b).

Computers: 1,500 computers/terminals and 500 ports are available on campus for general student use. Students can access the following: campus intranet, computer help desk, free student e-mail accounts, online (class) grades, online (class) registration, online (class) schedules, wireless networking, filesharing software, bursar billing information and payment, view and change personal information, order official and unofficial transcripts, check meal plan balance, apply for graduation. Campuswide network is available. 100% of college-owned or -operated housing units are wired for high-speed Internet access. Wireless service is available via entire campus.

Library: William T. Jerome Library. *Books:* 143,305 (physical), 104,852 (digital/electronic); *Serial titles:* 825 (physical), 11,511 (digital/electronic); *Databases:* 268. Weekly public service hours: 110; students can reserve study rooms.

STUDENT LIFE

Housing options: on-campus residence required through sophomore year; coed, men-only, women-only, special housing for students with disabilities. Campus housing is university owned. Freshman campus housing is guaranteed.

Activities and organizations: drama/theater group, student-run newspaper, radio and television station, choral group, marching band, Dance Marathon, Undergraduate Student Government, University Activities Organization, Alpha Phi Omega, Athletic Training Student Organization, national fraternities, national sororities.

Athletics Member NCAA. All Division I. ***Intercollegiate sports:*** baseball M(s), basketball M(s)/W(s), cross-country running M(s)/W(s), football M(s), golf M(s)/W(s), gymnastics W(s), ice hockey M(s), soccer M(s)/W(s), softball W(s), swimming and diving W(s), tennis W(s), track and field W(s), volleyball W(s). ***Intramural sports:*** badminton M/W, baseball M(c), basketball M/W, bowling M(c)/W(c), cross-country running M(c)/W(c), equestrian sports M(c)/W(c), football M/W, golf M/W, gymnastics M(c)/W(c), ice hockey M(c), lacrosse M(c)/W(c), rugby M(c)/W(c), sailing M(c)/W(c), skiing (downhill) M(c)/W(c), soccer M/W, softball W(c), swimming and diving M(c)/W(c), tennis M/W, track and field M(c)/W(c), ultimate Frisbee M/W, volleyball M/W, water polo M(c)/W(c), wrestling M(c)/W(c).

Campus security: 24-hour emergency response devices and patrols, late-night transport/escort service, controlled dormitory access.

Student services: health clinic, personal/psychological counseling, women's center, legal services.

COSTS & FINANCIAL AID

Costs (2016–17) ***Tuition:*** state resident $9096 full-time, $379 per credit hour part-time; nonresident $16,632 full-time, $693 per credit hour part-time. Full-time tuition and fees vary according to course load and location. Part-time tuition and fees vary according to course load and location. ***Required fees:*** $1961 full-time, $70 per credit hour part-time. ***Room and board:*** $8690. Room and board charges vary according to board plan and housing facility. ***Payment plan:*** installment. ***Waivers:*** senior citizens and employees or children of employees.

Financial Aid Of all full-time matriculated undergraduates who enrolled in 2016, 10,767 applied for aid, 8,548 were judged to have need, 1,227 had their need fully met. 371 Federal Work-Study jobs (averaging $1220). In 2016, 2636 non-need-based awards were made. ***Average percent of need met:*** 80. ***Average financial aid package:*** $14,013. ***Average need-based loan:*** $4143. ***Average need-based gift aid:*** $6920. ***Average non-need-based aid:*** $5186. ***Average indebtedness upon graduation:*** $30,801.

APPLYING

Standardized Tests *Required:* SAT or ACT (for admission).

Options: electronic application, deferred entrance.

Application fee: $45.

Required for some: high school transcript.

Application deadlines: 7/15 (freshmen), 8/1 (transfers).

Notification: continuous until 8/1 (freshmen), continuous (transfers).

CONTACT

Bowling Green State University, Admissions Office, 110 McFall, Bowling Green State University, Bowling Green, OH 43403-0085.
Phone: 419-372-2478. *Fax:* 419-372-6955.
E-mail: choosebgsu@bgsu.edu.

Bowling Green State University–Firelands College

Huron, Ohio

http://www.firelands.bgsu.edu/

- **State-supported** primarily 2-year, founded 1968, part of Bowling Green State University System
- **Rural** 216-acre campus with easy access to Cleveland, Toledo
- **Coed** 2,162 undergraduate students, 43% full-time, 64% women, 36% men
- **Noncompetitive** entrance level

UNDERGRAD STUDENTS

940 full-time, 1,222 part-time. Students come from 6 states and territories; 1 other country; 1% are from out of state; 5% Black or African American, non-Hispanic/Latino; 5% Hispanic/Latino; 0.7% Asian, non-Hispanic/Latino; 0.4% American Indian or Alaska Native, non-Hispanic/Latino; 4% Two or more races, non-Hispanic/Latino; 4% Race/ethnicity unknown; 0.1% international.

Freshmen:

Admission: 378 enrolled. ***Average high school GPA:*** 2.95.

Retention: 52% of full-time freshmen returned.

FACULTY

Total: 113, 44% full-time.

Student/faculty ratio: 19:1.

ACADEMICS

Calendar: semesters. *Degrees:* certificates, associate, and bachelor's (also offers some upper-level and graduate courses).

Special study options: academic remediation for entering students, adult/continuing education programs, advanced placement credit, cooperative education, distance learning, double majors, honors programs, independent study, internships, part-time degree program, services for LD students, student-designed majors, study abroad, summer session for credit. ***ROTC:*** Army (c), Air Force (c).

Computers: 300 computers/terminals are available on campus for general student use. Students can access the following: computer help desk, free student e-mail accounts, online (class) grades, online (class) registration, online (class) schedules. Campuswide network is available. Wireless service is available via entire campus.

Library: BGSU Firelands College Library.

STUDENT LIFE

Housing options: college housing not available.

Activities and organizations: drama/theater group, choral group, Society of Fandom and Gaming, Student Government, Student Theater Guild, Safe Space, Society of Leadership and Success.

Athletics ***Intramural sports:*** basketball M/W, bowling M/W, football M, table tennis M/W, volleyball M/W.

Campus security: 24-hour emergency response devices, late-night transport/escort service, patrols by trained security personnel.

COSTS
Costs (2017–18) ***Tuition:*** state resident $4706 full-time, $196 per credit hour part-time; nonresident $12,014 full-time, $501 per credit hour part-time. Full-time tuition and fees vary according to location and reciprocity agreements. Part-time tuition and fees vary according to location and reciprocity agreements. ***Required fees:*** $240 full-time, $9 per credit hour part-time, $120 per term part-time. ***Payment plan:*** installment. ***Waivers:*** children of alumni, senior citizens, and employees or children of employees.

APPLYING
Options: electronic application, early admission, deferred entrance.
Application fee: $45.
Required: high school transcript.
Application deadlines: 8/6 (freshmen), 8/6 (transfers).
Notification: continuous (freshmen), continuous (transfers).

CONTACT
Cheryl Chafee, Assistant Director of Admissions and Financial Aid, Bowling Green State University–Firelands College, One University Drive, Huron, OH 44839-9791. *Phone:* 419-433-5560. *Toll-free phone:* 800-322-4787. *Fax:* 419-372-0604. *E-mail:* cchafee@bgsu.edu.

Bryant & Stratton College–Akron Campus

Akron, Ohio

http://www.bryantstratton.edu/

CONTACT
Bryant & Stratton College–Akron Campus, 190 Montrose West Avenue, Akron, OH 44321.

Bryant & Stratton College–Cleveland Campus

Cleveland, Ohio

http://www.bryantstratton.edu/

CONTACT
Bryant & Stratton College–Cleveland Campus, Cleveland, OH 44114-3203. *Phone:* 216-771-1700. *Fax:* 216-771-7787.

Bryant & Stratton College–Eastlake Campus

Eastlake, Ohio

http://www.bryantstratton.edu/

CONTACT
Ms. Melanie Pettit, Director of Admissions, Bryant & Stratton College–Eastlake Campus, 35350 Curtis Boulevard, Eastlake, OH 44095. *Phone:* 440-510-1112.

Bryant & Stratton College–Parma Campus

Parma, Ohio

http://www.bryantstratton.edu/

CONTACT
Bryant & Stratton College–Parma Campus, 12955 Snow Road, Parma, OH 44130-1005. *Phone:* 216-265-3151. *Toll-free phone:* 866-948-0571.

Capital University

Columbus, Ohio

http://www.capital.edu/

- **Independent** comprehensive, founded 1830, affiliated with Evangelical Lutheran Church in America
- **Suburban** 48-acre campus with easy access to Columbus
- **Endowment** $71.5 million
- **Coed** 2,718 undergraduate students, 92% full-time, 61% women, 39% men
- **Moderately difficult** entrance level, 69% of applicants were admitted

UNDERGRAD STUDENTS
2,511 full-time, 207 part-time. Students come from 35 states and territories; 20 other countries; 10% are from out of state; 10% Black or African American, non-Hispanic/Latino; 4% Hispanic/Latino; 1% Asian, non-Hispanic/Latino; 0.1% Native Hawaiian or other Pacific Islander, non-Hispanic/Latino; 0.2% American Indian or Alaska Native, non-Hispanic/Latino; 5% Two or more races, non-Hispanic/Latino; 3% Race/ethnicity unknown; 2% international; 3% transferred in; 59% live on campus.

Freshmen:
Admission: 4,287 applied, 2,968 admitted, 613 enrolled. ***Average high school GPA:*** 3.52. ***Test scores:*** SAT critical reading scores over 500: 71%; SAT math scores over 500: 66%; SAT writing scores over 500: 63%; ACT scores over 18: 97%; SAT critical reading scores over 600: 28%; SAT math scores over 600: 31%; SAT writing scores over 600: 15%; ACT scores over 24: 62%; SAT critical reading scores over 700: 4%; SAT math scores over 700: 4%; ACT scores over 30: 15%.
Retention: 75% of full-time freshmen returned.

FACULTY
Total: 406, 39% full-time, 47% with terminal degrees.
Student/faculty ratio: 12:1.

ACADEMICS
Calendar: semesters. *Degrees:* bachelor's, master's, doctoral, and postbachelor's certificates.
Special study options: accelerated degree program, adult/continuing education programs, advanced placement credit, cooperative education, double majors, English as a second language, external degree program, freshman honors college, honors programs, independent study, internships, off-campus study, part-time degree program, services for LD students, student-designed majors, study abroad, summer session for credit. ***ROTC:*** Army (b), Air Force (c).
Unusual degree programs: 3-2 engineering with Washington University in St. Louis, Case Western Reserve University.
Computers: 457 computers/terminals and 1,400 ports are available on campus for general student use. Students can access the following: campus intranet, computer help desk, free student e-mail accounts, online (class) grades, online (class) registration, online (class) schedules. Campuswide network is available. 100% of college-owned or -operated housing units are wired for high-speed Internet access. Wireless service is available via entire campus.
Library: Blackmore Library.

STUDENT LIFE
Housing options: on-campus residence required through sophomore year; coed, special housing for students with disabilities. Campus housing is university owned. Freshman campus housing is guaranteed.
Activities and organizations: drama/theater group, student-run newspaper, radio and television station, choral group, Campus Crusade for Christ, student government, University Programming, College Republicans, American Marketing Association, national fraternities, national sororities.
Athletics Member NCAA. All Division III. ***Intercollegiate sports:*** baseball M, basketball M/W, cross-country running M/W, football M, golf M/W, lacrosse M/W, soccer M/W, softball W, tennis M/W, track and field M/W, volleyball W. ***Intramural sports:*** basketball M/W, cheerleading M(c)/W(c), fencing M(c)/W(c), football M/W, racquetball M/W, ultimate Frisbee M/W, volleyball M/W.
Campus security: 24-hour emergency response devices and patrols, late-night transport/escort service, controlled dormitory access.

Student services: health clinic, personal/psychological counseling.

COSTS & FINANCIAL AID

Costs (2017–18) ***Comprehensive fee:*** $44,778 includes full-time tuition ($34,280), mandatory fees ($320), and room and board ($10,178). Full-time tuition and fees vary according to course load. Part-time tuition: $1144 per credit hour. Part-time tuition and fees vary according to course load. ***Room and board:*** Room and board charges vary according to board plan and housing facility. ***Payment plan:*** installment. ***Waivers:*** senior citizens and employees or children of employees.

Financial Aid Of all full-time matriculated undergraduates who enrolled in 2015, 2,175 applied for aid, 2,014 were judged to have need, 551 had their need fully met. In 2015, 413 non-need-based awards were made. ***Average percent of need met:*** 81. ***Average financial aid package:*** $27,527. ***Average need-based loan:*** $4681. ***Average need-based gift aid:*** $22,547. ***Average non-need-based aid:*** $19,223. ***Average indebtedness upon graduation:*** $32,496.

APPLYING

Standardized Tests *Required:* SAT or ACT (for admission).

Options: electronic application, deferred entrance.

Application fee: $25.

Required: high school transcript, minimum 2.6 GPA. ***Required for some:*** 1 letter of recommendation, audition for Conservatory of Music. ***Recommended:*** interview.

Application deadlines: 5/1 (freshmen), rolling (transfers).

Notification: 9/30 (freshmen), continuous (transfers).

CONTACT

Ms. Sara Thompson, Interim Director of Admission, Capital University, 1 College and Main, Columbus, OH 43209. *Phone:* 614-236-6256. *Toll-free phone:* 866-544-6175. *Fax:* 614-236-6926. *E-mail:* sthompso@capital.edu.

Case Western Reserve University

Cleveland, Ohio

http://www.case.edu/

- **Independent** university, founded 1826
- **Urban** 267-acre campus
- **Endowment** $1.7 billion
- **Coed** 5,152 undergraduate students, 97% full-time, 45% women, 55% men
- **Very difficult** entrance level, 35% of applicants were admitted

UNDERGRAD STUDENTS

4,990 full-time, 162 part-time. Students come from 49 states and territories; 39 other countries; 68% are from out of state; 4% Black or African American, non-Hispanic/Latino; 6% Hispanic/Latino; 20% Asian, non-Hispanic/Latino; 0.1% Native Hawaiian or other Pacific Islander, non-Hispanic/Latino; 0.1% American Indian or Alaska Native, non-Hispanic/Latino; 5% Two or more races, non-Hispanic/Latino; 2% Race/ethnicity unknown; 12% international; 0.9% transferred in; 78% live on campus.

Freshmen:

Admission: 23,115 applied, 8,192 admitted, 1,264 enrolled. ***Test scores:*** SAT critical reading scores over 500: 99%; SAT math scores over 500: 100%; SAT writing scores over 500: 99%; ACT scores over 18: 100%; SAT critical reading scores over 600: 78%; SAT math scores over 600: 96%; SAT writing scores over 600: 85%; ACT scores over 24: 99%; SAT critical reading scores over 700: 37%; SAT math scores over 700: 69%; SAT writing scores over 700: 34%; ACT scores over 30: 76%.

Retention: 92% of full-time freshmen returned.

FACULTY

Total: 964, 80% full-time, 84% with terminal degrees.

Student/faculty ratio: 11:1.

ACADEMICS

Calendar: semesters. *Degrees:* bachelor's, master's, doctoral, post-master's, and postbachelor's certificates.

Special study options: accelerated degree program, adult/continuing education programs, advanced placement credit, cooperative education, double majors, English as a second language, honors programs, independent study, internships, off-campus study, part-time degree program, services for LD students, student-designed majors, study abroad, summer session for credit. ***ROTC:*** Army (b), Air Force (c).

Unusual degree programs: 3-2 engineering.

Computers: 254 computers/terminals and 50,000 ports are available on campus for general student use. Students can access the following: campus intranet, computer help desk, free student e-mail accounts, online (class) grades, online (class) registration, online (class) schedules, software library, online reference databases, electronic books and journals, research computing, training. Campuswide network is available. 100% of college-owned or -operated housing units are wired for high-speed Internet access. Wireless service is available via entire campus.

Library: Kelvin Smith Library plus 6 others. *Books:* 3.4 million (physical); *Serial titles:* 191,970 (physical); *Databases:* 423. Students can reserve study rooms.

STUDENT LIFE

Housing options: on-campus residence required through sophomore year; coed. Campus housing is university owned. Freshman campus housing is guaranteed.

Activities and organizations: drama/theater group, student-run newspaper, radio station, choral group, marching band, SpartaTHON, Quidditch Team, Spartans for Special Olympics, Undergraduate Indian Student Association, Footlighters, national fraternities, national sororities.

Athletics Member NCAA. All Division III. ***Intercollegiate sports:*** baseball M, basketball M/W, cross-country running M/W, football M, soccer M/W, softball W, swimming and diving M/W, tennis M/W, track and field M/W, volleyball W, wrestling M. ***Intramural sports:*** badminton M/W, basketball M/W, bowling M/W, football M/W, golf M/W, racquetball M/W, softball M/W, swimming and diving M/W, table tennis M/W, tennis M/W, ultimate Frisbee M/W, volleyball M/W, weight lifting M/W.

Campus security: 24-hour emergency response devices and patrols, student patrols, late-night transport/escort service, controlled dormitory access, crime prevention programs.

Student services: health clinic, personal/psychological counseling, women's center, legal services.

COSTS & FINANCIAL AID

Costs (2016–17) ***One-time required fee:*** $525. ***Comprehensive fee:*** $60,304 includes full-time tuition ($45,592), mandatory fees ($414), and room and board ($14,298). Part-time tuition: $1900 per credit hour. Part-time tuition and fees vary according to course load. ***College room only:*** $8280. Room and board charges vary according to board plan, housing facility, and student level. ***Payment plan:*** installment. ***Waivers:*** employees or children of employees.

Financial Aid Of all full-time matriculated undergraduates who enrolled in 2016, 2,858 applied for aid, 2,460 were judged to have need, 1,493 had their need fully met. 1,504 Federal Work-Study jobs (averaging $2629). In 2016, 1578 non-need-based awards were made. ***Average percent of need met:*** 83. ***Average financial aid package:*** $38,928. ***Average need-based loan:*** $4859. ***Average need-based gift aid:*** $28,156. ***Average non-need-based aid:*** $23,479. ***Average indebtedness upon graduation:*** $30,561. ***Financial aid deadline:*** 2/1.

APPLYING

Standardized Tests *Required:* SAT or ACT (for admission).

Options: electronic application, early admission, early decision, early action, deferred entrance.

Required: essay or personal statement, high school transcript, 2 letters of recommendation, school report, including a counselor recommendation. ***Recommended:*** interview.

Application deadlines: 1/15 (freshmen), 5/1 (transfers), 11/1 (early action).

Early decision deadline: 11/1 (for plan 1), 1/15 (for plan 2).

Notification: 3/20 (freshmen), continuous until 6/1 (transfers), 12/15 (early decision plan 1), 2/1 (early decision plan 2), 12/15 (early action).

CONTACT

Robert McCullough, Director of Undergraduate Admission, Case Western Reserve University, 10900 Euclid Avenue, Cleveland, OH 44106. *Phone:* 216-368-4450. *Fax:* 216-368-5111. *E-mail:* admission@case.edu.

Cedarville University
Cedarville, Ohio
http://www.cedarville.edu/

- **Independent Baptist** comprehensive, founded 1887
- **Small-town** 441-acre campus with easy access to Columbus, Dayton
- **Endowment** $25.8 million
- **Coed** 3,380 undergraduate students, 89% full-time, 52% women, 48% men
- **Moderately difficult** entrance level, 69% of applicants were admitted

UNDERGRAD STUDENTS
3,024 full-time, 356 part-time. Students come from 50 states and territories; 38 other countries; 63% are from out of state; 1% Black or African American, non-Hispanic/Latino; 3% Hispanic/Latino; 2% Asian, non-Hispanic/Latino; 0.4% American Indian or Alaska Native, non-Hispanic/Latino; 3% Two or more races, non-Hispanic/Latino; 4% Race/ethnicity unknown; 2% international; 3% transferred in; 83% live on campus.

Freshmen:
Admission: 4,092 applied, 2,826 admitted, 769 enrolled. ***Average high school GPA:*** 3.69. ***Test scores:*** SAT critical reading scores over 500: 88%; SAT math scores over 500: 84%; SAT writing scores over 500: 79%; ACT scores over 18: 99%; SAT critical reading scores over 600: 53%; SAT math scores over 600: 45%; SAT writing scores over 600: 38%; ACT scores over 24: 74%; SAT critical reading scores over 700: 14%; SAT math scores over 700: 10%; SAT writing scores over 700: 6%; ACT scores over 30: 20%.
Retention: 85% of full-time freshmen returned.

FACULTY
Total: 381, 50% full-time, 49% with terminal degrees.
Student/faculty ratio: 13:1.

ACADEMICS
Calendar: semesters. *Degrees:* certificates, bachelor's, master's, doctoral, post-master's, and postbachelor's certificates.
Special study options: academic remediation for entering students, adult/continuing education programs, advanced placement credit, cooperative education, distance learning, double majors, honors programs, independent study, internships, off-campus study, part-time degree program, services for LD students, student-designed majors, study abroad, summer session for credit. ***ROTC:*** Army (c), Air Force (c).
Computers: 1,500 computers/terminals and 4,000 ports are available on campus for general student use. Students can access the following: campus intranet, computer help desk, free student e-mail accounts, online (class) grades, online (class) registration, online (class) schedules, over 70 software packages. Campuswide network is available. 100% of college-owned or -operated housing units are wired for high-speed Internet access. Wireless service is available via entire campus.
Library: Centennial Library. *Books:* 183,128 (physical), 117,396 (digital/electronic); *Serial titles:* 763 (physical), 25,339 (digital/electronic); *Databases:* 199. Weekly public service hours: 91; students can reserve study rooms.

STUDENT LIFE
Housing options: on-campus residence required through senior year; men-only, women-only, special housing for students with disabilities. Campus housing is university owned. Freshman campus housing is guaranteed.
Activities and organizations: drama/theater group, student-run newspaper, radio station, choral group, Student Nurses Association, Tau Delta Kappa, Mu Kappa, AYO, MISO (Multicultural International Student Org).
Athletics Member NCAA, NCCAA. All NCAA Division II.
Intercollegiate sports: baseball M(s), basketball M(s)/W(s), cheerleading M/W, cross-country running M(s)/W(s), golf M(s), soccer M(s)/W(s), softball W(s), tennis M(s)/W(s), track and field M(s)/W(s), volleyball W(s). ***Intramural sports:*** badminton M/W, basketball M/W, football M/W, golf M/W, racquetball M/W, riflery M(c)/W(c), rock climbing M/W, rugby M(c)/W(c), soccer M/W, swimming and diving M(c)/W(c), table tennis M/W, tennis M/W, ultimate Frisbee M(c)/W(c), volleyball M/W.
Campus security: 24-hour emergency response devices and patrols, late-night transport/escort service, controlled dormitory access.
Student services: health clinic, personal/psychological counseling.

COSTS & FINANCIAL AID
Costs (2017–18) ***Comprehensive fee:*** $36,244 includes full-time tuition ($28,956), mandatory fees ($200), and room and board ($7088). Part-time tuition: $1096 per credit hour. Part-time tuition and fees vary according to course load. ***Required fees:*** $50 per term part-time. ***College room only:*** $4018. Room and board charges vary according to board plan and housing facility. ***Payment plan:*** installment. ***Waivers:*** adult students, senior citizens, and employees or children of employees.
Financial Aid Of all full-time matriculated undergraduates who enrolled in 2015, 2,370 applied for aid, 2,031 were judged to have need, 749 had their need fully met. 355 Federal Work-Study jobs (averaging $2363). 1,422 state and other part-time jobs (averaging $1862). In 2015, 788 non-need-based awards were made. ***Average percent of need met:*** 32. ***Average financial aid package:*** $18,493. ***Average need-based loan:*** $5494. ***Average need-based gift aid:*** $4831. ***Average non-need-based aid:*** $16,338. ***Average indebtedness upon graduation:*** $29,454.

APPLYING
Standardized Tests *Required:* SAT or ACT (for admission).
Options: electronic application, early admission, deferred entrance.
Application fee: $30.
Required: essay or personal statement, high school transcript, minimum 3.0 GPA, 1 letter of recommendation, clear testimony of faith in Jesus Christ and evidence of a consistent Christian lifestyle, minimum ACT score of 22 or SAT score of 1020, minimum 3.0 unweighted, cumulative GPA in college prep course work. ***Required for some:*** interview.
Application deadlines: rolling (freshmen), rolling (transfers).
Notification: continuous (freshmen), continuous (transfers).

CONTACT
Ms. Becky Hayes, Director of Enrollment Services, Cedarville University, 251 North Main Street, Cedarville, OH 45314-0601. *Phone:* 937-766-7700. *Toll-free phone:* 800-233-2784. *E-mail:* admissions@cedarville.edu.

Central State University
Wilberforce, Ohio
http://www.centralstate.edu/

- **State-supported** 4-year, founded 1887, part of Ohio Board of Regents
- **Rural** 60-acre campus with easy access to Dayton
- **Endowment** $4.4 million
- **Coed** 1,729 undergraduate students, 93% full-time, 55% women, 45% men
- **Minimally difficult** entrance level, 42% of applicants were admitted

UNDERGRAD STUDENTS
1,601 full-time, 128 part-time. Students come from 29 states and territories; 11 other countries; 45% are from out of state; 93% Black or African American, non-Hispanic/Latino; 0.8% Hispanic/Latino; 0.2% Asian, non-Hispanic/Latino; 0.1% American Indian or Alaska Native, non-Hispanic/Latino; 1% Two or more races, non-Hispanic/Latino; 2% Race/ethnicity unknown; 0.6% international; 6% transferred in; 60% live on campus.

Freshmen:
Admission: 7,669 applied, 3,222 admitted, 634 enrolled. ***Average high school GPA:*** 2.5.
Retention: 40% of full-time freshmen returned.

FACULTY
Total: 190, 51% full-time, 45% with terminal degrees.
Student/faculty ratio: 13:1.

ACADEMICS
Calendar: semesters. *Degrees:* bachelor's and master's.
Special study options: adult/continuing education programs, cooperative education, double majors, honors programs, independent study, internships, off-campus study, part-time degree program, services for LD students, study abroad, summer session for credit. ***ROTC:*** Army (b).
Computers: 680 computers/terminals and 1,200 ports are available on campus for general student use. Students can access the following: campus intranet, computer help desk, free student e-mail accounts, online

(class) grades, online (class) registration, online (class) schedules. Campuswide network is available. 100% of college-owned or -operated housing units are wired for high-speed Internet access. Wireless service is available via entire campus.

Library: Hallie Q. Brown Memorial Library plus 1 other. *Books:* 312,628 (physical), 8,242 (digital/electronic); *Serial titles:* 69 (physical); *Databases:* 179. Weekly public service hours: 77.

STUDENT LIFE

Housing options: on-campus residence required for freshman year; coed, men-only, women-only. Campus housing is university owned. Freshman campus housing is guaranteed.

Activities and organizations: drama/theater group, student-run newspaper, radio and television station, choral group, marching band, Student Ambassadors, student government, Make it Happen (Inter-Faith), Daughters of Nia Anaya (Social Group), Evolutions (Modeling Troupe), national fraternities, national sororities.

Athletics Member NCAA. All Division II. ***Intercollegiate sports:*** basketball M(s)/W(s), cheerleading M(s)/W(s), cross-country running M(s)/W(s), golf M(s)/W(s), tennis M(s)/W(s), track and field M(s)/W(s), volleyball W(s). ***Intramural sports:*** basketball M/W, bowling M/W, softball M/W, tennis M/W.

Campus security: 24-hour emergency response devices and patrols, controlled dormitory access.

Student services: health clinic, personal/psychological counseling.

COSTS & FINANCIAL AID

Costs (2016–17) ***Tuition:*** state resident $3926 full-time, $275 per credit hour part-time; nonresident $5776 full-time, $625 per credit hour part-time. Full-time tuition and fees vary according to reciprocity agreements. Part-time tuition and fees vary according to reciprocity agreements. ***Required fees:*** $2320 full-time. ***Room and board:*** $9934; room only: $5340. Room and board charges vary according to board plan and housing facility. ***Payment plan:*** installment. ***Waivers:*** senior citizens and employees or children of employees.

Financial Aid Of all full-time matriculated undergraduates who enrolled in 2012, 1,820 applied for aid, 1,820 were judged to have need. 337 Federal Work-Study jobs (averaging $1216). ***Average financial aid package:*** $6373. ***Average need-based loan:*** $2103. ***Average need-based gift aid:*** $3269.

APPLYING

Options: electronic application.

Application fee: $20.

Required: essay or personal statement, high school transcript. ***Required for some:*** minimum 2.2 GPA, 2 letters of recommendation.

Application deadlines: 6/15 (freshmen), 6/15 (transfers).

Notification: continuous (freshmen), continuous (transfers).

CONTACT

Mr. Stephen Williams, Director, Admissions, Central State University, PO Box 1004, 1400 Blush Row Road, Wilberforce, OH 45384. *Phone:* 937-376-6218. *Toll-free phone:* 800-388-CSU1 (in-state); 800-388-2781 (out-of-state). *Fax:* 937-376-6648. *E-mail:* admissions@centralstate.edu.

Chamberlain College of Nursing

Cleveland, Ohio

http://www.chamberlain.edu/

CONTACT

Chamberlain College of Nursing, 6700 Euclid Avenue, Cleveland, OH 44103. *Toll-free phone:* 877-751-5783.

Chamberlain College of Nursing

Columbus, Ohio

http://www.chamberlain.edu/

- **Proprietary** 4-year
- **Coed**

FACULTY

Student/faculty ratio: 13:1.

ACADEMICS

Calendar: semesters. *Degree:* bachelor's.

STUDENT LIFE

Housing options: college housing not available.

COSTS

Costs (2016–17) ***Tuition:*** $18,900 full-time, $675 per credit hour part-time. ***Required fees:*** $600 full-time.

APPLYING

Standardized Tests *Required:* SAT or ACT (for admission).

Options: deferred entrance.

Application fee: $95.

CONTACT

Admissions, Chamberlain College of Nursing, 1350 Alum Creek Drive, Columbus, OH 43209. *Phone:* 614-252-8890. *Toll-free phone:* 877-751-5783.

Cincinnati Christian University

Cincinnati, Ohio

http://www.ccuniversity.edu/

CONTACT

Cincinnati Christian University, 2700 Glenway Avenue, PO Box 04320, Cincinnati, OH 45204-3200. *Phone:* 513-244-8110. *Toll-free phone:* 800-949-4228 (in-state); 800-949-4CCU (out-of-state).

Cincinnati College of Mortuary Science

Cincinnati, Ohio

http://www.ccms.edu/

- **Independent** 4-year, founded 1882
- **Urban** 10-acre campus with easy access to Cincinnati
- **Endowment** $80,000
- **Coed**

FACULTY

Student/faculty ratio: 15:1.

ACADEMICS

Calendar: semesters. *Degrees:* associate and bachelor's.

Library: The Cincinnati College of Mortuary Science Library. *Books:* 2,000 (physical); *Serial titles:* 2,000 (physical). Weekly public service hours: 8.

STUDENT LIFE

Housing options: college housing not available.

Activities and organizations: national fraternities, national sororities.

Campus security: 24-hour emergency response devices.

COSTS

Costs (2016–17) ***Tuition:*** $23,250 full-time. No tuition increase for student's term of enrollment. ***Payment plans:*** tuition prepayment, installment.

APPLYING

Options: electronic application, deferred entrance.

Application fee: $50.

CONTACT

Cincinnati College of Mortuary Science, 645 West North Bend Road, Cincinnati, OH 45224-1462. *Phone:* 513-761-2020. *Toll-free phone:* 888-377-8433. *Fax:* 513-761-3333.

Cleveland Institute of Art

Cleveland, Ohio

http://www.cia.edu/

- **Independent** 4-year, founded 1882
- **Urban** 2-acre campus
- **Endowment** $27.1 million
- **Coed** 606 undergraduate students, 99% full-time, 57% women, 43% men
- **Moderately difficult** entrance level, 65% of applicants were admitted

UNDERGRAD STUDENTS
600 full-time, 6 part-time. Students come from 32 states and territories; 8 other countries; 35% are from out of state; 9% Black or African American, non-Hispanic/Latino; 5% Hispanic/Latino; 4% Asian, non-Hispanic/Latino; 0.2% American Indian or Alaska Native, non-Hispanic/Latino; 4% Two or more races, non-Hispanic/Latino; 10% international; 6% transferred in; 37% live on campus.

Freshmen:
Admission: 738 applied, 479 admitted, 168 enrolled. ***Average high school GPA:*** 3.06. ***Test scores:*** SAT critical reading scores over 500: 69%; SAT math scores over 500: 69%; SAT writing scores over 500: 57%; ACT scores over 18: 96%; SAT critical reading scores over 600: 29%; SAT math scores over 600: 19%; SAT writing scores over 600: 26%; ACT scores over 24: 42%; SAT critical reading scores over 700: 3%; SAT math scores over 700: 2%; ACT scores over 30: 6%.

Retention: 83% of full-time freshmen returned.

FACULTY
Total: 108, 43% full-time, 46% with terminal degrees.

Student/faculty ratio: 9:1.

ACADEMICS
Calendar: semesters. *Degree:* bachelor's.

Special study options: advanced placement credit, distance learning, double majors, independent study, internships, off-campus study, part-time degree program, services for LD students, study abroad.

Computers: 135 computers/terminals are available on campus for general student use. Students can access the following: campus intranet, computer help desk, free student e-mail accounts, online (class) grades, online (class) registration, online (class) schedules. Campuswide network is available. 100% of college-owned or -operated housing units are wired for high-speed Internet access. Wireless service is available via entire campus.

Library: Gund Library. *Books:* 51,594 (physical); *Serial titles:* 423 (physical), 11 (digital/electronic); *Databases:* 73. Weekly public service hours: 74; students can reserve study rooms.

STUDENT LIFE
Housing options: on-campus residence required for freshman year; coed. Campus housing is leased by the school. Freshman applicants given priority for college housing.

Activities and organizations: drama/theater group, choral group, marching band, Campus Activities Board, Student Independent Exhibition, International Interior Design Association, Student Leadership Council, Community Service Club, national fraternities, national sororities.

Athletics ***Intramural sports:*** basketball M/W, cross-country running M/W, football M/W, golf M/W, racquetball M/W, soccer M/W, softball M/W, swimming and diving M/W, tennis M/W, track and field M/W, ultimate Frisbee M/W, volleyball M/W.

Campus security: 24-hour emergency response devices and patrols, late-night transport/escort service, controlled dormitory access.

Student services: health clinic, personal/psychological counseling, women's center.

COSTS & FINANCIAL AID
Costs (2017–18) ***Comprehensive fee:*** $51,455 includes full-time tuition ($37,980), mandatory fees ($2675), and room and board ($10,800). Full-time tuition and fees vary according to reciprocity agreements. Part-time tuition: $1585 per credit. Part-time tuition and fees vary according to course load and reciprocity agreements. ***Required fees:*** $73 per semester hour part-time, $115 per semester part-time. ***College room only:*** $8150. Room and board charges vary according to board plan and housing facility. ***Payment plan:*** installment. ***Waivers:*** employees or children of employees.

Financial Aid Of all full-time matriculated undergraduates who enrolled in 2015, 504 applied for aid, 474 were judged to have need, 33 had their need fully met. 139 Federal Work-Study jobs (averaging $1203). In 2015, 94 non-need-based awards were made. ***Average percent of need met:*** 61. ***Average financial aid package:*** $27,354. ***Average need-based loan:*** $4627. ***Average need-based gift aid:*** $22,663. ***Average non-need-based aid:*** $13,768. ***Average indebtedness upon graduation:*** $35,136.

APPLYING
Standardized Tests *Required:* SAT or ACT (for admission).

Options: electronic application, early admission, early action.

Application fee: $40.

Required: essay or personal statement, high school transcript, minimum 2.0 GPA, 1 letter of recommendation, portfolio. ***Recommended:*** interview.

Application deadlines: 3/1 (freshmen), 6/1 (transfers).

Notification: continuous (freshmen), continuous (transfers).

CONTACT
Office of Admissions, Cleveland Institute of Art, 11610 Euclid Avenue, Cleveland, OH 44106. *Phone:* 216-421-7418.
Toll-free phone: 800-223-4700. *Fax:* 216-754-3634.
E-mail: admissions@cia.edu.

Cleveland Institute of Music

Cleveland, Ohio

http://www.cim.edu/

CONTACT
Mr. William Fay, Director of Admission, Cleveland Institute of Music, 11021 East Boulevard, Cleveland, OH 44106-1776. *Phone:* 216-795-3107. *Fax:* 216-791-1530. *E-mail:* william.fay@case.edu.

Cleveland State University

Cleveland, Ohio

http://www.csuohio.edu/

- **State-supported** university, founded 1964, part of University System of Ohio
- **Urban** 85-acre campus with easy access to Cleveland, OH
- **Endowment** $66.2 million
- **Coed** 12,433 undergraduate students, 74% full-time, 53% women, 47% men
- **Moderately difficult** entrance level, 88% of applicants were admitted

UNDERGRAD STUDENTS
9,218 full-time, 3,215 part-time. Students come from 33 states and territories; 96 other countries; 4% are from out of state; 17% Black or African American, non-Hispanic/Latino; 5% Hispanic/Latino; 3% Asian, non-Hispanic/Latino; 0.1% Native Hawaiian or other Pacific Islander, non-Hispanic/Latino; 0.2% American Indian or Alaska Native, non-Hispanic/Latino; 3% Two or more races, non-Hispanic/Latino; 2% Race/ethnicity unknown; 5% international; 10% transferred in; 6% live on campus.

Freshmen:
Admission: 8,351 applied, 7,359 admitted, 1,918 enrolled. ***Average high school GPA:*** 3.29. ***Test scores:*** ACT scores over 18: 86%; ACT scores over 24: 33%; ACT scores over 30: 4%.

Retention: 71% of full-time freshmen returned.

FACULTY
Total: 1,178, 46% full-time.

Student/faculty ratio: 17:1.

ACADEMICS
Calendar: semesters. *Degrees:* bachelor's, master's, doctoral, post-master's, and postbachelor's certificates.

Special study options: academic remediation for entering students, accelerated degree program, adult/continuing education programs, advanced placement credit, cooperative education, distance learning, double majors, English as a second language, freshman honors college, honors programs, independent study, internships, off-campus study, part-time degree program, services for LD students, study abroad, summer session for credit. ***ROTC:*** Army (c), Air Force (c).

Computers: 736 computers/terminals are available on campus for general student use. Students can access the following: campus intranet, computer help desk, free student e-mail accounts, online (class) grades, online (class) registration, online (class) schedules, each general purpose computer lab has a scanner and printer, students are allowed free black and white printing up to 2,000 pages per semester. Campuswide network is available. 100% of college-owned or -operated housing units are wired for high-speed Internet access. Wireless service is available via entire campus.

Library: Michael Schwartz Library plus 1 other. *Books:* 524,556 (physical), 228,146 (digital/electronic); *Serial titles:* 6,155 (physical), 194 (digital/electronic); *Databases:* 733. Students can reserve study rooms.

STUDENT LIFE

Housing options: coed, special housing for students with disabilities. Campus housing is university owned. Freshman campus housing is guaranteed.

Activities and organizations: drama/theater group, student-run newspaper, radio station, choral group, Black Student Union, Chinese Students and Scholars Association, Through the Cross Campus Ministries, Student Nurses Association, Joint Engineering Council, national fraternities, national sororities.

Athletics Member NCAA. All Division I. ***Intercollegiate sports:*** basketball M(s)/W(s), cheerleading M/W, cross-country running W(s), fencing M(s)/W(s), golf M(s)/W, lacrosse M, soccer M(s)/W, softball W(s), swimming and diving M(s)/W(s), tennis M/W(s), track and field W(s), volleyball W(s), wrestling M(s). ***Intramural sports:*** baseball M(c), basketball M/W, crew M(c)/W(c), cross-country running M/W, fencing M/W, golf M/W, ice hockey M(c), rock climbing M(c)/W(c), rugby M(c), soccer M(c)/W(c), track and field M/W, ultimate Frisbee M/W, volleyball W, wrestling M.

Campus security: 24-hour emergency response devices and patrols, late-night transport/escort service, controlled dormitory access, Campus Watch, CSU Alert Notification System, Community Emergency and Response Team (CERT).

Student services: health clinic, personal/psychological counseling, women's center.

COSTS & FINANCIAL AID

Costs (2016–17) ***Tuition:*** state resident $9636 full-time, $402 per credit hour part-time; nonresident $13,687 full-time, $570 per credit hour part-time. Full-time tuition and fees vary according to course load, degree level, and program. Part-time tuition and fees vary according to course load, degree level, and program. ***Required fees:*** $60 full-time, $30 per term part-time. ***Room and board:*** $12,000; room only: $8600. Room and board charges vary according to board plan and housing facility. ***Payment plan:*** installment. ***Waivers:*** senior citizens and employees or children of employees.

Financial Aid Of all full-time matriculated undergraduates who enrolled in 2016, 7,634 applied for aid, 6,709 were judged to have need, 566 had their need fully met. 233 Federal Work-Study jobs (averaging $3448). In 2016, 641 non-need-based awards were made. ***Average percent of need met:*** 43. ***Average financial aid package:*** $8777. ***Average need-based loan:*** $4209. ***Average need-based gift aid:*** $6600. ***Average non-need-based aid:*** $5145. ***Average indebtedness upon graduation:*** $25,504.

APPLYING

Standardized Tests *Required:* SAT or ACT (for admission).

Options: electronic application, early action, deferred entrance.

Application fee: $30.

Required: high school transcript, minimum 2.3 GPA, minimum ACT score of 16 or SAT of 770 (combined critical reading and math).

Application deadlines: 5/15 (freshmen), 5/15 (transfers), 5/1 (early action).

Notification: continuous (freshmen), continuous (transfers).

CONTACT

Undergraduate Admissions Office, Cleveland State University, 2121 Euclid Avenue, EC 100, Cleveland, OH 44115. *Phone:* 216-523-7416. *Toll-free phone:* 888-CSU-OHIO. *E-mail:* admissions@csuohio.edu.

The College of Wooster

Wooster, Ohio

http://www.wooster.edu/

- **Independent** 4-year, founded 1866, affiliated with Presbyterian Church (U.S.A.)
- **Small-town** 240-acre campus with easy access to Cleveland
- **Endowment** $280.5 million
- **Coed** 2,003 undergraduate students, 99% full-time, 55% women, 45% men
- **Moderately difficult** entrance level, 58% of applicants were admitted

UNDERGRAD STUDENTS

1,983 full-time, 20 part-time. Students come from 47 states and territories; 34 other countries; 62% are from out of state; 8% Black or African American, non-Hispanic/Latino; 5% Hispanic/Latino; 5% Asian, non-Hispanic/Latino; 0.1% Native Hawaiian or other Pacific Islander, non-Hispanic/Latino; 1% American Indian or Alaska Native, non-Hispanic/Latino; 2% Race/ethnicity unknown; 11% international; 0.9% transferred in; 99% live on campus.

Freshmen:

Admission: 5,667 applied, 3,296 admitted, 545 enrolled. ***Average high school GPA:*** 3.66. ***Test scores:*** SAT critical reading scores over 500: 87%; SAT math scores over 500: 91%; SAT writing scores over 500: 87%; ACT scores over 18: 99%; SAT critical reading scores over 600: 51%; SAT math scores over 600: 61%; SAT writing scores over 600: 52%; ACT scores over 24: 79%; SAT critical reading scores over 700: 20%; SAT math scores over 700: 19%; SAT writing scores over 700: 13%; ACT scores over 30: 30%.

Retention: 87% of full-time freshmen returned.

FACULTY

Total: 199, 82% full-time, 89% with terminal degrees.

Student/faculty ratio: 11:1.

ACADEMICS

Calendar: semesters. *Degree:* bachelor's.

Special study options: advanced placement credit, double majors, independent study, internships, off-campus study, services for LD students, student-designed majors, study abroad.

Unusual degree programs: 3-2 engineering with Case Western Reserve University, Washington University in St. Louis, University of Michigan; forestry with Duke University; nursing with Case Western Reserve University; social work with Case Western Reserve University; dentistry with Case Western Reserve University, architecture with Washington University in St. Louis.

Computers: 450 computers/terminals are available on campus for general student use. Students can access the following: campus intranet, computer help desk, free student e-mail accounts, online (class) grades, online (class) registration, online (class) schedules, learning management system, campus blogging site, campus wiki site. Campuswide network is available. 100% of college-owned or -operated housing units are wired for high-speed Internet access. Wireless service is available via entire campus.

Library: The College of Wooster Libraries plus 3 others. *Books:* 605,418 (physical), 585,473 (digital/electronic); *Serial titles:* 2,781 (physical), 117,940 (digital/electronic); *Databases:* 497. Students can reserve study rooms.

STUDENT LIFE

Housing options: on-campus residence required through senior year; coed, women-only. Campus housing is university owned. Freshman campus housing is guaranteed.

Activities and organizations: drama/theater group, student-run newspaper, radio station, choral group, marching band, Volunteer Network, International Student Association, Inter-Greek Council, Wooster Activities Crew, Women's Athletic and Recreation Association.

Athletics Member NCAA. All Division III. ***Intercollegiate sports:*** baseball M, basketball M/W, cheerleading W(c), cross-country running M/W, field hockey W, football M, golf M/W, lacrosse M/W, soccer M/W, softball W, swimming and diving M/W, tennis M/W, track and field M/W, volleyball W. ***Intramural sports:*** badminton M/W, equestrian sports M(c)/W(c), ice hockey M(c)/W(c), rugby M(c), table tennis M/W, ultimate Frisbee M(c)/W(c), volleyball M(c).

Campus security: 24-hour emergency response devices and patrols, student patrols, late-night transport/escort service, controlled dormitory access.

Student services: health clinic, personal/psychological counseling, women's center.

COSTS & FINANCIAL AID

Costs (2016–17) ***Comprehensive fee:*** $57,900 includes full-time tuition ($46,430), mandatory fees ($430), and room and board ($11,040). Full-time tuition and fees vary according to course load. Part-time tuition: $1440 per credit hour. Part-time tuition and fees vary according to course load. ***College room only:*** $5330. Room and board charges vary according to board plan and housing facility. ***Payment plan:*** installment. ***Waivers:*** employees or children of employees.

Financial Aid Of all full-time matriculated undergraduates who enrolled in 2016, 1,218 applied for aid, 1,083 were judged to have need, 539 had their need fully met. 820 Federal Work-Study jobs (averaging $2134). 145 state and other part-time jobs (averaging $3265). In 2016, 713 non-need-based awards were made. ***Average percent of need met:*** 92. ***Average financial aid package:*** $41,286. ***Average need-based loan:*** $6930. ***Average need-based gift aid:*** $31,599. ***Average non-need-based aid:*** $22,828. ***Average indebtedness upon graduation:*** $29,650.

APPLYING

Standardized Tests *Required:* SAT or ACT (for admission).

Options: electronic application, early admission, early decision, early action, deferred entrance.

Required: essay or personal statement, high school transcript. ***Recommended:*** interview.

Application deadlines: 2/15 (freshmen), 7/15 (transfers), 11/15 (early action).

Early decision deadline: 11/1 (for plan 1), 1/15 (for plan 2).

Notification: 4/1 (freshmen), continuous (transfers), 11/15 (early decision plan 1), 2/1 (early decision plan 2), 12/31 (early action).

CONTACT

Ms. Jennifer Winge, Dean of Admissions, The College of Wooster, 1189 Beall Avenue, Wooster, OH 44691-2363. *Phone:* 330-263-2270. *Toll-free phone:* 800-877-9905. *Fax:* 330-263-2621. *E-mail:* admissions@wooster.edu.

Columbus College of Art & Design

Columbus, Ohio

http://www.ccad.edu/

- **Independent** comprehensive, founded 1879
- **Urban** 17-acre campus
- **Endowment** $11.7 million
- **Coed** 1,060 undergraduate students, 94% full-time, 68% women, 32% men
- **Moderately difficult** entrance level, 79% of applicants were admitted

UNDERGRAD STUDENTS

999 full-time, 61 part-time. Students come from 38 states and territories; 23 other countries; 26% are from out of state; 10% Black or African American, non-Hispanic/Latino; 6% Hispanic/Latino; 4% Asian, non-Hispanic/Latino; 0.1% Native Hawaiian or other Pacific Islander, non-Hispanic/Latino; 0.2% American Indian or Alaska Native, non-Hispanic/Latino; 5% Two or more races, non-Hispanic/Latino; 3% Race/ethnicity unknown; 7% international; 1% transferred in; 35% live on campus.

Freshmen:

Admission: 612 applied, 485 admitted, 240 enrolled. ***Test scores:*** SAT critical reading scores over 500: 64%; SAT math scores over 500: 48%; SAT writing scores over 500: 58%; ACT scores over 18: 86%; SAT critical reading scores over 600: 32%; SAT math scores over 600: 15%; SAT writing scores over 600: 22%; ACT scores over 24: 43%; SAT critical reading scores over 700: 5%; SAT math scores over 700: 3%; SAT writing scores over 700: 3%; ACT scores over 30: 10%.

Retention: 79% of full-time freshmen returned.

FACULTY

Total: 190, 35% full-time, 51% with terminal degrees.

Student/faculty ratio: 10:1.

ACADEMICS

Calendar: semesters. *Degrees:* bachelor's and master's.

Special study options: academic remediation for entering students, advanced placement credit, distance learning, double majors, English as a second language, honors programs, independent study, internships, off-campus study, services for LD students, study abroad, summer session for credit.

Computers: 485 computers/terminals are available on campus for general student use. Students can access the following: campus intranet, computer help desk, free student e-mail accounts, online (class) grades, online (class) registration, online (class) schedules. Campuswide network is available. 100% of college-owned or -operated housing units are wired for high-speed Internet access. Wireless service is available via classrooms, computer centers, computer labs, dorm rooms, learning centers, libraries, student centers.

Library: Packard Library. *Books:* 40,836 (physical), 28,701 (digital/electronic); *Serial titles:* 434 (physical), 253,828 (digital/electronic).

STUDENT LIFE

Housing options: on-campus residence required for freshman year; coed, special housing for students with disabilities. Campus housing is university owned. Freshman campus housing is guaranteed.

Activities and organizations: Student Government Association, Student Collective, Student Programming Board, CCAD Battle Alliance.

Campus security: 24-hour emergency response devices and patrols, late-night transport/escort service, controlled dormitory access.

Student services: personal/psychological counseling.

COSTS & FINANCIAL AID

Costs (2017–18) ***Comprehensive fee:*** $44,745 includes full-time tuition ($33,960), mandatory fees ($1415), and room and board ($9370). Full-time tuition and fees vary according to course load. Part-time tuition: $1415 per credit hour. Part-time tuition and fees vary according to course load. ***Room and board:*** Room and board charges vary according to board plan, housing facility, location, and student level. ***Payment plans:*** installment, deferred payment. ***Waivers:*** employees or children of employees.

Financial Aid Of all full-time matriculated undergraduates who enrolled in 2015, 908 applied for aid, 848 were judged to have need, 71 had their need fully met. 137 Federal Work-Study jobs (averaging $3550). 297 state and other part-time jobs (averaging $3550). In 2015, 207 non-need-based awards were made. ***Average percent of need met:*** 55. ***Average financial aid package:*** $21,647. ***Average need-based loan:*** $6895. ***Average need-based gift aid:*** $15,539. ***Average non-need-based aid:*** $11,029. ***Average indebtedness upon graduation:*** $32,258.

APPLYING

Standardized Tests *Recommended:* SAT or ACT (for admission).

Options: electronic application, deferred entrance.

Application fee: $50.

Required: essay or personal statement, high school transcript, minimum 3.0 GPA, 2 letters of recommendation, portfolio. ***Required for some:*** interview.

Application deadlines: rolling (freshmen), rolling (transfers).

Notification: continuous (freshmen), continuous (transfers).

CONTACT

Columbus College of Art & Design, 60 Cleveland Avenue, Columbus, OH 43215-1758. *Phone:* 614-224-9101. *Toll-free phone:* 877-997-2223. *Fax:* 614-232-8344. *E-mail:* admissions@ccad.edu.

Defiance College

Defiance, Ohio

http://www.defiance.edu/

- **Independent** comprehensive, founded 1850, affiliated with United Church of Christ
- **Small-town** 150-acre campus with easy access to Toledo
- **Endowment** $12.2 million
- **Coed** 582 undergraduate students, 87% full-time, 46% women, 54% men
- **Moderately difficult** entrance level, 58% of applicants were admitted

UNDERGRAD STUDENTS
509 full-time, 73 part-time. Students come from 21 states and territories; 2 other countries; 27% are from out of state; 4% transferred in; 50% live on campus.

Freshmen:
Admission: 1,100 applied, 640 admitted, 138 enrolled. ***Average high school GPA:*** 3.12. ***Test scores:*** SAT critical reading scores over 500: 29%; SAT math scores over 500: 19%; SAT writing scores over 500: 20%; SAT critical reading scores over 600: 15%; SAT math scores over 600: 14%; SAT writing scores over 600: 10%; SAT critical reading scores over 700: 5%.

Retention: 59% of full-time freshmen returned.

FACULTY
Total: 79, 46% full-time, 43% with terminal degrees.

Student/faculty ratio: 11:1.

ACADEMICS
Calendar: semesters. *Degrees:* associate, bachelor's, and master's.

Special study options: academic remediation for entering students, adult/continuing education programs, advanced placement credit, double majors, honors programs, independent study, internships, off-campus study, part-time degree program, services for LD students, student-designed majors, study abroad, summer session for credit.

Computers: 200 computers/terminals are available on campus for general student use. Students can access the following: campus intranet, computer help desk, free student e-mail accounts, online (class) grades, online (class) registration, online (class) schedules. Campuswide network is available. 100% of college-owned or -operated housing units are wired for high-speed Internet access. Wireless service is available via entire campus.

Library: Pilgrim Library plus 1 other. *Books:* 64,765 (physical), 248,869 (digital/electronic); *Serial titles:* 308 (physical), 65,636 (digital/electronic); *Databases:* 146. Weekly public service hours: 83; students can reserve study rooms.

STUDENT LIFE
Housing options: on-campus residence required through junior year; coed. Campus housing is university owned. Freshman campus housing is guaranteed.

Activities and organizations: drama/theater group, student-run newspaper, choral group, marching band, Campus Activities Board, Criminal Justice Society, Student Senate, Black Action Student Association, Tau Kappa Epsilon, national fraternities, national sororities.

Athletics Member NCAA. All Division III. ***Intercollegiate sports:*** baseball M, basketball M/W, cross-country running M/W, football M, golf M/W, soccer M/W, softball W, tennis M/W, track and field M/W, volleyball W. ***Intramural sports:*** baseball M, basketball M/W, cheerleading M/W, football M/W, racquetball M/W, soccer M/W, softball M/W, volleyball M/W, weight lifting M.

Campus security: late-night transport/escort service, controlled dormitory access.

Student services: personal/psychological counseling.

COSTS & FINANCIAL AID
Costs (2017–18) ***Comprehensive fee:*** $42,240 includes full-time tuition ($31,480), mandatory fees ($710), and room and board ($10,050). Full-time tuition and fees vary according to course load. Part-time tuition: $495 per credit hour. Part-time tuition and fees vary according to course load. ***Required fees:*** $100 per term part-time. ***Room and board:*** Room and board charges vary according to board plan and housing facility. ***Payment plan:*** installment. ***Waivers:*** employees or children of employees.

Financial Aid Of all full-time matriculated undergraduates who enrolled in 2015, 535 applied for aid, 506 were judged to have need, 57 had their need fully met. In 2015, 67 non-need-based awards were made. ***Average percent of need met:*** 67. ***Average financial aid package:*** $22,809. ***Average need-based loan:*** $4566. ***Average need-based gift aid:*** $17,895. ***Average non-need-based aid:*** $14,680. ***Average indebtedness upon graduation:*** $19,554.

APPLYING
Standardized Tests *Required:* SAT or ACT (for admission).

Options: electronic application, deferred entrance.

Application fee: $25.

Required: high school transcript, minimum 2.3 GPA. ***Required for some:*** essay or personal statement, 1 letter of recommendation, interview. ***Recommended:*** interview.

Application deadlines: 8/15 (freshmen), 8/15 (transfers).

Notification: continuous (freshmen), continuous (out-of-state freshmen), continuous (transfers).

CONTACT
Mr. Brad Harsha, Dean of Admissions and Financial Aid, Defiance College, 701 North Clinton Street, Defiance, OH 43512. *Phone:* 419-783-2365. *Toll-free phone:* 800-520-4632. *Fax:* 419-783-2468. *E-mail:* bharsha@defiance.edu.

Denison University

Granville, Ohio

http://www.denison.edu/

- **Independent** 4-year, founded 1831
- **Suburban** 931-acre campus with easy access to Columbus
- **Endowment** $725.8 million
- **Coed** 2,277 undergraduate students, 99% full-time, 55% women, 45% men
- **Very difficult** entrance level, 44% of applicants were admitted

UNDERGRAD STUDENTS
2,259 full-time, 18 part-time. Students come from 50 states and territories; 34 other countries; 73% are from out of state; 7% Black or African American, non-Hispanic/Latino; 9% Hispanic/Latino; 4% Asian, non-Hispanic/Latino; 0.1% Native Hawaiian or other Pacific Islander, non-Hispanic/Latino; 4% Two or more races, non-Hispanic/Latino; 2% Race/ethnicity unknown; 8% international; 0.7% transferred in; 99% live on campus.

Freshmen:
Admission: 6,881 applied, 3,001 admitted, 637 enrolled. ***Average high school GPA:*** 3.7. ***Test scores:*** SAT critical reading scores over 500: 96%; SAT math scores over 500: 99%; ACT scores over 18: 100%; SAT critical reading scores over 600: 69%; SAT math scores over 600: 76%; ACT scores over 24: 100%; SAT critical reading scores over 700: 18%; SAT math scores over 700: 26%; ACT scores over 30: 50%.

Retention: 89% of full-time freshmen returned.

FACULTY
Total: 252, 88% full-time, 98% with terminal degrees.

Student/faculty ratio: 9:1.

ACADEMICS
Calendar: semesters plus optional May term. *Degree:* bachelor's.

Special study options: advanced placement credit, double majors, honors programs, independent study, internships, off-campus study, part-time degree program, services for LD students, student-designed majors, study abroad. ***ROTC:*** Army (c).

Unusual degree programs: engineering with Case Western Reserve University, Columbia University, Rensselaer Polytechnic Institute, Washington University in St. Louis; forestry with Duke University; natural resources with University of Michigan; occupational therapy with Washington University in St. Louis; environmental management, dentistry with Case Western Reserve University; medical technology with Rochester General Hospital.

Computers: 650 computers/terminals are available on campus for general student use. Students can access the following: campus intranet, computer help desk, free student e-mail accounts, online (class) grades, online (class) registration, online (class) schedules, eClassrooms; eSpaces; special purpose rooms and computer labs with specialized software; computers, digital video, audio and other media equipment may be checked out; software downloads. Campuswide network is available. 100% of college-owned or -operated housing units are wired for high-speed Internet access. Wireless service is available via entire campus.

Library: William Howard Doane Library. *Books:* 1.4 million (physical), 912,952 (digital/electronic); *Serial titles:* 540 (physical), 653 (digital/electronic); *Databases:* 464. Weekly public service hours: 104; students can reserve study rooms.

STUDENT LIFE
Housing options: on-campus residence required through senior year; coed, men-only, women-only, cooperative. Campus housing is university owned. Freshman campus housing is guaranteed.

Activities and organizations: drama/theater group, student-run newspaper, radio and television station, choral group, Community Association, Black Student Union, International Student Association, Student Activities Committee, Latina Fuerza, national fraternities, national sororities.

Athletics Member NCAA. All Division III. ***Intercollegiate sports:*** baseball M, basketball M/W, crew M(c), cross-country running M/W, equestrian sports M(c)/W(c), field hockey W, football M, golf M, ice hockey M(c), lacrosse M/W, riflery M(c)/W(c), rugby M(c)/W(c), sailing M(c)/W(c), skiing (downhill) M(c)/W(c), soccer M/W, softball W, squash M(c)/W(c), swimming and diving M/W, tennis M/W, track and field M/W, volleyball W. ***Intramural sports:*** badminton M(c)/W(c), basketball M/W, cheerleading M/W, crew W(c), fencing M(c)/W(c), football M/W, golf M/W, lacrosse M(c), racquetball M/W, soccer M/W, softball M/W, squash M/W, table tennis M/W, tennis M/W, ultimate Frisbee M/W, volleyball M(c)/W, water polo M/W, weight lifting M/W.

Campus security: 24-hour emergency response devices and patrols, student patrols, late-night transport/escort service, controlled dormitory access, security lighting, escort.

Student services: health clinic, personal/psychological counseling, women's center.

COSTS & FINANCIAL AID
Costs (2016–17) ***Comprehensive fee:*** $60,930 includes full-time tuition ($47,870), mandatory fees ($1090), and room and board ($11,970). Part-time tuition: $1495 per credit hour. Part-time tuition and fees vary according to course load. ***College room only:*** $6590. Room and board charges vary according to board plan and housing facility. ***Payment plan:*** installment. ***Waivers:*** employees or children of employees.

Financial Aid Of all full-time matriculated undergraduates who enrolled in 2016, 1,399 applied for aid, 1,198 were judged to have need, 506 had their need fully met. In 2016, 1015 non-need-based awards were made. ***Average percent of need met:*** 89. ***Average financial aid package:*** $40,586. ***Average need-based loan:*** $5103. ***Average need-based gift aid:*** $34,576. ***Average non-need-based aid:*** $20,710. ***Average indebtedness upon graduation:*** $28,833.

APPLYING
Options: early admission, early decision, deferred entrance.

Required: essay or personal statement, high school transcript, 2 letters of recommendation. ***Recommended:*** interview.

Application deadlines: 1/15 (freshmen), 6/1 (transfers).

Early decision deadline: 11/15 (for plan 1), 1/15 (for plan 2).

Notification: 4/1 (freshmen), continuous (transfers), 1/1 (early decision).

CONTACT
Mr. Michael S. Hills, Director of Admissions, Denison University, Granville, OH 43023. *Phone:* 740-587-6627. *Toll-free phone:* 800-DENISON. *E-mail:* hills@denison.edu.

DeVry University–Columbus Campus

Columbus, Ohio

http://www.devry.edu/

- **Proprietary** comprehensive, founded 1952
- **Urban** campus
- **Coed**
- **Minimally difficult** entrance level

FACULTY
Student/faculty ratio: 34:1.

ACADEMICS
Calendar: semesters. *Degrees:* associate, bachelor's, master's, and postbachelor's certificates.

COSTS
Costs (2016–17) ***Tuition:*** $17,502 full-time, $609 per credit hour part-time. ***Required fees:*** $460 full-time.

APPLYING
Application fee: $30.

CONTACT
Admissions Office, DeVry University–Columbus Campus, 1350 Alum Creek Drive, Columbus, OH 43209. *Phone:* 614-253-7291. *Toll-free phone:* 866-338-7934.

DeVry University–Seven Hills Campus

Seven Hills, Ohio

http://www.devry.edu/

CONTACT
Admissions Office, DeVry University–Seven Hills Campus, 4141 Rockside Road, Suite 110, Seven Hills, OH 44131. *Phone:* 216-328-8754. *Toll-free phone:* 866-338-7934.

Franciscan University of Steubenville

Steubenville, Ohio

http://www.franciscan.edu/

- **Independent Roman Catholic** comprehensive, founded 1946
- **Suburban** 235-acre campus with easy access to Pittsburg, PA
- **Coed** 2,090 undergraduate students, 95% full-time, 60% women, 40% men
- **Moderately difficult** entrance level, 79% of applicants were admitted

UNDERGRAD STUDENTS
1,995 full-time, 95 part-time. Students come from 50 states and territories; 10 other countries; 80% are from out of state; 0.7% Black or African American, non-Hispanic/Latino; 11% Hispanic/Latino; 2% Asian, non-Hispanic/Latino; 0.2% American Indian or Alaska Native, non-Hispanic/Latino; 2% Two or more races, non-Hispanic/Latino; 4% Race/ethnicity unknown; 0.6% international; 6% transferred in; 80% live on campus.

Freshmen:
Admission: 1,760 applied, 1,386 admitted, 456 enrolled. ***Average high school GPA:*** 3.63. ***Test scores:*** SAT critical reading scores over 500: 91%; SAT math scores over 500: 79%; SAT writing scores over 500: 82%; ACT scores over 18: 100%; SAT critical reading scores over 600: 49%; SAT math scores over 600: 35%; SAT writing scores over 600: 37%; ACT scores over 24: 68%; SAT critical reading scores over 700: 17%; SAT math scores over 700: 7%; SAT writing scores over 700: 7%; ACT scores over 30: 16%.

Retention: 84% of full-time freshmen returned.

FACULTY
Total: 240, 53% full-time, 52% with terminal degrees.
Student/faculty ratio: 14:1.

ACADEMICS
Calendar: semesters. *Degrees:* associate, bachelor's, and master's.

Special study options: accelerated degree program, advanced placement credit, cooperative education, distance learning, double majors, honors programs, independent study, internships, part-time degree program, services for LD students, study abroad, summer session for credit. ***ROTC:*** Army (b), Air Force (c).

Unusual degree programs: 3-2 engineering with University of Notre Dame.

Computers: 126 computers/terminals are available on campus for general student use. Students can access the following: campus intranet, computer help desk, free student e-mail accounts, online (class) grades, online (class) registration, online (class) schedules. Campuswide network is available. 100% of college-owned or -operated housing units are wired for high-speed Internet access. Wireless service is available via classrooms, computer centers, computer labs, dorm rooms, libraries, student centers.

Library: St. John Paul II Library. *Books:* 143,662 (physical), 254,496 (digital/electronic); *Serial titles:* 590 (physical), 51,894 (digital/electronic); *Databases:* 131. Weekly public service hours: 93.

STUDENT LIFE

Housing options: on-campus residence required through junior year; men-only, women-only. Campus housing is university owned. Freshman applicants given priority for college housing.

Activities and organizations: drama/theater group, student-run newspaper, radio station, choral group.

Athletics Member NCAA. All Division III. ***Intercollegiate sports:*** basketball M/W, cross-country running M/W, lacrosse M/W, rugby M(c), soccer M/W, softball W, swimming and diving W, tennis M/W, track and field M/W, volleyball W. ***Intramural sports:*** basketball M/W, football M/W, racquetball M/W, soccer M/W, softball M/W, ultimate Frisbee M/W, volleyball M/W, weight lifting M/W.

Campus security: 24-hour emergency response devices and patrols, student patrols, late-night transport/escort service, controlled dormitory access.

Student services: health clinic, personal/psychological counseling.

COSTS & FINANCIAL AID

Costs (2017–18) ***Comprehensive fee:*** $34,830 includes full-time tuition ($25,970), mandatory fees ($460), and room and board ($8400). Part-time tuition and fees vary according to class time and course load. ***College room only:*** $4800. Room and board charges vary according to board plan. ***Payment plan:*** installment. ***Waivers:*** employees or children of employees.

Financial Aid Of all full-time matriculated undergraduates who enrolled in 2015, 1,534 applied for aid, 1,267 were judged to have need, 194 had their need fully met. In 2015, 614 non-need-based awards were made. ***Average percent of need met:*** 60. ***Average financial aid package:*** $14,871. ***Average need-based loan:*** $4623. ***Average need-based gift aid:*** $10,727. ***Average non-need-based aid:*** $5917. ***Average indebtedness upon graduation:*** $30,879.

APPLYING

Standardized Tests *Required:* SAT or ACT (for admission).

Options: electronic application, deferred entrance.

Application fee: $20.

Required: high school transcript, minimum 2.4 GPA. ***Required for some:*** essay or personal statement, 3 letters of recommendation. ***Recommended:*** interview.

Application deadlines: rolling (freshmen), rolling (transfers).

Notification: continuous (freshmen), continuous (transfers).

CONTACT

Miss Victoria Kubicz, Assistant Director of Admissions, Franciscan University of Steubenville, 1235 University Boulevard, Steubenville, OH 43952-1763. *Phone:* 740-284-5863. *Toll-free phone:* 800-783-6220. *Fax:* 740-284-5456. *E-mail:* admissions@franciscan.edu.

Franklin University

Columbus, Ohio

http://www.franklin.edu/

CONTACT

Mrs. Lynne Hull, Director of New Student Enrollment, Franklin University, 201 South Grant Avenue, Columbus, OH 43215. *Phone:* 614-947-6046. *Toll-free phone:* 877-341-6300. *E-mail:* hulll@franklin.edu.

Galen College of Nursing

Cincinnati, Ohio

http://www.galencollege.edu/

CONTACT

Galen College of Nursing, 100 East Business Way, Suite 200, Cincinnati, OH 45241. *Toll-free phone:* 877-223-7040.

God's Bible School and College

Cincinnati, Ohio

http://www.gbs.edu/

CONTACT

Heather Couch, Director of Financial Aid and Admissions, God's Bible School and College, 1810 Young Street, Cincinnati, OH 45202-6838. *Phone:* 513-721-7944 Ext. 1161. *Toll-free phone:* 800-486-4637. *Fax:* 513-763-6649. *E-mail:* hcouch@gbs.edu.

Good Samaritan College of Nursing and Health Science

Cincinnati, Ohio

http://www.gscollege.edu/

CONTACT

Admissions Office, Good Samaritan College of Nursing and Health Science, 375 Dixmyth Avenue, Cincinnati, OH 45220. *Phone:* 513-862-2743. *Fax:* 513-862-3572.

Harrison College

Grove City, Ohio

http://www.harrison.edu/

CONTACT

Mr. Jason Howanec, Vice President of Enrollment, Harrison College, 500 N. Meridian Street, Indianapolis, IN 46204. *Phone:* 888-544-4422. *Toll-free phone:* 888-544-4422. *E-mail:* admissions@harrison.edu.

Heidelberg University

Tiffin, Ohio

http://www.heidelberg.edu/

- **Independent** comprehensive, founded 1850, affiliated with United Church of Christ
- **Small-town** 115-acre campus with easy access to Toledo, Cleveland, Columbus
- **Endowment** $45.8 million
- **Coed** 1,034 undergraduate students, 98% full-time, 48% women, 52% men
- **Moderately difficult** entrance level, 79% of applicants were admitted

UNDERGRAD STUDENTS

1,014 full-time, 20 part-time. Students come from 25 states and territories; 12 other countries; 19% are from out of state; 4% transferred in; 79% live on campus.

Freshmen:

Admission: 1,147 applied, 905 admitted, 272 enrolled. ***Average high school GPA:*** 3.28. ***Test scores:*** SAT critical reading scores over 500: 65%; SAT math scores over 500: 73%; ACT scores over 18: 92%; SAT critical reading scores over 600: 11%; SAT math scores over 600: 22%; ACT scores over 24: 35%; ACT scores over 30: 5%.

Retention: 67% of full-time freshmen returned.

FACULTY

Total: 152, 40% full-time, 48% with terminal degrees.

Student/faculty ratio: 13:1.

ACADEMICS

Calendar: semesters. *Degrees:* bachelor's and master's.

Special study options: academic remediation for entering students, accelerated degree program, adult/continuing education programs, advanced placement credit, cooperative education, double majors, English as a second language, honors programs, independent study, internships, off-campus study, part-time degree program, services for LD students, student-designed majors, study abroad, summer session for credit. ***ROTC:*** Army (c), Air Force (c).

Unusual degree programs: 3-2 nursing with Ursuline College.

Computers: 125 computers/terminals are available on campus for general student use. Students can access the following: campus intranet, computer help desk, free student e-mail accounts, online (class) grades, online (class) registration, online (class) schedules. Campuswide network is available. 100% of college-owned or -operated housing units are wired for high-speed Internet access. Wireless service is available via entire campus.

Library: Beeghly Library plus 1 other. *Books:* 103,000 (physical), 243,016 (digital/electronic); *Serial titles:* 1,300 (physical), 105,125 (digital/electronic); *Databases:* 150. Weekly public service hours: 83.

STUDENT LIFE

Housing options: on-campus residence required through junior year; coed, women-only, cooperative. Campus housing is university owned and leased by the school. Freshman campus housing is guaranteed.

Activities and organizations: drama/theater group, student-run newspaper, radio and television station, choral group, Alpha Phi Omega, BERG Events Council, Student Senate, Campus Fellowship, Black Student Union/World Student Union.

Athletics Member NCAA. All Division III. ***Intercollegiate sports:*** baseball M, basketball M/W, cheerleading M/W, cross-country running M/W, football M, golf M/W, lacrosse M/W, soccer M/W, softball W, tennis M/W, track and field M/W, volleyball M/W, wrestling M. ***Intramural sports:*** archery M/W, badminton M/W, football M/W, golf M/W, soccer M/W, softball M/W, table tennis M/W, volleyball M/W, weight lifting M/W.

Campus security: 24-hour emergency response devices and patrols, student patrols, late-night transport/escort service, controlled dormitory access.

Student services: health clinic, personal/psychological counseling.

COSTS & FINANCIAL AID

Costs (2017–18) ***Comprehensive fee:*** $40,400 includes full-time tuition ($29,600), mandatory fees ($600), and room and board ($10,200). Full-time tuition and fees vary according to course load and degree level. Part-time tuition: $822 per contact hour. Part-time tuition and fees vary according to course load and degree level. ***College room only:*** $5300. Room and board charges vary according to housing facility. ***Payment plan:*** installment. ***Waivers:*** employees or children of employees.

Financial Aid Of all full-time matriculated undergraduates who enrolled in 2016, 1,035 applied for aid, 949 were judged to have need, 288 had their need fully met. 703 Federal Work-Study jobs (averaging $2000). 61 state and other part-time jobs (averaging $1000). In 2016, 147 non-need-based awards were made. ***Average percent of need met:*** 79. ***Average financial aid package:*** $22,421. ***Average need-based loan:*** $4854. ***Average need-based gift aid:*** $19,536. ***Average non-need-based aid:*** $13,998. ***Average indebtedness upon graduation:*** $35,872.

APPLYING

Standardized Tests *Required:* SAT or ACT (for admission).

Options: electronic application, deferred entrance.

Required: high school transcript. ***Recommended:*** essay or personal statement, minimum 2.5 GPA, 1 letter of recommendation.

Application deadlines: 8/15 (freshmen), 8/15 (transfers).

Notification: 10/1 (freshmen), 8/15 (transfers).

CONTACT

Mr. Mike Brown, Director of Admission, Heidelberg University, 310 East Market Street, Tiffin, OH 44883. *Phone:* 419-448-2507. *Toll-free phone:* 800-434-3352. *Fax:* 419-448-2334. *E-mail:* mbrown@heidelberg.edu.

Herzing University

Akron, Ohio

http://www.herzing.edu/akron

CONTACT

Herzing University, 1600 South Arlington Street, Suite 100, Akron, OH 44306. *Toll-free phone:* 800-596-0724.

Herzing University

Toledo, Ohio

http://www.herzing.edu/toledo

CONTACT

Herzing University, 5212 Hill Avenue, Toledo, OH 43615. *Toll-free phone:* 800-596-0724.

Hiram College

Hiram, Ohio

http://www.hiram.edu/

- **Independent** comprehensive, founded 1850, affiliated with Christian Church (Disciples of Christ)
- **Rural** 110-acre campus with easy access to Cleveland
- **Endowment** $72.5 million
- **Coed** 1,090 undergraduate students, 79% full-time, 51% women, 49% men
- **Moderately difficult** entrance level, 54% of applicants were admitted

UNDERGRAD STUDENTS

856 full-time, 234 part-time. Students come from 31 states and territories; 14 other countries; 19% are from out of state; 15% Black or African American, non-Hispanic/Latino; 4% Hispanic/Latino; 1% Asian, non-Hispanic/Latino; 0.4% Native Hawaiian or other Pacific Islander, non-Hispanic/Latino; 0.1% American Indian or Alaska Native, non-Hispanic/Latino; 3% Two or more races, non-Hispanic/Latino; 15% Race/ethnicity unknown; 2% international; 2% transferred in; 79% live on campus.

Freshmen:

Admission: 2,521 applied, 1,366 admitted, 207 enrolled. ***Average high school GPA:*** 3.27. ***Test scores:*** SAT critical reading scores over 500: 45%; SAT math scores over 500: 37%; SAT writing scores over 500: 32%; ACT scores over 18: 88%; SAT critical reading scores over 600: 11%; SAT math scores over 600: 11%; SAT writing scores over 600: 6%; ACT scores over 24: 37%; SAT critical reading scores over 700: 3%; SAT math scores over 700: 3%; ACT scores over 30: 6%.

Retention: 70% of full-time freshmen returned.

FACULTY

Total: 126, 64% full-time.

Student/faculty ratio: 10:1.

ACADEMICS

Calendar: semesters. *Degrees:* bachelor's and master's.

Special study options: academic remediation for entering students, accelerated degree program, adult/continuing education programs, advanced placement credit, cooperative education, distance learning, double majors, English as a second language, honors programs, independent study, internships, off-campus study, part-time degree program, services for LD students, student-designed majors, study abroad, summer session for credit. ***ROTC:*** Army (c), Air Force (c).

Unusual degree programs: 3-2 engineering with Case Western Reserve University and Washington University in St. Louis; social work with Case Western Reserve University.

Computers: 75 computers/terminals and 3,500 ports are available on campus for general student use. Students can access the following: campus intranet, computer help desk, free student e-mail accounts, online (class) grades, online (class) registration, online (class) schedules. Campuswide network is available. 100% of college-owned or -operated housing units are wired for high-speed Internet access. Wireless service is available via entire campus.

Library: Hiram College Library. *Books:* 167,330 (physical), 144,662 (digital/electronic); *Serial titles:* 130 (physical), 10,214 (digital/electronic); *Databases:* 127. Weekly public service hours: 89.

STUDENT LIFE

Housing options: on-campus residence required through junior year; coed, men-only, women-only, special housing for students with disabilities. Campus housing is university owned. Freshman campus housing is guaranteed.

Activities and organizations: drama/theater group, student-run radio station, choral group, Greek Life, Intercultural Forum, Terrier Activities Board, Student-Athlete Advisory Committee, Hiram Climbers.

Athletics Member NCAA. All Division III. ***Intercollegiate sports:*** baseball M, basketball M/W, football M, golf M/W, lacrosse M/W, soccer M/W, softball W, swimming and diving M/W, volleyball M/W. ***Intramural sports:*** basketball M/W, cheerleading M/W, cross-country running M(c)/W(c), equestrian sports M(c)/W(c), football M/W, rugby M(c)/W(c), skiing (downhill) M(c)/W(c), soccer M/W, ultimate Frisbee M(c)/W(c), volleyball M/W.

Campus security: 24-hour emergency response devices, student patrols, late-night transport/escort service, controlled dormitory access, daytime services available M-F 8am-5pm and evenings 5pm-3am, weekend services from 5pm-3am.

Student services: health clinic, personal/psychological counseling.

COSTS & FINANCIAL AID
Costs (2016–17) ***Comprehensive fee:*** $43,230 includes full-time tuition ($31,440), mandatory fees ($1600), and room and board ($10,190). Part-time tuition: $455 per credit hour. No tuition increase for student's term of enrollment. ***Required fees:*** $125 per term part-time. ***College room only:*** $5150. Room and board charges vary according to housing facility. ***Payment plan:*** installment. ***Waivers:*** employees or children of employees.

Financial Aid Of all full-time matriculated undergraduates who enrolled in 2002, 790 applied for aid, 736 were judged to have need, 699 had their need fully met. 587 Federal Work-Study jobs (averaging $1600). 18 state and other part-time jobs (averaging $1580). In 2002, 114 non-need-based awards were made. ***Average percent of need met:*** 95. ***Average financial aid package:*** $21,218. ***Average need-based loan:*** $6960. ***Average need-based gift aid:*** $8163. ***Average non-need-based aid:*** $8635. ***Average indebtedness upon graduation:*** $17,125.

APPLYING
Standardized Tests *Required for some:* SAT or ACT for applicants with cumulative GPA below 2.8, nursing or education applicants, or Trustee and/or President's Scholarships applicants.

Options: electronic application, deferred entrance.

Application fee: $25.

Required: essay or personal statement, high school transcript. ***Recommended:*** minimum 2.8 GPA, interview.

Application deadlines: rolling (freshmen), rolling (transfers).

Notification: continuous (freshmen), continuous (transfers).

CONTACT
Sherman C. Dean II, Associate Director of Admission, Hiram College, PO Box 96, Hiram, OH 44234. *Phone:* 330-569-5169. *Toll-free phone:* 800-362-5280. *Fax:* 330-569-5944. *E-mail:* admission@hiram.edu.

John Carroll University

University Heights, Ohio

http://www.jcu.edu/

- **Independent Roman Catholic (Jesuit)** comprehensive, founded 1886
- **Suburban** 60-acre campus with easy access to Cleveland
- **Endowment** $200.4 million
- **Coed** 3,026 undergraduate students, 97% full-time, 49% women, 51% men
- **Moderately difficult** entrance level, 83% of applicants were admitted

UNDERGRAD STUDENTS
2,935 full-time, 91 part-time. Students come from 36 states and territories; 30 other countries; 31% are from out of state; 5% Black or African American, non-Hispanic/Latino; 4% Hispanic/Latino; 2% Asian, non-Hispanic/Latino; 0.1% American Indian or Alaska Native, non-Hispanic/Latino; 2% Two or more races, non-Hispanic/Latino; 1% Race/ethnicity unknown; 2% international; 2% transferred in; 54% live on campus.

Freshmen:
Admission: 3,857 applied, 3,201 admitted, 717 enrolled. ***Average high school GPA:*** 3.55. ***Test scores:*** SAT critical reading scores over 500: 75%; SAT math scores over 500: 78%; SAT writing scores over 500: 69%; ACT scores over 18: 99%; SAT critical reading scores over 600: 22%; SAT math scores over 600: 31%; SAT writing scores over 600: 18%; ACT scores over 24: 63%; SAT critical reading scores over 700: 3%; SAT math scores over 700: 3%; SAT writing scores over 700: 3%; ACT scores over 30: 12%.

Retention: 84% of full-time freshmen returned.

FACULTY
Total: 414, 45% full-time.

Student/faculty ratio: 14:1.

ACADEMICS
Calendar: semesters. *Degrees:* bachelor's, master's, and post-master's certificates.

Special study options: advanced placement credit, double majors, honors programs, independent study, internships, off-campus study, part-time degree program, services for LD students, student-designed majors, study abroad, summer session for credit. ***ROTC:*** Army (b).

Unusual degree programs: 3-2 business administration; engineering with Case Western Reserve University; nursing with Ursuline College.

Computers: 396 computers/terminals are available on campus for general student use. Students can access the following: campus intranet, computer help desk, free student e-mail accounts, online (class) grades, online (class) registration, online (class) schedules, billing, advising system, JCU mobile app, course management site, online financial aid and billing; online course sites; online housing selection. Campuswide network is available. 100% of college-owned or -operated housing units are wired for high-speed Internet access. Wireless service is available via entire campus.

Library: Grasselli Library. *Books:* 456,260 (physical), 91,554 (digital/electronic); *Serial titles:* 459,633 (physical), 115,548 (digital/electronic); *Databases:* 279. Weekly public service hours: 111; students can reserve study rooms.

STUDENT LIFE
Housing options: on-campus residence required through sophomore year; coed, women-only, special housing for students with disabilities. Campus housing is university owned. Freshman campus housing is guaranteed.

Activities and organizations: drama/theater group, student-run newspaper, radio and television station, choral group, Community Outreach/Volunteer Service Organization, Student Union, Club Sports, Fraternities and Sororities, Carroll News, national fraternities, national sororities.

Athletics Member NCAA. All Division III. ***Intercollegiate sports:*** baseball M, basketball M/W, cheerleading W(c), crew M(c)/W(c), cross-country running M/W, field hockey W(c), football M, golf M/W, ice hockey M(c), lacrosse M/W, rowing M(c)/W(c), rugby M(c)/W(c), sailing M(c)/W(c), skiing (cross-country) M(c)/W(c), skiing (downhill) M(c)/W(c), soccer M/W, softball W, swimming and diving M/W, tennis M/W, track and field M/W, ultimate Frisbee M(c), volleyball M(c)/W, wrestling M. ***Intramural sports:*** basketball M/W, football M/W, golf M/W, racquetball M/W, rock climbing M/W, soccer M/W, softball M/W, swimming and diving M/W, table tennis M/W, tennis M/W, ultimate Frisbee M/W, volleyball M/W, water polo M/W.

Campus security: 24-hour emergency response devices and patrols, late-night transport/escort service, controlled dormitory access, student-led EMS program.

Student services: health clinic, personal/psychological counseling, women's center.

COSTS & FINANCIAL AID
Costs (2017–18) ***One-time required fee:*** $325. ***Tuition:*** $38,490 full-time, $1275 per credit hour part-time. Full-time tuition and fees vary according to degree level. Part-time tuition and fees vary according to course load and degree level. ***Required fees:*** $1300 full-time. ***Room only:*** Room and board charges vary according to board plan and housing facility. ***Payment plan:*** installment. ***Waivers:*** senior citizens and employees or children of employees.

Financial Aid Of all full-time matriculated undergraduates who enrolled in 2015, 2,478 applied for aid, 2,079 were judged to have need, 506 had their need fully met. 441 Federal Work-Study jobs (averaging $1242). In 2015, 553 non-need-based awards were made. ***Average percent of need met:*** 80. ***Average financial aid package:*** $29,415. ***Average need-based loan:*** $4345. ***Average need-based gift aid:*** $23,696. ***Average non-need-based aid:*** $17,546. ***Average indebtedness upon graduation:*** $31,386. ***Financial aid deadline:*** 3/15.

APPLYING
Standardized Tests *Required:* SAT or ACT (for admission).

Options: electronic application, early admission, early action, deferred entrance.

Required: essay or personal statement, high school transcript, 1 letter of recommendation. ***Required for some:*** 2 letters of recommendation, interview.

Application deadlines: 2/1 (freshmen), 8/1 (transfers), 12/1 (early action).

Notification: continuous (freshmen), continuous (transfers), 12/20 (early action).

CONTACT

Mr. Steven P. Vitatoe, Asst VP Undergrad Admission, John Carroll University, 1 John Carroll Boulevard, University Heights, OH 44118. *Phone:* 216-397-4277. *Toll-free phone:* 888-335-6800. *Fax:* 216-397-4981. *E-mail:* svitatoe@jcu.edu.

Kent State University

Kent, Ohio

http://www.kent.edu/

- **State-supported** university, founded 1910, part of Kent State University System
- **Suburban** 866-acre campus with easy access to Cleveland, Akron, Canton
- **Endowment** $110.7 million
- **Coed** 23,684 undergraduate students, 87% full-time, 61% women, 39% men
- **Moderately difficult** entrance level, 85% of applicants were admitted

UNDERGRAD STUDENTS

20,687 full-time, 2,997 part-time. Students come from 49 states and territories; 78 other countries; 14% are from out of state; 9% Black or African American, non-Hispanic/Latino; 3% Hispanic/Latino; 2% Asian, non-Hispanic/Latino; 0.1% Native Hawaiian or other Pacific Islander, non-Hispanic/Latino; 0.2% American Indian or Alaska Native, non-Hispanic/Latino; 4% Two or more races, non-Hispanic/Latino; 3% Race/ethnicity unknown; 5% international; 5% transferred in; 28% live on campus.

Freshmen:

Admission: 16,145 applied, 13,782 admitted, 4,347 enrolled. ***Average high school GPA:*** 3.38. ***Test scores:*** SAT critical reading scores over 500: 37%; SAT math scores over 500: 35%; SAT writing scores over 500: 46%; ACT scores over 18: 99%; SAT critical reading scores over 600: 3%; SAT math scores over 600: 3%; SAT writing scores over 600: 8%; ACT scores over 24: 41%; ACT scores over 30: 5%.

Retention: 82% of full-time freshmen returned.

FACULTY

Total: 1,833, 53% full-time.

Student/faculty ratio: 21:1.

ACADEMICS

Calendar: semesters. *Degrees:* certificates, bachelor's, master's, doctoral, post-master's, and postbachelor's certificates.

Special study options: academic remediation for entering students, accelerated degree program, adult/continuing education programs, advanced placement credit, cooperative education, distance learning, double majors, English as a second language, freshman honors college, honors programs, independent study, internships, off-campus study, part-time degree program, services for LD students, student-designed majors, study abroad, summer session for credit. ***ROTC:*** Army (b), Air Force (b).

Unusual degree programs: 3-2 business administration; nursing; speech pathology and audiology, fashion merchandising and business administration.

Computers: 2,000 computers/terminals are available on campus for general student use. Students can access the following: computer help desk, free student e-mail accounts, online (class) grades, online (class) registration, online (class) schedules. Campuswide network is available. 100% of college-owned or -operated housing units are wired for high-speed Internet access. Wireless service is available via entire campus.

Library: Kent State University Main Library plus 4 others. *Books:* 2.5 million (physical), 220,834 (digital/electronic); *Serial titles:* 35,857 (physical), 14,996 (digital/electronic); *Databases:* 454. Weekly public service hours: 141; study areas open 24 hours, 5-7 days a week; students can reserve study rooms.

STUDENT LIFE

Housing options: on-campus residence required through sophomore year; coed, men-only, women-only, cooperative, special housing for students with disabilities. Campus housing is university owned. Freshman applicants given priority for college housing.

Activities and organizations: drama/theater group, student-run newspaper, radio and television station, choral group, marching band, Commuter and Off-Campus Student Organization (COSO), Pride Kent, Black United Students, Delta Sigma Pi, Kent International Students, national fraternities, national sororities.

Athletics Member NCAA. All Division I. ***Intercollegiate sports:*** baseball M(s), basketball M(s)/W(s), cross-country running M(s)/W(s), field hockey W(s), football M(s), golf M(s)/W(s), gymnastics W(s), soccer W(s), softball W(s), track and field M(s)/W(s), volleyball W(s), wrestling M(s). ***Intramural sports:*** badminton M/W, baseball M(c)/W(c), basketball M/W, bowling M(c)/W(c), equestrian sports M(c)/W(c), fencing M(c)/W(c), field hockey M(c)/W(c), golf M/W, gymnastics M(c)/W(c), ice hockey M(c)/W(c), lacrosse M(c)/W(c), rugby M(c)/W(c), sand volleyball M/W, soccer M/W, softball M/W, table tennis M/W, tennis M/W, ultimate Frisbee M/W, volleyball M/W.

Campus security: 24-hour emergency response devices and patrols, student patrols, late-night transport/escort service, controlled dormitory access, campus police and fire department, electronic locks on computer labs, studios and laboratory research areas.

Student services: health clinic, personal/psychological counseling, women's center, legal services.

COSTS & FINANCIAL AID

Costs (2016–17) ***One-time required fee:*** $150. ***Tuition:*** state resident $10,012 full-time, $456 per credit hour part-time; nonresident $18,376 full-time, $818 per credit hour part-time. Full-time tuition and fees vary according to course load. Part-time tuition and fees vary according to course load. ***Room and board:*** $10,720; room only: $6760. Room and board charges vary according to board plan and housing facility. ***Payment plan:*** installment. ***Waivers:*** senior citizens and employees or children of employees.

Financial Aid Of all full-time matriculated undergraduates who enrolled in 2016, 15,408 applied for aid, 12,603 were judged to have need, 1,385 had their need fully met. 329 Federal Work-Study jobs (averaging $3191). In 2016, 3526 non-need-based awards were made. ***Average percent of need met:*** 57. ***Average financial aid package:*** $10,292. ***Average need-based loan:*** $4516. ***Average need-based gift aid:*** $5437. ***Average non-need-based aid:*** $5064. ***Average indebtedness upon graduation:*** $33,234.

APPLYING

Standardized Tests *Required:* SAT or ACT (for admission).

Options: electronic application, deferred entrance.

Application fee: $45.

Required: high school transcript.

Application deadlines: 5/1 (freshmen), 5/1 (transfers).

Notification: continuous (freshmen), continuous (transfers).

CONTACT

Mr. Christopher Buttenschon, Senior Assistant Director of Admissions, Kent State University, 161 Michael Schwartz Center, Admissions Office, Kent, OH 44242-0001. *Phone:* 330-672-2444. *Toll-free phone:* 800-988-KENT. *Fax:* 330-672-2499. *E-mail:* cbuttens@kent.edu.

Kent State University at Ashtabula

Ashtabula, Ohio

http://www.ashtabula.kent.edu/

- **State-supported** primarily 2-year, founded 1958, part of Kent State University System
- **Small-town** 83-acre campus with easy access to Cleveland
- **Coed** 2,074 undergraduate students, 57% full-time, 63% women, 37% men
- **Noncompetitive** entrance level, 99% of applicants were admitted

UNDERGRAD STUDENTS

1,186 full-time, 888 part-time. Students come from 24 states and territories; 2 other countries; 5% are from out of state; 6% Black or African American, non-Hispanic/Latino; 4% Hispanic/Latino; 1% Asian, non-Hispanic/Latino; 0.2% Native Hawaiian or other Pacific Islander, non-Hispanic/Latino; 0.3% American Indian or Alaska Native, non-

Hispanic/Latino; 3% Two or more races, non-Hispanic/Latino; 2% Race/ethnicity unknown; 0.6% international; 5% transferred in.

Freshmen:
Admission: 292 applied, 289 admitted, 183 enrolled. ***Average high school GPA:*** 2.92. ***Test scores:*** SAT critical reading scores over 500: 100%; SAT math scores over 500: 100%; SAT writing scores over 500: 100%; ACT scores over 18: 62%; SAT critical reading scores over 600: 33%; SAT math scores over 600: 83%; SAT writing scores over 600: 80%; ACT scores over 24: 12%; SAT writing scores over 700: 40%.
Retention: 59% of full-time freshmen returned.

FACULTY
Total: 96, 51% full-time.
Student/faculty ratio: 23:1.

ACADEMICS
Calendar: semesters. *Degrees:* certificates, associate, and bachelor's (also offers some upper-level and graduate courses).
Special study options: academic remediation for entering students, advanced placement credit, distance learning, double majors, independent study, internships, part-time degree program, services for LD students, student-designed majors, study abroad, summer session for credit.
Computers: 70 computers/terminals are available on campus for general student use. Students can access the following: computer help desk, free student e-mail accounts, online (class) grades, online (class) registration, online (class) schedules. Campuswide network is available. Wireless service is available via entire campus.
Library: Kent State at Ashtabula Library. *Books:* 66,090 (physical); *Serial titles:* 454 (physical). Weekly public service hours: 56.

STUDENT LIFE
Housing options: college housing not available.
Activities and organizations: Student Government, Student Veterans Association, Student Nurses Association, Student Occupational Therapy Association, Media Club.
Athletics ***Intramural sports:*** volleyball M(c)/W(c).
Campus security: 24-hour emergency response devices.

COSTS & FINANCIAL AID
Costs (2016–17) ***One-time required fee:*** $150. ***Tuition:*** state resident $5664 full-time, $258 per credit hour part-time; nonresident $14,028 full-time, $620 per credit hour part-time. Full-time tuition and fees vary according to course level and course load. Part-time tuition and fees vary according to course level and course load. ***Payment plan:*** installment. ***Waivers:*** senior citizens and employees or children of employees.
Financial Aid Of all full-time matriculated undergraduates who enrolled in 2016, 536 applied for aid, 479 were judged to have need, 12 had their need fully met. In 2016, 9 non-need-based awards were made. ***Average percent of need met:*** 53. ***Average financial aid package:*** $7465. ***Average need-based loan:*** $3745. ***Average need-based gift aid:*** $4668. ***Average non-need-based aid:*** $1479.

APPLYING
Standardized Tests *Recommended:* SAT or ACT (for admission).
Options: electronic application, deferred entrance.
Application fee: $40.
Required: high school transcript.
Application deadlines: 8/15 (freshmen), 8/15 (transfers).
Notification: continuous (freshmen), continuous (transfers).

CONTACT
Megan Krippel, Admissions Coordinator, Kent State University at Ashtabula, 3300 Lake Road West, Ashtabula, OH 44004. *Phone:* 440-964-4217. *Fax:* 440-964-4269. *E-mail:* ashtabula_admissions@kent.edu.

Kent State University at East Liverpool

East Liverpool, Ohio

http://www.eliv.kent.edu/

- **State-supported** primarily 2-year, founded 1967, part of Kent State University System
- **Small-town** 3-acre campus with easy access to Pittsburgh, Youngstown
- **Coed** 1,302 undergraduate students, 55% full-time, 69% women, 31% men
- **Noncompetitive** entrance level, 100% of applicants were admitted

UNDERGRAD STUDENTS
710 full-time, 592 part-time. Students come from 3 states and territories; 7% are from out of state; 5% Black or African American, non-Hispanic/Latino; 2% Hispanic/Latino; 0.7% Asian, non-Hispanic/Latino; 0.1% Native Hawaiian or other Pacific Islander, non-Hispanic/Latino; 0.3% American Indian or Alaska Native, non-Hispanic/Latino; 3% Two or more races, non-Hispanic/Latino; 3% Race/ethnicity unknown; 0.4% international; 4% transferred in.

Freshmen:
Admission: 118 applied, 118 admitted, 83 enrolled. ***Average high school GPA:*** 3.01. ***Test scores:*** ACT scores over 18: 71%; ACT scores over 24: 11%.
Retention: 46% of full-time freshmen returned.

FACULTY
Total: 54, 41% full-time.
Student/faculty ratio: 28:1.

ACADEMICS
Calendar: semesters. *Degrees:* certificates, associate, and bachelor's.
Special study options: academic remediation for entering students, accelerated degree program, advanced placement credit, distance learning, double majors, freshman honors college, honors programs, independent study, internships, part-time degree program, services for LD students, student-designed majors, summer session for credit. ***ROTC:*** Army (c), Air Force (c).
Computers: 72 computers/terminals are available on campus for general student use. Students can access the following: computer help desk, free student e-mail accounts, online (class) grades, online (class) registration, online (class) schedules. Campuswide network is available. Wireless service is available via entire campus.
Library: Paul Blair Memorial Library. *Books:* 21,499 (physical); *Serial titles:* 238 (physical). Weekly public service hours: 46.

STUDENT LIFE
Housing options: college housing not available.
Activities and organizations: Undergraduate Student Government, Student Nurses Association, Environmental Club, Student Occupational Therapist Assistants, Physical Therapist Assistant Club.
Campus security: 24-hour emergency response devices, student patrols, late-night transport/escort service.
Student services: personal/psychological counseling.

COSTS & FINANCIAL AID
Costs (2016–17) ***One-time required fee:*** $150. ***Tuition:*** state resident $5664 full-time, $258 per credit hour part-time; nonresident $14,028 full-time, $620 per credit hour part-time. Full-time tuition and fees vary according to course level and course load. Part-time tuition and fees vary according to course level and course load. ***Payment plan:*** installment. ***Waivers:*** senior citizens and employees or children of employees.
Financial Aid Of all full-time matriculated undergraduates who enrolled in 2016, 204 applied for aid, 170 were judged to have need, 16 had their need fully met. In 2016, 7 non-need-based awards were made. ***Average percent of need met:*** 57. ***Average financial aid package:*** $7200. ***Average need-based loan:*** $3566. ***Average need-based gift aid:*** $4692. ***Average non-need-based aid:*** $2250.

APPLYING
Standardized Tests *Recommended:* SAT or ACT (for admission).
Options: electronic application, deferred entrance.
Application fee: $40.

Required: high school transcript.
Application deadlines: 8/15 (freshmen), 8/15 (transfers).
Notification: continuous (freshmen), continuous (transfers).

CONTACT
Office of Admissions, Kent State University at East Liverpool, 400 East 4th Street, East Liverpool, OH 43920-3497. *Phone:* 330-385-3805.

Kent State University at Geauga

Burton, Ohio

http://www.geauga.kent.edu/

- **State-supported** comprehensive, founded 1964, part of Kent State University System
- **Rural** 87-acre campus with easy access to Cleveland, Akron, Youngstown
- **Coed** 2,415 undergraduate students, 60% full-time, 63% women, 37% men
- **Noncompetitive** entrance level, 98% of applicants were admitted

UNDERGRAD STUDENTS
1,448 full-time, 967 part-time. Students come from 3 states and territories; 1 other country; 3% are from out of state; 10% Black or African American, non-Hispanic/Latino; 3% Hispanic/Latino; 2% Asian, non-Hispanic/Latino; 0.3% American Indian or Alaska Native, non-Hispanic/Latino; 3% Two or more races, non-Hispanic/Latino; 3% Race/ethnicity unknown; 0.6% international; 6% transferred in.

Freshmen:
Admission: 515 applied, 506 admitted, 339 enrolled. ***Average high school GPA:*** 2.75. ***Test scores:*** SAT critical reading scores over 500: 61%; SAT math scores over 500: 47%; SAT writing scores over 500: 67%; ACT scores over 18: 66%; SAT critical reading scores over 600: 28%; SAT math scores over 600: 16%; SAT writing scores over 600: 22%; ACT scores over 24: 12%; SAT critical reading scores over 700: 6%; ACT scores over 30: 1%.
Retention: 67% of full-time freshmen returned.

FACULTY
Total: 144, 27% full-time.
Student/faculty ratio: 24:1.

ACADEMICS
Calendar: semesters. *Degrees:* certificates, associate, bachelor's, and master's.
Special study options: academic remediation for entering students, advanced placement credit, distance learning, internships, part-time degree program, services for LD students, student-designed majors, summer session for credit.
Computers: Students can access the following: computer help desk, free student e-mail accounts, online (class) grades, online (class) registration, online (class) schedules. Campuswide network is available. Wireless service is available via entire campus.
Library: Kent State University at Geauga Library. *Books:* 12,083 (physical); *Serial titles:* 43 (physical). Weekly public service hours: 53.

STUDENT LIFE
Housing options: college housing not available.
Activities and organizations: National Student Nurse Association Twinsburg, Geauga Student Nurses Association, Alpha Delta Nu-Gamma Sigma Chapter, Kent State University Geauga College Republicans, Undergraduate Student Government.
Campus security: 24-hour emergency response devices.

COSTS & FINANCIAL AID
Costs (2016–17) ***One-time required fee:*** $150. ***Tuition:*** state resident $5664 full-time, $258 per credit hour part-time; nonresident $14,028 full-time, $620 per credit hour part-time. Full-time tuition and fees vary according to course level and course load. Part-time tuition and fees vary according to course level and course load. ***Payment plan:*** installment. ***Waivers:*** senior citizens and employees or children of employees.
Financial Aid Of all full-time matriculated undergraduates who enrolled in 2016, 567 applied for aid, 451 were judged to have need, 26 had their need fully met. In 2016, 8 non-need-based awards were made. ***Average percent of need met:*** 54. ***Average financial aid package:*** $6815. ***Average need-based loan:*** $3751. ***Average need-based gift aid:*** $4778. ***Average non-need-based aid:*** $773.

APPLYING
Standardized Tests *Recommended:* SAT or ACT (for admission).
Options: electronic application, deferred entrance.
Application fee: $40.
Required: high school transcript.
Application deadlines: 8/15 (freshmen), 8/15 (transfers).
Notification: continuous (freshmen), continuous (transfers).

CONTACT
Kent State University at Geauga, 14111 Claridon-Troy Road, Burton, OH 44021. *Phone:* 440-834-4187. *Fax:* 440-834-3786. *E-mail:* geaugaadmissions@kent.edu.

Kent State University at Salem

Salem, Ohio

http://www.salem.kent.edu/

- **State-supported** primarily 2-year, founded 1966, part of Kent State University System
- **Rural** 100-acre campus with easy access to Youngstown
- **Coed** 1,673 undergraduate students, 66% full-time, 69% women, 31% men
- **Noncompetitive** entrance level, 100% of applicants were admitted

UNDERGRAD STUDENTS
1,098 full-time, 575 part-time. Students come from 4 states and territories; 1 other country; 2% are from out of state; 3% Black or African American, non-Hispanic/Latino; 2% Hispanic/Latino; 0.8% Asian, non-Hispanic/Latino; 0.2% American Indian or Alaska Native, non-Hispanic/Latino; 2% Two or more races, non-Hispanic/Latino; 3% Race/ethnicity unknown; 0.5% international; 5% transferred in.

Freshmen:
Admission: 282 applied, 282 admitted, 176 enrolled. ***Average high school GPA:*** 3.01. ***Test scores:*** SAT critical reading scores over 500: 50%; SAT math scores over 500: 50%; SAT writing scores over 500: 50%; ACT scores over 18: 69%; SAT critical reading scores over 600: 50%; SAT math scores over 600: 50%; ACT scores over 24: 15%; ACT scores over 30: 1%.
Retention: 59% of full-time freshmen returned.

FACULTY
Total: 124, 31% full-time.
Student/faculty ratio: 19:1.

ACADEMICS
Calendar: semesters. *Degrees:* certificates, associate, and bachelor's (also offers some upper-level and graduate courses).
Special study options: academic remediation for entering students, accelerated degree program, adult/continuing education programs, advanced placement credit, cooperative education, distance learning, double majors, freshman honors college, honors programs, independent study, part-time degree program, services for LD students, student-designed majors, study abroad, summer session for credit. ***ROTC:*** Army (c), Air Force (c).
Computers: 85 computers/terminals are available on campus for general student use. Students can access the following: free student e-mail accounts, online (class) grades, online (class) registration, online (class) schedules. Campuswide network is available. Wireless service is available via entire campus.
Library: Kent State Salem Library. *Books:* 23,500 (physical); *Serial titles:* 4,500 (physical).

STUDENT LIFE
Housing options: college housing not available.
Campus security: 24-hour emergency response devices, late-night transport/escort service.
Student services: personal/psychological counseling.

COSTS & FINANCIAL AID
Costs (2016–17) ***One-time required fee:*** $150. ***Tuition:*** state resident $5664 full-time, $258 per credit hour part-time; nonresident $14,028 full-

time, $620 per credit hour part-time. Full-time tuition and fees vary according to course level and course load. Part-time tuition and fees vary according to course level and course load. ***Payment plan:*** installment. ***Waivers:*** senior citizens and employees or children of employees.

Financial Aid Of all full-time matriculated undergraduates who enrolled in 2016, 619 applied for aid, 523 were judged to have need, 31 had their need fully met. In 2016, 31 non-need-based awards were made. ***Average percent of need met:*** 55. ***Average financial aid package:*** $7059. ***Average need-based loan:*** $3896. ***Average need-based gift aid:*** $4665. ***Average non-need-based aid:*** $649.

APPLYING

Standardized Tests *Required for some:* SAT or ACT (for admission). *Recommended:* SAT or ACT (for admission).

Options: electronic application, deferred entrance.

Application fee: $40.

Required: high school transcript. ***Required for some:*** essay or personal statement.

Application deadlines: 12/15 (freshmen), 12/15 (transfers).

Notification: continuous (freshmen), continuous (transfers).

CONTACT

Office of Admissions, Kent State University at Salem, 2491 State Route 45 South, Salem, OH 44460-9412. *Phone:* 330-332-0361.

Kent State University at Stark

Canton, Ohio

http://www.stark.kent.edu/

- **State-supported** comprehensive, founded 1946, part of Kent State University System
- **Suburban** 200-acre campus with easy access to Cleveland, Akron, Canton
- **Coed** 4,998 undergraduate students, 64% full-time, 60% women, 40% men
- **Noncompetitive** entrance level, 100% of applicants were admitted

UNDERGRAD STUDENTS

3,219 full-time, 1,779 part-time. Students come from 10 states and territories; 5 other countries; 2% are from out of state; 6% Black or African American, non-Hispanic/Latino; 2% Hispanic/Latino; 0.9% Asian, non-Hispanic/Latino; 0.1% Native Hawaiian or other Pacific Islander, non-Hispanic/Latino; 0.3% American Indian or Alaska Native, non-Hispanic/Latino; 3% Two or more races, non-Hispanic/Latino; 4% Race/ethnicity unknown; 1% international; 7% transferred in.

Freshmen:

Admission: 1,076 applied, 1,075 admitted, 747 enrolled. ***Average high school GPA:*** 2.89. ***Test scores:*** SAT critical reading scores over 500: 40%; SAT math scores over 500: 50%; SAT writing scores over 500: 65%; ACT scores over 18: 74%; SAT critical reading scores over 600: 10%; SAT math scores over 600: 25%; SAT writing scores over 600: 20%; ACT scores over 24: 18%; SAT math scores over 700: 5%; ACT scores over 30: 1%.

Retention: 65% of full-time freshmen returned.

FACULTY

Total: 282, 39% full-time.

Student/faculty ratio: 23:1.

ACADEMICS

Calendar: semesters. *Degrees:* associate, bachelor's, and master's.

Special study options: academic remediation for entering students, adult/continuing education programs, advanced placement credit, distance learning, double majors, honors programs, independent study, internships, off-campus study, part-time degree program, services for LD students, student-designed majors, study abroad, summer session for credit. ***ROTC:*** Army (c), Air Force (c).

Computers: 605 computers/terminals are available on campus for general student use. Students can access the following: computer help desk, free student e-mail accounts, online (class) grades, online (class) registration, online (class) schedules. Campuswide network is available. Wireless service is available via entire campus.

Library: Kent State Stark Library. *Serial titles:* 600 (physical). Weekly public service hours: 72; students can reserve study rooms.

STUDENT LIFE

Housing options: college housing not available.

Activities and organizations: drama/theater group, choral group, Music Technology Club, Biology Club, SCRUBS (Nursing Organization), HDFS (Human Development Family Studies), Revive (Faith Based).

Athletics ***Intramural sports:*** basketball M/W, golf M/W, softball M/W, table tennis M/W, volleyball M/W, weight lifting M/W.

Campus security: 24-hour emergency response devices, student patrols, late-night transport/escort service.

Student services: personal/psychological counseling.

COSTS & FINANCIAL AID

Costs (2016–17) ***One-time required fee:*** $150. ***Tuition:*** state resident $5664 full-time, $258 per credit hour part-time; nonresident $14,028 full-time, $620 per credit hour part-time. Full-time tuition and fees vary according to course level and course load. Part-time tuition and fees vary according to course level and course load. ***Payment plan:*** installment. ***Waivers:*** senior citizens and employees or children of employees.

Financial Aid Of all full-time matriculated undergraduates who enrolled in 2016, 1,924 applied for aid, 1,582 were judged to have need, 139 had their need fully met. In 2016, 120 non-need-based awards were made. ***Average percent of need met:*** 59. ***Average financial aid package:*** $6840. ***Average need-based loan:*** $3823. ***Average need-based gift aid:*** $4228. ***Average non-need-based aid:*** $1843.

APPLYING

Standardized Tests *Recommended:* SAT or ACT (for admission).

Options: electronic application, deferred entrance.

Application fee: $40.

Required: high school transcript.

Application deadlines: 8/15 (freshmen), 8/15 (transfers).

Notification: continuous (freshmen), continuous (transfers).

CONTACT

Office of Admissions, Kent State University at Stark, 6000 Frank Avenue NW, North Canton, OH 44720. *Phone:* 330-244-3251. *Fax:* 330-499-0301. *E-mail:* starkadmissions@kent.edu.

Kent State University at Trumbull

Warren, Ohio

http://www.trumbull.kent.edu/

- **State-supported** primarily 2-year, founded 1954, part of Kent State University System
- **Suburban** 438-acre campus with easy access to Akron, Youngstown
- **Coed** 2,377 undergraduate students, 63% full-time, 61% women, 39% men
- **Noncompetitive** entrance level, 100% of applicants were admitted

UNDERGRAD STUDENTS

1,501 full-time, 876 part-time. Students come from 7 states and territories; 6 other countries; 3% are from out of state; 8% Black or African American, non-Hispanic/Latino; 2% Hispanic/Latino; 0.9% Asian, non-Hispanic/Latino; 0.1% Native Hawaiian or other Pacific Islander, non-Hispanic/Latino; 0.2% American Indian or Alaska Native, non-Hispanic/Latino; 2% Two or more races, non-Hispanic/Latino; 3% Race/ethnicity unknown; 0.4% international; 7% transferred in.

Freshmen:

Admission: 429 applied, 427 admitted, 272 enrolled. ***Average high school GPA:*** 2.82. ***Test scores:*** ACT scores over 18: 63%; ACT scores over 24: 10%.

Retention: 54% of full-time freshmen returned.

FACULTY

Total: 106, 49% full-time.

Student/faculty ratio: 26:1.

ACADEMICS

Calendar: semesters. *Degrees:* associate, bachelor's, and master's (also offers some upper-level and graduate courses).

Special study options: academic remediation for entering students, adult/continuing education programs, advanced placement credit, distance learning, double majors, freshman honors college, honors programs, independent study, internships, part-time degree program, services for LD students, student-designed majors, summer session for credit. ***ROTC:*** Army (c), Air Force (c).

Computers: 300 computers/terminals are available on campus for general student use. Students can access the following: computer help desk, free student e-mail accounts, online (class) grades, online (class) registration, online (class) schedules. Campuswide network is available. Wireless service is available via entire campus.

Library: Gelbke Library at Kent State Trumbull. *Books:* 40,000 (physical), 100,000 (digital/electronic); *Serial titles:* 40 (physical); *Databases:* 459. Weekly public service hours: 56.

STUDENT LIFE

Housing options: college housing not available.

Activities and organizations: drama/theater group, The National Society for Leadership and Success, Sigma Alpha Pi, Jurisprudence Organization, Student Nurses Association, Pride Alliance, S.E.E.D.S..

Campus security: 24-hour emergency response devices, late-night transport/escort service, patrols by trained security personnel during open hours.

Student services: personal/psychological counseling.

COSTS & FINANCIAL AID

Costs (2016–17) ***One-time required fee:*** $150. ***Tuition:*** state resident $5664 full-time, $258 per credit hour part-time; nonresident $14,028 full-time, $620 per credit hour part-time. Full-time tuition and fees vary according to course level and course load. Part-time tuition and fees vary according to course level and course load. ***Payment plan:*** installment. ***Waivers:*** senior citizens and employees or children of employees.

Financial Aid Of all full-time matriculated undergraduates who enrolled in 2016, 758 applied for aid, 655 were judged to have need, 39 had their need fully met. In 2016, 46 non-need-based awards were made. ***Average percent of need met:*** 57. ***Average financial aid package:*** $7387. ***Average need-based loan:*** $3851. ***Average need-based gift aid:*** $4655. ***Average non-need-based aid:*** $1468.

APPLYING

Standardized Tests *Recommended:* SAT or ACT (for admission).

Options: electronic application, deferred entrance.

Application fee: $40.

Required: high school transcript.

Application deadlines: 8/15 (freshmen), 8/15 (transfers).

Notification: continuous (freshmen), continuous (transfers).

CONTACT

Office of Enrollment Management, Kent State University at Trumbull, 4314 Mahoning Avenue, NW, Warren, OH 44483-1998. *Phone:* 330-675-8860. *E-mail:* trumbullinfo@kent.edu.

Kent State University at Tuscarawas

New Philadelphia, Ohio

http://www.tusc.kent.edu/

- **State-supported** primarily 2-year, founded 1962, part of Kent State University System
- **Small-town** 180-acre campus with easy access to Akron, Canton
- **Coed** 2,035 undergraduate students, 60% full-time, 58% women, 42% men
- **Noncompetitive** entrance level, 99% of applicants were admitted

UNDERGRAD STUDENTS

1,226 full-time, 809 part-time. Students come from 5 states and territories; 3 other countries; 2% are from out of state; 3% Black or African American, non-Hispanic/Latino; 2% Hispanic/Latino; 1% Asian, non-Hispanic/Latino; 0.0% Native Hawaiian or other Pacific Islander, non-Hispanic/Latino; 0.2% American Indian or Alaska Native, non-Hispanic/Latino; 2% Two or more races, non-Hispanic/Latino; 3% Race/ethnicity unknown; 0.2% international; 6% transferred in.

Freshmen:

Admission: 390 applied, 388 admitted, 267 enrolled. ***Average high school GPA:*** 2.98. ***Test scores:*** SAT writing scores over 500: 50%; ACT scores over 18: 76%; ACT scores over 24: 17%; ACT scores over 30: 1%.

Retention: 69% of full-time freshmen returned.

FACULTY

Total: 119, 39% full-time.

Student/faculty ratio: 22:1.

ACADEMICS

Calendar: semesters. *Degrees:* certificates, diplomas, associate, and bachelor's (also offers some upper-level and graduate courses).

Special study options: academic remediation for entering students, accelerated degree program, adult/continuing education programs, advanced placement credit, distance learning, double majors, freshman honors college, independent study, internships, part-time degree program, services for LD students, student-designed majors, study abroad, summer session for credit. ***ROTC:*** Army (c), Air Force (c).

Computers: 194 computers/terminals are available on campus for general student use. Students can access the following: computer help desk, free student e-mail accounts, online (class) grades, online (class) registration, online (class) schedules. Campuswide network is available. Wireless service is available via entire campus.

Library: Kent State Tuscarawas Library. *Books:* 52,500 (physical), 12 (digital/electronic); *Serial titles:* 540 (physical).

STUDENT LIFE

Housing options: college housing not available.

Activities and organizations: choral group, Student Nurses Association, Technology Club, Vet Tech Student Chapter, Realms of Roleplay, Vision.

Athletics Member USCAA. ***Intercollegiate sports:*** baseball M, basketball M/W, cross-country running M/W, golf M, soccer M/W, softball W, track and field M/W, volleyball W, wrestling M. ***Intramural sports:*** bowling M/W.

Campus security: 24-hour emergency response devices.

COSTS & FINANCIAL AID

Costs (2016–17) ***One-time required fee:*** $150. ***Tuition:*** state resident $5664 full-time, $258 per credit hour part-time; nonresident $14,028 full-time, $620 per credit hour part-time. Full-time tuition and fees vary according to course level and course load. Part-time tuition and fees vary according to course level and course load. ***Payment plan:*** installment. ***Waivers:*** senior citizens and employees or children of employees.

Financial Aid Of all full-time matriculated undergraduates who enrolled in 2016, 639 applied for aid, 538 were judged to have need, 52 had their need fully met. In 2016, 6 non-need-based awards were made. ***Average percent of need met:*** 59. ***Average financial aid package:*** $6682. ***Average need-based loan:*** $3737. ***Average need-based gift aid:*** $4331. ***Average non-need-based aid:*** $2977.

APPLYING

Standardized Tests *Recommended:* SAT or ACT (for admission).

Options: electronic application, deferred entrance.

Application fee: $40.

Required: high school transcript.

Application deadlines: 8/15 (freshmen), 8/15 (transfers).

Notification: continuous (freshmen), continuous (transfers).

CONTACT

Office of Admissions, Kent State University at Tuscarawas, 330 University Dr NE, New Philadelphia, OH 44663-9403. *Phone:* 330-339-3391. *E-mail:* infotusc@kent.edu.

Kenyon College

Gambier, Ohio

http://www.kenyon.edu/

- **Independent** 4-year, founded 1824
- **Rural** 1000-acre campus with easy access to Columbus
- **Endowment** $208.9 million
- **Coed** 1,708 undergraduate students, 99% full-time, 55% women, 45% men
- **Most difficult** entrance level, 29% of applicants were admitted

UNDERGRAD STUDENTS
1,688 full-time, 20 part-time. Students come from 50 states and territories; 45 other countries; 85% are from out of state; 3% Black or African American, non-Hispanic/Latino; 5% Hispanic/Latino; 4% Asian, non-Hispanic/Latino; 8% Two or more races, non-Hispanic/Latino; 3% Race/ethnicity unknown; 5% international; 0.5% transferred in; 100% live on campus.

Freshmen:
Admission: 5,927 applied, 1,702 admitted, 487 enrolled. ***Average high school GPA:*** 3.9. ***Test scores:*** SAT critical reading scores over 500: 98%; SAT math scores over 500: 98%; SAT writing scores over 500: 98%; ACT scores over 18: 100%; SAT critical reading scores over 600: 84%; SAT math scores over 600: 78%; SAT writing scores over 600: 85%; ACT scores over 24: 100%; SAT critical reading scores over 700: 45%; SAT math scores over 700: 28%; SAT writing scores over 700: 44%; ACT scores over 30: 72%.
Retention: 92% of full-time freshmen returned.

FACULTY
Total: 213, 78% full-time, 93% with terminal degrees.
Student/faculty ratio: 9:1.

ACADEMICS
Calendar: semesters. *Degree:* bachelor's.
Special study options: accelerated degree program, advanced placement credit, double majors, honors programs, independent study, internships, off-campus study, services for LD students, student-designed majors, study abroad.
Unusual degree programs: 3-2 engineering with Washington University in St. Louis, Case Western Reserve University, Rensselaer Polytechnic Institute; environmental science with Duke University, education with The Bank Street College of Education.
Computers: 715 computers/terminals are available on campus for general student use. Students can access the following: campus intranet, computer help desk, free student e-mail accounts, online (class) grades, online (class) registration, online (class) schedules, commercial databases. Campuswide network is available. 99% of college-owned or -operated housing units are wired for high-speed Internet access. Wireless service is available via entire campus.
Library: Olin Library plus 1 other. *Books:* 495,501 (physical), 42,965 (digital/electronic); *Serial titles:* 1,670 (physical), 43,534 (digital/electronic); *Databases:* 332. Weekly public service hours: 131; students can reserve study rooms.

STUDENT LIFE
Housing options: on-campus residence required through senior year; coed, women-only, special housing for students with disabilities. Campus housing is university owned. Freshman campus housing is guaranteed.
Activities and organizations: drama/theater group, student-run newspaper, radio station, choral group, student advisory groups, student radio station, musical groups, intramural sports and clubs, outdoors club, national fraternities, national sororities.
Athletics Member NCAA. All Division III. ***Intercollegiate sports:*** baseball M, basketball M/W, cross-country running M/W, equestrian sports M(c)/W(c), field hockey W, football M, golf M, lacrosse M/W, rugby M(c)/W(c), soccer M/W, softball W, squash M(c)/W(c), swimming and diving M/W, tennis M/W, track and field M/W, ultimate Frisbee M(c)/W(c), volleyball W. ***Intramural sports:*** archery M(c)/W(c), basketball M/W, fencing M(c)/W(c), racquetball M/W, soccer M(c)/W(c), tennis M(c)/W(c), volleyball M/W.
Campus security: 24-hour emergency response devices and patrols, student patrols, late-night transport/escort service, controlled dormitory access.
Student services: health clinic, personal/psychological counseling, women's center.

COSTS & FINANCIAL AID
Costs (2016–17) ***Comprehensive fee:*** $63,330 includes full-time tuition ($49,220), mandatory fees ($1980), and room and board ($12,130). Full-time tuition and fees vary according to reciprocity agreements. Part-time tuition and fees vary according to reciprocity agreements. ***College room only:*** $5340. Room and board charges vary according to housing facility and student level. ***Payment plan:*** installment. ***Waivers:*** employees or children of employees.

Financial Aid Of all full-time matriculated undergraduates who enrolled in 2015, 942 applied for aid, 778 were judged to have need, 487 had their need fully met. 259 Federal Work-Study jobs (averaging $1670). 157 state and other part-time jobs (averaging $1726). In 2015, 193 non-need-based awards were made. ***Average percent of need met:*** 100. ***Average financial aid package:*** $42,699. ***Average need-based loan:*** $4006. ***Average need-based gift aid:*** $39,628. ***Average non-need-based aid:*** $15,204. ***Average indebtedness upon graduation:*** $27,000.

APPLYING
Standardized Tests *Required:* SAT or ACT (for admission).
Options: electronic application, early admission, early decision, deferred entrance.
Required: essay or personal statement, high school transcript, counselor recommendation. ***Recommended:*** 2 letters of recommendation, interview.
Application deadlines: 1/15 (freshmen), 4/1 (transfers).
Early decision deadline: 11/15 (for plan 1), 1/15 (for plan 2).
Notification: 4/1 (freshmen), 5/15 (transfers), 12/15 (early decision plan 1), 2/1 (early decision plan 2).

CONTACT
Ms. Diane Anci, Vice President of Enrollment Management and Dean of Admissions and Financial Aid, Kenyon College, Ransom Hall, Gambier, OH 43022. *Phone:* 740-427-5776. *Toll-free phone:* 800-848-2468. *Fax:* 740-427-5770. *E-mail:* admissions@kenyon.edu.

Kettering College
Kettering, Ohio
http://www.kc.edu/

CONTACT
Mrs. Becky McDonald, Director of Enrollment Services, Kettering College, 3737 Southern Boulevard, Kettering, OH 45429-1299. *Phone:* 937-395-8628. *Toll-free phone:* 800-433-5262. *Fax:* 937-296-4238.

Lake Erie College
Painesville, Ohio
http://www.lec.edu/

- **Independent** comprehensive, founded 1856
- **Suburban** 46-acre campus with easy access to Cleveland
- **Endowment** $32.7 million
- **Coed** 955 undergraduate students, 78% full-time, 52% women, 48% men
- **Moderately difficult** entrance level, 63% of applicants were admitted

UNDERGRAD STUDENTS
745 full-time, 210 part-time. Students come from 27 states and territories; 14 other countries; 26% are from out of state; 14% Black or African American, non-Hispanic/Latino; 2% Hispanic/Latino; 0.8% Asian, non-Hispanic/Latino; 0.7% American Indian or Alaska Native, non-Hispanic/Latino; 3% Two or more races, non-Hispanic/Latino; 3% Race/ethnicity unknown; 4% international; 4% transferred in; 66% live on campus.

Freshmen:
Admission: 1,485 applied, 937 admitted, 219 enrolled. ***Average high school GPA:*** 3.09. ***Test scores:*** SAT critical reading scores over 500: 27%; SAT math scores over 500: 31%; SAT writing scores over 500: 19%; ACT scores over 18: 79%; SAT critical reading scores over 600: 4%; SAT math scores over 600: 7%; SAT writing scores over 600: 2%; ACT scores over 24: 15%; ACT scores over 30: 1%.
Retention: 70% of full-time freshmen returned.

FACULTY
Total: 103, 41% full-time, 41% with terminal degrees.
Student/faculty ratio: 14:1.

ACADEMICS
Calendar: semesters. *Degrees:* bachelor's, master's, and postbachelor's certificates.
Special study options: accelerated degree program, advanced placement credit, double majors, honors programs, independent study, internships,

off-campus study, part-time degree program, services for LD students, student-designed majors, study abroad, summer session for credit.

Computers: 78 computers/terminals are available on campus for general student use. Students can access the following: campus intranet, computer help desk, free student e-mail accounts, online (class) grades, online (class) registration, online (class) schedules. Campuswide network is available. 100% of college-owned or -operated housing units are wired for high-speed Internet access. Wireless service is available via entire campus.

Library: Lincoln Library. *Books:* 38,463 (physical), 299,340 (digital/electronic); *Serial titles:* 18,188 (digital/electronic); *Databases:* 107. Weekly public service hours: 56; students can reserve study rooms.

STUDENT LIFE

Housing options: on-campus residence required through sophomore year; coed, men-only, women-only. Campus housing is university owned and leased by the school. Freshman applicants given priority for college housing.

Activities and organizations: drama/theater group, choral group, Student Athlete Advisory Committee, Intercollegiate Horse Show Association, Gamma Phi Beta Sorority, Spanish Club, Student Government Association, national fraternities, national sororities.

Athletics Member NCAA. All Division II. ***Intercollegiate sports:*** baseball M(s), basketball M(s)/W(s), cross-country running M(s)/W(s), football M(s), lacrosse M(s)/W(s), soccer M(s)/W(s), softball W(s), track and field M(s)/W(s), volleyball W(s), wrestling M(s). ***Intramural sports:*** basketball M/W, equestrian sports M(c)/W(c), football M/W, racquetball M(c)/W(c), soccer M/W, softball M/W, ultimate Frisbee M/W, volleyball M/W.

Campus security: 24-hour emergency response devices and patrols, late-night transport/escort service.

COSTS & FINANCIAL AID

Costs (2017–18) ***One-time required fee:*** $350. ***Comprehensive fee:*** $39,994 includes full-time tuition ($29,426), mandatory fees ($1436), and room and board ($9132). Full-time tuition and fees vary according to course load, degree level, and program. Part-time tuition: $780 per credit hour. Part-time tuition and fees vary according to course load, degree level, and program. ***Required fees:*** $51 per credit hour part-time. ***College room only:*** $4508. Room and board charges vary according to board plan and housing facility. ***Payment plan:*** installment. ***Waivers:*** senior citizens and employees or children of employees.

Financial Aid Of all full-time matriculated undergraduates who enrolled in 2016, 633 applied for aid, 585 were judged to have need, 109 had their need fully met. In 2016, 91 non-need-based awards were made. ***Average percent of need met:*** 75. ***Average financial aid package:*** $23,882. ***Average need-based loan:*** $4342. ***Average need-based gift aid:*** $19,849. ***Average non-need-based aid:*** $13,855. ***Average indebtedness upon graduation:*** $38,234.

APPLYING

Standardized Tests *Required for some:* SAT or ACT (for admission), SAT and SAT Subject Tests or ACT (for admission). *Recommended:* AP, CLEP, institutional exam.

Options: electronic application, early action, deferred entrance.

Application fee: $30.

Required: high school transcript, minimum 2.5 GPA. ***Required for some:*** essay or personal statement, letters of recommendation. ***Recommended:*** essay or personal statement, interview.

Application deadlines: 8/1 (freshmen), rolling (transfers), 12/1 (early action).

Notification: continuous (freshmen), continuous (transfers), 12/14 (early action).

CONTACT

Mrs. Liz Sellers, Director of Admissions, Lake Erie College, 391 West Washington Street, Painesville, OH 44077-3389. *Phone:* 440-375-7251. *Toll-free phone:* 800-916-0904. *Fax:* 440-375-7058. *E-mail:* admissions@lec.edu.

Lourdes University

Sylvania, Ohio

http://www.lourdes.edu/

- **Independent Roman Catholic** comprehensive, founded 1958
- **Suburban** 113-acre campus with easy access to Toledo
- **Endowment** $11.0 million
- **Coed** 1,125 undergraduate students, 75% full-time, 64% women, 36% men
- **Moderately difficult** entrance level, 89% of applicants were admitted

UNDERGRAD STUDENTS

842 full-time, 283 part-time. Students come from 32 states and territories; 7 other countries; 25% are from out of state; 9% Black or African American, non-Hispanic/Latino; 9% Hispanic/Latino; 0.4% Asian, non-Hispanic/Latino; 0.1% Native Hawaiian or other Pacific Islander, non-Hispanic/Latino; 0.4% American Indian or Alaska Native, non-Hispanic/Latino; 4% Two or more races, non-Hispanic/Latino; 3% Race/ethnicity unknown; 0.9% international; 10% transferred in; 35% live on campus.

Freshmen:

Admission: 919 applied, 821 admitted, 213 enrolled.
Average high school GPA: 3.26.

Retention: 72% of full-time freshmen returned.

FACULTY

Total: 185, 32% full-time, 35% with terminal degrees.

Student/faculty ratio: 12:1.

ACADEMICS

Calendar: semesters. *Degrees:* certificates, associate, bachelor's, master's, and postbachelor's certificates.

Special study options: academic remediation for entering students, adult/continuing education programs, advanced placement credit, distance learning, double majors, freshman honors college, honors programs, independent study, internships, part-time degree program, services for LD students, student-designed majors, study abroad, summer session for credit. ***ROTC:*** Army (c), Air Force (c).

Computers: 264 computers/terminals are available on campus for general student use. Students can access the following: computer help desk, free student e-mail accounts, online (class) grades, online (class) registration, online (class) schedules, online course content, portfolio access, RRS news feeds, online polls, webcasting, business technologies. Campuswide network is available. 100% of college-owned or -operated housing units are wired for high-speed Internet access. Wireless service is available via entire campus.

Library: Duns Scotus Library plus 1 other. *Books:* 54,138 (physical), 325,641 (digital/electronic); *Serial titles:* 486 (physical), 2,057 (digital/electronic). Study areas open 24 hours, 5-7 days a week.

STUDENT LIFE

Housing options: on-campus residence required through senior year; coed. Campus housing is university owned. Freshman applicants given priority for college housing.

Activities and organizations: drama/theater group, choral group, Student Government Association, Student Nurses Association, Orbis Ars, Future Doctors of America, Active Minds.

Athletics Member NAIA. ***Intercollegiate sports:*** baseball M(s), basketball M(s)/W(s), cheerleading M(s)/W(s), cross-country running M(s)/W(s), golf M(s)/W(s), lacrosse M(s)/W(s), soccer M(s)/W(s), softball W(s), track and field M(s)/W(s), volleyball M(s)/W(s), wrestling M(s). ***Intramural sports:*** basketball M/W, bowling M/W, football M/W, golf M/W, ice hockey M/W, soccer M/W, tennis M/W, ultimate Frisbee M/W, volleyball M/W.

Campus security: 24-hour emergency response devices and patrols, late-night transport/escort service, controlled dormitory access.

Student services: health clinic, personal/psychological counseling.

COSTS & FINANCIAL AID

Costs (2017–18) ***One-time required fee:*** $250. ***Comprehensive fee:*** $26,640 includes full-time tuition ($20,800), mandatory fees ($740), and room and board ($5100). Full-time tuition and fees vary according to course load and location. Part-time tuition: $695 per credit hour. Part-time tuition and fees vary according to course load and location. ***Required fees:***

$220 per term part-time. ***College room only:*** $4600. Room and board charges vary according to board plan and housing facility. ***Payment plans:*** installment, deferred payment. ***Waivers:*** adult students, senior citizens, and employees or children of employees.

Financial Aid Of all full-time matriculated undergraduates who enrolled in 2013, 1,091 applied for aid, 938 were judged to have need. 68 Federal Work-Study jobs (averaging $1872). 128 state and other part-time jobs (averaging $1500). ***Average financial aid package:*** $13,172. ***Average need-based loan:*** $3988. ***Average need-based gift aid:*** $6089.

APPLYING

Standardized Tests *Required:* SAT or ACT (for admission).

Options: electronic application, early admission, deferred entrance.

Application fee: $25.

Required: high school transcript, minimum 2.5 GPA.

Application deadlines: rolling (freshmen), rolling (transfers).

Notification: continuous (freshmen), continuous (transfers).

CONTACT

Amy Houston, Associate Director of Admissions, Lourdes University, 6832 Convent Boulevard, Sylvania, OH 43560. *Phone:* 419-885-5291. *Toll-free phone:* 800-878-3210.

Malone University

Canton, Ohio

http://www.malone.edu/

- **Independent** comprehensive, founded 1892, affiliated with Evangelical Friends Church–Eastern Region
- **Suburban** 96-acre campus with easy access to Cleveland
- **Endowment** $17.6 million
- **Coed** 1,311 undergraduate students, 87% full-time, 59% women, 41% men
- **Moderately difficult** entrance level, 73% of applicants were admitted

UNDERGRAD STUDENTS

1,145 full-time, 166 part-time. Students come from 28 states and territories; 6 other countries; 14% are from out of state; 12% Black or African American, non-Hispanic/Latino; 3% Hispanic/Latino; 0.8% Asian, non-Hispanic/Latino; 0.2% American Indian or Alaska Native, non-Hispanic/Latino; 3% Two or more races, non-Hispanic/Latino; 0.2% Race/ethnicity unknown; 0.6% international; 5% transferred in; 63% live on campus.

Freshmen:

Admission: 1,762 applied, 1,283 admitted, 311 enrolled. ***Average high school GPA:*** 3.24. ***Test scores:*** SAT critical reading scores over 500: 81%; SAT math scores over 500: 42%; ACT scores over 18: 87%; SAT critical reading scores over 600: 45%; SAT math scores over 600: 9%; ACT scores over 24: 32%; SAT critical reading scores over 700: 11%; SAT math scores over 700: 4%; ACT scores over 30: 6%.

Retention: 78% of full-time freshmen returned.

FACULTY

Total: 190, 47% full-time, 50% with terminal degrees.

Student/faculty ratio: 11:1.

ACADEMICS

Calendar: semesters. *Degrees:* bachelor's and master's.

Special study options: academic remediation for entering students, accelerated degree program, adult/continuing education programs, advanced placement credit, distance learning, double majors, honors programs, independent study, internships, off-campus study, part-time degree program, services for LD students, student-designed majors, study abroad, summer session for credit.

Unusual degree programs: 3-2 engineering with The University of Akron.

Computers: 304 computers/terminals and 3,900 ports are available on campus for general student use. Students can access the following: campus intranet, computer help desk, free student e-mail accounts, online (class) grades, online (class) registration, online (class) schedules, online advising, online financial aid information, and online credit card payments. Campuswide network is available. 100% of college-owned or -operated housing units are wired for high-speed Internet access. Wireless service is available via entire campus.

Library: Everett L. Cattell Library plus 1 other. *Books:* 170,981 (physical), 382,388 (digital/electronic); *Serial titles:* 2,035 (physical), 38,355 (digital/electronic); *Databases:* 194. Weekly public service hours: 88.

STUDENT LIFE

Housing options: on-campus residence required through junior year; men-only, women-only, special housing for students with disabilities. Campus housing is university owned. Freshman applicants given priority for college housing.

Activities and organizations: drama/theater group, student-run newspaper, choral group, marching band, Celebration Worship Services (and other Spiritual Formation activities), Student Activities Council, Student Senate, FCA (Fellowship of Christian Athletes), intramural athletics.

Athletics Member NCAA. All Division II. ***Intercollegiate sports:*** baseball M(s), basketball M(s)/W(s), cheerleading M/W, cross-country running M(s)/W(s), football M(s), golf M(s)/W(s), soccer M(s)/W(s), softball W(s), swimming and diving M(s)/W(s), track and field M(s)/W(s), volleyball W(s). ***Intramural sports:*** basketball M/W, football M/W, soccer M/W, ultimate Frisbee M/W, volleyball M/W.

Campus security: 24-hour emergency response devices and patrols, late-night transport/escort service, controlled dormitory access.

Student services: health clinic, personal/psychological counseling.

COSTS & FINANCIAL AID

Costs (2017–18) ***Comprehensive fee:*** $39,200 includes full-time tuition ($29,000), mandatory fees ($900), and room and board ($9300). Part-time tuition: $500 per credit hour. Part-time tuition and fees vary according to course load. ***Required fees:*** $225 per term part-time. ***College room only:*** $4500. Room and board charges vary according to board plan. ***Payment plan:*** installment. ***Waivers:*** senior citizens and employees or children of employees.

Financial Aid Of all full-time matriculated undergraduates who enrolled in 2015, 1,063 applied for aid, 989 were judged to have need, 142 had their need fully met. 344 Federal Work-Study jobs (averaging $1983). In 2015, 129 non-need-based awards were made. ***Average percent of need met:*** 76. ***Average financial aid package:*** $22,543. ***Average need-based loan:*** $4710. ***Average need-based gift aid:*** $18,512. ***Average non-need-based aid:*** $10,202. ***Average indebtedness upon graduation:*** $33,069. ***Financial aid deadline:*** 7/31.

APPLYING

Standardized Tests *Required:* SAT or ACT (for admission).

Options: electronic application, early admission, deferred entrance.

Application fee: $20.

Required: high school transcript, minimum 2.0 GPA. ***Required for some:*** essay or personal statement. ***Recommended:*** interview.

Application deadlines: rolling (freshmen), rolling (transfers).

Notification: continuous (freshmen), continuous (transfers).

CONTACT

Mrs. Anissa D. Scott, Assistant Director - Admissions, Malone University, 2600 Cleveland Avenue NW, Canton, OH 44709-3308. *Phone:* 330-471-8153. *Toll-free phone:* 800-521-1146. *Fax:* 330-471-8149. *E-mail:* admissions@malone.edu.

Marietta College

Marietta, Ohio

http://www.marietta.edu/

- **Independent** comprehensive, founded 1835
- **Small-town** 90-acre campus
- **Endowment** $70.3 million
- **Coed** 1,144 undergraduate students, 92% full-time, 39% women, 61% men
- **Moderately difficult** entrance level, 61% of applicants were admitted

UNDERGRAD STUDENTS

1,053 full-time, 91 part-time. Students come from 32 states and territories; 7 other countries; 34% are from out of state; 5% Black or African American, non-Hispanic/Latino; 2% Hispanic/Latino; 1% Asian, non-

Hispanic/Latino; 0.2% Native Hawaiian or other Pacific Islander, non-Hispanic/Latino; 0.4% American Indian or Alaska Native, non-Hispanic/Latino; 3% Two or more races, non-Hispanic/Latino; 4% Race/ethnicity unknown; 17% international; 2% transferred in; 78% live on campus.

Freshmen:
Admission: 2,700 applied, 1,658 admitted, 245 enrolled. ***Average high school GPA:*** 3.45. ***Test scores:*** SAT critical reading scores over 500: 66%; SAT math scores over 500: 68%; ACT scores over 18: 94%; SAT critical reading scores over 600: 24%; SAT math scores over 600: 36%; ACT scores over 24: 47%; SAT critical reading scores over 700: 5%; SAT math scores over 700: 8%; ACT scores over 30: 8%.

Retention: 63% of full-time freshmen returned.

FACULTY
Total: 150, 61% full-time, 60% with terminal degrees.

Student/faculty ratio: 10:1.

ACADEMICS
Calendar: semesters. *Degrees:* certificates, associate, bachelor's, and master's.

Special study options: academic remediation for entering students, accelerated degree program, adult/continuing education programs, advanced placement credit, double majors, English as a second language, honors programs, independent study, internships, off-campus study, part-time degree program, services for LD students, student-designed majors, study abroad, summer session for credit.

Unusual degree programs: 3-2 engineering with Columbia University, Case Western Reserve University, Ohio University; forestry with Duke University.

Computers: 475 computers/terminals and 450 ports are available on campus for general student use. Students can access the following: campus intranet, computer help desk, free student e-mail accounts, online (class) grades, online (class) registration, online (class) schedules. Campuswide network is available. 100% of college-owned or -operated housing units are wired for high-speed Internet access. Wireless service is available via classrooms, computer centers, computer labs, dorm rooms, learning centers, libraries, student centers.

Library: Legacy Library. *Books:* 163,843 (physical), 126,903 (digital/electronic); *Serial titles:* 246 (physical), 15,186 (digital/electronic); *Databases:* 167. Weekly public service hours: 95; students can reserve study rooms.

STUDENT LIFE
Housing options: on-campus residence required through senior year; coed, men-only, women-only, special housing for students with disabilities. Campus housing is university owned, leased by the school and is provided by a third party. Freshman campus housing is guaranteed.

Activities and organizations: drama/theater group, student-run newspaper, radio and television station, choral group, Pioneer Activities Council, student government, Panhellenic Council, Inter-Varsity Christian Fellowship, Inter Fraternity Council, national fraternities, national sororities.

Athletics Member NCAA. All Division III. ***Intercollegiate sports:*** baseball M, basketball M/W, cheerleading M(c)/W(c), crew M/W, cross-country running M/W, football M, golf M/W, soccer M/W, softball W, tennis M/W, track and field M/W, volleyball W. ***Intramural sports:*** badminton M/W, basketball M/W, bowling M/W, cross-country running M/W, football M/W, golf M/W, racquetball M/W, rock climbing M/W, sand volleyball M/W, soccer M/W, softball M/W, swimming and diving M/W, tennis M/W, ultimate Frisbee M/W, volleyball M/W, weight lifting M/W.

Campus security: 24-hour emergency response devices and patrols, student patrols, late-night transport/escort service, controlled dormitory access.

Student services: health clinic, personal/psychological counseling.

COSTS & FINANCIAL AID
Costs (2017–18) ***Comprehensive fee:*** $47,380 includes full-time tuition ($35,050), mandatory fees ($1010), and room and board ($11,320). Full-time tuition and fees vary according to course load. Part-time tuition: $1170 per credit hour. Part-time tuition and fees vary according to course load. ***Room and board:*** Room and board charges vary according to board plan and housing facility. ***Payment plan:*** installment. ***Waivers:*** employees or children of employees.

Financial Aid Of all full-time matriculated undergraduates who enrolled in 2016, 804 applied for aid, 725 were judged to have need, 190 had their need fully met. 605 Federal Work-Study jobs (averaging $1909). In 2016, 114 non-need-based awards were made. ***Average percent of need met:*** 75. ***Average financial aid package:*** $29,627. ***Average need-based loan:*** $4733. ***Average need-based gift aid:*** $18,393. ***Average non-need-based aid:*** $15,236. ***Average indebtedness upon graduation:*** $40,196.

APPLYING
Standardized Tests *Required:* SAT or ACT (for admission). *Recommended:* SAT Subject Tests (for admission).

Options: electronic application, early admission, deferred entrance.

Required: essay or personal statement, high school transcript, minimum 2.5 GPA, 1 letter of recommendation. ***Recommended:*** minimum 3.4 GPA, interview.

Application deadlines: 7/1 (freshmen), rolling (transfers).

Notification: continuous until 7/1 (freshmen), continuous (transfers).

CONTACT
Mr. Scott McVicar, Director of Admission, Marietta College, 215 Fifth Street, Marietta, OH 45750. *Phone:* 740-376-4606.
Toll-free phone: 800-331-7896. *Fax:* 740-376-8888.
E-mail: admit@marietta.edu.

Mercy College of Ohio

Toledo, Ohio

http://www.mercycollege.edu/

- **Independent** 4-year, founded 1993, affiliated with Roman Catholic Church
- **Urban** campus with easy access to Toledo, OH
- **Endowment** $13.4 million
- **Coed, primarily women** 1,351 undergraduate students, 37% full-time, 86% women, 14% men
- **Moderately difficult** entrance level, 58% of applicants were admitted

UNDERGRAD STUDENTS
497 full-time, 854 part-time. Students come from 27 states and territories; 32% are from out of state; 10% Black or African American, non-Hispanic/Latino; 4% Hispanic/Latino; 1% Asian, non-Hispanic/Latino; 0.1% American Indian or Alaska Native, non-Hispanic/Latino; 5% Two or more races, non-Hispanic/Latino; 2% Race/ethnicity unknown; 26% transferred in; 2% live on campus.

Freshmen:
Admission: 245 applied, 141 admitted, 62 enrolled. ***Average high school GPA:*** 3.23. ***Test scores:*** ACT scores over 18: 76%; ACT scores over 24: 22%.

Retention: 79% of full-time freshmen returned.

FACULTY
Total: 208, 27% full-time, 13% with terminal degrees.

Student/faculty ratio: 7:1.

ACADEMICS
Calendar: semesters. *Degrees:* certificates, associate, and bachelor's.

Special study options: academic remediation for entering students, accelerated degree program, adult/continuing education programs, advanced placement credit, distance learning, double majors, independent study, internships, part-time degree program, services for LD students, summer session for credit.

Computers: 109 computers/terminals and 109 ports are available on campus for general student use. Students can access the following: computer help desk, free student e-mail accounts, online (class) grades, online (class) registration, online (class) schedules. Campuswide network is available. Wireless service is available via classrooms, computer centers, computer labs, learning centers, libraries, student centers.

Library: Mercy College of Ohio Library. *Books:* 7,587 (physical), 60,690 (digital/electronic); *Serial titles:* 65 (physical), 39,292 (digital/electronic); *Databases:* 17. Students can reserve study rooms.

STUDENT LIFE
Housing options: coed. Campus housing is leased by the school.

Activities and organizations: American Assembly of Men in Nursing, National Student Nurses Association, Student Government Association, Cardiovascular Technology Student Association, Gay Straight Alliance.

Campus security: 24-hour emergency response devices and patrols, late-night transport/escort service, controlled dormitory access.

Student services: personal/psychological counseling.

COSTS & FINANCIAL AID
Costs (2017–18) ***One-time required fee:*** $250. ***Tuition:*** $12,360 full-time, $454 per credit hour part-time. Full-time tuition and fees vary according to course load, location, and program. Part-time tuition and fees vary according to course load, location, and program. ***Required fees:*** $2250 full-time, $55 per credit hour part-time, $300 per term part-time. ***Room only:*** $5460. Room and board charges vary according to housing facility. ***Payment plans:*** installment, deferred payment. ***Waivers:*** employees or children of employees.

Financial Aid Of all full-time matriculated undergraduates who enrolled in 2015, 24 Federal Work-Study jobs (averaging $1744).

APPLYING
Standardized Tests *Required for some:* SAT or ACT (for admission). *Recommended:* SAT or ACT (for admission).

Options: electronic application, deferred entrance.

Application fee: $25.

Required: high school transcript, minimum 2.0 GPA.

Application deadlines: rolling (freshmen), rolling (transfers).

Notification: continuous (freshmen), continuous (transfers).

CONTACT
Ms. Kristen Porter, Admissions Officer, Mercy College of Ohio, 2221 Madison Avenue, Toledo, OH 43604. *Phone:* 419-251-1313. *Toll-free phone:* 888-80-MERCY. *Fax:* 419-251-1462.
E-mail: kristen.porter@mercycollege.edu.

Miami University
Oxford, Ohio
http://miamioh.edu/

- **State-related** university, founded 1809, part of Miami University System
- **Small-town** 2100-acre campus with easy access to Cincinnati
- **Endowment** $445.3 million
- **Coed** 16,981 undergraduate students, 97% full-time, 51% women, 49% men
- **Moderately difficult** entrance level, 64% of applicants were admitted

UNDERGRAD STUDENTS
16,434 full-time, 547 part-time. Students come from 50 states and territories; 92 other countries; 36% are from out of state; 3% Black or African American, non-Hispanic/Latino; 4% Hispanic/Latino; 2% Asian, non-Hispanic/Latino; 0.2% American Indian or Alaska Native, non-Hispanic/Latino; 3% Two or more races, non-Hispanic/Latino; 0.4% Race/ethnicity unknown; 13% international; 1% transferred in; 46% live on campus.

Freshmen:
Admission: 29,771 applied, 18,963 admitted, 3,799 enrolled. ***Average high school GPA:*** 3.8. ***Test scores:*** SAT critical reading scores over 500: 86%; SAT math scores over 500: 96%; ACT scores over 18: 100%; SAT critical reading scores over 600: 54%; SAT math scores over 600: 71%; ACT scores over 24: 95%; SAT critical reading scores over 700: 13%; SAT math scores over 700: 25%; ACT scores over 30: 40%.
Retention: 92% of full-time freshmen returned.

FACULTY
Total: 1,288, 76% full-time, 73% with terminal degrees.

Student/faculty ratio: 17:1.

ACADEMICS
Calendar: semesters. *Degrees:* certificates, associate, bachelor's, master's, doctoral, and post-master's certificates.

Special study options: advanced placement credit, cooperative education, distance learning, double majors, English as a second language, honors programs, independent study, internships, off-campus study, services for LD students, student-designed majors, study abroad, summer session for credit. ***ROTC:*** Army (c), Navy (b), Air Force (b).

Unusual degree programs: 3-2 engineering with Case Western Reserve University, Columbia University.

Computers: Students can access the following: campus intranet, computer help desk, free student e-mail accounts, online (class) grades, online (class) registration, online (class) schedules. Campuswide network is available. 100% of college-owned or -operated housing units are wired for high-speed Internet access. Wireless service is available via entire campus.

Library: King Library plus 3 others. *Books:* 2.4 million (physical), 658,343 (digital/electronic); *Serial titles:* 1,019 (physical), 25,772 (digital/electronic); *Databases:* 743. Weekly public service hours: 168; study areas open 24 hours, 5-7 days a week; students can reserve study rooms.

STUDENT LIFE
Housing options: on-campus residence required through sophomore year; coed, men-only, women-only, special housing for students with disabilities. Campus housing is university owned. Freshman campus housing is guaranteed.

Activities and organizations: drama/theater group, student-run newspaper, radio and television station, choral group, marching band, CRU (formerly Campus Crusade for Christ), Alpha Phi Omega, College Republicans, 4 Paws for Ability, Best Buddies, national fraternities, national sororities.

Athletics Member NCAA. All Division I except football (Division I-A). ***Intercollegiate sports:*** baseball M(s)/W(c), basketball M(s)/W(s), cross-country running M(s)/W(s), equestrian sports M(c)/W(c), fencing M(c)/W(c), field hockey M(c)/W(s), golf M(s), gymnastics M(c)/W(c), ice hockey M(s)/W(c), lacrosse M(c)/W(c), rugby M(c)/W(c), sailing M(c)/W(c), soccer M(c)/W(s), softball M(c)/W(s), swimming and diving M(s)/W(s), tennis M(c)/W(s), track and field M(s)/W(s), ultimate Frisbee M(c)/W(c), volleyball M(c)/W(s), water polo M(c)/W(c), weight lifting M(c)/W(c), wrestling M(c)/W(c). ***Intramural sports:*** badminton M(c)/W(c), baseball M/W, basketball M/W, golf M(c)/W(c), ice hockey M/W, racquetball M/W, soccer M/W, softball M/W, ultimate Frisbee M/W, volleyball M/W.

Campus security: 24-hour emergency response devices and patrols, student patrols, late-night transport/escort service, controlled dormitory access.

Student services: health clinic, personal/psychological counseling, women's center.

COSTS & FINANCIAL AID
Costs (2016–17) ***Tuition:*** state resident $13,534 full-time, $564 per credit hour part-time; nonresident $30,838 full-time, $1285 per credit hour part-time. Full-time tuition and fees vary according to location, program, and student level. Part-time tuition and fees vary according to course load, location, program, and student level. No tuition increase for student's term of enrollment. ***Required fees:*** $754 full-time, $29 per credit hour part-time. ***Room and board:*** $12,014; room only: $7314. Room and board charges vary according to board plan, housing facility, and student level. ***Payment plan:*** installment. ***Waivers:*** employees or children of employees.

Financial Aid Of all full-time matriculated undergraduates who enrolled in 2015, 8,309 applied for aid, 5,433 were judged to have need, 1,043 had their need fully met. 3,293 Federal Work-Study jobs (averaging $710). In 2015, 4757 non-need-based awards were made. ***Average percent of need met:*** 59. ***Average financial aid package:*** $13,240. ***Average need-based loan:*** $4580. ***Average need-based gift aid:*** $9543. ***Average non-need-based aid:*** $8001. ***Average indebtedness upon graduation:*** $30,015.

APPLYING
Standardized Tests *Required:* SAT or ACT (for admission).

Options: electronic application, early decision, early action, deferred entrance.

Application fee: $50.

Required: essay or personal statement, high school transcript, 1 letter of recommendation.

Application deadlines: 2/1 (freshmen), 6/1 (transfers), 12/1 (early action).

Early decision deadline: 11/15.

Notification: 3/15 (freshmen), continuous (transfers), 12/15 (early decision), 2/1 (early action).

CONTACT
Office of Admissions, Miami University, 301 South Campus Avenue, Oxford, OH 45056. *Phone:* 513-529-2531. *E-mail:* admission@miamioh.edu.

Miami University Hamilton

Hamilton, Ohio

http://regionals.miamioh.edu/

CONTACT
Mr. Archie Nelson, Director of Admission and Financial Aid, Miami University Hamilton, 1601 Peck Boulevard, Hamilton, OH 45011-3399. *Phone:* 513-785-3111. *Fax:* 513-785-1807. *E-mail:* nelsona3@muohio.edu.

Miami University Middletown

Middletown, Ohio

http://regionals.miamioh.edu/

CONTACT
Diane Cantonwine, Assistant Director of Admission and Financial Aid, Miami University Middletown, 4200 East University Boulevard, Middletown, OH 45042-3497. *Phone:* 513-727-3346. *Toll-free phone:* 866-426-4643. *Fax:* 513-727-3223. *E-mail:* cantondm@muohio.edu.

Mount Carmel College of Nursing

Columbus, Ohio

http://www.mccn.edu/

- **Independent** comprehensive, founded 1903
- **Urban** campus with easy access to Columbus
- **Endowment** $1.8 million
- **Coed, primarily women** 929 undergraduate students, 68% full-time, 90% women, 10% men
- **Moderately difficult** entrance level, 61% of applicants were admitted

UNDERGRAD STUDENTS
635 full-time, 291 part-time. 1% are from out of state; 8% Black or African American, non-Hispanic/Latino; 1% Hispanic/Latino; 1% Asian, non-Hispanic/Latino; 0.1% Native Hawaiian or other Pacific Islander, non-Hispanic/Latino; 2% Two or more races, non-Hispanic/Latino; 1% Race/ethnicity unknown; 8% transferred in; 13% live on campus.

Freshmen:
Admission: 254 applied, 154 admitted, 111 enrolled. ***Average high school GPA:*** 3.58. ***Test scores:*** ACT scores over 18: 96%; ACT scores over 24: 24%.
Retention: 84% of full-time freshmen returned.

FACULTY
Total: 94, 54% full-time, 17% with terminal degrees.
Student/faculty ratio: 15:1.

ACADEMICS
Calendar: semesters. *Degrees:* bachelor's, master's, doctoral, and post-master's certificates.
Special study options: accelerated degree program, adult/continuing education programs, advanced placement credit, distance learning, honors programs, off-campus study, summer session for credit. ***ROTC:*** Army (c), Navy (c), Air Force (c).
Computers: 25 computers/terminals are available on campus for general student use. Students can access the following: campus intranet, computer help desk, free student e-mail accounts, online (class) grades, online (class) registration, online (class) schedules. Campuswide network is available. 100% of college-owned or -operated housing units are wired for high-speed Internet access. Wireless service is available via entire campus.
Library: The Mount Carmel Health Sciences Library plus 1 other. *Books:* 8,187 (physical), 237,569 (digital/electronic); *Serial titles:* 1,951 (physical), 61,543 (digital/electronic); *Databases:* 50. Weekly public service hours: 65; study areas open 24 hours, 5-7 days a week; students can reserve study rooms.

STUDENT LIFE
Housing options: on-campus residence required through sophomore year; coed. Campus housing is leased by the school. Freshman applicants given priority for college housing.
Activities and organizations: Campus Ministry, Student Nurses Association of Mount Carmel (SNAM), Mount Carmel Rho Omicron Chapter of Sigma Theta Tau International Honor Society, Student Government Association (SGA), Student Ambassador Program.
Athletics ***Intramural sports:*** basketball W(c), softball W(c), volleyball M(c)/W(c).
Campus security: 24-hour emergency response devices and patrols, late-night transport/escort service, controlled dormitory access.
Student services: health clinic, personal/psychological counseling.

COSTS & FINANCIAL AID
Costs (2017–18) ***One-time required fee:*** $225. ***Tuition:*** $12,927 full-time, $417 per credit hour part-time. Full-time tuition and fees vary according to course level, course load, program, and student level. Part-time tuition and fees vary according to course level, course load, program, and student level. ***Required fees:*** $180 full-time. ***Room only:*** $5000. ***Payment plan:*** installment. ***Waivers:*** employees or children of employees.
Financial Aid Of all full-time matriculated undergraduates who enrolled in 2016, 458 applied for aid, 412 were judged to have need, 31 had their need fully met. In 2016, 30 non-need-based awards were made. ***Average percent of need met:*** 40. ***Average financial aid package:*** $11,070. ***Average need-based loan:*** $4584. ***Average need-based gift aid:*** $9230. ***Average non-need-based aid:*** $2950. ***Average indebtedness upon graduation:*** $35,713.

APPLYING
Standardized Tests *Required for some:* SAT or ACT (for admission).
Options: electronic application.
Application fee: $30.
Required: essay or personal statement, high school transcript, activities/interests resumé. ***Required for some:*** interview. ***Recommended:*** minimum 3.0 GPA.
Application deadlines: 4/1 (freshmen), 4/1 (transfers).
Notification: continuous (freshmen), continuous (out-of-state freshmen), continuous (transfers).

CONTACT
Dr. Kim Campbell, Director, Admissions and Recruitment, Mount Carmel College of Nursing, 127 South Davis Avenue, Columbus, OH 43222-1504. *Phone:* 614-234-5144. *Toll-free phone:* 800-556-6942. *Fax:* 614-234-5427. *E-mail:* kcampbell@mccn.edu.

Mount St. Joseph University

Cincinnati, Ohio

http://www.msj.edu/

- **Independent Roman Catholic** comprehensive, founded 1920
- **Suburban** 92-acre campus with easy access to Cincinnati, Ohio
- **Endowment** $36.2 million
- **Coed** 1,336 undergraduate students, 75% full-time, 59% women, 41% men
- **Minimally difficult** entrance level, 88% of applicants were admitted

UNDERGRAD STUDENTS
996 full-time, 340 part-time. Students come from 32 states and territories; 17% are from out of state; 11% Black or African American, non-Hispanic/Latino; 0.7% Hispanic/Latino; 0.5% Asian, non-Hispanic/Latino; 0.2% Native Hawaiian or other Pacific Islander, non-Hispanic/Latino; 0.3% American Indian or Alaska Native, non-Hispanic/Latino; 4% Two or more races, non-Hispanic/Latino; 3% Race/ethnicity unknown; 0.4% international; 6% transferred in; 27% live on campus.

Freshmen:
Admission: 1,029 applied, 906 admitted, 249 enrolled. ***Average high school GPA:*** 3.35. ***Test scores:*** SAT critical reading scores over 500: 46%; SAT math scores over 500: 44%; ACT scores over 18: 86%; SAT critical reading scores over 600: 9%; SAT math scores over 600: 20%; ACT scores over 24: 34%; SAT critical reading scores over 700: 4%; ACT scores over 30: 4%.

A ★ indicates that the school has detailed information with a Premium Profile on Petersons.com.

Retention: 73% of full-time freshmen returned.

FACULTY
Total: 215, 43% full-time, 32% with terminal degrees.

Student/faculty ratio: 11:1.

ACADEMICS
Calendar: semesters. *Degrees:* certificates, associate, bachelor's, master's, doctoral, and postbachelor's certificates.

Special study options: academic remediation for entering students, accelerated degree program, advanced placement credit, cooperative education, distance learning, double majors, honors programs, independent study, internships, off-campus study, part-time degree program, services for LD students, study abroad, summer session for credit. ***ROTC:*** Army (c).

Computers: 172 computers/terminals are available on campus for general student use. Students can access the following: computer help desk, free student e-mail accounts, online (class) grades, online (class) registration, online (class) schedules, wireless printing, storage space. Campuswide network is available. Wireless service is available via entire campus.
Library: Archbishop Alter Library. *Books:* 58,604 (physical), 149,341 (digital/electronic); *Serial titles:* 80 (physical), 30,599 (digital/electronic); *Databases:* 113. Weekly public service hours: 93.

STUDENT LIFE
Housing options: on-campus residence required through sophomore year; coed, special housing for students with disabilities. Campus housing is university owned. Freshman applicants given priority for college housing.

Activities and organizations: drama/theater group, student-run newspaper, choral group, Commuter Council, Campus Activities Board, Student Government Association, Student Alumni Association, Residence Hall Council, national fraternities.

Athletics Member NCAA. All Division III. ***Intercollegiate sports:*** baseball M, basketball M/W, cheerleading W, cross-country running M/W, football M, golf M/W, lacrosse M/W, soccer M/W, softball W, tennis M/W, track and field M/W, volleyball M/W, wrestling M. ***Intramural sports:*** basketball M/W, racquetball M/W, soccer M/W, volleyball M/W.

Campus security: 24-hour emergency response devices and patrols, late-night transport/escort service.

Student services: health clinic, personal/psychological counseling.

COSTS & FINANCIAL AID
Costs (2017–18) ***One-time required fee:*** $125. ***Comprehensive fee:*** $38,366 includes full-time tuition ($28,100), mandatory fees ($1000), and room and board ($9266). Full-time tuition and fees vary according to course load and reciprocity agreements. Part-time tuition: $525 per credit hour. Part-time tuition and fees vary according to course load and reciprocity agreements. ***Required fees:*** $500 per year part-time. ***Room and board:*** Room and board charges vary according to board plan and housing facility. ***Payment plans:*** installment, deferred payment. ***Waivers:*** senior citizens and employees or children of employees.

Financial Aid Of all full-time matriculated undergraduates who enrolled in 2016, 905 applied for aid, 796 were judged to have need, 131 had their need fully met. 187 Federal Work-Study jobs (averaging $1611). 192 state and other part-time jobs (averaging $1461). In 2016, 186 non-need-based awards were made. ***Average percent of need met:*** 72. ***Average financial aid package:*** $18,827. ***Average need-based loan:*** $3775. ***Average need-based gift aid:*** $15,762. ***Average non-need-based aid:*** $11,234.

APPLYING
Standardized Tests *Required:* SAT or ACT (for admission).

Options: electronic application, deferred entrance.

Application fee: $25.

Required: high school transcript. ***Recommended:*** minimum 3.0 GPA.

Application deadlines: 8/18 (freshmen), rolling (transfers).

Notification: continuous (freshmen), continuous (transfers).

CONTACT
Peggy Minnich, Director of Admission, Mount St. Joseph University, 5701 Delhi Road, Cincinnati, OH 45233-1670. *Phone:* 513-244-4531. *Toll-free phone:* 800-654-9314. *Fax:* 513-244-4629. *E-mail:* admissions@msj.edu.

Mount Vernon Nazarene University
Mount Vernon, Ohio
http://www.mvnu.edu/

- **Independent Nazarene** comprehensive, founded 1968
- **Small-town** 327-acre campus with easy access to Columbus
- **Endowment** $17.0 million
- **Coed** 1,831 undergraduate students, 82% full-time, 62% women, 38% men
- **Moderately difficult** entrance level, 74% of applicants were admitted

UNDERGRAD STUDENTS
1,509 full-time, 322 part-time. Students come from 24 states and territories; 10 other countries; 10% are from out of state; 3% Black or African American, non-Hispanic/Latino; 3% Hispanic/Latino; 0.8% Asian, non-Hispanic/Latino; 0.2% Native Hawaiian or other Pacific Islander, non-Hispanic/Latino; 3% Two or more races, non-Hispanic/Latino; 5% Race/ethnicity unknown; 1% international; 2% transferred in; 78% live on campus.

Freshmen:
Admission: 1,276 applied, 947 admitted, 387 enrolled. ***Average high school GPA:*** 3.5. ***Test scores:*** SAT critical reading scores over 500: 67%; SAT math scores over 500: 54%; ACT scores over 18: 93%; SAT critical reading scores over 600: 27%; SAT math scores over 600: 19%; ACT scores over 24: 43%; SAT critical reading scores over 700: 6%; ACT scores over 30: 7%.

Retention: 77% of full-time freshmen returned.

FACULTY
Total: 251, 31% full-time, 36% with terminal degrees.

Student/faculty ratio: 14:1.

ACADEMICS
Calendar: 4-1-4. *Degrees:* associate, bachelor's, and master's.

Special study options: academic remediation for entering students, adult/continuing education programs, advanced placement credit, distance learning, double majors, honors programs, independent study, internships, off-campus study, part-time degree program, services for LD students, study abroad, summer session for credit.

Unusual degree programs: pre-occupational therapy/physician assistant with Chatham University.

Computers: 220 computers/terminals and 1,200 ports are available on campus for general student use. Students can access the following: campus intranet, computer help desk, free student e-mail accounts, online (class) grades, online (class) schedules. Campuswide network is available. 100% of college-owned or -operated housing units are wired for high-speed Internet access. Wireless service is available via entire campus.
Library: Thorne Library/Learning Resource Center. *Books:* 100,799 (physical), 149,341 (digital/electronic); *Serial titles:* 62,880 (physical), 29,195 (digital/electronic); *Databases:* 235. Weekly public service hours: 93; study areas open 24 hours, 5-7 days a week; students can reserve study rooms.

STUDENT LIFE
Housing options: men-only, women-only, special housing for students with disabilities. Campus housing is university owned. Freshman campus housing is guaranteed.

Activities and organizations: drama/theater group, student-run newspaper, radio station, choral group, Campus Ministry Groups, Student Government Association, Student Education Association, Drama Club, Music Department Ensembles.

Athletics Member NAIA. ***Intercollegiate sports:*** baseball M(s), basketball M(s)/W(s), cross-country running M(s)/W(s), golf M(s)/W(s), soccer M(s)/W(s), softball W(s), tennis M(s)/W(s), track and field M(s)/W(s), volleyball W(s). ***Intramural sports:*** basketball M/W, bowling M/W, cheerleading M(c)/W(c), football M/W, soccer M/W, softball M/W, table tennis M/W, ultimate Frisbee M/W, volleyball M/W.

Campus security: 24-hour emergency response devices and patrols, late-night transport/escort service, controlled dormitory access.

Student services: health clinic, personal/psychological counseling.

COSTS & FINANCIAL AID
Costs (2017–18) ***Comprehensive fee:*** $35,944 includes full-time tuition ($27,840), mandatory fees ($250), and room and board ($7854). Full-time tuition and fees vary according to program. Part-time tuition: $773 per credit hour. Part-time tuition and fees vary according to course load and

program. ***College room only:*** $4388. ***Payment plan:*** installment. ***Waivers:*** senior citizens and employees or children of employees.

Financial Aid Of all full-time matriculated undergraduates who enrolled in 2015, 1,608 applied for aid, 1,355 were judged to have need, 394 had their need fully met. 232 Federal Work-Study jobs (averaging $1818). 15 state and other part-time jobs (averaging $1483). In 2015, 552 non-need-based awards were made. ***Average percent of need met:*** 67. ***Average financial aid package:*** $22,264. ***Average need-based loan:*** $4191. ***Average need-based gift aid:*** $18,829. ***Average non-need-based aid:*** $14,509. ***Average indebtedness upon graduation:*** $28,802.

APPLYING

Standardized Tests *Required:* SAT or ACT (for admission).

Options: electronic application, deferred entrance.

Application fee: $25.

Required: essay or personal statement, high school transcript, minimum 2.5 GPA, 2 letters of recommendation.

Notification: 9/1 (freshmen), continuous (transfers).

CONTACT

Mr. Tracy Waal, Director of Admissions and Student Recruitment, Mount Vernon Nazarene University, 800 Martinsburg Road, Mount Vernon, OH 43050. *Phone:* 740-392-6868 Ext. 4514. *Toll-free phone:* 866-462-6868. *Fax:* 740-393-0511. *E-mail:* admissions@mvnu.edu.

Muskingum University

New Concord, Ohio

http://www.muskingum.edu/

- **Independent** comprehensive, founded 1837, affiliated with Presbyterian Church (U.S.A.)
- **Small-town** 245-acre campus with easy access to Columbus
- **Endowment** $70.1 million
- **Coed** 1,549 undergraduate students, 85% full-time, 54% women, 46% men
- **Moderately difficult** entrance level, 77% of applicants were admitted

UNDERGRAD STUDENTS

1,310 full-time, 239 part-time. Students come from 23 states and territories; 6 other countries; 7% are from out of state; 5% Black or African American, non-Hispanic/Latino; 2% Hispanic/Latino; 0.9% Asian, non-Hispanic/Latino; 0.3% American Indian or Alaska Native, non-Hispanic/Latino; 4% Two or more races, non-Hispanic/Latino; 5% Race/ethnicity unknown; 4% international; 6% transferred in; 29% live on campus.

Freshmen:

Admission: 1,819 applied, 1,408 admitted, 319 enrolled. ***Average high school GPA:*** 3.28. ***Test scores:*** SAT critical reading scores over 500: 40%; SAT math scores over 500: 46%; SAT writing scores over 500: 33%; ACT scores over 18: 80%; SAT critical reading scores over 600: 13%; SAT math scores over 600: 13%; ACT scores over 24: 28%; ACT scores over 30: 3%.

Retention: 66% of full-time freshmen returned.

FACULTY

Total: 164, 59% full-time, 66% with terminal degrees.

ACADEMICS

Calendar: semesters. *Degrees:* bachelor's and master's.

Special study options: accelerated degree program, adult/continuing education programs, advanced placement credit, distance learning, double majors, English as a second language, external degree program, independent study, internships, off-campus study, part-time degree program, services for LD students, student-designed majors, study abroad, summer session for credit.

Unusual degree programs: engineering with Case Western Reserve University.

Computers: 167 computers/terminals are available on campus for general student use. Students can access the following: campus intranet, computer help desk, free student e-mail accounts, online (class) grades, online (class) registration, online (class) schedules. Campuswide network is available. 100% of college-owned or -operated housing units are wired for high-speed Internet access. Wireless service is available via entire campus.

Library: Roberta A. Smith Library. *Books:* 113,792 (physical), 279,915 (digital/electronic); *Serial titles:* 1,254 (physical), 60,228 (digital/electronic); *Databases:* 120. Weekly public service hours: 89; students can reserve study rooms.

STUDENT LIFE

Housing options: on-campus residence required through junior year; coed, men-only, women-only. Campus housing is university owned. Freshman campus housing is guaranteed.

Activities and organizations: drama/theater group, student-run newspaper, radio and television station, choral group, marching band, Campus Crusade for Christ (CRU), Equality Alliance, Muskingum Programming Board, Outdoor Initiative, Multicultural Association:Black Student Union, national fraternities, national sororities.

Athletics Member NCAA. All Division III. ***Intercollegiate sports:*** baseball M, basketball M/W, bowling M(c)/W(c), cheerleading M(c)/W(c), cross-country running M/W, football M, golf M/W, lacrosse M/W, soccer M/W, softball W, tennis M/W, track and field M/W, ultimate Frisbee M(c)/W(c), volleyball W, wrestling M. ***Intramural sports:*** badminton M/W, basketball M/W, cross-country running M/W, football M/W, golf M/W, racquetball M/W, rugby M/W, sand volleyball M/W, soccer M/W, softball M/W, swimming and diving M/W, table tennis M/W, tennis M/W, track and field M/W, volleyball M/W, water polo M/W, weight lifting M/W, wrestling M.

Campus security: 24-hour emergency response devices and patrols, late-night transport/escort service, controlled dormitory access.

Student services: health clinic, personal/psychological counseling, women's center.

COSTS & FINANCIAL AID

Costs (2017–18) ***One-time required fee:*** $250. ***Comprehensive fee:*** $38,852 includes full-time tuition ($26,900), mandatory fees ($912), and room and board ($11,040). Part-time tuition: $595 per credit hour. Part-time tuition and fees vary according to course load. ***College room only:*** $5720. Room and board charges vary according to board plan. ***Payment plan:*** installment. ***Waivers:*** children of alumni and employees or children of employees.

Financial Aid Of all full-time matriculated undergraduates who enrolled in 2016, 1,156 applied for aid, 1,094 were judged to have need, 186 had their need fully met. 394 Federal Work-Study jobs (averaging $1000). In 2016, 177 non-need-based awards were made. ***Average percent of need met:*** 77. ***Average financial aid package:*** $24,239. ***Average need-based loan:*** $5331. ***Average need-based gift aid:*** $19,222. ***Average non-need-based aid:*** $13,018. ***Average indebtedness upon graduation:*** $33,490.

APPLYING

Standardized Tests *Required:* SAT or ACT (for admission).

Options: electronic application, early admission, deferred entrance.

Required: high school transcript, minimum 2.0 GPA. ***Recommended:*** essay or personal statement, minimum 3.0 GPA, 1 letter of recommendation, interview.

Application deadlines: 6/1 (freshmen), 8/1 (transfers).

Notification: continuous (freshmen), continuous (transfers).

CONTACT

Mrs. Beth DaLonzo, Director of Admission, Muskingum University, 163 Stormont Street, New Concord, OH 43762. *Phone:* 740-826-8137. *Toll-free phone:* 800-752-6082. *Fax:* 740-826-8100. *E-mail:* adminfo@muskingum.edu.

★ Notre Dame College

South Euclid, Ohio

http://www.notredamecollege.edu/

CONTACT

Mr. David Armstrong, Dean of Admissions, Notre Dame College, 4545 College Road, South Euclid, OH 44121-4293. *Phone:* 216-373-5214. *Toll-free phone:* 877-NDC-OHIO. *Fax:* 216-381-3802. *E-mail:* admissinos@ndc.edu.

See page 1448 for the College Close-Up.

A ★ *indicates that the school has detailed information with a Premium Profile on Petersons.com.*

Oberlin College

Oberlin, Ohio

http://www.oberlin.edu/

- **Independent** comprehensive, founded 1833
- **Small-town** 440-acre campus with easy access to Cleveland
- **Endowment** $753.5 million
- **Coed** 2,895 undergraduate students, 99% full-time, 57% women, 43% men
- **Very difficult** entrance level, 28% of applicants were admitted

UNDERGRAD STUDENTS

2,869 full-time, 26 part-time. Students come from 51 states and territories; 42 other countries; 95% are from out of state; 5% Black or African American, non-Hispanic/Latino; 8% Hispanic/Latino; 4% Asian, non-Hispanic/Latino; 0.1% Native Hawaiian or other Pacific Islander, non-Hispanic/Latino; 42% Two or more races, non-Hispanic/Latino; 0.5% Race/ethnicity unknown; 9% international; 1% transferred in; 90% live on campus.

Freshmen:

Admission: 8,518 applied, 2,388 admitted, 762 enrolled. ***Average high school GPA:*** 3.58. ***Test scores:*** SAT critical reading scores over 500: 98%; SAT math scores over 500: 97%; SAT writing scores over 500: 98%; ACT scores over 18: 100%; SAT critical reading scores over 600: 88%; SAT math scores over 600: 82%; SAT writing scores over 600: 85%; ACT scores over 24: 96%; SAT critical reading scores over 700: 46%; SAT math scores over 700: 34%; SAT writing scores over 700: 40%; ACT scores over 30: 67%.

Retention: 89% of full-time freshmen returned.

FACULTY

Total: 381.

Student/faculty ratio: 10:1.

ACADEMICS

Calendar: 4-1-4. *Degrees:* diplomas, bachelor's, master's, and postbachelor's certificates.

Special study options: advanced placement credit, double majors, English as a second language, honors programs, independent study, internships, off-campus study, part-time degree program, services for LD students, student-designed majors, study abroad.

Unusual degree programs: 3-2 engineering with Washington University in St. Louis, Case Western Reserve University, California Institute of Technology, Columbia University.

Computers: 340 computers/terminals are available on campus for general student use. Students can access the following: campus intranet, computer help desk, free student e-mail accounts, online (class) grades, online (class) registration, online (class) schedules. Campuswide network is available. 100% of college-owned or -operated housing units are wired for high-speed Internet access. Wireless service is available via entire campus.

Library: Mudd Center Library plus 3 others. *Books:* 1.4 million (physical), 676,883 (digital/electronic); *Serial titles:* 181,044 (physical), 115,097 (digital/electronic). Students can reserve study rooms.

STUDENT LIFE

Housing options: on-campus residence required through senior year; coed, women-only, cooperative, special housing for students with disabilities. Campus housing is university owned. Freshman campus housing is guaranteed.

Activities and organizations: drama/theater group, student-run newspaper, radio station, choral group, Experimental College, Community Outreach, Student Government, Student Cooperative Association, student radio station.

Athletics Member NCAA. All Division III. ***Intercollegiate sports:*** archery M(c)/W(c), badminton M(c)/W(c), baseball M, basketball M/W, bowling M(c)/W(c), cross-country running M/W, equestrian sports M(c)/W(c), fencing M(c)/W(c), field hockey W, football M, golf M(c)/W(c), ice hockey M(c)/W(c), lacrosse M/W, rugby M(c)/W(c), soccer M/W, softball W, swimming and diving M/W, tennis M/W, track and field M/W, ultimate Frisbee M(c)/W(c), volleyball M(c)/W, water polo M(c)/W(c), wrestling M(c). ***Intramural sports:*** baseball M/W, basketball M/W, bowling M/W, cross-country running M/W, football M/W, gymnastics M(c)/W(c), racquetball M/W, rock climbing M/W, rugby M, soccer M/W, softball M/W, squash M/W, table tennis M(c)/W, tennis M/W, track and field M/W, volleyball M/W, water polo M/W, weight lifting M/W.

Campus security: 24-hour emergency response devices and patrols, student patrols, late-night transport/escort service, controlled dormitory access, crime prevention programs.

Student services: health clinic, personal/psychological counseling, women's center.

COSTS & FINANCIAL AID

Costs (2016–17) ***Comprehensive fee:*** $66,062 includes full-time tuition ($51,324), mandatory fees ($728), and room and board ($14,010). Part-time tuition: $2120 per credit. ***College room only:*** $7278. Room and board charges vary according to board plan and housing facility. ***Payment plan:*** installment. ***Waivers:*** employees or children of employees.

Financial Aid Of all full-time matriculated undergraduates who enrolled in 2015, 1,583 applied for aid, 1,348 were judged to have need, 1,348 had their need fully met. 1,500 Federal Work-Study jobs (averaging $2400). 600 state and other part-time jobs (averaging $2400). In 2015, 1065 non-need-based awards were made. ***Average percent of need met:*** 100. ***Average financial aid package:*** $39,414. ***Average need-based loan:*** $3322. ***Average need-based gift aid:*** $34,557. ***Average non-need-based aid:*** $13,671. ***Average indebtedness upon graduation:*** $25,018.

APPLYING

Standardized Tests *Required:* SAT or ACT (for admission). *Required for some:* SAT and SAT Subject Tests or ACT (for admission).

Options: electronic application, early admission, early decision, deferred entrance.

Required: essay or personal statement, high school transcript, 2 letters of recommendation. ***Required for some:*** interview, audition for the Conservatory of Music, detailed portfolio for homeschooled students. ***Recommended:*** interview.

Application deadlines: 1/15 (freshmen), 3/15 (transfers).

Early decision deadline: 11/15 (for plan 1), 1/2 (for plan 2).

Notification: 4/1 (freshmen), 5/15 (transfers), 12/15 (early decision plan 1), 2/1 (early decision plan 2).

CONTACT

Debra Chermonte, Vice President and Dean of Admissions and Financial Aid, Oberlin College, Admissions Office, Carnegie Building, 101 North Professor Street, Oberlin, OH 44074-1075. *Phone:* 440-775-8411. *Toll-free phone:* 800-622-OBIE. *Fax:* 440-775-6905.
E-mail: college.admissions@oberlin.edu.

Ohio Christian University

Circleville, Ohio

http://www.ohiochristian.edu/

- **Independent** comprehensive, founded 1948, affiliated with Churches of Christ in Christian Union
- **Small-town** 40-acre campus with easy access to Columbus
- **Endowment** $4.1 million
- **Coed** 3,738 undergraduate students, 43% full-time, 63% women, 37% men
- **Minimally difficult** entrance level, 65% of applicants were admitted

UNDERGRAD STUDENTS

1,613 full-time, 2,125 part-time. 26% Black or African American, non-Hispanic/Latino; 2% Hispanic/Latino; 0.6% Asian, non-Hispanic/Latino; 0.4% American Indian or Alaska Native, non-Hispanic/Latino; 2% Two or more races, non-Hispanic/Latino; 17% Race/ethnicity unknown; 0.4% international.

Freshmen:

Admission: 844 applied, 552 admitted, 744 enrolled.

FACULTY

Total: 349, 43% full-time, 34% with terminal degrees.

Student/faculty ratio: 10:1.

ACADEMICS

Calendar: semesters. *Degrees:* associate, bachelor's, and master's.

Special study options: academic remediation for entering students, adult/continuing education programs, advanced placement credit, double majors, honors programs, independent study, internships, off-campus study, part-time degree program, services for LD students, student-designed majors, summer session for credit. ***ROTC:*** Air Force (c).

Computers: 68 computers/terminals are available on campus for general student use. Students can access the following: campus intranet, computer help desk, free student e-mail accounts, online (class) grades, online (class) registration, online (class) schedules. Campuswide network is available. Wireless service is available via entire campus.

Library: Melvin Maxwell Memorial Library. *Books:* 59,755 (physical), 96,276 (digital/electronic); *Serial titles:* 143 (physical), 6,473 (digital/electronic). Weekly public service hours: 88; students can reserve study rooms.

STUDENT LIFE

Housing options: men-only, women-only. Campus housing is university owned.

Activities and organizations: drama/theater group, choral group.

Athletics Member NAIA. ***Intercollegiate sports:*** baseball M, basketball M/W, golf M, soccer M, softball W, volleyball W. ***Intramural sports:*** basketball M/W, soccer M/W, table tennis M/W, volleyball M/W.

Campus security: controlled dormitory access, security checks after midnight.

Student services: personal/psychological counseling, legal services.

COSTS & FINANCIAL AID

Costs (2017–18) ***Comprehensive fee:*** $19,597 includes full-time tuition ($10,849), mandatory fees ($1250), and room and board ($7498). Full-time tuition and fees vary according to course load and degree level.

Financial Aid Of all full-time matriculated undergraduates who enrolled in 2007, 480 applied for aid, 415 were judged to have need, 100 had their need fully met. 50 Federal Work-Study jobs (averaging $1700). In 2007, 80 non-need-based awards were made. ***Average percent of need met:*** 50. ***Average financial aid package:*** $9500. ***Average need-based loan:*** $4500. ***Average need-based gift aid:*** $4000. ***Average non-need-based aid:*** $1500. ***Average indebtedness upon graduation:*** $30,000.

APPLYING

Standardized Tests *Required for some:* ACT (for admission). *Recommended:* SAT (for admission).

Options: electronic application, early admission.

Application fee: $25.

Required: essay or personal statement, high school transcript, 4 letters of recommendation, medical form. ***Required for some:*** interview.

Application deadlines: rolling (freshmen), rolling (transfers).

Notification: continuous (freshmen), continuous (transfers).

CONTACT

Ohio Christian University, 1476 Lancaster Pike, PO Box 458, Circleville, OH 43113-9487. *Phone:* 740-477-7741. *Toll-free phone:* 877-762-8669.

★ Ohio Dominican University

Columbus, Ohio

http://www.ohiodominican.edu/

- **Independent Roman Catholic** comprehensive, founded 1911
- **Urban** 92-acre campus with easy access to Columbus, OH
- **Endowment** $25.1 million
- **Coed** 1,796 undergraduate students, 58% full-time, 56% women, 44% men
- **Moderately difficult** entrance level, 52% of applicants were admitted

UNDERGRAD STUDENTS

1,040 full-time, 756 part-time. Students come from 18 states and territories; 11 other countries; 5% are from out of state; 17% Black or African American, non-Hispanic/Latino; 3% Hispanic/Latino; 1% Asian, non-Hispanic/Latino; 0.2% American Indian or Alaska Native, non-Hispanic/Latino; 4% Two or more races, non-Hispanic/Latino; 11% Race/ethnicity unknown; 1% international; 4% transferred in; 42% live on campus.

Freshmen:

Admission: 1,969 applied, 1,027 admitted, 226 enrolled. ***Average high school GPA:*** 3.23. ***Test scores:*** SAT critical reading scores over 500: 31%; SAT math scores over 500: 38%; SAT writing scores over 500: 20%; ACT scores over 18: 95%; SAT critical reading scores over 600: 8%; SAT math scores over 600: 12%; SAT writing scores over 600: 8%; ACT scores over 24: 27%; ACT scores over 30: 2%.

Retention: 67% of full-time freshmen returned.

FACULTY

Total: 226, 31% full-time, 48% with terminal degrees.

Student/faculty ratio: 13:1.

ACADEMICS

Calendar: semesters. *Degrees:* certificates, associate, bachelor's, master's, and postbachelor's certificates.

Special study options: academic remediation for entering students, accelerated degree program, adult/continuing education programs, advanced placement credit, distance learning, double majors, honors programs, independent study, internships, off-campus study, part-time degree program, services for LD students, student-designed majors, study abroad, summer session for credit. ***ROTC:*** Army (c), Air Force (c).

Unusual degree programs: 3-2 business administration; sport management.

Computers: 350 computers/terminals and 2,300 ports are available on campus for general student use. Students can access the following: campus intranet, computer help desk, free student e-mail accounts, online (class) grades, online (class) registration, online (class) schedules. Campuswide network is available. 100% of college-owned or -operated housing units are wired for high-speed Internet access. Wireless service is available via classrooms, computer centers, computer labs, dorm rooms, learning centers, libraries, student centers.

Library: Ohio Dominican Library. *Books:* 78,234 (physical), 149,341 (digital/electronic); *Serial titles:* 611 (physical), 29,195 (digital/electronic); *Databases:* 264. Students can reserve study rooms.

STUDENT LIFE

Housing options: on-campus residence required through sophomore year; coed. Campus housing is university owned. Freshman campus housing is guaranteed.

Activities and organizations: drama/theater group, student-run radio station, choral group, marching band, Panther Activities Council, Student Athletic Advisory Committee, Black Student Union, World Student Club, Panther Players.

Athletics Member NCAA. All Division II except golf (Division I). ***Intercollegiate sports:*** baseball M(s), basketball M(s)/W(s), cross-country running M(s)/W(s), football M(s), golf M(s)/W(s), soccer M(s)/W(s), softball W(s), track and field M/W, volleyball W(s). ***Intramural sports:*** basketball M/W, sand volleyball M/W, table tennis M/W, ultimate Frisbee M/W.

Campus security: 24-hour emergency response devices and patrols, late-night transport/escort service, controlled dormitory access.

Student services: health clinic, personal/psychological counseling.

COSTS & FINANCIAL AID

Costs (2017–18) ***Comprehensive fee:*** $42,008 includes full-time tuition ($30,500), mandatory fees ($580), and room and board ($10,928). Part-time tuition: $720 per credit hour. Part-time tuition and fees vary according to course load. ***Required fees:*** $175 per term part-time. ***Room and board:*** Room and board charges vary according to board plan and housing facility. ***Payment plan:*** installment. ***Waivers:*** senior citizens and employees or children of employees.

Financial Aid Of all full-time matriculated undergraduates who enrolled in 2015, 200 Federal Work-Study jobs (averaging $2000). ***Average percent of need met:*** 92. ***Average financial aid package:*** $12,467. ***Average indebtedness upon graduation:*** $13,500.

APPLYING

Standardized Tests *Required:* SAT or ACT (for admission).

Options: electronic application, deferred entrance.

Required: high school transcript, minimum 2.3 GPA. ***Required for some:*** essay or personal statement. ***Recommended:*** interview.

Application deadlines: rolling (freshmen), rolling (transfers).

Notification: continuous (freshmen), continuous (transfers).

CONTACT

Ms. Jennifer Henley, Assistant Director of Admissions, Ohio Dominican University, 1216 Sunbury Road, Columbus, OH 43219. *Phone:* 614-251-

4605. *Toll-free phone:* 800-955-6446. *Fax:* 614-251-0156. *E-mail:* admissions@ohiodominican.edu.

Ohio Northern University

Ada, Ohio

http://www.onu.edu/

- **Independent** comprehensive, founded 1871, affiliated with United Methodist Church
- **Small-town** 342-acre campus
- **Coed**
- **Moderately difficult** entrance level

FACULTY

Student/faculty ratio: 11:1.

ACADEMICS

Calendar: semesters. *Degrees:* certificates, bachelor's, master's, doctoral, and postbachelor's certificates.

Library: Heterick Memorial Library plus 1 other. Students can reserve study rooms.

STUDENT LIFE

Housing options: on-campus residence required through junior year; coed, men-only, women-only, special housing for students with disabilities. Campus housing is university owned. Freshman campus housing is guaranteed.

Activities and organizations: drama/theater group, student-run newspaper, radio and television station, choral group, marching band, Habitat for Humanity, Student Planning Committee, Student Senate, Northern Christian Fellowship, Marching Band, national fraternities, national sororities.

Athletics Member NCAA. All Division III.

Campus security: 24-hour emergency response devices and patrols, controlled dormitory access.

Student services: health clinic, personal/psychological counseling, legal services.

COSTS

Costs (2016–17) ***Comprehensive fee:*** $40,870 includes full-time tuition ($29,240), mandatory fees ($580), and room and board ($11,050). Full-time tuition and fees vary according to course load, degree level, and program. Part-time tuition: $1220 per credit hour. Part-time tuition and fees vary according to course load, degree level, and program. ***Required fees:*** $125 per term part-time. ***Room and board:*** Room and board charges vary according to board plan, housing facility, and student level.

APPLYING

Standardized Tests *Required:* SAT or ACT (for admission).

Options: electronic application, deferred entrance.

Required: high school transcript. ***Required for some:*** 1 letter of recommendation. ***Recommended:*** essay or personal statement, interview.

CONTACT

Ms. Deborah Miller, Director of Admissions, Ohio Northern University, 525 South Main Street, Ada, OH 45810-1599. *Phone:* 419-772-2260 Ext. 2464. *Toll-free phone:* 888-408-4ONU. *Fax:* 419-772-2821. *E-mail:* admissions-ug@onu.edu.

See page 1450 for the College Close-Up.

The Ohio State University

Columbus, Ohio

http://www.osu.edu/

- **State-supported** university, founded 1870, part of The Ohio State University
- **Urban** 3996-acre campus with easy access to Columbus
- **Endowment** $3.6 billion
- **Coed** 45,831 undergraduate students, 91% full-time, 48% women, 52% men
- **Very difficult** entrance level, 54% of applicants were admitted

UNDERGRAD STUDENTS

41,862 full-time, 3,969 part-time. Students come from 58 states and territories; 66 other countries; 19% are from out of state; 5% Black or African American, non-Hispanic/Latino; 4% Hispanic/Latino; 6% Asian, non-Hispanic/Latino; 0.1% Native Hawaiian or other Pacific Islander, non-Hispanic/Latino; 0.1% American Indian or Alaska Native, non-Hispanic/Latino; 3% Two or more races, non-Hispanic/Latino; 4% Race/ethnicity unknown; 8% international; 5% transferred in; 34% live on campus.

Freshmen:

Admission: 44,845 applied, 24,265 admitted, 7,938 enrolled. ***Test scores:*** SAT critical reading scores over 500: 88%; SAT math scores over 500: 98%; SAT writing scores over 500: 94%; ACT scores over 18: 100%; SAT critical reading scores over 600: 53%; SAT math scores over 600: 84%; SAT writing scores over 600: 59%; ACT scores over 24: 94%; SAT critical reading scores over 700: 15%; SAT math scores over 700: 42%; SAT writing scores over 700: 12%; ACT scores over 30: 49%.

Retention: 94% of full-time freshmen returned.

FACULTY

Total: 5,453, 70% full-time.

Student/faculty ratio: 19:1.

ACADEMICS

Calendar: semesters. *Degrees:* certificates, diplomas, bachelor's, master's, doctoral, post-master's, and postbachelor's certificates.

Special study options: academic remediation for entering students, accelerated degree program, adult/continuing education programs, advanced placement credit, cooperative education, distance learning, double majors, English as a second language, freshman honors college, honors programs, independent study, internships, off-campus study, part-time degree program, services for LD students, student-designed majors, study abroad, summer session for credit. ***ROTC:*** Army (b), Navy (b), Air Force (b).

Unusual degree programs: 3-2 business administration.

Computers: Students can access the following: campus intranet, computer help desk, free student e-mail accounts, online (class) grades, online (class) registration, online (class) schedules, admission applications, fee payment. Campuswide network is available. 100% of college-owned or -operated housing units are wired for high-speed Internet access. Wireless service is available via entire campus.

Library: Thompson Library plus 12 others. Study areas open 24 hours, 5-7 days a week; students can reserve study rooms.

STUDENT LIFE

Housing options: on-campus residence required through sophomore year; coed, women-only, cooperative, special housing for students with disabilities. Campus housing is university owned. Freshman campus housing is guaranteed.

Activities and organizations: drama/theater group, student-run newspaper, radio and television station, choral group, marching band, h2o (faith-based), Scuba Club, Jazz Club, International Friendships, Nourish International, national fraternities, national sororities.

Athletics Member NCAA. All Division I except football (Division I-A). ***Intercollegiate sports:*** baseball M(s), basketball M(s)/W(s), cheerleading M/W, cross-country running M(s)/W(s), fencing M(s)/W(s), field hockey W(s), golf M(s)/W(s), gymnastics M(s)/W(s), ice hockey M(s)/W(s), lacrosse M(s)/W(s), riflery M/W, soccer M(s)/W(s), softball W(s), swimming and diving M(s)/W(s), tennis M(s)/W(s), track and field M(s)/W(s), volleyball M(s)/W(s), wrestling M(s). ***Intramural sports:*** badminton M(c)/W(c), baseball M(c), basketball M/W, bowling M(c)/W(c), crew M(c)/W, cross-country running M/W, equestrian sports M(c)/W(c), fencing M(c)/W(c), field hockey W, football M/W, golf M/W, gymnastics M(c)/W(c), ice hockey M(c)/W(c), lacrosse M(c)/W(c), racquetball M(c)/W(c), riflery M(c)/W(c), rock climbing M/W, rugby M(c)/W(c), sailing M(c)/W(c), skiing (downhill) M(c)/W(c), soccer M(c)/W(c), softball W(c), squash M(c)/W(c), swimming and diving M(c)/W(c), table tennis M/W, tennis M/W, track and field M(c)/W(c), ultimate Frisbee M(c)/W(c), volleyball M(c)/W(c), water polo M(c)/W(c), weight lifting M(c), wrestling M/W.

Campus security: 24-hour emergency response devices and patrols, student patrols, late-night transport/escort service, controlled dormitory access, dorm entrances locked after 9 pm, lighted pathways and sidewalks, self-defense education.

Student services: health clinic, personal/psychological counseling, women's center, legal services.

COSTS & FINANCIAL AID
Costs (2016–17) ***Tuition:*** state resident $10,037 full-time, $455 per credit hour part-time; nonresident $28,229 full-time, $1213 per credit hour part-time. Full-time tuition and fees vary according to course load, location, program, and reciprocity agreements. Part-time tuition and fees vary according to course load, location, program, and reciprocity agreements. ***Room and board:*** $11,666. Room and board charges vary according to board plan, housing facility, and location. ***Payment plan:*** installment. ***Waivers:*** senior citizens and employees or children of employees.

Financial Aid Of all full-time matriculated undergraduates who enrolled in 2016, 27,556 applied for aid, 19,681 were judged to have need, 3,651 had their need fully met. 1,926 Federal Work-Study jobs (averaging $2908). 3 state and other part-time jobs (averaging $1667). In 2016, 8137 non-need-based awards were made. ***Average percent of need met:*** 69. ***Average financial aid package:*** $13,354. ***Average need-based loan:*** $4742. ***Average need-based gift aid:*** $9548. ***Average non-need-based aid:*** $7034. ***Average indebtedness upon graduation:*** $27,930.

APPLYING
Standardized Tests *Required:* SAT or ACT (for admission).

Options: electronic application, early action.

Required: essay or personal statement, high school transcript.

Application deadlines: 2/1 (freshmen), 5/1 (transfers), 11/1 (early action).

Notification: continuous (freshmen), continuous (transfers), 1/15 (early action).

CONTACT
The Ohio State University, Student Academic Services Building, 281 West Lane Avenue, Columbus, OH 43210. *Phone:* 614-292-3980. *Fax:* 614-292-4818. *E-mail:* askabuckeye@osu.edu.

The Ohio State University at Lima

Lima, Ohio

http://lima.osu.edu/

- **State-supported** comprehensive, founded 1960, part of The Ohio State University
- **Suburban** 565-acre campus
- **Endowment** $6.2 million
- **Coed** 999 undergraduate students, 82% full-time, 57% women, 43% men
- **Noncompetitive** entrance level, 99% of applicants were admitted

UNDERGRAD STUDENTS
824 full-time, 175 part-time. Students come from 5 states and territories; 1 other country; 0.5% are from out of state; 4% Black or African American, non-Hispanic/Latino; 3% Hispanic/Latino; 2% Asian, non-Hispanic/Latino; 0.1% Native Hawaiian or other Pacific Islander, non-Hispanic/Latino; 0.3% American Indian or Alaska Native, non-Hispanic/Latino; 3% Two or more races, non-Hispanic/Latino; 2% Race/ethnicity unknown; 0.1% international; 7% transferred in.

Freshmen:
Admission: 1,078 applied, 1,064 admitted, 349 enrolled. ***Test scores:*** SAT critical reading scores over 500: 75%; SAT math scores over 500: 83%; SAT writing scores over 500: 42%; ACT scores over 18: 90%; SAT critical reading scores over 600: 16%; SAT math scores over 600: 25%; SAT writing scores over 600: 25%; ACT scores over 24: 39%; SAT critical reading scores over 700: 8%; ACT scores over 30: 3%.
Retention: 67% of full-time freshmen returned.

FACULTY
Total: 83, 41% full-time.

Student/faculty ratio: 18:1.

ACADEMICS
Calendar: semesters. *Degrees:* associate, bachelor's, and master's.

Special study options: academic remediation for entering students, accelerated degree program, adult/continuing education programs, advanced placement credit, cooperative education, distance learning, double majors, English as a second language, freshman honors college, honors programs, independent study, internships, off-campus study, part-time degree program, services for LD students, student-designed majors, study abroad, summer session for credit. ***ROTC:*** Army (c), Navy (c), Air Force (c).

Computers: Students can access the following: campus intranet, computer help desk, free student e-mail accounts, online (class) grades, online (class) registration, online (class) schedules. Campuswide network is available. 100% of college-owned or -operated housing units are wired for high-speed Internet access. Wireless service is available via entire campus.

Library: Lima Campus Library plus 1 other. Study areas open 24 hours, 5-7 days a week; students can reserve study rooms.

STUDENT LIFE
Housing options: college housing not available.

Activities and organizations: choral group, Student Senate, Psychology Club, Honors Club, Aggies, Newman Catholic Association.

Athletics ***Intramural sports:*** baseball M(c), basketball M(c)/W(c), football M/W, golf M(c)/W(c), soccer M/W, volleyball M(c)/W(c).

Campus security: 24-hour emergency response devices and patrols, student patrols, late-night transport/escort service, lighted pathways/sidewalks.

Student services: personal/psychological counseling.

COSTS
Costs (2016–17) ***Tuition:*** state resident $7140 full-time, $298 per credit hour part-time; nonresident $25,332 full-time, $1056 per credit hour part-time. Full-time tuition and fees vary according to course load, location, program, and reciprocity agreements. Part-time tuition and fees vary according to course load, location, program, and reciprocity agreements. ***Payment plan:*** installment. ***Waivers:*** senior citizens and employees or children of employees.

APPLYING
Standardized Tests *Required for some:* SAT or ACT (for admission).

Options: electronic application.

Application fee: $60.

Required: high school transcript.

Application deadlines: 6/1 (freshmen), 6/1 (transfers).

Notification: continuous (freshmen), continuous (out-of-state freshmen), continuous (transfers).

CONTACT
The Ohio State University at Lima, OH. *Phone:* 419-995-8434. *Fax:* 419-995-8483. *E-mail:* admissions@lima.ohio-state.edu.

The Ohio State University at Marion

Marion, Ohio

http://osumarion.osu.edu/

- **State-supported** comprehensive, founded 1958, part of The Ohio State University
- **Small-town** 188-acre campus with easy access to Columbus
- **Endowment** $6.1 million
- **Coed** 1,083 undergraduate students, 80% full-time, 53% women, 47% men
- **Noncompetitive** entrance level, 99% of applicants were admitted

UNDERGRAD STUDENTS
865 full-time, 218 part-time. Students come from 7 states and territories; 2 other countries; 0.6% are from out of state; 4% Black or African American, non-Hispanic/Latino; 4% Hispanic/Latino; 3% Asian, non-Hispanic/Latino; 0.2% Native Hawaiian or other Pacific Islander, non-Hispanic/Latino; 0.4% American Indian or Alaska Native, non-Hispanic/Latino; 3% Two or more races, non-Hispanic/Latino; 3% Race/ethnicity unknown; 0.3% international; 5% transferred in.

Freshmen:
Admission: 873 applied, 860 admitted, 388 enrolled. ***Test scores:*** SAT critical reading scores over 500: 65%; SAT math scores over 500: 73%; SAT writing scores over 500: 50%; ACT scores over 18: 89%; SAT critical reading scores over 600: 19%; SAT math scores over 600: 35%; SAT writing scores over 600: 12%; ACT scores over 24: 39%; SAT math scores over 700: 8%; ACT scores over 30: 4%.
Retention: 64% of full-time freshmen returned.

FACULTY
Total: 96, 36% full-time.

Student/faculty ratio: 17:1.

ACADEMICS
Calendar: semesters. *Degrees:* associate, bachelor's, and master's.

Special study options: academic remediation for entering students, accelerated degree program, adult/continuing education programs, advanced placement credit, cooperative education, distance learning, double majors, English as a second language, freshman honors college, honors programs, independent study, internships, off-campus study, part-time degree program, services for LD students, student-designed majors, study abroad, summer session for credit. ***ROTC:*** Army (c), Navy (c), Air Force (c).

Computers: Students can access the following: campus intranet, computer help desk, free student e-mail accounts, online (class) grades, online (class) registration, online (class) schedules. Campuswide network is available. Wireless service is available via classrooms, libraries.

Library: Marion Campus Library plus 1 other.

STUDENT LIFE
Housing options: college housing not available.

Activities and organizations: choral group.

Athletics Member USCAA. ***Intercollegiate sports:*** basketball M, golf M, volleyball W. ***Intramural sports:*** cheerleading M(c)/W(c), rugby M(c)/W(c), skiing (downhill) M(c)/W(c), soccer M(c)/W(c), softball M(c)/W(c), table tennis M/W.

Campus security: 24-hour emergency response devices.

Student services: personal/psychological counseling.

COSTS
Costs (2016–17) ***Tuition:*** state resident $7140 full-time, $298 per credit hour part-time; nonresident $25,332 full-time, $1056 per credit hour part-time. Full-time tuition and fees vary according to course load, location, program, and reciprocity agreements. Part-time tuition and fees vary according to course load, location, program, and reciprocity agreements. ***Payment plan:*** installment. ***Waivers:*** senior citizens and employees or children of employees.

APPLYING
Standardized Tests *Required for some:* SAT or ACT (for admission).

Options: electronic application.

Application fee: $60.

Required: high school transcript.

Application deadlines: 6/1 (freshmen), 6/1 (transfers).

Notification: continuous (freshmen), continuous (out-of-state freshmen), continuous (transfers).

CONTACT
Mr. Matthew Moreau, Admissions and Financial Aid Coordinator, The Ohio State University at Marion, 1465 Mount Vernon Avenue, Marion, OH 43302. *Phone:* 740-725-6337. *Fax:* 740-386-2439. *E-mail:* moreau.1@osu.edu.

The Ohio State University–Mansfield Campus

Mansfield, Ohio

http://www.mansfield.osu.edu/

- **State-supported** comprehensive, founded 1958, part of The Ohio State University
- **Small-town** 640-acre campus with easy access to Columbus, Cleveland
- **Endowment** $2.3 million
- **Coed** 1,189 undergraduate students, 83% full-time, 54% women, 46% men
- **Noncompetitive** entrance level, 99% of applicants were admitted

UNDERGRAD STUDENTS
990 full-time, 199 part-time. Students come from 4 states and territories; 1% are from out of state; 11% Black or African American, non-Hispanic/Latino; 3% Hispanic/Latino; 2% Asian, non-Hispanic/Latino; 0.1% American Indian or Alaska Native, non-Hispanic/Latino; 3% Two or more races, non-Hispanic/Latino; 2% Race/ethnicity unknown; 4% transferred in; 17% live on campus.

Freshmen:
Admission: 1,607 applied, 1,595 admitted, 522 enrolled. ***Test scores:*** SAT critical reading scores over 500: 54%; SAT math scores over 500: 62%; SAT writing scores over 500: 65%; ACT scores over 18: 86%; SAT critical reading scores over 600: 19%; SAT math scores over 600: 32%; SAT writing scores over 600: 14%; ACT scores over 24: 40%; SAT critical reading scores over 700: 3%; SAT math scores over 700: 5%; SAT writing scores over 700: 3%; ACT scores over 30: 3%.

Retention: 69% of full-time freshmen returned.

FACULTY
Total: 92, 41% full-time.

Student/faculty ratio: 19:1.

ACADEMICS
Calendar: semesters. *Degrees:* associate, bachelor's, and master's.

Special study options: academic remediation for entering students, accelerated degree program, adult/continuing education programs, advanced placement credit, cooperative education, distance learning, double majors, English as a second language, freshman honors college, honors programs, independent study, internships, off-campus study, part-time degree program, services for LD students, student-designed majors, study abroad, summer session for credit. ***ROTC:*** Army (c), Navy (c), Air Force (c).

Computers: Students can access the following: campus intranet, computer help desk, free student e-mail accounts, online (class) grades, online (class) registration, online (class) schedules. Campuswide network is available. 100% of college-owned or -operated housing units are wired for high-speed Internet access. Wireless service is available via computer centers, libraries, student centers.

Library: Bromfield Library plus 1 other.

STUDENT LIFE
Housing options: coed, special housing for students with disabilities. Campus housing is university owned.

Activities and organizations: drama/theater group, choral group, Campus Activities Board, Campus Crusader for Christ, Club Ed, Multicultural Student Association, Psychology Student Association.

Athletics ***Intramural sports:*** baseball M(c), basketball M(c)/W(c), bowling M/W, cheerleading M(c)/W(c), football M/W, golf M/W, soccer M(c), softball M/W, table tennis M/W, tennis M/W, volleyball M/W(c).

Campus security: 24-hour emergency response devices and patrols.

Student services: personal/psychological counseling.

COSTS
Costs (2016–17) ***Tuition:*** state resident $7140 full-time, $298 per credit hour part-time; nonresident $25,332 full-time, $1056 per credit hour part-time. Full-time tuition and fees vary according to course load, location, program, and reciprocity agreements. Part-time tuition and fees vary according to course load, location, program, and reciprocity agreements. ***Room and board:*** $4530; room only: $3730. Room and board charges vary according to housing facility and location. ***Payment plan:*** installment. ***Waivers:*** senior citizens and employees or children of employees.

APPLYING
Standardized Tests *Required for some:* SAT or ACT (for admission).

Options: electronic application.

Application fee: $60.

Required: high school transcript.

Application deadlines: 6/1 (freshmen), 6/1 (transfers).

Notification: continuous (freshmen), continuous (out-of-state freshmen), continuous (transfers).

CONTACT
The Ohio State University–Mansfield Campus, OH. *Phone:* 419-755-4225. *Fax:* 419-755-4241. *E-mail:* admissions@mansfield.ohio-state.edu.

The Ohio State University–Newark Campus

Newark, Ohio

http://www.newark.osu.edu/

- **State-supported** comprehensive, founded 1957, part of The Ohio State University
- **Small-town** 106-acre campus with easy access to Columbus
- **Endowment** $4.1 million
- **Coed** 2,448 undergraduate students, 84% full-time, 50% women, 50% men
- **Noncompetitive** entrance level, 99% of applicants were admitted

UNDERGRAD STUDENTS

2,054 full-time, 394 part-time. Students come from 11 states and territories; 0.5% are from out of state; 13% Black or African American, non-Hispanic/Latino; 3% Hispanic/Latino; 4% Asian, non-Hispanic/Latino; 0.1% Native Hawaiian or other Pacific Islander, non-Hispanic/Latino; 0.3% American Indian or Alaska Native, non-Hispanic/Latino; 4% Two or more races, non-Hispanic/Latino; 3% Race/ethnicity unknown; 5% transferred in; 8% live on campus.

Freshmen:

Admission: 2,831 applied, 2,793 admitted, 1,242 enrolled. ***Test scores:*** SAT critical reading scores over 500: 58%; SAT math scores over 500: 63%; SAT writing scores over 500: 49%; ACT scores over 18: 90%; SAT critical reading scores over 600: 13%; SAT math scores over 600: 16%; SAT writing scores over 600: 10%; ACT scores over 24: 38%; SAT critical reading scores over 700: 1%; ACT scores over 30: 2%.

Retention: 63% of full-time freshmen returned.

FACULTY

Total: 150, 33% full-time.

Student/faculty ratio: 26:1.

ACADEMICS

Calendar: semesters. *Degrees:* associate, bachelor's, and master's.

Special study options: academic remediation for entering students, accelerated degree program, adult/continuing education programs, advanced placement credit, cooperative education, distance learning, double majors, English as a second language, freshman honors college, honors programs, independent study, internships, off-campus study, part-time degree program, services for LD students, student-designed majors, study abroad, summer session for credit. ***ROTC:*** Army (b), Navy (c), Air Force (c).

Computers: Students can access the following: campus intranet, computer help desk, free student e-mail accounts, online (class) grades, online (class) registration, online (class) schedules. Campuswide network is available. 100% of college-owned or -operated housing units are wired for high-speed Internet access. Wireless service is available via entire campus.

Library: Newark Campus Library plus 1 other.

STUDENT LIFE

Housing options: coed. Campus housing is university owned.

Activities and organizations: choral group.

Athletics ***Intramural sports:*** baseball M(c), basketball M(c)/W(c), football M(c)/W(c), golf M(c)/W(c), soccer M(c)/W(c), softball W(c), volleyball M(c)/W(c), weight lifting M(c)/W(c).

Campus security: 24-hour emergency response devices and patrols, late-night transport/escort service, self-defense education.

Student services: personal/psychological counseling.

COSTS

Costs (2016–17) ***Tuition:*** state resident $7140 full-time, $298 per credit hour part-time; nonresident $25,332 full-time, $1056 per credit hour part-time. Full-time tuition and fees vary according to course load, location, program, and reciprocity agreements. Part-time tuition and fees vary according to course load, location, program, and reciprocity agreements. ***Room and board:*** Room and board charges vary according to board plan, housing facility, and location. ***Payment plan:*** installment. ***Waivers:*** senior citizens and employees or children of employees.

APPLYING

Standardized Tests *Required for some:* SAT or ACT (for admission).

Options: electronic application.

Application fee: $60.

Required: high school transcript.

Application deadlines: 6/1 (freshmen), 6/1 (transfers).

Notification: continuous (freshmen), continuous (out-of-state freshmen), continuous (transfers).

CONTACT

Ms. Ann Donahue, Director of Enrollment, The Ohio State University–Newark Campus, 1179 University Drive, Newark, OH 43055. *Phone:* 740-366-9333. *Fax:* 740-364-9645. *E-mail:* barclay.3@osu.edu.

Ohio University

Athens, Ohio

http://www.ohio.edu/

- **State-supported** university, founded 1804, part of Ohio Board of Regents
- **Small-town** 1774-acre campus
- **Endowment** $481.8 million
- **Coed** 23,788 undergraduate students, 76% full-time, 60% women, 40% men
- **Moderately difficult** entrance level, 75% of applicants were admitted

UNDERGRAD STUDENTS

18,012 full-time, 5,776 part-time. Students come from 48 states and territories; 75 other countries; 15% are from out of state; 5% Black or African American, non-Hispanic/Latino; 3% Hispanic/Latino; 1% Asian, non-Hispanic/Latino; 0.1% Native Hawaiian or other Pacific Islander, non-Hispanic/Latino; 0.2% American Indian or Alaska Native, non-Hispanic/Latino; 3% Two or more races, non-Hispanic/Latino; 1% Race/ethnicity unknown; 2% international; 2% transferred in; 40% live on campus.

Freshmen:

Admission: 20,623 applied, 15,437 admitted, 4,331 enrolled. ***Average high school GPA:*** 3.48. ***Test scores:*** SAT critical reading scores over 500: 74%; SAT math scores over 500: 76%; SAT writing scores over 500: 64%; ACT scores over 18: 99%; SAT critical reading scores over 600: 29%; SAT math scores over 600: 28%; SAT writing scores over 600: 18%; ACT scores over 24: 53%; SAT critical reading scores over 700: 5%; SAT math scores over 700: 4%; SAT writing scores over 700: 3%; ACT scores over 30: 7%.

Retention: 82% of full-time freshmen returned.

FACULTY

Total: 1,403, 71% full-time, 65% with terminal degrees.

Student/faculty ratio: 18:1.

ACADEMICS

Calendar: semesters. *Degrees:* certificates, associate, bachelor's, master's, and doctoral.

Special study options: academic remediation for entering students, accelerated degree program, adult/continuing education programs, advanced placement credit, cooperative education, distance learning, double majors, English as a second language, external degree program, freshman honors college, honors programs, independent study, internships, off-campus study, part-time degree program, services for LD students, student-designed majors, study abroad, summer session for credit. ***ROTC:*** Army (b), Air Force (b).

Computers: 1,000 computers/terminals and 22,000 ports are available on campus for general student use. Students can access the following: campus intranet, computer help desk, free student e-mail accounts, online (class) grades, online (class) registration, online (class) schedules. Campuswide network is available. 100% of college-owned or -operated housing units are wired for high-speed Internet access. Wireless service is available via entire campus.

Library: Alden Library plus 3 others. *Books:* 2.7 million (physical), 1.1 million (digital/electronic); *Serial titles:* 61,495 (physical), 77,421 (digital/electronic); *Databases:* 574. Weekly public service hours: 146; study areas open 24 hours, 5-7 days a week; students can reserve study rooms.

STUDENT LIFE

Housing options: on-campus residence required through sophomore year; coed, women-only, special housing for students with disabilities. Campus housing is university owned. Freshman campus housing is guaranteed.

Activities and organizations: drama/theater group, student-run newspaper, radio and television station, choral group, marching band, Student Senate, Student Alumni Board, International Student Union, University Program Council, Black Student Cultural Programming Board, national fraternities, national sororities.

Athletics Member NCAA. All Division I except football (Division I-A). ***Intercollegiate sports:*** baseball M(s), basketball M(s)/W(s), cheerleading M/W, cross-country running M(s)/W(s), field hockey W(s), golf M(s)/W(s), ice hockey M(c), soccer W(s), softball W(s), swimming and diving W(s), track and field W(s), volleyball W(s), wrestling M(s). ***Intramural sports:*** archery M(c)/W(c), badminton M/W, baseball M(c), basketball M/W, crew M(c)/W(c), equestrian sports M(c)/W(c), fencing M(c)/W(c), golf M(c)/W(c), gymnastics M(c)/W(c), lacrosse M(c)/W(c), rugby M(c)/W(c), soccer M(c)/W(c), softball M/W(c), swimming and diving M(c)/W(c), tennis M/W, ultimate Frisbee M(c)/W(c), volleyball M(c)/W(c), water polo M/W(c).

Campus security: 24-hour emergency response devices and patrols, student patrols, late-night transport/escort service, controlled dormitory access, electronic access to some dorms; fully sworn, 24/7 police department.

Student services: health clinic, personal/psychological counseling, women's center, legal services.

COSTS & FINANCIAL AID

Costs (2016–17) ***Tuition:*** state resident $11,744 full-time, $556 per semester hour part-time; nonresident $21,208 full-time, $1022 per semester hour part-time. Full-time tuition and fees vary according to degree level, location, program, and reciprocity agreements. Part-time tuition and fees vary according to course load, degree level, location, program, and reciprocity agreements. No tuition increase for student's term of enrollment. ***Room and board:*** $11,176. Room and board charges vary according to board plan. ***Payment plan:*** installment. ***Waivers:*** senior citizens and employees or children of employees.

Financial Aid Of all full-time matriculated undergraduates who enrolled in 2016, 12,709 applied for aid, 10,046 were judged to have need, 3,662 had their need fully met. 724 Federal Work-Study jobs (averaging $1684). In 2016, 1648 non-need-based awards were made. ***Average percent of need met:*** 47. ***Average financial aid package:*** $9240. ***Average need-based loan:*** $3751. ***Average need-based gift aid:*** $6510. ***Average non-need-based aid:*** $4231. ***Average indebtedness upon graduation:*** $27,879.

APPLYING

Standardized Tests *Required:* SAT or ACT (for admission).

Options: electronic application, early admission, early action, deferred entrance.

Application fee: $50.

Required for some: essay or personal statement, high school transcript, 2 letters of recommendation, audition for music and dance, interview and application supplement for Honors Tutorial College. ***Recommended:*** 2 letters of recommendation.

Application deadlines: 2/1 (freshmen), 6/15 (transfers), 12/1 (early action).

Notification: continuous (freshmen), continuous (transfers), rolling (early action).

CONTACT

Undergraduate Admissions, Ohio University, Athens, OH 45701-2979. *Phone:* 740-593-4100. *Fax:* 740-593-0560. *E-mail:* admissions@ohio.edu.

Ohio University–Chillicothe

Chillicothe, Ohio

http://www.chillicothe.ohiou.edu/

- **State-supported** comprehensive, founded 1946, part of Ohio University
- **Small-town** 124-acre campus with easy access to Columbus
- **Coed**
- **Noncompetitive** entrance level

ACADEMICS

Calendar: semesters. *Degrees:* associate, bachelor's, and master's (offers first 2 years of most bachelor's degree programs available at the main campus in Athens; also offers several bachelor's degree programs that can be completed at this campus and several programs exclusive to this campus; also offers some graduate programs).

Library: Quinn Library.

STUDENT LIFE

Housing options: college housing not available.

Activities and organizations: drama/theater group.

Campus security: 24-hour emergency response devices, patrols by city police.

Student services: personal/psychological counseling.

FINANCIAL AID

Financial Aid Of all full-time matriculated undergraduates who enrolled in 2016, 824 applied for aid, 680 were judged to have need, 91 had their need fully met. 18 Federal Work-Study jobs (averaging $1504). In 2016, 11 non-need-based awards were made. ***Average percent of need met:*** 54. ***Average financial aid package:*** $7323. ***Average need-based loan:*** $2675. ***Average need-based gift aid:*** $5439. ***Average non-need-based aid:*** $4111. ***Average indebtedness upon graduation:*** $27,879.

APPLYING

Standardized Tests *Required:* ACCUPLACER (for admission).

Options: electronic application, early admission, deferred entrance.

Application fee: $20.

Required: high school transcript.

CONTACT

Neeley Allen, Coordinator, Recruitment, Ohio University–Chillicothe, 101 University Drive, Chillicothe, OH 45601. *Phone:* 740-774-7241. *Toll-free phone:* 877-462-6824. *Fax:* 740-774-7214. *E-mail:* evelandt@ohio.edu.

Ohio University–Eastern

St. Clairsville, Ohio

http://www.eastern.ohiou.edu/

- **State-supported** comprehensive, founded 1957, part of Ohio Board of Regents
- **Rural** 300-acre campus
- **Coed** 751 undergraduate students
- **Noncompetitive** entrance level

ACADEMICS

Calendar: quarters. *Degrees:* associate, bachelor's, and master's (also offers some graduate courses).

Special study options: academic remediation for entering students, accelerated degree program, adult/continuing education programs, advanced placement credit, distance learning, double majors, external degree program, part-time degree program, student-designed majors, summer session for credit.

Computers: 15 computers/terminals and 50 ports are available on campus for general student use. Students can access the following: campus intranet, computer help desk, free student e-mail accounts, online (class) grades, online (class) registration, online (class) schedules. Campuswide network is available.

Library: The Library and Learning Commons. Weekly public service hours: 75; students can reserve study rooms.

STUDENT LIFE

Housing options: college housing not available.

Activities and organizations: drama/theater group.

Athletics ***Intercollegiate sports:*** basketball M/W, golf M/W, volleyball W. ***Intramural sports:*** basketball M, weight lifting M/W.

Campus security: late-night transport/escort service.

Student services: personal/psychological counseling.

COSTS & FINANCIAL AID

Costs (2017–18) ***Tuition:*** area resident $5084 full-time; state resident $219 per credit hour part-time; nonresident $305 per credit hour part-time. Full-time tuition and fees vary according to course load, location, program, reciprocity agreements, and student level. Part-time tuition and fees vary according to course load, location, program, reciprocity agreements, and student level. ***Required fees:*** $66 full-time, $3 per credit hour part-time. ***Payment plan:*** installment. ***Waivers:*** senior citizens and employees or children of employees.

Financial Aid Of all full-time matriculated undergraduates who enrolled in 2016, 275 applied for aid, 210 were judged to have need, 30 had their need fully met. 7 Federal Work-Study jobs (averaging $1781). In 2016, 5 non-need-based awards were made. ***Average percent of need met:*** 56. ***Average financial aid package:*** $6256. ***Average need-based loan:*** $2207. ***Average need-based gift aid:*** $5032. ***Average non-need-based aid:*** $3482. ***Average indebtedness upon graduation:*** $27,879.

APPLYING

Options: electronic application, early admission, deferred entrance.

Application fee: $20.

Required: high school transcript.

Application deadlines: rolling (freshmen), rolling (transfers).

CONTACT

Ms. Lisa Jeffries, Recruitment Coordinator, Ohio University–Eastern, 45425 National Road, St. Clairsville, OH 43950-9724. *Phone:* 740-699-2504. *Toll-free phone:* 800-648-3331. *E-mail:* jeffriee@ohio.edu.

Ohio University–Lancaster

Lancaster, Ohio

http://www.ohiou.edu/lancaster/

CONTACT

Pat Fox, Enrollment Manager, Ohio University–Lancaster, 1570 Granville Pike, Lancaster, OH 43130-1097. *Phone:* 740-654-6711 Ext. 215. *Toll-free phone:* 888-446-4468. *E-mail:* fox@ohio.edu.

Ohio University–Southern Campus

Ironton, Ohio

http://www.ohiou.edu/

CONTACT

Linda Harlow, Admission, Registration and Records Coordinator, Ohio University–Southern Campus, 1804 Liberty Avenue, Ironton, OH 45638-2214. *Phone:* 740-533-4584. *Toll-free phone:* 800-626-0513. *E-mail:* harlow@ohio.edu.

Ohio University–Zanesville

Zanesville, Ohio

http://www.ohio.edu/zanesville/

- **State-supported** 4-year, founded 1946
- **Rural** 179-acre campus with easy access to Columbus
- **Coed** 1,968 undergraduate students, 96% full-time, 69% women, 31% men
- **Noncompetitive** entrance level, 92% of applicants were admitted

UNDERGRAD STUDENTS

1,887 full-time, 81 part-time. 1% are from out of state; 3% Black or African American, non-Hispanic/Latino; 1% Hispanic/Latino; 0.5% Asian, non-Hispanic/Latino; 0.1% Native Hawaiian or other Pacific Islander, non-Hispanic/Latino; 0.1% American Indian or Alaska Native, non-Hispanic/Latino; 4% Two or more races, non-Hispanic/Latino; 2% Race/ethnicity unknown; 0.4% international.

Freshmen:

Admission: 552 applied, 508 admitted, 300 enrolled.

FACULTY

Total: 130, 24% full-time, 25% with terminal degrees.

Student/faculty ratio: 18:1.

ACADEMICS

Calendar: quarters. *Degrees:* associate and bachelor's (offers first 2 years of most bachelor's degree programs available at the main campus in Athens; also offers several bachelor's degree programs that can be completed at this campus; also offers some graduate courses).

Special study options: academic remediation for entering students, accelerated degree program, adult/continuing education programs, advanced placement credit, distance learning, double majors, external degree program, independent study, off-campus study, part-time degree program, services for LD students, student-designed majors, study abroad, summer session for credit.

Computers: 200 computers/terminals are available on campus for general student use. Students can access the following: computer help desk, free student e-mail accounts, online (class) grades, online (class) registration, online (class) schedules. Campuswide network is available. Wireless service is available via entire campus.

Library: Zanesville Campus Library plus 1 other. Students can reserve study rooms.

STUDENT LIFE

Activities and organizations: drama/theater group, student-run newspaper, radio station, Student Senate, Student Nurses Association, Good Intentions Group, Green Bobcats, Habitat for Humanity Club.

Athletics ***Intercollegiate sports:*** baseball M, basketball M/W, softball W.

Campus security: student patrols, late-night transport/escort service, night security.

Student services: personal/psychological counseling.

COSTS & FINANCIAL AID

Costs (2016–17) ***Tuition:*** state resident $4984 full-time, $234 per semester hour part-time; nonresident $8624 full-time, $413 per semester hour part-time. Full-time tuition and fees vary according to course load and student level. Part-time tuition and fees vary according to course load and student level. ***Required fees:*** $92 full-time, $6 per semester hour part-time, $8 per term part-time. ***Payment plan:*** installment. ***Waivers:*** senior citizens and employees or children of employees.

Financial Aid Of all full-time matriculated undergraduates who enrolled in 2016, 702 applied for aid, 547 were judged to have need, 78 had their need fully met. 3 Federal Work-Study jobs (averaging $1282). In 2016, 9 non-need-based awards were made. ***Average percent of need met:*** 55. ***Average financial aid package:*** $6619. ***Average need-based loan:*** $2259. ***Average need-based gift aid:*** $5229. ***Average non-need-based aid:*** $2778. ***Average indebtedness upon graduation:*** $27,879.

APPLYING

Standardized Tests *Required for some:* SAT or ACT (for admission).

Options: electronic application.

Application fee: $20.

Required: high school transcript.

Application deadlines: rolling (freshmen), rolling (transfers).

CONTACT

Ohio University–Zanesville, Office of Student Services, 1425 Newark Road, Zanesville, OH 43701. *Phone:* 740-588-1440. *Fax:* 740-588-1444. *E-mail:* ouzservices@ohio.edu.

Ohio Wesleyan University

Delaware, Ohio

http://www.owu.edu/

- **Independent United Methodist** 4-year, founded 1842
- **Small-town** 200-acre campus with easy access to Columbus
- **Coed** 1,639 undergraduate students, 99% full-time, 52% women, 48% men
- **Very difficult** entrance level, 72% of applicants were admitted

UNDERGRAD STUDENTS

1,624 full-time, 15 part-time. 47% are from out of state; 9% Black or African American, non-Hispanic/Latino; 5% Hispanic/Latino; 3% Asian, non-Hispanic/Latino; 0.1% Native Hawaiian or other Pacific Islander, non-Hispanic/Latino; 0.1% American Indian or Alaska Native, non-Hispanic/Latino; 5% Two or more races, non-Hispanic/Latino; 3% Race/ethnicity unknown; 6% international; 2% transferred in; 90% live on campus.

Freshmen:

Admission: 4,123 applied, 2,950 admitted, 489 enrolled. ***Average high school GPA:*** 3.42. ***Test scores:*** SAT critical reading scores over 500: 82%; SAT math scores over 500: 76%; SAT writing scores over 500: 71%; ACT scores over 18: 97%; SAT critical reading scores over 600: 38%; SAT math scores over 600: 38%; SAT writing scores over 600: 25%; ACT scores over 24: 64%; SAT critical reading scores over 700: 6%; SAT math

scores over 700: 4%; SAT writing scores over 700: 4%; ACT scores over 30: 16%.
Retention: 81% of full-time freshmen returned.

FACULTY
Total: 199, 67% full-time, 67% with terminal degrees.
Student/faculty ratio: 10:1.

ACADEMICS
Calendar: semesters. *Degree:* bachelor's.
Special study options: double majors, honors programs, internships, off-campus study, services for LD students, student-designed majors, study abroad, summer session for credit. ***ROTC:*** Army (c), Air Force (c).
Unusual degree programs: 3-2 engineering with Alfred University, California Institute of Technology, Case Western Reserve University, Polytechnic University, Rensselaer Polytechnic Institute, Washington University in St. Louis.
Computers: Students can access the following: campus intranet, computer help desk, free student e-mail accounts, online (class) grades, online (class) registration, online (class) schedules. Campuswide network is available. 100% of college-owned or -operated housing units are wired for high-speed Internet access. Wireless service is available via entire campus.
Library: [redacted]A. Beeghly Library.

STUDENT LIFE
Housing options: on-campus residence required through senior year; coed, women-only. Campus housing is university owned. Freshman campus housing is guaranteed.
Activities and organizations: drama/theater group, student-run newspaper, radio station, choral group, national fraternities, national sororities.
Athletics Member NCAA. All Division III. ***Intercollegiate sports:*** baseball M, basketball M/W, cross-country running M/W, equestrian sports M(c)/W(c), field hockey W, football M, golf M, ice hockey M(c)/W(c), lacrosse M/W, rugby M(c)/W(c), sailing M(c)/W(c), soccer M/W, softball W, swimming and diving M/W, tennis M/W, track and field M/W, ultimate Frisbee M(c)/W(c), volleyball M(c)/W(c). ***Intramural sports:*** badminton M/W, basketball M/W, football M/W, golf M/W, lacrosse M/W, racquetball M/W, skiing (cross-country) M/W, skiing (downhill) M/W, soccer M/W, softball M/W, squash M/W, swimming and diving M/W, tennis M/W, track and field M/W, volleyball M/W, water polo M/W.
Campus security: 24-hour emergency response devices and patrols, late-night transport/escort service, controlled dormitory access.
Student services: health clinic, personal/psychological counseling, women's center.

COSTS & FINANCIAL AID
Costs (2016–17) ***Comprehensive fee:*** $55,860 includes full-time tuition ($43,770), mandatory fees ($320), and room and board ($11,770). Full-time tuition and fees vary according to course load. Part-time tuition: $1267 per credit hour. Part-time tuition and fees vary according to course load. ***Room and board:*** Room and board charges vary according to board plan and housing facility. ***Payment plan:*** installment. ***Waivers:*** employees or children of employees.
Financial Aid Of all full-time matriculated undergraduates who enrolled in 2015, 1,269 applied for aid, 1,139 were judged to have need, 239 had their need fully met. In 2015, 503 non-need-based awards were made. ***Average percent of need met:*** 79. ***Average financial aid package:*** $34,662. ***Average need-based loan:*** $4766. ***Average need-based gift aid:*** $29,200. ***Average non-need-based aid:*** $22,895. ***Average indebtedness upon graduation:*** $34,666.

APPLYING
Standardized Tests *Required for some:* SAT or ACT (for admission).
Options: electronic application, early admission, early decision, early action, deferred entrance.
Required: essay or personal statement, high school transcript, minimum 2.5 GPA, 1 letter of recommendation. ***Recommended:*** 2 letters of recommendation, interview.
Application deadlines: 3/1 (freshmen), rolling (transfers), 12/15 (early action).
Early decision deadline: 11/15.
Notification: continuous (freshmen), continuous (out-of-state freshmen), continuous (transfers), 12/1 (early decision), 1/15 (early action).

CONTACT
Ms. Alisha Couch, Director of Admission, Ohio Wesleyan University, 61 South Sandusky Street, Delaware, OH 43015. *Phone:* 740-368-3099. *Toll-free phone:* 800-922-8953. *Fax:* 740-368-3314.
E-mail: amcouch@owu.edu.

See previous page for display ad and page 1452 for the College Close-Up.

Otterbein University

Westerville, Ohio

http://www.otterbein.edu/

- **Independent United Methodist** comprehensive, founded 1847
- **Suburban** 142-acre campus with easy access to Columbus
- **Endowment** $91.5 million
- **Coed** 2,485 undergraduate students, 92% full-time, 61% women, 39% men
- **Moderately difficult** entrance level, 75% of applicants were admitted

UNDERGRAD STUDENTS
2,282 full-time, 203 part-time. Students come from 38 states and territories; 10 other countries; 13% are from out of state; 6% Black or African American, non-Hispanic/Latino; 2% Hispanic/Latino; 2% Asian, non-Hispanic/Latino; 0.2% American Indian or Alaska Native, non-Hispanic/Latino; 4% Two or more races, non-Hispanic/Latino; 6% Race/ethnicity unknown; 2% international; 4% transferred in; 60% live on campus.

Freshmen:
Admission: 2,917 applied, 2,197 admitted, 647 enrolled. ***Average high school GPA:*** 3.6. ***Test scores:*** SAT critical reading scores over 500: 71%; SAT math scores over 500: 72%; SAT writing scores over 500: 64%; ACT scores over 18: 93%; SAT critical reading scores over 600: 34%; SAT math scores over 600: 35%; SAT writing scores over 600: 25%; ACT scores over 24: 50%; SAT critical reading scores over 700: 7%; SAT math scores over 700: 4%; SAT writing scores over 700: 4%; ACT scores over 30: 6%.

Retention: 84% of full-time freshmen returned.

FACULTY
Total: 317, 55% full-time, 51% with terminal degrees.
Student/faculty ratio: 12:1.

ACADEMICS
Calendar: semesters. *Degrees:* bachelor's, master's, doctoral, and post-master's certificates.
Special study options: academic remediation for entering students, adult/continuing education programs, advanced placement credit, cooperative education, distance learning, double majors, English as a second language, honors programs, internships, off-campus study, part-time degree program, services for LD students, student-designed majors, study abroad, summer session for credit. ***ROTC:*** Army (c), Air Force (c).
Computers: 198 computers/terminals are available on campus for general student use. Students can access the following: campus intranet, computer help desk, free student e-mail accounts, online (class) grades, online (class) registration, online (class) schedules. Campuswide network is available. 100% of college-owned or -operated housing units are wired for high-speed Internet access. Wireless service is available via entire campus.
Library: Courtright Memorial Library. *Books:* 281,721 (physical), 243,407 (digital/electronic); *Serial titles:* 11,978 (physical), 9,019 (digital/electronic). Weekly public service hours: 102; students can reserve study rooms.

STUDENT LIFE
Housing options: on-campus residence required through junior year; coed, men-only, women-only. Campus housing is university owned. Freshman campus housing is guaranteed.
Activities and organizations: drama/theater group, student-run newspaper, radio and television station, choral group, marching band, Musical groups, Honoraries, Academic interest clubs, Governance, national fraternities.
Athletics Member NCAA. All Division III. ***Intercollegiate sports:*** baseball M, basketball M/W, cheerleading M/W, cross-country running M/W, equestrian sports M/W, football M, golf M/W, lacrosse M/W, soccer M/W, softball W, tennis M/W, track and field M/W, volleyball W, wrestling M. ***Intramural sports:*** basketball M/W, football M, racquetball M/W, soccer M/W, softball M/W, ultimate Frisbee M/W, volleyball M/W.
Campus security: 24-hour emergency response devices and patrols, student patrols, late-night transport/escort service, controlled dormitory access, 24-hour locked residence hall entrances.
Student services: health clinic, personal/psychological counseling.

COSTS & FINANCIAL AID
Costs (2017–18) ***Comprehensive fee:*** $42,702 includes full-time tuition ($31,424), mandatory fees ($450), and room and board ($10,828). Part-time tuition: $564 per credit hour. ***College room only:*** $6256. Room and board charges vary according to board plan and housing facility. ***Waivers:*** employees or children of employees.
Financial Aid Of all full-time matriculated undergraduates who enrolled in 2015, 1,803 applied for aid, 1,604 were judged to have need, 297 had their need fully met. 868 Federal Work-Study jobs (averaging $1511). In 2015, 444 non-need-based awards were made. ***Average percent of need met:*** 75. ***Average financial aid package:*** $23,544. ***Average need-based loan:*** $4177. ***Average need-based gift aid:*** $17,851. ***Average non-need-based aid:*** $17,222. ***Average indebtedness upon graduation:*** $40,397.

APPLYING
Standardized Tests *Required:* SAT or ACT (for admission).
Options: electronic application, deferred entrance.
Application fee: $25.
Required: high school transcript. ***Required for some:*** essay or personal statement, 1 letter of recommendation. ***Recommended:*** minimum 2.5 GPA, interview.
Application deadlines: 3/1 (freshmen), rolling (transfers).
Notification: continuous (freshmen), continuous (transfers).

CONTACT
Mr. Mark Moffit, Director of Admissions, Otterbein University, 1 South Grove Street, Office Of Admission, Westerville, OH 43081-9924.
Phone: 614-823-1500. *Toll-free phone:* 800-488-8144.
Fax: 614-823-1200. *E-mail:* uotterb@otterbein.edu.

Pontifical College Josephinum

Columbus, Ohio

http://www.pcj.edu/

CONTACT
Mrs. Arminda Crawford, Secretary for Admissions, Pontifical College Josephinum, 7825 North High Street, Columbus, OH 43235. *Phone:* 614-985-2241. *Toll-free phone:* 888-252-5812. *Fax:* 614-885-2307.
E-mail: acrawford@pcj.edu.

Rabbinical College of Telshe

Wickliffe, Ohio

CONTACT
Admissions Office, Rabbinical College of Telshe, 28400 Euclid Avenue, Wickliffe, OH 44092-2523. *Phone:* 440-943-5300.

Ross College

Canton, Ohio

http://www.rosseducation.edu/

CONTACT
Ross College, 4300 Munson Street NW, Canton, OH 44718. *Phone:* 330-494-1214. *Toll-free phone:* 866-815-5578.

Shawnee State University

Portsmouth, Ohio

http://www.shawnee.edu/

- **State-supported** comprehensive, founded 1986, part of Ohio Higher Educational System
- **Small-town** 62-acre campus with easy access to Charleston-Huntington-Ashland Area
- **Endowment** $19.3 million
- **Coed** 3,603 undergraduate students, 84% full-time, 54% women, 46% men
- **Noncompetitive** entrance level, 74% of applicants were admitted

UNDERGRAD STUDENTS

3,036 full-time, 567 part-time. Students come from 21 states and territories; 19 other countries; 11% are from out of state; 6% Black or African American, non-Hispanic/Latino; 0.7% Hispanic/Latino; 0.5% Asian, non-Hispanic/Latino; 0.1% Native Hawaiian or other Pacific Islander, non-Hispanic/Latino; 0.8% American Indian or Alaska Native, non-Hispanic/Latino; 2% Two or more races, non-Hispanic/Latino; 4% Race/ethnicity unknown; 1% international; 5% transferred in; 24% live on campus.

Freshmen:

Admission: 3,614 applied, 2,659 admitted, 864 enrolled. *Average high school GPA:* 3.14.

Retention: 72% of full-time freshmen returned.

FACULTY

Total: 314, 48% full-time, 27% with terminal degrees.

Student/faculty ratio: 15:1.

ACADEMICS

Calendar: semesters. *Degrees:* certificates, associate, bachelor's, and master's.

Special study options: academic remediation for entering students, accelerated degree program, adult/continuing education programs, advanced placement credit, distance learning, double majors, English as a second language, honors programs, independent study, internships, off-campus study, part-time degree program, services for LD students, student-designed majors, study abroad, summer session for credit.

Unusual degree programs: 3-2 psychology/occupational therapy.

Computers: 620 computers/terminals are available on campus for general student use. Students can access the following: campus intranet, computer help desk, free student e-mail accounts, online (class) grades, online (class) registration, online (class) schedules, financial aid, student billing, courses, student service portal. Campuswide network is available. 100% of college-owned or -operated housing units are wired for high-speed Internet access. Wireless service is available via entire campus.

Library: Clark Memorial Library. *Books:* 122,670 (physical), 103,584 (digital/electronic); *Serial titles:* 140 (physical), 672 (digital/electronic); *Databases:* 543. Weekly public service hours: 91; students can reserve study rooms.

STUDENT LIFE

Housing options: on-campus residence required for freshman year; coed. Campus housing is university owned, leased by the school and is provided by a third party. Freshman applicants given priority for college housing.

Activities and organizations: drama/theater group, student-run newspaper, choral group, campus ministry, Health Executives and Administrators Learning Society, Student Programming Board, Student Government Association, national fraternities, national sororities.

Athletics Member NAIA. ***Intercollegiate sports:*** baseball M(s), basketball M(s)/W(s), cross-country running M(s)/W(s), golf M(s)/W(s), soccer M(s)/W(s), softball W(s), tennis W(s), track and field M(s)/W(s), volleyball W(s). ***Intramural sports:*** basketball M/W, bowling M/W, golf M/W, racquetball M/W, softball M, swimming and diving M/W, table tennis M/W, tennis M/W, volleyball M/W.

Campus security: 24-hour emergency response devices and patrols.

Student services: health clinic, personal/psychological counseling, women's center.

COSTS

Costs (2017–18) ***Tuition:*** state resident $7614 full-time, $297 per credit hour part-time; nonresident $13,396 full-time, $530 per credit hour part-time. Full-time tuition and fees vary according to course load, program, and reciprocity agreements. Part-time tuition and fees vary according to course load, program, and reciprocity agreements. ***Required fees:*** $3682 full-time, $46 per credit hour part-time. ***Room and board:*** $10,116; room only: $5645. Room and board charges vary according to board plan and housing facility. ***Payment plan:*** installment. ***Waivers:*** senior citizens and employees or children of employees.

APPLYING

Options: electronic application.

Required: high school transcript. ***Required for some:*** essay or personal statement, minimum 2.7 GPA, interview, If student is under 21, ACT/SAT scores are required.

Application deadlines: rolling (freshmen), rolling (transfers).

Notification: continuous (freshmen), continuous (transfers).

CONTACT

Amanda Means, Director of Admissions, Shawnee State University, 940 Second St, Portsmouth, OH 45662. *Phone:* 740-351-3229. *Toll-free phone:* 800-959-2778. *Fax:* 740-351-3111.
E-mail: ameans@shawnee.edu.

South University

Cleveland, Ohio

http://www.southuniversity.edu/cleveland.aspx

CONTACT

South University, 4743 Richmond Road, Cleveland, OH 44128.
Phone: 216-755-5000. *Toll-free phone:* 855-398-9280.

Tiffin University

Tiffin, Ohio

http://www.tiffin.edu/

- **Independent** comprehensive, founded 1888
- **Small-town** 135-acre campus with easy access to Toledo
- **Endowment** $9.1 million
- **Coed** 2,353 undergraduate students, 75% full-time, 47% women, 53% men
- **Moderately difficult** entrance level, 60% of applicants were admitted

UNDERGRAD STUDENTS

1,762 full-time, 591 part-time. Students come from 47 states and territories; 33 other countries; 26% are from out of state; 12% Black or African American, non-Hispanic/Latino; 3% Hispanic/Latino; 0.6% Asian, non-Hispanic/Latino; 0.1% American Indian or Alaska Native, non-Hispanic/Latino; 1% Two or more races, non-Hispanic/Latino; 29% Race/ethnicity unknown; 12% international; 7% transferred in; 42% live on campus.

Freshmen:

Admission: 3,653 applied, 2,204 admitted, 458 enrolled. ***Average high school GPA:*** 3.03. ***Test scores:*** SAT critical reading scores over 700: 16%.

Retention: 65% of full-time freshmen returned.

FACULTY

Total: 361, 20% full-time, 43% with terminal degrees.

Student/faculty ratio: 14:1.

ACADEMICS

Calendar: semesters. *Degrees:* certificates, associate, bachelor's, master's, post-master's, and postbachelor's certificates.

Special study options: academic remediation for entering students, accelerated degree program, adult/continuing education programs, advanced placement credit, distance learning, double majors, English as a second language, freshman honors college, independent study, internships, off-campus study, services for LD students, study abroad, summer session for credit. ***ROTC:*** Army (c), Air Force (c).

Computers: 280 computers/terminals are available on campus for general student use. Students can access the following: campus intranet, computer help desk, free student e-mail accounts, online (class) grades, online (class) registration, online (class) schedules. Campuswide network is available. 100% of college-owned or -operated housing units are wired for high-speed Internet access. Wireless service is available via classrooms,

computer centers, computer labs, dorm rooms, learning centers, libraries, student centers.
Library: Pfeiffer Library plus 1 other. *Books:* 40,849 (physical), 125,971 (digital/electronic); *Serial titles:* 120 (physical), 25,420 (digital/electronic); *Databases:* 187. Weekly public service hours: 73.

STUDENT LIFE
Housing options: on-campus residence required through sophomore year; coed, men-only, women-only, special housing for students with disabilities. Campus housing is university owned and leased by the school. Freshman campus housing is guaranteed.
Activities and organizations: drama/theater group, student-run newspaper, choral group, marching band, Student Government Association, H2O, International Student Association, Global Affairs Organization, Circle K, national fraternities, national sororities.
Athletics Member NCAA. All Division II. ***Intercollegiate sports:*** baseball M(s), basketball M(s)/W(s), cross-country running M(s)/W(s), football M(s), golf M(s)/W(s), lacrosse W(s), soccer M(s)/W(s), softball W(s), swimming and diving M(s)/W(s), tennis M(s)/W(s), track and field M(s)/W(s), volleyball W(s), wrestling M(s). ***Intramural sports:*** basketball M/W, bowling M/W, equestrian sports M(c)/W(c), football M, rugby M(c), soccer M/W, softball M/W, table tennis M/W, tennis M/W, ultimate Frisbee M/W, volleyball M/W, weight lifting M/W.
Campus security: 24-hour emergency response devices, student patrols, late-night transport/escort service, controlled dormitory access.
Student services: health clinic, personal/psychological counseling, women's center.

COSTS & FINANCIAL AID
Costs (2017–18) ***Comprehensive fee:*** $34,750 includes full-time tuition ($23,700), mandatory fees ($150), and room and board ($10,900). Full-time tuition and fees vary according to course load, degree level, location, program, and reciprocity agreements. Part-time tuition: $790 per credit hour. Part-time tuition and fees vary according to course load, degree level, location, program, and reciprocity agreements. ***College room only:*** $5900. Room and board charges vary according to board plan and housing facility. ***Payment plans:*** installment, deferred payment. ***Waivers:*** senior citizens and employees or children of employees.
Financial Aid Of all full-time matriculated undergraduates who enrolled in 2016, 1,380 applied for aid, 1,264 were judged to have need, 227 had their need fully met. 199 Federal Work-Study jobs (averaging $2095). ***Average percent of need met:*** 68. ***Average financial aid package:*** $17,797. ***Average need-based loan:*** $4066. ***Average need-based gift aid:*** $14,154. ***Average indebtedness upon graduation:*** $37,834.

APPLYING
Standardized Tests *Required for some:* SAT or ACT (for admission).
Options: electronic application.
Application fee: $20.
Required: high school transcript. ***Required for some:*** essay or personal statement, interview. ***Recommended:*** minimum 3.0 GPA.
Application deadlines: rolling (freshmen), rolling (transfers).
Notification: continuous (freshmen), continuous (transfers).

CONTACT
Mrs. Sarah Johnson, Director of Undergraduate Admissions, Tiffin University, 155 Miami Street, Tiffin, OH 44883. *Phone:* 419-448-3014. *Toll-free phone:* 800-968-6446. *Fax:* 419-443-5006. *E-mail:* depughst@tiffin.edu.

Tri-State Bible College

South Point, Ohio

http://www.tsbc.edu/

CONTACT
Tri-State Bible College, 506 Margaret Street, PO Box 445, South Point, OH 45680-8402. *Phone:* 740-377-2520.

Union Institute & University

Cincinnati, Ohio

http://www.myunion.edu/

- **Independent** university, founded 1964
- **Urban** 5-acre campus with easy access to Cincinnati
- **Endowment** $793,428
- **Coed** 837 undergraduate students, 48% full-time, 50% women, 50% men
- **Noncompetitive** entrance level

UNDERGRAD STUDENTS
399 full-time, 438 part-time. Students come from 40 states and territories; 13% are from out of state; 18% Black or African American, non-Hispanic/Latino; 25% Hispanic/Latino; 0.8% Asian, non-Hispanic/Latino; 0.7% Native Hawaiian or other Pacific Islander, non-Hispanic/Latino; 0.2% American Indian or Alaska Native, non-Hispanic/Latino; 3% Two or more races, non-Hispanic/Latino; 17% Race/ethnicity unknown; 29% transferred in.

Freshmen:
Admission: 13 enrolled.
Retention: 92% of full-time freshmen returned.

FACULTY
Total: 336, 10% full-time, 30% with terminal degrees.
Student/faculty ratio: 8:1.

ACADEMICS
Calendar: trimesters some programs offer split (8-week) sessions; some programs have two 6-month semesters. *Degrees:* bachelor's, master's, doctoral, and post-master's certificates.
Special study options: academic remediation for entering students, accelerated degree program, adult/continuing education programs, advanced placement credit, distance learning, double majors, external degree program, independent study, internships, off-campus study, part-time degree program, services for LD students, summer session for credit.
Computers: 65 computers/terminals are available on campus for general student use. Students can access the following: computer help desk, free student e-mail accounts, online (class) grades, online (class) registration, online (class) schedules, CampusWeb: access to basic information. Campuswide network is available. 100% of college-owned or -operated housing units are wired for high-speed Internet access. Wireless service is available via entire campus.
Library: Union Institute & University Library. *Books:* 3.0 million (digital/electronic); *Serial titles:* 77,317 (digital/electronic); *Databases:* 171. Weekly public service hours: 50.

STUDENT LIFE
Housing options: college housing not available.
Campus security: 24-hour emergency response devices, late-night transport/escort service, security personnel on site during business and class hours.

COSTS
Costs (2017–18) ***Tuition:*** $12,240 full-time, $510 per credit hour part-time. Full-time tuition and fees vary according to course load and program. Part-time tuition and fees vary according to course load and program. ***Required fees:*** $176 full-time, $88 per term part-time. ***Payment plan:*** installment. ***Waivers:*** employees or children of employees.

APPLYING
Options: electronic application, deferred entrance.
Required: essay or personal statement, recommendation from program faculty. ***Required for some:*** high school transcript, 1 letter of recommendation. ***Recommended:*** interview.
Application deadlines: rolling (freshmen), rolling (transfers).
Notification: continuous (freshmen), continuous (transfers).

CONTACT
Union Institute & University, 440 East McMillan Street, Cincinnati, OH 45206-1925. *Phone:* 513-487-1173. *Toll-free phone:* 800-486-3116.

The University of Akron

Akron, Ohio

http://www.uakron.edu/

- **State-supported** university, founded 1870
- **Urban** 223-acre campus with easy access to Cleveland
- **Endowment** $177.1 million
- **Coed** 17,416 undergraduate students, 79% full-time, 46% women, 54% men
- **Moderately difficult** entrance level, 96% of applicants were admitted

UNDERGRAD STUDENTS

13,827 full-time, 3,589 part-time. Students come from 39 states and territories; 67 other countries; 5% are from out of state; 12% Black or African American, non-Hispanic/Latino; 3% Hispanic/Latino; 2% Asian, non-Hispanic/Latino; 0.2% American Indian or Alaska Native, non-Hispanic/Latino; 4% Two or more races, non-Hispanic/Latino; 2% Race/ethnicity unknown; 2% international; 4% transferred in; 17% live on campus.

Freshmen:

Admission: 13,911 applied, 13,343 admitted, 3,090 enrolled. ***Average high school GPA:*** 3.34. ***Test scores:*** SAT critical reading scores over 500: 56%; SAT math scores over 500: 62%; ACT scores over 18: 85%; SAT critical reading scores over 600: 23%; SAT math scores over 600: 26%; ACT scores over 24: 40%; SAT critical reading scores over 700: 5%; SAT math scores over 700: 5%; ACT scores over 30: 7%.

Retention: 73% of full-time freshmen returned.

FACULTY

Total: 1,589, 48% full-time.

Student/faculty ratio: 17:1.

ACADEMICS

Calendar: semesters. *Degrees:* certificates, associate, bachelor's, master's, doctoral, post-master's, and postbachelor's certificates.

Special study options: academic remediation for entering students, accelerated degree program, adult/continuing education programs, advanced placement credit, cooperative education, distance learning, double majors, English as a second language, external degree program, freshman honors college, honors programs, independent study, internships, part-time degree program, services for LD students, student-designed majors, study abroad, summer session for credit. ***ROTC:*** Army (b), Air Force (c).

Unusual degree programs: 3-2 business administration; engineering; medicine, polymer chemistry.

Computers: 3,150 computers/terminals and 16,000 ports are available on campus for general student use. Students can access the following: campus intranet, computer help desk, free student e-mail accounts, online (class) grades, online (class) registration, online (class) schedules, library laptops for student checkout. Campuswide network is available. 100% of college-owned or -operated housing units are wired for high-speed Internet access. Wireless service is available via entire campus.

Library: Bierce Library plus 2 others. *Books:* 1.3 million (physical), 449,783 (digital/electronic); *Serial titles:* 28,058 (physical), 80,870 (digital/electronic); *Databases:* 389. Study areas open 24 hours, 5-7 days a week; students can reserve study rooms.

STUDENT LIFE

Housing options: on-campus residence required for freshman year; coed, special housing for students with disabilities. Campus housing is university owned. Freshman applicants given priority for college housing.

Activities and organizations: drama/theater group, student-run newspaper, radio and television station, choral group, marching band, AK-Rowdies, Akron Animation Association, National Society of Leadership and Success, Golden Key International Honor Society, Alpha Phi Omega, national fraternities, national sororities.

Athletics Member NCAA. All Division I except football (Division I-A). ***Intercollegiate sports:*** basketball M(s)/W(s), cheerleading M/W, cross-country running M(s)/W(s), golf M(s)/W(s), riflery M/W(s), soccer M(s)/W(s), softball W(s), swimming and diving W(s), tennis W(s), track and field M(s)/W(s), volleyball W(s). ***Intramural sports:*** badminton M/W, basketball M/W, bowling M/W, cross-country running M/W, golf M/W, racquetball M/W, skiing (cross-country) M/W, skiing (downhill) M/W, soccer M/W, softball M/W, swimming and diving M/W, table tennis M/W, track and field M/W, volleyball W, wrestling M.

Campus security: 24-hour emergency response devices and patrols, student patrols, late-night transport/escort service, controlled dormitory access.

Student services: health clinic, personal/psychological counseling, women's center, legal services.

COSTS & FINANCIAL AID

Costs (2017–18) ***Tuition:*** state resident $8618 full-time, $359 per credit hour part-time; nonresident $17,149 full-time, $715 per credit hour part-time. Full-time tuition and fees vary according to course load, degree level, location, and program. Part-time tuition and fees vary according to course load, degree level, location, and program. ***Required fees:*** $1652 full-time. ***Room and board:*** $10,684; room only: $7020. Room and board charges vary according to board plan and housing facility. ***Payment plan:*** installment. ***Waivers:*** senior citizens and employees or children of employees.

Financial Aid Of all full-time matriculated undergraduates who enrolled in 2015, 12,920 applied for aid, 10,182 were judged to have need, 1,037 had their need fully met. 424 Federal Work-Study jobs (averaging $2608). 3,460 state and other part-time jobs (averaging $4384). In 2015, 1969 non-need-based awards were made. ***Average percent of need met:*** 51. ***Average financial aid package:*** $7517. ***Average need-based loan:*** $3886. ***Average need-based gift aid:*** $5068. ***Average non-need-based aid:*** $4675. ***Average indebtedness upon graduation:*** $32,372.

APPLYING

Standardized Tests *Required:* SAT or ACT (for admission).

Options: electronic application, early action, deferred entrance.

Application fee: $45.

Required: high school transcript. ***Required for some:*** essay or personal statement, 3 letters of recommendation, interview.

Application deadlines: 8/11 (freshmen), rolling (transfers), 11/1 (early action).

Notification: 9/15 (freshmen), continuous (transfers).

CONTACT

Ms. Kimberley Gentile, Senior Associate Director of Admissions Outreach, The University of Akron, Office of Admissions, Simmons Hall 109N. *Phone:* 330-972-6345. *Toll-free phone:* 800-655-4884. *E-mail:* gentile@uakron.edu.

The University of Akron Wayne College

Orrville, Ohio

http://www.wayne.uakron.edu/

CONTACT

Ms. Alicia Broadus, Student Services Counselor, The University of Akron Wayne College, Orrville, OH 44667. *Phone:* 800-221-8308 Ext. 8901. *Toll-free phone:* 800-221-8308. *Fax:* 330-684-8989. *E-mail:* wayneadmissions@uakron.edu.

University of Cincinnati

Cincinnati, Ohio

http://www.uc.edu/

- **State-supported** university, founded 1819
- **Urban** 137-acre campus with easy access to Cincinnati
- **Endowment** $1.2 billion
- **Coed** 25,860 undergraduate students, 84% full-time, 50% women, 50% men
- **Moderately difficult** entrance level, 76% of applicants were admitted

UNDERGRAD STUDENTS

21,598 full-time, 4,262 part-time. Students come from 51 states and territories; 112 other countries; 15% are from out of state; 7% Black or African American, non-Hispanic/Latino; 3% Hispanic/Latino; 3% Asian, non-Hispanic/Latino; 0.1% Native Hawaiian or other Pacific Islander, non-Hispanic/Latino; 0.2% American Indian or Alaska Native, non-Hispanic/Latino; 3% Two or more races, non-Hispanic/Latino; 4%

Race/ethnicity unknown; 4% international; 8% transferred in; 22% live on campus.

Freshmen:
Admission: 19,370 applied, 14,803 admitted, 5,011 enrolled. ***Average high school GPA:*** 3.63. ***Test scores:*** SAT critical reading scores over 500: 80%; SAT math scores over 500: 85%; SAT writing scores over 500: 73%; ACT scores over 18: 100%; SAT critical reading scores over 600: 38%; SAT math scores over 600: 49%; SAT writing scores over 600: 30%; ACT scores over 24: 70%; SAT critical reading scores over 700: 9%; SAT math scores over 700: 13%; SAT writing scores over 700: 6%; ACT scores over 30: 17%.
Retention: 88% of full-time freshmen returned.

ACADEMICS
Calendar: semesters. *Degrees:* certificates, associate, bachelor's, master's, doctoral, post-master's, and postbachelor's certificates.

Special study options: academic remediation for entering students, accelerated degree program, adult/continuing education programs, advanced placement credit, cooperative education, distance learning, double majors, English as a second language, honors programs, independent study, internships, off-campus study, services for LD students, study abroad, summer session for credit. ***ROTC:*** Army (b), Air Force (b).

Computers: 406 computers/terminals are available on campus for general student use. Students can access the following: campus intranet, computer help desk, free student e-mail accounts, online (class) grades, online (class) registration, online (class) schedules. Campuswide network is available. 100% of college-owned or -operated housing units are wired for high-speed Internet access. Wireless service is available via entire campus.
Library: Walter C. Langsam Library plus 13 others. *Books:* 3.0 million (physical), 1.5 million (digital/electronic); *Serial titles:* 1,608 (physical), 154,043 (digital/electronic). Weekly public service hours: 107; study areas open 24 hours, 5-7 days a week; students can reserve study rooms.

STUDENT LIFE
Housing options: on-campus residence required for freshman year; coed, men-only, women-only. Campus housing is university owned, leased by the school and is provided by a third party. Freshman campus housing is guaranteed.

Activities and organizations: drama/theater group, student-run newspaper, radio station, choral group, marching band, Serve Beyond Cincinnati, University of Cincinnati Mountaineering Club, Rally Cats, Engineers Without Borders, UC League of Legends, national fraternities, national sororities.

Athletics Member NCAA. All Division I except football (Division I-A). ***Intercollegiate sports:*** baseball M(s), basketball M(s)/W(s), cheerleading M/W, cross-country running M(s)/W(s), golf M(s)/W(s), lacrosse W(s), soccer M(s)/W(s), swimming and diving M(s)/W(s), tennis W(s), track and field M(s)/W(s), volleyball W(s). ***Intramural sports:*** badminton M(c)/W(c), baseball M(c), basketball M/W, bowling M(c)/W(c), crew M(c)/W(c), cross-country running M(c)/W(c), equestrian sports M(c)/W(c), fencing M(c)/W(c), football M/W, golf M(c)/W(c), gymnastics M(c)/W(c), ice hockey M(c), lacrosse M(c)/W(c), racquetball M(c)/W(c), riflery M(c)/W(c), rugby M(c)/W(c), soccer M(c)/W(c), softball W(c), swimming and diving M(c)/W(c), table tennis M(c)/W(c), tennis M(c)/W(c), track and field W(c), ultimate Frisbee M(c)/W(c), volleyball M(c)/W(c), water polo M(c)/W(c), wrestling M(c).

Campus security: 24-hour emergency response devices and patrols, student patrols, late-night transport/escort service, controlled dormitory access.

Student services: health clinic, personal/psychological counseling, women's center.

COSTS & FINANCIAL AID
Costs (2016–17) ***Tuition:*** state resident $9322 full-time, $389 per credit hour part-time; nonresident $24,656 full-time, $1028 per credit hour part-time. Full-time tuition and fees vary according to course load, location, program, and reciprocity agreements. Part-time tuition and fees vary according to course load, location, program, and reciprocity agreements. ***Required fees:*** $1678 full-time, $70 per credit hour part-time. ***Room and board:*** $10,928; room only: $6558. Room and board charges vary according to board plan and housing facility. ***Payment plan:*** installment. ***Waivers:*** employees or children of employees.

Financial Aid Of all full-time matriculated undergraduates who enrolled in 2016, 14,457 applied for aid, 11,197 were judged to have need, 505 had their need fully met. 1,335 Federal Work-Study jobs (averaging $3045). In 2016, 3514 non-need-based awards were made. ***Average percent of need met:*** 44. ***Average financial aid package:*** $8489. ***Average need-based loan:*** $4424. ***Average need-based gift aid:*** $6192. ***Average non-need-based aid:*** $4847. ***Average indebtedness upon graduation:*** $28,970.

APPLYING
Standardized Tests *Required:* SAT or ACT (for admission).

Options: electronic application, early action, deferred entrance.

Application fee: $50.

Required: essay or personal statement, high school transcript. ***Required for some:*** 1 letter of recommendation, audition for performing arts majors.

Application deadlines: 3/1 (freshmen), 7/1 (transfers), 12/1 (early action).

Notification: continuous until 5/1 (freshmen), continuous (transfers), rolling (early action).

CONTACT
Dr. Thomas Canepa, Associate Vice President, Admissions, University of Cincinnati, Office of Admissions, PO Box210091, Cincinnati, OH 45221-0091. *Phone:* 513-556-1100. *Fax:* 513-556-1105.
E-mail: admissions@uc.edu.

University of Cincinnati Blue Ash College

Cincinnati, Ohio

http://www.ucblueash.edu/

- **State-supported** primarily 2-year, founded 1967, part of Ohio Department of Higher Education
- **Suburban** 120-acre campus with easy access to Cincinnati
- **Endowment** $457,000
- **Coed** 5,065 undergraduate students, 64% full-time, 58% women, 42% men
- **Noncompetitive** entrance level

UNDERGRAD STUDENTS
3,241 full-time, 1,824 part-time. Students come from 9 states and territories; 12 other countries; 3% are from out of state; 21% Black or African American, non-Hispanic/Latino; 3% Hispanic/Latino; 3% Asian, non-Hispanic/Latino; 0.1% Native Hawaiian or other Pacific Islander, non-Hispanic/Latino; 0.3% American Indian or Alaska Native, non-Hispanic/Latino; 3% Two or more races, non-Hispanic/Latino; 7% Race/ethnicity unknown; 2% international; 11% transferred in.

Freshmen:
Admission: 1,301 enrolled. ***Average high school GPA:*** 2.73.
Retention: 64% of full-time freshmen returned.

FACULTY
Total: 339, 50% full-time.

Student/faculty ratio: 16:1.

ACADEMICS
Calendar: semesters. *Degrees:* certificates, associate, bachelor's, and postbachelor's certificates.

Special study options: academic remediation for entering students, adult/continuing education programs, advanced placement credit, distance learning, double majors, off-campus study, part-time degree program, services for LD students, study abroad, summer session for credit. ***ROTC:*** Army (c), Air Force (c).

Computers: 150 computers/terminals are available on campus for general student use. Students can access the following: campus intranet, computer help desk, free student e-mail accounts, online (class) grades, online (class) registration, online (class) schedules. Campuswide network is available. Wireless service is available via entire campus.
Library: UC Blue Ash College Library. *Books:* 19,690 (physical). Weekly public service hours: 50; students can reserve study rooms.

STUDENT LIFE
Housing options: college housing not available.

Campus security: 24-hour emergency response devices and patrols, student patrols, late-night transport/escort service.

Student services: personal/psychological counseling.

COSTS & FINANCIAL AID

Costs (2017–18) ***Tuition:*** state resident $6010 full-time, $251 per credit hour part-time; nonresident $14,808 full-time, $617 per credit hour part-time. Full-time tuition and fees vary according to course load, degree level, location, program, and reciprocity agreements. Part-time tuition and fees vary according to course load, degree level, location, and reciprocity agreements. ***Required fees:*** $736 full-time. ***Payment plan:*** installment. ***Waivers:*** senior citizens and employees or children of employees.

Financial Aid Of all full-time matriculated undergraduates who enrolled in 2015, 285 Federal Work-Study jobs (averaging $2903).

APPLYING

Options: electronic application, deferred entrance.

Application fee: $50.

Required: high school transcript.

Application deadlines: rolling (freshmen), rolling (transfers).

Notification: continuous (freshmen), continuous (transfers).

CONTACT

University of Cincinnati Blue Ash College, 9555 Plainfield Road, Cincinnati, OH 45236-1007. *Phone:* 513-745-5700.

University of Cincinnati Clermont College

Batavia, Ohio

http://www.ucclermont.edu/

- **State-supported** primarily 2-year, founded 1972, part of University of Cincinnati System
- **Rural** 91-acre campus with easy access to Cincinnati
- **Coed** 2,883 undergraduate students, 55% full-time, 57% women, 43% men
- **Noncompetitive** entrance level, 48% of applicants were admitted

UNDERGRAD STUDENTS

1,595 full-time, 1,287 part-time. 4% are from out of state; 2% Black or African American, non-Hispanic/Latino; 3% Hispanic/Latino; 1% Asian, non-Hispanic/Latino; 0.1% Native Hawaiian or other Pacific Islander, non-Hispanic/Latino; 0.2% American Indian or Alaska Native, non-Hispanic/Latino; 2% Two or more races, non-Hispanic/Latino; 9% Race/ethnicity unknown; 0.3% international.

Freshmen:

Admission: 1,255 applied, 606 admitted, 606 enrolled. ***Average high school GPA:*** 2.93.

Retention: 61% of full-time freshmen returned.

FACULTY

Total: 293, 32% full-time.

Student/faculty ratio: 13:1.

ACADEMICS

Calendar: semesters. *Degrees:* certificates, associate, bachelor's, and postbachelor's certificates.

Special study options: academic remediation for entering students, adult/continuing education programs, advanced placement credit, cooperative education, distance learning, double majors, independent study, internships, off-campus study, part-time degree program, services for LD students, student-designed majors, study abroad, summer session for credit. ***ROTC:*** Army (c).

Computers: Students can access the following: campus intranet, computer help desk, free student e-mail accounts, online (class) grades, online (class) registration, online (class) schedules. Campuswide network is available. Wireless service is available via entire campus.

Library: UC Clermont College Library. Students can reserve study rooms.

STUDENT LIFE

Housing options: college housing not available.

Activities and organizations: student-run newspaper, Active Minds, PACE (Professionalism Academics Character Experiences), Phi Theta Kappa, Association of Paralegal Students, Cheerleading.

Athletics Member USCAA. ***Intercollegiate sports:*** baseball M, basketball M/W, cheerleading W, soccer M/W, softball W, volleyball W.

Campus security: 24-hour emergency response devices and patrols.

Student services: personal/psychological counseling.

COSTS

Costs (2016–17) ***Tuition:*** state resident $5316 full-time, $222 per credit part-time; nonresident $12,548 full-time, $523 per credit part-time. Full-time tuition and fees vary according to course level, degree level, program, and reciprocity agreements. Part-time tuition and fees vary according to course level, degree level, program, and reciprocity agreements. ***Payment plan:*** installment. ***Waivers:*** senior citizens and employees or children of employees.

APPLYING

Options: electronic application, deferred entrance.

Application fee: $50.

Required: high school transcript.

Application deadlines: 7/11 (freshmen), 7/11 (transfers).

Notification: continuous (freshmen), continuous (transfers).

CONTACT

Mrs. Jamie Adkins, University Services Associate, University of Cincinnati Clermont College, 4200 Clermont College Drive, Batavia, OH 45103. *Phone:* 513-732-5294. *Toll-free phone:* 866-446-2822. *Fax:* 513-732-5303. *E-mail:* jamie.adkins@uc.edu.

University of Dayton

Dayton, Ohio

http://www.udayton.edu/

- **Independent Roman Catholic** university, founded 1850
- **Suburban** 388-acre campus with easy access to Cincinnati
- **Endowment** $500.4 million
- **Coed** 8,665 undergraduate students, 95% full-time, 47% women, 53% men
- **Moderately difficult** entrance level, 58% of applicants were admitted

UNDERGRAD STUDENTS

8,205 full-time, 460 part-time. Students come from 50 states and territories; 39 other countries; 49% are from out of state; 3% Black or African American, non-Hispanic/Latino; 3% Hispanic/Latino; 1% Asian, non-Hispanic/Latino; 0.1% Native Hawaiian or other Pacific Islander, non-Hispanic/Latino; 0.1% American Indian or Alaska Native, non-Hispanic/Latino; 2% Two or more races, non-Hispanic/Latino; 2% Race/ethnicity unknown; 11% international; 2% transferred in; 72% live on campus.

Freshmen:

Admission: 16,968 applied, 9,760 admitted, 2,143 enrolled. ***Average high school GPA:*** 3.64. ***Test scores:*** SAT critical reading scores over 500: 84%; SAT math scores over 500: 84%; SAT writing scores over 500: 81%; ACT scores over 18: 100%; SAT critical reading scores over 600: 32%; SAT math scores over 600: 39%; SAT writing scores over 600: 33%; ACT scores over 24: 80%; SAT critical reading scores over 700: 6%; SAT math scores over 700: 6%; SAT writing scores over 700: 3%; ACT scores over 30: 24%.

Retention: 91% of full-time freshmen returned.

FACULTY

Total: 1,017, 53% full-time, 46% with terminal degrees.

Student/faculty ratio: 16:1.

ACADEMICS

Calendar: semesters plus 2 6-week summer terms. *Degrees:* bachelor's, master's, doctoral, post-master's, and postbachelor's certificates.

Special study options: academic remediation for entering students, accelerated degree program, adult/continuing education programs, advanced placement credit, cooperative education, distance learning, double majors, English as a second language, honors programs, independent study, internships, off-campus study, part-time degree program, services for LD students, student-designed majors, study abroad, summer session for credit. ***ROTC:*** Army (b), Air Force (c).

Unusual degree programs: 3-2 business administration; engineering.

Computers: 7,675 computers/terminals and 19,337 ports are available on campus for general student use. Students can access the following: campus intranet, computer help desk, free student e-mail accounts, online (class) grades, online (class) registration, online (class) schedules, admission/enrollment status, virtual orientation, online courses, assistive technology, learning management system, multimedia labs, payment, cyber cafes, downloadable software and training. Campuswide network is available. 100% of college-owned or -operated housing units are wired for high-speed Internet access. Wireless service is available via entire campus.

Library: Roesch Library plus 3 others. *Books:* 671,817 (physical), 1.3 million (digital/electronic); *Databases:* 301. Weekly public service hours: 131; students can reserve study rooms.

STUDENT LIFE

Housing options: on-campus residence required through sophomore year; coed, men-only, women-only, special housing for students with disabilities. Campus housing is university owned. Freshman campus housing is guaranteed.

Activities and organizations: drama/theater group, student-run newspaper, radio and television station, choral group, marching band, Student Government Association, marching band, Red Scare (basketball student cheering section), Campus Connection, Habitat for Humanity, national fraternities, national sororities.

Athletics Member NCAA. All Division I except football (Division I-AA). ***Intercollegiate sports:*** baseball M(s), basketball M(s)/W(s), cheerleading M/W, crew W, cross-country running M(s)/W(s), golf M(s)/W, soccer M(s)/W(s), softball W(s), tennis M(s)/W(s), track and field W(s), volleyball W(s). ***Intramural sports:*** baseball M(c), basketball M(c)/W(c), bowling M/W, crew M(c), cross-country running M(c)/W(c), field hockey M(c)/W(c), football M/W, golf M(c)/W(c), gymnastics M(c)/W(c), ice hockey M(c), lacrosse M(c)/W(c), racquetball M(c)/W(c), rugby M(c)/W(c), soccer M(c)/W(c), softball M/W(c), swimming and diving M(c)/W(c), tennis M(c)/W(c), ultimate Frisbee M(c)/W(c), volleyball M(c)/W(c), water polo M(c)/W(c), wrestling M(c)/W(c).

Campus security: 24-hour emergency response devices and patrols, student patrols, late-night transport/escort service, controlled dormitory access, approximately 1000 recording video cameras, automated external defibrillators in high density residential facilities and other areas.

Student services: health clinic, personal/psychological counseling, women's center.

COSTS & FINANCIAL AID

Costs (2016–17) ***Comprehensive fee:*** $53,620 includes full-time tuition ($40,940) and room and board ($12,680). Full-time tuition and fees vary according to degree level. Part-time tuition: $1360 per credit hour. Part-time tuition and fees vary according to course load and degree level. ***College room only:*** $7600. Room and board charges vary according to board plan and housing facility. ***Payment plans:*** tuition prepayment, installment, deferred payment. ***Waivers:*** adult students, senior citizens, and employees or children of employees.

Financial Aid Of all full-time matriculated undergraduates who enrolled in 2015, 5,199 applied for aid, 3,670 were judged to have need, 1,385 had their need fully met. In 2015, 2839 non-need-based awards were made. ***Average percent of need met:*** 83. ***Average financial aid package:*** $26,045. ***Average need-based loan:*** $3032. ***Average need-based gift aid:*** $23,166. ***Average non-need-based aid:*** $15,516. ***Average indebtedness upon graduation:*** $35,740.

APPLYING

Standardized Tests *Required:* SAT or ACT (for admission).

Options: electronic application, early action, deferred entrance.

Required: essay or personal statement, high school transcript, 1 letter of recommendation. ***Required for some:*** audition for music, music therapy, music education programs.

Application deadlines: 6/15 (transfers), 12/15 (early action).

Notification: continuous (transfers), 2/15 (early action).

CONTACT

Mr. Robert Durkle, Associate Vice President of Enrollment Management, University of Dayton, 300 College Park, Dayton, OH 45469-1310. *Phone:* 937-229-4411. *Toll-free phone:* 800-837-7433. *Fax:* 937-229-4729. *E-mail:* admission@udayton.edu.

★ The University of Findlay

Findlay, Ohio

http://www.findlay.edu/

- **Independent** comprehensive, founded 1882, affiliated with Church of God
- **Small-town** 390-acre campus with easy access to Toledo
- **Endowment** $32.8 million
- **Coed** 3,661 undergraduate students, 70% full-time, 64% women, 36% men
- **Moderately difficult** entrance level, 73% of applicants were admitted

UNDERGRAD STUDENTS

2,570 full-time, 1,091 part-time. Students come from 45 states and territories; 27 other countries; 19% are from out of state; 3% Black or African American, non-Hispanic/Latino; 2% Hispanic/Latino; 1% Asian, non-Hispanic/Latino; 0.1% American Indian or Alaska Native, non-Hispanic/Latino; 2% Two or more races, non-Hispanic/Latino; 1% Race/ethnicity unknown; 6% international; 3% transferred in; 30% live on campus.

Freshmen:

Admission: 2,976 applied, 2,172 admitted, 544 enrolled. ***Average high school GPA:*** 3.53. ***Test scores:*** SAT critical reading scores over 500: 57%; SAT math scores over 500: 65%; SAT writing scores over 500: 48%; ACT scores over 18: 97%; SAT critical reading scores over 600: 16%; SAT math scores over 600: 19%; SAT writing scores over 600: 16%; ACT scores over 24: 53%; SAT critical reading scores over 700: 1%; SAT math scores over 700: 3%; ACT scores over 30: 7%.

Retention: 80% of full-time freshmen returned.

FACULTY

Total: 274, 79% full-time, 60% with terminal degrees.

Student/faculty ratio: 16:1.

ACADEMICS

Calendar: semesters. *Degrees:* certificates, associate, bachelor's, master's, and doctoral.

Special study options: academic remediation for entering students, accelerated degree program, adult/continuing education programs, advanced placement credit, cooperative education, distance learning, double majors, English as a second language, honors programs, independent study, internships, off-campus study, part-time degree program, services for LD students, student-designed majors, study abroad, summer session for credit. ***ROTC:*** Army (c), Air Force (c).

Unusual degree programs: 3-2 athletic training, occupational therapy.

Computers: 151 computers/terminals are available on campus for general student use. Students can access the following: campus intranet, computer help desk, free student e-mail accounts, online (class) grades, online (class) registration, online (class) schedules. Campuswide network is available. 100% of college-owned or -operated housing units are wired for high-speed Internet access. Wireless service is available via entire campus.

Library: Shafer Library plus 4 others. *Books:* 98,669 (physical), 285,706 (digital/electronic); *Serial titles:* 361 (physical), 72,953 (digital/electronic); *Databases:* 173. Weekly public service hours: 94; study areas open 24 hours, 5-7 days a week.

STUDENT LIFE

Housing options: on-campus residence required through sophomore year; coed, men-only, women-only. Campus housing is university owned. Freshman campus housing is guaranteed.

Activities and organizations: drama/theater group, student-run newspaper, radio and television station, choral group, marching band, Habitat for Humanity, Pre-Vet Club, Horse Club, Stride, Black Student Union, national fraternities, national sororities.

Athletics Member NCAA. All Division II. ***Intercollegiate sports:*** baseball M(s), basketball M(s)/W(s), cross-country running M(s)/W(s), equestrian sports M(c)/W(c), football M(s), golf M(s)/W(s), lacrosse M(c)/W(s), rugby W(c), soccer M(s)/W(s), softball W(s), swimming and diving M(s)/W(s), tennis M(s)/W(s), track and field M(s)/W(s), volleyball

W(s), wrestling M(s). ***Intramural sports:*** basketball M/W, bowling M/W, golf M/W, soccer M/W, volleyball M/W.

Campus security: 24-hour emergency response devices and patrols, late-night transport/escort service, parking lot and building cameras (over 500), campus police.

Student services: health clinic, personal/psychological counseling, women's center.

COSTS & FINANCIAL AID

Costs (2017–18) ***Comprehensive fee:*** $43,040 includes full-time tuition ($32,330), mandatory fees ($990), and room and board ($9720). Full-time tuition and fees vary according to program. Part-time tuition: $715 per semester hour. Part-time tuition and fees vary according to course load and program. ***Required fees:*** $430 per term part-time. ***College room only:*** $4850. Room and board charges vary according to board plan and housing facility. ***Payment plan:*** installment. ***Waivers:*** senior citizens and employees or children of employees.

Financial Aid Of all full-time matriculated undergraduates who enrolled in 2015, 2,205 applied for aid, 1,764 were judged to have need, 333 had their need fully met. 1,284 Federal Work-Study jobs (averaging $1689). In 2015, 982 non-need-based awards were made. ***Average percent of need met:*** 73. ***Average financial aid package:*** $23,792. ***Average need-based loan:*** $4562. ***Average need-based gift aid:*** $19,065. ***Average non-need-based aid:*** $17,062. ***Average indebtedness upon graduation:*** $36,249. ***Financial aid deadline:*** 9/1.

APPLYING

Standardized Tests *Required:* SAT or ACT (for admission).

Options: electronic application, deferred entrance.

Required: essay or personal statement, high school transcript, minimum 2.5 GPA. ***Required for some:*** 1 letter of recommendation. ***Recommended:*** interview.

Application deadlines: rolling (freshmen), rolling (transfers).

Notification: continuous (freshmen), continuous (transfers).

CONTACT

Ms. Katie Ashcraft, Assistant Director of Undergraduate Admissions, The University of Findlay, 1000 North Main Street, Findlay, OH 45840-3653. *Phone:* 419-434-4707. *Toll-free phone:* 800-548-0932. *Fax:* 419-434-4898. *E-mail:* ashcraft@findlay.edu.

University of Mount Union

Alliance, Ohio

http://www.mountunion.edu/

- **Independent United Methodist** comprehensive, founded 1846
- **Suburban** 123-acre campus with easy access to Cleveland
- **Endowment** $131.9 million
- **Coed** 2,140 undergraduate students, 99% full-time, 48% women, 52% men
- **Moderately difficult** entrance level, 77% of applicants were admitted

UNDERGRAD STUDENTS

2,113 full-time, 27 part-time. Students come from 29 states and territories; 12 other countries; 18% are from out of state; 7% Black or African American, non-Hispanic/Latino; 3% Hispanic/Latino; 0.8% Asian, non-Hispanic/Latino; 0.1% Native Hawaiian or other Pacific Islander, non-Hispanic/Latino; 0.7% American Indian or Alaska Native, non-Hispanic/Latino; 3% Two or more races, non-Hispanic/Latino; 6% Race/ethnicity unknown; 0.4% international; 2% transferred in; 74% live on campus.

Freshmen:

Admission: 2,525 applied, 1,944 admitted, 642 enrolled. ***Average high school GPA:*** 3.44. ***Test scores:*** SAT critical reading scores over 500: 46%; SAT math scores over 500: 50%; SAT writing scores over 500: 31%; ACT scores over 18: 95%; SAT critical reading scores over 600: 12%; SAT math scores over 600: 15%; SAT writing scores over 600: 7%; ACT scores over 24: 46%; SAT critical reading scores over 700: 1%; ACT scores over 30: 4%.

Retention: 79% of full-time freshmen returned.

FACULTY

Total: 240, 56% full-time, 56% with terminal degrees.

Student/faculty ratio: 13:1.

ACADEMICS

Calendar: semesters. *Degrees:* bachelor's, master's, and doctoral.

Special study options: accelerated degree program, adult/continuing education programs, advanced placement credit, cooperative education, distance learning, double majors, English as a second language, honors programs, independent study, internships, off-campus study, part-time degree program, services for LD students, student-designed majors, study abroad, summer session for credit. ***ROTC:*** Army (b), Air Force (c).

Computers: 265 computers/terminals and 6,000 ports are available on campus for general student use. Students can access the following: campus intranet, computer help desk, free student e-mail accounts, online (class) grades, online (class) registration, online (class) schedules. Campuswide network is available. 100% of college-owned or -operated housing units are wired for high-speed Internet access. Wireless service is available via entire campus.

Library: University of Mount Union Library plus 1 other. Study areas open 24 hours, 5-7 days a week; students can reserve study rooms.

STUDENT LIFE

Housing options: on-campus residence required through sophomore year; coed, men-only, women-only, special housing for students with disabilities. Campus housing is university owned. Freshman campus housing is guaranteed.

Activities and organizations: drama/theater group, student-run newspaper, radio and television station, choral group, marching band, Alpha Phi Omega, Student Senate, FCA Fellowship of Christian Athletes, Black Student Union, Raider Programming Board, national fraternities, national sororities.

Athletics Member NCAA. All Division III. ***Intercollegiate sports:*** baseball M, basketball M/W, cheerleading W, cross-country running M/W, football M, golf M/W, lacrosse M/W, soccer M/W, softball W, swimming and diving M/W, tennis M/W, track and field M/W, volleyball W, wrestling M. ***Intramural sports:*** archery M/W, badminton M/W, basketball M/W, bowling M/W, football M, golf M/W, gymnastics M/W, racquetball M/W, soccer M/W, softball M/W, swimming and diving M/W, tennis M/W, track and field M/W, volleyball M/W, weight lifting M/W.

Campus security: 24-hour emergency response devices and patrols, late-night transport/escort service, controlled dormitory access, 24-hour locked residence hall entrances, outside phones.

Student services: health clinic, personal/psychological counseling.

COSTS & FINANCIAL AID

Costs (2017–18) ***Comprehensive fee:*** $39,990 includes full-time tuition ($29,560), mandatory fees ($330), and room and board ($10,100). Full-time tuition and fees vary according to course load and degree level. Part-time tuition: $1260 per credit hour. Part-time tuition and fees vary according to course load. ***Room and board:*** Room and board charges vary according to board plan and housing facility. ***Payment plans:*** tuition prepayment, installment. ***Waivers:*** children of alumni, senior citizens, and employees or children of employees.

Financial Aid Of all full-time matriculated undergraduates who enrolled in 2015, 1,778 applied for aid, 1,602 were judged to have need, 224 had their need fully met. 1,257 Federal Work-Study jobs (averaging $1074). 328 state and other part-time jobs (averaging $1487). In 2015, 367 non-need-based awards were made. ***Average percent of need met:*** 78. ***Average financial aid package:*** $22,577. ***Average need-based loan:*** $5877. ***Average need-based gift aid:*** $16,946. ***Average non-need-based aid:*** $12,016. ***Average indebtedness upon graduation:*** $32,680.

APPLYING

Standardized Tests *Required:* SAT or ACT (for admission).

Options: electronic application, early admission, deferred entrance.

Required: essay or personal statement, high school transcript, minimum 2.0 GPA, 1 letter of recommendation. ***Recommended:*** interview.

Application deadlines: rolling (freshmen), rolling (transfers).

Notification: continuous (freshmen), continuous (transfers).

CONTACT

Ms. Jess Canavan, Director of Admissions, University of Mount Union, 1972 Clark Avenue, Alliance, OH 44601. *Phone:* 330-823-2590. *Toll-free phone:* 800-334-6682. *Fax:* 330-823-5097. *E-mail:* admission@mountunion.edu.

University of Northwestern Ohio

Lima, Ohio

http://www.unoh.edu/

- **Independent** comprehensive, founded 1920
- **Small-town** 200-acre campus with easy access to Dayton, Toledo
- **Coed** 3,848 undergraduate students
- **Noncompetitive** entrance level

UNDERGRAD STUDENTS

Students come from 42 states and territories; 30 other countries; 51% are from out of state; 33% live on campus.

Freshmen:

Admission: 4,900 applied. ***Average high school GPA:*** 2.86.

FACULTY

Total: 127, 73% full-time, 3% with terminal degrees.

Student/faculty ratio: 20:1.

ACADEMICS

Calendar: quarters. *Degrees:* certificates, diplomas, associate, bachelor's, and master's.

Special study options: academic remediation for entering students, accelerated degree program, adult/continuing education programs, advanced placement credit, cooperative education, distance learning, double majors, internships, part-time degree program, services for LD students, summer session for credit. ***ROTC:*** Army (b).

Computers: 200 computers/terminals are available on campus for general student use. Students can access the following: campus intranet, computer help desk, free student e-mail accounts, online (class) grades, online (class) registration, online (class) schedules. Campuswide network is available. Wireless service is available via classrooms, computer centers, computer labs, learning centers, libraries, student centers.

Library: Dr. Cheryl Mueller Library. Students can reserve study rooms.

STUDENT LIFE

Housing options: men-only, women-only, special housing for students with disabilities. Campus housing is university owned and leased by the school. Freshman campus housing is guaranteed.

Activities and organizations: Business Professionals of America, ROTORAC, American Marketing Association, Optimist Club, Drag Club.

Athletics Member NAIA. ***Intercollegiate sports:*** baseball M(s), basketball M(s)/W(s), bowling M(s)/W(s), cheerleading W(s), golf M(s)/W(s), soccer M(s)/W(s), softball W(s), tennis M(s)/W(s), volleyball W(s). ***Intramural sports:*** basketball M/W, bowling M/W, sand volleyball M/W, soccer M/W, volleyball M/W.

Campus security: 24-hour emergency response devices and patrols, late-night transport/escort service.

Student services: personal/psychological counseling.

COSTS & FINANCIAL AID

Costs (2017–18) ***Tuition:*** $9900 full-time. Full-time tuition and fees vary according to class time, course load, and program. Part-time tuition and fees vary according to class time, course load, and program. ***Required fees:*** $250 full-time, $250 per term part-time. ***Room only:*** $2700. Room and board charges vary according to board plan and housing facility. ***Payment plan:*** installment. ***Waivers:*** employees or children of employees.

Financial Aid Of all full-time matriculated undergraduates who enrolled in 2015, 40 Federal Work-Study jobs (averaging $2000).

APPLYING

Options: electronic application, early admission, deferred entrance.

Application fee: $20.

Required: high school transcript.

Application deadlines: rolling (freshmen), rolling (transfers).

CONTACT

Mr. Don Lowden, Director of Admissions, University of Northwestern Ohio, 1441 North Cable Road, Lima, OH 45805-1498. *Phone:* 419-998-3120. *E-mail:* dmlowden@unoh.edu.

University of Rio Grande

Rio Grande, Ohio

http://www.rio.edu/

- **Independent** comprehensive, founded 1876
- **Rural** 170-acre campus
- **Endowment** $23.6 million
- **Coed**
- **Noncompetitive** entrance level

FACULTY

Student/faculty ratio: 19:1.

ACADEMICS

Calendar: semesters. *Degrees:* certificates, associate, bachelor's, and master's.

Library: Jeanette Albiez Davis Library.

STUDENT LIFE

Housing options: coed, men-only, women-only. Campus housing is university owned.

Activities and organizations: drama/theater group, student-run newspaper, radio and television station, choral group, Student Government, Honoraries, Bible studies, ENACTA, national fraternities, national sororities.

Athletics Member NAIA.

Campus security: 24-hour emergency response devices and patrols, late-night transport/escort service.

Student services: health clinic, personal/psychological counseling.

FINANCIAL AID

Financial Aid Of all full-time matriculated undergraduates who enrolled in 2014, 1,035 applied for aid, 1,035 were judged to have need, 736 had their need fully met. In 2014, 17 non-need-based awards were made. ***Average percent of need met:*** 87. ***Average financial aid package:*** $7030. ***Average need-based loan:*** $3191. ***Average need-based gift aid:*** $3778. ***Average non-need-based aid:*** $11,067. ***Average indebtedness upon graduation:*** $28,617.

APPLYING

Standardized Tests *Recommended:* ACT (for admission).

Options: electronic application.

Application fee: $25.

Required: high school transcript, medical history.

CONTACT

Kristie Russell, Assistant Director of Admissions, University of Rio Grande, PO Box 500, Rio Grande, OH 45674. *Phone:* 740-245-7208. *Toll-free phone:* 800-282-7201. *Fax:* 740-245-7260. *E-mail:* admissions@rio.edu.

The University of Toledo

Toledo, Ohio

http://www.utoledo.edu/

- **State-supported** university, founded 1872
- **Urban** 858-acre campus with easy access to Detroit
- **Endowment** $282.6 million
- **Coed** 16,064 undergraduate students, 79% full-time, 48% women, 52% men
- **Noncompetitive** entrance level, 93% of applicants were admitted

UNDERGRAD STUDENTS

12,714 full-time, 3,350 part-time. Students come from 47 states and territories; 67 other countries; 20% are from out of state; 12% Black or African American, non-Hispanic/Latino; 5% Hispanic/Latino; 2% Asian, non-Hispanic/Latino; 0.1% Native Hawaiian or other Pacific Islander, non-Hispanic/Latino; 0.2% American Indian or Alaska Native, non-Hispanic/Latino; 3% Two or more races, non-Hispanic/Latino; 3% Race/ethnicity unknown; 6% international; 7% transferred in; 19% live on campus.

Freshmen:

Admission: 10,678 applied, 9,952 admitted, 3,341 enrolled. ***Average high school GPA:*** 3.32. ***Test scores:*** ACT scores over 18: 88%; ACT scores over 24: 43%; ACT scores over 30: 7%.

Retention: 72% of full-time freshmen returned.

FACULTY
Total: 1,068, 73% full-time, 68% with terminal degrees.
Student/faculty ratio: 20:1.

ACADEMICS
Calendar: semesters. *Degrees:* certificates, associate, bachelor's, master's, doctoral, post-master's, and postbachelor's certificates.
Special study options: academic remediation for entering students, accelerated degree program, adult/continuing education programs, advanced placement credit, cooperative education, distance learning, double majors, English as a second language, freshman honors college, honors programs, independent study, internships, off-campus study, part-time degree program, services for LD students, student-designed majors, study abroad, summer session for credit. ***ROTC:*** Army (b), Air Force (c).
Unusual degree programs: 3-2 environmental sciences/public health.
Computers: 5,000 computers/terminals and 10,000 ports are available on campus for general student use. Students can access the following: campus intranet, computer help desk, free student e-mail accounts, online (class) grades, online (class) registration, online (class) schedules, online transcripts, student account. Campuswide network is available. 100% of college-owned or -operated housing units are wired for high-speed Internet access. Wireless service is available via entire campus.
Library: Carlson Library plus 3 others.

STUDENT LIFE
Housing options: on-campus residence required for freshman year; coed, special housing for students with disabilities. Campus housing is university owned. Freshman campus housing is guaranteed.
Activities and organizations: drama/theater group, student-run newspaper, radio and television station, choral group, marching band, Student Government, University YMCA, Newman Club, International Student Association, Campus Activities and Programming, national fraternities, national sororities.
Athletics Member NCAA. All Division I except football (Division I-A). ***Intercollegiate sports:*** baseball M(s), basketball M(s)/W(s), cross-country running M(s)/W(s), golf M(s)/W(s), soccer W(s), softball W(s), swimming and diving W(s), tennis M(s)/W(s), track and field W(s), volleyball W(s). ***Intramural sports:*** badminton M/W, basketball M/W, bowling M/W, cheerleading W, crew M(c)/W(c), fencing M(c)/W(c), football M/W, golf M/W, lacrosse M/W, racquetball M/W, sailing M(c)/W(c), skiing (cross-country) M(c)/W(c), skiing (downhill) M(c)/W(c), soccer M(c)/W(c), softball M/W, swimming and diving M/W, table tennis M/W, tennis M/W, track and field M/W, volleyball M/W, water polo M/W, weight lifting M/W, wrestling M.
Campus security: 24-hour emergency response devices and patrols, student patrols, late-night transport/escort service, controlled dormitory access, bicycle patrols by security staff, crime prevention officer.
Student services: health clinic, personal/psychological counseling, women's center, legal services.

COSTS & FINANCIAL AID
Costs (2016–17) ***Tuition:*** state resident $8052 full-time, $335 per credit hour part-time; nonresident $17,390 full-time, $725 per credit hour part-time. Full-time tuition and fees vary according to course load, program, reciprocity agreements, and student level. Part-time tuition and fees vary according to course load, program, reciprocity agreements, and student level. ***Required fees:*** $1508 full-time, $61 per credit hour part-time, $7 per term part-time. ***Room and board:*** $11,508; room only: $7864. Room and board charges vary according to board plan and housing facility. ***Payment plan:*** installment. ***Waivers:*** children of alumni and employees or children of employees.
Financial Aid Of all full-time matriculated undergraduates who enrolled in 2015, 10,380 applied for aid, 8,411 were judged to have need, 1,228 had their need fully met. 366 Federal Work-Study jobs (averaging $3435). In 2015, 2897 non-need-based awards were made. ***Average percent of need met:*** 59. ***Average financial aid package:*** $11,211. ***Average need-based loan:*** $4114. ***Average need-based gift aid:*** $8936. ***Average non-need-based aid:*** $6550. ***Average indebtedness upon graduation:*** $27,928.

APPLYING
Standardized Tests *Required:* SAT or ACT (for admission).
Options: electronic application, deferred entrance.
Application fee: $40.
Required: high school transcript. ***Required for some:*** minimum 2.0 GPA, core high school curriculum.
Application deadlines: rolling (freshmen), rolling (out-of-state freshmen), rolling (transfers).
Notification: continuous (freshmen), continuous (out-of-state freshmen), continuous (transfers).

CONTACT
William Pierce, Undergraduate Admissions Counselor, The University of Toledo, 2801 West Bancroft, Toledo, OH 43606-3390. *Phone:* 419-530-5445. *Toll-free phone:* 800-5TOLEDO. *Fax:* 419-530-5713. *E-mail:* william.pierce@utoledo.edu.

Urbana University

Urbana, Ohio

http://www.urbana.edu/

CONTACT
Mr. Donnel W. Wiggins, Director of Admissions, Urbana University, 579 College Way, Urbana, OH 43078. *Toll-free phone:* 800-7-URBANA. *E-mail:* admiss@urbana.edu.

Ursuline College

Pepper Pike, Ohio

http://www.ursuline.edu/

- **Independent Roman Catholic** comprehensive, founded 1871
- **Suburban** 62-acre campus with easy access to Cleveland
- **Endowment** $42.5 million
- **Coed, primarily women**
- **Minimally difficult** entrance level

FACULTY
Student/faculty ratio: 7:1.

ACADEMICS
Calendar: semesters. *Degrees:* certificates, bachelor's, master's, doctoral, post-master's, and postbachelor's certificates (applications from men are also accepted).
Library: Ralph M. Besse Library. *Books:* 134,397 (physical), 110,963 (digital/electronic); *Serial titles:* 880 (physical), 49,163 (digital/electronic); *Databases:* 161. Weekly public service hours: 91; students can reserve study rooms.

STUDENT LIFE
Housing options: coed, women-only, special housing for students with disabilities. Campus housing is university owned.
Activities and organizations: drama/theater group, Programming Board, Student Nurses of Ursuline College, U-Earth, Women's Circle, Anime Club.
Athletics Member NCAA. All Division II.
Campus security: 24-hour emergency response devices and patrols, late-night transport/escort service, controlled dormitory access.
Student services: personal/psychological counseling.

COSTS & FINANCIAL AID
Costs (2016–17) ***Comprehensive fee:*** $39,904 includes full-time tuition ($29,640), mandatory fees ($300), and room and board ($9964). Full-time tuition and fees vary according to class time, course load, degree level, location, and program. Part-time tuition: $988 per credit hour. Part-time tuition and fees vary according to class time, course load, degree level, location, and program. ***Required fees:*** $110 per term part-time. ***Room and board:*** Room and board charges vary according to board plan and housing facility.
Financial Aid Of all full-time matriculated undergraduates who enrolled in 2016, 410 applied for aid, 382 were judged to have need, 47 had their need fully met. In 2016, 51 non-need-based awards were made. ***Average percent of need met:*** 70. ***Average financial aid package:*** $22,926. ***Average need-based loan:*** $5302. ***Average need-based gift aid:*** $19,054. ***Average non-need-based aid:*** $8531. ***Average indebtedness upon graduation:*** $32,375.

APPLYING
Standardized Tests *Required:* SAT or ACT (for admission).
Options: electronic application, deferred entrance.
Application fee: $25.
Required: essay or personal statement, high school transcript, 1 letter of recommendation. ***Recommended:*** minimum 2.5 GPA, interview.

CONTACT
Ursuline College, 2550 Lander Road, Pepper Pike, OH 44124-4398. *Phone:* 440-449-4203. *Toll-free phone:* 888-URSULINE.

Walsh University
North Canton, Ohio
http://www.walsh.edu/

- **Independent Roman Catholic** comprehensive, founded 1958
- **Small-town** 134-acre campus with easy access to Cleveland
- **Endowment** $22.6 million
- **Coed** 2,112 undergraduate students, 84% full-time, 60% women, 40% men
- **Moderately difficult** entrance level, 78% of applicants were admitted

UNDERGRAD STUDENTS
1,778 full-time, 334 part-time. Students come from 34 states and territories; 24 other countries; 9% are from out of state; 7% Black or African American, non-Hispanic/Latino; 3% Hispanic/Latino; 0.8% Asian, non-Hispanic/Latino; 0.1% Native Hawaiian or other Pacific Islander, non-Hispanic/Latino; 0.3% American Indian or Alaska Native, non-Hispanic/Latino; 2% Two or more races, non-Hispanic/Latino; 10% Race/ethnicity unknown; 4% international; 5% transferred in; 48% live on campus.

Freshmen:
Admission: 1,693 applied, 1,315 admitted, 437 enrolled. ***Average high school GPA:*** 3.46. ***Test scores:*** SAT critical reading scores over 500: 59%; SAT math scores over 500: 62%; ACT scores over 18: 93%; SAT critical reading scores over 600: 16%; SAT math scores over 600: 20%; ACT scores over 24: 43%; SAT critical reading scores over 700: 1%; SAT math scores over 700: 1%; ACT scores over 30: 4%.
Retention: 83% of full-time freshmen returned.

FACULTY
Total: 242, 54% full-time, 43% with terminal degrees.
Student/faculty ratio: 13:1.

ACADEMICS
Calendar: semesters. *Degrees:* certificates, associate, bachelor's, master's, and doctoral.
Special study options: academic remediation for entering students, accelerated degree program, adult/continuing education programs, advanced placement credit, distance learning, double majors, English as a second language, external degree program, honors programs, independent study, internships, off-campus study, part-time degree program, services for LD students, study abroad, summer session for credit.
Unusual degree programs: 3-2 engineering with University of Dayton; behavioral science/counseling, biology/physical therapy.
Computers: 336 computers/terminals and 1,622 ports are available on campus for general student use. Students can access the following: campus intranet, computer help desk, free student e-mail accounts, online (class) grades, online (class) registration, online (class) schedules. Campuswide network is available. 100% of college-owned or -operated housing units are wired for high-speed Internet access. Wireless service is available via entire campus.
Library: Brother Edmond Drouin Library. *Books:* 97,575 (physical), 254,114 (digital/electronic); *Serial titles:* 995 (physical), 82,413 (digital/electronic); *Databases:* 167. Weekly public service hours: 79.

STUDENT LIFE
Housing options: on-campus residence required through senior year; coed, cooperative, special housing for students with disabilities. Campus housing is university owned. Freshman campus housing is guaranteed.
Activities and organizations: drama/theater group, student-run newspaper, radio station, choral group, marching band, Student Government, University Programming Board, Business and Communication Club, Behavioral Science Club, Education Club.
Athletics Member NCAA. All Division II. ***Intercollegiate sports:*** baseball M(s), basketball M(s)/W(s), cheerleading W(c), cross-country running M(s)/W(s), football M(s), golf M(s)/W(s), lacrosse M(s)/W(s), soccer M(s)/W(s), softball W(s), tennis M(s)/W(s), track and field M(s)/W(s), volleyball W(s). ***Intramural sports:*** basketball M/W, bowling M/W, football M, golf M/W, skiing (downhill) M(c)/W(c), soccer M/W, table tennis M/W, tennis M/W, ultimate Frisbee M(c)/W(c), volleyball M/W.
Campus security: 24-hour emergency response devices and patrols, late-night transport/escort service, controlled dormitory access.
Student services: health clinic, personal/psychological counseling.

COSTS & FINANCIAL AID
Costs (2017–18) ***Tuition:*** $28,720 full-time. Full-time tuition and fees vary according to location. Part-time tuition and fees vary according to location. ***Required fees:*** $1550 full-time. ***Room only:*** Room and board charges vary according to board plan and housing facility. ***Payment plan:*** installment. ***Waivers:*** children of alumni, senior citizens, and employees or children of employees.
Financial Aid Of all full-time matriculated undergraduates who enrolled in 2010, 1,726 applied for aid, 1,661 were judged to have need, 798 had their need fully met. In 2010, 180 non-need-based awards were made. ***Average percent of need met:*** 71. ***Average financial aid package:*** $18,133. ***Average need-based loan:*** $4850. ***Average need-based gift aid:*** $6844. ***Average non-need-based aid:*** $9372. ***Average indebtedness upon graduation:*** $24,753.

APPLYING
Standardized Tests *Required for some:* SAT or ACT (for admission).
Options: electronic application, early admission, deferred entrance.
Application fee: $25.
Required: high school transcript, minimum 2.4 GPA. ***Required for some:*** essay or personal statement, minimum 3.0 GPA, 2 letters of recommendation. ***Recommended:*** interview.
Application deadlines: rolling (freshmen), rolling (transfers).
Notification: continuous (freshmen), continuous (transfers).

CONTACT
Ms. Melissa Schoeppner, Campus Visit Coordinator, Walsh University, 2020 East Maple, North Canton, OH 44720. *Phone:* 330-490-7172. *Toll-free phone:* 800-362-9846 (in-state); 800-362-8846 (out-of-state). *Fax:* 330-490-7165. *E-mail:* admissions@walsh.edu.

Wilberforce University
Wilberforce, Ohio
http://www.wilberforce.edu/

CONTACT
Ms. Dadra Driscoll, Director, Office of Admissions, Wilberforce University, 1055 N. Bickett Road, PO Box 1001, Wolfe Administration, Wilberforce, OH 45384. *Phone:* 937-708-5556. *Toll-free phone:* 800-367-8568. *E-mail:* ddriscoll@wilberforce.edu.

Wilmington College
Wilmington, Ohio
http://www.wilmington.edu/

CONTACT
Ms. Tina Garland, Director of Admission and Financial Aid, Wilmington College, 1870 Quaker Way, Wilmington, OH 45177. *Phone:* 937-382-6661 Ext. 426. *Toll-free phone:* 800-341-9318. *Fax:* 937-383-8542. *E-mail:* admissions@wilmington.edu.

Wittenberg University
Springfield, Ohio
http://www.wittenberg.edu/

- **Independent** comprehensive, founded 1845, affiliated with Evangelical Lutheran Church
- **Suburban** 114-acre campus with easy access to Columbus, Dayton
- **Coed** 1,960 undergraduate students, 95% full-time, 56% women, 44% men
- **Moderately difficult** entrance level, 78% of applicants were admitted

UNDERGRAD STUDENTS
1,866 full-time, 94 part-time. Students come from 37 states and territories; 20 other countries; 25% are from out of state; 9% Black or African American, non-Hispanic/Latino; 4% Hispanic/Latino; 1% Asian, non-Hispanic/Latino; 0.1% Native Hawaiian or other Pacific Islander, non-Hispanic/Latino; 0.3% American Indian or Alaska Native, non-Hispanic/Latino; 5% Two or more races, non-Hispanic/Latino; 1% Race/ethnicity unknown; 1% international; 2% transferred in; 82% live on campus.

Freshmen:
Admission: 6,906 applied, 5,409 admitted, 553 enrolled. ***Average high school GPA:*** 3.4. ***Test scores:*** SAT critical reading scores over 500: 70%; SAT math scores over 500: 74%; ACT scores over 18: 98%; SAT critical reading scores over 600: 36%; SAT math scores over 600: 35%; ACT scores over 24: 65%; SAT critical reading scores over 700: 6%; SAT math scores over 700: 1%; ACT scores over 30: 12%.
Retention: 78% of full-time freshmen returned.

FACULTY
Total: 172, 68% full-time, 77% with terminal degrees.
Student/faculty ratio: 14:1.

ACADEMICS
Calendar: semesters. *Degrees:* bachelor's and master's.
Special study options: academic remediation for entering students, adult/continuing education programs, advanced placement credit, cooperative education, double majors, English as a second language, freshman honors college, honors programs, independent study, internships, off-campus study, part-time degree program, student-designed majors, study abroad, summer session for credit. ***ROTC:*** Army (c), Air Force (c).
Unusual degree programs: 3-2 engineering with Georgia Institute of Technology, Washington University in St. Louis, Case Western Reserve University; forestry with Duke University; nursing with Case Western Reserve University, Johns Hopkins University; occupational therapy with Washington University in St. Louis.
Computers: 900 computers/terminals and 1,200 ports are available on campus for general student use. Students can access the following: computer help desk, free student e-mail accounts, online (class) grades, online (class) registration, online (class) schedules. Campuswide network is available. Wireless service is available via entire campus.
Library: Thomas Library plus 1 other.

STUDENT LIFE
Housing options: on-campus residence required through sophomore year; coed, women-only. Campus housing is university owned, leased by the school and is provided by a third party. Freshman campus housing is guaranteed.
Activities and organizations: drama/theater group, student-run newspaper, radio station, choral group, Student Senate, Union Board, Choirs, Weaver Chapel Association, national fraternities, national sororities.
Athletics Member NCAA. All Division III. ***Intercollegiate sports:*** baseball M, basketball M/W, crew M(c)/W(c), cross-country running M/W, field hockey W, football M, golf M/W, lacrosse M/W, rugby M(c)/W(c), soccer M/W, softball W, swimming and diving M/W, tennis M/W, track and field M/W, volleyball M/W. ***Intramural sports:*** basketball M/W, football M, golf M/W, sailing M/W, soccer M/W, softball M/W, swimming and diving M/W, tennis M/W, track and field M/W, volleyball M/W.
Campus security: 24-hour emergency response devices and patrols, student patrols, late-night transport/escort service, controlled dormitory access, crime prevention programs.
Student services: health clinic, personal/psychological counseling, women's center.

COSTS & FINANCIAL AID
Costs (2017–18) ***Comprehensive fee:*** $48,856 includes full-time tuition ($37,930), mandatory fees ($800), and room and board ($10,126). Part-time tuition: $1264 per credit hour. Part-time tuition and fees vary according to course load. ***College room only:*** $5158. Room and board charges vary according to board plan and housing facility. ***Payment plan:*** installment. ***Waivers:*** minority students, children of alumni, adult students, senior citizens, and employees or children of employees.
Financial Aid Of all full-time matriculated undergraduates who enrolled in 2016, 1,664 applied for aid, 1,489 were judged to have need, 354 had their need fully met. In 2016, 348 non-need-based awards were made. ***Average percent of need met:*** 80. ***Average financial aid package:*** $27,498. ***Average need-based loan:*** $4724. ***Average need-based gift aid:*** $25,281. ***Average non-need-based aid:*** $19,277. ***Average indebtedness upon graduation:*** $35,034.

APPLYING
Standardized Tests *Recommended:* Test score optional.
Options: electronic application, early admission, early decision, early action, deferred entrance.
Application fee: $40.
Required: high school transcript, interview. ***Recommended:*** essay or personal statement.
Application deadlines: rolling (transfers), 12/1 (early action).
Early decision deadline: 11/15.
Notification: continuous (freshmen), continuous (transfers), 12/15 (early decision), 1/1 (early action).

CONTACT
Ms. Karen Hunt, Director of Admission, Wittenberg University, PO Box 720, Springfield, OH 45501-0720. *Phone:* 877-206-0332 Ext. 6377. *Toll-free phone:* 800-677-7558 Ext. 6314. *Fax:* 937-327-6379. *E-mail:* admission@wittenberg.edu.

Wright State University

Dayton, Ohio

http://www.wright.edu/

- **State-supported** university, founded 1964, part of University System of Ohio
- **Suburban** 557-acre campus with easy access to Dayton, Columbus, Cincinnati
- **Endowment** $84.8 million
- **Coed** 12,504 undergraduate students, 77% full-time, 52% women, 48% men
- **Minimally difficult** entrance level, 95% of applicants were admitted

UNDERGRAD STUDENTS
9,675 full-time, 2,829 part-time. Students come from 44 states and territories; 63 other countries; 2% are from out of state; 11% Black or African American, non-Hispanic/Latino; 3% Hispanic/Latino; 3% Asian, non-Hispanic/Latino; 0.1% Native Hawaiian or other Pacific Islander, non-Hispanic/Latino; 0.1% American Indian or Alaska Native, non-Hispanic/Latino; 4% Two or more races, non-Hispanic/Latino; 0.5% Race/ethnicity unknown; 4% international; 7% transferred in; 20% live on campus.

Freshmen:
Admission: 5,897 applied, 5,616 admitted, 2,174 enrolled. ***Average high school GPA:*** 3.3. ***Test scores:*** SAT critical reading scores over 500: 59%; SAT math scores over 500: 65%; SAT writing scores over 500: 44%; ACT scores over 18: 81%; SAT critical reading scores over 600: 25%; SAT math scores over 600: 31%; SAT writing scores over 600: 17%; ACT scores over 24: 37%; SAT critical reading scores over 700: 5%; SAT math scores over 700: 6%; SAT writing scores over 700: 3%; ACT scores over 30: 7%.
Retention: 66% of full-time freshmen returned.

FACULTY
Total: 1,110, 59% full-time, 42% with terminal degrees.
Student/faculty ratio: 17:1.

ACADEMICS
Calendar: semesters. *Degrees:* certificates, associate, bachelor's, master's, doctoral, post-master's, and postbachelor's certificates.
Special study options: academic remediation for entering students, adult/continuing education programs, advanced placement credit, cooperative education, distance learning, double majors, English as a second language, freshman honors college, honors programs, independent study, internships, off-campus study, part-time degree program, services for LD students, student-designed majors, study abroad, summer session for credit. ***ROTC:*** Army (b), Air Force (b).

Computers: 2,500 computers/terminals are available on campus for general student use. Students can access the following: campus intranet, computer help desk, free student e-mail accounts, online (class) grades, online (class) registration, online (class) schedules, student webpages, Lap tops 2 Go, office software programs. Campuswide network is available. 100% of college-owned or -operated housing units are wired for high-speed Internet access. Wireless service is available via entire campus.
Library: Paul Laurence Dunbar Library plus 1 other. *Books:* 870,406 (physical), 446,609 (digital/electronic); *Serial titles:* 520 (physical), 48,115 (digital/electronic); *Databases:* 130. Weekly public service hours: 105; students can reserve study rooms.

STUDENT LIFE

Housing options: coed, special housing for students with disabilities. Campus housing is university owned and leased by the school.

Activities and organizations: drama/theater group, student-run newspaper, radio and television station, choral group, Student Government, National Association for the Advancement of Colored People (NAACP), Interfraternity Council, Panhellenic Council, Golden Key International Honor Society, national fraternities, national sororities.

Athletics Member NCAA. All Division I. ***Intercollegiate sports:*** baseball M(s), basketball M(s)/W(s), cheerleading M(s)/W(s), cross-country running M(s)/W(s), golf M(s), soccer M(s)/W(s), softball W(s), swimming and diving M(s)/W(s), tennis M(s)/W(s), track and field W(s), volleyball W(s). ***Intramural sports:*** baseball M(c), basketball M, football M(c)/W(c), gymnastics M(c)/W(c), ice hockey M(c), rugby M(c)/W(c), skiing (downhill) M(c)/W(c), soccer M/W, softball M/W, swimming and diving M(c)/W(c), table tennis M, track and field M(c)/W(c), ultimate Frisbee M(c)/W(c), volleyball W, water polo M/W, wrestling M(c).

Campus security: 24-hour emergency response devices and patrols, student patrols, late-night transport/escort service, controlled dormitory access.

Student services: health clinic, personal/psychological counseling, women's center, legal services.

COSTS & FINANCIAL AID

Costs (2016–17) ***Tuition:*** state resident $8730 full-time, $394 per credit hour part-time; nonresident $17,098 full-time, $791 per credit hour part-time. Full-time tuition and fees vary according to course load, location, and reciprocity agreements. Part-time tuition and fees vary according to course load, location, and reciprocity agreements. ***Room and board:*** $11,376; room only: $7104. Room and board charges vary according to board plan, housing facility, and location. ***Payment plan:*** installment. ***Waivers:*** senior citizens and employees or children of employees.

Financial Aid Of all full-time matriculated undergraduates who enrolled in 2016, 7,340 applied for aid, 6,096 were judged to have need, 809 had their need fully met. 757 Federal Work-Study jobs (averaging $4371). In 2016, 1661 non-need-based awards were made. ***Average percent of need met:*** 58. ***Average financial aid package:*** $10,500. ***Average need-based loan:*** $4323. ***Average need-based gift aid:*** $6182. ***Average non-need-based aid:*** $4070. ***Average indebtedness upon graduation:*** $30,061.

APPLYING

Standardized Tests *Required:* SAT or ACT (for admission).

Options: electronic application, early admission, deferred entrance.

Application fee: $30.

Required: high school transcript. ***Recommended:*** minimum 2.0 GPA.

Application deadlines: rolling (freshmen), rolling (transfers).

Notification: continuous (freshmen), continuous (transfers).

CONTACT

Wright State University, 3640 Colonel Glenn Highway, E147 Student Union, Dayton, OH 45435. *Phone:* 937-775-5700. *Toll-free phone:* 800-247-1770. *Fax:* 937-775-5795. *E-mail:* admissions@wright.edu.

Wright State University–Lake Campus

Celina, Ohio

http://www.wright.edu/lake/

- **State-supported** comprehensive, founded 1969
- **Small-town** 211-acre campus
- **Coed** 1,302 undergraduate students, 70% full-time, 53% women, 47% men
- **Minimally difficult** entrance level, 99% of applicants were admitted

UNDERGRAD STUDENTS

915 full-time, 387 part-time. Students come from 18 states and territories; 4 other countries; 2% are from out of state; 3% Black or African American, non-Hispanic/Latino; 2% Hispanic/Latino; 0.5% Asian, non-Hispanic/Latino; 0.1% Native Hawaiian or other Pacific Islander, non-Hispanic/Latino; 1% Two or more races, non-Hispanic/Latino; 0.8% Race/ethnicity unknown; 0.8% international; 6% transferred in; 6% live on campus.

Freshmen:
Admission: 420 applied, 415 admitted, 284 enrolled. ***Average high school GPA:*** 3.1. ***Test scores:*** SAT critical reading scores over 500: 19%; SAT math scores over 500: 37%; SAT writing scores over 500: 16%; ACT scores over 18: 85%; SAT math scores over 600: 6%; SAT writing scores over 600: 8%; ACT scores over 24: 29%; ACT scores over 30: 2%.

FACULTY

Total: 98, 37% full-time, 28% with terminal degrees.

Student/faculty ratio: 19:1.

ACADEMICS

Calendar: semesters. *Degrees:* certificates, associate, bachelor's, and master's.

Special study options: academic remediation for entering students, accelerated degree program, adult/continuing education programs, advanced placement credit, cooperative education, distance learning, double majors, honors programs, independent study, internships, off-campus study, part-time degree program, services for LD students, student-designed majors, study abroad, summer session for credit. ***ROTC:*** Army (c), Air Force (c).

Computers: 130 computers/terminals are available on campus for general student use. Students can access the following: campus intranet, computer help desk, free student e-mail accounts, online (class) grades, online (class) registration, online (class) schedules. Campuswide network is available. 100% of college-owned or -operated housing units are wired for high-speed Internet access. Wireless service is available via entire campus.
Library: Lake Campus Library & Technology Center plus 1 other. *Books:* 870,406 (physical), 446,609 (digital/electronic); *Serial titles:* 520 (physical), 48,115 (digital/electronic); *Databases:* 130. Weekly public service hours: 44.

STUDENT LIFE

Housing options: coed. Campus housing is leased by the school.

Activities and organizations: Circle K, Engineering Club, Business and Graphics Professionals.

Athletics Member USCAA. ***Intercollegiate sports:*** baseball M, basketball M/W, softball W, volleyball W.

Campus security: 24-hour emergency response devices, WSU-Police Department presence, 40 hours per week.

Student services: health clinic, personal/psychological counseling.

COSTS & FINANCIAL AID

Costs (2016–17) ***Tuition:*** state resident $5842 full-time, $265 per credit hour part-time; nonresident $14,210 full-time, $662 per credit hour part-time. Full-time tuition and fees vary according to course load, location, and reciprocity agreements. Part-time tuition and fees vary according to course load, location, and reciprocity agreements. ***Room and board:*** $9674; room only: $4994. Room and board charges vary according to board plan, housing facility, and location. ***Payment plan:*** installment. ***Waivers:*** senior citizens and employees or children of employees.

Financial Aid Of all full-time matriculated undergraduates who enrolled in 2016, 702 applied for aid, 536 were judged to have need, 92 had their need fully met. 48 Federal Work-Study jobs (averaging $4192). In 2016, 189 non-need-based awards were made. ***Average percent of need met:*** 64. ***Average financial aid package:*** $8676. ***Average need-based loan:*** $3976. ***Average need-based gift aid:*** $4636. ***Average non-need-based aid:*** $2749. ***Average indebtedness upon graduation:*** $30,061.

APPLYING

Standardized Tests *Required:* SAT or ACT (for admission).

Options: electronic application, deferred entrance.

Application fee: $30.

Required: high school transcript. ***Recommended:*** minimum 2.0 GPA.

Application deadlines: rolling (freshmen), rolling (transfers).

Notification: continuous (freshmen), continuous (transfers).

CONTACT
Ms. Jill Puthoff, Admissions/Communications Coordinator, Wright State University–Lake Campus, 174 Dwyer Hall, Celina, OH 45822. *Phone:* 419-586-0363. *Toll-free phone:* 800-237-1477. *E-mail:* jill.puthoff@wright.edu.

Xavier University
Cincinnati, Ohio
http://www.xavier.edu/

CONTACT
Xavier University, 3800 Victory Parkway, Cincinnati, OH 45207-5311. *Phone:* 513-745-3301. *Toll-free phone:* 877-XUADMIT. *E-mail:* xuadmit@xavier.edu.

Youngstown State University
Youngstown, Ohio
http://www.ysu.edu/

- **State-supported** comprehensive, founded 1908
- **Urban** 160-acre campus with easy access to Cleveland, Pittsburgh
- **Endowment** $217.7 million
- **Coed** 11,391 undergraduate students, 77% full-time, 53% women, 47% men
- **Minimally difficult** entrance level, 67% of applicants were admitted

UNDERGRAD STUDENTS
8,786 full-time, 2,605 part-time. Students come from 61 states and territories; 49 other countries; 14% are from out of state; 10% Black or African American, non-Hispanic/Latino; 4% Hispanic/Latino; 1% Asian, non-Hispanic/Latino; 0.1% Native Hawaiian or other Pacific Islander, non-Hispanic/Latino; 0.1% American Indian or Alaska Native, non-Hispanic/Latino; 3% Two or more races, non-Hispanic/Latino; 4% Race/ethnicity unknown; 2% international; 5% transferred in; 11% live on campus.

Freshmen:
Admission: 9,010 applied, 6,071 admitted, 2,091 enrolled. ***Average high school GPA:*** 3.24. ***Test scores:*** SAT critical reading scores over 500: 41%; SAT math scores over 500: 46%; SAT writing scores over 500: 30%; ACT scores over 18: 82%; SAT critical reading scores over 600: 12%; SAT math scores over 600: 14%; SAT writing scores over 600: 8%; ACT scores over 24: 31%; SAT critical reading scores over 700: 2%; SAT math scores over 700: 2%; SAT writing scores over 700: 1%; ACT scores over 30: 5%.
Retention: 75% of full-time freshmen returned.

FACULTY
Total: 1,047, 38% full-time.
Student/faculty ratio: 17:1.

ACADEMICS
Calendar: semesters. *Degrees:* certificates, diplomas, associate, bachelor's, master's, doctoral, post-master's, and postbachelor's certificates.

Special study options: academic remediation for entering students, accelerated degree program, adult/continuing education programs, advanced placement credit, cooperative education, distance learning, double majors, English as a second language, freshman honors college, honors programs, independent study, internships, off-campus study, part-time degree program, services for LD students, student-designed majors, study abroad, summer session for credit. ***ROTC:*** Army (b), Air Force (c).

Unusual degree programs: 3-2 chemistry, medicine.

Computers: 500 computers/terminals are available on campus for general student use. Students can access the following: campus intranet, computer help desk, free student e-mail accounts, online (class) grades, online (class) registration, online (class) schedules. Campuswide network is available. 100% of college-owned or -operated housing units are wired for high-speed Internet access. Wireless service is available via entire campus.

Library: William F. Maag, Jr. Library plus 1 other. *Books:* 702,097 (physical), 87,658 (digital/electronic); *Serial titles:* 94,497 (physical), 42,590 (digital/electronic); *Databases:* 93. Weekly public service hours: 84.

STUDENT LIFE
Housing options: coed, women-only. Campus housing is university owned and is provided by a third party. Freshman applicants given priority for college housing.

Activities and organizations: drama/theater group, student-run newspaper, radio station, choral group, marching band, Honor Trustees, Society for Human Resource Management, Golden Key Honor Society, Fraternities/Sororities (IFC, NPHC and Panhellenic Council), Catholic Student Association, national fraternities, national sororities.

Athletics Member NCAA. All Division I except football (Division I-AA). ***Intercollegiate sports:*** baseball M(s), basketball M(s)/W(s), bowling W, cross-country running M(s)/W(s), golf M(s)/W(s), soccer W(s), softball W(s), swimming and diving W(s), tennis M(s)/W(s), track and field M(s)/W(s), volleyball W(s). ***Intramural sports:*** basketball M/W, bowling M(c), cross-country running M/W, equestrian sports W(c), fencing M(c)/W(c), football M, ice hockey M(c), lacrosse M(c)/W(c), racquetball M(c)/W(c), riflery M(c), rock climbing M/W, rugby W(c), soccer M, table tennis M/W, ultimate Frisbee M, volleyball M/W, weight lifting M/W.

Campus security: 24-hour emergency response devices and patrols, student patrols, late-night transport/escort service, controlled dormitory access, residence hall patrols.

Student services: health clinic, personal/psychological counseling.

COSTS & FINANCIAL AID
Costs (2016–17) ***Tuition:*** state resident $7847 full-time, $327 per credit hour part-time; nonresident $13,847 full-time, $577 per credit hour part-time. Full-time tuition and fees vary according to course load. Part-time tuition and fees vary according to course load. ***Required fees:*** $470 full-time, $10 per credit hour part-time, $115 per term part-time. ***Room and board:*** $8990. Room and board charges vary according to board plan and housing facility. ***Payment plan:*** installment. ***Waivers:*** senior citizens and employees or children of employees.

Financial Aid Of all full-time matriculated undergraduates who enrolled in 2015, 7,315 applied for aid, 6,303 were judged to have need, 515 had their need fully met. In 2015, 936 non-need-based awards were made. ***Average percent of need met:*** 32. ***Average financial aid package:*** $9007. ***Average need-based loan:*** $3791. ***Average need-based gift aid:*** $5380. ***Average non-need-based aid:*** $3165. ***Average indebtedness upon graduation:*** $30,403.

APPLYING
Standardized Tests *Required:* SAT or ACT (for admission).

Options: electronic application, early admission, deferred entrance.

Application fee: $45.

Required: high school transcript, minimum 2.0 GPA, minimum ACT composite score of 17 or combined SAT critical reading and math score of 820. ***Required for some:*** interview.

Application deadlines: 8/1 (freshmen), 8/1 (transfers).

Notification: continuous (freshmen), continuous (out-of-state freshmen), continuous (transfers).

CONTACT
Ms. Sue Davis, Director of Admissions, Youngstown State University, One University Plaza, Youngstown, OH 44555-0001. *Phone:* 330-941-2000. *Toll-free phone:* 877-468-6978. *Fax:* 330-941-3674. *E-mail:* enroll@ysu.edu.

OKLAHOMA

Bacone College
Muskogee, Oklahoma
http://www.bacone.edu/

CONTACT
Bacone College, 2299 Old Bacone Road, Muskogee, OK 74403-1597. *Phone:* 918-781-7342. *Toll-free phone:* 888-682-5514 Ext. 7340.

Cameron University

Lawton, Oklahoma

http://www.cameron.edu/

- **State-supported** comprehensive, founded 1908, part of Oklahoma State Regents for Higher Education
- **Small-town** 360-acre campus
- **Endowment** $17.3 million
- **Coed** 4,444 undergraduate students, 69% full-time, 60% women, 40% men
- **Noncompetitive** entrance level, 100% of applicants were admitted

UNDERGRAD STUDENTS

3,049 full-time, 1,395 part-time. Students come from 48 states and territories; 45 other countries; 13% are from out of state; 13% Black or African American, non-Hispanic/Latino; 12% Hispanic/Latino; 1% Asian, non-Hispanic/Latino; 0.6% Native Hawaiian or other Pacific Islander, non-Hispanic/Latino; 5% American Indian or Alaska Native, non-Hispanic/Latino; 9% Two or more races, non-Hispanic/Latino; 3% Race/ethnicity unknown; 4% international; 7% transferred in; 11% live on campus.

Freshmen:

Admission: 1,102 applied, 1,101 admitted, 726 enrolled. ***Average high school GPA:*** 3.16. ***Test scores:*** ACT scores over 18: 72%; ACT scores over 24: 18%; ACT scores over 30: 1%.

Retention: 62% of full-time freshmen returned.

FACULTY

Total: 279, 53% full-time, 47% with terminal degrees.

Student/faculty ratio: 19:1.

ACADEMICS

Calendar: semesters. *Degrees:* associate, bachelor's, and master's.

Special study options: academic remediation for entering students, accelerated degree program, adult/continuing education programs, advanced placement credit, distance learning, double majors, honors programs, independent study, internships, off-campus study, part-time degree program, services for LD students, student-designed majors, study abroad, summer session for credit. ***ROTC:*** Army (b).

Computers: 240 computers/terminals are available on campus for general student use. Students can access the following: computer help desk, free student e-mail accounts, online (class) grades, online (class) registration, online (class) schedules, online courses. Campuswide network is available. 100% of college-owned or -operated housing units are wired for high-speed Internet access. Wireless service is available via classrooms, computer centers, computer labs, dorm rooms, learning centers, libraries, student centers.

Library: Cameron University Library. *Books:* 155,124 (physical), 265,566 (digital/electronic); *Serial titles:* 10 (physical), 34,315 (digital/electronic); *Databases:* 76. Weekly public service hours: 94; students can reserve study rooms.

STUDENT LIFE

Housing options: men-only, women-only, special housing for students with disabilities. Campus housing is university owned.

Activities and organizations: drama/theater group, student-run newspaper, television station, choral group, Student Government Association, Programming Activities Council, Nigerian Student Association, International Club, Greek Life, national fraternities, national sororities.

Athletics Member NCAA. All Division II. ***Intercollegiate sports:*** baseball M(s), basketball M(s)/W(s), cross-country running M(s), golf M(s)/W(s), softball W(s), tennis M(s)/W(s), volleyball W(s). ***Intramural sports:*** badminton M/W, basketball M/W, bowling M/W, racquetball M/W, soccer M/W, softball M/W, table tennis M/W, tennis M/W, ultimate Frisbee M/W, volleyball M/W, weight lifting M/W.

Campus security: 24-hour emergency response devices and patrols, late-night transport/escort service, controlled dormitory access.

Student services: health clinic, personal/psychological counseling.

COSTS & FINANCIAL AID

Costs (2016–17) ***Tuition:*** state resident $4260 full-time, $142 per credit hour part-time; nonresident $13,500 full-time, $450 per credit hour part-time. Full-time tuition and fees vary according to course level, course load, location, and program. Part-time tuition and fees vary according to course level, course load, location, and program. ***Required fees:*** $1710 full-time, $57 per credit hour part-time. ***Room and board:*** $5102; room only: $1872. Room and board charges vary according to board plan and housing facility. ***Payment plan:*** installment. ***Waivers:*** senior citizens and employees or children of employees.

Financial Aid Of all full-time matriculated undergraduates who enrolled in 2015, 2,399 applied for aid, 2,071 were judged to have need, 219 had their need fully met. 65 Federal Work-Study jobs (averaging $1944). 309 state and other part-time jobs (averaging $2909). In 2015, 244 non-need-based awards were made. ***Average percent of need met:*** 61. ***Average financial aid package:*** $9499. ***Average need-based loan:*** $3902. ***Average need-based gift aid:*** $6296. ***Average non-need-based aid:*** $2139. ***Average indebtedness upon graduation:*** $20,019.

APPLYING

Standardized Tests *Required for some:* SAT or ACT (for admission).

Options: electronic application, deferred entrance.

Application fee: $25.

Required for some: high school transcript, minimum ACT composite score of 20 or SAT of 890 or rank in the top 50% of high school graduation class, minimum high school GPA of 2.7 for baccalaureate degrees; minimum high school curricular requirements and ACT or SAT for AS degree; ACT or SAT for AAS degree.

Application deadlines: rolling (freshmen), rolling (transfers).

Notification: continuous (freshmen), continuous (transfers).

CONTACT

Ms. Teresa Briggs, Administrative Assistant II, Cameron University, Admissions, 2800 West Gore Boulevard, Lawton, OK 73505-6377. *Phone:* 580-581-2987. *Toll-free phone:* 888-454-7600. *Fax:* 580-581-5416. *E-mail:* tbriggs@cameron.edu.

DeVry University–Oklahoma City Campus

Oklahoma City, Oklahoma

http://www.devry.edu/

CONTACT

Admissions Office, DeVry University–Oklahoma City Campus, Lakepointe Towers, 4013 Northwest Expressway Street, Suite 100, Oklahoma City, OK 73116. *Phone:* 405-767-9516. *Toll-free phone:* 866-338-7934.

East Central University

Ada, Oklahoma

http://www.ecok.edu/

- **State-supported** comprehensive, founded 1909, part of Oklahoma State Regents for Higher Education
- **Small-town** 140-acre campus with easy access to Oklahoma City
- **Endowment** $28.8 million
- **Coed** 3,455 undergraduate students, 77% full-time, 58% women, 42% men
- **Minimally difficult** entrance level, 58% of applicants were admitted

UNDERGRAD STUDENTS

2,667 full-time, 788 part-time. Students come from 22 states and territories; 36 other countries; 11% are from out of state; 3% Black or African American, non-Hispanic/Latino; 5% Hispanic/Latino; 0.4% Asian, non-Hispanic/Latino; 0.2% Native Hawaiian or other Pacific Islander, non-Hispanic/Latino; 14% American Indian or Alaska Native, non-Hispanic/Latino; 9% Two or more races, non-Hispanic/Latino; 2% Race/ethnicity unknown; 11% international; 7% transferred in; 35% live on campus.

Freshmen:

Admission: 1,423 applied, 822 admitted, 596 enrolled. ***Average high school GPA:*** 3.45. ***Test scores:*** SAT critical reading scores over 500: 5%; SAT math scores over 500: 70%; ACT scores over 18: 73%; SAT math scores over 600: 22%; ACT scores over 24: 20%; SAT math scores over 700: 4%; ACT scores over 30: 2%.

Retention: 55% of full-time freshmen returned.

FACULTY
Total: 239, 62% full-time, 49% with terminal degrees.
Student/faculty ratio: 19:1.

ACADEMICS
Calendar: semesters. *Degrees:* bachelor's, master's, post-master's, and postbachelor's certificates.
Special study options: academic remediation for entering students, adult/continuing education programs, advanced placement credit, double majors, English as a second language, honors programs, independent study, internships, off-campus study, part-time degree program, services for LD students, student-designed majors, study abroad, summer session for credit.
Computers: 800 computers/terminals are available on campus for general student use. Students can access the following: campus intranet, computer help desk, free student e-mail accounts, online (class) grades, online (class) registration, online (class) schedules. Campuswide network is available. 100% of college-owned or -operated housing units are wired for high-speed Internet access. Wireless service is available via entire campus.
Library: Linscheid Library. *Books:* 182,946 (physical), 25,981 (digital/electronic); *Serial titles:* 52,149 (physical), 2,648 (digital/electronic); *Databases:* 75. Weekly public service hours: 71; students can reserve study rooms.

STUDENT LIFE
Housing options: on-campus residence required for freshman year; coed. Campus housing is university owned.
Activities and organizations: drama/theater group, choral group, marching band, Campus Connection, F.A.T.E., GSA, Residence Hall Association, Tigers for Christ, national fraternities, national sororities.
Athletics Member NCAA. All Division II. ***Intercollegiate sports:*** baseball M(s), basketball M(s)/W(s), cross-country running M(s)/W(s), football M(s), soccer W(s), softball W(s), track and field M/W, volleyball W(s). ***Intramural sports:*** basketball M/W, cheerleading M/W, football M/W, racquetball M/W, soccer M/W, softball M/W, tennis M/W, ultimate Frisbee M/W, volleyball M/W.
Campus security: 24-hour emergency response devices and patrols, student patrols, late-night transport/escort service, controlled dormitory access, agreements with all local, state, federal, and tribal police departments for added crime and violation prevention.
Student services: health clinic, personal/psychological counseling.

COSTS & FINANCIAL AID
Costs (2017–18) ***Tuition:*** state resident $4980 full-time, $166 per semester hour part-time; nonresident $15,010 full-time, $470 per semester hour part-time. No tuition increase for student's term of enrollment. ***Required fees:*** $1299 full-time, $43 per semester hour part-time. ***Room and board:*** $5350; room only: $2200. Room and board charges vary according to board plan and housing facility. ***Waivers:*** employees or children of employees.
Financial Aid Of all full-time matriculated undergraduates who enrolled in 2014, 2,300 applied for aid, 1,992 were judged to have need. 534 Federal Work-Study jobs (averaging $3286). In 2014, 109 non-need-based awards were made. ***Average financial aid package:*** $6052. ***Average need-based loan:*** $64,449. ***Average need-based gift aid:*** $3900. ***Average non-need-based aid:*** $1836. ***Average indebtedness upon graduation:*** $25,308.

APPLYING
Standardized Tests *Required:* SAT or ACT (for admission).
Options: electronic application, early admission.
Application fee: $20.
Required: high school transcript. ***Required for some:*** minimum 2.7 GPA, rank in upper 50% of high school class.
Application deadlines: rolling (freshmen), rolling (transfers).
Notification: continuous (freshmen), continuous (transfers).

CONTACT
Ms. Kylie Stephens, Admissions Counselor, East Central University, 1100 East 14th Street, PMB R-8, Ada, OK 74820-6999. *Phone:* 580-559-5209. *E-mail:* kstephens@ecok.edu.

Family of Faith College
Shawnee, Oklahoma
http://www.familyoffaithcollege.edu/

CONTACT
Family of Faith College, 30 Kinville, Shawnee, OK 74802.

Langston University
Langston, Oklahoma
http://www.langston.edu/

- **State-supported** comprehensive, founded 1897, part of Oklahoma A&M System
- **Rural** 40-acre campus with easy access to Oklahoma City
- **Endowment** $3.9 million
- **Coed** 2,160 undergraduate students, 91% full-time, 64% women, 36% men
- **Moderately difficult** entrance level, 61% of applicants were admitted

UNDERGRAD STUDENTS
1,967 full-time, 193 part-time. Students come from 37 states and territories; 12 other countries; 38% are from out of state; 90% Black or African American, non-Hispanic/Latino; 1% Hispanic/Latino; 0.6% Asian, non-Hispanic/Latino; 0.2% Native Hawaiian or other Pacific Islander, non-Hispanic/Latino; 1% American Indian or Alaska Native, non-Hispanic/Latino; 0.7% Race/ethnicity unknown; 70% live on campus.

Freshmen:
Admission: 9,244 applied, 5,635 admitted, 645 enrolled. ***Average high school GPA:*** 2.81.
Retention: 47% of full-time freshmen returned.

FACULTY
Total: 231, 57% full-time, 37% with terminal degrees.
Student/faculty ratio: 22:1.

ACADEMICS
Calendar: semesters. *Degrees:* associate, bachelor's, master's, and doctoral.
Special study options: academic remediation for entering students, accelerated degree program, adult/continuing education programs, advanced placement credit, cooperative education, distance learning, double majors, English as a second language, external degree program, honors programs, independent study, internships, part-time degree program, services for LD students, study abroad, summer session for credit. ***ROTC:*** Army (c).
Computers: 300 computers/terminals and 1,600 ports are available on campus for general student use. Students can access the following: campus intranet, computer help desk, free student e-mail accounts, online (class) grades, online (class) registration, online (class) schedules. Campuswide network is available. 100% of college-owned or -operated housing units are wired for high-speed Internet access. Wireless service is available via entire campus.
Library: G. Lamar Harrison Library plus 2 others. *Books:* 188,852 (physical), 142,914 (digital/electronic); *Serial titles:* 956 (physical); *Databases:* 58. Students can reserve study rooms.

STUDENT LIFE
Housing options: on-campus residence required through sophomore year; coed, special housing for students with disabilities. Campus housing is university owned and is provided by a third party. Freshman campus housing is guaranteed.
Activities and organizations: drama/theater group, student-run newspaper, radio station, choral group, marching band, Student Government Association, Student Senate, Sorority and Fraternity (Greek Letter), NAACP, Pre- Alumni Council, national fraternities, national sororities.
Athletics Member NAIA. ***Intercollegiate sports:*** basketball M(s)/W(s), cheerleading W, cross-country running M/W, football M(s), softball W, track and field M(s)/W(s), volleyball W. ***Intramural sports:*** archery M/W, badminton M/W, basketball M/W, football M/W, golf M/W, soccer M, swimming and diving M/W, table tennis M/W, tennis M/W, track and field M/W, volleyball M/W.

Campus security: 24-hour emergency response devices and patrols, student patrols, late-night transport/escort service, controlled dormitory access.

Student services: health clinic, personal/psychological counseling, women's center.

COSTS & FINANCIAL AID

Costs (2016–17) ***Tuition:*** state resident $3707 full-time, $124 per credit hour part-time; nonresident $11,046 full-time, $368 per credit hour part-time. Full-time tuition and fees vary according to degree level, location, and program. Part-time tuition and fees vary according to degree level, location, and program. No tuition increase for student's term of enrollment. ***Required fees:*** $1681 full-time, $420 per term part-time, $420 per term part-time. ***Room and board:*** $10,050; room only: $6800. Room and board charges vary according to board plan and housing facility. ***Payment plans:*** tuition prepayment, installment. ***Waivers:*** children of alumni and employees or children of employees.

Financial Aid Of all full-time matriculated undergraduates who enrolled in 2015, 2,091 applied for aid, 1,972 were judged to have need, 309 had their need fully met. 171 Federal Work-Study jobs (averaging $1801). In 2015, 186 non-need-based awards were made. ***Average percent of need met:*** 53. ***Average financial aid package:*** $10,930. ***Average need-based loan:*** $28,655. ***Average need-based gift aid:*** $5144. ***Average non-need-based aid:*** $6759. ***Average indebtedness upon graduation:*** $39,681.

APPLYING

Standardized Tests *Required:* SAT or ACT (for admission).

Options: electronic application, deferred entrance.

Required: high school transcript, minimum 2.7 GPA.

Application deadlines: rolling (freshmen), rolling (transfers).

CONTACT

Mr. Jeremy Lane, Director of Admissions, Langston University, Box 1550, Langston, OK 73052. *Phone:* 405-466-3428. *Fax:* 466-2915. *E-mail:* jlane@langston.edu.

Mid-America Christian University

Oklahoma City, Oklahoma

http://www.macu.edu/

CONTACT

Mid-America Christian University, 3500 Southwest 119th Street, Oklahoma City, OK 73170-4504. *Phone:* 405-392-3180. *Toll-free phone:* 888-436-3035.

National American University

Tulsa, Oklahoma

http://www.national.edu/

CONTACT

National American University, 8040 South Sheridan Road, Tulsa, OK 74133. *Toll-free phone:* 800-209-0338.

Northeastern State University

Tahlequah, Oklahoma

http://www.nsuok.edu/

- **State-supported** comprehensive, founded 1846, part of Regional University System of Oklahoma
- **Small-town** 200-acre campus with easy access to Tulsa
- **Endowment** $3.7 million
- **Coed** 6,923 undergraduate students, 71% full-time, 60% women, 40% men
- **Moderately difficult** entrance level, 83% of applicants were admitted

UNDERGRAD STUDENTS

4,894 full-time, 2,029 part-time. Students come from 38 states and territories; 51 other countries; 6% are from out of state; 4% Black or African American, non-Hispanic/Latino; 6% Hispanic/Latino; 2% Asian, non-Hispanic/Latino; 0.1% Native Hawaiian or other Pacific Islander, non-Hispanic/Latino; 18% American Indian or Alaska Native, non-Hispanic/Latino; 19% Two or more races, non-Hispanic/Latino; 0.7% Race/ethnicity unknown; 2% international; 14% transferred in; 18% live on campus.

Freshmen:

Admission: 1,815 applied, 1,505 admitted, 878 enrolled. ***Average high school GPA:*** 3.4. ***Test scores:*** ACT scores over 18: 85%; ACT scores over 24: 27%; ACT scores over 30: 3%.

Retention: 65% of full-time freshmen returned.

FACULTY

Total: 472, 71% full-time, 60% with terminal degrees.

Student/faculty ratio: 17:1.

ACADEMICS

Calendar: semesters. *Degrees:* bachelor's, master's, doctoral, post-master's, and postbachelor's certificates.

Special study options: academic remediation for entering students, adult/continuing education programs, advanced placement credit, cooperative education, distance learning, double majors, honors programs, independent study, internships, part-time degree program, services for LD students, student-designed majors, summer session for credit. ***ROTC:*** Army (b).

Computers: 1,160 computers/terminals and 1,200 ports are available on campus for general student use. Students can access the following: campus intranet, computer help desk, free student e-mail accounts, online (class) grades, online (class) registration, online (class) schedules. Campuswide network is available. 100% of college-owned or -operated housing units are wired for high-speed Internet access. Wireless service is available via classrooms, computer centers, computer labs, libraries, student centers.

Library: John Vaughn Library. *Books:* 407,981 (physical), 56,335 (digital/electronic); *Serial titles:* 27,983 (physical), 58,449 (digital/electronic); *Databases:* 130. Weekly public service hours: 114.

STUDENT LIFE

Housing options: on-campus residence required for freshman year; coed, women-only, special housing for students with disabilities. Campus housing is university owned. Freshman applicants given priority for college housing.

Activities and organizations: drama/theater group, student-run newspaper, television station, choral group, marching band, national fraternities, national sororities.

Athletics Member NCAA. All Division II. ***Intercollegiate sports:*** baseball M(s), basketball M(s)/W(s), football M(s), golf M(s)/W(s), soccer M(s)/W(s), softball W(s), tennis W(s). ***Intramural sports:*** basketball M/W, football M/W, golf M/W, racquetball M/W, soccer M/W, softball M/W, tennis M/W, volleyball M/W.

Campus security: 24-hour emergency response devices and patrols, late-night transport/escort service, controlled dormitory access.

Student services: health clinic, personal/psychological counseling.

COSTS & FINANCIAL AID

Costs (2016–17) ***Tuition:*** state resident $5085 full-time, $170 per credit hour part-time; nonresident $12,585 full-time, $420 per credit hour part-time. Full-time tuition and fees vary according to course load and program. Part-time tuition and fees vary according to course load and program. No tuition increase for student's term of enrollment. ***Required fees:*** $1122 full-time, $37 per credit hour part-time. ***Room and board:*** $6650; room only: $2900. Room and board charges vary according to board plan and housing facility. ***Payment plan:*** installment. ***Waivers:*** employees or children of employees.

Financial Aid Of all full-time matriculated undergraduates who enrolled in 2016, 4,180 applied for aid, 3,266 were judged to have need, 2,281 had their need fully met. 210 Federal Work-Study jobs (averaging $1133). 776 state and other part-time jobs (averaging $1786). In 2016, 216 non-need-based awards were made. ***Average percent of need met:*** 95. ***Average financial aid package:*** $12,453. ***Average need-based loan:*** $6920. ***Average need-based gift aid:*** $6898. ***Average non-need-based aid:*** $2703. ***Average indebtedness upon graduation:*** $23,840.

APPLYING

Standardized Tests *Required:* ACT (for admission).

Options: electronic application, deferred entrance.

Application fee: $25.

Required: high school transcript, minimum 2.7 GPA, upper 50% of class or minimum ACT composite of 20. ***Required for some:*** interview.

Application deadlines: 8/1 (freshmen), 8/1 (transfers).

Notification: continuous (freshmen), continuous (transfers).

CONTACT
Ms. Jennifer McClendon, Director, Admissions and Recruitment, Northeastern State University, Case Building Room 220, 701 N Grand Avenue, Tahlequah, OK 74464. *Phone:* 918-449-6192. *Toll-free phone:* 800-722-9614. *E-mail:* mcclendo@nsuok.edu.

Northwestern Oklahoma State University

Alva, Oklahoma

http://www.nwosu.edu/

- **State-supported** comprehensive, founded 1897, part of Oklahoma State Regents for Higher Education
- **Rural** 70-acre campus
- **Endowment** $30.1 million
- **Coed** 1,982 undergraduate students, 71% full-time, 57% women, 43% men
- **Moderately difficult** entrance level, 81% of applicants were admitted

UNDERGRAD STUDENTS
1,412 full-time, 570 part-time. Students come from 38 states and territories; 22 other countries; 22% are from out of state; 7% Black or African American, non-Hispanic/Latino; 8% Hispanic/Latino; 0.6% Asian, non-Hispanic/Latino; 0.4% Native Hawaiian or other Pacific Islander, non-Hispanic/Latino; 7% American Indian or Alaska Native, non-Hispanic/Latino; 1% Two or more races, non-Hispanic/Latino; 7% Race/ethnicity unknown; 8% international; 10% transferred in; 30% live on campus.

Freshmen:
Admission: 1,078 applied, 872 admitted, 394 enrolled. ***Average high school GPA:*** 3.32.

Retention: 54% of full-time freshmen returned.

FACULTY
Total: 157, 57% full-time, 43% with terminal degrees.

Student/faculty ratio: 15:1.

ACADEMICS
Calendar: semesters. *Degrees:* bachelor's, master's, and doctoral.

Special study options: academic remediation for entering students, adult/continuing education programs, advanced placement credit, cooperative education, distance learning, honors programs, independent study, internships, off-campus study, part-time degree program, services for LD students, study abroad, summer session for credit.

Computers: 260 computers/terminals are available on campus for general student use. Students can access the following: campus intranet, free student e-mail accounts, online (class) grades, online (class) registration, online (class) schedules. Campuswide network is available. 100% of college-owned or -operated housing units are wired for high-speed Internet access. Wireless service is available via classrooms, computer centers, computer labs, learning centers, libraries, student centers.

Library: J. W. Martin Library plus 1 other. *Books:* 96,645 (physical), 141,500 (digital/electronic); *Serial titles:* 9 (physical), 34,500 (digital/electronic); *Databases:* 57. Weekly public service hours: 84; students can reserve study rooms.

STUDENT LIFE
Housing options: on-campus residence required for freshman year; men-only, women-only. Campus housing is university owned. Freshman campus housing is guaranteed.

Activities and organizations: drama/theater group, student-run newspaper, radio and television station, choral group, marching band, Student Government Association, Aggie Club, Delta Mu Delta, Baptist Student Union, SOEA.

Athletics Member NCAA. All Division II. ***Intercollegiate sports:*** baseball M(s), basketball M(s)/W(s), cheerleading M(s)/W(s), cross-country running M(s)/W(s), football M(s), golf M(s)/W(s), soccer W(s), softball W(s), volleyball W(s). ***Intramural sports:*** basketball M/W, football M, racquetball M/W, softball M/W, ultimate Frisbee M/W, volleyball M/W.

Campus security: 24-hour emergency response devices and patrols, late-night transport/escort service.

Student services: personal/psychological counseling.

COSTS & FINANCIAL AID
Costs (2016–17) ***Tuition:*** state resident $5738 full-time; nonresident $12,585 full-time. Full-time tuition and fees vary according to course load, degree level, location, and program. Part-time tuition and fees vary according to course load, degree level, location, and program. ***Required fees:*** $953 full-time. ***Room and board:*** $4480; room only: $1780. Room and board charges vary according to board plan. ***Payment plan:*** installment. ***Waivers:*** senior citizens and employees or children of employees.

Financial Aid Of all full-time matriculated undergraduates who enrolled in 2014, 1,149 applied for aid, 950 were judged to have need. ***Average indebtedness upon graduation:*** $16,932.

APPLYING
Standardized Tests *Required:* SAT or ACT (for admission).

Options: electronic application, early admission.

Application fee: $15.

Required: high school transcript. ***Required for some:*** essay or personal statement, minimum 2.7 GPA, 3 letters of recommendation.

Application deadlines: rolling (freshmen), rolling (transfers).

Notification: continuous (freshmen), continuous (transfers).

CONTACT
Ms. Paige Fischer, Director of Recruitment, Northwestern Oklahoma State University, 709 Oklahoma Boulevard, Alva, OK 73717-2799. *Phone:* 580-327-8545. *Fax:* 580-327-8699. *E-mail:* plfischer@nwosu.edu.

Oklahoma Baptist University

Shawnee, Oklahoma

http://www.okbu.edu/

- **Independent Southern Baptist** comprehensive, founded 1910
- **Small-town** 125-acre campus with easy access to Oklahoma City
- **Endowment** $116.2 million
- **Coed** 1,904 undergraduate students, 95% full-time, 61% women, 39% men
- **Moderately difficult** entrance level, 60% of applicants were admitted

UNDERGRAD STUDENTS
1,818 full-time, 86 part-time. Students come from 37 states and territories; 45 other countries; 34% are from out of state; 6% Black or African American, non-Hispanic/Latino; 2% Hispanic/Latino; 1% Asian, non-Hispanic/Latino; 0.2% Native Hawaiian or other Pacific Islander, non-Hispanic/Latino; 5% American Indian or Alaska Native, non-Hispanic/Latino; 11% Two or more races, non-Hispanic/Latino; 2% Race/ethnicity unknown; 4% international; 5% transferred in; 76% live on campus.

Freshmen:
Admission: 4,955 applied, 2,990 admitted, 582 enrolled. ***Average high school GPA:*** 3.68. ***Test scores:*** SAT critical reading scores over 500: 67%; SAT math scores over 500: 59%; ACT scores over 18: 95%; SAT critical reading scores over 600: 33%; SAT math scores over 600: 18%; ACT scores over 24: 44%; SAT critical reading scores over 700: 4%; SAT math scores over 700: 3%; ACT scores over 30: 11%.

Retention: 78% of full-time freshmen returned.

FACULTY
Total: 200, 63% full-time, 46% with terminal degrees.

Student/faculty ratio: 11:1.

ACADEMICS
Calendar: 4-1-4. *Degrees:* associate, bachelor's, and master's.

Special study options: academic remediation for entering students, advanced placement credit, cooperative education, double majors, honors programs, independent study, internships, off-campus study, part-time degree program, services for LD students, student-designed majors, study abroad, summer session for credit. ***ROTC:*** Air Force (c).

Unusual degree programs: medicine.

Computers: 175 computers/terminals are available on campus for general student use. Students can access the following: computer help desk, free student e-mail accounts, online (class) grades, online (class) registration, online (class) schedules, campus portal, online course work. Campuswide network is available. 100% of college-owned or -operated housing units are wired for high-speed Internet access. Wireless service is available via entire campus.

Library: Mabee Learning Center. *Books:* 164,341 (physical), 188,606 (digital/electronic); *Serial titles:* 1,140 (physical); *Databases:* 60. Weekly public service hours: 91; students can reserve study rooms.

STUDENT LIFE

Housing options: on-campus residence required through junior year; men-only, women-only. Campus housing is university owned. Freshman campus housing is guaranteed.

Activities and organizations: drama/theater group, student-run newspaper, television station, choral group, marching band, Campus Activities Board, University Concert Series, Student Foundation, Blitz Week Activities, Canterbury.

Athletics Member NCAA, NCCAA. All NCAA Division II except cross-country running (Division I), men's and women's swimming and diving (Division I). ***Intercollegiate sports:*** baseball M(s), basketball M(s)/W(s), cross-country running M(s)/W(s), football M(s), golf M(s)/W(s), lacrosse W(s), soccer M(s)/W(s), softball W(s), swimming and diving M(s)/W(s), tennis M(s)/W(s), track and field M(s)/W(s), volleyball W(s). ***Intramural sports:*** archery M/W, basketball M/W, bowling M/W, cheerleading W, football M/W, racquetball M/W, riflery M/W, rock climbing M/W, sand volleyball M/W, soccer M/W, softball M/W, table tennis M/W, tennis M/W, ultimate Frisbee M/W, volleyball M/W.

Campus security: 24-hour emergency response devices and patrols, late-night transport/escort service, controlled dormitory access, CLEET certified police officers.

Student services: health clinic, personal/psychological counseling.

COSTS & FINANCIAL AID

Costs (2017–18) ***Comprehensive fee:*** $33,990 includes full-time tuition ($23,940), mandatory fees ($2900), and room and board ($7150). Part-time tuition: $778 per credit hour. Part-time tuition and fees vary according to course load. ***Required fees:*** $2900 per term part-time. ***Room and board:*** Room and board charges vary according to housing facility. ***Payment plan:*** installment. ***Waivers:*** senior citizens and employees or children of employees.

Financial Aid Of all full-time matriculated undergraduates who enrolled in 2015, 1,442 applied for aid, 1,312 were judged to have need, 405 had their need fully met. 660 Federal Work-Study jobs (averaging $1772). In 2015, 442 non-need-based awards were made. ***Average percent of need met:*** 89. ***Average financial aid package:*** $21,800. ***Average need-based loan:*** $4154. ***Average need-based gift aid:*** $8275. ***Average non-need-based aid:*** $9477. ***Average indebtedness upon graduation:*** $24,451.

APPLYING

Standardized Tests *Required:* SAT or ACT (for admission).

Options: early admission, deferred entrance.

Required: high school transcript, minimum 3.0 GPA. ***Required for some:*** essay or personal statement, interview.

Application deadlines: rolling (freshmen), 8/1 (transfers).

Notification: continuous until 9/1 (freshmen), continuous until 9/1 (transfers).

CONTACT

Oklahoma Baptist University, 500 West University, Shawnee, OK 74804. *Phone:* 405-585-5000. *Toll-free phone:* 800-654-3285.

Oklahoma Christian University

Oklahoma City, Oklahoma

http://www.oc.edu/

- **Independent** comprehensive, founded 1950, affiliated with Church of Christ
- **Suburban** 200-acre campus with easy access to Oklahoma City
- **Coed** 1,974 undergraduate students, 93% full-time, 49% women, 51% men
- **Moderately difficult** entrance level, 61% of applicants were admitted

UNDERGRAD STUDENTS

1,845 full-time, 129 part-time. Students come from 42 states and territories; 34 other countries; 57% are from out of state; 5% Black or African American, non-Hispanic/Latino; 6% Hispanic/Latino; 1% Asian, non-Hispanic/Latino; 0.1% Native Hawaiian or other Pacific Islander, non-Hispanic/Latino; 2% American Indian or Alaska Native, non-Hispanic/Latino; 7% Two or more races, non-Hispanic/Latino; 7% international; 4% transferred in; 81% live on campus.

Freshmen:

Admission: 2,256 applied, 1,372 admitted, 458 enrolled. ***Average high school GPA:*** 3.57. ***Test scores:*** SAT critical reading scores over 500: 58%; SAT math scores over 500: 63%; SAT writing scores over 500: 50%; ACT scores over 18: 94%; SAT critical reading scores over 600: 34%; SAT math scores over 600: 27%; SAT writing scores over 600: 17%; ACT scores over 24: 59%; SAT critical reading scores over 700: 7%; SAT math scores over 700: 9%; SAT writing scores over 700: 4%; ACT scores over 30: 18%.

Retention: 79% of full-time freshmen returned.

FACULTY

Total: 224, 44% full-time, 45% with terminal degrees.

Student/faculty ratio: 13:1.

ACADEMICS

Calendar: semesters. *Degrees:* bachelor's, master's, and postbachelor's certificates.

Special study options: academic remediation for entering students, accelerated degree program, advanced placement credit, distance learning, double majors, English as a second language, honors programs, independent study, internships, off-campus study, services for LD students, study abroad, summer session for credit. ***ROTC:*** Army (c), Air Force (c).

Computers: 101 computers/terminals and 450 ports are available on campus for general student use. Students can access the following: campus intranet, computer help desk, free student e-mail accounts, online (class) grades, online (class) registration, online (class) schedules. Campuswide network is available. 100% of college-owned or -operated housing units are wired for high-speed Internet access. Wireless service is available via entire campus.

Library: Tom and Ada Beam Library plus 1 other. *Books:* 107,541 (physical), 65,297 (digital/electronic); *Serial titles:* 83 (physical), 42,000 (digital/electronic); *Databases:* 66. Weekly public service hours: 83; students can reserve study rooms.

STUDENT LIFE

Housing options: on-campus residence required through senior year; men-only, women-only, special housing for students with disabilities. Campus housing is university owned. Freshman campus housing is guaranteed.

Activities and organizations: drama/theater group, student-run newspaper, radio and television station, choral group, Outreach, Wishing Well Project, Student Government Association, Young Republicans, College Democrats.

Athletics Member NCAA. All Division II. ***Intercollegiate sports:*** baseball M(s), basketball M(s)/W(s), cross-country running M(s)/W(s), golf M(s)/W(s), soccer M(s)/W(s), softball W(s), swimming and diving M(s)/W(s), track and field M(s)/W(s). ***Intramural sports:*** basketball M/W, bowling M/W, cheerleading M/W, cross-country running M/W, football M/W, golf M/W, soccer M/W, softball M/W, swimming and diving M/W, table tennis M/W, tennis M/W, track and field M/W, volleyball M/W.

Campus security: 24-hour emergency response devices and patrols, late-night transport/escort service, controlled dormitory access.

Student services: health clinic, personal/psychological counseling.

COSTS & FINANCIAL AID

Costs (2017–18) ***Comprehensive fee:*** $29,260 includes full-time tuition ($21,600), mandatory fees ($70), and room and board ($7590). Full-time tuition and fees vary according to course load, program, and reciprocity agreements. Part-time tuition: $900 per credit hour. Part-time tuition and fees vary according to course load, program, and reciprocity agreements. ***Room and board:*** Room and board charges vary according to board plan and housing facility. ***Payment plans:*** tuition prepayment, installment. ***Waivers:*** employees or children of employees.

Financial Aid Of all full-time matriculated undergraduates who enrolled in 2014, 1,413 applied for aid, 1,198 were judged to have need, 501 had their need fully met. In 2014, 618 non-need-based awards were made. ***Average percent of need met:*** 77. ***Average financial aid package:*** $22,894. ***Average need-based loan:*** $2302. ***Average need-based gift aid:*** $3273. ***Average non-need-based aid:*** $7283. ***Average indebtedness upon graduation:*** $28,142. ***Financial aid deadline:*** 8/31.

APPLYING

Standardized Tests *Required:* SAT or ACT (for admission).

Options: electronic application, early admission, deferred entrance.

Application fee: $25.

Required: high school transcript, 1 letter of recommendation. ***Required for some:*** interview.

Application deadlines: rolling (freshmen), rolling (transfers).

Notification: continuous (freshmen), continuous (transfers).

CONTACT

Ms. Bonnie Howard, Associate Director of Admissions Records, Oklahoma Christian University, Box 11000, Oklahoma City, OK 73136-1100. *Phone:* 405-425-5000. *Toll-free phone:* 800-877-5010. *Fax:* 405-425-5208. *E-mail:* admissions@oc.edu.

Oklahoma City University

Oklahoma City, Oklahoma

http://www.okcu.edu/

- **Independent United Methodist** comprehensive, founded 1904
- **Urban** 104-acre campus with easy access to Oklahoma City
- **Endowment** $94.2 million
- **Coed** 1,764 undergraduate students, 90% full-time, 66% women, 34% men

UNDERGRAD STUDENTS

1,590 full-time, 174 part-time. Students come from 46 states and territories; 35 other countries; 49% are from out of state; 5% Black or African American, non-Hispanic/Latino; 9% Hispanic/Latino; 3% Asian, non-Hispanic/Latino; 0.2% Native Hawaiian or other Pacific Islander, non-Hispanic/Latino; 2% American Indian or Alaska Native, non-Hispanic/Latino; 8% Two or more races, non-Hispanic/Latino; 0.2% Race/ethnicity unknown; 11% international; 13% transferred in; 53% live on campus.

Freshmen:

Admission: 329 enrolled. ***Average high school GPA:*** 3.71. ***Test scores:*** SAT critical reading scores over 500: 77%; SAT math scores over 500: 72%; SAT writing scores over 500: 76%; ACT scores over 18: 98%; SAT critical reading scores over 600: 35%; SAT math scores over 600: 25%; SAT writing scores over 600: 30%; ACT scores over 24: 64%; SAT critical reading scores over 700: 6%; SAT math scores over 700: 1%; SAT writing scores over 700: 5%; ACT scores over 30: 16%.

Retention: 80% of full-time freshmen returned.

FACULTY

Total: 281, 69% full-time, 50% with terminal degrees.

Student/faculty ratio: 11:1.

ACADEMICS

Calendar: semesters. *Degrees:* bachelor's, master's, and doctoral.

Special study options: accelerated degree program, adult/continuing education programs, advanced placement credit, cooperative education, distance learning, double majors, English as a second language, honors programs, independent study, internships, off-campus study, part-time degree program, services for LD students, study abroad, summer session for credit. ***ROTC:*** Army (c), Air Force (c).

Unusual degree programs: 3-2 business administration; nursing.

Computers: 368 computers/terminals are available on campus for general student use. Students can access the following: campus intranet, computer help desk, free student e-mail accounts, online (class) grades, online (class) registration, online (class) schedules. Campuswide network is available. 100% of college-owned or -operated housing units are wired for high-speed Internet access. Wireless service is available via entire campus.

Library: Dulaney Browne Library plus 1 other. *Books:* 326,514 (physical), 240,741 (digital/electronic); *Serial titles:* 581 (physical), 3,060 (digital/electronic); *Databases:* 142. Weekly public service hours: 99; students can reserve study rooms.

STUDENT LIFE

Housing options: coed, special housing for students with disabilities. Campus housing is university owned and is provided by a third party. Freshman applicants given priority for college housing.

Activities and organizations: drama/theater group, student-run newspaper, television station, choral group, Tri-Beta, Multicultural Student Association, Student Nursing Associate, Fellowship of Christian Athletes, national fraternities, national sororities.

Athletics Member NAIA. ***Intercollegiate sports:*** baseball M(s), basketball M(s)/W(s), cheerleading M(s)/W(s), crew M(s)/W(s), golf M(s)/W(s), sailing M(c)/W(c), soccer M(s)/W(s), softball W(s), track and field M(s)/W(s), volleyball W(s), wrestling M(s)/W(s). ***Intramural sports:*** basketball M/W, golf M/W, softball M/W, table tennis M/W, volleyball M/W.

Campus security: 24-hour emergency response devices and patrols, late-night transport/escort service, controlled dormitory access.

Student services: health clinic, personal/psychological counseling.

COSTS & FINANCIAL AID

Costs (2017–18) ***One-time required fee:*** $300. ***Comprehensive fee:*** $39,350 includes full-time tuition ($27,276), mandatory fees ($3450), and room and board ($8624). Full-time tuition and fees vary according to course level, course load, degree level, program, and student level. Part-time tuition: $925 per credit hour. Part-time tuition and fees vary according to course level, degree level, program, and student level. ***Required fees:*** $115 per credit hour part-time. ***College room only:*** $4100. Room and board charges vary according to board plan and housing facility. ***Payment plans:*** installment, deferred payment. ***Waivers:*** employees or children of employees.

Financial Aid Of all full-time matriculated undergraduates who enrolled in 2016, 1,139 applied for aid, 984 were judged to have need, 821 had their need fully met. 239 Federal Work-Study jobs (averaging $1259). 351 state and other part-time jobs (averaging $1217). In 2016, 148 non-need-based awards were made. ***Average percent of need met:*** 60. ***Average financial aid package:*** $21,048. ***Average need-based loan:*** $4527. ***Average need-based gift aid:*** $17,061. ***Average non-need-based aid:*** $14,594. ***Average indebtedness upon graduation:*** $26,329.

APPLYING

Standardized Tests *Required:* SAT or ACT (for admission).

Required: essay or personal statement, high school transcript. ***Required for some:*** interview.

CONTACT

Ms. Michelle Cook, Senior Director of Admissions, Oklahoma City University, 2501 North Blackwelder, Oklahoma City, OK 73106. *Phone:* 405-208-5055. *Toll-free phone:* 800-633-7242. *Fax:* 405-208-5916. *E-mail:* michelle.cook@okcu.edu.

Oklahoma Panhandle State University

Goodwell, Oklahoma

http://www.opsu.edu/

CONTACT

Mr. Bobby Jenkins, Registrar and Director of Admissions, Oklahoma Panhandle State University, PO Box 430, 323 Eagle Boulevard, Goodwell, OK 73939-0430. *Phone:* 580-349-1376. *Toll-free phone:* 800-664-6778. *Fax:* 580-349-1371. *E-mail:* opsu@opsu.edu.

Oklahoma State University
Stillwater, Oklahoma
http://www.okstate.edu/

- **State-supported** university, founded 1890, part of Oklahoma State University
- **Small-town** 840-acre campus with easy access to Oklahoma City, Tulsa
- **Endowment** $766.7 million
- **Coed** 21,093 undergraduate students, 87% full-time, 49% women, 51% men
- **Moderately difficult** entrance level, 75% of applicants were admitted

UNDERGRAD STUDENTS
18,369 full-time, 2,724 part-time. Students come from 57 states and territories; 67 other countries; 27% are from out of state; 5% Black or African American, non-Hispanic/Latino; 7% Hispanic/Latino; 2% Asian, non-Hispanic/Latino; 0.1% Native Hawaiian or other Pacific Islander, non-Hispanic/Latino; 5% American Indian or Alaska Native, non-Hispanic/Latino; 9% Two or more races, non-Hispanic/Latino; 0.4% Race/ethnicity unknown; 4% international; 8% transferred in; 45% live on campus.

Freshmen:
Admission: 13,055 applied, 9,729 admitted, 4,096 enrolled. ***Average high school GPA:*** 3.54. ***Test scores:*** SAT critical reading scores over 500: 66%; SAT math scores over 500: 72%; ACT scores over 18: 96%; SAT critical reading scores over 600: 23%; SAT math scores over 600: 30%; ACT scores over 24: 55%; SAT critical reading scores over 700: 3%; SAT math scores over 700: 5%; ACT scores over 30: 12%.
Retention: 81% of full-time freshmen returned.

FACULTY
Total: 1,354, 77% full-time, 74% with terminal degrees.

Student/faculty ratio: 20:1.

ACADEMICS
Calendar: semesters. *Degrees:* bachelor's, master's, doctoral, post-master's, and postbachelor's certificates.

Special study options: accelerated degree program, advanced placement credit, distance learning, double majors, English as a second language, freshman honors college, honors programs, independent study, internships, off-campus study, part-time degree program, services for LD students, student-designed majors, study abroad, summer session for credit. ***ROTC:*** Army (b), Air Force (b).

Unusual degree programs: 3-2 business administration; accounting, special education, biochemistry, early childhood education.

Computers: Students can access the following: campus intranet, computer help desk, free student e-mail accounts, online (class) grades, online (class) registration, online (class) schedules. Campuswide network is available. 99% of college-owned or -operated housing units are wired for high-speed Internet access. Wireless service is available via classrooms, computer centers, computer labs, dorm rooms, learning centers, libraries, student centers.

Library: Edmon Low Library plus 3 others. Weekly public service hours: 146; study areas open 24 hours, 5-7 days a week; students can reserve study rooms.

STUDENT LIFE
Housing options: on-campus residence required for freshman year; coed, men-only, women-only, special housing for students with disabilities. Campus housing is university owned. Freshman applicants given priority for college housing.

Activities and organizations: drama/theater group, student-run newspaper, radio and television station, choral group, marching band, national fraternities, national sororities.

Athletics Member NCAA. All Division I. ***Intercollegiate sports:*** baseball M(s), basketball M(s)/W(s), cheerleading M(s)(c)/W(s)(c), cross-country running M(s)/W(s), equestrian sports W(s), football M(s), golf M(s)/W(s), soccer W(s), softball W(s), tennis M(s)/W(s), track and field M(s)/W(s), wrestling M(s). ***Intramural sports:*** archery M/W, badminton M/W, basketball M/W, bowling M/W, football M/W, golf M/W, racquetball M/W, soccer M/W, softball M/W, swimming and diving M/W, table tennis M/W, tennis M/W, ultimate Frisbee M/W, volleyball M/W, water polo M/W, weight lifting M/W, wrestling M/W.

Campus security: 24-hour emergency response devices and patrols, student patrols, late-night transport/escort service, controlled dormitory access.

Student services: health clinic, personal/psychological counseling, legal services.

COSTS & FINANCIAL AID
Costs (2016–17) ***One-time required fee:*** $95. ***Tuition:*** state resident $4943 full-time, $165 per credit hour part-time; nonresident $19,065 full-time, $636 per credit hour part-time. Full-time tuition and fees vary according to program. Part-time tuition and fees vary according to course load and program. No tuition increase for student's term of enrollment. ***Required fees:*** $3378 full-time, $113 per credit hour part-time. ***Room and board:*** $8443; room only: $4743. Room and board charges vary according to board plan and housing facility. ***Payment plan:*** installment. ***Waivers:*** children of alumni, senior citizens, and employees or children of employees.

Financial Aid Of all full-time matriculated undergraduates who enrolled in 2015, 12,120 applied for aid, 9,215 were judged to have need, 1,233 had their need fully met. 397 Federal Work-Study jobs (averaging $2112). 4,553 state and other part-time jobs (averaging $2868). In 2015, 5370 non-need-based awards were made. ***Average percent of need met:*** 77. ***Average financial aid package:*** $14,155. ***Average need-based loan:*** $4128. ***Average need-based gift aid:*** $7293. ***Average non-need-based aid:*** $5617. ***Average indebtedness upon graduation:*** $24,252.

APPLYING
Standardized Tests *Required:* SAT or ACT (for admission).

Options: electronic application, deferred entrance.

Application fee: $40.

Required: high school transcript, minimum 3.0 GPA, rank in top 33.3% of high school class. ***Required for some:*** essay or personal statement, letters of recommendation.

Application deadlines: rolling (freshmen), rolling (transfers).

Notification: continuous (freshmen), continuous (transfers).

CONTACT
Oklahoma State University, Stillwater, OK 74078. *Phone:* 405-744-3087. *Toll-free phone:* 800-233-5019.

Oklahoma State University Institute of Technology
Okmulgee, Oklahoma
http://www.osuit.edu/

- **State-supported** primarily 2-year, founded 1946, part of Oklahoma State University
- **Small-town** 160-acre campus with easy access to Tulsa
- **Endowment** $7.6 million
- **Coed** 2,397 undergraduate students, 71% full-time, 36% women, 64% men
- **Noncompetitive** entrance level, 100% of applicants were admitted

UNDERGRAD STUDENTS
1,713 full-time, 684 part-time. Students come from 25 states and territories; 16 other countries; 13% are from out of state; 5% Black or African American, non-Hispanic/Latino; 6% Hispanic/Latino; 0.7% Asian, non-Hispanic/Latino; 13% American Indian or Alaska Native, non-Hispanic/Latino; 10% Two or more races, non-Hispanic/Latino; 14% Race/ethnicity unknown; 2% international; 9% transferred in; 30% live on campus.

Freshmen:
Admission: 1,849 applied, 1,849 admitted, 627 enrolled. ***Average high school GPA:*** 3. ***Test scores:*** ACT scores over 18: 61%; ACT scores over 24: 11%; ACT scores over 30: 1%.
Retention: 56% of full-time freshmen returned.

FACULTY
Total: 164, 76% full-time, 5% with terminal degrees.

Student/faculty ratio: 14:1.

ACADEMICS
Calendar: trimesters. *Degrees:* associate and bachelor's.

Special study options: academic remediation for entering students, adult/continuing education programs, advanced placement credit, distance learning, double majors, independent study, internships, part-time degree program, services for LD students, summer session for credit.

Computers: 50 computers/terminals are available on campus for general student use. Students can access the following: computer help desk, free student e-mail accounts, online (class) grades, online (class) registration, online (class) schedules. Campuswide network is available. 100% of college-owned or -operated housing units are wired for high-speed Internet access. Wireless service is available via entire campus.
Library: Oklahoma State University Institute of Technology Library. *Books:* 9,743 (physical), 130,437 (digital/electronic); *Serial titles:* 77,907 (digital/electronic); *Databases:* 31. Weekly public service hours: 66; students can reserve study rooms.

STUDENT LIFE
Housing options: on-campus residence required for freshman year; coed, men-only. Campus housing is university owned. Freshman applicants given priority for college housing.

Activities and organizations: Phi Theta Kappa, Visual Communications Collective, Air Conditioning and Refrigeration Club, Future Chefs Association, Association of Information Technology Professionals.

Athletics ***Intramural sports:*** basketball M/W, football M/W, racquetball M/W, soccer M/W, softball M/W, table tennis M/W, volleyball M/W.

Campus security: 24-hour emergency response devices and patrols, late-night transport/escort service, controlled dormitory access.

Student services: health clinic, personal/psychological counseling.

COSTS & FINANCIAL AID
Costs (2017–18) ***Tuition:*** state resident $3900 full-time, $130 per credit hour part-time; nonresident $9510 full-time, $317 per credit hour part-time. Full-time tuition and fees vary according to course level, course load, location, program, and student level. Part-time tuition and fees vary according to course level, course load, location, program, and student level. ***Required fees:*** $1200 full-time, $40 per credit hour part-time. ***Room and board:*** $6724. Room and board charges vary according to board plan and housing facility. ***Payment plan:*** installment. ***Waivers:*** senior citizens and employees or children of employees.

Financial Aid Of all full-time matriculated undergraduates who enrolled in 2015, 1,857 applied for aid, 1,598 were judged to have need, 1,151 had their need fully met. In 2015, 217 non-need-based awards were made. ***Average percent of need met:*** 75. ***Average financial aid package:*** $7600. ***Average need-based loan:*** $4500. ***Average need-based gift aid:*** $7600. ***Average non-need-based aid:*** $500. ***Financial aid deadline:*** 6/30.

APPLYING
Standardized Tests *Required for some:* SAT or ACT (for admission). *Recommended:* ACT (for admission).

Options: deferred entrance.

Required: high school transcript.

Application deadlines: rolling (freshmen), rolling (transfers).

CONTACT
Kyle Gregorio, Assistant Registrar, Oklahoma State University Institute of Technology, 1801 E 4th Street, Okmulgee, OK 74447. *Phone:* 918-293-5274. *Toll-free phone:* 800-722-4471. *Fax:* 918-293-4643. *E-mail:* kyleg@okstate.edu.

Oklahoma State University–Oklahoma City

Oklahoma City, Oklahoma

http://www.osuokc.edu/

- **State-supported** primarily 2-year, founded 1961, part of Oklahoma State University
- **Urban** 110-acre campus with easy access to Oklahoma City, OK
- **Coed** 6,314 undergraduate students, 32% full-time, 60% women, 40% men
- **Noncompetitive** entrance level, 33% of applicants were admitted

UNDERGRAD STUDENTS
2,027 full-time, 4,287 part-time. Students come from 26 states and territories; 4% are from out of state; 13% Black or African American, non-Hispanic/Latino; 11% Hispanic/Latino; 3% Asian, non-Hispanic/Latino; 3% American Indian or Alaska Native, non-Hispanic/Latino; 12% Two or more races, non-Hispanic/Latino; 5% Race/ethnicity unknown; 13% transferred in.

Freshmen:
Admission: 2,412 applied, 795 admitted, 1,146 enrolled.

FACULTY
Total: 414, 21% full-time.

Student/faculty ratio: 14:1.

ACADEMICS
Calendar: semesters. *Degrees:* certificates, associate, and bachelor's.

Special study options: academic remediation for entering students, advanced placement credit, distance learning, double majors, honors programs, independent study, internships, part-time degree program, services for LD students, study abroad, summer session for credit.

Computers: 900 computers/terminals are available on campus for general student use. Students can access the following: campus intranet, computer help desk, free student e-mail accounts, online (class) grades, online (class) registration, online (class) schedules. Campuswide network is available. Wireless service is available via entire campus.
Library: Oklahoma State University, Oklahoma City Library. *Books:* 47,903 (physical); *Serial titles:* 237 (physical); *Databases:* 72. Weekly public service hours: 73; students can reserve study rooms.

STUDENT LIFE
Housing options: college housing not available.

Activities and organizations: OSU-OKC Chapter of the OK Student Nurse Association, Veterinary Technician Association, Hispanic Student Association, Student Leaders of Tomorrow, Student Government Association.

Campus security: 24-hour patrols, late-night transport/escort service.

COSTS & FINANCIAL AID
Costs (2017–18) ***Tuition:*** state resident $2938 full-time, $122 per credit hour part-time; nonresident $8171 full-time, $340 per credit hour part-time. Full-time tuition and fees vary according to class time, course level, and degree level. Part-time tuition and fees vary according to class time, course level, and degree level. No tuition increase for student's term of enrollment. ***Required fees:*** $70 full-time, $35 per term part-time, $35 per term part-time. ***Payment plans:*** tuition prepayment, installment. ***Waivers:*** senior citizens and employees or children of employees.

Financial Aid Of all full-time matriculated undergraduates who enrolled in 2015, 27 Federal Work-Study jobs.

APPLYING
Options: electronic application.

Required for some: high school transcript.

Application deadlines: rolling (freshmen), rolling (transfers).

Notification: continuous (freshmen), continuous (transfers).

CONTACT
Mr. Kyle Williams, Senior Director of Enrollment Management, Oklahoma State University–Oklahoma City, 900 North Portland Avenue, AD202, Oklahoma City, OK 73107. *Phone:* 405-945-9152. *Toll-free phone:* 800-560-4099. *E-mail:* wilkylw@osuokc.edu.

Oklahoma Wesleyan University

Bartlesville, Oklahoma

http://www.okwu.edu/

- **Independent** comprehensive, founded 1909, affiliated with Wesleyan Church
- **Small-town** 127-acre campus with easy access to Tulsa
- **Endowment** $3.5 million
- **Coed**
- **Minimally difficult** entrance level

FACULTY
Student/faculty ratio: 15:1.

ACADEMICS
Calendar: semesters. *Degrees:* associate, bachelor's, and master's.
Library: Janice and Charles Drake Library.

STUDENT LIFE
Housing options: men-only, women-only. Campus housing is university owned. Freshman campus housing is guaranteed.

Activities and organizations: drama/theater group, student-run newspaper, choral group, Operation Saturation (Community Service Opportunities), Fellowship of Christian Athletes, Missions Support Groups, intramurals, Student Government Groups.

Athletics Member NAIA, NCCAA.

Campus security: student patrols.

Student services: health clinic, personal/psychological counseling.

FINANCIAL AID
Financial Aid Of all full-time matriculated undergraduates who enrolled in 2016, 553 applied for aid, 491 were judged to have need, 66 had their need fully met. 129 Federal Work-Study jobs (averaging $1633). 30 state and other part-time jobs (averaging $1489). In 2016, 113 non-need-based awards were made. ***Average percent of need met:*** 61. ***Average financial aid package:*** $17,022. ***Average need-based loan:*** $4459. ***Average need-based gift aid:*** $12,875. ***Average non-need-based aid:*** $6515. ***Average indebtedness upon graduation:*** $25,234.

APPLYING
Standardized Tests *Required:* SAT or ACT (for admission).

Options: electronic application.

Application fee: $25.

Required: high school transcript, minimum ACT score of 18. ***Required for some:*** interview. ***Recommended:*** minimum 2.0 GPA.

CONTACT
Samantha Peterson, AVP of Enrollment, Oklahoma Wesleyan University, 2201 Silver Lake Road, Bartlesville, OK 74006. *Phone:* 866-222-8226. *Toll-free phone:* 866-222-8226. *Fax:* 918-335-6229. *E-mail:* admissions@okwu.edu.

Oral Roberts University

Tulsa, Oklahoma

http://www.oru.edu/

- **Independent interdenominational** comprehensive, founded 1963
- **Urban** 263-acre campus
- **Coed** 3,057 undergraduate students, 82% full-time, 58% women, 42% men
- **Moderately difficult** entrance level, 22% of applicants were admitted

UNDERGRAD STUDENTS
2,513 full-time, 544 part-time. 51% are from out of state; 15% Black or African American, non-Hispanic/Latino; 9% Hispanic/Latino; 2% Asian, non-Hispanic/Latino; 3% American Indian or Alaska Native, non-Hispanic/Latino; 6% Two or more races, non-Hispanic/Latino; 8% Race/ethnicity unknown; 8% international; 7% transferred in; 66% live on campus.

Freshmen:
Admission: 2,378 applied, 522 admitted, 449 enrolled. ***Average high school GPA:*** 3.45. ***Test scores:*** SAT critical reading scores over 500: 53%; SAT math scores over 500: 51%; ACT scores over 18: 84%; SAT critical reading scores over 600: 13%; SAT math scores over 600: 16%; ACT scores over 24: 30%; SAT critical reading scores over 700: 3%; SAT math scores over 700: 1%; ACT scores over 30: 6%.

Retention: 80% of full-time freshmen returned.

FACULTY
Total: 274, 58% full-time, 50% with terminal degrees.

Student/faculty ratio: 14:1.

ACADEMICS
Calendar: semesters. *Degrees:* certificates, diplomas, bachelor's, master's, and doctoral.

Special study options: adult/continuing education programs, external degree program, part-time degree program. ***ROTC:*** Air Force (c).

Computers: Students can access the following: free student e-mail accounts, online (class) registration. Campuswide network is available.

Library: John D. Messick Resources Center.

STUDENT LIFE
Housing options: on-campus residence required through senior year; men-only, women-only, special housing for students with disabilities.

Athletics Member NCAA. All Division I. ***Intercollegiate sports:*** baseball M(s), basketball M(s)/W(s), cross-country running M(s)/W(s), golf M(s)/W(s), soccer M(s)/W(s), tennis M(s)/W(s), track and field M(s)/W(s), volleyball W(s), wrestling M. ***Intramural sports:*** badminton M/W, basketball M/W, bowling M/W, cross-country running M/W, football M/W, golf M/W, racquetball M/W, softball M/W, swimming and diving M/W, table tennis M/W, tennis M/W, volleyball M/W.

Campus security: 24-hour emergency response devices and patrols, late-night transport/escort service.

COSTS & FINANCIAL AID
Costs (2017–18) ***Comprehensive fee:*** $35,542 includes full-time tuition ($25,800), mandatory fees ($992), and room and board ($8750). Full-time tuition and fees vary according to course load, degree level, and location. Part-time tuition: $1078 per contact hour. Part-time tuition and fees vary according to course load, degree level, and location. ***College room only:*** $3860. Room and board charges vary according to board plan and housing facility. ***Payment plan:*** installment. ***Waivers:*** employees or children of employees.

Financial Aid Of all full-time matriculated undergraduates who enrolled in 2016, 2,192 applied for aid, 2,001 were judged to have need, 912 had their need fully met. In 2016, 654 non-need-based awards were made. ***Average percent of need met:*** 90. ***Average financial aid package:*** $24,085. ***Average need-based loan:*** $7337. ***Average need-based gift aid:*** $16,966. ***Average non-need-based aid:*** $12,373. ***Average indebtedness upon graduation:*** $32,970.

APPLYING
Standardized Tests *Required:* SAT or ACT (for admission).

Options: deferred entrance.

Application fee: $35.

Required: essay or personal statement, high school transcript, minimum 2.0 GPA, 1 letter of recommendation, proof of immunization. ***Required for some:*** interview. ***Recommended:*** interview.

CONTACT
Chris Belcher, Director of Admissions, Oral Roberts University, 7777 South Lewis Avenue, Tulsa, OK 74171. *Phone:* 918-495-6529. *Toll-free phone:* 800-678-8876. *Fax:* 918-495-6222. *E-mail:* admissions@oru.edu.

Platt College

Oklahoma City, Oklahoma

http://www.plattcolleges.edu/

CONTACT
Platt College, 2727 West Memorial Road, Oklahoma City, OK 73134. *Toll-free phone:* 877-392-6616.

Randall University

Moore, Oklahoma

http://www.hc.edu/

CONTACT
Randall University, PO Box 7208, Moore, OK 73160. *Phone:* 405-912-9007. *Fax:* 405-912-9050. *E-mail:* recruitment@hc.edu.

Rogers State University

Claremore, Oklahoma

http://www.rsu.edu/

- **State-supported** comprehensive, founded 1909, part of Oklahoma State Regents for Higher Education
- **Small-town** 40-acre campus with easy access to Tulsa
- **Endowment** $13.1 million
- **Coed** 3,889 undergraduate students, 61% full-time, 61% women, 39% men
- **Noncompetitive** entrance level, 79% of applicants were admitted

UNDERGRAD STUDENTS
2,372 full-time, 1,517 part-time. Students come from 30 states and territories; 27 other countries; 5% are from out of state; 4% Black or African American, non-Hispanic/Latino; 3% Hispanic/Latino; 2% Asian, non-Hispanic/Latino; 0.2% Native Hawaiian or other Pacific Islander, non-Hispanic/Latino; 11% American Indian or Alaska Native, non-Hispanic/Latino; 21% Two or more races, non-Hispanic/Latino; 1% Race/ethnicity unknown; 9% transferred in; 20% live on campus.

Freshmen:
Admission: 1,169 applied, 924 admitted, 639 enrolled. ***Average high school GPA:*** 3.15. ***Test scores:*** ACT scores over 18: 73%; ACT scores over 24: 21%; ACT scores over 30: 2%.

Retention: 46% of full-time freshmen returned.

FACULTY
Total: 257, 40% full-time, 37% with terminal degrees.

Student/faculty ratio: 19:1.

ACADEMICS
Calendar: semesters. *Degrees:* associate, bachelor's, and master's.
Special study options: academic remediation for entering students, adult/continuing education programs, advanced placement credit, cooperative education, distance learning, double majors, honors programs, independent study, internships, off-campus study, part-time degree program, services for LD students, study abroad, summer session for credit.
Computers: 251 computers/terminals are available on campus for general student use. Students can access the following: computer help desk, free student e-mail accounts, online (class) grades, online (class) registration, online (class) schedules, software to support courses. Campuswide network is available. 100% of college-owned or -operated housing units are wired for high-speed Internet access. Wireless service is available via classrooms, computer labs, dorm rooms, learning centers, libraries, student centers.
Library: Stratton Taylor Library. *Books:* 79,336 (physical), 297,898 (digital/electronic); *Serial titles:* 491 (physical), 67,126 (digital/electronic); *Databases:* 81. Weekly public service hours: 86; students can reserve study rooms.

STUDENT LIFE
Housing options: coed. Campus housing is university owned.
Activities and organizations: drama/theater group, student-run radio station, choral group, Students Veterans Association, Student Nurses Association, President's Leadership Class, Pre-Professional Health Club (Pre-SOMA), Student Athlete Advisory Committee, national sororities.
Athletics Member NCAA. All Division II. ***Intercollegiate sports:*** baseball M(s), basketball M(s)/W(s), cheerleading M(s)/W(s), cross-country running M(s)/W(s), golf M(s)/W(s), soccer M(s)/W(s), softball W(s), track and field M(s)/W(s). ***Intramural sports:*** basketball M/W, soccer M/W, softball M/W, table tennis M/W, volleyball M/W.
Campus security: 24-hour patrols, student patrols, late-night transport/escort service, controlled dormitory access, state-certified law enforcement officers, comprehensive camera surveillance system.
Student services: health clinic, personal/psychological counseling.

COSTS & FINANCIAL AID
Costs (2017–18) ***Tuition:*** state resident $4170 full-time; nonresident $12,480 full-time. Full-time tuition and fees vary according to course level, course load, location, program, and student level. Part-time tuition and fees vary according to course level, course load, location, program, and student level. ***Required fees:*** $2830 full-time. ***Room and board:*** $9512; room only: $5354. Room and board charges vary according to housing facility. ***Payment plan:*** installment. ***Waivers:*** senior citizens and employees or children of employees.
Financial Aid Of all full-time matriculated undergraduates who enrolled in 2016, 2,041 applied for aid, 1,735 were judged to have need, 194 had their need fully met. 54 Federal Work-Study jobs (averaging $2035). 208 state and other part-time jobs (averaging $2027). In 2016, 85 non-need-based awards were made. ***Average percent of need met:*** 54. ***Average financial aid package:*** $9679. ***Average need-based loan:*** $3832. ***Average need-based gift aid:*** $7037. ***Average non-need-based aid:*** $7137. ***Average indebtedness upon graduation:*** $16,164.

APPLYING
Standardized Tests *Required:* SAT or ACT (for admission). *Recommended:* ACT (for admission).
Options: electronic application.
Application fee: $20.
Required: high school transcript. ***Required for some:*** minimum 2.8 GPA, minimum ACT composite of 20 or 2.75 GPA and top 50% rank for baccalaureate programs.
Application deadlines: rolling (freshmen), rolling (transfers).

CONTACT
Ms. Joy Lin Hall, Director of Admissions, Rogers State University, 1701 West Will Rogers Boulevard, Claremore, OK 74017. *Phone:* 918-343-7546. *Toll-free phone:* 800-256-7511. *Fax:* 918-343-7595. *E-mail:* admissions@rsu.edu.

St. Gregory's University
Shawnee, Oklahoma
http://www.stgregorys.edu/

- **Independent Roman Catholic** comprehensive, founded 1875
- **Small-town** 640-acre campus with easy access to Oklahoma City
- **Coed** 636 undergraduate students, 72% full-time, 58% women, 42% men
- **Minimally difficult** entrance level, 85% of applicants were admitted

UNDERGRAD STUDENTS
460 full-time, 176 part-time. Students come from 25 states and territories; 9 other countries; 30% are from out of state; 6% Black or African American, non-Hispanic/Latino; 11% Hispanic/Latino; 0.9% Asian, non-Hispanic/Latino; 0.2% Native Hawaiian or other Pacific Islander, non-Hispanic/Latino; 13% American Indian or Alaska Native, non-Hispanic/Latino; 9% Two or more races, non-Hispanic/Latino; 2% Race/ethnicity unknown; 3% international; 23% transferred in; 36% live on campus.

Freshmen:
Admission: 184 applied, 157 admitted, 102 enrolled. ***Average high school GPA:*** 3.37.

Retention: 58% of full-time freshmen returned.

FACULTY
Total: 192, 20% full-time.

Student/faculty ratio: 7:1.

ACADEMICS
Calendar: semesters. *Degrees:* certificates, associate, bachelor's, and master's.
Special study options: accelerated degree program, adult/continuing education programs, advanced placement credit, cooperative education, distance learning, double majors, external degree program, honors programs, independent study, internships, off-campus study, part-time degree program, services for LD students, summer session for credit.
Computers: 35 computers/terminals and 100 ports are available on campus for general student use. Students can access the following: campus intranet, computer help desk, free student e-mail accounts, online (class) grades, online (class) registration, online (class) schedules. Campuswide network is available. 100% of college-owned or -operated housing units are wired for high-speed Internet access. Wireless service is available via entire campus.
Library: James J. Kelly Library plus 1 other. *Books:* 88,444 (physical).

STUDENT LIFE
Housing options: on-campus residence required through senior year; men-only, women-only, special housing for students with disabilities. Campus housing is university owned. Freshman campus housing is guaranteed.
Activities and organizations: drama/theater group, choral group, Greek Life, Student Government Association, Pro-Life, Hispanic American Student Association, Campus Ministry.
Athletics Member NAIA. ***Intercollegiate sports:*** baseball M(s), basketball M(s)/W(s), cheerleading M/W, soccer M(s)/W(s), softball W(s), track and field M(s)/W(s), volleyball W(s). ***Intramural sports:*** basketball M/W, football M/W, racquetball M/W, soccer M/W, softball

M/W, swimming and diving M/W, table tennis M/W, tennis M/W, volleyball M/W.

Campus security: 24-hour emergency response devices and patrols, late-night transport/escort service, controlled dormitory access.

Student services: personal/psychological counseling.

COSTS & FINANCIAL AID

Costs (2016–17) ***Tuition:*** Full-time tuition and fees vary according to course level, degree level, program, and student level. Part-time tuition and fees vary according to course level, degree level, program, and student level. No tuition increase for student's term of enrollment. ***Room and board:*** $8578; room only: $4410. Room and board charges vary according to board plan and housing facility. ***Payment plans:*** tuition prepayment, installment. ***Waivers:*** employees or children of employees.

Financial Aid Of all full-time matriculated undergraduates who enrolled in 2015, 519 applied for aid, 435 were judged to have need, 54 had their need fully met. 34 Federal Work-Study jobs (averaging $900). 30 state and other part-time jobs (averaging $2000). In 2015, 76 non-need-based awards were made. ***Average percent of need met:*** 72. ***Average financial aid package:*** $19,328. ***Average need-based loan:*** $3500. ***Average need-based gift aid:*** $12,603. ***Average non-need-based aid:*** $3000. ***Average indebtedness upon graduation:*** $35,000.

APPLYING

Standardized Tests *Required:* SAT or ACT (for admission).

Options: electronic application, deferred entrance.

Required: minimum 2.8 GPA. ***Required for some:*** essay or personal statement, high school transcript, interview.

Application deadlines: rolling (freshmen), rolling (transfers).

Notification: continuous (freshmen), continuous (transfers).

CONTACT

Paul Carney, Director of Admissions, St. Gregory's University, 1900 West MacArthur Drive, Shawnee, OK 74804. *Phone:* 405-878-5161. *Toll-free phone:* 888-STGREGS. *Fax:* 405-878-5198. *E-mail:* admissions@stgregorys.edu.

Southeastern Oklahoma State University

Durant, Oklahoma

http://www.se.edu/

- **State-supported** comprehensive, founded 1909, part of Oklahoma State Regents for Higher Education
- **Small-town** 276-acre campus
- **Endowment** $22.4 million
- **Coed** 3,132 undergraduate students, 77% full-time, 54% women, 46% men
- **Moderately difficult** entrance level, 77% of applicants were admitted

UNDERGRAD STUDENTS

2,411 full-time, 721 part-time. Students come from 28 states and territories; 36 other countries; 25% are from out of state; 6% Black or African American, non-Hispanic/Latino; 6% Hispanic/Latino; 0.7% Asian, non-Hispanic/Latino; 0.3% Native Hawaiian or other Pacific Islander, non-Hispanic/Latino; 30% American Indian or Alaska Native, non-Hispanic/Latino; 3% Race/ethnicity unknown; 11% transferred in; 18% live on campus.

Freshmen:

Admission: 1,107 applied, 856 admitted, 517 enrolled. ***Average high school GPA:*** 3.36. ***Test scores:*** ACT scores over 18: 81%; ACT scores over 24: 18%; ACT scores over 30: 2%.

Retention: 55% of full-time freshmen returned.

FACULTY

Total: 227, 49% full-time, 60% with terminal degrees.

Student/faculty ratio: 20:1.

ACADEMICS

Calendar: semesters. *Degrees:* bachelor's, master's, and post-master's certificates.

Special study options: academic remediation for entering students, accelerated degree program, adult/continuing education programs, advanced placement credit, distance learning, double majors, honors programs, independent study, internships, off-campus study, part-time degree program, services for LD students, summer session for credit.

Computers: 598 computers/terminals and 598 ports are available on campus for general student use. Students can access the following: campus intranet, computer help desk, free student e-mail accounts, online (class) grades, online (class) registration, online (class) schedules, campus learning management system classes. Campuswide network is available. 100% of college-owned or -operated housing units are wired for high-speed Internet access. Wireless service is available via classrooms, computer labs, dorm rooms, learning centers, libraries, student centers.

Library: Henry G. Bennett Memorial Library plus 1 other. *Books:* 194,586 (physical), 17,613 (digital/electronic); *Serial titles:* 84 (physical), 2,260 (digital/electronic); *Databases:* 103. Weekly public service hours: 79; students can reserve study rooms.

STUDENT LIFE

Housing options: on-campus residence required for freshman year; coed, men-only, women-only, special housing for students with disabilities. Campus housing is university owned. Freshman campus housing is guaranteed.

Activities and organizations: drama/theater group, student-run newspaper, radio station, choral group, marching band, Baptist Collegiate Ministries, Greek Community, Student Government Association, Kappa Kappa Psi, Psychology Club, national fraternities, national sororities.

Athletics Member NCAA. All Division II. ***Intercollegiate sports:*** baseball M(s), basketball M(s)/W(s), cross-country running W(s), football M(s), golf M(s), softball W(s), tennis M(s)/W(s), volleyball W(s). ***Intramural sports:*** basketball M/W, football M.

Campus security: 24-hour emergency response devices and patrols, late-night transport/escort service, controlled dormitory access.

Student services: health clinic, personal/psychological counseling.

COSTS & FINANCIAL AID

Costs (2016–17) ***Tuition:*** state resident $5940 full-time, $198 per credit hour part-time; nonresident $15,210 full-time, $507 per credit hour part-time. Full-time tuition and fees vary according to course level, course load, degree level, location, and program. Part-time tuition and fees vary according to course level, course load, degree level, location, and program. No tuition increase for student's term of enrollment. ***Required fees:*** $510 full-time, $17 per credit hour part-time. ***Room and board:*** $6535; room only: $3435. Room and board charges vary according to board plan, housing facility, and student level. ***Payment plan:*** installment. ***Waivers:*** minority students, children of alumni, adult students, senior citizens, and employees or children of employees.

Financial Aid Of all full-time matriculated undergraduates who enrolled in 2015, 1,747 applied for aid, 1,565 were judged to have need, 112 had their need fully met. In 2015, 29 non-need-based awards were made. ***Average percent of need met:*** 8. ***Average financial aid package:*** $11,195. ***Average need-based loan:*** $2084. ***Average need-based gift aid:*** $1915. ***Average non-need-based aid:*** $1013. ***Average indebtedness upon graduation:*** $20,983.

APPLYING

Standardized Tests *Required:* SAT or ACT (for admission).

Options: electronic application.

Application fee: $20.

Required: high school transcript. ***Required for some:*** interview.

Application deadlines: rolling (freshmen), rolling (transfers).

Notification: continuous (freshmen), continuous (transfers).

CONTACT

Southeastern Oklahoma State University, 1405 North 4th Avenue, Durant, OK 74701-0609. *Phone:* 580-745-2061. *Toll-free phone:* 800-435-1327.

Southern Nazarene University

Bethany, Oklahoma

http://www.snu.edu/

- **Independent Nazarene** comprehensive, founded 1899
- **Suburban** 40-acre campus with easy access to Oklahoma City
- **Endowment** $21.6 million
- **Coed**
- **Noncompetitive** entrance level

FACULTY
Student/faculty ratio: 12:1.

ACADEMICS
Calendar: semesters. *Degrees:* associate, bachelor's, and master's.
Library: R. T. Williams Learning Resources Center. *Books:* 108,231 (physical), 125,507 (digital/electronic); *Serial titles:* 4,512 (physical), 21,217 (digital/electronic); *Databases:* 72. Students can reserve study rooms.

STUDENT LIFE
Housing options: on-campus residence required through senior year; men-only, women-only. Campus housing is university owned. Freshman campus housing is guaranteed.

Activities and organizations: drama/theater group, student-run newspaper, choral group, Business Gaming Team, Campus Social Life Committee, intramural sports societies, Choral Society, Inter-Club.

Athletics Member NCAA. All Division II.

Campus security: 24-hour emergency response devices, student patrols, late-night transport/escort service, controlled dormitory access.

Student services: health clinic, personal/psychological counseling.

FINANCIAL AID
Financial Aid Of all full-time matriculated undergraduates who enrolled in 2009, 1,485 applied for aid, 1,366 were judged to have need. 104 Federal Work-Study jobs (averaging $2125). 115 state and other part-time jobs (averaging $3000).

APPLYING
Standardized Tests *Required:* SAT or ACT (for admission). *Recommended:* ACT (for admission).

Options: electronic application, deferred entrance.

Application fee: $35.

Required: high school transcript, minimum 2.0 GPA, 2 letters of recommendation, interview.

CONTACT
Dr. Linda Cantwell, Director of Recruitment, Southern Nazarene University, 6729 Northwest 39th Expressway, Bethany, OK 73008. *Phone:* 405-491-6324. *Toll-free phone:* 800-648-9899. *Fax:* 405-491-6320. *E-mail:* admiss@snu.edu.

Southwestern Christian University

Bethany, Oklahoma

http://www.swcu.edu/

CONTACT
Ms. Jessie Burpo, Admissions Counselor, Southwestern Christian University, PO Box 340, Bethany, OK 73008-0340. *Phone:* 405-789-7661 Ext. 3432. *Fax:* 405-495-0078. *E-mail:* admissions@swcu.edu.

Southwestern Oklahoma State University

Weatherford, Oklahoma

http://www.swosu.edu/

- **State-supported** comprehensive, founded 1901
- **Small-town** 73-acre campus with easy access to Oklahoma City
- **Endowment** $22.3 million
- **Coed**
- **Minimally difficult** entrance level

FACULTY
Student/faculty ratio: 18:1.

ACADEMICS
Calendar: semesters. *Degrees:* certificates, associate, bachelor's, master's, and doctoral.
Library: Al Harris Library plus 1 other. *Books:* 301,353 (physical), 302,089 (digital/electronic); *Databases:* 150. Weekly public service hours: 84; students can reserve study rooms.

STUDENT LIFE
Housing options: men-only, women-only. Campus housing is university owned.

Activities and organizations: drama/theater group, student-run newspaper, choral group, marching band, Collegiate Activities Board, Chi Alpha, Sigma Sigma Chi, SWOSU Computer Club, Kappa Epsilon, national fraternities, national sororities.

Athletics Member NCAA. All Division II.

Campus security: late-night transport/escort service, police available 24-hours a day.

Student services: health clinic, personal/psychological counseling, legal services.

COSTS & FINANCIAL AID
Costs (2016–17) ***One-time required fee:*** $100. ***Tuition:*** state resident $5295 full-time, $177 per credit hour part-time; nonresident $12,045 full-time, $402 per credit hour part-time. Full-time tuition and fees vary according to degree level, location, and program. Part-time tuition and fees vary according to degree level, location, and program. ***Required fees:*** $1395 full-time, $47 per credit hour part-time, $47 per credit hour part-time. ***Room and board:*** $5400; room only: $2200. Room and board charges vary according to board plan and housing facility. ***Payment plans:*** installment, deferred payment.

Financial Aid Of all full-time matriculated undergraduates who enrolled in 2015, 2,590 applied for aid, 2,083 were judged to have need, 449 had their need fully met. In 2015, 1273 non-need-based awards were made. ***Average percent of need met:*** 94. ***Average financial aid package:*** $5667. ***Average need-based loan:*** $1672. ***Average need-based gift aid:*** $1710. ***Average non-need-based aid:*** $629. ***Average indebtedness upon graduation:*** $18,809. ***Financial aid deadline:*** 3/1.

APPLYING
Standardized Tests *Required:* SAT or ACT (for admission). *Recommended:* ACT (for admission).

Options: electronic application, deferred entrance.

Application fee: $15.

Required: high school transcript. ***Required for some:*** minimum 2.7 GPA, minimum ACT score of 20 (940 SAT) or rank in the upper 50% of high school graduating class or have a high school GPA of 2.7 in the 15-unit core curriculum.

CONTACT
Ms. Cassie Jones, Admissions Coordinator, Southwestern Oklahoma State University, Southwestern Oklahoma State University, John Hays Administration Building, Room 108-C, Weatherford, OK 73096. *Phone:* 580-774-3009. *Fax:* 580-774-3795. *E-mail:* cassie.jones@swosu.edu.

Spartan College of Aeronautics and Technology

Tulsa, Oklahoma

http://www.spartan.edu/

CONTACT
Mr. Mark Fowler, Vice President of Student Records and Finance, Spartan College of Aeronautics and Technology, 8820 East Pine Street, Tulsa, OK 74115. *Phone:* 918-836-6886. *Toll-free phone:* 800-331-1204.

University of Central Oklahoma

Edmond, Oklahoma

http://www.uco.edu/

- **State-supported** comprehensive, founded 1890, part of Oklahoma State Regents for Higher Education
- **Suburban** 200-acre campus with easy access to Oklahoma City
- **Endowment** $19.7 million
- **Coed**
- **Minimally difficult** entrance level

FACULTY
Student/faculty ratio: 19:1.

ACADEMICS
Calendar: semesters. *Degrees:* certificates, associate, bachelor's, and master's.
Library: Max Chambers Library plus 1 other. Weekly public service hours: 107; students can reserve study rooms.

STUDENT LIFE

Housing options: coed, men-only, women-only. Campus housing is university owned and leased by the school.

Activities and organizations: drama/theater group, student-run newspaper, radio and television station, choral group, marching band, Student Government Association, Student Programming Board, International Student Council, Panhellenic Council, Interfraternity Council, national fraternities, national sororities.

Athletics Member NCAA. All Division II.

Campus security: 24-hour emergency response devices and patrols, late-night transport/escort service.

Student services: health clinic, personal/psychological counseling, women's center.

COSTS & FINANCIAL AID

Costs (2016–17) ***Tuition:*** state resident $5157 full-time, $172 per credit hour part-time; nonresident $14,033 full-time, $468 per credit hour part-time. Full-time tuition and fees vary according to course load, degree level, location, and program. Part-time tuition and fees vary according to course load, degree level, location, and program. No tuition increase for student's term of enrollment. ***Required fees:*** $939 full-time, $31 per credit hour part-time. ***Room and board:*** $7130; room only: $3496. Room and board charges vary according to board plan and housing facility.

Financial Aid Of all full-time matriculated undergraduates who enrolled in 2014, 7,493 applied for aid, 1,193 had their need fully met. In 2014, 262 non-need-based awards were made. ***Average percent of need met:*** 52. ***Average financial aid package:*** $9073. ***Average need-based loan:*** $3973. ***Average need-based gift aid:*** $5909. ***Average non-need-based aid:*** $1421. ***Average indebtedness upon graduation:*** $21,770.

APPLYING

Standardized Tests *Required:* SAT or ACT (for admission). *Required for some:* SAT and SAT Subject Tests or ACT (for admission). *Recommended:* ACT (for admission).

Options: electronic application, deferred entrance.

Application fee: $90.

Required: high school transcript, minimum 2.7 GPA, rank in upper 50% of high school class; composite ACT score of 20; 2.7 GPA in core curriculum classes.

CONTACT

Mr. Dallas Caldwell, Director of Undergraduate Admissions, University of Central Oklahoma, Office of Enrollment Services, 100 North University Drive, Box 151, Edmond, OK 73034-5209. *Phone:* 405-974-2631. *Fax:* 405-974-3841. *E-mail:* onestop@uco.edu.

University of Oklahoma

Norman, Oklahoma

http://www.ou.edu/

- **State-supported** university, founded 1890
- **Suburban** 3337-acre campus with easy access to Oklahoma City
- **Endowment** $999.8 million
- **Coed** 21,609 undergraduate students, 85% full-time, 49% women, 51% men
- **Moderately difficult** entrance level, 70% of applicants were admitted

UNDERGRAD STUDENTS

18,424 full-time, 3,185 part-time. Students come from 52 states and territories; 111 other countries; 35% are from out of state; 5% Black or African American, non-Hispanic/Latino; 9% Hispanic/Latino; 6% Asian, non-Hispanic/Latino; 0.1% Native Hawaiian or other Pacific Islander, non-Hispanic/Latino; 4% American Indian or Alaska Native, non-Hispanic/Latino; 8% Two or more races, non-Hispanic/Latino; 2% Race/ethnicity unknown; 5% international; 5% transferred in; 31% live on campus.

Freshmen:

Admission: 14,522 applied, 10,228 admitted, 4,198 enrolled. ***Average high school GPA:*** 3.62. ***Test scores:*** SAT critical reading scores over 500: 86%; SAT math scores over 500: 90%; ACT scores over 18: 100%; SAT critical reading scores over 600: 45%; SAT math scores over 600: 53%; ACT scores over 24: 75%; SAT critical reading scores over 700: 18%; SAT math scores over 700: 19%; ACT scores over 30: 23%.

Retention: 90% of full-time freshmen returned.

FACULTY

Total: 1,459, 83% full-time, 81% with terminal degrees.

Student/faculty ratio: 18:1.

ACADEMICS

Calendar: semesters. *Degrees:* certificates, bachelor's, master's, doctoral, and postbachelor's certificates.

Special study options: academic remediation for entering students, accelerated degree program, adult/continuing education programs, advanced placement credit, cooperative education, distance learning, double majors, English as a second language, external degree program, freshman honors college, honors programs, independent study, internships, off-campus study, part-time degree program, services for LD students, student-designed majors, study abroad, summer session for credit. ***ROTC:*** Army (b), Navy (b), Air Force (b).

Unusual degree programs: 3-2 business administration; engineering; English, mathematics/biostatistics, computer science, international studies, political science/public administration.

Computers: 4,500 computers/terminals and 2,200 ports are available on campus for general student use. Students can access the following: campus intranet, computer help desk, free student e-mail accounts, online (class) grades, online (class) registration, online (class) schedules. Campuswide network is available. 100% of college-owned or -operated housing units are wired for high-speed Internet access. Wireless service is available via entire campus.

Library: Bizzell Memorial Library plus 5 others. *Books:* 5.7 million (physical), 1.3 million (digital/electronic); *Serial titles:* 116,374 (physical), 71,040 (digital/electronic); *Databases:* 310. Students can reserve study rooms.

STUDENT LIFE

Housing options: on-campus residence required for freshman year; coed, men-only, women-only, special housing for students with disabilities. Campus housing is university owned. Freshman campus housing is guaranteed.

Activities and organizations: drama/theater group, student-run newspaper, radio and television station, choral group, marching band, Campus Activities Council Soonerthon, Campus Activities Council Homecoming, Engineers Club, Relay For Life, The Big Event, national fraternities, national sororities.

Athletics Member NCAA. All Division I except football (Division I-A). ***Intercollegiate sports:*** baseball M(s), basketball M(s)/W(s), cheerleading M(s)/W(s), crew W(s), cross-country running M(s)/W(s), golf M(s)/W(s), gymnastics M(s)/W(s), rowing W(s), soccer W(s), softball W(s), tennis M(s)/W(s), track and field M(s)/W(s), volleyball W(s), wrestling M(s). ***Intramural sports:*** badminton M(c)/W(c), basketball M/W, crew M(c)/W(c), cross-country running M/W, equestrian sports W(c), field hockey M(c)/W(c), golf M(c)/W(c), ice hockey M(c), lacrosse M(c), racquetball M/W, rowing M(c)/W(c), rugby M(c)/W(c), sand volleyball M/W, soccer M(c)/W, softball M/W, table tennis M/W, tennis M/W, triathlon M(c)/W(c), ultimate Frisbee M(c)/W(c), volleyball M(c)/W(c).

Campus security: 24-hour emergency response devices and patrols, late-night transport/escort service, controlled dormitory access, crime prevention programs, police bicycle patrols, self-defense classes.

Student services: health clinic, personal/psychological counseling, women's center, legal services.

COSTS & FINANCIAL AID

Costs (2016–17) ***Tuition:*** state resident $4575 full-time, $153 per credit hour part-time; nonresident $18,897 full-time, $630 per credit hour part-time. Full-time tuition and fees vary according to course load, location, program, and student level. Part-time tuition and fees vary according to course load, location, program, and student level. No tuition increase for student's term of enrollment. ***Required fees:*** $4056 full-time, $127 per credit hour part-time, $127 per term part-time. ***Room and board:*** $10,280; room only: $6012. Room and board charges vary according to board plan and housing facility. ***Payment plan:*** installment. ***Waivers:*** senior citizens and employees or children of employees.

Financial Aid Of all full-time matriculated undergraduates who enrolled in 2015, 10,536 applied for aid, 7,880 were judged to have need, 6,460 had their need fully met. 627 Federal Work-Study jobs (averaging $2723). 101 state and other part-time jobs (averaging $7404). In 2015, 2493 non-need-based awards were made. ***Average percent of need met:*** 84. ***Average financial aid package:*** $12,746. ***Average need-based loan:*** $4229. ***Average need-based gift aid:*** $6098. ***Average non-need-based aid:*** $2625. ***Average indebtedness upon graduation:*** $28,444.

APPLYING

Standardized Tests *Required:* SAT or ACT (for admission).

Options: electronic application.

Application fee: $40.

Required: essay or personal statement, high school transcript, 15 specified curricular units.

Application deadlines: 2/1 (freshmen), 6/1 (transfers).

Notification: continuous (freshmen), continuous (transfers).

CONTACT

Mr. Jeff Blahnik, Director of Admissions, University of Oklahoma, 1000 Asp Avenue, Rm 127, Norman, OK 73019-3032. *Phone:* 405-325-2151. *Toll-free phone:* 800-234-6868. *Fax:* 405-325-7478. *E-mail:* ou-pss@ou.edu.

University of Oklahoma Health Sciences Center

Oklahoma City, Oklahoma

http://www.ouhsc.edu/

- **State-supported** upper-level, founded 1890, part of University of Oklahoma
- **Urban** 200-acre campus with easy access to Oklahoma City
- **Endowment** $312.6 million
- **Coed** 827 undergraduate students, 94% full-time, 89% women, 11% men

UNDERGRAD STUDENTS

776 full-time, 51 part-time. Students come from 43 states and territories; 14 other countries; 14% are from out of state; 4% Black or African American, non-Hispanic/Latino; 8% Hispanic/Latino; 7% Asian, non-Hispanic/Latino; 0.1% Native Hawaiian or other Pacific Islander, non-Hispanic/Latino; 4% American Indian or Alaska Native, non-Hispanic/Latino; 2% Two or more races, non-Hispanic/Latino; 9% Race/ethnicity unknown; 0.7% international; 39% transferred in; 13% live on campus.

FACULTY

Total: 408, 73% full-time, 71% with terminal degrees.

Student/faculty ratio: 10:1.

ACADEMICS

Calendar: semesters. *Degrees:* bachelor's, master's, doctoral, post-master's, and postbachelor's certificates.

Special study options: advanced placement credit, distance learning, honors programs, internships, part-time degree program, summer session for credit. ***ROTC:*** Army (c), Air Force (c).

Computers: 140 computers/terminals are available on campus for general student use. Students can access the following: campus intranet, computer help desk, free student e-mail accounts, online (class) grades, online (class) registration, online (class) schedules, online bursar bill and payment. Campuswide network is available. 100% of college-owned or -operated housing units are wired for high-speed Internet access. Wireless service is available via classrooms, computer centers, computer labs, learning centers, libraries, student centers.

Library: Robert M. Bird Health Sciences Library plus 1 other. *Books:* 286,469 (physical), 19,136 (digital/electronic); *Serial titles:* 158 (physical), 26,678 (digital/electronic); *Databases:* 157. Weekly public service hours: 111.

STUDENT LIFE

Housing options: coed. Campus housing is university owned.

Activities and organizations: student-run radio station, OU Health Sciences Center Student Association, OU College of Nursing Student Association, OU College of Medicine Student Association, OU College of Pharmacy Student Counsel, OU College of Allied Health Student Association.

Campus security: 24-hour emergency response devices and patrols, late-night transport/escort service.

Student services: health clinic, personal/psychological counseling, women's center.

COSTS

Costs (2016–17) ***Tuition:*** state resident $4575 full-time, $153 per credit hour part-time; nonresident $18,897 full-time, $630 per credit hour part-time. Full-time tuition and fees vary according to course level, course load, degree level, location, program, and student level. Part-time tuition and fees vary according to course level, course load, degree level, location, program, and student level. ***Required fees:*** $2290 full-time, $60 per credit hour part-time, $250 per term part-time. ***Room and board:*** Room and board charges vary according to location. ***Payment plan:*** installment. ***Waivers:*** employees or children of employees.

APPLYING

Options: electronic application, deferred entrance.

Notification: continuous (transfers).

CONTACT

University of Oklahoma Health Sciences Center, PO Box 26901, Oklahoma City, OK 73190. *Phone:* 405-271-2347 Ext. 48916.

★ University of Science and Arts of Oklahoma

Chickasha, Oklahoma

http://www.usao.edu/

- **State-supported** 4-year, founded 1908, part of Oklahoma State Regents for Higher Education
- **Small-town** 75-acre campus with easy access to Oklahoma City
- **Endowment** $13.1 million
- **Coed** 888 undergraduate students, 89% full-time, 66% women, 34% men
- **Moderately difficult** entrance level, 66% of applicants were admitted

UNDERGRAD STUDENTS

787 full-time, 101 part-time. Students come from 16 states and territories; 22 other countries; 14% are from out of state; 5% Black or African American, non-Hispanic/Latino; 7% Hispanic/Latino; 0.9% Asian, non-Hispanic/Latino; 14% American Indian or Alaska Native, non-Hispanic/Latino; 2% Race/ethnicity unknown; 8% international; 9% transferred in; 44% live on campus.

Freshmen:

Admission: 706 applied, 466 admitted, 223 enrolled. ***Average high school GPA:*** 3.43. ***Test scores:*** SAT critical reading scores over 500: 22%; SAT math scores over 500: 26%; ACT scores over 18: 81%; SAT critical reading scores over 600: 4%; SAT math scores over 600: 9%; ACT scores over 24: 23%; ACT scores over 30: 4%.

Retention: 77% of full-time freshmen returned.

FACULTY

Total: 87, 62% full-time, 60% with terminal degrees.

Student/faculty ratio: 12:1.

ACADEMICS

Calendar: trimesters. *Degree:* bachelor's.

Special study options: academic remediation for entering students, accelerated degree program, advanced placement credit, double majors, independent study, internships, off-campus study, part-time degree program, services for LD students, student-designed majors, summer session for credit.

Computers: 185 computers/terminals are available on campus for general student use. Students can access the following: computer help desk, free student e-mail accounts, online (class) schedules. Campuswide network is available. 100% of college-owned or -operated housing units are wired for high-speed Internet access. Wireless service is available via entire campus.

Library: Nash Library plus 1 other. *Books:* 87,603 (physical), 4,798 (digital/electronic); *Serial titles:* 22 (physical), 10,500 (digital/electronic); *Databases:* 60. Weekly public service hours: 81.

STUDENT LIFE

Housing options: on-campus residence required for freshman year; coed. Campus housing is university owned. Freshman campus housing is guaranteed.

Activities and organizations: drama/theater group, student-run newspaper, television station, choral group, Student Activities Board, Volunteer Action Council, Psychology Club, Young Democrats, Young Conservatives, national fraternities.

Athletics Member NAIA. ***Intercollegiate sports:*** baseball M(s), basketball M(s)/W(s), cheerleading M(s)/W(s), cross-country running M/W, soccer M(s)/W(s), softball W(s), volleyball W. ***Intramural sports:*** basketball M/W, football M/W, golf M/W, softball M/W, volleyball M/W.

Campus security: 24-hour emergency response devices and patrols, controlled dormitory access.

Student services: health clinic, personal/psychological counseling.

COSTS & FINANCIAL AID

Costs (2016–17) ***Tuition:*** state resident $201 per credit hour part-time; nonresident $546 per credit hour part-time. No tuition increase for student's term of enrollment. ***Room and board:*** Room and board charges vary according to board plan and housing facility. ***Payment plan:*** installment. ***Waivers:*** senior citizens and employees or children of employees.

Financial Aid Of all full-time matriculated undergraduates who enrolled in 2016, 589 applied for aid, 506 were judged to have need, 88 had their need fully met. 158 Federal Work-Study jobs (averaging $1420). In 2016, 99 non-need-based awards were made. ***Average percent of need met:*** 68. ***Average financial aid package:*** $11,157. ***Average need-based loan:*** $3126. ***Average need-based gift aid:*** $9357. ***Average non-need-based aid:*** $3104. ***Average indebtedness upon graduation:*** $22,760.

APPLYING

Standardized Tests *Required:* SAT or ACT (for admission).

Options: electronic application, deferred entrance.

Application fee: $40.

Required for some: high school transcript, minimum 3.0 GPA, minimum ACT score of 24 and 3.0 GPA/top 50% high school class, 3.0 GPA and top 25% high school class, or minimum ACT score of 22 and 3.0 GPA in 15-unit high school core. ***Recommended:*** minimum ACT score of 24 and 3.0 GPA/top 50% high school class, 3.0 GPA and top 25% high school class, or minimum ACT score of 22 and 3.0 GPA in 15-unit high school core.

Application deadlines: 9/2 (freshmen), rolling (out-of-state freshmen), 9/2 (transfers).

Notification: continuous until 1/2 (freshmen), continuous until 1/2 (out-of-state freshmen), continuous (transfers).

CONTACT

Mrs. Laura Coponiti, Dean of Admissions and Financial Aid, University of Science and Arts of Oklahoma, 1727 West Alabama, Chickasha, OK 73018-5322. *Phone:* 405-574-1350. *Toll-free phone:* 800-933-8726. *Fax:* 405-574-1220. *E-mail:* usao-admissions@usao.edu.

The University of Tulsa

Tulsa, Oklahoma

http://www.utulsa.edu/

- **Independent** university, founded 1894, affiliated with Presbyterian Church (U.S.A.)
- **Urban** 209-acre campus with easy access to Tulsa
- **Endowment** $975.6 million
- **Coed** 3,406 undergraduate students, 96% full-time, 43% women, 57% men
- **Very difficult** entrance level, 37% of applicants were admitted

UNDERGRAD STUDENTS

3,259 full-time, 147 part-time. Students come from 43 states and territories; 57 other countries; 42% are from out of state; 5% Black or African American, non-Hispanic/Latino; 5% Hispanic/Latino; 4% Asian, non-Hispanic/Latino; 0.2% Native Hawaiian or other Pacific Islander, non-Hispanic/Latino; 3% American Indian or Alaska Native, non-Hispanic/Latino; 0.5% Two or more races, non-Hispanic/Latino; 2% Race/ethnicity unknown; 24% international; 4% transferred in; 69% live on campus.

Freshmen:

Admission: 8,089 applied, 2,990 admitted, 717 enrolled. ***Average high school GPA:*** 3.9. ***Test scores:*** SAT critical reading scores over 500: 86%; SAT math scores over 500: 89%; SAT writing scores over 500: 78%; ACT scores over 18: 100%; SAT critical reading scores over 600: 61%; SAT math scores over 600: 62%; SAT writing scores over 600: 46%; ACT

scores over 24: 90%; SAT critical reading scores over 700: 28%; SAT math scores over 700: 25%; SAT writing scores over 700: 16%; ACT scores over 30: 53%.

Retention: 91% of full-time freshmen returned.

FACULTY
Total: 448, 78% full-time, 95% with terminal degrees.

Student/faculty ratio: 11:1.

ACADEMICS
Calendar: semesters. *Degrees:* bachelor's, master's, doctoral, and postbachelor's certificates.

Special study options: accelerated degree program, adult/continuing education programs, advanced placement credit, double majors, English as a second language, honors programs, independent study, internships, part-time degree program, services for LD students, student-designed majors, study abroad, summer session for credit. ***ROTC:*** Air Force (c).

Unusual degree programs: 3-2 business administration; engineering; accountancy, mathematics, athletic training, biochemistry, biology, chemistry, computer science, cyber security, geosciences, geophysics, history, physics, women's and gender studies.

Computers: 710 computers/terminals and 250 ports are available on campus for general student use. Students can access the following: campus intranet, computer help desk, free student e-mail accounts, online (class) grades, online (class) registration, online (class) schedules. Campuswide network is available. 100% of college-owned or -operated housing units are wired for high-speed Internet access. Wireless service is available via entire campus.

Library: McFarlin Library plus 1 other. *Books:* 1.2 million (physical), 460,240 (digital/electronic); *Serial titles:* 59,171 (digital/electronic); *Databases:* 289. Weekly public service hours: 94; study areas open 24 hours, 5-7 days a week; students can reserve study rooms.

STUDENT LIFE
Housing options: on-campus residence required through sophomore year; coed, men-only, women-only, special housing for students with disabilities. Campus housing is university owned. Freshman campus housing is guaranteed.

Activities and organizations: drama/theater group, student-run newspaper, radio and television station, choral group, marching band, Student Association, Residence Hall Association, Pre-Professional organizations, intramural sports, Greek life, national fraternities, national sororities.

Athletics Member NCAA. All Division I except football (Division I-A). ***Intercollegiate sports:*** basketball M(s)/W(s), cheerleading M/W, crew W(s), cross-country running M(s)/W(s), golf W(s), soccer M(s)/W(s), softball W(s), tennis M(s)/W(s), track and field M(s)/W(s), volleyball W(s). ***Intramural sports:*** badminton M/W, basketball M/W, bowling M/W, crew M(c), cross-country running M/W, football M/W, golf W, lacrosse M(c), racquetball M/W, rugby M(c), soccer M/W, softball M/W, squash M/W, table tennis M/W, tennis M/W, track and field M/W, volleyball M/W, weight lifting M/W.

Campus security: 24-hour emergency response devices and patrols, late-night transport/escort service, controlled dormitory access.

Student services: health clinic, personal/psychological counseling.

COSTS & FINANCIAL AID
Costs (2017–18) ***One-time required fee:*** $485. ***Comprehensive fee:*** $52,140 includes full-time tuition ($40,484), mandatory fees ($540), and room and board ($11,116). Full-time tuition and fees vary according to course load and program. Part-time tuition: $1453 per credit hour. Part-time tuition and fees vary according to course load and program. ***College room only:*** $6394. Room and board charges vary according to board plan and housing facility. ***Payment plan:*** installment. ***Waivers:*** employees or children of employees.

Financial Aid Of all full-time matriculated undergraduates who enrolled in 2016, 1,596 applied for aid, 1,377 were judged to have need, 584 had their need fully met. 275 Federal Work-Study jobs (averaging $2612). In 2016, 1385 non-need-based awards were made. ***Average percent of need met:*** 81. ***Average financial aid package:*** $29,644. ***Average need-based loan:*** $6621. ***Average need-based gift aid:*** $5679. ***Average non-need-based aid:*** $19,520. ***Average indebtedness upon graduation:*** $37,136.

APPLYING
Standardized Tests *Required:* SAT or ACT (for admission).

Options: electronic application, early admission, early action, deferred entrance.

Application fee: $50.

Required: essay or personal statement, high school transcript, 1 letter of recommendation. ***Recommended:*** minimum 3.0 GPA, interview.

Application deadlines: rolling (freshmen), rolling (transfers), 11/1 (early action).

Notification: continuous (freshmen), continuous (transfers), 12/15 (early action).

CONTACT
Ms. Casey Reed, Dean of Admission, The University of Tulsa, 800 South Tucker Drive, Tulsa, OK 74104. *Phone:* 918-631-2307. *Toll-free phone:* 800-331-3050. *Fax:* 918-631-5003. *E-mail:* admission@utulsa.edu.

See previous page for display ad and page 1580 for the College Close-Up.

OREGON

The Art Institute of Portland
Portland, Oregon
http://www.artinstitutes.edu/portland/

CONTACT
The Art Institute of Portland, 1122 NW Davis Street, Portland, OR 97209. *Phone:* 503-228-6528. *Toll-free phone:* 888-228-6528.

Birthingway College of Midwifery
Portland, Oregon
http://www.birthingway.edu/

CONTACT
Director of Admission, Birthingway College of Midwifery, 12113 SE Foster Road, Portland, OR 97299. *Phone:* 503-760-3131. *E-mail:* info@birthingway.edu.

Concordia University
Portland, Oregon
http://www.cu-portland.edu/

CONTACT
Ms. Bobi Swan, Dean of Admission, Concordia University, 2811 Northeast Holman, Portland, OR 97211-6099. *Phone:* 503-493-6526. *Toll-free phone:* 800-321-9371. *Fax:* 503-280-8531. *E-mail:* admissions@cu-portland.edu.

★ Corban University
Salem, Oregon
http://www.corban.edu/

- **Independent Christian** comprehensive, founded 1935
- **Suburban** 145-acre campus with easy access to Portland
- **Coed** 1,022 undergraduate students, 95% full-time, 60% women, 40% men
- **Moderately difficult** entrance level, 35% of applicants were admitted

UNDERGRAD STUDENTS
973 full-time, 49 part-time. Students come from 32 states and territories; 12 other countries; 54% are from out of state; 1% Black or African American, non-Hispanic/Latino; 3% Hispanic/Latino; 2% Asian, non-Hispanic/Latino; 0.4% Native Hawaiian or other Pacific Islander, non-Hispanic/Latino; 0.9% American Indian or Alaska Native, non-Hispanic/Latino; 8% Two or more races, non-Hispanic/Latino; 5% Race/ethnicity unknown; 6% international; 6% transferred in; 63% live on campus.

Freshmen:
Admission: 2,474 applied, 855 admitted, 239 enrolled. ***Average high school GPA:*** 3.53. ***Test scores:*** SAT critical reading scores over 500: 71%; SAT math scores over 500: 61%; SAT writing scores over 500: 52%; ACT scores over 18: 96%; SAT critical reading scores over 600: 23%;

SAT math scores over 600: 18%; SAT writing scores over 600: 15%; ACT scores over 24: 44%; SAT critical reading scores over 700: 3%; SAT math scores over 700: 2%; SAT writing scores over 700: 2%; ACT scores over 30: 4%.

Retention: 80% of full-time freshmen returned.

FACULTY

Total: 131, 42% full-time, 37% with terminal degrees.

Student/faculty ratio: 13:1.

ACADEMICS

Calendar: semesters. *Degrees:* associate, bachelor's, master's, doctoral, and postbachelor's certificates.

Special study options: accelerated degree program, adult/continuing education programs, advanced placement credit, cooperative education, distance learning, double majors, external degree program, freshman honors college, honors programs, independent study, internships, off-campus study, services for LD students, student-designed majors, study abroad, summer session for credit. ***ROTC:*** Army (c), Air Force (c).

Computers: Students can access the following: computer help desk, free student e-mail accounts, online (class) grades, online (class) schedules. Campuswide network is available. 100% of college-owned or -operated housing units are wired for high-speed Internet access. Wireless service is available via entire campus.

Library: Corban University Library. *Books:* 84,327 (physical), 140,737 (digital/electronic); *Databases:* 15. Students can reserve study rooms.

STUDENT LIFE

Housing options: on-campus residence required through sophomore year; men-only, women-only. Campus housing is university owned. Freshman campus housing is guaranteed.

Activities and organizations: drama/theater group, student-run newspaper, choral group, Student Fellowship Groups, Poetry Club, Worship Teams, Drama Club, Westrek Hiking Club.

Athletics Member NAIA, NCCAA. ***Intercollegiate sports:*** baseball M(s), basketball M(s)/W(s), cross-country running M(s)/W(s), golf M(s)/W(s), soccer M(s)/W(s), softball W(s), track and field M(s)/W(s), volleyball W(s). ***Intramural sports:*** basketball M/W, football M, soccer M/W, table tennis M/W, volleyball M/W.

Campus security: 24-hour emergency response devices and patrols, student patrols, late-night transport/escort service, controlled dormitory access.

Student services: health clinic, personal/psychological counseling.

COSTS & FINANCIAL AID

Costs (2017–18) ***One-time required fee:*** $100. ***Comprehensive fee:*** $41,700 includes full-time tuition ($30,980), mandatory fees ($660), and room and board ($10,060). Full-time tuition and fees vary according to course load, degree level, program, and reciprocity agreements. Part-time tuition: $1291 per credit hour. Part-time tuition and fees vary according to course load, degree level, program, and reciprocity agreements. ***Required fees:*** $330 per term part-time. ***College room only:*** $5852. Room and board charges vary according to board plan. ***Payment plan:*** installment. ***Waivers:*** children of alumni, senior citizens, and employees or children of employees.

Financial Aid Of all full-time matriculated undergraduates who enrolled in 2015, 820 applied for aid, 756 were judged to have need, 119 had their need fully met. 248 Federal Work-Study jobs (averaging $1159). In 2015, 95 non-need-based awards were made. ***Average percent of need met:*** 68. ***Average financial aid package:*** $21,751. ***Average need-based loan:*** $4392. ***Average need-based gift aid:*** $17,920. ***Average non-need-based aid:*** $9516. ***Average indebtedness upon graduation:*** $27,325.

APPLYING

Standardized Tests *Required:* SAT or ACT (for admission).

Options: electronic application.

Application fee: $40.

Required: essay or personal statement, high school transcript, minimum 2.7 GPA, 2 letters of recommendation.

Application deadlines: 8/1 (freshmen), 8/1 (transfers).

Notification: continuous (freshmen), continuous (transfers).

CONTACT

Jordan Lindsey, Associate Director of Admissions, Corban University, 5000 Deer Park Drive, SE, Salem, OR 97301-9392. *Phone:* 503-375-7156. *Toll-free phone:* 800-845-3005. *Fax:* 503-585-4316.
E-mail: admissions@corban.edu.

Eastern Oregon University

La Grande, Oregon

http://www.eou.edu/

- **State-supported** comprehensive, founded 1929
- **Rural** 121-acre campus
- **Endowment** $10.7 million
- **Coed** 3,128 undergraduate students, 56% full-time, 62% women, 38% men
- **Minimally difficult** entrance level, 97% of applicants were admitted

UNDERGRAD STUDENTS

1,759 full-time, 1,369 part-time. Students come from 45 states and territories; 13 other countries; 27% are from out of state; 2% Black or African American, non-Hispanic/Latino; 5% Hispanic/Latino; 2% Asian, non-Hispanic/Latino; 1% Native Hawaiian or other Pacific Islander, non-Hispanic/Latino; 2% American Indian or Alaska Native, non-Hispanic/Latino; 2% Two or more races, non-Hispanic/Latino; 11% Race/ethnicity unknown; 0.9% international; 16% transferred in; 11% live on campus.

Freshmen:

Admission: 994 applied, 967 admitted, 325 enrolled. ***Average high school GPA:*** 3.29. ***Test scores:*** SAT critical reading scores over 500: 39%; SAT math scores over 500: 34%; SAT writing scores over 500: 24%; ACT scores over 18: 75%; SAT critical reading scores over 600: 8%; SAT math scores over 600: 7%; SAT writing scores over 600: 4%; ACT scores over 24: 17%; SAT critical reading scores over 700: 1%.

Retention: 57% of full-time freshmen returned.

FACULTY

Total: 215, 45% full-time, 56% with terminal degrees.

Student/faculty ratio: 18:1.

ACADEMICS

Calendar: quarters. *Degrees:* certificates, associate, bachelor's, and master's.

Special study options: academic remediation for entering students, adult/continuing education programs, advanced placement credit, cooperative education, distance learning, double majors, external degree program, honors programs, independent study, internships, off-campus study, part-time degree program, services for LD students, student-designed majors, study abroad, summer session for credit. ***ROTC:*** Army (b).

Computers: 120 computers/terminals are available on campus for general student use. Students can access the following: free student e-mail accounts, online (class) grades, online (class) registration, online (class) schedules. Campuswide network is available. 95% of college-owned or -operated housing units are wired for high-speed Internet access. Wireless service is available via entire campus.

Library: Pierce Library. *Books:* 169,456 (physical), 6,790 (digital/electronic); *Serial titles:* 996 (physical), 1,454 (digital/electronic); *Databases:* 158. Weekly public service hours: 89; students can reserve study rooms.

STUDENT LIFE

Housing options: on-campus residence required for freshman year; coed, special housing for students with disabilities. Campus housing is university owned. Freshman applicants given priority for college housing.

Activities and organizations: drama/theater group, student-run newspaper, radio station, choral group, Outdoor Program, Pre-Professional Health Club, Student Government, International Student Association, Chemistry Club.

Athletics Member NAIA. ***Intercollegiate sports:*** basketball M(s)/W(s), cross-country running M(s)/W(s), football M(s), soccer M(s)/W(s), softball W(s), track and field M(s)/W(s), volleyball W(s). ***Intramural sports:*** basketball M/W, football M, rock climbing M(c)/W(c), soccer M/W, softball M/W, volleyball M/W.

Campus security: 24-hour emergency response devices, late-night transport/escort service, controlled dormitory access.

Student services: health clinic, personal/psychological counseling, women's center.

COSTS & FINANCIAL AID

Costs (2016–17) ***Tuition:*** state resident $6570 full-time, $146 per credit hour part-time; nonresident $17,213 full-time, $383 per credit hour part-time. Full-time tuition and fees vary according to course load, location, and reciprocity agreements. Part-time tuition and fees vary according to course load, location, and reciprocity agreements. ***Required fees:*** $1434 full-time, $306 per term part-time. ***Room and board:*** $8930; room only: $5375. Room and board charges vary according to board plan and housing facility. ***Payment plans:*** installment, deferred payment. ***Waivers:*** senior citizens and employees or children of employees.

Financial Aid Of all full-time matriculated undergraduates who enrolled in 2015, 1,535 applied for aid, 1,346 were judged to have need, 136 had their need fully met. 164 Federal Work-Study jobs (averaging $2113). In 2015, 120 non-need-based awards were made. ***Average percent of need met:*** 55. ***Average financial aid package:*** $9506. ***Average need-based loan:*** $4154. ***Average need-based gift aid:*** $8241. ***Average non-need-based aid:*** $2254. ***Average indebtedness upon graduation:*** $28,942.

APPLYING

Standardized Tests *Required:* SAT or ACT (for admission).

Options: electronic application, early admission, early action, deferred entrance.

Application fee: $50.

Required: high school transcript, minimum 2.8 GPA. ***Required for some:*** essay or personal statement, 2 letters of recommendation.

Application deadlines: 9/1 (freshmen), 9/1 (transfers), 2/1 (early action).

Notification: continuous (freshmen), continuous (out-of-state freshmen), continuous (transfers), rolling (early action).

CONTACT

Admissions Department, Eastern Oregon University, One University Boulevard, La Grande, OR. *Phone:* 800-452-8639. *Toll-free phone:* 800-452-8639. *Fax:* 541-962-3418. *E-mail:* admissions@eou.edu.

George Fox University

Newberg, Oregon

http://www.georgefox.edu/

- **Independent Friends** university, founded 1891
- **Small-town** 108-acre campus with easy access to Portland
- **Coed** 2,591 undergraduate students, 91% full-time, 55% women, 44% men
- **Moderately difficult** entrance level, 78% of applicants were admitted

UNDERGRAD STUDENTS

2,348 full-time, 221 part-time. 49% are from out of state; 2% Black or African American, non-Hispanic/Latino; 11% Hispanic/Latino; 4% Asian, non-Hispanic/Latino; 0.4% Native Hawaiian or other Pacific Islander, non-Hispanic/Latino; 0.6% American Indian or Alaska Native, non-Hispanic/Latino; 6% Two or more races, non-Hispanic/Latino; 3% Race/ethnicity unknown; 4% international; 1% transferred in; 55% live on campus.

Freshmen:

Admission: 2,980 applied, 2,334 admitted, 634 enrolled. ***Average high school GPA:*** 3.56. ***Test scores:*** SAT critical reading scores over 500: 69%; SAT math scores over 500: 69%; SAT writing scores over 500: 59%; ACT scores over 18: 92%; SAT critical reading scores over 600: 26%; SAT math scores over 600: 26%; SAT writing scores over 600: 22%; ACT scores over 24: 52%; SAT critical reading scores over 700: 6%; SAT math scores over 700: 5%; SAT writing scores over 700: 5%; ACT scores over 30: 8%.

Retention: 80% of full-time freshmen returned.

FACULTY

Total: 604, 32% full-time, 27% with terminal degrees.

Student/faculty ratio: 14:1.

ACADEMICS

Calendar: semesters. *Degrees:* bachelor's, master's, doctoral, post-master's, and postbachelor's certificates.

Special study options: academic remediation for entering students, accelerated degree program, adult/continuing education programs, advanced placement credit, distance learning, double majors, English as a second language, honors programs, independent study, internships, off-campus study, part-time degree program, services for LD students, student-designed majors, study abroad, summer session for credit. ***ROTC:*** Air Force (c).

Unusual degree programs: 3-2 engineering; nursing.

Computers: Students can access the following: campus intranet, computer help desk, free student e-mail accounts, online (class) grades, online (class) registration, online (class) schedules, online acceptance of financial aid. Campuswide network is available. 100% of college-owned or -operated housing units are wired for high-speed Internet access. Wireless service is available via classrooms, computer centers, computer labs, dorm rooms, learning centers, libraries, student centers.

Library: Murdock Learning Resource Center plus 1 other. *Books:* 463,450 (physical); *Serial titles:* 101,027 (digital/electronic); *Databases:* 209. Weekly public service hours: 93; study areas open 24 hours, 5-7 days a week; students can reserve study rooms.

STUDENT LIFE

Housing options: on-campus residence required through junior year; men-only, women-only, cooperative, special housing for students with disabilities. Campus housing is university owned. Freshman applicants given priority for college housing.

Activities and organizations: drama/theater group, student-run newspaper, radio station, choral group, Student Government, Christian Ministries, Orientation Committee, Outdoor Club and Bruin Ambassadors, Blue Zone.

Athletics Member NCAA. All Division III. ***Intercollegiate sports:*** baseball M, basketball M/W, cross-country running M/W, football M, golf M/W, lacrosse W, soccer M/W, softball W, tennis M/W, track and field M/W, volleyball W. ***Intramural sports:*** badminton M/W, basketball M/W, football M/W, golf M/W, racquetball M/W, rock climbing M/W, soccer M/W, table tennis M/W, tennis M/W, ultimate Frisbee M/W, volleyball M/W.

Campus security: 24-hour emergency response devices and patrols, student patrols, late-night transport/escort service, controlled dormitory access, parking lot cameras, video surveillance of key buildings.

Student services: health clinic, personal/psychological counseling.

COSTS & FINANCIAL AID

Costs (2017–18) ***Comprehensive fee:*** $45,752 includes full-time tuition ($34,500), mandatory fees ($366), and room and board ($10,886). Full-time tuition and fees vary according to reciprocity agreements. Part-time tuition and fees vary according to course load. ***Room and board:*** Room and board charges vary according to board plan. ***Payment plan:*** installment. ***Waivers:*** senior citizens and employees or children of employees.

Financial Aid Of all full-time matriculated undergraduates who enrolled in 2016, 2,135 applied for aid, 1,912 were judged to have need, 749 had their need fully met. 1,364 Federal Work-Study jobs (averaging $2198). In 2016, 570 non-need-based awards were made. ***Average percent of need met:*** 85. ***Average financial aid package:*** $22,722. ***Average need-based loan:*** $4045. ***Average need-based gift aid:*** $17,611. ***Average non-need-based aid:*** $12,945. ***Average indebtedness upon graduation:*** $22,799.

APPLYING

Standardized Tests *Required:* SAT or ACT (for admission).

Options: electronic application, early action, deferred entrance.

Application fee: $40.

Required: essay or personal statement, 1 letter of recommendation. ***Required for some:*** high school transcript. ***Recommended:*** high school transcript.

Application deadlines: rolling (freshmen), 6/1 (transfers), 11/15 (early action).

Notification: continuous until 10/1 (freshmen), continuous (transfers), 12/15 (early action).

CONTACT
Ms. Lindsay Knox, Director of Undergraduate Admissions, George Fox University, 414 North Meridian Street, Newberg, OR 97132. *Phone:* 503-554-2240. *Toll-free phone:* 800-765-4369. *Fax:* 503-554-3110. *E-mail:* admissions@georgefox.edu.

Gutenberg College

Eugene, Oregon

http://www.gutenberg.edu/

CONTACT
Mr. Terry Stollar, Director of Admissions and Development, Gutenberg College, 1883 University Street, Eugene, OR 97403. *Phone:* 541-736-9071. *Fax:* 541-683-6997. *E-mail:* tstollar@gutenberg.edu.

Lewis & Clark College

Portland, Oregon

http://www.lclark.edu/

- **Independent** comprehensive, founded 1867
- **Urban** 137-acre campus with easy access to Portland
- **Endowment** $202.3 million
- **Coed** 2,134 undergraduate students, 99% full-time, 61% women, 39% men
- **Very difficult** entrance level, 55% of applicants were admitted

UNDERGRAD STUDENTS
2,102 full-time, 32 part-time. Students come from 48 states and territories; 75 other countries; 89% are from out of state; 2% Black or African American, non-Hispanic/Latino; 10% Hispanic/Latino; 6% Asian, non-Hispanic/Latino; 0.5% Native Hawaiian or other Pacific Islander, non-Hispanic/Latino; 1% American Indian or Alaska Native, non-Hispanic/Latino; 3% Two or more races, non-Hispanic/Latino; 6% Race/ethnicity unknown; 8% international; 2% transferred in; 69% live on campus.

Freshmen:
Admission: 7,796 applied, 4,284 admitted, 506 enrolled. ***Average high school GPA:*** 3.93. ***Test scores:*** SAT critical reading scores over 500: 97%; SAT math scores over 500: 99%; SAT writing scores over 500: 97%; ACT scores over 18: 100%; SAT critical reading scores over 600: 76%; SAT math scores over 600: 71%; SAT writing scores over 600: 66%; ACT scores over 24: 97%; SAT critical reading scores over 700: 23%; SAT math scores over 700: 17%; SAT writing scores over 700: 15%; ACT scores over 30: 39%.

Retention: 85% of full-time freshmen returned.

FACULTY
Total: 528, 40% full-time, 45% with terminal degrees.
Student/faculty ratio: 11:1.

ACADEMICS
Calendar: semesters. *Degrees:* bachelor's, master's, doctoral, and post-master's certificates.

Special study options: advanced placement credit, double majors, English as a second language, honors programs, independent study, internships, off-campus study, services for LD students, student-designed majors, study abroad, summer session for credit. ***ROTC:*** Army (c).

Unusual degree programs: 3-2 engineering with Columbia University in New York, Washington University in St. Louis, University of Southern California in Los Angeles.

Computers: 440 computers/terminals are available on campus for general student use. Students can access the following: campus intranet, computer help desk, free student e-mail accounts, online (class) grades, online (class) registration, online (class) schedules. Campuswide network is available. 100% of college-owned or -operated housing units are wired for high-speed Internet access. Wireless service is available via entire campus.

Library: Aubrey Watzek Library plus 1 other. *Books:* 523,517 (physical), 275,318 (digital/electronic); *Serial titles:* 7,568 (physical), 6,299 (digital/electronic); *Databases:* 327. Weekly public service hours: 141; study areas open 24 hours, 5-7 days a week; students can reserve study rooms.

STUDENT LIFE

Housing options: on-campus residence required through sophomore year; coed, women-only. Campus housing is university owned. Freshman campus housing is guaranteed.

Activities and organizations: drama/theater group, student-run newspaper, radio station, choral group, International Students of Lewis & Clark, Campus Activities Board, MOSAIC (Multicultural Organizations Seeking An Inclusive Community), Bacchus Men's Ultimate Frisbee, Hillel.

Athletics Member NCAA. All Division III. ***Intercollegiate sports:*** baseball M, basketball M/W, crew M/W, cross-country running M/W, football M, golf M/W, lacrosse W(c), rugby M(c)/W(c), soccer M(c)/W, softball W, swimming and diving M/W, tennis M/W, track and field M/W, ultimate Frisbee M(c)/W(c), volleyball W. ***Intramural sports:*** football M/W, soccer M/W, water polo M/W.

Campus security: 24-hour emergency response devices and patrols, late-night transport/escort service, controlled dormitory access.

Student services: health clinic, personal/psychological counseling.

COSTS & FINANCIAL AID

Costs (2016–17) ***Comprehensive fee:*** $58,434 includes full-time tuition ($46,534), mandatory fees ($360), and room and board ($11,540). Part-time tuition: $2327 per credit hour. Part-time tuition and fees vary according to course load. ***Required fees:*** $18 per credit hour part-time. ***College room only:*** $6376. Room and board charges vary according to board plan and housing facility. ***Payment plan:*** installment. ***Waivers:*** employees or children of employees.

Financial Aid Of all full-time matriculated undergraduates who enrolled in 2016, 1,407 applied for aid, 1,153 were judged to have need, 623 had their need fully met. 935 Federal Work-Study jobs (averaging $2443). 190 state and other part-time jobs (averaging $4742). In 2016, 709 non-need-based awards were made. ***Average percent of need met:*** 91. ***Average financial aid package:*** $42,109. ***Average need-based loan:*** $7597. ***Average need-based gift aid:*** $31,828. ***Average non-need-based aid:*** $15,538. ***Average indebtedness upon graduation:*** $29,913.

APPLYING

Standardized Tests *Required:* SAT or ACT scores or Test-Optional Portfolio Path materials (for admission).

Options: electronic application, early decision, early action, deferred entrance.

Required: essay or personal statement, high school transcript, 1 letter of recommendation. ***Required for some:*** 2 letters of recommendation, graded writing sample, math or science sample, 2 letters of recommendation for Test Optional Portfolio Path. ***Recommended:*** interview.

Application deadlines: 1/15 (freshmen), 4/1 (transfers), 11/1 (early action).

Early decision deadline: 11/1.

Notification: 4/1 (freshmen), continuous (transfers), 12/15 (early decision), 12/31 (early action).

CONTACT

Erica Johnson, Director of Admissions, Lewis & Clark College, 0615 SW Palatine Hill Road, Portland, OR 97219. *Phone:* 503-768-7040. *Toll-free phone:* 800-444-4111. *Fax:* 503-768-7055. *E-mail:* admissions@lclark.edu.

See below for display ad and page 1396 for the College Close-Up.

★ Linfield College

McMinnville, Oregon

http://www.linfield.edu/

- **Independent American Baptist Churches in the USA** 4-year, founded 1858, part of Linfield College
- **Small-town** 189-acre campus with easy access to Portland
- **Endowment** $101.6 million
- **Coed** 1,632 undergraduate students, 98% full-time, 62% women, 38% men
- **Moderately difficult** entrance level, 81% of applicants were admitted

UNDERGRAD STUDENTS

1,602 full-time, 30 part-time. Students come from 54 states and territories; 19 other countries; 45% are from out of state; 2% Black or African

American, non-Hispanic/Latino; 14% Hispanic/Latino; 5% Asian, non-Hispanic/Latino; 0.7% Native Hawaiian or other Pacific Islander, non-Hispanic/Latino; 0.7% American Indian or Alaska Native, non-Hispanic/Latino; 12% Two or more races, non-Hispanic/Latino; 3% Race/ethnicity unknown; 3% international; 4% transferred in; 77% live on campus.

Freshmen:
Admission: 2,296 applied, 1,854 admitted, 393 enrolled. ***Average high school GPA:*** 3.65. ***Test scores:*** SAT critical reading scores over 500: 60%; SAT math scores over 500: 61%; SAT writing scores over 500: 57%; ACT scores over 18: 57%; SAT critical reading scores over 600: 23%; SAT math scores over 600: 17%; SAT writing scores over 600: 17%; ACT scores over 24: 17%; SAT critical reading scores over 700: 3%; SAT math scores over 700: 2%; SAT writing scores over 700: 2%; ACT scores over 30: 2%.

Retention: 82% of full-time freshmen returned.

FACULTY
Total: 199, 59% full-time, 70% with terminal degrees.

Student/faculty ratio: 11:1.

ACADEMICS
Calendar: 4-1-4. *Degrees:* bachelor's and postbachelor's certificates (Linfield College includes the Linfield College McMinnville Campus in McMinnville, Oregon; the Linfield-Good Samaritan School of Nursing in Portland, Oregon(Portland Campus) and the Linfield College Adult Degree Program online).

Special study options: accelerated degree program, adult/continuing education programs, advanced placement credit, distance learning, double majors, English as a second language, external degree program, independent study, internships, off-campus study, part-time degree program, services for LD students, student-designed majors, study abroad, summer session for credit. ***ROTC:*** Air Force (c).

Unusual degree programs: 3-2 engineering with Washington State University, Oregon State University, University of Southern California.

Computers: 250 computers/terminals are available on campus for general student use. Students can access the following: computer help desk, free student e-mail accounts, online (class) grades, online (class) registration, online (class) schedules. Campuswide network is available. 100% of college-owned or -operated housing units are wired for high-speed Internet access. Wireless service is available via classrooms, computer centers, computer labs, dorm rooms, learning centers, libraries, student centers.

Library: Jereld R. Nicholson Library. *Books:* 189,314 (physical), 5,719 (digital/electronic); *Serial titles:* 19,573 (physical), 2 (digital/electronic); *Databases:* 186. Weekly public service hours: 95.

STUDENT LIFE
Housing options: on-campus residence required through junior year; coed, men-only, women-only, special housing for students with disabilities. Campus housing is university owned. Freshman campus housing is guaranteed.

Activities and organizations: drama/theater group, student-run newspaper, radio station, choral group, Fellowship of Christian Athletes, Linfield Ultimate Players Association, Hawaiian Club, International Club, Outdoor Club, national fraternities, national sororities.

Athletics Member NCAA. All Division III. ***Intercollegiate sports:*** baseball M, basketball M/W, cross-country running M/W, football M, golf M/W, lacrosse W, soccer M/W, softball W, swimming and diving M/W, tennis M/W, track and field M/W, volleyball W. ***Intramural sports:*** basketball M/W, bowling M/W, football M/W, soccer M/W, softball M/W, tennis M/W, ultimate Frisbee M/W, volleyball M/W.

Campus security: 24-hour emergency response devices and patrols, late-night transport/escort service, controlled dormitory access.

Student services: health clinic, personal/psychological counseling.

COSTS & FINANCIAL AID
Costs (2017–18) ***Comprehensive fee:*** $53,346 includes full-time tuition ($41,100), mandatory fees ($476), and room and board ($11,770). Full-time tuition and fees vary according to course load, location, and program. Part-time tuition: $1285 per semester hour. Part-time tuition and fees vary according to course load, location, and program. ***Required fees:*** $132 per term part-time. ***College room only:*** $6400. Room and board charges vary according to board plan, housing facility, and location. ***Payment plan:*** installment. ***Waivers:*** senior citizens and employees or children of employees.

Financial Aid Of all full-time matriculated undergraduates who enrolled in 2016, 1,360 applied for aid, 1,208 were judged to have need, 256 had their need fully met. 584 Federal Work-Study jobs (averaging $1153). 544 state and other part-time jobs (averaging $1328). In 2016, 343 non-need-based awards were made. ***Average percent of need met:*** 82. ***Average financial aid package:*** $32,663. ***Average need-based loan:*** $4896. ***Average need-based gift aid:*** $26,818. ***Average non-need-based aid:*** $18,275. ***Average indebtedness upon graduation:*** $34,320.

APPLYING
Standardized Tests *Required:* SAT or ACT (for admission).

Options: electronic application, early action, deferred entrance.

Required: essay or personal statement, high school transcript, 1 letter of recommendation. ***Recommended:*** interview.

Application deadlines: 2/1 (freshmen), 4/15 (transfers), 11/1 (early action).

Notification: 4/1 (freshmen), 5/15 (transfers), 1/15 (early action).

CONTACT
Ms. Lisa Knodle-Bragiel, Director of Admission, Linfield College, 900 SE Baker Street, McMinnville, OR 97128. *Phone:* 503-883-2213. *Toll-free phone:* 800-640-2287. *Fax:* 503-883-2472. *E-mail:* admission@linfield.edu.

See previous page for display ad and page 1400 for the College Close-Up.

Marylhurst University

Marylhurst, Oregon

http://www.marylhurst.edu/

- **Independent Roman Catholic** comprehensive, founded 1893
- **Suburban** 63-acre campus with easy access to Portland
- **Coed** 398 undergraduate students, 34% full-time, 71% women, 29% men
- **Noncompetitive** entrance level, 100% of applicants were admitted

UNDERGRAD STUDENTS
135 full-time, 263 part-time. Students come from 38 states and territories; 8 other countries; 21% are from out of state; 3% Black or African American, non-Hispanic/Latino; 7% Hispanic/Latino; 3% Asian, non-Hispanic/Latino; 1% American Indian or Alaska Native, non-Hispanic/Latino; 4% Two or more races, non-Hispanic/Latino; 9% Race/ethnicity unknown; 2% international.

Freshmen:
Admission: 2 applied, 2 admitted, 2 enrolled.

ACADEMICS
Calendar: quarters. *Degrees:* certificates, bachelor's, master's, post-master's, and postbachelor's certificates.

Special study options: accelerated degree program, adult/continuing education programs, advanced placement credit, distance learning, double majors, English as a second language, honors programs, independent study, internships, off-campus study, part-time degree program, services for LD students, student-designed majors, study abroad, summer session for credit.

Computers: Students can access the following: campus intranet, computer help desk, free student e-mail accounts, online (class) grades, online (class) registration, online (class) schedules. Campuswide network is available. Wireless service is available via entire campus.

Library: Shoen Library. *Books:* 105,004 (physical), 11,479 (digital/electronic); *Serial titles:* 156 (physical).

STUDENT LIFE
Housing options: college housing not available.

Activities and organizations: choral group.

Campus security: security is available during campus hours.

Student services: personal/psychological counseling.

COSTS & FINANCIAL AID
Costs (2016–17) ***Tuition:*** $20,835 full-time, $463 per credit hour part-time. Full-time tuition and fees vary according to program. Part-time tuition and fees vary according to program. ***Payment plan:*** installment. ***Waivers:*** employees or children of employees.

Financial Aid Of all full-time matriculated undergraduates who enrolled in 2016, 123 applied for aid, 117 were judged to have need, 2 had their need fully met. 111 Federal Work-Study jobs (averaging $5728). In 2016, 25 non-need-based awards were made. ***Average percent of need met:*** 52. ***Average financial aid package:*** $17,455. ***Average need-based loan:*** $4030. ***Average need-based gift aid:*** $11,607. ***Average non-need-based aid:*** $4553. ***Average indebtedness upon graduation:*** $51,833.

APPLYING

Options: electronic application, deferred entrance.

Application fee: $50.

Required: essay or personal statement, high school transcript. ***Required for some:*** 2 letters of recommendation, interview.

Application deadlines: rolling (freshmen), rolling (transfers).

Notification: continuous (freshmen), continuous (transfers).

CONTACT

Rachel Dixon, Interim Director of Admissions, Marylhurst University, 17600 Pacific Highway, PO Box 261, Marylhurst, OR 97036-0261. *Phone:* 503-699-6268. *Toll-free phone:* 800-634-9982. *E-mail:* admissions@marylhurst.edu.

Mount Angel Seminary

Saint Benedict, Oregon

http://www.mountangelabbey.org/seminary/

CONTACT

Registrar/Admissions Officer, Mount Angel Seminary, Saint Benedict, OR 97373. *Phone:* 503-845-3951 Ext. 14. *E-mail:* admissions@mtangel.edu.

Multnomah University

Portland, Oregon

http://www.multnomah.edu/

- **Independent interdenominational** comprehensive, founded 1936
- **Urban** 22-acre campus with easy access to Portland, OR
- **Endowment** $6.9 million
- **Coed** 417 undergraduate students, 87% full-time, 48% women, 52% men
- **Moderately difficult** entrance level, 70% of applicants were admitted

UNDERGRAD STUDENTS

364 full-time, 53 part-time. Students come from 18 states and territories; 57% are from out of state; 3% Black or African American, non-Hispanic/Latino; 8% Hispanic/Latino; 1% Asian, non-Hispanic/Latino; 1% Native Hawaiian or other Pacific Islander, non-Hispanic/Latino; 0.7% American Indian or Alaska Native, non-Hispanic/Latino; 9% Two or more races, non-Hispanic/Latino; 1% Race/ethnicity unknown; 14% transferred in; 59% live on campus.

Freshmen:

Admission: 198 applied, 139 admitted, 72 enrolled. ***Average high school GPA:*** 3.2. ***Test scores:*** SAT critical reading scores over 500: 66%; SAT math scores over 500: 54%; SAT writing scores over 500: 75%; ACT scores over 18: 100%; SAT critical reading scores over 600: 29%; SAT math scores over 600: 25%; SAT writing scores over 600: 14%; ACT scores over 24: 45%; SAT critical reading scores over 700: 4%; SAT math scores over 700: 7%; ACT scores over 30: 18%.

Retention: 63% of full-time freshmen returned.

FACULTY

Total: 100, 26% full-time, 42% with terminal degrees.

Student/faculty ratio: 12:1.

ACADEMICS

Calendar: semesters. *Degrees:* bachelor's, master's, doctoral, and postbachelor's certificates.

Special study options: academic remediation for entering students, adult/continuing education programs, advanced placement credit, distance learning, double majors, internships, part-time degree program, services for LD students, summer session for credit.

Computers: 36 computers/terminals are available on campus for general student use. Students can access the following: campus intranet, computer help desk, free student e-mail accounts, online (class) grades, online (class) registration, online (class) schedules. Campuswide network is available. 80% of college-owned or -operated housing units are wired for high-speed Internet access. Wireless service is available via entire campus.

Library: John Mitchell Library. *Books:* 109,731 (physical), 133,470 (digital/electronic); *Serial titles:* 294 (physical), 20,000 (digital/electronic); *Databases:* 42. Weekly public service hours: 88; students can reserve study rooms.

STUDENT LIFE

Housing options: on-campus residence required through sophomore year; men-only, women-only, special housing for students with disabilities. Campus housing is university owned. Freshman campus housing is guaranteed.

Activities and organizations: choral group, Student Government, Commuter Life, Poetry Club, Brunch Chats, Fitness Club.

Athletics Member NAIA. ***Intercollegiate sports:*** basketball M(s)/W(s), cross-country running M(s)/W(s), golf M(s)/W(s), soccer M(s), track and field M(s)/W(s), volleyball W.

Campus security: 24-hour emergency response devices and patrols, late-night transport/escort service, controlled dormitory access.

Student services: personal/psychological counseling.

COSTS & FINANCIAL AID

Costs (2017–18) ***Comprehensive fee:*** $33,240 includes full-time tuition ($24,100), mandatory fees ($580), and room and board ($8560). Full-time tuition and fees vary according to course load, degree level, location, and program. Part-time tuition: $730 per credit hour. Part-time tuition and fees vary according to course load, degree level, location, and program. ***Room and board:*** Room and board charges vary according to housing facility. ***Payment plan:*** installment. ***Waivers:*** employees or children of employees.

Financial Aid Of all full-time matriculated undergraduates who enrolled in 2009, 503 applied for aid, 441 were judged to have need, 11 had their need fully met. 75 Federal Work-Study jobs (averaging $1500). In 2009, 36 non-need-based awards were made. ***Average percent of need met:*** 50. ***Average financial aid package:*** $9211. ***Average need-based loan:*** $4094. ***Average need-based gift aid:*** $5846. ***Average non-need-based aid:*** $1848. ***Average indebtedness upon graduation:*** $21,020.

APPLYING

Standardized Tests *Recommended:* SAT or ACT (for admission).

Options: electronic application, deferred entrance.

Application fee: $40.

Required: essay or personal statement, high school transcript, minimum 2.5 GPA, 2 letters of recommendation.

Notification: continuous (freshmen), continuous (transfers).

CONTACT

Ms. Jenae Johnson, Admissions Counselor, Multnomah University, 8435 Northeast Glisan Street, Portland, OR 97220-5898. *Phone:* 503-251-6467. *Toll-free phone:* 877-251-6560. *Fax:* 503-254-1268. *E-mail:* admiss@multnomah.edu.

New Hope Christian College

Eugene, Oregon

http://www.newhope.edu/

CONTACT

Sarah Slater, Director of Admissions, New Hope Christian College, 2155 Bailey Hill Road, Eugene, OR 97405. *Phone:* 541-485-1780 Ext. 3115. *Toll-free phone:* 800-322-2638. *Fax:* 541-343-5801. *E-mail:* sarahslater@newhope.edu.

Northwest Christian University

Eugene, Oregon

http://www.nwcu.edu/

- **Independent Christian** comprehensive, founded 1895
- **Urban** 8-acre campus with easy access to Portland
- **Endowment** $12.4 million
- **Coed** 566 undergraduate students, 74% full-time, 62% women, 38% men
- **Minimally difficult** entrance level, 67% of applicants were admitted

UNDERGRAD STUDENTS
421 full-time, 145 part-time. Students come from 22 states and territories; 2 other countries; 24% are from out of state; 5% Black or African American, non-Hispanic/Latino; 7% Hispanic/Latino; 3% Asian, non-Hispanic/Latino; 1% Native Hawaiian or other Pacific Islander, non-Hispanic/Latino; 4% American Indian or Alaska Native, non-Hispanic/Latino; 3% Two or more races, non-Hispanic/Latino; 2% Race/ethnicity unknown; 10% transferred in; 34% live on campus.

Freshmen:
Admission: 427 applied, 285 admitted, 81 enrolled. ***Average high school GPA:*** 3.39. ***Test scores:*** SAT critical reading scores over 500: 45%; SAT math scores over 500: 42%; SAT writing scores over 500: 44%; ACT scores over 18: 74%; SAT critical reading scores over 600: 16%; SAT math scores over 600: 6%; SAT writing scores over 600: 9%; ACT scores over 24: 26%; SAT critical reading scores over 700: 2%.
Retention: 77% of full-time freshmen returned.

FACULTY
Total: 87, 30% full-time, 23% with terminal degrees.

Student/faculty ratio: 13:1.

ACADEMICS
Calendar: quarters. *Degrees:* associate, bachelor's, master's, and postbachelor's certificates.

Special study options: academic remediation for entering students, accelerated degree program, adult/continuing education programs, advanced placement credit, cooperative education, distance learning, double majors, English as a second language, independent study, internships, part-time degree program, services for LD students, study abroad, summer session for credit.

Computers: 16 computers/terminals are available on campus for general student use. Students can access the following: campus intranet, computer help desk, free student e-mail accounts, online (class) grades, online (class) registration, online (class) schedules. Campuswide network is available. Wireless service is available via entire campus.

Library: Edward P. Kellenberger Library. *Books:* 59,536 (physical), 14 (digital/electronic); *Serial titles:* 156 (physical), 105,706 (digital/electronic); *Databases:* 105. Weekly public service hours: 70.

STUDENT LIFE
Housing options: on-campus residence required for freshman year; men-only, women-only. Campus housing is university owned. Freshman campus housing is guaranteed.

Activities and organizations: student-run newspaper, choral group, Embrace the City (community service), FeMystique (Social justice club), Beacon Boards (game board club), History Club, Psychology Club.

Athletics Member NAIA. ***Intercollegiate sports:*** basketball M(s)/W(s), cross-country running M(s)/W(s), golf M(s)/W(s), soccer M(s)/W(s), softball W(s), track and field M(s)/W(s), volleyball W(s). ***Intramural sports:*** basketball M/W, volleyball M/W.

Campus security: 24-hour emergency response devices and patrols, late-night transport/escort service, controlled dormitory access.

Student services: personal/psychological counseling.

COSTS & FINANCIAL AID
Costs (2017–18) ***Comprehensive fee:*** $37,480 includes full-time tuition ($28,500), mandatory fees ($180), and room and board ($8800). Full-time tuition and fees vary according to course load. Part-time tuition: $950 per credit hour. Part-time tuition and fees vary according to course load. ***Room and board:*** Room and board charges vary according to housing facility. ***Payment plan:*** installment. ***Waivers:*** employees or children of employees.

Financial Aid Of all full-time matriculated undergraduates who enrolled in 2016, 371 applied for aid, 338 were judged to have need, 54 had their need fully met. 108 Federal Work-Study jobs (averaging $2750). 8 state and other part-time jobs (averaging $2750). In 2016, 63 non-need-based awards were made. ***Average percent of need met:*** 70. ***Average financial aid package:*** $21,401. ***Average need-based loan:*** $4631. ***Average need-based gift aid:*** $17,468. ***Average non-need-based aid:*** $8803. ***Average indebtedness upon graduation:*** $23,279.

APPLYING
Standardized Tests *Required:* SAT or ACT (for admission).

Options: electronic application, deferred entrance.

Required: essay or personal statement, minimum 2.5 GPA. ***Required for some:*** high school transcript. ***Recommended:*** interview.

Application deadlines: rolling (freshmen), rolling (transfers).

Notification: continuous (freshmen), continuous (transfers).

CONTACT
Kassia Galick, Assistant Director of Admissions, Northwest Christian University, 828 E. 11th Avenue, Eugene, OR 97401-3745. *Phone:* 541-684-7334. *Toll-free phone:* 877-463-6622. *Fax:* 541-684-7317. *E-mail:* kgalick@nwcu.edu.

Oregon College of Art and Craft
Portland, Oregon
http://www.ocac.edu/

- **Independent** comprehensive, founded 1907
- **Urban** 10-acre campus with easy access to Portland
- **Endowment** $1.9 million
- **Coed** 123 undergraduate students, 87% full-time, 80% women, 20% men
- **Moderately difficult** entrance level, 58% of applicants were admitted

UNDERGRAD STUDENTS
107 full-time, 16 part-time. Students come from 24 states and territories; 1 other country; 64% are from out of state; 2% Black or African American, non-Hispanic/Latino; 7% Hispanic/Latino; 2% Asian, non-Hispanic/Latino; 0.8% Native Hawaiian or other Pacific Islander, non-Hispanic/Latino; 2% American Indian or Alaska Native, non-Hispanic/Latino; 11% Two or more races, non-Hispanic/Latino; 2% Race/ethnicity unknown; 0.8% international; 8% transferred in; 16% live on campus.

Freshmen:
Admission: 142 applied, 83 admitted, 27 enrolled. ***Average high school GPA:*** 3.28. ***Test scores:*** ACT scores over 18: 90%; ACT scores over 24: 40%; ACT scores over 30: 20%.
Retention: 69% of full-time freshmen returned.

FACULTY
Total: 37, 30% full-time, 84% with terminal degrees.

Student/faculty ratio: 7:1.

ACADEMICS
Calendar: semesters. *Degrees:* certificates, bachelor's, master's, and postbachelor's certificates.

Special study options: adult/continuing education programs, advanced placement credit, independent study, internships, off-campus study, part-time degree program, services for LD students, study abroad.

Computers: 15 computers/terminals are available on campus for general student use. Students can access the following: free student e-mail accounts. Campuswide network is available. Wireless service is available via entire campus.

Library: Oregon College of Art and Craft Library plus 1 other. *Books:* 11,673 (physical); *Serial titles:* 111 (physical); *Databases:* 3. Weekly public service hours: 40.

STUDENT LIFE
Housing options: coed. Campus housing is university owned. Freshman applicants given priority for college housing.

Activities and organizations: Student Commonwealth, Ceramics Club, Photo Society, Film Club, Figure Drawing Club.

Campus security: 24-hour emergency response devices.

Student services: personal/psychological counseling.

COSTS & FINANCIAL AID
Costs (2017–18) ***One-time required fee:*** $40. ***Comprehensive fee:*** $43,060 includes full-time tuition ($31,500), mandatory fees ($1660), and room and board ($9900). Full-time tuition and fees vary according to course load and degree level. Part-time tuition: $1315 per credit hour. Part-time tuition and fees vary according to course load and degree level. ***Required fees:*** $47 per credit hour part-time, $365 per term part-time. ***College room only:*** $6400. Room and board charges vary according to board plan and housing facility. ***Payment plan:*** installment. ***Waivers:*** employees or children of employees.

Financial Aid Of all full-time matriculated undergraduates who enrolled in 2012, 116 applied for aid, 112 were judged to have need, 8 had their

need fully met. In 2012, 15 non-need-based awards were made. ***Average percent of need met:*** 73. ***Average financial aid package:*** $22,239. ***Average need-based loan:*** $4332. ***Average need-based gift aid:*** $6986. ***Average non-need-based aid:*** $7533. ***Average indebtedness upon graduation:*** $22,500.

APPLYING
Standardized Tests *Recommended:* SAT (for admission), ACT (for admission).
Options: electronic application, deferred entrance.
Application fee: $45.
Required: essay or personal statement, high school transcript, minimum 2.0 GPA, portfolio including 12 to 20 pieces of studio artwork. ***Required for some:*** interview. ***Recommended:*** letters of recommendation.
Application deadlines: rolling (freshmen), rolling (transfers).
Notification: continuous (freshmen), continuous (transfers).

CONTACT
Oregon College of Art and Craft, 8245 Southwest Barnes Road, Portland, OR 97225. *Phone:* 971-255-4192. *Toll-free phone:* 800-390-0632.

Oregon Health & Science University
Portland, Oregon
http://www.ohsu.edu/

- **State-related** upper-level, founded 1974
- **Urban** 120-acre campus
- **Coed**

ACADEMICS
Calendar: quarters. *Degrees:* certificates, bachelor's, master's, doctoral, post-master's, and postbachelor's certificates.
Library: OHSU Main Library.

STUDENT LIFE
Housing options: college housing not available.
Activities and organizations: student-run newspaper, choral group.
Campus security: 24-hour emergency response devices and patrols, late-night transport/escort service.
Student services: health clinic, personal/psychological counseling.

FINANCIAL AID
Financial Aid Of all full-time matriculated undergraduates who enrolled in 2016, 287 applied for aid, 270 were judged to have need, 14 had their need fully met. 23 Federal Work-Study jobs (averaging $1000). ***Average percent of need met:*** 38. ***Average financial aid package:*** $14,386. ***Average need-based loan:*** $6369. ***Average need-based gift aid:*** $9563.

APPLYING
Options: electronic application.
Application fee: $120.

CONTACT
Oregon Health & Science University, 3181 Southwest Sam Jackson Park Road, Portland, OR 97239-3098. *Phone:* 503-494-0954.

Oregon Institute of Technology
Klamath Falls, Oregon
http://www.oit.edu/

CONTACT
Oregon Institute of Technology, 3201 Campus Drive, Klamath Falls, OR 97601-8801. *Phone:* 541-885-1151. *Toll-free phone:* 800-422-2017.

Oregon State University
Corvallis, Oregon
http://www.oregonstate.edu/

- **State-supported** university, founded 1868
- **Small-town** 422-acre campus
- **Endowment** $562.8 million
- **Coed** 25,327 undergraduate students, 74% full-time, 46% women, 54% men
- **Moderately difficult** entrance level, 77% of applicants were admitted

UNDERGRAD STUDENTS
18,852 full-time, 6,475 part-time. Students come from 57 states and territories; 77 other countries; 30% are from out of state; 1% Black or African American, non-Hispanic/Latino; 9% Hispanic/Latino; 7% Asian, non-Hispanic/Latino; 0.3% Native Hawaiian or other Pacific Islander, non-Hispanic/Latino; 0.5% American Indian or Alaska Native, non-Hispanic/Latino; 7% Two or more races, non-Hispanic/Latino; 2% Race/ethnicity unknown; 7% international; 8% transferred in; 17% live on campus.

Freshmen:
Admission: 14,595 applied, 11,308 admitted, 3,814 enrolled. ***Average high school GPA:*** 3.67. ***Test scores:*** SAT critical reading scores over 500: 74%; SAT math scores over 500: 75%; SAT writing scores over 500: 65%; ACT scores over 18: 96%; SAT critical reading scores over 600: 32%; SAT math scores over 600: 35%; SAT writing scores over 600: 23%; ACT scores over 24: 61%; SAT critical reading scores over 700: 7%; SAT math scores over 700: 8%; SAT writing scores over 700: 3%; ACT scores over 30: 17%.
Retention: 83% of full-time freshmen returned.

FACULTY
Total: 1,665, 71% full-time, 77% with terminal degrees.
Student/faculty ratio: 18:1.

ACADEMICS
Calendar: quarters. *Degrees:* certificates, bachelor's, master's, doctoral, post-master's, and postbachelor's certificates.
Special study options: academic remediation for entering students, accelerated degree program, advanced placement credit, cooperative education, distance learning, double majors, English as a second language, freshman honors college, honors programs, independent study, internships, off-campus study, part-time degree program, services for LD students, student-designed majors, study abroad, summer session for credit. ***ROTC:*** Army (b), Navy (b), Air Force (b).
Computers: 2,179 computers/terminals are available on campus for general student use. Students can access the following: campus intranet, computer help desk, free student e-mail accounts, online (class) grades, online (class) registration, online (class) schedules. Campuswide network is available. 100% of college-owned or -operated housing units are wired for high-speed Internet access. Wireless service is available via entire campus.
Library: Valley Library plus 2 others. *Books:* 1.8 million (physical), 403,777 (digital/electronic); *Databases:* 196. Weekly public service hours: 144; study areas open 24 hours, 5-7 days a week; students can reserve study rooms.

STUDENT LIFE
Housing options: on-campus residence required for freshman year; coed, special housing for students with disabilities. Campus housing is university owned. Freshman applicants given priority for college housing.
Activities and organizations: drama/theater group, student-run newspaper, radio and television station, choral group, marching band, Ballroom Dance Club, Gaming Club, Organic Growers Club, Blood Drive Association, Residence Hall Association, national fraternities, national sororities.
Athletics Member NCAA. All Division I except football (Division I-A). ***Intercollegiate sports:*** baseball M(s), basketball M(s)/W(s), crew M/W, cross-country running W(s), golf M(s)/W(s), gymnastics W(s), soccer M(s)/W(s), softball W(s), swimming and diving W(s), track and field W(s), volleyball W(s), wrestling M(s). ***Intramural sports:*** archery M/W, badminton M/W, baseball M, basketball M/W, bowling M/W, crew M/W, cross-country running M/W, equestrian sports M(c)/W(c), fencing M(c)/W(c), football M, golf M/W, gymnastics M(c)/W(c), lacrosse M(c)/W(c), racquetball M/W, riflery M(c)/W(c), rock climbing M/W, rugby M(c)/W(c), sailing M(c)/W(c), skiing (cross-country) M(c)/W(c), skiing (downhill) M(c)/W(c), soccer M/W, softball M/W, squash M(c), swimming and diving M/W, table tennis M(c)/W(c), tennis M/W, track and field M/W, ultimate Frisbee M/W, volleyball M/W, water polo M(c)/W(c), wrestling M.
Campus security: 24-hour emergency response devices and patrols, student patrols, late-night transport/escort service, controlled dormitory access, crime prevention office.

Student services: health clinic, personal/psychological counseling, women's center, legal services.

COSTS & FINANCIAL AID

Costs (2016–17) ***One-time required fee:*** $350. ***Tuition:*** state resident $8715 full-time, $187 per credit hour part-time; nonresident $27,195 full-time, $582 per credit hour part-time. Full-time tuition and fees vary according to course load, location, and program. Part-time tuition and fees vary according to course load, location, and program. ***Required fees:*** $1651 full-time, $505 per term part-time. ***Room and board:*** $12,153; room only: $8340. Room and board charges vary according to board plan and housing facility. ***Waivers:*** employees or children of employees.

Financial Aid Of all full-time matriculated undergraduates who enrolled in 2015, 12,585 applied for aid, 9,943 were judged to have need, 814 had their need fully met. 1,164 Federal Work-Study jobs (averaging $2983). In 2015, 2573 non-need-based awards were made. ***Average percent of need met:*** 65. ***Average financial aid package:*** $13,267. ***Average need-based loan:*** $4642. ***Average need-based gift aid:*** $7295. ***Average non-need-based aid:*** $4660. ***Average indebtedness upon graduation:*** $26,453.

APPLYING

Standardized Tests *Required:* SAT or ACT (for admission). *Required for some:* SAT Subject Tests (for admission).

Options: electronic application, early action, deferred entrance.

Application fee: $60.

Required: essay or personal statement, high school transcript, minimum 3.0 GPA.

Application deadlines: 2/1 (freshmen), 6/1 (transfers), 11/1 (early action).

Notification: continuous (freshmen), continuous (transfers), 12/20 (early action).

CONTACT

Oregon State University, Corvallis, OR 97331. *Phone:* 541-737-4411. *Toll-free phone:* 800-291-4192.

Oregon State University–Cascades

Bend, Oregon

http://www.osucascades.edu/

CONTACT

Admissions Department, Oregon State University–Cascades, 2600 Northwest College Way, Bend, OR 97701. *Phone:* 541-322-3150. *E-mail:* cascadeadmit@osucascades.edu.

Pacific Northwest College of Art

Portland, Oregon

http://www.pnca.edu/

- **Independent** comprehensive, founded 1909
- **Urban** 2-acre campus with easy access to Portland
- **Endowment** $12.9 million
- **Coed** 405 undergraduate students, 90% full-time, 68% women, 32% men
- **Minimally difficult** entrance level, 95% of applicants were admitted

UNDERGRAD STUDENTS

363 full-time, 42 part-time. Students come from 41 states and territories; 4 other countries; 54% are from out of state; 2% Black or African American, non-Hispanic/Latino; 5% Hispanic/Latino; 4% Asian, non-Hispanic/Latino; 0.5% Native Hawaiian or other Pacific Islander, non-Hispanic/Latino; 1% American Indian or Alaska Native, non-Hispanic/Latino; 11% Two or more races, non-Hispanic/Latino; 12% Race/ethnicity unknown; 2% international; 11% transferred in; 25% live on campus.

Freshmen:

Admission: 312 applied, 297 admitted, 81 enrolled.

Retention: 61% of full-time freshmen returned.

FACULTY

Total: 98, 27% full-time, 27% with terminal degrees.

Student/faculty ratio: 9:1.

ACADEMICS

Calendar: semesters. *Degrees:* bachelor's and master's.

Special study options: advanced placement credit, cooperative education, independent study, internships, off-campus study, part-time degree program, services for LD students, student-designed majors, study abroad, summer session for credit.

Computers: 300 computers/terminals are available on campus for general student use. Students can access the following: campus intranet, computer help desk, free student e-mail accounts, online (class) grades, online (class) registration, online (class) schedules. Campuswide network is available. 100% of college-owned or -operated housing units are wired for high-speed Internet access. Wireless service is available via entire campus.

Library: Albert Solheim Library. *Books:* 34,806 (physical); *Serial titles:* 270 (physical); *Databases:* 52. Weekly public service hours: 87; students can reserve study rooms.

STUDENT LIFE

Housing options: on-campus residence required for freshman year; coed, men-only, women-only, special housing for students with disabilities. Campus housing is provided by a third party. Freshman campus housing is guaranteed.

Campus security: 24-hour emergency response devices, late-night transport/escort service, controlled dormitory access, entrance security guards and patrols during open hours.

Student services: personal/psychological counseling.

COSTS & FINANCIAL AID

Costs (2017–18) ***Comprehensive fee:*** $49,510 includes full-time tuition ($35,740), mandatory fees ($700), and room and board ($13,070). Full-time tuition and fees vary according to degree level. Part-time tuition: $1489 per credit hour. Part-time tuition and fees vary according to course load and degree level. ***Required fees:*** $17 per credit hour part-time, $150 per year part-time. ***Payment plan:*** installment. ***Waivers:*** employees or children of employees.

Financial Aid Of all full-time matriculated undergraduates who enrolled in 2006, 264 applied for aid, 238 were judged to have need, 13 had their need fully met. 33 Federal Work-Study jobs (averaging $1200). 33 state and other part-time jobs (averaging $1200). In 2006, 10 non-need-based awards were made. ***Average percent of need met:*** 54. ***Average financial aid package:*** $11,845. ***Average need-based loan:*** $4040. ***Average need-based gift aid:*** $4699. ***Average non-need-based aid:*** $2442. ***Average indebtedness upon graduation:*** $22,155.

APPLYING

Options: electronic application.

Application fee: $45.

Required: essay or personal statement, portfolio of artwork. ***Required for some:*** high school transcript. ***Recommended:*** minimum 2.3 GPA.

Application deadlines: rolling (freshmen), rolling (transfers).

Notification: continuous (freshmen), continuous (transfers).

CONTACT

Pacific Northwest College of Art, 511 NW Broadway, Portland, OR 97209. *Phone:* 503-821-8926.

Pacific University

Forest Grove, Oregon

http://www.pacificu.edu/

- **Independent** comprehensive, founded 1849
- **Small-town** 60-acre campus with easy access to Portland
- **Coed**
- **Moderately difficult** entrance level

ACADEMICS

Calendar: semesters. *Degrees:* bachelor's, master's, doctoral, post-master's, and postbachelor's certificates.

Library: Pacific University Library.

STUDENT LIFE

Housing options: on-campus residence required through sophomore year; coed, special housing for students with disabilities. Campus housing is university owned. Freshman campus housing is guaranteed.

Athletics Member NCAA, NAIA. All NCAA Division III.

Campus security: 24-hour emergency response devices and patrols, late-night transport/escort service, controlled dormitory access.

COSTS & FINANCIAL AID

Costs (2016–17) ***Comprehensive fee:*** $52,876 includes full-time tuition ($40,120), mandatory fees ($934), and room and board ($11,822). Part-time tuition: $1672 per credit hour. Part-time tuition and fees vary according to course load. ***College room only:*** $6528. Room and board charges vary according to board plan and housing facility. ***Payment plans:*** installment, deferred payment.

Financial Aid Of all full-time matriculated undergraduates who enrolled in 2016, 1,597 applied for aid, 1,475 were judged to have need, 237 had their need fully met. In 2016, 295 non-need-based awards were made. ***Average percent of need met:*** 72. ***Average financial aid package:*** $30,945. ***Average need-based loan:*** $4991. ***Average need-based gift aid:*** $10,383. ***Average non-need-based aid:*** $19,350. ***Average indebtedness upon graduation:*** $34,282.

APPLYING

Standardized Tests *Required:* SAT or ACT (for admission).

Options: electronic application, deferred entrance.

Application fee: $40.

Required: essay or personal statement, high school transcript, minimum 3.0 GPA, 1 letter of recommendation. ***Recommended:*** interview.

CONTACT

Ms. Karen Dunston, Executive Director, Pacific University, 2043 College Way, Forest Grove, OR 97116-1797. *Phone:* 503-352-2218. *Toll-free phone:* 877-722-8648. *Fax:* 503-352-2975. *E-mail:* admissions@pacificu.edu.

See page 1456 for the College Close-Up.

Pioneer Pacific College

Wilsonville, Oregon

http://www.pioneerpacific.edu/

CONTACT

Elizabeth Cox, Director of Admissions, Pioneer Pacific College, 27501 SW Parkway Avenue, Wilsonville, OR 97070. *Phone:* 503-688-2178. *Toll-free phone:* 866-PPC-INFO. *Fax:* 503-682-1514. *E-mail:* wil-info@pioneerpacific.edu.

Portland State University

Portland, Oregon

http://www.pdx.edu/

- **State-supported** university, founded 1946
- **Urban** 49-acre campus with easy access to Portland
- **Endowment** $81.3 million
- **Coed** 21,633 undergraduate students, 66% full-time, 53% women, 47% men
- **Moderately difficult** entrance level, 89% of applicants were admitted

UNDERGRAD STUDENTS

14,208 full-time, 7,425 part-time. Students come from 50 states and territories; 89 other countries; 17% are from out of state; 3% Black or African American, non-Hispanic/Latino; 12% Hispanic/Latino; 9% Asian, non-Hispanic/Latino; 0.6% Native Hawaiian or other Pacific Islander, non-Hispanic/Latino; 1% American Indian or Alaska Native, non-Hispanic/Latino; 6% Two or more races, non-Hispanic/Latino; 5% Race/ethnicity unknown; 7% international; 13% transferred in; 10% live on campus.

Freshmen:

Admission: 6,373 applied, 5,699 admitted, 1,758 enrolled. ***Average high school GPA:*** 3.37. ***Test scores:*** SAT critical reading scores over 500: 65%; SAT math scores over 500: 60%; SAT writing scores over 500: 55%; ACT scores over 18: 82%; SAT critical reading scores over 600: 24%; SAT math scores over 600: 18%; SAT writing scores over 600: 17%; ACT scores over 24: 39%; SAT critical reading scores over 700: 5%; SAT math scores over 700: 2%; SAT writing scores over 700: 2%; ACT scores over 30: 5%.

Retention: 73% of full-time freshmen returned.

FACULTY

Total: 1,595, 56% full-time, 47% with terminal degrees.

Student/faculty ratio: 20:1.

ACADEMICS

Calendar: quarters. *Degrees:* certificates, bachelor's, master's, doctoral, and postbachelor's certificates.

Special study options: academic remediation for entering students, accelerated degree program, adult/continuing education programs, advanced placement credit, cooperative education, distance learning, double majors, English as a second language, freshman honors college, honors programs, independent study, internships, off-campus study, part-time degree program, services for LD students, study abroad, summer session for credit. ***ROTC:*** Army (c), Air Force (c).

Computers: Students can access the following: campus intranet, computer help desk, free student e-mail accounts, online (class) grades, online (class) registration, online (class) schedules. Campuswide network is available. Wireless service is available via entire campus.

Library: Branford P. Millar Library plus 1 other. Students can reserve study rooms.

STUDENT LIFE

Housing options: coed, cooperative, special housing for students with disabilities. Campus housing is university owned. Freshman campus housing is guaranteed.

Activities and organizations: drama/theater group, student-run newspaper, radio station, choral group, national fraternities, national sororities.

Athletics Member NCAA. All Division I except football (Division I-AA). ***Intercollegiate sports:*** basketball M/W, cross-country running M/W, golf W, soccer W, softball W, tennis M/W, track and field M/W, volleyball W.

Campus security: 24-hour emergency response devices and patrols, late-night transport/escort service, controlled dormitory access.

Student services: health clinic, personal/psychological counseling, women's center, legal services.

COSTS & FINANCIAL AID

Costs (2016–17) ***Tuition:*** state resident $5616 full-time, $156 per credit hour part-time; nonresident $18,828 full-time, $523 per credit hour part-time. Full-time tuition and fees vary according to program and reciprocity agreements. Part-time tuition and fees vary according to program and reciprocity agreements. ***Required fees:*** $1317 full-time, $17 per credit hour part-time, $106 per term part-time. ***Room and board:*** $12,822; room only: $9204. Room and board charges vary according to board plan and housing facility. ***Payment plan:*** installment. ***Waivers:*** senior citizens and employees or children of employees.

Financial Aid Of all full-time matriculated undergraduates who enrolled in 2015, 10,901 applied for aid, 9,710 were judged to have need, 418 had their need fully met. In 2015, 112 non-need-based awards were made. ***Average percent of need met:*** 52. ***Average financial aid package:*** $9293. ***Average need-based loan:*** $4188. ***Average need-based gift aid:*** $5798. ***Average non-need-based aid:*** $2652. ***Average indebtedness upon graduation:*** $27,213.

APPLYING

Standardized Tests *Required for some:* SAT or ACT (for admission).

Options: electronic application, early admission, deferred entrance.

Application fee: $50.

Required: high school transcript, minimum 3.0 GPA.

Application deadlines: rolling (freshmen), rolling (transfers).

Notification: continuous (freshmen), continuous (transfers).

CONTACT

Shannon Carr, Executive Director, Admissions and New Student Programs, Portland State University, PO Box 751, Portland, OR 97207. *Phone:* 503-725-3511. *Toll-free phone:* 800-547-8887. *Fax:* 503-725-5525. *E-mail:* shannon.carr@pdx.edu.

★ Reed College

Portland, Oregon

http://www.reed.edu/

- **Independent** comprehensive, founded 1908
- **Urban** 116-acre campus with easy access to Portland
- **Coed** 1,410 undergraduate students, 98% full-time, 55% women, 45% men
- **Very difficult** entrance level, 31% of applicants were admitted

UNDERGRAD STUDENTS
1,379 full-time, 31 part-time. 92% are from out of state; 2% Black or African American, non-Hispanic/Latino; 11% Hispanic/Latino; 6% Asian, non-Hispanic/Latino; 0.3% Native Hawaiian or other Pacific Islander, non-Hispanic/Latino; 0.4% American Indian or Alaska Native, non-Hispanic/Latino; 8% Two or more races, non-Hispanic/Latino; 4% Race/ethnicity unknown; 9% international; 3% transferred in; 67% live on campus.

Freshmen:
Admission: 5,705 applied, 1,786 admitted, 354 enrolled. ***Average high school GPA:*** 3.9. ***Test scores:*** SAT critical reading scores over 500: 100%; SAT math scores over 500: 98%; SAT writing scores over 500: 99%; ACT scores over 18: 99%; SAT critical reading scores over 600: 94%; SAT math scores over 600: 85%; SAT writing scores over 600: 87%; ACT scores over 24: 97%; SAT critical reading scores over 700: 59%; SAT math scores over 700: 39%; SAT writing scores over 700: 42%; ACT scores over 30: 73%.

Retention: 87% of full-time freshmen returned.

FACULTY
Total: 149, 99% full-time, 94% with terminal degrees.

Student/faculty ratio: 9:1.

ACADEMICS
Calendar: semesters. *Degrees:* bachelor's and master's.

Special study options: academic remediation for entering students, advanced placement credit, cooperative education, independent study, internships, off-campus study, services for LD students, student-designed majors, study abroad.

Unusual degree programs: 3-2 forestry with Duke University; computer science with University of Washington, engineering with California Institute of Technology, Columbia University, Rensselaer Polytechnic Institute.

Computers: 434 computers/terminals are available on campus for general student use. Students can access the following: campus intranet, computer help desk, free student e-mail accounts, online (class) registration, online (class) schedules. Campuswide network is available. 100% of college-owned or -operated housing units are wired for high-speed Internet access. Wireless service is available via entire campus.

Library: Eric V. Hauser Memorial Library plus 1 other.

STUDENT LIFE
Housing options: coed, women-only, cooperative, special housing for students with disabilities. Campus housing is university owned. Freshman campus housing is guaranteed.

Activities and organizations: drama/theater group, student-run newspaper, radio station, choral group.

Athletics ***Intramural sports:*** basketball M/W, fencing M/W, rugby M/W, soccer M/W, squash M/W, ultimate Frisbee M/W.

Campus security: 24-hour emergency response devices and patrols, student patrols, late-night transport/escort service, controlled dormitory access.

Student services: health clinic, personal/psychological counseling, women's center, legal services.

COSTS & FINANCIAL AID
Costs (2016–17) ***Comprehensive fee:*** $65,300 includes full-time tuition ($51,850), mandatory fees ($300), and room and board ($13,150). Full-time tuition and fees vary according to degree level. Part-time tuition: $8790 per unit. Part-time tuition and fees vary according to course load and degree level. ***Required fees:*** $150 per term part-time. ***College room only:*** $6890. Room and board charges vary according to board plan and housing facility. ***Payment plan:*** installment. ***Waivers:*** employees or children of employees.

Financial Aid Of all full-time matriculated undergraduates who enrolled in 2016, 799 applied for aid, 741 were judged to have need, 611 had their need fully met. ***Average percent of need met:*** 100. ***Average financial aid package:*** $45,050. ***Average need-based loan:*** $3298. ***Average need-based gift aid:*** $39,915. ***Average indebtedness upon graduation:*** $19,627. ***Financial aid deadline:*** 2/1.

APPLYING
Standardized Tests *Required:* SAT or ACT (for admission).

Options: electronic application, early admission, early decision, deferred entrance.

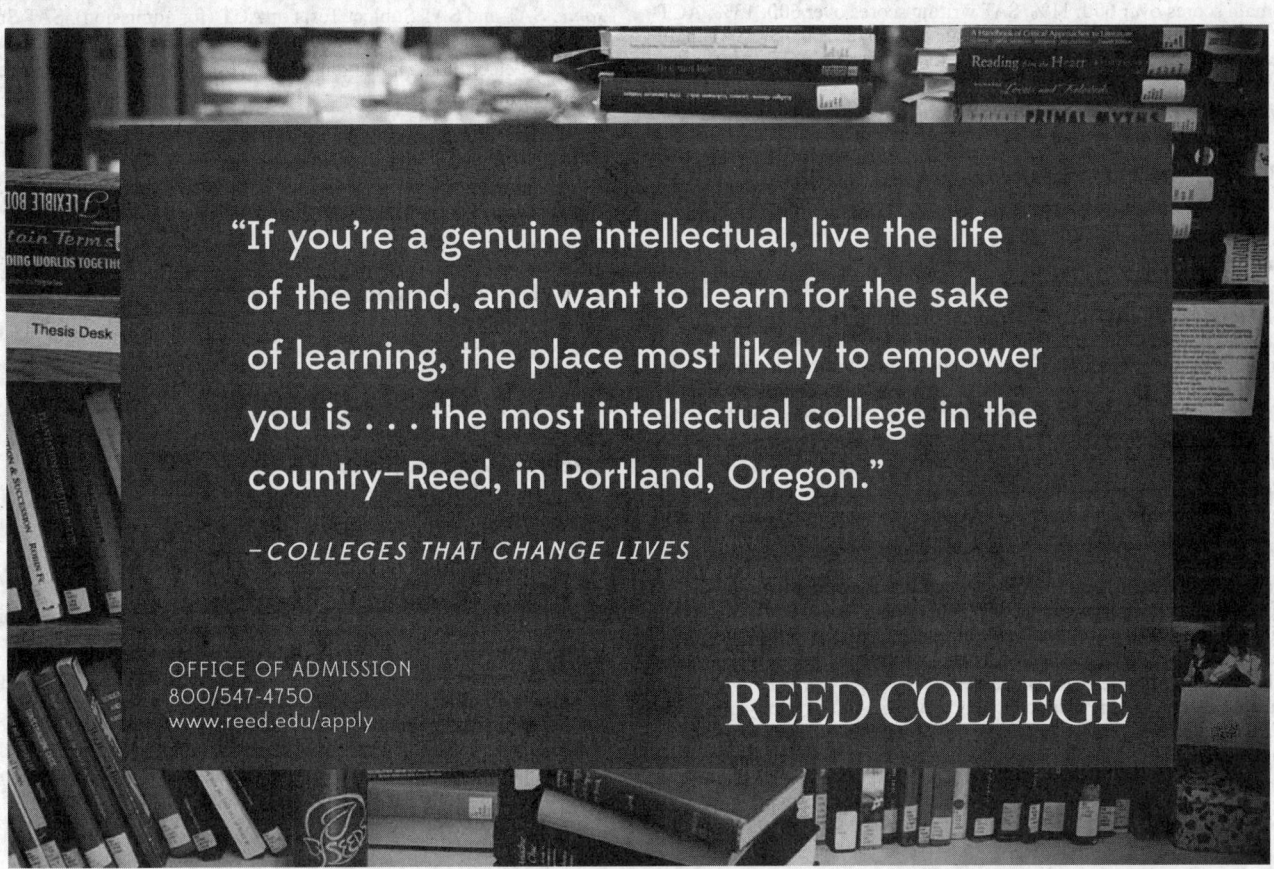

Required: essay or personal statement, high school transcript, 2 letters of recommendation. ***Recommended:*** interview.

Application deadlines: 1/1 (freshmen), 3/1 (transfers).

Early decision deadline: 11/15 (for plan 1), 12/20 (for plan 2).

Notification: 4/1 (freshmen), 5/1 (transfers), 12/15 (early decision plan 1), 2/1 (early decision plan 2).

CONTACT
Office of Admission, Reed College, 3203 Southeast Woodstock Boulevard, Portland, OR 97202-8199. *Phone:* 800-547-4750. *Toll-free phone:* 800-547-4750. *Fax:* 503-777-7553. *E-mail:* admission@reed.edu.

See previous page for display ad and page 1468 for the College Close-Up.

Southern Oregon University

Ashland, Oregon

http://www.sou.edu/

- **State-supported** comprehensive, founded 1926
- **Small-town** 175-acre campus
- **Endowment** $24.6 million
- **Coed** 5,314 undergraduate students, 68% full-time, 59% women, 41% men
- **Moderately difficult** entrance level, 78% of applicants were admitted

UNDERGRAD STUDENTS
3,598 full-time, 1,716 part-time. Students come from 41 states and territories; 15 other countries; 40% are from out of state; 2% Black or African American, non-Hispanic/Latino; 12% Hispanic/Latino; 2% Asian, non-Hispanic/Latino; 0.7% Native Hawaiian or other Pacific Islander, non-Hispanic/Latino; 1% American Indian or Alaska Native, non-Hispanic/Latino; 10% Two or more races, non-Hispanic/Latino; 9% Race/ethnicity unknown; 3% international; 10% transferred in; 26% live on campus.

Freshmen:
Admission: 2,766 applied, 2,163 admitted, 675 enrolled. ***Average high school GPA:*** 3.32. ***Test scores:*** SAT critical reading scores over 500: 59%; SAT math scores over 500: 50%; SAT writing scores over 500: 44%; ACT scores over 18: 86%; SAT critical reading scores over 600: 21%; SAT math scores over 600: 11%; SAT writing scores over 600: 13%; ACT scores over 24: 36%; SAT critical reading scores over 700: 4%; SAT math scores over 700: 1%; SAT writing scores over 700: 1%; ACT scores over 30: 3%.

Retention: 68% of full-time freshmen returned.

FACULTY
Total: 283, 59% full-time, 42% with terminal degrees.

Student/faculty ratio: 21:1.

ACADEMICS
Calendar: quarters. *Degrees:* certificates, bachelor's, master's, and postbachelor's certificates.

Special study options: academic remediation for entering students, accelerated degree program, adult/continuing education programs, advanced placement credit, cooperative education, distance learning, double majors, English as a second language, freshman honors college, honors programs, independent study, internships, off-campus study, part-time degree program, services for LD students, student-designed majors, study abroad, summer session for credit. ***ROTC:*** Army (b).

Computers: 750 computers/terminals are available on campus for general student use. Students can access the following: campus intranet, computer help desk, free student e-mail accounts, online (class) grades, online (class) registration, online (class) schedules, online account information including bill payment, online employee records for student workers. Campuswide network is available. 100% of college-owned or -operated housing units are wired for high-speed Internet access. Wireless service is available via classrooms, computer centers, computer labs, dorm rooms, learning centers, libraries, student centers.

Library: Lenn and Dixie Hannon Library. *Books:* 340,015 (physical), 135,298 (digital/electronic); *Databases:* 80. Students can reserve study rooms.

STUDENT LIFE
Housing options: on-campus residence required for freshman year; coed, special housing for students with disabilities. Campus housing is university owned. Freshman campus housing is guaranteed.

Activities and organizations: drama/theater group, student-run newspaper, radio and television station, choral group, Native American Student Union, International Student Association, Impact (religious club), Ho`opa`a Hawaii Club, Omicron Delta Kappa.

Athletics Member NAIA. ***Intercollegiate sports:*** basketball M(s)/W(s), cheerleading W, football M(s), lacrosse M(c), rugby M(c)/W(c), soccer M(c)/W(s), softball W(s), tennis M(c)/W(c), track and field M(s)/W(s), volleyball W(s), wrestling M(s). ***Intramural sports:*** basketball M/W, bowling M(c)/W(c), football M, rock climbing M(c)/W(c), soccer M/W, softball M/W, volleyball M/W.

Campus security: 24-hour emergency response devices and patrols, student patrols, late-night transport/escort service, controlled dormitory access.

Student services: health clinic, personal/psychological counseling, women's center, legal services.

COSTS & FINANCIAL AID
Costs (2016–17) ***Tuition:*** state resident $6813 full-time, $151 per credit hour part-time; nonresident $21,460 full-time, $477 per credit hour part-time. Full-time tuition and fees vary according to course load, program, and reciprocity agreements. Part-time tuition and fees vary according to course load, program, and reciprocity agreements. ***Required fees:*** $1710 full-time, $61 per credit hour part-time. ***Room and board:*** $12,756; room only: $7065. Room and board charges vary according to board plan and housing facility. ***Payment plans:*** installment, deferred payment. ***Waivers:*** senior citizens and employees or children of employees.

Financial Aid Of all full-time matriculated undergraduates who enrolled in 2016, 2,729 applied for aid, 2,129 were judged to have need, 495 had their need fully met. 195 Federal Work-Study jobs (averaging $2977). ***Average percent of need met:*** 77. ***Average financial aid package:*** $11,131. ***Average need-based loan:*** $7371. ***Average need-based gift aid:*** $6825. ***Average indebtedness upon graduation:*** $27,375.

APPLYING
Standardized Tests *Required:* SAT or ACT (for admission). *Required for some:* SAT and SAT Subject Tests or ACT (for admission), SAT Subject Tests (for admission).

Options: electronic application, early admission, deferred entrance.

Application fee: $60.

Required: high school transcript, minimum 3.0 GPA. ***Required for some:*** essay or personal statement.

Application deadlines: rolling (freshmen), rolling (transfers).

Notification: continuous (freshmen), continuous (transfers).

CONTACT
Mr. Kelly Moutsatson, Director of Admissions, Southern Oregon University, 1250 Siskiyou Boulevard, Ashland, OR 97520. *Phone:* 541-552-6411. *Toll-free phone:* 855-470-3377. *Fax:* 541-552-6614. *E-mail:* admissions@sou.edu.

University of Oregon

Eugene, Oregon

http://www.uoregon.edu/

- **State-supported** university, founded 1876
- **Suburban** 295-acre campus
- **Endowment** $758.7 million
- **Coed** 20,047 undergraduate students, 91% full-time, 53% women, 47% men
- **Moderately difficult** entrance level, 78% of applicants were admitted

UNDERGRAD STUDENTS
18,328 full-time, 1,719 part-time. Students come from 52 states and territories; 72 other countries; 42% are from out of state; 2% Black or African American, non-Hispanic/Latino; 11% Hispanic/Latino; 6% Asian, non-Hispanic/Latino; 0.4% Native Hawaiian or other Pacific Islander, non-Hispanic/Latino; 0.5% American Indian or Alaska Native, non-Hispanic/Latino; 7% Two or more races, non-Hispanic/Latino; 2% Race/ethnicity unknown; 13% international; 6% transferred in; 19% live on campus.

Freshmen:
Admission: 21,821 applied, 16,992 admitted, 4,041 enrolled. ***Average high school GPA:*** 3.58. ***Test scores:*** SAT critical reading scores over 500: 74%; SAT math scores over 500: 73%; SAT writing scores over 500: 70%; ACT scores over 18: 96%; SAT critical reading scores over 600: 33%; SAT math scores over 600: 31%; SAT writing scores over 600: 27%; ACT scores over 24: 62%; SAT critical reading scores over 700: 5%; SAT math scores over 700: 4%; SAT writing scores over 700: 4%; ACT scores over 30: 12%.

Retention: 87% of full-time freshmen returned.

FACULTY
Total: 1,701, 67% full-time, 90% with terminal degrees.

Student/faculty ratio: 17:1.

ACADEMICS
Calendar: quarters. *Degrees:* bachelor's, master's, doctoral, post-master's, and postbachelor's certificates.

Special study options: advanced placement credit, cooperative education, distance learning, double majors, English as a second language, honors programs, independent study, internships, off-campus study, part-time degree program, services for LD students, student-designed majors, study abroad, summer session for credit. ***ROTC:*** Army (b), Air Force (c).

Unusual degree programs: 3-2 engineering with Oregon State University.

Computers: 480 computers/terminals and 480 ports are available on campus for general student use. Students can access the following: campus intranet, computer help desk, free student e-mail accounts, online (class) grades, online (class) registration, online (class) schedules. Campuswide network is available. 100% of college-owned or -operated housing units are wired for high-speed Internet access. Wireless service is available via entire campus.

Library: Knight Library plus 6 others. *Books:* 2.2 million (physical), 617,137 (digital/electronic); *Serial titles:* 2,374 (physical), 104,383 (digital/electronic); *Databases:* 457. Weekly public service hours: 120; study areas open 24 hours, 5-7 days a week; students can reserve study rooms.

STUDENT LIFE
Housing options: on-campus residence required for freshman year; coed, cooperative. Campus housing is university owned. Freshman applicants given priority for college housing.

Activities and organizations: drama/theater group, student-run newspaper, radio and television station, choral group, marching band, political and environmental action, cultural organizations, major-specific organizations, community service organizations, club sports, national fraternities, national sororities.

Athletics Member NCAA. All Division I except football (Division I-A). ***Intercollegiate sports:*** baseball M(s), basketball M(s)/W(s), cross-country running M(s)/W(s), golf M(s)/W(s), lacrosse W(s), soccer W(s), softball W(s), tennis M(s)/W(s), track and field M(s)/W(s), volleyball W(s). ***Intramural sports:*** badminton M(c)/W(c), baseball M(c), basketball M/W, crew M(c)/W(c), cross-country running M(c)/W(c), equestrian sports M(c)/W(c), fencing M(c)/W(c), field hockey M/W, football M/W, golf M(c)/W(c), ice hockey M(c)/W(c), lacrosse M(c)/W(c), racquetball M/W, rock climbing M(c)/W(c), rowing M(c)/W(c), rugby M(c)/W(c), sailing M(c)/W(c), sand volleyball M/W, skiing (cross-country) M(c)/W(c), skiing (downhill) M(c)/W(c), soccer M(c)/W(c), softball M(c)/W(c), squash M(c)/W(c), swimming and diving M(c)/W(c), table tennis M(c)/W(c), tennis M/W, track and field M/W, triathlon M(c)/W(c), ultimate Frisbee M(c)/W(c), volleyball M(c)/W(c), water polo M(c)/W(c), weight lifting M(c)/W(c).

Campus security: 24-hour emergency response devices and patrols, late-night transport/escort service, controlled dormitory access.

Student services: health clinic, personal/psychological counseling, women's center, legal services.

COSTS & FINANCIAL AID
Costs (2016–17) ***One-time required fee:*** $389. ***Tuition:*** state resident $8910 full-time, $198 per credit hour part-time; nonresident $31,590 full-time, $702 per credit hour part-time. Full-time tuition and fees vary according to course load and program. Part-time tuition and fees vary according to course load and program. ***Required fees:*** $1852 full-time. ***Room and board:*** $12,210. Room and board charges vary according to board plan and housing facility. ***Payment plan:*** installment. ***Waivers:*** employees or children of employees.

Financial Aid Of all full-time matriculated undergraduates who enrolled in 2015, 10,783 applied for aid, 8,245 were judged to have need, 509 had their need fully met. 2,420 Federal Work-Study jobs (averaging $1765). 79 state and other part-time jobs (averaging $2519). In 2015, 2517 non-need-based awards were made. ***Average percent of need met:*** 63. ***Average financial aid package:*** $10,879. ***Average need-based loan:*** $4658. ***Average need-based gift aid:*** $8320. ***Average non-need-based aid:*** $5434. ***Average indebtedness upon graduation:*** $25,542.

APPLYING
Standardized Tests *Required:* SAT or ACT (for admission). *Required for some:* SAT and SAT Subject Tests or ACT (for admission).

Options: electronic application, early action.

Application fee: $65.

Required: essay or personal statement, high school transcript, C+ or better in 15 college preparatory units. ***Required for some:*** 2 letters of recommendation.

Application deadlines: 1/15 (freshmen), 5/15 (transfers), 11/1 (early action).

Notification: 4/1 (freshmen), 12/15 (early action).

CONTACT
University of Oregon, Eugene, OR 97403. *Phone:* 541-346-3201. *Toll-free phone:* 800-232-3825.

University of Portland

Portland, Oregon

http://www.up.edu/

- **Independent Roman Catholic** comprehensive, founded 1901
- **Urban** 150-acre campus
- **Endowment** $147.0 million
- **Coed**
- **Moderately difficult** entrance level

FACULTY
Student/faculty ratio: 14:1.

ACADEMICS
Calendar: semesters. *Degrees:* bachelor's, master's, doctoral, and post-master's certificates.

Library: Wilson M. Clark Library plus 1 other. *Books:* 191,219 (physical), 138,108 (digital/electronic); *Serial titles:* 1,080 (digital/electronic); *Databases:* 153. Weekly public service hours: 117; students can reserve study rooms.

STUDENT LIFE
Housing options: on-campus residence required for freshman year; coed, men-only, women-only. Campus housing is university owned. Freshman campus housing is guaranteed.

Activities and organizations: drama/theater group, student-run newspaper, radio station, choral group, Hawaii Club, International Club, Student Nurses Association, Feminist Discussion Group, The Bluffoons (Improv Club).

Athletics Member NCAA. All Division I.

Campus security: 24-hour emergency response devices and patrols, student patrols, late-night transport/escort service, controlled dormitory access.

Student services: health clinic, personal/psychological counseling.

FINANCIAL AID
Financial Aid Of all full-time matriculated undergraduates who enrolled in 2015, 2,702 applied for aid, 2,278 were judged to have need, 165 had their need fully met. 444 Federal Work-Study jobs (averaging $1030). 1,437 state and other part-time jobs (averaging $1413). In 2015, 1264 non-need-based awards were made. ***Average percent of need met:*** 73. ***Average financial aid package:*** $29,493. ***Average need-based loan:*** $5099. ***Average need-based gift aid:*** $22,439. ***Average non-need-based aid:*** $15,787. ***Average indebtedness upon graduation:*** $28,307. ***Financial aid deadline:*** 3/1.

APPLYING
Standardized Tests *Required:* SAT or ACT (for admission). *Recommended:* SAT (for admission), ACT (for admission).

Options: electronic application, deferred entrance.

Application fee: $50.

Required: essay or personal statement, high school transcript, 1 letter of recommendation.

CONTACT
Mr. Jason McDonald, Dean of Admissions, University of Portland, 5000 North Willamette Boulevard, Portland, OR 97203-5798. *Phone:* 503-943-7147. *Toll-free phone:* 888-627-5601. *Fax:* 503-943-7315. *E-mail:* admissions@up.edu.

Warner Pacific College

Portland, Oregon

http://www.warnerpacific.edu/

- **Independent** comprehensive, founded 1937, affiliated with Church of God
- **Urban** 15-acre campus with easy access to Portland
- **Endowment** $10.2 million
- **Coed**
- **Moderately difficult** entrance level

FACULTY
Student/faculty ratio: 12:1.

ACADEMICS
Calendar: semesters. *Degrees:* certificates, associate, bachelor's, and master's.
Library: Otto F. Linn Library.

STUDENT LIFE
Housing options: on-campus residence required through junior year; men-only, women-only, special housing for students with disabilities. Campus housing is university owned. Freshman applicants given priority for college housing.

Activities and organizations: drama/theater group, student-run newspaper, choral group, Associated Students of Warner Pacific College, yearbook, College Activities Board, Fellowship of Christian Athletes.

Athletics Member NAIA, NCCAA.

Campus security: 24-hour emergency response devices and patrols, student patrols, late-night transport/escort service, controlled dormitory access.

Student services: health clinic, personal/psychological counseling.

COSTS & FINANCIAL AID
Costs (2016–17) ***Comprehensive fee:*** $31,610 includes full-time tuition ($22,050), mandatory fees ($660), and room and board ($8900). Part-time tuition: $1005 per semester hour. Part-time tuition and fees vary according to course load. ***Required fees:*** $330 per term part-time. ***College room only:*** $3680. Room and board charges vary according to board plan and housing facility. ***Payment plans:*** installment, deferred payment.

Financial Aid Of all full-time matriculated undergraduates who enrolled in 2016, 419 applied for aid, 386 were judged to have need, 73 had their need fully met. 319 Federal Work-Study jobs (averaging $1985). In 2016, 71 non-need-based awards were made. ***Average percent of need met:*** 67. ***Average financial aid package:*** $18,736. ***Average need-based loan:*** $4462. ***Average need-based gift aid:*** $6715. ***Average non-need-based aid:*** $7383. ***Average indebtedness upon graduation:*** $36,916.

APPLYING
Standardized Tests *Required:* SAT or ACT (for admission).

Options: electronic application.

Required: essay or personal statement, high school transcript, minimum 2.5 GPA. ***Required for some:*** 1 letter of recommendation, interview. ***Recommended:*** minimum 3.0 GPA, interview.

CONTACT
Dale Seipp, Vice President for Enrollment Management, Warner Pacific College, 2219 Southeast 68th Avenue, Portland, OR 97215. *Phone:* 503-517-1020. *Toll-free phone:* 800-804-1510. *Fax:* 503-517-1540. *E-mail:* admiss@warnerpacific.edu.

Western Oregon University

Monmouth, Oregon

http://www.wou.edu/

- **State-supported** comprehensive, founded 1856
- **Rural** 157-acre campus with easy access to Portland
- **Coed** 4,833 undergraduate students, 84% full-time, 61% women, 39% men
- **Moderately difficult** entrance level, 88% of applicants were admitted

UNDERGRAD STUDENTS
4,081 full-time, 752 part-time. Students come from 33 states and territories; 22 other countries; 19% are from out of state; 4% Black or African American, non-Hispanic/Latino; 14% Hispanic/Latino; 4% Asian, non-Hispanic/Latino; 3% Native Hawaiian or other Pacific Islander, non-Hispanic/Latino; 2% American Indian or Alaska Native, non-Hispanic/Latino; 0.1% Two or more races, non-Hispanic/Latino; 4% Race/ethnicity unknown; 6% international; 12% transferred in; 26% live on campus.

Freshmen:
Admission: 2,901 applied, 2,546 admitted, 886 enrolled. ***Average high school GPA:*** 3.26. ***Test scores:*** SAT critical reading scores over 500: 45%; SAT math scores over 500: 43%; SAT writing scores over 500: 33%; ACT scores over 18: 72%; SAT critical reading scores over 600: 10%; SAT math scores over 600: 9%; SAT writing scores over 600: 6%; ACT scores over 24: 20%; SAT critical reading scores over 700: 1%; SAT math scores over 700: 1%; ACT scores over 30: 3%.
Retention: 74% of full-time freshmen returned.

FACULTY
Total: 400, 73% full-time, 55% with terminal degrees.
Student/faculty ratio: 14:1.

ACADEMICS
Calendar: quarters. *Degrees:* bachelor's, master's, and postbachelor's certificates.

Special study options: academic remediation for entering students, advanced placement credit, distance learning, double majors, English as a second language, freshman honors college, honors programs, independent study, internships, off-campus study, part-time degree program, services for LD students, student-designed majors, study abroad, summer session for credit. ***ROTC:*** Army (c).

Unusual degree programs: nursing.

Computers: 411 computers/terminals are available on campus for general student use. Students can access the following: computer help desk, free student e-mail accounts, online (class) grades, online (class) registration, online (class) schedules. Campuswide network is available. 100% of college-owned or -operated housing units are wired for high-speed Internet access. Wireless service is available via entire campus.

Library: Wayne and Lynn Hamersly Library. *Books:* 164,610 (physical), 193,700 (digital/electronic); *Serial titles:* 33,400 (physical), 223,223 (digital/electronic); *Databases:* 291. Students can reserve study rooms.

STUDENT LIFE
Housing options: on-campus residence required for freshman year; coed, men-only, women-only, special housing for students with disabilities. Campus housing is university owned. Freshman campus housing is guaranteed.

Activities and organizations: drama/theater group, student-run newspaper, radio station, choral group, Model United Nations, Multicultural Student Union, Oregon Student Association, Alternative Spring Break (community service), M.E.Ch.A, national fraternities, national sororities.

Athletics Member NCAA. All Division II. ***Intercollegiate sports:*** baseball M(s), basketball M(s)/W(s), cross-country running M(s)/W(s), football M(s), soccer W(s), softball W(s), track and field M(s)/W(s), volleyball W(s). ***Intramural sports:*** badminton M/W, basketball M/W, bowling M/W, cross-country running M(c)/W(c), football M/W, golf M/W, lacrosse M(c), racquetball M(c)/W(c), rugby M(c)/W(c), soccer M(c)/W(c), softball M/W, swimming and diving M(c)/W(c), tennis M/W, track and field M/W, volleyball M(c)/W(c), water polo M(c)/W(c).

Campus security: 24-hour emergency response devices and patrols, late-night transport/escort service, controlled dormitory access.

Student services: health clinic, personal/psychological counseling, women's center.

COSTS & FINANCIAL AID

Costs (2016–17) ***Tuition:*** state resident $9285 full-time; nonresident $23,445 full-time. Full-time tuition and fees vary according to course load. Part-time tuition and fees vary according to course load. No tuition increase for student's term of enrollment. ***Room and board:*** $9798; room only: $8148. Room and board charges vary according to board plan and housing facility.

Financial Aid Of all full-time matriculated undergraduates who enrolled in 2015, 3,171 applied for aid, 2,685 were judged to have need, 228 had their need fully met. 260 Federal Work-Study jobs (averaging $1048). In 2015, 295 non-need-based awards were made. ***Average percent of need met:*** 55. ***Average financial aid package:*** $9924. ***Average need-based loan:*** $3966. ***Average need-based gift aid:*** $6807. ***Average non-need-based aid:*** $1212. ***Average indebtedness upon graduation:*** $30,586.

APPLYING

Options: electronic application.

Application fee: $60.

Required: high school transcript, minimum 2.8 GPA, general college preparatory program completion.

Application deadlines: rolling (freshmen), rolling (transfers).

Notification: continuous (freshmen), continuous (transfers).

CONTACT

Mr. David Compton, Assistant Director of Admissions for Recruitment, Western Oregon University, 345 North Monmouth Avenue, Monmouth, OR 97361. *Phone:* 503-838-8211. *Toll-free phone:* 877-877-1593. *Fax:* 503-838-8067. *E-mail:* wolfgram@wou.edu.

Willamette University

Salem, Oregon

http://www.willamette.edu/

- **Independent United Methodist** comprehensive, founded 1842
- **Urban** 72-acre campus with easy access to Portland
- **Endowment** $214.3 million
- **Coed** 2,002 undergraduate students, 93% full-time, 57% women, 43% men
- **Very difficult** entrance level, 78% of applicants were admitted

UNDERGRAD STUDENTS

1,862 full-time, 140 part-time. Students come from 37 states and territories; 9 other countries; 79% are from out of state; 3% Black or African American, non-Hispanic/Latino; 13% Hispanic/Latino; 8% Asian, non-Hispanic/Latino; 0.3% Native Hawaiian or other Pacific Islander, non-Hispanic/Latino; 0.5% American Indian or Alaska Native, non-Hispanic/Latino; 9% Two or more races, non-Hispanic/Latino; 3% Race/ethnicity unknown; 6% international; 1% transferred in; 66% live on campus.

Freshmen:

Admission: 6,181 applied, 4,825 admitted, 474 enrolled. ***Average high school GPA:*** 3.93. ***Test scores:*** SAT critical reading scores over 500: 92%; SAT math scores over 500: 91%; SAT writing scores over 500: 89%; ACT scores over 18: 100%; SAT critical reading scores over 600: 62%; SAT math scores over 600: 52%; SAT writing scores over 600: 52%; ACT scores over 24: 85%; SAT critical reading scores over 700: 19%; SAT math scores over 700: 9%; SAT writing scores over 700: 12%; ACT scores over 30: 31%.

Retention: 86% of full-time freshmen returned.

FACULTY

Total: 270, 79% full-time, 89% with terminal degrees.

Student/faculty ratio: 10:1.

ACADEMICS

Calendar: semesters. *Degrees:* bachelor's, master's, and doctoral.

Special study options: accelerated degree program, advanced placement credit, double majors, independent study, internships, off-campus study, part-time degree program, services for LD students, student-designed majors, study abroad. ***ROTC:*** Army (c), Air Force (c).

Unusual degree programs: 3-2 engineering with University of Southern California, Washington University in St. Louis, Columbia University; forestry with Duke University.

Computers: Students can access the following: computer help desk, free student e-mail accounts, online (class) grades, online (class) registration, online (class) schedules. Campuswide network is available. 100% of college-owned or -operated housing units are wired for high-speed Internet access. Wireless service is available via entire campus.

Library: Mark O. Hatfield Library plus 1 other. Study areas open 24 hours, 5-7 days a week; students can reserve study rooms.

STUDENT LIFE

Housing options: on-campus residence required through sophomore year; coed. Campus housing is university owned. Freshman campus housing is guaranteed.

Activities and organizations: drama/theater group, student-run newspaper, radio station, choral group, national fraternities, national sororities.

Athletics Member NCAA. All Division III. ***Intercollegiate sports:*** baseball M, basketball M/W, crew M/W, cross-country running M/W, football M, golf M/W, lacrosse M(c), soccer M/W, softball W, swimming and diving M/W, tennis M/W, track and field M/W, volleyball W. ***Intramural sports:*** badminton M/W, basketball M/W, bowling M/W, cross-country running M/W, football M/W, golf M/W, racquetball M/W, skiing (cross-country) M(c)/W(c), skiing (downhill) M(c)/W(c), soccer M/W, softball M/W, table tennis M/W, tennis M/W, ultimate Frisbee M/W, volleyball M/W, water polo M/W, weight lifting M/W.

Campus security: 24-hour emergency response devices and patrols, student patrols, late-night transport/escort service, controlled dormitory access.

Student services: health clinic, personal/psychological counseling, women's center.

COSTS & FINANCIAL AID

Costs (2017–18) ***Comprehensive fee:*** $59,994 includes full-time tuition ($47,840), mandatory fees ($324), and room and board ($11,830). Full-time tuition and fees vary according to course load. Part-time tuition: $5980 per credit. Part-time tuition and fees vary according to course load. ***Room and board:*** Room and board charges vary according to board plan and housing facility. ***Payment plans:*** tuition prepayment, installment. ***Waivers:*** employees or children of employees.

Financial Aid Of all full-time matriculated undergraduates who enrolled in 2016, 1,354 applied for aid, 1,161 were judged to have need, 304 had their need fully met. In 2016, 668 non-need-based awards were made. ***Average percent of need met:*** 80. ***Average financial aid package:*** $35,895. ***Average need-based loan:*** $5473. ***Average need-based gift aid:*** $29,689. ***Average non-need-based aid:*** $21,056. ***Average indebtedness upon graduation:*** $29,958.

APPLYING

Standardized Tests *Recommended:* SAT or ACT (for admission), SAT and SAT Subject Tests or ACT (for admission), SAT Subject Tests (for admission).

Options: electronic application, early action, deferred entrance.

Application fee: $50.

Required: essay or personal statement, high school transcript, minimum 2.0 GPA, 1 letter of recommendation. ***Required for some:*** interview. ***Recommended:*** interview.

Application deadlines: 1/15 (freshmen), 2/1 (transfers), 11/15 (early action).

Notification: continuous until 5/1 (freshmen), 3/15 (transfers), 12/31 (early action).

CONTACT

Sue Corner, Senior Associate Director of Admission, Willamette University, 900 State Street, Salem, OR 97301. *Phone:* 503-375-5337. *Toll-free phone:* 877-542-2787. *E-mail:* bearcat@willamette.edu.

PENNSYLVANIA

Albright College

Reading, Pennsylvania

http://www.albright.edu/

- **Independent** comprehensive, founded 1856, affiliated with United Methodist Church
- **Suburban** 118-acre campus with easy access to Philadelphia
- **Endowment** $62.9 million
- **Coed** 2,304 undergraduate students, 99% full-time, 60% women, 40% men
- **Moderately difficult** entrance level, 51% of applicants were admitted

UNDERGRAD STUDENTS
2,284 full-time, 20 part-time. Students come from 30 states and territories; 14 other countries; 41% are from out of state; 24% Black or African American, non-Hispanic/Latino; 12% Hispanic/Latino; 3% Asian, non-Hispanic/Latino; 0.9% American Indian or Alaska Native, non-Hispanic/Latino; 2% Two or more races, non-Hispanic/Latino; 2% Race/ethnicity unknown; 2% international; 2% transferred in; 65% live on campus.

Freshmen:
Admission: 8,832 applied, 4,514 admitted, 596 enrolled. ***Average high school GPA:*** 3.35. ***Test scores:*** SAT critical reading scores over 500: 67%; SAT math scores over 500: 62%; ACT scores over 18: 97%; SAT critical reading scores over 600: 18%; SAT math scores over 600: 17%; ACT scores over 24: 31%; SAT critical reading scores over 700: 3%; SAT math scores over 700: 1%; ACT scores over 30: 1%.

Retention: 71% of full-time freshmen returned.

FACULTY
Total: 178, 62% full-time, 62% with terminal degrees.

Student/faculty ratio: 14:1.

ACADEMICS
Calendar: 4-1-4. *Degrees:* certificates, bachelor's, and master's.

Special study options: accelerated degree program, adult/continuing education programs, advanced placement credit, distance learning, double majors, honors programs, independent study, internships, off-campus study, services for LD students, student-designed majors, study abroad, summer session for credit. ***ROTC:*** Army (c).

Computers: 450 computers/terminals are available on campus for general student use. Students can access the following: campus intranet, computer help desk, free student e-mail accounts, online (class) grades, online (class) registration, online (class) schedules, online financial statements, housing choices, course management systems. Campuswide network is available. 100% of college-owned or -operated housing units are wired for high-speed Internet access. Wireless service is available via entire campus.

Library: F. W. Gingrich Library plus 1 other. *Books:* 210,904 (physical), 296,145 (digital/electronic); *Serial titles:* 1,210 (physical), 35,708 (digital/electronic); *Databases:* 70. Students can reserve study rooms.

STUDENT LIFE
Housing options: on-campus residence required through senior year; coed, special housing for students with disabilities. Campus housing is university owned. Freshman campus housing is guaranteed.

Activities and organizations: drama/theater group, student-run newspaper, radio and television station, choral group, Greek Organizations (combined), Alpha Phi Omega (service organization), Student Government Association, Albright College Activities Council, Albrightian (newspaper), national fraternities, national sororities.

Athletics Member NCAA. All Division III. ***Intercollegiate sports:*** badminton W(c), baseball M, basketball M/W, cheerleading M/W, cross-country running M/W, field hockey W, football M, golf M/W, lacrosse M/W, rugby M(c)/W(c), soccer M/W, softball W, swimming and diving M/W, tennis M/W, track and field M/W, ultimate Frisbee M(c)/W(c), volleyball W. ***Intramural sports:*** badminton W, basketball M/W, football M, racquetball M/W, soccer M/W, softball M/W, volleyball M/W.

Campus security: 24-hour emergency response devices and patrols, student patrols, late-night transport/escort service, controlled dormitory access, E2 Campus Text messaging, Rape Aggression Defense Training, marked patrol cars, partnership with local and state police.

Student services: health clinic, personal/psychological counseling, women's center.

COSTS & FINANCIAL AID
Costs (2017–18) ***Comprehensive fee:*** $54,910 includes full-time tuition ($42,404), mandatory fees ($900), and room and board ($11,606). Full-time tuition and fees vary according to degree level. Part-time tuition: $5300 per course. Part-time tuition and fees vary according to degree level. ***College room only:*** $6408. Room and board charges vary according to board plan and housing facility. ***Payment plan:*** installment. ***Waivers:*** adult students, senior citizens, and employees or children of employees.

Financial Aid Of all full-time matriculated undergraduates who enrolled in 2016, 1,742 applied for aid, 1,684 were judged to have need, 197 had their need fully met. In 2016, 155 non-need-based awards were made. ***Average percent of need met:*** 80. ***Average financial aid package:*** $36,812. ***Average need-based loan:*** $5224. ***Average need-based gift aid:*** $31,045. ***Average non-need-based aid:*** $19,738. ***Average indebtedness upon graduation:*** $38,196. ***Financial aid deadline:*** 2/1.

APPLYING
Options: electronic application, deferred entrance.

Application fee: $35.

Required: high school transcript, minimum 2.5 GPA. ***Required for some:*** essay or personal statement, 1 letter of recommendation, interview, secondary school report (guidance department), interview for students applying test-optional.

Application deadlines: rolling (freshmen), rolling (transfers).
Notification: continuous (freshmen), continuous (transfers).

CONTACT
Mr. Paul Cramer, Vice President for Enrollment Management, Albright College, PO Box 15234, 13th and Bern Streets, Reading, PA 19612-5234. *Phone:* 610-921-7260. *Toll-free phone:* 800-252-1856. *Fax:* 610-921-7294. *E-mail:* admission@albright.edu.

Allegheny College

Meadville, Pennsylvania

http://www.allegheny.edu/

- **Independent** 4-year, founded 1815
- **Suburban** 565-acre campus
- **Endowment** $181.6 million
- **Coed** 1,920 undergraduate students, 97% full-time, 53% women, 47% men
- **Very difficult** entrance level, 68% of applicants were admitted

UNDERGRAD STUDENTS
1,869 full-time, 51 part-time. Students come from 43 states and territories; 51 other countries; 49% are from out of state; 7% Black or African American, non-Hispanic/Latino; 8% Hispanic/Latino; 2% Asian, non-Hispanic/Latino; 0.1% Native Hawaiian or other Pacific Islander, non-Hispanic/Latino; 0.1% American Indian or Alaska Native, non-Hispanic/Latino; 4% Two or more races, non-Hispanic/Latino; 2% Race/ethnicity unknown; 3% international; 2% transferred in; 95% live on campus.

Freshmen:
Admission: 4,724 applied, 3,201 admitted, 553 enrolled. ***Average high school GPA:*** 3.71. ***Test scores:*** SAT critical reading scores over 500: 84%; SAT math scores over 500: 84%; SAT writing scores over 500: 74%; ACT scores over 18: 98%; SAT critical reading scores over 600: 43%; SAT math scores over 600: 41%; SAT writing scores over 600: 34%; ACT scores over 24: 76%; SAT critical reading scores over 700: 10%; SAT math scores over 700: 7%; SAT writing scores over 700: 6%; ACT scores over 30: 20%.

Retention: 83% of full-time freshmen returned.

FACULTY
Total: 203, 82% full-time, 79% with terminal degrees.

Student/faculty ratio: 11:1.

ACADEMICS
Calendar: semesters. *Degree:* bachelor's.

Special study options: advanced placement credit, double majors, English as a second language, independent study, internships, off-campus study, services for LD students, student-designed majors, study abroad.

Unusual degree programs: 3-2 engineering with Columbia University, Case Western Reserve University, Duke University, Washington University, University of Pittsburgh; arts management, public policy and management, health care with Carnegie Mellon University; physician assistant and occupational therapy with Chatham University.

Computers: 207 computers/terminals and 200 ports are available on campus for general student use. Students can access the following: campus intranet, computer help desk, free student e-mail accounts, online (class) grades, online (class) registration, online (class) schedules, placement testing, course catalog, class lists, book buy, repair service, transcript review and ordering, billing, payroll time cards, internet kiosks, dataports for laptops, education applications, campus organizations, financial aid. Campuswide network is available. 100% of college-owned or -operated housing units are wired for high-speed Internet access. Wireless service is available via entire campus.

Library: Lawrence Lee Pelletier Library. *Books:* 735,583 (physical), 271,259 (digital/electronic); *Serial titles:* 76 (physical), 20,600 (digital/electronic). Weekly public service hours: 115; students can reserve study rooms.

STUDENT LIFE

Housing options: on-campus residence required through senior year; coed, men-only, women-only, special housing for students with disabilities. Campus housing is university owned and leased by the school. Freshman campus housing is guaranteed.

Activities and organizations: drama/theater group, student-run newspaper, radio and television station, choral group, Student Government, Gators Activity Programming, Alpha Phi Omega (service fraternity), Outing Club, Greek life, national fraternities, national sororities.

Athletics Member NCAA. All Division III. ***Intercollegiate sports:*** baseball M, basketball M/W, cheerleading M(c)/W(c), cross-country running M/W, equestrian sports M(c)/W(c), fencing M(c)/W(c), football M, golf M/W, ice hockey M(c), lacrosse M(c)/W, rugby M(c)/W(c), soccer M/W, softball W, swimming and diving M/W, tennis M/W, track and field M/W, ultimate Frisbee M(c)/W(c), volleyball M(c)/W. ***Intramural sports:*** basketball M/W, soccer M/W, volleyball M/W.

Campus security: 24-hour emergency response devices and patrols, student patrols, late-night transport/escort service, controlled dormitory access, local police patrol, emergency alert system, self defense education, compliance program, property engraving, CCTV system for parking.

Student services: health clinic, personal/psychological counseling.

COSTS & FINANCIAL AID

Costs (2017–18) ***Comprehensive fee:*** $57,620 includes full-time tuition ($45,470), mandatory fees ($500), and room and board ($11,650). Part-time tuition: $1895 per credit hour. Part-time tuition and fees vary according to course load. ***Required fees:*** $250 per term part-time. ***College room only:*** $6130. Room and board charges vary according to board plan and housing facility. ***Payment plan:*** installment. ***Waivers:*** employees or children of employees.

Financial Aid Of all full-time matriculated undergraduates who enrolled in 2016, 1,529 applied for aid, 1,387 were judged to have need, 431 had their need fully met. 948 Federal Work-Study jobs (averaging $2470). 130 state and other part-time jobs (averaging $5282). In 2016, 444 non-need-based awards were made. ***Average percent of need met:*** 90. ***Average financial aid package:*** $39,415. ***Average need-based loan:*** $5259. ***Average need-based gift aid:*** $31,814. ***Average non-need-based aid:*** $18,569.

APPLYING

Options: electronic application, early admission, early decision, early action, deferred entrance.

Required: essay or personal statement, high school transcript, 2 letters of recommendation, college preparatory program. ***Recommended:*** interview.

Application deadlines: 2/15 (freshmen), 7/1 (transfers), 12/1 (early action).

Early decision deadline: 11/1 (for plan 1), 2/1 (for plan 2).

Notification: 3/15 (freshmen), 8/1 (transfers), 11/15 (early decision plan 1), 2/15 (early decision plan 2), 1/1 (early action).

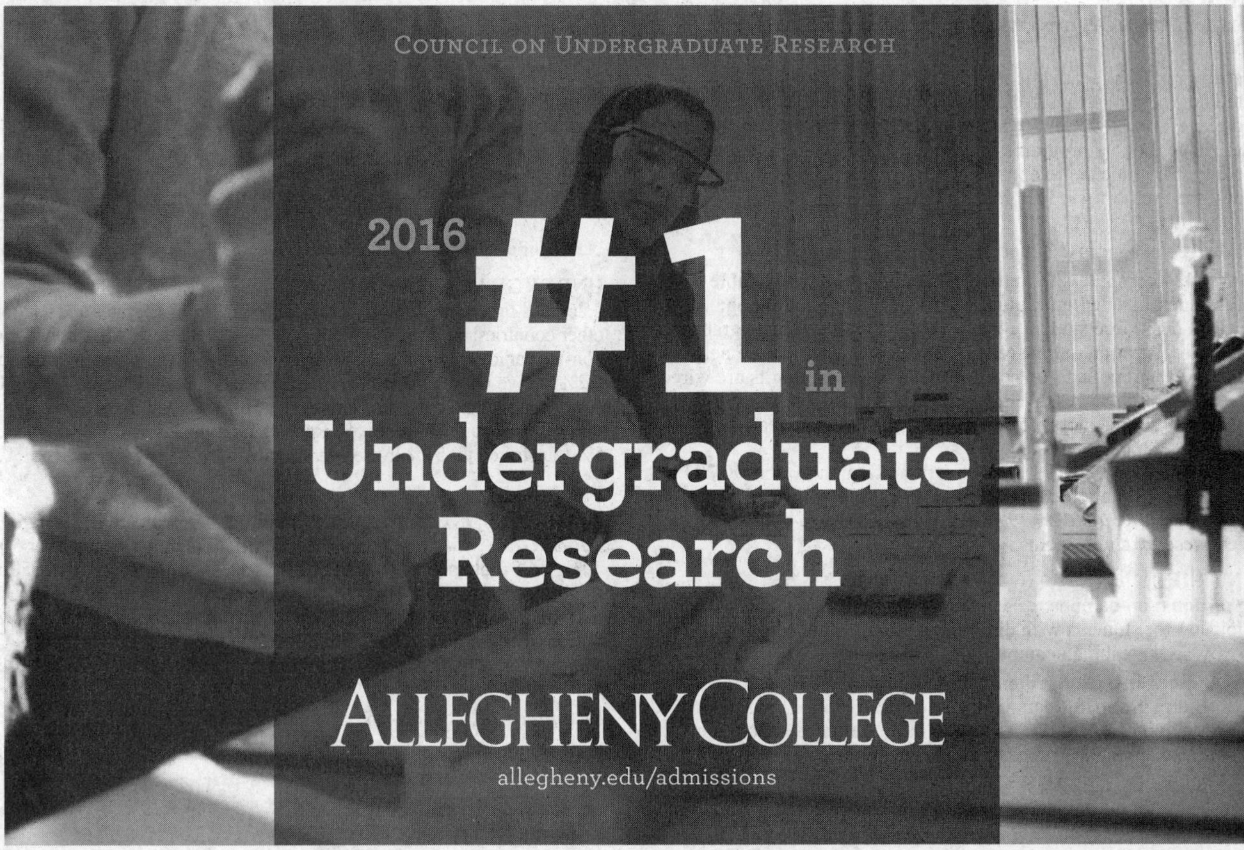

CONTACT
Ms. Linda Clune, Senior Associate Director of Admissions, Allegheny College, 520 North Main Street, Box 5, Meadville, PA 16335. *Phone:* 814-332-4351. *Toll-free phone:* 800-521-5293. *Fax:* 814-337-0431. *E-mail:* admissions@allegheny.edu.

See previous page for display ad and page 1276 for the College Close-Up.

Alvernia University

Reading, Pennsylvania

http://www.alvernia.edu/

- **Independent Roman Catholic** comprehensive, founded 1958
- **Suburban** 121-acre campus with easy access to Philadelphia
- **Endowment** $22.4 million
- **Coed** 2,323 undergraduate students, 74% full-time, 74% women, 26% men
- **Moderately difficult** entrance level, 74% of applicants were admitted

UNDERGRAD STUDENTS
1,719 full-time, 604 part-time. Students come from 18 states and territories; 6 other countries; 20% are from out of state; 10% Black or African American, non-Hispanic/Latino; 9% Hispanic/Latino; 2% Asian, non-Hispanic/Latino; 0.1% Native Hawaiian or other Pacific Islander, non-Hispanic/Latino; 0.3% American Indian or Alaska Native, non-Hispanic/Latino; 2% Two or more races, non-Hispanic/Latino; 10% Race/ethnicity unknown; 0.4% international; 3% transferred in; 59% live on campus.

Freshmen:
Admission: 1,788 applied, 1,332 admitted, 345 enrolled. ***Average high school GPA:*** 3.33. ***Test scores:*** SAT critical reading scores over 500: 43%; SAT math scores over 500: 50%; SAT writing scores over 500: 34%; SAT critical reading scores over 600: 7%; SAT math scores over 600: 10%; SAT writing scores over 600: 5%.

Retention: 82% of full-time freshmen returned.

FACULTY
Total: 319, 34% full-time, 43% with terminal degrees.

Student/faculty ratio: 12:1.

ACADEMICS
Calendar: semesters. *Degrees:* associate, bachelor's, master's, and doctoral.

Special study options: academic remediation for entering students, accelerated degree program, adult/continuing education programs, advanced placement credit, distance learning, double majors, English as a second language, honors programs, independent study, internships, off-campus study, part-time degree program, services for LD students, student-designed majors, study abroad, summer session for credit. ***ROTC:*** Army (c).

Unusual degree programs: 3-2 occupational therapy.

Computers: 424 computers/terminals and 2,016 ports are available on campus for general student use. Students can access the following: computer help desk, free student e-mail accounts, online (class) grades, online (class) registration, online (class) schedules. Campuswide network is available. 100% of college-owned or -operated housing units are wired for high-speed Internet access. Wireless service is available via classrooms, computer centers, computer labs, dorm rooms, learning centers, libraries, student centers.

Library: Dr. Frank A. Franco Library Learning Center. *Books:* 90,227 (physical), 7,907 (digital/electronic); *Serial titles:* 599 (physical), 45,037 (digital/electronic); *Databases:* 39. Weekly public service hours: 107; students can reserve study rooms.

STUDENT LIFE
Housing options: on-campus residence required for freshman year; coed, special housing for students with disabilities. Campus housing is university owned. Freshman campus housing is guaranteed.

Activities and organizations: drama/theater group, student-run newspaper, choral group, Student Government Association, Student Nurses Association of Alvernia (ASNA), Criminal Justice Association (CJA), Sport Management Association (SMA), Science Association.

Athletics Member NCAA. All Division III. ***Intercollegiate sports:*** baseball M, basketball M/W, cheerleading W(c), cross-country running M/W, field hockey W, golf M/W, ice hockey M(c), lacrosse M/W, soccer M/W, softball W, tennis M/W, track and field M/W, volleyball W. ***Intramural sports:*** basketball M/W, football M, soccer M/W, volleyball M/W.

Campus security: 24-hour patrols, late-night transport/escort service, controlled dormitory access.

Student services: health clinic, personal/psychological counseling.

COSTS & FINANCIAL AID
Costs (2017–18) ***Comprehensive fee:*** $45,530 includes full-time tuition ($32,840), mandatory fees ($800), and room and board ($11,890). Full-time tuition and fees vary according to class time and reciprocity agreements. Part-time tuition and fees vary according to class time and course load. ***College room only:*** $6030. Room and board charges vary according to board plan and housing facility. ***Payment plan:*** installment. ***Waivers:*** senior citizens and employees or children of employees.

Financial Aid Of all full-time matriculated undergraduates who enrolled in 2016, 1,582 applied for aid, 1,434 were judged to have need, 192 had their need fully met. 981 Federal Work-Study jobs (averaging $1592). In 2016, 207 non-need-based awards were made. ***Average percent of need met:*** 65. ***Average financial aid package:*** $20,349. ***Average need-based loan:*** $4113. ***Average need-based gift aid:*** $16,212. ***Average non-need-based aid:*** $13,054. ***Average indebtedness upon graduation:*** $51,958.

APPLYING
Standardized Tests *Required:* SAT or ACT (for admission).

Options: electronic application, deferred entrance.

Application fee: $25.

Required: essay or personal statement, high school transcript. ***Required for some:*** 2 letters of recommendation, interview. ***Recommended:*** minimum 2.0 GPA, 1 letter of recommendation.

Application deadlines: rolling (freshmen), rolling (transfers).

Notification: continuous (freshmen), continuous (transfers).

CONTACT
Mr. Dan Hartzman, Director of Undergraduate Admissions, Alvernia University, 400 Saint Bernardine Street, Reading, PA 19607-1799. *Phone:* 610-568-1530. *Toll-free phone:* 888-ALVERNIA. *Fax:* 610-796-2873. *E-mail:* admissions@alvernia.edu.

Arcadia University

Glenside, Pennsylvania

http://www.arcadia.edu/

- **Independent** comprehensive, founded 1853, affiliated with Presbyterian Church (U.S.A.)
- **Suburban** 71-acre campus with easy access to Philadelphia
- **Coed** 2,473 undergraduate students, 92% full-time, 69% women, 31% men
- **Moderately difficult** entrance level, 63% of applicants were admitted

UNDERGRAD STUDENTS
2,266 full-time, 207 part-time. Students come from 42 states and territories; 23 other countries; 41% are from out of state; 9% Black or African American, non-Hispanic/Latino; 8% Hispanic/Latino; 5% Asian, non-Hispanic/Latino; 0.2% Native Hawaiian or other Pacific Islander, non-Hispanic/Latino; 0.2% American Indian or Alaska Native, non-Hispanic/Latino; 4% Two or more races, non-Hispanic/Latino; 5% Race/ethnicity unknown; 4% international; 5% transferred in; 51% live on campus.

Freshmen:
Admission: 8,987 applied, 5,685 admitted, 606 enrolled. ***Average high school GPA:*** 3.64. ***Test scores:*** SAT critical reading scores over 500: 79%; SAT math scores over 500: 80%; SAT writing scores over 500: 67%; ACT scores over 18: 99%; SAT critical reading scores over 600: 30%; SAT math scores over 600: 29%; SAT writing scores over 600: 26%; ACT scores over 24: 66%; SAT critical reading scores over 700: 5%; SAT math scores over 700: 3%; SAT writing scores over 700: 3%; ACT scores over 30: 14%.

Retention: 77% of full-time freshmen returned.

FACULTY
Total: 493, 36% full-time.

Student/faculty ratio: 10:1.

ACADEMICS

Calendar: semesters. *Degrees:* bachelor's, master's, doctoral, and postbachelor's certificates.

Special study options: accelerated degree program, advanced placement credit, cooperative education, distance learning, double majors, English as a second language, honors programs, independent study, internships, off-campus study, part-time degree program, services for LD students, student-designed majors, study abroad, summer session for credit.

Unusual degree programs: 3-2 engineering with Columbia University, University of Pittsburgh, and Washington University in Saint Louis; forensic science, international peace and conflict resolution.

Computers: Students can access the following: campus intranet, computer help desk, free student e-mail accounts, online (class) grades, online (class) registration, online (class) schedules. Campuswide network is available. 100% of college-owned or -operated housing units are wired for high-speed Internet access. Wireless service is available via entire campus.

Library: Bette E. Landman Library. Students can reserve study rooms.

STUDENT LIFE

Housing options: coed, women-only. Campus housing is university owned and leased by the school. Freshman applicants given priority for college housing.

Activities and organizations: drama/theater group, student-run newspaper, radio station, choral group, Student Program Board, Residence Hall Council, Student Government, Arcadia Christian Fellowship, Student Alumni Association.

Athletics Member NCAA. All Division III. ***Intercollegiate sports:*** baseball M, basketball M/W, cross-country running M/W, field hockey W, golf M/W, lacrosse M/W, soccer M/W, softball W, swimming and diving M/W, tennis M/W, volleyball M/W. ***Intramural sports:*** basketball M/W, cheerleading M(c)/W(c), equestrian sports M/W, soccer M/W, volleyball M/W.

Campus security: 24-hour emergency response devices and patrols, student patrols, late-night transport/escort service, controlled dormitory access.

Student services: health clinic, personal/psychological counseling.

COSTS & FINANCIAL AID

Costs (2017–18) ***Comprehensive fee:*** $55,990 includes full-time tuition ($41,630), mandatory fees ($700), and room and board ($13,660). Part-time tuition: $700 per credit hour. ***College room only:*** $9000. Room and board charges vary according to board plan and housing facility. ***Payment plan:*** installment. ***Waivers:*** employees or children of employees.

Financial Aid Of all full-time matriculated undergraduates who enrolled in 2016, 2,054 applied for aid, 1,863 were judged to have need, 558 had their need fully met. 1,362 Federal Work-Study jobs (averaging $1363). 140 state and other part-time jobs (averaging $1671). In 2016, 354 non-need-based awards were made. ***Average percent of need met:*** 83. ***Average financial aid package:*** $30,072. ***Average need-based loan:*** $3894. ***Average need-based gift aid:*** $26,516. ***Average non-need-based aid:*** $17,060.

APPLYING

Standardized Tests *Required:* SAT or ACT (for admission).

Options: electronic application, deferred entrance.

Application fee: $30.

Required: essay or personal statement, high school transcript, 2 letters of recommendation. ***Required for some:*** portfolio, audition. ***Recommended:*** minimum 3.0 GPA.

Application deadlines: 3/1 (freshmen), 6/15 (transfers).

Notification: continuous until 9/1 (freshmen), continuous until 9/1 (transfers).

CONTACT

Colleen Pernicello, Director of Undergraduate Admissions, Arcadia University, 450 South Easton Road, Glenside, PA 19038. *Phone:* 215-572-2910. *Toll-free phone:* 877-ARCADIA. *Fax:* 215-572-4049. *E-mail:* admiss@arcadia.edu.

The Art Institute of Philadelphia

Philadelphia, Pennsylvania

http://www.artinstitutes.edu/philadelphia/

CONTACT

The Art Institute of Philadelphia, 1622 Chestnut Street, Philadelphia, PA 19103. *Phone:* 215-567-7080. *Toll-free phone:* 800-275-2474.

The Art Institute of Pittsburgh

Pittsburgh, Pennsylvania

http://www.artinstitutes.edu/pittsburgh/

CONTACT

The Art Institute of Pittsburgh, 420 Boulevard of the Allies, Pittsburgh, PA 15219. *Phone:* 412-263-6600. *Toll-free phone:* 800-275-2470.

Bloomsburg University of Pennsylvania

Bloomsburg, Pennsylvania

http://www.bloomu.edu/

- **State-supported** comprehensive, founded 1839, part of Pennsylvania State System of Higher Education
- **Small-town** 366-acre campus
- **Endowment** $31.9 million
- **Coed** 8,995 undergraduate students, 92% full-time, 57% women, 43% men
- **Minimally difficult** entrance level, 78% of applicants were admitted

UNDERGRAD STUDENTS

8,274 full-time, 721 part-time. Students come from 22 states and territories; 20 other countries; 9% are from out of state; 9% Black or African American, non-Hispanic/Latino; 7% Hispanic/Latino; 1% Asian, non-Hispanic/Latino; 0.1% Native Hawaiian or other Pacific Islander, non-Hispanic/Latino; 0.2% American Indian or Alaska Native, non-Hispanic/Latino; 3% Two or more races, non-Hispanic/Latino; 1% Race/ethnicity unknown; 0.3% international; 5% transferred in; 41% live on campus.

Freshmen:

Admission: 9,330 applied, 7,236 admitted, 1,902 enrolled. ***Average high school GPA:*** 3.3. ***Test scores:*** SAT critical reading scores over 500: 43%; SAT math scores over 500: 47%; SAT writing scores over 500: 33%; ACT scores over 18: 75%; SAT critical reading scores over 600: 7%; SAT math scores over 600: 9%; SAT writing scores over 600: 5%; ACT scores over 24: 20%; SAT math scores over 700: 1%; ACT scores over 30: 1%.

Retention: 76% of full-time freshmen returned.

FACULTY

Total: 499, 82% full-time, 73% with terminal degrees.

Student/faculty ratio: 20:1.

ACADEMICS

Calendar: semesters. *Degrees:* certificates, bachelor's, master's, doctoral, and postbachelor's certificates.

Special study options: academic remediation for entering students, advanced placement credit, cooperative education, distance learning, double majors, English as a second language, honors programs, independent study, internships, off-campus study, part-time degree program, services for LD students, student-designed majors, study abroad, summer session for credit. ***ROTC:*** Army (b), Air Force (c).

Unusual degree programs: 3-2 engineering with Penn State University.

Computers: 1,571 computers/terminals are available on campus for general student use. Students can access the following: computer help desk, free student e-mail accounts, online (class) grades, online (class) registration, online (class) schedules. Campuswide network is available. 100% of college-owned or -operated housing units are wired for high-speed Internet access. Wireless service is available via entire campus.

Library: Andruss Library. *Books:* 473,456 (physical), 229,760 (digital/electronic); *Serial titles:* 5,900 (physical), 451,151 (digital/electronic); *Databases:* 154. Weekly public service hours: 98; students can reserve study rooms.

STUDENT LIFE

Housing options: on-campus residence required for freshman year; coed. Campus housing is university owned and leased by the school. Freshman campus housing is guaranteed.

Activities and organizations: drama/theater group, student-run newspaper, radio and television station, choral group, marching band, Living and Learning Communities, Band and Music Groups, Greek Organizations, Residence Hall Councils, Club Sports, national fraternities, national sororities.

Athletics Member NCAA. All Division II except wrestling (Division I). ***Intercollegiate sports:*** baseball M(s), basketball M(s)/W(s), cross-country running M(s)/W(s), field hockey W(s), football M(s), lacrosse W(s), soccer M(s)/W(s), softball W(s), swimming and diving M(s)/W(s), tennis M(s)/W(s), track and field M(s)/W(s), wrestling M(s). ***Intramural sports:*** baseball M(c), basketball M/W, cheerleading M(c)/W(c), equestrian sports M(c)/W(c), field hockey W, football M, ice hockey M(c), lacrosse M(c)/W(c), racquetball M/W, rugby M(c)/W(c), sand volleyball M/W, skiing (downhill) M(c)/W(c), soccer M(c)/W(c), softball M/W, swimming and diving M(c)/W(c), table tennis M(c)/W(c), tennis M(c)/W(c), ultimate Frisbee M(c)/W(c), volleyball M(c)/W(c), wrestling M(c).

Campus security: 24-hour emergency response devices and patrols, late-night transport/escort service, controlled dormitory access, monitored surveillance cameras.

Student services: health clinic, personal/psychological counseling, women's center, legal services.

COSTS & FINANCIAL AID

Costs (2016–17) ***Tuition:*** state resident $7238 full-time, $302 per credit part-time; nonresident $18,096 full-time, $754 per credit part-time. Full-time tuition and fees vary according to course load and location. Part-time tuition and fees vary according to course load and location. ***Required fees:*** $2916 full-time, $106 per credit part-time, $75 per term part-time. ***Room and board:*** $8912; room only: $5736. Room and board charges vary according to board plan and housing facility. ***Payment plan:*** installment. ***Waivers:*** senior citizens and employees or children of employees.

Financial Aid Of all full-time matriculated undergraduates who enrolled in 2016, 7,363 applied for aid, 5,327 were judged to have need, 646 had their need fully met. 907 Federal Work-Study jobs (averaging $3251). 1,195 state and other part-time jobs (averaging $3834). In 2016, 207 non-need-based awards were made. ***Average percent of need met:*** 57. ***Average financial aid package:*** $9232. ***Average need-based loan:*** $4172. ***Average need-based gift aid:*** $5924. ***Average non-need-based aid:*** $2269. ***Average indebtedness upon graduation:*** $36,915.

APPLYING

Standardized Tests *Required:* SAT or ACT (for admission).

Options: electronic application, early admission, early action, deferred entrance.

Application fee: $35.

Required: high school transcript.

Application deadlines: rolling (freshmen), rolling (transfers).

Notification: continuous until 9/18 (freshmen), continuous (transfers), 5/1 (early action).

CONTACT

Mr. Christopher Lapos, Director of Admissions, Bloomsburg University of Pennsylvania, 104 Student Services Center, Bloomsburg, PA 17815-1905. *Phone:* 570-389-4316. *Fax:* 570-389-4741. *E-mail:* buadmiss@bloomu.edu.

Bryn Athyn College of the New Church

Bryn Athyn, Pennsylvania

http://www.brynathyn.edu/

- **Independent Christian** comprehensive, founded 1877, affiliated with Church of the New Jerusalem, part of The Academy of the New Church
- **Suburban** 130-acre campus with easy access to Philadelphia
- **Endowment** $55.9 million
- **Coed** 295 undergraduate students, 98% full-time, 50% women, 50% men
- **Minimally difficult** entrance level, 42% of applicants were admitted

UNDERGRAD STUDENTS

289 full-time, 6 part-time. Students come from 16 states and territories; 3 other countries; 24% are from out of state; 19% Black or African American, non-Hispanic/Latino; 9% Hispanic/Latino; 2% Asian, non-Hispanic/Latino; 0.3% Native Hawaiian or other Pacific Islander, non-Hispanic/Latino; 0.7% American Indian or Alaska Native, non-Hispanic/Latino; 0.3% Two or more races, non-Hispanic/Latino; 3% international; 10% transferred in; 61% live on campus.

Freshmen:

Admission: 439 applied, 185 admitted, 71 enrolled. ***Average high school GPA:*** 3.1. ***Test scores:*** SAT critical reading scores over 500: 35%; SAT math scores over 500: 35%; SAT writing scores over 500: 41%; SAT critical reading scores over 600: 18%; SAT math scores over 600: 15%; SAT writing scores over 600: 13%; SAT critical reading scores over 700: 4%; SAT math scores over 700: 1%.

Retention: 37% of full-time freshmen returned.

FACULTY

Total: 81, 41% full-time, 30% with terminal degrees.

Student/faculty ratio: 7:1.

ACADEMICS

Calendar: trimesters. *Degrees:* associate, bachelor's, master's, and doctoral.

Special study options: academic remediation for entering students, accelerated degree program, advanced placement credit, cooperative education, English as a second language, independent study, internships, part-time degree program, services for LD students, student-designed majors, study abroad. ***ROTC:*** Army (c), Air Force (c).

Computers: 18 computers/terminals are available on campus for general student use. Students can access the following: computer help desk, free student e-mail accounts, online (class) registration, online (class) schedules. Campuswide network is available. 100% of college-owned or -operated housing units are wired for high-speed Internet access. Wireless service is available via entire campus.

Library: Swedenborg Library plus 1 other. *Books:* 70,742 (physical), 252 (digital/electronic); *Serial titles:* 834 (physical), 74 (digital/electronic); *Databases:* 13.

STUDENT LIFE

Housing options: men-only, women-only. Campus housing is university owned. Freshman campus housing is guaranteed.

Activities and organizations: drama/theater group, student-run newspaper, choral group, C.A.R.E. (Community Service), Social council, International Student Organization, Peer Advisory Council, Student Government.

Athletics Member NCAA. All Division III. ***Intercollegiate sports:*** basketball M/W, cross-country running M/W, field hockey W, golf M, ice hockey M, lacrosse M/W, soccer M/W, tennis M/W, volleyball W.

Campus security: 24-hour emergency response devices, controlled dormitory access, 18-hour patrols by trained personnel.

Student services: health clinic, personal/psychological counseling.

COSTS & FINANCIAL AID

Costs (2017–18) ***Comprehensive fee:*** $32,664 includes full-time tuition ($19,671), mandatory fees ($1455), and room and board ($11,538). ***College room only:*** $5769. ***Payment plan:*** installment. ***Waivers:*** senior citizens.

Financial Aid Of all full-time matriculated undergraduates who enrolled in 2008, 92 applied for aid, 66 were judged to have need, 30 had their need fully met. In 2008, 22 non-need-based awards were made. ***Average percent of need met:*** 95. ***Average financial aid package:*** $9987. ***Average need-based loan:*** $3329. ***Average need-based gift aid:*** $8358. ***Average non-need-based aid:*** $2232. ***Average indebtedness upon graduation:*** $8299. ***Financial aid deadline:*** 7/1.

APPLYING

Standardized Tests *Required:* SAT or ACT (for admission).

Options: electronic application, deferred entrance.

Required: essay or personal statement, high school transcript, minimum 2.0 GPA, 1 letter of recommendation, interest in the writings of Emanuel Swedenborg. ***Required for some:*** interview.

Notification: continuous (freshmen), continuous (out-of-state freshmen), continuous (transfers), rolling (early decision plan 1), rolling (early decision plan 2), rolling (early action).

CONTACT
Admissions Office, Bryn Athyn College of the New Church, 2945 College Drive, Box 717, Bryn Athyn, PA 19009. *Phone:* 267-502-6000. *Toll-free phone:* 800-767-9552. *Fax:* 267-502-2593.
E-mail: admissions@brynathyn.edu.

★ Bryn Mawr College
Bryn Mawr, Pennsylvania
http://www.brynmawr.edu/

- **Independent** university, founded 1885
- **Suburban** 111-acre campus with easy access to Philadelphia
- **Endowment** $797.1 million
- **Undergraduate: women only; graduate: coed** 1,381 undergraduate students, 99% full-time, 100% women, 0% men
- **Most difficult** entrance level, 40% of applicants were admitted

UNDERGRAD STUDENTS
1,361 full-time, 20 part-time. Students come from 50 states and territories; 60 other countries; 84% are from out of state; 6% Black or African American, non-Hispanic/Latino; 9% Hispanic/Latino; 12% Asian, non-Hispanic/Latino; 0.1% Native Hawaiian or other Pacific Islander, non-Hispanic/Latino; 0.1% American Indian or Alaska Native, non-Hispanic/Latino; 6% Two or more races, non-Hispanic/Latino; 8% Race/ethnicity unknown; 23% international; 0.5% transferred in; 92% live on campus.

Freshmen:
Admission: 3,012 applied, 1,203 admitted, 407 enrolled. ***Test scores:*** SAT critical reading scores over 500: 98%; SAT math scores over 500: 99%; SAT writing scores over 500: 98%; ACT scores over 18: 100%; SAT critical reading scores over 600: 79%; SAT math scores over 600: 79%; SAT writing scores over 600: 84%; ACT scores over 24: 99%; SAT critical reading scores over 700: 37%; SAT math scores over 700: 34%; SAT writing scores over 700: 37%; ACT scores over 30: 64%.

Retention: 94% of full-time freshmen returned.

FACULTY
Total: 218, 70% full-time, 86% with terminal degrees.
Student/faculty ratio: 8:1.

ACADEMICS
Calendar: semesters. *Degrees:* bachelor's, master's, doctoral, and postbachelor's certificates.
Special study options: academic remediation for entering students, accelerated degree program, advanced placement credit, double majors, independent study, internships, off-campus study, services for LD students, student-designed majors, study abroad, summer session for credit. ***ROTC:*** Air Force (c).
Unusual degree programs: 3-2 engineering with California Institute of Technology.
Computers: 125 computers/terminals are available on campus for general student use. Students can access the following: computer help desk, free student e-mail accounts, online (class) grades, online (class) registration, online (class) schedules. Campuswide network is available. 100% of college-owned or -operated housing units are wired for high-speed Internet access. Wireless service is available via entire campus.
Library: Canaday Library plus 3 others. *Books:* 731,197 (physical), 700,741 (digital/electronic); *Serial titles:* 9,382 (physical), 96,451 (digital/electronic); *Databases:* 184. Weekly public service hours: 105; study areas open 24 hours, 5-7 days a week.

STUDENT LIFE
Housing options: on-campus residence required for freshman year; coed, women-only, cooperative. Campus housing is university owned. Freshman campus housing is guaranteed.
Activities and organizations: drama/theater group, student-run newspaper, radio station, choral group, Student Government Association.
Athletics Member NCAA. All Division III. ***Intercollegiate sports:*** badminton W, basketball W, crew W, cross-country running W, field hockey W, lacrosse W, soccer W, swimming and diving W, tennis W, track and field W, volleyball W.

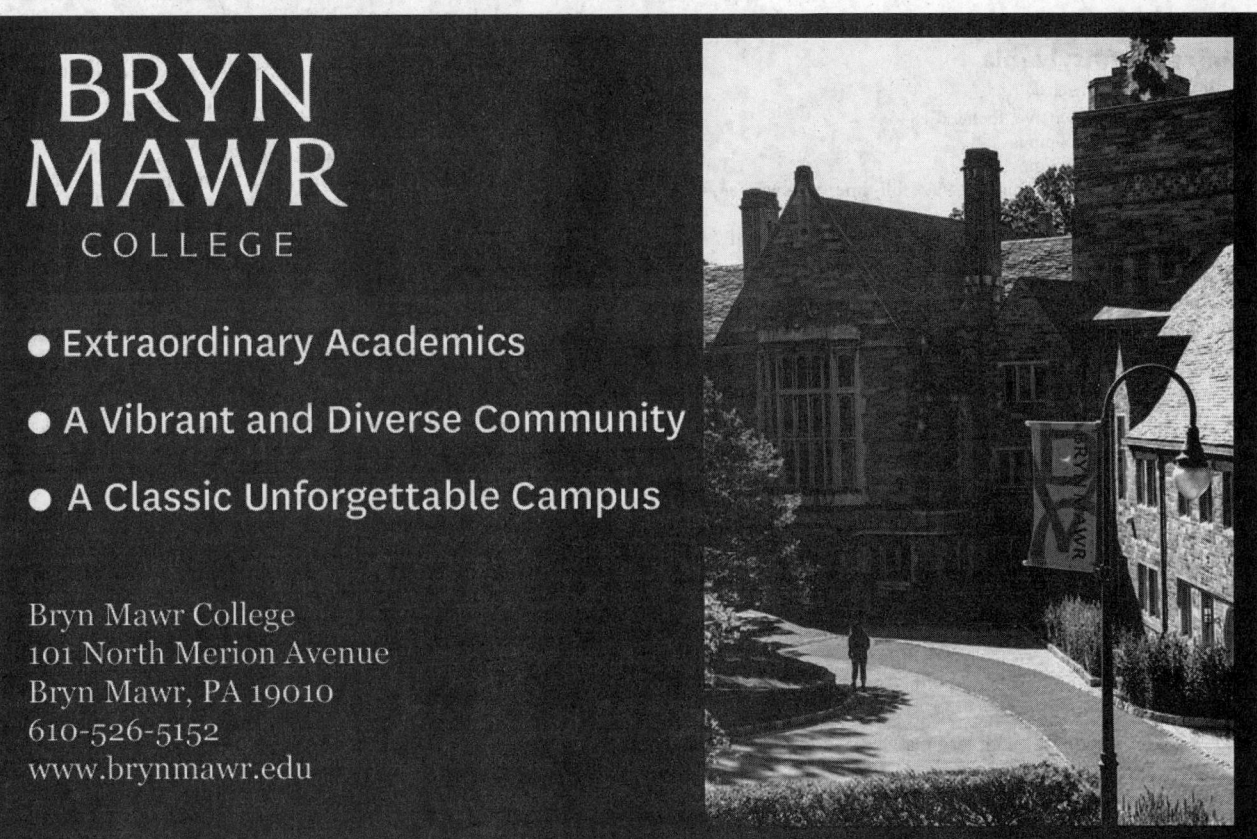

Campus security: 24-hour emergency response devices and patrols, late-night transport/escort service, controlled dormitory access, shuttle bus service, awareness programs, bicycle registration, security Web site.

Student services: health clinic, personal/psychological counseling, women's center.

COSTS & FINANCIAL AID
Costs (2017–18) ***Comprehensive fee:*** $66,410 includes full-time tuition ($49,310), mandatory fees ($1190), and room and board ($15,910). Part-time tuition: $6165 per course. ***College room only:*** $9080. ***Payment plan:*** installment.

Financial Aid Of all full-time matriculated undergraduates who enrolled in 2016, 803 applied for aid, 734 were judged to have need, 721 had their need fully met. In 2016, 228 non-need-based awards were made. ***Average percent of need met:*** 100. ***Average financial aid package:*** $45,900. ***Average need-based loan:*** $4437. ***Average need-based gift aid:*** $40,315. ***Average non-need-based aid:*** $14,533. ***Average indebtedness upon graduation:*** $23,081. ***Financial aid deadline:*** 1/15.

APPLYING
Standardized Tests *Required for some:* SAT and SAT Subject Tests or ACT (for admission).

Options: electronic application, early admission, early decision, deferred entrance.

Application fee: $50.

Required: essay or personal statement, high school transcript, 3 letters of recommendation. ***Recommended:*** interview.

Application deadlines: 1/15 (freshmen), 3/1 (transfers).

Early decision deadline: 11/15 (for plan 1), 1/1 (for plan 2).

Notification: 4/1 (freshmen), 6/1 (transfers), 12/15 (early decision plan 1), 2/1 (early decision plan 2).

CONTACT
Ms. Peaches Valdes, Director of Admissions, Bryn Mawr College, 101 North Merion Avenue, Bryn Mawr, PA 19010. *Phone:* 610-526-5152. *Toll-free phone:* 800-BMC-1885. *Fax:* 610-526-7471. *E-mail:* admissions@brynmawr.edu.

See previous page for display ad and page 1308 for the College Close-Up.

Bucknell University
Lewisburg, Pennsylvania
http://www.bucknell.edu/

- **Independent** comprehensive, founded 1846
- **Small-town** 446-acre campus
- **Endowment** $722.4 million
- **Coed** 3,571 undergraduate students, 99% full-time, 51% women, 49% men
- **Most difficult** entrance level, 30% of applicants were admitted

UNDERGRAD STUDENTS
3,530 full-time, 41 part-time. Students come from 45 states and territories; 46 other countries; 78% are from out of state; 3% Black or African American, non-Hispanic/Latino; 6% Hispanic/Latino; 5% Asian, non-Hispanic/Latino; 4% Two or more races, non-Hispanic/Latino; 0.2% Race/ethnicity unknown; 6% international; 0.7% transferred in; 92% live on campus.

Freshmen:

Admission: 10,487 applied, 3,138 admitted, 950 enrolled. ***Average high school GPA:*** 3.52. ***Test scores:*** SAT critical reading scores over 500: 97%; SAT math scores over 500: 98%; SAT writing scores over 500: 97%; ACT scores over 18: 100%; SAT critical reading scores over 600: 70%; SAT math scores over 600: 84%; SAT writing scores over 600: 75%; ACT scores over 24: 99%; SAT critical reading scores over 700: 18%; SAT math scores over 700: 33%; SAT writing scores over 700: 21%; ACT scores over 30: 58%.

Retention: 92% of full-time freshmen returned.

FACULTY
Total: 431, 88% full-time, 93% with terminal degrees.

Student/faculty ratio: 9:1.

ACADEMICS
Calendar: semesters. *Degrees:* bachelor's and master's.

Special study options: advanced placement credit, double majors, honors programs, independent study, internships, off-campus study, part-time degree program, services for LD students, student-designed majors, study abroad, summer session for credit. ***ROTC:*** Army (b).

Unusual degree programs: 3-2 engineering; biology, chemistry.

Computers: 1,031 computers/terminals and 190 ports are available on campus for general student use. Students can access the following: campus intranet, computer help desk, free student e-mail accounts, online (class) grades, online (class) registration, online (class) schedules. Campuswide network is available. 100% of college-owned or -operated housing units are wired for high-speed Internet access. Wireless service is available via entire campus.

Library: Ellen Clarke Bertrand Library. *Books:* 721,500 (physical), 360,572 (digital/electronic); *Serial titles:* 351 (physical), 52,048 (digital/electronic); *Databases:* 221. Weekly public service hours: 125.

STUDENT LIFE
Housing options: on-campus residence required through senior year; coed, women-only, cooperative, special housing for students with disabilities. Campus housing is university owned. Freshman campus housing is guaranteed.

Activities and organizations: drama/theater group, student-run newspaper, radio station, choral group, Habitat for Humanity, Outing Club, Activities and Campus Events, Catholic Campus Ministries, CALVIN and HOBBES, national fraternities, national sororities.

Athletics Member NCAA. All Division I except football (Division I-AA). ***Intercollegiate sports:*** baseball M, basketball M(s)/W(s), cheerleading M(c)/W(c), crew M(c)/W, cross-country running M/W(s), equestrian sports M(c)/W(c), field hockey W(s), golf M/W, ice hockey M(c), lacrosse M(s)/W(s), rock climbing M(c)/W(c), rugby M(c)/W(c), sailing M(c)/W(c), skiing (downhill) M(c)/W(c), soccer M(s)/W, softball W(s), squash M(c)/W(c), swimming and diving M(s)/W, tennis M/W, track and field M/W(s), ultimate Frisbee M(c)/W(c), volleyball M(c)/W(s), water polo M/W, weight lifting M(c)/W(c), wrestling M(s). ***Intramural sports:*** basketball M/W, cross-country running M/W, golf M/W, racquetball M/W, soccer M/W, softball M/W, squash M/W, table tennis M/W, tennis M/W, ultimate Frisbee M/W, volleyball M/W, weight lifting M, wrestling M.

Campus security: 24-hour emergency response devices and patrols, student patrols, late-night transport/escort service, controlled dormitory access, well-lit pathways, self-defense education, safety/security orientation.

Student services: health clinic, personal/psychological counseling, women's center.

COSTS & FINANCIAL AID
Costs (2016–17) ***Comprehensive fee:*** $64,616 includes full-time tuition ($51,676), mandatory fees ($284), and room and board ($12,656). Part-time tuition: $5672 per course. ***College room only:*** $7718. Room and board charges vary according to board plan and housing facility. ***Payment plans:*** tuition prepayment, installment. ***Waivers:*** employees or children of employees.

Financial Aid Of all full-time matriculated undergraduates who enrolled in 2016, 1,490 applied for aid, 1,326 were judged to have need, 1,219 had their need fully met. 600 Federal Work-Study jobs (averaging $1500). 50 state and other part-time jobs (averaging $1500). In 2016, 412 non-need-based awards were made. ***Average percent of need met:*** 91. ***Average financial aid package:*** $32,500. ***Average need-based loan:*** $5500. ***Average need-based gift aid:*** $28,900. ***Average non-need-based aid:*** $11,817. ***Average indebtedness upon graduation:*** $22,600. ***Financial aid deadline:*** 1/15.

APPLYING
Standardized Tests *Required:* SAT or ACT (for admission).

Options: electronic application, early decision, deferred entrance.

Application fee: $40.

Required: essay or personal statement, high school transcript, 1 letter of recommendation.

Application deadlines: 1/15 (freshmen), 3/15 (transfers).

Early decision deadline: 11/15 (for plan 1), 1/15 (for plan 2).

Notification: 4/1 (freshmen), 5/1 (transfers), 12/15 (early decision plan 1), 2/15 (early decision plan 2).

CONTACT
Dean Robert Springall, Dean of Admissions, Bucknell University, 1 Dent Drive, Lewisburg, PA 17837. *Phone:* 570-577-3000. *Fax:* 570-577-3538. *E-mail:* admissions@bucknell.edu.

Cabrini University

Radnor, Pennsylvania

http://www.cabrini.edu/

- **Independent Roman Catholic** comprehensive, founded 1957
- **Suburban** 112-acre campus with easy access to Philadelphia
- **Endowment** $43.7 million
- **Coed** 1,650 undergraduate students, 84% full-time, 61% women, 39% men
- **Moderately difficult** entrance level, 71% of applicants were admitted

UNDERGRAD STUDENTS
1,384 full-time, 266 part-time. Students come from 24 states and territories; 1 other country; 29% are from out of state; 20% Black or African American, non-Hispanic/Latino; 10% Hispanic/Latino; 2% Asian, non-Hispanic/Latino; 0.2% Native Hawaiian or other Pacific Islander, non-Hispanic/Latino; 0.1% American Indian or Alaska Native, non-Hispanic/Latino; 4% Two or more races, non-Hispanic/Latino; 5% Race/ethnicity unknown; 0.3% international; 4% transferred in; 62% live on campus.

Freshmen:
Admission: 3,186 applied, 2,264 admitted, 486 enrolled. ***Average high school GPA:*** 3.06. ***Test scores:*** SAT critical reading scores over 500: 43%; SAT writing scores over 500: 36%; SAT critical reading scores over 600: 6%; SAT writing scores over 600: 6%; SAT writing scores over 700: 1%.

Retention: 70% of full-time freshmen returned.

FACULTY
Total: 231, 36% full-time.

Student/faculty ratio: 13:1.

ACADEMICS
Calendar: semesters. *Degrees:* bachelor's, master's, and doctoral.

Special study options: academic remediation for entering students, adult/continuing education programs, advanced placement credit, cooperative education, distance learning, double majors, honors programs, independent study, internships, off-campus study, part-time degree program, services for LD students, student-designed majors, study abroad, summer session for credit. ***ROTC:*** Army (c), Navy (c), Air Force (c).

Unusual degree programs: 3-2 physical therapy, occupational therapy with Thomas Jefferson University.

Computers: 575 computers/terminals and 2,922 ports are available on campus for general student use. Students can access the following: campus intranet, computer help desk, free student e-mail accounts, online (class) grades, online (class) registration, online (class) schedules, account balances. Campuswide network is available. 100% of college-owned or -operated housing units are wired for high-speed Internet access. Wireless service is available via entire campus.

Library: Holy Spirit Library. *Books:* 143,980 (digital/electronic); *Serial titles:* 67 (physical), 68,500 (digital/electronic); *Databases:* 47. Weekly public service hours: 97.

STUDENT LIFE
Housing options: coed, women-only, special housing for students with disabilities. Campus housing is university owned and leased by the school. Freshman applicants given priority for college housing.

Activities and organizations: drama/theater group, student-run newspaper, radio and television station, choral group, Campus Activities and Programming (CAP) Board, Student Government Association (SGA), Black Student Union, Catholic Relief Services (CRS) Ambassadors, Cabrini Friends of Exceptional Children (CFEC), national fraternities, national sororities.

Athletics Member NCAA. All Division III. ***Intercollegiate sports:*** baseball M, basketball M/W, cross-country running M/W, field hockey W, golf M, lacrosse M/W, rowing W, soccer M/W, softball W, swimming and diving M/W, tennis M/W, volleyball W. ***Intramural sports:*** archery M/W, basketball M/W, cheerleading M(c)/W(c), football M/W, lacrosse M(c), rock climbing M/W, sand volleyball M/W, skiing (downhill) M/W, soccer M/W, volleyball M/W.

Campus security: 24-hour emergency response devices and patrols, student patrols, late-night transport/escort service, controlled dormitory access, Resident Assistants and Directors on nightly duty.

Student services: health clinic, personal/psychological counseling.

COSTS & FINANCIAL AID
Costs (2017–18) ***Comprehensive fee:*** $43,690 includes full-time tuition ($30,400), mandatory fees ($950), and room and board ($12,340). Part-time tuition: $550 per credit hour. Part-time tuition and fees vary according to course load. ***Required fees:*** $45 per term part-time. ***Room and board:*** Room and board charges vary according to board plan and housing facility. ***Payment plan:*** installment. ***Waivers:*** children of alumni, senior citizens, and employees or children of employees.

Financial Aid Of all full-time matriculated undergraduates who enrolled in 2015, 1,197 applied for aid, 1,006 were judged to have need, 258 had their need fully met. 226 Federal Work-Study jobs (averaging $1141). In 2015, 221 non-need-based awards were made. ***Average financial aid package:*** $16,988. ***Average need-based loan:*** $3257. ***Average need-based gift aid:*** $7627. ***Average non-need-based aid:*** $10,210. ***Average indebtedness upon graduation:*** $43,437.

APPLYING
Standardized Tests *Recommended:* SAT or ACT (for admission).

Options: electronic application, deferred entrance.

Application fee: $20.

Required: essay or personal statement, high school transcript, minimum 2.0 GPA. ***Recommended:*** minimum 2.0 GPA, 1 letter of recommendation, interview.

Application deadlines: rolling (freshmen), rolling (transfers).

CONTACT
Ms. Shannon Zottola, Assistant Vice President for Enrollment Management, Cabrini University, 610 King of Prussia Road, Radnor, PA 19087-3698. *Phone:* 610-902-1027. *Toll-free phone:* 800-848-1003. *Fax:* 610-902-8508. *E-mail:* admit@cabrini.edu.

Cairn University

Langhorne, Pennsylvania

http://cairn.edu/

- **Independent nondenominational** comprehensive, founded 1913
- **Suburban** 115-acre campus with easy access to Philadelphia
- **Endowment** $10.1 million
- **Coed** 744 undergraduate students, 94% full-time, 55% women, 45% men
- **Moderately difficult** entrance level, 98% of applicants were admitted

UNDERGRAD STUDENTS
703 full-time, 41 part-time. Students come from 30 states and territories; 16 other countries; 45% are from out of state; 13% Black or African American, non-Hispanic/Latino; 8% Hispanic/Latino; 4% Asian, non-Hispanic/Latino; 0.3% American Indian or Alaska Native, non-Hispanic/Latino; 2% Two or more races, non-Hispanic/Latino; 2% international; 9% transferred in; 66% live on campus.

Freshmen:
Admission: 338 applied, 331 admitted, 147 enrolled. ***Average high school GPA:*** 3.39. ***Test scores:*** SAT critical reading scores over 500: 63%; SAT math scores over 500: 53%; SAT writing scores over 500: 50%; ACT scores over 18: 85%; SAT critical reading scores over 600: 18%; SAT math scores over 600: 18%; SAT writing scores over 600: 19%; ACT scores over 24: 26%; SAT critical reading scores over 700: 3%; SAT math scores over 700: 3%; SAT writing scores over 700: 3%; ACT scores over 30: 7%.

Retention: 74% of full-time freshmen returned.

FACULTY
Total: 117, 34% full-time, 40% with terminal degrees.

Student/faculty ratio: 12:1.

ACADEMICS
Calendar: semesters. *Degrees:* bachelor's, master's, and postbachelor's certificates.

Special study options: academic remediation for entering students, accelerated degree program, adult/continuing education programs, advanced placement credit, double majors, honors programs, independent study, internships, off-campus study, part-time degree program, services for LD students, study abroad, summer session for credit. ***ROTC:*** Air Force (c).

Computers: 66 computers/terminals are available on campus for general student use. Students can access the following: campus intranet, computer help desk, free student e-mail accounts, online (class) grades, online (class) registration, online (class) schedules. Campuswide network is available. 100% of college-owned or -operated housing units are wired for high-speed Internet access. Wireless service is available via entire campus.

Library: Masland Learning Resource Center. *Books:* 104,860 (physical), 421,604 (digital/electronic); *Serial titles:* 945 (physical), 53,295 (digital/electronic); *Databases:* 177. Weekly public service hours: 86; students can reserve study rooms.

STUDENT LIFE

Housing options: on-campus residence required through senior year; men-only, women-only, special housing for students with disabilities. Campus housing is university owned. Freshman campus housing is guaranteed.

Activities and organizations: drama/theater group, student-run newspaper, choral group, Ascend (outdoor adventure club), Chi Beta Sigma (Social Work Club), Enactus (Business), Student Missionary Fellowship, Visual Arts Society.

Athletics Member NCAA, NCCAA. All NCAA Division III. ***Intercollegiate sports:*** baseball M, basketball M/W, cross-country running M/W, golf M, soccer M/W, softball W, tennis W, volleyball M/W. ***Intramural sports:*** badminton M/W, basketball M/W, soccer M/W, table tennis M/W, tennis M/W, ultimate Frisbee M/W, volleyball M/W.

Campus security: 24-hour emergency response devices and patrols, student patrols, late-night transport/escort service, controlled dormitory access.

Student services: health clinic, personal/psychological counseling.

COSTS & FINANCIAL AID

Costs (2017–18) ***Comprehensive fee:*** $36,296 includes full-time tuition ($26,193), mandatory fees ($300), and room and board ($9803). Full-time tuition and fees vary according to course load. Part-time tuition: $777 per credit. Part-time tuition and fees vary according to course load. ***College room only:*** $5132. Room and board charges vary according to board plan and location. ***Payment plan:*** installment. ***Waivers:*** employees or children of employees.

Financial Aid Of all full-time matriculated undergraduates who enrolled in 2016, 623 applied for aid, 567 were judged to have need, 75 had their need fully met. In 2016, 125 non-need-based awards were made. ***Average percent of need met:*** 75. ***Average financial aid package:*** $20,983. ***Average need-based loan:*** $4991. ***Average need-based gift aid:*** $16,025. ***Average non-need-based aid:*** $11,286. ***Average indebtedness upon graduation:*** $31,166.

APPLYING

Standardized Tests *Required:* SAT or ACT (for admission).

Options: electronic application, early admission, deferred entrance.

Application fee: $25.

Required: essay or personal statement, high school transcript, minimum 2.0 GPA, interview.

Application deadlines: rolling (freshmen), rolling (transfers).

Notification: continuous (freshmen), continuous (transfers).

CONTACT

Ms. Rebecca Lippert, Director of Undergraduate Admissions, Cairn University, 200 Manor Avenue, Langhorne, PA 19047. *Phone:* 215-702-4250. *Toll-free phone:* 800-366-0049. *Fax:* 215-702-4248. *E-mail:* admissions@cairn.edu.

California University of Pennsylvania

California, Pennsylvania

http://www.calu.edu/

- **State-supported** comprehensive, founded 1852, part of Pennsylvania State System of Higher Education
- **Small-town** 188-acre campus with easy access to Pittsburgh
- **Endowment** $29.9 million
- **Coed** 5,522 undergraduate students, 83% full-time, 54% women, 46% men
- **Moderately difficult** entrance level, 94% of applicants were admitted

UNDERGRAD STUDENTS

4,606 full-time, 916 part-time. Students come from 47 states and territories; 23 other countries; 11% are from out of state; 13% Black or African American, non-Hispanic/Latino; 3% Hispanic/Latino; 1% Asian, non-Hispanic/Latino; 0.1% Native Hawaiian or other Pacific Islander, non-Hispanic/Latino; 0.2% American Indian or Alaska Native, non-Hispanic/Latino; 4% Two or more races, non-Hispanic/Latino; 2% Race/ethnicity unknown; 0.8% international; 13% transferred in; 34% live on campus.

Freshmen:

Admission: 3,202 applied, 2,994 admitted, 904 enrolled. ***Average high school GPA:*** 3.1. ***Test scores:*** SAT critical reading scores over 500: 32%; SAT math scores over 500: 29%; SAT writing scores over 500: 22%; ACT scores over 18: 66%; SAT critical reading scores over 600: 7%; SAT math scores over 600: 7%; SAT writing scores over 600: 5%; ACT scores over 24: 25%; SAT critical reading scores over 700: 1%; SAT math scores over 700: 1%; SAT writing scores over 700: 1%; ACT scores over 30: 8%. ***Retention:*** 72% of full-time freshmen returned.

FACULTY

Total: 381, 67% full-time, 69% with terminal degrees.

Student/faculty ratio: 19:1.

ACADEMICS

Calendar: semesters. *Degrees:* certificates, associate, bachelor's, master's, doctoral, post-master's, and postbachelor's certificates.

Special study options: academic remediation for entering students, accelerated degree program, adult/continuing education programs, advanced placement credit, cooperative education, distance learning, double majors, English as a second language, external degree program, honors programs, independent study, internships, off-campus study, part-time degree program, services for LD students, study abroad, summer session for credit. ***ROTC:*** Army (b).

Computers: 1,300 computers/terminals and 18,000 ports are available on campus for general student use. Students can access the following: campus intranet, computer help desk, free student e-mail accounts, online (class) grades, online (class) registration, online (class) schedules. Campuswide network is available. 100% of college-owned or -operated housing units are wired for high-speed Internet access. Wireless service is available via entire campus.

Library: Manderino Library. *Books:* 236,664 (physical), 83,157 (digital/electronic); *Databases:* 107. Students can reserve study rooms.

STUDENT LIFE

Housing options: on-campus residence required for freshman year; coed, men-only, women-only, cooperative, special housing for students with disabilities. Campus housing is university owned, leased by the school and is provided by a third party. Freshman campus housing is guaranteed.

Activities and organizations: drama/theater group, student-run newspaper, radio and television station, choral group, marching band, national fraternities, national sororities.

Athletics Member NCAA. All Division II. ***Intercollegiate sports:*** baseball M, basketball M/W, cross-country running M/W, football M, golf M/W, soccer M/W, softball W, swimming and diving W, tennis W, track and field M/W, volleyball W.

Campus security: 24-hour emergency response devices and patrols, student patrols, late-night transport/escort service, controlled dormitory access, residence hall entrances staffed 24/7, fire suppression and smoke detection systems, security staff are trained police officers.

Student services: health clinic, personal/psychological counseling, women's center, legal services.

COSTS & FINANCIAL AID

Costs (2016–17) ***Tuition:*** state resident $7238 full-time, $302 per credit hour part-time; nonresident $10,858 full-time, $452 per credit hour part-time. Full-time tuition and fees vary according to course load, location, and student level. Part-time tuition and fees vary according to course load, location, and student level. ***Required fees:*** $3101 full-time. ***Room and board:*** $10,086; room only: $6592. Room and board charges vary according to board plan and housing facility. ***Payment plan:*** installment. ***Waivers:*** employees or children of employees.

Financial Aid Of all full-time matriculated undergraduates who enrolled in 2015, 4,510 applied for aid, 3,763 were judged to have need, 275 had their need fully met. 400 Federal Work-Study jobs (averaging $900). 1,035 state and other part-time jobs (averaging $1400). In 2015, 87 non-need-based awards were made. ***Average percent of need met:*** 53. ***Average financial aid package:*** $9863. ***Average need-based loan:*** $4043. ***Average need-based gift aid:*** $6145. ***Average non-need-based aid:*** $3943. ***Average indebtedness upon graduation:*** $25,683. ***Financial aid deadline:*** 3/1.

APPLYING

Standardized Tests *Required:* SAT or ACT (for admission).

Options: electronic application, early admission, deferred entrance.

Application fee: $25.

Required: high school transcript.

Application deadlines: rolling (freshmen), 5/1 (transfers).

Notification: continuous (freshmen), continuous (transfers).

CONTACT

Dr. Tracey Sheetz, Dean of Undergraduate Admissions, California University of Pennsylvania, 250 University Avenue, California, PA 15419. *Phone:* 724-938-4404. *Toll-free phone:* 888-412-0479. *Fax:* 724-938-4564.

See below for display ad and page 1310 for the College Close-Up.

Carlow University

Pittsburgh, Pennsylvania

http://www.carlow.edu/

- **Independent Roman Catholic** comprehensive, founded 1929
- **Urban** 13-acre campus with easy access to Pittsburgh
- **Coed, primarily women** 1,399 undergraduate students, 74% full-time, 88% women, 12% men
- **Minimally difficult** entrance level, 81% of applicants were admitted

UNDERGRAD STUDENTS

1,040 full-time, 359 part-time. 5% are from out of state; 22% Black or African American, non-Hispanic/Latino; 2% Hispanic/Latino; 1% Asian, non-Hispanic/Latino; 0.2% Native Hawaiian or other Pacific Islander, non-Hispanic/Latino; 0.4% American Indian or Alaska Native, non-Hispanic/Latino; 5% Two or more races, non-Hispanic/Latino; 8% Race/ethnicity unknown; 0.2% international; 19% transferred in; 31% live on campus.

Freshmen:

Admission: 945 applied, 763 admitted, 222 enrolled. ***Average high school GPA:*** 3.38. ***Test scores:*** SAT critical reading scores over 500: 43%; SAT math scores over 500: 43%; SAT writing scores over 500: 35%; ACT scores over 18: 88%; SAT critical reading scores over 600: 10%; SAT math scores over 600: 2%; SAT writing scores over 600: 5%; ACT scores over 24: 19%; SAT critical reading scores over 700: 1%; SAT math scores over 700: 1%; ACT scores over 30: 2%.

Retention: 77% of full-time freshmen returned.

FACULTY

Total: 266, 36% full-time, 43% with terminal degrees.

Student/faculty ratio: 11:1.

ACADEMICS

Calendar: semesters. *Degrees:* bachelor's, master's, doctoral, post-master's, and postbachelor's certificates.

Special study options: academic remediation for entering students, accelerated degree program, advanced placement credit, cooperative education, distance learning, double majors, honors programs,

independent study, internships, off-campus study, part-time degree program, services for LD students, study abroad, summer session for credit. ***ROTC:*** Army (c), Navy (c), Air Force (c).

Unusual degree programs: 3-2 biology/environmental science and management with Duquesne University.

Computers: Students can access the following: campus intranet, computer help desk, free student e-mail accounts, online (class) grades, online (class) registration, online (class) schedules. Campuswide network is available. 100% of college-owned or -operated housing units are wired for high-speed Internet access. Wireless service is available via entire campus.

Library: Grace Library.

STUDENT LIFE

Housing options: coed, men-only, women-only. Campus housing is university owned. Freshman applicants given priority for college housing.

Activities and organizations: drama/theater group, student-run newspaper, choral group, Student Government Association, Campus Activities Board, SPiRiT (Student Ambassadors), SNAP (Student Nursing Association), PSEA (School Education Association), national fraternities.

Athletics Member NAIA, USCAA. ***Intercollegiate sports:*** basketball M(s)/W(s), cross-country running M(s)/W(s), soccer W(s), softball W(s), tennis W(s), volleyball W(s).

Campus security: 24-hour emergency response devices and patrols, late-night transport/escort service, controlled dormitory access.

Student services: health clinic, personal/psychological counseling.

COSTS & FINANCIAL AID

Costs (2016–17) ***Comprehensive fee:*** $38,548 includes full-time tuition ($27,136), mandatory fees ($628), and room and board ($10,784). Full-time tuition and fees vary according to course load, program, and reciprocity agreements. Part-time tuition: $863 per credit hour. Part-time tuition and fees vary according to course load, program, and reciprocity agreements. ***Required fees:*** $13 per credit hour part-time. ***College room only:*** $5514. Room and board charges vary according to board plan. ***Payment plan:*** installment. ***Waivers:*** children of alumni, adult students, and employees or children of employees.

Financial Aid Of all full-time matriculated undergraduates who enrolled in 2003, 431 Federal Work-Study jobs (averaging $776).

APPLYING

Standardized Tests *Required:* SAT or ACT (for admission). *Recommended:* SAT (for admission).

Options: electronic application, deferred entrance.

Application fee: $20.

Required: high school transcript. ***Recommended:*** essay or personal statement, minimum 2.5 GPA, interview.

Application deadlines: rolling (freshmen), rolling (transfers).

Notification: continuous (freshmen), continuous (transfers).

CONTACT

Ms. Wivina Chmura, Director of Undergraduate Admissions, Carlow University, 3333 Fifth Avenue, Pittsburgh, PA 15213. *Phone:* 412-578-8762. *Toll-free phone:* 800-333-CARLOW. *Fax:* 412-578-6668. *E-mail:* admissions@carlow.edu.

Carnegie Mellon University

Pittsburgh, Pennsylvania

http://www.cmu.edu/

- **Independent** university, founded 1900
- **Urban** 148-acre campus with easy access to Pittsburgh
- **Endowment** $1.3 billion
- **Coed** 6,673 undergraduate students, 96% full-time, 47% women, 53% men
- **Most difficult** entrance level, 22% of applicants were admitted

UNDERGRAD STUDENTS

6,439 full-time, 234 part-time. Students come from 53 states and territories; 68 other countries; 85% are from out of state; 4% Black or African American, non-Hispanic/Latino; 8% Hispanic/Latino; 28% Asian, non-Hispanic/Latino; 4% Two or more races, non-Hispanic/Latino; 5% Race/ethnicity unknown; 23% international; 0.6% transferred in; 60% live on campus.

Freshmen:

Admission: 21,189 applied, 4,601 admitted, 1,552 enrolled. ***Average high school GPA:*** 3.76. ***Test scores:*** SAT critical reading scores over 500: 100%; SAT math scores over 500: 99%; SAT writing scores over 500: 100%; ACT scores over 18: 100%; SAT critical reading scores over 600: 94%; SAT math scores over 600: 97%; SAT writing scores over 600: 94%; ACT scores over 24: 99%; SAT critical reading scores over 700: 57%; SAT math scores over 700: 81%; SAT writing scores over 700: 63%; ACT scores over 30: 86%.

Retention: 96% of full-time freshmen returned.

FACULTY

Total: 1,023, 97% full-time, 92% with terminal degrees.

Student/faculty ratio: 13:1.

ACADEMICS

Calendar: semesters. *Degrees:* bachelor's, master's, doctoral, post-master's, and postbachelor's certificates.

Special study options: accelerated degree program, advanced placement credit, cooperative education, distance learning, double majors, independent study, internships, off-campus study, part-time degree program, services for LD students, student-designed majors, study abroad, summer session for credit. ***ROTC:*** Army (c), Navy (b), Air Force (c).

Unusual degree programs: 3-2 business administration; engineering; public management and policy.

Computers: 462 computers/terminals are available on campus for general student use. Students can access the following: campus intranet, computer help desk, free student e-mail accounts, online (class) grades, online (class) registration, online (class) schedules. Campuswide network is available. 100% of college-owned or -operated housing units are wired for high-speed Internet access. Wireless service is available via entire campus.

Library: Hunt Library plus 2 others. Weekly public service hours: 168; study areas open 24 hours, 5-7 days a week; students can reserve study rooms.

STUDENT LIFE

Housing options: on-campus residence required for freshman year; coed, special housing for students with disabilities. Campus housing is university owned. Freshman campus housing is guaranteed.

Activities and organizations: drama/theater group, student-run newspaper, radio station, choral group, marching band, national fraternities, national sororities.

Athletics Member NCAA. All Division III. ***Intercollegiate sports:*** baseball M(c), basketball M/W, cross-country running M/W, fencing M(c)/W(c), football M, golf M/W, ice hockey M(c)/W(c), lacrosse M(c)/W(c), rowing M(c)/W(c), rugby M(c)/W(c), skiing (downhill) M(c)/W(c), soccer M/W, swimming and diving M/W, tennis M/W, track and field M/W, ultimate Frisbee M(c)/W(c), volleyball M(c)/W, water polo M(c)/W(c). ***Intramural sports:*** badminton M/W, basketball M/W, racquetball M/W, soccer M/W, softball M/W, squash M/W, table tennis M/W, tennis M/W, ultimate Frisbee M/W, volleyball M/W, water polo M/W.

Campus security: 24-hour emergency response devices and patrols, late-night transport/escort service, controlled dormitory access, Safe Walk.

Student services: health clinic, personal/psychological counseling, legal services.

COSTS & FINANCIAL AID

Costs (2017–18) ***Tuition:*** $733 per unit part-time. ***Room only:*** Room and board charges vary according to board plan and housing facility. ***Payment plan:*** installment. ***Waivers:*** employees or children of employees.

Financial Aid Of all full-time matriculated undergraduates who enrolled in 2016, 3,243 applied for aid, 2,735 were judged to have need, 733 had their need fully met. In 2016, 249 non-need-based awards were made. ***Average percent of need met:*** 85. ***Average financial aid package:*** $40,347. ***Average need-based loan:*** $5764. ***Average need-based gift aid:*** $34,632. ***Average non-need-based aid:*** $11,763. ***Average indebtedness upon graduation:*** $30,866.

APPLYING

Standardized Tests *Required:* SAT or ACT (for admission), SAT Subject Tests (for admission).

Options: electronic application, early admission, early decision, deferred entrance.

Application fee: $75.

Required: essay or personal statement, high school transcript. ***Required for some:*** audition/portfolio for fine arts. ***Recommended:*** interview.

Application deadlines: 1/1 (freshmen), 2/15 (transfers).

Early decision deadline: 11/1.

Notification: 4/15 (freshmen), 5/15 (transfers), 12/15 (early decision).

CONTACT

Mr. Greg Edleman, Director of Admission, Carnegie Mellon University, 5000 Forbes Avenue, Pittsburgh, PA 15213. *Phone:* 412-268-2082. *Fax:* 412-268-7838. *E-mail:* admission@andrew.cmu.edu.

Cedar Crest College

Allentown, Pennsylvania

http://www.cedarcrest.edu/

- **Independent** comprehensive, founded 1867, affiliated with United Church of Christ
- **Suburban** 84-acre campus with easy access to Philadelphia
- **Endowment** $27.8 million
- **Coed, primarily women** 1,428 undergraduate students, 62% full-time, 87% women, 13% men
- **Moderately difficult** entrance level, 66% of applicants were admitted

UNDERGRAD STUDENTS

884 full-time, 544 part-time. Students come from 28 states and territories; 25 other countries; 18% are from out of state; 9% Black or African American, non-Hispanic/Latino; 14% Hispanic/Latino; 3% Asian, non-Hispanic/Latino; 0.1% Native Hawaiian or other Pacific Islander, non-Hispanic/Latino; 0.4% American Indian or Alaska Native, non-Hispanic/Latino; 1% Two or more races, non-Hispanic/Latino; 5% Race/ethnicity unknown; 10% international; 3% transferred in; 28% live on campus.

Freshmen:

Admission: 1,193 applied, 793 admitted, 181 enrolled. ***Average high school GPA:*** 3.38. ***Test scores:*** SAT critical reading scores over 500: 40%; SAT math scores over 500: 41%; SAT writing scores over 500: 38%; ACT scores over 18: 78%; SAT critical reading scores over 600: 10%; SAT math scores over 600: 10%; SAT writing scores over 600: 11%; ACT scores over 24: 41%; SAT math scores over 700: 2%; SAT writing scores over 700: 1%; ACT scores over 30: 4%.

Retention: 79% of full-time freshmen returned.

FACULTY

Total: 212, 35% full-time, 48% with terminal degrees.

Student/faculty ratio: 10:1.

ACADEMICS

Calendar: semesters. *Degrees:* certificates, bachelor's, master's, and postbachelor's certificates.

Special study options: academic remediation for entering students, advanced placement credit, double majors, honors programs, independent study, internships, off-campus study, part-time degree program, services for LD students, student-designed majors, summer session for credit. ***ROTC:*** Army (c).

Computers: 285 computers/terminals and 587 ports are available on campus for general student use. Students can access the following: campus intranet, computer help desk, free student e-mail accounts, online (class) grades, online (class) registration, online (class) schedules. Campuswide network is available. 100% of college-owned or -operated housing units are wired for high-speed Internet access. Wireless service is available via entire campus.

Library: Frank M. Cressman Library.

STUDENT LIFE

Housing options: women-only, special housing for students with disabilities. Campus housing is university owned. Freshman campus housing is guaranteed.

Activities and organizations: drama/theater group, student-run newspaper, radio station, choral group, Student Activities Board, Student Government Association, Commuter Awareness Board, Student Nurse Association, Forensic Student Science organization, national fraternities.

Athletics Member NCAA. All Division III. ***Intercollegiate sports:*** basketball W, cross-country running W, equestrian sports W(c), field hockey W, lacrosse W, soccer W, softball W, swimming and diving W, tennis W, track and field W(c), volleyball W. ***Intramural sports:*** badminton W, basketball W, soccer W, softball W, tennis W, volleyball W.

Campus security: 24-hour emergency response devices and patrols, late-night transport/escort service, controlled dormitory access, crime prevention programs.

Student services: health clinic, personal/psychological counseling.

COSTS & FINANCIAL AID

Costs (2017–18) ***Comprehensive fee:*** $49,300 includes full-time tuition ($37,492), mandatory fees ($600), and room and board ($11,208). Full-time tuition and fees vary according to class time, course load, and program. Part-time tuition: $1250 per credit hour. Part-time tuition and fees vary according to class time, course load, and program. ***Required fees:*** $150 per term part-time. ***College room only:*** $5262. Room and board charges vary according to board plan and housing facility. ***Payment plans:*** installment, deferred payment. ***Waivers:*** employees or children of employees.

Financial Aid Of all full-time matriculated undergraduates who enrolled in 2016, 606 applied for aid, 571 were judged to have need, 75 had their need fully met. In 2016, 49 non-need-based awards were made. ***Average percent of need met:*** 75. ***Average financial aid package:*** $29,244. ***Average need-based loan:*** $4461. ***Average need-based gift aid:*** $25,125. ***Average non-need-based aid:*** $16,296. ***Average indebtedness upon graduation:*** $38,726.

APPLYING

Standardized Tests *Required:* SAT or ACT (for admission).

Options: electronic application, early admission, deferred entrance.

Required: essay or personal statement, high school transcript. ***Required for some:*** 2 letters of recommendation. ***Recommended:*** minimum 2.0 GPA, interview.

Application deadlines: rolling (freshmen), rolling (transfers).

Notification: continuous (freshmen), continuous (transfers).

CONTACT

Jonathan Squire, Associate Director of Admissions, Cedar Crest College, 100 College Drive, Allentown, PA 18104. *Phone:* 610-606-4666. *Toll-free phone:* 800-360-1222. *E-mail:* admissions@cedarcrest.edu.

Central Penn College

Summerdale, Pennsylvania

http://www.centralpenn.edu/

- **Proprietary** comprehensive, founded 1881
- **Small-town** 35-acre campus with easy access to Harrisburg
- **Coed** 1,337 undergraduate students, 24% full-time, 64% women, 36% men
- **Minimally difficult** entrance level, 22% of applicants were admitted

UNDERGRAD STUDENTS

326 full-time, 1,011 part-time. 5% are from out of state; 26% Black or African American, non-Hispanic/Latino; 6% Hispanic/Latino; 2% Asian, non-Hispanic/Latino; 0.3% Native Hawaiian or other Pacific Islander, non-Hispanic/Latino; 2% American Indian or Alaska Native, non-Hispanic/Latino; 5% Race/ethnicity unknown; 20% transferred in; 17% live on campus.

Freshmen:

Admission: 1,086 applied, 238 admitted, 239 enrolled.

Retention: 52% of full-time freshmen returned.

FACULTY

Total: 131, 34% full-time, 13% with terminal degrees.

Student/faculty ratio: 9:1.

ACADEMICS

Calendar: quarters. *Degrees:* associate, bachelor's, and master's.

Special study options: academic remediation for entering students, adult/continuing education programs, advanced placement credit, distance learning, honors programs, independent study, internships, part-time degree program, services for LD students, summer session for credit.

Computers: 100 computers/terminals are available on campus for general student use. Students can access the following: campus intranet, computer help desk, free student e-mail accounts, online (class) grades, online (class) registration, online (class) schedules. Campuswide network is available. 100% of college-owned or -operated housing units are wired for high-speed Internet access. Wireless service is available via entire campus.

Library: Charles T Jones Leadership Library plus 1 other. *Books:* 23,949 (physical), 126,485 (digital/electronic); *Serial titles:* 60 (physical), 2 (digital/electronic); *Databases:* 34. Weekly public service hours: 74.

STUDENT LIFE

Housing options: coed, men-only, women-only, special housing for students with disabilities. Campus housing is university owned. Freshman applicants given priority for college housing.

Activities and organizations: drama/theater group, student-run newspaper, PTA Club, Student Government Association, Central Penn Players, Student Ambassadors, Colleges Against Cancer.

Athletics Member USCAA. ***Intercollegiate sports:*** baseball M, basketball M/W, cross-country running M/W, soccer M/W, volleyball W. ***Intramural sports:*** badminton M/W, basketball M/W, bowling M/W, cheerleading W, football M/W, sand volleyball M/W, soccer M/W, wrestling M.

Campus security: 24-hour emergency response devices and patrols, student patrols, late-night transport/escort service, controlled dormitory access.

Student services: personal/psychological counseling.

COSTS & FINANCIAL AID

Costs (2017–18) ***One-time required fee:*** $100. ***Comprehensive fee:*** $25,590 includes full-time tuition ($17,280), mandatory fees ($894), and room and board ($7416). Part-time tuition: $480 per credit hour. ***Required fees:*** $290 per term part-time. ***College room only:*** $5346. Room and board charges vary according to board plan and housing facility. ***Payment plan:*** installment. ***Waivers:*** employees or children of employees.

Financial Aid ***Financial aid deadline:*** 5/1.

APPLYING

Standardized Tests *Required for some:* SAT or ACT (for admission).

Options: electronic application.

Required: essay or personal statement, high school transcript, minimum 2.0 GPA, interview. ***Required for some:*** 1 letter of recommendation. ***Recommended:*** 1 letter of recommendation.

Application deadlines: rolling (freshmen), rolling (transfers).

Notification: continuous (freshmen), continuous (transfers).

CONTACT

Ms. Rebecca Bowman, Director of Admissions, Central Penn College, College Hill and Valley Roads, Mechanicsburg, PA 17093. *Phone:* 717-728-2267. *Toll-free phone:* 800-759-2727. *Fax:* 717-728-2505. *E-mail:* rebeccabowman@centralpenn.edu.

Chatham University

Pittsburgh, Pennsylvania

http://www.chatham.edu/

- **Independent** university, founded 1869
- **Urban** 427-acre campus
- **Endowment** $75.0 million
- **Coed, primarily women** 1,002 undergraduate students, 74% full-time, 81% women, 19% men
- **Moderately difficult** entrance level, 53% of applicants were admitted

UNDERGRAD STUDENTS

745 full-time, 257 part-time. Students come from 33 states and territories; 20 other countries; 19% are from out of state; 10% Black or African American, non-Hispanic/Latino; 4% Hispanic/Latino; 3% Asian, non-Hispanic/Latino; 0.3% Native Hawaiian or other Pacific Islander, non-Hispanic/Latino; 0.5% American Indian or Alaska Native, non-Hispanic/Latino; 2% Two or more races, non-Hispanic/Latino; 4% Race/ethnicity unknown; 3% international; 8% transferred in; 57% live on campus.

Freshmen:

Admission: 1,926 applied, 1,016 admitted, 194 enrolled. ***Average high school GPA:*** 3.72. ***Test scores:*** SAT critical reading scores over 500: 68%; SAT math scores over 500: 66%; SAT writing scores over 500: 61%; ACT scores over 18: 96%; SAT critical reading scores over 600: 31%; SAT math scores over 600: 15%; SAT writing scores over 600: 16%; ACT scores over 24: 51%; SAT critical reading scores over 700: 4%; SAT math scores over 700: 1%; SAT writing scores over 700: 3%; ACT scores over 30: 5%.

Retention: 81% of full-time freshmen returned.

FACULTY

Total: 324, 34% full-time, 38% with terminal degrees.

Student/faculty ratio: 10:1.

ACADEMICS

Calendar: 4-4-1. *Degrees:* bachelor's, master's, doctoral, post-master's, and postbachelor's certificates.

Special study options: accelerated degree program, adult/continuing education programs, advanced placement credit, cooperative education, distance learning, double majors, English as a second language, honors programs, independent study, internships, off-campus study, part-time degree program, services for LD students, student-designed majors, study abroad, summer session for credit. ***ROTC:*** Army (c), Navy (c), Air Force (c).

Unusual degree programs: 3-2 business administration; engineering with Carnegie Mellon University, Penn State University, University of Pittsburgh; arts management with Carnegie Mellon, biology, counseling psychology, film/digital technology, leadership/organizational transformation, occupational therapy, physician assistant studies, business, teaching, writing and creative writing, architecture (landscape and interior), global/public policy.

Computers: 180 computers/terminals and 150 ports are available on campus for general student use. Students can access the following: campus intranet, computer help desk, free student e-mail accounts, online (class) grades, online (class) registration, online (class) schedules. Campuswide network is available. 100% of college-owned or -operated housing units are wired for high-speed Internet access. Wireless service is available via entire campus.

Library: Jennie King Mellon Library. *Books:* 88,368 (physical), 1,200 (digital/electronic); *Serial titles:* 92 (physical), 32,874 (digital/electronic); *Databases:* 65. Weekly public service hours: 99; study areas open 24 hours, 5-7 days a week; students can reserve study rooms.

STUDENT LIFE

Housing options: on-campus residence required through sophomore year; coed, women-only. Campus housing is university owned. Freshman campus housing is guaranteed.

Activities and organizations: drama/theater group, student-run newspaper, choral group, Chatham Student Government, Residence Hall Council, Student Athletic Advisory Council (SAAC), Creative Writing Club and MFA Writing Council, Graduate Student Assembly.

Athletics Member NCAA. All Division III. ***Intercollegiate sports:*** baseball M, basketball M/W, cross-country running M/W, ice hockey M/W, lacrosse M/W, soccer W, softball W, swimming and diving M/W, track and field M/W, volleyball W. ***Intramural sports:*** basketball W, bowling M/W, cheerleading M/W, soccer M/W, squash M/W, volleyball M/W.

Campus security: 24-hour emergency response devices and patrols, late-night transport/escort service, controlled dormitory access, self-defense education, well-lighted pathways and sidewalks.

Student services: health clinic, personal/psychological counseling, women's center.

COSTS & FINANCIAL AID

Costs (2016–17) ***Comprehensive fee:*** $46,517 includes full-time tuition ($34,195), mandatory fees ($1280), and room and board ($11,042). Part-time tuition: $829 per credit. Part-time tuition and fees vary according to course load. ***College room only:*** $5634. Room and board charges vary according to board plan and housing facility. ***Payment plan:*** installment. ***Waivers:*** employees or children of employees.

Financial Aid Of all full-time matriculated undergraduates who enrolled in 2016, 687 applied for aid, 579 were judged to have need, 128 had their need fully met. 220 Federal Work-Study jobs (averaging $2200). In 2016,

28 non-need-based awards were made. ***Average percent of need met:*** 83. ***Average financial aid package:*** $25,627. ***Average need-based loan:*** $4670. ***Average need-based gift aid:*** $8938. ***Average non-need-based aid:*** $15,576. ***Average indebtedness upon graduation:*** $37,734. ***Financial aid deadline:*** 3/1.

APPLYING
Options: electronic application, early admission, deferred entrance.

Application fee: $35.

Required: essay or personal statement, high school transcript, minimum 2.0 GPA, 1 letter of recommendation. ***Recommended:*** interview.

Application deadlines: 8/1 (freshmen), rolling (transfers).

Notification: continuous (freshmen), continuous (transfers).

CONTACT
Ms. Amy M. Becher, Vice President for Enrollment Management, Chatham University, Woodland, Berry Hall, Pittsburgh, PA 15232. *Phone:* 800-837-1290. *Toll-free phone:* 800-837-1290. *Fax:* 412-365-1609. *E-mail:* admission@chatham.edu.

Chestnut Hill College

Philadelphia, Pennsylvania

http://www.chc.edu/

- **Independent Roman Catholic** comprehensive, founded 1924
- **Suburban** 75-acre campus with easy access to Philadelphia
- **Endowment** $9.2 million
- **Coed** 1,369 undergraduate students, 81% full-time, 65% women, 35% men
- **Moderately difficult** entrance level, 94% of applicants were admitted

UNDERGRAD STUDENTS
1,103 full-time, 266 part-time. Students come from 26 states and territories; 35 other countries; 37% are from out of state; 34% Black or African American, non-Hispanic/Latino; 9% Hispanic/Latino; 2% Asian, non-Hispanic/Latino; 0.2% Native Hawaiian or other Pacific Islander, non-Hispanic/Latino; 0.1% American Indian or Alaska Native, non-Hispanic/Latino; 4% Two or more races, non-Hispanic/Latino; 8% Race/ethnicity unknown; 2% international; 6% transferred in; 52% live on campus.

Freshmen:
Admission: 1,242 applied, 1,165 admitted, 244 enrolled. ***Average high school GPA:*** 3.21. ***Test scores:*** SAT critical reading scores over 500: 40%; SAT math scores over 500: 38%; SAT writing scores over 500: 36%; ACT scores over 18: 65%; SAT critical reading scores over 600: 10%; SAT math scores over 600: 7%; SAT writing scores over 600: 8%; ACT scores over 24: 11%; SAT critical reading scores over 700: 1%; SAT writing scores over 700: 1%; ACT scores over 30: 2%.

Retention: 79% of full-time freshmen returned.

FACULTY
Total: 303, 29% full-time, 45% with terminal degrees.

Student/faculty ratio: 10:1.

ACADEMICS
Calendar: semesters. *Degrees:* certificates, associate, bachelor's, master's, doctoral, post-master's, and postbachelor's certificates (profile includes figures from both traditional and accelerated (part-time) programs).

Special study options: academic remediation for entering students, accelerated degree program, adult/continuing education programs, advanced placement credit, cooperative education, double majors, English as a second language, honors programs, independent study, internships, off-campus study, part-time degree program, services for LD students, student-designed majors, study abroad, summer session for credit.

Unusual degree programs: 3-2 computer science/instructional technology, early education, biology/chemistry with Thomas Jefferson University; biology/chemistry and physician assistant with Arcadia University; human services administration; counseling psychology; international business, language, and culture.

Computers: 70 computers/terminals and 150 ports are available on campus for general student use. Students can access the following: campus intranet, computer help desk, free student e-mail accounts, online (class) grades, online (class) registration, online (class) schedules. Campuswide network is available. 90% of college-owned or -operated housing units are wired for high-speed Internet access. Wireless service is available via classrooms, dorm rooms.

Library: Logue Library. *Books:* 120,388 (physical), 161,204 (digital/electronic); *Serial titles:* 671 (physical), 230,922 (digital/electronic); *Databases:* 424. Weekly public service hours: 99; students can reserve study rooms.

STUDENT LIFE
Housing options: coed. Campus housing is university owned and leased by the school.

Activities and organizations: drama/theater group, student-run newspaper, radio and television station, choral group, Student Government, Mask and Foil Drama Club, Association for Musical Performance, Campus Ministry Community Service Group, Business Club.

Athletics Member NCAA. All Division II. ***Intercollegiate sports:*** baseball M(s), basketball M(s)/W(s), bowling W(s), cross-country running M(s)/W(s), football M(s)(c), golf M(s)(c)/W(c), lacrosse M(s)/W(s), soccer M(s)/W(s), softball W(s), tennis M(s)/W(s), track and field M(s)/W(s), volleyball W(s).

Campus security: 24-hour emergency response devices and patrols, late-night transport/escort service, controlled dormitory access.

Student services: health clinic, personal/psychological counseling.

COSTS & FINANCIAL AID
Costs (2017–18) ***One-time required fee:*** $425. ***Comprehensive fee:*** $45,560 includes full-time tuition ($34,950), mandatory fees ($210), and room and board ($10,400). Part-time tuition: $745 per credit hour. ***Room and board:*** Room and board charges vary according to board plan and housing facility. ***Payment plans:*** installment, deferred payment. ***Waivers:*** senior citizens and employees or children of employees.

Financial Aid Of all full-time matriculated undergraduates who enrolled in 2016, 972 applied for aid, 924 were judged to have need, 62 had their need fully met. 386 Federal Work-Study jobs (averaging $1224). In 2016, 112 non-need-based awards were made. ***Average percent of need met:*** 56. ***Average financial aid package:*** $23,919. ***Average need-based loan:*** $4298. ***Average need-based gift aid:*** $19,979. ***Average non-need-based aid:*** $14,926. ***Average indebtedness upon graduation:*** $42,527.

APPLYING
Standardized Tests *Required:* SAT or ACT (for admission).

Options: electronic application, deferred entrance.

Application fee: $35.

Required: high school transcript. ***Required for some:*** interview. ***Recommended:*** essay or personal statement, minimum 2.0 GPA.

Application deadlines: rolling (freshmen), rolling (transfers).

Notification: continuous (freshmen), continuous (transfers).

CONTACT
Ms. Stephanie Williams, Chestnut Hill College, 9601 Germantown Avenue, Philadelphia, PA 19118-2693. *Phone:* 215-248-7001. *Toll-free phone:* 800-248-0052. *Fax:* 215-248-7082. *E-mail:* williamss@chc.edu.

Cheyney University of Pennsylvania

Cheyney, Pennsylvania

http://www.cheyney.edu/

CONTACT
Shon Jeffery, Associate Director of Enrollment Management, Cheyney University of Pennsylvania, 1837 University Circle, PO Box 200, Cheyney, PA 19319. *Phone:* 610-399-2255. *Toll-free phone:* 800-CHEYNEY. *E-mail:* spjeffery@cheyney.edu.

Clarion University of Pennsylvania

Clarion, Pennsylvania

http://www.clarion.edu/

- **State-supported** comprehensive, founded 1867, part of Pennsylvania State System of Higher Education
- **Rural** 201-acre campus
- **Endowment** $30.7 million
- **Coed** 4,911 undergraduate students, 82% full-time, 63% women, 37% men

UNDERGRAD STUDENTS
4,018 full-time, 893 part-time. Students come from 12 states and territories; 1 other country; 7% are from out of state; 7% Black or African American, non-Hispanic/Latino; 2% Hispanic/Latino; 0.6% Asian, non-Hispanic/Latino; 0.1% Native Hawaiian or other Pacific Islander, non-Hispanic/Latino; 0.1% American Indian or Alaska Native, non-Hispanic/Latino; 2% Two or more races, non-Hispanic/Latino; 3% Race/ethnicity unknown; 2% international; 7% transferred in; 35% live on campus.

Freshmen:
Admission: 989 enrolled. ***Average high school GPA:*** 3.21. ***Test scores:*** SAT critical reading scores over 500: 31%; SAT math scores over 500: 33%; SAT writing scores over 500: 23%; ACT scores over 18: 59%; SAT critical reading scores over 600: 6%; SAT math scores over 600: 7%; SAT writing scores over 600: 4%; ACT scores over 24: 17%; ACT scores over 30: 2%.

Retention: 74% of full-time freshmen returned.

FACULTY
Total: 294, 74% full-time, 67% with terminal degrees.

Student/faculty ratio: 19:1.

ACADEMICS
Calendar: semesters. *Degrees:* certificates, associate, bachelor's, master's, doctoral, post-master's, and postbachelor's certificates.

Special study options: academic remediation for entering students, accelerated degree program, adult/continuing education programs, advanced placement credit, cooperative education, distance learning, double majors, English as a second language, honors programs, independent study, internships, off-campus study, part-time degree program, services for LD students, study abroad, summer session for credit. ***ROTC:*** Army (c).

Unusual degree programs: 3-2 engineering with University of Pittsburgh, Case Western Reserve University.

Computers: 1,208 computers/terminals and 2,436 ports are available on campus for general student use. Students can access the following: campus intranet, computer help desk, free student e-mail accounts, online (class) grades, online (class) registration, online (class) schedules, learning management system, Web-based personal disk space, online student services (financial aid, billing). Campuswide network is available. 100% of college-owned or -operated housing units are wired for high-speed Internet access. Wireless service is available via entire campus.
Library: Carlson Library plus 1 other.

STUDENT LIFE
Housing options: on-campus residence required through sophomore year; coed, men-only, women-only, special housing for students with disabilities. Campus housing is university owned. Freshman campus housing is guaranteed.

Activities and organizations: drama/theater group, student-run newspaper, radio and television station, choral group, marching band, Circle K, Psychology Club, Council for Exceptional Children, Animae Club, Allies, national fraternities, national sororities.

Athletics Member NCAA. All Division II except wrestling (Division I). ***Intercollegiate sports:*** baseball M(s), basketball M(s)/W(s), cross-country running W(s), football M(s), golf M(s)/W(s), soccer W(s), softball W(s), swimming and diving M(s)/W(s), tennis W(s), track and field W(s), volleyball W(s), wrestling M(s). ***Intramural sports:*** badminton M/W, basketball M/W, cheerleading M(c)/W(c), cross-country running M/W, equestrian sports M(c)/W(c), football M/W, golf M/W, racquetball M/W, rock climbing M(c)/W(c), rugby M(c)/W(c), soccer M(c)/W(c), softball M/W, swimming and diving M/W, table tennis M/W, tennis M/W, track and field M(c)/W(c), ultimate Frisbee M(c)/W(c), volleyball M(c)/W, water polo M/W, weight lifting M/W, wrestling M/W.

Campus security: 24-hour emergency response devices and patrols, student patrols, late-night transport/escort service, controlled dormitory access.

Student services: health clinic, personal/psychological counseling, women's center.

FINANCIAL AID
Financial Aid Of all full-time matriculated undergraduates who enrolled in 2016, 3,263 applied for aid, 2,849 were judged to have need, 153 had their need fully met. 139 Federal Work-Study jobs (averaging $2442). 634 state and other part-time jobs (averaging $1726). In 2016, 185 non-need-based awards were made. ***Average percent of need met:*** 45. ***Average financial aid package:*** $9580. ***Average need-based loan:*** $4159. ***Average need-based gift aid:*** $5716. ***Average non-need-based aid:*** $2187. ***Average indebtedness upon graduation:*** $33,346.

APPLYING
Standardized Tests *Required:* SAT or ACT (for admission). *Required for some:* TOEFL, TSE or IELTS for international students.

Required: high school transcript. ***Required for some:*** essay or personal statement, interview, NLN Test for ASN program. ***Recommended:*** essay or personal statement, 2 letters of recommendation, interview.

CONTACT
Clarion University of Pennsylvania, 840 Wood Street, Clarion, PA 16214. *Phone:* 814-393-2306. *Toll-free phone:* 800-672-7171.

Clarks Summit University

South Abington Township, Pennsylvania

http://www.clarkssummitu.edu/

CONTACT
Ms. Kellyn Lovell, Supervisor, Support Services, Clarks Summit University, 538 Venard Road, Clarks Summit, PA 18411-1297. *Phone:* 800-451-7664. *Toll-free phone:* 800-451-7664. *Fax:* 570-585-9271. *E-mail:* admissions@bbc.edu.

Curtis Institute of Music

Philadelphia, Pennsylvania

http://www.curtis.edu/

CONTACT
Mr. Christopher Hodges, Admissions Officer, Curtis Institute of Music, 1726 Locust Street, Philadelphia, PA 19103-6107. *Phone:* 215-893-5262. *E-mail:* chris.hodges@curtis.edu.

Delaware Valley University

Doylestown, Pennsylvania

http://www.delval.edu/

- **Independent** comprehensive, founded 1896
- **Suburban** 600-acre campus with easy access to Philadelphia
- **Endowment** $28.3 million
- **Coed** 1,967 undergraduate students, 90% full-time, 59% women, 41% men
- **Moderately difficult** entrance level, 68% of applicants were admitted

UNDERGRAD STUDENTS
1,767 full-time, 200 part-time. Students come from 22 states and territories; 4 other countries; 41% are from out of state; 8% Black or African American, non-Hispanic/Latino; 8% Hispanic/Latino; 1% Asian, non-Hispanic/Latino; 0.1% Native Hawaiian or other Pacific Islander, non-Hispanic/Latino; 0.7% American Indian or Alaska Native, non-Hispanic/Latino; 0.2% Two or more races, non-Hispanic/Latino; 6% Race/ethnicity unknown; 0.4% international; 7% transferred in; 57% live on campus.

Freshmen:
Admission: 2,233 applied, 1,527 admitted, 451 enrolled. ***Average high school GPA:*** 3.3. ***Test scores:*** SAT critical reading scores over 500: 46%; SAT math scores over 500: 47%; SAT writing scores over 500: 40%; ACT scores over 18: 83%; SAT critical reading scores over 600: 13%; SAT

math scores over 600: 12%; SAT writing scores over 600: 7%; ACT scores over 24: 36%; SAT critical reading scores over 700: 1%; SAT math scores over 700: 1%; SAT writing scores over 700: 1%; ACT scores over 30: 6%.

Retention: 67% of full-time freshmen returned.

FACULTY

Total: 273, 32% full-time.

Student/faculty ratio: 14:1.

ACADEMICS

Calendar: semesters. *Degrees:* certificates, associate, bachelor's, master's, and doctoral.

Special study options: academic remediation for entering students, accelerated degree program, adult/continuing education programs, advanced placement credit, distance learning, double majors, honors programs, independent study, internships, part-time degree program, services for LD students, study abroad, summer session for credit.

Computers: 200 computers/terminals are available on campus for general student use. Students can access the following: campus intranet, computer help desk, free student e-mail accounts, online (class) grades, online (class) registration, online (class) schedules. Campuswide network is available. 100% of college-owned or -operated housing units are wired for high-speed Internet access. Wireless service is available via entire campus.

Library: Joseph Krauskopf Memorial Library. *Books:* 46,060 (physical), 4,386 (digital/electronic); *Serial titles:* 124 (physical), 105,529 (digital/electronic); *Databases:* 51. Weekly public service hours: 92.

STUDENT LIFE

Housing options: coed, special housing for students with disabilities. Campus housing is university owned and is provided by a third party.

Activities and organizations: drama/theater group, choral group, Dairy Society, Pre-Vet club, Equestrian Team, American Association of Zookeepers, FFA, national fraternities, national sororities.

Athletics Member NCAA. All Division III. ***Intercollegiate sports:*** baseball M, basketball M/W, cross-country running M/W, equestrian sports M(c)/W(c), field hockey W, football M, golf M/W, lacrosse M/W, soccer M/W, softball W, tennis M/W, track and field M/W, volleyball W, wrestling M. ***Intramural sports:*** basketball M/W, cheerleading W, ultimate Frisbee M/W, volleyball M/W.

Campus security: 24-hour emergency response devices and patrols, late-night transport/escort service, controlled dormitory access.

Student services: health clinic, personal/psychological counseling.

COSTS & FINANCIAL AID

Costs (2016–17) ***Comprehensive fee:*** $50,078 includes full-time tuition ($34,440), mandatory fees ($2310), and room and board ($13,328). Full-time tuition and fees vary according to class time, degree level, and program. Part-time tuition: $950 per credit hour. Part-time tuition and fees vary according to class time, course load, degree level, and program. ***Required fees:*** $116 per course part-time. ***College room only:*** $6234. Room and board charges vary according to board plan and housing facility. ***Payment plan:*** installment. ***Waivers:*** employees or children of employees.

Financial Aid Of all full-time matriculated undergraduates who enrolled in 2016, 1,549 applied for aid, 1,398 were judged to have need, 174 had their need fully met. 154 Federal Work-Study jobs (averaging $1767). In 2016, 330 non-need-based awards were made. ***Average percent of need met:*** 64. ***Average financial aid package:*** $24,129. ***Average need-based loan:*** $3593. ***Average need-based gift aid:*** $21,111. ***Average non-need-based aid:*** $16,925. ***Average indebtedness upon graduation:*** $47,640.

APPLYING

Standardized Tests *Required:* SAT or ACT (for admission). *Required for some:* SAT and SAT Subject Tests or ACT (for admission).

Options: electronic application, deferred entrance.

Application fee: $50.

Required: high school transcript, 1 letter of recommendation. ***Recommended:*** interview.

Notification: continuous (freshmen).

CONTACT

Mr. Dwayne Walker, Associate Vice President of Enrollment Management and Director of Admission, Delaware Valley University, 700 E. Butler Avenue, Doylestown, PA 18901. *Phone:* 215-489-2372. *Toll-free phone:* 800-2DELVAL. *Fax:* 215-230-2968. *E-mail:* dwayne.walker@delval.edu.

DeSales University

Center Valley, Pennsylvania

http://www.desales.edu/

- **Independent Roman Catholic** comprehensive, founded 1964
- **Suburban** 480-acre campus with easy access to Philadelphia, PA
- **Endowment** $69.3 million
- **Coed** 2,388 undergraduate students, 78% full-time, 60% women, 40% men
- **Moderately difficult** entrance level, 76% of applicants were admitted

UNDERGRAD STUDENTS

1,854 full-time, 534 part-time. Students come from 27 states and territories; 9 other countries; 24% are from out of state; 4% Black or African American, non-Hispanic/Latino; 12% Hispanic/Latino; 2% Asian, non-Hispanic/Latino; 3% Two or more races, non-Hispanic/Latino; 7% Race/ethnicity unknown; 0.5% international; 3% transferred in; 46% live on campus.

Freshmen:

Admission: 2,861 applied, 2,181 admitted, 500 enrolled. ***Average high school GPA:*** 3.25. ***Test scores:*** SAT critical reading scores over 500: 65%; SAT math scores over 500: 59%; SAT writing scores over 500: 60%; SAT critical reading scores over 600: 23%; SAT math scores over 600: 21%; SAT writing scores over 600: 20%; SAT critical reading scores over 700: 3%; SAT math scores over 700: 3%; SAT writing scores over 700: 3%.

Retention: 81% of full-time freshmen returned.

FACULTY

Total: 370, 34% full-time.

Student/faculty ratio: 13:1.

ACADEMICS

Calendar: semesters. *Degrees:* certificates, bachelor's, master's, doctoral, post-master's, and postbachelor's certificates.

Special study options: academic remediation for entering students, accelerated degree program, adult/continuing education programs, advanced placement credit, cooperative education, distance learning, double majors, external degree program, honors programs, independent study, internships, off-campus study, part-time degree program, services for LD students, student-designed majors, study abroad, summer session for credit. ***ROTC:*** Army (c).

Unusual degree programs: 3-2 medical studies/physician assistant studies.

Computers: 245 computers/terminals are available on campus for general student use. Students can access the following: campus intranet, computer help desk, free student e-mail accounts, online (class) grades, online (class) registration, online (class) schedules. Campuswide network is available. 100% of college-owned or -operated housing units are wired for high-speed Internet access. Wireless service is available via entire campus.

Library: Trexler Library. *Books:* 167,111 (physical), 134,000 (digital/electronic); *Serial titles:* 207 (physical), 12,125 (digital/electronic); *Databases:* 88. Weekly public service hours: 102; students can reserve study rooms.

STUDENT LIFE

Housing options: on-campus residence required for freshman year; coed, men-only, women-only, special housing for students with disabilities. Campus housing is university owned. Freshman campus housing is guaranteed.

Activities and organizations: drama/theater group, student-run newspaper, radio and television station, choral group, marching band, College Against Cancer, Outdoor Adventure Club, Student Nursing Association, Criminal Justice Association, Natural Science Club.

Athletics Member NCAA. All Division III. ***Intercollegiate sports:*** baseball M, basketball M/W, cross-country running M/W, field hockey W, golf M, lacrosse M, soccer M/W, softball W, tennis M/W, track and field

M/W, volleyball W. ***Intramural sports:*** cheerleading M(c)/W(c), ice hockey M(c), rugby M(c), swimming and diving M(c)/W(c), tennis M(c)/W(c), volleyball M(c).

Campus security: 24-hour emergency response devices and patrols, late-night transport/escort service, controlled dormitory access.

Student services: health clinic, personal/psychological counseling.

COSTS & FINANCIAL AID
Costs (2016–17) ***Comprehensive fee:*** $47,450 includes full-time tuition ($33,500), mandatory fees ($1550), and room and board ($12,400). Full-time tuition and fees vary according to class time and course load. Part-time tuition: $1400 per credit hour. Part-time tuition and fees vary according to class time and course load. ***College room only:*** $6400. Room and board charges vary according to board plan and housing facility. ***Payment plans:*** installment, deferred payment. ***Waivers:*** adult students, senior citizens, and employees or children of employees.

Financial Aid Of all full-time matriculated undergraduates who enrolled in 2016, 1,612 applied for aid, 1,431 were judged to have need, 302 had their need fully met. 468 Federal Work-Study jobs (averaging $1996). 355 state and other part-time jobs (averaging $1992). In 2016, 339 non-need-based awards were made. ***Average percent of need met:*** 69. ***Average financial aid package:*** $24,563. ***Average need-based loan:*** $4579. ***Average need-based gift aid:*** $19,165. ***Average non-need-based aid:*** $14,996. ***Average indebtedness upon graduation:*** $40,194.

APPLYING
Standardized Tests *Required:* SAT or ACT (for admission).

Options: electronic application, early admission, deferred entrance.

Required: essay or personal statement, high school transcript, letters of recommendation. ***Recommended:*** interview.

Notification: continuous until 10/6 (freshmen).

CONTACT
Mr. Derrick Wetzel, Director of Admissions, DeSales University, 2755 Station Avenue, Center Valley, PA 18034-9568. *Phone:* 610-282-4443. *Fax:* 610-282-0131. *E-mail:* derrick.wetzell@desales.edu.

DeVry University–Ft. Washington Campus

Fort Washington, Pennsylvania

http://www.devry.edu/

CONTACT
DeVry University–Ft. Washington Campus, 1140 Virginia Drive, Fort Washington, PA 19034. *Phone:* 215-591-5700. *Toll-free phone:* 866-338-7934.

Dickinson College

Carlisle, Pennsylvania

http://www.dickinson.edu/

- **Independent** 4-year, founded 1773
- **Suburban** 144-acre campus with easy access to Harrisburg
- **Endowment** $381.0 million
- **Coed** 2,420 undergraduate students, 98% full-time, 59% women, 41% men
- **Very difficult** entrance level, 43% of applicants were admitted

UNDERGRAD STUDENTS
2,376 full-time, 44 part-time. Students come from 41 states and territories; 43 other countries; 78% are from out of state; 5% Black or African American, non-Hispanic/Latino; 7% Hispanic/Latino; 3% Asian, non-Hispanic/Latino; 0.1% Native Hawaiian or other Pacific Islander, non-Hispanic/Latino; 0.1% American Indian or Alaska Native, non-Hispanic/Latino; 4% Two or more races, non-Hispanic/Latino; 1% Race/ethnicity unknown; 10% international; 0.4% transferred in; 94% live on campus.

Freshmen:
Admission: 6,172 applied, 2,667 admitted, 610 enrolled. ***Test scores:*** SAT critical reading scores over 500: 98%; SAT math scores over 500: 99%; SAT writing scores over 500: 97%; ACT scores over 18: 100%; SAT critical reading scores over 600: 74%; SAT math scores over 600: 79%; SAT writing scores over 600: 77%; ACT scores over 24: 97%; SAT critical reading scores over 700: 20%; SAT math scores over 700: 28%; SAT writing scores over 700: 23%; ACT scores over 30: 48%.
Retention: 90% of full-time freshmen returned.

FACULTY
Total: 276, 82% full-time, 87% with terminal degrees.
Student/faculty ratio: 9:1.

ACADEMICS
Calendar: semesters. *Degree:* bachelor's.

Special study options: accelerated degree program, adult/continuing education programs, advanced placement credit, double majors, English as a second language, independent study, internships, off-campus study, part-time degree program, services for LD students, student-designed majors, study abroad, summer session for credit. ***ROTC:*** Army (b).

Unusual degree programs: 3-2 engineering with Case Western Reserve University, Rensselaer Polytechnic Institute, Columbia University; nursing with Johns Hopkins University; international studies with Johns Hopkins University.

Computers: 1,730 computers/terminals and 5,000 ports are available on campus for general student use. Students can access the following: campus intranet, computer help desk, free student e-mail accounts, online (class) grades, online (class) registration, online (class) schedules. Campuswide network is available. 100% of college-owned or -operated housing units are wired for high-speed Internet access. Wireless service is available via classrooms, computer centers, computer labs, dorm rooms, libraries, student centers.
Library: Waidner-Spahr Library. *Books:* 522,704 (physical), 693,013 (digital/electronic); *Serial titles:* 3,708 (physical), 67,219 (digital/electronic); *Databases:* 484. Weekly public service hours: 114; students can reserve study rooms.

STUDENT LIFE
Housing options: on-campus residence required through senior year; coed, special housing for students with disabilities. Campus housing is university owned. Freshman campus housing is guaranteed.

Activities and organizations: drama/theater group, student-run newspaper, radio station, choral group, Multi-Organization Board, Outing Club, Student Senate, Admissions Volunteers, WDCV Radio Station, national fraternities, national sororities.

Athletics Member NCAA. All Division III. ***Intercollegiate sports:*** baseball M, basketball M/W, cheerleading M(c)/W(c), cross-country running M/W, equestrian sports M(c)/W(c), fencing M(c)/W(c), field hockey W, football M, golf M/W, ice hockey M(c)/W(c), lacrosse M/W, skiing (downhill) M(c)/W(c), soccer M/W, softball W, squash M/W, swimming and diving M/W, tennis M/W, track and field M/W, ultimate Frisbee M(c)/W(c), volleyball M(c)/W. ***Intramural sports:*** badminton M/W, basketball M/W, field hockey W, football M/W, racquetball M/W, sand volleyball M/W, soccer M/W, softball M, squash M/W, tennis M/W, volleyball M/W.

Campus security: 24-hour emergency response devices and patrols, student patrols, late-night transport/escort service, controlled dormitory access.

Student services: health clinic, personal/psychological counseling, women's center.

COSTS & FINANCIAL AID
Costs (2016–17) ***One-time required fee:*** $25. ***Comprehensive fee:*** $63,974 includes full-time tuition ($50,730), mandatory fees ($450), and room and board ($12,794). Part-time tuition: $6342 per course. ***Required fees:*** $56 per course part-time. ***College room only:*** $6598. Room and board charges vary according to board plan and housing facility. ***Payment plan:*** installment. ***Waivers:*** senior citizens and employees or children of employees.

Financial Aid Of all full-time matriculated undergraduates who enrolled in 2016, 1,395 applied for aid, 1,292 were judged to have need, 1,094 had their need fully met. 964 Federal Work-Study jobs (averaging $2271). 196 state and other part-time jobs (averaging $3821). In 2016, 404 non-need-based awards were made. ***Average percent of need met:*** 99. ***Average financial aid package:*** $43,737. ***Average need-based loan:*** $4834. ***Average need-based gift aid:*** $37,817. ***Average non-need-based aid:*** $10,918. ***Average indebtedness upon graduation:*** $26,908. ***Financial aid deadline:*** 2/1.

APPLYING
Standardized Tests *Recommended:* SAT or ACT (for admission).

Options: electronic application, early decision, early action, deferred entrance.

Application fee: $65.

Required: essay or personal statement, high school transcript, 2 letters of recommendation. ***Recommended:*** minimum 3.0 GPA, interview.

Application deadlines: 2/1 (freshmen), 4/1 (transfers), 12/1 (early action).

Early decision deadline: 11/15 (for plan 1), 1/15 (for plan 2).

Notification: 3/23 (freshmen), 3/23 (out-of-state freshmen), continuous until 5/15 (transfers), 12/15 (early decision plan 1), 2/15 (early decision plan 2), 2/15 (early action).

CONTACT
Catherine Davenport, Dean of Admissions, Dickinson College, PO Box 1773, Admissions Office, Carlisle, PA 17013-2896. *Phone:* 717-245-1231. *Toll-free phone:* 800-644-1773. *Fax:* 717-245-1442.
E-mail: admissions@dickinson.edu.

★ Drexel University
Philadelphia, Pennsylvania
http://www.drexel.edu/

- **Independent** university, founded 1891
- **Urban** 96-acre campus with easy access to Philadelphia
- **Endowment** $668.4 million
- **Coed** 15,499 undergraduate students, 86% full-time, 47% women, 53% men
- **Moderately difficult** entrance level, 75% of applicants were admitted

UNDERGRAD STUDENTS
13,296 full-time, 2,203 part-time. Students come from 48 states and territories; 115 other countries; 47% are from out of state; 6% Black or African American, non-Hispanic/Latino; 6% Hispanic/Latino; 16% Asian, non-Hispanic/Latino; 0.7% Native Hawaiian or other Pacific Islander, non-Hispanic/Latino; 0.1% American Indian or Alaska Native, non-Hispanic/Latino; 4% Two or more races, non-Hispanic/Latino; 2% Race/ethnicity unknown; 14% international; 5% transferred in; 26% live on campus.

Freshmen:
Admission: 28,535 applied, 21,298 admitted, 2,327 enrolled. ***Average high school GPA:*** 3.56. ***Test scores:*** SAT critical reading scores over 500: 86%; SAT math scores over 500: 94%; ACT scores over 18: 100%; SAT critical reading scores over 600: 41%; SAT math scores over 600: 60%; ACT scores over 24: 84%; SAT critical reading scores over 700: 8%; SAT math scores over 700: 17%; ACT scores over 30: 30%.

Retention: 89% of full-time freshmen returned.

FACULTY
Total: 2,079, 56% full-time, 49% with terminal degrees.

Student/faculty ratio: 10:1.

ACADEMICS
Calendar: quarters. *Degrees:* certificates, bachelor's, master's, doctoral, post-master's, and postbachelor's certificates.

Special study options: academic remediation for entering students, accelerated degree program, adult/continuing education programs, advanced placement credit, cooperative education, distance learning, double majors, English as a second language, freshman honors college, honors programs, independent study, internships, part-time degree program, services for LD students, student-designed majors, study abroad, summer session for credit. ***ROTC:*** Army (b), Navy (c), Air Force (c).

Unusual degree programs: 3-2 business administration; engineering; nursing.

Computers: Students can access the following: campus intranet, computer help desk, free student e-mail accounts, online (class) grades, online (class) registration, online (class) schedules. Campuswide network is available. 100% of college-owned or -operated housing units are wired for high-speed Internet access. Wireless service is available via entire campus.

Library: W. W. Hagerty Library plus 3 others. *Books:* 286,613 (physical), 215,379 (digital/electronic); *Serial titles:* 126 (physical), 51,775 (digital/electronic); *Databases:* 465. Weekly public service hours: 87;

study areas open 24 hours, 5-7 days a week; students can reserve study rooms.

STUDENT LIFE

Housing options: on-campus residence required for freshman year; coed, special housing for students with disabilities. Campus housing is university owned. Freshman campus housing is guaranteed.

Activities and organizations: drama/theater group, student-run newspaper, radio and television station, choral group, Student Government, Black Student Union, Society of Hispanic Professional Engineers, Society of Minority Engineers and Scientists, Campus Activities Board, national fraternities, national sororities.

Athletics Member NCAA. All Division I. ***Intercollegiate sports:*** basketball M(s)/W(s), crew M(s)/W(s), field hockey W(s), golf M(s), lacrosse M(s)/W(s), soccer M(s)/W(s), softball W(s), squash M(s)/W(s), swimming and diving M(s)/W(s), tennis M(s)/W(s), wrestling M(s). ***Intramural sports:*** basketball M/W, fencing M/W, football M, ice hockey M, riflery M/W, sailing M/W, soccer M/W, softball M/W, squash M/W, table tennis M/W, tennis M/W, volleyball M/W, water polo M/W.

Campus security: 24-hour emergency response devices and patrols, late-night transport/escort service, controlled dormitory access.

Student services: health clinic, personal/psychological counseling, women's center.

COSTS & FINANCIAL AID

Costs (2017–18) ***Comprehensive fee:*** $65,892 includes full-time tuition ($49,632), mandatory fees ($2370), and room and board ($13,890). Full-time tuition and fees vary according to course load, location, program, and student level. Part-time tuition and fees vary according to course load and program. ***Room and board:*** Room and board charges vary according to board plan and housing facility. ***Payment plan:*** installment. ***Waivers:*** children of alumni and employees or children of employees.

Financial Aid Of all full-time matriculated undergraduates who enrolled in 2015, 9,578 applied for aid, 8,525 were judged to have need, 1,667 had their need fully met. In 2015, 4130 non-need-based awards were made. ***Average percent of need met:*** 68. ***Average financial aid package:*** $34,747. ***Average need-based loan:*** $10,979. ***Average need-based gift aid:*** $24,565. ***Average non-need-based aid:*** $14,589. ***Financial aid deadline:*** 3/1.

APPLYING

Standardized Tests *Required:* SAT or ACT (for admission).

Options: electronic application, early admission, early decision, early action, deferred entrance.

Application fee: $50.

Required: essay or personal statement, high school transcript, minimum 2.0 GPA. ***Recommended:*** 2 letters of recommendation, interview.

Application deadlines: 1/15 (freshmen), rolling (transfers), 11/1 (early action).

Early decision deadline: 11/1.

Notification: continuous until 4/1 (freshmen), continuous (transfers), 12/15 (early decision), 12/15 (early action).

CONTACT

Evelyn Thimba, Vice President, Dean of Admissions, Drexel University, 3141 Chestnut Street, Philadelphia, PA 19104-2875. *Phone:* 215-895-6712. *Toll-free phone:* 800-2-DREXEL.
E-mail: evelyn.k.thimba@drexel.edu.

See previous page for display ad and page 1336 for the College Close-Up.

Duquesne University

Pittsburgh, Pennsylvania

http://www.duq.edu/

- **Independent Roman Catholic** university, founded 1878
- **Urban** 50-acre campus with easy access to Pittsburgh
- **Endowment** $280.0 million
- **Coed** 6,039 undergraduate students, 97% full-time, 63% women, 37% men
- **Moderately difficult** entrance level, 73% of applicants were admitted

UNDERGRAD STUDENTS

5,851 full-time, 188 part-time. Students come from 44 states and territories; 45 other countries; 29% are from out of state; 5% Black or African American, non-Hispanic/Latino; 3% Hispanic/Latino; 3% Asian, non-Hispanic/Latino; 0.1% Native Hawaiian or other Pacific Islander, non-Hispanic/Latino; 0.1% American Indian or Alaska Native, non-Hispanic/Latino; 3% Two or more races, non-Hispanic/Latino; 1% Race/ethnicity unknown; 4% international; 3% transferred in; 57% live on campus.

Freshmen:

Admission: 7,655 applied, 5,560 admitted, 1,556 enrolled. ***Average high school GPA:*** 3.72. ***Test scores:*** SAT critical reading scores over 500: 91%; SAT math scores over 500: 88%; SAT writing scores over 500: 81%; ACT scores over 18: 100%; SAT critical reading scores over 600: 31%; SAT math scores over 600: 36%; SAT writing scores over 600: 25%; ACT scores over 24: 84%; SAT critical reading scores over 700: 3%; SAT math scores over 700: 4%; SAT writing scores over 700: 2%; ACT scores over 30: 20%.

Retention: 87% of full-time freshmen returned.

FACULTY

Total: 983, 50% full-time.

Student/faculty ratio: 14:1.

ACADEMICS

Calendar: semesters. *Degrees:* bachelor's, master's, doctoral, post-master's, and postbachelor's certificates.

Special study options: academic remediation for entering students, accelerated degree program, adult/continuing education programs, advanced placement credit, distance learning, double majors, English as a second language, external degree program, freshman honors college, honors programs, independent study, internships, off-campus study, part-time degree program, services for LD students, student-designed majors, study abroad, summer session for credit. ***ROTC:*** Army (b), Navy (c), Air Force (c).

Unusual degree programs: 3-2 engineering with Case Western Reserve University, University of Pittsburgh.

Computers: 1,000 computers/terminals are available on campus for general student use. Students can access the following: campus intranet, computer help desk, free student e-mail accounts, online (class) grades, online (class) registration, online (class) schedules. Campuswide network is available. 100% of college-owned or -operated housing units are wired for high-speed Internet access. Wireless service is available via classrooms, computer centers, computer labs, dorm rooms, learning centers, libraries, student centers.

Library: Gumberg Library plus 1 other. *Books:* 647,175 (physical), 306,412 (digital/electronic); *Serial titles:* 203 (physical), 117,733 (digital/electronic); *Databases:* 205. Weekly public service hours: 111; students can reserve study rooms.

STUDENT LIFE

Housing options: on-campus residence required through sophomore year; coed, men-only, women-only, special housing for students with disabilities. Campus housing is university owned. Freshman campus housing is guaranteed.

Activities and organizations: drama/theater group, student-run newspaper, radio and television station, choral group, marching band, Duquesne University Volunteers (DUV), Red and Blue Crew, Student Government Association, Duquesne Program Council, Residence Hall Association, national fraternities, national sororities.

Athletics Member NCAA. All Division I except football (Division I-AA). ***Intercollegiate sports:*** basketball M(s)/W(s), bowling W(s), crew W(s), cross-country running M(s)/W(s), lacrosse W(s), soccer M(s)/W(s), swimming and diving W(s), tennis M(s)/W(s), track and field M(s)/W(s), volleyball W(s). ***Intramural sports:*** baseball M(c)/W(c), basketball M/W, cheerleading W(c), crew W(c), equestrian sports M(c)/W(c), golf M(c)/W(c), ice hockey M(c)/W(c), lacrosse M(c)/W(c), racquetball M/W, rugby M(c)/W(c), soccer M/W, tennis M(c)/W(c), ultimate Frisbee M/W, volleyball M/W.

Campus security: 24-hour emergency response devices and patrols, late-night transport/escort service, controlled dormitory access, cameras monitor exterior 24-hours/day, card access for buildings, outside warning siren system.

Student services: health clinic, personal/psychological counseling.

COSTS & FINANCIAL AID

Costs (2016–17) ***Comprehensive fee:*** $46,822 includes full-time tuition ($35,062) and room and board ($11,760). Full-time tuition and fees vary according to course load and program. Part-time tuition: $1162 per credit hour. Part-time tuition and fees vary according to course load and program. ***College room only:*** $6412. Room and board charges vary according to board plan and housing facility. ***Payment plans:*** installment, deferred payment. ***Waivers:*** senior citizens and employees or children of employees.

Financial Aid Of all full-time matriculated undergraduates who enrolled in 2015, 4,581 applied for aid, 3,862 were judged to have need, 725 had their need fully met. 1,777 Federal Work-Study jobs (averaging $2400). In 2015, 1552 non-need-based awards were made. ***Average percent of need met:*** 71. ***Average financial aid package:*** $24,000. ***Average need-based loan:*** $4802. ***Average need-based gift aid:*** $19,267. ***Average non-need-based aid:*** $12,168. ***Average indebtedness upon graduation:*** $41,272. ***Financial aid deadline:*** 5/1.

APPLYING

Standardized Tests *Required for some:* SAT or ACT (for admission).

Options: electronic application, early admission, early decision, early action, deferred entrance.

Application fee: $50.

Required: high school transcript. ***Required for some:*** essay or personal statement, 1 letter of recommendation, audition for School of Music; 40 hours of volunteer, paid, or shadowing experience for physical therapy. ***Recommended:*** minimum 3.0 GPA, interview.

Application deadlines: 7/1 (freshmen), 7/1 (transfers), 12/1 (early action).

Early decision deadline: 11/1.

Notification: continuous until 10/1 (freshmen), 11/15 (early decision), 1/15 (early action).

CONTACT

Ms. Debra Zugates, Director of Admissions, Duquesne University, Administration Building, 600 Forbes Avenue, Pittsburgh, PA 15282-0201. *Phone:* 412-396-5211. *Toll-free phone:* 800-456-0590. *Fax:* 412-396-5644. *E-mail:* admissions@duq.edu.

Eastern University

St. Davids, Pennsylvania

http://www.eastern.edu/

- **Independent Christian** comprehensive, founded 1952
- **Suburban** 114-acre campus with easy access to Philadelphia
- **Endowment** $26.5 million
- **Coed** 2,082 undergraduate students, 85% full-time, 70% women, 30% men
- **Moderately difficult** entrance level, 61% of applicants were admitted

UNDERGRAD STUDENTS

1,760 full-time, 322 part-time. Students come from 35 states and territories; 18 other countries; 42% are from out of state; 21% Black or African American, non-Hispanic/Latino; 20% Hispanic/Latino; 2% Asian, non-Hispanic/Latino; 0.1% American Indian or Alaska Native, non-Hispanic/Latino; 1% Two or more races, non-Hispanic/Latino; 7% Race/ethnicity unknown; 2% international; 9% transferred in; 75% live on campus.

Freshmen:

Admission: 1,992 applied, 1,219 admitted, 442 enrolled. ***Average high school GPA:*** 3.47. ***Test scores:*** SAT critical reading scores over 500: 61%; SAT math scores over 500: 58%; SAT writing scores over 500: 54%; ACT scores over 18: 93%; SAT critical reading scores over 600: 21%; SAT math scores over 600: 18%; SAT writing scores over 600: 17%; ACT scores over 24: 24%; SAT critical reading scores over 700: 5%; SAT math scores over 700: 2%; SAT writing scores over 700: 2%; ACT scores over 30: 2%.

Retention: 78% of full-time freshmen returned.

FACULTY

Total: 486, 26% full-time, 20% with terminal degrees.

Student/faculty ratio: 10:1.

ACADEMICS

Calendar: semesters. *Degrees:* certificates, diplomas, associate, bachelor's, master's, doctoral, and post-master's certificates.

Special study options: academic remediation for entering students, accelerated degree program, adult/continuing education programs, advanced placement credit, distance learning, double majors, English as a second language, external degree program, honors programs, independent study, internships, off-campus study, part-time degree program, services for LD students, student-designed majors, study abroad, summer session for credit. ***ROTC:*** Army (c), Air Force (c).

Computers: 98 computers/terminals and 300 ports are available on campus for general student use. Students can access the following: campus intranet, computer help desk, free student e-mail accounts, online (class) grades, online (class) registration, online (class) schedules. Campuswide network is available. 100% of college-owned or -operated housing units are wired for high-speed Internet access. Wireless service is available via entire campus.

Library: Warner Memorial Library plus 4 others. *Books:* 183,941 (physical), 600,000 (digital/electronic); *Serial titles:* 100 (physical), 30,000 (digital/electronic); *Databases:* 130. Weekly public service hours: 83; students can reserve study rooms.

STUDENT LIFE

Housing options: on-campus residence required through senior year; men-only, women-only, special housing for students with disabilities. Campus housing is university owned and leased by the school. Freshman campus housing is guaranteed.

Activities and organizations: drama/theater group, student-run newspaper, choral group, Kappa Delta Pi - Education Honor Society, ETHELS - Swing Club, Black Student League (BSL), SPSEA - Students of Pennsylvania State Education Association, Psi Chi - Psychology Honor Society.

Athletics Member NCAA. All Division III. ***Intercollegiate sports:*** baseball M, basketball M/W, cross-country running M/W, field hockey W, golf M/W, lacrosse M/W, soccer M/W, softball W, tennis M/W, track and field M/W, volleyball W. ***Intramural sports:*** basketball M/W, soccer M/W, volleyball M/W.

Campus security: 24-hour emergency response devices and patrols, late-night transport/escort service, controlled dormitory access, emergency call boxes.

Student services: health clinic, personal/psychological counseling.

COSTS & FINANCIAL AID

Costs (2017–18) ***One-time required fee:*** $60. ***Comprehensive fee:*** $43,060 includes full-time tuition ($31,700), mandatory fees ($380), and room and board ($10,980). Full-time tuition and fees vary according to course load, degree level, and program. Part-time tuition: $695 per credit. Part-time tuition and fees vary according to course load, degree level, and program. ***Required fees:*** $180 per term part-time. ***College room only:*** $5840. Room and board charges vary according to housing facility and location. ***Payment plan:*** installment. ***Waivers:*** children of alumni and employees or children of employees.

Financial Aid Of all full-time matriculated undergraduates who enrolled in 2015, 1,823 applied for aid, 1,704 were judged to have need, 168 had their need fully met. 348 Federal Work-Study jobs (averaging $1037). In 2015, 85 non-need-based awards were made. ***Average percent of need met:*** 66. ***Average financial aid package:*** $20,007. ***Average need-based loan:*** $3941. ***Average need-based gift aid:*** $7241. ***Average non-need-based aid:*** $11,293. ***Average indebtedness upon graduation:*** $38,904.

APPLYING

Standardized Tests *Required:* SAT or ACT (for admission).

Options: electronic application, early admission, deferred entrance.

Application fee: $35.

Required: essay or personal statement, high school transcript, minimum 2.0 GPA, 1 letter of recommendation. ***Recommended:*** 2 letters of recommendation, interview.

Application deadlines: rolling (freshmen), rolling (transfers).

Notification: continuous (freshmen), continuous (transfers).

CONTACT

Mr. Michael Dziedziak, Executive Director of Enrollment, Eastern University, 1300 Eagle Road, St Davids, PA 19087-3696. *Phone:* 610-

341-1376. *Toll-free phone:* 800-452-0996. *Fax:* 610-341-1723. *E-mail:* ugadm@eastern.edu.

East Stroudsburg University of Pennsylvania

East Stroudsburg, Pennsylvania

http://www.esu.edu/

- **State-supported** comprehensive, founded 1893, part of Pennsylvania State System of Higher Education
- **Rural** 258-acre campus
- **Endowment** $14,319
- **Coed** 6,159 undergraduate students, 92% full-time, 57% women, 43% men
- **Moderately difficult** entrance level, 73% of applicants were admitted

UNDERGRAD STUDENTS

5,642 full-time, 517 part-time. Students come from 21 states and territories; 19 other countries; 22% are from out of state; 16% Black or African American, non-Hispanic/Latino; 11% Hispanic/Latino; 2% Asian, non-Hispanic/Latino; 0.1% Native Hawaiian or other Pacific Islander, non-Hispanic/Latino; 0.2% American Indian or Alaska Native, non-Hispanic/Latino; 5% Two or more races, non-Hispanic/Latino; 1% Race/ethnicity unknown; 0.7% international; 10% transferred in; 46% live on campus.

Freshmen:

Admission: 7,449 applied, 5,420 admitted, 1,307 enrolled. ***Average high school GPA:*** 3.2. ***Test scores:*** SAT critical reading scores over 500: 33%; SAT math scores over 500: 35%; SAT writing scores over 500: 24%; ACT scores over 18: 66%; SAT critical reading scores over 600: 5%; SAT math scores over 600: 6%; SAT writing scores over 600: 2%; ACT scores over 24: 11%; SAT critical reading scores over 700: 1%; ACT scores over 30: 1%.

Retention: 72% of full-time freshmen returned.

FACULTY

Total: 351, 79% full-time, 66% with terminal degrees.

Student/faculty ratio: 19:1.

ACADEMICS

Calendar: semesters. *Degrees:* associate, bachelor's, master's, doctoral, and postbachelor's certificates.

Special study options: academic remediation for entering students, accelerated degree program, adult/continuing education programs, advanced placement credit, distance learning, double majors, honors programs, independent study, internships, off-campus study, part-time degree program, services for LD students, student-designed majors, study abroad, summer session for credit. ***ROTC:*** Army (b), Air Force (c).

Unusual degree programs: 3-2 engineering with Penn State University Park.

Computers: 500 computers/terminals and 1,500 ports are available on campus for general student use. Students can access the following: campus intranet, computer help desk, free student e-mail accounts, online (class) grades, online (class) registration, online (class) schedules, online classes. Campuswide network is available. 100% of college-owned or -operated housing units are wired for high-speed Internet access. Wireless service is available via classrooms, computer labs, dorm rooms, libraries, student centers.

Library: Kemp Library. *Books:* 591,746 (physical), 215,088 (digital/electronic); *Serial titles:* 110,974 (physical); *Databases:* 82. Weekly public service hours: 99.

STUDENT LIFE

Housing options: on-campus residence required for freshman year; coed, special housing for students with disabilities. Campus housing is university owned and is provided by a third party. Freshman campus housing is guaranteed.

Activities and organizations: drama/theater group, student-run newspaper, radio station, choral group, marching band, Student Senate, Stage II, Council for Exceptional Children, Environmental Club, National Speech/Hearing/Language Association, national fraternities, national sororities.

Athletics Member NCAA. All Division II. ***Intercollegiate sports:*** baseball M(s), basketball M(s)/W(s), cheerleading M/W, cross-country running M(s)/W(s), equestrian sports M(c)/W(c), field hockey W(s), football M(s), golf M(c)/W, ice hockey M(c)/W(c), lacrosse M(c)/W(s), rugby M(c)/W(c), soccer M(s)/W(s), softball W(s), swimming and diving W(s), tennis M(c)/W(s), track and field M(s)/W(s), ultimate Frisbee M(c)/W(c), volleyball M(c)/W(s), wrestling M(s). ***Intramural sports:*** basketball M/W, racquetball M(c)/W(c), soccer M(c)/W(c), softball M/W.

Campus security: 24-hour emergency response devices and patrols, late-night transport/escort service, controlled dormitory access, self-defense education, shuttle buses, lighted pathways/sidewalks, controlled building access.

Student services: health clinic, personal/psychological counseling, women's center, legal services.

COSTS & FINANCIAL AID

Costs (2016–17) ***Tuition:*** state resident $7238 full-time, $302 per credit hour part-time; nonresident $18,096 full-time, $754 per credit hour part-time. Full-time tuition and fees vary according to course load, location, and program. Part-time tuition and fees vary according to location and program. ***Required fees:*** $2706 full-time, $143 per credit hour part-time, $683 per term part-time. ***Room and board:*** $8280; room only: $5680. Room and board charges vary according to board plan and housing facility. ***Payment plan:*** installment. ***Waivers:*** senior citizens and employees or children of employees.

Financial Aid Of all full-time matriculated undergraduates who enrolled in 2015, 3,883 applied for aid, 3,221 were judged to have need, 1,406 had their need fully met. In 2015, 58 non-need-based awards were made. ***Average percent of need met:*** 43. ***Average financial aid package:*** $8213. ***Average need-based loan:*** $4123. ***Average need-based gift aid:*** $5814. ***Average non-need-based aid:*** $1272. ***Average indebtedness upon graduation:*** $28,500. ***Financial aid deadline:*** 2/16.

APPLYING

Standardized Tests *Required for some:* SAT or ACT (for admission).

Options: electronic application, deferred entrance.

Application fee: $25.

Required: high school transcript.

Application deadlines: 5/1 (freshmen), 6/1 (transfers).

Notification: 5/1 (freshmen), continuous (transfers).

CONTACT

Mr. Jeff Jones, Director of Admissions, East Stroudsburg University of Pennsylvania, 200 Prospect Street, East Stroudsburg, PA 18301. *Phone:* 570-422-3542. *Toll-free phone:* 877-230-5547. *Fax:* 570-422-3933. *E-mail:* undergrads@po-box.esu.edu.

Edinboro University of Pennsylvania

Edinboro, Pennsylvania

http://www.edinboro.edu/

CONTACT

Ms. Melissa Manning, Associate Director of Undergraduate Admissions, Edinboro University of Pennsylvania, Academy Hall, Edinboro, PA 16444. *Phone:* 814-732-2761. *Toll-free phone:* 888-846-2676. *Fax:* 814-732-2420. *E-mail:* eup_admissions@edinboro.edu.

Elizabethtown College

Elizabethtown, Pennsylvania

http://www.etown.edu/

- **Independent** comprehensive, founded 1899, affiliated with Church of the Brethren
- **Small-town** 204-acre campus with easy access to Philadelphia, Baltimore, Harrisburg, Lancaster
- **Endowment** $69.7 million
- **Coed** 1,737 undergraduate students, 98% full-time, 61% women, 39% men
- **Moderately difficult** entrance level, 73% of applicants were admitted

UNDERGRAD STUDENTS

1,707 full-time, 30 part-time. Students come from 30 states and territories; 26 other countries; 36% are from out of state; 3% Black or African American, non-Hispanic/Latino; 4% Hispanic/Latino; 3% Asian, non-

Hispanic/Latino; 0.1% Native Hawaiian or other Pacific Islander, non-Hispanic/Latino; 0.2% American Indian or Alaska Native, non-Hispanic/Latino; 2% Two or more races, non-Hispanic/Latino; 3% international; 1% transferred in; 85% live on campus.

Freshmen:
Admission: 2,904 applied, 2,134 admitted, 442 enrolled. ***Test scores:*** SAT critical reading scores over 500: 76%; SAT math scores over 500: 72%; SAT writing scores over 500: 67%; ACT scores over 18: 94%; SAT critical reading scores over 600: 28%; SAT math scores over 600: 31%; SAT writing scores over 600: 22%; ACT scores over 24: 55%; SAT critical reading scores over 700: 5%; SAT math scores over 700: 5%; SAT writing scores over 700: 3%; ACT scores over 30: 16%.

Retention: 87% of full-time freshmen returned.

FACULTY
Total: 188, 69% full-time, 76% with terminal degrees.

Student/faculty ratio: 12:1.

ACADEMICS
Calendar: semesters. *Degrees:* bachelor's and master's.

Special study options: advanced placement credit, distance learning, double majors, English as a second language, honors programs, independent study, internships, off-campus study, services for LD students, study abroad, summer session for credit.

Unusual degree programs: 3-2 forestry with Duke University; allied health with Thomas Jefferson University, Widener University; environmental management with Duke University.

Computers: 230 computers/terminals and 200 ports are available on campus for general student use. Students can access the following: campus intranet, computer help desk, free student e-mail accounts, online (class) grades, online (class) registration, online (class) schedules, file space, personal Web page, financial aid, student billing, residence hall selection, personal and group blogs. Campuswide network is available. 100% of college-owned or -operated housing units are wired for high-speed Internet access. Wireless service is available via entire campus.

Library: High Library plus 1 other. *Books:* 264,124 (physical), 5,305 (digital/electronic); *Serial titles:* 1,455 (physical), 49,133 (digital/electronic); *Databases:* 83. Weekly public service hours: 80; students can reserve study rooms.

STUDENT LIFE
Housing options: on-campus residence required through senior year; coed, women-only, special housing for students with disabilities. Campus housing is university owned and leased by the school. Freshman campus housing is guaranteed.

Activities and organizations: drama/theater group, student-run newspaper, radio and television station, choral group, Enactus, Emotion Dance Club, Student Senate, Acappella groups, Religious groups.

Athletics Member NCAA. All Division III. ***Intercollegiate sports:*** baseball M, basketball M/W, cross-country running M/W, field hockey W, golf M/W, lacrosse M/W, soccer M/W, softball W, swimming and diving M/W, tennis M/W, track and field M/W, volleyball W, wrestling M. ***Intramural sports:*** basketball M/W, bowling M/W, cheerleading M(c)/W(c), equestrian sports M(c)/W(c), golf M/W, ice hockey M(c), soccer M/W, softball M/W, tennis M/W, triathlon M(c)/W(c), ultimate Frisbee M(c)/W(c), volleyball M(c)/W(c).

Campus security: 24-hour emergency response devices and patrols, student patrols, late-night transport/escort service, controlled dormitory access, self-defense workshops, crime prevention program.

Student services: health clinic, personal/psychological counseling.

COSTS & FINANCIAL AID
Costs (2017–18) ***Comprehensive fee:*** $56,340 includes full-time tuition ($45,350) and room and board ($10,990). Full-time tuition and fees vary according to course load. Part-time tuition: $1100 per credit hour. Part-time tuition and fees vary according to course load. ***College room only:*** $5440. Room and board charges vary according to board plan and housing facility. ***Payment plan:*** installment. ***Waivers:*** employees or children of employees.

Financial Aid Of all full-time matriculated undergraduates who enrolled in 2015, 1,443 applied for aid, 1,310 were judged to have need, 257 had their need fully met. 836 Federal Work-Study jobs (averaging $1296). In 2015, 417 non-need-based awards were made. ***Average percent of need met:*** 79. ***Average financial aid package:*** $29,704. ***Average need-based***

loan: $4537. ***Average need-based gift aid:*** $25,140. ***Average non-need-based aid:*** $19,675. ***Average indebtedness upon graduation:*** $30,355.

APPLYING

Standardized Tests *Required:* SAT or ACT (for admission).

Options: electronic application, deferred entrance.

Application fee: $30.

Required: essay or personal statement, high school transcript, minimum 2.0 GPA, 2 letters of recommendation. ***Required for some:*** interview. ***Recommended:*** minimum 3.0 GPA, interview.

Application deadlines: 3/1 (freshmen), 8/1 (transfers).

Notification: continuous (freshmen), continuous (transfers).

CONTACT

Ms. Lauren Deibler, Director of Admissions and Coordinator of International Recruitment, Elizabethtown College, One Alpha Drive, Elizabethtown, PA 17022. *Phone:* 717-361-1400. *Fax:* 717-361-1365. *E-mail:* admissions@etown.edu.

See previous page for display ad and page 1338 for the College Close-Up.

Elizabethtown College School of Continuing and Professional Studies

Elizabethtown, Pennsylvania

http://www.etowndegrees.com/

CONTACT

Ms. Barbara A. Randazzo, Assistant Dean of Enrollment Management, Elizabethtown College School of Continuing and Professional Studies, One Alpha Drive, Elizabethtown College, PA 17022. *Phone:* 717-361-3750. *Toll-free phone:* 800-877-2694. *Fax:* 717-361-1466. *E-mail:* randazzob@etown.edu.

Franklin & Marshall College

Lancaster, Pennsylvania

http://www.fandm.edu/

- **Independent** 4-year, founded 1787
- **Suburban** 209-acre campus with easy access to Philadelphia
- **Coed** 2,255 undergraduate students, 99% full-time, 53% women, 47% men
- **Very difficult** entrance level, 36% of applicants were admitted

UNDERGRAD STUDENTS

2,225 full-time, 30 part-time. Students come from 45 states and territories; 55 other countries; 73% are from out of state; 6% Black or African American, non-Hispanic/Latino; 9% Hispanic/Latino; 5% Asian, non-Hispanic/Latino; 2% Two or more races, non-Hispanic/Latino; 6% Race/ethnicity unknown; 15% international; 1% transferred in; 99% live on campus.

Freshmen:

Admission: 6,953 applied, 2,529 admitted, 639 enrolled. ***Test scores:*** SAT critical reading scores over 500: 96%; SAT math scores over 500: 99%; ACT scores over 18: 100%; SAT critical reading scores over 600: 64%; SAT math scores over 600: 86%; ACT scores over 24: 98%; SAT critical reading scores over 700: 22%; SAT math scores over 700: 34%; ACT scores over 30: 46%.

Retention: 91% of full-time freshmen returned.

FACULTY

Total: 293, 83% full-time, 87% with terminal degrees.

Student/faculty ratio: 9:1.

ACADEMICS

Calendar: semesters. *Degree:* bachelor's.

Special study options: accelerated degree program, advanced placement credit, double majors, independent study, internships, off-campus study, services for LD students, student-designed majors, study abroad, summer session for credit. ***ROTC:*** Army (c).

Unusual degree programs: 3-2 engineering with Rensselaer Polytechnic Institute, Washington University in St. Louis, Columbia University, Case Western Reserve University, Penn State University College of Engineering; forestry with Duke University; environmental studies with Duke University.

Computers: 125 computers/terminals are available on campus for general student use. Students can access the following: campus intranet, computer help desk, free student e-mail accounts, online (class) grades, online (class) registration, online (class) schedules, online degree audit, unofficial transcripts, course material. Campuswide network is available. 100% of college-owned or -operated housing units are wired for high-speed Internet access. Wireless service is available via entire campus.

Library: Shadek-Fackenthal Library plus 1 other. *Books:* 468,748 (physical), 135,071 (digital/electronic); *Serial titles:* 2,680 (physical), 167,874 (digital/electronic). Weekly public service hours: 110; students can reserve study rooms.

STUDENT LIFE

Housing options: on-campus residence required through senior year; coed, men-only, women-only, cooperative, special housing for students with disabilities. Campus housing is university owned and is provided by a third party. Freshman campus housing is guaranteed.

Activities and organizations: drama/theater group, student-run newspaper, radio station, choral group, Intervarsity, Hillel, Mi Gente Latina, Cia Bella, F&M Players, national fraternities, national sororities.

Athletics Member NCAA. All Division III except wrestling (Division I). ***Intercollegiate sports:*** baseball M, basketball M/W, crew M(c)/W, cross-country running M/W, equestrian sports W(c), field hockey W, football M, golf M/W, ice hockey M(c), lacrosse M/W, rugby M(c)/W(c), soccer M/W, softball W, squash M/W, swimming and diving M/W, tennis M/W, track and field M/W, ultimate Frisbee M(c)/W(c), volleyball M(c)/W, wrestling M. ***Intramural sports:*** basketball M/W, football M, soccer M/W, softball M/W, squash M/W, tennis M/W, volleyball M/W, wrestling M.

Campus security: 24-hour emergency response devices and patrols, late-night transport/escort service, controlled dormitory access, residence hall security, campus security connected to city police and fire company.

Student services: health clinic, personal/psychological counseling, women's center.

COSTS & FINANCIAL AID

Costs (2017–18) ***One-time required fee:*** $200. ***Comprehensive fee:*** $65,610 includes full-time tuition ($52,190), mandatory fees ($300), and room and board ($13,120). Part-time tuition and fees vary according to course load. ***College room only:*** $7760. Room and board charges vary according to board plan and housing facility. ***Payment plans:*** installment, deferred payment. ***Waivers:*** employees or children of employees.

Financial Aid Of all full-time matriculated undergraduates who enrolled in 2016, 1,326 applied for aid, 1,189 were judged to have need, 1,189 had their need fully met. In 2016, 29 non-need-based awards were made. ***Average percent of need met:*** 100. ***Average financial aid package:*** $47,144. ***Average need-based loan:*** $4154. ***Average need-based gift aid:*** $42,719. ***Average non-need-based aid:*** $6820. ***Average indebtedness upon graduation:*** $27,133. ***Financial aid deadline:*** 2/1.

APPLYING

Options: electronic application, early admission, early decision, deferred entrance.

Application fee: $60.

Required: essay or personal statement, high school transcript, 2 letters of recommendation, Common Application Supplement. ***Required for some:*** interview.

Application deadlines: 1/15 (freshmen), 5/15 (transfers).

Early decision deadline: 11/15 (for plan 1), 1/15 (for plan 2).

Notification: 4/1 (freshmen), 4/1 (out-of-state freshmen), 12/15 (early decision plan 1), 2/15 (early decision plan 2).

CONTACT

Julie Kerich, Director of Admissions, Franklin & Marshall College, PO Box 3003, Lancaster, PA 17604-3003. *Phone:* 717-358-47433. *Toll-free phone:* 877-678-9111. *Fax:* 717-291-4389. *E-mail:* julie.kerich@fandm.edu.

★ Gannon University

Erie, Pennsylvania

http://www.gannon.edu/

- **Independent Roman Catholic** university, founded 1925
- **Urban** 38-acre campus with easy access to Cleveland, Buffalo, Pittsburgh
- **Endowment** $56.6 million
- **Coed** 3,098 undergraduate students, 80% full-time, 56% women, 44% men
- **Moderately difficult** entrance level, 78% of applicants were admitted

UNDERGRAD STUDENTS

2,481 full-time, 617 part-time. Students come from 31 states and territories; 39 other countries; 29% are from out of state; 5% Black or African American, non-Hispanic/Latino; 3% Hispanic/Latino; 2% Asian, non-Hispanic/Latino; 0.2% Native Hawaiian or other Pacific Islander, non-Hispanic/Latino; 0.2% American Indian or Alaska Native, non-Hispanic/Latino; 2% Two or more races, non-Hispanic/Latino; 5% Race/ethnicity unknown; 9% international; 3% transferred in; 44% live on campus.

Freshmen:

Admission: 4,710 applied, 3,662 admitted, 631 enrolled. ***Average high school GPA:*** 3.55. ***Test scores:*** SAT critical reading scores over 500: 56%; SAT math scores over 500: 63%; ACT scores over 18: 91%; SAT critical reading scores over 600: 14%; SAT math scores over 600: 17%; ACT scores over 24: 47%; SAT critical reading scores over 700: 2%; SAT math scores over 700: 1%; ACT scores over 30: 5%.

Retention: 78% of full-time freshmen returned.

FACULTY

Total: 403, 59% full-time, 57% with terminal degrees.

Student/faculty ratio: 12:1.

ACADEMICS

Calendar: semesters plus 2 summer sessions. *Degrees:* certificates, associate, bachelor's, master's, doctoral, post-master's, and postbachelor's certificates.

Special study options: academic remediation for entering students, accelerated degree program, adult/continuing education programs, advanced placement credit, cooperative education, distance learning, double majors, English as a second language, honors programs, independent study, internships, off-campus study, part-time degree program, services for LD students, study abroad, summer session for credit. ***ROTC:*** Army (b).

Unusual degree programs: 3-2 business administration; engineering with University of Pittsburgh; occupational therapy, physician assistant, sport and exercise science.

Computers: 386 computers/terminals and 1,425 ports are available on campus for general student use. Students can access the following: campus intranet, computer help desk, free student e-mail accounts, online (class) grades, online (class) registration, online (class) schedules. Campuswide network is available. 100% of college-owned or -operated housing units are wired for high-speed Internet access. Wireless service is available via entire campus.

Library: Nash Library. *Books:* 213,041 (physical), 252,244 (digital/electronic); *Serial titles:* 37 (physical), 52,805 (digital/electronic); *Databases:* 45. Weekly public service hours: 97; students can reserve study rooms.

STUDENT LIFE

Housing options: on-campus residence required through sophomore year; coed, special housing for students with disabilities. Campus housing is university owned and leased by the school. Freshman campus housing is guaranteed.

Activities and organizations: drama/theater group, student-run newspaper, radio station, choral group, GU Society of Physician Assistant, GU Habitat for Humanity, Activities Programming Board, Student Occupational Therapy Association, Organization of Women Leaders, national fraternities, national sororities.

Athletics Member NCAA. All Division II. ***Intercollegiate sports:*** baseball M(s), basketball M(s)/W(s), cheerleading W(s)(c), cross-country running M(s)/W(s), football M(s), golf M(s)/W(s), gymnastics W(s)(c), lacrosse W(s), rugby M(c), soccer M(s)/W(s), softball W(s), swimming and diving M(s)/W(s), volleyball W(s), water polo M(s)/W(s), wrestling M(s). ***Intramural sports:*** basketball M/W, football M/W, ice hockey M(c), lacrosse M(c), racquetball M/W, rugby M(c)/W(c), sailing M(c)/W(c), soccer M/W(c), ultimate Frisbee M(c)/W(c), volleyball M(c)/W(c).

Campus security: 24-hour emergency response devices and patrols, late-night transport/escort service, controlled dormitory access, security cameras in and outside of campus facilities, including streets and sidewalks..

Student services: health clinic, personal/psychological counseling.

COSTS & FINANCIAL AID

Costs (2016–17) ***Comprehensive fee:*** $42,032 includes full-time tuition ($29,300), mandatory fees ($742), and room and board ($11,990). Full-time tuition and fees vary according to course load and program. Part-time tuition: $710 per credit hour. Part-time tuition and fees vary according to course load and program. ***Required fees:*** $25 per credit hour part-time. ***College room only:*** $6370. Room and board charges vary according to board plan and housing facility. ***Payment plans:*** installment, deferred payment. ***Waivers:*** senior citizens and employees or children of employees.

Financial Aid Of all full-time matriculated undergraduates who enrolled in 2016, 2,091 applied for aid, 1,915 were judged to have need, 467 had their need fully met. In 2016, 390 non-need-based awards were made. ***Average percent of need met:*** 73. ***Average financial aid package:*** $24,832. ***Average need-based loan:*** $4322. ***Average need-based gift aid:*** $20,924. ***Average non-need-based aid:*** $14,266.

APPLYING

Standardized Tests *Required:* SAT or ACT (for admission).

Options: electronic application, deferred entrance.

Application fee: $25.

Required: high school transcript, minimum 2.0 GPA, counselor's recommendation. ***Required for some:*** minimum 3.0 GPA, 2 letters of recommendation, interview. ***Recommended:*** essay or personal statement.

Application deadlines: rolling (freshmen), rolling (transfers).

Notification: continuous (freshmen), continuous (transfers).

CONTACT

Office of Admissions, Gannon University, 109 University Square, Erie, PA 16541. *Phone:* 814-871-7240. *Toll-free phone:* 800-GANNONU. *Fax:* 814-871-5803. *E-mail:* admissions@gannon.edu.

See next page for display ad and page 1358 for the College Close-Up.

Geneva College

Beaver Falls, Pennsylvania

http://www.geneva.edu/

- **Independent** comprehensive, founded 1848, affiliated with Reformed Presbyterian Church of North America
- **Small-town** 55-acre campus with easy access to Pittsburgh
- **Endowment** $36.9 million
- **Coed** 1,457 undergraduate students, 90% full-time, 51% women, 49% men
- **Moderately difficult** entrance level, 71% of applicants were admitted

UNDERGRAD STUDENTS

1,305 full-time, 152 part-time. Students come from 35 states and territories; 10 other countries; 25% are from out of state; 9% Black or African American, non-Hispanic/Latino; 1% Hispanic/Latino; 1% Asian, non-Hispanic/Latino; 0.1% Native Hawaiian or other Pacific Islander, non-Hispanic/Latino; 0.1% American Indian or Alaska Native, non-Hispanic/Latino; 3% Two or more races, non-Hispanic/Latino; 2% Race/ethnicity unknown; 0.5% international; 3% transferred in; 74% live on campus.

Freshmen:

Admission: 1,587 applied, 1,120 admitted, 292 enrolled. ***Average high school GPA:*** 3.59. ***Test scores:*** SAT critical reading scores over 500: 64%; SAT math scores over 500: 69%; SAT writing scores over 500: 53%; ACT scores over 18: 92%; SAT critical reading scores over 600: 30%; SAT math scores over 600: 25%; SAT writing scores over 600: 18%; ACT scores over 24: 57%; SAT critical reading scores over 700: 6%; SAT math

scores over 700: 4%; SAT writing scores over 700: 3%; ACT scores over 30: 16%.

Retention: 81% of full-time freshmen returned.

FACULTY

Total: 155, 52% full-time, 49% with terminal degrees.

Student/faculty ratio: 13:1.

ACADEMICS

Calendar: semesters. *Degrees:* associate, bachelor's, and master's (also offers non-traditional programs in Philadelphia and western Pennsylvania with significant enrollment not reflected in profile).

Special study options: academic remediation for entering students, accelerated degree program, adult/continuing education programs, advanced placement credit, cooperative education, double majors, English as a second language, honors programs, independent study, internships, off-campus study, part-time degree program, services for LD students, student-designed majors, study abroad, summer session for credit. ***ROTC:*** Army (c).

Unusual degree programs: 3-2 divinity with Reformed Presbyterian Theological Seminary.

Computers: 150 computers/terminals and 400 ports are available on campus for general student use. Students can access the following: campus intranet, computer help desk, free student e-mail accounts, online (class) grades, online (class) registration, online (class) schedules. Campuswide network is available. 100% of college-owned or -operated housing units are wired for high-speed Internet access. Wireless service is available via entire campus.

Library: McCartney Library plus 3 others. *Books:* 138,989 (physical), 15,997 (digital/electronic); *Serial titles:* 438 (physical), 20 (digital/electronic); *Databases:* 44. Weekly public service hours: 84.

STUDENT LIFE

Housing options: on-campus residence required through senior year; men-only, women-only. Campus housing is university owned. Freshman campus housing is guaranteed.

Activities and organizations: drama/theater group, student-run newspaper, choral group, marching band, marching band, Genevans Choir, Intramural sports, ministry groups, discipleship groups.

Athletics Member NCAA, NCCAA. All NCAA Division III. ***Intercollegiate sports:*** baseball M, basketball M/W, cross-country running M/W, football M, golf M/W, soccer M/W, softball W, tennis M/W, track and field M/W, volleyball M(c)/W. ***Intramural sports:*** basketball M/W, cheerleading W(c), football M/W, ice hockey M(c), racquetball M/W, rugby M(c)/W(c), skiing (downhill) M(c)/W(c), soccer M/W, softball M/W, table tennis M/W, ultimate Frisbee M/W, volleyball M/W.

Campus security: 24-hour emergency response devices and patrols, late-night transport/escort service, controlled dormitory access.

Student services: health clinic, personal/psychological counseling.

COSTS & FINANCIAL AID

Costs (2017–18) ***Comprehensive fee:*** $36,490 includes full-time tuition ($26,570) and room and board ($9920). Full-time tuition and fees vary according to course load. Part-time tuition: $880 per credit hour. Part-time tuition and fees vary according to course load. ***Room and board:*** Room and board charges vary according to board plan. ***Payment plan:*** installment. ***Waivers:*** employees or children of employees.

Financial Aid Of all full-time matriculated undergraduates who enrolled in 2016, 1,095 applied for aid, 977 were judged to have need, 200 had their need fully met. 170 Federal Work-Study jobs (averaging $2000). In 2016, 199 non-need-based awards were made. ***Average percent of need met:*** 79. ***Average financial aid package:*** $21,000. ***Average need-based loan:*** $3795. ***Average need-based gift aid:*** $16,926. ***Average non-need-based aid:*** $10,707. ***Average indebtedness upon graduation:*** $10,549.

APPLYING

Standardized Tests *Required:* SAT or ACT (for admission).

Options: electronic application, early admission, deferred entrance.

Application fee: $40.

Required: essay or personal statement, high school transcript, minimum 2.0 GPA. ***Required for some:*** interview, 1 unit of chemistry and physics and 4 units of college-prep mathematics (including trigonometry and pre-calculus) for engineering. ***Recommended:*** minimum 3.0 GPA, 2 letters of recommendation, interview.

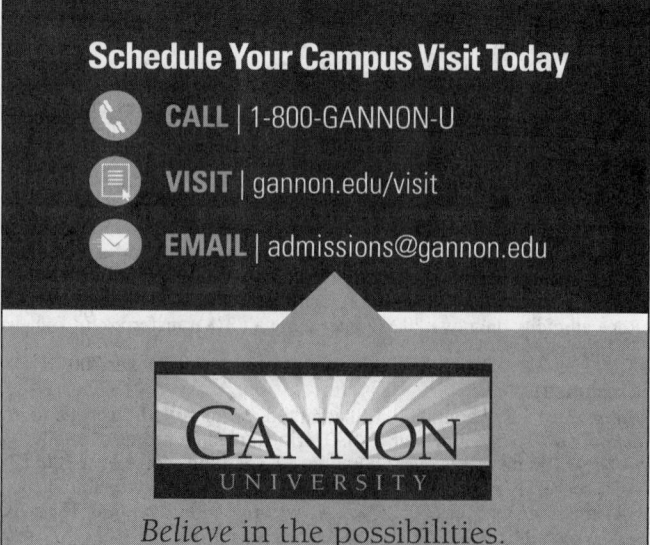

Application deadlines: rolling (freshmen), rolling (transfers).

Notification: continuous (freshmen), continuous (transfers).

CONTACT
Mr. David Layton, Associate Vice President for Enrollment, Geneva College, 3200 College Avenue, Beaver Falls, PA 15010-3599.
Phone: 724-847-6500. *Toll-free phone:* 800-847-8255.
E-mail: admissions@geneva.edu.

★ Gettysburg College
Gettysburg, Pennsylvania
http://www.gettysburg.edu/

- **Independent** 4-year, founded 1832, affiliated with Evangelical Lutheran Church in America
- **Suburban** 200-acre campus with easy access to Baltimore and Washington, DC
- **Endowment** $336.5 million
- **Coed** 2,384 undergraduate students, 99% full-time, 53% women, 47% men
- **Most difficult** entrance level, 43% of applicants were admitted

UNDERGRAD STUDENTS
2,371 full-time, 13 part-time. Students come from 39 states and territories; 39 other countries; 75% are from out of state; 3% Black or African American, non-Hispanic/Latino; 6% Hispanic/Latino; 2% Asian, non-Hispanic/Latino; 0.2% American Indian or Alaska Native, non-Hispanic/Latino; 3% Two or more races, non-Hispanic/Latino; 2% Race/ethnicity unknown; 7% international; 0.5% transferred in; 94% live on campus.

Freshmen:
Admission: 6,816 applied, 2,906 admitted, 698 enrolled. ***Test scores:*** SAT critical reading scores over 500: 100%; SAT math scores over 500: 100%; SAT critical reading scores over 600: 76%; SAT math scores over 600: 79%; SAT critical reading scores over 700: 18%; SAT math scores over 700: 17%.

Retention: 90% of full-time freshmen returned.

FACULTY
Total: 305, 73% full-time, 83% with terminal degrees.

Student/faculty ratio: 9:1.

ACADEMICS
Calendar: semesters. *Degree:* bachelor's.

Special study options: adult/continuing education programs, advanced placement credit, double majors, independent study, internships, off-campus study, student-designed majors, study abroad. ***ROTC:*** Army (c).

Unusual degree programs: 3-2 engineering with Rensselaer Polytechnic Institute, Washington University, Columbia University, University of Pittsburgh; forestry with Duke University; nursing with Johns Hopkins University; optometry with Pennsylvania College of Optometry.

Computers: 295 computers/terminals are available on campus for general student use. Students can access the following: campus intranet, computer help desk, free student e-mail accounts, online (class) grades, online (class) registration, online (class) schedules. Campuswide network is available. 100% of college-owned or -operated housing units are wired for high-speed Internet access. Wireless service is available via entire campus.
Library: Musselman Library. *Books:* 412,379 (physical), 307,926 (digital/electronic). Study areas open 24 hours, 5-7 days a week.

STUDENT LIFE
Housing options: on-campus residence required through senior year; coed, men-only, women-only. Campus housing is university owned. Freshman campus housing is guaranteed.

Activities and organizations: drama/theater group, student-run newspaper, radio and television station, choral group, marching band, community service, music, athletics, student government, national fraternities, national sororities.

Athletics Member NCAA. All Division III. ***Intercollegiate sports:*** baseball M, basketball M/W, cheerleading M/W, cross-country running M/W, equestrian sports M(c)/W(c), field hockey W, football M, golf M/W, ice hockey M(c), lacrosse M/W, rugby M(c)/W(c), soccer M/W, softball W, swimming and diving M/W, tennis M/W, track and field M/W, ultimate Frisbee M(c)/W(c), volleyball W, wrestling M. ***Intramural sports:*** basketball M/W, fencing M(c)/W(c), football M/W, soccer M/W, softball M/W, volleyball M/W, water polo M/W.

Campus security: 24-hour emergency response devices and patrols, late-night transport/escort service, controlled dormitory access.

Student services: health clinic, personal/psychological counseling, women's center.

COSTS & FINANCIAL AID
Costs (2016–17) ***Comprehensive fee:*** $63,000 includes full-time tuition ($50,860) and room and board ($12,140). ***College room only:*** $6510. Room and board charges vary according to board plan and housing facility. ***Payment plan:*** installment.

Financial Aid Of all full-time matriculated undergraduates who enrolled in 2016, 1,627 applied for aid, 1,448 were judged to have need, 1,275 had their need fully met. 366 Federal Work-Study jobs (averaging $903). 1,223 state and other part-time jobs (averaging $1084). In 2016, 420 non-need-based awards were made. ***Average percent of need met:*** 90. ***Average financial aid package:*** $41,554. ***Average need-based loan:*** $6599. ***Average need-based gift aid:*** $34,208. ***Average non-need-based aid:*** $12,279. ***Average indebtedness upon graduation:*** $31,169. ***Financial aid deadline:*** 2/1.

APPLYING
Standardized Tests *Required for some:* SAT or ACT (for admission).

Options: electronic application, early admission, early decision, deferred entrance.

Application fee: $60.

Required: essay or personal statement, high school transcript, 2 letters of recommendation. ***Recommended:*** minimum 3.0 GPA, interview, extracurricular activities.

Application deadlines: 1/15 (freshmen), 11/1 (transfers).

Early decision deadline: 11/15 (for plan 1), 1/15 (for plan 2).

Notification: 4/1 (freshmen), continuous (transfers), 12/15 (early decision plan 1), 2/15 (early decision plan 2).

CONTACT
Ms. Gail Sweezey, Director of Admissions, Gettysburg College, 300 North Washington Street, Gettysburg, PA 17325. *Phone:* 717-337-6100. *Toll-free phone:* 800-431-0803. *Fax:* 717-337-6145.
E-mail: admiss@gettysburg.edu.

★ Grove City College
Grove City, Pennsylvania
http://www.gcc.edu/

- **Independent Presbyterian** 4-year, founded 1876
- **Small-town** 180-acre campus with easy access to Pittsburgh
- **Endowment** $103.5 million
- **Coed** 2,392 undergraduate students, 98% full-time, 50% women, 50% men
- **Moderately difficult** entrance level, 82% of applicants were admitted

UNDERGRAD STUDENTS
2,334 full-time, 58 part-time. Students come from 45 states and territories; 13 other countries; 46% are from out of state; 0.4% Black or African American, non-Hispanic/Latino; 1% Hispanic/Latino; 2% Asian, non-Hispanic/Latino; 3% Two or more races, non-Hispanic/Latino; 1% international; 1% transferred in; 96% live on campus.

Freshmen:
Admission: 1,517 applied, 1,251 admitted, 583 enrolled. ***Average high school GPA:*** 3.68. ***Test scores:*** SAT critical reading scores over 500: 89%; SAT math scores over 500: 88%; ACT scores over 18: 99%; SAT critical reading scores over 600: 47%; SAT math scores over 600: 48%; ACT scores over 24: 73%; SAT critical reading scores over 700: 13%; SAT math scores over 700: 10%; ACT scores over 30: 22%.

Retention: 94% of full-time freshmen returned.

FACULTY
Total: 235, 65% full-time, 62% with terminal degrees.

Student/faculty ratio: 13:1.

ACADEMICS
Calendar: semesters. *Degree:* bachelor's.

Special study options: accelerated degree program, advanced placement credit, distance learning, double majors, independent study, internships, off-campus study, services for LD students, study abroad, summer session for credit.

Computers: 50 computers/terminals and 8,000 ports are available on campus for general student use. Students can access the following: campus intranet, computer help desk, free student e-mail accounts, online (class) grades, online (class) registration, online (class) schedules. Campuswide network is available. 100% of college-owned or -operated housing units are wired for high-speed Internet access. Wireless service is available via entire campus.

Library: Henry Buhl Library plus 1 other. *Books:* 148,000 (physical), 150,300 (digital/electronic); *Serial titles:* 44 (physical), 125,000 (digital/electronic); *Databases:* 123. Weekly public service hours: 103.

STUDENT LIFE

Housing options: on-campus residence required through senior year; men-only, women-only. Campus housing is university owned. Freshman campus housing is guaranteed.

Activities and organizations: drama/theater group, student-run newspaper, radio and television station, choral group, marching band, Warriors for Christ, Orchesis, Orientation Board, Accounting Society, Association for Women Students (AWS).

Athletics Member NCAA. All Division III. ***Intercollegiate sports:*** baseball M, basketball M/W, cross-country running M/W, fencing M(c)/W(c), football M, golf M/W, lacrosse M(c)/W(c), rugby M(c)/W(c), soccer M/W, softball W, swimming and diving M/W, tennis M/W, track and field M/W, volleyball M(c)/W, water polo M(c)/W. ***Intramural sports:*** badminton M/W, basketball M/W, bowling M/W, football M/W, racquetball M/W, soccer M/W, softball M, table tennis M/W, tennis M/W, ultimate Frisbee M/W, volleyball M/W.

Campus security: 24-hour emergency response devices and patrols, student patrols, late-night transport/escort service, controlled dormitory access, security cameras located around campus and in parking lots.

Student services: health clinic, personal/psychological counseling.

COSTS & FINANCIAL AID

Costs (2016–17) ***Comprehensive fee:*** $25,692 includes full-time tuition ($16,630) and room and board ($9062). Part-time tuition: $540 per credit hour. ***Room and board:*** Room and board charges vary according to housing facility. ***Waivers:*** employees or children of employees.

Financial Aid Of all full-time matriculated undergraduates who enrolled in 2016, 1,292 applied for aid, 1,053 were judged to have need, 90 had their need fully met. In 2016, 404 non-need-based awards were made. ***Average percent of need met:*** 51. ***Average financial aid package:*** $7206. ***Average need-based gift aid:*** $7206. ***Average non-need-based aid:*** $2247. ***Average indebtedness upon graduation:*** $37,655. ***Financial aid deadline:*** 4/15.

APPLYING

Standardized Tests *Required:* SAT or ACT (for admission).

Options: electronic application, early admission, early decision, deferred entrance.

Application fee: $50.

Required: essay or personal statement, high school transcript, 2 letters of recommendation. ***Recommended:*** interview.

Application deadlines: 2/1 (freshmen), 8/15 (transfers).

Early decision deadline: 11/15.

Notification: 3/1 (freshmen), continuous (transfers), 12/15 (early decision).

CONTACT

Sarah E. Gibbs, Director of Admissions, Grove City College, 100 Campus Drive, Grove City, PA 16127-2104. *Phone:* 724-458-2100. *Fax:* 724-458-3395. *E-mail:* admissions@gcc.edu.

See below for display ad and page 1368 for the College Close-Up.

Gwynedd Mercy University
Gwynedd Valley, Pennsylvania
http://www.gmercyu.edu/

- **Independent Roman Catholic** comprehensive, founded 1948
- **Suburban** 170-acre campus with easy access to Philadelphia
- **Endowment** $23.3 million
- **Coed** 2,035 undergraduate students, 93% full-time, 76% women, 24% men
- **Moderately difficult** entrance level, 91% of applicants were admitted

UNDERGRAD STUDENTS
1,886 full-time, 149 part-time. Students come from 15 states and territories; 34 other countries; 13% are from out of state; 20% Black or African American, non-Hispanic/Latino; 4% Hispanic/Latino; 5% Asian, non-Hispanic/Latino; 0.2% American Indian or Alaska Native, non-Hispanic/Latino; 21% Race/ethnicity unknown; 0.2% international; 13% transferred in; 19% live on campus.

Freshmen:
Admission: 904 applied, 821 admitted, 225 enrolled. ***Average high school GPA:*** 3.22. ***Test scores:*** SAT critical reading scores over 500: 33%; SAT math scores over 500: 37%; SAT writing scores over 500: 31%; ACT scores over 18: 66%; SAT critical reading scores over 600: 2%; SAT math scores over 600: 7%; SAT writing scores over 600: 2%; ACT scores over 24: 17%.
Retention: 84% of full-time freshmen returned.

FACULTY
Total: 262, 31% full-time, 27% with terminal degrees.
Student/faculty ratio: 11:1.

ACADEMICS
Calendar: semesters. *Degrees:* bachelor's, master's, doctoral, and post-master's certificates.
Special study options: academic remediation for entering students, accelerated degree program, adult/continuing education programs, advanced placement credit, cooperative education, distance learning, double majors, external degree program, honors programs, independent study, internships, part-time degree program, services for LD students, study abroad, summer session for credit.
Computers: 250 computers/terminals and 1,000 ports are available on campus for general student use. Students can access the following: campus intranet, computer help desk, free student e-mail accounts, online (class) grades, online (class) registration, online (class) schedules. Campuswide network is available. 100% of college-owned or -operated housing units are wired for high-speed Internet access. Wireless service is available via entire campus.
Library: Keiss Library plus 1 other. *Books:* 84,372 (physical), 150,948 (digital/electronic); *Serial titles:* 172 (physical), 32,373 (digital/electronic); *Databases:* 45. Weekly public service hours: 76; students can reserve study rooms.

STUDENT LIFE
Housing options: coed, special housing for students with disabilities. Campus housing is university owned. Freshman applicants given priority for college housing.
Activities and organizations: student-run newspaper, choral group, Voices of Gwynedd, Athletic Association, Student Government, Program Board, Peer Mentors.
Athletics Member NCAA. All Division III. ***Intercollegiate sports:*** baseball M, basketball M/W, cheerleading W(c), cross-country running M/W, field hockey W, golf M, lacrosse W, soccer M/W, softball W, tennis M/W, track and field M/W, ultimate Frisbee M(c)/W(c), volleyball W. ***Intramural sports:*** baseball M/W, basketball M/W, cross-country running M/W, field hockey W, golf M, lacrosse M/W, soccer M/W, softball W, tennis M/W, track and field M/W, volleyball W.
Campus security: 24-hour emergency response devices and patrols, late-night transport/escort service, controlled dormitory access.
Student services: health clinic, personal/psychological counseling.

COSTS & FINANCIAL AID
Costs (2017–18) ***Comprehensive fee:*** $45,150 includes full-time tuition ($32,820), mandatory fees ($700), and room and board ($11,630). Full-time tuition and fees vary according to location and program. Part-time tuition: $725 per credit hour. Part-time tuition and fees vary according to location and program. ***College room only:*** $5360. Room and board

charges vary according to board plan and housing facility. ***Payment plan:*** installment. ***Waivers:*** employees or children of employees.

Financial Aid Of all full-time matriculated undergraduates who enrolled in 2016, 1,504 applied for aid, 1,377 were judged to have need, 168 had their need fully met. In 2016, 155 non-need-based awards were made. ***Average percent of need met:*** 60. ***Average financial aid package:*** $20,302. ***Average need-based loan:*** $4134. ***Average need-based gift aid:*** $18,273. ***Average non-need-based aid:*** $12,507. ***Average indebtedness upon graduation:*** $43,789. ***Financial aid deadline:*** 5/1.

APPLYING

Standardized Tests *Required:* SAT or ACT (for admission).

Options: electronic application, deferred entrance.

Required: high school transcript. ***Required for some:*** essay or personal statement, interview. ***Recommended:*** letters of recommendation.

Application deadlines: rolling (freshmen), 8/20 (transfers).

Notification: continuous (freshmen), continuous (transfers).

CONTACT

Ms. Michelle Diehl, Director of Admissions, Gwynedd Mercy University, 1325 Sumneytown Pike, Gwynedd Valley, PA 19437-0901. *Phone:* 215-646-7300. *Toll-free phone:* 800-342-5462. *Fax:* 215-641-5556. *E-mail:* admissions@gmercyu.edu.

See previous page for display ad and page 1370 for the College Close-Up.

Harrisburg University of Science and Technology

Harrisburg, Pennsylvania

http://www.HarrisburgU.edu/

- **Independent** comprehensive, founded 2005
- **Urban** campus
- **Coed** 387 undergraduate students, 83% full-time, 47% women, 53% men
- **Minimally difficult** entrance level

UNDERGRAD STUDENTS

323 full-time, 64 part-time. Students come from 6 states and territories; 3 other countries; 11% are from out of state; 42% Black or African American, non-Hispanic/Latino; 10% Hispanic/Latino; 4% Asian, non-Hispanic/Latino; 0.3% Native Hawaiian or other Pacific Islander, non-Hispanic/Latino; 0.5% American Indian or Alaska Native, non-Hispanic/Latino; 5% Two or more races, non-Hispanic/Latino; 0.5% Race/ethnicity unknown; 1% international; 2% transferred in.

Freshmen:

Admission: 153 enrolled. ***Average high school GPA:*** 2.79.

Retention: 48% of full-time freshmen returned.

FACULTY

Total: 130, 19% full-time, 15% with terminal degrees.

Student/faculty ratio: 28:1.

ACADEMICS

Calendar: semesters. *Degrees:* bachelor's and master's.

Special study options: academic remediation for entering students, adult/continuing education programs, advanced placement credit, double majors, independent study, internships, part-time degree program, services for LD students, student-designed majors, summer session for credit.

Computers: 10 computers/terminals and 240 ports are available on campus for general student use. Students can access the following: campus intranet, computer help desk, free student e-mail accounts. Campuswide network is available. Wireless service is available via entire campus.

Library: Information Commons. *Books:* 4,130 (physical), 26 (digital/electronic); *Serial titles:* 103 (physical), 126 (digital/electronic); *Databases:* 24. Study areas open 24 hours, 5-7 days a week.

STUDENT LIFE

Housing options: college housing not available.

Campus security: 24-hour emergency response devices and patrols, trained security personnel during hours of operation.

Student services: personal/psychological counseling.

COSTS & FINANCIAL AID

Costs (2017–18) ***Tuition:*** $1000 per semester hour part-time. Full-time tuition and fees vary according to class time, course level, course load, degree level, location, program, reciprocity agreements, and student level. Part-time tuition and fees vary according to class time, course level, course load, degree level, location, program, reciprocity agreements, and student level. ***Room only:*** Room and board charges vary according to housing facility. ***Payment plans:*** installment, deferred payment.

Financial Aid Of all full-time matriculated undergraduates who enrolled in 2016, 335 applied for aid, 320 were judged to have need, 56 had their need fully met. 15 Federal Work-Study jobs (averaging $2000). In 2016, 22 non-need-based awards were made. ***Average percent of need met:*** 65. ***Average financial aid package:*** $19,814. ***Average need-based loan:*** $3923. ***Average need-based gift aid:*** $16,857. ***Average non-need-based aid:*** $15,789. ***Average indebtedness upon graduation:*** $34,547.

APPLYING

Options: electronic application.

Required: high school transcript. ***Recommended:*** essay or personal statement, interview.

Notification: continuous (freshmen).

CONTACT

Harrisburg University of Science and Technology, 326 Market Street, Harrisburg, PA 17101. *Phone:* 717-901-5150. *Toll-free phone:* 866-HBG-UNIV.

Haverford College

Haverford, Pennsylvania

http://www.haverford.edu/

- **Independent** 4-year, founded 1833
- **Suburban** 216-acre campus with easy access to Philadelphia
- **Endowment** $464.6 million
- **Coed** 1,268 undergraduate students, 100% full-time, 52% women, 48% men
- **Most difficult** entrance level, 21% of applicants were admitted

UNDERGRAD STUDENTS

1,268 full-time. Students come from 45 states and territories; 37 other countries; 88% are from out of state; 7% Black or African American, non-Hispanic/Latino; 8% Hispanic/Latino; 10% Asian, non-Hispanic/Latino; 0.2% American Indian or Alaska Native, non-Hispanic/Latino; 4% Two or more races, non-Hispanic/Latino; 3% Race/ethnicity unknown; 9% international; 0.7% transferred in; 99% live on campus.

Freshmen:

Admission: 4,066 applied, 870 admitted, 349 enrolled. ***Test scores:*** SAT critical reading scores over 500: 100%; SAT math scores over 500: 100%; SAT writing scores over 500: 100%; SAT critical reading scores over 600: 93%; SAT math scores over 600: 93%; SAT writing scores over 600: 97%; ACT scores over 24: 100%; SAT critical reading scores over 700: 59%; SAT math scores over 700: 61%; SAT writing scores over 700: 59%; ACT scores over 30: 88%.

Retention: 97% of full-time freshmen returned.

FACULTY

Total: 158, 84% full-time, 96% with terminal degrees.

Student/faculty ratio: 9:1.

ACADEMICS

Calendar: semesters. *Degree:* bachelor's.

Special study options: advanced placement credit, double majors, independent study, internships, off-campus study, services for LD students, student-designed majors, study abroad.

Unusual degree programs: 3-2 engineering with California Institute of Technology; city planning with University of Pennsylvania.

Computers: 300 computers/terminals and 1,600 ports are available on campus for general student use. Students can access the following: campus intranet, computer help desk, free student e-mail accounts, online (class) grades, online (class) registration, online (class) schedules. Campuswide network is available. 100% of college-owned or -operated housing units are wired for high-speed Internet access. Wireless service is available via entire campus.

Library: James P. Magill Library plus 3 others. *Books:* 475,604 (physical), 702,593 (digital/electronic); *Serial titles:* 18,525 (physical), 135,312 (digital/electronic); *Databases:* 91. Study areas open 24 hours, 5-7 days a week; students can reserve study rooms.

STUDENT LIFE

Housing options: on-campus residence required for freshman year; coed, special housing for students with disabilities. Campus housing is university owned. Freshman campus housing is guaranteed.

Activities and organizations: drama/theater group, student-run newspaper, radio station, choral group, Volunteer Programs, Student government, Choral groups, Multicultural Groups, Orientation Team/Residential Life Leaders.

Athletics Member NCAA. All Division III. ***Intercollegiate sports:*** badminton W(c), baseball M, basketball M/W, crew M(c)/W(c), cross-country running M/W, fencing M/W, field hockey W, golf M(c)/W(c), lacrosse M/W, rugby M(c), soccer M/W, softball W, squash M/W, tennis M/W, track and field M/W, ultimate Frisbee M(c)/W(c), volleyball M(c)/W, wrestling M(c). ***Intramural sports:*** basketball M/W, ice hockey M(c)/W(c), sailing M(c)/W(c), soccer M/W, softball M/W, tennis M/W, volleyball W.

Campus security: 24-hour emergency response devices and patrols, late-night transport/escort service, controlled dormitory access.

Student services: health clinic, personal/psychological counseling, women's center.

COSTS & FINANCIAL AID

Costs (2016–17) ***One-time required fee:*** $235. ***Comprehensive fee:*** $66,490 includes full-time tuition ($50,564), mandatory fees ($460), and room and board ($15,466). ***College room only:*** $8826. ***Payment plans:*** tuition prepayment, installment. ***Waivers:*** employees or children of employees.

Financial Aid Of all full-time matriculated undergraduates who enrolled in 2015, 644 applied for aid, 628 were judged to have need, 628 had their need fully met. ***Average percent of need met:*** 100. ***Average financial aid package:*** $46,600. ***Average need-based loan:*** $930. ***Average need-based gift aid:*** $45,390. ***Average indebtedness upon graduation:*** $14,750.

APPLYING

Standardized Tests *Required:* SAT or ACT (for admission).

Options: electronic application, early admission, early decision, deferred entrance.

Application fee: $65.

Required: essay or personal statement. ***Required for some:*** high school transcript. ***Recommended:*** interview.

Application deadlines: 1/15 (freshmen), 3/31 (transfers).

Early decision deadline: 11/15.

Notification: 4/1 (freshmen), 5/15 (transfers), 12/15 (early decision).

CONTACT

Mr. Jess Lord, Dean of Admissions and Financial Aid, Haverford College, 370 Lancaster Avenue, Haverford, PA 19041-1392. *Phone:* 610-896-1350. *Fax:* 610-896-1338. *E-mail:* admission@haverford.edu.

Holy Family University

Philadelphia, Pennsylvania

http://www.holyfamily.edu/

- **Independent Roman Catholic** comprehensive, founded 1954
- **Suburban** 47-acre campus with easy access to Philadelphia
- **Endowment** $16.7 million
- **Coed** 1,950 undergraduate students, 73% full-time, 74% women, 26% men
- **Minimally difficult** entrance level, 68% of applicants were admitted

UNDERGRAD STUDENTS

1,424 full-time, 526 part-time. Students come from 20 states and territories; 7 other countries; 14% are from out of state; 11% Black or African American, non-Hispanic/Latino; 5% Hispanic/Latino; 5% Asian, non-Hispanic/Latino; 0.1% Native Hawaiian or other Pacific Islander, non-Hispanic/Latino; 0.2% American Indian or Alaska Native, non-Hispanic/Latino; 22% Race/ethnicity unknown; 0.4% international; 7% transferred in; 17% live on campus.

Freshmen:

Admission: 1,441 applied, 987 admitted, 328 enrolled. ***Average high school GPA:*** 3.13. ***Test scores:*** SAT critical reading scores over 500: 32%; SAT writing scores over 500: 28%; SAT critical reading scores over 600: 4%; SAT writing scores over 600: 4%.

Retention: 76% of full-time freshmen returned.

FACULTY

Total: 329, 23% full-time, 33% with terminal degrees.

Student/faculty ratio: 13:1.

ACADEMICS

Calendar: semesters. *Degrees:* certificates, associate, bachelor's, master's, doctoral, post-master's, and postbachelor's certificates.

Special study options: academic remediation for entering students, accelerated degree program, adult/continuing education programs, advanced placement credit, cooperative education, double majors, honors programs, independent study, internships, off-campus study, part-time degree program, services for LD students, study abroad, summer session for credit. ***ROTC:*** Army (c).

Unusual degree programs: 3-2 criminal justice; psychology, sociology/criminal justice; business administration/human resources management, information systems management.

Computers: 300 computers/terminals and 388 ports are available on campus for general student use. Students can access the following: campus intranet, computer help desk, free student e-mail accounts, online (class) grades, online (class) registration, online (class) schedules, online course syllabi, online course evaluations. Campuswide network is available. 100% of college-owned or -operated housing units are wired for high-speed Internet access. Wireless service is available via entire campus.

Library: Holy Family University Library plus 1 other. *Books:* 124,616 (physical), 18,080 (digital/electronic); *Databases:* 50. Weekly public service hours: 113; students can reserve study rooms.

STUDENT LIFE

Housing options: coed, special housing for students with disabilities. Campus housing is university owned. Freshman campus housing is guaranteed.

Activities and organizations: drama/theater group, student-run newspaper, choral group, Students at Your Service (S.A.Y.S.), Green Team, Campus Ministry Team, Habitat for Humanity, Student Nurses Association of Holy Family.

Athletics Member NCAA. All Division II. ***Intercollegiate sports:*** basketball M(s)/W(s), cross-country running M(s)/W(s), lacrosse W(s), soccer M(s)/W(s), softball W(s), tennis W(s), track and field M(s)/W(s), volleyball W(s). ***Intramural sports:*** baseball M(c), basketball M/W, cheerleading M(c)/W(c), rugby M(c), volleyball M/W.

Campus security: 24-hour emergency response devices and patrols, late-night transport/escort service, controlled dormitory access, video surveillance.

Student services: health clinic, personal/psychological counseling.

COSTS & FINANCIAL AID

Costs (2017–18) ***Comprehensive fee:*** $42,914 includes full-time tuition ($28,350), mandatory fees ($988), and room and board ($13,576). Full-time tuition and fees vary according to class time, course level, course load, degree level, program, and reciprocity agreements. Part-time tuition: $615 per credit hour. Part-time tuition and fees vary according to class time, course level, course load, degree level, program, and reciprocity agreements. ***Required fees:*** $110 per term part-time. ***College room only:*** $7140. Room and board charges vary according to board plan and housing facility. ***Payment plans:*** installment, deferred payment. ***Waivers:*** senior citizens and employees or children of employees.

Financial Aid Of all full-time matriculated undergraduates who enrolled in 2016, 1,308 applied for aid, 1,222 were judged to have need, 204 had their need fully met. 414 Federal Work-Study jobs (averaging $1143). In 2016, 151 non-need-based awards were made. ***Average percent of need met:*** 77. ***Average financial aid package:*** $22,642. ***Average need-based loan:*** $4440. ***Average need-based gift aid:*** $14,458. ***Average non-need-based aid:*** $13,021. ***Average indebtedness upon graduation:*** $39,664.

APPLYING

Standardized Tests *Required:* SAT or ACT (for admission).

Options: electronic application, deferred entrance.

Application fee: $25.

Required: essay or personal statement, high school transcript, minimum 2.0 GPA, 2 letters of recommendation. ***Recommended:*** interview.

Application deadlines: rolling (freshmen), rolling (transfers).

Notification: continuous (freshmen), continuous (transfers).

CONTACT

Ms. Lauren Campbell, Director of Admissions, Holy Family University, 9801 Frankford Avenue, Philadelphia, PA 19114-2009. *Phone:* 215-637-3050. *Fax:* 215-281-1022. *E-mail:* admissions@holyfamily.edu.

Hussian College, School of Art

Philadelphia, Pennsylvania

http://www.hussiancollege.edu/

- **Proprietary** primarily 2-year, founded 1946
- **Urban** 1-acre campus with easy access to Philadelphia
- **Coed**
- **Minimally difficult** entrance level

ACADEMICS

Calendar: semesters. *Degree:* bachelor's.

Library: Hussian Library. *Books:* 4,000 (physical); *Serial titles:* 15 (physical); *Databases:* 100.

STUDENT LIFE

Housing options: Campus housing is provided by a third party.

Campus security: 24-hour patrols.

COSTS

Costs (2016–17) ***One-time required fee:*** $100. ***Tuition:*** $18,600 full-time. Full-time tuition and fees vary according to course load. Part-time tuition and fees vary according to course load. ***Required fees:*** $2000 full-time.

APPLYING

Options: electronic application, deferred entrance.

Required: high school transcript, interview, portfolio evaluation, creative assessment activity or portfolio development drawing workshop. ***Recommended:*** minimum 2.5 GPA.

CONTACT

Mr. Mark Cernero, Director of Admissions, Hussian College, School of Art, The Bourse, Suite 300, 111 South Independence Mall East, Philadelphia, PA 19106. *Phone:* 215-574-9600. *Fax:* 215-574-9800. *E-mail:* mcernero@hussianart.edu.

Immaculata University

Immaculata, Pennsylvania

http://www.immaculata.edu/

- **Independent Roman Catholic** university, founded 1920
- **Suburban** 375-acre campus with easy access to Philadelphia
- **Endowment** $16.9 million
- **Coed** 1,555 undergraduate students, 61% full-time, 75% women, 25% men
- **Moderately difficult** entrance level, 82% of applicants were admitted

UNDERGRAD STUDENTS

943 full-time, 612 part-time. Students come from 16 states and territories; 2 other countries; 28% are from out of state; 14% Black or African American, non-Hispanic/Latino; 6% Hispanic/Latino; 2% Asian, non-Hispanic/Latino; 0.1% Native Hawaiian or other Pacific Islander, non-Hispanic/Latino; 0.1% American Indian or Alaska Native, non-Hispanic/Latino; 2% Two or more races, non-Hispanic/Latino; 4% Race/ethnicity unknown; 0.9% international; 3% transferred in; 33% live on campus.

Freshmen:

Admission: 1,582 applied, 1,304 admitted, 219 enrolled. ***Average high school GPA:*** 3.27. ***Test scores:*** SAT critical reading scores over 500: 45%; SAT math scores over 500: 47%; SAT writing scores over 500: 45%; ACT scores over 18: 82%; SAT critical reading scores over 600: 10%; SAT math scores over 600: 11%; SAT writing scores over 600: 14%; ACT scores over 24: 24%; SAT critical reading scores over 700: 1%; SAT math scores over 700: 2%; SAT writing scores over 700: 2%.

Retention: 80% of full-time freshmen returned.

FACULTY

Total: 344, 27% full-time, 47% with terminal degrees.

Student/faculty ratio: 8:1.

ACADEMICS

Calendar: semesters. *Degrees:* certificates, associate, bachelor's, master's, and doctoral.

Special study options: academic remediation for entering students, accelerated degree program, adult/continuing education programs, advanced placement credit, distance learning, double majors, honors programs, independent study, internships, off-campus study, part-time degree program, services for LD students, study abroad, summer session for credit. ***ROTC:*** Army (c).

Unusual degree programs: 3-2 business administration with DeSales University; occupational therapy with Thomas Jefferson University.

Computers: 600 computers/terminals are available on campus for general student use. Students can access the following: campus intranet, computer help desk, free student e-mail accounts, online (class) grades, online (class) registration, online (class) schedules. Campuswide network is available. Wireless service is available via entire campus.

Library: Gabriele Library. *Books:* 117,104 (physical), 10,441 (digital/electronic); *Databases:* 53. Students can reserve study rooms.

STUDENT LIFE

Housing options: coed, men-only, women-only, special housing for students with disabilities. Campus housing is university owned. Freshman campus housing is guaranteed.

Activities and organizations: drama/theater group, student-run newspaper, choral group, National Society of Leadership and Success, Student Dietetic Association, Immaculata University Chorale, College of Undergraduate Studies Honor Society, Immaculata University Pre-Med.

Athletics Member NCAA. All Division III. ***Intercollegiate sports:*** baseball M, basketball M/W, cross-country running M/W, field hockey W, golf M/W, lacrosse M/W, soccer M/W, softball W, tennis M/W, track and field M/W, volleyball W. ***Intramural sports:*** basketball M/W, cheerleading W(c), soccer M/W, softball M/W, volleyball M/W.

Campus security: 24-hour emergency response devices and patrols, late-night transport/escort service, controlled dormitory access.

Student services: health clinic, personal/psychological counseling.

COSTS

Costs (2017–18) ***Comprehensive fee:*** $39,970 includes full-time tuition ($26,500), mandatory fees ($850), and room and board ($12,620). Full-time tuition and fees vary according to course load. Part-time tuition: $540 per credit hour. Part-time tuition and fees vary according to course load. ***College room only:*** $6390. Room and board charges vary according to board plan and housing facility. ***Payment plan:*** installment. ***Waivers:*** senior citizens and employees or children of employees.

APPLYING

Standardized Tests *Required for some:* SAT or ACT (for admission).

Options: electronic application, deferred entrance.

Application fee: $35.

Required: essay or personal statement, high school transcript, minimum 2.0 GPA, 1 letter of recommendation. ***Required for some:*** 2 letters of recommendation, audition for music students. ***Recommended:*** minimum 3.0 GPA, interview.

Application deadlines: rolling (freshmen), rolling (transfers).

Notification: continuous (freshmen), continuous (transfers).

CONTACT

Nicola DiFronzo-Heitzer, Director of Admissions, Immaculata University, PO Box 642, Immaculata, PA 19345-0702. *Phone:* 610-647-4400 Ext. 3046. *Toll-free phone:* 877-428-6329. *Fax:* 610-640-0836. *E-mail:* admiss@immaculata.edu.

Indiana University of Pennsylvania

Indiana, Pennsylvania

http://www.iup.edu/

- **State-supported** university, founded 1875, part of Pennsylvania State System of Higher Education
- **Small-town** 374-acre campus with easy access to Pittsburgh
- **Endowment** $60.9 million
- **Coed** 10,618 undergraduate students, 92% full-time, 56% women, 44% men
- **Minimally difficult** entrance level, 92% of applicants were admitted

UNDERGRAD STUDENTS

9,819 full-time, 799 part-time. Students come from 29 states and territories; 36 other countries; 5% are from out of state; 12% Black or African American, non-Hispanic/Latino; 4% Hispanic/Latino; 1% Asian, non-Hispanic/Latino; 0.1% American Indian or Alaska Native, non-Hispanic/Latino; 4% Two or more races, non-Hispanic/Latino; 1% Race/ethnicity unknown; 4% international; 5% transferred in; 32% live on campus.

Freshmen:

Admission: 8,943 applied, 8,186 admitted, 2,203 enrolled. ***Test scores:*** SAT critical reading scores over 500: 40%; SAT math scores over 500: 39%; SAT writing scores over 500: 30%; SAT critical reading scores over 600: 8%; SAT math scores over 600: 6%; SAT writing scores over 600: 5%; SAT critical reading scores over 700: 1%.

Retention: 75% of full-time freshmen returned.

FACULTY

Total: 681, 85% full-time.

Student/faculty ratio: 16:1.

ACADEMICS

Calendar: semesters. *Degrees:* certificates, associate, bachelor's, master's, doctoral, post-master's, and postbachelor's certificates.

Special study options: academic remediation for entering students, accelerated degree program, adult/continuing education programs, advanced placement credit, cooperative education, distance learning, double majors, English as a second language, external degree program, freshman honors college, honors programs, independent study, internships, off-campus study, part-time degree program, services for LD students, student-designed majors, study abroad, summer session for credit. ***ROTC:*** Army (b).

Unusual degree programs: 3-2 engineering with Drexel University, University of Pittsburgh; chiropractic with Logan College of Chiropractic, New York Chiropractic College, Parker College, Sherman College of Straight Chiropractic; dentistry with Temple University School of Dentistry; optometry with Pennsylvania College of Optometry.

Computers: 2,363 computers/terminals and 5,000 ports are available on campus for general student use. Students can access the following: computer help desk, free student e-mail accounts, online (class) grades, online (class) registration, online (class) schedules. Campuswide network is available. 100% of college-owned or -operated housing units are wired for high-speed Internet access. Wireless service is available via entire campus.

Library: Stapleton Library. *Books:* 547,640 (physical), 277,326 (digital/electronic); *Serial titles:* 125,517 (physical). Weekly public service hours: 134; study areas open 24 hours, 5-7 days a week; students can reserve study rooms.

STUDENT LIFE

Housing options: on-campus residence required for freshman year; coed, women-only, special housing for students with disabilities. Campus housing is university owned and is provided by a third party. Freshman campus housing is guaranteed.

Activities and organizations: drama/theater group, student-run newspaper, radio and television station, choral group, marching band, Student Government Association, Panhellenic Association, Interfraternity Council, Student Association of Nutrition and Dietetics, NAACP, national fraternities, national sororities.

Athletics Member NCAA. All Division II. ***Intercollegiate sports:*** baseball M(s), basketball M(s)/W(s), cross-country running M(s)/W(s), field hockey W(s), football M(s), golf M(s), lacrosse W(s), soccer W(s), softball W(s), swimming and diving M(s)/W(s), tennis W(s), track and field M(s)/W(s), volleyball W(s). ***Intramural sports:*** baseball M(c), basketball M/W, cheerleading M/W, equestrian sports M(c)/W(c), fencing M(c)/W(c), golf M(c)/W(c), ice hockey M(c)/W(c), lacrosse M(c)/W(c), riflery M(c)/W(c), rugby M(c)/W(c), sailing M(c)/W(c), soccer M(c)/W(c), swimming and diving M(c)/W(c), tennis M(c)/W(c), ultimate Frisbee M(c)/W(c), volleyball M/W.

Campus security: 24-hour emergency response devices and patrols, late-night transport/escort service, controlled dormitory access.

Student services: health clinic, personal/psychological counseling, legal services.

COSTS & FINANCIAL AID

Costs (2016–17) ***Tuition:*** state resident $8430 full-time, $281 per credit hour part-time; nonresident $18,096 full-time, $754 per credit hour part-time. Full-time tuition and fees vary according to course load and reciprocity agreements. Part-time tuition and fees vary according to course load and reciprocity agreements. ***Required fees:*** $2938 full-time, $109 per credit hour part-time, $50 per term part-time. ***Room and board:*** $12,402; room only: $8950. Room and board charges vary according to board plan, housing facility, and location. ***Payment plans:*** installment, deferred payment. ***Waivers:*** senior citizens and employees or children of employees.

Financial Aid Of all full-time matriculated undergraduates who enrolled in 2015, 9,198 applied for aid, 7,583 were judged to have need, 637 had their need fully met. 881 Federal Work-Study jobs (averaging $1881). 1,534 state and other part-time jobs (averaging $2763). In 2015, 347 non-need-based awards were made. ***Average percent of need met:*** 58. ***Average financial aid package:*** $9845. ***Average need-based loan:*** $4196. ***Average need-based gift aid:*** $6004. ***Average non-need-based aid:*** $1880. ***Average indebtedness upon graduation:*** $36,514.

APPLYING

Standardized Tests *Required:* SAT or ACT (for admission).

Options: electronic application, early admission, deferred entrance.

Application fee: $25.

Required: high school transcript. ***Recommended:*** essay or personal statement, 2 letters of recommendation.

Application deadlines: rolling (freshmen), rolling (transfers).

Notification: 9/1 (freshmen), continuous (transfers).

CONTACT

Office of Admissions, Indiana University of Pennsylvania, 1011 South Drive, Sutton Hall, Suite120, Indiana, PA 15705. *Phone:* 724-357-2230. *Toll-free phone:* 800-442-6830. *Fax:* 724-357-6281. *E-mail:* admissions-inquiry@iup.edu.

Juniata College

Huntingdon, Pennsylvania

http://www.juniata.edu/

- **Independent** comprehensive, founded 1876, affiliated with Church of the Brethren
- **Small-town** 110-acre campus
- **Endowment** $108.0 million
- **Coed** 3,796 undergraduate students
- **Moderately difficult** entrance level, 75% of applicants were admitted

UNDERGRAD STUDENTS

Students come from 38 states and territories; 37 other countries; 34% are from out of state; 3% Black or African American, non-Hispanic/Latino; 4% Hispanic/Latino; 4% Asian, non-Hispanic/Latino; 0.1% American Indian or Alaska Native, non-Hispanic/Latino; 3% Two or more races, non-Hispanic/Latino; 5% Race/ethnicity unknown; 7% international; 82% live on campus.

Freshmen:

Admission: 2,386 applied, 1,780 admitted. ***Average high school GPA:*** 3.71. ***Test scores:*** SAT critical reading scores over 500: 82%; SAT math scores over 500: 83%; SAT writing scores over 500: 70%; ACT scores over 18: 100%; SAT critical reading scores over 600: 34%; SAT math scores over 600: 36%; SAT writing scores over 600: 29%; ACT scores over 24: 75%; SAT critical reading scores over 700: 7%; SAT math scores over 700: 3%; SAT writing scores over 700: 3%; ACT scores over 30: 20%.

Retention: 85% of full-time freshmen returned.

FACULTY
Total: 154, 76% full-time, 75% with terminal degrees.

Student/faculty ratio: 12:1.

ACADEMICS
Calendar: semesters. *Degrees:* bachelor's and master's.

Special study options: advanced placement credit, double majors, English as a second language, honors programs, independent study, internships, off-campus study, part-time degree program, services for LD students, student-designed majors, study abroad, summer session for credit.

Unusual degree programs: 3-2 engineering with Columbia University, Penn State University, Washington University in St. Louis, Clarkson University; nursing with Case Western University, Johns Hopkins University.

Computers: 150 computers/terminals and 257 ports are available on campus for general student use. Students can access the following: computer help desk, free student e-mail accounts, online (class) grades, online (class) registration, online (class) schedules, access to bills. Campuswide network is available. 100% of college-owned or -operated housing units are wired for high-speed Internet access. Wireless service is available via classrooms, computer centers, computer labs, dorm rooms, learning centers, libraries, student centers.

Library: Beeghly Library. *Books:* 52,000 (physical); *Serial titles:* 12,000 (physical). Weekly public service hours: 107.

STUDENT LIFE
Housing options: on-campus residence required through senior year; coed, women-only. Campus housing is university owned. Freshman campus housing is guaranteed.

Activities and organizations: drama/theater group, student-run radio station, choral group, Student Government Association, Juniata Activities Board (JAB), Habitat for Humanity, National Society of Leadership and Success.

Athletics Member NCAA. All Division III. ***Intercollegiate sports:*** baseball M, basketball M/W, cross-country running M/W, field hockey W, football M, golf M(c)/W(c), lacrosse M(c), rugby M(c)/W(c), soccer M/W, softball W, swimming and diving W, tennis M/W, track and field M/W, ultimate Frisbee M(c)/W(c), volleyball M/W. ***Intramural sports:*** basketball M/W, cheerleading W(c), equestrian sports M(c)/W(c), field hockey M(c)/W(c), lacrosse W(c), racquetball M/W, skiing (downhill) M(c)/W(c), soccer M/W, swimming and diving M/W, table tennis M(c)/W(c), volleyball M(c)/W(c).

Campus security: 24-hour emergency response devices and patrols, student patrols, late-night transport/escort service, controlled dormitory access, fire safety training, adopt-an-officer program, security Website, weather/terror alerts, travel forecast, crime statistics.

Student services: health clinic, personal/psychological counseling, women's center.

COSTS & FINANCIAL AID
Costs (2017–18) ***Comprehensive fee:*** $55,915 includes full-time tuition ($43,050), mandatory fees ($825), and room and board ($12,040). Full-time tuition and fees vary according to course load, degree level, and program. Part-time tuition: $1765 per credit. Part-time tuition and fees vary according to course load and degree level. ***College room only:*** $6410. Room and board charges vary according to board plan and housing facility. ***Payment plan:*** installment. ***Waivers:*** senior citizens and employees or children of employees.

Financial Aid Of all full-time matriculated undergraduates who enrolled in 2016, 1,197 applied for aid, 1,111 were judged to have need, 274 had their need fully met. 310 Federal Work-Study jobs (averaging $435). 720 state and other part-time jobs (averaging $837). In 2016, 349 non-need-based awards were made. ***Average percent of need met:*** 82. ***Average financial aid package:*** $35,585. ***Average need-based loan:*** $4534. ***Average need-based gift aid:*** $29,430. ***Average non-need-based aid:*** $19,992. ***Average indebtedness upon graduation:*** $36,338.

APPLYING
Standardized Tests *Recommended:* SAT or ACT (for admission).

Options: electronic application, early admission, early decision, deferred entrance.

Required: essay or personal statement, high school transcript, minimum 3.0 GPA, 1 letter of recommendation. ***Recommended:*** interview.

Application deadlines: 2/15 (freshmen), 6/15 (transfers).

Early decision deadline: 11/15 (for plan 1), 2/15 (for plan 2).

Notification: 2/1 (freshmen), continuous (transfers), 12/23 (early decision plan 1), rolling (early decision plan 2).

CONTACT
Terri Bollman-Dalansky, Senior Associate Dean of Admission, Juniata College, 1700 Moore Street, Huntingdon, PA 16652-2119. *Phone:* 814-641-3424. *Toll-free phone:* 877-JUNIATA. *Fax:* 814-641-3100. *E-mail:* bollmat@juniata.edu.

Keystone College
La Plume, Pennsylvania
http://www.keystone.edu/

CONTACT
Jessica Lopez, Senior Administrative Assistant, Keystone College, One College Green, PO Box 50, La Plume, PA 18440-1099. *Phone:* 570-945-8111. *Toll-free phone:* 877-4-COLLEGE. *Fax:* 570-945-7916. *E-mail:* admissions@keystone.edu.

See next page for display ad and page 1388 for the College Close-Up.

★ King's College
Wilkes-Barre, Pennsylvania
http://www.kings.edu/

- **Independent Roman Catholic** comprehensive, founded 1946
- **Urban** 48-acre campus
- **Endowment** $67.0 million
- **Coed** 2,082 undergraduate students, 92% full-time, 48% women, 52% men
- **Moderately difficult** entrance level, 71% of applicants were admitted

UNDERGRAD STUDENTS
1,907 full-time, 175 part-time. Students come from 16 states and territories; 5 other countries; 30% are from out of state; 3% Black or African American, non-Hispanic/Latino; 7% Hispanic/Latino; 2% Asian, non-Hispanic/Latino; 0.2% American Indian or Alaska Native, non-Hispanic/Latino; 2% Two or more races, non-Hispanic/Latino; 5% Race/ethnicity unknown; 6% international; 3% transferred in; 49% live on campus.

Freshmen:
Admission: 3,852 applied, 2,731 admitted, 573 enrolled. ***Average high school GPA:*** 3.4. ***Test scores:*** SAT critical reading scores over 500: 61%; SAT math scores over 500: 68%; ACT scores over 18: 93%; SAT critical reading scores over 600: 15%; SAT math scores over 600: 21%; ACT scores over 24: 45%; SAT critical reading scores over 700: 1%; SAT math scores over 700: 1%; ACT scores over 30: 3%.

Retention: 77% of full-time freshmen returned.

FACULTY
Total: 227, 58% full-time, 60% with terminal degrees.

Student/faculty ratio: 13:1.

ACADEMICS
Calendar: semesters. *Degrees:* bachelor's, master's, and postbachelor's certificates.

Special study options: accelerated degree program, adult/continuing education programs, advanced placement credit, distance learning, double majors, English as a second language, honors programs, independent study, internships, off-campus study, part-time degree program, services for LD students, student-designed majors, study abroad, summer session for credit. ***ROTC:*** Army (b), Air Force (c).

Unusual degree programs: 3-2 engineering with University of Notre Dame.

Computers: 470 computers/terminals are available on campus for general student use. Students can access the following: computer help desk, free student e-mail accounts, online (class) grades, online (class) registration, online (class) schedules. Campuswide network is available. 100% of college-owned or -operated housing units are wired for high-speed Internet access. Wireless service is available via classrooms, computer labs, dorm rooms, libraries, student centers.

Library: D. Leonard Corgan Library. *Books:* 185,069 (physical); *Databases:* 52. Weekly public service hours: 86; study areas open 24 hours, 5-7 days a week.

STUDENT LIFE

Housing options: on-campus residence required through sophomore year; coed, men-only, women-only, cooperative, special housing for students with disabilities. Campus housing is university owned. Freshman campus housing is guaranteed.

Activities and organizations: drama/theater group, student-run newspaper, radio station, choral group, Association of Campus Events, Student Government Association, Accounting Association, International/Multicultural Club, Biology Club.

Athletics Member NCAA. All Division III. ***Intercollegiate sports:*** baseball M, basketball M/W, cross-country running M/W, field hockey W, football M, golf M, ice hockey M/W, lacrosse M/W, soccer M/W, softball W, swimming and diving M/W, tennis M/W, track and field M/W, volleyball W, wrestling M. ***Intramural sports:*** basketball M/W, ice hockey M(c), soccer M/W.

Campus security: 24-hour emergency response devices and patrols, late-night transport/escort service, controlled dormitory access.

Student services: health clinic, personal/psychological counseling.

COSTS & FINANCIAL AID

Costs (2016–17) ***Comprehensive fee:*** $46,858 includes full-time tuition ($33,620), mandatory fees ($1100), and room and board ($12,138). Part-time tuition: $550 per credit hour. ***College room only:*** $6060. Room and board charges vary according to board plan. ***Payment plan:*** installment. ***Waivers:*** senior citizens and employees or children of employees.

Financial Aid Of all full-time matriculated undergraduates who enrolled in 2016, 1,645 applied for aid, 1,500 were judged to have need, 268 had their need fully met. 313 Federal Work-Study jobs (averaging $1542). 284 state and other part-time jobs (averaging $1122). In 2016, 272 non-need-based awards were made. ***Average percent of need met:*** 73. ***Average financial aid package:*** $24,694. ***Average need-based loan:*** $4760. ***Average need-based gift aid:*** $19,407. ***Average non-need-based aid:*** $14,708. ***Average indebtedness upon graduation:*** $37,874.

APPLYING

Standardized Tests *Recommended:* SAT or ACT (for admission).

Options: electronic application, early action, deferred entrance.

Application fee: $30.

Required: essay or personal statement, high school transcript. ***Recommended:*** interview.

Application deadlines: rolling (freshmen), rolling (transfers), 12/1 (early action).

Notification: continuous (freshmen), continuous (transfers), 12/15 (early action).

CONTACT

Mr. Corry Unis, Vice President for Enrollment Management, King's College, 133 North River Street, Wilkes-Barre, PA 18711-0801. *Phone:* 570-208-5858. *Toll-free phone:* 888-KINGSPA. *Fax:* 570-208-5971. *E-mail:* admissions@kings.edu.

See page 1390 for the College Close-Up.

★ Kutztown University of Pennsylvania

Kutztown, Pennsylvania

http://www.kutztown.edu/

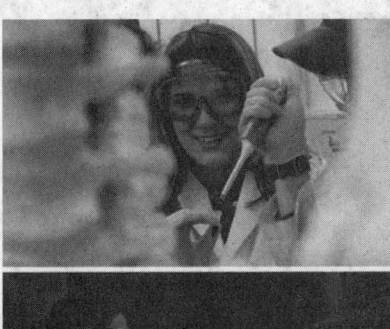

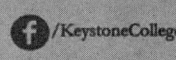

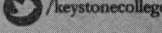

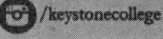

- **State-supported** comprehensive, founded 1866, part of Pennsylvania State System of Higher Education
- **Rural** 289-acre campus with easy access to Philadelphia
- **Endowment** $19.0 million
- **Coed** 7,718 undergraduate students, 94% full-time, 54% women, 46% men
- **Moderately difficult** entrance level, 80% of applicants were admitted

UNDERGRAD STUDENTS
7,288 full-time, 430 part-time. Students come from 29 states and territories; 26 other countries; 12% are from out of state; 8% Black or African American, non-Hispanic/Latino; 8% Hispanic/Latino; 1% Asian, non-Hispanic/Latino; 0.1% Native Hawaiian or other Pacific Islander, non-Hispanic/Latino; 0.1% American Indian or Alaska Native, non-Hispanic/Latino; 3% Two or more races, non-Hispanic/Latino; 1% Race/ethnicity unknown; 0.7% international; 7% transferred in; 45% live on campus.

Freshmen:
Admission: 7,668 applied, 6,117 admitted, 1,695 enrolled. ***Average high school GPA:*** 3.2. ***Test scores:*** SAT critical reading scores over 500: 42%; SAT math scores over 500: 43%; SAT writing scores over 500: 34%; ACT scores over 18: 80%; SAT critical reading scores over 600: 10%; SAT math scores over 600: 9%; SAT writing scores over 600: 6%; ACT scores over 24: 18%; SAT critical reading scores over 700: 1%; SAT math scores over 700: 1%; ACT scores over 30: 2%.
Retention: 73% of full-time freshmen returned.

FACULTY
Total: 441, 93% full-time, 83% with terminal degrees.
Student/faculty ratio: 18:1.

ACADEMICS
Calendar: semesters. *Degrees:* bachelor's, master's, doctoral, post-master's, and postbachelor's certificates.
Special study options: academic remediation for entering students, accelerated degree program, adult/continuing education programs, advanced placement credit, distance learning, double majors, honors programs, independent study, internships, off-campus study, part-time degree program, services for LD students, student-designed majors, study abroad, summer session for credit. ***ROTC:*** Army (c).
Unusual degree programs: business administration; social work.
Computers: 1,075 computers/terminals and 100 ports are available on campus for general student use. Students can access the following: computer help desk, free student e-mail accounts, online (class) grades, online (class) registration, online (class) schedules. Campuswide network is available. 100% of college-owned or -operated housing units are wired for high-speed Internet access. Wireless service is available via classrooms, computer centers, computer labs, dorm rooms, learning centers, libraries, student centers.
Library: Rohrbach Library. *Books:* 379,570 (physical), 385,501 (digital/electronic); *Serial titles:* 5,277 (physical), 142,078 (digital/electronic); *Databases:* 119. Weekly public service hours: 92; students can reserve study rooms.

STUDENT LIFE
Housing options: coed, women-only, cooperative. Campus housing is university owned and leased by the school. Freshman campus housing is guaranteed.
Activities and organizations: drama/theater group, student-run newspaper, radio and television station, choral group, marching band, Marching Unit, Honors Club, American Marketing Association Kutztown Chapter, Humans versus Zombies: Kutztown Chapter, Paws for Love, national fraternities, national sororities.
Athletics Member NCAA. All Division II. ***Intercollegiate sports:*** baseball M(s), basketball M(s)/W(s), bowling W(s), cheerleading W(c), cross-country running M(s)/W(s), equestrian sports M(c)/W(c), fencing M(c)/W(c), field hockey W(s), football M(s), golf M(c)/W(s), ice hockey M(c), lacrosse M(c)/W(s), rugby M(c)/W(c), soccer M(c)/W(s), softball W(s), swimming and diving W(s), tennis M(s)/W(s), track and field M(s)/W(s), ultimate Frisbee M(c)/W(c), volleyball M(c)/W(s), wrestling M(s). ***Intramural sports:*** basketball M/W, football M/W, racquetball M/W, rock climbing M/W, soccer M/W, softball M/W, table tennis M/W, tennis M/W, volleyball M/W.
Campus security: 24-hour emergency response devices and patrols, student patrols, late-night transport/escort service, controlled dormitory access, secondary door electronic alarm system in residence halls, 24-hour student desk personnel at main entrance of residence halls.
Student services: health clinic, personal/psychological counseling, women's center.

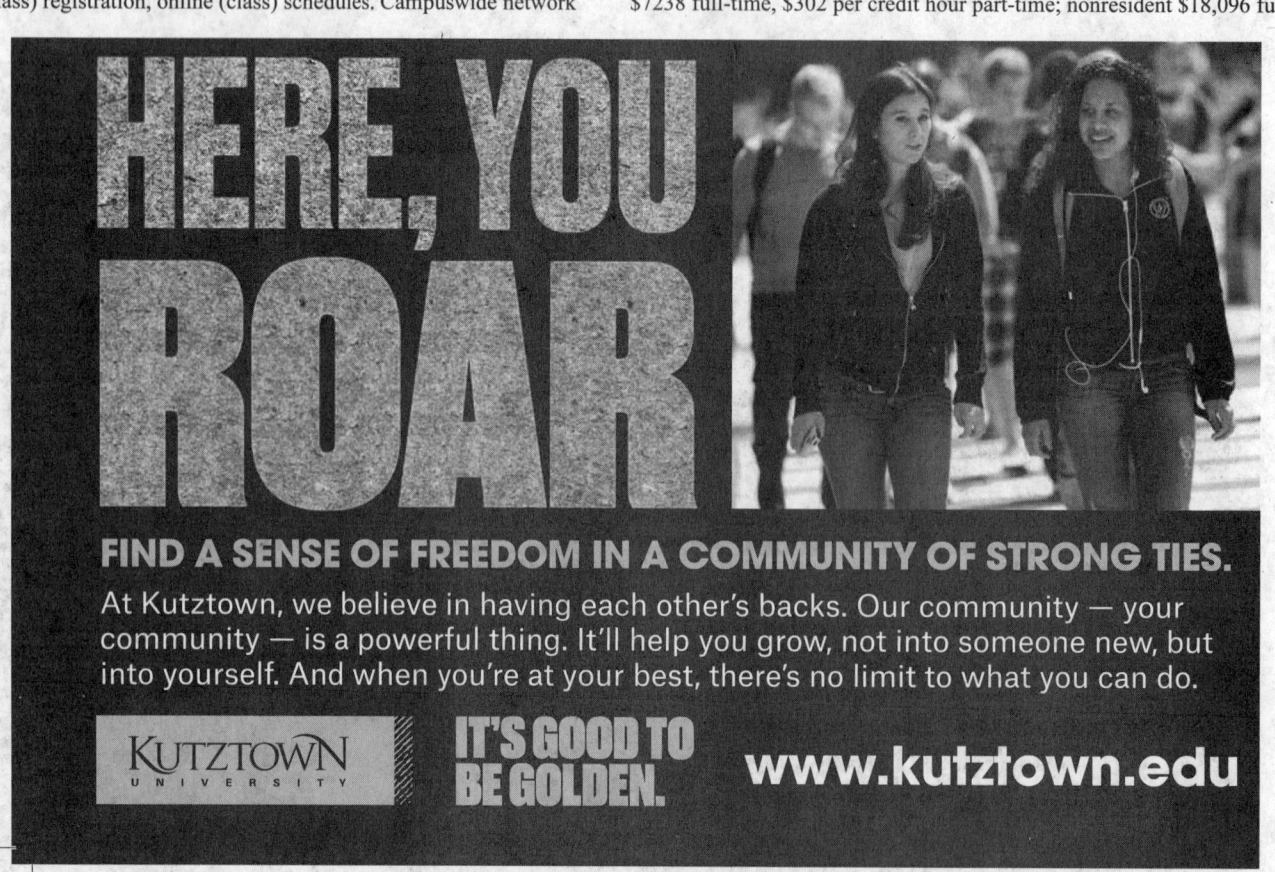

COSTS & FINANCIAL AID
Costs (2016–17) ***One-time required fee:*** $238. ***Tuition:*** state resident $7238 full-time, $302 per credit hour part-time; nonresident $18,096 full-

time, $754 per credit hour part-time. Full-time tuition and fees vary according to course load. Part-time tuition and fees vary according to course load. ***Required fees:*** $2380 full-time, $100 per credit hour part-time. ***Room and board:*** $9438; room only: $5720. Room and board charges vary according to board plan and housing facility. ***Payment plans:*** installment, deferred payment. ***Waivers:*** senior citizens and employees or children of employees.

Financial Aid Of all full-time matriculated undergraduates who enrolled in 2015, 6,724 applied for aid, 5,561 were judged to have need, 367 had their need fully met. 447 Federal Work-Study jobs (averaging $2587). In 2015, 288 non-need-based awards were made. ***Average percent of need met:*** 47. ***Average financial aid package:*** $8699. ***Average need-based loan:*** $4172. ***Average need-based gift aid:*** $5726. ***Average non-need-based aid:*** $776. ***Average indebtedness upon graduation:*** $39,230.

APPLYING

Standardized Tests *Required:* SAT or ACT (for admission). *Required for some:* SAT Subject Tests (for admission).

Options: electronic application, early admission, deferred entrance.

Application fee: $35.

Required: high school transcript, minimum 2.0 GPA. ***Required for some:*** audition for music, portfolio and/or art test for arts.

Application deadlines: rolling (freshmen), rolling (transfers).

Notification: continuous (freshmen), continuous (transfers).

CONTACT

Kutztown University of Pennsylvania, 15200 Kutztown Road, Kutztown, PA 19530-0730. *Phone:* 610-683-4060. *Toll-free phone:* 877-628-1915.

See previous page for display ad and page 1392 for the College Close-Up.

Lafayette College

Easton, Pennsylvania

http://www.lafayette.edu/

- **Independent** 4-year, founded 1826, affiliated with Presbyterian Church (U.S.A.)
- **Suburban** 340-acre campus with easy access to New York City, Philadelphia
- **Endowment** $774.7 million
- **Coed** 2,550 undergraduate students, 98% full-time, 51% women, 49% men

UNDERGRAD STUDENTS

2,505 full-time, 45 part-time. Students come from 45 states and territories; 59 other countries; 82% are from out of state; 5% Black or African American, non-Hispanic/Latino; 6% Hispanic/Latino; 4% Asian, non-Hispanic/Latino; 2% Two or more races, non-Hispanic/Latino; 6% Race/ethnicity unknown; 10% international; 0.4% transferred in; 93% live on campus.

Freshmen:

Admission: 649 enrolled. ***Average high school GPA:*** 3.53. ***Test scores:*** SAT critical reading scores over 500: 96%; SAT math scores over 500: 100%; SAT writing scores over 500: 96%; ACT scores over 18: 100%; SAT critical reading scores over 600: 68%; SAT math scores over 600: 83%; SAT writing scores over 600: 74%; ACT scores over 24: 96%; SAT critical reading scores over 700: 17%; SAT math scores over 700: 31%; SAT writing scores over 700: 22%; ACT scores over 30: 52%.

Retention: 94% of full-time freshmen returned.

FACULTY

Total: 276, 83% full-time, 90% with terminal degrees.

Student/faculty ratio: 10:1.

ACADEMICS

Calendar: semesters plus interim January program. *Degree:* bachelor's.

Special study options: academic remediation for entering students, accelerated degree program, advanced placement credit, double majors, honors programs, independent study, internships, off-campus study, part-time degree program, services for LD students, student-designed majors, study abroad, summer session for credit. ***ROTC:*** Army (c).

Computers: 690 computers/terminals and 690 ports are available on campus for general student use. Students can access the following: campus intranet, computer help desk, free student e-mail accounts, online (class) grades, online (class) registration, online (class) schedules. Campuswide network is available. 100% of college-owned or -operated housing units are wired for high-speed Internet access. Wireless service is available via entire campus.

Library: Skillman Library plus 2 others. *Books:* 603,599 (physical), 344,469 (digital/electronic); *Serial titles:* 306 (physical), 68,298 (digital/electronic); *Databases:* 132. Weekly public service hours: 106.

STUDENT LIFE

Housing options: on-campus residence required through senior year; coed, men-only, women-only, special housing for students with disabilities. Campus housing is university owned. Freshman campus housing is guaranteed.

Activities and organizations: drama/theater group, student-run newspaper, radio station, choral group, LAF (Lafayette Activities Forum), Student Government, Crew, International Students Association, Leopards Lair, national fraternities, national sororities.

Athletics Member NCAA. All Division I except football (Division I-AA). ***Intercollegiate sports:*** baseball M, basketball M/W, crew M(c)/W(c), cross-country running M/W, equestrian sports M(c)/W(c), fencing M/W, field hockey W, golf M, ice hockey M(c), lacrosse M/W, rugby M(c)/W(c), skiing (downhill) M(c)/W(c), soccer M/W, softball W, squash M(c), swimming and diving M/W, tennis M/W, track and field M/W, volleyball W, weight lifting M(c)/W(c), wrestling M(c). ***Intramural sports:*** badminton M/W, baseball M, basketball M/W, bowling M/W, cross-country running M/W, fencing M/W, field hockey W, football M, golf M/W, lacrosse M/W, racquetball M/W, sailing M(c)/W(c), skiing (cross-country) M(c)/W(c), soccer M/W, softball M/W, squash M/W, swimming and diving M/W, table tennis M/W, tennis M/W, track and field M/W, volleyball M/W, weight lifting M/W, wrestling M.

Campus security: 24-hour emergency response devices and patrols, student patrols, late-night transport/escort service, controlled dormitory access.

Student services: health clinic, personal/psychological counseling, women's center.

COSTS & FINANCIAL AID

Costs (2017–18) ***One-time required fee:*** $450. ***Comprehensive fee:*** $65,890. No tuition increase for student's term of enrollment.

Financial Aid Of all full-time matriculated undergraduates who enrolled in 2016, 1,299 applied for aid, 764 were judged to have need, 764 had their need fully met. 448 Federal Work-Study jobs (averaging $1287). In 2016, 223 non-need-based awards were made. ***Average percent of need met:*** 100. ***Average financial aid package:*** $45,615. ***Average need-based loan:*** $4417. ***Average need-based gift aid:*** $40,285. ***Average non-need-based aid:*** $27,358. ***Average indebtedness upon graduation:*** $29,324. ***Financial aid deadline:*** 1/15.

APPLYING

Standardized Tests *Required:* SAT or ACT (for admission). *Recommended:* SAT Subject Tests (for admission).

Required: essay or personal statement, high school transcript, 1 letter of recommendation. ***Recommended:*** interview.

CONTACT

Mr. Matthew Hyde, Director of Admissions, Lafayette College, 118 Markle Hall, 730 High Street, Easton, PA 18042-1798. *Phone:* 610-330-5100. *Fax:* 610-330-5355. *E-mail:* hydem@lafayette.edu.

Lancaster Bible College

Lancaster, Pennsylvania

http://www.lbc.edu/

CONTACT

Mrs. Joanne M. Roper, Associate Vice President for Admissions, Lancaster Bible College, PO Box 83403, Lancaster, PA 17608. *Phone:* 717-560-8271. *Toll-free phone:* 800-544-7335. *Fax:* 717-560-8213. *E-mail:* admissions@lbc.edu.

La Roche College

Pittsburgh, Pennsylvania

http://www.laroche.edu/

- **Independent** comprehensive, founded 1963, affiliated with Roman Catholic Church
- **Suburban** 43-acre campus
- **Endowment** $5.3 million
- **Coed** 1,406 undergraduate students, 82% full-time, 55% women, 45% men
- **Minimally difficult** entrance level, 92% of applicants were admitted

UNDERGRAD STUDENTS

1,151 full-time, 255 part-time. Students come from 23 states and territories; 28 other countries; 9% are from out of state; 10% Black or African American, non-Hispanic/Latino; 3% Hispanic/Latino; 1% Asian, non-Hispanic/Latino; 0.2% Native Hawaiian or other Pacific Islander, non-Hispanic/Latino; 0.3% American Indian or Alaska Native, non-Hispanic/Latino; 2% Two or more races, non-Hispanic/Latino; 8% Race/ethnicity unknown; 16% international; 12% transferred in; 44% live on campus.

Freshmen:

Admission: 1,320 applied, 1,218 admitted, 265 enrolled. ***Average high school GPA:*** 3.2. ***Test scores:*** SAT critical reading scores over 500: 30%; SAT math scores over 500: 30%; SAT writing scores over 500: 27%; ACT scores over 18: 66%; SAT critical reading scores over 600: 7%; SAT math scores over 600: 5%; SAT writing scores over 600: 3%; ACT scores over 24: 15%; SAT critical reading scores over 700: 1%; SAT math scores over 700: 1%.

Retention: 68% of full-time freshmen returned.

FACULTY

Total: 194, 31% full-time, 41% with terminal degrees.

Student/faculty ratio: 13:1.

ACADEMICS

Calendar: semesters plus summer term. *Degrees:* certificates, associate, bachelor's, master's, and postbachelor's certificates.

Special study options: academic remediation for entering students, accelerated degree program, adult/continuing education programs, advanced placement credit, distance learning, double majors, English as a second language, freshman honors college, honors programs, independent study, internships, off-campus study, part-time degree program, services for LD students, student-designed majors, study abroad, summer session for credit. ***ROTC:*** Army (c), Air Force (c).

Unusual degree programs: 3-2 engineering with University of Pittsburgh; physical therapy, physician's assistant, speech language pathologist, athletic trainer, occupational therapy with Duquesne University; pharmacy, dental and medical with Lake Erie College of Osteopathic Medicine; software engineering with Gannon University.

Computers: Students can access the following: campus intranet, computer help desk, free student e-mail accounts, online (class) grades, online (class) registration, online (class) schedules. Campuswide network is available. 100% of college-owned or -operated housing units are wired for high-speed Internet access. Wireless service is available via classrooms, computer labs, learning centers, libraries, student centers.

Library: John J. Wright Library plus 1 other. *Books:* 75,803 (physical), 221,000 (digital/electronic); *Databases:* 1,248.

STUDENT LIFE

Housing options: coed. Campus housing is university owned. Freshman campus housing is guaranteed.

Activities and organizations: student-run newspaper, radio station, American Society of Interior Design, student government, Visions (environmental club).

Athletics Member NCAA. All Division III. ***Intercollegiate sports:*** baseball M, basketball M/W, cross-country running M/W, golf M, lacrosse M/W, soccer M/W, softball W, tennis W, volleyball W. ***Intramural sports:*** basketball M/W, weight lifting M/W.

Campus security: 24-hour emergency response devices and patrols, student patrols, late-night transport/escort service, controlled dormitory access.

Student services: health clinic, personal/psychological counseling.

COSTS & FINANCIAL AID

Costs (2016–17) ***Comprehensive fee:*** $37,924 includes full-time tuition ($26,200), mandatory fees ($800), and room and board ($10,924). Part-time tuition: $665 per credit hour. ***College room only:*** $6916. Room and board charges vary according to board plan and housing facility. ***Payment plan:*** installment. ***Waivers:*** senior citizens and employees or children of employees.

Financial Aid Of all full-time matriculated undergraduates who enrolled in 2016, 835 applied for aid, 774 were judged to have need, 516 had their need fully met. 132 Federal Work-Study jobs (averaging $1573). In 2016, 61 non-need-based awards were made. ***Average percent of need met:*** 92. ***Average financial aid package:*** $29,356. ***Average need-based loan:*** $5791. ***Average need-based gift aid:*** $8538. ***Average non-need-based aid:*** $23,179. ***Average indebtedness upon graduation:*** $34,992.

APPLYING

Standardized Tests *Required:* SAT or ACT (for admission).

Options: electronic application, early admission, deferred entrance.

Application fee: $50.

Required: high school transcript, minimum 2.0 GPA, 2 letters of recommendation. ***Recommended:*** essay or personal statement, minimum 3.0 GPA, interview.

Application deadlines: rolling (freshmen), rolling (transfers).

Notification: 9/15 (freshmen).

CONTACT

La Roche College, 9000 Babcock Boulevard, Pittsburgh, PA 15237. *Phone:* 412-536-1272. *Toll-free phone:* 800-838-4LRC. *Fax:* 412-536-1048. *E-mail:* admissions@laroche.edu.

La Salle University

Philadelphia, Pennsylvania

http://www.lasalle.edu/

- **Independent Roman Catholic** comprehensive, founded 1863
- **Urban** 133-acre campus with easy access to Philadelphia
- **Endowment** $84.5 million
- **Coed** 3,652 undergraduate students, 87% full-time, 62% women, 38% men
- **Moderately difficult** entrance level, 77% of applicants were admitted

UNDERGRAD STUDENTS

3,181 full-time, 471 part-time. Students come from 35 states and territories; 31 other countries; 33% are from out of state; 19% Black or African American, non-Hispanic/Latino; 14% Hispanic/Latino; 5% Asian, non-Hispanic/Latino; 0.2% Native Hawaiian or other Pacific Islander, non-Hispanic/Latino; 0.2% American Indian or Alaska Native, non-Hispanic/Latino; 3% Two or more races, non-Hispanic/Latino; 6% Race/ethnicity unknown; 2% international; 3% transferred in; 52% live on campus.

Freshmen:

Admission: 5,673 applied, 4,359 admitted, 869 enrolled. ***Average high school GPA:*** 3.32. ***Test scores:*** SAT critical reading scores over 500: 46%; SAT math scores over 500: 43%; ACT scores over 18: 85%; SAT critical reading scores over 600: 12%; SAT math scores over 600: 10%; ACT scores over 24: 33%; SAT critical reading scores over 700: 1%; SAT math scores over 700: 2%; ACT scores over 30: 6%.

Retention: 75% of full-time freshmen returned.

FACULTY

Total: 430, 53% full-time.

Student/faculty ratio: 11:1.

ACADEMICS

Calendar: semesters. *Degrees:* associate, bachelor's, master's, doctoral, post-master's, and postbachelor's certificates.

Special study options: academic remediation for entering students, accelerated degree program, adult/continuing education programs, advanced placement credit, cooperative education, distance learning, double majors, English as a second language, freshman honors college, honors programs, independent study, internships, off-campus study, part-time degree program, services for LD students, student-designed majors, study abroad, summer session for credit. ***ROTC:*** Army (c), Air Force (c).

Unusual degree programs: 3-2 business administration; communication sciences and disorders/speech language pathology, communication/professional business communication, computer information science, history, elementary/special education, occupational therapy program with Thomas Jefferson University.

Computers: 1,100 computers/terminals are available on campus for general student use. Students can access the following: campus intranet, computer help desk, free student e-mail accounts, online (class) grades, online (class) registration, online (class) schedules, course management system. Campuswide network is available. 100% of college-owned or -operated housing units are wired for high-speed Internet access. Wireless service is available via classrooms, computer centers, computer labs, dorm rooms, learning centers, libraries, student centers.

Library: Connelly Library. *Books:* 274,998 (physical), 172,068 (digital/electronic); *Serial titles:* 1,470 (physical), 127,163 (digital/electronic); *Databases:* 88. Weekly public service hours: 96; students can reserve study rooms.

STUDENT LIFE

Housing options: on-campus residence required through sophomore year; coed, men-only, women-only, special housing for students with disabilities. Campus housing is university owned. Freshman campus housing is guaranteed.

Activities and organizations: drama/theater group, student-run newspaper, radio and television station, choral group, Student Government Association, community service organization, La Salle Entertainment Organization, The Explorer (yearbook), The Masque (theater group), national fraternities, national sororities.

Athletics Member NCAA. All Division I. ***Intercollegiate sports:*** baseball M(s), basketball M(s)/W(s), cheerleading M/W, crew M(s)/W(s), cross-country running M(s)/W(s), field hockey W(s), golf M(s)/W(s), lacrosse W(s), soccer M(s)/W(s), softball W(s), swimming and diving M(s)/W(s), tennis M(s)/W(s), track and field M(s)/W(s), volleyball W(s), water polo M(s)/W(s). ***Intramural sports:*** basketball M/W, football M/W, ice hockey M(c), lacrosse M(c), rugby M(c)/W(c), softball M/W, ultimate Frisbee M(c)/W(c), volleyball M/W.

Campus security: 24-hour emergency response devices and patrols, student patrols, late-night transport/escort service, controlled dormitory access.

Student services: health clinic, personal/psychological counseling, women's center.

COSTS & FINANCIAL AID

Costs (2017–18) ***One-time required fee:*** $150. ***Comprehensive fee:*** $44,580 includes full-time tuition ($28,800), mandatory fees ($700), and room and board ($15,080). Full-time tuition and fees vary according to course load and program. Part-time tuition: $570 per credit hour. Part-time tuition and fees vary according to course load and program. ***Required fees:*** $175 per term part-time. ***College room only:*** $7530. Room and board charges vary according to board plan and housing facility. ***Payment plans:*** installment, deferred payment. ***Waivers:*** employees or children of employees.

Financial Aid Of all full-time matriculated undergraduates who enrolled in 2015, 2,912 applied for aid, 2,739 were judged to have need, 358 had their need fully met. 394 Federal Work-Study jobs (averaging $1807). In 2015, 509 non-need-based awards were made. ***Average percent of need met:*** 74. ***Average financial aid package:*** $31,356. ***Average need-based loan:*** $4720. ***Average need-based gift aid:*** $25,297. ***Average non-need-based aid:*** $18,533. ***Average indebtedness upon graduation:*** $36,907.

APPLYING

Standardized Tests *Required:* SAT or ACT (for admission).

Options: electronic application, early admission, early action, deferred entrance.

Application fee: $35.

Required: essay or personal statement, high school transcript, 1 letter of recommendation. ***Recommended:*** interview.

Application deadlines: 8/15 (transfers), 11/15 (early action).

Notification: continuous (freshmen), continuous (transfers), 12/15 (early action).

CONTACT

Mr. James Plunkett, Executive Director of Undergraduate Admission, La Salle University, 1900 West Olney Avenue, Philadelphia, PA 19141-1199. *Phone:* 215-951-1500. *Toll-free phone:* 800-328-1910. *Fax:* 215-951-1656. *E-mail:* admiss@lasalle.edu.

Lebanon Valley College

Annville, Pennsylvania

http://www.lvc.edu/

- **Independent United Methodist** comprehensive, founded 1866
- **Small-town** 357-acre campus
- **Endowment** $60.3 million
- **Coed** 1,712 undergraduate students, 94% full-time, 54% women, 46% men
- **Moderately difficult** entrance level, 76% of applicants were admitted

UNDERGRAD STUDENTS

1,602 full-time, 110 part-time. Students come from 20 states and territories; 4 other countries; 20% are from out of state; 3% Black or African American, non-Hispanic/Latino; 5% Hispanic/Latino; 2% Asian, non-Hispanic/Latino; 0.1% Native Hawaiian or other Pacific Islander, non-Hispanic/Latino; 0.1% American Indian or Alaska Native, non-Hispanic/Latino; 3% Two or more races, non-Hispanic/Latino; 3% Race/ethnicity unknown; 0.4% international; 3% transferred in; 78% live on campus.

Freshmen:

Admission: 2,561 applied, 1,948 admitted, 423 enrolled. ***Average high school GPA:*** 3.7. ***Test scores:*** SAT critical reading scores over 500: 69%; SAT math scores over 500: 72%; SAT writing scores over 500: 62%; ACT scores over 18: 86%; SAT critical reading scores over 600: 26%; SAT math scores over 600: 31%; SAT writing scores over 600: 18%; ACT scores over 24: 56%; SAT critical reading scores over 700: 4%; SAT math scores over 700: 6%; SAT writing scores over 700: 2%; ACT scores over 30: 14%.

Retention: 82% of full-time freshmen returned.

FACULTY

Total: 253, 45% full-time, 56% with terminal degrees.

Student/faculty ratio: 11:1.

ACADEMICS

Calendar: semesters. *Degrees:* bachelor's, master's, doctoral, and postbachelor's certificates.

Special study options: academic remediation for entering students, adult/continuing education programs, advanced placement credit, distance learning, double majors, English as a second language, independent study, internships, off-campus study, part-time degree program, services for LD students, student-designed majors, study abroad, summer session for credit.

Unusual degree programs: 3-2 engineering with Case Western Reserve University, The Penn State University.

Computers: 198 computers/terminals are available on campus for general student use. Students can access the following: campus intranet, computer help desk, free student e-mail accounts, online (class) grades, online (class) registration, online (class) schedules. Campuswide network is available. 100% of college-owned or -operated housing units are wired for high-speed Internet access. Wireless service is available via entire campus.

Library: Vernon and Doris Bishop Library. *Books:* 158,734 (physical), 198,403 (digital/electronic); *Databases:* 129. Weekly public service hours: 101; students can reserve study rooms.

STUDENT LIFE

Housing options: on-campus residence required through senior year; coed, special housing for students with disabilities. Campus housing is university owned. Freshman campus housing is guaranteed.

Activities and organizations: drama/theater group, student-run newspaper, choral group, marching band, Mini-THON, Outdoors Club, Colleges Against Cancer, Wig and Buckle Theater Group, Valleyfest, national fraternities, national sororities.

Athletics Member NCAA. All Division III. ***Intercollegiate sports:*** baseball M, basketball M/W, cross-country running M/W, field hockey W, football M, golf M/W, ice hockey M/W, lacrosse M/W, soccer M/W, softball W, swimming and diving M/W, tennis M/W, track and field M/W, volleyball W. ***Intramural sports:*** basketball M/W, cheerleading W(c), equestrian sports M(c)/W(c), football M/W, soccer M(c)/W(c), ultimate Frisbee M(c)/W(c), volleyball M/W, weight lifting W(c).

Campus security: 24-hour emergency response devices and patrols, late-night transport/escort service, controlled dormitory access.

Student services: health clinic, personal/psychological counseling, women's center.

COSTS & FINANCIAL AID

Costs (2017–18) ***Comprehensive fee:*** $53,590 includes full-time tuition ($40,990), mandatory fees ($1190), and room and board ($11,410). Part-time tuition: $650 per credit hour. Part-time tuition and fees vary according to class time and degree level. ***College room only:*** $5520. Room and board charges vary according to board plan and housing facility. ***Payment plan:*** installment. ***Waivers:*** senior citizens and employees or children of employees.

Financial Aid Of all full-time matriculated undergraduates who enrolled in 2015, 1,480 applied for aid, 1,388 were judged to have need, 273 had their need fully met. 1,048 Federal Work-Study jobs (averaging $1467). In 2015, 247 non-need-based awards were made. ***Average percent of need met:*** 78. ***Average financial aid package:*** $30,078. ***Average need-based loan:*** $4405. ***Average need-based gift aid:*** $24,641. ***Average non-need-based aid:*** $16,129. ***Average indebtedness upon graduation:*** $37,865.

APPLYING

Options: electronic application, early decision.

Required: high school transcript. ***Required for some:*** audition for music majors, specific requirements for physical therapy and athletic training programs. ***Recommended:*** 2 letters of recommendation, interview.

Application deadlines: rolling (freshmen), rolling (transfers).

Early decision deadline: 11/1.

Notification: continuous until 11/15 (freshmen), continuous (transfers), 11/1 (early decision).

CONTACT

Mr. Edwin Wright, Vice President of Enrollment Management, Lebanon Valley College, 101 North College Avenue, Annville, PA 17003. *Phone:* 717-867-6181. *Toll-free phone:* 866-LVC-4ADM. *Fax:* 717-867-6026. *E-mail:* admission@lvc.edu.

Lehigh University

Bethlehem, Pennsylvania

http://www.lehigh.edu/

- **Independent** university, founded 1865
- **Suburban** 2355-acre campus with easy access to Philadelphia
- **Endowment** $1.2 billion
- **Coed** 5,080 undergraduate students, 98% full-time, 44% women, 56% men
- **Most difficult** entrance level, 26% of applicants were admitted

UNDERGRAD STUDENTS

5,003 full-time, 77 part-time. Students come from 52 states and territories; 60 other countries; 74% are from out of state; 4% Black or African American, non-Hispanic/Latino; 9% Hispanic/Latino; 8% Asian, non-Hispanic/Latino; 0.1% Native Hawaiian or other Pacific Islander, non-Hispanic/Latino; 0.2% American Indian or Alaska Native, non-Hispanic/Latino; 3% Two or more races, non-Hispanic/Latino; 3% Race/ethnicity unknown; 8% international; 0.6% transferred in; 66% live on campus.

Freshmen:

Admission: 13,403 applied, 3,499 admitted, 1,249 enrolled. ***Test scores:*** SAT critical reading scores over 500: 97%; SAT math scores over 500: 99%; ACT scores over 18: 100%; SAT critical reading scores over 600: 72%; SAT math scores over 600: 89%; ACT scores over 24: 98%; SAT critical reading scores over 700: 17%; SAT math scores over 700: 42%; ACT scores over 30: 67%.

Retention: 95% of full-time freshmen returned.

FACULTY

Total: 711, 76% full-time, 80% with terminal degrees.

Student/faculty ratio: 9:1.

ACADEMICS

Calendar: semesters. *Degrees:* bachelor's, master's, doctoral, post-master's, and postbachelor's certificates.

Special study options: accelerated degree program, advanced placement credit, cooperative education, distance learning, double majors, English as a second language, external degree program, honors programs, independent study, internships, off-campus study, services for LD students, study abroad, summer session for credit. ***ROTC:*** Army (b).

Unusual degree programs: 3-2 engineering; education.

Computers: 597 computers/terminals are available on campus for general student use. Students can access the following: campus intranet, computer help desk, free student e-mail accounts, online (class) grades, online (class) registration, online (class) schedules. Campuswide network is available. 100% of college-owned or -operated housing units are wired for high-speed Internet access. Wireless service is available via classrooms, computer centers, computer labs, dorm rooms, learning centers, libraries, student centers.

Library: E. W. Fairchild-Martindale Library plus 1 other. *Books:* 887,151 (physical), 402,005 (digital/electronic); *Serial titles:* 2,010 (physical), 61,305 (digital/electronic); *Databases:* 189. Weekly public service hours: 80; students can reserve study rooms.

STUDENT LIFE

Housing options: on-campus residence required through sophomore year; coed, special housing for students with disabilities. Campus housing is university owned. Freshman campus housing is guaranteed.

Activities and organizations: drama/theater group, student-run newspaper, radio station, choral group, marching band, WLVR Radio Station, Marching 97, University Productions, Accounting Club, Phi Sigma Pi, national fraternities, national sororities.

Athletics Member NCAA. All Division I. ***Intercollegiate sports:*** baseball M, basketball M(s)/W(s), crew M(c)/W(s), cross-country running M(s)/W(s), equestrian sports M(c)/W(c), fencing M(c)/W(c), field hockey W(s), football M(s), golf M(s)/W(s), ice hockey M(c), lacrosse M(s)/W(s), rugby M(c)/W(c), skiing (downhill) M(c)/W(c), soccer M/W(s), softball W(s), squash M(c)/W(c), swimming and diving M(s)/W(s), tennis M(s)/W(s), track and field M(s)/W(s), ultimate Frisbee M(c)/W(c), volleyball M(c)/W(s), water polo M(c)/W(c), wrestling M(s). ***Intramural sports:*** badminton M(c)/W(c), baseball M(c), basketball M/W, cheerleading M(c)/W(c), cross-country running M/W, field hockey W(c), football M/W, golf M(c)/W(c), gymnastics M(c)/W(c), lacrosse M(c)/W(c), skiing (downhill) M(c)/W(c), soccer M/W, softball M/W, volleyball M/W, wrestling M(c).

Campus security: 24-hour emergency response devices and patrols, student patrols, late-night transport/escort service, controlled dormitory access, self defense training.

Student services: health clinic, personal/psychological counseling, women's center.

COSTS & FINANCIAL AID

Costs (2016–17) ***Comprehensive fee:*** $61,010 includes full-time tuition ($47,920), mandatory fees ($400), and room and board ($12,690). Part-time tuition: $2000 per credit hour. ***College room only:*** $7320. Room and board charges vary according to board plan and housing facility. ***Payment plans:*** tuition prepayment, installment. ***Waivers:*** employees or children of employees.

Financial Aid Of all full-time matriculated undergraduates who enrolled in 2016, 2,640 applied for aid, 1,926 were judged to have need, 1,584 had their need fully met. 1,107 Federal Work-Study jobs (averaging $1893). 75 state and other part-time jobs (averaging $1713). In 2016, 254 non-need-based awards were made. ***Average percent of need met:*** 97. ***Average financial aid package:*** $43,376. ***Average need-based loan:*** $4320. ***Average need-based gift aid:*** $37,699. ***Average non-need-based aid:*** $12,914. ***Average indebtedness upon graduation:*** $34,215. ***Financial aid deadline:*** 2/15.

APPLYING

Standardized Tests *Required:* SAT or ACT (for admission). *Recommended:* SAT (for admission), ACT (for admission).

Options: electronic application, early admission, early decision, deferred entrance.

Application fee: $70.

Required: essay or personal statement, high school transcript, 2 letters of recommendation.

Application deadlines: 1/1 (freshmen), 3/1 (transfers).

Early decision deadline: 11/15 (for plan 1), 1/1 (for plan 2).

Notification: 3/31 (freshmen), 5/15 (transfers), 12/15 (early decision plan 1), 2/15 (early decision plan 2).

CONTACT

Krista Evans, Interim Director of Admissions, Lehigh University, 27 Memorial Drive West, Bethlehem, PA 18015. *Phone:* 610-758-3100. *Fax:* 610-758-4361. *E-mail:* admissions@lehigh.edu.

Lincoln University

Lincoln University, Pennsylvania

http://www.lincoln.edu/

- **State-related** comprehensive, founded 1854
- **Rural** 422-acre campus with easy access to Philadelphia
- **Endowment** $34.5 million
- **Coed** 1,824 undergraduate students, 91% full-time, 63% women, 37% men
- **Minimally difficult** entrance level, 87% of applicants were admitted

UNDERGRAD STUDENTS

1,668 full-time, 156 part-time. Students come from 30 states and territories; 13 other countries; 55% are from out of state; 83% Black or African American, non-Hispanic/Latino; 2% Hispanic/Latino; 0.1% Asian, non-Hispanic/Latino; 0.4% American Indian or Alaska Native, non-Hispanic/Latino; 1% Two or more races, non-Hispanic/Latino; 7% Race/ethnicity unknown; 4% international; 8% transferred in; 84% live on campus.

Freshmen:

Admission: 3,685 applied, 3,211 admitted, 526 enrolled. ***Average high school GPA:*** 2.86. ***Test scores:*** SAT critical reading scores over 500: 16%; SAT math scores over 500: 18%; SAT writing scores over 500: 16%; ACT scores over 18: 43%; SAT critical reading scores over 600: 1%; SAT math scores over 600: 3%; SAT writing scores over 600: 1%; ACT scores over 24: 8%.

Retention: 75% of full-time freshmen returned.

FACULTY

Total: 227, 41% full-time.

Student/faculty ratio: 12:1.

ACADEMICS

Calendar: semesters. *Degrees:* certificates, bachelor's, and master's.

Special study options: academic remediation for entering students, accelerated degree program, adult/continuing education programs, advanced placement credit, double majors, English as a second language, honors programs, independent study, internships, off-campus study, part-time degree program, services for LD students, study abroad, summer session for credit. ***ROTC:*** Army (c).

Computers: 155 computers/terminals are available on campus for general student use. Students can access the following: campus intranet, computer help desk, free student e-mail accounts, online (class) grades, online (class) registration, online (class) schedules. Campuswide network is available. 100% of college-owned or -operated housing units are wired for high-speed Internet access. Wireless service is available via entire campus.

Library: Langston Hughes Memorial Library. *Books:* 179,155 (physical), 161,264 (digital/electronic); *Databases:* 17. Weekly public service hours: 80; study areas open 24 hours, 5-7 days a week; students can reserve study rooms.

STUDENT LIFE

Housing options: on-campus residence required for freshman year; coed, men-only, women-only. Campus housing is university owned. Freshman applicants given priority for college housing.

Activities and organizations: drama/theater group, student-run newspaper, radio and television station, choral group, marching band, Student Government: Class sections, We R "1" Family, Residence Hall Association, International Students Association, Onyx Dance Troupe, national fraternities, national sororities.

Athletics Member NCAA. All Division II. ***Intercollegiate sports:*** baseball M(s), basketball M(s), cheerleading W(s), cross-country running M(s)/W, football M(s), soccer W(s), softball W(s), track and field M(s)/W(s), volleyball W(s). ***Intramural sports:*** basketball M/W, bowling M/W, football M, swimming and diving M/W, volleyball M/W.

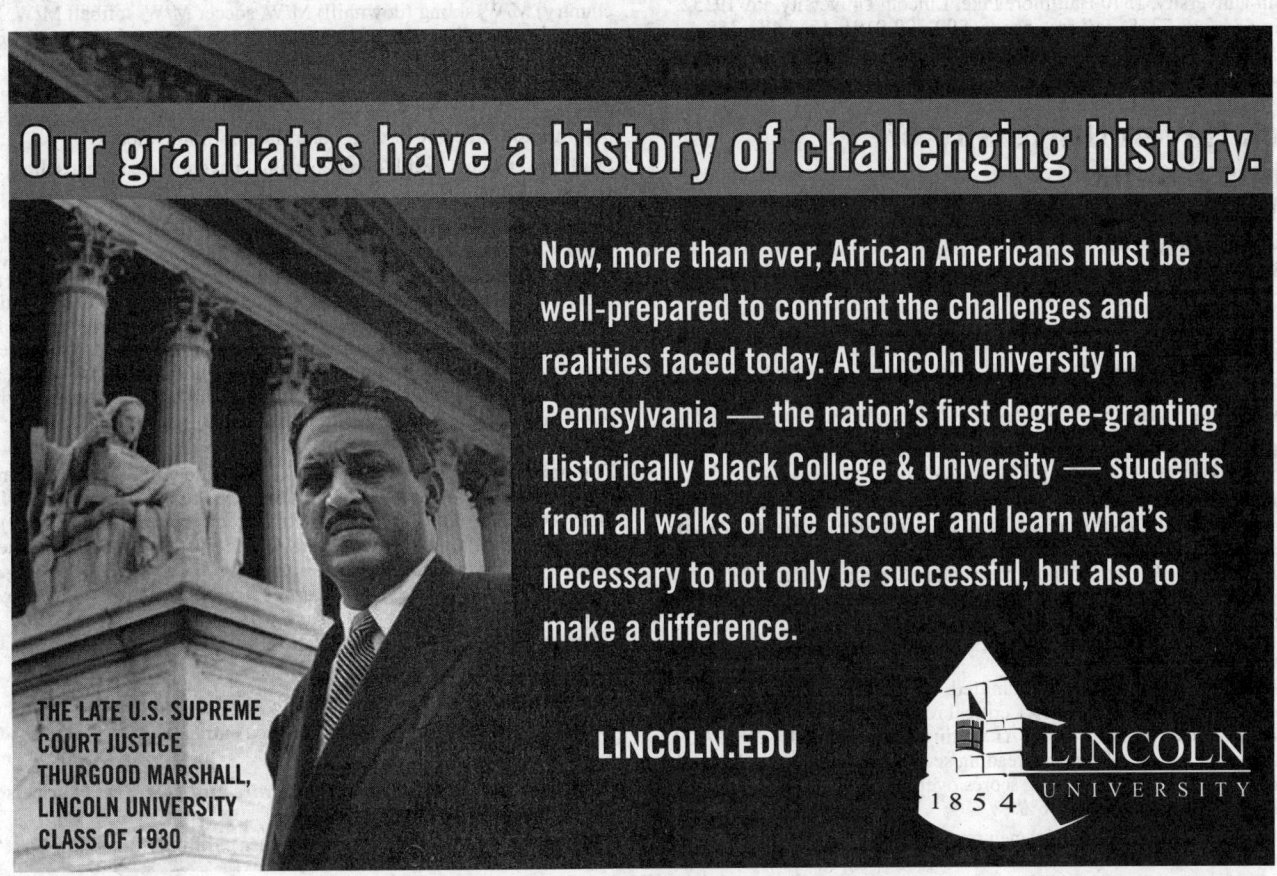

Campus security: 24-hour emergency response devices and patrols, late-night transport/escort service, controlled dormitory access, 24-hour command center, gated entrance/exit, medical transports.

Student services: health clinic, personal/psychological counseling, women's center.

COSTS & FINANCIAL AID
Costs (2016–17) ***One-time required fee:*** $100. ***Tuition:*** state resident $7487 full-time, $315 per credit hour part-time; nonresident $12,375 full-time, $519 per credit hour part-time. Full-time tuition and fees vary according to course load, degree level, location, program, and student level. Part-time tuition and fees vary according to course load, degree level, location, program, and student level. No tuition increase for student's term of enrollment. ***Required fees:*** $3615 full-time, $135 per credit hour part-time. ***Room and board:*** $9268; room only: $5010. Room and board charges vary according to board plan and housing facility. ***Payment plans:*** installment, deferred payment. ***Waivers:*** children of alumni and employees or children of employees.

Financial Aid Of all full-time matriculated undergraduates who enrolled in 2015, 1,489 applied for aid, 1,396 were judged to have need, 92 had their need fully met. 1,248 Federal Work-Study jobs (averaging $4381). In 2015, 50 non-need-based awards were made. ***Average percent of need met:*** 47. ***Average financial aid package:*** $12,451. ***Average need-based loan:*** $4249. ***Average need-based gift aid:*** $7112. ***Average non-need-based aid:*** $6045. ***Average indebtedness upon graduation:*** $31,555.

APPLYING
Standardized Tests *Required:* SAT or ACT (for admission).

Options: electronic application, deferred entrance.

Application fee: $20.

Required: high school transcript, minimum 2.2 GPA. ***Required for some:*** interview. ***Recommended:*** essay or personal statement, 2 letters of recommendation.

Application deadlines: rolling (freshmen), rolling (transfers).

Notification: continuous (freshmen), continuous (transfers).

CONTACT
Ms. Nikoia Fredericksen, Associate Director, Undergraduate Admissions, Lincoln University, 1570 Baltimore Pike, Lincoln University, PA 19352. *Phone:* 484-365-7275. *Toll-free phone:* 800-790-0191. *Fax:* 484-365-8109. *E-mail:* nfredericksen@lincoln.edu.

See previous page for display ad and page 1398 for the College Close-Up.

Lock Haven University of Pennsylvania

Lock Haven, Pennsylvania

http://www.lhup.edu/

- **State-supported** comprehensive, founded 1870, part of Pennsylvania State System of Higher Education
- **Rural** 165-acre campus
- **Endowment** $10.7 million
- **Coed** 3,845 undergraduate students, 92% full-time, 57% women, 43% men
- **Moderately difficult** entrance level, 88% of applicants were admitted

UNDERGRAD STUDENTS
3,538 full-time, 307 part-time. Students come from 31 states and territories; 17 other countries; 5% are from out of state; 9% Black or African American, non-Hispanic/Latino; 2% Hispanic/Latino; 1% Asian, non-Hispanic/Latino; 0.5% American Indian or Alaska Native, non-Hispanic/Latino; 1% Two or more races, non-Hispanic/Latino; 1% Race/ethnicity unknown; 1% international; 4% transferred in; 54% live on campus.

Freshmen:
Admission: 3,750 applied, 3,294 admitted, 828 enrolled. ***Average high school GPA:*** 3.3. ***Test scores:*** SAT critical reading scores over 500: 33%; SAT math scores over 500: 40%; SAT writing scores over 500: 26%; ACT scores over 18: 63%; SAT critical reading scores over 600: 6%; SAT math scores over 600: 8%; SAT writing scores over 600: 3%; ACT scores over 24: 24%; ACT scores over 30: 6%.

Retention: 73% of full-time freshmen returned.

FACULTY
Total: 232, 88% full-time, 78% with terminal degrees.

Student/faculty ratio: 18:1.

ACADEMICS
Calendar: semesters. *Degrees:* associate, bachelor's, and master's.

Special study options: academic remediation for entering students, adult/continuing education programs, advanced placement credit, cooperative education, distance learning, double majors, English as a second language, freshman honors college, honors programs, independent study, internships, off-campus study, part-time degree program, services for LD students, student-designed majors, study abroad, summer session for credit. ***ROTC:*** Army (b).

Unusual degree programs: 3-2 engineering with Penn State University Park.

Computers: 290 computers/terminals are available on campus for general student use. Students can access the following: online (class) registration. Campuswide network is available.

Library: Stevenson Library plus 1 other. *Books:* 226,712 (physical), 18,288 (digital/electronic); *Databases:* 7. Weekly public service hours: 87; students can reserve study rooms.

STUDENT LIFE
Housing options: on-campus residence required through sophomore year; coed. Campus housing is university owned and is provided by a third party. Freshman applicants given priority for college housing.

Activities and organizations: drama/theater group, student-run newspaper, radio and television station, choral group, marching band, Student Government, Residence Hall Association, national fraternities, national sororities.

Athletics Member NCAA. All Division II except field hockey (Division I), wrestling (Division I). ***Intercollegiate sports:*** baseball M(s), basketball M(s)/W(s), cross-country running M(s)/W(s), field hockey W(s), football M(s), lacrosse W(s), soccer M(s)/W(s), softball W(s), swimming and diving W(s), track and field M(s)/W(s), volleyball W(s), wrestling M(s). ***Intramural sports:*** badminton M/W, basketball M/W, cross-country running M/W, fencing M/W, field hockey W, football M, golf M/W, ice hockey M, lacrosse M/W, racquetball M/W, rugby M/W, skiing (cross-country) M/W, skiing (downhill) M/W, soccer M/W, softball M/W, swimming and diving M/W, tennis M/W, track and field M/W, ultimate Frisbee M/W, volleyball M/W, water polo M, weight lifting M/W, wrestling M.

Campus security: 24-hour emergency response devices and patrols, late-night transport/escort service, controlled dormitory access.

Student services: health clinic, personal/psychological counseling, women's center.

COSTS & FINANCIAL AID
Costs (2016–17) ***Tuition:*** state resident $7238 full-time, $302 per credit hour part-time; nonresident $16,096 full-time, $671 per credit hour part-time. Full-time tuition and fees vary according to course load, location, and program. Part-time tuition and fees vary according to course load, location, and program. ***Required fees:*** $2991 full-time, $156 per credit hour part-time. ***Room and board:*** $9588; room only: $6144. Room and board charges vary according to board plan and housing facility. ***Payment plan:*** installment. ***Waivers:*** minority students, senior citizens, and employees or children of employees.

Financial Aid Of all full-time matriculated undergraduates who enrolled in 2016, 3,095 applied for aid, 2,644 were judged to have need, 2,441 had their need fully met. 244 Federal Work-Study jobs (averaging $649). 330 state and other part-time jobs (averaging $1350). In 2016, 38 non-need-based awards were made. ***Average percent of need met:*** 73. ***Average financial aid package:*** $8046. ***Average need-based loan:*** $4258. ***Average need-based gift aid:*** $6187. ***Average non-need-based aid:*** $1486. ***Average indebtedness upon graduation:*** $34,192.

APPLYING
Standardized Tests *Required:* SAT or ACT (for admission).

Options: electronic application, deferred entrance.

Application fee: $25.

Required: high school transcript. ***Required for some:*** essay or personal statement. ***Recommended:*** interview.

Application deadlines: rolling (freshmen), rolling (transfers).

Notification: continuous (freshmen), continuous (transfers).

CONTACT
Lock Haven University of Pennsylvania, Office of Admission, Lock Haven University - DACC, Lock Haven, PA 17745. *Phone:* 570-484-2109. *Toll-free phone:* 800-332-8900 (in-state); 800-233-8978 (out-of-state). *Fax:* 570-484-2201. *E-mail:* admissions@lhup.edu.

Lycoming College

Williamsport, Pennsylvania

http://www.lycoming.edu/

- **Independent United Methodist** 4-year, founded 1812
- **Small-town** 35-acre campus
- **Endowment** $183.4 million
- **Coed** 1,272 undergraduate students, 98% full-time, 52% women, 48% men
- **Moderately difficult** entrance level, 70% of applicants were admitted

UNDERGRAD STUDENTS
1,245 full-time, 27 part-time. Students come from 29 states and territories; 26 other countries; 39% are from out of state; 10% Black or African American, non-Hispanic/Latino; 9% Hispanic/Latino; 0.9% Asian, non-Hispanic/Latino; 0.2% American Indian or Alaska Native, non-Hispanic/Latino; 3% Two or more races, non-Hispanic/Latino; 5% Race/ethnicity unknown; 5% international; 2% transferred in; 88% live on campus.

Freshmen:
Admission: 1,876 applied, 1,305 admitted, 343 enrolled. ***Average high school GPA:*** 3.39. ***Test scores:*** SAT critical reading scores over 500: 60%; SAT math scores over 500: 63%; SAT writing scores over 500: 44%; ACT scores over 18: 96%; SAT critical reading scores over 600: 11%; SAT math scores over 600: 15%; SAT writing scores over 600: 9%; ACT scores over 24: 39%; SAT critical reading scores over 700: 2%; SAT math scores over 700: 1%; ACT scores over 30: 6%.
Retention: 79% of full-time freshmen returned.

FACULTY
Total: 122, 74% full-time, 80% with terminal degrees.
Student/faculty ratio: 12:1.

ACADEMICS
Calendar: semesters. *Degree:* bachelor's.
Special study options: accelerated degree program, adult/continuing education programs, advanced placement credit, cooperative education, double majors, honors programs, independent study, internships, off-campus study, part-time degree program, services for LD students, student-designed majors, study abroad, summer session for credit. ***ROTC:*** Army (c).
Unusual degree programs: 3-2 engineering with Binghamton University, State University of New York; forestry with Duke University; environmental management with Duke University.
Computers: 188 computers/terminals and 3,408 ports are available on campus for general student use. Students can access the following: campus intranet, computer help desk, free student e-mail accounts, online (class) grades, online (class) registration, online financial aid, free printing up to a limit, password management. Campuswide network is available. 100% of college-owned or -operated housing units are wired for high-speed Internet access. Wireless service is available via entire campus.
Library: Snowden Library. *Books:* 133,194 (physical), 129,088 (digital/electronic); *Serial titles:* 832 (physical), 35,574 (digital/electronic); *Databases:* 87. Weekly public service hours: 107.

STUDENT LIFE
Housing options: on-campus residence required through senior year; coed, women-only. Campus housing is university owned. Freshman campus housing is guaranteed.
Activities and organizations: drama/theater group, student-run newspaper, radio station, choral group, Campus Activities Board, Lycoming Dance Club, Habitat for Humanity, Circle K, United Campus Ministry, national fraternities, national sororities.
Athletics Member NCAA. All Division III. ***Intercollegiate sports:*** badminton M(c)/W(c), basketball M/W, cheerleading M(c)/W(c), crew M(c)/W(c), cross-country running M/W, equestrian sports M(c)/W(c), fencing M(c)/W(c), football M, golf M/W, lacrosse M/W, rugby M(c), soccer M/W, softball W, swimming and diving M/W, tennis M/W, ultimate Frisbee M(c)/W(c), volleyball W, water polo M(c)/W(c), wrestling M. ***Intramural sports:*** basketball M/W, football M/W, soccer M/W, softball M/W, table tennis M/W, volleyball M/W.
Campus security: 24-hour emergency response devices and patrols, student patrols, late-night transport/escort service, controlled dormitory access.
Student services: health clinic, personal/psychological counseling.

COSTS & FINANCIAL AID
Costs (2016–17) ***One-time required fee:*** $225. ***Comprehensive fee:*** $48,580 includes full-time tuition ($36,432), mandatory fees ($730), and room and board ($11,418). Part-time tuition: $1139 per credit hour. Part-time tuition and fees vary according to course load. ***Room and board:*** Room and board charges vary according to board plan and housing facility. ***Payment plan:*** installment. ***Waivers:*** employees or children of employees.
Financial Aid Of all full-time matriculated undergraduates who enrolled in 2016, 1,106 applied for aid, 1,048 were judged to have need, 298 had their need fully met. In 2016, 186 non-need-based awards were made. ***Average percent of need met:*** 85. ***Average financial aid package:*** $35,046. ***Average need-based loan:*** $4630. ***Average need-based gift aid:*** $29,394. ***Average non-need-based aid:*** $22,873.

APPLYING
Standardized Tests *Recommended:* SAT or ACT (for admission).
Options: electronic application, early decision, early action, deferred entrance.
Required: essay or personal statement, high school transcript, 2 letters of recommendation. ***Recommended:*** minimum 2.3 GPA, interview.
Application deadlines: 8/1 (freshmen), 7/1 (transfers), 11/15 (early action).
Early decision deadline: 11/1.
Notification: continuous until 12/15 (freshmen), continuous until 12/15 (transfers), 11/15 (early decision), 12/1 (early action).

CONTACT
Jessica Hess, Director of Admissions, Lycoming College, 700 College Place, Williamsport, PA 17701. *Phone:* 570-321-4318. *Toll-free phone:* 800-345-3920 Ext. 4026. *Fax:* 570-321-4317.
E-mail: admissions@lycoming.edu.

Mansfield University of Pennsylvania

Mansfield, Pennsylvania

http://www.mansfield.edu/

- **State-supported** comprehensive, founded 1857, part of Pennsylvania State System of Higher Education
- **Small-town** 174-acre campus
- **Coed** 2,195 undergraduate students, 91% full-time, 61% women, 39% men
- **Moderately difficult** entrance level, 86% of applicants were admitted

UNDERGRAD STUDENTS
1,988 full-time, 207 part-time. 17% are from out of state; 9% Black or African American, non-Hispanic/Latino; 3% Hispanic/Latino; 0.8% Asian, non-Hispanic/Latino; 0.3% American Indian or Alaska Native, non-Hispanic/Latino; 2% Two or more races, non-Hispanic/Latino; 1% Race/ethnicity unknown; 0.4% international; 6% transferred in; 51% live on campus.

Freshmen:
Admission: 2,017 applied, 1,742 admitted, 356 enrolled. ***Average high school GPA:*** 3.33. ***Test scores:*** SAT critical reading scores over 500: 39%; SAT math scores over 500: 42%; SAT writing scores over 500: 29%; SAT critical reading scores over 600: 8%; SAT math scores over 600: 8%; SAT writing scores over 600: 5%; SAT math scores over 700: 1%.
Retention: 76% of full-time freshmen returned.

FACULTY
Total: 157, 72% full-time, 66% with terminal degrees.
Student/faculty ratio: 17:1.

ACADEMICS
Calendar: semesters. *Degrees:* associate, bachelor's, and master's.
Special study options: adult/continuing education programs, part-time degree program. ***ROTC:*** Army (c).
Computers: Students can access the following: campus intranet, computer help desk, free student e-mail accounts, online (class) grades, online (class) registration, online (class) schedules. Campuswide network is available. 100% of college-owned or -operated housing units are wired for high-speed Internet access. Wireless service is available via classrooms, computer centers, computer labs, dorm rooms, learning centers, libraries, student centers.
Library: North Hall Library.

STUDENT LIFE
Housing options: on-campus residence required through sophomore year; coed. Campus housing is university owned. Freshman campus housing is guaranteed.
Activities and organizations: drama/theater group, student-run newspaper, radio and television station, choral group, marching band, national fraternities, national sororities.
Athletics Member NCAA. All Division II. ***Intercollegiate sports:*** baseball M(s), basketball M(s)/W(s), cross-country running M(s)/W(s), field hockey W(s), football M(c), soccer W(s), softball W(s), swimming and diving W, track and field M(s)/W(s). ***Intramural sports:*** badminton M/W, basketball M/W, bowling M/W, cheerleading W, cross-country running M/W, equestrian sports M/W, football M/W, golf M/W, racquetball M/W, skiing (cross-country) M/W, skiing (downhill) M/W, soccer M/W, softball M/W, swimming and diving M/W, tennis M/W, track and field M/W, volleyball M/W, water polo M/W, weight lifting M/W.
Campus security: 24-hour emergency response devices and patrols, student patrols, late-night transport/escort service, controlled dormitory access.
Student services: health clinic, personal/psychological counseling, women's center.

COSTS & FINANCIAL AID
Costs (2017–18) ***Tuition:*** state resident $9150 full-time, $305 per credit hour part-time; nonresident $15,090 full-time, $610 per credit hour part-time. Part-time tuition and fees vary according to course load. ***Required fees:*** $2758 full-time. ***Room and board:*** $11,468; room only: $8142. Room and board charges vary according to board plan and housing facility. ***Payment plans:*** installment, deferred payment. ***Waivers:*** senior citizens and employees or children of employees.
Financial Aid Of all full-time matriculated undergraduates who enrolled in 2015, 1,950 applied for aid, 1,729 were judged to have need, 155 had their need fully met. In 2015, 59 non-need-based awards were made. ***Average percent of need met:*** 63. ***Average financial aid package:*** $10,187. ***Average need-based loan:*** $3097. ***Average need-based gift aid:*** $2952. ***Average non-need-based aid:*** $2069. ***Average indebtedness upon graduation:*** $41,816. ***Financial aid deadline:*** 6/30.

APPLYING
Standardized Tests *Required for some:* SAT or ACT (for admission).
Options: electronic application, early admission, deferred entrance.
Application fee: $25.
Required: high school transcript. ***Required for some:*** interview. ***Recommended:*** essay or personal statement, minimum 2.5 GPA.

CONTACT
Ms. Rachel Green, Director of Admissions, Mansfield University of Pennsylvania, Academy Street, Mansfield, PA 16933. *Phone:* 570-662-4813. *Toll-free phone:* 800-577-6826. *E-mail:* admissions@mnsfld.edu.

★ Marywood University
Scranton, Pennsylvania
http://www.marywood.edu/

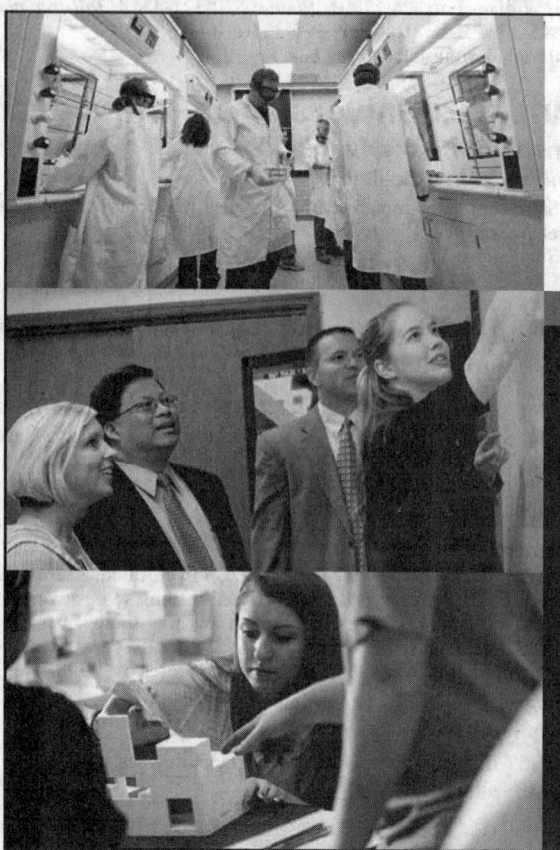

- **Independent Roman Catholic** comprehensive, founded 1915
- **Suburban** 123-acre campus
- **Endowment** $35.4 million
- **Coed** 1,931 undergraduate students, 91% full-time, 69% women, 31% men
- **Moderately difficult** entrance level, 69% of applicants were admitted

UNDERGRAD STUDENTS
1,753 full-time, 178 part-time. Students come from 20 states and territories; 10 other countries; 31% are from out of state; 2% Black or African American, non-Hispanic/Latino; 6% Hispanic/Latino; 2% Asian, non-Hispanic/Latino; 0.1% American Indian or Alaska Native, non-Hispanic/Latino; 2% Two or more races, non-Hispanic/Latino; 9% Race/ethnicity unknown; 3% international; 7% transferred in; 37% live on campus.

Freshmen:
Admission: 2,202 applied, 1,518 admitted, 325 enrolled. ***Average high school GPA:*** 3.42. ***Test scores:*** SAT math scores over 500: 66%; SAT writing scores over 500: 57%; SAT math scores over 600: 13%; SAT writing scores over 600: 10%; SAT math scores over 700: 1%.
Retention: 84% of full-time freshmen returned.

FACULTY
Total: 394, 37% full-time.
Student/faculty ratio: 12:1.

ACADEMICS
Calendar: semesters. *Degrees:* certificates, bachelor's, master's, doctoral, post-master's, and postbachelor's certificates.
Special study options: adult/continuing education programs, advanced placement credit, double majors, English as a second language, honors programs, independent study, internships, off-campus study, part-time degree program, services for LD students, student-designed majors, study abroad, summer session for credit. ***ROTC:*** Army (c), Air Force (c).
Unusual degree programs: 3-2 physician assistant, communication sciences disorders, criminal justice, biotechnology, health services administration.
Computers: 359 computers/terminals are available on campus for general student use. Students can access the following: computer help desk, free student e-mail accounts, online (class) grades, online (class) registration, online (class) schedules, degree audit, student account management, financial aid self-service, student planning. Campuswide network is available. 100% of college-owned or -operated housing units are wired for high-speed Internet access. Wireless service is available via entire campus.
Library: Learning Commons plus 2 others. *Books:* 204,320 (physical), 50,560 (digital/electronic); *Serial titles:* 97 (physical), 31,831 (digital/electronic); *Databases:* 54. Weekly public service hours: 111; students can reserve study rooms.

STUDENT LIFE
Housing options: on-campus residence required through sophomore year; men-only, women-only, special housing for students with disabilities. Campus housing is university owned. Freshman campus housing is guaranteed.
Activities and organizations: drama/theater group, student-run newspaper, radio and television station, choral group, Student Nurses Association, Health Professions Club, Speech and Hearing Club, Volunteers in Action (VIA), American Institute of Architects.
Athletics Member NCAA. All Division III. ***Intercollegiate sports:*** baseball M, basketball M/W, cross-country running M/W, field hockey W, golf M, lacrosse M/W, soccer M/W, softball W, swimming and diving M/W, tennis M/W, track and field M/W, volleyball W. ***Intramural sports:*** badminton M/W, basketball M/W, cheerleading M(c)/W(c), football M/W, golf W(c), racquetball M/W, rock climbing M(c)/W(c), soccer M/W, softball M/W, swimming and diving M/W, table tennis M/W, tennis M/W, volleyball M/W, water polo M/W.
Campus security: 24-hour emergency response devices and patrols, late-night transport/escort service, controlled dormitory access, apartments with deadbolts, self-defense education, lighted pathways, seminars on safety.
Student services: health clinic, personal/psychological counseling.

COSTS & FINANCIAL AID
Costs (2016–17) ***Comprehensive fee:*** $46,900 includes full-time tuition ($31,250), mandatory fees ($1750), and room and board ($13,900). Full-time tuition and fees vary according to course load. Part-time tuition: $630 per credit. Part-time tuition and fees vary according to course load.
Required fees: $450 per term part-time. ***College room only:*** $7822. Room and board charges vary according to board plan and housing facility.
Payment plans: installment, deferred payment. ***Waivers:*** senior citizens and employees or children of employees.
Financial Aid Of all full-time matriculated undergraduates who enrolled in 2016, 1,561 applied for aid, 1,427 were judged to have need, 235 had their need fully met. 584 Federal Work-Study jobs (averaging $1917). In 2016, 251 non-need-based awards were made. ***Average percent of need met:*** 69. ***Average financial aid package:*** $24,643. ***Average need-based loan:*** $4509. ***Average need-based gift aid:*** $19,504. ***Average non-need-based aid:*** $13,963. ***Average indebtedness upon graduation:*** $42,603.

APPLYING
Standardized Tests *Required:* SAT or ACT (for admission).
Options: electronic application, early admission, deferred entrance.
Application fee: $35.
Required: essay or personal statement, high school transcript, minimum 2.3 GPA, 1 letter of recommendation. ***Required for some:*** interview, portfolio for art majors, audition for music majors. ***Recommended:*** interview.
Application deadlines: rolling (freshmen), rolling (transfers).
Notification: continuous (freshmen), continuous (transfers).

CONTACT
Mr. Christian DiGregorio, Director of University Admissions, Marywood University, 2300 Adams Avenue, Scranton, PA 18509. *Phone:* 570-348-6234. *Toll-free phone:* 866-279-9663. *Fax:* 570-961-4763.
E-mail: yourfuture@marywood.edu.

See previous page for display ad and page 1414 for the College Close-Up.

Mercyhurst North East
North East, Pennsylvania
http://northeast.mercyhurst.edu/

CONTACT
Travis Lindahl, Director of Admissions, Mercyhurst North East, 16 West Division Street, North East, PA 16428. *Phone:* 814-725-6217. *Toll-free phone:* 866-846-6042. *Fax:* 814-725-6251.
E-mail: neadmiss@mercyhurst.edu.

Mercyhurst University
Erie, Pennsylvania
http://www.mercyhurst.edu/

- **Independent Roman Catholic** comprehensive, founded 1926
- **Suburban** 88-acre campus with easy access to Buffalo
- **Endowment** $31.9 million
- **Coed** 2,494 undergraduate students, 97% full-time, 56% women, 44% men
- **Moderately difficult** entrance level, 75% of applicants were admitted

UNDERGRAD STUDENTS
2,424 full-time, 70 part-time. Students come from 42 states and territories; 31 other countries; 58% are from out of state; 5% Black or African American, non-Hispanic/Latino; 4% Hispanic/Latino; 1% Asian, non-Hispanic/Latino; 0.2% Native Hawaiian or other Pacific Islander, non-Hispanic/Latino; 0.6% American Indian or Alaska Native, non-Hispanic/Latino; 18% Two or more races, non-Hispanic/Latino; 2% Race/ethnicity unknown; 10% international; 2% transferred in; 68% live on campus.

Freshmen:
Admission: 3,254 applied, 2,448 admitted, 718 enrolled. ***Average high school GPA:*** 3.3.
Retention: 78% of full-time freshmen returned.

FACULTY
Total: 135.
Student/faculty ratio: 15:1.

ACADEMICS
Calendar: semesters. *Degrees:* bachelor's, master's, and postbachelor's certificates.
Special study options: academic remediation for entering students, accelerated degree program, adult/continuing education programs, advanced placement credit, distance learning, double majors, honors

programs, independent study, internships, off-campus study, part-time degree program, services for LD students, student-designed majors, study abroad, summer session for credit. ***ROTC:*** Army (b), Air Force (c).

Unusual degree programs: 3-2 business administration.

Computers: 350 computers/terminals and 150 ports are available on campus for general student use. Students can access the following: campus intranet, computer help desk, free student e-mail accounts, online (class) grades, online (class) registration, online (class) schedules. Campuswide network is available. 100% of college-owned or -operated housing units are wired for high-speed Internet access. Wireless service is available via entire campus.

Library: Hammermill Library. *Books:* 149,867 (physical), 143,272 (digital/electronic); *Databases:* 49. Study areas open 24 hours, 5-7 days a week; students can reserve study rooms.

STUDENT LIFE

Housing options: on-campus residence required through sophomore year; coed, men-only, women-only. Campus housing is university owned and leased by the school. Freshman campus housing is guaranteed.

Activities and organizations: drama/theater group, student-run newspaper, radio and television station, choral group, marching band, Student Government, chorus, Admission Ambassadors, Amnesty International, The Merciad.

Athletics Member NCAA. All Division II except men's and women's ice hockey (Division I). ***Intercollegiate sports:*** baseball M(s), basketball M(s)/W(s), crew M(s)/W(s), cross-country running M(s)/W(s), field hockey W(s), football M(s), golf M(s)/W(s), ice hockey M(s)/W(s), lacrosse M(s)/W(s), soccer M(s)/W(s), softball W(s), tennis M(s)/W(s), volleyball W(s), water polo M(s)/W(s), wrestling M(s). ***Intramural sports:*** basketball M/W, football M, skiing (cross-country) M/W, skiing (downhill) M/W, volleyball M/W.

Campus security: 24-hour emergency response devices and patrols, campus-wide camera system.

Student services: health clinic, personal/psychological counseling.

COSTS & FINANCIAL AID

Costs (2016–17) ***Comprehensive fee:*** $46,104 includes full-time tuition ($32,430), mandatory fees ($2050), and room and board ($11,624). Full-time tuition and fees vary according to class time, course load, degree level, location, and program. Part-time tuition: $3243 per course. Part-time tuition and fees vary according to class time, course load, degree level, location, and program. ***Required fees:*** $616 per term part-time. ***College room only:*** $5732. Room and board charges vary according to board plan, housing facility, and location. ***Payment plan:*** installment. ***Waivers:*** adult students and employees or children of employees.

Financial Aid Of all full-time matriculated undergraduates who enrolled in 2015, 1,866 applied for aid, 1,686 were judged to have need, 104 had their need fully met. In 2015, 411 non-need-based awards were made. ***Average percent of need met:*** 50. ***Average financial aid package:*** $26,019. ***Average need-based loan:*** $4360. ***Average need-based gift aid:*** $16,089. ***Average non-need-based aid:*** $15,583. ***Average indebtedness upon graduation:*** $24,739. ***Financial aid deadline:*** 5/1.

APPLYING

Options: electronic application, deferred entrance.

Required: essay or personal statement, high school transcript. ***Required for some:*** 1 letter of recommendation. ***Recommended:*** interview.

Application deadlines: rolling (freshmen), rolling (transfers).

Notification: continuous until 11/1 (freshmen), continuous until 12/1 (transfers).

CONTACT

Christian Beyer, Director of Undergraduate Admissions, Mercyhurst University, 501 East 38th Street, Erie, PA 16546-0001. *Phone:* 814-824-2202. *Toll-free phone:* 800-825-1926. *Fax:* 814-824-2071. *E-mail:* cbeyer@mercyhurst.edu.

Messiah College
Mechanicsburg, Pennsylvania
http://www.messiah.edu/

- **Independent interdenominational** comprehensive, founded 1909
- **Small-town** 485-acre campus
- **Endowment** $126.0 million
- **Coed** 2,788 undergraduate students, 95% full-time, 61% women, 39% men
- **Moderately difficult** entrance level, 80% of applicants were admitted

UNDERGRAD STUDENTS

2,648 full-time, 140 part-time. Students come from 38 states and territories; 29 other countries; 36% are from out of state; 2% Black or African American, non-Hispanic/Latino; 4% Hispanic/Latino; 2% Asian, non-Hispanic/Latino; 0.1% American Indian or Alaska Native, non-Hispanic/Latino; 4% Two or more races, non-Hispanic/Latino; 0.9% Race/ethnicity unknown; 5% international; 3% transferred in; 85% live on campus.

Freshmen:

Admission: 2,596 applied, 2,064 admitted, 685 enrolled. ***Average high school GPA:*** 3.77. ***Test scores:*** SAT critical reading scores over 500: 81%; SAT math scores over 500: 82%; SAT writing scores over 500: 74%; ACT scores over 18: 99%; SAT critical reading scores over 600: 39%; SAT math scores over 600: 40%; SAT writing scores over 600: 30%; ACT scores over 24: 69%; SAT critical reading scores over 700: 9%; SAT math scores over 700: 10%; SAT writing scores over 700: 5%; ACT scores over 30: 21%.

Retention: 85% of full-time freshmen returned.

FACULTY

Total: 361, 52% full-time, 48% with terminal degrees.

Student/faculty ratio: 13:1.

ACADEMICS

Calendar: semesters. *Degrees:* bachelor's, master's, doctoral, post-master's, and postbachelor's certificates.

Special study options: academic remediation for entering students, accelerated degree program, adult/continuing education programs, advanced placement credit, cooperative education, distance learning, double majors, English as a second language, freshman honors college, honors programs, independent study, internships, off-campus study, part-time degree program, services for LD students, student-designed majors, study abroad, summer session for credit.

Unusual degree programs: 3-2 applied health science or biopsychology/occupational therapy with Thomas Jefferson University, biochemistry/pharmacy with the University of the Sciences in Philadelphia, politics/public policy and management with Carnegie Mellon University.

Computers: 571 computers/terminals are available on campus for general student use. Students can access the following: campus intranet, computer help desk, free student e-mail accounts, online (class) grades, online (class) registration, online (class) schedules, access to software. Campuswide network is available. 100% of college-owned or -operated housing units are wired for high-speed Internet access. Wireless service is available via entire campus.

Library: Murray Library. *Books:* 250,939 (physical), 142,235 (digital/electronic); *Serial titles:* 144 (physical), 115,506 (digital/electronic); *Databases:* 105. Weekly public service hours: 96; students can reserve study rooms.

STUDENT LIFE

Housing options: on-campus residence required through senior year; coed, men-only, women-only, special housing for students with disabilities. Campus housing is university owned. Freshman campus housing is guaranteed.

Activities and organizations: drama/theater group, student-run newspaper, radio station, choral group, Outreach teams, student government, choral groups and ensembles, Small Group Program, Outdoors Club.

Athletics Member NCAA. All Division III. ***Intercollegiate sports:*** baseball M, basketball M/W, cross-country running M/W, field hockey W, golf M, lacrosse M/W, soccer M/W, softball W, swimming and diving M/W, tennis M/W, track and field M/W, volleyball W, wrestling M.

Intramural sports: basketball M/W, field hockey W(c), football M/W, ice hockey M(c), soccer M/W, softball M/W, ultimate Frisbee M(c)/W(c), volleyball M(c)/W.

Campus security: 24-hour emergency response devices and patrols, student patrols, late-night transport/escort service, controlled dormitory access, bicycle patrols, security lighting, self-defense classes, prevention/awareness programs.

Student services: health clinic, personal/psychological counseling.

COSTS & FINANCIAL AID

Costs (2016–17) ***Comprehensive fee:*** $43,100 includes full-time tuition ($32,350), mandatory fees ($830), and room and board ($9920). Part-time tuition: $1350 per credit hour. ***College room only:*** $5250. Room and board charges vary according to board plan and housing facility. ***Payment plan:*** installment. ***Waivers:*** adult students, senior citizens, and employees or children of employees.

Financial Aid Of all full-time matriculated undergraduates who enrolled in 2016, 2,134 applied for aid, 1,916 were judged to have need, 364 had their need fully met. 851 Federal Work-Study jobs (averaging $2131). 821 state and other part-time jobs (averaging $2046). In 2016, 678 non-need-based awards were made. ***Average percent of need met:*** 72. ***Average financial aid package:*** $23,627. ***Average need-based loan:*** $4861. ***Average need-based gift aid:*** $17,599. ***Average non-need-based aid:*** $14,515. ***Average indebtedness upon graduation:*** $39,617.

APPLYING

Standardized Tests *Required:* SAT or ACT (for admission).

Options: electronic application.

Application fee: $50.

Required: essay or personal statement, high school transcript. ***Required for some:*** interview.

Application deadlines: rolling (freshmen), rolling (transfers).

Notification: continuous (freshmen), continuous (transfers).

CONTACT

Dr. John Chopka, Vice President for Enrollment Management, Messiah College, One College Avenue, Suite 3005, Mechanicsburg, PA 17055. *Phone:* 717-691-6000. *Toll-free phone:* 800-233-4220. *Fax:* 717-691-2307. *E-mail:* admiss@messiah.edu.

★ Millersville University of Pennsylvania

Millersville, Pennsylvania

http://www.millersville.edu/

- **State-supported** comprehensive, founded 1855, part of Pennsylvania State System of Higher Education
- **Small-town** 250-acre campus
- **Endowment** $8.3 million
- **Coed** 6,980 undergraduate students, 85% full-time, 56% women, 44% men
- **Moderately difficult** entrance level, 69% of applicants were admitted

UNDERGRAD STUDENTS

5,941 full-time, 1,039 part-time. Students come from 34 states and territories; 55 other countries; 6% are from out of state; 9% Black or African American, non-Hispanic/Latino; 9% Hispanic/Latino; 3% Asian, non-Hispanic/Latino; 0.1% Native Hawaiian or other Pacific Islander, non-Hispanic/Latino; 0.2% American Indian or Alaska Native, non-Hispanic/Latino; 2% Two or more races, non-Hispanic/Latino; 1% Race/ethnicity unknown; 0.5% international; 8% transferred in; 31% live on campus.

Freshmen:

Admission: 6,943 applied, 4,794 admitted, 1,327 enrolled. ***Test scores:*** SAT critical reading scores over 500: 57%; SAT math scores over 500: 58%; SAT writing scores over 500: 44%; ACT scores over 18: 86%; SAT critical reading scores over 600: 14%; SAT math scores over 600: 14%; SAT writing scores over 600: 8%; ACT scores over 24: 34%; SAT critical reading scores over 700: 2%; SAT math scores over 700: 1%; ACT scores over 30: 5%.

Retention: 77% of full-time freshmen returned.

FACULTY

Total: 489, 60% full-time, 69% with terminal degrees.

Student/faculty ratio: 19:1.

ACADEMICS
Calendar: 4-1-4. *Degrees:* associate, bachelor's, master's, doctoral, post-master's, and postbachelor's certificates.

Special study options: academic remediation for entering students, accelerated degree program, adult/continuing education programs, advanced placement credit, cooperative education, distance learning, double majors, freshman honors college, honors programs, independent study, internships, off-campus study, part-time degree program, services for LD students, student-designed majors, study abroad, summer session for credit. ***ROTC:*** Army (b).

Unusual degree programs: 3-2 engineering with Penn State University, University of Delaware.

Computers: 430 computers/terminals and 2,500 ports are available on campus for general student use. Students can access the following: campus intranet, computer help desk, free student e-mail accounts, online (class) grades, online (class) registration, online (class) schedules. Campuswide network is available. 100% of college-owned or -operated housing units are wired for high-speed Internet access. Wireless service is available via entire campus.
Library: The Francine G. McNairy Library and Learning Forum at Ganser Hall. *Books:* 317,945 (physical), 53,341 (digital/electronic); *Serial titles:* 4,191 (physical), 372,826 (digital/electronic); *Databases:* 179. Weekly public service hours: 94; students can reserve study rooms.

STUDENT LIFE
Housing options: on-campus residence required through sophomore year; coed, special housing for students with disabilities. Campus housing is university owned and leased by the school. Freshman campus housing is guaranteed.

Activities and organizations: drama/theater group, student-run newspaper, radio and television station, choral group, marching band, MUTV 99, Marching Band, University Activities Board, Student Senate, University Christian Fellowship, national fraternities, national sororities.

Athletics Member NCAA. All Division II. ***Intercollegiate sports:*** baseball M(s), basketball M(s)/W(s), cross-country running W(s), field hockey W(s), football M(s), golf M(s)/W(s), lacrosse W(s), soccer M(s)/W(s), softball W(s), swimming and diving W(s), tennis M(s)/W(s), track and field W(s), volleyball W(s), wrestling M(s). ***Intramural sports:*** badminton M/W, baseball M(c)/W(c), basketball M/W, bowling M(c)/W(c), cheerleading M(c)/W(c), cross-country running M(c)/W(c), equestrian sports M(c)/W(c), fencing M(c)/W(c), football M/W, golf M/W, ice hockey M(c)/W(c), lacrosse M(c), rugby M(c)/W(c), soccer M/W, softball M/W, table tennis M/W, tennis M/W, ultimate Frisbee M/W, volleyball M/W, water polo M(c)/W(c).

Campus security: 24-hour emergency response devices and patrols, student patrols, late-night transport/escort service, controlled dormitory access, emergency notification system, crime awareness programs, self-defense education, shuttle buses, lighted paths, LiveSafe app, TAT.

Student services: health clinic, personal/psychological counseling, women's center.

COSTS & FINANCIAL AID
Costs (2016–17) ***Tuition:*** state resident $8970 full-time, $299 per credit part-time; nonresident $18,096 full-time, $754 per credit part-time. Full-time tuition and fees vary according to course load and program. Part-time tuition and fees vary according to course load and program. ***Required fees:*** $2524 full-time, $87 per credit part-time, $19 per credit part-time. ***Room and board:*** $12,228; room only: $8274. Room and board charges vary according to board plan and housing facility. ***Payment plan:*** installment. ***Waivers:*** senior citizens and employees or children of employees.

Financial Aid Of all full-time matriculated undergraduates who enrolled in 2015, 5,151 applied for aid, 4,220 were judged to have need, 195 had their need fully met. 198 Federal Work-Study jobs (averaging $1494). 1,601 state and other part-time jobs (averaging $1518). In 2015, 172 non-need-based awards were made. ***Average percent of need met:*** 63. ***Average financial aid package:*** $8501. ***Average need-based loan:*** $4072. ***Average need-based gift aid:*** $5823. ***Average non-need-based aid:*** $3238. ***Average indebtedness upon graduation:*** $29,481.

APPLYING
Standardized Tests *Required:* SAT or ACT (for admission).

Options: electronic application, early admission, deferred entrance.
Application fee: $50.

Required: essay or personal statement, high school transcript, minimum 2.0 GPA. ***Required for some:*** 1 letter of recommendation, interview, audition for music applicants, portfolio for art applicants, Associate degree in nursing or Diploma and RN license for nursing. ***Recommended:*** minimum 3.0 GPA, 2 letters of recommendation.

Application deadlines: rolling (freshmen), rolling (transfers).

Notification: continuous (freshmen), continuous (transfers).

CONTACT
Ms. Katy A. Ferrier, Director of Admissions, Millersville University of Pennsylvania, PO Box 1002, Millersville, PA 17551-0302. *Phone:* 717-871-4625. *Toll-free phone:* 800-MU-ADMIT. *Fax:* 717-871-2147. *E-mail:* admissions@millersville.edu.

See previous page for display ad and page 1418 for the College Close-Up.

★ Misericordia University
Dallas, Pennsylvania
http://www.misericordia.edu/

- **Independent Roman Catholic** comprehensive, founded 1924
- **Small-town** 120-acre campus
- **Endowment** $43.5 million
- **Coed** 2,195 undergraduate students, 75% full-time, 67% women, 33% men
- **Moderately difficult** entrance level, 74% of applicants were admitted

UNDERGRAD STUDENTS
1,641 full-time, 554 part-time. Students come from 26 states and territories; 1 other country; 25% are from out of state; 3% Black or African American, non-Hispanic/Latino; 3% Hispanic/Latino; 1% Asian, non-Hispanic/Latino; 0.1% Native Hawaiian or other Pacific Islander, non-Hispanic/Latino; 0.2% American Indian or Alaska Native, non-Hispanic/Latino; 2% Two or more races, non-Hispanic/Latino; 1% Race/ethnicity unknown; 0.1% international; 3% transferred in; 43% live on campus.

Freshmen:
Admission: 1,823 applied, 1,357 admitted, 430 enrolled. ***Average high school GPA:*** 3.33. ***Test scores:*** SAT critical reading scores over 500: 65%; SAT math scores over 500: 69%; ACT scores over 18: 96%; SAT critical reading scores over 600: 15%; SAT math scores over 600: 19%; ACT scores over 24: 54%; SAT critical reading scores over 700: 1%; SAT math scores over 700: 1%; ACT scores over 30: 6%.

Retention: 82% of full-time freshmen returned.

FACULTY
Total: 320, 43% full-time, 44% with terminal degrees.

Student/faculty ratio: 11:1.

ACADEMICS
Calendar: semesters. *Degrees:* certificates, bachelor's, master's, doctoral, post-master's, and postbachelor's certificates.

Special study options: accelerated degree program, adult/continuing education programs, advanced placement credit, cooperative education, distance learning, double majors, honors programs, independent study, internships, off-campus study, part-time degree program, services for LD students, student-designed majors, study abroad, summer session for credit. ***ROTC:*** Army (c), Air Force (c).

Computers: 150 computers/terminals and 1,000 ports are available on campus for general student use. Students can access the following: campus intranet, computer help desk, free student e-mail accounts, online (class) grades, online (class) registration, online (class) schedules. Campuswide network is available. 100% of college-owned or -operated housing units are wired for high-speed Internet access. Wireless service is available via entire campus.
Library: Mary Kintz Bevevino Library. *Books:* 80,036 (physical), 13,154 (digital/electronic); *Serial titles:* 8,153 (physical), 28,230 (digital/electronic); *Databases:* 111. Students can reserve study rooms.

STUDENT LIFE
Housing options: coed. Campus housing is university owned and is provided by a third party. Freshman applicants given priority for college housing.

Activities and organizations: drama/theater group, student-run newspaper, radio station, choral group, Physical Therapy club, MSOTA, Colleges against Cancer, Dance Ensemble, Medical Imaging club.

Athletics Member NCAA. All Division III except tennis (Division II). ***Intercollegiate sports:*** baseball M, basketball M/W, cross-country running M/W, field hockey W, football M, golf M/W, lacrosse M/W, soccer M/W, softball W, swimming and diving M/W, tennis M/W, track and field M/W, volleyball M/W. ***Intramural sports:*** basketball M/W, football M/W, soccer M/W, softball M/W, tennis M/W, ultimate Frisbee M/W, volleyball M/W.

Campus security: 24-hour emergency response devices and patrols, late-night transport/escort service, controlled dormitory access.

Student services: health clinic, personal/psychological counseling, women's center.

COSTS & FINANCIAL AID

Costs (2017–18) ***Comprehensive fee:*** $45,210 includes full-time tuition ($30,030), mandatory fees ($1630), and room and board ($13,550). Full-time tuition and fees vary according to degree level. Part-time tuition: $595 per credit. Part-time tuition and fees vary according to class time and location. ***College room only:*** $7380. Room and board charges vary according to board plan and housing facility. ***Payment plans:*** installment, deferred payment. ***Waivers:*** employees or children of employees.

Financial Aid Of all full-time matriculated undergraduates who enrolled in 2016, 1,508 applied for aid, 1,335 were judged to have need, 308 had their need fully met. In 2016, 173 non-need-based awards were made. ***Average percent of need met:*** 79. ***Average financial aid package:*** $22,829. ***Average need-based loan:*** $8709. ***Average need-based gift aid:*** $16,553. ***Average non-need-based aid:*** $12,739. ***Average indebtedness upon graduation:*** $42,686. ***Financial aid deadline:*** 5/1.

APPLYING

Standardized Tests *Required:* SAT or ACT (for admission).

Options: electronic application, early admission, deferred entrance.

Application fee: $35.

Required: high school transcript. ***Required for some:*** essay or personal statement, minimum 2.5 GPA, 2 letters of recommendation. ***Recommended:*** interview.

Application deadlines: rolling (freshmen), rolling (transfers).

Notification: continuous (freshmen), continuous (transfers).

CONTACT

Mr. Glenn Bozinski, Director of Admissions, Misericordia University, 301 Lake Street, Dallas, PA 18612-1098. *Phone:* 570-675-6264. *Toll-free phone:* 866-262-6363. *Fax:* 570-674-6232. *E-mail:* admiss@misericordia.edu.

See below for display ad and page 1422 for the College Close-Up.

Moore College of Art & Design

Philadelphia, Pennsylvania

http://www.moore.edu/

- **Independent** comprehensive, founded 1848
- **Urban** 3-acre campus with easy access to Philadelphia
- **Endowment** $21.7 million
- **Undergraduate: women only; graduate: coed**
- **Moderately difficult** entrance level

FACULTY

Student/faculty ratio: 7:1.

ACADEMICS

Calendar: semesters. *Degrees:* certificates, bachelor's, master's, and postbachelor's certificates.

Library: Connelly Library plus 1 other. *Books:* 50,000 (physical); *Serial titles:* 110 (physical); *Databases:* 12.

STUDENT LIFE

Housing options: women-only. Campus housing is university owned. Freshman campus housing is guaranteed.

Activities and organizations: Student Government Association, Student Orientation Staff, Student-run Gallery, Visionary Women Honors Program, Yearbook.

Campus security: 24-hour emergency response devices and patrols, late-night transport/escort service, controlled dormitory access, RD and professional staff on call 24 /7.

Student services: health clinic, personal/psychological counseling.

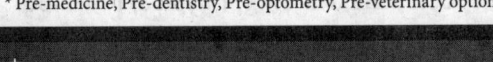

COSTS
Costs (2016–17) ***Comprehensive fee:*** $52,690 includes full-time tuition ($37,032), mandatory fees ($1269), and room and board ($14,389). Full-time tuition and fees vary according to course load. Part-time tuition: $1545 per credit. Part-time tuition and fees vary according to course load. ***College room only:*** $8663. Room and board charges vary according to board plan.

APPLYING
Standardized Tests *Recommended:* SAT or ACT (for admission).

Options: electronic application, deferred entrance.

Application fee: $60.

Required: high school transcript, minimum 2.5 GPA, 1 letter of recommendation, portfolio review. ***Required for some:*** minimum 3.0 GPA. ***Recommended:*** essay or personal statement, interview.

CONTACT
Ms. Jasmine Zateeny, Assistant Director of Admissions, Recruitment Coordinator, Moore College of Art & Design, 20th and The Parkway, Philadelphia, PA 19103. *Phone:* 215-965-4015. *Toll-free phone:* 800-523-2025. *Fax:* 215-965-8544. *E-mail:* enroll@moore.edu.

Moravian College

Bethlehem, Pennsylvania

http://www.moravian.edu/

- **Independent** comprehensive, founded 1742, affiliated with Moravian Church
- **Suburban** 85-acre campus with easy access to Philadelphia
- **Endowment** $102.4 million
- **Coed** 2,006 undergraduate students, 89% full-time, 59% women, 41% men
- **Moderately difficult** entrance level, 80% of applicants were admitted

UNDERGRAD STUDENTS
1,794 full-time, 212 part-time. Students come from 24 states and territories; 19 other countries; 31% are from out of state; 5% Black or African American, non-Hispanic/Latino; 10% Hispanic/Latino; 2% Asian, non-Hispanic/Latino; 0.1% Native Hawaiian or other Pacific Islander, non-Hispanic/Latino; 0.2% American Indian or Alaska Native, non-Hispanic/Latino; 2% Two or more races, non-Hispanic/Latino; 6% Race/ethnicity unknown; 7% international; 5% transferred in; 67% live on campus.

Freshmen:
Admission: 2,512 applied, 2,005 admitted, 488 enrolled. ***Average high school GPA:*** 3.47. ***Test scores:*** SAT critical reading scores over 500: 55%; SAT math scores over 500: 55%; SAT writing scores over 500: 50%; ACT scores over 18: 92%; SAT critical reading scores over 600: 13%; SAT math scores over 600: 15%; SAT writing scores over 600: 10%; ACT scores over 24: 40%; SAT critical reading scores over 700: 1%; SAT writing scores over 700: 1%; ACT scores over 30: 3%.
Retention: 78% of full-time freshmen returned.

FACULTY
Total: 339, 40% full-time.

Student/faculty ratio: 12:1.

ACADEMICS
Calendar: semesters. *Degrees:* bachelor's, master's, post-master's, and postbachelor's certificates.

Special study options: accelerated degree program, adult/continuing education programs, advanced placement credit, cooperative education, distance learning, double majors, honors programs, independent study, internships, off-campus study, part-time degree program, services for LD students, student-designed majors, study abroad, summer session for credit. ***ROTC:*** Army (c).

Unusual degree programs: 3-2 engineering with Lehigh University, Washington University in St. Louis.

Computers: 306 computers/terminals and 1,700 ports are available on campus for general student use. Students can access the following: campus intranet, computer help desk, free student e-mail accounts, online (class) grades, online (class) registration, online (class) schedules. Campuswide network is available. 100% of college-owned or -operated housing units are wired for high-speed Internet access. Wireless service is available via entire campus.

Library: Reeves Library. *Books:* 253,908 (physical), 154,565 (digital/electronic); *Serial titles:* 3 (physical), 75,717 (digital/electronic); *Databases:* 50. Weekly public service hours: 86.

STUDENT LIFE

Housing options: on-campus residence required through sophomore year; coed, men-only, women-only, special housing for students with disabilities. Campus housing is university owned. Freshman campus housing is guaranteed.

Activities and organizations: drama/theater group, student-run newspaper, radio station, choral group, marching band, American Association of University Women, International Club, Latin Student Union, Black Student Union, Saudi Students Club, national fraternities, national sororities.

Athletics Member NCAA. All Division III. ***Intercollegiate sports:*** baseball M, basketball M/W, cheerleading W(c), cross-country running M/W, equestrian sports W(c), field hockey W, football M, golf M, ice hockey M(c), lacrosse M/W, rugby M(c), soccer M/W, softball W, tennis M/W, track and field M/W, ultimate Frisbee W(c), volleyball W. ***Intramural sports:*** basketball M/W, soccer M/W, softball M/W, table tennis M/W, tennis M/W, volleyball M/W.

Campus security: 24-hour emergency response devices and patrols, late-night transport/escort service, controlled dormitory access.

Student services: health clinic, personal/psychological counseling.

COSTS & FINANCIAL AID

Costs (2017–18) ***One-time required fee:*** $140. ***Comprehensive fee:*** $54,718 includes full-time tuition ($40,293), mandatory fees ($1731), and room and board ($12,694). Part-time tuition: $1120 per credit. Part-time tuition and fees vary according to class time. ***College room only:*** $7132. Room and board charges vary according to board plan and housing facility. ***Payment plan:*** installment. ***Waivers:*** employees or children of employees.

Financial Aid Of all full-time matriculated undergraduates who enrolled in 2016, 1,553 applied for aid, 1,443 were judged to have need, 203 had their need fully met. 1,200 Federal Work-Study jobs (averaging $2400). 140 state and other part-time jobs (averaging $1100). In 2016, 336 non-need-based awards were made. ***Average percent of need met:*** 74. ***Average financial aid package:*** $29,554. ***Average need-based loan:*** $4448. ***Average need-based gift aid:*** $23,904. ***Average non-need-based aid:*** $12,336. ***Average indebtedness upon graduation:*** $33,377.

APPLYING

Standardized Tests *Required:* SAT or ACT (for admission).

Options: electronic application, deferred entrance.

Required: essay or personal statement, high school transcript, 1 letter of recommendation, interview. ***Required for some:*** portfolio for art majors; audition for music majors; 3.3 high school GPA, minimum SAT combined score of 1500 (with no section less than 500) or ACT score of 23 for nursing.

Application deadlines: 3/1 (freshmen), 3/1 (transfers).

Notification: continuous until 10/15 (freshmen), continuous (transfers).

CONTACT

Alyson Remsing, Moravian College, 1200 Main Street, Bethlehem, PA 18018. *Phone:* 610-861-1320. *Toll-free phone:* 800-441-3191. *Fax:* 610-625-7930. *E-mail:* admission@moravian.edu.

See previous page for display ad and page 1428 for the College Close-Up.

★ Mount Aloysius College

Cresson, Pennsylvania

http://www.mtaloy.edu/

- **Independent Roman Catholic** comprehensive, founded 1939
- **Small-town** 193-acre campus
- **Coed** 1,803 undergraduate students, 65% full-time, 71% women, 29% men
- **Minimally difficult** entrance level, 73% of applicants were admitted

UNDERGRAD STUDENTS

1,176 full-time, 627 part-time. 6% are from out of state; 3% Black or African American, non-Hispanic/Latino; 0.7% Hispanic/Latino; 0.3% Asian, non-Hispanic/Latino; 0.1% American Indian or Alaska Native, non-Hispanic/Latino; 16% Race/ethnicity unknown; 2% international; 3% transferred in; 34% live on campus.

Freshmen:

Admission: 1,485 applied, 1,082 admitted, 376 enrolled. ***Average high school GPA:*** 3.2. ***Test scores:*** SAT critical reading scores over 500: 34%; SAT math scores over 500: 35%; SAT writing scores over 500: 28%; ACT scores over 18: 70%; SAT critical reading scores over 600: 5%; SAT math scores over 600: 5%; SAT writing scores over 600: 2%; ACT scores over 24: 13%; ACT scores over 30: 2%.

FACULTY

Total: 203, 35% full-time.

Student/faculty ratio: 12:1.

ACADEMICS

Calendar: semesters. *Degrees:* certificates, associate, bachelor's, and master's.

Special study options: academic remediation for entering students, accelerated degree program, advanced placement credit, distance learning, double majors, external degree program, honors programs, independent study, internships, part-time degree program, student-designed majors, study abroad, summer session for credit.

Computers: Students can access the following: campus intranet, computer help desk, free student e-mail accounts, online (class) grades, online (class) registration, online (class) schedules. Campuswide network is available. 100% of college-owned or -operated housing units are wired for high-speed Internet access. Wireless service is available via entire campus.

Library: Mount Aloysius College Library.

STUDENT LIFE

Housing options: on-campus residence required through sophomore year; coed. Campus housing is university owned. Freshman campus housing is guaranteed.

Activities and organizations: drama/theater group, student-run newspaper, choral group, Student Government, Campus Activity Board, Student Athletic Advisory Committee, Spirit Team, Dance Team.

Athletics Member NCAA. All Division III. ***Intercollegiate sports:*** baseball M, basketball M/W, cross-country running M/W, golf M/W, soccer M/W, softball W, tennis M/W, volleyball W. ***Intramural sports:*** basketball M/W, bowling M/W, cheerleading M(c)/W(c), football M/W, skiing (cross-country) M/W, skiing (downhill) M/W, table tennis M/W, ultimate Frisbee M/W, volleyball M/W, weight lifting M/W.

Campus security: 24-hour emergency response devices and patrols, student patrols, late-night transport/escort service, controlled dormitory access.

Student services: health clinic, personal/psychological counseling.

COSTS & FINANCIAL AID

Costs (2016–17) ***Comprehensive fee:*** $31,790 includes full-time tuition ($20,710), mandatory fees ($1140), and room and board ($9940). Part-time tuition: $770 per credit hour. ***College room only:*** $5000.

Financial Aid Of all full-time matriculated undergraduates who enrolled in 2016, 1,075 applied for aid, 898 were judged to have need. In 2016, 178 non-need-based awards were made. ***Average percent of need met:*** 38. ***Average financial aid package:*** $14,140. ***Average need-based loan:*** $4260. ***Average need-based gift aid:*** $2650. ***Average non-need-based aid:*** $5200.

APPLYING

Standardized Tests *Required:* SAT or ACT (for admission). *Recommended:* SAT (for admission), ACT (for admission).

Options: electronic application, early admission, deferred entrance.

Application fee: $30.

Required: high school transcript. ***Required for some:*** essay or personal statement, interview. ***Recommended:*** interview.

Application deadlines: rolling (freshmen), rolling (transfers).

Notification: continuous (freshmen), continuous (transfers).

CONTACT

Mr. Frank C. Crouse Jr., Vice President for Enrollment Management/Dean of Admissions, Mount Aloysius College, 7373 Admiral Peary Highway,

Cresson, PA 16630-1999. *Phone:* 814-886-6383. *Toll-free phone:* 888-823-2220. *Fax:* 814-886-6441. *E-mail:* admissions@mtaloy.edu.

See page 1430 for the College Close-Up.

★ Muhlenberg College
Allentown, Pennsylvania
http://www.muhlenberg.edu/

- **Independent** 4-year, founded 1848, affiliated with Lutheran Church
- **Suburban** 75-acre campus with easy access to Philadelphia
- **Endowment** $246.9 million
- **Coed** 2,408 undergraduate students, 96% full-time, 60% women, 40% men
- **Very difficult** entrance level, 48% of applicants were admitted

UNDERGRAD STUDENTS
2,318 full-time, 90 part-time. Students come from 35 states and territories; 13 other countries; 76% are from out of state; 3% Black or African American, non-Hispanic/Latino; 7% Hispanic/Latino; 3% Asian, non-Hispanic/Latino; 1% Two or more races, non-Hispanic/Latino; 6% Race/ethnicity unknown; 3% international; 0.8% transferred in; 92% live on campus.

Freshmen:
Admission: 4,862 applied, 2,346 admitted, 593 enrolled. ***Average high school GPA:*** 3.31. ***Test scores:*** SAT critical reading scores over 500: 93%; SAT math scores over 500: 94%; SAT writing scores over 500: 91%; ACT scores over 18: 100%; SAT critical reading scores over 600: 55%; SAT math scores over 600: 61%; SAT writing scores over 600: 59%; ACT scores over 24: 91%; SAT critical reading scores over 700: 15%; SAT math scores over 700: 14%; SAT writing scores over 700: 15%; ACT scores over 30: 28%.
Retention: 90% of full-time freshmen returned.

FACULTY
Total: 289, 64% full-time, 62% with terminal degrees.
Student/faculty ratio: 11:1.

ACADEMICS
Calendar: semesters. *Degrees:* certificates, associate, and bachelor's.
Special study options: accelerated degree program, adult/continuing education programs, advanced placement credit, double majors, honors programs, independent study, internships, off-campus study, part-time degree program, services for LD students, student-designed majors, study abroad, summer session for credit. ***ROTC:*** Army (c).
Unusual degree programs: 3-2 engineering with Columbia University; forestry with Duke University; dentistry with University of Pennsylvania, medicine with Drexel University, optometry with State University of New York (SUNY) State College of Optometry, occupational and physical therapy with Thomas Jefferson University.
Computers: 450 computers/terminals and 100 ports are available on campus for general student use. Students can access the following: campus intranet, computer help desk, free student e-mail accounts, online (class) grades, online (class) registration, online (class) schedules. Campuswide network is available. 100% of college-owned or -operated housing units are wired for high-speed Internet access. Wireless service is available via entire campus.
Library: Trexler Library. *Books:* 236,297 (physical), 108,619 (digital/electronic); *Serial titles:* 964 (physical), 41,709 (digital/electronic); *Databases:* 73. Weekly public service hours: 105; students can reserve study rooms.

STUDENT LIFE
Housing options: on-campus residence required through senior year; coed, women-only, special housing for students with disabilities. Campus housing is university owned and leased by the school. Freshman campus housing is guaranteed.
Activities and organizations: drama/theater group, student-run newspaper, radio and television station, choral group, Theater Association, Environmental Action Team, Jefferson School Partnership, Select Choir, Habitat for Humanity, national fraternities, national sororities.
Athletics Member NCAA. All Division III. ***Intercollegiate sports:*** baseball M, basketball M/W, cheerleading M/W, cross-country running M/W, field hockey W, football M, golf M/W, lacrosse M/W, soccer M/W, softball W, tennis M/W, track and field M/W, volleyball W, wrestling M.

Intramural sports: basketball M/W, cross-country running M/W, football M/W, ice hockey M, racquetball M/W, rugby M/W, soccer M/W, softball M, swimming and diving M/W, tennis M/W, ultimate Frisbee M/W, volleyball M/W.

Campus security: 24-hour emergency response devices and patrols, late-night transport/escort service, controlled dormitory access.

Student services: health clinic, personal/psychological counseling.

COSTS & FINANCIAL AID

Costs (2016–17) ***Comprehensive fee:*** $59,400 includes full-time tuition ($47,825), mandatory fees ($485), and room and board ($11,090). Part-time tuition and fees vary according to program. ***College room only:*** $6025. Room and board charges vary according to board plan, housing facility, and location. ***Payment plan:*** installment. ***Waivers:*** employees or children of employees.

Financial Aid Of all full-time matriculated undergraduates who enrolled in 2016, 1,491 applied for aid, 1,268 were judged to have need, 358 had their need fully met. In 2016, 829 non-need-based awards were made. ***Average percent of need met:*** 87. ***Average financial aid package:*** $33,371. ***Average need-based loan:*** $4514. ***Average need-based gift aid:*** $29,760. ***Average non-need-based aid:*** $12,817. ***Average indebtedness upon graduation:*** $31,063. ***Financial aid deadline:*** 3/1.

APPLYING

Standardized Tests *Required for some:* SAT or ACT (for admission).

Options: electronic application, early admission, early decision, deferred entrance.

Application fee: $50.

Required: essay or personal statement, high school transcript, 2 letters of recommendation. ***Required for some:*** interview, graded paper. ***Recommended:*** interview.

Application deadlines: 2/15 (freshmen), 6/15 (transfers).

Early decision deadline: 2/15.

Notification: 3/15 (freshmen), continuous until 7/1 (transfers), rolling (early decision).

CONTACT

Mr. Christopher Hooker-Haring, Director of Undergraduate Admissions, Muhlenberg College, 2400 Chew Street, Allentown, PA 18104. *Phone:* 484-664-3245. *Fax:* 484-664-3234. *E-mail:* adm@muhlenberg.edu.

See previous page for display ad and page 1432 for the College Close-Up.

★ Neumann University
Aston, Pennsylvania
http://www.neumann.edu/

- **Independent Roman Catholic** comprehensive, founded 1965
- **Suburban** 68-acre campus with easy access to Philadelphia
- **Endowment** $28.0 million
- **Coed** 2,278 undergraduate students, 71% full-time, 65% women, 35% men
- **Minimally difficult** entrance level, 94% of applicants were admitted

UNDERGRAD STUDENTS

1,608 full-time, 670 part-time. Students come from 21 states and territories; 14 other countries; 31% are from out of state; 23% Black or African American, non-Hispanic/Latino; 5% Hispanic/Latino; 1% Asian, non-Hispanic/Latino; 0.1% Native Hawaiian or other Pacific Islander, non-Hispanic/Latino; 2% Two or more races, non-Hispanic/Latino; 14% Race/ethnicity unknown; 1% international; 4% transferred in; 31% live on campus.

Freshmen:

Admission: 1,486 applied, 1,393 admitted, 375 enrolled. ***Average high school GPA:*** 3.1. ***Test scores:*** SAT critical reading scores over 500: 22%; SAT math scores over 500: 22%; SAT writing scores over 500: 19%; ACT scores over 18: 59%; SAT critical reading scores over 600: 3%; SAT math scores over 600: 4%; SAT writing scores over 600: 2%; ACT scores over 24: 12%; SAT writing scores over 700: 1%.

Retention: 69% of full-time freshmen returned.

FACULTY

Total: 276, 36% full-time, 50% with terminal degrees.

Student/faculty ratio: 14:1.

ACADEMICS
Calendar: semesters. *Degrees:* associate, bachelor's, master's, doctoral, and post-master's certificates.

Special study options: academic remediation for entering students, accelerated degree program, adult/continuing education programs, advanced placement credit, cooperative education, distance learning, double majors, honors programs, independent study, internships, off-campus study, part-time degree program, services for LD students, study abroad, summer session for credit. ***ROTC:*** Army (c), Air Force (c).

Computers: 550 computers/terminals and 1,500 ports are available on campus for general student use. Students can access the following: campus intranet, computer help desk, free student e-mail accounts, online (class) grades, online (class) registration, online (class) schedules. Campuswide network is available. 100% of college-owned or -operated housing units are wired for high-speed Internet access. Wireless service is available via entire campus.

Library: Neumann University Library plus 1 other. *Books:* 46,200 (physical), 160,882 (digital/electronic); *Serial titles:* 25 (physical), 100,000 (digital/electronic); *Databases:* 51. Weekly public service hours: 80; students can reserve study rooms.

STUDENT LIFE
Housing options: coed, special housing for students with disabilities. Campus housing is university owned and leased by the school. Freshman applicants given priority for college housing.

Activities and organizations: drama/theater group, student-run newspaper, radio and television station, choral group, Black Student Union, Student Activities Board, Boogie Nights, Student Nurses Association, Neumann Media.

Athletics Member NCAA. All Division III. ***Intercollegiate sports:*** baseball M, basketball M/W, cross-country running M/W, field hockey W, golf M/W, ice hockey M/W, lacrosse M/W, rugby M(c)/W(c), soccer M/W, softball W, tennis M/W, track and field M/W, volleyball W. ***Intramural sports:*** baseball M(c), basketball M(c)/W, cheerleading W(c), ice hockey M(c), soccer M/W, softball M/W, table tennis M/W, volleyball M/W.

Campus security: 24-hour emergency response devices and patrols, late-night transport/escort service, controlled dormitory access.

Student services: health clinic, personal/psychological counseling.

COSTS & FINANCIAL AID
Costs (2016–17) ***Comprehensive fee:*** $40,738 includes full-time tuition ($27,340), mandatory fees ($1240), and room and board ($12,158). Full-time tuition and fees vary according to degree level. Part-time tuition: $625 per credit hour. Part-time tuition and fees vary according to degree level. ***Required fees:*** $80 per term part-time. ***College room only:*** $7314. Room and board charges vary according to board plan and housing facility. ***Payment plans:*** installment, deferred payment. ***Waivers:*** employees or children of employees.

Financial Aid Of all full-time matriculated undergraduates who enrolled in 2016, 1,495 applied for aid, 1,338 were judged to have need. In 2016, 239 non-need-based awards were made. ***Average percent of need met:*** 70. ***Average financial aid package:*** $16,971. ***Average need-based loan:*** $4462. ***Average need-based gift aid:*** $7460. ***Average non-need-based aid:*** $9707.

APPLYING
Standardized Tests *Required:* SAT or ACT (for admission).

Options: electronic application, deferred entrance.

Application fee: $35.

Required: high school transcript, minimum 2.0 GPA. ***Required for some:*** 1 letter of recommendation. ***Recommended:*** essay or personal statement, interview.

Application deadlines: rolling (freshmen), rolling (transfers).

Notification: continuous (freshmen), continuous (transfers).

CONTACT
Mr. Kevin Maccarella, Associate Dean of Enrollment Management/Director of Undergraduate Admissions, Neumann University, One Neumann Drive, Aston, PA 19014-1298. *Phone:* 610-361-2583. *Toll-free phone:* 800-963-8626. *Fax:* 610-361-2548. *E-mail:* neumann@neumann.edu.

See previous page for display ad and page 1434 for the College Close-Up.

Peirce College
Philadelphia, Pennsylvania
http://www.peirce.edu/

- **Independent** comprehensive, founded 1865
- **Urban** 1-acre campus
- **Coed, primarily women** 1,643 undergraduate students, 19% full-time, 72% women, 28% men
- **Noncompetitive** entrance level

UNDERGRAD STUDENTS
304 full-time, 1,339 part-time. 8% are from out of state; 69% Black or African American, non-Hispanic/Latino; 7% Hispanic/Latino; 2% Asian, non-Hispanic/Latino; 0.2% Native Hawaiian or other Pacific Islander, non-Hispanic/Latino; 0.1% American Indian or Alaska Native, non-Hispanic/Latino; 0.4% Two or more races, non-Hispanic/Latino; 0.9% Race/ethnicity unknown; 0.2% international.

Freshmen:

Admission: 81 enrolled.

Retention: 50% of full-time freshmen returned.

FACULTY
Total: 121, 25% full-time, 37% with terminal degrees.

Student/faculty ratio: 13:1.

ACADEMICS
Calendar: semesters. *Degrees:* certificates, associate, bachelor's, and master's.

Special study options: accelerated degree program, adult/continuing education programs, advanced placement credit, cooperative education, distance learning, internships, part-time degree program, services for LD students, summer session for credit.

Computers: Students can access the following: campus intranet, computer help desk, free student e-mail accounts, online (class) grades, online (class) registration, online (class) schedules. Campuswide network is available. Wireless service is available via entire campus.

Library: Peirce College Library.

STUDENT LIFE
Housing options: college housing not available.

Campus security: 24-hour emergency response devices and patrols, late-night transport/escort service, 24-hour security cameras.

COSTS & FINANCIAL AID
Costs (2016–17) ***Tuition:*** $13,872 full-time, $578 per credit part-time. Full-time tuition and fees vary according to course load and reciprocity agreements. Part-time tuition and fees vary according to course load and reciprocity agreements. ***Required fees:*** $600 full-time. ***Payment plans:*** installment, deferred payment. ***Waivers:*** children of alumni and employees or children of employees.

Financial Aid Of all full-time matriculated undergraduates who enrolled in 2014, 300 applied for aid, 271 were judged to have need, 2 had their need fully met. In 2014, 8 non-need-based awards were made. ***Average percent of need met:*** 41. ***Average financial aid package:*** $10,928. ***Average need-based loan:*** $3384. ***Average need-based gift aid:*** $6226. ***Average non-need-based aid:*** $4462.

APPLYING
Options: electronic application.

Application fee: $50.

Required: high school transcript.

CONTACT
Mr. Paul Ballentine, Manager, Admissions, Peirce College, 1420 Pine Street, Philadelphia, PA 19102. *Phone:* 215-670-9214. *Toll-free phone:* 888-467-3472. *Fax:* 215-670-9366. *E-mail:* info@peirce.edu.

Penn State Abington

Abington, Pennsylvania

http://www.abington.psu.edu/

- **State-related** 4-year, founded 1950, part of Pennsylvania State University
- **Small-town** campus
- **Coed** 3,961 undergraduate students, 79% full-time, 53% women, 47% men
- **Very difficult** entrance level, 82% of applicants were admitted

UNDERGRAD STUDENTS
3,113 full-time, 848 part-time. 7% are from out of state; 13% Black or African American, non-Hispanic/Latino; 10% Hispanic/Latino; 17% Asian, non-Hispanic/Latino; 0.2% Native Hawaiian or other Pacific Islander, non-Hispanic/Latino; 0.2% American Indian or Alaska Native, non-Hispanic/Latino; 2% Two or more races, non-Hispanic/Latino; 3% Race/ethnicity unknown; 5% international; 6% transferred in.

Freshmen:
Admission: 3,946 applied, 3,251 admitted, 872 enrolled. ***Average high school GPA:*** 3.11. ***Test scores:*** SAT critical reading scores over 500: 37%; SAT math scores over 500: 52%; SAT writing scores over 500: 33%; ACT scores over 18: 87%; SAT critical reading scores over 600: 9%; SAT math scores over 600: 20%; SAT writing scores over 600: 9%; ACT scores over 24: 38%; SAT critical reading scores over 700: 1%; SAT math scores over 700: 6%; SAT writing scores over 700: 1%; ACT scores over 30: 8%.
Retention: 80% of full-time freshmen returned.

FACULTY
Total: 304, 45% full-time, 46% with terminal degrees.
Student/faculty ratio: 18:1.

ACADEMICS
Calendar: semesters. *Degrees:* certificates, associate, bachelor's, and postbachelor's certificates (enrollment figures include students enrolled at The Graduate School at Penn State who are taking courses at this location).
Special study options: adult/continuing education programs, external degree program, part-time degree program. ***ROTC:*** Army (c), Air Force (c).
Computers: Students can access the following: campus intranet, computer help desk, free student e-mail accounts, online (class) grades, online (class) registration, online (class) schedules. Campuswide network is available.
Library: Penn State Abington Library.

STUDENT LIFE
Housing options: college housing not available.
Athletics ***Intercollegiate sports:*** baseball M, basketball M/W, golf M, soccer M/W, softball W, tennis M/W, volleyball W. ***Intramural sports:*** basketball M/W, cross-country running M/W, football M, soccer M/W, softball M, tennis M/W, volleyball M/W.
Campus security: 24-hour emergency response devices and patrols.

COSTS & FINANCIAL AID
Costs (2016–17) ***Tuition:*** state resident $13,212 full-time, $543 per credit hour part-time; nonresident $20,782 full-time, $866 per credit hour part-time. Full-time tuition and fees vary according to course level, degree level, location, program, and student level. Part-time tuition and fees vary according to course level, course load, degree level, location, program, and student level. ***Required fees:*** $960 full-time. ***Payment plans:*** installment, deferred payment. ***Waivers:*** senior citizens and employees or children of employees.
Financial Aid Of all full-time matriculated undergraduates who enrolled in 2015, 2,526 applied for aid, 2,193 were judged to have need, 66 had their need fully met. In 2015, 152 non-need-based awards were made. ***Average percent of need met:*** 59. ***Average financial aid package:*** $10,520. ***Average need-based loan:*** $4125. ***Average need-based gift aid:*** $7588. ***Average non-need-based aid:*** $3591. ***Average indebtedness upon graduation:*** $35,758.

APPLYING
Standardized Tests *Required:* SAT or ACT (for admission).
Options: electronic application, early admission, deferred entrance.
Application fee: $50.
Required: high school transcript. ***Required for some:*** interview. ***Recommended:*** essay or personal statement.
Application deadlines: rolling (freshmen), rolling (transfers).
Notification: continuous (freshmen), continuous (transfers).

CONTACT
Admissions Office, Penn State Abington, 1600 Woodland Road, Abington, PA 19001. *Phone:* 215-881-7600. *Fax:* 215-881-7655. *E-mail:* abingtonadmissions@psu.edu.

Penn State Altoona

Altoona, Pennsylvania

http://www.altoona.psu.edu/

- **State-related** 4-year, founded 1939, part of Pennsylvania State University
- **Suburban** campus
- **Coed** 3,838 undergraduate students, 96% full-time, 44% women, 56% men
- **Very difficult** entrance level, 89% of applicants were admitted

UNDERGRAD STUDENTS
3,684 full-time, 154 part-time. 17% are from out of state; 7% Black or African American, non-Hispanic/Latino; 6% Hispanic/Latino; 3% Asian, non-Hispanic/Latino; 0.1% Native Hawaiian or other Pacific Islander, non-Hispanic/Latino; 0.1% American Indian or Alaska Native, non-Hispanic/Latino; 2% Two or more races, non-Hispanic/Latino; 1% Race/ethnicity unknown; 5% international; 3% transferred in; 25% live on campus.

Freshmen:
Admission: 5,738 applied, 5,129 admitted, 1,379 enrolled. ***Average high school GPA:*** 3.05. ***Test scores:*** SAT critical reading scores over 500: 48%; SAT math scores over 500: 56%; SAT writing scores over 500: 41%; ACT scores over 18: 93%; SAT critical reading scores over 600: 8%; SAT math scores over 600: 14%; SAT writing scores over 600: 7%; ACT scores over 24: 31%; SAT math scores over 700: 2%; ACT scores over 30: 3%.
Retention: 84% of full-time freshmen returned.

FACULTY
Total: 302, 67% full-time, 52% with terminal degrees.
Student/faculty ratio: 16:1.

ACADEMICS
Calendar: semesters. *Degrees:* certificates, associate, and bachelor's (enrollment figures include students enrolled at The Graduate School at Penn State who are taking courses at this location).
Special study options: independent study. ***ROTC:*** Army (b), Air Force (b).
Computers: Students can access the following: campus intranet, computer help desk, free student e-mail accounts, online (class) grades, online (class) registration, online (class) schedules.
Library: Robert E. Eiche Library.

STUDENT LIFE
Housing options: coed, special housing for students with disabilities. Campus housing is university owned.
Athletics Member NCAA. All Division III. ***Intercollegiate sports:*** baseball M, basketball M/W, cross-country running M/W, golf M/W, soccer M/W, softball W, swimming and diving M/W, tennis M/W. ***Intramural sports:*** badminton M/W, baseball M/W, basketball M/W, football M/W, golf M/W, racquetball M/W, soccer M/W, softball M/W, table tennis M/W, tennis M/W, track and field M/W, volleyball M/W, weight lifting M/W.
Campus security: 24-hour emergency response devices and patrols, late-night transport/escort service.

COSTS & FINANCIAL AID
Costs (2016–17) ***Tuition:*** state resident $13,868 full-time, $578 per credit hour part-time; nonresident $21,874 full-time, $911 per credit hour part-time. Full-time tuition and fees vary according to course level, degree level, location, program, and student level. Part-time tuition and fees vary according to course level, course load, degree level, location, program,

and student level. ***Required fees:*** $960 full-time. ***Room and board:*** $11,860; room only: $5940. Room and board charges vary according to board plan, housing facility, and location. ***Payment plans:*** installment, deferred payment. ***Waivers:*** senior citizens and employees or children of employees.

Financial Aid Of all full-time matriculated undergraduates who enrolled in 2015, 2,910 applied for aid, 2,437 were judged to have need, 122 had their need fully met. In 2015, 274 non-need-based awards were made. ***Average percent of need met:*** 59. ***Average financial aid package:*** $10,460. ***Average need-based loan:*** $4042. ***Average need-based gift aid:*** $6704. ***Average non-need-based aid:*** $3096. ***Average indebtedness upon graduation:*** $41,435.

APPLYING

Standardized Tests *Required:* SAT or ACT (for admission).

Options: electronic application, early admission, deferred entrance.

Application fee: $50.

Required: high school transcript. ***Required for some:*** interview. ***Recommended:*** essay or personal statement.

Application deadlines: rolling (freshmen), rolling (transfers).

Notification: continuous (freshmen), continuous (transfers).

CONTACT

Admissions Office, Penn State Altoona, 3000 Ivyside Park, Altoona, PA 16601. *Phone:* 814-949-5466. *Toll-free phone:* 800-848-9843. *Fax:* 814-949-5564. *E-mail:* aaadmit@psu.edu.

Penn State Beaver

Monaca, Pennsylvania

http://www.beaver.psu.edu/

- **State-related** 4-year, founded 1964, part of Pennsylvania State University
- **Small-town** campus
- **Coed** 705 undergraduate students, 88% full-time, 41% women, 59% men
- **Moderately difficult** entrance level, 82% of applicants were admitted

UNDERGRAD STUDENTS

619 full-time, 86 part-time. 9% are from out of state; 9% Black or African American, non-Hispanic/Latino; 5% Hispanic/Latino; 3% Asian, non-Hispanic/Latino; 0.2% Native Hawaiian or other Pacific Islander, non-Hispanic/Latino; 0.3% American Indian or Alaska Native, non-Hispanic/Latino; 2% Two or more races, non-Hispanic/Latino; 1% Race/ethnicity unknown; 3% international; 4% transferred in; 23% live on campus.

Freshmen:

Admission: 753 applied, 620 admitted, 210 enrolled. ***Average high school GPA:*** 3.12. ***Test scores:*** SAT critical reading scores over 500: 46%; SAT math scores over 500: 55%; SAT writing scores over 500: 38%; ACT scores over 18: 75%; SAT critical reading scores over 600: 11%; SAT math scores over 600: 18%; SAT writing scores over 600: 9%; ACT scores over 24: 30%; SAT critical reading scores over 700: 1%; SAT math scores over 700: 4%; ACT scores over 30: 5%.

Retention: 78% of full-time freshmen returned.

FACULTY

Total: 59, 54% full-time, 39% with terminal degrees.

Student/faculty ratio: 16:1.

ACADEMICS

Calendar: semesters. *Degree:* certificates and bachelor's.

Special study options: adult/continuing education programs.

STUDENT LIFE

Housing options: coed, special housing for students with disabilities. Campus housing is university owned. Freshman campus housing is guaranteed.

Athletics Member NJCAA. ***Intercollegiate sports:*** baseball M, basketball M, softball M/W, volleyball W. ***Intramural sports:*** basketball M/W, cheerleading M(c)/W(c), cross-country running M/W, football M, golf M/W, soccer M/W, softball M/W, table tennis M/W.

COSTS & FINANCIAL AID

Costs (2016–17) ***Tuition:*** state resident $12,718 full-time, $524 per credit hour part-time; nonresident $19,598 full-time, $817 per credit hour part-time. Full-time tuition and fees vary according to course level, degree level, location, program, and student level. Part-time tuition and fees vary according to course level, course load, degree level, location, program, and student level. ***Required fees:*** $960 full-time. ***Room and board:*** $11,860; room only: $5940. Room and board charges vary according to board plan, housing facility, and location. ***Payment plan:*** deferred payment. ***Waivers:*** senior citizens and employees or children of employees.

Financial Aid Of all full-time matriculated undergraduates who enrolled in 2015, 534 applied for aid, 437 were judged to have need, 23 had their need fully met. In 2015, 75 non-need-based awards were made. ***Average percent of need met:*** 66. ***Average financial aid package:*** $11,692. ***Average need-based loan:*** $4201. ***Average need-based gift aid:*** $7378. ***Average non-need-based aid:*** $2886. ***Average indebtedness upon graduation:*** $32,739.

APPLYING

Standardized Tests *Required:* SAT or ACT (for admission).

Options: electronic application, early admission, deferred entrance.

Application fee: $50.

Required: high school transcript. ***Required for some:*** interview. ***Recommended:*** essay or personal statement.

Application deadlines: rolling (freshmen), rolling (transfers).

Notification: continuous (freshmen), continuous (transfers).

CONTACT

Admissions Office, Penn State Beaver, 100 University Drive, Monaca, PA 15061. *Phone:* 724-773-3800. *Fax:* 724-773-3658. *E-mail:* br-admissions@psu.edu.

Penn State Berks

Reading, Pennsylvania

http://www.berks.psu.edu/

- **State-related** 4-year, founded 1924, part of Pennsylvania State University
- **Suburban** campus
- **Coed** 2,906 undergraduate students, 90% full-time, 43% women, 57% men
- **Very difficult** entrance level, 85% of applicants were admitted

UNDERGRAD STUDENTS

2,602 full-time, 304 part-time. 8% are from out of state; 9% Black or African American, non-Hispanic/Latino; 11% Hispanic/Latino; 5% Asian, non-Hispanic/Latino; 0.1% Native Hawaiian or other Pacific Islander, non-Hispanic/Latino; 2% Two or more races, non-Hispanic/Latino; 1% Race/ethnicity unknown; 3% international; 5% transferred in; 28% live on campus.

Freshmen:

Admission: 2,413 applied, 2,048 admitted, 793 enrolled. ***Average high school GPA:*** 3.06. ***Test scores:*** SAT critical reading scores over 500: 43%; SAT math scores over 500: 51%; SAT writing scores over 500: 34%; ACT scores over 18: 85%; SAT critical reading scores over 600: 8%; SAT math scores over 600: 15%; SAT writing scores over 600: 6%; ACT scores over 24: 33%; SAT critical reading scores over 700: 1%; SAT math scores over 700: 2%; ACT scores over 30: 5%.

Retention: 82% of full-time freshmen returned.

FACULTY

Total: 220, 62% full-time, 50% with terminal degrees.

Student/faculty ratio: 17:1.

ACADEMICS

Calendar: semesters. *Degrees:* certificates, associate, bachelor's, and postbachelor's certificates (enrollment figures include students enrolled at The Graduate School at Penn State who are taking courses at this location).

Special study options: adult/continuing education programs, part-time degree program. ***ROTC:*** Army (c).

Computers: Students can access the following: campus intranet, computer help desk, free student e-mail accounts, online (class) grades, online (class) registration, online (class) schedules. Campuswide network is available.

Library: Thun Library.

STUDENT LIFE

Housing options: coed, special housing for students with disabilities. Campus housing is university owned.

Athletics Member NJCAA. ***Intercollegiate sports:*** baseball M, basketball M/W, cheerleading M/W, cross-country running M/W, golf M, soccer M/W, softball W, tennis M/W, volleyball W. ***Intramural sports:*** badminton M/W, basketball M/W, football M/W, golf M/W, table tennis M/W, volleyball M/W.

Campus security: 24-hour emergency response devices and patrols, late-night transport/escort service, controlled dormitory access.

COSTS & FINANCIAL AID

Costs (2016–17) ***Tuition:*** state resident $13,868 full-time, $578 per credit hour part-time; nonresident $21,874 full-time, $911 per credit hour part-time. Full-time tuition and fees vary according to course level, degree level, location, program, and student level. Part-time tuition and fees vary according to course level, course load, degree level, location, program, and student level. ***Required fees:*** $960 full-time. ***Room and board:*** $12,940; room only: $7020. Room and board charges vary according to board plan, housing facility, and location. ***Payment plan:*** deferred payment. ***Waivers:*** senior citizens and employees or children of employees.

Financial Aid Of all full-time matriculated undergraduates who enrolled in 2015, 2,173 applied for aid, 1,806 were judged to have need, 86 had their need fully met. In 2015, 144 non-need-based awards were made. ***Average percent of need met:*** 60. ***Average financial aid package:*** $10,537. ***Average need-based loan:*** $4241. ***Average need-based gift aid:*** $7087. ***Average non-need-based aid:*** $2378. ***Average indebtedness upon graduation:*** $38,227.

APPLYING

Standardized Tests *Required:* SAT or ACT (for admission).

Options: electronic application, early admission, deferred entrance.

Application fee: $50.

Required: high school transcript. ***Required for some:*** interview. ***Recommended:*** essay or personal statement.

Application deadlines: rolling (freshmen), rolling (transfers).

Notification: continuous (freshmen), continuous (transfers).

CONTACT

Admissions Office, Penn State Berks, Tulpehocken Road, PO Box 7009, Reading, PA 19610. *Phone:* 610-396-6060. *Fax:* 610-396-6077. *E-mail:* admissionsbk@psu.edu.

Penn State Brandywine

Media, Pennsylvania

http://www.brandywine.psu.edu/

- **State-related** 4-year, founded 1966, part of Pennsylvania State University
- **Small-town** campus
- **Coed** 1,457 undergraduate students, 86% full-time, 43% women, 57% men
- **Moderately difficult** entrance level, 83% of applicants were admitted

UNDERGRAD STUDENTS

1,250 full-time, 207 part-time. 5% are from out of state; 15% Black or African American, non-Hispanic/Latino; 5% Hispanic/Latino; 11% Asian, non-Hispanic/Latino; 0.2% Native Hawaiian or other Pacific Islander, non-Hispanic/Latino; 0.3% American Indian or Alaska Native, non-Hispanic/Latino; 2% Two or more races, non-Hispanic/Latino; 2% Race/ethnicity unknown; 1% international; 4% transferred in.

Freshmen:

Admission: 1,265 applied, 1,051 admitted, 374 enrolled. ***Average high school GPA:*** 2.98. ***Test scores:*** SAT critical reading scores over 500: 39%; SAT math scores over 500: 47%; SAT writing scores over 500: 31%; ACT scores over 18: 75%; SAT critical reading scores over 600: 7%; SAT math scores over 600: 14%; SAT writing scores over 600: 5%; ACT scores over 24: 40%; SAT math scores over 700: 2%.

Retention: 74% of full-time freshmen returned.

FACULTY

Total: 135, 50% full-time, 47% with terminal degrees.

Student/faculty ratio: 15:1.

ACADEMICS

Calendar: semesters. *Degrees:* certificates, associate, and bachelor's.

Special study options: adult/continuing education programs. ***ROTC:*** Army (c), Air Force (c).

Computers: Students can access the following: online (class) registration. Campuswide network is available.

STUDENT LIFE

Housing options: college housing not available.

Athletics Member NJCAA. ***Intercollegiate sports:*** baseball M, basketball M/W, soccer M/W, tennis M/W, volleyball W. ***Intramural sports:*** basketball M/W, cheerleading M(c)/W(c), golf M/W, ice hockey M(c)/W(c), lacrosse M/W, soccer M/W, softball W(c), tennis M/W, volleyball M(c)/W.

Campus security: late-night transport/escort service, part-time trained security personnel.

COSTS & FINANCIAL AID

Costs (2016–17) ***Tuition:*** state resident $13,174 full-time, $542 per credit hour part-time; nonresident $20,608 full-time, $859 per credit hour part-time. Full-time tuition and fees vary according to course level, degree level, location, program, and student level. Part-time tuition and fees vary according to course level, course load, degree level, location, program, and student level. ***Required fees:*** $960 full-time. ***Payment plan:*** deferred payment. ***Waivers:*** senior citizens and employees or children of employees.

Financial Aid Of all full-time matriculated undergraduates who enrolled in 2015, 984 applied for aid, 760 were judged to have need, 41 had their need fully met. In 2015, 121 non-need-based awards were made. ***Average percent of need met:*** 63. ***Average financial aid package:*** $10,682. ***Average need-based loan:*** $3961. ***Average need-based gift aid:*** $7185. ***Average non-need-based aid:*** $3796. ***Average indebtedness upon graduation:*** $32,742.

APPLYING

Standardized Tests *Required:* SAT or ACT (for admission).

Options: electronic application, early admission, deferred entrance.

Application fee: $50.

Required: high school transcript.

Application deadlines: rolling (freshmen), rolling (transfers).

Notification: continuous (freshmen), continuous (transfers).

CONTACT

Admissions Office, Penn State Brandywine, 25 Yearsley Mill Road, Media, PA 19063. *Phone:* 610-892-1200. *Fax:* 610-892-1320. *E-mail:* bwadmissions@psu.edu.

Penn State DuBois

DuBois, Pennsylvania

http://www.dubois.psu.edu/

- **State-related** primarily 2-year, founded 1935, part of Pennsylvania State University
- **Small-town** campus
- **Coed** 602 undergraduate students, 83% full-time, 45% women, 55% men
- **Moderately difficult** entrance level, 85% of applicants were admitted

UNDERGRAD STUDENTS

497 full-time, 105 part-time. 3% are from out of state; 2% Black or African American, non-Hispanic/Latino; 2% Hispanic/Latino; 0.6% Asian, non-Hispanic/Latino; 0.2% Native Hawaiian or other Pacific Islander, non-Hispanic/Latino; 0.4% Two or more races, non-Hispanic/Latino; 1% Race/ethnicity unknown; 0.4% international; 4% transferred in.

Freshmen:
Admission: 394 applied, 335 admitted, 163 enrolled. ***Average high school GPA:*** 3.13. ***Test scores:*** SAT critical reading scores over 500: 40%; SAT math scores over 500: 52%; SAT writing scores over 500: 22%; ACT scores over 18: 100%; SAT critical reading scores over 600: 10%; SAT math scores over 600: 12%; SAT writing scores over 600: 1%; ACT scores over 24: 33%; SAT critical reading scores over 700: 1%; SAT math scores over 700: 1%; SAT writing scores over 700: 1%.

Retention: 87% of full-time freshmen returned.

FACULTY
Total: 58, 72% full-time, 52% with terminal degrees.

Student/faculty ratio: 11:1.

ACADEMICS
Calendar: semesters. *Degrees:* certificates, associate, and bachelor's.

Special study options: adult/continuing education programs, external degree program.

Computers: Students can access the following: online (class) registration. Campuswide network is available.

STUDENT LIFE
Housing options: college housing not available.

Athletics Member NJCAA. ***Intercollegiate sports:*** basketball M, cross-country running M/W, golf M/W, volleyball W. ***Intramural sports:*** basketball M/W, football M, soccer M/W, table tennis M/W, volleyball M/W.

COSTS & FINANCIAL AID
Costs (2016–17) ***Tuition:*** state resident $12,718 full-time, $524 per credit hour part-time; nonresident $19,598 full-time, $817 per credit hour part-time. Full-time tuition and fees vary according to course level, degree level, location, program, and student level. Part-time tuition and fees vary according to course level, course load, degree level, location, program, and student level. ***Required fees:*** $898 full-time. ***Payment plan:*** deferred payment. ***Waivers:*** senior citizens and employees or children of employees.

Financial Aid Of all full-time matriculated undergraduates who enrolled in 2015, 447 applied for aid, 391 were judged to have need, 23 had their need fully met. In 2015, 17 non-need-based awards were made. ***Average percent of need met:*** 65. ***Average financial aid package:*** $11,311. ***Average need-based loan:*** $3865. ***Average need-based gift aid:*** $6450. ***Average non-need-based aid:*** $2741. ***Average indebtedness upon graduation:*** $36,818.

APPLYING
Standardized Tests *Required:* SAT or ACT (for admission).

Options: electronic application, early admission, deferred entrance.

Application fee: $50.

Required: high school transcript. ***Required for some:*** interview. ***Recommended:*** essay or personal statement.

Application deadlines: rolling (freshmen), rolling (transfers).

Notification: continuous (freshmen), continuous (transfers).

CONTACT
Admissions Office, Penn State DuBois, 1 College Place, DuBois, PA 15801. *Phone:* 814-375-4720. *Toll-free phone:* 800-346-7627. *Fax:* 814-375-4784. *E-mail:* duboisinfo@psi.edu.

Penn State Erie, The Behrend College

Erie, Pennsylvania

http://www.psbehrend.psu.edu/

- **State-related** comprehensive, founded 1948, part of Pennsylvania State University
- **Suburban** 725-acre campus
- **Coed** 4,175 undergraduate students, 95% full-time, 35% women, 65% men
- **Very difficult** entrance level, 87% of applicants were admitted

UNDERGRAD STUDENTS
3,955 full-time, 220 part-time. 10% are from out of state; 4% Black or African American, non-Hispanic/Latino; 2% Hispanic/Latino; 3% Asian, non-Hispanic/Latino; 0.1% American Indian or Alaska Native, non-Hispanic/Latino; 2% Two or more races, non-Hispanic/Latino; 1% Race/ethnicity unknown; 9% international; 3% transferred in; 41% live on campus.

Freshmen:
Admission: 4,079 applied, 3,552 admitted, 1,176 enrolled. ***Average high school GPA:*** 3.3. ***Test scores:*** SAT critical reading scores over 500: 58%; SAT math scores over 500: 71%; SAT writing scores over 500: 49%; ACT scores over 18: 88%; SAT critical reading scores over 600: 13%; SAT math scores over 600: 31%; SAT writing scores over 600: 10%; ACT scores over 24: 43%; SAT critical reading scores over 700: 2%; SAT math scores over 700: 9%; SAT writing scores over 700: 1%; ACT scores over 30: 3%.

Retention: 85% of full-time freshmen returned.

FACULTY
Total: 330, 79% full-time, 55% with terminal degrees.

Student/faculty ratio: 15:1.

ACADEMICS
Calendar: semesters. *Degrees:* certificates, associate, bachelor's, and master's.

Special study options: adult/continuing education programs, part-time degree program. ***ROTC:*** Army (b).

Computers: Students can access the following: campus intranet, computer help desk, free student e-mail accounts, online (class) grades, online (class) registration, online (class) schedules. Campuswide network is available.

Library: John M. Lilley Library.

STUDENT LIFE
Housing options: coed, men-only, women-only, special housing for students with disabilities. Campus housing is university owned.

Athletics Member NCAA. All Division III. ***Intercollegiate sports:*** baseball M, basketball M/W, cheerleading M/W, cross-country running M/W, golf M/W, ice hockey M(c), lacrosse M(c), skiing (downhill) M(c)/W(c), soccer M/W, softball W, swimming and diving M/W, tennis M/W, track and field M/W, volleyball M(c)/W, water polo M/W. ***Intramural sports:*** badminton M/W, basketball M/W, bowling M/W, cross-country running M/W, football M/W, golf M/W, skiing (downhill) M/W, soccer M/W, softball M/W, swimming and diving M/W, table tennis M/W, tennis M/W, volleyball M/W.

Campus security: 24-hour emergency response devices and patrols, student patrols, late-night transport/escort service, controlled dormitory access.

COSTS & FINANCIAL AID
Costs (2016–17) ***Tuition:*** state resident $13,868 full-time, $578 per credit hour part-time; nonresident $21,874 full-time, $911 per credit hour part-time. Full-time tuition and fees vary according to course level, degree level, location, program, and student level. Part-time tuition and fees vary according to course level, course load, degree level, location, program, and student level. ***Required fees:*** $960 full-time. ***Room and board:*** $11,860; room only: $5940. Room and board charges vary according to board plan, housing facility, and location. ***Payment plan:*** deferred payment. ***Waivers:*** senior citizens and employees or children of employees.

Financial Aid Of all full-time matriculated undergraduates who enrolled in 2015, 3,132 applied for aid, 2,657 were judged to have need, 121 had their need fully met. In 2015, 230 non-need-based awards were made. ***Average percent of need met:*** 61. ***Average financial aid package:*** $11,015. ***Average need-based loan:*** $4381. ***Average need-based gift aid:*** $7241. ***Average non-need-based aid:*** $3368. ***Average indebtedness upon graduation:*** $39,209.

APPLYING
Standardized Tests *Required:* SAT or ACT (for admission).

Options: electronic application, early admission, deferred entrance.

Application fee: $50.

Required: high school transcript. ***Required for some:*** interview. ***Recommended:*** essay or personal statement.

Application deadlines: rolling (freshmen), rolling (transfers).

Notification: continuous (freshmen), continuous (transfers).

CONTACT
Admissions Office, Penn State Erie, The Behrend College, 4701 College Drive, Erie, PA 16563. *Phone:* 814-898-6100. *Toll-free phone:* 866-374-3378. *Fax:* 814-898-6044. *E-mail:* behrend.admissions@psu.edu.

Penn State Fayette, The Eberly Campus

Lemont Furnace, Pennsylvania

http://www.fayette.psu.edu/

- **State-related** primarily 2-year, founded 1934, part of Pennsylvania State University
- **Small-town** campus
- **Coed** 704 undergraduate students, 84% full-time, 58% women, 42% men
- **Moderately difficult** entrance level, 81% of applicants were admitted

UNDERGRAD STUDENTS
592 full-time, 112 part-time. 5% are from out of state; 6% transferred in.

Freshmen:
Admission: 659 applied, 533 admitted, 193 enrolled. ***Average high school GPA:*** 3.19. ***Test scores:*** SAT critical reading scores over 500: 29%; SAT math scores over 500: 35%; SAT writing scores over 500: 18%; ACT scores over 18: 70%; SAT critical reading scores over 600: 3%; SAT math scores over 600: 7%; SAT writing scores over 600: 5%; ACT scores over 24: 10%; SAT math scores over 700: 3%; ACT scores over 30: 10%.

Retention: 77% of full-time freshmen returned.

FACULTY
Total: 69, 64% full-time, 35% with terminal degrees.

Student/faculty ratio: 12:1.

ACADEMICS
Calendar: semesters. *Degrees:* certificates, associate, and bachelor's.

Special study options: adult/continuing education programs, external degree program.

Computers: Students can access the following: online (class) registration. Campuswide network is available.

STUDENT LIFE
Housing options: college housing not available.

Athletics Member NJCAA. ***Intercollegiate sports:*** baseball M, basketball M, softball W, volleyball W. ***Intramural sports:*** badminton M/W, basketball M/W, cheerleading M(c)/W(c), equestrian sports M(c)/W(c), football M/W, golf M(c)/W(c), softball M/W, tennis M/W, volleyball M/W, weight lifting M/W.

Campus security: student patrols, 8-hour patrols by trained security personnel.

COSTS & FINANCIAL AID
Costs (2016–17) ***Tuition:*** state resident $12,718 full-time, $524 per credit hour part-time; nonresident $19,598 full-time, $817 per credit hour part-time. Full-time tuition and fees vary according to course level, degree level, location, program, and student level. Part-time tuition and fees vary according to course level, course load, degree level, location, program, and student level. ***Required fees:*** $898 full-time. ***Payment plan:*** deferred payment. ***Waivers:*** senior citizens and employees or children of employees.

Financial Aid Of all full-time matriculated undergraduates who enrolled in 2015, 546 applied for aid, 472 were judged to have need, 26 had their need fully met. In 2015, 51 non-need-based awards were made. ***Average percent of need met:*** 65. ***Average financial aid package:*** $10,865. ***Average need-based loan:*** $3854. ***Average need-based gift aid:*** $6633. ***Average non-need-based aid:*** $2743. ***Average indebtedness upon graduation:*** $35,525.

APPLYING
Standardized Tests *Required:* SAT or ACT (for admission).

Options: electronic application, early admission, deferred entrance.

Application fee: $50.

Required: high school transcript. ***Required for some:*** interview. ***Recommended:*** essay or personal statement.

Application deadlines: rolling (freshmen), rolling (transfers).

Notification: continuous (freshmen), continuous (transfers).

CONTACT
Admissions Office, Penn State Fayette, The Eberly Campus, 2201 University Drive, Lemont Furnace, PA 15456. *Phone:* 724-430-4130. *Toll-free phone:* 877-568-4130. *Fax:* 724-430-4175. *E-mail:* feadm@psu.edu.

Penn State Greater Allegheny

McKeesport, Pennsylvania

http://www.greaterallegheny.psu.edu/

- **State-related** comprehensive, founded 1947, part of Pennsylvania State University
- **Small-town** campus
- **Coed** 577 undergraduate students, 87% full-time, 42% women, 58% men
- **Moderately difficult** entrance level, 79% of applicants were admitted

UNDERGRAD STUDENTS
504 full-time, 73 part-time. 7% are from out of state; 19% Black or African American, non-Hispanic/Latino; 7% Hispanic/Latino; 5% Asian, non-Hispanic/Latino; 3% Two or more races, non-Hispanic/Latino; 1% Race/ethnicity unknown; 4% international; 6% transferred in; 22% live on campus.

Freshmen:
Admission: 594 applied, 468 admitted, 158 enrolled. ***Average high school GPA:*** 3.06. ***Test scores:*** SAT critical reading scores over 500: 39%; SAT math scores over 500: 38%; SAT writing scores over 500: 28%; ACT scores over 18: 91%; SAT critical reading scores over 600: 10%; SAT math scores over 600: 15%; SAT writing scores over 600: 7%; ACT scores over 24: 55%; SAT critical reading scores over 700: 1%; SAT math scores over 700: 3%; SAT writing scores over 700: 1%.

Retention: 80% of full-time freshmen returned.

FACULTY
Total: 77, 44% full-time, 42% with terminal degrees.

Student/faculty ratio: 11:1.

ACADEMICS
Calendar: semesters. *Degrees:* certificates, associate, bachelor's, and master's.

Special study options: adult/continuing education programs.

Computers: Students can access the following: online (class) registration. Campuswide network is available.

STUDENT LIFE
Housing options: special housing for students with disabilities. Campus housing is university owned. Freshman campus housing is guaranteed.

Athletics Member NJCAA. ***Intercollegiate sports:*** baseball M, basketball M, softball W, volleyball W. ***Intramural sports:*** basketball M/W, cheerleading M(c)/W(c), football M/W, ice hockey M(c), racquetball M/W, skiing (cross-country) M(c)/W(c), skiing (downhill) M(c)/W(c), soccer M(c)/W(c), softball M/W, tennis M/W, volleyball M/W.

Campus security: 24-hour patrols, controlled dormitory access.

COSTS & FINANCIAL AID
Costs (2016–17) ***Tuition:*** state resident $12,718 full-time, $524 per credit hour part-time; nonresident $19,598 full-time, $817 per credit hour part-time. Full-time tuition and fees vary according to course level, degree level, location, program, and student level. Part-time tuition and fees vary according to course level, course load, degree level, location, program, and student level. ***Required fees:*** $948 full-time. ***Room and board:*** $11,860; room only: $5940. Room and board charges vary according to board plan, housing facility, and location. ***Payment plan:*** deferred payment. ***Waivers:*** senior citizens and employees or children of employees.

Financial Aid Of all full-time matriculated undergraduates who enrolled in 2015, 447 applied for aid, 394 were judged to have need, 24 had their need fully met. In 2015, 31 non-need-based awards were made. ***Average percent of need met:*** 67. ***Average financial aid package:*** $12,576. ***Average need-based loan:*** $3983. ***Average need-based gift aid:*** $7570. ***Average non-need-based aid:*** $3332. ***Average indebtedness upon graduation:*** $42,291.

APPLYING
Standardized Tests *Required:* SAT or ACT (for admission).

Options: electronic application, early admission, deferred entrance.
Application fee: $50.
Required: high school transcript.
Application deadlines: rolling (freshmen), rolling (transfers).
Notification: continuous (freshmen), continuous (transfers).

CONTACT
Admissions Office, Penn State Greater Allegheny, 4000 University Drive, McKeesport, PA 15132. *Phone:* 412-675-9010. *Fax:* 412-675-9046. *E-mail:* psuga@psu.edu.

Penn State Harrisburg

Middletown, Pennsylvania

http://www.harrisburg.psu.edu/

- **State-related** comprehensive, founded 1966, part of Pennsylvania State University
- **Small-town** campus
- **Coed** 3,866 undergraduate students, 89% full-time, 39% women, 61% men
- **Very difficult** entrance level, 85% of applicants were admitted

UNDERGRAD STUDENTS
3,439 full-time, 427 part-time. 16% are from out of state; 11% Black or African American, non-Hispanic/Latino; 6% Hispanic/Latino; 9% Asian, non-Hispanic/Latino; 0.2% Native Hawaiian or other Pacific Islander, non-Hispanic/Latino; 0.2% American Indian or Alaska Native, non-Hispanic/Latino; 3% Two or more races, non-Hispanic/Latino; 2% Race/ethnicity unknown; 10% international; 9% transferred in; 11% live on campus.

Freshmen:
Admission: 3,938 applied, 3,342 admitted, 858 enrolled. ***Average high school GPA:*** 3.14. ***Test scores:*** SAT critical reading scores over 500: 51%; SAT math scores over 500: 65%; SAT writing scores over 500: 45%; ACT scores over 18: 89%; SAT critical reading scores over 600: 13%; SAT math scores over 600: 32%; SAT writing scores over 600: 12%; ACT scores over 24: 41%; SAT critical reading scores over 700: 1%; SAT math scores over 700: 10%; SAT writing scores over 700: 2%; ACT scores over 30: 8%.
Retention: 87% of full-time freshmen returned.

FACULTY
Total: 371, 62% full-time, 65% with terminal degrees.
Student/faculty ratio: 15:1.

ACADEMICS
Calendar: semesters. *Degrees:* certificates, associate, bachelor's, master's, doctoral, and postbachelor's certificates.
Special study options: adult/continuing education programs, part-time degree program. ***ROTC:*** Army (c).
Computers: Students can access the following: campus intranet, computer help desk, free student e-mail accounts, online (class) grades, online (class) registration, online (class) schedules. Campuswide network is available.
Library: Penn State Harrisburg Library.

STUDENT LIFE
Housing options: special housing for students with disabilities. Campus housing is university owned.
Athletics ***Intercollegiate sports:*** baseball M, basketball M/W, cross-country running M/W, golf M/W, soccer M/W, softball W, tennis M/W, volleyball W. ***Intramural sports:*** badminton M/W, basketball M/W, racquetball M/W, tennis M/W.
Campus security: 24-hour emergency response devices and patrols, student patrols, late-night transport/escort service, controlled dormitory access.

COSTS & FINANCIAL AID
Costs (2016–17) ***Tuition:*** state resident $13,868 full-time, $578 per credit hour part-time; nonresident $21,874 full-time, $911 per credit hour part-time. Full-time tuition and fees vary according to course level, degree level, location, program, and student level. Part-time tuition and fees vary according to course level, course load, degree level, location, program, and student level. ***Required fees:*** $960 full-time. ***Room and board:*** $13,460; room only: $7540. Room and board charges vary according to board plan, housing facility, and location. ***Payment plan:*** deferred payment. ***Waivers:*** senior citizens and employees or children of employees.
Financial Aid Of all full-time matriculated undergraduates who enrolled in 2015, 2,592 applied for aid, 2,245 were judged to have need, 139 had their need fully met. In 2015, 311 non-need-based awards were made. ***Average percent of need met:*** 57. ***Average financial aid package:*** $11,083. ***Average need-based loan:*** $4433. ***Average need-based gift aid:*** $6886. ***Average non-need-based aid:*** $1997. ***Average indebtedness upon graduation:*** $42,149.

APPLYING
Standardized Tests *Required:* SAT or ACT (for admission).
Options: electronic application, early admission, deferred entrance.
Application fee: $50.
Required: high school transcript. ***Required for some:*** interview. ***Recommended:*** essay or personal statement.
Application deadlines: rolling (freshmen), rolling (transfers).
Notification: continuous (freshmen), continuous (transfers).

CONTACT
Admissions Office, Penn State Harrisburg, 777 West Harrisburg Pike, Middletown, PA 17057. *Phone:* 717-948-6250. *Toll-free phone:* 800-222-2056. *Fax:* 717-948-6325. *E-mail:* hbgadmit@psu.edu.

Penn State Hazleton

Hazleton, Pennsylvania

http://www.hazleton.psu.edu/

- **State-related** 4-year, founded 1934, part of Pennsylvania State University
- **Small-town** campus
- **Coed** 831 undergraduate students, 87% full-time, 42% women, 58% men
- **Moderately difficult** entrance level, 84% of applicants were admitted

UNDERGRAD STUDENTS
725 full-time, 106 part-time. 19% are from out of state; 12% Black or African American, non-Hispanic/Latino; 19% Hispanic/Latino; 3% Asian, non-Hispanic/Latino; 0.3% Native Hawaiian or other Pacific Islander, non-Hispanic/Latino; 0.4% American Indian or Alaska Native, non-Hispanic/Latino; 3% Two or more races, non-Hispanic/Latino; 0.7% Race/ethnicity unknown; 2% international; 5% transferred in; 41% live on campus.

Freshmen:
Admission: 763 applied, 640 admitted, 262 enrolled. ***Average high school GPA:*** 3.1. ***Test scores:*** SAT critical reading scores over 500: 36%; SAT math scores over 500: 45%; SAT writing scores over 500: 27%; ACT scores over 18: 73%; SAT critical reading scores over 600: 7%; SAT math scores over 600: 9%; SAT writing scores over 600: 5%; ACT scores over 24: 33%; SAT critical reading scores over 700: 1%; SAT math scores over 700: 1%.
Retention: 79% of full-time freshmen returned.

FACULTY
Total: 71, 70% full-time, 54% with terminal degrees.
Student/faculty ratio: 13:1.

ACADEMICS
Calendar: semesters. *Degrees:* certificates, associate, bachelor's, and postbachelor's certificates.
Special study options: adult/continuing education programs. ***ROTC:*** Air Force (c).
Computers: Students can access the following: online (class) registration. Campuswide network is available.

STUDENT LIFE
Housing options: coed. Campus housing is university owned. Freshman campus housing is guaranteed.
Athletics Member NJCAA. ***Intercollegiate sports:*** baseball M, basketball M/W, cheerleading M/W, soccer M, softball W(s), tennis M/W, volleyball M/W. ***Intramural sports:*** basketball M/W, skiing (downhill) M(c)/W(c), soccer M/W, volleyball M/W.

Campus security: 24-hour patrols, late-night transport/escort service, controlled dormitory access.

COSTS & FINANCIAL AID

Costs (2016–17) ***Tuition:*** state resident $13,174 full-time, $542 per credit hour part-time; nonresident $20,608 full-time, $859 per credit hour part-time. Full-time tuition and fees vary according to course level, degree level, location, program, and student level. Part-time tuition and fees vary according to course level, course load, degree level, location, program, and student level. ***Required fees:*** $898 full-time. ***Room and board:*** $11,860; room only: $5940. Room and board charges vary according to board plan, housing facility, and location. ***Payment plan:*** deferred payment. ***Waivers:*** senior citizens and employees or children of employees.

Financial Aid Of all full-time matriculated undergraduates who enrolled in 2015, 643 applied for aid, 579 were judged to have need, 19 had their need fully met. In 2015, 70 non-need-based awards were made. ***Average percent of need met:*** 62. ***Average financial aid package:*** $11,533. ***Average need-based loan:*** $4032. ***Average need-based gift aid:*** $7452. ***Average non-need-based aid:*** $3241. ***Average indebtedness upon graduation:*** $43,579.

APPLYING

Standardized Tests *Required:* SAT or ACT (for admission).

Options: electronic application, early admission, deferred entrance.

Application fee: $50.

Required: high school transcript. ***Required for some:*** interview. ***Recommended:*** essay or personal statement.

Application deadlines: rolling (freshmen), rolling (transfers).

Notification: continuous (freshmen), continuous (transfers).

CONTACT

Admissions Office, Penn State Hazleton, 76 University Drive, Hazleton, PA 18202. *Phone:* 570-450-3142. *Toll-free phone:* 800-279-8495. *Fax:* 570-450-3182. *E-mail:* admissions-hn@psu.edu.

Penn State Lehigh Valley

Center Valley, Pennsylvania

http://www.lehighvalley.psu.edu/

- **State-related** 4-year, founded 1912, part of Pennsylvania State University
- **Rural** campus
- **Coed** 862 undergraduate students, 83% full-time, 49% women, 51% men
- **Moderately difficult** entrance level, 86% of applicants were admitted

UNDERGRAD STUDENTS

712 full-time, 150 part-time. 3% are from out of state; 6% Black or African American, non-Hispanic/Latino; 16% Hispanic/Latino; 10% Asian, non-Hispanic/Latino; 0.3% Native Hawaiian or other Pacific Islander, non-Hispanic/Latino; 2% Two or more races, non-Hispanic/Latino; 1% Race/ethnicity unknown; 0.3% international; 9% transferred in.

Freshmen:

Admission: 843 applied, 728 admitted, 208 enrolled. ***Average high school GPA:*** 3.03. ***Test scores:*** SAT critical reading scores over 500: 51%; SAT math scores over 500: 57%; SAT writing scores over 500: 43%; ACT scores over 18: 88%; SAT critical reading scores over 600: 15%; SAT math scores over 600: 18%; SAT writing scores over 600: 8%; ACT scores over 24: 44%; SAT critical reading scores over 700: 2%; SAT math scores over 700: 1%; SAT writing scores over 700: 1%; ACT scores over 30: 6%.

Retention: 78% of full-time freshmen returned.

FACULTY

Total: 84, 51% full-time, 44% with terminal degrees.

Student/faculty ratio: 14:1.

ACADEMICS

Calendar: semesters. *Degrees:* certificates, associate, bachelor's, and postbachelor's certificates (enrollment figures include students enrolled at The Graduate School at Penn State who are taking courses at this location).

Special study options: adult/continuing education programs, external degree program, part-time degree program. ***ROTC:*** Army (c).

Computers: Students can access the following: online (class) registration. Campuswide network is available.

STUDENT LIFE

Housing options: college housing not available.

Athletics Member NJCAA. ***Intercollegiate sports:*** baseball M, basketball M/W, bowling M(c)/W(c), cheerleading M/W, cross-country running M/W, football M(c), golf M(c)/W(c), ice hockey M(c)/W(c), skiing (downhill) M(c)/W(c), soccer M(c)/W, tennis M/W, volleyball M(c)/W. ***Intramural sports:*** badminton M/W, basketball M/W, football M/W, golf M/W, soccer M/W, volleyball M/W.

COSTS & FINANCIAL AID

Costs (2016–17) ***Tuition:*** state resident $13,174 full-time, $542 per credit hour part-time; nonresident $20,608 full-time, $859 per credit hour part-time. Full-time tuition and fees vary according to course level, degree level, location, program, and student level. Part-time tuition and fees vary according to course level, course load, degree level, location, program, and student level. ***Required fees:*** $960 full-time. ***Payment plan:*** deferred payment. ***Waivers:*** senior citizens and employees or children of employees.

Financial Aid Of all full-time matriculated undergraduates who enrolled in 2015, 566 applied for aid, 448 were judged to have need, 15 had their need fully met. In 2015, 77 non-need-based awards were made. ***Average percent of need met:*** 61. ***Average financial aid package:*** $10,792. ***Average need-based loan:*** $4203. ***Average need-based gift aid:*** $7528. ***Average non-need-based aid:*** $1814. ***Average indebtedness upon graduation:*** $34,713.

APPLYING

Standardized Tests *Required:* SAT or ACT (for admission).

Options: electronic application, early admission, deferred entrance.

Application fee: $50.

Required: high school transcript.

CONTACT

Admissions Office, Penn State Lehigh Valley, 2809 Saucon Valley Road, Center Valley, PA 18034. *Phone:* 610-285-5000. *Fax:* 610-285-5220. *E-mail:* admissions-lv@psu.edu.

Penn State Mont Alto

Mont Alto, Pennsylvania

http://www.montalto.psu.edu/

- **State-related** primarily 2-year, founded 1929, part of Pennsylvania State University
- **Small-town** campus
- **Coed** 893 undergraduate students, 74% full-time, 57% women, 43% men
- **Moderately difficult** entrance level, 79% of applicants were admitted

UNDERGRAD STUDENTS

661 full-time, 232 part-time. 12% are from out of state; 8% Black or African American, non-Hispanic/Latino; 5% Hispanic/Latino; 2% Asian, non-Hispanic/Latino; 0.1% Native Hawaiian or other Pacific Islander, non-Hispanic/Latino; 3% Two or more races, non-Hispanic/Latino; 0.9% Race/ethnicity unknown; 0.4% international; 4% transferred in; 26% live on campus.

Freshmen:

Admission: 688 applied, 546 admitted, 246 enrolled. ***Average high school GPA:*** 3.11. ***Test scores:*** SAT critical reading scores over 500: 43%; SAT math scores over 500: 42%; SAT writing scores over 500: 29%; ACT scores over 18: 57%; SAT critical reading scores over 600: 5%; SAT math scores over 600: 11%; SAT writing scores over 600: 2%; ACT scores over 24: 29%.

Retention: 77% of full-time freshmen returned.

FACULTY

Total: 92, 61% full-time, 30% with terminal degrees.

Student/faculty ratio: 11:1.

ACADEMICS

Calendar: semesters. *Degrees:* certificates, associate, and bachelor's.

Special study options: adult/continuing education programs, external degree program. ***ROTC:*** Army (c).

Computers: Students can access the following: online (class) registration. Campuswide network is available.

STUDENT LIFE

Housing options: coed, special housing for students with disabilities. Campus housing is university owned. Freshman campus housing is guaranteed.

Athletics Member NJCAA. ***Intercollegiate sports:*** basketball M/W, cheerleading M/W, cross-country running M/W, golf M/W, soccer M/W, softball W, tennis M/W, volleyball W. ***Intramural sports:*** badminton M/W, basketball M/W, cheerleading M(c)/W(c), racquetball M/W, soccer M/W, softball W, volleyball M/W.

Campus security: 24-hour patrols, controlled dormitory access.

COSTS & FINANCIAL AID

Costs (2016–17) ***Tuition:*** state resident $12,718 full-time, $524 per credit hour part-time; nonresident $19,598 full-time, $817 per credit hour part-time. Full-time tuition and fees vary according to course level, degree level, location, program, and student level. Part-time tuition and fees vary according to course level, course load, degree level, location, program, and student level. ***Required fees:*** $960 full-time. ***Room and board:*** $11,860; room only: $5940. Room and board charges vary according to board plan, housing facility, and location. ***Payment plan:*** deferred payment. ***Waivers:*** senior citizens and employees or children of employees.

Financial Aid Of all full-time matriculated undergraduates who enrolled in 2015, 602 applied for aid, 522 were judged to have need, 28 had their need fully met. In 2015, 34 non-need-based awards were made. ***Average percent of need met:*** 62. ***Average financial aid package:*** $11,228. ***Average need-based loan:*** $4068. ***Average need-based gift aid:*** $6419. ***Average non-need-based aid:*** $3498. ***Average indebtedness upon graduation:*** $43,317.

APPLYING

Standardized Tests *Required:* SAT or ACT (for admission).

Options: electronic application, early admission, deferred entrance.

Application fee: $50.

Required: high school transcript. ***Required for some:*** interview. ***Recommended:*** essay or personal statement.

Application deadlines: rolling (freshmen), rolling (transfers).

Notification: continuous (freshmen), continuous (transfers).

CONTACT

Admissions Office, Penn State Mont Alto, 1 Campus Drive, Mont Alto, PA 17237. *Phone:* 717-749-6130. *Toll-free phone:* 800-392-6173. *Fax:* 717-749-6132. *E-mail:* psuma@psu.edu.

Penn State New Kensington

New Kensington, Pennsylvania

http://www.newkensington.psu.edu/

- **State-related** 4-year, founded 1958, part of Pennsylvania State University
- **Small-town** campus
- **Coed** 656 undergraduate students, 78% full-time, 43% women, 57% men
- **Moderately difficult** entrance level, 79% of applicants were admitted

UNDERGRAD STUDENTS

512 full-time, 144 part-time. 2% are from out of state; 5% Black or African American, non-Hispanic/Latino; 2% Hispanic/Latino; 2% Asian, non-Hispanic/Latino; 0.3% American Indian or Alaska Native, non-Hispanic/Latino; 1% Two or more races, non-Hispanic/Latino; 0.8% Race/ethnicity unknown; 2% international; 7% transferred in.

Freshmen:

Admission: 508 applied, 402 admitted, 178 enrolled. ***Average high school GPA:*** 3.13. ***Test scores:*** SAT critical reading scores over 500: 43%; SAT math scores over 500: 48%; SAT writing scores over 500: 36%; ACT scores over 18: 88%; SAT critical reading scores over 600: 7%; SAT math scores over 600: 11%; SAT writing scores over 600: 3%; ACT scores over 24: 25%; SAT math scores over 700: 2%; ACT scores over 30: 13%.

Retention: 67% of full-time freshmen returned.

FACULTY

Total: 72, 49% full-time, 43% with terminal degrees.

Student/faculty ratio: 12:1.

ACADEMICS

Calendar: semesters. *Degrees:* certificates, associate, and bachelor's.

Special study options: adult/continuing education programs, external degree program. ***ROTC:*** Air Force (c).

Computers: Students can access the following: online (class) registration. Campuswide network is available.

STUDENT LIFE

Athletics Member NJCAA. ***Intercollegiate sports:*** baseball M, basketball M/W, cheerleading M/W, golf M/W, softball W, volleyball W. ***Intramural sports:*** badminton M/W, basketball M/W, bowling M/W, cheerleading M(c)/W(c), football M/W, ice hockey M(c)/W(c), racquetball M/W, skiing (downhill) M(c)/W(c), soccer M/W, softball W, volleyball M/W.

Campus security: part-time trained security personnel.

COSTS & FINANCIAL AID

Costs (2016–17) ***Tuition:*** state resident $12,718 full-time, $524 per credit hour part-time; nonresident $19,598 full-time, $817 per credit hour part-time. Full-time tuition and fees vary according to course level, degree level, location, program, and student level. Part-time tuition and fees vary according to course level, course load, degree level, location, program, and student level. ***Required fees:*** $898 full-time. ***Payment plan:*** deferred payment. ***Waivers:*** senior citizens and employees or children of employees.

Financial Aid Of all full-time matriculated undergraduates who enrolled in 2015, 423 applied for aid, 349 were judged to have need, 33 had their need fully met. In 2015, 59 non-need-based awards were made. ***Average percent of need met:*** 67. ***Average financial aid package:*** $10,679. ***Average need-based loan:*** $4020. ***Average need-based gift aid:*** $6292. ***Average non-need-based aid:*** $2862. ***Average indebtedness upon graduation:*** $34,024.

APPLYING

Standardized Tests *Required:* SAT or ACT (for admission).

Options: electronic application, early admission, deferred entrance.

Application fee: $50.

Required: high school transcript. ***Required for some:*** interview. ***Recommended:*** essay or personal statement.

Application deadlines: rolling (freshmen), rolling (transfers).

Notification: continuous (freshmen), continuous (transfers).

CONTACT

Admissions Office, Penn State New Kensington, 3550 Seventh Street Road, New Kensington, PA 15068. *Phone:* 724-334-5466. *Toll-free phone:* 888-968-7297. *Fax:* 724-334-6111. *E-mail:* nkadmissions@psu.edu.

Penn State Schuylkill

Schuylkill Haven, Pennsylvania

http://www.schuylkill.psu.edu/

- **State-related** 4-year, founded 1934, part of Pennsylvania State University
- **Small-town** campus
- **Coed** 783 undergraduate students, 80% full-time, 60% women, 40% men
- **Moderately difficult** entrance level, 73% of applicants were admitted

UNDERGRAD STUDENTS

626 full-time, 157 part-time. 12% are from out of state; 18% Black or African American, non-Hispanic/Latino; 7% Hispanic/Latino; 1% Asian, non-Hispanic/Latino; 0.1% Native Hawaiian or other Pacific Islander, non-Hispanic/Latino; 0.1% American Indian or Alaska Native, non-Hispanic/Latino; 1% Two or more races, non-Hispanic/Latino; 2% Race/ethnicity unknown; 1% international; 5% transferred in; 30% live on campus.

Freshmen:

Admission: 690 applied, 504 admitted, 220 enrolled. ***Average high school GPA:*** 2.9. ***Test scores:*** SAT critical reading scores over 500: 36%; SAT math scores over 500: 32%; SAT writing scores over 500: 26%; ACT scores over 18: 36%; SAT critical reading scores over 600: 8%; SAT math scores over 600: 6%; SAT writing scores over 600: 3%; ACT scores over 24: 4%; SAT critical reading scores over 700: 1%; SAT math scores over 700: 1%; ACT scores over 30: 4%.

Retention: 76% of full-time freshmen returned.

FACULTY

Total: 71, 61% full-time, 56% with terminal degrees.

Student/faculty ratio: 13:1.

ACADEMICS

Calendar: semesters. *Degrees:* certificates, associate, and bachelor's (bachelor's degree programs completed at the Harrisburg campus).

Special study options: adult/continuing education programs, external degree program.

Computers: Students can access the following: online (class) registration. Campuswide network is available.

STUDENT LIFE

Housing options: special housing for students with disabilities.

Athletics Member NJCAA. ***Intercollegiate sports:*** basketball M, cross-country running M/W, golf M, soccer M, softball W, volleyball W. ***Intramural sports:*** basketball M/W, football M, soccer M/W, softball M/W, table tennis M/W, volleyball M/W.

Campus security: 24-hour patrols, controlled dormitory access.

COSTS & FINANCIAL AID

Costs (2016–17) ***Tuition:*** state resident $13,174 full-time, $542 per credit hour part-time; nonresident $20,608 full-time, $859 per credit hour part-time. Full-time tuition and fees vary according to course level, degree level, location, program, and student level. Part-time tuition and fees vary according to course level, course load, degree level, location, program, and student level. ***Required fees:*** $898 full-time. ***Room and board:*** $8240; room only: $6240. Room and board charges vary according to board plan, housing facility, and location. ***Payment plan:*** deferred payment. ***Waivers:*** senior citizens and employees or children of employees.

Financial Aid Of all full-time matriculated undergraduates who enrolled in 2015, 571 applied for aid, 520 were judged to have need, 34 had their need fully met. In 2015, 38 non-need-based awards were made. ***Average percent of need met:*** 66. ***Average financial aid package:*** $12,117. ***Average need-based loan:*** $4022. ***Average need-based gift aid:*** $7340. ***Average non-need-based aid:*** $2760. ***Average indebtedness upon graduation:*** $41,345.

APPLYING

Standardized Tests *Required:* SAT or ACT (for admission).

Options: electronic application, early admission, deferred entrance.

Application fee: $50.

Required: high school transcript.

Application deadlines: rolling (freshmen), rolling (transfers).

Notification: continuous (freshmen), continuous (transfers).

CONTACT

Admissions Office, Penn State Schuylkill, 200 University Drive, Schuylkill Haven, PA 17972. *Phone:* 570-385-6252. *Fax:* 570-385-6272. *E-mail:* sl-admissions@psu.edu.

Penn State Shenango

Sharon, Pennsylvania

http://www.shenango.psu.edu/

- **State-related** primarily 2-year, founded 1965, part of Pennsylvania State University
- **Small-town** campus
- **Coed** 508 undergraduate students, 55% full-time, 72% women, 28% men
- **Moderately difficult** entrance level, 68% of applicants were admitted

UNDERGRAD STUDENTS

280 full-time, 228 part-time. 22% are from out of state; 7% Black or African American, non-Hispanic/Latino; 2% Hispanic/Latino; 0.7% Asian, non-Hispanic/Latino; 3% Two or more races, non-Hispanic/Latino; 3% Race/ethnicity unknown; 9% transferred in.

Freshmen:

Admission: 154 applied, 105 admitted, 57 enrolled. ***Average high school GPA:*** 3.04. ***Test scores:*** SAT critical reading scores over 500: 36%; SAT math scores over 500: 44%; SAT writing scores over 500: 28%; ACT scores over 18: 80%; SAT critical reading scores over 600: 3%; SAT math scores over 600: 5%; SAT writing scores over 600: 5%; ACT scores over 24: 10%.

Retention: 66% of full-time freshmen returned.

FACULTY

Total: 44, 64% full-time, 39% with terminal degrees.

Student/faculty ratio: 11:1.

ACADEMICS

Calendar: semesters. *Degrees:* certificates, associate, and bachelor's.

Special study options: adult/continuing education programs, external degree program.

Computers: Students can access the following: online (class) registration. Campuswide network is available.

STUDENT LIFE

Housing options: college housing not available.

Athletics ***Intramural sports:*** basketball M(c)/W, bowling M/W, football M(c), golf M/W, softball M/W, tennis M/W, volleyball M/W.

COSTS & FINANCIAL AID

Costs (2016–17) ***Tuition:*** state resident $12,474 full-time, $504 per credit hour part-time; nonresident $19,220 full-time, $801 per credit hour part-time. Full-time tuition and fees vary according to course level, degree level, location, program, and student level. Part-time tuition and fees vary according to course level, course load, degree level, location, program, and student level. ***Required fees:*** $822 full-time. ***Payment plan:*** deferred payment. ***Waivers:*** senior citizens and employees or children of employees.

Financial Aid Of all full-time matriculated undergraduates who enrolled in 2015, 259 applied for aid, 247 were judged to have need, 12 had their need fully met. In 2015, 15 non-need-based awards were made. ***Average percent of need met:*** 62. ***Average financial aid package:*** $13,323. ***Average need-based loan:*** $3902. ***Average need-based gift aid:*** $7384. ***Average non-need-based aid:*** $2366. ***Average indebtedness upon graduation:*** $39,706.

APPLYING

Standardized Tests *Required:* SAT or ACT (for admission).

Options: electronic application, early admission, deferred entrance.

Application fee: $50.

Required: high school transcript.

Application deadlines: rolling (freshmen), rolling (transfers).

Notification: continuous (freshmen), continuous (transfers).

CONTACT

Admissions Office, Penn State Shenango, 147 Shenango Avenue, Sharon, PA 16146. *Phone:* 724-983-2803. *Fax:* 724-983-2820. *E-mail:* psushenango@psu.edu.

Penn State University Park

State College, Pennsylvania

http://www.psu.edu/

- **State-related** university, founded 1855, part of The Pennsylvania State University
- **Small-town** 8556-acre campus with easy access to Harrisburg
- **Endowment** $2.5 billion
- **Coed** 41,359 undergraduate students, 97% full-time, 46% women, 54% men
- **Very difficult** entrance level, 56% of applicants were admitted

UNDERGRAD STUDENTS

40,139 full-time, 1,220 part-time. Students come from 53 states and territories; 117 other countries; 33% are from out of state; 4% Black or African American, non-Hispanic/Latino; 6% Hispanic/Latino; 6% Asian, non-Hispanic/Latino; 0.1% Native Hawaiian or other Pacific Islander, non-Hispanic/Latino; 0.1% American Indian or Alaska Native, non-Hispanic/Latino; 3% Two or more races, non-Hispanic/Latino; 2%

Race/ethnicity unknown; 12% international; 0.8% transferred in; 35% live on campus.

Freshmen:
Admission: 52,974 applied, 29,878 admitted, 8,499 enrolled. ***Average high school GPA:*** 3.59. ***Test scores:*** SAT critical reading scores over 500: 87%; SAT math scores over 500: 93%; ACT scores over 18: 100%; SAT critical reading scores over 600: 40%; SAT math scores over 600: 59%; ACT scores over 24: 86%; SAT critical reading scores over 700: 7%; SAT math scores over 700: 15%; ACT scores over 30: 23%.
Retention: 93% of full-time freshmen returned.

FACULTY
Total: 3,156, 87% full-time, 76% with terminal degrees.
Student/faculty ratio: 16:1.

ACADEMICS
Calendar: semesters. *Degrees:* certificates, associate, bachelor's, master's, doctoral, and postbachelor's certificates.
Special study options: academic remediation for entering students, accelerated degree program, adult/continuing education programs, advanced placement credit, cooperative education, distance learning, double majors, English as a second language, external degree program, freshman honors college, honors programs, independent study, internships, off-campus study, part-time degree program, services for LD students, student-designed majors, study abroad, summer session for credit. ***ROTC:*** Army (b), Navy (b), Air Force (b).
Unusual degree programs: 3-2 engineering; geoscience.
Computers: 6,200 computers/terminals and 23,250 ports are available on campus for general student use. Students can access the following: campus intranet, computer help desk, free student e-mail accounts, online (class) grades, online (class) registration, online (class) schedules. Campuswide network is available. 100% of college-owned or -operated housing units are wired for high-speed Internet access. Wireless service is available via classrooms, computer centers, computer labs, dorm rooms, learning centers, libraries, student centers.
Library: Pattee and Paterno Libraries plus 4 others. *Books:* 4.2 million (physical), 421,000 (digital/electronic); *Serial titles:* 85,765 (physical), 115,000 (digital/electronic); *Databases:* 779. Weekly public service hours: 148; study areas open 24 hours, 5-7 days a week; students can reserve study rooms.

STUDENT LIFE
Housing options: on-campus residence required for freshman year; coed, women-only, special housing for students with disabilities. Campus housing is university owned. Freshman campus housing is guaranteed.
Activities and organizations: drama/theater group, student-run newspaper, radio and television station, choral group, marching band, national fraternities, national sororities.
Athletics Member NCAA, USCAA. All Division I except football (Division I-A). ***Intercollegiate sports:*** baseball M(s), basketball M(s)/W(s), cross-country running M(s)/W(s), fencing M(s)/W(s), field hockey W(s), golf M(s)/W(s), gymnastics M(s)/W(s), ice hockey M(s)(c)/W(s)(c), lacrosse M(s)/W(s), soccer M(s)/W(s), softball W(s), swimming and diving M(s)/W(s), tennis M(s)/W(s), track and field M(s)/W(s), volleyball M(s)/W(s), wrestling M(s). ***Intramural sports:*** archery M(c)/W(c), badminton M/W, baseball M(c)/W(c), basketball M/W, bowling M(c)/W(c), cheerleading M(c)/W(c), crew M(c)/W(c), cross-country running M/W, equestrian sports M/W, fencing M(c)/W(c), field hockey M(c)/W(c), football M, golf M/W, gymnastics M(c)/W(c), ice hockey M(c)/W(c), lacrosse M(c)/W(c), racquetball M/W, riflery M(c)/W(c), rowing M(c)/W(c), sailing M(c)/W(c), skiing (downhill) M(c)/W(c), soccer M/W, softball M/W, squash M/W, swimming and diving M/W, table tennis M/W, tennis M/W, track and field M/W, triathlon M(c)/W(c), ultimate Frisbee M(c)/W(c), volleyball M/W, water polo M(c)/W(c), weight lifting M(c)/W(c), wrestling M(c)/W(c).
Campus security: 24-hour emergency response devices and patrols, student patrols, late-night transport/escort service, controlled dormitory access.
Student services: health clinic, personal/psychological counseling, women's center, legal services.

COSTS & FINANCIAL AID
Costs (2016–17) ***Tuition:*** state resident $16,952 full-time, $706 per credit hour part-time; nonresident $31,434 full-time, $1310 per credit hour part-time. Full-time tuition and fees vary according to course level, degree level, location, program, and student level. Part-time tuition and fees vary according to course level, course load, degree level, location, program, and student level. ***Required fees:*** $948 full-time. ***Room and board:*** $11,860; room only: $5940. Room and board charges vary according to board plan, housing facility, and location. ***Payment plan:*** deferred payment. ***Waivers:*** senior citizens and employees or children of employees.
Financial Aid Of all full-time matriculated undergraduates who enrolled in 2015, 23,999 applied for aid, 18,369 were judged to have need, 1,423 had their need fully met. 994 Federal Work-Study jobs (averaging $3144). In 2015, 3891 non-need-based awards were made. ***Average percent of need met:*** 59. ***Average financial aid package:*** $11,498. ***Average need-based loan:*** $4712. ***Average need-based gift aid:*** $7685. ***Average non-need-based aid:*** $3933. ***Average indebtedness upon graduation:*** $37,213.

APPLYING
Standardized Tests *Required:* SAT or ACT (for admission).
Options: electronic application, early admission, deferred entrance.
Application fee: $65.
Required: high school transcript. ***Recommended:*** essay or personal statement.
Application deadlines: rolling (freshmen), rolling (transfers).
Notification: continuous (freshmen), continuous (transfers).

CONTACT
Clark V. Brigger, Executive Director for Undergraduate Admissions, Penn State University Park, 201 Shields Building, University Park, PA 16802. *Phone:* 814-865-5471. *Fax:* 814-863-7590. *E-mail:* admissions@psu.edu.

Penn State Wilkes-Barre
Lehman, Pennsylvania
http://www.wb.psu.edu/

- **State-related** 4-year, founded 1916, part of Pennsylvania State University
- **Rural** campus
- **Coed** 493 undergraduate students, 89% full-time, 34% women, 66% men
- **Moderately difficult** entrance level, 88% of applicants were admitted

UNDERGRAD STUDENTS
440 full-time, 53 part-time. 5% are from out of state; 3% Black or African American, non-Hispanic/Latino; 5% Hispanic/Latino; 1% Asian, non-Hispanic/Latino; 0.2% American Indian or Alaska Native, non-Hispanic/Latino; 2% Two or more races, non-Hispanic/Latino; 1% Race/ethnicity unknown; 0.4% international; 4% transferred in.

Freshmen:
Admission: 411 applied, 360 admitted, 143 enrolled. ***Average high school GPA:*** 3.1. ***Test scores:*** SAT critical reading scores over 500: 45%; SAT math scores over 500: 50%; SAT writing scores over 500: 38%; ACT scores over 18: 100%; SAT critical reading scores over 600: 12%; SAT math scores over 600: 15%; SAT writing scores over 600: 5%; ACT scores over 24: 33%; SAT critical reading scores over 700: 1%; SAT math scores over 700: 2%.
Retention: 84% of full-time freshmen returned.

FACULTY
Total: 49, 61% full-time, 43% with terminal degrees.
Student/faculty ratio: 13:1.

ACADEMICS
Calendar: semesters. *Degrees:* certificates, associate, bachelor's, and postbachelor's certificates (enrollment figures include students enrolled at The Graduate School at Penn State who are taking courses at this location).
Special study options: adult/continuing education programs, external degree program. ***ROTC:*** Army (c), Air Force (c).
Computers: Students can access the following: online (class) registration. Campuswide network is available.

STUDENT LIFE
Housing options: college housing not available.

Athletics Member NJCAA. ***Intercollegiate sports:*** baseball M, basketball M, cross-country running M/W, golf M/W, soccer M/W, volleyball W. ***Intramural sports:*** basketball M/W, bowling M(c)/W(c), cheerleading M(c)/W(c), football M, racquetball M/W, softball W, volleyball M(c)/W.

COSTS & FINANCIAL AID
Costs (2016–17) ***Tuition:*** state resident $12,718 full-time, $524 per credit hour part-time; nonresident $19,598 full-time, $817 per credit hour part-time. Full-time tuition and fees vary according to course level, degree level, location, program, and student level. Part-time tuition and fees vary according to course level, course load, degree level, location, program, and student level. ***Required fees:*** $822 full-time. ***Payment plans:*** installment, deferred payment. ***Waivers:*** senior citizens and employees or children of employees.
Financial Aid Of all full-time matriculated undergraduates who enrolled in 2015, 400 applied for aid, 312 were judged to have need, 21 had their need fully met. In 2015, 44 non-need-based awards were made. ***Average percent of need met:*** 66. ***Average financial aid package:*** $11,107. ***Average need-based loan:*** $4224. ***Average need-based gift aid:*** $7239. ***Average non-need-based aid:*** $2626. ***Average indebtedness upon graduation:*** $35,984.

APPLYING
Standardized Tests *Required:* SAT or ACT (for admission).
Options: electronic application, early admission, deferred entrance.
Application fee: $50.
Required: high school transcript.
Application deadlines: rolling (freshmen), rolling (transfers).
Notification: continuous (freshmen), continuous (transfers).

CONTACT
Admissions Office, Penn State Wilkes-Barre, Old Route 115, PO Box PSU, Lehman, PA 18627. *Phone:* 570-675-9238. *Fax:* 570-675-9113. *E-mail:* wbadmissions@psu.edu.

Penn State Worthington Scranton
Dunmore, Pennsylvania
http://www.sn.psu.edu/

- **State-related** 4-year, founded 1923, part of Pennsylvania State University
- **Small-town** campus
- **Coed** 1,034 undergraduate students, 85% full-time, 52% women, 48% men
- **Moderately difficult** entrance level, 81% of applicants were admitted

UNDERGRAD STUDENTS
880 full-time, 154 part-time. 1% are from out of state; 3% Black or African American, non-Hispanic/Latino; 6% Hispanic/Latino; 5% Asian, non-Hispanic/Latino; 2% Two or more races, non-Hispanic/Latino; 2% Race/ethnicity unknown; 0.3% international; 5% transferred in.

Freshmen:
Admission: 733 applied, 591 admitted, 230 enrolled. ***Average high school GPA:*** 3.03. ***Test scores:*** SAT critical reading scores over 500: 42%; SAT math scores over 500: 46%; SAT writing scores over 500: 31%; ACT scores over 18: 57%; SAT critical reading scores over 600: 7%; SAT math scores over 600: 10%; SAT writing scores over 600: 6%; ACT scores over 24: 14%; SAT math scores over 700: 1%.
Retention: 75% of full-time freshmen returned.

FACULTY
Total: 97, 52% full-time, 42% with terminal degrees.
Student/faculty ratio: 14:1.

ACADEMICS
Calendar: semesters. *Degrees:* certificates, associate, and bachelor's.
Special study options: adult/continuing education programs, external degree program. ***ROTC:*** Army (c), Air Force (c).
Computers: Students can access the following: online (class) registration. Campuswide network is available.

STUDENT LIFE
Housing options: college housing not available.

Athletics Member NJCAA. ***Intercollegiate sports:*** baseball M, basketball M/W, cheerleading M/W, cross-country running M/W, soccer M, softball W, volleyball W. ***Intramural sports:*** basketball M/W, bowling M(c)/W(c), skiing (downhill) M(c)/W(c), soccer M/W, softball M/W, volleyball M/W(c), weight lifting M(c)/W(c).

COSTS & FINANCIAL AID
Costs (2016–17) ***Tuition:*** state resident $13,174 full-time, $542 per credit hour part-time; nonresident $20,608 full-time, $859 per credit hour part-time. Full-time tuition and fees vary according to course level, degree level, location, program, and student level. Part-time tuition and fees vary according to course level, course load, degree level, location, program, and student level. ***Required fees:*** $898 full-time. ***Payment plans:*** installment, deferred payment. ***Waivers:*** senior citizens and employees or children of employees.
Financial Aid Of all full-time matriculated undergraduates who enrolled in 2015, 778 applied for aid, 674 were judged to have need, 34 had their need fully met. In 2015, 39 non-need-based awards were made. ***Average percent of need met:*** 61. ***Average financial aid package:*** $10,523. ***Average need-based loan:*** $3918. ***Average need-based gift aid:*** $7043. ***Average non-need-based aid:*** $3412. ***Average indebtedness upon graduation:*** $37,098.

APPLYING
Standardized Tests *Required:* SAT or ACT (for admission).
Options: electronic application, early admission, deferred entrance.
Application fee: $50.
Required: high school transcript. ***Required for some:*** interview. ***Recommended:*** essay or personal statement.
Application deadlines: rolling (freshmen), rolling (transfers).
Notification: continuous (freshmen), continuous (transfers).

CONTACT
Admissions Office, Penn State Worthington Scranton, 120 Ridge View Drive, Dunmore, PA 18512. *Phone:* 570-963-2500. *Fax:* 570-963-2524. *E-mail:* wsadmissions@psu.edu.

Penn State York
York, Pennsylvania
http://www.yk.psu.edu/

- **State-related** comprehensive, founded 1926, part of Pennsylvania State University
- **Suburban** campus
- **Coed** 1,087 undergraduate students, 77% full-time, 44% women, 56% men
- **Moderately difficult** entrance level, 86% of applicants were admitted

UNDERGRAD STUDENTS
841 full-time, 246 part-time. 9% are from out of state; 6% Black or African American, non-Hispanic/Latino; 6% Hispanic/Latino; 5% Asian, non-Hispanic/Latino; 0.1% Native Hawaiian or other Pacific Islander, non-Hispanic/Latino; 0.1% American Indian or Alaska Native, non-Hispanic/Latino; 3% Two or more races, non-Hispanic/Latino; 2% Race/ethnicity unknown; 15% international; 4% transferred in.

Freshmen:
Admission: 1,397 applied, 1,196 admitted, 320 enrolled. ***Average high school GPA:*** 3.11. ***Test scores:*** SAT critical reading scores over 500: 48%; SAT math scores over 500: 65%; SAT writing scores over 500: 45%; ACT scores over 18: 90%; SAT critical reading scores over 600: 13%; SAT math scores over 600: 36%; SAT writing scores over 600: 10%; ACT scores over 24: 65%; SAT critical reading scores over 700: 1%; SAT math scores over 700: 14%; ACT scores over 30: 6%.
Retention: 80% of full-time freshmen returned.

FACULTY
Total: 93, 54% full-time, 56% with terminal degrees.
Student/faculty ratio: 15:1.

ACADEMICS
Calendar: semesters. *Degrees:* certificates, associate, bachelor's, master's, and postbachelor's certificates (also offers up to 2 years of most bachelor's degree programs offered at University Park campus).

Special study options: adult/continuing education programs, external degree program.

Computers: Students can access the following: online (class) registration. Campuswide network is available.

STUDENT LIFE
Housing options: college housing not available.

Athletics Member NJCAA.

COSTS & FINANCIAL AID
Costs (2016–17) ***Tuition:*** state resident $13,174 full-time, $542 per credit hour part-time; nonresident $20,608 full-time, $859 per credit hour part-time. Full-time tuition and fees vary according to course level, degree level, location, program, and student level. Part-time tuition and fees vary according to course level, course load, degree level, location, program, and student level. ***Required fees:*** $960 full-time. ***Payment plans:*** installment, deferred payment. ***Waivers:*** senior citizens and employees or children of employees.

Financial Aid Of all full-time matriculated undergraduates who enrolled in 2015, 570 applied for aid, 449 were judged to have need, 34 had their need fully met. In 2015, 114 non-need-based awards were made. ***Average percent of need met:*** 62. ***Average financial aid package:*** $10,704. ***Average need-based loan:*** $4008. ***Average need-based gift aid:*** $6597. ***Average non-need-based aid:*** $2381. ***Average indebtedness upon graduation:*** $36,176.

APPLYING
Standardized Tests *Required:* SAT or ACT (for admission).

Options: electronic application, early admission, deferred entrance.

Application fee: $50.

Required: high school transcript.

Application deadlines: rolling (freshmen), rolling (transfers).

Notification: continuous (freshmen), continuous (transfers).

CONTACT
Admissions Office, Penn State York, 1031 Edgecomb Avenue, York, PA 17403. *Phone:* 717-771-4040. *Toll-free phone:* 800-778-6227. *Fax:* 717-771-4005. *E-mail:* ykadmission@psu.edu.

Pennsylvania Academy of the Fine Arts

Philadelphia, Pennsylvania

http://www.pafa.edu/

CONTACT
Andr? van de Putte, Dean of Enrollment, Pennsylvania Academy of the Fine Arts, 128 North Broad Street, Philadelphia, PA 19102. *E-mail:* avandeputte@pafa.edu.

Pennsylvania College of Art & Design

Lancaster, Pennsylvania

http://www.pcad.edu/

- **Independent** 4-year, founded 1982
- **Urban** campus with easy access to Philadelphia, Baltimore
- **Coed** 232 undergraduate students, 96% full-time, 67% women, 33% men
- **Moderately difficult** entrance level, 45% of applicants were admitted

UNDERGRAD STUDENTS
222 full-time, 10 part-time. 26% are from out of state; 8% Black or African American, non-Hispanic/Latino; 4% Hispanic/Latino; 4% Asian, non-Hispanic/Latino; 1% American Indian or Alaska Native, non-Hispanic/Latino; 4% Two or more races, non-Hispanic/Latino; 8% Race/ethnicity unknown; 7% transferred in.

Freshmen:
Admission: 419 applied, 187 admitted, 75 enrolled. ***Average high school GPA:*** 3.01.

Retention: 74% of full-time freshmen returned.

FACULTY
Total: 51, 20% full-time, 41% with terminal degrees.

Student/faculty ratio: 12:1.

ACADEMICS
Calendar: semesters. *Degree:* certificates and bachelor's.

Special study options: advanced placement credit, internships.

Computers: 90 computers/terminals are available on campus for general student use. Students can access the following: campus intranet, computer help desk, free student e-mail accounts, online (class) grades, online (class) registration, online (class) schedules. Campuswide network is available. Wireless service is available via entire campus.

Library: Pennsylvania College of Art & Design Library.

STUDENT LIFE
Housing options: college housing not available.

Activities and organizations: Student Council, Anime Club, Student AIGA, Society of Illustrators - Student Group.

Campus security: late-night transport/escort service, trained evening/weekend security personnel.

COSTS
Costs (2017–18) ***Tuition:*** $23,500 full-time, $979 per credit part-time. Full-time tuition and fees vary according to course load and program. Part-time tuition and fees vary according to course load and program. ***Required fees:*** $1500 full-time, $1500 per year part-time. ***Room only:*** Room and board charges vary according to housing facility. ***Payment plan:*** installment. ***Waivers:*** employees or children of employees.

APPLYING
Options: electronic application, deferred entrance.

Application fee: $40.

Required: essay or personal statement, high school transcript, minimum 2.5 GPA, portfolio. ***Required for some:*** 2 letters of recommendation, interview. ***Recommended:*** interview.

Application deadlines: rolling (freshmen), rolling (transfers).

Notification: continuous (freshmen), continuous (transfers).

CONTACT
Admissions Department, Pennsylvania College of Art & Design, 204 North Prince Street, PO Box 59, Lancaster, PA 17608. *Phone:* 717-396-7833. *Toll-free phone:* 800-689-0379 Ext. 1001. *Fax:* 717-396-1339. *E-mail:* admissions@pcad.edu.

Pennsylvania College of Health Sciences

Lancaster, Pennsylvania

http://www.pacollege.edu/

- **Independent** comprehensive, founded 1903
- **Urban** 25-acre campus with easy access to Harrisburg
- **Endowment** $5.0 million
- **Coed, primarily women** 1,454 undergraduate students, 33% full-time, 87% women, 13% men
- **Moderately difficult** entrance level, 73% of applicants were admitted

UNDERGRAD STUDENTS
484 full-time, 970 part-time. Students come from 15 states and territories; 2% are from out of state; 6% Black or African American, non-Hispanic/Latino; 7% Hispanic/Latino; 2% Asian, non-Hispanic/Latino; 2% Two or more races, non-Hispanic/Latino; 5% Race/ethnicity unknown; 18% transferred in.

Freshmen:
Admission: 347 applied, 252 admitted, 82 enrolled.

Retention: 73% of full-time freshmen returned.

FACULTY
Total: 250, 31% full-time.

Student/faculty ratio: 6:1.

ACADEMICS
Calendar: semesters. *Degrees:* certificates, associate, bachelor's, and master's.

Special study options: accelerated degree program, adult/continuing education programs, advanced placement credit, distance learning, part-time degree program, services for LD students, summer session for credit.

Computers: 200 computers/terminals are available on campus for general student use. Students can access the following: campus intranet, computer help desk, free student e-mail accounts, online (class) grades, online (class) registration, online (class) schedules. Campuswide network is available. Wireless service is available via entire campus.
Library: Health Sciences Library. *Books:* 1,245 (physical), 570 (digital/electronic); *Serial titles:* 121 (physical), 1,390 (digital/electronic); *Databases:* 43. Students can reserve study rooms.

STUDENT LIFE
Housing options: college housing not available.

Athletics ***Intramural sports:*** cross-country running M(c)/W(c), soccer M(c)/W(c).

Campus security: 24-hour emergency response devices and patrols, late-night transport/escort service.

Student services: health clinic, personal/psychological counseling.

APPLYING
Standardized Tests *Required for some:* SAT or ACT (for admission).

Options: electronic application, deferred entrance.

Application fee: $35.

Required: minimum 3.0 GPA, 2 letters of recommendation, transcripts of all institutions attended. ***Required for some:*** essay or personal statement.

Notification: continuous (freshmen).

CONTACT
Admissions Office, Pennsylvania College of Health Sciences, 850 Greenfield Rd, Lancaster, PA 17601. *Phone:* 800-622-5443. *Toll-free phone:* 800-622-5443. *E-mail:* admission@pacollege.edu.

Pennsylvania College of Technology

Williamsport, Pennsylvania

http://www.pct.edu/

- **State-related** 4-year, founded 1965
- **Suburban** 994-acre campus
- **Coed** 5,432 undergraduate students, 84% full-time, 36% women, 64% men
- **Noncompetitive** entrance level, 67% of applicants were admitted

UNDERGRAD STUDENTS
4,583 full-time, 849 part-time. Students come from 27 states and territories; 12 other countries; 11% are from out of state; 3% Black or African American, non-Hispanic/Latino; 4% Hispanic/Latino; 0.9% Asian, non-Hispanic/Latino; 0.1% Native Hawaiian or other Pacific Islander, non-Hispanic/Latino; 0.2% American Indian or Alaska Native, non-Hispanic/Latino; 2% Two or more races, non-Hispanic/Latino; 1% international; 8% transferred in; 31% live on campus.

Freshmen:
Admission: 6,366 applied, 4,239 admitted, 1,227 enrolled. ***Average high school GPA:*** 3.05.
Retention: 75% of full-time freshmen returned.

FACULTY
Total: 472, 62% full-time.

Student/faculty ratio: 14:1.

ACADEMICS
Calendar: semesters. *Degrees:* certificates, associate, and bachelor's.

Special study options: academic remediation for entering students, advanced placement credit, cooperative education, distance learning, English as a second language, independent study, internships, off-campus study, part-time degree program, services for LD students, student-designed majors, study abroad, summer session for credit.
ROTC: Army (b).

Computers: 1,800 computers/terminals are available on campus for general student use. Students can access the following: campus intranet, computer help desk, free student e-mail accounts, online (class) grades, online (class) registration, online (class) schedules. Campuswide network is available. 100% of college-owned or -operated housing units are wired for high-speed Internet access. Wireless service is available via entire campus.
Library: Penn College Madigan Library plus 1 other. *Books:* 89,038 (physical), 18,813 (digital/electronic); *Serial titles:* 9,190 (physical), 50,347 (digital/electronic); *Databases:* 83. Weekly public service hours: 90; students can reserve study rooms.

STUDENT LIFE
Housing options: coed, special housing for students with disabilities. Campus housing is university owned.

Activities and organizations: Student Government Association, Residence Hall Association, Wildcats Event Board, Association of Computing Machinery, Campus Ministry International, national fraternities.

Athletics Member NCAA, USCAA. All Division III. ***Intercollegiate sports:*** archery M/W, baseball M, basketball M/W, bowling M/W, cross-country running M/W, golf M/W, soccer M/W, softball W, tennis M/W, volleyball M/W, wrestling M. ***Intramural sports:*** archery M/W, badminton M/W, basketball M/W, bowling M/W, football M, golf M/W, lacrosse M, soccer M/W, softball M/W, table tennis M/W, tennis M/W, ultimate Frisbee M/W, volleyball M/W, weight lifting M/W.

Campus security: 24-hour emergency response devices and patrols, late-night transport/escort service, controlled dormitory access.

Student services: health clinic, personal/psychological counseling.

COSTS & FINANCIAL AID
Costs (2017–18) ***Tuition:*** state resident $16,080 full-time, $536 per credit hour part-time; nonresident $22,890 full-time, $763 per credit hour part-time. Full-time tuition and fees vary according to course load and program. Part-time tuition and fees vary according to course load and program. ***Required fees:*** $2490 full-time. ***Room and board:*** $11,244; room only: $6456. Room and board charges vary according to board plan and housing facility. ***Payment plan:*** deferred payment. ***Waivers:*** employees or children of employees.

Financial Aid Of all full-time matriculated undergraduates who enrolled in 2014, 4,556 applied for aid, 4,365 were judged to have need. 129 Federal Work-Study jobs (averaging $1650). ***Average percent of need met:*** 23. ***Average financial aid package:*** $12,668. ***Average need-based loan:*** $4160. ***Average need-based gift aid:*** $7907.

APPLYING
Standardized Tests *Required for some:* SAT (for admission).

Options: electronic application, early admission, deferred entrance.

Application fee: $50.

Required for some: high school transcript, college transcripts for transfers.

Application deadlines: 7/1 (freshmen), rolling (transfers).

CONTACT
Mr. Dennis L. Correll, Associate Dean for Financial Aid/Admissions, Pennsylvania College of Technology, One College Avenue, DIF #119, Williamsport, PA 17701. *Phone:* 570-327-4761 Ext. 7337. *Toll-free phone:* 800-367-9222. *Fax:* 570-321-5551. *E-mail:* admissions@pct.edu.

Philadelphia University

Philadelphia, Pennsylvania

http://www.philau.edu/

- **Independent** comprehensive, founded 1884
- **Suburban** 100-acre campus
- **Coed**
- **Moderately difficult** entrance level

ACADEMICS
Calendar: semesters. *Degrees:* certificates, associate, bachelor's, master's, doctoral, post-master's, and postbachelor's certificates.
Library: Paul J. Gutman Library.

STUDENT LIFE
Housing options: coed, women-only, special housing for students with disabilities. Campus housing is university owned and leased by the school. Freshman campus housing is guaranteed.

Athletics Member NCAA. All Division II.

Campus security: 24-hour emergency response devices and patrols, late-night transport/escort service, controlled dormitory access.

COSTS & FINANCIAL AID
Costs (2016–17) ***Comprehensive fee:*** $50,370 includes full-time tuition ($36,870), mandatory fees ($930), and room and board ($12,570). Full-

time tuition and fees vary according to course load, degree level, program, and student level. Part-time tuition: $605 per credit hour. Part-time tuition and fees vary according to class time, course load, degree level, program, and reciprocity agreements. ***Required fees:*** $25 per credit hour part-time. ***College room only:*** $5870. Room and board charges vary according to board plan and housing facility. ***Payment plans:*** installment, deferred payment.

Financial Aid Of all full-time matriculated undergraduates who enrolled in 2016, 2,095 applied for aid, 1,893 were judged to have need, 203 had their need fully met. In 2016, 356 non-need-based awards were made. ***Average percent of need met:*** 70. ***Average financial aid package:*** $27,325. ***Average need-based loan:*** $4449. ***Average need-based gift aid:*** $23,340. ***Average non-need-based aid:*** $11,952. ***Average indebtedness upon graduation:*** $40,227. ***Financial aid deadline:*** 4/15.

APPLYING
Standardized Tests *Required:* SAT or ACT (for admission).
Options: electronic application, deferred entrance.
Application fee: $40.
Required: high school transcript. ***Recommended:*** essay or personal statement, 2 letters of recommendation, interview.

CONTACT
Greg Potts, Director of Admissions, Philadelphia University, 4201 Henry Avenue, Philadelphia, PA 19144-5497. *Phone:* 215-951-2800. *Fax:* 215-951-2907. *E-mail:* admissions@philau.edu.

See this page for display ad and page 1460 for the College Close-Up.

Pittsburgh Technical College

Oakdale, Pennsylvania

http://www.ptcollege.edu/

- **Proprietary** primarily 2-year, founded 1946
- **Suburban** 180-acre campus with easy access to Pittsburgh
- **Coed** 1,875 undergraduate students, 100% full-time, 42% women, 58% men
- 87% of applicants were admitted

UNDERGRAD STUDENTS
1,875 full-time. Students come from 11 states and territories; 19% are from out of state; 8% Black or African American, non-Hispanic/Latino; 0.5% Hispanic/Latino; 0.9% Asian, non-Hispanic/Latino; 0.1% Native Hawaiian or other Pacific Islander, non-Hispanic/Latino; 0.3% American Indian or Alaska Native, non-Hispanic/Latino; 5% Two or more races, non-Hispanic/Latino; 17% Race/ethnicity unknown; 10% transferred in; 44% live on campus.

Freshmen:
Admission: 1,865 applied, 1,615 admitted, 663 enrolled. ***Average high school GPA:*** 2.47.

FACULTY
Total: 133, 57% full-time, 5% with terminal degrees.
Student/faculty ratio: 14:1.

ACADEMICS
Calendar: quarters. *Degrees:* certificates, associate, and bachelor's.
Special study options: academic remediation for entering students, adult/continuing education programs, advanced placement credit, cooperative education, distance learning, double majors, internships, services for LD students.
Computers: 393 computers/terminals are available on campus for general student use. Students can access the following: campus intranet, computer help desk, free student e-mail accounts, online (class) grades, online (class) schedules. Campuswide network is available. 100% of college-owned or -operated housing units are wired for high-speed Internet access. Wireless service is available via entire campus.
Library: Library Resource Center. *Books:* 6,529 (physical), 53 (digital/electronic); *Serial titles:* 133 (physical), 2 (digital/electronic); *Databases:* 7. Weekly public service hours: 58.

STUDENT LIFE
Housing options: coed. Campus housing is university owned and leased by the school.

Activities and organizations: drama/theater group, Software Development Club, Drama Club, DECA, Gay-Straight Alliance, Magic Club.

Athletics ***Intramural sports:*** basketball M/W, sand volleyball M/W, soccer M/W, softball M/W, ultimate Frisbee M/W, volleyball M/W.

Campus security: 24-hour emergency response devices and patrols, student patrols, late-night transport/escort service, controlled dormitory access.

Student services: personal/psychological counseling.

COSTS

Costs (2017–18) ***Comprehensive fee:*** $25,811 includes full-time tuition ($16,361) and room and board ($9450). Full-time tuition and fees vary according to degree level and program. No tuition increase for student's term of enrollment. ***College room only:*** $6993. Room and board charges vary according to housing facility. ***Payment plans:*** installment, deferred payment. ***Waivers:*** children of alumni and employees or children of employees.

APPLYING

Standardized Tests *Required:* entrance exam for practical nursing certificate as well as nursing and surgical technology Associate degrees (for admission). *Required for some:* SAT or ACT (for admission).

Options: electronic application, deferred entrance.

Required: high school transcript. ***Required for some:*** essay or personal statement, criminal background check, minimum rank in top 80% of class. ***Recommended:*** interview.

Application deadlines: rolling (freshmen), rolling (transfers).

Notification: continuous (freshmen), continuous (transfers).

CONTACT

Ms. Nancy Goodlin, Admissions Office Assistant, Pittsburgh Technical College, 1111 McKee Road, Oakdale, PA 15071. *Phone:* 412-809-5100. *Toll-free phone:* 800-784-9675. *Fax:* 412-809-5351. *E-mail:* goodlin.nancy@ptcollege.edu.

Point Park University

Pittsburgh, Pennsylvania

http://www.pointpark.edu/

- **Independent** comprehensive, founded 1960
- **Urban** campus
- **Endowment** $31.0 million
- **Coed** 3,226 undergraduate students, 79% full-time, 57% women, 43% men
- **Moderately difficult** entrance level, 74% of applicants were admitted

UNDERGRAD STUDENTS

2,551 full-time, 675 part-time. Students come from 49 states and territories; 37 other countries; 21% are from out of state; 16% Black or African American, non-Hispanic/Latino; 3% Hispanic/Latino; 1% Asian, non-Hispanic/Latino; 0.1% American Indian or Alaska Native, non-Hispanic/Latino; 4% Two or more races, non-Hispanic/Latino; 0.8% Race/ethnicity unknown; 3% international; 14% transferred in; 25% live on campus.

Freshmen:

Admission: 3,237 applied, 2,393 admitted, 548 enrolled. ***Average high school GPA:*** 3.22. ***Test scores:*** SAT critical reading scores over 500: 55%; SAT math scores over 500: 43%; SAT writing scores over 500: 49%; ACT scores over 18: 86%; SAT critical reading scores over 600: 16%; SAT math scores over 600: 9%; SAT writing scores over 600: 14%; ACT scores over 24: 36%; SAT critical reading scores over 700: 2%; SAT math scores over 700: 1%; SAT writing scores over 700: 2%; ACT scores over 30: 4%.

Retention: 76% of full-time freshmen returned.

FACULTY

Total: 454, 30% full-time.

Student/faculty ratio: 13:1.

ACADEMICS

Calendar: semesters. *Degrees:* certificates, associate, bachelor's, master's, and postbachelor's certificates.

Special study options: academic remediation for entering students, accelerated degree program, adult/continuing education programs, advanced placement credit, cooperative education, distance learning, double majors, English as a second language, honors programs, independent study, internships, off-campus study, part-time degree program, services for LD students, student-designed majors, study abroad, summer session for credit. ***ROTC:*** Army (c), Air Force (c).

Computers: 309 computers/terminals and 112 ports are available on campus for general student use. Students can access the following: campus intranet, computer help desk, free student e-mail accounts, online (class) grades, online (class) registration, online (class) schedules. Campuswide network is available. 100% of college-owned or -operated housing units are wired for high-speed Internet access. Wireless service is available via entire campus.

Library: Point Park University Library.

STUDENT LIFE

Housing options: coed, women-only, special housing for students with disabilities. Campus housing is university owned and leased by the school. Freshman campus housing is guaranteed.

Activities and organizations: drama/theater group, student-run newspaper, radio and television station, student radio station, The Body Christian Fellowship, Dance Club, Campus Activities Board, Action Sports Club.

Athletics Member NAIA. ***Intercollegiate sports:*** baseball M(s), basketball M(s)/W(s), cross-country running M(s)/W(s), golf M(s)/W(s), soccer M(s)/W(s), softball W(s), volleyball W(s). ***Intramural sports:*** basketball M, bowling M/W, football M, golf M, tennis M/W, volleyball M/W, weight lifting M/W.

Campus security: 24-hour emergency response devices and patrols, late-night transport/escort service, controlled dormitory access, campus patrolled by accredited law enforcement agency, 24-hour security desk, video security.

Student services: health clinic, personal/psychological counseling.

COSTS & FINANCIAL AID

Costs (2017–18) ***Comprehensive fee:*** $42,090 includes full-time tuition ($28,860), mandatory fees ($1270), and room and board ($11,960). Full-time tuition and fees vary according to program. Part-time tuition: $819 per credit. Part-time tuition and fees vary according to program. ***Required fees:*** $55 per credit part-time. ***College room only:*** $5220. Room and board charges vary according to board plan and housing facility. ***Payment plans:*** installment, deferred payment. ***Waivers:*** employees or children of employees.

Financial Aid Of all full-time matriculated undergraduates who enrolled in 2014, 2,388 applied for aid, 2,181 were judged to have need, 264 had their need fully met. In 2014, 194 non-need-based awards were made. ***Average percent of need met:*** 67. ***Average financial aid package:*** $21,099. ***Average need-based loan:*** $5244. ***Average need-based gift aid:*** $15,569. ***Average non-need-based aid:*** $10,246. ***Average indebtedness upon graduation:*** $28,753.

APPLYING

Standardized Tests *Required:* SAT or ACT (for admission).

Options: electronic application, deferred entrance.

Application fee: $40.

Required: high school transcript. ***Required for some:*** 2 letters of recommendation, interview, audition. ***Recommended:*** essay or personal statement, minimum 2.5 GPA.

Application deadlines: rolling (freshmen), rolling (transfers).

Notification: continuous (freshmen), continuous (transfers).

CONTACT

Point Park University, 201 Wood Street, Pittsburgh, PA 15222-1984. *Phone:* 412-392-3430. *Toll-free phone:* 800-321-0129.

The Restaurant School at Walnut Hill College

Philadelphia, Pennsylvania

http://www.walnuthillcollege.edu/

- **Proprietary** primarily 2-year, founded 1974
- **Urban** 2-acre campus
- **Coed**
- 97% of applicants were admitted

FACULTY

Student/faculty ratio: 22:1.

ACADEMICS

Calendar: quarters. *Degrees:* associate and bachelor's.

Library: Alumni Resource Center plus 1 other. Weekly public service hours: 61.

STUDENT LIFE

Housing options: coed. Campus housing is leased by the school.

Activities and organizations: Wine Club, Book Club, Coffee and Tea Club, Craft Club, Flair Bartending.

Campus security: 24-hour emergency response devices and patrols, student patrols, controlled dormitory access.

COSTS

Costs (2016–17) ***One-time required fee:*** $200. ***Tuition:*** $19,050 full-time. ***Required fees:*** $3850 full-time. ***Room only:*** $5400. Room and board charges vary according to housing facility. ***Payment plans:*** installment, deferred payment.

APPLYING

Standardized Tests *Recommended:* SAT or ACT (for admission).

Options: electronic application, early admission, early decision, deferred entrance.

Application fee: $50.

Required: essay or personal statement, high school transcript, 2 letters of recommendation, interview. ***Recommended:*** minimum 2.0 GPA.

CONTACT

Mr. John English, Director of Admissions, The Restaurant School at Walnut Hill College, 4207 Walnut Street, Philadelphia, PA 19104-3518. *Phone:* 267-295-2353. *Fax:* 215-222-4219. *E-mail:* jenglish@walnuthillcollege.edu.

See below for display ad and page 1472 for the College Close-Up.

★ Robert Morris University

Moon Township, Pennsylvania

http://www.rmu.edu/

- **Independent** university, founded 1921
- **Suburban** 230-acre campus with easy access to Pittsburgh
- **Endowment** $30.3 million
- **Coed** 4,384 undergraduate students, 90% full-time, 42% women, 58% men
- **Minimally difficult** entrance level, 80% of applicants were admitted

UNDERGRAD STUDENTS

3,940 full-time, 444 part-time. Students come from 49 states and territories; 39 other countries; 14% are from out of state; 6% Black or African American, non-Hispanic/Latino; 2% Hispanic/Latino; 1% Asian, non-Hispanic/Latino; 0.1% Native Hawaiian or other Pacific Islander, non-Hispanic/Latino; 0.1% American Indian or Alaska Native, non-Hispanic/Latino; 3% Two or more races, non-Hispanic/Latino; 2% Race/ethnicity unknown; 12% international; 7% transferred in; 46% live on campus.

Freshmen:

Admission: 7,164 applied, 5,720 admitted, 880 enrolled. ***Average high school GPA:*** 3.46. ***Test scores:*** SAT critical reading scores over 500: 58%; SAT math scores over 500: 64%; SAT writing scores over 500: 44%; ACT scores over 18: 94%; SAT critical reading scores over 600: 14%; SAT math scores over 600: 20%; SAT writing scores over 600: 8%; ACT scores over 24: 48%; SAT critical reading scores over 700: 2%; SAT math scores over 700: 3%; SAT writing scores over 700: 1%; ACT scores over 30: 4%.

Retention: 80% of full-time freshmen returned.

FACULTY

Total: 486, 42% full-time, 65% with terminal degrees.

Student/faculty ratio: 15:1.

ACADEMICS

Calendar: semesters. *Degrees:* bachelor's, master's, doctoral, and postbachelor's certificates.

Special study options: academic remediation for entering students, accelerated degree program, adult/continuing education programs, cooperative education, distance learning, double majors, honors programs, independent study, internships, off-campus study, part-time degree program, services for LD students, study abroad, summer session for credit. ***ROTC:*** Army (b), Navy (c), Air Force (c).

Computers: 300 computers/terminals are available on campus for general student use. Students can access the following: campus intranet, computer help desk, free student e-mail accounts, online (class) grades, online (class) registration, online (class) schedules, online payment. Campuswide network is available. 100% of college-owned or -operated housing units are wired for high-speed Internet access. Wireless service is available via entire campus.

Library: Robert Morris University Library. *Books:* 87,233 (physical), 172,931 (digital/electronic); *Serial titles:* 244 (physical), 2,810 (digital/electronic); *Databases:* 75. Weekly public service hours: 101; study areas open 24 hours, 5-7 days a week; students can reserve study rooms.

STUDENT LIFE

Housing options: on-campus residence required for freshman year; coed, men-only, women-only, special housing for students with disabilities. Campus housing is university owned. Freshman applicants given priority for college housing.

Activities and organizations: drama/theater group, student-run newspaper, radio and television station, choral group, marching band, Student Government Association, Residence Hall Association, The Saudi Student Club, National Society of Collegiate Scholars, Top Secret Colonials, national fraternities, national sororities.

Athletics Member NCAA. All Division I. ***Intercollegiate sports:*** basketball M(s)/W(s), crew W(s), cross-country running W(s), football M(s), golf M(s), ice hockey M(s)/W, lacrosse M(s)/W, rowing W(s), soccer M(s)/W(s), softball W(s), track and field W(s), volleyball W(s). ***Intramural sports:*** baseball M(c), basketball M(c), bowling M(c)/W(c), golf M(c), ice hockey M(c), rugby M(c)/W(c), soccer M(c)/W(c), table tennis M(c)/W(c), tennis M(c)/W(c), ultimate Frisbee M(c)/W(c), volleyball M(c)/W(c), weight lifting M(c)/W(c), wrestling M(c).

Campus security: 24-hour emergency response devices and patrols, late-night transport/escort service, controlled dormitory access.

Student services: health clinic, personal/psychological counseling.

COSTS & FINANCIAL AID

Costs (2016–17) ***Comprehensive fee:*** $39,160 includes full-time tuition ($27,320), mandatory fees ($930), and room and board ($10,910). Full-time tuition and fees vary according to degree level and program. Part-time tuition: $875 per credit hour. Part-time tuition and fees vary according to course load, degree level, and program. ***Required fees:*** $75 per credit hour part-time. ***College room only:*** $6070. Room and board charges vary according to board plan and housing facility. ***Payment plans:*** installment, deferred payment. ***Waivers:*** employees or children of employees.

Financial Aid Of all full-time matriculated undergraduates who enrolled in 2016, 3,096 applied for aid, 2,768 were judged to have need, 373 had their need fully met. In 2016, 703 non-need-based awards were made. ***Average percent of need met:*** 71. ***Average financial aid package:*** $21,873. ***Average need-based loan:*** $6302. ***Average need-based gift aid:*** $15,789. ***Average non-need-based aid:*** $11,540. ***Average indebtedness upon graduation:*** $39,431.

APPLYING

Standardized Tests *Required:* SAT or ACT (for admission).

Options: electronic application, deferred entrance.

Application fee: $30.

Required: high school transcript, minimum 2.0 GPA. ***Required for some:*** interview. ***Recommended:*** essay or personal statement, minimum 3.0 GPA, interview.

Notification: continuous until 8/1 (freshmen), continuous (transfers).

CONTACT
Enrollment Services Department, Robert Morris University, 6001 University Boulevard, Moon Township, PA 15108-1189. *Phone:* 412-397-5200. *Toll-free phone:* 800-762-0097. *Fax:* 412-397-2425.
E-mail: admissionsoffice@rmu.edu.

See previous page for display ad and page 1482 for the College Close-Up.

Rosemont College

Rosemont, Pennsylvania

http://www.rosemont.edu/

- **Independent Roman Catholic** comprehensive, founded 1921
- **Suburban** 56-acre campus with easy access to Philadelphia
- **Endowment** $13.0 million
- **Coed** 646 undergraduate students, 81% full-time, 62% women, 38% men
- **Moderately difficult** entrance level, 69% of applicants were admitted

UNDERGRAD STUDENTS
523 full-time, 123 part-time. Students come from 12 states and territories; 4 other countries; 27% are from out of state; 39% Black or African American, non-Hispanic/Latino; 7% Hispanic/Latino; 3% Asian, non-Hispanic/Latino; 0.3% Native Hawaiian or other Pacific Islander, non-Hispanic/Latino; 0.3% American Indian or Alaska Native, non-Hispanic/Latino; 5% Two or more races, non-Hispanic/Latino; 6% Race/ethnicity unknown; 8% transferred in; 88% live on campus.

Freshmen:
Admission: 1,404 applied, 970 admitted, 158 enrolled. ***Average high school GPA:*** 3.05.

Retention: 65% of full-time freshmen returned.

FACULTY
Total: 126, 22% full-time, 81% with terminal degrees.

Student/faculty ratio: 11:1.

ACADEMICS
Calendar: semesters. *Degrees:* bachelor's, master's, post-master's, and postbachelor's certificates.

Special study options: accelerated degree program, advanced placement credit, distance learning, double majors, external degree program, honors programs, independent study, internships, off-campus study, part-time degree program, services for LD students, student-designed majors, study abroad, summer session for credit.

Computers: 100 computers/terminals and 200 ports are available on campus for general student use. Students can access the following: campus intranet, computer help desk, free student e-mail accounts, online (class) grades, online (class) registration, online (class) schedules. Campuswide network is available. 100% of college-owned or -operated housing units are wired for high-speed Internet access. Wireless service is available via classrooms, computer centers, computer labs, dorm rooms, learning centers, libraries, student centers.
Library: Gertrude Kistler Memorial Library plus 1 other. *Books:* 151,475 (physical), 11,106 (digital/electronic); *Serial titles:* 20 (physical), 16,261 (digital/electronic); *Databases:* 50. Weekly public service hours: 90; students can reserve study rooms.

STUDENT LIFE
Housing options: coed. Campus housing is university owned. Freshman applicants given priority for college housing.

Activities and organizations: drama/theater group, student-run newspaper, choral group, Book Club, International Club, Organization of African American Students, Ram Squad, Ambassadors.

Athletics Member NCAA. All Division III. ***Intercollegiate sports:*** basketball M/W, cross-country running M/W, golf M, lacrosse M/W, soccer M/W, softball W, tennis M/W, volleyball W.

Campus security: 24-hour emergency response devices and patrols, late-night transport/escort service.

Student services: health clinic, personal/psychological counseling.

COSTS & FINANCIAL AID
Costs (2017–18) ***Tuition:*** $18,500 full-time. ***Required fees:*** $980 full-time. ***Room only:*** Room and board charges vary according to board plan and housing facility. ***Payment plan:*** installment. ***Waivers:*** employees or children of employees.

Financial Aid Of all full-time matriculated undergraduates who enrolled in 2016, 275 applied for aid, 275 were judged to have need, 48 had their need fully met. 130 Federal Work-Study jobs (averaging $910). 6 state and other part-time jobs (averaging $2000). In 2016, 27 non-need-based awards were made. ***Average percent of need met:*** 84. ***Average financial aid package:*** $18,171. ***Average need-based loan:*** $4500. ***Average need-based gift aid:*** $16,152. ***Average non-need-based aid:*** $8000. ***Average indebtedness upon graduation:*** $40,792.

APPLYING
Standardized Tests *Required:* SAT or ACT (for admission).

Options: electronic application, deferred entrance.

Required: high school transcript, minimum 2.0 GPA. ***Required for some:*** essay or personal statement. ***Recommended:*** interview.

Application deadlines: rolling (freshmen), rolling (transfers).

Notification: continuous (transfers).

CONTACT
Ms. Bettsy Thommen, Associate Director of Admissions, Undergraduate College, Rosemont College, 1400 Montgomery Avenue, Rosemont, PA 19010. *Phone:* 610-527-0200 Ext. 2601.
Toll-free phone: 888-2-ROSEMONT. *Fax:* 610-520-4399.
E-mail: bettsy.thommen@rosemont.edu.

Saint Charles Borromeo Seminary, Overbrook

Wynnewood, Pennsylvania

http://www.scs.edu/

CONTACT
Rev. Joseph Shenosky, Vice Rector, Saint Charles Borromeo Seminary, Overbrook, 100 East Wynnewood Road, Wynnewood, PA 19096.
Phone: 610-785-6520. *E-mail:* jshenosky@scs.edu.

★ Saint Francis University

Loretto, Pennsylvania

http://www.francis.edu/

- **Independent Roman Catholic** comprehensive, founded 1847
- **Rural** 600-acre campus
- **Endowment** $43.1 million
- **Coed** 1,707 undergraduate students, 90% full-time, 63% women, 37% men
- **Moderately difficult** entrance level, 74% of applicants were admitted

UNDERGRAD STUDENTS
1,530 full-time, 177 part-time. Students come from 41 states and territories; 38 other countries; 21% are from out of state; 6% Black or African American, non-Hispanic/Latino; 1% Hispanic/Latino; 2% Asian, non-Hispanic/Latino; 0.2% Native Hawaiian or other Pacific Islander, non-Hispanic/Latino; 0.2% American Indian or Alaska Native, non-Hispanic/Latino; 2% Two or more races, non-Hispanic/Latino; 5% Race/ethnicity unknown; 1% international; 2% transferred in; 88% live on campus.

Freshmen:
Admission: 1,932 applied, 1,432 admitted, 352 enrolled. ***Average high school GPA:*** 3.63. ***Test scores:*** SAT critical reading scores over 500: 60%; SAT math scores over 500: 65%; SAT writing scores over 500: 56%; ACT scores over 18: 89%; SAT critical reading scores over 600: 16%; SAT math scores over 600: 24%; SAT writing scores over 600: 15%; ACT scores over 24: 40%; SAT critical reading scores over 700: 2%; SAT math scores over 700: 2%; SAT writing scores over 700: 2%; ACT scores over 30: 2%.

Retention: 89% of full-time freshmen returned.

FACULTY
Total: 236, 55% full-time.

Student/faculty ratio: 14:1.

ACADEMICS
Calendar: semesters. *Degrees:* certificates, associate, bachelor's, master's, and doctoral.

Special study options: academic remediation for entering students, accelerated degree program, adult/continuing education programs, advanced placement credit, cooperative education, distance learning, double majors, English as a second language, external degree program, freshman honors college, honors programs, independent study, internships, off-campus study, part-time degree program, services for LD students, student-designed majors, study abroad, summer session for credit. ***ROTC:*** Army (b).

Unusual degree programs: 3-2 engineering with Penn State University Park, University of Pittsburgh, Clarkson University; forestry with Duke University; Pennsylvania College of Optometry, Lake Erie College of Osteopathic Medicine (LECOM), Temple University.

Computers: 75 computers/terminals are available on campus for general student use. Students can access the following: campus intranet, computer help desk, free student e-mail accounts, online (class) grades, online (class) registration, online (class) schedules. Campuswide network is available. 95% of college-owned or -operated housing units are wired for high-speed Internet access. Wireless service is available via entire campus.

Library: Saint Francis University Library. *Books:* 76,787 (physical), 153,616 (digital/electronic); *Databases:* 74.

STUDENT LIFE

Housing options: on-campus residence required through junior year; men-only, women-only. Campus housing is university owned and leased by the school. Freshman campus housing is guaranteed.

Activities and organizations: drama/theater group, student-run newspaper, radio station, choral group, marching band, Student Activities Organization, Club Baseball, Student Government Association, Best Buddies, Ultimate Frisbee Club, national fraternities, national sororities.

Athletics Member NCAA. All Division I. ***Intercollegiate sports:*** basketball M(s)/W(s), bowling W, cross-country running M(s)/W(s), field hockey W(s), football M, golf M(s)/W(s), lacrosse W(s), soccer M(s)/W(s), softball W(s), swimming and diving M(s)/W(s), tennis M(s)/W(s), track and field M(s)/W(s), volleyball M(s)/W(s). ***Intramural sports:*** baseball M(c), basketball M/W, cheerleading M/W, cross-country running M/W, football M, golf M/W, ice hockey M(c), lacrosse W, racquetball M/W, skiing (cross-country) M/W, skiing (downhill) M/W, soccer M/W, softball W, swimming and diving M/W, table tennis M/W, tennis M/W, track and field M/W, ultimate Frisbee M/W, volleyball M/W.

Campus security: 24-hour emergency response devices and patrols, late-night transport/escort service, controlled dormitory access.

Student services: health clinic, personal/psychological counseling.

COSTS & FINANCIAL AID

Costs (2016–17) ***One-time required fee:*** $100. ***Comprehensive fee:*** $44,868 includes full-time tuition ($32,244), mandatory fees ($1100), and room and board ($11,524). Full-time tuition and fees vary according to course load, degree level, program, and student level. Part-time tuition: $1007 per credit hour. Part-time tuition and fees vary according to class time, degree level, and program. ***College room only:*** $5734. Room and board charges vary according to board plan and housing facility. ***Payment plan:*** installment. ***Waivers:*** employees or children of employees.

Financial Aid Of all full-time matriculated undergraduates who enrolled in 2015, 1,497 applied for aid, 1,247 were judged to have need, 347 had their need fully met. 285 Federal Work-Study jobs (averaging $1000). 780 state and other part-time jobs (averaging $1000). In 2015, 289 non-need-based awards were made. ***Average percent of need met:*** 52. ***Average financial aid package:*** $20,018. ***Average need-based loan:*** $4207. ***Average need-based gift aid:*** $16,858. ***Average non-need-based aid:*** $17,963. ***Average indebtedness upon graduation:*** $36,656.

APPLYING

Standardized Tests *Required:* SAT or ACT (for admission).

Options: electronic application, deferred entrance.

Application fee: $30.

Required: essay or personal statement, high school transcript, 1 letter of recommendation. ***Required for some:*** interview. ***Recommended:*** interview.

Application deadlines: rolling (freshmen), rolling (transfers).

Notification: continuous (transfers).

CONTACT

Robert Beener, Dean for Enrollment Management, Saint Francis University, 117 Evergreen Drive, PO Box 600, Loretto, PA 15940-0600. *Phone:* 814-472-3100. *Toll-free phone:* 866-DIAL-SFU. *E-mail:* rbeener@francis.edu.

See below for display ad and page 1488 for the College Close-Up.

Saint Joseph's University
Philadelphia, Pennsylvania
http://www.sju.edu/

- **Independent Roman Catholic (Jesuit)** comprehensive, founded 1851
- **Suburban** 113-acre campus with easy access to Philadelphia
- **Endowment** $202.2 million
- **Coed** 5,377 undergraduate students, 87% full-time, 55% women, 45% men
- **Moderately difficult** entrance level, 78% of applicants were admitted

UNDERGRAD STUDENTS
4,654 full-time, 723 part-time. Students come from 43 states and territories; 27 other countries; 52% are from out of state; 6% Black or African American, non-Hispanic/Latino; 6% Hispanic/Latino; 3% Asian, non-Hispanic/Latino; 0.1% Native Hawaiian or other Pacific Islander, non-Hispanic/Latino; 0.1% American Indian or Alaska Native, non-Hispanic/Latino; 2% Two or more races, non-Hispanic/Latino; 2% Race/ethnicity unknown; 2% international; 1% transferred in; 55% live on campus.

Freshmen:
Admission: 8,914 applied, 6,947 admitted, 1,271 enrolled. ***Average high school GPA:*** 3.6. ***Test scores:*** SAT critical reading scores over 500: 81%; SAT math scores over 500: 86%; ACT scores over 18: 100%; SAT critical reading scores over 600: 33%; SAT math scores over 600: 35%; ACT scores over 24: 71%; SAT critical reading scores over 700: 3%; SAT math scores over 700: 4%; ACT scores over 30: 16%.

Retention: 91% of full-time freshmen returned.

FACULTY
Total: 647, 47% full-time.

Student/faculty ratio: 12:1.

ACADEMICS
Calendar: semesters. *Degrees:* associate, bachelor's, master's, doctoral, post-master's, and postbachelor's certificates.

Special study options: accelerated degree program, adult/continuing education programs, advanced placement credit, cooperative education, distance learning, double majors, English as a second language, honors programs, independent study, internships, off-campus study, part-time degree program, services for LD students, student-designed majors, study abroad, summer session for credit. ***ROTC:*** Army (c), Navy (c), Air Force (b).

Computers: 521 computers/terminals are available on campus for general student use. Students can access the following: campus intranet, computer help desk, free student e-mail accounts, online (class) grades, online (class) registration, online (class) schedules. Campuswide network is available. 100% of college-owned or -operated housing units are wired for high-speed Internet access. Wireless service is available via entire campus.

Library: Post Learning Commons and Drexel Library. *Books:* 260,000 (physical), 9,511 (digital/electronic); *Serial titles:* 590 (physical), 57,790 (digital/electronic); *Databases:* 203. Weekly public service hours: 107; students can reserve study rooms.

STUDENT LIFE
Housing options: on-campus residence required through sophomore year; coed, men-only, women-only, special housing for students with disabilities. Campus housing is university owned, leased by the school and is provided by a third party. Freshman campus housing is guaranteed.

Activities and organizations: drama/theater group, student-run newspaper, radio station, choral group, Student Union Board, Hand-in-Hand, 54th Airborne / Booster Club, Appalachian Experience, Weekly Service, national fraternities, national sororities.

Athletics Member NCAA. All Division I. ***Intercollegiate sports:*** baseball M(s), basketball M(s)/W(s), cheerleading M(c)/W(c), crew M(s)/W(s), cross-country running M(s)/W(s), field hockey W(s), golf M(s), lacrosse M(s)/W(s), soccer M(s)/W(s), softball W(s), tennis M(s)/W(s), track and field M(s)/W(s). ***Intramural sports:*** baseball M(c), basketball M(c)/W(c), field hockey W(c), football M/W, golf M(c)/W(c), ice hockey M(c)/W(c), lacrosse M(c)/W(c), rugby M(c)/W(c), soccer M(c)/W(c), softball W, swimming and diving M(c)/W(c), tennis M(c)/W(c), ultimate Frisbee M(c)/W(c), volleyball M(c)/W(c), water polo M(c)/W(c).

Campus security: 24-hour emergency response devices and patrols, late-night transport/escort service, controlled dormitory access, 24-hour shuttle/escort service, bicycle patrols.

Student services: health clinic, personal/psychological counseling.

COSTS & FINANCIAL AID

Costs (2016–17) ***Comprehensive fee:*** $57,544 includes full-time tuition ($42,840), mandatory fees ($180), and room and board ($14,524). Full-time tuition and fees vary according to course load. Part-time tuition: $573 per credit. Part-time tuition and fees vary according to course load. ***College room only:*** $9240. Room and board charges vary according to board plan and housing facility. ***Payment plan:*** installment. ***Waivers:*** employees or children of employees.

Financial Aid Of all full-time matriculated undergraduates who enrolled in 2016, 3,404 applied for aid, 2,807 were judged to have need, 637 had their need fully met. In 2016, 1653 non-need-based awards were made. ***Average percent of need met:*** 72. ***Average financial aid package:*** $27,253. ***Average need-based loan:*** $9601. ***Average need-based gift aid:*** $22,112. ***Average non-need-based aid:*** $12,083.

APPLYING

Options: electronic application, early action, deferred entrance.

Application fee: $50.

Required: essay or personal statement, high school transcript, 1 letter of recommendation.

Application deadlines: 2/1 (freshmen), 3/1 (transfers), 11/15 (early action).

Notification: 3/15 (freshmen), continuous (transfers), 12/25 (early action).

CONTACT

Office of Admissions, Saint Joseph's University, 5600 City Avenue, Philadelphia, PA 19131-1395. *Phone:* 610-660-1300. *Toll-free phone:* 888-BE-A-HAWK (in-state); 800-BE-A-HAWK (out-of-state). *Fax:* 610-660-1314. *E-mail:* admit@sju.edu.

See previous page for display ad and page 1490 for the College Close-Up.

★ Saint Vincent College

Latrobe, Pennsylvania

http://www.stvincent.edu/

- **Independent Roman Catholic** comprehensive, founded 1846
- **Suburban** 200-acre campus with easy access to Pittsburgh
- **Endowment** $84.9 million
- **Coed** 1,646 undergraduate students, 96% full-time, 48% women, 52% men
- **Moderately difficult** entrance level, 66% of applicants were admitted

UNDERGRAD STUDENTS

1,586 full-time, 60 part-time. Students come from 26 states and territories; 5 other countries; 19% are from out of state; 5% Black or African American, non-Hispanic/Latino; 3% Hispanic/Latino; 2% Asian, non-Hispanic/Latino; 0.1% Native Hawaiian or other Pacific Islander, non-Hispanic/Latino; 0.3% American Indian or Alaska Native, non-Hispanic/Latino; 0.7% Two or more races, non-Hispanic/Latino; 4% Race/ethnicity unknown; 0.6% international; 3% transferred in; 74% live on campus.

Freshmen:

Admission: 2,256 applied, 1,486 admitted, 393 enrolled. ***Average high school GPA:*** 3.56. ***Test scores:*** SAT critical reading scores over 500: 62%; SAT math scores over 500: 62%; SAT writing scores over 500: 50%; ACT scores over 18: 91%; SAT critical reading scores over 600: 21%; SAT math scores over 600: 21%; SAT writing scores over 600: 16%; ACT scores over 24: 44%; SAT critical reading scores over 700: 5%; SAT math scores over 700: 2%; SAT writing scores over 700: 2%; ACT scores over 30: 7%.

Retention: 83% of full-time freshmen returned.

FACULTY

Total: 224, 46% full-time, 61% with terminal degrees.

Student/faculty ratio: 12:1.

ACADEMICS

Calendar: semesters. *Degrees:* certificates, bachelor's, master's, doctoral, and postbachelor's certificates.

Special study options: advanced placement credit, cooperative education, distance learning, double majors, English as a second language, external degree program, honors programs, independent study, internships, part-time degree program, services for LD students, student-designed majors, study abroad, summer session for credit. ***ROTC:*** Army (c), Air Force (c).

Unusual degree programs: engineering with University of Pittsburgh, Penn State University, The Catholic University of America; physical therapy, physician assistant, occupational therapy, pharmacy with Duquesne University.

Computers: 272 computers/terminals are available on campus for general student use. Students can access the following: campus intranet, computer help desk, free student e-mail accounts, online (class) grades, online (class) registration, online (class) schedules, program requirement evaluation. Campuswide network is available. 100% of college-owned or -operated housing units are wired for high-speed Internet access. Wireless service is available via entire campus.

Library: Latimer Family Library plus 1 other. *Books:* 289,773 (physical); *Serial titles:* 258 (physical). Weekly public service hours: 84.

STUDENT LIFE

Housing options: coed. Campus housing is university owned. Freshman applicants given priority for college housing.

Activities and organizations: drama/theater group, student-run newspaper, choral group, marching band, Activities Programming Board, Orientation Committee, Campus Ministry, Visionaries of Hope.

Athletics Member NCAA. All Division III. ***Intercollegiate sports:*** baseball M, basketball M/W, cheerleading W(c), cross-country running M/W, equestrian sports M(c)/W(c), fencing M(c)/W(c), football M, golf M/W, ice hockey M(c), lacrosse M/W, rugby M(c)/W(c), soccer M/W, softball W, swimming and diving M/W, tennis M/W, track and field M/W, volleyball W. ***Intramural sports:*** basketball M/W, football M/W, ultimate Frisbee M/W, volleyball M/W.

Campus security: 24-hour emergency response devices and patrols, late-night transport/escort service, controlled dormitory access, limited access to residence halls on weekends.

Student services: health clinic, personal/psychological counseling.

COSTS & FINANCIAL AID

Costs (2016–17) ***Comprehensive fee:*** $44,919 includes full-time tuition ($32,540), mandatory fees ($1274), and room and board ($11,105). Full-time tuition and fees vary according to course load and degree level. Part-time tuition: $1018 per credit hour. Part-time tuition and fees vary according to course load and degree level. ***College room only:*** $5973. Room and board charges vary according to board plan and housing facility. ***Payment plan:*** installment. ***Waivers:*** employees or children of employees.

Financial Aid Of all full-time matriculated undergraduates who enrolled in 2016, 1,341 applied for aid, 1,239 were judged to have need, 350 had their need fully met. In 2016, 330 non-need-based awards were made. ***Average percent of need met:*** 82. ***Average financial aid package:*** $29,677. ***Average need-based loan:*** $4296. ***Average need-based gift aid:*** $6405. ***Average non-need-based aid:*** $19,530. ***Average indebtedness upon graduation:*** $38,493.

APPLYING

Standardized Tests *Required:* SAT or ACT (for admission).

Options: electronic application, early admission, deferred entrance.

Application fee: $25.

Required: essay or personal statement, high school transcript, minimum 2.5 GPA. ***Required for some:*** interview. ***Recommended:*** minimum 3.2 GPA, 3 letters of recommendation, interview.

Application deadlines: 5/1 (freshmen), 7/1 (transfers).

Notification: continuous until 10/1 (freshmen), continuous (transfers).

CONTACT

Mr. Stephen Neitz, Dean of Admission, Saint Vincent College, 300 Fraser Purchase Road, Latrobe, PA 15650-2690. *Phone:* 800-782-5549. *Toll-free phone:* 800-782-5549. *Fax:* 724-532-5069.
E-mail: admission@stvincent.edu.

See previous page for display ad and page 1502 for the College Close-Up.

Seton Hill University

Greensburg, Pennsylvania

http://www.setonhill.edu/

- **Independent Roman Catholic** comprehensive, founded 1883
- **Small-town** 200-acre campus with easy access to Pittsburgh
- **Coed** 1,606 undergraduate students, 92% full-time, 65% women, 35% men
- **Moderately difficult** entrance level, 73% of applicants were admitted

UNDERGRAD STUDENTS

1,483 full-time, 123 part-time. Students come from 36 states and territories; 17 other countries; 24% are from out of state; 8% Black or African American, non-Hispanic/Latino; 4% Hispanic/Latino; 1% Asian, non-Hispanic/Latino; 0.1% Native Hawaiian or other Pacific Islander, non-Hispanic/Latino; 3% Two or more races, non-Hispanic/Latino; 2% Race/ethnicity unknown; 3% international; 4% transferred in; 546% live on campus.

Freshmen:

Admission: 2,206 applied, 1,612 admitted, 367 enrolled. ***Average high school GPA:*** 3.7. ***Test scores:*** SAT critical reading scores over 500: 63%; SAT math scores over 500: 64%; SAT writing scores over 500: 57%; ACT scores over 18: 93%; SAT critical reading scores over 600: 21%; SAT math scores over 600: 19%; SAT writing scores over 600: 18%; ACT scores over 24: 51%; SAT critical reading scores over 700: 5%; SAT math scores over 700: 2%; SAT writing scores over 700: 3%; ACT scores over 30: 10%.

Retention: 79% of full-time freshmen returned.

FACULTY

Total: 199, 51% full-time, 57% with terminal degrees.

Student/faculty ratio: 12:1.

ACADEMICS

Calendar: semesters. *Degrees:* certificates, bachelor's, master's, and postbachelor's certificates.

Special study options: academic remediation for entering students, adult/continuing education programs, advanced placement credit, distance learning, double majors, English as a second language, honors programs, independent study, internships, off-campus study, part-time degree program, services for LD students, student-designed majors, study abroad, summer session for credit. ***ROTC:*** Army (c).

Unusual degree programs: 3-2 engineering with University of Pittsburgh, Penn State University Park, Georgia Institute of Technology; physician assistant with Seton Hill University, osteopatchic medicine or pharmacy with Lake Erie College of Osteopathic Medicine.

Computers: 66 computers/terminals and 66 ports are available on campus for general student use. Students can access the following: campus intranet, computer help desk, free student e-mail accounts, online (class) grades, online (class) registration, online (class) schedules. Campuswide network is available. 100% of college-owned or -operated housing units are wired for high-speed Internet access. Wireless service is available via entire campus.

Library: Reeves Memorial Library. *Books:* 72,274 (physical), 127,160 (digital/electronic); *Serial titles:* 2,919 (physical); *Databases:* 37. Students can reserve study rooms.

STUDENT LIFE

Housing options: on-campus residence required for freshman year; coed. Campus housing is university owned. Freshman campus housing is guaranteed.

Activities and organizations: drama/theater group, student-run newspaper, choral group, marching band, Student Body Activities Council, Future Greek leaders, Dietetics Club, Biology Club, intramurals.

Athletics Member NCAA. All Division II. ***Intercollegiate sports:*** baseball M(s), basketball M(s)/W(s), cross-country running M(s)/W(s), equestrian sports W(s), field hockey W(s), football M(s), golf W(s), lacrosse M(s)/W(s), soccer M(s)/W(s), softball W(s), tennis W(s), track and field M(s)/W(s), volleyball W(s), wrestling M(s).

Campus security: 24-hour emergency response devices and patrols, late-night transport/escort service, controlled dormitory access, emergency phones throughout camps, campus alert system, safety committee.

Student services: health clinic, personal/psychological counseling.

COSTS & FINANCIAL AID
Costs (2016–17) ***Comprehensive fee:*** $44,520 includes full-time tuition ($32,520), mandatory fees ($1000), and room and board ($11,000). Full-time tuition and fees vary according to course load, degree level, and program. Part-time tuition: $872 per credit. Part-time tuition and fees vary according to course load, degree level, and program. ***Required fees:*** $25 per credit part-time. ***Room and board:*** Room and board charges vary according to board plan and housing facility. ***Payment plan:*** installment. ***Waivers:*** employees or children of employees.

Financial Aid Of all full-time matriculated undergraduates who enrolled in 2015, 1,354 applied for aid, 1,248 were judged to have need, 214 had their need fully met. 602 Federal Work-Study jobs (averaging $1500). 107 state and other part-time jobs (averaging $303). In 2015, 222 non-need-based awards were made. ***Average percent of need met:*** 73. ***Average financial aid package:*** $24,866. ***Average need-based loan:*** $6309. ***Average need-based gift aid:*** $19,244. ***Average non-need-based aid:*** $13,432. ***Average indebtedness upon graduation:*** $38,414.

APPLYING
Standardized Tests *Recommended:* SAT or ACT (for admission).

Options: electronic application, deferred entrance.

Application fee: $35.

Required: essay or personal statement, high school transcript, 1 letter of recommendation. ***Required for some:*** portfolio for art, audition for music and theatre. ***Recommended:*** interview.

Application deadlines: rolling (freshmen), rolling (transfers).

Notification: continuous (freshmen), continuous (transfers).

CONTACT
Mrs. Allison Sasso, Assistant Director of Admissions, Seton Hill University, Seton Hill Drive, Greensburg, PA 15601. *Phone:* 724-838-4255. *Toll-free phone:* 800-826-6234. *Fax:* 724-830-1294. *E-mail:* admit@setonhill.edu.

Shippensburg University of Pennsylvania

Shippensburg, Pennsylvania

http://www.ship.edu/

- **State-supported** comprehensive, founded 1871, part of Pennsylvania State System of Higher Education
- **Rural** 200-acre campus
- **Endowment** $34.5 million
- **Coed** 5,912 undergraduate students, 94% full-time, 50% women, 50% men
- 88% of applicants were admitted

UNDERGRAD STUDENTS
5,545 full-time, 367 part-time. Students come from 24 states and territories; 18 other countries; 8% are from out of state; 11% Black or African American, non-Hispanic/Latino; 5% Hispanic/Latino; 2% Asian, non-Hispanic/Latino; 0.1% Native Hawaiian or other Pacific Islander,-non-Hispanic/Latino; 0.2% American Indian or Alaska Native, non-Hispanic/Latino; 3% Two or more races, non-Hispanic/Latino; 1% Race/ethnicity unknown; 0.6% international; 5% transferred in; 33% live on campus.

Freshmen:
Admission: 5,799 applied, 5,121 admitted, 1,381 enrolled. ***Average high school GPA:*** 3.2. ***Test scores:*** SAT critical reading scores over 500: 40%; SAT math scores over 500: 44%; SAT writing scores over 500: 29%; ACT scores over 18: 75%; SAT critical reading scores over 600: 9%; SAT math scores over 600: 8%; SAT writing scores over 600: 5%; ACT scores over 24: 22%; SAT critical reading scores over 700: 1%; ACT scores over 30: 1%.
Retention: 75% of full-time freshmen returned.

FACULTY
Total: 366, 79% full-time, 77% with terminal degrees.

Student/faculty ratio: 20:1.

ACADEMICS
Calendar: semesters. *Degrees:* certificates, bachelor's, master's, doctoral, post-master's, and postbachelor's certificates.

Special study options: academic remediation for entering students, accelerated degree program, advanced placement credit, cooperative education, distance learning, double majors, honors programs, independent study, internships, off-campus study, part-time degree program, services for LD students, study abroad, summer session for credit. ***ROTC:*** Army (b).

Unusual degree programs: 3-2 engineering with Penn State University Park, Penn State Harrisburg.

Computers: 1,100 computers/terminals are available on campus for general student use. Students can access the following: campus intranet, computer help desk, free student e-mail accounts, online (class) grades, online (class) registration, online (class) schedules, personal Web pages. Campuswide network is available. 100% of college-owned or -operated housing units are wired for high-speed Internet access. Wireless service is available via classrooms, computer centers, computer labs, dorm rooms, learning centers, libraries, student centers.

Library: Ezra Lehman Memorial Library plus 1 other. *Books:* 357,662 (physical), 57,973 (digital/electronic); *Serial titles:* 50 (physical), 255 (digital/electronic); *Databases:* 109. Weekly public service hours: 97.

STUDENT LIFE
Housing options: on-campus residence required for freshman year; coed. Campus housing is university owned and leased by the school. Freshman campus housing is guaranteed.

Activities and organizations: drama/theater group, student-run newspaper, radio and television station, choral group, marching band, national fraternities, national sororities.

Athletics Member NCAA. All Division II. ***Intercollegiate sports:*** baseball M(s), basketball M(s)/W(s), cross-country running M(s)/W(s), field hockey W(s), football M(s), lacrosse W(s), soccer M(s)/W(s), softball W(s), swimming and diving M(s)/W(s), tennis W(s), track and field M(s)/W(s), volleyball W(s), wrestling M(s). ***Intramural sports:*** basketball M/W, equestrian sports M(c)/W(c), fencing M(c), ice hockey M(c), lacrosse M(c), rugby W(c), soccer M/W, softball M/W, ultimate Frisbee M(c)/W(c), volleyball M/W.

Campus security: 24-hour emergency response devices and patrols, late-night transport/escort service, controlled dormitory access, surveillance cameras in certain parking lots and buildings; foot, vehicular and bicycle patrols by security officers.

Student services: health clinic, personal/psychological counseling, women's center.

COSTS & FINANCIAL AID
Costs (2016–17) ***Tuition:*** state resident $8430 full-time, $281 per credit hour part-time; nonresident $16,286 full-time, $679 per credit hour part-time. Full-time tuition and fees vary according to course load and location. Part-time tuition and fees vary according to course load and location. ***Required fees:*** $3022 full-time, $126 per credit hour part-time. ***Room and board:*** $11,756; room only: $7706. Room and board charges vary according to board plan and housing facility. ***Payment plan:*** installment. ***Waivers:*** senior citizens and employees or children of employees.

Financial Aid Of all full-time matriculated undergraduates who enrolled in 2016, 4,789 applied for aid, 3,840 were judged to have need, 323 had their need fully met. 125 Federal Work-Study jobs (averaging $1190). 602 state and other part-time jobs (averaging $2031). In 2016, 400 non-need-based awards were made. ***Average percent of need met:*** 53. ***Average financial aid package:*** $8971. ***Average need-based loan:*** $4003. ***Average need-based gift aid:*** $6554. ***Average non-need-based aid:*** $5565. ***Average indebtedness upon graduation:*** $33,673.

APPLYING
Standardized Tests *Required:* SAT or ACT (for admission).

Options: electronic application, early admission, early action, deferred entrance.

Application fee: $45.

Required: high school transcript. ***Required for some:*** interview. ***Recommended:*** essay or personal statement, class rank, letters of recommendation.

Application deadlines: rolling (freshmen), rolling (transfers).

Notification: continuous (freshmen), continuous (transfers).

CONTACT
Mr. William H. Washabaugh, Associate Dean of Admissions, Shippensburg University of Pennsylvania, 1871 Old Main Drive, Shippensburg, PA 17257-2299. *Phone:* 717-477-1231. *Toll-free phone:* 800-822-8028. *Fax:* 717-477-4016. *E-mail:* admiss@ship.edu.

Slippery Rock University of Pennsylvania

Slippery Rock, Pennsylvania

http://www.sru.edu/

- **State-supported** comprehensive, founded 1889, part of Pennsylvania State System of Higher Education
- **Small-town** 660-acre campus with easy access to Pittsburgh
- **Endowment** $27.0 million
- **Coed** 7,664 undergraduate students, 93% full-time, 57% women, 43% men
- **Moderately difficult** entrance level, 69% of applicants were admitted

UNDERGRAD STUDENTS
7,161 full-time, 503 part-time. Students come from 38 states and territories; 37 other countries; 10% are from out of state; 5% Black or African American, non-Hispanic/Latino; 2% Hispanic/Latino; 0.8% Asian, non-Hispanic/Latino; 0.1% Native Hawaiian or other Pacific Islander, non-Hispanic/Latino; 0.2% American Indian or Alaska Native, non-Hispanic/Latino; 4% Two or more races, non-Hispanic/Latino; 1% Race/ethnicity unknown; 1% international; 8% transferred in; 36% live on campus.

Freshmen:
Admission: 5,889 applied, 4,092 admitted, 1,564 enrolled. ***Average high school GPA:*** 3.46. ***Test scores:*** SAT critical reading scores over 500: 47%; SAT math scores over 500: 53%; SAT writing scores over 500: 38%; ACT scores over 18: 88%; SAT critical reading scores over 600: 9%; SAT math scores over 600: 10%; SAT writing scores over 600: 6%; ACT scores over 24: 23%; SAT critical reading scores over 700: 1%; SAT math scores over 700: 1%; SAT writing scores over 700: 1%; ACT scores over 30: 2%.
Retention: 83% of full-time freshmen returned.

FACULTY
Total: 405, 83% full-time, 78% with terminal degrees.
Student/faculty ratio: 22:1.

ACADEMICS
Calendar: semesters. *Degrees:* certificates, bachelor's, master's, doctoral, and postbachelor's certificates.
Special study options: academic remediation for entering students, adult/continuing education programs, advanced placement credit, distance learning, double majors, English as a second language, honors programs, independent study, internships, off-campus study, part-time degree program, services for LD students, student-designed majors, study abroad, summer session for credit. ***ROTC:*** Army (b).
Unusual degree programs: 3-2 engineering with Penn State University Park, Youngstown State University, West Virginia University, University of Pittsburg.
Computers: 1,654 computers/terminals are available on campus for general student use. Students can access the following: computer help desk, free student e-mail accounts, online (class) grades, online (class) registration, online (class) schedules. Campuswide network is available. 100% of college-owned or -operated housing units are wired for high-speed Internet access. Wireless service is available via classrooms, computer labs, dorm rooms, libraries, student centers.
Library: Bailey Library. *Books:* 314,860 (physical), 280,458 (digital/electronic); *Serial titles:* 248 (physical), 46,495 (digital/electronic); *Databases:* 125. Weekly public service hours: 96; students can reserve study rooms.

STUDENT LIFE
Housing options: on-campus residence required for freshman year; coed, special housing for students with disabilities. Campus housing is university owned. Freshman campus housing is guaranteed.
Activities and organizations: drama/theater group, student-run newspaper, radio and television station, choral group, marching band, SRU Pre-Physical Therapy Club, American Society of Safety Engineers, Therapeutic Recreation Club, Sport Management Alliance, University Program Board, national fraternities, national sororities.
Athletics Member NCAA. All Division II. ***Intercollegiate sports:*** baseball M(s), basketball M(s)/W(s), cheerleading M(c)/W(c), cross-country running M(s)/W(s), equestrian sports M(c)/W(c), field hockey W(s), football M(s), ice hockey M(c)/W(c), lacrosse M(c)/W(s), rugby M(c)/W(c), soccer M(s)/W(s), softball W(s), tennis M(c)/W(s), track and field M(s)/W(s), volleyball M(c)/W(s). ***Intramural sports:*** badminton M/W, baseball M(c), basketball M/W, football M/W, golf M(c)/W(c), gymnastics M(c)/W(c), soccer M/W, softball M/W, swimming and diving M(c)/W(c), ultimate Frisbee M/W, volleyball M/W, water polo M/W, wrestling M(c).
Campus security: 24-hour emergency response devices and patrols, late-night transport/escort service, controlled dormitory access.
Student services: health clinic, personal/psychological counseling, women's center, legal services.

COSTS & FINANCIAL AID
Costs (2016–17) ***Tuition:*** state resident $7238 full-time, $302 per credit hour part-time; nonresident $10,858 full-time, $452 per credit hour part-time. Full-time tuition and fees vary according to course load. Part-time tuition and fees vary according to course load. ***Required fees:*** $2624 full-time, $110 per credit hour part-time. ***Room and board:*** $10,110; room only: $6620. Room and board charges vary according to board plan and housing facility. ***Payment plan:*** installment. ***Waivers:*** minority students, senior citizens, and employees or children of employees.
Financial Aid Of all full-time matriculated undergraduates who enrolled in 2016, 6,142 applied for aid, 4,826 were judged to have need, 427 had their need fully met. 554 Federal Work-Study jobs (averaging $1572). 906 state and other part-time jobs (averaging $1960). In 2016, 565 non-need-based awards were made. ***Average percent of need met:*** 60. ***Average financial aid package:*** $9251. ***Average need-based loan:*** $4383. ***Average need-based gift aid:*** $5945. ***Average non-need-based aid:*** $2749. ***Average indebtedness upon graduation:*** $33,303.

APPLYING
Standardized Tests *Required:* SAT or ACT (for admission).
Options: electronic application, deferred entrance.
Application fee: $30.
Required: high school transcript. ***Recommended:*** minimum 3.0 GPA.
Application deadlines: rolling (freshmen), rolling (transfers).
Notification: continuous until 6/15 (freshmen), continuous (transfers).

CONTACT
Slippery Rock University of Pennsylvania, 1 Morrow Way, Slippery Rock, PA 16057-1383. *Phone:* 724-738-2015.
Toll-free phone: 800-SRU-9111.

Strayer University–Allentown Campus

Center Valley, Pennsylvania

http://www.strayer.edu/pennsylvania/allentown/

CONTACT
Strayer University–Allentown Campus, 3800 Sierra Circle, Suite 300, Center Valley, PA 18034.

Strayer University–Center City Campus

Philadelphia, Pennsylvania

http://www.strayer.edu/pennsylvania/center-city/

CONTACT
Strayer University–Center City Campus, 1601 Cherry Street, Suite 100, Philadelphia, PA 19102.

Strayer University–Delaware County Campus

Springfield, Pennsylvania

http://www.strayer.edu/pennsylvania/delaware-county/

CONTACT
Strayer University–Delaware County Campus, 760 West Sproul Road, Suite 200, Springfield, PA 19064-1215.

Strayer University–King of Prussia Campus

King of Prussia, Pennsylvania

http://www.strayer.edu/pennsylvania/king-prussia/

CONTACT
Strayer University–King of Prussia Campus, 234 Mall Boulevard, Suite G-50, King of Prussia, PA 19406.

Strayer University–Lower Bucks County Campus

Trevose, Pennsylvania

http://www.strayer.edu/pennsylvania/lower-bucks-county/

CONTACT
Strayer University–Lower Bucks County Campus, 3800 Horizon Boulevard, Suite 100, Trevose, PA 19053.

Strayer University–Warrendale Campus

Warrendale, Pennsylvania

http://www.strayer.edu/pennsylvania/warrendale/

CONTACT
Strayer University–Warrendale Campus, 802 Warrendale Village Drive, Warrendale, PA 15086.

Susquehanna University

Selinsgrove, Pennsylvania

http://www.susqu.edu/

- **Independent** 4-year, founded 1858, affiliated with Evangelical Lutheran Church in America
- **Small-town** 325-acre campus
- **Endowment** $143.2 million
- **Coed** 2,195 undergraduate students, 97% full-time, 56% women, 44% men
- **Moderately difficult** entrance level, 68% of applicants were admitted

UNDERGRAD STUDENTS
2,129 full-time, 66 part-time. Students come from 34 states and territories; 22 other countries; 51% are from out of state; 7% Black or African American, non-Hispanic/Latino; 6% Hispanic/Latino; 2% Asian, non-Hispanic/Latino; 0.1% American Indian or Alaska Native, non-Hispanic/Latino; 3% Two or more races, non-Hispanic/Latino; 0.2% Race/ethnicity unknown; 2% international; 1% transferred in; 92% live on campus.

Freshmen:
Admission: 6,629 applied, 4,488 admitted, 637 enrolled. ***Average high school GPA:*** 3.49. ***Test scores:*** SAT critical reading scores over 500: 79%; SAT math scores over 500: 80%; ACT scores over 18: 100%; SAT critical reading scores over 600: 32%; SAT math scores over 600: 29%; ACT scores over 24: 67%; SAT critical reading scores over 700: 5%; SAT math scores over 700: 3%; ACT scores over 30: 6%.
Retention: 83% of full-time freshmen returned.

FACULTY
Total: 249, 53% full-time, 62% with terminal degrees.
Student/faculty ratio: 13:1.

ACADEMICS
Calendar: semesters. *Degrees:* bachelor's (also offers evening associate degree program limited to local adult students).
Special study options: accelerated degree program, advanced placement credit, distance learning, double majors, honors programs, independent study, internships, off-campus study, part-time degree program, services for LD students, student-designed majors, study abroad, summer session for credit. ***ROTC:*** Army (c).
Unusual degree programs: 3-2 engineering with Columbia University.
Computers: 183 computers/terminals are available on campus for general student use. Students can access the following: campus intranet, computer help desk, free student e-mail accounts, online (class) grades, online (class) registration, online (class) schedules, online voting booth. Campuswide network is available. 100% of college-owned or -operated housing units are wired for high-speed Internet access. Wireless service is available via classrooms, computer centers, computer labs, dorm rooms, learning centers, libraries, student centers.
Library: Blough-Weis Library. *Books:* 155,190 (physical), 268,174 (digital/electronic); *Serial titles:* 612 (physical), 94,180 (digital/electronic); *Databases:* 108. Weekly public service hours: 106; students can reserve study rooms.

STUDENT LIFE
Housing options: on-campus residence required through senior year; coed. Campus housing is university owned. Freshman campus housing is guaranteed.
Activities and organizations: drama/theater group, student-run newspaper, radio station, choral group, Student Government Association, Alpha Phi Omega, Student Activities Committee, SU Dance Corps, Intramural Sports, national fraternities, national sororities.
Athletics Member NCAA. All Division III. ***Intercollegiate sports:*** baseball M, basketball M/W, cheerleading M(c)/W(c), crew M(c)/W(c), cross-country running M/W, equestrian sports M(c)/W(c), field hockey W, football M, golf M/W, lacrosse M/W, rugby M(c)/W(c), soccer M/W, softball W, swimming and diving M/W, tennis M/W, track and field M/W, volleyball M(c)/W. ***Intramural sports:*** basketball M/W, racquetball M/W, soccer M/W, softball M/W, tennis M/W, volleyball M/W.
Campus security: 24-hour emergency response devices and patrols, late-night transport/escort service, controlled dormitory access.
Student services: health clinic, personal/psychological counseling.

COSTS & FINANCIAL AID
Costs (2017–18) ***Comprehensive fee:*** $57,560 includes full-time tuition ($44,890), mandatory fees ($580), and room and board ($12,090). Part-time tuition: $1430 per credit hour. ***College room only:*** $6320. Room and board charges vary according to board plan. ***Payment plans:*** tuition prepayment, installment. ***Waivers:*** employees or children of employees.
Financial Aid Of all full-time matriculated undergraduates who enrolled in 2016, 1,877 applied for aid, 1,692 were judged to have need, 340 had their need fully met. In 2016, 473 non-need-based awards were made. ***Average percent of need met:*** 81. ***Average financial aid package:*** $34,622. ***Average need-based loan:*** $4246. ***Average need-based gift aid:*** $29,983. ***Average non-need-based aid:*** $20,454. ***Average indebtedness upon graduation:*** $36,882.

APPLYING
Options: electronic application, early admission, early decision, early action, deferred entrance.
Required: essay or personal statement, high school transcript, minimum 2.5 GPA, 1 letter of recommendation. ***Required for some:*** writing portfolio, audition for music programs. ***Recommended:*** minimum 3.0 GPA, interview.
Application deadlines: rolling (freshmen), 8/1 (transfers), 11/1 (early action).
Early decision deadline: 11/15 (for plan 1), 2/15 (for plan 2).
Notification: 11/1 (freshmen), continuous until 8/1 (transfers), 12/1 (early decision plan 1), 3/1 (early decision plan 2), 12/1 (early action).

CONTACT
Mr. Philip Betz, Director of Admissions, Susquehanna University, 514 University Avenue, Selinsgrove, PA 17870. *Phone:* 570-372-4260. *Toll-free phone:* 800-326-9672. *Fax:* 570-372-2722. *E-mail:* suadmiss@susqu.edu.

Swarthmore College

Swarthmore, Pennsylvania

http://www.swarthmore.edu/

- **Independent** 4-year, founded 1864
- **Suburban** 425-acre campus with easy access to Philadelphia
- **Endowment** $180.0 million
- **Coed** 1,581 undergraduate students, 99% full-time, 50% women, 50% men

UNDERGRAD STUDENTS

1,571 full-time, 10 part-time. 87% are from out of state; 6% Black or African American, non-Hispanic/Latino; 13% Hispanic/Latino; 17% Asian, non-Hispanic/Latino; 0.1% Native Hawaiian or other Pacific Islander, non-Hispanic/Latino; 0.1% American Indian or Alaska Native, non-Hispanic/Latino; 8% Two or more races, non-Hispanic/Latino; 3% Race/ethnicity unknown; 11% international; 0.4% transferred in; 95% live on campus.

Freshmen:

Admission: 407 enrolled. ***Test scores:*** SAT critical reading scores over 500: 100%; SAT math scores over 500: 100%; SAT writing scores over 500: 100%; ACT scores over 18: 100%; SAT critical reading scores over 600: 96%; SAT math scores over 600: 97%; SAT writing scores over 600: 96%; ACT scores over 24: 100%; SAT critical reading scores over 700: 62%; SAT math scores over 700: 62%; SAT writing scores over 700: 67%; ACT scores over 30: 78%.

Retention: 98% of full-time freshmen returned.

FACULTY

Total: 212, 86% full-time, 95% with terminal degrees.

Student/faculty ratio: 8:1.

ACADEMICS

Calendar: semesters. *Degree:* bachelor's.

Special study options: accelerated degree program, double majors, honors programs, independent study, internships, services for LD students, student-designed majors, study abroad. ***ROTC:*** Army (c), Navy (c), Air Force (c).

Computers: Students can access the following: computer help desk, free student e-mail accounts, online (class) grades, online (class) registration, online (class) schedules, online course materials and academic software. Campuswide network is available. Wireless service is available via entire campus.

Library: McCabe Library plus 6 others.

STUDENT LIFE

Housing options: on-campus residence required for freshman year; coed, men-only, women-only, special housing for students with disabilities. Campus housing is university owned. Freshman campus housing is guaranteed.

Activities and organizations: drama/theater group, student-run newspaper, radio station, choral group, Boy Meets Tractor (sketch comedy troupe), Mock Trial, Rhythm N' Motion (performing dance styles of the African Diaspora), Multi (community for people who self-identify as multiracial, multiethnic, multicultural, and/or multireligious), Mixed Company (a capella group), national fraternities, national sororities.

Athletics Member NCAA. All Division III. ***Intercollegiate sports:*** badminton M(c)/W, baseball M, basketball M/W, cross-country running M/W, fencing M(c)/W(c), field hockey W, golf M, ice hockey M(c)/W(c), lacrosse M/W, rugby M(c)/W(c), soccer M/W, softball W, squash M(c)/W(c), swimming and diving M/W, tennis M/W, track and field M/W, ultimate Frisbee M(c)/W(c), volleyball M(c)/W, water polo M(c)/W(c). ***Intramural sports:*** basketball M/W, football M/W, soccer M/W, softball M/W, table tennis M/W, tennis M/W, volleyball M/W.

Campus security: 24-hour emergency response devices and patrols, late-night transport/escort service.

Student services: health clinic, personal/psychological counseling, women's center.

COSTS & FINANCIAL AID

Costs (2017–18) ***Comprehensive fee:*** $65,774 includes full-time tuition ($50,424), mandatory fees ($398), and room and board ($14,952). ***College room only:*** $7670. Room and board charges vary according to board plan. ***Payment plan:*** installment.

Financial Aid Of all full-time matriculated undergraduates who enrolled in 2016, 985 applied for aid, 867 were judged to have need, 867 had their need fully met. 765 Federal Work-Study jobs (averaging $1949). In 2016, 12 non-need-based awards were made. ***Average percent of need met:*** 100. ***Average financial aid package:*** $47,255. ***Average need-based gift aid:*** $45,536. ***Average non-need-based aid:*** $48,720. ***Average indebtedness upon graduation:*** $22,957. ***Financial aid deadline:*** 1/1.

APPLYING

Standardized Tests *Required:* SAT and SAT Subject Tests or ACT (for admission).

Required: essay or personal statement, high school transcript, 3 letters of recommendation.

CONTACT

Swarthmore College, 500 College Avenue, Swarthmore, PA 19081-1397. *Toll-free phone:* 800-667-3110.

Talmudical Yeshiva of Philadelphia

Philadelphia, Pennsylvania

CONTACT

Rabbi Shmuel Kamenetsky, Co-Dean, Talmudical Yeshiva of Philadelphia, 6063 Drexel Road, Philadelphia, PA 19131-1296. *Phone:* 215-473-1212.

★ Temple University

Philadelphia, Pennsylvania

http://www.temple.edu/

- **State-related** university, founded 1884, part of Commonwealth System of Higher Education
- **Urban** 384-acre campus with easy access to Philadelphia
- **Endowment** $386.2 million
- **Coed** 29,275 undergraduate students, 90% full-time, 52% women, 48% men
- **Moderately difficult** entrance level, 52% of applicants were admitted

UNDERGRAD STUDENTS

26,277 full-time, 2,998 part-time. Students come from 49 states and territories; 129 other countries; 20% are from out of state; 13% Black or African American, non-Hispanic/Latino; 6% Hispanic/Latino; 11% Asian, non-Hispanic/Latino; 0.1% Native Hawaiian or other Pacific Islander, non-Hispanic/Latino; 0.1% American Indian or Alaska Native, non-Hispanic/Latino; 3% Two or more races, non-Hispanic/Latino; 4% Race/ethnicity unknown; 7% international; 9% transferred in; 19% live on campus.

Freshmen:

Admission: 33,139 applied, 17,295 admitted, 5,162 enrolled. ***Average high school GPA:*** 3.56. ***Test scores:*** SAT critical reading scores over 500: 85%; SAT math scores over 500: 87%; SAT writing scores over 500: 81%; ACT scores over 18: 98%; SAT critical reading scores over 600: 41%; SAT math scores over 600: 47%; SAT writing scores over 600: 37%; ACT scores over 24: 77%; SAT critical reading scores over 700: 10%; SAT math scores over 700: 11%; SAT writing scores over 700: 8%; ACT scores over 30: 27%.

Retention: 90% of full-time freshmen returned.

FACULTY

Total: 2,898, 50% full-time, 44% with terminal degrees.

Student/faculty ratio: 15:1.

ACADEMICS

Calendar: semesters. *Degrees:* certificates, diplomas, associate, bachelor's, master's, doctoral, post-master's, and postbachelor's certificates.

Special study options: academic remediation for entering students, accelerated degree program, adult/continuing education programs, advanced placement credit, cooperative education, distance learning, double majors, English as a second language, external degree program, honors programs, independent study, internships, off-campus study, part-time degree program, services for LD students, study abroad, summer session for credit. ***ROTC:*** Army (b), Navy (c), Air Force (c).

Computers: 8,324 computers/terminals and 68,334 ports are available on campus for general student use. Students can access the following: computer help desk, free student e-mail accounts, online (class) grades, online (class) registration, online (class) schedules, student accounts, Web hosting. Campuswide network is available. 100% of college-owned or -operated housing units are wired for high-speed Internet access. Wireless service is available via entire campus.

Library: Paley Library plus 6 others. *Books:* 3.8 million (physical), 1.2 million (digital/electronic); *Serial titles:* 1,080 (physical), 51,077 (digital/electronic); *Databases:* 1,939. Students can reserve study rooms.

STUDENT LIFE

Housing options: coed, special housing for students with disabilities. Campus housing is university owned, leased by the school and is provided by a third party.

Activities and organizations: drama/theater group, student-run newspaper, radio and television station, choral group, marching band, Temple Slavic Association, Alpha Epsilon Delta (Pre-professional students with interests in pursuing careers in healthcare), Habitat for Humanity, National Student Speech Language and Hearing Association, Queer Student Union, national fraternities, national sororities.

Athletics Member NCAA. All Division I except football (Division I-A). ***Intercollegiate sports:*** basketball M(s)/W(s), crew M(s)/W(s), cross-country running M(s)/W(s), fencing W(s), field hockey W(s), golf M(s), gymnastics W(s), lacrosse W(s), soccer M(s)/W(s), tennis M(s)/W(s), track and field W(s), volleyball W(s). ***Intramural sports:*** badminton M(c)/W(c), baseball M(c), basketball M/W, equestrian sports M(c)/W(c), fencing M(c)/W(c), field hockey W(c), football M/W, gymnastics M(c)/W(c), ice hockey M, lacrosse M(c)/W(c), racquetball M(c)/W(c), rugby M(c)/W(c), skiing (downhill) M(c)/W(c), soccer M/W, softball M/W, swimming and diving M(c)/W(c), tennis M(c)/W(c), track and field M(c)/W(c), ultimate Frisbee M(c)/W(c), volleyball M/W, weight lifting M(c)/W(c), wrestling M(c).

Campus security: 24-hour emergency response devices and patrols, late-night transport/escort service, controlled dormitory access.

Student services: health clinic, personal/psychological counseling, legal services.

COSTS & FINANCIAL AID

Costs (2016–17) ***Tuition:*** state resident $15,384 full-time, $641 per credit hour part-time; nonresident $26,376 full-time, $1099 per credit hour part-time. Full-time tuition and fees vary according to course load, degree level, location, program, reciprocity agreements, and student level. Part-time tuition and fees vary according to course load, degree level, location, program, reciprocity agreements, and student level. ***Required fees:*** $890 full-time. ***Room and board:*** $11,298; room only: $7540. Room and board charges vary according to board plan and housing facility. ***Payment plan:*** installment. ***Waivers:*** employees or children of employees.

Financial Aid Of all full-time matriculated undergraduates who enrolled in 2015, 19,887 applied for aid, 17,261 were judged to have need, 4,262 had their need fully met. 1,377 Federal Work-Study jobs (averaging $1438). In 2015, 3055 non-need-based awards were made. ***Average percent of need met:*** 66. ***Average financial aid package:*** $17,767. ***Average need-based loan:*** $4497. ***Average need-based gift aid:*** $6812. ***Average non-need-based aid:*** $7109. ***Average indebtedness upon graduation:*** $37,708.

APPLYING

Options: electronic application, early action, deferred entrance.

Application fee: $55.

Required: essay or personal statement, high school transcript. ***Recommended:*** minimum 3.0 GPA, 1 letter of recommendation.

Application deadlines: 3/1 (freshmen), 6/1 (transfers).

Notification: continuous (freshmen), continuous (transfers).

CONTACT

Temple University, 1801 North Broad Street, Philadelphia, PA 19122-6096. *Phone:* 215-204-7200. *Toll-free phone:* 888-340-2222.

See this page for display ad and page 1532 for the College Close-Up.

Thiel College

Greenville, Pennsylvania

http://www.thiel.edu/

- **Independent** 4-year, founded 1866, affiliated with Evangelical Lutheran Church in America
- **Rural** 135-acre campus with easy access to Cleveland, Pittsburgh
- **Endowment** $31.4 million
- **Coed**
- **Moderately difficult** entrance level

FACULTY

Student/faculty ratio: 13:1.

ACADEMICS

Calendar: semesters. *Degrees:* associate and bachelor's.
Library: Langenheim Memorial Library.

STUDENT LIFE

Housing options: on-campus residence required through senior year; coed. Campus housing is university owned. Freshman campus housing is guaranteed.

Activities and organizations: drama/theater group, student-run newspaper, radio and television station, choral group, marching band, Thiel Players Theatre Group, student government, Thiel Choir, Ski Club, Thiel Christian Fellowship, national fraternities, national sororities.

Athletics Member NCAA. All Division III.

Campus security: 24-hour emergency response devices and patrols, late-night transport/escort service, controlled dormitory access.

Student services: health clinic, personal/psychological counseling.

COSTS & FINANCIAL AID

Costs (2016–17) ***Comprehensive fee:*** $41,440 includes full-time tuition ($27,910), mandatory fees ($1830), and room and board ($11,700). Full-time tuition and fees vary according to course load. Part-time tuition: $900 per credit hour. Part-time tuition and fees vary according to course load. ***Required fees:*** $915 per term part-time. ***College room only:*** $5850. Room and board charges vary according to housing facility.

Financial Aid Of all full-time matriculated undergraduates who enrolled in 2014, 913 applied for aid, 867 were judged to have need, 92 had their need fully met. 60 Federal Work-Study jobs (averaging $1475). 300 state and other part-time jobs (averaging $2063). In 2014, 82 non-need-based awards were made. ***Average percent of need met:*** 70. ***Average financial aid package:*** $23,041. ***Average need-based loan:*** $4654. ***Average need-based gift aid:*** $18,846. ***Average non-need-based aid:*** $11,816. ***Average indebtedness upon graduation:*** $37,932.

APPLYING

Standardized Tests *Required:* SAT or ACT (for admission).

Options: electronic application, deferred entrance.

Required: essay or personal statement, high school transcript, minimum 2.0 GPA, 1 letter of recommendation. ***Required for some:*** interview.

CONTACT

Mr. Stephen Lazowski, Vice President for Enrollment Management, Thiel College, 75 College Avenue, Greenville, PA 16125. *Phone:* 724-589-2182. *Toll-free phone:* 800-248-4435. *Fax:* 724-589-2013. *E-mail:* admissions@thiel.edu.

Thomas Jefferson University

Philadelphia, Pennsylvania

http://www.jefferson.edu/university.html

CONTACT

Ms. Karen Jacobs, Director of Admissions, Thomas Jefferson University, Edison Building, 130 South Ninth Street, Philadelphia, PA 19107. *Phone:* 215-503-8890. *Toll-free phone:* 877-533-3247. *Fax:* 215-503-7241. *E-mail:* chpadmissions@mail.tju.edu.

University of Pennsylvania

Philadelphia, Pennsylvania

http://www.upenn.edu/

- **Independent** university, founded 1740
- **Urban** 299-acre campus
- **Endowment** $10.7 billion
- **Coed** 10,019 undergraduate students, 97% full-time, 50% women, 50% men
- **Most difficult** entrance level, 9% of applicants were admitted

UNDERGRAD STUDENTS

9,706 full-time, 313 part-time. Students come from 54 states and territories; 102 other countries; 81% are from out of state; 7% Black or African American, non-Hispanic/Latino; 10% Hispanic/Latino; 21% Asian, non-Hispanic/Latino; 0.1% American Indian or Alaska Native, non-Hispanic/Latino; 4% Two or more races, non-Hispanic/Latino; 2% Race/ethnicity unknown; 12% international; 2% transferred in; 54% live on campus.

Freshmen:

Admission: 38,918 applied, 3,674 admitted, 2,428 enrolled. ***Average high school GPA:*** 3.91. ***Test scores:*** SAT critical reading scores over 500: 99%; SAT math scores over 500: 101%; SAT writing scores over 500: 100%; ACT scores over 18: 100%; SAT critical reading scores over 600: 96%; SAT math scores over 600: 99%; SAT writing scores over 600: 97%; ACT scores over 24: 100%; SAT critical reading scores over 700: 69%; SAT math scores over 700: 77%; SAT writing scores over 700: 73%; ACT scores over 30: 89%.

Retention: 98% of full-time freshmen returned.

FACULTY

Total: 2,150, 69% full-time, 100% with terminal degrees.

Student/faculty ratio: 6:1.

ACADEMICS

Calendar: semesters plus 2 5-week summer sessions. *Degrees:* certificates, associate, bachelor's, master's, doctoral, post-master's, and postbachelor's certificates (also offers evening program with significant enrollment not reflected in profile).

Special study options: academic remediation for entering students, accelerated degree program, adult/continuing education programs, advanced placement credit, cooperative education, distance learning, double majors, English as a second language, honors programs, independent study, internships, off-campus study, part-time degree program, services for LD students, student-designed majors, study abroad, summer session for credit. ***ROTC:*** Army (c), Navy (b), Air Force (c).

Computers: Students can access the following: campus intranet, computer help desk, free student e-mail accounts, online (class) grades, online (class) registration, online (class) schedules, billing information, financial aid application, status, academic records, student services. Campuswide network is available. 100% of college-owned or -operated housing units are wired for high-speed Internet access. Wireless service is available via entire campus.

Library: Van Pelt Library plus 14 others. *Books:* 6.4 million (physical); *Serial titles:* 188,604 (physical). Study areas open 24 hours, 5-7 days a week; students can reserve study rooms.

STUDENT LIFE

Housing options: coed, men-only, special housing for students with disabilities. Campus housing is university owned. Freshman campus housing is guaranteed.

Activities and organizations: drama/theater group, student-run newspaper, radio and television station, choral group, marching band, Kite and Key Society, Social Planning and Events Committee, Hillel at Penn, Sports Club Council, Interfraternity Council, national fraternities, national sororities.

Athletics Member NCAA. All Division I except football (Division I-AA). ***Intercollegiate sports:*** baseball M, basketball M/W, crew M/W, cross-country running M/W, fencing M/W, field hockey W, golf M/W, gymnastics W, lacrosse M/W, soccer M/W, softball W, squash M/W, swimming and diving M/W, tennis M/W, track and field M/W, volleyball W, wrestling M. ***Intramural sports:*** badminton M(c)/W(c), baseball M(c)/W(c), basketball M(c)/W(c), cheerleading M/W, equestrian sports M(c)/W(c), field hockey M(c)/W(c), golf M(c)/W(c), gymnastics

M(c)/W(c), ice hockey M(c)/W(c), lacrosse M/W, rugby M(c)/W(c), sailing M(c)/W(c), skiing (downhill) M(c)/W(c), soccer M/W, softball M/W, squash M/W, swimming and diving M/W, table tennis M/W, tennis M/W, ultimate Frisbee M(c)/W(c), volleyball M/W, water polo M(c)/W(c).

Campus security: 24-hour emergency response devices and patrols, late-night transport/escort service, controlled dormitory access.

Student services: health clinic, personal/psychological counseling, women's center, legal services.

COSTS & FINANCIAL AID
Costs (2017–18) ***Comprehensive fee:*** $68,600 includes full-time tuition ($47,416), mandatory fees ($6118), and room and board ($15,066). Part-time tuition and fees vary according to course load. ***Room and board:*** Room and board charges vary according to board plan and housing facility. ***Payment plans:*** tuition prepayment, installment. ***Waivers:*** employees or children of employees.

Financial Aid Of all full-time matriculated undergraduates who enrolled in 2014, 4,861 applied for aid, 4,453 were judged to have need, 4,453 had their need fully met. 3,395 Federal Work-Study jobs (averaging $2945). 1,394 state and other part-time jobs (averaging $2655). ***Average percent of need met:*** 100. ***Average financial aid package:*** $43,542. ***Average need-based loan:*** $242. ***Average need-based gift aid:*** $41,598. ***Average indebtedness upon graduation:*** $26,157.

APPLYING
Standardized Tests *Required:* SAT or ACT (for admission). *Recommended:* SAT Subject Tests (for admission).

Options: electronic application, early admission, early decision, deferred entrance.

Application fee: $75.

Required: essay or personal statement, high school transcript, 2 letters of recommendation.

Application deadlines: 1/5 (freshmen), 3/15 (transfers).

Early decision deadline: 11/1.

Notification: continuous until 4/1 (freshmen), 5/15 (transfers), 12/15 (early decision).

CONTACT
Office of Undergraduate Admissions, University of Pennsylvania, 1 College Hall, Room 1, Philadelphia, PA 19104. *Phone:* 215-898-7507.

University of Pittsburgh

Pittsburgh, Pennsylvania

http://www.pitt.edu/

- **State-related** university, founded 1787, part of Commonwealth System of Higher Education
- **Urban** 145-acre campus with easy access to Pittsburgh
- **Endowment** $3.5 billion
- **Coed** 19,123 undergraduate students, 95% full-time, 52% women, 48% men
- **Very difficult** entrance level, 55% of applicants were admitted

UNDERGRAD STUDENTS
18,163 full-time, 960 part-time. Students come from 50 states and territories; 49 other countries; 28% are from out of state; 5% Black or African American, non-Hispanic/Latino; 3% Hispanic/Latino; 10% Asian, non-Hispanic/Latino; 0.1% American Indian or Alaska Native, non-Hispanic/Latino; 4% Two or more races, non-Hispanic/Latino; 1% Race/ethnicity unknown; 4% international; 4% transferred in; 43% live on campus.

Freshmen:
Admission: 29,175 applied, 16,165 admitted, 3,954 enrolled. ***Average high school GPA:*** 4.14. ***Test scores:*** SAT critical reading scores over 500: 98%; SAT math scores over 500: 99%; SAT writing scores over 500: 97%; ACT scores over 18: 100%; SAT critical reading scores over 600: 70%; SAT math scores over 600: 79%; SAT writing scores over 600: 63%; ACT scores over 24: 96%; SAT critical reading scores over 700: 20%; SAT math scores over 700: 26%; SAT writing scores over 700: 16%; ACT scores over 30: 42%.

Retention: 92% of full-time freshmen returned.

FACULTY
Total: 2,283, 77% full-time.

Student/faculty ratio: 15:1.

ACADEMICS
Calendar: semesters plus summer term. *Degrees:* certificates, bachelor's, master's, doctoral, post-master's, and postbachelor's certificates.

Special study options: academic remediation for entering students, accelerated degree program, adult/continuing education programs, advanced placement credit, cooperative education, distance learning, double majors, English as a second language, external degree program, freshman honors college, honors programs, independent study, internships, off-campus study, part-time degree program, services for LD students, student-designed majors, study abroad, summer session for credit. ***ROTC:*** Army (b), Navy (c), Air Force (b).

Unusual degree programs: 3-2 engineering; computer science/statistics, pharmaceutical sciences, pharmaceutical sciences/pharmacy.

Computers: 1,200 computers/terminals and 17,782 ports are available on campus for general student use. Students can access the following: campus intranet, computer help desk, free student e-mail accounts, online (class) grades, online (class) registration, online (class) schedules, online class listings, online tuition payment. Campuswide network is available. 100% of college-owned or -operated housing units are wired for high-speed Internet access. Wireless service is available via entire campus.

Library: Hillman Library plus 16 others. *Books:* 5.9 million (physical), 1.5 million (digital/electronic); *Serial titles:* 110,789 (physical), 223,301 (digital/electronic); *Databases:* 570. Weekly public service hours: 145; study areas open 24 hours, 5-7 days a week; students can reserve study rooms.

STUDENT LIFE
Housing options: coed, women-only, special housing for students with disabilities. Campus housing is university owned. Freshman campus housing is guaranteed.

Activities and organizations: drama/theater group, student-run newspaper, radio and television station, choral group, marching band, Resident Student Association, Black Action Society, Pitt Program Council, Interfraternity Council, Panhellenic Association, national fraternities, national sororities.

Athletics Member NCAA. All Division I except football (Division I-A). ***Intercollegiate sports:*** baseball M(s), basketball M(s)/W(s), cross-country running M(s)/W(s), gymnastics W(s), soccer M(s)/W(s), softball W(s), swimming and diving M(s)/W(s), tennis W(s), track and field M(s)/W(s), volleyball W(s), wrestling M(s). ***Intramural sports:*** badminton M/W, baseball M(c), basketball M/W, crew M(c)/W(c), cross-country running M(c)/W(c), equestrian sports M(c)/W(c), fencing M(c), field hockey M(c), football M, gymnastics W(c), ice hockey M(c)/W(c), lacrosse M(c), rugby M(c)/W(c), soccer M/W, softball W(c), squash M/W, swimming and diving M(c)/W(c), table tennis M/W, tennis M(c)/W(c), ultimate Frisbee M/W, volleyball M/W, water polo M(c)/W(c).

Campus security: 24-hour emergency response devices and patrols, late-night transport/escort service, controlled dormitory access, on-call van transportation.

Student services: health clinic, personal/psychological counseling.

COSTS & FINANCIAL AID
Costs (2016–17) ***Tuition:*** state resident $17,688 full-time, $737 per credit hour part-time; nonresident $28,828 full-time, $1201 per credit hour part-time. Full-time tuition and fees vary according to location and program. Part-time tuition and fees vary according to location and program. ***Required fees:*** $930 full-time, $274 per term part-time. ***Room and board:*** $10,950; room only: $6300. Room and board charges vary according to board plan, housing facility, and location. ***Payment plans:*** installment, deferred payment. ***Waivers:*** employees or children of employees.

Financial Aid Of all full-time matriculated undergraduates who enrolled in 2015, 12,340 applied for aid, 9,486 were judged to have need, 1,123 had their need fully met. In 2015, 540 non-need-based awards were made. ***Average percent of need met:*** 52. ***Average financial aid package:*** $12,286. ***Average need-based loan:*** $5125. ***Average need-based gift aid:*** $9289. ***Average non-need-based aid:*** $10,081. ***Average indebtedness upon graduation:*** $38,612.

APPLYING
Standardized Tests *Required:* SAT or ACT (for admission).

Options: electronic application.

Application fee: $45.

Required: high school transcript. ***Recommended:*** essay or personal statement, interview.

Application deadlines: rolling (freshmen), rolling (transfers).

Notification: continuous (freshmen), continuous (transfers).

CONTACT

Marc L. Harding, Chief Enrollment Officer, University of Pittsburgh, 4227 Fifth Avenue, First Floor, Alumni Hall, Pittsburgh, PA 15260. *Phone:* 412-624-7488. *Fax:* 412-648-8815. *E-mail:* oafa@pitt.edu.

★ University of Pittsburgh at Bradford

Bradford, Pennsylvania

http://www.upb.pitt.edu/

- **State-related** 4-year, founded 1963, part of University of Pittsburgh System
- **Small-town** 317-acre campus with easy access to Buffalo
- **Endowment** $22.6 million
- **Coed** 1,476 undergraduate students, 92% full-time, 54% women, 46% men
- **Minimally difficult** entrance level, 53% of applicants were admitted

UNDERGRAD STUDENTS

1,360 full-time, 116 part-time. Students come from 24 states and territories; 19 other countries; 22% are from out of state; 12% Black or African American, non-Hispanic/Latino; 5% Hispanic/Latino; 2% Asian, non-Hispanic/Latino; 0.1% Native Hawaiian or other Pacific Islander, non-Hispanic/Latino; 0.5% American Indian or Alaska Native, non-Hispanic/Latino; 2% Two or more races, non-Hispanic/Latino; 7% Race/ethnicity unknown; 3% international; 7% transferred in; 69% live on campus.

Freshmen:

Admission: 2,955 applied, 1,566 admitted, 398 enrolled. ***Average high school GPA:*** 3.22. ***Test scores:*** SAT critical reading scores over 500: 46%; SAT math scores over 500: 47%; SAT writing scores over 500: 28%; ACT scores over 18: 88%; SAT critical reading scores over 600: 9%; SAT math scores over 600: 10%; SAT writing scores over 600: 3%; ACT scores over 24: 24%; SAT critical reading scores over 700: 1%; SAT math scores over 700: 1%; ACT scores over 30: 3%.

Retention: 66% of full-time freshmen returned.

FACULTY

Total: 166, 45% full-time, 41% with terminal degrees.

Student/faculty ratio: 17:1.

ACADEMICS

Calendar: semesters. *Degrees:* associate and bachelor's.

Special study options: academic remediation for entering students, accelerated degree program, adult/continuing education programs, advanced placement credit, cooperative education, distance learning, double majors, independent study, internships, off-campus study, part-time degree program, services for LD students, student-designed majors, study abroad, summer session for credit. ***ROTC:*** Army (c).

Computers: 136 computers/terminals and 1,200 ports are available on campus for general student use. Students can access the following: computer help desk, free student e-mail accounts, online (class) grades, online (class) registration, online (class) schedules, online bills. Campuswide network is available. 100% of college-owned or -operated housing units are wired for high-speed Internet access. Wireless service is available via entire campus.

Library: T. Edward and Tullah Hanley Library. *Books:* 101,404 (physical), 1.5 million (digital/electronic); *Serial titles:* 84 (physical), 10,000 (digital/electronic); *Databases:* 550. Weekly public service hours: 86; students can reserve study rooms.

STUDENT LIFE

Housing options: on-campus residence required for freshman year; coed, special housing for students with disabilities. Campus housing is university owned. Freshman campus housing is guaranteed.

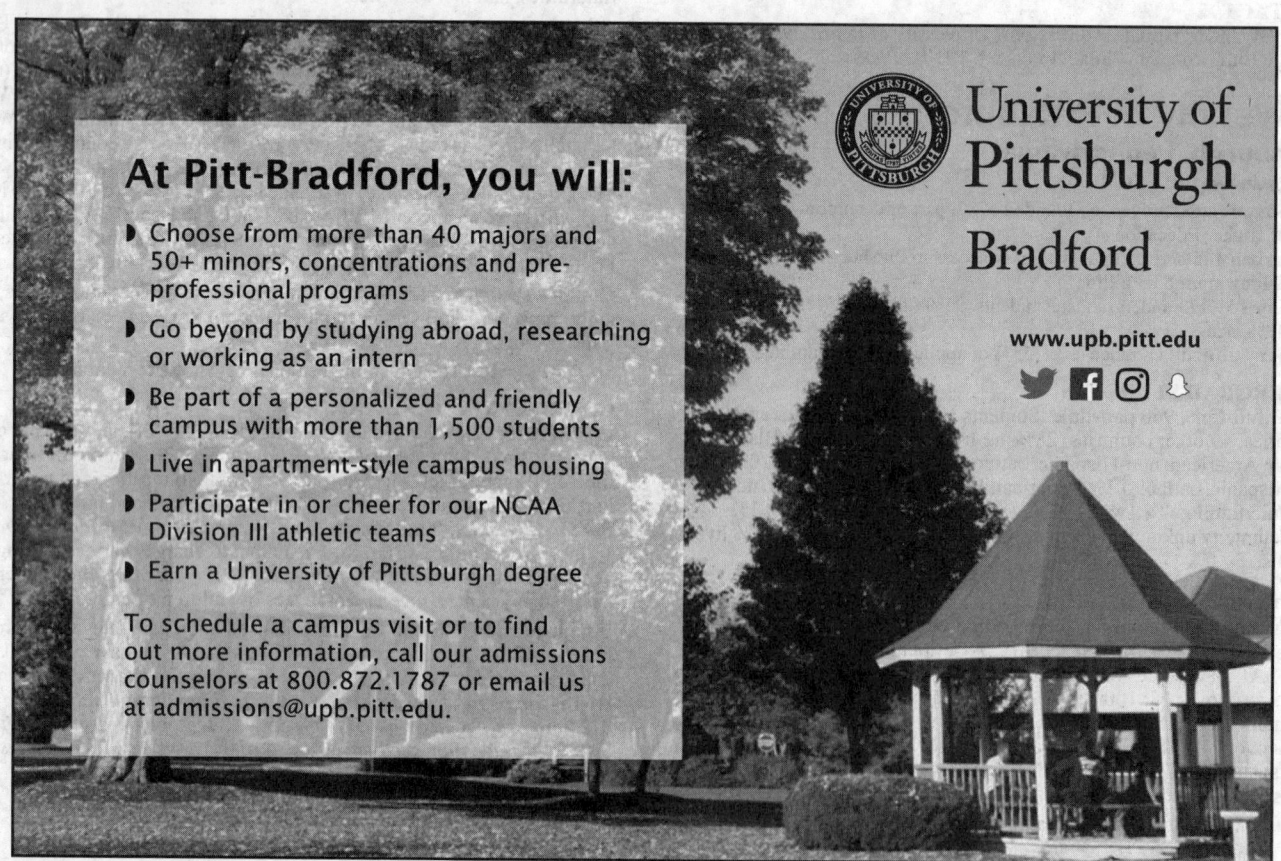

Activities and organizations: drama/theater group, student-run newspaper, radio station, choral group, Student Government Association, Student Activities Board, The Source (student newspaper), Alpha Phi

Omega, WDRQ (student radio station), national fraternities, national sororities.

Athletics Member NCAA. All Division III. ***Intercollegiate sports:*** baseball M, basketball M/W, bowling W, golf M, soccer M/W, softball W, swimming and diving M/W, tennis M/W, volleyball W. ***Intramural sports:*** basketball M/W, cheerleading W(c), football M/W, golf M/W, ice hockey M(c)/W(c), rock climbing M/W, sand volleyball M/W, skiing (downhill) M/W, soccer M/W, softball M/W, swimming and diving M/W, tennis M/W, ultimate Frisbee M/W, volleyball M/W, water polo M/W, wrestling M(c).

Campus security: 24-hour emergency response devices and patrols, late-night transport/escort service, controlled dormitory access, Resident Assistants do nightly rounds of residence halls.

Student services: health clinic, personal/psychological counseling.

COSTS & FINANCIAL AID

Costs (2016–17) ***One-time required fee:*** $90. ***Tuition:*** state resident $12,688 full-time, $528 per credit hour part-time; nonresident $23,710 full-time, $987 per credit hour part-time. Full-time tuition and fees vary according to course load and program. Part-time tuition and fees vary according to course load and program. ***Required fees:*** $920 full-time, $155 per term part-time. ***Room and board:*** $8794; room only: $5330. Room and board charges vary according to board plan and housing facility. ***Payment plan:*** installment. ***Waivers:*** employees or children of employees.

Financial Aid Of all full-time matriculated undergraduates who enrolled in 2016, 1,228 applied for aid, 1,133 were judged to have need, 195 had their need fully met. 180 Federal Work-Study jobs (averaging $1980). 44 state and other part-time jobs (averaging $1857). In 2016, 74 non-need-based awards were made. ***Average percent of need met:*** 68. ***Average financial aid package:*** $16,539. ***Average need-based loan:*** $7398. ***Average need-based gift aid:*** $9968. ***Average non-need-based aid:*** $6339. ***Average indebtedness upon graduation:*** $32,816.

APPLYING

Standardized Tests *Required:* SAT or ACT (for admission).

Options: electronic application, deferred entrance.

Application fee: $45.

Required: high school transcript, minimum 2.0 GPA. ***Required for some:*** minimum 3.0 GPA. ***Recommended:*** essay or personal statement, 2 letters of recommendation, interview.

Application deadlines: rolling (freshmen), rolling (transfers).

Notification: continuous (freshmen), continuous (transfers).

CONTACT

Ms. Vicky Pingie, Associate Director of Admissions, University of Pittsburgh at Bradford, 300 Campus Drive, Bradford, PA 16701. *Phone:* 814-362-7552. *Toll-free phone:* 800-872-1787. *Fax:* 814-362-5150. *E-mail:* monti@pitt.edu.

See previous page for display ad and page 1574 for the College Close-Up.

University of Pittsburgh at Greensburg

Greensburg, Pennsylvania

http://www.greensburg.pitt.edu/

- **State-related** 4-year, founded 1963, part of University of Pittsburgh System
- **Small-town** 219-acre campus with easy access to Pittsburgh
- **Coed** 1,562 undergraduate students, 94% full-time, 52% women, 48% men
- **Moderately difficult** entrance level, 71% of applicants were admitted

UNDERGRAD STUDENTS

1,471 full-time, 91 part-time. Students come from 18 states and territories; 4 other countries; 3% are from out of state; 6% Black or African American, non-Hispanic/Latino; 6% Hispanic/Latino; 4% Asian, non-Hispanic/Latino; 0.1% Native Hawaiian or other Pacific Islander, non-Hispanic/Latino; 0.1% American Indian or Alaska Native, non-Hispanic/Latino; 3% Two or more races, non-Hispanic/Latino; 2% Race/ethnicity unknown; 1% international; 7% transferred in; 40% live on campus.

Freshmen:

Admission: 2,044 applied, 1,461 admitted, 409 enrolled. ***Average high school GPA:*** 3.48. ***Test scores:*** SAT critical reading scores over 500: 56%; SAT math scores over 500: 62%; SAT writing scores over 500: 43%; ACT scores over 18: 86%; SAT critical reading scores over 600: 12%; SAT math scores over 600: 14%; SAT writing scores over 600: 8%; ACT scores over 24: 35%; SAT critical reading scores over 700: 1%; SAT math scores over 700: 1%; ACT scores over 30: 2%.

Retention: 78% of full-time freshmen returned.

FACULTY

Total: 158, 48% full-time, 37% with terminal degrees.

Student/faculty ratio: 15:1.

ACADEMICS

Calendar: semesters. *Degree:* certificates and bachelor's.

Special study options: academic remediation for entering students, accelerated degree program, adult/continuing education programs, advanced placement credit, distance learning, double majors, independent study, internships, off-campus study, part-time degree program, services for LD students, student-designed majors, study abroad, summer session for credit. ***ROTC:*** Army (c), Air Force (c).

Computers: 216 computers/terminals and 201 ports are available on campus for general student use. Students can access the following: campus intranet, computer help desk, free student e-mail accounts, online (class) grades, online (class) registration, online (class) schedules. Campuswide network is available. 100% of college-owned or -operated housing units are wired for high-speed Internet access. Wireless service is available via classrooms, computer centers, computer labs, dorm rooms, learning centers, libraries, student centers.

Library: Millstein Library.

STUDENT LIFE

Housing options: coed. Campus housing is university owned.

Activities and organizations: drama/theater group, student-run newspaper, choral group, Habitat for Humanity, Student Government Association, Student Activities Board, Outdoor Adventure and Community Service, Freshmen Honor Society - Phi Eta Sigma.

Athletics Member NCAA. All Division III. ***Intercollegiate sports:*** baseball M, basketball M/W, cross-country running M/W, golf M, soccer M/W, softball W, tennis M/W, volleyball W. ***Intramural sports:*** baseball M, basketball M/W, bowling M/W, football M/W, golf M/W, racquetball M/W, skiing (cross-country) M/W, skiing (downhill) M/W, soccer M/W, softball M/W, table tennis M/W, tennis M/W, volleyball M/W, weight lifting M/W.

Campus security: 24-hour emergency response devices and patrols, late-night transport/escort service, controlled dormitory access.

Student services: health clinic, personal/psychological counseling.

COSTS & FINANCIAL AID

Costs (2016–17) ***Tuition:*** state resident $12,688 full-time, $528 per credit hour part-time; nonresident $23,710 full-time, $987 per credit hour part-time. ***Required fees:*** $930 full-time, $174 per term part-time. ***Room and board:*** $9990; room only: $6110. Room and board charges vary according to board plan and housing facility. ***Payment plan:*** installment. ***Waivers:*** senior citizens and employees or children of employees.

Financial Aid Of all full-time matriculated undergraduates who enrolled in 2015, 1,266 applied for aid, 1,084 were judged to have need, 103 had their need fully met. In 2015, 70 non-need-based awards were made. ***Average percent of need met:*** 59. ***Average financial aid package:*** $10,873. ***Average need-based loan:*** $4315. ***Average need-based gift aid:*** $8221. ***Average non-need-based aid:*** $4301. ***Average indebtedness upon graduation:*** $32,987.

APPLYING

Standardized Tests *Required:* SAT or ACT (for admission).

Options: electronic application, early admission, deferred entrance.

Application fee: $45.

Required: high school transcript, minimum 2.5 GPA. ***Recommended:*** essay or personal statement, interview.

Application deadlines: rolling (freshmen), rolling (out-of-state freshmen), rolling (transfers).

Notification: continuous (freshmen), continuous (transfers).

CONTACT
Ms. Heather Kabala, Director of Admissions, University of Pittsburgh at Greensburg, 150 Finoli Drive, Greensburg, PA 15601. *Phone:* 724-836-9880. *Fax:* 724-836-7471. *E-mail:* upgadmit@pitt.edu.

University of Pittsburgh at Johnstown

Johnstown, Pennsylvania

http://www.upj.pitt.edu/

- **State-related** 4-year, founded 1927, part of University of Pittsburgh System
- **Suburban** 655-acre campus with easy access to Pittsburgh
- **Coed** 2,769 undergraduate students, 98% full-time, 44% women, 56% men
- **Moderately difficult** entrance level, 88% of applicants were admitted

UNDERGRAD STUDENTS
2,708 full-time, 61 part-time. Students come from 14 states and territories; 12 other countries; 2% are from out of state; 4% Black or African American, non-Hispanic/Latino; 2% Hispanic/Latino; 2% Asian, non-Hispanic/Latino; 0.1% Native Hawaiian or other Pacific Islander, non-Hispanic/Latino; 0.2% American Indian or Alaska Native, non-Hispanic/Latino; 2% Two or more races, non-Hispanic/Latino; 3% Race/ethnicity unknown; 2% international; 4% transferred in; 59% live on campus.

Freshmen:
Admission: 1,613 applied, 1,418 admitted, 715 enrolled. ***Average high school GPA:*** 3.51. ***Test scores:*** SAT critical reading scores over 500: 52%; SAT math scores over 500: 64%; SAT writing scores over 500: 37%; ACT scores over 18: 90%; SAT critical reading scores over 600: 11%; SAT math scores over 600: 19%; SAT writing scores over 600: 4%; ACT scores over 24: 37%; SAT critical reading scores over 700: 1%; SAT math scores over 700: 2%; ACT scores over 30: 2%.

Retention: 79% of full-time freshmen returned.

FACULTY
Total: 151, 91% full-time, 74% with terminal degrees.

Student/faculty ratio: 20:1.

ACADEMICS
Calendar: semesters. *Degrees:* certificates, associate, and bachelor's.

Special study options: accelerated degree program, adult/continuing education programs, advanced placement credit, cooperative education, distance learning, double majors, independent study, internships, off-campus study, part-time degree program, services for LD students, student-designed majors, study abroad, summer session for credit.

Computers: 222 computers/terminals and 100 ports are available on campus for general student use. Students can access the following: computer help desk, free student e-mail accounts, online (class) grades, online (class) registration, online (class) schedules. Campuswide network is available. 100% of college-owned or -operated housing units are wired for high-speed Internet access. Wireless service is available via entire campus.

Library: Owen Library. Study areas open 24 hours, 5-7 days a week.

STUDENT LIFE
Housing options: coed, special housing for students with disabilities. Campus housing is university owned. Freshman campus housing is guaranteed.

Activities and organizations: drama/theater group, student-run newspaper, radio and television station, choral group, Dance Ensemble, Student Senate, Programming Board, academic clubs, national fraternities, national sororities.

Athletics Member NCAA. All Division II. ***Intercollegiate sports:*** baseball M(s), basketball M(s)/W(s), cheerleading W(c), cross-country running M(s)/W(s), golf M(s), ice hockey M(c)/W(c), lacrosse M(c)/W(c), rugby M(c)/W(c), soccer M(s)/W(s), softball W(s), track and field M(s)/W(s), ultimate Frisbee M(c)/W(c), volleyball W(s), wrestling M(s). ***Intramural sports:*** basketball M/W, football M/W, rock climbing M/W, skiing (downhill) M(c)/W(c), soccer M/W, softball M/W, volleyball M/W.

Campus security: 24-hour emergency response devices and patrols, late-night transport/escort service, controlled dormitory access.

Student services: health clinic, personal/psychological counseling.

COSTS & FINANCIAL AID
Costs (2017–18) ***Tuition:*** state resident $12,452 full-time, $518 per credit part-time; nonresident $23,268 full-time, $969 per credit part-time. Full-time tuition and fees vary according to program. Part-time tuition and fees vary according to program. ***Required fees:*** $936 full-time, $127 per term part-time. ***Room and board:*** $9684; room only: $5470. Room and board charges vary according to board plan and housing facility. ***Payment plan:*** installment. ***Waivers:*** employees or children of employees.

Financial Aid Of all full-time matriculated undergraduates who enrolled in 2015, 2,434 applied for aid, 2,063 were judged to have need, 322 had their need fully met. In 2015, 151 non-need-based awards were made. ***Average percent of need met:*** 60. ***Average financial aid package:*** $10,567. ***Average need-based loan:*** $4301. ***Average need-based gift aid:*** $7769. ***Average non-need-based aid:*** $3588. ***Average indebtedness upon graduation:*** $39,145.

APPLYING
Standardized Tests *Required:* SAT or ACT (for admission).

Options: electronic application, early admission, deferred entrance.

Required: high school transcript, minimum 2.0 GPA. ***Recommended:*** essay or personal statement, 3 letters of recommendation, interview.

Application deadlines: rolling (freshmen), rolling (transfers).

Notification: continuous (freshmen), continuous (transfers).

CONTACT
Mr. Ryan Clancy, Office of Admissions, University of Pittsburgh at Johnstown, 157 Blackington Hall, Johnstown, PA 15904. *Phone:* 814-269-7050. *Toll-free phone:* 800-765-4875. *E-mail:* upjadmit@pitt.edu.

The University of Scranton

Scranton, Pennsylvania

http://www.scranton.edu/

- **Independent Roman Catholic (Jesuit)** comprehensive, founded 1888
- **Urban** 50-acre campus
- **Endowment** $165.0 million
- **Coed** 3,867 undergraduate students, 95% full-time, 59% women, 41% men
- **Moderately difficult** entrance level, 75% of applicants were admitted

UNDERGRAD STUDENTS
3,678 full-time, 189 part-time. Students come from 25 states and territories; 23 other countries; 60% are from out of state; 2% Black or African American, non-Hispanic/Latino; 9% Hispanic/Latino; 3% Asian, non-Hispanic/Latino; 0.2% Native Hawaiian or other Pacific Islander, non-Hispanic/Latino; 0.1% American Indian or Alaska Native, non-Hispanic/Latino; 2% Two or more races, non-Hispanic/Latino; 2% Race/ethnicity unknown; 1% international; 1% transferred in; 64% live on campus.

Freshmen:
Admission: 10,114 applied, 7,540 admitted, 1,006 enrolled. ***Average high school GPA:*** 3.49. ***Test scores:*** SAT critical reading scores over 500: 81%; SAT math scores over 500: 85%; ACT scores over 18: 97%; SAT critical reading scores over 600: 29%; SAT math scores over 600: 39%; ACT scores over 24: 70%; SAT critical reading scores over 700: 4%; SAT math scores over 700: 4%; ACT scores over 30: 13%.

Retention: 87% of full-time freshmen returned.

FACULTY
Total: 481, 60% full-time, 60% with terminal degrees.

Student/faculty ratio: 12:1.

ACADEMICS
Calendar: 4-1-4. *Degrees:* certificates, bachelor's, master's, doctoral, post-master's, and postbachelor's certificates.

Special study options: academic remediation for entering students, accelerated degree program, adult/continuing education programs, advanced placement credit, distance learning, double majors, honors programs, independent study, internships, off-campus study, part-time degree program, services for LD students, student-designed majors, study abroad, summer session for credit. ***ROTC:*** Army (b), Air Force (c).

Computers: 988 computers/terminals are available on campus for general student use. Students can access the following: computer help desk, free student e-mail accounts, online (class) grades, online (class) registration, online (class) schedules. Campuswide network is available. 100% of college-owned or -operated housing units are wired for high-speed Internet access. Wireless service is available via classrooms, computer centers, computer labs, dorm rooms, learning centers, libraries, student centers.

Library: Harry and Jeanette Weinberg Memorial Library. *Books:* 331,804 (physical), 212,028 (digital/electronic); *Serial titles:* 2,677 (physical), 53,194 (digital/electronic); *Databases:* 120. Weekly public service hours: 95; study areas open 24 hours, 5-7 days a week; students can reserve study rooms.

STUDENT LIFE

Housing options: on-campus residence required through sophomore year; coed, men-only, women-only, special housing for students with disabilities. Campus housing is university owned. Freshman campus housing is guaranteed.

Activities and organizations: drama/theater group, student-run newspaper, radio and television station, choral group, Service-oriented student clubs, United Colors, Retreat Programs, Biology/Pre-Medicine clubs, Pre-Law Society.

Athletics Member NCAA. All Division III. ***Intercollegiate sports:*** baseball M, basketball M/W, crew M(c)/W(c), cross-country running M/W, equestrian sports M(c)/W(c), fencing M(c)/W(c), field hockey W, golf M/W, ice hockey M(c), lacrosse M/W, rugby M(c)/W(c), soccer M/W, softball W, swimming and diving M/W, tennis M/W, ultimate Frisbee M(c)/W(c), volleyball M(c)/W, wrestling M. ***Intramural sports:*** badminton M/W, basketball M/W, cheerleading M(c)/W(c), football M/W, skiing (downhill) M(c)/W(c), soccer M/W, softball M/W, ultimate Frisbee M/W, volleyball M/W.

Campus security: 24-hour emergency response devices and patrols, student patrols, late-night transport/escort service, controlled dormitory access, sprinkler systems in all University-owned housing.

Student services: health clinic, personal/psychological counseling, women's center.

COSTS & FINANCIAL AID

Costs (2016–17) ***Comprehensive fee:*** $56,426 includes full-time tuition ($41,762), mandatory fees ($400), and room and board ($14,264). ***College room only:*** $8354. Room and board charges vary according to board plan and housing facility. ***Payment plan:*** installment. ***Waivers:*** senior citizens and employees or children of employees.

Financial Aid Of all full-time matriculated undergraduates who enrolled in 2014, 3,169 applied for aid, 2,768 were judged to have need, 321 had their need fully met. 892 Federal Work-Study jobs (averaging $1959). 543 state and other part-time jobs (averaging $2018). In 2014, 687 non-need-based awards were made. ***Average percent of need met:*** 68. ***Average financial aid package:*** $25,053. ***Average need-based loan:*** $8363. ***Average need-based gift aid:*** $21,367. ***Average non-need-based aid:*** $13,699. ***Average indebtedness upon graduation:*** $40,640.

APPLYING

Standardized Tests *Required:* SAT or ACT (for admission).

Options: electronic application, early admission, early action, deferred entrance.

Required: essay or personal statement, high school transcript, 1 letter of recommendation. ***Required for some:*** interview.

Application deadlines: 3/1 (freshmen), rolling (transfers), 11/15 (early action).

Notification: continuous until 1/5 (freshmen), continuous (transfers), 12/15 (early action).

CONTACT

Mr. Joseph Roback, Associate Vice Provost, Admissions and Enrollment, The University of Scranton, The Estate Room 208, Scranton, PA 18510-4501. *Phone:* 570-941-7540. *Toll-free phone:* 888-SCRANTON. *Fax:* 570-941-5928. *E-mail:* admissions@scranton.edu.

The University of the Arts

Philadelphia, Pennsylvania

http://www.uarts.edu/

- **Independent** comprehensive, founded 1870
- **Urban** 21-acre campus
- **Coed** 1,712 undergraduate students, 98% full-time, 60% women, 40% men
- **Moderately difficult** entrance level, 74% of applicants were admitted

UNDERGRAD STUDENTS

1,671 full-time, 41 part-time. Students come from 43 states and territories; 21 other countries; 59% are from out of state; 13% Black or African American, non-Hispanic/Latino; 10% Hispanic/Latino; 3% Asian, non-Hispanic/Latino; 0.5% Native Hawaiian or other Pacific Islander, non-Hispanic/Latino; 0.4% American Indian or Alaska Native, non-Hispanic/Latino; 5% Two or more races, non-Hispanic/Latino; 2% Race/ethnicity unknown; 6% international; 5% transferred in; 34% live on campus.

Freshmen:

Admission: 1,608 applied, 1,185 admitted, 404 enrolled.

Retention: 76% of full-time freshmen returned.

FACULTY

Total: 511, 19% full-time.

Student/faculty ratio: 8:1.

ACADEMICS

Calendar: semesters. *Degrees:* diplomas, bachelor's, master's, and postbachelor's certificates.

Special study options: academic remediation for entering students, advanced placement credit, double majors, English as a second language, honors programs, independent study, internships, off-campus study, part-time degree program, services for LD students, study abroad, summer session for credit.

Computers: Students can access the following: campus intranet, computer help desk, free student e-mail accounts, online (class) grades, online (class) registration, online (class) schedules. Campuswide network is available. 100% of college-owned or -operated housing units are wired for high-speed Internet access. Wireless service is available via entire campus.

Library: Albert M. Greenfield Library plus 1 other.

STUDENT LIFE

Housing options: coed. Campus housing is university owned and leased by the school. Freshman applicants given priority for college housing.

Activities and organizations: drama/theater group, choral group, National Society of College Scholars, Students of Creative Action, African Diaspora Collective, Blurring Edges, Ladies of Service (open to female identifying students).

Athletics ***Intramural sports:*** fencing M/W.

Campus security: 24-hour emergency response devices and patrols, crime prevention workshops and seminars.

Student services: health clinic, personal/psychological counseling.

COSTS & FINANCIAL AID

Costs (2017–18) ***Comprehensive fee:*** $58,810 includes full-time tuition ($43,100) and room and board ($15,710). Part-time tuition: $1795 per credit hour. Part-time tuition and fees vary according to course load. ***College room only:*** $10,150. Room and board charges vary according to board plan and housing facility. ***Payment plan:*** installment. ***Waivers:*** children of alumni and employees or children of employees.

Financial Aid In 2002, 561 non-need-based awards were made. ***Average percent of need met:*** 65. ***Average financial aid package:*** $16,500. ***Average indebtedness upon graduation:*** $17,000.

APPLYING

Standardized Tests *Required:* SAT or ACT (for admission).

Options: electronic application, deferred entrance.

Application fee: $60.

Required: essay or personal statement, high school transcript, 1 letter of recommendation. ***Required for some:*** interview, audition or portfolio required for performing arts programs; portfolio for design, visual arts, film programs. ***Recommended:*** minimum 2.0 GPA, interview.

COLLEGES AT-A-GLANCE

Application deadlines: rolling (freshmen), rolling (out-of-state freshmen), rolling (transfers).

Notification: continuous (freshmen), continuous (out-of-state freshmen), continuous (transfers).

CONTACT

Ms. Liz Gensemer, Assistant Director, Admissions, The University of the Arts, 320 South Broad Street, Philadelphia, PA 19102-4944. *Phone:* 215-717-6041. *Toll-free phone:* 800-616-ARTS. *Fax:* 215-717-6045. *E-mail:* admissions@uarts.edu.

University of the Sciences

Philadelphia, Pennsylvania

http://www.usciences.edu/

- **Independent** university, founded 1821
- **Urban** 35-acre campus with easy access to Philadelphia
- **Endowment** $174.5 million
- **Coed**
- **Moderately difficult** entrance level

FACULTY

Student/faculty ratio: 9:1.

ACADEMICS

Calendar: semesters. *Degrees:* certificates, bachelor's, master's, doctoral, and postbachelor's certificates.

Library: Joseph W. England Library.

STUDENT LIFE

Housing options: on-campus residence required through sophomore year; coed. Campus housing is university owned and leased by the school. Freshman campus housing is guaranteed.

Activities and organizations: drama/theater group, student-run newspaper, choral group, Student Government Association, Hillel: Jewish Student Association, Pre-Medical Society, Society of Physics Students, American Chemical Society, national fraternities, national sororities.

Athletics Member NCAA, NAIA. All NCAA Division II.

Campus security: 24-hour emergency response devices and patrols, late-night transport/escort service, controlled dormitory access.

Student services: health clinic, personal/psychological counseling.

COSTS & FINANCIAL AID

Costs (2016–17) ***Comprehensive fee:*** $54,038 includes full-time tuition ($36,962), mandatory fees ($1888), and room and board ($15,188). Full-time tuition and fees vary according to program and student level. Part-time tuition: $1540 per contact hour. ***College room only:*** $9280. Room and board charges vary according to board plan and housing facility.

Financial Aid Of all full-time matriculated undergraduates who enrolled in 2014, 1,422 applied for aid, 1,324 were judged to have need, 523 had their need fully met. In 2014, 171 non-need-based awards were made. ***Average percent of need met:*** 30. ***Average financial aid package:*** $29,235. ***Average need-based loan:*** $5083. ***Average need-based gift aid:*** $9565. ***Average non-need-based aid:*** $14,098.

APPLYING

Standardized Tests *Required:* SAT or ACT (for admission). *Required for some:* TOEFL or IELTS for non-English as first language applicants.

Options: electronic application, deferred entrance.

Application fee: $45.

Required: essay or personal statement, high school transcript, minimum 3.0 GPA, 1 letter of recommendation. ***Required for some:*** interview.

CONTACT

Executive Director of Admission and Enrollment Services, University of the Sciences, 600 South 43rd Street, Philadelphia, PA 19104-4495. *Phone:* 888-996-8747. *Toll-free phone:* 888-996-8747. *Fax:* 215-596-8821. *E-mail:* admit@usciences.edu.

University of Valley Forge

Phoenixville, Pennsylvania

http://www.valleyforge.edu/

- **Independent Assemblies of God** comprehensive, founded 1939
- **Small-town** 150-acre campus with easy access to Philadelphia
- **Endowment** $1.9 million
- **Coed** 810 undergraduate students, 77% full-time, 52% women, 48% men
- **Minimally difficult** entrance level, 79% of applicants were admitted

UNDERGRAD STUDENTS

625 full-time, 185 part-time. Students come from 35 states and territories; 1 other country; 56% are from out of state; 16% Black or African American, non-Hispanic/Latino; 17% Hispanic/Latino; 1% Asian, non-Hispanic/Latino; 0.1% Native Hawaiian or other Pacific Islander, non-Hispanic/Latino; 0.4% American Indian or Alaska Native, non-Hispanic/Latino; 4% Two or more races, non-Hispanic/Latino; 6% Race/ethnicity unknown; 0.2% international; 8% transferred in; 89% live on campus.

Freshmen:

Admission: 465 applied, 366 admitted, 139 enrolled. ***Average high school GPA:*** 2.96.

Retention: 76% of full-time freshmen returned.

FACULTY

Total: 115, 30% full-time, 33% with terminal degrees.

Student/faculty ratio: 13:1.

ACADEMICS

Calendar: semesters. *Degrees:* associate, bachelor's, and master's.

Special study options: academic remediation for entering students, accelerated degree program, adult/continuing education programs, advanced placement credit, distance learning, double majors, external degree program, honors programs, independent study, internships, part-time degree program, services for LD students, study abroad, summer session for credit.

Computers: 64 computers/terminals and 3,000 ports are available on campus for general student use. Students can access the following: campus intranet, computer help desk, free student e-mail accounts, online (class) grades, online (class) registration, online (class) schedules. Campuswide network is available. 100% of college-owned or -operated housing units are wired for high-speed Internet access. Wireless service is available via entire campus.

Library: Storms Research Center. *Books:* 65,000 (physical), 280,000 (digital/electronic); *Serial titles:* 44 (physical), 110,000 (digital/electronic); *Databases:* 47. Weekly public service hours: 85; students can reserve study rooms.

STUDENT LIFE

Housing options: on-campus residence required through senior year; men-only, women-only. Campus housing is university owned. Freshman campus housing is guaranteed.

Activities and organizations: drama/theater group, choral group, Homeless Ministry, The Art Of, Noteworthy, Inspire India, Audience of One.

Athletics Member NCAA, NCCAA. All NCAA Division III. ***Intercollegiate sports:*** baseball M, basketball M/W, cross-country running M/W, golf M, soccer M/W, softball W, volleyball W. ***Intramural sports:*** basketball M/W, soccer M/W, softball M/W, ultimate Frisbee M/W.

Campus security: 24-hour emergency response devices and patrols, student patrols, late-night transport/escort service, controlled dormitory access.

Student services: health clinic, personal/psychological counseling.

COSTS & FINANCIAL AID

Costs (2017–18) ***Comprehensive fee:*** $29,880 includes full-time tuition ($19,820), mandatory fees ($1450), and room and board ($8610). Full-time tuition and fees vary according to course load and location. Part-time tuition: $744 per credit hour. Part-time tuition and fees vary according to course load and location. ***Required fees:*** $250 per semester part-time. ***College room only:*** $4212. Room and board charges vary according to board plan, housing facility, and location. ***Payment plan:*** installment. ***Waivers:*** senior citizens and employees or children of employees.

Financial Aid Of all full-time matriculated undergraduates who enrolled in 2016, 640 applied for aid, 583 were judged to have need, 69 had their need fully met. 18 Federal Work-Study jobs (averaging $2671). In 2016, 64 non-need-based awards were made. ***Average percent of need met:*** 56. ***Average financial aid package:*** $13,961. ***Average need-based loan:*** $4059. ***Average need-based gift aid:*** $10,584. ***Average non-need-based aid:*** $8222. ***Average indebtedness upon graduation:*** $34,920.

APPLYING
Standardized Tests *Recommended:* SAT or ACT (for admission).

Options: electronic application, deferred entrance.

Application fee: $25.

Required: essay or personal statement, high school transcript. ***Required for some:*** interview. ***Recommended:*** minimum 2.0 GPA.

Application deadlines: 8/1 (freshmen), 8/1 (transfers).

Notification: continuous (freshmen), continuous (transfers).

CONTACT
Mr. Mark S. Cernero II, Director of Admissions, University of Valley Forge, 1401 Charlestown Road, Phoenixville, PA 19460. *Phone:* 610-935-0450 Ext. 1430. *Toll-free phone:* 800-432-8322. *Fax:* 610-917-2069. *E-mail:* admissions@valleyforge.edu.

Ursinus College

Collegeville, Pennsylvania

http://www.ursinus.edu/

- **Independent** 4-year, founded 1869
- **Suburban** 170-acre campus with easy access to Philadelphia
- **Endowment** $137.0 million
- **Coed** 1,556 undergraduate students, 99% full-time, 53% women, 47% men
- **Moderately difficult** entrance level, 82% of applicants were admitted

UNDERGRAD STUDENTS
1,542 full-time, 14 part-time. Students come from 35 states and territories; 23 other countries; 44% are from out of state; 6% Black or African American, non-Hispanic/Latino; 7% Hispanic/Latino; 4% Asian, non-Hispanic/Latino; 0.1% American Indian or Alaska Native, non-Hispanic/Latino; 4% Two or more races, non-Hispanic/Latino; 2% Race/ethnicity unknown; 2% international; 1% transferred in; 96% live on campus.

Freshmen:
Admission: 2,491 applied, 2,053 admitted, 382 enrolled. ***Average high school GPA:*** 3.21. ***Test scores:*** SAT critical reading scores over 500: 82%; SAT math scores over 500: 83%; SAT writing scores over 500: 83%; ACT scores over 18: 96%; SAT critical reading scores over 600: 44%; SAT math scores over 600: 44%; SAT writing scores over 600: 35%; ACT scores over 24: 73%; SAT critical reading scores over 700: 10%; SAT math scores over 700: 10%; SAT writing scores over 700: 8%; ACT scores over 30: 21%.

Retention: 84% of full-time freshmen returned.

FACULTY
Total: 181, 67% full-time, 77% with terminal degrees.

Student/faculty ratio: 11:1.

ACADEMICS
Calendar: semesters. *Degree:* bachelor's.

Special study options: advanced placement credit, cooperative education, double majors, English as a second language, honors programs, independent study, internships, off-campus study, services for LD students, student-designed majors, study abroad.

Unusual degree programs: 3-2 engineering with Columbia University.

Computers: Students can access the following: campus intranet, computer help desk, free student e-mail accounts, online (class) grades, online (class) registration, online (class) schedules. Campuswide network is available. 100% of college-owned or -operated housing units are wired for high-speed Internet access. Wireless service is available via entire campus.

Library: Myrin Library. *Books:* 186,419 (physical), 120,298 (digital/electronic); *Serial titles:* 1,089 (physical), 21,302 (digital/electronic); *Databases:* 47. Weekly public service hours: 113.

STUDENT LIFE
Housing options: coed, men-only, women-only, special housing for students with disabilities. Campus housing is university owned. Freshman campus housing is guaranteed.

Activities and organizations: drama/theater group, student-run newspaper, radio and television station, choral group, Campus Activities Board, Men's Rugby, Women's Rugby, Ursinus College Student Government, Best Buddies, national fraternities, national sororities.

Athletics Member NCAA. All Division III. ***Intercollegiate sports:*** baseball M, basketball M/W, cross-country running M/W, field hockey W, football M, golf M/W, gymnastics W, lacrosse M/W, soccer M/W, softball W, swimming and diving M/W, tennis M/W, track and field M/W, volleyball W, wrestling M. ***Intramural sports:*** badminton M(c)/W(c), cheerleading M(c)/W(c), cross-country running M(c)/W(c), rugby M(c)/W(c), sand volleyball M(c)/W(c), soccer M(c)/W(c), ultimate Frisbee M(c)/W(c), volleyball M(c).

Campus security: 24-hour emergency response devices and patrols, student patrols, late-night transport/escort service, controlled dormitory access.

Student services: health clinic, personal/psychological counseling.

COSTS & FINANCIAL AID
Costs (2017–18) ***Comprehensive fee:*** $62,920 includes full-time tuition ($50,360) and room and board ($12,560). Part-time tuition: $1574 per credit hour. ***Waivers:*** employees or children of employees.

Financial Aid Of all full-time matriculated undergraduates who enrolled in 2016, 1,316 applied for aid, 1,183 were judged to have need, 321 had their need fully met. In 2016, 356 non-need-based awards were made. ***Average percent of need met:*** 83. ***Average financial aid package:*** $36,770. ***Average need-based loan:*** $4660. ***Average need-based gift aid:*** $34,028. ***Average non-need-based aid:*** $22,886. ***Average indebtedness upon graduation:*** $38,537. ***Financial aid deadline:*** 2/1.

APPLYING
Standardized Tests *Recommended:* SAT or ACT (for admission).

Options: electronic application, early decision, early action, deferred entrance.

Required: essay or personal statement, high school transcript, 1 letter of recommendation.

Application deadlines: rolling (freshmen), 11/1 (early action).

Early decision deadline: 12/1.

Notification: continuous (freshmen), continuous (transfers), 12/15 (early decision), 12/15 (early action).

CONTACT
Scott Myers, Director of Admission, Ursinus College, 601 E Main Street, Collegeville, PA 19426. *Phone:* 610-409-3200. *Fax:* 610-409-3197. *E-mail:* admissions@ursinus.edu.

Villanova University

Villanova, Pennsylvania

http://www.villanova.edu/

- **Independent Roman Catholic** comprehensive, founded 1842
- **Suburban** 254-acre campus with easy access to Philadelphia
- **Endowment** $552.0 million
- **Coed** 6,999 undergraduate students, 93% full-time, 53% women, 47% men
- **Very difficult** entrance level, 44% of applicants were admitted

UNDERGRAD STUDENTS
6,490 full-time, 509 part-time. Students come from 52 states and territories; 49 other countries; 78% are from out of state; 5% Black or African American, non-Hispanic/Latino; 7% Hispanic/Latino; 7% Asian, non-Hispanic/Latino; 2% Two or more races, non-Hispanic/Latino; 2% Race/ethnicity unknown; 2% international; 3% transferred in; 66% live on campus.

Freshmen:
Admission: 17,272 applied, 7,514 admitted, 1,678 enrolled. ***Average high school GPA:*** 4.02. ***Test scores:*** SAT critical reading scores over 500: 97%; SAT math scores over 500: 98%; SAT writing scores over 500: 96%; ACT scores over 18: 100%; SAT critical reading scores over 600: 78%; SAT math scores over 600: 83%; SAT writing scores over 600: 76%; ACT

scores over 24: 98%; SAT critical reading scores over 700: 26%; SAT math scores over 700: 36%; SAT writing scores over 700: 25%; ACT scores over 30: 75%.

Retention: 95% of full-time freshmen returned.

FACULTY

Total: 1,037, 61% full-time, 64% with terminal degrees.

Student/faculty ratio: 12:1.

ACADEMICS

Calendar: semesters. *Degrees:* bachelor's, master's, doctoral, post-master's, and postbachelor's certificates.

Special study options: accelerated degree program, adult/continuing education programs, advanced placement credit, cooperative education, distance learning, double majors, English as a second language, external degree program, honors programs, independent study, internships, off-campus study, part-time degree program, services for LD students, study abroad, summer session for credit. ***ROTC:*** Army (b), Navy (b), Air Force (c).

Unusual degree programs: 3-2 engineering; arts/liberal studies, classical studies, communication, criminal justice, political science, psychology, Spanish, religious studies, computer science, biology, chemistry, mathematics, mathematics/applied statistics, human resources development, business information systems/software engineering.

Computers: 700 computers/terminals and 15,000 ports are available on campus for general student use. Students can access the following: campus intranet, computer help desk, free student e-mail accounts, online (class) grades, online (class) registration, online (class) schedules, learning management system with anti-plagiarism software, testing software, online faculty hours, videoconferencing, electronic portfolios, data vaulting/backup service, software. Campuswide network is available. 100% of college-owned or -operated housing units are wired for high-speed Internet access. Wireless service is available via classrooms, computer centers, computer labs, dorm rooms, learning centers, libraries, student centers.

Library: Falvey Memorial Library plus 1 other. Study areas open 24 hours, 5-7 days a week; students can reserve study rooms.

STUDENT LIFE

Housing options: coed, women-only, special housing for students with disabilities. Campus housing is university owned. Freshman campus housing is guaranteed.

Activities and organizations: drama/theater group, student-run newspaper, radio and television station, choral group, marching band, Blue Key Society, New Student Orientation Counselor Program, Special Olympics, Campus Activities Team, Student Government Association, national fraternities, national sororities.

Athletics Member NCAA. All Division I except football (Division I-AA). ***Intercollegiate sports:*** baseball M(s), basketball M(s)/W(s), cheerleading M/W, crew M(c)/W, cross-country running M(s)/W(s), equestrian sports W(c), field hockey W(s), golf M, ice hockey M(c)/W(c), lacrosse M(s)/W(s), sailing M(c)/W(c), skiing (downhill) M(c)/W(c), soccer M(s)/W(s), softball W(s), swimming and diving M/W(s), tennis M/W, track and field M(s)/W(s), volleyball M(c)/W(s), water polo M(c)/W. ***Intramural sports:*** badminton M(c)/W(c), baseball M(c), basketball M(c)/W(c), crew M(c), cross-country running M(c)/W(c), equestrian sports W(c), field hockey W(c), football M, golf M(c)/W(c), ice hockey M(c)/W(c), lacrosse M(c)/W(c), rugby M(c), sailing M(c)/W(c), skiing (downhill) M(c)/W(c), soccer M(c)/W(c), softball M/W, swimming and diving M(c)/W(c), tennis M(c)/W(c), ultimate Frisbee M(c)/W(c), volleyball M(c)/W(c), water polo M(c).

Campus security: 24-hour emergency response devices and patrols, late-night transport/escort service, controlled dormitory access, Nova Alert: email, text messaging for emergency situations.

Student services: health clinic, personal/psychological counseling.

COSTS & FINANCIAL AID

Costs (2016–17) ***Comprehensive fee:*** $62,373 includes full-time tuition ($48,610), mandatory fees ($670), and room and board ($13,093). Full-time tuition and fees vary according to degree level, location, and student level. Part-time tuition: $2701 per credit hour. Part-time tuition and fees vary according to class time, course load, degree level, location, and program. ***Required fees:*** $37 per credit hour part-time. ***Room and board:*** Room and board charges vary according to board plan and housing facility. ***Payment plan:*** installment. ***Waivers:*** senior citizens and employees or children of employees.

Financial Aid Of all full-time matriculated undergraduates who enrolled in 2016, 3,859 applied for aid, 3,135 were judged to have need, 514 had their need fully met. 2,149 Federal Work-Study jobs (averaging $2818). 35 state and other part-time jobs (averaging $2852). In 2016, 488 non-need-based awards were made. ***Average percent of need met:*** 79. ***Average financial aid package:*** $36,074. ***Average need-based loan:*** $5064. ***Average need-based gift aid:*** $30,497. ***Average non-need-based aid:*** $15,614. ***Average indebtedness upon graduation:*** $35,545. ***Financial aid deadline:*** 1/15.

APPLYING
Standardized Tests *Required:* SAT or ACT (for admission).

Options: electronic application, early admission, early action, deferred entrance.

Application fee: $80.

Required: essay or personal statement, high school transcript, 1 letter of recommendation.

Application deadlines: 1/15 (freshmen), 6/1 (transfers), 11/1 (early action).

Notification: 4/1 (freshmen), continuous (transfers), 12/20 (early action).

CONTACT
Mr. Michael Gaynor, Director of University Admission, Villanova University, 800 Lancaster Avenue, Villanova, PA 19085-1672. *Phone:* 610-519-4000. *Fax:* 610-519-6450. *E-mail:* gotovu@villanova.edu.

See previous page for display ad and page 1586 for the College Close-Up.

Washington & Jefferson College

Washington, Pennsylvania

http://www.washjeff.edu/

- **Independent** comprehensive, founded 1781
- **Suburban** 60-acre campus with easy access to Pittsburgh
- **Endowment** $132.1 million
- **Coed** 1,396 undergraduate students, 99% full-time, 49% women, 51% men
- **Very difficult** entrance level, 46% of applicants were admitted

UNDERGRAD STUDENTS
1,386 full-time, 10 part-time. Students come from 36 states and territories; 37 other countries; 22% are from out of state; 5% Black or African American, non-Hispanic/Latino; 3% Hispanic/Latino; 2% Asian, non-Hispanic/Latino; 0.1% Native Hawaiian or other Pacific Islander, non-Hispanic/Latino; 0.1% American Indian or Alaska Native, non-Hispanic/Latino; 3% Two or more races, non-Hispanic/Latino; 5% Race/ethnicity unknown; 5% international; 0.7% transferred in; 95% live on campus.

Freshmen:
Admission: 7,155 applied, 3,258 admitted, 429 enrolled. ***Average high school GPA:*** 3.66. ***Test scores:*** SAT critical reading scores over 500: 92%; SAT math scores over 500: 91%; SAT writing scores over 500: 58%; ACT scores over 18: 99%; SAT critical reading scores over 600: 40%; SAT math scores over 600: 44%; SAT writing scores over 600: 15%; ACT scores over 24: 77%; SAT critical reading scores over 700: 8%; SAT math scores over 700: 5%; SAT writing scores over 700: 2%; ACT scores over 30: 22%.

FACULTY
Total: 155, 72% full-time, 80% with terminal degrees.

Student/faculty ratio: 11:1.

ACADEMICS
Calendar: 4-1-4. *Degrees:* bachelor's, master's, and postbachelor's certificates.

Special study options: academic remediation for entering students, accelerated degree program, advanced placement credit, double majors, English as a second language, freshman honors college, honors programs, independent study, internships, off-campus study, part-time degree program, services for LD students, student-designed majors, study abroad, summer session for credit. ***ROTC:*** Army (b), Air Force (c).

Unusual degree programs: 3-2 engineering with Columbia University, Case Western Reserve University, Washington University in St. Louis.

Computers: 450 computers/terminals and 2,000 ports are available on campus for general student use. Students can access the following: campus intranet, computer help desk, free student e-mail accounts, online (class) grades, online (class) registration, online (class) schedules. Campuswide network is available. 100% of college-owned or -operated housing units are wired for high-speed Internet access. Wireless service is available via entire campus.

Library: U. Grant Miller Library plus 4 others. *Books:* 128,212 (physical), 6,368 (digital/electronic); *Serial titles:* 296 (physical), 46,374 (digital/electronic); *Databases:* 74. Weekly public service hours: 107.

STUDENT LIFE
Housing options: on-campus residence required through senior year; coed, men-only, women-only, special housing for students with disabilities. Campus housing is university owned. Freshman campus housing is guaranteed.

Activities and organizations: drama/theater group, student-run newspaper, radio station, choral group, Student Government Association, Student Activities Board, Black Student Union, Asian Culture Association, Student Christian Association, national fraternities, national sororities.

Athletics Member NCAA. All Division III. ***Intercollegiate sports:*** baseball M, basketball M/W, cheerleading M(c)/W(c), cross-country running M/W, equestrian sports M(c)/W(c), field hockey W, football M, golf M/W, ice hockey M(c), lacrosse M/W, rugby M(c)/W(c), soccer M/W, softball W, swimming and diving M/W, tennis M/W, track and field M/W, ultimate Frisbee M(c)/W(c), volleyball M(c)/W, water polo M/W, wrestling M. ***Intramural sports:*** basketball M/W, fencing M/W, soccer M/W, softball M/W, tennis M/W, triathlon M/W, volleyball M/W.

Campus security: 24-hour emergency response devices and patrols, late-night transport/escort service, controlled dormitory access, blue light emergency phones, security cameras monitored 24/7 throughout campus.

Student services: health clinic, personal/psychological counseling, women's center.

COSTS & FINANCIAL AID
Costs (2016–17) ***Comprehensive fee:*** $56,754 includes full-time tuition ($44,320), mandatory fees ($580), and room and board ($11,854). Full-time tuition and fees vary according to reciprocity agreements. Part-time tuition: $1113 per credit hour. Part-time tuition and fees vary according to course load. ***College room only:*** $6956. Room and board charges vary according to board plan and housing facility. ***Payment plans:*** tuition prepayment, installment. ***Waivers:*** employees or children of employees.

Financial Aid Of all full-time matriculated undergraduates who enrolled in 2016, 1,187 applied for aid, 1,078 were judged to have need, 175 had their need fully met. 594 Federal Work-Study jobs (averaging $1568). 130 state and other part-time jobs (averaging $1000). In 2016, 267 non-need-based awards were made. ***Average percent of need met:*** 80. ***Average financial aid package:*** $34,948. ***Average need-based loan:*** $4517. ***Average need-based gift aid:*** $13,627. ***Average non-need-based aid:*** $19,612.

APPLYING
Options: electronic application, early admission, early decision, early action, deferred entrance.

Application fee: $25.

Required: essay or personal statement, high school transcript, 1 letter of recommendation. ***Required for some:*** interview. ***Recommended:*** interview.

Application deadlines: 3/1 (freshmen), 1/15 (early action).

Early decision deadline: 12/1.

Notification: 4/1 (freshmen), 12/15 (early decision), 2/15 (early action).

CONTACT
Mr. Robert J. Gould, Vice President for Enrollment, Washington & Jefferson College, 60 South Lincoln Street, Washington, PA 15301. *Phone:* 724-223-6025. *Toll-free phone:* 888-WANDJAY. *Fax:* 724-223-6534. *E-mail:* admission@washjeff.edu.

Waynesburg University

Waynesburg, Pennsylvania

http://www.waynesburg.edu/

- **Independent** comprehensive, founded 1849, affiliated with Presbyterian Church (U.S.A.)
- **Small-town** 30-acre campus with easy access to Pittsburgh
- **Coed** 1,400 undergraduate students, 95% full-time, 59% women, 41% men
- **Moderately difficult** entrance level, 94% of applicants were admitted

UNDERGRAD STUDENTS

1,332 full-time, 68 part-time. Students come from 31 states and territories; 2 other countries; 17% are from out of state; 4% Black or African American, non-Hispanic/Latino; 2% Hispanic/Latino; 0.5% Asian, non-Hispanic/Latino; 3% Two or more races, non-Hispanic/Latino; 0.6% Race/ethnicity unknown; 0.2% international; 2% transferred in; 74% live on campus.

Freshmen:
Admission: 1,478 applied, 1,385 admitted, 401 enrolled.
Average high school GPA: 3.52.
Retention: 77% of full-time freshmen returned.

FACULTY

Total: 234, 34% full-time, 39% with terminal degrees.

Student/faculty ratio: 12:1.

ACADEMICS

Calendar: semesters. *Degrees:* bachelor's, master's, and doctoral.

Special study options: accelerated degree program, adult/continuing education programs, advanced placement credit, distance learning, double majors, honors programs, independent study, internships, part-time degree program, services for LD students, study abroad, summer session for credit. ***ROTC:*** Army (c).

Unusual degree programs: 3-2 engineering with Penn State University Park.

Computers: 150 computers/terminals are available on campus for general student use. Students can access the following: campus intranet, computer help desk, free student e-mail accounts, online (class) grades, online (class) registration, online (class) schedules. Campuswide network is available. 100% of college-owned or -operated housing units are wired for high-speed Internet access. Wireless service is available via classrooms, computer labs, libraries.

Library: Eberly Library. *Books:* 85,861 (physical), 133,921 (digital/electronic); *Serial titles:* 7,083 (physical); *Databases:* 62.

STUDENT LIFE

Housing options: on-campus residence required through junior year; men-only, women-only, special housing for students with disabilities. Campus housing is university owned. Freshman campus housing is guaranteed.

Activities and organizations: drama/theater group, student-run newspaper, radio and television station, choral group, Student-Pennsylvania State Education Association, Lamplighter Choir, Student Nurses Association, Christian Fellowship.

Athletics Member NCAA. All Division III. ***Intercollegiate sports:*** baseball M, basketball M/W, cross-country running M/W, football M, golf M/W, lacrosse W, soccer M/W, softball W, tennis M/W, track and field M/W, volleyball W, wrestling M. ***Intramural sports:*** basketball M/W, bowling M/W, racquetball M/W, softball M/W, table tennis M/W, volleyball M/W.

Campus security: 24-hour emergency response devices and patrols, late-night transport/escort service, controlled dormitory access.

Student services: health clinic, personal/psychological counseling.

COSTS & FINANCIAL AID

Costs (2016–17) ***Comprehensive fee:*** $32,290 includes full-time tuition ($22,380), mandatory fees ($420), and room and board ($9490). Full-time tuition and fees vary according to class time. Part-time tuition: $930 per credit hour. Part-time tuition and fees vary according to class time, course load, and location. ***Required fees:*** $16 per credit hour part-time. ***College room only:*** $4800. Room and board charges vary according to board plan and housing facility. ***Payment plan:*** installment. ***Waivers:*** employees or children of employees.

Financial Aid Of all full-time matriculated undergraduates who enrolled in 2016, 1,255 applied for aid, 1,115 were judged to have need, 365 had their need fully met. 600 Federal Work-Study jobs (averaging $1500). In 2016, 206 non-need-based awards were made. ***Average percent of need met:*** 80. ***Average financial aid package:*** $18,776. ***Average need-based loan:*** $5114. ***Average need-based gift aid:*** $14,082. ***Average non-need-based aid:*** $10,885. ***Average indebtedness upon graduation:*** $30,850.

APPLYING

Standardized Tests *Required:* SAT or ACT (for admission).

Options: electronic application, early admission.

Application fee: $20.

Required: high school transcript, minimum 2.8 GPA. ***Required for some:*** essay or personal statement, 2 letters of recommendation. ***Recommended:*** minimum 3.0 GPA, interview.

Application deadlines: rolling (freshmen), rolling (transfers).

Notification: continuous (freshmen), continuous (transfers).

CONTACT

Mrs. Jacqueline Palko, Director of Admissions, Waynesburg University, 51 West College Street, Waynesburg, PA 15370. *Phone:* 724-852-3216. *Toll-free phone:* 800-225-7393. *Fax:* 724-627-8124.
E-mail: admissions@waynesburg.edu.

West Chester University of Pennsylvania

West Chester, Pennsylvania

http://www.wcupa.edu/

- **State-supported** comprehensive, founded 1871, part of Pennsylvania State System of Higher Education
- **Suburban** 409-acre campus with easy access to Philadelphia
- **Endowment** $21.0 million
- **Coed** 14,398 undergraduate students, 89% full-time, 59% women, 41% men
- **Moderately difficult** entrance level, 64% of applicants were admitted

UNDERGRAD STUDENTS

12,824 full-time, 1,574 part-time. Students come from 31 states and territories; 74 other countries; 12% are from out of state; 11% Black or African American, non-Hispanic/Latino; 5% Hispanic/Latino; 2% Asian, non-Hispanic/Latino; 0.1% Native Hawaiian or other Pacific Islander, non-Hispanic/Latino; 0.1% American Indian or Alaska Native, non-Hispanic/Latino; 3% Two or more races, non-Hispanic/Latino; 0.7% Race/ethnicity unknown; 0.5% international; 10% transferred in; 40% live on campus.

Freshmen:
Admission: 12,609 applied, 8,127 admitted, 2,454 enrolled. ***Average high school GPA:*** 3.44. ***Test scores:*** SAT critical reading scores over 500: 66%; SAT math scores over 500: 70%; SAT writing scores over 500: 61%; ACT scores over 18: 95%; SAT critical reading scores over 600: 15%; SAT math scores over 600: 18%; SAT writing scores over 600: 13%; ACT scores over 24: 45%; SAT critical reading scores over 700: 2%; SAT math scores over 700: 1%; SAT writing scores over 700: 1%; ACT scores over 30: 4%.
Retention: 86% of full-time freshmen returned.

ACADEMICS

Calendar: semesters. *Degrees:* bachelor's, master's, doctoral, and postbachelor's certificates.

Special study options: academic remediation for entering students, accelerated degree program, adult/continuing education programs, advanced placement credit, distance learning, double majors, English as a second language, freshman honors college, honors programs, independent study, internships, off-campus study, part-time degree program, services for LD students, student-designed majors, study abroad, summer session for credit. ***ROTC:*** Army (b), Air Force (c).

Unusual degree programs: 3-2 engineering with Pennsylvania State University, Philadelphia University.

Computers: 2,500 computers/terminals are available on campus for general student use. Students can access the following: campus intranet, computer help desk, free student e-mail accounts, online (class) grades, online (class) registration, online (class) schedules, virtual software.

Campuswide network is available. 100% of college-owned or -operated housing units are wired for high-speed Internet access. Wireless service is available via entire campus.
Library: Francis Harvey Green Library plus 1 other. *Books:* 734,356 (physical), 1.0 million (digital/electronic); *Serial titles:* 2,066 (physical), 100,390 (digital/electronic); *Databases:* 314. Weekly public service hours: 107.

STUDENT LIFE
Housing options: coed, special housing for students with disabilities. Campus housing is university owned and is provided by a third party. Freshman applicants given priority for college housing.

Activities and organizations: drama/theater group, student-run newspaper, radio and television station, choral group, marching band, Student Government Association, Residence Hall Association, Inter-Greek Council, Sports Club Council, CRU, national fraternities, national sororities.

Athletics Member NCAA. All Division II. ***Intercollegiate sports:*** baseball M(s), basketball M(s)/W(s), bowling M(c)/W(c), cheerleading W, cross-country running M(s)/W(s), equestrian sports M(c)/W(c), fencing M(c)/W(c), field hockey W(s), football M(s), golf M(s)/W(s), gymnastics W(s), ice hockey M(c)/W(c), lacrosse M(c)/W(s), rugby M(c)/W(s), skiing (downhill) M(c)/W(c), soccer M(s)/W(s), softball W(s), swimming and diving M(s)/W(s), tennis M(s)/W(s), track and field M(s)/W(s), ultimate Frisbee M(c), volleyball M(c)/W(s), water polo M(c)/W(c), wrestling M(c). ***Intramural sports:*** badminton M/W, basketball M/W, football M/W, racquetball M/W, rock climbing M/W, soccer M/W, softball M/W, squash M/W, table tennis M/W, tennis M/W, volleyball M/W.

Campus security: 24-hour emergency response devices and patrols, late-night transport/escort service, controlled dormitory access, camera systems in campus residence halls, recreational and classroom facilities and outdoor areas.

Student services: health clinic, personal/psychological counseling, women's center, legal services.

COSTS & FINANCIAL AID
Costs (2016–17) ***Tuition:*** state resident $7238 full-time, $302 per credit hour part-time; nonresident $18,096 full-time, $754 per credit hour part-time. Full-time tuition and fees vary according to course load and location. Part-time tuition and fees vary according to course load and location. ***Required fees:*** $2482 full-time, $103 per credit hour part-time. ***Room and board:*** $8736; room only: $5276. Room and board charges vary according to board plan and housing facility. ***Payment plan:*** installment. ***Waivers:*** senior citizens and employees or children of employees.

Financial Aid Of all full-time matriculated undergraduates who enrolled in 2015, 10,042 applied for aid, 7,547 were judged to have need, 714 had their need fully met. 286 Federal Work-Study jobs (averaging $1571). In 2015, 211 non-need-based awards were made. ***Average percent of need met:*** 48. ***Average financial aid package:*** $7871. ***Average need-based loan:*** $4133. ***Average need-based gift aid:*** $5587. ***Average non-need-based aid:*** $4180. ***Average indebtedness upon graduation:*** $33,814.

APPLYING
Standardized Tests *Required:* SAT or ACT (for admission).

Options: electronic application.

Application fee: $45.

Required: essay or personal statement, high school transcript. ***Required for some:*** interview. ***Recommended:*** minimum 3.0 GPA.

Application deadlines: rolling (freshmen), rolling (transfers).

Notification: continuous (freshmen), continuous (transfers).

CONTACT
West Chester University of Pennsylvania, University Avenue and High Street, West Chester, PA 19383. *Phone:* 610-436-3414. *Toll-free phone:* 877-315-2165.

Westminster College
New Wilmington, Pennsylvania
http://www.westminster.edu/

- **Independent** comprehensive, founded 1852, affiliated with Presbyterian Church (U.S.A.)
- **Small-town** 350-acre campus with easy access to Pittsburgh
- **Endowment** $110.1 million
- **Coed** 1,168 undergraduate students, 98% full-time, 54% women, 46% men
- **Moderately difficult** entrance level, 91% of applicants were admitted

UNDERGRAD STUDENTS
1,148 full-time, 20 part-time. Students come from 18 states and territories; 1 other country; 27% are from out of state; 5% Black or African American, non-Hispanic/Latino; 1% Hispanic/Latino; 1% Asian, non-Hispanic/Latino; 0.3% American Indian or Alaska Native, non-Hispanic/Latino; 2% Two or more races, non-Hispanic/Latino; 18% Race/ethnicity unknown; 0.6% international; 2% transferred in; 75% live on campus.

Freshmen:
Admission: 2,125 applied, 1,937 admitted, 371 enrolled. ***Average high school GPA:*** 3.53. ***Test scores:*** SAT critical reading scores over 500: 55%; SAT math scores over 500: 60%; SAT writing scores over 500: 54%; ACT scores over 18: 90%; SAT critical reading scores over 600: 19%; SAT math scores over 600: 15%; SAT writing scores over 600: 13%; ACT scores over 24: 44%; SAT critical reading scores over 700: 1%; SAT math scores over 700: 1%; SAT writing scores over 700: 1%; ACT scores over 30: 10%.

Retention: 83% of full-time freshmen returned.

FACULTY
Total: 145, 62% full-time, 65% with terminal degrees.
Student/faculty ratio: 11:1.

ACADEMICS
Calendar: semesters. *Degrees:* bachelor's and master's.

Special study options: adult/continuing education programs, advanced placement credit, distance learning, double majors, honors programs, independent study, internships, off-campus study, part-time degree program, services for LD students, student-designed majors, study abroad, summer session for credit. ***ROTC:*** Army (c).

Unusual degree programs: 3-2 engineering with Penn State University Park, Washington University in St. Louis, Case Western Reserve University.

Computers: 144 computers/terminals and 1,175 ports are available on campus for general student use. Students can access the following: campus intranet, computer help desk, free student e-mail accounts, online (class) grades, online (class) registration, online (class) schedules. Campuswide network is available. 100% of college-owned or -operated housing units are wired for high-speed Internet access. Wireless service is available via entire campus.
Library: McGill Memorial Library plus 1 other. *Books:* 160,296 (physical), 771,138 (digital/electronic); *Serial titles:* 89 (physical), 30,100 (digital/electronic); *Databases:* 70. Weekly public service hours: 104; students can reserve study rooms.

STUDENT LIFE
Housing options: on-campus residence required through junior year; coed, men-only, women-only. Campus housing is university owned. Freshman campus housing is guaranteed.

Activities and organizations: drama/theater group, student-run newspaper, radio and television station, choral group, marching band, Student Government Association, Interfraternity Council/Panhellenic Council, Dance Theatre, Habitat for Humanity, Campus Programming Council, national fraternities, national sororities.

Athletics Member NCAA. All Division III. ***Intercollegiate sports:*** baseball M, basketball M/W, cross-country running M/W, equestrian sports M(c)/W(c), football M, golf M/W, ice hockey M(c), lacrosse M/W, rock climbing M(c)/W(c), skiing (downhill) M(c)/W(c), soccer M/W, softball W, swimming and diving M/W, tennis M/W, track and field M/W, ultimate Frisbee M(c)/W(c), volleyball W. ***Intramural sports:*** archery M/W, badminton M/W, basketball M/W, cross-country running M/W, football M, golf M/W, racquetball M/W, skiing (cross-country) M/W, skiing (downhill) M/W, softball M, swimming and diving M/W, tennis M/W, track and field W, volleyball W, weight lifting M/W.

Campus security: 24-hour emergency response devices and patrols, late-night transport/escort service, controlled dormitory access.

Student services: health clinic, personal/psychological counseling.

COSTS & FINANCIAL AID

Costs (2017–18) ***Comprehensive fee:*** $47,250 includes full-time tuition ($34,830), mandatory fees ($1400), and room and board ($11,020). Part-time tuition: $1125 per credit hour. ***Room and board:*** Room and board charges vary according to board plan and housing facility. ***Payment plan:*** installment. ***Waivers:*** employees or children of employees.

Financial Aid Of all full-time matriculated undergraduates who enrolled in 2015, 1,017 applied for aid, 943 were judged to have need, 196 had their need fully met. 292 Federal Work-Study jobs (averaging $1671). 80 state and other part-time jobs (averaging $1563). In 2015, 176 non-need-based awards were made. ***Average percent of need met:*** 83. ***Average financial aid package:*** $28,042. ***Average need-based loan:*** $4600. ***Average need-based gift aid:*** $23,612. ***Average non-need-based aid:*** $17,887. ***Average indebtedness upon graduation:*** $36,692.

APPLYING

Standardized Tests *Required:* SAT or ACT (for admission).

Options: electronic application, deferred entrance.

Application fee: $35.

Required: essay or personal statement, high school transcript, minimum 2.0 GPA, 2 letters of recommendation. ***Recommended:*** minimum 3.0 GPA, interview.

Application deadlines: 5/1 (freshmen), rolling (transfers).

Notification: continuous (freshmen), continuous (transfers).

CONTACT

Dr. Thomas H. Stein, Vice President for Enrollment Management, Westminster College, Remick House, 319 S. Market Street, New Wilmington, PA 16172. *Phone:* 724-946-7105. *Toll-free phone:* 800-942-8033. *Fax:* 724-946-7171. *E-mail:* steinth@westminster.edu.

Widener University

Chester, Pennsylvania

http://www.widener.edu/

- **Independent** comprehensive, founded 1821
- **Suburban** 110-acre campus with easy access to Philadelphia
- **Endowment** $86.8 million
- **Coed** 3,591 undergraduate students, 83% full-time, 56% women, 44% men
- **Moderately difficult** entrance level, 70% of applicants were admitted

UNDERGRAD STUDENTS

2,978 full-time, 613 part-time. 43% are from out of state; 11% Black or African American, non-Hispanic/Latino; 5% Hispanic/Latino; 4% Asian, non-Hispanic/Latino; 0.3% American Indian or Alaska Native, non-Hispanic/Latino; 3% Two or more races, non-Hispanic/Latino; 2% Race/ethnicity unknown; 4% international; 3% transferred in; 58% live on campus.

Freshmen:

Admission: 5,175 applied, 3,608 admitted, 729 enrolled. ***Average high school GPA:*** 3.52. ***Test scores:*** SAT critical reading scores over 500: 46%; SAT math scores over 500: 56%; ACT scores over 18: 94%; SAT critical reading scores over 600: 9%; SAT math scores over 600: 16%; ACT scores over 24: 50%; SAT critical reading scores over 700: 1%; SAT math scores over 700: 1%; ACT scores over 30: 6%.

Retention: 82% of full-time freshmen returned.

FACULTY

Total: 611, 46% full-time, 60% with terminal degrees.

Student/faculty ratio: 13:1.

ACADEMICS

Calendar: semesters. *Degrees:* associate, bachelor's, master's, doctoral, and post-master's certificates.

Special study options: academic remediation for entering students, accelerated degree program, adult/continuing education programs, advanced placement credit, cooperative education, distance learning, double majors, English as a second language, honors programs, independent study, internships, off-campus study, part-time degree program, services for LD students, student-designed majors, study abroad, summer session for credit. ***ROTC:*** Army (b), Navy (c), Air Force (c).

Unusual degree programs: 3-2 business administration; engineering; social work; physical therapy, education.

Computers: 710 computers/terminals are available on campus for general student use. Students can access the following: campus intranet, computer help desk, free student e-mail accounts, online (class) grades, online (class) registration, online (class) schedules. Campuswide network is available. 100% of college-owned or -operated housing units are wired for high-speed Internet access. Wireless service is available via classrooms, computer centers, computer labs, dorm rooms, learning centers, libraries, student centers.

Library: Wolfgram Memorial Library.

STUDENT LIFE

Housing options: on-campus residence required through junior year; coed, men-only, women-only, cooperative. Campus housing is university owned. Freshman campus housing is guaranteed.

Activities and organizations: drama/theater group, student-run television station, choral group, marching band, national fraternities, national sororities.

Athletics Member NCAA. All Division III. ***Intercollegiate sports:*** baseball M, basketball M/W, cheerleading W, cross-country running M/W, field hockey W, football M, golf M, lacrosse M/W, soccer M/W, softball W, swimming and diving M/W, track and field M/W, volleyball W. ***Intramural sports:*** crew M, ice hockey M(c), rock climbing M(c)/W(c), rugby M(c), skiing (downhill) M(c)/W(c), soccer M, volleyball M(c).

Campus security: 24-hour emergency response devices and patrols, late-night transport/escort service, controlled dormitory access.

Student services: health clinic, personal/psychological counseling.

COSTS & FINANCIAL AID

Costs (2016–17) ***Comprehensive fee:*** $56,486 includes full-time tuition ($42,034), mandatory fees ($836), and room and board ($13,616). Full-time tuition and fees vary according to class time, course load, and program. Part-time tuition: $1400 per credit. ***College room only:*** $7088. Room and board charges vary according to board plan and housing facility. ***Payment plan:*** installment. ***Waivers:*** senior citizens and employees or children of employees.

Financial Aid Of all full-time matriculated undergraduates who enrolled in 2016, 2,593 applied for aid, 2,343 were judged to have need, 521 had their need fully met. 1,565 Federal Work-Study jobs (averaging $1960). In 2016, 216 non-need-based awards were made. ***Average percent of need met:*** 80. ***Average financial aid package:*** $32,580. ***Average need-based loan:*** $4680. ***Average need-based gift aid:*** $26,700. ***Average non-need-based aid:*** $23,800.

APPLYING

Standardized Tests *Required:* SAT or ACT (for admission).

Options: electronic application, deferred entrance.

Required: essay or personal statement, high school transcript. ***Required for some:*** minimum 2.9 GPA. ***Recommended:*** interview.

Application deadlines: rolling (freshmen), rolling (transfers).

Notification: continuous (freshmen), continuous (transfers).

CONTACT

Office of Admissions, Widener University, One University Place, Chester, PA 19013. *Phone:* 610-499-4126. *Toll-free phone:* 888-WIDENER. *Fax:* 610-499-4676. *E-mail:* admissions.office@widener.edu.

Wilkes University

Wilkes-Barre, Pennsylvania

http://www.wilkes.edu/

- **Independent** comprehensive, founded 1933
- **Urban** 25-acre campus
- **Endowment** $40.6 million
- **Coed** 2,561 undergraduate students, 90% full-time, 48% women, 52% men
- **Moderately difficult** entrance level, 76% of applicants were admitted

UNDERGRAD STUDENTS
2,303 full-time, 258 part-time. Students come from 25 states and territories; 10 other countries; 19% are from out of state; 5% Black or African American, non-Hispanic/Latino; 7% Hispanic/Latino; 3% Asian, non-Hispanic/Latino; 0.5% American Indian or Alaska Native, non-Hispanic/Latino; 3% Two or more races, non-Hispanic/Latino; 2% Race/ethnicity unknown; 8% international; 7% transferred in; 39% live on campus.

Freshmen:
Admission: 4,245 applied, 3,223 admitted, 664 enrolled. ***Average high school GPA:*** 3.52. ***Test scores:*** SAT critical reading scores over 500: 54%; SAT math scores over 500: 60%; SAT writing scores over 500: 44%; ACT scores over 18: 89%; SAT critical reading scores over 600: 14%; SAT math scores over 600: 21%; SAT writing scores over 600: 9%; ACT scores over 24: 42%; SAT critical reading scores over 700: 1%; SAT math scores over 700: 1%; ACT scores over 30: 4%.
Retention: 76% of full-time freshmen returned.

FACULTY
Total: 454, 40% full-time.
Student/faculty ratio: 14:1.

ACADEMICS
Calendar: semesters. *Degrees:* bachelor's, master's, and doctoral.
Special study options: academic remediation for entering students, accelerated degree program, adult/continuing education programs, advanced placement credit, cooperative education, distance learning, double majors, English as a second language, honors programs, independent study, internships, off-campus study, part-time degree program, services for LD students, student-designed majors, study abroad, summer session for credit. ***ROTC:*** Army (c), Air Force (b).
Computers: 817 computers/terminals are available on campus for general student use. Students can access the following: campus intranet, computer help desk, free student e-mail accounts, online (class) grades, online (class) registration, online (class) schedules. Campuswide network is available. Wireless service is available via libraries, student centers.
Library: Eugene S. Farley Library. *Books:* 168,516 (physical), 7,880 (digital/electronic); *Serial titles:* 55,000 (digital/electronic); *Databases:* 55. Students can reserve study rooms.

STUDENT LIFE
Housing options: on-campus residence required through sophomore year; coed, men-only, women-only. Campus housing is university owned. Freshman campus housing is guaranteed.
Activities and organizations: drama/theater group, student-run newspaper, radio and television station, choral group, marching band.
Athletics Member NCAA. All Division III. ***Intercollegiate sports:*** baseball M, basketball M/W, cross-country running M/W, field hockey W, football M, golf M/W, lacrosse M/W, soccer M/W, softball W, swimming and diving M/W, tennis M/W, volleyball M/W, wrestling M. ***Intramural sports:*** basketball M/W, bowling M/W, cheerleading W(c), cross-country running M(c)/W(c), football M, racquetball M(c)/W(c), rock climbing M(c)/W(c), skiing (downhill) M(c)/W(c), soccer M/W, softball M/W, ultimate Frisbee M(c)/W(c), volleyball M/W.
Campus security: 24-hour emergency response devices and patrols, late-night transport/escort service, controlled dormitory access.
Student services: health clinic, personal/psychological counseling.

COSTS & FINANCIAL AID
Costs (2016–17) ***Comprehensive fee:*** $47,314 includes full-time tuition ($31,946), mandatory fees ($1622), and room and board ($13,746). Part-time tuition: $887 per credit hour. ***Required fees:*** $72 per credit hour part-time. ***College room only:*** $8274. Room and board charges vary according to board plan and housing facility. ***Payment plans:*** installment, deferred payment. ***Waivers:*** employees or children of employees.
Financial Aid Of all full-time matriculated undergraduates who enrolled in 2016, 1,986 applied for aid, 1,841 were judged to have need, 193 had their need fully met. In 2016, 114 non-need-based awards were made. ***Average percent of need met:*** 69. ***Average financial aid package:*** $24,604. ***Average need-based loan:*** $4405. ***Average need-based gift aid:*** $20,242. ***Average non-need-based aid:*** $13,090. ***Average indebtedness upon graduation:*** $43,241.

APPLYING
Standardized Tests *Required:* SAT or ACT (for admission).

Options: electronic application, early admission, deferred entrance.
Application fee: $40.
Required: high school transcript. ***Recommended:*** interview.
Application deadlines: rolling (freshmen), rolling (transfers).
Notification: 8/30 (freshmen), continuous until 8/30 (transfers).

CONTACT
Brian Dalton, Vice President of Enrollment Services, Wilkes University, 84 West South Street, Wilkes-Barre, PA 18766. *Phone:* 570-408-4400. *Toll-free phone:* 800-945-5378 Ext. 4400. *Fax:* 570-408-4904. *E-mail:* admissions@wilkes.edu.

See previous page for display ad and page 1604 for the College Close-Up.

Wilson College

Chambersburg, Pennsylvania

http://www.wilson.edu/

- **Independent** comprehensive, founded 1869, affiliated with Presbyterian Church (U.S.A.)
- **Small-town** 300-acre campus
- **Endowment** $51.3 million
- **Coed, primarily women** 571 undergraduate students, 58% full-time, 88% women, 12% men
- **Moderately difficult** entrance level, 53% of applicants were admitted

UNDERGRAD STUDENTS
330 full-time, 241 part-time. Students come from 19 states and territories; 12 other countries; 23% are from out of state; 3% Black or African American, non-Hispanic/Latino; 3% Hispanic/Latino; 0.4% Asian, non-Hispanic/Latino; 0.2% American Indian or Alaska Native, non-Hispanic/Latino; 2% Two or more races, non-Hispanic/Latino; 18% Race/ethnicity unknown; 5% international; 3% transferred in; 66% live on campus.

Freshmen:
Admission: 450 applied, 237 admitted, 70 enrolled. ***Average high school GPA:*** 3.45. ***Test scores:*** SAT critical reading scores over 500: 53%; SAT math scores over 500: 56%; SAT writing scores over 500: 42%; SAT critical reading scores over 600: 15%; SAT math scores over 600: 10%; SAT writing scores over 600: 10%.
Retention: 53% of full-time freshmen returned.

FACULTY
Total: 94, 41% full-time, 51% with terminal degrees.
Student/faculty ratio: 8:1.

ACADEMICS
Calendar: 4-1-4. *Degrees:* associate, bachelor's, and master's.
Special study options: academic remediation for entering students, adult/continuing education programs, advanced placement credit, distance learning, double majors, honors programs, independent study, internships, off-campus study, part-time degree program, services for LD students, student-designed majors, study abroad, summer session for credit. ***ROTC:*** Army (c).
Computers: 96 computers/terminals and 1,200 ports are available on campus for general student use. Students can access the following: campus intranet, computer help desk, free student e-mail accounts, online (class) grades, online (class) registration, online (class) schedules, online databases. Campuswide network is available. 100% of college-owned or -operated housing units are wired for high-speed Internet access. Wireless service is available via entire campus.
Library: Stewart Library. Weekly public service hours: 88; students can reserve study rooms.

STUDENT LIFE
Housing options: on-campus residence required through junior year; women-only. Campus housing is university owned. Freshman campus housing is guaranteed.
Activities and organizations: drama/theater group, student-run newspaper, choral group, Muhibbah Club, Orchesis Club, student newspaper, Student Government, Campus Activity Board.
Athletics Member NCAA. All Division III. ***Intercollegiate sports:*** basketball M/W, cross-country running M/W, field hockey W, golf M, lacrosse W, soccer M/W, softball W, volleyball M. ***Intramural sports:*** archery W, baseball M, equestrian sports W, golf M, soccer M, tennis W, volleyball M.
Campus security: 24-hour emergency response devices and patrols, late-night transport/escort service, controlled dormitory access.
Student services: health clinic, personal/psychological counseling, women's center.

COSTS & FINANCIAL AID
Costs (2017–18) ***Comprehensive fee:*** $35,620 includes full-time tuition ($23,745), mandatory fees ($685), and room and board ($11,190). Full-time tuition and fees vary according to location and program. Part-time tuition: $792 per credit hour. Part-time tuition and fees vary according to course load, location, and program. ***Required fees:*** $35 per credit hour part-time. ***College room only:*** $5390. Room and board charges vary according to board plan and housing facility. ***Payment plan:*** installment. ***Waivers:*** employees or children of employees.
Financial Aid Of all full-time matriculated undergraduates who enrolled in 2015, 449 applied for aid, 422 were judged to have need, 68 had their need fully met. 37 Federal Work-Study jobs (averaging $2000). 140 state and other part-time jobs (averaging $2000). In 2015, 14 non-need-based awards were made. ***Average percent of need met:*** 75. ***Average financial aid package:*** $21,589. ***Average need-based loan:*** $4857. ***Average need-based gift aid:*** $17,520. ***Average non-need-based aid:*** $9367. ***Average indebtedness upon graduation:*** $31,613.

APPLYING
Standardized Tests *Required for some:* SAT or ACT (for admission), TOEFL/IELTS/STEP for international students.
Options: electronic application, early admission, deferred entrance.
Required: essay or personal statement, high school transcript, 1 letter of recommendation, college preparatory program that includes 4 units of English, 4 units of history/civics, 3 units of mathematics, 2 units of same foreign language, and 2 units of natural sciences with lab. ***Recommended:*** minimum 2.8 GPA, interview.
Application deadlines: rolling (freshmen), rolling (transfers).
Notification: continuous (freshmen), continuous (transfers).

CONTACT
Mr. Michael Montana, Director of Admissions, Wilson College, 1015 Philadelphia Avenue, Chambersburg, PA 17201. *Phone:* 717-262-2002 Ext. 3197. *Toll-free phone:* 800-421-8402. *Fax:* 717-262-2546. *E-mail:* admissions@wilson.edu.

Yeshiva Beth Moshe

Scranton, Pennsylvania

CONTACT
Dean, Yeshiva Beth Moshe, 930 Hickory Street, PO Box 1141, Scranton, PA 18505-2124. *Phone:* 717-346-1747.

York College of Pennsylvania

York, Pennsylvania

http://www.ycp.edu/

- **Independent** comprehensive, founded 1787
- **Suburban** 190-acre campus with easy access to Baltimore
- **Coed** 4,537 undergraduate students, 90% full-time, 55% women, 45% men
- **Moderately difficult** entrance level, 43% of applicants were admitted

UNDERGRAD STUDENTS
4,077 full-time, 460 part-time. 42% are from out of state; 5% Black or African American, non-Hispanic/Latino; 6% Hispanic/Latino; 2% Asian, non-Hispanic/Latino; 0.1% Native Hawaiian or other Pacific Islander, non-Hispanic/Latino; 0.1% American Indian or Alaska Native, non-Hispanic/Latino; 4% Two or more races, non-Hispanic/Latino; 1% Race/ethnicity unknown; 0.4% international; 4% transferred in; 57% live on campus.

Freshmen:
Admission: 13,235 applied, 5,694 admitted, 896 enrolled. ***Average high school GPA:*** 3.52. ***Test scores:*** SAT critical reading scores over 500: 63%; SAT math scores over 500: 70%; SAT writing scores over 500: 50%; ACT scores over 18: 95%; SAT critical reading scores over 600: 14%;

SAT math scores over 600: 20%; SAT writing scores over 600: 11%; ACT scores over 24: 39%; SAT critical reading scores over 700: 1%; SAT math scores over 700: 1%; SAT writing scores over 700: 1%; ACT scores over 30: 3%.

Retention: 78% of full-time freshmen returned.

FACULTY

Total: 469, 37% full-time, 44% with terminal degrees.

Student/faculty ratio: 16:1.

ACADEMICS

Calendar: semesters. *Degrees:* associate, bachelor's, master's, doctoral, and post-master's certificates.

Special study options: academic remediation for entering students, advanced placement credit, cooperative education, double majors, honors programs, independent study, internships, part-time degree program, services for LD students, student-designed majors, study abroad, summer session for credit.

Unusual degree programs: 3-2 business administration.

Computers: Students can access the following: campus intranet, computer help desk, free student e-mail accounts, online (class) grades, online (class) registration, online (class) schedules. Campuswide network is available. 100% of college-owned or -operated housing units are wired for high-speed Internet access. Wireless service is available via entire campus.

Library: Schmidt Library.

STUDENT LIFE

Housing options: on-campus residence required through senior year; coed, special housing for students with disabilities. Campus housing is university owned. Freshman campus housing is guaranteed.

Activities and organizations: drama/theater group, student-run newspaper, radio and television station, choral group, Pre-Med Society, Ski and Outdoor Club, Habitat for Humanity, Students in Free Enterprise (SIFE), WVYC Radio Station, national fraternities, national sororities.

Athletics Member NCAA. All Division III. ***Intercollegiate sports:*** baseball M, basketball M/W, cheerleading M/W, cross-country running M/W, field hockey W, golf M, lacrosse M/W, soccer M/W, softball W, swimming and diving M/W, tennis M/W, track and field M/W, volleyball W, wrestling M. ***Intramural sports:*** badminton M/W, basketball M/W, equestrian sports M(c)/W(c), football M/W, lacrosse M(c)/W(c), racquetball M/W, rugby M(c)/W(c), soccer M/W, softball M/W, table tennis M/W, tennis M/W, ultimate Frisbee M(c)/W(c), volleyball M/W.

Campus security: 24-hour emergency response devices and patrols, student patrols, late-night transport/escort service, controlled dormitory access.

Student services: health clinic, personal/psychological counseling.

COSTS & FINANCIAL AID

Costs (2016–17) ***Comprehensive fee:*** $29,240 includes full-time tuition ($16,970), mandatory fees ($1810), and room and board ($10,460). Full-time tuition and fees vary according to program. Part-time tuition: $525 per credit hour. ***Room and board:*** Room and board charges vary according to board plan and housing facility. ***Payment plan:*** installment. ***Waivers:*** employees or children of employees.

Financial Aid Of all full-time matriculated undergraduates who enrolled in 2015, 3,393 applied for aid, 2,724 were judged to have need, 704 had their need fully met. 421 Federal Work-Study jobs (averaging $1513). 12 state and other part-time jobs (averaging $1575). In 2015, 1063 non-need-based awards were made. ***Average percent of need met:*** 68. ***Average financial aid package:*** $14,371. ***Average need-based loan:*** $7471. ***Average need-based gift aid:*** $5458. ***Average non-need-based aid:*** $4925. ***Average indebtedness upon graduation:*** $39,334.

APPLYING

Standardized Tests *Required:* SAT or ACT (for admission).

Options: electronic application, deferred entrance.

Required: high school transcript, minimum 2.0 GPA. ***Required for some:*** interview. ***Recommended:*** essay or personal statement, 1 letter of recommendation.

Notification: continuous (freshmen), continuous (transfers).

CONTACT

York College of Pennsylvania, 441 Country Club Road, York, PA 17403-3651. *Phone:* 717-849-1600. *Toll-free phone:* 800-455-8018.

RHODE ISLAND

Brown University

Providence, Rhode Island

http://www.brown.edu/

- **Independent** university, founded 1764
- **Urban** 154-acre campus with easy access to Boston
- **Endowment** $3.3 billion
- **Coed**
- **Most difficult** entrance level

FACULTY

Student/faculty ratio: 9:1.

ACADEMICS

Calendar: semesters. *Degrees:* bachelor's, master's, and doctoral.

Library: John D. Rockefeller Library plus 6 others. Students can reserve study rooms.

STUDENT LIFE

Housing options: on-campus residence required through junior year; coed, cooperative, special housing for students with disabilities. Campus housing is university owned. Freshman campus housing is guaranteed.

Activities and organizations: drama/theater group, student-run newspaper, radio and television station, choral group, marching band, national fraternities, national sororities.

Athletics Member NCAA. All Division I except football (Division I-AA).

Campus security: 24-hour emergency response devices and patrols, student patrols, late-night transport/escort service, controlled dormitory access.

Student services: health clinic, personal/psychological counseling, women's center.

COSTS & FINANCIAL AID

Costs (2016–17) ***Comprehensive fee:*** $64,566 includes full-time tuition ($50,224), mandatory fees ($1142), and room and board ($13,200). Part-time tuition: $6278 per course. ***College room only:*** $8284. Room and board charges vary according to board plan.

Financial Aid Of all full-time matriculated undergraduates who enrolled in 2016, 3,291 applied for aid, 2,868 were judged to have need, 2,868 had their need fully met. 1,646 Federal Work-Study jobs (averaging $2489). 395 state and other part-time jobs (averaging $2564). In 2016, 8 non-need-based awards were made. ***Average percent of need met:*** 100. ***Average financial aid package:*** $48,420. ***Average need-based loan:*** $4059. ***Average need-based gift aid:*** $44,105. ***Average non-need-based aid:*** $8704. ***Average indebtedness upon graduation:*** $23,810. ***Financial aid deadline:*** 2/1.

APPLYING

Standardized Tests *Required:* SAT and SAT Subject Tests or ACT (for admission).

Options: electronic application, early decision, deferred entrance.

Application fee: $75.

Required: essay or personal statement, high school transcript, 2 letters of recommendation, Common Application, Brown University Supplement. ***Recommended:*** interview.

CONTACT

Mr. James Miller, Dean of Admission, Brown University, Box 1876, Providence, RI 02912. *Phone:* 401-863-2378. *Fax:* 401-863-9300. *E-mail:* admission_undergraduate@brown.edu.

★ Bryant University
Smithfield, Rhode Island
http://www.bryant.edu/

- **Independent** comprehensive, founded 1863
- **Suburban** 435-acre campus with easy access to Boston, Providence
- **Endowment** $170.1 million
- **Coed** 3,459 undergraduate students, 98% full-time, 41% women, 59% men
- **Moderately difficult** entrance level, 72% of applicants were admitted

UNDERGRAD STUDENTS
3,379 full-time, 80 part-time. Students come from 36 states and territories; 59 other countries; 88% are from out of state; 4% Black or African American, non-Hispanic/Latino; 7% Hispanic/Latino; 5% Asian, non-Hispanic/Latino; 0.2% Native Hawaiian or other Pacific Islander, non-Hispanic/Latino; 0.4% American Indian or Alaska Native, non-Hispanic/Latino; 1% Two or more races, non-Hispanic/Latino; 2% Race/ethnicity unknown; 8% international; 3% transferred in; 82% live on campus.

Freshmen:
Admission: 6,705 applied, 4,849 admitted, 908 enrolled. ***Average high school GPA:*** 3.42. ***Test scores:*** SAT critical reading scores over 500: 88%; SAT math scores over 500: 96%; SAT writing scores over 500: 85%; ACT scores over 18: 100%; SAT critical reading scores over 600: 33%; SAT math scores over 600: 51%; SAT writing scores over 600: 31%; ACT scores over 24: 75%; SAT critical reading scores over 700: 2%; SAT math scores over 700: 7%; SAT writing scores over 700: 3%; ACT scores over 30: 10%.
Retention: 90% of full-time freshmen returned.

FACULTY
Total: 281, 59% full-time, 52% with terminal degrees.
Student/faculty ratio: 13:1.

ACADEMICS
Calendar: semesters. *Degrees:* bachelor's, master's, and postbachelor's certificates.
Special study options: adult/continuing education programs, advanced placement credit, double majors, English as a second language, honors programs, independent study, internships, off-campus study, part-time degree program, study abroad, summer session for credit. ***ROTC:*** Army (c).
Computers: 574 computers/terminals and 3,585 ports are available on campus for general student use. Students can access the following: campus intranet, computer help desk, free student e-mail accounts, online (class) grades, online (class) registration, online (class) schedules, e-mail, student Web hosts. Campuswide network is available. 100% of college-owned or -operated housing units are wired for high-speed Internet access. Wireless service is available via entire campus.
Library: Douglas and Judith Krupp Library plus 1 other. Students can reserve study rooms.

STUDENT LIFE
Housing options: coed, special housing for students with disabilities. Campus housing is university owned. Freshman campus housing is guaranteed.
Activities and organizations: drama/theater group, student-run newspaper, radio and television station, choral group, Big Brothers and Big Sisters, Bryant Fishing Club, Collegiate Entrepreneurs Organization, WJMF Radio Station, Bryant Outdoor Adventure Club, national fraternities, national sororities.
Athletics Member NCAA. All Division I except football (Division I-AA). ***Intercollegiate sports:*** baseball M(s), basketball M(s)/W(s), bowling M(c)/W(c), cheerleading W(c), crew W(c), cross-country running M(s)/W(s), field hockey W(s), golf M(s), ice hockey M(c), lacrosse M(s)/W(s), racquetball M(c)/W(c), rowing W(c), rugby M(c)/W(c), soccer M(s)/W(s), softball W(s), squash M(c)/W(c), swimming and diving M(s)/W(s), tennis M(s)/W(s), track and field M(s)/W(s), ultimate Frisbee M(c)/W(c), volleyball M(c)/W(s). ***Intramural sports:*** basketball M/W, soccer M/W, softball M/W, tennis M/W, volleyball M/W, wrestling M.
Campus security: 24-hour emergency response devices and patrols, late-night transport/escort service, controlled dormitory access, 24 full-time staff; 20 patrol officers on foot, bike, golf cart, and car; Entry Control Station staffed 24/7 at only campus entry point.
Student services: health clinic, personal/psychological counseling, women's center.

COSTS & FINANCIAL AID
Costs (2017–18) ***Comprehensive fee:*** $57,503 includes full-time tuition ($41,700), mandatory fees ($409), and room and board ($15,394). Part-time tuition: $1033 per credit hour. Part-time tuition and fees vary according to course load. ***College room only:*** $9036. Room and board charges vary according to board plan and housing facility. ***Payment plan:*** installment. ***Waivers:*** employees or children of employees.
Financial Aid Of all full-time matriculated undergraduates who enrolled in 2015, 2,390 applied for aid, 2,106 were judged to have need, 477 had their need fully met. In 2015, 816 non-need-based awards were made. ***Average percent of need met:*** 51. ***Average financial aid package:*** $24,591. ***Average need-based loan:*** $4998. ***Average need-based gift aid:*** $9864. ***Average non-need-based aid:*** $14,240. ***Average indebtedness upon graduation:*** $39,283.

APPLYING
Options: electronic application, early decision, early action, deferred entrance.
Application fee: $50.
Required: essay or personal statement, high school transcript, 1 letter of recommendation, senior year first-quarter grades, three short essay questions in place of test scores. ***Recommended:*** minimum 3.3 GPA, 2 letters of recommendation, interview.
Application deadlines: 2/1 (freshmen), 5/1 (transfers), 12/1 (early action).
Early decision deadline: 11/15 (for plan 1), 1/15 (for plan 2).
Notification: 3/20 (freshmen), 3/20 (out-of-state freshmen), continuous (transfers), 12/15 (early decision plan 1), 2/15 (early decision plan 2), 1/15 (early action).

CONTACT
Ms. Michelle Cloutier, Executive Director of Admission, Bryant University, 1150 Douglas Pike, Smithfield, RI 02917. *Phone:* 401-232-6100. *Toll-free phone:* 800-622-7001. *Fax:* 401-232-6741. *E-mail:* admission@bryant.edu.

Johnson & Wales University
Providence, Rhode Island
http://www.jwu.edu/providence/

- **Independent** comprehensive, founded 1914
- **Urban** 47-acre campus with easy access to Boston
- **Coed**
- **Moderately difficult** entrance level

FACULTY
Student/faculty ratio: 20:1.

ACADEMICS
Calendar: quarters. *Degrees:* certificates, diplomas, associate, bachelor's, master's, and doctoral (branch locations in Charlotte, NC; Denver, CO; North Miami, FL).
Library: Johnson & Wales University Library.

STUDENT LIFE
Housing options: on-campus residence required for freshman year; coed, special housing for students with disabilities. Campus housing is university owned. Freshman campus housing is guaranteed.
Activities and organizations: student-run newspaper, national fraternities, national sororities.
Athletics Member NCAA. All Division III.
Campus security: 24-hour emergency response devices and patrols, student patrols, late-night transport/escort service.
Student services: health clinic, personal/psychological counseling, women's center.

COSTS & FINANCIAL AID
Costs (2016–17) ***Tuition:*** $30,396 full-time. ***Required fees:*** $350 full-time. ***Room only:*** $8268.

Financial Aid Of all full-time matriculated undergraduates who enrolled in 2015, 7,814 applied for aid, 5,787 were judged to have need, 711 had their need fully met. In 2015, 1481 non-need-based awards were made. ***Average percent of need met:*** 67. ***Average financial aid package:*** $20,636. ***Average need-based loan:*** $5038. ***Average need-based gift aid:*** $8553. ***Average non-need-based aid:*** $7305.

APPLYING

Options: electronic application, early admission, deferred entrance.

Required: high school transcript. ***Required for some:*** essay or personal statement, minimum 2.8 GPA, interview. ***Recommended:*** minimum 2.0 GPA.

CONTACT

Amy Podbelski, Dean of Undergraduate Admissions, Johnson & Wales University, 8 Abbott Park Place, Providence, RI 02903-3703. *Phone:* 401-598-2310. *Toll-free phone:* 800-342-5598. *Fax:* 401-598-2948. *E-mail:* pvd@admissions.jwu.edu.

New England Institute of Technology

East Greenwich, Rhode Island

http://www.neit.edu/

- **Independent** comprehensive, founded 1940
- **Suburban** 225-acre campus with easy access to Boston
- **Coed** 2,853 undergraduate students, 83% full-time, 33% women, 67% men
- **Minimally difficult** entrance level

UNDERGRAD STUDENTS

2,377 full-time, 476 part-time. Students come from 10 states and territories; 19 other countries; 53% are from out of state; 5% Black or African American, non-Hispanic/Latino; 12% Hispanic/Latino; 2% Asian, non-Hispanic/Latino; 0.1% Native Hawaiian or other Pacific Islander, non-Hispanic/Latino; 0.5% American Indian or Alaska Native, non-Hispanic/Latino; 2% Two or more races, non-Hispanic/Latino; 12% Race/ethnicity unknown; 3% international.

Freshmen:

Admission: 444 enrolled.

FACULTY

Total: 359, 39% full-time, 13% with terminal degrees.

Student/faculty ratio: 13:1.

ACADEMICS

Calendar: quarters. *Degrees:* associate, bachelor's, and master's.

Special study options: academic remediation for entering students, accelerated degree program, advanced placement credit, cooperative education, distance learning, double majors, English as a second language, internships, part-time degree program, services for LD students, student-designed majors, summer session for credit.

Computers: 1,000 computers/terminals are available on campus for general student use. Students can access the following: campus intranet, computer help desk, free student e-mail accounts, online (class) grades, online (class) registration, online (class) schedules. Campuswide network is available. Wireless service is available via entire campus.

Library: New England Institute of Technology Library. *Books:* 46,744 (physical), 24,454 (digital/electronic); *Serial titles:* 109 (physical), 30,789 (digital/electronic); *Databases:* 64. Weekly public service hours: 67; students can reserve study rooms.

STUDENT LIFE

Housing options: coed. Campus housing is university owned.

Activities and organizations: Rotaract Club, Student Physical Therapist Assistant Club, Student Nurses Association, Video Club, Criminal Justice Club.

Athletics ***Intramural sports:*** basketball M(c)/W(c), golf M(c)/W(c), soccer M(c)/W(c).

Campus security: security is currently available during hours of operation and will be expanded once the new residence hall opens in mid 2017..

COSTS & FINANCIAL AID

Costs (2017–18) ***Tuition:*** $27,000 full-time. Full-time tuition and fees vary according to program. Part-time tuition and fees vary according to program. No tuition increase for student's term of enrollment. ***Required fees:*** $1740 full-time. ***Payment plans:*** tuition prepayment, installment. ***Waivers:*** employees or children of employees.

Financial Aid Of all full-time matriculated undergraduates who enrolled in 2015, 250 Federal Work-Study jobs (averaging $2290).

APPLYING

Standardized Tests *Recommended:* SAT or ACT (for admission).

Options: electronic application, early admission, deferred entrance.

Application fee: $25.

Required: high school transcript, interview. ***Required for some:*** portfolio for advanced standing.

Application deadlines: rolling (freshmen), rolling (transfers).

Notification: continuous (freshmen), continuous (transfers).

CONTACT

Mr. Michael Caruso, Director of Admissions, New England Institute of Technology, One New England Tech Boulevard, East Greenwich, RI 02818. *Phone:* 401-739-5000 Ext. 3411. *Toll-free phone:* 800-736-7744. *Fax:* 401-886-0868. *E-mail:* mcaruso@neit.edu.

Providence College

Providence, Rhode Island

http://www.providence.edu/

- **Independent Roman Catholic** comprehensive, founded 1917
- **Suburban** 105-acre campus with easy access to Boston
- **Endowment** $198.6 million
- **Coed** 4,270 undergraduate students, 94% full-time, 56% women, 44% men

UNDERGRAD STUDENTS

4,008 full-time, 262 part-time. Students come from 43 states and territories; 29 other countries; 90% are from out of state; 4% Black or African American, non-Hispanic/Latino; 9% Hispanic/Latino; 1% Asian, non-Hispanic/Latino; 0.3% Native Hawaiian or other Pacific Islander, non-Hispanic/Latino; 0.3% American Indian or Alaska Native, non-Hispanic/Latino; 2% Two or more races, non-Hispanic/Latino; 5% Race/ethnicity unknown; 2% international; 1% transferred in; 74% live on campus.

Freshmen:

Admission: 1,058 enrolled. ***Average high school GPA:*** 3.41. ***Test scores:*** SAT critical reading scores over 500: 80%; SAT math scores over 500: 84%; SAT writing scores over 500: 82%; ACT scores over 18: 98%; SAT critical reading scores over 600: 32%; SAT math scores over 600: 39%; SAT writing scores over 600: 35%; ACT scores over 24: 71%; SAT critical reading scores over 700: 5%; SAT math scores over 700: 6%; SAT writing scores over 700: 5%; ACT scores over 30: 16%.

Retention: 93% of full-time freshmen returned.

FACULTY

Total: 523, 57% full-time, 72% with terminal degrees.

Student/faculty ratio: 12:1.

ACADEMICS

Calendar: semesters. *Degrees:* certificates, bachelor's, and master's.

Special study options: adult/continuing education programs, advanced placement credit, distance learning, double majors, honors programs, independent study, internships, off-campus study, part-time degree program, services for LD students, student-designed majors, study abroad, summer session for credit. ***ROTC:*** Army (b).

Unusual degree programs: 3-2 engineering with Columbia University, Washington University in St. Louis; biology/optometry with New England School of Optometry.

Computers: 440 computers/terminals and 5,000 ports are available on campus for general student use. Students can access the following: campus intranet, computer help desk, free student e-mail accounts, online (class) grades, online (class) registration, online (class) schedules. Campuswide network is available. 100% of college-owned or -operated housing units are wired for high-speed Internet access. Wireless service is available via entire campus.

Library: Phillips Memorial Library. *Books:* 391,000 (physical), 1.3 million (digital/electronic); *Serial titles:* 565 (physical), 42,609

(digital/electronic); *Databases:* 394. Weekly public service hours: 116; students can reserve study rooms.

STUDENT LIFE
Housing options: on-campus residence required through sophomore year; coed, men-only, women-only, special housing for students with disabilities. Campus housing is university owned. Freshman campus housing is guaranteed.

Activities and organizations: drama/theater group, student-run newspaper, radio and television station, choral group, Student Congress, Board of Multicultural Student Affairs, Dance Club, Student Alumni Association, Board of Programmers.

Athletics Member NCAA. All Division I. ***Intercollegiate sports:*** basketball M(s)/W(s), cross-country running M(s)/W(s), field hockey W(s), ice hockey M(s)/W(s), lacrosse M(s), soccer M(s)/W(s), softball W(s), swimming and diving M/W, tennis W, track and field M(s)/W(s), volleyball W(s). ***Intramural sports:*** badminton M/W, basketball M(c)/W(c), cheerleading M(c)/W(c), cross-country running M/W, field hockey W, football M/W, golf M(c)/W(c), ice hockey M(c)/W, lacrosse M/W(c), racquetball M(c)/W(c), rugby M(c)/W(c), sailing M(c)/W(c), soccer M/W, softball M/W, table tennis M/W, track and field M/W, ultimate Frisbee M(c)/W(c), volleyball M(c)/W(c), water polo M/W, wrestling M(c)/W(c).

Campus security: 24-hour emergency response devices and patrols, late-night transport/escort service, controlled dormitory access.

Student services: health clinic, personal/psychological counseling, legal services.

COSTS & FINANCIAL AID
Costs (2016–17) ***Comprehensive fee:*** $60,760 includes full-time tuition ($46,080), mandatory fees ($890), and room and board ($13,790). Full-time tuition and fees vary according to class time and degree level. Part-time tuition: $1646 per credit hour. Part-time tuition and fees vary according to class time and degree level. ***College room only:*** $7950. Room and board charges vary according to board plan and housing facility. ***Payment plan:*** installment. ***Waivers:*** employees or children of employees.

Financial Aid Of all full-time matriculated undergraduates who enrolled in 2015, 2,558 applied for aid, 2,193 were judged to have need, 490 had their need fully met. In 2015, 682 non-need-based awards were made. ***Average percent of need met:*** 82. ***Average financial aid package:*** $27,900. ***Average need-based loan:*** $5135. ***Average need-based gift aid:*** $23,825. ***Average non-need-based aid:*** $19,280. ***Average indebtedness upon graduation:*** $37,740. ***Financial aid deadline:*** 2/1.

APPLYING
Standardized Tests *Required for some:* TOEFL or IELTS if English is not the applicant's first language.

Required: essay or personal statement, high school transcript, 2 letters of recommendation.

CONTACT
Providence College, 1 Cunningham Square, Providence, RI 02918.
Phone: 401-865-2535. *Toll-free phone:* 800-721-6444.

Rhode Island College
Providence, Rhode Island
http://www.ric.edu/

- **State-supported** comprehensive, founded 1854
- **Suburban** 180-acre campus with easy access to Boston
- **Endowment** $16.4 million
- **Coed** 7,398 undergraduate students, 76% full-time, 68% women, 32% men
- **Moderately difficult** entrance level, 75% of applicants were admitted

UNDERGRAD STUDENTS
5,598 full-time, 1,800 part-time. Students come from 26 states and territories; 15% are from out of state; 9% Black or African American, non-Hispanic/Latino; 17% Hispanic/Latino; 3% Asian, non-Hispanic/Latino; 0.1% Native Hawaiian or other Pacific Islander, non-Hispanic/Latino; 0.4% American Indian or Alaska Native, non-Hispanic/Latino; 2% Two or more races, non-Hispanic/Latino; 7% Race/ethnicity unknown; 0.2% international; 9% transferred in; 15% live on campus.

Freshmen:
Admission: 5,148 applied, 3,845 admitted, 1,170 enrolled. ***Test scores:*** SAT critical reading scores over 500: 28%; SAT math scores over 500: 29%; SAT writing scores over 500: 25%; ACT scores over 18: 57%; SAT critical reading scores over 600: 5%; SAT math scores over 600: 4%; SAT writing scores over 600: 3%; ACT scores over 24: 5%; SAT critical reading scores over 700: 1%.
Retention: 74% of full-time freshmen returned.

FACULTY
Total: 764, 45% full-time.

Student/faculty ratio: 14:1.

ACADEMICS
Calendar: semesters. *Degrees:* certificates, bachelor's, master's, doctoral, post-master's, and postbachelor's certificates.

Special study options: academic remediation for entering students, adult/continuing education programs, advanced placement credit, double majors, honors programs, independent study, internships, off-campus study, part-time degree program, services for LD students, student-designed majors, study abroad, summer session for credit.
ROTC: Army (c).

Unusual degree programs: 3-2 public administration with University of Rhode Island.

Computers: 250 computers/terminals are available on campus for general student use. Students can access the following: campus intranet, computer help desk, free student e-mail accounts, online (class) grades, online (class) registration, online (class) schedules. Campuswide network is available. 100% of college-owned or -operated housing units are wired for high-speed Internet access. Wireless service is available via classrooms, computer centers, computer labs, dorm rooms, learning centers, libraries, student centers.

Library: Adams Library. *Books:* 545,755 (physical), 151,873 (digital/electronic); *Serial titles:* 1,195 (physical), 54,116 (digital/electronic); *Databases:* 101. Weekly public service hours: 79.

STUDENT LIFE
Housing options: coed, women-only, special housing for students with disabilities. Campus housing is university owned. Freshman applicants given priority for college housing.

Activities and organizations: drama/theater group, student-run newspaper, radio and television station, choral group, Sojourn Collegiate Ministries, Asian Student Association, Delta Phi Epsilon, Resident Student Association, Student Community Government, national fraternities, national sororities.

Athletics Member NCAA. All Division III. ***Intercollegiate sports:*** baseball M, basketball M/W, cross-country running M/W, golf M/W, gymnastics W, lacrosse W, soccer M/W, softball W, swimming and diving W, tennis M/W, track and field M/W, volleyball W, wrestling M. ***Intramural sports:*** badminton M/W, basketball M/W, football M, soccer M/W, softball M/W, swimming and diving M/W, tennis M/W, volleyball M/W, water polo M/W.

Campus security: 24-hour emergency response devices and patrols, late-night transport/escort service, controlled dormitory access.

Student services: health clinic, personal/psychological counseling, women's center, legal services.

COSTS & FINANCIAL AID
Costs (2017–18) ***Tuition:*** state resident $7118 full-time, $280 per credit part-time; nonresident $18,779 full-time, $690 per credit part-time. Part-time tuition and fees vary according to course load. ***Required fees:*** $1088 full-time, $32 per credit part-time, $74 per term part-time. ***Room and board:*** $10,794; room only: $6180. Room and board charges vary according to housing facility. ***Payment plan:*** installment. ***Waivers:*** employees or children of employees.

Financial Aid Of all full-time matriculated undergraduates who enrolled in 2016, 4,693 applied for aid, 3,818 were judged to have need, 758 had their need fully met. In 2016, 134 non-need-based awards were made. ***Average percent of need met:*** 68. ***Average financial aid package:*** $9027. ***Average need-based loan:*** $3856. ***Average need-based gift aid:*** $6532. ***Average non-need-based aid:*** $2342. ***Average indebtedness upon graduation:*** $26,519.

APPLYING
Standardized Tests *Required:* SAT or ACT (for admission).

Options: electronic application, early admission.

Application fee: $50.

Required: essay or personal statement, high school transcript, 1 letter of recommendation, one letter from guidance counselor. ***Required for some:*** interview. ***Recommended:*** minimum 3.0 GPA.

Application deadlines: 3/15 (freshmen), 6/1 (transfers).

Notification: continuous until 12/15 (freshmen), continuous (out-of-state freshmen), continuous (transfers).

CONTACT
Jason Anthony, Interim Director of Admissions, Rhode Island College, 600 Mount Pleasant Avenue, Providence, RI 02908-1927. *Phone:* 401-456-8234. *Toll-free phone:* 800-669-5760. *Fax:* 401-456-8817. *E-mail:* admissions@ric.edu.

Rhode Island School of Design
Providence, Rhode Island
http://www.risd.edu/

- **Independent** comprehensive, founded 1877
- **Urban** 23-acre campus with easy access to Boston, MA
- **Endowment** $303.4 million
- **Coed** 2,000 undergraduate students, 100% full-time, 69% women, 31% men

UNDERGRAD STUDENTS
2,000 full-time. Students come from 48 states and territories; 48 other countries; 94% are from out of state; 3% Black or African American, non-Hispanic/Latino; 8% Hispanic/Latino; 20% Asian, non-Hispanic/Latino; 0.2% American Indian or Alaska Native, non-Hispanic/Latino; 5% Two or more races, non-Hispanic/Latino; 5% Race/ethnicity unknown; 27% international; 3% transferred in; 60% live on campus.

Freshmen:

Admission: 456 enrolled. ***Average high school GPA:*** 3.5.

Retention: 93% of full-time freshmen returned.

FACULTY
Total: 425, 37% full-time, 65% with terminal degrees.

Student/faculty ratio: 10:1.

ACADEMICS
Calendar: 4-1-4. *Degrees:* bachelor's and master's.

Special study options: advanced placement credit, double majors, honors programs, independent study, internships, off-campus study, services for LD students, study abroad. ***ROTC:*** Army (c).

Computers: 65 computers/terminals and 400 ports are available on campus for general student use. Students can access the following: campus intranet, computer help desk, free student e-mail accounts, online (class) grades, online (class) registration, online (class) schedules. Campuswide network is available. 100% of college-owned or -operated housing units are wired for high-speed Internet access. Wireless service is available via entire campus.

Library: Fleet Library. *Books:* 160,296 (physical), 144,887 (digital/electronic); *Serial titles:* 1,200 (digital/electronic); *Databases:* 62. Weekly public service hours: 89; students can reserve study rooms.

STUDENT LIFE
Housing options: on-campus residence required through sophomore year; coed, special housing for students with disabilities. Campus housing is university owned and leased by the school. Freshman campus housing is guaranteed.

Activities and organizations: drama/theater group, student-run radio station, choral group, athletic clubs, Religious clubs, South Asian Student Association, RISD Global Initiative, Community Service Club.

Athletics ***Intercollegiate sports:*** basketball M(c)/W(c), ice hockey M(c)/W(c). ***Intramural sports:*** badminton M(c)/W(c), equestrian sports M(c)/W(c), fencing M(c)/W(c), football M(c)/W(c), sailing M(c)/W(c), skiing (downhill) M(c)/W(c), soccer M(c)/W(c), softball M(c)/W(c), squash M(c)/W(c), swimming and diving M(c)/W(c), tennis M(c)/W(c), ultimate Frisbee M(c)/W(c), volleyball M(c)/W(c), water polo M(c)/W(c).

Campus security: 24-hour emergency response devices and patrols, late-night transport/escort service, controlled dormitory access.

Student services: health clinic, personal/psychological counseling, legal services.

COSTS & FINANCIAL AID
Costs (2016–17) ***Comprehensive fee:*** $59,960 includes full-time tuition ($46,800), mandatory fees ($310), and room and board ($12,850). ***College room only:*** $7350. Room and board charges vary according to board plan and housing facility. ***Payment plan:*** installment. ***Waivers:*** employees or children of employees.

Financial Aid Of all full-time matriculated undergraduates who enrolled in 2016, 900 applied for aid, 774 were judged to have need, 10 had their need fully met. In 2016, 20 non-need-based awards were made. ***Average percent of need met:*** 65. ***Average financial aid package:*** $29,371. ***Average need-based loan:*** $5216. ***Average need-based gift aid:*** $22,934. ***Average non-need-based aid:*** $7500. ***Average indebtedness upon graduation:*** $31,037. ***Financial aid deadline:*** 2/15.

APPLYING
Standardized Tests *Required:* SAT or ACT (for admission).

Required: essay or personal statement, high school transcript, portfolio, drawing assignments. ***Recommended:*** 3 letters of recommendation.

CONTACT
Mr. Edward Newhall, Associate Vice President for Enrollment, Rhode Island School of Design, 2 College Street, Providence, RI 02903-2784. *Phone:* 401-454-6300. *Toll-free phone:* 800-364-7473. *Fax:* 401-454-6309. *E-mail:* admissions@risd.edu.

★ Roger Williams University
Bristol, Rhode Island
http://www.rwu.edu/

- **Independent** comprehensive, founded 1956
- **Small-town** 140-acre campus with easy access to Boston
- **Endowment** $63.5 million
- **Coed** 4,902 undergraduate students, 84% full-time, 54% women, 46% men
- **Moderately difficult** entrance level, 79% of applicants were admitted

UNDERGRAD STUDENTS
4,124 full-time, 778 part-time. Students come from 48 states and territories; 52 other countries; 77% are from out of state; 3% Black or African American, non-Hispanic/Latino; 6% Hispanic/Latino; 1% Asian, non-Hispanic/Latino; 0.1% Native Hawaiian or other Pacific Islander, non-Hispanic/Latino; 0.2% American Indian or Alaska Native, non-Hispanic/Latino; 2% Two or more races, non-Hispanic/Latino; 7% Race/ethnicity unknown; 4% international; 2% transferred in; 75% live on campus.

Freshmen:

Admission: 9,829 applied, 7,790 admitted, 1,211 enrolled. ***Average high school GPA:*** 3.34. ***Test scores:*** SAT critical reading scores over 500: 79%; SAT math scores over 500: 84%; SAT writing scores over 500: 77%; ACT scores over 18: 99%; SAT critical reading scores over 600: 24%; SAT math scores over 600: 30%; SAT writing scores over 600: 21%; ACT scores over 24: 75%; SAT critical reading scores over 700: 3%; SAT math scores over 700: 2%; SAT writing scores over 700: 1%; ACT scores over 30: 9%.

Retention: 83% of full-time freshmen returned.

FACULTY
Total: 533, 40% full-time, 38% with terminal degrees.

Student/faculty ratio: 14:1.

ACADEMICS
Calendar: semesters. *Degrees:* certificates, associate, bachelor's, master's, doctoral, and postbachelor's certificates.

Special study options: accelerated degree program, adult/continuing education programs, advanced placement credit, cooperative education, distance learning, double majors, English as a second language, freshman honors college, honors programs, independent study, internships, part-time degree program, services for LD students, student-designed majors, study abroad, summer session for credit. ***ROTC:*** Army (b).

A ★ *indicates that the school has detailed information with a Premium Profile on Petersons.com.*

Computers: 105 computers/terminals and 3,690 ports are available on campus for general student use. Students can access the following: campus intranet, computer help desk, free student e-mail accounts, online (class) registration, online (class) schedules. Campuswide network is available. 100% of college-owned or -operated housing units are wired for high-speed Internet access. Wireless service is available via classrooms, computer centers, computer labs, dorm rooms, learning centers, libraries, student centers.

Library: Roger Williams University Library plus 1 other. *Books:* 201,390 (physical), 236,803 (digital/electronic); *Databases:* 104. Weekly public service hours: 111; students can reserve study rooms.

STUDENT LIFE

Housing options: on-campus residence required through sophomore year; coed, special housing for students with disabilities. Campus housing is university owned. Freshman campus housing is guaranteed.

Activities and organizations: drama/theater group, student-run newspaper, radio station, choral group, Campus Entertainment Network, Dance Club, WQRI 88.3 Radio Station, Habitat for Humanity.

Athletics Member NCAA. All Division III. ***Intercollegiate sports:*** baseball M, basketball M/W, cheerleading W(c), crew M(c)/W(c), cross-country running M/W, equestrian sports M/W, field hockey W, golf M, lacrosse M/W, rugby M(c)/W(c), sailing M/W, soccer M/W, softball W, swimming and diving M/W, tennis M/W, track and field M/W, volleyball W, wrestling M. ***Intramural sports:*** basketball M/W, football M, ice hockey M(c), soccer M/W, softball M, tennis M/W, ultimate Frisbee M(c)/W(c), volleyball M.

Campus security: 24-hour emergency response devices and patrols, student patrols, late-night transport/escort service, controlled dormitory access.

Student services: health clinic, personal/psychological counseling, women's center.

COSTS & FINANCIAL AID

Costs (2017–18) ***One-time required fee:*** $250. ***Comprehensive fee:*** $47,262 includes full-time tuition ($29,976), mandatory fees ($1874), and room and board ($15,412). Full-time tuition and fees vary according to class time, course load, degree level, and program. Part-time tuition: $1249 per credit hour. Part-time tuition and fees vary according to class time, course load, degree level, and program. No tuition increase for student's term of enrollment. ***College room only:*** $8230. Room and board charges vary according to board plan and housing facility. ***Payment plan:*** deferred payment. ***Waivers:*** employees or children of employees.

Financial Aid Of all full-time matriculated undergraduates who enrolled in 2016, 3,124 applied for aid, 2,566 were judged to have need, 270 had their need fully met. 1,353 Federal Work-Study jobs (averaging $2056). In 2016, 527 non-need-based awards were made. ***Average percent of need met:*** 81. ***Average financial aid package:*** $21,104. ***Average need-based loan:*** $3730. ***Average need-based gift aid:*** $14,200. ***Average non-need-based aid:*** $12,612. ***Average indebtedness upon graduation:*** $41,632. ***Financial aid deadline:*** 2/1.

APPLYING

Options: electronic application, early action, deferred entrance.

Application fee: $50.

Required: essay or personal statement, high school transcript, 1 letter of recommendation. ***Required for some:*** portfolio review, audition, specific preparatory courses for visual arts studies, graphic design communications, architecture, creative writing, dance and theater.

Application deadlines: 2/1 (freshmen), rolling (transfers), 11/1 (early action).

Notification: continuous (freshmen), continuous (out-of-state freshmen), continuous (transfers).

CONTACT

Admissions Office (Undergraduate), Roger Williams University, 1 Old Ferry Road, Bristol, RI 02809. *Phone:* 401-254-3500. *Toll-free phone:* 800-458-7144. *Fax:* 401-254-3557. *E-mail:* admit@rwu.edu.

Salve Regina University

Newport, Rhode Island

http://www.salve.edu/

- **Independent Roman Catholic** comprehensive, founded 1934
- **Suburban** 80-acre campus with easy access to Boston, Providence
- **Endowment** $54.0 million
- **Coed** 2,124 undergraduate students, 93% full-time, 70% women, 30% men
- **Moderately difficult** entrance level, 68% of applicants were admitted

UNDERGRAD STUDENTS

1,975 full-time, 149 part-time. Students come from 32 states and territories; 17 other countries; 78% are from out of state; 2% Black or African American, non-Hispanic/Latino; 6% Hispanic/Latino; 1% Asian, non-Hispanic/Latino; 0.1% Native Hawaiian or other Pacific Islander, non-Hispanic/Latino; 0.2% American Indian or Alaska Native, non-Hispanic/Latino; 2% Two or more races, non-Hispanic/Latino; 6% Race/ethnicity unknown; 1% international; 1% transferred in; 60% live on campus.

Freshmen:

Admission: 5,158 applied, 3,526 admitted, 548 enrolled. ***Average high school GPA:*** 3.25.

Retention: 82% of full-time freshmen returned.

FACULTY

Total: 279, 45% full-time, 49% with terminal degrees.

Student/faculty ratio: 13:1.

ACADEMICS

Calendar: semesters. *Degrees:* certificates, associate, bachelor's, master's, doctoral, post-master's, and postbachelor's certificates.

Special study options: accelerated degree program, adult/continuing education programs, advanced placement credit, distance learning, double majors, English as a second language, honors programs, independent study, internships, off-campus study, part-time degree program, services for LD students, study abroad, summer session for credit. ***ROTC:*** Army (c).

Unusual degree programs: 3-2 business administration; administration of justice, business administration, holistic counseling, international relations, management, rehabilitation counseling.

Computers: 163 computers/terminals are available on campus for general student use. Students can access the following: campus intranet, computer help desk, free student e-mail accounts, online (class) grades, online (class) registration, online (class) schedules. Campuswide network is available. 100% of college-owned or -operated housing units are wired for high-speed Internet access. Wireless service is available via entire campus.

Library: McKillop Library. *Books:* 158,092 (physical), 266,078 (digital/electronic); *Serial titles:* 18,762 (physical), 46,067 (digital/electronic); *Databases:* 53. Weekly public service hours: 52; students can reserve study rooms.

STUDENT LIFE

Housing options: on-campus residence required through sophomore year; coed, men-only, women-only, special housing for students with disabilities. Campus housing is university owned and leased by the school. Freshman campus housing is guaranteed.

Activities and organizations: drama/theater group, student-run newspaper, radio station, choral group, Orpheus Musical Society, Student Government Association, Student Outdoor Adventures, Student Nurse Organization, Stagefright Theatre Company.

Athletics Member NCAA. All Division III. ***Intercollegiate sports:*** baseball M, basketball M/W, cross-country running M/W, field hockey W, football M, ice hockey M/W, lacrosse M/W, rugby M(c)/W(c), sailing M/W, soccer M/W, softball W, tennis M/W, track and field W, volleyball W. ***Intramural sports:*** baseball M, basketball M/W, cheerleading W(c), equestrian sports W(c), football M/W, golf M/W, rugby M(c)/W(c), soccer M/W, softball M/W, swimming and diving M(c)/W(c), tennis M/W, ultimate Frisbee M/W, volleyball M/W, weight lifting M/W.

Campus security: 24-hour emergency response devices and patrols, late-night transport/escort service, controlled dormitory access.

Student services: health clinic, personal/psychological counseling.

COSTS & FINANCIAL AID
Costs (2016–17) ***Comprehensive fee:*** $51,470 includes full-time tuition ($37,270), mandatory fees ($550), and room and board ($13,650). Full-time tuition and fees vary according to location. Part-time tuition: $1242 per credit. Part-time tuition and fees vary according to course load and location. ***Required fees:*** $50 per term part-time. ***Room and board:*** Room and board charges vary according to board plan and housing facility. ***Payment plan:*** installment. ***Waivers:*** employees or children of employees.

Financial Aid Of all full-time matriculated undergraduates who enrolled in 2016, 1,698 applied for aid, 1,529 were judged to have need, 188 had their need fully met. In 2016, 372 non-need-based awards were made. ***Average percent of need met:*** 68. ***Average financial aid package:*** $26,402. ***Average need-based loan:*** $4498. ***Average need-based gift aid:*** $21,395. ***Average non-need-based aid:*** $14,506. ***Average indebtedness upon graduation:*** $29,192.

APPLYING
Options: electronic application, early action, deferred entrance.

Application fee: $50.

Required: essay or personal statement, high school transcript, 2 letters of recommendation. ***Recommended:*** minimum 2.7 GPA.

Application deadlines: 2/1 (freshmen), rolling (transfers), 11/1 (early action).

Notification: 12/25 (freshmen), continuous (transfers), 12/25 (early action).

CONTACT
Dean Colleen Emerson, Dean of Undergraduate Admissions, Salve Regina University, 100 Ochre Point Avenue, Newport, RI 02840-4192. *Phone:* 401-341-2908. *Toll-free phone:* 888-GO SALVE. *Fax:* 401-848-2823. *E-mail:* sruadmis@salve.edu.

★ University of Rhode Island
Kingston, Rhode Island
http://www.uri.edu/

- **State-supported** university, founded 1892
- **Small-town** 1200-acre campus
- **Endowment** $107.8 million
- **Coed** 14,801 undergraduate students, 84% full-time, 56% women, 44% men
- **Moderately difficult** entrance level, 71% of applicants were admitted

UNDERGRAD STUDENTS
12,475 full-time, 2,326 part-time. Students come from 44 states and territories; 41 other countries; 46% are from out of state; 5% Black or African American, non-Hispanic/Latino; 10% Hispanic/Latino; 3% Asian, non-Hispanic/Latino; 0.2% American Indian or Alaska Native, non-Hispanic/Latino; 2% Two or more races, non-Hispanic/Latino; 7% Race/ethnicity unknown; 2% international; 4% transferred in; 44% live on campus.

Freshmen:
Admission: 21,797 applied, 15,485 admitted, 3,257 enrolled. ***Average high school GPA:*** 3.45. ***Test scores:*** SAT critical reading scores over 500: 75%; SAT math scores over 500: 78%; SAT writing scores over 500: 70%; ACT scores over 18: 98%; SAT critical reading scores over 600: 23%; SAT math scores over 600: 28%; SAT writing scores over 600: 21%; ACT scores over 24: 62%; SAT critical reading scores over 700: 2%; SAT math scores over 700: 3%; SAT writing scores over 700: 1%; ACT scores over 30: 8%.
Retention: 83% of full-time freshmen returned.

FACULTY
Total: 1,106, 63% full-time, 57% with terminal degrees.

Student/faculty ratio: 16:1.

ACADEMICS
Calendar: semesters. *Degrees:* bachelor's, master's, doctoral, and postbachelor's certificates.

Special study options: academic remediation for entering students, accelerated degree program, adult/continuing education programs, advanced placement credit, cooperative education, distance learning, double majors, English as a second language, honors programs, independent study, internships, off-campus study, part-time degree program, services for LD students, study abroad, summer session for credit. ***ROTC:*** Army (b).

Unusual degree programs: 3-2 engineering; nursing; accounting, pharmacy, chemistry, education, psychology.

Computers: 2,500 computers/terminals are available on campus for general student use. Students can access the following: campus intranet, computer help desk, free student e-mail accounts, online (class) grades, online (class) registration, online (class) schedules. Campuswide network is available. 100% of college-owned or -operated housing units are wired for high-speed Internet access. Wireless service is available via entire campus.

Library: Robert L. Carothers Library and Learning Commons plus 3 others.

STUDENT LIFE
Housing options: coed, cooperative, special housing for students with disabilities. Campus housing is university owned and leased by the school. Freshman campus housing is guaranteed.

Activities and organizations: drama/theater group, student-run newspaper, radio and television station, choral group, marching band, Student Entertainment Committee, student radio station, Intramural sport clubs, Student Alumni Association, student newspaper, national fraternities, national sororities.

Athletics Member NCAA. All Division I. ***Intercollegiate sports:*** baseball M(s), basketball M(s), crew M(s), cross-country running M(s)/W(s), football M(s), golf M(s), soccer M(s)/W(s), softball W(s), swimming and diving W(s), tennis W(s), track and field M(s)/W(s), volleyball W(s). ***Intramural sports:*** equestrian sports M(c)/W(c), gymnastics W(c), ice hockey M(c)/W(c), lacrosse M(c)/W(c), rugby M(c)/W(c), sailing M(c)/W(c), skiing (downhill) M(c)/W(c), swimming and diving M(c), ultimate Frisbee M(c)/W(c), volleyball M(c), wrestling M(c).

Campus security: 24-hour emergency response devices and patrols, student patrols, late-night transport/escort service, controlled dormitory access.

Student services: health clinic, personal/psychological counseling, women's center.

COSTS & FINANCIAL AID
Costs (2016–17) ***Tuition:*** state resident $11,128 full-time, $464 per credit hour part-time; nonresident $27,118 full-time, $1130 per term part-time. Full-time tuition and fees vary according to course load, location, and reciprocity agreements. Part-time tuition and fees vary according to course load, location, and reciprocity agreements. ***Required fees:*** $1756 full-time, $44 per credit hour part-time, $58 per term part-time. ***Room and board:*** $7622; room only: $4400. Room and board charges vary according to board plan and housing facility. ***Payment plan:*** installment. ***Waivers:*** minority students, senior citizens, and employees or children of employees.

Financial Aid Of all full-time matriculated undergraduates who enrolled in 2016, 12,459 applied for aid, 10,699 were judged to have need, 350 had their need fully met. In 2016, 1007 non-need-based awards were made. ***Average percent of need met:*** 57. ***Average financial aid package:*** $15,768. ***Average need-based loan:*** $6042. ***Average need-based gift aid:*** $10,125. ***Average non-need-based aid:*** $6683. ***Average indebtedness upon graduation:*** $32,750.

APPLYING
Standardized Tests *Required:* SAT or ACT (for admission).

Options: electronic application, early admission, early action, deferred entrance.

Application fee: $65.

Required: essay or personal statement, high school transcript, 1 letter of recommendation, list of senior courses. ***Required for some:*** 2 letters of recommendation.

Application deadlines: 2/1 (freshmen), 6/1 (transfers), 12/1 (early action).

Notification: 3/31 (freshmen), continuous (transfers), 1/31 (early action).

CONTACT
Ms. Joanne Lynch, Assistant Dean of Admissions, University of Rhode Island, Undergraduate Admission Office, Newman Hall, 14 Upper College Road, Kingston, RI 02881. *Phone:* 401-874-7110. *Fax:* 401-874-5523. *E-mail:* lynch@uri.edu.

SOUTH CAROLINA

Allen University

Columbia, South Carolina

http://www.allenuniversity.edu/

CONTACT

Terri Parker, Director of Admission, Allen University, 1530 Harden Street, Columbia, SC 29204. *Phone:* 803-376-5733. *Toll-free phone:* 877-625-5368. *E-mail:* tparker@allenuniversity.edu.

Anderson University

Anderson, South Carolina

http://www.andersonuniversity.edu/

- **Independent Baptist** comprehensive, founded 1911
- **Urban** 271-acre campus with easy access to Greenville
- **Endowment** $41.2 million
- **Coed** 2,940 undergraduate students, 84% full-time, 69% women, 31% men
- **Minimally difficult** entrance level, 54% of applicants were admitted

UNDERGRAD STUDENTS

2,480 full-time, 460 part-time. Students come from 41 states and territories; 20 other countries; 19% are from out of state; 8% Black or African American, non-Hispanic/Latino; 3% Hispanic/Latino; 1% Asian, non-Hispanic/Latino; 0.9% American Indian or Alaska Native, non-Hispanic/Latino; 4% Race/ethnicity unknown; 0.9% international; 5% transferred in; 46% live on campus.

Freshmen:

Admission: 3,316 applied, 1,788 admitted, 670 enrolled. ***Average high school GPA:*** 3.55. ***Test scores:*** SAT critical reading scores over 500: 60%; SAT math scores over 500: 57%; SAT writing scores over 500: 52%; ACT scores over 18: 94%; SAT critical reading scores over 600: 16%; SAT math scores over 600: 13%; SAT writing scores over 600: 11%; ACT scores over 24: 46%; SAT critical reading scores over 700: 3%; SAT writing scores over 700: 1%; ACT scores over 30: 6%.

Retention: 76% of full-time freshmen returned.

FACULTY

Total: 413, 31% full-time, 39% with terminal degrees.

Student/faculty ratio: 14:1.

ACADEMICS

Calendar: semesters. *Degrees:* bachelor's, master's, and doctoral.

Special study options: academic remediation for entering students, accelerated degree program, adult/continuing education programs, advanced placement credit, cooperative education, distance learning, double majors, honors programs, independent study, internships, part-time degree program, services for LD students, study abroad, summer session for credit. ***ROTC:*** Army (c), Air Force (c).

Computers: 192 computers/terminals are available on campus for general student use. Students can access the following: campus intranet, computer help desk, free student e-mail accounts, online (class) grades, online (class) registration, online (class) schedules. Campuswide network is available. 100% of college-owned or -operated housing units are wired for high-speed Internet access. Wireless service is available via entire campus.

Library: Thrift Library. *Books:* 90,729 (physical), 99,204 (digital/electronic); *Serial titles:* 14,268 (physical), 174,052 (digital/electronic); *Databases:* 200. Weekly public service hours: 88; students can reserve study rooms.

STUDENT LIFE

Housing options: on-campus residence required through sophomore year; men-only, women-only. Campus housing is university owned. Freshman campus housing is guaranteed.

Activities and organizations: drama/theater group, student-run newspaper, choral group, Baptist Collegiate Ministries, Gamma Beta Phi, Anderson University Education Club, Ducks Unlimited, Council of Exceptional Children.

Athletics Member NCAA. All Division II. ***Intercollegiate sports:*** baseball M(s), basketball M(s)/W(s), cheerleading W(s), cross-country running M(s)/W(s), golf M(s)/W(s), soccer M(s)/W(s), softball W(s), tennis M(s)/W(s), track and field M(s)/W(s), volleyball W(s). ***Intramural sports:*** basketball M/W, football M/W, racquetball M/W, softball M/W, table tennis M/W, ultimate Frisbee M/W, volleyball M/W, weight lifting M.

Campus security: 24-hour emergency response devices and patrols, late-night transport/escort service, controlled dormitory access.

Student services: health clinic, personal/psychological counseling.

COSTS & FINANCIAL AID

Costs (2016–17) ***Comprehensive fee:*** $35,054 includes full-time tuition ($23,470), mandatory fees ($2410), and room and board ($9174). Full-time tuition and fees vary according to course load and program. Part-time tuition: $585 per credit hour. Part-time tuition and fees vary according to course load and program. ***College room only:*** $4670. Room and board charges vary according to board plan and housing facility. ***Payment plan:*** installment. ***Waivers:*** employees or children of employees.

Financial Aid Of all full-time matriculated undergraduates who enrolled in 2015, 2,221 applied for aid, 1,912 were judged to have need, 514 had their need fully met. 261 Federal Work-Study jobs (averaging $2000). 317 state and other part-time jobs (averaging $3622). In 2015, 427 non-need-based awards were made. ***Average percent of need met:*** 70. ***Average financial aid package:*** $18,176. ***Average need-based loan:*** $4993. ***Average need-based gift aid:*** $14,959. ***Average non-need-based aid:*** $10,641. ***Average indebtedness upon graduation:*** $29,846. ***Financial aid deadline:*** 7/30.

APPLYING

Standardized Tests *Required:* SAT or ACT (for admission).

Options: electronic application, deferred entrance.

Application fee: $25.

Required: high school transcript. ***Required for some:*** essay or personal statement, 2 letters of recommendation, interview. ***Recommended:*** minimum 2.9 GPA.

Notification: continuous (freshmen), continuous (transfers).

CONTACT

Mr. Jacob Queen, Director of Admission, Anderson University, 316 Boulevard, Anderson, SC 29621. *Phone:* 864-231-5795. *Toll-free phone:* 800-542-3594. *E-mail:* jqueen@andersonuniversity.edu.

The Art Institute of Charleston, a branch of The Art Institute of Atlanta

Charleston, South Carolina

http://www.artinstitutes.edu/charleston/

CONTACT

The Art Institute of Charleston, a branch of The Art Institute of Atlanta, 24 North Market Street, Charleston, SC 29401. *Phone:* 843-727-3500. *Toll-free phone:* 866-211-0107.

Benedict College

Columbia, South Carolina

http://www.benedict.edu/

CONTACT

Benedict College, 1600 Harden Street, Columbia, SC 29204. *Phone:* 803-705-4491. *Toll-free phone:* 800-868-6598.

Bob Jones University

Greenville, South Carolina

http://www.bju.edu/

CONTACT

Mr. Gary Deedrick, Director of Admission, Bob Jones University, 1700 Wade Hampton Boulevard, Greenville, SC 29614. *Phone:* 864-242-5100. *Toll-free phone:* 800-252-6363. *Fax:* 800-232-9258. *E-mail:* admission@bju.edu.

Charleston Southern University

Charleston, South Carolina

http://www.charlestonsouthern.edu/

- **Independent Baptist** comprehensive, founded 1964
- **Suburban** 500-acre campus
- **Endowment** $17.1 million
- **Coed** 3,181 undergraduate students, 88% full-time, 63% women, 37% men
- **Moderately difficult** entrance level, 60% of applicants were admitted

UNDERGRAD STUDENTS

2,796 full-time, 385 part-time. Students come from 47 states and territories; 16 other countries; 15% are from out of state; 26% Black or African American, non-Hispanic/Latino; 3% Hispanic/Latino; 2% Asian, non-Hispanic/Latino; 0.2% Native Hawaiian or other Pacific Islander, non-Hispanic/Latino; 0.8% American Indian or Alaska Native, non-Hispanic/Latino; 2% Two or more races, non-Hispanic/Latino; 4% Race/ethnicity unknown; 0.7% international; 11% transferred in; 42% live on campus.

Freshmen:

Admission: 4,390 applied, 2,643 admitted, 756 enrolled.
Average high school GPA: 3.63.

Retention: 65% of full-time freshmen returned.

FACULTY

Total: 292, 56% full-time.

Student/faculty ratio: 15:1.

ACADEMICS

Calendar: 4-4-1. *Degrees:* bachelor's, master's, and post-master's certificates.

Special study options: academic remediation for entering students, accelerated degree program, advanced placement credit, double majors, honors programs, internships, off-campus study, part-time degree program, services for LD students, summer session for credit. ***ROTC:*** Army (b), Air Force (b).

Unusual degree programs: 3-2 engineering with University of South Carolina.

Computers: 250 computers/terminals are available on campus for general student use. Students can access the following: computer help desk, free student e-mail accounts, online (class) grades, online (class) registration, online (class) schedules, online course work. Campuswide network is available. 100% of college-owned or -operated housing units are wired for high-speed Internet access. Wireless service is available via entire campus.

Library: L. Mendel Rivers Library.

STUDENT LIFE

Housing options: on-campus residence required for freshman year; men-only, women-only. Campus housing is university owned. Freshman applicants given priority for college housing.

Activities and organizations: drama/theater group, student-run newspaper, choral group, marching band, Student Government, Baptist Student Union, Fellowship of Christian Athletes, national fraternities, national sororities.

Athletics Member NCAA. All Division I except football (Division I-AA). ***Intercollegiate sports:*** baseball M(s), basketball M(s)/W(s), cheerleading M/W, cross-country running M(s)/W(s), golf M(s)/W(s), soccer W(s), softball W(s), tennis W(s), track and field M(s)/W(s), volleyball W(s). ***Intramural sports:*** basketball M/W, football M/W, soccer M/W, softball M/W, volleyball M/W.

Campus security: 24-hour emergency response devices and patrols, late-night transport/escort service, controlled dormitory access.

Student services: personal/psychological counseling.

FINANCIAL AID

Financial Aid Of all full-time matriculated undergraduates who enrolled in 2007, 1,968 applied for aid, 1,749 were judged to have need, 421 had their need fully met. 614 Federal Work-Study jobs (averaging $1406). In 2007, 306 non-need-based awards were made. ***Average percent of need met:*** 73. ***Average financial aid package:*** $15,036. ***Average need-based loan:*** $4804. ***Average need-based gift aid:*** $11,008. ***Average non-need-based aid:*** $10,832. ***Average indebtedness upon graduation:*** $20,252.

APPLYING

Standardized Tests *Required:* SAT or ACT (for admission).

Options: electronic application.

Application fee: $40.

Required: high school transcript, minimum 2.0 GPA. ***Required for some:*** essay or personal statement, 1 letter of recommendation, interview.

Application deadlines: rolling (freshmen), rolling (transfers).

Notification: continuous (freshmen), continuous (transfers).

CONTACT

Mr. Jim Rhoden, Director of Enrollment Management, Charleston Southern University, Charleston, SC 29423-8087. *Phone:* 843-863-7050. *Toll-free phone:* 800-947-7474. *E-mail:* enroll@csuniv.edu.

The Citadel, The Military College of South Carolina

Charleston, South Carolina

http://www.citadel.edu/

- **State-supported** comprehensive, founded 1842
- **Suburban** 300-acre campus
- **Endowment** $244.5 million
- **Coed, primarily men** 2,773 undergraduate students, 90% full-time, 11% women, 89% men
- **Moderately difficult** entrance level, 82% of applicants were admitted

UNDERGRAD STUDENTS

2,504 full-time, 269 part-time. Students come from 42 states and territories; 8 other countries; 35% are from out of state; 9% Black or African American, non-Hispanic/Latino; 7% Hispanic/Latino; 2% Asian, non-Hispanic/Latino; 0.3% Native Hawaiian or other Pacific Islander, non-Hispanic/Latino; 0.5% American Indian or Alaska Native, non-Hispanic/Latino; 4% Two or more races, non-Hispanic/Latino; 0.3% Race/ethnicity unknown; 0.9% international; 4% transferred in; 100% live on campus.

Freshmen:

Admission: 2,620 applied, 2,156 admitted, 734 enrolled. ***Average high school GPA:*** 3.58. ***Test scores:*** SAT critical reading scores over 500: 61%; SAT math scores over 500: 69%; ACT scores over 18: 95%; SAT critical reading scores over 600: 21%; SAT math scores over 600: 20%; ACT scores over 24: 39%; SAT critical reading scores over 700: 3%; SAT math scores over 700: 1%; ACT scores over 30: 5%.

Retention: 85% of full-time freshmen returned.

FACULTY

Total: 304, 63% full-time, 73% with terminal degrees.

Student/faculty ratio: 12:1.

ACADEMICS

Calendar: semesters. *Degrees:* bachelor's, master's, post-master's, and postbachelor's certificates.

Special study options: advanced placement credit, cooperative education, distance learning, double majors, English as a second language, honors programs, independent study, internships, off-campus study, part-time degree program, services for LD students, study abroad, summer session for credit. ***ROTC:*** Army (b), Navy (b), Air Force (b).

Computers: 350 computers/terminals are available on campus for general student use. Students can access the following: campus intranet, computer help desk, free student e-mail accounts, online (class) grades, online (class) registration, online (class) schedules. Campuswide network is available. 100% of college-owned or -operated housing units are wired for high-speed Internet access. Wireless service is available via entire campus.

Library: Daniel Library. *Books:* 201,000 (physical), 190,000 (digital/electronic). Students can reserve study rooms.

STUDENT LIFE

Housing options: on-campus residence required through senior year; coed. Campus housing is university owned. Freshman campus housing is guaranteed.

Activities and organizations: student-run newspaper, choral group, marching band, The Republican Society, Semper Fi Society, American Society of Civil Engineers, Campus Outreach, Criminal Justice Society.

Athletics Member NCAA. All Division I except football (Division I-AA). ***Intercollegiate sports:*** baseball M(s), basketball M(s), cross-country running M(s)/W(s), golf W(s), riflery M(s)/W(s), soccer W(s), tennis M(s), track and field M(s)/W(s), volleyball W(s), wrestling M(s). ***Intramural sports:*** badminton M/W, football M/W, golf M(c), ice hockey M(c)/W(c), lacrosse M(c), racquetball M/W, riflery M/W, rugby M(c)/W(c), sailing M(c)/W(c), sand volleyball M/W, soccer M/W, softball M/W, swimming and diving M/W, table tennis M/W, tennis M/W, track and field M/W, triathlon M(c)/W(c), ultimate Frisbee M/W, volleyball M(c)/W(c), weight lifting M/W, wrestling M/W.

Campus security: 24-hour patrols.

Student services: health clinic, personal/psychological counseling.

COSTS & FINANCIAL AID

Costs (2017–18) ***Tuition:*** state resident $12,755 full-time; nonresident $34,518 full-time. Full-time tuition and fees vary according to class time, degree level, program, and student level. Part-time tuition and fees vary according to class time and program. ***Room and board:*** $7924. ***Payment plan:*** installment. ***Waivers:*** senior citizens and employees or children of employees.

Financial Aid Of all full-time matriculated undergraduates who enrolled in 2016, 1,869 applied for aid, 1,424 were judged to have need, 373 had their need fully met. 96 Federal Work-Study jobs (averaging $4476). In 2016, 593 non-need-based awards were made. ***Average percent of need met:*** 61. ***Average financial aid package:*** $16,428. ***Average need-based loan:*** $4314. ***Average need-based gift aid:*** $16,154. ***Average non-need-based aid:*** $13,354. ***Average indebtedness upon graduation:*** $27,872.

APPLYING

Standardized Tests *Required:* SAT or ACT (for admission).

Options: electronic application.

Application fee: $40.

Required: high school transcript. ***Recommended:*** interview.

Application deadlines: rolling (freshmen), rolling (transfers).

Notification: continuous (freshmen), continuous (transfers).

CONTACT

Lt. Col. John W. Powell Jr., Director of Admissions, The Citadel, The Military College of South Carolina, 171 Moultrie Street, Charleston, SC 29409. *Phone:* 843-953-5230. *Toll-free phone:* 800-868-1842. *Fax:* 843-953-7036. *E-mail:* john.powell@citadel.edu.

Claflin University

Orangeburg, South Carolina

http://www.claflin.edu/

CONTACT

Claflin University, 400 Magnolia Street, Orangeburg, SC 29115. *Phone:* 803-535-5340. *Toll-free phone:* 800-922-1276.

★ Clemson University

Clemson, South Carolina

http://www.clemson.edu/

- **State-supported** university, founded 1889
- **Small-town** 1400-acre campus
- **Endowment** $518.6 million
- **Coed** 18,599 undergraduate students, 96% full-time, 48% women, 52% men
- **Very difficult** entrance level, 51% of applicants were admitted

UNDERGRAD STUDENTS

17,883 full-time, 716 part-time. Students come from 53 states and territories; 84 other countries; 29% are from out of state; 7% Black or African American, non-Hispanic/Latino; 3% Hispanic/Latino; 2% Asian, non-Hispanic/Latino; 0.2% American Indian or Alaska Native, non-Hispanic/Latino; 3% Two or more races, non-Hispanic/Latino; 0.5% Race/ethnicity unknown; 0.9% international; 8% transferred in; 37% live on campus.

Freshmen:

Admission: 23,506 applied, 11,881 admitted, 3,684 enrolled. ***Test scores:*** SAT critical reading scores over 500: 92%; SAT math scores over 500: 96%; ACT scores over 18: 100%; SAT critical reading scores over 600:

59%; SAT math scores over 600: 73%; ACT scores over 24: 91%; SAT critical reading scores over 700: 14%; SAT math scores over 700: 18%; ACT scores over 30: 41%.

Retention: 93% of full-time freshmen returned.

FACULTY

Total: 1,264, 93% full-time, 84% with terminal degrees.

Student/faculty ratio: 18:1.

ACADEMICS

Calendar: semesters. *Degrees:* bachelor's, master's, doctoral, and post-master's certificates.

Special study options: academic remediation for entering students, advanced placement credit, cooperative education, distance learning, double majors, English as a second language, freshman honors college, honors programs, independent study, internships, off-campus study, part-time degree program, services for LD students, study abroad, summer session for credit. ***ROTC:*** Army (b), Air Force (b).

Computers: 1,250 computers/terminals are available on campus for general student use. Students can access the following: online (class) registration. Campuswide network is available. 100% of college-owned or -operated housing units are wired for high-speed Internet access. Wireless service is available via entire campus.

Library: Robert Muldrow Cooper Library plus 1 other.

STUDENT LIFE

Housing options: on-campus residence required for freshman year; coed, men-only, women-only. Campus housing is university owned. Freshman campus housing is guaranteed.

Activities and organizations: drama/theater group, student-run newspaper, radio and television station, choral group, marching band, Student Government, Fellowship of Christian Athletes, Tiger Band, national fraternities, national sororities.

Athletics Member NCAA. All Division I except football (Division I-A). ***Intercollegiate sports:*** baseball M(s), basketball M(s)/W(s), bowling M(c)/W(c), cheerleading M/W, crew M(c)/W(s), cross-country running M(s)/W(s), equestrian sports M(c)/W(c), fencing M(c)/W(c), field hockey M(c)/W(c), golf M(s), ice hockey M(c)/W(c), lacrosse M(c)/W(c), riflery M(c)/W(c), rugby M(c)/W(c), sailing M(c)/W(c), soccer M(s)/W(s), softball W(c), tennis M(s)/W(s), track and field M(s)/W(s), ultimate Frisbee M(c)/W(c), volleyball M(c)/W(s), weight lifting M(c)/W(c), wrestling M(c). ***Intramural sports:*** basketball M/W, golf M/W, racquetball M/W, soccer M/W, softball M/W, swimming and diving M(c)/W(c), table tennis M/W, tennis M(c)/W(c), volleyball M/W, water polo M/W.

Campus security: 24-hour emergency response devices and patrols, late-night transport/escort service, controlled dormitory access.

Student services: health clinic, personal/psychological counseling, legal services.

COSTS & FINANCIAL AID

Costs (2016–17) ***Tuition:*** state resident $13,186 full-time, $613 per credit hour part-time; nonresident $32,738 full-time, $1477 per credit hour part-time. Full-time tuition and fees vary according to course level, course load, location, program, and student level. Part-time tuition and fees vary according to course level, course load, location, program, and student level. ***Required fees:*** $1132 full-time. ***Room and board:*** $9144. Room and board charges vary according to board plan, housing facility, and location. ***Payment plan:*** installment. ***Waivers:*** senior citizens.

Financial Aid Of all full-time matriculated undergraduates who enrolled in 2016, 11,865 applied for aid, 8,502 were judged to have need, 1,397 had their need fully met. 1,177 Federal Work-Study jobs (averaging $3.9 million). In 2016, 4805 non-need-based awards were made. ***Average percent of need met:*** 55. ***Average financial aid package:*** $11,511. ***Average need-based loan:*** $4544. ***Average need-based gift aid:*** $9062. ***Average non-need-based aid:*** $5122.

APPLYING

Standardized Tests *Required:* SAT or ACT (for admission).

Options: electronic application.

Application fee: $70.

Required: high school transcript. ***Recommended:*** essay or personal statement.

Application deadlines: 5/1 (freshmen), 7/1 (transfers).

Notification: continuous (freshmen), continuous (transfers).

CONTACT

Ms. Audrey R. Bodell, Associate Director of Admissions, Clemson University, PO Box 345124, 105 Sikes Hall, Clemson, SC 29634. *Phone:* 864-656-2287. *Fax:* 864-656-2464. *E-mail:* cuadmissions@clemson.edu.

See previous page for display ad and page 1318 for the College Close-Up.

Coastal Carolina University

Conway, South Carolina

http://www.coastal.edu/

- **State-supported** comprehensive, founded 1954
- **Suburban** 633-acre campus
- **Endowment** $33.4 million
- **Coed** 9,747 undergraduate students, 91% full-time, 53% women, 47% men
- **Moderately difficult** entrance level, 61% of applicants were admitted

UNDERGRAD STUDENTS

8,864 full-time, 883 part-time. Students come from 49 states and territories; 63 other countries; 50% are from out of state; 20% Black or African American, non-Hispanic/Latino; 4% Hispanic/Latino; 0.7% Asian, non-Hispanic/Latino; 0.1% Native Hawaiian or other Pacific Islander, non-Hispanic/Latino; 0.3% American Indian or Alaska Native, non-Hispanic/Latino; 5% Two or more races, non-Hispanic/Latino; 0.9% Race/ethnicity unknown; 2% international; 8% transferred in; 42% live on campus.

Freshmen:

Admission: 17,768 applied, 10,871 admitted, 2,249 enrolled. ***Average high school GPA:*** 3.48. ***Test scores:*** SAT critical reading scores over 500: 50%; SAT math scores over 500: 58%; ACT scores over 18: 99%; SAT critical reading scores over 600: 10%; SAT math scores over 600: 11%; ACT scores over 24: 34%; SAT critical reading scores over 700: 1%; SAT math scores over 700: 1%; ACT scores over 30: 3%.

Retention: 69% of full-time freshmen returned.

FACULTY

Total: 738, 61% full-time, 56% with terminal degrees.

Student/faculty ratio: 17:1.

ACADEMICS

Calendar: semesters. *Degrees:* certificates, bachelor's, master's, doctoral, post-master's, and postbachelor's certificates.

Special study options: accelerated degree program, adult/continuing education programs, advanced placement credit, cooperative education, distance learning, double majors, honors programs, independent study, internships, part-time degree program, services for LD students, student-designed majors, study abroad, summer session for credit. ***ROTC:*** Army (b).

Computers: 1,322 computers/terminals are available on campus for general student use. Students can access the following: computer help desk, free student e-mail accounts, online (class) grades, online (class) registration, online (class) schedules. Campuswide network is available. Wireless service is available via classrooms, computer centers, computer labs, dorm rooms, learning centers, libraries, student centers.

Library: Kimbel Library. *Books:* 138,355 (physical), 375,066 (digital/electronic); *Serial titles:* 588 (physical), 45,000 (digital/electronic); *Databases:* 175. Weekly public service hours: 168; study areas open 24 hours, 5-7 days a week.

STUDENT LIFE

Housing options: on-campus residence required through sophomore year; coed, special housing for students with disabilities. Campus housing is university owned. Freshman campus housing is guaranteed.

Activities and organizations: drama/theater group, student-run newspaper, radio station, choral group, marching band, National Society of Leadership and Success, Leadership Challenge, Alpha Delta Pi, Salt Water Anglers, Aqua League (Scuba Club), national fraternities, national sororities.

Athletics Member NCAA. All Division I. ***Intercollegiate sports:*** baseball M(s), basketball M(s)/W(s), bowling M(c)/W(c), cheerleading M(c)/W(c), cross-country running M(s)/W(s), equestrian sports M(c)/W(c), field hockey M(c)/W(c), football M(s), golf M(s)/W(s), lacrosse M(c)/W(s), rugby M(c)/W(c), sailing M(c)/W(c), sand volleyball W(s), soccer M(s)/W(s), softball W(s), swimming and diving M(c)/W(c), tennis M(s)/W(s), track and field M(s)/W(s), volleyball M(c)/W(s), weight lifting M(c)/W(c), wrestling M(c). ***Intramural sports:*** badminton M/W, basketball M/W, sand volleyball M/W, soccer M/W, softball M/W, table tennis M/W, tennis M/W, volleyball M/W.

Campus security: 24-hour emergency response devices and patrols, late-night transport/escort service.

Student services: health clinic, personal/psychological counseling, women's center.

COSTS & FINANCIAL AID

Costs (2016–17) ***Tuition:*** state resident $10,696 full-time, $451 per credit hour part-time; nonresident $24,940 full-time, $1039 per credit hour part-time. Full-time tuition and fees vary according to course load, degree level, and reciprocity agreements. Part-time tuition and fees vary according to course load, degree level, and reciprocity agreements. ***Required fees:*** $180 full-time, $5 per credit hour part-time. ***Room and board:*** $8890; room only: $5440. Room and board charges vary according to board plan and housing facility. ***Payment plan:*** installment. ***Waivers:*** senior citizens and employees or children of employees.

Financial Aid Of all full-time matriculated undergraduates who enrolled in 2015, 7,324 applied for aid, 6,150 were judged to have need, 497 had their need fully met. 184 Federal Work-Study jobs (averaging $2335). 1,404 state and other part-time jobs (averaging $2012). In 2015, 1546 non-need-based awards were made. ***Average percent of need met:*** 47. ***Average financial aid package:*** $10,093. ***Average need-based loan:*** $9136. ***Average need-based gift aid:*** $4846. ***Average non-need-based aid:*** $13,723. ***Average indebtedness upon graduation:*** $38,897.

APPLYING

Standardized Tests *Required:* SAT or ACT (for admission).

Options: electronic application, deferred entrance.

Application fee: $45.

Required: high school transcript, minimum 2.0 GPA. ***Recommended:*** essay or personal statement, 1 letter of recommendation, interview.

Application deadlines: rolling (freshmen), rolling (transfers).

Notification: continuous until 10/1 (freshmen), continuous until 10/1 (transfers).

CONTACT

Coastal Carolina University, PO Box 261954, Conway, SC 29528-6054. *Phone:* 843-349-2037. *Toll-free phone:* 800-277-7000.

Coker College

Hartsville, South Carolina

http://www.coker.edu/

CONTACT

Mr. Adam Connolly, Associate Vice President Enrollment Management, Coker College, 300 E. College Avenue, Hartsville, SC 29550. *Phone:* 843-383-8050. *Toll-free phone:* 800-950-1908. *Fax:* 843-383-8056. *E-mail:* admissions@coker.edu.

College of Charleston

Charleston, South Carolina

http://www.cofc.edu/

- **State-supported** comprehensive, founded 1770
- **Urban** 52-acre campus
- **Endowment** $71.0 million
- **Coed** 10,375 undergraduate students, 92% full-time, 63% women, 37% men
- **Moderately difficult** entrance level, 84% of applicants were admitted

UNDERGRAD STUDENTS

9,524 full-time, 851 part-time. Students come from 51 states and territories; 62 other countries; 33% are from out of state; 8% Black or African American, non-Hispanic/Latino; 5% Hispanic/Latino; 2% Asian, non-Hispanic/Latino; 0.2% Native Hawaiian or other Pacific Islander, non-Hispanic/Latino; 0.3% American Indian or Alaska Native, non-Hispanic/Latino; 4% Two or more races, non-Hispanic/Latino; 1% Race/ethnicity unknown; 1% international; 7% transferred in; 32% live on campus.

Freshmen:

Admission: 10,828 applied, 9,110 admitted, 2,349 enrolled. ***Average high school GPA:*** 3.9. ***Test scores:*** SAT critical reading scores over 500: 76%; SAT math scores over 500: 76%; ACT scores over 18: 98%; SAT critical reading scores over 600: 27%; SAT math scores over 600: 22%; ACT scores over 24: 58%; SAT critical reading scores over 700: 5%; SAT math scores over 700: 2%; ACT scores over 30: 11%.

Retention: 79% of full-time freshmen returned.

FACULTY

Total: 952, 58% full-time, 69% with terminal degrees.

Student/faculty ratio: 15:1.

ACADEMICS

Calendar: semesters. *Degrees:* bachelor's, master's, post-master's, and postbachelor's certificates (also offers graduate degree programs through University of Charleston, South Carolina).

Special study options: accelerated degree program, adult/continuing education programs, advanced placement credit, cooperative education, distance learning, double majors, English as a second language, honors programs, independent study, internships, off-campus study, part-time degree program, services for LD students, study abroad, summer session for credit. ***ROTC:*** Air Force (c).

Unusual degree programs: 3-2 computer science, mathematics.

Computers: 1,024 computers/terminals and 2,053 ports are available on campus for general student use. Students can access the following: campus intranet, computer help desk, free student e-mail accounts, online (class) grades, online (class) registration, online (class) schedules. Campuswide network is available. 80% of college-owned or -operated housing units are wired for high-speed Internet access. Wireless service is available via entire campus.

Library: Marlene and Nathan Addlestone Library plus 3 others. *Books:* 700,910 (physical), 573,884 (digital/electronic); *Serial titles:* 2,721 (physical), 84,039 (digital/electronic); *Databases:* 328. Weekly public service hours: 121; students can reserve study rooms.

STUDENT LIFE

Housing options: coed, men-only, women-only, special housing for students with disabilities. Campus housing is university owned and leased by the school. Freshman applicants given priority for college housing.

Activities and organizations: drama/theater group, student-run newspaper, radio and television station, choral group, Student Government Association, Cougar Activities Board, Intramural Basketball, Black Student Union, Committed to Charleston Society, national fraternities, national sororities.

Athletics Member NCAA. All Division I. ***Intercollegiate sports:*** baseball M(s), basketball M(s)/W(s), cheerleading M/W, cross-country running M(s)/W(s), equestrian sports W, golf M(s)/W(s), sailing M/W, soccer M(s)/W(s), softball W(s), tennis M(s)/W(s), volleyball W(s). ***Intramural sports:*** badminton M/W, basketball M/W, crew M(c)/W(c), golf M(c)/W(c), gymnastics M(c)/W(c), ice hockey M(c)/W(c), lacrosse M(c)/W(c), racquetball M/W, rock climbing M/W, rowing M(c)/W(c), rugby M(c)/W(c), soccer M/W, softball M/W, squash M(c)/W(c), swimming and diving M(c)/W(c), table tennis M/W, tennis M(c)/W(c), ultimate Frisbee M(c)/W(c), volleyball M(c)/W(c), weight lifting M/W.

Campus security: 24-hour emergency response devices and patrols, student patrols, late-night transport/escort service, controlled dormitory access, shuttle service.

Student services: health clinic, personal/psychological counseling, women's center.

COSTS & FINANCIAL AID

Costs (2016–17) ***Tuition:*** state resident $11,386 full-time, $474 per credit hour part-time; nonresident $29,544 full-time, $1231 per credit hour part-time. Full-time tuition and fees vary according to student level. Part-time tuition and fees vary according to course load and student level. ***Required fees:*** $460 full-time, $16 per term part-time, $15 per term part-time. ***Room and board:*** $12,048; room only: $7828. Room and board charges vary according to board plan and housing facility. ***Payment plan:*** installment. ***Waivers:*** senior citizens and employees or children of employees.

Financial Aid Of all full-time matriculated undergraduates who enrolled in 2016, 6,219 applied for aid, 4,786 were judged to have need, 773 had their need fully met. In 2016, 1794 non-need-based awards were made.

Average percent of need met: 54. ***Average financial aid package:*** $13,505. ***Average need-based loan:*** $3587. ***Average need-based gift aid:*** $2609. ***Average non-need-based aid:*** $11,630. ***Average indebtedness upon graduation:*** $26,203.

APPLYING

Standardized Tests *Required:* SAT or ACT (for admission).

Options: electronic application, early action, deferred entrance.

Application fee: $50.

Required: essay or personal statement, high school transcript. ***Required for some:*** letters of recommendation for Honors College.

Application deadlines: 2/1 (freshmen), 6/1 (transfers), 11/1 (early action).

Notification: 4/1 (freshmen), continuous (transfers), 1/1 (early action).

CONTACT

Ms. Suzette Stille, Executive Director of Admissions, College of Charleston, 66 George Street, Charleston, SC 29424-0001. *Phone:* 843-953-5670. *Fax:* 843-953-6322. *E-mail:* admissions@cofc.edu.

Columbia College

Columbia, South Carolina

http://www.columbiasc.edu/

- **Independent United Methodist** comprehensive, founded 1854
- **Suburban** campus
- **Coed, primarily women**
- **Moderately difficult** entrance level

FACULTY

Student/faculty ratio: 13:1.

ACADEMICS

Calendar: semesters. *Degrees:* bachelor's, master's, and doctoral.

Library: J. Edens Drake Library plus 1 other.

STUDENT LIFE

Housing options: on-campus residence required through sophomore year; women-only. Campus housing is university owned. Freshman campus housing is guaranteed.

Activities and organizations: drama/theater group, student-run newspaper, choral group.

Athletics Member NAIA.

Campus security: 24-hour emergency response devices and patrols, late-night transport/escort service, controlled dormitory access.

Student services: health clinic, personal/psychological counseling, women's center.

FINANCIAL AID

Financial Aid Of all full-time matriculated undergraduates who enrolled in 2005, 794 applied for aid, 698 were judged to have need, 310 had their need fully met. 200 Federal Work-Study jobs (averaging $1000). In 2005, 152 non-need-based awards were made. ***Average percent of need met:*** 70. ***Average financial aid package:*** $20,052. ***Average need-based loan:*** $3810. ***Average need-based gift aid:*** $8495. ***Average non-need-based aid:*** $7775. ***Average indebtedness upon graduation:*** $25,333.

APPLYING

Standardized Tests *Required:* SAT or ACT (for admission).

Options: electronic application.

Required: high school transcript. ***Required for some:*** interview. ***Recommended:*** essay or personal statement.

CONTACT

Ms. Julie King, Director of Admissions, Columbia College, 1301 Columbia College Drive, Columbia, SC 29203. *Phone:* 803-786-3871. *Toll-free phone:* 800-277-1301. *E-mail:* juking@columbiasc.edu.

Columbia International University

Columbia, South Carolina

http://www.ciu.edu/

- **Independent nondenominational** university, founded 1923
- **Suburban** 400-acre campus with easy access to Columbia, SC
- **Endowment** $21.1 million
- **Coed** 497 undergraduate students, 91% full-time, 48% women, 52% men
- **Moderately difficult** entrance level, 36% of applicants were admitted

UNDERGRAD STUDENTS

454 full-time, 43 part-time. Students come from 27 states and territories; 15 other countries; 48% are from out of state; 11% Black or African American, non-Hispanic/Latino; 4% Hispanic/Latino; 2% Asian, non-Hispanic/Latino; 2% Two or more races, non-Hispanic/Latino; 3% Race/ethnicity unknown; 5% international; 10% transferred in; 68% live on campus.

Freshmen:

Admission: 518 applied, 185 admitted, 80 enrolled. ***Average high school GPA:*** 3.65. ***Test scores:*** SAT critical reading scores over 500: 66%; SAT math scores over 500: 58%; ACT scores over 18: 88%; SAT critical reading scores over 600: 30%; SAT math scores over 600: 19%; ACT scores over 24: 48%; SAT critical reading scores over 700: 6%; SAT math scores over 700: 4%; ACT scores over 30: 13%.

Retention: 78% of full-time freshmen returned.

FACULTY

Total: 63, 60% full-time.

Student/faculty ratio: 16:1.

ACADEMICS

Calendar: semesters. *Degrees:* certificates, associate, bachelor's, master's, doctoral, post-master's, and postbachelor's certificates.

Special study options: academic remediation for entering students, accelerated degree program, advanced placement credit, cooperative education, distance learning, double majors, honors programs, independent study, internships, off-campus study, part-time degree program, services for LD students, study abroad, summer session for credit.

Unusual degree programs: 3-2 teaching or dvinity.

Computers: 106 computers/terminals and 374 ports are available on campus for general student use. Students can access the following: campus intranet, computer help desk, free student e-mail accounts, online (class) grades, online (class) registration, online (class) schedules. Campuswide network is available. 100% of college-owned or -operated housing units are wired for high-speed Internet access. Wireless service is available via classrooms, computer centers, computer labs, dorm rooms, learning centers, libraries, student centers.

Library: G. Allen Fleece Library. *Books:* 32,000 (physical), 100,000 (digital/electronic); *Databases:* 133. Weekly public service hours: 81; students can reserve study rooms.

STUDENT LIFE

Housing options: on-campus residence required through senior year; men-only, women-only. Campus housing is university owned. Freshman campus housing is guaranteed.

Activities and organizations: drama/theater group, student-run newspaper, choral group, Student Union, Mu Kappa, Student Missions Connection, GradLife, African American Fellowship Ministries.

Athletics Member NCCAA. ***Intercollegiate sports:*** basketball M(s)/W(s), cross-country running M(s)/W(s), soccer M(s)/W(s). ***Intramural sports:*** basketball M/W, football M/W, soccer M/W, ultimate Frisbee M/W, volleyball M/W.

Campus security: 24-hour emergency response devices and patrols, late-night transport/escort service, controlled dormitory access.

Student services: health clinic, personal/psychological counseling, legal services.

COSTS & FINANCIAL AID

Costs (2017–18) ***Comprehensive fee:*** $30,380 includes full-time tuition ($21,720), mandatory fees ($670), and room and board ($7990). Full-time tuition and fees vary according to course load, program, and reciprocity agreements. Part-time tuition: $905 per semester hour. Part-time tuition and fees vary according to course load, program, and reciprocity agreements. ***Required fees:*** $10 per semester hour part-time, $185 per term part-time. ***Room and board:*** Room and board charges vary according to board plan and housing facility. ***Payment plan:*** installment. ***Waivers:*** employees or children of employees.

Financial Aid Of all full-time matriculated undergraduates who enrolled in 2015, 417 applied for aid, 371 were judged to have need, 50 had their need fully met. 95 Federal Work-Study jobs (averaging $1157). 243 state and other part-time jobs (averaging $1799). In 2015, 123 non-need-based awards were made. ***Average percent of need met:*** 63. ***Average financial aid package:*** $17,615. ***Average need-based loan:*** $4132. ***Average need-based gift aid:*** $13,771. ***Average non-need-based aid:*** $5306. ***Average indebtedness upon graduation:*** $22,405.

APPLYING

Standardized Tests *Required:* SAT or ACT (for admission).

Options: electronic application, deferred entrance.

Required: essay or personal statement, minimum 2.0 GPA, 1 letter of recommendation. ***Required for some:*** interview. ***Recommended:*** high school transcript.

Application deadlines: 8/1 (freshmen), 8/1 (transfers).

Notification: continuous (freshmen), continuous (out-of-state freshmen), continuous (transfers).

CONTACT

Ms. Jen Johnson, Undergraduate Admissions Office, Columbia International University, Columbia, SC 29230-3122. *Phone:* 803-777-2227. *Toll-free phone:* 800-777-2227 Ext. 5024. *Fax:* 803-786-4041. *E-mail:* yesciu@ciu.edu.

Converse College

Spartanburg, South Carolina

http://www.converse.edu/

- **Independent** comprehensive, founded 1889
- **Urban** 70-acre campus
- **Endowment** $81.0 million
- **Undergraduate: women only; graduate: coed** 794 undergraduate students, 94% full-time, 100% women
- **Moderately difficult** entrance level, 58% of applicants were admitted

UNDERGRAD STUDENTS

745 full-time, 49 part-time. Students come from 29 states and territories; 12 other countries; 9% Black or African American, non-Hispanic/Latino; 5% Hispanic/Latino; 0.6% Asian, non-Hispanic/Latino; 4% Two or more races, non-Hispanic/Latino; 10% Race/ethnicity unknown; 2% international; 6% transferred in; 80% live on campus.

Freshmen:

Admission: 1,316 applied, 760 admitted, 212 enrolled. ***Average high school GPA:*** 3.89. ***Test scores:*** SAT critical reading scores over 500: 66%; SAT math scores over 500: 60%; ACT scores over 18: 97%; SAT critical reading scores over 600: 21%; SAT math scores over 600: 14%; ACT scores over 24: 50%; SAT critical reading scores over 700: 3%; SAT math scores over 700: 2%; ACT scores over 30: 5%.

Retention: 66% of full-time freshmen returned.

FACULTY

Total: 82, 96% full-time.

Student/faculty ratio: 12:1.

ACADEMICS

Calendar: 4-2-4. *Degrees:* bachelor's, master's, and post-master's certificates.

Special study options: adult/continuing education programs, advanced placement credit, cooperative education, distance learning, double majors, English as a second language, honors programs, independent study, internships, off-campus study, part-time degree program, services for LD students, student-designed majors, study abroad, summer session for credit. ***ROTC:*** Army (c).

Computers: 140 computers/terminals are available on campus for general student use. Students can access the following: campus intranet, computer help desk, free student e-mail accounts, online (class) grades, online (class) registration, online (class) schedules. Campuswide network is available. 100% of college-owned or -operated housing units are wired for high-speed Internet access. Wireless service is available via entire campus.

Library: Mickel Library. *Books:* 165,873 (physical), 252,047 (digital/electronic); *Databases:* 30.

STUDENT LIFE

Housing options: on-campus residence required through senior year; women-only. Campus housing is university owned. Freshman campus housing is guaranteed.

Activities and organizations: drama/theater group, student-run newspaper, choral group, Student Government, student volunteer services, Student Christian Organization, Student Activities Committee, Athletic Association.

Athletics Member NCAA. All Division II. ***Intercollegiate sports:*** basketball W(s), cross-country running W(s), equestrian sports W(s), golf W(s), lacrosse W(s), soccer W(s), swimming and diving W(s), tennis W(s), track and field W(s), volleyball W(s). ***Intramural sports:*** archery W, basketball W, bowling W, equestrian sports W, fencing W, field hockey W, soccer W, softball W, swimming and diving W, tennis W, volleyball W, weight lifting W.

Campus security: 24-hour emergency response devices and patrols, late-night transport/escort service, controlled dormitory access.

Student services: health clinic, personal/psychological counseling, women's center.

COSTS & FINANCIAL AID

Costs (2017–18) ***Comprehensive fee:*** $28,640 includes full-time tuition ($17,680), mandatory fees ($350), and room and board ($10,610). Full-time tuition and fees vary according to course load and program. Part-time tuition: $875 per credit. Part-time tuition and fees vary according to course load and program. ***Room and board:*** Room and board charges vary according to board plan. ***Payment plan:*** installment. ***Waivers:*** employees or children of employees.

Financial Aid Of all full-time matriculated undergraduates who enrolled in 2015, 703 applied for aid, 589 were judged to have need, 113 had their need fully met. 65 Federal Work-Study jobs (averaging $1128). 87 state and other part-time jobs (averaging $1316). In 2015, 99 non-need-based awards were made. ***Average percent of need met:*** 67. ***Average financial aid package:*** $14,856. ***Average need-based loan:*** $4818. ***Average need-based gift aid:*** $11,182. ***Average non-need-based aid:*** $4785. ***Average indebtedness upon graduation:*** $28,036.

APPLYING

Standardized Tests *Required:* SAT or ACT (for admission).

Options: electronic application, deferred entrance.

Required: high school transcript. ***Recommended:*** essay or personal statement, minimum 3.0 GPA.

Application deadlines: rolling (freshmen), rolling (out-of-state freshmen), rolling (transfers).

Notification: continuous (freshmen), continuous (out-of-state freshmen), continuous (transfers).

CONTACT

Admissions, Converse College, 580 East Main Street, Spartanburg, SC 29302. *Phone:* 864-596-9040. *Toll-free phone:* 800-766-1125. *E-mail:* admissions@converse.edu.

Erskine College

Due West, South Carolina

http://www.erskine.edu/

- **Independent** comprehensive, founded 1839, affiliated with Associate Reformed Presbyterian Church
- **Rural** 90-acre campus
- **Endowment** $39.8 million
- **Coed**
- **Moderately difficult** entrance level

FACULTY

Student/faculty ratio: 12:1.

ACADEMICS

Calendar: 4-1-4. *Degrees:* certificates, bachelor's, master's, and doctoral.

Library: McCain Library. Students can reserve study rooms.

STUDENT LIFE

Housing options: on-campus residence required through senior year; men-only, women-only. Campus housing is university owned. Freshman campus housing is guaranteed.

Activities and organizations: drama/theater group, student-run newspaper, radio station, choral group, literary societies, religious organizations, Student Government Organization, publications, honor societies.

Athletics Member NCAA. All Division II.

Campus security: 24-hour patrols, late-night transport/escort service, controlled dormitory access.

Student services: health clinic, personal/psychological counseling.

COSTS & FINANCIAL AID

Costs (2016–17) ***Comprehensive fee:*** $44,210 includes full-time tuition ($31,345), mandatory fees ($2365), and room and board ($10,500). Full-time tuition and fees vary according to program. Part-time tuition and fees vary according to program. ***College room only:*** $5400. Room and board charges vary according to board plan.

Financial Aid Of all full-time matriculated undergraduates who enrolled in 2009, 498 applied for aid, 400 were judged to have need, 156 had their need fully met. In 2009, 121 non-need-based awards were made. ***Average percent of need met:*** 86. ***Average financial aid package:*** $21,093. ***Average need-based loan:*** $4750. ***Average need-based gift aid:*** $16,222. ***Average non-need-based aid:*** $10,725. ***Average indebtedness upon graduation:*** $24,450.

APPLYING

Standardized Tests *Required:* SAT or ACT (for admission).

Options: electronic application, early admission, early action, deferred entrance.

Required: essay or personal statement, high school transcript, 1 letter of recommendation. ***Recommended:*** interview.

CONTACT

Ms. Tobe Frierson, Senior Admissions Specialist, Erskine College, 2 Washington Street, PO Box 338, Due West, SC 29639.
Phone: 864-379-8838. *Toll-free phone:* 800-241-8721.

Francis Marion University

Florence, South Carolina

http://www.fmarion.edu/

- **State-supported** comprehensive, founded 1970
- **Rural** 400-acre campus
- **Endowment** $27.6 million
- **Coed** 3,559 undergraduate students, 88% full-time, 69% women, 31% men
- **Moderately difficult** entrance level, 62% of applicants were admitted

UNDERGRAD STUDENTS

3,133 full-time, 426 part-time. Students come from 29 states and territories; 24 other countries; 4% are from out of state; 43% Black or African American, non-Hispanic/Latino; 2% Hispanic/Latino; 1% Asian, non-Hispanic/Latino; 0.3% American Indian or Alaska Native, non-Hispanic/Latino; 3% Two or more races, non-Hispanic/Latino; 0.5% Race/ethnicity unknown; 2% international; 6% transferred in; 44% live on campus.

Freshmen:

Admission: 3,738 applied, 2,301 admitted, 729 enrolled. ***Average high school GPA:*** 3.79. ***Test scores:*** SAT critical reading scores over 500: 34%; SAT math scores over 500: 30%; ACT scores over 18: 69%; SAT critical reading scores over 600: 5%; SAT math scores over 600: 5%; ACT scores over 24: 17%.

Retention: 68% of full-time freshmen returned.

FACULTY

Total: 279, 73% full-time, 69% with terminal degrees.

Student/faculty ratio: 15:1.

ACADEMICS

Calendar: semesters. *Degrees:* bachelor's, master's, and post-master's certificates.

Special study options: accelerated degree program, adult/continuing education programs, advanced placement credit, distance learning, double majors, honors programs, independent study, internships, off-campus study, part-time degree program, services for LD students, study abroad, summer session for credit. ***ROTC:*** Army (b).

Unusual degree programs: 3-2 engineering with Clemson University; forestry with Clemson University; wildlife and fisheries with Clemson University.

Computers: 634 computers/terminals are available on campus for general student use. Students can access the following: computer help desk, free student e-mail accounts, online (class) grades, online (class) registration, online (class) schedules, learning management system. Campuswide network is available. 100% of college-owned or -operated housing units are wired for high-speed Internet access. Wireless service is available via entire campus.

Library: James A. Rogers Library plus 1 other. *Books:* 343,000 (digital/electronic).

STUDENT LIFE

Housing options: men-only, women-only, special housing for students with disabilities. Campus housing is university owned and is provided by a third party. Freshman applicants given priority for college housing.

Activities and organizations: drama/theater group, student-run newspaper, choral group, Baptist Collegiate Ministries, University Programming Board, Psychology Club, Student Alumni Association, Young Gifted and Blessed Chorus, national fraternities, national sororities.

Athletics Member NCAA. All Division II except golf (Division I), soccer (Division I). ***Intercollegiate sports:*** baseball M(s), basketball M(s)/W(s), cheerleading W, cross-country running M(s)/W(s), golf M(s), soccer M(s)/W(s), softball W(s), tennis M(s)/W(s), track and field M/W, volleyball W(s). ***Intramural sports:*** basketball M/W, football M, racquetball M/W, soccer M/W, softball M/W, table tennis M/W, tennis M/W, volleyball M/W.

Campus security: 24-hour emergency response devices and patrols, late-night transport/escort service, controlled dormitory access.

Student services: health clinic, personal/psychological counseling.

COSTS & FINANCIAL AID

Costs (2016–17) ***Tuition:*** state resident $9880 full-time, $494 per credit hour part-time; nonresident $19,760 full-time, $988 per credit hour part-time. Full-time tuition and fees vary according to degree level and program. Part-time tuition and fees vary according to course load, degree level, and program. ***Required fees:*** $548 full-time, $15 per credit hour part-time, $73 per term part-time. ***Room and board:*** $7716; room only: $4360. Room and board charges vary according to board plan and housing facility. ***Payment plan:*** installment. ***Waivers:*** senior citizens and employees or children of employees.

Financial Aid Of all full-time matriculated undergraduates who enrolled in 2016, 2,129 applied for aid, 1,907 were judged to have need, 203 had their need fully met. In 2016, 61 non-need-based awards were made. ***Average percent of need met:*** 82. ***Average financial aid package:*** $16,226. ***Average need-based loan:*** $8697. ***Average need-based gift aid:*** $5239. ***Average non-need-based aid:*** $4245. ***Average indebtedness upon graduation:*** $36,587.

APPLYING

Standardized Tests *Required:* SAT or ACT (for admission).

Options: electronic application, deferred entrance.

Application fee: $39.

Required: minimum 2.0 GPA. ***Required for some:*** essay or personal statement, high school transcript.

Application deadlines: 8/15 (freshmen), rolling (transfers).

Notification: 9/1 (freshmen).

CONTACT

Perry Wilson, Director of Admissions, Francis Marion University, PO Box 100547, Florence, SC 29502-0547. *Phone:* 843-661-1231. *Toll-free phone:* 800-368-7551. *Fax:* 843-661-4635. *E-mail:* admissions@fmarion.edu.

Furman University
Greenville, South Carolina
http://www.furman.edu/

- **Independent** comprehensive, founded 1826
- **Suburban** 800-acre campus
- **Endowment** $609.7 million
- **Coed** 2,797 undergraduate students, 96% full-time, 58% women, 42% men
- **Moderately difficult** entrance level, 68% of applicants were admitted

UNDERGRAD STUDENTS
2,696 full-time, 101 part-time. Students come from 45 states and territories; 49 other countries; 71% are from out of state; 5% Black or African American, non-Hispanic/Latino; 5% Hispanic/Latino; 2% Asian, non-Hispanic/Latino; 0.1% American Indian or Alaska Native, non-Hispanic/Latino; 3% Two or more races, non-Hispanic/Latino; 3% Race/ethnicity unknown; 5% international; 1% transferred in; 96% live on campus.

Freshmen:
Admission: 5,232 applied, 3,545 admitted, 748 enrolled. ***Test scores:*** SAT critical reading scores over 500: 93%; SAT math scores over 500: 93%; SAT writing scores over 500: 90%; ACT scores over 18: 100%; SAT critical reading scores over 600: 62%; SAT math scores over 600: 62%; SAT writing scores over 600: 53%; ACT scores over 24: 88%; SAT critical reading scores over 700: 16%; SAT math scores over 700: 14%; SAT writing scores over 700: 17%; ACT scores over 30: 37%.

Retention: 90% of full-time freshmen returned.

FACULTY
Total: 254, 92% full-time, 93% with terminal degrees.

Student/faculty ratio: 11:1.

ACADEMICS
Calendar: 3-2-3. *Degrees:* bachelor's and master's.

Special study options: accelerated degree program, adult/continuing education programs, advanced placement credit, double majors, independent study, internships, part-time degree program, services for LD students, student-designed majors, study abroad, summer session for credit. ***ROTC:*** Army (b).

Unusual degree programs: 3-2 engineering with Georgia Institute of Technology, Clemson University, Auburn University, North Carolina State University, Washington University in St. Louis; forestry with Duke University.

Computers: 500 computers/terminals and 3,500 ports are available on campus for general student use. Students can access the following: campus intranet, computer help desk, free student e-mail accounts, online (class) grades, online (class) registration, online (class) schedules. Campuswide network is available. 100% of college-owned or -operated housing units are wired for high-speed Internet access. Wireless service is available via entire campus.

Library: James Buchanan Duke Library plus 3 others. *Books:* 494,912 (physical), 633,142 (digital/electronic); *Serial titles:* 588 (physical), 197,182 (digital/electronic); *Databases:* 275. Weekly public service hours: 99; study areas open 24 hours, 5-7 days a week.

STUDENT LIFE
Housing options: on-campus residence required through senior year; coed, men-only, women-only, special housing for students with disabilities. Campus housing is university owned. Freshman campus housing is guaranteed.

Activities and organizations: drama/theater group, student-run newspaper, radio and television station, choral group, marching band, Collegiate Educational Service Corps, Fellowship of Christian Athletes, Baptist Student Union, Student Activities Board, Furman Singers, national fraternities, national sororities.

Athletics Member NCAA. All Division I except football (Division I-AA). ***Intercollegiate sports:*** baseball M(s), basketball M(s)/W(s), cheerleading M/W, crew M(c)/W(c), cross-country running M(s)/W(s), equestrian sports W(c), fencing M(c)/W(c), golf M(c)/W(s), ice hockey M(c), lacrosse M/W, rugby M(c)/W(c), soccer M(s)/W(s), softball W(s), swimming and diving M(c)/W(c), tennis M(s)/W(s), track and field M(s)/W(s), ultimate Frisbee M(c)/W(c), volleyball W(s), weight lifting M(c)/W(c), wrestling M(c). ***Intramural sports:*** basketball M/W, bowling M/W, cross-country running M/W, football M/W, golf M/W, racquetball M/W, soccer M/W, softball M/W, swimming and diving M/W, tennis M/W, track and field M/W, volleyball M/W.

Campus security: 24-hour emergency response devices and patrols, student patrols, late-night transport/escort service, controlled dormitory access.

Student services: health clinic, personal/psychological counseling, women's center.

COSTS & FINANCIAL AID
Costs (2016–17) ***Comprehensive fee:*** $59,028 includes full-time tuition ($46,784), mandatory fees ($380), and room and board ($11,864). Part-time tuition: $1462 per credit. Part-time tuition and fees vary according to course load. ***College room only:*** $6358. Room and board charges vary according to board plan and housing facility. ***Payment plan:*** installment. ***Waivers:*** employees or children of employees.

Financial Aid Of all full-time matriculated undergraduates who enrolled in 2016, 1,521 applied for aid, 1,255 were judged to have need, 434 had their need fully met. 598 Federal Work-Study jobs (averaging $1530). In 2016, 1176 non-need-based awards were made. ***Average percent of need met:*** 79. ***Average financial aid package:*** $39,063. ***Average need-based loan:*** $4884. ***Average need-based gift aid:*** $35,508. ***Average non-need-based aid:*** $20,472. ***Average indebtedness upon graduation:*** $36,846. ***Financial aid deadline:*** 1/15.

APPLYING
Standardized Tests *Recommended:* SAT or ACT (for admission).

Options: electronic application, early decision, early action.

Application fee: $50.

Required: essay or personal statement, high school transcript. ***Required for some:*** interview.

Application deadlines: 1/15 (freshmen), 1/15 (transfers), 11/1 (early action).

Early decision deadline: 11/1.

Notification: 3/1 (freshmen), 3/1 (transfers), 11/15 (early decision), 12/20 (early action).

CONTACT
Mr. Brad Pochard, Dean of Admission, Furman University, 3300 Poinsett Highway, Greenville, SC 29613. *Phone:* 864-294-2034. *Fax:* 864-294-2018. *E-mail:* admissions@furman.edu.

Lander University
Greenwood, South Carolina
http://www.lander.edu/

CONTACT
Ms. Jennifer M. Mathis, Director of Admissions, Lander University, 320 Stanley Avenue, Greenwood, SC 29649. *Phone:* 864-388-8307. *Toll-free phone:* 888-452-6337. *Fax:* 864-388-8125. *E-mail:* admissions@lander.edu.

Limestone College
Gaffney, South Carolina
http://www.limestone.edu/

- **Independent** comprehensive, founded 1845
- **Suburban** 123-acre campus with easy access to Charlotte
- **Endowment** $17.0 million
- **Coed** 1,227 undergraduate students, 100% full-time, 37% women, 63% men
- **Minimally difficult** entrance level, 52% of applicants were admitted

UNDERGRAD STUDENTS
1,227 full-time. Students come from 30 states and territories; 31 other countries; 42% are from out of state; 34% Black or African American, non-Hispanic/Latino; 4% Hispanic/Latino; 0.2% American Indian or Alaska Native, non-Hispanic/Latino; 3% Two or more races, non-Hispanic/Latino; 1% Race/ethnicity unknown; 9% international; 3% transferred in; 74% live on campus.

Freshmen:
Admission: 3,195 applied, 1,653 admitted, 416 enrolled. ***Average high school GPA:*** 3.24. ***Test scores:*** SAT critical reading scores over 500:

23%; SAT math scores over 500: 33%; ACT scores over 18: 58%; SAT critical reading scores over 600: 3%; SAT math scores over 600: 6%; ACT scores over 24: 10%; ACT scores over 30: 2%.

Retention: 56% of full-time freshmen returned.

FACULTY

Total: 117, 69% full-time.

Student/faculty ratio: 13:1.

ACADEMICS

Calendar: semesters. *Degrees:* associate, bachelor's, and master's.

Special study options: academic remediation for entering students, accelerated degree program, adult/continuing education programs, advanced placement credit, distance learning, double majors, honors programs, independent study, internships, part-time degree program, services for LD students, student-designed majors, summer session for credit. ***ROTC:*** Army (c).

Computers: 137 computers/terminals are available on campus for general student use. Students can access the following: campus intranet, computer help desk, free student e-mail accounts, online (class) grades, online (class) registration, online (class) schedules. Campuswide network is available. 100% of college-owned or -operated housing units are wired for high-speed Internet access. Wireless service is available via classrooms, dorm rooms, learning centers, libraries, student centers.

Library: A. J. Eastwood Library plus 1 other. *Books:* 67,000 (physical), 239,537 (digital/electronic); *Serial titles:* 111 (physical), 482,082 (digital/electronic); *Databases:* 156. Weekly public service hours: 70.

STUDENT LIFE

Housing options: on-campus residence required through junior year; men-only, women-only. Campus housing is university owned. Freshman applicants given priority for college housing.

Activities and organizations: drama/theater group, choral group, marching band, Fellowship of Christian Athletes, Student Government Association, Student Alumni Leadership Council, Campus Crusade (CRU), Limestone Activities Board (LAB), national fraternities, national sororities.

Athletics Member NCAA. All Division II. ***Intercollegiate sports:*** baseball M(s), basketball M(s)/W(s), cheerleading M(s)/W(s), cross-country running M(s)/W(s), field hockey W(s), football M(s), golf M(s)/W(s), lacrosse M(s)/W(s), soccer M(s)/W(s), softball W(s), swimming and diving M(s)/W(s), tennis M(s)/W(s), track and field M(s)/W(s), volleyball M(s)/W(s), wrestling M(s). ***Intramural sports:*** badminton M/W, basketball M/W, bowling M/W, racquetball M/W, soccer M/W, table tennis M/W, ultimate Frisbee M/W, volleyball M/W, weight lifting M/W.

Campus security: 24-hour emergency response devices and patrols, late-night transport/escort service, controlled dormitory access.

Student services: health clinic, personal/psychological counseling.

COSTS & FINANCIAL AID

Costs (2017–18) ***Comprehensive fee:*** $34,482 includes full-time tuition ($24,900) and room and board ($9582). Full-time tuition and fees vary according to class time and course load. Part-time tuition: $996 per semester hour. Part-time tuition and fees vary according to class time. ***College room only:*** $5204. Room and board charges vary according to board plan and housing facility. ***Payment plan:*** installment. ***Waivers:*** employees or children of employees.

Financial Aid Of all full-time matriculated undergraduates who enrolled in 2015, 819 applied for aid, 749 were judged to have need, 117 had their need fully met. 105 Federal Work-Study jobs (averaging $1101). 90 state and other part-time jobs (averaging $673). In 2015, 192 non-need-based awards were made. ***Average percent of need met:*** 66. ***Average financial aid package:*** $19,841. ***Average need-based loan:*** $3850. ***Average need-based gift aid:*** $16,403. ***Average non-need-based aid:*** $5980. ***Average indebtedness upon graduation:*** $30,856.

APPLYING

Standardized Tests *Required:* SAT or ACT (for admission). *Required for some:* minimum score of 500 on TOEFL or proof of successfully completed ESL program for students whose native language is not English.

Options: electronic application.

Application fee: $25.

Required: high school transcript, minimum 2.0 GPA. ***Recommended:*** 2 letters of recommendation, interview.

Application deadlines: rolling (freshmen), rolling (transfers).

Notification: continuous (freshmen), continuous (transfers).

CONTACT

Ms. Lisa Hobbs, Admissions Office Manager, Limestone College, 1115 College Drive, Gaffney, SC 29340-3799. *Phone:* 864-488-4554. *Toll-free phone:* 800-795-7151. *Fax:* 864-487-8706. *E-mail:* lhobbs@limestone.edu.

Medical University of South Carolina

Charleston, South Carolina

http://www.musc.edu/

CONTACT

Lyla E. Hudson, Director of Admissions, Medical University of South Carolina, 41 Bee Street MSC203, Charleston, SC 29425-2030. *Phone:* 843-792-7408. *E-mail:* hudsonly@musc.edu.

Morris College

Sumter, South Carolina

http://www.morris.edu/

- **Independent** 4-year, founded 1908, affiliated with Baptist Educational and Missionary Convention of South Carolina
- **Urban** 34-acre campus with easy access to Columbia, SC
- **Endowment** $12.1 million
- **Coed** 754 undergraduate students, 97% full-time, 59% women, 41% men
- **Noncompetitive** entrance level, 78% of applicants were admitted

UNDERGRAD STUDENTS

735 full-time, 19 part-time. Students come from 21 states and territories; 18% are from out of state; 98% Black or African American, non-Hispanic/Latino; 0.5% Hispanic/Latino; 0.1% Asian, non-Hispanic/Latino; 0.1% American Indian or Alaska Native, non-Hispanic/Latino; 0.8% Two or more races, non-Hispanic/Latino; 6% transferred in; 78% live on campus.

Freshmen:

Admission: 2,551 applied, 2,002 admitted, 219 enrolled. ***Average high school GPA:*** 2.53.

Retention: 55% of full-time freshmen returned.

FACULTY

Total: 56, 70% full-time, 59% with terminal degrees.

Student/faculty ratio: 13:1.

ACADEMICS

Calendar: semesters. *Degree:* bachelor's.

Special study options: academic remediation for entering students, accelerated degree program, adult/continuing education programs, advanced placement credit, cooperative education, double majors, honors programs, internships, study abroad, summer session for credit. ***ROTC:*** Army (b).

Unusual degree programs: 3-2 engineering with North Carolina Agricultural and Technical State University.

Computers: 292 computers/terminals are available on campus for general student use. Students can access the following: free student e-mail accounts, online (class) grades, online (class) schedules, online financial aid Information, learning management system. Campuswide network is available. 100% of college-owned or -operated housing units are wired for high-speed Internet access. Wireless service is available via entire campus.

Library: Richardson-Johnson Learning Resources Center plus 1 other. *Books:* 96,146 (physical), 36,880 (digital/electronic); *Serial titles:* 427 (physical), 36,880 (digital/electronic); *Databases:* 74. Weekly public service hours: 76.

STUDENT LIFE

Housing options: men-only, women-only. Campus housing is university owned.

Activities and organizations: drama/theater group, student-run newspaper, radio station, choral group, Student Government Association,

New Emphasis on Nontraditional Students (NEONS), Block M Club, Pre Alumni Council, Baptist Student Union.

Athletics Member NAIA. ***Intercollegiate sports:*** baseball M(s), basketball M(s)/W(s), cheerleading M(s)/W(s), cross-country running M(s)/W(s), softball W(s), track and field M(s)/W(s), volleyball W(s). ***Intramural sports:*** basketball M/W, table tennis M/W.

Campus security: 24-hour emergency response devices and patrols.

Student services: personal/psychological counseling.

COSTS & FINANCIAL AID

Costs (2016–17) ***Comprehensive fee:*** $18,500 includes full-time tuition ($11,690), mandatory fees ($1355), and room and board ($5455). Part-time tuition: $487 per credit hour. ***Required fees:*** $1355 per semester hour part-time, $1355 per semester part-time. ***College room only:*** $2358. ***Payment plan:*** installment.

Financial Aid Of all full-time matriculated undergraduates who enrolled in 2015, 887 applied for aid, 859 were judged to have need, 10 had their need fully met. 300 Federal Work-Study jobs (averaging $818). ***Average percent of need met:*** 85. ***Average financial aid package:*** $12,100. ***Average need-based loan:*** $3900. ***Average need-based gift aid:*** $7400. ***Average indebtedness upon graduation:*** $17,125.

APPLYING

Options: electronic application, deferred entrance.

Required: high school transcript. ***Required for some:*** interview.

Application deadlines: rolling (freshmen), rolling (transfers).

Notification: continuous (freshmen), continuous (transfers).

CONTACT

Ms. Gloria Scriven, Assistant Director of Admissions and Records, Morris College, 100 West College Street, Sumter, SC 29150-3502. *Phone:* 803-934-3239. *Toll-free phone:* 866-853-1345. *Fax:* 803-773-8241. *E-mail:* gscriven@morris.edu.

Newberry College

Newberry, South Carolina

http://www.newberry.edu/

- **Independent Evangelical Lutheran** 4-year, founded 1856
- **Small-town** 90-acre campus with easy access to Columbia and Greenville, SC
- **Endowment** $18.8 million
- **Coed** 1,070 undergraduate students, 98% full-time, 46% women, 54% men
- **Moderately difficult** entrance level, 60% of applicants were admitted

UNDERGRAD STUDENTS

1,052 full-time, 18 part-time. Students come from 30 states and territories; 19 other countries; 21% are from out of state; 26% Black or African American, non-Hispanic/Latino; 4% Hispanic/Latino; 0.7% Asian, non-Hispanic/Latino; 0.4% American Indian or Alaska Native, non-Hispanic/Latino; 3% Two or more races, non-Hispanic/Latino; 5% Race/ethnicity unknown; 4% international; 7% transferred in; 82% live on campus.

Freshmen:

Admission: 1,445 applied, 862 admitted, 285 enrolled. ***Average high school GPA:*** 3.5. ***Test scores:*** SAT critical reading scores over 500: 31%; SAT math scores over 500: 40%; ACT scores over 18: 72%; SAT critical reading scores over 600: 6%; SAT math scores over 600: 6%; ACT scores over 24: 19%; SAT critical reading scores over 700: 1%; ACT scores over 30: 1%.

Retention: 66% of full-time freshmen returned.

FACULTY

Total: 128, 50% full-time, 52% with terminal degrees.

Student/faculty ratio: 12:1.

ACADEMICS

Calendar: semesters. *Degree:* bachelor's.

Special study options: academic remediation for entering students, adult/continuing education programs, advanced placement credit, double majors, honors programs, independent study, internships, part-time degree program, services for LD students, student-designed majors, study abroad, summer session for credit. ***ROTC:*** Army (b).

Unusual degree programs: 3-2 engineering with Clemson University; forestry with Duke University; pharmacy with Presbyterian College.

Computers: 21 computers/terminals are available on campus for general student use. Students can access the following: campus intranet, computer help desk, free student e-mail accounts, online (class) grades, online (class) registration, online (class) schedules. Campuswide network is available. 100% of college-owned or -operated housing units are wired for high-speed Internet access. Wireless service is available via entire campus.

Library: Wessels Library. *Books:* 36,525 (physical), 295,982 (digital/electronic); *Serial titles:* 33 (physical), 10,000 (digital/electronic); *Databases:* 108. Weekly public service hours: 91.

STUDENT LIFE

Housing options: on-campus residence required through senior year; coed, men-only, women-only. Campus housing is university owned and is provided by a third party. Freshman applicants given priority for college housing.

Activities and organizations: drama/theater group, student-run radio station, choral group, marching band, National Society of Leadership and Success, Kappa Delta, Sigma Sigma Sigma, Alpha Xi Delta, Kappa Alpha Order, national fraternities, national sororities.

Athletics Member NCAA. All Division II. ***Intercollegiate sports:*** baseball M(s), basketball M(s)/W(s), cheerleading M(s)/W(s), cross-country running M(s)/W(s), field hockey W(s), football M(s), golf M(s)/W(s), lacrosse W(s), soccer M(s)/W(s), softball W(s), tennis M(s)/W(s), volleyball W(s), wrestling M(s). ***Intramural sports:*** basketball M/W, soccer M/W, volleyball M/W.

Campus security: 24-hour emergency response devices and patrols, late-night transport/escort service, controlled dormitory access.

Student services: health clinic, personal/psychological counseling.

COSTS & FINANCIAL AID

Costs (2016–17) ***Comprehensive fee:*** $35,444 includes full-time tuition ($23,500), mandatory fees ($2100), and room and board ($9844). Full-time tuition and fees vary according to course load and student level. Part-time tuition: $735 per credit hour. Part-time tuition and fees vary according to course load and student level. No tuition increase for student's term of enrollment. ***Required fees:*** $68 per credit hour part-time. ***Room and board:*** Room and board charges vary according to board plan and housing facility. ***Payment plan:*** installment. ***Waivers:*** employees or children of employees.

Financial Aid Of all full-time matriculated undergraduates who enrolled in 2015, 985 applied for aid, 911 were judged to have need, 118 had their need fully met. 120 Federal Work-Study jobs (averaging $1100). In 2015, 116 non-need-based awards were made. ***Average percent of need met:*** 68. ***Average financial aid package:*** $22,608. ***Average need-based loan:*** $4400. ***Average need-based gift aid:*** $19,005. ***Average non-need-based aid:*** $10,886. ***Average indebtedness upon graduation:*** $31,015.

APPLYING

Standardized Tests *Required:* SAT or ACT (for admission).

Options: electronic application, deferred entrance.

Application fee: $30.

Required: high school transcript, minimum 2.0 GPA. ***Required for some:*** essay or personal statement, interview.

Application deadlines: rolling (freshmen), rolling (transfers).

Notification: continuous (freshmen), continuous (transfers).

CONTACT

Mr. Joel Vander Horst, Dean of Enrollment Management, Newberry College, 2100 College Street, Newberry, SC 29108. *Phone:* 803-947-2110. *Toll-free phone:* 800-845-4955. *Fax:* 803-321-5138. *E-mail:* admissions@newberry.edu.

North Greenville University

Tigerville, South Carolina

http://www.ngu.edu/

- **Independent Southern Baptist** comprehensive, founded 1892
- **Rural** 380-acre campus with easy access to Greenville
- **Endowment** $28.2 million
- **Coed** 2,481 undergraduate students, 89% full-time, 50% women, 50% men
- **Minimally difficult** entrance level, 59% of applicants were admitted

UNDERGRAD STUDENTS

2,209 full-time, 272 part-time. Students come from 35 states and territories; 27 other countries; 33% are from out of state; 8% Black or African American, non-Hispanic/Latino; 3% Hispanic/Latino; 0.6% Asian, non-Hispanic/Latino; 0.1% Native Hawaiian or other Pacific Islander, non-Hispanic/Latino; 0.3% American Indian or Alaska Native, non-Hispanic/Latino; 2% Two or more races, non-Hispanic/Latino; 8% Race/ethnicity unknown; 0.4% international; 5% transferred in; 65% live on campus.

Freshmen:
Admission: 1,617 applied, 956 admitted, 531 enrolled. ***Average high school GPA:*** 3.5. ***Test scores:*** SAT writing scores over 500: 76%; ACT scores over 18: 95%; SAT writing scores over 600: 27%; ACT scores over 24: 49%; SAT writing scores over 700: 6%; ACT scores over 30: 8%.

Retention: 73% of full-time freshmen returned.

FACULTY

Total: 244, 67% full-time, 49% with terminal degrees.

Student/faculty ratio: 14:1.

ACADEMICS

Calendar: semesters. *Degrees:* bachelor's, master's, and doctoral.

Special study options: academic remediation for entering students, accelerated degree program, advanced placement credit, cooperative education, distance learning, double majors, English as a second language, freshman honors college, honors programs, independent study, internships, part-time degree program, services for LD students, student-designed majors, study abroad, summer session for credit. ***ROTC:*** Army (c).

Unusual degree programs: 3-2 engineering with Clemson University.

Computers: 95 computers/terminals and 6 ports are available on campus for general student use. Students can access the following: campus intranet, computer help desk, free student e-mail accounts, online (class) grades, online (class) schedules. Campuswide network is available. 100% of college-owned or -operated housing units are wired for high-speed Internet access. Wireless service is available via entire campus.

Library: Hester Memorial Library. *Books:* 70,000 (physical), 250,000 (digital/electronic); *Serial titles:* 250 (physical), 150 (digital/electronic); *Databases:* 103. Weekly public service hours: 85.

STUDENT LIFE

Housing options: on-campus residence required through sophomore year; men-only, women-only. Campus housing is university owned. Freshman campus housing is guaranteed.

Activities and organizations: drama/theater group, student-run radio station, choral group, marching band, Baptist Student Union, Fellowship of Christians in Service, Fellowship of Christian Athletes, Black Student Fellowship, Education Club.

Athletics Member NCAA, NCCAA. All NCAA Division II. ***Intercollegiate sports:*** baseball M(s), basketball M(s)/W(s), cheerleading M(s)/W(s), cross-country running M(s)/W(s), football M(s), golf M(s)/W(s), lacrosse M(s)/W(s), soccer M(s)/W(s), softball W(s), tennis M(s)/W(s), track and field M(s)/W(s), volleyball M(s)/W(s). ***Intramural sports:*** basketball M/W, bowling M/W, football M, golf M/W, sand volleyball M/W, soccer M/W, softball M/W, table tennis M/W, tennis M/W, ultimate Frisbee M/W, volleyball W, weight lifting M/W.

Campus security: 24-hour emergency response devices and patrols, late-night transport/escort service, controlled dormitory access.

Student services: personal/psychological counseling.

COSTS & FINANCIAL AID

Costs (2016–17) ***Comprehensive fee:*** $27,486 includes full-time tuition ($17,594) and room and board ($9892). Full-time tuition and fees vary according to course load. Part-time tuition: $425 per credit. ***Room and board:*** Room and board charges vary according to housing facility. ***Payment plan:*** installment. ***Waivers:*** employees or children of employees.

Financial Aid Of all full-time matriculated undergraduates who enrolled in 2015, 1,143 applied for aid, 1,143 were judged to have need, 1,143 had their need fully met. In 2015, 1989 non-need-based awards were made. ***Average financial aid package:*** $5783. ***Average need-based gift aid:*** $5783. ***Average non-need-based aid:*** $7081.

APPLYING

Standardized Tests *Required:* SAT or ACT (for admission). *Required for some:* CPT. *Recommended:* CPT.

Options: electronic application, early admission, deferred entrance.

Application fee: $30.

Required: high school transcript. ***Required for some:*** interview. ***Recommended:*** minimum 2.0 GPA.

Application deadlines: 8/22 (freshmen), 8/26 (transfers).

Notification: continuous (freshmen), continuous (transfers).

CONTACT

North Greenville University, PO Box 1892, Tigerville, SC 29688-1892. *Phone:* 864-977-7052. *Toll-free phone:* 800-468-6642 Ext. 7001.

Presbyterian College

Clinton, South Carolina

http://www.presby.edu/

- **Independent** comprehensive, founded 1880, affiliated with Presbyterian Church (U.S.A.)
- **Small-town** 240-acre campus with easy access to Greenville, Spartanburg
- **Endowment** $92.0 million
- **Coed**
- **Very difficult** entrance level

FACULTY

Student/faculty ratio: 12:1.

ACADEMICS

Calendar: semesters. *Degrees:* bachelor's and doctoral.

Library: James H. Thomason Library.

STUDENT LIFE

Housing options: on-campus residence required through senior year; coed, men-only, women-only. Campus housing is university owned. Freshman campus housing is guaranteed.

Activities and organizations: drama/theater group, student-run newspaper, choral group, Student Volunteer Services, Intramural sports, Student Union Board, Fellowship of Christian Athletes, Student Government Association, national fraternities, national sororities.

Athletics Member NCAA. All Division I.

Campus security: 24-hour emergency response devices and patrols, late-night transport/escort service, controlled dormitory access.

Student services: health clinic, personal/psychological counseling.

COSTS & FINANCIAL AID

Costs (2016–17) ***Comprehensive fee:*** $47,186 includes full-time tuition ($34,282), mandatory fees ($2860), and room and board ($10,044). Full-time tuition and fees vary according to course load and reciprocity agreements. Part-time tuition: $1428 per credit hour. Part-time tuition and fees vary according to course load and program. ***Required fees:*** $27 per credit hour part-time. ***College room only:*** $4894. Room and board charges vary according to board plan and housing facility.

Financial Aid Of all full-time matriculated undergraduates who enrolled in 2015, 853 applied for aid, 738 were judged to have need. In 2015, 201 non-need-based awards were made. ***Average percent of need met:*** 30. ***Average financial aid package:*** $34,081. ***Average need-based loan:*** $4670. ***Average need-based gift aid:*** $26,877. ***Average non-need-based aid:*** $17,000. ***Average indebtedness upon graduation:*** $27,169. ***Financial aid deadline:*** 6/30.

APPLYING

Standardized Tests *Required for some:* SAT or ACT (for admission).

Options: electronic application, early decision, early action, deferred entrance.

A ★ indicates that the school has detailed information with a Premium Profile on Petersons.com.

Required: essay or personal statement, high school transcript, minimum 2.0 GPA, 1 letter of recommendation. ***Recommended:*** interview.

CONTACT
Mr. Brian J. Fortman, Dean for Enrollment Management, Presbyterian College, 503 South Broad Street, Clinton, SC 29325. *Phone:* 864-833-8258. *Toll-free phone:* 800-960-7583. *Fax:* 864-833-8481. *E-mail:* bjfortman@presby.edu.

South Carolina State University

Orangeburg, South Carolina

http://www.scsu.edu/

- **State-supported** comprehensive, founded 1896, part of South Carolina Commission on Higher Education
- **Small-town** 160-acre campus
- **Coed** 2,529 undergraduate students, 90% full-time, 50% women, 50% men
- **Minimally difficult** entrance level, 86% of applicants were admitted

UNDERGRAD STUDENTS
2,282 full-time, 247 part-time. Students come from 31 states and territories; 13 other countries; 15% are from out of state; 96% Black or African American, non-Hispanic/Latino; 0.5% Hispanic/Latino; 0.4% Asian, non-Hispanic/Latino; 0.2% American Indian or Alaska Native, non-Hispanic/Latino; 0.3% Two or more races, non-Hispanic/Latino; 0.2% international; 5% transferred in; 68% live on campus.

Freshmen:
Admission: 2,847 applied, 2,455 admitted, 628 enrolled. ***Average high school GPA:*** 2.85. ***Test scores:*** SAT critical reading scores over 500: 11%; SAT math scores over 500: 11%; ACT scores over 18: 24%; SAT critical reading scores over 600: 2%; SAT math scores over 600: 1%; ACT scores over 24: 4%; SAT critical reading scores over 700: 1%; ACT scores over 30: 1%.

Retention: 70% of full-time freshmen returned.

FACULTY
Total: 191, 72% full-time, 64% with terminal degrees.

Student/faculty ratio: 17:1.

ACADEMICS
Calendar: semesters. *Degrees:* bachelor's, master's, doctoral, and postbachelor's certificates.

Special study options: adult/continuing education programs, advanced placement credit, cooperative education, distance learning, double majors, honors programs, independent study, internships, off-campus study, part-time degree program, services for LD students, study abroad, summer session for credit. ***ROTC:*** Army (b).

Computers: 600 computers/terminals and 600 ports are available on campus for general student use. Students can access the following: campus intranet, computer help desk, free student e-mail accounts, online (class) grades, online (class) registration, online (class) schedules. Campuswide network is available. 70% of college-owned or -operated housing units are wired for high-speed Internet access. Wireless service is available via classrooms, computer centers, computer labs, dorm rooms, learning centers, libraries, student centers.

Library: Miller F. Whittaker Library. *Books:* 317,233 (physical), 195,578 (digital/electronic); *Serial titles:* 18,334 (digital/electronic); *Databases:* 114. Weekly public service hours: 74; students can reserve study rooms.

STUDENT LIFE
Housing options: coed, men-only, women-only, special housing for students with disabilities. Campus housing is university owned, leased by the school and is provided by a third party. Freshman applicants given priority for college housing.

Activities and organizations: drama/theater group, student-run newspaper, radio station, choral group, marching band, Student Government Association, Campus Activity Board, NAACP, United Voices of Christ, Student Media, national fraternities, national sororities.

Athletics Member NCAA. All Division I except football (Division I-AA). ***Intercollegiate sports:*** basketball M(s)/W(s), cross-country running M(s)/W(s), soccer W(s), softball W(s), tennis M(s)/W(s), track and field M(s)/W(s), volleyball W(s). ***Intramural sports:*** basketball M/W, softball M/W.

Campus security: 24-hour emergency response devices and patrols, late-night transport/escort service, controlled dormitory access.

Student services: health clinic, personal/psychological counseling.

COSTS
Costs (2016–17) ***Tuition:*** state resident $8938 full-time, $434 per credit hour part-time; nonresident $19,018 full-time, $854 per credit hour part-time. Full-time tuition and fees vary according to course load, program, and reciprocity agreements. Part-time tuition and fees vary according to course load, program, and reciprocity agreements. ***Required fees:*** $1482 full-time. ***Room and board:*** $9890; room only: $6600. Room and board charges vary according to board plan and housing facility. ***Payment plan:*** installment. ***Waivers:*** senior citizens.

APPLYING
Standardized Tests *Required:* SAT or ACT (for admission).

Options: electronic application, deferred entrance.

Application fee: $25.

Required: high school transcript, minimum 2.0 GPA.

Application deadlines: 7/31 (freshmen), 7/31 (transfers).

Notification: continuous (freshmen), continuous (transfers).

CONTACT
Mrs. Gennifer Bookhardt, South Carolina State University, PO Box 7127, 300 College Street NE, Orangeburg, SC 29117. *Phone:* 803-536-7186. *Toll-free phone:* 800-260-5956. *Fax:* 803-536-8990. *E-mail:* admissions@scsu.edu.

Southern Wesleyan University

Central, South Carolina

http://www.swu.edu/

CONTACT
Mrs. Beth Roe, Director of First Year Experience, Southern Wesleyan University, PO Box 1020, 907 Wesleyan Drive, Central, SC 29630-1020. *Phone:* 864-644-5149. *Toll-free phone:* 800-CU-AT-SWU. *Fax:* 864-644-5901. *E-mail:* broe@swu.edu.

South University

Columbia, South Carolina

http://www.southuniversity.edu/columbia/

CONTACT
South University, 9 Science Court, Columbia, SC 29203. *Phone:* 803-799-9082. *Toll-free phone:* 866-629-3031.

Strayer University–Charleston Campus

North Charleston, South Carolina

http://www.strayer.edu/south-carolina/charleston/

CONTACT
Strayer University–Charleston Campus, 5010 Wetland Crossing, North Charleston, SC 29418.

Strayer University–Columbia Campus

Columbia, South Carolina

http://www.strayer.edu/south-carolina/columbia/

CONTACT
Strayer University–Columbia Campus, 200 Center Point Circle, Suite 300, Columbia, SC 29210.

Strayer University–Greenville Campus

Greenville, South Carolina

http://www.strayer.edu/south-carolina/greenville/

CONTACT

Strayer University–Greenville Campus, 555 North Pleasantburg Drive, Suite 300, Greenville, SC 29607.

University of South Carolina

Columbia, South Carolina

http://www.sc.edu/

- **State-supported** university, founded 1801, part of University of South Carolina System
- **Urban** 444-acre campus
- **Coed** 25,556 undergraduate students, 94% full-time, 53% women, 47% men
- **Moderately difficult** entrance level, 65% of applicants were admitted

UNDERGRAD STUDENTS

23,926 full-time, 1,630 part-time. 48% are from out of state; 9% Black or African American, non-Hispanic/Latino; 4% Hispanic/Latino; 3% Asian, non-Hispanic/Latino; 0.1% Native Hawaiian or other Pacific Islander, non-Hispanic/Latino; 0.2% American Indian or Alaska Native, non-Hispanic/Latino; 4% Two or more races, non-Hispanic/Latino; 1% Race/ethnicity unknown; 3% international; 6% transferred in; 29% live on campus.

Freshmen:

Admission: 23,341 applied, 15,219 admitted, 5,110 enrolled. ***Average high school GPA:*** 4.07. ***Test scores:*** SAT critical reading scores over 500: 96%; SAT math scores over 500: 96%; ACT scores over 18: 100%; SAT critical reading scores over 600: 54%; SAT math scores over 600: 59%; ACT scores over 24: 87%; SAT critical reading scores over 700: 10%; SAT math scores over 700: 10%; ACT scores over 30: 26%.

Retention: 87% of full-time freshmen returned.

FACULTY

Total: 2,373, 64% full-time, 65% with terminal degrees.

Student/faculty ratio: 18:1.

ACADEMICS

Calendar: semesters. *Degrees:* associate, bachelor's, master's, doctoral, post-master's, and postbachelor's certificates.

Special study options: accelerated degree program, adult/continuing education programs, advanced placement credit, cooperative education, distance learning, double majors, English as a second language, freshman honors college, honors programs, independent study, internships, part-time degree program, services for LD students, student-designed majors, study abroad, summer session for credit. ***ROTC:*** Army (b), Navy (b), Air Force (b).

Computers: Students can access the following: computer help desk, free student e-mail accounts, online (class) grades, online (class) registration, online (class) schedules. Campuswide network is available. Wireless service is available via entire campus.

Library: Thomas Cooper Library.

STUDENT LIFE

Housing options: on-campus residence required for freshman year; coed, men-only, women-only, special housing for students with disabilities. Campus housing is university owned. Freshman campus housing is guaranteed.

Activities and organizations: drama/theater group, student-run newspaper, radio and television station, choral group, marching band, Social Work Student Association, Friendship Association of Chinese Students and Scholars, Alpha Lambda Delta, Residence Hall Association, Student Bar Association, national fraternities, national sororities.

Athletics Member NCAA. All Division I except football (Division I-A). ***Intercollegiate sports:*** baseball M(s), basketball M(s)/W(s), cross-country running W(s), equestrian sports W(s), golf M(s)/W(s), soccer M(s)/W(s), softball W(s), swimming and diving M(s)/W(s), tennis M(s)/W(s), track and field M(s)/W(s), volleyball W(s). ***Intramural sports:*** badminton M(c)/W(c), baseball M(c), basketball M/W, bowling M/W, equestrian sports M(c)/W(c), fencing M(c)/W(c), field hockey W(c), football M/W, golf M/W, gymnastics W(c), ice hockey M(c), lacrosse M(c)/W(c), racquetball M/W, rock climbing M(c)/W(c), rugby M(c)/W(c), sailing M(c)/W(c), soccer M/W, softball M/W, swimming and diving M/W, table tennis M/W, tennis M/W, ultimate Frisbee M(c)/W(c), volleyball M/W, water polo M(c)/W(c), weight lifting M/W, wrestling M(c).

Campus security: 24-hour emergency response devices and patrols, student patrols, late-night transport/escort service, controlled dormitory access.

Student services: health clinic, personal/psychological counseling, women's center.

COSTS & FINANCIAL AID

Costs (2016–17) ***Tuition:*** state resident $11,454 full-time, $477 per credit hour part-time; nonresident $30,882 full-time, $1287 per credit hour part-time. Full-time tuition and fees vary according to program and reciprocity agreements. Part-time tuition and fees vary according to course load. ***Required fees:*** $400 full-time, $17 per term part-time. ***Room and board:*** $9700; room only: $6040. Room and board charges vary according to board plan, housing facility, and location. ***Payment plan:*** deferred payment. ***Waivers:*** senior citizens and employees or children of employees.

Financial Aid Of all full-time matriculated undergraduates who enrolled in 2016, 16,266 applied for aid, 12,181 were judged to have need, 2,905 had their need fully met. In 2016, 7821 non-need-based awards were made. ***Average percent of need met:*** 75. ***Average financial aid package:*** $9400. ***Average need-based loan:*** $4351. ***Average need-based gift aid:*** $5148. ***Average non-need-based aid:*** $6707. ***Average indebtedness upon graduation:*** $29,012.

APPLYING

Standardized Tests *Required:* SAT or ACT (for admission).

Options: electronic application, early action.

Application fee: $65.

Required: high school transcript, minimum 2.0 GPA.

CONTACT

Dr. Mary Wagner, Senior Associate Director, Undergraduate Admissions, University of South Carolina, Columbia, SC 29208. *Phone:* 803-777-7700. *Toll-free phone:* 800-868-5872. *Fax:* 803-777-0101. *E-mail:* admissions-ugrad@sc.edu.

University of South Carolina Aiken

Aiken, South Carolina

http://www.usca.edu/

- **State-supported** comprehensive, founded 1961, part of University of South Carolina System
- **Suburban** 453-acre campus with easy access to Columbia
- **Endowment** $22.5 million
- **Coed** 3,374 undergraduate students, 79% full-time, 64% women, 36% men
- **Moderately difficult** entrance level, 61% of applicants were admitted

UNDERGRAD STUDENTS

2,680 full-time, 694 part-time. Students come from 33 states and territories; 30 other countries; 11% are from out of state; 27% Black or African American, non-Hispanic/Latino; 4% Hispanic/Latino; 1% Asian, non-Hispanic/Latino; 0.1% Native Hawaiian or other Pacific Islander, non-Hispanic/Latino; 0.5% American Indian or Alaska Native, non-Hispanic/Latino; 4% Two or more races, non-Hispanic/Latino; 1% Race/ethnicity unknown; 4% international; 9% transferred in; 27% live on campus.

Freshmen:

Admission: 2,177 applied, 1,318 admitted, 623 enrolled. ***Average high school GPA:*** 3.75. ***Test scores:*** SAT critical reading scores over 500: 42%; SAT math scores over 500: 44%; SAT writing scores over 500: 28%; ACT scores over 18: 82%; SAT critical reading scores over 600: 9%; SAT math scores over 600: 9%; SAT writing scores over 600: 4%; ACT scores over 24: 21%; SAT math scores over 700: 1%; ACT scores over 30: 2%.

Retention: 72% of full-time freshmen returned.

FACULTY

Total: 295, 52% full-time, 54% with terminal degrees.

Student/faculty ratio: 15:1.

ACADEMICS
Calendar: semesters. *Degrees:* bachelor's and master's.

Special study options: adult/continuing education programs, advanced placement credit, cooperative education, distance learning, double majors, English as a second language, honors programs, independent study, internships, off-campus study, part-time degree program, services for LD students, student-designed majors, study abroad, summer session for credit.

Computers: 550 computers/terminals and 1,400 ports are available on campus for general student use. Students can access the following: computer help desk, free student e-mail accounts, online (class) grades, online (class) registration, online (class) schedules. Campuswide network is available. 100% of college-owned or -operated housing units are wired for high-speed Internet access. Wireless service is available via entire campus.

Library: Gregg-Graniteville Library. *Books:* 138,795 (physical), 349,394 (digital/electronic); *Serial titles:* 2,277 (physical), 104,068 (digital/electronic); *Databases:* 236. Weekly public service hours: 78; students can reserve study rooms.

STUDENT LIFE
Housing options: coed, special housing for students with disabilities. Campus housing is university owned. Freshman applicants given priority for college housing.

Activities and organizations: drama/theater group, student-run newspaper, choral group, National Society of Leadership and Success, Pacer Fanatics, Alpha Omicron Pi, Zeta Tau Alpha, Phi Mu, national fraternities, national sororities.

Athletics Member NCAA. All Division II except bowling (Division I). ***Intercollegiate sports:*** baseball M(s), basketball M(s)/W(s), bowling W, cross-country running W(s), golf M(s), soccer M(s)/W(s), softball W(s), tennis M(s)/W(s), volleyball W(s). ***Intramural sports:*** basketball M/W, cheerleading M(c)/W(c), equestrian sports M(c)/W(c), rugby M(c)/W(c), soccer M/W, swimming and diving M(c)/W(c), table tennis M(c)/W(c), ultimate Frisbee M/W, volleyball M/W.

Campus security: 24-hour emergency response devices and patrols, late-night transport/escort service, controlled dormitory access.

Student services: health clinic, personal/psychological counseling.

COSTS & FINANCIAL AID
Costs (2016–17) ***Tuition:*** state resident $9882 full-time, $412 per credit hour part-time; nonresident $19,788 full-time, $825 per credit hour part-time. Full-time tuition and fees vary according to reciprocity agreements. Part-time tuition and fees vary according to course load and reciprocity agreements. ***Required fees:*** $314 full-time, $11 per credit hour part-time, $25 per term part-time. ***Room and board:*** $7466. Room and board charges vary according to board plan and housing facility. ***Payment plan:*** deferred payment. ***Waivers:*** senior citizens and employees or children of employees.

Financial Aid Of all full-time matriculated undergraduates who enrolled in 2015, 2,591 applied for aid, 1,859 were judged to have need, 316 had their need fully met. 78 Federal Work-Study jobs (averaging $1776). 399 state and other part-time jobs (averaging $1469). In 2015, 138 non-need-based awards were made. ***Average percent of need met:*** 61. ***Average financial aid package:*** $10,964. ***Average need-based loan:*** $4164. ***Average need-based gift aid:*** $6751. ***Average non-need-based aid:*** $1866. ***Average indebtedness upon graduation:*** $31,289.

APPLYING
Standardized Tests *Required:* SAT or ACT (for admission).

Options: electronic application, early admission, deferred entrance.

Application fee: $45.

Required: high school transcript.

Application deadlines: 8/1 (freshmen), 8/1 (transfers).

Notification: continuous (freshmen), continuous (out-of-state freshmen), continuous (transfers).

CONTACT
Mr. Andrew Hendrix, Director of Admissions, University of South Carolina Aiken, 471 University Parkway, Aiken, SC 29801-6309. *Phone:* 803-641-3366. *Toll-free phone:* 888-WOW-USCA. *Fax:* 803-641-3727. *E-mail:* admit@usca.edu.

University of South Carolina Beaufort
Bluffton, South Carolina
http://www.uscb.edu/

- **State-supported** 4-year, founded 1959, part of University of South Carolina system
- **Suburban** 200-acre campus
- **Endowment** $4.2 million
- **Coed**
- **Minimally difficult** entrance level

ACADEMICS
Calendar: semesters. *Degrees:* associate and bachelor's.
Library: University of South Carolina Beaufort Library plus 1 other. *Books:* 90,519 (physical), 505,463 (digital/electronic); *Serial titles:* 1,861 (physical), 7,031 (digital/electronic); *Databases:* 235. Students can reserve study rooms.

STUDENT LIFE
Housing options: on-campus residence required for freshman yearCampus housing is university owned and leased by the school.

Activities and organizations: drama/theater group, choral group, Student Government Association, Gamma Beta Phi, Black Student Organization, Business Club, Environmental Awareness Club, national fraternities, national sororities.

Athletics Member NAIA.

Campus security: 24-hour emergency response devices, controlled dormitory access, evening security service.

Student services: personal/psychological counseling.

COSTS & FINANCIAL AID
Costs (2016–17) ***One-time required fee:*** $175. ***Tuition:*** state resident $9780 full-time, $408 per credit hour part-time; nonresident $20,244 full-time, $844 per credit hour part-time. Full-time tuition and fees vary according to course load, program, and reciprocity agreements. Part-time tuition and fees vary according to course load, program, and reciprocity agreements. ***Required fees:*** $386 full-time, $14 per credit hour part-time, $25 per credit hour part-time. ***Room and board:*** $7800; room only: $5200. Room and board charges vary according to board plan, housing facility, location, and student level. ***Payment plans:*** installment, deferred payment.

Financial Aid Of all full-time matriculated undergraduates who enrolled in 2015, 21 Federal Work-Study jobs (averaging $2800).

APPLYING
Standardized Tests *Required:* SAT or ACT (for admission).

Options: electronic application, deferred entrance.

Application fee: $40.

Required: high school transcript, prerequisite high school courses. ***Recommended:*** minimum 2.0 GPA.

CONTACT
Ms. Monica Williams, University of South Carolina Beaufort, 1 University Boulevard, Bluffton, SC 29909. *Phone:* 843-208-8112. *Fax:* 843-208-8015. *E-mail:* monicaw@sc.edu.

University of South Carolina Union
Union, South Carolina
http://uscunion.sc.edu/

- **State-supported** primarily 2-year, founded 1965, part of University of South Carolina System
- **Small-town** campus with easy access to Charlotte
- **Coed** 757 undergraduate students, 57% full-time, 60% women, 40% men
- **Minimally difficult** entrance level

UNDERGRAD STUDENTS
435 full-time, 322 part-time.

Freshmen:
Average high school GPA: 3.2.

FACULTY
Total: 38, 26% full-time.
Student/faculty ratio: 18:1.

ACADEMICS
Calendar: semesters. *Degrees:* associate and bachelor's.

Special study options: cooperative education, part-time degree program.

Computers: 60 computers/terminals are available on campus for general student use. Students can access the following: campus intranet, computer help desk, free student e-mail accounts, online (class) grades, online (class) registration, online (class) schedules. Campuswide network is available. Wireless service is available via entire campus.
Library: USC Union Campus Library plus 1 other.

STUDENT LIFE
Housing options: college housing not available.

Activities and organizations: drama/theater group, choral group.

Athletics ***Intramural sports:*** baseball M(c), softball W(c).

COSTS & FINANCIAL AID
Costs (2017–18) ***One-time required fee:*** $50. ***Tuition:*** state resident $3500 full-time, $280 per credit hour part-time; nonresident $8400 full-time, $700 per credit hour part-time. Full-time tuition and fees vary according to class time, course load, degree level, location, program, and student level. Part-time tuition and fees vary according to class time, location, program, and student level. ***Required fees:*** $315 full-time, $40 per credit hour part-time. ***Payment plan:*** deferred payment. ***Waivers:*** senior citizens.
Financial Aid Of all full-time matriculated undergraduates who enrolled in 2015, 16 Federal Work-Study jobs (averaging $3400).

APPLYING
Standardized Tests *Required:* SAT or ACT (for admission).

Options: electronic application.

Application fee: $40.

Required: high school transcript.

CONTACT
Mr. Michael B. Greer, Director of Enrollment Services, University of South Carolina Union, PO Drawer 729, Union, SC 29379-0729. *Phone:* 864-424-8039. *E-mail:* tyoung@gwm.sc.edu.

University of South Carolina Upstate

Spartanburg, South Carolina

http://www.uscupstate.edu/

CONTACT
Ms. Donette Stewart, Associate Vice Chancellor for Enrollment Services, University of South Carolina Upstate, 800 University Way, Spartanburg, SC 29303. *Phone:* 864-503-5280. *Toll-free phone:* 800-277-8727. *Fax:* 864-503-5727. *E-mail:* dstewart@uscupstate.edu.

Voorhees College

Denmark, South Carolina

http://www.voorhees.edu/

CONTACT
Adrain West, Dean of Enrollment Management, Voorhees College, PO Box 678, Denmark, SC 29042. *Phone:* 803-780-1269. *Toll-free phone:* 866-237-4570. *E-mail:* west@voorhees.edu.

Winthrop University

Rock Hill, South Carolina

http://www.winthrop.edu/

- **State-supported** comprehensive, founded 1886, part of South Carolina Commission on Higher Education
- **Suburban** 456-acre campus with easy access to Charlotte
- **Coed** 5,091 undergraduate students, 89% full-time, 69% women, 31% men
- **Moderately difficult** entrance level, 69% of applicants were admitted

UNDERGRAD STUDENTS
4,545 full-time, 546 part-time. Students come from 40 states and territories; 82 other countries; 9% are from out of state; 30% Black or African American, non-Hispanic/Latino; 5% Hispanic/Latino; 1% Asian, non-Hispanic/Latino; 0.1% Native Hawaiian or other Pacific Islander, non-Hispanic/Latino; 0.4% American Indian or Alaska Native, non-Hispanic/Latino; 3% Two or more races, non-Hispanic/Latino; 2% international; 7% transferred in; 47% live on campus.

Freshmen:
Admission: 4,940 applied, 3,384 admitted, 1,072 enrolled. ***Average high school GPA:*** 3.91. ***Test scores:*** SAT critical reading scores over 500: 60%; SAT math scores over 500: 52%; ACT scores over 18: 93%; SAT critical reading scores over 600: 20%; SAT math scores over 600: 14%; ACT scores over 24: 41%; SAT critical reading scores over 700: 2%; SAT math scores over 700: 1%; ACT scores over 30: 5%.
Retention: 73% of full-time freshmen returned.

FACULTY
Total: 549, 51% full-time, 59% with terminal degrees.

Student/faculty ratio: 14:1.

ACADEMICS
Calendar: semesters. *Degrees:* certificates, bachelor's, master's, post-master's, and postbachelor's certificates.

Special study options: adult/continuing education programs, advanced placement credit, cooperative education, distance learning, double majors, honors programs, independent study, internships, off-campus study, part-time degree program, services for LD students, student-designed majors, study abroad, summer session for credit. ***ROTC:*** Army (c), Air Force (c).

Computers: 620 computers/terminals are available on campus for general student use. Students can access the following: campus intranet, computer help desk, free student e-mail accounts, online (class) grades, online (class) registration, online (class) schedules, university services. Campuswide network is available. 100% of college-owned or -operated housing units are wired for high-speed Internet access. Wireless service is available via entire campus.
Library: Dacus Library plus 1 other. *Books:* 438,816 (physical), 15,746 (digital/electronic); *Serial titles:* 12,205 (physical), 15,873 (digital/electronic); *Databases:* 127. Weekly public service hours: 49; study areas open 24 hours, 5-7 days a week; students can reserve study rooms.

STUDENT LIFE
Housing options: on-campus residence required through sophomore year; coed, women-only, special housing for students with disabilities. Campus housing is university owned. Freshman campus housing is guaranteed.

Activities and organizations: drama/theater group, student-run newspaper, radio station, choral group, Association of Ebonites, WU Crew, Greek Life, DiGiorgio Student Union, Campus Ministries, national fraternities, national sororities.

Athletics Member NCAA. All Division I. ***Intercollegiate sports:*** baseball M(s), basketball M(s)/W(s), cheerleading M(c)/W(c), cross-country running M(s)/W(s), fencing M(c)/W(c), golf M(s)/W(s), lacrosse M(c)/W, rugby M(c), soccer M(s)/W(s), softball W(s), tennis M(s)/W(s), track and field M(s)/W(s), volleyball W(s). ***Intramural sports:*** badminton M/W, basketball M/W, cross-country running M/W, equestrian sports M(c)/W(c), football M/W, golf M/W, racquetball M/W, soccer M/W, softball M/W, swimming and diving M/W, table tennis M/W, tennis M/W, ultimate Frisbee M/W, volleyball M/W, water polo M/W, weight lifting M/W.

Campus security: 24-hour emergency response devices and patrols, late-night transport/escort service, controlled dormitory access.

Student services: health clinic, personal/psychological counseling.

COSTS & FINANCIAL AID
Costs (2016–17) ***Tuition:*** state resident $14,510 full-time, $605 per credit hour part-time; nonresident $28,090 full-time, $1170 per credit hour part-time. Full-time tuition and fees vary according to degree level, reciprocity agreements, and student level. Part-time tuition and fees vary according to degree level and student level. ***Room and board:*** $8572; room only: $5242. Room and board charges vary according to board plan and housing facility. ***Payment plan:*** installment. ***Waivers:*** senior citizens and employees or children of employees.

Financial Aid Of all full-time matriculated undergraduates who enrolled in 2016, 3,891 applied for aid, 3,385 were judged to have need, 492 had their need fully met. 165 Federal Work-Study jobs (averaging $1964). In 2016, 549 non-need-based awards were made. ***Average percent of need met:*** 56. ***Average financial aid package:*** $13,080. ***Average need-based***

loan: $4361. ***Average need-based gift aid:*** $8744. ***Average non-need-based aid:*** $5268. ***Average indebtedness upon graduation:*** $30,061.

APPLYING

Standardized Tests *Required:* SAT or ACT (for admission).

Options: electronic application, deferred entrance.

Application fee: $40.

Required: high school transcript, minimum 3.0 GPA. ***Required for some:*** essay or personal statement.

Application deadlines: 5/1 (freshmen), 5/1 (transfers).

Notification: continuous (freshmen), continuous (transfers).

CONTACT

Winthrop University, 701 Oakland Avenue, Rock Hill, SC 29733. *Phone:* 803-323-2191. *Toll-free phone:* 800-763-0230.

Wofford College

Spartanburg, South Carolina

http://www.wofford.edu/

- **Independent** 4-year, founded 1854, affiliated with United Methodist Church
- **Urban** 170-acre campus
- **Endowment** $172.0 million
- **Coed** 1,622 undergraduate students, 98% full-time, 51% women, 49% men
- **Very difficult** entrance level, 70% of applicants were admitted

UNDERGRAD STUDENTS

1,582 full-time, 40 part-time. Students come from 36 states and territories; 18 other countries; 46% are from out of state; 8% Black or African American, non-Hispanic/Latino; 4% Hispanic/Latino; 2% Asian, non-Hispanic/Latino; 0.2% Native Hawaiian or other Pacific Islander, non-Hispanic/Latino; 0.2% American Indian or Alaska Native, non-Hispanic/Latino; 3% Two or more races, non-Hispanic/Latino; 1% Race/ethnicity unknown; 2% international; 1% transferred in; 93% live on campus.

Freshmen:

Admission: 2,937 applied, 2,059 admitted, 440 enrolled. ***Average high school GPA:*** 3.6. ***Test scores:*** SAT critical reading scores over 500: 84%; SAT math scores over 500: 87%; SAT writing scores over 500: 79%; ACT scores over 18: 99%; SAT critical reading scores over 600: 45%; SAT math scores over 600: 44%; SAT writing scores over 600: 36%; ACT scores over 24: 76%; SAT critical reading scores over 700: 8%; SAT math scores over 700: 7%; SAT writing scores over 700: 5%; ACT scores over 30: 16%.

Retention: 87% of full-time freshmen returned.

FACULTY

Total: 169, 83% full-time, 89% with terminal degrees.

Student/faculty ratio: 11:1.

ACADEMICS

Calendar: 4-1-4. *Degree:* bachelor's.

Special study options: accelerated degree program, advanced placement credit, double majors, independent study, internships, off-campus study, part-time degree program, student-designed majors, study abroad, summer session for credit. ***ROTC:*** Army (b).

Unusual degree programs: 3-2 engineering with Clemson University.

Computers: 233 computers/terminals are available on campus for general student use. Students can access the following: campus intranet, computer help desk, free student e-mail accounts, online (class) grades, online (class) registration, online (class) schedules. Campuswide network is available. Wireless service is available via entire campus.

Library: Sandor Teszler Library. *Books:* 590,175 (digital/electronic).

STUDENT LIFE

Housing options: on-campus residence required through senior year; coed. Campus housing is university owned. Freshman applicants given priority for college housing.

Activities and organizations: drama/theater group, student-run newspaper, radio station, choral group, W.A.R. - Wofford Athletics and Recreation, W.A.C. - Wofford Activities Council, Twin Towers - Service Organization, Math Academy, Arcadia Volunteer Corp, national fraternities, national sororities.

Athletics Member NCAA. All Division I except football (Division I-AA). ***Intercollegiate sports:*** baseball M(s), basketball M(s)/W(s), cheerleading W, cross-country running M(s)/W(s), golf M(s)/W(s), lacrosse W(s), riflery M(s)/W(s), soccer M(s)/W(s), tennis M(s)/W(s), track and field M(s)/W(s), volleyball W(s). ***Intramural sports:*** basketball M/W, football M/W, soccer M/W, softball M/W, table tennis M/W, tennis M/W, ultimate Frisbee M/W.

Campus security: 24-hour emergency response devices and patrols, late-night transport/escort service, controlled dormitory access.

Student services: health clinic, personal/psychological counseling.

COSTS & FINANCIAL AID

Costs (2017–18) ***Comprehensive fee:*** $54,095 includes full-time tuition ($41,955) and room and board ($12,140). ***Payment plan:*** installment. ***Waivers:*** employees or children of employees.

Financial Aid Of all full-time matriculated undergraduates who enrolled in 2016, 1,224 applied for aid, 1,009 were judged to have need, 413 had their need fully met. 138 Federal Work-Study jobs (averaging $990). In 2016, 433 non-need-based awards were made. ***Average percent of need met:*** 89. ***Average financial aid package:*** $34,662. ***Average need-based loan:*** $4331. ***Average need-based gift aid:*** $30,783. ***Average non-need-based aid:*** $16,243. ***Average indebtedness upon graduation:*** $31,102.

APPLYING

Standardized Tests *Required:* SAT or ACT (for admission).

Options: electronic application, early admission, early decision, early action, deferred entrance.

Application fee: $35.

Required: essay or personal statement, high school transcript. ***Recommended:*** 2 letters of recommendation, interview.

Application deadlines: 1/15 (freshmen), rolling (transfers), 11/15 (early action).

Early decision deadline: 11/1.

Notification: 3/1 (freshmen), continuous (transfers), 12/1 (early decision), 2/1 (early action).

CONTACT

Ms. Chelsea Pagliuca, Visit Coordinator, Wofford College, 429 N. Church Street, Spartanburg, SC 29303. *Phone:* 864-597-4132. *Fax:* 864-597-4147. *E-mail:* admission@wofford.edu.

SOUTH DAKOTA

Augustana University

Sioux Falls, South Dakota

http://www.augie.edu/

- **Independent** comprehensive, founded 1860, affiliated with Evangelical Lutheran Church in America
- **Urban** 100-acre campus
- **Endowment** $72.0 million
- **Coed** 1,665 undergraduate students, 95% full-time, 59% women, 41% men
- **Moderately difficult** entrance level, 69% of applicants were admitted

UNDERGRAD STUDENTS

1,574 full-time, 91 part-time. Students come from 35 states and territories; 38 other countries; 50% are from out of state; 3% transferred in; 71% live on campus.

Freshmen:

Admission: 1,464 applied, 1,012 admitted, 424 enrolled. ***Average high school GPA:*** 3.76. ***Test scores:*** ACT scores over 18: 100%; ACT scores over 24: 71%; ACT scores over 30: 18%.

Retention: 84% of full-time freshmen returned.

FACULTY

Total: 190, 69% full-time, 64% with terminal degrees.

Student/faculty ratio: 11:1.

ACADEMICS
Calendar: 4-1-4. *Degrees:* bachelor's and master's.

Special study options: academic remediation for entering students, accelerated degree program, advanced placement credit, distance learning, double majors, external degree program, honors programs, independent study, internships, off-campus study, part-time degree program, services for LD students, student-designed majors, study abroad, summer session for credit. ***ROTC:*** Army (c), Air Force (c).

Unusual degree programs: 3-2 engineering with Columbia University, Washington University in St. Louis.

Computers: 250 computers/terminals are available on campus for general student use. Students can access the following: campus intranet, computer help desk, free student e-mail accounts, online (class) grades, online (class) registration, online (class) schedules. Campuswide network is available. 100% of college-owned or -operated housing units are wired for high-speed Internet access. Wireless service is available via entire campus.

Library: Mikkelsen Library. Students can reserve study rooms.

STUDENT LIFE
Housing options: on-campus residence required through sophomore year; coed, special housing for students with disabilities. Campus housing is university owned. Freshman campus housing is guaranteed.

Activities and organizations: drama/theater group, student-run newspaper, choral group, Augieholics (student athletics support organization), intramurals, Union Board of Governors (student union), Augie Green, Campus Ministries.

Athletics Member NCAA. All Division II. ***Intercollegiate sports:*** baseball M(s), basketball M(s)/W(s), cheerleading M/W, cross-country running M(s)/W(s), football M(s), golf M(s)/W(s), rugby W(c), soccer M(c)/W(s), softball W(s), swimming and diving W(s), tennis M(s)/W(s), track and field M(s)/W(s), ultimate Frisbee M(c)/W(c), volleyball W(s), wrestling M(s). ***Intramural sports:*** basketball M/W, bowling M/W, cross-country running M/W, football M/W, golf M/W, racquetball M/W, rock climbing M/W, skiing (cross-country) M/W, soccer M/W, softball M/W, swimming and diving M/W, table tennis M/W, tennis M/W, ultimate Frisbee M/W, volleyball M(c)/W(c), weight lifting M/W.

Campus security: 24-hour emergency response devices and patrols, late-night transport/escort service, controlled dormitory access, special "day lighting" night lights throughout the campus grounds.

Student services: health clinic, personal/psychological counseling.

COSTS & FINANCIAL AID
Costs (2016–17) ***Comprehensive fee:*** $38,424 includes full-time tuition ($30,454), mandatory fees ($490), and room and board ($7480). Full-time tuition and fees vary according to course load and degree level. Part-time tuition: $450 per credit hour. Part-time tuition and fees vary according to course load and degree level. ***College room only:*** $3360. Room and board charges vary according to board plan and housing facility. ***Payment plan:*** installment. ***Waivers:*** employees or children of employees.

Financial Aid Of all full-time matriculated undergraduates who enrolled in 2016, 1,108 applied for aid, 943 were judged to have need, 177 had their need fully met. 327 Federal Work-Study jobs (averaging $1815). 117 state and other part-time jobs (averaging $922). In 2016, 592 non-need-based awards were made. ***Average percent of need met:*** 94. ***Average financial aid package:*** $25,553. ***Average need-based loan:*** $5002. ***Average need-based gift aid:*** $21,864. ***Average non-need-based aid:*** $15,673. ***Average indebtedness upon graduation:*** $36,950.

APPLYING
Standardized Tests *Required:* SAT or ACT (for admission).

Options: electronic application, deferred entrance.

Required: high school transcript, minimum 2.7 GPA, minimum ACT score of 20. ***Recommended:*** essay or personal statement, 1 letter of recommendation, interview.

Application deadlines: rolling (freshmen), rolling (transfers).

Notification: continuous until 10/1 (freshmen), continuous (transfers).

CONTACT
Nancy Davidson, Vice President for Enrollment, Augustana University, 2001 South Summit Avenue, Sioux Falls, SD 57197. *Phone:* 605-274-5516. *Toll-free phone:* 800-727-2844. *Fax:* 605-274-5518. *E-mail:* admission@augie.edu.

Black Hills State University

Spearfish, South Dakota

http://www.bhsu.edu/

- **State-supported** comprehensive, founded 1883, part of South Dakota Board of Regents
- **Small-town** 123-acre campus
- **Coed** 4,020 undergraduate students, 57% full-time, 64% women, 36% men

UNDERGRAD STUDENTS
2,279 full-time, 1,741 part-time. Students come from 44 states and territories; 22 other countries; 28% are from out of state; 1% Black or African American, non-Hispanic/Latino; 5% Hispanic/Latino; 0.4% Asian, non-Hispanic/Latino; 0.2% Native Hawaiian or other Pacific Islander, non-Hispanic/Latino; 4% American Indian or Alaska Native, non-Hispanic/Latino; 4% Two or more races, non-Hispanic/Latino; 0.8% Race/ethnicity unknown; 1% international; 8% transferred in.

Freshmen:
Admission: 507 enrolled. ***Average high school GPA:*** 3.09. ***Test scores:*** ACT scores over 18: 83%; ACT scores over 24: 23%; ACT scores over 30: 1%.

Retention: 63% of full-time freshmen returned.

FACULTY
Total: 235, 37% with terminal degrees.

Student/faculty ratio: 19:1.

ACADEMICS
Calendar: semesters. *Degrees:* associate, bachelor's, master's, post-master's, and postbachelor's certificates.

Special study options: academic remediation for entering students, accelerated degree program, advanced placement credit, cooperative education, distance learning, double majors, English as a second language, honors programs, independent study, internships, off-campus study, part-time degree program, services for LD students, study abroad, summer session for credit. ***ROTC:*** Army (b).

Computers: Students can access the following: campus intranet, computer help desk, free student e-mail accounts, online (class) grades, online (class) registration, online (class) schedules. Campuswide network is available. 100% of college-owned or -operated housing units are wired for high-speed Internet access. Wireless service is available via classrooms, computer centers, computer labs, dorm rooms, learning centers, libraries, student centers.

Library: E. Y. Berry Library. Students can reserve study rooms.

STUDENT LIFE
Housing options: on-campus residence required through sophomore year; coed, men-only, women-only, special housing for students with disabilities. Campus housing is university owned. Freshman applicants given priority for college housing.

Activities and organizations: drama/theater group, student-run newspaper, radio and television station, choral group, Student Activities Committee, Student Government, national fraternities, national sororities.

Athletics Member NCAA. All Division II. ***Intercollegiate sports:*** basketball M(s)/W(s), cross-country running M(s)/W(s), football M(s), golf W, track and field M(s)/W(s), volleyball W(s). ***Intramural sports:*** archery M/W, badminton M/W, basketball M/W, bowling M/W, football M, golf M/W, racquetball M/W, skiing (cross-country) M/W, skiing (downhill) M/W, soccer M/W, softball M/W, tennis M/W, volleyball M/W, weight lifting M/W.

Campus security: 24-hour patrols, late-night transport/escort service, controlled dormitory access.

Student services: health clinic, personal/psychological counseling.

COSTS & FINANCIAL AID
Costs (2017–18) ***Tuition:*** state resident $6984 full-time, $267 per credit hour part-time; nonresident $9900 full-time, $364 per credit hour part-time. Full-time tuition and fees vary according to course load, location, program, and reciprocity agreements. Part-time tuition and fees vary according to course load, location, program, and reciprocity agreements. ***Required fees:*** $1020 full-time. ***Room and board:*** $6695. Room and board charges vary according to board plan and housing facility. ***Payment***

plan: installment. ***Waivers:*** children of alumni, senior citizens, and employees or children of employees.

Financial Aid ***Average indebtedness upon graduation:*** $25,628.

APPLYING

Standardized Tests *Required:* SAT or ACT (for admission).

Required: high school transcript, minimum 2.0 high school GPA in core curriculum.

CONTACT

Mrs. Beth Oaks, Director of Admissions, Black Hills State University, 1200 University Station, Unit 9502, Spearfish, SD 57799-9502. *Phone:* 605-642-6343. *Toll-free phone:* 800-255-2478. *Fax:* 605-642-6254. *E-mail:* admissions@bhsu.edu.

Dakota State University

Madison, South Dakota

http://www.dsu.edu/

- **State-supported** comprehensive, founded 1881, part of South Dakota Board of Regents
- **Rural** 56-acre campus with easy access to Sioux Falls
- **Endowment** $10.1 million
- **Coed** 2,844 undergraduate students, 45% full-time, 44% women, 56% men
- **Minimally difficult** entrance level, 81% of applicants were admitted

UNDERGRAD STUDENTS

1,293 full-time, 1,551 part-time. Students come from 47 states and territories; 18 other countries; 32% are from out of state; 4% Black or African American, non-Hispanic/Latino; 4% Hispanic/Latino; 2% Asian, non-Hispanic/Latino; 0.2% Native Hawaiian or other Pacific Islander, non-Hispanic/Latino; 1% American Indian or Alaska Native, non-Hispanic/Latino; 4% Two or more races, non-Hispanic/Latino; 0.7% Race/ethnicity unknown; 1% international; 10% transferred in; 32% live on campus.

Freshmen:

Admission: 911 applied, 740 admitted, 329 enrolled. ***Average high school GPA:*** 3.17. ***Test scores:*** SAT critical reading scores over 500: 43%; SAT math scores over 500: 48%; ACT scores over 18: 89%; SAT critical reading scores over 600: 14%; SAT math scores over 600: 24%; ACT scores over 24: 42%; SAT critical reading scores over 700: 5%; SAT math scores over 700: 10%; ACT scores over 30: 4%.

Retention: 72% of full-time freshmen returned.

FACULTY

Total: 141, 65% full-time, 54% with terminal degrees.

Student/faculty ratio: 18:1.

ACADEMICS

Calendar: semesters. *Degrees:* certificates, associate, bachelor's, master's, doctoral, and postbachelor's certificates.

Special study options: academic remediation for entering students, advanced placement credit, cooperative education, distance learning, double majors, honors programs, independent study, internships, off-campus study, part-time degree program, services for LD students, study abroad, summer session for credit. ***ROTC:*** Army (c), Air Force (c).

Computers: 165 computers/terminals and 356 ports are available on campus for general student use. Students can access the following: campus intranet, computer help desk, free student e-mail accounts, online (class) grades, online (class) registration, online (class) schedules. Campuswide network is available. 100% of college-owned or -operated housing units are wired for high-speed Internet access. Wireless service is available via entire campus.

Library: Karl E. Mundt Library & Learning Commons plus 1 other. *Books:* 67,151 (physical), 162,866 (digital/electronic); *Serial titles:* 243 (physical), 104,900 (digital/electronic); *Databases:* 121. Weekly public service hours: 85.

STUDENT LIFE

Housing options: on-campus residence required through sophomore year; coed, men-only. Campus housing is university owned and leased by the school. Freshman campus housing is guaranteed.

Activities and organizations: drama/theater group, student-run newspaper, radio station, choral group, Gaming Club, KDSU, Computer Club, Student Senate, PBL Business Club.

Athletics Member NAIA. ***Intercollegiate sports:*** baseball M(s), basketball M(s)/W(s), cheerleading M/W, cross-country running M(s)/W(s), football M(s), softball W(s), track and field M(s)/W(s), volleyball W(s). ***Intramural sports:*** basketball M/W, softball M/W, volleyball M/W.

Campus security: controlled dormitory access.

Student services: health clinic, personal/psychological counseling.

COSTS & FINANCIAL AID

Costs (2016–17) ***Tuition:*** state resident $6984 full-time, $233 per credit hour part-time; nonresident $9900 full-time, $330 per credit hour part-time. Full-time tuition and fees vary according to location and reciprocity agreements. Part-time tuition and fees vary according to location and reciprocity agreements. ***Required fees:*** $1943 full-time, $39 per credit part-time. ***Room and board:*** $6411; room only: $3494. Room and board charges vary according to board plan and housing facility. ***Payment plan:*** installment. ***Waivers:*** senior citizens and employees or children of employees.

Financial Aid Of all full-time matriculated undergraduates who enrolled in 2015, 1,042 applied for aid, 848 were judged to have need, 86 had their need fully met. 131 Federal Work-Study jobs (averaging $2263). 19 state and other part-time jobs (averaging $6405). In 2015, 103 non-need-based awards were made. ***Average percent of need met:*** 74. ***Average financial aid package:*** $8117. ***Average need-based loan:*** $4108. ***Average need-based gift aid:*** $4374. ***Average non-need-based aid:*** $5138. ***Average indebtedness upon graduation:*** $24,444.

APPLYING

Standardized Tests *Required:* SAT or ACT (for admission).

Options: electronic application, deferred entrance.

Application fee: $20.

Required: high school transcript, minimum 2.6 GPA, GPA of 2.6, rank in top 60% of high school class, or minimum ACT score of 18 or SAT score of 870 (combined math and critical reading).

Application deadlines: rolling (freshmen), rolling (out-of-state freshmen), rolling (transfers).

Notification: continuous (freshmen), continuous (out-of-state freshmen), continuous (transfers).

CONTACT

Ms. Tory Bickett, Admissions Senior Secretary, Dakota State University, 820 North Washington, Madison, SD 57042-1799. *Phone:* 605-256-5139. *Toll-free phone:* 888-DSU-9988. *Fax:* 605-256-5020. *E-mail:* admissions@dsu.edu.

Dakota Wesleyan University

Mitchell, South Dakota

http://www.dwu.edu/

CONTACT

Mrs. Melissa Herr-Valburg, Director of Admissions, Dakota Wesleyan University, 1200 West University Avenue, Mitchell, SD 57301-4398. *Phone:* 605-995-2600 Ext. 2652. *Toll-free phone:* 800-333-8506. *Fax:* 605-995-2699. *E-mail:* admissions@dwu.edu.

Mount Marty College

Yankton, South Dakota

http://www.mtmc.edu/

- **Independent Roman Catholic** comprehensive, founded 1936
- **Small-town** 80-acre campus
- **Endowment** $20.4 million
- **Coed** 1,006 undergraduate students, 47% full-time, 59% women, 41% men
- **Minimally difficult** entrance level, 65% of applicants were admitted

UNDERGRAD STUDENTS

468 full-time, 538 part-time. Students come from 24 states and territories; 2 other countries; 41% are from out of state; 3% Black or African American, non-Hispanic/Latino; 5% Hispanic/Latino; 0.9% Asian, non-

Hispanic/Latino; 0.4% Native Hawaiian or other Pacific Islander, non-Hispanic/Latino; 2% American Indian or Alaska Native, non-Hispanic/Latino; 0.7% Two or more races, non-Hispanic/Latino; 0.8% Race/ethnicity unknown; 3% transferred in; 64% live on campus.

Freshmen:
Admission: 473 applied, 306 admitted, 117 enrolled. ***Average high school GPA:*** 3.41.
Retention: 74% of full-time freshmen returned.

FACULTY
Total: 51, 82% full-time, 63% with terminal degrees.
Student/faculty ratio: 10:1.

ACADEMICS
Calendar: semesters. *Degrees:* certificates, associate, bachelor's, master's, doctoral, and post-master's certificates.
Special study options: academic remediation for entering students, accelerated degree program, adult/continuing education programs, advanced placement credit, cooperative education, distance learning, double majors, honors programs, independent study, internships, off-campus study, part-time degree program, services for LD students, student-designed majors, summer session for credit. ***ROTC:*** Army (c).
Computers: 12 computers/terminals are available on campus for general student use. Students can access the following: campus intranet, computer help desk, free student e-mail accounts, online (class) grades, online (class) registration, online (class) schedules. Campuswide network is available. 100% of college-owned or -operated housing units are wired for high-speed Internet access. Wireless service is available via entire campus.
Library: Mount Marty College Library. Study areas open 24 hours, 5-7 days a week; students can reserve study rooms.

STUDENT LIFE
Housing options: on-campus residence required through senior year; coed, men-only, women-only. Campus housing is university owned. Freshman campus housing is guaranteed.
Activities and organizations: drama/theater group, choral group, Campus Ministry, Student Government Association, Nursing Club, Education Club, Theater Club.
Athletics Member NAIA. ***Intercollegiate sports:*** archery M(c)/W(c), baseball M(s), basketball M(s)/W(s), cross-country running M(s)/W(s), golf M(s)/W(s), riflery M(c)/W(c), soccer M(s)/W(s), softball W(s), tennis W(s), track and field M(s)/W(s), volleyball W(s). ***Intramural sports:*** archery M/W, basketball M/W, soccer M/W, softball W, volleyball M/W.
Campus security: 24-hour emergency response devices and patrols, late-night transport/escort service.
Student services: health clinic, personal/psychological counseling.

COSTS & FINANCIAL AID
Costs (2017–18) ***Comprehensive fee:*** $34,156 includes full-time tuition ($24,160), mandatory fees ($2150), and room and board ($7846). Full-time tuition and fees vary according to degree level, location, and program. Part-time tuition: $530 per credit hour. Part-time tuition and fees vary according to course load, degree level, location, and program. ***Required fees:*** $45 per credit hour part-time. ***Room and board:*** Room and board charges vary according to board plan. ***Payment plan:*** installment. ***Waivers:*** employees or children of employees.
Financial Aid Of all full-time matriculated undergraduates who enrolled in 2016, 429 applied for aid, 364 were judged to have need, 154 had their need fully met. 119 Federal Work-Study jobs (averaging $1771). 60 state and other part-time jobs (averaging $1800). In 2016, 55 non-need-based awards were made. ***Average percent of need met:*** 83. ***Average financial aid package:*** $24,755. ***Average need-based loan:*** $4888. ***Average need-based gift aid:*** $14,929. ***Average non-need-based aid:*** $9298. ***Average indebtedness upon graduation:*** $30,083.

APPLYING
Standardized Tests *Required:* SAT or ACT (for admission).
Options: electronic application, early admission, deferred entrance.
Application fee: $35.
Required: high school transcript, minimum 2.0 GPA.
Recommended: interview.
Application deadlines: rolling (freshmen), rolling (transfers).
Notification: continuous (freshmen), continuous (transfers).

CONTACT
Stephanie Moser, Dean of Enrollment, Mount Marty College, 1105 W. 8th Street, Yankton, SD 57078. *Phone:* 605-668-1545.
Toll-free phone: 800-658-4552. *E-mail:* stephanie.moser@mtmc.edu.

National American University
Ellsworth AFB, South Dakota
http://www.national.edu/

CONTACT
Admissions Office, National American University, 1000 Ellsworth Street, Rushmore Center, Suite 2400B, Ellsworth AFB, SD 57706.

National American University
Rapid City, South Dakota
http://www.national.edu/

CONTACT
Ms. Angela Beck, Director of Enrollment Management, National American University, 321 Kansas City Street, Rapid City, SD 57701. *Phone:* 605-394-4902. *Toll-free phone:* 800-209-0490. *Fax:* 605-394-4871. *E-mail:* abeck@national.edu.

National American University
Sioux Falls, South Dakota
http://www.national.edu/

CONTACT
Ms. Lisa Houtsma, Director of Admissions, National American University, 5801 South Corporate Place, Sioux Falls, SD 57108. *Phone:* 605-336-4600. *Toll-free phone:* 800-388-5430. *Fax:* 605-336-4605. *E-mail:* lhoutsma@national.edu.

Northern State University
Aberdeen, South Dakota
http://www.northern.edu/

- **State-supported** comprehensive, founded 1901, part of South Dakota Board of Regents
- **Small-town** 72-acre campus
- **Endowment** $25.1 million
- **Coed** 3,001 undergraduate students, 49% full-time, 58% women, 42% men
- **Minimally difficult** entrance level, 83% of applicants were admitted

UNDERGRAD STUDENTS
1,477 full-time, 1,524 part-time. Students come from 41 states and territories; 35 other countries; 18% are from out of state; 4% transferred in; 41% live on campus.

Freshmen:
Admission: 1,379 applied, 1,143 admitted, 363 enrolled. ***Average high school GPA:*** 3.25. ***Test scores:*** SAT critical reading scores over 500: 42%; SAT math scores over 500: 52%; ACT scores over 18: 83%; SAT critical reading scores over 600: 12%; SAT math scores over 600: 14%; ACT scores over 24: 31%; SAT critical reading scores over 700: 4%; SAT math scores over 700: 3%; ACT scores over 30: 2%.
Retention: 67% of full-time freshmen returned.

FACULTY
Total: 169, 53% full-time, 46% with terminal degrees.
Student/faculty ratio: 21:1.

ACADEMICS
Calendar: semesters. *Degrees:* certificates, associate, bachelor's, master's, and postbachelor's certificates.
Special study options: academic remediation for entering students, accelerated degree program, adult/continuing education programs, advanced placement credit, cooperative education, distance learning, double majors, English as a second language, freshman honors college, honors programs, independent study, internships, off-campus study, part-time degree program, services for LD students, student-designed majors, study abroad, summer session for credit.

Computers: 135 computers/terminals are available on campus for general student use. Students can access the following: campus intranet, computer help desk, free student e-mail accounts, online (class) grades, online (class) registration, online (class) schedules. Campuswide network is available. 100% of college-owned or -operated housing units are wired for high-speed Internet access. Wireless service is available via entire campus.

Library: Beulah Williams Library.

STUDENT LIFE

Housing options: on-campus residence required through sophomore year; coed, special housing for students with disabilities. Campus housing is university owned.

Activities and organizations: drama/theater group, student-run newspaper, television station, choral group, marching band, Student Ambassadors, Choices, honor society, Native American Student Association, International Student Association.

Athletics Member NCAA. All Division II. ***Intercollegiate sports:*** baseball M(s), basketball M(s)/W(s), cross-country running M(s)/W(s), football M(s), soccer W(s), softball W(s), swimming and diving W(s), track and field M(s)/W(s), volleyball W(s), wrestling M(s). ***Intramural sports:*** badminton M(c)/W(c), basketball M/W, football M/W, racquetball M/W, rugby M(c)/W(c), soccer M/W, softball M/W, table tennis M/W, ultimate Frisbee M/W, volleyball M/W.

Campus security: 24-hour emergency response devices, controlled dormitory access, evening patrols.

Student services: health clinic, personal/psychological counseling, women's center, legal services.

COSTS & FINANCIAL AID

Costs (2017–18) ***Tuition:*** state resident $7191 full-time, $240 per credit hour part-time; nonresident $10,120 full-time, $337 per credit hour part-time. ***Required fees:*** $1089 full-time, $36 per credit hour part-time. ***Room and board:*** $7850; room only: $3640. Room and board charges vary according to board plan and housing facility. ***Payment plan:*** installment. ***Waivers:*** children of alumni, senior citizens, and employees or children of employees.

Financial Aid Of all full-time matriculated undergraduates who enrolled in 2016, 988 applied for aid, 749 were judged to have need, 232 had their need fully met. 334 Federal Work-Study jobs (averaging $2504). 369 state and other part-time jobs (averaging $1009). In 2016, 127 non-need-based awards were made. ***Average percent of need met:*** 77. ***Average financial aid package:*** $10,128. ***Average need-based loan:*** $5346. ***Average need-based gift aid:*** $4230. ***Average non-need-based aid:*** $1702. ***Average indebtedness upon graduation:*** $28,142.

APPLYING

Standardized Tests *Required:* SAT or ACT (for admission).

Options: electronic application, early admission, deferred entrance.

Application fee: $20.

Required: high school transcript, minimum 2.6 GPA.

Notification: continuous (freshmen), continuous (transfers).

CONTACT

Ms. Joellen Lindner, Vice President for Student Affairs and Enrollment Management, Northern State University, 1200 South Jay Street, Aberdeen, SD 57401. *Phone:* 605-626-2530. *Toll-free phone:* 800-678-5330. *Fax:* 605-626-2531. *E-mail:* admission2@northern.edu.

Oglala Lakota College

Kyle, South Dakota

http://www.olc.edu/

CONTACT

Director of Admissions, Oglala Lakota College, 490 Piya Wiconi Road, Kyle, SD 57752-0490. *Phone:* 605-455-2321 Ext. 236.
E-mail: lmeseteth@olc.edu.

Presentation College

Aberdeen, South Dakota

http://www.presentation.edu/

CONTACT

Mr. Robert Schuchardt, Vice President for Student Services, Presentation College, 1500 North Main Street, Aberdeen, SD 57401. *Phone:* 605-229-8406. *Toll-free phone:* 800-437-6060. *Fax:* 605-229-8425.
E-mail: admit@presentation.edu.

Sinte Gleska University

Mission, South Dakota

http://www.sintegleska.edu/

CONTACT

Mr. Jack Herman, Registrar and Director of Admissions, Sinte Gleska University, 101 Antelope Lake Circle, PO Box 105, Mission, SD 57555. *Phone:* 605-856-8100 Ext. 8479.

South Dakota School of Mines and Technology

Rapid City, South Dakota

http://www.sdsmt.edu/

- **State-supported** university, founded 1885, part of South Dakota Board of Regents
- **Suburban** 120-acre campus
- **Endowment** $53.7 million
- **Coed** 2,485 undergraduate students, 81% full-time, 22% women, 78% men
- **Moderately difficult** entrance level, 85% of applicants were admitted

UNDERGRAD STUDENTS

2,018 full-time, 467 part-time. Students come from 42 states and territories; 27 other countries; 53% are from out of state; 2% Black or African American, non-Hispanic/Latino; 5% Hispanic/Latino; 1% Asian, non-Hispanic/Latino; 0.1% Native Hawaiian or other Pacific Islander, non-Hispanic/Latino; 2% American Indian or Alaska Native, non-Hispanic/Latino; 3% Two or more races, non-Hispanic/Latino; 0.7% Race/ethnicity unknown; 3% international; 4% transferred in; 60% live on campus.

Freshmen:

Admission: 1,368 applied, 1,156 admitted, 497 enrolled. ***Average high school GPA:*** 3.57. ***Test scores:*** SAT critical reading scores over 500: 74%; SAT math scores over 500: 87%; SAT writing scores over 500: 63%; ACT scores over 18: 100%; SAT critical reading scores over 600: 38%; SAT math scores over 600: 54%; SAT writing scores over 600: 23%; ACT scores over 24: 80%; SAT critical reading scores over 700: 9%; SAT math scores over 700: 7%; SAT writing scores over 700: 2%; ACT scores over 30: 25%.

Retention: 78% of full-time freshmen returned.

FACULTY

Total: 177, 85% full-time, 80% with terminal degrees.

Student/faculty ratio: 15:1.

ACADEMICS

Calendar: semesters. *Degrees:* certificates, associate, bachelor's, master's, doctoral, and postbachelor's certificates.

Special study options: academic remediation for entering students, adult/continuing education programs, advanced placement credit, cooperative education, distance learning, double majors, English as a second language, honors programs, independent study, internships, off-campus study, part-time degree program, services for LD students, study abroad, summer session for credit. ***ROTC:*** Army (b).

Computers: 105 computers/terminals and 1,246 ports are available on campus for general student use. Students can access the following: campus intranet, computer help desk, free student e-mail accounts, online (class) grades, online (class) registration, online (class) schedules. Campuswide network is available. 100% of college-owned or -operated housing units are wired for high-speed Internet access. Wireless service is available via entire campus.

Library: Devereaux Library plus 1 other. *Books:* 130,971 (physical), 142,661 (digital/electronic); *Serial titles:* 1,663 (physical), 23,896 (digital/electronic); *Databases:* 200. Weekly public service hours: 32; students can reserve study rooms.

STUDENT LIFE

Housing options: on-campus residence required through sophomore year; coed, men-only, women-only, special housing for students with disabilities. Campus housing is university owned and leased by the school. Freshman campus housing is guaranteed.

Activities and organizations: drama/theater group, student-run newspaper, radio station, choral group, eSports 144, ASME (American Society of Mechanical Engineers), Skid Snowboard Club 115, AIChe 107, ASCE 105, national fraternities, national sororities.

Athletics Member NCAA. All Division II. ***Intercollegiate sports:*** basketball M(s)/W(s), cross-country running M(s)/W(s), football M(s), golf M(s)/W(s), soccer M, track and field M(s)/W(s), volleyball W(s). ***Intramural sports:*** badminton M(c)/W(c), cheerleading M(c)/W(c), racquetball M/W, riflery M(c)/W(c), rock climbing M(c)/W(c), skiing (downhill) M(c)/W(c), soccer M(c)/W(c), squash M(c), tennis M(c)/W(c), ultimate Frisbee M(c)/W(c), volleyball M/W, water polo M/W.

Campus security: 24-hour emergency response devices and patrols, student patrols, late-night transport/escort service, controlled dormitory access.

Student services: health clinic, personal/psychological counseling.

COSTS & FINANCIAL AID

Costs (2016–17) ***Tuition:*** state resident $4530 full-time, $245 per credit hour part-time; nonresident $7590 full-time, $383 per credit hour part-time. Full-time tuition and fees vary according to course level, course load, program, and reciprocity agreements. Part-time tuition and fees vary according to course level, course load, program, and reciprocity agreements. ***Required fees:*** $6640 full-time, $127 per credit hour part-time. ***Room and board:*** $7300; room only: $3800. Room and board charges vary according to board plan and housing facility. ***Payment plan:*** installment. ***Waivers:*** children of alumni, senior citizens, and employees or children of employees.

Financial Aid Of all full-time matriculated undergraduates who enrolled in 2015, 1,812 applied for aid, 1,095 were judged to have need, 334 had their need fully met. 148 Federal Work-Study jobs (averaging $1718). In 2015, 405 non-need-based awards were made. ***Average percent of need met:*** 71. ***Average financial aid package:*** $14,262. ***Average need-based loan:*** $4106. ***Average need-based gift aid:*** $4616. ***Average non-need-based aid:*** $3360. ***Average indebtedness upon graduation:*** $32,995.

APPLYING

Standardized Tests *Required:* SAT or ACT (for admission).

Options: electronic application.

Application fee: $20.

Required: high school transcript. ***Recommended:*** minimum 2.8 GPA.

Application deadlines: rolling (freshmen), rolling (transfers).

Notification: continuous (freshmen), continuous (transfers).

CONTACT

Genene Sigler, Applications Processor, South Dakota School of Mines and Technology, 501 East Saint Joseph Street, Rapid City, SD 57701-3995. *Phone:* 605-394-2414 Ext. 5209. *Toll-free phone:* 800-544-8162. *Fax:* 605-394-1979. *E-mail:* admissions@sdsmt.edu.

South Dakota State University

Brookings, South Dakota

http://www.sdstate.edu/

- **State-supported** university, founded 1881, part of South Dakota Board of Regents
- **Small-town** 363-acre campus
- **Coed** 10,959 undergraduate students, 77% full-time, 53% women, 47% men
- **Minimally difficult** entrance level, 91% of applicants were admitted

UNDERGRAD STUDENTS

8,474 full-time, 2,485 part-time. 2% Black or African American, non-Hispanic/Latino; 2% Hispanic/Latino; 0.9% Asian, non-Hispanic/Latino; 0.1% Native Hawaiian or other Pacific Islander, non-Hispanic/Latino; 0.9% American Indian or Alaska Native, non-Hispanic/Latino; 2% Two or more races, non-Hispanic/Latino; 0.4% Race/ethnicity unknown; 4% international; 6% transferred in.

Freshmen:

Admission: 5,173 applied, 4,695 admitted, 2,273 enrolled. ***Average high school GPA:*** 3.37. ***Test scores:*** SAT critical reading scores over 500: 39%; SAT math scores over 500: 64%; ACT scores over 18: 93%; SAT critical reading scores over 600: 20%; SAT math scores over 600: 20%; ACT scores over 24: 44%; SAT critical reading scores over 700: 3%; SAT math scores over 700: 3%; ACT scores over 30: 6%.

Retention: 79% of full-time freshmen returned.

FACULTY

Total: 696, 79% full-time, 67% with terminal degrees.

Student/faculty ratio: 17:1.

ACADEMICS

Calendar: semesters. *Degrees:* certificates, associate, bachelor's, master's, doctoral, post-master's, and postbachelor's certificates.

Special study options: academic remediation for entering students, accelerated degree program, adult/continuing education programs, advanced placement credit, cooperative education, distance learning, double majors, English as a second language, freshman honors college, honors programs, independent study, internships, off-campus study, part-time degree program, services for LD students, study abroad, summer session for credit. ***ROTC:*** Army (b), Air Force (b).

Unusual degree programs: 3-2 economics.

Computers: 120 computers/terminals and 100 ports are available on campus for general student use. Students can access the following: campus intranet, computer help desk, free student e-mail accounts, online (class) grades, online (class) registration, online (class) schedules. Campuswide network is available. 100% of college-owned or -operated housing units are wired for high-speed Internet access. Wireless service is available via entire campus.

Library: H. M. Briggs Library. *Books:* 778,376 (physical), 134,615 (digital/electronic); *Serial titles:* 19,899 (physical), 19,850 (digital/electronic); *Databases:* 108. Students can reserve study rooms.

STUDENT LIFE

Housing options: on-campus residence required through sophomore year; coed, special housing for students with disabilities. Campus housing is university owned. Freshman campus housing is guaranteed.

Activities and organizations: drama/theater group, student-run newspaper, radio station, choral group, marching band, national fraternities, national sororities.

Athletics Member NCAA. All Division I. ***Intercollegiate sports:*** baseball M(s), basketball M(s)/W(s), bowling M(c)/W(c), cheerleading M(c)/W(c), cross-country running M(s)/W(s), equestrian sports W(s), football M(s), golf M(s)/W(s), ice hockey M(c)/W(c), soccer W(s), softball W(s), swimming and diving M(s)/W(s), tennis M(s)/W(s), track and field M(s)/W(s), volleyball W(s), wrestling M(s). ***Intramural sports:*** badminton M/W, baseball M, basketball M/W, cross-country running M/W, football M/W, golf M/W, rock climbing M/W, rugby M(c)/W(c), soccer W, softball M/W, swimming and diving M/W, table tennis M/W, tennis M/W, track and field M/W, ultimate Frisbee M/W, volleyball M/W, wrestling M.

Campus security: 24-hour emergency response devices and patrols, student patrols, late-night transport/escort service, controlled dormitory access.

Student services: health clinic, personal/psychological counseling, legal services.

FINANCIAL AID

Financial Aid Of all full-time matriculated undergraduates who enrolled in 2014, 7,135 applied for aid, 5,684 were judged to have need, 575 had their need fully met. In 2014, 1322 non-need-based awards were made. ***Average percent of need met:*** 44. ***Average financial aid package:*** $8636. ***Average need-based loan:*** $3709. ***Average need-based gift aid:*** $3755. ***Average non-need-based aid:*** $1949. ***Average indebtedness upon graduation:*** $28,769.

APPLYING

Standardized Tests *Required:* SAT or ACT (for admission).

Options: electronic application.

Application fee: $20.
Required: high school transcript, minimum 2.6 GPA.
Application deadlines: rolling (freshmen), rolling (transfers).
Notification: continuous (freshmen), continuous (transfers).

CONTACT

Ms. Michelle Kuebler, Assistant Director of Admissions, South Dakota State University, PO Box 2201, Brookings, SD 57007. *Phone:* 605-688-4121. *Toll-free phone:* 800-952-3541. *Fax:* 605-688-6891.
E-mail: sdsu.admissions@sdstate.edu.

University of Sioux Falls

Sioux Falls, South Dakota

http://www.usiouxfalls.edu/

CONTACT

Aimee Vander Feen, Director of Admissions, University of Sioux Falls, 1101 West 22nd Street, Sioux Falls, SD 57105. *Phone:* 605-331-6602.
Toll-free phone: 800-888-1047. *Fax:* 605-331-6615.
E-mail: admissions@usiouxfalls.edu.

The University of South Dakota

Vermillion, South Dakota

http://www.usd.edu/

- **State-supported**university, founded 1862, part of South Dakota Board of Regents
- **Small-town**275-acre campus
- **Endowment**$17.8 million
- **Coed**7,500 undergraduate students, 66% full-time, 62% women, 38% men
- **Moderately difficult** entrance level, 88% of applicants were admitted

UNDERGRAD STUDENTS

4,943 full-time, 2557 part-time. Students come from 46 states and territories; 29 other countries; 33% are from out of state; 3% Black or African American, non-Hispanic/Latino; 4% Hispanic/Latino; 1% Asian, non-Hispanic/Latino; 2% American Indian or Alaska Native, non-Hispanic/Latino; 3% Two or more races, non-Hispanic/Latino; .4% Race/ethnicity unknown; 2% international; 27% live on campus.

Freshmen:
Admission:3,607 applied, 3,179 admitted, 1,243 enrolled.***Average high school GPA:***3.03.***Test scores:***SAT critical reading scores over 500: 44%; SAT math scores over 500: 54%; ACT scores over 18: 78%; SAT critical reading scores over 600: 20%; SAT math scores over 600: 22%; ACT scores over 24: 31%; SAT critical reading scores over 700: 3%; SAT math scores over 700: 6%; ACT scores over 30: 4%.
Retention:76% of full-time freshmen returned.

FACULTY

Total:635, 69% full-time, 53% with terminal degrees.
Student/faculty ratio:18:1.

ACADEMICS

Calendar:semesters.*Degrees:*certificates, associate, bachelor's, master's, doctoral, post-master's, and postbachelor's certificates.
Special study options:academic remediation for entering students, accelerated degree program, adult/continuing education programs, advanced placement credit, cooperative education, distance learning, double majors, English as a second language, external degree program, honors programs, independent
study, internships, off-campus study, part-time degree program, services for LD students, student-designed majors, study abroad
summer session for credit.***ROTC:***Army (b).
Computers:975 computers/terminals are available on
campus for general student use. Students can access the following: campus intranet, computer help desk, free student e-mail accounts, online (class) registration. Campuswide network is available. Wireless service is available..
Library:I. D. Weeks Library plus 2 others.

STUDENT LIFE

Housing options: coed, special housing for students with disabilities. Campus housing is university owned.
Activities and organizations: drama/theater group, student-run newspaper, radio station, choral group, marching band, Program Council, Residence Hall Association, Student Ambassadors, Delta Sigma Pi, national fraternities, national sororities.
Athletics Member NCAA. All Division I.***Intercollegiate sports:*** basketball M(s)/W(s), cross-country running M(s)/W(s), football M(s), golf M/W(s), soccer W(s), softball W(s), swimming and diving M(s)/W(s), tennis W(s), track and field M(s)/W(s), volleyball W(s).***Intramural sports:*** baseball M(c),basketball M/W, bowling M/W, crew M(c)/W(c), Fencing M(c)/W(c), football M, ice hockey M(c), lacrosse M(c)/W(c), rock climbing M(c)/W(c), rugby M(c)/W(c), soccer M(c)/W(c), softball M(c)/W(c), tennis M/W.
Campus security:24-hour emergency response devices and patrols, student patrols, late-night transport/escort service, controlled dormitory access.
Student services: health clinic, personal/psychological counseling, legal services, women's center.

COSTS & FINANCIAL AID

Costs (2017–18)***Tuition:*** state resident
$7155 full-time, $239 per credit hour part-time; nonresident $10,386 full-time, $346 per credit hour part-time. Full-time tuition and fees vary according to course load. Part-time tuition and fees vary according to course load.
Required fees:$1302 full-time, $53 per term part-time.***Room and board:***$7535; room only: $4086. Room and board charges vary according to board plan and housing facility.***Payment plan:*** deferred payment.***Waivers:***children of alumni, senior citizens, employees or children of employees.

APPLYING

Standardized Tests *Required:* SAT and SAT Subject Tests or ACT (for admission).
Options: electronic application, early admission.
Application fee:$20.
Required: high school transcript.
Recommended: minimum 2.0 GPA.
Application deadlines: continuous (freshmen), continuous (transfers).
Notification: continuous (freshmen), continuous (transfers).

CONTACT

Mr. Travis Vlasman, Director of Enrollment Services, The University of South Dakota, 414 East Clark Street, Vermillion, SD 57069-2390.
Phone: 605-677-5434. *Toll-free phone:* 877-269-6837.
Fax: 605-677-6753. *E-mail:* admiss@usd.edu.

TENNESSEE

American Baptist College

Nashville, Tennessee

http://www.abcnash.edu/

- **Independent Baptist** 4-year, founded 1924
- **Urban** 52-acre campus with easy access to Nashville
- **Endowment** $626,121
- **Coed**
- **Noncompetitive** entrance level

FACULTY

Student/faculty ratio: 12:1.

ACADEMICS
Calendar: semesters. *Degrees:* diplomas, associate, and bachelor's.
Library: T. L. Holcolm Library. *Books:* 14,290 (physical); *Serial titles:* 2 (physical); *Databases:* 2. Weekly public service hours: 2; students can reserve study rooms.

STUDENT LIFE
Housing options: coed, men-only, women-only. Campus housing is university owned.

Activities and organizations: choral group, Student Government Association, Vespers Service, Baptist Student Union, Choir, Greek Letter Fraternity and Hoi Adelphoi Fraternity, national fraternities.

Campus security: 24-hour emergency response devices and patrols, controlled dormitory access.

Student services: health clinic.

COSTS & FINANCIAL AID
Costs (2016–17) ***Comprehensive fee:*** $13,800 includes full-time tuition ($8760) and room and board ($5040). Part-time tuition: $380 per credit hour. ***College room only:*** $3840. Room and board charges vary according to board plan and housing facility.

Financial Aid Of all full-time matriculated undergraduates who enrolled in 2014, 128 applied for aid, 128 were judged to have need. 5 Federal Work-Study jobs (averaging $7452). ***Average percent of need met:*** 40. ***Average financial aid package:*** $10,412. ***Average need-based loan:*** $3823. ***Average need-based gift aid:*** $8263. ***Average indebtedness upon graduation:*** $9743. ***Financial aid deadline:*** 7/23.

APPLYING
Standardized Tests *Required:* (for admission).

Options: electronic application, deferred entrance.

Application fee: $30.

Required: essay or personal statement, high school transcript, minimum 2.0 GPA, 2 letters of recommendation, official transcript(s). ***Required for some:*** interview.

CONTACT
Recruiter, American Baptist College, 1800 Baptist World Center Drive, Nashville, TN 37207. *Phone:* 615-687-6907. *Fax:* 615-226-7855.
E-mail: admissions@abcnash.edu.

Aquinas College
Nashville, Tennessee
http://www.aquinascollege.edu/

- **Independent Roman Catholic** comprehensive, founded 1961
- **Urban** 83-acre campus
- **Endowment** $16.5 million
- **Coed** 337 undergraduate students, 58% full-time, 80% women, 20% men
- **Minimally difficult** entrance level, 52% of applicants were admitted

UNDERGRAD STUDENTS
196 full-time, 141 part-time. Students come from 26 states and territories; 5 other countries; 23% are from out of state; 6% Black or African American, non-Hispanic/Latino; 4% Hispanic/Latino; 4% Asian, non-Hispanic/Latino; 2% Native Hawaiian or other Pacific Islander, non-Hispanic/Latino; 0.3% American Indian or Alaska Native, non-Hispanic/Latino; 2% Two or more races, non-Hispanic/Latino; 9% Race/ethnicity unknown; 4% international; 17% transferred in; 15% live on campus.

Freshmen:
Admission: 183 applied, 95 admitted, 29 enrolled. ***Average high school GPA:*** 3.55. ***Test scores:*** SAT critical reading scores over 500: 90%; SAT math scores over 500: 70%; ACT scores over 18: 100%; SAT critical reading scores over 600: 60%; SAT math scores over 600: 40%; ACT scores over 24: 50%; SAT critical reading scores over 700: 30%; SAT math scores over 700: 10%; ACT scores over 30: 9%.

Retention: 73% of full-time freshmen returned.

FACULTY
Total: 73, 38% full-time, 34% with terminal degrees.

Student/faculty ratio: 8:1.

ACADEMICS
Calendar: semesters. *Degrees:* associate, bachelor's, master's, and post-master's certificates.

Special study options: academic remediation for entering students, accelerated degree program, advanced placement credit, cooperative education, double majors, independent study, internships, part-time degree program, study abroad, summer session for credit.

Computers: 59 computers/terminals are available on campus for general student use. Students can access the following: computer help desk, free student e-mail accounts, online (class) grades, online (class) registration, online (class) schedules. Campuswide network is available. Wireless service is available via dorm rooms, libraries, student centers.
Library: Aquinas College Library. *Books:* 55,934 (physical), 71,042 (digital/electronic); *Serial titles:* 381 (physical), 17,998 (digital/electronic); *Databases:* 95. Weekly public service hours: 64.

STUDENT LIFE
Housing options: on-campus residence required through sophomore year; men-only, women-only. Campus housing is leased by the school. Freshman applicants given priority for college housing.

Activities and organizations: choral group, Campus Ministry, Student Activities Board, Association for Supervision and Curriculum Development, Association of Student Nurses, Socratic Club.

Campus security: 24-hour patrols, late-night transport/escort service.

Student services: personal/psychological counseling.

COSTS
Costs (2016–17) ***Comprehensive fee:*** $30,800 includes full-time tuition ($21,350), mandatory fees ($600), and room and board ($8850). Full-time tuition and fees vary according to course load and program. Part-time tuition: $730 per credit hour. Part-time tuition and fees vary according to course load and program. ***College room only:*** $5700. ***Payment plan:*** installment. ***Waivers:*** employees or children of employees.

APPLYING
Standardized Tests *Required:* SAT or ACT (for admission).

Options: electronic application, deferred entrance.

Required: high school transcript, minimum 2.4 GPA. ***Required for some:*** essay or personal statement.

Application deadlines: rolling (freshmen), rolling (out-of-state freshmen), rolling (transfers).

Notification: continuous (freshmen), continuous (out-of-state freshmen), continuous (transfers).

CONTACT
Ms. Connie Hansom, Director of Admissions, Aquinas College, 4210 Harding Pike, Nashville, TN 37205-2005. *Phone:* 615-297-7545 Ext. 411. *Toll-free phone:* 800-649-9956. *Fax:* 615-279-3893.
E-mail: hansomc@aquinascollege.edu.

Argosy University, Nashville
Nashville, Tennessee
http://www.argosy.edu/locations/nashville/

CONTACT
Argosy University, Nashville, 100 Centerview Drive, Suite 225, Nashville, TN 37214. *Phone:* 615-525-2800.
Toll-free phone: 866-833-6598.

The Art Institute of Tennessee–Nashville, a branch of The Art Institute of Atlanta
Nashville, Tennessee
http://www.artinstitutes.edu/nashville/

CONTACT
The Art Institute of Tennessee–Nashville, a branch of The Art Institute of Atlanta, 100 Centerview Drive, Suite 250, Nashville, TN 37214.
Phone: 615-874-1067. *Toll-free phone:* 866-747-5770.

Austin Peay State University

Clarksville, Tennessee

http://www.apsu.edu/

- **State-supported** comprehensive, founded 1927, part of Tennessee Board of Regents
- **Suburban** 169-acre campus with easy access to Nashville
- **Endowment** $8.6 million
- **Coed** 9,513 undergraduate students, 73% full-time, 58% women, 42% men
- **Moderately difficult** entrance level, 89% of applicants were admitted

UNDERGRAD STUDENTS

6,956 full-time, 2,557 part-time. Students come from 43 states and territories; 17 other countries; 10% are from out of state; 21% Black or African American, non-Hispanic/Latino; 6% Hispanic/Latino; 2% Asian, non-Hispanic/Latino; 0.3% Native Hawaiian or other Pacific Islander, non-Hispanic/Latino; 0.4% American Indian or Alaska Native, non-Hispanic/Latino; 6% Two or more races, non-Hispanic/Latino; 3% Race/ethnicity unknown; 0.4% international; 10% transferred in; 17% live on campus.

Freshmen:

Admission: 6,255 applied, 5,569 admitted, 1,963 enrolled. ***Average high school GPA:*** 3.24. ***Test scores:*** SAT critical reading scores over 500: 56%; SAT math scores over 500: 56%; ACT scores over 18: 88%; SAT critical reading scores over 600: 6%; ACT scores over 24: 27%; ACT scores over 30: 3%.

Retention: 66% of full-time freshmen returned.

FACULTY

Total: 640, 58% full-time.

Student/faculty ratio: 18:1.

ACADEMICS

Calendar: semesters. *Degrees:* certificates, associate, bachelor's, master's, post-master's, and postbachelor's certificates.

Special study options: academic remediation for entering students, accelerated degree program, adult/continuing education programs, advanced placement credit, cooperative education, distance learning, double majors, English as a second language, honors programs, independent study, internships, part-time degree program, services for LD students, study abroad, summer session for credit. ***ROTC:*** Army (b), Air Force (c).

Computers: 1,062 computers/terminals are available on campus for general student use. Students can access the following: campus intranet, computer help desk, free student e-mail accounts, online (class) grades, online (class) registration, online (class) schedules. Campuswide network is available. Wireless service is available via entire campus.

Library: Felix G. Woodward Library. *Books:* 219,393 (physical), 302,794 (digital/electronic); *Serial titles:* 2,800 (physical), 54,016 (digital/electronic); *Databases:* 281. Weekly public service hours: 109.

STUDENT LIFE

Housing options: on-campus residence required for freshman year; coed, men-only, women-only, special housing for students with disabilities. Campus housing is university owned.

Activities and organizations: drama/theater group, student-run newspaper, radio and television station, choral group, marching band, national fraternities, national sororities.

Athletics Member NCAA. All Division I except football (Division I-AA). ***Intercollegiate sports:*** baseball M(s), basketball M(s)/W(s), cheerleading M(s)/W(s), cross-country running M(s)/W(s), golf M(s)/W(s), soccer W(s), softball W(s), tennis M(s)/W(s), track and field W(s), volleyball W(s). ***Intramural sports:*** badminton M/W, basketball M/W, football M/W, golf M/W, racquetball M/W, soccer M/W, softball M/W, table tennis M/W, ultimate Frisbee M/W, volleyball M/W.

Campus security: 24-hour emergency response devices and patrols, student patrols, late-night transport/escort service, controlled dormitory access.

Student services: health clinic, personal/psychological counseling.

COSTS & FINANCIAL AID

Costs (2017–18) ***One-time required fee:*** $75. ***Tuition:*** state resident $6216 full-time, $259 per credit hour part-time; nonresident $21,456 full-time, $894 per credit hour part-time. Full-time tuition and fees vary according to location and program. Part-time tuition and fees vary according to location and program. ***Required fees:*** $1473 full-time. ***Room and board:*** $8708; room only: $5360. Room and board charges vary according to board plan and housing facility. ***Payment plan:*** installment. ***Waivers:*** senior citizens and employees or children of employees.

Financial Aid Of all full-time matriculated undergraduates who enrolled in 2015, 6,267 applied for aid, 5,519 were judged to have need. 137 Federal Work-Study jobs (averaging $2482). 486 state and other part-time jobs (averaging $1551). In 2015, 515 non-need-based awards were made. ***Average financial aid package:*** $10,840. ***Average need-based loan:*** $3863. ***Average need-based gift aid:*** $7480. ***Average non-need-based aid:*** $4808. ***Average indebtedness upon graduation:*** $23,808.

APPLYING

Standardized Tests *Required for some:* SAT or ACT (for admission).

Options: electronic application, deferred entrance.

Application fee: $25.

Required: high school transcript. ***Required for some:*** minimum 2.8 GPA.

Application deadlines: 8/9 (freshmen), rolling (transfers).

Notification: continuous (freshmen), continuous (transfers).

CONTACT

Ms. Amy Corlew, Director of Admissions, Austin Peay State University, 601 College Street, Clarksville, TN 37044. *Phone:* 931-221-7661. *Toll-free phone:* 800-844-2778. *Fax:* 931-221-6168. *E-mail:* admissions@apsu.edu.

Baptist College of Health Sciences

Memphis, Tennessee

http://www.bchs.edu/

CONTACT

Baptist College of Health Sciences, 1003 Monroe Avenue, Memphis, TN 38104. *Phone:* 901-572-2441. *Toll-free phone:* 866-575-2247.

Belhaven University

Memphis, Tennessee

http://memphis.belhaven.edu/

CONTACT

Don Jones, Director of Admission, Belhaven University, 5100 Poplar Avenue, Suite 200, Memphis, TN 38137. *Phone:* 901-888-3343. *Fax:* 901-888-0771. *E-mail:* memphisadmission@belhaven.edu.

Belmont University

Nashville, Tennessee

http://www.belmont.edu/

- **Independent Christian** university, founded 1951
- **Urban** 77-acre campus
- **Endowment** $107.8 million
- **Coed** 6,293 undergraduate students, 95% full-time, 63% women, 37% men
- **Moderately difficult** entrance level, 87% of applicants were admitted

UNDERGRAD STUDENTS

5,951 full-time, 342 part-time. Students come from 51 states and territories; 33 other countries; 70% are from out of state; 5% Black or African American, non-Hispanic/Latino; 5% Hispanic/Latino; 2% Asian, non-Hispanic/Latino; 0.1% Native Hawaiian or other Pacific Islander, non-Hispanic/Latino; 0.3% American Indian or Alaska Native, non-Hispanic/Latino; 3% Two or more races, non-Hispanic/Latino; 3% Race/ethnicity unknown; 1% international; 5% transferred in; 56% live on campus.

Freshmen:

Admission: 6,765 applied, 5,886 admitted, 1,568 enrolled. ***Average high school GPA:*** 3.7. ***Test scores:*** SAT critical reading scores over 500: 87%; SAT math scores over 500: 81%; ACT scores over 18: 99%; SAT critical reading scores over 600: 40%; SAT math scores over 600: 36%; ACT scores over 24: 75%; SAT critical reading scores over 700: 9%; SAT math scores over 700: 4%; ACT scores over 30: 19%.

Retention: 83% of full-time freshmen returned.

FACULTY

Total: 847, 41% full-time, 54% with terminal degrees.

Student/faculty ratio: 13:1.

ACADEMICS

Calendar: semesters. *Degrees:* bachelor's, master's, doctoral, and post-master's certificates.

Special study options: accelerated degree program, adult/continuing education programs, advanced placement credit, cooperative education, distance learning, double majors, English as a second language, honors programs, independent study, internships, off-campus study, part-time degree program, student-designed majors, study abroad, summer session for credit. ***ROTC:*** Army (c), Navy (c), Air Force (c).

Unusual degree programs: 3-2 engineering with Auburn University, Georgia Institute of Technology, University of Tennessee.

Computers: 500 computers/terminals are available on campus for general student use. Students can access the following: campus intranet, free student e-mail accounts, online (class) grades, online (class) registration, online (class) schedules, individual student information via course management system. Campuswide network is available. 100% of college-owned or -operated housing units are wired for high-speed Internet access. Wireless service is available via entire campus.

Library: Lila D. Bunch Library plus 1 other. *Books:* 236,551 (physical), 78,431 (digital/electronic); *Serial titles:* 35,012 (physical), 800,919 (digital/electronic); *Databases:* 299. Weekly public service hours: 127; students can reserve study rooms.

STUDENT LIFE

Housing options: on-campus residence required through sophomore year; men-only, women-only. Campus housing is university owned. Freshman campus housing is guaranteed.

Activities and organizations: drama/theater group, student-run newspaper, radio and television station, choral group, marching band, Service Corp, Alpha Sigma Tau, Phi Mu, Phi Kappa Tau, MOB, national fraternities, national sororities.

Athletics Member NCAA. All Division I. ***Intercollegiate sports:*** baseball M(s), basketball M(s)/W(s), cross-country running M(s)/W(s), golf M(s)/W(s), soccer M(s)/W(s), softball W(s), tennis M(s)/W(s), track and field M(s)/W(s), volleyball W(s). ***Intramural sports:*** baseball M, basketball M/W, bowling M/W, cheerleading M/W, football M, golf M, ice hockey M/W, racquetball M/W, soccer M/W, softball M/W, table tennis M/W, tennis M/W, volleyball M/W.

Campus security: 24-hour emergency response devices and patrols, late-night transport/escort service, controlled dormitory access, bicycle patrol.

Student services: health clinic, personal/psychological counseling, women's center.

COSTS & FINANCIAL AID

Costs (2017–18) ***Comprehensive fee:*** $44,500 includes full-time tuition ($31,300), mandatory fees ($1520), and room and board ($11,680). Full-time tuition and fees vary according to course load. Part-time tuition: $1190 per credit hour. Part-time tuition and fees vary according to course load. ***College room only:*** $6440. Room and board charges vary according to board plan and housing facility. ***Payment plans:*** installment, deferred payment. ***Waivers:*** senior citizens and employees or children of employees.

Financial Aid Of all full-time matriculated undergraduates who enrolled in 2016, 3,990 applied for aid, 3,037 were judged to have need, 318 had their need fully met. In 2016, 1446 non-need-based awards were made. ***Average percent of need met:*** 50. ***Average financial aid package:*** $18,276. ***Average need-based loan:*** $4501. ***Average need-based gift aid:*** $14,857. ***Average non-need-based aid:*** $7561. ***Average indebtedness upon graduation:*** $31,020.

APPLYING

Standardized Tests *Required:* SAT or ACT (for admission).

Options: electronic application, early admission, deferred entrance.

Application fee: $50.

Required: essay or personal statement, high school transcript, minimum 3.0 GPA, 2 letters of recommendation, resumé of activities. ***Required for some:*** interview.

Application deadlines: 8/1 (freshmen), 8/1 (transfers).

Notification: continuous (freshmen), continuous (transfers).

CONTACT

Mr. David Mee, Associate Provost and Dean of Enrollment, Belmont University, 1900 Belmont Boulevard, Nashville, TN 37212-3757.
Phone: 615-460-5479. *Fax:* 615-460-5434. *E-mail:* david.mee@belmont.edu.

Bethel University

McKenzie, Tennessee

http://www.bethelu.edu/

CONTACT

Tina Hodges, Enrollment Director of Admissions and Financial Aid, Bethel University, 325 Cherry Avenue, McKenzie, TN 38201.
Phone: 731-352-4030. *Fax:* 731-352-4069.
E-mail: hodgest@bethelu.edu.

Bryan College

Dayton, Tennessee

http://www.bryan.edu/

- **Independent interdenominational** comprehensive, founded 1930
- **Small-town** 130-acre campus
- **Coed** 1,420 undergraduate students, 59% full-time, 54% women, 46% men
- **Moderately difficult** entrance level, 46% of applicants were admitted

UNDERGRAD STUDENTS

838 full-time, 582 part-time. 64% are from out of state; 5% Black or African American, non-Hispanic/Latino; 4% Hispanic/Latino; 0.3% Asian, non-Hispanic/Latino; 0.2% American Indian or Alaska Native, non-Hispanic/Latino; 4% Two or more races, non-Hispanic/Latino; 0.2% Race/ethnicity unknown; 5% international; 5% transferred in; 74% live on campus.

Freshmen:

Admission: 716 applied, 326 admitted, 158 enrolled. ***Average high school GPA:*** 3.56. ***Test scores:*** SAT critical reading scores over 500: 50%; SAT math scores over 500: 37%; SAT writing scores over 500: 42%; ACT scores over 18: 93%; SAT critical reading scores over 600: 16%; SAT math scores over 600: 8%; SAT writing scores over 600: 18%; ACT scores over 24: 40%; SAT critical reading scores over 700: 3%; ACT scores over 30: 4%.

Retention: 66% of full-time freshmen returned.

FACULTY

Total: 124, 30% full-time, 35% with terminal degrees.

ACADEMICS

Calendar: semesters. *Degrees:* certificates, associate, bachelor's, and master's.

Special study options: academic remediation for entering students, adult/continuing education programs, advanced placement credit, distance learning, double majors, honors programs, independent study, internships, off-campus study, part-time degree program, services for LD students, study abroad, summer session for credit.

Unusual degree programs: 3-2 nursing with Vanderbilt University; psychology with Richmont Graduate University.

Computers: Students can access the following: campus intranet, computer help desk, free student e-mail accounts, online (class) grades, online (class) registration, online (class) schedules. Campuswide network is available. Wireless service is available via entire campus.

Library: Bryan College Library.

STUDENT LIFE

Housing options: on-campus residence required through senior year; men-only, women-only, special housing for students with disabilities. Campus housing is university owned. Freshman campus housing is guaranteed.

Activities and organizations: drama/theater group, student-run newspaper, choral group, Practical Christian Involvement (PCI), International Students Association, Rugby club, Nutella Club, Navigators.

Athletics Member NAIA. ***Intercollegiate sports:*** baseball M(s), basketball M(s)/W(s), cross-country running M(s)/W(s), golf M(s)/W(s), soccer M(s)/W(s), softball W(s), track and field M(s)/W(s), volleyball M(s)/W(s). ***Intramural sports:*** basketball M/W, cheerleading M(c)/W(c), football M, rugby M(c), soccer M/W, softball M/W, table tennis M/W, ultimate Frisbee M/W, volleyball M/W.

Campus security: controlled dormitory access, police patrols, night watch.

Student services: health clinic, personal/psychological counseling.

COSTS & FINANCIAL AID

Costs (2017–18) ***Comprehensive fee:*** $32,900 includes full-time tuition ($25,600) and room and board ($7300). Part-time tuition: $1100 per credit hour. ***College room only:*** $4550. Room and board charges vary according to housing facility. ***Payment plan:*** installment. ***Waivers:*** employees or children of employees.

Financial Aid Of all full-time matriculated undergraduates who enrolled in 2015, 534 applied for aid, 435 were judged to have need, 285 had their need fully met. ***Average percent of need met:*** 50. ***Average financial aid package:*** $25,450. ***Average need-based loan:*** $4100. ***Average need-based gift aid:*** $15,700. ***Average indebtedness upon graduation:*** $16,992.

APPLYING

Standardized Tests *Required:* SAT or ACT (for admission).

Options: electronic application, early action, deferred entrance.

Application fee: $35.

Required: essay or personal statement, high school transcript, minimum 2.0 GPA, 3 letters of recommendation, minimum ACT score of 18 or SAT of 860. ***Required for some:*** interview.

Application deadlines: rolling (freshmen), rolling (out-of-state freshmen), rolling (transfers), 5/1 (early action).

Notification: continuous (freshmen), continuous (out-of-state freshmen), rolling (early action).

CONTACT

Mr. Andrew Smith, Senior Enrollment Counselor, Bryan College, 721 Bryan Drive, Dayton, TN 37321-7000. *Phone:* 423-775-2041 Ext. 218. *Toll-free phone:* 800-277-9522. *Fax:* 423-775-7199. *E-mail:* admissions@bryan.edu.

★ Carson-Newman University

Jefferson City, Tennessee

http://www.cn.edu/

- **Independent Southern Baptist** comprehensive, founded 1851
- **Small-town** 90-acre campus with easy access to Knoxville
- **Endowment** $53.6 million
- **Coed** 1,752 undergraduate students, 97% full-time, 58% women, 42% men
- **Moderately difficult** entrance level, 59% of applicants were admitted

UNDERGRAD STUDENTS

1,691 full-time, 61 part-time. Students come from 38 states and territories; 31 other countries; 23% are from out of state; 8% Black or African American, non-Hispanic/Latino; 2% Hispanic/Latino; 0.5% Asian, non-Hispanic/Latino; 0.4% American Indian or Alaska Native, non-Hispanic/Latino; 3% Two or more races, non-Hispanic/Latino; 0.4% Race/ethnicity unknown; 3% international; 5% transferred in; 56% live on campus.

Freshmen:

Admission: 5,871 applied, 3,454 admitted, 497 enrolled. ***Average high school GPA:*** 3.49. ***Test scores:*** SAT critical reading scores over 500: 52%; SAT math scores over 500: 51%; ACT scores over 18: 87%; SAT critical reading scores over 600: 14%; SAT math scores over 600: 10%; ACT scores over 24: 42%; SAT math scores over 700: 2%; ACT scores over 30: 9%.

Retention: 65% of full-time freshmen returned.

FACULTY

Total: 215, 55% full-time, 56% with terminal degrees.

Student/faculty ratio: 11:1.

ACADEMICS

Calendar: semesters. *Degrees:* associate, bachelor's, master's, doctoral, and postbachelor's certificates.

Special study options: academic remediation for entering students, accelerated degree program, adult/continuing education programs, advanced placement credit, English as a second language, honors programs, internships, off-campus study, part-time degree program, services for LD students, student-designed majors, study abroad, summer session for credit. ***ROTC:*** Army (b).

Unusual degree programs: 3-2 engineering with Georgia Institute of Technology, University of Tennessee, Tennessee Technological University; pharmacy with Campbell University, Mercer University, University of Georgia.

Computers: 200 computers/terminals and 200 ports are available on campus for general student use. Students can access the following: campus intranet, computer help desk, free student e-mail accounts, online (class) grades, online (class) registration, online (class) schedules. Campuswide network is available. 100% of college-owned or -operated housing units are wired for high-speed Internet access. Wireless service is available via entire campus.

Library: Stephens-Burnett Library plus 3 others. *Books:* 216,676 (physical), 435,957 (digital/electronic); *Serial titles:* 315 (physical); *Databases:* 143. Weekly public service hours: 90; study areas open 24 hours, 5-7 days a week; students can reserve study rooms.

STUDENT LIFE

Housing options: on-campus residence required through junior year; men-only, women-only, special housing for students with disabilities. Campus housing is university owned. Freshman campus housing is guaranteed.

Activities and organizations: drama/theater group, student-run newspaper, choral group, marching band, Baptist Student Union, Fellowship of Christian Athletes, Student Government Association, Student Ambassadors Association, Columbians, national fraternities, national sororities.

Athletics Member NCAA. All Division II. ***Intercollegiate sports:*** baseball M(s), basketball M(s)/W(s), cross-country running M(s)/W(s), football M(s), golf M(s)/W, soccer M(s)/W(s), softball W(s), swimming and diving M(s)/W(s), tennis M(s)/W(s), track and field M(s)/W(s), volleyball W(s). ***Intramural sports:*** badminton M/W, baseball M/W, basketball M/W, football M/W, golf M/W, racquetball M/W, skiing (downhill) M/W, soccer M/W, softball M/W, swimming and diving M/W, table tennis M/W, tennis M/W, volleyball M/W.

Campus security: 24-hour emergency response devices and patrols, late-night transport/escort service, controlled dormitory access.

Student services: health clinic, personal/psychological counseling.

COSTS & FINANCIAL AID

Costs (2017–18) ***Comprehensive fee:*** $36,030 includes full-time tuition ($26,200), mandatory fees ($1200), and room and board ($8630). Full-time tuition and fees vary according to class time and course load. Part-time tuition: $1092 per credit hour. ***College room only:*** $4030. Room and board charges vary according to board plan, gender, and housing facility. ***Payment plans:*** installment, deferred payment. ***Waivers:*** senior citizens and employees or children of employees.

Financial Aid Of all full-time matriculated undergraduates who enrolled in 2014, 1,383 applied for aid, 1,383 were judged to have need, 304 had their need fully met. 279 Federal Work-Study jobs (averaging $1879). 7 state and other part-time jobs (averaging $1314). In 2014, 172 non-need-based awards were made. ***Average percent of need met:*** 78. ***Average financial aid package:*** $22,399. ***Average need-based loan:*** $3655. ***Average need-based gift aid:*** $16,939. ***Average non-need-based aid:*** $9434. ***Average indebtedness upon graduation:*** $26,851.

APPLYING

Standardized Tests *Required:* SAT or ACT (for admission).

Options: electronic application, deferred entrance.

Required: high school transcript, minimum 2.3 GPA, medical history. ***Required for some:*** essay or personal statement, interview. ***Recommended:*** interview.

Application deadlines: 8/1 (freshmen), 8/1 (transfers).

Notification: continuous (freshmen), continuous (transfers).

CONTACT
Mr. Aaron Porter, Dean of Enrollment Management, Carson-Newman University, 1646 Russell Avenue, PO Box 557, Jefferson City, TN 37760. *Phone:* 865-471-3223. *Toll-free phone:* 800-678-9061. *Fax:* 865-471-4817. *E-mail:* cnadmiss@cn.edu.

Christian Brothers University

Memphis, Tennessee

http://www.cbu.edu/

- **Independent Roman Catholic** comprehensive, founded 1871
- **Urban** 75-acre campus with easy access to Memphis
- **Endowment** $33.3 million
- **Coed** 1,410 undergraduate students, 92% full-time, 53% women, 47% men
- **Moderately difficult** entrance level, 46% of applicants were admitted

UNDERGRAD STUDENTS
1,300 full-time, 110 part-time. Students come from 26 states and territories; 21 other countries; 19% are from out of state; 29% Black or African American, non-Hispanic/Latino; 6% Hispanic/Latino; 5% Asian, non-Hispanic/Latino; 0.1% Native Hawaiian or other Pacific Islander, non-Hispanic/Latino; 0.5% American Indian or Alaska Native, non-Hispanic/Latino; 3% Two or more races, non-Hispanic/Latino; 6% Race/ethnicity unknown; 7% international; 7% transferred in; 40% live on campus.

Freshmen:
Admission: 2,321 applied, 1,063 admitted, 312 enrolled. ***Average high school GPA:*** 3.63. ***Test scores:*** ACT scores over 18: 99%; ACT scores over 24: 51%; ACT scores over 30: 8%.
Retention: 80% of full-time freshmen returned.

FACULTY
Total: 179, 58% full-time, 65% with terminal degrees.
Student/faculty ratio: 10:1.

ACADEMICS
Calendar: semesters. *Degrees:* associate, bachelor's, and master's.
Special study options: accelerated degree program, adult/continuing education programs, advanced placement credit, cooperative education, distance learning, double majors, honors programs, independent study, internships, off-campus study, part-time degree program, services for LD students, study abroad, summer session for credit. ***ROTC:*** Army (c), Navy (c), Air Force (c).
Unusual degree programs: 3-2 engineering with Rhodes College.
Computers: 310 computers/terminals are available on campus for general student use. Students can access the following: campus intranet, computer help desk, free student e-mail accounts, online (class) grades, online (class) registration, online (class) schedules. Campuswide network is available. 100% of college-owned or -operated housing units are wired for high-speed Internet access. Wireless service is available via entire campus.
Library: Plough Memorial Library and Media Center. *Books:* 77,766 (physical), 97,153 (digital/electronic); *Databases:* 27. Students can reserve study rooms.

STUDENT LIFE
Housing options: on-campus residence required through sophomore year; coed, men-only, women-only. Campus housing is university owned. Freshman campus housing is guaranteed.
Activities and organizations: drama/theater group, choral group, Black Student Association, BACCHUS Alcohol Awareness Group, Intercultural Club, The Chosen Generation, Lasallian Collegians, national fraternities, national sororities.
Athletics Member NCAA. All Division II. ***Intercollegiate sports:*** baseball M(s), basketball M(s)/W(s), cross-country running M(s)/W(s), golf M(s)/W(s), soccer M(s)/W(s), softball W(s), tennis M(s)/W(s), track and field M(s)/W(s), volleyball W(s). ***Intramural sports:*** basketball M/W, lacrosse W(c), soccer M/W, softball M/W, ultimate Frisbee M(c)/W(c), volleyball M/W.
Campus security: 24-hour emergency response devices and patrols, student patrols, late-night transport/escort service, controlled dormitory access.
Student services: health clinic, personal/psychological counseling.

COSTS & FINANCIAL AID
Costs (2017–18) ***Comprehensive fee:*** $37,860 includes full-time tuition ($29,990), mandatory fees ($870), and room and board ($7000). Full-time tuition and fees vary according to class time, course load, and program. Part-time tuition: $1070 per credit hour. Part-time tuition and fees vary according to class time, course load, and program. ***Required fees:*** $205 per term part-time. ***Room and board:*** Room and board charges vary according to board plan and housing facility. ***Payment plan:*** installment. ***Waivers:*** employees or children of employees.
Financial Aid Of all full-time matriculated undergraduates who enrolled in 2014, 1,178 applied for aid, 920 were judged to have need, 186 had their need fully met. In 2014, 258 non-need-based awards were made. ***Average percent of need met:*** 74. ***Average financial aid package:*** $22,486. ***Average need-based loan:*** $3754. ***Average need-based gift aid:*** $18,357. ***Average non-need-based aid:*** $14,626. ***Average indebtedness upon graduation:*** $27,892.

APPLYING
Standardized Tests *Required:* SAT or ACT (for admission).
Options: electronic application, deferred entrance.
Application fee: $25.
Required: essay or personal statement, high school transcript, minimum 2.0 GPA. ***Required for some:*** 2 letters of recommendation. ***Recommended:*** interview.
Application deadlines: 8/1 (freshmen), 8/23 (transfers).
Notification: 12/1 (freshmen), continuous (transfers).

CONTACT
Ms. Kristi Forman, Director of Admissions, Christian Brothers University, 650 East Parkway South, Memphis, TN 38104. *Phone:* 901-321-3205. *Toll-free phone:* 877-321-4CBU. *Fax:* 901-321-3202. *E-mail:* admissions@cbu.edu.

Cumberland University

Lebanon, Tennessee

http://www.cumberland.edu/

CONTACT
Ms. Beatrice LaChance, Director of Enrollment Services, Cumberland University, One Cumberland Square, Lebanon, TN 37087. *Phone:* 615-547-1244. *Toll-free phone:* 800-467-0562. *Fax:* 615-444-2569. *E-mail:* admissions@cumberland.edu.

Daymar College

Clarksville, Tennessee

http://www.daymarcollege.edu/

CONTACT
Daymar College, 2691 Trenton Road, Clarksville, TN 37040. *Phone:* 931-552-7600 Ext. 204.

Daymar College

Murfreesboro, Tennessee

http://www.daymarcollege.edu/

CONTACT
Daymar College, 415 Golden Bear Court, Murfreesboro, TN 37128.

DeVry University–Nashville Campus

Nashville, Tennessee

http://www.devry.edu/

CONTACT
Admissions Office, DeVry University–Nashville Campus, 3343 Perimeter Hill Drive, Suite 200, Nashville, TN 37211-4147. *Phone:* 615-445-3456. *Toll-free phone:* 866-338-7934.

East Tennessee State University

Johnson City, Tennessee

http://www.etsu.edu/

- **State-supported** university, founded 1911, part of State University and Community College System of Tennessee; Tennessee Board of Regents
- **Small-town** 366-acre campus
- **Endowment** $113.3 million
- **Coed** 11,065 undergraduate students, 85% full-time, 56% women, 44% men
- **Moderately difficult** entrance level, 80% of applicants were admitted

UNDERGRAD STUDENTS

9,371 full-time, 1,694 part-time. Students come from 42 states and territories; 60 other countries; 14% are from out of state; 6% Black or African American, non-Hispanic/Latino; 2% Hispanic/Latino; 1% Asian, non-Hispanic/Latino; 0.1% Native Hawaiian or other Pacific Islander, non-Hispanic/Latino; 0.2% American Indian or Alaska Native, non-Hispanic/Latino; 3% Two or more races, non-Hispanic/Latino; 1% Race/ethnicity unknown; 4% international; 9% transferred in; 25% live on campus.

Freshmen:

Admission: 6,835 applied, 5,467 admitted, 1,886 enrolled. ***Average high school GPA:*** 3.4. ***Test scores:*** ACT scores over 18: 88%; ACT scores over 24: 40%; ACT scores over 30: 7%.

Retention: 71% of full-time freshmen returned.

FACULTY

Total: 1,069, 55% full-time.

Student/faculty ratio: 16:1.

ACADEMICS

Calendar: semesters. *Degrees:* certificates, bachelor's, master's, doctoral, post-master's, and postbachelor's certificates.

Special study options: adult/continuing education programs, advanced placement credit, cooperative education, distance learning, double majors, English as a second language, external degree program, freshman honors college, honors programs, independent study, internships, off-campus study, part-time degree program, services for LD students, student-designed majors, study abroad, summer session for credit.
ROTC: Army (b).

Computers: 1,400 computers/terminals are available on campus for general student use. Students can access the following: computer help desk, free student e-mail accounts, online (class) grades, online (class) registration, online (class) schedules. Campuswide network is available. Wireless service is available via entire campus.

Library: Charles C. Sherrod Library plus 2 others. *Books:* 731,960 (physical), 98,312 (digital/electronic); *Databases:* 212. Study areas open 24 hours, 5-7 days a week; students can reserve study rooms.

STUDENT LIFE

Housing options: coed, men-only, women-only, special housing for students with disabilities. Campus housing is university owned.

Activities and organizations: drama/theater group, student-run newspaper, radio and television station, choral group, marching band, honor societies, Volunteer ETSU, religious groups, residence hall councils, national fraternities, national sororities.

Athletics Member NCAA. All Division I except football (Division I-AA). ***Intercollegiate sports:*** baseball M(s), basketball M(s)/W(s), cross-country running M(s)/W(s), golf M(s)/W(s), soccer M(s)/W(s), softball W(s), tennis M(s)/W(s), track and field M(s)/W(s), volleyball W(s). ***Intramural sports:*** basketball M/W, cross-country running M/W, football M/W, golf M/W, racquetball M/W, softball M/W, tennis M/W, volleyball W, weight lifting M.

Campus security: 24-hour emergency response devices and patrols, student patrols, late-night transport/escort service, controlled dormitory access.

Student services: health clinic, personal/psychological counseling, women's center.

COSTS & FINANCIAL AID

Costs (2016–17) ***Tuition:*** state resident $7002 full-time, $278 per credit hour part-time; nonresident $25,098 full-time, $996 per credit hour part-time. Full-time tuition and fees vary according to course load and program. Part-time tuition and fees vary according to course load and program. ***Required fees:*** $1669 full-time, $105 per credit hour part-time. ***Room and board:*** $7952; room only: $4602. Room and board charges vary according to board plan and housing facility. ***Payment plans:*** tuition prepayment, installment. ***Waivers:*** senior citizens and employees or children of employees.

Financial Aid Of all full-time matriculated undergraduates who enrolled in 2014, 8,285 applied for aid, 7,209 were judged to have need, 493 had their need fully met. In 2014, 1104 non-need-based awards were made. ***Average percent of need met:*** 52. ***Average financial aid package:*** $9840. ***Average need-based loan:*** $4179. ***Average need-based gift aid:*** $6222. ***Average non-need-based aid:*** $10,678. ***Average indebtedness upon graduation:*** $27,866.

APPLYING

Standardized Tests *Required:* SAT or ACT (for admission).

Options: electronic application, early admission.

Application fee: $25.

Required: high school transcript, minimum 2.3 GPA, 2.3 high school GPA or 19 ACT.

Application deadlines: rolling (freshmen), rolling (transfers).

Notification: continuous (freshmen), continuous (transfers).

CONTACT

Mr. Brian Henley, Director of Admissions, East Tennessee State University, PO Box 70731, Johnson City, TN 37614-0734. *Phone:* 423-439-4213. *Toll-free phone:* 800-462-3878. *Fax:* 423-439-4630. *E-mail:* go2etsu@etsu.edu.

Fisk University

Nashville, Tennessee

http://www.fisk.edu/

- **Independent** comprehensive, founded 1866, affiliated with United Church of Christ
- **Urban** 40-acre campus
- **Endowment** $20.6 million
- **Coed**
- **Moderately difficult** entrance level

FACULTY

Student/faculty ratio: 13:1.

ACADEMICS

Calendar: semesters. *Degrees:* certificates, bachelor's, master's, and postbachelor's certificates.

Library: John Hope and Aurelia E. Franklin Library. *Books:* 228,832 (physical); *Databases:* 97.

STUDENT LIFE

Housing options: coed, men-only, women-only, special housing for students with disabilities. Campus housing is university owned. Freshman applicants given priority for college housing.

Activities and organizations: drama/theater group, student-run newspaper, choral group, Student Government Association, State Clubs, Class organizations, Greek Fraternities and Sororities, University Choir, national fraternities, national sororities.

Athletics Member NAIA.

Campus security: 24-hour emergency response devices and patrols, late-night transport/escort service, controlled dormitory access.

Student services: health clinic, personal/psychological counseling.

COSTS & FINANCIAL AID

Costs (2016–17) ***Comprehensive fee:*** $32,270 includes full-time tuition ($19,624), mandatory fees ($1856), and room and board ($10,790). Full-time tuition and fees vary according to course load and degree level. Part-time tuition: $827 per semester hour. No tuition increase for student's term of enrollment. ***College room only:*** $6162. Room and board charges vary according to board plan. ***Payment plans:*** tuition prepayment, installment.

Financial Aid Of all full-time matriculated undergraduates who enrolled in 2011, 554 applied for aid, 499 were judged to have need, 160 had their need fully met. ***Average percent of need met:*** 75. ***Average financial aid package:*** $12,920. ***Average need-based loan:*** $3780. ***Average need-based***

gift aid: $10,417. ***Average indebtedness upon graduation:*** $6147. ***Financial aid deadline:*** 6/1.

APPLYING
Standardized Tests *Required:* SAT or ACT (for admission).

Options: electronic application, early admission, early decision.

Application fee: $25.

Required: essay or personal statement, high school transcript, 2 letters of recommendation.

CONTACT
Ms. Loretta McDonald, Dean of the Office of Recruitment and Admission, Fisk University, 1000 17th Avenue North, Nashville, TN 37208-3051. *Phone:* 615-329-8503. *Toll-free phone:* 888-702-0022. *Fax:* 615-329-8774. *E-mail:* lmcdonald@fisk.edu.

Fountainhead College of Technology
Knoxville, Tennessee
http://www.fountainheadcollege.edu/

CONTACT
Mr. Joel B. Southern, Director of Admissions, Fountainhead College of Technology, 10208 Technology Drive, Knoxville, TN 37932. *Phone:* 865-688-9422. *Toll-free phone:* 888-218-7335. *Fax:* 865-688-2419. *E-mail:* joel.southern@fountainheadcollege.edu.

Freed-Hardeman University
Henderson, Tennessee
http://www.fhu.edu/

- **Independent** comprehensive, founded 1869, affiliated with Church of Christ
- **Small-town** 120-acre campus
- **Coed** 1,402 undergraduate students, 88% full-time, 58% women, 42% men
- **Moderately difficult** entrance level, 96% of applicants were admitted

UNDERGRAD STUDENTS
1,228 full-time, 174 part-time. 41% are from out of state; 4% Black or African American, non-Hispanic/Latino; 2% Hispanic/Latino; 1% Asian, non-Hispanic/Latino; 0.1% Native Hawaiian or other Pacific Islander, non-Hispanic/Latino; 0.1% American Indian or Alaska Native, non-Hispanic/Latino; 1% Two or more races, non-Hispanic/Latino; 14% Race/ethnicity unknown; 1% international; 7% transferred in; 78% live on campus.

Freshmen:
Admission: 791 applied, 762 admitted, 325 enrolled. ***Average high school GPA:*** 3.64. ***Test scores:*** SAT critical reading scores over 500: 64%; SAT math scores over 500: 46%; ACT scores over 18: 95%; SAT critical reading scores over 600: 9%; SAT math scores over 600: 5%; ACT scores over 24: 51%; ACT scores over 30: 15%.
Retention: 78% of full-time freshmen returned.

FACULTY
Total: 157, 59% full-time, 62% with terminal degrees.

Student/faculty ratio: 13:1.

ACADEMICS
Calendar: semesters. *Degrees:* diplomas, bachelor's, master's, doctoral, post-master's, and postbachelor's certificates.

Special study options: academic remediation for entering students, accelerated degree program, advanced placement credit, cooperative education, distance learning, double majors, freshman honors college, honors programs, independent study, internships, off-campus study, part-time degree program, services for LD students, student-designed majors, study abroad, summer session for credit.

Unusual degree programs: 3-2 engineering.

Computers: Students can access the following: computer help desk, free student e-mail accounts, online (class) grades, online (class) registration, online (class) schedules. Campuswide network is available. 100% of college-owned or -operated housing units are wired for high-speed Internet access. Wireless service is available via entire campus.

Library: Hope Barber Shull Academic Resource Center plus 1 other. Students can reserve study rooms.

STUDENT LIFE
Housing options: on-campus residence required through senior year; men-only, women-only, special housing for students with disabilities. Campus housing is university owned. Freshman campus housing is guaranteed.

Activities and organizations: drama/theater group, student-run newspaper, radio station, choral group.

Athletics Member NAIA. ***Intercollegiate sports:*** baseball M(s), basketball M(s)/W(s), cheerleading W(s), cross-country running M(s)/W(s), golf M(s)/W(s), soccer M(s)/W(s), softball W(s), track and field M(s)/W(s), volleyball W(s). ***Intramural sports:*** basketball M/W, football M/W, softball M/W, volleyball M/W.

Campus security: 24-hour patrols, controlled dormitory access.

Student services: health clinic, personal/psychological counseling.

COSTS & FINANCIAL AID
Costs (2017–18) ***Comprehensive fee:*** $29,900 includes full-time tuition ($21,950) and room and board ($7950). Full-time tuition and fees vary according to location. Part-time tuition: $725 per credit hour. Part-time tuition and fees vary according to location. ***College room only:*** $4320. Room and board charges vary according to board plan and housing facility. ***Payment plan:*** installment. ***Waivers:*** employees or children of employees.

Financial Aid Of all full-time matriculated undergraduates who enrolled in 2014, 1,188 applied for aid, 997 were judged to have need, 213 had their need fully met. In 2014, 231 non-need-based awards were made. ***Average percent of need met:*** 68. ***Average financial aid package:*** $17,710. ***Average need-based loan:*** $3839. ***Average need-based gift aid:*** $11,999. ***Average non-need-based aid:*** $10,285. ***Average indebtedness upon graduation:*** $31,185.

APPLYING
Standardized Tests *Required:* SAT or ACT (for admission).

Options: electronic application, deferred entrance.

Required: high school transcript, minimum 2.3 GPA. ***Required for some:*** interview.

Application deadlines: rolling (freshmen), rolling (transfers).

Notification: continuous (freshmen), continuous until 9/1 (transfers).

CONTACT
Freed-Hardeman University, 158 East Main Street, Henderson, TN 38340-2399. *Phone:* 731-989-6557. *Toll-free phone:* 800-FHU-FHU-1.

Huntington College of Health Sciences
Knoxville, Tennessee
http://www.hchs.edu/

- **Proprietary** comprehensive, founded 1984
- **Suburban** campus
- **Coed** 288 undergraduate students, 62% women, 38% men
- **Noncompetitive** entrance level, 52% of applicants were admitted

UNDERGRAD STUDENTS
288 part-time. Students come from 44 states and territories; 7 other countries; 99% are from out of state; 5% Black or African American, non-Hispanic/Latino; 5% Hispanic/Latino; 2% Race/ethnicity unknown; 3% international; 9% transferred in.

Freshmen:
Admission: 220 applied, 114 admitted.
Retention: 85% of full-time freshmen returned.

FACULTY
Total: 22, 14% full-time, 41% with terminal degrees.

Student/faculty ratio: 13:1.

ACADEMICS
Calendar: continuous. *Degrees:* certificates, diplomas, associate, bachelor's, master's, doctoral, and postbachelor's certificates (offers only external degree programs conducted through home study).

Special study options: academic remediation for entering students, accelerated degree program, adult/continuing education programs, distance learning, external degree program, independent study, part-time degree program, summer session for credit.
Library: HCHS Online Library.

COSTS
Costs (2016–17) ***Tuition:*** $5880 full-time, $245 per credit hour part-time. Full-time tuition and fees vary according to course load, degree level, and program. Part-time tuition and fees vary according to course load, degree level, and program. ***Required fees:*** $200 full-time. ***Payment plan:*** installment.

APPLYING
Options: deferred entrance.

Application fee: $75.

Required for some: high school transcript, interview. ***Recommended:*** minimum 2.0 GPA.

Application deadlines: rolling (freshmen), rolling (transfers).

Notification: continuous (freshmen), continuous (transfers).

CONTACT
Kimberly Marquis, Director of Admissions, Huntington College of Health Sciences, 117 Legacy View Way, Knoxville, TN 37918. *Phone:* 800-290-4226 Ext. 1. *Toll-free phone:* 800-290-4226. *Fax:* 865-524-8339. *E-mail:* admissions@hchs.edu.

Johnson University
Knoxville, Tennessee
http://www.johnsonu.edu/

- **Independent** comprehensive, founded 1893, affiliated with Christian Churches and Churches of Christ
- **Rural** 175-acre campus with easy access to Knoxville
- **Coed** 842 undergraduate students, 82% full-time, 47% women, 53% men
- **Moderately difficult** entrance level, 53% of applicants were admitted

UNDERGRAD STUDENTS
689 full-time, 153 part-time. Students come from 33 states and territories; 7 other countries; 35% are from out of state; 3% Black or African American, non-Hispanic/Latino; 2% Hispanic/Latino; 0.1% Asian, non-Hispanic/Latino; 0.2% American Indian or Alaska Native, non-Hispanic/Latino; 1% Two or more races, non-Hispanic/Latino; 2% Race/ethnicity unknown; 3% international; 9% transferred in; 80% live on campus.

Freshmen:
Admission: 370 applied, 196 admitted, 139 enrolled. ***Test scores:*** SAT critical reading scores over 500: 49%; SAT math scores over 500: 56%; SAT writing scores over 500: 36%; ACT scores over 18: 80%; SAT critical reading scores over 600: 16%; SAT math scores over 600: 18%; SAT writing scores over 600: 10%; ACT scores over 24: 20%; SAT critical reading scores over 700: 3%; SAT math scores over 700: 5%.
Retention: 75% of full-time freshmen returned.

FACULTY
Total: 172, 38% full-time, 71% with terminal degrees.

Student/faculty ratio: 13:1.

ACADEMICS
Calendar: semesters. *Degrees:* certificates, associate, bachelor's, master's, and doctoral.

Special study options: academic remediation for entering students, accelerated degree program, adult/continuing education programs, advanced placement credit, cooperative education, distance learning, double majors, English as a second language, honors programs, independent study, internships, part-time degree program, services for LD students, study abroad, summer session for credit.

Computers: 70 computers/terminals are available on campus for general student use. Students can access the following: campus intranet, computer help desk, free student e-mail accounts, online (class) grades, online (class) registration, online (class) schedules. Campuswide network is available. 100% of college-owned or -operated housing units are wired for high-speed Internet access. Wireless service is available via entire campus.

Library: Glass Memorial Library plus 1 other. *Books:* 117,967 (physical), 245,630 (digital/electronic); *Serial titles:* 4,698 (physical), 27 (digital/electronic); *Databases:* 125. Weekly public service hours: 80.

STUDENT LIFE
Housing options: on-campus residence required through senior year; men-only, women-only. Campus housing is university owned.

Activities and organizations: drama/theater group, student-run newspaper, radio station, choral group, Student Government Association, International student Association, Harvesters (Missions), International Justice Mission, Students Promoting Social Unity.

Athletics Member NCCAA. ***Intercollegiate sports:*** baseball M, basketball M/W, cheerleading M/W, cross-country running M/W, soccer M/W, volleyball W. ***Intramural sports:*** basketball M, tennis M/W, ultimate Frisbee M/W, volleyball M/W.

Campus security: 24-hour emergency response devices and patrols, student patrols, controlled dormitory access.

Student services: health clinic, personal/psychological counseling.

COSTS & FINANCIAL AID
Costs (2016–17) ***One-time required fee:*** $195. ***Comprehensive fee:*** $19,770 includes full-time tuition ($13,000), mandatory fees ($950), and room and board ($5820). Full-time tuition and fees vary according to course load and location. Part-time tuition: $410 per credit hour. Part-time tuition and fees vary according to course load and location. ***Required fees:*** $40 per credit hour part-time. ***College room only:*** $3602. Room and board charges vary according to board plan, housing facility, and location. ***Payment plan:*** installment. ***Waivers:*** employees or children of employees.

Financial Aid Of all full-time matriculated undergraduates who enrolled in 2010, 649 applied for aid, 543 were judged to have need, 51 had their need fully met. 64 Federal Work-Study jobs (averaging $1602). 335 state and other part-time jobs (averaging $1611). ***Average percent of need met:*** 63. ***Average financial aid package:*** $11,642. ***Average need-based loan:*** $3414. ***Average need-based gift aid:*** $6471. ***Average indebtedness upon graduation:*** $18,494.

APPLYING
Standardized Tests *Required:* SAT or ACT (for admission). *Required for some:* ACT (for admission).

Options: electronic application, early admission, early decision, deferred entrance.

Application fee: $35.

Required: essay or personal statement, high school transcript, minimum 2.5 GPA, 3 letters of recommendation. ***Required for some:*** interview.

Application deadlines: 7/1 (freshmen), 7/1 (transfers).

Notification: continuous (freshmen), continuous (transfers).

CONTACT
Ms. Julee Schultz, Director of Admissions, Johnson University, 7900 Johnson Drive, Knoxville, TN 37998. *Phone:* 865-251-2233. *Toll-free phone:* 800-827-2122. *Fax:* 865-251-2336. *E-mail:* jschultz@johnsonu.edu.

King University
Bristol, Tennessee
http://www.king.edu/

- **Independent** comprehensive, founded 1867, affiliated with Presbyterian Church (U.S.A.)
- **Suburban** 135-acre campus
- **Endowment** $34.3 million
- **Coed** 2,343 undergraduate students, 90% full-time, 63% women, 37% men
- **Moderately difficult** entrance level, 55% of applicants were admitted

UNDERGRAD STUDENTS
2,120 full-time, 223 part-time. Students come from 41 states and territories; 30 other countries; 66% are from out of state; 6% Black or African American, non-Hispanic/Latino; 3% Hispanic/Latino; 0.6% Asian, non-Hispanic/Latino; 2% Two or more races, non-Hispanic/Latino; 5% Race/ethnicity unknown; 3% international; 25% transferred in; 42% live on campus.

Freshmen:
Admission: 343 applied, 189 admitted, 159 enrolled. ***Average high school GPA:*** 3.58. ***Test scores:*** SAT critical reading scores over 500: 45%; SAT math scores over 500: 47%; ACT scores over 18: 91%; SAT critical reading scores over 600: 9%; SAT math scores over 600: 14%; ACT scores over 24: 40%; ACT scores over 30: 5%.

Retention: 73% of full-time freshmen returned.

FACULTY
Total: 355, 36% full-time, 39% with terminal degrees.

Student/faculty ratio: 13:1.

ACADEMICS
Calendar: semesters. *Degrees:* associate, bachelor's, master's, doctoral, and post-master's certificates.

Special study options: academic remediation for entering students, accelerated degree program, adult/continuing education programs, advanced placement credit, cooperative education, distance learning, double majors, honors programs, independent study, internships, off-campus study, part-time degree program, services for LD students, student-designed majors, study abroad, summer session for credit.

Computers: 90 computers/terminals and 500 ports are available on campus for general student use. Students can access the following: campus intranet, computer help desk, free student e-mail accounts, online (class) grades, online (class) registration, online (class) schedules, student portal. Campuswide network is available. 100% of college-owned or -operated housing units are wired for high-speed Internet access. Wireless service is available via entire campus.

Library: E. W. King Library plus 3 others. *Books:* 71,757 (physical), 320,815 (digital/electronic); *Serial titles:* 179 (physical); *Databases:* 97. Weekly public service hours: 91.

STUDENT LIFE
Housing options: on-campus residence required through junior year; men-only, women-only. Campus housing is university owned. Freshman campus housing is guaranteed.

Activities and organizations: drama/theater group, student-run newspaper, choral group, Student Government Association, Fellowship of Christian Athletes, King Security and Intelligence Studies Student Group, Enactus (formerly Students in Free Enterprise).

Athletics Member NCAA. All Division II. ***Intercollegiate sports:*** baseball M(s), basketball M(s)/W(s), cheerleading M(s)/W(s), cross-country running M(s)/W(s), golf M(s)/W(s), soccer M(s)/W(s), softball W(s), swimming and diving M(s)/W(s), tennis M(s)/W(s), track and field M(s)/W(s), volleyball M(s)/W(s), wrestling M(s)/W(s). ***Intramural sports:*** badminton M/W, basketball M/W, gymnastics M(c)/W(c), soccer M/W, softball M/W, table tennis M/W, tennis M/W, ultimate Frisbee M/W, volleyball M/W, weight lifting M.

Campus security: 24-hour emergency response devices and patrols, late-night transport/escort service, controlled dormitory access, Emergency Notification System.

Student services: personal/psychological counseling.

COSTS & FINANCIAL AID
Costs (2016–17) ***One-time required fee:*** $125. ***Comprehensive fee:*** $35,456 includes full-time tuition ($25,798), mandatory fees ($1478), and room and board ($8180). Full-time tuition and fees vary according to class time, course load, degree level, location, and program. Part-time tuition: $600 per credit. Part-time tuition and fees vary according to class time, course load, degree level, location, and program. ***Required fees:*** $120 per term part-time. ***College room only:*** $4108. Room and board charges vary according to board plan and housing facility. ***Payment plan:*** installment. ***Waivers:*** senior citizens and employees or children of employees.

Financial Aid Of all full-time matriculated undergraduates who enrolled in 2016, 1,877 applied for aid, 1,704 were judged to have need, 216 had their need fully met. 138 Federal Work-Study jobs (averaging $1123). 105 state and other part-time jobs (averaging $1268). In 2016, 107 non-need-based awards were made. ***Average percent of need met:*** 63. ***Average financial aid package:*** $14,306. ***Average need-based loan:*** $4509. ***Average need-based gift aid:*** $12,095. ***Average non-need-based aid:*** $10,036. ***Average indebtedness upon graduation:*** $23,950.

APPLYING
Options: electronic application, deferred entrance.

Application fee: $25.

Required: high school transcript. ***Required for some:*** essay or personal statement. ***Recommended:*** minimum 3.0 GPA.

Application deadlines: rolling (freshmen), rolling (out-of-state freshmen), rolling (transfers).

Notification: continuous (freshmen), continuous (out-of-state freshmen), continuous (transfers).

CONTACT
Mr. Tom VerDow, Director of Undergraduate Recruitment, King University, 1350 King College Road, Bristol, TN 37620. *Phone:* 423-652-4149. *Toll-free phone:* 800-362-0014. *Fax:* 423-652-4727.
E-mail: admissions@king.edu.

Lane College

Jackson, Tennessee

http://www.lanecollege.edu/

- **Independent** 4-year, founded 1882, affiliated with Christian Methodist Episcopal Church
- **Suburban** 55-acre campus with easy access to Memphis
- **Coed** 1,376 undergraduate students, 98% full-time, 46% women, 54% men
- **Minimally difficult** entrance level, 55% of applicants were admitted

UNDERGRAD STUDENTS
1,351 full-time, 25 part-time. 42% are from out of state; 97% Black or African American, non-Hispanic/Latino; 0.3% Hispanic/Latino; 0.1% Asian, non-Hispanic/Latino; 0.1% American Indian or Alaska Native, non-Hispanic/Latino; 2% Two or more races, non-Hispanic/Latino; 0.2% international; 10% transferred in; 63% live on campus.

Freshmen:
Admission: 4,729 applied, 2,579 admitted, 444 enrolled. ***Average high school GPA:*** 2.42. ***Test scores:*** SAT critical reading scores over 500: 20%; ACT scores over 18: 15%; ACT scores over 24: 2%; ACT scores over 30: 1%.

Retention: 53% of full-time freshmen returned.

FACULTY
Total: 73, 89% full-time, 36% with terminal degrees.

Student/faculty ratio: 21:1.

ACADEMICS
Calendar: semesters. *Degree:* bachelor's.

Special study options: academic remediation for entering students, accelerated degree program, adult/continuing education programs, advanced placement credit, cooperative education, honors programs, independent study, internships, off-campus study, part-time degree program, services for LD students, study abroad, summer session for credit. ***ROTC:*** Army (b).

Computers: 258 computers/terminals and 258 ports are available on campus for general student use. Students can access the following: campus intranet, computer help desk, free student e-mail accounts, online (class) grades, online (class) schedules, online admissions and advising. Campuswide network is available. 100% of college-owned or -operated housing units are wired for high-speed Internet access. Wireless service is available via classrooms, computer centers, computer labs, dorm rooms, learning centers, libraries, student centers.

Library: Chambers-McClure Academic Center.

STUDENT LIFE
Housing options: on-campus residence required for freshman year; men-only, women-only. Campus housing is university owned. Freshman applicants given priority for college housing.

Activities and organizations: drama/theater group, choral group, marching band, Student Government Association, Pre-Law Club, Student Christian Association, Drama Club, Sociology Club, national fraternities, national sororities.

Athletics Member NCAA. All Division II. ***Intercollegiate sports:*** baseball M(s), basketball M(s)/W(s), cheerleading W, cross-country running M(s)/W(s), football M(s), softball W(s), tennis M(s)/W(s), track and field M(s)/W(s), volleyball W(s).

Campus security: 24-hour emergency response devices and patrols, late-night transport/escort service, surveillance cameras, lighted parking areas.

Student services: health clinic, personal/psychological counseling, legal services.

COSTS & FINANCIAL AID

Costs (2017–18) ***Tuition:*** $9000 full-time, $375 per credit hour part-time. Full-time tuition and fees vary according to course load. Part-time tuition and fees vary according to course load. ***Required fees:*** $1690 full-time. ***Room only:*** $4570. ***Payment plans:*** installment, deferred payment. ***Waivers:*** adult students and employees or children of employees.

Financial Aid Of all full-time matriculated undergraduates who enrolled in 2016, 1,365 applied for aid, 1,365 were judged to have need. In 2016, 2 non-need-based awards were made. ***Average financial aid package:*** $12,240. ***Average need-based loan:*** $3568. ***Average need-based gift aid:*** $13,527. ***Average non-need-based aid:*** $4761.

APPLYING

Standardized Tests *Required:* SAT or ACT (for admission).

Options: electronic application, deferred entrance.

Required: high school transcript, 2 letters of recommendation.

Application deadlines: rolling (freshmen), rolling (out-of-state freshmen), rolling (transfers).

Notification: continuous (freshmen), continuous (transfers).

CONTACT

Dr. Monica C. Scott, Director of Enrollment Management, Lane College, 545 Lane Avenue, Jackson, TN 38301. *Phone:* 731-426-7533. *Toll-free phone:* 800-960-7533. *Fax:* 731-426-7559.
E-mail: mclayborne@lanecollege.edu.

Lee University

Cleveland, Tennessee

http://www.leeuniversity.edu/

- **Independent** comprehensive, founded 1918, affiliated with Church of God
- **Small-town** 110-acre campus with easy access to Chattanooga, TN
- **Endowment** $18.3 million
- **Coed** 4,821 undergraduate students, 79% full-time, 61% women, 39% men

UNDERGRAD STUDENTS

3,828 full-time, 993 part-time. Students come from 52 states and territories; 53 other countries; 56% are from out of state; 6% Black or African American, non-Hispanic/Latino; 3% Hispanic/Latino; 0.9% Asian, non-Hispanic/Latino; 0.2% Native Hawaiian or other Pacific Islander, non-Hispanic/Latino; 0.5% American Indian or Alaska Native, non-Hispanic/Latino; 2% Two or more races, non-Hispanic/Latino; 4% Race/ethnicity unknown; 4% international; 5% transferred in; 47% live on campus.

Freshmen:

Admission: 889 enrolled. ***Average high school GPA:*** 3.6. ***Test scores:*** SAT critical reading scores over 500: 65%; SAT math scores over 500: 60%; ACT scores over 18: 92%; SAT critical reading scores over 600: 27%; SAT math scores over 600: 19%; ACT scores over 24: 62%; SAT critical reading scores over 700: 5%; SAT math scores over 700: 2%; ACT scores over 30: 14%.

Retention: 76% of full-time freshmen returned.

FACULTY

Total: 439, 40% full-time, 47% with terminal degrees.

Student/faculty ratio: 17:1.

ACADEMICS

Calendar: semesters. *Degrees:* bachelor's, master's, and post-master's certificates.

Special study options: academic remediation for entering students, adult/continuing education programs, advanced placement credit, cooperative education, distance learning, double majors, English as a second language, external degree program, honors programs, independent study, internships, off-campus study, part-time degree program, services for LD students, student-designed majors, study abroad, summer session for credit.

Computers: 350 computers/terminals and 2,500 ports are available on campus for general student use. Students can access the following: campus intranet, computer help desk, free student e-mail accounts, online (class) grades, online (class) registration, online (class) schedules. Campuswide network is available. 95% of college-owned or -operated housing units are wired for high-speed Internet access. Wireless service is available via entire campus.

Library: William G. Squires Library plus 2 others. *Books:* 158,647 (physical), 231,120 (digital/electronic); *Serial titles:* 242 (physical), 23,216 (digital/electronic); *Databases:* 137. Weekly public service hours: 91; students can reserve study rooms.

STUDENT LIFE

Housing options: on-campus residence required through sophomore year; men-only, women-only. Campus housing is university owned and leased by the school. Freshman campus housing is guaranteed.

Activities and organizations: drama/theater group, student-run newspaper, choral group, Student Leadership Council, CRU, Big Pal Little Pal, Delta Zeta Tau, Crossover.

Athletics Member NCAA, NCCAA. All NCAA Division II. ***Intercollegiate sports:*** baseball M(s), basketball M(s)/W(s), cross-country running M(s)/W(s), golf M(s)/W(s), lacrosse W(s), soccer M(s)/W(s), softball W(s), tennis M(s)/W(s), track and field M(s)/W(s), volleyball W(s). ***Intramural sports:*** basketball M/W, bowling M/W, football M/W, golf M/W, racquetball M/W, rugby M(c)/W(c), soccer M/W, softball M/W, table tennis M/W, tennis M/W, ultimate Frisbee M/W, volleyball M/W.

Campus security: 24-hour emergency response devices and patrols, late-night transport/escort service, controlled dormitory access.

Student services: health clinic, personal/psychological counseling.

COSTS & FINANCIAL AID

Costs (2017–18) ***Comprehensive fee:*** $24,810 includes full-time tuition ($16,080), mandatory fees ($650), and room and board ($8080). Full-time tuition and fees vary according to course load, location, and program. Part-time tuition: $670 per credit hour. Part-time tuition and fees vary according to course load, location, and program. ***Required fees:*** $35 per term part-time. ***College room only:*** $4420. Room and board charges vary according to board plan and housing facility. ***Payment plan:*** deferred payment. ***Waivers:*** senior citizens and employees or children of employees.

Financial Aid Of all full-time matriculated undergraduates who enrolled in 2016, 3,326 applied for aid, 2,619 were judged to have need, 560 had their need fully met. 240 Federal Work-Study jobs (averaging $1643). 714 state and other part-time jobs (averaging $1410). In 2016, 673 non-need-based awards were made. ***Average percent of need met:*** 54. ***Average financial aid package:*** $11,437. ***Average need-based loan:*** $4286. ***Average need-based gift aid:*** $8732. ***Average non-need-based aid:*** $7425. ***Average indebtedness upon graduation:*** $31,630.

APPLYING

Standardized Tests *Required:* SAT or ACT (for admission). *Recommended:* SAT (for admission), ACT (for admission).

Required: high school transcript, minimum 2.0 GPA, MMR immunization record. ***Required for some:*** 3 letters of recommendation.

CONTACT

Mr. Phillip Cook, Vice President for Enrollment, Lee University, 1120 N. Ocoee Street, Cleveland, TN 37311. *Phone:* 423-614-8500.
Toll-free phone: 800-533-9930. *Fax:* 423-614-8533.
E-mail: admissions@leeuniversity.edu.

LeMoyne-Owen College

Memphis, Tennessee

http://www.loc.edu/

- **Independent** 4-year, founded 1862, affiliated with United Church of Christ
- **Urban** 15-acre campus
- **Endowment** $15.1 million
- **Coed**
- **Minimally difficult** entrance level

FACULTY

Student/faculty ratio: 14:1.

ACADEMICS
Calendar: semesters. *Degrees:* bachelor's and postbachelor's certificates.
Library: Hollis F. Price Library.

STUDENT LIFE
Housing options: men-only, women-only. Campus housing is university owned.

Activities and organizations: drama/theater group, student-run newspaper, choral group, Greek Fraternities and Sororities, Black Business Students Association, National Black Student Accountant Club, Gospel Choir, Pre-Alumni organization, national fraternities, national sororities.

Athletics Member NCAA, NAIA. All NCAA Division I except baseball (Division II), men's and women's basketball (Division II), men's and women's cross-country running (Division II), men's and women's golf (Division II), softball (Division II), men's and women's tennis (Division II).

Campus security: 24-hour patrols, late-night transport/escort service, controlled dormitory access.

Student services: health clinic, personal/psychological counseling.

COSTS & FINANCIAL AID
Costs (2016–17) ***Comprehensive fee:*** $17,400 includes full-time tuition ($10,880), mandatory fees ($420), and room and board ($6100). Full-time tuition and fees vary according to course load. Part-time tuition: $436 per credit hour. ***College room only:*** $3600. Room and board charges vary according to housing facility.

Financial Aid Of all full-time matriculated undergraduates who enrolled in 2014, 773 applied for aid, 762 were judged to have need, 17 had their need fully met. 145 Federal Work-Study jobs (averaging $1670). In 2014, 9 non-need-based awards were made. ***Average percent of need met:*** 47. ***Average financial aid package:*** $10,423. ***Average need-based loan:*** $3603. ***Average need-based gift aid:*** $7384. ***Average non-need-based aid:*** $11,002. ***Average indebtedness upon graduation:*** $27,441.

APPLYING
Standardized Tests *Required:* SAT or ACT (for admission).

Options: electronic application.

Application fee: $25.

Required: high school transcript, minimum 2.0 GPA. ***Recommended:*** essay or personal statement, 2 letters of recommendation, interview.

CONTACT
LeMoyne-Owen College, 807 Walker Avenue, Memphis, TN 38126-6595. *Phone:* 901-435-1500. *Toll-free phone:* 800-737-7778.

Lincoln Memorial University
Harrogate, Tennessee
http://www.lmunet.edu/

CONTACT
Lincoln Memorial University, 6965 Cumberland Gap Parkway, Harrogate, TN 37752-1901. *Phone:* 423-869-6280. *Toll-free phone:* 800-325-0900.

Lipscomb University
Nashville, Tennessee
http://www.lipscomb.edu/

- **Independent** comprehensive, founded 1891, affiliated with Church of Christ
- **Suburban** 89-acre campus
- **Endowment** $68.8 million
- **Coed** 2,986 undergraduate students, 89% full-time, 62% women, 38% men
- **Moderately difficult** entrance level, 61% of applicants were admitted

UNDERGRAD STUDENTS
2,656 full-time, 330 part-time. Students come from 47 states and territories; 44 other countries; 35% are from out of state; 7% Black or African American, non-Hispanic/Latino; 6% Hispanic/Latino; 3% Asian, non-Hispanic/Latino; 0.1% Native Hawaiian or other Pacific Islander, non-Hispanic/Latino; 0.2% American Indian or Alaska Native, non-Hispanic/Latino; 3% Two or more races, non-Hispanic/Latino; 2% Race/ethnicity unknown; 3% international; 5% transferred in; 50% live on campus.

Freshmen:
Admission: 3,464 applied, 2,108 admitted, 637 enrolled. ***Average high school GPA:*** 3.56. ***Test scores:*** SAT critical reading scores over 500: 78%; SAT math scores over 500: 73%; ACT scores over 18: 99%; SAT critical reading scores over 600: 42%; SAT math scores over 600: 39%; ACT scores over 24: 65%; SAT critical reading scores over 700: 8%; SAT math scores over 700: 8%; ACT scores over 30: 17%.

Retention: 85% of full-time freshmen returned.

FACULTY
Total: 593, 37% full-time, 56% with terminal degrees.

Student/faculty ratio: 12:1.

ACADEMICS
Calendar: semesters. *Degrees:* associate, bachelor's, master's, doctoral, and postbachelor's certificates.

Special study options: academic remediation for entering students, accelerated degree program, adult/continuing education programs, advanced placement credit, distance learning, double majors, English as a second language, honors programs, independent study, internships, part-time degree program, services for LD students, student-designed majors, study abroad, summer session for credit. ***ROTC:*** Army (c), Air Force (c).

Computers: 150 computers/terminals are available on campus for general student use. Students can access the following: campus intranet, computer help desk, free student e-mail accounts, online (class) grades, online (class) registration, online (class) schedules. Campuswide network is available. 100% of college-owned or -operated housing units are wired for high-speed Internet access. Wireless service is available via entire campus.

Library: Beaman Library plus 1 other. *Books:* 157,824 (physical), 167,520 (digital/electronic); *Serial titles:* 253 (physical), 489 (digital/electronic); *Databases:* 100. Students can reserve study rooms.

STUDENT LIFE
Housing options: on-campus residence required through junior year; men-only, women-only. Campus housing is university owned. Freshman applicants given priority for college housing.

Activities and organizations: drama/theater group, student-run newspaper, radio and television station, choral group, Sigma Pi Beta, business fraternities, Multicultural Association, Alpha Phi Chi men's service club, Pi Kappa Sigma women's service club.

Athletics Member NCAA. All Division I. ***Intercollegiate sports:*** baseball M(s), basketball M(s)/W(s), cross-country running M(s)/W(s), golf M(s)/W(s), soccer M(s)/W(s), softball W(s), tennis M(s)/W(s), track and field M(s)/W(s), volleyball W(s). ***Intramural sports:*** basketball M/W, football M/W, golf M/W, racquetball M/W, sand volleyball M/W, soccer M/W, softball M/W, table tennis M/W, ultimate Frisbee M/W, volleyball M/W.

Campus security: 24-hour emergency response devices and patrols, late-night transport/escort service, controlled dormitory access.

Student services: health clinic, personal/psychological counseling.

COSTS & FINANCIAL AID
Costs (2017–18) ***Comprehensive fee:*** $42,966 includes full-time tuition ($28,556), mandatory fees ($2376), and room and board ($12,034). Part-time tuition: $1194 per credit hour. ***College room only:*** $6834. Room and board charges vary according to board plan and housing facility. ***Payment plan:*** installment. ***Waivers:*** employees or children of employees.

Financial Aid Of all full-time matriculated undergraduates who enrolled in 2016, 2,565 applied for aid, 1,655 were judged to have need, 462 had their need fully met. 239 Federal Work-Study jobs (averaging $2320). In 2016, 836 non-need-based awards were made. ***Average percent of need met:*** 65. ***Average financial aid package:*** $24,556. ***Average need-based loan:*** $5436. ***Average need-based gift aid:*** $4195. ***Average non-need-based aid:*** $15,231. ***Average indebtedness upon graduation:*** $31,082.

APPLYING
Standardized Tests *Required:* SAT or ACT (for admission).

Options: electronic application, early admission, deferred entrance.

Application fee: $50.

Required: essay or personal statement, high school transcript, minimum 2.5 GPA, 1 letter of recommendation. ***Recommended:*** interview.

Application deadlines: rolling (freshmen), rolling (transfers).

Notification: continuous (freshmen), continuous (transfers).

CONTACT

Mr. Johnathan Akin, Senior Director of Admissions, Lipscomb University, One University Park Drive, Nashville, TN 37204-3951. *Phone:* 615-966-1776. *Toll-free phone:* 877-582-4766. *Fax:* 615-966-1804. *E-mail:* admissions@lipscomb.edu.

Martin Methodist College

Pulaski, Tennessee

http://www.martinmethodist.edu/

CONTACT

Lisa Smith, Director of Admissions, Martin Methodist College, 433 West Madison Street, Pulaski, TN 38478-2716. *Phone:* 931-363-9868. *Toll-free phone:* 800-467-1273. *Fax:* 931-363-9818. *E-mail:* admit@martinmethodist.edu.

Maryville College

Maryville, Tennessee

http://www.maryvillecollege.edu/

- **Independent Presbyterian** 4-year, founded 1819
- **Suburban** 263-acre campus
- **Endowment** $66.0 million
- **Coed**
- **Moderately difficult** entrance level

FACULTY

Student/faculty ratio: 13:1.

ACADEMICS

Calendar: 4-1-4. *Degree:* bachelor's.

Library: Lamar Memorial Library plus 1 other. *Books:* 126,681 (physical), 115,843 (digital/electronic); *Serial titles:* 200 (physical), 43,452 (digital/electronic); *Databases:* 138. Weekly public service hours: 93; students can reserve study rooms.

STUDENT LIFE

Housing options: on-campus residence required through senior year; coed, men-only, women-only, special housing for students with disabilities. Campus housing is university owned. Freshman campus housing is guaranteed.

Activities and organizations: drama/theater group, student-run newspaper, choral group, Voices of Praise, student government, Student Programming Board, Global Citizenship, Peer Mentors.

Athletics Member NCAA. All Division III.

Campus security: 24-hour emergency response devices and patrols, late-night transport/escort service, controlled dormitory access, campus-wide emergency alert system via cell phones, home phones, and email.

Student services: health clinic, personal/psychological counseling.

COSTS & FINANCIAL AID

Costs (2016–17) ***Comprehensive fee:*** $44,392 includes full-time tuition ($32,746), mandatory fees ($778), and room and board ($10,868). Full-time tuition and fees vary according to course load. Part-time tuition and fees vary according to course load. ***College room only:*** $5450. Room and board charges vary according to board plan and housing facility.

Financial Aid Of all full-time matriculated undergraduates who enrolled in 2015, 1,175 applied for aid, 1,005 were judged to have need, 245 had their need fully met. 622 Federal Work-Study jobs (averaging $1710). 37 state and other part-time jobs (averaging $1981). In 2015, 171 non-need-based awards were made. ***Average percent of need met:*** 85. ***Average financial aid package:*** $34,507. ***Average need-based loan:*** $4817. ***Average need-based gift aid:*** $26,268. ***Average non-need-based aid:*** $21,433. ***Average indebtedness upon graduation:*** $27,571.

APPLYING

Standardized Tests *Required:* SAT or ACT (for admission).

Options: electronic application, early admission, deferred entrance.

Required: high school transcript, minimum 2.5 GPA, 1 letter of recommendation. ***Required for some:*** essay or personal statement, interview. ***Recommended:*** minimum 3.0 GPA.

CONTACT

Ms. Linda L. Moore, Administrative Assistant of Admissions, Maryville College, 502 East Lamar Alexander Parkway, Maryville, TN 37804-5907. *Phone:* 865-981-8096. *Toll-free phone:* 800-597-2687. *Fax:* 865-981-8005. *E-mail:* admissions@maryvillecollege.edu.

Memphis College of Art

Memphis, Tennessee

http://www.mca.edu/

- **Independent** comprehensive, founded 1936
- **Urban** 200-acre campus
- **Coed** 366 undergraduate students, 91% full-time, 65% women, 35% men
- **Moderately difficult** entrance level, 38% of applicants were admitted

UNDERGRAD STUDENTS

332 full-time, 34 part-time. Students come from 23 states and territories; 1 other country; 52% are from out of state; 25% Black or African American, non-Hispanic/Latino; 8% Hispanic/Latino; 2% Asian, non-Hispanic/Latino; 0.3% American Indian or Alaska Native, non-Hispanic/Latino; 5% Two or more races, non-Hispanic/Latino; 0.3% Race/ethnicity unknown; 0.3% international; 8% transferred in; 44% live on campus.

Freshmen:

Admission: 958 applied, 360 admitted, 100 enrolled. ***Average high school GPA:*** 3.14. ***Test scores:*** ACT scores over 18: 91%; ACT scores over 24: 26%; ACT scores over 30: 3%.

Retention: 68% of full-time freshmen returned.

FACULTY

Total: 52, 52% full-time, 65% with terminal degrees.

Student/faculty ratio: 10:1.

ACADEMICS

Calendar: semesters. *Degrees:* bachelor's and master's.

Special study options: adult/continuing education programs, advanced placement credit, double majors, independent study, internships, off-campus study, part-time degree program, services for LD students, study abroad, summer session for credit.

Computers: 100 computers/terminals and 20 ports are available on campus for general student use. Students can access the following: computer help desk, free student e-mail accounts. Campuswide network is available. 100% of college-owned or -operated housing units are wired for high-speed Internet access. Wireless service is available via entire campus.

Library: G. Pillow Lewis Library. *Books:* 20,972 (physical); *Serial titles:* 162 (physical); *Databases:* 66.

STUDENT LIFE

Housing options: on-campus residence required for freshman yearCampus housing is university owned. Freshman campus housing is guaranteed.

Activities and organizations: drama/theater group, Student Alliance, Photo Club, Design Club-AIGA, Clay Club, Swiftness (Running Club).

Campus security: 24-hour emergency response devices and patrols, late-night transport/escort service, controlled dormitory access.

Student services: personal/psychological counseling.

COSTS & FINANCIAL AID

Costs (2016–17) ***Comprehensive fee:*** $40,450 includes full-time tuition ($31,000), mandatory fees ($700), and room and board ($8750). Full-time tuition and fees vary according to degree level and reciprocity agreements. Part-time tuition: $3875 per course. Part-time tuition and fees vary according to course load and degree level. ***Required fees:*** $350 per term part-time. ***College room only:*** $6750. Room and board charges vary according to housing facility. ***Payment plans:*** tuition prepayment, installment. ***Waivers:*** employees or children of employees.

Financial Aid Of all full-time matriculated undergraduates who enrolled in 2015, 290 applied for aid, 267 were judged to have need, 29 had their need fully met. 95 Federal Work-Study jobs (averaging $520). 22 state and other part-time jobs (averaging $539). In 2015, 42 non-need-based awards were made. ***Average percent of need met:*** 61. ***Average financial aid package:*** $22,858. ***Average need-based loan:*** $4484. ***Average need-based gift aid:*** $19,009. ***Average non-need-based aid:*** $14,439. ***Average indebtedness upon graduation:*** $34,828.

APPLYING

Standardized Tests *Required:* SAT or ACT (for admission).

Options: electronic application, deferred entrance.

Required: minimum 2.0 GPA, portfolio.

Application deadlines: rolling (freshmen), rolling (out-of-state freshmen), rolling (transfers).

Notification: continuous (freshmen), continuous (out-of-state freshmen), continuous (transfers).

CONTACT

Katey Henriksen, Director of Admissions, Memphis College of Art, 1930 Poplar Avenue, Memphis, TN 38104. *Phone:* 901-272-5151. *Toll-free phone:* 800-727-1088. *Fax:* 901-272-5158. *E-mail:* khenriksen@mca.edu.

Mid-America Baptist Theological Seminary

Cordova, Tennessee

http://www.mabts.edu/

CONTACT

Mr. Duffy Guyton, Director of Admissions, Mid-America Baptist Theological Seminary, PO Box 2350, Cordova, TN 38016. *Phone:* 901-751-8453 Ext. 3066. *Toll-free phone:* 800-968-4508. *Fax:* 901-751-8454. *E-mail:* info@mabts.edu.

Middle Tennessee State University

Murfreesboro, Tennessee

http://www.mtsu.edu/

- **State-supported** university, founded 1911, part of Tennessee Board of Regents
- **Urban** 500-acre campus with easy access to Nashville
- **Coed**
- **Moderately difficult** entrance level

FACULTY

Student/faculty ratio: 18:1.

ACADEMICS

Calendar: semesters. *Degrees:* certificates, bachelor's, master's, doctoral, post-master's, and postbachelor's certificates.

Library: James E. Walker Library.

STUDENT LIFE

Housing options: coed, men-only, women-only, special housing for students with disabilities. Campus housing is university owned.

Activities and organizations: drama/theater group, student-run newspaper, radio and television station, choral group, marching band, national fraternities, national sororities.

Athletics Member NCAA. All Division I except football (Division I-A).

Campus security: 24-hour emergency response devices and patrols, student patrols, late-night transport/escort service, controlled dormitory access.

Student services: health clinic, personal/psychological counseling, women's center, legal services.

COSTS & FINANCIAL AID

Costs (2016–17) ***Tuition:*** state resident $6930 full-time, $275 per credit hour part-time; nonresident $24,930 full-time, $989 per credit hour part-time. Full-time tuition and fees vary according to course load. Part-time tuition and fees vary according to course load. ***Required fees:*** $1680 full-time, $70 per credit hour part-time. ***Room and board:*** $8850. Room and board charges vary according to board plan and housing facility.

Financial Aid Of all full-time matriculated undergraduates who enrolled in 2016, 13,665 applied for aid, 10,921 were judged to have need, 1,125 had their need fully met. 249 Federal Work-Study jobs (averaging $2339). In 2016, 1957 non-need-based awards were made. ***Average percent of need met:*** 62. ***Average financial aid package:*** $9552. ***Average need-based loan:*** $4027. ***Average need-based gift aid:*** $5667. ***Average non-need-based aid:*** $8032. ***Average indebtedness upon graduation:*** $25,456.

APPLYING

Standardized Tests *Required:* SAT or ACT (for admission).

Application fee: $25.

Required: high school transcript, minimum 3.0 GPA. ***Required for some:*** essay or personal statement.

CONTACT

Director of Admissions, Middle Tennessee State University, 1301 East Main Street, Murfreesboro, TN 37132. *Phone:* 615-898-2111. *Toll-free phone:* 800-331-MTSU. *Fax:* 615-898-5478. *E-mail:* admissions@mtsu.edu.

Mid-South Christian College

Memphis, Tennessee

http://www.midsouthchristian.edu/

- **Independent** 4-year
- **Urban** 12-acre campus with easy access to Memphis, TN
- **Endowment** $138,731
- **Coed**

FACULTY

Student/faculty ratio: 4:1.

ACADEMICS

Calendar: semesters. *Degrees:* certificates, associate, and bachelor's.

Library: W. H. Griffin Memorial Resource Center. *Books:* 27,214 (physical). Weekly public service hours: 42; students can reserve study rooms.

STUDENT LIFE

Housing options: on-campus residence required for freshman year; men-only, women-only, special housing for students with disabilities. Campus housing is university owned.

Campus security: controlled dormitory access.

COSTS

Costs (2016–17) ***Comprehensive fee:*** $10,058 includes full-time tuition ($5568), mandatory fees ($1090), and room and board ($3400). No tuition increase for student's term of enrollment. ***College room only:*** $1800.

APPLYING

Standardized Tests *Required:* ACT (for admission).

Required: essay or personal statement, high school transcript, minimum 2.3 GPA, 3 letters of recommendation. ***Recommended:*** interview.

CONTACT

Mrs. Wendy Lambert, Student Recruiter, Mid-South Christian College, PO Box 181056, Memphis, TN 38181. *Phone:* 901-375-4400 Ext. 103. *Fax:* 901-375-4085. *E-mail:* wendylambert@midsouthcc.org.

Milligan College

Milligan College, Tennessee

http://www.milligan.edu/

- **Independent Christian** comprehensive, founded 1866
- **Suburban** 181-acre campus
- **Endowment** $21.0 million
- **Coed** 892 undergraduate students, 88% full-time, 63% women, 37% men
- **Moderately difficult** entrance level, 65% of applicants were admitted

UNDERGRAD STUDENTS

785 full-time, 107 part-time. Students come from 36 states and territories; 19 other countries; 30% are from out of state; 4% Black or African American, non-Hispanic/Latino; 5% Hispanic/Latino; 2% Asian, non-Hispanic/Latino; 0.1% Native Hawaiian or other Pacific Islander, non-Hispanic/Latino; 0.4% American Indian or Alaska Native, non-Hispanic/Latino; 2% Two or more races, non-Hispanic/Latino; 0.4% Race/ethnicity unknown; 3% international; 6% transferred in; 74% live on campus.

Freshmen:
Admission: 603 applied, 393 admitted, 187 enrolled. ***Average high school GPA:*** 3.75. ***Test scores:*** SAT critical reading scores over 500: 67%; SAT writing scores over 500: 61%; ACT scores over 18: 96%; SAT critical reading scores over 600: 24%; SAT writing scores over 600: 23%; ACT scores over 24: 54%; SAT critical reading scores over 700: 5%; SAT writing scores over 700: 2%; ACT scores over 30: 12%.

Retention: 78% of full-time freshmen returned.

FACULTY
Total: 150, 53% full-time, 57% with terminal degrees.

Student/faculty ratio: 9:1.

ACADEMICS
Calendar: semesters. *Degrees:* bachelor's, master's, and doctoral.

Special study options: academic remediation for entering students, adult/continuing education programs, advanced placement credit, cooperative education, distance learning, double majors, honors programs, independent study, internships, off-campus study, part-time degree program, study abroad, summer session for credit.

Unusual degree programs: 3-2 pharmacy with Gatton College of Pharmacy at East Tennessee State University.

Computers: 97 computers/terminals are available on campus for general student use. Students can access the following: campus intranet, computer help desk, free student e-mail accounts, online (class) grades, online (class) registration, online (class) schedules. Campuswide network is available. 100% of college-owned or -operated housing units are wired for high-speed Internet access. Wireless service is available via classrooms, computer centers, computer labs, dorm rooms, libraries, student centers.

Library: P. H. Welshimer Memorial Library plus 1 other. *Books:* 171,308 (physical), 224,015 (digital/electronic); *Serial titles:* 945 (physical), 33,520 (digital/electronic); *Databases:* 83. Weekly public service hours: 89; students can reserve study rooms.

STUDENT LIFE
Housing options: on-campus residence required through senior year; men-only, women-only. Campus housing is university owned. Freshman campus housing is guaranteed.

Activities and organizations: drama/theater group, student-run newspaper, radio and television station, choral group, Social Affairs Committee, Buffalo Ramblers, Concert Council, Volunteer Milligan, Students for Life.

Athletics Member NAIA. ***Intercollegiate sports:*** baseball M(s), basketball M(s)/W(s), cross-country running M(s)/W(s), golf M(s)/W(s), soccer M(s)/W(s), softball W(s), swimming and diving M(s)/W(s), tennis M(s)/W(s), track and field M(s)/W(s), volleyball W(s). ***Intramural sports:*** basketball M/W, cheerleading W, football M/W, softball M/W, swimming and diving M/W, table tennis M/W, tennis M/W, ultimate Frisbee M/W, volleyball M/W, weight lifting M/W.

Campus security: 24-hour emergency response devices and patrols, late-night transport/escort service, controlled dormitory access.

Student services: health clinic, personal/psychological counseling.

COSTS & FINANCIAL AID
Costs (2016–17) ***One-time required fee:*** $75. ***Comprehensive fee:*** $38,150 includes full-time tuition ($30,250), mandatory fees ($1200), and room and board ($6700). Full-time tuition and fees vary according to course load and degree level. Part-time tuition: $840 per credit. Part-time tuition and fees vary according to course load and degree level. ***Required fees:*** $375 per term part-time. ***Room and board:*** Room and board charges vary according to housing facility. ***Payment plan:*** installment. ***Waivers:*** employees or children of employees.

Financial Aid Of all full-time matriculated undergraduates who enrolled in 2016, 710 applied for aid, 626 were judged to have need, 171 had their need fully met. 100 Federal Work-Study jobs (averaging $1200). 149 state and other part-time jobs (averaging $1594). In 2016, 10 non-need-based awards were made. ***Average percent of need met:*** 77. ***Average financial aid package:*** $23,410. ***Average need-based loan:*** $4895. ***Average need-based gift aid:*** $19,771. ***Average non-need-based aid:*** $10,939. ***Average indebtedness upon graduation:*** $28,510.

APPLYING
Standardized Tests *Required:* SAT or ACT (for admission).

Options: electronic application, deferred entrance.

Application fee: $30.

Required: essay or personal statement, high school transcript, minimum 2.0 GPA, 2 letters of recommendation. ***Required for some:*** interview. ***Recommended:*** minimum 3.0 GPA.

Application deadlines: 8/1 (freshmen), rolling (transfers).

Notification: continuous (freshmen), continuous (transfers).

CONTACT
Ms. Kristin Wright, Director of Enrollment Management, Milligan College, PO Box 210, Milligan College, TN 37682. *Phone:* 423-461-8730. *Toll-free phone:* 800-262-8337. *Fax:* 423-461-8982.
E-mail: admissions@milligan.edu.

National College

Bristol, Tennessee

http://www.national-college.edu/

CONTACT
National College, 1328 Highway 11 West, Bristol, TN 37620. *Phone:* 423-878-4440. *Toll-free phone:* 888-9-JOBREADY.

Nossi College of Art

Nashville, Tennessee

http://www.nossi.edu/

- **Proprietary** 4-year
- **Urban** 10-acre campus with easy access to Nashville
- **Coed** 354 undergraduate students, 100% full-time, 53% women, 47% men

UNDERGRAD STUDENTS
354 full-time. Students come from 8 states and territories; 23% are from out of state; 15% Black or African American, non-Hispanic/Latino; 3% Hispanic/Latino; 1% Asian, non-Hispanic/Latino; 1% Native Hawaiian or other Pacific Islander, non-Hispanic/Latino; 0.3% American Indian or Alaska Native, non-Hispanic/Latino; 1% Two or more races, non-Hispanic/Latino; 1% Race/ethnicity unknown; 0.3% international; 11% transferred in.

Freshmen:
Admission: 123 enrolled.

Retention: 86% of full-time freshmen returned.

FACULTY
Total: 38, 11% full-time.

Student/faculty ratio: 8:1.

ACADEMICS
Calendar: semesters. *Degrees:* associate and bachelor's.

Special study options: independent study, internships, off-campus study, part-time degree program.

Computers: 22 computers/terminals are available on campus for general student use. Students can access the following: campus intranet, free student e-mail accounts, online (class) grades, online (class) schedules. Wireless service is available via entire campus.

Library: Learning Resource Center.

STUDENT LIFE
Housing options: college housing not available.

Activities and organizations: Kappa Pi, CMA.EDU, Fashion Alliance, national fraternities, national sororities.

Campus security: gated entrance, ID badges for building accesss, doors are locked at all times.

COSTS
Costs (2017–18) ***Tuition:*** $17,700 full-time. No tuition increase for student's term of enrollment. ***Required fees:*** $100 full-time. ***Payment plan:*** installment.

APPLYING
Standardized Tests *Required for some:* ACT (for admission).

Options: electronic application, early admission.

Application fee: $100.

Required: essay or personal statement, high school transcript, interview, portfolio of work.

Notification: continuous (freshmen).

CONTACT

Ms. Mary Alexander, Admissions Director, Nossi College of Art, 590 Cheron Road, Madison, TN 37115. *Phone:* 615-514-2787 (ARTS). *Toll-free phone:* 888-986-ARTS. *Fax:* 615-514-2788. *E-mail:* admissions@nossi.edu.

O'More College of Design

Franklin, Tennessee

http://www.omorecollege.edu/

- **Independent** 4-year, founded 1970
- **Small-town** 7-acre campus with easy access to Nashville
- **Coed** 170 undergraduate students, 89% full-time, 87% women, 13% men
- **Moderately difficult** entrance level, 80% of applicants were admitted

UNDERGRAD STUDENTS

152 full-time, 18 part-time. Students come from 20 states and territories; 1 other country; 22% are from out of state; 11% Black or African American, non-Hispanic/Latino; 3% Hispanic/Latino; 2% Asian, non-Hispanic/Latino; 0.6% Native Hawaiian or other Pacific Islander, non-Hispanic/Latino; 0.6% American Indian or Alaska Native, non-Hispanic/Latino; 3% Two or more races, non-Hispanic/Latino; 0.6% Race/ethnicity unknown; 0.6% international; 9% transferred in.

Freshmen:

Admission: 132 applied, 105 admitted, 34 enrolled. ***Average high school GPA:*** 3.28. ***Test scores:*** ACT scores over 18: 70%; ACT scores over 24: 10%; ACT scores over 30: 1%.

Retention: 81% of full-time freshmen returned.

FACULTY

Total: 42, 33% full-time, 52% with terminal degrees.

Student/faculty ratio: 7:1.

ACADEMICS

Calendar: semesters. *Degree:* bachelor's.

Special study options: advanced placement credit, cooperative education, double majors, independent study, internships, off-campus study, part-time degree program, study abroad, summer session for credit.

Computers: 19 computers/terminals and 15 ports are available on campus for general student use. Students can access the following: campus intranet, computer help desk, free student e-mail accounts, online (class) grades, online (class) registration, online (class) schedules. Campuswide network is available. Wireless service is available via entire campus.

Library: McAfee Library. *Books:* 3,618 (physical); *Serial titles:* 3 (physical); *Databases:* 30. Weekly public service hours: 40.

STUDENT LIFE

Housing options: college housing not available.

Activities and organizations: American Society for Interior Design, Student Government Association, O'More Fashion Merchandising Association, Magnolia Social, International Interior Design Association.

Campus security: on-campus security during business hours; studio key card access after hours.

Student services: personal/psychological counseling.

COSTS & FINANCIAL AID

Costs (2016–17) ***Tuition:*** $28,176 full-time, $1174 per credit hour part-time. Full-time tuition and fees vary according to course load. ***Payment plan:*** installment. ***Waivers:*** employees or children of employees.

Financial Aid Of all full-time matriculated undergraduates who enrolled in 2015, 147 applied for aid, 130 were judged to have need, 18 had their need fully met. 13 Federal Work-Study jobs (averaging $1285). 17 state and other part-time jobs (averaging $2130). In 2015, 34 non-need-based awards were made. ***Average percent of need met:*** 76. ***Average financial aid package:*** $16,617. ***Average need-based loan:*** $4762. ***Average need-based gift aid:*** $13,756. ***Average non-need-based aid:*** $5934. ***Average indebtedness upon graduation:*** $31,773.

APPLYING

Standardized Tests *Required:* SAT or ACT (for admission).

Options: electronic application, deferred entrance.

Application fee: $50.

Required: high school transcript, interview, 2.70 GPA or minimum ACT score of 20. ***Required for some:*** essay or personal statement. ***Recommended:*** 10 letters of recommendation.

Application deadlines: 7/31 (freshmen), 7/31 (transfers).

Notification: continuous (freshmen), continuous (out-of-state freshmen), continuous (transfers).

CONTACT

Mrs. Tori Bagsby, Director of Admissions, O'More College of Design, 423 South Margin Street, Franklin, TN 37064-2816. *Phone:* 615-794-4254 Ext. 230. *Toll-free phone:* 888-662-1970. *Fax:* 615-790-1662. *E-mail:* tbagsby@omorecollege.edu.

Remington College–Memphis Campus

Memphis, Tennessee

http://www.remingtoncollege.edu/

CONTACT

Randal Hayes, Director of Recruitment, Remington College–Memphis Campus, 2710 Nonconnah Boulevard, Memphis, TN 38132. *Phone:* 901-345-1000. *Toll-free phone:* 800-323-8122. *Fax:* 901-396-8310. *E-mail:* randal.hayes@remingtoncollege.edu.

Rhodes College

Memphis, Tennessee

http://www.rhodes.edu/

- **Independent** comprehensive, founded 1848
- **Urban** 100-acre campus with easy access to Memphis
- **Endowment** $318.1 million
- **Coed** 1,999 undergraduate students, 99% full-time, 56% women, 44% men
- **Very difficult** entrance level, 54% of applicants were admitted

UNDERGRAD STUDENTS

1,984 full-time, 15 part-time. Students come from 46 states and territories; 35 other countries; 73% are from out of state; 8% Black or African American, non-Hispanic/Latino; 5% Hispanic/Latino; 6% Asian, non-Hispanic/Latino; 0.1% Native Hawaiian or other Pacific Islander, non-Hispanic/Latino; 0.4% American Indian or Alaska Native, non-Hispanic/Latino; 4% Two or more races, non-Hispanic/Latino; 2% Race/ethnicity unknown; 3% international; 0.6% transferred in; 70% live on campus.

Freshmen:

Admission: 4,481 applied, 2,434 admitted, 507 enrolled. ***Average high school GPA:*** 3.87. ***Test scores:*** SAT critical reading scores over 500: 97%; SAT math scores over 500: 98%; ACT scores over 18: 100%; SAT critical reading scores over 600: 70%; SAT math scores over 600: 71%; ACT scores over 24: 96%; SAT critical reading scores over 700: 19%; SAT math scores over 700: 24%; ACT scores over 30: 48%.

Retention: 93% of full-time freshmen returned.

FACULTY

Total: 220, 80% full-time, 92% with terminal degrees.

Student/faculty ratio: 10:1.

ACADEMICS

Calendar: semesters. *Degrees:* bachelor's and master's (master's degree in accounting only).

Special study options: advanced placement credit, cooperative education, double majors, honors programs, independent study, internships, off-campus study, part-time degree program, services for LD students, student-designed majors, study abroad, summer session for credit. ***ROTC:*** Army (c), Navy (c), Air Force (c).

Unusual degree programs: 3-2 engineering with Washington University in St. Louis, Christian Brothers University, University of Memphis, The University of Tennessee.

Computers: 220 computers/terminals are available on campus for general student use. Students can access the following: campus intranet, computer help desk, free student e-mail accounts, online (class) grades, online (class) registration, online (class) schedules. Campuswide network is available. 100% of college-owned or -operated housing units are wired for high-speed Internet access. Wireless service is available via entire campus.

Library: Paul Barret, Jr. Library. *Books:* 359,746 (physical); *Serial titles:* 95,955 (digital/electronic); *Databases:* 153. Weekly public service hours: 113.

STUDENT LIFE

Housing options: on-campus residence required through sophomore year; coed, men-only, women-only. Campus housing is university owned. Freshman campus housing is guaranteed.

Activities and organizations: drama/theater group, student-run newspaper, radio and television station, choral group, Health Professions Society, Rhodes Outdoors Club, Kinney, RhodeKill (ultimate Frisbee), Reformed University Fellowship, national fraternities, national sororities.

Athletics Member NCAA. All Division III. ***Intercollegiate sports:*** badminton M(c)/W(c), baseball M, basketball M/W, cheerleading W(c), crew M(c)/W(c), cross-country running M/W, fencing M(c)/W(c), field hockey W, football M, golf M/W, lacrosse M(c)/W(c), rugby M(c), soccer M/W, softball W, swimming and diving M/W, tennis M/W, track and field M/W, ultimate Frisbee M(c)/W(c), volleyball W. ***Intramural sports:*** basketball M/W, racquetball M/W, soccer M/W, squash M, volleyball M/W.

Campus security: 24-hour emergency response devices and patrols, student patrols, late-night transport/escort service, 24-hour monitored security cameras in parking areas, fenced campus with monitored access at night.

Student services: health clinic, personal/psychological counseling, women's center.

COSTS & FINANCIAL AID

Costs (2017–18) ***Comprehensive fee:*** $56,010 includes full-time tuition ($44,632), mandatory fees ($310), and room and board ($11,068). ***College room only:*** $5534. Room and board charges vary according to board plan and housing facility. ***Payment plan:*** installment. ***Waivers:*** employees or children of employees.

Financial Aid Of all full-time matriculated undergraduates who enrolled in 2016, 1,286 applied for aid, 702 were judged to have need, 292 had their need fully met. In 2016, 1136 non-need-based awards were made. ***Average percent of need met:*** 88. ***Average financial aid package:*** $37,616. ***Average need-based loan:*** $4534. ***Average need-based gift aid:*** $31,002. ***Average non-need-based aid:*** $22,703. ***Average indebtedness upon graduation:*** $25,859. ***Financial aid deadline:*** 3/1.

APPLYING

Standardized Tests *Required:* SAT or ACT (for admission).

Options: electronic application, early admission, early decision, early action, deferred entrance.

Required: essay or personal statement, high school transcript, 2 letters of recommendation. ***Recommended:*** interview.

Application deadlines: 1/15 (freshmen), 1/15 (transfers), 11/15 (early action).

Early decision deadline: 11/1 (for plan 1), 1/1 (for plan 2).

Notification: 4/1 (freshmen), 4/1 (transfers), 12/1 (early decision plan 1), 2/1 (early decision plan 2), 1/15 (early action).

CONTACT

Mr. Carey Thompson, Vice President of Enrollment and Communications, Dean of Admissions, Rhodes College, 2000 N. Parkway, Memphis, TN 38112. *Phone:* 901-843-3700. *Toll-free phone:* 800-844-5969. *Fax:* 901-843-3631. *E-mail:* adminfo@rhodes.edu.

Sewanee: The University of the South

Sewanee, Tennessee

http://www.sewanee.edu/

- **Independent Episcopal** comprehensive, founded 1857
- **Small-town** 13,000-acre campus with easy access to Chattanooga
- **Coed** 1,731 undergraduate students, 99% full-time, 53% women, 47% men
- **Very difficult** entrance level, 44% of applicants were admitted

UNDERGRAD STUDENTS

1,718 full-time, 13 part-time. Students come from 48 states and territories; 26 other countries; 79% are from out of state; 4% Black or African American, non-Hispanic/Latino; 6% Hispanic/Latino; 2% Asian, non-Hispanic/Latino; 0.1% American Indian or Alaska Native, non-Hispanic/Latino; 3% Two or more races, non-Hispanic/Latino; 3% international; 0.7% transferred in; 98% live on campus.

Freshmen:

Admission: 4,423 applied, 1,930 admitted, 514 enrolled. ***Average high school GPA:*** 3.69. ***Test scores:*** SAT critical reading scores over 500: 96%; SAT math scores over 500: 95%; SAT writing scores over 500: 95%; ACT scores over 18: 100%; SAT critical reading scores over 600: 72%; SAT math scores over 600: 62%; SAT writing scores over 600: 60%; ACT scores over 24: 95%; SAT critical reading scores over 700: 16%; SAT math scores over 700: 16%; SAT writing scores over 700: 16%; ACT scores over 30: 36%.

Retention: 88% of full-time freshmen returned.

FACULTY

Total: 243, 66% full-time, 84% with terminal degrees.

Student/faculty ratio: 10:1.

ACADEMICS

Calendar: semesters. *Degrees:* bachelor's, master's, doctoral, post-master's, and postbachelor's certificates.

Special study options: advanced placement credit, double majors, independent study, internships, off-campus study, services for LD students, student-designed majors, study abroad, summer session for credit.

Unusual degree programs: 3-2 engineering with Washington University in St. Louis, Vanderbilt University, Columbia University.

Computers: Students can access the following: computer help desk, free student e-mail accounts, online (class) grades, online (class) registration, online (class) schedules. Campuswide network is available. 100% of college-owned or -operated housing units are wired for high-speed Internet access. Wireless service is available via entire campus.

Library: Jessie Ball duPont Library. *Books:* 784,306 (physical), 622,710 (digital/electronic); *Serial titles:* 4,508 (physical), 10,570 (digital/electronic); *Databases:* 342. Study areas open 24 hours, 5-7 days a week; students can reserve study rooms.

STUDENT LIFE

Housing options: on-campus residence required through senior year; coed, men-only, women-only. Campus housing is university owned. Freshman campus housing is guaranteed.

Activities and organizations: drama/theater group, student-run newspaper, radio station, choral group, Sewanee Outing Program, Sewanee Outreach, Organization for Cross Cultural Understanding, Alpha Phi Omega (APO) National Service Fraternity, African American Alliance, national fraternities, national sororities.

Athletics Member NCAA. All Division III. ***Intercollegiate sports:*** baseball M, basketball M/W, cheerleading W, crew M(c)/W(c), cross-country running M/W, equestrian sports M/W, fencing M(c)/W(c), field hockey W, football M, golf M/W, ice hockey M(c)/W(c), lacrosse M/W, rugby M(c)/W(c), soccer M/W, softball W, squash M(c)/W(c), swimming and diving M/W, tennis M/W, track and field M/W, volleyball W. ***Intramural sports:*** basketball M/W, football M/W, soccer M/W, table tennis M/W.

Campus security: 24-hour emergency response devices and patrols, late-night transport/escort service, controlled dormitory access, security lighting.

Student services: health clinic, personal/psychological counseling, women's center.

COSTS & FINANCIAL AID
Costs (2017–18) ***Comprehensive fee:*** $58,000 includes full-time tuition ($44,848), mandatory fees ($272), and room and board ($12,880). Part-time tuition: $1425 per credit hour. No tuition increase for student's term of enrollment. ***College room only:*** $6675. ***Payment plan:*** installment. ***Waivers:*** employees or children of employees.

Financial Aid Of all full-time matriculated undergraduates who enrolled in 2016, 1,042 applied for aid, 802 were judged to have need, 303 had their need fully met. 426 Federal Work-Study jobs (averaging $1602). 153 state and other part-time jobs (averaging $2985). In 2016, 604 non-need-based awards were made. ***Average percent of need met:*** 93. ***Average financial aid package:*** $33,055. ***Average need-based loan:*** $4290. ***Average need-based gift aid:*** $27,341. ***Average non-need-based aid:*** $12,275. ***Average indebtedness upon graduation:*** $24,431. ***Financial aid deadline:*** 12/1.

APPLYING
Standardized Tests *Required for some:* TOEFL for international students. *Recommended:* SAT or ACT (for admission).

Options: electronic application, early admission, early decision, early action, deferred entrance.

Required: essay or personal statement, high school transcript, 2 letters of recommendation. ***Recommended:*** interview.

Application deadlines: 2/1 (freshmen), 4/1 (transfers), 12/1 (early action).

Early decision deadline: 11/15 (for plan 1), 1/15 (for plan 2).

Notification: continuous (transfers), 12/15 (early decision plan 1), 2/15 (early decision plan 2).

CONTACT
Ms. Lisa Burns, Associate Dean of Admission, Sewanee: The University of the South, 735 University Avenue, Sewanee, TN 37383-1000. *Phone:* 931-598-1238. *Toll-free phone:* 800-522-2234. *Fax:* 931-598-3248. *E-mail:* admiss@sewanee.edu.

South College

Knoxville, Tennessee

http://www.southcollegetn.edu/

CONTACT
Mr. Walter Hosea, Director of Admissions, South College, 720 North Fifth Avenue, Knoxville, TN 37917. *Phone:* 865-524-3043 Ext. 1825. *E-mail:* whosea@southcollegetn.edu.

Southern Adventist University

Collegedale, Tennessee

http://www.southern.edu/

- **Independent Seventh-day Adventist** comprehensive, founded 1892
- **Small-town** 1000-acre campus with easy access to Chattanooga
- **Endowment** $33.2 million
- **Coed**
- **Moderately difficult** entrance level

FACULTY
Student/faculty ratio: 15:1.

ACADEMICS
Calendar: semesters. *Degrees:* certificates, associate, bachelor's, master's, doctoral, and post-master's certificates.

Library: McKee Library plus 7 others. *Books:* 173,284 (physical), 107,663 (digital/electronic); *Serial titles:* 510 (physical), 170 (digital/electronic); *Databases:* 160. Weekly public service hours: 82; students can reserve study rooms.

STUDENT LIFE
Housing options: on-campus residence required through junior year; men-only, women-only. Campus housing is university owned. Freshman campus housing is guaranteed.

Activities and organizations: drama/theater group, student-run newspaper, radio and television station, choral group, Asian Club, Black Christian Union, Business Society, School of Nursing, Student Ministerial Association.

Campus security: 24-hour emergency response devices and patrols, student patrols, late-night transport/escort service, controlled dormitory access.

Student services: health clinic, personal/psychological counseling.

COSTS & FINANCIAL AID
Costs (2016–17) ***Comprehensive fee:*** $27,600 includes full-time tuition ($20,300), mandatory fees ($850), and room and board ($6450). Full-time tuition and fees vary according to course load. Part-time tuition: $850 per credit hour. Part-time tuition and fees vary according to course load. ***Required fees:*** $850 per term part-time. ***College room only:*** $4050. Room and board charges vary according to board plan.

Financial Aid Of all full-time matriculated undergraduates who enrolled in 2016, 1,671 applied for aid, 1,435 were judged to have need, 19 had their need fully met. In 2016, 519 non-need-based awards were made. ***Average percent of need met:*** 67. ***Average financial aid package:*** $16,232. ***Average need-based loan:*** $4521. ***Average need-based gift aid:*** $10,431. ***Average non-need-based aid:*** $6926. ***Average indebtedness upon graduation:*** $33,320.

APPLYING
Standardized Tests *Required:* SAT or ACT (for admission).

Options: electronic application, deferred entrance.

Application fee: $25.

Required: high school transcript, minimum 2.5 GPA. ***Required for some:*** essay or personal statement, minimum 2.3 GPA.

CONTACT
Emily Freck, Applications Manager, Southern Adventist University, PO Box 370, Collegedale, TN 37315-0370. *Phone:* 423-236-2655. *Toll-free phone:* 800-768-8437. *Fax:* 423-236-1835. *E-mail:* emilyfreck@southern.edu.

Strayer University–Knoxville Campus

Knoxville, Tennessee

http://www.strayer.edu/tennessee/knoxville/

CONTACT
Strayer University–Knoxville Campus, 10118 Parkside Drive, Suite 200, Knoxville, TN 37922.

Strayer University–Nashville Campus

Nashville, Tennessee

http://www.strayer.edu/tennessee/nashville/

CONTACT
Strayer University–Nashville Campus, 1809 Dabbs Avenue, Nashville, TN 37210.

Strayer University–Shelby Campus

Memphis, Tennessee

http://www.strayer.edu/tennessee/shelby/

CONTACT
Strayer University–Shelby Campus, 7275 Appling Farms Parkway, Memphis, TN 38133.

Strayer University–Thousand Oaks Campus

Memphis, Tennessee

http://www.strayer.edu/tennessee/thousand-oaks/

CONTACT
Strayer University–Thousand Oaks Campus, 2620 Thousand Oaks Boulevard, Suite 1100, Memphis, TN 38118.

Tennessee State University

Nashville, Tennessee

http://www.tnstate.edu/

- **State-supported** comprehensive, founded 1912, part of Tennessee Board of Regents
- **Urban** 450-acre campus with easy access to Nashville
- **Coed** 7,264 undergraduate students, 82% full-time, 60% women, 40% men
- **Minimally difficult** entrance level, 61% of applicants were admitted

UNDERGRAD STUDENTS

5,975 full-time, 1,289 part-time. Students come from 46 states and territories; 21 other countries; 33% are from out of state; 70% Black or African American, non-Hispanic/Latino; 1% Hispanic/Latino; 0.9% Asian, non-Hispanic/Latino; 0.2% American Indian or Alaska Native, non-Hispanic/Latino; 3% Two or more races, non-Hispanic/Latino; 0.5% Race/ethnicity unknown; 11% international; 8% transferred in.

Freshmen:

Admission: 8,826 applied, 5,356 admitted, 1,405 enrolled. ***Average high school GPA:*** 2.82. ***Test scores:*** ACT scores over 18: 49%; ACT scores over 24: 6%.

Retention: 59% of full-time freshmen returned.

FACULTY

Total: 538, 74% full-time.

Student/faculty ratio: 17:1.

ACADEMICS

Calendar: semesters. *Degrees:* associate, bachelor's, master's, doctoral, post-master's, and postbachelor's certificates.

Special study options: academic remediation for entering students, accelerated degree program, adult/continuing education programs, cooperative education, external degree program, freshman honors college, honors programs, independent study, internships, off-campus study, part-time degree program, services for LD students, summer session for credit. ***ROTC:*** Army (c), Navy (c), Air Force (b).

Computers: 1,025 computers/terminals are available on campus for general student use. Students can access the following: campus intranet, computer help desk, free student e-mail accounts, online (class) grades, online (class) registration, online (class) schedules. Campuswide network is available. Wireless service is available via entire campus.

Library: Martha M. Brown/Lois H. Daniel Library plus 1 other.

STUDENT LIFE

Housing options: coed, men-only, women-only. Campus housing is university owned. Freshman applicants given priority for college housing.

Activities and organizations: drama/theater group, student-run newspaper, radio and television station, choral group, marching band, national fraternities, national sororities.

Athletics Member NCAA. All Division I except football (Division I-AA). ***Intercollegiate sports:*** basketball M(s)/W(s), cross-country running M(s)/W(s), golf M(s), softball W, tennis M(s)/W(s), track and field M(s)/W(s), volleyball W. ***Intramural sports:*** baseball M, basketball M/W, cheerleading M/W, football M, softball W, track and field M/W, volleyball M/W.

Campus security: 24-hour patrols, controlled dormitory access.

Student services: health clinic, personal/psychological counseling, women's center.

FINANCIAL AID

Financial Aid Of all full-time matriculated undergraduates who enrolled in 2014, 5,534 applied for aid, 5,236 were judged to have need, 271 had their need fully met. In 2014, 232 non-need-based awards were made. ***Average percent of need met:*** 53. ***Average financial aid package:*** $10,539. ***Average need-based loan:*** $4060. ***Average need-based gift aid:*** $5332. ***Average non-need-based aid:*** $14,290. ***Average indebtedness upon graduation:*** $35,214.

APPLYING

Standardized Tests *Required:* SAT or ACT (for admission).

Options: electronic application.

Application fee: $25.

Required: high school transcript, minimum 2.3 GPA. ***Required for some:*** 3 letters of recommendation.

Application deadlines: 8/1 (freshmen), 8/1 (transfers).

Notification: continuous until 8/15 (freshmen), continuous until 8/15 (transfers).

CONTACT

Dr. John Cade, Associate Vice President/Interim Vice President, Tennessee State University, 3500 John A. Merritt Boulevard, Nashville, TN 37209. *Phone:* 615-963-5101. *E-mail:* jcade@tnstate.edu.

Tennessee Technological University

Cookeville, Tennessee

http://www.tntech.edu/

CONTACT

Mr. Alexis Pope, Director of Admissions, Tennessee Technological University, PO Box 5006, Cookeville, TN 38505. *Phone:* 931-372-3888. *Toll-free phone:* 800-255-8881. *Fax:* 931-372-6250. *E-mail:* admissions@tntech.edu.

Tennessee Wesleyan University

Athens, Tennessee

http://www.tnwesleyan.edu/

- **Independent United Methodist** comprehensive, founded 1857
- **Small-town** 40-acre campus with easy access to Knoxville, Chattanooga
- **Endowment** $9.4 million
- **Coed** 1,015 undergraduate students, 90% full-time, 63% women, 37% men
- **Minimally difficult** entrance level, 58% of applicants were admitted

UNDERGRAD STUDENTS

911 full-time, 104 part-time. Students come from 25 states and territories; 30 other countries; 13% are from out of state; 4% Black or African American, non-Hispanic/Latino; 1% Hispanic/Latino; 0.4% Asian, non-Hispanic/Latino; 2% Two or more races, non-Hispanic/Latino; 44% Race/ethnicity unknown; 12% transferred in; 35% live on campus.

Freshmen:

Admission: 988 applied, 570 admitted, 199 enrolled. ***Average high school GPA:*** 3.36. ***Test scores:*** SAT critical reading scores over 500: 30%; SAT math scores over 500: 45%; ACT scores over 18: 93%; SAT critical reading scores over 600: 3%; SAT math scores over 600: 9%; ACT scores over 24: 36%; ACT scores over 30: 2%.

Retention: 68% of full-time freshmen returned.

FACULTY

Total: 121, 47% full-time, 55% with terminal degrees.

Student/faculty ratio: 12:1.

ACADEMICS

Calendar: semesters. *Degrees:* bachelor's and master's (profile includes information for both the main and branch campuses).

Special study options: academic remediation for entering students, accelerated degree program, adult/continuing education programs, advanced placement credit, distance learning, double majors, honors programs, independent study, internships, off-campus study, part-time degree program, services for LD students, student-designed majors, study abroad, summer session for credit.

Computers: 205 computers/terminals and 350 ports are available on campus for general student use. Students can access the following: campus intranet, computer help desk, free student e-mail accounts, online (class) grades, online (class) registration, online (class) schedules. Campuswide network is available. 100% of college-owned or -operated housing units are wired for high-speed Internet access. Wireless service is available via entire campus.

Library: Merner-Pfeiffer Library plus 1 other. *Books:* 52,369 (physical), 156,820 (digital/electronic); *Serial titles:* 82 (physical); *Databases:* 76. Weekly public service hours: 69.

STUDENT LIFE

Housing options: men-only, women-only. Campus housing is university owned. Freshman campus housing is guaranteed.

Activities and organizations: drama/theater group, student-run newspaper, choral group, Student Government Association, national sororities.

Athletics Member NAIA. ***Intercollegiate sports:*** baseball M(s), basketball M(s)/W(s), bowling M(s)/W(s), cheerleading M(s)/W(s), cross-country running M(s)/W(s), golf M(s)/W(s), lacrosse M(s)/W(s), soccer M(s)/W(s), softball W(s), tennis M(s)/W(s), track and field M(s)/W(s), volleyball W(s).

Campus security: 24-hour patrols, late-night transport/escort service, controlled dormitory access, night patrols by trained security personnel.

Student services: health clinic.

COSTS & FINANCIAL AID

Costs (2017–18) ***Comprehensive fee:*** $31,550 includes full-time tuition ($22,800), mandatory fees ($1000), and room and board ($7750). Full-time tuition and fees vary according to class time and degree level. Part-time tuition: $570 per credit hour. Part-time tuition and fees vary according to class time, course load, degree level, location, and program. ***Required fees:*** $10 per contact hour part-time. ***Room and board:*** Room and board charges vary according to board plan and housing facility. ***Payment plan:*** installment. ***Waivers:*** employees or children of employees.

Financial Aid Of all full-time matriculated undergraduates who enrolled in 2014, 904 applied for aid, 815 were judged to have need, 135 had their need fully met. In 2014, 75 non-need-based awards were made. ***Average percent of need met:*** 65. ***Average financial aid package:*** $17,663. ***Average need-based loan:*** $3879. ***Average need-based gift aid:*** $15,178. ***Average non-need-based aid:*** $10,198. ***Average indebtedness upon graduation:*** $21,644.

APPLYING

Standardized Tests *Required:* SAT or ACT (for admission).

Options: electronic application, deferred entrance.

Application fee: $30.

Required: high school transcript, minimum 2.3 GPA, 1 letter of recommendation. ***Required for some:*** essay or personal statement, interview. ***Recommended:*** essay or personal statement.

Application deadlines: rolling (freshmen), rolling (transfers).

Notification: continuous (freshmen), continuous (transfers).

CONTACT

Ms. Joanne Landers, Vice President for Admissions, Tennessee Wesleyan University, 204 East College Street, Athens, TN 37303. *Phone:* 423-746-7504. *Toll-free phone:* 800-PICK-TWU. *Fax:* 423-745-9335. *E-mail:* admissions@twcnet.edu.

Trevecca Nazarene University

Nashville, Tennessee

http://www.trevecca.edu/

- **Independent Nazarene** comprehensive, founded 1901
- **Urban** 75-acre campus
- **Endowment** $25.8 million
- **Coed** 2,092 undergraduate students, 60% full-time, 60% women, 40% men
- **Moderately difficult** entrance level, 72% of applicants were admitted

UNDERGRAD STUDENTS

1,251 full-time, 841 part-time. Students come from 43 states and territories; 16 other countries; 33% are from out of state; 13% Black or African American, non-Hispanic/Latino; 12% Hispanic/Latino; 1% Asian, non-Hispanic/Latino; 0.2% Native Hawaiian or other Pacific Islander, non-Hispanic/Latino; 0.4% American Indian or Alaska Native, non-Hispanic/Latino; 2% Two or more races, non-Hispanic/Latino; 6% Race/ethnicity unknown; 2% international; 4% transferred in; 41% live on campus.

Freshmen:

Admission: 1,417 applied, 1,024 admitted, 414 enrolled. ***Average high school GPA:*** 3.37. ***Test scores:*** SAT critical reading scores over 500: 60%; SAT math scores over 500: 45%; ACT scores over 18: 88%; SAT critical reading scores over 600: 18%; SAT math scores over 600: 18%; ACT scores over 24: 37%; SAT critical reading scores over 700: 1%; SAT math scores over 700: 1%; ACT scores over 30: 7%.

Retention: 82% of full-time freshmen returned.

FACULTY

Total: 252, 33% full-time, 54% with terminal degrees.

Student/faculty ratio: 17:1.

ACADEMICS

Calendar: semesters. *Degrees:* certificates, associate, bachelor's, master's, doctoral, post-master's, and postbachelor's certificates.

Special study options: academic remediation for entering students, adult/continuing education programs, advanced placement credit, distance learning, double majors, internships, services for LD students, study abroad, summer session for credit. ***ROTC:*** Army (c).

Computers: 200 computers/terminals and 1,460 ports are available on campus for general student use. Students can access the following: campus intranet, computer help desk, free student e-mail accounts, online (class) grades, online (class) registration, online (class) schedules. Campuswide network is available. 100% of college-owned or -operated housing units are wired for high-speed Internet access. Wireless service is available via entire campus.

Library: Waggoner Library. *Books:* 87,390 (physical), 48,974 (digital/electronic); *Serial titles:* 431 (physical); *Databases:* 3,346. Weekly public service hours: 95; students can reserve study rooms.

STUDENT LIFE

Housing options: on-campus residence required through senior year; men-only, women-only. Campus housing is university owned.

Activities and organizations: drama/theater group, student-run newspaper, choral group, marching band.

Athletics Member NCAA. All Division II. ***Intercollegiate sports:*** baseball M(s), basketball M(s)/W(s), cross-country running M(s)/W(s), golf M(s)/W(s), soccer M(s)/W(s), softball W(s), track and field M(s)/W(s), volleyball W(s). ***Intramural sports:*** basketball M/W, football M/W, soccer M/W, softball M/W, tennis M/W, ultimate Frisbee M/W, volleyball M/W.

Campus security: 24-hour patrols, late-night transport/escort service, weather alert warning system (phone, email, siren).

Student services: health clinic, personal/psychological counseling.

COSTS & FINANCIAL AID

Costs (2017–18) ***Comprehensive fee:*** $33,908 includes full-time tuition ($24,200), mandatory fees ($900), and room and board ($8808). Full-time tuition and fees vary according to course load and program. Part-time tuition: $935 per credit hour. Part-time tuition and fees vary according to course load and program. ***College room only:*** $4404. Room and board charges vary according to board plan. ***Payment plans:*** tuition prepayment, installment. ***Waivers:*** senior citizens and employees or children of employees.

Financial Aid ***Average indebtedness upon graduation:*** $29,291.

APPLYING

Standardized Tests *Required:* SAT or ACT (for admission).

Options: electronic application, early admission, deferred entrance.

Application fee: $25.

Required: high school transcript, minimum 2.5 GPA, minimum ACT composite score of 18, OLD SAT Critical Reading and Math score of 860, or NEW RSAT Evidence-Based Reading and Writing and Math score of 940; enrollment fee; medical history and immunization records.

Application deadlines: 8/1 (freshmen), rolling (transfers).

Notification: continuous (freshmen), continuous (transfers).

CONTACT

Ms. Melinda Miller, Director of Undergraduate Admissions, Trevecca Nazarene University, 333 Murfreesboro Road, Nashville, TN 37210. *Phone:* 615-248-1320. *Toll-free phone:* 888-210-4TNU. *Fax:* 615-248-7406. *E-mail:* admissions_und@trevecca.edu.

Tusculum College

Greeneville, Tennessee

http://www.tusculum.edu/

- **Independent Presbyterian** comprehensive, founded 1794
- **Small-town** 140-acre campus
- **Endowment** $18.6 million
- **Coed** 1,585 undergraduate students, 89% full-time, 53% women, 47% men
- **Moderately difficult** entrance level, 74% of applicants were admitted

UNDERGRAD STUDENTS

1,417 full-time, 168 part-time. Students come from 28 states and territories; 15 other countries; 27% are from out of state; 14% Black or African American, non-Hispanic/Latino; 3% Hispanic/Latino; 0.4% Asian, non-Hispanic/Latino; 0.1% Native Hawaiian or other Pacific Islander, non-Hispanic/Latino; 0.4% American Indian or Alaska Native, non-Hispanic/Latino; 2% Two or more races, non-Hispanic/Latino; 4% Race/ethnicity unknown; 4% international; 4% transferred in; 50% live on campus.

Freshmen:

Admission: 2,238 applied, 1,665 admitted, 324 enrolled. ***Average high school GPA:*** 3.17. ***Test scores:*** SAT critical reading scores over 500: 32%; SAT math scores over 500: 44%; ACT scores over 18: 81%; SAT critical reading scores over 600: 3%; SAT math scores over 600: 7%; ACT scores over 24: 19%; ACT scores over 30: 1%.

Retention: 68% of full-time freshmen returned.

FACULTY

Total: 185, 39% full-time.

Student/faculty ratio: 15:1.

ACADEMICS

Calendar: semesters. *Degrees:* associate, bachelor's, and master's.

Special study options: academic remediation for entering students, adult/continuing education programs, advanced placement credit, double majors, honors programs, independent study, internships, part-time degree program, services for LD students, student-designed majors, study abroad, summer session for credit.

Computers: 200 computers/terminals are available on campus for general student use. Students can access the following: campus intranet, computer help desk, free student e-mail accounts, online (class) grades, online (class) registration, online (class) schedules. Campuswide network is available. 100% of college-owned or -operated housing units are wired for high-speed Internet access. Wireless service is available via entire campus.

Library: Thomas J. Garland Library plus 2 others. *Books:* 47,855 (physical), 432,852 (digital/electronic); *Databases:* 152. Students can reserve study rooms.

STUDENT LIFE

Housing options: on-campus residence required through senior year; coed, men-only, women-only, special housing for students with disabilities. Campus housing is university owned. Freshman campus housing is guaranteed.

Activities and organizations: drama/theater group, student-run newspaper, radio and television station, choral group, marching band, Pioneer Newspaper, Bonwondi, Campus Activities Board, Fellowship of Christian Athletes, Tusculana (yearbook).

Athletics Member NCAA. All Division II. ***Intercollegiate sports:*** baseball M(s), basketball M(s)/W(s), cheerleading M(s)/W(s), cross-country running M(s)/W(s), football M(s), golf M(s)/W, lacrosse M(s)/W(s), soccer M(s)/W(s), softball W(s), tennis M(s)/W(s), track and field M(s)/W(s), volleyball W(s). ***Intramural sports:*** baseball M, basketball M/W, football M, softball M, tennis M/W, volleyball M/W.

Campus security: 24-hour emergency response devices and patrols, student patrols, late-night transport/escort service, controlled dormitory access, trained security personnel on duty.

Student services: health clinic, personal/psychological counseling, women's center.

COSTS & FINANCIAL AID

Costs (2017–18) ***Comprehensive fee:*** $32,400 includes full-time tuition ($23,700) and room and board ($8700). Part-time tuition: $736 per credit hour. ***College room only:*** $5810. ***Payment plan:*** installment. ***Waivers:*** employees or children of employees.

Financial Aid Of all full-time matriculated undergraduates who enrolled in 2015, 1,367 applied for aid, 1,283 were judged to have need, 239 had their need fully met. 56 Federal Work-Study jobs (averaging $971). In 2015, 73 non-need-based awards were made. ***Average percent of need met:*** 59. ***Average financial aid package:*** $16,087. ***Average need-based loan:*** $4241. ***Average need-based gift aid:*** $8067. ***Average non-need-based aid:*** $7670. ***Average indebtedness upon graduation:*** $31,806.

APPLYING

Standardized Tests *Required:* SAT or ACT (for admission).

Options: electronic application, early admission, early decision, deferred entrance.

Required: essay or personal statement, high school transcript, minimum 2.0 GPA. ***Required for some:*** 3 letters of recommendation. ***Recommended:*** interview.

Application deadlines: rolling (freshmen), rolling (transfers).

CONTACT

Mr. Andrew Starnes, Assistant Director of Residential Admissions, Tusculum College, PO Box 50627, Greeneville, TN 37743-9997.
Phone: 423-636-7300 Ext. 5627. *Toll-free phone:* 800-729-0256.
Fax: 423-798-1622. *E-mail:* admissions@tusculum.edu.

Union University

Jackson, Tennessee

http://www.uu.edu/

- **Independent Southern Baptist** comprehensive, founded 1823
- **Small-town** 360-acre campus with easy access to Memphis
- **Endowment** $35.6 million
- **Coed** 2,214 undergraduate students, 80% full-time, 65% women, 35% men
- **Moderately difficult** entrance level, 63% of applicants were admitted

UNDERGRAD STUDENTS

1,779 full-time, 435 part-time. 23% are from out of state; 18% Black or African American, non-Hispanic/Latino; 2% Hispanic/Latino; 1% Asian, non-Hispanic/Latino; 0.1% Native Hawaiian or other Pacific Islander, non-Hispanic/Latino; 0.1% American Indian or Alaska Native, non-Hispanic/Latino; 2% Two or more races, non-Hispanic/Latino; 6% Race/ethnicity unknown; 1% international; 3% transferred in.

Freshmen:

Admission: 2,012 applied, 1,259 admitted, 336 enrolled. ***Average high school GPA:*** 3.76. ***Test scores:*** SAT critical reading scores over 500: 83%; SAT math scores over 500: 70%; ACT scores over 18: 100%; SAT critical reading scores over 600: 50%; SAT math scores over 600: 35%; ACT scores over 24: 68%; SAT critical reading scores over 700: 15%; SAT math scores over 700: 5%; ACT scores over 30: 26%.

Retention: 89% of full-time freshmen returned.

FACULTY

Total: 236, 100% full-time, 82% with terminal degrees.

Student/faculty ratio: 11:1.

ACADEMICS

Calendar: 4-1-4. *Degrees:* certificates, diplomas, associate, bachelor's, master's, doctoral, and post-master's certificates.

Special study options: academic remediation for entering students, accelerated degree program, adult/continuing education programs, advanced placement credit, cooperative education, distance learning, double majors, English as a second language, honors programs, independent study, internships, off-campus study, part-time degree program, services for LD students, study abroad, summer session for credit. ***ROTC:*** Army (c).

Unusual degree programs: 3-2 pharmacy.

Computers: Students can access the following: campus intranet, computer help desk, free student e-mail accounts, online (class) grades, online (class) registration, online (class) schedules. Campuswide network is available. 100% of college-owned or -operated housing units are wired for high-speed Internet access. Wireless service is available via entire campus.

Library: The Logos Library plus 1 other. *Books:* 133,129 (physical), 265,144 (digital/electronic); *Serial titles:* 1,272 (physical), 42,526 (digital/electronic); *Databases:* 123. Weekly public service hours: 94; students can reserve study rooms.

STUDENT LIFE

Housing options: on-campus residence required through junior year; men-only, women-only, special housing for students with disabilities. Campus housing is university owned. Freshman applicants given priority for college housing.

Activities and organizations: drama/theater group, student-run newspaper, choral group, Campus Ministries, Student Government Association, Student Activities Council, Students in Free Enterprise (SIFE), national fraternities, national sororities.

Athletics Member NCAA, NCCAA. All NCAA Division II. ***Intercollegiate sports:*** baseball M(s), basketball M(s)/W(s), cheerleading W(s), cross-country running M/W(s), golf M(s), soccer M(s)/W(s), softball W(s), track and field M/W, volleyball W(s). ***Intramural sports:*** basketball M/W, bowling M/W, cross-country running M/W, football M/W, golf M/W, racquetball M/W, soccer W, softball M/W, swimming and diving M/W, table tennis M/W, track and field M/W, ultimate Frisbee M/W, volleyball M/W.

Campus security: 24-hour emergency response devices and patrols, student patrols, late-night transport/escort service.

Student services: health clinic, personal/psychological counseling.

COSTS & FINANCIAL AID

Costs (2017–18) ***Comprehensive fee:*** $42,130 includes full-time tuition ($30,480), mandatory fees ($1300), and room and board ($10,350). Full-time tuition and fees vary according to class time, course load, degree level, location, and program. Part-time tuition: $980 per semester hour. Part-time tuition and fees vary according to class time, course load, degree level, location, and program. ***Required fees:*** $45 per credit hour part-time. ***College room only:*** $7800. Room and board charges vary according to board plan and housing facility. ***Payment plans:*** installment, deferred payment. ***Waivers:*** children of alumni and employees or children of employees.

Financial Aid Of all full-time matriculated undergraduates who enrolled in 2016, 1,504 applied for aid, 1,139 were judged to have need, 294 had their need fully met. 55 Federal Work-Study jobs (averaging $2906). 56 state and other part-time jobs (averaging $2777). In 2016, 160 non-need-based awards were made. ***Average percent of need met:*** 68. ***Average financial aid package:*** $26,410. ***Average need-based loan:*** $4470. ***Average need-based gift aid:*** $6137. ***Average non-need-based aid:*** $15,077. ***Average indebtedness upon graduation:*** $31,784.

APPLYING

Standardized Tests *Required:* SAT or ACT (for admission).

Options: electronic application, early admission, deferred entrance.

Application fee: $35.

Required: high school transcript, minimum 2.5 GPA. ***Required for some:*** 3 letters of recommendation. ***Recommended:*** essay or personal statement, interview.

Application deadlines: rolling (freshmen), rolling (out-of-state freshmen), rolling (transfers).

Notification: continuous (freshmen), continuous (out-of-state freshmen), continuous (transfers).

CONTACT

Mr. Robbie Graves, Director of Enrollment Services, Union University, 1050 Union University Drive, Jackson, TN 38305-3697.
Phone: 731-661-5590. *Toll-free phone:* 800-33-UNION.
Fax: 731-661-5589.
E-mail: rgraves@uu.edu.

University of Memphis

Memphis, Tennessee

http://www.memphis.edu/

- **State-supported** university, founded 1912, part of Tennessee Board of Regents
- **Urban** 1160-acre campus with easy access to Memphis
- **Endowment** $199.4 million
- **Coed**
- **Moderately difficult** entrance level

FACULTY

Student/faculty ratio: 15:1.

ACADEMICS

Calendar: semesters. *Degrees:* bachelor's, master's, doctoral, post-master's, and postbachelor's certificates.

Library: McWherter Library plus 4 others. *Books:* 2.3 million (physical), 113,204 (digital/electronic); *Serial titles:* 288 (physical), 1,098 (digital/electronic); *Databases:* 739. Weekly public service hours: 83; students can reserve study rooms.

STUDENT LIFE

Housing options: coed, men-only, women-only, cooperative, special housing for students with disabilities. Campus housing is university owned.

Activities and organizations: drama/theater group, student-run newspaper, radio station, choral group, marching band, Student Activities Council, Fraternity and Sorority Life, Black Student Association, Student Government Association, Up 'til Dawn- St. Jude Philanthropy, national fraternities, national sororities.

Athletics Member NCAA. All Division I except football (Division I-A).

Campus security: 24-hour emergency response devices and patrols, student patrols, late-night transport/escort service, controlled dormitory access.

Student services: health clinic, personal/psychological counseling, women's center.

COSTS & FINANCIAL AID

Costs (2016–17) ***Tuition:*** state resident $7860 full-time, $312 per credit hour part-time; nonresident $19,572 full-time, $800 per credit hour part-time. Full-time tuition and fees vary according to course load, degree level, program, and reciprocity agreements. Part-time tuition and fees vary according to course load, degree level, and program. ***Required fees:*** $1637 full-time. ***Room and board:*** $9153; room only: $5456. Room and board charges vary according to board plan, housing facility, and location.

Financial Aid Of all full-time matriculated undergraduates who enrolled in 2016, 12,358 applied for aid, 10,384 were judged to have need, 1,412 had their need fully met. 150 Federal Work-Study jobs (averaging $2754). In 2016, 1341 non-need-based awards were made. ***Average percent of need met:*** 72. ***Average financial aid package:*** $9985. ***Average need-based loan:*** $4292. ***Average need-based gift aid:*** $6370. ***Average non-need-based aid:*** $6229. ***Average indebtedness upon graduation:*** $27,155.

APPLYING

Standardized Tests *Required:* SAT or ACT (for admission).

Options: electronic application, early admission.

Application fee: $25.

Required: high school transcript. ***Required for some:*** minimum 2.0 GPA, 2 letters of recommendation, interview.

CONTACT

Gloria W. Moore, Associate Director of Admissions, University of Memphis, Office of Admissions, 101 Wilder Tower, Memphis, TN 38152.
Phone: 901-678-2111. *Toll-free phone:* 800-669-2678.
Fax: 901-678-5318. *E-mail:* admissions@memphis.edu.

The University of Tennessee

Knoxville, Tennessee

http://www.utk.edu/

- **State-supported** university, founded 1794, part of University of Tennessee System
- **Urban** 600-acre campus
- **Endowment** $461.5 million
- **Coed** 22,139 undergraduate students, 94% full-time, 49% women, 51% men
- **Moderately difficult** entrance level, 77% of applicants were admitted

UNDERGRAD STUDENTS
20,778 full-time, 1,361 part-time. Students come from 48 states and territories; 63 other countries; 11% are from out of state; 7% Black or African American, non-Hispanic/Latino; 4% Hispanic/Latino; 4% Asian, non-Hispanic/Latino; 0.2% American Indian or Alaska Native, non-Hispanic/Latino; 3% Two or more races, non-Hispanic/Latino; 3% Race/ethnicity unknown; 2% international; 6% transferred in; 33% live on campus.

Freshmen:
Admission: 17,583 applied, 13,578 admitted, 4,851 enrolled. ***Average high school GPA:*** 3.89. ***Test scores:*** SAT critical reading scores over 500: 84%; SAT math scores over 500: 86%; ACT scores over 18: 99%; SAT critical reading scores over 600: 37%; SAT math scores over 600: 38%; ACT scores over 24: 80%; SAT critical reading scores over 700: 7%; SAT math scores over 700: 7%; ACT scores over 30: 29%.

Retention: 86% of full-time freshmen returned.

FACULTY
Total: 1,739, 88% full-time, 83% with terminal degrees.

Student/faculty ratio: 17:1.

ACADEMICS
Calendar: semesters. *Degrees:* bachelor's, master's, doctoral, and postbachelor's certificates.

Special study options: accelerated degree program, advanced placement credit, cooperative education, distance learning, double majors, English as a second language, external degree program, freshman honors college, honors programs, independent study, internships, off-campus study, part-time degree program, services for LD students, student-designed majors, study abroad, summer session for credit. ***ROTC:*** Army (b), Air Force (b).

Computers: 1,200 computers/terminals are available on campus for general student use. Students can access the following: campus intranet, computer help desk, free student e-mail accounts, online (class) grades, online (class) registration, online (class) schedules, course management system. Campuswide network is available. 100% of college-owned or -operated housing units are wired for high-speed Internet access. Wireless service is available via entire campus.

Library: John C. Hodges Library plus 5 others. *Books:* 1.5 million (physical), 687,998 (digital/electronic); *Serial titles:* 51,677 (physical), 92,682 (digital/electronic); *Databases:* 678. Weekly public service hours: 160; study areas open 24 hours, 5-7 days a week; students can reserve study rooms.

STUDENT LIFE
Housing options: on-campus residence required for freshman year; coed, men-only, women-only, special housing for students with disabilities. Campus housing is university owned. Freshman campus housing is guaranteed.

Activities and organizations: drama/theater group, student-run newspaper, radio and television station, choral group, marching band, Fraternities/Sororities, Religious organizations, Campus Events Board, Black Cultural Programming Committee, Student Government Association, national fraternities, national sororities.

Athletics Member NCAA. All Division I. ***Intercollegiate sports:*** baseball M(s), basketball M(s)/W(s), crew W(s), cross-country running M/W, football M(s), golf M(s)/W(s), soccer W(s), softball W(s), swimming and diving M(s)/W(s), tennis M(s)/W(s), track and field M(s)/W(s), volleyball W(s). ***Intramural sports:*** badminton M/W, baseball M(c), basketball M/W, crew M(c)/W(c), cross-country running M(c)/W(c), equestrian sports M(c)/W(c), fencing M(c)/W(c), field hockey M/W, football M/W, golf M(c)/W(c), gymnastics M(c)/W(c), ice hockey M(c)/W(c), lacrosse M(c)/W(c), racquetball M/W, rock climbing M(c)/W(c), rowing M(c)/W(c), rugby M(c)/W(c), sailing M(c)/W(c), sand volleyball M/W, skiing (downhill) M(c)/W(c), soccer M/W, softball M/W, swimming and diving M(c)/W(c), table tennis M/W, tennis M/W, triathlon M(c)/W(c), ultimate Frisbee M/W, volleyball M/W, water polo M/W, weight lifting M/W, wrestling M(c)/W(c).

Campus security: 24-hour emergency response devices and patrols, late-night transport/escort service, controlled dormitory access, security cameras on all building entrances.

Student services: health clinic, personal/psychological counseling, women's center.

COSTS & FINANCIAL AID
Costs (2016–17) ***Tuition:*** state resident $10,914 full-time, $362 per credit hour part-time; nonresident $29,104 full-time, $1121 per credit hour part-time. Full-time tuition and fees vary according to course level, location, program, reciprocity agreements, and student level. Part-time tuition and fees vary according to course level, location, program, reciprocity agreements, and student level. ***Required fees:*** $1810 full-time, $87 per credit hour part-time. ***Room and board:*** $10,238. Room and board charges vary according to board plan and housing facility. ***Payment plan:*** installment. ***Waivers:*** senior citizens and employees or children of employees.

Financial Aid Of all full-time matriculated undergraduates who enrolled in 2016, 18,288 applied for aid, 12,057 were judged to have need, 2,214 had their need fully met. 772 Federal Work-Study jobs (averaging $2502). In 2016, 2420 non-need-based awards were made. ***Average percent of need met:*** 57. ***Average financial aid package:*** $13,012. ***Average need-based loan:*** $6755. ***Average need-based gift aid:*** $9760. ***Average non-need-based aid:*** $5348. ***Average indebtedness upon graduation:*** $24,420.

APPLYING
Standardized Tests *Required:* SAT or ACT (for admission).

Options: electronic application.

Application fee: $50.

Required: essay or personal statement, high school transcript, high school prerequisite units. ***Recommended:*** letters of recommendation.

Notification: continuous until 10/1 (freshmen), continuous until 10/1 (transfers).

CONTACT
Ms. Norma Harrington, Senior Associate Director, The University of Tennessee, 320 Student Services Building, Knoxville, TN 37996-0230. *Phone:* 865-974-2184. *E-mail:* admissions@utk.edu.

The University of Tennessee at Chattanooga

Chattanooga, Tennessee

http://www.utc.edu/

- **State-supported** comprehensive, founded 1886, part of University of Tennessee System
- **Urban** 425-acre campus
- **Coed** 10,170 undergraduate students, 87% full-time, 56% women, 44% men
- **Moderately difficult** entrance level, 78% of applicants were admitted

UNDERGRAD STUDENTS
8,875 full-time, 1,295 part-time. Students come from 34 states and territories; 30 other countries; 5% are from out of state; 11% Black or African American, non-Hispanic/Latino; 4% Hispanic/Latino; 2% Asian, non-Hispanic/Latino; 0.0% Native Hawaiian or other Pacific Islander, non-Hispanic/Latino; 0.2% American Indian or Alaska Native, non-Hispanic/Latino; 5% Two or more races, non-Hispanic/Latino; 0.9% Race/ethnicity unknown; 0.9% international; 8% transferred in; 31% live on campus.

Freshmen:
Admission: 7,628 applied, 5,970 admitted, 2,080 enrolled. ***Average high school GPA:*** 3.51. ***Test scores:*** SAT critical reading scores over 500: 68%; SAT math scores over 500: 60%; ACT scores over 18: 99%; SAT critical reading scores over 600: 25%; SAT math scores over 600: 20%; ACT scores over 24: 49%; SAT critical reading scores over 700: 6%; SAT math scores over 700: 1%; ACT scores over 30: 7%.

Retention: 74% of full-time freshmen returned.

FACULTY

Total: 689, 65% full-time, 62% with terminal degrees.

Student/faculty ratio: 19:1.

ACADEMICS

Calendar: semesters. *Degrees:* certificates, bachelor's, master's, doctoral, post-master's, and postbachelor's certificates.

Special study options: accelerated degree program, advanced placement credit, cooperative education, distance learning, double majors, English as a second language, freshman honors college, honors programs, independent study, internships, off-campus study, part-time degree program, services for LD students, student-designed majors, study abroad, summer session for credit. ***ROTC:*** Army (b).

Computers: Students can access the following: campus intranet, computer help desk, free student e-mail accounts, online (class) grades, online (class) registration, online (class) schedules. Campuswide network is available. 100% of college-owned or -operated housing units are wired for high-speed Internet access. Wireless service is available via entire campus.

Library: UTC Library plus 1 other. *Books:* 799,387 (physical); *Databases:* 154. Study areas open 24 hours, 5-7 days a week; students can reserve study rooms.

STUDENT LIFE

Housing options: on-campus residence required for freshman year; coed, special housing for students with disabilities. Campus housing is university owned. Freshman applicants given priority for college housing.

Activities and organizations: drama/theater group, student-run newspaper, choral group, marching band, national fraternities, national sororities.

Athletics Member NCAA. All Division I except football (Division I-AA). ***Intercollegiate sports:*** basketball M(s)/W(s), cross-country running M(s)/W(s), golf M(s)/W(s), soccer W(s), softball W(s), tennis M(s)/W(s), track and field M(s)/W(s), volleyball W(s), wrestling M(s). ***Intramural sports:*** badminton M/W, baseball M(c), basketball M/W, crew M(c)/W(c), cross-country running M/W, fencing M(c)/W(c), golf M/W, racquetball M/W, soccer M/W, swimming and diving M/W, tennis M/W, ultimate Frisbee M(c)/W(c), volleyball W, wrestling M.

Campus security: 24-hour emergency response devices.

Student services: health clinic, personal/psychological counseling, women's center.

COSTS & FINANCIAL AID

Costs (2016–17) ***Tuition:*** state resident $6768 full-time, $282 per credit hour part-time; nonresident $22,886 full-time, $954 per credit hour part-time. Full-time tuition and fees vary according to degree level. Part-time tuition and fees vary according to degree level. ***Required fees:*** $1776 full-time, $264 per credit hour part-time. ***Room and board:*** $8676; room only: $5226. Room and board charges vary according to board plan, housing facility, and location. ***Payment plan:*** installment. ***Waivers:*** senior citizens and employees or children of employees.

Financial Aid Of all full-time matriculated undergraduates who enrolled in 2016, 7,926 applied for aid, 5,519 were judged to have need, 777 had their need fully met. In 2016, 986 non-need-based awards were made. ***Average percent of need met:*** 64. ***Average financial aid package:*** $9747. ***Average need-based loan:*** $3998. ***Average need-based gift aid:*** $7658. ***Average non-need-based aid:*** $2994. ***Average indebtedness upon graduation:*** $22,917. ***Financial aid deadline:*** 5/1.

APPLYING

Standardized Tests *Required:* SAT or ACT (for admission).

Options: electronic application, early admission, deferred entrance.

Application fee: $30.

Required: high school transcript, 2.5 GPA with minimum ACT score of 21/SAT of 990 or minimum GPA of 2.85 with minimum ACT score of 18/SAT score of 870.

Application deadlines: 5/1 (freshmen), 7/1 (transfers).

CONTACT

Ms. Lee Pierce, Director of Admissions, The University of Tennessee at Chattanooga, 615 McCallie Ave, 101 University Center, Dept. 5105, Chattanooga, TN 37403. *Phone:* 423-425-4662. *Toll-free phone:* 800-882-6627. *Fax:* 423-425-4157. *E-mail:* admissions@utc.edu.

The University of Tennessee at Martin

Martin, Tennessee

http://www.utm.edu/

- **State-supported** comprehensive, founded 1900, part of University of Tennessee System
- **Small-town** 250-acre campus
- **Endowment** $30.3 million
- **Coed** 6,279 undergraduate students, 79% full-time, 58% women, 42% men
- **Moderately difficult** entrance level, 67% of applicants were admitted

UNDERGRAD STUDENTS

4,955 full-time, 1,324 part-time. Students come from 43 states and territories; 19 other countries; 7% are from out of state; 14% Black or African American, non-Hispanic/Latino; 2% Hispanic/Latino; 0.6% Asian, non-Hispanic/Latino; 0.2% American Indian or Alaska Native, non-Hispanic/Latino; 2% Two or more races, non-Hispanic/Latino; 3% international; 7% transferred in; 29% live on campus.

Freshmen:

Admission: 3,547 applied, 2,366 admitted, 946 enrolled. ***Average high school GPA:*** 3.56. ***Test scores:*** ACT scores over 18: 99%; ACT scores over 24: 40%; ACT scores over 30: 4%.

Retention: 75% of full-time freshmen returned.

FACULTY

Total: 506, 58% full-time, 49% with terminal degrees.

Student/faculty ratio: 15:1.

ACADEMICS

Calendar: semesters. *Degrees:* bachelor's and master's.

Special study options: accelerated degree program, adult/continuing education programs, advanced placement credit, cooperative education, distance learning, double majors, English as a second language, honors programs, independent study, internships, off-campus study, part-time degree program, services for LD students, student-designed majors, study abroad, summer session for credit. ***ROTC:*** Army (b).

Unusual degree programs: veterinary medicine, dentistry, medicine, pharmacy.

Computers: 1,119 computers/terminals and 7,203 ports are available on campus for general student use. Students can access the following: campus intranet, computer help desk, free student e-mail accounts, online (class) grades, online (class) registration, online (class) schedules, online fee payments, degree progress, financial aid data, housing applications, transcripts. Campuswide network is available. 100% of college-owned or -operated housing units are wired for high-speed Internet access. Wireless service is available via entire campus.

Library: Paul Meek Library. *Books:* 345,939 (physical), 156,902 (digital/electronic); *Serial titles:* 156 (physical), 99,944 (digital/electronic); *Databases:* 79. Weekly public service hours: 92; study areas open 24 hours, 5-7 days a week.

STUDENT LIFE

Housing options: on-campus residence required for freshman year; men-only, women-only, special housing for students with disabilities. Campus housing is university owned. Freshman applicants given priority for college housing.

Activities and organizations: drama/theater group, student-run newspaper, radio and television station, choral group, marching band, Student Government Association, Black Student Association, National Society for Leadership and Success, Gamma Beta Phi, Student Tennessee Education Association, national fraternities, national sororities.

Athletics Member NCAA. All Division I except football (Division I-AA). ***Intercollegiate sports:*** baseball M(s), basketball M(s)/W(s), cheerleading W(s), cross-country running M(s)/W(s), equestrian sports W(s), golf M(s), riflery M(s)/W(s), sand volleyball W(s), soccer W(s), softball W(s), tennis W(s), volleyball W(s). ***Intramural sports:*** basketball M/W, football M/W, golf M/W, racquetball M/W, soccer M/W, softball M/W, tennis M/W, ultimate Frisbee M/W, volleyball M/W, water polo M/W.

Campus security: 24-hour emergency response devices and patrols, student patrols, controlled dormitory access.

Student services: health clinic, personal/psychological counseling, women's center.

COSTS & FINANCIAL AID

Costs (2016–17) ***Tuition:*** state resident $7680 full-time, $294 per credit hour part-time; nonresident $13,440 full-time, $534 per credit hour part-time. Full-time tuition and fees vary according to student level. Part-time tuition and fees vary according to course level and course load. ***Required fees:*** $1408 full-time, $59 per credit hour part-time. ***Room and board:*** $5788; room only: $2600. Room and board charges vary according to board plan and housing facility. ***Payment plans:*** installment, deferred payment. ***Waivers:*** senior citizens and employees or children of employees.

Financial Aid Of all full-time matriculated undergraduates who enrolled in 2016, 4,504 applied for aid, 3,694 were judged to have need, 669 had their need fully met. 324 Federal Work-Study jobs (averaging $2566). In 2016, 253 non-need-based awards were made. ***Average percent of need met:*** 44. ***Average financial aid package:*** $11,218. ***Average need-based loan:*** $4396. ***Average need-based gift aid:*** $6286. ***Average non-need-based aid:*** $2024. ***Average indebtedness upon graduation:*** $28,077.

APPLYING

Standardized Tests *Required:* SAT or ACT (for admission).

Options: electronic application, early admission, deferred entrance.

Application fee: $30.

Required: high school transcript, minimum 2.7 GPA.

Application deadlines: rolling (freshmen), rolling (transfers).

Notification: continuous until 8/1 (freshmen), continuous until 8/1 (transfers).

CONTACT

Dr. James Mantooth, Executive Director of Enrollment Services and Student Engagement, The University of Tennessee at Martin, 200 Hall-Moody Administration Building, Martin, TN 38238.
Phone: 731-881-7053. *Toll-free phone:* 800-829-8861.
Fax: 731-881-7055. *E-mail:* jdmantooth@utm.edu.

Vanderbilt University

Nashville, Tennessee

http://www.vanderbilt.edu/

- **Independent** university, founded 1873
- **Urban** 330-acre campus with easy access to Nashville, TN
- **Endowment** $3.8 billion
- **Coed** 6,871 undergraduate students, 99% full-time, 51% women, 49% men
- **Most difficult** entrance level, 11% of applicants were admitted

UNDERGRAD STUDENTS

6,817 full-time, 54 part-time. Students come from 53 states and territories; 47 other countries; 90% are from out of state; 9% Black or African American, non-Hispanic/Latino; 9% Hispanic/Latino; 12% Asian, non-Hispanic/Latino; 0.2% Native Hawaiian or other Pacific Islander, non-Hispanic/Latino; 0.5% American Indian or Alaska Native, non-Hispanic/Latino; 5% Two or more races, non-Hispanic/Latino; 5% Race/ethnicity unknown; 7% international; 3% transferred in; 90% live on campus.

Freshmen:

Admission: 32,442 applied, 3,487 admitted, 1,601 enrolled. ***Average high school GPA:*** 3.8. ***Test scores:*** SAT critical reading scores over 500: 99%; SAT math scores over 500: 99%; SAT writing scores over 500: 98%; ACT scores over 18: 100%; SAT critical reading scores over 600: 96%; SAT math scores over 600: 96%; SAT writing scores over 600: 95%; ACT scores over 24: 98%; SAT critical reading scores over 700: 79%; SAT math scores over 700: 83%; SAT writing scores over 700: 69%; ACT scores over 30: 91%.

Retention: 97% of full-time freshmen returned.

FACULTY

Total: 1,225, 78% full-time.

Student/faculty ratio: 8:1.

ACADEMICS

Calendar: semesters. *Degrees:* bachelor's, master's, and doctoral.

Special study options: accelerated degree program, advanced placement credit, cooperative education, double majors, English as a second language, honors programs, independent study, internships, off-campus study, services for LD students, student-designed majors, study abroad, summer session for credit. ***ROTC:*** Army (b), Navy (b), Air Force (c).

Unusual degree programs: 3-2 business administration; engineering; nursing; English, French, German, history, Latin American Studies, mathematics, philosophy, political science, psychology, and medicine, health and society.

Computers: Students can access the following: campus intranet, computer help desk, free student e-mail accounts, online (class) grades, online (class) registration, online (class) schedules, productivity and educational software. Campuswide network is available. Wireless service is available via entire campus.

Library: Jean and Alexander Heard Library plus 7 others. *Books:* 3.1 million (physical), 1.7 million (digital/electronic); *Databases:* 3,700.

STUDENT LIFE

Housing options: on-campus residence required for freshman year; coed, men-only, women-only, special housing for students with disabilities. Campus housing is university owned. Freshman campus housing is guaranteed.

Activities and organizations: drama/theater group, student-run newspaper, radio and television station, choral group, marching band, national fraternities, national sororities.

Athletics Member NCAA. All Division I except football (Division I-A). ***Intercollegiate sports:*** baseball M(s), basketball M(s)/W(s), bowling W(s), cross-country running M(s)/W(s), golf M(s)/W(s), lacrosse W(s), soccer W(s), swimming and diving W(s), tennis M(s)/W(s), track and field W(s). ***Intramural sports:*** badminton M(c)/W(c), baseball M(c), basketball M(c)/W(c), bowling M(c)/W(c), crew M(c)/W(c), cross-country running M(c)/W(c), equestrian sports M(c)/W(c), fencing M(c)/W(c), field hockey M(c)/W(c), golf M(c)/W(c), ice hockey M(c), lacrosse M(c)/W(c), racquetball M(c)/W(c), rowing M(c)/W(c), rugby M(c), sailing M(c)/W(c), sand volleyball M/W, soccer M(c)/W(c), softball M/W, squash M(c)/W(c), swimming and diving M(c)/W(c), table tennis M(c)/W(c), tennis M(c)/W(c), track and field M(c)/W(c), triathlon M(c)/W(c), ultimate Frisbee M/W, volleyball M(c)/W(c), water polo M(c)/W(c).

Campus security: 24-hour emergency response devices and patrols, student patrols, late-night transport/escort service, controlled dormitory access.

Student services: health clinic, personal/psychological counseling, women's center.

COSTS & FINANCIAL AID

Costs (2016–17) ***Comprehensive fee:*** $60,572 includes full-time tuition ($44,496), mandatory fees ($1114), and room and board ($14,962). Part-time tuition: $1854 per credit hour. ***College room only:*** $9772. Room and board charges vary according to board plan. ***Payment plans:*** tuition prepayment, installment. ***Waivers:*** employees or children of employees.

Financial Aid Of all full-time matriculated undergraduates who enrolled in 2016, 3,836 applied for aid, 3,406 were judged to have need, 3,383 had their need fully met. 1,466 Federal Work-Study jobs (averaging $2383). In 2016, 720 non-need-based awards were made. ***Average percent of need met:*** 100. ***Average financial aid package:*** $46,938. ***Average need-based loan:*** $3375. ***Average need-based gift aid:*** $41,331. ***Average non-need-based aid:*** $22,357. ***Average indebtedness upon graduation:*** $24,122.

APPLYING

Standardized Tests *Required:* SAT or ACT (for admission).

Options: electronic application, early admission, early decision, deferred entrance.

Application fee: $50.

Required: essay or personal statement, high school transcript, 3 letters of recommendation, 3 letters of recommendation (2 from teachers in core subject areas and 1 from counselor).

Application deadlines: 1/1 (freshmen), 3/15 (transfers).

Early decision deadline: 11/1 (for plan 1), 1/1 (for plan 2).

Notification: 4/1 (freshmen), 4/15 (transfers), 12/15 (early decision plan 1), 2/15 (early decision plan 2).

CONTACT
Mr. John O. Gaines, Director of Undergraduate Admissions, Vanderbilt University, 2305 West End Avenue, Nashville, TN 37203. *Phone:* 615-936-2811. *Toll-free phone:* 800-288-0432. *Fax:* 615-343-8326. *E-mail:* admissions@vanderbilt.edu.

See page 1584 for the College Close-Up.

Visible Music College

Memphis, Tennessee

http://visible.edu/

CONTACT
Visible Music College, 200 Madison Avenue, Memphis, TN 38103.

Watkins College of Art, Design, & Film

Nashville, Tennessee

http://www.watkins.edu/

- **Independent** comprehensive, founded 1885
- **Urban** 13-acre campus
- **Endowment** $1.8 million
- **Coed** 246 undergraduate students, 79% full-time, 59% women, 41% men
- **Moderately difficult** entrance level, 94% of applicants were admitted

UNDERGRAD STUDENTS
194 full-time, 52 part-time. Students come from 26 states and territories; 2 other countries; 27% are from out of state; 14% Black or African American, non-Hispanic/Latino; 6% Hispanic/Latino; 2% Asian, non-Hispanic/Latino; 0.4% Native Hawaiian or other Pacific Islander, non-Hispanic/Latino; 0.4% American Indian or Alaska Native, non-Hispanic/Latino; 6% Two or more races, non-Hispanic/Latino; 0.4% Race/ethnicity unknown; 0.8% international; 9% transferred in; 24% live on campus.

Freshmen:
Admission: 89 applied, 84 admitted, 43 enrolled. ***Test scores:*** SAT writing scores over 500: 50%; ACT scores over 18: 79%; SAT writing scores over 600: 10%; ACT scores over 24: 20%.
Retention: 58% of full-time freshmen returned.

FACULTY
Total: 56, 36% full-time, 64% with terminal degrees.
Student/faculty ratio: 13:1.

ACADEMICS
Calendar: semesters. *Degrees:* bachelor's and master's.
Special study options: advanced placement credit, cooperative education, independent study, internships, part-time degree program, services for LD students, summer session for credit.
Computers: 200 computers/terminals and 175 ports are available on campus for general student use. Students can access the following: campus intranet, computer help desk, free student e-mail accounts, online (class) grades, online (class) registration, online (class) schedules. Campuswide network is available. 100% of college-owned or -operated housing units are wired for high-speed Internet access. Wireless service is available via entire campus.
Library: The Watkins Library plus 1 other.

STUDENT LIFE
Housing options: on-campus residence required for freshman year; men-only, women-only, special housing for students with disabilities. Campus housing is university owned. Freshman applicants given priority for college housing.
Activities and organizations: Company Q (art society), Film club, sports club, Student Government.
Campus security: 24-hour emergency response devices and patrols, late-night transport/escort service, controlled dormitory access, monitored 24 hour camera security.
Student services: health clinic, personal/psychological counseling.

COSTS & FINANCIAL AID
Costs (2016–17) ***Tuition:*** $21,750 full-time, $725 per credit hour part-time. ***Required fees:*** $1950 full-time, $65 per credit hour part-time. ***Room only:*** $6500. ***Payment plan:*** installment. ***Waivers:*** employees or children of employees.
Financial Aid ***Average indebtedness upon graduation:*** $15,000.

APPLYING
Standardized Tests *Required:* SAT or ACT (for admission).
Options: electronic application, early admission, deferred entrance.
Application fee: $50.
Required: essay or personal statement, high school transcript, minimum 2.6 GPA, 1 letter of recommendation. ***Required for some:*** artistic exercises, optional portfolio. ***Recommended:*** interview.
Application deadlines: 7/15 (freshmen), 7/15 (transfers).
Notification: 8/1 (freshmen), 8/1 (transfers).

CONTACT
Ms. Jaime Raybin, Recruiter, Watkins College of Art, Design, & Film, 2298 Rosa L. Parks Boulevard, Nashville, TN 37228. *Phone:* 615-383-4848 Ext. 5397. *Fax:* 615-383-4849. *E-mail:* admissions@watkins.edu.

Welch College

Nashville, Tennessee

http://www.welch.edu/

- **Independent Free Will Baptist** 4-year, founded 1942
- **Urban** 8-acre campus with easy access to Nashville
- **Endowment** $1.5 million
- **Coed** 327 undergraduate students, 67% full-time, 47% women, 53% men
- **Noncompetitive** entrance level, 69% of applicants were admitted

UNDERGRAD STUDENTS
220 full-time, 107 part-time. Students come from 23 states and territories; 1 other country; 58% are from out of state; 9% Black or African American, non-Hispanic/Latino; 3% Hispanic/Latino; 1% Asian, non-Hispanic/Latino; 0.3% American Indian or Alaska Native, non-Hispanic/Latino; 1% Two or more races, non-Hispanic/Latino; 8% international; 6% transferred in; 52% live on campus.

Freshmen:
Admission: 115 applied, 79 admitted, 45 enrolled. ***Average high school GPA:*** 3.34. ***Test scores:*** SAT critical reading scores over 500: 76%; SAT math scores over 500: 44%; SAT writing scores over 500: 55%; SAT critical reading scores over 600: 24%; SAT math scores over 600: 22%; SAT writing scores over 600: 33%; SAT critical reading scores over 700: 12%.
Retention: 66% of full-time freshmen returned.

FACULTY
Total: 58, 28% full-time, 43% with terminal degrees.
Student/faculty ratio: 8:1.

ACADEMICS
Calendar: semesters. *Degrees:* associate and bachelor's.
Special study options: academic remediation for entering students, adult/continuing education programs, advanced placement credit, distance learning, double majors, external degree program, independent study, internships, part-time degree program, student-designed majors, summer session for credit. ***ROTC:*** Army (c), Air Force (c).
Unusual degree programs: nursing.
Computers: 41 computers/terminals are available on campus for general student use. Students can access the following: campus intranet, computer help desk, free student e-mail accounts, online (class) grades, online (class) schedules. Campuswide network is available. 100% of college-owned or -operated housing units are wired for high-speed Internet access. Wireless service is available via computer centers, computer labs, dorm rooms, libraries, student centers.
Library: Welch Library. *Books:* 66,170 (physical), 48,564 (digital/electronic); *Databases:* 56.

STUDENT LIFE
Housing options: on-campus residence required through senior year; men-only, women-only. Campus housing is university owned. Freshman campus housing is guaranteed.

Activities and organizations: drama/theater group, choral group, GMF-Global Missions Fellowship, Four Women's Societies, Four Men's Societies.

Athletics Member NCCAA. ***Intercollegiate sports:*** basketball M/W, golf M/W, volleyball W. ***Intramural sports:*** basketball M/W, tennis M/W, ultimate Frisbee M/W, volleyball M/W.

Campus security: 24-hour emergency response devices, student patrols, late-night transport/escort service, controlled dormitory access.

Student services: personal/psychological counseling.

COSTS & FINANCIAL AID

Costs (2017–18) ***Comprehensive fee:*** $25,936 includes full-time tuition ($18,458) and room and board ($7478). Part-time tuition: $630 per unit. ***College room only:*** $2840. Room and board charges vary according to board plan. ***Payment plans:*** installment, deferred payment. ***Waivers:*** employees or children of employees.

Financial Aid Of all full-time matriculated undergraduates who enrolled in 2011, 178 applied for aid, 172 were judged to have need. 7 Federal Work-Study jobs (averaging $1871). 101 state and other part-time jobs (averaging $1960). ***Average percent of need met:*** 71. ***Average financial aid package:*** $5331. ***Average need-based loan:*** $2195. ***Average need-based gift aid:*** $4214. ***Average indebtedness upon graduation:*** $19,688.

APPLYING

Standardized Tests *Required:* SAT or ACT (for admission).

Options: electronic application, early admission, deferred entrance.

Application fee: $35.

Required: essay or personal statement, high school transcript, 3 letters of recommendation, medical history.

Application deadlines: rolling (freshmen), rolling (out-of-state freshmen), rolling (transfers).

Notification: continuous (freshmen), continuous (out-of-state freshmen), continuous (transfers).

CONTACT

Mrs. Debbie Mouser, Director of Enrollment Services, Welch College, 3606 West End Avenue, Nashville, TN 37205. *Phone:* 615-844-5222. *Toll-free phone:* 800-763-9222. *Fax:* 615-269-6028. *E-mail:* dmouser@welch.edu.

Williamson College

Franklin, Tennessee

http://www.williamsoncc.edu/

- **Independent interdenominational** comprehensive, founded 1997
- **Suburban** 1-acre campus with easy access to Nashville
- **Coed** 41 undergraduate students, 95% full-time, 44% women, 56% men
- **Noncompetitive** entrance level, 100% of applicants were admitted

UNDERGRAD STUDENTS

39 full-time, 2 part-time. Students come from 3 states and territories; 4 other countries; 7% Black or African American, non-Hispanic/Latino; 12% Hispanic/Latino; 2% Asian, non-Hispanic/Latino; 22% transferred in.

Freshmen:

Admission: 11 applied, 11 admitted, 3 enrolled. ***Average high school GPA:*** 3.25.

Retention: 73% of full-time freshmen returned.

FACULTY

Total: 17, 29% full-time.

Student/faculty ratio: 7:1.

ACADEMICS

Calendar: semesters. *Degrees:* associate, bachelor's, and master's.

Special study options: accelerated degree program, adult/continuing education programs, advanced placement credit, distance learning, double majors, external degree program, independent study, internships, part-time degree program.

Computers: 3 computers/terminals are available on campus for general student use. Students can access the following: free student e-mail accounts, online (class) grades, online (class) schedules. Campuswide network is available. Wireless service is available via entire campus.

Library: John W. Neth, Jr. Library plus 1 other. *Books:* 4,836 (physical); *Serial titles:* 11,203 (digital/electronic); *Databases:* 70. Weekly public service hours: 40; students can reserve study rooms.

STUDENT LIFE

Housing options: college housing not available.

Activities and organizations: Student Government Association.

Campus security: 24-hour emergency response devices.

Student services: health clinic, personal/psychological counseling.

COSTS & FINANCIAL AID

Costs (2017–18) ***One-time required fee:*** $150. ***Tuition:*** $12,150 full-time, $425 per semester hour part-time. ***Required fees:*** $600 full-time.

Financial Aid Of all full-time matriculated undergraduates who enrolled in 2003, 11 applied for aid, 10 were judged to have need, 1 had their need fully met. 2 Federal Work-Study jobs (averaging $2000). ***Average percent of need met:*** 50. ***Average financial aid package:*** $4858. ***Average need-based gift aid:*** $2556.

APPLYING

Standardized Tests *Required for some:* SAT or ACT (for admission).

Options: early admission, deferred entrance.

Application fee: $25.

Required: essay or personal statement, high school transcript, minimum 2.0 GPA, 1 letter of recommendation. ***Required for some:*** interview.

Application deadlines: 9/1 (freshmen), 9/1 (transfers).

Notification: continuous until 10/1 (freshmen), continuous until 10/1 (transfers).

CONTACT

Ms. Laura Flowers, Admissions Coordinator, Williamson College, 274 Mallory Station Road, Franklin, TN 37067. *Phone:* 615-771-7821. *Fax:* 615-771-7810. *E-mail:* laura@williamsoncc.edu.

TEXAS

Abilene Christian University

Abilene, Texas

http://www.acu.edu/

- **Independent** university, founded 1906, affiliated with Church of Christ
- **Urban** 208-acre campus
- **Endowment** $351.0 million
- **Coed** 3,758 undergraduate students, 95% full-time, 59% women, 41% men
- **Moderately difficult** entrance level, 51% of applicants were admitted

UNDERGRAD STUDENTS

3,562 full-time, 196 part-time. Students come from 51 states and territories; 40 other countries; 13% are from out of state; 9% Black or African American, non-Hispanic/Latino; 16% Hispanic/Latino; 1% Asian, non-Hispanic/Latino; 0.1% Native Hawaiian or other Pacific Islander, non-Hispanic/Latino; 0.3% American Indian or Alaska Native, non-Hispanic/Latino; 5% Two or more races, non-Hispanic/Latino; 0.2% Race/ethnicity unknown; 4% international; 3% transferred in; 49% live on campus.

Freshmen:

Admission: 10,252 applied, 5,217 admitted, 1,047 enrolled. ***Average high school GPA:*** 3.64. ***Test scores:*** SAT critical reading scores over 500: 64%; SAT math scores over 500: 62%; SAT writing scores over 500: 51%; ACT scores over 18: 95%; SAT critical reading scores over 600: 22%; SAT math scores over 600: 22%; SAT writing scores over 600: 16%; ACT scores over 24: 54%; SAT critical reading scores over 700: 4%; SAT math scores over 700: 2%; SAT writing scores over 700: 2%; ACT scores over 30: 13%.

Retention: 76% of full-time freshmen returned.

FACULTY

Total: 416, 61% full-time, 67% with terminal degrees.

Student/faculty ratio: 14:1.

ACADEMICS
Calendar: semesters. *Degrees:* certificates, associate, bachelor's, master's, doctoral, post-master's, and postbachelor's certificates.

Special study options: advanced placement credit, distance learning, double majors, English as a second language, honors programs, independent study, internships, off-campus study, part-time degree program, services for LD students, student-designed majors, study abroad, summer session for credit.

Computers: 466 computers/terminals and 3,900 ports are available on campus for general student use. Students can access the following: campus intranet, computer help desk, free student e-mail accounts, online (class) grades, online (class) registration, online (class) schedules. Campuswide network is available. 100% of college-owned or -operated housing units are wired for high-speed Internet access. Wireless service is available via entire campus.
Library: Brown Library. *Books:* 543,851 (physical), 281,582 (digital/electronic); *Serial titles:* 4,182 (physical), 51,856 (digital/electronic); *Databases:* 116. Weekly public service hours: 97; students can reserve study rooms.

STUDENT LIFE
Housing options: on-campus residence required through sophomore year; men-only, women-only. Campus housing is university owned. Freshman campus housing is guaranteed.
Activities and organizations: drama/theater group, student-run newspaper, radio and television station, choral group, marching band, Student Association, Graduate Students Association, Spring Break Campaigns, International Students Association, LYNAY.

Athletics Member NCAA. All Division I. ***Intercollegiate sports:*** baseball M(s), basketball M(s)/W(s), cross-country running M(s)/W(s), football M(s), golf M(s), soccer W(s), softball W(s), tennis M(s)/W(s), track and field M(s)/W(s), volleyball W(s). ***Intramural sports:*** basketball M/W, football M/W, golf M(c)/W(c), lacrosse M(c), racquetball M/W, rugby M(c), soccer M(c)/W, softball M/W, table tennis M/W, tennis M/W, volleyball M/W.

Campus security: 24-hour emergency response devices and patrols, student patrols, late-night transport/escort service, controlled dormitory access.
Student services: health clinic, personal/psychological counseling.

COSTS & FINANCIAL AID
Costs (2016–17) ***Comprehensive fee:*** $41,800 includes full-time tuition ($32,020), mandatory fees ($50), and room and board ($9730). Full-time tuition and fees vary according to course load. Part-time tuition: $1334 per credit hour. Part-time tuition and fees vary according to course load. ***College room only:*** $4690. Room and board charges vary according to board plan and housing facility. ***Payment plans:*** tuition prepayment, installment. ***Waivers:*** employees or children of employees.

Financial Aid Of all full-time matriculated undergraduates who enrolled in 2016, 2,770 applied for aid, 2,391 were judged to have need, 613 had their need fully met. In 2016, 1219 non-need-based awards were made. ***Average percent of need met:*** 68. ***Average financial aid package:*** $22,694. ***Average need-based loan:*** $4404. ***Average need-based gift aid:*** $19,776. ***Average non-need-based aid:*** $12,246.

APPLYING
Standardized Tests *Required:* SAT or ACT (for admission).

Options: electronic application, early admission, early action.

Application fee: $50.

Required: high school transcript. ***Required for some:*** essay or personal statement.

Application deadlines: 2/15 (freshmen), rolling (transfers).

Notification: 3/15 (freshmen), continuous until 9/1 (transfers).

CONTACT
Admissions, Abilene Christian University, ACU Box 29000, Abilene, TX 79699-9000. *Phone:* 325-674-2650. *Toll-free phone:* 800-460-6228. *Fax:* 325-674-2130. *E-mail:* info@admissions.acu.edu.

Amberton University
Garland, Texas
http://www.amberton.edu/

- **Independent nondenominational** upper-level, founded 1971
- **Suburban** 5-acre campus with easy access to Dallas-Fort Worth
- **Endowment** $10.0 million
- **Coed**
- **Minimally difficult** entrance level

FACULTY
Student/faculty ratio: 25:1.

ACADEMICS
Calendar: 4 10-week terms. *Degrees:* bachelor's and master's.
Library: Library Resource Center plus 1 other.

STUDENT LIFE
Housing options: college housing not available.

Campus security: 24-hour emergency response devices and patrols.

COSTS
Costs (2016–17) ***Tuition:*** $12,000 full-time, $250 per credit hour part-time.

APPLYING
Options: electronic application, deferred entrance.

CONTACT
Academic Dean, Amberton University, 1700 Eastgate Drive, Garland, TX 75041-5595. *Phone:* 972-279-6511. *E-mail:* advisor@amberton.edu.

American InterContinental University Houston
Houston, Texas
http://www.aiuniv.edu/

CONTACT
American InterContinental University Houston, 9999 Richmond Avenue, Houston, TX 77042. *Phone:* 877-564-6248. *Toll-free phone:* 888-607-9888.

Angelo State University
San Angelo, Texas
http://www.angelo.edu/

- **State-supported** comprehensive, founded 1928, part of Texas Tech University System
- **Urban** 268-acre campus
- **Endowment** $158.8 million
- **Coed** 8,094 undergraduate students, 64% full-time, 55% women, 45% men
- **Moderately difficult** entrance level, 74% of applicants were admitted

UNDERGRAD STUDENTS
5,198 full-time, 2,896 part-time. Students come from 42 states and territories; 22 other countries; 2% are from out of state; 7% Black or African American, non-Hispanic/Latino; 32% Hispanic/Latino; 1% Asian, non-Hispanic/Latino; 0.1% Native Hawaiian or other Pacific Islander, non-Hispanic/Latino; 0.4% American Indian or Alaska Native, non-Hispanic/Latino; 3% Two or more races, non-Hispanic/Latino; 0.1% Race/ethnicity unknown; 3% international; 5% transferred in; 38% live on campus.

Freshmen:
Admission: 4,368 applied, 3,248 admitted, 1,583 enrolled. ***Test scores:*** SAT critical reading scores over 500: 63%; SAT math scores over 500: 59%; ACT scores over 18: 70%; SAT critical reading scores over 600: 14%; SAT math scores over 600: 12%; ACT scores over 24: 34%; ACT scores over 30: 2%.
Retention: 67% of full-time freshmen returned.

FACULTY
Total: 381, 70% full-time, 61% with terminal degrees.
Student/faculty ratio: 21:1.

ACADEMICS
Calendar: semesters. *Degrees:* bachelor's, master's, and doctoral.

Special study options: academic remediation for entering students, advanced placement credit, distance learning, double majors, English as a second language, honors programs, independent study, internships, part-time degree program, study abroad, summer session for credit. ***ROTC:*** Air Force (b).

Unusual degree programs: 3-2 business administration.

Computers: 750 computers/terminals and 3,900 ports are available on campus for general student use. Students can access the following: campus intranet, computer help desk, free student e-mail accounts, online (class) grades, online (class) registration, online (class) schedules, online courses, tuition payments, book purchase, parking permits, university calendar, discounted hardware and software. Campuswide network is available. 100% of college-owned or -operated housing units are wired for high-speed Internet access. Wireless service is available via entire campus.

Library: Porter Henderson Library. *Books:* 484,935 (physical), 85,670 (digital/electronic); *Serial titles:* 128 (physical), 61,918 (digital/electronic); *Databases:* 154. Weekly public service hours: 130; study areas open 24 hours, 5-7 days a week; students can reserve study rooms.

STUDENT LIFE
Housing options: on-campus residence required through sophomore year; coed, special housing for students with disabilities. Campus housing is university owned.

Activities and organizations: drama/theater group, student-run newspaper, radio and television station, choral group, marching band, Association of Mexican-American Students, Block and Bridle Club, Air force ROTC, University Center Program Council, Baptist Student Union, national fraternities, national sororities.

Athletics Member NCAA. All Division II. ***Intercollegiate sports:*** baseball M(s), basketball M(s)/W(s), cross-country running M(s)/W(s), football M(s), golf W(s), soccer W(s), softball W(s), track and field M(s)/W(s), volleyball W(s). ***Intramural sports:*** badminton M/W, basketball M/W, bowling M/W, football M/W, golf M/W, racquetball M/W, soccer M/W, softball M/W, swimming and diving M/W, table tennis M/W, tennis M/W, ultimate Frisbee M/W, volleyball M/W, weight lifting M/W.

Campus security: 24-hour emergency response devices and patrols, student patrols, late-night transport/escort service, controlled dormitory access.

Student services: health clinic, personal/psychological counseling.

COSTS & FINANCIAL AID
Costs (2016–17) ***Tuition:*** state resident $4956 full-time, $165 per credit hour part-time; nonresident $17,196 full-time, $573 per credit hour part-time. Full-time tuition and fees vary according to course load. Part-time tuition and fees vary according to course load. No tuition increase for student's term of enrollment. ***Required fees:*** $3082 full-time. ***Room and board:*** $7666. Room and board charges vary according to board plan and housing facility. ***Payment plan:*** installment.

Financial Aid Of all full-time matriculated undergraduates who enrolled in 2015, 3,675 applied for aid, 2,805 were judged to have need, 482 had their need fully met. In 2015, 910 non-need-based awards were made. ***Average percent of need met:*** 83. ***Average financial aid package:*** $11,500. ***Average need-based loan:*** $3786. ***Average need-based gift aid:*** $3220. ***Average non-need-based aid:*** $3781. ***Average indebtedness upon graduation:*** $24,099.

APPLYING
Standardized Tests *Required:* SAT or ACT (for admission).

Options: electronic application, early admission, deferred entrance.

Application fee: $35.

Required: high school transcript, high school class rank.

Application deadlines: rolling (freshmen), rolling (transfers).

Notification: continuous (freshmen), continuous (transfers).

CONTACT
Ms. Sharla Adam, Director of Admissions, Angelo State University, 2601 West Avenue N., San Angelo, TX 76909. *Phone:* 325-942-2185. *Toll-free phone:* 800-946-8627. *Fax:* 325-942-2078.
E-mail: admissions@angelo.edu.

Argosy University, Dallas
Farmers Branch, Texas
http://www.argosy.edu/dallas-texas/default.aspx

CONTACT
Argosy University, Dallas, 5001 Lyndon B. Johnson Freeway, Heritage Square, Farmers Branch, TX 75244. *Phone:* 214-890-9900.
Toll-free phone: 866-954-9900.

Arlington Baptist College
Arlington, Texas
http://www.arlingtonbaptistcollege.edu/

- **Independent Baptist** comprehensive, founded 1939
- **Urban** 32-acre campus with easy access to Dallas-Fort Worth
- **Endowment** $17,000
- **Coed** 184 undergraduate students, 84% full-time, 45% women, 55% men
- **Noncompetitive** entrance level, 100% of applicants were admitted

UNDERGRAD STUDENTS
154 full-time, 30 part-time. Students come from 7 states and territories; 1 other country; 6% are from out of state; 24% Black or African American, non-Hispanic/Latino; 10% Hispanic/Latino; 0.5% Asian, non-Hispanic/Latino; 0.5% Native Hawaiian or other Pacific Islander, non-Hispanic/Latino; 3% American Indian or Alaska Native, non-Hispanic/Latino; 1% Race/ethnicity unknown; 20% transferred in; 46% live on campus.

Freshmen:
Admission: 80 applied, 80 admitted, 28 enrolled.

Retention: 42% of full-time freshmen returned.

FACULTY
Total: 28, 43% full-time, 29% with terminal degrees.

Student/faculty ratio: 10:1.

ACADEMICS
Calendar: semesters. *Degrees:* bachelor's and master's.

Special study options: academic remediation for entering students, advanced placement credit, distance learning, double majors, independent study, internships, part-time degree program, summer session for credit.

Computers: 25 computers/terminals are available on campus for general student use. Students can access the following: online (class) grades, online (class) registration, online (class) schedules. Campuswide network is available. Wireless service is available via classrooms, computer labs, dorm rooms, libraries, student centers.

Library: Earl K. Oldham Library.

STUDENT LIFE
Housing options: on-campus residence required through senior year; men-only, women-only. Campus housing is university owned. Freshman campus housing is guaranteed.

Activities and organizations: drama/theater group, choral group, Collegians.

Athletics Member NCCAA. ***Intercollegiate sports:*** baseball M, basketball M/W, cross-country running M/W, volleyball W.

Campus security: controlled dormitory access, night security guards.

Student services: personal/psychological counseling.

COSTS & FINANCIAL AID
Costs (2017–18) ***One-time required fee:*** $250. ***Comprehensive fee:*** $20,430 includes full-time tuition ($13,100), mandatory fees ($930), and room and board ($6400). Full-time tuition and fees vary according to course load and degree level. Part-time tuition: $400 per credit hour. Part-time tuition and fees vary according to course load and degree level. ***Required fees:*** $445 per term part-time. ***Payment plan:*** installment. ***Waivers:*** employees or children of employees.

Financial Aid Of all full-time matriculated undergraduates who enrolled in 2006, 164 applied for aid, 118 were judged to have need, 93 had their need fully met. ***Average financial aid package:*** $6847. ***Average indebtedness upon graduation:*** $4838.

APPLYING
Options: electronic application, early admission, deferred entrance.

Application fee: $25.

Required: essay or personal statement, high school transcript, 1 letter of recommendation, pastoral recommendation, medical examination. ***Required for some:*** interview.

Application deadlines: rolling (freshmen), rolling (transfers).

Notification: continuous (freshmen), continuous (transfers).

CONTACT

Mrs. Kim Marvin, Admissions, Arlington Baptist College, 3001 West Division, Arlington, TX 76012-3425. *Phone:* 817-461-8741. *Fax:* 817-274-1138. *E-mail:* kmarvin@arlingtonbaptistcollege.edu.

The Art Institute of Austin, a branch of The Art Institute of Houston

Austin, Texas

http://www.artinstitutes.edu/austin

CONTACT

The Art Institute of Austin, a branch of The Art Institute of Houston, 101 W. Louis Henna Boulevard, Suite 100, Austin, TX 78728. *Phone:* 512-691-1707. *Toll-free phone:* 866-583-7952.

The Art Institute of Dallas, a branch of Miami International University of Art & Design

Dallas, Texas

http://www.artinstitutes.edu/dallas/

CONTACT

The Art Institute of Dallas, a branch of Miami International University of Art & Design, 8080 Park Lane, Suite 100, Dallas, TX 75231-5993. *Phone:* 214-692-8080. *Toll-free phone:* 800-275-4243.

The Art Institute of Houston

Houston, Texas

http://www.artinstitutes.edu/houston/

CONTACT

The Art Institute of Houston, 4140 Southwest Freeway, Houston, TX 77027. *Phone:* 713-623-2040. *Toll-free phone:* 800-275-4244.

The Art Institute of San Antonio, a branch of The Art Institute of Houston

San Antonio, Texas

http://www.artinstitutes.edu/san-antonio/

CONTACT

The Art Institute of San Antonio, a branch of The Art Institute of Houston, 1000 IH-10 West, Suite 200, San Antonio, TX 78230. *Phone:* 210-338-7320. *Toll-free phone:* 888-222-0040.

Austin College

Sherman, Texas

http://www.austincollege.edu/

- **Independent Presbyterian** comprehensive, founded 1849
- **Small-town** 60-acre campus with easy access to Dallas-Fort Worth
- **Endowment** $125.6 million
- **Coed** 1,278 undergraduate students, 100% full-time, 52% women, 48% men
- **Very difficult** entrance level, 53% of applicants were admitted

UNDERGRAD STUDENTS

1,273 full-time, 5 part-time. Students come from 37 states and territories; 24 other countries; 9% are from out of state; 8% Black or African American, non-Hispanic/Latino; 19% Hispanic/Latino; 14% Asian, non-Hispanic/Latino; 0.2% Native Hawaiian or other Pacific Islander, non-Hispanic/Latino; 1% American Indian or Alaska Native, non-Hispanic/Latino; 3% Two or more races, non-Hispanic/Latino; 0.1% Race/ethnicity unknown; 3% international; 3% transferred in; 82% live on campus.

Freshmen:
Admission: 3,352 applied, 1,791 admitted, 345 enrolled. ***Average high school GPA:*** 3.52. ***Test scores:*** SAT critical reading scores over 500: 91%; SAT math scores over 500: 87%; SAT writing scores over 500: 80%; ACT scores over 18: 99%; SAT critical reading scores over 600: 55%; SAT math scores over 600: 55%; SAT writing scores over 600: 39%; ACT scores over 24: 74%; SAT critical reading scores over 700: 13%; SAT math scores over 700: 14%; SAT writing scores over 700: 9%; ACT scores over 30: 20%.

Retention: 83% of full-time freshmen returned.

FACULTY

Total: 106, 89% full-time, 93% with terminal degrees.

Student/faculty ratio: 13:1.

ACADEMICS

Calendar: 4-1-4. *Degrees:* bachelor's and master's.

Special study options: advanced placement credit, double majors, honors programs, independent study, internships, off-campus study, part-time degree program, services for LD students, student-designed majors, study abroad, summer session for credit.

Unusual degree programs: 3-2 engineering with University of Texas at Dallas, Texas A&M University, Washington University in St. Louis, Columbia University.

Computers: 160 computers/terminals are available on campus for general student use. Students can access the following: campus intranet, computer help desk, free student e-mail accounts, online (class) grades, online (class) registration, online (class) schedules. Campuswide network is available. 100% of college-owned or -operated housing units are wired for high-speed Internet access. Wireless service is available via entire campus.

Library: Abell Library. *Books:* 227,390 (physical). Study areas open 24 hours, 5-7 days a week; students can reserve study rooms.

STUDENT LIFE

Housing options: on-campus residence required through junior year; coed, men-only, women-only, special housing for students with disabilities. Campus housing is university owned. Freshman campus housing is guaranteed.

Activities and organizations: drama/theater group, student-run newspaper, choral group, Inter-Varsity Christian Fellowship (IVCF), Campus Activity Board (CAB), Indian Cultural Association, Students Today Alumni Tomorrow (STAT), ACtivators.

Athletics Member NCAA. All Division III. ***Intercollegiate sports:*** baseball M, basketball M/W, cheerleading M(c)/W(c), cross-country running M/W, football M, soccer M/W, softball W, swimming and diving M/W, tennis M/W, volleyball W. ***Intramural sports:*** basketball M/W, football M/W, soccer M/W, softball M/W, ultimate Frisbee M/W, volleyball M/W.

Campus security: 24-hour emergency response devices and patrols, late-night transport/escort service, controlled dormitory access.

Student services: health clinic, personal/psychological counseling.

COSTS & FINANCIAL AID

Costs (2017–18) ***One-time required fee:*** $25. ***Comprehensive fee:*** $51,344 includes full-time tuition ($38,825), mandatory fees ($185), and room and board ($12,334). Full-time tuition and fees vary according to student level. ***Room and board:*** Room and board charges vary according to board plan and housing facility. ***Payment plan:*** installment. ***Waivers:*** employees or children of employees.

Financial Aid Of all full-time matriculated undergraduates who enrolled in 2016, 952 applied for aid, 834 were judged to have need, 354 had their need fully met. 345 Federal Work-Study jobs (averaging $1844). 119 state and other part-time jobs (averaging $1464). In 2016, 423 non-need-based awards were made. ***Average percent of need met:*** 94. ***Average financial aid package:*** $34,859. ***Average need-based loan:*** $4792. ***Average need-based gift aid:*** $29,091. ***Average non-need-based aid:*** $22,355.

APPLYING

Standardized Tests *Required:* SAT or ACT (for admission).

Options: electronic application, early admission, early decision, early action, deferred entrance.

Required: essay or personal statement, high school transcript, 2 letters of recommendation. ***Recommended:*** minimum 3.0 GPA, interview.

Application deadlines: 3/1 (freshmen), 8/1 (transfers), 12/1 (early action).

Early decision deadline: 11/1 (for plan 1), 1/15 (for plan 2).

Notification: 4/1 (freshmen), 12/4 (early decision plan 1), 3/1 (early decision plan 2), 1/15 (early action).

CONTACT

Mrs. Nan Davis, Vice President for Institutional Enrollment, Austin College, 900 North Grand Avenue, Suite 6N, Sherman, TX 75090-4400. *Phone:* 903-813-3000. *Toll-free phone:* 800-596-4276 (in-state); 800-526.4276 (out-of-state). *Fax:* 903-813-3198.
E-mail: admission@austincollege.edu.

Austin Graduate School of Theology

Austin, Texas

http://www.austingrad.edu/

- **Independent** upper-level, founded 1917, affiliated with Church of Christ
- **Urban** 2-acre campus with easy access to Austin
- **Endowment** $4.0 million
- **Coed** 20 undergraduate students, 20% full-time, 45% women, 55% men
- **Minimally difficult** entrance level

UNDERGRAD STUDENTS

4 full-time, 16 part-time. Students come from 1 other state; 1 other country; 1% are from out of state; 60% Black or African American, non-Hispanic/Latino; 5% Hispanic/Latino.

FACULTY

Total: 10, 40% full-time, 80% with terminal degrees.

Student/faculty ratio: 4:1.

ACADEMICS

Calendar: semesters. *Degrees:* bachelor's and master's.

Special study options: adult/continuing education programs, part-time degree program, summer session for credit.

Computers: 6 computers/terminals are available on campus for general student use. Campuswide network is available. Wireless service is available via entire campus.

Library: David Worley Library.

STUDENT LIFE

Housing options: college housing not available.

Activities and organizations: Student Association (government).

COSTS

Costs (2017–18) ***Tuition:*** $8400 full-time, $350 per credit hour part-time. ***Required fees:*** $350 full-time, $175 per term part-time. ***Payment plan:*** installment.

APPLYING

Options: electronic application, early admission, deferred entrance.

CONTACT

Dawn Bond, Director of Admissions, Austin Graduate School of Theology, 7640 Guadalupe Street, Austin, TX 78752.
Phone: 512-476-2772. *Toll-free phone:* 866-AUS-GRAD.
Fax: 512-476-3919.
E-mail: registrar@austingrad.edu.

Baptist Health System School of Health Professions

San Antonio, Texas

http://www.bshp.edu/

CONTACT

Baptist Health System School of Health Professions, 8400 Datapoint Drive, San Antonio, TX 78229.

Baptist Missionary Association Theological Seminary

Jacksonville, Texas

http://www.bmats.edu/

CONTACT

Baptist Missionary Association Theological Seminary, 1530 East Pine Street, Jacksonville, TX 75766-5407. *Phone:* 903-586-2501 Ext. 229. *Toll-free phone:* 800-259-5673.

Baptist University of the Americas

San Antonio, Texas

http://www.bua.edu/

- **Independent Baptist** 4-year, founded 1947
- **Urban** 75-acre campus with easy access to San Antonio
- **Endowment** $3.2 million
- **Coed** 195 undergraduate students, 66% full-time, 48% women, 52% men

UNDERGRAD STUDENTS

128 full-time, 67 part-time. Students come from 3 states and territories; 14 other countries; 21% are from out of state; 2% Black or African American, non-Hispanic/Latino; 70% Hispanic/Latino; 1% Asian, non-Hispanic/Latino; 21% international; 9% transferred in; 40% live on campus.

Freshmen:

Admission: 30 enrolled.

Retention: 87% of full-time freshmen returned.

FACULTY

Total: 40, 23% full-time, 35% with terminal degrees.

Student/faculty ratio: 7:1.

ACADEMICS

Calendar: semesters May term is a two week intensive course. *Degrees:* certificates, diplomas, associate, bachelor's, and postbachelor's certificates (associate degree in Cross-Cultural Studies).

Special study options: academic remediation for entering students, advanced placement credit, double majors, English as a second language, honors programs, independent study, internships, off-campus study, part-time degree program, services for LD students.

Computers: 122 computers/terminals and 328 ports are available on campus for general student use. Students can access the following: campus intranet, computer help desk, free student e-mail accounts, online (class) grades, online (class) registration, online (class) schedules. Campuswide network is available. 100% of college-owned or -operated housing units are wired for high-speed Internet access. Wireless service is available via entire campus.

Library: Baptist University of the Americas Learning Resource Center. *Books:* 21,947 (physical), 362 (digital/electronic); *Serial titles:* 252 (physical), 252 (digital/electronic); *Databases:* 8. Weekly public service hours: 72; students can reserve study rooms.

STUDENT LIFE

Housing options: coed, men-only, women-only, special housing for students with disabilities. Campus housing is university owned. Freshman campus housing is guaranteed.

Activities and organizations: choral group, Called Club, Spanish Club, Missions Society, Business Society, BUA Band.

Athletics ***Intramural sports:*** soccer M(c).

Campus security: 24-hour emergency response devices, student patrols, late-night transport/escort service, gate code is required to enter the residence area.

Student services: personal/psychological counseling.

COSTS & FINANCIAL AID

Costs (2017–18) ***Tuition:*** $5520 full-time, $230 per credit hour part-time. ***Required fees:*** $720 full-time, $30 per credit hour part-time. ***Room only:*** $2500. Room and board charges vary according to housing facility. ***Payment plan:*** installment. ***Waivers:*** employees or children of employees.

Financial Aid Of all full-time matriculated undergraduates who enrolled in 2015, 4 Federal Work-Study jobs (averaging $1265). 114 state and other part-time jobs (averaging $2740).

APPLYING

Standardized Tests *Required:* SAT and SAT Subject Tests or ACT (for admission), ACCUPLACER, THEA, CPT and TSI (for admission). *Recommended:* SAT (for admission), ACT (for admission), SAT or ACT (for admission).

Required: essay or personal statement, high school transcript, minimum 2.0 GPA, 2 letters of recommendation, meningitis vaccination for students under 22 years. ***Required for some:*** minimum 2.0 GPA, 2 letters of recommendation, interview. ***Recommended:*** minimum 2.0 GPA, 2 letters of recommendation.

CONTACT

Admissions Counselor, Baptist University of the Americas, 8019 Pan Am Expressway, San Antonio, TX 78224. *Phone:* 210-924-4338 Ext. 229. *Toll-free phone:* 800-721-1396. *Fax:* 210-924-2701. *E-mail:* admissions@bua.edu.

Baylor University

Waco, Texas

http://www.baylor.edu/

- **Independent Baptist** university, founded 1845
- **Urban** 1000-acre campus with easy access to Dallas-Fort Worth
- **Endowment** $1.2 billion
- **Coed** 14,348 undergraduate students, 98% full-time, 58% women, 42% men
- **Moderately difficult** entrance level, 40% of applicants were admitted

UNDERGRAD STUDENTS

14,109 full-time, 239 part-time. Students come from 51 states and territories; 86 other countries; 29% are from out of state; 7% Black or African American, non-Hispanic/Latino; 15% Hispanic/Latino; 6% Asian, non-Hispanic/Latino; 0.3% American Indian or Alaska Native, non-Hispanic/Latino; 5% Two or more races, non-Hispanic/Latino; 0.3% Race/ethnicity unknown; 3% international; 3% transferred in; 34% live on campus.

Freshmen:

Admission: 34,636 applied, 13,758 admitted, 3,503 enrolled. ***Test scores:*** SAT critical reading scores over 500: 93%; SAT math scores over 500: 97%; SAT writing scores over 500: 87%; ACT scores over 18: 100%; SAT critical reading scores over 600: 51%; SAT math scores over 600: 60%; SAT writing scores over 600: 41%; ACT scores over 24: 91%; SAT critical reading scores over 700: 12%; SAT math scores over 700: 15%; SAT writing scores over 700: 8%; ACT scores over 30: 34%.

Retention: 89% of full-time freshmen returned.

FACULTY

Total: 1,290, 79% full-time.

Student/faculty ratio: 15:1.

ACADEMICS

Calendar: semesters. *Degrees:* certificates, bachelor's, master's, doctoral, and post-master's certificates.

Special study options: accelerated degree program, advanced placement credit, double majors, honors programs, internships, part-time degree program, services for LD students, student-designed majors, study abroad, summer session for credit. ***ROTC:*** Army (b), Air Force (b).

Unusual degree programs: 3-2 clinical laboratory science.

Computers: Students can access the following: campus intranet, computer help desk, free student e-mail accounts, online (class) grades, online (class) registration, online (class) schedules. Campuswide network is available. 99% of college-owned or -operated housing units are wired for high-speed Internet access. Wireless service is available via entire campus.

Library: Moody Memorial Library plus 8 others.

STUDENT LIFE

Housing options: on-campus residence required for freshman year; coed, men-only, women-only, special housing for students with disabilities. Campus housing is university owned. Freshman campus housing is guaranteed.

Activities and organizations: drama/theater group, student-run newspaper, radio and television station, choral group, marching band, The Bear Pit, Alpha Lambda Delta, Delta Epsilon Iota, National Society of Collegiate Scholars, American Medical Student Association, national fraternities, national sororities.

Athletics Member NCAA. All Division I except football (Division I-A). ***Intercollegiate sports:*** baseball M(s), basketball M(s)/W(s), cheerleading M(s)/W(s), cross-country running M(s)/W(s), equestrian sports W(s), golf M(s)/W(s), soccer W(s), softball W(s), tennis M(s)/W(s), track and field M(s)/W(s), volleyball W(s). ***Intramural sports:*** baseball M(c), basketball M/W, bowling M/W, crew M(c)/W(c), cross-country running M/W, fencing M(c)/W(c), football M/W, golf M(c)/W(c), gymnastics M(c)/W(c), lacrosse M(c)/W(c), racquetball M/W, rock climbing M(c)/W(c), rugby M(c), sailing M(c)/W(c), skiing (downhill) M(c)/W(c), soccer M(c)/W(c), softball M/W, swimming and diving M(c)/W(c), table tennis M/W, tennis M(c)/W(c), track and field M/W, triathlon M(c)/W(c), ultimate Frisbee M(c)/W(c), volleyball M(c)/W(c), water polo M(c)/W(c).

Campus security: 24-hour emergency response devices and patrols, late-night transport/escort service, controlled dormitory access, bicycle patrols.

Student services: health clinic, personal/psychological counseling, legal services.

COSTS & FINANCIAL AID

Costs (2017–18) ***Comprehensive fee:*** $55,953 includes full-time tuition ($39,610), mandatory fees ($4180), and room and board ($12,163). Part-time tuition: $1650 per semester hour. ***Required fees:*** $174 per semester hour part-time. ***College room only:*** $6650. Room and board charges vary according to board plan and housing facility. ***Payment plan:*** installment. ***Waivers:*** employees or children of employees.

Financial Aid Of all full-time matriculated undergraduates who enrolled in 2016, 9,090 applied for aid, 7,660 were judged to have need, 1,154 had their need fully met. 5,154 Federal Work-Study jobs (averaging $2930). In 2016, 5263 non-need-based awards were made. ***Average percent of need met:*** 65. ***Average financial aid package:*** $28,278. ***Average need-based loan:*** $3537. ***Average need-based gift aid:*** $22,291. ***Average non-need-based aid:*** $13,976. ***Average indebtedness upon graduation:*** $44,540.

APPLYING

Standardized Tests *Required:* SAT or ACT (for admission).

Options: electronic application, early admission, early action.

Required: high school transcript. ***Required for some:*** essay or personal statement, minimum 2.5 GPA, 2 letters of recommendation.

Application deadlines: 2/1 (freshmen), rolling (transfers), 11/1 (early action).

Notification: 4/10 (freshmen), continuous (transfers), 1/15 (early action).

CONTACT

Ms. Jessica King Gereghty, Assistant Vice President of Undergraduate Admissions, Baylor University, PO Box 97056, Waco, TX 76798. *Phone:* 254-710-3435. *Toll-free phone:* 800-BAYLORU. *Fax:* 254-710-3436. *E-mail:* admissions@baylor.edu.

Brazosport College

Lake Jackson, Texas

http://www.brazosport.edu/

CONTACT

Brazosport College, 500 College Drive, Lake Jackson, TX 77566-3199. *Phone:* 979-230-3020.

Chamberlain College of Nursing

Houston, Texas

http://www.chamberlain.edu/

- **Proprietary** 4-year
- **Coed**
- **Moderately difficult** entrance level

FACULTY

Student/faculty ratio: 9:1.

ACADEMICS

Degree: bachelor's.

STUDENT LIFE
Housing options: college housing not available.

COSTS
Costs (2016–17) ***Tuition:*** $18,900 full-time, $675 per credit hour part-time. ***Required fees:*** $600 full-time.

APPLYING
Standardized Tests *Required:* SAT or ACT (for admission).
Options: deferred entrance.
Application fee: $95.

CONTACT
Director of Recruitment, Chamberlain College of Nursing, 11025 Equity Drive, Houston, TX 77041. *Phone:* 713-277-9800. *Toll-free phone:* 877-751-5783.

Chamberlain College of Nursing

Pearland, Texas

http://www.chamberlain.edu/

- **Proprietary** 4-year
- **Coed**

FACULTY
Student/faculty ratio: 11:1.

ACADEMICS
Degree: bachelor's.

STUDENT LIFE
Housing options: college housing not available.

COSTS
Costs (2016–17) ***Tuition:*** $18,900 full-time, $675 per credit hour part-time. ***Required fees:*** $600 full-time.

APPLYING
Standardized Tests *Required:* SAT or ACT (for admission).
Options: deferred entrance.
Application fee: $95.

CONTACT
Chamberlain College of Nursing, 12000 Shadow Creek Parkway, Pearland, TX 77584. *Toll-free phone:* 877-751-5783.

College of Biblical Studies–Houston

Houston, Texas

http://www.cbshouston.edu/

- **Independent nondenominational** 4-year, founded 1979
- **Urban** 12-acre campus with easy access to Houston
- **Endowment** $1.4 million
- **Coed**
- **Noncompetitive** entrance level

ACADEMICS
Calendar: semesters. *Degrees:* certificates, associate, and bachelor's.
Library: College of Biblical Studies Library. *Books:* 88,005 (physical), 161,601 (digital/electronic); *Serial titles:* 476 (physical), 5,325 (digital/electronic). Weekly public service hours: 53; students can reserve study rooms.

STUDENT LIFE
Housing options: college housing not available.
Activities and organizations: choral group, Student Ministries.
Campus security: 24-hour emergency response devices, late-night transport/escort service, hourly patrols by trained security guards and police.
Student services: personal/psychological counseling.

COSTS & FINANCIAL AID
Costs (2016–17) ***Tuition:*** $6946 full-time, $274 per credit hour part-time. Full-time tuition and fees vary according to program. Part-time tuition and fees vary according to program. ***Required fees:*** $370 full-time, $185 per term part-time. ***Payment plans:*** installment, deferred payment.
Financial Aid ***Financial aid deadline:*** 8/5.

APPLYING
Options: electronic application.
Application fee: $40.
Required: essay or personal statement, high school transcript. ***Required for some:*** interview.

CONTACT
Mrs. Maggie Rodriguez, Admissions, College of Biblical Studies–Houston, 7000 Regency Square Boulevard, Houston, TX 77036. *Phone:* 832-252-3377. *Toll-free phone:* 844-227-9673. *Fax:* 713-532-8150. *E-mail:* admissions@cbshouston.edu.

★ Concordia University Texas

Austin, Texas

http://www.concordia.edu/

CONTACT
Ms. Kristin Coulter, Director of Admissions, Concordia University Texas, 11400 Concordia University Drive, Austin, TX 78726. *Phone:* 800-865-4282. *Toll-free phone:* 800-865-4282. *Fax:* 512-313-3999. *E-mail:* admissions@concordia.edu.

Criswell College

Dallas, Texas

http://www.criswell.edu/

- **Independent** comprehensive, founded 1970, affiliated with Southern Baptist Convention
- **Urban** 1-acre campus
- **Coed**
- **Minimally difficult** entrance level

ACADEMICS
Calendar: semesters. *Degrees:* associate, bachelor's, and master's.
Special study options: part-time degree program, summer session for credit.
Library: Wallace Library.

STUDENT LIFE
Housing options: college housing not available.
Campus security: 24-hour emergency response devices and patrols, late-night transport/escort service.

COSTS & FINANCIAL AID
Costs (2017–18) ***Tuition:*** $9120 full-time, $380 per credit hour part-time. Full-time tuition and fees vary according to course load. Part-time tuition and fees vary according to course load. ***Required fees:*** $738 full-time, $738 per year part-time. ***Payment plan:*** installment. ***Waivers:*** employees or children of employees.
Financial Aid Of all full-time matriculated undergraduates who enrolled in 2015, 209 applied for aid, 177 were judged to have need, 164 had their need fully met. 16 state and other part-time jobs (averaging $7200). In 2015, 15 non-need-based awards were made. ***Average percent of need met:*** 87. ***Average financial aid package:*** $26,154. ***Average need-based loan:*** $161. ***Average need-based gift aid:*** $3500. ***Average non-need-based aid:*** $1400. ***Average indebtedness upon graduation:*** $38,285.

APPLYING
Application fee: $35.

CONTACT
Criswell College, 4010 Gaston Avenue, Dallas, TX 75246-1537. *Toll-free phone:* 800-899-0012.

Dallas Baptist University

Dallas, Texas

http://www.dbu.edu/

- **Independent** comprehensive, founded 1965, affiliated with Baptist General Convention of Texas
- **Suburban** 293-acre campus with easy access to Dallas-Fort Worth
- **Endowment** $41.7 million
- **Coed** 3,223 undergraduate students, 75% full-time, 59% women, 41% men
- **Moderately difficult** entrance level, 43% of applicants were admitted

UNDERGRAD STUDENTS
2,408 full-time, 815 part-time. Students come from 39 states and territories; 39 other countries; 8% are from out of state; 13% Black or African American, non-Hispanic/Latino; 16% Hispanic/Latino; 2% Asian, non-Hispanic/Latino; 0.3% Native Hawaiian or other Pacific Islander, non-Hispanic/Latino; 0.8% American Indian or Alaska Native, non-Hispanic/Latino; 9% international; 8% transferred in; 60% live on campus.

Freshmen:
Admission: 3,259 applied, 1,405 admitted, 527 enrolled. ***Average high school GPA:*** 3.72. ***Test scores:*** SAT critical reading scores over 500: 83%; SAT math scores over 500: 84%; ACT scores over 18: 90%; SAT critical reading scores over 600: 32%; SAT math scores over 600: 24%; ACT scores over 24: 30%; SAT critical reading scores over 700: 4%; SAT math scores over 700: 1%; ACT scores over 30: 4%.

Retention: 77% of full-time freshmen returned.

FACULTY
Total: 659, 19% full-time, 53% with terminal degrees.

Student/faculty ratio: 12:1.

ACADEMICS
Calendar: 4-1-4. *Degrees:* certificates, associate, bachelor's, master's, doctoral, post-master's, and postbachelor's certificates.

Special study options: academic remediation for entering students, accelerated degree program, adult/continuing education programs, advanced placement credit, distance learning, double majors, English as a second language, honors programs, independent study, internships, off-campus study, part-time degree program, services for LD students, study abroad, summer session for credit. ***ROTC:*** Army (c), Air Force (c).

Unusual degree programs: 3-2 business administration.

Computers: 199 computers/terminals are available on campus for general student use. Students can access the following: computer help desk, free student e-mail accounts, online (class) grades, online (class) registration, online (class) schedules. Campuswide network is available. 100% of college-owned or -operated housing units are wired for high-speed Internet access. Wireless service is available via entire campus.

Library: Vance Memorial Library plus 3 others. *Books:* 233,126 (physical), 95,122 (digital/electronic); *Serial titles:* 597 (physical), 35,689 (digital/electronic); *Databases:* 189. Weekly public service hours: 108.

STUDENT LIFE
Housing options: men-only, women-only, special housing for students with disabilities. Campus housing is university owned and leased by the school. Freshman applicants given priority for college housing.

Activities and organizations: drama/theater group, choral group, Ministry Fellowship, Baptist Student Ministry, Student Government Association, Student Education Association, International Student Organization.

Athletics Member NCAA, NCCAA. All NCAA Division II except baseball (Division I). ***Intercollegiate sports:*** baseball M(s), basketball M(s), cheerleading W(c), cross-country running M/W(s), golf M/W(s), ice hockey M(c), lacrosse M(c), soccer M/W(s), tennis M/W(s), track and field M/W(s), volleyball W(s). ***Intramural sports:*** badminton M/W, basketball M/W, football M/W, golf M/W, soccer M/W, softball M/W, table tennis M/W, tennis M/W, ultimate Frisbee M/W, volleyball M/W.

Campus security: 24-hour emergency response devices and patrols, late-night transport/escort service, controlled dormitory access.

Student services: health clinic, personal/psychological counseling.

COSTS & FINANCIAL AID
Costs (2016–17) ***Comprehensive fee:*** $33,713 includes full-time tuition ($25,380), mandatory fees ($800), and room and board ($7533). Full-time tuition and fees vary according to course load. Part-time tuition: $846 per credit hour. Part-time tuition and fees vary according to course load. ***Required fees:*** $400 per term part-time. ***College room only:*** $3685. Room and board charges vary according to board plan and housing facility. ***Payment plans:*** installment, deferred payment. ***Waivers:*** employees or children of employees.

Financial Aid Of all full-time matriculated undergraduates who enrolled in 2016, 2,067 applied for aid, 1,601 were judged to have need, 532 had their need fully met. 118 Federal Work-Study jobs (averaging $2433). 11 state and other part-time jobs (averaging $2139). In 2016, 503 non-need-based awards were made. ***Average percent of need met:*** 57. ***Average financial aid package:*** $15,416. ***Average need-based loan:*** $4126. ***Average need-based gift aid:*** $3975. ***Average non-need-based aid:*** $9026. ***Average indebtedness upon graduation:*** $22,568.

APPLYING
Standardized Tests *Required:* SAT or ACT (for admission).

Options: electronic application, early admission, deferred entrance.

Application fee: $25.

Required: essay or personal statement, high school transcript, minimum 2.5 GPA, rank in upper 50% of high school class. ***Recommended:*** interview.

Application deadlines: rolling (freshmen), rolling (transfers).

Notification: continuous (freshmen), continuous (transfers).

CONTACT
Mr. Bobby Soto, Director of Admissions, Dallas Baptist University, 3000 Mountain Creek Parkway, Dallas, TX 75211-9299. *Phone:* 214-333-6894. *Toll-free phone:* 800-460-1328. *Fax:* 214-333-5447.
E-mail: admiss@dbu.edu.

Dallas Christian College
Dallas, Texas
http://www.dallas.edu/

- **Independent** 4-year, founded 1950, affiliated with Christian Churches and Churches of Christ
- **Suburban** 22-acre campus with easy access to Dallas-Fort Worth
- **Endowment** $169,907
- **Coed** 252 undergraduate students, 75% full-time, 42% women, 58% men
- **Moderately difficult** entrance level, 23% of applicants were admitted

UNDERGRAD STUDENTS
189 full-time, 63 part-time. Students come from 13 states and territories; 6 other countries; 45% are from out of state; 23% Black or African American, non-Hispanic/Latino; 17% Hispanic/Latino; 0.8% Asian, non-Hispanic/Latino; 0.4% Native Hawaiian or other Pacific Islander, non-Hispanic/Latino; 0.8% American Indian or Alaska Native, non-Hispanic/Latino; 6% Two or more races, non-Hispanic/Latino; 4% Race/ethnicity unknown; 2% international; 19% transferred in; 46% live on campus.

Freshmen:
Admission: 225 applied, 51 admitted, 32 enrolled. ***Average high school GPA:*** 3.04.

Retention: 47% of full-time freshmen returned.

FACULTY
Total: 56, 14% full-time, 29% with terminal degrees.

Student/faculty ratio: 16:1.

ACADEMICS
Calendar: semesters. *Degrees:* associate, bachelor's, and postbachelor's certificates.

Special study options: academic remediation for entering students, accelerated degree program, adult/continuing education programs, advanced placement credit, distance learning, double majors, independent study, internships, part-time degree program, summer session for credit.

Computers: 16 computers/terminals are available on campus for general student use. Students can access the following: free student e-mail accounts, online (class) grades, online (class) registration, online (class) schedules. Campuswide network is available. Wireless service is available via entire campus.

Library: The Crawford Library. *Books:* 35,000 (physical), 26,000 (digital/electronic); *Serial titles:* 100 (physical); *Databases:* 60.

STUDENT LIFE
Housing options: on-campus residence required through sophomore year; men-only, women-only. Campus housing is university owned.

Activities and organizations: drama/theater group, choral group.

Athletics Member NCCAA. ***Intercollegiate sports:*** baseball M, basketball M/W, soccer M/W, volleyball W. ***Intramural sports:*** basketball M/W, sand volleyball M/W, soccer M/W, table tennis M/W, volleyball M/W.

Campus security: controlled dormitory access.
Student services: personal/psychological counseling.

COSTS & FINANCIAL AID
Costs (2016–17) ***Comprehensive fee:*** $23,806 includes full-time tuition ($14,476), mandatory fees ($910), and room and board ($8420). Full-time tuition and fees vary according to program. Part-time tuition: $517 per credit hour. Part-time tuition and fees vary according to program. ***Required fees:*** $285 per term part-time. ***Payment plan:*** installment. ***Waivers:*** children of alumni and employees or children of employees.
Financial Aid Of all full-time matriculated undergraduates who enrolled in 2005, 189 applied for aid, 132 were judged to have need. 36 Federal Work-Study jobs (averaging $1404). In 2005, 26 non-need-based awards were made. ***Average percent of need met:*** 43. ***Average financial aid package:*** $3940. ***Average need-based loan:*** $3589. ***Average need-based gift aid:*** $1282. ***Average non-need-based aid:*** $3664. ***Average indebtedness upon graduation:*** $15,000.

APPLYING
Standardized Tests *Required:* SAT or ACT (for admission).
Options: electronic application, deferred entrance.
Application fee: $30.
Required: essay or personal statement, high school transcript, minimum 2.0 GPA, interview. ***Required for some:*** letters of recommendation.
Application deadlines: rolling (freshmen), rolling (transfers).

CONTACT
Mr. Brian Condra, Admissions Counselor, Dallas Christian College, 2700 Christian Parkway, Dallas, TX 75234-7299. *Phone:* 972-241-3371 Ext. 104. *Toll-free phone:* 800-688-1029. *Fax:* 972-241-8021.
E-mail: bcondra@dallas.edu.

Dallas Nursing Institute
Dallas, Texas
http://www.dni.edu/

CONTACT
Dallas Nursing Institute, 12170 N. Abrams Road, Suite 200, Dallas, TX 75243.

DeVry University–Irving Campus
Irving, Texas
http://www.devry.edu/

- **Proprietary** comprehensive, founded 1969, part of DeVry University
- **Suburban** campus
- **Coed**
- **Minimally difficult** entrance level

FACULTY
Student/faculty ratio: 15:1.

ACADEMICS
Calendar: semesters. *Degrees:* associate, bachelor's, master's, and postbachelor's certificates.
Library: Learning Resource Center.

STUDENT LIFE
Housing options: college housing not available.

COSTS
Costs (2016–17) ***Tuition:*** $17,052 full-time, $609 per credit hour part-time. ***Required fees:*** $460 full-time.

APPLYING
Options: deferred entrance.
Application fee: $30.
Required: high school transcript, interview.

CONTACT
DeVry University–Irving Campus, 4800 Regent Boulevard, Suite 200, Irving, TX 75063. *Phone:* 972-929-6777. *Toll-free phone:* 866-338-7934.

East Texas Baptist University
Marshall, Texas
http://www.etbu.edu/

- **Independent Baptist** comprehensive, founded 1912
- **Small-town** 250-acre campus
- **Endowment** $66.3 million
- **Coed** 1,339 undergraduate students, 88% full-time, 53% women, 47% men
- **Moderately difficult** entrance level, 51% of applicants were admitted

UNDERGRAD STUDENTS
1,177 full-time, 162 part-time. Students come from 18 states and territories; 9 other countries; 10% are from out of state; 19% Black or African American, non-Hispanic/Latino; 8% Hispanic/Latino; 0.2% Asian, non-Hispanic/Latino; 0.3% Native Hawaiian or other Pacific Islander, non-Hispanic/Latino; 0.2% American Indian or Alaska Native, non-Hispanic/Latino; 4% Two or more races, non-Hispanic/Latino; 0.2% Race/ethnicity unknown; 0.9% international; 9% transferred in; 83% live on campus.

Freshmen:
Admission: 1,397 applied, 709 admitted, 346 enrolled. ***Average high school GPA:*** 3.37. ***Test scores:*** SAT critical reading scores over 500: 36%; SAT math scores over 500: 41%; ACT scores over 18: 81%; SAT critical reading scores over 600: 6%; SAT math scores over 600: 6%; ACT scores over 24: 20%; SAT critical reading scores over 700: 1%; ACT scores over 30: 1%.
Retention: 68% of full-time freshmen returned.

FACULTY
Total: 141, 48% full-time, 52% with terminal degrees.
Student/faculty ratio: 15:1.

ACADEMICS
Calendar: semesters. *Degrees:* certificates, bachelor's, and master's.
Special study options: accelerated degree program, adult/continuing education programs, advanced placement credit, distance learning, double majors, English as a second language, honors programs, independent study, internships, off-campus study, part-time degree program, services for LD students, student-designed majors, study abroad, summer session for credit.
Computers: 200 computers/terminals and 800 ports are available on campus for general student use. Students can access the following: campus intranet, free student e-mail accounts, online (class) grades, online (class) registration, online (class) schedules. Campuswide network is available. 100% of college-owned or -operated housing units are wired for high-speed Internet access. Wireless service is available via entire campus.
Library: Mamye Jarrett Library. *Books:* 94,074 (physical), 3.5 million (digital/electronic); *Serial titles:* 21 (physical), 24,044 (digital/electronic); *Databases:* 228. Weekly public service hours: 89.

STUDENT LIFE
Housing options: on-campus residence required through senior year; men-only, women-only. Campus housing is university owned. Freshman campus housing is guaranteed.
Activities and organizations: drama/theater group, choral group, marching band, Baptist Student Ministry, Student Foundation, Freshman Class Council (FCC), Student Government Association (SGA), Fellowship of Christian Athletes (FCA), national fraternities, national sororities.
Athletics Member NCAA. All Division III. ***Intercollegiate sports:*** baseball M, basketball M/W, cross-country running M/W, football M, soccer M/W, softball W, tennis M/W, track and field M/W, volleyball W. ***Intramural sports:*** basketball M/W, football M/W, sand volleyball M/W, soccer M/W, softball M/W, table tennis W, ultimate Frisbee M/W, volleyball M/W.
Campus security: 24-hour emergency response devices and patrols, student patrols, late-night transport/escort service, controlled dormitory access.
Student services: personal/psychological counseling.

COSTS & FINANCIAL AID
Costs (2016–17) ***Comprehensive fee:*** $33,409 includes full-time tuition ($23,700), mandatory fees ($1000), and room and board ($8709). Part-time tuition: $790 per credit hour. ***Required fees:*** $43 per credit hour part-time. ***College room only:*** $4576. Room and board charges vary according to board plan and housing facility. ***Payment plan:*** installment. ***Waivers:*** employees or children of employees.

Financial Aid Of all full-time matriculated undergraduates who enrolled in 2015, 1,038 applied for aid, 937 were judged to have need, 100 had their need fully met. 104 Federal Work-Study jobs (averaging $985). 278 state and other part-time jobs (averaging $1290). In 2015, 153 non-need-based awards were made. ***Average percent of need met:*** 30. ***Average financial aid package:*** $18,227. ***Average need-based loan:*** $4011. ***Average need-based gift aid:*** $6178. ***Average non-need-based aid:*** $10,502. ***Average indebtedness upon graduation:*** $34,048.

APPLYING
Standardized Tests *Required:* SAT or ACT (for admission).

Options: electronic application.

Application fee: $25.

Required: high school transcript. ***Required for some:*** interview.

Application deadlines: 8/29 (freshmen), 8/29 (transfers).

Notification: continuous (freshmen), continuous (transfers).

CONTACT
Mr. Kevin Caffey, Vice President for Enrollment and Administrative Affairs, East Texas Baptist University, One Tiger Drive, Marshall, TX 75670. *Phone:* 903-923-2000. *Toll-free phone:* 800-804-ETBU. *Fax:* 903-923-2001. *E-mail:* admissions@etbu.edu.

Grace School of Theology

Conroe, Texas

http://www.gsot.edu/

CONTACT
Grace School of Theology, 3705 College Park Drive Suite 140, Conroe, TX 77384-4894.

Hallmark University

San Antonio, Texas

http://www.hallmarkuniversity.edu/

- **Independent** comprehensive, founded 1969
- **Suburban** 2-acre campus with easy access to San Antonio
- **Coed** 854 undergraduate students, 100% full-time, 36% women, 64% men
- **Moderately difficult** entrance level

UNDERGRAD STUDENTS
854 full-time. Students come from 16 states and territories; 3% are from out of state; 12% Black or African American, non-Hispanic/Latino; 49% Hispanic/Latino; 3% Asian, non-Hispanic/Latino; 0.5% Native Hawaiian or other Pacific Islander, non-Hispanic/Latino; 2% American Indian or Alaska Native, non-Hispanic/Latino; 5% Two or more races, non-Hispanic/Latino; 0.1% Race/ethnicity unknown; 0.1% international; 2% transferred in.

Freshmen:
Admission: 79 enrolled.

FACULTY
Total: 70, 41% full-time, 14% with terminal degrees.

Student/faculty ratio: 20:1.

ACADEMICS
Calendar: continuous. *Degrees:* bachelor's and master's.

Special study options: academic remediation for entering students, accelerated degree program, advanced placement credit, distance learning, internships.

Computers: 250 computers/terminals and 250 ports are available on campus for general student use. Students can access the following: campus intranet, computer help desk, free student e-mail accounts, online (class) grades, online (class) registration, online (class) schedules. Campuswide network is available. Wireless service is available via entire campus.

Library: Randall K. Williams Assessment Center/ Virtual Library plus 1 other.

STUDENT LIFE
Housing options: college housing not available.

Activities and organizations: Alpha Beta Kappa Honor Society, Student Veteran's Organization.

Campus security: 24-hour emergency response devices and patrols, security guard on duty during hours when students are on campus.

APPLYING
Standardized Tests *Required:* Wonderlic aptitude test for Main Campus, Aviation Assessment for Satellite Campus, SAT/ACT is used for some degree programs (for admission).

Options: electronic application, early admission.

Required: high school transcript, interview, hybrid readiness test (main campus only). ***Required for some:*** essay or personal statement, letters of recommendation.

Application deadlines: rolling (freshmen), rolling (transfers).

Notification: continuous (freshmen), continuous (transfers).

CONTACT
Ms. Jennifer Sanchez, Director of Admissions, Hallmark University, 10401 IH-10 West, San Antonio, TX 78230. *Phone:* 210-690-9000 Ext. 212. *Toll-free phone:* 800-880-6600. *Fax:* 210-697-8225. *E-mail:* jsanchez@hallmarkuniversity.edu.

Hardin-Simmons University

Abilene, Texas

http://www.hsutx.edu/

- **Independent Baptist** comprehensive, founded 1891
- **Urban** 220-acre campus
- **Endowment** $125.2 million
- **Coed** 1,721 undergraduate students, 88% full-time, 55% women, 45% men
- **Moderately difficult** entrance level, 88% of applicants were admitted

UNDERGRAD STUDENTS
1,523 full-time, 198 part-time. Students come from 26 states and territories; 19 other countries; 4% are from out of state; 7% Black or African American, non-Hispanic/Latino; 17% Hispanic/Latino; 1% Asian, non-Hispanic/Latino; 0.2% Native Hawaiian or other Pacific Islander, non-Hispanic/Latino; 0.2% American Indian or Alaska Native, non-Hispanic/Latino; 4% Two or more races, non-Hispanic/Latino; 1% Race/ethnicity unknown; 1% international; 8% transferred in; 47% live on campus.

Freshmen:
Admission: 1,149 applied, 1,011 admitted, 393 enrolled. ***Average high school GPA:*** 3.65. ***Test scores:*** SAT critical reading scores over 500: 48%; SAT math scores over 500: 62%; SAT writing scores over 500: 41%; ACT scores over 18: 91%; SAT critical reading scores over 600: 13%; SAT math scores over 600: 14%; SAT writing scores over 600: 8%; ACT scores over 24: 35%; SAT critical reading scores over 700: 3%; SAT math scores over 700: 1%; SAT writing scores over 700: 1%; ACT scores over 30: 5%.

Retention: 71% of full-time freshmen returned.

FACULTY
Total: 207, 66% full-time, 76% with terminal degrees.

Student/faculty ratio: 12:1.

ACADEMICS
Calendar: semesters. *Degrees:* bachelor's, master's, doctoral, post-master's, and postbachelor's certificates.

Special study options: academic remediation for entering students, accelerated degree program, adult/continuing education programs, advanced placement credit, distance learning, double majors, honors programs, independent study, internships, off-campus study, part-time degree program, services for LD students, study abroad, summer session for credit.

Computers: 114 computers/terminals and 1,200 ports are available on campus for general student use. Students can access the following: campus intranet, computer help desk, free student e-mail accounts, online (class) grades, online (class) registration, online (class) schedules. Campuswide network is available. 100% of college-owned or -operated housing units are wired for high-speed Internet access. Wireless service is available via entire campus.

Library: Richardson Library plus 1 other. *Books:* 515,254 (physical), 194,276 (digital/electronic); *Serial titles:* 1,040 (physical), 45,534 (digital/electronic); *Databases:* 137. Weekly public service hours: 89.

STUDENT LIFE

Housing options: on-campus residence required through sophomore year; men-only, women-only, special housing for students with disabilities. Campus housing is university owned. Freshman campus housing is guaranteed.

Activities and organizations: drama/theater group, student-run newspaper, choral group, marching band, Baptist Student Ministries, Student Government, Alpha Phi Omega, Student Activities Board, Fellowship of Christian Athletes.

Athletics Member NCAA. All Division III. ***Intercollegiate sports:*** baseball M, basketball M/W, cheerleading M(c)/W(c), cross-country running M/W, football M, golf M/W, soccer M/W, softball W, tennis M/W, track and field M/W, volleyball W. ***Intramural sports:*** badminton M/W, basketball M/W, bowling M/W, football M/W, golf M/W, racquetball M/W, rock climbing M(c)/W(c), soccer M/W, softball M/W, table tennis M(c)/W(c), tennis M(c)/W(c), ultimate Frisbee M/W, volleyball M/W.

Campus security: 24-hour emergency response devices and patrols, late-night transport/escort service, controlled dormitory access.

Student services: health clinic, personal/psychological counseling.

COSTS & FINANCIAL AID

Costs (2017–18) ***Comprehensive fee:*** $35,860 includes full-time tuition ($26,240), mandatory fees ($1200), and room and board ($8420). Full-time tuition and fees vary according to program. Part-time tuition: $800 per credit hour. Part-time tuition and fees vary according to course load and program. No tuition increase for student's term of enrollment. ***Required fees:*** $545 per term part-time. ***College room only:*** $3900. Room and board charges vary according to board plan and housing facility. ***Payment plan:*** installment. ***Waivers:*** employees or children of employees.

Financial Aid Of all full-time matriculated undergraduates who enrolled in 2016, 1,490 applied for aid, 1,098 were judged to have need, 265 had their need fully met. In 2016, 396 non-need-based awards were made. ***Average percent of need met:*** 80. ***Average financial aid package:*** $25,683. ***Average need-based loan:*** $4170. ***Average need-based gift aid:*** $7318. ***Average non-need-based aid:*** $11,983. ***Average indebtedness upon graduation:*** $39,597.

APPLYING

Standardized Tests *Required:* SAT or ACT (for admission).

Options: electronic application, deferred entrance.

Required: high school transcript, minimum 2.0 GPA. ***Required for some:*** 3 letters of recommendation.

Application deadlines: rolling (freshmen), rolling (transfers).

Notification: continuous (freshmen), continuous (transfers).

CONTACT

Ms. Bobbie Turner, Campus Guest Coordinator, Hardin-Simmons University, Box 16050, Abilene, TX 79698-0001. *Phone:* 325-670-5890. *Toll-free phone:* 877-464-7889. *Fax:* 325-671-2115. *E-mail:* visit@hsutx.edu.

Houston Baptist University

Houston, Texas

http://www.hbu.edu/

- **Independent Baptist** comprehensive, founded 1960
- **Suburban** 100-acre campus with easy access to Houston
- **Endowment** $94.6 million
- **Coed** 2,332 undergraduate students, 93% full-time, 62% women, 38% men
- **Moderately difficult** entrance level, 35% of applicants were admitted

UNDERGRAD STUDENTS

2,161 full-time, 171 part-time. Students come from 31 states and territories; 29 other countries; 4% are from out of state; 18% Black or African American, non-Hispanic/Latino; 33% Hispanic/Latino; 10% Asian, non-Hispanic/Latino; 0.3% Native Hawaiian or other Pacific Islander, non-Hispanic/Latino; 0.3% American Indian or Alaska Native, non-Hispanic/Latino; 4% Two or more races, non-Hispanic/Latino; 5% Race/ethnicity unknown; 3% international; 10% transferred in; 39% live on campus.

Freshmen:

Admission: 15,256 applied, 5,273 admitted, 577 enrolled. ***Average high school GPA:*** 3.43. ***Test scores:*** SAT critical reading scores over 500: 58%; SAT math scores over 500: 64%; SAT writing scores over 500: 47%; ACT scores over 18: 96%; SAT critical reading scores over 600: 15%; SAT math scores over 600: 18%; SAT writing scores over 600: 9%; ACT scores over 24: 42%; SAT critical reading scores over 700: 2%; SAT math scores over 700: 1%; SAT writing scores over 700: 2%; ACT scores over 30: 5%.

Retention: 68% of full-time freshmen returned.

FACULTY

Total: 255, 53% full-time, 67% with terminal degrees.

Student/faculty ratio: 16:1.

ACADEMICS

Calendar: semesters. *Degrees:* bachelor's, master's, and doctoral.

Special study options: academic remediation for entering students, accelerated degree program, adult/continuing education programs, advanced placement credit, distance learning, double majors, freshman honors college, honors programs, independent study, internships, off-campus study, part-time degree program, services for LD students, study abroad, summer session for credit. ***ROTC:*** Army (c), Navy (c), Air Force (c).

Unusual degree programs: 3-2 business administration.

Computers: 100 computers/terminals are available on campus for general student use. Students can access the following: campus intranet, computer help desk, free student e-mail accounts, online (class) grades, online (class) registration, online (class) schedules, office software for 5 devices for each student. Campuswide network is available. 100% of college-owned or -operated housing units are wired for high-speed Internet access. Wireless service is available via entire campus.

Library: Moody Library. *Books:* 109,121 (physical); *Serial titles:* 237 (physical), 41,354 (digital/electronic); *Databases:* 119. Weekly public service hours: 88; students can reserve study rooms.

STUDENT LIFE

Housing options: on-campus residence required for freshman year; coed, men-only, women-only, special housing for students with disabilities. Campus housing is university owned. Freshman campus housing is guaranteed.

Activities and organizations: drama/theater group, student-run newspaper, choral group, marching band, Filipino Student Association, Alpha Chi Omega, Alpha Epsilon Delta, American Red Cross, Phi Mu, national fraternities, national sororities.

Athletics Member NCAA. All Division I. ***Intercollegiate sports:*** baseball M(s), basketball M(s)/W(s), cheerleading M(s)/W(s), cross-country running M(s)/W(s), football M(s), golf M(s)/W(s), soccer M(s)/W(s), softball W(s), track and field M(s)/W(s), volleyball W(s). ***Intramural sports:*** basketball M/W, golf M/W, soccer M/W, softball M/W, tennis M/W, ultimate Frisbee M/W, volleyball M/W.

Campus security: 24-hour emergency response devices and patrols, late-night transport/escort service, controlled dormitory access.

Student services: health clinic, personal/psychological counseling.

COSTS & FINANCIAL AID

Costs (2016–17) ***Comprehensive fee:*** $38,658 includes full-time tuition ($28,850), mandatory fees ($1950), and room and board ($7858). Part-time tuition: $1200 per credit hour. Part-time tuition and fees vary according to course load. ***Required fees:*** $975 per term part-time. ***College room only:*** $4770. Room and board charges vary according to board plan and housing facility. ***Payment plan:*** installment. ***Waivers:*** senior citizens and employees or children of employees.

Financial Aid Of all full-time matriculated undergraduates who enrolled in 2016, 1,680 applied for aid, 1,594 were judged to have need, 443 had their need fully met. 1,029 Federal Work-Study jobs (averaging $1944). In 2016, 511 non-need-based awards were made. ***Average percent of need met:*** 74. ***Average financial aid package:*** $30,060. ***Average need-based loan:*** $5934. ***Average need-based gift aid:*** $19,431. ***Average non-need-based aid:*** $14,164. ***Average indebtedness upon graduation:*** $32,027.

APPLYING
Standardized Tests *Required:* SAT or ACT (for admission).

Options: electronic application, early admission.

Application fee: $25.

Required: high school transcript. ***Required for some:*** essay or personal statement, interview.

Application deadlines: rolling (freshmen), rolling (transfers).
Notification: continuous (freshmen), continuous (transfers).

CONTACT
Mr. Clint Strickland, Director of Admissions, Houston Baptist University, 7502 Fondren Road, Houston, TX 77074-3298. *Phone:* 281-649-3211. *Toll-free phone:* 800-696-3210. *Fax:* 281-649-3217.

Howard Payne University

Brownwood, Texas

http://www.hputx.edu/

- **Independent** comprehensive, founded 1889, affiliated with Baptist General Convention of Texas
- **Small-town** 80-acre campus
- **Endowment** $52.2 million
- **Coed** 1,098 undergraduate students, 87% full-time, 47% women, 53% men
- **Moderately difficult** entrance level, 88% of applicants were admitted

UNDERGRAD STUDENTS
959 full-time, 139 part-time. Students come from 9 states and territories; 2% are from out of state; 9% Black or African American, non-Hispanic/Latino; 20% Hispanic/Latino; 0.5% Asian, non-Hispanic/Latino; 0.4% Native Hawaiian or other Pacific Islander, non-Hispanic/Latino; 0.6% American Indian or Alaska Native, non-Hispanic/Latino; 12% Race/ethnicity unknown; 5% transferred in; 59% live on campus.

Freshmen:
Admission: 953 applied, 836 admitted, 330 enrolled. ***Average high school GPA:*** 3.23. ***Test scores:*** SAT critical reading scores over 500: 33%; SAT math scores over 500: 30%; ACT scores over 18: 82%; SAT critical reading scores over 600: 10%; SAT math scores over 600: 10%; ACT scores over 24: 18%; SAT critical reading scores over 700: 2%; SAT math scores over 700: 1%; ACT scores over 30: 2%.
Retention: 51% of full-time freshmen returned.

FACULTY
Total: 148, 54% full-time, 49% with terminal degrees.

Student/faculty ratio: 10:1.

ACADEMICS
Calendar: semesters. *Degrees:* certificates, bachelor's, and master's.

Special study options: academic remediation for entering students, accelerated degree program, advanced placement credit, distance learning, double majors, honors programs, independent study, internships, off-campus study, part-time degree program, services for LD students, study abroad, summer session for credit.

Computers: 260 computers/terminals and 200 ports are available on campus for general student use. Students can access the following: campus intranet, computer help desk, free student e-mail accounts, online (class) grades, online (class) schedules. Campuswide network is available. 100% of college-owned or -operated housing units are wired for high-speed Internet access. Wireless service is available via entire campus.
Library: Walker Memorial Library. *Books:* 125,784 (physical), 144,053 (digital/electronic); *Serial titles:* 27,347 (physical). Weekly public service hours: 84.

STUDENT LIFE
Housing options: on-campus residence required through sophomore year; men-only, women-only. Campus housing is university owned. Freshman campus housing is guaranteed.

Activities and organizations: drama/theater group, student-run newspaper, choral group, marching band, Baptist Student Ministry, Fellowship of Christian Athletes, Gaming Guild, Spanish Club, Social Work Club, national fraternities, national sororities.

Athletics Member NCAA. All Division III. ***Intercollegiate sports:*** baseball M, basketball M/W, football M, soccer M/W, softball W, tennis M/W, volleyball W. ***Intramural sports:*** basketball M/W, football M/W, soccer M/W, softball M/W, table tennis M/W, tennis M/W, ultimate Frisbee M/W, volleyball M/W.

Campus security: 24-hour emergency response devices and patrols, late-night transport/escort service, controlled dormitory access.

Student services: health clinic, personal/psychological counseling.

COSTS & FINANCIAL AID
Costs (2017–18) ***Comprehensive fee:*** $35,994 includes full-time tuition ($25,290), mandatory fees ($2400), and room and board ($8304). Full-time tuition and fees vary according to course load, location, and program. Part-time tuition: $820 per credit hour. Part-time tuition and fees vary according to location and program. ***Room and board:*** Room and board charges vary according to board plan and housing facility. ***Payment plan:*** installment. ***Waivers:*** employees or children of employees.

Financial Aid Of all full-time matriculated undergraduates who enrolled in 2016, 871 applied for aid, 811 were judged to have need, 158 had their need fully met. In 2016, 142 non-need-based awards were made. ***Average percent of need met:*** 78. ***Average financial aid package:*** $20,390. ***Average need-based loan:*** $5129. ***Average need-based gift aid:*** $16,195. ***Average non-need-based aid:*** $12,984. ***Average indebtedness upon graduation:*** $34,875.

APPLYING
Standardized Tests *Required:* SAT or ACT (for admission). *Required for some:* ACCUPLACER.

Options: electronic application, early admission.

Required: high school transcript. ***Required for some:*** 3 letters of recommendation, interview. ***Recommended:*** essay or personal statement, minimum 3.0 GPA.

Application deadlines: rolling (freshmen), rolling (transfers).
Notification: continuous (freshmen), continuous (transfers).

CONTACT
Mrs. P. J. Gramling, Director of Admission, Howard Payne University, 1000 Fisk Street, Brownwood, TX 76801. *Phone:* 325-649-8406. *Toll-free phone:* 800-880-4478. *Fax:* 325-649-8901. *E-mail:* enroll@hputx.edu.

Huston-Tillotson University

Austin, Texas

http://www.htu.edu/

- **Independent interdenominational** comprehensive, founded 1875
- **Urban** 23-acre campus
- **Coed** 968 undergraduate students, 95% full-time, 56% women, 44% men
- **Moderately difficult** entrance level, 60% of applicants were admitted

UNDERGRAD STUDENTS
923 full-time, 45 part-time. Students come from 24 states and territories; 3 other countries; 6% are from out of state; 67% Black or African American, non-Hispanic/Latino; 23% Hispanic/Latino; 0.2% Asian, non-Hispanic/Latino; 0.2% American Indian or Alaska Native, non-Hispanic/Latino; 0.3% Two or more races, non-Hispanic/Latino; 0.6% Race/ethnicity unknown; 4% international; 9% transferred in; 37% live on campus.

Freshmen:
Admission: 2,042 applied, 1,219 admitted, 146 enrolled. ***Average high school GPA:*** 2.91. ***Test scores:*** SAT critical reading scores over 500: 10%; ACT scores over 18: 38%; ACT scores over 24: 6%; ACT scores over 30: 2%.
Retention: 54% of full-time freshmen returned.

FACULTY
Total: 96, 52% full-time, 59% with terminal degrees.
Student/faculty ratio: 15:1.

ACADEMICS
Calendar: semesters. *Degrees:* associate, bachelor's, and master's.
Special study options: academic remediation for entering students, advanced placement credit, cooperative education, distance learning, double majors, English as a second language, honors programs, independent study, internships, part-time degree program, services for LD students, study abroad, summer session for credit. ***ROTC:*** Army (c), Navy (c), Air Force (c).
Unusual degree programs: 3-2 engineering with Prairie View A&M University.
Computers: Students can access the following: campus intranet, computer help desk, free student e-mail accounts, online (class) grades, online (class) registration, online (class) schedules. Campuswide network is available. Wireless service is available via entire campus.
Library: Downs-Jones Library.

STUDENT LIFE
Housing options: on-campus residence required for freshman year; men-only, women-only. Campus housing is university owned. Freshman campus housing is guaranteed.
Activities and organizations: drama/theater group, choral group, Campus Ministries, Zeta Phi Beta Sorority, Inc, Alpha Phi Alpha Fraternity, Inc, The Gentlemen's Club, Pre-Alumni Council, national fraternities, national sororities.
Athletics Member NAIA. ***Intercollegiate sports:*** baseball M(s), basketball M(s)/W(s), cross-country running M(s), soccer M(s)/W(s), softball W(s), track and field M(s)/W(s), volleyball W(s). ***Intramural sports:*** cheerleading W.
Campus security: 24-hour emergency response devices and patrols, late-night transport/escort service, controlled dormitory access.
Student services: health clinic, personal/psychological counseling.

COSTS
Costs (2016–17) ***Comprehensive fee:*** $21,914 includes full-time tuition ($12,262), mandatory fees ($2084), and room and board ($7568). Full-time tuition and fees vary according to course load. Part-time tuition: $410 per credit hour. Part-time tuition and fees vary according to course load. ***College room only:*** $3642. Room and board charges vary according to housing facility. ***Payment plans:*** installment, deferred payment. ***Waivers:*** employees or children of employees.

APPLYING
Standardized Tests *Required:* SAT or ACT (for admission). *Recommended:* SAT (for admission), ACT (for admission), SAT and SAT Subject Tests or ACT (for admission).
Options: electronic application, deferred entrance.
Application fee: $25.
Required: high school transcript, minimum 2.5 GPA. ***Required for some:*** interview.

CONTACT
Ms. Shakitha Stinson, Director of Admission, Huston-Tillotson University, 900 Chicon Street, Austin, TX 78702. *Phone:* 512-505-3029. *Fax:* 512-505-3192. *E-mail:* slstinson@htu.edu.

Jarvis Christian College
Hawkins, Texas
http://www.jarvis.edu/

- **Independent** 4-year, founded 1912, affiliated with Christian Church (Disciples of Christ)
- **Rural** 465-acre campus
- **Endowment** $11.5 million
- **Coed**
- **Minimally difficult** entrance level

FACULTY
Student/faculty ratio: 26:1.

ACADEMICS
Calendar: semesters. *Degree:* bachelor's.
Library: Olin Library. *Books:* 85,971 (physical); *Serial titles:* 432 (physical); *Databases:* 63.

STUDENT LIFE
Housing options: coed, men-only, women-only. Campus housing is university owned.
Activities and organizations: drama/theater group, choral group, Student Government Association, Pre-Alumni Club, Student Ministers' Association, Women 2 Women, Panhellenic Council, national fraternities, national sororities.
Athletics Member NAIA.
Campus security: 24-hour emergency response devices and patrols.
Student services: health clinic.

FINANCIAL AID
Financial Aid Of all full-time matriculated undergraduates who enrolled in 2011, 476 applied for aid, 476 were judged to have need, 30 had their need fully met. 149 Federal Work-Study jobs (averaging $1538). 2 state and other part-time jobs (averaging $2315). In 2011, 5 non-need-based awards were made. ***Average percent of need met:*** 80. ***Average financial aid package:*** $12,115. ***Average need-based loan:*** $5392. ***Average need-based gift aid:*** $8062. ***Average non-need-based aid:*** $17,192. ***Average indebtedness upon graduation:*** $29,296.

APPLYING
Standardized Tests *Required:* SAT or ACT (for admission).
Options: electronic application.
Application fee: $50.
Required: high school transcript. ***Recommended:*** minimum 2.0 GPA.

CONTACT
Mr. Brandon Byrd, Director of Admissions and Enrollment, Jarvis Christian College, PO Box 1470, Hawkins, TX 75765-9989. *Phone:* 903-730-4890 Ext. 2201. *Fax:* 903-769-4842.

The King's University
Southlake, Texas
http://www.tku.edu/

CONTACT
Tyler Maxey, Director of Admissions, The King's University, 2121 E. Southlake Boulevard, Southlake, TX 76092. *Phone:* 817-552-7570. *Toll-free phone:* 888-779-8040. *E-mail:* tyler.maxey@tku.edu.

Lamar University
Beaumont, Texas
http://www.lamar.edu/

- **State-supported** university, founded 1923, part of Texas State University System
- **Suburban** 292-acre campus with easy access to Houston
- **Endowment** $95.9 million
- **Coed** 9,326 undergraduate students, 66% full-time, 58% women, 42% men
- **Minimally difficult** entrance level, 76% of applicants were admitted

UNDERGRAD STUDENTS
6,193 full-time, 3,133 part-time. Students come from 34 states and territories; 46 other countries; 3% are from out of state; 27% Black or African American, non-Hispanic/Latino; 15% Hispanic/Latino; 5% Asian, non-Hispanic/Latino; 0.1% Native Hawaiian or other Pacific Islander, non-Hispanic/Latino; 0.4% American Indian or Alaska Native, non-Hispanic/Latino; 2% Two or more races, non-Hispanic/Latino; 1% Race/ethnicity unknown; 1% international; 9% transferred in; 24% live on campus.

Freshmen:
Admission: 5,613 applied, 4,276 admitted, 1,467 enrolled. ***Test scores:*** SAT critical reading scores over 500: 36%; SAT math scores over 500: 39%; SAT writing scores over 500: 25%; ACT scores over 18: 77%; SAT critical reading scores over 600: 9%; SAT math scores over 600: 8%; SAT writing scores over 600: 5%; ACT scores over 24: 23%; SAT critical reading scores over 700: 1%; SAT math scores over 700: 1%; SAT writing scores over 700: 1%; ACT scores over 30: 3%.

Retention: 64% of full-time freshmen returned.

FACULTY

Total: 598, 80% full-time, 60% with terminal degrees.

Student/faculty ratio: 15:1.

ACADEMICS

Calendar: semesters. *Degrees:* bachelor's, master's, doctoral, post-master's, and postbachelor's certificates.

Special study options: academic remediation for entering students, accelerated degree program, advanced placement credit, cooperative education, distance learning, double majors, English as a second language, honors programs, independent study, internships, off-campus study, part-time degree program, services for LD students, student-designed majors, study abroad, summer session for credit. ***ROTC:*** Air Force (c).

Computers: 644 computers/terminals and 50 ports are available on campus for general student use. Students can access the following: campus intranet, computer help desk, free student e-mail accounts, online (class) grades, online (class) registration, online (class) schedules. Campuswide network is available. 100% of college-owned or -operated housing units are wired for high-speed Internet access. Wireless service is available via entire campus.

Library: Mary and John Gray Library plus 1 other. *Books:* 529,806 (physical), 83,153 (digital/electronic); *Serial titles:* 42,694 (physical), 47,629 (digital/electronic); *Databases:* 141. Weekly public service hours: 94; students can reserve study rooms.

STUDENT LIFE

Housing options: on-campus residence required for freshman year; coed, special housing for students with disabilities. Campus housing is university owned. Freshman campus housing is guaranteed.

Activities and organizations: drama/theater group, student-run newspaper, television station, choral group, marching band, national fraternities, national sororities.

Athletics Member NCAA. All Division I except football (Division I-AA). ***Intercollegiate sports:*** baseball M(s), basketball M(s)/W(s), cheerleading M/W, cross-country running M(s)/W(s), golf M(s)/W(s), soccer W(s), softball W, tennis M(s)/W(s), track and field M(s)/W(s), volleyball W(s). ***Intramural sports:*** badminton M/W, basketball M/W, cross-country running M/W, football M, golf M/W, racquetball M/W, rugby M/W, sailing M/W, soccer M/W, softball M/W, swimming and diving M/W, table tennis M/W, tennis M/W, track and field M/W, volleyball M/W, weight lifting M/W.

Campus security: 24-hour emergency response devices and patrols, student patrols, late-night transport/escort service, controlled dormitory access.

Student services: health clinic, personal/psychological counseling.

COSTS & FINANCIAL AID

Costs (2017–18) ***One-time required fee:*** $10. ***Tuition:*** state resident $7080 full-time, $336 per credit hour part-time; nonresident $19,320 full-time, $744 per credit hour part-time. Full-time tuition and fees vary according to course load, location, and program. Part-time tuition and fees vary according to course load, location, and program. No tuition increase for student's term of enrollment. ***Required fees:*** $2821 full-time, $382 per credit hour part-time. ***Room and board:*** $8450; room only: $5350. Room and board charges vary according to board plan. ***Payment plan:*** installment. ***Waivers:*** senior citizens and employees or children of employees.

Financial Aid Of all full-time matriculated undergraduates who enrolled in 2015, 5,289 applied for aid, 4,307 were judged to have need, 545 had their need fully met. 230 Federal Work-Study jobs (averaging $3140). 64 state and other part-time jobs (averaging $1878). In 2015, 744 non-need-based awards were made. ***Average percent of need met:*** 49. ***Average financial aid package:*** $5009. ***Average need-based loan:*** $3930. ***Average need-based gift aid:*** $6657. ***Average non-need-based aid:*** $4090. ***Average indebtedness upon graduation:*** $11,878.

APPLYING

Standardized Tests *Required:* SAT or ACT (for admission).

Options: electronic application, early admission.

Application fee: $25.

Required: high school transcript. ***Required for some:*** essay or personal statement.

Application deadlines: 8/8 (freshmen), 8/8 (transfers).

Notification: continuous (freshmen).

CONTACT

Deidre Mayer, Interim Director of Admissions, Lamar University, PO Box 10009, Beaumont, TX 77710. *Phone:* 409-880-8888. *Fax:* 409-880-8463. *E-mail:* admissions@lamar.edu.

LeTourneau University

Longview, Texas

http://www.letu.edu/

- **Independent nondenominational** comprehensive, founded 1946
- **Suburban** 162-acre campus
- **Coed** 2,253 undergraduate students, 56% full-time, 47% women, 53% men
- **Moderately difficult** entrance level, 44% of applicants were admitted

UNDERGRAD STUDENTS

1,262 full-time, 991 part-time. 31% are from out of state; 9% Black or African American, non-Hispanic/Latino; 10% Hispanic/Latino; 1% Asian, non-Hispanic/Latino; 0.5% American Indian or Alaska Native, non-Hispanic/Latino; 4% Two or more races, non-Hispanic/Latino; 10% Race/ethnicity unknown; 3% international; 9% transferred in; 70% live on campus.

Freshmen:

Admission: 1,842 applied, 814 admitted, 280 enrolled. ***Average high school GPA:*** 3.64. ***Test scores:*** SAT critical reading scores over 500: 79%; SAT math scores over 500: 84%; SAT writing scores over 500: 65%; ACT scores over 18: 95%; SAT critical reading scores over 600: 39%; SAT math scores over 600: 44%; SAT writing scores over 600: 25%; ACT scores over 24: 62%; SAT critical reading scores over 700: 10%; SAT math scores over 700: 11%; SAT writing scores over 700: 3%; ACT scores over 30: 19%.

Retention: 78% of full-time freshmen returned.

FACULTY

Total: 216, 38% full-time, 61% with terminal degrees.

Student/faculty ratio: 14:1.

ACADEMICS

Calendar: semesters. *Degrees:* associate, bachelor's, and master's.

Special study options: accelerated degree program, advanced placement credit, cooperative education, distance learning, double majors, English as a second language, freshman honors college, honors programs, independent study, internships, part-time degree program, services for LD students, study abroad, summer session for credit.

Computers: 210 computers/terminals are available on campus for general student use. Students can access the following: campus intranet, computer help desk, free student e-mail accounts, online (class) grades, online (class) registration, online (class) schedules. Campuswide network is available. 100% of college-owned or -operated housing units are wired for high-speed Internet access. Wireless service is available via entire campus.

Library: Margaret Estes Library plus 1 other. *Books:* 46,700 (physical), 234,328 (digital/electronic); *Serial titles:* 200 (physical), 46,450 (digital/electronic); *Databases:* 90.

STUDENT LIFE

Housing options: on-campus residence required through junior year; men-only, women-only, special housing for students with disabilities. Campus housing is university owned. Freshman campus housing is guaranteed.

Activities and organizations: drama/theater group, choral group.

Athletics Member NCAA. All Division III. ***Intercollegiate sports:*** baseball M, basketball M/W, cross-country running M/W, golf M/W, rugby M(c), soccer M/W, softball W, tennis M/W, track and field M/W, volleyball W. ***Intramural sports:*** basketball M/W, football M/W, sand volleyball M/W, soccer M/W, softball M/W, tennis M/W, ultimate Frisbee M/W, volleyball M/W.

Campus security: 24-hour emergency response devices and patrols, student patrols, late-night transport/escort service, controlled dormitory access, University police department.

Student services: personal/psychological counseling.

COSTS & FINANCIAL AID
Costs (2017–18) ***Comprehensive fee:*** $39,190 includes full-time tuition ($28,770), mandatory fees ($550), and room and board ($9870). Full-time tuition and fees vary according to course level, course load, location, and program. Part-time tuition and fees vary according to course level, course load, location, and program. ***Room and board:*** Room and board charges vary according to board plan and housing facility. ***Payment plan:*** installment. ***Waivers:*** employees or children of employees.

Financial Aid Of all full-time matriculated undergraduates who enrolled in 2016, 995 applied for aid, 907 were judged to have need, 141 had their need fully met. In 2016, 283 non-need-based awards were made. ***Average percent of need met:*** 70. ***Average financial aid package:*** $22,747. ***Average need-based loan:*** $5335. ***Average need-based gift aid:*** $17,265. ***Average non-need-based aid:*** $13,316. ***Average indebtedness upon graduation:*** $38,988.

APPLYING
Standardized Tests *Required for some:* SAT or ACT (for admission).

Options: electronic application, deferred entrance.

Application deadlines: rolling (freshmen), rolling (transfers).

Notification: continuous (freshmen), continuous (transfers).

CONTACT
LeTourneau University, TX. *Toll-free phone:* 800-759-8811.

Lubbock Christian University

Lubbock, Texas

http://www.lcu.edu/

- **Independent** comprehensive, founded 1957, affiliated with Church of Christ
- **Suburban** 120-acre campus
- **Endowment** $19.0 million
- **Coed** 1,471 undergraduate students, 86% full-time, 60% women, 40% men
- **Moderately difficult** entrance level, 100% of applicants were admitted

UNDERGRAD STUDENTS
1,267 full-time, 204 part-time. Students come from 35 states and territories; 20 other countries; 10% are from out of state; 5% Black or African American, non-Hispanic/Latino; 22% Hispanic/Latino; 0.6% Asian, non-Hispanic/Latino; 0.4% Native Hawaiian or other Pacific Islander, non-Hispanic/Latino; 1% American Indian or Alaska Native, non-Hispanic/Latino; 2% international; 13% transferred in; 37% live on campus.

Freshmen:
Admission: 815 applied, 812 admitted, 320 enrolled. ***Average high school GPA:*** 3.46. ***Test scores:*** SAT critical reading scores over 500: 53%; SAT math scores over 500: 43%; SAT writing scores over 500: 33%; ACT scores over 18: 90%; SAT critical reading scores over 600: 26%; SAT math scores over 600: 16%; SAT writing scores over 600: 33%; ACT scores over 24: 42%; SAT critical reading scores over 700: 11%; SAT math scores over 700: 5%; ACT scores over 30: 4%.

Retention: 65% of full-time freshmen returned.

FACULTY
Total: 186, 54% full-time, 55% with terminal degrees.

Student/faculty ratio: 12:1.

ACADEMICS
Calendar: semesters. *Degrees:* bachelor's and master's.

Special study options: academic remediation for entering students, adult/continuing education programs, advanced placement credit, cooperative education, distance learning, double majors, honors programs, internships, part-time degree program, services for LD students, study abroad, summer session for credit. ***ROTC:*** Army (c), Air Force (c).

Unusual degree programs: 3-2 engineering with Texas Tech University.

Computers: 169 computers/terminals are available on campus for general student use. Students can access the following: campus intranet, computer help desk, free student e-mail accounts, online (class) grades, online (class) registration, online (class) schedules. Campuswide network is available. 100% of college-owned or -operated housing units are wired for high-speed Internet access. Wireless service is available via entire campus.

Library: University Library. *Books:* 125,715 (physical), 73,557 (digital/electronic); *Serial titles:* 6 (digital/electronic); *Databases:* 78.

STUDENT LIFE
Housing options: on-campus residence required through sophomore year; men-only, women-only. Campus housing is university owned. Freshman campus housing is guaranteed.

Activities and organizations: drama/theater group, student-run newspaper, radio station, choral group, Student Senate, Enactus, Ag Club, Behavioral Science Society, International Student Association.

Athletics Member NCAA. All Division II. ***Intercollegiate sports:*** baseball M(s), basketball M(s)/W(s), cheerleading M/W, cross-country running M(s)/W(s), golf M(s)/W(s), soccer M(s)/W(s), softball W(s), track and field M/W, volleyball W(s). ***Intramural sports:*** badminton M/W, basketball M/W, cross-country running M/W, football M/W, golf M/W, racquetball M/W, rock climbing M/W, soccer M/W, softball M/W, table tennis M/W, tennis M/W, track and field M/W, ultimate Frisbee M/W, volleyball M/W.

Campus security: 24-hour patrols, late-night transport/escort service, controlled dormitory access.

Student services: health clinic, personal/psychological counseling.

COSTS & FINANCIAL AID
Costs (2016–17) ***Comprehensive fee:*** $28,426 includes full-time tuition ($21,166) and room and board ($7260). Full-time tuition and fees vary according to degree level and program. Part-time tuition: $685 per credit hour. Part-time tuition and fees vary according to course load, degree level, and program. ***Required fees:*** $60 per term part-time. ***Room and board:*** Room and board charges vary according to board plan and housing facility. ***Payment plan:*** installment. ***Waivers:*** employees or children of employees.

Financial Aid Of all full-time matriculated undergraduates who enrolled in 2016, 1,087 applied for aid, 948 were judged to have need, 82 had their need fully met. 642 Federal Work-Study jobs (averaging $1716). 13 state and other part-time jobs (averaging $781). In 2016, 206 non-need-based awards were made. ***Average percent of need met:*** 65. ***Average financial aid package:*** $15,385. ***Average need-based loan:*** $4512. ***Average need-based gift aid:*** $10,846. ***Average non-need-based aid:*** $5813. ***Average indebtedness upon graduation:*** $31,089.

APPLYING
Standardized Tests *Required:* SAT or ACT (for admission).

Options: electronic application, early decision.

Application fee: $25.

Required: high school transcript.

Application deadlines: 8/1 (freshmen), rolling (transfers).

Early decision deadline: 10/31.

Notification: continuous (freshmen), continuous (transfers), 12/15 (early decision).

CONTACT
Mr. Chris Hayes, Director of Admissions, Lubbock Christian University, 5601 19th Street, Lubbock, TX 79407. *Phone:* 806-720-7156. *Toll-free phone:* 800-933-7601. *Fax:* 806-720-7162. *E-mail:* admissions@lcu.edu.

McMurry University

Abilene, Texas

http://www.mcm.edu/

- **Independent United Methodist** comprehensive, founded 1923
- **Suburban** 52-acre campus
- **Endowment** $72.3 million
- **Coed** 1,073 undergraduate students, 87% full-time, 44% women, 56% men
- **Moderately difficult** entrance level, 48% of applicants were admitted

UNDERGRAD STUDENTS
932 full-time, 141 part-time. Students come from 23 states and territories; 8 other countries; 5% are from out of state; 17% Black or African American, non-Hispanic/Latino; 25% Hispanic/Latino; 0.8% Asian, non-Hispanic/Latino; 0.1% Native Hawaiian or other Pacific Islander, non-Hispanic/Latino; 0.7% American Indian or Alaska Native, non-Hispanic/Latino; 2% Two or more races, non-Hispanic/Latino; 0.3%

Race/ethnicity unknown; 7% international; 11% transferred in; 49% live on campus.

Freshmen:
Admission: 1,884 applied, 905 admitted, 284 enrolled. ***Average high school GPA:*** 3.5. ***Test scores:*** SAT critical reading scores over 500: 28%; SAT math scores over 500: 39%; SAT writing scores over 500: 16%; ACT scores over 18: 76%; SAT critical reading scores over 600: 6%; SAT math scores over 600: 10%; SAT writing scores over 600: 2%; ACT scores over 24: 16%; SAT critical reading scores over 700: 1%; SAT math scores over 700: 1%; ACT scores over 30: 2%.

Retention: 52% of full-time freshmen returned.

FACULTY
Total: 109, 68% full-time, 64% with terminal degrees.

Student/faculty ratio: 12:1.

ACADEMICS
Calendar: semesters plus May term. *Degrees:* bachelor's and master's.

Special study options: academic remediation for entering students, accelerated degree program, adult/continuing education programs, advanced placement credit, double majors, honors programs, independent study, internships, off-campus study, part-time degree program, services for LD students, student-designed majors, study abroad, summer session for credit.

Computers: 50 computers/terminals and 705 ports are available on campus for general student use. Students can access the following: campus intranet, computer help desk, free student e-mail accounts, online (class) grades, online (class) registration, online (class) schedules, learning management system. Campuswide network is available. 100% of college-owned or -operated housing units are wired for high-speed Internet access. Wireless service is available via entire campus.

Library: Jay-Rollins Library. *Books:* 128,774 (physical), 175,090 (digital/electronic); *Serial titles:* 115 (physical), 378 (digital/electronic); *Databases:* 87. Weekly public service hours: 76.

STUDENT LIFE
Housing options: on-campus residence required through junior year; coed, men-only, women-only. Campus housing is university owned and is provided by a third party. Freshman campus housing is guaranteed.

Activities and organizations: drama/theater group, student-run newspaper, choral group, marching band, Alpha Phi Omega, Religious Life Council, McMurry Student Government, Campus Activity Board, Servant Leadership.

Athletics Member NCAA, NCCAA. All NCAA Division III. ***Intercollegiate sports:*** baseball M, basketball M/W, cross-country running M/W, football M, golf M/W, soccer M/W, swimming and diving M/W, tennis M/W, track and field M/W, volleyball W. ***Intramural sports:*** basketball M/W, football M/W, soccer M/W, softball M/W, ultimate Frisbee M/W, volleyball M/W.

Campus security: 24-hour emergency response devices and patrols, late-night transport/escort service, controlled dormitory access.

Student services: health clinic, personal/psychological counseling.

COSTS & FINANCIAL AID
Costs (2017–18) ***One-time required fee:*** $175. ***Comprehensive fee:*** $35,036 includes full-time tuition ($26,622), mandatory fees ($90), and room and board ($8324). Full-time tuition and fees vary according to course load. Part-time tuition: $887 per credit hour. Part-time tuition and fees vary according to course load. ***Required fees:*** $3 per credit hour part-time. ***College room only:*** $4104. Room and board charges vary according to board plan and housing facility. ***Payment plan:*** installment. ***Waivers:*** employees or children of employees.

Financial Aid Of all full-time matriculated undergraduates who enrolled in 2014, 770 applied for aid, 719 were judged to have need, 94 had their need fully met. 164 Federal Work-Study jobs (averaging $1440). 58 state and other part-time jobs (averaging $1321). In 2014, 120 non-need-based awards were made. ***Average percent of need met:*** 70. ***Average financial aid package:*** $21,153. ***Average need-based loan:*** $4773. ***Average need-based gift aid:*** $15,669. ***Average non-need-based aid:*** $10,626. ***Average indebtedness upon graduation:*** $35,701.

APPLYING
Standardized Tests *Required:* SAT or ACT (for admission).

Options: electronic application, deferred entrance.

Application fee: $25.

Required: essay or personal statement, high school transcript, minimum 2.0 GPA. ***Required for some:*** 3 letters of recommendation, interview.

Application deadlines: 8/15 (freshmen), 8/15 (transfers).

Notification: continuous (freshmen), continuous (transfers).

CONTACT
Ms. Teresa Bridwell, Admission Counselor, McMurry University, 1 McMurry University, #278, Abilene, TX 79697. *Phone:* 325-793-4700. *Toll-free phone:* 800-460-2392. *Fax:* 325-793-4701.
E-mail: admissions@mcm.edu.

Messenger College

Euless, Texas

http://www.messengercollege.edu/

- **Independent Pentecostal** 4-year, founded 1987
- **Suburban** 16-acre campus with easy access to Springfield
- **Endowment** $319,026
- **Coed** 70 undergraduate students, 83% full-time, 50% women, 50% men
- **Moderately difficult** entrance level, 77% of applicants were admitted

UNDERGRAD STUDENTS
58 full-time, 12 part-time. 23% transferred in.

Freshmen:
Admission: 13 applied, 10 admitted, 9 enrolled. ***Test scores:*** ACT scores over 18: 57%; ACT scores over 24: 21%.

Retention: 77% of full-time freshmen returned.

FACULTY
Total: 14, 43% full-time, 21% with terminal degrees.

ACADEMICS
Calendar: semesters. *Degrees:* associate and bachelor's.

Special study options: academic remediation for entering students, cooperative education, distance learning, double majors, external degree program, honors programs, independent study, internships, part-time degree program.

Computers: 5 computers/terminals are available on campus for general student use. Students can access the following: campus intranet, free student e-mail accounts, online (class) grades. Campuswide network is available. Wireless service is available via entire campus.

Library: McDole-McDonald Library.

STUDENT LIFE
Housing options: on-campus residence required through sophomore year; men-only, women-only. Campus housing is university owned.

Activities and organizations: choral group.

Campus security: 24-hour emergency response devices, student patrols.

Student services: personal/psychological counseling.

COSTS & FINANCIAL AID
Costs (2017–18) ***Tuition:*** $325 per credit hour part-time. Full-time tuition and fees vary according to location. Part-time tuition and fees vary according to location. ***Required fees:*** $630 per term part-time. ***Room only:*** Room and board charges vary according to location. ***Payment plans:*** installment, deferred payment. ***Waivers:*** employees or children of employees.

Financial Aid Of all full-time matriculated undergraduates who enrolled in 2010, 64 applied for aid, 64 were judged to have need. 16 Federal Work-Study jobs (averaging $460). ***Average percent of need met:*** 44. ***Average financial aid package:*** $8338. ***Average need-based loan:*** $3791. ***Average need-based gift aid:*** $5198. ***Average indebtedness upon graduation:*** $20,805.

APPLYING
Standardized Tests *Required:* SAT or ACT (for admission).

Options: electronic application.

Application fee: $35.

Required: essay or personal statement, high school transcript, minimum 2.0 GPA, 3 letters of recommendation, health form. ***Required for some:*** interview.

Application deadlines: 8/14 (freshmen), 8/14 (transfers).

Notification: 8/25 (freshmen), continuous until 8/25 (transfers).

CONTACT
Ron Cannon, Vice President of Academic Affairs, Messenger College, 400 South Industrial Boulevard, Suite 300, Euless, TX 76040. *Phone:* 417-624-7070 Ext. 108. *Toll-free phone:* 800-385-8940. *Fax:* 417-624-5070. *E-mail:* info@messengercollege.edu.

Midland College
Midland, Texas
http://www.midland.edu/

- **State and locally supported** 4-year, founded 1969
- **Suburban** 163-acre campus
- **Endowment** $5.3 million
- **Coed** 4,618 undergraduate students, 32% full-time, 58% women, 42% men
- **Noncompetitive** entrance level

UNDERGRAD STUDENTS
1,495 full-time, 3,123 part-time. Students come from 19 states and territories; 31 other countries; 38% are from out of state; 7% Black or African American, non-Hispanic/Latino; 52% Hispanic/Latino; 2% Asian, non-Hispanic/Latino; 0.2% Native Hawaiian or other Pacific Islander, non-Hispanic/Latino; 0.2% American Indian or Alaska Native, non-Hispanic/Latino; 2% Two or more races, non-Hispanic/Latino; 3% Race/ethnicity unknown; 0.1% international; 6% transferred in.

Freshmen:
Admission: 810 enrolled.

FACULTY
Total: 255, 53% full-time, 13% with terminal degrees.
Student/faculty ratio: 26:1.

ACADEMICS
Calendar: semesters. *Degrees:* certificates, associate, and bachelor's.
Special study options: academic remediation for entering students, advanced placement credit, cooperative education, distance learning, English as a second language, honors programs, off-campus study, services for LD students, summer session for credit.
Computers: 950 computers/terminals are available on campus for general student use. Students can access the following: computer help desk, free student e-mail accounts, online (class) grades, online (class) registration, online (class) schedules. Campuswide network is available. 100% of college-owned or -operated housing units are wired for high-speed Internet access. Wireless service is available via entire campus.
Library: Murray Fasken Learning Resource Center. Weekly public service hours: 84.

STUDENT LIFE
Housing options: coed, men-only, women-only. Campus housing is university owned.
Activities and organizations: drama/theater group, student-run newspaper, choral group, OIKOS, Midland College Latin American Student Society, Student Government Association, Student Nurses Association, Baptist Student Ministries.
Athletics Member NJCAA. ***Intercollegiate sports:*** baseball M(s), basketball M(s)/W(s), cheerleading M(s)/W(s), golf M(s), softball W(s), volleyball W(s). ***Intramural sports:*** basketball M/W, cheerleading M/W, volleyball M/W.
Campus security: 24-hour patrols, controlled dormitory access.
Student services: personal/psychological counseling.

COSTS
Costs (2017–18) ***Tuition:*** area resident $2064 full-time; state resident $3264 full-time; nonresident $4224 full-time. Full-time tuition and fees vary according to class time, course level, course load, degree level, location, program, reciprocity agreements, and student level. Part-time tuition and fees vary according to class time, course level, course load, degree level, location, program, reciprocity agreements, and student level. ***Room and board:*** $5015. Room and board charges vary according to board plan and housing facility. ***Payment plan:*** installment. ***Waivers:*** senior citizens and employees or children of employees.

APPLYING
Options: electronic application.
Application deadlines: rolling (freshmen), rolling (transfers).
Notification: continuous (freshmen), continuous (transfers).

CONTACT
Mr. Jeremy Martinez, Director of Admissions, Midland College, 3600 North Garfield, Midland, TX 79705-6399. *Phone:* 432-685-5523. *Fax:* 432-685-6887. *E-mail:* jmartinez@midland.edu.

Midwestern State University
Wichita Falls, Texas
http://www.mwsu.edu/

- **State-supported** comprehensive, founded 1922
- **Urban** 255-acre campus
- **Endowment** $20.9 million
- **Coed**
- **Moderately difficult** entrance level

FACULTY
Student/faculty ratio: 18:1.

ACADEMICS
Calendar: semesters. *Degrees:* associate, bachelor's, master's, and postbachelor's certificates.
Library: Moffett Library plus 1 other. *Books:* 331,562 (physical), 193,374 (digital/electronic); *Databases:* 123.

STUDENT LIFE
Housing options: on-campus residence required through sophomore year; coed, men-only, women-only, special housing for students with disabilities. Campus housing is university owned. Freshman applicants given priority for college housing.
Activities and organizations: drama/theater group, student-run newspaper, television station, choral group, marching band, Caribbean Students Organization, Baptist Student Ministry, Catholic Campus Ministry, African Students Organization, University Programming Board, national fraternities, national sororities.
Athletics Member NCAA. All Division II.
Campus security: 24-hour emergency response devices and patrols, controlled dormitory access.
Student services: health clinic, personal/psychological counseling, legal services.

FINANCIAL AID
Financial Aid Of all full-time matriculated undergraduates who enrolled in 2016, 3,619 applied for aid, 2,545 were judged to have need, 1,448 had their need fully met. In 2016, 754 non-need-based awards were made. ***Average percent of need met:*** 65. ***Average financial aid package:*** $10,027. ***Average need-based loan:*** $6768. ***Average need-based gift aid:*** $7005. ***Average non-need-based aid:*** $2085. ***Average indebtedness upon graduation:*** $28,468.

APPLYING
Standardized Tests *Required:* SAT or ACT (for admission). *Required for some:* SAT and SAT Subject Tests or ACT (for admission).
Options: electronic application.
Application fee: $25.
Required: high school transcript.

CONTACT
Ms. Leah Vineyard, Interim Director of Admissions, Midwestern State University, 3410 Taft Boulevard, Wichita Falls, TX 76308. *Phone:* 940-397-4343. *Toll-free phone:* 800-842-1922. *Fax:* 940-397-4672. *E-mail:* leah.vineyard@mwsu.edu.

National American University
Mesquite, Texas
http://www.national.edu/

CONTACT
National American University, 18600 LBJ Freeway, Mesquite, TX 75150. *Toll-free phone:* 800-548-0605.

North American University

Stafford, Texas

http://www.na.edu/

- **Independent** comprehensive
- **Urban** 12-acre campus with easy access to Houston, TX
- **Coed** 437 undergraduate students, 97% full-time, 36% women, 64% men
- **Minimally difficult** entrance level, 57% of applicants were admitted

UNDERGRAD STUDENTS
424 full-time, 13 part-time. Students come from 12 states and territories; 52 other countries; 12% are from out of state; 16% Black or African American, non-Hispanic/Latino; 19% Hispanic/Latino; 4% Asian, non-Hispanic/Latino; 2% Two or more races, non-Hispanic/Latino; 4% Race/ethnicity unknown; 47% international; 11% transferred in.

Freshmen:
Admission: 215 applied, 123 admitted, 95 enrolled.

Retention: 58% of full-time freshmen returned.

FACULTY
Total: 38, 42% full-time.

Student/faculty ratio: 19:1.

ACADEMICS
Calendar: semesters. *Degrees:* bachelor's and master's.

Special study options: academic remediation for entering students, advanced placement credit, distance learning, English as a second language, internships, part-time degree program, summer session for credit.

Computers: 150 computers/terminals are available on campus for general student use. Students can access the following: campus intranet, computer help desk, free student e-mail accounts, online (class) grades, online (class) registration, online (class) schedules. Campuswide network is available. 100% of college-owned or -operated housing units are wired for high-speed Internet access. Wireless service is available via entire campus.

Library: North American University Library. *Books:* 4,604 (physical), 168,629 (digital/electronic); *Serial titles:* 7 (physical), 16,591 (digital/electronic); *Databases:* 8. Weekly public service hours: 61; students can reserve study rooms.

STUDENT LIFE
Housing options: men-only, women-only. Campus housing is leased by the school.

Activities and organizations: Computer Science, Women's Computer Science, NAU Care Services, Student Athlete Association, Harmony Stallions Association.

Student services: personal/psychological counseling.

COSTS
Costs (2017–18) ***One-time required fee:*** $110. ***Comprehensive fee:*** $18,800 includes full-time tuition ($9450), mandatory fees ($450), and room and board ($8900). Full-time tuition and fees vary according to course load, degree level, and program. Part-time tuition: $475 per credit hour. Part-time tuition and fees vary according to course load, degree level, and program. No tuition increase for student's term of enrollment. ***Required fees:*** $225 per term part-time. ***College room only:*** $4500. Room and board charges vary according to board plan. ***Payment plan:*** installment. ***Waivers:*** employees or children of employees.

APPLYING
Standardized Tests *Recommended:* SAT or ACT (for admission).

Options: electronic application, early admission, deferred entrance.

Required: high school transcript, interview. ***Required for some:*** essay or personal statement, 1 letter of recommendation. ***Recommended:*** minimum 2.7 GPA.

Application deadlines: rolling (freshmen), rolling (out-of-state freshmen), rolling (transfers).

Early decision deadline: rolling (for plan 1), rolling (for plan 2).

Notification: continuous (freshmen), continuous (out-of-state freshmen), continuous (transfers).

CONTACT
Mr. Shawn Washington, Associate Director of Admissions, North American University, 11929 West Airport Blvd., Stafford, TX 77477. *Phone:* 832-230-5555. *E-mail:* Admissions@na.edu.

Our Lady of the Lake University of San Antonio

San Antonio, Texas

http://www.ollusa.edu/

- **Independent Roman Catholic** comprehensive, founded 1895
- **Urban** 75-acre campus with easy access to San Antonio, TX
- **Endowment** $23.7 million
- **Coed** 1,528 undergraduate students, 88% full-time, 69% women, 31% men

UNDERGRAD STUDENTS
1,343 full-time, 185 part-time. Students come from 20 states and territories; 7 other countries; 3% are from out of state; 9% Black or African American, non-Hispanic/Latino; 70% Hispanic/Latino; 0.7% Asian, non-Hispanic/Latino; 0.1% Native Hawaiian or other Pacific Islander, non-Hispanic/Latino; 0.6% American Indian or Alaska Native, non-Hispanic/Latino; 2% Two or more races, non-Hispanic/Latino; 4% Race/ethnicity unknown; 1% international; 12% transferred in; 41% live on campus.

Freshmen:
Admission: 308 enrolled. ***Average high school GPA:*** 3.23. ***Test scores:*** SAT critical reading scores over 500: 28%; SAT math scores over 500: 30%; ACT scores over 18: 81%; SAT critical reading scores over 600: 4%; SAT math scores over 600: 4%; ACT scores over 24: 11%.

Retention: 59% of full-time freshmen returned.

FACULTY
Total: 335, 30% full-time, 67% with terminal degrees.

Student/faculty ratio: 13:1.

ACADEMICS
Calendar: semesters plus summer sessions. *Degrees:* bachelor's, master's, and doctoral.

Special study options: accelerated degree program, adult/continuing education programs, advanced placement credit, cooperative education, distance learning, double majors, honors programs, independent study, internships, off-campus study, part-time degree program, services for LD students, study abroad, summer session for credit. ***ROTC:*** Army (c).

Computers: 230 computers/terminals are available on campus for general student use. Students can access the following: computer help desk, free student e-mail accounts, online (class) grades, online (class) registration, online (class) schedules. Campuswide network is available. 100% of college-owned or -operated housing units are wired for high-speed Internet access. Wireless service is available via entire campus.

Library: The Sueltenfuss Library. *Books:* 71,610 (physical), 51,161 (digital/electronic); *Serial titles:* 416 (physical), 60,823 (digital/electronic); *Databases:* 53. Weekly public service hours: 95; study areas open 24 hours, 5-7 days a week.

STUDENT LIFE
Housing options: coed, women-only, special housing for students with disabilities. Campus housing is university owned.

Activities and organizations: drama/theater group, student-run newspaper, television station, choral group, First Year Connection, Kappa Delta Chi, Epsilon Sigma Alpha, Social Justice Organization, Higher Achievement Through Leadership Opportunities, national sororities.

Athletics Member NAIA. ***Intercollegiate sports:*** baseball M(s), basketball M(s)/W(s), cross-country running M(s)/W(s), golf M(s), soccer M(s)/W(s), softball W(s), tennis M(s)/W(s), track and field M(s)/W(s), volleyball W(s). ***Intramural sports:*** cheerleading W, football M/W, volleyball M.

Campus security: 24-hour emergency response devices and patrols, late-night transport/escort service, controlled dormitory access.

Student services: health clinic, personal/psychological counseling, women's center.

COSTS & FINANCIAL AID

Costs (2017–18) ***Comprehensive fee:*** $37,580 includes full-time tuition ($27,364), mandatory fees ($828), and room and board ($9388). Full-time tuition and fees vary according to course load and location. Part-time tuition: $877 per credit hour. Part-time tuition and fees vary according to course load and location. ***College room only:*** $5600. Room and board charges vary according to board plan and housing facility. ***Payment plans:*** installment, deferred payment. ***Waivers:*** employees or children of employees.

Financial Aid Of all full-time matriculated undergraduates who enrolled in 2015, 1,247 applied for aid, 1,164 were judged to have need, 270 had their need fully met. In 2015, 109 non-need-based awards were made. ***Average percent of need met:*** 77. ***Average financial aid package:*** $21,000. ***Average need-based loan:*** $4716. ***Average need-based gift aid:*** $15,658. ***Average non-need-based aid:*** $8743. ***Average indebtedness upon graduation:*** $31,438.

APPLYING

Standardized Tests *Required:* SAT or ACT (for admission).

Required: high school transcript, minimum 2.0 GPA.

CONTACT

Shannon Tijerina, Assistant Director of Traditional Admissions, Our Lady of the Lake University of San Antonio, 411 Southwest 24th Street, San Antonio, TX 78207-4689. *Phone:* 210-434-6711 Ext. 4133. *Toll-free phone:* 800-436-6558. *Fax:* 210-431-4036. *E-mail:* sytijeria@lake.ollusa.edu.

Paul Quinn College

Dallas, Texas

http://www.pqc.edu/

CONTACT

Paul Quinn College, 3837 Simpson-Stuart Road, Dallas, TX 75241-4331. *Phone:* 214-379-5494. *Toll-free phone:* 877-346-1063.

Prairie View A&M University

Prairie View, Texas

http://www.pvamu.edu/

- **State-supported** university, founded 1878, part of Texas A&M University System
- **Small-town** 1502-acre campus with easy access to Houston
- **Endowment** $71.2 million
- **Coed** 7,455 undergraduate students, 91% full-time, 60% women, 40% men
- **Moderately difficult** entrance level, 85% of applicants were admitted

UNDERGRAD STUDENTS

6,820 full-time, 635 part-time. Students come from 42 states and territories; 31 other countries; 7% are from out of state; 85% Black or African American, non-Hispanic/Latino; 7% Hispanic/Latino; 3% Asian, non-Hispanic/Latino; 0.1% Native Hawaiian or other Pacific Islander, non-Hispanic/Latino; 0.4% American Indian or Alaska Native, non-Hispanic/Latino; 0.9% Two or more races, non-Hispanic/Latino; 0.2% Race/ethnicity unknown; 2% international; 6% transferred in; 51% live on campus.

Freshmen:

Admission: 5,660 applied, 4,838 admitted, 1,839 enrolled. ***Average high school GPA:*** 3.04. ***Test scores:*** SAT critical reading scores over 500: 14%; SAT math scores over 500: 17%; SAT writing scores over 500: 12%; ACT scores over 18: 48%; SAT critical reading scores over 600: 2%; SAT math scores over 600: 2%; SAT writing scores over 600: 1%; ACT scores over 24: 9%; ACT scores over 30: 1%.

Retention: 69% of full-time freshmen returned.

FACULTY

Total: 481, 81% full-time, 57% with terminal degrees.

Student/faculty ratio: 18:1.

ACADEMICS

Calendar: semesters. *Degrees:* bachelor's, master's, doctoral, post-master's, and postbachelor's certificates.

Special study options: academic remediation for entering students, accelerated degree program, advanced placement credit, cooperative education, distance learning, double majors, honors programs, independent study, internships, off-campus study, part-time degree program, services for LD students, study abroad, summer session for credit. ***ROTC:*** Army (b), Navy (b), Air Force (c).

Computers: 341 computers/terminals and 1,000 ports are available on campus for general student use. Students can access the following: campus intranet, computer help desk, free student e-mail accounts, online (class) grades, online (class) registration, online (class) schedules. Campuswide network is available. 100% of college-owned or -operated housing units are wired for high-speed Internet access. Wireless service is available via entire campus.

Library: John B. Coleman Library plus 4 others. *Books:* 345,971 (physical), 16,626 (digital/electronic); *Serial titles:* 199 (physical); *Databases:* 81. Weekly public service hours: 97; students can reserve study rooms.

STUDENT LIFE

Housing options: men-only, women-only, special housing for students with disabilities. Campus housing is provided by a third party. Freshman applicants given priority for college housing.

Activities and organizations: drama/theater group, student-run newspaper, radio station, choral group, marching band, National Society of Black Engineers, National Association of Black Accountants, National Organization of Black Chemists and Chemical Engineers, Toastmasters International, Baptist Student Movement, national fraternities, national sororities.

Athletics Member NCAA, NAIA. All NCAA Division I except football (Division I-AA). ***Intercollegiate sports:*** baseball M(s), basketball M(s)/W(s), bowling W(s), cross-country running M(s)/W(s), golf M(s)/W(s), soccer W(s), softball W(s), tennis M(s)/W(s), track and field M(s)/W(s), volleyball W(s). ***Intramural sports:*** baseball M, basketball M/W, bowling W, cross-country running M/W, golf M/W, soccer W, softball W, tennis M/W, track and field M/W, volleyball M/W.

Campus security: 24-hour emergency response devices and patrols, late-night transport/escort service, controlled dormitory access.

Student services: health clinic, personal/psychological counseling.

COSTS & FINANCIAL AID

Costs (2016–17) ***Tuition:*** state resident $6216 full-time, $241 per credit hour part-time; nonresident $19,535 full-time, $684 per credit hour part-time. Full-time tuition and fees vary according to course load, degree level, program, and reciprocity agreements. Part-time tuition and fees vary according to course load, degree level, program, and reciprocity agreements. No tuition increase for student's term of enrollment. ***Required fees:*** $3843 full-time. ***Room and board:*** $8626; room only: $5922. Room and board charges vary according to board plan, housing facility, and student level. ***Payment plan:*** installment. ***Waivers:*** senior citizens and employees or children of employees.

Financial Aid Of all full-time matriculated undergraduates who enrolled in 2015, 5,923 applied for aid, 5,549 were judged to have need, 636 had their need fully met. 453 Federal Work-Study jobs (averaging $2796). 18 state and other part-time jobs (averaging $3217). In 2015, 137 non-need-based awards were made. ***Average percent of need met:*** 74. ***Average financial aid package:*** $15,280. ***Average need-based loan:*** $7695. ***Average need-based gift aid:*** $7742. ***Average non-need-based aid:*** $5649. ***Average indebtedness upon graduation:*** $34,752. ***Financial aid deadline:*** 3/15.

APPLYING

Standardized Tests *Required:* SAT or ACT (for admission).

Options: electronic application, early admission, deferred entrance.

Application fee: $40.

Required: high school transcript, minimum 2.5 GPA.

Application deadlines: 6/1 (freshmen), 6/1 (transfers).

CONTACT

Ms. Nicole Woods, Administrative Assistant, Prairie View A&M University, PO Box 519, MS #1009, Prairie View, TX 77446-0188. *Phone:* 936-261-1000. *E-mail:* admissions@pvamu.edu.

Rice University

Houston, Texas

http://www.rice.edu/

- **Independent** university, founded 1912
- **Urban** 300-acre campus with easy access to Houston
- **Endowment** $5.3 billion
- **Coed** 3,893 undergraduate students, 99% full-time, 48% women, 52% men
- **Most difficult** entrance level, 15% of applicants were admitted

UNDERGRAD STUDENTS
3,836 full-time, 57 part-time. Students come from 51 states and territories; 42 other countries; 50% are from out of state; 7% Black or African American, non-Hispanic/Latino; 14% Hispanic/Latino; 24% Asian, non-Hispanic/Latino; 0.1% Native Hawaiian or other Pacific Islander, non-Hispanic/Latino; 0.1% American Indian or Alaska Native, non-Hispanic/Latino; 4% Two or more races, non-Hispanic/Latino; 2% Race/ethnicity unknown; 12% international; 0.9% transferred in; 72% live on campus.

Freshmen:
Admission: 18,236 applied, 2,785 admitted, 978 enrolled. ***Test scores:*** SAT critical reading scores over 500: 99%; SAT math scores over 500: 99%; SAT writing scores over 500: 99%; ACT scores over 18: 100%; SAT critical reading scores over 600: 95%; SAT math scores over 600: 96%; SAT writing scores over 600: 95%; ACT scores over 24: 97%; SAT critical reading scores over 700: 72%; SAT math scores over 700: 82%; SAT writing scores over 700: 68%; ACT scores over 30: 89%.
Retention: 96% of full-time freshmen returned.

FACULTY
Total: 881, 76% full-time, 90% with terminal degrees.

Student/faculty ratio: 6:1.

ACADEMICS
Calendar: semesters. *Degrees:* bachelor's, master's, and doctoral.

Special study options: accelerated degree program, advanced placement credit, double majors, English as a second language, honors programs, independent study, internships, off-campus study, services for LD students, student-designed majors, study abroad, summer session for credit. ***ROTC:*** Army (c), Navy (b), Air Force (c).

Computers: 253 computers/terminals are available on campus for general student use. Students can access the following: campus intranet, computer help desk, free student e-mail accounts, online (class) grades, online (class) registration, online (class) schedules. Campuswide network is available. 100% of college-owned or -operated housing units are wired for high-speed Internet access. Wireless service is available via entire campus.

Library: Fondren Library. *Books:* 291,925 (physical), 48,983 (digital/electronic); *Serial titles:* 153,652 (digital/electronic).

STUDENT LIFE
Housing options: coed. Campus housing is university owned. Freshman applicants given priority for college housing.

Activities and organizations: drama/theater group, student-run newspaper, radio and television station, choral group, marching band, Drama Club, Community service/volunteer program, intramural sports, College government, Marching Owl Band.

Athletics Member NCAA. All Division I except football (Division I-A). ***Intercollegiate sports:*** badminton M(c)/W(c), baseball M(s), basketball M(s)/W(s), cheerleading M(c)/W(c), crew M(c)/W(c), cross-country running M(s)/W(s), equestrian sports M(c)/W(c), fencing M(c)/W(c), field hockey W(c), golf M(s), lacrosse M(c)/W(c), riflery M(c)/W(c), rugby M(c)/W(c), sailing M(c)/W(c), soccer M(c)/W(s), softball W(c), swimming and diving W(s), tennis M(s)/W(s), track and field M(s)/W(s), ultimate Frisbee M(c)/W(c), volleyball M(c)/W(s), water polo M(c)/W(c). ***Intramural sports:*** badminton M/W, basketball M/W, cross-country running M/W, football M/W, racquetball M/W, soccer M/W, softball M/W, swimming and diving M/W, table tennis M/W, tennis M/W, track and field M/W, ultimate Frisbee M/W, volleyball M/W.

Campus security: 24-hour emergency response devices and patrols, late-night transport/escort service, controlled dormitory access.

Student services: health clinic, personal/psychological counseling, women's center.

COSTS & FINANCIAL AID
Costs (2016–17) ***One-time required fee:*** $635. ***Comprehensive fee:*** $57,668 includes full-time tuition ($43,220), mandatory fees ($698), and room and board ($13,750). Part-time tuition: $1801 per credit hour. ***College room only:*** $9415. Room and board charges vary according to board plan. ***Payment plan:*** installment. ***Waivers:*** employees or children of employees.

Financial Aid Of all full-time matriculated undergraduates who enrolled in 2015, 2,738 applied for aid, 1,480 were judged to have need, 1,464 had their need fully met. In 2015, 440 non-need-based awards were made. ***Average percent of need met:*** 100. ***Average financial aid package:*** $40,421. ***Average need-based loan:*** $3581. ***Average need-based gift aid:*** $36,025. ***Average non-need-based aid:*** $16,399. ***Average indebtedness upon graduation:*** $25,528.

APPLYING
Standardized Tests *Required:* SAT and SAT Subject Tests or ACT (for admission).

Options: electronic application, early decision, deferred entrance.

Application fee: $75.

Required: essay or personal statement, high school transcript, 2 letters of recommendation. ***Required for some:*** portfolio for architecture, audition for music. ***Recommended:*** interview.

Application deadlines: 1/1 (freshmen), 3/15 (transfers).

Early decision deadline: 11/1.

Notification: 4/1 (freshmen), continuous until 5/15 (transfers), 12/15 (early decision).

CONTACT
Office of Admission, Rice University, Office of Admission, PO Box 1892, MS 17, Houston, TX 77251-1892. *Phone:* 713-348-RICE.
E-mail: admi@rice.edu.

Rio Grande Bible Institute

Edinburg, Texas

http://www.riogrande.edu/

CONTACT
David Loyola, Director of Admissions, Rio Grande Bible Institute, 4300 S US Hwy 281, Edinburg, TX 78539. *Phone:* 956-380-8100.
Fax: 956-380-8256. *E-mail:* admisiones@riogrande.edu.

St. Edward's University

Austin, Texas

http://www.stedwards.edu/

- **Independent Roman Catholic** comprehensive, founded 1885
- **Urban** 160-acre campus with easy access to Austin
- **Endowment** $94.9 million
- **Coed** 4,056 undergraduate students, 89% full-time, 61% women, 39% men
- **Moderately difficult** entrance level, 74% of applicants were admitted

UNDERGRAD STUDENTS
3,610 full-time, 446 part-time. Students come from 49 states and territories; 54 other countries; 14% are from out of state; 4% Black or African American, non-Hispanic/Latino; 41% Hispanic/Latino; 3% Asian, non-Hispanic/Latino; 0.1% Native Hawaiian or other Pacific Islander, non-Hispanic/Latino; 0.4% American Indian or Alaska Native, non-Hispanic/Latino; 3% Two or more races, non-Hispanic/Latino; 2% Race/ethnicity unknown; 8% international; 6% transferred in; 37% live on campus.

Freshmen:
Admission: 6,046 applied, 4,468 admitted, 864 enrolled. ***Test scores:*** SAT critical reading scores over 500: 81%; SAT math scores over 500: 79%; SAT writing scores over 500: 69%; ACT scores over 18: 99%; SAT critical reading scores over 600: 32%; SAT math scores over 600: 23%; SAT writing scores over 600: 22%; ACT scores over 24: 65%; SAT critical reading scores over 700: 5%; SAT math scores over 700: 3%; SAT writing scores over 700: 2%; ACT scores over 30: 8%.
Retention: 81% of full-time freshmen returned.

FACULTY
Total: 481, 41% full-time, 64% with terminal degrees.
Student/faculty ratio: 14:1.

ACADEMICS
Calendar: semesters. *Degrees:* bachelor's, master's, and postbachelor's certificates.
Special study options: academic remediation for entering students, adult/continuing education programs, advanced placement credit, double majors, honors programs, independent study, internships, part-time degree program, services for LD students, study abroad, summer session for credit. ***ROTC:*** Army (c), Air Force (c).
Computers: 928 computers/terminals and 7,200 ports are available on campus for general student use. Students can access the following: computer help desk, free student e-mail accounts, online (class) grades, online (class) registration, online (class) schedules, access to address and biographical data, transcripts, statements of account, online progress reports and degree audit, campus job postings, student timesheets, financial aid information. Campuswide network is available. 100% of college-owned or -operated housing units are wired for high-speed Internet access. Wireless service is available via entire campus.
Library: Munday Library. *Books:* 71,983 (physical), 273,440 (digital/electronic); *Serial titles:* 202 (physical), 121,477 (digital/electronic); *Databases:* 230. Weekly public service hours: 103; students can reserve study rooms.

STUDENT LIFE
Housing options: on-campus residence required for freshman year; coed, special housing for students with disabilities. Campus housing is university owned. Freshman campus housing is guaranteed.
Activities and organizations: drama/theater group, student-run newspaper, radio and television station, choral group, American Medical Student Association, Students for Sustainability, Academy of Science, PRIDE, Asian Student Association.
Athletics Member NCAA. All Division II. ***Intercollegiate sports:*** baseball M(s), basketball M(s)/W(s), cheerleading M/W, cross-country running M/W, golf M(s)/W(s), soccer M(s)/W(s), softball W(s), tennis M(s)/W(s), volleyball W(s). ***Intramural sports:*** basketball M(c)/W, crew M(c)/W(c), soccer M(c)/W(c), swimming and diving M(c)/W(c), tennis M(c)/W(c), ultimate Frisbee M(c)/W(c), volleyball M(c)/W(c), weight lifting M/W.
Campus security: 24-hour emergency response devices and patrols, late-night transport/escort service, controlled dormitory access, self-defense education, informal discussions, pamphlets, posters, alcohol awareness meetings, lighted pathways and sidewalks.
Student services: health clinic, personal/psychological counseling.

COSTS & FINANCIAL AID
Costs (2017–18) ***Comprehensive fee:*** $55,990 includes full-time tuition ($42,550), mandatory fees ($500), and room and board ($12,940). Full-time tuition and fees vary according to degree level. Part-time tuition: $1419 per credit hour. Part-time tuition and fees vary according to course load and degree level. ***Required fees:*** $150 per year part-time. ***Room and board:*** Room and board charges vary according to board plan and housing facility. ***Payment plan:*** installment. ***Waivers:*** employees or children of employees.
Financial Aid Of all full-time matriculated undergraduates who enrolled in 2016, 2,714 applied for aid, 2,473 were judged to have need, 258 had their need fully met. 233 Federal Work-Study jobs (averaging $1974). 18 state and other part-time jobs (averaging $2000). In 2016, 161 non-need-based awards were made. ***Average percent of need met:*** 68. ***Average financial aid package:*** $32,523. ***Average need-based loan:*** $4517. ***Average need-based gift aid:*** $20,681. ***Average non-need-based aid:*** $16,563. ***Average indebtedness upon graduation:*** $37,377.

APPLYING
Standardized Tests *Required:* SAT or ACT (for admission).
Options: electronic application, deferred entrance.
Application fee: $50.
Required: essay or personal statement, high school transcript, 1 letter of recommendation. ***Recommended:*** interview.
Application deadlines: 5/1 (freshmen), 7/1 (transfers).
Notification: continuous (freshmen), continuous (transfers).

CONTACT
Ms. Kelsey McClure, Administrative Coordinator, St. Edward's University, 3001 South Congress Avenue, Austin, TX 78704. *Phone:* 512-448-8500. *Toll-free phone:* 800-555-0164. *Fax:* 512-464-8877. *E-mail:* seu.admit@stedwards.edu.

★ St. Mary's University
San Antonio, Texas
http://www.stmarytx.edu/

- **Independent Roman Catholic** comprehensive, founded 1852
- **Urban** 135-acre campus with easy access to San Antonio
- **Endowment** $183,000
- **Coed**
- **Moderately difficult** entrance level

FACULTY
Student/faculty ratio: 11:1.

ACADEMICS
Calendar: semesters. *Degrees:* bachelor's, master's, and doctoral.
Library: Louis J. Blume Library plus 1 other. *Books:* 195,486 (physical), 84,385 (digital/electronic); *Serial titles:* 498 (physical), 32,005 (digital/electronic); *Databases:* 137. Weekly public service hours: 100.

STUDENT LIFE
Housing options: on-campus residence required for freshman year; coed, special housing for students with disabilities. Campus housing is university owned. Freshman applicants given priority for college housing.
Activities and organizations: drama/theater group, student-run newspaper, choral group, Alpha Phi Omega (service), Beta Beta Beta Biological Honor Society, Delta Sigma Pi (business), Pre-Dental Society, Pre-Medical Society, national fraternities, national sororities.
Athletics Member NCAA. All Division II.
Campus security: 24-hour emergency response devices and patrols, late-night transport/escort service, controlled dormitory access.
Student services: health clinic, personal/psychological counseling.

FINANCIAL AID
Financial Aid Of all full-time matriculated undergraduates who enrolled in 2015, 1,708 applied for aid, 1,589 were judged to have need, 204 had their need fully met. 436 Federal Work-Study jobs (averaging $2127). 48 state and other part-time jobs (averaging $2033). In 2015, 406 non-need-based awards were made. ***Average percent of need met:*** 71. ***Average financial aid package:*** $24,223. ***Average need-based loan:*** $5016. ***Average need-based gift aid:*** $18,310. ***Average non-need-based aid:*** $17,244. ***Average indebtedness upon graduation:*** $39,883. ***Financial aid deadline:*** 6/1.

APPLYING
Standardized Tests *Required:* SAT or ACT (for admission).
Options: electronic application, deferred entrance.
Required: essay or personal statement, high school transcript, minimum 2.5 GPA, 1 letter of recommendation. ***Required for some:*** interview.

CONTACT
Mr. Nelson Delgado, Dean of Admission, St. Mary's University, One Camino Santa Maria, Box #3, San Antonio, TX 78228. *Phone:* 210-436-3126. *Toll-free phone:* 800-367-7868. *Fax:* 210-431-6742. *E-mail:* uadm@stmarytx.edu.

Sam Houston State University
Huntsville, Texas
http://www.shsu.edu/

- **State-supported** university, founded 1879, part of Texas State University System
- **Small-town** campus with easy access to Houston
- **Endowment** $96.5 million
- **Coed** 17,902 undergraduate students, 81% full-time, 62% women, 38% men
- **Moderately difficult** entrance level, 72% of applicants were admitted

UNDERGRAD STUDENTS
14,497 full-time, 3,405 part-time. Students come from 44 states and territories; 49 other countries; 2% are from out of state; 18% Black or

African American, non-Hispanic/Latino; 22% Hispanic/Latino; 2% Asian, non-Hispanic/Latino; 0.5% American Indian or Alaska Native, non-Hispanic/Latino; 3% Two or more races, non-Hispanic/Latino; 2% Race/ethnicity unknown; 1% international; 15% transferred in; 23% live on campus.

Freshmen:
Admission: 12,540 applied, 9,034 admitted, 2,758 enrolled. ***Test scores:*** ACT scores over 18: 86%; ACT scores over 24: 22%; ACT scores over 30: 2%.
Retention: 77% of full-time freshmen returned.

FACULTY
Total: 958, 64% full-time, 74% with terminal degrees.
Student/faculty ratio: 23:1.

ACADEMICS
Calendar: semesters. *Degrees:* bachelor's, master's, doctoral, and postbachelor's certificates.
Special study options: academic remediation for entering students, advanced placement credit, distance learning, double majors, English as a second language, honors programs, independent study, internships, off-campus study, part-time degree program, services for LD students, study abroad, summer session for credit. ***ROTC:*** Army (b).
Computers: 1,600 computers/terminals and 5,544 ports are available on campus for general student use. Students can access the following: computer help desk, free student e-mail accounts, online (class) grades, online (class) registration, online (class) schedules. Campuswide network is available. 100% of college-owned or -operated housing units are wired for high-speed Internet access. Wireless service is available via entire campus.
Library: Newton Gresham Library. Students can reserve study rooms.

STUDENT LIFE
Housing options: on-campus residence required for freshman year; coed, men-only, women-only, special housing for students with disabilities. Campus housing is university owned and is provided by a third party. Freshman campus housing is guaranteed.
Activities and organizations: drama/theater group, student-run newspaper, radio and television station, choral group, marching band, Kinesiology, Health, Recreation Association for Sam Houston, Student Alumni Association, Gamma Sigma Kappa, Chi Alpha Christian Fellowship, Campus Outreach, national fraternities, national sororities.
Athletics Member NCAA. All Division I except football (Division I-AA). ***Intercollegiate sports:*** baseball M(s), basketball M(s)/W(s), bowling W(s), cheerleading M(s)/W(s), cross-country running M(s)/W(s), equestrian sports M/W, golf M(s)/W(s), lacrosse M(c)/W(c), soccer W(s), softball W(s), tennis W(s), track and field M(s)/W(s), ultimate Frisbee M(c)/W(c), volleyball W(s). ***Intramural sports:*** basketball M/W, football M/W, racquetball M/W, riflery M(c), rugby M(c)/W(c), soccer M/W, softball M/W, tennis M(c)/W(c), volleyball M/W.
Campus security: 24-hour emergency response devices and patrols, student patrols, late-night transport/escort service, controlled dormitory access.
Student services: health clinic, personal/psychological counseling, legal services.

COSTS & FINANCIAL AID
Costs (2017–18) ***Tuition:*** state resident $6465 full-time, $216 per credit hour part-time; nonresident $18,705 full-time, $624 per credit hour part-time. Full-time tuition and fees vary according to course load and location. Part-time tuition and fees vary according to course load and location. No tuition increase for student's term of enrollment. ***Required fees:*** $3051 full-time. ***Room and board:*** $8780; room only: $4920. Room and board charges vary according to board plan and housing facility. ***Payment plan:*** installment. ***Waivers:*** employees or children of employees.
Financial Aid Of all full-time matriculated undergraduates who enrolled in 2015, 10,811 applied for aid, 9,315 were judged to have need, 968 had their need fully met. In 2015, 1170 non-need-based awards were made. ***Average percent of need met:*** 79. ***Average financial aid package:*** $11,140. ***Average need-based loan:*** $7610. ***Average need-based gift aid:*** $7387. ***Average non-need-based aid:*** $2530. ***Average indebtedness upon graduation:*** $26,135.

APPLYING
Standardized Tests *Required:* SAT or ACT (for admission).
Options: electronic application, early admission.
Application fee: $45.
Required: high school transcript.
Application deadlines: 8/1 (freshmen), 8/1 (transfers).
Notification: continuous (freshmen), continuous (transfers).

CONTACT
Ms. Angie Taylor, Director of Admissions, Sam Houston State University, Box 2418, Huntsville, TX 77341. *Phone:* 936-294-1845. *Toll-free phone:* 866-232-7528 Ext. 1828. *Fax:* 936-294-3758. *E-mail:* agb003@shsu.edu.

Schreiner University

Kerrville, Texas

http://www.schreiner.edu/

- **Independent Presbyterian** comprehensive, founded 1923
- **Small-town** 211-acre campus with easy access to San Antonio, Austin
- **Endowment** $57.9 million
- **Coed** 1,237 undergraduate students, 87% full-time, 58% women, 42% men
- **Moderately difficult** entrance level, 91% of applicants were admitted

UNDERGRAD STUDENTS
1,075 full-time, 162 part-time. Students come from 15 states and territories; 14 other countries; 3% are from out of state; 3% Black or African American, non-Hispanic/Latino; 37% Hispanic/Latino; 1% Asian, non-Hispanic/Latino; 0.3% American Indian or Alaska Native, non-Hispanic/Latino; 2% Two or more races, non-Hispanic/Latino; 7% Race/ethnicity unknown; 0.8% international; 5% transferred in; 61% live on campus.

Freshmen:
Admission: 998 applied, 906 admitted, 302 enrolled. ***Average high school GPA:*** 3.63. ***Test scores:*** SAT critical reading scores over 500: 53%; SAT math scores over 500: 54%; SAT writing scores over 500: 40%; ACT scores over 18: 90%; SAT critical reading scores over 600: 13%; SAT math scores over 600: 11%; SAT writing scores over 600: 7%; ACT scores over 24: 25%; SAT critical reading scores over 700: 1%; SAT math scores over 700: 1%; SAT writing scores over 700: 2%; ACT scores over 30: 3%.
Retention: 69% of full-time freshmen returned.

FACULTY
Total: 125, 50% full-time, 38% with terminal degrees.
Student/faculty ratio: 13:1.

ACADEMICS
Calendar: semesters. *Degrees:* certificates, associate, bachelor's, and master's.
Special study options: academic remediation for entering students, accelerated degree program, advanced placement credit, cooperative education, distance learning, double majors, honors programs, independent study, internships, part-time degree program, services for LD students, student-designed majors, study abroad, summer session for credit.
Unusual degree programs: 3-2 engineering with University of Texas at Austin, Texas A&M University, University of North Dakota.
Computers: 120 computers/terminals are available on campus for general student use. Students can access the following: campus intranet, computer help desk, free student e-mail accounts, online (class) grades, online (class) registration, online (class) schedules. Campuswide network is available. 100% of college-owned or -operated housing units are wired for high-speed Internet access. Wireless service is available via entire campus.
Library: W. M. Logan Library. *Books:* 80,478 (physical); *Serial titles:* 404 (physical). Weekly public service hours: 30; students can reserve study rooms.

STUDENT LIFE
Housing options: on-campus residence required through junior year; coed, special housing for students with disabilities. Campus housing is university owned. Freshman campus housing is guaranteed.

Activities and organizations: drama/theater group, student-run newspaper, choral group, Student Senate, Greek Life, Campus Ministry, honor societies, Hall Councils, national fraternities, national sororities.

Athletics Member NCAA. All Division III. ***Intercollegiate sports:*** baseball M, basketball M/W, cross-country running M/W, golf M/W, soccer M/W, softball W, tennis M/W, volleyball W. ***Intramural sports:*** cheerleading W, riflery M/W.

Campus security: 24-hour emergency response devices and patrols, student patrols, late-night transport/escort service.

Student services: health clinic, personal/psychological counseling.

COSTS & FINANCIAL AID

Costs (2017–18) ***Comprehensive fee:*** $37,662 includes full-time tuition ($24,990), mandatory fees ($1760), and room and board ($10,912). Full-time tuition and fees vary according to course load, location, program, and student level. Part-time tuition: $1069 per credit hour. Part-time tuition and fees vary according to course load and program. ***Required fees:*** $830 per year part-time. ***College room only:*** $5740. Room and board charges vary according to board plan and housing facility. ***Payment plan:*** installment. ***Waivers:*** employees or children of employees.

Financial Aid Of all full-time matriculated undergraduates who enrolled in 2015, 869 applied for aid, 765 were judged to have need, 107 had their need fully met. In 2015, 219 non-need-based awards were made. ***Average percent of need met:*** 71. ***Average financial aid package:*** $19,712. ***Average need-based loan:*** $3892. ***Average need-based gift aid:*** $16,250. ***Average non-need-based aid:*** $9654. ***Average indebtedness upon graduation:*** $29,020.

APPLYING

Standardized Tests *Required:* SAT or ACT (for admission).

Options: electronic application, deferred entrance.

Application fee: $25.

Required: high school transcript.

Application deadlines: 5/1 (freshmen), 5/1 (transfers).

Notification: continuous (freshmen), continuous (transfers).

CONTACT

Caroline Randall, Director of Admissions, Schreiner University, 2100 Memorial Boulevard, Kerrville, TX 78028. *Phone:* 800-343-4919. *Toll-free phone:* 800-343-4919. *E-mail:* carandall@schreiner.edu.

Southern Methodist University

Dallas, Texas

http://www.smu.edu/

- **Independent** university, founded 1911, affiliated with United Methodist Church
- **Urban** 234-acre campus with easy access to Dallas-Fort Worth
- **Endowment** $1.4 billion
- **Coed** 6,521 undergraduate students, 97% full-time, 50% women, 50% men
- **Moderately difficult** entrance level, 49% of applicants were admitted

UNDERGRAD STUDENTS

6,296 full-time, 225 part-time. Students come from 50 states and territories; 70 other countries; 54% are from out of state; 5% Black or African American, non-Hispanic/Latino; 11% Hispanic/Latino; 7% Asian, non-Hispanic/Latino; 0.1% Native Hawaiian or other Pacific Islander, non-Hispanic/Latino; 0.3% American Indian or Alaska Native, non-Hispanic/Latino; 4% Two or more races, non-Hispanic/Latino; 0.1% Race/ethnicity unknown; 8% international; 4% transferred in; 54% live on campus.

Freshmen:

Admission: 13,250 applied, 6,482 admitted, 1,522 enrolled. ***Average high school GPA:*** 3.65. ***Test scores:*** SAT critical reading scores over 500: 97%; SAT math scores over 500: 99%; SAT writing scores over 500: 96%; ACT scores over 18: 99%; SAT critical reading scores over 600: 79%; SAT math scores over 600: 85%; SAT writing scores over 600: 73%; ACT scores over 24: 96%; SAT critical reading scores over 700: 25%; SAT math scores over 700: 35%; SAT writing scores over 700: 22%; ACT scores over 30: 53%.

Retention: 91% of full-time freshmen returned.

FACULTY
Total: 1,142, 65% full-time, 65% with terminal degrees.

Student/faculty ratio: 11:1.

ACADEMICS
Calendar: semesters. *Degrees:* bachelor's, master's, doctoral, post-master's, and postbachelor's certificates.

Special study options: academic remediation for entering students, accelerated degree program, adult/continuing education programs, advanced placement credit, cooperative education, distance learning, double majors, English as a second language, honors programs, independent study, internships, part-time degree program, services for LD students, student-designed majors, study abroad, summer session for credit. ***ROTC:*** Army (b), Air Force (c).

Computers: 758 computers/terminals and 758 ports are available on campus for general student use. Students can access the following: campus intranet, computer help desk, free student e-mail accounts, online (class) grades, online (class) registration, online (class) schedules, online billing/payment processing. Campuswide network is available. 100% of college-owned or -operated housing units are wired for high-speed Internet access. Wireless service is available via classrooms, computer centers, computer labs, dorm rooms, learning centers, libraries, student centers.

Library: Central University Library plus 7 others. *Books:* 3.0 million (physical), 1.1 million (digital/electronic); *Serial titles:* 16,595 (physical), 175,717 (digital/electronic); *Databases:* 487. Weekly public service hours: 150; study areas open 24 hours, 5-7 days a week; students can reserve study rooms.

STUDENT LIFE
Housing options: on-campus residence required through sophomore year; coed, special housing for students with disabilities. Campus housing is university owned, leased by the school and is provided by a third party. Freshman campus housing is guaranteed.

Activities and organizations: drama/theater group, student-run newspaper, radio and television station, choral group, marching band, Program Council, Student Senate, Student Foundation, Residence Hall Association, SPARC (Students Promoting Awareness, Responsibility, and Citizenship), national fraternities, national sororities.

Athletics Member NCAA. All Division I except football (Division I-A). ***Intercollegiate sports:*** baseball M(c), basketball M(s)/W(s), cheerleading M(s)(c)/W(s)(c), crew W(s), cross-country running W(s), equestrian sports W(s), fencing M(c)/W(c), golf M(s)/W(s), ice hockey M(c), lacrosse M(c), rugby M(c)/W(c), soccer M(s)/W(s), swimming and diving M(s)/W(s), tennis M(s)/W(s), track and field W, volleyball W(s), wrestling M(c). ***Intramural sports:*** basketball M/W, bowling M/W, football M, golf M/W, racquetball M/W, rock climbing M(c)/W(c), soccer M/W, softball M/W, swimming and diving M/W, table tennis M(c)/W(c), tennis M/W, ultimate Frisbee M/W, volleyball M/W, water polo M/W, weight lifting M(c)/W(c).

Campus security: 24-hour emergency response devices and patrols, late-night transport/escort service, controlled dormitory access.

Student services: health clinic, personal/psychological counseling, women's center.

COSTS & FINANCIAL AID
Costs (2017–18) ***Comprehensive fee:*** $69,408 includes full-time tuition ($46,594), mandatory fees ($5904), and room and board ($16,910). Part-time tuition: $1946 per credit hour. Part-time tuition and fees vary according to course load. ***Room and board:*** Room and board charges vary according to board plan and housing facility. ***Payment plans:*** tuition prepayment, installment. ***Waivers:*** employees or children of employees.

Financial Aid Of all full-time matriculated undergraduates who enrolled in 2016, 2,497 applied for aid, 2,063 were judged to have need, 623 had their need fully met. In 2016, 2239 non-need-based awards were made. ***Average percent of need met:*** 85. ***Average financial aid package:*** $41,761. ***Average need-based loan:*** $4278. ***Average need-based gift aid:*** $22,210. ***Average non-need-based aid:*** $23,323. ***Average indebtedness upon graduation:*** $29,601.

APPLYING
Standardized Tests *Required:* SAT or ACT (for admission). *Required for some:* SAT Subject Tests (for admission).

Options: electronic application, early decision, early action, deferred entrance.

Application fee: $60.

Required: high school transcript, minimum 2.0 GPA, 1 letter of recommendation, statement of good standing from prior institution(s). ***Recommended:*** essay or personal statement, minimum 2.7 GPA.

Application deadlines: 1/15 (freshmen), 4/1 (transfers), 11/1 (early action).

Early decision deadline: 11/1 (for plan 1), 1/15 (for plan 2).

Notification: continuous (freshmen), 12/31 (early decision plan 1), 4/1 (early decision plan 2), 12/31 (early action).

CONTACT
Ms. Elena Hicks, Dean of Undergraduate Admission, Southern Methodist University, PO Box 750181, Dallas, TX 75275-0181. *Phone:* 214-768-3417. *Toll-free phone:* 800-323-0672. *Fax:* 214-768-1083. *E-mail:* ugadmission@smu.edu.

See previous page for display ad and page 1512 for the College Close-Up.

South Texas College
McAllen, Texas
http://www.southtexascollege.edu/

CONTACT
Mr. Matthew Hebbard, Director of Enrollment Services and Registrar, South Texas College, 3201 West Pecan, McAllen, TX 78501. *Phone:* 956-872-2147. *Toll-free phone:* 800-742-7822. *E-mail:* mshebbar@southtexascollege.edu.

South University
Round Rock, Texas
http://www.southuniversity.edu/austin.aspx

CONTACT
Director of Admissions, South University, 1220 West Louis Henna Boulevard, Round Rock, TX 78681. *Phone:* 512-516-8800. *Toll-free phone:* 877-659-5706. *Fax:* 512-516-8680.

Southwestern Adventist University
Keene, Texas
http://www.swau.edu/

- **Independent Seventh-day Adventist** comprehensive, founded 1894
- **Small-town** 150-acre campus with easy access to Dallas-Fort Worth
- **Endowment** $10.6 million
- **Coed** 789 undergraduate students, 85% full-time, 58% women, 42% men
- **Moderately difficult** entrance level, 50% of applicants were admitted

UNDERGRAD STUDENTS
671 full-time, 118 part-time. Students come from 15 states and territories; 32 other countries; 20% are from out of state; 16% Black or African American, non-Hispanic/Latino; 45% Hispanic/Latino; 4% Asian, non-Hispanic/Latino; 2% Native Hawaiian or other Pacific Islander, non-Hispanic/Latino; 0.1% American Indian or Alaska Native, non-Hispanic/Latino; 4% Two or more races, non-Hispanic/Latino; 1% Race/ethnicity unknown; 7% international; 8% transferred in; 47% live on campus.

Freshmen:
Admission: 1,551 applied, 775 admitted, 134 enrolled. ***Average high school GPA:*** 3.2.

Retention: 72% of full-time freshmen returned.

FACULTY
Total: 83, 59% full-time, 48% with terminal degrees.

Student/faculty ratio: 11:1.

ACADEMICS
Calendar: semesters. *Degrees:* associate, bachelor's, and master's.

Special study options: academic remediation for entering students, accelerated degree program, adult/continuing education programs, advanced placement credit, distance learning, double majors, English as a second language, external degree program, honors programs, independent study, internships, off-campus study, part-time degree program, services for LD students, student-designed majors, study abroad, summer session for credit.

Computers: 100 computers/terminals are available on campus for general student use. Students can access the following: campus intranet, computer help desk, free student e-mail accounts, online (class) grades, online (class) registration, online (class) schedules. Campuswide network is available. 100% of college-owned or -operated housing units are wired for high-speed Internet access. Wireless service is available via entire campus.

Library: Chan Shun Centennial Library. *Books:* 109,332 (physical), 29,515 (digital/electronic); *Serial titles:* 5,000 (digital/electronic); *Databases:* 86. Weekly public service hours: 60.

STUDENT LIFE

Housing options: men-only, women-only, cooperative. Campus housing is university owned. Freshman campus housing is guaranteed.

Activities and organizations: drama/theater group, student-run newspaper, radio and television station, choral group, Student Association, Enactus (to enable progress through entrepreneurial action), Education/Psychology Club, Theology Club, Nursing Club.

Athletics Member USCAA. ***Intercollegiate sports:*** basketball M/W, soccer M/W, volleyball W. ***Intramural sports:*** badminton M/W, basketball M/W, football M/W, racquetball M/W, soccer M/W, softball M/W, table tennis M/W, tennis M/W, volleyball M/W(c).

Campus security: 24-hour emergency response devices, student patrols, controlled dormitory access.

Student services: health clinic, personal/psychological counseling.

COSTS

Costs (2016–17) ***Comprehensive fee:*** $27,776 includes full-time tuition ($19,656), mandatory fees ($620), and room and board ($7500). Full-time tuition and fees vary according to course load and program. Part-time tuition: $819 per semester hour. Part-time tuition and fees vary according to course load and program. ***Required fees:*** $620 per term part-time. ***Room and board:*** Room and board charges vary according to board plan. ***Payment plan:*** installment. ***Waivers:*** senior citizens and employees or children of employees.

APPLYING

Standardized Tests *Required:* SAT or ACT (for admission).

Options: electronic application, early admission, deferred entrance.

Application fee: $25.

Required: high school transcript, minimum 2.5 GPA. ***Required for some:*** essay or personal statement, 1 letter of recommendation, interview.

Application deadlines: 8/1 (freshmen), 8/7 (transfers).

Notification: continuous (freshmen), continuous until 9/1 (transfers).

CONTACT

Ms. Rahneeka Hazelton, Director of Admissions, Southwestern Adventist University, 100 West Hillcrest, Keene, TX 76059. *Phone:* 817-202-6733. *Toll-free phone:* 800-433-2240. *E-mail:* rahneeka@swau.edu.

Southwestern Assemblies of God University

Waxahachie, Texas

http://www.sagu.edu/

- **Independent** comprehensive, founded 1927, affiliated with Assemblies of God
- **Small-town** 70-acre campus with easy access to Dallas-Fort Worth
- **Endowment** $9.1 million
- **Coed** 1,774 undergraduate students, 85% full-time, 52% women, 48% men
- **Noncompetitive** entrance level, 23% of applicants were admitted

UNDERGRAD STUDENTS

1,506 full-time, 268 part-time. Students come from 9 other countries; 42% are from out of state; 12% Black or African American, non-Hispanic/Latino; 20% Hispanic/Latino; 0.9% Asian, non-Hispanic/Latino; 0.6% Native Hawaiian or other Pacific Islander, non-Hispanic/Latino; 4% American Indian or Alaska Native, non-Hispanic/Latino; 2% Two or more races, non-Hispanic/Latino; 0.6% Race/ethnicity unknown; 0.6% international; 12% transferred in.

Freshmen:
Admission: 2,097 applied, 492 admitted, 331 enrolled. ***Test scores:*** SAT critical reading scores over 500: 50%; SAT math scores over 500: 43%; SAT writing scores over 500: 46%; ACT scores over 18: 89%; SAT critical reading scores over 600: 10%; SAT math scores over 600: 3%; SAT writing scores over 600: 13%; ACT scores over 24: 30%; ACT scores over 30: 7%.
Retention: 75% of full-time freshmen returned.

FACULTY
Total: 175, 50% full-time, 38% with terminal degrees.
Student/faculty ratio: 14:1.

ACADEMICS
Calendar: semesters. *Degrees:* associate, bachelor's, and master's.
Special study options: academic remediation for entering students, adult/continuing education programs, advanced placement credit, distance learning, double majors, external degree program, independent study, internships, part-time degree program, services for LD students, summer session for credit. ***ROTC:*** Air Force (c).
Computers: 80 computers/terminals and 1,000 ports are available on campus for general student use. Students can access the following: computer help desk, free student e-mail accounts, online (class) grades, online (class) registration, online (class) schedules. Campuswide network is available. 95% of college-owned or -operated housing units are wired for high-speed Internet access. Wireless service is available via entire campus.
Library: P. C. Nelson Memorial Library plus 1 other. *Books:* 100,582 (physical), 256 (digital/electronic); *Serial titles:* 414 (physical), 13,284 (digital/electronic); *Databases:* 70. Weekly public service hours: 90; students can reserve study rooms.

STUDENT LIFE
Housing options: on-campus residence required through senior year; coed, women-only. Campus housing is university owned. Freshman campus housing is guaranteed.
Activities and organizations: drama/theater group, student-run newspaper, choral group, Student Congress, Southwestern Missions Association, Street Hope, Gold Jackets, Women in Ministry.
Athletics Member NAIA, NCCAA. ***Intercollegiate sports:*** baseball M(s), basketball M(s)/W(s), football M(s), soccer M(s)/W(s), softball W(s), volleyball W(s). ***Intramural sports:*** basketball M/W, cheerleading W, football M/W, soccer M(c)/W, softball M/W, table tennis M/W, tennis M/W, ultimate Frisbee M/W, volleyball M/W.
Campus security: 24-hour patrols, late-night transport/escort service, controlled dormitory access, electronic and key access in dorms, camera surveillance, 24-hour dispatch monitored fire alarm systems (offsite).
Student services: health clinic, personal/psychological counseling.

COSTS & FINANCIAL AID
Costs (2017–18) ***Comprehensive fee:*** $27,470 includes full-time tuition ($19,450), mandatory fees ($960), and room and board ($7060). Full-time tuition and fees vary according to course load, degree level, and location. Part-time tuition: $810 per credit hour. Part-time tuition and fees vary according to course load, degree level, and location. ***College room only:*** $3500. Room and board charges vary according to board plan, housing facility, and location. ***Payment plan:*** deferred payment. ***Waivers:*** employees or children of employees.
Financial Aid Of all full-time matriculated undergraduates who enrolled in 2000, 1,116 applied for aid, 1,002 were judged to have need, 110 had their need fully met. 178 Federal Work-Study jobs, 7 state and other part-time jobs (averaging $890). In 2000, 316 non-need-based awards were made. ***Average percent of need met:*** 64. ***Average financial aid package:*** $6728. ***Average need-based loan:*** $3177. ***Average need-based gift aid:*** $3511. ***Average indebtedness upon graduation:*** $13,938. ***Financial aid deadline:*** 7/1.

APPLYING
Standardized Tests *Required:* SAT or ACT (for admission). *Recommended:* ACT (for admission).
Options: electronic application.
Application fee: $35.
Required: essay or personal statement, high school transcript, minimum 2.0 GPA, 1 letter of recommendation.
Application deadlines: rolling (freshmen), rolling (transfers).
Notification: continuous (freshmen), continuous (transfers).

CONTACT
Mr. Joshua Martin, Assistant Dean of Admissions, Southwestern Assemblies of God University, 1200 Sycamore Street, Waxahachie, TX 75165. *Phone:* 972-825-4821. *Toll-free phone:* 888-937-7248. *Fax:* 972-923-8131. *E-mail:* jmartin@sagu.edu.

See previous page for display ad and page 1516 for the College Close-Up.

Southwestern Christian College

Terrell, Texas

http://www.swcc.edu/

CONTACT
Admissions Department, Southwestern Christian College, Box 10, 200 Bowser Street, Terrell, TX 75160. *Phone:* 214-524-3341.

Southwestern University

Georgetown, Texas

http://www.southwestern.edu/

- **Independent Methodist** 4-year, founded 1840
- **Suburban** 700-acre campus with easy access to Austin
- **Endowment** $239.9 million
- **Coed** 1,486 undergraduate students, 99% full-time, 57% women, 43% men
- **Very difficult** entrance level, 45% of applicants were admitted

UNDERGRAD STUDENTS
1,464 full-time, 22 part-time. Students come from 35 states and territories; 14 other countries; 10% are from out of state; 6% Black or African American, non-Hispanic/Latino; 21% Hispanic/Latino; 4% Asian, non-Hispanic/Latino; 0.2% Native Hawaiian or other Pacific Islander, non-Hispanic/Latino; 0.4% American Indian or Alaska Native, non-Hispanic/Latino; 4% Two or more races, non-Hispanic/Latino; 1% Race/ethnicity unknown; 2% international; 2% transferred in; 72% live on campus.

Freshmen:
Admission: 3,773 applied, 1,699 admitted, 381 enrolled. ***Test scores:*** SAT critical reading scores over 500: 87%; SAT math scores over 500: 87%; ACT scores over 18: 98%; SAT critical reading scores over 600: 47%; SAT math scores over 600: 38%; ACT scores over 24: 69%; SAT critical reading scores over 700: 12%; SAT math scores over 700: 7%; ACT scores over 30: 20%.
Retention: 85% of full-time freshmen returned.

FACULTY
Total: 151, 73% full-time, 90% with terminal degrees.
Student/faculty ratio: 12:1.

ACADEMICS
Calendar: semesters. *Degree:* bachelor's.
Special study options: advanced placement credit, double majors, honors programs, independent study, internships, off-campus study, services for LD students, student-designed majors, study abroad, summer session for credit. ***ROTC:*** Air Force (c).
Unusual degree programs: 3-2 engineering.
Computers: 410 computers/terminals are available on campus for general student use. Students can access the following: campus intranet, computer help desk, free student e-mail accounts, online (class) grades, online (class) registration, online (class) schedules, transcripts. Campuswide network is available. 100% of college-owned or -operated housing units are wired for high-speed Internet access. Wireless service is available via entire campus.
Library: A. Frank Smith, Jr. Library Center. *Books:* 268,745 (physical), 473,268 (digital/electronic); *Serial titles:* 312 (physical), 98,835 (digital/electronic); *Databases:* 123. Weekly public service hours: 90; study areas open 24 hours, 5-7 days a week.

STUDENT LIFE
Housing options: on-campus residence required through sophomore year; coed, men-only, women-only, special housing for students with

disabilities. Campus housing is university owned. Freshman campus housing is guaranteed.

Activities and organizations: drama/theater group, student-run newspaper, radio station, choral group, Student Peace Alliance (SPA), Students for Environmental Activism and Knowledge (SEAK), Alpha Phi Omega, Men's IFC, Women's Panhellenic, national fraternities, national sororities.

Athletics Member NCAA. All Division III. ***Intercollegiate sports:*** baseball M, basketball M/W, cross-country running M/W, football M, golf M/W, lacrosse M/W, soccer M/W, softball W, swimming and diving M/W, tennis M/W, track and field M/W, volleyball W. ***Intramural sports:*** basketball M/W, cheerleading M(c)/W(c), fencing M(c)/W(c), football M/W, racquetball M/W, sand volleyball M/W, soccer M/W, table tennis M/W, ultimate Frisbee M(c)/W(c), volleyball M/W.

Campus security: 24-hour emergency response devices and patrols, late-night transport/escort service, controlled dormitory access.

Student services: health clinic, personal/psychological counseling, women's center.

COSTS & FINANCIAL AID

Costs (2017–18) ***Comprehensive fee:*** $52,370 includes full-time tuition ($40,560) and room and board ($11,810). Part-time tuition: $1690 per credit hour. Part-time tuition and fees vary according to course load. ***College room only:*** $6290. Room and board charges vary according to board plan and housing facility. ***Payment plan:*** installment. ***Waivers:*** employees or children of employees.

Financial Aid Of all full-time matriculated undergraduates who enrolled in 2016, 1,053 applied for aid, 919 were judged to have need, 261 had their need fully met. 112 Federal Work-Study jobs (averaging $2134). 601 state and other part-time jobs (averaging $2392). In 2016, 525 non-need-based awards were made. ***Average percent of need met:*** 89. ***Average financial aid package:*** $34,758. ***Average need-based loan:*** $5263. ***Average need-based gift aid:*** $28,975. ***Average non-need-based aid:*** $20,622. ***Average indebtedness upon graduation:*** $32,801.

APPLYING

Standardized Tests *Required:* SAT or ACT (for admission).

Options: electronic application, early admission, early decision, early action, deferred entrance.

Required: essay or personal statement, high school transcript, 1 letter of recommendation, counselor recommendation. ***Required for some:*** interview. ***Recommended:*** interview.

Application deadlines: 5/1 (freshmen), 4/1 (transfers), 12/1 (early action).

Early decision deadline: 11/1.

Notification: continuous (freshmen), continuous (out-of-state freshmen), 7/15 (transfers), 12/1 (early decision), 3/1 (early action).

CONTACT

Mr. Bob Baldwin, Director of Admission, Southwestern University, 1001 East University Avenue, Georgetown, TX 78626. *Phone:* 512-863-1200. *Toll-free phone:* 800-252-3166. *Fax:* 512-863-9601. *E-mail:* admission@southwestern.edu.

Southwest University at El Paso

El Paso, Texas

http://southwestuniversity.edu/

CONTACT

Southwest University at El Paso, 1414 Geronimo Drive, El Paso, TX 79925.

Stephen F. Austin State University

Nacogdoches, Texas

http://www.sfasu.edu/

- **State-supported** comprehensive, founded 1923
- **Small-town** 419-acre campus
- **Endowment** $77.3 million
- **Coed** 11,140 undergraduate students, 87% full-time, 64% women, 36% men
- **Moderately difficult** entrance level, 62% of applicants were admitted

UNDERGRAD STUDENTS

9,637 full-time, 1,503 part-time. Students come from 37 states and territories; 36 other countries; 2% are from out of state; 18% Black or African American, non-Hispanic/Latino; 18% Hispanic/Latino; 1% Asian, non-Hispanic/Latino; 0.1% Native Hawaiian or other Pacific Islander, non-Hispanic/Latino; 0.5% American Indian or Alaska Native, non-Hispanic/Latino; 3% Two or more races, non-Hispanic/Latino; 0.8% Race/ethnicity unknown; 0.6% international; 8% transferred in; 44% live on campus.

Freshmen:

Admission: 11,382 applied, 7,108 admitted, 2,173 enrolled. ***Test scores:*** SAT critical reading scores over 500: 46%; SAT math scores over 500: 47%; SAT writing scores over 500: 34%; ACT scores over 18: 88%; SAT critical reading scores over 600: 10%; SAT math scores over 600: 10%; SAT writing scores over 600: 6%; ACT scores over 24: 27%; SAT critical reading scores over 700: 1%; ACT scores over 30: 2%.

Retention: 71% of full-time freshmen returned.

FACULTY

Total: 710, 72% full-time, 66% with terminal degrees.

Student/faculty ratio: 20:1.

ACADEMICS

Calendar: semesters. *Degrees:* bachelor's, master's, and doctoral.

Special study options: academic remediation for entering students, accelerated degree program, adult/continuing education programs, advanced placement credit, cooperative education, distance learning, double majors, freshman honors college, honors programs, independent study, internships, off-campus study, part-time degree program, services for LD students, student-designed majors, study abroad, summer session for credit. ***ROTC:*** Army (b).

Unusual degree programs: 3-2 professional accountancy.

Computers: 1,000 computers/terminals are available on campus for general student use. Students can access the following: campus intranet, computer help desk, free student e-mail accounts, online (class) grades, online (class) registration, online (class) schedules. Campuswide network is available. 100% of college-owned or -operated housing units are wired for high-speed Internet access. Wireless service is available via classrooms, computer centers, computer labs, dorm rooms, learning centers, libraries, student centers.

Library: Ralph W. Steen Library. *Books:* 898,719 (physical), 206,432 (digital/electronic); *Serial titles:* 5,863 (physical), 106,272 (digital/electronic); *Databases:* 259. Weekly public service hours: 99; students can reserve study rooms.

STUDENT LIFE

Housing options: on-campus residence required through sophomore year; coed, men-only, women-only, special housing for students with disabilities. Campus housing is university owned and is provided by a third party. Freshman campus housing is guaranteed.

Activities and organizations: drama/theater group, student-run newspaper, radio and television station, choral group, marching band, Residence Hall Association, Baptist Student Ministries, Greek Life, Student Activities Association, Student Government Association, national fraternities, national sororities.

Athletics Member NCAA. All Division I except football (Division I-AA). ***Intercollegiate sports:*** baseball M(s), basketball M(s)/W(s), bowling W(s), cheerleading M(s)/W(s), cross-country running M(s)/W(s), golf M(s)/W(s), lacrosse M(c), rugby M(c)/W, soccer M(c)/W(s), softball W(s), tennis M(c)/W(s), track and field M(s)/W(s), volleyball W(s). ***Intramural sports:*** baseball M(c), basketball M(c)/W(c), football M/W, golf M/W, racquetball M/W, rock climbing M/W, soccer M/W, softball M/W, swimming and diving M(c)/W(c), table tennis M/W, tennis M/W, ultimate Frisbee M/W, volleyball M/W, water polo M/W.

Campus security: 24-hour emergency response devices and patrols, student patrols, late-night transport/escort service, controlled dormitory access.

Student services: health clinic, personal/psychological counseling.

COSTS & FINANCIAL AID

Costs (2016–17) ***Tuition:*** state resident $7260 full-time, $242 per credit hour part-time; nonresident $19,500 full-time, $650 per credit hour part-time. Full-time tuition and fees vary according to course load, degree level, and location. Part-time tuition and fees vary according to course load, degree level, and location. No tuition increase for student's term of enrollment. ***Required fees:*** $2277 full-time, $158 per credit hour part-time. ***Room and board:*** $8868. Room and board charges vary according to board plan and housing facility. ***Payment plan:*** installment. ***Waivers:*** senior citizens and employees or children of employees.

Financial Aid Of all full-time matriculated undergraduates who enrolled in 2015, 8,036 applied for aid, 6,520 were judged to have need, 961 had their need fully met. In 2015, 951 non-need-based awards were made. ***Average percent of need met:*** 60. ***Average financial aid package:*** $11,866. ***Average need-based loan:*** $4764. ***Average need-based gift aid:*** $7373. ***Average non-need-based aid:*** $2445. ***Average indebtedness upon graduation:*** $29,574.

APPLYING

Standardized Tests *Required:* SAT or ACT (for admission).

Options: electronic application.

Application fee: $45.

Required: high school transcript.

Application deadlines: rolling (freshmen), rolling (transfers).

Notification: continuous (freshmen), continuous (transfers).

CONTACT

Mr. Kevin Davis, Associate Director of Admissions, Stephen F. Austin State University, PO Box 13051, SFA Station, Nacogdoches, TX 75962. *Phone:* 936-468-2504. *Toll-free phone:* 800-731-2902. *Fax:* 936-468-3849. *E-mail:* admissions@sfasu.edu.

Strayer University–Cedar Hill Campus

Cedar Hill, Texas

http://www.strayer.edu/texas/cedar-hill/

CONTACT

Strayer University–Cedar Hill Campus, 610 Uptown Boulevard, Suite 3500, Cedar Hill, TX 75104.

Strayer University–Irving Campus

Irving, Texas

http://www.strayer.edu/texas/irving/

CONTACT

Strayer University–Irving Campus, 7701 Las Colinas Ridge, Suite 450, Irving, TX 75063.

Strayer University–Katy Campus

Houston, Texas

http://www.strayer.edu/texas/katy/

CONTACT

Strayer University–Katy Campus, 14511 Old Katy Road, Suite 200, Houston, TX 77079.

Strayer University–North Austin Campus

Austin, Texas

http://www.strayer.edu/texas/north-austin/

CONTACT

Strayer University–North Austin Campus, 8501 North Mopac Expressway, Suite 100, Austin, TX 78759.

Strayer University–Northwest Houston Campus

Houston, Texas

http://www.strayer.edu/texas/northwest-houston/

CONTACT

Strayer University–Northwest Houston Campus, 10940 W. Sam Houston Parkway N., Suite 200, Houston, TX 77064.

Strayer University–Plano Campus

Plano, Texas

http://www.strayer.edu/texas/plano/

CONTACT

Strayer University–Plano Campus, 2701 North Dallas Parkway, Suite 300, Plano, TX 75093.

Sul Ross State University

Alpine, Texas

http://www.sulross.edu/

- **State-supported** comprehensive, founded 1920, part of Texas State University System
- **Rural** 640-acre campus
- **Coed**
- **Noncompetitive** entrance level

FACULTY

Student/faculty ratio: 13:1.

ACADEMICS

Calendar: semesters. *Degrees:* bachelor's and master's.

Library: Bryan Wildenthal Memorial Library.

STUDENT LIFE

Housing options: on-campus residence required through sophomore year; coed. Campus housing is university owned. Freshman campus housing is guaranteed.

Activities and organizations: drama/theater group, student-run newspaper, marching band.

Athletics Member NCAA. All Division III.

Campus security: 24-hour patrols, late-night transport/escort service.

Student services: health clinic, personal/psychological counseling.

FINANCIAL AID

Financial Aid Of all full-time matriculated undergraduates who enrolled in 2014, 924 were judged to have need. ***Average financial aid package:*** $11,152. ***Average need-based loan:*** $3285. ***Average need-based gift aid:*** $6427. ***Financial aid deadline:*** 4/1.

APPLYING

Standardized Tests *Required:* SAT or ACT (for admission).

Options: deferred entrance.

Required: high school transcript. ***Recommended:*** interview.

CONTACT

Sul Ross State University, PO Box C - 114, Alpine, TX 79832. *Phone:* 432-837-8050. *Toll-free phone:* 888-722-7778.

Tarleton State University

Stephenville, Texas

http://www.tarleton.edu/

- **State-supported** comprehensive, founded 1899, part of Texas A&M University System
- **Small-town** 175-acre campus with easy access to Fort Worth
- **Endowment** $37.0 million
- **Coed** 11,463 undergraduate students, 70% full-time, 55% women, 45% men
- **Moderately difficult** entrance level, 74% of applicants were admitted

UNDERGRAD STUDENTS

8,059 full-time, 3,404 part-time. 2% are from out of state; 8% Black or African American, non-Hispanic/Latino; 19% Hispanic/Latino; 1% Asian, non-Hispanic/Latino; 0.1% Native Hawaiian or other Pacific Islander, non-Hispanic/Latino; 0.6% American Indian or Alaska Native, non-Hispanic/Latino; 3% Two or more races, non-Hispanic/Latino; 0.7% Race/ethnicity unknown; 0.3% international; 14% transferred in; 28% live on campus.

Freshmen:

Admission: 6,433 applied, 4,740 admitted, 2,032 enrolled. ***Test scores:*** SAT critical reading scores over 500: 37%; SAT math scores over 500: 42%; SAT writing scores over 500: 27%; ACT scores over 18: 69%; SAT critical reading scores over 600: 8%; SAT math scores over 600: 7%; SAT writing scores over 600: 3%; ACT scores over 24: 23%; ACT scores over 30: 1%.

FACULTY

Total: 666, 55% full-time.

Student/faculty ratio: 19:1.

ACADEMICS

Calendar: semesters. *Degrees:* associate, bachelor's, master's, and doctoral.

Special study options: academic remediation for entering students, accelerated degree program, adult/continuing education programs, advanced placement credit, cooperative education, distance learning, double majors, honors programs, independent study, internships, off-campus study, part-time degree program, services for LD students, study abroad, summer session for credit. ***ROTC:*** Army (b).

Computers: 1,200 computers/terminals are available on campus for general student use. Students can access the following: campus intranet, computer help desk, free student e-mail accounts, online (class) grades, online (class) registration, online (class) schedules. Campuswide network is available. 100% of college-owned or -operated housing units are wired for high-speed Internet access. Wireless service is available via entire campus.

Library: Dick Smith Library plus 1 other. Students can reserve study rooms.

STUDENT LIFE

Housing options: on-campus residence required through sophomore year; coed, men-only, women-only. Campus housing is university owned and leased by the school. Freshman campus housing is guaranteed.

Activities and organizations: drama/theater group, student-run newspaper, radio station, choral group, marching band, Student Government Association, Student Programming Association, Kappa Delta Rho, Delta Zeta, Chi Alpha, national fraternities, national sororities.

Athletics Member NCAA. All Division II. ***Intercollegiate sports:*** baseball M(s), basketball M(s)/W(s), cheerleading M(s)/W(s), cross-country running M(s)/W(s), football M(s), golf W(s), softball W(s), tennis W(s), track and field M(s)/W(s), volleyball W(s). ***Intramural sports:*** archery M/W, basketball M/W, football M/W, golf M/W, racquetball M/W, soccer M/W, softball M/W, table tennis M/W, tennis M/W, volleyball M/W.

Campus security: 24-hour emergency response devices and patrols, student patrols, late-night transport/escort service, controlled dormitory access.

Student services: health clinic, personal/psychological counseling, legal services.

COSTS & FINANCIAL AID

Costs (2017–18) ***Tuition:*** state resident $4876 full-time, $154 per credit hour part-time; nonresident $16,858 full-time, $562 per credit hour part-time. Full-time tuition and fees vary according to course load, degree level, program, and student level. Part-time tuition and fees vary according to course load, degree level, program, and student level. No tuition increase for student's term of enrollment. ***Required fees:*** $3827 full-time. ***Room and board:*** $9970; room only: $6220. Room and board charges vary according to board plan and housing facility. ***Payment plan:*** installment.

Financial Aid Of all full-time matriculated undergraduates who enrolled in 2015, 6,524 applied for aid, 5,319 were judged to have need, 204 had their need fully met. ***Average percent of need met:*** 53. ***Average financial aid package:*** $9221. ***Average need-based loan:*** $3940. ***Average need-based gift aid:*** $6874. ***Average indebtedness upon graduation:*** $25,725. ***Financial aid deadline:*** 11/1.

APPLYING

Standardized Tests *Required:* SAT or ACT (for admission).

Options: electronic application, early action.

Application fee: $45.

Required: high school transcript.

Application deadlines: 7/21 (freshmen), 7/21 (transfers), 3/1 (early action).

CONTACT

Ms. Cindy Hess, Director of Undergraduate Admissions, Tarleton State University, Box T-0030, Tarleton Station, Stephenville, TX 76402. *Phone:* 254-968-9123. *Toll-free phone:* 800-687-8236. *Fax:* 254-968-9951. *E-mail:* uadm@tarleton.edu.

Texas A&M International University

Laredo, Texas

http://www.tamiu.edu/

- **State-supported** comprehensive, founded 1969, part of Texas A&M University System
- **Urban** 300-acre campus
- **Endowment** $46.0 million
- **Coed** 6,591 undergraduate students, 74% full-time, 60% women, 40% men
- **Moderately difficult** entrance level, 54% of applicants were admitted

UNDERGRAD STUDENTS

4,860 full-time, 1,731 part-time. Students come from 21 states and territories; 24 other countries; 0.9% are from out of state; 0.3% Black or African American, non-Hispanic/Latino; 95% Hispanic/Latino; 0.4% Asian, non-Hispanic/Latino; 0.1% American Indian or Alaska Native, non-Hispanic/Latino; 0.3% Two or more races, non-Hispanic/Latino; 0.2% Race/ethnicity unknown; 2% international; 8% transferred in; 9% live on campus.

Freshmen:

Admission: 6,306 applied, 3,379 admitted, 1,026 enrolled. ***Average high school GPA:*** 3.6. ***Test scores:*** SAT critical reading scores over 500: 27%; SAT math scores over 500: 34%; SAT writing scores over 500: 21%; ACT scores over 18: 55%; SAT critical reading scores over 600: 3%; SAT math scores over 600: 7%; SAT writing scores over 600: 3%; ACT scores over 24: 12%.

Retention: 77% of full-time freshmen returned.

FACULTY

Total: 366, 62% full-time, 55% with terminal degrees.

Student/faculty ratio: 20:1.

ACADEMICS

Calendar: semesters. *Degrees:* bachelor's, master's, and doctoral.

Special study options: academic remediation for entering students, advanced placement credit, distance learning, double majors, English as a second language, honors programs, independent study, internships, part-time degree program, services for LD students, study abroad, summer session for credit. ***ROTC:*** Army (b).

Computers: 970 computers/terminals are available on campus for general student use. Students can access the following: free student e-mail accounts, online (class) grades, online (class) registration, online (class) schedules. Campuswide network is available. 100% of college-owned or -operated housing units are wired for high-speed Internet access. Wireless service is available via entire campus.

Library: Sue and Radcliff Killam Library. *Books:* 261,216 (physical), 497,827 (digital/electronic); *Serial titles:* 213 (physical), 65,322 (digital/electronic); *Databases:* 302. Weekly public service hours: 94; students can reserve study rooms.

STUDENT LIFE

Housing options: coed. Campus housing is university owned and is provided by a third party.

Activities and organizations: student-run newspaper, choral group, TAMIU Trailblazers, Student Nurses Association, National Student Speech Language Hearing Association (NSSLHA), University Honor Program, American Medical Student Association, national fraternities, national sororities.

Athletics Member NCAA. All Division II. ***Intercollegiate sports:*** baseball M(s), basketball M(s)/W(s), cross-country running M(s)/W(s), golf M(s)/W(s), soccer M(s)/W(s), softball W(s), volleyball W(s). ***Intramural sports:*** badminton M/W, basketball M/W, soccer M/W, softball M/W, table tennis M/W, ultimate Frisbee M/W, volleyball M/W.

Campus security: 24-hour emergency response devices and patrols, late-night transport/escort service, controlled dormitory access, active shooter response training for faculty, staff, and new students; timely on-going threat information dissemination.

Student services: health clinic, personal/psychological counseling.

COSTS & FINANCIAL AID

Costs (2017–18) ***Tuition:*** state resident $8320 full-time; nonresident $20,704 full-time. Full-time tuition and fees vary according to course load. Part-time tuition and fees vary according to course load and reciprocity agreements. ***Required fees:*** $3136 full-time. ***Room and board:*** $7882; room only: $5126. Room and board charges vary according to board plan and housing facility. ***Payment plan:*** installment. ***Waivers:*** senior citizens.

Financial Aid Of all full-time matriculated undergraduates who enrolled in 2015, 4,374 applied for aid, 3,897 were judged to have need, 5 had their need fully met. 100 Federal Work-Study jobs (averaging $2400). 25 state and other part-time jobs (averaging $2507). In 2015, 181 non-need-based awards were made. ***Average percent of need met:*** 66. ***Average financial aid package:*** $11,567. ***Average need-based loan:*** $3937. ***Average need-based gift aid:*** $6891. ***Average non-need-based aid:*** $3467. ***Average indebtedness upon graduation:*** $17,394. ***Financial aid deadline:*** 7/30.

APPLYING

Standardized Tests *Required:* SAT or ACT (for admission).

Options: electronic application, early admission, deferred entrance.

Required: high school transcript.

Application deadlines: 7/1 (freshmen), 7/1 (transfers).

Notification: 7/15 (freshmen), 7/15 (transfers).

CONTACT

Ms. Rosa Dickinson, Director of Admissions, Texas A&M International University, 5201 University Boulevard, Laredo, TX 78041-1900. *Phone:* 956-326-2200. *Toll-free phone:* 888-489-2648. *E-mail:* adms@tamiu.edu.

Texas A&M University

College Station, Texas

http://www.tamu.edu/

- **State-supported** university, founded 1876, part of Texas A&M University System
- **Suburban** campus with easy access to Houston
- **Endowment** $10.5 billion
- **Coed** 50,735 undergraduate students, 88% full-time, 48% women, 52% men
- **Moderately difficult** entrance level, 66% of applicants were admitted

UNDERGRAD STUDENTS

44,818 full-time, 5,917 part-time. Students come from 53 states and territories; 96 other countries; 4% are from out of state; 3% Black or African American, non-Hispanic/Latino; 23% Hispanic/Latino; 6% Asian, non-Hispanic/Latino; 0.1% Native Hawaiian or other Pacific Islander, non-Hispanic/Latino; 0.3% American Indian or Alaska Native, non-Hispanic/Latino; 3% Two or more races, non-Hispanic/Latino; 0.2% Race/ethnicity unknown; 1% international; 5% transferred in; 23% live on campus.

Freshmen:

Admission: 35,494 applied, 23,594 admitted, 10,145 enrolled. ***Test scores:*** SAT critical reading scores over 500: 83%; SAT math scores over 500: 90%; SAT writing scores over 500: 73%; ACT scores over 18: 99%; SAT critical reading scores over 600: 45%; SAT math scores over 600: 58%; SAT writing scores over 600: 31%; ACT scores over 24: 81%; SAT critical reading scores over 700: 10%; SAT math scores over 700: 16%; SAT writing scores over 700: 5%; ACT scores over 30: 31%.

Retention: 91% of full-time freshmen returned.

FACULTY

Total: 3,886, 78% full-time, 85% with terminal degrees.

Student/faculty ratio: 21:1.

ACADEMICS

Calendar: semesters. *Degrees:* bachelor's, master's, doctoral, post-master's, and postbachelor's certificates.

Special study options: academic remediation for entering students, accelerated degree program, advanced placement credit, cooperative education, distance learning, double majors, English as a second language, honors programs, independent study, internships, off-campus study, part-time degree program, services for LD students, study abroad, summer session for credit. ***ROTC:*** Army (b), Navy (b), Air Force (b).

Computers: 2,666 computers/terminals and 500 ports are available on campus for general student use. Students can access the following: campus intranet, computer help desk, free student e-mail accounts, online (class) grades, online (class) registration, online (class) schedules. Campuswide network is available. 100% of college-owned or -operated housing units are wired for high-speed Internet access. Wireless service is available via entire campus.

Library: Sterling C. Evans Library plus 6 others. *Books:* 3.8 million (physical), 1.8 million (digital/electronic); *Serial titles:* 7,647 (physical), 121,167 (digital/electronic); *Databases:* 1,712. Weekly public service hours: 144; study areas open 24 hours, 5-7 days a week; students can reserve study rooms.

STUDENT LIFE

Housing options: coed, men-only, women-only, special housing for students with disabilities. Campus housing is university owned, leased by the school and is provided by a third party.

Activities and organizations: drama/theater group, student-run newspaper, radio and television station, choral group, marching band, Memorial Student Center, Corps of Cadets, Fish Camp, Student Government, national fraternities, national sororities.

Athletics Member NCAA. All Division I except football (Division I-A). ***Intercollegiate sports:*** baseball M(s), basketball M(s)/W(s), cross-country running M/W, equestrian sports W(s), golf M(s)/W(s), soccer W(s), softball W(s), swimming and diving M(s)/W(s), tennis M(s)/W(s), track and field M(s)/W(s), volleyball W(s). ***Intramural sports:*** archery M(c)/W(c), baseball M(c), basketball M/W, bowling M(c)/W(c), equestrian sports M(c)/W(c), fencing M(c)/W(c), football M/W, golf M/W, lacrosse M(c)/W(c), racquetball M(c)/W(c), riflery M(c)/W(c), rowing M(c)/W(c), rugby M(c)/W(c), sailing M(c)/W(c), soccer M/W, softball M/W, table tennis M/W, tennis M/W, triathlon M(c)/W(c), ultimate Frisbee M(c), volleyball M(c)/W(c), water polo M(c)/W(c), weight lifting M(c)/W(c), wrestling M(c)/W(c).

Campus security: 24-hour emergency response devices and patrols, late-night transport/escort service, controlled dormitory access, student escorts.

Student services: health clinic, personal/psychological counseling, women's center, legal services.

COSTS & FINANCIAL AID

Costs (2017–18) ***Tuition:*** state resident $6679 full-time, $223 per credit hour part-time; nonresident $26,857 full-time, $895 per credit hour part-time. Full-time tuition and fees vary according to program. Part-time tuition and fees vary according to program. No tuition increase for student's term of enrollment. ***Required fees:*** $3351 full-time. ***Room and board:*** $10,368. Room and board charges vary according to board plan, housing facility, and location. ***Payment plan:*** installment.

Financial Aid Of all full-time matriculated undergraduates who enrolled in 2014, 26,167 applied for aid, 18,915 were judged to have need, 5,330 had their need fully met. 907 Federal Work-Study jobs (averaging $2171). 150 state and other part-time jobs (averaging $2426). In 2014, 2485 non-need-based awards were made. ***Average percent of need met:*** 66. ***Average financial aid package:*** $15,849. ***Average need-based loan:*** $7428. ***Average need-based gift aid:*** $9818. ***Average non-need-based aid:*** $3580. ***Average indebtedness upon graduation:*** $24,276.

APPLYING

Standardized Tests *Required:* SAT or ACT (for admission).

Options: electronic application.

Application fee: $75.

Required: essay or personal statement, high school transcript. ***Required for some:*** Apply Texas application, minimum SAT math score of 550 or ACT math score of 24 for the Dwight Look College of Engineering.

Application deadlines: 12/1 (freshmen), 3/15 (transfers).

Notification: continuous (freshmen), continuous (transfers).

CONTACT

Office of Admissions, Texas A&M University, Freshman Admissions, PO Box 30014, College Station, TX 77842-3014. *Phone:* 979-845-1060. *Fax:* 979-845-1808.

Texas A&M University–Central Texas

Killeen, Texas

http://www.tamuct.edu/

- **State-supported** upper-level, founded 2009, part of Texas A&M University System
- **Rural** 662-acre campus
- **Coed** 2,021 undergraduate students, 31% full-time, 60% women, 40% men

UNDERGRAD STUDENTS
633 full-time, 1,388 part-time. Students come from 30 states and territories; 3 other countries; 3% are from out of state; 99% transferred in.

FACULTY
Total: 190, 33% full-time, 49% with terminal degrees.

Student/faculty ratio: 20:1.

ACADEMICS
Calendar: semesters. *Degrees:* certificates, bachelor's, master's, and post-master's certificates.

Special study options: accelerated degree program, advanced placement credit, cooperative education, distance learning, double majors, independent study, internships, off-campus study, part-time degree program, services for LD students, study abroad, summer session for credit. ***ROTC:*** Army (b).

Computers: 48 computers/terminals are available on campus for general student use. Students can access the following: computer help desk, free student e-mail accounts, online (class) grades, online (class) registration, online (class) schedules. Campuswide network is available. Wireless service is available via entire campus.

Library: University Library. *Books:* 79,788 (physical), 440,601 (digital/electronic); *Serial titles:* 155 (physical), 116,827 (digital/electronic); *Databases:* 175. Weekly public service hours: 81; students can reserve study rooms.

STUDENT LIFE
Housing options: college housing not available.

Activities and organizations: student-run newspaper.

Athletics ***Intramural sports:*** rugby M(c)/W(c).

Campus security: 24-hour emergency response devices and patrols.

Student services: personal/psychological counseling.

COSTS
Costs (2016–17) ***Tuition:*** state resident $21,318 full-time, $175 per credit hour part-time; nonresident $31,797 full-time, $620 per credit hour part-time. Full-time tuition and fees vary according to course load. Part-time tuition and fees vary according to course load. No tuition increase for student's term of enrollment. ***Required fees:*** $2085 full-time, $211 per credit hour part-time. ***Payment plan:*** installment.

APPLYING
Options: electronic application, deferred entrance.

Notification: continuous (transfers).

CONTACT
Texas A&M University–Central Texas, 1001 Leadership Place, Killeen, TX 76549. *Phone:* 254-519-5438.

Texas A&M University–Commerce

Commerce, Texas

http://www.tamuc.edu/

- **State-supported** university, founded 1889, part of Texas A&M University System
- **Small-town** 1883-acre campus with easy access to Dallas-Fort Worth
- **Coed** 7,642 undergraduate students, 71% full-time, 59% women, 41% men
- **Moderately difficult** entrance level, 47% of applicants were admitted

UNDERGRAD STUDENTS
5,445 full-time, 2,197 part-time. 2% are from out of state; 21% Black or African American, non-Hispanic/Latino; 17% Hispanic/Latino; 1% Asian, non-Hispanic/Latino; 0.2% Native Hawaiian or other Pacific Islander, non-Hispanic/Latino; 0.7% American Indian or Alaska Native, non-Hispanic/Latino; 5% Two or more races, non-Hispanic/Latino; 0.9% Race/ethnicity unknown; 3% international; 15% transferred in; 30% live on campus.

Freshmen:
Admission: 7,195 applied, 3,413 admitted, 1,097 enrolled. ***Average high school GPA:*** 3.23. ***Test scores:*** SAT critical reading scores over 500: 40%; SAT math scores over 500: 45%; ACT scores over 18: 81%; SAT critical reading scores over 600: 11%; SAT math scores over 600: 10%; ACT scores over 24: 27%; SAT critical reading scores over 700: 1%; ACT scores over 30: 3%.

Retention: 72% of full-time freshmen returned.

FACULTY
Total: 705, 50% full-time, 57% with terminal degrees.

Student/faculty ratio: 19:1.

ACADEMICS
Calendar: semesters. *Degrees:* bachelor's, master's, doctoral, and postbachelor's certificates.

Special study options: academic remediation for entering students, accelerated degree program, adult/continuing education programs, advanced placement credit, cooperative education, distance learning, double majors, English as a second language, freshman honors college, honors programs, independent study, internships, off-campus study, part-time degree program, services for LD students, student-designed majors, study abroad, summer session for credit. ***ROTC:*** Air Force (c).

Computers: Students can access the following: campus intranet, computer help desk, free student e-mail accounts, online (class) grades, online (class) registration, online (class) schedules. Campuswide network is available. 100% of college-owned or -operated housing units are wired for high-speed Internet access. Wireless service is available via entire campus.

Library: Gee Library.

STUDENT LIFE
Housing options: on-campus residence required for freshman year; coed, women-only, special housing for students with disabilities. Campus housing is university owned. Freshman campus housing is guaranteed.

Activities and organizations: drama/theater group, student-run newspaper, radio and television station, choral group, marching band, National Society for Leadership and Success, Residence Hall Association, Indian Students Association, The Pride Alliance, National Association of Colored Women's Club, Inc, national fraternities, national sororities.

Athletics Member NCAA. All Division II. ***Intercollegiate sports:*** basketball M(s)/W(s), cheerleading M(s)/W(s), cross-country running M(s)/W(s), football M(s), golf M(s)/W(s), soccer W(s), softball W, track and field M(s)/W(s), volleyball W(s). ***Intramural sports:*** archery M/W, badminton M/W, basketball M/W, bowling M/W, cross-country running M/W, equestrian sports M/W, football M/W, golf M/W, racquetball M/W, soccer M, softball M/W, swimming and diving M/W, table tennis M/W, tennis M/W, track and field M/W, volleyball W.

Campus security: 24-hour emergency response devices and patrols, controlled dormitory access.

Student services: health clinic, personal/psychological counseling, legal services.

COSTS & FINANCIAL AID
Costs (2017–18) ***Tuition:*** state resident $4790 full-time, $50 per credit hour part-time; nonresident $20,129 full-time, $458 per credit hour part-time. Full-time tuition and fees vary according to course load, location, program, and reciprocity agreements. Part-time tuition and fees vary according to course load, location, program, and reciprocity agreements. No tuition increase for student's term of enrollment. ***Required fees:*** $3098 full-time. ***Room and board:*** $8326. Room and board charges vary according to board plan and housing facility. ***Payment plan:*** installment. ***Waivers:*** senior citizens and employees or children of employees.

Financial Aid Of all full-time matriculated undergraduates who enrolled in 2016, 4,840 applied for aid, 4,265 were judged to have need, 281 had their need fully met. 122 Federal Work-Study jobs (averaging $1850). 15 state and other part-time jobs (averaging $1952). In 2016, 204 non-need-based awards were made. ***Average percent of need met:*** 58. ***Average financial aid package:*** $10,155. ***Average need-based loan:*** $3686. ***Average need-based gift aid:*** $8593. ***Average non-need-based aid:*** $1986. ***Average indebtedness upon graduation:*** $28,054.

APPLYING

Standardized Tests *Required:* SAT or ACT (for admission).

Options: electronic application, deferred entrance.

Required: high school transcript. ***Required for some:*** interview for honors college.

CONTACT

Mr. Jody Todhunter, Director of Admissions, Texas A&M University–Commerce, PO Box 3011, Commerce, TX 75429. *Phone:* 903-886-5072. *Toll-free phone:* 888-868-2682. *Fax:* 903-468-8698. *E-mail:* admissions@tamu-commerce.edu.

Texas A&M University–Corpus Christi

Corpus Christi, Texas

http://www.tamucc.edu/

- **State-supported** university, founded 1947, part of Texas A&M University System
- **Suburban** 317-acre campus
- **Endowment** $12.4 million
- **Coed** 10,212 undergraduate students, 82% full-time, 59% women, 41% men
- **Moderately difficult** entrance level, 86% of applicants were admitted

UNDERGRAD STUDENTS

8,363 full-time, 1,849 part-time. Students come from 37 states and territories; 34 other countries; 2% are from out of state; 7% Black or African American, non-Hispanic/Latino; 49% Hispanic/Latino; 3% Asian, non-Hispanic/Latino; 0.2% American Indian or Alaska Native, non-Hispanic/Latino; 1% Two or more races, non-Hispanic/Latino; 2% Race/ethnicity unknown; 2% international; 10% transferred in; 22% live on campus.

Freshmen:

Admission: 9,002 applied, 7,773 admitted, 2,267 enrolled. ***Average high school GPA:*** 3.26. ***Test scores:*** SAT critical reading scores over 500: 39%; SAT math scores over 500: 41%; SAT writing scores over 500: 29%; ACT scores over 18: 73%; SAT critical reading scores over 600: 8%; SAT math scores over 600: 9%; SAT writing scores over 600: 3%; ACT scores over 24: 21%; SAT critical reading scores over 700: 1%; ACT scores over 30: 1%.

Retention: 58% of full-time freshmen returned.

FACULTY

Total: 622, 69% full-time, 65% with terminal degrees.

Student/faculty ratio: 20:1.

ACADEMICS

Calendar: semesters. *Degrees:* bachelor's, master's, and doctoral.

Special study options: academic remediation for entering students, advanced placement credit, cooperative education, distance learning, double majors, English as a second language, honors programs, independent study, internships, off-campus study, part-time degree program, services for LD students, study abroad, summer session for credit. ***ROTC:*** Army (b).

Unusual degree programs: 3-2 business administration; engineering; nursing.

Computers: 1,236 computers/terminals are available on campus for general student use. Students can access the following: campus intranet, computer help desk, free student e-mail accounts, online (class) grades, online (class) registration, online (class) schedules. Campuswide network is available. 100% of college-owned or -operated housing units are wired for high-speed Internet access. Wireless service is available via entire campus.

Library: Mary and Jeff Bell Library. *Books:* 342,196 (physical), 163,385 (digital/electronic); *Serial titles:* 1,691 (physical), 64,357 (digital/electronic); *Databases:* 276. Weekly public service hours: 106; students can reserve study rooms.

STUDENT LIFE

Housing options: coed. Campus housing is provided by a third party.

Activities and organizations: drama/theater group, student-run newspaper, choral group, Student Accounting Society: Alpha Epsilon Delta, Student Art Association: Golden Key, Islander Cultural Alliance: Kinesiology Club, Graduate Student Association: Sea Turtle Club, Student Nurses Association, national fraternities, national sororities.

Athletics Member NCAA. All Division I. ***Intercollegiate sports:*** baseball M(s), basketball M(s)/W(s), cheerleading M/W, cross-country running M(s)/W(s), golf W(s), sand volleyball W, soccer W(s), softball W(s), tennis M(s)/W(s), track and field M(s)/W(s), volleyball W(s). ***Intramural sports:*** badminton M/W, basketball M/W, fencing M/W, football M/W, lacrosse M/W, riflery M/W, rock climbing M/W, rugby M/W, sailing M/W, sand volleyball M/W, soccer M/W, softball M/W, swimming and diving M/W, table tennis M/W, tennis M/W, track and field M/W, ultimate Frisbee M/W, volleyball M/W, weight lifting M/W.

Campus security: 24-hour emergency response devices and patrols, late-night transport/escort service, controlled dormitory access.

Student services: health clinic, personal/psychological counseling.

COSTS & FINANCIAL AID

Costs (2016–17) ***Tuition:*** state resident $4979 full-time, $176 per credit part-time; nonresident $16,567 full-time, $578 per credit part-time. Full-time tuition and fees vary according to course load, degree level, location, program, and student level. Part-time tuition and fees vary according to course load, degree level, location, program, and student level. No tuition increase for student's term of enrollment. ***Required fees:*** $3641 full-time, $402 per credit part-time. ***Room and board:*** $9195; room only: $5484. Room and board charges vary according to board plan and housing facility. ***Payment plan:*** installment. ***Waivers:*** senior citizens.

Financial Aid Of all full-time matriculated undergraduates who enrolled in 2016, 6,457 applied for aid, 5,287 were judged to have need, 150 had their need fully met. 303 Federal Work-Study jobs (averaging $3121). 248 state and other part-time jobs (averaging $2742). In 2016, 390 non-need-based awards were made. ***Average percent of need met:*** 53. ***Average financial aid package:*** $9234. ***Average need-based loan:*** $3756. ***Average need-based gift aid:*** $6540. ***Average non-need-based aid:*** $2517. ***Average indebtedness upon graduation:*** $17,804.

APPLYING

Standardized Tests *Required:* SAT or ACT (for admission).

Options: electronic application.

Application fee: $50.

Required: high school transcript, minimum 2.0 GPA.

Application deadlines: 7/1 (freshmen), 7/1 (transfers).

Notification: continuous (freshmen), continuous (out-of-state freshmen), continuous (transfers).

CONTACT

Mrs. Monica Martinez, Assistant Director of Admissions, Texas A&M University–Corpus Christi, SSC 107, 6300 Ocean Drive, Unit 5774, Corpus Christi, TX 78412-5774. *Phone:* 361-825-2624. *Toll-free phone:* 800-482-6822. *Fax:* 361-825-5887. *E-mail:* monica.martinez@tamucc.edu.

Texas A&M University–Kingsville

Kingsville, Texas

http://www.tamuk.edu/

- **State-supported** university, founded 1925, part of Texas A&M University System
- **Small-town** 250-acre campus
- **Endowment** $21.3 million
- **Coed** 6,605 undergraduate students, 77% full-time, 47% women, 53% men
- **Moderately difficult** entrance level, 82% of applicants were admitted

UNDERGRAD STUDENTS

5,077 full-time, 1,528 part-time. Students come from 27 states and territories; 30 other countries; 1% are from out of state; 7% Black or African American, non-Hispanic/Latino; 70% Hispanic/Latino; 0.8% Asian, non-Hispanic/Latino; 0.1% Native Hawaiian or other Pacific Islander, non-Hispanic/Latino; 0.1% American Indian or Alaska Native, non-Hispanic/Latino; 0.6% Two or more races, non-Hispanic/Latino; 0.6% Race/ethnicity unknown; 3% international; 7% transferred in; 32% live on campus.

Freshmen:
Admission: 7,344 applied, 6,049 admitted, 1,300 enrolled. ***Average high school GPA:*** 3.35. ***Test scores:*** SAT critical reading scores over 500: 34%; SAT math scores over 500: 45%; SAT writing scores over 500: 18%; ACT scores over 18: 71%; SAT critical reading scores over 600: 6%; SAT math scores over 600: 10%; SAT writing scores over 600: 2%; ACT scores over 24: 19%; SAT critical reading scores over 700: 1%; SAT math scores over 700: 1%; ACT scores over 30: 1%.

Retention: 69% of full-time freshmen returned.

ACADEMICS
Calendar: semesters. *Degrees:* bachelor's, master's, doctoral, and postbachelor's certificates.

Special study options: academic remediation for entering students, adult/continuing education programs, advanced placement credit, distance learning, double majors, English as a second language, honors programs, independent study, internships, off-campus study, part-time degree program, services for LD students, study abroad, summer session for credit. ***ROTC:*** Army (b).

Computers: 400 computers/terminals are available on campus for general student use. Students can access the following: campus intranet, computer help desk, free student e-mail accounts, online (class) grades, online (class) registration, online (class) schedules. Campuswide network is available.

Library: James C. Jernigan Library. *Books:* 655,779 (physical), 207,818 (digital/electronic); *Serial titles:* 467 (physical), 40,228 (digital/electronic); *Databases:* 142. Weekly public service hours: 100; students can reserve study rooms.

STUDENT LIFE
Housing options: on-campus residence required for freshman year; coed, men-only, women-only, special housing for students with disabilities. Campus housing is university owned. Freshman campus housing is guaranteed.

Activities and organizations: drama/theater group, student-run newspaper, radio and television station, choral group, marching band, national fraternities, national sororities.

Athletics Member NCAA. All Division II. ***Intercollegiate sports:*** baseball M, basketball M/W, cross-country running M/W, football M, golf W, softball W, tennis W, track and field M/W, volleyball W. ***Intramural sports:*** badminton M/W, basketball M/W, racquetball M/W, soccer M/W, softball M/W, tennis M/W, ultimate Frisbee M/W, volleyball W.

Campus security: controlled dormitory access.

Student services: health clinic, personal/psychological counseling.

COSTS & FINANCIAL AID
Costs (2016–17) ***Tuition:*** $3851 per year part-time; state resident $8050 full-time, $120 per credit hour part-time; nonresident $21,356 full-time, $458 per credit hour part-time. Full-time tuition and fees vary according to course load and degree level. Part-time tuition and fees vary according to course load and degree level. No tuition increase for student's term of enrollment. ***Room and board:*** $8530. Room and board charges vary according to board plan and housing facility. ***Payment plan:*** installment. ***Waivers:*** senior citizens and employees or children of employees.

Financial Aid Of all full-time matriculated undergraduates who enrolled in 2005, 4,449 applied for aid, 4,214 were judged to have need, 2,899 had their need fully met. ***Average financial aid package:*** $6500. ***Average need-based loan:*** $3875. ***Average need-based gift aid:*** $6500. ***Average indebtedness upon graduation:*** $2867.

APPLYING
Standardized Tests *Required:* SAT or ACT (for admission).

Options: electronic application.

Application fee: $25.

Required for some: essay or personal statement, high school transcript, minimum 2.0 GPA, 2 letters of recommendation, written statement and two letters of recommendation for alternate admissions process.

Application deadlines: 8/1 (freshmen), rolling (out-of-state freshmen), rolling (transfers).

CONTACT
Laura Knippers, Associate Director of Admissions, Texas A&M University–Kingsville, MSC 128, 700 University Boulevard, Kingsville, TX 78363. *Phone:* 361-593-2311. *Toll-free phone:* 800-687-6000. *E-mail:* laura.knippers@tamuk.edu.

Texas A&M University–San Antonio

San Antonio, Texas

http://www.tamusa.tamus.edu/

CONTACT
Ms. Jennifer Zamarripa, Director of Admissions and Registrar, Texas A&M University–San Antonio, One University Way, San Antonio, TX 78224. *Phone:* 210-932-6201. *E-mail:* jennifer.zamarripa@tamusa.tamus.edu.

Texas A&M University–Texarkana

Texarkana, Texas

http://www.tamut.edu/

CONTACT
Mrs. Patricia Black, Director of Admissions and Registrar, Texas A&M University–Texarkana, PO Box 5518, Texarkana, TX 75505-5518. *Phone:* 903-223-3068. *Fax:* 903-223-3140. *E-mail:* admissions@tamut.edu.

Texas Christian University

Fort Worth, Texas

http://www.tcu.edu/

- **Independent** university, founded 1873, affiliated with Christian Church (Disciples of Christ)
- **Suburban** 289-acre campus with easy access to Dallas-Fort Worth
- **Endowment** $1.4 billion
- **Coed** 8,891 undergraduate students, 97% full-time, 60% women, 40% men
- **Very difficult** entrance level, 38% of applicants were admitted

UNDERGRAD STUDENTS
8,608 full-time, 283 part-time. Students come from 50 states and territories; 72 other countries; 46% are from out of state; 5% Black or African American, non-Hispanic/Latino; 12% Hispanic/Latino; 3% Asian, non-Hispanic/Latino; 0.2% Native Hawaiian or other Pacific Islander, non-Hispanic/Latino; 0.8% American Indian or Alaska Native, non-Hispanic/Latino; 0.3% Two or more races, non-Hispanic/Latino; 2% Race/ethnicity unknown; 5% international; 5% transferred in; 49% live on campus.

Freshmen:
Admission: 19,972 applied, 7,506 admitted, 1,888 enrolled.
Retention: 91% of full-time freshmen returned.

FACULTY
Total: 1,031, 62% full-time, 69% with terminal degrees.
Student/faculty ratio: 13:1.

ACADEMICS
Calendar: semesters. *Degrees:* certificates, diplomas, bachelor's, master's, doctoral, post-master's, and postbachelor's certificates.

Special study options: accelerated degree program, advanced placement credit, distance learning, double majors, English as a second language, honors programs, independent study, internships, part-time degree program, services for LD students, student-designed majors, study abroad, summer session for credit. ***ROTC:*** Army (b), Air Force (b).

Computers: 1,400 computers/terminals and 10,000 ports are available on campus for general student use. Students can access the following: campus intranet, computer help desk, free student e-mail accounts, online (class) grades, online (class) registration, online (class) schedules. Campuswide network is available. 100% of college-owned or -operated housing units are wired for high-speed Internet access. Wireless service is available via entire campus.

Library: Mary Couts Burnett Library. *Books:* 1.4 million (physical), 903,006 (digital/electronic); *Serial titles:* 10,139 (physical), 120,885 (digital/electronic); *Databases:* 475. Study areas open 24 hours, 5-7 days a week; students can reserve study rooms.

STUDENT LIFE

Housing options: on-campus residence required through sophomore year; coed, men-only, women-only, special housing for students with disabilities. Campus housing is university owned and leased by the school. Freshman campus housing is guaranteed.

Activities and organizations: drama/theater group, student-run newspaper, radio and television station, choral group, marching band, the Crew, Catholic Community, Ignite, LEAPS, Business School organizations, national fraternities, national sororities.

Athletics Member NCAA. All Division I. ***Intercollegiate sports:*** baseball M(s), basketball M(s)/W(s), cross-country running M(s)/W(s), equestrian sports W(s), football M(s), golf M(s)/W(s), gymnastics M(c)/W(c), ice hockey M(c), lacrosse M(c)/W(c), riflery W(s), rock climbing M(c)/W(c), rowing M(c)/W(c), rugby M(c)/W(c), sand volleyball W(s), soccer M(c)/W(s), swimming and diving M(s)/W(s), tennis M(s)/W(s), track and field M(s)/W(s), triathlon M(c)/W(c), ultimate Frisbee M(c)/W(c), volleyball M(c)/W(s), water polo M(c)/W(c). ***Intramural sports:*** baseball M(c), basketball M/W, bowling M/W, football M/W, golf M(c)/W(c), racquetball M/W, sand volleyball M/W, soccer M/W(c), table tennis M/W, tennis M(c)/W(c), ultimate Frisbee M/W, volleyball M/W(c).

Campus security: 24-hour emergency response devices and patrols, late-night transport/escort service, controlled dormitory access, emergency call boxes, video surveillance in parking lots, self-defense education, lighted sidewalks, Emergency Mass Notification System.

Student services: health clinic, personal/psychological counseling, women's center.

COSTS & FINANCIAL AID

Costs (2016–17) ***Comprehensive fee:*** $54,670 includes full-time tuition ($42,580), mandatory fees ($90), and room and board ($12,000). Part-time tuition: $1800 per credit hour. Part-time tuition and fees vary according to course load. ***Required fees:*** $45 per term part-time. ***College room only:*** $7300. Room and board charges vary according to board plan and housing facility. ***Payment plan:*** installment. ***Waivers:*** employees or children of employees.

Financial Aid Of all full-time matriculated undergraduates who enrolled in 2016, 4,115 applied for aid, 3,248 were judged to have need, 905 had their need fully met. 1,244 Federal Work-Study jobs (averaging $2076). In 2016, 2371 non-need-based awards were made. ***Average percent of need met:*** 66. ***Average financial aid package:*** $29,456. ***Average need-based loan:*** $4537. ***Average need-based gift aid:*** $26,467. ***Average non-need-based aid:*** $16,838. ***Average indebtedness upon graduation:*** $36,550. ***Financial aid deadline:*** 5/1.

APPLYING

Standardized Tests *Required:* SAT or ACT (for admission).

Options: electronic application, early decision, early action, deferred entrance.

Application fee: $40.

Required: essay or personal statement, high school transcript, 2 letters of recommendation.

Application deadlines: 2/15 (freshmen), 8/1 (transfers), 11/1 (early action).

Early decision deadline: 11/1.

Notification: 4/1 (freshmen), continuous (transfers), 12/5 (early decision), 12/15 (early action).

CONTACT

Mr. Mike Mooneyham, Director of Freshman Admission, Texas Christian University, TCU Office of Admission, TCU Box 297013, Fort Worth, TX 76129. *Phone:* 817-257-7490. *Toll-free phone:* 800-828-3764. *Fax:* 817-257-7268. *E-mail:* frogmail@tcu.edu.

Texas College

Tyler, Texas

http://www.texascollege.edu/

- **Independent** 4-year, founded 1894, affiliated with Christian Methodist Episcopal Church
- **Urban** 25-acre campus
- **Endowment** $1.3 million
- **Coed** 960 undergraduate students, 97% full-time, 41% women, 59% men
- 32% of applicants were admitted

UNDERGRAD STUDENTS

932 full-time, 28 part-time. Students come from 26 states and territories; 6 other countries; 14% are from out of state; 87% Black or African American, non-Hispanic/Latino; 7% Hispanic/Latino; 0.1% Asian, non-Hispanic/Latino; 0.1% American Indian or Alaska Native, non-Hispanic/Latino; 2% Race/ethnicity unknown; 2% international; 18% transferred in; 48% live on campus.

Freshmen:

Admission: 4,190 applied, 1,337 admitted, 271 enrolled. ***Average high school GPA:*** 2.9.

Retention: 70% of full-time freshmen returned.

FACULTY

Total: 46, 83% full-time, 46% with terminal degrees.

Student/faculty ratio: 20:1.

ACADEMICS

Calendar: semesters. *Degrees:* associate and bachelor's.

Special study options: academic remediation for entering students, adult/continuing education programs, advanced placement credit, distance learning, internships, services for LD students, summer session for credit.

Computers: 300 computers/terminals and 300 ports are available on campus for general student use. Students can access the following: campus intranet, computer help desk, free student e-mail accounts, online (class) grades, online (class) schedules. Campuswide network is available. 100% of college-owned or -operated housing units are wired for high-speed Internet access. Wireless service is available via entire campus.

Library: D. R. Glass Library. *Books:* 40,000 (physical), 155,000 (digital/electronic); *Serial titles:* 500 (physical); *Databases:* 73. Weekly public service hours: 69; students can reserve study rooms.

STUDENT LIFE

Housing options: men-only, women-only, special housing for students with disabilities. Campus housing is university owned.

Activities and organizations: choral group, marching band, national fraternities, national sororities.

Athletics Member NAIA. ***Intercollegiate sports:*** baseball M, basketball M/W, cheerleading M/W, football M, soccer M/W, softball W, track and field M/W, volleyball W. ***Intramural sports:*** basketball M/W, football M.

Campus security: 24-hour emergency response devices and patrols.

Student services: health clinic.

COSTS & FINANCIAL AID

Costs (2017–18) ***Comprehensive fee:*** $13,604 includes full-time tuition ($8204), mandatory fees ($1800), and room and board ($3600). ***Payment plan:*** installment. ***Waivers:*** employees or children of employees.

Financial Aid Of all full-time matriculated undergraduates who enrolled in 2011, 928 applied for aid, 906 were judged to have need, 26 had their need fully met. 160 Federal Work-Study jobs (averaging $1320). 17 state and other part-time jobs (averaging $1010). In 2011, 16 non-need-based awards were made. ***Average percent of need met:*** 53. ***Average financial aid package:*** $9329. ***Average need-based loan:*** $3288. ***Average need-based gift aid:*** $6285. ***Average non-need-based aid:*** $2433. ***Average indebtedness upon graduation:*** $21,147.

APPLYING

Options: electronic application, early admission.

Application fee: $20.

Required: high school transcript, minimum 2.0 GPA.

Application deadlines: rolling (freshmen), rolling (transfers).

Notification: continuous (freshmen), continuous (transfers).

CONTACT

Mr. Ronald MsDowell, Director of Financial Aid, Texas College, 2404 North Grand Avenue, Tyler, TX 75702. *Phone:* 903-593-8311 Ext. 2297. *Toll-free phone:* 800-306-6299. *Fax:* 903-593-6551. *E-mail:* rmcdowell@texascollege.edu.

Texas Lutheran University
Seguin, Texas
http://www.tlu.edu/

- **Independent** comprehensive, founded 1891, affiliated with Evangelical Lutheran Church
- **Suburban** 196-acre campus with easy access to San Antonio, Austin
- **Endowment** $87.7 million
- **Coed** 1,283 undergraduate students, 95% full-time, 51% women, 49% men

UNDERGRAD STUDENTS
1,213 full-time, 70 part-time. Students come from 17 states and territories; 13 other countries; 2% are from out of state; 10% Black or African American, non-Hispanic/Latino; 32% Hispanic/Latino; 0.6% Asian, non-Hispanic/Latino; 0.3% American Indian or Alaska Native, non-Hispanic/Latino; 1% Two or more races, non-Hispanic/Latino; 2% Race/ethnicity unknown; 0.5% international; 4% transferred in; 60% live on campus.

Freshmen:
Admission: 377 enrolled. ***Average high school GPA:*** 3.32. ***Test scores:*** SAT critical reading scores over 500: 45%; SAT math scores over 500: 47%; SAT writing scores over 500: 28%; ACT scores over 18: 87%; SAT critical reading scores over 600: 10%; SAT math scores over 600: 11%; SAT writing scores over 600: 4%; ACT scores over 24: 23%; ACT scores over 30: 1%.

Retention: 68% of full-time freshmen returned.

FACULTY
Total: 135, 61% full-time, 61% with terminal degrees.

Student/faculty ratio: 16:1.

ACADEMICS
Calendar: semesters. *Degrees:* bachelor's and master's.

Special study options: advanced placement credit, double majors, external degree program, honors programs, independent study, internships, part-time degree program, services for LD students, study abroad, summer session for credit. ***ROTC:*** Army (c), Air Force (c).

Unusual degree programs: 3-2 engineering with Texas A&M University, Texas Tech University, Texas State University.

Computers: 264 computers/terminals and 57 ports are available on campus for general student use. Students can access the following: campus intranet, computer help desk, free student e-mail accounts, online (class) grades, online (class) registration, online (class) schedules, free printing. Campuswide network is available. 100% of college-owned or -operated housing units are wired for high-speed Internet access. Wireless service is available via entire campus.

Library: Blumberg Memorial Library plus 1 other. *Books:* 107,981 (physical), 54,856 (digital/electronic); *Serial titles:* 937 (physical), 58,647 (digital/electronic); *Databases:* 56. Weekly public service hours: 86; students can reserve study rooms.

STUDENT LIFE
Housing options: on-campus residence required through sophomore year; coed, special housing for students with disabilities. Campus housing is university owned. Freshman campus housing is guaranteed.

Activities and organizations: drama/theater group, student-run newspaper, choral group, Alpha Lambda Delta, Pre Health Professions Club, Xi Tau, Sigma Phi Theta, Mexican American Student Association.

Athletics Member NCAA. All Division III. ***Intercollegiate sports:*** baseball M, basketball M/W, cross-country running M/W, football M, golf M/W, soccer M/W, softball W, tennis M/W, track and field M/W, volleyball W. ***Intramural sports:*** basketball M/W, bowling M/W, football M, racquetball M/W, softball M/W, tennis M/W, volleyball M/W.

Campus security: 24-hour emergency response devices and patrols, late-night transport/escort service, controlled dormitory access.

Student services: health clinic, personal/psychological counseling, women's center.

COSTS & FINANCIAL AID
Costs (2017–18) ***Comprehensive fee:*** $38,720 includes full-time tuition ($28,600), mandatory fees ($400), and room and board ($9720). Full-time tuition and fees vary according to course load. Part-time tuition: $945 per semester hour. ***Required fees:*** $155 per term part-time. ***College room only:*** $5600. Room and board charges vary according to board plan and housing facility. ***Payment plan:*** installment. ***Waivers:*** children of alumni and employees or children of employees.

Financial Aid Of all full-time matriculated undergraduates who enrolled in 2016, 1,115 applied for aid, 980 were judged to have need. In 2016, 6 non-need-based awards were made. ***Average financial aid package:*** $25,676. ***Average need-based loan:*** $4232. ***Average need-based gift aid:*** $20,868. ***Average non-need-based aid:*** $14,746. ***Average indebtedness upon graduation:*** $37,337.

APPLYING
Standardized Tests *Required:* SAT or ACT (for admission).

Required: high school transcript, 2 letters of recommendation. ***Required for some:*** minimum 2.0 GPA. ***Recommended:*** essay or personal statement, interview.

CONTACT
Mr. Tom Oliver, Vice President for Enrollment Services, Texas Lutheran University, 1000 West Court Street, Seguin, TX 78155-5999. *Phone:* 830-372-8053. *Toll-free phone:* 800-771-8521. *Fax:* 830-372-8096. *E-mail:* toliver@tlu.edu.

Texas Southern University
Houston, Texas
http://www.tsu.edu/

CONTACT
Enrollment Services Customer Service Center, Texas Southern University, 3100 Cleburne Street, Houston, TX 77004-4598. *Phone:* 713-313-7071. *Fax:* 713-313-7851. *E-mail:* eservices@em.tsu.edu.

Texas State University
San Marcos, Texas
http://www.txstate.edu/

- **State-supported** university, founded 1899, part of Texas State University System
- **Suburban** 491-acre campus with easy access to San Antonio, Austin
- **Endowment** $167.1 million
- **Coed** 34,244 undergraduate students, 82% full-time, 57% women, 43% men
- **Moderately difficult** entrance level, 71% of applicants were admitted

UNDERGRAD STUDENTS
28,180 full-time, 6,064 part-time. Students come from 51 states and territories; 49 other countries; 2% are from out of state; 10% Black or African American, non-Hispanic/Latino; 36% Hispanic/Latino; 2% Asian, non-Hispanic/Latino; 0.2% Native Hawaiian or other Pacific Islander, non-Hispanic/Latino; 0.3% American Indian or Alaska Native, non-Hispanic/Latino; 3% Two or more races, non-Hispanic/Latino; 0.4% Race/ethnicity unknown; 0.5% international; 11% transferred in; 19% live on campus.

Freshmen:
Admission: 21,524 applied, 15,239 admitted, 5,732 enrolled. ***Test scores:*** SAT critical reading scores over 500: 56%; SAT math scores over 500: 59%; SAT writing scores over 500: 42%; ACT scores over 18: 97%; SAT critical reading scores over 600: 14%; SAT math scores over 600: 13%; SAT writing scores over 600: 7%; ACT scores over 24: 40%; SAT critical reading scores over 700: 2%; SAT math scores over 700: 1%; SAT writing scores over 700: 1%; ACT scores over 30: 5%.

Retention: 77% of full-time freshmen returned.

FACULTY
Total: 1,934, 71% full-time, 68% with terminal degrees.

Student/faculty ratio: 19:1.

ACADEMICS
Calendar: semesters. *Degrees:* bachelor's, master's, doctoral, and postbachelor's certificates.

Special study options: academic remediation for entering students, accelerated degree program, adult/continuing education programs, advanced placement credit, distance learning, double majors, English as a second language, external degree program, freshman honors college, honors programs, independent study, internships, off-campus study, part-time degree program, services for LD students, study abroad, summer session for credit. ***ROTC:*** Army (b), Air Force (b).

Unusual degree programs: 3-2 business administration; engineering with University of Texas at Austin, Texas A&M University, Texas Tech University, University of Texas at San Antonio.

Computers: 3,233 computers/terminals are available on campus for general student use. Students can access the following: computer help desk, free student e-mail accounts, online (class) grades, online (class) registration, online (class) schedules. Campuswide network is available. 100% of college-owned or -operated housing units are wired for high-speed Internet access. Wireless service is available via entire campus.

Library: Alkek Library plus 1 other. *Books:* 1.5 million (physical), 664,569 (digital/electronic); *Serial titles:* 32,501 (physical), 129,479 (digital/electronic); *Databases:* 503. Students can reserve study rooms.

STUDENT LIFE

Housing options: on-campus residence required for freshman year; coed, men-only, women-only. Campus housing is university owned. Freshman campus housing is guaranteed.

Activities and organizations: drama/theater group, student-run newspaper, radio station, choral group, marching band, Veterans Alliance of Texas State, Texas State Strutters (Dance performance group), Student Foundation, Sport Clubs Alliance, Student Association for Campus Activities, national fraternities, national sororities.

Athletics Member NCAA. All Division I. ***Intercollegiate sports:*** baseball M(s), basketball M(s)/W(s), cheerleading M/W, cross-country running M(s)/W(s), equestrian sports M(c)/W(c), fencing M(c)/W(c), football M(s), golf M(s)/W(s), gymnastics M(c)/W(c), lacrosse M(c)/W(c), rugby M(c)/W(c), soccer M(c)/W(s), softball M(c)/W(s), tennis M(c)/W(s), track and field M(s)/W(s), ultimate Frisbee M(c)/W(c), volleyball W(s), water polo M(c)/W(c), weight lifting M(c)/W(c), wrestling M(c)/W(c). ***Intramural sports:*** basketball M/W, bowling M/W, cross-country running M/W, football M/W, golf M/W, racquetball M/W, rock climbing M/W, soccer M/W, softball M/W, tennis M/W, ultimate Frisbee M/W, volleyball M/W.

Campus security: 24-hour emergency response devices and patrols, late-night transport/escort service, controlled dormitory access, Emergency Notification System (electronic signs) within classrooms and offices.

Student services: health clinic, personal/psychological counseling, legal services.

COSTS & FINANCIAL AID

Costs (2017–18) ***Tuition:*** state resident $8055 full-time, $269 per credit hour part-time; nonresident $20,295 full-time, $677 per credit hour part-time. Full-time tuition and fees vary according to course load and degree level. Part-time tuition and fees vary according to course load and degree level. No tuition increase for student's term of enrollment. ***Required fees:*** $2565 full-time, $51 per credit hour part-time, $523 per term part-time. ***Room and board:*** $9490; room only: $6778. Room and board charges vary according to board plan and housing facility. ***Payment plans:*** tuition prepayment, installment. ***Waivers:*** employees or children of employees.

Financial Aid Of all full-time matriculated undergraduates who enrolled in 2016, 23,799 applied for aid, 16,534 were judged to have need, 2,930 had their need fully met. 443 Federal Work-Study jobs (averaging $2958). 122 state and other part-time jobs (averaging $3279). In 2016, 683 non-need-based awards were made. ***Average percent of need met:*** 63. ***Average financial aid package:*** $10,311. ***Average need-based loan:*** $4043. ***Average need-based gift aid:*** $6993. ***Average non-need-based aid:*** $3770. ***Average indebtedness upon graduation:*** $27,840.

APPLYING

Standardized Tests *Required:* SAT or ACT (for admission). *Required for some:* TOEFL for international students. *Recommended:* SAT (for admission), ACT (for admission).

Options: electronic application, early admission, deferred entrance.

Application fee: $75.

Required: essay or personal statement, high school transcript.

Application deadlines: 3/1 (freshmen), 7/1 (transfers).

Notification: continuous (freshmen), continuous (transfers).

CONTACT

Texas State University, 429 N. Guadalupe Street, San Marcos, TX 78666.
Phone: 512-245-2364. *Fax:* 512-245-8100.
E-mail: admissions@txstate.edu.

Texas Tech University

Lubbock, Texas

http://www.ttu.edu/

- **State-supported** university, founded 1923, part of Texas Tech University System
- **Urban** 1839-acre campus
- **Endowment** $662.6 million
- **Coed** 29,963 undergraduate students, 89% full-time, 45% women, 55% men
- **Moderately difficult** entrance level, 63% of applicants were admitted

UNDERGRAD STUDENTS

26,627 full-time, 3,336 part-time. Students come from 53 states and territories; 90 other countries; 6% are from out of state; 6% Black or African American, non-Hispanic/Latino; 24% Hispanic/Latino; 3% Asian, non-Hispanic/Latino; 0.1% Native Hawaiian or other Pacific Islander, non-Hispanic/Latino; 0.3% American Indian or Alaska Native, non-Hispanic/Latino; 2% Two or more races, non-Hispanic/Latino; 0.4% Race/ethnicity unknown; 5% international; 10% transferred in; 24% live on campus.

Freshmen:

Admission: 23,311 applied, 14,592 admitted, 4,762 enrolled. ***Average high school GPA:*** 3.5. ***Test scores:*** SAT critical reading scores over 500: 78%; SAT math scores over 500: 87%; SAT writing scores over 500: 63%; ACT scores over 18: 99%; SAT critical reading scores over 600: 25%; SAT math scores over 600: 33%; SAT writing scores over 600: 15%; ACT scores over 24: 60%; SAT critical reading scores over 700: 3%; SAT math scores over 700: 4%; SAT writing scores over 700: 1%; ACT scores over 30: 9%.

Retention: 84% of full-time freshmen returned.

FACULTY

Total: 1,766, 86% full-time.

Student/faculty ratio: 21:1.

ACADEMICS

Calendar: semesters. *Degrees:* certificates, bachelor's, master's, doctoral, and postbachelor's certificates.

Special study options: academic remediation for entering students, accelerated degree program, advanced placement credit, cooperative education, distance learning, double majors, English as a second language, external degree program, freshman honors college, honors programs, independent study, internships, off-campus study, part-time degree program, services for LD students, student-designed majors, study abroad, summer session for credit. ***ROTC:*** Army (b), Air Force (b).

Unusual degree programs: 3-2 business administration; engineering; agribusiness, agriculture and applied economics, architecture, classics, French, German, music education, personal and financial planning, political science, psychology, romance languages, Spanish.

Computers: 2,728 computers/terminals and 3,000 ports are available on campus for general student use. Students can access the following: campus intranet, computer help desk, free student e-mail accounts, online (class) grades, online (class) registration, online (class) schedules, online degree plans, accounts, transcripts, financial aid, course and instructor evaluations. Campuswide network is available. 100% of college-owned or -operated housing units are wired for high-speed Internet access. Wireless service is available via classrooms, computer centers, computer labs, dorm rooms, learning centers, libraries, student centers.

Library: Texas Tech Library plus 3 others. *Books:* 2.9 million (physical), 157,061 (digital/electronic); *Serial titles:* 3,340 (physical), 155,013 (digital/electronic); *Databases:* 399. Weekly public service hours: 146; study areas open 24 hours, 5-7 days a week; students can reserve study rooms.

STUDENT LIFE

Housing options: on-campus residence required for freshman year; coed, men-only, women-only, special housing for students with disabilities. Campus housing is university owned. Freshman campus housing is guaranteed.

Activities and organizations: drama/theater group, student-run newspaper, radio station, choral group, marching band, Society of Petroleum Engineers, Double T Health Service Corps, Pre-Nursing

Association, Alpha Lambda Delta & PES, Gamma Beta Phi, national fraternities, national sororities.

Athletics Member NCAA. All Division I except football (Division I-A). ***Intercollegiate sports:*** baseball M(s), basketball M(s)/W(s), cross-country running M(s)/W(s), golf M(s)/W(s), soccer W(s), softball W(s), tennis M(s)/W(s), track and field M(s)/W(s), volleyball W(s). ***Intramural sports:*** badminton M(c)/W(c), baseball M/W, basketball M/W, bowling M/W, equestrian sports M(c)/W(c), fencing M(c)/W(c), golf M/W, gymnastics M(c)/W(c), ice hockey M(c), lacrosse M(c)/W(c), racquetball M/W, rock climbing M(c)/W(c), rugby M(c)/W(c), sand volleyball M/W, soccer M/W, softball M/W, table tennis M/W, tennis M/W, triathlon M(c)/W(c), ultimate Frisbee M(c)/W(c), volleyball M/W, water polo M(c)/W(c), weight lifting M, wrestling M(c)/W(c).

Campus security: 24-hour emergency response devices and patrols, late-night transport/escort service, controlled dormitory access, TechAlert system, bike registration, crime prevention programs.

Student services: health clinic, personal/psychological counseling, legal services.

COSTS & FINANCIAL AID

Costs (2016–17) ***Tuition:*** state resident $7050 full-time, $235 per credit hour part-time; nonresident $19,290 full-time, $643 per credit hour part-time. Full-time tuition and fees vary according to course level, course load, degree level, location, program, reciprocity agreements, and student level. Part-time tuition and fees vary according to course level, course load, degree level, location, program, reciprocity agreements, and student level. ***Required fees:*** $2731 full-time, $51 per credit hour part-time, $608 per term part-time. ***Room and board:*** $8505; room only: $4510. Room and board charges vary according to board plan and housing facility. ***Payment plan:*** installment. ***Waivers:*** senior citizens and employees or children of employees.

Financial Aid Of all full-time matriculated undergraduates who enrolled in 2015, 12,542 applied for aid, 10,380 were judged to have need, 718 had their need fully met. 328 Federal Work-Study jobs (averaging $2513). In 2015, 2245 non-need-based awards were made. ***Average percent of need met:*** 68. ***Average financial aid package:*** $14,932. ***Average need-based loan:*** $5338. ***Average need-based gift aid:*** $7579. ***Average non-need-based aid:*** $3495. ***Average indebtedness upon graduation:*** $29,214.

APPLYING

Standardized Tests *Required:* SAT or ACT (for admission).

Options: electronic application.

Application fee: $75.

Required: high school transcript. ***Recommended:*** essay or personal statement, letters of recommendation.

Application deadlines: 8/1 (freshmen), rolling (transfers).

Notification: 10/1 (freshmen), continuous (transfers).

CONTACT

Texas Tech University, 2500 Broadway, Lubbock, TX 79409.
Phone: 806-742-1480.

Texas Wesleyan University

Fort Worth, Texas

http://www.txwes.edu/

- **Independent United Methodist** comprehensive, founded 1890
- **Urban** 74-acre campus with easy access to Dallas-Fort Worth
- **Endowment** $59.7 million
- **Coed** 1,905 undergraduate students, 78% full-time, 51% women, 49% men
- **Moderately difficult** entrance level, 41% of applicants were admitted

UNDERGRAD STUDENTS

1,487 full-time, 418 part-time. Students come from 28 states and territories; 48 other countries; 6% are from out of state; 15% Black or African American, non-Hispanic/Latino; 29% Hispanic/Latino; 1% Asian, non-Hispanic/Latino; 0.8% American Indian or Alaska Native, non-Hispanic/Latino; 6% Two or more races, non-Hispanic/Latino; 1% Race/ethnicity unknown; 16% international; 18% transferred in; 30% live on campus.

Freshmen:
Admission: 2,959 applied, 1,218 admitted, 301 enrolled. ***Average high school GPA:*** 3.35. ***Test scores:*** SAT critical reading scores over 500: 50%; SAT math scores over 500: 54%; SAT writing scores over 500: 26%; ACT scores over 18: 97%; SAT critical reading scores over 600: 8%; SAT math scores over 600: 6%; SAT writing scores over 600: 4%; ACT scores over 24: 20%; SAT critical reading scores over 700: 1%; SAT writing scores over 700: 1%; ACT scores over 30: 2%.
Retention: 41% of full-time freshmen returned.

FACULTY

Total: 234, 58% full-time, 51% with terminal degrees.

Student/faculty ratio: 13:1.

ACADEMICS

Calendar: semesters. *Degrees:* bachelor's, master's, and doctoral.

Special study options: academic remediation for entering students, accelerated degree program, advanced placement credit, distance learning, double majors, honors programs, independent study, internships, off-campus study, part-time degree program, services for LD students, study abroad, summer session for credit. ***ROTC:*** Army (c), Air Force (c).

Unusual degree programs: 3-2 business administration; education with Texas Wesleyan University, dentistry with the University of Texas Health Science Center.

Computers: 507 computers/terminals and 487 ports are available on campus for general student use. Students can access the following: campus intranet, computer help desk, free student e-mail accounts, online (class) grades, online (class) registration, online (class) schedules. Campuswide network is available. 100% of college-owned or -operated housing units are wired for high-speed Internet access. Wireless service is available via entire campus.

Library: Eunice and James L. West Library plus 1 other. *Books:* 185,461 (physical), 171,492 (digital/electronic); *Serial titles:* 1,500 (physical), 150,836 (digital/electronic); *Databases:* 104. Weekly public service hours: 101.

STUDENT LIFE

Housing options: on-campus residence required for freshman year; coed, special housing for students with disabilities. Campus housing is university owned.

Activities and organizations: drama/theater group, student-run newspaper, radio and television station, choral group, Mortar Board, Delta Sigma Phi, Alpha Xi Delta, Bilingual Education Student Organization, Alpha Lambda Delta, national fraternities, national sororities.

Athletics Member NAIA. ***Intercollegiate sports:*** baseball M(s), basketball M(s)/W(s), cheerleading M(s)/W(s), cross-country running M(s)/W(s), football M(s), golf M(s)/W(s), soccer M(s)/W(s), softball W(s), table tennis M(s)/W(s), tennis W, track and field M(s)/W(s), volleyball W(s).

Campus security: 24-hour emergency response devices and patrols, student patrols, late-night transport/escort service, controlled dormitory access.

Student services: health clinic, personal/psychological counseling.

COSTS & FINANCIAL AID

Costs (2017–18) ***Comprehensive fee:*** $37,314 includes full-time tuition ($24,178), mandatory fees ($3506), and room and board ($9630). Full-time tuition and fees vary according to course level, course load, degree level, program, and student level. Part-time tuition: $828 per credit hour. Part-time tuition and fees vary according to course level, course load, degree level, program, and student level. ***Required fees:*** $120 per credit hour part-time. ***College room only:*** $5646. Room and board charges vary according to housing facility. ***Payment plans:*** installment, deferred payment. ***Waivers:*** employees or children of employees.

Financial Aid Of all full-time matriculated undergraduates who enrolled in 2015, 1,059 applied for aid, 950 were judged to have need, 148 had their need fully met. 93 Federal Work-Study jobs (averaging $4000). 7 state and other part-time jobs (averaging $4000). In 2015, 420 non-need-based awards were made. ***Average percent of need met:*** 72. ***Average financial aid package:*** $24,260. ***Average need-based loan:*** $3890. ***Average need-based gift aid:*** $16,801. ***Average non-need-based aid:*** $10,635. ***Average indebtedness upon graduation:*** $12,164.

APPLYING

Standardized Tests *Required:* SAT or ACT (for admission).

Options: electronic application, deferred entrance.

Required: minimum 2.5 GPA, minimum ACT score of 19 or SAT of 920. ***Required for some:*** essay or personal statement, high school transcript.

Application deadlines: rolling (freshmen), rolling (transfers).

Notification: continuous (freshmen), continuous (transfers).

CONTACT

Mrs. Djuana Young, Associate Vice President for Enrollment, Admissions, Texas Wesleyan University, 1201 Wesleyan Street, Fort Worth, TX 76105-1536. *Phone:* 817-531-4422. *Toll-free phone:* 800-580-8980. *Fax:* 817-531-7515. *E-mail:* admissions@txwes.edu.

Texas Woman's University

Denton, Texas

http://www.twu.edu/

- **State-supported** university, founded 1901
- **Suburban** 270-acre campus with easy access to Dallas-Fort Worth
- **Endowment** $49.1 million
- **Coed, primarily women** 10,408 undergraduate students, 67% full-time, 87% women, 13% men
- **Minimally difficult** entrance level, 86% of applicants were admitted

UNDERGRAD STUDENTS

7,014 full-time, 3,394 part-time. Students come from 34 states and territories; 52 other countries; 1% are from out of state; 18% Black or African American, non-Hispanic/Latino; 28% Hispanic/Latino; 8% Asian, non-Hispanic/Latino; 0.1% Native Hawaiian or other Pacific Islander, non-Hispanic/Latino; 0.4% American Indian or Alaska Native, non-Hispanic/Latino; 4% Two or more races, non-Hispanic/Latino; 0.8% Race/ethnicity unknown; 0.7% international; 13% transferred in; 21% live on campus.

Freshmen:

Admission: 5,414 applied, 4,648 admitted, 1,317 enrolled. ***Average high school GPA:*** 3.1. ***Test scores:*** SAT critical reading scores over 500: 34%; SAT math scores over 500: 38%; ACT scores over 18: 72%; SAT critical reading scores over 600: 8%; SAT math scores over 600: 8%; ACT scores over 24: 20%; SAT critical reading scores over 700: 1%; SAT math scores over 700: 1%; ACT scores over 30: 2%.

Retention: 76% of full-time freshmen returned.

FACULTY

Total: 910, 56% full-time, 57% with terminal degrees.

Student/faculty ratio: 18:1.

ACADEMICS

Calendar: semesters. *Degrees:* bachelor's, master's, doctoral, post-master's, and postbachelor's certificates.

Special study options: academic remediation for entering students, accelerated degree program, adult/continuing education programs, advanced placement credit, cooperative education, distance learning, double majors, honors programs, independent study, internships, off-campus study, part-time degree program, services for LD students, study abroad, summer session for credit. ***ROTC:*** Army (c), Navy (c), Air Force (c).

Computers: 1,000 computers/terminals and 1,000 ports are available on campus for general student use. Students can access the following: campus intranet, computer help desk, free student e-mail accounts, online (class) grades, online (class) registration, online (class) schedules. Campuswide network is available. 100% of college-owned or -operated housing units are wired for high-speed Internet access. Wireless service is available via entire campus.

Library: Blagg-Huey Library. *Books:* 523,507 (physical), 336,902 (digital/electronic); *Databases:* 223. Weekly public service hours: 116; students can reserve study rooms.

STUDENT LIFE

Housing options: on-campus residence required through sophomore year; coed, men-only, women-only, special housing for students with disabilities. Campus housing is university owned, leased by the school and is provided by a third party. Freshman campus housing is guaranteed.

Activities and organizations: drama/theater group, student-run newspaper, choral group, Helping Hands, Athenian Honor Society, Campus Activities Board, Nursing Student Organization, Graduate Library and Information Studies Association, national fraternities, national sororities.

Athletics Member NCAA. All Division II. ***Intercollegiate sports:*** basketball W(s), gymnastics W(s), soccer W(s), softball W(s), volleyball W(s). ***Intramural sports:*** badminton M/W, basketball M(c)/W(c), football M/W, golf M(c)/W(c), soccer M(c)/W(c), softball M(c)/W(c), tennis M/W, track and field M(c)/W(c), volleyball M/W, weight lifting M(c)/W(c), wrestling M(c)/W(c).

Campus security: 24-hour emergency response devices and patrols, late-night transport/escort service, controlled dormitory access.

Student services: health clinic, personal/psychological counseling, women's center, legal services.

COSTS & FINANCIAL AID

Costs (2017–18) ***Tuition:*** state resident $6180 full-time, $206 per credit hour part-time; nonresident $19,920 full-time, $614 per credit hour part-time. Full-time tuition and fees vary according to course level, course load, program, and reciprocity agreements. Part-time tuition and fees vary according to course level, course load, program, and reciprocity agreements. No tuition increase for student's term of enrollment. ***Required fees:*** $2610 full-time, $78 per credit hour part-time, $287 per term part-time. ***Room and board:*** $7578; room only: $4140. Room and board charges vary according to board plan and housing facility. ***Payment plan:*** installment. ***Waivers:*** senior citizens.

Financial Aid Of all full-time matriculated undergraduates who enrolled in 2016, 5,368 applied for aid, 4,852 were judged to have need, 1,400 had their need fully met. In 2016, 383 non-need-based awards were made. ***Average percent of need met:*** 84. ***Average financial aid package:*** $14,764. ***Average need-based loan:*** $7334. ***Average need-based gift aid:*** $7335. ***Average non-need-based aid:*** $5390. ***Average indebtedness upon graduation:*** $24,916.

APPLYING

Standardized Tests *Required for some:* SAT or ACT (for admission).

Options: electronic application, early admission, deferred entrance.

Application fee: $50.

Required: minimum 2.0 GPA. ***Required for some:*** high school transcript.

Application deadlines: 7/15 (freshmen), 7/15 (transfers).

Notification: continuous (freshmen), continuous (out-of-state freshmen), continuous (transfers).

CONTACT

Ms. Erma Nieto-Brecht, Director of Admissions, Texas Woman's University, 304 Administration Drive, Denton, TX 76201. *Phone:* 940-898-3188. *Toll-free phone:* 866-809-6130. *Fax:* 940-898-3081. *E-mail:* admissions@twu.edu.

Trinity University

San Antonio, Texas

http://www.trinity.edu/

- **Independent** comprehensive, founded 1869, affiliated with Presbyterian Church
- **Urban** 117-acre campus
- **Endowment** $1.2 billion
- **Coed** 2,334 undergraduate students, 98% full-time, 53% women, 47% men
- **Very difficult** entrance level, 27% of applicants were admitted

UNDERGRAD STUDENTS

2,283 full-time, 51 part-time. Students come from 48 states and territories; 44 other countries; 16% are from out of state; 4% Black or African American, non-Hispanic/Latino; 21% Hispanic/Latino; 6% Asian, non-Hispanic/Latino; 0.3% American Indian or Alaska Native, non-Hispanic/Latino; 5% Two or more races, non-Hispanic/Latino; 2% Race/ethnicity unknown; 7% international; 1% transferred in; 77% live on campus.

Freshmen:

Admission: 7,255 applied, 1,950 admitted, 662 enrolled. ***Average high school GPA:*** 3.56. ***Test scores:*** SAT critical reading scores over 500:

97%; SAT math scores over 500: 99%; SAT writing scores over 500: 94%; ACT scores over 18: 100%; SAT critical reading scores over 600: 69%; SAT math scores over 600: 70%; SAT writing scores over 600: 59%; ACT scores over 24: 98%; SAT critical reading scores over 700: 21%; SAT math scores over 700: 18%; SAT writing scores over 700: 14%; ACT scores over 30: 47%.

Retention: 89% of full-time freshmen returned.

FACULTY

Total: 348, 76% full-time, 83% with terminal degrees.

Student/faculty ratio: 8:1.

ACADEMICS

Calendar: semesters. *Degrees:* bachelor's and master's.

Special study options: accelerated degree program, advanced placement credit, double majors, honors programs, independent study, internships, off-campus study, part-time degree program, services for LD students, student-designed majors, study abroad, summer session for credit. ***ROTC:*** Army (c), Air Force (c).

Computers: 500 computers/terminals and 2,000 ports are available on campus for general student use. Students can access the following: campus intranet, computer help desk, free student e-mail accounts, online (class) grades, online (class) registration, online (class) schedules. Campuswide network is available. 100% of college-owned or -operated housing units are wired for high-speed Internet access. Wireless service is available via entire campus.

Library: Elizabeth Huth Coates Library plus 1 other. *Books:* 819,196 (physical); *Serial titles:* 2,176 (physical), 95,000 (digital/electronic); *Databases:* 304. Weekly public service hours: 96.

STUDENT LIFE

Housing options: on-campus residence required through junior year; coed. Campus housing is university owned. Freshman campus housing is guaranteed.

Activities and organizations: drama/theater group, student-run newspaper, radio and television station, choral group, Tiger Stand Band, Alpha Phi Omega, Association of Student Representatives, Acabellas/Trinitones, Multicultural Network.

Athletics Member NCAA. All Division III. ***Intercollegiate sports:*** baseball M, basketball M/W, cross-country running M/W, fencing M(c)/W(c), football M, golf M/W, lacrosse M(c)/W(c), soccer M/W, softball W, swimming and diving M/W, tennis M/W, track and field M/W, volleyball W. ***Intramural sports:*** basketball M/W, cross-country running M/W, equestrian sports M(c)/W(c), football M, racquetball M/W, soccer M/W, softball M/W, swimming and diving M/W, table tennis M/W, tennis M/W, ultimate Frisbee M/W, volleyball M/W.

Campus security: 24-hour emergency response devices and patrols, late-night transport/escort service, controlled dormitory access.

Student services: health clinic, personal/psychological counseling.

COSTS & FINANCIAL AID

Costs (2017–18) ***Comprehensive fee:*** $54,480 includes full-time tuition ($40,728), mandatory fees ($616), and room and board ($13,136). Full-time tuition and fees vary according to course load. Part-time tuition: $1697 per credit hour. Part-time tuition and fees vary according to course load. ***Required fees:*** $13 per credit hour part-time. ***College room only:*** $8478. Room and board charges vary according to board plan. ***Payment plan:*** installment. ***Waivers:*** employees or children of employees.

Financial Aid Of all full-time matriculated undergraduates who enrolled in 2016, 1,287 applied for aid, 1,041 were judged to have need, 521 had their need fully met. In 2016, 1099 non-need-based awards were made. ***Average percent of need met:*** 93. ***Average financial aid package:*** $36,123. ***Average need-based loan:*** $5077. ***Average need-based gift aid:*** $28,826. ***Average non-need-based aid:*** $19,042. ***Average indebtedness upon graduation:*** $38,605.

APPLYING

Standardized Tests *Required:* SAT or ACT (for admission).

Options: electronic application, early decision, early action, deferred entrance.

Required: essay or personal statement, high school transcript, 2 letters of recommendation. ***Recommended:*** interview.

Application deadlines: 2/1 (freshmen), 3/1 (transfers), 11/1 (early action).

Early decision deadline: 11/1 (for plan 1), 1/1 (for plan 2).

Notification: 4/1 (freshmen), 5/1 (transfers), 12/15 (early decision plan 1), 2/15 (early decision plan 2), 12/15 (early action).

CONTACT

Office of Admissions, Trinity University, One Trinity Place, Northrup Hall 140, San Antonio, TX 78212-7200. *Phone:* 210-999-7207. *Toll-free phone:* 800-TRINITY. *Fax:* 210-999-8164. *E-mail:* admissions@trinity.edu.

Tyler Junior College

Tyler, Texas

http://www.tjc.edu/

- **State and locally supported** primarily 2-year, founded 1926
- **Suburban** 137-acre campus
- **Endowment** $42.2 million
- **Coed** 11,478 undergraduate students, 51% full-time, 58% women, 42% men
- **Noncompetitive** entrance level, 100% of applicants were admitted

UNDERGRAD STUDENTS

5,904 full-time, 5,574 part-time. Students come from 27 states and territories; 31 other countries; 3% are from out of state; 20% Black or African American, non-Hispanic/Latino; 20% Hispanic/Latino; 1% Asian, non-Hispanic/Latino; 0.2% Native Hawaiian or other Pacific Islander, non-Hispanic/Latino; 0.5% American Indian or Alaska Native, non-Hispanic/Latino; 3% Two or more races, non-Hispanic/Latino; 1% Race/ethnicity unknown; 0.8% international; 5% transferred in; 11% live on campus.

Freshmen:

Admission: 10,778 applied, 10,778 admitted, 2,995 enrolled.

Retention: 54% of full-time freshmen returned.

FACULTY

Total: 559, 56% full-time, 9% with terminal degrees.

Student/faculty ratio: 20:1.

ACADEMICS

Calendar: semesters. *Degrees:* certificates, diplomas, associate, and bachelor's.

Special study options: academic remediation for entering students, accelerated degree program, adult/continuing education programs, advanced placement credit, distance learning, freshman honors college, honors programs, part-time degree program, services for LD students, study abroad, summer session for credit.

Computers: Students can access the following: campus intranet, computer help desk, free student e-mail accounts, online (class) grades, online (class) registration, online (class) schedules. Campuswide network is available. 100% of college-owned or -operated housing units are wired for high-speed Internet access. Wireless service is available via entire campus.

Library: Vaughn Library and Learning Resource Center. *Books:* 85,418 (physical), 135,816 (digital/electronic); *Databases:* 100. Weekly public service hours: 74.

STUDENT LIFE

Housing options: coed, men-only, women-only. Campus housing is university owned and is provided by a third party.

Activities and organizations: drama/theater group, student-run newspaper, choral group, marching band, Student Government, Religious Affiliation Clubs, Phi Theta Kappa, national sororities.

Athletics Member NJCAA. ***Intercollegiate sports:*** baseball M, basketball M(s)/W(s), cheerleading W(s), football M(s), golf M/W, soccer M(s)/W(s), softball W(s), tennis M(s)/W(s), volleyball W(s). ***Intramural sports:*** basketball M/W, cheerleading W, racquetball M/W, volleyball M/W, weight lifting M/W.

Campus security: 24-hour emergency response devices and patrols, controlled dormitory access.

Student services: health clinic, personal/psychological counseling.

COSTS & FINANCIAL AID

Costs (2016–17) ***Tuition:*** area resident $900 full-time, $30 per credit hour part-time; state resident $2550 full-time, $85 per credit hour part-time;

nonresident $3240 full-time, $108 per credit hour part-time. ***Required fees:*** $1538 full-time, $7 per credit hour part-time, $106 per term part-time. ***Room and board:*** $8320; room only: $5940. Room and board charges vary according to housing facility. ***Payment plan:*** installment. ***Waivers:*** senior citizens and employees or children of employees.

Financial Aid Of all full-time matriculated undergraduates who enrolled in 2014, 4,922 applied for aid, 4,010 were judged to have need, 73 had their need fully met. 45 Federal Work-Study jobs (averaging $1411). 27 state and other part-time jobs (averaging $2297). In 2014, 37 non-need-based awards were made. ***Average percent of need met:*** 56. ***Average financial aid package:*** $7014. ***Average need-based loan:*** $3349. ***Average need-based gift aid:*** $5569. ***Average non-need-based aid:*** $2956. ***Average indebtedness upon graduation:*** $14,743.

APPLYING
Options: electronic application, early admission.

Required: high school transcript.

Application deadlines: rolling (freshmen), rolling (transfers).

Notification: continuous (freshmen), continuous (transfers).

CONTACT
Ms. Janna Chancey, Director of Enrollment Management, Tyler Junior College, PO Box 9020, Tyler, TX 75711-9020. *Phone:* 903-510-3325. *Toll-free phone:* 800-687-5680. *E-mail:* jcha@tjc.edu.

University of Dallas
Irving, Texas
http://www.udallas.edu/

- **Independent Roman Catholic** university, founded 1955
- **Suburban** 215-acre campus with easy access to Dallas-Fort Worth
- **Endowment** $54.9 million
- **Coed**
- **Moderately difficult** entrance level

FACULTY
Student/faculty ratio: 10:1.

ACADEMICS
Calendar: semesters. *Degrees:* bachelor's, master's, doctoral, post-master's, and postbachelor's certificates.

Library: William A. Blakley Library.

STUDENT LIFE
Housing options: on-campus residence required through junior year; men-only, women-only. Campus housing is university owned. Freshman campus housing is guaranteed.

Activities and organizations: drama/theater group, student-run newspaper, choral group, SPUD (Programming Board), Residence Hall Association, Student Government, Best Buddies, Alpha Phi Omega.

Athletics Member NCAA. All Division III.

Campus security: 24-hour emergency response devices and patrols, late-night transport/escort service, controlled dormitory access.

Student services: health clinic, personal/psychological counseling.

COSTS & FINANCIAL AID
Costs (2016–17) ***Comprehensive fee:*** $48,770 includes full-time tuition ($34,650), mandatory fees ($2580), and room and board ($11,540). Full-time tuition and fees vary according to course load. Part-time tuition: $1430 per credit. Part-time tuition and fees vary according to course load. ***Required fees:*** $2580 per year part-time. ***College room only:*** $6450. Room and board charges vary according to board plan and housing facility.

Financial Aid Of all full-time matriculated undergraduates who enrolled in 2015, 922 applied for aid, 816 were judged to have need, 194 had their need fully met. In 2015, 467 non-need-based awards were made. ***Average percent of need met:*** 80. ***Average financial aid package:*** $30,216. ***Average need-based loan:*** $5748. ***Average need-based gift aid:*** $25,113. ***Average non-need-based aid:*** $18,397. ***Average indebtedness upon graduation:*** $33,511. ***Financial aid deadline:*** 11/15.

APPLYING
Standardized Tests *Required:* SAT or ACT (for admission).

Options: electronic application, early action, deferred entrance.

Application fee: $50.

Required: essay or personal statement, high school transcript, 2 letters of recommendation. ***Required for some:*** interview.

CONTACT
Elizabeth Griffin-Smith, Director of Admissions, University of Dallas, 1845 East Northgate Drive, Irving, TX 75062-4736. *Phone:* 800-628-6999. *Toll-free phone:* 800-628-6999. *Fax:* 972-721-5017. *E-mail:* ugadmis@udallas.edu.

University of Houston
Houston, Texas
http://www.uh.edu/

- **State-supported** university, founded 1927, part of University of Houston System
- **Urban** 594-acre campus with easy access to Houston
- **Endowment** $679.2 million
- **Coed** 35,871 undergraduate students, 72% full-time, 49% women, 51% men
- **Moderately difficult** entrance level, 59% of applicants were admitted

UNDERGRAD STUDENTS
25,794 full-time, 10,077 part-time. Students come from 47 states and territories; 114 other countries; 2% are from out of state; 10% Black or African American, non-Hispanic/Latino; 33% Hispanic/Latino; 22% Asian, non-Hispanic/Latino; 0.2% Native Hawaiian or other Pacific Islander, non-Hispanic/Latino; 0.1% American Indian or Alaska Native, non-Hispanic/Latino; 3% Two or more races, non-Hispanic/Latino; 1% Race/ethnicity unknown; 4% international; 15% transferred in; 19% live on campus.

Freshmen:

Admission: 19,860 applied, 11,627 admitted, 4,463 enrolled. ***Test scores:*** SAT critical reading scores over 500: 80%; SAT math scores over 500: 88%; ACT scores over 18: 98%; SAT critical reading scores over 600: 32%; SAT math scores over 600: 44%; ACT scores over 24: 67%; SAT critical reading scores over 700: 6%; SAT math scores over 700: 8%; ACT scores over 30: 15%.

Retention: 85% of full-time freshmen returned.

FACULTY
Total: 2,349, 65% full-time, 75% with terminal degrees.

Student/faculty ratio: 21:1.

ACADEMICS
Calendar: semesters. *Degrees:* bachelor's, master's, and doctoral.

Special study options: academic remediation for entering students, adult/continuing education programs, advanced placement credit, cooperative education, distance learning, double majors, freshman honors college, honors programs, independent study, internships, off-campus study, part-time degree program, services for LD students, study abroad, summer session for credit. ***ROTC:*** Army (b), Navy (c), Air Force (b).

Unusual degree programs: 3-2 business administration.

Computers: 1,006 computers/terminals and 40,000 ports are available on campus for general student use. Students can access the following: campus intranet, computer help desk, free student e-mail accounts, online (class) grades, online (class) registration, online (class) schedules, online Bus Loop schedule. Campuswide network is available. 100% of college-owned or -operated housing units are wired for high-speed Internet access. Wireless service is available via entire campus.

Library: M. D. Anderson Library plus 4 others. *Books:* 1.9 million (physical), 807,736 (digital/electronic); *Serial titles:* 53,165 (physical), 123,894 (digital/electronic); *Databases:* 543. Weekly public service hours: 116; study areas open 24 hours, 5-7 days a week; students can reserve study rooms.

STUDENT LIFE
Housing options: coed, special housing for students with disabilities. Campus housing is university owned and is provided by a third party.

Activities and organizations: drama/theater group, student-run newspaper, radio and television station, choral group, marching band, Metropolitan Volunteer Program, Interfraternity Council, Delta Omega Chi Medical Service Society, Health Occupation Students of America, Pre-Pharmacy Association, national fraternities, national sororities.

Athletics Member NCAA. All Division I except football (Division I-A). ***Intercollegiate sports:*** baseball M(s), basketball M(s)/W(s), cross-country running M(s)/W(s), golf M(s)/W(s), soccer W(s), softball W(s), swimming and diving W(s), tennis W(s), track and field M(s)/W(s), volleyball W(s). ***Intramural sports:*** badminton M/W, basketball M/W, bowling M(c)/W, fencing M(c)/W(c), golf M/W, racquetball M/W, rock climbing M/W, soccer M/W, softball M/W, swimming and diving M/W, table tennis M/W, tennis M/W, track and field M/W, ultimate Frisbee M(c)/W(c), volleyball M/W(c), water polo M(c)/W(c), weight lifting M/W.

Campus security: 24-hour emergency response devices and patrols, student patrols, late-night transport/escort service, controlled dormitory access, vehicle assistance.

Student services: health clinic, personal/psychological counseling, women's center, legal services.

COSTS & FINANCIAL AID

Costs (2016–17) ***Tuition:*** state resident $10,671 full-time, $356 per credit hour part-time; nonresident $25,911 full-time, $864 per credit hour part-time. Full-time tuition and fees vary according to course level, course load, degree level, program, and student level. Part-time tuition and fees vary according to course level, course load, degree level, program, and student level. No tuition increase for student's term of enrollment. ***Required fees:*** $982 full-time. ***Room and board:*** $9830. Room and board charges vary according to board plan and housing facility. ***Payment plans:*** installment, deferred payment.

Financial Aid Of all full-time matriculated undergraduates who enrolled in 2016, 17,691 applied for aid, 15,649 were judged to have need, 2,007 had their need fully met. 858 Federal Work-Study jobs (averaging $3909). In 2016, 758 non-need-based awards were made. ***Average percent of need met:*** 58. ***Average financial aid package:*** $12,167. ***Average need-based loan:*** $7389. ***Average need-based gift aid:*** $8121. ***Average non-need-based aid:*** $5233. ***Average indebtedness upon graduation:*** $23,665.

APPLYING

Standardized Tests *Required:* SAT or ACT (for admission).

Options: electronic application.

Application fee: $75.

Required: high school transcript.

Application deadlines: 6/30 (freshmen), 6/30 (transfers).

Notification: continuous (freshmen), continuous (transfers).

CONTACT

Jeff Fuller, Director, Student Recruitment, University of Houston, Welcome Center, 4400 University Boulevard, Houston, TX 77204-2023. *Phone:* 713-743-1010. *Fax:* 713-743-9633. *E-mail:* jdfuller@central.uh.edu.

University of Houston–Clear Lake

Houston, Texas

http://www.uhcl.edu/

- **State-supported** comprehensive, founded 1971, part of University of Houston System
- **Suburban** 524-acre campus with easy access to Houston
- **Endowment** $27.7 million
- **Coed** 5,570 undergraduate students, 48% full-time, 64% women, 36% men
- **Minimally difficult** entrance level, 95% of applicants were admitted

UNDERGRAD STUDENTS

2,693 full-time, 2,877 part-time. Students come from 21 other countries; 8% Black or African American, non-Hispanic/Latino; 38% Hispanic/Latino; 6% Asian, non-Hispanic/Latino; 0.1% Native Hawaiian or other Pacific Islander, non-Hispanic/Latino; 0.2% American Indian or Alaska Native, non-Hispanic/Latino; 3% Two or more races, non-Hispanic/Latino; 1% Race/ethnicity unknown; 2% international; 21% transferred in; 3% live on campus.

Freshmen:

Admission: 1,056 applied, 1,003 admitted, 196 enrolled. ***Average high school GPA:*** 3.39. ***Test scores:*** SAT critical reading scores over 500: 51%; SAT math scores over 500: 61%; SAT writing scores over 500: 39%; ACT scores over 18: 90%; SAT critical reading scores over 600: 13%; SAT math scores over 600: 10%; SAT writing scores over 600: 6%; ACT scores over 24: 17%; SAT critical reading scores over 700: 2%; SAT math scores over 700: 1%; ACT scores over 30: 1%.

Retention: 76% of full-time freshmen returned.

FACULTY

Total: 535, 56% full-time.

Student/faculty ratio: 15:1.

ACADEMICS

Calendar: semesters. *Degrees:* bachelor's, master's, doctoral, post-master's, and postbachelor's certificates.

Special study options: academic remediation for entering students, advanced placement credit, cooperative education, distance learning, double majors, English as a second language, independent study, internships, off-campus study, part-time degree program, services for LD students, study abroad, summer session for credit.

Computers: 723 computers/terminals are available on campus for general student use. Students can access the following: campus intranet, computer help desk, free student e-mail accounts, online (class) grades, online (class) registration, online (class) schedules. Campuswide network is available. Wireless service is available via entire campus.

Library: Alfred R. Neuman Library. *Books:* 515,000 (physical), 457,000 (digital/electronic); *Serial titles:* 5,546 (physical), 84,700 (digital/electronic); *Databases:* 239. Weekly public service hours: 85; students can reserve study rooms.

STUDENT LIFE

Housing options: special housing for students with disabilities. Campus housing is provided by a third party. Freshman applicants given priority for college housing.

Activities and organizations: drama/theater group, student-run newspaper, National Society of Leadership and Success, Student Government Association, Texas State Student Association, Indian Students Association, Communication and Digital Media Association.

Athletics ***Intramural sports:*** weight lifting M(c).

Campus security: 24-hour emergency response devices and patrols, student patrols, late-night transport/escort service.

Student services: health clinic, personal/psychological counseling, women's center.

FINANCIAL AID

Financial Aid Of all full-time matriculated undergraduates who enrolled in 2014, 1,701 applied for aid, 1,615 were judged to have need, 65 had their need fully met. In 2014, 288 non-need-based awards were made. ***Average percent of need met:*** 44. ***Average financial aid package:*** $8496. ***Average need-based loan:*** $4462. ***Average need-based gift aid:*** $6561. ***Average non-need-based aid:*** $1699.

APPLYING

Standardized Tests *Required:* SAT or ACT (for admission).

Options: electronic application, early admission, deferred entrance.

Application fee: $45.

Required: high school transcript, State of Texas Uniform Admission Policy criteria. ***Required for some:*** essay or personal statement, 2 letters of recommendation.

Application deadlines: 6/1 (freshmen), rolling (transfers).

Notification: continuous (transfers).

CONTACT

Ms. Rauchelle Jones, Executive Director of Admissions, University of Houston–Clear Lake, 2700 Bay Area Boulevard, Box 13, Houston, TX 77058-1002. *Phone:* 281-283-2518. *Fax:* 281-283-2530. *E-mail:* admissions@uhcl.edu.

University of Houston–Downtown

Houston, Texas

http://www.uhd.edu/

- **State-supported** comprehensive, founded 1974, part of University of Houston System
- **Urban** 24-acre campus
- **Coed** 13,245 undergraduate students, 50% full-time, 60% women, 40% men
- **Noncompetitive** entrance level, 78% of applicants were admitted

UNDERGRAD STUDENTS

6,643 full-time, 6,602 part-time. 1% are from out of state; 23% Black or African American, non-Hispanic/Latino; 43% Hispanic/Latino; 9% Asian, non-Hispanic/Latino; 0.2% Native Hawaiian or other Pacific Islander, non-Hispanic/Latino; 0.5% American Indian or Alaska Native, non-Hispanic/Latino; 1% Two or more races, non-Hispanic/Latino; 1% Race/ethnicity unknown; 5% international; 14% transferred in.

Freshmen:

Admission: 3,460 applied, 2,686 admitted, 877 enrolled. ***Test scores:*** SAT critical reading scores over 500: 18%; SAT math scores over 500: 34%; SAT writing scores over 500: 15%; ACT scores over 18: 59%; SAT critical reading scores over 600: 2%; SAT math scores over 600: 2%; SAT writing scores over 600: 1%; ACT scores over 24: 3%.

Retention: 66% of full-time freshmen returned.

FACULTY

Total: 717, 49% full-time, 63% with terminal degrees.

Student/faculty ratio: 20:1.

ACADEMICS

Calendar: semesters. *Degrees:* bachelor's, master's, and postbachelor's certificates.

Special study options: academic remediation for entering students, advanced placement credit, distance learning, double majors, English as a second language, independent study, internships, off-campus study, part-time degree program, services for LD students, study abroad, summer session for credit. ***ROTC:*** Army (c), Air Force (c).

Computers: Students can access the following: computer help desk, free student e-mail accounts, online (class) grades, online (class) registration, online (class) schedules. Campuswide network is available. Wireless service is available via entire campus.

Library: W. I. Dykes Library.

STUDENT LIFE

Housing options: college housing not available.

Activities and organizations: drama/theater group, student-run newspaper, national fraternities, national sororities.

Athletics ***Intramural sports:*** badminton M/W, baseball M(c), basketball M(c)/W(c), bowling M/W, cheerleading M(c)/W(c), soccer M(c)/W(c), tennis M/W, volleyball M(c)/W(c), weight lifting M(c)/W(c).

Campus security: 24-hour emergency response devices and patrols, late-night transport/escort service.

Student services: health clinic, personal/psychological counseling, legal services.

COSTS & FINANCIAL AID

Costs (2017–18) ***Tuition:*** state resident $203 per credit hour part-time; nonresident $611 per credit hour part-time. Full-time tuition and fees vary according to course load and program. Part-time tuition and fees vary according to course load and program. ***Payment plan:*** installment. ***Waivers:*** senior citizens.

Financial Aid Of all full-time matriculated undergraduates who enrolled in 2016, 5,080 applied for aid, 4,579 were judged to have need, 191 had their need fully met. In 2016, 322 non-need-based awards were made. ***Average percent of need met:*** 57. ***Average financial aid package:*** $9191. ***Average need-based loan:*** $8177. ***Average need-based gift aid:*** $4679. ***Average non-need-based aid:*** $1987. ***Average indebtedness upon graduation:*** $23,874.

APPLYING

Standardized Tests *Required:* SAT or ACT (for admission).

Options: electronic application.

Application fee: $35.

Required: high school transcript.

CONTACT

Ms. Kecia Osbourne, Assistant Director of Admissions-Outreach Services, University of Houston–Downtown, One Main Street, Suite 350-S, Houston, TX 77002. *Phone:* 713-221-8522. *Fax:* 713-221-8157. *E-mail:* uhdadmit@uhd.edu.

University of Houston–Victoria

Victoria, Texas

http://www.uhv.edu/

CONTACT

Mrs. Trudy Wortham, Registrar, University of Houston–Victoria, 3007 North Ben Wilson, Victoria, TX 77901. *Phone:* 361-485-4521 Ext. 4184. *Toll-free phone:* 877-970-4848 Ext. 110. *E-mail:* worthamt@uhv.edu.

University of Mary Hardin-Baylor

Belton, Texas

http://www.umhb.edu/

- **Independent Southern Baptist** comprehensive, founded 1845
- **Small-town** 340-acre campus with easy access to Austin
- **Endowment** $75.0 million
- **Coed** 3,278 undergraduate students, 91% full-time, 63% women, 37% men
- **Moderately difficult** entrance level, 79% of applicants were admitted

UNDERGRAD STUDENTS

2,996 full-time, 282 part-time. Students come from 35 states and territories; 22 other countries; 2% are from out of state; 15% Black or African American, non-Hispanic/Latino; 21% Hispanic/Latino; 2% Asian, non-Hispanic/Latino; 0.4% Native Hawaiian or other Pacific Islander, non-Hispanic/Latino; 0.8% American Indian or Alaska Native, non-Hispanic/Latino; 3% Two or more races, non-Hispanic/Latino; 2% Race/ethnicity unknown; 1% international; 8% transferred in; 57% live on campus.

Freshmen:

Admission: 8,954 applied, 7,056 admitted, 750 enrolled. ***Average high school GPA:*** 3.51. ***Test scores:*** SAT critical reading scores over 500: 56%; SAT math scores over 500: 59%; SAT writing scores over 500: 39%; ACT scores over 18: 95%; SAT critical reading scores over 600: 13%; SAT math scores over 600: 13%; SAT writing scores over 600: 7%; ACT scores over 24: 45%; SAT critical reading scores over 700: 2%; SAT math scores over 700: 1%; SAT writing scores over 700: 1%; ACT scores over 30: 7%.

Retention: 71% of full-time freshmen returned.

FACULTY

Total: 278, 60% full-time, 68% with terminal degrees.

Student/faculty ratio: 19:1.

ACADEMICS

Calendar: semesters. *Degrees:* bachelor's, master's, doctoral, and post-master's certificates.

Special study options: academic remediation for entering students, adult/continuing education programs, advanced placement credit, distance learning, double majors, English as a second language, honors programs, independent study, internships, off-campus study, part-time degree program, services for LD students, study abroad, summer session for credit. ***ROTC:*** Army (b), Air Force (c).

Unusual degree programs: 3-2 business administration; engineering.

Computers: 275 computers/terminals and 1,000 ports are available on campus for general student use. Students can access the following: campus intranet, computer help desk, free student e-mail accounts, online (class) grades, online (class) registration, online (class) schedules. Campuswide network is available. 100% of college-owned or -operated housing units are wired for high-speed Internet access. Wireless service is available via entire campus.

Library: Townsend Memorial Library. *Books:* 188,001 (physical), 27,676 (digital/electronic); *Serial titles:* 720 (physical), 140,549 (digital/electronic); *Databases:* 128. Weekly public service hours: 99; students can reserve study rooms.

STUDENT LIFE

Housing options: men-only, women-only, special housing for students with disabilities. Campus housing is university owned. Freshman applicants given priority for college housing.

Activities and organizations: drama/theater group, student-run newspaper, choral group, Baptist Student Ministry, Student Government Association, Nursing Student Association, Campus Activities Board, Search Cru.

Athletics Member NCAA. All Division III. ***Intercollegiate sports:*** baseball M, basketball M/W, football M, golf M/W, soccer M/W, softball W, tennis M/W, volleyball W. ***Intramural sports:*** basketball M/W, football M/W, golf M/W, soccer M/W, softball M/W, table tennis M/W, tennis M/W, ultimate Frisbee M/W, volleyball M/W.

Campus security: 24-hour emergency response devices and patrols, late-night transport/escort service, controlled dormitory access, campus police force, lighted pathways and sidewalks.

Student services: health clinic, personal/psychological counseling.

COSTS & FINANCIAL AID

Costs (2017–18) ***Comprehensive fee:*** $33,452 includes full-time tuition ($23,660), mandatory fees ($2200), and room and board ($7592). Full-time tuition and fees vary according to course load and degree level. Part-time tuition: $845 per credit hour. Part-time tuition and fees vary according to course load and degree level. ***Room and board:*** Room and board charges vary according to board plan and housing facility. ***Payment plan:*** installment. ***Waivers:*** employees or children of employees.

Financial Aid Of all full-time matriculated undergraduates who enrolled in 2016, 2,635 applied for aid, 2,355 were judged to have need, 214 had their need fully met. In 2016, 377 non-need-based awards were made. ***Average percent of need met:*** 57. ***Average financial aid package:*** $17,171. ***Average need-based loan:*** $4467. ***Average need-based gift aid:*** $13,293. ***Average non-need-based aid:*** $8153. ***Average indebtedness upon graduation:*** $38,726.

APPLYING

Standardized Tests *Required:* SAT or ACT (for admission).

Options: electronic application, early admission, deferred entrance.

Application fee: $35.

Required: high school transcript. ***Required for some:*** essay or personal statement, interview.

Application deadlines: rolling (freshmen), rolling (transfers).

Notification: continuous (freshmen), continuous (transfers).

CONTACT

Dr. Brent Burks, Director of Admissions, University of Mary Hardin-Baylor, UMHB Station Box 8004, 900 College Street, Belton, TX 76513-2599. *Phone:* 254-295-4520. *Toll-free phone:* 800-727-8642. *Fax:* 254-295-5049. *E-mail:* admission@umhb.edu.

University of North Texas

Denton, Texas

http://www.unt.edu/

- **State-supported** university, founded 1890, part of University of North Texas System
- **Suburban** 875-acre campus with easy access to Dallas-Fort Worth
- **Endowment** $144.4 million
- **Coed** 31,209 undergraduate students, 82% full-time, 52% women, 48% men
- **Moderately difficult** entrance level, 72% of applicants were admitted

UNDERGRAD STUDENTS

25,513 full-time, 5,696 part-time. Students come from 50 states and territories; 133 other countries; 3% are from out of state; 14% Black or African American, non-Hispanic/Latino; 24% Hispanic/Latino; 6% Asian, non-Hispanic/Latino; 0.1% Native Hawaiian or other Pacific Islander, non-Hispanic/Latino; 0.3% American Indian or Alaska Native, non-Hispanic/Latino; 4% Two or more races, non-Hispanic/Latino; 0.7% Race/ethnicity unknown; 3% international; 13% transferred in; 20% live on campus.

Freshmen:

Admission: 16,826 applied, 12,046 admitted, 4,774 enrolled. ***Test scores:*** SAT critical reading scores over 500: 71%; SAT math scores over 500: 72%; SAT writing scores over 500: 58%; ACT scores over 18: 88%; SAT critical reading scores over 600: 28%; SAT math scores over 600: 27%; SAT writing scores over 600: 16%; ACT scores over 24: 46%; SAT critical reading scores over 700: 4%; SAT math scores over 700: 5%; SAT writing scores over 700: 2%; ACT scores over 30: 5%.

Retention: 80% of full-time freshmen returned.

FACULTY

Total: 1,554, 67% full-time, 58% with terminal degrees.

Student/faculty ratio: 26:1.

ACADEMICS

Calendar: semesters. *Degrees:* bachelor's, master's, doctoral, and postbachelor's certificates.

Special study options: academic remediation for entering students, accelerated degree program, advanced placement credit, cooperative education, distance learning, double majors, English as a second language, freshman honors college, honors programs, independent study, internships, off-campus study, part-time degree program, services for LD students, study abroad, summer session for credit. ***ROTC:*** Army (b), Air Force (b).

Computers: 1,078 computers/terminals are available on campus for general student use. Students can access the following: campus intranet, computer help desk, free student e-mail accounts, online (class) grades, online (class) registration, online (class) schedules. Campuswide network is available. 100% of college-owned or -operated housing units are wired for high-speed Internet access. Wireless service is available via entire campus.

Library: Willis Library plus 5 others. *Books:* 3.8 million (physical), 867,204 (digital/electronic); *Serial titles:* 595 (physical), 133,294 (digital/electronic); *Databases:* 528. Weekly public service hours: 168; study areas open 24 hours, 5-7 days a week; students can reserve study rooms.

STUDENT LIFE

Housing options: on-campus residence required for freshman year; coed, special housing for students with disabilities. Campus housing is university owned. Freshman applicants given priority for college housing.

Activities and organizations: drama/theater group, student-run newspaper, radio and television station, choral group, marching band, Student Government Association, Residence Hall Association, Panhellenic Association, Interfraternity Council, College Life, national fraternities, national sororities.

Athletics Member NCAA. All Division I except football (Division I-A). ***Intercollegiate sports:*** archery M(c)/W(c), badminton M(c)/W(c), baseball M(c), basketball M(s)/W(s), bowling M(c)/W(c), cross-country running M(s)/W(s), equestrian sports M(c)/W(c), fencing M(c)/W(c), golf M(s)/W(s), ice hockey M(c)/W(c), lacrosse M(c)/W(c), racquetball M(c)/W(c), rugby M(c), sailing M(c)/W(c), soccer M(c)/W(s), softball M/W(s), swimming and diving W(s), table tennis M(c)/W(c), tennis M(c)/W, track and field M(s)/W(s), ultimate Frisbee M(c)/W(c), volleyball M(c)/W(s), wrestling M(c)/W(c). ***Intramural sports:*** basketball M/W, football M, racquetball M/W, soccer M/W, softball M/W, table tennis M/W, tennis M/W, ultimate Frisbee M/W, volleyball M/W.

Campus security: 24-hour emergency response devices and patrols, late-night transport/escort service, controlled dormitory access.

Student services: health clinic, personal/psychological counseling, women's center, legal services.

COSTS & FINANCIAL AID

Costs (2016–17) ***Tuition:*** state resident $7988 full-time, $266 per credit hour part-time; nonresident $20,228 full-time, $674 per credit hour part-time. No tuition increase for student's term of enrollment. ***Required fees:*** $2532 full-time. ***Room and board:*** $8679. Room and board charges vary according to board plan and housing facility. ***Payment plan:*** installment. ***Waivers:*** senior citizens and employees or children of employees.

Financial Aid Of all full-time matriculated undergraduates who enrolled in 2016, 18,666 applied for aid, 15,454 were judged to have need, 1,523 had their need fully met. In 2016, 3110 non-need-based awards were made. ***Average percent of need met:*** 53. ***Average financial aid package:*** $10,759. ***Average need-based loan:*** $4124. ***Average need-based gift aid:*** $7815. ***Average non-need-based aid:*** $5636. ***Average indebtedness upon graduation:*** $25,249.

APPLYING
Standardized Tests *Required:* SAT or ACT (for admission).
Options: electronic application, early admission, deferred entrance.
Application fee: $75.
Required: high school transcript. ***Required for some:*** essay or personal statement.
Application deadlines: 8/1 (freshmen), rolling (transfers).
Notification: continuous (freshmen), continuous (transfers).

CONTACT
Mr. Randall Nunn, Associate Director of Admissions, University of North Texas, Denton, TX 76203. *Phone:* 940-565-3920. *Toll-free phone:* 800-868-8211. *E-mail:* randall.nunn@unt.edu.

University of North Texas at Dallas

Dallas, Texas

http://untdallas.edu/

- **State-supported** comprehensive, founded 2001, part of University of North Texas System
- **Urban** 264-acre campus with easy access to Dallas-Fort Worth
- **Endowment** $823,724
- **Coed** 2,295 undergraduate students, 60% full-time, 68% women, 32% men
- 68% of applicants were admitted

UNDERGRAD STUDENTS
1,375 full-time, 920 part-time. Students come from 11 states and territories; 17 other countries; 0.8% are from out of state; 34% Black or African American, non-Hispanic/Latino; 50% Hispanic/Latino; 2% Asian, non-Hispanic/Latino; 0.1% Native Hawaiian or other Pacific Islander, non-Hispanic/Latino; 0.3% American Indian or Alaska Native, non-Hispanic/Latino; 2% Two or more races, non-Hispanic/Latino; 0.8% Race/ethnicity unknown; 1% international; 24% transferred in.

Freshmen:
Admission: 1,863 applied, 1,270 admitted, 280 enrolled. ***Test scores:*** SAT math scores over 500: 30%; ACT scores over 18: 57%; SAT math scores over 600: 1%; ACT scores over 24: 10%; ACT scores over 30: 1%.
Retention: 66% of full-time freshmen returned.

FACULTY
Total: 167, 56% full-time.
Student/faculty ratio: 15:1.

ACADEMICS
Degrees: bachelor's, master's, and doctoral.
Special study options: accelerated degree program, advanced placement credit, cooperative education, distance learning, independent study, internships, off-campus study, part-time degree program, services for LD students, summer session for credit.
Computers: Students can access the following: computer help desk, free student e-mail accounts, online (class) grades. Campuswide network is available.
Library: UNTD Library. *Books:* 3,980 (physical), 44,401 (digital/electronic); *Serial titles:* 330 (physical), 10,899 (digital/electronic); *Databases:* 281.

STUDENT LIFE
Activities and organizations: national fraternities, national sororities.
Athletics ***Intramural sports:*** basketball M/W, soccer M/W, volleyball M/W.
Campus security: 24-hour emergency response devices, late-night transport/escort service.
Student services: personal/psychological counseling.

COSTS & FINANCIAL AID
Costs (2016–17) ***Tuition:*** state resident $7548 full-time, $252 per credit hour part-time; nonresident $19,788 full-time, $660 per credit hour part-time. Full-time tuition and fees vary according to degree level. Part-time tuition and fees vary according to degree level. No tuition increase for student's term of enrollment. ***Required fees:*** $300 full-time, $10 per credit hour part-time, $10 per credit hour part-time. ***Room and board:*** Room and board charges vary according to board plan and housing facility. ***Waivers:*** senior citizens and employees or children of employees.
Financial Aid Of all full-time matriculated undergraduates who enrolled in 2016, 958 applied for aid, 908 were judged to have need, 32 had their need fully met. In 2016, 228 non-need-based awards were made. ***Average percent of need met:*** 40. ***Average financial aid package:*** $8143. ***Average need-based loan:*** $4110. ***Average need-based gift aid:*** $5620. ***Average non-need-based aid:*** $1924. ***Average indebtedness upon graduation:*** $6927.

APPLYING
Standardized Tests *Required:* SAT or ACT (for admission).
Options: electronic application.
Application fee: $50.
Required: high school transcript.

CONTACT
Mr. Jason Faulk, Director of Undergraduate Admission, University of North Texas at Dallas, 7300 University Hill Drive, Admin (B1)105, Dallas 76039. *Phone:* 972-780-3642. *E-mail:* admissions@untdallas.edu.

University of Phoenix–Dallas Campus

Dallas, Texas

http://www.phoenix.edu/

CONTACT
Marc Booker, Sr. Director, Office of Admissions and Evaluation, University of Phoenix–Dallas Campus, 4035 South Riverpoint Parkway, Mail Stop CF-L101, Phoenix, AZ 85040. *Phone:* 602-557-4609. *Toll-free phone:* 866-766-0766. *Fax:* 480-643-1156.

University of Phoenix–Houston Campus

Houston, Texas

http://www.phoenix.edu/

CONTACT
Marc Booker, Sr. Director, Office of Admissions and Evaluation, University of Phoenix–Houston Campus, 4305 South Riverpoint Parkway, Mail Stop CF-L101, Phoenix, AZ 85040. *Phone:* 602-557-4609. *Toll-free phone:* 866-766-0766. *Fax:* 480-643-1156.

University of Phoenix–San Antonio Campus

San Antonio, Texas

http://www.phoenix.edu/

CONTACT
University of Phoenix–San Antonio Campus, 8200 IH-10 West, San Antonio, TX 78230. *Toll-free phone:* 866-766-0766.

University of St. Thomas

Houston, Texas

http://www.stthom.edu/

- **Independent Roman Catholic** comprehensive, founded 1947
- **Urban** 23-acre campus with easy access to Houston, TX
- **Endowment** $81.8 million
- **Coed** 1,814 undergraduate students, 77% full-time, 60% women, 40% men
- **Moderately difficult** entrance level, 77% of applicants were admitted

UNDERGRAD STUDENTS
1,391 full-time, 423 part-time. Students come from 26 states and territories; 59 other countries; 3% are from out of state; 7% Black or African American, non-Hispanic/Latino; 43% Hispanic/Latino; 11% Asian, non-Hispanic/Latino; 0.2% Native Hawaiian or other Pacific Islander, non-Hispanic/Latino; 0.2% American Indian or Alaska Native, non-Hispanic/Latino; 3% Two or more races, non-Hispanic/Latino; 2% Race/ethnicity unknown; 9% international; 10% transferred in; 22% live on campus.

Freshmen:
Admission: 942 applied, 729 admitted, 277 enrolled. ***Average high school GPA:*** 3.61. ***Test scores:*** SAT critical reading scores over 500: 72%; SAT math scores over 500: 76%; SAT writing scores over 500: 66%; ACT scores over 18: 98%; SAT critical reading scores over 600: 20%; SAT math scores over 600: 23%; SAT writing scores over 600: 19%; ACT scores over 24: 55%; SAT critical reading scores over 700: 4%; SAT math scores over 700: 4%; SAT writing scores over 700: 3%; ACT scores over 30: 10%.

Retention: 82% of full-time freshmen returned.

FACULTY
Total: 350, 51% full-time, 62% with terminal degrees.

Student/faculty ratio: 10:1.

ACADEMICS
Calendar: semesters. *Degrees:* diplomas, bachelor's, master's, and doctoral.

Special study options: accelerated degree program, adult/continuing education programs, advanced placement credit, distance learning, double majors, honors programs, independent study, internships, off-campus study, part-time degree program, services for LD students, student-designed majors, study abroad, summer session for credit. ***ROTC:*** Army (c), Air Force (c).

Unusual degree programs: 3-2 business administration; engineering with University of Notre Dame, University of Houston, Texas A&M University, The Catholic University of America.

Computers: 390 computers/terminals and 400 ports are available on campus for general student use. Students can access the following: campus intranet, computer help desk, free student e-mail accounts, online (class) grades, online (class) registration, online (class) schedules. Campuswide network is available. 95% of college-owned or -operated housing units are wired for high-speed Internet access. Wireless service is available via entire campus.

Library: Doherty Library. *Books:* 262,422 (physical), 2,491 (digital/electronic); *Serial titles:* 78,316 (physical), 78,316 (digital/electronic); *Databases:* 265. Weekly public service hours: 100.

STUDENT LIFE
Housing options: coed, men-only, women-only, special housing for students with disabilities. Campus housing is university owned. Freshman applicants given priority for college housing.

Activities and organizations: drama/theater group, student-run newspaper, choral group, Health Occupations Students of America (HOSA), Filipino Student Association (FSA), Student Activities Board (SAB), American Chemical Society, Ultimate Frisbee.

Athletics Member NAIA. ***Intercollegiate sports:*** basketball M(s)/W(s), cheerleading M(c)/W(c), fencing M(c)/W(c), golf M(s)/W(s), soccer M(s)/W(s), tennis M(c)/W(c), track and field M(c)/W(c), volleyball W(s). ***Intramural sports:*** basketball M/W, football M(c)/W(c), soccer M(c)/W(c), table tennis M/W, ultimate Frisbee M(c)/W(c), volleyball M(c)/W(c).

Campus security: 24-hour emergency response devices and patrols, late-night transport/escort service, controlled dormitory access.

Student services: personal/psychological counseling.

COSTS & FINANCIAL AID
Costs (2017–18) ***Comprehensive fee:*** $41,510 includes full-time tuition ($32,100), mandatory fees ($560), and room and board ($8850). Full-time tuition and fees vary according to course load. Part-time tuition: $1070 per credit hour. Part-time tuition and fees vary according to course load. ***College room only:*** $5360. Room and board charges vary according to board plan and housing facility. ***Payment plans:*** installment, deferred payment. ***Waivers:*** senior citizens and employees or children of employees.

Financial Aid Of all full-time matriculated undergraduates who enrolled in 2016, 931 applied for aid, 888 were judged to have need, 86 had their need fully met. 97 Federal Work-Study jobs (averaging $3959). 2 state and other part-time jobs (averaging $4000). In 2016, 367 non-need-based awards were made. ***Average percent of need met:*** 67. ***Average financial aid package:*** $24,458. ***Average need-based loan:*** $4778. ***Average need-based gift aid:*** $21,027. ***Average non-need-based aid:*** $11,769. ***Average indebtedness upon graduation:*** $26,455.

APPLYING
Standardized Tests *Required:* SAT or ACT (for admission).

Options: electronic application, early action, deferred entrance.

Required: essay or personal statement, high school transcript, minimum 2.8 GPA, minimum 1070 SAT (Critical Reading and Math) or 23 ACT.

Application deadlines: 5/1 (freshmen), rolling (transfers), 12/1 (early action).

Notification: continuous until 11/1 (freshmen), continuous until 11/1 (out-of-state freshmen), continuous (transfers), 12/15 (early action).

CONTACT
Mr. Arthur Ortiz, Assistant Vice President of Enrollment, University of St. Thomas, 3800 Montrose Boulevard, Houston, TX 77006-4696. *Phone:* 713-525-3848. *Toll-free phone:* 800-856-8565. *Fax:* 713-525-3558. *E-mail:* admissions@stthom.edu.

The University of Texas at Arlington
Arlington, Texas
http://www.uta.edu/

CONTACT
Dr. Hans Gatterdam, Executive Director of Admissions, Records and Registration, The University of Texas at Arlington, UTA Box 19088, 701 South Nedderman Drive, Arlington, TX 76019-0088. *Phone:* 817-272-3275. *Fax:* 817-272-5114.

The University of Texas at Austin
Austin, Texas
http://www.utexas.edu/

- **State-supported** university, founded 1883, part of University of Texas System
- **Urban** 437-acre campus with easy access to Austin
- **Endowment** $3.4 billion
- **Coed** 40,168 undergraduate students, 93% full-time, 53% women, 47% men
- **Moderately difficult** entrance level, 40% of applicants were admitted

UNDERGRAD STUDENTS
37,234 full-time, 2,934 part-time. Students come from 54 states and territories; 118 other countries; 5% are from out of state; 4% Black or African American, non-Hispanic/Latino; 23% Hispanic/Latino; 21% Asian, non-Hispanic/Latino; 0.1% Native Hawaiian or other Pacific Islander, non-Hispanic/Latino; 0.1% American Indian or Alaska Native, non-Hispanic/Latino; 4% Two or more races, non-Hispanic/Latino; 0.9% Race/ethnicity unknown; 5% international; 6% transferred in; 18% live on campus.

Freshmen:
Admission: 47,501 applied, 19,182 admitted, 8,719 enrolled. ***Test scores:*** SAT critical reading scores over 500: 91%; SAT math scores over 500: 94%; SAT writing scores over 500: 88%; ACT scores over 18: 99%; SAT critical reading scores over 600: 62%; SAT math scores over 600: 71%; SAT writing scores over 600: 59%; ACT scores over 24: 88%; SAT critical reading scores over 700: 22%; SAT math scores over 700: 34%; SAT writing scores over 700: 21%; ACT scores over 30: 51%.

Retention: 95% of full-time freshmen returned.

FACULTY
Total: 3,071, 83% full-time, 86% with terminal degrees.

Student/faculty ratio: 18:1.

ACADEMICS
Calendar: semesters. *Degrees:* certificates, bachelor's, master's, doctoral, and postbachelor's certificates.

Special study options: academic remediation for entering students, accelerated degree program, advanced placement credit, cooperative education, distance learning, double majors, English as a second language, honors programs, independent study, internships, off-campus study, part-time degree program, services for LD students, student-designed majors, study abroad, summer session for credit. ***ROTC:*** Army (b), Navy (b), Air Force (b).

Unusual degree programs: 3-2 business administration; engineering; nursing; social work; computer science.

Computers: 550 computers/terminals and 1,650 ports are available on campus for general student use. Students can access the following: campus intranet, computer help desk, free student e-mail accounts, online (class) grades, online (class) registration, online (class) schedules. Campuswide network is available. 100% of college-owned or -operated housing units are wired for high-speed Internet access. Wireless service is available via entire campus.

Library: PCL (Perry Castaneda Library) plus 23 others. *Books:* 11.5 million (physical), 1.4 million (digital/electronic); *Serial titles:* 3,554 (physical), 224,040 (digital/electronic); *Databases:* 1,570. Weekly public service hours: 94; study areas open 24 hours, 5-7 days a week; students can reserve study rooms.

STUDENT LIFE

Housing options: coed, men-only, women-only, special housing for students with disabilities. Campus housing is university owned. Freshman applicants given priority for college housing.

Activities and organizations: drama/theater group, student-run newspaper, radio and television station, choral group, marching band, Alpha Phi Omega, University Panhellenic Council, Asian Business Students Association, Longhorn Band Student Organization, Campus Events + Entertainment, national fraternities, national sororities.

Athletics Member NCAA. All Division I except football (Division I-A). ***Intercollegiate sports:*** archery M(c)/W(c), badminton M(c)/W(c), baseball M(s)/W(c), basketball M(s)/W(s), crew M(c)/W(s), cross-country running M(s)/W(s), fencing M(c)/W(c), golf M(s)/W(s), gymnastics M(c)/W(c), ice hockey M(c)/W(c), lacrosse M(c)/W(c), racquetball M(c)/W(c), rock climbing M(c)/W(c), rugby M(c)/W(c), sailing M(c)/W(c), soccer M(c)/W(s), softball W(s), swimming and diving M(s)/W(s), table tennis M(c)/W(c), tennis M(s)/W(s), track and field M(s)/W(s), ultimate Frisbee M(c)/W(c), volleyball M(c)/W(s), water polo M(c)/W(c), weight lifting M(c)/W(c), wrestling M(c)/W(c). ***Intramural sports:*** basketball M/W, football M/W, golf M/W, racquetball M/W, rock climbing M/W, soccer M/W, softball M/W, swimming and diving M/W, table tennis M/W, tennis M/W, track and field M/W, ultimate Frisbee M/W, volleyball M/W.

Campus security: 24-hour emergency response devices and patrols, late-night transport/escort service, controlled dormitory access.

Student services: health clinic, personal/psychological counseling, women's center, legal services.

COSTS & FINANCIAL AID

Costs (2016–17) ***Tuition:*** state resident $10,144 full-time; nonresident $35,796 full-time. Full-time tuition and fees vary according to course load and program. Part-time tuition and fees vary according to course load and program. No tuition increase for student's term of enrollment. ***Room and board:*** $10,070. Room and board charges vary according to housing facility. ***Payment plan:*** installment. ***Waivers:*** senior citizens and employees or children of employees.

Financial Aid Of all full-time matriculated undergraduates who enrolled in 2016, 21,887 applied for aid, 14,944 were judged to have need, 3,210 had their need fully met. In 2016, 169 non-need-based awards were made. ***Average percent of need met:*** 70. ***Average financial aid package:*** $12,283. ***Average need-based loan:*** $4767. ***Average need-based gift aid:*** $9587. ***Average non-need-based aid:*** $2502. ***Average indebtedness upon graduation:*** $25,338.

APPLYING

Standardized Tests *Required:* SAT or ACT (for admission).

Options: electronic application.

Application fee: $75.

Required: essay or personal statement, high school transcript. *Recommended:* letters of recommendation.

Application deadlines: 12/1 (freshmen), 3/1 (transfers).

Notification: continuous (freshmen), continuous (transfers).

CONTACT

Susan Kearns, Director of Admissions, The University of Texas at Austin, Office of Admissions, Freshman Admissions Center, PO Box 8058, Austin, TX 78713-8058. *Phone:* 512-475-7368. *Fax:* 512-232-4241. *E-mail:* susan.kearns@austin.utexas.edu.

The University of Texas at Dallas

Richardson, Texas

http://www.utdallas.edu/

- **State-supported** university, founded 1969, part of University of Texas System
- **Suburban** 500-acre campus with easy access to Dallas-Fort Worth
- **Endowment** $436.1 million
- **Coed** 17,350 undergraduate students, 83% full-time, 43% women, 57% men
- **Very difficult** entrance level, 68% of applicants were admitted

UNDERGRAD STUDENTS

14,323 full-time, 3,027 part-time. Students come from 48 states and territories; 76 other countries; 4% are from out of state; 6% Black or African American, non-Hispanic/Latino; 18% Hispanic/Latino; 29% Asian, non-Hispanic/Latino; 0.2% Native Hawaiian or other Pacific Islander, non-Hispanic/Latino; 0.2% American Indian or Alaska Native, non-Hispanic/Latino; 4% Two or more races, non-Hispanic/Latino; 2% Race/ethnicity unknown; 4% international; 12% transferred in; 25% live on campus.

Freshmen:

Admission: 12,686 applied, 8,625 admitted, 3,229 enrolled. ***Test scores:*** SAT critical reading scores over 500: 91%; SAT math scores over 500: 97%; SAT writing scores over 500: 84%; ACT scores over 18: 100%; SAT critical reading scores over 600: 56%; SAT math scores over 600: 73%; SAT writing scores over 600: 45%; ACT scores over 24: 87%; SAT critical reading scores over 700: 18%; SAT math scores over 700: 29%; SAT writing scores over 700: 13%; ACT scores over 30: 39%.

Retention: 87% of full-time freshmen returned.

FACULTY

Total: 1,227, 70% full-time, 84% with terminal degrees.

Student/faculty ratio: 23:1.

ACADEMICS

Calendar: semesters. *Degrees:* bachelor's, master's, doctoral, and postbachelor's certificates.

Special study options: academic remediation for entering students, accelerated degree program, adult/continuing education programs, advanced placement credit, cooperative education, distance learning, double majors, freshman honors college, honors programs, independent study, internships, part-time degree program, services for LD students, student-designed majors, study abroad, summer session for credit. ***ROTC:*** Army (c), Air Force (c).

Unusual degree programs: 3-2 engineering with Abilene Christian University, Austin College, Paul Quinn College, Texas Woman's University.

Computers: 170 computers/terminals are available on campus for general student use. Students can access the following: computer help desk, free student e-mail accounts, online (class) grades, online (class) registration, online (class) schedules. Campuswide network is available. 100% of college-owned or -operated housing units are wired for high-speed Internet access. Wireless service is available via classrooms, computer centers, dorm rooms, libraries, student centers.

Library: Eugene McDermott Library plus 1 other. *Books:* 593,907 (physical), 1.6 million (digital/electronic); *Serial titles:* 93,747 (physical), 171,102 (digital/electronic); *Databases:* 517. Weekly public service hours: 152; study areas open 24 hours, 5-7 days a week; students can reserve study rooms.

STUDENT LIFE

Housing options: coed. Campus housing is university owned and is provided by a third party. Freshman applicants given priority for college housing.

Activities and organizations: drama/theater group, student-run newspaper, radio and television station, choral group, Student Government Association, Golden Key National Honor Society, Muslim Students Association, Indian Student Association, Friendship Association of Chinese Students and Scholars, national fraternities, national sororities.

Athletics Member NCAA. All Division III. ***Intercollegiate sports:*** baseball M, basketball M/W, cross-country running M/W, golf M/W, soccer M/W, softball W, tennis M/W, volleyball W. ***Intramural sports:*** archery M(c)/W(c), badminton M(c)/W(c), basketball M(c)/W(c), cheerleading M/W, cross-country running M(c)/W(c), fencing M(c)/W(c), gymnastics M(c)/W(c), lacrosse M(c), racquetball M(c)/W(c), rock climbing M(c)/W(c), rugby M(c)/W(c), soccer M(c)/W(c), swimming and diving M(c)/W(c), table tennis M(c)/W(c), tennis M(c)/W(c), ultimate Frisbee M(c)/W(c), volleyball M(c)/W(c), weight lifting M(c)/W(c), wrestling M(c)/W(c).

Campus security: 24-hour emergency response devices and patrols, student patrols, late-night transport/escort service, controlled dormitory access.

Student services: health clinic, personal/psychological counseling, women's center, legal services.

COSTS & FINANCIAL AID

Costs (2016–17) ***Tuition:*** state resident $12,162 full-time, $405 per credit hour part-time; nonresident $33,654 full-time, $1122 per credit hour part-time. Full-time tuition and fees vary according to course load and degree level. Part-time tuition and fees vary according to course load and degree level. No tuition increase for student's term of enrollment. ***Room and board:*** $10,668. Room and board charges vary according to board plan and housing facility. ***Payment plan:*** installment. ***Waivers:*** senior citizens and employees or children of employees.

Financial Aid Of all full-time matriculated undergraduates who enrolled in 2015, 8,095 applied for aid, 6,772 were judged to have need, 1,089 had their need fully met. In 2015, 2681 non-need-based awards were made. ***Average percent of need met:*** 65. ***Average financial aid package:*** $12,888. ***Average need-based loan:*** $4375. ***Average need-based gift aid:*** $9119. ***Average non-need-based aid:*** $11,894. ***Average indebtedness upon graduation:*** $20,432.

APPLYING

Standardized Tests *Required:* SAT or ACT (for admission). *Required for some:* THEA.

Options: electronic application, deferred entrance.

Application fee: $50.

Required: essay or personal statement, high school transcript. ***Required for some:*** interview. ***Recommended:*** 3 letters of recommendation.

Notification: continuous (freshmen), continuous (transfers).

CONTACT

Enrollment Services, The University of Texas at Dallas, 800 West Campbell Road, Mail Station ROC12, Richardson, TX 75083-0688. *Phone:* 972-883-2270. *Toll-free phone:* 800-889-2443. *Fax:* 972-883-2599. *E-mail:* interest@utdallas.edu.

The University of Texas at El Paso

El Paso, Texas

http://www.utep.edu/

- **State-supported** university, founded 1913, part of University of Texas System
- **Urban** 360-acre campus
- **Coed** 20,220 undergraduate students, 65% full-time, 54% women, 46% men
- **Minimally difficult** entrance level, 100% of applicants were admitted

UNDERGRAD STUDENTS

13,079 full-time, 7,141 part-time. Students come from 50 states and territories; 51 other countries; 4% are from out of state; 3% Black or African American, non-Hispanic/Latino; 83% Hispanic/Latino; 0.8% Asian, non-Hispanic/Latino; 0.1% Native Hawaiian or other Pacific Islander, non-Hispanic/Latino; 0.2% American Indian or Alaska Native, non-Hispanic/Latino; 0.7% Two or more races, non-Hispanic/Latino; 0.5% Race/ethnicity unknown; 5% international; 10% transferred in.

Freshmen:

Admission: 7,134 applied, 7,133 admitted, 2,957 enrolled. ***Average high school GPA:*** 3.22. ***Test scores:*** SAT critical reading scores over 500: 29%; SAT math scores over 500: 43%; ACT scores over 18: 72%; SAT critical reading scores over 600: 6%; SAT math scores over 600: 11%; ACT scores over 24: 16%; SAT math scores over 700: 1%; ACT scores over 30: 1%.

Retention: 72% of full-time freshmen returned.

FACULTY

Total: 1,260, 59% full-time.

Student/faculty ratio: 21:1.

ACADEMICS

Calendar: semesters. *Degrees:* certificates, bachelor's, master's, doctoral, and post-master's certificates.

Special study options: academic remediation for entering students, accelerated degree program, adult/continuing education programs, advanced placement credit, cooperative education, distance learning, double majors, English as a second language, honors programs, independent study, internships, off-campus study, part-time degree program, services for LD students, study abroad, summer session for credit.

Computers: Students can access the following: computer help desk, free student e-mail accounts, online (class) grades, online (class) registration, online (class) schedules. Campuswide network is available. Wireless service is available via entire campus.

Library: University Library.

STUDENT LIFE

Housing options: coed. Campus housing is university owned.

Activities and organizations: drama/theater group, student-run newspaper, radio station, choral group, marching band, national fraternities, national sororities.

Athletics Member NCAA. All Division I except football (Division I-A). ***Intercollegiate sports:*** basketball M(s)/W(s), cross-country running M(s)/W(s), golf M(s), riflery M/W, tennis W(s), track and field M(s)/W(s), volleyball W(s). ***Intramural sports:*** archery M/W, badminton M/W, basketball M/W, bowling M/W, fencing M/W, field hockey M, golf M/W, gymnastics M/W, racquetball M/W, skiing (downhill) M, soccer M/W, squash M/W, swimming and diving M/W, tennis M/W, track and field M/W, volleyball M/W, water polo M/W, weight lifting M, wrestling M/W.

Campus security: 24-hour emergency response devices and patrols, late-night transport/escort service.

Student services: health clinic, personal/psychological counseling, women's center, legal services.

COSTS & FINANCIAL AID

Costs (2017–18) ***Tuition:*** state resident $5769 full-time, $192 per credit hour part-time; nonresident $18,744 full-time, $625 per credit hour part-time. No tuition increase for student's term of enrollment. ***Required fees:*** $1779 full-time. ***Room and board:*** $9496; room only: $4914. ***Payment plan:*** installment.

Financial Aid Of all full-time matriculated undergraduates who enrolled in 2015, 11,695 applied for aid, 10,365 were judged to have need, 729 had their need fully met. 400 Federal Work-Study jobs (averaging $3113). 103 state and other part-time jobs (averaging $2052). In 2015, 542 non-need-based awards were made. ***Average percent of need met:*** 61. ***Average financial aid package:*** $14,511. ***Average need-based loan:*** $6675. ***Average need-based gift aid:*** $8196. ***Average non-need-based aid:*** $4391. ***Average indebtedness upon graduation:*** $21,840.

APPLYING

Standardized Tests *Required:* SAT or ACT (for admission).

Options: deferred entrance.

Application fee: $40.

Required: high school transcript.

CONTACT

Mr. Michael J. Talamantes, Director of Admissions and Recruitment, The University of Texas at El Paso, Academic Services Building, Room 102, El Paso, TX 779968. *Phone:* 915-747-5890. *Toll-free phone:* 877-74MINER. *Fax:* 915-747-5890. *E-mail:* futureminer@utep.edu.

The University of Texas at San Antonio

San Antonio, Texas

http://www.utsa.edu/

- **State-supported** university, founded 1969, part of University of Texas System
- **Suburban** 725-acre campus with easy access to San Antonio
- **Endowment** $134.5 million
- **Coed** 24,724 undergraduate students, 82% full-time, 50% women, 50% men
- **Moderately difficult** entrance level, 76% of applicants were admitted

UNDERGRAD STUDENTS

20,222 full-time, 4,502 part-time. Students come from 51 states and territories; 75 other countries; 2% are from out of state; 9% Black or African American, non-Hispanic/Latino; 54% Hispanic/Latino; 6% Asian, non-Hispanic/Latino; 0.2% Native Hawaiian or other Pacific Islander, non-Hispanic/Latino; 0.2% American Indian or Alaska Native, non-Hispanic/Latino; 3% Two or more races, non-Hispanic/Latino; 0.8% Race/ethnicity unknown; 2% international; 9% transferred in; 17% live on campus.

Freshmen:

Admission: 15,500 applied, 11,843 admitted, 4,377 enrolled. ***Test scores:*** SAT critical reading scores over 500: 55%; SAT math scores over 500: 63%; SAT writing scores over 500: 43%; ACT scores over 18: 90%; SAT critical reading scores over 600: 16%; SAT math scores over 600: 17%; SAT writing scores over 600: 8%; ACT scores over 24: 36%; SAT critical reading scores over 700: 2%; SAT math scores over 700: 2%; SAT writing scores over 700: 1%; ACT scores over 30: 4%.

Retention: 71% of full-time freshmen returned.

FACULTY

Total: 1,328, 69% full-time, 73% with terminal degrees.

Student/faculty ratio: 23:1.

ACADEMICS

Calendar: semesters. *Degrees:* bachelor's, master's, and doctoral.

Special study options: academic remediation for entering students, adult/continuing education programs, advanced placement credit, cooperative education, distance learning, double majors, English as a second language, honors programs, independent study, internships, off-campus study, part-time degree program, services for LD students, student-designed majors, study abroad, summer session for credit. ***ROTC:*** Army (b), Air Force (b).

Computers: 510 computers/terminals and 104 ports are available on campus for general student use. Students can access the following: campus intranet, computer help desk, free student e-mail accounts, online (class) grades, online (class) registration, online (class) schedules. Campuswide network is available. 100% of college-owned or -operated housing units are wired for high-speed Internet access. Wireless service is available via entire campus.

Library: John Peace Library plus 3 others. Students can reserve study rooms.

STUDENT LIFE

Housing options: coed, special housing for students with disabilities. Campus housing is university owned and is provided by a third party.

Activities and organizations: student-run newspaper, radio and television station, choral group, marching band, Student Government, VOICES, Chi Alpha Christian Fellowship, Hispanic Student Association, Panhellenic Council, national fraternities, national sororities.

Athletics Member NCAA. All Division I. ***Intercollegiate sports:*** badminton M(c)/W(c), baseball M(s), basketball M(s)/W(s), cross-country running M(s)/W(s), fencing M(c)/W(c), football M(s), golf M(s)/W(s), ice hockey M(c), lacrosse M(c)/W(c), racquetball M(c)/W(c), rock climbing M(c)/W(c), rugby M(c)/W(c), soccer M(c)/W(s), softball W(s), swimming and diving M(c)/W(c), table tennis M(c)/W(c), tennis M(s)/W(s), track and field M(s)/W(s), ultimate Frisbee M(c)/W(c), volleyball M(c)/W(s), weight lifting M(c)/W(c), wrestling M(c). ***Intramural sports:*** badminton M/W, baseball M(c), basketball M/W, cross-country running M/W, football M, golf M/W, racquetball M/W, soccer M/W, softball M/W, table tennis M/W, tennis M/W, track and field M/W, ultimate Frisbee M/W, volleyball M/W.

Campus security: 24-hour emergency response devices and patrols, late-night transport/escort service, controlled dormitory access, close to 1000 security cameras, Reverse 911 emergency telephone notification system, warning speaker arrays.

Student services: health clinic, personal/psychological counseling, women's center.

COSTS & FINANCIAL AID

Costs (2016–17) ***Tuition:*** state resident $6299 full-time, $210 per credit hour part-time; nonresident $19,545 full-time, $652 per credit hour part-time. Full-time tuition and fees vary according to course load and degree level. Part-time tuition and fees vary according to course load and degree level. No tuition increase for student's term of enrollment. ***Required fees:*** $2745 full-time. ***Room and board:*** $8074; room only: $5190. Room and board charges vary according to board plan and housing facility. ***Payment plans:*** installment, deferred payment. ***Waivers:*** employees or children of employees.

Financial Aid Of all full-time matriculated undergraduates who enrolled in 2015, 15,632 applied for aid, 13,304 were judged to have need, 609 had their need fully met. 366 Federal Work-Study jobs (averaging $2877). 900 state and other part-time jobs (averaging $2133). In 2015, 707 non-need-based awards were made. ***Average percent of need met:*** 53. ***Average financial aid package:*** $9751. ***Average need-based loan:*** $4109. ***Average need-based gift aid:*** $7147. ***Average non-need-based aid:*** $3418. ***Average indebtedness upon graduation:*** $26,763.

APPLYING

Standardized Tests *Required:* SAT or ACT (for admission).

Options: electronic application.

Application fee: $60.

Required: high school transcript. ***Required for some:*** transfer applicants with less than 30 hours must meet freshman requirements and have a 2.25 GPA on a 4.0 scale and submit all college transcripts; transfer applicants with 30 or more completed hours must have a 2.25 GPA on a 4.0 scale and submit all college transcripts. ***Recommended:*** essay or personal statement, 1 letter of recommendation.

Application deadlines: 6/1 (freshmen), 6/1 (transfers).

Notification: continuous (freshmen), continuous (out-of-state freshmen), continuous (transfers).

CONTACT

Mrs. Beverly Woodson Day, Director of Admissions, The University of Texas at San Antonio, One UTSA Circle, San Antonio, TX 78249. *Phone:* 210-458-4536. *Toll-free phone:* 800-669-0919. *Fax:* 210-458-2001. *E-mail:* prospects@utsa.edu.

The University of Texas at Tyler

Tyler, Texas

http://www.uttyler.edu/

- **State-supported** comprehensive, founded 1971, part of University of Texas System
- **Urban** 200-acre campus
- **Coed**
- **Moderately difficult** entrance level

ACADEMICS

Calendar: semesters. *Degrees:* bachelor's, master's, doctoral, post-master's, and postbachelor's certificates.

Library: Robert Muntz Library.

STUDENT LIFE

Housing options: on-campus residence required for freshman year; coed. Campus housing is university owned and is provided by a third party. Freshman applicants given priority for college housing.

Activities and organizations: student-run newspaper, choral group, national fraternities, national sororities.

Athletics Member NCAA. All Division III.

Campus security: 24-hour emergency response devices and patrols, late-night transport/escort service, controlled dormitory access.

FINANCIAL AID
Financial Aid Of all full-time matriculated undergraduates who enrolled in 2012, 3,220 applied for aid, 3,098 were judged to have need, 90 had their need fully met. In 2012, 8 non-need-based awards were made. ***Average percent of need met:*** 41. ***Average financial aid package:*** $7962. ***Average need-based loan:*** $3654. ***Average need-based gift aid:*** $6395. ***Average non-need-based aid:*** $2563. ***Average indebtedness upon graduation:*** $20,151.

APPLYING
Standardized Tests *Required:* SAT or ACT (for admission).

Options: electronic application, deferred entrance.

Application fee: $40.

Required: high school transcript.

CONTACT
Ms. Sarah Bowdin, Interim Assistant Vice President for Enrollment Management, The University of Texas at Tyler, 3900 University Boulevard, Tyler, TX 75799-0001. *Phone:* 903-566-7057. *Toll-free phone:* 800-UTTYLER. *Fax:* 903-566-7068.
E-mail: admissions@uttyler.edu.

The University of Texas Health Science Center at Houston

Houston, Texas

http://www.uthouston.edu/

- **State-supported** upper-level, founded 1972, part of University of Texas System
- **Urban** campus with easy access to Houston
- **Endowment** $217.5 million
- **Coed**
- **Moderately difficult** entrance level

FACULTY
Student/faculty ratio: 9:1.

ACADEMICS
Calendar: semesters. *Degrees:* certificates, bachelor's, master's, doctoral, post-master's, and postbachelor's certificates.
Library: The Texas Medical Center Library plus 1 other.

STUDENT LIFE
Housing options: college housing not available.

Activities and organizations: student-run newspaper, Student Intercouncil (SIC), School of Nursing Student Government Organization (School of Nursing), Student Council (Dental Branch), Student Senate (Medical School), SPH Student Association (School of Public Health).

Campus security: 24-hour emergency response devices and patrols, late-night transport/escort service, controlled access to all buildings.

Student services: health clinic, personal/psychological counseling.

FINANCIAL AID
Financial Aid Of all full-time matriculated undergraduates who enrolled in 2015, 660 applied for aid, 656 were judged to have need, 218 had their need fully met. In 2015, 3 non-need-based awards were made. ***Average percent of need met:*** 42. ***Average financial aid package:*** $9034. ***Average need-based loan:*** $6318. ***Average need-based gift aid:*** $5678. ***Average non-need-based aid:*** $3333.

APPLYING
Standardized Tests *Required:* HESI A2-Nursing Entrance Test for BSN programs (for admission).

Options: electronic application.

Application fee: $60.

CONTACT
The University of Texas Health Science Center at Houston, PO Box 20036, Houston, TX 77225-0036. *Phone:* 713-500-3388.

The University of Texas Health Science Center at San Antonio

San Antonio, Texas

http://www.uthscsa.edu/

CONTACT
The University of Texas Health Science Center at San Antonio, 7703 Floyd Curl Drive, San Antonio, TX 78229-3900. *Phone:* 210-567-2659.

The University of Texas MD Anderson Cancer Center

Houston, Texas

http://www.mdanderson.org/education-and-research/

CONTACT
The University of Texas MD Anderson Cancer Center, 1515 Holcombe Boulevard, Houston, TX 77030.

The University of Texas Medical Branch

Galveston, Texas

http://www.utmb.edu/

CONTACT
The University of Texas Medical Branch, 301 University Boulevard, Galveston, TX 77555. *Phone:* 409-772-1215.

The University of Texas of the Permian Basin

Odessa, Texas

http://www.utpb.edu/

- **State-supported** comprehensive, founded 1969, part of The University of Texas System
- **Urban** 600-acre campus
- **Endowment** $38.6 million
- **Coed** 5,663 undergraduate students, 38% full-time, 57% women, 43% men
- **Moderately difficult** entrance level, 81% of applicants were admitted

UNDERGRAD STUDENTS
2,168 full-time, 3,495 part-time. Students come from 37 states and territories; 33 other countries; 4% are from out of state; 5% Black or African American, non-Hispanic/Latino; 46% Hispanic/Latino; 3% Asian, non-Hispanic/Latino; 0.2% Native Hawaiian or other Pacific Islander, non-Hispanic/Latino; 0.7% American Indian or Alaska Native, non-Hispanic/Latino; 1% Two or more races, non-Hispanic/Latino; 7% Race/ethnicity unknown; 2% international; 7% transferred in; 21% live on campus.

Freshmen:
Admission: 1,307 applied, 1,065 admitted, 427 enrolled. ***Test scores:*** SAT critical reading scores over 500: 36%; SAT math scores over 500: 43%; ACT scores over 18: 77%; SAT critical reading scores over 600: 5%; SAT math scores over 600: 5%; ACT scores over 24: 17%; SAT critical reading scores over 700: 1%; ACT scores over 30: 3%.
Retention: 70% of full-time freshmen returned.

FACULTY
Total: 256, 55% full-time, 55% with terminal degrees.
Student/faculty ratio: 24:1.

ACADEMICS
Calendar: semesters. *Degrees:* bachelor's, master's, and postbachelor's certificates.
Special study options: academic remediation for entering students, accelerated degree program, advanced placement credit, cooperative education, distance learning, double majors, English as a second language, honors programs, independent study, internships, part-time degree program, services for LD students, study abroad, summer session for credit.

Unusual degree programs: 3-2 business administration.

Computers: 511 computers/terminals are available on campus for general student use. Students can access the following: campus intranet, computer help desk, free student e-mail accounts, online (class) grades, online (class) registration, online (class) schedules. Campuswide network is available. 100% of college-owned or -operated housing units are wired for high-speed Internet access. Wireless service is available via entire campus.

Library: J. Conrad Dunagan Library. *Books:* 236,956 (physical), 192,640 (digital/electronic); *Serial titles:* 364 (physical), 574 (digital/electronic); *Databases:* 231. Weekly public service hours: 90; students can reserve study rooms.

STUDENT LIFE

Housing options: coed. Campus housing is university owned.

Activities and organizations: drama/theater group, student-run newspaper, choral group, marching band, The American Society for Mechanical Engineers, The Student Veteran Association, Marketing Experiences, The National Society for Leadership and Success, Students in Free Enterprise, national fraternities.

Athletics Member NCAA. All Division II. ***Intercollegiate sports:*** baseball M(s), basketball M(s)/W(s), cheerleading M(s)/W(s), cross-country running M(s)/W(s), football M(s), soccer M(s)/W(s), softball W(s), swimming and diving M(s)/W(s), tennis M(s)/W(s), volleyball W(s). ***Intramural sports:*** basketball M/W, bowling M/W, cross-country running M/W, golf M/W, soccer M/W, softball W, swimming and diving M/W, tennis M/W, volleyball M/W.

Campus security: 24-hour emergency response devices and patrols, late-night transport/escort service, controlled dormitory access.

Student services: health clinic, personal/psychological counseling.

COSTS & FINANCIAL AID

Costs (2017–18) ***Tuition:*** state resident $5598 full-time, $186 per credit hour part-time; nonresident $18,078 full-time, $603 per credit hour part-time. Full-time tuition and fees vary according to course load, degree level, and location. Part-time tuition and fees vary according to course load, degree level, and location. No tuition increase for student's term of enrollment. ***Required fees:*** $1462 full-time, $70 per credit hour part-time. ***Room and board:*** $10,800; room only: $7200. Room and board charges vary according to board plan and housing facility. ***Payment plan:*** installment.

Financial Aid Of all full-time matriculated undergraduates who enrolled in 2015, 1,946 applied for aid, 1,646 were judged to have need, 1,170 had their need fully met. In 2015, 906 non-need-based awards were made. ***Average percent of need met:*** 65. ***Average financial aid package:*** $10,560. ***Average need-based loan:*** $3750. ***Average need-based gift aid:*** $7926. ***Average non-need-based aid:*** $2447. ***Average indebtedness upon graduation:*** $17,578.

APPLYING

Standardized Tests *Required:* SAT or ACT (for admission).

Options: electronic application.

Application fee: $40.

Required: high school transcript.

Application deadlines: 8/26 (freshmen), 8/26 (transfers).

Notification: continuous (freshmen), continuous (transfers).

CONTACT

The University of Texas of the Permian Basin, 4901 East University Boulevard, Odessa, TX 79762-0001. *Phone:* 432-552-2605. *Toll-free phone:* 866-552-UTPB.

The University of Texas Rio Grande Valley

Edinburg, Texas

http://www.utrgv.edu/

- **State-supported** comprehensive, founded 1927, part of University of Texas System
- **Small-town** 414-acre campus with easy access to McAllen, Edinburg, Mission
- **Coed** 24,433 undergraduate students, 74% full-time, 56% women, 44% men
- **Noncompetitive** entrance level, 64% of applicants were admitted

UNDERGRAD STUDENTS

17,959 full-time, 6,474 part-time. Students come from 34 states and territories; 47 other countries; 0.2% are from out of state; 0.5% Black or African American, non-Hispanic/Latino; 91% Hispanic/Latino; 1% Asian, non-Hispanic/Latino; 0.1% Native Hawaiian or other Pacific Islander, non-Hispanic/Latino; 0.3% Two or more races, non-Hispanic/Latino; 2% Race/ethnicity unknown; 2% international; 5% transferred in; 4% live on campus.

Freshmen:

Admission: 9,998 applied, 6,392 admitted, 3,944 enrolled.

ACADEMICS

Calendar: semesters. *Degrees:* bachelor's, master's, doctoral, and postbachelor's certificates.

Special study options: academic remediation for entering students, accelerated degree program, adult/continuing education programs, advanced placement credit, cooperative education, distance learning, double majors, English as a second language, honors programs, independent study, internships, off-campus study, part-time degree program, services for LD students, study abroad, summer session for credit. ***ROTC:*** Army (b).

Unusual degree programs: 3-2 business administration.

Computers: Students can access the following: campus intranet, computer help desk, free student e-mail accounts, online (class) grades, online (class) registration, online (class) schedules. Campuswide network is available. 66% of college-owned or -operated housing units are wired for high-speed Internet access. Wireless service is available via entire campus.

Library: University Library. Students can reserve study rooms.

STUDENT LIFE

Housing options: men-only, women-only, special housing for students with disabilities. Campus housing is university owned.

Activities and organizations: drama/theater group, student-run newspaper, radio and television station, choral group, Alpha Lambda Delta National Honor Society for First-Year Students, The National Society of Collegiate Scholars, Golden Key International Honor Society, Pre-Medical Bio-Medical Society, Environmental Awareness Club, national fraternities, national sororities.

Athletics Member NCAA. All Division I. ***Intercollegiate sports:*** baseball M(s), basketball M(s)/W(s), cross-country running M(s)/W(s), golf M(s)/W(s), tennis M(s)/W(s), track and field M(s)/W(s), volleyball W(s). ***Intramural sports:*** badminton M/W, basketball M/W, bowling M/W, cheerleading M/W, football M/W, racquetball M/W, soccer M/W, softball M/W, table tennis M/W, tennis M/W, ultimate Frisbee M/W, volleyball M/W.

Campus security: 24-hour emergency response devices and patrols, late-night transport/escort service.

Student services: health clinic, personal/psychological counseling.

COSTS & FINANCIAL AID

Costs (2016–17) ***Tuition:*** state resident $5970 full-time, $361 per credit hour part-time; nonresident $15,762 full-time, $769 per credit hour part-time. Full-time tuition and fees vary according to course load, degree level, program, and student level. Part-time tuition and fees vary according to course load, degree level, program, and student level. No tuition increase for student's term of enrollment. ***Required fees:*** $1468 full-time, $185 per credit hour part-time. ***Room and board:*** $7950; room only: $4232. Room and board charges vary according to board plan, housing facility, and location. ***Payment plan:*** installment.

Financial Aid Of all full-time matriculated undergraduates who enrolled in 2015, 11,996 applied for aid, 11,492 were judged to have need, 317 had their need fully met. 749 Federal Work-Study jobs (averaging $2640). 406 state and other part-time jobs (averaging $1883). In 2015, 325 non-need-based awards were made. ***Average percent of need met:*** 79. ***Average financial aid package:*** $10,172. ***Average need-based loan:*** $4691. ***Average need-based gift aid:*** $10,688. ***Average non-need-based aid:*** $3357. ***Average indebtedness upon graduation:*** $15,731.

APPLYING

Standardized Tests *Required:* SAT or ACT (for admission).

Options: electronic application.

Required: high school transcript, minimum 2.0 GPA. ***Required for some:*** interview.

Application deadlines: 7/1 (freshmen), 7/1 (transfers).

Notification: continuous (freshmen), continuous (transfers).

CONTACT

Dr. Debbie Gilchrist, Interim Registrar, The University of Texas Rio Grande Valley, Office of Enrollment Services, 1201 West University Drive, Edinburg, TX 78539. *Phone:* 956-665-2926. *Toll-free phone:* 888-882-4026. *Fax:* 956-665-2212. *E-mail:* debbie.gilchrist@utrgv.edu.

University of the Incarnate Word

San Antonio, Texas

http://www.uiw.edu/

- **Independent Roman Catholic** comprehensive, founded 1881
- **Urban** 200-acre campus with easy access to San Antonio
- **Endowment** $124.2 million
- **Coed** 6,423 undergraduate students, 71% full-time, 60% women, 40% men
- **Moderately difficult** entrance level, 93% of applicants were admitted

UNDERGRAD STUDENTS

4,532 full-time, 1,891 part-time. Students come from 46 states and territories; 57 other countries; 6% are from out of state; 7% Black or African American, non-Hispanic/Latino; 57% Hispanic/Latino; 2% Asian, non-Hispanic/Latino; 0.3% Native Hawaiian or other Pacific Islander, non-Hispanic/Latino; 0.2% American Indian or Alaska Native, non-Hispanic/Latino; 1% Two or more races, non-Hispanic/Latino; 6% Race/ethnicity unknown; 6% international; 13% transferred in; 13% live on campus.

Freshmen:

Admission: 3,887 applied, 3,613 admitted, 788 enrolled. ***Average high school GPA:*** 3.5. ***Test scores:*** SAT critical reading scores over 500: 35%; SAT math scores over 500: 37%; SAT writing scores over 500: 30%; ACT scores over 18: 73%; SAT critical reading scores over 600: 6%; SAT math scores over 600: 5%; SAT writing scores over 600: 3%; ACT scores over 24: 17%; ACT scores over 30: 1%.

Retention: 77% of full-time freshmen returned.

FACULTY

Total: 773, 41% full-time.

Student/faculty ratio: 13:1.

ACADEMICS

Calendar: semesters. *Degrees:* diplomas, associate, bachelor's, master's, and doctoral.

Special study options: academic remediation for entering students, accelerated degree program, adult/continuing education programs, advanced placement credit, cooperative education, distance learning, double majors, English as a second language, freshman honors college, honors programs, independent study, internships, off-campus study, part-time degree program, services for LD students, study abroad, summer session for credit. ***ROTC:*** Army (c).

Unusual degree programs: 3-2 business administration.

Computers: 185 computers/terminals are available on campus for general student use. Students can access the following: computer help desk, free student e-mail accounts, online (class) grades, online (class) registration, online (class) schedules. Campuswide network is available. 100% of college-owned or -operated housing units are wired for high-speed Internet access. Wireless service is available via entire campus.

Library: J. E. and M. E. Mabee Library plus 1 other. *Books:* 270,398 (physical), 31,458 (digital/electronic); *Serial titles:* 103 (physical), 224 (digital/electronic); *Databases:* 167. Weekly public service hours: 105.

STUDENT LIFE

Housing options: coed, men-only, women-only, special housing for students with disabilities. Campus housing is university owned.

Activities and organizations: drama/theater group, student-run newspaper, radio and television station, choral group, marching band, Society of Leadership and Success, Pre-Pharmacy Association, Alpha Sigma Alpha, Lambda Chi Alpha, Student Government Association, national fraternities, national sororities.

Athletics Member NCAA. All Division I except football (Division I-AA), softball (Division II). ***Intercollegiate sports:*** baseball M(s), basketball M(s)/W(s), cross-country running M(s)/W(s), golf M(s)/W(s), soccer M(s)/W(s), softball W(s), swimming and diving M(s)/W(s), tennis M(s)/W(s), track and field M(s)/W(s), volleyball W(s). ***Intramural sports:*** basketball M/W, cheerleading M/W, football M/W, racquetball M/W, soccer M/W, softball M/W, tennis M/W, ultimate Frisbee M/W, volleyball M/W, water polo M/W.

Campus security: 24-hour emergency response devices and patrols, late-night transport/escort service, controlled dormitory access.

Student services: health clinic, personal/psychological counseling.

COSTS & FINANCIAL AID

Costs (2017–18) ***Comprehensive fee:*** $42,426 includes full-time tuition ($27,900), mandatory fees ($2090), and room and board ($12,436). Full-time tuition and fees vary according to course load, degree level, location, program, and reciprocity agreements. Part-time tuition: $915 per credit hour. Part-time tuition and fees vary according to course load, degree level, location, program, and reciprocity agreements. ***Room and board:*** Room and board charges vary according to board plan and housing facility. ***Payment plan:*** installment. ***Waivers:*** senior citizens and employees or children of employees.

Financial Aid Of all full-time matriculated undergraduates who enrolled in 2015, 3,376 applied for aid, 3,161 were judged to have need, 266 had their need fully met. In 2015, 930 non-need-based awards were made. ***Average percent of need met:*** 76. ***Average financial aid package:*** $20,196. ***Average need-based loan:*** $3541. ***Average need-based gift aid:*** $16,738. ***Average non-need-based aid:*** $7979. ***Average indebtedness upon graduation:*** $19,243.

APPLYING

Standardized Tests *Required:* SAT or ACT (for admission).

Options: electronic application, deferred entrance.

Application fee: $20.

Required: high school transcript. ***Required for some:*** essay or personal statement, interview. ***Recommended:*** minimum 2.0 GPA, interview.

Application deadlines: rolling (freshmen), rolling (transfers).

Notification: continuous (freshmen), continuous (transfers).

CONTACT

Mr. Javier Lara, Director of Undergraduate Admissions, University of the Incarnate Word, 4301 Broadway Avenue, San Antonio, TX 78209. *Phone:* 210-829-6005. *Toll-free phone:* 800-749-WORD. *Fax:* 210-829-3921. *E-mail:* jdlara@uiwtx.edu.

Wade College

Dallas, Texas

http://www.wadecollege.edu/

CONTACT

Wade College, INFOMart, 1950 Stemmons Freeway, Suite 4080, LB 562, Dallas, TX 75207. *Phone:* 214-637-3530. *Toll-free phone:* 800-624-4850.

Wayland Baptist University

Plainview, Texas

http://www.wbu.edu/

- **Independent Baptist** comprehensive, founded 1908
- **Small-town** 80-acre campus
- **Endowment** $82.5 million
- **Coed** 3,776 undergraduate students, 28% full-time, 49% women, 51% men
- **Minimally difficult** entrance level, 100% of applicants were admitted

UNDERGRAD STUDENTS
1,070 full-time, 2,706 part-time. Students come from 41 states and territories; 23 other countries; 32% are from out of state; 17% Black or African American, non-Hispanic/Latino; 30% Hispanic/Latino; 2% Asian, non-Hispanic/Latino; 1% Native Hawaiian or other Pacific Islander, non-Hispanic/Latino; 1% American Indian or Alaska Native, non-Hispanic/Latino; 4% Two or more races, non-Hispanic/Latino; 3% Race/ethnicity unknown; 2% international; 9% transferred in; 19% live on campus.

Freshmen:
Admission: 651 applied, 648 admitted, 342 enrolled. ***Average high school GPA:*** 3.26. ***Test scores:*** SAT critical reading scores over 500: 29%; SAT math scores over 500: 37%; SAT writing scores over 500: 19%; ACT scores over 18: 68%; SAT critical reading scores over 600: 6%; SAT math scores over 600: 9%; SAT writing scores over 600: 2%; ACT scores over 24: 14%; SAT critical reading scores over 700: 1%; SAT math scores over 700: 1%; SAT writing scores over 700: 1%; ACT scores over 30: 2%.

Retention: 51% of full-time freshmen returned.

FACULTY
Total: 593, 26% full-time, 52% with terminal degrees.

Student/faculty ratio: 8:1.

ACADEMICS
Calendar: semesters. *Degrees:* associate, bachelor's, master's, and doctoral (branch locations in Anchorage, AK; Amarillo, TX; Luke Air Force Base, AZ; Glorieta, NM; Aiea, HI; Lubbock, TX; San Antonio, TX; Wichita Falls, TX).

Special study options: academic remediation for entering students, accelerated degree program, adult/continuing education programs, advanced placement credit, distance learning, double majors, external degree program, honors programs, part-time degree program, services for LD students, study abroad, summer session for credit. ***ROTC:*** Army (c), Air Force (c).

Unusual degree programs: 3-2 engineering with Texas Tech University.

Computers: 840 computers/terminals are available on campus for general student use. Students can access the following: computer help desk, free student e-mail accounts, online (class) grades, online (class) registration, online (class) schedules. Campuswide network is available. 100% of college-owned or -operated housing units are wired for high-speed Internet access. Wireless service is available via classrooms, computer labs, dorm rooms, libraries, student centers.

Library: J.E. and L.E. Mabee Learning Resource Center. *Books:* 129,396 (physical), 48,643 (digital/electronic); *Serial titles:* 3,139 (digital/electronic); *Databases:* 132.

STUDENT LIFE
Housing options: on-campus residence required through junior year; men-only, women-only. Campus housing is university owned. Freshman campus housing is guaranteed.

Activities and organizations: drama/theater group, student-run newspaper, radio and television station, choral group, marching band, Student Government, Wayland Singers, Baptist Student Ministries, International Choir, President's Ambassadors, national fraternities, national sororities.

Athletics Member NAIA. ***Intercollegiate sports:*** baseball M(s), basketball M(s)/W(s), cheerleading M(s)/W(s), cross-country running M(s)/W(s), football M(s), golf M(s)/W(s), soccer M(s)/W(s), track and field M(s)/W(s), volleyball W(s), wrestling M(s)/W(s). ***Intramural sports:*** basketball M/W, football M, soccer M/W, softball M/W, table tennis M/W, volleyball M/W.

Campus security: 24-hour emergency response devices and patrols, security lighting, campus police department.

Student services: health clinic, personal/psychological counseling.

COSTS & FINANCIAL AID
Costs (2016–17) ***Comprehensive fee:*** $25,686 includes full-time tuition ($17,250), mandatory fees ($1260), and room and board ($7176). Full-time tuition and fees vary according to course load and location. Part-time tuition: $575 per credit hour. Part-time tuition and fees vary according to course load and location. ***College room only:*** $2900. Room and board charges vary according to board plan and housing facility. ***Payment plan:*** installment.

Financial Aid Of all full-time matriculated undergraduates who enrolled in 2016, 879 applied for aid, 813 were judged to have need, 78 had their need fully met. 130 Federal Work-Study jobs (averaging $1650). 351 state and other part-time jobs (averaging $1368). In 2016, 95 non-need-based awards were made. ***Average percent of need met:*** 58. ***Average financial aid package:*** $13,894. ***Average need-based loan:*** $4245. ***Average need-based gift aid:*** $10,622. ***Average non-need-based aid:*** $5344. ***Average indebtedness upon graduation:*** $23,764.

APPLYING
Standardized Tests *Required:* SAT or ACT (for admission).

Options: electronic application.

Application fee: $35.

Required: high school transcript. ***Required for some:*** interview.

Application deadlines: 8/1 (freshmen), rolling (transfers).

Notification: continuous (freshmen), continuous (transfers).

CONTACT
Ms. Debbie Stennett, Director of Student Admissions, Wayland Baptist University, 1900 West 7th Street, CMB 1294, Plainview, TX 79072. *Phone:* 806-291-3500. *Toll-free phone:* 800-588-1928. *Fax:* 806-291-1973. *E-mail:* admityou@wbu.edu.

West Coast University

Dallas, Texas

http://www.westcoastuniversity.edu/

- **Proprietary** 4-year
- **Urban** campus with easy access to Dallas-Fort Worth
- **Coed**

ACADEMICS
Degree: bachelor's.

CONTACT
West Coast University, 8435 N. Stemmons Freeway, Dallas, TX 75247. *Toll-free phone:* 866-508-2684.

West Texas A&M University

Canyon, Texas

http://www.wtamu.edu/

- **State-supported** comprehensive, founded 1909, part of Texas A&M University System
- **Small-town** 128-acre campus
- **Endowment** $74.5 million
- **Coed** 7,389 undergraduate students, 76% full-time, 56% women, 44% men
- **Moderately difficult** entrance level, 60% of applicants were admitted

UNDERGRAD STUDENTS
5,650 full-time, 1,739 part-time. Students come from 50 states and territories; 55 other countries; 13% are from out of state; 5% Black or African American, non-Hispanic/Latino; 27% Hispanic/Latino; 1% Asian, non-Hispanic/Latino; 0.1% Native Hawaiian or other Pacific Islander, non-Hispanic/Latino; 0.5% American Indian or Alaska Native, non-Hispanic/Latino; 2% Two or more races, non-Hispanic/Latino; 2% Race/ethnicity unknown; 2% international; 13% transferred in; 33% live on campus.

Freshmen:
Admission: 6,163 applied, 3,686 admitted, 1,330 enrolled. ***Test scores:*** SAT critical reading scores over 500: 61%; SAT math scores over 500: 58%; ACT scores over 18: 80%; SAT critical reading scores over 600: 16%; SAT math scores over 600: 14%; ACT scores over 24: 26%; SAT

critical reading scores over 700: 1%; SAT math scores over 700: 1%; ACT scores over 30: 2%.

Retention: 66% of full-time freshmen returned.

FACULTY

Total: 441, 75% full-time, 51% with terminal degrees.

Student/faculty ratio: 20:1.

ACADEMICS

Calendar: semesters. *Degrees:* bachelor's, master's, and doctoral.

Special study options: academic remediation for entering students, adult/continuing education programs, advanced placement credit, cooperative education, distance learning, double majors, English as a second language, honors programs, independent study, internships, part-time degree program, services for LD students, study abroad, summer session for credit.

Computers: 1,200 computers/terminals and 1,200 ports are available on campus for general student use. Students can access the following: campus intranet, computer help desk, free student e-mail accounts, online (class) grades, online (class) registration, online (class) schedules. Campuswide network is available. 100% of college-owned or -operated housing units are wired for high-speed Internet access. Wireless service is available via entire campus.

Library: Cornette Library plus 3 others. *Books:* 305,487 (physical), 516,531 (digital/electronic); *Serial titles:* 12,207 (physical), 12,592 (digital/electronic); *Databases:* 181. Weekly public service hours: 91; students can reserve study rooms.

STUDENT LIFE

Housing options: on-campus residence required through sophomore year; coed, men-only, women-only, special housing for students with disabilities. Campus housing is university owned. Freshman campus housing is guaranteed.

Activities and organizations: drama/theater group, student-run newspaper, radio station, choral group, marching band, Residence Hall Association, Wesley, Student Government, SAGE, Baptist Student Ministries, national fraternities, national sororities.

Athletics Member NCAA. All Division II. ***Intercollegiate sports:*** baseball M(s), basketball M(s)/W(s), bowling M(s)(c)/W(s)(c), cross-country running M(s)/W(s), equestrian sports M(c)/W(s), football M(s), golf M(s)/W(s), soccer M(s)/W(s), softball W(s), track and field M(s)/W(s), volleyball W(s). ***Intramural sports:*** badminton M/W, basketball M/W, bowling M/W, football M/W, golf M/W, racquetball M/W, soccer M/W, softball M/W, swimming and diving M/W, table tennis M/W, tennis M/W, volleyball M/W, wrestling M.

Campus security: 24-hour emergency response devices and patrols, late-night transport/escort service, controlled dormitory access.

Student services: health clinic, personal/psychological counseling.

COSTS & FINANCIAL AID

Costs (2016–17) ***Tuition:*** state resident $5289 full-time, $50 per credit hour part-time; nonresident $6279 full-time, $80 per credit hour part-time. Full-time tuition and fees vary according to course load, degree level, program, and student level. Part-time tuition and fees vary according to course load, degree level, program, and student level. No tuition increase for student's term of enrollment. ***Required fees:*** $2392 full-time, $229 per credit hour part-time, $238 per term part-time. ***Room and board:*** $7196. Room and board charges vary according to board plan and housing facility. ***Payment plan:*** installment. ***Waivers:*** employees or children of employees.

Financial Aid Of all full-time matriculated undergraduates who enrolled in 2014, 4,462 applied for aid, 3,751 were judged to have need, 167 had their need fully met. 157 Federal Work-Study jobs (averaging $1817). 61 state and other part-time jobs (averaging $901). In 2014, 583 non-need-based awards were made. ***Average percent of need met:*** 56. ***Average financial aid package:*** $8344. ***Average need-based loan:*** $4002. ***Average need-based gift aid:*** $5346. ***Average non-need-based aid:*** $2020. ***Average indebtedness upon graduation:*** $24,282.

APPLYING

Standardized Tests *Required:* SAT or ACT (for admission).

Options: electronic application, deferred entrance.

Application fee: $40.

Required: high school transcript, class rank and Texas high school curriculum or equivalent.

Application deadlines: rolling (freshmen), rolling (transfers).

Notification: continuous (freshmen), continuous (transfers).

CONTACT

Mr. Kyle Moore, Director of Admissions, West Texas A&M University, WT Box 60907, Canyon, TX 79016-0001. *Phone:* 806-651-5288. *Toll-free phone:* 800-99-WTAMU. *Fax:* 806-651-5285. *E-mail:* kmoore@mail.wtamu.edu.

Wiley College

Marshall, Texas

http://www.wileyc.edu/

CONTACT

Ms. Alvena Jones, Interim Director of Admissions/Recruitment, Wiley College, 711 Wiley Avenue, Marshall, TX 75670-5199. *Phone:* 903-927-3222. *Toll-free phone:* 800-658-6889. *Fax:* 903-923-8878. *E-mail:* ajones@wileyc.edu.

UTAH

AmeriTech College

Draper, Utah

http://www.ameritech.edu/

- **Proprietary** primarily 2-year
- **Coed**

ACADEMICS

Degrees: associate and bachelor's.

CONTACT

AmeriTech College, 12257 South Business Park Drive, Suite 108, Draper, UT 84020-6545.

Argosy University, Salt Lake City

Draper, Utah

http://www.argosy.edu/locations/salt-lake-city/

CONTACT

Argosy University, Salt Lake City, 121 Election Road, Suite 300, Draper, UT 84020. *Phone:* 801-601-5000. *Toll-free phone:* 888-639-4756.

Brigham Young University

Provo, Utah

http://www.byu.edu/

- **Independent** university, founded 1875, affiliated with The Church of Jesus Christ of Latter-day Saints, part of Church Education System (CES) of The Church of Jesus Christ of Latter-day Saints
- **Suburban** 557-acre campus with easy access to Salt Lake City
- **Coed** 30,221 undergraduate students, 90% full-time, 48% women, 52% men
- **Moderately difficult** entrance level, 48% of applicants were admitted

UNDERGRAD STUDENTS

27,339 full-time, 2,882 part-time. 66% are from out of state; 0.5% Black or African American, non-Hispanic/Latino; 6% Hispanic/Latino; 2% Asian, non-Hispanic/Latino; 0.6% Native Hawaiian or other Pacific Islander, non-Hispanic/Latino; 0.3% American Indian or Alaska Native, non-Hispanic/Latino; 4% Two or more races, non-Hispanic/Latino; 1% Race/ethnicity unknown; 3% international; 3% transferred in; 19% live on campus.

Freshmen:

Admission: 13,376 applied, 6,427 admitted, 5,127 enrolled. ***Average high school GPA:*** 3.83. ***Test scores:*** SAT critical reading scores over 500: 94%; SAT math scores over 500: 96%; SAT writing scores over 500: 90%; ACT scores over 18: 100%; SAT critical reading scores over 600: 65%; SAT math scores over 600: 69%; SAT writing scores over 600: 55%; ACT

scores over 24: 93%; SAT critical reading scores over 700: 21%; SAT math scores over 700: 21%; SAT writing scores over 700: 11%; ACT scores over 30: 41%.

Retention: 86% of full-time freshmen returned.

FACULTY

Total: 1,766, 71% full-time, 74% with terminal degrees.

Student/faculty ratio: 20:1.

ACADEMICS

Calendar: semesters. *Degrees:* bachelor's, master's, doctoral, post-master's, and postbachelor's certificates.

Special study options: adult/continuing education programs, external degree program, off-campus study, part-time degree program. ***ROTC:*** Army (b), Air Force (b).

Computers: Students can access the following: campus intranet, computer help desk, online (class) grades, online (class) registration, online (class) schedules. Campuswide network is available.

Library: Harold B. Lee Library plus 2 others.

STUDENT LIFE

Housing options: men-only, women-only, special housing for students with disabilities. Campus housing is university owned.

Athletics Member NCAA. All Division I except football (Division I-A). ***Intercollegiate sports:*** baseball M(s), basketball M(s)/W(s), cheerleading M(s)/W(s), cross-country running M(s)/W(s), golf M(s)/W(s), gymnastics W(s), lacrosse M(c), racquetball M/W, rugby M(c), soccer M(c)/W(s), softball W(s), swimming and diving M(s)/W(s), tennis M(s)/W(s), track and field M(s)/W(s), volleyball M(s)/W(s). ***Intramural sports:*** badminton W, basketball M/W, field hockey M, football M/W, golf M/W, racquetball M/W, soccer M/W, softball M/W, table tennis M/W, tennis M/W, ultimate Frisbee M/W, volleyball M/W, water polo M/W, wrestling M.

Campus security: 24-hour emergency response devices and patrols, late-night transport/escort service, controlled dormitory access.

COSTS & FINANCIAL AID

Costs (2016–17) ***Comprehensive fee:*** $12,748 includes full-time tuition ($5300) and room and board ($7448). Part-time tuition: $276 per credit hour. Part-time tuition and fees vary according to course load. ***Room and board:*** Room and board charges vary according to board plan, housing facility, and location. ***Waivers:*** employees or children of employees.

Financial Aid Of all full-time matriculated undergraduates who enrolled in 2015, 15,451 applied for aid, 13,019 were judged to have need, 244 had their need fully met. In 2015, 7096 non-need-based awards were made. ***Average percent of need met:*** 33. ***Average financial aid package:*** $7436. ***Average need-based loan:*** $4111. ***Average need-based gift aid:*** $4874. ***Average non-need-based aid:*** $4338. ***Average indebtedness upon graduation:*** $15,158.

APPLYING

Standardized Tests *Required:* SAT or ACT (for admission).

Options: electronic application, early admission, deferred entrance.

Application fee: $35.

Required: essay or personal statement, high school transcript, 1 letter of recommendation, interview.

CONTACT

Mr. Tom Gourley, Dean of Admissions and Records, Brigham Young University, A-153 Abraham Smoot Building, Provo, UT 84602. *Phone:* 801-422-2507. *Fax:* 801-422-0005. *E-mail:* admissions@byu.edu.

Broadview Entertainment Arts University

Salt Lake City, Utah

http://www.broadviewuniversity.edu/

CONTACT

Broadview Entertainment Arts University, 240 East Morris Avenue, Salt Lake City, UT 84115. *Toll-free phone:* 877-801-8889.

Broadview University–West Jordan

West Jordan, Utah

http://www.broadviewuniversity.edu/

CONTACT

Broadview University–West Jordan, 1902 West 7800 South, West Jordan, UT 84088. *Toll-free phone:* 866-304-4224.

Careers Unlimited

Orem, Utah

http://www.ucdh.edu/

CONTACT

Careers Unlimited, 1176 South 1480 West, Orem, UT 84058.

Dixie State University

St. George, Utah

http://www.dixie.edu/

- **State-supported** 4-year, founded 1911, part of Utah System of Higher Education
- **Small-town** 117-acre campus
- **Endowment** $33.0 million
- **Coed** 8,503 undergraduate students, 63% full-time, 53% women, 47% men
- **Noncompetitive** entrance level, 100% of applicants were admitted

UNDERGRAD STUDENTS

5,324 full-time, 3,179 part-time. Students come from 44 states and territories; 32 other countries; 19% are from out of state; 3% Black or African American, non-Hispanic/Latino; 11% Hispanic/Latino; 0.9% Asian, non-Hispanic/Latino; 1% Native Hawaiian or other Pacific Islander, non-Hispanic/Latino; 1% American Indian or Alaska Native, non-Hispanic/Latino; 3% Two or more races, non-Hispanic/Latino; 1% Race/ethnicity unknown; 3% international; 6% transferred in; 4% live on campus.

Freshmen:

Admission: 4,041 applied, 4,041 admitted, 1,700 enrolled. ***Average high school GPA:*** 3.22. ***Test scores:*** SAT critical reading scores over 500: 27%; SAT math scores over 500: 30%; SAT writing scores over 500: 20%; ACT scores over 18: 74%; SAT critical reading scores over 600: 5%; SAT math scores over 600: 6%; SAT writing scores over 600: 2%; ACT scores over 24: 24%; SAT math scores over 700: 1%; ACT scores over 30: 2%.

Retention: 55% of full-time freshmen returned.

FACULTY

Total: 582, 36% full-time, 36% with terminal degrees.

Student/faculty ratio: 19:1.

ACADEMICS

Calendar: semesters. *Degrees:* certificates, diplomas, associate, and bachelor's.

Special study options: academic remediation for entering students, accelerated degree program, adult/continuing education programs, advanced placement credit, cooperative education, distance learning, double majors, English as a second language, honors programs, independent study, internships, off-campus study, part-time degree program, services for LD students, student-designed majors, study abroad, summer session for credit. ***ROTC:*** Army (b).

Computers: 400 computers/terminals and 350 ports are available on campus for general student use. Students can access the following: computer help desk, free student e-mail accounts, online (class) grades, online (class) registration, online (class) schedules. Campuswide network is available. 100% of college-owned or -operated housing units are wired for high-speed Internet access. Wireless service is available via entire campus.

Library: Val A. Browning Library.

STUDENT LIFE

Housing options: coed, men-only. Campus housing is university owned.

Activities and organizations: drama/theater group, student-run newspaper, radio and television station, choral group, marching band,

Dixie Spirit, Outdoor Club, Association of Women Students, intramurals, Futbol Club.

Athletics Member NCAA. except baseball (Division II), men's and women's basketball (Division II), men's and women's cross-country running (Division II), football (Division II), men's and women's golf (Division II), men's and women's soccer (Division II), softball (Division II), tennis (Division II), volleyball (Division II)***Intercollegiate sports:*** baseball M(s), basketball M(s)/W(s), cross-country running M(s)/W(s), football M(s), golf M(s)/W(s), soccer M(s)/W(s), softball W(s), tennis W(s), volleyball W(s). ***Intramural sports:*** basketball M/W, football M, soccer M/W, table tennis M/W, tennis M/W, volleyball M/W.

Campus security: 24-hour emergency response devices and patrols.

Student services: health clinic, personal/psychological counseling, women's center.

COSTS & FINANCIAL AID

Costs (2017–18) ***Tuition:*** state resident $4308 full-time, $180 per credit hour part-time; nonresident $13,776 full-time, $574 per credit hour part-time. Full-time tuition and fees vary according to course load. Part-time tuition and fees vary according to course load. ***Required fees:*** $772 full-time, $32 per credit hour part-time, $32 per credit hour part-time. ***Room and board:*** $5615. Room and board charges vary according to board plan, housing facility, and location. ***Payment plan:*** installment. ***Waivers:*** senior citizens and employees or children of employees.

Financial Aid Of all full-time matriculated undergraduates who enrolled in 2016, 3,994 applied for aid, 3,624 were judged to have need, 364 had their need fully met. 132 Federal Work-Study jobs (averaging $3678). 42 state and other part-time jobs (averaging $3702). In 2016, 93 non-need-based awards were made. ***Average percent of need met:*** 60. ***Average financial aid package:*** $10,256. ***Average need-based loan:*** $4261. ***Average need-based gift aid:*** $6657. ***Average non-need-based aid:*** $2348. ***Average indebtedness upon graduation:*** $15,882. ***Financial aid deadline:*** 6/30.

APPLYING

Standardized Tests *Recommended:* SAT or ACT (for admission).

Options: electronic application, early admission, deferred entrance.

Application fee: $35.

Required: high school transcript.

Application deadlines: 8/15 (freshmen), rolling (out-of-state freshmen), 8/15 (transfers).

Notification: continuous (freshmen), continuous (out-of-state freshmen), continuous (transfers).

CONTACT

Dixie State University, 225 South 700 East, St. George, UT 84770-3876. *Phone:* 435-652-7698.

Eagle Gate College

Layton, Utah

http://eaglegatecollege.edu/

CONTACT

Eagle Gate College, 915 North 400 West, Layton, UT 84041. *Phone:* 801-546-7500. *Toll-free phone:* 866-29-EAGLE.

Eagle Gate College

Murray, Utah

http://eaglegatecollege.edu/

CONTACT

Eagle Gate College, 5588 South Green Street, Murray, UT 84123. *Phone:* 801-333-8100. *Toll-free phone:* 866-29-EAGLE.

Independence University

Salt Lake City, Utah

http://www.independence.edu/

CONTACT

Ms. Deborah Hopkins, Enrollment Manager, Independence University, 4021 South 700 East, Suite 400, Salt Lake City, UT 84107. *Toll-free phone:* 800-917-6391.

Midwives College of Utah

Salt Lake City, Utah

http://www.midwifery.edu/

CONTACT

Kristi Ridd-Young, President, Midwives College of Utah, 1174 East 2700 South, Suite 2, Salt Lake City, UT 84106. *Phone:* 801-649-5230. *Toll-free phone:* 866-680-2756. *Fax:* 866-207-2024. *E-mail:* office@midwifery.edu.

Neumont University

Salt Lake City, Utah

http://www.neumont.edu/

- **Proprietary** 4-year, founded 2002
- **Urban** campus with easy access to Salt Lake City
- **Coed**
- **Moderately difficult** entrance level

FACULTY

Student/faculty ratio: 21:1.

ACADEMICS

Calendar: quarters. *Degree:* bachelor's.

Library: Neumont University Library.

STUDENT LIFE

Housing options: men-only, women-only, special housing for students with disabilities. Campus housing is university owned and leased by the school. Freshman campus housing is guaranteed.

Activities and organizations: Unified Student Government, Society of Women Engineers, Pathfinder- (RPG group), Game Gurus, Bowling Club.

Student services: health clinic, personal/psychological counseling.

COSTS & FINANCIAL AID

Costs (2016–17) ***Tuition:*** $22,950 full-time. ***Required fees:*** $1500 full-time. ***Room only:*** $5670. Room and board charges vary according to housing facility.

Financial Aid Of all full-time matriculated undergraduates who enrolled in 2014, 221 applied for aid, 221 were judged to have need. In 2014, 213 non-need-based awards were made. ***Average percent of need met:*** 16. ***Average financial aid package:*** $11,060. ***Average need-based gift aid:*** $2356. ***Average non-need-based aid:*** $1250. ***Average indebtedness upon graduation:*** $39,623. ***Financial aid deadline:*** 8/1.

APPLYING

Standardized Tests *Required:* SAT or ACT (for admission).

Options: electronic application.

Application fee: $35.

Required: essay or personal statement, high school transcript. ***Recommended:*** 2 letters of recommendation, interview.

CONTACT

Karick Heaton, Director of Enrollment, Neumont University, 143 South Main Street, Salt Lake City, UT 84111. *Phone:* 801-302-2879. *Toll-free phone:* 888-NEUMONT. *Fax:* 801-302-2811. *E-mail:* karick.heaton@neumont.edu.

See next page for display ad and page 1436 for the College Close-Up.

New Charter University

Salt Lake City, Utah

http://www.new.edu/

CONTACT

Ms. Tammy J. Kassner, Director of Admissions, New Charter University, 2919 John Hawkins Parkway, Birmingham, AL 35244. *Phone:* 205-871-9288 Ext. 107. *Toll-free phone:* 888-639-1388. *Fax:* 800-871-9294. *E-mail:* admissions@aju.edu.

Nightingale College

Ogden, Utah

http://www.nightingale.edu/

- **Proprietary** primarily 2-year
- **Suburban** campus with easy access to Salt Lake City
- **Coed**
- 75% of applicants were admitted

ACADEMICS
Calendar: semesters. *Degree:* diplomas and bachelor's.

COSTS
Costs (2016–17) ***Tuition:*** $20,040 full-time, $835 per credit hour part-time. Full-time tuition and fees vary according to class time, course load, degree level, location, and program. Part-time tuition and fees vary according to class time, course load, degree level, location, and program. ***Required fees:*** $2200 full-time.

APPLYING
Standardized Tests *Required:* Nightingale Entrance Exam (for admission).

Options: electronic application, early admission.

Application fee: $100.

Required: essay or personal statement, high school transcript, interview.

CONTACT
Nightingale College, 4155 Harrison Boulevard #100, Ogden, UT 84403.

Southern Utah University

Cedar City, Utah

http://www.suu.edu/

- **State-supported** comprehensive, founded 1897, part of Utah System of Higher Education
- **Small-town** 130-acre campus
- **Endowment** $25.4 million
- **Coed** 8,407 undergraduate students, 70% full-time, 57% women, 43% men
- **Moderately difficult** entrance level, 72% of applicants were admitted

UNDERGRAD STUDENTS
5,879 full-time, 2,528 part-time. Students come from 48 states and territories; 37 other countries; 23% are from out of state; 2% Black or African American, non-Hispanic/Latino; 6% Hispanic/Latino; 1% Asian, non-Hispanic/Latino; 2% Native Hawaiian or other Pacific Islander, non-Hispanic/Latino; 1% American Indian or Alaska Native, non-Hispanic/Latino; 0.6% Two or more races, non-Hispanic/Latino; 6% Race/ethnicity unknown; 4% international; 5% transferred in; 8% live on campus.

Freshmen:
Admission: 10,573 applied, 7,642 admitted, 1,526 enrolled. ***Average high school GPA:*** 3.5. ***Test scores:*** SAT critical reading scores over 500: 58%; SAT math scores over 500: 52%; SAT writing scores over 500: 47%; ACT scores over 18: 93%; SAT critical reading scores over 600: 19%; SAT math scores over 600: 18%; SAT writing scores over 600: 11%; ACT scores over 24: 47%; SAT critical reading scores over 700: 3%; SAT math scores over 700: 3%; SAT writing scores over 700: 1%; ACT scores over 30: 6%.
Retention: 69% of full-time freshmen returned.

FACULTY
Total: 578, 49% full-time, 42% with terminal degrees.
Student/faculty ratio: 19:1.

ACADEMICS
Calendar: semesters. *Degrees:* certificates, diplomas, associate, bachelor's, and master's.
Special study options: academic remediation for entering students, adult/continuing education programs, advanced placement credit, cooperative education, distance learning, double majors, English as a second language, honors programs, independent study, internships, part-time degree program, services for LD students, study abroad, summer session for credit. ***ROTC:*** Army (b).
Computers: Students can access the following: campus intranet, computer help desk, free student e-mail accounts, online (class) grades, online (class) registration, online (class) schedules. Campuswide network is available. 100% of college-owned or -operated housing units are wired for high-speed Internet access. Wireless service is available via entire campus.
Library: Gerald R Sherratt Library. *Books:* 239,788 (physical), 420,411 (digital/electronic); *Databases:* 218. Students can reserve study rooms.

STUDENT LIFE
Housing options: coed, special housing for students with disabilities. Campus housing is university owned.
Activities and organizations: drama/theater group, student-run newspaper, radio and television station, choral group, national fraternities, national sororities.
Athletics Member NCAA. All Division I. ***Intercollegiate sports:*** basketball M(s)/W(s), cross-country running M(s)/W(s), football M(s), golf M(s)/W(s), gymnastics W(s), soccer W(s), softball W(s), tennis M(s)/W(s), track and field M(s)/W(s), volleyball W(s). ***Intramural sports:*** basketball M/W, cheerleading M(c)/W(c), golf M/W, soccer M/W, tennis M/W, volleyball M/W.
Campus security: 24-hour emergency response devices, student patrols, late-night transport/escort service, controlled dormitory access.
Student services: health clinic, personal/psychological counseling, women's center.

COSTS & FINANCIAL AID
Costs (2016–17) ***Tuition:*** state resident $5774 full-time, $271 per credit part-time; nonresident $19,054 full-time, $897 per credit part-time. Full-time tuition and fees vary according to program. Part-time tuition and fees vary according to course load and program. ***Required fees:*** $756 full-time, $378 per term part-time. ***Room and board:*** $7067; room only: $3167. Room and board charges vary according to board plan and housing facility. ***Payment plan:*** installment. ***Waivers:*** children of alumni, senior citizens, and employees or children of employees.
Financial Aid Of all full-time matriculated undergraduates who enrolled in 2015, 3,849 applied for aid, 3,331 were judged to have need, 253 had their need fully met. In 2015, 1246 non-need-based awards were made. ***Average percent of need met:*** 56. ***Average financial aid package:*** $8958. ***Average need-based loan:*** $3746. ***Average need-based gift aid:*** $4469. ***Average non-need-based aid:*** $6146. ***Average indebtedness upon graduation:*** $16,892.

APPLYING
Standardized Tests *Required:* SAT or ACT (for admission).
Options: electronic application, deferred entrance.
Application fee: $50.
Required: high school transcript.
Notification: continuous (freshmen), continuous (out-of-state freshmen).

CONTACT
Southern Utah University, 351 West University Boulevard, Cedar City, UT 84720-2498. *Phone:* 435-586-7740.

Stevens-Henager College
Logan, Utah
http://www.stevenshenager.edu/

CONTACT
Stevens-Henager College, 755 South Main Street, Logan, UT 84321. *Toll-free phone:* 800-622-2640.

Stevens-Henager College
Orem, Utah
http://www.stevenshenager.edu/

CONTACT
Stevens-Henager College, 1476 South Sandhill Road, Orem, UT 84058. *Toll-free phone:* 800-622-2640.

Stevens-Henager College
St. George, Utah
http://www.stevenshenager.edu/

CONTACT
Stevens-Henager College, 720 South River Road, Suite C-130, St. George, UT 84790. *Toll-free phone:* 800-622-2640.

Stevens-Henager College
Salt Lake City, Utah
http://www.stevenshenager.edu/

CONTACT
Stevens-Henager College, 383 West Vine Street, Salt Lake City, UT 84123. *Toll-free phone:* 800-622-2640.

Stevens-Henager College
West Haven, Utah
http://www.stevenshenager.edu/

CONTACT
Admissions Office, Stevens-Henager College, 1890 South 1350 West, West Haven, UT 84401. *Phone:* 801-394-7791. *Toll-free phone:* 800-622-2640.

University of Phoenix–Utah Campus
Salt Lake City, Utah
http://www.phoenix.edu/

CONTACT
Marc Booker, Sr. Director, Office of Admissions and Evaluation, University of Phoenix–Utah Campus, 4615 East Elwood Street, Mail Stop AA-K101, Phoenix, AZ 85040-1958. *Phone:* 602-557-4609. *Toll-free phone:* 866-766-0766. *Fax:* 480-643-1156.

University of Utah
Salt Lake City, Utah
http://www.utah.edu/

- **State-supported** university, founded 1850, part of Utah System of Higher Education
- **Urban** 1535-acre campus with easy access to Salt Lake City
- **Endowment** $958.0 million
- **Coed** 23,789 undergraduate students, 72% full-time, 46% women, 54% men
- **Moderately difficult** entrance level, 76% of applicants were admitted

UNDERGRAD STUDENTS
17,197 full-time, 6,592 part-time. Students come from 51 states and territories; 87 other countries; 20% are from out of state; 1% Black or African American, non-Hispanic/Latino; 12% Hispanic/Latino; 6% Asian, non-Hispanic/Latino; 0.4% Native Hawaiian or other Pacific Islander, non-Hispanic/Latino; 0.5% American Indian or Alaska Native, non-Hispanic/Latino; 5% Two or more races, non-Hispanic/Latino; 2% Race/ethnicity unknown; 5% international; 7% transferred in; 13% live on campus.

Freshmen:
Admission: 14,308 applied, 10,934 admitted, 3,601 enrolled. ***Average high school GPA:*** 3.61. ***Test scores:*** SAT critical reading scores over 500: 81%; SAT math scores over 500: 89%; SAT writing scores over 500: 76%; ACT scores over 18: 96%; SAT critical reading scores over 600: 40%; SAT math scores over 600: 49%; SAT writing scores over 600: 35%; ACT scores over 24: 62%; SAT critical reading scores over 700: 11%; SAT math scores over 700: 14%; SAT writing scores over 700: 7%; ACT scores over 30: 19%.

Retention: 90% of full-time freshmen returned.

FACULTY
Total: 2,209, 68% full-time, 68% with terminal degrees.

Student/faculty ratio: 16:1.

ACADEMICS
Calendar: semesters. *Degrees:* bachelor's, master's, doctoral, post-master's, and postbachelor's certificates.

Special study options: academic remediation for entering students, accelerated degree program, advanced placement credit, cooperative education, distance learning, double majors, English as a second language, freshman honors college, honors programs, independent study, internships, off-campus study, part-time degree program, services for LD students, student-designed majors, study abroad, summer session for credit. ***ROTC:*** Army (b), Navy (b), Air Force (b).

Unusual degree programs: 3-2 engineering; nursing; computer science, chemistry, math, public policy.

Computers: 1,099 computers/terminals are available on campus for general student use. Students can access the following: campus intranet, computer help desk, free student e-mail accounts, online (class) grades, online (class) registration, online (class) schedules, online classes. Campuswide network is available. 100% of college-owned or -operated housing units are wired for high-speed Internet access. Wireless service is available via entire campus.

Library: J. Willard Marriott Library plus 3 others. *Books:* 3.2 million (physical), 460,000 (digital/electronic); *Serial titles:* 530 (physical), 11,500 (digital/electronic); *Databases:* 320. Weekly public service hours: 111; students can reserve study rooms.

STUDENT LIFE
Housing options: coed, men-only, women-only, special housing for students with disabilities. Campus housing is university owned.

Activities and organizations: drama/theater group, student-run newspaper, radio station, choral group, marching band, TEK Club, International Business Club, Golden Key International Honours Society, Tennis Club, Thai Student Association, national fraternities, national sororities.

Athletics Member NCAA. All Division I. ***Intercollegiate sports:*** baseball M(s), basketball M(s)/W(s), cheerleading M(s)/W(s), cross-country running W(s), fencing M(c)/W(c), football M(s), golf M(s), gymnastics W(s), ice hockey M(c), lacrosse M(c)/W(c), racquetball M(c)/W(c), riflery M(c)/W(c), rugby M(c), skiing (cross-country) M(s)/W(s), skiing (downhill) M(s)/W(s), soccer M(c)/W(s), softball W(s), swimming and diving M(s)/W(s), table tennis M(c)/W(c), tennis M(s)/W(s), track and field W(s), ultimate Frisbee M(c)/W(c), volleyball M(c)/W(s), water polo M(c)/W(c), weight lifting M(c)/W(c), wrestling M(c). ***Intramural sports:*** basketball M/W, fencing M/W, football M, racquetball M/W, soccer M/W, softball M/W, tennis M/W, ultimate Frisbee M/W, volleyball M/W, water polo M/W, weight lifting M/W.

Campus security: 24-hour emergency response devices and patrols, student patrols, late-night transport/escort service, controlled dormitory access.

Student services: health clinic, personal/psychological counseling, women's center.

COSTS & FINANCIAL AID
Costs (2016–17) ***Tuition:*** state resident $7408 full-time, $208 per credit hour part-time; nonresident $25,929 full-time, $715 per credit hour part-time. Full-time tuition and fees vary according to course level, course load, degree level, location, program, and student level. Part-time tuition and fees vary according to course level, course load, degree level, location, program, and student level. ***Required fees:*** $1110 full-time, $455 per term part-time. ***Room and board:*** $9406; room only: $4874. Room and board charges vary according to board plan, housing facility, and location. ***Payment plans:*** installment, deferred payment. ***Waivers:*** senior citizens and employees or children of employees.

Financial Aid Of all full-time matriculated undergraduates who enrolled in 2016, 10,102 applied for aid, 8,164 were judged to have need, 1,262 had their need fully met. 320 Federal Work-Study jobs (averaging $4194). In 2016, 4592 non-need-based awards were made. ***Average percent of need met:*** 65. ***Average financial aid package:*** $18,758. ***Average need-based loan:*** $4235. ***Average need-based gift aid:*** $7029. ***Average non-need-based aid:*** $6212. ***Average indebtedness upon graduation:*** $21,081.

APPLYING
Standardized Tests *Required:* SAT or ACT (for admission).

Options: electronic application, early admission, early action, deferred entrance.

Application fee: $45.

Required: high school transcript.

Application deadlines: 4/1 (freshmen), 4/1 (transfers), 12/1 (early action).

Notification: continuous (freshmen), continuous (out-of-state freshmen), continuous (transfers).

CONTACT
Mateo Remsburg, Associate Director, Office of Admissions, University of Utah, 201 S. 1460 E., Room 250 S., Salt Lake City, UT 84112.
Phone: 801-581-8761. *Toll-free phone:* 800-685-8856.
Fax: 801-585-3257. *E-mail:* mremsburg@sa.utah.edu.

Utah State University
Logan, Utah
http://www.usu.edu/

- **State-supported** university, founded 1888, part of Utah System of Higher Education
- **Urban** 456-acre campus
- **Endowment** $326.0 million
- **Coed** 24,838 undergraduate students, 68% full-time, 53% women, 47% men
- **Moderately difficult** entrance level, 90% of applicants were admitted

UNDERGRAD STUDENTS
16,991 full-time, 7,847 part-time. Students come from 53 states and territories; 64 other countries; 26% are from out of state; 0.8% Black or African American, non-Hispanic/Latino; 6% Hispanic/Latino; 1% Asian, non-Hispanic/Latino; 0.4% Native Hawaiian or other Pacific Islander, non-Hispanic/Latino; 2% American Indian or Alaska Native, non-Hispanic/Latino; 2% Two or more races, non-Hispanic/Latino; 4% Race/ethnicity unknown; 1% international; 7% transferred in.

Freshmen:
Admission: 15,401 applied, 13,899 admitted, 4,466 enrolled. ***Test scores:*** SAT critical reading scores over 500: 72%; SAT math scores over 500: 72%; ACT scores over 18: 90%; SAT critical reading scores over 600: 31%; SAT math scores over 600: 29%; ACT scores over 24: 51%; SAT critical reading scores over 700: 6%; SAT math scores over 700: 6%; ACT scores over 30: 14%.

Retention: 73% of full-time freshmen returned.

FACULTY
Total: 1,197, 77% full-time, 69% with terminal degrees.

ACADEMICS
Calendar: semesters. *Degrees:* certificates, associate, bachelor's, master's, doctoral, and postbachelor's certificates.

Special study options: academic remediation for entering students, accelerated degree program, adult/continuing education programs, advanced placement credit, cooperative education, distance learning, double majors, English as a second language, freshman honors college, honors programs, independent study, internships, off-campus study, part-time degree program, services for LD students, student-designed majors, study abroad, summer session for credit. ***ROTC:*** Army (b), Air Force (b).

Computers: 1,000 computers/terminals are available on campus for general student use. Students can access the following: computer help desk, free student e-mail accounts, online (class) grades, online (class) registration, online (class) schedules. Campuswide network is available. 100% of college-owned or -operated housing units are wired for high-

speed Internet access. Wireless service is available via classrooms, computer centers, computer labs, dorm rooms, learning centers, libraries, student centers.
Library: Merrill-Cazier Library plus 4 others.

STUDENT LIFE
Housing options: coed, men-only, women-only, special housing for students with disabilities. Campus housing is university owned.

Activities and organizations: drama/theater group, student-run newspaper, radio station, choral group, marching band, Latter-Day Saints Student Association, multicultural clubs, volunteer groups, college councils, national fraternities, national sororities.

Athletics Member NCAA. All Division I except football (Division I-A). ***Intercollegiate sports:*** baseball M(c), basketball M(s)/W(s), cross-country running M(s)/W(s), equestrian sports M(c)/W(c), golf M(s), gymnastics W(s), ice hockey M(c), racquetball M(c)/W(c), rugby M(c)/W(c), soccer M(c)/W(s), softball W(s), tennis M(s)/W(s), track and field M(s)/W(s), ultimate Frisbee M(c)/W(c), volleyball M(c)/W(s). ***Intramural sports:*** badminton M/W, basketball M/W, football M/W, lacrosse M(c)/W(c), racquetball M/W, rock climbing M(c)/W(c), soccer M/W, softball M/W, swimming and diving M(c)/W(c), table tennis M/W, tennis M/W, ultimate Frisbee M/W, volleyball M/W.

Campus security: 24-hour emergency response devices and patrols, student patrols, late-night transport/escort service, video monitors in pedestrian tunnels.

Student services: health clinic, personal/psychological counseling, women's center, legal services.

COSTS & FINANCIAL AID
Costs (2016–17) ***Tuition:*** state resident $5817 full-time; nonresident $18,720 full-time. Full-time tuition and fees vary according to course level, course load, program, and reciprocity agreements. Part-time tuition and fees vary according to course level, course load, program, and reciprocity agreements. ***Required fees:*** $1052 full-time. ***Room and board:*** $5870; room only: $2090. Room and board charges vary according to board plan and housing facility. ***Payment plan:*** deferred payment. ***Waivers:*** minority students, children of alumni, adult students, senior citizens, and employees or children of employees.

Financial Aid Of all full-time matriculated undergraduates who enrolled in 2016, 10,972 applied for aid, 9,298 were judged to have need, 818 had their need fully met. 465 Federal Work-Study jobs (averaging $3567). In 2016, 2145 non-need-based awards were made. ***Average percent of need met:*** 57. ***Average financial aid package:*** $9705. ***Average need-based loan:*** $4282. ***Average need-based gift aid:*** $4553. ***Average non-need-based aid:*** $3252. ***Average indebtedness upon graduation:*** $23,000.

APPLYING
Standardized Tests *Required:* SAT or ACT (for admission).

Options: electronic application, deferred entrance.

Application fee: $50.

Required: high school transcript. ***Recommended:*** minimum 2.8 GPA.

Application deadlines: rolling (freshmen), rolling (transfers).

Notification: continuous (freshmen), continuous (transfers).

CONTACT
Mr. Jeff Sorenson, Assistant Director, Admissions Office, Utah State University, 0160 Old Main Hill, Logan, UT 84322-0160. *Phone:* 435-797-1079. *Toll-free phone:* 800-488-8108. *Fax:* 435-797-3708.
E-mail: admit@usu.edu.

Utah Valley University

Orem, Utah

http://www.uvu.edu/

- **State-supported** comprehensive, founded 1941, affiliated with Advent Christian Church, part of Utah System of Higher Education
- **Suburban** 537-acre campus with easy access to Salt Lake City
- **Coed** 33,026 undergraduate students, 52% full-time, 45% women, 55% men
- **Noncompetitive** entrance level, 100% of applicants were admitted

UNDERGRAD STUDENTS
17,173 full-time, 15,853 part-time. Students come from 50 states and territories; 72 other countries; 16% are from out of state; 0.8% Black or African American, non-Hispanic/Latino; 10% Hispanic/Latino; 1% Asian, non-Hispanic/Latino; 0.7% Native Hawaiian or other Pacific Islander, non-Hispanic/Latino; 0.6% American Indian or Alaska Native, non-Hispanic/Latino; 3% Two or more races, non-Hispanic/Latino; 5% Race/ethnicity unknown; 2% international; 6% transferred in.

Freshmen:
Admission: 9,183 applied, 9,178 admitted, 4,245 enrolled. ***Average high school GPA:*** 3.31. ***Test scores:*** ACT scores over 18: 81%; ACT scores over 24: 34%; ACT scores over 30: 3%.

Retention: 61% of full-time freshmen returned.

FACULTY
Total: 1,846, 35% full-time, 29% with terminal degrees.

Student/faculty ratio: 22:1.

ACADEMICS
Calendar: semesters. *Degrees:* certificates, diplomas, associate, bachelor's, master's, and postbachelor's certificates.

Special study options: academic remediation for entering students, advanced placement credit, cooperative education, distance learning, double majors, English as a second language, honors programs, independent study, internships, off-campus study, part-time degree program, services for LD students, student-designed majors, study abroad, summer session for credit. ***ROTC:*** Army (b), Air Force (c).

Computers: 1,000 computers/terminals are available on campus for general student use. Students can access the following: campus intranet, computer help desk, free student e-mail accounts, online (class) grades, online (class) registration, online (class) schedules. Campuswide network is available. Wireless service is available via entire campus.
Library: Utah Valley University Library plus 1 other.

STUDENT LIFE
Housing options: college housing not available.

Activities and organizations: drama/theater group, student-run newspaper, television station, choral group, LDSSA Orem Institute, Center for the Advancement of Leadership, national fraternities, national sororities.

Athletics Member NCAA. All Division I. ***Intercollegiate sports:*** baseball M(s), basketball M(s)/W(s), cross-country running M(s)/W(s), golf M(s)/W(s), soccer W(s), softball W(s), track and field M(s)/W(s), volleyball W(s), wrestling M(s).

Campus security: 24-hour patrols.

Student services: health clinic, personal/psychological counseling, women's center, legal services.

COSTS & FINANCIAL AID
Costs (2016–17) ***Tuition:*** state resident $4840 full-time, $207 per credit part-time; nonresident $15,000 full-time, $640 per credit part-time. Full-time tuition and fees vary according to course load and degree level. Part-time tuition and fees vary according to course load and degree level. ***Required fees:*** $690 full-time, $345 per term part-time, $345 per term part-time. ***Payment plans:*** installment, deferred payment. ***Waivers:*** employees or children of employees.

Financial Aid Of all full-time matriculated undergraduates who enrolled in 2016, 11,403 applied for aid, 10,008 were judged to have need, 954 had their need fully met. In 2016, 202 non-need-based awards were made. ***Average percent of need met:*** 65. ***Average financial aid package:*** $7730. ***Average need-based loan:*** $2927. ***Average need-based gift aid:*** $4825. ***Average non-need-based aid:*** $1788. ***Average indebtedness upon graduation:*** $22,259.

APPLYING
Standardized Tests *Required:* ACT, SAT, or ACCUPLACER (for admission).

Options: electronic application, deferred entrance.

Application fee: $35.

Required: high school transcript.

Application deadlines: 8/1 (freshmen), 8/1 (transfers).

Notification: continuous (freshmen), continuous (out-of-state freshmen), continuous (transfers).

CONTACT

Mr. Kristopher Coles, Director of Admissions, Utah Valley University, 800 West University Parkway, Orem, UT 84058-5999. *Phone:* 801-863-6368. *Fax:* 801-863-7229. *E-mail:* coleskr@uvu.edu.

Weber State University

Ogden, Utah

http://www.weber.edu/

- **State-supported** comprehensive, founded 1889, part of Utah System of Higher Education
- **Urban** 504-acre campus with easy access to Salt Lake City
- **Endowment** $110.6 million
- **Coed** 26,112 undergraduate students, 42% full-time, 54% women, 46% men
- **Noncompetitive** entrance level, 100% of applicants were admitted

UNDERGRAD STUDENTS

10,980 full-time, 15,132 part-time. Students come from 54 states and territories; 56 other countries; 8% are from out of state; 1% Black or African American, non-Hispanic/Latino; 10% Hispanic/Latino; 2% Asian, non-Hispanic/Latino; 0.5% Native Hawaiian or other Pacific Islander, non-Hispanic/Latino; 0.5% American Indian or Alaska Native, non-Hispanic/Latino; 3% Two or more races, non-Hispanic/Latino; 6% Race/ethnicity unknown; 1% international; 7% transferred in; 4% live on campus.

Freshmen:

Admission: 6,199 applied, 6,199 admitted, 2,940 enrolled. ***Average high school GPA:*** 3.27. ***Test scores:*** ACT scores over 18: 77%; ACT scores over 24: 28%; ACT scores over 30: 4%.

Retention: 62% of full-time freshmen returned.

FACULTY

Total: 1,359, 37% full-time, 39% with terminal degrees.

Student/faculty ratio: 20:1.

ACADEMICS

Calendar: semesters. *Degrees:* certificates, associate, bachelor's, master's, post-master's, and postbachelor's certificates.

Special study options: academic remediation for entering students, accelerated degree program, adult/continuing education programs, advanced placement credit, cooperative education, distance learning, double majors, English as a second language, external degree program, freshman honors college, honors programs, independent study, internships, off-campus study, part-time degree program, services for LD students, student-designed majors, study abroad, summer session for credit. ***ROTC:*** Army (b), Navy (c), Air Force (c).

Computers: 650 computers/terminals are available on campus for general student use. Students can access the following: campus intranet, computer help desk, free student e-mail accounts, online (class) grades, online (class) registration, online (class) schedules. Campuswide network is available. 100% of college-owned or -operated housing units are wired for high-speed Internet access. Wireless service is available via entire campus.

Library: Stewart Library. *Books:* 411,661 (physical); *Serial titles:* 370 (physical).

STUDENT LIFE

Housing options: men-only, women-only, cooperative, special housing for students with disabilities. Campus housing is university owned and is provided by a third party.

Activities and organizations: drama/theater group, student-run newspaper, radio and television station, choral group, marching band, LDSSA (Latter-day Saint Student Association), SAA (Student Alumni Association), GSA (Gay-Straight Alliance), Chinese Club, Golden Key Honor Society, national fraternities, national sororities.

Athletics Member NCAA. All Division I. ***Intercollegiate sports:*** archery M(c)/W(c), baseball M(c), basketball M(s)/W(s), bowling M(c)/W(c), cheerleading M(s)/W(s), cross-country running M/W, football M(s), golf M(s)/W(s), ice hockey M(c), lacrosse M(c), rugby M(c), skiing (downhill) W(c), soccer M(c)/W(s), softball W(s), swimming and diving M(c)/W(c), tennis M(s)/W(s), track and field M(s)/W(s), volleyball M(c)/W(s), weight lifting M(c)/W(c), wrestling M(c). ***Intramural sports:*** racquetball M(c)/W(c), rock climbing M/W, tennis M(c)/W(c), ultimate Frisbee M(c)/W(c), volleyball M(c)/W(c).

Campus security: 24-hour emergency response devices and patrols, student patrols, late-night transport/escort service, controlled dormitory access.

Student services: health clinic, personal/psychological counseling, women's center, legal services.

COSTS & FINANCIAL AID

Costs (2016–17) ***Tuition:*** state resident $4611 full-time, $2721 per year part-time; nonresident $13,837 full-time, $8164 per year part-time. Full-time tuition and fees vary according to course level, course load, degree level, and program. Part-time tuition and fees vary according to course level, course load, degree level, and program. ***Required fees:*** $914 full-time, $560 per year part-time. ***Room and board:*** $5400. Room and board charges vary according to board plan and housing facility. ***Payment plan:*** installment. ***Waivers:*** senior citizens and employees or children of employees.

Financial Aid Of all full-time matriculated undergraduates who enrolled in 2016, 7,060 applied for aid, 6,062 were judged to have need, 3,938 had their need fully met. In 2016, 2128 non-need-based awards were made. ***Average financial aid package:*** $5920. ***Average need-based loan:*** $3384. ***Average need-based gift aid:*** $4112. ***Average non-need-based aid:*** $3755. ***Average indebtedness upon graduation:*** $22,029.

APPLYING

Standardized Tests *Required for some:* ACCUPLACER. *Recommended:* SAT or ACT (for admission).

Options: electronic application, early admission, deferred entrance.

Application fee: $30.

Required: high school transcript.

Application deadlines: 8/31 (freshmen), rolling (transfers).

Notification: continuous (freshmen), continuous (out-of-state freshmen), continuous (transfers).

CONTACT

Brant Brown, Associate Director of Admissions, Weber State University, 1137 University Circle, Ogden, UT 84408-1137. *Phone:* 801-626-6050. *Toll-free phone:* 800-848-7700 (in-state); 800-848-7770 (out-of-state). *Fax:* 801-626-6747. *E-mail:* admissions@weber.edu.

Western Governors University

Salt Lake City, Utah

http://www.wgu.edu/

CONTACT

Western Governors University, 4001 South 700 East, Suite 700, Salt Lake City, UT 84107. *Phone:* 801-274-3280 Ext. 336. *Toll-free phone:* 866-225-5948.

Westminster College

Salt Lake City, Utah

http://www.westminstercollege.edu/

- **Independent** comprehensive, founded 1875
- **Suburban** 27-acre campus
- **Endowment** $68.7 million
- **Coed** 2,127 undergraduate students, 95% full-time, 56% women, 44% men
- **Moderately difficult** entrance level, 94% of applicants were admitted

UNDERGRAD STUDENTS

2,013 full-time, 114 part-time. 2% Black or African American, non-Hispanic/Latino; 10% Hispanic/Latino; 3% Asian, non-Hispanic/Latino; 0.1% Native Hawaiian or other Pacific Islander, non-Hispanic/Latino; 0.7% American Indian or Alaska Native, non-Hispanic/Latino; 4% Two or more races, non-Hispanic/Latino; 4% Race/ethnicity unknown; 5% international; 8% transferred in; 32% live on campus.

Freshmen:
Admission: 1,938 applied, 1,820 admitted, 434 enrolled. ***Average high school GPA:*** 3.53. ***Test scores:*** SAT critical reading scores over 500: 76%; SAT math scores over 500: 76%; ACT scores over 18: 98%; SAT critical reading scores over 600: 31%; SAT math scores over 600: 28%; ACT scores over 24: 56%; SAT critical reading scores over 700: 4%; SAT math scores over 700: 4%; ACT scores over 30: 12%.
Retention: 79% of full-time freshmen returned.

FACULTY
Total: 367, 42% full-time, 39% with terminal degrees.
Student/faculty ratio: 9:1.

ACADEMICS
Calendar: 4-4-1. *Degrees:* bachelor's, master's, and postbachelor's certificates.
Special study options: academic remediation for entering students, accelerated degree program, adult/continuing education programs, advanced placement credit, cooperative education, distance learning, double majors, English as a second language, external degree program, freshman honors college, honors programs, independent study, internships, off-campus study, part-time degree program, services for LD students, student-designed majors, study abroad, summer session for credit. ***ROTC:*** Army (c), Navy (c), Air Force (c).
Unusual degree programs: 3-2 engineering with University of Southern California, Washington University in St. Louis.
Computers: 200 computers/terminals are available on campus for general student use. Students can access the following: campus intranet, computer help desk, free student e-mail accounts, online (class) grades, online (class) registration, online (class) schedules. Campuswide network is available. 100% of college-owned or -operated housing units are wired for high-speed Internet access. Wireless service is available via entire campus.
Library: Giovale Library plus 1 other. *Books:* 95,039 (physical), 364,687 (digital/electronic); *Databases:* 56. Students can reserve study rooms.

STUDENT LIFE
Housing options: on-campus residence required through sophomore year; coed, special housing for students with disabilities. Campus housing is university owned and leased by the school. Freshman campus housing is guaranteed.
Activities and organizations: drama/theater group, student-run newspaper, choral group, Westminster Ski and Snowboard Club (WSSC), Residence Hall Association (Residential Government), Feminist Club, Latin X, Love Your Melon.
Athletics Member NCAA. All Division II. ***Intercollegiate sports:*** basketball M(s)/W(s), cross-country running M(s)/W(s), golf M(s)/W(s), lacrosse M(s)/W(s), skiing (downhill) M(s)/W(s), soccer M(s)/W(s), track and field M(s)/W(s), volleyball W(s). ***Intramural sports:*** badminton M/W, basketball M/W, rock climbing M/W, skiing (cross-country) M/W, soccer M/W, volleyball M/W.
Campus security: 24-hour emergency response devices and patrols, student patrols, late-night transport/escort service, controlled dormitory access.
Student services: health clinic, personal/psychological counseling.

COSTS & FINANCIAL AID
Costs (2016–17) ***Comprehensive fee:*** $41,722 includes full-time tuition ($31,584), mandatory fees ($520), and room and board ($9618). Full-time tuition and fees vary according to course load and program. Part-time tuition: $1316 per credit hour. Part-time tuition and fees vary according to course load and program. ***Room and board:*** Room and board charges vary according to board plan. ***Payment plans:*** installment, deferred payment. ***Waivers:*** employees or children of employees.
Financial Aid Of all full-time matriculated undergraduates who enrolled in 2016, 1,381 applied for aid, 1,195 were judged to have need, 273 had their need fully met. 662 Federal Work-Study jobs (averaging $2253). In 2016, 594 non-need-based awards were made. ***Average percent of need met:*** 78. ***Average financial aid package:*** $26,199. ***Average need-based loan:*** $5123. ***Average need-based gift aid:*** $20,755. ***Average non-need-based aid:*** $13,402. ***Average indebtedness upon graduation:*** $30,442.

APPLYING
Standardized Tests *Required:* SAT or ACT (for admission).
Options: electronic application, deferred entrance.
Application fee: $50.
Required: essay or personal statement, high school transcript, minimum 2.5 GPA, 1 letter of recommendation. ***Recommended:*** interview.
Application deadlines: rolling (freshmen), rolling (transfers).
Notification: continuous (freshmen), continuous (transfers).

CONTACT
Darlene Dilley, Interim Chief Enrollment Officer, Westminster College, 1840 South 1300 East, Salt Lake City, UT 84105-3697. *Phone:* 801-832-2200. *Toll-free phone:* 800-748-4753. *Fax:* 801-832-3101.
E-mail: admission@westminstercollege.edu.

VERMONT

Bennington College
Bennington, Vermont
http://www.bennington.edu/

- **Independent** comprehensive, founded 1932
- **Small-town** 440-acre campus with easy access to Albany, NY
- **Endowment** $16.5 million
- **Coed** 711 undergraduate students, 96% full-time, 64% women, 36% men
- **Very difficult** entrance level, 60% of applicants were admitted

UNDERGRAD STUDENTS
682 full-time, 29 part-time. Students come from 42 states and territories; 47 other countries; 97% are from out of state; 3% Black or African American, non-Hispanic/Latino; 9% Hispanic/Latino; 2% Asian, non-Hispanic/Latino; 1% American Indian or Alaska Native, non-Hispanic/Latino; 5% Two or more races, non-Hispanic/Latino; 6% Race/ethnicity unknown; 14% international; 1% transferred in; 98% live on campus.

Freshmen:
Admission: 1,236 applied, 741 admitted, 216 enrolled. ***Test scores:*** SAT critical reading scores over 500: 94%; SAT math scores over 500: 89%; SAT writing scores over 500: 96%; ACT scores over 18: 100%; SAT critical reading scores over 600: 86%; SAT math scores over 600: 61%; SAT writing scores over 600: 69%; ACT scores over 24: 82%; SAT critical reading scores over 700: 37%; SAT math scores over 700: 16%; SAT writing scores over 700: 19%; ACT scores over 30: 41%.
Retention: 80% of full-time freshmen returned.

FACULTY
Total: 125, 48% full-time, 62% with terminal degrees.
Student/faculty ratio: 11:1.

ACADEMICS
Calendar: semesters plus winter work term in January and February. *Degrees:* bachelor's, master's, and postbachelor's certificates.
Special study options: advanced placement credit, double majors, independent study, internships, off-campus study, services for LD students, student-designed majors, study abroad.
Computers: 40 computers/terminals are available on campus for general student use. Students can access the following: campus intranet, computer help desk, free student e-mail accounts, online (class) grades, online (class) registration, online (class) schedules. Campuswide network is available. 100% of college-owned or -operated housing units are wired for high-speed Internet access. Wireless service is available via entire campus.

Library: Crossett Library plus 1 other. *Books:* 89,000 (physical), 162,000 (digital/electronic); *Serial titles:* 200 (physical), 48,000 (digital/electronic); *Databases:* 56. Weekly public service hours: 103; students can reserve study rooms.

STUDENT LIFE

Housing options: on-campus residence required through senior year; coed. Campus housing is university owned. Freshman campus housing is guaranteed.

Activities and organizations: drama/theater group, student-run newspaper, choral group, Program Activity Council, Bennington Free Press, Student Endowment for the Arts, SILO: Student Journal of Arts and Letters, Bennington Zombie Defense: Humans vs. Zombies Game.

Athletics ***Intercollegiate sports:*** basketball M(c)/W(c), fencing M(c)/W(c), soccer M(c)/W(c), ultimate Frisbee M(c)/W(c), volleyball M(c)/W(c). ***Intramural sports:*** archery M/W, badminton M/W, basketball M/W, bowling M/W, cheerleading M/W, cross-country running M/W, equestrian sports M/W, golf M/W, skiing (cross-country) M/W, skiing (downhill) M/W, softball M/W, table tennis M/W, tennis M/W, volleyball M/W, weight lifting M/W.

Campus security: 24-hour emergency response devices and patrols, late-night transport/escort service, controlled dormitory access, prevention/awareness program.

Student services: health clinic, personal/psychological counseling.

COSTS & FINANCIAL AID

Costs (2017–18) ***One-time required fee:*** $2135. ***Comprehensive fee:*** $67,460 includes full-time tuition ($51,240), mandatory fees ($1180), and room and board ($15,040). Full-time tuition and fees vary according to degree level and program. Part-time tuition: $2135 per credit hour. ***College room only:*** $8150. Room and board charges vary according to board plan. ***Payment plan:*** installment. ***Waivers:*** employees or children of employees.

Financial Aid Of all full-time matriculated undergraduates who enrolled in 2015, 650 applied for aid, 423 were judged to have need, 59 had their need fully met. 310 Federal Work-Study jobs (averaging $1713). 82 state and other part-time jobs (averaging $2300). In 2015, 145 non-need-based awards were made. ***Average percent of need met:*** 79. ***Average financial aid package:*** $38,260. ***Average need-based loan:*** $3601. ***Average need-based gift aid:*** $33,968. ***Average non-need-based aid:*** $10,098. ***Average indebtedness upon graduation:*** $28,263. ***Financial aid deadline:*** 2/15.

APPLYING

Options: electronic application, early admission, early decision, early action, deferred entrance.

Required: essay or personal statement, high school transcript, 2 letters of recommendation, graded analytic paper. ***Recommended:*** interview.

Application deadlines: 1/15 (freshmen), 3/15 (transfers), 12/1 (early action).

Early decision deadline: 11/15 (for plan 1), 1/3 (for plan 2).

Notification: 3/30 (freshmen), 5/1 (transfers), 12/20 (early decision plan 1), 2/1 (early decision plan 2), 12/1 (early action).

CONTACT

Mr. Fumio Sugihara, Director of Admissions, Bennington College, One College Drive, Bennington, VT 05201-6003. *Phone:* 802-440-4316. *Toll-free phone:* 800-833-6845. *Fax:* 802-440-4320. *E-mail:* admissions@bennington.edu.

Castleton University

Castleton, Vermont

http://www.castleton.edu/

CONTACT

Mr. Maurice Ouimet Jr., Dean of Enrollment, Castleton University, 62 Alumni Drive, Woodruff Hall, Castleton, VT 05735. *Phone:* 802-468-1213. *Toll-free phone:* 800-639-8521. *Fax:* 802-468-1476. *E-mail:* info@castleton.edu.

See below for display ad and page 1312 for the College Close-Up.

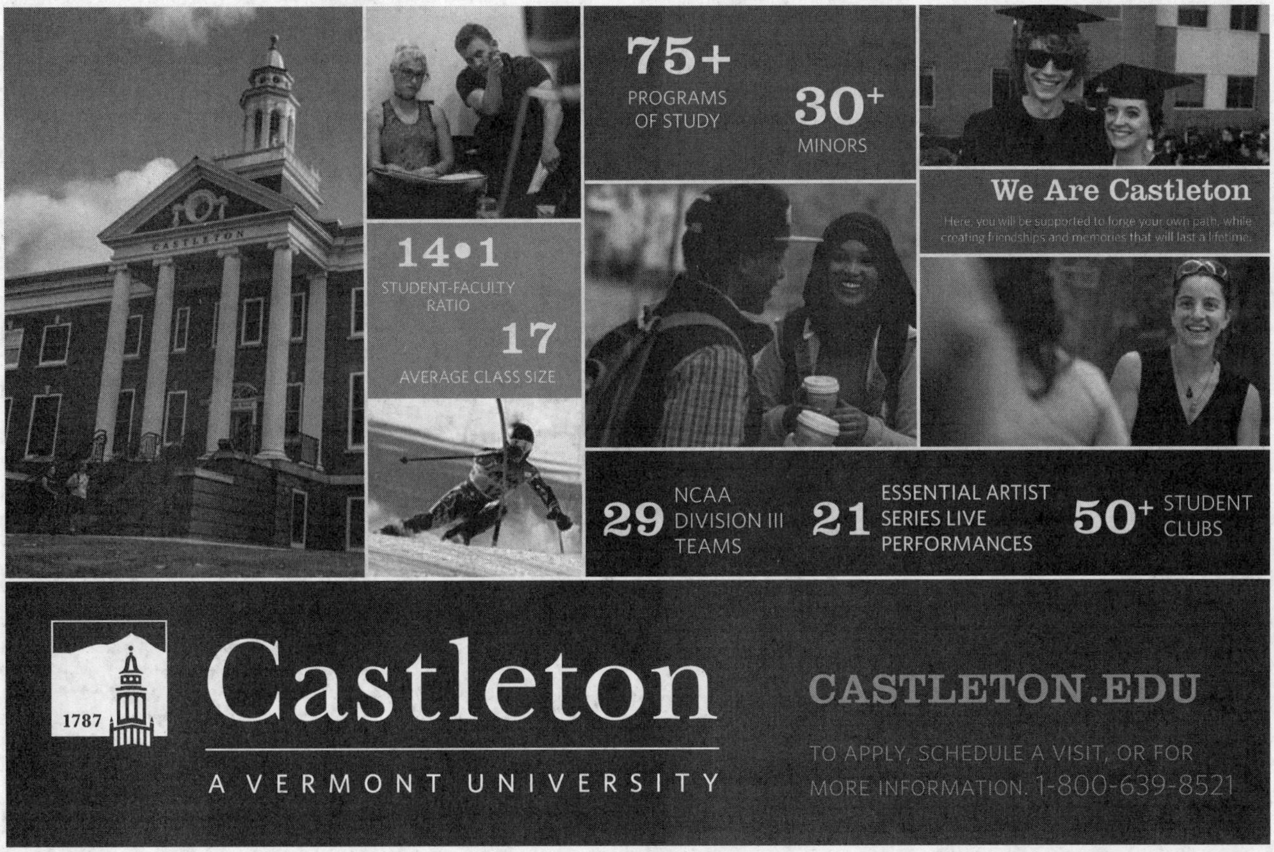

Champlain College

Burlington, Vermont

http://www.champlain.edu/

- **Independent** comprehensive, founded 1878
- **Urban** 22-acre campus with easy access to Montreal
- **Endowment** $17.4 million
- **Coed** 2,267 undergraduate students, 98% full-time, 38% women, 62% men
- **Moderately difficult** entrance level, 70% of applicants were admitted

UNDERGRAD STUDENTS

2,225 full-time, 42 part-time. Students come from 46 states and territories; 16 other countries; 78% are from out of state; 2% Black or African American, non-Hispanic/Latino; 5% Hispanic/Latino; 2% Asian, non-Hispanic/Latino; 0.2% American Indian or Alaska Native, non-Hispanic/Latino; 3% Two or more races, non-Hispanic/Latino; 14% Race/ethnicity unknown; 0.8% international; 3% transferred in; 69% live on campus.

Freshmen:

Admission: 4,576 applied, 3,201 admitted, 650 enrolled. ***Average high school GPA:*** 3.23. ***Test scores:*** SAT critical reading scores over 500: 82%; SAT math scores over 500: 78%; SAT writing scores over 500: 73%; ACT scores over 18: 96%; SAT critical reading scores over 600: 39%; SAT math scores over 600: 33%; SAT writing scores over 600: 28%; ACT scores over 24: 67%; SAT critical reading scores over 700: 6%; SAT math scores over 700: 6%; SAT writing scores over 700: 3%; ACT scores over 30: 18%.

Retention: 82% of full-time freshmen returned.

FACULTY

Total: 279, 39% full-time.

Student/faculty ratio: 14:1.

ACADEMICS

Calendar: semesters. *Degrees:* certificates, associate, bachelor's, master's, and postbachelor's certificates.

Special study options: adult/continuing education programs, advanced placement credit, cooperative education, distance learning, double majors, independent study, internships, off-campus study, part-time degree program, services for LD students, study abroad, summer session for credit. ***ROTC:*** Army (c).

Computers: 640 computers/terminals are available on campus for general student use. Students can access the following: campus intranet, computer help desk, free student e-mail accounts, online (class) grades, online (class) registration, online (class) schedules. Campuswide network is available. 100% of college-owned or -operated housing units are wired for high-speed Internet access. Wireless service is available via entire campus.

Library: Miller Information Commons. *Books:* 49,324 (physical), 208,755 (digital/electronic); *Serial titles:* 150 (physical), 66,446 (digital/electronic); *Databases:* 148. Weekly public service hours: 105; students can reserve study rooms.

STUDENT LIFE

Housing options: coed, women-only, special housing for students with disabilities. Campus housing is university owned and leased by the school. Freshman campus housing is guaranteed.

Activities and organizations: drama/theater group, student-run newspaper, radio station, choral group, Diversity Champlain, International Club, community service organization, Champlain Players (theater group), Outing Club/Skiing Snowboarding Club.

Athletics *Intramural sports:* basketball M/W, cross-country running M(c)/W(c), equestrian sports M(c)/W(c), field hockey W, football M/W, ice hockey M, lacrosse M, rock climbing M/W, rugby M(c)/W(c), skiing (cross-country) M/W, skiing (downhill) M(c)/W(c), soccer M/W, table tennis M/W, tennis M/W, ultimate Frisbee M/W, volleyball M/W.

Campus security: 24-hour emergency response devices and patrols, late-night transport/escort service, controlled dormitory access.

Student services: health clinic, personal/psychological counseling, women's center.

COSTS & FINANCIAL AID

Costs (2016–17) ***Comprehensive fee:*** $53,132 includes full-time tuition ($38,560), mandatory fees ($100), and room and board ($14,472). Part-time tuition: $1608 per credit hour. ***Room and board:*** Room and board charges vary according to housing facility. ***Payment plans:*** tuition prepayment, installment. ***Waivers:*** employees or children of employees.

Financial Aid Of all full-time matriculated undergraduates who enrolled in 2016, 2,028 applied for aid, 1,788 were judged to have need, 252 had their need fully met. In 2016, 605 non-need-based awards were made. ***Average percent of need met:*** 67. ***Average financial aid package:*** $25,134. ***Average need-based loan:*** $4230. ***Average need-based gift aid:*** $19,364. ***Average non-need-based aid:*** $10,330. ***Average indebtedness upon graduation:*** $34,582. ***Financial aid deadline:*** 1/15.

APPLYING

Standardized Tests *Required:* SAT or ACT (for admission).

Options: electronic application, early admission, early decision, deferred entrance.

Required: essay or personal statement, high school transcript. ***Required for some:*** portfolio for creative media, filmmaking, game art and animation, game design, and graphic design and digital media majors. ***Recommended:*** 2 letters of recommendation.

Application deadlines: 1/15 (freshmen), rolling (transfers).

Early decision deadline: 11/1 (for plan 1), 12/15 (for plan 2).

Notification: 3/15 (freshmen), continuous (transfers), 12/15 (early decision plan 1), 2/1 (early decision plan 2).

CONTACT

Chris Perlongo, Director of Undergraduate Admissions, Champlain College, PO Box 670, Burlington, VT 05401. *Phone:* 802-860-5740. *Toll-free phone:* 800-570-5858. *Fax:* 802-860-2767. *E-mail:* admission@champlain.edu.

See previous page for display ad and page 1316 for the College Close-Up.

College of St. Joseph

Rutland, Vermont

http://www.csj.edu/

CONTACT

Mr. Alan Young, Dean of Admissions, College of St. Joseph, 71 Clement Road, Rutland, VT 05701-3899. *Phone:* 802-773-5227. *Toll-free phone:* 877-270-9998. *Fax:* 802-776-5310. *E-mail:* admissions@csj.edu.

★ Goddard College

Plainfield, Vermont

http://www.goddard.edu/

- **Independent** comprehensive, founded 1938
- **Rural** 200-acre campus
- **Coed** 194 undergraduate students, 94% full-time, 72% women, 28% men
- **Minimally difficult** entrance level, 56% of applicants were admitted

UNDERGRAD STUDENTS

182 full-time, 12 part-time. Students come from 24 states and territories; 1 other country; 69% are from out of state; 1% Black or African American, non-Hispanic/Latino; 2% Hispanic/Latino; 3% Asian, non-Hispanic/Latino; 4% American Indian or Alaska Native, non-Hispanic/Latino; 5% Two or more races, non-Hispanic/Latino; 18% Race/ethnicity unknown; 40% transferred in.

Freshmen:

Admission: 16 applied, 9 admitted, 9 enrolled.

Retention: 66% of full-time freshmen returned.

FACULTY

Total: 89, 13% full-time, 83% with terminal degrees.

ACADEMICS

Calendar: semesters. *Degrees:* bachelor's and master's.

Special study options: accelerated degree program, adult/continuing education programs, advanced placement credit, distance learning, double majors, external degree program, independent study, internships, off-campus study, part-time degree program, services for LD students, student-designed majors, study abroad.

Computers: 55 computers/terminals are available on campus for general student use. Students can access the following: campus intranet, computer help desk, free student e-mail accounts, online (class) registration, online (class) schedules. Campuswide network is available. 80% of college-owned or -operated housing units are wired for high-speed Internet access. Wireless service is available via entire campus.

Library: Eliot Pratt Center. *Books:* 34,000 (physical), 151,000 (digital/electronic); *Databases:* 21.

STUDENT LIFE

Housing options: coed, women-only, special housing for students with disabilities. Campus housing is university owned.

Activities and organizations: student-run radio station.

Campus security: 24-hour patrols, patrols by trained security personnel 9 pm to 6 am.

Student services: personal/psychological counseling.

FINANCIAL AID

Financial Aid Of all full-time matriculated undergraduates who enrolled in 2015, 147 applied for aid, 141 were judged to have need, 1 had their need fully met. In 2015, 4 non-need-based awards were made. ***Average percent of need met:*** 35. ***Average financial aid package:*** $8211. ***Average need-based loan:*** $4379. ***Average need-based gift aid:*** $4622. ***Average non-need-based aid:*** $1062.

APPLYING

Options: electronic application, deferred entrance.

Application fee: $65.

Required: essay or personal statement, 2 letters of recommendation, interview. ***Required for some:*** high school transcript, 3 letters of recommendation. ***Recommended:*** 4 years of English, mathematics, social studies, natural sciences; 3 years of lab science; 2 years of a foreign language; creative portfolio for arts.

Application deadlines: rolling (freshmen), rolling (transfers).

Notification: continuous (freshmen), continuous (transfers).

CONTACT

Admissions Office, Goddard College, 123 Pitkin Road, Plainfield, VT 05667-9432. *Phone:* 800-906-8312. *Toll-free phone:* 800-906-8312. *Fax:* 802-454-1029. *E-mail:* admissions@goddard.edu.

See page 1362 for the College Close-Up.

Green Mountain College

Poultney, Vermont

http://www.greenmtn.edu/

- **Independent** comprehensive, founded 1834
- **Small-town** 155-acre campus
- **Endowment** $3.7 million
- **Coed** 515 undergraduate students, 93% full-time, 55% women, 45% men
- **Moderately difficult** entrance level, 79% of applicants were admitted

UNDERGRAD STUDENTS

479 full-time, 36 part-time. Students come from 41 states and territories; 11 other countries; 83% are from out of state; 5% Black or African American, non-Hispanic/Latino; 3% Hispanic/Latino; 0.8% Asian, non-Hispanic/Latino; 1% American Indian or Alaska Native, non-Hispanic/Latino; 2% Two or more races, non-Hispanic/Latino; 28% Race/ethnicity unknown; 2% international; 7% transferred in; 85% live on campus.

Freshmen:

Admission: 881 applied, 692 admitted, 125 enrolled. ***Average high school GPA:*** 3.

Retention: 54% of full-time freshmen returned.

FACULTY

Total: 71, 56% full-time, 68% with terminal degrees.

Student/faculty ratio: 14:1.

ACADEMICS
Calendar: semesters. *Degrees:* certificates, bachelor's, and master's.

Special study options: accelerated degree program, advanced placement credit, cooperative education, distance learning, double majors, honors programs, independent study, internships, off-campus study, part-time degree program, services for LD students, student-designed majors, study abroad, summer session for credit.

Unusual degree programs: 3-2 environmental law and policy, energy regulation and law with Vermont Law School.

Computers: 102 computers/terminals are available on campus for general student use. Students can access the following: campus intranet, computer help desk, free student e-mail accounts, online (class) grades, online (class) registration, online (class) schedules, personal network folders, electronic course folders. Campuswide network is available. 100% of college-owned or -operated housing units are wired for high-speed Internet access. Wireless service is available via entire campus.
Library: Griswold Library. *Books:* 77,500 (physical), 144,000 (digital/electronic); *Serial titles:* 220 (physical), 38,500 (digital/electronic); *Databases:* 35. Weekly public service hours: 98; study areas open 24 hours, 5-7 days a week.

STUDENT LIFE
Housing options: on-campus residence required through senior year; coed. Campus housing is university owned. Freshman campus housing is guaranteed.

Activities and organizations: drama/theater group, student-run newspaper, choral group, Student Government Association, Green Mountain College Ultimate Frisbee, Diversity, College Programming Board, International Awareness Club.

Athletics Member NCAA. All Division III. ***Intercollegiate sports:*** basketball M/W, cross-country running M/W, golf M/W, lacrosse M/W, soccer M/W, tennis M, track and field M/W, volleyball W. ***Intramural sports:*** rugby M(c)/W(c), ultimate Frisbee M(c)/W(c).

Campus security: 24-hour emergency response devices and patrols, late-night transport/escort service.

Student services: personal/psychological counseling.

COSTS & FINANCIAL AID
Costs (2017–18) ***One-time required fee:*** $250. ***Comprehensive fee:*** $48,724 includes full-time tuition ($35,560), mandatory fees ($1442), and room and board ($11,722). Full-time tuition and fees vary according to degree level, location, and program. Part-time tuition: $1185 per credit hour. Part-time tuition and fees vary according to degree level and location. No tuition increase for student's term of enrollment. ***Required fees:*** $30 per course part-time, $741 per term part-time. ***Room and board:*** Room and board charges vary according to location. ***Payment plan:*** installment. ***Waivers:*** employees or children of employees.

Financial Aid Of all full-time matriculated undergraduates who enrolled in 2012, 520 applied for aid, 486 were judged to have need, 52 had their need fully met. 188 Federal Work-Study jobs (averaging $1700). 122 state and other part-time jobs (averaging $1700). In 2012, 110 non-need-based awards were made. ***Average percent of need met:*** 67. ***Average financial aid package:*** $23,458. ***Average need-based loan:*** $3753. ***Average need-based gift aid:*** $19,712. ***Average non-need-based aid:*** $13,191. ***Average indebtedness upon graduation:*** $42,269.

APPLYING
Standardized Tests *Required for some:* SAT or ACT (for admission).

Options: electronic application, early action, deferred entrance.

Required: essay or personal statement, high school transcript, 1 letter of recommendation. ***Required for some:*** interview. ***Recommended:*** minimum 2.5 GPA, interview.

Application deadlines: rolling (freshmen), rolling (transfers), rolling (early action).

Notification: continuous until 9/1 (freshmen), continuous until 9/1 (transfers), 12/14 (early action).

CONTACT
Green Mountain College, One Brennan Circle, Poultney, VT 05764. *Phone:* 802-287-8219. *Toll-free phone:* 800-776-6675.

Johnson State College

Johnson, Vermont

http://www.jsc.edu/

- **State-supported** comprehensive, founded 1828, part of Vermont State Colleges System
- **Rural** 350-acre campus with easy access to Montreal
- **Endowment** $2.3 million
- **Coed**
- **Moderately difficult** entrance level

FACULTY
Student/faculty ratio: 14:1.

ACADEMICS
Calendar: semesters. *Degrees:* certificates, associate, bachelor's, master's, and post-master's certificates.
Library: Willey Library plus 1 other. *Books:* 111,100 (physical), 6,500 (digital/electronic). Study areas open 24 hours, 5-7 days a week.

STUDENT LIFE
Housing options: on-campus residence required through sophomore year; coed. Campus housing is university owned. Freshman applicants given priority for college housing.
Activities and organizations: drama/theater group, student-run newspaper, radio station, choral group, SERVE (Break Away), A Global partnership: Students for Children's Right, Ski/Snowboarding Club, Dance Club, Christian Fellowship Club.

Athletics Member NCAA. All Division III.

Campus security: 24-hour emergency response devices and patrols, student patrols, late-night transport/escort service, controlled dormitory access.

Student services: health clinic, personal/psychological counseling, women's center.

COSTS & FINANCIAL AID
Costs (2016–17) ***One-time required fee:*** $600. ***Tuition:*** state resident $10,224 full-time, $426 per credit hour part-time; nonresident $22,680 full-time, $945 per credit hour part-time. Full-time tuition and fees vary according to reciprocity agreements and student level. Part-time tuition and fees vary according to course load, reciprocity agreements, and student level. ***Room and board:*** $9696; room only: $5774. Room and board charges vary according to board plan.
Financial Aid Of all full-time matriculated undergraduates who enrolled in 2013, 901 applied for aid, 812 were judged to have need, 337 had their need fully met. In 2013, 57 non-need-based awards were made. ***Average percent of need met:*** 83. ***Average financial aid package:*** $16,372. ***Average need-based loan:*** $4273. ***Average need-based gift aid:*** $8225. ***Average non-need-based aid:*** $6379. ***Average indebtedness upon graduation:*** $31,595.

APPLYING
Standardized Tests *Recommended:* SAT or ACT (for admission).
Options: electronic application, early admission, early action, deferred entrance.

Application fee: $40.

Required: essay or personal statement, high school transcript, minimum 2.0 GPA, 1 letter of recommendation. ***Recommended:*** minimum 3.0 GPA, interview.

CONTACT
Bethany Harrington, Admissions Specialist, Johnson State College, 337 College Hill, Johnson, VT 05656. *Phone:* 802-635-1219. *Toll-free phone:* 800-635-2356. *Fax:* 802-635-1230. *E-mail:* admissions@jsc.edu.

Landmark College

Putney, Vermont

http://www.landmark.edu/

CONTACT
Admissions Main Desk, Landmark College, Admissions Office, River Road South, Putney, VT 05346. *Phone:* 802-387-6718. *Fax:* 802-387-6868. *E-mail:* admissions@landmark.edu.

Lyndon State College
Lyndonville, Vermont
http://www.lyndonstate.edu/

CONTACT
Ms. Cheri Goldrick, Admissions Assistant, Lyndon State College, 1001 College Road, PO Box 919, Lyndonville, VT 05851. *Phone:* 802-626-6451. *Toll-free phone:* 800-225-1998. *Fax:* 802-626-6335. *E-mail:* admissions@lyndonstate.edu.

See this page for display ad and page 1406 for the College Close-Up.

★ Marlboro College
Marlboro, Vermont
http://www.marlboro.edu/

- **Independent** comprehensive, founded 1946
- **Rural** 350-acre campus
- **Endowment** $39.4 million
- **Coed**
- **Moderately difficult** entrance level

FACULTY
Student/faculty ratio: 4:1.

ACADEMICS
Calendar: semesters. *Degrees:* bachelor's and master's.
Library: Rice-Aron Library. *Books:* 88,500 (physical), 137,548 (digital/electronic); *Serial titles:* 5,400 (physical), 150 (digital/electronic); *Databases:* 75. Study areas open 24 hours, 5-7 days a week.

STUDENT LIFE
Housing options: on-campus residence required for freshman year; coed, women-only, cooperative, special housing for students with disabilities. Campus housing is university owned. Freshman campus housing is guaranteed.

Activities and organizations: drama/theater group, student-run newspaper, radio station, choral group, outdoor program, theater, farm program, Gay/Lesbian/Bisexual Alliance, madrigal and a cappella groups.

Campus security: 24-hour emergency response devices and patrols.

Student services: health clinic, personal/psychological counseling, women's center.

COSTS & FINANCIAL AID
Costs (2016–17) ***Comprehensive fee:*** $50,832 includes full-time tuition ($39,086), mandatory fees ($944), and room and board ($10,802). Full-time tuition and fees vary according to reciprocity agreements. Part-time tuition: $1305 per credit. Part-time tuition and fees vary according to course load. ***Required fees:*** $105 per term part-time. ***College room only:*** $5948.

Financial Aid Of all full-time matriculated undergraduates who enrolled in 2015, 157 applied for aid, 148 were judged to have need. In 2015, 27 non-need-based awards were made. ***Average percent of need met:*** 79. ***Average financial aid package:*** $31,863. ***Average need-based loan:*** $4660. ***Average need-based gift aid:*** $25,443. ***Average non-need-based aid:*** $13,688. ***Average indebtedness upon graduation:*** $36,805. ***Financial aid deadline:*** 3/1.

APPLYING
Standardized Tests *Recommended:* SAT or ACT (for admission).

Options: electronic application, early admission, early decision, early action, deferred entrance.

Application fee: $50.

Required: essay or personal statement, high school transcript, 2 letters of recommendation, analytical essay. ***Required for some:*** interview. ***Recommended:*** interview.

CONTACT
Marlboro College, VT. *Phone:* 802-258-9261. *Toll-free phone:* 800-343-0049.

See next page for display ad and page 1412 for the College Close-Up.

Middlebury College

Middlebury, Vermont

http://www.middlebury.edu/

- **Independent** comprehensive, founded 1800
- **Small-town** 350-acre campus
- **Coed** 2,532 undergraduate students, 99% full-time, 52% women, 48% men
- **Most difficult** entrance level, 16% of applicants were admitted

UNDERGRAD STUDENTS

2,506 full-time, 26 part-time. Students come from 52 states and territories; 69 other countries; 86% are from out of state; 3% Black or African American, non-Hispanic/Latino; 9% Hispanic/Latino; 7% Asian, non-Hispanic/Latino; 0.2% American Indian or Alaska Native, non-Hispanic/Latino; 5% Two or more races, non-Hispanic/Latino; 1% Race/ethnicity unknown; 9% international; 0.8% transferred in; 95% live on campus.

Freshmen:

Admission: 8,819 applied, 1,423 admitted, 606 enrolled. ***Test scores:*** SAT critical reading scores over 500: 99%; SAT math scores over 500: 100%; SAT writing scores over 500: 100%; ACT scores over 18: 99%; SAT critical reading scores over 600: 89%; SAT math scores over 600: 90%; SAT writing scores over 600: 91%; ACT scores over 24: 99%; SAT critical reading scores over 700: 50%; SAT math scores over 700: 50%; SAT writing scores over 700: 54%; ACT scores over 30: 76%.

Retention: 94% of full-time freshmen returned.

FACULTY

Total: 341, 83% full-time, 92% with terminal degrees.

Student/faculty ratio: 8:1.

ACADEMICS

Calendar: 4-1-4. *Degrees:* bachelor's, master's, and doctoral.

Special study options: accelerated degree program, advanced placement credit, double majors, honors programs, independent study, internships, off-campus study, services for LD students, student-designed majors, study abroad, summer session for credit. ***ROTC:*** Army (c).

Unusual degree programs: 3-2 engineering with Columbia University, Dartmouth College.

Computers: 250 computers/terminals are available on campus for general student use. Students can access the following: campus intranet, computer help desk, free student e-mail accounts, online (class) grades, online (class) registration, online (class) schedules, personal Web pages, file servers. Campuswide network is available. Wireless service is available via entire campus.

Library: Davis Family Library plus 2 others. *Books:* 764,667 (physical), 644,056 (digital/electronic); *Databases:* 695. Weekly public service hours: 112; students can reserve study rooms.

STUDENT LIFE

Housing options: on-campus residence required through junior year; coed, special housing for students with disabilities. Campus housing is university owned. Freshman campus housing is guaranteed.

Activities and organizations: drama/theater group, student-run newspaper, radio station, choral group, Middlebury College Activities Board, Middlebury Mountain Club, Student Government Association, International Students Organization, WRMC.

Athletics Member NCAA. All Division III except men's and women's skiing (cross-country) (Division I), men's and women's skiing (downhill) (Division I). ***Intercollegiate sports:*** baseball M, basketball M/W, cross-country running M/W, field hockey W, football M, golf M/W, ice hockey M/W, lacrosse M/W, skiing (cross-country) M/W, skiing (downhill) M/W, soccer M/W, softball W, squash M/W, swimming and diving M/W, tennis M/W, track and field M/W, volleyball W. ***Intramural sports:*** badminton M(c)/W(c), basketball M/W, crew M(c)/W(c), equestrian sports M(c)/W(c), fencing M(c)/W(c), football M/W, golf M/W, ice hockey M/W, rugby M(c)/W(c), sailing M(c)/W(c), soccer M/W, softball M/W, squash M/W, tennis M/W, ultimate Frisbee M(c)/W(c), volleyball M(c), water polo M(c)/W(c).

Campus security: 24-hour emergency response devices and patrols, student patrols, late-night transport/escort service, controlled dormitory access.

Student services: health clinic, personal/psychological counseling, women's center.

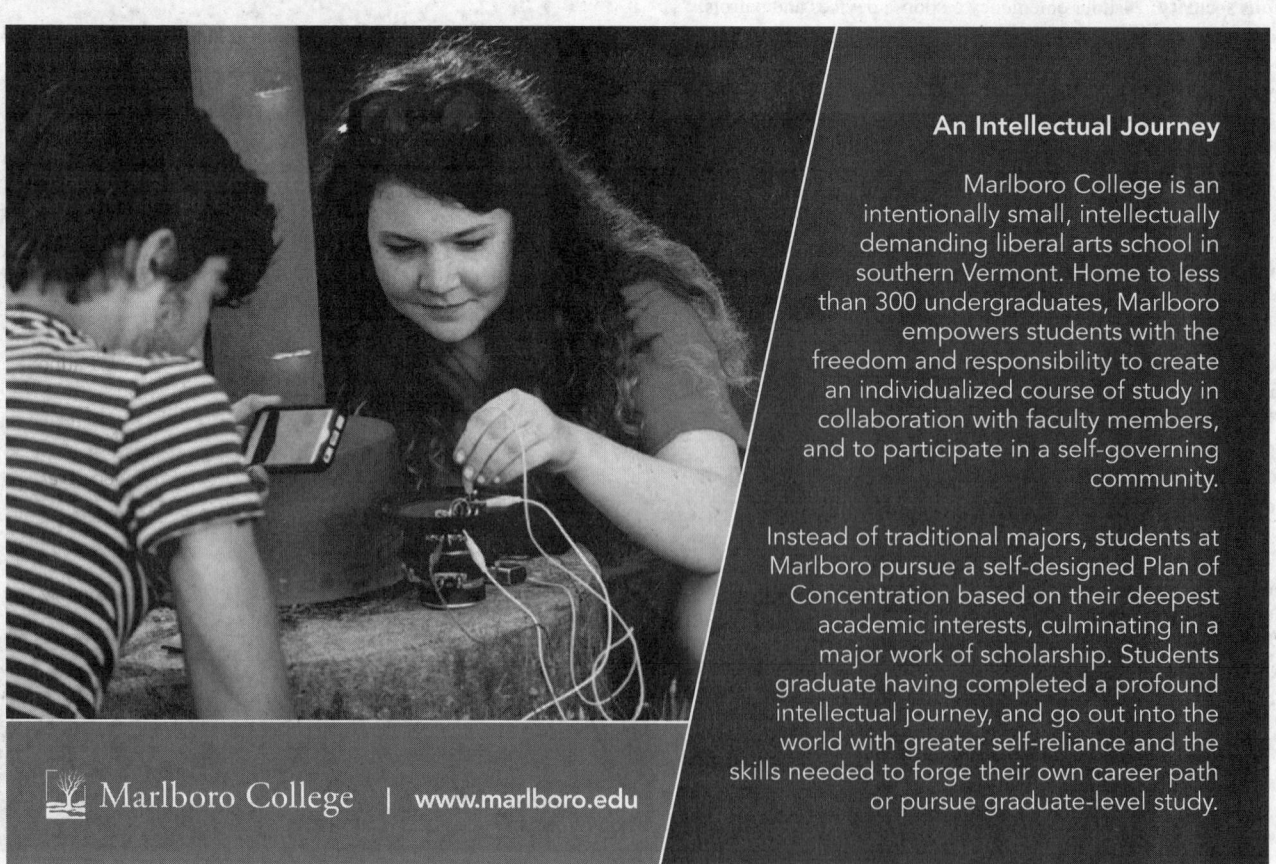

COSTS & FINANCIAL AID
Costs (2016–17) ***Comprehensive fee:*** $64,332 includes full-time tuition ($49,648), mandatory fees ($415), and room and board ($14,269). ***Payment plan:*** tuition prepayment. ***Waivers:*** employees or children of employees.

Financial Aid Of all full-time matriculated undergraduates who enrolled in 2016, 1,291 applied for aid, 1,104 were judged to have need, 1,104 had their need fully met. In 2016, 4 non-need-based awards were made. ***Average percent of need met:*** 100. ***Average financial aid package:*** $48,000. ***Average need-based loan:*** $3509. ***Average need-based gift aid:*** $45,035. ***Average non-need-based aid:*** $5000. ***Average indebtedness upon graduation:*** $18,736. ***Financial aid deadline:*** 2/1.

APPLYING
Standardized Tests *Required:* SAT and SAT Subject Tests or ACT (for admission).

Options: electronic application, early admission, early decision, deferred entrance.

Application fee: $65.

Required: essay or personal statement, high school transcript, 2 letters of recommendation. ***Recommended:*** interview.

Application deadlines: 1/1 (freshmen), 3/1 (transfers).

Early decision deadline: 11/1 (for plan 1), 1/1 (for plan 2).

Notification: 3/31 (freshmen), 4/10 (transfers), 12/15 (early decision plan 1), 2/15 (early decision plan 2).

CONTACT
Mr. Greg Buckles, Dean of Admissions, Middlebury College, Emma Willard House, Middlebury, VT 05753-6002. *Phone:* 802-443-3000. *Fax:* 802-443-2056. *E-mail:* admissions@middlebury.edu.

New England Culinary Institute
Montpelier, Vermont
http://www.neci.edu/

- **Proprietary** primarily 2-year, founded 1980
- **Small-town** campus
- **Coed** 300 undergraduate students, 86% full-time, 45% women, 55% men
- **Moderately difficult** entrance level

UNDERGRAD STUDENTS
257 full-time, 43 part-time. Students come from 39 states and territories; 6 other countries; 80% are from out of state; 8% Black or African American, non-Hispanic/Latino; 5% Hispanic/Latino; 4% Asian, non-Hispanic/Latino; 1% American Indian or Alaska Native, non-Hispanic/Latino; 1% Two or more races, non-Hispanic/Latino; 13% Race/ethnicity unknown; 6% transferred in; 80% live on campus.

Freshmen:
Admission: 52 enrolled.
Retention: 86% of full-time freshmen returned.

FACULTY
Total: 27, 59% full-time.
Student/faculty ratio: 15:1.

ACADEMICS
Calendar: quarters. *Degrees:* certificates, associate, and bachelor's.

Special study options: academic remediation for entering students, accelerated degree program, advanced placement credit, cooperative education, distance learning, honors programs, internships, services for LD students.

Computers: Students can access the following: computer help desk, free student e-mail accounts, online (class) grades, online learning platform. Campuswide network is available. 100% of college-owned or -operated housing units are wired for high-speed Internet access. Wireless service is available via entire campus.
Library: New England Culinary Institute Library.

STUDENT LIFE
Housing options: on-campus residence required for freshman year; coed, men-only, women-only. Campus housing is leased by the school. Freshman applicants given priority for college housing.

Activities and organizations: American Culinary Federation, Slow Food, Student Council, Special Guest Lecture Series, Student Ambassadors (leadership program).

Campus security: 24-hour emergency response devices, student patrols.

COSTS & FINANCIAL AID
Costs (2016–17) ***Comprehensive fee:*** $31,165 includes full-time tuition ($20,625), mandatory fees ($2540), and room and board ($8000). Full-time tuition and fees vary according to course load, degree level, program, reciprocity agreements, and student level. Part-time tuition and fees vary according to course load, degree level, program, reciprocity agreements, and student level. ***Payment plan:*** installment. ***Waivers:*** employees or children of employees.

Financial Aid Of all full-time matriculated undergraduates who enrolled in 2015, 320 Federal Work-Study jobs (averaging $1000).

APPLYING
Standardized Tests *Recommended:* SAT or ACT (for admission).

Options: electronic application, early admission, deferred entrance.

Application fee: $35.

Required: essay or personal statement, high school transcript, 1 letter of recommendation, interview. ***Recommended:*** culinary experience.

CONTACT
Adonica Williams, New England Culinary Institute, 7 School Street, Montpelier, VT 05602-3115. *Phone:* 802-225-3210. *Toll-free phone:* 877-223-6324. *Fax:* 802-225-3280. *E-mail:* admissions@neci.edu.

Norwich University
Northfield, Vermont
http://www.norwich.edu/

CONTACT
Norwich University, 158 Harmon Drive, Northfield, VT 05663. *Phone:* 802-485-2658. *Toll-free phone:* 800-468-6679.

Saint Michael's College
Colchester, Vermont
http://www.smcvt.edu/

- **Independent Roman Catholic** comprehensive, founded 1904
- **Suburban** 440-acre campus with easy access to Montreal
- **Endowment** $91.4 million
- **Coed** 1,902 undergraduate students, 98% full-time, 56% women, 44% men
- **Moderately difficult** entrance level, 77% of applicants were admitted

UNDERGRAD STUDENTS
1,868 full-time, 34 part-time. Students come from 33 states and territories; 20 other countries; 84% are from out of state; 2% Black or African American, non-Hispanic/Latino; 4% Hispanic/Latino; 2% Asian, non-Hispanic/Latino; 0.1% Native Hawaiian or other Pacific Islander, non-Hispanic/Latino; 0.2% American Indian or Alaska Native, non-Hispanic/Latino; 2% Two or more races, non-Hispanic/Latino; 1% Race/ethnicity unknown; 4% international; 2% transferred in; 95% live on campus.

Freshmen:
Admission: 5,013 applied, 3,860 admitted, 461 enrolled. ***Average high school GPA:*** 3.18. ***Test scores:*** SAT critical reading scores over 500: 96%; SAT math scores over 500: 94%; SAT writing scores over 500: 94%; ACT scores over 18: 97%; SAT critical reading scores over 600: 51%; SAT math scores over 600: 41%; SAT writing scores over 600: 43%; ACT scores over 24: 79%; SAT critical reading scores over 700: 9%; SAT math scores over 700: 4%; SAT writing scores over 700: 4%; ACT scores over 30: 15%.
Retention: 89% of full-time freshmen returned.

FACULTY
Total: 225, 66% full-time, 70% with terminal degrees.
Student/faculty ratio: 11:1.

ACADEMICS
Calendar: semesters. *Degrees:* bachelor's, master's, post-master's, and postbachelor's certificates.

Special study options: advanced placement credit, distance learning, double majors, English as a second language, honors programs, independent study, internships, off-campus study, part-time degree program, services for LD students, student-designed majors, study abroad, summer session for credit. ***ROTC:*** Army (c), Air Force (c).

Unusual degree programs: 3-2 business administration with Clarkson University, Syracuse University, Northeastern University, Boston College; engineering with University of Vermont, Clarkson University; pharmacy with Albany College of Pharmacy and Health Sciences.

Computers: 79 computers/terminals and 5,000 ports are available on campus for general student use. Students can access the following: campus intranet, computer help desk, free student e-mail accounts, online (class) grades, online (class) registration, online (class) schedules. Campuswide network is available. 100% of college-owned or -operated housing units are wired for high-speed Internet access. Wireless service is available via entire campus.

Library: Durick Library. *Books:* 231,540 (physical), 230,090 (digital/electronic); *Serial titles:* 1,621 (physical), 128,515 (digital/electronic); *Databases:* 142. Weekly public service hours: 102.

STUDENT LIFE

Housing options: on-campus residence required through senior year; coed, men-only, women-only, special housing for students with disabilities. Campus housing is university owned. Freshman campus housing is guaranteed.

Activities and organizations: drama/theater group, student-run newspaper, radio station, choral group, Student Association (governing board), Mobilization of Volunteer Efforts (MOVE), Wilderness Program, Martin Luther King Society, ShredMC.

Athletics Member NCAA. All Division II. ***Intercollegiate sports:*** baseball M, basketball M(s)/W(s), cross-country running M/W, field hockey W, golf M, ice hockey M/W, lacrosse M/W, rugby M(c)/W(c), skiing (cross-country) M/W, skiing (downhill) M/W, soccer M/W, softball W, swimming and diving M/W, tennis M/W, volleyball W. ***Intramural sports:*** basketball M/W, ice hockey M/W, racquetball M/W, rock climbing M/W, skiing (cross-country) M/W, skiing (downhill) M/W, soccer M/W, softball M/W, table tennis M/W, tennis M/W, track and field M(c)/W(c), ultimate Frisbee M(c)/W(c), volleyball M/W, water polo M/W.

Campus security: 24-hour emergency response devices and patrols, student patrols, late-night transport/escort service, controlled dormitory access, bicycle patrols, fire and rescue squad with professionals and trained student volunteers.

Student services: health clinic, personal/psychological counseling, women's center.

COSTS & FINANCIAL AID

Costs (2016–17) ***Comprehensive fee:*** $53,275 includes full-time tuition ($41,650), mandatory fees ($325), and room and board ($11,300). Full-time tuition and fees vary according to course load. Part-time tuition: $1340 per credit hour. Part-time tuition and fees vary according to course load. ***Room and board:*** Room and board charges vary according to board plan and housing facility. ***Payment plan:*** installment. ***Waivers:*** employees or children of employees.

Financial Aid Of all full-time matriculated undergraduates who enrolled in 2016, 1,369 applied for aid, 1,168 were judged to have need, 343 had their need fully met. 250 Federal Work-Study jobs (averaging $1750). 280 state and other part-time jobs (averaging $1750). In 2016, 637 non-need-based awards were made. ***Average percent of need met:*** 77. ***Average financial aid package:*** $30,235. ***Average need-based loan:*** $5563. ***Average need-based gift aid:*** $24,498. ***Average non-need-based aid:*** $17,355. ***Average indebtedness upon graduation:*** $38,226.

APPLYING

Options: electronic application, early action, deferred entrance.

Application fee: $50.

Required: essay or personal statement, high school transcript. ***Recommended:*** minimum 3.0 GPA, 3 letters of recommendation, interview.

Application deadlines: 2/1 (freshmen), 3/15 (transfers), 11/1 (early action).

Notification: 4/1 (freshmen), 4/15 (transfers), 1/1 (early action).

CONTACT

Mr. Michael Stefanowicz, Director of Admission, Saint Michael's College, One Winooski Park, Colchester, VT 05452. *Phone:* 802-654-2108. *Toll-free phone:* 800-762-8000. *Fax:* 802-654-2906. *E-mail:* admission@smcvt.edu.

Southern Vermont College

Bennington, Vermont

http://www.svc.edu/

- **Independent** 4-year, founded 1926
- **Small-town** 371-acre campus with easy access to Albany, NY
- **Endowment** $3.5 million
- **Coed**
- **Noncompetitive** entrance level

FACULTY

Student/faculty ratio: 14:1.

ACADEMICS

Calendar: semesters. *Degrees:* certificates, associate, and bachelor's.

Library: Southern Vermont College Library. *Books:* 10,025 (physical), 8,818 (digital/electronic); *Serial titles:* 792 (physical); *Databases:* 70. Students can reserve study rooms.

STUDENT LIFE

Housing options: on-campus residence required through sophomore year; coed. Campus housing is university owned. Freshman campus housing is guaranteed.

Activities and organizations: drama/theater group, Student Government Association, Mountaineer Event Board, Japanese Culture and Anime Club, Big Brothers Big Sisters, Moosecorps.

Athletics Member NCAA. All Division III.

Campus security: 24-hour patrols, late-night transport/escort service, controlled dormitory access.

Student services: personal/psychological counseling.

FINANCIAL AID

Financial Aid Of all full-time matriculated undergraduates who enrolled in 2015, 100 Federal Work-Study jobs (averaging $1000).

APPLYING

Standardized Tests *Required:* SAT or ACT (for admission).

Options: electronic application, early admission, deferred entrance.

Application fee: $30.

Required: essay or personal statement, high school transcript, 2 letters of recommendation. ***Required for some:*** interview, Dean's report and college transcripts for transfer students. ***Recommended:*** minimum 2.0 GPA, interview.

CONTACT

Southern Vermont College, 897 Monument Avenue, Bennington, VT 05201. *Phone:* 802-447-6300. *Fax:* 802-681-2868. *E-mail:* admissions@svc.edu.

Sterling College

Craftsbury Common, Vermont

http://www.sterlingcollege.edu/

- **Independent** 4-year, founded 1958
- **Rural** 430-acre campus
- **Endowment** $1.3 million
- **Coed**

FACULTY

Student/faculty ratio: 7:1.

ACADEMICS

Calendar: semesters. *Degree:* bachelor's.

Library: Brown Library plus 1 other. *Books:* 11,773 (physical), 959 (digital/electronic); *Serial titles:* 28,324 (physical); *Databases:* 27. Weekly public service hours: 45; study areas open 24 hours, 5-7 days a week.

STUDENT LIFE

Housing options: on-campus residence required for freshman year; coed, women-only, cooperative. Campus housing is university owned. Freshman campus housing is guaranteed.

Activities and organizations: drama/theater group, Nordic Ski Team, Trail Running Team, Shooting Club, Environmental and Social Justice Club, Outdoor Club.

Campus security: 24-hour emergency response devices, 24-hour pager.

Student services: personal/psychological counseling, women's center.

COSTS & FINANCIAL AID

Costs (2016–17) ***One-time required fee:*** $285. ***Comprehensive fee:*** $41,072 includes full-time tuition ($32,592), mandatory fees ($3700), and room and board ($4780). Full-time tuition and fees vary according to course load. Part-time tuition: $8148 per term. Part-time tuition and fees vary according to course load. ***College room only:*** $4354. Room and board charges vary according to board plan.

Financial Aid Of all full-time matriculated undergraduates who enrolled in 2014, 105 applied for aid, 72 were judged to have need, 8 had their need fully met. In 2014, 5 non-need-based awards were made. ***Average percent of need met:*** 87. ***Average financial aid package:*** $29,124. ***Average need-based loan:*** $5300. ***Average need-based gift aid:*** $11,200. ***Average non-need-based aid:*** $12,889. ***Average indebtedness upon graduation:*** $35,937.

APPLYING

Required: essay or personal statement, high school transcript, 2 letters of recommendation, interview. ***Recommended:*** minimum 2.0 GPA.

CONTACT

Tim Patterson, Director of Admission and Financial Aid, Sterling College, PO Box 72, Craftsbury Common, VT 05827. *Phone:* 802-586-7711 Ext. 135. *Toll-free phone:* 800-648-3591 Ext. 100. *Fax:* 802-586-2596. *E-mail:* tpatterson@sterlingcollege.edu.

See below for display ad and page 1524 for the College Close-Up.

University of Vermont

Burlington, Vermont

http://www.uvm.edu/

- **State-supported** university, founded 1791
- **Suburban** 459-acre campus
- **Endowment** $408.9 million
- **Coed** 11,159 undergraduate students, 91% full-time, 57% women, 43% men
- **Moderately difficult** entrance level, 69% of applicants were admitted

UNDERGRAD STUDENTS

10,183 full-time, 976 part-time. Students come from 48 states and territories; 72% are from out of state; 1% Black or African American, non-Hispanic/Latino; 4% Hispanic/Latino; 3% Asian, non-Hispanic/Latino; 0.1% American Indian or Alaska Native, non-Hispanic/Latino; 3% Two or more races, non-Hispanic/Latino; 2% Race/ethnicity unknown; 5% international; 4% transferred in; 62% live on campus.

Freshmen:

Admission: 22,476 applied, 15,495 admitted, 2,496 enrolled. ***Average high school GPA:*** 3.62. ***Test scores:*** SAT critical reading scores over 500: 93%; SAT math scores over 500: 94%; SAT writing scores over 500: 93%; ACT scores over 18: 99%; SAT critical reading scores over 600: 56%; SAT math scores over 600: 56%; SAT writing scores over 600: 52%; ACT scores over 24: 85%; SAT critical reading scores over 700: 12%; SAT math scores over 700: 10%; SAT writing scores over 700: 9%; ACT scores over 30: 27%.

Retention: 86% of full-time freshmen returned.

FACULTY

Total: 785, 80% full-time, 72% with terminal degrees.

Student/faculty ratio: 17:1.

ACADEMICS

Calendar: semesters. *Degrees:* bachelor's, master's, doctoral, post-master's, and postbachelor's certificates.

Special study options: adult/continuing education programs, advanced placement credit, cooperative education, distance learning, double majors, freshman honors college, honors programs, independent study, internships, off-campus study, part-time degree program, services for LD students, student-designed majors, study abroad, summer session for credit. ***ROTC:*** Army (b).

Unusual degree programs: 3-2 computer science, law with Vermont Law School.

Computers: 850 computers/terminals and 299 ports are available on campus for general student use. Students can access the following: campus intranet, computer help desk, free student e-mail accounts, online (class) grades, online (class) registration, online (class) schedules, Web pages, online course support. Campuswide network is available. 100% of college-owned or -operated housing units are wired for high-speed Internet access. Wireless service is available via entire campus.

Library: Bailey-Howe Library plus 2 others. *Books:* 3.3 million (physical), 351,994 (digital/electronic); *Serial titles:* 90,542 (physical). Weekly public service hours: 104; students can reserve study rooms.

STUDENT LIFE

Housing options: on-campus residence required through sophomore year; coed. Campus housing is university owned. Freshman campus housing is guaranteed.

Activities and organizations: drama/theater group, student-run newspaper, radio and television station, choral group, Volunteers in Action, Outing Club, Ski and Snowboard Club, national fraternities, national sororities.

Athletics Member NCAA. All Division I. ***Intercollegiate sports:*** basketball M(s)/W(s), cheerleading M(c)/W(c), crew M(c)/W(c), cross-country running M(s)/W(s), equestrian sports M(c)/W(c), fencing M(c)/W(c), field hockey W(s), gymnastics M(c)/W(c), ice hockey M(s)/W(s), lacrosse M(s)/W(s), rugby M(c)/W(c), sailing M(c)/W(c), skiing (cross-country) M(s)/W(s), skiing (downhill) M(s)/W(s), soccer M(s)/W(s), swimming and diving W(s), table tennis M(c)/W(c), track and field M(s)/W(s), ultimate Frisbee M(c)/W(c), volleyball M(c)/W(c), water polo M(c)/W(c). ***Intramural sports:*** basketball M/W, bowling M/W, football M(c)/W, ice hockey M/W, lacrosse M/W, racquetball M/W, soccer M/W, softball M/W, tennis M/W, volleyball M/W, water polo M/W.

Campus security: 24-hour emergency response devices and patrols, late-night transport/escort service, controlled dormitory access, campus alert system (via phone, email, text).

Student services: health clinic, personal/psychological counseling, women's center, legal services.

COSTS & FINANCIAL AID

Costs (2016–17) ***Tuition:*** state resident $15,096 full-time, $611 per credit hour part-time; nonresident $38,160 full-time, $1544 per credit hour part-time. Part-time tuition and fees vary according to course load. ***Required fees:*** $2174 full-time. ***Room and board:*** $11,608; room only: $7788. Room and board charges vary according to board plan and housing facility. ***Payment plan:*** installment. ***Waivers:*** employees or children of employees.

Financial Aid Of all full-time matriculated undergraduates who enrolled in 2015, 6,569 applied for aid, 5,315 were judged to have need, 738 had their need fully met. 1,415 Federal Work-Study jobs (averaging $1600). In 2015, 3046 non-need-based awards were made. ***Average percent of need met:*** 65. ***Average financial aid package:*** $23,942. ***Average need-based loan:*** $4454. ***Average need-based gift aid:*** $15,647. ***Average non-need-based aid:*** $10,950. ***Average indebtedness upon graduation:*** $26,964.

APPLYING

Standardized Tests *Required:* SAT or ACT (for admission).

Options: electronic application, early admission, early action, deferred entrance.

Application fee: $55.

Required: essay or personal statement, high school transcript, 1 letter of recommendation. ***Required for some:*** audition for music or music education.

Application deadlines: 1/15 (freshmen), 4/15 (transfers), 11/1 (early action).

Notification: 3/15 (freshmen), continuous (transfers), 12/15 (early action).

CONTACT

Dr. Beth A. Wiser, Director of Admissions, University of Vermont, Office of Admissions, 194 South Prospect Street, Burlington, VT 05401. *Phone:* 802-656-3370. *Fax:* 802-656-8611. *E-mail:* admissions@uvm.edu.

Vermont Technical College

Randolph Center, Vermont

http://www.vtc.edu/

- **State-supported** comprehensive, founded 1866, part of Vermont State Colleges System
- **Rural** 544-acre campus
- **Endowment** $5.0 million
- **Coed** 1,625 undergraduate students, 68% full-time, 48% women, 52% men
- **Moderately difficult** entrance level, 70% of applicants were admitted

UNDERGRAD STUDENTS

1,104 full-time, 521 part-time. Students come from 24 states and territories; 5 other countries; 16% are from out of state; 2% Black or African American, non-Hispanic/Latino; 2% Hispanic/Latino; 2% Asian, non-Hispanic/Latino; 0.7% American Indian or Alaska Native, non-Hispanic/Latino; 3% Two or more races, non-Hispanic/Latino; 2% Race/ethnicity unknown; 2% international; 19% transferred in.

Freshmen:

Admission: 584 applied, 406 admitted, 218 enrolled. ***Test scores:*** SAT critical reading scores over 500: 32%; SAT math scores over 500: 42%; ACT scores over 18: 68%; SAT critical reading scores over 600: 8%; SAT math scores over 600: 11%; ACT scores over 24: 21%; SAT critical reading scores over 700: 1%.

Retention: 63% of full-time freshmen returned.

FACULTY

Total: 146, 56% full-time, 55% with terminal degrees.

Student/faculty ratio: 13:1.

ACADEMICS

Calendar: semesters. *Degrees:* certificates, associate, bachelor's, and master's.

Special study options: academic remediation for entering students, accelerated degree program, advanced placement credit, cooperative education, distance learning, double majors, English as a second language, honors programs, independent study, internships, part-time degree program, services for LD students, summer session for credit. ***ROTC:*** Army (c).

Computers: 480 computers/terminals and 600 ports are available on campus for general student use. Students can access the following: campus intranet, computer help desk, free student e-mail accounts, online (class) grades, online (class) registration, online (class) schedules, online (network) file storage. Campuswide network is available. 98% of college-owned or -operated housing units are wired for high-speed Internet access. Wireless service is available via entire campus.

Library: Hartness Library. *Books:* 59,000 (physical).

STUDENT LIFE

Housing options: on-campus residence required through sophomore year; coed. Campus housing is university owned.

Activities and organizations: student-run radio and television station, choral group, Student Council (student government), Adventurer's Guild (board and video gaming), WVTC (student radio station), Outing Club, Veterinary Technology Club.

Athletics Member USCAA. ***Intercollegiate sports:*** baseball M, basketball M/W, golf M/W, soccer M/W, softball W. ***Intramural sports:*** basketball M/W, bowling M(c)/W(c), cross-country running M/W, fencing M(c)/W(c), football M/W, golf M(c)/W(c), ice hockey M(c)/W(c), racquetball M/W, riflery M(c)/W(c), rock climbing M(c)/W(c), rugby M(c), skiing (cross-country) M(c)/W(c), skiing (downhill) M(c)/W(c), soccer M/W, softball M/W, swimming and diving M/W, table tennis M/W, tennis M/W, volleyball M/W, water polo M/W, weight lifting M(c)/W(c).

Campus security: 24-hour emergency response devices and patrols, late-night transport/escort service, controlled dormitory access.

Student services: health clinic.

COSTS & FINANCIAL AID

Costs (2017–18) ***Tuition:*** state resident $13,512 full-time, $563 per credit hour part-time; nonresident $25,824 full-time, $1076 per credit hour part-time. Full-time tuition and fees vary according to course load and program. Part-time tuition and fees vary according to program. ***Required fees:*** $1488 full-time, $47 per credit hour part-time. ***Room and board:*** $10,290; room only: $6128. Room and board charges vary according to board plan. ***Payment plan:*** installment. ***Waivers:*** employees or children of employees.

Financial Aid Of all full-time matriculated undergraduates who enrolled in 2016, 902 applied for aid, 816 were judged to have need, 71 had their need fully met. 177 Federal Work-Study jobs (averaging $1260). In 2016, 66 non-need-based awards were made. ***Average percent of need met:*** 61. ***Average financial aid package:*** $14,736. ***Average need-based loan:*** $3920. ***Average need-based gift aid:*** $5648. ***Average non-need-based aid:*** $4740. ***Average indebtedness upon graduation:*** $29,988.

APPLYING

Standardized Tests *Required for some:* SAT or ACT (for admission).

Options: electronic application.

Application fee: $47.

Required: high school transcript. ***Required for some:*** essay or personal statement, 2 letters of recommendation, interview. ***Recommended:*** minimum 3.0 GPA, 2 letters of recommendation, interview.

Application deadlines: rolling (freshmen), rolling (transfers).

Notification: continuous (freshmen), continuous (transfers).

CONTACT

Jessica Van Deren, Director of Admissions, Vermont Technical College, PO Box 500, Randolph Center, VT 05061. *Phone:* 802-728-1244. *Toll-free phone:* 800-442-VTC1. *Fax:* 802-728-1390. *E-mail:* admissions@vtc.edu.

VIRGINIA

American National University

Danville, Virginia

http://www.an.edu/

CONTACT

Admissions Office, American National University, 336 Old Riverside Drive, Danville, VA 24541. *Phone:* 434-793-6822. *Toll-free phone:* 888-9-JOBREADY.

American National University

Harrisonburg, Virginia

http://www.an.edu/

CONTACT

Jack Evey, Campus Director, American National University, 1515 Country Club Road, Harrisonburg, VA 22802. *Phone:* 540-432-0943. *Toll-free phone:* 888-9-JOBREADY.

American National University

Lynchburg, Virginia

http://www.an.edu/

CONTACT

Admissions Representative, American National University, 104 Candlewood Court, Lynchburg, VA 24502. *Phone:* 804-239-3500. *Toll-free phone:* 888-9-JOBREADY.

American National University

Salem, Virginia

http://www.an.edu/

CONTACT

Director of Admissions, American National University, 1813 East Main Street, Salem, VA 24153. *Phone:* 540-986-1800. *Toll-free phone:* 888-9-JOBREADY. *Fax:* 540-444-4198.

Argosy University, Northern Virginia

Arlington, Virginia

http://www.argosy.edu/locations/washington-dc/

CONTACT

Argosy University, Northern Virginia, 1550 Wilson Boulevard, Suite 600, Arlington, VA 22209. *Phone:* 703-526-5800. *Toll-free phone:* 866-703-2777.

The Art Institute of Virginia Beach, a branch of The Art Institute of Atlanta

Virginia Beach, Virginia

http://www.artinstitutes.edu/virginia-beach/

CONTACT

The Art Institute of Virginia Beach, a branch of The Art Institute of Atlanta, Two Columbus Center, 4500 Main Street, Suite 100, Virginia Beach, VA 23462. *Phone:* 757-493-6700. *Toll-free phone:* 877-437-4428.

The Art Institute of Washington, a branch of The Art Institute of Atlanta

Arlington, Virginia

http://www.artinstitutes.edu/arlington/

CONTACT

The Art Institute of Washington, a branch of The Art Institute of Atlanta, 1820 North Fort Meyer Drive, Arlington, VA 22209. *Phone:* 703-358-9550. *Toll-free phone:* 877-303-3771.

Averett University

Danville, Virginia

http://www.averett.edu/

- **Independent** comprehensive, founded 1859, affiliated with Baptist General Association of Virginia
- **Small-town** 252-acre campus with easy access to Greensboro, NC
- **Endowment** $19.8 million
- **Coed** 859 undergraduate students, 97% full-time, 49% women, 51% men
- **Moderately difficult** entrance level, 55% of applicants were admitted

UNDERGRAD STUDENTS

831 full-time, 28 part-time. Students come from 22 states and territories; 14 other countries; 36% are from out of state; 32% Black or African American, non-Hispanic/Latino; 3% Hispanic/Latino; 1% Asian, non-Hispanic/Latino; 0.2% Native Hawaiian or other Pacific Islander, non-Hispanic/Latino; 0.8% American Indian or Alaska Native, non-Hispanic/Latino; 5% international; 8% transferred in; 77% live on campus.

Freshmen:

Admission: 2,238 applied, 1,228 admitted, 237 enrolled. ***Average high school GPA:*** 3.24. ***Test scores:*** SAT critical reading scores over 500: 28%; SAT math scores over 500: 29%; SAT writing scores over 500: 19%; ACT scores over 18: 59%; SAT critical reading scores over 600: 4%; SAT math scores over 600: 3%; SAT writing scores over 600: 2%; ACT scores over 24: 14%; SAT critical reading scores over 700: 1%.

Retention: 55% of full-time freshmen returned.

FACULTY

Total: 106, 58% full-time, 47% with terminal degrees.

Student/faculty ratio: 11:1.

ACADEMICS
Calendar: semesters. *Degrees:* bachelor's and master's.

Special study options: academic remediation for entering students, accelerated degree program, adult/continuing education programs, advanced placement credit, cooperative education, distance learning, double majors, external degree program, honors programs, independent study, internships, off-campus study, part-time degree program, services for LD students, student-designed majors, study abroad, summer session for credit.

Computers: 150 computers/terminals and 25 ports are available on campus for general student use. Students can access the following: computer help desk, free student e-mail accounts, online (class) grades, online (class) registration, online (class) schedules. Campuswide network is available. 100% of college-owned or -operated housing units are wired for high-speed Internet access. Wireless service is available via entire campus.

Library: Mary B. Blount Library. *Books:* 87,139 (physical), 184,225 (digital/electronic); *Serial titles:* 284 (physical), 34,278 (digital/electronic); *Databases:* 124. Weekly public service hours: 81; students can reserve study rooms.

STUDENT LIFE
Housing options: on-campus residence required through junior year; coed, men-only, women-only. Campus housing is university owned. Freshman campus housing is guaranteed.

Activities and organizations: drama/theater group, student-run newspaper, choral group, Cougar Activities Board (CAB), Student Athletic Advisory Committee (SAAC), Student Government Association (SGA), IMPACT, Christian Student Union, national fraternities.

Athletics Member NCAA. All Division III. ***Intercollegiate sports:*** baseball M, basketball M/W, cheerleading M(c)/W(c), cross-country running M/W, equestrian sports M(c)/W(c), football M, golf M, soccer M/W, softball W, tennis M/W, volleyball W. ***Intramural sports:*** basketball M/W, soccer M/W, volleyball M/W.

Campus security: 24-hour emergency response devices and patrols, late-night transport/escort service, controlled dormitory access.

Student services: health clinic, personal/psychological counseling.

COSTS & FINANCIAL AID
Costs (2016–17) ***Comprehensive fee:*** $40,970 includes full-time tuition ($31,980) and room and board ($8990). Full-time tuition and fees vary according to class time, course load, degree level, location, and program. Part-time tuition: $1000 per credit. Part-time tuition and fees vary according to class time, course load, degree level, location, and program. ***College room only:*** $6070. Room and board charges vary according to board plan and housing facility. ***Payment plan:*** installment. ***Waivers:*** senior citizens and employees or children of employees.

Financial Aid Of all full-time matriculated undergraduates who enrolled in 2016, 749 applied for aid, 715 were judged to have need, 109 had their need fully met. 163 Federal Work-Study jobs (averaging $918). In 2016, 117 non-need-based awards were made. ***Average percent of need met:*** 73. ***Average financial aid package:*** $25,270. ***Average need-based loan:*** $4358. ***Average need-based gift aid:*** $21,485. ***Average non-need-based aid:*** $14,110. ***Average indebtedness upon graduation:*** $35,659.

APPLYING
Standardized Tests *Required:* SAT or ACT (for admission), TOEFL for international students (for admission).

Options: electronic application, deferred entrance.

Required: high school transcript, minimum 2.5 GPA. ***Recommended:*** essay or personal statement, 1 letter of recommendation.

Application deadlines: 9/1 (freshmen), 8/15 (transfers).

Notification: continuous (freshmen), continuous (out-of-state freshmen), continuous (transfers).

CONTACT
Mr. Joel Nester, Director of Admissions and International Counselor, Averett University, 420 West Main Street, English Hall, Danville, VA 24541. *Phone:* 434-791-5663. *Toll-free phone:* 800-AVERETT. *E-mail:* joel.nester@averett.edu.

Bethel College
Hampton, Virginia
http://www.bcva.edu/

- **Independent** 4-year, founded 1996, affiliated with Assembly of God Church
- **Suburban** campus
- **Coed**
- **Minimally difficult** entrance level

ACADEMICS
Calendar: semesters. *Degrees:* diplomas, associate, and bachelor's.

STUDENT LIFE
Housing options: men-only, women-only. Campus housing is university owned.

Activities and organizations: drama/theater group, choral group.

Campus security: controlled dormitory access.

Student services: personal/psychological counseling.

COSTS
Costs (2016–17) ***Tuition:*** $250 per credit part-time.

APPLYING
Standardized Tests *Required:* SAT or ACT (for admission).

Options: early admission.

CONTACT
Ms. Nanette Bartholomew, Student Affairs, Bethel College, 1705 Todds Lane, Hampton, VA 23666. *Phone:* 757-826-1883 Ext. 215.

Bluefield College
Bluefield, Virginia
http://www.bluefield.edu/

- **Independent Southern Baptist** comprehensive, founded 1922
- **Small-town** 82-acre campus
- **Endowment** $6.8 million
- **Coed** 969 undergraduate students, 83% full-time, 53% women, 47% men

UNDERGRAD STUDENTS
805 full-time, 164 part-time. Students come from 27 states and territories; 24 other countries; 24% are from out of state; 23% Black or African American, non-Hispanic/Latino; 4% Hispanic/Latino; 0.3% Asian, non-Hispanic/Latino; 0.2% Native Hawaiian or other Pacific Islander, non-Hispanic/Latino; 3% Two or more races, non-Hispanic/Latino; 1% Race/ethnicity unknown; 4% international; 15% transferred in; 61% live on campus.

Freshmen:
Admission: 179 enrolled. ***Average high school GPA:*** 3.16. ***Test scores:*** SAT critical reading scores over 500: 31%; SAT math scores over 500: 35%; ACT scores over 18: 70%; SAT critical reading scores over 600: 8%; SAT math scores over 600: 8%; ACT scores over 24: 14%; ACT scores over 30: 2%.

Retention: 61% of full-time freshmen returned.

FACULTY
Total: 92, 41% full-time, 47% with terminal degrees.

Student/faculty ratio: 15:1.

ACADEMICS
Calendar: semesters. *Degrees:* bachelor's and master's.

Special study options: academic remediation for entering students, adult/continuing education programs, advanced placement credit, cooperative education, distance learning, double majors, honors programs, independent study, internships, off-campus study, part-time degree program, services for LD students, study abroad, summer session for credit.

Computers: 110 computers/terminals are available on campus for general student use. Students can access the following: campus intranet, free student e-mail accounts, online (class) grades, online (class) registration, online (class) schedules. Campuswide network is available. 100% of college-owned or -operated housing units are wired for high-speed Internet access. Wireless service is available via entire campus.

Library: Easley Library. *Books:* 44,352 (physical), 165,829 (digital/electronic); *Serial titles:* 7,976 (physical), 334 (digital/electronic); *Databases:* 72. Students can reserve study rooms.

STUDENT LIFE

Housing options: on-campus residence required through junior year; men-only, women-only. Campus housing is university owned. Freshman applicants given priority for college housing.

Activities and organizations: drama/theater group, student-run newspaper, choral group, Baptist Collegiate Ministries, Fellowship of Christian Athletes, Student Union Board, Student Government Association, Arts Club.

Athletics Member NAIA, NCCAA. ***Intercollegiate sports:*** baseball M(s), basketball M(s)/W(s), cheerleading M(s)/W(s), cross-country running M(s)/W(s), football M(s), golf M(s), skiing (cross-country) M(s)/W(s), soccer M(s)/W(s), softball W(s), tennis M(s)/W(s), volleyball M(s)/W(s). ***Intramural sports:*** baseball M, basketball M/W, football M/W, softball M/W, table tennis M/W, tennis M/W, volleyball M/W.

Campus security: controlled dormitory access, night security patrols.

Student services: personal/psychological counseling.

COSTS & FINANCIAL AID

Costs (2017–18) ***Comprehensive fee:*** $34,403 includes full-time tuition ($24,800), mandatory fees ($760), and room and board ($8843). Full-time tuition and fees vary according to course load and program. Part-time tuition: $970 per credit. Part-time tuition and fees vary according to course load and program. ***Required fees:*** $28 per credit hour part-time. ***College room only:*** $3692. Room and board charges vary according to housing facility. ***Payment plan:*** installment. ***Waivers:*** senior citizens and employees or children of employees.

Financial Aid Of all full-time matriculated undergraduates who enrolled in 2016, 728 applied for aid, 687 were judged to have need, 69 had their need fully met. 57 Federal Work-Study jobs (averaging $1137). 16 state and other part-time jobs (averaging $375). In 2016, 85 non-need-based awards were made. ***Average percent of need met:*** 62. ***Average financial aid package:*** $16,515. ***Average need-based loan:*** $4343. ***Average need-based gift aid:*** $12,876. ***Average non-need-based aid:*** $5819. ***Average indebtedness upon graduation:*** $30,487.

APPLYING

Standardized Tests *Required:* SAT or ACT (for admission).

Required: high school transcript, minimum 2.0 GPA. ***Required for some:*** essay or personal statement.

CONTACT

Mr. Evan Sherman, Director of Traditional Admissions, Bluefield College, 3000 College Avenue, Bluefield, VA 24605-1799. *Phone:* 276-326-4602. *Toll-free phone:* 800-872-0175. *Fax:* 276-326-4395. *E-mail:* esherman@bluefield.edu.

Bon Secours Memorial College of Nursing

Richmond, Virginia

http://www.bsmcon.edu/

CONTACT

Bon Secours Memorial College of Nursing, 8550 Magellan Parkway, Suite 1100, Richmond, VA 23227-1149. *Toll-free phone:* 866-238-7414.

Bridgewater College

Bridgewater, Virginia

http://www.bridgewater.edu/

- **Independent** comprehensive, founded 1880, affiliated with Church of the Brethren
- **Small-town** 300-acre campus
- **Endowment** $82.1 million
- **Coed** 1,882 undergraduate students, 100% full-time, 53% women, 47% men
- **Moderately difficult** entrance level, 53% of applicants were admitted

UNDERGRAD STUDENTS

1,876 full-time, 6 part-time. Students come from 28 states and territories; 17 other countries; 27% are from out of state; 13% Black or African American, non-Hispanic/Latino; 6% Hispanic/Latino; 1% Asian, non-Hispanic/Latino; 0.1% Native Hawaiian or other Pacific Islander, non-Hispanic/Latino; 0.3% American Indian or Alaska Native, non-Hispanic/Latino; 6% Two or more races, non-Hispanic/Latino; 4% Race/ethnicity unknown; 1% international; 3% transferred in; 82% live on campus.

Freshmen:

Admission: 7,486 applied, 3,949 admitted, 600 enrolled. ***Average high school GPA:*** 3.53. ***Test scores:*** SAT critical reading scores over 500: 55%; SAT math scores over 500: 56%; SAT writing scores over 500: 40%; ACT scores over 18: 93%; SAT critical reading scores over 600: 13%; SAT math scores over 600: 12%; SAT writing scores over 600: 9%; ACT scores over 24: 47%; SAT critical reading scores over 700: 2%; SAT math scores over 700: 2%; SAT writing scores over 700: 1%; ACT scores over 30: 8%.

Retention: 78% of full-time freshmen returned.

FACULTY

Total: 163, 71% full-time, 69% with terminal degrees.

Student/faculty ratio: 14:1.

ACADEMICS

Calendar: 4-1-4. *Degree:* bachelor's.

Special study options: adult/continuing education programs, advanced placement credit, distance learning, double majors, honors programs, independent study, internships, off-campus study, part-time degree program, services for LD students, study abroad, summer session for credit.

Unusual degree programs: 3-2 engineering with Virginia Polytechnic Institute and State University; nursing with Vanderbilt University.

Computers: 158 computers/terminals and 700 ports are available on campus for general student use. Students can access the following: campus intranet, computer help desk, free student e-mail accounts, online (class) grades, online (class) registration, online (class) schedules, course management system, campus bulletin board system. Campuswide network is available. 100% of college-owned or -operated housing units are wired for high-speed Internet access. Wireless service is available via entire campus.

Library: Alexander Mack Memorial Library. *Books:* 133,901 (physical), 23,752 (digital/electronic); *Serial titles:* 395 (physical), 51,417 (digital/electronic); *Databases:* 102. Weekly public service hours: 107.

STUDENT LIFE

Housing options: on-campus residence required through junior year; coed, men-only, women-only, special housing for students with disabilities. Campus housing is university owned.

Activities and organizations: drama/theater group, student-run newspaper, radio station, choral group, Eagle Productions (program board), Physics Club, Active Minds, BC Allies.

Athletics Member NCAA. All Division III. ***Intercollegiate sports:*** baseball M, basketball M/W, cheerleading M(c)/W(c), cross-country running M/W, equestrian sports M(c)/W(c), field hockey W, football M, golf M/W, lacrosse M/W, soccer M/W, softball W, swimming and diving W, tennis M/W, track and field M/W, volleyball W, wrestling M(c). ***Intramural sports:*** badminton M/W, basketball M/W, bowling M/W, football M/W, golf M/W, racquetball M/W, sand volleyball M/W, soccer M/W, softball M/W, table tennis M/W, tennis M/W, ultimate Frisbee M/W, volleyball M/W.

Campus security: 24-hour emergency response devices and patrols, controlled dormitory access, emergency alert system.

Student services: health clinic, personal/psychological counseling.

COSTS & FINANCIAL AID

Costs (2017–18) ***Comprehensive fee:*** $46,260 includes full-time tuition ($33,000), mandatory fees ($820), and room and board ($12,440). Part-time tuition: $1150 per credit hour. ***Required fees:*** $40 per term part-time. ***Room and board:*** Room and board charges vary according to housing facility. ***Payment plan:*** installment. ***Waivers:*** employees or children of employees.

Financial Aid Of all full-time matriculated undergraduates who enrolled in 2016, 1,661 applied for aid, 1,508 were judged to have need, 443 had their need fully met. 407 Federal Work-Study jobs (averaging $1454). 103 state and other part-time jobs (averaging $1145). In 2016, 363 non-need-

based awards were made. ***Average percent of need met:*** 85. ***Average financial aid package:*** $29,897. ***Average need-based loan:*** $4579. ***Average need-based gift aid:*** $26,156. ***Average non-need-based aid:*** $19,563. ***Average indebtedness upon graduation:*** $34,035.

APPLYING
Standardized Tests *Required:* SAT or ACT (for admission).
Options: electronic application, deferred entrance.
Required: high school transcript. ***Recommended:*** minimum 3.0 GPA.
Application deadlines: 5/1 (freshmen), 5/1 (transfers).
Notification: continuous (freshmen), continuous (transfers).

CONTACT
Mr. Jarret L. Smith, Director of Admissions, Bridgewater College, 402 East College Street, Bridgewater, VA 22812. *Phone:* 540-828-5469. *Toll-free phone:* 800-759-8328. *Fax:* 540-828-5481. *E-mail:* admissions@bridgewater.edu.

Bryant & Stratton College–Hampton Campus
Hampton, Virginia
http://www.bryantstratton.edu/

CONTACT
Bryant & Stratton College–Hampton Campus, 4410 East Claiborne Square, Suite 233, Hampton, VA 23666.

Bryant & Stratton College–Richmond Campus
Richmond, Virginia
http://www.bryantstratton.edu/

CONTACT
Mr. David K. Mayle, Director of Admissions, Bryant & Stratton College–Richmond Campus, 8141 Hull Street Road, Richmond, VA 23235-6411. *Phone:* 804-745-2444. *Fax:* 804-745-6884. *E-mail:* tlawson@bryanstratton.edu.

Bryant & Stratton College–Virginia Beach Campus
Virginia Beach, Virginia
http://www.bryantstratton.edu/

CONTACT
Bryant & Stratton College–Virginia Beach Campus, 301 Centre Pointe Drive, Virginia Beach, VA 23462. *Phone:* 757-499-7900 Ext. 173.

Centura College
Virginia Beach, Virginia
http://www.centuracollege.edu/

CONTACT
Admissions Office, Centura College, 2697 Dean Drive, Suite 100, Virginia Beach, VA 23452. *Phone:* 757-340-2121. *Toll-free phone:* 877-575-5627. *Fax:* 757-340-9704.

Chamberlain College of Nursing
Arlington, Virginia
http://www.chamberlain.edu/

- **Proprietary** 4-year
- **Coed**

FACULTY
Student/faculty ratio: 15:1.

ACADEMICS
Calendar: semesters. *Degree:* bachelor's.

STUDENT LIFE
Housing options: college housing not available.

COSTS
Costs (2016–17) ***Tuition:*** $18,900 full-time, $675 per credit hour part-time. ***Required fees:*** $600 full-time.

APPLYING
Standardized Tests *Required:* SAT or ACT (for admission).
Options: deferred entrance.
Application fee: $95.

CONTACT
Admissions, Chamberlain College of Nursing, 2450 Crystal Drive, Suite 319, Arlington, VA 22202. *Phone:* 703-416-7300. *Toll-free phone:* 877-751-5783.

Christendom College
Front Royal, Virginia
http://www.christendom.edu/

- **Independent Roman Catholic** comprehensive, founded 1977
- **Rural** 200-acre campus with easy access to Washington, DC
- **Endowment** $12.6 million
- **Coed** 477 undergraduate students, 100% full-time, 57% women, 43% men
- **Moderately difficult** entrance level, 87% of applicants were admitted

UNDERGRAD STUDENTS
475 full-time, 2 part-time. Students come from 45 states and territories; 4 other countries; 75% are from out of state; 6% Hispanic/Latino; 1% Asian, non-Hispanic/Latino; 92% Race/ethnicity unknown; 1% international; 1% transferred in; 90% live on campus.

Freshmen:
Admission: 323 applied, 281 admitted, 119 enrolled. ***Average high school GPA:*** 3.6. ***Test scores:*** SAT critical reading scores over 500: 98%; SAT math scores over 500: 81%; SAT writing scores over 500: 87%; SAT critical reading scores over 600: 58%; SAT math scores over 600: 34%; SAT writing scores over 600: 51%; SAT critical reading scores over 700: 27%; SAT math scores over 700: 6%; SAT writing scores over 700: 15%.
Retention: 85% of full-time freshmen returned.

FACULTY
Total: 48, 54% full-time.
Student/faculty ratio: 14:1.

ACADEMICS
Calendar: semesters. *Degrees:* associate, bachelor's, and master's.
Special study options: academic remediation for entering students, accelerated degree program, advanced placement credit, cooperative education, double majors, independent study, internships, services for LD students, study abroad, summer session for credit.
Computers: 60 computers/terminals are available on campus for general student use. Students can access the following: campus intranet, computer help desk, free student e-mail accounts. Campuswide network is available. Wireless service is available via computer centers, computer labs, learning centers, libraries, student centers.
Library: St. John the Evangelist Library. *Books:* 100,000 (physical), 1,000 (digital/electronic); *Serial titles:* 250 (physical), 1,000 (digital/electronic); *Databases:* 45. Weekly public service hours: 97.

STUDENT LIFE
Housing options: on-campus residence required through senior year; men-only, women-only. Campus housing is university owned. Freshman campus housing is guaranteed.
Activities and organizations: drama/theater group, student-run newspaper, choral group, drama, choir, Chester-Belloc Debate Society, Swing Dance Club, Shields of Rose Pro-life group.
Athletics Member USCAA. ***Intercollegiate sports:*** baseball M, basketball M/W, cross-country running M/W, rugby M, soccer M/W, softball W, volleyball W. ***Intramural sports:*** basketball M/W, equestrian sports M/W, football M/W, racquetball M/W, soccer M/W, table tennis M/W, tennis M/W, ultimate Frisbee M/W, volleyball M/W.
Campus security: 24-hour emergency response devices, late-night transport/escort service, night patrols by trained security personnel.
Student services: health clinic, personal/psychological counseling.

COSTS & FINANCIAL AID

Costs (2016–17) ***Comprehensive fee:*** $34,570 includes full-time tuition ($23,990), mandatory fees ($850), and room and board ($9730). ***Payment plan:*** installment. ***Waivers:*** employees or children of employees.

Financial Aid Of all full-time matriculated undergraduates who enrolled in 2016, 287 applied for aid, 258 were judged to have need. 150 state and other part-time jobs (averaging $2168). In 2016, 92 non-need-based awards were made. ***Average percent of need met:*** 75. ***Average financial aid package:*** $19,472. ***Average need-based loan:*** $7343. ***Average need-based gift aid:*** $12,511. ***Average non-need-based aid:*** $10,452. ***Average indebtedness upon graduation:*** $27,005.

APPLYING

Standardized Tests *Required:* SAT or ACT (for admission).

Options: electronic application, early admission, early action.

Required: essay or personal statement, high school transcript, 1 letter of recommendation. ***Required for some:*** 2 letters of recommendation. ***Recommended:*** minimum 2.0 GPA, interview.

Application deadlines: 3/1 (freshmen), 3/1 (transfers), 12/1 (early action).

Notification: 4/1 (freshmen), continuous until 4/1 (transfers), 12/15 (early action).

CONTACT

Christendom College, 134 Christendom Drive, Front Royal, VA 22630-5103. *Phone:* 540-636-2900 Ext. 1290. *Toll-free phone:* 800-877-5456.

Christopher Newport University

Newport News, Virginia

http://www.cnu.edu/

- **State-supported** comprehensive, founded 1960
- **Suburban** 260-acre campus with easy access to Virginia Beach
- **Endowment** $24.1 million
- **Coed** 4,930 undergraduate students, 98% full-time, 57% women, 43% men
- **Moderately difficult** entrance level, 62% of applicants were admitted

UNDERGRAD STUDENTS

4,856 full-time, 74 part-time. Students come from 31 states and territories; 36 other countries; 8% are from out of state; 8% Black or African American, non-Hispanic/Latino; 5% Hispanic/Latino; 3% Asian, non-Hispanic/Latino; 0.1% Native Hawaiian or other Pacific Islander, non-Hispanic/Latino; 0.4% American Indian or Alaska Native, non-Hispanic/Latino; 5% Two or more races, non-Hispanic/Latino; 5% Race/ethnicity unknown; 0.4% international; 3% transferred in; 78% live on campus.

Freshmen:

Admission: 7,532 applied, 4,682 admitted, 1,228 enrolled. ***Average high school GPA:*** 3.79. ***Test scores:*** SAT critical reading scores over 500: 91%; SAT math scores over 500: 89%; ACT scores over 18: 99%; SAT critical reading scores over 600: 43%; SAT math scores over 600: 38%; ACT scores over 24: 74%; SAT critical reading scores over 700: 6%; SAT math scores over 700: 4%; ACT scores over 30: 13%.

Retention: 86% of full-time freshmen returned.

FACULTY

Total: 456, 61% full-time, 64% with terminal degrees.

Student/faculty ratio: 15:1.

ACADEMICS

Calendar: semesters. *Degrees:* bachelor's and master's.

Special study options: advanced placement credit, double majors, honors programs, independent study, internships, off-campus study, services for LD students, student-designed majors, study abroad, summer session for credit. ***ROTC:*** Army (b).

Computers: 540 computers/terminals and 1,000 ports are available on campus for general student use. Students can access the following: campus intranet, computer help desk, free student e-mail accounts, online (class) grades, online (class) registration, online (class) schedules. Campuswide network is available. 100% of college-owned or -operated housing units are wired for high-speed Internet access. Wireless service is available via entire campus.

Library: Paul and Rosemary Trible Library. *Books:* 226,712 (physical), 567,490 (digital/electronic); *Serial titles:* 760 (physical), 64,477 (digital/electronic); *Databases:* 282. Weekly public service hours: 101; study areas open 24 hours, 5-7 days a week; students can reserve study rooms.

STUDENT LIFE

Housing options: on-campus residence required through junior year; coed. Campus housing is university owned. Freshman campus housing is guaranteed.

Activities and organizations: drama/theater group, student-run newspaper, radio and television station, choral group, marching band, Intervarsity, Alpha Delta Pi, Delta Gamma, Gamma Phi Beta, Phi Mu, national fraternities, national sororities.

Athletics Member NCAA. All Division III. ***Intercollegiate sports:*** baseball M, basketball M/W, cheerleading M/W, crew M(c)/W(c), cross-country running M/W, equestrian sports M(c)/W(c), field hockey W, football M, golf M/W, gymnastics M(c)/W(c), ice hockey M(c), lacrosse M/W, rowing M(c)/W(c), rugby M(c), sailing M(c)/W(c), skiing (cross-country) M(c)/W(c), skiing (downhill) M(c)/W(c), soccer M/W, softball W, swimming and diving M(c)/W(c), tennis M/W, track and field M/W, ultimate Frisbee M(c)/W(c), volleyball M(c)/W. ***Intramural sports:*** basketball M/W, equestrian sports M(c)/W(c), field hockey W(c), football M/W, golf M(c), lacrosse M(c)/W(c), rock climbing M(c)/W(c), sailing M(c)/W(c), sand volleyball M/W, soccer M/W, softball M/W, table tennis M(c)/W(c), tennis M/W, ultimate Frisbee M/W, volleyball M/W.

Campus security: 24-hour emergency response devices and patrols, late-night transport/escort service, controlled dormitory access, campus-based University Police, Emergency Notification System, crime prevention programs.

Student services: health clinic, personal/psychological counseling.

COSTS & FINANCIAL AID

Costs (2016–17) ***Tuition:*** state resident $7836 full-time, $327 per credit hour part-time; nonresident $19,062 full-time, $794 per credit hour part-time. Full-time tuition and fees vary according to course load. Part-time tuition and fees vary according to course load. ***Required fees:*** $5218 full-time, $217 per credit hour part-time. ***Room and board:*** $10,914; room only: $6764. Room and board charges vary according to board plan and housing facility. ***Payment plan:*** installment. ***Waivers:*** senior citizens and employees or children of employees.

Financial Aid Of all full-time matriculated undergraduates who enrolled in 2016, 3,150 applied for aid, 2,160 were judged to have need, 438 had their need fully met. 58 Federal Work-Study jobs (averaging $1822). 1,629 state and other part-time jobs (averaging $1849). In 2016, 692 non-need-based awards were made. ***Average percent of need met:*** 69. ***Average financial aid package:*** $9195. ***Average need-based loan:*** $4279. ***Average need-based gift aid:*** $6731. ***Average non-need-based aid:*** $2460. ***Average indebtedness upon graduation:*** $30,451.

APPLYING

Standardized Tests *Required for some:* SAT or ACT (for admission).

Options: electronic application, early admission, early decision, early action, deferred entrance.

Application fee: $65.

Required: essay or personal statement, high school transcript. ***Required for some:*** interview. ***Recommended:*** minimum 3.5 GPA, 2 letters of recommendation.

Application deadlines: 2/1 (freshmen), 3/1 (transfers), 12/1 (early action).

Early decision deadline: 11/15.

Notification: 3/15 (freshmen), 4/15 (transfers), 12/15 (early decision), 1/15 (early action).

CONTACT

Mr. Rob J. Lange III, Dean of Admission, Christopher Newport University, Office of Admission, 1 Avenue of the Arts, Newport News, VA 23606-3072. *Phone:* 757-594-7015. *Toll-free phone:* 800-333-4268. *Fax:* 757-594-7333. *E-mail:* admit@cnu.edu.

The College of William and Mary

Williamsburg, Virginia

http://www.wm.edu/

- **State-supported** university, founded 1693
- **Small-town** 1200-acre campus with easy access to Richmond
- **Endowment** $803.7 million
- **Coed** 6,276 undergraduate students, 99% full-time, 58% women, 42% men
- **Most difficult** entrance level, 37% of applicants were admitted

UNDERGRAD STUDENTS
6,209 full-time, 67 part-time. Students come from 55 states and territories; 67 other countries; 30% are from out of state; 7% Black or African American, non-Hispanic/Latino; 9% Hispanic/Latino; 8% Asian, non-Hispanic/Latino; 0.2% American Indian or Alaska Native, non-Hispanic/Latino; 5% Two or more races, non-Hispanic/Latino; 6% Race/ethnicity unknown; 6% international; 3% transferred in; 74% live on campus.

Freshmen:
Admission: 14,382 applied, 5,253 admitted, 1,507 enrolled. ***Average high school GPA:*** 4.2. ***Test scores:*** SAT critical reading scores over 500: 99%; SAT math scores over 500: 99%; SAT writing scores over 500: 97%; ACT scores over 18: 100%; SAT critical reading scores over 600: 87%; SAT math scores over 600: 84%; SAT writing scores over 600: 82%; ACT scores over 24: 96%; SAT critical reading scores over 700: 46%; SAT math scores over 700: 42%; SAT writing scores over 700: 37%; ACT scores over 30: 64%.

Retention: 95% of full-time freshmen returned.

ACADEMICS
Calendar: semesters. *Degrees:* bachelor's, master's, doctoral, post-master's, and postbachelor's certificates.

Special study options: accelerated degree program, advanced placement credit, distance learning, double majors, honors programs, independent study, internships, off-campus study, part-time degree program, services for LD students, student-designed majors, study abroad, summer session for credit. ***ROTC:*** Army (b).

Unusual degree programs: 3-2 engineering with Columbia University; elementary education, secondary education, special education, chemistry.

Computers: 400 computers/terminals and 8,000 ports are available on campus for general student use. Students can access the following: campus intranet, computer help desk, free student e-mail accounts, online (class) grades, online (class) registration, online (class) schedules. Campuswide network is available. 100% of college-owned or -operated housing units are wired for high-speed Internet access. Wireless service is available via entire campus.

Library: Earl Gregg Swem Library plus 7 others. *Books:* 1.3 million (physical), 1.6 million (digital/electronic); *Serial titles:* 37,434 (physical), 143,090 (digital/electronic); *Databases:* 505. Weekly public service hours: 107; study areas open 24 hours, 5-7 days a week; students can reserve study rooms.

STUDENT LIFE
Housing options: on-campus residence required for freshman year; coed, special housing for students with disabilities. Campus housing is university owned and leased by the school. Freshman campus housing is guaranteed.

Activities and organizations: drama/theater group, student-run newspaper, radio and television station, choral group, Alma Mater Productions, Student Assembly, Residence Hall Association, Alpha Phi Omega, International Relations Club, national fraternities, national sororities.

Athletics Member NCAA. All Division I except football (Division I-AA). ***Intercollegiate sports:*** baseball M(s), basketball M(s)/W(s), cross-country running M(s)/W(s), field hockey W(s), golf M(s)/W(s), gymnastics M(s)/W(s), lacrosse W(s), soccer M(s)/W(s), swimming and diving M/W, tennis M(s)/W(s), track and field M(s)/W(s), volleyball W(s). ***Intramural sports:*** badminton M(c)/W(c), baseball M(c), basketball M/W, bowling M/W, cheerleading M(c)/W(c), crew M(c)/W(c), cross-country running M(c)/W(c), equestrian sports M(c)/W(c), fencing M(c)/W(c), field hockey M(c)/W(c), football M/W, golf M(c)/W(c), gymnastics M(c)/W(c), ice hockey M(c), lacrosse M(c)/W(c), racquetball M(c)/W(c), rock climbing M(c)/W(c), rugby M(c)/W(c), sailing M(c)/W(c), soccer M/W, softball M/W, swimming and diving M(c)/W(c), table tennis M(c)/W(c), tennis M(c)/W(c), ultimate Frisbee M(c)/W(c), volleyball M/W, water polo M(c)/W(c), weight lifting M/W, wrestling M(c).

Campus security: 24-hour emergency response devices and patrols, late-night transport/escort service, controlled dormitory access, state-certified law enforcement officers.

Student services: health clinic, personal/psychological counseling, legal services.

COSTS & FINANCIAL AID
Costs (2016–17) ***Tuition:*** state resident $15,674 full-time, $400 per credit hour part-time; nonresident $36,158 full-time, $1150 per credit hour part-time. ***Required fees:*** $5560 full-time. ***Room and board:*** $11,382; room only: $6944. Room and board charges vary according to board plan and housing facility. ***Payment plan:*** installment. ***Waivers:*** senior citizens and employees or children of employees.

Financial Aid Of all full-time matriculated undergraduates who enrolled in 2015, 3,090 applied for aid, 2,141 were judged to have need, 481 had their need fully met. 297 Federal Work-Study jobs (averaging $990). In 2015, 406 non-need-based awards were made. ***Average percent of need met:*** 80. ***Average financial aid package:*** $21,243. ***Average need-based loan:*** $3946. ***Average need-based gift aid:*** $15,892. ***Average non-need-based aid:*** $6288. ***Average indebtedness upon graduation:*** $26,400.

APPLYING
Standardized Tests *Required:* SAT or ACT (for admission).

Options: electronic application, early admission, early decision, deferred entrance.

Application fee: $70.

Required: essay or personal statement, high school transcript, 1 letter of recommendation. ***Recommended:*** 2 letters of recommendation.

Application deadlines: 1/1 (freshmen), 3/1 (transfers).

Early decision deadline: 11/1.

Notification: 4/1 (freshmen), 5/1 (transfers), 12/1 (early decision).

CONTACT
Ms. Deborah Basket, Associate Dean of Admission, The College of William and Mary, PO Box 8795, Williamsburg, VA 23187-8795. *Phone:* 757-221-4223. *Fax:* 757-221-1242. *E-mail:* admission@wm.edu.

Culinary Institute of Virginia

Norfolk, Virginia

http://www.chefva.com/

CONTACT
Director of Admissions, Culinary Institute of Virginia, 2428 Almeda Avenue, Suite 316, Norfolk, VA 23513. *Phone:* 757-858-2433. *Toll-free phone:* 866-619-CHEF. *E-mail:* hsadmissions@chefva.com.

DeVry University–Arlington Campus

Arlington, Virginia

http://www.devry.edu/

- **Proprietary** comprehensive, founded 2001, part of DeVry University
- **Coed**
- **Minimally difficult** entrance level

FACULTY
Student/faculty ratio: 15:1.

ACADEMICS
Calendar: semesters. *Degrees:* associate, bachelor's, master's, and postbachelor's certificates.

Library: Learning Resource Center.

STUDENT LIFE
Housing options: college housing not available.

COSTS & FINANCIAL AID
Costs (2016–17) ***Tuition:*** $17,052 full-time, $609 per credit hour part-time. ***Required fees:*** $460 full-time.

Financial Aid Of all full-time matriculated undergraduates who enrolled in 2007, 175 applied for aid, 164 were judged to have need, 9 had their need fully met. In 2007, 21 non-need-based awards were made. ***Average***

percent of need met: 38. ***Average financial aid package:*** $11,581. ***Average need-based loan:*** $7979. ***Average need-based gift aid:*** $5610. ***Average non-need-based aid:*** $18,172. ***Average indebtedness upon graduation:*** $12,479.

APPLYING
Options: deferred entrance.
Application fee: $30.
Required: high school transcript, interview.

CONTACT
DeVry University–Arlington Campus, 2450 Crystal Drive, Arlington, VA 22202. *Phone:* 703-414-4000. *Toll-free phone:* 866-338-7934.

DeVry University–Chesapeake Campus

Chesapeake, Virginia

http://www.devry.edu/

CONTACT
Admissions Office, DeVry University–Chesapeake Campus, 1317 Executive Boulevard, Suite 100, Chesapeake, VA 23320-3671. *Phone:* 757-382-5680. *Toll-free phone:* 866-338-7934.

Eastern Mennonite University

Harrisonburg, Virginia

http://www.emu.edu/

- **Independent Mennonite** comprehensive, founded 1917
- **Small-town** 93-acre campus
- **Endowment** $24.2 million
- **Coed** 1,259 undergraduate students, 86% full-time, 65% women, 35% men
- **Moderately difficult** entrance level, 61% of applicants were admitted

UNDERGRAD STUDENTS
1,082 full-time, 177 part-time. Students come from 33 states and territories; 32 other countries; 44% are from out of state; 9% Black or African American, non-Hispanic/Latino; 8% Hispanic/Latino; 2% Asian, non-Hispanic/Latino; 0.3% American Indian or Alaska Native, non-Hispanic/Latino; 3% Two or more races, non-Hispanic/Latino; 3% Race/ethnicity unknown; 3% international; 12% transferred in; 44% live on campus.

Freshmen:
Admission: 1,215 applied, 743 admitted, 227 enrolled. ***Average high school GPA:*** 3.56. ***Test scores:*** SAT critical reading scores over 500: 51%; SAT math scores over 500: 54%; ACT scores over 18: 90%; SAT critical reading scores over 600: 23%; SAT math scores over 600: 18%; ACT scores over 24: 53%; SAT critical reading scores over 700: 6%; SAT math scores over 700: 7%; ACT scores over 30: 18%.
Retention: 74% of full-time freshmen returned.

FACULTY
Total: 222, 50% full-time.
Student/faculty ratio: 10:1.

ACADEMICS
Calendar: semesters. *Degrees:* certificates, associate, bachelor's, master's, and postbachelor's certificates.
Special study options: adult/continuing education programs, advanced placement credit, distance learning, double majors, English as a second language, honors programs, independent study, internships, off-campus study, part-time degree program, services for LD students, study abroad, summer session for credit.
Unusual degree programs: 3-2 engineering with The Catholic University of America.
Computers: 154 computers/terminals are available on campus for general student use. Students can access the following: campus intranet, computer help desk, free student e-mail accounts, online (class) grades, online (class) registration, online (class) schedules. Campuswide network is available. 98% of college-owned or -operated housing units are wired for high-speed Internet access. Wireless service is available via classrooms, dorm rooms, learning centers, libraries, student centers.
Library: Sadie Hartzler Library. *Books:* 172,730 (physical), 168,108 (digital/electronic); *Serial titles:* 70,933 (physical), 27,384 (digital/electronic); *Databases:* 93. Weekly public service hours: 92.

STUDENT LIFE
Housing options: on-campus residence required through junior year; coed, cooperative, special housing for students with disabilities. Campus housing is university owned. Freshman campus housing is guaranteed.
Activities and organizations: drama/theater group, student-run newspaper, choral group, Young People's Christian Association, Student Government Association, Student Education Association, Creation Care Council, Black Student Union.
Athletics Member NCAA. All Division III. ***Intercollegiate sports:*** baseball M, basketball M/W, cross-country running M/W, field hockey W, golf M/W, soccer M/W, softball W, track and field M/W, volleyball M/W. ***Intramural sports:*** basketball M/W, football M/W, golf M/W, lacrosse M(c), rock climbing M/W, soccer M/W, softball M/W, table tennis M/W, tennis M/W, volleyball M/W.
Campus security: 24-hour emergency response devices, controlled dormitory access, night watchman.
Student services: health clinic, personal/psychological counseling.

COSTS & FINANCIAL AID
Costs (2016–17) ***Comprehensive fee:*** $44,860 includes full-time tuition ($34,060), mandatory fees ($140), and room and board ($10,660). Part-time tuition: $1350 per credit hour. Part-time tuition and fees vary according to course load. ***Required fees:*** $6 per credit hour part-time. ***Room and board:*** Room and board charges vary according to board plan and housing facility. ***Payment plan:*** installment. ***Waivers:*** employees or children of employees.
Financial Aid Of all full-time matriculated undergraduates who enrolled in 2003, 735 applied for aid, 652 were judged to have need, 246 had their need fully met. 326 Federal Work-Study jobs (averaging $1787). In 2003, 82 non-need-based awards were made. ***Average percent of need met:*** 87. ***Average financial aid package:*** $15,530. ***Average need-based loan:*** $5665. ***Average need-based gift aid:*** $5520. ***Average non-need-based aid:*** $7765. ***Average indebtedness upon graduation:*** $18,208.

APPLYING
Standardized Tests *Required:* SAT or ACT (for admission).
Options: electronic application, deferred entrance.
Application fee: $25.
Required: high school transcript, minimum 2.2 GPA, Community Lifestyle Commitment. ***Required for some:*** 2 letters of recommendation. ***Recommended:*** interview.
Application deadlines: rolling (freshmen), rolling (transfers).
Notification: continuous (freshmen), continuous (transfers).

CONTACT
Matthew Ruth, Director of Admissions, Eastern Mennonite University, 1200 Park Road, Harrisonburg, VA 22802. *Phone:* 540-432-4118. *Toll-free phone:* 800-368-2665. *Fax:* 540-432-4444. *E-mail:* admiss@emu.edu.

ECPI University

Virginia Beach, Virginia

http://www.ecpi.edu/

CONTACT
Mrs. Bernadette Rozman Bellas, Vice President, Accreditation and Regulatory Affairs, ECPI University, 5555 Greenwich Road, Suite 100, Virginia Beach, VA 23462. *Phone:* 757-671-7171. *Toll-free phone:* 844-611-0766. *Fax:* 757-671-8661. *E-mail:* rballance@ecpi.edu.

Emory & Henry College

Emory, Virginia

http://www.ehc.edu/

- **Independent United Methodist** comprehensive, founded 1836
- **Rural** 330-acre campus
- **Endowment** $81.8 million
- **Coed** 1,024 undergraduate students, 98% full-time, 51% women, 49% men
- 70% of applicants were admitted

UNDERGRAD STUDENTS

1,001 full-time, 23 part-time. 58% are from out of state; 9% Black or African American, non-Hispanic/Latino; 5% Hispanic/Latino; 1% Asian, non-Hispanic/Latino; 0.1% Native Hawaiian or other Pacific Islander, non-Hispanic/Latino; 0.5% American Indian or Alaska Native, non-Hispanic/Latino; 2% Two or more races, non-Hispanic/Latino; 6% Race/ethnicity unknown; 1% international; 6% transferred in; 78% live on campus.

Freshmen:

Admission: 1,455 applied, 1,017 admitted, 284 enrolled. ***Average high school GPA:*** 3.58. ***Test scores:*** SAT critical reading scores over 500: 54%; SAT math scores over 500: 46%; SAT writing scores over 500: 34%; ACT scores over 18: 90%; SAT critical reading scores over 600: 14%; SAT math scores over 600: 8%; SAT writing scores over 600: 9%; ACT scores over 24: 35%; SAT critical reading scores over 700: 2%; ACT scores over 30: 5%.

Retention: 70% of full-time freshmen returned.

FACULTY

Total: 148, 57% full-time, 63% with terminal degrees.

Student/faculty ratio: 11:1.

ACADEMICS

Calendar: semesters. *Degrees:* bachelor's, master's, and doctoral.

Special study options: academic remediation for entering students, advanced placement credit, cooperative education, double majors, honors programs, independent study, internships, part-time degree program, services for LD students, student-designed majors, study abroad, summer session for credit.

Computers: 200 computers/terminals are available on campus for general student use. Students can access the following: campus intranet, computer help desk, free student e-mail accounts, online (class) grades, online (class) registration, online (class) schedules. Campuswide network is available. 100% of college-owned or -operated housing units are wired for high-speed Internet access. Wireless service is available via entire campus.

Library: Kelly Library plus 1 other. *Books:* 225,739 (physical), 126,654 (digital/electronic); *Serial titles:* 728 (physical), 113,345 (digital/electronic); *Databases:* 105. Weekly public service hours: 90; students can reserve study rooms.

STUDENT LIFE

Housing options: on-campus residence required through junior year; coed, men-only, women-only, special housing for students with disabilities. Campus housing is university owned. Freshman campus housing is guaranteed.

Activities and organizations: drama/theater group, student-run newspaper, radio and television station, choral group, marching band, E&H Outdoor Program, Alpha Psi Omega Honors Fraternity, Alpha Phi Omega Honors Fraternity, Blue Key/ Cardinal Key Honors Society, The Emory Activities Board.

Athletics Member NCAA. All Division III. ***Intercollegiate sports:*** baseball M, basketball M/W, cheerleading M(c)/W(c), cross-country running M/W, equestrian sports M/W, football M, golf M/W, soccer M/W, softball W, swimming and diving W, tennis M/W, volleyball W. ***Intramural sports:*** basketball M/W, football M/W, racquetball M/W, rugby M(c)/W(c), sand volleyball M/W, soccer M/W, table tennis M/W, tennis M/W, ultimate Frisbee M/W, volleyball M/W.

Campus security: 24-hour emergency response devices and patrols, late-night transport/escort service, controlled dormitory access.

Student services: health clinic, personal/psychological counseling.

COSTS & FINANCIAL AID

Costs (2016–17) ***Comprehensive fee:*** $44,900 includes full-time tuition ($33,500), mandatory fees ($200), and room and board ($11,200). Full-

time tuition and fees vary according to degree level, location, and student level. Part-time tuition: $1250 per credit. Part-time tuition and fees vary according to course load, degree level, location, and student level. No tuition increase for student's term of enrollment. ***College room only:*** $6000. Room and board charges vary according to board plan and housing facility. ***Payment plans:*** installment, deferred payment. ***Waivers:*** employees or children of employees.

Financial Aid Of all full-time matriculated undergraduates who enrolled in 2016, 934 applied for aid, 835 were judged to have need, 193 had their need fully met. 149 Federal Work-Study jobs (averaging $1774). 147 state and other part-time jobs (averaging $1835). In 2016, 151 non-need-based awards were made. ***Average percent of need met:*** 84. ***Average financial aid package:*** $29,365. ***Average need-based loan:*** $3296. ***Average need-based gift aid:*** $25,207. ***Average non-need-based aid:*** $16,857. ***Average indebtedness upon graduation:*** $30,514.

APPLYING

Standardized Tests *Required:* SAT or ACT (for admission).

Options: electronic application, early decision.

Required: high school transcript. ***Recommended:*** essay or personal statement, interview.

Application deadlines: rolling (freshmen), rolling (transfers).

Early decision deadline: 11/15 (for plan 1), 1/15 (for plan 2).

Notification: continuous (freshmen), continuous (transfers), 12/15 (early decision).

CONTACT

Mr. Matt Crisman, Director of Admissions, Emory & Henry College, PO Box 947, Emory, VA 24327-0947. *Phone:* 276-944-6491. *Toll-free phone:* 800-848-5493. *E-mail:* mcrisman@ehc.edu.

See previous page for display ad and page 1350 for the College Close-Up.

Ferrum College

Ferrum, Virginia

http://www.ferrum.edu/

CONTACT

Ms. Gilda Q. Woods, Associate Vice President for Enrollment Management and Dean of Admissions, Ferrum College, Spilman-Daniel House, PO Box 1000, Ferrum, VA 24088-9001. *Phone:* 540-365-4290. *Toll-free phone:* 800-868-9797. *Fax:* 540-365-4266. *E-mail:* admissions@ferrum.edu.

George Mason University

Fairfax, Virginia

http://www.gmu.edu/

- **State-supported** university, founded 1957
- **Suburban** 817-acre campus with easy access to Washington, DC
- **Endowment** $72.2 million
- **Coed**

FACULTY

Student/faculty ratio: 16:1.

ACADEMICS

Calendar: semesters. *Degrees:* bachelor's, master's, doctoral, post-master's, and postbachelor's certificates.

Library: Fenwick Library plus 3 others. *Books:* 1.3 million (physical), 1.5 million (digital/electronic); *Serial titles:* 1,244 (physical), 102,222 (digital/electronic); *Databases:* 793. Weekly public service hours: 87; study areas open 24 hours, 5-7 days a week; students can reserve study rooms.

STUDENT LIFE

Housing options: coed, special housing for students with disabilities. Campus housing is university owned and leased by the school. Freshman campus housing is guaranteed.

Activities and organizations: drama/theater group, student-run newspaper, radio and television station, choral group, Catholic Campus Ministry, Muslim Student Association, National Society of Collegiate Scholars, Campus Crusade for Christ, The Gathering, national fraternities, national sororities.

Athletics Member NCAA. All Division I.

Campus security: 24-hour emergency response devices and patrols, student patrols, late-night transport/escort service, controlled dormitory access.

Student services: health clinic, personal/psychological counseling, women's center.

COSTS & FINANCIAL AID

Costs (2016–17) ***Tuition:*** state resident $8204 full-time, $342 per credit hour part-time; nonresident $29,486 full-time, $1229 per credit hour part-time. Full-time tuition and fees vary according to course load. Part-time tuition and fees vary according to course load. ***Required fees:*** $3096 full-time, $129 per credit hour part-time. ***Room and board:*** $10,730; room only: $6400. Room and board charges vary according to board plan and housing facility. ***Payment plans:*** installment, deferred payment.

Financial Aid Of all full-time matriculated undergraduates who enrolled in 2015, 12,561 applied for aid, 10,220 were judged to have need, 505 had their need fully met. 499 Federal Work-Study jobs (averaging $2162). In 2015, 1078 non-need-based awards were made. ***Average percent of need met:*** 57. ***Average financial aid package:*** $12,890. ***Average need-based loan:*** $4450. ***Average need-based gift aid:*** $6413. ***Average non-need-based aid:*** $4513. ***Average indebtedness upon graduation:*** $30,132.

APPLYING

Standardized Tests *Required for some:* SAT or ACT (for admission).

Required: high school transcript. ***Required for some:*** audition for dance and music, portfolio for art and visual technology and computer game design, interview and audition or portfolio for theater. ***Recommended:*** essay or personal statement, 3 letters of recommendation.

CONTACT

Matthew Boyce, Director, Undergraduate Admissions, George Mason University, 4400 University Drive, MSN 3A4, Fairfax, VA 22030-4444. *Phone:* 703-993-5304. *Toll-free phone:* 888-627-6612. *Fax:* 703-993-2392. *E-mail:* mboyce3@gmu.edu.

Hampden-Sydney College

Hampden-Sydney, Virginia

http://www.hsc.edu/

- **Independent** 4-year, founded 1776, affiliated with Presbyterian Church (U.S.A.)
- **Rural** 1340-acre campus with easy access to Richmond, Lynchburg, Charlottesville
- **Endowment** $145.4 million
- **Men only** 1,027 undergraduate students, 100% full-time
- **Moderately difficult** entrance level, 56% of applicants were admitted

UNDERGRAD STUDENTS

1,027 full-time. Students come from 27 states and territories; 9 other countries; 30% are from out of state; 5% Black or African American, non-Hispanic/Latino; 4% Hispanic/Latino; 0.9% Asian, non-Hispanic/Latino; 0.2% Native Hawaiian or other Pacific Islander, non-Hispanic/Latino; 0.4% American Indian or Alaska Native, non-Hispanic/Latino; 4% Two or more races, non-Hispanic/Latino; 2% Race/ethnicity unknown; 0.6% international; 1% transferred in; 95% live on campus.

Freshmen:

Admission: 3,403 applied, 1,892 admitted, 283 enrolled. ***Average high school GPA:*** 3.56. ***Test scores:*** SAT critical reading scores over 500: 76%; SAT math scores over 500: 78%; SAT writing scores over 500: 62%; ACT scores over 18: 96%; SAT critical reading scores over 600: 30%; SAT math scores over 600: 32%; SAT writing scores over 600: 18%; ACT scores over 24: 56%; SAT critical reading scores over 700: 9%; SAT math scores over 700: 5%; SAT writing scores over 700: 1%; ACT scores over 30: 15%.

Retention: 83% of full-time freshmen returned.

FACULTY

Total: 110, 79% full-time, 86% with terminal degrees.

Student/faculty ratio: 10:1.

ACADEMICS

Calendar: semesters. *Degree:* bachelor's.

Special study options: academic remediation for entering students, advanced placement credit, cooperative education, double majors, honors programs, independent study, internships, off-campus study, study abroad, summer session for credit. ***ROTC:*** Army (c).

Unusual degree programs: 3-2 engineering with University of Virginia, Old Dominion University.

Computers: 200 computers/terminals are available on campus for general student use. Students can access the following: campus intranet, computer help desk, free student e-mail accounts, online (class) grades, online (class) registration, online (class) schedules. Campuswide network is available. 100% of college-owned or -operated housing units are wired for high-speed Internet access. Wireless service is available via entire campus.

Library: Walter M. Bortz III Library. *Books:* 274,361 (physical), 141,894 (digital/electronic); *Serial titles:* 52 (physical), 113,070 (digital/electronic); *Databases:* 100. Weekly public service hours: 99; students can reserve study rooms.

STUDENT LIFE

Housing options: on-campus residence required through senior year; men-only, special housing for students with disabilities. Campus housing is university owned. Freshman campus housing is guaranteed.

Activities and organizations: drama/theater group, student-run newspaper, radio station, choral group, Republican Society, Pre-Health Society, Outdoors Club, Tiger Athletic Club, Pre-Law Society, national fraternities.

Athletics Member NCAA. All Division III. ***Intercollegiate sports:*** baseball M, basketball M, crew M(c), cross-country running M, fencing M(c), football M, golf M, lacrosse M, riflery M(c), rugby M(c), soccer M, swimming and diving M, tennis M, ultimate Frisbee M(c), wrestling M(c). ***Intramural sports:*** archery M(c), basketball M, fencing M(c), football M, lacrosse M(c), racquetball M(c), riflery M(c), soccer M, softball M, swimming and diving M(c), volleyball M, water polo M(c), wrestling M(c).

Campus security: 24-hour emergency response devices and patrols.

Student services: health clinic, personal/psychological counseling.

COSTS & FINANCIAL AID

Costs (2017–18) ***Comprehensive fee:*** $57,360 includes full-time tuition ($42,470), mandatory fees ($1470), and room and board ($13,420). Full-time tuition and fees vary according to course load and student level. Part-time tuition: $1330 per credit hour. Part-time tuition and fees vary according to course load and student level. ***College room only:*** $6012. Room and board charges vary according to board plan and housing facility. ***Payment plan:*** installment. ***Waivers:*** employees or children of employees.

Financial Aid Of all full-time matriculated undergraduates who enrolled in 2016, 754 applied for aid, 659 were judged to have need, 147 had their need fully met. 227 Federal Work-Study jobs (averaging $1272). In 2016, 350 non-need-based awards were made. ***Average percent of need met:*** 79. ***Average financial aid package:*** $32,430. ***Average need-based loan:*** $4837. ***Average need-based gift aid:*** $28,432. ***Average non-need-based aid:*** $17,333. ***Average indebtedness upon graduation:*** $34,344.

APPLYING

Standardized Tests *Required:* SAT or ACT (for admission). *Recommended:* SAT and SAT Subject Tests or ACT (for admission).

Options: electronic application, early admission, early decision, early action.

Application fee: $30.

Required: essay or personal statement, high school transcript, 2 letters of recommendation. ***Recommended:*** interview.

Application deadlines: 3/1 (freshmen), 7/1 (transfers), 1/15 (early action).

Early decision deadline: 11/1.

Notification: 4/15 (freshmen), 7/31 (transfers), 12/1 (early decision), 2/15 (early action).

CONTACT

Dean Anita Garland, Dean of Admissions, Hampden-Sydney College, PO Box 667, Hampden-Sydney, VA 23943-0667. *Phone:* 434-223-6120. *Toll-free phone:* 800-755-0733. *Fax:* 434-223-6346. *E-mail:* hsapp@hsc.edu.

Hampton University

Hampton, Virginia

http://www.hamptonu.edu/

- **Independent** comprehensive, founded 1868
- **Urban** 314-acre campus with easy access to Norfolk
- **Coed** 3,836 undergraduate students, 95% full-time, 67% women, 33% men
- **Moderately difficult** entrance level, 65% of applicants were admitted

UNDERGRAD STUDENTS

3,652 full-time, 184 part-time. Students come from 44 states and territories; 26 other countries; 71% are from out of state; 96% Black or African American, non-Hispanic/Latino; 1% Hispanic/Latino; 0.2% Asian, non-Hispanic/Latino; 0.1% Native Hawaiian or other Pacific Islander, non-Hispanic/Latino; 0.3% American Indian or Alaska Native, non-Hispanic/Latino; 0.8% international; 4% transferred in; 65% live on campus.

Freshmen:

Admission: 11,165 applied, 7,237 admitted, 1,278 enrolled. ***Average high school GPA:*** 3.3. ***Test scores:*** SAT critical reading scores over 500: 53%; SAT math scores over 500: 49%; ACT scores over 18: 79%; SAT critical reading scores over 600: 8%; SAT math scores over 600: 8%; ACT scores over 24: 22%; SAT critical reading scores over 700: 1%; SAT math scores over 700: 1%; ACT scores over 30: 1%.

Retention: 80% of full-time freshmen returned.

FACULTY

Total: 378, 80% full-time, 65% with terminal degrees.

Student/faculty ratio: 13:1.

ACADEMICS

Calendar: semesters. *Degrees:* certificates, associate, bachelor's, master's, doctoral, and post-master's certificates.

Special study options: academic remediation for entering students, accelerated degree program, adult/continuing education programs, advanced placement credit, cooperative education, distance learning, double majors, English as a second language, honors programs, independent study, internships, off-campus study, part-time degree program, services for LD students, study abroad, summer session for credit. ***ROTC:*** Army (b), Navy (b).

Computers: 1,500 computers/terminals are available on campus for general student use. Students can access the following: campus intranet, computer help desk, free student e-mail accounts, online (class) grades, online (class) registration, online (class) schedules, learning management system. Campuswide network is available. 100% of college-owned or -operated housing units are wired for high-speed Internet access. Wireless service is available via entire campus.

Library: William R. and Norma B. Harvey Library plus 4 others. *Books:* 307,143 (physical), 91,991 (digital/electronic); *Serial titles:* 8,240 (physical); *Databases:* 115. Study areas open 24 hours, 5-7 days a week; students can reserve study rooms.

STUDENT LIFE

Housing options: on-campus residence required for freshman year; coed, men-only, women-only, special housing for students with disabilities. Campus housing is university owned. Freshman applicants given priority for college housing.

Activities and organizations: drama/theater group, student-run newspaper, radio station, choral group, marching band, Student Government, student leaders, Student Union Board, student recruitment team, resident assistants, national fraternities, national sororities.

Athletics Member NCAA. All Division I. ***Intercollegiate sports:*** basketball M(s)/W(s), bowling W(s), cheerleading W, cross-country running M(s)/W(s), football M(s), golf M(s)/W(s), lacrosse M(s), sailing M(s)/W(s), soccer W, softball W(s), tennis M(s)/W(s), track and field M(s)/W(s), volleyball W(s). ***Intramural sports:*** badminton M/W, basketball M/W, bowling W, football M, lacrosse M/W, soccer M, softball W, swimming and diving M/W, table tennis M/W, volleyball W.

Campus security: 24-hour emergency response devices and patrols.

Student services: health clinic, personal/psychological counseling, women's center.

COSTS & FINANCIAL AID

Costs (2016–17) ***Comprehensive fee:*** $34,926 includes full-time tuition ($21,552), mandatory fees ($2690), and room and board ($10,684). Full-time tuition and fees vary according to course load, degree level, location, program, and reciprocity agreements. Part-time tuition: $548 per credit hour. Part-time tuition and fees vary according to class time, course load, location, and reciprocity agreements. ***College room only:*** $5556. Room and board charges vary according to board plan, housing facility, and location. ***Payment plans:*** installment, deferred payment. ***Waivers:*** employees or children of employees.

Financial Aid Of all full-time matriculated undergraduates who enrolled in 2015, 2,131 applied for aid, 1,675 were judged to have need, 659 had their need fully met. 226 Federal Work-Study jobs (averaging $1452). 44 state and other part-time jobs (averaging $1769). In 2015, 607 non-need-based awards were made. ***Average percent of need met:*** 41. ***Average financial aid package:*** $5613. ***Average need-based loan:*** $5707. ***Average need-based gift aid:*** $5145. ***Average non-need-based aid:*** $10,956. ***Average indebtedness upon graduation:*** $34,367. ***Financial aid deadline:*** 4/15.

APPLYING

Standardized Tests *Required for some:* SAT or ACT (for admission).

Options: electronic application, early admission, early action, deferred entrance.

Application fee: $35.

Required: essay or personal statement, high school transcript, minimum 2.5 GPA, 1 letter of recommendation. ***Required for some:*** interview, audition for music.

Application deadlines: 3/1 (freshmen), 11/1 (early action).

Notification: 12/15 (early action).

CONTACT

Mr. Derrick Boone, Director, Freshman Studies, Hampton University, 204 Student Center, Hampton University, Hampton, VA 23668. *Phone:* 757-727-5901. *Toll-free phone:* 800-624-3328. *Fax:* 757-727-5095. *E-mail:* derrick.boone@hamptonu.edu.

Hollins University

Roanoke, Virginia

http://www.hollins.edu/

- **Independent** comprehensive, founded 1842
- **Suburban** 475-acre campus
- **Endowment** $160.8 million
- **Undergraduate: women only; graduate: coed** 654 undergraduate students, 98% full-time, 100% women, 0% men
- **Moderately difficult** entrance level, 60% of applicants were admitted

UNDERGRAD STUDENTS

644 full-time, 10 part-time. Students come from 38 states and territories; 21 other countries; 54% are from out of state; 12% Black or African American, non-Hispanic/Latino; 7% Hispanic/Latino; 2% Asian, non-Hispanic/Latino; 0.2% Native Hawaiian or other Pacific Islander, non-Hispanic/Latino; 1% American Indian or Alaska Native, non-Hispanic/Latino; 5% Two or more races, non-Hispanic/Latino; 4% Race/ethnicity unknown; 5% international; 3% transferred in; 84% live on campus.

Freshmen:

Admission: 2,901 applied, 1,737 admitted, 224 enrolled. ***Average high school GPA:*** 3.7. ***Test scores:*** SAT critical reading scores over 500: 87%; SAT math scores over 500: 70%; SAT writing scores over 500: 73%; ACT scores over 18: 99%; SAT critical reading scores over 600: 43%; SAT math scores over 600: 24%; SAT writing scores over 600: 27%; ACT scores over 24: 68%; SAT critical reading scores over 700: 11%; SAT math scores over 700: 1%; SAT writing scores over 700: 6%; ACT scores over 30: 14%.

Retention: 69% of full-time freshmen returned.

FACULTY

Total: 96, 73% full-time, 86% with terminal degrees.

Student/faculty ratio: 9:1.

ACADEMICS

Calendar: 4-1-4. *Degrees:* bachelor's, master's, and post-master's certificates.

Special study options: accelerated degree program, adult/continuing education programs, advanced placement credit, double majors, honors programs, independent study, internships, off-campus study, part-time degree program, services for LD students, student-designed majors, study abroad.

Computers: 120 computers/terminals and 3,000 ports are available on campus for general student use. Students can access the following: campus intranet, computer help desk, free student e-mail accounts, online (class) grades, online (class) registration, online (class) schedules. Campuswide network is available. 100% of college-owned or -operated housing units are wired for high-speed Internet access. Wireless service is available via entire campus.

Library: Wyndham Robertson Library plus 1 other. *Books:* 315,214 (physical), 56,164 (digital/electronic); *Serial titles:* 682 (physical), 49,619 (digital/electronic); *Databases:* 131. Weekly public service hours: 94.

STUDENT LIFE

Housing options: on-campus residence required through senior year; women-only, special housing for students with disabilities. Campus housing is university owned. Freshman campus housing is guaranteed.

Activities and organizations: drama/theater group, choral group, Hollins Activity Board, Black Student Alliance, Hollins Repertory Dance Club, Arts Association, Voices for Unity.

Athletics Member NCAA. All Division III. ***Intercollegiate sports:*** basketball W, cross-country running W, equestrian sports W, fencing W(c), golf W, lacrosse W, soccer W, swimming and diving W, tennis W, volleyball W.

Campus security: 24-hour emergency response devices and patrols, late-night transport/escort service, controlled dormitory access, emergency call boxes.

Student services: health clinic, personal/psychological counseling, women's center.

COSTS & FINANCIAL AID

Costs (2016–17) ***Comprehensive fee:*** $49,635 includes full-time tuition ($36,200), mandatory fees ($635), and room and board ($12,800). Part-time tuition: $1132 per credit hour. Part-time tuition and fees vary according to course load. ***Required fees:*** $323 per year part-time. ***Payment plans:*** tuition prepayment, installment. ***Waivers:*** employees or children of employees.

Financial Aid Of all full-time matriculated undergraduates who enrolled in 2016, 568 applied for aid, 525 were judged to have need, 120 had their need fully met. In 2016, 112 non-need-based awards were made. ***Average percent of need met:*** 84. ***Average financial aid package:*** $35,508. ***Average need-based loan:*** $5026. ***Average need-based gift aid:*** $29,001. ***Average non-need-based aid:*** $26,663. ***Average indebtedness upon graduation:*** $34,414.

APPLYING

Standardized Tests *Required:* SAT or ACT (for admission).

Options: electronic application, early admission, early decision, early action, deferred entrance.

Required: essay or personal statement, high school transcript, 2 letters of recommendation. ***Recommended:*** interview.

Application deadlines: rolling (freshmen), 11/15 (early action).

Early decision deadline: 11/1.

Notification: continuous (freshmen), 11/15 (early decision), 12/1 (early action).

CONTACT

Ms. Ashley Browning, Director of Admission, Hollins University, Hollins University, 7916 Williamson Rd, Box 9707, Roanoke, VA 24020. *Phone:* 540-362-6401. *Toll-free phone:* 800-456-9595. *Fax:* 540-362-6218. *E-mail:* huadm@hollins.edu.

IGlobal University

Vienna, Virginia

http://www.iglobal.edu/

CONTACT

IGlobal University, 8133 Leesburg Pike, #230, Vienna, VA 22182.

James Madison University

Harrisonburg, Virginia

http://www.jmu.edu/

- **State-supported** comprehensive, founded 1908
- **Small-town** 721-acre campus
- **Endowment** $80.0 million
- **Coed** 19,548 undergraduate students, 95% full-time, 59% women, 41% men
- **Very difficult** entrance level, 72% of applicants were admitted

UNDERGRAD STUDENTS

18,554 full-time, 994 part-time. 23% are from out of state; 5% Black or African American, non-Hispanic/Latino; 6% Hispanic/Latino; 5% Asian, non-Hispanic/Latino; 0.1% Native Hawaiian or other Pacific Islander, non-Hispanic/Latino; 0.1% American Indian or Alaska Native, non-Hispanic/Latino; 4% Two or more races, non-Hispanic/Latino; 3% Race/ethnicity unknown; 3% international; 4% transferred in; 12% live on campus.

Freshmen:

Admission: 21,304 applied, 15,366 admitted, 4,505 enrolled. ***Test scores:*** SAT critical reading scores over 500: 84%; SAT math scores over 500: 86%; ACT scores over 18: 98%; SAT critical reading scores over 600: 31%; SAT math scores over 600: 34%; ACT scores over 24: 68%; SAT critical reading scores over 700: 3%; SAT math scores over 700: 3%; ACT scores over 30: 8%.

Retention: 91% of full-time freshmen returned.

FACULTY

Total: 1,500, 69% full-time, 60% with terminal degrees.

Student/faculty ratio: 16:1.

ACADEMICS

Calendar: semesters. *Degrees:* bachelor's, master's, and doctoral (also offers specialist in education degree).

Special study options: accelerated degree program, adult/continuing education programs, advanced placement credit, distance learning, double majors, English as a second language, freshman honors college, honors programs, independent study, internships, off-campus study, part-time degree program, services for LD students, student-designed majors, study abroad, summer session for credit. ***ROTC:*** Army (b), Air Force (c).

Unusual degree programs: 3-2 forestry with Virginia Polytechnic Institute and State University.

Computers: Students can access the following: campus intranet, computer help desk, free student e-mail accounts, online (class) grades, online (class) registration, online (class) schedules. Campuswide network is available. Wireless service is available via entire campus.

Library: Carrier Library plus 2 others. Students can reserve study rooms.

STUDENT LIFE

Housing options: on-campus residence required for freshman year; coed, special housing for students with disabilities. Campus housing is university owned and leased by the school. Freshman campus housing is guaranteed.

Activities and organizations: drama/theater group, student-run newspaper, radio station, choral group, marching band, national fraternities, national sororities.

Athletics Member NCAA. All Division I except football (Division I-AA). ***Intercollegiate sports:*** baseball M(s), basketball M(s)/W(s), cheerleading M/W, cross-country running W(s), field hockey W(s), golf M(s)/W(s), lacrosse W(s), soccer M(s)/W(s), softball W(s), swimming and diving W(s), tennis M(s)/W(s), track and field W(s), volleyball W(s). ***Intramural sports:*** archery M(c)/W(c), baseball M(c), basketball M/W, bowling M/W, cheerleading W(c), crew M(c)/W(c), cross-country running M(c)/W(c), equestrian sports M(c)/W(c), fencing M(c)/W(c), field hockey W(c), football M/W, golf M/W, gymnastics M(c)/W(c), ice hockey M(c)/W(c), lacrosse M(c)/W(c), racquetball M/W, rugby M(c)/W(c), skiing (downhill) M(c)/W(c), soccer M/W, softball M/W, squash M(c)/W(c), swimming and diving M(c)/W(c), table tennis M/W, tennis M/W, track and field M(c)/W(c), ultimate Frisbee M(c)/W(c), volleyball M/W, water polo M(c)/W(c), wrestling M(c).

Campus security: 24-hour emergency response devices and patrols, student patrols, late-night transport/escort service, controlled dormitory access, lighted pathways.

Student services: health clinic, personal/psychological counseling, women's center.

COSTS & FINANCIAL AID

Costs (2016–17) ***Tuition:*** state resident $5896 full-time, $196 per credit hour part-time; nonresident $21,670 full-time, $703 per credit hour part-time. ***Required fees:*** $4446 full-time. ***Room and board:*** $9334; room only: $4786. Room and board charges vary according to board plan. ***Waivers:*** employees or children of employees.

Financial Aid Of all full-time matriculated undergraduates who enrolled in 2016, 10,856 applied for aid, 7,457 were judged to have need, 4,988 had their need fully met. In 2016, 209 non-need-based awards were made. ***Average percent of need met:*** 43. ***Average financial aid package:*** $8528. ***Average need-based loan:*** $3767. ***Average need-based gift aid:*** $7300. ***Average non-need-based aid:*** $4418. ***Average indebtedness upon graduation:*** $28,407.

APPLYING

Standardized Tests *Required:* SAT or ACT (for admission).

Options: electronic application, early action, deferred entrance.

Application fee: $70.

Required: high school transcript. ***Recommended:*** minimum 3.0 GPA.

CONTACT

James Madison University, 800 South Main Street, Harrisonburg, VA 22807. *Phone:* 540-568-5681.

Jefferson College of Health Sciences

Roanoke, Virginia

http://www.jchs.edu/

- **Independent** comprehensive, founded 1982
- **Urban** 1-acre campus
- **Endowment** $2.3 million
- **Coed**
- **Moderately difficult** entrance level

ACADEMICS

Calendar: semesters. *Degrees:* certificates, associate, bachelor's, and master's.

Library: JCHS Library. *Books:* 5,265 (physical), 41,000 (digital/electronic); *Serial titles:* 99 (physical), 65 (digital/electronic); *Databases:* 29.

STUDENT LIFE

Housing options: coed. Campus housing is university owned.

Activities and organizations: student-run newspaper, choral group, Jefferson Activities Group (JAG), Student Ambassadors, Hands of Healing, American Medical Students Association (AMSA), Student Nurses Association.

Campus security: 24-hour emergency response devices and patrols, late-night transport/escort service, controlled dormitory access.

Student services: personal/psychological counseling.

COSTS

Costs (2016–17) ***Comprehensive fee:*** $34,664 includes full-time tuition ($24,700), mandatory fees ($450), and room and board ($9514). Full-time tuition and fees vary according to course load. Part-time tuition: $715 per credit hour. Part-time tuition and fees vary according to course load. ***Required fees:*** $150 per year part-time. ***Room and board:*** Room and board charges vary according to location.

APPLYING

Standardized Tests *Required:* SAT or ACT (for admission). *Recommended:* SAT (for admission).

Options: electronic application, deferred entrance.

Application fee: $35.

Required: high school transcript, minimum 2.0 GPA. ***Required for some:*** interview.

CONTACT
Jefferson College of Health Sciences, 101 Elm Avenue SE, Roanoke, VA 24013. *Phone:* 540-985-9083. *Toll-free phone:* 888-985-8483.

★ Liberty University
Lynchburg, Virginia
http://www.liberty.edu/

- **Independent nondenominational** comprehensive, founded 1971
- **Suburban** 6500-acre campus
- **Coed** 13,646 undergraduate students, 97% full-time, 53% women, 47% men
- **Minimally difficult** entrance level, 28% of applicants were admitted

UNDERGRAD STUDENTS
13,202 full-time, 444 part-time. Students come from 52 states and territories; 78 other countries; 60% are from out of state; 5% Black or African American, non-Hispanic/Latino; 5% Hispanic/Latino; 2% Asian, non-Hispanic/Latino; 0.1% Native Hawaiian or other Pacific Islander, non-Hispanic/Latino; 0.5% American Indian or Alaska Native, non-Hispanic/Latino; 2% Two or more races, non-Hispanic/Latino; 15% Race/ethnicity unknown; 5% international; 10% transferred in; 59% live on campus.

Freshmen:
Admission: 22,984 applied, 6,369 admitted, 2,917 enrolled. ***Average high school GPA:*** 3.51. ***Test scores:*** SAT critical reading scores over 500: 70%; SAT math scores over 500: 64%; SAT writing scores over 500: 61%; ACT scores over 18: 96%; SAT critical reading scores over 600: 27%; SAT math scores over 600: 24%; SAT writing scores over 600: 21%; ACT scores over 24: 53%; SAT critical reading scores over 700: 5%; SAT math scores over 700: 4%; SAT writing scores over 700: 4%; ACT scores over 30: 16%.

Retention: 88% of full-time freshmen returned.

ACADEMICS
Calendar: semesters. *Degrees:* certificates, associate, bachelor's, master's, doctoral, post-master's, and postbachelor's certificates (also offers external degree program with significant enrollment not reflected in profile).

Special study options: academic remediation for entering students, accelerated degree program, advanced placement credit, cooperative education, distance learning, double majors, English as a second language, external degree program, honors programs, independent study, internships, off-campus study, part-time degree program, services for LD students, student-designed majors, study abroad, summer session for credit. ***ROTC:*** Army (b), Air Force (c).

Computers: 820 computers/terminals are available on campus for general student use. Students can access the following: computer help desk, free student e-mail accounts, online (class) grades, online (class) registration, online (class) schedules. Campuswide network is available. 100% of college-owned or -operated housing units are wired for high-speed Internet access. Wireless service is available via entire campus.

Library: Jerry Falwell Library plus 1 other. *Books:* 405,620 (physical), 283,195 (digital/electronic); *Serial titles:* 120 (physical), 78,253 (digital/electronic); *Databases:* 589. Students can reserve study rooms.

STUDENT LIFE
Housing options: on-campus residence required through senior year; men-only, women-only, special housing for students with disabilities. Campus housing is university owned. Freshman campus housing is guaranteed.

Activities and organizations: drama/theater group, student-run newspaper, radio station, choral group, marching band, Campus Serve.

Athletics Member NCAA. All Division I except football (Division I-AA). ***Intercollegiate sports:*** baseball M(s), basketball M(s)/W(s), cheerleading M(s)/W(s), crew M(c)/W(c), cross-country running M(s)/W(s), equestrian sports W(c), field hockey W(s), golf M(s), ice hockey M(c)/W(c), lacrosse W(s), soccer M(s)/W(s), softball W(s), swimming and diving W(s), tennis M(s)/W(s), track and field M(s)/W(s), volleyball M(c)/W(s). ***Intramural sports:*** archery M(c)/W(c), basketball M/W, football M/W, gymnastics M(c)/W(c), lacrosse M(c), racquetball M(c)/W(c), skiing (downhill) M(c)/W(c), soccer M/W, softball M/W, table tennis M/W, tennis M/W, ultimate Frisbee M(c)/W(c), wrestling M(c).

Campus security: 24-hour patrols, late-night transport/escort service, 24-hour emergency dispatch.

Student services: health clinic, personal/psychological counseling.

COSTS & FINANCIAL AID
Costs (2016–17) ***Comprehensive fee:*** $32,326 includes full-time tuition ($22,000), mandatory fees ($1020), and room and board ($9306). Full-time tuition and fees vary according to course load. Part-time tuition: $917 per credit hour. Part-time tuition and fees vary according to course load. ***College room only:*** $5806. Room and board charges vary according to housing facility. ***Payment plan:*** installment. ***Waivers:*** employees or children of employees.

Financial Aid Of all full-time matriculated undergraduates who enrolled in 2016, 12,050 applied for aid, 9,465 were judged to have need, 1,187 had their need fully met. In 2016, 2533 non-need-based awards were made. ***Average percent of need met:*** 60. ***Average financial aid package:*** $15,118. ***Average need-based loan:*** $4219. ***Average need-based gift aid:*** $10,831. ***Average non-need-based aid:*** $8343. ***Average indebtedness upon graduation:*** $21,474. ***Financial aid deadline:*** 3/1.

APPLYING
Standardized Tests *Required:* SAT or ACT (for admission).

Options: electronic application.

Application fee: $50.

Required: essay or personal statement, high school transcript, minimum 2.0 GPA. ***Recommended:*** minimum 2.0 GPA.

Application deadlines: rolling (freshmen), rolling (transfers).

Notification: continuous (freshmen), continuous (transfers).

CONTACT
Dr. Terry Elam, Director of Admissions, Liberty University, 1971 University Boulevard, Lynchburg, VA 24515. *Phone:* 434-592-3966. *Toll-free phone:* 800-543-5317. *Fax:* 800-542-2311. *E-mail:* admissions@liberty.edu.

Longwood University
Farmville, Virginia
http://www.longwood.edu/

- **State-supported** comprehensive, founded 1839
- **Small-town** 60-acre campus with easy access to Richmond
- **Endowment** $53.2 million
- **Coed** 4,386 undergraduate students, 90% full-time, 67% women, 33% men
- **Moderately difficult** entrance level, 79% of applicants were admitted

UNDERGRAD STUDENTS
3,952 full-time, 434 part-time. Students come from 35 states and territories; 18 other countries; 4% are from out of state; 9% Black or African American, non-Hispanic/Latino; 5% Hispanic/Latino; 1% Asian, non-Hispanic/Latino; 0.1% Native Hawaiian or other Pacific Islander, non-Hispanic/Latino; 0.4% American Indian or Alaska Native, non-Hispanic/Latino; 4% Two or more races, non-Hispanic/Latino; 4% Race/ethnicity unknown; 1% international; 5% transferred in; 78% live on campus.

Freshmen:
Admission: 4,716 applied, 3,721 admitted, 929 enrolled. ***Average high school GPA:*** 3.46. ***Test scores:*** SAT critical reading scores over 500: 46%; SAT math scores over 500: 40%; ACT scores over 18: 80%; SAT critical reading scores over 600: 9%; SAT math scores over 600: 6%; ACT scores over 24: 19%; ACT scores over 30: 1%.

Retention: 80% of full-time freshmen returned.

FACULTY
Total: 310, 82% full-time, 75% with terminal degrees.

Student/faculty ratio: 16:1.

ACADEMICS
Calendar: semesters. *Degrees:* bachelor's, master's, post-master's, and postbachelor's certificates.

Special study options: accelerated degree program, distance learning, double majors, English as a second language, honors programs, independent study, internships, off-campus study, services for LD students, study abroad, summer session for credit. ***ROTC:*** Army (b).

Unusual degree programs: 3-2 engineering with University of Virginia, Old Dominion University, Virginia Polytechnic Institute and State University.

Computers: 325 computers/terminals and 650 ports are available on campus for general student use. Students can access the following: campus intranet, computer help desk, free student e-mail accounts, online (class) grades, online (class) registration, online (class) schedules. Campuswide network is available. 100% of college-owned or -operated housing units are wired for high-speed Internet access. Wireless service is available via entire campus.

Library: The Janet D. Greenwood Library. *Books:* 280,777 (physical), 333,714 (digital/electronic); *Serial titles:* 2,473 (physical), 206 (digital/electronic); *Databases:* 294. Weekly public service hours: 93.

STUDENT LIFE

Housing options: on-campus residence required through sophomore year; coed, women-only, special housing for students with disabilities. Campus housing is university owned. Freshman campus housing is guaranteed.

Activities and organizations: drama/theater group, student-run newspaper, radio station, choral group, Student Government Association, Alpha Phi Omega, Baptist Campus Ministries, Longwood Ambassadors, Chi Alpha, national fraternities, national sororities.

Athletics Member NCAA. All Division I. ***Intercollegiate sports:*** baseball M(s), basketball M(s)/W(s), cross-country running M(s)/W(s), field hockey W(s), football M(c), golf M(s)/W(s), lacrosse W(s), soccer M(s)/W(s), softball W(s), tennis M(s)/W(s). ***Intramural sports:*** baseball M(c), basketball M(c)/W(c), cheerleading M/W, equestrian sports M(c)/W(c), field hockey M(c)/W(c), football M/W, golf M/W, lacrosse M(c)/W(c), racquetball M/W, rock climbing M/W, rugby W(c), sand volleyball M/W, soccer M(c)/W(c), softball M/W(c), swimming and diving M(c)/W(c), table tennis M/W, tennis M/W, ultimate Frisbee M/W, volleyball M/W, weight lifting M/W, wrestling M(c).

Campus security: 24-hour emergency response devices and patrols, late-night transport/escort service, controlled dormitory access.

Student services: health clinic, personal/psychological counseling.

COSTS & FINANCIAL AID

Costs (2016–17) ***Tuition:*** state resident $7350 full-time, $245 per credit part-time; nonresident $21,780 full-time, $706 per credit part-time. Full-time tuition and fees vary according to course load and program. Part-time tuition and fees vary according to course load and program. ***Required fees:*** $4890 full-time, $163 per credit hour part-time. ***Room and board:*** $10,685; room only: $6650. Room and board charges vary according to board plan, housing facility, and location. ***Payment plan:*** installment. ***Waivers:*** senior citizens and employees or children of employees.

Financial Aid Of all full-time matriculated undergraduates who enrolled in 2014, 3,052 applied for aid, 2,354 were judged to have need, 699 had their need fully met. 260 Federal Work-Study jobs (averaging $1414). 493 state and other part-time jobs (averaging $1312). In 2014, 150 non-need-based awards were made. ***Average percent of need met:*** 83. ***Average financial aid package:*** $13,973. ***Average need-based loan:*** $4716. ***Average need-based gift aid:*** $7359. ***Average non-need-based aid:*** $3919. ***Average indebtedness upon graduation:*** $28,047.

APPLYING

Standardized Tests *Required:* SAT or ACT (for admission).

Options: electronic application, early admission, early action, deferred entrance.

Application fee: $50.

Required: essay or personal statement, high school transcript. ***Recommended:*** 3 letters of recommendation.

Application deadlines: 3/1 (freshmen), 3/1 (transfers), 12/1 (early action).

Notification: 6/1 (freshmen), continuous until 6/1 (transfers), 1/15 (early action).

CONTACT

Mr. Jason Faulk, Dean of Admissions, Longwood University, 201 High Street, Farmville, VA 23909. *Phone:* 434-395-2809. *Toll-free phone:* 800-281-4677. *Fax:* 434-395-2332. *E-mail:* faulkjc@longwood.edu.

Mary Baldwin University

Staunton, Virginia

http://www.marybaldwin.edu/

- **Independent** comprehensive, founded 1842
- **Small-town** 59-acre campus
- **Endowment** $35.1 million
- **Coed, primarily women** 1,310 undergraduate students, 66% full-time, 92% women, 8% men
- **Moderately difficult** entrance level, 99% of applicants were admitted

UNDERGRAD STUDENTS

866 full-time, 444 part-time. Students come from 40 states and territories; 7 other countries; 25% are from out of state; 22% Black or African American, non-Hispanic/Latino; 7% Hispanic/Latino; 2% Asian, non-Hispanic/Latino; 0.3% Native Hawaiian or other Pacific Islander, non-Hispanic/Latino; 0.9% American Indian or Alaska Native, non-Hispanic/Latino; 4% Two or more races, non-Hispanic/Latino; 5% Race/ethnicity unknown; 2% international; 10% transferred in; 84% live on campus.

Freshmen:

Admission: 2,706 applied, 2,692 admitted, 227 enrolled. ***Average high school GPA:*** 3.51. ***Test scores:*** SAT critical reading scores over 500: 52%; SAT math scores over 500: 39%; SAT writing scores over 500: 43%; ACT scores over 18: 82%; SAT critical reading scores over 600: 18%; SAT math scores over 600: 9%; SAT writing scores over 600: 17%; ACT scores over 24: 38%; SAT critical reading scores over 700: 3%; SAT math scores over 700: 1%; SAT writing scores over 700: 1%; ACT scores over 30: 3%.

Retention: 65% of full-time freshmen returned.

FACULTY

Total: 211, 42% full-time, 82% with terminal degrees.

Student/faculty ratio: 10:1.

ACADEMICS

Calendar: 4-1-4. *Degrees:* certificates, bachelor's, master's, and doctoral.

Special study options: academic remediation for entering students, accelerated degree program, adult/continuing education programs, advanced placement credit, distance learning, double majors, English as a second language, external degree program, freshman honors college, honors programs, independent study, internships, off-campus study, part-time degree program, services for LD students, student-designed majors, study abroad, summer session for credit. ***ROTC:*** Army (c), Navy (c), Air Force (c).

Unusual degree programs: 3-2 engineering with University of Virginia; nursing with Vanderbilt University, Jefferson College of Health Sciences; osteopathy with Edward Via College of Osteopathic Medicine.

Computers: 247 computers/terminals are available on campus for general student use. Students can access the following: computer help desk, free student e-mail accounts, online (class) grades, online (class) registration, online (class) schedules. Campuswide network is available. 100% of college-owned or -operated housing units are wired for high-speed Internet access. Wireless service is available via entire campus.

Library: Grafton Library. *Books:* 108,444 (physical), 271,803 (digital/electronic); *Serial titles:* 368 (physical), 31,879 (digital/electronic); *Databases:* 88. Weekly public service hours: 92; students can reserve study rooms.

STUDENT LIFE

Housing options: on-campus residence required through senior year; women-only. Campus housing is university owned. Freshman campus housing is guaranteed.

Activities and organizations: drama/theater group, student-run television station, choral group, marching band, Black Student Alliance, Minority Clubs United, Math Club, Illusion Dance Company, Resident Hall Association.

Athletics Member NCAA. All Division III. ***Intercollegiate sports:*** basketball W, cross-country running W, soccer W, softball W, tennis W, track and field W, volleyball W. ***Intramural sports:*** equestrian sports W(c), fencing W(c).

Campus security: 24-hour emergency response devices and patrols, late-night transport/escort service, controlled dormitory access.

Student services: health clinic, personal/psychological counseling.

COSTS & FINANCIAL AID

Costs (2017–18) ***Comprehensive fee:*** $40,495 includes full-time tuition ($30,690), mandatory fees ($395), and room and board ($9410). Full-time tuition and fees vary according to degree level. Part-time tuition: $460 per semester hour. Part-time tuition and fees vary according to degree level. ***Required fees:*** $58 per term part-time. ***Room and board:*** Room and board charges vary according to housing facility and student level. ***Payment plan:*** installment. ***Waivers:*** employees or children of employees.

Financial Aid Of all full-time matriculated undergraduates who enrolled in 2016, 786 applied for aid, 757 were judged to have need, 106 had their need fully met. 214 Federal Work-Study jobs (averaging $1463). 104 state and other part-time jobs (averaging $1553). In 2016, 59 non-need-based awards were made. ***Average percent of need met:*** 70. ***Average financial aid package:*** $24,347. ***Average need-based loan:*** $4317. ***Average need-based gift aid:*** $20,360. ***Average non-need-based aid:*** $16,960. ***Average indebtedness upon graduation:*** $35,169.

APPLYING

Standardized Tests *Required:* SAT or ACT (for admission).

Options: electronic application, deferred entrance.

Required: high school transcript. ***Required for some:*** essay or personal statement, 1 letter of recommendation, interview. ***Recommended:*** 1 letter of recommendation.

Application deadlines: rolling (freshmen), rolling (transfers).

Notification: continuous (freshmen), continuous (transfers).

CONTACT

Ms. Amber Wilkins, Interim Director of Admissions, Mary Baldwin University, Frederick and New Streets, Staunton, VA 24401. *Phone:* 540-887-7211. *Toll-free phone:* 800-468-2262. *Fax:* 540-887-7292. *E-mail:* awilkins@marybaldwin.edu.

Marymount University

Arlington, Virginia

http://www.marymount.edu/

- **Independent** comprehensive, founded 1950, affiliated with Roman Catholic Church
- **Suburban** 21-acre campus with easy access to Washington, DC
- **Endowment** $37.4 million
- **Coed** 2,323 undergraduate students, 91% full-time, 64% women, 36% men
- **Moderately difficult** entrance level, 91% of applicants were admitted

UNDERGRAD STUDENTS

2,124 full-time, 199 part-time. Students come from 42 states and territories; 65 other countries; 39% are from out of state; 15% Black or African American, non-Hispanic/Latino; 18% Hispanic/Latino; 7% Asian, non-Hispanic/Latino; 0.4% Native Hawaiian or other Pacific Islander, non-Hispanic/Latino; 0.5% American Indian or Alaska Native, non-Hispanic/Latino; 3% Two or more races, non-Hispanic/Latino; 3% Race/ethnicity unknown; 14% international; 11% transferred in; 34% live on campus.

Freshmen:

Admission: 2,476 applied, 2,242 admitted, 442 enrolled. ***Average high school GPA:*** 3.24. ***Test scores:*** SAT critical reading scores over 500: 46%; SAT math scores over 500: 41%; SAT writing scores over 500: 39%; ACT scores over 18: 77%; SAT critical reading scores over 600: 8%; SAT math scores over 600: 10%; SAT writing scores over 600: 5%; ACT scores over 24: 20%; SAT critical reading scores over 700: 1%.

Retention: 79% of full-time freshmen returned.

FACULTY

Total: 353, 44% full-time, 65% with terminal degrees.

Student/faculty ratio: 13:1.

ACADEMICS

Calendar: semesters plus 2 summer terms. *Degrees:* certificates, bachelor's, master's, doctoral, post-master's, and postbachelor's certificates.

Special study options: academic remediation for entering students, accelerated degree program, advanced placement credit, distance learning, double majors, honors programs, independent study, internships, off-campus study, part-time degree program, services for LD students, student-designed majors, study abroad, summer session for credit. ***ROTC:*** Army (c).

Unusual degree programs: 3-2 business administration; information technology.

Computers: 250 computers/terminals are available on campus for general student use. Students can access the following: campus intranet, computer help desk, free student e-mail accounts, online (class) grades, online (class) registration, online (class) schedules, online drive space. Campuswide network is available. 100% of college-owned or -operated housing units are wired for high-speed Internet access. Wireless service is available via entire campus.

Library: Emerson C. Reinsch Library plus 1 other. *Books:* 242,577 (physical), 330,705 (digital/electronic); *Databases:* 227. Weekly public service hours: 104; students can reserve study rooms.

STUDENT LIFE

Housing options: on-campus residence required through sophomore year; coed, men-only, women-only. Campus housing is university owned and leased by the school. Freshman applicants given priority for college housing.

Activities and organizations: drama/theater group, student-run newspaper, choral group, Fashion Club, Student Nurses Association, International Club, Association for Campus Events, Blue Harmony (show choir).

Athletics Member NCAA. All Division III. ***Intercollegiate sports:*** baseball M, basketball M/W, cross-country running M/W, golf M/W, lacrosse M/W, soccer M/W, swimming and diving M/W, triathlon M/W, volleyball M/W. ***Intramural sports:*** basketball M/W, cheerleading W, football M/W, ice hockey M, soccer M/W, ultimate Frisbee M/W, volleyball M/W, water polo M/W.

Campus security: 24-hour emergency response devices and patrols, late-night transport/escort service, controlled dormitory access.

Student services: health clinic, personal/psychological counseling.

COSTS & FINANCIAL AID

Costs (2017–18) ***One-time required fee:*** $450. ***Comprehensive fee:*** $43,231 includes full-time tuition ($29,950), mandatory fees ($476), and room and board ($12,805). Part-time tuition: $975 per credit hour. ***Required fees:*** $11 per credit hour part-time. ***Room and board:*** Room and board charges vary according to housing facility. ***Payment plan:*** installment. ***Waivers:*** senior citizens and employees or children of employees.

Financial Aid Of all full-time matriculated undergraduates who enrolled in 2016, 1,447 applied for aid, 1,316 were judged to have need, 168 had their need fully met. 574 Federal Work-Study jobs (averaging $1940). In 2016, 426 non-need-based awards were made. ***Average percent of need met:*** 55. ***Average financial aid package:*** $19,015. ***Average need-based loan:*** $4459. ***Average need-based gift aid:*** $6568. ***Average non-need-based aid:*** $12,782. ***Average indebtedness upon graduation:*** $35,545.

APPLYING

Standardized Tests *Required for some:* SAT or ACT (for admission).

Options: electronic application, deferred entrance.

Application fee: $40.

Required: essay or personal statement, high school transcript, minimum 2.6 GPA, 1 letter of recommendation. ***Required for some:*** interview. ***Recommended:*** interview.

Application deadlines: rolling (freshmen), rolling (transfers).

Notification: continuous (freshmen), continuous (transfers).

CONTACT

Ms. Dana Matassino, Director of Undergraduate Admissions, Marymount University, 2807 North Glebe Road, Arlington, VA 22207-4299. *Phone:* 703-284-1500. *Toll-free phone:* 800-548-7638. *Fax:* 703-522-0349. *E-mail:* admissions@marymount.edu.

Norfolk State University

Norfolk, Virginia

http://www.nsu.edu/

CONTACT

Mr. Kevin M. Holmes, Director of Recruitment and Admissions, Norfolk State University, 700 Park Avenue, Norfolk, VA 23504. *Phone:* 757-823-9222. *Toll-free phone:* 800-274-1821. *Fax:* 757-823-2078. *E-mail:* admissions@nsu.edu.

Old Dominion University

Norfolk, Virginia

http://www.odu.edu/

- **State-supported** university, founded 1930
- **Urban** 251-acre campus with easy access to Virginia Beach
- **Endowment** $205.8 million
- **Coed** 19,793 undergraduate students, 77% full-time, 54% women, 46% men
- **Moderately difficult** entrance level, 85% of applicants were admitted

UNDERGRAD STUDENTS

15,203 full-time, 4,590 part-time. Students come from 49 states and territories; 88 other countries; 7% are from out of state; 29% Black or African American, non-Hispanic/Latino; 8% Hispanic/Latino; 4% Asian, non-Hispanic/Latino; 0.3% Native Hawaiian or other Pacific Islander, non-Hispanic/Latino; 0.3% American Indian or Alaska Native, non-Hispanic/Latino; 7% Two or more races, non-Hispanic/Latino; 3% Race/ethnicity unknown; 1% international; 11% transferred in; 23% live on campus.

Freshmen:

Admission: 11,352 applied, 9,608 admitted, 2,757 enrolled. ***Average high school GPA:*** 3.28. ***Test scores:*** SAT critical reading scores over 500: 55%; SAT math scores over 500: 53%; ACT scores over 18: 80%; SAT critical reading scores over 600: 15%; SAT math scores over 600: 16%; ACT scores over 24: 31%; SAT critical reading scores over 700: 2%; SAT math scores over 700: 2%; ACT scores over 30: 4%.

Retention: 78% of full-time freshmen returned.

FACULTY

Total: 1,511, 55% full-time, 59% with terminal degrees.

Student/faculty ratio: 18:1.

ACADEMICS

Calendar: semesters. *Degrees:* bachelor's, master's, doctoral, post-master's, and postbachelor's certificates.

Special study options: accelerated degree program, adult/continuing education programs, advanced placement credit, cooperative education, distance learning, double majors, English as a second language, freshman honors college, honors programs, independent study, internships, off-campus study, part-time degree program, services for LD students, student-designed majors, study abroad, summer session for credit. ***ROTC:*** Army (b), Navy (b).

Unusual degree programs: 3-2 business administration; engineering; nursing; international studies, dental hygiene, communications/humanities, English, English/applied linguistics, history, interdisciplinary studies/humanities, computer science, women's studies/humanities, philosophy/humanities, health science/public health, environmental health/public health.

Computers: 2,025 computers/terminals and 6,100 ports are available on campus for general student use. Students can access the following: campus intranet, computer help desk, free student e-mail accounts, online (class) grades, online (class) registration, online (class) schedules, online courses. Campuswide network is available. 100% of college-owned or -operated housing units are wired for high-speed Internet access. Wireless service is available via entire campus.

Library: Patricia W. and Douglas Perry Library plus 3 others. *Books:* 1.3 million (physical), 1.3 million (digital/electronic); *Serial titles:* 18,082 (physical), 70,169 (digital/electronic); *Databases:* 383. Weekly public service hours: 146; study areas open 24 hours, 5-7 days a week; students can reserve study rooms.

STUDENT LIFE

Housing options: coed, women-only, special housing for students with disabilities. Campus housing is university owned and leased by the school. Freshman campus housing is guaranteed.

Activities and organizations: drama/theater group, student-run newspaper, radio station, choral group, marching band, Student Activities Council, Student Government Association, Student Veterans Association, Colleges Against Cancer, Ebony Impact Gospel Choir, national fraternities, national sororities.

Athletics Member NCAA. All Division I. ***Intercollegiate sports:*** baseball M(s), basketball M(s)/W(s), cheerleading M(s)/W(s), crew M(c)/W(s), cross-country running M(c)/W(c), equestrian sports M(c)/W(c), fencing M(c)/W(c), field hockey W(s), football M(s), golf M(s)/W(s), ice hockey M(c)/W(c), lacrosse M(c)/W(s), rugby M(c)/W(c), sailing M/W, soccer M(s)/W(s), softball W(c), swimming and diving M(s)/W(s), table tennis M(c)/W(c), tennis M(s)/W(s), triathlon M(c)/W(c), ultimate Frisbee M(c)/W(c), volleyball M(c)/W(c), wrestling M(s). ***Intramural sports:*** badminton M/W, basketball M/W, golf M/W, racquetball M/W, soccer M/W, softball M/W, table tennis M/W, ultimate Frisbee M/W, volleyball M/W.

Campus security: 24-hour emergency response devices and patrols, student patrols, late-night transport/escort service, controlled dormitory access, lighted pathways, video cameras, on-campus EMTs, emergency notification system.

Student services: health clinic, personal/psychological counseling, women's center.

COSTS & FINANCIAL AID

Costs (2016–17) ***Tuition:*** state resident $9750 full-time, $325 per credit hour part-time; nonresident $26,730 full-time, $891 per credit hour part-time. ***Required fees:*** $296 full-time, $66 per term part-time. ***Room and board:*** $10,864; room only: $6094. Room and board charges vary according to board plan and housing facility. ***Payment plans:*** installment, deferred payment. ***Waivers:*** senior citizens and employees or children of employees.

Financial Aid Of all full-time matriculated undergraduates who enrolled in 2016, 12,174 applied for aid, 10,275 were judged to have need, 1,366 had their need fully met. 200 Federal Work-Study jobs (averaging $2400). In 2016, 922 non-need-based awards were made. ***Average percent of need met:*** 46. ***Average financial aid package:*** $10,584. ***Average need-based loan:*** $4315. ***Average need-based gift aid:*** $7011. ***Average non-need-based aid:*** $4842. ***Average indebtedness upon graduation:*** $30,410. ***Financial aid deadline:*** 3/15.

APPLYING

Standardized Tests *Required for some:* SAT or ACT (for admission).

Options: electronic application, early admission, early action, deferred entrance.

Application fee: $50.

Required: high school transcript, minimum 2.7 GPA. ***Recommended:*** essay or personal statement, 1 letter of recommendation.

Application deadlines: 2/1 (freshmen), 5/1 (transfers), 12/1 (early action).

Notification: continuous (freshmen), continuous (out-of-state freshmen), continuous (transfers), 1/15 (early action).

CONTACT

Ms. Shereen Williams, Customer Service Manager, Admissions Office, Old Dominion University, 108 Rollins Hall, 5215 Hampton Boulevard, Norfolk, VA 23529. *Phone:* 757-683-3648. *Toll-free phone:* 800-348-7926. *Fax:* 757-683-3255. *E-mail:* admissions@odu.edu.

Patrick Henry College

Purcellville, Virginia

http://www.phc.edu/

- **Independent nondenominational** 4-year, founded 2000
- **Small-town** 119-acre campus with easy access to Washington, DC
- **Endowment** $1.2 million
- **Coed** 277 undergraduate students, 88% full-time, 47% women, 53% men
- **Moderately difficult** entrance level, 95% of applicants were admitted

UNDERGRAD STUDENTS
245 full-time, 32 part-time. Students come from 35 states and territories; 80% are from out of state; 0.4% Black or African American, non-Hispanic/Latino; 5% Hispanic/Latino; 3% Asian, non-Hispanic/Latino; 0.4% Native Hawaiian or other Pacific Islander, non-Hispanic/Latino; 10% Race/ethnicity unknown; 3% transferred in; 83% live on campus.

Freshmen:
Admission: 227 applied, 216 admitted, 51 enrolled. ***Average high school GPA:*** 3.75. ***Test scores:*** SAT critical reading scores over 500: 95%; SAT math scores over 500: 87%; SAT writing scores over 500: 84%; ACT scores over 18: 100%; SAT critical reading scores over 600: 74%; SAT math scores over 600: 37%; SAT writing scores over 600: 50%; ACT scores over 24: 84%; SAT critical reading scores over 700: 37%; SAT math scores over 700: 5%; SAT writing scores over 700: 16%; ACT scores over 30: 47%.

Retention: 83% of full-time freshmen returned.

FACULTY
Total: 41, 46% full-time, 71% with terminal degrees.

Student/faculty ratio: 10:1.

ACADEMICS
Calendar: semesters. *Degree:* bachelor's.

Special study options: advanced placement credit, cooperative education, distance learning, double majors, independent study, internships, off-campus study, summer session for credit.

Computers: 10 computers/terminals and 100 ports are available on campus for general student use. Students can access the following: campus intranet, computer help desk, free student e-mail accounts, online (class) grades, online (class) registration, online (class) schedules. Campuswide network is available. 100% of college-owned or -operated housing units are wired for high-speed Internet access. Wireless service is available via entire campus.
Library: Patrick Henry College Library. *Books:* 38,995 (physical), 387,798 (digital/electronic); *Serial titles:* 240 (physical), 42,361 (digital/electronic); *Databases:* 33. Weekly public service hours: 80; students can reserve study rooms.

STUDENT LIFE
Housing options: on-campus residence required through sophomore year; men-only, women-only. Campus housing is university owned. Freshman applicants given priority for college housing.

Activities and organizations: drama/theater group, student-run newspaper, choral group, Drama Club, Eden Troupe, Student Government, Chorale, College Republicans, Debate/Moot Court.

Athletics Member USCAA. ***Intercollegiate sports:*** basketball M, soccer M/W. ***Intramural sports:*** baseball M, basketball M/W, fencing M(c)/W(c), football M(c)/W(c), racquetball M(c)/W(c), sand volleyball M(c)/W(c), table tennis M(c)/W(c), tennis M/W, ultimate Frisbee M/W, volleyball M/W, weight lifting M.

Campus security: 24-hour emergency response devices and patrols, student patrols, late-night transport/escort service, controlled dormitory access, after hours patrols by trained security personnel.

Student services: health clinic, personal/psychological counseling.

COSTS & FINANCIAL AID
Costs (2017–18) ***Comprehensive fee:*** $38,900 includes full-time tuition ($27,922), mandatory fees ($250), and room and board ($10,728). Full-time tuition and fees vary according to course load. Part-time tuition: $1163 per credit hour. Part-time tuition and fees vary according to course level and course load. ***Room and board:*** Room and board charges vary according to board plan and housing facility. ***Payment plans:*** installment, deferred payment. ***Waivers:*** employees or children of employees.

Financial Aid Of all full-time matriculated undergraduates who enrolled in 2016, 94 applied for aid, 70 were judged to have need. In 2016, 140 non-need-based awards were made. ***Average percent of need met:*** 35. ***Average financial aid package:*** $14,600. ***Average need-based gift aid:*** $7000. ***Average non-need-based aid:*** $9100. ***Average indebtedness upon graduation:*** $44,000. ***Financial aid deadline:*** 6/15.

APPLYING
Standardized Tests *Required:* SAT or ACT (for admission).

Options: electronic application, early action, deferred entrance.

Application fee: $20.

Required: essay or personal statement, high school transcript, 2 letters of recommendation, interview, official transcripts from all colleges attended, reading list.

Application deadlines: 6/15 (freshmen), 6/15 (transfers), 11/1 (early action).

Notification: continuous (freshmen), continuous (transfers), rolling (early action).

CONTACT
Mr. Stephen C. Allen, Director of Admissions and Communications, Patrick Henry College, 10 Patrick Henry Circle, Purcellville, VA 20132. *Phone:* 540-338-1776. *Toll-free phone:* 888-338-1776. *Fax:* 540-441-8119. *E-mail:* admissions@phc.edu.

Radford University

Radford, Virginia

http://www.radford.edu/

- **State-supported** comprehensive, founded 1910
- **Small-town** 204-acre campus
- **Endowment** $44.9 million
- **Coed** 8,453 undergraduate students, 96% full-time, 57% women, 43% men
- **Minimally difficult** entrance level, 81% of applicants were admitted

UNDERGRAD STUDENTS
8,104 full-time, 349 part-time. Students come from 35 states and territories; 56 other countries; 5% are from out of state; 15% Black or African American, non-Hispanic/Latino; 7% Hispanic/Latino; 1% Asian, non-Hispanic/Latino; 0.2% Native Hawaiian or other Pacific Islander, non-Hispanic/Latino; 0.2% American Indian or Alaska Native, non-Hispanic/Latino; 5% Two or more races, non-Hispanic/Latino; 0.9% Race/ethnicity unknown; 0.9% international; 9% transferred in; 35% live on campus.

Freshmen:
Admission: 7,447 applied, 6,047 admitted, 1,751 enrolled. ***Average high school GPA:*** 3.17. ***Test scores:*** SAT critical reading scores over 500: 39%; SAT math scores over 500: 36%; SAT writing scores over 500: 29%; ACT scores over 18: 72%; SAT critical reading scores over 600: 8%; SAT math scores over 600: 5%; SAT writing scores over 600: 4%; ACT scores over 24: 19%; SAT critical reading scores over 700: 1%; ACT scores over 30: 2%.

Retention: 74% of full-time freshmen returned.

FACULTY
Total: 735, 64% full-time, 60% with terminal degrees.

Student/faculty ratio: 16:1.

ACADEMICS
Calendar: semesters. *Degrees:* certificates, bachelor's, master's, doctoral, post-master's, and postbachelor's certificates.

Special study options: accelerated degree program, adult/continuing education programs, advanced placement credit, distance learning, double majors, honors programs, independent study, internships, off-campus study, part-time degree program, services for LD students, student-designed majors, study abroad, summer session for credit. ***ROTC:*** Army (b).

Computers: 900 computers/terminals are available on campus for general student use. Students can access the following: campus intranet, computer help desk, free student e-mail accounts, online (class) grades, online (class) registration, online (class) schedules, online financial aid status and student accounts payable. Campuswide network is available. 100% of college-owned or -operated housing units are wired for high-speed Internet access. Wireless service is available via entire campus.
Library: McConnell Library. *Books:* 271,383 (physical), 332,165 (digital/electronic); *Serial titles:* 558 (physical), 28,298 (digital/electronic); *Databases:* 535. Students can reserve study rooms.

STUDENT LIFE
Housing options: on-campus residence required through sophomore year; coed, special housing for students with disabilities. Campus housing is university owned and leased by the school. Freshman campus housing is guaranteed.

Activities and organizations: drama/theater group, student-run newspaper, radio station, choral group, Radford Crafty, American Sign Language Club, Radford Student Programming and Campus Events (R-SPaCE), National Society for Collegiate Scholars, Scholar-Citizen Initiative Student Organization, national fraternities, national sororities.

Athletics Member NCAA. All Division I. ***Intercollegiate sports:*** baseball M(s), basketball M(s)/W(s), cross-country running M(s)/W(s), golf M(s)/W(s), lacrosse W(s), soccer M(s)/W(s), softball W(s), tennis M(s)/W(s), track and field W(s), volleyball W(s). ***Intramural sports:*** basketball M/W, bowling M(c)/W(c), cheerleading M(c)/W(c), cross-country running M/W, equestrian sports M(c)/W(c), field hockey W(c), football M/W, ice hockey M(c)/W(c), lacrosse M(c)/W(c), riflery M(c)/W(c), rugby M(c)/W(c), skiing (downhill) M(c)/W(c), soccer M(c)/W(c), softball M/W, swimming and diving M(c)/W(c), table tennis M/W, tennis M/W, ultimate Frisbee M/W, volleyball M/W, wrestling M(c)/W(c).

Campus security: 24-hour emergency response devices and patrols, late-night transport/escort service, controlled dormitory access.

Student services: health clinic, personal/psychological counseling.

COSTS & FINANCIAL AID

Costs (2016–17) ***Tuition:*** state resident $6991 full-time, $291 per credit hour part-time; nonresident $18,626 full-time, $776 per credit hour part-time. Part-time tuition and fees vary according to course load. ***Required fees:*** $3090 full-time, $130 per credit hour part-time. ***Room and board:*** $8946; room only: $4962. Room and board charges vary according to board plan and housing facility. ***Payment plan:*** installment. ***Waivers:*** senior citizens and employees or children of employees.

Financial Aid Of all full-time matriculated undergraduates who enrolled in 2016, 6,144 applied for aid, 4,878 were judged to have need, 1,300 had their need fully met. 377 Federal Work-Study jobs (averaging $2432). 407 state and other part-time jobs (averaging $2330). In 2016, 319 non-need-based awards were made. ***Average percent of need met:*** 80. ***Average financial aid package:*** $10,116. ***Average need-based loan:*** $4221. ***Average need-based gift aid:*** $8110. ***Average non-need-based aid:*** $4230. ***Average indebtedness upon graduation:*** $29,103.

APPLYING

Standardized Tests *Recommended:* SAT or ACT (for admission).

Options: electronic application, early admission, early action, deferred entrance.

Required: high school transcript. ***Recommended:*** essay or personal statement, letters of recommendation.

Application deadlines: 2/1 (freshmen), 6/1 (transfers), 12/1 (early action).

Notification: 4/1 (freshmen), continuous (transfers), 1/15 (early action).

CONTACT

Mr. James A. Pennix, Dean of Admissions and Enrollment Management, Radford University, PO Box 6903, Radford, VA 24142. *Phone:* 540-831-5371. *Fax:* 540-831-5038. *E-mail:* admissions@radford.edu.

Randolph College

Lynchburg, Virginia

http://www.randolphcollege.edu/

- **Independent Methodist** comprehensive, founded 1891
- **Suburban** 100-acre campus
- **Coed** 672 undergraduate students, 99% full-time, 66% women, 34% men
- **Moderately difficult** entrance level, 81% of applicants were admitted

UNDERGRAD STUDENTS

664 full-time, 8 part-time. 40% are from out of state; 12% Black or African American, non-Hispanic/Latino; 5% Hispanic/Latino; 2% Asian, non-Hispanic/Latino; 0.3% Native Hawaiian or other Pacific Islander, non-Hispanic/Latino; 0.6% American Indian or Alaska Native, non-Hispanic/Latino; 5% Two or more races, non-Hispanic/Latino; 0.5% Race/ethnicity unknown; 8% international; 6% transferred in; 84% live on campus.

Freshmen:

Admission: 1,207 applied, 972 admitted, 184 enrolled. ***Average high school GPA:*** 3.48. ***Test scores:*** SAT critical reading scores over 500: 58%; SAT math scores over 500: 54%; SAT writing scores over 500: 47%; ACT scores over 18: 91%; SAT critical reading scores over 600: 18%; SAT math scores over 600: 13%; SAT writing scores over 600: 15%; ACT scores over 24: 32%; SAT critical reading scores over 700: 2%; SAT math scores over 700: 2%; SAT writing scores over 700: 2%; ACT scores over 30: 4%.

Retention: 78% of full-time freshmen returned.

FACULTY

Total: 72, 94% full-time, 92% with terminal degrees.

Student/faculty ratio: 10:1.

ACADEMICS

Calendar: semesters. *Degrees:* bachelor's and master's.

Special study options: adult/continuing education programs, part-time degree program.

Computers: Students can access the following: campus intranet, computer help desk, free student e-mail accounts, online (class) grades, online (class) registration, online (class) schedules. Campuswide network is available. Wireless service is available via entire campus.

Library: Lipscomb Library.

STUDENT LIFE

Housing options: on-campus residence required through senior year; coed. Campus housing is university owned. Freshman campus housing is guaranteed.

Athletics Member NCAA. All Division III. ***Intercollegiate sports:*** basketball M/W, cross-country running M/W, equestrian sports M/W, lacrosse M/W, soccer M/W, softball W, tennis M/W, volleyball W.

Campus security: 24-hour emergency response devices and patrols, late-night transport/escort service.

COSTS & FINANCIAL AID

Costs (2016–17) ***Comprehensive fee:*** $49,350 includes full-time tuition ($36,160), mandatory fees ($610), and room and board ($12,580). Part-time tuition: $1500 per credit hour. Part-time tuition and fees vary according to course load. ***Required fees:*** $53 per term part-time. ***Payment plan:*** installment. ***Waivers:*** adult students and employees or children of employees.

Financial Aid Of all full-time matriculated undergraduates who enrolled in 2016, 531 applied for aid, 476 were judged to have need, 105 had their need fully met. In 2016, 158 non-need-based awards were made. ***Average percent of need met:*** 77. ***Average financial aid package:*** $30,377. ***Average need-based loan:*** $4687. ***Average need-based gift aid:*** $25,987. ***Average non-need-based aid:*** $21,877. ***Average indebtedness upon graduation:*** $35,199.

APPLYING

Standardized Tests *Required:* SAT or ACT (for admission).

Options: electronic application, early admission, early action, deferred entrance.

Required: essay or personal statement, high school transcript, 2 letters of recommendation. ***Recommended:*** interview.

CONTACT

Ms. Margaret Blount, Director of Admissions, Randolph College, 2500 Rivermont Avenue, Lynchburg, VA 24503-1555. *Phone:* 434-947-8100. *Toll-free phone:* 800-745-7692. *Fax:* 434-947-8996. *E-mail:* admissions@randolphcollege.edu.

Randolph-Macon College

Ashland, Virginia

http://www.rmc.edu/

- **Independent United Methodist** 4-year, founded 1830
- **Suburban** 116-acre campus with easy access to Richmond
- **Endowment** $140.4 million
- **Coed** 1,446 undergraduate students, 98% full-time, 53% women, 47% men
- **Moderately difficult** entrance level, 61% of applicants were admitted

UNDERGRAD STUDENTS

1,415 full-time, 31 part-time. Students come from 26 states and territories; 20 other countries; 26% are from out of state; 8% Black or African American, non-Hispanic/Latino; 4% Hispanic/Latino; 2% Asian, non-Hispanic/Latino; 0.1% Native Hawaiian or other Pacific Islander, non-

Hispanic/Latino; 0.3% American Indian or Alaska Native, non-Hispanic/Latino; 4% Two or more races, non-Hispanic/Latino; 0.9% Race/ethnicity unknown; 2% international; 3% transferred in; 85% live on campus.

Freshmen:
Admission: 2,842 applied, 1,745 admitted, 396 enrolled. ***Average high school GPA:*** 3.69. ***Test scores:*** SAT critical reading scores over 500: 72%; SAT math scores over 500: 71%; SAT writing scores over 500: 58%; ACT scores over 18: 99%; SAT critical reading scores over 600: 27%; SAT math scores over 600: 22%; SAT writing scores over 600: 16%; ACT scores over 24: 58%; SAT critical reading scores over 700: 4%; SAT math scores over 700: 3%; SAT writing scores over 700: 3%; ACT scores over 30: 11%.
Retention: 85% of full-time freshmen returned.

FACULTY
Total: 162, 63% full-time, 79% with terminal degrees.
Student/faculty ratio: 12:1.

ACADEMICS
Calendar: 4-1-4. *Degree:* bachelor's.
Special study options: academic remediation for entering students, accelerated degree program, advanced placement credit, double majors, honors programs, independent study, internships, off-campus study, part-time degree program, services for LD students, study abroad, summer session for credit. ***ROTC:*** Army (c).
Unusual degree programs: 3-2 business administration with Virginia Commonwealth University; engineering with Columbia University, University of Virginia; forestry with Duke University.
Computers: 345 computers/terminals and 1,500 ports are available on campus for general student use. Students can access the following: campus intranet, computer help desk, free student e-mail accounts, online (class) registration, online (class) schedules. Campuswide network is available. 100% of college-owned or -operated housing units are wired for high-speed Internet access. Wireless service is available via classrooms, computer centers, computer labs, dorm rooms, learning centers, libraries, student centers.
Library: McGraw-Page Library. *Books:* 161,104 (physical), 70,003 (digital/electronic); *Serial titles:* 873 (physical), 111,507 (digital/electronic); *Databases:* 111. Study areas open 24 hours, 5-7 days a week; students can reserve study rooms.

STUDENT LIFE
Housing options: on-campus residence required through junior year; coed, men-only, women-only, special housing for students with disabilities. Campus housing is university owned. Freshman campus housing is guaranteed.
Activities and organizations: drama/theater group, student-run newspaper, radio and television station, choral group, marching band, Habitat for Humanity, Macon Outdoors, Relay for Life, College Panhellenic Council, R-MC Angler's Club, national fraternities, national sororities.
Athletics Member NCAA. All Division III. ***Intercollegiate sports:*** baseball M, basketball M/W, cheerleading W(c), equestrian sports M(c)/W(c), field hockey W, football M, golf M/W, lacrosse M/W, soccer M/W, softball W, swimming and diving M/W, tennis M/W, volleyball W. ***Intramural sports:*** badminton M/W, basketball M/W, cheerleading M(c)/W(c), cross-country running M(c)/W(c), football M/W, lacrosse M/W, racquetball M/W, rugby M/W, sand volleyball M(c)/W, soccer M/W, softball M/W, table tennis M/W, tennis M/W, ultimate Frisbee M/W, volleyball M/W, water polo M/W.
Campus security: 24-hour emergency response devices and patrols, late-night transport/escort service, controlled dormitory access.
Student services: health clinic, personal/psychological counseling, women's center.

COSTS & FINANCIAL AID
Costs (2017–18) ***One-time required fee:*** $100. ***Comprehensive fee:*** $51,480 includes full-time tuition ($38,750), mandatory fees ($1250), and room and board ($11,480). Full-time tuition and fees vary according to reciprocity agreements. ***College room only:*** $6390. Room and board charges vary according to board plan and housing facility. ***Payment plan:*** installment. ***Waivers:*** employees or children of employees.
Financial Aid Of all full-time matriculated undergraduates who enrolled in 2016, 1,234 applied for aid, 1,037 were judged to have need, 318 had their need fully met. In 2016, 370 non-need-based awards were made. ***Average percent of need met:*** 82. ***Average financial aid package:*** $28,588. ***Average need-based loan:*** $5271. ***Average need-based gift aid:*** $24,444. ***Average non-need-based aid:*** $17,939. ***Average indebtedness upon graduation:*** $33,015.

APPLYING
Standardized Tests *Required:* SAT or ACT (for admission). *Recommended:* SAT Subject Tests (for admission).
Options: electronic application, early admission, early action, deferred entrance.
Application fee: $30.
Required: essay or personal statement, high school transcript, minimum 2.0 GPA, 1 letter of recommendation. ***Recommended:*** interview.
Application deadlines: 3/1 (freshmen), 4/1 (transfers), 11/15 (early action).
Notification: 4/1 (freshmen), 5/1 (transfers), 1/1 (early action).

CONTACT
Anthony Ambrogi, Director of Admissions and Enrollment Research, Randolph-Macon College, PO Box 5005, Ashland, VA 23005-5505. *Phone:* 804-752-7305. *Toll-free phone:* 800-888-1762. *Fax:* 804-752-4707. *E-mail:* admissions@rmc.edu.

Regent University

Virginia Beach, Virginia

http://www.regent.edu/

- **Independent Christian** comprehensive, founded 1977
- **Suburban** 70-acre campus
- **Endowment** $107.6 million
- **Coed** 3,806 undergraduate students, 58% full-time, 62% women, 38% men
- **Minimally difficult** entrance level, 83% of applicants were admitted

UNDERGRAD STUDENTS
2,206 full-time, 1,600 part-time. Students come from 50 states and territories; 31 other countries; 54% are from out of state; 27% Black or African American, non-Hispanic/Latino; 7% Hispanic/Latino; 2% Asian, non-Hispanic/Latino; 0.4% Native Hawaiian or other Pacific Islander, non-Hispanic/Latino; 0.7% American Indian or Alaska Native, non-Hispanic/Latino; 5% Two or more races, non-Hispanic/Latino; 2% Race/ethnicity unknown; 0.9% international; 29% transferred in; 17% live on campus.

Freshmen:
Admission: 1,953 applied, 1,616 admitted, 453 enrolled. ***Average high school GPA:*** 3.52. ***Test scores:*** SAT critical reading scores over 500: 65%; SAT math scores over 500: 51%; SAT writing scores over 500: 54%; ACT scores over 18: 86%; SAT critical reading scores over 600: 23%; SAT math scores over 600: 15%; SAT writing scores over 600: 17%; ACT scores over 24: 39%; SAT critical reading scores over 700: 4%; SAT math scores over 700: 2%; SAT writing scores over 700: 3%; ACT scores over 30: 6%.
Retention: 77% of full-time freshmen returned.

FACULTY
Total: 696, 22% full-time, 72% with terminal degrees.
Student/faculty ratio: 21:1.

ACADEMICS
Calendar: trimesters. *Degrees:* certificates, associate, bachelor's, master's, doctoral, post-master's, and postbachelor's certificates.
Special study options: academic remediation for entering students, adult/continuing education programs, advanced placement credit, distance learning, double majors, external degree program, freshman honors college, honors programs, internships, off-campus study, part-time degree program, services for LD students, study abroad, summer session for credit. ***ROTC:*** Army (c), Navy (c).
Computers: 70 computers/terminals and 75 ports are available on campus for general student use. Students can access the following: campus intranet, computer help desk, free student e-mail accounts, online (class) grades, online (class) registration, online (class) schedules. Campuswide

network is available. 100% of college-owned or -operated housing units are wired for high-speed Internet access. Wireless service is available via entire campus.

Library: Regent University Library plus 1 other. *Books:* 321,520 (physical), 454,079 (digital/electronic); *Serial titles:* 133 (physical), 380,580 (digital/electronic); *Databases:* 174. Weekly public service hours: 102; students can reserve study rooms.

STUDENT LIFE

Housing options: on-campus residence required for freshman year; men-only, women-only, special housing for students with disabilities. Campus housing is university owned. Freshman applicants given priority for college housing.

Activities and organizations: drama/theater group, student-run newspaper, choral group, College Student Leadership Board, Student Activities Board, Psychology Club, Student Alumni Ambassadors (SAA), Undergraduate Debate Association, national fraternities, national sororities.

Athletics Member NCCAA. ***Intercollegiate sports:*** cross-country running M/W. ***Intramural sports:*** basketball M/W, soccer M/W, ultimate Frisbee M/W, volleyball M/W.

Campus security: 24-hour emergency response devices and patrols, student patrols, late-night transport/escort service, controlled dormitory access.

Student services: personal/psychological counseling.

COSTS & FINANCIAL AID

Costs (2016–17) ***Comprehensive fee:*** $25,180 includes full-time tuition ($15,900), mandatory fees ($800), and room and board ($8480). Full-time tuition and fees vary according to course load. Part-time tuition: $530 per credit hour. Part-time tuition and fees vary according to course load. ***Required fees:*** $489 per term part-time. ***College room only:*** $5960. Room and board charges vary according to board plan and housing facility. ***Payment plan:*** installment. ***Waivers:*** employees or children of employees.

Financial Aid Of all full-time matriculated undergraduates who enrolled in 2016, 1,879 applied for aid, 1,690 were judged to have need, 168 had their need fully met. In 2016, 341 non-need-based awards were made. ***Average percent of need met:*** 54. ***Average financial aid package:*** $10,870. ***Average need-based loan:*** $3886. ***Average need-based gift aid:*** $7610. ***Average non-need-based aid:*** $6596. ***Average indebtedness upon graduation:*** $28,780.

APPLYING

Standardized Tests *Required for some:* SAT or ACT (for admission).

Options: electronic application, deferred entrance.

Application fee: $50.

Required: high school transcript. ***Required for some:*** essay or personal statement, minimum 3.0 GPA.

Application deadlines: 8/1 (freshmen), 8/1 (transfers).

Notification: continuous (freshmen), continuous (transfers).

CONTACT

Mrs. Heidi Cece, Executive Director of University Admissions, Regent University, 1000 Regent University Drive, Virginia Beach, VA 23464. *Phone:* 800-373-5504. *Toll-free phone:* 800-373-5504. *Fax:* 757-352-4839. *E-mail:* admissions@regent.edu.

Roanoke College

Salem, Virginia

http://www.roanoke.edu/

- **Independent** 4-year, founded 1842, affiliated with Evangelical Lutheran Church in America
- **Suburban** 80-acre campus
- **Endowment** $121.1 million
- **Coed** 1,992 undergraduate students, 97% full-time, 59% women, 41% men
- **Moderately difficult** entrance level, 73% of applicants were admitted

UNDERGRAD STUDENTS

1,933 full-time, 59 part-time. Students come from 43 states and territories; 31 other countries; 46% are from out of state; 6% Black or African American, non-Hispanic/Latino; 4% Hispanic/Latino; 1% Asian, non-Hispanic/Latino; 0.1% Native Hawaiian or other Pacific Islander, non-Hispanic/Latino; 0.3% American Indian or Alaska Native, non-Hispanic/Latino; 4% Two or more races, non-Hispanic/Latino; 0.1% Race/ethnicity unknown; 3% international; 4% transferred in; 78% live on campus.

Freshmen:

Admission: 4,459 applied, 3,257 admitted, 508 enrolled. ***Average high school GPA:*** 3.53. ***Test scores:*** SAT critical reading scores over 500: 74%; SAT math scores over 500: 70%; SAT writing scores over 500: 63%; ACT scores over 18: 95%; SAT critical reading scores over 600: 29%; SAT math scores over 600: 25%; SAT writing scores over 600: 19%; ACT scores over 24: 58%; SAT critical reading scores over 700: 5%; SAT math scores over 700: 2%; SAT writing scores over 700: 2%; ACT scores over 30: 10%.

Retention: 83% of full-time freshmen returned.

FACULTY

Total: 222, 74% full-time, 73% with terminal degrees.

Student/faculty ratio: 11:1.

ACADEMICS

Calendar: semesters. *Degree:* bachelor's.

Special study options: accelerated degree program, adult/continuing education programs, advanced placement credit, distance learning, double majors, English as a second language, honors programs, independent study, internships, off-campus study, part-time degree program, services for LD students, study abroad, summer session for credit.

Unusual degree programs: 3-2 engineering with Virginia Polytechnic Institute and State University.

Computers: 270 computers/terminals and 1,600 ports are available on campus for general student use. Students can access the following: campus intranet, computer help desk, free student e-mail accounts, online (class) grades, online (class) registration, online (class) schedules, discounts on computer hardware and software purchases, free office software, free security software. Campuswide network is available. 100% of college-owned or -operated housing units are wired for high-speed Internet access. Wireless service is available via entire campus.

Library: Fintel Library. *Books:* 164,291 (physical), 190,250 (digital/electronic); *Serial titles:* 313 (physical), 58,378 (digital/electronic); *Databases:* 200. Weekly public service hours: 100; study areas open 24 hours, 5-7 days a week; students can reserve study rooms.

STUDENT LIFE

Housing options: on-campus residence required through senior year; coed, women-only, special housing for students with disabilities. Campus housing is university owned. Freshman campus housing is guaranteed.

Activities and organizations: drama/theater group, student-run newspaper, radio station, choral group, Catholic Campus Ministry, Roanoke College Lutherans, International Club, Colleges Against Cancer, College Republicans, national fraternities, national sororities.

Athletics Member NCAA. All Division III. ***Intercollegiate sports:*** baseball M, basketball M/W, cross-country running M/W, field hockey W, golf M, lacrosse M/W, soccer M/W, softball W, swimming and diving M/W, tennis M/W, track and field M/W, volleyball W. ***Intramural sports:*** baseball M(c), basketball M(c)/W, cheerleading M(c)/W(c), equestrian sports M(c)/W(c), football M/W, golf M(c)/W(c), ice hockey M(c)/W(c), rugby M(c), soccer M(c)/W(c), softball M/W, tennis M(c)/W(c), ultimate Frisbee M(c)/W(c), volleyball M/W, weight lifting M(c).

Campus security: 24-hour emergency response devices and patrols, late-night transport/escort service, controlled dormitory access, campus emergency phones, Maroon Alert system.

Student services: health clinic, personal/psychological counseling.

COSTS & FINANCIAL AID

Costs (2017–18) ***One-time required fee:*** $125. ***Comprehensive fee:*** $55,952 includes full-time tuition ($41,110), mandatory fees ($1584), and room and board ($13,258). Part-time tuition: $1964 per course. Part-time tuition and fees vary according to course load and reciprocity agreements. ***Required fees:*** $60 per term part-time. ***College room only:*** $6156. Room and board charges vary according to board plan and housing facility. ***Payment plan:*** installment. ***Waivers:*** adult students, senior citizens, and employees or children of employees.

Financial Aid Of all full-time matriculated undergraduates who enrolled in 2016, 1,611 applied for aid, 1,436 were judged to have need, 345 had their need fully met. In 2016, 473 non-need-based awards were made. ***Average percent of need met:*** 81. ***Average financial aid package:*** $32,685. ***Average need-based loan:*** $4930. ***Average need-based gift aid:*** $27,005. ***Average non-need-based aid:*** $18,442. ***Average indebtedness upon graduation:*** $39,175.

APPLYING

Standardized Tests *Required:* SAT or ACT (for admission).

Options: electronic application, early admission, early decision, deferred entrance.

Application fee: $30.

Required: high school transcript. ***Recommended:*** essay or personal statement, 1 letter of recommendation, interview.

Application deadlines: 3/15 (freshmen), 8/1 (transfers).

Early decision deadline: 11/15.

Notification: continuous until 4/1 (freshmen), continuous until 8/15 (transfers), 12/15 (early decision).

CONTACT

Admissions Office, Roanoke College, 221 College Lane, Salem, VA 24153. *Phone:* 540-375-2270. *Toll-free phone:* 800-388-2276. *Fax:* 540-375-2267. *E-mail:* admissions@roanoke.edu.

Sentara College of Health Sciences

Chesapeake, Virginia

http://www.sentara.edu/

- **Independent** 4-year
- **Urban** campus with easy access to Virginia Beach
- **Coed** 383 undergraduate students, 39% full-time, 89% women, 11% men

UNDERGRAD STUDENTS

148 full-time, 235 part-time. Students come from 2 states and territories; 9% Black or African American, non-Hispanic/Latino; 3% Hispanic/Latino; 10% Asian, non-Hispanic/Latino; 1% Native Hawaiian or other Pacific Islander, non-Hispanic/Latino; 6% Race/ethnicity unknown.

FACULTY

Total: 51, 57% full-time, 25% with terminal degrees.

Student/faculty ratio: 5:1.

ACADEMICS

Calendar: semesters. *Degrees:* associate and bachelor's.

Special study options: academic remediation for entering students, adult/continuing education programs, distance learning, honors programs, part-time degree program, services for LD students, summer session for credit.

Computers: 13 computers/terminals are available on campus for general student use. Students can access the following: free student e-mail accounts, online (class) grades. Campuswide network is available. Wireless service is available via entire campus.

Library: Sentara Healthcare Library. *Books:* 2,846 (physical), 965 (digital/electronic); *Serial titles:* 204 (physical), 5,804 (digital/electronic); *Databases:* 26.

STUDENT LIFE

Housing options: college housing not available.

Activities and organizations: Sentara Nursing Student Association, Student Association of Allied Health Professionals.

Campus security: 24-hour emergency response devices.

Student services: personal/psychological counseling.

COSTS

Costs (2016–17) ***One-time required fee:*** $85. ***Tuition:*** $9604 full-time, $343 per credit hour part-time. Full-time tuition and fees vary according to course level, course load, degree level, and program. Part-time tuition and fees vary according to course level, course load, degree level, and program. ***Required fees:*** $1725 full-time, $1725 per year part-time.

APPLYING

Standardized Tests *Required for some:* TEAS for BSN, TEAS V for allied health programs, ATI TEAS (BSN/CVT/ST.

Required: minimum 3.5 GPA, general education prerequisite courses, cumulative GPA of 3.3 on all college transcripts.

CONTACT

Sentara College of Health Sciences, 1441 Crossways Boulevard, Crossways I, Suite 105, Chesapeake, VA 23320.

Shenandoah University

Winchester, Virginia

http://www.su.edu/

- **Independent United Methodist** comprehensive, founded 1875
- **Small-town** 315-acre campus with easy access to Washington, D.C.
- **Endowment** $60.3 million
- **Coed** 2,099 undergraduate students, 96% full-time, 60% women, 40% men

UNDERGRAD STUDENTS

2,024 full-time, 75 part-time. Students come from 37 states and territories; 38 other countries; 39% are from out of state; 12% Black or African American, non-Hispanic/Latino; 7% Hispanic/Latino; 3% Asian, non-Hispanic/Latino; 0.1% Native Hawaiian or other Pacific Islander, non-Hispanic/Latino; 0.7% American Indian or Alaska Native, non-Hispanic/Latino; 3% Two or more races, non-Hispanic/Latino; 15% Race/ethnicity unknown; 4% international; 9% transferred in; 48% live on campus.

Freshmen:

Admission: 460 enrolled. ***Average high school GPA:*** 3.42. ***Test scores:*** SAT critical reading scores over 500: 51%; SAT math scores over 500: 49%; ACT scores over 18: 84%; SAT critical reading scores over 600: 19%; SAT math scores over 600: 12%; ACT scores over 24: 40%; SAT critical reading scores over 700: 3%; SAT math scores over 700: 1%; ACT scores over 30: 7%.

Retention: 82% of full-time freshmen returned.

FACULTY

Total: 447, 56% full-time, 59% with terminal degrees.

Student/faculty ratio: 10:1.

ACADEMICS

Calendar: semesters. *Degrees:* certificates, bachelor's, master's, doctoral, post-master's, and postbachelor's certificates.

Special study options: accelerated degree program, adult/continuing education programs, advanced placement credit, distance learning, double majors, English as a second language, independent study, internships, off-campus study, part-time degree program, services for LD students, student-designed majors, study abroad, summer session for credit.

Unusual degree programs: 3-2 occupational therapy, athletic training.

Computers: 32 computers/terminals and 218 ports are available on campus for general student use. Students can access the following: campus intranet, computer help desk, free student e-mail accounts, online (class) grades, online (class) registration, online (class) schedules, online student account information. Campuswide network is available. 100% of college-owned or -operated housing units are wired for high-speed Internet access. Wireless service is available via entire campus.

Library: Alson H. Smith, Jr. Library plus 1 other. *Books:* 122,422 (physical), 217,000 (digital/electronic); *Serial titles:* 700 (physical), 86,500 (digital/electronic); *Databases:* 135. Weekly public service hours: 96; students can reserve study rooms.

STUDENT LIFE

Housing options: on-campus residence required through sophomore year; coed, special housing for students with disabilities. Campus housing is university owned and leased by the school. Freshman campus housing is guaranteed.

Activities and organizations: drama/theater group, student-run newspaper, radio station, choral group, Student Government Association, Graduate Student Assembly, Campus Activities Network, Colleges Against Cancer, Variety of Groups for Professional Fraternities.

Athletics Member NCAA. All Division III. ***Intercollegiate sports:*** baseball M, basketball M/W, cross-country running M/W, field hockey W, football M, golf M/W, lacrosse M/W, soccer M/W, softball W, tennis M/W, track and field M/W, volleyball W. ***Intramural sports:*** basketball M/W, cheerleading M(c)/W(c), equestrian sports M(c)/W(c), football

M/W, sand volleyball M/W, soccer M/W, softball M/W, table tennis M/W, ultimate Frisbee M/W, volleyball M/W.

Campus security: 24-hour emergency response devices and patrols, late-night transport/escort service, controlled dormitory access, LiveSafe mobile app, anonymous reporting, side-door alarms, campus shuttle, Safe in Sixty Seconds Program, Safe Walk/Safe Ride Program.

Student services: health clinic, personal/psychological counseling, women's center.

COSTS & FINANCIAL AID

Costs (2017–18) ***Comprehensive fee:*** $42,100 includes full-time tuition ($30,700), mandatory fees ($1220), and room and board ($10,180). Full-time tuition and fees vary according to course load and program. Part-time tuition: $895 per credit hour. Part-time tuition and fees vary according to course load and program. ***Required fees:*** $370 per term part-time. ***Room and board:*** Room and board charges vary according to board plan and housing facility. ***Payment plan:*** installment. ***Waivers:*** employees or children of employees.

Financial Aid Of all full-time matriculated undergraduates who enrolled in 2016, 1,697 applied for aid, 1,495 were judged to have need, 125 had their need fully met. In 2016, 204 non-need-based awards were made. ***Average percent of need met:*** 22. ***Average financial aid package:*** $19,949. ***Average need-based loan:*** $4061. ***Average need-based gift aid:*** $6758. ***Average non-need-based aid:*** $7916. ***Average indebtedness upon graduation:*** $22,392.

APPLYING

Standardized Tests *Required:* SAT or ACT (for admission).

Required: high school transcript. ***Required for some:*** interview, audition for conservatory applicants, interview for some Conservatory programs and for Guaranteed Admission for Health Professions programs.

CONTACT

Mr. Thomas McKenna, Associate Director of Admissions, Shenandoah University, 1460 University Drive, Wilkins Building, Admissions Office, Winchester, VA 22601-5195. *Phone:* 540-545-7327. *Toll-free phone:* 800-432-2266. *Fax:* 540-665.4627. *E-mail:* admit@su.edu.

Southern Virginia University

Buena Vista, Virginia

http://www.svu.edu/

CONTACT

Mr. Tony Caputo, Dean of Admissions, Southern Virginia University, One University Hill Drive, Buena Vista, VA 24416. *Phone:* 540-261-2756. *Toll-free phone:* 800-229-8420. *Fax:* 540-261-8559. *E-mail:* admissions@southernvirginia.edu.

South University

Glen Allen, Virginia

http://www.southuniversity.edu/richmond

CONTACT

South University, 2151 Old Brick Road, Glen Allen, VA 23060. *Phone:* 804-727-6800. *Toll-free phone:* 888-422-5076.

South University

Virginia Beach, Virginia

http://www.southuniversity.edu/virginia-beach

CONTACT

South University, 301 Bendix Road, Suite 100, Virginia Beach, VA 23452. *Phone:* 757-493-6900. *Toll-free phone:* 877-206-1845.

Stratford University

Alexandria, Virginia

http://www.stratford.edu/

- **Proprietary** comprehensive
- **Urban** campus with easy access to Washington DC
- **Coed** 292 undergraduate students, 21% full-time, 66% women, 34% men

UNDERGRAD STUDENTS

61 full-time, 231 part-time. Students come from 3 states and territories; 60% are from out of state; 63% Black or African American, non-Hispanic/Latino; 7% Hispanic/Latino; 4% Asian, non-Hispanic/Latino; 0.3% Native Hawaiian or other Pacific Islander, non-Hispanic/Latino; 5% American Indian or Alaska Native, non-Hispanic/Latino; 1% Two or more races, non-Hispanic/Latino; 9% Race/ethnicity unknown; 64% transferred in.

Freshmen:

Admission: 25 enrolled.

FACULTY

Total: 45, 20% full-time.

ACADEMICS

Calendar: quarters. *Degrees:* associate, bachelor's, and master's.

Special study options: academic remediation for entering students, accelerated degree program, adult/continuing education programs, cooperative education, distance learning, internships, off-campus study, part-time degree program, services for LD students, summer session for credit.

Computers: Students can access the following: campus intranet, computer help desk, free student e-mail accounts, online (class) grades, online (class) registration, online (class) schedules. Campuswide network is available. Wireless service is available via entire campus.

Library: Learning Resource Center.

STUDENT LIFE

Housing options: college housing not available.

COSTS

Costs (2017–18) ***One-time required fee:*** $100. ***Tuition:*** $14,985 full-time, $1665 per course part-time. Full-time tuition and fees vary according to course level, course load, degree level, and program. Part-time tuition and fees vary according to course level, course load, degree level, and program. ***Payment plan:*** installment. ***Waivers:*** employees or children of employees.

APPLYING

Options: electronic application.

Application fee: $50.

Required: high school transcript, interview. ***Recommended:*** essay or personal statement.

Application deadlines: rolling (freshmen), rolling (transfers).

Notification: continuous (freshmen), continuous (transfers).

CONTACT

Admissions, Stratford University, 2900 Eisenhower Avenue, Alexandria, VA 22314. *Phone:* 571-699-3200. *Toll-free phone:* 800-444-0804. *E-mail:* alexandriaadmissions@stratford.edu.

★ Stratford University

Falls Church, Virginia

http://www.stratford.edu/

- **Proprietary** comprehensive, founded 1976
- **Urban** campus with easy access to Washington, DC
- **Coed** 407 undergraduate students, 29% full-time, 76% women, 24% men
- **Noncompetitive** entrance level

UNDERGRAD STUDENTS

118 full-time, 289 part-time. 57% Black or African American, non-Hispanic/Latino; 15% Hispanic/Latino; 13% Asian, non-Hispanic/Latino; 0.3% Native Hawaiian or other Pacific Islander, non-Hispanic/Latino; 0.6% American Indian or Alaska Native, non-Hispanic/Latino; 0.8% Two or more races, non-Hispanic/Latino.

Freshmen:

Admission: 11 enrolled.

FACULTY

Total: 128, 20% full-time.

ACADEMICS

Calendar: quarters. *Degrees:* diplomas, associate, bachelor's, master's, and doctoral.

Special study options: academic remediation for entering students, accelerated degree program, adult/continuing education programs, cooperative education, distance learning, English as a second language, independent study, internships, off-campus study, part-time degree program, services for LD students, summer session for credit.

Computers: Students can access the following: campus intranet, computer help desk, free student e-mail accounts, online (class) grades, online (class) registration, online (class) schedules. Campuswide network is available. Wireless service is available via entire campus.
Library: Learning Resource Center.

STUDENT LIFE
Housing options: college housing not available.

COSTS
Costs (2016–17) ***One-time required fee:*** $100. ***Tuition:*** $14,985 full-time, $1665 per course part-time. Full-time tuition and fees vary according to course level, course load, degree level, and program. Part-time tuition and fees vary according to course level, course load, degree level, and program. ***Payment plan:*** installment. ***Waivers:*** employees or children of employees.

APPLYING
Options: electronic application.
Application fee: $50.
Required: high school transcript, interview. ***Recommended:*** essay or personal statement.
Application deadlines: rolling (freshmen), rolling (transfers).
Notification: continuous (freshmen), continuous (transfers).

CONTACT
Admissions, Stratford University, 7777 Leesburg Pike, Falls Church, VA 22043. *Phone:* 703-821-8570. *Toll-free phone:* 800-444-0804. *E-mail:* fcadmissions@stratford.edu.

Stratford University

Glen Allen, Virginia

http://www.stratford.edu/

- **Proprietary** comprehensive
- **Suburban** campus with easy access to Richmond, VA
- **Coed** 176 undergraduate students, 13% full-time, 62% women, 38% men

UNDERGRAD STUDENTS
23 full-time, 153 part-time. 69% Black or African American, non-Hispanic/Latino; 5% Hispanic/Latino; 0.6% Asian, non-Hispanic/Latino; 0.6% Native Hawaiian or other Pacific Islander, non-Hispanic/Latino; 1% American Indian or Alaska Native, non-Hispanic/Latino; 1% Two or more races, non-Hispanic/Latino.

Freshmen:
Admission: 6 enrolled.

FACULTY
Total: 57, 16% full-time.

ACADEMICS
Calendar: quarters. *Degrees:* associate, bachelor's, and master's.

Special study options: academic remediation for entering students, accelerated degree program, adult/continuing education programs, cooperative education, distance learning, independent study, internships, off-campus study, part-time degree program, services for LD students, summer session for credit.

Computers: Students can access the following: campus intranet, computer help desk, free student e-mail accounts, online (class) grades, online (class) registration, online (class) schedules. Campuswide network is available. Wireless service is available via entire campus.
Library: Learning Resource Center.

STUDENT LIFE
Housing options: college housing not available.

COSTS
Costs (2016–17) ***One-time required fee:*** $100. ***Tuition:*** $14,985 full-time, $1665 per course part-time. Full-time tuition and fees vary according to course level, course load, degree level, and program. Part-time tuition and fees vary according to course level, course load, degree level, and program. ***Payment plan:*** installment. ***Waivers:*** employees or children of employees.

APPLYING
Required: high school transcript, interview. ***Recommended:*** essay or personal statement.

CONTACT
Admissions, Stratford University, 11104 West Broad Street, Glen Allen, VA 23060. *Phone:* 804-290-4231. *Toll-free phone:* 877-373-5173. *E-mail:* gaadmissions@stratford.edu.

Stratford University

Newport News, Virginia

http://www.stratford.edu/

- **Proprietary** comprehensive
- **Urban** campus with easy access to Richmond
- **Coed** 265 undergraduate students, 26% full-time, 66% women, 34% men

UNDERGRAD STUDENTS
70 full-time, 195 part-time. Students come from 2 states and territories; 1% are from out of state; 71% Black or African American, non-Hispanic/Latino; 4% Hispanic/Latino; 2% Asian, non-Hispanic/Latino; 0.4% Native Hawaiian or other Pacific Islander, non-Hispanic/Latino; 0.8% American Indian or Alaska Native, non-Hispanic/Latino; 2% Two or more races, non-Hispanic/Latino; 0.4% Race/ethnicity unknown; 47% transferred in.

Freshmen:
Admission: 16 enrolled.
Retention: 71% of full-time freshmen returned.

FACULTY
Total: 62, 19% full-time.

ACADEMICS
Calendar: quarters. *Degrees:* associate, bachelor's, and master's.

Special study options: academic remediation for entering students, accelerated degree program, adult/continuing education programs, cooperative education, distance learning, independent study, internships, part-time degree program, services for LD students, summer session for credit.

Computers: Students can access the following: campus intranet, computer help desk, free student e-mail accounts, online (class) grades, online (class) registration, online (class) schedules. Campuswide network is available. Wireless service is available via entire campus.
Library: Learning Resource Center.

STUDENT LIFE
Housing options: college housing not available.

COSTS
Costs (2017–18) ***One-time required fee:*** $100. ***Tuition:*** $14,985 full-time, $1665 per course part-time. Full-time tuition and fees vary according to course level, course load, degree level, and program. Part-time tuition and fees vary according to course level, course load, degree level, and program. ***Payment plan:*** installment. ***Waivers:*** employees or children of employees.

APPLYING
Required: high school transcript, interview. ***Recommended:*** essay or personal statement.

CONTACT
Admissions, Stratford University, 836 J. Clyde Morris Boulevard, Newport News, VA 23601. *Phone:* 757-873-4235. *Toll-free phone:* 855-873-4235. *E-mail:* newportnewsadmissions@stratford.edu.

Stratford University

Virginia Beach, Virginia

http://www.stratford.edu/

- **Proprietary** comprehensive
- **Urban** campus
- **Coed** 245 undergraduate students, 38% full-time, 62% women, 38% men

UNDERGRAD STUDENTS
93 full-time, 152 part-time. Students come from 3 states and territories; 2% are from out of state; 54% Black or African American, non-Hispanic/Latino; 7% Hispanic/Latino; 3% Asian, non-Hispanic/Latino; 0.8% Native Hawaiian or other Pacific Islander, non-Hispanic/Latino; 3% American Indian or Alaska Native, non-Hispanic/Latino; 2% Two or more races, non-Hispanic/Latino; 2% Race/ethnicity unknown; 10% transferred in.

Freshmen:
Admission: 13 enrolled.

FACULTY
Total: 56, 20% full-time.

ACADEMICS
Calendar: quarters. *Degrees:* associate, bachelor's, and master's.
Special study options: academic remediation for entering students, accelerated degree program, adult/continuing education programs, cooperative education, distance learning, internships, part-time degree program, summer session for credit.
Computers: Students can access the following: campus intranet, computer help desk, free student e-mail accounts, online (class) grades, online (class) registration, online (class) schedules. Campuswide network is available. Wireless service is available via entire campus.
Library: Learning Resource Center.

STUDENT LIFE
Housing options: college housing not available.

COSTS
Costs (2017–18) ***One-time required fee:*** $100. ***Tuition:*** $14,985 full-time, $1665 per course part-time. Full-time tuition and fees vary according to course level, course load, degree level, and program. Part-time tuition and fees vary according to course level, course load, degree level, and program. ***Payment plan:*** installment. ***Waivers:*** employees or children of employees.

APPLYING
Options: electronic application.
Application fee: $50.
Required: high school transcript, interview. ***Recommended:*** essay or personal statement.
Application deadlines: rolling (freshmen), rolling (transfers).
Notification: continuous (freshmen), continuous (transfers).

CONTACT
Admissions, Stratford University, 555 South Independence Boulevard, Virginia Beach, VA 23452. *Phone:* 757-497-4466.
Toll-free phone: 866-528-8363.
E-mail: virginiabeachadmissions@stratford.edu.

Stratford University
Woodbridge, Virginia
http://www.stratford.edu/

- **Proprietary** comprehensive
- **Suburban** campus with easy access to Washington DC
- **Coed** 361 undergraduate students, 27% full-time, 69% women, 31% men

UNDERGRAD STUDENTS
97 full-time, 264 part-time. Students come from 8 states and territories; 7% are from out of state; 44% Black or African American, non-Hispanic/Latino; 12% Hispanic/Latino; 6% Asian, non-Hispanic/Latino; 0.3% Native Hawaiian or other Pacific Islander, non-Hispanic/Latino; 6% American Indian or Alaska Native, non-Hispanic/Latino; 1% Two or more races, non-Hispanic/Latino; 6% Race/ethnicity unknown; 60% transferred in.

Freshmen:
Admission: 8 enrolled.

FACULTY
Total: 77, 23% full-time.

ACADEMICS
Calendar: quarters. *Degrees:* diplomas, associate, bachelor's, and master's.
Special study options: academic remediation for entering students, accelerated degree program, adult/continuing education programs, cooperative education, distance learning, independent study, internships, part-time degree program, summer session for credit.
Computers: Students can access the following: campus intranet, computer help desk, free student e-mail accounts, online (class) registration, online (class) schedules. Campuswide network is available. Wireless service is available via entire campus.
Library: Learning Resource Center.

STUDENT LIFE
Housing options: college housing not available.

COSTS
Costs (2017–18) ***One-time required fee:*** $100. ***Tuition:*** $14,985 full-time, $1665 per course part-time. Full-time tuition and fees vary according to course level, course load, degree level, and program. Part-time tuition and fees vary according to course level, course load, degree level, and program. ***Payment plan:*** installment. ***Waivers:*** employees or children of employees.

APPLYING
Options: electronic application.
Application fee: $50.
Required: high school transcript, interview. ***Required for some:*** letters of recommendation. ***Recommended:*** essay or personal statement.
Application deadlines: rolling (freshmen), rolling (transfers).
Notification: continuous (freshmen), continuous (transfers).

CONTACT
Admissions, Stratford University, 14349 Gideon Drive, Woodbridge, VA 22192. *Phone:* 703-897-1982. *Toll-free phone:* 888-546-1250. *E-mail:* woodbridgeadmissions@stratford.edu.

Strayer University–Alexandria Campus
Alexandria, Virginia
http://www.strayer.edu/virginia/alexandria/

CONTACT
Strayer University–Alexandria Campus, 2730 Eisenhower Avenue, Alexandria, VA 22314.

Strayer University–Arlington Campus
Arlington, Virginia
http://www.strayer.edu/virginia/arlington/

CONTACT
Strayer University–Arlington Campus, 2121 15th Street North, Arlington, VA 22201.

Strayer University–Chesapeake Campus
Chesapeake, Virginia
http://www.strayer.edu/virginia/chesapeake/

CONTACT
Strayer University–Chesapeake Campus, 676 Independence Parkway, Suite 300, Chesapeake, VA 23320.

Strayer University–Chesterfield Campus
Midlothian, Virginia
http://www.strayer.edu/virginia/chesterfield/

CONTACT
Strayer University–Chesterfield Campus, 2820 Waterford Lake Drive, Suite 100, Midlothian, VA 23112.

Strayer University–Fredericksburg Campus

Fredericksburg, Virginia

http://www.strayer.edu/virginia/fredericksburg/

CONTACT
Strayer University–Fredericksburg Campus, 150 Riverside Parkway, Suite 100, Fredericksburg, VA 22406.

Strayer University–Henrico Campus

Glen Allen, Virginia

http://www.strayer.edu/virginia/henrico/

CONTACT
Strayer University–Henrico Campus, 11501 Nuckols Road, Glen Allen, VA 23059.

Strayer University–Loudoun Campus

Ashburn, Virginia

http://www.strayer.edu/virginia/loudoun/

CONTACT
Strayer University–Loudoun Campus, 45150 Russell Branch Parkway, Suite 200, Ashburn, VA 20147.

Strayer University–Manassas Campus

Manassas, Virginia

http://www.strayer.edu/virginia/manassas/

CONTACT
Strayer University–Manassas Campus, 9990 Battleview Parkway, Manassas, VA 20109.

Strayer University–Newport News Campus

Newport News, Virginia

http://www.strayer.edu/virginia/newport-news/

CONTACT
Strayer University–Newport News Campus, 99 Old Oyster Point Road, Unit 1, Newport News, VA 23602.

Strayer University–Virginia Beach Campus

Virginia Beach, Virginia

http://www.strayer.edu/virginia/virginia-beach/

CONTACT
Strayer University–Virginia Beach Campus, 249 Central Park Avenue, Suite 350, Virginia Beach, VA 23462.

Strayer University–Woodbridge Campus

Woodbridge, Virginia

http://www.strayer.edu/virginia/woodbridge/

CONTACT
Strayer University–Woodbridge Campus, 13385 Minnieville Road, Woodbridge, VA 22192.

Sweet Briar College

Sweet Briar, Virginia

http://www.sbc.edu/

- **Independent** comprehensive, founded 1901
- **Rural** 3250-acre campus
- **Endowment** $68.0 million
- **Women only** 365 undergraduate students, 98% full-time
- **Minimally difficult** entrance level, 93% of applicants were admitted

UNDERGRAD STUDENTS
356 full-time, 9 part-time. Students come from 31 states and territories; 5 other countries; 49% are from out of state; 10% Black or African American, non-Hispanic/Latino; 10% Hispanic/Latino; 2% Asian, non-Hispanic/Latino; 0.3% Native Hawaiian or other Pacific Islander, non-Hispanic/Latino; 0.3% American Indian or Alaska Native, non-Hispanic/Latino; 4% Two or more races, non-Hispanic/Latino; 0.6% Race/ethnicity unknown; 2% international; 6% transferred in; 93% live on campus.

Freshmen:
Admission: 950 applied, 884 admitted, 134 enrolled. ***Average high school GPA:*** 3.5. ***Test scores:*** SAT critical reading scores over 500: 61%; SAT math scores over 500: 47%; SAT writing scores over 500: 58%; ACT scores over 18: 77%; SAT critical reading scores over 600: 31%; SAT math scores over 600: 19%; SAT writing scores over 600: 19%; ACT scores over 24: 42%; SAT critical reading scores over 700: 4%; SAT math scores over 700: 2%; SAT writing scores over 700: 2%; ACT scores over 30: 12%.
Retention: 50% of full-time freshmen returned.

FACULTY
Total: 79, 75% full-time, 72% with terminal degrees.
Student/faculty ratio: 5:1.

ACADEMICS
Calendar: semesters. *Degrees:* bachelor's and master's.
Special study options: adult/continuing education programs, advanced placement credit, double majors, honors programs, independent study, internships, off-campus study, part-time degree program, services for LD students, student-designed majors, study abroad, summer session for credit.
Unusual degree programs: 3-2 engineering with Virginia Polytechnic Institute and State University, University of Virginia, Columbia University, Washington University in St. Louis.
Computers: 111 computers/terminals and 3,000 ports are available on campus for general student use. Students can access the following: campus intranet, computer help desk, free student e-mail accounts, online (class) grades, online (class) registration, online (class) schedules. Campuswide network is available. 100% of college-owned or -operated housing units are wired for high-speed Internet access. Wireless service is available via entire campus.
Library: Mary Helen Cochran Library plus 1 other. *Books:* 254,573 (physical), 787,753 (digital/electronic); *Serial titles:* 1,273 (physical), 46,683 (digital/electronic); *Databases:* 118. Weekly public service hours: 96; study areas open 24 hours, 5-7 days a week.

STUDENT LIFE
Housing options: on-campus residence required through senior year; women-only. Campus housing is university owned. Freshman campus housing is guaranteed.
Activities and organizations: drama/theater group, student-run newspaper, radio station, choral group, Student Government Association, Campus Events Organization, Interclub Council, MInority Student Union, Paint and Patches - Theater Group.
Athletics Member NCAA. All Division III. ***Intercollegiate sports:*** cross-country running W, equestrian sports W, field hockey W, golf W, lacrosse W, soccer W, softball W, swimming and diving W, tennis W.
Campus security: 24-hour emergency response devices and patrols, student patrols, late-night transport/escort service, controlled dormitory access, front gate security.
Student services: health clinic, personal/psychological counseling, women's center.

COSTS & FINANCIAL AID
Costs (2017–18) ***Comprehensive fee:*** $50,060 includes full-time tuition ($36,520), mandatory fees ($640), and room and board ($12,900). Part-time tuition: $1070 per credit hour. ***Room and board:*** Room and board charges vary according to board plan. ***Payment plan:*** installment. ***Waivers:*** adult students, senior citizens, and employees or children of employees.

Financial Aid Of all full-time matriculated undergraduates who enrolled in 2015, 199 applied for aid, 180 were judged to have need, 44 had their need fully met. In 2015, 51 non-need-based awards were made. ***Average percent of need met:*** 83. ***Average financial aid package:*** $33,548. ***Average need-based loan:*** $4973. ***Average need-based gift aid:*** $28,394. ***Average non-need-based aid:*** $20,074. ***Average indebtedness upon graduation:*** $33,026.

APPLYING
Standardized Tests *Required:* SAT or ACT (for admission).

Options: electronic application, deferred entrance.

Required: essay or personal statement, high school transcript, 2 letters of recommendation.

Notification: continuous (freshmen).

CONTACT
Bill Allen, Vice President for Enrollment Management, Sweet Briar College, PO Box 1052, Sweet Briar, VA 24595. *Phone:* 434-381-6142. *Toll-free phone:* 800-381-6142. *Fax:* 434-381-6152. *E-mail:* admissions@sbc.edu.

University of Lynchburg
Lynchburg, Virginia
http://www.lynchburg.edu/

- **Independent** comprehensive, founded 1903, affiliated with Christian Church (Disciples of Christ)
- **Suburban** 264-acre campus
- **Endowment** $96.6 million
- **Coed** 2,079 undergraduate students, 93% full-time, 61% women, 39% men
- **Moderately difficult** entrance level, 64% of applicants were admitted

UNDERGRAD STUDENTS
1,938 full-time, 141 part-time. Students come from 37 states and territories; 15 other countries; 30% are from out of state; 12% Black or African American, non-Hispanic/Latino; 5% Hispanic/Latino; 1% Asian, non-Hispanic/Latino; 0.4% American Indian or Alaska Native, non-Hispanic/Latino; 4% Two or more races, non-Hispanic/Latino; 3% Race/ethnicity unknown; 3% international; 3% transferred in; 75% live on campus.

Freshmen:
Admission: 5,223 applied, 3,331 admitted, 521 enrolled. ***Average high school GPA:*** 3.5. ***Test scores:*** SAT critical reading scores over 500: 55%; SAT math scores over 500: 56%; ACT scores over 18: 86%; SAT critical reading scores over 600: 15%; SAT math scores over 600: 13%; ACT scores over 24: 37%; SAT critical reading scores over 700: 1%; SAT math scores over 700: 1%; ACT scores over 30: 2%.

Retention: 81% of full-time freshmen returned.

FACULTY
Total: 288, 63% full-time, 64% with terminal degrees.

Student/faculty ratio: 10:1.

ACADEMICS
Calendar: semesters. *Degrees:* bachelor's, master's, doctoral, post-master's, and postbachelor's certificates.

Special study options: accelerated degree program, adult/continuing education programs, advanced placement credit, distance learning, double majors, English as a second language, honors programs, independent study, internships, off-campus study, part-time degree program, services for LD students, student-designed majors, study abroad, summer session for credit.

Unusual degree programs: 3-2 engineering with Old Dominion University, University of Virginia.

Computers: 300 computers/terminals are available on campus for general student use. Students can access the following: campus intranet, computer help desk, free student e-mail accounts, online (class) grades, online (class) registration, online (class) schedules. Campuswide network is available. 100% of college-owned or -operated housing units are wired for high-speed Internet access. Wireless service is available via entire campus.

Library: Knight-Capron Library. *Books:* 122,870 (physical), 306,584 (digital/electronic). Study areas open 24 hours, 5-7 days a week.

STUDENT LIFE
Housing options: on-campus residence required through junior year; coed, special housing for students with disabilities. Campus housing is university owned. Freshman campus housing is guaranteed.

Activities and organizations: drama/theater group, student-run newspaper, choral group, Student Government Association, Student Activities Board, Enrollment Student Ambassadors, Emergency Services, Greek Life, national fraternities, national sororities.

Athletics Member NCAA. All Division III. ***Intercollegiate sports:*** baseball M, basketball M/W, cheerleading M/W, cross-country running M/W, equestrian sports M/W, field hockey W, golf M, lacrosse M/W, soccer M/W, softball W, tennis M/W, track and field M/W, volleyball W. ***Intramural sports:*** basketball M(c)/W(c), golf M(c)/W(c), lacrosse M(c)/W(c), rugby M/W, soccer M(c)/W(c), tennis M(c)/W(c), volleyball M/W, wrestling M(c).

Campus security: 24-hour emergency response devices and patrols, late-night transport/escort service, controlled dormitory access.

Student services: health clinic, personal/psychological counseling.

COSTS & FINANCIAL AID
Costs (2016–17) ***Comprehensive fee:*** $46,740 includes full-time tuition ($35,650), mandatory fees ($970), and room and board ($10,120). Part-time tuition: $490 per credit hour. Part-time tuition and fees vary according to course load. ***Required fees:*** $5 per credit hour part-time. ***College room only:*** $5160. Room and board charges vary according to board plan and housing facility. ***Payment plans:*** tuition prepayment, installment. ***Waivers:*** adult students, senior citizens, and employees or children of employees.

Financial Aid Of all full-time matriculated undergraduates who enrolled in 2016, 1,611 applied for aid, 1,482 were judged to have need, 302 had their need fully met. In 2016, 393 non-need-based awards were made. ***Average percent of need met:*** 76. ***Average financial aid package:*** $27,341. ***Average need-based loan:*** $3578. ***Average need-based gift aid:*** $23,781. ***Average non-need-based aid:*** $17,162. ***Average indebtedness upon graduation:*** $35,614.

APPLYING
Standardized Tests *Required:* SAT or ACT (for admission).

Options: electronic application, early admission, early decision, deferred entrance.

Application fee: $30.

Required: high school transcript. ***Recommended:*** essay or personal statement, 2 letters of recommendation, interview.

Application deadlines: rolling (freshmen), rolling (transfers).

Early decision deadline: 11/15.

Notification: continuous (freshmen), continuous (transfers), 12/15 (early decision).

CONTACT
University of Lynchburg , 1501 Lakeside Drive, Lynchburg, VA 24501-3199. *Phone:* 434-544-8300. *Toll-free phone:* 800-426-8101.

See next page for display ad and page 1560 for the College Close-Up.

University of Management and Technology
Arlington, Virginia
http://www.umtweb.edu/

- **Proprietary** comprehensive, founded 1998
- **Urban** campus with easy access to Washington, DC
- **Coed** 1,029 undergraduate students, 46% full-time, 26% women, 74% men

UNDERGRAD STUDENTS
476 full-time, 553 part-time.

FACULTY
Student/faculty ratio: 25:1.

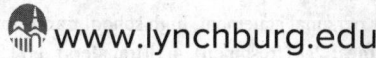

ACADEMICS
Calendar: continuous. *Degrees:* certificates, associate, bachelor's, master's, doctoral, post-master's, and postbachelor's certificates.

Special study options: adult/continuing education programs, part-time degree program.

Computers: Students can access the following: campus intranet, online (class) grades, online (class) registration, online (class) schedules. Campuswide network is available. Wireless service is available via entire campus.

Library: ***Books:*** 9,149 (physical), 35 (digital/electronic).

COSTS & FINANCIAL AID
Costs (2016–17) ***Tuition:*** $9360 full-time, $390 per credit hour part-time. ***Required fees:*** $90 full-time, $30 per term part-time. ***Payment plans:*** installment, deferred payment. ***Waivers:*** employees or children of employees.

Financial Aid Of all full-time matriculated undergraduates who enrolled in 2014, 71 applied for aid, 67 were judged to have need, 67 had their need fully met. ***Average percent of need met:*** 100. ***Average financial aid package:*** $16,980. ***Average need-based loan:*** $3414. ***Average need-based gift aid:*** $3989. ***Average indebtedness upon graduation:*** $15,415.

APPLYING
Application fee: $30.

CONTACT
Mr. Kenny Hickey, University of Management and Technology, 1901 Fort Myers Drive, Suite 700, Arlington, VA 22209. *Phone:* 703-516-0035. *Toll-free phone:* 800-924-4883. *Fax:* 703-516-0985. *E-mail:* admissions@umtweb.edu.

University of Mary Washington
Fredericksburg, Virginia

http://www.umw.edu/

- **State-supported** comprehensive, founded 1908
- **Small-town** 234-acre campus with easy access to Richmond, Washington, D.C.
- **Endowment** $44.9 million
- **Coed** 4,357 undergraduate students, 89% full-time, 64% women, 36% men
- **Very difficult** entrance level, 74% of applicants were admitted

UNDERGRAD STUDENTS
3,859 full-time, 498 part-time. Students come from 34 states and territories; 25 other countries; 10% are from out of state; 7% Black or African American, non-Hispanic/Latino; 8% Hispanic/Latino; 4% Asian, non-Hispanic/Latino; 0.1% Native Hawaiian or other Pacific Islander, non-Hispanic/Latino; 0.3% American Indian or Alaska Native, non-Hispanic/Latino; 5% Two or more races, non-Hispanic/Latino; 4% Race/ethnicity unknown; 1% international; 8% transferred in; 57% live on campus.

Freshmen:
Admission: 6,270 applied, 4,668 admitted, 972 enrolled. ***Average high school GPA:*** 3.59. ***Test scores:*** SAT critical reading scores over 500: 81%; SAT math scores over 500: 75%; SAT writing scores over 500: 72%; ACT scores over 18: 100%; SAT critical reading scores over 600: 36%; SAT math scores over 600: 24%; SAT writing scores over 600: 25%; ACT scores over 24: 64%; SAT critical reading scores over 700: 5%; SAT math scores over 700: 1%; SAT writing scores over 700: 2%; ACT scores over 30: 11%.

Retention: 83% of full-time freshmen returned.

FACULTY
Total: 389, 64% full-time, 71% with terminal degrees.
Student/faculty ratio: 14:1.

ACADEMICS
Calendar: semesters. *Degrees:* certificates, bachelor's, master's, and postbachelor's certificates.

Special study options: adult/continuing education programs, advanced placement credit, distance learning, double majors, honors programs, independent study, internships, part-time degree program, services for LD students, student-designed majors, study abroad, summer session for credit. ***ROTC:*** Army (c).

Computers: 579 computers/terminals are available on campus for general student use. Students can access the following: campus intranet, computer help desk, free student e-mail accounts, online (class) grades, online (class) registration, online (class) schedules, student Web hosting. Campuswide network is available. 100% of college-owned or -operated housing units are wired for high-speed Internet access. Wireless service is available via entire campus.
Library: Simpson Library plus 2 others. *Books:* 338,183 (physical), 201,723 (digital/electronic); *Serial titles:* 3,272 (physical), 77,774 (digital/electronic); *Databases:* 208. Weekly public service hours: 90; students can reserve study rooms.

STUDENT LIFE
Housing options: on-campus residence required through sophomore year; coed, women-only, special housing for students with disabilities. Campus housing is university owned. Freshman campus housing is guaranteed.
Activities and organizations: drama/theater group, student-run newspaper, radio station, choral group, Class Council, Campus Programming Board, Community Outreach and Participation, Association of Residence Halls, Student Government Association.
Athletics Member NCAA. All Division III. ***Intercollegiate sports:*** baseball M, basketball M/W, crew M(c)/W(c), cross-country running M/W, equestrian sports M/W, field hockey W, golf M/W, lacrosse M/W, rugby M(c)/W(c), soccer M/W, softball W, swimming and diving M/W, tennis M/W, track and field M/W, volleyball W. ***Intramural sports:*** badminton M/W, baseball M(c), basketball M/W, cheerleading M(c)/W(c), fencing M(c)/W(c), field hockey W(c), football M/W, lacrosse M(c)/W(c), sand volleyball M/W, soccer M(c)/W(c), softball W, swimming and diving M(c)/W(c), tennis M(c)/W(c), ultimate Frisbee M(c)/W(c), volleyball M(c)/W(c).

Campus security: 24-hour emergency response devices and patrols, student patrols, late-night transport/escort service, controlled dormitory access, self-defense and safety classes. Guardian App.

Student services: health clinic, personal/psychological counseling.

COSTS & FINANCIAL AID
Costs (2016–17) ***One-time required fee:*** $60. ***Tuition:*** state resident $5772 full-time, $248 per credit hour part-time; nonresident $20,362 full-time, $853 per credit hour part-time. Full-time tuition and fees vary according to course load, degree level, and location. Part-time tuition and fees vary according to course load, degree level, and location. ***Required fees:*** $5798 full-time, $165 per credit hour part-time, $30 per term part-time. ***Room and board:*** $11,118; room only: $7326. Room and board charges vary according to board plan and housing facility. ***Payment plan:*** installment. ***Waivers:*** senior citizens.

Financial Aid Of all full-time matriculated undergraduates who enrolled in 2014, 2,305 applied for aid, 1,517 were judged to have need, 179 had their need fully met. 47 Federal Work-Study jobs (averaging $1408). 646 state and other part-time jobs (averaging $976). In 2014, 464 non-need-based awards were made. ***Average percent of need met:*** 49. ***Average financial aid package:*** $8596. ***Average need-based loan:*** $4236. ***Average need-based gift aid:*** $3269. ***Average non-need-based aid:*** $2768. ***Average indebtedness upon graduation:*** $18,029. ***Financial aid deadline:*** 6/1.

APPLYING
Standardized Tests *Required for some:* SAT or ACT (for admission).

Options: electronic application, early admission, early decision, early action, deferred entrance.

Application fee: $50.

Required: essay or personal statement, high school transcript.

Application deadlines: 2/1 (freshmen), 4/1 (transfers), 11/15 (early action).

Early decision deadline: 11/1.

Notification: 4/1 (freshmen), 5/15 (transfers), 1/31 (early decision), 1/31 (early action).

CONTACT
Ms. Melissa Yakabouski, Director of Undergraduate Admissions, University of Mary Washington, 1301 College Avenue, Fredericksburg, VA 22401-5358. *Phone:* 540-654-1669. *Toll-free phone:* 800-468-5614. *Fax:* 540-654-1857. *E-mail:* myak@umw.edu.

University of Richmond
Richmond, Virginia
http://www.richmond.edu/

- **Independent** comprehensive, founded 1830
- **Suburban** 350-acre campus
- **Endowment** $2.2 billion
- **Coed** 3,036 undergraduate students, 99% full-time, 52% women, 48% men
- **Very difficult** entrance level, 32% of applicants were admitted

UNDERGRAD STUDENTS
3,000 full-time, 36 part-time. Students come from 47 states and territories; 74 other countries; 81% are from out of state; 6% Black or African American, non-Hispanic/Latino; 8% Hispanic/Latino; 8% Asian, non-Hispanic/Latino; 0.2% American Indian or Alaska Native, non-Hispanic/Latino; 4% Two or more races, non-Hispanic/Latino; 6% Race/ethnicity unknown; 9% international; 2% transferred in; 91% live on campus.

Freshmen:
Admission: 10,422 applied, 3,385 admitted, 815 enrolled. ***Test scores:*** SAT critical reading scores over 500: 97%; SAT math scores over 500: 98%; SAT writing scores over 500: 96%; ACT scores over 18: 100%; SAT critical reading scores over 600: 78%; SAT math scores over 600: 81%; SAT writing scores over 600: 80%; ACT scores over 24: 97%; SAT critical reading scores over 700: 25%; SAT math scores over 700: 38%; SAT writing scores over 700: 26%; ACT scores over 30: 72%.
Retention: 93% of full-time freshmen returned.

FACULTY
Total: 441, 76% full-time, 86% with terminal degrees.
Student/faculty ratio: 8:1.

ACADEMICS
Calendar: semesters. *Degrees:* bachelor's, master's, and doctoral.
Special study options: advanced placement credit, double majors, English as a second language, honors programs, independent study, internships, off-campus study, part-time degree program, services for LD students, student-designed majors, study abroad, summer session for credit. ***ROTC:*** Army (b).
Unusual degree programs: 3-2 engineering with Columbia University School of Engineering and Applied Science; forestry with Duke University, Virginia Commonwealth University.
Computers: 1,151 computers/terminals and 3,300 ports are available on campus for general student use. Students can access the following: campus intranet, computer help desk, free student e-mail accounts, online (class) grades, online (class) registration, online (class) schedules. Campuswide network is available. 100% of college-owned or -operated housing units are wired for high-speed Internet access. Wireless service is available via entire campus.
Library: Boatwright Memorial Library plus 2 others. *Books:* 555,452 (physical), 299,190 (digital/electronic); *Serial titles:* 630 (physical), 123,863 (digital/electronic); *Databases:* 356. Weekly public service hours: 100; study areas open 24 hours, 5-7 days a week; students can reserve study rooms.

STUDENT LIFE
Housing options: coed, men-only, women-only, special housing for students with disabilities. Campus housing is university owned. Freshman campus housing is guaranteed.
Activities and organizations: drama/theater group, student-run newspaper, radio station, choral group, Greek Life, Sport Clubs, SpiderBoard, InterVarsity Christian Fellowship, Alpha Phi Omega Service Fraternity, national fraternities, national sororities.

Athletics Member NCAA. All Division I except football (Division I-AA). ***Intercollegiate sports:*** baseball M(s), basketball M(s)/W(s), crew M(c)/W(c), cross-country running M/W(s), equestrian sports M(c)/W(c), field hockey W(s), golf M(s)/W(s), ice hockey M(c), lacrosse M(s)/W(s), rugby M(c)/W(c), soccer M(c)/W(c), squash M(c)/W(c), swimming and diving W(s), tennis M(s)/W(s), track and field W(s), ultimate Frisbee M(c)/W(c), volleyball M(c)/W(c), water polo M(c)/W(c). ***Intramural sports:*** archery M(c)/W(c), badminton M(c)/W(c), baseball M(c), basketball M(c)/W, field hockey M(c)/W(c), golf M/W, lacrosse M(c)/W(c), racquetball M/W, soccer M/W, softball M/W, squash M/W, table tennis M/W, tennis M/W, volleyball M/W.

Campus security: 24-hour emergency response devices and patrols, late-night transport/escort service, controlled dormitory access, campus police.

Student services: health clinic, personal/psychological counseling, women's center.

COSTS & FINANCIAL AID

Costs (2017–18) ***Comprehensive fee:*** $62,730 includes full-time tuition ($50,910) and room and board ($11,820). Full-time tuition and fees vary according to course load. Part-time tuition: $2546 per credit hour. Part-time tuition and fees vary according to course load. ***College room only:*** $5440. Room and board charges vary according to board plan and housing facility. ***Payment plan:*** installment. ***Waivers:*** employees or children of employees.

Financial Aid Of all full-time matriculated undergraduates who enrolled in 2016, 1,637 applied for aid, 1,339 were judged to have need, 1,114 had their need fully met. 609 Federal Work-Study jobs (averaging $1395). In 2016, 545 non-need-based awards were made. ***Average percent of need met:*** 100. ***Average financial aid package:*** $45,784. ***Average need-based loan:*** $3730. ***Average need-based gift aid:*** $39,874. ***Average non-need-based aid:*** $22,658. ***Average indebtedness upon graduation:*** $27,670. ***Financial aid deadline:*** 2/1.

APPLYING

Standardized Tests *Required:* SAT or ACT (for admission).

Options: electronic application, early decision, early action, deferred entrance.

Application fee: $50.

Required: essay or personal statement, high school transcript, 1 letter of recommendation.

Application deadlines: 1/15 (freshmen), 2/15 (transfers), 11/1 (early action).

Early decision deadline: 11/1 (for plan 1), 1/15 (for plan 2).

Notification: 4/1 (freshmen), 4/15 (transfers), 12/1 (early decision plan 1), 2/15 (early decision plan 2), 1/15 (early action).

CONTACT

Mr. Gil Villanueva, Dean of Admission, University of Richmond, Brunet Memorial Hall, 28 Westhampton Way, University of Richmond, VA 23173. *Phone:* 804-289-8640. *Toll-free phone:* 800-700-1662. *Fax:* 804-287-6003. *E-mail:* admissions@richmond.edu.

University of Valley Forge Virginia Campus

Woodbridge, Virginia

http://www.valleyforge.edu/

CONTACT

Admissions Coordinator, University of Valley Forge Virginia Campus, 13909 Smoketown Road, Woodbridge, VA 22192. *Phone:* 703-580-4810 Ext. 210. *Toll-free phone:* 800-432-8322.

University of Virginia

Charlottesville, Virginia

http://www.virginia.edu/

- **State-supported** university, founded 1819
- **Suburban** 1167-acre campus with easy access to Richmond
- **Endowment** $5.9 billion
- **Coed** 16,736 undergraduate students, 95% full-time, 56% women, 44% men
- **Very difficult** entrance level, 30% of applicants were admitted

UNDERGRAD STUDENTS

15,816 full-time, 920 part-time. Students come from 54 states and territories; 118 other countries; 28% are from out of state; 6% Black or African American, non-Hispanic/Latino; 6% Hispanic/Latino; 13% Asian, non-Hispanic/Latino; 0.1% American Indian or Alaska Native, non-Hispanic/Latino; 5% Two or more races, non-Hispanic/Latino; 6% Race/ethnicity unknown; 5% international; 4% transferred in; 40% live on campus.

Freshmen:

Admission: 30,840 applied, 9,186 admitted, 3,685 enrolled. ***Test scores:*** SAT critical reading scores over 500: 98%; SAT math scores over 500: 98%; SAT writing scores over 500: 97%; ACT scores over 18: 100%; SAT critical reading scores over 600: 83%; SAT math scores over 600: 86%; SAT writing scores over 600: 83%; ACT scores over 24: 97%; SAT critical reading scores over 700: 35%; SAT math scores over 700: 44%; SAT writing scores over 700: 37%; ACT scores over 30: 64%.

Retention: 97% of full-time freshmen returned.

FACULTY

Total: 1,465, 93% full-time, 89% with terminal degrees.

Student/faculty ratio: 15:1.

ACADEMICS

Calendar: semesters. *Degrees:* bachelor's, master's, doctoral, and post-master's certificates.

Special study options: accelerated degree program, adult/continuing education programs, advanced placement credit, cooperative education, double majors, English as a second language, honors programs, independent study, internships, part-time degree program, services for LD students, student-designed majors, study abroad, summer session for credit. ***ROTC:*** Army (b), Navy (b), Air Force (b).

Unusual degree programs: 3-2 education.

Computers: 250 computers/terminals are available on campus for general student use. Students can access the following: campus intranet, computer help desk, free student e-mail accounts, online (class) grades, online (class) registration, online (class) schedules, online course management tool. Campuswide network is available. 100% of college-owned or -operated housing units are wired for high-speed Internet access. Wireless service is available via classrooms, computer centers, computer labs, dorm rooms, learning centers, libraries, student centers.

Library: Alderman Library plus 14 others. *Books:* 4.7 million (physical), 521,356 (digital/electronic); *Serial titles:* 11,783 (physical), 188,351 (digital/electronic); *Databases:* 1,191. Weekly public service hours: 149; study areas open 24 hours, 5-7 days a week; students can reserve study rooms.

STUDENT LIFE

Housing options: on-campus residence required for freshman year; coed. Campus housing is university owned. Freshman campus housing is guaranteed.

Activities and organizations: drama/theater group, student-run newspaper, radio and television station, choral group, marching band, Madison House, student government, university guides, University Union, The Cavalier Daily, national fraternities, national sororities.

Athletics Member NCAA. All Division I except football (Division I-A). ***Intercollegiate sports:*** baseball M(s), basketball M(s)/W(s), crew W(s), cross-country running M(s)/W(s), field hockey W(s), golf M(s)/W(s), lacrosse M(s)/W(s), soccer M(s)/W(s), softball W(s), swimming and diving M(s)/W(s), tennis M(s)/W(s), track and field M(s)/W(s), volleyball W(s), wrestling M(s). ***Intramural sports:*** archery M(c)/W(c), badminton M(c)/W(c), baseball M(c), basketball M(c)/W(c), cheerleading M(c)/W(c), crew M(c)/W, cross-country running M(c)/W(c), equestrian sports M(c)/W(c), fencing M(c)/W(c), field hockey W(c), football M, golf M(c)/W(c), gymnastics M(c)/W(c), ice hockey M(c), lacrosse W(c), racquetball M(c)/W(c), riflery M(c)/W(c), rock climbing M(c)/W(c), rugby M(c)/W(c), sailing M(c)/W(c), skiing (downhill) M(c)/W(c), soccer M(c)/W(c), softball W(c), squash M(c)/W(c), swimming and diving M(c)/W(c), tennis M(c)/W(c), track and field M(c)/W(c), ultimate Frisbee M(c)/W(c), volleyball M(c)/W(c), water polo M(c)/W(c), wrestling M(c)/W(c).

Campus security: 24-hour emergency response devices and patrols, student patrols, late-night transport/escort service, controlled dormitory access.

Student services: health clinic, personal/psychological counseling, women's center, legal services.

COSTS & FINANCIAL AID

Costs (2016–17) ***Tuition:*** state resident $12,494 full-time, $415 per credit hour part-time; nonresident $42,642 full-time, $1420 per credit hour part-time. Full-time tuition and fees vary according to location, program, and student level. Part-time tuition and fees vary according to location, program, and student level. ***Required fees:*** $2668 full-time, $2654 per year part-time. ***Room and board:*** $10,726; room only: $5876. Room and board charges vary according to board plan and housing facility. ***Payment plan:*** installment. ***Waivers:*** senior citizens and employees or children of employees.

Financial Aid Of all full-time matriculated undergraduates who enrolled in 2016, 8,961 applied for aid, 5,001 were judged to have need, 5,001 had their need fully met. In 2016, 690 non-need-based awards were made. ***Average percent of need met:*** 100. ***Average financial aid package:*** $26,422. ***Average need-based loan:*** $5756. ***Average need-based gift aid:*** $20,980. ***Average non-need-based aid:*** $5966. ***Average indebtedness upon graduation:*** $24,598.

APPLYING

Standardized Tests *Required:* SAT or ACT (for admission). *Recommended:* SAT Subject Tests (for admission).

Options: electronic application, early action, deferred entrance.

Application fee: $60.

Required: essay or personal statement, high school transcript, 2 letters of recommendation.

Application deadlines: 1/1 (freshmen), 3/1 (transfers), 11/1 (early action).

Notification: 4/1 (freshmen), 5/1 (transfers), 1/31 (early action).

CONTACT

Mr. Gregory W. Roberts, Dean of Admission, University of Virginia, PO Box 400160, Charlottesville, VA 22904-4727. *Phone:* 434-982-3200. *Fax:* 434-924-3587. *E-mail:* undergrad-admission@virginia.edu.

The University of Virginia's College at Wise

Wise, Virginia

http://www.uvawise.edu/

- **State-supported** 4-year, founded 1954, part of University of Virginia
- **Small-town** 396-acre campus
- **Endowment** $60.4 million
- **Coed** 2,221 undergraduate students, 59% full-time, 59% women, 41% men
- **Moderately difficult** entrance level, 76% of applicants were admitted

UNDERGRAD STUDENTS

1,300 full-time, 921 part-time. Students come from 17 states and territories; 9 other countries; 5% are from out of state; 11% Black or African American, non-Hispanic/Latino; 2% Hispanic/Latino; 0.8% Asian, non-Hispanic/Latino; 0.3% American Indian or Alaska Native, non-Hispanic/Latino; 0.3% Two or more races, non-Hispanic/Latino; 9% Race/ethnicity unknown; 5% transferred in; 23% live on campus.

Freshmen:

Admission: 1,068 applied, 816 admitted, 334 enrolled. ***Average high school GPA:*** 3.42. ***Test scores:*** SAT critical reading scores over 500: 41%; SAT math scores over 500: 39%; SAT writing scores over 500: 30%; ACT scores over 18: 75%; SAT critical reading scores over 600: 13%; SAT math scores over 600: 9%; SAT writing scores over 600: 6%; ACT scores over 24: 20%; SAT critical reading scores over 700: 1%; ACT scores over 30: 3%.

Retention: 62% of full-time freshmen returned.

FACULTY

Total: 162, 63% full-time, 54% with terminal degrees.

Student/faculty ratio: 13:1.

ACADEMICS

Calendar: semesters. *Degree:* bachelor's.

Special study options: academic remediation for entering students, accelerated degree program, adult/continuing education programs, advanced placement credit, cooperative education, distance learning, double majors, honors programs, independent study, internships, part-time degree program, services for LD students, student-designed majors, summer session for credit. ***ROTC:*** Army (b).

Computers: 330 computers/terminals are available on campus for general student use. Students can access the following: campus intranet, computer help desk, free student e-mail accounts, online (class) grades, online (class) registration, online (class) schedules. Campuswide network is available. 100% of college-owned or -operated housing units are wired for high-speed Internet access. Wireless service is available via learning centers, libraries, student centers.

Library: University of Virginia's College at Wise Library. *Books:* 147,677 (physical), 159,701 (digital/electronic); *Serial titles:* 984 (physical), 2,949 (digital/electronic); *Databases:* 124. Weekly public service hours: 77; study areas open 24 hours, 5-7 days a week; students can reserve study rooms.

STUDENT LIFE

Housing options: on-campus residence required for freshman year; coed, men-only, women-only, special housing for students with disabilities. Campus housing is university owned.

Activities and organizations: drama/theater group, student-run newspaper, radio and television station, choral group, marching band, Student Government, Student Activities Board, Multicultural Association, Residence Hall Association, intramurals, national fraternities, national sororities.

Athletics Member NCAA. All Division II. ***Intercollegiate sports:*** baseball M(s), basketball M(s)/W(s), cross-country running M(s)/W(s), football M(s), golf M/W, lacrosse W(s), softball W(s), tennis M(s)/W(s), track and field M/W, volleyball W(s). ***Intramural sports:*** badminton M/W, basketball M/W, football M/W, golf M/W, racquetball M/W, soccer M/W, softball M/W, table tennis M/W, tennis M/W, ultimate Frisbee M/W, volleyball M/W, water polo M/W.

Campus security: 24-hour emergency response devices and patrols, student patrols, late-night transport/escort service, self-defense, informal discussions, pamphlets/posters/films, and crime prevention office.

Student services: health clinic, personal/psychological counseling.

COSTS & FINANCIAL AID

Costs (2016–17) ***Tuition:*** state resident $5210 full-time, $222 per credit hour part-time; nonresident $21,278 full-time, $900 per credit hour part-time. Part-time tuition and fees vary according to course load. ***Required fees:*** $4329 full-time, $51 per credit hour part-time, $51 per credit hour part-time. ***Room and board:*** $10,346. Room and board charges vary according to board plan and housing facility. ***Payment plans:*** installment, deferred payment. ***Waivers:*** senior citizens and employees or children of employees.

Financial Aid Of all full-time matriculated undergraduates who enrolled in 2015, 1,067 applied for aid, 941 were judged to have need, 368 had their need fully met. In 2015, 112 non-need-based awards were made. ***Average percent of need met:*** 82. ***Average financial aid package:*** $17,477. ***Average need-based loan:*** $3832. ***Average need-based gift aid:*** $7907. ***Average non-need-based aid:*** $5284. ***Average indebtedness upon graduation:*** $14,424.

APPLYING

Standardized Tests *Required:* SAT or ACT (for admission).

Options: early admission, early action.

Application fee: $25.

Required: high school transcript, minimum 2.3 GPA. ***Recommended:*** 2 letters of recommendation.

Application deadlines: 8/1 (freshmen), 8/15 (transfers), 12/1 (early action).

Notification: 8/20 (freshmen), continuous until 8/20 (transfers), 12/15 (early action).

CONTACT

Mr. Russell D. Necessary, Vice Chancellor for Enrollment Management and Student Life, The University of Virginia's College at Wise, 1 College Avenue, Wise, VA 24293. *Phone:* 276-328-0322. *Toll-free phone:* 888-282-9324. *Fax:* 276-328-0251. *E-mail:* admissions@uvawise.edu.

Virginia Baptist College
Fredericksburg, Virginia
http://www.vbc.edu/

CONTACT
Virginia Baptist College, 4111 Plank Road, Fredericksburg, VA 22407.

Virginia Commonwealth University
Richmond, Virginia
http://www.vcu.edu/

- **State-supported** university, founded 1838
- **Urban** 158-acre campus
- **Endowment** $48.0 million
- **Coed** 24,212 undergraduate students, 85% full-time, 59% women, 41% men
- 75% of applicants were admitted

UNDERGRAD STUDENTS
20,554 full-time, 3,658 part-time. Students come from 46 states and territories; 79 other countries; 7% are from out of state; 19% Black or African American, non-Hispanic/Latino; 9% Hispanic/Latino; 13% Asian, non-Hispanic/Latino; 0.1% Native Hawaiian or other Pacific Islander, non-Hispanic/Latino; 0.2% American Indian or Alaska Native, non-Hispanic/Latino; 6% Two or more races, non-Hispanic/Latino; 3% Race/ethnicity unknown; 3% international; 9% transferred in.

Freshmen:
Admission: 17,176 applied, 12,805 admitted, 4,279 enrolled. ***Average high school GPA:*** 3.63. ***Test scores:*** SAT critical reading scores over 500: 75%; SAT math scores over 500: 71%; SAT writing scores over 500: 65%; ACT scores over 18: 97%; SAT critical reading scores over 600: 29%; SAT math scores over 600: 24%; SAT writing scores over 600: 22%; ACT scores over 24: 53%; SAT critical reading scores over 700: 6%; SAT math scores over 700: 4%; SAT writing scores over 700: 3%; ACT scores over 30: 13%.
Retention: 86% of full-time freshmen returned.

FACULTY
Total: 2,093, 58% full-time.
Student/faculty ratio: 18:1.

ACADEMICS
Calendar: semesters. *Degrees:* certificates, bachelor's, master's, doctoral, post-master's, and postbachelor's certificates.
Special study options: academic remediation for entering students, accelerated degree program, adult/continuing education programs, advanced placement credit, cooperative education, distance learning, double majors, English as a second language, freshman honors college, honors programs, independent study, internships, off-campus study, part-time degree program, services for LD students, student-designed majors, study abroad, summer session for credit. ***ROTC:*** Army (c).
Computers: 450 computers/terminals and 210 ports are available on campus for general student use. Students can access the following: campus intranet, computer help desk, free student e-mail accounts, online (class) grades, online (class) registration, online (class) schedules. Campuswide network is available. 100% of college-owned or -operated housing units are wired for high-speed Internet access. Wireless service is available via entire campus.
Library: Cabell Library and Thompkins McCaw Library plus 3 others. *Books:* 1.9 million (physical), 1.0 million (digital/electronic); *Serial titles:* 260,501 (physical), 116,369 (digital/electronic); *Databases:* 471. Weekly public service hours: 146; study areas open 24 hours, 5-7 days a week; students can reserve study rooms.

STUDENT LIFE
Housing options: coed. Campus housing is university owned.
Activities and organizations: drama/theater group, student-run newspaper, radio and television station, choral group, national fraternities, national sororities.
Athletics Member NCAA. All Division I. ***Intercollegiate sports:*** baseball M(s), basketball M(s)/W(s), cross-country running M(s)/W(s), field hockey W(s), golf M(s), lacrosse W(s), soccer M(s)/W(s), tennis M(s)/W(s), track and field M(s)/W(s), volleyball W(s). ***Intramural sports:*** badminton M(c)/W(c), baseball M(c), basketball M(c)/W(c), bowling M(c)/W(c), equestrian sports M(c)/W(c), field hockey M(c)/W(c), ice hockey M(c), lacrosse M(c)/W(c), rowing M(c)/W(c), rugby M(c)/W(c), soccer M(c)/W(c), softball W(c), swimming and diving M(c)/W(c), table tennis M(c)/W(c), tennis M(c)/W(c), triathlon M(c)/W(c), ultimate Frisbee M(c)/W(c), volleyball M(c)/W(c).
Campus security: 24-hour emergency response devices and patrols, student patrols, late-night transport/escort service, controlled dormitory access, security personnel in residence halls, RAD classes/special event coverage, more than 90 sworn officers and 200 security personnel.
Student services: health clinic, personal/psychological counseling, women's center.

COSTS & FINANCIAL AID
Costs (2016–17) ***Tuition:*** state resident $10,846 full-time, $374 per credit hour part-time; nonresident $29,378 full-time, $1013 per credit hour part-time. ***Required fees:*** $2230 full-time. ***Room and board:*** $9919. Room and board charges vary according to board plan and housing facility. ***Payment plan:*** installment. ***Waivers:*** employees or children of employees.
Financial Aid Of all full-time matriculated undergraduates who enrolled in 2015, 14,130 applied for aid, 11,619 were judged to have need, 1,241 had their need fully met. 772 Federal Work-Study jobs (averaging $1714). 8 state and other part-time jobs (averaging $100). In 2015, 1902 non-need-based awards were made. ***Average percent of need met:*** 48. ***Average financial aid package:*** $10,342. ***Average need-based loan:*** $4236. ***Average need-based gift aid:*** $6435. ***Average non-need-based aid:*** $12,666. ***Average indebtedness upon graduation:*** $31,512.

APPLYING
Standardized Tests *Required for some:* SAT or ACT (for admission).
Options: electronic application, early admission, deferred entrance.
Application fee: $65.
Required: high school transcript.
Notification: 11/1 (freshmen).

CONTACT
Office of Admissions, Virginia Commonwealth University, 821 West Franklin Street, Richmond, VA 23284-2526. *Phone:* 800-841-3638. *Toll-free phone:* 800-841-3638. *Fax:* 804-828-1899. *E-mail:* ugrad@vcu.edu.

Virginia International University
Fairfax, Virginia
http://www.viu.edu/

CONTACT
Admissions Department, Virginia International University, 4401 Village Drive, Fairfax, VA 22030. *Phone:* 703-591-7042 Ext. 313. *Toll-free phone:* 800-514-6848. *Fax:* 703-591-7048. *E-mail:* admissions@viu.edu.

★ Virginia Military Institute
Lexington, Virginia
http://www.vmi.edu/

- **State-supported** 4-year, founded 1839
- **Small-town** 134-acre campus
- **Endowment** $381.9 million
- **Coed, primarily men** 1,713 undergraduate students, 100% full-time, 11% women, 89% men
- **Moderately difficult** entrance level, 51% of applicants were admitted

UNDERGRAD STUDENTS
1,713 full-time. Students come from 46 states and territories; 6 other countries; 41% are from out of state; 6% Black or African American, non-Hispanic/Latino; 6% Hispanic/Latino; 4% Asian, non-Hispanic/Latino; 0.4% Native Hawaiian or other Pacific Islander, non-Hispanic/Latino; 0.6% American Indian or Alaska Native, non-Hispanic/Latino; 1% Two or more races, non-Hispanic/Latino; 0.1% Race/ethnicity unknown; 2% international; 2% transferred in; 100% live on campus.

Freshmen:
Admission: 1,843 applied, 939 admitted, 454 enrolled. ***Average high school GPA:*** 3.65. ***Test scores:*** SAT critical reading scores over 500: 87%; SAT math scores over 500: 89%; ACT scores over 18: 100%; SAT critical reading scores over 600: 38%; SAT math scores over 600: 37%;

ACT scores over 24: 71%; SAT critical reading scores over 700: 6%; SAT math scores over 700: 5%; ACT scores over 30: 15%.

Retention: 84% of full-time freshmen returned.

FACULTY

Total: 208, 64% full-time, 76% with terminal degrees.

Student/faculty ratio: 11:1.

ACADEMICS

Calendar: semesters. *Degree:* bachelor's.

Special study options: advanced placement credit, double majors, honors programs, independent study, internships, services for LD students, study abroad, summer session for credit. ***ROTC:*** Army (b), Navy (b), Air Force (b).

Computers: 200 computers/terminals are available on campus for general student use. Students can access the following: campus intranet, computer help desk, free student e-mail accounts, online (class) registration, online (class) schedules. Campuswide network is available. 100% of college-owned or -operated housing units are wired for high-speed Internet access. Wireless service is available via classrooms, dorm rooms, libraries, student centers.

Library: Preston Library. *Books:* 280,000 (physical), 240,000 (digital/electronic); *Databases:* 150. Weekly public service hours: 113.

STUDENT LIFE

Housing options: on-campus residence required through senior year; coed. Campus housing is university owned. Freshman campus housing is guaranteed.

Activities and organizations: drama/theater group, student-run newspaper, choral group, marching band, Newman Club, Officers Christian Fellowship, strength and fitness organizations, Promaji, Pre-Law Society.

Athletics Member NCAA. All Division I. ***Intercollegiate sports:*** baseball M(s), basketball M(s), cross-country running M(s)/W(s), football M(s), lacrosse M(s), riflery M(s)/W(s), soccer M(s)/W, swimming and diving M(s)/W, track and field M(s)/W(s), water polo W, wrestling M(s).

Campus security: 24-hour emergency response devices and patrols, student patrols.

Student services: health clinic, personal/psychological counseling.

COSTS & FINANCIAL AID

Costs (2016–17) ***Tuition:*** state resident $8461 full-time, $328 per credit hour part-time; nonresident $32,770 full-time, $1024 per credit hour part-time. ***Required fees:*** $9031 full-time. ***Room and board:*** $8968. ***Payment plan:*** installment.

Financial Aid Of all full-time matriculated undergraduates who enrolled in 2014, 1,146 applied for aid, 879 were judged to have need, 445 had their need fully met. In 2014, 227 non-need-based awards were made. ***Average percent of need met:*** 85. ***Average financial aid package:*** $16,281. ***Average need-based loan:*** $4456. ***Average need-based gift aid:*** $14,959. ***Average non-need-based aid:*** $4754. ***Average indebtedness upon graduation:*** $27,621. ***Financial aid deadline:*** 3/1.

APPLYING

Standardized Tests *Required:* SAT or ACT (for admission).

Options: electronic application, early admission, early decision.

Application fee: $40.

Required: high school transcript. ***Recommended:*** essay or personal statement, 2 letters of recommendation, interview.

Early decision deadline: 11/15.

Notification: continuous (freshmen), 12/15 (early decision).

CONTACT

Office of Admissions, Virginia Military Institute, Lexington, VA 24450. *Phone:* 800-767-4207. *Toll-free phone:* 800-767-4207. *Fax:* 540-464-7746. *E-mail:* admissions@vmi.edu.

Virginia Polytechnic Institute and State University

Blacksburg, Virginia

http://www.vt.edu/

- **State-supported** university, founded 1872
- **Small-town** 2600-acre campus
- **Endowment** $843.0 million
- **Coed** 25,791 undergraduate students, 98% full-time, 43% women, 57% men
- **Moderately difficult** entrance level, 71% of applicants were admitted

UNDERGRAD STUDENTS

25,213 full-time, 578 part-time. 23% are from out of state; 4% Black or African American, non-Hispanic/Latino; 6% Hispanic/Latino; 10% Asian, non-Hispanic/Latino; 0.1% Native Hawaiian or other Pacific Islander, non-Hispanic/Latino; 0.2% American Indian or Alaska Native, non-Hispanic/Latino; 4% Two or more races, non-Hispanic/Latino; 3% Race/ethnicity unknown; 6% international; 4% transferred in; 37% live on campus.

Freshmen:

Admission: 25,000 applied, 17,718 admitted, 5,929 enrolled. ***Test scores:*** SAT critical reading scores over 500: 91%; SAT math scores over 500: 94%; SAT writing scores over 500: 87%; SAT critical reading scores over 600: 49%; SAT math scores over 600: 62%; SAT writing scores over 600: 43%; SAT critical reading scores over 700: 9%; SAT math scores over 700: 18%; SAT writing scores over 700: 6%.

Retention: 93% of full-time freshmen returned.

FACULTY

Total: 1,958, 89% full-time, 85% with terminal degrees.

Student/faculty ratio: 14:1.

ACADEMICS

Calendar: semesters. *Degrees:* associate, bachelor's, master's, doctoral, and post-master's certificates.

Special study options: accelerated degree program, adult/continuing education programs, advanced placement credit, cooperative education, distance learning, double majors, English as a second language, honors programs, independent study, internships, part-time degree program, services for LD students, study abroad, summer session for credit. ***ROTC:*** Army (b), Navy (b), Air Force (b).

Computers: Students can access the following: campus intranet, computer help desk, free student e-mail accounts, online (class) grades, online (class) registration, online (class) schedules. Campuswide network is available. Wireless service is available via entire campus.

Library: Newman Library plus 2 others.

STUDENT LIFE

Housing options: on-campus residence required for freshman year; coed, men-only, women-only. Campus housing is university owned. Freshman campus housing is guaranteed.

Activities and organizations: drama/theater group, student-run newspaper, radio and television station, choral group, marching band, Virginia Tech Union, Student Government Association, International student organizations, national fraternities, national sororities.

Athletics Member NCAA. All Division I except football (Division I-A). ***Intercollegiate sports:*** baseball M, basketball M, cross-country running M/W, golf M(s), lacrosse W(s), soccer M(s)/W(s), swimming and diving M(s)/W(s), tennis M(s)/W(s), track and field M(s)/W(s), ultimate Frisbee M/W, volleyball W. ***Intramural sports:*** baseball M(c), basketball M, bowling M/W, crew M(c)/W(c), cross-country running M/W, equestrian sports M(c)/W(c), fencing M(c)/W(c), field hockey M(c)/W(c), football M/W, golf M/W, gymnastics M(c)/W(c), ice hockey M/W, lacrosse M(c)/W(c), racquetball M/W, riflery M(c)/W(c), rugby M(c)/W(c), soccer M/W, softball M/W, swimming and diving M/W, table tennis M/W, tennis M/W, volleyball M/W, water polo M/W.

Campus security: 24-hour emergency response devices and patrols, student patrols, late-night transport/escort service, controlled dormitory access.

Student services: health clinic, personal/psychological counseling, women's center, legal services.

COSTS & FINANCIAL AID

Costs (2016–17) ***Tuition:*** state resident $10,787 full-time; nonresident $27,306 full-time. ***Required fees:*** $2065 full-time. ***Room and board:*** $8564.

Financial Aid Of all full-time matriculated undergraduates who enrolled in 2015, 15,848 applied for aid, 10,484 were judged to have need, 1,853 had their need fully met. In 2015, 2862 non-need-based awards were made. ***Average percent of need met:*** 65. ***Average financial aid package:*** $17,594. ***Average need-based loan:*** $4655. ***Average need-based gift aid:*** $7003. ***Average non-need-based aid:*** $3808. ***Average indebtedness upon graduation:*** $28,884. ***Financial aid deadline:*** 1/1.

APPLYING

Standardized Tests *Required:* SAT or ACT (for admission).

Options: electronic application, early admission, early decision, deferred entrance.

Application fee: $60.

Required: high school transcript.

Application deadlines: 1/15 (freshmen), 2/15 (transfers).

Early decision deadline: 11/1.

Notification: 4/1 (freshmen), 5/1 (transfers), 12/15 (early decision).

CONTACT

Virginia Polytechnic Institute and State University, Blacksburg, VA 24061. *Phone:* 540-231-6267.

Virginia State University

Petersburg, Virginia

http://www.vsu.edu/

- **State-supported** comprehensive, founded 1882, part of State Council of Higher Education for Virginia
- **Suburban** 236-acre campus with easy access to Richmond
- **Endowment** $32.5 million
- **Coed** 4,165 undergraduate students, 97% full-time, 57% women, 43% men
- **Minimally difficult** entrance level, 94% of applicants were admitted

UNDERGRAD STUDENTS

4,023 full-time, 142 part-time. Students come from 39 states and territories; 25% are from out of state; 61% Black or African American, non-Hispanic/Latino; 1% Hispanic/Latino; 0.5% Asian, non-Hispanic/Latino; 0.3% American Indian or Alaska Native, non-Hispanic/Latino; 35% Race/ethnicity unknown; 0.2% international; 6% transferred in.

Freshmen:

Admission: 5,722 applied, 5,406 admitted, 1,024 enrolled. ***Average high school GPA:*** 2.85. ***Test scores:*** SAT critical reading scores over 500: 13%; SAT math scores over 500: 14%; ACT scores over 18: 38%; SAT critical reading scores over 600: 1%; SAT math scores over 600: 2%; ACT scores over 24: 11%.

Retention: 74% of full-time freshmen returned.

FACULTY

Total: 480, 59% full-time.

Student/faculty ratio: 13:1.

ACADEMICS

Calendar: semesters. *Degrees:* bachelor's, master's, doctoral, and postbachelor's certificates.

Special study options: adult/continuing education programs, advanced placement credit, cooperative education, double majors, honors programs, independent study, internships, off-campus study, part-time degree program, services for LD students, student-designed majors, study abroad, summer session for credit. ***ROTC:*** Army (b).

Computers: 1,400 computers/terminals and 1,650 ports are available on campus for general student use. Students can access the following: computer help desk, free student e-mail accounts, online (class) grades, online (class) registration, online (class) schedules. Campuswide network is available. 100% of college-owned or -operated housing units are wired for high-speed Internet access. Wireless service is available via entire campus.

Library: Johnston Memorial Library. *Books:* 434,496 (physical); *Serial titles:* 5,805 (physical); *Databases:* 245. Weekly public service hours: 82.

STUDENT LIFE

Housing options: on-campus residence required for freshman year; coed, men-only, women-only. Campus housing is university owned. Freshman applicants given priority for college housing.

Activities and organizations: drama/theater group, student-run newspaper, choral group, marching band, AbstraKt Entertainment, Golden Key Honor Society, The Betterment of Brothers and Sisters, Diversified Virtue Entertainment, Sankofa, national fraternities, national sororities.

Athletics Member NCAA. All Division II. ***Intercollegiate sports:*** baseball M(s), basketball M(s)/W(s), bowling W(s), cheerleading M/W, cross-country running M(s)/W(s), football M(s), golf M(s)/W(s), softball W(s), tennis M(s)/W(s), track and field M(s)/W(s), volleyball W(s). ***Intramural sports:*** basketball M/W, football M, tennis M/W, track and field M/W, volleyball W.

Campus security: 24-hour emergency response devices and patrols, late-night transport/escort service, controlled dormitory access.

Student services: health clinic, personal/psychological counseling.

COSTS & FINANCIAL AID

Costs (2016–17) ***Tuition:*** state resident $5172 full-time, $369 per credit hour part-time; nonresident $14,992 full-time, $817 per credit hour part-time. Full-time tuition and fees vary according to course load. Part-time tuition and fees vary according to course load. ***Required fees:*** $3300 full-time, $10 per credit hour part-time. ***Room and board:*** $10,562; room only: $6170. Room and board charges vary according to board plan and housing facility. ***Payment plan:*** installment. ***Waivers:*** senior citizens.

Financial Aid Of all full-time matriculated undergraduates who enrolled in 2015, 3,817 applied for aid, 3,817 were judged to have need, 572 had their need fully met. 300 Federal Work-Study jobs (averaging $2000). 150 state and other part-time jobs (averaging $3000). In 2015, 427 non-need-based awards were made. ***Average percent of need met:*** 58. ***Average financial aid package:*** $11,586. ***Average need-based loan:*** $5500. ***Average need-based gift aid:*** $6940. ***Average non-need-based aid:*** $1000. ***Average indebtedness upon graduation:*** $28,250.

APPLYING

Standardized Tests *Required:* SAT or ACT (for admission).

Options: electronic application.

Application fee: $25.

Required: high school transcript, minimum 2.2 GPA, 2 letters of recommendation. ***Recommended:*** essay or personal statement.

Application deadlines: 5/1 (freshmen), 5/1 (transfers).

Notification: continuous (freshmen), continuous (transfers).

CONTACT

Mr. Rodney Hall, Director of Enrollment Services, Virginia State University, Office of Admissions, Petersburg, VA 23806. *Phone:* 804-524-2954. *Toll-free phone:* 800-871-7611. *Fax:* 804-524-5055. *E-mail:* rhall@vsu.edu.

Virginia Union University

Richmond, Virginia

http://www.vuu.edu/

- **Independent Baptist** comprehensive, founded 1865
- **Urban** 100-acre campus
- **Coed** 1,509 undergraduate students, 94% full-time, 58% women, 42% men
- **Moderately difficult** entrance level, 49% of applicants were admitted

UNDERGRAD STUDENTS

1,419 full-time, 90 part-time. Students come from 22 states and territories; 19 other countries; 46% are from out of state; 92% Black or African American, non-Hispanic/Latino; 0.9% Hispanic/Latino; 0.3% Asian, non-Hispanic/Latino; 0.7% American Indian or Alaska Native, non-Hispanic/Latino; 4% Race/ethnicity unknown; 0.4% international; 6% transferred in; 72% live on campus.

Freshmen:
Admission: 7,337 applied, 3,598 admitted, 456 enrolled. ***Average high school GPA:*** 2.71.
Retention: 60% of full-time freshmen returned.

FACULTY
Total: 138, 54% full-time, 36% with terminal degrees.
Student/faculty ratio: 15:1.

ACADEMICS
Calendar: semesters. *Degrees:* bachelor's, master's, and doctoral.
Special study options: academic remediation for entering students, adult/continuing education programs, advanced placement credit, cooperative education, double majors, English as a second language, honors programs, internships, off-campus study, summer session for credit. ***ROTC:*** Army (c).
Unusual degree programs: 3-2 engineering with Howard University, Virginia Commonwealth University,Michigan State.
Computers: 237 computers/terminals are available on campus for general student use. Students can access the following: campus intranet, computer help desk, free student e-mail accounts, online (class) grades, online (class) registration, online (class) schedules. Campuswide network is available. Wireless service is available via entire campus.
Library: L. Douglas Wilder Learning Resource Center and Library plus 1 other. *Books:* 123,475 (physical), 66,271 (digital/electronic); *Databases:* 100. Weekly public service hours: 41; students can reserve study rooms.

STUDENT LIFE
Housing options: coed, men-only, women-only. Campus housing is university owned and leased by the school. Freshman applicants given priority for college housing.
Activities and organizations: drama/theater group, student-run newspaper, choral group, marching band, Student Government Association, Panther PALS (Peer Advisory Leadership Students), Men About Positive Purpose, NAACP, Student Athlete Advisory Committee, national fraternities, national sororities.
Athletics Member NCAA. All Division II. ***Intercollegiate sports:*** basketball M(s)/W(s), bowling M(s)/W(s), cross-country running M(s)/W(s), football M(s), golf M(s), softball W(s), tennis M(s)/W(s), track and field M(s)/W(s), volleyball W(s). ***Intramural sports:*** basketball M, softball W.
Campus security: 24-hour emergency response devices and patrols, controlled dormitory access.
Student services: health clinic, personal/psychological counseling.

COSTS & FINANCIAL AID
Costs (2017–18) ***One-time required fee:*** $200. ***Comprehensive fee:*** $25,833 includes full-time tuition ($15,152), mandatory fees ($1381), and room and board ($9300). Full-time tuition and fees vary according to course level, course load, and reciprocity agreements. Part-time tuition: $470 per credit hour. Part-time tuition and fees vary according to course level, course load, and reciprocity agreements. ***Required fees:*** $42 per credit hour part-time, $250 per credit hour part-time. ***College room only:*** $3876. Room and board charges vary according to housing facility. ***Payment plans:*** installment, deferred payment. ***Waivers:*** employees or children of employees.
Financial Aid Of all full-time matriculated undergraduates who enrolled in 2015, 1,257 applied for aid, 1,210 were judged to have need, 78 had their need fully met. 217 Federal Work-Study jobs (averaging $2422). In 2015, 26 non-need-based awards were made. ***Average percent of need met:*** 52. ***Average financial aid package:*** $13,242. ***Average need-based loan:*** $3882. ***Average need-based gift aid:*** $9724. ***Average non-need-based aid:*** $5928. ***Average indebtedness upon graduation:*** $35,789.

APPLYING
Standardized Tests *Required:* SAT or ACT (for admission).
Options: electronic application, deferred entrance.
Application fee: $25.
Required: high school transcript. ***Required for some:*** interview. ***Recommended:*** essay or personal statement.
Application deadlines: rolling (freshmen), rolling (transfers).
Notification: continuous (freshmen), continuous (transfers).

CONTACT
Ms. Danitra Morrison, Assistant Director of Admissions, Virginia Union University, 1500 North Lombardy Street, Richmond, VA 23220-1170. *Phone:* 804-257-5853. *Toll-free phone:* 800-368-3227. *Fax:* 804-342-3511. *E-mail:* dvmorrison@vuu.edu.

Virginia University of Lynchburg

Lynchburg, Virginia

http://www.vul.edu/

CONTACT
Ms. Cheryl Glass, Director of Admissions, Virginia University of Lynchburg, 2058 Garfield Avenue, Lynchburg, VA 24501. *Phone:* 434-528-5276 Ext. 106. *Fax:* 434-528-4275. *E-mail:* cglass@vul.edu.

Virginia Wesleyan College

Norfolk, Virginia

http://www.vwc.edu/

- **Independent United Methodist** comprehensive, founded 1961
- **Urban** 300-acre campus with easy access to Norfolk, Virginia Beach
- **Endowment** $52.6 million
- **Coed** 1,374 undergraduate students, 96% full-time, 62% women, 38% men
- **Moderately difficult** entrance level, 90% of applicants were admitted

UNDERGRAD STUDENTS
1,319 full-time, 55 part-time. Students come from 31 states and territories; 10 other countries; 26% are from out of state; 25% Black or African American, non-Hispanic/Latino; 8% Hispanic/Latino; 1% Asian, non-Hispanic/Latino; 0.1% Native Hawaiian or other Pacific Islander, non-Hispanic/Latino; 1% American Indian or Alaska Native, non-Hispanic/Latino; 6% Two or more races, non-Hispanic/Latino; 6% Race/ethnicity unknown; 2% international; 6% transferred in; 65% live on campus.

Freshmen:
Admission: 1,654 applied, 1,488 admitted, 368 enrolled. ***Average high school GPA:*** 3.21. ***Test scores:*** SAT critical reading scores over 500: 41%; SAT math scores over 500: 35%; SAT writing scores over 500: 31%; ACT scores over 18: 73%; SAT critical reading scores over 600: 10%; SAT math scores over 600: 10%; SAT writing scores over 600: 7%; ACT scores over 24: 28%; SAT critical reading scores over 700: 2%; SAT math scores over 700: 1%; SAT writing scores over 700: 1%; ACT scores over 30: 5%.
Retention: 61% of full-time freshmen returned.

FACULTY
Total: 120, 76% full-time, 78% with terminal degrees.
Student/faculty ratio: 13:1.

ACADEMICS
Calendar: 4-1-4. *Degrees:* certificates, bachelor's, and master's.
Special study options: academic remediation for entering students, adult/continuing education programs, advanced placement credit, double majors, freshman honors college, honors programs, independent study, internships, off-campus study, part-time degree program, services for LD students, student-designed majors, study abroad, summer session for credit. ***ROTC:*** Army (c).
Unusual degree programs: 3-2 engineering with Old Dominion University; forestry with Duke University.
Computers: 137 computers/terminals are available on campus for general student use. Students can access the following: campus intranet, computer help desk, free student e-mail accounts, online (class) grades, online (class) registration, online (class) schedules. Campuswide network is available. 100% of college-owned or -operated housing units are wired for high-speed Internet access. Wireless service is available via entire campus.
Library: H. C. Hofheimer II Library plus 1 other. *Books:* 132,158 (physical), 70,925 (digital/electronic). Study areas open 24 hours, 5-7 days a week; students can reserve study rooms.

STUDENT LIFE
Housing options: on-campus residence required through senior year; coed, women-only, special housing for students with disabilities. Campus housing is university owned. Freshman campus housing is guaranteed.

Activities and organizations: drama/theater group, student-run newspaper, radio station, choral group, Wesleyan Activities Council, community service, Student Government Association, student newspaper, Black Student Union, national fraternities, national sororities.

Athletics Member NCAA. All Division III. ***Intercollegiate sports:*** baseball M, basketball M/W, cheerleading W, cross-country running M/W, field hockey W, golf M/W, lacrosse M/W, soccer M/W, softball W, swimming and diving M/W, tennis M/W, track and field M/W, volleyball W. ***Intramural sports:*** basketball M/W, crew M(c)/W(c), fencing M(c)/W(c), field hockey W, football M/W, racquetball M/W, soccer M/W, softball M/W, table tennis M/W, ultimate Frisbee M/W, volleyball M/W.

Campus security: 24-hour emergency response devices and patrols, late-night transport/escort service, controlled dormitory access, well-lit pathways.

Student services: health clinic, personal/psychological counseling, women's center.

COSTS & FINANCIAL AID
Costs (2017–18) ***One-time required fee:*** $350. ***Comprehensive fee:*** $45,604 includes full-time tuition ($36,010), mandatory fees ($650), and room and board ($8944). Full-time tuition and fees vary according to course load. Part-time tuition: $1500 per credit hour. Part-time tuition and fees vary according to course load. ***Room and board:*** Room and board charges vary according to board plan and housing facility. ***Payment plan:*** installment. ***Waivers:*** adult students, senior citizens, and employees or children of employees.

Financial Aid Of all full-time matriculated undergraduates who enrolled in 2015, 1,336 applied for aid, 1,092 were judged to have need, 176 had their need fully met. 187 Federal Work-Study jobs (averaging $975). In 2015, 242 non-need-based awards were made. ***Average percent of need met:*** 69. ***Average financial aid package:*** $24,802. ***Average need-based loan:*** $7519. ***Average need-based gift aid:*** $21,149. ***Average non-need-based aid:*** $20,584. ***Average indebtedness upon graduation:*** $36,255.

APPLYING
Standardized Tests *Required:* SAT or ACT (for admission).

Options: electronic application.

Required: high school transcript, minimum 2.5 GPA. ***Required for some:*** interview. ***Recommended:*** essay or personal statement, letters of recommendation.

Application deadlines: rolling (freshmen), rolling (transfers).

Notification: continuous (freshmen), continuous (transfers).

CONTACT
Virginia Wesleyan College, 1584 Wesleyan Drive, Norfolk, VA 23502-5599. *Phone:* 757-455-3208. *Toll-free phone:* 800-737-8684.

Washington and Lee University

Lexington, Virginia

http://www.wlu.edu/

- **Independent** comprehensive, founded 1749
- **Small-town** 415-acre campus
- **Endowment** $1.5 billion
- **Coed** 1,830 undergraduate students, 100% full-time, 48% women, 52% men
- **Most difficult** entrance level, 24% of applicants were admitted

UNDERGRAD STUDENTS
1,824 full-time, 6 part-time. Students come from 49 states and territories; 30 other countries; 85% are from out of state; 2% Black or African American, non-Hispanic/Latino; 4% Hispanic/Latino; 3% Asian, non-Hispanic/Latino; 3% Two or more races, non-Hispanic/Latino; 0.9% Race/ethnicity unknown; 4% international; 0.5% transferred in; 74% live on campus.

Freshmen:
Admission: 5,101 applied, 1,203 admitted, 466 enrolled. ***Test scores:*** SAT critical reading scores over 500: 100%; SAT math scores over 500: 100%; SAT writing scores over 500: 100%; ACT scores over 18: 100%; SAT critical reading scores over 600: 95%; SAT math scores over 600: 98%; SAT writing scores over 600: 95%; ACT scores over 24: 100%; SAT critical reading scores over 700: 47%; SAT math scores over 700: 48%; SAT writing scores over 700: 40%; ACT scores over 30: 88%.
Retention: 95% of full-time freshmen returned.

FACULTY
Total: 313, 74% full-time, 91% with terminal degrees.

Student/faculty ratio: 9:1.

ACADEMICS
Calendar: 4-4-2. *Degrees:* bachelor's, master's, and doctoral.

Special study options: advanced placement credit, double majors, honors programs, independent study, internships, off-campus study, services for LD students, student-designed majors, study abroad. ***ROTC:*** Army (c).

Computers: 176 computers/terminals and 1,200 ports are available on campus for general student use. Students can access the following: campus intranet, computer help desk, free student e-mail accounts, online (class) grades, online (class) registration, online (class) schedules. Campuswide network is available. 100% of college-owned or -operated housing units are wired for high-speed Internet access. Wireless service is available via entire campus.

Library: James G. Leyburn Library plus 2 others. *Books:* 1.0 million (physical), 321,493 (digital/electronic); *Serial titles:* 66,967 (digital/electronic); *Databases:* 441. Study areas open 24 hours, 5-7 days a week; students can reserve study rooms.

STUDENT LIFE
Housing options: on-campus residence required through junior year; coed, men-only, women-only, special housing for students with disabilities. Campus housing is university owned. Freshman campus housing is guaranteed.

Activities and organizations: drama/theater group, student-run newspaper, radio and television station, choral group, Mock Convention, General Activities Board, Nabors Service League, Outing Club, Sports Clubs, national fraternities, national sororities.

Athletics Member NCAA. All Division III. ***Intercollegiate sports:*** baseball M, basketball M/W, cross-country running M/W, equestrian sports M/W, field hockey W, football M, golf M/W, lacrosse M/W, rugby M(c), soccer M/W, swimming and diving M/W, tennis M/W, track and field M/W, volleyball W, wrestling M. ***Intramural sports:*** badminton M/W, baseball M(c), cheerleading M/W, equestrian sports W(c), golf M/W, ice hockey M(c), rock climbing M(c)/W(c), table tennis M/W, tennis M/W, track and field M/W, ultimate Frisbee M/W, volleyball W.

Campus security: 24-hour emergency response devices and patrols, late-night transport/escort service, controlled dormitory access, Emergency Alert System.

Student services: health clinic, personal/psychological counseling.

COSTS & FINANCIAL AID
Costs (2016–17) ***Comprehensive fee:*** $60,634 includes full-time tuition ($48,267), mandatory fees ($987), and room and board ($11,380). Full-time tuition and fees vary according to degree level. Part-time tuition: $1689 per credit hour. Part-time tuition and fees vary according to course load and degree level. ***College room only:*** $5250. Room and board charges vary according to board plan and housing facility. ***Payment plan:*** installment. ***Waivers:*** employees or children of employees.

Financial Aid Of all full-time matriculated undergraduates who enrolled in 2016, 832 applied for aid, 772 were judged to have need, 772 had their need fully met. 222 Federal Work-Study jobs (averaging $2000). 368 state and other part-time jobs (averaging $2000). In 2016, 148 non-need-based awards were made. ***Average percent of need met:*** 100. ***Average financial aid package:*** $48,392. ***Average need-based loan:*** $783. ***Average need-based gift aid:*** $42,292. ***Average non-need-based aid:*** $34,766. ***Average indebtedness upon graduation:*** $26,397. ***Financial aid deadline:*** 2/15.

APPLYING
Standardized Tests *Required:* SAT or ACT (for admission).

Options: electronic application, early decision, deferred entrance.

Application fee: $60.

Required: high school transcript, 3 letters of recommendation.
Recommended: essay or personal statement, interview.

Application deadlines: 1/1 (freshmen), 4/1 (transfers).

Early decision deadline: 11/1 (for plan 1), 1/1 (for plan 2).

Notification: 4/1 (freshmen), continuous (transfers), 12/22 (early decision plan 1), 2/1 (early decision plan 2).

CONTACT
Sally S. Richmond, VP for Admissions and Financial Aid, Washington and Lee University, 204 West Washington Street, Lexington, VA 24450-2116. *Phone:* 540-458-8710. *Fax:* 540-458-8062.
E-mail: admissions@wlu.edu.

WASHINGTON

Antioch University Seattle

Seattle, Washington

http://www.antiochsea.edu/

- **Independent** university, founded 1975, part of Antioch University
- **Urban** campus
- **Coed** 103 undergraduate students
- **Noncompetitive** entrance level

UNDERGRAD STUDENTS
Students come from 9 states and territories; 1 other country; 3% Black or African American, non-Hispanic/Latino; 8% Hispanic/Latino; 4% Asian, non-Hispanic/Latino; 3% Two or more races, non-Hispanic/Latino; 41% Race/ethnicity unknown.

ACADEMICS
Calendar: quarters. *Degrees:* certificates, bachelor's, master's, and doctoral.

Special study options: summer session for credit.
Library: Antioch Seattle Library. *Books:* 8,425 (physical), 264,631 (digital/electronic); *Serial titles:* 40,950 (digital/electronic); *Databases:* 222.

STUDENT LIFE
Housing options: college housing not available.

FINANCIAL AID
Financial Aid Of all full-time matriculated undergraduates who enrolled in 2006, 259 applied for aid, 150 had their need fully met. 18 Federal Work-Study jobs (averaging $6000). 2 state and other part-time jobs (averaging $5000). ***Average percent of need met:*** 75. ***Average financial aid package:*** $6701. ***Average need-based loan:*** $5500. ***Average need-based gift aid:*** $4000. ***Average indebtedness upon graduation:*** $15,999.

APPLYING
Options: electronic application, deferred entrance.

Application fee: $75.

CONTACT
Admissions Office, Antioch University Seattle, 2326 Sixth Avenue, Seattle, WA 98121-1814. *Phone:* 206-268-4202. *Toll-free phone:* 888-268-4477. *E-mail:* admissions@antiochseattle.edu.

Argosy University, Seattle

Seattle, Washington

http://www.argosy.edu/locations/seattle/

CONTACT
Argosy University, Seattle, 2601-A Elliott Avenue, Seattle, WA 98121.
Phone: 206-283-4500. *Toll-free phone:* 866-283-2777.

The Art Institute of Seattle

Seattle, Washington

http://www.artinstitutes.edu/seattle/

CONTACT
The Art Institute of Seattle, 2323 Elliott Avenue, Seattle, WA 98121-1642.
Phone: 206-448-6600. *Toll-free phone:* 800-275-2471.

Bastyr University

Kenmore, Washington

http://www.bastyr.edu/

- **Independent** upper-level, founded 1978
- **Suburban** 51-acre campus with easy access to Seattle
- **Coed**

ACADEMICS
Calendar: quarters. *Degrees:* certificates, bachelor's, master's, doctoral, and post-master's certificates.
Library: Bastyr University Library.

STUDENT LIFE
Housing options: coed, special housing for students with disabilities. Campus housing is university owned.

Activities and organizations: Naturopaths Without Borders, Nature Club, Multicultural Student Association of Natural Medicine, Environmental Action Team, Venture Grant.

Campus security: student patrols, late-night transport/escort service, controlled dormitory access.

Student services: health clinic, personal/psychological counseling.

FINANCIAL AID
Financial Aid Of all full-time matriculated undergraduates who enrolled in 2014, 30 applied for aid, 29 were judged to have need. ***Average percent of need met:*** 54. ***Average financial aid package:*** $14,865. ***Average need-based loan:*** $11,000. ***Average need-based gift aid:*** $7568.

APPLYING
Options: electronic application, deferred entrance.

Application fee: $60.

CONTACT
Ms. Lauren Marani, Assistant Director of Admissions, Bastyr University, 14500 Juanita Drive NE, Kenmore, WA 98028-4966. *Phone:* 425-602-1300. *Fax:* 425-602-3090. *E-mail:* admissions@bastyr.edu.

Bellevue College

Bellevue, Washington

http://www.bcc.ctc.edu/

CONTACT
Morenika Jacobs, Associate Dean of Enrollment Services, Bellevue College, 3000 Landerholm Circle, SE, Bellevue, WA 98007-6484.
Phone: 425-564-2205. *Fax:* 425-564-4065.

Cascadia College

Bothell, Washington

http://www.cascadia.edu/

- **State-supported** primarily 2-year, founded 1999, part of Washington State Board for Community and Technical Colleges
- **Suburban** 128-acre campus
- **Coed**
- **Noncompetitive** entrance level

ACADEMICS
Calendar: quarters. *Degrees:* certificates, diplomas, associate, and bachelor's.
Library: Campus Library. *Books:* 90,000 (physical), 600,000 (digital/electronic); *Serial titles:* 600 (physical), 100,000 (digital/electronic); *Databases:* 600. Weekly public service hours: 86; students can reserve study rooms.

STUDENT LIFE
Housing options: college housing not available.

Activities and organizations: drama/theater group, student-run newspaper.

Campus security: 24-hour emergency response devices, late-night transport/escort service.

Student services: personal/psychological counseling.

COSTS
Costs (2016–17) ***One-time required fee:*** $30. ***Tuition:*** state resident $3852 full-time, $103 per credit hour part-time; nonresident $4265 full-time, $116 per credit hour part-time. Full-time tuition and fees vary according to course load, degree level, and program. Part-time tuition and fees vary according to course load, degree level, and program. ***Required fees:*** $420 full-time, $11 per credit hour part-time.

APPLYING
Options: electronic application.

Application fee: $30.

CONTACT
Ms. Erin Blakeney, Dean for Student Success, Cascadia College, 18345 Campus Way, NE, Bothell, WA 98011. *Phone:* 425-352-8000. *Fax:* 425-352-8137. *E-mail:* admissions@cascadia.edu.

Central Washington University

Ellensburg, Washington

http://www.cwu.edu/

- **State-supported** comprehensive, founded 1891
- **Small-town** 380-acre campus with easy access to Seattle
- **Endowment** $5.7 million
- **Coed** 11,047 undergraduate students, 86% full-time, 51% women, 49% men
- **Moderately difficult** entrance level, 79% of applicants were admitted

UNDERGRAD STUDENTS
9,473 full-time, 1,574 part-time. Students come from 36 states and territories; 17 other countries; 5% are from out of state; 4% Black or African American, non-Hispanic/Latino; 15% Hispanic/Latino; 4% Asian, non-Hispanic/Latino; 0.7% Native Hawaiian or other Pacific Islander, non-Hispanic/Latino; 0.6% American Indian or Alaska Native, non-Hispanic/Latino; 7% Two or more races, non-Hispanic/Latino; 11% Race/ethnicity unknown; 3% international; 12% transferred in; 31% live on campus.

Freshmen:
Admission: 7,340 applied, 5,823 admitted, 1,665 enrolled. ***Average high school GPA:*** 3.16. ***Test scores:*** SAT critical reading scores over 500: 67%; SAT math scores over 500: 66%; SAT writing scores over 500: 35%; ACT scores over 18: 79%; SAT critical reading scores over 600: 21%; SAT math scores over 600: 14%; SAT writing scores over 600: 6%; ACT scores over 24: 28%; SAT critical reading scores over 700: 3%; SAT math scores over 700: 3%; SAT writing scores over 700: 1%; ACT scores over 30: 3%.
Retention: 76% of full-time freshmen returned.

FACULTY
Total: 724, 69% full-time.

Student/faculty ratio: 18:1.

ACADEMICS
Calendar: quarters. *Degrees:* certificates, bachelor's, master's, post-master's, and postbachelor's certificates.

Special study options: academic remediation for entering students, advanced placement credit, cooperative education, distance learning, double majors, English as a second language, freshman honors college, honors programs, independent study, internships, off-campus study, part-time degree program, services for LD students, student-designed majors, study abroad, summer session for credit. ***ROTC:*** Army (b), Air Force (b).

Computers: 791 computers/terminals and 3,100 ports are available on campus for general student use. Students can access the following: campus intranet, computer help desk, free student e-mail accounts, online (class) grades, online (class) registration, online (class) schedules, online data storage, office software. Campuswide network is available. 100% of college-owned or -operated housing units are wired for high-speed Internet access. Wireless service is available via entire campus.

Library: James E. Brooks Library plus 2 others. *Books:* 900,981 (physical), 251,073 (digital/electronic); *Serial titles:* 327 (physical), 72,453 (digital/electronic); *Databases:* 112. Weekly public service hours: 101; students can reserve study rooms.

STUDENT LIFE
Housing options: on-campus residence required for freshman year; coed, cooperative, special housing for students with disabilities. Campus housing is university owned. Freshman campus housing is guaranteed.

Activities and organizations: drama/theater group, student-run newspaper, radio and television station, choral group, marching band, SISTERS, Brother 2 Brother, Cosplay, Alpha Kappa Si, Society of Human Resource Management.

Athletics Member NCAA. All Division II. ***Intercollegiate sports:*** archery M(c)/W(c), baseball M(s), basketball M(s)/W(s), bowling M(c)/W(c), cheerleading M/W, cross-country running M(s)/W(s), equestrian sports M(c)/W(c), fencing M(c)/W(c), football M(s), golf M(c)/W(c), ice hockey M(c)/W(c), lacrosse M(c)/W(c), rock climbing M(c)/W(c), rugby M(s)/W(s), soccer M(c)/W(s), softball W(s), swimming and diving M(c)/W(c), tennis M(c)/W(c), track and field M(s)/W(s), ultimate Frisbee M(c)/W(c), volleyball W(s), water polo M(c)/W(c), wrestling M(c)/W(c). ***Intramural sports:*** badminton M/W, basketball M/W, rock climbing M/W, skiing (cross-country) M/W, soccer M/W, softball M/W, table tennis M/W, tennis M/W, volleyball M/W.

Campus security: 24-hour emergency response devices and patrols, late-night transport/escort service, controlled dormitory access, alert update system: emergency notification across digital platforms, Rape Aggression Defense System: realistic self-defense for women.

Student services: health clinic, personal/psychological counseling.

COSTS & FINANCIAL AID
Costs (2017–18) ***Tuition:*** state resident $6037 full-time; nonresident $20,144 full-time. Full-time tuition and fees vary according to course load, degree level, location, and reciprocity agreements. Part-time tuition and fees vary according to course load, degree level, location, and reciprocity agreements. ***Required fees:*** $1812 full-time. ***Room and board:*** $10,684. Room and board charges vary according to board plan, housing facility, and location. ***Payment plan:*** installment. ***Waivers:*** senior citizens and employees or children of employees.

Financial Aid Of all full-time matriculated undergraduates who enrolled in 2015, 7,422 applied for aid, 5,859 were judged to have need, 1,674 had their need fully met. In 2015, 14 non-need-based awards were made. ***Average percent of need met:*** 80. ***Average financial aid package:*** $11,434. ***Average need-based loan:*** $4376. ***Average need-based gift aid:*** $8841. ***Average non-need-based aid:*** $821. ***Average indebtedness upon graduation:*** $22,827.

APPLYING
Standardized Tests *Required:* SAT or ACT (for admission).

Options: electronic application.

Application fee: $50.

Required: high school transcript, minimum 2.0 GPA. ***Required for some:*** essay or personal statement, interview.

Application deadlines: 3/1 (freshmen), rolling (out-of-state freshmen), 3/1 (transfers).

Notification: continuous (freshmen), continuous (out-of-state freshmen), continuous (transfers).

CONTACT
Ms. Kathy Gaer-Carlton, Director of Admissions, Central Washington University, 400 East University Way, Ellensburg, WA 98926-7463. *Phone:* 509-963-1211. *Fax:* 509-963-3065. *E-mail:* admissions@cwu.edu.

City University of Seattle

Seattle, Washington

http://www.cityu.edu/

CONTACT
Student Services Center, City University of Seattle, 11900 NE First Street, Bellevue, WA 98005. *Phone:* 888-422-4898. *Toll-free phone:* 800-426-5596. *E-mail:* info@cityu.edu.

Clark College
Vancouver, Washington
http://www.clark.edu/

- **State-supported** primarily 2-year, founded 1933, part of Washington State Board for Community and Technical Colleges
- **Urban** 101-acre campus with easy access to Portland
- **Coed**
- **Noncompetitive** entrance level

FACULTY
Student/faculty ratio: 24:1.

ACADEMICS
Calendar: quarters. *Degrees:* certificates, diplomas, associate, and bachelor's.
Library: Lewis D. Cannell Library.

STUDENT LIFE
Housing options: college housing not available.
Campus security: 24-hour patrols, late-night transport/escort service, security staff during hours of operation.

COSTS
Costs (2016–17) ***Tuition:*** area resident $4023 full-time, $107 per credit hour part-time; state resident $5436 full-time, $153 per credit hour part-time; nonresident $9432 full-time, $283 per credit hour part-time. Full-time tuition and fees vary according to course level, course load, degree level, program, and reciprocity agreements. Part-time tuition and fees vary according to course level, course load, degree level, program, and reciprocity agreements.

APPLYING
Options: electronic application, early admission, deferred entrance.
Application fee: $25.

CONTACT
Ms. Sheryl Anderson, Director of Admissions, Clark College, Vancouver, WA 98663. *Phone:* 360-992-2308. *Fax:* 360-992-2867.
E-mail: admissions@clark.edu.

Cornish College of the Arts
Seattle, Washington
http://www.cornish.edu/

- **Independent** 4-year, founded 1914
- **Urban** 4-acre campus with easy access to Seattle
- **Coed**
- **Moderately difficult** entrance level

FACULTY
Student/faculty ratio: 4:1.

ACADEMICS
Calendar: semesters. *Degrees:* bachelor's and postbachelor's certificates.
Library: Cornish Library.

STUDENT LIFE
Housing options: on-campus residence required for freshman year; coed. Campus housing is university owned. Freshman campus housing is guaranteed.
Activities and organizations: drama/theater group, student-run radio station, choral group, Student Leadership Council, Black Student Alliance, Sigma Alpha Phi, AIGA, Cheese Tasting.
Campus security: 24-hour emergency response devices and patrols, late-night transport/escort service, controlled dormitory access.
Student services: personal/psychological counseling.

FINANCIAL AID
Financial Aid Of all full-time matriculated undergraduates who enrolled in 2015, 629 applied for aid, 559 were judged to have need, 45 had their need fully met. In 2015, 142 non-need-based awards were made. ***Average percent of need met:*** 59. ***Average financial aid package:*** $24,566. ***Average need-based loan:*** $4930. ***Average need-based gift aid:*** $18,098. ***Average non-need-based aid:*** $9626. ***Average indebtedness upon graduation:*** $37,686.

APPLYING
Standardized Tests *Recommended:* SAT or ACT (for admission).
Options: electronic application, early action, deferred entrance.
Application fee: $40.
Required: essay or personal statement, high school transcript, minimum 2.5 GPA, portfolio or audition. ***Required for some:*** 2 letters of recommendation. ***Recommended:*** 2 letters of recommendation, interview.

CONTACT
Ms. Sharron Starling, Director of Admissions, Cornish College of the Arts, 1000 Lenora Street, Seattle, WA 98121. *Phone:* 206-726-5017. *Toll-free phone:* 800-726-ARTS. *Fax:* 206-720-1011.
E-mail: admissions@cornish.edu.

DigiPen Institute of Technology
Redmond, Washington
http://www.digipen.edu/

- **Proprietary** comprehensive, founded 1988
- **Suburban** 3-acre campus with easy access to Seattle
- **Coed** 976 undergraduate students
- **Minimally difficult** entrance level, 54% of applicants were admitted

UNDERGRAD STUDENTS
Students come from 52 states and territories; 45 other countries; 55% are from out of state; 0.5% Black or African American, non-Hispanic/Latino; 5% Hispanic/Latino; 5% Asian, non-Hispanic/Latino; 0.2% Native Hawaiian or other Pacific Islander, non-Hispanic/Latino; 0.2% American Indian or Alaska Native, non-Hispanic/Latino; 4% Two or more races, non-Hispanic/Latino; 31% Race/ethnicity unknown; 13% international.

Freshmen:
Admission: 767 applied, 415 admitted. ***Average high school GPA:*** 3.26.
Retention: 65% of full-time freshmen returned.

FACULTY
Total: 128, 51% full-time, 34% with terminal degrees.
Student/faculty ratio: 11:1.

ACADEMICS
Calendar: semesters. *Degrees:* bachelor's and master's.
Special study options: academic remediation for entering students, accelerated degree program, advanced placement credit, English as a second language, independent study, internships, services for LD students, study abroad, summer session for credit.
Computers: 794 computers/terminals are available on campus for general student use. Students can access the following: campus intranet, computer help desk, free student e-mail accounts, online (class) grades, online (class) registration, online (class) schedules. Campuswide network is available. 100% of college-owned or -operated housing units are wired for high-speed Internet access. Wireless service is available via entire campus.
Library: DigiPen Library. *Books:* 5,024 (physical), 138,729 (digital/electronic); *Serial titles:* 29 (physical); *Databases:* 10. Weekly public service hours: 81.

STUDENT LIFE
Housing options: coed, men-only, women-only, special housing for students with disabilities. Campus housing is leased by the school and is provided by a third party. Freshman applicants given priority for college housing.
Activities and organizations: choral group, Tabletop Club, Counterstrike Club, Ping Pong Club, Pokemon Club, SMASH Club.
Campus security: late-night transport/escort service, controlled dormitory access, on-site security during campus hours.
Student services: personal/psychological counseling.

COSTS & FINANCIAL AID
Costs (2017–18) ***One-time required fee:*** $150. ***Tuition:*** $29,800 full-time, $960 per credit part-time. Full-time tuition and fees vary according to course load, degree level, and program. Part-time tuition and fees vary according to course load, degree level, and program. ***Required fees:*** $200 full-time. ***Room only:*** Room and board charges vary according to board plan and housing facility. ***Payment plan:*** installment. ***Waivers:*** employees or children of employees.

Financial Aid Of all full-time matriculated undergraduates who enrolled in 2015, 628 applied for aid, 550 were judged to have need, 106 had their need fully met. 77 Federal Work-Study jobs (averaging $1098). In 2015, 5 non-need-based awards were made. ***Average percent of need met:*** 70. ***Average financial aid package:*** $11,409. ***Average need-based loan:*** $4054. ***Average need-based gift aid:*** $8614. ***Average non-need-based aid:*** $7200. ***Average indebtedness upon graduation:*** $27,403.

APPLYING
Standardized Tests *Required for some:* SAT or ACT (for admission).

Options: electronic application, deferred entrance.

Application fee: $35.

Required: essay or personal statement, high school transcript, minimum 2.5 GPA. ***Required for some:*** precalculus for Bachelor of Science, art portfolio for digital art and animation, audition portfolio for music and sound design. ***Recommended:*** 2 letters of recommendation.

Application deadlines: rolling (freshmen), rolling (transfers).

Notification: continuous (freshmen), continuous (transfers).

CONTACT
Ms. Danial Powers, Director of Admissions, DigiPen Institute of Technology, 9931 Willows Road NE, Redmond, WA 98052. *Phone:* 425-629-5071. *Toll-free phone:* 866-478-5236. *Fax:* 425-558-0378. *E-mail:* admissions@digipen.edu.

Eastern Washington University
Cheney, Washington
http://www.ewu.edu/

- **State-supported** comprehensive, founded 1882
- **Suburban** 335-acre campus with easy access to Spokane
- **Coed** 11,217 undergraduate students, 89% full-time, 54% women, 46% men

UNDERGRAD STUDENTS
10,032 full-time, 1,185 part-time. 6% are from out of state; 4% Black or African American, non-Hispanic/Latino; 15% Hispanic/Latino; 3% Asian, non-Hispanic/Latino; 0.4% Native Hawaiian or other Pacific Islander, non-Hispanic/Latino; 1% American Indian or Alaska Native, non-Hispanic/Latino; 6% Two or more races, non-Hispanic/Latino; 2% Race/ethnicity unknown; 5% international; 12% transferred in; 17% live on campus.

Freshmen:
Admission: 1,697 enrolled. ***Average high school GPA:*** 3.19. ***Test scores:*** SAT critical reading scores over 500: 43%; SAT math scores over 500: 45%; SAT writing scores over 500: 33%; ACT scores over 18: 72%; SAT critical reading scores over 600: 11%; SAT math scores over 600: 12%; SAT writing scores over 600: 5%; ACT scores over 24: 23%; SAT critical reading scores over 700: 2%; SAT math scores over 700: 1%; ACT scores over 30: 5%.

Retention: 76% of full-time freshmen returned.

FACULTY
Total: 678, 71% full-time, 63% with terminal degrees.

Student/faculty ratio: 21:1.

ACADEMICS
Calendar: quarters. *Degrees:* certificates, bachelor's, master's, doctoral, and postbachelor's certificates.

Special study options: academic remediation for entering students, accelerated degree program, adult/continuing education programs, advanced placement credit, cooperative education, distance learning, double majors, English as a second language, honors programs, independent study, internships, off-campus study, part-time degree program, services for LD students, student-designed majors, study abroad, summer session for credit. ***ROTC:*** Army (b).

Unusual degree programs: 3-2 exercise science/occupational therapy, therapeutic recreation, interdisciplinary studies.

Computers: Students can access the following: campus intranet, computer help desk, free student e-mail accounts, online (class) grades, online (class) registration, online (class) schedules, network disk storage; discounted software; laptops, still and video cameras, projectors for checkout; print credit; black white laser, color laser, and color photo options, large format print service. Campuswide network is available. 100% of college-owned or -operated housing units are wired for high-speed Internet access. Wireless service is available via entire campus.
Library: John F. Kennedy Library. Students can reserve study rooms.

STUDENT LIFE
Housing options: on-campus residence required for freshman year; coed, special housing for students with disabilities. Campus housing is university owned. Freshman campus housing is guaranteed.

Activities and organizations: drama/theater group, student-run newspaper, radio station, choral group, marching band, national fraternities, national sororities.

Athletics Member NCAA. All Division I except football (Division I-AA). ***Intercollegiate sports:*** archery M(c)/W(c), baseball M(c), basketball M(s)/W(s), cheerleading W(c), cross-country running M(s)/W(s), equestrian sports M(c)/W(c), fencing M(c)/W(c), golf W(s), ice hockey M(c)/W(c), rugby M(c)/W(c), soccer M(c)/W(s), softball W(c), tennis M(s)/W(s), track and field M(s)/W(s), volleyball W(s). ***Intramural sports:*** baseball M/W, basketball M/W, bowling M/W, cross-country running M/W, football M/W, golf W, racquetball M/W, soccer M/W, softball M/W, tennis M/W, track and field M/W, ultimate Frisbee M(c)/W(c), volleyball M/W, wrestling M(c)/W(c).

Campus security: 24-hour emergency response devices and patrols, student patrols, late-night transport/escort service, controlled dormitory access, emergency call boxes.

Student services: health clinic, personal/psychological counseling, women's center.

COSTS & FINANCIAL AID
Costs (2016–17) ***Tuition:*** state resident $6110 full-time, $204 per credit hour part-time; nonresident $22,502 full-time, $750 per credit hour part-time. Full-time tuition and fees vary according to course level, course load, degree level, program, reciprocity agreements, and student level. Part-time tuition and fees vary according to course level, course load, degree level, program, reciprocity agreements, and student level. ***Required fees:*** $841 full-time. ***Room and board:*** $10,941; room only: $6100. Room and board charges vary according to board plan and housing facility. ***Payment plan:*** installment. ***Waivers:*** employees or children of employees.

Financial Aid Of all full-time matriculated undergraduates who enrolled in 2015, 7,973 applied for aid, 5,699 were judged to have need, 708 had their need fully met. In 2015, 507 non-need-based awards were made. ***Average percent of need met:*** 58. ***Average financial aid package:*** $13,877. ***Average need-based loan:*** $4210. ***Average need-based gift aid:*** $8175. ***Average non-need-based aid:*** $3824. ***Average indebtedness upon graduation:*** $24,109.

APPLYING
Standardized Tests *Required:* SAT or ACT (for admission).

Required: high school transcript, minimum 2.0 GPA. ***Required for some:*** essay or personal statement. ***Recommended:*** minimum 3.0 GPA.

CONTACT
Mr. Catherine Sleeth, Director of Admissions, Eastern Washington University, 304 Sutton Hall, Cheney, WA 99004-2447. *Phone:* 509-359-6582. *Fax:* 509-359-6692. *E-mail:* admissions@ewu.edu.

★ The Evergreen State College
Olympia, Washington
http://www.evergreen.edu/

- **State-supported** comprehensive, founded 1967, part of Washington State Public Baccalaureate Institution
- **Rural** 1000-acre campus with easy access to Seattle
- **Endowment** $12.7 million
- **Coed** 3,787 undergraduate students, 91% full-time, 56% women, 44% men
- **Moderately difficult** entrance level, 97% of applicants were admitted

UNDERGRAD STUDENTS
3,458 full-time, 329 part-time. Students come from 48 states and territories; 19 other countries; 25% are from out of state; 5% Black or African American, non-Hispanic/Latino; 11% Hispanic/Latino; 3% Asian, non-Hispanic/Latino; 0.3% Native Hawaiian or other Pacific Islander, non-Hispanic/Latino; 2% American Indian or Alaska Native, non-

Hispanic/Latino; 8% Two or more races, non-Hispanic/Latino; 4% Race/ethnicity unknown; 0.7% international; 18% transferred in; 23% live on campus.

Freshmen:
Admission: 1,901 applied, 1,853 admitted, 572 enrolled. ***Average high school GPA:*** 3.02. ***Test scores:*** SAT critical reading scores over 500: 68%; SAT math scores over 500: 51%; SAT writing scores over 500: 59%; ACT scores over 18: 87%; SAT critical reading scores over 600: 33%; SAT math scores over 600: 14%; SAT writing scores over 600: 16%; ACT scores over 24: 50%; SAT critical reading scores over 700: 6%; SAT math scores over 700: 1%; SAT writing scores over 700: 2%; ACT scores over 30: 10%.

Retention: 65% of full-time freshmen returned.

FACULTY
Total: 229, 71% full-time, 78% with terminal degrees.

Student/faculty ratio: 21:1.

ACADEMICS
Calendar: quarters. *Degrees:* bachelor's and master's.

Special study options: accelerated degree program, advanced placement credit, double majors, independent study, internships, off-campus study, part-time degree program, services for LD students, student-designed majors, study abroad, summer session for credit.

Computers: 556 computers/terminals are available on campus for general student use. Students can access the following: campus intranet, computer help desk, free student e-mail accounts, online (class) grades, online (class) registration, online (class) schedules, online payment, student accounts history, financial aid records, academic history, housing application, evaluations. Campuswide network is available. 100% of college-owned or -operated housing units are wired for high-speed Internet access. Wireless service is available via entire campus.

Library: Daniel J. Evans Library. *Books:* 322,238 (physical), 158,542 (digital/electronic); *Serial titles:* 79 (physical), 54,617 (digital/electronic); *Databases:* 54. Weekly public service hours: 83; students can reserve study rooms.

STUDENT LIFE
Housing options: coed, special housing for students with disabilities. Campus housing is university owned. Freshman campus housing is guaranteed.

Activities and organizations: drama/theater group, student-run newspaper, radio and television station, choral group, Black Focus, Cooper Point Journal, Embodied Arts Tribe, Movimiento Estudiantil Xican@ de Aztlan (MEXA), Chemistry and Other Sciences (CHAOS).

Athletics Member NAIA. ***Intercollegiate sports:*** basketball M(s)/W(s), soccer M(s)/W(s), track and field M(s)/W(s), volleyball W(s). ***Intramural sports:*** archery M(c)/W(c), badminton M/W, basketball M/W, crew M(c)/W(c), fencing M(c)/W(c), soccer M/W, volleyball M/W.

Campus security: 24-hour emergency response devices and patrols, student patrols, late-night transport/escort service, controlled dormitory access, car lockouts, jump-starts.

Student services: health clinic, personal/psychological counseling, women's center.

COSTS & FINANCIAL AID
Costs (2016–17) ***Tuition:*** state resident $6534 full-time, $218 per credit hour part-time; nonresident $23,007 full-time, $767 per credit hour part-time. Full-time tuition and fees vary according to course load, location, and program. Part-time tuition and fees vary according to course load, location, and program. ***Required fees:*** $705 full-time, $9 per credit hour part-time, $5 per term part-time. ***Room and board:*** $9360; room only: $6195. Room and board charges vary according to board plan, housing facility, location, and student level. ***Payment plan:*** installment. ***Waivers:*** senior citizens and employees or children of employees.

Financial Aid Of all full-time matriculated undergraduates who enrolled in 2015, 2,727 applied for aid, 2,410 were judged to have need, 150 had their need fully met. In 2015, 20 non-need-based awards were made. ***Average percent of need met:*** 60. ***Average financial aid package:*** $12,646. ***Average need-based loan:*** $4279. ***Average need-based gift aid:*** $9826. ***Average non-need-based aid:*** $3062. ***Average indebtedness upon graduation:*** $21,215.

APPLYING
Standardized Tests *Required:* SAT or ACT (for admission).

Options: electronic application, deferred entrance.

Application fee: $50.

Required: high school transcript, minimum 2.0 GPA. ***Required for some:*** essay or personal statement. ***Recommended:*** essay or personal statement.

Application deadlines: 2/1 (freshmen), 2/1 (transfers).

Notification: continuous until 11/1 (freshmen), continuous until 11/1 (transfers).

CONTACT

The Evergreen State College, 2700 Evergreen Parkway, NW, Olympia, WA 98505. *Phone:* 360-867-6170.

See previous page for display ad and page 1352 for the College Close-Up.

Gonzaga University

Spokane, Washington

http://www.gonzaga.edu/

- **Independent Roman Catholic** comprehensive, founded 1887
- **Urban** 152-acre campus
- **Endowment** $181.4 million
- **Coed** 5,160 undergraduate students, 98% full-time, 53% women, 47% men
- **Moderately difficult** entrance level, 67% of applicants were admitted

UNDERGRAD STUDENTS

5,073 full-time, 87 part-time. Students come from 42 states and territories; 29 other countries; 51% are from out of state; 1% Black or African American, non-Hispanic/Latino; 10% Hispanic/Latino; 5% Asian, non-Hispanic/Latino; 0.3% Native Hawaiian or other Pacific Islander, non-Hispanic/Latino; 0.7% American Indian or Alaska Native, non-Hispanic/Latino; 6% Two or more races, non-Hispanic/Latino; 3% Race/ethnicity unknown; 1% international; 2% transferred in; 59% live on campus.

Freshmen:

Admission: 7,324 applied, 4,928 admitted, 1,271 enrolled. ***Average high school GPA:*** 3.76. ***Test scores:*** SAT critical reading scores over 500: 94%; SAT math scores over 500: 94%; ACT scores over 18: 100%; SAT critical reading scores over 600: 48%; SAT math scores over 600: 55%; ACT scores over 24: 89%; SAT critical reading scores over 700: 10%; SAT math scores over 700: 10%; ACT scores over 30: 25%.

Retention: 92% of full-time freshmen returned.

FACULTY

Total: 745, 59% full-time, 52% with terminal degrees.

Student/faculty ratio: 12:1.

ACADEMICS

Calendar: semesters. *Degrees:* bachelor's, master's, and doctoral.

Special study options: accelerated degree program, adult/continuing education programs, advanced placement credit, distance learning, double majors, English as a second language, honors programs, independent study, internships, off-campus study, part-time degree program, services for LD students, study abroad, summer session for credit. ***ROTC:*** Army (b).

Unusual degree programs: 3-2 nursing.

Computers: 500 computers/terminals and 900 ports are available on campus for general student use. Students can access the following: computer help desk, free student e-mail accounts, online (class) grades, online (class) registration, online (class) schedules. Campuswide network is available. 100% of college-owned or -operated housing units are wired for high-speed Internet access. Wireless service is available via entire campus.

Library: Ralph E. and Helen Higgins Foley Center plus 1 other. *Books:* 264,009 (physical), 68,637 (digital/electronic); *Serial titles:* 7,690 (physical), 74,520 (digital/electronic); *Databases:* 206. Weekly public service hours: 112; study areas open 24 hours, 5-7 days a week; students can reserve study rooms.

STUDENT LIFE

Housing options: on-campus residence required through sophomore year; coed, men-only, women-only, special housing for students with disabilities. Campus housing is university owned and leased by the school. Freshman campus housing is guaranteed.

Activities and organizations: drama/theater group, student-run newspaper, radio and television station, choral group, Student Body Association, Kennel Club, Search, Circle K, Encore.

Athletics Member NCAA. All Division I. ***Intercollegiate sports:*** baseball M(s), basketball M(s)/W(s), cross-country running M(s)/W(s), golf M(s)/W(s), ice hockey M(c), lacrosse M(c)/W(c), rowing M(s)/W(s), rugby M(c)/W(c), skiing (downhill) M(c)/W(c), soccer M(s)/W(s), tennis M(s)/W(s), track and field M(s)/W(s), ultimate Frisbee M(c)/W(c), volleyball M(c)/W(s). ***Intramural sports:*** badminton M/W, basketball M/W, cheerleading M(c)/W(c), football M/W, racquetball M/W, soccer M(c)/W(c), softball M/W, swimming and diving M(c)/W(c), tennis M/W, triathlon M/W, ultimate Frisbee M/W, volleyball M/W, weight lifting M/W.

Campus security: 24-hour emergency response devices and patrols, late-night transport/escort service.

Student services: health clinic, personal/psychological counseling.

COSTS & FINANCIAL AID

Costs (2017–18) ***Comprehensive fee:*** $52,880 includes full-time tuition ($40,540), mandatory fees ($790), and room and board ($11,550). Full-time tuition and fees vary according to course load, location, program, reciprocity agreements, and student level. Part-time tuition: $1110 per credit. Part-time tuition and fees vary according to course load, location, program, reciprocity agreements, and student level. ***Required fees:*** $180 per term part-time. ***College room only:*** $5900. Room and board charges vary according to board plan, housing facility, and location. ***Payment plans:*** installment, deferred payment. ***Waivers:*** senior citizens and employees or children of employees.

Financial Aid Of all full-time matriculated undergraduates who enrolled in 2015, 3,357 applied for aid, 2,660 were judged to have need, 677 had their need fully met. In 2015, 2042 non-need-based awards were made. ***Average percent of need met:*** 79. ***Average financial aid package:*** $29,293. ***Average need-based loan:*** $5840. ***Average need-based gift aid:*** $21,408. ***Average non-need-based aid:*** $14,545. ***Average indebtedness upon graduation:*** $30,700.

APPLYING

Standardized Tests *Required:* SAT or ACT (for admission).

Options: electronic application, early action, deferred entrance.

Application fee: $50.

Required: essay or personal statement, high school transcript, minimum 3.2 GPA, 1 letter of recommendation. ***Recommended:*** interview.

Application deadlines: 2/1 (freshmen), 6/1 (transfers), 11/15 (early action).

Notification: 3/15 (freshmen), continuous (transfers), 1/15 (early action).

CONTACT

Ms. Julie McCulloh, Dean of Admission, Gonzaga University, 502 East Boone Avenue, Spokane, WA 99258-0102. *Phone:* 800-322-2584. *Toll-free phone:* 800-322-2584 Ext. 6572. *Fax:* 509-313-6572. *E-mail:* admissions@gonzaga.edu.

Heritage University

Toppenish, Washington

http://www.heritage.edu/

CONTACT

Olivia Gutierrez, Director of Admissions, Heritage University, 3240 Fort Road, Toppenish, WA 98948-9599. *Phone:* 509-865-8697. *Toll-free phone:* 888-272-6190. *Fax:* 509-865-4469. *E-mail:* admissions@heritage.edu.

Northwest College of Art & Design

Poulsbo, Washington

http://www.ncad.edu/

- **Proprietary** 4-year, founded 1982
- **Small-town** 26-acre campus with easy access to Seattle
- **Coed** 114 undergraduate students, 100% full-time, 69% women, 31% men

UNDERGRAD STUDENTS
114 full-time. Students come from 5 states and territories; 3% Black or African American, non-Hispanic/Latino; 7% Hispanic/Latino; 5% Asian, non-Hispanic/Latino; 6% American Indian or Alaska Native, non-Hispanic/Latino; 4% Two or more races, non-Hispanic/Latino; 6% Race/ethnicity unknown.

Freshmen:
Average high school GPA: 2.91.
Retention: 50% of full-time freshmen returned.

FACULTY
Total: 17.
Student/faculty ratio: 5:1.

ACADEMICS
Calendar: semesters. *Degree:* bachelor's.
Special study options: accelerated degree program, double majors, internships, services for LD students, summer session for credit.
Computers: 76 computers/terminals are available on campus for general student use. Students can access the following: campus intranet, computer help desk, free student e-mail accounts, online (class) grades, online (class) schedules. Campuswide network is available. Wireless service is available via entire campus.
Library: Northwest College of Art & Design Library. *Books:* 600 (physical); *Serial titles:* 500 (physical). Weekly public service hours: 48.

COSTS & FINANCIAL AID
Costs (2017–18) ***One-time required fee:*** $200. ***Tuition:*** $18,975 full-time, $825 per credit hour part-time. Part-time tuition and fees vary according to course load. ***Required fees:*** $100 full-time, $100 per year part-time. ***Payment plans:*** installment, deferred payment. ***Waivers:*** children of alumni and employees or children of employees.
Financial Aid Of all full-time matriculated undergraduates who enrolled in 2014, 87 applied for aid, 87 were judged to have need. ***Average percent of need met:*** 61. ***Average financial aid package:*** $9025. ***Average need-based gift aid:*** $3967. ***Average indebtedness upon graduation:*** $20,426.

APPLYING
Required: essay or personal statement, high school transcript, interview, 5 piece portfolio.

CONTACT
Mrs. Ashley Miller, Admissions Representative, Northwest College of Art & Design, 16301 Creative Drive NE, Poulsbo, WA 98370. *Phone:* 360-779-9993. *Toll-free phone:* 800-769-ARTS. *Fax:* 360-7799933. *E-mail:* amiller@ncad.edu.

Northwest Indian College
Bellingham, Washington
http://www.nwic.edu/

CONTACT
Office of Admissions, Northwest Indian College, 2522 Kwina Road, Bellingham, WA 98226. *Phone:* 360-676-2772. *Toll-free phone:* 866-676-2772. *Fax:* 360-392-4333. *E-mail:* admissions@nwic.edu.

Northwest University
Kirkland, Washington
http://www.northwestu.edu/

- **Independent** comprehensive, founded 1934, affiliated with Assemblies of God
- **Suburban** 56-acre campus with easy access to Seattle
- **Endowment** $5.7 million
- **Coed** 1,820 undergraduate students, 72% full-time, 59% women, 41% men
- **Moderately difficult** entrance level, 99% of applicants were admitted

UNDERGRAD STUDENTS
1,316 full-time, 504 part-time. Students come from 33 states and territories; 16 other countries; 26% are from out of state; 7% Black or African American, non-Hispanic/Latino; 10% Hispanic/Latino; 6% Asian, non-Hispanic/Latino; 1% Native Hawaiian or other Pacific Islander, non-Hispanic/Latino; 2% American Indian or Alaska Native, non-Hispanic/Latino; 5% Two or more races, non-Hispanic/Latino; 6% Race/ethnicity unknown; 1% international; 13% transferred in; 55% live on campus.

Freshmen:
Admission: 525 applied, 520 admitted, 186 enrolled. ***Average high school GPA:*** 3.33. ***Test scores:*** SAT critical reading scores over 500: 44%; SAT math scores over 500: 39%; SAT writing scores over 500: 36%; ACT scores over 18: 76%; SAT critical reading scores over 600: 6%; SAT math scores over 600: 7%; SAT writing scores over 600: 8%; ACT scores over 24: 26%; SAT critical reading scores over 700: 1%; ACT scores over 30: 3%.
Retention: 53% of full-time freshmen returned.

FACULTY
Total: 252, 33% full-time, 15% with terminal degrees.
Student/faculty ratio: 14:1.

ACADEMICS
Calendar: semesters. *Degrees:* certificates, diplomas, associate, bachelor's, master's, and doctoral.
Special study options: academic remediation for entering students, accelerated degree program, adult/continuing education programs, advanced placement credit, cooperative education, double majors, English as a second language, independent study, internships, part-time degree program, study abroad, summer session for credit. ***ROTC:*** Army (c), Air Force (c).
Computers: 134 computers/terminals are available on campus for general student use. Students can access the following: campus intranet, computer help desk, free student e-mail accounts, online (class) grades, online (class) registration, online (class) schedules, online classes. Campuswide network is available. 100% of college-owned or -operated housing units are wired for high-speed Internet access. Wireless service is available via entire campus.
Library: Hurst Library. *Books:* 170,000 (physical); *Serial titles:* 7,000 (physical); *Databases:* 81. Weekly public service hours: 91; study areas open 24 hours, 5-7 days a week; students can reserve study rooms.

STUDENT LIFE
Housing options: on-campus residence required through sophomore year; men-only, women-only. Campus housing is university owned. Freshman campus housing is guaranteed.
Activities and organizations: drama/theater group, choral group, Student Ministries, Pursuit (worship service), Northwest University Business Club, Environmental Stewardship Club.
Athletics Member NAIA. ***Intercollegiate sports:*** basketball M(s)/W(s), cross-country running M(s)/W(s), soccer M(s)/W(s), softball W(s), track and field M(s)/W(s), volleyball W(s).
Campus security: 24-hour emergency response devices and patrols, late-night transport/escort service, controlled dormitory access.
Student services: health clinic, personal/psychological counseling.

COSTS & FINANCIAL AID
Costs (2017–18) ***Comprehensive fee:*** $36,977 includes full-time tuition ($28,800), mandatory fees ($387), and room and board ($7790). Full-time tuition and fees vary according to class time, course load, location, program, and reciprocity agreements. Part-time tuition: $1200 per credit hour. Part-time tuition and fees vary according to class time, course load, and location. ***College room only:*** $4660. Room and board charges vary according to housing facility and student level. ***Payment plan:*** installment. ***Waivers:*** employees or children of employees.
Financial Aid Of all full-time matriculated undergraduates who enrolled in 2015, 1,116 applied for aid, 961 were judged to have need, 110 had their need fully met. 5 state and other part-time jobs (averaging $2611). In 2015, 175 non-need-based awards were made. ***Average percent of need met:*** 69. ***Average financial aid package:*** $17,538. ***Average need-based loan:*** $3831. ***Average need-based gift aid:*** $14,107. ***Average non-need-based aid:*** $9290. ***Average indebtedness upon graduation:*** $23,516.

APPLYING
Standardized Tests *Required:* SAT or ACT (for admission).
Options: electronic application, early action, deferred entrance.
Application fee: $30.

Required: essay or personal statement, high school transcript, minimum 2.3 GPA, 2 letters of recommendation. ***Required for some:*** interview.

Application deadlines: 8/1 (freshmen), 8/1 (transfers), 1/15 (early action).

Notification: continuous (freshmen), continuous (transfers), 2/15 (early action).

CONTACT
Andy Hall, Northwest University, 5520 108th Avenue NE, PO Box 579, Kirkland, WA 98083-0579. *Phone:* 425-889-5212. *Toll-free phone:* 800-669-3781. *Fax:* 425-889-5224. *E-mail:* admissions@northwestu.edu.

Olympic College

Bremerton, Washington

http://www.olympic.edu/

- **State-supported** primarily 2-year, founded 1946, part of Washington State Board for Community and Technical Colleges
- **Suburban** 33-acre campus with easy access to Seattle, Tacoma
- **Coed** 7,253 undergraduate students
- **Noncompetitive** entrance level

UNDERGRAD STUDENTS
5% Black or African American, non-Hispanic/Latino; 8% Hispanic/Latino; 10% Asian, non-Hispanic/Latino; 2% American Indian or Alaska Native, non-Hispanic/Latino; 2% international; 1% live on campus.

FACULTY
Total: 473, 27% full-time.

ACADEMICS
Calendar: quarters. *Degrees:* certificates, diplomas, associate, and bachelor's.

Special study options: academic remediation for entering students, adult/continuing education programs, advanced placement credit, cooperative education, distance learning, English as a second language, independent study, internships, off-campus study, part-time degree program, services for LD students, study abroad, summer session for credit.

Computers: 1,300 computers/terminals are available on campus for general student use. Students can access the following: campus intranet, computer help desk, free student e-mail accounts, online (class) grades, online (class) registration, online (class) schedules. Campuswide network is available. Wireless service is available via entire campus.
Library: Haselwood Library plus 1 other. Students can reserve study rooms.

STUDENT LIFE
Housing options: coed. Campus housing is university owned.

Activities and organizations: drama/theater group, student-run newspaper, choral group, International Club, Armed Forces Club, Gay/Straight Alliance, Engineering Club, Clay Club.

Athletics ***Intercollegiate sports:*** baseball M(s), basketball M(s)/W(s), cross-country running M(s)/W(s), golf M(s)/W(s), softball W(s), track and field M(s)/W, volleyball W(s). ***Intramural sports:*** basketball M/W.

Campus security: 24-hour emergency response devices and patrols, student patrols, late-night transport/escort service.

Student services: personal/psychological counseling.

FINANCIAL AID
Financial Aid Of all full-time matriculated undergraduates who enrolled in 2015, 105 Federal Work-Study jobs (averaging $2380). 31 state and other part-time jobs (averaging $2880).

APPLYING
Options: electronic application.

Required for some: essay or personal statement, high school transcript, 2 letters of recommendation.

Application deadlines: rolling (freshmen), rolling (transfers).

CONTACT
Ms. Nora Downard, Program Manager, Olympic College, 1600 Chester Avenue, Bremerton, WA 98337-1699. *Phone:* 360-475-7445. *Toll-free phone:* 800-259-6718. *Fax:* 360-475-7202.
E-mail: ndownard@olympic.edu.

Pacific Lutheran University

Tacoma, Washington

http://www.plu.edu/

- **Independent** comprehensive, founded 1890, affiliated with Evangelical Lutheran Church in America
- **Suburban** 156-acre campus with easy access to Seattle
- **Endowment** $80.5 million
- **Coed** 2,783 undergraduate students, 97% full-time, 63% women, 37% men
- **Moderately difficult** entrance level, 77% of applicants were admitted

UNDERGRAD STUDENTS
2,702 full-time, 80 part-time. Students come from 43 states and territories; 19 other countries; 24% are from out of state; 3% Black or African American, non-Hispanic/Latino; 9% Hispanic/Latino; 10% Asian, non-Hispanic/Latino; 1% Native Hawaiian or other Pacific Islander, non-Hispanic/Latino; 0.7% American Indian or Alaska Native, non-Hispanic/Latino; 8% Two or more races, non-Hispanic/Latino; 1% Race/ethnicity unknown; 3% international; 6% transferred in; 48% live on campus.

Freshmen:
Admission: 3,770 applied, 2,896 admitted, 678 enrolled. ***Average high school GPA:*** 3.68. ***Test scores:*** SAT critical reading scores over 500: 73%; SAT math scores over 500: 75%; SAT writing scores over 500: 66%; ACT scores over 18: 94%; SAT critical reading scores over 600: 32%; SAT math scores over 600: 33%; SAT writing scores over 600: 20%; ACT scores over 24: 64%; SAT critical reading scores over 700: 6%; SAT math scores over 700: 5%; SAT writing scores over 700: 2%; ACT scores over 30: 16%.

Retention: 79% of full-time freshmen returned.

FACULTY
Total: 343, 66% full-time, 73% with terminal degrees.
Student/faculty ratio: 11:1.

ACADEMICS
Calendar: 4-1-4. *Degrees:* certificates, bachelor's, master's, doctoral, and post-master's certificates.

Special study options: advanced placement credit, cooperative education, distance learning, double majors, English as a second language, honors programs, independent study, internships, part-time degree program, services for LD students, student-designed majors, study abroad, summer session for credit. ***ROTC:*** Army (b).

Unusual degree programs: 3-2 engineering with Columbia University (New York), Washington University in St. Louis.

Computers: 810 computers/terminals and 3,500 ports are available on campus for general student use. Students can access the following: campus intranet, computer help desk, free student e-mail accounts, online (class) grades, online (class) registration, online (class) schedules. Campuswide network is available. 100% of college-owned or -operated housing units are wired for high-speed Internet access. Wireless service is available via entire campus.
Library: Robert A. L. Mortvedt Library. *Books:* 256,165 (physical), 43,611 (digital/electronic); *Databases:* 118. Weekly public service hours: 80; students can reserve study rooms.

STUDENT LIFE
Housing options: on-campus residence required through sophomore year; coed, women-only, special housing for students with disabilities. Campus housing is university owned. Freshman campus housing is guaranteed.

Activities and organizations: drama/theater group, student-run newspaper, radio and television station, choral group, Delta Iota Chi, Swing Club, Club Keithly, Young Life College Club, ROTC Cadet Activities Council.

Athletics Member NCAA. All Division III. ***Intercollegiate sports:*** baseball M, basketball M/W, cheerleading M(c)/W(c), crew M(c)/W, cross-country running M/W, football M, golf M/W, lacrosse M(c)/W(c), rowing M(c)/W, soccer M/W, softball W, swimming and diving M/W, tennis M/W, track and field M/W, ultimate Frisbee M(c)/W(c), volleyball W. ***Intramural sports:*** badminton M/W, basketball M/W, bowling M/W, cross-country running M/W, football M/W, soccer M/W, softball M/W, swimming and diving M/W, table tennis M/W, tennis M/W, ultimate Frisbee M/W, volleyball M/W, water polo M/W.

Campus security: 24-hour emergency response devices and patrols, student patrols, late-night transport/escort service, controlled dormitory access, over 60 surveillance camera monitoring stations. Emergency notification system with indoor/outdoor speakers and text/phone/email alerts.

Student services: health clinic, personal/psychological counseling, women's center.

COSTS & FINANCIAL AID

Costs (2017–18) ***Comprehensive fee:*** $51,242 includes full-time tuition ($40,352), mandatory fees ($370), and room and board ($10,520). Full-time tuition and fees vary according to course load and degree level. Part-time tuition: $1261 per semester hour. Part-time tuition and fees vary according to course load and degree level. ***Required fees:*** $370 per year part-time. ***College room only:*** $4940. Room and board charges vary according to board plan and housing facility. ***Payment plan:*** installment. ***Waivers:*** children of alumni and employees or children of employees.

Financial Aid Of all full-time matriculated undergraduates who enrolled in 2015, 2,269 applied for aid, 2,048 were judged to have need, 406 had their need fully met. 675 Federal Work-Study jobs (averaging $3189). 477 state and other part-time jobs (averaging $3808). In 2015, 640 non-need-based awards were made. ***Average percent of need met:*** 84. ***Average financial aid package:*** $35,634. ***Average need-based loan:*** $9177. ***Average need-based gift aid:*** $23,228. ***Average non-need-based aid:*** $16,755. ***Average indebtedness upon graduation:*** $29,866.

APPLYING

Standardized Tests *Required:* SAT or ACT (for admission).

Options: electronic application, deferred entrance.

Application fee: $40.

Required: essay or personal statement, high school transcript, 1 letter of recommendation. ***Required for some:*** interview. ***Recommended:*** minimum 2.5 GPA.

Application deadlines: rolling (freshmen), rolling (transfers).

Notification: continuous (freshmen), continuous (transfers).

CONTACT

Melody A. Ferguson, Director of Admission, Pacific Lutheran University, Tacoma, WA 98447. *Phone:* 253-535-7151. *Toll-free phone:* 800-274-6758. *Fax:* 253-536-5136. *E-mail:* admission@plu.edu.

Peninsula College

Port Angeles, Washington

http://www.pc.ctc.edu/

CONTACT

Ms. Pauline Marvin, Peninsula College, 1502 East Lauridsen Boulevard, Port Angeles, WA 98362. *Phone:* 360-417-6596. *Toll-free phone:* 877-452-9277. *Fax:* 360-457-8100. *E-mail:* admissions@pencol.edu.

Pima Medical Institute

Seattle, Washington

http://www.pmi.edu/

CONTACT

Admissions Office, Pima Medical Institute, 9709 Third Avenue NE, Suite 400, Seattle, WA 98115. *Phone:* 206-322-6100. *Toll-free phone:* 800-477-PIMA.

Renton Technical College

Renton, Washington

http://www.rtc.edu/

- **State-supported** primarily 2-year, founded 1942, part of Washington State Board for Community and Technical Colleges
- **Suburban** 30-acre campus with easy access to Seattle
- **Endowment** $818,276
- **Coed** 3,961 undergraduate students, 31% full-time, 30% women, 70% men
- **Noncompetitive** entrance level

UNDERGRAD STUDENTS

1,238 full-time, 2,720 part-time. Students come from 8 states and territories; 0.1% are from out of state; 8% Black or African American, non-Hispanic/Latino; 7% Hispanic/Latino; 11% Asian, non-Hispanic/Latino; 0.5% Native Hawaiian or other Pacific Islander, non-Hispanic/Latino; 0.9% American Indian or Alaska Native, non-Hispanic/Latino; 3% Two or more races, non-Hispanic/Latino; 34% Race/ethnicity unknown; 0.2% international; 15% transferred in.

Freshmen:

Admission: 184 enrolled.

Retention: 73% of full-time freshmen returned.

FACULTY

Total: 247, 37% full-time.

Student/faculty ratio: 17:1.

ACADEMICS

Calendar: quarters. *Degrees:* certificates, diplomas, associate, and bachelor's.

Special study options: academic remediation for entering students, adult/continuing education programs, advanced placement credit, cooperative education, distance learning, English as a second language, internships, off-campus study, part-time degree program, services for LD students, summer session for credit.

Computers: 96 computers/terminals are available on campus for general student use. Campuswide network is available.

Library: Renton Technical College Library.

STUDENT LIFE

Housing options: college housing not available.

Campus security: patrols by security, security system.

Student services: personal/psychological counseling.

COSTS

Costs (2016–17) ***Tuition:*** state resident $4167 full-time, $110 per credit hour part-time; nonresident $4580 full-time, $123 per credit hour part-time. Full-time tuition and fees vary according to course load, degree level, and program. Part-time tuition and fees vary according to course load, degree level, and program. ***Payment plan:*** installment.

APPLYING

Standardized Tests *Required for some:* ACT ASSET, CLEP, ACCUPLACER, DSP.

Options: electronic application, early admission.

Application fee: $30.

Required for some: essay or personal statement, high school transcript, interview.

Application deadlines: rolling (freshmen), rolling (transfers).

Notification: continuous (freshmen), continuous (transfers).

CONTACT

Linh Bracking, Student Success Advisor, Renton Technical College, 3000 NE 4th Street, Renton, WA 98056. *Phone:* 425-235-2352 Ext. 5543. *E-mail:* lbracking@rtc.edu.

Saint Martin's University

Lacey, Washington

http://www.stmartin.edu/

- **Independent Roman Catholic** comprehensive, founded 1895
- **Suburban** 300-acre campus with easy access to Seattle
- **Endowment** $17.5 million
- **Coed** 1,281 undergraduate students, 84% full-time, 50% women, 50% men
- **Moderately difficult** entrance level, 95% of applicants were admitted

UNDERGRAD STUDENTS

1,073 full-time, 208 part-time. Students come from 28 states and territories; 16 other countries; 28% are from out of state; 6% Black or African American, non-Hispanic/Latino; 14% Hispanic/Latino; 6% Asian, non-Hispanic/Latino; 3% Native Hawaiian or other Pacific Islander, non-Hispanic/Latino; 1% American Indian or Alaska Native, non-Hispanic/Latino; 6% Two or more races, non-Hispanic/Latino; 5%

Race/ethnicity unknown; 5% international; 13% transferred in; 38% live on campus.

Freshmen:
Admission: 1,344 applied, 1,281 admitted, 241 enrolled. ***Average high school GPA:*** 3.4. ***Test scores:*** SAT critical reading scores over 500: 51%; SAT math scores over 500: 51%; SAT writing scores over 500: 45%; ACT scores over 18: 93%; SAT critical reading scores over 600: 18%; SAT math scores over 600: 22%; SAT writing scores over 600: 11%; ACT scores over 24: 35%; SAT critical reading scores over 700: 4%; SAT math scores over 700: 2%; SAT writing scores over 700: 3%; ACT scores over 30: 7%.

Retention: 81% of full-time freshmen returned.

FACULTY
Total: 184, 44% full-time, 55% with terminal degrees.
Student/faculty ratio: 12:1.

ACADEMICS
Calendar: semesters. *Degrees:* certificates, bachelor's, master's, post-master's, and postbachelor's certificates.
Special study options: academic remediation for entering students, adult/continuing education programs, advanced placement credit, cooperative education, distance learning, double majors, English as a second language, honors programs, independent study, internships, off-campus study, part-time degree program, services for LD students, study abroad, summer session for credit. ***ROTC:*** Army (c), Air Force (c).
Computers: 80 computers/terminals and 130 ports are available on campus for general student use. Students can access the following: campus intranet, computer help desk, free student e-mail accounts, online (class) grades, online (class) registration, online (class) schedules. Campuswide network is available. 100% of college-owned or -operated housing units are wired for high-speed Internet access. Wireless service is available via entire campus.
Library: O'Grady Library. *Books:* 82,453 (physical), 199,324 (digital/electronic); *Serial titles:* 100 (physical), 46,874 (digital/electronic); *Databases:* 110. Weekly public service hours: 88; students can reserve study rooms.

STUDENT LIFE
Housing options: on-campus residence required through sophomore year; coed. Campus housing is university owned. Freshman campus housing is guaranteed.
Activities and organizations: drama/theater group, student-run newspaper, choral group.
Athletics Member NCAA. All Division II. ***Intercollegiate sports:*** baseball M(s), basketball M(s)/W(s), cross-country running M(s)/W(s), golf M(s)/W(s), soccer M/W(s), softball W(s), track and field M(s)/W(s), volleyball W(s). ***Intramural sports:*** basketball M/W, bowling M/W, golf M/W, soccer M/W, softball M/W, table tennis M/W, tennis M/W, ultimate Frisbee M/W, volleyball M/W.
Campus security: 24-hour emergency response devices and patrols, student patrols, late-night transport/escort service, controlled dormitory access, close-circuit TV cameras throughout campus, emergency text messaging/notification.
Student services: health clinic, personal/psychological counseling.

COSTS & FINANCIAL AID
Costs (2017–18) ***Comprehensive fee:*** $46,686 includes full-time tuition ($35,250), mandatory fees ($406), and room and board ($11,030). Full-time tuition and fees vary according to course load, degree level, location, and program. Part-time tuition: $1190 per credit. Part-time tuition and fees vary according to degree level, location, and program. ***College room only:*** $5410. Room and board charges vary according to board plan and housing facility. ***Payment plan:*** installment. ***Waivers:*** children of alumni and employees or children of employees.
Financial Aid Of all full-time matriculated undergraduates who enrolled in 2015, 808 applied for aid, 740 were judged to have need, 169 had their need fully met. 120 Federal Work-Study jobs (averaging $1667). 26 state and other part-time jobs (averaging $7110). In 2015, 124 non-need-based awards were made. ***Average percent of need met:*** 76. ***Average financial aid package:*** $25,969. ***Average need-based loan:*** $4191. ***Average need-based gift aid:*** $22,929. ***Average non-need-based aid:*** $12,771. ***Average indebtedness upon graduation:*** $27,807.

APPLYING
Standardized Tests *Required:* SAT or ACT (for admission).
Options: electronic application, deferred entrance.
Required: essay or personal statement, high school transcript, 1 letter of recommendation.
Application deadlines: 7/31 (freshmen), 8/1 (transfers).
Notification: continuous (freshmen), continuous (out-of-state freshmen), continuous (transfers).

CONTACT
Ms. Emilie Schnabel, Associate Director of Admissions, Saint Martin's University, 5000 Abbey Way SE, Lacey, WA 98503-7500. *Phone:* 360-688-2104. *Toll-free phone:* 800-368-8803. *Fax:* 360-412-6189. *E-mail:* admissions@stmartin.edu.

Seattle Pacific University

Seattle, Washington

http://www.spu.edu/

- **Independent Free Methodist** comprehensive, founded 1891
- **Urban** 40-acre campus
- **Coed** 3,095 undergraduate students, 97% full-time, 67% women, 33% men
- **Moderately difficult** entrance level, 87% of applicants were admitted

UNDERGRAD STUDENTS
2,998 full-time, 97 part-time. 36% are from out of state; 4% Black or African American, non-Hispanic/Latino; 10% Hispanic/Latino; 11% Asian, non-Hispanic/Latino; 0.6% Native Hawaiian or other Pacific Islander, non-Hispanic/Latino; 0.4% American Indian or Alaska Native, non-Hispanic/Latino; 9% Two or more races, non-Hispanic/Latino; 2% Race/ethnicity unknown; 4% international; 7% transferred in; 53% live on campus.

Freshmen:
Admission: 4,034 applied, 3,521 admitted, 685 enrolled. ***Average high school GPA:*** 3.53. ***Test scores:*** SAT critical reading scores over 500: 79%; SAT math scores over 500: 78%; ACT scores over 18: 97%; SAT critical reading scores over 600: 40%; SAT math scores over 600: 33%; ACT scores over 24: 66%; SAT critical reading scores over 700: 9%; SAT math scores over 700: 7%; ACT scores over 30: 15%.

Retention: 82% of full-time freshmen returned.

FACULTY
Total: 402, 53% full-time, 50% with terminal degrees.
Student/faculty ratio: 14:1.

ACADEMICS
Calendar: quarters. *Degrees:* bachelor's, master's, doctoral, and post-master's certificates.
Special study options: academic remediation for entering students, adult/continuing education programs, advanced placement credit, distance learning, double majors, external degree program, honors programs, independent study, internships, off-campus study, part-time degree program, services for LD students, student-designed majors, study abroad, summer session for credit. ***ROTC:*** Army (c), Navy (c), Air Force (c).
Computers: 150 computers/terminals are available on campus for general student use. Students can access the following: campus intranet, computer help desk, free student e-mail accounts, online (class) grades, online (class) registration, online (class) schedules. Campuswide network is available. Wireless service is available via entire campus.
Library: University Library.

STUDENT LIFE
Housing options: on-campus residence required through sophomore year; coed, special housing for students with disabilities. Campus housing is university owned. Freshman campus housing is guaranteed.
Activities and organizations: drama/theater group, student-run newspaper, radio station, choral group, Centurions, Falconettes, forensics organization, Amnesty International, University Players.
Athletics Member NCAA. All Division II. ***Intercollegiate sports:*** basketball M(s)/W(s), crew M/W(s), cross-country running M(s)/W(s), gymnastics W(s), soccer M(s)/W(s), track and field M(s)/W(s), volleyball W(s). ***Intramural sports:*** archery M/W, basketball M/W, bowling M/W,

cross-country running M/W, football M/W, soccer M/W(c), softball M/W, tennis M/W, volleyball M(c)/W(c), weight lifting M/W.

Campus security: 24-hour emergency response devices and patrols, student patrols, late-night transport/escort service, closed-circuit TV monitors.

Student services: health clinic, personal/psychological counseling.

COSTS & FINANCIAL AID

Costs (2016–17) ***Comprehensive fee:*** $49,764 includes full-time tuition ($38,520), mandatory fees ($420), and room and board ($10,824). Part-time tuition: $1070 per credit hour. Part-time tuition and fees vary according to course load. ***College room only:*** $5883. Room and board charges vary according to board plan and housing facility. ***Payment plans:*** installment, deferred payment. ***Waivers:*** senior citizens and employees or children of employees.

Financial Aid Of all full-time matriculated undergraduates who enrolled in 2016, 2,422 applied for aid, 2,083 were judged to have need, 138 had their need fully met. 425 Federal Work-Study jobs (averaging $2396). 140 state and other part-time jobs (averaging $2156). In 2016, 707 non-need-based awards were made. ***Average percent of need met:*** 79. ***Average financial aid package:*** $32,869. ***Average need-based loan:*** $5088. ***Average need-based gift aid:*** $30,163. ***Average non-need-based aid:*** $22,062. ***Average indebtedness upon graduation:*** $28,880.

APPLYING

Standardized Tests *Required:* SAT or ACT (for admission). *Required for some:* SAT and SAT Subject Tests or ACT (for admission), SAT Subject Tests (for admission).

Options: electronic application, early admission, early action.

Application fee: $50.

Required: essay or personal statement, high school transcript, minimum 2.5 GPA, 2 letters of recommendation. ***Recommended:*** interview.

Application deadlines: 2/1 (freshmen), 8/1 (transfers), 11/15 (early action).

Notification: 3/1 (freshmen), continuous (transfers), 1/5 (early action).

CONTACT

Ineliz Soto-Fuller, Director of Undergraduate Admissions, Seattle Pacific University, 3307 3rd Avenue, West, Seattle, WA 98119-1997. *Phone:* 206-281-2021. *Toll-free phone:* 800-366-3344. *Fax:* 206-281-2669. *E-mail:* admissions@spu.edu.

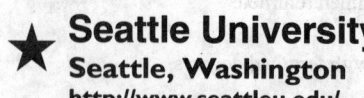

★ Seattle University

Seattle, Washington

http://www.seattleu.edu/

- **Independent Roman Catholic** comprehensive, founded 1891
- **Urban** 50-acre campus with easy access to Seattle
- **Coed** 4,776 undergraduate students, 95% full-time, 61% women, 39% men
- **Moderately difficult** entrance level, 74% of applicants were admitted

UNDERGRAD STUDENTS

4,528 full-time, 248 part-time. Students come from 50 states and territories; 102 other countries; 69% are from out of state; 3% Black or African American, non-Hispanic/Latino; 10% Hispanic/Latino; 16% Asian, non-Hispanic/Latino; 0.9% Native Hawaiian or other Pacific Islander, non-Hispanic/Latino; 0.4% American Indian or Alaska Native, non-Hispanic/Latino; 8% Two or more races, non-Hispanic/Latino; 8% Race/ethnicity unknown; 11% international; 8% transferred in; 45% live on campus.

Freshmen:

Admission: 8,149 applied, 6,001 admitted, 982 enrolled. ***Average high school GPA:*** 3.61. ***Test scores:*** SAT critical reading scores over 500: 88%; SAT math scores over 500: 89%; SAT writing scores over 500: 84%; ACT scores over 18: 100%; SAT critical reading scores over 600: 45%; SAT math scores over 600: 47%; SAT writing scores over 600: 39%; ACT scores over 24: 85%; SAT critical reading scores over 700: 9%; SAT math scores over 700: 8%; SAT writing scores over 700: 7%; ACT scores over 30: 27%.

Retention: 87% of full-time freshmen returned.

FACULTY

Total: 767, 66% full-time, 75% with terminal degrees.

Student/faculty ratio: 12:1.

ACADEMICS

Calendar: quarters. *Degrees:* bachelor's, master's, doctoral, post-master's, and postbachelor's certificates.

Special study options: accelerated degree program, adult/continuing education programs, advanced placement credit, double majors, English as a second language, freshman honors college, honors programs, independent study, internships, off-campus study, part-time degree program, services for LD students, student-designed majors, study abroad, summer session for credit. ***ROTC:*** Army (b), Navy (c), Air Force (c).

Computers: 467 computers/terminals are available on campus for general student use. Students can access the following: campus intranet, computer help desk, free student e-mail accounts, online (class) grades, online (class) registration, online (class) schedules. Campuswide network is available. 99% of college-owned or -operated housing units are wired for high-speed Internet access. Wireless service is available via entire campus.

Library: Lemieux Library & McGoldrick Learning Commons plus 1 other. *Books:* 472,572 (physical), 257,641 (digital/electronic); *Serial titles:* 118,353 (physical), 8,597 (digital/electronic); *Databases:* 235. Students can reserve study rooms.

STUDENT LIFE

Housing options: on-campus residence required through sophomore year; coed, special housing for students with disabilities. Campus housing is university owned and leased by the school. Freshman campus housing is guaranteed.

Activities and organizations: drama/theater group, student-run newspaper, radio station, choral group, Student Government of Seattle University (SGSU), Student Events and Activities Council (SEAC), Redzone, Dance Marathon, Hui 'O Nani Hawaii Club.

Athletics Member NCAA. All Division I. ***Intercollegiate sports:*** baseball M, basketball M(s)/W(s), cheerleading M(c)/W(c), crew W(c), cross-country running M(s)/W(s), golf M(s)/W(s), soccer M(s)/W(s), softball W(s), swimming and diving M(s)/W(s), tennis M/W, track and field M(s)/W(s), volleyball W(s). ***Intramural sports:*** archery M(c)/W(c), basketball M/W, crew M(c)/W(c), field hockey M/W, football M/W, riflery M(c)/W(c), rock climbing M/W, skiing (downhill) M(c)/W(c), soccer M/W, softball M/W, tennis M/W, ultimate Frisbee M/W, volleyball M/W, water polo M/W.

Campus security: 24-hour emergency response devices and patrols, late-night transport/escort service, controlled dormitory access, bicycle patrols.

Student services: health clinic, personal/psychological counseling, women's center.

COSTS & FINANCIAL AID

Costs (2016–17) ***Comprehensive fee:*** $52,764 includes full-time tuition ($40,500), mandatory fees ($765), and room and board ($11,499). Full-time tuition and fees vary according to course load. Part-time tuition: $900 per credit hour. Part-time tuition and fees vary according to course load. ***College room only:*** $7059. Room and board charges vary according to board plan and housing facility. ***Payment plans:*** installment, deferred payment. ***Waivers:*** employees or children of employees.

Financial Aid Of all full-time matriculated undergraduates who enrolled in 2016, 3,093 applied for aid, 2,490 were judged to have need, 291 had their need fully met. 484 Federal Work-Study jobs (averaging $3893). 599 state and other part-time jobs (averaging $5179). In 2016, 179 non-need-based awards were made. ***Average percent of need met:*** 70. ***Average financial aid package:*** $33,772. ***Average need-based loan:*** $5659. ***Average need-based gift aid:*** $23,620. ***Average non-need-based aid:*** $13,344. ***Average indebtedness upon graduation:*** $28,297.

APPLYING

Standardized Tests *Required:* SAT or ACT (for admission).

Options: electronic application, early action, deferred entrance.

Application fee: $50.

Required: essay or personal statement, high school transcript, minimum 2.5 GPA, 2 letters of recommendation.

Application deadlines: rolling (freshmen), 3/1 (transfers), 11/15 (early action).

Notification: continuous until 3/1 (freshmen), continuous (transfers), 12/23 (early action).

CONTACT
Melore Nielsen, Dean of Undergraduate Admissions, Seattle University, 901 12th Avenue, PO Box 222000, Seattle, WA 98122-1090. *Phone:* 206-296-2000. *Toll-free phone:* 800-542-0833 (in-state); 800-426-7123 (out-of-state). *Fax:* 206-296-5656. *E-mail:* admissions@seattleu.edu.

University of Phoenix–Western Washington Campus

Tukwila, Washington

http://www.phoenix.edu/

CONTACT
Marc Booker, Sr. Director, Office of Admissions and Evaluation, University of Phoenix–Western Washington Campus, 4615 East Elwood Street, Mail Stop AA-K101, Phoenix, AZ 85040-1958. *Phone:* 602-557-4609. *Toll-free phone:* 866-766-0766. *Fax:* 480-643-1156.

University of Puget Sound

Tacoma, Washington

http://www.pugetsound.edu/

- **Independent** comprehensive, founded 1888
- **Urban** 97-acre campus with easy access to Seattle
- **Coed** 2,476 undergraduate students, 99% full-time, 59% women, 41% men
- **Moderately difficult** entrance level, 79% of applicants were admitted

UNDERGRAD STUDENTS
2,459 full-time, 17 part-time. 79% are from out of state; 0.9% Black or African American, non-Hispanic/Latino; 7% Hispanic/Latino; 6% Asian, non-Hispanic/Latino; 0.2% Native Hawaiian or other Pacific Islander, non-Hispanic/Latino; 0.1% American Indian or Alaska Native, non-Hispanic/Latino; 8% Two or more races, non-Hispanic/Latino; 2% Race/ethnicity unknown; 0.4% international; 2% transferred in; 66% live on campus.

Freshmen:
Admission: 5,827 applied, 4,616 admitted, 652 enrolled. ***Average high school GPA:*** 3.53. ***Test scores:*** SAT critical reading scores over 500: 93%; SAT math scores over 500: 88%; SAT writing scores over 500: 91%; ACT scores over 18: 99%; SAT critical reading scores over 600: 60%; SAT math scores over 600: 50%; SAT writing scores over 600: 54%; ACT scores over 24: 83%; SAT critical reading scores over 700: 18%; SAT math scores over 700: 10%; SAT writing scores over 700: 14%; ACT scores over 30: 30%.
Retention: 86% of full-time freshmen returned.

FACULTY
Total: 281, 84% full-time.
Student/faculty ratio: 11:1.

ACADEMICS
Calendar: semesters. *Degrees:* bachelor's, master's, and doctoral.
Special study options: advanced placement credit, cooperative education, double majors, honors programs, independent study, internships, part-time degree program, services for LD students, student-designed majors, study abroad, summer session for credit. ***ROTC:*** Army (c).
Unusual degree programs: 3-2 engineering with Washington University in St. Louis, Columbia University, University of Southern California.
Computers: Students can access the following: campus intranet, computer help desk, free student e-mail accounts, online (class) grades, online (class) registration, online (class) schedules, financial aid, admission, student employment. Campuswide network is available. 100% of college-owned or -operated housing units are wired for high-speed Internet access. Wireless service is available via entire campus.
Library: Collins Memorial Library.

STUDENT LIFE
Housing options: on-campus residence required through sophomore year; coed, special housing for students with disabilities. Campus housing is university owned. Freshman campus housing is guaranteed.
Activities and organizations: drama/theater group, student-run newspaper, radio station, choral group, Puget Sound Outdoors, Repertory Dance Group, Hui-O-Hawaii, Student Theatre Productions, Relay for Life, national fraternities, national sororities.
Athletics Member NCAA. All Division III. ***Intercollegiate sports:*** baseball M, basketball M/W, cheerleading M/W, crew M/W, cross-country running M/W, fencing M(c)/W(c), football M, golf M/W, lacrosse M(c)/W, rugby M(c)/W(c), sailing M(c)/W(c), skiing (downhill) M(c)/W(c), soccer M/W, softball W, swimming and diving M/W, tennis M/W, track and field M/W, ultimate Frisbee M(c)/W(c), volleyball W, water polo M(c)/W(c). ***Intramural sports:*** basketball M/W, football M/W, soccer M/W, softball M/W, volleyball M/W.
Campus security: 24-hour emergency response devices and patrols, student patrols, late-night transport/escort service, controlled dormitory access, 24-hour locked residence hall entrances, surveillance cameras, and emergency telephone towers.
Student services: health clinic, personal/psychological counseling.

COSTS & FINANCIAL AID
Costs (2017–18) ***Comprehensive fee:*** $60,210 includes full-time tuition ($47,840), mandatory fees ($250), and room and board ($12,120). Full-time tuition and fees vary according to course load. Part-time tuition: $6040 per unit. Part-time tuition and fees vary according to course load. ***College room only:*** $6620. Room and board charges vary according to board plan and housing facility. ***Payment plans:*** installment, deferred payment. ***Waivers:*** employees or children of employees.
Financial Aid Of all full-time matriculated undergraduates who enrolled in 2016, 1,506 applied for aid, 1,212 were judged to have need, 196 had their need fully met. 528 Federal Work-Study jobs (averaging $3092). 841 state and other part-time jobs (averaging $2557). In 2016, 1233 non-need-based awards were made. ***Average percent of need met:*** 76. ***Average financial aid package:*** $31,725. ***Average need-based loan:*** $6466. ***Average need-based gift aid:*** $24,456. ***Average non-need-based aid:*** $15,870. ***Average indebtedness upon graduation:*** $34,140.

APPLYING
Standardized Tests *Required:* SAT or ACT (for admission).
Options: electronic application, early admission, early decision, deferred entrance.
Application fee: $50.
Required: essay or personal statement, high school transcript, 2 letters of recommendation. ***Recommended:*** minimum 3.0 GPA, interview.

CONTACT
Dr. Jenny Rickard, Vice President for Enrollment, University of Puget Sound, 1500 North Warner Street, CMB 1062, Tacoma, WA 98416. *Phone:* 253-879-3211. *Toll-free phone:* 800-396-7191. *Fax:* 253-879-3993. *E-mail:* admission@pugetsound.edu.

University of Washington

Seattle, Washington

http://www.washington.edu/

- **State-supported** university, founded 1861, part of University of Washington
- **Urban** 703-acre campus
- **Endowment** $3.0 billion
- **Coed** 30,933 undergraduate students, 92% full-time, 52% women, 48% men
- **Very difficult** entrance level, 45% of applicants were admitted

UNDERGRAD STUDENTS
28,380 full-time, 2,553 part-time. Students come from 51 states and territories; 87 other countries; 17% are from out of state; 3% Black or African American, non-Hispanic/Latino; 8% Hispanic/Latino; 25% Asian, non-Hispanic/Latino; 0.5% Native Hawaiian or other Pacific Islander, non-Hispanic/Latino; 0.4% American Indian or Alaska Native, non-Hispanic/Latino; 7% Two or more races, non-Hispanic/Latino; 1% Race/ethnicity unknown; 15% international; 5% transferred in; 27% live on campus.

Freshmen:
Admission: 43,517 applied, 19,733 admitted, 6,475 enrolled. ***Average high school GPA:*** 3.78. ***Test scores:*** SAT critical reading scores over 500: 87%; SAT math scores over 500: 92%; SAT writing scores over 500: 86%; ACT scores over 18: 98%; SAT critical reading scores over 600: 53%; SAT math scores over 600: 70%; SAT writing scores over 600: 54%; ACT

scores over 24: 87%; SAT critical reading scores over 700: 16%; SAT math scores over 700: 30%; SAT writing scores over 700: 15%; ACT scores over 30: 44%.

Retention: 94% of full-time freshmen returned.

FACULTY
Total: 3,206, 66% full-time, 74% with terminal degrees.

Student/faculty ratio: 17:1.

ACADEMICS
Calendar: quarters. *Degrees:* bachelor's, master's, doctoral, and post-master's certificates.

Special study options: adult/continuing education programs, advanced placement credit, cooperative education, distance learning, double majors, English as a second language, external degree program, honors programs, independent study, internships, off-campus study, part-time degree program, services for LD students, student-designed majors, study abroad, summer session for credit. ***ROTC:*** Army (b), Navy (b), Air Force (b).

Computers: 450 computers/terminals are available on campus for general student use. Students can access the following: computer help desk, free student e-mail accounts, online (class) grades, online (class) registration, online (class) schedules. Campuswide network is available. 100% of college-owned or -operated housing units are wired for high-speed Internet access. Wireless service is available via entire campus.

Library: Odegaard Undergraduate libraray plus 12 others. *Books:* 8.7 million (physical), 833,635 (digital/electronic); *Serial titles:* 25,000 (physical), 100,000 (digital/electronic); *Databases:* 500. Weekly public service hours: 124; study areas open 24 hours, 5-7 days a week; students can reserve study rooms.

STUDENT LIFE
Housing options: coed, special housing for students with disabilities. Campus housing is university owned, leased by the school and is provided by a third party.

Activities and organizations: drama/theater group, student-run newspaper, radio and television station, choral group, marching band, Interfraternity Council/Pan-Hellenic Council, Taiwanese Student Association, Chinese Student Association, Yacht Club, Asian American Intervarsity Christian Fellowship/Muslim Students Association, national sororities.

Athletics Member NCAA, NAIA. All NCAA Division I except football (Division I-A). ***Intercollegiate sports:*** baseball M(s), basketball M(s)/W(s), cheerleading M(s)/W(s), crew M(s)/W(s), cross-country running M(s)/W(s), golf M(s)/W(s), gymnastics W(s), rowing M(s)/W(s), soccer M(s)/W(s), softball W(s), tennis M(s)/W(s), track and field M(s)/W(s), volleyball W(s). ***Intramural sports:*** archery M(c)/W(c), badminton M/W, baseball M(c)/W(c), basketball M/W, bowling M/W(c), crew M(c)/W(c), equestrian sports M(c)/W(c), football M/W, ice hockey M(c)/W(c), lacrosse M(c)/W(c), racquetball M/W, rock climbing M/W, rowing M/W, rugby M(c)/W(c), sailing M(c)/W(c), skiing (cross-country) M(c)/W(c), skiing (downhill) M(c)/W(c), soccer M/W, softball M/W, squash M(c)/W(c), swimming and diving M/W, table tennis M(c)/W(c), tennis M/W, triathlon M(c)/W(c), ultimate Frisbee M/W, volleyball M/W, water polo M(c)/W(c), wrestling M(c)/W(c).

Campus security: 24-hour emergency response devices and patrols, late-night transport/escort service, controlled dormitory access.

Student services: health clinic, personal/psychological counseling, women's center, legal services.

COSTS & FINANCIAL AID
Costs (2017–18) ***Tuition:*** state resident $9694 full-time, $323 per credit part-time; nonresident $33,732 full-time, $1124 per credit part-time. Full-time tuition and fees vary according to course load and location. Part-time tuition and fees vary according to course load and location. ***Required fees:*** $1059 full-time, $27 per credit part-time, $84 per term part-time. ***Room and board:*** $11,691. Room and board charges vary according to board plan and housing facility. ***Payment plan:*** tuition prepayment. ***Waivers:*** senior citizens and employees or children of employees.

Financial Aid Of all full-time matriculated undergraduates who enrolled in 2016, 11,770 applied for aid, 11,700 were judged to have need, 3,100 had their need fully met. 540 Federal Work-Study jobs (averaging $4146). 145 state and other part-time jobs (averaging $4841). In 2016, 1000 non-need-based awards were made. ***Average percent of need met:*** 82. ***Average financial aid package:*** $19,100. ***Average need-based loan:*** $7000. ***Average need-based gift aid:*** $15,000. ***Average non-need-based aid:*** $6000. ***Average indebtedness upon graduation:*** $21,900.

APPLYING
Standardized Tests *Required:* SAT or ACT (for admission).

Options: electronic application.

Application fee: $70.

Required: essay or personal statement. ***Required for some:*** high school transcript.

Application deadlines: 12/1 (freshmen), 2/15 (transfers).

Notification: 3/15 (freshmen), 6/30 (transfers).

CONTACT
Office of Admissions, University of Washington, 1410 NE Campus Parkway, Seattle, WA 98195. *Phone:* 206-543-9686. *Fax:* 206-685-3655.

University of Washington, Bothell
Bothell, Washington
http://www.uwb.edu/

- **State-supported** comprehensive, founded 1990, part of University of Washington
- **Suburban** 127-acre campus with easy access to Seattle
- **Endowment** $4.1 million
- **Coed** 5,112 undergraduate students, 87% full-time, 49% women, 51% men
- **Moderately difficult** entrance level, 80% of applicants were admitted

UNDERGRAD STUDENTS
4,426 full-time, 686 part-time. Students come from 28 states and territories; 29 other countries; 2% are from out of state; 6% Black or African American, non-Hispanic/Latino; 9% Hispanic/Latino; 27% Asian, non-Hispanic/Latino; 0.8% Native Hawaiian or other Pacific Islander, non-Hispanic/Latino; 0.3% American Indian or Alaska Native, non-Hispanic/Latino; 6% Two or more races, non-Hispanic/Latino; 1% Race/ethnicity unknown; 10% international; 17% transferred in; 5% live on campus.

Freshmen:
Admission: 3,071 applied, 2,466 admitted, 820 enrolled. ***Average high school GPA:*** 3.3. ***Test scores:*** SAT critical reading scores over 500: 55%; SAT math scores over 500: 65%; SAT writing scores over 500: 47%; ACT scores over 18: 85%; SAT critical reading scores over 600: 17%; SAT math scores over 600: 27%; SAT writing scores over 600: 13%; ACT scores over 24: 40%; SAT critical reading scores over 700: 3%; SAT math scores over 700: 5%; SAT writing scores over 700: 2%; ACT scores over 30: 6%.

Retention: 84% of full-time freshmen returned.

FACULTY
Total: 362, 59% full-time, 75% with terminal degrees.

Student/faculty ratio: 19:1.

ACADEMICS
Calendar: quarters. *Degrees:* bachelor's and master's.

Special study options: adult/continuing education programs, advanced placement credit, cooperative education, double majors, English as a second language, independent study, distance learning, internships, off-campus study, part-time degree program, honors program, services for LD students, student-designed majors, study abroad, summer session for credit. ***ROTC:*** Army (c), Navy (c), Air Force (c).

Computers: 498 computers/terminals are available on campus for general student use. Students can access the following: campus intranet, computer help desk, free student e-mail accounts, online (class) grades, online (class) registration, online (class) schedules. Campuswide network is available. 100% of college-owned or -operated housing units are wired for high-speed Internet access. Wireless service is available via entire campus.

Library: Campus Library. *Books:* 118,611 (physical), 833,635 (digital/electronic); *Serial titles:* 100,000 (digital/electronic); *Databases:* 500. Weekly public service hours: 86; students can reserve study rooms.

STUDENT LIFE

Housing options: coed, men-only, women-only, special housing for students with disabilities. Campus housing is university owned and leased by the school. Freshman applicants given priority for college housing.

Activities and organizations: student-run newspaper, radio station, Campus Events Board, Social Justice Organizers, Associated Students of University of Washington Bothell (ASUWB), Recreation and Intramurals Program, Club Council.

Athletics *Intramural sports:* basketball M/W, football M/W, soccer M/W, softball M/W, tennis M/W, ultimate Frisbee M(c)/W(c), volleyball M/W.

Campus security: 24-hour emergency response devices and patrols, late-night transport/escort service.

Student services: personal/psychological counseling.

COSTS & FINANCIAL AID

Costs (2017–18) *Tuition:* state resident $9695 full-time, $323 per credit part-time; nonresident $33,732 full-time, $1124 per credit part-time. Full-time tuition and fees vary according to course load. Part-time tuition and fees vary according to course load. ***Required fees:*** $996 full-time, $33 per credit part-time. ***Room and board:*** $10,833. Room and board charges vary according to board plan, housing facility, and location. ***Payment plans:*** tuition prepayment, installment. ***Waivers:*** senior citizens and employees or children of employees.

Financial Aid Of all full-time matriculated undergraduates who enrolled in 2016, 2,956 applied for aid, 2,488 were judged to have need, 650 had their need fully met. 70 Federal Work-Study jobs (averaging $4187). 22 state and other part-time jobs (averaging $4407). In 2016, 170 non-need-based awards were made. ***Average percent of need met:*** 82. ***Average financial aid package:*** $14,900. ***Average need-based loan:*** $7000. ***Average need-based gift aid:*** $15,500. ***Average non-need-based aid:*** $7300. ***Average indebtedness upon graduation:*** $19,640.

APPLYING

Standardized Tests *Required:* SAT or ACT (for admission).

Options: electronic application.

Application fee: $60.

Required: essay or personal statement, high school transcript, minimum 2.0 GPA. ***Required for some:*** 1 letter of recommendation.

Application deadlines: 1/15 (freshmen), 1/15 (transfers).

Notification: continuous (freshmen), continuous (transfers).

CONTACT

Office of Admissions, University of Washington, Bothell, 18115 Campus Way NE, Box 358500, Bothell, WA 8011-8246. *Phone:* 425-352-5000. *Fax:* 425-352-5455. *E-mail:* uwbinfo@uw.edu.

University of Washington, Tacoma

Tacoma, Washington

http://www.tacoma.washington.edu/

- **State-supported** comprehensive, founded 1990, part of University of Washington
- **Urban** 31-acre campus with easy access to Seattle
- **Endowment** $40.5 million
- **Coed** 4,285 undergraduate students, 88% full-time, 52% women, 48% men
- **Moderately difficult** entrance level, 84% of applicants were admitted

UNDERGRAD STUDENTS

3,761 full-time, 524 part-time. Students come from 28 states and territories; 24 other countries; 1% are from out of state; 7% Black or African American, non-Hispanic/Latino; 14% Hispanic/Latino; 19% Asian, non-Hispanic/Latino; 1% Native Hawaiian or other Pacific Islander, non-Hispanic/Latino; 0.7% American Indian or Alaska Native, non-Hispanic/Latino; 9% Two or more races, non-Hispanic/Latino; 2% Race/ethnicity unknown; 5% international; 22% transferred in; 3% live on campus.

Freshmen:

Admission: 1,878 applied, 1,574 admitted, 534 enrolled. ***Average high school GPA:*** 3.24. ***Test scores:*** SAT critical reading scores over 500: 45%; SAT math scores over 500: 46%; SAT writing scores over 500: 36%; ACT scores over 18: 71%; SAT critical reading scores over 600: 11%; SAT math scores over 600: 15%; SAT writing scores over 600: 6%; ACT scores over 24: 21%; SAT critical reading scores over 700: 2%; SAT math scores over 700: 2%; ACT scores over 30: 1%.

Retention: 76% of full-time freshmen returned.

FACULTY

Total: 331, 73% full-time, 70% with terminal degrees.

Student/faculty ratio: 16:1.

ACADEMICS

Calendar: quarters. *Degrees:* bachelor's, master's, doctoral, and postbachelor's certificates.

Special study options: academic remediation for entering students, advanced placement credit, part-time degree program, distance learning, double majors, external degree program, honors programs, independent study, internships, off-campus study, part-time degree program, services for LD students, student-designed majors, study abroad, summer session for credit. ***ROTC:*** Army (c), Navy (c), Air Force (c).

Computers: 166 computers/terminals are available on campus for general student use. Students can access the following: campus intranet, computer help desk, free student e-mail accounts, online (class) grades, online (class) registration, online (class) schedules, learning management system, course management system. Campuswide network is available. 100% of college-owned or -operated housing units are wired for high-speed Internet access. Wireless service is available via entire campus.

Library: University of Washington Tacoma Library. *Books:* 123,187 (physical), 833,635 (digital/electronic); *Serial titles:* 100,000 (digital/electronic); *Databases:* 500. Weekly public service hours: 84; students can reserve study rooms.

STUDENT LIFE

Housing options: Campus housing is leased by the school. Freshman applicants given priority for college housing.

Activities and organizations: drama/theater group, student-run newspaper, choral group, Accounting Student Association, International Student Association, Partners in Action to Transform Healthcare (PATH), Asian Pacific Islander Student Union (APISU).

Athletics *Intramural sports:* badminton M/W, basketball M/W, soccer M(c)/W(c), wrestling M(c)/W(c).

Campus security: 24-hour emergency response devices and patrols, late-night transport/escort service, key card access to buildings after hours.

Student services: health clinic, personal/psychological counseling.

COSTS & FINANCIAL AID

Costs (2017–18) *Tuition:* state resident $9694 full-time, $323 per credit part-time; nonresident $33,732 full-time, $1124 per credit part-time. Full-time tuition and fees vary according to course load. Part-time tuition and fees vary according to course load. ***Required fees:*** $1137 full-time, $38 per credit part-time. ***Room and board:*** $10,230. Room and board charges vary according to housing facility and location. ***Payment plans:*** tuition prepayment, installment. ***Waivers:*** senior citizens and employees or children of employees.

Financial Aid Of all full-time matriculated undergraduates who enrolled in 2016, 3,053 applied for aid, 2,694 were judged to have need, 780 had their need fully met. 110 Federal Work-Study jobs (averaging $4083). 7 state and other part-time jobs (averaging $4386). In 2016, 400 non-need-based awards were made. ***Average percent of need met:*** 82. ***Average financial aid package:*** $15,700. ***Average need-based loan:*** $7000. ***Average need-based gift aid:*** $15,500. ***Average non-need-based aid:*** $3075. ***Average indebtedness upon graduation:*** $18,420.

APPLYING

Standardized Tests *Required:* SAT or ACT (for admission).

Options: electronic application, deferred entrance.

Application fee: $60.

Required: essay or personal statement. ***Required for some:*** high school transcript, 3 letters of recommendation.

Application deadlines: 6/30 (freshmen), 3/15 (transfers).

Notification: continuous (freshmen), continuous (transfers).

CONTACT

Ms. Megan Beresford, Associate Director of University Recruitment, University of Washington, Tacoma, 1900 Commerce Street, Tacoma, WA 98402-3100. *Phone:* 253-692-4738. *Toll-free phone:* 800-736-7750. *Fax:* 253-692-4414. *E-mail:* megan61@uw.edu.

Walla Walla University

College Place, Washington

http://www.wallawalla.edu/

- **Independent Seventh-day Adventist** comprehensive, founded 1892
- **Small-town** 77-acre campus
- **Coed** 1,700 undergraduate students, 93% full-time, 50% women, 50% men
- **Moderately difficult** entrance level

UNDERGRAD STUDENTS
1,585 full-time, 115 part-time. 62% are from out of state; 3% Black or African American, non-Hispanic/Latino; 15% Hispanic/Latino; 6% Asian, non-Hispanic/Latino; 0.7% Native Hawaiian or other Pacific Islander, non-Hispanic/Latino; 0.6% American Indian or Alaska Native, non-Hispanic/Latino; 0.7% Two or more races, non-Hispanic/Latino; 5% Race/ethnicity unknown; 3% international; 7% transferred in; 72% live on campus.

Freshmen:
Admission: 387 enrolled. ***Average high school GPA:*** 3.53. ***Test scores:*** SAT critical reading scores over 500: 67%; SAT math scores over 500: 63%; SAT writing scores over 500: 58%; ACT scores over 18: 67%; SAT critical reading scores over 600: 26%; SAT math scores over 600: 26%; SAT writing scores over 600: 18%; ACT scores over 24: 26%; SAT critical reading scores over 700: 6%; SAT math scores over 700: 3%; SAT writing scores over 700: 1%; ACT scores over 30: 6%.

FACULTY
Total: 171, 58% full-time, 44% with terminal degrees.

Student/faculty ratio: 15:1.

ACADEMICS
Calendar: quarters. *Degrees:* associate, bachelor's, and master's.

Special study options: academic remediation for entering students, advanced placement credit, cooperative education, distance learning, double majors, freshman honors college, honors programs, independent study, internships, off-campus study, part-time degree program, services for LD students, study abroad, summer session for credit.

Computers: Students can access the following: campus intranet, computer help desk, free student e-mail accounts, online (class) grades, online (class) registration, online (class) schedules, online forum, online classifieds, online student directory. Campuswide network is available. 100% of college-owned or -operated housing units are wired for high-speed Internet access. Wireless service is available via entire campus.

Library: Peterson Memorial Library plus 3 others.

STUDENT LIFE
Housing options: on-campus residence required through junior year; men-only, women-only, special housing for students with disabilities. Campus housing is university owned and leased by the school. Freshman campus housing is guaranteed.

Activities and organizations: drama/theater group, student-run newspaper, choral group, Associated Students of Walla Walla University, Campus Ministries, Village Club, OPS Club (Men's residence hall club), AGA Club (women's residence hall club).

Athletics Member NAIA. ***Intercollegiate sports:*** basketball M/W, soccer M, softball W, volleyball W. ***Intramural sports:*** basketball M/W, football M/W, ice hockey M, softball W, table tennis M/W, volleyball M/W.

Campus security: 24-hour emergency response devices and patrols, student patrols, late-night transport/escort service, controlled dormitory access.

Student services: health clinic, personal/psychological counseling.

COSTS & FINANCIAL AID
Costs (2017–18) ***Comprehensive fee:*** $34,845 includes full-time tuition ($26,595), mandatory fees ($900), and room and board ($7350). Part-time tuition: $738 per quarter hour. ***College room only:*** $4185.

Financial Aid Of all full-time matriculated undergraduates who enrolled in 2015, 1,138 applied for aid, 962 were judged to have need, 378 had their need fully met. In 2015, 437 non-need-based awards were made. ***Average percent of need met:*** 92. ***Average financial aid package:*** $22,193. ***Average need-based loan:*** $4160. ***Average need-based gift aid:*** $6334. ***Average non-need-based aid:*** $8677. ***Average indebtedness upon graduation:*** $33,018.

APPLYING
Standardized Tests *Required:* SAT or ACT (for admission).

Options: electronic application.

Application fee: $40.

Required: high school transcript, minimum 2.5 GPA.

Application deadlines: rolling (freshmen), rolling (transfers).

Notification: continuous (freshmen), continuous (transfers).

CONTACT
Mr. Dallas Weis, Director of Admissions, Walla Walla University, Marketing and Enrollment Services, 204 S. College Avenue, College Place, WA 99324. *Phone:* 509-527-2327.
Toll-free phone: 800-541-8900. *Fax:* 509-527-2397.

Washington State University

Pullman, Washington

http://www.wsu.edu/

- **State-supported** university, founded 1890
- **Small-town** 620-acre campus with easy access to Spokane
- **Endowment** $907.8 million
- **Coed** 17,716 undergraduate students, 95% full-time, 49% women, 51% men
- **Moderately difficult** entrance level, 73% of applicants were admitted

UNDERGRAD STUDENTS
16,784 full-time, 932 part-time. Students come from 49 states and territories; 70 other countries; 14% are from out of state; 4% Black or African American, non-Hispanic/Latino; 14% Hispanic/Latino; 6% Asian, non-Hispanic/Latino; 0.4% Native Hawaiian or other Pacific Islander, non-Hispanic/Latino; 0.8% American Indian or Alaska Native, non-Hispanic/Latino; 8% Two or more races, non-Hispanic/Latino; 1% Race/ethnicity unknown; 5% international; 7% transferred in; 24% live on campus.

Freshmen:
Admission: 21,410 applied, 15,608 admitted, 3,988 enrolled. ***Average high school GPA:*** 3.4. ***Test scores:*** SAT critical reading scores over 500: 58%; SAT math scores over 500: 66%; SAT writing scores over 500: 50%; ACT scores over 18: 90%; SAT critical reading scores over 600: 19%; SAT math scores over 600: 22%; SAT writing scores over 600: 12%; ACT scores over 24: 49%; SAT critical reading scores over 700: 3%; SAT math scores over 700: 3%; SAT writing scores over 700: 1%; ACT scores over 30: 7%.

Retention: 80% of full-time freshmen returned.

FACULTY
Total: 1,871, 72% full-time, 78% with terminal degrees.

Student/faculty ratio: 15:1.

ACADEMICS
Calendar: semesters. *Degrees:* certificates, bachelor's, master's, doctoral, post-master's, and postbachelor's certificates.

Special study options: academic remediation for entering students, accelerated degree program, adult/continuing education programs, advanced placement credit, cooperative education, distance learning, double majors, English as a second language, external degree program, freshman honors college, honors programs, independent study, internships, off-campus study, part-time degree program, services for LD students, student-designed majors, study abroad, summer session for credit. ***ROTC:*** Army (b), Navy (c), Air Force (b).

Computers: 2,500 computers/terminals and 2,500 ports are available on campus for general student use. Students can access the following: campus intranet, computer help desk, free student e-mail accounts, online (class) grades, online (class) registration, online (class) schedules. Campuswide network is available. 100% of college-owned or -operated housing units are wired for high-speed Internet access. Wireless service is available via classrooms, computer centers, computer labs, dorm rooms, learning centers, libraries, student centers.

Library: Holland and Terrell Libraries plus 3 others. *Books:* 2.4 million (physical), 677,302 (digital/electronic); *Serial titles:* 75,442 (physical), 58,249 (digital/electronic); *Databases:* 216. Weekly public service hours: 140; students can reserve study rooms.

STUDENT LIFE

Housing options: on-campus residence required for freshman year; coed, men-only, women-only, cooperative, special housing for students with disabilities. Campus housing is university owned. Freshman campus housing is guaranteed.

Activities and organizations: drama/theater group, student-run newspaper, radio and television station, choral group, marching band, Panhellenic Association - Sororities, Interfraternity Council - Fraternities, Student Entertainment Board, International Students Council, ChiLaStAl (Chicana/o Latina/o Student Alliance), national fraternities, national sororities.

Athletics Member NCAA. All Division I except football (Division I-A). ***Intercollegiate sports:*** baseball M(s), basketball M(s)/W(s), bowling M(c)/W(c), cheerleading M/W, crew M(c)/W(s), cross-country running M(s)/W(s), equestrian sports W(c), fencing M(c)/W(c), golf M(s)/W(s), ice hockey M(c)/W(c), lacrosse M(c)/W(c), rowing M(c)/W, rugby M(c)/W(c), skiing (cross-country) M(c)/W(c), skiing (downhill) M(c)/W(c), soccer M(c)/W(s), softball W(c), swimming and diving W(s), tennis M(c)/W(s), track and field M(s)/W(s), triathlon M(c)/W(c), ultimate Frisbee M(c)/W(c), volleyball M(c)/W(s), water polo W(c), weight lifting M(c)/W(c), wrestling M(c). ***Intramural sports:*** badminton M/W, basketball M/W, football M/W, golf M/W, racquetball M/W, rock climbing M/W, soccer M/W, softball M/W, table tennis M/W, tennis M/W, triathlon M/W, ultimate Frisbee M/W, volleyball M/W.

Campus security: 24-hour emergency response devices and patrols, student patrols, late-night transport/escort service, controlled dormitory access.

Student services: health clinic, personal/psychological counseling, women's center, legal services.

COSTS & FINANCIAL AID

Costs (2016–17) ***Tuition:*** state resident $9324 full-time, $497 per credit part-time; nonresident $23,956 full-time, $1226 per credit part-time. Full-time tuition and fees vary according to course load, location, and reciprocity agreements. Part-time tuition and fees vary according to course load, location, and reciprocity agreements. ***Required fees:*** $1717 full-time. ***Room and board:*** $11,356; room only: $6858. Room and board charges vary according to board plan, housing facility, and location. ***Waivers:*** senior citizens and employees or children of employees.

Financial Aid Of all full-time matriculated undergraduates who enrolled in 2015, 16,012 applied for aid, 12,986 were judged to have need, 1,323 had their need fully met. In 2015, 3036 non-need-based awards were made. ***Average percent of need met:*** 64. ***Average financial aid package:*** $13,465. ***Average need-based loan:*** $4509. ***Average need-based gift aid:*** $11,337. ***Average non-need-based aid:*** $3935. ***Average indebtedness upon graduation:*** $25,874. ***Financial aid deadline:*** 1/31.

APPLYING

Standardized Tests *Required:* SAT or ACT (for admission).

Options: electronic application.

Application fee: $50.

Required: high school transcript, minimum 2.0 GPA. ***Recommended:*** essay or personal statement.

Application deadlines: 1/31 (freshmen), rolling (out-of-state freshmen), 1/31 (transfers).

Notification: continuous until 11/1 (freshmen), continuous until 11/1 (out-of-state freshmen), continuous until 11/1 (transfers).

CONTACT

Ms. Wendy Peterson, Director of Admissions, Washington State University, PO Box 641067, Pullman, WA 99164-1067. *Phone:* 888-468-6978. *Toll-free phone:* 888-468-6978. *Fax:* 509-335-4902. *E-mail:* admissions@wsu.edu.

Washington State University–Global Campus

Pullman, Washington

http://www.globalcampus.wsu.edu/

- **State-supported** comprehensive
- **Coed** 2,007 undergraduate students, 40% full-time, 68% women, 32% men
- **Moderately difficult** entrance level, 48% of applicants were admitted

UNDERGRAD STUDENTS

804 full-time, 1,203 part-time. Students come from 40 states and territories; 33 other countries; 14% are from out of state; 4% Black or African American, non-Hispanic/Latino; 10% Hispanic/Latino; 5% Asian, non-Hispanic/Latino; 0.5% Native Hawaiian or other Pacific Islander, non-Hispanic/Latino; 1% American Indian or Alaska Native, non-Hispanic/Latino; 5% Two or more races, non-Hispanic/Latino; 4% Race/ethnicity unknown; 8% international; 23% transferred in.

Freshmen:

Admission: 109 applied, 52 admitted, 26 enrolled. ***Average high school GPA:*** 3.24. ***Test scores:*** SAT critical reading scores over 500: 67%; SAT math scores over 500: 53%; SAT writing scores over 500: 87%; ACT scores over 18: 80%; SAT critical reading scores over 600: 33%; SAT math scores over 600: 27%; SAT writing scores over 600: 67%; ACT scores over 24: 20%; SAT critical reading scores over 700: 13%; SAT writing scores over 700: 13%.

ACADEMICS

Calendar: semesters. *Degrees:* certificates, bachelor's, master's, post-master's, and postbachelor's certificates.

Special study options: adult/continuing education programs, distance learning, part-time degree program.

COSTS

Costs (2016–17) ***Tuition:*** state resident $9836 full-time, $494 per credit part-time; nonresident $11,386 full-time, $569 per credit part-time. Full-time tuition and fees vary according to course load, location, and reciprocity agreements. Part-time tuition and fees vary according to course load, location, and reciprocity agreements. ***Waivers:*** employees or children of employees.

APPLYING

Standardized Tests *Required:* SAT or ACT (for admission).

Options: electronic application.

Application fee: $50.

Required: high school transcript, minimum 2.0 GPA. ***Recommended:*** essay or personal statement.

Application deadlines: 7/24 (freshmen), 7/24 (transfers).

CONTACT

Ms. Wendy Peterson, Director of Admissions, Washington State University–Global Campus, 370 Lighty Student Services Building, PO Box 641067, Pullman, WA 99164-1067. *Phone:* 509-335-5586. *Toll-free phone:* 800-222-4978. *Fax:* 509-335-4902. *E-mail:* admissions@wsu.edu.

Washington State University–Spokane

Spokane, Washington

http://www.spokane.wsu.edu/

- **State-supported** upper-level, founded 1989
- **Urban** 48-acre campus
- **Coed** 583 undergraduate students, 94% full-time, 86% women, 14% men
- **Moderately difficult** entrance level, 75% of applicants were admitted

UNDERGRAD STUDENTS

547 full-time, 36 part-time. Students come from 10 states and territories; 5 other countries; 6% are from out of state; 3% Black or African American, non-Hispanic/Latino; 11% Hispanic/Latino; 4% Asian, non-Hispanic/Latino; 0.2% Native Hawaiian or other Pacific Islander, non-Hispanic/Latino; 0.3% American Indian or Alaska Native, non-Hispanic/Latino; 5% Two or more races, non-Hispanic/Latino; 4% Race/ethnicity unknown; 0.9% international; 15% transferred in.

Freshmen:

Admission: 4 applied, 3 admitted.

ACADEMICS

Calendar: semesters. *Degrees:* bachelor's, master's, and doctoral.

Special study options: accelerated degree program, adult/continuing education programs, advanced placement credit, cooperative education, distance learning, double majors, English as a second language, external degree program, freshman honors college, honors programs, independent study, internships, off-campus study, part-time degree program, services for LD students, student-designed majors, study abroad, summer session for credit.

Computers: Campuswide network is available. Wireless service is available via entire campus.

STUDENT LIFE

Housing options: college housing not available.

Activities and organizations: ASWSU Spokane, Simulation Club, Multicultural Club, IHI Open School (Interprofessional Club), Diversity Club.

Campus security: 24-hour emergency response devices and patrols.

Student services: personal/psychological counseling.

COSTS

Costs (2016–17) ***Tuition:*** state resident $9324 full-time, $497 per credit part-time; nonresident $23,956 full-time, $1226 per credit part-time. Full-time tuition and fees vary according to course load, location, and reciprocity agreements. Part-time tuition and fees vary according to course load, location, and reciprocity agreements. ***Required fees:*** $733 full-time. ***Waivers:*** senior citizens and employees or children of employees.

APPLYING

Standardized Tests *Required:* SAT or ACT (for admission).

Options: electronic application.

Application fee: $50.

Notification: continuous until 11/1 (transfers).

CONTACT

Washington State University–Spokane, 412 East Spokane Falls Boulevard, PO Box 1495, Spokane, WA 99210-1495.
Phone: 509-335-5586.

Washington State University–Tri-Cities

Richland, Washington

http://www.tricity.wsu.edu/

- **State-supported** comprehensive, founded 1989
- **Urban** 84-acre campus
- **Coed** 1,636 undergraduate students, 74% full-time, 59% women, 41% men
- **Moderately difficult** entrance level, 66% of applicants were admitted

UNDERGRAD STUDENTS

1,210 full-time, 426 part-time. Students come from 8 states and territories; 6 other countries; 3% are from out of state; 1% Black or African American, non-Hispanic/Latino; 28% Hispanic/Latino; 3% Asian, non-Hispanic/Latino; 0.2% American Indian or Alaska Native, non-Hispanic/Latino; 4% Two or more races, non-Hispanic/Latino; 20% Race/ethnicity unknown; 0.6% international; 17% transferred in.

Freshmen:

Admission: 521 applied, 342 admitted, 177 enrolled. ***Average high school GPA:*** 3.36. ***Test scores:*** SAT critical reading scores over 500: 45%; SAT math scores over 500: 46%; SAT writing scores over 500: 38%; ACT scores over 18: 82%; SAT critical reading scores over 600: 14%; SAT math scores over 600: 17%; SAT writing scores over 600: 8%; ACT scores over 24: 34%; SAT critical reading scores over 700: 1%; SAT math scores over 700: 4%; ACT scores over 30: 5%.

Retention: 71% of full-time freshmen returned.

ACADEMICS

Calendar: semesters. *Degrees:* certificates, bachelor's, master's, doctoral, and postbachelor's certificates.

Special study options: accelerated degree program, adult/continuing education programs, advanced placement credit, cooperative education, distance learning, double majors, English as a second language, external degree program, independent study, internships, part-time degree program, services for LD students, study abroad, summer session for credit.

Computers: Students can access the following: campus intranet, computer help desk, free student e-mail accounts, online (class) grades, online (class) registration. Campuswide network is available. Wireless service is available via entire campus.

Library: Max E. Benitz Memorial Library plus 2 others.

STUDENT LIFE

Housing options: Campus housing is provided by a third party.

Activities and organizations: American Society of Civil Engineers, Environmental Club, Gaming Club, Pre-Health Club, Robotics Club.

Athletics ***Intercollegiate sports:*** rugby M(c), soccer M(c)/W(c), volleyball W(c).

Campus security: 24-hour emergency response devices.

Student services: personal/psychological counseling.

COSTS

Costs (2016–17) ***Tuition:*** state resident $9324 full-time, $494 per credit part-time; nonresident $23,956 full-time, $1223 per credit part-time. Full-time tuition and fees vary according to course load, location, and reciprocity agreements. Part-time tuition and fees vary according to course load, location, and reciprocity agreements. ***Required fees:*** $812 full-time. ***Room and board:*** Room and board charges vary according to housing facility and location. ***Waivers:*** senior citizens and employees or children of employees.

APPLYING

Standardized Tests *Required:* SAT or ACT (for admission).

Options: electronic application.

Application fee: $50.

Required: high school transcript, minimum 2.0 GPA. ***Recommended:*** essay or personal statement.

Application deadlines: 1/31 (freshmen), 1/7 (out-of-state freshmen), 1/31 (transfers).

Notification: continuous until 11/1 (freshmen), continuous until 11/1 (out-of-state freshmen), continuous until 11/1 (transfers).

CONTACT

Ms. Mika McAskill, Director of Admissions, Washington State University–Tri-Cities, 2710 Crimson Way, Richland, WA 99354. *Phone:* 509-372-7250. *E-mail:* admissions@tricity.wsu.edu.

Washington State University–Vancouver

Vancouver, Washington

http://www.vancouver.wsu.edu/

- **State-supported** comprehensive, founded 1989
- **Suburban** 351-acre campus with easy access to Portland, OR
- **Coed** 2,962 undergraduate students, 78% full-time, 51% women, 49% men
- **Moderately difficult** entrance level, 62% of applicants were admitted

UNDERGRAD STUDENTS

2,307 full-time, 655 part-time. Students come from 18 states and territories; 10 other countries; 4% are from out of state; 1% Black or African American, non-Hispanic/Latino; 10% Hispanic/Latino; 6% Asian, non-Hispanic/Latino; 0.5% Native Hawaiian or other Pacific Islander, non-Hispanic/Latino; 0.8% American Indian or Alaska Native, non-Hispanic/Latino; 7% Two or more races, non-Hispanic/Latino; 4% Race/ethnicity unknown; 0.8% international; 21% transferred in.

Freshmen:

Admission: 1,179 applied, 726 admitted, 333 enrolled. ***Average high school GPA:*** 3.39. ***Test scores:*** SAT critical reading scores over 500: 62%; SAT math scores over 500: 59%; SAT writing scores over 500: 50%; ACT scores over 18: 95%; SAT critical reading scores over 600: 25%; SAT math scores over 600: 20%; SAT writing scores over 600: 14%; ACT scores over 24: 53%; SAT critical reading scores over 700: 5%; SAT math scores over 700: 2%; SAT writing scores over 700: 1%; ACT scores over 30: 11%.

Retention: 76% of full-time freshmen returned.

ACADEMICS

Calendar: semesters. *Degrees:* certificates, bachelor's, master's, and doctoral.

Special study options: accelerated degree program, adult/continuing education programs, advanced placement credit, cooperative education, distance learning, double majors, English as a second language, external degree program, honors programs, independent study, internships, off-campus study, part-time degree program, services for LD students, student-designed majors, study abroad, summer session for credit. ***ROTC:*** Army (c), Air Force (c).

Computers: Students can access the following: free student e-mail accounts, online (class) grades, online (class) registration, online (class) schedules. Campuswide network is available. Wireless service is available via classrooms, computer centers, computer labs, learning centers, libraries, student centers.

Library: WSU Vancouver Library plus 1 other. Students can reserve study rooms.

STUDENT LIFE

Housing options: college housing not available.

Activities and organizations: student-run newspaper, radio station.

Athletics ***Intramural sports:*** basketball M/W, soccer M/W, volleyball M/W.

Campus security: 24-hour emergency response devices and patrols, student patrols.

Student services: personal/psychological counseling.

COSTS

Costs (2016–17) ***Tuition:*** state resident $9324 full-time, $495 per credit part-time; nonresident $23,956 full-time, $1224 per credit part-time. Full-time tuition and fees vary according to course load, location, and reciprocity agreements. Part-time tuition and fees vary according to course load, location, and reciprocity agreements. ***Required fees:*** $559 full-time. ***Waivers:*** senior citizens and employees or children of employees.

APPLYING

Standardized Tests *Required:* SAT or ACT (for admission).

Options: electronic application.

Application fee: $50.

Required: high school transcript, minimum 2.0 GPA. ***Recommended:*** essay or personal statement.

Application deadlines: 1/31 (freshmen), 1/7 (out-of-state freshmen), 1/31 (transfers).

Notification: continuous until 11/1 (freshmen), continuous until 11/1 (out-of-state freshmen), continuous until 11/1 (transfers).

CONTACT

Ms. Kim Hiatt, Associate Director of Admissions, Washington State University–Vancouver, 14204 NE Salmon Creek Avenue, Vancouver, WA 98686. *Phone:* 360-546-9779. *Fax:* 360-546-9032.
E-mail: van.admissions@wsu.edu.

Western Washington University

Bellingham, Washington

http://www.wwu.edu/

- **State-supported** comprehensive, founded 1893
- **Small-town** 223-acre campus with easy access to Seattle, WA and Vancouver, BC Canada
- **Endowment** $70.9 million
- **Coed** 14,592 undergraduate students, 92% full-time, 56% women, 44% men
- **Moderately difficult** entrance level, 83% of applicants were admitted

UNDERGRAD STUDENTS

13,413 full-time, 1,179 part-time. Students come from 52 states and territories; 37 other countries; 11% are from out of state; 2% Black or African American, non-Hispanic/Latino; 9% Hispanic/Latino; 7% Asian, non-Hispanic/Latino; 0.2% Native Hawaiian or other Pacific Islander, non-Hispanic/Latino; 0.4% American Indian or Alaska Native, non-Hispanic/Latino; 9% Two or more races, non-Hispanic/Latino; 0.8% Race/ethnicity unknown; 1% international; 8% transferred in; 27% live on campus.

Freshmen:
Admission: 10,519 applied, 8,743 admitted, 2,888 enrolled. ***Average high school GPA:*** 3.41. ***Test scores:*** SAT critical reading scores over 500: 77%; SAT math scores over 500: 75%; SAT writing scores over 500: 65%; ACT scores over 18: 97%; SAT critical reading scores over 600: 36%; SAT math scores over 600: 28%; SAT writing scores over 600: 21%; ACT scores over 24: 66%; SAT critical reading scores over 700: 7%; SAT math scores over 700: 4%; SAT writing scores over 700: 2%; ACT scores over 30: 14%.

Retention: 82% of full-time freshmen returned.

FACULTY

Total: 937, 66% full-time, 73% with terminal degrees.

Student/faculty ratio: 19:1.

ACADEMICS

Calendar: quarters. *Degrees:* certificates, bachelor's, master's, and post-master's certificates.

Special study options: accelerated degree program, advanced placement credit, cooperative education, distance learning, double majors, English as a second language, honors programs, independent study, internships, off-campus study, part-time degree program, services for LD students, student-designed majors, study abroad, summer session for credit.

Computers: 2,708 computers/terminals are available on campus for general student use. Students can access the following: free student e-mail accounts, online (class) registration. Campuswide network is available. 99% of college-owned or -operated housing units are wired for high-speed Internet access. Wireless service is available via classrooms, computer centers, computer labs, dorm rooms, learning centers, libraries, student centers.

Library: Wilson Library plus 2 others. *Books:* 633,295 (physical), 307,457 (digital/electronic); *Serial titles:* 22,077 (physical), 180,049 (digital/electronic); *Databases:* 110. Weekly public service hours: 97; students can reserve study rooms.

STUDENT LIFE

Housing options: coed, special housing for students with disabilities. Campus housing is university owned. Freshman campus housing is guaranteed.

Activities and organizations: drama/theater group, student-run newspaper, radio and television station, choral group, intramurals, Residence Hall Association, Associated Students, Outdoor Center, Ethnic Student Center.

Athletics Member NCAA. All Division II. ***Intercollegiate sports:*** basketball M(s)/W(s), cheerleading M/W, crew M(s)(c)/W(s), cross-country running M(s)/W(s), golf M(s)/W(s), soccer M(s)/W(s), softball W(s), track and field M(s)/W(s), volleyball W(s). ***Intramural sports:*** badminton M/W, baseball M, basketball M/W, equestrian sports M(c)/W(c), fencing M/W, ice hockey M, lacrosse M/W, racquetball M/W, rock climbing M/W, sailing M/W, skiing (downhill) M/W, soccer M/W, softball M/W, swimming and diving M/W, table tennis M/W, tennis M/W, ultimate Frisbee M/W, volleyball M/W, water polo M/W, wrestling M.

Campus security: 24-hour emergency response devices and patrols, student patrols, late-night transport/escort service, controlled dormitory access.

Student services: health clinic, personal/psychological counseling, women's center, legal services.

COSTS & FINANCIAL AID

Costs (2016–17) ***Tuition:*** state resident $6116 full-time; nonresident $20,060 full-time. Full-time tuition and fees vary according to course load, location, and reciprocity agreements. Part-time tuition and fees vary according to course load, location, and reciprocity agreements. ***Required fees:*** $1537 full-time, $224 per credit hour part-time. ***Room and board:*** $10,755. Room and board charges vary according to board plan, housing facility, and location. ***Payment plan:*** installment. ***Waivers:*** minority students, senior citizens, and employees or children of employees.

Financial Aid Of all full-time matriculated undergraduates who enrolled in 2016, 8,977 applied for aid, 6,470 were judged to have need, 1,030 had their need fully met. 238 Federal Work-Study jobs (averaging $3510). 423 state and other part-time jobs (averaging $3472). In 2016, 299 non-need-based awards were made. ***Average percent of need met:*** 87. ***Average financial aid package:*** $14,074. ***Average need-based loan:*** $4490.

Average need-based gift aid: $8999. ***Average non-need-based aid:*** $2068. ***Average indebtedness upon graduation:*** $19,727.

APPLYING

Standardized Tests *Required:* SAT or ACT (for admission).

Options: electronic application, deferred entrance.

Application fee: $55.

Required: high school transcript. ***Recommended:*** essay or personal statement.

Application deadlines: 1/31 (freshmen), 3/1 (transfers).

Notification: continuous until 11/1 (freshmen), continuous until 5/1 (transfers).

CONTACT

Mr. Cezar Mesquita, Assistant Vice President, Enrollment and Student Services, Western Washington University, 516 High Street, Bellingham, WA 98225-9009. *Phone:* 360-650-3440. *Fax:* 360-650-7369. *E-mail:* admit@wwu.edu.

Whitman College

Walla Walla, Washington

http://www.whitman.edu/

- **Independent** 4-year, founded 1859
- **Small-town** 117-acre campus
- **Endowment** $477.8 million
- **Coed** 1,493 undergraduate students, 97% full-time, 57% women, 43% men
- **Very difficult** entrance level, 51% of applicants were admitted

UNDERGRAD STUDENTS

1,453 full-time, 40 part-time. Students come from 47 states and territories; 26 other countries; 65% are from out of state; 1% Black or African American, non-Hispanic/Latino; 7% Hispanic/Latino; 5% Asian, non-Hispanic/Latino; 0.3% Native Hawaiian or other Pacific Islander, non-Hispanic/Latino; 0.3% American Indian or Alaska Native, non-Hispanic/Latino; 7% Two or more races, non-Hispanic/Latino; 2% Race/ethnicity unknown; 6% international; 1% transferred in; 64% live on campus.

Freshmen:

Admission: 3,749 applied, 1,915 admitted, 405 enrolled. ***Average high school GPA:*** 3.69. ***Test scores:*** SAT critical reading scores over 500: 97%; SAT math scores over 500: 98%; SAT writing scores over 500: 98%; ACT scores over 18: 100%; SAT critical reading scores over 600: 77%; SAT math scores over 600: 77%; SAT writing scores over 600: 77%; ACT scores over 24: 96%; SAT critical reading scores over 700: 30%; SAT math scores over 700: 28%; SAT writing scores over 700: 22%; ACT scores over 30: 56%.

Retention: 94% of full-time freshmen returned.

FACULTY

Total: 205, 68% full-time, 81% with terminal degrees.

Student/faculty ratio: 8:1.

ACADEMICS

Calendar: semesters. *Degree:* bachelor's.

Special study options: advanced placement credit, cooperative education, double majors, honors programs, independent study, internships, off-campus study, services for LD students, student-designed majors, study abroad.

Unusual degree programs: 3-2 engineering with California Institute of Technology, Columbia University, University of Washington, Washington University in St. Louis; forestry with Duke University; oceanography with University of Washington, law with Columbia University.

Computers: 127 computers/terminals are available on campus for general student use. Students can access the following: computer help desk, free student e-mail accounts, online (class) grades, online (class) registration. Campuswide network is available. 100% of college-owned or -operated housing units are wired for high-speed Internet access. Wireless service is available via classrooms, computer centers, computer labs, dorm rooms, learning centers, libraries, student centers.

Library: Penrose Library plus 1 other. *Books:* 406,675 (physical), 305,306 (digital/electronic); *Serial titles:* 5,082 (physical), 98,012 (digital/electronic); *Databases:* 206. Weekly public service hours: 168; study areas open 24 hours, 5-7 days a week; students can reserve study rooms.

STUDENT LIFE

Housing options: on-campus residence required through sophomore year; coed, women-only. Campus housing is university owned. Freshman campus housing is guaranteed.

Activities and organizations: drama/theater group, student-run newspaper, radio station, choral group, national fraternities, national sororities.

Athletics Member NCAA. All Division III. ***Intercollegiate sports:*** baseball M, basketball M/W, cross-country running M/W, football M(c)/W(c), golf M/W, lacrosse W, soccer M/W, softball M(c)/W(c), swimming and diving M/W, table tennis M(c)/W(c), tennis M/W, ultimate Frisbee M(c)/W(c), volleyball M(c)/W. ***Intramural sports:*** basketball M(c)/W(c), fencing M/W, football M/W, lacrosse M(c)/W(c), racquetball M/W, rock climbing M/W, rugby M(c)/W(c), skiing (downhill) M(c)/W(c), soccer M(c)/W(c), tennis M(c)/W(c), ultimate Frisbee M(c)/W(c), volleyball M(c)/W(c).

Campus security: 24-hour emergency response devices and patrols, student patrols, late-night transport/escort service, controlled dormitory access.

Student services: health clinic, personal/psychological counseling, women's center.

COSTS & FINANCIAL AID

Costs (2017–18) ***Comprehensive fee:*** $62,290 includes full-time tuition ($49,390), mandatory fees ($376), and room and board ($12,524). Part-time tuition: $2058 per credit. Part-time tuition and fees vary according to course load. ***College room only:*** $5674. Room and board charges vary according to board plan and housing facility. ***Payment plan:*** deferred payment. ***Waivers:*** employees or children of employees.

Financial Aid Of all full-time matriculated undergraduates who enrolled in 2015, 1,208 applied for aid, 652 were judged to have need, 277 had their need fully met. 450 Federal Work-Study jobs (averaging $1983). 158 state and other part-time jobs (averaging $1957). In 2015, 427 non-need-based awards were made. ***Average percent of need met:*** 89. ***Average financial aid package:*** $36,130. ***Average need-based loan:*** $5031. ***Average need-based gift aid:*** $30,721. ***Average non-need-based aid:*** $9595. ***Average indebtedness upon graduation:*** $21,192. ***Financial aid deadline:*** 2/1.

APPLYING

Standardized Tests *Required for some:* SAT or ACT (for admission).

Options: electronic application, early decision, deferred entrance.

Application fee: $50.

Required: essay or personal statement, high school transcript, 1 letter of recommendation. ***Recommended:*** interview.

Application deadlines: 1/15 (freshmen), 3/1 (transfers).

Early decision deadline: 11/15 (for plan 1), 1/1 (for plan 2).

Notification: 4/1 (freshmen), 4/20 (transfers), 12/20 (early decision plan 1), 2/1 (early decision plan 2).

CONTACT

Mr. Tony Cabasco, Dean of Admission and Financial Aid, Whitman College, 515 Boyer Avenue, Walla Walla, WA 99362-2083. *Phone:* 509-527-5176. *Toll-free phone:* 877-462-9448. *Fax:* 509-527-4967. *E-mail:* admission@whitman.edu.

Whitworth University

Spokane, Washington

http://www.whitworth.edu/

- **Independent Presbyterian** comprehensive, founded 1890
- **Suburban** 200-acre campus
- **Endowment** $127.4 million
- **Coed** 2,308 undergraduate students, 98% full-time, 60% women, 40% men
- **Moderately difficult** entrance level, 89% of applicants were admitted

UNDERGRAD STUDENTS

2,258 full-time, 50 part-time. Students come from 33 states and territories; 41 other countries; 29% are from out of state; 2% Black or African

American, non-Hispanic/Latino; 9% Hispanic/Latino; 5% Asian, non-Hispanic/Latino; 0.3% Native Hawaiian or other Pacific Islander, non-Hispanic/Latino; 0.6% American Indian or Alaska Native, non-Hispanic/Latino; 7% Two or more races, non-Hispanic/Latino; 1% Race/ethnicity unknown; 3% international; 4% transferred in; 54% live on campus.

Freshmen:
Admission: 3,262 applied, 2,889 admitted, 595 enrolled. ***Average high school GPA:*** 3.76. ***Test scores:*** SAT critical reading scores over 500: 75%; SAT math scores over 500: 77%; SAT writing scores over 500: 71%; ACT scores over 18: 94%; SAT critical reading scores over 600: 41%; SAT math scores over 600: 34%; SAT writing scores over 600: 34%; ACT scores over 24: 66%; SAT critical reading scores over 700: 11%; SAT math scores over 700: 5%; SAT writing scores over 700: 7%; ACT scores over 30: 20%.
Retention: 85% of full-time freshmen returned.

FACULTY
Total: 306, 59% full-time, 46% with terminal degrees.
Student/faculty ratio: 11:1.

ACADEMICS
Calendar: 4-1-4. *Degrees:* bachelor's, master's, post-master's, and postbachelor's certificates.
Special study options: adult/continuing education programs, advanced placement credit, double majors, honors programs, independent study, internships, off-campus study, part-time degree program, services for LD students, student-designed majors, study abroad, summer session for credit. ***ROTC:*** Army (c).
Unusual degree programs: 3-2 engineering with Seattle Pacific University, University of Southern California, Washington University in St. Louis, Columbia University, Washington State University; nursing with Washington State University; athletic training.
Computers: 280 computers/terminals and 1,355 ports are available on campus for general student use. Students can access the following: campus intranet, computer help desk, free student e-mail accounts, online (class) grades, online (class) registration, online (class) schedules, learning management system. Campuswide network is available. 100% of college-owned or -operated housing units are wired for high-speed Internet access. Wireless service is available via entire campus.
Library: Harriet Cheney Cowles Library. *Books:* 210,113 (physical), 160,000 (digital/electronic); *Serial titles:* 278 (physical), 36,239 (digital/electronic); *Databases:* 153. Weekly public service hours: 97; students can reserve study rooms.

STUDENT LIFE
Housing options: on-campus residence required through sophomore year; coed, men-only, women-only. Campus housing is university owned. Freshman campus housing is guaranteed.
Activities and organizations: drama/theater group, student-run newspaper, radio station, choral group, International Club, Whitworth Student Investment Group, En Christo, Hawaiian Club, Swing and Ballroom Dance Club.
Athletics Member NCAA, USCAA. All Division III. ***Intercollegiate sports:*** baseball M, basketball M/W, cross-country running M/W, football M, golf M/W, soccer M/W, softball W, swimming and diving M/W, tennis M/W, track and field M/W, volleyball W. ***Intramural sports:*** badminton M/W, basketball M(c)/W, football M/W, soccer M/W, softball M/W, table tennis M/W, tennis M/W, ultimate Frisbee M(c)/W(c), volleyball M/W.
Campus security: 24-hour emergency response devices and patrols, late-night transport/escort service, controlled dormitory access.
Student services: health clinic, personal/psychological counseling.

COSTS & FINANCIAL AID
Costs (2017–18) ***Comprehensive fee:*** $53,682 includes full-time tuition ($41,086), mandatory fees ($1100), and room and board ($11,496). Part-time tuition: $1712 per credit. Part-time tuition and fees vary according to course load. ***Required fees:*** $490 per term part-time. ***College room only:*** $6250. Room and board charges vary according to board plan and housing facility. ***Payment plan:*** installment. ***Waivers:*** senior citizens and employees or children of employees.
Financial Aid Of all full-time matriculated undergraduates who enrolled in 2016, 1,731 applied for aid, 1,523 were judged to have need, 220 had their need fully met. 844 Federal Work-Study jobs (averaging $2351). 101 state and other part-time jobs (averaging $3195). In 2016, 641 non-need-based awards were made. ***Average percent of need met:*** 79. ***Average financial aid package:*** $34,546. ***Average need-based loan:*** $4737. ***Average need-based gift aid:*** $25,948. ***Average non-need-based aid:*** $19,334. ***Average indebtedness upon graduation:*** $28,294.

APPLYING
Standardized Tests *Recommended:* SAT or ACT (for admission).
Options: electronic application, early admission, early action, deferred entrance.
Required: essay or personal statement, high school transcript, 1 letter of recommendation. ***Required for some:*** minimum 3.0 GPA, 2 letters of recommendation, interview.
Application deadlines: 8/1 (freshmen), 11/30 (early action).
Notification: continuous (freshmen), 12/20 (early action).

CONTACT
Ms. Marianne Hansen, Director of Admission, Whitworth University, 300 West, Hawthorne Road, Spokane, WA 99251. *Phone:* 509-777-4347. *Toll-free phone:* 800-533-4668. *Fax:* 509-777-3758.
E-mail: admission@whitworth.edu.

WEST VIRGINIA

Alderson Broaddus University

Philippi, West Virginia

http://www.ab.edu/

- **Independent** comprehensive, founded 1871, affiliated with American Baptist Churches in the U.S.A.
- **Rural** 170-acre campus
- **Endowment** $17.6 million
- **Coed** 981 undergraduate students, 95% full-time, 46% women, 54% men
- **Moderately difficult** entrance level, 41% of applicants were admitted

UNDERGRAD STUDENTS
934 full-time, 47 part-time. Students come from 52 states and territories; 18 other countries; 63% are from out of state; 18% Black or African American, non-Hispanic/Latino; 4% Hispanic/Latino; 1% Asian, non-Hispanic/Latino; 0.4% Native Hawaiian or other Pacific Islander, non-Hispanic/Latino; 0.7% American Indian or Alaska Native, non-Hispanic/Latino; 0.9% Two or more races, non-Hispanic/Latino; 5% international; 6% transferred in; 84% live on campus.

Freshmen:
Admission: 4,103 applied, 1,698 admitted, 261 enrolled. ***Average high school GPA:*** 3.2. ***Test scores:*** SAT critical reading scores over 500: 32%; SAT math scores over 500: 38%; SAT writing scores over 500: 19%; ACT scores over 18: 84%; SAT critical reading scores over 600: 2%; SAT math scores over 600: 6%; SAT writing scores over 600: 3%; ACT scores over 24: 21%; SAT math scores over 700: 2%; ACT scores over 30: 1%.
Retention: 55% of full-time freshmen returned.

FACULTY
Total: 87, 64% full-time, 48% with terminal degrees.
Student/faculty ratio: 17:1.

ACADEMICS
Calendar: semesters. *Degrees:* associate, bachelor's, and master's.
Special study options: advanced placement credit, double majors, honors programs, independent study, internships, part-time degree program, services for LD students, study abroad, summer session for credit.
Computers: 100 computers/terminals and 750 ports are available on campus for general student use. Students can access the following: campus intranet, computer help desk, free student e-mail accounts, online (class) grades, online (class) registration, online (class) schedules, course materials, student record information. Campuswide network is available. 100% of college-owned or -operated housing units are wired for high-speed Internet access. Wireless service is available via entire campus.
Library: Pickett Library. *Books:* 40,000 (physical), 160,000 (digital/electronic); *Serial titles:* 8 (physical), 11,000 (digital/electronic);

Databases: 31. Weekly public service hours: 78; study areas open 24 hours, 5-7 days a week; students can reserve study rooms.

STUDENT LIFE

Housing options: on-campus residence required through senior year; coed, special housing for students with disabilities. Campus housing is university owned. Freshman campus housing is guaranteed.

Activities and organizations: drama/theater group, student-run newspaper, radio and television station, choral group, marching band, AAPA/Hu C. Myers Society, Alpha Beta Nu, Student Athletic Advisory Committee, Sigma Alpha Iota, Kappa Xi Omega.

Athletics Member NCAA. All Division II. ***Intercollegiate sports:*** baseball M(s), basketball M(s)/W(s), cheerleading M(s)/W(s), cross-country running M(s)/W(s), football M(s), golf M(s)/W(s), gymnastics W(s), lacrosse M(s)/W(s), soccer M(s)/W(s), softball W(s), swimming and diving M(s)/W(s), tennis W(s), track and field M(s)/W(s), volleyball M(s)/W(s), wrestling M(s). ***Intramural sports:*** badminton M/W, basketball M/W, bowling M/W, football M/W, golf M/W, racquetball M/W, soccer M/W, softball W, table tennis M/W, tennis M/W, ultimate Frisbee M/W, volleyball M/W, water polo M/W.

Campus security: 24-hour patrols, controlled dormitory access, emergency notification system, lighted pathways and sidewalks.

Student services: health clinic, personal/psychological counseling.

COSTS & FINANCIAL AID

Costs (2016–17) ***Comprehensive fee:*** $33,340 includes full-time tuition ($25,140), mandatory fees ($210), and room and board ($7990). Part-time tuition: $838 per credit hour. ***Required fees:*** $53 per term part-time. ***Room and board:*** Room and board charges vary according to housing facility. ***Payment plan:*** installment. ***Waivers:*** employees or children of employees.

Financial Aid Of all full-time matriculated undergraduates who enrolled in 2016, 887 applied for aid, 787 were judged to have need, 260 had their need fully met. 430 Federal Work-Study jobs (averaging $1435). 95 state and other part-time jobs (averaging $2410). In 2016, 126 non-need-based awards were made. ***Average percent of need met:*** 90. ***Average financial aid package:*** $22,284. ***Average need-based loan:*** $4047. ***Average need-based gift aid:*** $20,274. ***Average non-need-based aid:*** $9505. ***Average indebtedness upon graduation:*** $24,079.

APPLYING

Standardized Tests *Required:* SAT and SAT Subject Tests or ACT (for admission).

Options: electronic application, deferred entrance.

Required: high school transcript, minimum 2.0 GPA. ***Required for some:*** 3 letters of recommendation, interview.

Application deadlines: rolling (freshmen), rolling (transfers).

Notification: 8/31 (freshmen), continuous until 8/31 (transfers).

CONTACT

Mr. Erika L. Thon, Director of Admissions, Alderson Broaddus University, 101 College Hill Drive, Campus Box 2003, Philippi, WV 26416. *Phone:* 304-457-6256. *Toll-free phone:* 800-263-1549. *Fax:* 304-457-6239. *E-mail:* thonel@ab.edu.

American Public University System

Charles Town, West Virginia

http://www.apus.edu/

- **Proprietary** comprehensive, founded 1991
- **Rural** campus with easy access to Washington, DC
- **Coed** 39,662 undergraduate students, 6% full-time, 36% women, 64% men
- **Noncompetitive** entrance level

UNDERGRAD STUDENTS

2,451 full-time, 37,211 part-time. Students come from 64 states and territories; 50 other countries; 99% are from out of state; 17% Black or African American, non-Hispanic/Latino; 11% Hispanic/Latino; 2% Asian, non-Hispanic/Latino; 0.9% Native Hawaiian or other Pacific Islander, non-Hispanic/Latino; 0.6% American Indian or Alaska Native, non-Hispanic/Latino; 4% Two or more races, non-Hispanic/Latino; 6% Race/ethnicity unknown; 0.8% international; 13% transferred in.

Freshmen:

Admission: 1,340 enrolled.

FACULTY

Total: 2,104, 19% full-time, 57% with terminal degrees.

Student/faculty ratio: 19:1.

ACADEMICS

Calendar: courses start on the first Monday of each month. *Degrees:* certificates, associate, bachelor's, master's, and postbachelor's certificates (profile includes American Public University, American Military University and American Community College).

Special study options: advanced placement credit, distance learning, external degree program, independent study, internships, part-time degree program, services for LD students, summer session for credit.

Computers: Students can access the following: free student e-mail accounts, online (class) grades, online (class) registration, online (class) schedules.

Library: APUS Online Library.

STUDENT LIFE

Housing options: college housing not available.

Activities and organizations: Student Veterans of America, Saber and Scroll Historical Club, Regional-Southeast, Veterans Connect-Army, Regional-Northeast.

COSTS

Costs (2016–17) ***Tuition:*** $6480 full-time, $270 per credit hour part-time. ***Required fees:*** $400 full-time, $50 per course part-time. ***Payment plan:*** installment. ***Waivers:*** employees or children of employees.

APPLYING

Options: electronic application, deferred entrance.

Required: high school transcript.

Application deadlines: rolling (freshmen), rolling (transfers).

CONTACT

Ms. Terry Grant, Vice President, Enrollment Management and Student Support, American Public University System, 111 West Congress Street, Charles Town, WV 25414. *Phone:* 877-468-6268. *Toll-free phone:* 877-755-2787. *Fax:* 304-724-3788. *E-mail:* info@apus.edu.

Appalachian Bible College

Mount Hope, West Virginia

http://www.abc.edu/

- **Independent nondenominational** comprehensive, founded 1950
- **Small-town** 110-acre campus
- **Endowment** $316,677
- **Coed**
- **Noncompetitive** entrance level

FACULTY

Student/faculty ratio: 17:1.

ACADEMICS

Calendar: semesters. *Degrees:* certificates, diplomas, associate, bachelor's, master's, and postbachelor's certificates.

Library: John Van Pufflen Library.

STUDENT LIFE

Housing options: on-campus residence required through senior year; men-only, women-only. Campus housing is university owned. Freshman campus housing is guaranteed.

Activities and organizations: drama/theater group, choral group.

Athletics Member NCCAA.

Campus security: 24-hour emergency response devices, controlled dormitory access, patrols by trained security personnel.

Student services: health clinic, personal/psychological counseling.

COSTS & FINANCIAL AID

Costs (2016–17) ***Comprehensive fee:*** $20,840 includes full-time tuition ($12,380), mandatory fees ($890), and room and board ($7570). Full-time tuition and fees vary according to class time, course level, course load, degree level, location, program, and student level. Part-time tuition: $375 per credit hour. Part-time tuition and fees vary according to class time, course level, degree level, location, program, and student level. ***Required fees:*** $40 per credit hour part-time, $150 per year part-time. ***Room and board:*** Room and board charges vary according to housing facility.

Financial Aid Of all full-time matriculated undergraduates who enrolled in 2011, 188 applied for aid, 176 were judged to have need, 10 had their need fully met. 26 Federal Work-Study jobs (averaging $630). In 2011, 12 non-need-based awards were made. ***Average percent of need met:*** 56. ***Average financial aid package:*** $9337. ***Average need-based loan:*** $2910. ***Average need-based gift aid:*** $7851. ***Average non-need-based aid:*** $1709. ***Average indebtedness upon graduation:*** $8618. ***Financial aid deadline:*** 6/15.

APPLYING

Standardized Tests *Required:* SAT or ACT (for admission).

Options: electronic application, early admission.

Application fee: $20.

Required: essay or personal statement, high school transcript, 3 letters of recommendation, interview. ***Required for some:*** interview.
Recommended: minimum 2.5 GPA.

CONTACT

Miss Elisabeth Anderson, Admissions Assistant, Appalachian Bible College, 161 College Drive, Mount Hope, WV 25880. *Phone:* 304-877-6428 Ext. 313. *Toll-free phone:* 800-678-9ABC. *Fax:* 304-877-5082. *E-mail:* admissions2@abc.edu.

Bethany College

Bethany, West Virginia

http://www.bethanywv.edu/

- **Independent** comprehensive, founded 1840, affiliated with Christian Church (Disciples of Christ)
- **Rural** 1300-acre campus with easy access to Pittsburgh
- **Endowment** $49.8 million
- **Coed**
- **Moderately difficult** entrance level

FACULTY

Student/faculty ratio: 12:1.

ACADEMICS

Calendar: semesters. *Degrees:* bachelor's and master's.
Library: T. W. Phillips Memorial Library. *Books:* 126,369 (physical), 135,500 (digital/electronic); *Serial titles:* 3,975 (physical); *Databases:* 50. Weekly public service hours: 88.

STUDENT LIFE

Housing options: on-campus residence required through senior year; coed, men-only, women-only, special housing for students with disabilities. Campus housing is university owned. Freshman campus housing is guaranteed.

Activities and organizations: drama/theater group, student-run newspaper, radio and television station, choral group, marching band, Student Government Association, Culture Clubs, Equestrian Club, Outdoors Club, Black Alliance, national fraternities, national sororities.

Athletics Member NCAA. All Division III.

Campus security: 24-hour emergency response devices and patrols, late-night transport/escort service, controlled dormitory access.

Student services: health clinic, personal/psychological counseling.

COSTS & FINANCIAL AID

Costs (2016–17) ***One-time required fee:*** $125. ***Comprehensive fee:*** $37,362 includes full-time tuition ($26,496), mandatory fees ($1142), and room and board ($9724). Full-time tuition and fees vary according to course load. Part-time tuition: $1104 per credit hour. Part-time tuition and fees vary according to course load. ***Required fees:*** $39 per credit hour part-time. ***College room only:*** $4800. Room and board charges vary according to board plan and housing facility.

Financial Aid Of all full-time matriculated undergraduates who enrolled in 2016, 282,000 Federal Work-Study jobs (averaging $2000). 248,481 state and other part-time jobs (averaging $1500). ***Average indebtedness upon graduation:*** $27,057.

APPLYING

Standardized Tests *Required:* SAT or ACT (for admission). *Required for some:* TOEFL/IELTS.

Options: electronic application, deferred entrance.

Required: essay or personal statement, high school transcript.
Recommended: minimum 2.5 GPA, 2 letters of recommendation, interview, documentation of student involvement in extracurricular activities.

CONTACT

Ms. Mollie Cecere, Director of Enrollment, Bethany College, Bethany College Center for Enrollment and Financial Aid, 31 E Campus Drive #4, Bethany, WV 26032. *Phone:* 304-829-7611. *Toll-free phone:* 800-922-7611. *Fax:* 304-829-7142. *E-mail:* enrollment@bethanywv.edu.

Bluefield State College

Bluefield, West Virginia

http://www.bluefieldstate.edu/

- **State-supported** 4-year, founded 1895, part of West Virginia Higher Education Policy Commission
- **Small-town** 45-acre campus
- **Coed** 1,486 undergraduate students, 82% full-time, 60% women, 40% men
- **Noncompetitive** entrance level, 77% of applicants were admitted

UNDERGRAD STUDENTS

1,217 full-time, 269 part-time. 3% are from out of state; 9% Black or African American, non-Hispanic/Latino; 0.9% Hispanic/Latino; 0.6% Asian, non-Hispanic/Latino; 0.3% American Indian or Alaska Native, non-Hispanic/Latino; 2% Two or more races, non-Hispanic/Latino; 3% international; 10% transferred in.

Freshmen:

Admission: 618 applied, 475 admitted, 273 enrolled. ***Average high school GPA:*** 3.29. ***Test scores:*** SAT critical reading scores over 500: 35%; SAT math scores over 500: 44%; ACT scores over 18: 71%; SAT critical reading scores over 600: 9%; SAT math scores over 600: 6%; ACT scores over 24: 16%; SAT critical reading scores over 700: 3%; ACT scores over 30: 1%.

Retention: 58% of full-time freshmen returned.

FACULTY

Total: 129, 60% full-time, 29% with terminal degrees.

Student/faculty ratio: 14:1.

ACADEMICS

Calendar: semesters. *Degrees:* associate and bachelor's.

Special study options: adult/continuing education programs, part-time degree program.

Computers: Students can access the following: computer help desk, free student e-mail accounts, online (class) grades, online (class) registration. Campuswide network is available. Wireless service is available via entire campus.

Library: Hardway Library.

STUDENT LIFE

Housing options: college housing not available.

Activities and organizations: drama/theater group, student-run newspaper, radio station, choral group, national fraternities, national sororities.

Athletics Member NCAA. All Division II. ***Intercollegiate sports:*** baseball M(s), basketball M(s)/W(s), cheerleading W, cross-country running M(s)/W(s), golf M(s), softball W(s), tennis M(s)/W(s).
Intramural sports: badminton M/W, basketball M/W, football M, soccer M, swimming and diving M/W, table tennis M/W, volleyball M/W, water polo M/W.

Campus security: 24-hour emergency response devices and patrols, student patrols.

Student services: health clinic, personal/psychological counseling.

COSTS & FINANCIAL AID

Costs (2016–17) ***Tuition:*** state resident $6408 full-time, $267 per credit hour part-time; nonresident $12,876 full-time, $537 per credit hour part-time. ***Payment plan:*** installment. ***Waivers:*** adult students and senior citizens.

Financial Aid Of all full-time matriculated undergraduates who enrolled in 2016, 1,300 applied for aid, 1,200 were judged to have need, 145 had their need fully met. 50 Federal Work-Study jobs (averaging $2950). In 2016, 12 non-need-based awards were made. ***Average percent of need met:*** 67. ***Average financial aid package:*** $3600. ***Average need-based loan:*** $4300. ***Average need-based gift aid:*** $3800. ***Average non-need-based aid:*** $900. ***Average indebtedness upon graduation:*** $29,000.

APPLYING

Standardized Tests *Required:* SAT or ACT (for admission).

Options: early admission, deferred entrance.

Required: high school transcript, minimum 2.0 GPA.

CONTACT

Bluefield State College, 219 Rock Street, Bluefield, WV 24701-2198. *Phone:* 304-327-4067. *Toll-free phone:* 800-344-8892 Ext. 4065 (in-state); 800-654-7798 Ext. 4065 (out-of-state).

Concord University

Athens, West Virginia

http://www.concord.edu/

- **State-supported** comprehensive, founded 1872, part of State College System of West Virginia
- **Rural** 100-acre campus
- **Endowment** $24.2 million
- **Coed** 2,102 undergraduate students, 89% full-time, 59% women, 41% men
- **Minimally difficult** entrance level, 81% of applicants were admitted

UNDERGRAD STUDENTS

1,878 full-time, 224 part-time. Students come from 30 states and territories; 30 other countries; 14% are from out of state; 6% Black or African American, non-Hispanic/Latino; 1% Hispanic/Latino; 0.7% Asian, non-Hispanic/Latino; 0.2% Native Hawaiian or other Pacific Islander, non-Hispanic/Latino; 0.4% American Indian or Alaska Native, non-Hispanic/Latino; 2% Two or more races, non-Hispanic/Latino; 0.4% Race/ethnicity unknown; 4% international; 7% transferred in; 38% live on campus.

Freshmen:

Admission: 2,960 applied, 2,402 admitted, 471 enrolled. ***Average high school GPA:*** 3.39. ***Test scores:*** SAT critical reading scores over 500: 45%; SAT math scores over 500: 41%; SAT writing scores over 500: 33%; ACT scores over 18: 87%; SAT critical reading scores over 600: 8%; SAT math scores over 600: 9%; SAT writing scores over 600: 8%; ACT scores over 24: 28%; SAT critical reading scores over 700: 3%; SAT math scores over 700: 1%; ACT scores over 30: 2%.

Retention: 68% of full-time freshmen returned.

FACULTY

Total: 187, 61% full-time, 55% with terminal degrees.

Student/faculty ratio: 16:1.

ACADEMICS

Calendar: semesters. *Degrees:* certificates, bachelor's, master's, and post-master's certificates.

Special study options: academic remediation for entering students, accelerated degree program, adult/continuing education programs, advanced placement credit, cooperative education, distance learning, double majors, English as a second language, external degree program, honors programs, independent study, internships, off-campus study, part-time degree program, services for LD students, student-designed majors, study abroad, summer session for credit.

Computers: 350 computers/terminals and 1,100 ports are available on campus for general student use. Students can access the following: campus intranet, computer help desk, free student e-mail accounts, online (class) grades, online (class) registration, online (class) schedules. Campuswide network is available. 100% of college-owned or -operated housing units are wired for high-speed Internet access. Wireless service is available via entire campus.

Library: J. Frank Marsh Library. *Books:* 156,138 (physical), 3,029 (digital/electronic); *Serial titles:* 86 (physical), 110 (digital/electronic); *Databases:* 21. Weekly public service hours: 77; study areas open 24 hours, 5-7 days a week; students can reserve study rooms.

STUDENT LIFE

Housing options: coed, men-only, women-only. Campus housing is university owned. Freshman campus housing is guaranteed.

Activities and organizations: drama/theater group, student-run newspaper, radio and television station, choral group, marching band, Service Groups, student government, student-run publications, intramurals, Student Activities Committee, national fraternities, national sororities.

Athletics Member NCAA. All Division II. ***Intercollegiate sports:*** baseball M(s), basketball M(s)/W(s), cheerleading M/W, cross-country running M(s)/W(s), football M(s), golf M(s)/W(s), soccer M(s)/W(s), softball W(s), tennis M(s)/W(s), track and field M(s)/W(s), volleyball W(s). ***Intramural sports:*** basketball M/W, football M, soccer M/W, tennis M/W, volleyball M/W.

Campus security: 24-hour emergency response devices and patrols, student patrols, late-night transport/escort service, controlled dormitory access.

Student services: health clinic, personal/psychological counseling.

COSTS & FINANCIAL AID

Costs (2016–17) ***Tuition:*** state resident $7080 full-time, $295 per credit hour part-time; nonresident $15,564 full-time, $649 per credit hour part-time. Full-time tuition and fees vary according to course load and program. Part-time tuition and fees vary according to course load and program. ***Room and board:*** $8350. Room and board charges vary according to board plan. ***Payment plan:*** installment. ***Waivers:*** employees or children of employees.

Financial Aid Of all full-time matriculated undergraduates who enrolled in 2016, 1,685 applied for aid, 1,409 were judged to have need, 473 had their need fully met. 182 Federal Work-Study jobs (averaging $1246). In 2016, 197 non-need-based awards were made. ***Average percent of need met:*** 80. ***Average financial aid package:*** $8425. ***Average need-based loan:*** $3569. ***Average need-based gift aid:*** $5629. ***Average non-need-based aid:*** $3434. ***Average indebtedness upon graduation:*** $21,176. ***Financial aid deadline:*** 4/15.

APPLYING

Standardized Tests *Required:* SAT or ACT (for admission).

Options: electronic application, early admission.

Required: high school transcript, minimum 2.0 GPA. ***Required for some:*** essay or personal statement, interview. ***Recommended:*** interview.

Application deadlines: rolling (freshmen), rolling (transfers).

Notification: continuous (freshmen), continuous (transfers).

CONTACT

Ms. Sarah Wambe, Director of Admissions, Concord University, 1000 Vermillion Street, Athens, WV 24712. *Phone:* 304-384-6294. *Toll-free phone:* 888-384-5249. *Fax:* 304-384-9044.
E-mail: admissions@concord.edu.

Davis & Elkins College

Elkins, West Virginia

http://www.dewv.edu/

CONTACT

Ms. Rene? Heckel, Director of Enrollment Management, Davis & Elkins College, 100 Campus Drive, Elkins, WV 26241. *Phone:* 304-637-1974. *Toll-free phone:* 800-624-3157. *Fax:* 304-637-1800.
E-mail: admiss@davisandelkins.edu.

Fairmont State University

Fairmont, West Virginia

http://www.fairmontstate.edu/

- **State-supported** comprehensive, founded 1865, part of State College System of West Virginia
- **Small-town** 120-acre campus
- **Endowment** $22.6 million
- **Coed**
- **Minimally difficult** entrance level

FACULTY
Student/faculty ratio: 15:1.

ACADEMICS
Calendar: semesters. *Degrees:* associate, bachelor's, and master's.
Library: Musick Library. Study areas open 24 hours, 5-7 days a week.

STUDENT LIFE
Housing options: on-campus residence required through sophomore year; coed, men-only, women-only. Campus housing is university owned. Freshman campus housing is guaranteed.

Activities and organizations: drama/theater group, student-run newspaper, choral group, marching band, Alpha Phi Omega, Circle K, Society for Non-traditional Students, Criminal Justice Club, Honors Association, national fraternities, national sororities.

Athletics Member NCAA. All Division II.

Campus security: 24-hour emergency response devices and patrols, student patrols, controlled dormitory access.

Student services: health clinic, personal/psychological counseling, legal services.

COSTS & FINANCIAL AID
Costs (2016–17) ***Tuition:*** state resident $6950 full-time, $281 per credit hour part-time; nonresident $14,666 full-time, $603 per credit hour part-time. Full-time tuition and fees vary according to location. Part-time tuition and fees vary according to course load and location. ***Required fees:*** $1734 full-time. ***Room and board:*** $9640; room only: $5096. Room and board charges vary according to board plan and housing facility.

Financial Aid Of all full-time matriculated undergraduates who enrolled in 2014, 2,940 applied for aid, 2,385 were judged to have need, 160 had their need fully met. 139 Federal Work-Study jobs (averaging $1347). 674 state and other part-time jobs (averaging $2074). In 2014, 253 non-need-based awards were made. ***Average percent of need met:*** 67. ***Average financial aid package:*** $8934. ***Average need-based loan:*** $3762. ***Average need-based gift aid:*** $6198. ***Average non-need-based aid:*** $5593. ***Average indebtedness upon graduation:*** $25,473.

APPLYING
Standardized Tests *Required:* SAT or ACT (for admission).

Options: electronic application.

Required: high school transcript. ***Recommended:*** minimum 2.0 GPA.

CONTACT
Mrs. Amie Fazalare, Director of Recruiting, Fairmont State University, 1201 Locust Avenue, Fairmont, WV 26554. *Phone:* 304-367-4892. *Toll-free phone:* 800-641-5678. *Fax:* 304-367-4789. *E-mail:* admit@fairmontstate.edu.

Glenville State College

Glenville, West Virginia

http://www.glenville.edu/

- **State-supported** 4-year, founded 1872, part of West Virginia Higher Education Policy Commission
- **Rural** 331-acre campus
- **Endowment** $8.7 million
- **Coed**
- **Noncompetitive** entrance level

FACULTY
Student/faculty ratio: 15:1.

ACADEMICS
Calendar: semesters. *Degrees:* associate and bachelor's.
Library: Robert F. Kidd Library plus 1 other. *Books:* 117,347 (physical), 64,412 (digital/electronic); *Serial titles:* 3,857 (physical), 10,004 (digital/electronic); *Databases:* 62. Weekly public service hours: 71.

STUDENT LIFE
Housing options: on-campus residence required through sophomore year; coed, men-only, women-only, special housing for students with disabilities. Campus housing is university owned. Freshman campus housing is guaranteed.

Activities and organizations: drama/theater group, student-run newspaper, choral group, marching band, Music Educators National Conference, Student Government Association, Student Support Services, Student Advisory Committee, Glenville Student Action, national fraternities.

Athletics Member NCAA. All Division II.

Campus security: 24-hour emergency response devices and patrols, student patrols, late-night transport/escort service, controlled dormitory access.

Student services: health clinic, personal/psychological counseling.

COSTS & FINANCIAL AID
Costs (2016–17) ***Tuition:*** state resident $7344 full-time, $306 per credit hour part-time; nonresident $16,560 full-time, $692 per credit hour part-time. Full-time tuition and fees vary according to course load. ***Required fees:*** $1752 full-time. ***Room and board:*** $10,042. Room and board charges vary according to board plan and housing facility.

Financial Aid Of all full-time matriculated undergraduates who enrolled in 2016, 1,020 applied for aid, 892 were judged to have need, 171 had their need fully met. 119 Federal Work-Study jobs (averaging $1152). 273 state and other part-time jobs (averaging $1720). In 2016, 37 non-need-based awards were made. ***Average percent of need met:*** 76. ***Average financial aid package:*** $14,500. ***Average need-based loan:*** $3715. ***Average need-based gift aid:*** $6437. ***Average non-need-based aid:*** $2124. ***Average indebtedness upon graduation:*** $28,930.

APPLYING
Standardized Tests *Required:* SAT or ACT (for admission).

Options: electronic application, deferred entrance.

Application fee: $20.

Required: high school transcript, minimum 3.0 GPA, college preparatory program. ***Required for some:*** interview.

CONTACT
Ms. Ashley Weir, Admission Counselor, Glenville State College, 200 High Street, Glenville, WV 26351-1200. *Phone:* 304-462-4128 Ext. 6133. *Toll-free phone:* 800-924-2010. *Fax:* 304-462-8619. *E-mail:* ashley.weir@glenville.edu.

Marshall University

Huntington, West Virginia

http://www.marshall.edu/

- **State-supported** university, founded 1837, part of University System of West Virginia
- **Urban** 100-acre campus
- **Coed** 9,615 undergraduate students, 83% full-time, 57% women, 43% men
- **Moderately difficult** entrance level, 89% of applicants were admitted

UNDERGRAD STUDENTS
7,997 full-time, 1,618 part-time. Students come from 43 states and territories; 42 other countries; 20% are from out of state; 6% Black or African American, non-Hispanic/Latino; 2% Hispanic/Latino; 0.8% Asian, non-Hispanic/Latino; 0.1% Native Hawaiian or other Pacific Islander, non-Hispanic/Latino; 0.3% American Indian or Alaska Native, non-Hispanic/Latino; 3% Two or more races, non-Hispanic/Latino; 4% Race/ethnicity unknown; 2% international; 6% transferred in.

Freshmen:
Admission: 4,891 applied, 4,374 admitted, 1,888 enrolled. ***Average high school GPA:*** 3.4. ***Test scores:*** SAT critical reading scores over 500: 35%; SAT math scores over 500: 45%; ACT scores over 18: 89%; SAT critical reading scores over 600: 8%; SAT math scores over 600: 8%; ACT scores over 24: 33%; SAT critical reading scores over 700: 2%; SAT math scores over 700: 1%; ACT scores over 30: 5%.

Retention: 75% of full-time freshmen returned.

FACULTY
Total: 724, 70% full-time, 58% with terminal degrees.
Student/faculty ratio: 18:1.

ACADEMICS
Calendar: semesters. *Degrees:* certificates, associate, bachelor's, master's, doctoral, post-master's, and postbachelor's certificates.

Special study options: academic remediation for entering students, accelerated degree program, adult/continuing education programs, advanced placement credit, cooperative education, distance learning, double majors, English as a second language, honors programs, independent study, internships, off-campus study, part-time degree program, services for LD students, study abroad, summer session for credit. ***ROTC:*** Army (b).

Unusual degree programs: 3-2 forestry with Duke University.

Computers: 1,200 computers/terminals and 500 ports are available on campus for general student use. Students can access the following: campus intranet, computer help desk, free student e-mail accounts, online (class) grades, online (class) registration, online (class) schedules, virtual computer lab: remote and Web conferencing. Campuswide network is available. 100% of college-owned or -operated housing units are wired for high-speed Internet access. Wireless service is available via classrooms, computer centers, computer labs, dorm rooms, learning centers, libraries, student centers.

Library: John Deaver Drinko Library plus 1 other. *Books:* 394,886 (physical), 115,843 (digital/electronic); *Serial titles:* 1,987 (physical), 50,182 (digital/electronic); *Databases:* 254. Weekly public service hours: 133; study areas open 24 hours, 5-7 days a week; students can reserve study rooms.

STUDENT LIFE

Housing options: on-campus residence required through sophomore year; coed, women-only, special housing for students with disabilities. Campus housing is university owned and is provided by a third party. Freshman campus housing is guaranteed.

Activities and organizations: drama/theater group, student-run newspaper, radio and television station, choral group, marching band, Campus Crusade for Christ, Gamma Beta Phi, The International Students' Organization, Newman Association, Phi Alpha Theta, national fraternities, national sororities.

Athletics Member NCAA. All Division I except football (Division I-A). ***Intercollegiate sports:*** baseball M(s), basketball M(s)/W(s), cross-country running M(s)/W(s), golf M(s)/W(s), lacrosse M(c), rugby M(c)/W(c), soccer M(s)/W(s), softball W(s), swimming and diving W(s), tennis W(s), track and field M(s)/W(s), volleyball W(s). ***Intramural sports:*** basketball M/W, bowling M/W, football M/W, golf M/W, racquetball M/W, soccer M/W, softball M/W, swimming and diving M/W, tennis M/W, track and field M/W, volleyball M/W.

Campus security: 24-hour emergency response devices and patrols, student patrols, late-night transport/escort service, controlled dormitory access.

Student services: health clinic, personal/psychological counseling, women's center, legal services.

COSTS & FINANCIAL AID

Costs (2016–17) ***Tuition:*** state resident $6032 full-time, $252 per credit hour part-time; nonresident $15,260 full-time, $636 per credit hour part-time. Full-time tuition and fees vary according to degree level, location, program, and reciprocity agreements. Part-time tuition and fees vary according to course load, degree level, location, program, and reciprocity agreements. ***Required fees:*** $1122 full-time, $47 per credit hour part-time, $47 per credit hour part-time. ***Room and board:*** $10,126; room only: $6266. Room and board charges vary according to board plan and housing facility. ***Payment plan:*** installment. ***Waivers:*** children of alumni, senior citizens, and employees or children of employees.

Financial Aid Of all full-time matriculated undergraduates who enrolled in 2016, 7,039 applied for aid, 5,595 were judged to have need, 1,546 had their need fully met. In 2016, 1062 non-need-based awards were made. ***Average percent of need met:*** 49. ***Average financial aid package:*** $10,625. ***Average need-based loan:*** $6843. ***Average need-based gift aid:*** $6326. ***Average non-need-based aid:*** $2230. ***Average indebtedness upon graduation:*** $27,121.

APPLYING

Standardized Tests *Required:* SAT or ACT (for admission).

Options: electronic application, deferred entrance.

Application fee: $30.

Required for some: high school transcript.

Application deadlines: rolling (freshmen), rolling (transfers).

Notification: continuous (freshmen), continuous (transfers).

CONTACT

Dr. Tammy Johnson, Director of Admissions, Marshall University, 1 John Marshall Drive, Huntington, WV 25755. *Phone:* 800-642-3499. *Toll-free phone:* 800-642-3499. *Fax:* 304-696-3135. *E-mail:* admissions@marshall.edu.

Ohio Valley University

Vienna, West Virginia

http://www.ovu.edu/

- **Independent** comprehensive, founded 1960, affiliated with Church of Christ
- **Small-town** 299-acre campus
- **Coed** 418 undergraduate students, 95% full-time, 47% women, 53% men
- **Minimally difficult** entrance level, 47% of applicants were admitted

UNDERGRAD STUDENTS

396 full-time, 22 part-time. Students come from 27 states and territories; 25 other countries; 61% are from out of state; 12% Black or African American, non-Hispanic/Latino; 5% Hispanic/Latino; 0.2% Asian, non-Hispanic/Latino; 3% Two or more races, non-Hispanic/Latino; 10% Race/ethnicity unknown; 9% international; 8% transferred in; 60% live on campus.

Freshmen:

Admission: 882 applied, 415 admitted, 121 enrolled. ***Average high school GPA:*** 2.85. ***Test scores:*** SAT critical reading scores over 500: 25%; SAT math scores over 500: 41%; SAT writing scores over 500: 22%; ACT scores over 18: 66%; SAT critical reading scores over 600: 3%; SAT math scores over 600: 9%; ACT scores over 24: 15%; ACT scores over 30: 2%.

Retention: 56% of full-time freshmen returned.

FACULTY

Total: 88, 23% full-time, 28% with terminal degrees.

Student/faculty ratio: 10:1.

ACADEMICS

Calendar: semesters. *Degrees:* associate, bachelor's, master's, and postbachelor's certificates.

Special study options: academic remediation for entering students, adult/continuing education programs, advanced placement credit, distance learning, double majors, English as a second language, honors programs, independent study, internships, off-campus study, part-time degree program, services for LD students, student-designed majors, study abroad, summer session for credit.

Computers: Students can access the following: campus intranet, computer help desk, free student e-mail accounts, online (class) grades, online (class) registration, online (class) schedules. Campuswide network is available. Wireless service is available via entire campus.

Library: Icy Belle Library.

STUDENT LIFE

Housing options: on-campus residence required through sophomore year; men-only, women-only, special housing for students with disabilities. Campus housing is university owned. Freshman campus housing is guaranteed.

Activities and organizations: drama/theater group, student-run newspaper, choral group, Social Clubs, intramural sports, Theatre Production, Acappella Choir, Ambassadors.

Athletics Member NCAA. All Division II. ***Intercollegiate sports:*** baseball M(s), basketball M(s)/W(s), cross-country running M(s)/W(s), golf M(s)/W(s), lacrosse M(s), soccer M(s)/W(s), softball W(s), volleyball W(s), wrestling M(s). ***Intramural sports:*** basketball M/W, bowling M/W, football M/W, golf M/W, soccer M/W, softball M/W, volleyball M/W.

Campus security: 24-hour emergency response devices and patrols, controlled dormitory access.

COSTS & FINANCIAL AID

Costs (2017–18) ***Comprehensive fee:*** $28,800 includes full-time tuition ($21,100) and room and board ($7700). Full-time tuition and fees vary according to course load. Part-time tuition: $700 per credit hour. Part-time tuition and fees vary according to course load. ***College room only:*** $3850. Room and board charges vary according to board plan. ***Payment plan:*** installment. ***Waivers:*** employees or children of employees.

Financial Aid Of all full-time matriculated undergraduates who enrolled in 2014, 346 applied for aid, 306 were judged to have need, 72 had their need fully met. In 2014, 52 non-need-based awards were made. ***Average percent of need met:*** 71. ***Average financial aid package:*** $14,737.

Average need-based loan: $3826. ***Average need-based gift aid:*** $11,693. ***Average non-need-based aid:*** $6015. ***Average indebtedness upon graduation:*** $34,373.

APPLYING
Standardized Tests *Required for some:* SAT or ACT (for admission).

Options: electronic application.

Required: high school transcript. ***Required for some:*** essay or personal statement, interview.

CONTACT
Mrs. Valerie Wright, Admissions Office Manager, Ohio Valley University, 1 Campus View Drive, Vienna, WV 26105. *Phone:* 304-865-6200. *Toll-free phone:* 877-446-8668. *Fax:* 304-865-6001. *E-mail:* admissions@ovu.edu.

Potomac State College of West Virginia University

Keyser, West Virginia

http://www.potomacstatecollege.edu/

- **State-supported** primarily 2-year, founded 1901, part of West Virginia Higher Education Policy Commission
- **Small-town** 18-acre campus
- **Coed**
- **Noncompetitive** entrance level

FACULTY
Student/faculty ratio: 22:1.

ACADEMICS
Calendar: semesters. *Degrees:* associate and bachelor's.
Library: Mary F. Shipper Library.

STUDENT LIFE
Housing options: on-campus residence required through sophomore year; coed. Campus housing is university owned. Freshman applicants given priority for college housing.

Activities and organizations: drama/theater group, student-run newspaper, choral group, Agriculture and Forestry Club, Black Student Alliance, Gamers and Geeks Club, Campus and Community Ministries.

Athletics Member NJCAA.

Campus security: 24-hour patrols, late-night transport/escort service, controlled dormitory access.

Student services: health clinic, personal/psychological counseling.

COSTS & FINANCIAL AID
Costs (2016–17) ***Tuition:*** state resident $4056 full-time, $169 per credit hour part-time; nonresident $10,416 full-time, $434 per credit hour part-time. Full-time tuition and fees vary according to course load and degree level. Part-time tuition and fees vary according to course load and degree level. ***Room and board:*** $8752; room only: $4620. Room and board charges vary according to board plan and housing facility.

Financial Aid Of all full-time matriculated undergraduates who enrolled in 2015, 70 Federal Work-Study jobs (averaging $1300).

APPLYING
Standardized Tests *Recommended:* SAT or ACT (for admission).

Options: electronic application.

Required: high school transcript.

CONTACT
Ms. Beth Little, Director of Enrollment Services, Potomac State College of West Virginia University, 75 Arnold Street, Keyser, WV 26726. *Phone:* 304-788-6820. *Toll-free phone:* 800-262-7332 Ext. 6820. *Fax:* 304-788-6939. *E-mail:* go2psc@mail.wvu.edu.

Salem International University

Salem, West Virginia

http://www.salemu.edu/

CONTACT
Mrs. Brenda Davis, Admissions Representative, Salem International University, PO Box 500, Salem, WV 26426-0500. *Phone:* 304-326-1359. *Toll-free phone:* 888-235-5024. *Fax:* 304-326-1592. *E-mail:* admissions@salemiu.edu.

Shepherd University

Shepherdstown, West Virginia

http://www.shepherd.edu/

- **State-supported** comprehensive, founded 1871, part of West Virginia Higher Education Policy Commission
- **Small-town** 325-acre campus with easy access to Washington, DC
- **Endowment** $25.2 million
- **Coed** 3,436 undergraduate students, 79% full-time, 58% women, 42% men
- **Moderately difficult** entrance level, 92% of applicants were admitted

UNDERGRAD STUDENTS
2,700 full-time, 736 part-time. Students come from 49 states and territories; 9 other countries; 35% are from out of state; 25% Black or African American, non-Hispanic/Latino; 4% Hispanic/Latino; 2% Asian, non-Hispanic/Latino; 0.1% Native Hawaiian or other Pacific Islander, non-Hispanic/Latino; 0.4% American Indian or Alaska Native, non-Hispanic/Latino; 2% Two or more races, non-Hispanic/Latino; 1% Race/ethnicity unknown; 0.4% international; 11% transferred in; 34% live on campus.

Freshmen:
Admission: 1,546 applied, 1,421 admitted, 564 enrolled. ***Average high school GPA:*** 3.34. ***Test scores:*** SAT critical reading scores over 500: 53%; SAT math scores over 500: 44%; ACT scores over 18: 89%; SAT critical reading scores over 600: 9%; SAT math scores over 600: 7%; ACT scores over 24: 32%; SAT critical reading scores over 700: 1%; ACT scores over 30: 3%.

Retention: 60% of full-time freshmen returned.

FACULTY
Total: 350, 40% full-time, 49% with terminal degrees.

Student/faculty ratio: 15:1.

ACADEMICS
Calendar: semesters. *Degrees:* bachelor's and master's.

Special study options: academic remediation for entering students, adult/continuing education programs, advanced placement credit, cooperative education, distance learning, double majors, English as a second language, honors programs, independent study, internships, part-time degree program, services for LD students, study abroad, summer session for credit. ***ROTC:*** Air Force (c).

Unusual degree programs: 3-2 business administration; biochemistry (biopharmaceutical science) with West Virginia University.

Computers: 611 computers/terminals and 150 ports are available on campus for general student use. Students can access the following: computer help desk, free student e-mail accounts, online (class) grades, online (class) registration, online (class) schedules, virtual labs. Campuswide network is available. 100% of college-owned or -operated housing units are wired for high-speed Internet access. Wireless service is available via entire campus.

Library: Scarborough Library. *Books:* 140,072 (physical), 6,727 (digital/electronic); *Serial titles:* 434 (physical), 62,786 (digital/electronic); *Databases:* 71. Weekly public service hours: 87; study areas open 24 hours, 5-7 days a week; students can reserve study rooms.

STUDENT LIFE
Housing options: on-campus residence required through senior year; coed, special housing for students with disabilities. Campus housing is university owned. Freshman campus housing is guaranteed.

Activities and organizations: drama/theater group, student-run newspaper, radio station, choral group, marching band, Relay for Life, Student Government Association, Ram Marching Band, Sigma Sigma Sigma, Alpha Phi Omega, national fraternities, national sororities.

Athletics Member NCAA. All Division II. ***Intercollegiate sports:*** baseball M(s), basketball M(s)/W(s), football M(s), golf M(s), lacrosse W(s), soccer M(s)/W(s), softball W(s), tennis M(s)/W(s), volleyball W(s). ***Intramural sports:*** basketball M/W, football M/W, racquetball M/W, sand volleyball M/W, soccer M/W, volleyball M/W.

Campus security: 24-hour emergency response devices and patrols, late-night transport/escort service, controlled dormitory access, student security in academic buildings, RAVE emergency alert system.

Student services: health clinic, personal/psychological counseling.

COSTS & FINANCIAL AID
Costs (2016–17) ***Tuition:*** state resident $7170 full-time, $293 per credit hour part-time; nonresident $17,482 full-time, $722 per credit hour part-time. Full-time tuition and fees vary according to program and reciprocity agreements. Part-time tuition and fees vary according to program. ***Room and board:*** $10,054. Room and board charges vary according to board plan and housing facility. ***Payment plan:*** installment. ***Waivers:*** minority students, senior citizens, and employees or children of employees.

Financial Aid Of all full-time matriculated undergraduates who enrolled in 2016, 2,573 applied for aid, 1,756 were judged to have need, 503 had their need fully met. 47 Federal Work-Study jobs (averaging $205). 455 state and other part-time jobs (averaging $1503). In 2016, 605 non-need-based awards were made. ***Average percent of need met:*** 77. ***Average financial aid package:*** $12,398. ***Average need-based loan:*** $3859. ***Average need-based gift aid:*** $5100. ***Average non-need-based aid:*** $10,451. ***Average indebtedness upon graduation:*** $30,526.

APPLYING
Standardized Tests *Required:* SAT or ACT (for admission).

Options: electronic application, early admission, early action, deferred entrance.

Application fee: $45.

Required: high school transcript, minimum 2.0 GPA. ***Recommended:*** essay or personal statement, minimum 3.0 GPA, 2 letters of recommendation.

Application deadlines: rolling (freshmen), rolling (transfers), 11/15 (early action).

Notification: continuous until 8/15 (freshmen), continuous until 8/15 (transfers), 12/15 (early action).

CONTACT
Ms. Kristen Lorenz, Director of Admissions, Shepherd University, PO Box 5000, Shepherdstown, WV 25443-5000. *Phone:* 304-876-5212. *Toll-free phone:* 800-344-5231. *Fax:* 304-876-5165. *E-mail:* admission@shepherd.edu.

Strayer University–Teays Valley Campus

Scott Depot, West Virginia

http://www.strayer.edu/west-virginia/teays-valley/

CONTACT
Strayer University–Teays Valley Campus, 100 Corporate Center Drive, Scott Depot, WV 25560.

University of Charleston

Charleston, West Virginia

http://www.ucwv.edu/

- **Independent** comprehensive, founded 1888
- **Small-town** 40-acre campus
- **Coed** 1,761 undergraduate students, 69% full-time, 45% women, 55% men
- **Moderately difficult** entrance level, 52% of applicants were admitted

UNDERGRAD STUDENTS
1,218 full-time, 543 part-time. Students come from 44 states and territories; 44 other countries; 46% are from out of state; 7% Black or African American, non-Hispanic/Latino; 2% Hispanic/Latino; 0.6% Asian, non-Hispanic/Latino; 0.3% Native Hawaiian or other Pacific Islander, non-Hispanic/Latino; 0.3% American Indian or Alaska Native, non-Hispanic/Latino; 2% Two or more races, non-Hispanic/Latino; 27% Race/ethnicity unknown; 9% international; 17% transferred in; 47% live on campus.

Freshmen:
Admission: 1,801 applied, 934 admitted, 304 enrolled. ***Average high school GPA:*** 3.3. ***Test scores:*** SAT critical reading scores over 500: 26%; SAT math scores over 500: 35%; ACT scores over 18: 84%; SAT critical reading scores over 600: 3%; SAT math scores over 600: 9%; ACT scores over 24: 28%; SAT math scores over 700: 1%; ACT scores over 30: 3%. ***Retention:*** 66% of full-time freshmen returned.

ACADEMICS
Calendar: semesters. *Degrees:* associate, bachelor's, master's, and doctoral.

Special study options: academic remediation for entering students, accelerated degree program, adult/continuing education programs, advanced placement credit, cooperative education, distance learning, double majors, English as a second language, freshman honors college, honors programs, independent study, internships, off-campus study, part-time degree program, services for LD students, student-designed majors, study abroad, summer session for credit. ***ROTC:*** Army (b).

Computers: 200 computers/terminals are available on campus for general student use. Students can access the following: campus intranet, computer help desk, free student e-mail accounts, online (class) grades, online (class) registration, online (class) schedules. Campuswide network is available. Wireless service is available via entire campus.

Library: Schoenbaum Library plus 1 other. *Books:* 189,000 (physical), 210,000 (digital/electronic); *Databases:* 56. Students can reserve study rooms.

STUDENT LIFE
Housing options: on-campus residence required through sophomore year; coed, special housing for students with disabilities. Campus housing is university owned. Freshman campus housing is guaranteed.

Activities and organizations: student-run newspaper, choral group, Student Activities Board, American Society of Interior Designers, Student Government Association, Capito Association of Nursing Students, International Student Organization, national fraternities, national sororities.

Athletics Member NCAA. All Division II. ***Intercollegiate sports:*** baseball M(s), basketball M(s)/W(s), cheerleading W(s), crew W(s), cross-country running W(s), football M(s), golf M(s)/W(s), lacrosse W(s), soccer M(s)/W(s), softball W(s), swimming and diving M(s)/W(s), tennis M(s)/W(s), track and field M(s)/W(s), volleyball M(s)/W(s). ***Intramural sports:*** basketball M/W, bowling M/W, football M/W, tennis M/W, volleyball M/W, water polo M/W.

Campus security: 24-hour emergency response devices and patrols, student patrols, late-night transport/escort service, controlled dormitory access, radio connection to city police and ambulance.

Student services: health clinic, personal/psychological counseling.

COSTS & FINANCIAL AID
Costs (2016–17) ***Comprehensive fee:*** $39,200 includes full-time tuition ($28,900), mandatory fees ($1200), and room and board ($9100). Full-time tuition and fees vary according to location and program. Part-time tuition: $380 per credit. Part-time tuition and fees vary according to course load, location, and program. ***College room only:*** $5000. Room and board charges vary according to board plan and housing facility. ***Payment plan:*** installment. ***Waivers:*** children of alumni, senior citizens, and employees or children of employees.

Financial Aid Of all full-time matriculated undergraduates who enrolled in 2015, 1,162 applied for aid, 1,083 were judged to have need, 197 had their need fully met. In 2015, 85 non-need-based awards were made. ***Average percent of need met:*** 52. ***Average financial aid package:*** $19,719. ***Average need-based loan:*** $5500. ***Average need-based gift aid:*** $5025. ***Average non-need-based aid:*** $10,250. ***Financial aid deadline:*** 8/15.

APPLYING
Standardized Tests *Required:* SAT or ACT (for admission).

Options: electronic application, early admission, deferred entrance.

Application fee: $25.

Required: high school transcript, minimum 2.3 GPA. ***Required for some:*** interview. ***Recommended:*** essay or personal statement.

Application deadlines: rolling (freshmen), rolling (transfers).

Notification: continuous (freshmen), continuous (transfers).

CONTACT
Sandy Dolin, Application Coordinator, University of Charleston, 2300 MacCorkle Avenue, SE, Charleston, WV 25304. *Phone:* 304-357-4752. *Toll-free phone:* 800-995-GOUC. *E-mail:* admissions@ucwv.edu.

West Liberty University

West Liberty, West Virginia

http://www.westliberty.edu/

- **State-supported** comprehensive, founded 1837, part of West Virginia Higher Education Policy Commission
- **Rural** campus
- **Coed**
- **Minimally difficult** entrance level

ACADEMICS
Calendar: semesters. *Degrees:* associate, bachelor's, and master's.
Library: Paul N. Elbin Library.

STUDENT LIFE
Housing options: coed, men-only, women-only, special housing for students with disabilities. Campus housing is university owned.
Athletics Member NCAA. All Division II.
Campus security: 24-hour emergency response devices and patrols, controlled dormitory access.

COSTS & FINANCIAL AID
Costs (2016–17) ***Tuition:*** state resident $7038 full-time, $287 per credit hour part-time; nonresident $14,394 full-time, $593 per credit hour part-time. Full-time tuition and fees vary according to course load, degree level, and program. Part-time tuition and fees vary according to course load, degree level, and program. ***Room and board:*** $9120; room only: $5050. Room and board charges vary according to housing facility and location. ***Payment plans:*** installment, deferred payment.
Financial Aid Of all full-time matriculated undergraduates who enrolled in 2010, 2,138 applied for aid, 1,799 were judged to have need, 391 had their need fully met. In 2010, 43 non-need-based awards were made. ***Average percent of need met:*** 70. ***Average financial aid package:*** $7990. ***Average need-based loan:*** $3974. ***Average need-based gift aid:*** $5196. ***Average non-need-based aid:*** $1507. ***Average indebtedness upon graduation:*** $25,000.

APPLYING
Standardized Tests *Required:* SAT or ACT (for admission).
Options: electronic application.
Required: high school transcript, minimum 2.0 GPA. ***Recommended:*** interview.

CONTACT
Ms. Stephanie North, Admissions Counselor, West Liberty University, 208 University Drive, West Liberty, WV 26074. *Phone:* 304-336-8078. *Toll-free phone:* 800-732-6204 (in-state); 866-WESTLIB (out-of-state). *Fax:* 304-336-8403. *E-mail:* wladmsn1@westliberty.edu.

West Virginia State University

Institute, West Virginia

http://www.wvstateu.edu/

- **State-supported** comprehensive, founded 1891, part of West Virginia four-year public higher education system
- **Small-town** 98-acre campus
- **Coed** 3,391 undergraduate students, 53% full-time, 56% women, 44% men
- **Minimally difficult** entrance level, 96% of applicants were admitted

UNDERGRAD STUDENTS
1,797 full-time, 1,594 part-time. Students come from 22 states and territories; 14 other countries; 12% are from out of state; 15% Black or African American, non-Hispanic/Latino; 2% Hispanic/Latino; 0.2% Asian, non-Hispanic/Latino; 0.1% Native Hawaiian or other Pacific Islander, non-Hispanic/Latino; 6% American Indian or Alaska Native, non-Hispanic/Latino; 10% Two or more races, non-Hispanic/Latino; 5% Race/ethnicity unknown; 1% international; 15% live on campus.

Freshmen:
Admission: 3,462 applied, 3,333 admitted. ***Average high school GPA:*** 3.13. ***Test scores:*** ACT scores over 18: 72%; ACT scores over 24: 17%; ACT scores over 30: 1%.
Retention: 57% of full-time freshmen returned.

FACULTY
Total: 192, 55% full-time, 48% with terminal degrees.
Student/faculty ratio: 17:1.

ACADEMICS
Calendar: semesters. *Degrees:* bachelor's, master's, and postbachelor's certificates.
Special study options: academic remediation for entering students, accelerated degree program, adult/continuing education programs, advanced placement credit, cooperative education, double majors, external degree program, honors programs, internships, part-time degree program, services for LD students, summer session for credit. ***ROTC:*** Army (b).
Computers: 625 computers/terminals and 5,500 ports are available on campus for general student use. Students can access the following: campus intranet, computer help desk, free student e-mail accounts, online (class) grades, online (class) registration, online (class) schedules. Campuswide network is available. 100% of college-owned or -operated housing units are wired for high-speed Internet access. Wireless service is available via entire campus.
Library: Drain-Jordan Library. *Books:* 168,009 (physical), 20,776 (digital/electronic); *Databases:* 27. Weekly public service hours: 82.

STUDENT LIFE
Housing options: on-campus residence required through sophomore year; coed, special housing for students with disabilities. Campus housing is university owned.
Activities and organizations: drama/theater group, student-run newspaper, radio station, choral group, marching band, Student Social Work Organization 20, WVSU College Chapter - NAACP 17, CHOICES Peer Educators 13, WVSU International Student Services 13, C.E. Jones Historical Society 12, national fraternities, national sororities.
Athletics Member NCAA. All Division II. ***Intercollegiate sports:*** baseball M(s), basketball M(s)/W(s), cross-country running W(s), football M(s), golf M(s), softball W(s), tennis M(s)/W(s), volleyball W(s). ***Intramural sports:*** baseball M, basketball M/W, cheerleading W, cross-country running W, football M, golf M, softball W, tennis M/W, volleyball W.
Campus security: 24-hour emergency response devices and patrols, student patrols, controlled dormitory access.
Student services: health clinic, personal/psychological counseling.

COSTS & FINANCIAL AID
Costs (2016–17) ***Tuition:*** state resident $6996 full-time, $287 per credit hour part-time; nonresident $15,572 full-time, $644 per semester hour part-time. Full-time tuition and fees vary according to course load and program. Part-time tuition and fees vary according to course load and program. ***Room and board:*** $11,388; room only: $6834. Room and board charges vary according to board plan and housing facility. ***Payment plan:*** installment.
Financial Aid ***Financial aid deadline:*** 6/15.

APPLYING
Standardized Tests *Required:* SAT or ACT (for admission).
Options: electronic application.
Application fee: $20.
Required: high school transcript, minimum 2.0 GPA, mimum ACT composite score of 18 (870 SAT).
Application deadlines: 8/17 (freshmen), 8/10 (transfers).
Notification: continuous (freshmen), continuous (out-of-state freshmen), continuous (transfers).

CONTACT
Ashley Weir, Director of Admissions, West Virginia State University, PO Box 1000, Ferrell Hall, Room 106, Institute, WV 25112-1000. *Phone:* 304-204-4340. *Toll-free phone:* 800-987-2112. *Fax:* 304-766-5182. *E-mail:* ashley.weir@wvstateu.edu.

West Virginia University

Morgantown, West Virginia

http://www.wvu.edu/

- **State-supported** university, founded 1867, part of West Virginia Higher Education Policy Commission
- **Small-town** 1892-acre campus with easy access to Pittsburgh
- **Endowment** $403.6 million
- **Coed** 22,350 undergraduate students, 92% full-time, 46% women, 54% men
- **Moderately difficult** entrance level, 76% of applicants were admitted

UNDERGRAD STUDENTS

20,524 full-time, 1,826 part-time. Students come from 50 states and territories; 75 other countries; 48% are from out of state; 5% Black or African American, non-Hispanic/Latino; 4% Hispanic/Latino; 2% Asian, non-Hispanic/Latino; 0.1% Native Hawaiian or other Pacific Islander, non-Hispanic/Latino; 0.1% American Indian or Alaska Native, non-Hispanic/Latino; 4% Two or more races, non-Hispanic/Latino; 0.3% Race/ethnicity unknown; 6% international; 4% transferred in; 15% live on campus.

Freshmen:

Admission: 21,558 applied, 16,411 admitted, 5,124 enrolled. ***Average high school GPA:*** 3.49. ***Test scores:*** SAT critical reading scores over 500: 50%; SAT math scores over 500: 53%; ACT scores over 18: 90%; SAT critical reading scores over 600: 12%; SAT math scores over 600: 16%; ACT scores over 24: 40%; SAT critical reading scores over 700: 1%; SAT math scores over 700: 3%; ACT scores over 30: 5%.

Retention: 79% of full-time freshmen returned.

FACULTY

Total: 1,596, 74% full-time, 68% with terminal degrees.

Student/faculty ratio: 19:1.

ACADEMICS

Calendar: semesters. *Degrees:* bachelor's, master's, and doctoral.

Special study options: academic remediation for entering students, accelerated degree program, adult/continuing education programs, advanced placement credit, distance learning, double majors, English as a second language, external degree program, honors programs, independent study, internships, off-campus study, part-time degree program, services for LD students, student-designed majors, study abroad, summer session for credit. ***ROTC:*** Army (b), Air Force (b).

Unusual degree programs: 3-2 education, business/foreign language, occupational therapy, physical therapy, social work.

Computers: 1,800 computers/terminals and 900 ports are available on campus for general student use. Students can access the following: campus intranet, computer help desk, free student e-mail accounts, online (class) grades, online (class) registration, online (class) schedules. Campuswide network is available. 100% of college-owned or -operated housing units are wired for high-speed Internet access. Wireless service is available via entire campus.

Library: Downtown Library Complex plus 5 others. *Books:* 2.4 million (physical); *Serial titles:* 89,824 (physical); *Databases:* 390,341. Study areas open 24 hours, 5-7 days a week; students can reserve study rooms.

STUDENT LIFE

Housing options: on-campus residence required for freshman year; coed, men-only, women-only, cooperative, special housing for students with disabilities. Campus housing is university owned and leased by the school. Freshman campus housing is guaranteed.

Activities and organizations: drama/theater group, student-run newspaper, radio station, choral group, marching band, Residential Hall Association, Alpha Phi Omega, WVU Greek System, Mountaineer Maniacs, Campus Crusade for Christ, national fraternities, national sororities.

Athletics Member NCAA. All Division I except football (Division I-A). ***Intercollegiate sports:*** baseball M(s), basketball M(s)/W(s), crew W(s), cross-country running W(s), golf M(s), gymnastics W(s), riflery M(s)/W(s), soccer M(s)/W(s), swimming and diving M(s)/W(s), tennis W(s), track and field W(s), volleyball W(s), wrestling M(s). ***Intramural sports:*** archery M(c)/W(c), baseball M(c), basketball M(c)/W(c), bowling M(c)/W(c), cheerleading M(c)/W(c), crew M(c)/W(c), cross-country running M(c)/W(c), equestrian sports M(c)/W(c), fencing M(c)/W(c), field hockey M(c)/W(c), football M, golf M(c), ice hockey M(c), lacrosse M(c)/W(c), racquetball M(c)/W(c), riflery M(c)/W(c), rock climbing M(c)/W(c), rugby M(c)/W(c), skiing (cross-country) M(c)/W(c), skiing (downhill) M(c)/W(c), soccer M(c)/W(c), softball M(c)/W(c), swimming and diving M(c)/W(c), table tennis M(c)/W(c), tennis M(c)/W(c), track and field M(c)/W(c), ultimate Frisbee M(c)/W(c), volleyball M(c)/W(c), weight lifting M(c), wrestling M(c).

Campus security: 24-hour emergency response devices and patrols, student patrols, late-night transport/escort service, controlled dormitory access, patrol officers just for housing.

Student services: health clinic, personal/psychological counseling, women's center, legal services.

COSTS & FINANCIAL AID

Costs (2016–17) ***Tuition:*** state resident $7992 full-time, $333 per credit hour part-time; nonresident $22,488 full-time, $937 per credit hour part-time. Full-time tuition and fees vary according to location, program, and reciprocity agreements. Part-time tuition and fees vary according to course load, location, program, and reciprocity agreements. ***Room and board:*** $10,218. Room and board charges vary according to board plan, housing facility, and location. ***Payment plan:*** installment. ***Waivers:*** senior citizens and employees or children of employees.

Financial Aid Of all full-time matriculated undergraduates who enrolled in 2015, 15,727 applied for aid, 10,957 were judged to have need, 3,977 had their need fully met. 1,142 Federal Work-Study jobs (averaging $1505). In 2015, 3289 non-need-based awards were made. ***Average percent of need met:*** 75. ***Average financial aid package:*** $6839. ***Average need-based loan:*** $3553. ***Average need-based gift aid:*** $4790. ***Average non-need-based aid:*** $2437. ***Average indebtedness upon graduation:*** $27,993. ***Financial aid deadline:*** 3/1.

APPLYING

Standardized Tests *Required:* SAT or ACT (for admission).

Options: electronic application.

Application fee: $45.

Required: high school transcript, minimum 2.0 GPA. ***Required for some:*** essay or personal statement, minimum 2.3 GPA.

Application deadlines: 8/1 (freshmen), 8/1 (transfers).

Notification: continuous (transfers).

CONTACT

Ms. Marilyn Potts, Director of Admissions, West Virginia University, PO Box 6009, Morgantown, WV 26506-6009. *Phone:* 304-293-2121. *Toll-free phone:* 800-344-9881. *Fax:* 304-293-3080. *E-mail:* marilyn.potts@mail.wvu.edu.

West Virginia University at Parkersburg

Parkersburg, West Virginia

http://www.wvup.edu/

CONTACT

Christine Post, Associate Dean of Enrollment Management, West Virginia University at Parkersburg, 300 Campus Drive, Parkersburg, WV 26104. *Phone:* 304-424-8223 Ext. 223. *Toll-free phone:* 800-WVA-WVUP. *Fax:* 304-424-8332. *E-mail:* christine.post@mail.wvu.edu.

West Virginia University Institute of Technology

Montgomery, West Virginia

http://www.wvutech.edu/

- **State-supported** 4-year, founded 1895
- **Small-town** 114-acre campus
- **Endowment** $532.6 million
- **Coed** 1,347 undergraduate students, 72% full-time, 44% women, 56% men
- **Minimally difficult** entrance level, 53% of applicants were admitted

UNDERGRAD STUDENTS

975 full-time, 372 part-time. Students come from 35 states and territories; 26 other countries; 6% Black or African American, non-Hispanic/Latino;

3% Hispanic/Latino; 0.7% Asian, non-Hispanic/Latino; 0.4% American Indian or Alaska Native, non-Hispanic/Latino; 3% Two or more races, non-Hispanic/Latino; 3% Race/ethnicity unknown; 7% international; 8% transferred in; 35% live on campus.

Freshmen:
Admission: 1,613 applied, 850 admitted, 307 enrolled. ***Average high school GPA:*** 3.35. ***Test scores:*** SAT math scores over 500: 53%; ACT scores over 18: 75%; SAT math scores over 600: 22%; ACT scores over 24: 24%; SAT math scores over 700: 2%; ACT scores over 30: 1%.

Retention: 57% of full-time freshmen returned.

FACULTY
Total: 93, 86% full-time, 72% with terminal degrees.

ACADEMICS
Calendar: semesters. *Degrees:* bachelor's and postbachelor's certificates.

Special study options: academic remediation for entering students, advanced placement credit, cooperative education, distance learning, double majors, independent study, internships, part-time degree program, services for LD students, student-designed majors, study abroad, summer session for credit. ***ROTC:*** Army (b).

Unusual degree programs: 3-2 teacher education with West Virginia University.

Computers: 200 computers/terminals are available on campus for general student use. Students can access the following: computer help desk, free student e-mail accounts, online (class) grades, online (class) registration, online (class) schedules, electronic course materials. Campuswide network is available. 100% of college-owned or -operated housing units are wired for high-speed Internet access. Wireless service is available via classrooms, computer centers, computer labs, dorm rooms, learning centers, libraries, student centers.

Library: Vining Library plus 1 other. *Books:* 147,685 (physical), 11 (digital/electronic); *Serial titles:* 16,253 (physical). Students can reserve study rooms.

STUDENT LIFE
Housing options: on-campus residence required through sophomore year; coed. Campus housing is university owned. Freshman campus housing is guaranteed.

Activities and organizations: drama/theater group, student-run newspaper, Christian Student Union, Student Activities Board, Alpha Phi Omega, Student Government Association, American Society of Mechanical Engineers, national fraternities, national sororities.

Athletics Member NAIA, USCAA. ***Intercollegiate sports:*** baseball M(s), basketball M(s)/W(s), cross-country running M(s)/W(s), golf M(s), soccer M(s)/W(s), softball W(s), swimming and diving M(s)/W(s), volleyball W(s), wrestling M(s). ***Intramural sports:*** badminton M(c)/W(c), basketball M(c)/W(c), cheerleading M(c)/W(c), soccer M(c)/W(c), ultimate Frisbee M(c)/W(c), volleyball M(c)/W(c).

Campus security: 24-hour emergency response devices and patrols.

Student services: health clinic, personal/psychological counseling.

COSTS & FINANCIAL AID
Costs (2016–17) ***Tuition:*** state resident $6648 full-time, $277 per credit hour part-time; nonresident $16,728 full-time, $697 per credit hour part-time. Full-time tuition and fees vary according to program. Part-time tuition and fees vary according to course load and program. ***Room and board:*** $9814. Room and board charges vary according to board plan and housing facility. ***Payment plan:*** installment. ***Waivers:*** senior citizens.

Financial Aid Of all full-time matriculated undergraduates who enrolled in 2015, 829 applied for aid, 684 were judged to have need, 176 had their need fully met. In 2015, 58 non-need-based awards were made. ***Average percent of need met:*** 75. ***Average financial aid package:*** $7200. ***Average need-based loan:*** $2746. ***Average need-based gift aid:*** $5341. ***Average non-need-based aid:*** $2775. ***Average indebtedness upon graduation:*** $27,364.

APPLYING
Standardized Tests *Required:* SAT or ACT (for admission). *Required for some:* TOEFL or IELTS.

Options: electronic application, early admission.

Required: high school transcript, minimum 2.0 GPA, minimum ACT composite score of 18 or 870 SAT math and verbal or minimum 3.0 high school GPA.

Application deadlines: rolling (freshmen), rolling (out-of-state freshmen), rolling (transfers).

Notification: continuous until 8/15 (freshmen), continuous (out-of-state freshmen), continuous until 8/15 (transfers).

CONTACT
William Allen Jr., Dean of Enrollment Services, West Virginia University Institute of Technology, Old Main Box 80, 405 Fayette Pike, Montgomery, WV 25136. *Phone:* 304-442-3146. *Toll-free phone:* 888-554-8324. *Fax:* 304-442-3067. *E-mail:* tech-admissions@mail.wvu.edu.

West Virginia Wesleyan College

Buckhannon, West Virginia

http://www.wvwc.edu/

- **Independent** comprehensive, founded 1890, affiliated with United Methodist Church
- **Small-town** 180-acre campus
- **Endowment** $44.8 million
- **Coed** 1,396 undergraduate students, 98% full-time, 55% women, 45% men
- **Moderately difficult** entrance level, 77% of applicants were admitted

UNDERGRAD STUDENTS
1,367 full-time, 29 part-time. Students come from 38 states and territories; 20 other countries; 37% are from out of state; 8% Black or African American, non-Hispanic/Latino; 3% Hispanic/Latino; 0.1% Asian, non-Hispanic/Latino; 0.1% Native Hawaiian or other Pacific Islander, non-Hispanic/Latino; 0.4% American Indian or Alaska Native, non-Hispanic/Latino; 4% Two or more races, non-Hispanic/Latino; 0.9% Race/ethnicity unknown; 6% international; 3% transferred in; 79% live on campus.

Freshmen:
Admission: 1,730 applied, 1,337 admitted, 387 enrolled. ***Average high school GPA:*** 3.54. ***Test scores:*** SAT critical reading scores over 500: 43%; SAT math scores over 500: 52%; SAT writing scores over 500: 39%; ACT scores over 18: 90%; SAT critical reading scores over 600: 10%; SAT math scores over 600: 13%; SAT writing scores over 600: 4%; ACT scores over 24: 40%; SAT critical reading scores over 700: 1%; SAT math scores over 700: 1%; ACT scores over 30: 4%.

Retention: 70% of full-time freshmen returned.

FACULTY
Total: 156, 58% full-time, 53% with terminal degrees.

Student/faculty ratio: 13:1.

ACADEMICS
Calendar: semesters. *Degrees:* bachelor's, master's, post-master's, and postbachelor's certificates.

Special study options: academic remediation for entering students, advanced placement credit, distance learning, double majors, English as a second language, honors programs, independent study, internships, off-campus study, part-time degree program, services for LD students, student-designed majors, study abroad, summer session for credit.

Unusual degree programs: 3-2 engineering with University of Virginia, West Virginia University, Virginia Polytechnic Institute and State University.

Computers: Students can access the following: campus intranet, computer help desk, free student e-mail accounts, online (class) grades, online (class) registration, online (class) schedules. Campuswide network is available. 100% of college-owned or -operated housing units are wired for high-speed Internet access. Wireless service is available via entire campus.

Library: Annie Merner Pfeifer Library plus 1 other. *Books:* 122,495 (physical), 271,641 (digital/electronic); *Serial titles:* 11,057 (physical), 112,139 (digital/electronic); *Databases:* 110. Students can reserve study rooms.

STUDENT LIFE
Housing options: on-campus residence required through senior year; coed, men-only, women-only, special housing for students with disabilities. Campus housing is university owned. Freshman campus housing is guaranteed.

Activities and organizations: drama/theater group, student-run newspaper, radio station, choral group, marching band, Campus Activities Board, Green Club, WE LEAD, Wesleyan Ambassadors, Enactus, national fraternities, national sororities.

Athletics Member NCAA. All Division II. ***Intercollegiate sports:*** baseball M(s), basketball M(s)/W(s), cheerleading M/W, cross-country running M(s)/W(s), football M(s), golf M(s)/W(s), lacrosse M(c)/W(s), skiing (downhill) M(c)/W(c), soccer M(s)/W(s), softball W(s), swimming and diving M(s)/W(s), tennis M(s)/W(s), track and field M(s)/W(s), volleyball W(s). ***Intramural sports:*** basketball M/W, bowling M/W, football M/W, golf M/W, racquetball M/W, soccer M/W, softball M/W, table tennis M/W, volleyball M/W, water polo M/W.

Campus security: 24-hour emergency response devices and patrols, student patrols, late-night transport/escort service, controlled dormitory access.

Student services: health clinic, personal/psychological counseling.

COSTS & FINANCIAL AID

Costs (2016–17) ***Comprehensive fee:*** $34,032 includes full-time tuition ($28,574), mandatory fees ($1378), and room and board ($4080). Full-time tuition and fees vary according to course load and student level. Part-time tuition and fees vary according to course load. ***College room only:*** $4168. Room and board charges vary according to housing facility. ***Payment plan:*** installment. ***Waivers:*** employees or children of employees.

Financial Aid Of all full-time matriculated undergraduates who enrolled in 2016, 1,198 applied for aid, 1,081 were judged to have need, 303 had their need fully met. In 2016, 178 non-need-based awards were made. ***Average percent of need met:*** 83. ***Average financial aid package:*** $27,645. ***Average need-based loan:*** $3827. ***Average need-based gift aid:*** $24,490. ***Average non-need-based aid:*** $16,317. ***Average indebtedness upon graduation:*** $31,996.

APPLYING

Standardized Tests *Required:* SAT or ACT (for admission). *Required for some:* SAT Subject Tests (for admission).

Options: electronic application, deferred entrance.

Application fee: $35.

Required: high school transcript. ***Required for some:*** letters of recommendation. ***Recommended:*** essay or personal statement, interview.

Notification: continuous (freshmen), continuous (transfers).

CONTACT

John Waltz, VP for Enrollment Management, West Virginia Wesleyan College, 59 College Avenue, Buckhannon, WV 26201. *Phone:* 304-473-8510. *Toll-free phone:* 800-722-9933. *Fax:* 304-473-8108.
E-mail: admission@wvwc.edu.

See below for display ad and page 1598 for the College Close-Up.

Wheeling Jesuit University

Wheeling, West Virginia

http://www.wju.edu/

- **Independent Roman Catholic (Jesuit)** comprehensive, founded 1954
- **Suburban** 65-acre campus with easy access to Pittsburgh
- **Endowment** $12.5 million
- **Coed** 945 undergraduate students, 84% full-time, 51% women, 49% men
- **Moderately difficult** entrance level, 93% of applicants were admitted

UNDERGRAD STUDENTS

790 full-time, 155 part-time. Students come from 37 states and territories; 26 other countries; 66% are from out of state; 8% Black or African American, non-Hispanic/Latino; 3% Hispanic/Latino; 0.9% Asian, non-Hispanic/Latino; 0.9% Native Hawaiian or other Pacific Islander, non-Hispanic/Latino; 0.5% American Indian or Alaska Native, non-Hispanic/Latino; 2% Two or more races, non-Hispanic/Latino; 5% Race/ethnicity unknown; 5% international; 3% transferred in; 68% live on campus.

Freshmen:

Admission: 1,020 applied, 951 admitted, 222 enrolled. ***Average high school GPA:*** 3.33. ***Test scores:*** SAT critical reading scores over 500: 34%; SAT math scores over 500: 50%; SAT writing scores over 500: 21%; ACT scores over 18: 85%; SAT critical reading scores over 600: 9%; SAT math scores over 600: 7%; ACT scores over 24: 25%; ACT scores over 30: 3%.

Retention: 71% of full-time freshmen returned.

FACULTY

Total: 155, 50% full-time, 63% with terminal degrees.

Student/faculty ratio: 10:1.

ACADEMICS

Calendar: semesters. *Degrees:* bachelor's, master's, doctoral, post-master's, and postbachelor's certificates.

Special study options: academic remediation for entering students, accelerated degree program, adult/continuing education programs, advanced placement credit, distance learning, double majors, English as a second language, honors programs, independent study, internships, off-campus study, part-time degree program, services for LD students, student-designed majors, study abroad, summer session for credit.

Unusual degree programs: 3-2 engineering with Case Western Reserve University, West Virginia University.

Computers: 215 computers/terminals are available on campus for general student use. Students can access the following: campus intranet, computer help desk, free student e-mail accounts, online (class) grades, online (class) registration, online (class) schedules. Campuswide network is available. 100% of college-owned or -operated housing units are wired for high-speed Internet access. Wireless service is available via entire campus.

Library: Bishop Hodges Library. *Books:* 134,540 (physical), 165,927 (digital/electronic); *Serial titles:* 107 (physical), 42 (digital/electronic); *Databases:* 69. Weekly public service hours: 85; students can reserve study rooms.

STUDENT LIFE

Housing options: on-campus residence required through sophomore year; coed, women-only, special housing for students with disabilities. Campus housing is university owned and is provided by a third party. Freshman campus housing is guaranteed.

Activities and organizations: drama/theater group, student-run newspaper, choral group, Campus Activity Board (CAB), Theater Guild, Student Senate, International Student Club, Campus Ministry.

Athletics Member NCAA. All Division II except rugby (Division I). ***Intercollegiate sports:*** baseball M(s), basketball M(s)/W(s), cheerleading M(c)/W(c), cross-country running M(s)/W(s), golf M(s)/W(s), ice hockey M(c), lacrosse M(s)/W(s), rugby M(s), soccer M(s)/W(s), softball W(s), swimming and diving M(s)/W(s), track and field M(s)/W(s), volleyball W(s), wrestling M(s). ***Intramural sports:*** basketball M/W, volleyball M/W.

Campus security: 24-hour patrols, late-night transport/escort service, controlled dormitory access, cameras at residence hall entrances.

Student services: health clinic, personal/psychological counseling.

COSTS & FINANCIAL AID

Costs (2017–18) ***Comprehensive fee:*** $37,106 includes full-time tuition ($27,000), mandatory fees ($1110), and room and board ($8996). Part-time tuition: $735 per credit hour. ***College room only:*** $5006. Room and board charges vary according to board plan, housing facility, and student level. ***Waivers:*** employees or children of employees.

Financial Aid Of all full-time matriculated undergraduates who enrolled in 2016, 688 applied for aid, 607 were judged to have need, 146 had their need fully met. 155 Federal Work-Study jobs (averaging $2800). 93 state and other part-time jobs (averaging $2800). In 2016, 176 non-need-based awards were made. ***Average percent of need met:*** 80. ***Average financial aid package:*** $25,276. ***Average need-based loan:*** $4554. ***Average need-based gift aid:*** $9454. ***Average non-need-based aid:*** $17,196. ***Average indebtedness upon graduation:*** $37,762. ***Financial aid deadline:*** 8/1.

APPLYING

Standardized Tests *Required:* SAT or ACT (for admission).

Options: electronic application, deferred entrance.

Application fee: $25.

Required: high school transcript. ***Required for some:*** interview. ***Recommended:*** essay or personal statement, minimum 3.0 GPA, 2 letters of recommendation, interview.

Application deadlines: rolling (freshmen), rolling (transfers).

Notification: continuous (freshmen), continuous (transfers).

CONTACT

Mr. Christopher Rouhier, Senior Admissions Representative, Wheeling Jesuit University, 316 Washington Avenue, Wheeling, WV 26003. *Phone:* 304-243-2106. *Toll-free phone:* 800-624-6992 Ext. 2359. *Fax:* 304-243-2397. *E-mail:* crouhier@wju.edu.

WISCONSIN

Alverno College

Milwaukee, Wisconsin

http://www.alverno.edu/

- **Independent Roman Catholic** comprehensive, founded 1887
- **Urban** 46-acre campus
- **Endowment** $23.9 million
- **Undergraduate: women only; graduate: coed** 1,413 undergraduate students, 76% full-time, 100% women, 0% men
- **Moderately difficult** entrance level, 74% of applicants were admitted

UNDERGRAD STUDENTS

1,080 full-time, 333 part-time. Students come from 13 states and territories; 10 other countries; 6% are from out of state; 13% Black or African American, non-Hispanic/Latino; 23% Hispanic/Latino; 5% Asian, non-Hispanic/Latino; 0.4% Native Hawaiian or other Pacific Islander, non-Hispanic/Latino; 0.8% American Indian or Alaska Native, non-Hispanic/Latino; 4% Two or more races, non-Hispanic/Latino; 0.3% international; 9% transferred in; 16% live on campus.

Freshmen:

Admission: 698 applied, 516 admitted, 168 enrolled. ***Average high school GPA:*** 3.11. ***Test scores:*** ACT scores over 18: 76%; ACT scores over 24: 17%; ACT scores over 30: 3%.

Retention: 72% of full-time freshmen returned.

FACULTY

Total: 218, 43% full-time, 62% with terminal degrees.

Student/faculty ratio: 10:1.

ACADEMICS

Calendar: semesters. *Degrees:* associate, bachelor's, master's, post-master's, and postbachelor's certificates (also offers weekend program with significant enrollment not reflected in profile).

Special study options: academic remediation for entering students, accelerated degree program, adult/continuing education programs, advanced placement credit, double majors, honors programs, independent study, internships, part-time degree program, services for LD students, student-designed majors, study abroad, summer session for credit. ***ROTC:*** Army (c), Air Force (c).

Computers: 735 computers/terminals are available on campus for general student use. Students can access the following: campus intranet, computer help desk, free student e-mail accounts, online (class) registration, online (class) schedules. Campuswide network is available. 100% of college-owned or -operated housing units are wired for high-speed Internet access. Wireless service is available via classrooms, computer centers, computer labs, dorm rooms, libraries.

Library: Alverno College Library. *Books:* 69,144 (physical), 146,724 (digital/electronic); *Serial titles:* 2,509 (physical), 74,275 (digital/electronic); *Databases:* 75.

STUDENT LIFE

Housing options: women-only. Campus housing is university owned. Freshman campus housing is guaranteed.

Activities and organizations: drama/theater group, student-run newspaper, radio station, choral group, R.A.I.S.E., CHICA, Love Your Melon Crew, Circle K, Gay-Straight Alliance.

Athletics Member NCAA. All Division III. ***Intercollegiate sports:*** basketball W, cross-country running W, golf W, soccer W, softball W, tennis W, volleyball W.

Campus security: 24-hour emergency response devices and patrols, late-night transport/escort service, controlled dormitory access, well-lit parking lots and pathways, emergency first-aid and CPR, crisis intervention team and plan in place.

Student services: health clinic, personal/psychological counseling.

COSTS & FINANCIAL AID
Costs (2016–17) ***Comprehensive fee:*** $34,816 includes full-time tuition ($26,232), mandatory fees ($700), and room and board ($7884). Full-time tuition and fees vary according to program. Part-time tuition: $1093 per credit hour. Part-time tuition and fees vary according to program. ***Room and board:*** Room and board charges vary according to board plan and housing facility. ***Payment plans:*** installment, deferred payment. ***Waivers:*** employees or children of employees.

Financial Aid Of all full-time matriculated undergraduates who enrolled in 2016, 1,011 applied for aid, 962 were judged to have need. 444 Federal Work-Study jobs (averaging $1998). In 2016, 88 non-need-based awards were made. ***Average financial aid package:*** $23,988. ***Average need-based loan:*** $3830. ***Average need-based gift aid:*** $15,461. ***Average non-need-based aid:*** $10,670. ***Average indebtedness upon graduation:*** $41,044.

APPLYING
Standardized Tests *Required:* SAT or ACT (for admission).

Options: electronic application, deferred entrance.

Required: essay or personal statement, high school transcript, minimum 2.0 college GPA. ***Recommended:*** minimum 2.0 GPA, interview.

Application deadlines: rolling (freshmen), rolling (transfers).

Notification: continuous (freshmen), continuous (transfers).

CONTACT
Ms. Becky Kurter, Associate Director of Undergraduate Admissions & Recruitment, Alverno College, 3400 South 43 Street, PO Box 343922, Milwaukee, WI 53234-3922. *Phone:* 414-382-6110. *Toll-free phone:* 800-933-3401. *Fax:* 414-382-6055. *E-mail:* admissions@alverno.edu.

Bellin College

Green Bay, Wisconsin

http://www.bellincollege.edu/

- **Independent** comprehensive, founded 1909
- **Urban** campus
- **Coed, primarily women** 259 undergraduate students
- **Moderately difficult** entrance level

Freshmen:
Admission: 92 applied.

ACADEMICS
Calendar: semesters. *Degrees:* bachelor's and master's.

Special study options: accelerated degree program, advanced placement credit, distance learning, independent study, off-campus study, part-time degree program, summer session for credit. ***ROTC:*** Army (c).

Computers: Campuswide network is available.

Library: Meredith B. and John M. Rose Library.

STUDENT LIFE
Housing options: college housing not available.

Campus security: 24-hour patrols, late-night transport/escort service, electronically operated building access after hours.

Student services: health clinic, personal/psychological counseling.

COSTS & FINANCIAL AID
Costs (2017–18) ***Tuition:*** $998 per credit hour part-time. ***Payment plan:*** installment.

Financial Aid Of all full-time matriculated undergraduates who enrolled in 2012, 122 applied for aid, 117 were judged to have need, 2 had their need fully met. In 2012, 1 non-need-based awards were made. ***Average percent of need met:*** 67. ***Average financial aid package:*** $21,230. ***Average need-based loan:*** $4979. ***Average need-based gift aid:*** $5448. ***Average non-need-based aid:*** $857. ***Average indebtedness upon graduation:*** $33,961.

APPLYING
Standardized Tests *Required:* ACT (for admission).

Options: electronic application.

Application fee: $30.

Required: high school transcript, minimum 3.3 GPA, 3 letters of recommendation, interview. ***Recommended:*** minimum 3.3 GPA.

Application deadlines: rolling (freshmen), rolling (transfers).

Notification: continuous (freshmen), continuous (transfers).

CONTACT
Dr. Penny Croghan, Admissions Director, Bellin College, 3201 Eaton Road, Green Bay, WI 54305. *Phone:* 920-433-5803. *Toll-free phone:* 800-236-8707. *Fax:* 920-433-7416. *E-mail:* admissio@bcon.edu.

Beloit College

Beloit, Wisconsin

http://www.beloit.edu/

- **Independent** 4-year, founded 1846
- **Small-town** 84-acre campus with easy access to Chicago, Milwaukee
- **Endowment** $145.3 million
- **Coed** 1,394 undergraduate students, 96% full-time, 54% women, 46% men

UNDERGRAD STUDENTS
1,337 full-time, 57 part-time. Students come from 48 states and territories; 41 other countries; 83% are from out of state; 5% Black or African American, non-Hispanic/Latino; 9% Hispanic/Latino; 3% Asian, non-Hispanic/Latino; 0.2% Native Hawaiian or other Pacific Islander, non-Hispanic/Latino; 0.4% American Indian or Alaska Native, non-Hispanic/Latino; 3% Two or more races, non-Hispanic/Latino; 4% Race/ethnicity unknown; 14% international; 2% transferred in; 87% live on campus.

Freshmen:
Admission: 382 enrolled. ***Average high school GPA:*** 3.32. ***Test scores:*** SAT critical reading scores over 500: 80%; SAT math scores over 500: 91%; ACT scores over 18: 97%; SAT critical reading scores over 600: 57%; SAT math scores over 600: 61%; ACT scores over 24: 75%; SAT critical reading scores over 700: 20%; SAT math scores over 700: 22%; ACT scores over 30: 27%.

Retention: 86% of full-time freshmen returned.

ACADEMICS
Calendar: semesters. *Degree:* bachelor's.

Special study options: adult/continuing education programs, advanced placement credit, double majors, English as a second language, independent study, internships, off-campus study, services for LD students, student-designed majors, study abroad, summer session for credit.

Unusual degree programs: 3-2 engineering with Columbia University, University of Illinois at Urbana–Champaign, University of Michigan, Rensselaer Polytechnic Institute, Washington University in St. Louis; forestry with Duke University.

Computers: 300 computers/terminals are available on campus for general student use. Students can access the following: campus intranet, computer help desk, free student e-mail accounts, online (class) grades, online (class) registration, online (class) schedules. Campuswide network is available. 100% of college-owned or -operated housing units are wired for high-speed Internet access. Wireless service is available via entire campus.

Library: Morse Library and Black Information Center. Weekly public service hours: 109; students can reserve study rooms.

STUDENT LIFE
Housing options: on-campus residence required through junior year; coed, women-only, cooperative. Campus housing is university owned. Freshman campus housing is guaranteed.

Activities and organizations: drama/theater group, student-run newspaper, radio and television station, choral group, BSFFA - Beloit Science Fiction and Fantasy Association, Ceramics Club, Anthropology Club, Yoga Club, Outdoor Environmental Club, national fraternities, national sororities.

Athletics Member NCAA. All Division III. ***Intercollegiate sports:*** baseball M, basketball M/W, cross-country running M/W, football M, ice hockey M(c)/W(c), lacrosse M/W, soccer M/W, softball W, swimming and diving M/W, tennis W, track and field M/W, volleyball W. ***Intramural sports:*** archery M(c)/W(c), badminton M/W, basketball M/W, fencing M(c)/W(c), football M, golf M(c)/W(c), racquetball M/W, sailing M(c)/W(c), skiing (downhill) M(c)/W(c), soccer M/W, ultimate Frisbee M/W, volleyball M/W.

Campus security: 24-hour emergency response devices and patrols, late-night transport/escort service, controlled dormitory access.

Student services: health clinic, personal/psychological counseling, women's center.

COSTS & FINANCIAL AID

Costs (2016–17) ***Comprehensive fee:*** $55,206 includes full-time tuition ($46,596), mandatory fees ($464), and room and board ($8146). Part-time tuition: $1456 per credit hour. ***College room only:*** $4626. Room and board charges vary according to board plan. ***Payment plan:*** installment. ***Waivers:*** employees or children of employees.

Financial Aid Of all full-time matriculated undergraduates who enrolled in 2016, 925 applied for aid, 830 were judged to have need, 280 had their need fully met. In 2016, 450 non-need-based awards were made. ***Average percent of need met:*** 94. ***Average financial aid package:*** $39,976. ***Average need-based loan:*** $6497. ***Average need-based gift aid:*** $30,133. ***Average non-need-based aid:*** $22,962. ***Average indebtedness upon graduation:*** $31,308. ***Financial aid deadline:*** 3/1.

APPLYING

Standardized Tests *Required for some:* SAT or ACT (for admission).

Required: essay or personal statement, high school transcript, 1 letter of recommendation. ***Recommended:*** interview.

CONTACT

Mr. Pat Walsh, Director of Admissions and Recruitment, Beloit College, 700 College Street, Beloit, WI 53511-5596. *Phone:* 608-561-9724. *Toll-free phone:* 800-9-BELOIT. *Fax:* 608-363-2075.
E-mail: walshpj@beloit.edu.

Bryant & Stratton College–Bayshore Campus

Glendale, Wisconsin

http://www.bryantstratton.edu/

CONTACT

Bryant & Stratton College–Bayshore Campus, 500 West Silver Spring Drive, Bayshore Town Center, Suite K340, Glendale, WI 53217.

Bryant & Stratton College–Milwaukee Campus

Milwaukee, Wisconsin

http://www.bryantstratton.edu/

CONTACT

Mr. Dan Basile, Director of Admissions, Bryant & Stratton College–Milwaukee Campus, 310 West Wisconsin Avenue, Suite 500 East, Milwaukee, WI 53203-2214. *Phone:* 414-276-5200.

Bryant & Stratton College–Wauwatosa Campus

Wauwatosa, Wisconsin

http://www.bryantstratton.edu/

CONTACT

Bryant & Stratton College–Wauwatosa Campus, 10950 West Potter Road, Wauwatosa, WI 53226. *Phone:* 414-302-7000 Ext. 502.

Cardinal Stritch University

Milwaukee, Wisconsin

http://www.stritch.edu/

- **Independent Roman Catholic** university, founded 1937
- **Suburban** 40-acre campus with easy access to Milwaukee
- **Endowment** $18.6 million
- **Coed** 1,534 undergraduate students, 79% full-time, 66% women, 34% men
- **Moderately difficult** entrance level, 82% of applicants were admitted

UNDERGRAD STUDENTS

1,205 full-time, 329 part-time. Students come from 28 states and territories; 39 other countries; 13% are from out of state; 19% Black or African American, non-Hispanic/Latino; 14% Hispanic/Latino; 3% Asian, non-Hispanic/Latino; 0.2% Native Hawaiian or other Pacific Islander, non-Hispanic/Latino; 0.5% American Indian or Alaska Native, non-Hispanic/Latino; 3% Two or more races, non-Hispanic/Latino; 3% Race/ethnicity unknown; 10% international; 13% transferred in; 19% live on campus.

Freshmen:

Admission: 774 applied, 631 admitted, 155 enrolled. ***Average high school GPA:*** 3.09. ***Test scores:*** ACT scores over 18: 86%; ACT scores over 24: 18%; ACT scores over 30: 2%.

Retention: 73% of full-time freshmen returned.

FACULTY

Total: 204, 40% full-time.

Student/faculty ratio: 15:1.

ACADEMICS

Calendar: semesters. *Degrees:* certificates, associate, bachelor's, master's, doctoral, post-master's, and postbachelor's certificates.

Special study options: academic remediation for entering students, accelerated degree program, adult/continuing education programs, advanced placement credit, cooperative education, distance learning, double majors, independent study, internships, off-campus study, part-time degree program, services for LD students, study abroad, summer session for credit.

Computers: 454 computers/terminals and 1,283 ports are available on campus for general student use. Students can access the following: computer help desk, free student e-mail accounts, online (class) grades, online (class) registration, online (class) schedules. Campuswide network is available. 100% of college-owned or -operated housing units are wired for high-speed Internet access. Wireless service is available via entire campus.

Library: Cardinal Stritch University Library. *Books:* 123,152 (physical), 146,127 (digital/electronic); *Serial titles:* 121 (physical), 71 (digital/electronic); *Databases:* 74. Weekly public service hours: 90.

STUDENT LIFE

Housing options: on-campus residence required for freshman year; coed. Campus housing is university owned and leased by the school. Freshman campus housing is guaranteed.

Activities and organizations: drama/theater group, choral group, Student Government, Student Programming Board, Hispanic Club, University Ministry, Black Student Union, national fraternities, national sororities.

Athletics Member NAIA. ***Intercollegiate sports:*** basketball M(s)/W(s), cross-country running M(s)/W(s), golf M(s)/W(s), soccer M(s)/W(s), softball W(s), tennis M(s)/W(s), track and field M(s)/W(s), volleyball M(s)/W(s).

Campus security: 24-hour emergency response devices and patrols, controlled dormitory access.

Student services: health clinic, personal/psychological counseling.

COSTS & FINANCIAL AID

Costs (2016–17) ***Comprehensive fee:*** $36,152 includes full-time tuition ($28,212) and room and board ($7940). Full-time tuition and fees vary according to degree level, program, and reciprocity agreements. Part-time tuition: $880 per credit. Part-time tuition and fees vary according to course load, degree level, program, and reciprocity agreements. ***Room and board:*** Room and board charges vary according to board plan and housing facility. ***Payment plan:*** installment. ***Waivers:*** employees or children of employees.

Financial Aid Of all full-time matriculated undergraduates who enrolled in 2016, 882 applied for aid, 753 were judged to have need, 89 had their need fully met. 380 Federal Work-Study jobs (averaging $2168). In 2016, 229 non-need-based awards were made. ***Average percent of need met:*** 67. ***Average financial aid package:*** $20,277. ***Average need-based loan:*** $4055. ***Average need-based gift aid:*** $16,610. ***Average non-need-based aid:*** $17,945. ***Average indebtedness upon graduation:*** $27,997.

APPLYING

Standardized Tests *Required for some:* SAT or ACT (for admission), TOEFL for international students.

Options: electronic application, deferred entrance.

Required for some: high school transcript, minimum 2.0 GPA.

Application deadlines: rolling (freshmen), rolling (transfers).

Notification: continuous (freshmen), continuous (transfers).

CONTACT

Sarah C. Blake, Associate Director of Admissions, Cardinal Stritch University, 6801 N. Yates Road, Milwaukee, WI 53217. *Phone:* 414-410-4052. *Toll-free phone:* 800-347-8822 Ext. 4040. *Fax:* 414-410-4058. *E-mail:* admissions@stritch.edu.

Carroll University

Waukesha, Wisconsin

http://www.carrollu.edu/

CONTACT

Mr. James Wiseman, Vice President of Enrollment, Carroll University, 100 North East Avenue, Waukesha, WI 53186-5593. *Phone:* 262-524-7221. *Toll-free phone:* 800-CARROLL. *Fax:* 262-524-7139. *E-mail:* info@carrollu.edu.

Carthage College

Kenosha, Wisconsin

http://www.carthage.edu/

- **Independent** comprehensive, founded 1847, affiliated with Evangelical Lutheran Church in America
- **Suburban** 72-acre campus with easy access to Chicago, Milwaukee
- **Endowment** $48.6 million
- **Coed** 2,660 undergraduate students, 84% full-time, 58% women, 42% men
- **Moderately difficult** entrance level, 77% of applicants were admitted

UNDERGRAD STUDENTS

2,233 full-time, 427 part-time. Students come from 31 states and territories; 16 other countries; 72% are from out of state; 3% transferred in; 68% live on campus.

Freshmen:

Admission: 4,687 applied, 3,611 admitted, 686 enrolled. ***Average high school GPA:*** 3.24. ***Test scores:*** SAT critical reading scores over 500: 73%; SAT math scores over 500: 75%; ACT scores over 18: 97%; SAT critical reading scores over 600: 32%; SAT math scores over 600: 37%; ACT scores over 24: 52%; SAT critical reading scores over 700: 7%; SAT math scores over 700: 7%; ACT scores over 30: 8%.

Retention: 75% of full-time freshmen returned.

FACULTY

Total: 137.

Student/faculty ratio: 15:1.

ACADEMICS

Calendar: 4-1-4. *Degrees:* bachelor's and master's.

Special study options: accelerated degree program, adult/continuing education programs, advanced placement credit, cooperative education, double majors, honors programs, independent study, internships, off-campus study, part-time degree program, services for LD students, student-designed majors, study abroad, summer session for credit. ***ROTC:*** Army (c), Air Force (c).

Unusual degree programs: 3-2 engineering with Case Western Reserve University, University of Wisconsin–Madison, University of Minnesota; occupational therapy with Washington University in St. Louis.

Computers: 250 computers/terminals and 400 ports are available on campus for general student use. Students can access the following: campus intranet, computer help desk, free student e-mail accounts, online (class) grades, online (class) registration, online (class) schedules. Campuswide network is available. 96% of college-owned or -operated housing units are wired for high-speed Internet access. Wireless service is available via entire campus.

Library: Hedberg Library.

STUDENT LIFE

Housing options: on-campus residence required through junior year; coed, men-only, women-only. Campus housing is university owned and leased by the school. Freshman campus housing is guaranteed.

Activities and organizations: drama/theater group, student-run newspaper, radio station, choral group, Residence Life Council, Alpha Lambda Delta, Circle K, Inter-Varsity Christian Fellowship, Pals-n-Partners, national fraternities, national sororities.

Athletics Member NCAA. All Division III. ***Intercollegiate sports:*** baseball M, basketball M/W, bowling M(c)/W(c), cross-country running M/W, football M, golf M/W, ice hockey M(c)/W(c), lacrosse M/W, soccer M/W, softball W, swimming and diving M/W, tennis M/W, track and field M/W, volleyball M/W, water polo W. ***Intramural sports:*** badminton M/W, basketball M/W, bowling W, cheerleading M/W, football M/W, racquetball M/W, rock climbing M/W, soccer M/W, softball M/W, table tennis M/W, tennis M/W, ultimate Frisbee M/W, volleyball M/W, weight lifting M/W.

Campus security: 24-hour emergency response devices and patrols, student patrols, late-night transport/escort service, controlled dormitory access.

Student services: health clinic, personal/psychological counseling.

COSTS & FINANCIAL AID

Costs (2017–18) ***Comprehensive fee:*** $53,550 includes full-time tuition ($41,950) and room and board ($11,600). Part-time tuition: $575 per credit. Part-time tuition and fees vary according to class time. ***Room and board:*** Room and board charges vary according to board plan and housing facility. ***Payment plan:*** installment. ***Waivers:*** minority students, children of alumni, and employees or children of employees.

Financial Aid Of all full-time matriculated undergraduates who enrolled in 2009, 2,172 applied for aid, 1,855 were judged to have need, 264 had their need fully met. 843 Federal Work-Study jobs (averaging $4000). In 2009, 571 non-need-based awards were made. ***Average percent of need met:*** 65. ***Average financial aid package:*** $18,268. ***Average need-based loan:*** $4266. ***Average need-based gift aid:*** $13,416. ***Average non-need-based aid:*** $9564. ***Average indebtedness upon graduation:*** $29,075.

APPLYING

Standardized Tests *Required:* SAT or ACT (for admission).

Options: electronic application, early admission, early action, deferred entrance.

Application fee: $25.

Required: high school transcript. ***Required for some:*** essay or personal statement, 2 letters of recommendation, interview. ***Recommended:*** essay or personal statement, interview.

Application deadlines: rolling (freshmen), rolling (transfers), 7/26 (early action).

Notification: continuous (freshmen), continuous (transfers), 9/15 (early action).

CONTACT

Mr. Bradley J. Andrews, Vice President for Enrollment and Student Life, Carthage College, 2001 Alford Park Drive, Kenosha, WI 53140. *Phone:* 262-551-6000. *Toll-free phone:* 800-351-4058. *Fax:* 262-551-5762. *E-mail:* admissions@carthage.edu.

Columbia College of Nursing

Glendale, Wisconsin

http://www.ccon.edu/

CONTACT

Columbia College of Nursing, 4425 North Port Washington Road, Glendale, WI 53212. *Phone:* 414-326-2336.

Concordia University Wisconsin

Mequon, Wisconsin

http://www.cuw.edu/

- **Independent** comprehensive, founded 1881, affiliated with Lutheran Church–Missouri Synod, part of Concordia University System
- **Suburban** 192-acre campus with easy access to Milwaukee
- **Coed** 4,338 undergraduate students, 69% full-time, 64% women, 36% men
- **Moderately difficult** entrance level, 69% of applicants were admitted

UNDERGRAD STUDENTS

3,005 full-time, 1,333 part-time. 24% are from out of state; 15% Black or African American, non-Hispanic/Latino; 2% Hispanic/Latino; 2% Asian, non-Hispanic/Latino; 0.1% Native Hawaiian or other Pacific Islander, non-Hispanic/Latino; 0.9% American Indian or Alaska Native, non-Hispanic/Latino; 3% Two or more races, non-Hispanic/Latino; 2% Race/ethnicity unknown; 2% international; 6% transferred in; 58% live on campus.

Freshmen:

Admission: 2,837 applied, 1,959 admitted, 627 enrolled. ***Average high school GPA:*** 3.46. ***Test scores:*** SAT critical reading scores over 500: 61%; SAT math scores over 500: 59%; SAT writing scores over 500: 43%; ACT scores over 18: 98%; SAT critical reading scores over 600: 13%; SAT math scores over 600: 22%; SAT writing scores over 600: 9%; ACT scores over 24: 44%; SAT writing scores over 700: 2%; ACT scores over 30: 7%.

Retention: 76% of full-time freshmen returned.

FACULTY

Total: 582, 34% full-time, 42% with terminal degrees.

Student/faculty ratio: 12:1.

ACADEMICS

Calendar: 4-1-4. *Degrees:* certificates, associate, bachelor's, master's, doctoral, and post-master's certificates.

Special study options: academic remediation for entering students, accelerated degree program, adult/continuing education programs, advanced placement credit, distance learning, double majors, English as a second language, independent study, internships, off-campus study, part-time degree program, services for LD students, student-designed majors, study abroad, summer session for credit.

Computers: Students can access the following: computer help desk, free student e-mail accounts. Campuswide network is available.

Library: Rinker Memorial Library.

STUDENT LIFE

Housing options: men-only, women-only. Campus housing is university owned. Freshman applicants given priority for college housing.

Activities and organizations: drama/theater group, student-run newspaper, radio station, choral group.

Athletics Member NCAA. All Division III. ***Intercollegiate sports:*** baseball M, basketball M/W, cross-country running M/W, football M, golf M/W, ice hockey M/W, soccer M/W, softball W, tennis M/W, track and field M/W, volleyball W, wrestling M. ***Intramural sports:*** basketball M/W, softball M/W, volleyball M/W.

Campus security: 24-hour patrols, student patrols, late-night transport/escort service, controlled dormitory access.

Student services: health clinic, personal/psychological counseling.

COSTS & FINANCIAL AID

Costs (2017–18) ***Comprehensive fee:*** $39,130 includes full-time tuition ($28,330), mandatory fees ($270), and room and board ($10,530). Full-time tuition and fees vary according to program. Part-time tuition and fees vary according to program. ***College room only:*** $7970. Room and board charges vary according to board plan.

Financial Aid Of all full-time matriculated undergraduates who enrolled in 2015, 2,545 applied for aid, 2,243 were judged to have need, 505 had their need fully met. In 2015, 430 non-need-based awards were made. ***Average percent of need met:*** 70. ***Average financial aid package:*** $20,416. ***Average need-based loan:*** $7015. ***Average need-based gift aid:*** $13,437. ***Average non-need-based aid:*** $11,007.

APPLYING

Standardized Tests *Required:* SAT or ACT (for admission).

Application fee: $35.

Required: high school transcript, minimum 2.0 GPA. ***Required for some:*** essay or personal statement, minimum 3.0 GPA, 3 letters of recommendation. ***Recommended:*** interview.

Application deadlines: 8/15 (freshmen), rolling (transfers).

Notification: continuous (freshmen).

CONTACT

Ms. Julie Schroeder, Concordia University Wisconsin, Admissions Office, 12800 North Lake Drive, Mequon, WI 53097. *Phone:* 262-243-4305 Ext. 4305. *Toll-free phone:* 888-628-9472. *E-mail:* admission@cuw.edu.

Edgewood College

Madison, Wisconsin

http://www.edgewood.edu/

- **Independent Roman Catholic** comprehensive, founded 1927
- **Urban** 55-acre campus
- **Endowment** $31.8 million
- **Coed** 1,661 undergraduate students, 87% full-time, 72% women, 28% men
- **Moderately difficult** entrance level, 78% of applicants were admitted

UNDERGRAD STUDENTS

1,450 full-time, 211 part-time. Students come from 18 states and territories; 24 other countries; 8% are from out of state; 3% Black or African American, non-Hispanic/Latino; 6% Hispanic/Latino; 3% Asian, non-Hispanic/Latino; 0.2% Native Hawaiian or other Pacific Islander, non-Hispanic/Latino; 0.2% American Indian or Alaska Native, non-Hispanic/Latino; 3% Two or more races, non-Hispanic/Latino; 3% Race/ethnicity unknown; 4% international; 10% transferred in; 34% live on campus.

Freshmen:

Admission: 1,035 applied, 808 admitted, 263 enrolled. ***Average high school GPA:*** 3.4. ***Test scores:*** ACT scores over 18: 95%; ACT scores over 24: 40%; ACT scores over 30: 3%.

Retention: 78% of full-time freshmen returned.

FACULTY

Total: 290, 56% full-time, 53% with terminal degrees.

Student/faculty ratio: 10:1.

ACADEMICS

Calendar: semesters. *Degrees:* certificates, bachelor's, master's, doctoral, and postbachelor's certificates.

Special study options: academic remediation for entering students, accelerated degree program, adult/continuing education programs, advanced placement credit, cooperative education, distance learning, double majors, honors programs, independent study, internships, off-campus study, part-time degree program, services for LD students, student-designed majors, study abroad, summer session for credit. ***ROTC:*** Army (c), Navy (c), Air Force (c).

Computers: 180 computers/terminals and 200 ports are available on campus for general student use. Students can access the following: campus intranet, computer help desk, free student e-mail accounts, online (class) grades, online (class) registration, online (class) schedules. Campuswide network is available. 100% of college-owned or -operated housing units are wired for high-speed Internet access. Wireless service is available via entire campus.

Library: Oscar Rennebohm Library. *Books:* 102,707 (physical), 135,379 (digital/electronic); *Serial titles:* 80 (physical), 31,600 (digital/electronic); *Databases:* 81. Weekly public service hours: 98.

STUDENT LIFE

Housing options: on-campus residence required through sophomore year; coed, cooperative, special housing for students with disabilities. Campus housing is university owned. Freshman campus housing is guaranteed.

Activities and organizations: drama/theater group, student-run newspaper, choral group, Circle K, Student Education Association, Student Government Association, Rotaract, Ambassadors.

Athletics Member NCAA. All Division III. ***Intercollegiate sports:*** baseball M, basketball M/W, cross-country running M/W, golf M/W, soccer M/W, softball W, tennis M/W, track and field M/W, volleyball W. ***Intramural sports:*** basketball M/W, soccer M/W, swimming and diving M/W, volleyball M/W.

Campus security: 24-hour emergency response devices and patrols, student patrols, late-night transport/escort service, controlled dormitory access, lighted pathways/sidewalks, Eagle Alert System, Public Address System, Safe Ride Shuttle, extensive video surveillance system.

Student services: health clinic, personal/psychological counseling.

COSTS & FINANCIAL AID

Costs (2016–17) ***Comprehensive fee:*** $37,400 includes full-time tuition ($27,530) and room and board ($9870). Full-time tuition and fees vary according to degree level. Part-time tuition: $866 per credit. Part-time tuition and fees vary according to course load and degree level. ***Room and board:*** Room and board charges vary according to housing facility. ***Payment plan:*** installment. ***Waivers:*** employees or children of employees.

Financial Aid Of all full-time matriculated undergraduates who enrolled in 2015, 1,277 applied for aid, 1,145 were judged to have need, 146 had their need fully met. 546 Federal Work-Study jobs (averaging $1992). 688 state and other part-time jobs (averaging $1930). In 2015, 263 non-need-based awards were made. ***Average percent of need met:*** 74. ***Average financial aid package:*** $20,707. ***Average need-based loan:*** $5558. ***Average need-based gift aid:*** $14,227. ***Average non-need-based aid:*** $6048. ***Average indebtedness upon graduation:*** $33,104.

APPLYING

Standardized Tests *Required:* SAT or ACT (for admission).

Options: electronic application, deferred entrance.

Application fee: $30.

Required: high school transcript, minimum 2.5 GPA, cumulative high school GPA of 2.5 on a 4.0 scale, a rank in the top 50% of high school graduating class and/or ACT Composite score of 18 or the equivalent SAT score. ***Required for some:*** essay or personal statement, 2 letters of recommendation, interview.

Application deadlines: 8/15 (freshmen), rolling (transfers).

Notification: continuous until 9/1 (freshmen), continuous (transfers).

CONTACT

Ms. Christine Benedict, Vice President for Enrollment Management, Admissions Office, Edgewood College, 1000 Edgewood College Drive, Madison, WI 53711-1997. *Phone:* 608-663-2294. *Toll-free phone:* 800-444-4861 Ext. 2294. *Fax:* 608-663-2214.
E-mail: admissions@edgewood.edu.

Herzing University

Brookfield, Wisconsin

http://www.herzing.edu/brookfield

CONTACT

Herzing University, 555 South Executive Drive, Brookfield, WI 53005. *Toll-free phone:* 800-596-0724.

Herzing University

Kenosha, Wisconsin

http://www.herzing.edu/kenosha

CONTACT

Herzing University, 4006 Washington Road, Kenosha, WI 53144. *Toll-free phone:* 800-596-0724.

Herzing University

Madison, Wisconsin

http://www.herzing.edu/madison/

CONTACT

Herzing University, 5218 East Terrace Drive, Madison, WI 53718. *Toll-free phone:* 800-596-0724.

Herzing University Online

Menomonee Falls, Wisconsin

http://www.herzingonline.edu/

CONTACT

Herzing University Online, W140N8917 Lilly Road, Menomonee Falls, WI 53051. *Toll-free phone:* 866-508-0748.

Lakeland University

Plymouth, Wisconsin

http://www.lakeland.edu/

CONTACT

Mr. Nick Spaeth, Director of Admissions, Lakeland University, PO Box 359, Nash Visitors Center, Sheboygan, WI 53082-0359. *Phone:* 920-565-1007. *Toll-free phone:* 800-569-2166. *Fax:* 920-565-1215. *E-mail:* admissions@lakeland.edu.

★ Lawrence University

Appleton, Wisconsin

http://www.lawrence.edu/

- **Independent** 4-year, founded 1847
- **Small-town** 84-acre campus
- **Coed** 1,532 undergraduate students, 98% full-time, 54% women, 46% men
- **Very difficult** entrance level, 63% of applicants were admitted

UNDERGRAD STUDENTS

1,503 full-time, 29 part-time. 71% are from out of state; 4% Black or African American, non-Hispanic/Latino; 8% Hispanic/Latino; 5% Asian, non-Hispanic/Latino; 0.1% Native Hawaiian or other Pacific Islander, non-Hispanic/Latino; 0.3% American Indian or Alaska Native, non-Hispanic/Latino; 3% Two or more races, non-Hispanic/Latino; 0.6% Race/ethnicity unknown; 11% international; 2% transferred in; 96% live on campus.

Freshmen:

Admission: 3,579 applied, 2,254 admitted, 374 enrolled. ***Average high school GPA:*** 3.66. ***Test scores:*** SAT critical reading scores over 500: 87%; SAT math scores over 500: 95%; SAT writing scores over 500: 90%; ACT scores over 18: 100%; SAT critical reading scores over 600: 66%; SAT math scores over 600: 72%; SAT writing scores over 600: 65%; ACT scores over 24: 87%; SAT critical reading scores over 700: 26%; SAT math scores over 700: 35%; SAT writing scores over 700: 23%; ACT scores over 30: 47%.

Retention: 91% of full-time freshmen returned.

FACULTY

Total: 201, 82% full-time, 86% with terminal degrees.

Student/faculty ratio: 9:1.

ACADEMICS

Calendar: trimesters. *Degree:* bachelor's.

Special study options: advanced placement credit, double majors, independent study, internships, off-campus study, part-time degree program, services for LD students, student-designed majors, study abroad.

Unusual degree programs: 3-2 engineering with Columbia University, Rensselaer Polytechnic Institute, Washington University in St. Louis; forestry with Duke University; occupational therapy with Washington University in St. Louis.

Computers: Students can access the following: campus intranet, computer help desk, free student e-mail accounts, online (class) grades, online (class) registration, online (class) schedules, online transcripts, financial aid, financial account information. Campuswide network is available. 100% of college-owned or -operated housing units are wired for high-speed Internet access. Wireless service is available via classrooms, computer centers, computer labs, dorm rooms, learning centers, libraries, student centers.

Library: Seeley G. Mudd Library.

STUDENT LIFE

Housing options: on-campus residence required through senior year; coed, men-only, women-only, cooperative, special housing for students with disabilities. Campus housing is university owned. Freshman campus housing is guaranteed.

Activities and organizations: drama/theater group, student-run newspaper, radio station, choral group, Lawrence Swing Dancers, Lawrence International, Outdoor Recreation Club, Sustainable Lawrence University Gardens (SLUG), Greenfire, national fraternities, national sororities.

Athletics Member NCAA. All Division III. ***Intercollegiate sports:*** baseball M, basketball M/W, crew M(c)/W(c), cross-country running M/W, fencing M/W, football M, golf M, ice hockey M/W(c), soccer M/W, softball W, swimming and diving M/W, tennis M/W, track and field M/W, ultimate Frisbee M(c)/W(c), volleyball M(c)/W. ***Intramural sports:*** badminton M/W, basketball M/W, fencing M/W, racquetball M/W, skiing (downhill) M/W, soccer M/W, softball M/W, table tennis M/W, tennis M/W, volleyball M/W, water polo M/W.

Campus security: 24-hour emergency response devices and patrols, student patrols, late-night transport/escort service, controlled dormitory access, evening patrols by trained security personnel.

Student services: health clinic, personal/psychological counseling.

COSTS & FINANCIAL AID

Costs (2017–18) ***Comprehensive fee:*** $56,133 includes full-time tuition ($45,801), mandatory fees ($300), and room and board ($10,032). ***College room only:*** $4989. ***Payment plan:*** installment. ***Waivers:*** employees or children of employees.

Financial Aid Of all full-time matriculated undergraduates who enrolled in 2016, 1,056 applied for aid, 887 were judged to have need, 450 had their need fully met. In 2016, 560 non-need-based awards were made. ***Average percent of need met:*** 93. ***Average financial aid package:*** $38,487. ***Average need-based loan:*** $5658. ***Average need-based gift aid:*** $31,617. ***Average non-need-based aid:*** $21,124. ***Average indebtedness upon graduation:*** $34,750.

APPLYING

Standardized Tests *Required for some:* English Language Proficiency Exam (SAT/TOEFL/IELTS/ACT).

Options: electronic application, early admission, early action, deferred entrance.

Required: essay or personal statement, high school transcript, 1 letter of recommendation. ***Required for some:*** audition for music majors. ***Recommended:*** minimum 3.0 GPA, interview.

CONTACT

Mr. Ken Anselment, Dean of Admissions and Financial Aid, Lawrence University, 711 East Boldt Way SPC 29, Appleton, WI 54911-5699. *Phone:* 920-832-6500. *Toll-free phone:* 800-227-0982. *Fax:* 920-832-6782. *E-mail:* ken.anselment@lawrence.edu.

Maranatha Baptist University

Watertown, Wisconsin

http://www.mbu.edu/

- **Independent Baptist** comprehensive, founded 1968
- **Small-town** 60-acre campus with easy access to Milwaukee
- **Coed** 905 undergraduate students, 70% full-time, 57% women, 43% men
- **Noncompetitive** entrance level, 69% of applicants were admitted

UNDERGRAD STUDENTS

633 full-time, 272 part-time. 73% are from out of state; 1% Black or African American, non-Hispanic/Latino; 3% Hispanic/Latino; 1% Asian, non-Hispanic/Latino; 0.3% Native Hawaiian or other Pacific Islander, non-Hispanic/Latino; 0.1% American Indian or Alaska Native, non-Hispanic/Latino; 4% Two or more races, non-Hispanic/Latino; 2% Race/ethnicity unknown; 1% international; 5% transferred in; 69% live on campus.

Freshmen:

Admission: 338 applied, 232 admitted, 179 enrolled. ***Test scores:*** SAT critical reading scores over 500: 42%; SAT math scores over 500: 54%; SAT writing scores over 500: 42%; ACT scores over 18: 92%; SAT critical reading scores over 600: 25%; SAT math scores over 600: 4%; SAT writing scores over 600: 8%; ACT scores over 24: 42%; SAT math scores over 700: 4%; ACT scores over 30: 6%.

Retention: 66% of full-time freshmen returned.

FACULTY

Total: 110, 35% full-time, 34% with terminal degrees.

Student/faculty ratio: 13:1.

ACADEMICS

Calendar: semesters. *Degrees:* certificates, associate, bachelor's, master's, and doctoral.

Special study options: academic remediation for entering students, advanced placement credit, distance learning, double majors, independent study, internships, off-campus study, part-time degree program, study abroad, summer session for credit. ***ROTC:*** Army (b), Air Force (c).

Computers: Students can access the following: campus intranet, computer help desk, free student e-mail accounts, online (class) grades, online (class) registration, online (class) schedules. Campuswide network is available. 100% of college-owned or -operated housing units are wired for high-speed Internet access. Wireless service is available via entire campus.

Library: Cedarholm Library and Resource Center.

STUDENT LIFE

Housing options: on-campus residence required through senior year; men-only, women-only. Campus housing is university owned. Freshman campus housing is guaranteed.

Activities and organizations: drama/theater group, choral group.

Athletics Member NCAA, NCCAA. All NCAA Division III. ***Intercollegiate sports:*** baseball M, basketball M/W, cross-country running M/W, football M, soccer M/W, softball W, volleyball W, wrestling M. ***Intramural sports:*** basketball M/W.

Campus security: student patrols, late-night transport/escort service, controlled dormitory access.

Student services: health clinic, personal/psychological counseling.

COSTS & FINANCIAL AID

Costs (2017–18) ***Comprehensive fee:*** $20,980 includes full-time tuition ($13,100), mandatory fees ($1160), and room and board ($6720). Full-time tuition and fees vary according to location and program. Part-time tuition: $546 per credit hour. Part-time tuition and fees vary according to course load. ***Payment plan:*** installment. ***Waivers:*** employees or children of employees.

Financial Aid Of all full-time matriculated undergraduates who enrolled in 2015, 523 applied for aid, 478 were judged to have need, 53 had their need fully met. In 2015, 55 non-need-based awards were made. ***Average percent of need met:*** 52. ***Average financial aid package:*** $10,139. ***Average need-based loan:*** $4129. ***Average need-based gift aid:*** $6718. ***Average non-need-based aid:*** $3962. ***Average indebtedness upon graduation:*** $20,965.

APPLYING

Standardized Tests *Required:* SAT or ACT (for admission).

Options: electronic application.

Application fee: $50.

Required: essay or personal statement, high school transcript, 4 letters of recommendation.

CONTACT

Dr. James Harrison, Director of Admissions, Maranatha Baptist University, 745 West Main Street, Watertown, WI 53094. *Phone:* 920-206-2327. *Toll-free phone:* 800-622-2947. *Fax:* 920-261-9109. *E-mail:* admissions@mbbc.edu.

Marian University

Fond du Lac, Wisconsin

http://www.marianuniversity.edu/

- **Independent Roman Catholic** comprehensive, founded 1936
- **Small-town** 78-acre campus with easy access to Milwaukee
- **Endowment** $11.7 million
- **Coed** 1,487 undergraduate students, 80% full-time, 70% women, 30% men
- **Moderately difficult** entrance level, 77% of applicants were admitted

UNDERGRAD STUDENTS

1,184 full-time, 303 part-time. Students come from 23 states and territories; 12 other countries; 16% are from out of state; 6% Black or

African American, non-Hispanic/Latino; 6% Hispanic/Latino; 1% Asian, non-Hispanic/Latino; 0.2% Native Hawaiian or other Pacific Islander, non-Hispanic/Latino; 0.5% American Indian or Alaska Native, non-Hispanic/Latino; 0.6% Two or more races, non-Hispanic/Latino; 2% Race/ethnicity unknown; 2% international; 6% transferred in; 24% live on campus.

Freshmen:
Admission: 1,245 applied, 961 admitted, 267 enrolled. ***Average high school GPA:*** 3. ***Test scores:*** ACT scores over 18: 74%; ACT scores over 24: 23%; ACT scores over 30: 1%.
Retention: 70% of full-time freshmen returned.

FACULTY
Total: 232, 41% full-time, 37% with terminal degrees.
Student/faculty ratio: 12:1.

ACADEMICS
Calendar: semesters. *Degrees:* certificates, bachelor's, master's, doctoral, post-master's, and postbachelor's certificates.
Special study options: academic remediation for entering students, accelerated degree program, advanced placement credit, cooperative education, distance learning, double majors, honors programs, independent study, internships, part-time degree program, services for LD students, student-designed majors, study abroad, summer session for credit. ***ROTC:*** Army (c).
Computers: 500 computers/terminals are available on campus for general student use. Students can access the following: campus intranet, computer help desk, free student e-mail accounts, online (class) grades, online (class) registration, online (class) schedules. Campuswide network is available. 100% of college-owned or -operated housing units are wired for high-speed Internet access. Wireless service is available via entire campus.
Library: Cardinal Meyer Library plus 1 other. *Books:* 210,079 (physical), 147,236 (digital/electronic); *Databases:* 1,805.

STUDENT LIFE
Housing options: on-campus residence required through sophomore year; coed, special housing for students with disabilities. Campus housing is university owned. Freshman campus housing is guaranteed.
Activities and organizations: student-run newspaper, choral group, Student Senate, Student Nurses Association, Student Education Association, Science and Math Association, Business Club, national sororities.
Athletics Member NCAA. All Division III. ***Intercollegiate sports:*** baseball M, basketball M/W, cross-country running M/W, golf M/W, ice hockey M/W, lacrosse M, soccer M/W, softball W, tennis M/W, track and field M/W, volleyball M/W. ***Intramural sports:*** badminton M/W, basketball M/W, bowling M/W, football M, skiing (downhill) M/W, softball M, tennis M/W, volleyball M/W.
Campus security: 24-hour emergency response devices and patrols, student patrols, late-night transport/escort service, controlled dormitory access.
Student services: health clinic, personal/psychological counseling.

COSTS & FINANCIAL AID
Costs (2017–18) ***One-time required fee:*** $100. ***Comprehensive fee:*** $34,370 includes full-time tuition ($26,950), mandatory fees ($420), and room and board ($7000). Full-time tuition and fees vary according to course load and program. Part-time tuition: $450 per credit hour. Part-time tuition and fees vary according to course load and program. ***College room only:*** $4220. Room and board charges vary according to board plan. ***Payment plan:*** installment. ***Waivers:*** senior citizens and employees or children of employees.
Financial Aid Of all full-time matriculated undergraduates who enrolled in 2015, 1,271 applied for aid, 1,176 were judged to have need, 66 had their need fully met. 146 Federal Work-Study jobs (averaging $443). 342 state and other part-time jobs (averaging $1465). In 2015, 87 non-need-based awards were made. ***Average percent of need met:*** 60. ***Average financial aid package:*** $16,769. ***Average need-based loan:*** $3444. ***Average need-based gift aid:*** $12,996. ***Average non-need-based aid:*** $6038. ***Average indebtedness upon graduation:*** $30,565.

APPLYING
Standardized Tests *Required:* SAT or ACT (for admission). *Recommended:* ACT (for admission).
Options: electronic application, deferred entrance.
Application fee: $20.
Required: high school transcript. ***Required for some:*** interview. ***Recommended:*** interview.
Application deadlines: rolling (freshmen), rolling (transfers).
Notification: 8/15 (freshmen), continuous until 8/15 (transfers).

CONTACT
Shannon LaLuzerne, Dean of Admission, Marian University, 45 S. National Avenue, Fond du Lac, WI 54935-4699. *Phone:* 920-923-7650. *Toll-free phone:* 800-2-MARIAN. *E-mail:* admission@marianuniversity.edu.

Marquette University
Milwaukee, Wisconsin
http://www.marquette.edu/

- **Independent Roman Catholic (Jesuit)** university, founded 1881
- **Urban** 107-acre campus with easy access to Milwaukee
- **Endowment** $551.6 million
- **Coed**
- **Moderately difficult** entrance level

FACULTY
Student/faculty ratio: 15:1.

ACADEMICS
Calendar: semesters. *Degrees:* bachelor's, master's, doctoral, post-master's, and postbachelor's certificates.
Library: Raynor Memorial Libraries plus 1 other. *Books:* 1.8 million (physical), 3,492 (digital/electronic); *Serial titles:* 1,596 (physical), 46,519 (digital/electronic); *Databases:* 231. Weekly public service hours: 166; study areas open 24 hours, 5-7 days a week; students can reserve study rooms.

STUDENT LIFE
Housing options: on-campus residence required through sophomore year; coed, men-only, women-only, cooperative, special housing for students with disabilities. Campus housing is university owned. Freshman campus housing is guaranteed.
Activities and organizations: drama/theater group, student-run newspaper, radio and television station, choral group, Student Government, club sports, community service organizations, band/jazz/orchestra, Residence Hall Association, national fraternities, national sororities.
Athletics Member NCAA. All Division I.
Campus security: 24-hour emergency response devices and patrols, student patrols, late-night transport/escort service, 24-hour desk attendants in residence halls.
Student services: health clinic, personal/psychological counseling.

COSTS & FINANCIAL AID
Costs (2016–17) ***Comprehensive fee:*** $49,910 includes full-time tuition ($38,000), mandatory fees ($470), and room and board ($11,440). Full-time tuition and fees vary according to course load and program. Part-time tuition: $995 per credit. Part-time tuition and fees vary according to program. ***College room only:*** $7420. Room and board charges vary according to housing facility.
Financial Aid Of all full-time matriculated undergraduates who enrolled in 2016, 5,641 applied for aid, 4,477 were judged to have need, 1,189 had their need fully met. In 2016, 3202 non-need-based awards were made. ***Average percent of need met:*** 80. ***Average financial aid package:*** $27,906. ***Average need-based loan:*** $7646. ***Average need-based gift aid:*** $20,324. ***Average non-need-based aid:*** $11,877. ***Average indebtedness upon graduation:*** $35,421.

APPLYING
Standardized Tests *Required:* SAT or ACT (for admission).
Options: electronic application, deferred entrance.
Required: essay or personal statement, high school transcript, minimum 2.5 GPA. ***Recommended:*** minimum 3.4 GPA.

CONTACT
Ms. Jean Burke, Interim Dean of Admissions, Marquette University, PO Box 1881, Milwaukee, WI 53201-1881. *Phone:* 414-288-7004. *Toll-free phone:* 800-222-6544. *Fax:* 414-288-3764.
E-mail: admissions@marquette.edu.

Milwaukee Institute of Art and Design

Milwaukee, Wisconsin

http://www.miad.edu/

- **Independent** 4-year, founded 1974
- **Urban** campus with easy access to Milwaukee
- **Coed** 630 undergraduate students, 98% full-time, 55% women, 45% men
- **Moderately difficult** entrance level, 53% of applicants were admitted

UNDERGRAD STUDENTS
617 full-time, 13 part-time. 33% are from out of state; 7% Black or African American, non-Hispanic/Latino; 14% Hispanic/Latino; 3% Asian, non-Hispanic/Latino; 0.2% Native Hawaiian or other Pacific Islander, non-Hispanic/Latino; 0.5% American Indian or Alaska Native, non-Hispanic/Latino; 6% Two or more races, non-Hispanic/Latino; 2% Race/ethnicity unknown; 1% international; 7% transferred in.

Freshmen:
Admission: 921 applied, 492 admitted, 174 enrolled. ***Average high school GPA:*** 3.04.
Retention: 81% of full-time freshmen returned.

FACULTY
Student/faculty ratio: 15:1.

ACADEMICS
Calendar: semesters. *Degree:* bachelor's.
Special study options: academic remediation for entering students, adult/continuing education programs, advanced placement credit, cooperative education, double majors, independent study, internships, off-campus study, services for LD students, study abroad, summer session for credit.
Computers: Campuswide network is available.

STUDENT LIFE
Housing options: on-campus residence required through sophomore year; coed. Campus housing is provided by a third party. Freshman applicants given priority for college housing.
Activities and organizations: drama/theater group.
Campus security: 24-hour emergency response devices, late-night transport/escort service.
Student services: health clinic, personal/psychological counseling.

COSTS & FINANCIAL AID
Costs (2017–18) ***Tuition:*** $34,820 full-time. ***Required fees:*** $1700 full-time. ***Room only:*** $7730. ***Payment plan:*** installment. ***Waivers:*** employees or children of employees.
Financial Aid Of all full-time matriculated undergraduates who enrolled in 2008, 566 applied for aid, 530 were judged to have need, 58 had their need fully met. In 2008, 81 non-need-based awards were made. ***Average percent of need met:*** 68. ***Average financial aid package:*** $19,455. ***Average need-based loan:*** $6236. ***Average need-based gift aid:*** $12,888. ***Average non-need-based aid:*** $9611. ***Average indebtedness upon graduation:*** $24,162. ***Financial aid deadline:*** 2/15.

APPLYING
Options: electronic application, deferred entrance.
Required: high school transcript, portfolio. ***Recommended:*** essay or personal statement, minimum 2.0 GPA, interview.
Application deadlines: rolling (freshmen), rolling (transfers).

CONTACT
David Sigman, Director of Admissions, Milwaukee Institute of Art and Design, 273 East Erie Street, Milwaukee, WI 53202. *Phone:* 414-847-3200. *Toll-free phone:* 888-749-MIAD. *Fax:* 414-291-8077. *E-mail:* admissions@miad.edu.

Milwaukee School of Engineering

Milwaukee, Wisconsin

http://www.msoe.edu/

- **Independent** comprehensive, founded 1903
- **Urban** 22-acre campus
- **Endowment** $58.7 million
- **Coed, primarily men** 2,675 undergraduate students, 96% full-time, 26% women, 74% men
- **Moderately difficult** entrance level, 66% of applicants were admitted

UNDERGRAD STUDENTS
2,561 full-time, 114 part-time. Students come from 37 states and territories; 29 other countries; 35% are from out of state; 2% Black or African American, non-Hispanic/Latino; 5% Hispanic/Latino; 4% Asian, non-Hispanic/Latino; 0.1% Native Hawaiian or other Pacific Islander, non-Hispanic/Latino; 0.2% American Indian or Alaska Native, non-Hispanic/Latino; 2% Two or more races, non-Hispanic/Latino; 8% Race/ethnicity unknown; 11% international; 8% transferred in; 30% live on campus.

Freshmen:
Admission: 2,686 applied, 1,781 admitted, 555 enrolled. ***Average high school GPA:*** 3.62. ***Test scores:*** SAT critical reading scores over 500: 94%; SAT math scores over 500: 100%; ACT scores over 18: 100%; SAT critical reading scores over 600: 25%; SAT math scores over 600: 69%; ACT scores over 24: 98%; SAT critical reading scores over 700: 6%; SAT math scores over 700: 13%; ACT scores over 30: 32%.
Retention: 83% of full-time freshmen returned.

FACULTY
Total: 260, 53% full-time, 58% with terminal degrees.
Student/faculty ratio: 16:1.

ACADEMICS
Calendar: quarters. *Degrees:* bachelor's and master's.
Special study options: academic remediation for entering students, adult/continuing education programs, advanced placement credit, double majors, English as a second language, honors programs, independent study, internships, part-time degree program, services for LD students, study abroad, summer session for credit. ***ROTC:*** Army (c), Navy (c), Air Force (c).
Computers: 50 computers/terminals are available on campus for general student use. Students can access the following: campus intranet, computer help desk, free student e-mail accounts, online (class) grades, online (class) registration, online (class) schedules. Campuswide network is available. 100% of college-owned or -operated housing units are wired for high-speed Internet access. Wireless service is available via entire campus.
Library: Walter Schroeder. *Books:* 68,970 (physical), 305,378 (digital/electronic); *Serial titles:* 2,000 (physical), 2,431 (digital/electronic); *Databases:* 98. Weekly public service hours: 96; students can reserve study rooms.

STUDENT LIFE
Housing options: on-campus residence required through sophomore year; coed, special housing for students with disabilities. Campus housing is university owned. Freshman campus housing is guaranteed.
Activities and organizations: drama/theater group, student-run radio station, choral group, Student Union Board, Greek Council, Student Government Association, Residence Hall Association, Intervarsity Christian Fellowship, national fraternities, national sororities.
Athletics Member NCAA. All Division III. ***Intercollegiate sports:*** baseball M, basketball M/W, cheerleading M/W, crew M/W, cross-country running M/W, golf M, ice hockey M, lacrosse M, soccer M/W, softball W, tennis M/W, track and field M/W, volleyball M/W, wrestling M. ***Intramural sports:*** badminton M(c)/W(c), basketball M/W, bowling M(c)/W(c), fencing M(c)/W(c), football M/W, rugby M(c), soccer M/W, softball M/W, ultimate Frisbee M(c)/W(c), volleyball M/W, weight lifting M(c)/W(c).
Campus security: 24-hour emergency response devices and patrols, late-night transport/escort service, controlled dormitory access.
Student services: health clinic, personal/psychological counseling, women's center.

COSTS & FINANCIAL AID
Costs (2017–18) ***Comprehensive fee:*** $48,531 includes full-time tuition ($37,719), mandatory fees ($1710), and room and board ($9102). Full-time tuition and fees vary according to course load. Part-time tuition: $655 per credit hour. Part-time tuition and fees vary according to course load. ***Required fees:*** $420 per credit hour part-time. ***College room only:*** $5718. Room and board charges vary according to board plan and housing facility. ***Payment plan:*** installment. ***Waivers:*** employees or children of employees.

Financial Aid Of all full-time matriculated undergraduates who enrolled in 2015, 2,123 applied for aid, 1,919 were judged to have need, 416 had their need fully met. 269 Federal Work-Study jobs (averaging $1120). In 2015, 404 non-need-based awards were made. ***Average percent of need met:*** 76. ***Average financial aid package:*** $27,296. ***Average need-based loan:*** $4279. ***Average need-based gift aid:*** $23,666. ***Average non-need-based aid:*** $14,232. ***Average indebtedness upon graduation:*** $38,745.

APPLYING
Standardized Tests *Required:* SAT or ACT (for admission).

Options: electronic application, deferred entrance.

Required: high school transcript. ***Required for some:*** essay or personal statement, interview.

Application deadlines: 1/1 (freshmen), 1/1 (transfers).

Notification: continuous until 10/1 (freshmen), continuous until 10/1 (transfers).

CONTACT
Seandra Mitchell, Director, Undergraduate Admission, Milwaukee School of Engineering, 1025 N. Broadway, Milwaukee, WI 53202. *Phone:* 414-277-6762. *Toll-free phone:* 800-332-6763. *E-mail:* mitchell@msoe.edu.

Mount Mary University

Milwaukee, Wisconsin

http://www.mtmary.edu/

- **Independent Roman Catholic** comprehensive, founded 1913
- **Urban** 80-acre campus with easy access to Milwaukee
- **Endowment** $17.0 million
- **Undergraduate: women only; graduate: coed** 807 undergraduate students, 88% full-time, 99% women, 1% men
- **Moderately difficult** entrance level, 56% of applicants were admitted

UNDERGRAD STUDENTS
714 full-time, 93 part-time. Students come from 14 states and territories; 11 other countries; 7% are from out of state; 17% Black or African American, non-Hispanic/Latino; 16% Hispanic/Latino; 8% Asian, non-Hispanic/Latino; 0.1% American Indian or Alaska Native, non-Hispanic/Latino; 4% Two or more races, non-Hispanic/Latino; 0.4% Race/ethnicity unknown; 2% international; 10% transferred in; 30% live on campus.

Freshmen:
Admission: 689 applied, 388 admitted, 118 enrolled. ***Average high school GPA:*** 3.17. ***Test scores:*** ACT scores over 18: 79%; ACT scores over 24: 24%; ACT scores over 30: 2%.

Retention: 77% of full-time freshmen returned.

FACULTY
Total: 186, 33% full-time, 50% with terminal degrees.

Student/faculty ratio: 12:1.

ACADEMICS
Calendar: semesters. *Degrees:* bachelor's, master's, doctoral, post-master's, and postbachelor's certificates.

Special study options: academic remediation for entering students, accelerated degree program, advanced placement credit, double majors, honors programs, independent study, internships, part-time degree program, services for LD students, student-designed majors, study abroad, summer session for credit.

Unusual degree programs: 3-2 occupational therapy, public health.

Computers: 177 computers/terminals and 10 ports are available on campus for general student use. Students can access the following: campus intranet, computer help desk, free student e-mail accounts, online (class) grades, online (class) registration, online (class) schedules. Campuswide network is available. 100% of college-owned or -operated housing units are wired for high-speed Internet access. Wireless service is available via entire campus.

Library: The Patrick and Beatrice Haggerty Library. *Books:* 65,458 (physical), 130,464 (digital/electronic); *Serial titles:* 5,483 (physical), 160,422 (digital/electronic); *Databases:* 89. Students can reserve study rooms.

STUDENT LIFE
Housing options: on-campus residence required for freshman year; women-only. Campus housing is university owned. Freshman applicants given priority for college housing.

Activities and organizations: student-run newspaper, choral group, Programming and Activities Council, Student Government Association, International Club, Caroline Hall Council, Department Affiliated Clubs.

Athletics Member NCAA. All Division III. ***Intercollegiate sports:*** basketball W, cross-country running W, golf W, soccer W, softball W, tennis W, volleyball W.

Campus security: 24-hour emergency response devices and patrols, late-night transport/escort service, controlled dormitory access.

Student services: personal/psychological counseling.

COSTS & FINANCIAL AID
Costs (2017–18) ***Comprehensive fee:*** $38,040 includes full-time tuition ($28,940), mandatory fees ($570), and room and board ($8530). Full-time tuition and fees vary according to degree level and program. Part-time tuition: $860 per credit. Part-time tuition and fees vary according to course load, degree level, and program. ***Required fees:*** $350 per year part-time. ***Room and board:*** Room and board charges vary according to board plan. ***Payment plan:*** installment. ***Waivers:*** senior citizens and employees or children of employees.

Financial Aid Of all full-time matriculated undergraduates who enrolled in 2016, 677 applied for aid, 639 were judged to have need, 55 had their need fully met. 97 Federal Work-Study jobs (averaging $1442). 114 state and other part-time jobs (averaging $1756). In 2016, 45 non-need-based awards were made. ***Average percent of need met:*** 71. ***Average financial aid package:*** $23,785. ***Average need-based loan:*** $4532. ***Average need-based gift aid:*** $18,915. ***Average non-need-based aid:*** $12,425. ***Average indebtedness upon graduation:*** $27,811.

APPLYING
Standardized Tests *Required:* SAT or ACT (for admission).

Options: electronic application, deferred entrance.

Required: high school transcript. ***Required for some:*** essay or personal statement, 1 letter of recommendation. ***Recommended:*** minimum 2.5 GPA.

Application deadlines: rolling (freshmen), rolling (transfers).

Notification: continuous (freshmen), continuous (transfers).

CONTACT
Liz Saffold, Admission Counselor Assistant/Receptionist, Mount Mary University, 2900 North Menomonee River Parkway, Milwaukee, WI 53222. *Phone:* 414-930-3000 Ext. 219. *Toll-free phone:* 800-321-6265. *Fax:* 414-256-0180. *E-mail:* mmu-admiss@mtmary.edu.

Northland College

Ashland, Wisconsin

http://www.northland.edu/

- **Independent** 4-year, founded 1892, affiliated with United Church of Christ
- **Small-town** 130-acre campus
- **Endowment** $22.9 million
- **Coed** 582 undergraduate students, 96% full-time, 51% women, 49% men
- **Moderately difficult** entrance level, 54% of applicants were admitted

UNDERGRAD STUDENTS
560 full-time, 22 part-time. Students come from 35 states and territories; 3 other countries; 50% are from out of state; 1% Black or African American, non-Hispanic/Latino; 5% Hispanic/Latino; 0.4% Asian, non-Hispanic/Latino; 3% American Indian or Alaska Native, non-Hispanic/Latino; 1% Two or more races, non-Hispanic/Latino; 3% Race/ethnicity unknown; 3% international; 6% transferred in; 75% live on campus.

Freshmen:
Admission: 1,335 applied, 721 admitted, 168 enrolled. ***Average high school GPA:*** 3.3. ***Test scores:*** ACT scores over 18: 95%; ACT scores over 24: 47%; ACT scores over 30: 8%.
Retention: 77% of full-time freshmen returned.

FACULTY
Total: 65, 82% full-time, 72% with terminal degrees.
Student/faculty ratio: 10:1.

ACADEMICS
Calendar: 4-4-1. *Degree:* bachelor's.
Special study options: advanced placement credit, double majors, honors programs, independent study, internships, off-campus study, part-time degree program, services for LD students, student-designed majors, study abroad, summer session for credit.
Unusual degree programs: 3-2 engineering with Washington University in St. Louis.
Computers: 125 computers/terminals are available on campus for general student use. Students can access the following: campus intranet, computer help desk, free student e-mail accounts, online (class) grades, online (class) registration, online (class) schedules. Campuswide network is available. 100% of college-owned or -operated housing units are wired for high-speed Internet access. Wireless service is available via entire campus.
Library: Dexter Library. *Books:* 75,000 (physical); *Serial titles:* 82 (physical), 50 (digital/electronic); *Databases:* 40. Weekly public service hours: 86; students can reserve study rooms.

STUDENT LIFE
Housing options: on-campus residence required through junior year; coed, women-only, special housing for students with disabilities. Campus housing is university owned. Freshman campus housing is guaranteed.
Activities and organizations: drama/theater group, student-run newspaper, radio station, choral group, Northland Volunteer Program, Northland College Student Association, Native American Student Association, Environmental Council, SAAC (Student Athlete Organization).
Athletics Member NCAA. All Division III. ***Intercollegiate sports:*** baseball M, basketball M/W, cross-country running M/W, golf M/W, ice hockey M/W, lacrosse M/W, soccer M/W, softball W, volleyball W.
Campus security: 24-hour emergency response devices and patrols, late-night transport/escort service, controlled dormitory access.
Student services: health clinic, personal/psychological counseling.

COSTS & FINANCIAL AID
Costs (2017–18) ***Comprehensive fee:*** $44,043 includes full-time tuition ($33,640), mandatory fees ($1517), and room and board ($8886). Full-time tuition and fees vary according to course load. Part-time tuition: $650 per credit. Part-time tuition and fees vary according to course load. ***College room only:*** $4069. Room and board charges vary according to board plan and housing facility. ***Payment plan:*** installment. ***Waivers:*** employees or children of employees.
Financial Aid Of all full-time matriculated undergraduates who enrolled in 2016, 517 applied for aid, 466 were judged to have need, 111 had their need fully met. 266 Federal Work-Study jobs (averaging $1649). 236 state and other part-time jobs (averaging $1572). In 2016, 82 non-need-based awards were made. ***Average percent of need met:*** 85. ***Average financial aid package:*** $37,720. ***Average need-based loan:*** $4773. ***Average need-based gift aid:*** $23,487. ***Average non-need-based aid:*** $18,605. ***Average indebtedness upon graduation:*** $34,144.

APPLYING
Standardized Tests *Required:* SAT or ACT (for admission). *Required for some:* SAT (for admission), ACT (for admission), SAT or ACT (for admission).
Options: electronic application, deferred entrance.
Required: high school transcript. ***Recommended:*** minimum 2.0 GPA.
Application deadlines: rolling (freshmen), rolling (transfers).
Notification: continuous (freshmen), continuous (transfers).

CONTACT
Teege Mettille, Executive Director of Admissions, Northland College, 1411 Ellis Avenue, Ashland, WI 54806. *Phone:* 715-682-1224. *Toll-free phone:* 800-753-1840 (in-state); 800-753-1040 (out-of-state). *Fax:* 715-682-1258. *E-mail:* admit@northland.edu.

Rasmussen College Green Bay

Green Bay, Wisconsin

http://www.rasmussen.edu/

- **Proprietary** 4-year, part of Rasmussen College System
- **Suburban** campus
- **Coed** 449 undergraduate students, 53% full-time, 82% women, 18% men
- **Minimally difficult** entrance level, 81% of applicants were admitted

UNDERGRAD STUDENTS
238 full-time, 211 part-time.

Freshmen:
Admission: 31 applied, 25 admitted, 27 enrolled.

FACULTY
Total: 53, 23% full-time.
Student/faculty ratio: 22:1.

ACADEMICS
Calendar: quarters. *Degrees:* certificates, diplomas, associate, and bachelor's.
Special study options: academic remediation for entering students, accelerated degree program, adult/continuing education programs, distance learning, double majors, internships, part-time degree program, summer session for credit.
Computers: 137 computers/terminals are available on campus for general student use. Students can access the following: computer help desk, free student e-mail accounts, online (class) grades, online (class) schedules. Campuswide network is available. Wireless service is available via entire campus.
Library: Rasmussen College Library - Green Bay.

STUDENT LIFE
Housing options: college housing not available.

COSTS
Costs (2017–18) ***Tuition:*** $11,055 full-time. Full-time tuition and fees vary according to course level, course load, degree level, location, and program. Part-time tuition and fees vary according to course level, course load, degree level, location, and program. No tuition increase for student's term of enrollment. ***Required fees:*** $1695 full-time. ***Payment plans:*** installment, deferred payment. ***Waivers:*** employees or children of employees.

APPLYING
Standardized Tests *Required:* institutional exam (for admission).
Options: electronic application, early admission, deferred entrance.
Required: high school transcript, minimum 2.0 GPA. ***Required for some:*** interview.
Application deadlines: rolling (freshmen), rolling (transfers).

CONTACT
Ms. Susan Hammerstrom, Director of Admissions, Rasmussen College Green Bay, 904 South Taylor Street, Suite 100, Green Bay, WI 54303. *Phone:* 920-593-8400. *Toll-free phone:* 888-549-6755. *E-mail:* susan.hammerstrom@rasmussen.edu.

Rasmussen College Wausau

Wausau, Wisconsin

http://www.rasmussen.edu/

- **Proprietary** 4-year, part of Rasmussen College System
- **Suburban** campus
- **Coed** 254 undergraduate students, 62% full-time, 76% women, 24% men
- **Minimally difficult** entrance level, 93% of applicants were admitted

UNDERGRAD STUDENTS
158 full-time, 96 part-time.

Freshmen:
Admission: 15 applied, 14 admitted, 14 enrolled.

FACULTY
Total: 48, 17% full-time.
Student/faculty ratio: 22:1.

ACADEMICS
Calendar: quarters. *Degrees:* certificates, diplomas, associate, and bachelor's.
Special study options: academic remediation for entering students, accelerated degree program, adult/continuing education programs, distance learning, double majors, internships, part-time degree program, summer session for credit.
Computers: 74 computers/terminals are available on campus for general student use. Students can access the following: computer help desk, free student e-mail accounts, online (class) grades, online (class) schedules. Campuswide network is available. Wireless service is available via entire campus.
Library: Rasmussen College Library - Wausau.

STUDENT LIFE
Housing options: college housing not available.

COSTS
Costs (2017–18) ***Tuition:*** $11,055 full-time. Full-time tuition and fees vary according to course level, course load, degree level, location, and program. Part-time tuition and fees vary according to course level, course load, degree level, location, and program. No tuition increase for student's term of enrollment. ***Required fees:*** $1695 full-time. ***Payment plans:*** installment, deferred payment. ***Waivers:*** employees or children of employees.

APPLYING
Standardized Tests *Required:* institutional exam (for admission).
Options: electronic application, early admission, deferred entrance.
Required: high school transcript, minimum 2.0 GPA. ***Required for some:*** interview.
Application deadlines: rolling (freshmen), rolling (transfers).

CONTACT
Ms. Susan Hammerstrom, Director of Admissions, Rasmussen College Wausau, 1101 Westwood Drive, Wausau, WI 54401. *Phone:* 715-841-8000. *Toll-free phone:* 888-549-6755.
E-mail: susan.hammerstrom@rasmussen.edu.

Ripon College
Ripon, Wisconsin
http://www.ripon.edu/

- **Independent** 4-year, founded 1851
- **Small-town** 250-acre campus with easy access to Milwaukee
- **Endowment** $76.7 million
- **Coed** 793 undergraduate students, 99% full-time, 52% women, 48% men
- **Moderately difficult** entrance level, 65% of applicants were admitted

UNDERGRAD STUDENTS
783 full-time, 10 part-time. Students come from 32 states and territories; 6 other countries; 30% are from out of state; 2% Black or African American, non-Hispanic/Latino; 6% Hispanic/Latino; 1% Asian, non-Hispanic/Latino; 0.3% American Indian or Alaska Native, non-Hispanic/Latino; 2% Two or more races, non-Hispanic/Latino; 0.5% Race/ethnicity unknown; 4% international; 0.9% transferred in; 93% live on campus.

Freshmen:
Admission: 2,553 applied, 1,666 admitted, 214 enrolled. ***Average high school GPA:*** 3.4. ***Test scores:*** SAT critical reading scores over 500: 35%; SAT math scores over 500: 64%; ACT scores over 18: 97%; SAT critical reading scores over 600: 21%; SAT math scores over 600: 14%; ACT scores over 24: 47%; ACT scores over 30: 13%.
Retention: 81% of full-time freshmen returned.

FACULTY
Total: 78, 79% full-time, 85% with terminal degrees.
Student/faculty ratio: 12:1.

ACADEMICS
Calendar: semesters. *Degree:* bachelor's.

Special study options: accelerated degree program, advanced placement credit, double majors, internships, off-campus study, part-time degree program, services for LD students, student-designed majors, study abroad. ***ROTC:*** Army (b).

Unusual degree programs: 3-2 engineering with Rensselaer Polytechnic Institute, Washington University in St. Louis, University of Wisconsin–Madison; forestry with Duke University; nursing with Rush University; environmental studies with Duke University.

Computers: 150 computers/terminals are available on campus for general student use. Students can access the following: campus intranet, computer help desk, free student e-mail accounts, online (class) grades, online (class) schedules. Campuswide network is available. 100% of college-owned or -operated housing units are wired for high-speed Internet access. Wireless service is available via entire campus.

Library: Lane Library. *Books:* 160,664 (physical), 142,427 (digital/electronic); *Serial titles:* 86 (physical), 61,132 (digital/electronic); *Databases:* 26. Weekly public service hours: 52; students can reserve study rooms.

STUDENT LIFE

Housing options: on-campus residence required through senior year; coed, men-only, women-only. Campus housing is university owned. Freshman campus housing is guaranteed.

Activities and organizations: drama/theater group, student-run newspaper, radio station, choral group, Environmental Group, Student Senate, Community Service Coalition, SMAC (Student Media and Activities Committee), national fraternities, national sororities.

Athletics Member NCAA. All Division III. ***Intercollegiate sports:*** baseball M, basketball M/W, cheerleading M(c)/W, cross-country running M/W, football M, rugby M(c)/W(c), soccer M/W, softball W, swimming and diving M/W, tennis M/W, track and field M/W, volleyball W. ***Intramural sports:*** basketball M/W, bowling M/W, equestrian sports M(c)/W(c), fencing M/W, football M/W, racquetball M/W, soccer M/W, softball M/W, table tennis M/W, tennis M/W, ultimate Frisbee M/W, volleyball M/W.

Campus security: 24-hour emergency response devices and patrols, student patrols, late-night transport/escort service, controlled dormitory access.

Student services: health clinic, personal/psychological counseling.

COSTS & FINANCIAL AID

Costs (2017–18) ***Comprehensive fee:*** $49,991 includes full-time tuition ($41,535), mandatory fees ($300), and room and board ($8156). Part-time tuition: $1300 per credit. ***Payment plan:*** installment. ***Waivers:*** employees or children of employees.

Financial Aid Of all full-time matriculated undergraduates who enrolled in 2012, 840 applied for aid, 760 were judged to have need, 135 had their need fully met. 437 Federal Work-Study jobs (averaging $1777). 326 state and other part-time jobs (averaging $1727). In 2012, 124 non-need-based awards were made. ***Average percent of need met:*** 84. ***Average financial aid package:*** $25,418. ***Average need-based loan:*** $5329. ***Average need-based gift aid:*** $19,763. ***Average non-need-based aid:*** $10,803. ***Average indebtedness upon graduation:*** $31,216.

APPLYING

Options: electronic application, deferred entrance.

Application fee: $30.

Required: high school transcript, minimum 2.0 GPA, 1 letter of recommendation. ***Required for some:*** essay or personal statement, interview. ***Recommended:*** essay or personal statement, interview.

Application deadlines: rolling (freshmen), rolling (transfers).

Notification: continuous (freshmen), continuous (transfers).

CONTACT

Office of Admission, Ripon College, 300 Seward Street, PO Box 248, Ripon, WI 54971. *Phone:* 920-748-8337. *Toll-free phone:* 800-947-4766. *Fax:* 920-748-8335. *E-mail:* adminfo@ripon.edu.

See previous page for display ad and page 1478 for the College Close-Up.

St. Norbert College

De Pere, Wisconsin

http://www.snc.edu/

- **Independent Roman Catholic** comprehensive, founded 1898
- **Suburban** 112-acre campus
- **Endowment** $99.6 million
- **Coed** 2,102 undergraduate students, 98% full-time, 57% women, 43% men
- **Moderately difficult** entrance level, 81% of applicants were admitted

UNDERGRAD STUDENTS

2,054 full-time, 48 part-time. Students come from 26 states and territories; 22 other countries; 21% are from out of state; 1% Black or African American, non-Hispanic/Latino; 4% Hispanic/Latino; 1% Asian, non-Hispanic/Latino; 0.9% American Indian or Alaska Native, non-Hispanic/Latino; 2% Two or more races, non-Hispanic/Latino; 0.3% Race/ethnicity unknown; 3% international; 1% transferred in; 84% live on campus.

Freshmen:

Admission: 3,605 applied, 2,934 admitted, 584 enrolled. ***Average high school GPA:*** 3.52. ***Test scores:*** ACT scores over 18: 98%; ACT scores over 24: 57%; ACT scores over 30: 10%.

Retention: 86% of full-time freshmen returned.

FACULTY

Total: 204, 69% full-time, 74% with terminal degrees.

Student/faculty ratio: 13:1.

ACADEMICS

Calendar: semesters. *Degrees:* bachelor's and master's.

Special study options: academic remediation for entering students, advanced placement credit, distance learning, double majors, English as a second language, honors programs, independent study, internships, off-campus study, part-time degree program, services for LD students, student-designed majors, study abroad, summer session for credit. ***ROTC:*** Army (b).

Computers: 214 computers/terminals are available on campus for general student use. Students can access the following: campus intranet, computer help desk, free student e-mail accounts, online (class) grades, online (class) registration, online (class) schedules. Campuswide network is available. 100% of college-owned or -operated housing units are wired for high-speed Internet access. Wireless service is available via classrooms, computer centers, computer labs, dorm rooms, learning centers, libraries, student centers.

Library: Miriam B. and James J. Mulva Library plus 1 other. *Books:* 246,257 (physical), 89,569 (digital/electronic); *Serial titles:* 100,047 (physical), 99,843 (digital/electronic). Weekly public service hours: 116; students can reserve study rooms.

STUDENT LIFE

Housing options: on-campus residence required through senior year; coed, women-only, special housing for students with disabilities. Campus housing is university owned. Freshman campus housing is guaranteed.

Activities and organizations: drama/theater group, student-run newspaper, radio and television station, choral group, Pre-Health Sciences Club, Dance Marathon, SNC Law Club, Omicron Delta Kappa, CC Hams, national fraternities, national sororities.

Athletics Member NCAA. All Division III. ***Intercollegiate sports:*** baseball M, basketball M/W, cross-country running M/W, football M, golf M/W, ice hockey M/W, soccer M/W, softball W, tennis M/W, track and field M/W, volleyball W. ***Intramural sports:*** badminton M/W, basketball M/W, cheerleading W, crew M(c)/W(c), football M/W, skiing (downhill) M(c)/W(c), soccer M/W, ultimate Frisbee M(c)/W(c), volleyball M/W.

Campus security: 24-hour emergency response devices and patrols, student patrols, late-night transport/escort service, controlled dormitory access, ConnectED emergency information system, crime prevention programs.

Student services: health clinic, personal/psychological counseling, women's center.

COSTS & FINANCIAL AID

Costs (2017–18) ***Comprehensive fee:*** $46,060 includes full-time tuition ($35,878), mandatory fees ($715), and room and board ($9467). Full-time

tuition and fees vary according to course load. Part-time tuition: $1121 per credit hour. Part-time tuition and fees vary according to course load. ***College room only:*** $5077. Room and board charges vary according to board plan and housing facility. ***Payment plans:*** installment, deferred payment. ***Waivers:*** employees or children of employees.

Financial Aid Of all full-time matriculated undergraduates who enrolled in 2015, 1,741 applied for aid, 1,533 were judged to have need, 382 had their need fully met. 377 Federal Work-Study jobs (averaging $1227). In 2015, 453 non-need-based awards were made. ***Average percent of need met:*** 83. ***Average financial aid package:*** $25,511. ***Average need-based loan:*** $4938. ***Average need-based gift aid:*** $19,617. ***Average non-need-based aid:*** $12,234. ***Average indebtedness upon graduation:*** $33,948.

APPLYING

Standardized Tests *Required:* SAT or ACT (for admission).

Options: electronic application, deferred entrance.

Application fee: $10.

Required: high school transcript, 1 letter of recommendation. ***Required for some:*** interview. ***Recommended:*** essay or personal statement.

Application deadlines: rolling (freshmen), rolling (transfers).

Notification: continuous (freshmen), continuous (transfers).

CONTACT

Mr. Mark Selin, Executive Director of Enrollment and Marketing, St. Norbert College, 100 Grant Street, De Pere, WI 54115-2099. *Phone:* 920-403-3005. *Toll-free phone:* 800-236-4878. *Fax:* 920-403-4072.
E-mail: admit@snc.edu.

See below for display ad and page 1498 for the College Close-Up.

Silver Lake College of the Holy Family

Manitowoc, Wisconsin

http://www.sl.edu/

- **Independent Roman Catholic** comprehensive, founded 1869
- **Rural** 30-acre campus with easy access to Milwaukee
- **Endowment** $7.2 million
- **Coed** 357 undergraduate students, 60% full-time, 66% women, 34% men
- **Minimally difficult** entrance level, 55% of applicants were admitted

UNDERGRAD STUDENTS

214 full-time, 143 part-time. Students come from 12 states and territories; 11 other countries; 15% are from out of state; 13% Black or African American, non-Hispanic/Latino; 8% Hispanic/Latino; 3% Asian, non-Hispanic/Latino; 0.3% Native Hawaiian or other Pacific Islander, non-Hispanic/Latino; 0.3% American Indian or Alaska Native, non-Hispanic/Latino; 1% Two or more races, non-Hispanic/Latino; 6% Race/ethnicity unknown; 5% international; 7% transferred in; 50% live on campus.

Freshmen:

Admission: 481 applied, 264 admitted, 56 enrolled. ***Average high school GPA:*** 2.49. ***Test scores:*** ACT scores over 18: 39%; ACT scores over 24: 11%; ACT scores over 30: 2%.

Retention: 70% of full-time freshmen returned.

FACULTY

Total: 72, 36% full-time.

Student/faculty ratio: 8:1.

ACADEMICS

Calendar: semesters. *Degrees:* certificates, bachelor's, master's, and postbachelor's certificates.

Special study options: academic remediation for entering students, accelerated degree program, adult/continuing education programs, advanced placement credit, distance learning, double majors, independent study, internships, off-campus study, part-time degree program, services for LD students, student-designed majors, summer session for credit.

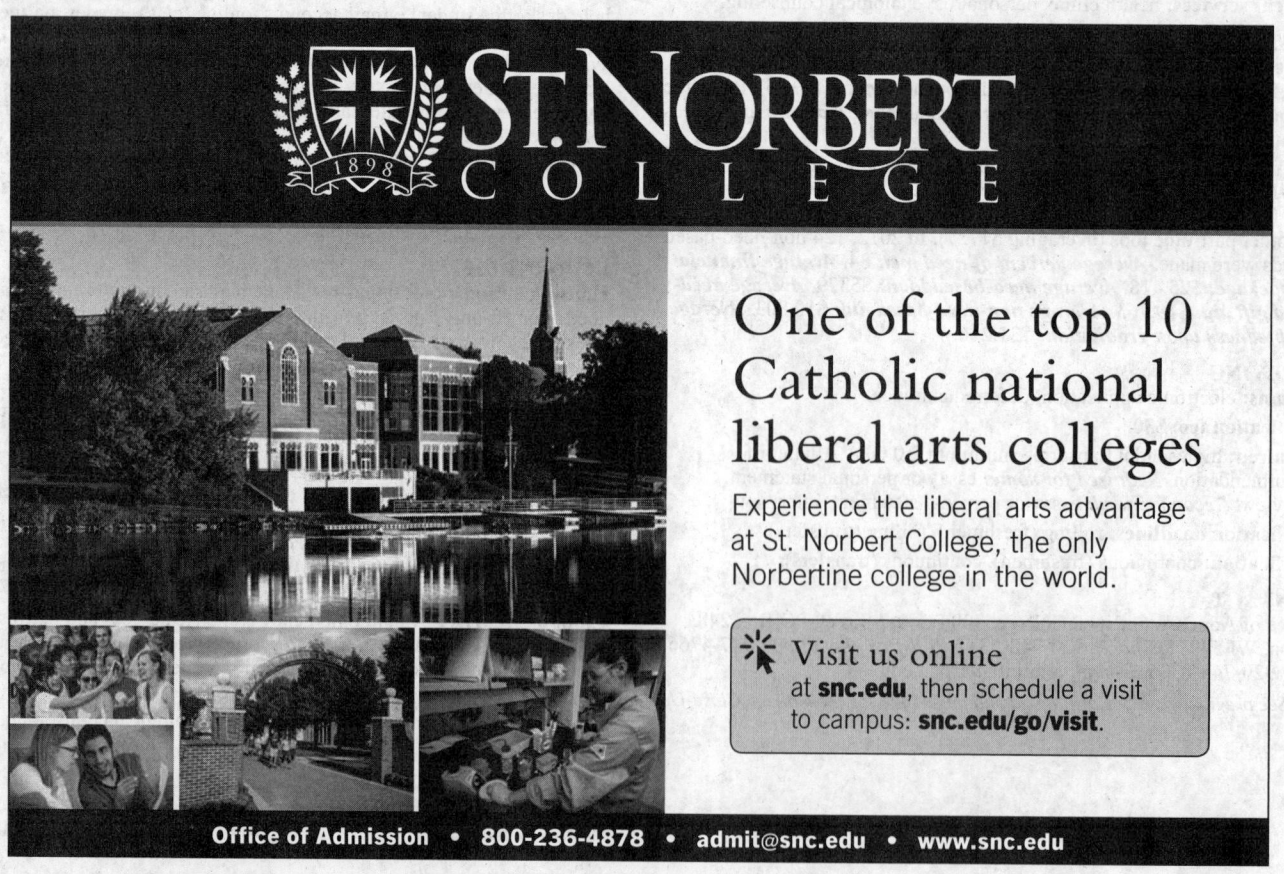

Computers: 120 computers/terminals are available on campus for general student use. Students can access the following: campus intranet, computer help desk, free student e-mail accounts, online (class) grades, online (class) registration, online (class) schedules. Campuswide network is available. 100% of college-owned or -operated housing units are wired for high-speed Internet access. Wireless service is available via entire campus.

Library: The Erma M. and Theodore M. Zigmunt Library. Study areas open 24 hours, 5-7 days a week; students can reserve study rooms.

STUDENT LIFE

Housing options: on-campus residence required through junior year; coed, men-only, women-only, special housing for students with disabilities. Campus housing is university owned. Freshman campus housing is guaranteed.

Activities and organizations: choral group, Wellness Club, Card and Game Club, Student For Life, Campus Activity Board, Silver Lake Serves.

Athletics Member NAIA, USCAA. ***Intercollegiate sports:*** basketball M(s)/W(s), cross-country running M(s)/W(s), golf M(s)/W(s), soccer M(s)/W(s), softball W(s), volleyball W(s). ***Intramural sports:*** table tennis M/W, ultimate Frisbee M/W, volleyball M/W.

Campus security: 24-hour emergency response devices, student patrols, late-night transport/escort service, controlled dormitory access.

Student services: health clinic, personal/psychological counseling.

COSTS & FINANCIAL AID

Costs (2017–18) ***One-time required fee:*** $270. ***Comprehensive fee:*** $270. Full-time tuition and fees vary according to course load and degree level. Part-time tuition: $545 per credit hour. Part-time tuition and fees vary according to course load and degree level. ***Required fees:*** $270 per year part-time, $270 per year part-time. ***Room and board:*** Room and board charges vary according to board plan. ***Payment plan:*** installment. ***Waivers:*** senior citizens and employees or children of employees.

Financial Aid Of all full-time matriculated undergraduates who enrolled in 2011, 157 applied for aid, 149 were judged to have need, 17 had their need fully met. 97 Federal Work-Study jobs (averaging $1429). 3 state and other part-time jobs (averaging $2450). In 2011, 7 non-need-based awards were made. ***Average percent of need met:*** 77. ***Average financial aid package:*** $18,970. ***Average need-based loan:*** $4210. ***Average need-based gift aid:*** $14,197. ***Average non-need-based aid:*** $10,140. ***Average indebtedness upon graduation:*** $35,164.

APPLYING

Standardized Tests *Required:* SAT or ACT (for admission).

Options: electronic application, deferred entrance.

Application fee: $50.

Required: high school transcript, minimum 2.0 GPA, 1 letter of recommendation. ***Required for some:*** essay or personal statement, interview.

Application deadlines: rolling (freshmen), 9/1 (transfers).

Notification: continuous until 9/1 (freshmen), continuous (transfers).

CONTACT

Jamie A. Grant, Executive Director of Enrollment Management, Silver Lake College of the Holy Family, 2406 South Alverno Road, Manitowoc, WI 54220-9319. *Phone:* 920-686-6206. *Toll-free phone:* 800-236-4752 Ext. 175. *Fax:* 920-686-6322. *E-mail:* jamie.grant@sl.edu.

University of Wisconsin–Eau Claire

Eau Claire, Wisconsin

http://www.uwec.edu/

- **State-supported** comprehensive, founded 1916, part of University of Wisconsin System
- **Small-town** 337-acre campus with easy access to Minneapolis-St. Paul
- **Endowment** $67.5 million
- **Coed** 9,981 undergraduate students, 93% full-time, 62% women, 38% men
- **Moderately difficult** entrance level, 89% of applicants were admitted

UNDERGRAD STUDENTS

9,311 full-time, 670 part-time. Students come from 37 states and territories; 31 other countries; 29% are from out of state; 0.9% Black or African American, non-Hispanic/Latino; 3% Hispanic/Latino; 4% Asian, non-Hispanic/Latino; 0.1% Native Hawaiian or other Pacific Islander, non-Hispanic/Latino; 0.2% American Indian or Alaska Native, non-Hispanic/Latino; 2% Two or more races, non-Hispanic/Latino; 0.2% Race/ethnicity unknown; 2% international; 5% transferred in; 41% live on campus.

Freshmen:

Admission: 5,706 applied, 5,079 admitted, 2,302 enrolled. ***Test scores:*** SAT critical reading scores over 500: 94%; SAT math scores over 500: 94%; ACT scores over 18: 98%; SAT critical reading scores over 600: 56%; SAT math scores over 600: 44%; ACT scores over 24: 52%; SAT critical reading scores over 700: 19%; SAT math scores over 700: 13%; ACT scores over 30: 6%.

Retention: 84% of full-time freshmen returned.

FACULTY

Total: 551, 70% full-time, 70% with terminal degrees.

Student/faculty ratio: 22:1.

ACADEMICS

Calendar: semesters. *Degrees:* certificates, associate, bachelor's, master's, doctoral, post-master's, and postbachelor's certificates.

Special study options: academic remediation for entering students, accelerated degree program, adult/continuing education programs, advanced placement credit, cooperative education, distance learning, double majors, English as a second language, external degree program, honors programs, independent study, internships, off-campus study, part-time degree program, services for LD students, student-designed majors, study abroad, summer session for credit. ***ROTC:*** Army (b).

Computers: 900 computers/terminals are available on campus for general student use. Students can access the following: campus intranet, computer help desk, free student e-mail accounts, online (class) grades, online (class) registration, online (class) schedules, course management system, ability to check where there are open seats in the general access computer labs, laptop check. Campuswide network is available. 100% of college-owned or -operated housing units are wired for high-speed Internet access. Wireless service is available via entire campus.

Library: William D. McIntyre Library plus 1 other. *Books:* 715,318 (physical), 325,928 (digital/electronic); *Serial titles:* 829 (physical), 83,513 (digital/electronic); *Databases:* 227. Weekly public service hours: 112; study areas open 24 hours, 5-7 days a week; students can reserve study rooms.

STUDENT LIFE

Housing options: on-campus residence required through sophomore year; coed, men-only. Campus housing is university owned. Freshman campus housing is guaranteed.

Activities and organizations: drama/theater group, student-run newspaper, radio and television station, choral group, marching band, Student Wisconsin Education Association, Pre- Professional Health Club, Kinesiology Club, RHA (Residence Hall Association), Blugold Beginnings, national fraternities, national sororities.

Athletics Member NCAA. All Division III. ***Intercollegiate sports:*** basketball M/W, cross-country running M/W, football M, golf M/W, gymnastics W, ice hockey M/W, soccer W, softball W, swimming and diving M/W, tennis M/W, track and field M/W, volleyball W, wrestling M. ***Intramural sports:*** baseball M(c)/W(c), basketball M/W, bowling M(c)/W(c), cheerleading M(c)/W(c), equestrian sports M(c)/W(c), football M/W, ice hockey M(c), lacrosse M(c)/W(c), rugby M(c)/W(c), sand volleyball M/W, skiing (cross-country) M(c)/W(c), soccer M/W, softball M/W, table tennis M(c)/W(c), tennis M/W, triathlon M(c)/W(c), ultimate Frisbee M/W, volleyball M/W.

Campus security: 24-hour emergency response devices and patrols, student patrols, late-night transport/escort service, controlled dormitory access.

Student services: health clinic, personal/psychological counseling, women's center, legal services.

COSTS & FINANCIAL AID

Costs (2016–17) ***Tuition:*** state resident $7361 full-time, $307 per credit part-time; nonresident $14,934 full-time, $622 per credit part-time. Full-time tuition and fees vary according to program and reciprocity agreements. Part-time tuition and fees vary according to program and reciprocity agreements. ***Required fees:*** $1452 full-time, $61 per credit part-time. ***Room and board:*** $6984; room only: $4184. Room and board charges vary according to board plan and housing facility. ***Payment plan:*** installment.

Financial Aid Of all full-time matriculated undergraduates who enrolled in 2015, 7,002 applied for aid, 4,935 were judged to have need, 1,000 had their need fully met. 3,942 Federal Work-Study jobs (averaging $1249). In 2015, 466 non-need-based awards were made. ***Average percent of need met:*** 84. ***Average financial aid package:*** $9403. ***Average need-based loan:*** $4363. ***Average need-based gift aid:*** $5872. ***Average non-need-based aid:*** $2127. ***Average indebtedness upon graduation:*** $26,295.

APPLYING

Standardized Tests *Required:* SAT or ACT (for admission).

Options: electronic application, early admission.

Application fee: $50.

Required: essay or personal statement, high school transcript.

Application deadlines: 8/20 (freshmen), 8/20 (transfers).

Notification: continuous (freshmen), continuous (transfers).

CONTACT

Heather Kretz, Director of Admissions, University of Wisconsin–Eau Claire, PO Box 4004, Eau Claire, WI 54702-4004. *Phone:* 715-836-5188. *Fax:* 715-836-2409. *E-mail:* admissions@uwec.edu.

University of Wisconsin–Green Bay

Green Bay, Wisconsin

http://www.uwgb.edu/

- **State-supported** comprehensive, founded 1968, part of University of Wisconsin System
- **Suburban** 700-acre campus with easy access to Milwaukee
- **Endowment** $28.0 million
- **Coed** 6,758 undergraduate students, 59% full-time, 67% women, 33% men
- **Moderately difficult** entrance level, 92% of applicants were admitted

UNDERGRAD STUDENTS

4,009 full-time, 2,749 part-time. Students come from 40 states and territories; 38 other countries; 8% are from out of state; 2% Black or African American, non-Hispanic/Latino; 4% Hispanic/Latino; 3% Asian, non-Hispanic/Latino; 0.1% Native Hawaiian or other Pacific Islander, non-Hispanic/Latino; 1% American Indian or Alaska Native, non-Hispanic/Latino; 3% Two or more races, non-Hispanic/Latino; 0.1% Race/ethnicity unknown; 1% international; 10% transferred in; 33% live on campus.

Freshmen:

Admission: 2,126 applied, 1,966 admitted, 872 enrolled. ***Average high school GPA:*** 3.33. ***Test scores:*** SAT critical reading scores over 500: 52%; SAT math scores over 500: 63%; SAT writing scores over 500: 47%; ACT scores over 18: 94%; SAT critical reading scores over 600: 26%; SAT math scores over 600: 21%; SAT writing scores over 600: 31%; ACT scores over 24: 38%; SAT math scores over 700: 5%; SAT writing scores over 700: 5%; ACT scores over 30: 2%.

Retention: 74% of full-time freshmen returned.

FACULTY

Total: 308, 60% full-time.

Student/faculty ratio: 22:1.

ACADEMICS

Calendar: semesters. *Degrees:* associate, bachelor's, and master's.

Special study options: academic remediation for entering students, adult/continuing education programs, advanced placement credit, distance learning, double majors, external degree program, independent study, internships, off-campus study, part-time degree program, services for LD students, student-designed majors, study abroad, summer session for credit. ***ROTC:*** Army (c).

Unusual degree programs: 3-2 business administration; engineering with University of Wisconsin–Milwaukee; nursing; social work.

Computers: 550 computers/terminals are available on campus for general student use. Students can access the following: computer help desk, free student e-mail accounts, online (class) grades, online (class) registration, online (class) schedules, online degree progress, online financial records and bill paying. Campuswide network is available. 100% of college-owned or -operated housing units are wired for high-speed Internet access. Wireless service is available via entire campus.

Library: Cofrin Library. *Books:* 353,331 (physical); *Serial titles:* 7,592 (physical); *Databases:* 179. Weekly public service hours: 100; students can reserve study rooms.

STUDENT LIFE

Housing options: coed. Campus housing is university owned and is provided by a third party. Freshman applicants given priority for college housing.

Activities and organizations: drama/theater group, student-run newspaper, radio station, choral group, Good Times, Psychology and Human Development Club, Student Ambassadors, Residence Hall Apartment Association, Student Government Association.

Athletics Member NCAA. All Division I. ***Intercollegiate sports:*** basketball M(s)/W(s), cross-country running M(s)/W(s), golf M(s)/W(s), skiing (cross-country) M(s)/W(s), soccer M(s)/W(s), softball W(s), swimming and diving M(s)/W(s), tennis M(s)/W(s), volleyball W(s). ***Intramural sports:*** basketball M/W, bowling M/W, cheerleading M/W, football M/W, golf M/W, racquetball M/W, sailing M/W, skiing (cross-country) M/W, soccer M/W, softball M/W, swimming and diving M/W, tennis M/W, ultimate Frisbee M/W, volleyball M/W, weight lifting M/W.

Campus security: 24-hour emergency response devices and patrols, late-night transport/escort service, controlled dormitory access.

Student services: health clinic, personal/psychological counseling.

COSTS & FINANCIAL AID

Costs (2017–18) ***One-time required fee:*** $225. ***Tuition:*** state resident $6298 full-time, $262 per credit hour part-time; nonresident $13,871 full-time, $578 per credit hour part-time. Full-time tuition and fees vary according to course load and reciprocity agreements. Part-time tuition and fees vary according to reciprocity agreements. ***Required fees:*** $1650 full-time, $57 per credit hour part-time. ***Room and board:*** $7200; room only: $4300. Room and board charges vary according to board plan and housing facility. ***Payment plan:*** installment. ***Waivers:*** senior citizens.

Financial Aid Of all full-time matriculated undergraduates who enrolled in 2016, 3,282 applied for aid, 2,678 were judged to have need, 922 had their need fully met. 289 Federal Work-Study jobs (averaging $1893). In 2016, 173 non-need-based awards were made. ***Average percent of need met:*** 76. ***Average financial aid package:*** $10,328. ***Average need-based loan:*** $6565. ***Average need-based gift aid:*** $5976. ***Average non-need-based aid:*** $1226. ***Average indebtedness upon graduation:*** $28,940.

APPLYING

Standardized Tests *Required:* SAT or ACT (for admission).

Options: electronic application, deferred entrance.

Application fee: $50.

Required: essay or personal statement, high school transcript. ***Required for some:*** interview.

Application deadlines: rolling (freshmen), rolling (transfers).

Notification: continuous (freshmen), continuous (transfers).

CONTACT

Ms. Jen Jones, Director of Admissions, University of Wisconsin–Green Bay, 2420 Nicolet Drive, Green Bay, WI 54311-7001. *Phone:* 920-465-2111. *Fax:* 920-465-5754. *E-mail:* uwgb@uwgb.edu.

University of Wisconsin–La Crosse

La Crosse, Wisconsin

http://www.uwlax.edu/

- **State-supported** comprehensive, founded 1909, part of University of Wisconsin System
- **Suburban** 121-acre campus
- **Endowment** $20.6 million
- **Coed** 9,699 undergraduate students, 95% full-time, 56% women, 44% men
- **Moderately difficult** entrance level, 82% of applicants were admitted

UNDERGRAD STUDENTS

9,175 full-time, 524 part-time. Students come from 31 states and territories; 26 other countries; 18% are from out of state; 0.8% Black or African American, non-Hispanic/Latino; 4% Hispanic/Latino; 2% Asian, non-Hispanic/Latino; 0.1% Native Hawaiian or other Pacific Islander, non-Hispanic/Latino; 0.1% American Indian or Alaska Native, non-Hispanic/Latino; 3% Two or more races, non-Hispanic/Latino; 1% international; 5% transferred in; 36% live on campus.

Freshmen:
Admission: 5,801 applied, 4,782 admitted, 2,086 enrolled. ***Test scores:*** SAT critical reading scores over 500: 92%; SAT math scores over 500: 92%; SAT writing scores over 500: 83%; ACT scores over 18: 100%; SAT critical reading scores over 600: 33%; SAT math scores over 600: 50%; SAT writing scores over 600: 42%; ACT scores over 24: 63%; SAT math scores over 700: 17%; SAT writing scores over 700: 8%; ACT scores over 30: 7%.

Retention: 86% of full-time freshmen returned.

FACULTY
Total: 588, 79% full-time, 69% with terminal degrees.

Student/faculty ratio: 19:1.

ACADEMICS
Calendar: semesters. *Degrees:* certificates, associate, bachelor's, master's, doctoral, and postbachelor's certificates.

Special study options: academic remediation for entering students, adult/continuing education programs, advanced placement credit, cooperative education, distance learning, double majors, English as a second language, independent study, internships, off-campus study, part-time degree program, services for LD students, study abroad, summer session for credit. ***ROTC:*** Army (b).

Unusual degree programs: 3-2 engineering with University of Wisconsin–Madison, University of Wisconsin–Milwaukee, University of Wisconsin–Platteville, University of Minnesota; physical therapy and physics, physical therapy and biology, occupational therapy and psychology.

Computers: 200 computers/terminals are available on campus for general student use. Students can access the following: campus intranet, computer help desk, free student e-mail accounts, online (class) grades, online (class) registration, online (class) schedules. Campuswide network is available. 100% of college-owned or -operated housing units are wired for high-speed Internet access. Wireless service is available via entire campus.

Library: Murphy Library plus 6 others. Weekly public service hours: 55; students can reserve study rooms.

STUDENT LIFE
Housing options: on-campus residence required for freshman year; coed, special housing for students with disabilities. Campus housing is university owned. Freshman applicants given priority for college housing.

Activities and organizations: drama/theater group, student-run newspaper, radio and television station, choral group, marching band, Sports and Activities Club, Residential Hall Council, religious/spiritual organizations, Human Diversity Organizations, departmental/professional, national fraternities, national sororities.

Athletics Member NCAA. All Division III. ***Intercollegiate sports:*** baseball M, basketball M/W, cross-country running M/W, football M, gymnastics W, soccer W, softball W, swimming and diving M/W, tennis M/W, track and field M/W, volleyball W, wrestling M. ***Intramural sports:*** archery M(c)/W(c), basketball M/W, cheerleading M/W, equestrian sports M(c)/W(c), football M/W, ice hockey M(c)/W(c), lacrosse M(c)/W(c), racquetball M/W, rugby M(c)/W(c), skiing (cross-country) M(c)/W(c), skiing (downhill) M(c)/W(c), soccer M(c)/W(c), softball M/W, table tennis M/W, tennis M/W, ultimate Frisbee M(c)/W(c), volleyball M(c)/W(c), weight lifting M(c)/W(c).

Campus security: 24-hour emergency response devices and patrols, late-night transport/escort service, controlled dormitory access.

Student services: health clinic, personal/psychological counseling, women's center, legal services.

COSTS & FINANCIAL AID
Costs (2016–17) ***Tuition:*** state resident $7585 full-time, $370 per credit part-time; nonresident $16,106 full-time, $725 per credit part-time. ***Required fees:*** $1506 full-time, $54 per credit part-time. ***Room and board:*** $6156; room only: $3606. Room and board charges vary according to board plan and housing facility. ***Payment plan:*** installment.

Financial Aid Of all full-time matriculated undergraduates who enrolled in 2015, 6,902 applied for aid, 4,454 were judged to have need, 812 had their need fully met. 472 Federal Work-Study jobs (averaging $1679). 1,706 state and other part-time jobs (averaging $1401). In 2015, 328 non-need-based awards were made. ***Average percent of need met:*** 70. ***Average financial aid package:*** $7577. ***Average need-based loan:*** $4141. ***Average need-based gift aid:*** $4812. ***Average non-need-based aid:*** $1733. ***Average indebtedness upon graduation:*** $26,487.

APPLYING
Standardized Tests *Required:* SAT or ACT (for admission).

Options: electronic application.

Application fee: $50.

Required: essay or personal statement, high school transcript. ***Required for some:*** interview.

Application deadlines: rolling (freshmen), rolling (transfers).

Notification: continuous (freshmen), continuous (transfers).

CONTACT
Mr. Corey Sjoquist, Director of Admissions, University of Wisconsin–La Crosse, 1725 State Street, La Crosse, WI 54601. *Phone:* 608-785-8939. *Fax:* 608-785-8940. *E-mail:* admissions@uwlax.edu.

University of Wisconsin–Madison

Madison, Wisconsin

http://www.wisc.edu/

- **State-supported** university, founded 1848, part of University of Wisconsin System
- **Urban** 936-acre campus with easy access to Milwaukee
- **Endowment** $2.4 billion
- **Coed** 31,710 undergraduate students, 90% full-time, 51% women, 49% men
- **Very difficult** entrance level, 53% of applicants were admitted

UNDERGRAD STUDENTS
28,608 full-time, 3,102 part-time. Students come from 52 states and territories; 102 other countries; 33% are from out of state; 2% Black or African American, non-Hispanic/Latino; 5% Hispanic/Latino; 6% Asian, non-Hispanic/Latino; 0.1% Native Hawaiian or other Pacific Islander, non-Hispanic/Latino; 0.2% American Indian or Alaska Native, non-Hispanic/Latino; 3% Two or more races, non-Hispanic/Latino; 0.3% Race/ethnicity unknown; 8% international; 3% transferred in; 26% live on campus.

Freshmen:
Admission: 32,887 applied, 17,304 admitted, 6,430 enrolled. ***Average high school GPA:*** 3.84. ***Test scores:*** SAT critical reading scores over 500: 96%; SAT math scores over 500: 99%; ACT scores over 18: 100%; SAT critical reading scores over 600: 62%; SAT math scores over 600: 90%; ACT scores over 24: 96%; SAT critical reading scores over 700: 13%; SAT math scores over 700: 55%; ACT scores over 30: 41%.

Retention: 95% of full-time freshmen returned.

FACULTY
Total: 2,843, 84% full-time, 87% with terminal degrees.

Student/faculty ratio: 18:1.

ACADEMICS
Calendar: semesters. *Degrees:* bachelor's, master's, doctoral, and postbachelor's certificates.

Special study options: accelerated degree program, adult/continuing education programs, advanced placement credit, cooperative education, distance learning, double majors, English as a second language, honors programs, independent study, internships, part-time degree program, services for LD students, student-designed majors, study abroad, summer session for credit. ***ROTC:*** Army (b), Navy (b), Air Force (b).

Computers: 1,000 computers/terminals are available on campus for general student use. Students can access the following: computer help desk, free student e-mail accounts, online (class) grades, online (class) registration, online (class) schedules. Campuswide network is available. 100% of college-owned or -operated housing units are wired for high-speed Internet access. Wireless service is available via entire campus.

Library: Memorial Library plus 40 others. Study areas open 24 hours, 5-7 days a week; students can reserve study rooms.

STUDENT LIFE
Housing options: coed, men-only, women-only, cooperative. Campus housing is university owned. Freshman applicants given priority for college housing.

Activities and organizations: drama/theater group, student-run newspaper, radio station, choral group, marching band, national fraternities, national sororities.

Athletics Member NCAA. All Division I except football (Division I-A). ***Intercollegiate sports:*** basketball M(s)/W(s), cheerleading M/W, crew M/W, cross-country running M(s)/W(s), fencing M(c)/W(c), golf M(s)/W(s), ice hockey M(s)/W(s), lacrosse M(c)/W(c), racquetball M(c)/W(c), rugby M(c)/W(c), sailing M(c)/W(c), soccer M(s)/W(s), softball W(s), swimming and diving M(s)/W(s), tennis M(s)/W(s), track and field M(s)/W(s), ultimate Frisbee M(c)/W(c), volleyball M(c)/W(s), water polo M(c)/W(c), wrestling M(s). ***Intramural sports:*** badminton M(c)/W(c), basketball M/W, fencing M(c)/W(c), racquetball M/W, softball M/W, tennis M/W, ultimate Frisbee M/W, volleyball M/W.

Campus security: 24-hour emergency response devices and patrols, late-night transport/escort service, controlled dormitory access.

Student services: health clinic, personal/psychological counseling, women's center.

COSTS & FINANCIAL AID
Costs (2016–17) ***Tuition:*** state resident $9273 full-time, $386 per credit hour part-time; nonresident $31,523 full-time, $1313 per credit hour part-time. Full-time tuition and fees vary according to program and reciprocity agreements. Part-time tuition and fees vary according to course load, program, and reciprocity agreements. ***Required fees:*** $1215 full-time, $97 per credit hour part-time. ***Room and board:*** $10,446. Room and board charges vary according to board plan and housing facility.

Financial Aid Of all full-time matriculated undergraduates who enrolled in 2016, 15,028 applied for aid, 10,302 were judged to have need, 3,820 had their need fully met. In 2016, 2106 non-need-based awards were made. ***Average percent of need met:*** 79. ***Average financial aid package:*** $14,981. ***Average need-based loan:*** $6130. ***Average need-based gift aid:*** $10,943. ***Average non-need-based aid:*** $4452. ***Average indebtedness upon graduation:*** $27,831.

APPLYING
Standardized Tests *Required:* SAT or ACT (for admission).

Options: electronic application, early action, deferred entrance.

Application fee: $60.

Required: essay or personal statement, high school transcript. ***Recommended:*** 2 letters of recommendation.

Application deadlines: 2/1 (freshmen), 3/1 (transfers), 11/1 (early action).

Notification: 3/31 (freshmen), 4/30 (transfers), 1/31 (early action).

CONTACT
Office of Admissions and Recruitment, University of Wisconsin–Madison, 702 West Johnson Street, Suite 101, Madison, WI 53706-1481. *Phone:* 608-262-3961. *Fax:* 608-262-7706.
E-mail: onwisconsin@admissions.wisc.edu.

University of Wisconsin–Milwaukee

Milwaukee, Wisconsin

http://www.uwm.edu/

- **State-supported** university, founded 1956, part of University of Wisconsin System
- **Urban** 104-acre campus with easy access to Milwaukee
- **Endowment** $94.5 million
- **Coed** 21,375 undergraduate students, 82% full-time, 52% women, 48% men
- **Moderately difficult** entrance level, 72% of applicants were admitted

UNDERGRAD STUDENTS
17,578 full-time, 3,797 part-time. Students come from 52 states and territories; 89 other countries; 11% are from out of state; 8% Black or African American, non-Hispanic/Latino; 10% Hispanic/Latino; 7% Asian, non-Hispanic/Latino; 0.1% Native Hawaiian or other Pacific Islander, non-Hispanic/Latino; 0.4% American Indian or Alaska Native, non-Hispanic/Latino; 4% Two or more races, non-Hispanic/Latino; 0.2% Race/ethnicity unknown; 4% international; 7% transferred in; 18% live on campus.

Freshmen:
Admission: 9,834 applied, 7,124 admitted, 3,118 enrolled. ***Average high school GPA:*** 3.11. ***Test scores:*** ACT scores over 18: 92%; ACT scores over 24: 35%; ACT scores over 30: 4%.

Retention: 72% of full-time freshmen returned.

FACULTY
Total: 1,497, 67% full-time, 56% with terminal degrees.

Student/faculty ratio: 19:1.

ACADEMICS
Calendar: semesters. *Degrees:* certificates, bachelor's, master's, doctoral, post-master's, and postbachelor's certificates.

Special study options: academic remediation for entering students, accelerated degree program, adult/continuing education programs, advanced placement credit, cooperative education, distance learning, double majors, English as a second language, external degree program, freshman honors college, honors programs, independent study, internships, off-campus study, part-time degree program, services for LD students, student-designed majors, study abroad, summer session for credit. ***ROTC:*** Army (c), Navy (c), Air Force (c).

Computers: 500 computers/terminals are available on campus for general student use. Students can access the following: campus intranet, computer help desk, free student e-mail accounts, online (class) grades, online (class) registration, online (class) schedules. Campuswide network is available. 100% of college-owned or -operated housing units are wired for high-speed Internet access. Wireless service is available via classrooms, computer centers, computer labs, dorm rooms, learning centers, libraries, student centers.

Library: Golda Meir Library. *Books:* 2.5 million (physical), 178,268 (digital/electronic); *Serial titles:* 112,752 (physical). Students can reserve study rooms.

STUDENT LIFE
Housing options: on-campus residence required for freshman year; coed, special housing for students with disabilities. Campus housing is university owned. Freshman applicants given priority for college housing.

Activities and organizations: drama/theater group, student-run newspaper, choral group, national fraternities, national sororities.

Athletics Member NCAA. All Division I. ***Intercollegiate sports:*** baseball M(s), basketball M(s)/W(s), bowling M(c)/W(c), cross-country running M(s)/W(s), equestrian sports M(c)/W(c), football M(c)/W(c), ice hockey M(c)/W(c), lacrosse M(c)/W(c), rugby M(c)/W(c), sailing M(c)/W(c), soccer M(s)/W(s), swimming and diving M(s)/W(s), tennis W(s), track and field M(s)/W(s), ultimate Frisbee M(c)/W(c), volleyball M(c)/W(s). ***Intramural sports:*** badminton M/W, baseball M(c)/W(c), basketball M/W, cross-country running M/W, football M/W, racquetball M/W, skiing (downhill) M(c)/W(c), soccer M/W, swimming and diving M/W, tennis M(c)/W(c), track and field M(c)/W(c), volleyball M/W.

Campus security: 24-hour emergency response devices and patrols, student patrols, late-night transport/escort service, controlled dormitory access.

Student services: health clinic, personal/psychological counseling, women's center, legal services.

COSTS & FINANCIAL AID
Costs (2017–18) ***Tuition:*** state resident $8090 full-time. Full-time tuition and fees vary according to course load, degree level, location, program, and reciprocity agreements. Part-time tuition and fees vary according to course load, degree level, location, program, and reciprocity agreements. ***Required fees:*** $1444 full-time. ***Room and board:*** $10,560; room only: $6640. Room and board charges vary according to board plan, housing facility, and location. ***Payment plan:*** installment. ***Waivers:*** senior citizens.

Financial Aid Of all full-time matriculated undergraduates who enrolled in 2014, 19,189 applied for aid, 16,510 were judged to have need, 3,150 had their need fully met. In 2014, 89 non-need-based awards were made. ***Average percent of need met:*** 43. ***Average financial aid package:*** $7434. ***Average need-based loan:*** $4148. ***Average need-based gift aid:*** $5692. ***Average non-need-based aid:*** $2115. ***Average indebtedness upon graduation:*** $32,009.

APPLYING

Standardized Tests *Required:* SAT or ACT (for admission). *Required for some:* TOEFL for students whose native language is not English and who were not educated in an entirely English-speaking country.

Options: electronic application, deferred entrance.

Application fee: $50.

Required: high school transcript. ***Recommended:*** essay or personal statement.

Application deadlines: rolling (freshmen), 7/1 (transfers).

Notification: continuous (freshmen), continuous (transfers).

CONTACT

Katie Miota, Interim Director, Undergraduate Admissions, University of Wisconsin–Milwaukee, PO Box 413, Milwaukee, WI 53201-0413. *Phone:* 414-229-4445. *E-mail:* uwmlook@uwm.edu.

University of Wisconsin–Oshkosh

Oshkosh, Wisconsin

http://www.uwosh.edu/

CONTACT

Associate Director of Admissions, University of Wisconsin–Oshkosh, 800 Algoma Boulevard, Oshkosh, WI 54901. *Phone:* 920-424-0202. *E-mail:* oshadmuw@uwosh.edu.

University of Wisconsin–Parkside

Kenosha, Wisconsin

http://www.uwp.edu/

- **State-supported** comprehensive, founded 1968, part of University of Wisconsin System
- **Suburban** 700-acre campus with easy access to Chicago, Milwaukee
- **Coed** 4,276 undergraduate students, 76% full-time, 53% women, 47% men
- **Moderately difficult** entrance level, 82% of applicants were admitted

UNDERGRAD STUDENTS

3,247 full-time, 1,029 part-time. Students come from 26 states and territories; 27 other countries; 17% are from out of state; 9% Black or African American, non-Hispanic/Latino; 14% Hispanic/Latino; 3% Asian, non-Hispanic/Latino; 0.2% Native Hawaiian or other Pacific Islander, non-Hispanic/Latino; 0.2% American Indian or Alaska Native, non-Hispanic/Latino; 4% Two or more races, non-Hispanic/Latino; 0.2% Race/ethnicity unknown; 1% international; 9% transferred in; 17% live on campus.

Freshmen:

Admission: 1,629 applied, 1,328 admitted, 666 enrolled. ***Average high school GPA:*** 3.06. ***Test scores:*** SAT critical reading scores over 500: 27%; SAT math scores over 500: 64%; SAT writing scores over 500: 36%; ACT scores over 18: 84%; SAT critical reading scores over 600: 9%; SAT writing scores over 600: 9%; ACT scores over 24: 22%; ACT scores over 30: 1%.

Retention: 71% of full-time freshmen returned.

FACULTY

Total: 248, 66% full-time, 59% with terminal degrees.

Student/faculty ratio: 19:1.

ACADEMICS

Calendar: semesters. *Degrees:* certificates, associate, bachelor's, and master's.

Special study options: academic remediation for entering students, adult/continuing education programs, advanced placement credit, cooperative education, distance learning, double majors, external degree program, honors programs, independent study, internships, off-campus study, part-time degree program, services for LD students, study abroad, summer session for credit. ***ROTC:*** Army (c), Air Force (c).

Unusual degree programs: 3-2 molecular biology; pharmacy with Rosalind-Franklin University.

Computers: 173 computers/terminals are available on campus for general student use. Students can access the following: campus intranet, computer help desk, free student e-mail accounts, online (class) grades, online (class) registration, online (class) schedules. Campuswide network is available. 100% of college-owned or -operated housing units are wired for high-speed Internet access. Wireless service is available via entire campus.

Library: UWP Library. Students can reserve study rooms.

STUDENT LIFE

Housing options: on-campus residence required through sophomore year; coed, special housing for students with disabilities. Campus housing is university owned.

Activities and organizations: drama/theater group, student-run newspaper, radio station, choral group, Black Student Union, Parkside Asian Organization, Parkside Activities Board, Latinos Unidos, Men's Rugby Club, national fraternities, national sororities.

Athletics Member NCAA. All Division II. ***Intercollegiate sports:*** baseball M(s), basketball M(s)/W(s), cross-country running M(s)/W(s), golf M(s), soccer M(s)/W(s), softball W(s), track and field M(s)/W(s), volleyball W(s), wrestling M(s). ***Intramural sports:*** badminton M/W, basketball M/W, football M/W, racquetball M/W, rugby M(c), soccer M/W, softball M/W, table tennis M/W, tennis M/W, volleyball M/W.

Campus security: 24-hour emergency response devices and patrols, late-night transport/escort service, controlled dormitory access.

Student services: health clinic, personal/psychological counseling, women's center.

COSTS & FINANCIAL AID

Costs (2017–18) ***One-time required fee:*** $140. ***Tuition:*** state resident $6298 full-time, $262 per credit hour part-time; nonresident $14,287 full-time, $595 per credit hour part-time. Full-time tuition and fees vary according to course load and reciprocity agreements. Part-time tuition and fees vary according to course load and reciprocity agreements. ***Required fees:*** $1069 full-time, $45 per credit hour part-time. ***Room and board:*** $7736; room only: $4406. Room and board charges vary according to board plan and housing facility. ***Payment plan:*** installment. ***Waivers:*** senior citizens.

Financial Aid Of all full-time matriculated undergraduates who enrolled in 2014, 2,626 applied for aid, 2,235 were judged to have need, 305 had their need fully met. 76 Federal Work-Study jobs (averaging $1284). 34 state and other part-time jobs (averaging $2012). In 2014, 206 non-need-based awards were made. ***Average percent of need met:*** 63. ***Average financial aid package:*** $9119. ***Average need-based loan:*** $4412. ***Average need-based gift aid:*** $6219. ***Average non-need-based aid:*** $3923. ***Average indebtedness upon graduation:*** $29,362.

APPLYING

Standardized Tests *Required for some:* SAT or ACT (for admission).

Options: electronic application.

Application fee: $44.

Required: high school transcript, minimum of 17 high school units distribution.

Application deadlines: rolling (freshmen), rolling (transfers).

Notification: continuous (freshmen), continuous (transfers).

CONTACT

Troy Moldenhauer, Director, Admissions and Recruitment, University of Wisconsin–Parkside, PO Box 2000, 900 Wood Road, Kenosha, WI 53141-2000. *Phone:* 262-595-2355. *Fax:* 262-595-2006. *E-mail:* moldenht@uwp.edu.

University of Wisconsin–Platteville

Platteville, Wisconsin

http://www.uwplatt.edu/

- **State-supported** comprehensive, founded 1866, part of University of Wisconsin System
- **Small-town** 821-acre campus
- **Endowment** $21.7 million
- **Coed** 7,793 undergraduate students, 90% full-time, 34% women, 66% men

UNDERGRAD STUDENTS

7,001 full-time, 792 part-time. Students come from 26 other countries; 24% are from out of state; 1% Black or African American, non-Hispanic/Latino; 3% Hispanic/Latino; 1% Asian, non-Hispanic/Latino;

0.1% Native Hawaiian or other Pacific Islander, non-Hispanic/Latino; 3% Two or more races, non-Hispanic/Latino; 0.7% Race/ethnicity unknown; 1% international; 7% transferred in; 41% live on campus.

Freshmen:
Admission: 1,541 enrolled. ***Test scores:*** SAT critical reading scores over 500: 42%; SAT math scores over 500: 67%; ACT scores over 18: 93%; SAT critical reading scores over 600: 8%; SAT math scores over 600: 25%; ACT scores over 24: 44%; SAT critical reading scores over 700: 8%; ACT scores over 30: 6%.
Retention: 77% of full-time freshmen returned.

FACULTY
Total: 402, 81% full-time, 62% with terminal degrees.
Student/faculty ratio: 22:1.

ACADEMICS
Calendar: semesters. *Degrees:* certificates, associate, bachelor's, master's, and postbachelor's certificates.
Special study options: academic remediation for entering students, adult/continuing education programs, advanced placement credit, cooperative education, distance learning, double majors, English as a second language, external degree program, independent study, internships, off-campus study, part-time degree program, services for LD students, student-designed majors, study abroad, summer session for credit. ***ROTC:*** Army (c).
Computers: 228 computers/terminals and 250 ports are available on campus for general student use. Students can access the following: campus intranet, computer help desk, free student e-mail accounts, online (class) grades, online (class) registration, online (class) schedules. Campuswide network is available. 100% of college-owned or -operated housing units are wired for high-speed Internet access. Wireless service is available via entire campus.
Library: Karrmann Library plus 1 other. *Books:* 199,895 (physical), 61,518 (digital/electronic); *Serial titles:* 14,246 (physical), 264 (digital/electronic); *Databases:* 172. Weekly public service hours: 87.

STUDENT LIFE
Housing options: on-campus residence required through sophomore year; coed, men-only, women-only, cooperative, special housing for students with disabilities. Campus housing is university owned. Freshman campus housing is guaranteed.
Activities and organizations: drama/theater group, student-run newspaper, radio and television station, choral group, marching band, Criminal Justice Association, Platteville Gaming Association, Dodgeball, American Society of Mechanical Engineers, Outdoor Adventure Club, national fraternities, national sororities.
Athletics Member NCAA. All Division III. ***Intercollegiate sports:*** baseball M, basketball M/W, bowling M(c)/W(c), cross-country running M/W, football M, golf W, ice hockey M(c)/W(c), lacrosse M(c)/W(c), rugby M(c)/W(c), soccer M/W, softball W, track and field M/W, ultimate Frisbee M(c)/W(c), volleyball M(c)/W, wrestling M. ***Intramural sports:*** badminton M/W, basketball M/W, bowling M(c)/W(c), cheerleading M(c)/W(c), football M/W, racquetball M/W, soccer M/W, softball M/W, tennis M/W, ultimate Frisbee M/W, volleyball M/W, water polo M/W.
Campus security: 24-hour emergency response devices and patrols, student patrols, late-night transport/escort service, controlled dormitory access.
Student services: health clinic, personal/psychological counseling, women's center.

COSTS & FINANCIAL AID
Costs (2016–17) ***Tuition:*** state resident $6298 full-time, $262 per credit hour part-time; nonresident $14,149 full-time, $590 per credit hour part-time. Full-time tuition and fees vary according to course load, degree level, and reciprocity agreements. Part-time tuition and fees vary according to course load, degree level, and reciprocity agreements. ***Required fees:*** $1186 full-time, $49 per credit hour part-time. ***Room and board:*** $7160; room only: $3970. Room and board charges vary according to board plan and housing facility. ***Payment plan:*** installment. ***Waivers:*** senior citizens.
Financial Aid Of all full-time matriculated undergraduates who enrolled in 2002, 3,289 applied for aid, 2,468 were judged to have need. 382 Federal Work-Study jobs (averaging $1392). In 2002, 652 non-need-based awards were made. ***Average financial aid package:*** $6161. ***Average need-based loan:*** $3499. ***Average need-based gift aid:*** $3599. ***Average non-need-based aid:*** $1427. ***Average indebtedness upon graduation:*** $15,785.

APPLYING
Standardized Tests *Required:* SAT or ACT (for admission).
Required: high school transcript. ***Recommended:*** essay or personal statement.

CONTACT
Ms. Heidi Tuescher-Gille, Director of Admission and Enrollment Services, University of Wisconsin–Platteville, 1 University Plaza, 1300 Ullsvik Hall, Platteville, WI 53818-3099. *Phone:* 608-342-1125. *Toll-free phone:* 877-897-5288. *Fax:* 608-342-1122. *E-mail:* tuescheh@uwplatt.edu.

University of Wisconsin–River Falls

River Falls, Wisconsin

http://www.uwrf.edu/

- **State-supported** comprehensive, founded 1874, part of University of Wisconsin System
- **Suburban** 303-acre campus with easy access to Minneapolis-St. Paul
- **Endowment** $14.9 million
- **Coed**
- **Moderately difficult** entrance level

FACULTY
Student/faculty ratio: 23:1.

ACADEMICS
Calendar: semesters. *Degrees:* certificates, bachelor's, master's, post-master's, and postbachelor's certificates.
Library: Chalmer Davee Library plus 1 other. *Books:* 301,138 (physical), 159,542 (digital/electronic); *Serial titles:* 149 (physical), 8,350 (digital/electronic); *Databases:* 162. Weekly public service hours: 89; study areas open 24 hours, 5-7 days a week; students can reserve study rooms.

STUDENT LIFE
Housing options: on-campus residence required through sophomore year; coed, women-only, special housing for students with disabilities. Campus housing is university owned. Freshman campus housing is guaranteed.
Activities and organizations: drama/theater group, student-run newspaper, radio and television station, choral group, Pre-Vet Society, Dairy Club, Tomorrow's Educators, Block and Bridle, Agriculture Education Society, national fraternities, national sororities.
Athletics Member NCAA. All Division III.
Campus security: 24-hour emergency response devices and patrols, student patrols, late-night transport/escort service, controlled dormitory access.
Student services: health clinic, personal/psychological counseling.

COSTS & FINANCIAL AID
Costs (2016–17) ***Tuition:*** state resident $6428 full-time, $268 per credit hour part-time; nonresident $14,401 full-time, $583 per credit hour part-time. Full-time tuition and fees vary according to course load, degree level, program, and reciprocity agreements. Part-time tuition and fees vary according to course load, degree level, program, and reciprocity agreements. ***Required fees:*** $1553 full-time, $166 per credit hour part-time. ***Room and board:*** $6576; room only: $4136. Room and board charges vary according to board plan and housing facility.
Financial Aid Of all full-time matriculated undergraduates who enrolled in 2014, 3,978 applied for aid, 3,978 were judged to have need, 40 had their need fully met. 364 Federal Work-Study jobs (averaging $1013). In 2014, 173 non-need-based awards were made. ***Average percent of need met:*** 53. ***Average financial aid package:*** $6900. ***Average need-based loan:*** $4270. ***Average need-based gift aid:*** $4771. ***Average non-need-based aid:*** $1467. ***Average indebtedness upon graduation:*** $26,295.

APPLYING
Standardized Tests *Required:* SAT or ACT (for admission). *Recommended:* ACT (for admission).
Options: electronic application, deferred entrance.
Application fee: $44.

Required: essay or personal statement, high school transcript. ***Recommended:*** rank in upper 40% of high school class.

CONTACT

Sarah Egerstrom, Director of Admissions, University of Wisconsin–River Falls, 410 South Third Street, River Falls, WI 54022.
Phone: 715-425-3500. *Fax:* 715-425-0676. *E-mail:* admit@uwrf.edu.

University of Wisconsin–Stevens Point

Stevens Point, Wisconsin

http://www.uwsp.edu/

- **State-supported** comprehensive, founded 1894, part of University of Wisconsin System
- **Small-town** 400-acre campus
- **Endowment** $25.3 million
- **Coed** 8,296 undergraduate students, 92% full-time, 53% women, 47% men
- **Moderately difficult** entrance level, 77% of applicants were admitted

UNDERGRAD STUDENTS

7,644 full-time, 652 part-time. 12% are from out of state; 2% Black or African American, non-Hispanic/Latino; 4% Hispanic/Latino; 3% Asian, non-Hispanic/Latino; 0.4% American Indian or Alaska Native, non-Hispanic/Latino; 2% Two or more races, non-Hispanic/Latino; 0.1% Race/ethnicity unknown; 2% international; 7% transferred in; 37% live on campus.

Freshmen:

Admission: 4,005 applied, 3,068 admitted, 1,591 enrolled. ***Average high school GPA:*** 3.18. ***Test scores:*** SAT critical reading scores over 500: 52%; SAT math scores over 500: 38%; SAT writing scores over 500: 48%; ACT scores over 18: 93%; SAT critical reading scores over 600: 9%; SAT math scores over 600: 5%; SAT writing scores over 600: 15%; ACT scores over 24: 35%; ACT scores over 30: 4%.

Retention: 73% of full-time freshmen returned.

FACULTY

Total: 463, 77% full-time, 63% with terminal degrees.

Student/faculty ratio: 20:1.

ACADEMICS

Calendar: semesters. *Degrees:* associate, bachelor's, master's, and doctoral.

Special study options: academic remediation for entering students, accelerated degree program, advanced placement credit, cooperative education, distance learning, double majors, English as a second language, independent study, internships, off-campus study, part-time degree program, services for LD students, student-designed majors, study abroad, summer session for credit. ***ROTC:*** Army (b).

Computers: 1,233 computers/terminals and 3,963 ports are available on campus for general student use. Students can access the following: computer help desk, free student e-mail accounts, online (class) grades, online (class) registration, online (class) schedules. Campuswide network is available. 100% of college-owned or -operated housing units are wired for high-speed Internet access. Wireless service is available via entire campus.

Library: Learning Resources Center plus 1 other. Study areas open 24 hours, 5-7 days a week; students can reserve study rooms.

STUDENT LIFE

Housing options: on-campus residence required through sophomore year; coed, men-only, women-only. Campus housing is university owned. Freshman applicants given priority for college housing.

Activities and organizations: drama/theater group, student-run newspaper, radio and television station, choral group, The Wildlife Society, Student Impact, WWSP 90-FM radio station, Gender and Sexuality Alliance, Student Wisconsin Education Association, national fraternities, national sororities.

Athletics Member NCAA. All Division III. ***Intercollegiate sports:*** baseball M, basketball M/W, cheerleading M/W, cross-country running M/W, football M, golf W, ice hockey M/W, soccer W, softball W, swimming and diving M/W, tennis W, track and field M/W, volleyball W, wrestling M. ***Intramural sports:*** archery M(c)/W(c), badminton M/W, basketball M/W, football M, golf M/W, ice hockey M/W, lacrosse M(c), racquetball M/W, rock climbing M/W, rugby M(c)/W(c), skiing (downhill) M(c)/W(c), soccer M/W, softball M/W, table tennis M/W, tennis M/W, ultimate Frisbee M/W, volleyball M/W.

Campus security: 24-hour emergency response devices and patrols, student patrols, late-night transport/escort service, controlled dormitory access.

Student services: health clinic, personal/psychological counseling, women's center.

COSTS & FINANCIAL AID

Costs (2017–18) ***Tuition:*** state resident $7687 full-time, $403 per credit part-time; nonresident $15,954 full-time, $747 per credit part-time. Full-time tuition and fees vary according to course load, location, program, reciprocity agreements, and student level. Part-time tuition and fees vary according to course load, location, program, reciprocity agreements, and student level. ***Required fees:*** $1996 full-time. ***Room and board:*** $7180; room only: $4240. Room and board charges vary according to board plan and housing facility. ***Payment plans:*** installment, deferred payment. ***Waivers:*** senior citizens.

Financial Aid Of all full-time matriculated undergraduates who enrolled in 2015, 6,953 applied for aid, 5,032 were judged to have need, 677 had their need fully met. In 2015, 570 non-need-based awards were made. ***Average percent of need met:*** 72. ***Average financial aid package:*** $9069. ***Average need-based loan:*** $5320. ***Average need-based gift aid:*** $5177. ***Average non-need-based aid:*** $1483. ***Average indebtedness upon graduation:*** $25,646. ***Financial aid deadline:*** 5/1.

APPLYING

Standardized Tests *Required:* SAT or ACT (for admission).

Options: electronic application, deferred entrance.

Application fee: $50.

Required: high school transcript. ***Recommended:*** essay or personal statement, 3 letters of recommendation.

Application deadlines: rolling (freshmen), rolling (transfers).

Notification: continuous (freshmen), continuous (transfers).

CONTACT

Mr. William Jordan, Director of Admissions, University of Wisconsin–Stevens Point, 102 Student Services Center, Stevens Point, WI 54481.
Phone: 715-346-4021. *Fax:* 715-346-3296. *E-mail:* bjordan@uwsp.edu.

University of Wisconsin–Stout

Menomonie, Wisconsin

http://www.uwstout.edu/

- **State-supported** comprehensive, founded 1891, part of University of Wisconsin System
- **Small-town** 120-acre campus with easy access to Minneapolis-St. Paul
- **Coed** 8,398 undergraduate students, 81% full-time, 45% women, 55% men
- **Moderately difficult** entrance level, 88% of applicants were admitted

UNDERGRAD STUDENTS

6,831 full-time, 1,567 part-time. 33% are from out of state; 2% Black or African American, non-Hispanic/Latino; 0.7% Hispanic/Latino; 0.1% Asian, non-Hispanic/Latino; 87% Native Hawaiian or other Pacific Islander, non-Hispanic/Latino; 3% American Indian or Alaska Native, non-Hispanic/Latino; 4% Two or more races, non-Hispanic/Latino; 0.2% Race/ethnicity unknown; 2% international; 9% transferred in; 40% live on campus.

Freshmen:

Admission: 3,445 applied, 3,023 admitted, 1,588 enrolled. ***Average high school GPA:*** 3.2. ***Test scores:*** ACT scores over 18: 90%; ACT scores over 24: 34%; ACT scores over 30: 4%.

Retention: 73% of full-time freshmen returned.

FACULTY

Total: 503, 80% full-time, 67% with terminal degrees.

Student/faculty ratio: 19:1.

ACADEMICS

Calendar: 4-1-4. *Degrees:* certificates, bachelor's, master's, doctoral, post-master's, and postbachelor's certificates.

Special study options: accelerated degree program, adult/continuing education programs, cooperative education, distance learning, double majors, English as a second language, external degree program, honors programs, independent study, internships, off-campus study, part-time degree program, services for LD students, study abroad, summer session for credit. ***ROTC:*** Army (b), Air Force (c).

Computers: Students can access the following: computer help desk, free student e-mail accounts, online (class) grades, online (class) registration, online (class) schedules. Campuswide network is available. 100% of college-owned or -operated housing units are wired for high-speed Internet access. Wireless service is available via entire campus.

Library: Library Learning Center.

STUDENT LIFE

Housing options: on-campus residence required through sophomore year; coed, special housing for students with disabilities. Campus housing is university owned. Freshman campus housing is guaranteed.

Activities and organizations: drama/theater group, student-run newspaper, radio station, choral group, marching band, national fraternities, national sororities.

Athletics Member NCAA. All Division III. ***Intercollegiate sports:*** baseball M, basketball M/W, cross-country running M/W, football M, gymnastics W, ice hockey M/W(c), soccer M(c)/W, softball W, tennis W, track and field M/W, volleyball M(c)/W. ***Intramural sports:*** baseball M, basketball M/W, bowling M(c)/W(c), football M/W, golf M/W, ice hockey M/W, racquetball M/W, rugby M(c)/W(c), skiing (cross-country) M(c)/W(c), skiing (downhill) M(c)/W(c), softball M/W, ultimate Frisbee M/W, volleyball M/W.

Campus security: 24-hour emergency response devices and patrols, student patrols, controlled dormitory access.

Student services: health clinic, personal/psychological counseling, legal services.

FINANCIAL AID

Financial Aid Of all full-time matriculated undergraduates who enrolled in 2016, 5,324 applied for aid, 3,801 were judged to have need, 654 had their need fully met. 1,399 Federal Work-Study jobs (averaging $1592). In 2016, 153 non-need-based awards were made. ***Average percent of need met:*** 84. ***Average financial aid package:*** $11,000. ***Average need-based loan:*** $4596. ***Average need-based gift aid:*** $4719. ***Average non-need-based aid:*** $1882. ***Average indebtedness upon graduation:*** $30,563.

APPLYING

Standardized Tests *Required:* SAT or ACT (for admission).

Options: electronic application.

Application fee: $50.

Required: high school transcript. ***Required for some:*** minimum 2.8 GPA. ***Recommended:*** minimum 2.5 GPA.

Application deadlines: rolling (freshmen), rolling (out-of-state freshmen), rolling (transfers).

Notification: continuous until 9/1 (freshmen), continuous (out-of-state freshmen), continuous (transfers).

CONTACT

Dr. Pamela Holsinger-Fuchs, Executive Director of Enrollment Services, University of Wisconsin–Stout, Admissions, Bowman Hall, Menomonie, WI 54751. *Phone:* 715-232-2639. *Toll-free phone:* 800-HI-STOUT. *Fax:* 715-232-1667. *E-mail:* admissions@uwstout.edu.

University of Wisconsin–Superior

Superior, Wisconsin

http://www.uwsuper.edu/

- **State-supported** comprehensive, founded 1893, part of University of Wisconsin System
- **Suburban** 230-acre campus
- **Coed** 2,365 undergraduate students, 76% full-time, 61% women, 39% men
- **Minimally difficult** entrance level, 69% of applicants were admitted

UNDERGRAD STUDENTS

1,806 full-time, 559 part-time. Students come from 35 states and territories; 46 other countries; 41% are from out of state; 2% Black or African American, non-Hispanic/Latino; 2% Hispanic/Latino; 1% Asian, non-Hispanic/Latino; 0.1% Native Hawaiian or other Pacific Islander, non-Hispanic/Latino; 2% American Indian or Alaska Native, non-Hispanic/Latino; 4% Two or more races, non-Hispanic/Latino; 0.4% Race/ethnicity unknown; 9% international; 11% transferred in; 33% live on campus.

Freshmen:

Admission: 1,148 applied, 797 admitted, 376 enrolled. ***Average high school GPA:*** 3.14. ***Test scores:*** ACT scores over 18: 88%; ACT scores over 24: 29%; ACT scores over 30: 3%.

Retention: 68% of full-time freshmen returned.

FACULTY

Total: 228, 51% full-time, 39% with terminal degrees.

Student/faculty ratio: 13:1.

ACADEMICS

Calendar: semesters. *Degrees:* certificates, associate, bachelor's, master's, post-master's, and postbachelor's certificates.

Special study options: academic remediation for entering students, accelerated degree program, adult/continuing education programs, advanced placement credit, cooperative education, distance learning, double majors, English as a second language, external degree program, freshman honors college, independent study, internships, off-campus study, part-time degree program, services for LD students, student-designed majors, study abroad, summer session for credit. ***ROTC:*** Air Force (c).

Unusual degree programs: 3-2 engineering with Michigan Technological University, University of Wisconsin%-Madison; forestry with Michigan Technological University.

Computers: 375 computers/terminals are available on campus for general student use. Students can access the following: campus intranet, computer help desk, free student e-mail accounts, online (class) grades, online (class) registration, online (class) schedules. Campuswide network is available. 100% of college-owned or -operated housing units are wired for high-speed Internet access. Wireless service is available via entire campus.

Library: Jim Dan Hill Library.

STUDENT LIFE

Housing options: on-campus residence required through sophomore year; coed, women-only, special housing for students with disabilities. Campus housing is university owned. Freshman campus housing is guaranteed.

Activities and organizations: drama/theater group, student-run newspaper, radio station, choral group, Student Senate, Student Activities Board, Residence Hall Association, Inter-Varsity Christian Fellowship, World Student Association.

Athletics Member NCAA. All Division III. ***Intercollegiate sports:*** baseball M, basketball M/W, cross-country running M/W, ice hockey M/W, soccer M/W, softball W, tennis M/W, track and field M/W, volleyball W. ***Intramural sports:*** badminton M/W, baseball M(c), basketball M/W, bowling M/W, football M/W, ice hockey M(c)/W(c), racquetball M/W, riflery M/W, rock climbing M/W, soccer M/W, softball M/W, swimming and diving M/W, table tennis M/W, tennis M(c)/W(c), ultimate Frisbee M(c)/W(c), volleyball M(c)/W(c).

Campus security: 24-hour emergency response devices and patrols, student patrols, late-night transport/escort service, controlled dormitory access.

Student services: health clinic, personal/psychological counseling, women's center.

COSTS & FINANCIAL AID

Costs (2016–17) ***Tuition:*** state resident $6535 full-time, $272 per credit hour part-time; nonresident $14,108 full-time, $588 per credit hour part-time. Full-time tuition and fees vary according to course load and reciprocity agreements. Part-time tuition and fees vary according to course load and reciprocity agreements. ***Required fees:*** $1552 full-time. ***Room and board:*** $6520; room only: $3490. Room and board charges vary according to board plan and housing facility. ***Payment plan:*** installment.

Financial Aid Of all full-time matriculated undergraduates who enrolled in 2016, 1,398 applied for aid, 1,136 were judged to have need, 184 had their need fully met. In 2016, 54 non-need-based awards were made. ***Average percent of need met:*** 85. ***Average financial aid package:***

$11,428. ***Average need-based loan:*** $4308. ***Average need-based gift aid:*** $5623. ***Average non-need-based aid:*** $1789. ***Average indebtedness upon graduation:*** $27,382.

APPLYING

Standardized Tests *Required:* SAT or ACT (for admission).

Options: electronic application, early admission, deferred entrance.

Application fee: $44.

Required: high school transcript. ***Required for some:*** essay or personal statement. ***Recommended:*** interview.

Application deadlines: 8/1 (freshmen), 8/1 (transfers).

Notification: continuous until 9/16 (freshmen), continuous (transfers).

CONTACT

University of Wisconsin–Superior, Belknap and Catlin, PO Box 2000, Superior, WI 54880-4500. *Phone:* 715-394-8230. *Fax:* 715-394-8407. *E-mail:* admissions@uwsuper.edu.

University of Wisconsin–Waukesha

Waukesha, Wisconsin

http://www.waukesha.uwc.edu/

CONTACT

Ms. Deb Kusick, Sr. Admission Specialist, University of Wisconsin–Waukesha, 1500 North University Drive, Waukesha, WI 53188-2799. *Phone:* 262-521-5040. *Fax:* 262-521-5530. *E-mail:* deborah.kusick@uwc.edu.

University of Wisconsin–Whitewater

Whitewater, Wisconsin

http://www.uww.edu/

- **State-supported** comprehensive, founded 1868, part of University of Wisconsin System
- **Small-town** 400-acre campus with easy access to Milwaukee
- **Endowment** $207.7 million
- **Coed** 11,380 undergraduate students, 89% full-time, 49% women, 51% men
- **Moderately difficult** entrance level, 81% of applicants were admitted

UNDERGRAD STUDENTS

10,088 full-time, 1,292 part-time. Students come from 35 states and territories; 35 other countries; 20% are from out of state; 4% Black or African American, non-Hispanic/Latino; 6% Hispanic/Latino; 2% Asian, non-Hispanic/Latino; 0.1% Native Hawaiian or other Pacific Islander, non-Hispanic/Latino; 0.2% American Indian or Alaska Native, non-Hispanic/Latino; 5% Two or more races, non-Hispanic/Latino; 0.1% Race/ethnicity unknown; 1% international; 7% transferred in; 39% live on campus.

Freshmen:

Admission: 6,228 applied, 5,056 admitted, 2,163 enrolled. ***Average high school GPA:*** 3.26. ***Test scores:*** ACT scores over 18: 94%; ACT scores over 24: 36%; ACT scores over 30: 3%.

Retention: 81% of full-time freshmen returned.

FACULTY

Total: 611, 79% full-time.

Student/faculty ratio: 21:1.

ACADEMICS

Calendar: semesters. *Degrees:* associate, bachelor's, master's, and doctoral.

Special study options: academic remediation for entering students, accelerated degree program, adult/continuing education programs, advanced placement credit, cooperative education, distance learning, double majors, English as a second language, external degree program, honors programs, independent study, internships, part-time degree program, services for LD students, student-designed majors, study abroad, summer session for credit. ***ROTC:*** Army (b), Air Force (b).

Unusual degree programs: 3-2 engineering with University of Wisconsin–Madison, University of Wisconsin–Milwaukee.

Computers: 1,920 computers/terminals are available on campus for general student use. Students can access the following: campus intranet, computer help desk, free student e-mail accounts, online (class) grades, online (class) registration, online (class) schedules. Campuswide network is available. 100% of college-owned or -operated housing units are wired for high-speed Internet access. Wireless service is available via entire campus.

Library: Andersen Library. *Books:* 594,628 (physical), 113,484 (digital/electronic); *Serial titles:* 20,731 (physical), 118,443 (digital/electronic); *Databases:* 243. Weekly public service hours: 110; students can reserve study rooms.

STUDENT LIFE

Housing options: on-campus residence required through sophomore year; coed. Campus housing is university owned. Freshman campus housing is guaranteed.

Activities and organizations: drama/theater group, student-run newspaper, radio and television station, choral group, marching band, Adult Student Connection, Pan Hellenic Council, Sigma Alpha Lambda (Academic Honors), Cru (Faith-Related Organization), National Society of Leadership and Success, national fraternities, national sororities.

Athletics Member NCAA. All Division III. ***Intercollegiate sports:*** baseball M, basketball M/W, bowling M(c)/W, cheerleading M(c)/W(c), cross-country running M/W, football M, golf W, gymnastics W, soccer M/W, softball W, swimming and diving M/W, tennis M/W, track and field M/W, volleyball M(c)/W, weight lifting M(c), wrestling M. ***Intramural sports:*** badminton M/W, baseball M(c), basketball M/W, bowling M/W, fencing M(c)/W(c), football M/W, golf M/W, lacrosse M(c)/W(c), racquetball M/W, rock climbing M(c)/W(c), rugby M(c)/W(c), skiing (downhill) M(c)/W(c), soccer M/W, softball M/W, table tennis M/W, tennis M/W, ultimate Frisbee M(c)/W(c), volleyball M/W, wrestling M/W.

Campus security: 24-hour emergency response devices and patrols, student patrols, late-night transport/escort service, controlled dormitory access.

Student services: health clinic, personal/psychological counseling, women's center, legal services.

COSTS & FINANCIAL AID

Costs (2016–17) ***Tuition:*** state resident $6519 full-time, $272 per credit hour part-time; nonresident $15,092 full-time, $628 per credit hour part-time. Full-time tuition and fees vary according to course load, degree level, and reciprocity agreements. ***Required fees:*** $1131 full-time. ***Room and board:*** $7204. Room and board charges vary according to board plan and housing facility. ***Payment plans:*** installment, deferred payment. ***Waivers:*** senior citizens.

Financial Aid Of all full-time matriculated undergraduates who enrolled in 2016, 8,026 applied for aid, 5,740 were judged to have need, 2,534 had their need fully met. 542 Federal Work-Study jobs (averaging $1296). 2,468 state and other part-time jobs (averaging $1904). In 2016, 492 non-need-based awards were made. ***Average percent of need met:*** 63. ***Average financial aid package:*** $8347. ***Average need-based loan:*** $4223. ***Average need-based gift aid:*** $5466. ***Average non-need-based aid:*** $2297. ***Average indebtedness upon graduation:*** $28,345.

APPLYING

Standardized Tests *Required:* SAT or ACT (for admission).

Options: electronic application, deferred entrance.

Application fee: $50.

Required: high school transcript. ***Recommended:*** essay or personal statement.

Application deadlines: rolling (freshmen), rolling (transfers).

Notification: continuous (freshmen), continuous (transfers).

CONTACT

Mr. Jeremy Reed, Director of Admissions, University of Wisconsin–Whitewater, 800 West Main Street, Whitewater, WI 53190-1790. *Phone:* 262-472-1440. *E-mail:* uwwadmit@uww.edu.

Viterbo University

La Crosse, Wisconsin

http://www.viterbo.edu/

- **Independent Roman Catholic** comprehensive, founded 1890
- **Suburban** 72-acre campus
- **Coed** 1,875 undergraduate students, 79% full-time, 74% women, 26% men
- **Moderately difficult** entrance level, 63% of applicants were admitted

UNDERGRAD STUDENTS
1,483 full-time, 392 part-time. Students come from 35 states and territories; 6 other countries; 27% are from out of state; 2% Black or African American, non-Hispanic/Latino; 3% Hispanic/Latino; 0.9% Asian, non-Hispanic/Latino; 0.1% Native Hawaiian or other Pacific Islander, non-Hispanic/Latino; 0.2% American Indian or Alaska Native, non-Hispanic/Latino; 2% Two or more races, non-Hispanic/Latino; 0.4% Race/ethnicity unknown; 2% international; 11% transferred in; 24% live on campus.

Freshmen:
Admission: 1,770 applied, 1,107 admitted, 320 enrolled. ***Average high school GPA:*** 3.51. ***Test scores:*** ACT scores over 18: 97%; ACT scores over 24: 44%; ACT scores over 30: 6%.
Retention: 80% of full-time freshmen returned.

FACULTY
Total: 324, 37% full-time, 31% with terminal degrees.
Student/faculty ratio: 11:1.

ACADEMICS
Calendar: semesters. *Degrees:* certificates, associate, bachelor's, master's, doctoral, post-master's, and postbachelor's certificates.
Special study options: accelerated degree program, adult/continuing education programs, distance learning, double majors, English as a second language, honors programs, independent study, internships, part-time degree program, student-designed majors, study abroad. ***ROTC:*** Army (c).
Unusual degree programs: 3-2 English, history, philosophy, religious studies, or Spanish/ business or servant leadership.
Computers: 400 computers/terminals are available on campus for general student use. Students can access the following: campus intranet, computer help desk, free student e-mail accounts, online (class) grades, online (class) registration, online (class) schedules, learning management system courses. Campuswide network is available. 100% of college-owned or -operated housing units are wired for high-speed Internet access. Wireless service is available via entire campus.
Library: Todd Wehr Memorial Library. *Books:* 69,288 (physical), 236 (digital/electronic); *Serial titles:* 105 (physical), 75 (digital/electronic); *Databases:* 36. Weekly public service hours: 97; study areas open 24 hours, 5-7 days a week; students can reserve study rooms.

STUDENT LIFE
Housing options: on-campus residence required for freshman year; coed. Campus housing is university owned. Freshman campus housing is guaranteed.
Activities and organizations: drama/theater group, student-run newspaper, choral group, Student Activities Board (SAB), Viterbo Student Nurses Association (VSNA), Education Club, Colleges Against Cancer (CAL), Residence Hall Association.
Athletics Member NAIA. ***Intercollegiate sports:*** baseball M(s), basketball M(s)/W(s), bowling M(s)/W(s), cross-country running M(s)/W(s), golf M(s)/W(s), soccer M(s)/W(s), softball W(s), track and field M/W, volleyball W(s). ***Intramural sports:*** basketball M/W, bowling M/W, soccer M/W, softball M/W, ultimate Frisbee M/W, volleyball M/W.
Campus security: 24-hour emergency response devices and patrols, late-night transport/escort service, controlled dormitory access, lighted pathways, emergency evacuation plan, self-defense education programs, security cameras.
Student services: health clinic, personal/psychological counseling.

COSTS & FINANCIAL AID
Costs (2017–18) ***Comprehensive fee:*** $35,680 includes full-time tuition ($26,230), mandatory fees ($690), and room and board ($8760). Full-time tuition and fees vary according to program. Part-time tuition and fees vary according to program. ***College room only:*** $3870. Room and board charges vary according to board plan and housing facility. ***Waivers:*** employees or children of employees.
Financial Aid Of all full-time matriculated undergraduates who enrolled in 2003, 1,311 applied for aid, 1,208 were judged to have need, 309 had their need fully met. 387 Federal Work-Study jobs (averaging $1680). 19 state and other part-time jobs (averaging $1615). In 2003, 223 non-need-based awards were made. ***Average percent of need met:*** 71. ***Average financial aid package:*** $13,534. ***Average need-based loan:*** $4317. ***Average need-based gift aid:*** $8859. ***Average non-need-based aid:*** $5629. ***Average indebtedness upon graduation:*** $16,619.

APPLYING
Standardized Tests *Required:* SAT or ACT (for admission).
Options: electronic application, deferred entrance.
Required: high school transcript, minimum 2.0 GPA. ***Required for some:*** essay or personal statement, interview, audition for theater and music, portfolio for art.
Application deadlines: 8/15 (freshmen), 8/1 (transfers).
Notification: continuous (freshmen), continuous (transfers).

CONTACT
Mr. Eric Schmidt, Freshman Admission Counselor/Associate Director for Admission, Viterbo University, 900 Viterbo Drive, La Crosse, WI 54601.
Phone: 608-796-3017. *Toll-free phone:* 800-VITERBO.
E-mail: admission@viterbo.edu.

Wisconsin Lutheran College

Milwaukee, Wisconsin

http://www.wlc.edu/

CONTACT
Mr. Cameron Teske, Admissions Office Coordinator, Wisconsin Lutheran College, 8800 West Bluemound Road, Milwaukee, WI 53226-9942.
Phone: 414-443-8811. *Fax:* 414-443-8547.
E-mail: cameron.teske@wlc.edu.

WYOMING

CollegeAmerica–Cheyenne

Cheyenne, Wyoming

http://www.collegeamerica.edu/

CONTACT
CollegeAmerica–Cheyenne, 6101 Yellowstone Road, Cheyenne, WY 82009.

University of Wyoming

Laramie, Wyoming

http://www.uwyo.edu/

- **State-supported** university, founded 1886
- **Small-town** 785-acre campus
- **Endowment** $437.6 million
- **Coed**
- **Moderately difficult** entrance level

FACULTY
Student/faculty ratio: 14:1.

ACADEMICS
Calendar: semesters. *Degrees:* certificates, bachelor's, master's, doctoral, post-master's, and postbachelor's certificates.
Library: William Robertson Coe Library plus 5 others. *Books:* 1.7 million (physical), 922,041 (digital/electronic); *Serial titles:* 14,119 (physical), 126,027 (digital/electronic); *Databases:* 1,000. Students can reserve study rooms.

STUDENT LIFE
Housing options: on-campus residence required for freshman year; coed, men-only, women-only, special housing for students with disabilities.

Campus housing is university owned. Freshman campus housing is guaranteed.

Activities and organizations: drama/theater group, student-run newspaper, television station, choral group, marching band, national fraternities, national sororities.

Athletics Member NCAA. All Division I except football (Division I-A).

Campus security: 24-hour emergency response devices and patrols, student patrols, late-night transport/escort service, controlled dormitory access, 24-hour front desk coverage at campus housing and at campus police.

Student services: health clinic, personal/psychological counseling, women's center, legal services.

COSTS & FINANCIAL AID

Costs (2016–17) ***One-time required fee:*** $40. ***Tuition:*** state resident $3720 full-time, $124 per credit hour part-time; nonresident $14,880 full-time, $496 per credit hour part-time. Full-time tuition and fees vary according to course load, location, and reciprocity agreements. Part-time tuition and fees vary according to course load, location, and reciprocity agreements. ***Required fees:*** $1335 full-time, $321 per term part-time. ***Room and board:*** $10,320; room only: $4493. Room and board charges vary according to board plan and housing facility.

Financial Aid Of all full-time matriculated undergraduates who enrolled in 2015, 5,349 applied for aid, 3,831 were judged to have need, 592 had their need fully met. 289 Federal Work-Study jobs (averaging $1972). In 2015, 1895 non-need-based awards were made. ***Average percent of need met:*** 59. ***Average financial aid package:*** $9742. ***Average need-based loan:*** $4139. ***Average need-based gift aid:*** $5226. ***Average non-need-based aid:*** $4821. ***Average indebtedness upon graduation:*** $25,378.

APPLYING

Standardized Tests *Required:* SAT or ACT (for admission).

Options: electronic application, deferred entrance.

Application fee: $40.

Required: high school transcript, minimum 3.0 GPA, pre-college curriculum, minimum ACT composite score of 21 or SAT of 980.

CONTACT

Ryan Goeken, Assistant Director of Admissions, University of Wyoming, 1000 E. University Avenue, Dept 3435, Laramie, WY 82071. *Phone:* 307-766-4138. *Toll-free phone:* 800-342-5996. *Fax:* 307-766-4042. *E-mail:* admissions@uwyo.edu.

AMERICAN SAMOA

American Samoa Community College

Pago Pago, American Samoa

http://www.amsamoa.edu/

- **Territory-supported** primarily 2-year, founded 1969
- **Rural** 20-acre campus
- **Endowment** $3.1 million
- **Coed** 1,253 undergraduate students, 56% full-time, 67% women, 33% men
- **Noncompetitive** entrance level, 100% of applicants were admitted

UNDERGRAD STUDENTS

702 full-time, 551 part-time. Students come from 5 other countries; 0.1% Hispanic/Latino; 0.4% Asian, non-Hispanic/Latino; 89% Native Hawaiian or other Pacific Islander, non-Hispanic/Latino; 0.2% Race/ethnicity unknown; 10% international; 0.2% transferred in.

Freshmen:

Admission: 407 applied, 407 admitted, 407 enrolled. ***Test scores:*** SAT critical reading scores over 500: 17%; SAT math scores over 500: 19%; SAT critical reading scores over 600: 5%; SAT math scores over 600: 2%. ***Retention:*** 100% of full-time freshmen returned.

FACULTY

Total: 82, 78% full-time, 9% with terminal degrees.

Student/faculty ratio: 20:1.

ACADEMICS

Calendar: semesters. *Degrees:* certificates, associate, and bachelor's.

Special study options: academic remediation for entering students, adult/continuing education programs, cooperative education, double majors, English as a second language, honors programs, independent study, internships, off-campus study, part-time degree program, services for LD students, student-designed majors, summer session for credit. ***ROTC:*** Army (b).

Computers: 300 computers/terminals and 300 ports are available on campus for general student use. Students can access the following: campus intranet, computer help desk, online (class) grades, online (class) registration, online (class) schedules. Campuswide network is available. Wireless service is available via entire campus.

Library: ASCC Learning Resource Center/Library plus 1 other. *Books:* 40,000 (physical); *Serial titles:* 236 (physical). Weekly public service hours: 42.

STUDENT LIFE

Housing options: college housing not available.

Activities and organizations: student-run newspaper, Student Government Association, Phi Theta Kappa, ASCC Research Foundation Student Club, Fa'aSamoa (Samoan culture) Club, Journalism Club.

Athletics ***Intramural sports:*** basketball M/W, football M/W, golf M/W, rugby M, soccer M, tennis M/W, track and field M/W, volleyball M/W.

Campus security: 24-hour patrols.

Student services: personal/psychological counseling.

COSTS & FINANCIAL AID

Costs (2017–18) ***Tuition:*** territory resident $3300 full-time; nonresident $3600 full-time. Full-time tuition and fees vary according to course load. Part-time tuition and fees vary according to course load. ***Required fees:*** $250 full-time. ***Payment plan:*** installment. ***Waivers:*** employees or children of employees.

Financial Aid Of all full-time matriculated undergraduates who enrolled in 2015, 588 applied for aid, 588 were judged to have need.

APPLYING

Standardized Tests *Recommended:* SAT (for admission), ACT (for admission), SAT or ACT (for admission), SAT and SAT Subject Tests or ACT (for admission), SAT Subject Tests (for admission).

Options: electronic application, early admission, deferred entrance.

Notification: continuous (freshmen).

CONTACT

Elizabeth Leuma, Admissions Officer, American Samoa Community College, PO Box 2609, Pago Pago 96799, American Samoa. *Phone:* 684-699-9155 Ext. 411. *Fax:* 684-699-1083.

GUAM

Pacific Islands University

Mangilao, Guam

http://www.piu.edu/

CONTACT

Ethel Laco, Admissions Office, Pacific Islands University, 172 Kinney's Road, Mangilao, GU 96913. *Phone:* 671-734-1812. *Fax:* 671-734-1813. *E-mail:* guamcampus@pibc.edu.

University of Guam

Mangilao, Guam

http://www.uog.edu/

CONTACT

Ms. Angelica Anthonio, Admissions Supervisor, University of Guam, Admissions and Records Office, UOG Station, Mangilao, GU 96923. *Phone:* 671-735-2201. *Fax:* 671-735-2203. *E-mail:* admitme@uguam.uog.edu.

NORTHERN MARIANA ISLANDS

Northern Marianas College

Saipan, Northern Mariana Islands
http://www.marianas.edu/

CONTACT
Ms. Leilani M. Basa-Alam, Admission Specialist, Northern Marianas College, PO Box 501250, Saipan, MP 96950-1250. *Phone:* 670-234-3690 Ext. 1539. *Fax:* 670-235-4967. *E-mail:* leilanib@nmcnet.edu.

PUERTO RICO

American University of Puerto Rico

Bayamon, Puerto Rico
http://www.aupr.edu/

CONTACT
Ms. Keren Llanos Figueroa, Director of Admissions, American University of Puerto Rico, PO Box 2037, Bayamon, PR 00960-2037. *Phone:* 787-620-2040 Ext. 2020. *Fax:* 787-785-7377. *E-mail:* kllanos@aupr.edu.

American University of Puerto Rico

Manati, Puerto Rico
http://www.aupr.edu/

CONTACT
American University of Puerto Rico, Carretera Estatal #2 Km. 48.7, PO Box 1082, Manati, PR 00674-1082.

Atenas College

Manati, Puerto Rico
http://www.atenascollege.edu/

CONTACT
Atenas College, Paseo de La Atenas #101 Altos, Manati, PR 00674.

Atlantic University College

Guaynabo, Puerto Rico
http://www.atlanticu.edu/

CONTACT
Ms. Zaida Perez, Admission's Officer, Atlantic University College, PO Box 3918, Guaynabo, PR 00970. *Phone:* 787-720-1022 Ext. 13. *E-mail:* admisiones@atlanticcollege.edu.

Bayamón Central University

Bayamón, Puerto Rico
http://www.ucb.edu.pr/

- **Independent Roman Catholic** comprehensive, founded 1970
- **Urban** 55-acre campus with easy access to San Juan
- **Endowment** $439,784
- **Coed** 1,722 undergraduate students
- 45% of applicants were admitted

UNDERGRAD STUDENTS
Students come from 1 other state; 2 other countries; 100% Hispanic/Latino; 0.3% international.

Freshmen:
Admission: 517 applied, 232 admitted. ***Average high school GPA:*** 2.95.
Retention: 91% of full-time freshmen returned.

FACULTY
Total: 145, 26% full-time, 18% with terminal degrees.
Student/faculty ratio: 23:1.

ACADEMICS
Calendar: semesters for undergraduate programs, trimesters for graduate programs. *Degrees:* certificates, associate, bachelor's, master's, post-master's, and postbachelor's certificates.
Special study options: academic remediation for entering students, accelerated degree program, cooperative education, distance learning, honors programs, part-time degree program, services for LD students, summer session for credit. ***ROTC:*** Army (c), Air Force (c).
Computers: 150 computers/terminals are available on campus for general student use. Students can access the following: computer help desk, free student e-mail accounts, online (class) grades. Campuswide network is available. Wireless service is available via entire campus.
Library: Bliblioteca Dra. Margot Arce de Vazquez plus 1 other. Weekly public service hours: 50; students can reserve study rooms.

STUDENT LIFE
Housing options: college housing not available.
Campus security: 24-hour patrols.
Student services: health clinic, personal/psychological counseling.

COSTS
Costs (2017–18) ***Tuition:*** $6568 full-time, $185 per credit part-time. ***Required fees:*** $950 full-time. ***Payment plans:*** installment, deferred payment. ***Waivers:*** employees or children of employees.

APPLYING
Standardized Tests *Required:* CEEB (for admission).
Options: electronic application.
Application fee: $25.
Required: high school transcript. ***Recommended:*** minimum 2.0 GPA.
Application deadlines: rolling (freshmen), rolling (transfers).
Notification: continuous (freshmen), continuous (transfers).

CONTACT
Bayamón Central University, PO Box 1725, Bayamón, PR 00960-1725. *Phone:* 787-786-3030 Ext. 2102.

Caribbean University

Bayamón, Puerto Rico
http://www.caribbean.edu/

- **Independent** comprehensive, founded 1969
- **Urban** 16-acre campus with easy access to San Juan
- **Coed** 2,920 undergraduate students, 72% full-time, 56% women, 44% men
- **Minimally difficult** entrance level, 57% of applicants were admitted

UNDERGRAD STUDENTS
2,099 full-time, 821 part-time. 100% Hispanic/Latino.

Freshmen:
Admission: 1,020 applied, 581 admitted, 293 enrolled. ***Average high school GPA:*** 2.64.
Retention: 72% of full-time freshmen returned.

FACULTY
Total: 361, 24% full-time, 19% with terminal degrees.
Student/faculty ratio: 14:1.

ACADEMICS
Calendar: semesters. *Degrees:* certificates, associate, bachelor's, master's, and doctoral.
Special study options: academic remediation for entering students, accelerated degree program, adult/continuing education programs, English as a second language, part-time degree program, services for LD students, summer session for credit. ***ROTC:*** Army (c).
Computers: 378 computers/terminals are available on campus for general student use. Students can access the following: campus intranet, computer help desk, free student e-mail accounts, online (class) grades, online (class) registration, online (class) schedules. Campuswide network is available. Wireless service is available via entire campus.
Library: Biblioteca Virgilio Davila, Recinto de Bayamon plus 4 others. *Books:* 76,606 (physical), 139,981 (digital/electronic); *Databases:* 2,346.

STUDENT LIFE
Housing options: college housing not available.

Activities and organizations: drama/theater group, choral group, Engineering Student Association, Nursing, Social Work, Speech Therapy, Criminal Justices.

Athletics ***Intercollegiate sports:*** baseball M, basketball M/W, cheerleading M/W, cross-country running M/W, soccer M/W, softball W, table tennis M, track and field M/W, volleyball M/W, wrestling M/W. ***Intramural sports:*** basketball M/W, volleyball M/W.

Campus security: 24-hour patrols.

Student services: health clinic, personal/psychological counseling.

COSTS
Costs (2016–17) ***Tuition:*** $4392 full-time. Full-time tuition and fees vary according to class time, degree level, location, and program. Part-time tuition and fees vary according to class time, degree level, location, and program. ***Required fees:*** $790 full-time. ***Payment plan:*** installment. ***Waivers:*** employees or children of employees.

APPLYING
Standardized Tests *Required for some:* College Board math/verbal tes for engineering.

Options: deferred entrance.

Application fee: $30.

Required: high school transcript. ***Required for some:*** minimum 2.0 GPA, 1 letter of recommendation, interview.

CONTACT
Caribbean University, Box 493, Bayamón, PR 00960-0493. *Phone:* 787-780-0070 Ext. 1129.

Caribbean University–Carolina

Carolina, Puerto Rico

http://www.caribbean.edu/

CONTACT
Caribbean University–Carolina, Calle Ignacio Arzuaga #208, Carolina, PR 00985.

Caribbean University–Ponce

Ponce, Puerto Rico

http://www.caribbean.edu/

CONTACT
Caribbean University–Ponce, Ave. Ednita Nazario #1015, Ponce, PR 00716-7733.

Caribbean University–Vega Baja

Vega Baja, Puerto Rico

http://www.caribbean.edu/

CONTACT
Caribbean University–Vega Baja, Carr 671 K.M. 5, Sector El Criollo, Bo. Algarrobo, Vega Baja, PR 00964.

Carlos Albizu University

San Juan, Puerto Rico

http://www.albizu.edu/

CONTACT
Carlos Albizu University, 151 Tanca Street, San Juan, PR 00901. *Phone:* 787-725-6500 Ext. 1521.

Centro de Estudios Multidisciplinarios

Bayamon, Puerto Rico

http://www.cempr.edu/

CONTACT
Centro de Estudios Multidisciplinarios, Calle Degetau #25, Bayamon, PR 00961.

Centro de Estudios Multidisciplinarios

Humacao, Puerto Rico

http://www.cempr.edu/

- **Proprietary** 4-year
- **Urban** 1-acre campus
- **Coed**

FACULTY
Student/faculty ratio: 5:1.

ACADEMICS
Calendar: quarters. *Degrees:* certificates, diplomas, associate, and bachelor's.
Library: Students can reserve study rooms.

STUDENT LIFE
Campus security: 24-hour emergency response devices and patrols.
Student services: personal/psychological counseling.

APPLYING
Required: high school transcript, minimum 2.0 GPA, interview.

CONTACT
Centro de Estudios Multidisciplinarios, Calle Dr. Vidal #8 y #53, Humacao, PR 00791. *Phone:* 787-850-8333.

Centro de Estudios Multidisciplinarios

Mayaguez, Puerto Rico

http://www.cempr.edu/

CONTACT
Centro de Estudios Multidisciplinarios, Calle Cristy #56, Mayaguez, PR 00680.

Centro de Estudios Multidisciplinarios

Rio Piedras, Puerto Rico

http://www.cempr.edu/

CONTACT
Admissions Department, Centro de Estudios Multidisciplinarios, Calle 13 #1206, Ext. San Agustin, Rio Piedras, PR 00926. *Phone:* 787-765-4210 Ext. 115. *Toll-free phone:* 877-779-CDEM.

Colegio Universitario de San Juan

San Juan, Puerto Rico

http://www.cunisanjuan.edu/

CONTACT
Colegio Universitario de San Juan, Jose R. Oliver Street, Hato Rey, PR 00918. *Phone:* 787-250-7111 Ext. 2227.

Columbia Centro Universitario

Caguas, Puerto Rico

http://www.columbiacentral.edu/

CONTACT
Mrs. Linette J. Miletti, Admission and Recruitment Coordinator, Columbia Centro Universitario, PO Box 8517, Caguas, PR 00726. *Phone:* 787-743-4041 Ext. 239. *Fax:* 787-744-7031. *E-mail:* lmiletti@columbiaco.edu.

Columbia Centro Universitario

Yauco, Puerto Rico

http://www.columbiacentral.edu/

CONTACT
Mrs. Carmen Ivette Pabon MSC, Admissions Coordinator, Columbia Centro Universitario, PO Box 3062, Yauco, PR 00698. *Phone:* 787-856-0845 Ext. 118. *Fax:* 787-267-0994. *E-mail:* cipabon@columbiaco.edu.

Conservatorio de Musica de Puerto Rico

San Juan, Puerto Rico

http://www.cmpr.edu/

- **Commonwealth-supported** comprehensive
- **Urban** 4-acre campus with easy access to Old San Juan
- **Endowment** $1.0 million
- **Coed**
- **Moderately difficult** entrance level

FACULTY
Student/faculty ratio: 6:1.

ACADEMICS
Calendar: semesters. *Degrees:* bachelor's, master's, and postbachelor's certificates.
Library: Biblioteca Amaury Veray plus 1 other.

STUDENT LIFE
Activities and organizations: choral group.
Campus security: 24-hour patrols.

COSTS
Costs (2016–17) ***Tuition:*** commonwealth resident $2520 full-time, $105 per credit part-time; nonresident $2520 full-time, $105 per credit part-time. Full-time tuition and fees vary according to program. Part-time tuition and fees vary according to program. ***Required fees:*** $850 full-time, $850 per term part-time, $850 per term part-time.

APPLYING
Application fee: $75.
Required: high school transcript, minimum 2.0 GPA, instrument audition, ear training test. ***Required for some:*** essay or personal statement, minimum 3.0 GPA. ***Recommended:*** interview.

CONTACT
Mrs. Ana Marta Arraiza, Admission Coordinator, Conservatorio de Musica de Puerto Rico, 951 Ponce de Leon Avenue, San Juan, PR 00907-3373. *Phone:* 787-751-0160 Ext. 275. *Fax:* 787-7589511. *E-mail:* aarraiza2@cmpr.gobierno.pr.

Dewey University–Carolina

Carolina, Puerto Rico

http://www.dewey.edu/

CONTACT
Dewey University–Carolina, Carr. #3, Km. 11, Parque Industrial de Carolina, Lote 7, Carolina, PR 00986.

Dewey University–Hato Rey

Hato Rey, Puerto Rico

http://www.dewey.edu/

CONTACT
Dewey University–Hato Rey, 427 Avenida Barbosa, Hato Rey, PR 00923.

Dewey University–Manati

Manati, Puerto Rico

http://www.dewey.edu/

CONTACT
Dewey University–Manati, Carr. 604, Km. 49.1 Barrio Tierras Nuevas, Salientes, Manati, PR 00674. *Toll-free phone:* 866-773-3939.

EDIC College

Caguas, Puerto Rico

http://www.ediccollege.edu/

CONTACT
EDIC College, Ave. Rafael Cordero Calle G?nova Urb. Caguas Norte, Caguas, PR 00726.

EDP University of Puerto Rico

Hato Rey, Puerto Rico

http://www.edpuniversity.edu/

- **Independent** comprehensive, founded 1968
- **Urban** 1-acre campus with easy access to San Juan
- **Coed** 1,574 undergraduate students, 62% full-time, 67% women, 33% men
- **Noncompetitive** entrance level, 61% of applicants were admitted

UNDERGRAD STUDENTS
971 full-time, 603 part-time. Students come from 19 states and territories; 27% are from out of state; 24% transferred in.

Freshmen:
Admission: 342 applied, 209 admitted, 97 enrolled. ***Average high school GPA:*** 2.93.
Retention: 89% of full-time freshmen returned.

FACULTY
Total: 198, 25% full-time, 17% with terminal degrees.
Student/faculty ratio: 12:1.

ACADEMICS
Calendar: semesters. *Degrees:* associate, bachelor's, master's, and postbachelor's certificates.
Special study options: academic remediation for entering students, accelerated degree program, adult/continuing education programs, advanced placement credit, cooperative education, distance learning, English as a second language, independent study, internships, part-time degree program, services for LD students, summer session for credit.
Computers: 205 computers/terminals and 230 ports are available on campus for general student use. Students can access the following: campus intranet, computer help desk, free student e-mail accounts, online (class) grades, online (class) registration, online (class) schedules. Campuswide network is available. Wireless service is available via classrooms, computer centers, computer labs, learning centers, libraries, student centers.
Library: Centro de Recursos para la Informacion plus 2 others. *Books:* 15,975 (physical), 300 (digital/electronic); *Serial titles:* 67 (physical), 13,800 (digital/electronic); *Databases:* 15. Weekly public service hours: 87; students can reserve study rooms.

STUDENT LIFE
Housing options: college housing not available.
Activities and organizations: choral group, Student Council, Graduate Student Association, Dance Group.
Campus security: 24-hour emergency response devices, student patrols, late-night transport/escort service, security and emergency telephones during working hours.

Student services: personal/psychological counseling.

COSTS & FINANCIAL AID

Costs (2017–18) ***Tuition:*** $5100 full-time, $170 per credit hour part-time. Full-time tuition and fees vary according to course load and program. Part-time tuition and fees vary according to course load and program. No tuition increase for student's term of enrollment. ***Required fees:*** $840 full-time, $420 per credit hour part-time. ***Payment plans:*** tuition prepayment, installment. ***Waivers:*** employees or children of employees.

Financial Aid Of all full-time matriculated undergraduates who enrolled in 2011, 1,028 applied for aid, 1,028 were judged to have need. 35 Federal Work-Study jobs (averaging $1972). ***Average percent of need met:*** 90. ***Average financial aid package:*** $5587. ***Average need-based loan:*** $3137. ***Average need-based gift aid:*** $5416. ***Average indebtedness upon graduation:*** $4256.

APPLYING

Standardized Tests *Required:* CEEB, institutional admission exam (for admission).

Options: electronic application, early admission, early decision, deferred entrance.

Application fee: $15.

Required: high school transcript, minimum 1.6 GPA, vaccination certificate. ***Required for some:*** essay or personal statement, minimum 2.5 GPA, 3 letters of recommendation, interview. ***Recommended:*** minimum 2.0 GPA.

Application deadlines: rolling (freshmen), rolling (transfers).

CONTACT

Mr. Oscar Morales, Dean of Student Affairs, EDP University of Puerto Rico, Avenue Ponce de Leon, #560, Hato Rey, PR 00918, Puerto Rico. *Phone:* 787-765-3560 Ext. 2272. *Fax:* 787-777-0024. *E-mail:* oscarmorales@edpuniversity.edu.

EDP University of Puerto Rico–San Sebastian

San Sebastian, Puerto Rico

http://www.edpuniversity.edu/

- **Independent** comprehensive, founded 1976
- **Rural** campus
- **Coed** 1,049 undergraduate students, 70% full-time, 68% women, 32% men
- **Minimally difficult** entrance level, 94% of applicants were admitted

UNDERGRAD STUDENTS

734 full-time, 315 part-time. Students come from 8 states and territories; 1 other country; 15% are from out of state; 100% Hispanic/Latino; 0.1% international; 11% transferred in.

Freshmen:

Admission: 113 applied, 106 admitted, 156 enrolled. ***Average high school GPA:*** 3.

FACULTY

Total: 94, 32% full-time, 12% with terminal degrees.

Student/faculty ratio: 17:1.

ACADEMICS

Calendar: semesters. *Degrees:* associate, bachelor's, and master's.

Special study options: academic remediation for entering students, accelerated degree program, adult/continuing education programs, cooperative education, distance learning, external degree program, independent study, internships, services for LD students, summer session for credit.

Computers: 168 computers/terminals are available on campus for general student use. Students can access the following: computer help desk, free student e-mail accounts, online (class) grades, online (class) registration, online (class) schedules. Campuswide network is available. Wireless service is available via entire campus.

Library: Juan S. Robles Library. *Books:* 11,871 (physical), 222,189 (digital/electronic); *Serial titles:* 11 (physical), 25,540 (digital/electronic); *Databases:* 12. Weekly public service hours: 85; students can reserve study rooms.

STUDENT LIFE

Housing options: college housing not available.

Activities and organizations: Nursing, Physical Therapy, Information Systems (SITA), Pharmacy, Digital Fashion Design.

Campus security: private security.

Student services: personal/psychological counseling.

COSTS & FINANCIAL AID

Costs (2017–18) ***Tuition:*** $5100 full-time, $170 per credit hour part-time. Full-time tuition and fees vary according to course load and program. Part-time tuition and fees vary according to course load and program. ***Required fees:*** $840 full-time, $420 per term part-time. ***Payment plan:*** installment. ***Waivers:*** employees or children of employees.

Financial Aid Of all full-time matriculated undergraduates who enrolled in 2012, 1,098 applied for aid, 1,097 were judged to have need. 32 Federal Work-Study jobs (averaging $1714). ***Average percent of need met:*** 92. ***Average financial aid package:*** $5000. ***Average need-based loan:*** $2601. ***Average need-based gift aid:*** $4545.

APPLYING

Standardized Tests *Required:* College Board exam or institutional entrance test (for admission).

Application fee: $15.

Required: high school transcript, minimum 1.6 GPA. ***Required for some:*** essay or personal statement, minimum 2.5 GPA, interview.

Application deadlines: rolling (freshmen), rolling (transfers).

CONTACT

Dra. Damarys Varela Velez, Student Affairs Dean, EDP University of Puerto Rico–San Sebastian, Avenue Betances #49, San Sebastian, PR 00685. *Phone:* 787-896-2252 Ext. 3313. *Fax:* 787-896-0066. *E-mail:* dvarela@edpuniversity.edu.

Escuela de Artes Plasticas y Diseño de Puerto Rico

San Juan, Puerto Rico

http://www.eap.edu/

- **Commonwealth-supported** 4-year, founded 1966
- **Urban** campus
- **Endowment** $2.4 million
- **Coed** 555 undergraduate students, 75% full-time, 65% women, 35% men
- **Moderately difficult** entrance level, 84% of applicants were admitted

UNDERGRAD STUDENTS

414 full-time, 141 part-time. Students come from 1 other state; 1 other country; 100% Hispanic/Latino; 4% transferred in.

Freshmen:

Admission: 91 applied, 76 admitted, 72 enrolled. ***Average high school GPA:*** 3.23.

Retention: 92% of full-time freshmen returned.

FACULTY

Total: 73, 22% full-time, 52% with terminal degrees.

Student/faculty ratio: 13:1.

ACADEMICS

Calendar: semesters 3 semesters each calendar year; participant in Year Round Pell. *Degree:* bachelor's.

Special study options: academic remediation for entering students, adult/continuing education programs, advanced placement credit, independent study, internships, part-time degree program, services for LD students, summer session for credit.

Computers: 110 computers/terminals and 110 ports are available on campus for general student use. Students can access the following: computer help desk, free student e-mail accounts. Wireless service is available via entire campus.

Library: Francisco Oller Library. *Books:* 31,789 (physical); *Databases:* 2. Weekly public service hours: 59.

STUDENT LIFE

Housing options: college housing not available.

Activities and organizations: Student government, CINEAP, Arte-Sanacion.

Campus security: 24-hour emergency response devices and patrols, security cameras.

Student services: personal/psychological counseling.

COSTS & FINANCIAL AID

Costs (2016–17) ***Tuition:*** commonwealth resident $2860 full-time, $90 per credit hour part-time; nonresident $5020 full-time, $180 per credit hour part-time. Part-time tuition and fees vary according to course load. ***Required fees:*** $602 full-time, $602 per year part-time. ***Room and board:*** $8144. ***Payment plan:*** installment.

Financial Aid Of all full-time matriculated undergraduates who enrolled in 2007, 276 applied for aid, 276 were judged to have need. 10 Federal Work-Study jobs (averaging $1850). ***Average percent of need met:*** 82. ***Financial aid deadline:*** 5/25.

APPLYING

Standardized Tests *Recommended:* SAT (for admission).

Application fee: $25.

Required: high school transcript, minimum 2.0 GPA, evaluation regarding artistic skills through a portfolio or seminar.

Application deadlines: 3/18 (freshmen), 3/18 (transfers).

Notification: 5/1 (freshmen), 5/1 (out-of-state freshmen), 5/1 (transfers).

CONTACT

Mrs. Nitza Melendez, Officer of Admissions, Escuela de Artes Plasticas y Diseño de Puerto Rico, PO Box 902112, San Juan, PR 00902-1112. *Phone:* 787-725-8120 Ext. 333. *Fax:* 787-721-3798. *E-mail:* nmelendez@eap.edu.

Humacao Community College

Humacao, Puerto Rico

http://www.hccpr.edu/

- **Independent** primarily 2-year
- **Urban** campus
- **Endowment** $865,348
- **Coed** 516 undergraduate students, 75% full-time, 67% women, 33% men
- **Noncompetitive** entrance level, 89% of applicants were admitted

UNDERGRAD STUDENTS

388 full-time, 128 part-time. Students come from 1 other state; 100% Hispanic/Latino; 29% transferred in.

Freshmen:

Admission: 140 applied, 124 admitted, 94 enrolled. ***Average high school GPA:*** 2.89.

Retention: 54% of full-time freshmen returned.

FACULTY

Total: 27, 48% full-time, 100% with terminal degrees.

Student/faculty ratio: 30:1.

ACADEMICS

Calendar: trimesters. *Degrees:* certificates, diplomas, associate, and bachelor's.

Special study options: academic remediation for entering students, adult/continuing education programs, cooperative education, distance learning, internships, part-time degree program, services for LD students.

Computers: 294 computers/terminals are available on campus for general student use. Students can access the following: campus intranet, computer help desk, free student e-mail accounts, online (class) grades, online (class) registration. Wireless service is available via entire campus.

Library: Santiago N. Manuez Educational Resources Center plus 1 other. *Books:* 5,320 (physical); *Serial titles:* 43 (physical), 2 (digital/electronic); *Databases:* 5. Weekly public service hours: 56.

STUDENT LIFE

Housing options: college housing not available.

Activities and organizations: Enactus Humacao Community College, Students Council.

Campus security: 24-hour emergency response devices and patrols.

Student services: personal/psychological counseling.

COSTS & FINANCIAL AID

Costs (2017–18) ***One-time required fee:*** $140. ***Tuition:*** $4932 full-time, $2466 per year part-time. Full-time tuition and fees vary according to course load and degree level. Part-time tuition and fees vary according to course load and degree level. ***Required fees:*** $450 full-time, $450 per year part-time. ***Payment plan:*** installment. ***Waivers:*** employees or children of employees.

Financial Aid Of all full-time matriculated undergraduates who enrolled in 2015, 64 Federal Work-Study jobs (averaging $546).

APPLYING

Application fee: $15.

Required: high school transcript, interview. ***Required for some:*** certificate of Immunization for students under 21 years.

Notification: continuous (freshmen).

CONTACT

Mrs. Adela Aponte, Director of Admissions, Humacao Community College, PO Box 9139, Humacao, PR 00792, Puerto Rico. *Phone:* 787-852-1430 Ext. 225. *Fax:* 787-850-1577. *E-mail:* adela.aponte@hccpr.edu.

Inter American University of Puerto Rico, Aguadilla Campus

Aguadilla, Puerto Rico

http://www.aguadilla.inter.edu/

- **Independent** comprehensive, founded 1957, part of Inter American University of Puerto Rico
- **Small-town** 50-acre campus
- **Endowment** $1.7 million
- **Coed** 3,964 undergraduate students, 85% full-time, 55% women, 45% men
- **Moderately difficult** entrance level, 47% of applicants were admitted

UNDERGRAD STUDENTS

3,355 full-time, 609 part-time. Students come from 24 states and territories; 1 other country; 2% are from out of state; 0.1% Black or African American, non-Hispanic/Latino; 100% Hispanic/Latino; 0.1% Asian, non-Hispanic/Latino; 0.1% American Indian or Alaska Native, non-Hispanic/Latino; 3% transferred in.

Freshmen:

Admission: 1,728 applied, 806 admitted, 787 enrolled. ***Average high school GPA:*** 2.95.

Retention: 74% of full-time freshmen returned.

FACULTY

Total: 263, 30% full-time, 100% with terminal degrees.

Student/faculty ratio: 30:1.

ACADEMICS

Calendar: semesters. *Degrees:* certificates, associate, bachelor's, master's, and postbachelor's certificates.

Special study options: academic remediation for entering students, accelerated degree program, adult/continuing education programs, advanced placement credit, cooperative education, distance learning, double majors, English as a second language, external degree program, honors programs, independent study, internships, part-time degree program, services for LD students, study abroad, summer session for credit. ***ROTC:*** Army (b), Air Force (b).

Computers: 861 computers/terminals are available on campus for general student use. Students can access the following: campus intranet, free student e-mail accounts, online (class) grades, online (class) registration, online (class) schedules. Campuswide network is available. Wireless service is available via entire campus.

Library: Manuel Mendez Ballester Information Access Center. *Books:* 63,637 (physical), 128 (digital/electronic); *Serial titles:* 199 (digital/electronic); *Databases:* 80. Weekly public service hours: 80; students can reserve study rooms.

STUDENT LIFE

Housing options: college housing not available.

Activities and organizations: drama/theater group, student-run newspaper, choral group, Criminal Justice Association, Microbiot Science

Association, Social Workers Association, Nursing Association, Psychology Association.

Athletics ***Intercollegiate sports:*** baseball M(s), basketball M(s)/W(s), cheerleading M(s)/W(s), cross-country running M(s)/W(s), soccer M(s)/W(s), softball M(s)/W(s), swimming and diving M(s)/W(s), table tennis M(s)/W(s), tennis M(s)/W(s), track and field M(s)/W(s), volleyball M(s)/W(s), weight lifting M(s)/W(s), wrestling M(s). ***Intramural sports:*** basketball M/W, cross-country running M/W, soccer M/W, softball M/W, table tennis M/W, tennis M/W, track and field M/W, volleyball M/W, weight lifting M/W.

Campus security: 24-hour emergency response devices and patrols.

Student services: personal/psychological counseling.

COSTS

Costs (2017–18) ***Tuition:*** $4488 full-time, $187 per semester hour part-time. Full-time tuition and fees vary according to course load and program. Part-time tuition and fees vary according to course load and program. ***Required fees:*** $652 full-time. ***Payment plan:*** deferred payment.

APPLYING

Standardized Tests *Required:* SAT or ACT (for admission), PAA (for admission).

Options: electronic application.

Required: high school transcript, minimum 2.0 GPA.

Application deadlines: rolling (freshmen), rolling (transfers).

CONTACT

Mrs. Daisy Irizarry, Administrative Assistant, Inter American University of Puerto Rico, Aguadilla Campus, PO Box 20,000, Road 459 Intersection 463, Aguadilla, PR 00605. *Phone:* 787-891-0925 Ext. 2181. *Fax:* 787-882-3020.

Inter American University of Puerto Rico, Arecibo Campus

Arecibo, Puerto Rico

http://www.arecibo.inter.edu/

CONTACT

Ms. Provi Montalvo, Admission Director, Inter American University of Puerto Rico, Arecibo Campus, PO Box 4050, Arecibo, PR 00614-4050. *Phone:* 787-878-5475. *Fax:* 787-880-1624. *E-mail:* pmontalvo@arecibo.inter.edu.

Inter American University of Puerto Rico, Barranquitas Campus

Barranquitas, Puerto Rico

http://www.br.inter.edu/

- **Independent** comprehensive, founded 1957, part of Inter American University of Puerto Rico
- **Small-town** campus with easy access to San Juan
- **Endowment** $1.0 million
- **Coed** 2,067 undergraduate students, 88% full-time, 62% women, 38% men

UNDERGRAD STUDENTS

1,824 full-time, 243 part-time. 100% Hispanic/Latino.

Freshmen:

Admission: 570 enrolled. ***Average high school GPA:*** 2.97.

Retention: 79% of full-time freshmen returned.

FACULTY

Total: 143, 22% full-time, 22% with terminal degrees.

Student/faculty ratio: 24:1.

ACADEMICS

Calendar: semesters. *Degrees:* associate, bachelor's, master's, and postbachelor's certificates.

Special study options: academic remediation for entering students, adult/continuing education programs, advanced placement credit, cooperative education, distance learning, English as a second language, external degree program, freshman honors college, honors programs, off-campus study, part-time degree program, services for LD students, study abroad, summer session for credit. ***ROTC:*** Army (c).

Computers: 450 computers/terminals and 450 ports are available on campus for general student use. Students can access the following: campus intranet, computer help desk, free student e-mail accounts, online (class) grades, online (class) registration, online (class) schedules. Campuswide network is available. Wireless service is available via entire campus.

Library: Centro de Accoso a la Informacio, Recinto de Barranquitas. Students can reserve study rooms.

STUDENT LIFE

Activities and organizations: Alumni Student Chapter.

Athletics ***Intercollegiate sports:*** baseball M(s), basketball M/W, cross-country running M/W, softball M/W, table tennis M/W, tennis M/W, track and field M/W, volleyball M/W, weight lifting M/W, wrestling M/W. ***Intramural sports:*** basketball M/W, cross-country running M/W, softball M/W, table tennis M/W, track and field M/W, volleyball M/W.

Campus security: 24-hour patrols.

Student services: health clinic, personal/psychological counseling.

COSTS

Costs (2017–18) ***One-time required fee:*** $100. ***Tuition:*** $6039 full-time, $3020 per year part-time. Full-time tuition and fees vary according to course load, degree level, and program. Part-time tuition and fees vary according to course load, degree level, and program. ***Required fees:*** $652 full-time, $524 per year part-time, $262 per term part-time. ***Room only:*** Room and board charges vary according to housing facility. ***Payment plan:*** deferred payment. ***Waivers:*** minority students and employees or children of employees.

APPLYING

Standardized Tests *Required:* CEEB (for admission). *Required for some:* SAT or ACT (for admission).

Required: high school transcript, interview. ***Recommended:*** letters of recommendation.

CONTACT

Dra. Maribel Lopez, Decana de Estudiantes, Inter American University of Puerto Rico, Barranquitas Campus, PO Box 517, Barranquitas, PR 00794. *Phone:* 787-857-3600 Ext. 2009. *Fax:* 787-857-2125. *E-mail:* mlopez@br.inter.edu.

Inter American University of Puerto Rico, Bayamón Campus

Bayamón, Puerto Rico

http://bayamon.inter.edu/

- **Independent** comprehensive, founded 1912, part of Inter American University of Puerto Rico
- **Urban** 51-acre campus with easy access to San Juan
- **Endowment** $201.4 million
- **Coed** 4,328 undergraduate students, 87% full-time, 42% women, 58% men
- 43% of applicants were admitted

UNDERGRAD STUDENTS

3,772 full-time, 556 part-time. Students come from 4 states and territories; 8 other countries; 0.2% are from out of state; 0.4% Black or African American, non-Hispanic/Latino; 99% Hispanic/Latino; 0.1% Asian, non-Hispanic/Latino; 0.1% Native Hawaiian or other Pacific Islander, non-Hispanic/Latino; 3% transferred in.

Freshmen:

Admission: 2,227 applied, 950 admitted, 910 enrolled. ***Average high school GPA:*** 3.09.

Retention: 72% of full-time freshmen returned.

FACULTY

Total: 291, 33% full-time, 30% with terminal degrees.

Student/faculty ratio: 24:1.

ACADEMICS
Calendar: semesters. *Degrees:* certificates, associate, bachelor's, and master's.
Special study options: accelerated degree program, adult/continuing education programs, advanced placement credit, cooperative education, distance learning, external degree program, honors programs, independent study, internships, part-time degree program, services for LD students, summer session for credit. ***ROTC:*** Army (c).
Computers: 730 computers/terminals are available on campus for general student use. Students can access the following: computer help desk, free student e-mail accounts, online (class) grades, online (class) registration. Campuswide network is available. Wireless service is available via entire campus.
Library: Centro de Acceso a la Informacion plus 1 other. *Books:* 33,638 (physical), 224,713 (digital/electronic); *Serial titles:* 147 (physical), 2 (digital/electronic); *Databases:* 56. Weekly public service hours: 79; students can reserve study rooms.

STUDENT LIFE
Housing options: men-only, women-only. Campus housing is university owned.
Activities and organizations: drama/theater group, student-run radio station, choral group, Consejo de Estudiantes, Asociacion Estudiantes de Ingenieria, Asociacion Estudiantes de Aviacion, Estudiantes Unidos por la Ciencia, Asociacion de Estudiantes de Administracion de Empresas.
Athletics ***Intercollegiate sports:*** baseball M(s), basketball M(s)/W(s), cross-country running M(s)/W(s), softball M(s)/W(s), swimming and diving M(s)/W(s), table tennis M(s)/W(s), track and field M(s)/W(s), volleyball M(s)/W(s), weight lifting M(s). ***Intramural sports:*** basketball M/W, cross-country running M/W, softball M/W, swimming and diving M/W, table tennis M/W, tennis M/W, track and field M/W, volleyball M/W, weight lifting M.
Campus security: 24-hour patrols.
Student services: health clinic, personal/psychological counseling.

COSTS & FINANCIAL AID
Costs (2017–18) ***Comprehensive fee:*** $11,292 includes full-time tuition ($4488), mandatory fees ($690), and room and board ($6114). Full-time tuition and fees vary according to course load and program. Part-time tuition: $1122 per credit hour. Part-time tuition and fees vary according to course load and program. ***Required fees:*** $187 per credit part-time, $305 per semester part-time. ***College room only:*** $3113. ***Payment plan:*** deferred payment.
Financial Aid Of all full-time matriculated undergraduates who enrolled in 2016, 2,592 applied for aid, 2,558 were judged to have need, 7 had their need fully met. ***Average percent of need met:*** 28. ***Average financial aid package:*** $3755. ***Average need-based loan:*** $2904. ***Average need-based gift aid:*** $3231.

APPLYING
Standardized Tests *Required:* CEEB (for admission). *Required for some:* SAT (for admission).
Options: electronic application.
Required: high school transcript, minimum 2.0 GPA. ***Required for some:*** 2.5 GPA for engineering.
Notification: continuous (freshmen), continuous (transfers).

CONTACT
Inter American University of Puerto Rico, Bayamón Campus, 500 Dr. John Will Harris Road, Bayamón, PR 00957. *Phone:* 787-279-1912 Ext. 2017.

Inter American University of Puerto Rico, Fajardo Campus

Fajardo, Puerto Rico

http://www.fajardo.inter.edu/

- **Independent** comprehensive, founded 1965, part of Inter American University of Puerto Rico
- **Small-town** 11-acre campus with easy access to San Juan
- **Endowment** $4.3 million
- **Coed** 1,986 undergraduate students, 87% full-time, 58% women, 42% men
- **Moderately difficult** entrance level, 82% of applicants were admitted

UNDERGRAD STUDENTS
1,727 full-time, 259 part-time. Students come from 3 states and territories; 100% Hispanic/Latino.

Freshmen:
Admission: 663 applied, 545 admitted, 487 enrolled. ***Average high school GPA:*** 2.
Retention: 74% of full-time freshmen returned.

FACULTY
Total: 113, 36% full-time, 27% with terminal degrees.
Student/faculty ratio: 11:1.

ACADEMICS
Calendar: semesters. *Degrees:* certificates, associate, bachelor's, and master's.
Special study options: academic remediation for entering students, adult/continuing education programs, advanced placement credit, cooperative education, distance learning, English as a second language, external degree program, honors programs, independent study, internships, off-campus study, part-time degree program, services for LD students, summer session for credit. ***ROTC:*** Army (c).
Computers: 280 computers/terminals are available on campus for general student use. Students can access the following: free student e-mail accounts, online (class) grades, online (class) registration, online (class) schedules. Campuswide network is available. Wireless service is available via entire campus.
Library: Antonio S. Belaval Library plus 1 other. *Books:* 46,756 (physical), 185,479 (digital/electronic); *Serial titles:* 22,085 (physical), 49,284 (digital/electronic); *Databases:* 26. Weekly public service hours: 79; students can reserve study rooms.

STUDENT LIFE
Housing options: college housing not available.
Activities and organizations: choral group, Future Teachers Association, Criminal Justice Student Association, Honor Program Association, Computer Science Association, Social Work Association.
Athletics ***Intercollegiate sports:*** baseball M, basketball M(s)/W, cheerleading W, softball W, track and field M(s)/W(s), volleyball M/W.
Campus security: 24-hour patrols.
Student services: personal/psychological counseling.

COSTS
Costs (2017–18) ***Tuition:*** $4392 full-time, $183 per credit part-time. Full-time tuition and fees vary according to class time, course level, course load, degree level, location, program, and student level. Part-time tuition and fees vary according to class time, course level, course load, degree level, location, program, and student level. ***Required fees:*** $710 full-time, $281 per term part-time. ***Room only:*** Room and board charges vary according to location. ***Payment plans:*** installment, deferred payment. ***Waivers:*** employees or children of employees.

APPLYING
Standardized Tests *Required:* College Board exam (for admission).
Options: electronic application, early admission, deferred entrance.
Required: high school transcript. ***Required for some:*** interview.
Application deadlines: 5/15 (freshmen), rolling (transfers).

CONTACT
Ms. Ghisita M. Garcia, Administrative Assistant II, Inter American University of Puerto Rico, Fajardo Campus, Call Box 70003, Fajardo, PR

00738-7003. *Phone:* 787-863-2390 Ext. 2210. *Fax:* 787-860-3470. *E-mail:* ghisita.garcia@fajardo.inter.edu.

Inter American University of Puerto Rico, Guayama Campus

Guayama, Puerto Rico

http://www.guayama.inter.edu/

- **Independent** comprehensive, founded 1958, part of Inter American University of Puerto Rico
- **Small-town** 50-acre campus with easy access to San Juan
- **Coed** 1,815 undergraduate students, 80% full-time, 66% women, 34% men
- **Moderately difficult** entrance level, 48% of applicants were admitted

UNDERGRAD STUDENTS

1,443 full-time, 372 part-time. 0.1% Black or African American, non-Hispanic/Latino; 100% Hispanic/Latino; 0.1% Native Hawaiian or other Pacific Islander, non-Hispanic/Latino; 0.1% American Indian or Alaska Native, non-Hispanic/Latino; 9% transferred in.

Freshmen:

Admission: 536 applied, 259 admitted, 245 enrolled. ***Average high school GPA:*** 3.08.

Retention: 71% of full-time freshmen returned.

FACULTY

Total: 165, 27% full-time, 20% with terminal degrees.

Student/faculty ratio: 12:1.

ACADEMICS

Calendar: semesters. *Degrees:* certificates, associate, bachelor's, and master's.

Special study options: academic remediation for entering students, adult/continuing education programs, advanced placement credit, cooperative education, distance learning, English as a second language, honors programs, independent study, internships, off-campus study, part-time degree program, services for LD students, summer session for credit. ***ROTC:*** Army (c).

Computers: 252 computers/terminals are available on campus for general student use. Students can access the following: campus intranet, computer help desk, free student e-mail accounts, online (class) grades, online (class) registration, online (class) schedules. Campuswide network is available. Wireless service is available via entire campus.

Library: Information Access Center. Weekly public service hours: 60.

STUDENT LIFE

Housing options: college housing not available.

Activities and organizations: student-run radio station, Natural Science and Technology, Nursing Student Association, Office Professionals, Medical Billers Organization, Pharmacy Technicians.

Athletics ***Intercollegiate sports:*** baseball M, basketball M(s)/W(s), cross-country running M(s)/W(s), swimming and diving M. ***Intramural sports:*** baseball M, basketball M/W, cross-country running M/W, soccer M, softball M/W, swimming and diving M, table tennis W, tennis W, track and field M/W.

Campus security: 24-hour patrols.

Student services: health clinic, personal/psychological counseling.

COSTS & FINANCIAL AID

Costs (2017–18) ***One-time required fee:*** $55. ***Tuition:*** $5610 full-time. ***Required fees:*** $815 full-time. ***Payment plan:*** deferred payment. ***Waivers:*** employees or children of employees.

Financial Aid Of all full-time matriculated undergraduates who enrolled in 2015, 1,039 applied for aid, 1,036 were judged to have need, 1 had their need fully met. ***Average percent of need met:*** 29. ***Average financial aid package:*** $4163. ***Average need-based loan:*** $2279. ***Average need-based gift aid:*** $3301.

APPLYING

Standardized Tests *Required:* PAA (for admission). *Recommended:* SAT (for admission).

Options: electronic application.

Required: high school transcript, minimum 2.0 GPA. ***Required for some:*** interview.

Application deadlines: 8/1 (freshmen), 8/1 (transfers).

CONTACT

Mrs. Laura E. Ferrer, Director of Admissions, Inter American University of Puerto Rico, Guayama Campus, Call Box 10004, Guayama, PR 00785. *Phone:* 787-864-2222 Ext. 2220. *Fax:* 787-864-8232. *E-mail:* laura.ferrer@guayama.inter.edu.

Inter American University of Puerto Rico, Metropolitan Campus

San Juan, Puerto Rico

http://metro.inter.edu/

- **Independent** comprehensive, founded 1960, part of Inter American University of Puerto Rico
- **Urban** campus
- **Endowment** $201.4 million
- **Coed** 6,307 undergraduate students, 81% full-time, 56% women, 44% men
- **Moderately difficult** entrance level, 16% of applicants were admitted

UNDERGRAD STUDENTS

5,087 full-time, 1,220 part-time. 0.8% Black or African American, non-Hispanic/Latino; 98% Hispanic/Latino; 0.2% Asian, non-Hispanic/Latino; 0.1% Native Hawaiian or other Pacific Islander, non-Hispanic/Latino; 0.3% American Indian or Alaska Native, non-Hispanic/Latino.

Freshmen:

Admission: 4,102 applied, 647 admitted, 641 enrolled. ***Average high school GPA:*** 3.12.

Retention: 71% of full-time freshmen returned.

FACULTY

Total: 604, 32% full-time, 45% with terminal degrees.

ACADEMICS

Calendar: semesters. *Degrees:* certificates, associate, bachelor's, master's, doctoral, post-master's, and postbachelor's certificates.

Special study options: accelerated degree program, adult/continuing education programs, cooperative education, distance learning, English as a second language, external degree program, honors programs, independent study, internships, part-time degree program, services for LD students, study abroad, summer session for credit. ***ROTC:*** Army (c), Navy (c), Air Force (c).

Computers: 637 computers/terminals are available on campus for general student use. Students can access the following: campus intranet, computer help desk, free student e-mail accounts, online (class) grades, online (class) registration, online (class) schedules. Campuswide network is available. Wireless service is available via classrooms, computer centers, computer labs, learning centers, libraries, student centers.

Library: Centro de Acceso a la Informacion plus 1 other. *Books:* 121,223 (physical); *Serial titles:* 311 (physical); *Databases:* 24. Students can reserve study rooms.

STUDENT LIFE

Housing options: college housing not available.

Activities and organizations: drama/theater group, student-run newspaper, choral group, Intercultural Student Association, Club Rotaract, Roots and Shoots Inter Metro, Chemical Students Association, Social Work Students Association.

Athletics ***Intercollegiate sports:*** basketball M, soccer M, table tennis M/W, tennis M/W, volleyball M/W.

Campus security: 24-hour emergency response devices and patrols, Video Security System.

Student services: personal/psychological counseling, women's center.

FINANCIAL AID

Financial Aid Of all full-time matriculated undergraduates who enrolled in 1999, 4,328 applied for aid, 3,935 were judged to have need, 29 had their need fully met. ***Average percent of need met:*** 11. ***Average financial aid package:*** $2144. ***Average need-based loan:*** $1149. ***Average need-based gift aid:*** $1617. ***Financial aid deadline:*** 4/30.

APPLYING
Standardized Tests *Required:* CEEB (for admission). *Required for some:* SAT (for admission).
Options: electronic application.
Required: high school transcript, minimum 2.0 GPA.
Application deadlines: 5/15 (freshmen), 5/15 (transfers).

CONTACT
Inter American University of Puerto Rico, Metropolitan Campus, PO Box 191293, San Juan, PR 00919-1293. *Phone:* 787-250-1912 Ext. 2418.

Inter American University of Puerto Rico, Ponce Campus

Mercedita, Puerto Rico

http://www.ponce.inter.edu/

- **Independent** comprehensive, founded 1962, part of Inter American University of Puerto Rico
- **Urban** 50-acre campus with easy access to San Juan
- **Endowment** $14.5 million
- **Coed** 4,868 undergraduate students, 85% full-time, 59% women, 41% men
- **Moderately difficult** entrance level, 56% of applicants were admitted

UNDERGRAD STUDENTS
4,151 full-time, 717 part-time. 100% Hispanic/Latino; 0.1% American Indian or Alaska Native, non-Hispanic/Latino; 4% transferred in.

Freshmen:
Admission: 1,646 applied, 925 admitted, 894 enrolled. *Average high school GPA:* 2.75.
Retention: 76% of full-time freshmen returned.

FACULTY
Total: 284, 35% full-time, 34% with terminal degrees.
Student/faculty ratio: 30:1.

ACADEMICS
Calendar: semesters. *Degrees:* certificates, associate, bachelor's, master's, and doctoral.
Special study options: academic remediation for entering students, adult/continuing education programs, cooperative education, distance learning, English as a second language, honors programs, internships, off-campus study, part-time degree program, services for LD students, study abroad, summer session for credit.
Computers: 376 computers/terminals and 447 ports are available on campus for general student use. Students can access the following: free student e-mail accounts, online (class) grades, online (class) registration. Campuswide network is available. Wireless service is available via entire campus.
Library: Centro de Acceso a la Informacion plus 1 other. *Books:* 54,043 (physical), 243,183 (digital/electronic); *Serial titles:* 109 (physical); *Databases:* 130. Weekly public service hours: 56; students can reserve study rooms.

STUDENT LIFE
Housing options: college housing not available.
Activities and organizations: drama/theater group, choral group, Association of Future Teachers of Special Education, Hotel Management Association, American Chemical Society (ACS), Criminal Justice Association, Students Board of Honor Program, national fraternities.
Athletics *Intercollegiate sports:* baseball M(s), basketball M(s)/W(s), cheerleading M/W, cross-country running M(s)/W(s), soccer M(s)/W(s), softball M(s)/W(s), table tennis M(s)/W(s), tennis M(s)/W(s), track and field M(s)/W(s), volleyball M(s)/W(s), weight lifting M(s)/W(s).
Intramural sports: basketball M/W, cross-country running M/W, soccer M/W, softball M/W, swimming and diving M/W, table tennis M/W, tennis M/W, track and field M/W, volleyball M/W, weight lifting M/W, wrestling M/W.
Campus security: 24-hour emergency response devices and patrols.
Student services: health clinic, personal/psychological counseling.

COSTS & FINANCIAL AID
Costs (2016–17) *Tuition:* $4392 full-time, $183 per credit hour part-time. Full-time tuition and fees vary according to course load and program. Part-time tuition and fees vary according to course load and program. *Required fees:* $690 full-time, $183 per credit hour part-time. *Payment plan:* deferred payment.
Financial Aid Of all full-time matriculated undergraduates who enrolled in 2012, 3,337 applied for aid, 3,323 were judged to have need, 2 had their need fully met. *Average percent of need met:* 8. *Average financial aid package:* $1160. *Average need-based loan:* $1476. *Average need-based gift aid:* $533.

APPLYING
Standardized Tests *Required:* CEEB (for admission). *Required for some:* SAT (for admission).
Options: deferred entrance.
Required: high school transcript, minimum 2.0 GPA.
Application deadlines: 5/15 (freshmen), 5/15 (transfers).

CONTACT
Mr. Franco Diaz, Admissions Officer, Inter American University of Puerto Rico, Ponce Campus, 104 Turpo Industrial Park, Road #1, Mercedita, PR 00715-1602. *Phone:* 787-284-1912 Ext. 2025. *Fax:* 787-841-0103. *E-mail:* fidiaz@ponce.inter.edu.

Inter American University of Puerto Rico, San Germán Campus

San Germán, Puerto Rico

http://www.sg.inter.edu/

- **Independent** university, founded 1912, part of Inter American University of Puerto Rico
- **Small-town** 274-acre campus with easy access to Ponce, Aguadilla, Mayaguez
- **Endowment** $38.9 million
- **Coed** 4,031 undergraduate students, 90% full-time, 53% women, 47% men
- **Moderately difficult** entrance level, 69% of applicants were admitted

UNDERGRAD STUDENTS
3,618 full-time, 413 part-time. Students come from 16 states and territories; 3 other countries; 1% are from out of state; 0.2% Black or African American, non-Hispanic/Latino; 99% Hispanic/Latino; 2% transferred in; 5% live on campus.

Freshmen:
Admission: 1,453 applied, 1,004 admitted, 942 enrolled. *Average high school GPA:* 3.
Retention: 71% of full-time freshmen returned.

FACULTY
Total: 298, 35% full-time, 36% with terminal degrees.
Student/faculty ratio: 17:1.

ACADEMICS
Calendar: semesters. *Degrees:* certificates, associate, bachelor's, master's, doctoral, and postbachelor's certificates.
Special study options: academic remediation for entering students, accelerated degree program, adult/continuing education programs, advanced placement credit, cooperative education, distance learning, double majors, English as a second language, external degree program, honors programs, independent study, internships, off-campus study, part-time degree program, services for LD students, summer session for credit. *ROTC:* Army (c), Navy (c), Air Force (c).
Computers: 1,200 computers/terminals and 1,300 ports are available on campus for general student use. Students can access the following: campus intranet, computer help desk, free student e-mail accounts, online (class) grades, online (class) registration, online (class) schedules. Campuswide network is available. Wireless service is available via computer centers, computer labs, dorm rooms, learning centers, libraries, student centers.
Library: Juan Cancio Ortiz Library. *Books:* 159,511 (physical), 3,850 (digital/electronic); *Serial titles:* 2,025 (physical), 594,924

(digital/electronic); *Databases:* 96. Weekly public service hours: 86; students can reserve study rooms.

STUDENT LIFE

Housing options: men-only, women-only, special housing for students with disabilities. Campus housing is university owned. Freshman applicants given priority for college housing.

Activities and organizations: drama/theater group, student-run newspaper, choral group, Asociacion de Pre-Medica-Caduceus, Business Professionals of America, Sociedad de Honor en Biologia Beta Beta Beta (TriBeta, Asociacion de Estudiantes de Futuros Exalumnos, Asociacion de Estudiantes del Programa de Honor, national fraternities, national sororities.

Athletics ***Intercollegiate sports:*** baseball M(s), basketball M(s)/W(s), cross-country running M(s)/W(s), sand volleyball M/W, soccer M(s)/W, softball M/W, swimming and diving M/W, table tennis M(s)/W(s), tennis M(s)/W(s), track and field M(s)/W(s), volleyball M(s)/W(s), weight lifting M(s)/W(s). ***Intramural sports:*** badminton M/W, basketball M/W, cross-country running M/W, softball M/W, table tennis M/W, tennis M/W, track and field M/W, volleyball M/W.

Campus security: 24-hour emergency response devices and patrols, late-night transport/escort service, electronic vigilance systems with nonstop digital video cameras, access control permits, periodic surveillance.

Student services: health clinic, personal/psychological counseling, women's center.

COSTS & FINANCIAL AID

Costs (2017–18) ***Comprehensive fee:*** $8880 includes full-time tuition ($5490), mandatory fees ($690), and room and board ($2700). Full-time tuition and fees vary according to degree level. Part-time tuition: $183 per credit hour. Part-time tuition and fees vary according to degree level. ***College room only:*** $1200. Room and board charges vary according to board plan and housing facility. ***Payment plan:*** installment. ***Waivers:*** employees or children of employees.

Financial Aid Of all full-time matriculated undergraduates who enrolled in 2009, 2,797 applied for aid, 2,755 were judged to have need, 4 had their need fully met. ***Average percent of need met:*** 12. ***Average financial aid package:*** $2009. ***Average need-based loan:*** $3080. ***Average need-based gift aid:*** $642.

APPLYING

Standardized Tests *Required:* CEEB (for admission). *Required for some:* SAT or ACT (for admission).

Options: electronic application, early admission.

Required: high school transcript, medical history, vaccination. ***Required for some:*** 1 letter of recommendation, interview. ***Recommended:*** essay or personal statement, minimum 2.0 GPA.

Application deadlines: 5/15 (freshmen), 5/15 (transfers).

Notification: continuous (freshmen), continuous (transfers).

CONTACT

Prof. Mildred Camacho, Director of Admissions, Inter American University of Puerto Rico, San Germán Campus, PO Box 5100, San German, PR 00683-5008. *Phone:* 787-264-1912 Ext. 7283. *Toll-free phone:* 800-981-8075. *Fax:* 787-892-7020. *E-mail:* milcama@intersg.edu.

National University College

Bayamón, Puerto Rico

http://www.nuc.edu/

CONTACT

Admissions, National University College, PO Box 2036, National College Plaza Building, Bayamón, PR 00960. *Toll-free phone:* 800-780-5134.

National University College

Caguas, Puerto Rico

http://www.nuc.edu/

CONTACT

National University College, 190 Avenida Gautier Benitez Esquina Avenida Federico Degatau, Caguas, PR 00725. *Toll-free phone:* 800-780-5134.

National University College

Ponce, Puerto Rico

http://www.nuc.edu/

CONTACT

National University College, PO Box 801243, Ponce, PR 00716.

National University College

Rio Grande, Puerto Rico

http://www.nuc.edu/

CONTACT

National University College, Carretera #3 Km. 22.1, Bo. Ci naga Baja, Rio Grande, PR 00745. *Toll-free phone:* 800-981-0812.

Polytechnic University of Puerto Rico

Hato Rey, Puerto Rico

http://www.pupr.edu/

- **Independent** comprehensive, founded 1966
- **Urban** 10-acre campus with easy access to San Juan
- **Endowment** $14.1 million
- **Coed** 3,493 undergraduate students, 46% full-time, 20% women, 80% men
- **Minimally difficult** entrance level, 85% of applicants were admitted

UNDERGRAD STUDENTS

1,592 full-time, 1,901 part-time. Students come from 9 states and territories; 4 other countries; 100% Hispanic/Latino; 0.1% Asian, non-Hispanic/Latino; 0.1% Race/ethnicity unknown; 6% transferred in.

Freshmen:

Admission: 611 applied, 521 admitted, 361 enrolled. ***Average high school GPA:*** 3.25.

Retention: 77% of full-time freshmen returned.

FACULTY

Total: 226, 59% full-time, 29% with terminal degrees.

Student/faculty ratio: 21:1.

ACADEMICS

Calendar: trimesters. *Degrees:* associate, bachelor's, master's, and doctoral.

Special study options: academic remediation for entering students, advanced placement credit, distance learning, English as a second language, honors programs, independent study, internships, student-designed majors, summer session for credit. ***ROTC:*** Army (c).

Computers: 800 computers/terminals and 800 ports are available on campus for general student use. Students can access the following: campus intranet, computer help desk, free student e-mail accounts, online (class) grades, online (class) registration, online (class) schedules. Campuswide network is available. 100% of college-owned or -operated housing units are wired for high-speed Internet access. Wireless service is available via entire campus.

Library: Biblioteca de la Unidersidad Politecnica de Puerto Rico. *Books:* 66,393 (physical), 59,171 (digital/electronic); *Serial titles:* 1,759 (physical), 16,160 (digital/electronic); *Databases:* 46. Weekly public service hours: 82; study areas open 24 hours, 5-7 days a week; students can reserve study rooms.

STUDENT LIFE

Housing options: Campus housing is university owned.

Activities and organizations: choral group, ASCE (American Society of Civil Engineering), PRWEA (Puerto Rico Water and Environment Association), ACI (American Concrete Institute), SAE PUPR AERO DESIGN TEAM, SHPE (Society of Hispanic Professional Engineers).

Campus security: 24-hour emergency response devices and patrols, late-night transport/escort service, over 250 security cameras on campus.

Student services: health clinic, personal/psychological counseling.

COSTS & FINANCIAL AID

Costs (2017–18) ***Comprehensive fee:*** $20,165 includes full-time tuition ($7488), mandatory fees ($840), and room and board ($11,837). Full-time tuition and fees vary according to course level, course load, degree level, and program. Part-time tuition and fees vary according to course level, course load, degree level, and program. ***Payment plan:*** deferred payment. ***Waivers:*** employees or children of employees.

Financial Aid Of all full-time matriculated undergraduates who enrolled in 2013, 1,918 applied for aid, 1,865 were judged to have need, 8 had their need fully met. ***Average percent of need met:*** 45. ***Average financial aid package:*** $7698. ***Average need-based loan:*** $2665. ***Average need-based gift aid:*** $2535. ***Average non-need-based aid:*** $245. ***Financial aid deadline:*** 5/15.

APPLYING

Standardized Tests *Recommended:* CEEB or PEAU.

Options: electronic application.

Application fee: $30.

Required: high school transcript, minimum 2.0 GPA.

CONTACT

Ms. Teresa Cardona, Director of Admissions, Polytechnic University of Puerto Rico, PO Box 192017, San Juan, PR 00919-2017. *Phone:* 787-622-8000 Ext. 240. *Fax:* 787-764-8712. *E-mail:* tcardona@pupr.edu.

Pontifical Catholic University of Puerto Rico

Ponce, Puerto Rico

http://www.pucpr.edu/

CONTACT

Sra. Ana O. Bonilla, Director of Admissions, Pontifical Catholic University of Puerto Rico, 2250 Avenida Las Americas Avenue, Suite 584, Ponce, PR 00717-9777. *Phone:* 787-841-2000 Ext. 1004. *Toll-free phone:* 800-961-7696. *Fax:* 787-840-4295. *E-mail:* admissions@email.pucpr.edu.

Pontifical Catholic University of Puerto Rico–Arecibo Campus

Arecibo, Puerto Rico

http://www.pucpr.edu/arecibo/

CONTACT

Pontifical Catholic University of Puerto Rico–Arecibo Campus, PO Box 144045, Arecibo, PR 00614-4045.

Pontifical Catholic University of Puerto Rico–Mayaguez Campus

Mayaguez, Puerto Rico

http://www.pucpr.edu/mayaguez/

CONTACT

Pontifical Catholic University of Puerto Rico–Mayaguez Campus, 482 Sur Calle Ramon Emerito Betances, Mayaguez, PR 00680.

Theological University of the Caribbean

Saint Just, Puerto Rico

http://www.utcpr.edu/

- **Independent Pentecostal** comprehensive, founded 1956
- **Suburban** 4-acre campus with easy access to San Juan
- **Endowment** $1.0 million
- **Coed** 267 undergraduate students, 61% full-time, 44% women, 56% men
- 100% of applicants were admitted

UNDERGRAD STUDENTS

162 full-time, 105 part-time. Students come from 1 other state; 100% Hispanic/Latino.

Freshmen:

Admission: 53 applied, 53 admitted, 53 enrolled.

Retention: 67% of full-time freshmen returned.

FACULTY

Total: 64, 23% full-time, 38% with terminal degrees.

Student/faculty ratio: 6:1.

ACADEMICS

Calendar: semesters. *Degrees:* certificates, diplomas, associate, bachelor's, master's, and doctoral.

Special study options: distance learning, honors programs, independent study, internships, off-campus study, part-time degree program, services for LD students, summer session for credit.

Computers: 8 computers/terminals and 8 ports are available on campus for general student use. Students can access the following: free student e-mail accounts, online (class) grades, online (class) registration, online (class) schedules. Campuswide network is available. 90% of college-owned or -operated housing units are wired for high-speed Internet access. Wireless service is available via entire campus.

Library: Juan L. Lugo Library plus 1 other. *Books:* 16,871 (physical). Weekly public service hours: 60; students can reserve study rooms.

STUDENT LIFE

Housing options: coed. Campus housing is university owned.

Activities and organizations: Student Council, Missionary Evangelistic Association, Ministerial Association, FESI, Free Night.

Campus security: patrols by security personnel at night from 6:00 pm-midnight.

Student services: personal/psychological counseling.

COSTS & FINANCIAL AID

Costs (2017–18) ***Comprehensive fee:*** $7568 includes full-time tuition ($4168), mandatory fees ($1000), and room and board ($2400). Full-time tuition and fees vary according to course load. Part-time tuition: $18 per credit hour. Part-time tuition and fees vary according to course load. ***Required fees:*** $137 per credit hour part-time, $3288 per term part-time. ***College room only:*** $1200. Room and board charges vary according to board plan. ***Payment plan:*** deferred payment. ***Waivers:*** employees or children of employees.

Financial Aid Of all full-time matriculated undergraduates who enrolled in 2015, 243 applied for aid, 243 were judged to have need. ***Financial aid deadline:*** 6/30.

APPLYING

Options: early admission.

Application fee: $45.

Required: medical certificate, certificate of immunization, 1 2x2 photo, Bible content exam. ***Required for some:*** high school transcript.

CONTACT

Avianny Paulino, Recruitment Officer, Theological University of the Caribbean, PO Box 901, Saint Just, PR 00978-901. *Phone:* 787-761-0640 Ext. 246. *Fax:* 787-748-9220. *E-mail:* promociones@utcpr.edu.

Universidad Adventista de las Antillas

Mayagüez, Puerto Rico

http://www.uaa.edu/

- **Independent Seventh-day Adventist** comprehensive, founded 1957
- **Rural** 284-acre campus
- **Endowment** $134,104
- **Coed** 1,256 undergraduate students, 91% full-time, 63% women, 37% men
- **Minimally difficult** entrance level, 81% of applicants were admitted

UNDERGRAD STUDENTS

1,138 full-time, 118 part-time. Students come from 23 other countries; 19% are from out of state; 1% Black or African American, non-Hispanic/Latino; 96% Hispanic/Latino; 0.2% Asian, non-Hispanic/Latino; 0.1% American Indian or Alaska Native, non-Hispanic/Latino; 2% international; 7% transferred in; 28% live on campus.

Freshmen:

Admission: 513 applied, 415 admitted, 158 enrolled.

Retention: 77% of full-time freshmen returned.

FACULTY

Total: 107, 40% full-time, 44% with terminal degrees.

Student/faculty ratio: 20:1.

ACADEMICS

Calendar: semesters. *Degrees:* associate, bachelor's, and master's.

Special study options: academic remediation for entering students, advanced placement credit, cooperative education, double majors, English as a second language, internships, part-time degree program, services for LD students, summer session for credit.

Computers: 50 computers/terminals are available on campus for general student use. Students can access the following: campus intranet, computer help desk, free student e-mail accounts, online (class) grades, online (class) registration, online (class) schedules. Campuswide network is available. 95% of college-owned or -operated housing units are wired for high-speed Internet access. Wireless service is available via classrooms, computer centers, computer labs, dorm rooms, learning centers, libraries, student centers.

Library: Dennis Soto Library. *Books:* 67,322 (physical); *Databases:* 42. Weekly public service hours: 67; students can reserve study rooms.

STUDENT LIFE

Housing options: on-campus residence required for freshman year; men-only, women-only. Campus housing is university owned. Freshman applicants given priority for college housing.

Activities and organizations: student-run newspaper, choral group, Score Group, Gymnastic Club, Student Council, Green Movement, 3AM.

Athletics ***Intramural sports:*** basketball M/W, soccer M, volleyball M/W.

Campus security: 24-hour emergency response devices and patrols, student patrols, controlled dormitory access.

Student services: health clinic, personal/psychological counseling.

COSTS & FINANCIAL AID

Costs (2017–18) ***One-time required fee:*** $20. ***Comprehensive fee:*** $11,770 includes full-time tuition ($5370), mandatory fees ($1100), and room and board ($5300). Full-time tuition and fees vary according to course load and program. Part-time tuition: $179 per credit hour. Part-time tuition and fees vary according to course load and program. ***Required fees:*** $1100 per term part-time. ***College room only:*** $1800. Room and board charges vary according to board plan and housing facility. ***Payment plan:*** installment. ***Waivers:*** employees or children of employees.

Financial Aid Of all full-time matriculated undergraduates who enrolled in 2013, 1,249 applied for aid, 1,124 were judged to have need. 179 Federal Work-Study jobs (averaging $756). 278 state and other part-time jobs (averaging $961). ***Average percent of need met:*** 78. ***Average financial aid package:*** $2422. ***Average need-based loan:*** $1900. ***Average need-based gift aid:*** $2422. ***Average indebtedness upon graduation:*** $4801.

APPLYING

Standardized Tests *Recommended:* SAT or ACT (for admission), CEEB.

Options: electronic application, early admission.

Application fee: $20.

Required: high school transcript, minimum 2.0 GPA, 1 letter of recommendation. ***Required for some:*** essay or personal statement, interview.

Application deadlines: 7/15 (freshmen), 7/15 (transfers).

CONTACT

Mrs. Yolanda Ferrer, Director of Admissions, Universidad Adventista de las Antillas, Oficina de Admisiones, PO Box 118, Mayaguez, PR 00681-0118. *Phone:* 787-834-9595 Ext. 2208. *Fax:* 787-834-9597. *E-mail:* admissions@uaa.edu.

Universidad Central del Caribe

Bayamón, Puerto Rico

http://www.uccaribe.edu/

CONTACT

Admissions Department, Universidad Central del Caribe, PO Box 60-327, Bayamón, PR 00960-6032. *Phone:* 787-740-1611.

Universidad del Este

Carolina, Puerto Rico

http://www.suagm.edu/une/

- **Independent** comprehensive, founded 1949, part of Ana G. Mendez University System
- **Small-town** campus with easy access to San Juan
- **Coed**
- **Noncompetitive** entrance level

FACULTY

Student/faculty ratio: 21:1.

ACADEMICS

Calendar: semesters. *Degrees:* certificates, associate, bachelor's, and master's.

STUDENT LIFE

Housing options: college housing not available.

Campus security: 24-hour patrols.

APPLYING

Standardized Tests *Required for some:* College Board exam.

Options: electronic application, deferred entrance.

Application fee: $15.

Required: high school transcript. ***Required for some:*** essay or personal statement, interview.

CONTACT

Universidad del Este, PO Box 2010, Carolina, PR 00984. *Phone:* 787-257-7373 Ext. 3401.

Universidad del Turabo

Gurabo, Puerto Rico

http://www.suagm.edu/ut/

- **Independent** university, founded 1972, part of Ana G. Mendez University System
- **Urban** 140-acre campus with easy access to San Juan
- **Coed**
- **Minimally difficult** entrance level

FACULTY

Student/faculty ratio: 22:1.

ACADEMICS

Calendar: semesters. *Degrees:* certificates, associate, bachelor's, master's, doctoral, post-master's, and postbachelor's certificates.

STUDENT LIFE

Housing options: college housing not available.

Activities and organizations: drama/theater group, student-run newspaper, radio station, choral group.

Campus security: 24-hour patrols.

Student services: health clinic, personal/psychological counseling.

FINANCIAL AID

Financial Aid Of all full-time matriculated undergraduates who enrolled in 2013, 10,405 applied for aid, 10,405 were judged to have need. 493 Federal Work-Study jobs (averaging $634). ***Financial aid deadline:*** 6/30.

APPLYING

Standardized Tests *Required for some:* College Board exam. *Recommended:* SAT (for admission).

Options: electronic application.

Application fee: $15.

Required: high school transcript. ***Required for some:*** essay or personal statement, interview.

CONTACT

Universidad del Turabo, PO Box 3030, Gurabo, PR 00778-3030. *Phone:* 787-743-7979 Ext. 4351.

Universidad Metropolitana

San Juan, Puerto Rico

http://www.suagm.edu/umet/

- **Independent** comprehensive, founded 1980, part of Ana G. Mendez University System
- **Urban** campus with easy access to San Juan
- **Coed**
- **Moderately difficult** entrance level

FACULTY
Student/faculty ratio: 22:1.

ACADEMICS
Calendar: semesters. *Degrees:* certificates, associate, bachelor's, master's, doctoral, and postbachelor's certificates.

STUDENT LIFE
Housing options: college housing not available.

Activities and organizations: drama/theater group, student-run newspaper, radio and television station, choral group.

Campus security: 24-hour patrols.

Student services: health clinic, personal/psychological counseling.

APPLYING
Standardized Tests *Required:* College Board exam (for admission). *Recommended:* SAT (for admission).

Options: electronic application, early admission.

Application fee: $15.

Required: high school transcript. ***Required for some:*** essay or personal statement, interview.

CONTACT
Mrs. Yadira Rivera Lugo, Director of Admissions, Universidad Metropolitana, Box 21150, San Juan, PR 00928-1150. *Phone:* 787-766-1717 Ext. 6683. *Toll-free phone:* 800-747-8362. *E-mail:* yrivera@suagm.edu.

Universidad Pentecostal Mizpa

San Juan, Puerto Rico

http://www.mizpa.edu/

CONTACT
Omar Alicea, Recruitment, Universidad Pentecostal Mizpa, Bo Caimito Road 199, Apartado 20966, San Juan, PR 00928-0966. *Phone:* 787-720-4476. *Fax:* 787-720-2012.

University of Puerto Rico in Aguadilla

Aguadilla, Puerto Rico

http://www.uprag.edu/

CONTACT
Ms. Melba Serrano Lugo, Admissions Officer, University of Puerto Rico in Aguadilla, PO Box 6150, Aguadilla, PR 00604. *Phone:* 787-890-2681 Ext. 280.

University of Puerto Rico in Arecibo

Arecibo, Puerto Rico

http://www.upra.edu/

CONTACT
University of Puerto Rico in Arecibo, Carretera 653 Km. 0.8, Sector Las Dunas, PO Box 4010, Arecibo, PR 00614. *Phone:* 787-878-2830 Ext. 4101.

University of Puerto Rico in Bayamón

Bayamón, Puerto Rico

http://www.uprb.edu/

- **Commonwealth-supported** 4-year, founded 1971, part of University of Puerto Rico System
- **Urban** 78-acre campus with easy access to San Juan
- **Coed** 4,927 undergraduate students, 87% full-time, 51% women, 49% men
- **Very difficult** entrance level, 23% of applicants were admitted

UNDERGRAD STUDENTS
4,301 full-time, 626 part-time. Students come from 6 other countries; 1% are from out of state; 100% Hispanic/Latino; 11% transferred in.

Freshmen:
Admission: 5,443 applied, 1,238 admitted, 1,246 enrolled. ***Average high school GPA:*** 3.6.

Retention: 85% of full-time freshmen returned.

FACULTY
Total: 254, 77% full-time, 54% with terminal degrees.

Student/faculty ratio: 20:1.

ACADEMICS
Calendar: semesters. *Degrees:* associate and bachelor's.

Special study options: academic remediation for entering students, adult/continuing education programs, advanced placement credit, cooperative education, honors programs, independent study, internships, part-time degree program, services for LD students, summer session for credit.

Computers: 496 computers/terminals and 496 ports are available on campus for general student use. Students can access the following: campus intranet, free student e-mail accounts, online (class) grades, online (class) registration, online (class) schedules. Campuswide network is available. Wireless service is available via entire campus.

Library: Centro Recursos para el Aprendizaje. *Books:* 162,227 (physical), 3,399 (digital/electronic); *Serial titles:* 386 (physical), 2,947 (digital/electronic); *Databases:* 111. Weekly public service hours: 78; students can reserve study rooms.

STUDENT LIFE
Housing options: college housing not available.

Activities and organizations: drama/theater group, choral group, The National Society of Collegiate Scholars at UPRB (NSCS), American Medical Student Association (AMSA), Med Life Capitulo Vaquero, Asociacion de Estudiantes de Computadoras (AECC), Asociacion de Estudiantes de Contabilidad (ASEC).

Athletics Member NCAA. All Division II. ***Intercollegiate sports:*** basketball M(s)/W(s), cross-country running M(s)/W(s), tennis M(s)/W(s), track and field M(s)/W(s), volleyball M(s)/W(s).

Campus security: 24-hour patrols.

Student services: health clinic, personal/psychological counseling.

COSTS & FINANCIAL AID
Costs (2016–17) ***Tuition:*** commonwealth resident $1904 full-time, $56 per credit part-time; nonresident $3892 full-time, $114 per credit part-time. Full-time tuition and fees vary according to class time, course load, and program. Part-time tuition and fees vary according to class time, course load, and program. No tuition increase for student's term of enrollment. ***Required fees:*** $144 full-time. ***Payment plan:*** deferred payment. ***Waivers:*** employees or children of employees.

Financial Aid Of all full-time matriculated undergraduates who enrolled in 2015, 238 Federal Work-Study jobs (averaging $1473).

APPLYING
Standardized Tests *Required:* College Board exam (for admission).

Options: electronic application.

Application fee: $30.

Required: high school transcript.

Application deadlines: 1/6 (freshmen), 2/15 (transfers).

Notification: 5/1 (freshmen), continuous until 7/1 (transfers).

CONTACT
Ms. Carmen I. Montes Burgos, Director, Office of Admissions, University of Puerto Rico in Bayamón, OPEI Office, Street 174 #170 Minillas Industrial Park, Bayamon, PR 00959-1919, Puerto Rico. *Phone:* 787-993-8952 Ext. 4016. *Fax:* 787-993-8929. *E-mail:* carmen.montes1@upr.edu.

University of Puerto Rico in Carolina

Carolina, Puerto Rico

http://www.uprc.edu/

CONTACT
Ms. Celia Mendez, Admissions Officer, University of Puerto Rico in Carolina, PO Box 4800, Carolina, PR 00984-4800. *Phone:* 787-757-1485.

University of Puerto Rico in Cayey

Cayey, Puerto Rico

http://www.cayey.upr.edu/

CONTACT
University of Puerto Rico in Cayey, 205 Avenue Antonio R. Barcelo, Cayey, PR 00736. *Phone:* 787-738-2161 Ext. 2233.

University of Puerto Rico in Humacao

Humacao, Puerto Rico

http://www.uprh.edu/

CONTACT
Mrs. Elizabeth Gerena, Director of Admissions, University of Puerto Rico in Humacao, Call Box 860, Humacao, PR 00792. *Phone:* 787-850-9301. *Fax:* 787-850-9428. *E-mail:* elizabeth.gerena@upr.edu.

University of Puerto Rico in Ponce

Ponce, Puerto Rico

http://www.uprp.edu/

CONTACT
University of Puerto Rico in Ponce, PO Box 7186, Ponce, PR 00732-7186. *Phone:* 787-844-8181 Ext. 2533.

University of Puerto Rico in Utuado

Utuado, Puerto Rico

http://www.uprutuado.edu/

CONTACT
Mrs. Maria Robles Serrano, Admissions Officer, University of Puerto Rico in Utuado, PO Box 2500, Utuado, PR 00641-2500. *Phone:* 787-894-2828 Ext. 2240.

University of Puerto Rico, Mayagüez Campus

Mayagüez, Puerto Rico

http://www.uprm.edu/

CONTACT
Ms. Sheila Marty-Rodriquez, Director, Admissions Office, University of Puerto Rico, Mayagüez Campus, PO Box 9000, Mayagüez, PR 00681-9000. *Phone:* 787-265-5465. *Fax:* 787-265-5465. *E-mail:* smarty@uprm.edu.

University of Puerto Rico, Medical Sciences Campus

San Juan, Puerto Rico

http://www.rcm.upr.edu/

CONTACT
University of Puerto Rico, Medical Sciences Campus, PO Box 365067, San Juan, PR 00936-5067. *Phone:* 787-758-2525 Ext. 5214.

University of Puerto Rico, Río Piedras Campus

San Juan, Puerto Rico

http://www.uprrp.edu/

- **Commonwealth-supported** university, founded 1903, part of University of Puerto Rico System
- **Urban** 281-acre campus
- **Coed**
- **Very difficult** entrance level

FACULTY
Student/faculty ratio: 16:1.

ACADEMICS
Calendar: semesters. *Degrees:* bachelor's, master's, doctoral, post-master's, and postbachelor's certificates.
Library: Jose M. Lazaro Library plus 10 others.

STUDENT LIFE
Housing options: coed. Campus housing is university owned.
Activities and organizations: drama/theater group, student-run radio station, choral group, national fraternities, national sororities.
Athletics Member NCAA, NAIA. All NCAA Division II.
Campus security: 24-hour emergency response devices, late-night transport/escort service.
Student services: health clinic, personal/psychological counseling, legal services.

FINANCIAL AID
Financial Aid ***Financial aid deadline:*** 4/25.

APPLYING
Standardized Tests *Required:* SAT (for admission), College Entrance Examination Board (CEEB) Aptitude Test in mathematics and verbal reasoning and the Academic Achievement Test in English, mathematics and Spanish (for admission).
Options: electronic application.
Application fee: $20.
Required: high school transcript. ***Required for some:*** interview.

CONTACT
Mrs. Cruz B. Valentìn, Director of Admissions, University of Puerto Rico, Río Piedras Campus, PO Box 23300, San Juan, PR 00931-3300. *Phone:* 787-764-0000 Ext. 85700.

University of the Sacred Heart

San Juan, Puerto Rico

http://www.sagrado.edu/

CONTACT
Mr. Luis Heviquez, Director of Admissions, University of the Sacred Heart, PO Box 12383, San Juan, PR 00914-0383. *Phone:* 787-728-1515 Ext. 3237.

VIRGIN ISLANDS

University of the Virgin Islands

St. Thomas, Virgin Islands

http://www.uvi.edu/

- **Territory-supported** comprehensive, founded 1962
- **Small-town** 518-acre campus
- **Coed** 2,132 undergraduate students, 67% full-time, 67% women, 33% men
- **Noncompetitive** entrance level, 92% of applicants were admitted

UNDERGRAD STUDENTS
1,422 full-time, 710 part-time. Students come from 35 states and territories; 14 other countries; 4% are from out of state; 72% Black or African American, non-Hispanic/Latino; 9% Hispanic/Latino; 0.5% Asian, non-Hispanic/Latino; 0.2% American Indian or Alaska Native,

non-Hispanic/Latino; 0.8% Two or more races, non-Hispanic/Latino; 6% Race/ethnicity unknown; 6% international; 4% transferred in.

Freshmen:
Admission: 1,789 applied, 1,645 admitted, 345 enrolled. ***Average high school GPA:*** 3.14.
Retention: 75% of full-time freshmen returned.

FACULTY
Total: 239, 46% full-time.
Student/faculty ratio: 12:1.

ACADEMICS
Calendar: semesters. *Degrees:* associate, bachelor's, master's, doctoral, and post-master's certificates.
Special study options: academic remediation for entering students, adult/continuing education programs, advanced placement credit, cooperative education, distance learning, double majors, English as a second language, external degree program, honors programs, independent study, internships, off-campus study, part-time degree program, services for LD students, study abroad, summer session for credit.
ROTC: Army (b).
Unusual degree programs: 3-2 engineering with Columbia University, University of Florida, University of South Carolina.
Computers: 500 computers/terminals are available on campus for general student use. Students can access the following: campus intranet, computer help desk, free student e-mail accounts, online (class) grades, online (class) registration, online (class) schedules. Campuswide network is available. 100% of college-owned or -operated housing units are wired for high-speed Internet access. Wireless service is available via entire campus.
Library: Ralph M. Paiewonsky Library.

STUDENT LIFE
Housing options: coed, men-only, women-only. Campus housing is university owned.
Activities and organizations: drama/theater group, student-run newspaper, radio station, choral group, Student Government Association, Golden Key Honor Society, Student Nurses Association, National Student Exchange Club, St. Kitts and Nevis, national sororities.
Athletics Member NAIA. ***Intercollegiate sports:*** basketball M(s)/W(s)(c), cross-country running M(c)/W(c), soccer M(s)(c), track and field M(c)/W(c), volleyball M(c)/W(c).
Campus security: 24-hour emergency response devices and patrols.
Student services: health clinic, personal/psychological counseling.

COSTS & FINANCIAL AID
Costs (2017–18) ***Tuition:*** territory resident $4631 full-time, $154 per credit part-time; nonresident $13,892 full-time, $463 per credit part-time. Full-time tuition and fees vary according to reciprocity agreements. Part-time tuition and fees vary according to course load and reciprocity agreements. ***Required fees:*** $604 full-time, $254 per term part-time. ***Room and board:*** $9900; room only: $4120. Room and board charges vary according to board plan and housing facility. ***Payment plan:*** installment. ***Waivers:*** senior citizens and employees or children of employees.
Financial Aid Of all full-time matriculated undergraduates who enrolled in 2007, 1,202 applied for aid, 1,118 were judged to have need, 10 had their need fully met. 39 Federal Work-Study jobs (averaging $2130). 28 state and other part-time jobs (averaging $1900). In 2007, 5 non-need-based awards were made. ***Average financial aid package:*** $4450. ***Average need-based loan:*** $3240. ***Average need-based gift aid:*** $3440. ***Average non-need-based aid:*** $8500. ***Average indebtedness upon graduation:*** $9480.

APPLYING
Options: electronic application, early admission, deferred entrance.
Application fee: $25.
Recommended: high school transcript, minimum 2.0 GPA.
Application deadlines: 4/30 (freshmen), 4/30 (transfers).
Notification: continuous until 10/1 (freshmen).

CONTACT
Dr. Xuri Maurice Allen, Director of Admissions/Recruitment, University of the Virgin Islands, #2 John Brewers Bay, St. Thomas, VI 00802. *Phone:* 340-693-1224. *Toll-free phone:* 877-468-6884. *Fax:* 340-693-1167. *E-mail:* xallen@uvi.edu.

CANADA

CANADA

Acadia University
Wolfville, Nova Scotia, Canada
http://www.acadiau.ca/

- **Province-supported** comprehensive, founded 1838
- **Small-town** 250-acre campus with easy access to Halifax, Nova Scotia
- **Coed**
- **Moderately difficult** entrance level

FACULTY
Student/faculty ratio: 15:1.

ACADEMICS
Calendar: Canadian standard year. *Degrees:* bachelor's, master's, and doctoral.
Library: Vaughan Memorial Library.

STUDENT LIFE
Housing options: coed, women-only. Campus housing is university owned. Freshman campus housing is guaranteed.

Activities and organizations: drama/theater group, student-run newspaper, radio station, choral group, Dance Acadia, Power Cheerleading, Water Watch Canada, LINC, Biology.

Athletics Member CIS.

Campus security: 24-hour emergency response devices and patrols, student patrols, late-night transport/escort service, controlled dormitory access, video surveillance, emergency response, emergency notification, emergency management planning.

Student services: health clinic, personal/psychological counseling, women's center, legal services.

COSTS
Costs (2016–17) ***One-time required fee:*** $426 Canadian dollars. ***Tuition:*** province resident $7476 Canadian dollars full-time, $935 Canadian dollars per course part-time; nonresident $8759 Canadian dollars full-time, $1063 Canadian dollars per course part-time; International tuition $16,718 Canadian dollars full-time. Full-time tuition and fees vary according to course level, course load, degree level, and program. Part-time tuition and fees vary according to course level, course load, degree level, and program. ***Required fees:*** $300 Canadian dollars full-time, $10 Canadian dollars per course part-time. ***Room and board:*** $9929 Canadian dollars; room only: $5560 Canadian dollars. Room and board charges vary according to board plan and housing facility.

APPLYING
Options: electronic application, deferred entrance.

Application fee: $40 Canadian dollars.

Required: high school transcript, minimum 2.5 GPA. ***Required for some:*** essay or personal statement, 1 letter of recommendation, interview.

CONTACT
Ms. Anne Scott, Manager of Admissions, Acadia University, Wolfville, NS B4P 2R6, Canada. *Phone:* 902-585-1016. *Toll-free phone:* 877-585-1121. *Fax:* 902-585-1092. *E-mail:* admissions@acadiau.ca.

Alberta College of Art & Design
Calgary, Alberta, Canada
http://www.acad.ca/

CONTACT
Ms. Katie Potapoff, Admissions Officer, Alberta College of Art & Design, 1407-14 Avenue NW, Calgary, AB T2N 4R3, Canada. *Phone:* 403-284-7617. *Toll-free phone:* 800-251-8290. *Fax:* 403-284-7644. *E-mail:* admissions@acad.ca.

Ambrose University
Calgary, Alberta, Canada
http://www.ambrose.edu/

- **Independent** comprehensive, founded 1941, affiliated with The Christian and Missionary Alliance
- **Urban** 37-acre campus
- **Endowment** $6.0 million
- **Coed** 713 undergraduate students, 90% full-time, 58% women, 42% men

UNDERGRAD STUDENTS
644 full-time, 69 part-time. Students come from 11 provinces and territories; 13 other countries; 13% are from out of state; 2% Black or African American, non-Hispanic/Latino; 1% Hispanic/Latino; 9% Asian, non-Hispanic/Latino; 2% American Indian or Alaska Native, non-Hispanic/Latino; 10% Race/ethnicity unknown; 6% transferred in; 18% live on campus.

Freshmen:
Admission: 298 enrolled.

FACULTY
Total: 84, 52% full-time, 44% with terminal degrees.
Student/faculty ratio: 13:1.

ACADEMICS
Calendar: semesters. *Degrees:* certificates, diplomas, bachelor's, and master's (graduate and professional degrees are offered by Canadian Theological Seminary).

Special study options: academic remediation for entering students, accelerated degree program, adult/continuing education programs, advanced placement credit, cooperative education, distance learning, double majors, independent study, internships, off-campus study, part-time degree program, services for LD students, study abroad, summer session for credit.

Unusual degree programs: 3-2 elementary education.

Computers: 20 computers/terminals are available on campus for general student use. Students can access the following: campus intranet, computer help desk, free student e-mail accounts, online (class) grades, online (class) registration, online (class) schedules. Campuswide network is available. 50% of college-owned or -operated housing units are wired for high-speed Internet access. Wireless service is available via entire campus.

Library: Archibald Foundation Library. *Books:* 125,000 (physical), 150,000 (digital/electronic); *Serial titles:* 185,000 (physical), 65,704 (digital/electronic); *Databases:* 42. Weekly public service hours: 81; students can reserve study rooms.

STUDENT LIFE
Housing options: on-campus residence required for freshman year; men-only, women-only. Campus housing is university owned. Freshman applicants given priority for college housing.

Activities and organizations: drama/theater group, student-run newspaper, choral group, Coffee Club, Business Society, Hockey Club, Biology Club, Outdoors Club.

Athletics ***Intercollegiate sports:*** basketball M(s)/W(s), soccer M(s)/W(s), volleyball M(s)/W(s). ***Intramural sports:*** basketball M/W, cross-country running M(c)/W(c), ice hockey M(c)/W(c), soccer M/W, volleyball M/W.

Campus security: 24-hour emergency response devices, student patrols, late-night transport/escort service, controlled dormitory access.

Student services: personal/psychological counseling.

COSTS & FINANCIAL AID
Costs (2017–18) ***Comprehensive fee:*** $18,528 includes full-time tuition ($10,920), mandatory fees ($908), and room and board ($6700). Full-time tuition and fees vary according to course load, degree level, and program. Part-time tuition: $364 per credit hour. Part-time tuition and fees vary according to course load, degree level, and program. ***Required fees:*** $30 per credit hour part-time. ***College room only:*** $3600. Room and board charges vary according to board plan and housing facility. ***Payment plans:***

installment, deferred payment. ***Waivers:*** employees or children of employees.

Financial Aid Of all full-time matriculated undergraduates who enrolled in 2016, 275 applied for aid, 250 were judged to have need. ***Average financial aid package:*** $1200. ***Average need-based gift aid:*** $700. ***Financial aid deadline:*** 6/1.

APPLYING

Standardized Tests *Required for some:* SAT or ACT (for admission).

Required: high school transcript, 1 letter of recommendation. ***Required for some:*** essay or personal statement, 3 letters of recommendation, interview, minimum 60% overall average on 5 grade-12 level courses.

CONTACT

Kalie Eeles, Enrolment Coordinator, Ambrose University, 150 Ambrose Circle SW, Calgary, AB T3H 0L5, Canada. *Phone:* 403-410-2000 Ext. 2954. *Toll-free phone:* 800-461-1222. *Fax:* 403-571-6556. *E-mail:* enrolment@ambrose.edu.

Athabasca University

Athabasca, Alberta, Canada

http://www.athabascau.ca/

CONTACT

Information Centre, Athabasca University, 1 University Drive, Athabasca, AB T9S 3A3, Canada. *Phone:* 800-788-9041. *Toll-free phone:* 800-788-9041. *Fax:* 780-675-6437.

Bishop's University

Sherbrooke, Quebec, Canada

http://www.ubishops.ca/

- **Province-supported** comprehensive, founded 1843, part of Association of Universities and Colleges of Canada (AUCC)
- **Small-town** 550-acre campus with easy access to Montreal
- **Coed**
- **Moderately difficult** entrance level

UNDERGRAD STUDENTS

Students come from 22 provinces and territories; 59 other countries; 51% are from out of state.

FACULTY

Student/faculty ratio: 16:1.

ACADEMICS

Calendar: semesters most students study from September to late April. Spring semester is May-June. *Degrees:* certificates, bachelor's, master's, and postbachelor's certificates.

Special study options: adult/continuing education programs, advanced placement credit, cooperative education, double majors, honors programs, independent study, internships, off-campus study, part-time degree program, services for LD students, study abroad, summer session for credit.

Computers: 650 computers/terminals are available on campus for general student use. Students can access the following: campus intranet, computer help desk, free student e-mail accounts, online (class) grades, online (class) registration, online (class) schedules, Web course management systems, individualized Web access. Campuswide network is available. 100% of college-owned or -operated housing units are wired for high-speed Internet access. Wireless service is available via entire campus.

Library: John Bassett Memorial Library plus 1 other. Students can reserve study rooms.

STUDENT LIFE

Housing options: coed, special housing for students with disabilities. Campus housing is university owned. Freshman campus housing is guaranteed.

Activities and organizations: drama/theater group, student-run newspaper, radio station, choral group, Ski and Snowboard Club, Bishop's University Commerce Society, BU Model UN, Big Buddies, Bishop's Psychology Club, national sororities.

Athletics Member CIS. ***Intercollegiate sports:*** basketball M(s)/W(s), cheerleading W(c), field hockey W(c), football M(s), golf M/W, ice hockey W, lacrosse M(s)/W(c), rugby M(s)/W(s), soccer W, volleyball W(c). ***Intramural sports:*** badminton M/W, baseball M, basketball M/W, cross-country running M/W, equestrian sports M(c)/W(c), football M, golf M/W, ice hockey M/W, riflery M(c)/W(c), soccer M/W, softball M/W, squash M/W, swimming and diving M/W, table tennis M/W, tennis M/W, ultimate Frisbee M/W, volleyball M/W, water polo M/W, weight lifting M/W.

Campus security: 24-hour emergency response devices and patrols, student patrols, late-night transport/escort service, controlled dormitory access.

Student services: health clinic, personal/psychological counseling.

COSTS

Costs (2017–18) ***Tuition:*** province resident $2328 full-time, $78 per credit part-time; nonresident $7227 full-time, $241 per credit part-time; International tuition $17,807 full-time. Full-time tuition and fees vary according to course load, program, and reciprocity agreements. Part-time tuition and fees vary according to course load and program. No tuition increase for student's term of enrollment. ***Required fees:*** $1385 full-time, $1385 per year part-time. ***Room and board:*** $9000; room only: $4500. Room and board charges vary according to board plan and housing facility. ***Payment plan:*** installment. ***Waivers:*** employees or children of employees.

APPLYING

Options: electronic application, early admission, deferred entrance.

Application fee: $85 Canadian dollars.

Required: high school transcript, minimum 3.4 GPA, birth certificate, copy of student visa. ***Required for some:*** essay or personal statement, 2 letters of recommendation.

Application deadlines: 4/1 (freshmen), 3/1 (out-of-state freshmen), 3/1 (transfers).

Notification: continuous (freshmen), continuous (out-of-state freshmen), continuous (transfers).

CONTACT

Mr. Doug McCooeye, Manager Student Recruitment, Admissions and Student Exchange, Bishop's University, 2600 College Street, Sherbrooke, QC J1M 1Z7, Canada. *Phone:* 819-822-9600 Ext. 2206. *Toll-free phone:* 877-822-8200. *E-mail:* admissions@ubishops.ca.

Booth University College

Winnipeg, Manitoba, Canada

http://www.boothuc.ca/

CONTACT

Chantel Burt, Director of Admission, Booth University College, 447 Webb Place, Winnipeg, MB R3B 2P2, Canada. *Phone:* 204-924-4867. *Toll-free phone:* 877-942-6684. *E-mail:* cburt@boothcollege.ca.

Brandon University

Brandon, Manitoba, Canada

http://www.brandonu.ca/

CONTACT

Murray Kerr, Director of Admissions, Brandon University, 270 18th Street, Brandon, MB R7A 6A9, Canada. *Phone:* 204-727-7352. *Toll-free phone:* 800-644-7644. *Fax:* 204-728-3221. *E-mail:* kerr@brandonu.ca.

Briercrest College

Caronport, Saskatchewan, Canada

http://www.briercrest.ca/

CONTACT

Mr. Ralph Troshke, Director of Enrolment, Briercrest College, 510 College Drive, Caronport, SK S0H 0S0, Canada. *Phone:* 306-756-3200. *Toll-free phone:* 800-667-5199. *Fax:* 800-667.5199. *E-mail:* admissions@briercrest.ca.

British Columbia Institute of Technology

Burnaby, British Columbia, Canada

http://www.bcit.ca/

CONTACT
Ms. Anna Dosen, Supervisor of Admissions, British Columbia Institute of Technology, 3700 Willingdon Avenue, Burnaby, BC V5G 3H2, Canada. *Phone:* 604-432-8496. *Toll-free phone:* 866-434-1610. *Fax:* 604-431-6917.

Brock University

St. Catharines, Ontario, Canada

http://www.brocku.ca/

CONTACT
Mrs. Lynn Thompson-Dovi, International Admissions Officer, Brock University, 500 Glenridge Avenue, L2S 3A1, Canada. *Phone:* 905-688-5550 Ext. 3431. *Fax:* 905-688-5488. *E-mail:* admissns@brocku.ca.

Cape Breton University

Sydney, Nova Scotia, Canada

http://www.cbu.ca/

- **Province-supported** comprehensive, founded 1974
- **Urban** campus
- **Coed**
- **Moderately difficult** entrance level

ACADEMICS
Calendar: semesters. *Degrees:* certificates, diplomas, bachelor's, and master's.
Library: Cape Breton University Library plus 1 other. Weekly public service hours: 110; students can reserve study rooms.

STUDENT LIFE
Housing options: coed. Campus housing is university owned. Freshman applicants given priority for college housing.
Activities and organizations: drama/theater group, student-run newspaper, radio station.
Athletics Member CIS.
Campus security: 24-hour emergency response devices and patrols, student patrols, late-night transport/escort service, controlled dormitory access.
Student services: health clinic, personal/psychological counseling, women's center, legal services.

FINANCIAL AID
Financial Aid Of all full-time matriculated undergraduates who enrolled in 2013, 2 applied for aid, 2 were judged to have need, 2 had their need fully met. ***Average percent of need met:*** 100. ***Average financial aid package:*** $5000. ***Average need-based loan:*** $5000.

APPLYING
Options: electronic application, early admission, deferred entrance.
Application fee: $36 Canadian dollars.
Required: high school transcript. ***Required for some:*** essay or personal statement, 2 letters of recommendation, interview, overall average of 65%.

CONTACT
Cape Breton University, Box 5300, 1250 Grand Lake Road, Sydney, NS B1P 6L2, Canada. *Phone:* 902-563-1844. *Toll-free phone:* 888-959-9995.

Capilano University

North Vancouver, British Columbia, Canada

http://www.capilanou.ca/

- **Public** 4-year, part of British Columbia's Advanced Education system
- **Suburban** 44-hectare campus with easy access to Vancouver
- **Endowment** $7.3 million
- **Coed** 6,766 undergraduate students, 72% full-time, 60% women, 40% men
- **Noncompetitive** entrance level, 23% of applicants were admitted

UNDERGRAD STUDENTS
4,879 full-time, 1,887 part-time. Students come from 15 provinces and territories; 64 other countries; 3% are from out of state.

Freshmen:
Admission: 2,200 applied, 511 admitted, 573 enrolled.
Retention: 68% of full-time freshmen returned.

FACULTY
Total: 620, 27% full-time, 25% with terminal degrees.
Student/faculty ratio: 17:1.

ACADEMICS
Calendar: semesters. *Degrees:* certificates, diplomas, associate, bachelor's, and postbachelor's certificates.
Special study options: academic remediation for entering students, advanced placement credit, cooperative education, distance learning, English as a second language, independent study, internships, part-time degree program, services for LD students, study abroad, summer session for credit.
Computers: 100 computers/terminals are available on campus for general student use. Students can access the following: campus intranet, computer help desk, free student e-mail accounts, online (class) grades, online (class) registration, online (class) schedules. Campuswide network is available. Wireless service is available via entire campus.
Library: Capilano University Library. *Books:* 80,330 (physical), 174,658 (digital/electronic); *Serial titles:* 163 (physical), 56,969 (digital/electronic); *Databases:* 55. Weekly public service hours: 73; students can reserve study rooms.

STUDENT LIFE
Housing options: college housing not available.
Activities and organizations: drama/theater group, student-run newspaper, choral group, Pen & Paper Club, Enactus Capilano, Psychology Club, Music Therapy Student Association, Learn and Connect.
Athletics *Intercollegiate sports:* basketball M(s)/W(s), soccer M(s)/W(s), volleyball M(s)/W(s).
Campus security: 24-hour emergency response devices and patrols, late-night transport/escort service.
Student services: health clinic, personal/psychological counseling, women's center.

COSTS
Costs (2017–18) *Tuition:* province resident $3651 full-time, $128 per credit part-time; nonresident $3651 full-time, $128 per credit part-time. Full-time tuition and fees vary according to course level, degree level, and program. Part-time tuition and fees vary according to course level, degree level, and program. ***Required fees:*** $254 full-time, $12 per credit part-time, $28 per term part-time. ***Payment plan:*** deferred payment. ***Waivers:*** senior citizens and employees or children of employees.

APPLYING
Options: electronic application, early admission.
Required: high school transcript. ***Required for some:*** essay or personal statement, letters of recommendation, interview.
Application deadlines: 3/31 (freshmen), 3/31 (transfers).

CONTACT
Capilano University, 2055 Purcell Way, North Vancouver, BC V7J 3H5, Canada.

Carleton University

Ottawa, Ontario, Canada

http://www.carleton.ca/

CONTACT
Ms. Jean Mullan, Director, Undergraduate Recruitment Office, Carleton University, 1125 Colonel By Drive, Ottawa, ON K1S 5B6, Canada. *Phone:* 613-520-3663. *Toll-free phone:* 888-354-4414. *E-mail:* liaison@admissions.carleton.ca.

Centennial College

Scarborough, Ontario, Canada

http://www.centennialcollege.ca/

- **Province-supported** 4-year, part of Ontario College Application System
- **Urban** campus with easy access to Greater Toronto Area
- **Coed**

ACADEMICS

Calendar: semesters. *Degrees:* certificates, diplomas, bachelor's, and postbachelor's certificates.

Library: Centennial College Libraries. Study areas open 24 hours, 5-7 days a week; students can reserve study rooms.

STUDENT LIFE

Housing options: Campus housing is university owned. Freshman applicants given priority for college housing.

Athletics Member CIS.

Campus security: 24-hour emergency response devices and patrols, late-night transport/escort service.

Student services: personal/psychological counseling.

APPLYING

Options: electronic application.

Application fee: $95 Canadian dollars.

Required: high school transcript.

CONTACT

Enrolment Services, Centennial College, PO Box 631, Station 'A', Scarborough, ON M1K 5E9, Canada. *Phone:* 416-289-5325. *Toll-free phone:* 800-268-4419. *E-mail:* success@centennialcollege.ca.

Columbia Bible College

Abbotsford, British Columbia, Canada

http://www.columbiabc.edu/

CONTACT

Nathan Martin, Admissions Coordinator, Columbia Bible College, 2940 Clearbrook Road, Abbotsford, BC V2T 2Z8, Canada. *Phone:* 604-853-3358 Ext. 309. *Toll-free phone:* 800-283-0881. *Fax:* 604-853-3063. *E-mail:* nathan.martin@columbiabc.edu.

Concordia University

Montréal, Quebec, Canada

http://www.concordia.ca/

- **Province-supported** university, founded 1974, part of Quebec University Network
- **Urban** 52-acre campus with easy access to Montreal
- **Coed** 31,244 undergraduate students, 67% full-time, 52% women, 48% men
- **Moderately difficult** entrance level, 73% of applicants were admitted

UNDERGRAD STUDENTS

21,066 full-time, 10,178 part-time. Students come from 12 provinces and territories; 156 other countries; 8% are from out of state; 2% live on campus.

Freshmen:

Admission: 13,734 applied, 10,013 admitted, 5,714 enrolled.

Retention: 85% of full-time freshmen returned.

FACULTY

Total: 1,654, 63% full-time.

Student/faculty ratio: 24:1.

ACADEMICS

Calendar: semesters. *Degrees:* certificates, diplomas, bachelor's, master's, doctoral, and postbachelor's certificates.

Special study options: academic remediation for entering students, accelerated degree program, adult/continuing education programs, advanced placement credit, cooperative education, distance learning, double majors, English as a second language, honors programs, independent study, internships, off-campus study, part-time degree program, services for LD students, student-designed majors, study abroad, summer session for credit.

Computers: 350 computers/terminals are available on campus for general student use. Students can access the following: campus intranet, computer help desk, free student e-mail accounts, online (class) grades, online (class) registration, online (class) schedules, specialized software applications. Campuswide network is available. 100% of college-owned or -operated housing units are wired for high-speed Internet access. Wireless service is available via entire campus.

Library: Webster Library plus 1 other. *Books:* 9.9 million (physical), 522,287 (digital/electronic); *Serial titles:* 18,806 (physical), 112,295 (digital/electronic); *Databases:* 1,000. Weekly public service hours: 70; study areas open 24 hours, 5-7 days a week; students can reserve study rooms.

STUDENT LIFE

Housing options: coed, special housing for students with disabilities. Campus housing is university owned. Freshman applicants given priority for college housing.

Activities and organizations: drama/theater group, student-run newspaper, radio and television station, choral group, Undergraduate Student Union, departmental clubs, religious clubs, ethnic clubs, social action groups, national fraternities, national sororities.

Athletics Member CIS. ***Intercollegiate sports:*** baseball M(s), basketball M(s)/W(s), cross-country running M(c)/W(c), football M(s), golf M(c)/W(c), ice hockey M(s)/W(s), rugby M(s)/W(s), skiing (downhill) M(c)/W(c), soccer M(s)/W(s), wrestling M(s)/W(s). ***Intramural sports:*** basketball M/W, cross-country running M/W, ice hockey M/W, lacrosse M, soccer M/W, ultimate Frisbee M/W, volleyball M/W, wrestling M/W.

Campus security: 24-hour emergency response devices and patrols, student patrols, late-night transport/escort service, controlled dormitory access.

Student services: health clinic, personal/psychological counseling, women's center.

COSTS & FINANCIAL AID

Costs (2017–18) ***Tuition:*** province resident $2328 full-time, $78 per credit part-time; nonresident $7728 full-time, $241 per credit part-time; International tuition $17,808 full-time. Full-time tuition and fees vary according to course load. Part-time tuition and fees vary according to course load. ***Required fees:*** $1406 full-time, $49 per credit part-time. ***Room and board:*** $9758; room only: $5608. Room and board charges vary according to housing facility and location. ***Payment plan:*** installment. ***Waivers:*** senior citizens and employees or children of employees.

Financial Aid Of all full-time matriculated undergraduates who enrolled in 2015, 349 state and other part-time jobs (averaging $1286). ***Financial aid deadline:*** 3/31.

APPLYING

Options: electronic application, deferred entrance.

Application fee: $100 Canadian dollars.

Required: high school transcript, minimum 2.5 GPA. ***Required for some:*** essay or personal statement, minimum 3.7 GPA, 2 letters of recommendation, interview, portfolio and/or auditions are for performing and visual arts, interview/essay/portfolio for communications, letter of intent and interview for some education programs.

Application deadlines: 3/1 (freshmen), 3/1 (transfers).

Notification: continuous (freshmen), continuous (transfers).

CONTACT

Dr. Matthew Stiegemeyer, Director, Student Recruitment (Enrolment and Student Services), Concordia University, 1455 de Maisonneuve Boulevard West, Building LB-718, Montreal, QC H3G 1M8, Canada. *Phone:* 514-848-2424 Ext. 4781. *Fax:* 514-848-2837. *E-mail:* matthew.stiegemeyer@concordia.ca.

Concordia University of Edmonton

Edmonton, Alberta, Canada

http://www.concordia.ab.ca/

CONTACT

Student and Enrollment Services, Concordia University of Edmonton, 7128 Ada Boulevard, Edmonton, AB T5B 4E4, Canada. *Phone:* 780-479-9220. *Toll-free phone:* 866-479-5200. *Fax:* 780-378-8460. *E-mail:* admits@concordia.ab.ca.

Crandall University

Moncton, New Brunswick, Canada

http://www.crandallu.ca/

- **Independent Baptist** comprehensive, founded 1949
- **Urban** 220-acre campus
- **Coed** 428 undergraduate students
- **Minimally difficult** entrance level

UNDERGRAD STUDENTS

30% live on campus.

FACULTY

Total: 61, 43% full-time, 52% with terminal degrees.

Student/faculty ratio: 13:1.

ACADEMICS

Calendar: trimesters. *Degrees:* certificates, bachelor's, and master's.

Special study options: accelerated degree program, adult/continuing education programs, advanced placement credit, cooperative education, double majors, English as a second language, honors programs, independent study, internships, off-campus study, part-time degree program, services for LD students, study abroad, summer session for credit.

Computers: Students can access the following: computer help desk, free student e-mail accounts, online (class) grades, online (class) registration, online (class) schedules. Campuswide network is available. 100% of college-owned or -operated housing units are wired for high-speed Internet access. Wireless service is available via entire campus.

Library: George A. Rawlyk Library.

STUDENT LIFE

Housing options: men-only, women-only, special housing for students with disabilities. Campus housing is university owned.

Activities and organizations: student-run newspaper, choral group, Crandall Student Association, Worship Ministry Teams, Community Service Teams, Student Newspaper, Student Ambassadors.

Athletics ***Intercollegiate sports:*** baseball M, basketball M/W, cross-country running M/W, soccer M/W. ***Intramural sports:*** basketball M/W, ice hockey M, soccer M/W, volleyball M/W, weight lifting M/W.

Campus security: student patrols, controlled dormitory access, trained security personnel on campus for specific times.

Student services: health clinic, personal/psychological counseling.

COSTS & FINANCIAL AID

Costs (2016–17) ***One-time required fee:*** $50 Canadian dollars. ***Comprehensive fee:*** $17,690 Canadian dollars includes full-time tuition ($8100 Canadian dollars), mandatory fees ($1200 Canadian dollars), and room and board ($8390 Canadian dollars). Full-time tuition and fees vary according to course load, degree level, and program. Part-time tuition: $810 Canadian dollars per course. Part-time tuition and fees vary according to course load, degree level, and program. ***Required fees:*** $120 Canadian dollars per course part-time. ***College room only:*** $4200 Canadian dollars. Room and board charges vary according to board plan and housing facility. ***Payment plan:*** installment. ***Waivers:*** senior citizens and employees or children of employees.

Financial Aid ***Financial aid deadline:*** 5/15.

APPLYING

Options: electronic application, early admission, early decision, deferred entrance.

Application fee: $35 Canadian dollars.

Required: high school transcript, minimum 2.7 GPA. ***Required for some:*** essay or personal statement, minimum 3.0 GPA, 3 letters of recommendation, interview.

Application deadlines: rolling (freshmen), rolling (transfers).

Early decision deadline: 11/30.

Notification: continuous (freshmen), continuous (transfers), rolling (early decision).

CONTACT

Mrs. Lorrie Weir, Admissions Administrative Assistant, Crandall University, Box 6004, Moncton, NB E1C 9L7, Canada. *Phone:* 506-858-8970 Ext. 434. *Toll-free phone:* 888-968-6228. *Fax:* 506-863-6460. *E-mail:* admissions@crandallu.ca.

Dalhousie University

Halifax, Nova Scotia, Canada

http://www.dal.ca/

- **Province-supported** university, founded 1818
- **Urban** 80-acre campus
- **Endowment** $537.8 million
- **Coed** 14,685 undergraduate students, 89% full-time, 55% women, 45% men
- **Moderately difficult** entrance level, 63% of applicants were admitted

UNDERGRAD STUDENTS

13,023 full-time, 1,662 part-time. Students come from 36 provinces and territories; 124 other countries.

Freshmen:

Admission: 11,721 applied, 7,360 admitted.

FACULTY

Student/faculty ratio: 14:1.

ACADEMICS

Calendar: semesters. *Degrees:* certificates, diplomas, bachelor's, master's, doctoral, and postbachelor's certificates.

Special study options: academic remediation for entering students, accelerated degree program, advanced placement credit, cooperative education, distance learning, double majors, English as a second language, honors programs, internships, off-campus study, part-time degree program, services for LD students, study abroad, summer session for credit.

Computers: 710 computers/terminals are available on campus for general student use. Students can access the following: campus intranet, computer help desk, free student e-mail accounts, online (class) grades, online (class) registration, online (class) schedules. Campuswide network is available. 100% of college-owned or -operated housing units are wired for high-speed Internet access. Wireless service is available via entire campus.

Library: The Killam Library plus 5 others.

STUDENT LIFE

Housing options: coed, women-only, special housing for students with disabilities. Campus housing is university owned. Freshman applicants given priority for college housing.

Activities and organizations: drama/theater group, student-run newspaper, radio station, choral group, International Students Association, Arts Society, Science Society, Commerce Society, Dalhousie Outdoors Club, national fraternities, national sororities.

Athletics Member CIS. ***Intercollegiate sports:*** basketball M/W, cross-country running M/W, field hockey W(c), ice hockey M/W, soccer M/W, swimming and diving M/W, track and field M/W, volleyball M/W. ***Intramural sports:*** badminton M(c)/W(c), baseball M(c), basketball M/W, cheerleading W(c), crew M(c)/W(c), cross-country running M/W, fencing M(c)/W(c), field hockey W, football M(c)/W, golf M/W, gymnastics M/W, ice hockey M, lacrosse M(c)/W(c), racquetball M/W, rugby M(c)/W(c), sailing M(c)/W(c), skiing (cross-country) M/W, skiing (downhill) M/W, soccer M/W, softball M/W, squash M(c)/W(c), swimming and diving M(c)/W(c), tennis M/W, track and field M/W, ultimate Frisbee M/W, volleyball M/W, water polo M/W, weight lifting M/W, wrestling M(c)/W(c).

Campus security: 24-hour emergency response devices and patrols, student patrols, late-night transport/escort service, controlled dormitory access.

Student services: health clinic, personal/psychological counseling, women's center, legal services.

COSTS

Costs (2017–18) ***Tuition:*** province resident $8265 full-time; nonresident $8265 full-time; International tuition $17,730 full-time. Full-time tuition and fees vary according to course load, degree level, location, and program. Part-time tuition and fees vary according to course load, degree level, location, and program. ***Required fees:*** $1066 full-time. ***Room and board:*** $10,880; room only: $7325. Room and board charges vary according to board plan, housing facility, and location. ***Waivers:*** senior citizens and employees or children of employees.

APPLYING

Standardized Tests *Required:* SAT or ACT (for admission).

Options: electronic application, early admission, deferred entrance.

Application fee: $70 Canadian dollars.

Required: high school transcript, minimum 3.0 GPA. ***Required for some:*** essay or personal statement, 1 letter of recommendation, interview.

Application deadlines: 6/1 (freshmen), 6/1 (transfers).

Notification: continuous (freshmen), continuous (transfers).

CONTACT

Ashley Jordan, Assistant Registrar, Associate Director Admissions, Dalhousie University, Office of the Registrar, Halifax, NS B3H 4H6, Canada. *Phone:* 902-494-1833. *Fax:* 902-494-1630. *E-mail:* admissions@dal.ca.

École Polytechnique de Montréal

Montréal, Quebec, Canada

http://www.polymtl.ca/

CONTACT

École Polytechnique de Montréal, CP 6079, Succursale Centre-Ville, Montréal, QC H3C 3A7, Canada.

Emily Carr University of Art + Design

Vancouver, British Columbia, Canada

http://www.ecuad.ca/

- **Province-supported** comprehensive, founded 1925
- **Urban** campus
- **Coed** 1,800 undergraduate students
- **Moderately difficult** entrance level

FACULTY

Total: 220, 25% full-time.

Student/faculty ratio: 18:1.

ACADEMICS

Degrees: bachelor's and master's.

Special study options: advanced placement credit, cooperative education, part-time degree program, services for LD students, study abroad.

Computers: Students can access the following: campus intranet, computer help desk, free student e-mail accounts, online (class) grades, online (class) registration, online (class) schedules. Campuswide network is available. Wireless service is available via entire campus.

STUDENT LIFE

Housing options: college housing not available.

Activities and organizations: student-run newspaper, radio station.

Campus security: 24-hour emergency response devices and patrols.

Student services: personal/psychological counseling.

COSTS

Costs (2016–17) ***Tuition:*** province resident $3942 Canadian dollars full-time; International tuition $14,904 Canadian dollars full-time. Full-time tuition and fees vary according to course load. Part-time tuition and fees vary according to course load. ***Required fees:*** $425 Canadian dollars full-time.

APPLYING

Options: electronic application.

Application fee: $70 Canadian dollars.

Required: essay or personal statement, high school transcript, minimum 2.7 GPA, portfolio and questionnaire.

Application deadlines: 1/15 (freshmen), 1/15 (transfers).

Notification: 3/1 (freshmen), 3/1 (transfers).

CONTACT

Admissions, Emily Carr University of Art + Design, 1399 Johnston Street, Vancouver, BC V6H 3R9, Canada. *Phone:* 604-844-3800. *Toll-free phone:* 800-832-7788. *Fax:* 604-844-3801. *E-mail:* admissions@ecuad.ca.

Emmanuel Bible College

Kitchener, Ontario, Canada

http://www.emmanuelbiblecollege.ca/

CONTACT

Emmanuel Bible College, 100 Fergus Avenue, Kitchener, ON N2A 2H2, Canada. *Phone:* 519-894-8900 Ext. 224.

Eston College

Eston, Saskatchewan, Canada

http://www.estoncollege.ca/

CONTACT

Admissions, Eston College, 730 1st Street E., Box 579, Eston, SK S0L 1A0, Canada. *Phone:* 306-962-3621. *Toll-free phone:* 888-440-3424. *Fax:* 306-962-3810. *E-mail:* admissions@estoncollege.ca.

HEC Montreal

Montréal, Quebec, Canada

http://www.hec.ca/

- **Province-supported** comprehensive, founded 1910, part of Universite de Montreal
- **Urban** 9-acre campus with easy access to Montreal, QC
- **Coed** 10,276 undergraduate students, 48% full-time, 51% women, 49% men
- **Moderately difficult** entrance level, 73% of applicants were admitted

UNDERGRAD STUDENTS

4,973 full-time, 5,303 part-time. Students come from 5 provinces and territories; 65 other countries; 31% are from out of state.

Freshmen:

Admission: 2,643 applied, 1,924 admitted, 952 enrolled.

Retention: 1% of full-time freshmen returned.

FACULTY

Total: 753, 39% full-time, 36% with terminal degrees.

Student/faculty ratio: 21:1.

ACADEMICS

Calendar: trimesters. *Degrees:* certificates, bachelor's, master's, doctoral, and postbachelor's certificates.

Special study options: academic remediation for entering students, adult/continuing education programs, English as a second language, honors programs, independent study, off-campus study, part-time degree program, student-designed majors, study abroad, summer session for credit.

Computers: 161 computers/terminals and 9,000 ports are available on campus for general student use. Students can access the following: campus intranet, computer help desk, free student e-mail accounts, online (class) grades, online (class) registration, online (class) schedules, learning management system, corporate calendar and Web sites for resources available for classes. Campuswide network is available. 100% of college-owned or -operated housing units are wired for high-speed Internet access. Wireless service is available via entire campus.

Library: Myriam et J.-Robert Ouimet Library plus 1 other. *Books:* 111,403 (physical), 299,595 (digital/electronic); *Serial titles:* 1,050 (physical), 118,890 (digital/electronic); *Databases:* 156. Weekly public service hours: 85; students can reserve study rooms.

STUDENT LIFE

Housing options: coed. Campus housing is university owned. Freshman applicants given priority for college housing.

Activities and organizations: student-run newspaper, AEMBA (MBA Students' Association), AEHEC (BBA Students' Association), AEPC (Certificate Students' Association), AECS (Graduate Students' Association).

Campus security: 24-hour emergency response devices and patrols.

Student services: health clinic, personal/psychological counseling.

COSTS & FINANCIAL AID

Costs (2016–17) ***Tuition:*** province resident $2328 Canadian dollars full-time, $78 Canadian dollars per credit part-time; nonresident $7228 Canadian dollars full-time, $234 Canadian dollars per credit part-time; International tuition $23,000 Canadian dollars full-time. Full-time tuition and fees vary according to program. Part-time tuition and fees vary according to program. ***Required fees:*** $1469 Canadian dollars full-time, $46 Canadian dollars per credit part-time, $82 Canadian dollars per credit part-time. ***Room and board:*** $3850 Canadian dollars. Room and board charges vary according to board plan and housing facility. ***Waivers:*** employees or children of employees.

Financial Aid Of all full-time matriculated undergraduates who enrolled in 2015, 2,600 applied for aid, 2,600 were judged to have need. 10 state and other part-time jobs (averaging $2000). ***Average financial aid package:*** $8300. ***Average need-based loan:*** $3200. ***Average need-based gift aid:*** $6600. ***Average indebtedness upon graduation:*** $3200.

APPLYING

Options: electronic application, deferred entrance.

Application fee: $85 Canadian dollars.

Required: high school transcript. ***Required for some:*** R score, collegial/college performance rating.

Application deadlines: 3/1 (freshmen), 2/15 (out-of-state freshmen).

CONTACT

Mrs. Virginie Lefebvre, Director of Admission Services, HEC Montreal, 3000 Chemin de la Cote-Sainte-Catherine, Montreal, QC H3T 2A7, Canada. *Phone:* 514-340-6112. *Fax:* 514-340-5640. *E-mail:* registraire.info@hec.ca.

Heritage College and Seminary

Cambridge, Ontario, Canada

http://www.heritagecambridge.com/

CONTACT

Mr. Mark Walther, Assistant Dean of Students, Heritage College and Seminary, New York, NY 10023-6588. *Phone:* 519-651-2869 Ext. 251. *Toll-free phone:* 800-465-1961. *Fax:* 519-651-2870. *E-mail:* mwalther@heritagecollege.net.

Horizon College & Seminary

Saskatoon, Saskatchewan, Canada

http://www.horizon.edu/

CONTACT

Mrs. Jenn Lundy, Assistant Registrar, Horizon College & Seminary, 1303 Jackson Avenue, Saskatoon, SK S7H 2M9, Canada. *Phone:* 306-374-6655 Ext. 225. *Toll-free phone:* 877-374-6655. *Fax:* 306-373-6968. *E-mail:* admissions@horizon.edu.

The King's University

Edmonton, Alberta, Canada

http://www.kingsu.ca/

- **Independent interdenominational** 4-year, founded 1979
- **Suburban** 20-acre campus
- **Endowment** $3.1 million
- **Coed** 718 undergraduate students, 91% full-time, 56% women, 44% men
- **Moderately difficult** entrance level, 88% of applicants were admitted

UNDERGRAD STUDENTS

651 full-time, 67 part-time. Students come from 6 provinces and territories; 12 other countries; 10% are from out of state; 14% transferred in; 31% live on campus.

Freshmen:

Admission: 417 applied, 368 admitted, 205 enrolled. ***Average high school GPA:*** 3.

Retention: 70% of full-time freshmen returned.

FACULTY

Total: 108, 42% full-time, 69% with terminal degrees.

Student/faculty ratio: 11:1.

ACADEMICS

Calendar: Canadian standard year. *Degrees:* certificates, diplomas, bachelor's, and postbachelor's certificates.

Special study options: adult/continuing education programs, advanced placement credit, double majors, English as a second language, independent study, internships, off-campus study, part-time degree program, services for LD students, study abroad, summer session for credit.

Unusual degree programs: 3-2 elementary education, secondary education.

Computers: 76 computers/terminals are available on campus for general student use. Students can access the following: campus intranet, computer help desk, free student e-mail accounts, online (class) grades, online (class) registration, online (class) schedules. Campuswide network is available. 100% of college-owned or -operated housing units are wired for high-speed Internet access. Wireless service is available via entire campus.

Library: Simona Maaskant. *Books:* 80,000 (physical), 301,000 (digital/electronic); *Serial titles:* 166 (physical), 130,000 (digital/electronic); *Databases:* 50. Weekly public service hours: 63.

STUDENT LIFE

Housing options: coed, women-only. Campus housing is university owned. Freshman applicants given priority for college housing.

Activities and organizations: drama/theater group, student-run newspaper, choral group, Micah Action and Awareness Students' Society, King';s Eagles Hockey Club, King's Rugby Club, King's Science Society, The King's Commerce Association.

Athletics ***Intercollegiate sports:*** badminton M(s)/W(s), basketball M(s)/W(s), soccer M(s)/W(s), volleyball M(s)/W(s). ***Intramural sports:*** basketball M/W, ice hockey M, soccer M/W, volleyball M/W.

Campus security: 24-hour emergency response devices, student patrols, controlled dormitory access.

Student services: personal/psychological counseling.

COSTS & FINANCIAL AID

Costs (2017–18) ***Comprehensive fee:*** $19,427 includes full-time tuition ($11,780), mandatory fees ($857), and room and board ($6790). Full-time tuition and fees vary according to course load. Part-time tuition: $380 per credit hour. Part-time tuition and fees vary according to course load. ***Required fees:*** $530 per term part-time. ***College room only:*** $3700. Room and board charges vary according to board plan and housing facility. ***Payment plan:*** installment. ***Waivers:*** employees or children of employees.

Financial Aid ***Financial aid deadline:*** 3/31.

APPLYING

Options: electronic application.

Application fee: $70 Canadian dollars.

Required: high school transcript, minimum 2.0 GPA, 1 letter of recommendation. ***Required for some:*** essay or personal statement, interview.

Application deadlines: rolling (freshmen), rolling (transfers).

Notification: 8/15 (freshmen), 8/15 (transfers).

CONTACT

Ms. Hilda Buisman, Director of Admissions, The King's University, 9125-50 Street, Edmonton, AB T6B 2H3, Canada. *Phone:* 780-465-3500 Ext. 8031. *Toll-free phone:* 800-661-8582. *Fax:* 780-465-3534. *E-mail:* admissions@kingsu.ca.

Kingswood University
Sussex, New Brunswick, Canada
http://www.kingswood.edu/

CONTACT
Mrs. Shelley Vail, Associate Director for Admissions and Financial Aid, Kingswood University, PO Box 5125, Sussex, NB E4E 5L2, Canada. *Phone:* 506-432-4422. *Toll-free phone:* 888-432-4422. *Fax:* 506-432.4442. *E-mail:* vails@kingswood.edu.

Lakehead University
Thunder Bay, Ontario, Canada
http://www.lakeheadu.ca/

CONTACT
Mr. Nicholas Chamut, Manager of Undergraduate Admissions, Lakehead University, 955 Oliver Road, Thunder Bay, ON P7B 5E1, Canada. *Phone:* 807-343-8676. *Toll-free phone:* 800-465-3959. *Fax:* 807-766-7209. *E-mail:* admissions@lakeheadu.ca.

Laurentian University
Sudbury, Ontario, Canada
http://www.laurentian.ca/

- **Province-supported** comprehensive, founded 1960
- **Suburban** 700-acre campus
- **Endowment** $40.8 million
- **Coed**

FACULTY
Student/faculty ratio: 18:1.

ACADEMICS
Calendar: Canadian standard year (fall, winter, spring sessions). *Degrees:* certificates, diplomas, bachelor's, master's, doctoral, and postbachelor's certificates.
Library: J. N. Desmarais Library plus 9 others. *Books:* 1.0 million (physical), 331,212 (digital/electronic); *Serial titles:* 14,439 (physical), 56,000 (digital/electronic). Students can reserve study rooms.

STUDENT LIFE
Housing options: coed. Campus housing is university owned. Freshman campus housing is guaranteed.
Activities and organizations: drama/theater group, student-run newspaper, radio station, choral group, Students General Association, Association des Étudiantes/Étudiants francophones, Association of Mature and Part-time Students, Graduate Students Association.
Athletics Member CIS.
Campus security: 24-hour emergency response devices and patrols, late-night transport/escort service, controlled dormitory access.
Student services: health clinic, personal/psychological counseling, women's center.

COSTS & FINANCIAL AID
Costs (2016–17) ***Tuition:*** province resident $6102 Canadian dollars full-time, $1220 Canadian dollars per course part-time; International tuition $19,407 Canadian dollars full-time. Full-time tuition and fees vary according to degree level and program. Part-time tuition and fees vary according to course load and degree level. ***Required fees:*** $800 Canadian dollars full-time, $41 Canadian dollars per course part-time. ***Room and board:*** $9835 Canadian dollars; room only: $5760 Canadian dollars. Room and board charges vary according to board plan and housing facility.
Financial Aid Of all full-time matriculated undergraduates who enrolled in 2015, 241 state and other part-time jobs (averaging $1563).

APPLYING
Required: high school transcript. ***Required for some:*** essay or personal statement, 2 letters of recommendation, interview.

CONTACT
Laurentian University, 935 Ramsey Lake Road, P3E 2C6, Canada. *Phone:* 800-263-4188. *Toll-free phone:* 800-263-4188. *E-mail:* explore@laurentian.ca.

Master's College and Seminary
Peterborough, Ontario, Canada
http://www.mcs.edu/

- **Independent Pentecostal** 4-year, founded 1939
- **Suburban** campus with easy access to Toronto
- **Endowment** $934,661
- **Coed** 221 undergraduate students
- **Noncompetitive** entrance level, 94% of applicants were admitted

UNDERGRAD STUDENTS
Students come from 7 provinces and territories; 2 other countries; 20% are from out of state; 65% live on campus.

Freshmen:
Admission: 70 applied, 66 admitted.
Retention: 90% of full-time freshmen returned.

FACULTY
Total: 25, 16% full-time, 20% with terminal degrees.
Student/faculty ratio: 16:1.

ACADEMICS
Calendar: semesters. *Degree:* certificates, diplomas, and bachelor's.
Special study options: academic remediation for entering students, distance learning, independent study, internships, off-campus study, part-time degree program, services for LD students, summer session for credit.
Computers: 6 computers/terminals are available on campus for general student use. Students can access the following: computer help desk, free student e-mail accounts, online (class) grades, online (class) registration, online (class) schedules. Campuswide network is available. Wireless service is available via entire campus.
Library: Robert and Shirley Taitinger Learning Commons. *Books:* 35,757 (physical), 5,272 (digital/electronic); *Serial titles:* 565 (physical). Weekly public service hours: 71.

STUDENT LIFE
Housing options: on-campus residence required for freshman year; men-only, women-only. Campus housing is leased by the school. Freshman campus housing is guaranteed.
Campus security: 24-hour emergency response devices, controlled dormitory access.

COSTS
Costs (2017–18) ***One-time required fee:*** $510. ***Comprehensive fee:*** $15,280 includes full-time tuition ($6656), mandatory fees ($1424), and room and board ($7200). Full-time tuition and fees vary according to course load, location, and program. Part-time tuition: $208 per credit hour. Part-time tuition and fees vary according to course load, location, and program. ***Required fees:*** $28 per credit hour part-time. ***Room and board:*** Room and board charges vary according to board plan. ***Payment plan:*** deferred payment. ***Waivers:*** senior citizens and employees or children of employees.

APPLYING
Options: electronic application, deferred entrance.
Application fee: $75 Canadian dollars.
Required: essay or personal statement, high school transcript, 3 letters of recommendation, Christian commitment. ***Required for some:*** interview. ***Recommended:*** minimum 2.0 GPA.
Application deadlines: 6/1 (freshmen), 6/1 (transfers).
Notification: continuous (freshmen), continuous (transfers).

CONTACT
Ms. Jessica Nelder, Recruiter/Admissions Counsellor, Master's College and Seminary, 780 Argyle Street, Peterborough, ON K9H 5T2, Canada. *Phone:* 800-295-6368 Ext. 237. *Toll-free phone:* 800-295-6368. *Fax:* 705-749-0417. *E-mail:* jessica.nelder@mcs.edu.

McGill University

Montréal, Quebec, Canada

http://www.mcgill.ca/

CONTACT
Enrollment Services, McGill University, 845 Sherbrooke Street West, James Administration Building, Room 205, Montreal, QC H3A 2T5, Canada. *Phone:* 514-398-3910. *Fax:* 514-398-4193. *E-mail:* admissions@mcgill.ca.

McMaster University

Hamilton, Ontario, Canada

http://www.mcmaster.ca/

- **Province-supported** university, founded 1887
- **Suburban** 300-acre campus with easy access to Toronto
- **Coed** 22,493 undergraduate students
- **Very difficult** entrance level, 68% of applicants were admitted

UNDERGRAD STUDENTS
Students come from 12 provinces and territories; 79 other countries; 20% live on campus.

Freshmen:
Admission: 30,589 applied, 20,918 admitted.
Retention: 88% of full-time freshmen returned.

FACULTY
Total: 894, 100% full-time, 92% with terminal degrees.
Student/faculty ratio: 25:1.

ACADEMICS
Calendar: Canadian standard year. *Degrees:* certificates, diplomas, bachelor's, master's, and doctoral.

Special study options: academic remediation for entering students, accelerated degree program, adult/continuing education programs, advanced placement credit, cooperative education, double majors, English as a second language, honors programs, independent study, internships, off-campus study, part-time degree program, services for LD students, study abroad, summer session for credit.

Computers: 400 computers/terminals are available on campus for general student use. Students can access the following: campus intranet, computer help desk, free student e-mail accounts, online (class) grades, online (class) registration, online (class) schedules. Campuswide network is available. 100% of college-owned or -operated housing units are wired for high-speed Internet access. Wireless service is available via classrooms, computer centers, computer labs, learning centers, libraries, student centers.
Library: Mills Memorial Library plus 4 others.

STUDENT LIFE
Housing options: coed, women-only, special housing for students with disabilities. Campus housing is university owned. Freshman applicants given priority for college housing.

Activities and organizations: drama/theater group, student-run newspaper, radio station, choral group, Inter-Varsity Christian Fellowship, African-Caribbean Student Association, Chinese Students' Association, AIESEC (international leadership organization), Southeast Asian-American Society.

Athletics Member CIS. ***Intercollegiate sports:*** badminton M/W, baseball M, basketball M/W, cross-country running M/W, fencing M/W, football M, golf M/W, lacrosse M/W, rugby M/W, soccer M/W, squash M/W, swimming and diving M/W, tennis M/W, track and field M/W, volleyball M/W, water polo M/W, wrestling M/W. ***Intramural sports:*** badminton M/W, baseball M/W, basketball M/W, cross-country running M/W, football M/W, golf M, gymnastics M/W, ice hockey M/W, lacrosse M/W, soccer M/W, softball M/W, squash M/W, table tennis M/W, tennis M/W, volleyball M/W, water polo M/W.

Campus security: 24-hour emergency response devices and patrols, student patrols, late-night transport/escort service, controlled dormitory access.

Student services: health clinic, personal/psychological counseling, women's center, legal services.

APPLYING
Standardized Tests *Required:* SAT or ACT (for admission).
Options: electronic application, deferred entrance.
Application fee: $95 Canadian dollars.
Required: high school transcript. ***Required for some:*** essay or personal statement, interview.
Application deadlines: 6/1 (freshmen), 6/1 (transfers).
Notification: 5/28 (freshmen), continuous until 9/1 (transfers).

CONTACT
Olivia Demerling, Admissions Officer, McMaster University, 1280 Main Street West, Hamilton, ON L8S 4M2, Canada. *Phone:* 905-525-4600. *Fax:* 905-527-1105. *E-mail:* admitmac@mcmaster.ca.

Memorial University of Newfoundland

St. John's, Newfoundland and Labrador, Canada

http://www.mun.ca/

CONTACT
Ms. Marian Abbott, Admissions Office, Memorial University of Newfoundland, Elizabeth Avenue, St. John's, NL A1C 5S7, Canada. *Phone:* 709-737-3705. *E-mail:* sturecru@morgan.ucs.mun.ca.

Mount Allison University

Sackville, New Brunswick, Canada

http://www.mta.ca/

- **Province-supported** comprehensive, founded 1839
- **Small-town** 50-acre campus
- **Endowment** $65.0 million
- **Coed** 2,517 undergraduate students, 96% full-time, 58% women, 42% men
- **Moderately difficult** entrance level, 90% of applicants were admitted

UNDERGRAD STUDENTS
2,411 full-time, 106 part-time. Students come from 22 provinces and territories; 44 other countries; 58% are from out of state; 4% transferred in; 50% live on campus.

Freshmen:
Admission: 1,628 applied, 1,464 admitted, 701 enrolled. ***Average high school GPA:*** 3.31.
Retention: 80% of full-time freshmen returned.

FACULTY
Total: 187, 71% full-time, 88% with terminal degrees.
Student/faculty ratio: 16:1.

ACADEMICS
Calendar: Canadian standard year. *Degrees:* certificates, bachelor's, and master's.

Special study options: academic remediation for entering students, adult/continuing education programs, advanced placement credit, distance learning, double majors, honors programs, independent study, internships, off-campus study, part-time degree program, services for LD students, student-designed majors, study abroad, summer session for credit.

Computers: 100 computers/terminals and 240 ports are available on campus for general student use. Students can access the following: computer help desk, free student e-mail accounts, online (class) grades, online (class) registration, online (class) schedules, online student account/Websis. Campuswide network is available. 100% of college-owned or -operated housing units are wired for high-speed Internet access. Wireless service is available via entire campus.
Library: Ralph Pickard Bell Library plus 3 others. Students can reserve study rooms.

STUDENT LIFE
Housing options: coed, women-only, cooperative. Campus housing is university owned. Freshman campus housing is guaranteed.

Activities and organizations: drama/theater group, student-run newspaper, radio station, choral group, Commerce Society, Windsor Theatre, Presiden's Leadership Development Certificate, Leadership Mount Allison, Garnet and Gold Society.

Athletics Member CIS. ***Intercollegiate sports:*** basketball M/W, football M, ice hockey W, rugby M/W, soccer M/W, swimming and diving M/W. ***Intramural sports:*** archery M(c)/W(c), badminton M/W, baseball M/W, basketball M/W, football M/W, golf M/W, ice hockey M/W, rugby M/W, skiing (cross-country) M/W, skiing (downhill) M/W, soccer M/W, softball M/W, tennis M/W, ultimate Frisbee M/W, volleyball M/W, weight lifting M/W.

Campus security: 24-hour emergency response devices, late-night transport/escort service.

Student services: health clinic, personal/psychological counseling.

COSTS

Costs (2016–17) ***Tuition:*** province resident $7765 Canadian dollars full-time, $1675 Canadian dollars per course part-time; nonresident $7765 Canadian dollars full-time, $1675 Canadian dollars per course part-time; International tuition $16,750 Canadian dollars full-time. Full-time tuition and fees vary according to course load and degree level. Part-time tuition and fees vary according to course load and degree level. ***Required fees:*** $956 Canadian dollars full-time, $194 Canadian dollars per year part-time. ***Room and board:*** $9227 Canadian dollars; room only: $4605 Canadian dollars. Room and board charges vary according to board plan and housing facility. ***Waivers:*** employees or children of employees.

APPLYING

Options: electronic application, deferred entrance.

Application fee: $50 Canadian dollars.

Required: high school transcript, minimum 2.5 GPA. ***Required for some:*** essay or personal statement, interview. ***Recommended:*** 2 letters of recommendation.

Application deadlines: rolling (freshmen), rolling (transfers).

Notification: continuous (freshmen), continuous (transfers).

CONTACT

Mr. Curtis Michaelis, Manager of Admissions, Mount Allison University, 65 York Street, Sackville, NB E4L 1E4, Canada. *Phone:* 506-364-3294. *Fax:* 506-364-2272. *E-mail:* admissions@mta.ca.

Mount Royal University

Calgary, Alberta, Canada

http://www.mtroyal.ca/

CONTACT

Admissions Office, Mount Royal University, 4825 Mount Royal Gate SW, Calgary, AB T3E 6K6, Canada. *Phone:* 403-440-5000. *Toll-free phone:* 877-440-5001.

Mount Saint Vincent University

Halifax, Nova Scotia, Canada

http://www.msvu.ca/

CONTACT

Ms. Heidi Tattrie, Assistant Registrar/Admissions, Mount Saint Vincent University, 166 Bedford Highway, Halifax, NS B3M2J6, Canada. *Phone:* 902-457-6117. *Toll-free phone:* 877-733-6788. *Fax:* 902-457-6498. *E-mail:* admissions@msvu.ca.

Ner Israel Yeshiva College of Toronto

Thornhill, Ontario, Canada

http://www.neryisroel.info/

CONTACT

Rabbi Y. Kravetz, Director of Admissions, Ner Israel Yeshiva College of Toronto, 8950 Bathurst Street, Thornhill, ON L4J 8A7, Canada. *Phone:* 905-731-1224.

Nipissing University

North Bay, Ontario, Canada

http://www.nipissingu.ca/

CONTACT

Ms. Lori-Ann Beckford, Assistant Registrar, Liaison, Nipissing University, 100 College Drive, Box 5002, North Bay, ON P1B 8L7, Canada. *Phone:* 705-474-3461 Ext. 4518. *Fax:* 705-474-1947. *E-mail:* liaison@nipissingu.ca.

NSCAD University

Halifax, Nova Scotia, Canada

http://www.nscad.ca/

CONTACT

Mr. Terry Bailey, Director of Admissions and Enrollment Services, NSCAD University, 5163 Duke Street, Halifax, NS B3J 3J6, Canada. *Phone:* 902-494-8129. *Toll-free phone:* 888-444-5989. *Fax:* 902-425-2987. *E-mail:* admissions@nscad.ca.

Okanagan College

Kelowna, British Columbia, Canada

http://www.okanagan.bc.ca/

CONTACT

Mr. Allan Hickey, Associate Registrar Systems, Okanagan College, 1000 K.L.O. Road, Kelowna, BC V1Y 4X8, Canada. *Phone:* 250-762-5445 Ext. 4332. *Toll-free phone:* 877-755-2266. *E-mail:* ahickey@okanagan.bc.ca.

Prairie Bible Institute

Three Hills, Alberta, Canada

http://www.prairie.edu/

CONTACT

Mr. Kevin Kirk, Vice President, Marketing and Enrollment Management, Prairie Bible Institute, 330 Sixth Avenue North, PO Box 4000, Three Hills, AB T0M 2N0, Canada. *Phone:* 403-443-5511 Ext. 3007. *Toll-free phone:* 800-661-2425. *E-mail:* admissions@prairie.edu.

Providence University College & Theological Seminary

Otterburne, Manitoba, Canada

http://www.providenceuc.ca/

CONTACT

Mr. Adrian Enns, Director of College Enrollment, Providence University College & Theological Seminary, 10 College Crescent, Otterburne, MB R0A 1G0, Canada. *Phone:* 204-433-7488. *Toll-free phone:* 800-668-7768. *Fax:* 204-433-7158. *E-mail:* info@prov.ca.

Queen's University at Kingston

Kingston, Ontario, Canada

http://www.queensu.ca/

CONTACT

Ms. Iveta Reinikovaite, Admission Coordinator, Queen's University at Kingston, Undergraduate Admissions, Gordon Hall, 74 Union Street, Kingston, ON K7L 3N6, Canada. *Phone:* 613-533-2218. *Fax:* 613-533-6810. *E-mail:* admission@queensu.ca.

Redeemer University College

Ancaster, Ontario, Canada

http://www.redeemer.ca/

- **Independent interdenominational** 4-year, founded 1980
- **Small-town** 86-acre campus with easy access to Toronto
- **Endowment** $4.1 million
- **Coed** 697 undergraduate students, 91% full-time, 62% women, 38% men
- 94% of applicants were admitted

UNDERGRAD STUDENTS

636 full-time, 61 part-time. Students come from 7 provinces and territories; 16 other countries; 4% are from out of state.

Freshmen:

Admission: 210 applied, 198 admitted.

Retention: 81% of full-time freshmen returned.

FACULTY
Total: 99, 46% full-time, 60% with terminal degrees.
Student/faculty ratio: 10:1.

ACADEMICS
Calendar: semesters. *Degree:* certificates and bachelor's.
Special study options: academic remediation for entering students, cooperative education, double majors, honors programs, independent study, internships, off-campus study, part-time degree program, services for LD students, study abroad, summer session for credit.
Computers: 81 computers/terminals are available on campus for general student use. Students can access the following: campus intranet, computer help desk, free student e-mail accounts, online (class) grades, online (class) schedules. Campuswide network is available. 100% of college-owned or -operated housing units are wired for high-speed Internet access. Wireless service is available via entire campus.
Library: Peter Turkstra Library. *Books:* 92,733 (physical); *Serial titles:* 93 (physical), 9,387 (digital/electronic); *Databases:* 21. Students can reserve study rooms.

STUDENT LIFE
Housing options: on-campus residence required through sophomore year; men-only, women-only. Campus housing is university owned. Freshman campus housing is guaranteed.
Activities and organizations: drama/theater group, student-run newspaper, choral group, Church in the Box, Service Learning Trips, Deedz, Athletics and Recreation, Concert Choir.
Athletics ***Intercollegiate sports:*** badminton M/W, basketball M(s)/W(s), cross-country running M/W, soccer M/W, volleyball M/W. ***Intramural sports:*** basketball M/W, ice hockey M, soccer M/W, squash M/W, tennis M/W, ultimate Frisbee M/W, volleyball M/W.
Campus security: 24-hour emergency response devices, student patrols, late-night transport/escort service, controlled dormitory access, path lighting.
Student services: personal/psychological counseling.

COSTS & FINANCIAL AID
Costs (2016–17) ***Comprehensive fee:*** $23,728 Canadian dollars includes full-time tuition ($15,982 Canadian dollars), mandatory fees ($524 Canadian dollars), and room and board ($7222 Canadian dollars). Full-time tuition and fees vary according to course load. Part-time tuition: $1602 Canadian dollars per course. Part-time tuition and fees vary according to course load. ***Required fees:*** $39 Canadian dollars per course part-time. ***College room only:*** $4944 Canadian dollars. Room and board charges vary according to board plan and housing facility. ***Payment plan:*** installment. ***Waivers:*** senior citizens and employees or children of employees.
Financial Aid Of all full-time matriculated undergraduates who enrolled in 2010, 640 applied for aid, 607 were judged to have need, 200 had their need fully met. 385 state and other part-time jobs (averaging $1238). In 2010, 99 non-need-based awards were made. ***Average percent of need met:*** 82. ***Average financial aid package:*** $12,582. ***Average need-based loan:*** $7464. ***Average need-based gift aid:*** $4587. ***Average non-need-based aid:*** $3061. ***Average indebtedness upon graduation:*** $23,598. ***Financial aid deadline:*** 3/31.

APPLYING
Standardized Tests *Required for some:* SAT or ACT (for admission).
Options: electronic application, deferred entrance.
Application fee: $40 Canadian dollars.
Required: essay or personal statement, high school transcript, minimum 2.0 GPA, 1 letter of recommendation. ***Required for some:*** interview.
Application deadlines: rolling (freshmen), rolling (transfers).
Notification: continuous (freshmen), continuous (transfers).

CONTACT
Recruitment, Redeemer University College, 777 Garner Road East, Ancaster, ON L9K 1J4, Canada. *Phone:* 905-648-2131 Ext. 4280. *Toll-free phone:* 800-263-6467. *Fax:* 905-648-9545. *E-mail:* recruitment@redeemer.ca.

Rocky Mountain College

Calgary, Alberta, Canada

http://www.rockymountaincollege.ca/

- **Independent** 4-year, founded 1992, affiliated with Missionary Church
- **Urban** 1-acre campus with easy access to Calgary
- **Endowment** $343,200
- **Coed**
- **Noncompetitive** entrance level

ACADEMICS
Calendar: semesters. *Degree:* certificates, diplomas, and bachelor's.
Library: Main Library plus 1 other.

STUDENT LIFE
Student services: personal/psychological counseling.

APPLYING
Options: electronic application, early decision, deferred entrance.
Application fee: $50 Canadian dollars.
Required: essay or personal statement, high school transcript, 2 letters of recommendation. ***Required for some:*** interview.

CONTACT
Rocky Mountain College, 4039 Brentwood Road, NW, Calgary, AB T2L 1L1, Canada. *Phone:* 403-284-5100 Ext. 222. *Toll-free phone:* 877-YOUnRMC.

Royal Military College of Canada

Kingston, Ontario, Canada

http://www.rmc.ca/

- **Federally supported** university, founded 1876, part of Council of Ontario Universities
- **Urban** 90-acre campus
- **Coed** 1,969 undergraduate students, 63% full-time, 17% women, 83% men

UNDERGRAD STUDENTS
1,246 full-time, 723 part-time. Students come from 13 provinces and territories; 51% are from out of state; 95% live on campus.

FACULTY
Total: 520, 45% full-time.
Student/faculty ratio: 5:1.

ACADEMICS
Calendar: Canadian standard year. *Degrees:* certificates, diplomas, bachelor's, master's, and doctoral.
Special study options: academic remediation for entering students, advanced placement credit, distance learning, double majors, English as a second language, honors programs, off-campus study, part-time degree program, services for LD students, study abroad.
Computers: 1,200 computers/terminals are available on campus for general student use. Students can access the following: campus intranet, computer help desk, free student e-mail accounts, online (class) grades, online (class) registration, online (class) schedules. Campuswide network is available. 100% of college-owned or -operated housing units are wired for high-speed Internet access. Wireless service is available via entire campus.
Library: Massey Library plus 1 other. Study areas open 24 hours, 5-7 days a week.

STUDENT LIFE
Housing options: on-campus residence required through senior year; coed. Campus housing is provided by a third party. Freshman campus housing is guaranteed.
Activities and organizations: drama/theater group, student-run newspaper, choral group, marching band.
Athletics Member CIS. ***Intercollegiate sports:*** basketball M, fencing M/W, ice hockey M, rugby M, soccer M/W, volleyball M/W. ***Intramural sports:*** badminton M/W, basketball M/W, crew M(c)/W(c), cross-country running M(c)/W(c), football M/W, golf M/W, ice hockey M/W, racquetball M/W, riflery M(c)/W(c), rock climbing M(c)/W(c), rowing M(c)/W(c), rugby M/W, sailing M(c)/W(c), skiing (cross-country) M(c)/W(c), skiing (downhill) M(c)/W(c), soccer M/W, squash M/W,

swimming and diving M(c)/W(c), tennis M(c)/W(c), track and field M(c)/W(c), triathlon M(c)/W(c), ultimate Frisbee M/W, volleyball M/W, water polo M/W, weight lifting M(c), wrestling M(c).

Campus security: 24-hour emergency response devices and patrols, late-night transport/escort service, controlled dormitory access.

Student services: health clinic, personal/psychological counseling, legal services.

COSTS

Costs (2017–18) ***Required fees:*** $75 per degree program part-time.

APPLYING

Required: essay or personal statement, high school transcript, interview, medical, aptitude test, security screening.

CONTACT

Royal Military College of Canada, PO Box 17000, Station Forces, Kingston, ON K7K 7B4, Canada. *Phone:* 613-541-6000 Ext. 6579.

Royal Roads University

Victoria, British Columbia, Canada

http://www.royalroads.ca/

- **Province-supported** upper-level, founded 1995
- **Suburban** 565-acre campus
- **Coed** 1,010 undergraduate students
- **Moderately difficult** entrance level

FACULTY

Total: 50.

Student/faculty ratio: 12:1.

ACADEMICS

Calendar: continuous. *Degrees:* certificates, diplomas, bachelor's, master's, and doctoral.

Special study options: accelerated degree program, adult/continuing education programs, distance learning, study abroad, summer session for credit.

Computers: Students can access the following: computer help desk, free student e-mail accounts, online (class) grades, online (class) registration, online (class) schedules, free file storage. Campuswide network is available. 100% of college-owned or -operated housing units are wired for high-speed Internet access. Wireless service is available via classrooms, computer centers, computer labs, learning centers, libraries, student centers.

Library: Coronel Memorial Library.

STUDENT LIFE

Housing options: college housing not available.

Athletics ***Intramural sports:*** badminton M/W, basketball M/W, crew M/W, cross-country running M/W, racquetball M/W, sailing M/W, soccer M/W, softball M/W, squash M/W, swimming and diving M/W, tennis M/W, ultimate Frisbee M/W, volleyball M/W, weight lifting M/W.

Campus security: 24-hour emergency response devices and patrols, late-night transport/escort service.

APPLYING

Options: electronic application.

Application fee: $110 Canadian dollars.

Application deadlines: rolling (transfers), rolling (early action).

Early decision deadline: rolling (for plan 1), rolling (for plan 2).

Notification: continuous (transfers), rolling (early decision plan 1), rolling (early decision plan 2), rolling (early action).

CONTACT

Royal Roads University, 2005 Sooke Road, Victoria, BC V9B 5Y2, Canada. *Phone:* 250-391-2511. *Toll-free phone:* 800-788-8028.

Ryerson University

Toronto, Ontario, Canada

http://www.ryerson.ca/

CONTACT

Michelle Beaton, Manager of International Student Recruitment, Ryerson University, 350 Victoria Street, Toronto, ON M5B 2K3, Canada. *Phone:* 416-979-5080. *Fax:* 416-979-5067. *E-mail:* inquire@ryerson.ca.

St. Francis Xavier University

Antigonish, Nova Scotia, Canada

http://www.stfx.ca/

CONTACT

Ms. Sarah Murray, Admissions Officer, St. Francis Xavier University, PO Box 5000, Antigonish, NS B2G 2W5, Canada. *Phone:* 902-867-2219. *Toll-free phone:* 877-867-7839 (in-state); 877-867-STFX (out-of-state). *Fax:* 902-867-2329. *E-mail:* mbarry@stfx.ca.

Saint Mary's University

Halifax, Nova Scotia, Canada

http://www.smu.ca/

CONTACT

Mr. Greg Ferguson, Director of Admissions, Saint Mary's University, Halifax, NS B3H 3C3, Canada. *Phone:* 902-420-5415. *Fax:* 902-496-8100. *E-mail:* greg.ferguson@smu.ca.

Saint Paul University

Ottawa, Ontario, Canada

http://www.ustpaul.ca/

CONTACT

Admission and Recruitment Office, Saint Paul University, 223 Main Street, Ottawa, ON K1S 1C4, Canada. *Phone:* 613-236-1393 Ext. 8990. *Toll-free phone:* 800-637-6859. *Fax:* 613-782-3014. *E-mail:* admission@ustpaul.ca.

St. Thomas University

Fredericton, New Brunswick, Canada

http://www.stu.ca/

- **Independent Roman Catholic** 4-year, founded 1910
- **Small-town** 16-acre campus
- **Endowment** $19.3 million
- **Coed** 1,827 undergraduate students, 95% full-time, 73% women, 27% men
- **Moderately difficult** entrance level, 91% of applicants were admitted

UNDERGRAD STUDENTS

1,740 full-time, 87 part-time. Students come from 10 provinces and territories; 38 other countries; 20% are from out of state; 94% Race/ethnicity unknown; 6% international; 5% transferred in; 29% live on campus.

Freshmen:

Admission: 897 applied, 816 admitted, 559 enrolled. ***Average high school GPA:*** 3.4.

Retention: 70% of full-time freshmen returned.

FACULTY

Total: 188, 54% full-time, 66% with terminal degrees.

Student/faculty ratio: 16:1.

ACADEMICS

Calendar: semesters. *Degrees:* certificates, bachelor's, and postbachelor's certificates.

Special study options: academic remediation for entering students, accelerated degree program, advanced placement credit, double majors, English as a second language, honors programs, independent study, internships, off-campus study, part-time degree program, services for LD students, student-designed majors, study abroad, summer session for credit.

Computers: 59 computers/terminals are available on campus for general student use. Students can access the following: computer help desk, free student e-mail accounts, online (class) grades, online (class) registration, online (class) schedules, learning management system. Campuswide network is available. 100% of college-owned or -operated housing units are wired for high-speed Internet access. Wireless service is available via entire campus.

Library: Harriet Irving Library plus 2 others.

STUDENT LIFE

Housing options: coed, women-only, special housing for students with disabilities. Campus housing is university owned. Freshman campus housing is guaranteed.

Activities and organizations: drama/theater group, student-run newspaper, radio station, choral group, Theatre St. Thomas, St. Thomas Student Union, Criminology Society, Model UN, International Students' Association.

Athletics Member CIS. ***Intercollegiate sports:*** basketball M/W, cross-country running M/W, golf M/W, soccer M/W, volleyball M/W. ***Intramural sports:*** badminton M/W, basketball M/W, cross-country running M/W, fencing M/W, football M, ice hockey M/W, rock climbing M/W, soccer M/W, softball M/W, squash M/W, swimming and diving M/W, table tennis M/W, track and field M/W, ultimate Frisbee M/W, volleyball M/W, water polo M/W.

Campus security: 24-hour emergency response devices and patrols, student patrols, late-night transport/escort service, controlled dormitory access.

Student services: health clinic, personal/psychological counseling, women's center.

COSTS & FINANCIAL AID

Costs (2016–17) ***Comprehensive fee:*** $15,387 Canadian dollars includes full-time tuition ($6276 Canadian dollars), mandatory fees ($500 Canadian dollars), and room and board ($8611 Canadian dollars). Full-time tuition and fees vary according to course load, degree level, and program. Part-time tuition and fees vary according to course load. ***Required fees:*** $633 Canadian dollars per course part-time. ***Room and board:*** Room and board charges vary according to board plan, housing facility, and location. ***Payment plans:*** installment, deferred payment. ***Waivers:*** senior citizens and employees or children of employees.

Financial Aid ***Financial aid deadline:*** 3/1.

APPLYING

Standardized Tests *Recommended:* SAT (for admission).

Options: electronic application, early action.

Application fee: $55 Canadian dollars.

Required: essay or personal statement, high school transcript, minimum 3.0 GPA. ***Required for some:*** interview.

Application deadlines: 8/31 (freshmen), 8/31 (transfers), 12/7 (early action).

Notification: continuous (freshmen), continuous (transfers).

CONTACT

Ms. Kathryn Monti, Director of Admissions, St. Thomas University, Duffie Hall, Fredericton, NB E3B 5G3, Canada. *Phone:* 506-452-0532. *Fax:* 506-452-0617. *E-mail:* admissions@stu.ca.

Simon Fraser University

Burnaby, British Columbia, Canada

http://www.sfu.ca/

- **Province-supported** university, founded 1965
- **Suburban** 174-hectare campus with easy access to Vancouver
- **Coed** 25,366 undergraduate students, 51% full-time, 54% women, 46% men
- **Moderately difficult** entrance level, 65% of applicants were admitted

UNDERGRAD STUDENTS

12,884 full-time, 12,482 part-time. Students come from 84 other countries; 7% are from out of state; 4% transferred in.

Freshmen:

Admission: 16,052 applied, 10,450 admitted, 3,581 enrolled. ***Average high school GPA:*** 3.35.

Retention: 85% of full-time freshmen returned.

FACULTY

Total: 984, 99% full-time, 89% with terminal degrees.

Student/faculty ratio: 22:1.

ACADEMICS

Calendar: trimesters. *Degrees:* certificates, diplomas, bachelor's, master's, doctoral, post-master's, and postbachelor's certificates.

Special study options: academic remediation for entering students, adult/continuing education programs, advanced placement credit, cooperative education, distance learning, double majors, English as a second language, honors programs, independent study, internships, off-campus study, part-time degree program, services for LD students, study abroad, summer session for credit.

Computers: 200 computers/terminals and 30 ports are available on campus for general student use. Students can access the following: computer help desk, free student e-mail accounts, online (class) grades, online (class) registration, online (class) schedules. Campuswide network is available. 100% of college-owned or -operated housing units are wired for high-speed Internet access. Wireless service is available via entire campus.

Library: Bennett Library plus 2 others. *Books:* 1.5 million (physical), 1.1 million (digital/electronic); *Serial titles:* 2,500 (physical), 98,000 (digital/electronic). Weekly public service hours: 103; students can reserve study rooms.

STUDENT LIFE

Housing options: coed, special housing for students with disabilities. Campus housing is university owned. Freshman applicants given priority for college housing.

Activities and organizations: drama/theater group, student-run newspaper, radio station, The Peak Newspaper, orientation/peer leaders, Crisis line, Women's Centre, Simon Fraser Public Interest Research Group.

Athletics Member NCAA. All Division II. ***Intercollegiate sports:*** basketball M(s)/W(s), cross-country running M(s)/W(s), football M(s), golf M(s)/W, gymnastics M, soccer M(s)/W(s), softball W(s), swimming and diving M(s)/W(s), track and field M(s)/W(s), volleyball W(s), wrestling M(s)/W(s). ***Intramural sports:*** archery M(c)/W(c), badminton M(c)/W(c), basketball M/W, cheerleading M(c)/W(c), crew M(c)/W(c), fencing M(c)/W(c), field hockey W(c), football M/W, golf W(c), gymnastics W(c), ice hockey M(c)/W(c), lacrosse M(c), rugby M(c)/W(c), soccer M/W, softball M/W, squash M(c)/W(c), table tennis M(c)/W(c), tennis M/W, ultimate Frisbee M(c)/W(c), volleyball M(c)/W(c), water polo M(c)/W(c).

Campus security: 24-hour emergency response devices and patrols, student patrols, late-night transport/escort service, controlled dormitory access, safe-walk stations, 24-hour safe study area.

Student services: health clinic, personal/psychological counseling, women's center.

COSTS & FINANCIAL AID

Costs (2016–17) ***Tuition:*** province resident $5428 Canadian dollars full-time, $181 Canadian dollars per credit hour part-time; nonresident $5428 Canadian dollars full-time, $181 Canadian dollars per credit hour part-time; International tuition $22,046 Canadian dollars full-time. Full-time tuition and fees vary according to course level and program. Part-time tuition and fees vary according to course level and program. ***Required fees:*** $764 Canadian dollars full-time, $342 Canadian dollars per term part-time. ***Room and board:*** $9356 Canadian dollars; room only: $5736 Canadian dollars. Room and board charges vary according to board plan and housing facility. ***Waivers:*** employees or children of employees.

Financial Aid ***Financial aid deadline:*** 11/15.

APPLYING

Standardized Tests *Required for some:* SAT or ACT (for admission).

Options: electronic application, early admission, early action, deferred entrance.

Application fee: $75 Canadian dollars.

Required: high school transcript, minimum 3.0 GPA. ***Required for some:*** essay or personal statement, interview.

Application deadlines: 2/28 (freshmen), 2/28 (transfers).

Notification: continuous until 6/30 (freshmen), continuous until 5/30 (transfers).

CONTACT
Louise Legris, Director of Admissions, Simon Fraser University, 8888 University Drive, MBC 3100, Burnaby, BC V5A 1S6, Canada. *Phone:* 778-782-3498. *Fax:* 778-782-4969. *E-mail:* admissionsteam@sfu.ca.

Southern Alberta Institute of Technology

Calgary, Alberta, Canada
http://www.sait.ca/

CONTACT
Southern Alberta Institute of Technology, 1301 16th Avenue NW, Calgary, AB T2M 0L4, Canada. *Phone:* 403-284-8857. *Toll-free phone:* 877-284-SAIT.

Steinbach Bible College

Steinbach, Manitoba, Canada
http://www.sbcollege.ca/

CONTACT
Mrs. Kaylene Buhler, Admissions Counselor, Steinbach Bible College, 50 PTH 12 North, Steinbach, MB R5G 1T4, Canada. *Phone:* 204-326-6451 Ext. 232. *Toll-free phone:* 800-230-8478. *Fax:* 204-326-6908. *E-mail:* info@sbcollege.ca.

Summit Pacific College

Abbotsford, British Columbia, Canada
http://www.summitpacific.ca/

CONTACT
Ms. Melody Deeley, Admissions and Registration, Summit Pacific College, Box 1700, Abbotsford, BC V2S 7E7, Canada. *Phone:* 604-851-7225. *Toll-free phone:* 800-976-8388. *E-mail:* registrar@summitpacific.ca.

Télé-université

Québec, Quebec, Canada
http://www.teluq.uquebec.ca/

CONTACT
Ms. Louise Bertrand, Registraire, Télé-université, 455, rue de l'Église, C.P. 4800, succ. Terminus, Québec, QC G1K 9H5, Canada. *Phone:* 418-657-2262 Ext. 5307. *Toll-free phone:* 888-843-4333.

Thompson Rivers University

Kamloops, British Columbia, Canada
http://www.tru.ca/

CONTACT
Mr. Josh Keller, Director, Student Recruitment and Liaison, Thompson Rivers University, 900 McGill Road, Kamloops, BC V2C 0C8, Canada. *Phone:* 250-828-5008. *Fax:* 250-828-5159. *E-mail:* jkeller@tru.ca.

Trent University

Peterborough, Ontario, Canada
http://www.trentu.ca/

- **Province-supported** university, founded 1963
- **Suburban** 1400-acre campus with easy access to Toronto
- **Coed** 8,445 undergraduate students
- **Moderately difficult** entrance level, 22% of applicants were admitted

UNDERGRAD STUDENTS
Students come from 13 provinces and territories; 86 other countries; 2% are from out of state; 17% live on campus.

Freshmen:
Admission: 7,300 applied, 1,600 admitted, 1,869 enrolled.
Retention: 84% of full-time freshmen returned.

FACULTY
Total: 207.

ACADEMICS
Calendar: Canadian standard year. *Degrees:* certificates, diplomas, bachelor's, master's, and doctoral.
Special study options: academic remediation for entering students, accelerated degree program, advanced placement credit, cooperative education, distance learning, double majors, English as a second language, honors programs, independent study, internships, off-campus study, part-time degree program, services for LD students, student-designed majors, study abroad, summer session for credit.
Computers: Students can access the following: campus intranet, computer help desk, free student e-mail accounts, online (class) grades, online (class) registration, online (class) schedules, online tuition payment. Campuswide network is available. 100% of college-owned or -operated housing units are wired for high-speed Internet access. Wireless service is available via entire campus.
Library: Thomas J. Bata Library plus 1 other. Students can reserve study rooms.

STUDENT LIFE
Housing options: coed, women-only. Campus housing is university owned. Freshman applicants given priority for college housing.
Activities and organizations: drama/theater group, student-run newspaper, radio station, choral group, Trent Radio, Trent International Program, Trent Central Student Association, Arthur (student newspaper), Excalibur (yearbook).
Athletics Member CIS. ***Intercollegiate sports:*** crew M/W, cross-country running M/W, golf M, lacrosse M/W, rugby M/W, soccer M/W, track and field M/W, volleyball M/W. ***Intramural sports:*** badminton M/W, baseball M/W, basketball M/W, cross-country running M/W, football M/W, ice hockey M/W, soccer M/W, softball M/W, squash M/W, swimming and diving M/W, tennis M/W, track and field M/W, ultimate Frisbee M/W, volleyball M/W, water polo M/W.
Campus security: 24-hour emergency response devices and patrols, student patrols, late-night transport/escort service, controlled dormitory access.
Student services: health clinic, personal/psychological counseling, women's center.

COSTS
Costs (2016–17) ***Tuition:*** province resident $6408 Canadian dollars full-time, $1282 Canadian dollars per credit part-time; nonresident $3766 Canadian dollars per credit part-time; International tuition $18,832 Canadian dollars full-time. Full-time tuition and fees vary according to course load, location, program, and student level. Part-time tuition and fees vary according to course load, location, program, and student level. ***Required fees:*** $1600 Canadian dollars full-time, $124 Canadian dollars per credit part-time. ***Room and board:*** $9563 Canadian dollars. Room and board charges vary according to board plan, housing facility, and location. ***Payment plans:*** installment, deferred payment. ***Waivers:*** employees or children of employees.

APPLYING
Options: electronic application, deferred entrance.
Application fee: $150 Canadian dollars.
Required: high school transcript, minimum 2.8 GPA. ***Required for some:*** essay or personal statement, interview.
Application deadlines: 6/1 (freshmen), 9/1 (transfers).
Notification: continuous (freshmen), continuous (transfers).

CONTACT
Mr. Kevin Whitmore, Manager, Admissions, Trent University, 1600 West Bank Drive, Peterborough, ON K9J 7B8, Canada. *Phone:* 705-748-1011 Ext. 7748. *Fax:* 705-748-1629. *E-mail:* admissions@trentu.ca.

Trinity Western University

Langley, British Columbia, Canada

http://www.twu.ca/

CONTACT
Trinity Western University, 7600 Glover Road, Langley, BC V2Y 1Y1, Canada. *Toll-free phone:* 888-468-6898.

Tyndale University College & Seminary

Toronto, Ontario, Canada

http://www.tyndale.ca/

CONTACT
Tricia McKenley, Admissions Office Coordinator, Tyndale University College & Seminary, 25 Ballyconnor Court, Toronto, ON M2M 4B3, Canada. *Phone:* 416-218-6757 Ext. 6738. *Toll-free phone:* 877-896-3253. *E-mail:* admissions@tydale.ca.

Université de Moncton

Moncton, New Brunswick, Canada

http://www.umoncton.ca/

CONTACT
Miss Nicole Savois, Chief Admission Officer, Université de Moncton, Moncton, NB E1A 3E9, Canada. *Phone:* 506-858-4115. *Toll-free phone:* 800-363-8336. *E-mail:* gallanrm@umoncton.ca.

Université de Montréal

Montréal, Quebec, Canada

http://www.umontreal.ca/

- **Province-supported** university, founded 1920
- **Urban** 160-acre campus with easy access to Montreal
- **Endowment** $300.1 million
- **Coed** 35,907 undergraduate students, 73% full-time, 68% women, 32% men
- **Moderately difficult** entrance level, 76% of applicants were admitted

UNDERGRAD STUDENTS
26,104 full-time, 9,803 part-time. Students come from 13 provinces and territories; 130 other countries; 2% are from out of state.

Freshmen:
Admission: 28,856 applied, 21,987 admitted.

FACULTY
Total: 6,100, 25% full-time, 74% with terminal degrees.

ACADEMICS
Calendar: trimesters. *Degrees:* certificates, diplomas, bachelor's, master's, doctoral, post-master's, and postbachelor's certificates.

Special study options: accelerated degree program, adult/continuing education programs, cooperative education, distance learning, double majors, English as a second language, honors programs, independent study, internships, off-campus study, part-time degree program, services for LD students, student-designed majors, study abroad, summer session for credit.

Computers: 1,500 computers/terminals are available on campus for general student use. Students can access the following: campus intranet, computer help desk, free student e-mail accounts, online (class) registration, online (class) schedules. Campuswide network is available. Wireless service is available via entire campus.

Library: Bibliotheque des lettres et sciences humaines plus 18 others. *Books:* 1.5 million (physical), 366,149 (digital/electronic); *Serial titles:* 42,537 (physical), 88,591 (digital/electronic); *Databases:* 245. Weekly public service hours: 93; study areas open 24 hours, 5-7 days a week; students can reserve study rooms.

STUDENT LIFE
Housing options: coed, women-only, special housing for students with disabilities. Campus housing is university owned.

Activities and organizations: drama/theater group, student-run newspaper, radio station, choral group, Federation des Associations Etudiantes du Campus (FAECUM), Amnistie Internationale UdeM, Action humanitaire et communautaire (AHC), Groupe de recherche et d'interet en developpement durable et en agriculture urbaine (GRIDDAU), Association generale des Etudiants de la Faculte de l'education permanente (AGEEFEP), national sororities.

Athletics Member CIS. ***Intercollegiate sports:*** badminton M(s)/W(s), baseball M/W, cheerleading M/W, cross-country running M/W, football M(s), golf M(s)/W(s), ice hockey W(s), rowing M/W, rugby M/W, skiing (downhill) M(s)/W(s), soccer M(s)/W(s), swimming and diving M(s)/W(s), tennis M(s)/W(s), track and field M(s)/W(s), triathlon M/W, ultimate Frisbee M/W, volleyball M(s)/W(s). ***Intramural sports:*** basketball M/W, ice hockey M/W, skiing (cross-country) M/W, soccer M/W, squash M/W, volleyball M/W, water polo M/W.

Campus security: 24-hour emergency response devices and patrols, student patrols, late-night transport/escort service, controlled dormitory access, cameras, alarm systems, access control system, crime prevention programs.

Student services: health clinic, personal/psychological counseling, legal services.

COSTS & FINANCIAL AID
Costs (2017–18) ***One-time required fee:*** $54. ***Tuition:*** province resident $163 per credit part-time; nonresident $326 per credit part-time. Full-time tuition and fees vary according to course load, location, and program. Part-time tuition and fees vary according to course load, location, and program. ***Required fees:*** $341 per year part-time. ***Payment plan:*** installment. ***Waivers:*** employees or children of employees.

Financial Aid Of all full-time matriculated undergraduates who enrolled in 2006, 400 state and other part-time jobs.

APPLYING
Options: electronic application.

Application fee: $94.

Required: Diploma of Collegiate Studies (and transcript) or equivalent. ***Required for some:*** interview.

Application deadlines: 3/1 (freshmen), 3/1 (transfers).

Notification: 5/15 (freshmen), 5/15 (transfers).

CONTACT
Mme. Marie-Claude Binette, Registrar, Université de Montréal, Bureau du registraire, CP 6128, Succursale Centre-Ville, Montreal, QC H3C 3J7, Canada. *Phone:* 514-343-2214. *Toll-free phone:* 866-977-7076 (in-state); 800-977-0761 (out-of-state). *Fax:* 514-343-2097. *E-mail:* marie-claude.binette@umontreal.ca.

Université de Saint-Boniface

Saint-Boniface, Manitoba, Canada

http://www.ustboniface.mb.ca/

CONTACT
Université de Saint-Boniface, 200 avenue de la Cathèdrale, Saint-Boniface, MB R2H 0H7, Canada.

Université de Sherbrooke

Sherbrooke, Quebec, Canada

http://www.usherbrooke.ca/

- **Independent** university, founded 1954
- **Urban** 800-acre campus with easy access to Montreal
- **Coed** 14,619 undergraduate students, 81% full-time, 55% women, 45% men
- **Moderately difficult** entrance level, 58% of applicants were admitted

UNDERGRAD STUDENTS
11,818 full-time, 2,801 part-time. Students come from 8 provinces and territories; 72 other countries; 1% are from out of state.

Freshmen:
Admission: 17,697 applied, 10,296 admitted, 3,279 enrolled.

FACULTY
Total: 3,053, 37% full-time.

ACADEMICS
Calendar: Canadian standard year. *Degrees:* certificates, diplomas, bachelor's, master's, and doctoral.

Special study options: accelerated degree program, adult/continuing education programs, cooperative education, English as a second language, internships, off-campus study, part-time degree program, services for LD students, student-designed majors, study abroad, summer session for credit.

Computers: 300 computers/terminals are available on campus for general student use. Students can access the following: computer help desk, free student e-mail accounts, online (class) registration, online (class) schedules. Campuswide network is available. Wireless service is available via entire campus.

Library: Bibliotheque Roger-Maltais plus 5 others. Weekly public service hours: 73; students can reserve study rooms.

STUDENT LIFE
Housing options: coed. Campus housing is university owned.

Activities and organizations: drama/theater group, student-run newspaper, radio station.

Athletics Member CIS. ***Intercollegiate sports:*** badminton M/W, cheerleading M/W, golf M/W, rugby M/W. ***Intramural sports:*** badminton M/W, basketball M/W, field hockey M/W, ice hockey M, racquetball M/W, soccer M/W, squash M/W, track and field M/W, ultimate Frisbee M/W, volleyball M/W, water polo M/W.

Campus security: 24-hour emergency response devices and patrols.

Student services: health clinic, personal/psychological counseling, legal services.

COSTS & FINANCIAL AID
Costs (2016–17) ***Tuition:*** Full-time tuition and fees vary according to course load, location, and reciprocity agreements. Part-time tuition and fees vary according to course load, location, and reciprocity agreements. ***Required fees:*** $71,964 Canadian dollars full-time, $1328 Canadian dollars per credit part-time, $10,812 Canadian dollars per term part-time. ***Room only:*** $3300 Canadian dollars. Room and board charges vary according to location. ***Waivers:*** employees or children of employees.

Financial Aid ***Financial aid deadline:*** 3/31.

APPLYING
Options: electronic application, early admission.

Application fee: $70 Canadian dollars.

Required: high school transcript. ***Required for some:*** interview.

Notification: continuous until 5/15 (freshmen).

CONTACT
Mme. Lisa BEDARD, Admissions Officer, Université de Sherbrooke, 2500 boulevard de l'Universite, Sherbrooke, QC J1K 2R1, Canada. *Phone:* 819-821-7687. *Toll-free phone:* 800-267-UDES.

Université du Québec à Chicoutimi

Chicoutimi, Quebec, Canada
http://www.uqac.ca/

CONTACT
Jean Wauthier, Admissions Officer, Université du Québec à Chicoutimi, 555, boulevard de L'Université, Chicoutimi, QC G7H 2B1, Canada. *Phone:* 418-545-5005. *E-mail:* czoccast@uqac.uquebec.ca.

Université du Québec à Montréal

Montréal, Quebec, Canada
http://www.uqam.ca/

CONTACT
Ms. Lucille Boisselle-Roy, Admissions Officer, Université du Québec à Montréal, CP 8888, Succursale Centreville, Montréal, QC H2L 4S8, Canada. *Phone:* 514-987-3132. *E-mail:* admission@uqam.ca.

Université du Québec à Rimouski

Rimouski, Quebec, Canada
http://www.uqar.ca/

CONTACT
Ms. Marie Saint-Laurent, Admissions Officer, Université du Québec à Rimouski, 300 Allee des Ursulines, CP3300, Rimouski QC G5L 3A1, Canada. *Phone:* 418-724-1433. *E-mail:* philippe_horth@uqar.uquebec.ca.

Université du Québec à Trois-Rivières

Trois-Rivières, Quebec, Canada
http://www.uqtr.ca/

CONTACT
Ms. Jean Bois, Admissions Officer, Université du Québec à Trois-Rivières, 3351 blvd des Forges, Case post 500, Trois-Rivières, QC G9A 5H7, Canada. *Phone:* 819-376-5011. *Toll-free phone:* 800-365-0922. *Fax:* 819-376-5232. *E-mail:* registraire@uqtr.ca.

Université du Québec, École de technologie supérieure

Montréal, Quebec, Canada
http://www.etsmtl.ca/

CONTACT
Mme. Francine Gamache, Registraire, Université du Québec, École de technologie supérieure, 1100, rue Notre Dame Ouest, Montréal, QC H3C 1K3, Canada. *Phone:* 514-396-8885. *E-mail:* admission@ets.mtl.ca.

Université du Québec en Abitibi-Témiscamingue

Rouyn-Noranda, Quebec, Canada
http://www.uqat.ca/

CONTACT
Mrs. Monique Fay, Admissions Officer, Université du Québec en Abitibi-Témiscamingue, 445 boulevard de l'Université, Rouyn-Noranda, QC J9X 5E4, Canada. *Phone:* 819-762-0971. *E-mail:* micheline.chevalier@uqat.uquebec.ca.

Université du Québec en Outaouais

Gatineau, Quebec, Canada
http://www.uqo.ca/

CONTACT
Registrar's Office, Université du Québec en Outaouais, CP 1250, Succursale Hull, 101 Saint-Jean-Bosco, 101 rue Saint-Jean-Bosco, Gatineau, QC J8X 3X7, Canada. *Phone:* 819-595-3900 Ext. 1850. *Toll-free phone:* 800-567-1283. *Fax:* 819-773-1835. *E-mail:* registraire@uqo.ca.

Université Laval

Québec, Quebec, Canada
http://www.ulaval.ca/

CONTACT
Promotion and Recruitment Division, Université Laval, Quebec, QC G1K 7P4, Canada. *Phone:* 418-656-2764. *Toll-free phone:* 877-785-2825. *Fax:* 418-656-5216. *E-mail:* info@dap.ulaval.ca.

Université Sainte-Anne

Church Point, Nova Scotia, Canada
http://www.usainteanne.ca/

CONTACT
Mrs. Blanche Theriault, Admissions Officer, Université Sainte-Anne, Church Point, NS B0W 1M0, Canada. *Phone:* 902-769-2114 Ext. 116. *E-mail:* admission@usainteanne.ca.

University of Alberta
Edmonton, Alberta, Canada
http://www.ualberta.ca/

CONTACT
Melissa Padfield, Deputy Registrar, University of Alberta, Administration Building, University of Alberta, Edmonton, AB T6G 2M7, Canada. *Phone:* 780-492-3113. *Toll-free phone:* 855-492-3113. *Fax:* 780-492-7172.

The University of British Columbia
Vancouver, British Columbia, Canada
http://www.ubc.ca/

CONTACT
The University of British Columbia, 2075 Westbrook Mall, Vancouver, BC V6T 1Z1, Canada. *Phone:* 604-822-3014.

The University of British Columbia–Okanagan Campus
Kelowna, British Columbia, Canada
http://www.ubc.ca/okanagan/welcome.html

CONTACT
International Student Recruitment, The University of British Columbia–Okanagan Campus, UC222 University Centre, 3333 University Way, Kelowna, BC V1V 1V7, Canada. *Phone:* 250-807-9447. *Fax:* 250-807-8552.

★ University of Calgary
Calgary, Alberta, Canada
http://www.ucalgary.ca/

- **Province-supported** university, founded 1945
- **Urban** 213-hectare campus
- **Endowment** $790.6 million
- **Coed**
- **Moderately difficult** entrance level

FACULTY
Student/faculty ratio: 21:1.

ACADEMICS
Calendar: semesters. *Degrees:* diplomas, bachelor's, master's, doctoral, post-master's, and postbachelor's certificates.
Library: Taylor Family Digital Library plus 8 others. *Books:* 3.0 million (physical), 944,517 (digital/electronic); *Databases:* 88,743. Weekly public service hours: 99; students can reserve study rooms.

STUDENT LIFE
Housing options: coed, special housing for students with disabilities. Campus housing is university owned. Freshman applicants given priority for college housing.

Activities and organizations: drama/theater group, student-run newspaper, radio and television station, choral group, Muslim Students' Association, Snowboard Club, Ski Club, Video Game Club, Student Dance Club, national fraternities, national sororities.

Athletics Member CIS.

Campus security: 24-hour emergency response devices and patrols, late-night transport/escort service, controlled dormitory access.

Student services: health clinic, personal/psychological counseling, women's center, legal services.

COSTS & FINANCIAL AID
Costs (2016–17) ***Tuition:*** province resident $5386 Canadian dollars full-time; nonresident $5386 Canadian dollars full-time; International tuition $18,338 Canadian dollars full-time. Full-time tuition and fees vary according to course load and program. Part-time tuition and fees vary

according to course load and program. ***Required fees:*** $1204 Canadian dollars full-time. ***Room and board:*** Room and board charges vary according to board plan and housing facility.

Financial Aid ***Financial aid deadline:*** 6/15.

APPLYING

Standardized Tests *Required for some:* SAT or ACT (for admission).

Options: electronic application, early admission.

Application fee: $145 Canadian dollars.

Required: high school transcript. ***Required for some:*** essay or personal statement, minimum 3.7 GPA, 3 letters of recommendation.

CONTACT

Mr. Kaili Xu, Associate Registrar, Undergraduate Admissions, University of Calgary, 2500 University Drive NW, Calgary, AB T2N 1N4, Canada. *Phone:* 403-210-7625. *E-mail:* future.students@ucalgary.ca.

See previous page for display ad and page 1542 for the College Close-Up.

University of Guelph

Guelph, Ontario, Canada

http://www.uoguelph.ca/

- **Province-supported** university, founded 1964
- **Suburban** 1017-acre campus with easy access to Toronto
- **Endowment** $263.4 million
- **Coed** 20,393 undergraduate students
- **Moderately difficult** entrance level, 66% of applicants were admitted

UNDERGRAD STUDENTS

Students come from 13 provinces and territories; 100 other countries; 28% live on campus.

Freshmen:

Admission: 23,750 applied, 15,564 admitted. ***Average high school GPA:*** 3.5.

Retention: 91% of full-time freshmen returned.

FACULTY

Total: 756, 99% with terminal degrees.

Student/faculty ratio: 23:1.

ACADEMICS

Calendar: trimesters. *Degrees:* certificates, diplomas, associate, bachelor's, master's, and doctoral.

Special study options: academic remediation for entering students, accelerated degree program, advanced placement credit, cooperative education, distance learning, double majors, English as a second language, honors programs, independent study, internships, off-campus study, part-time degree program, services for LD students, student-designed majors, study abroad, summer session for credit.

Computers: 8,000 computers/terminals and 24,000 ports are available on campus for general student use. Students can access the following: campus intranet, computer help desk, free student e-mail accounts, online (class) grades, online (class) registration, online (class) schedules. Campuswide network is available. 100% of college-owned or -operated housing units are wired for high-speed Internet access. Wireless service is available via entire campus.

Library: University of Guelph Library plus 1 other. *Books:* 1.2 million (physical), 344,256 (digital/electronic); *Serial titles:* 1,617 (physical), 21,287 (digital/electronic). Students can reserve study rooms.

STUDENT LIFE

Housing options: coed, women-only, cooperative, special housing for students with disabilities. Campus housing is university owned and is provided by a third party. Freshman campus housing is guaranteed.

Activities and organizations: drama/theater group, student-run newspaper, radio station, choral group, Guelph Gryphon Athletics, Habitat for Humanity, Curtain Call Productions, West Indian Students Association, OXFAM-Guelph Chapter.

Athletics Member CIS. ***Intercollegiate sports:*** baseball M, basketball M(s)/W(s), crew M/W, cross-country running M(s)/W(s), field hockey W(s), football M, golf M/W, ice hockey M(s)/W(s), lacrosse M/W, rowing M/W, rugby M(s)/W(s), skiing (cross-country) M/W, skiing (downhill) M/W, soccer M(s)/W(s), swimming and diving M(s)/W(s), track and field M(s)/W(s), volleyball M(s)/W(s), wrestling M(s)/W(s). ***Intramural sports:*** badminton M/W, basketball M/W, cheerleading M(c)/W(c), equestrian sports M(c)/W(c), fencing M(c)/W(c), football M/W, ice

hockey M/W, rock climbing M(c)/W(c), sand volleyball M/W, soccer M/W, softball M/W(c), squash M(c)/W(c), table tennis M(c)/W(c), ultimate Frisbee M/W, volleyball M/W, water polo M(c)/W(c).

Campus security: 24-hour emergency response devices and patrols, student patrols, late-night transport/escort service, controlled dormitory access, video camera surveillance in parking lots, alarms in women's locker room.

Student services: health clinic, personal/psychological counseling, women's center, legal services.

COSTS

Costs (2017–18) ***Tuition:*** province resident $6380 full-time, $825 per course part-time; International tuition $20,234 full-time. Full-time tuition and fees vary according to degree level and program. Part-time tuition and fees vary according to course load, degree level, and program. No tuition increase for student's term of enrollment. ***Room and board:*** $10,924; room only: $5974. Room and board charges vary according to board plan, housing facility, and location. ***Payment plan:*** installment. ***Waivers:*** senior citizens and employees or children of employees.

APPLYING

Standardized Tests *Required:* SAT or ACT (for admission).

Options: electronic application, early admission, deferred entrance.

Application fee: $150 Canadian dollars.

Required: high school transcript, minimum 3.0 GPA. ***Required for some:*** essay or personal statement.

Application deadlines: 3/1 (freshmen), 5/1 (transfers).

Notification: continuous until 5/27 (freshmen), continuous (transfers).

CONTACT

Ms. Janette Hogan, Assistant Registrar, Admissions, University of Guelph, L-3 University Centre, Guelph, ON N1G 2W1, Canada. *Phone:* 519-824-4120 Ext. 58529. *Fax:* 519-766-9481. *E-mail:* jhogan@uoguelph.ca.

See previous page for display ad and page 1556 for the College Close-Up.

University of King's College

Halifax, Nova Scotia, Canada

http://www.ukings.ca/

- **Province-supported** comprehensive, founded 1789
- **Urban** 4-acre campus
- **Endowment** $41.3 million
- **Coed** 869 undergraduate students, 97% full-time, 62% women, 38% men
- **Moderately difficult** entrance level, 87% of applicants were admitted

UNDERGRAD STUDENTS

845 full-time, 22 part-time. Students come from 12 provinces and territories; 19 other countries; 65% are from out of state; 5% transferred in; 23% live on campus.

Freshmen:
Admission: 510 applied, 446 admitted, 199 enrolled.

FACULTY

Total: 45, 100% full-time, 87% with terminal degrees.

Student/faculty ratio: 21:1.

ACADEMICS

Calendar: Canadian standard year. *Degrees:* bachelor's and master's.

Special study options: accelerated degree program, advanced placement credit, cooperative education, double majors, honors programs, independent study, internships, off-campus study, services for LD students, student-designed majors, study abroad, summer session for credit.

Computers: Students can access the following: online (class) grades, online (class) registration, online (class) schedules. Campuswide network is available. Wireless service is available via libraries, student centers.

Library: University of King's College Library. Students can reserve study rooms.

STUDENT LIFE

Housing options: coed, women-only. Campus housing is university owned. Freshman applicants given priority for college housing.

Activities and organizations: drama/theater group, student-run newspaper, radio station, choral group, King's Theatrical Society, student newspaper, King's College Dance Collective, St. Andrew's Missionary Society, King's Independent Film-Makers Society.

Athletics ***Intercollegiate sports:*** badminton M/W, basketball M/W, rugby M/W, soccer M/W, volleyball M/W. ***Intramural sports:*** badminton M/W, basketball M/W, soccer M/W, softball M/W, tennis M/W, ultimate Frisbee M/W, volleyball M/W, water polo M/W.

Campus security: student patrols, late-night transport/escort service, controlled dormitory access.

Student services: health clinic, personal/psychological counseling, women's center, legal services.

APPLYING

Standardized Tests *Required for some:* SAT or ACT (for admission).

Options: electronic application, early admission, early decision, deferred entrance.

Application fee: $65 Canadian dollars.

Required: high school transcript, minimum 3.0 GPA. ***Required for some:*** essay or personal statement, writing sample.

Application deadlines: 3/1 (freshmen), 6/1 (transfers).

Notification: continuous until 4/15 (freshmen), continuous (transfers).

CONTACT

Ms. Tara Wigglesworth-Hines, Assistant Registrar/Admissions, University of King's College, Registrar's Office, Halifax, NS B3H 3A1, Canada. *Phone:* 902-422-1271. *Fax:* 902-425-8183. *E-mail:* admissions@ukings.ns.ca.

University of Lethbridge

Lethbridge, Alberta, Canada

http://www.uleth.ca/

- **Province-supported** university, founded 1967
- **Urban** 576-acre campus
- **Coed** 7,891 undergraduate students, 90% full-time, 58% women, 42% men
- **Moderately difficult** entrance level, 84% of applicants were admitted

UNDERGRAD STUDENTS

7,083 full-time, 808 part-time. Students come from 13 provinces and territories; 53 other countries; 10% are from out of state; 11% live on campus.

Freshmen:
Admission: 3,185 applied, 2,660 admitted.
Retention: 79% of full-time freshmen returned.

ACADEMICS

Calendar: semesters. *Degrees:* certificates, diplomas, bachelor's, master's, doctoral, post-master's, and postbachelor's certificates.

Special study options: academic remediation for entering students, accelerated degree program, advanced placement credit, cooperative education, distance learning, double majors, English as a second language, independent study, internships, off-campus study, part-time degree program, services for LD students, student-designed majors, study abroad, summer session for credit.

Unusual degree programs: 3-2 education.

Computers: Students can access the following: computer help desk, free student e-mail accounts, online (class) grades, online (class) registration, online (class) schedules. Campuswide network is available. 100% of college-owned or -operated housing units are wired for high-speed Internet access. Wireless service is available via entire campus.

Library: The University of Lethbridge Library. Students can reserve study rooms.

STUDENT LIFE

Housing options: coed. Campus housing is university owned.

Activities and organizations: drama/theater group, student-run newspaper, radio station, choral group, national fraternities.

Athletics Member CIS. ***Intercollegiate sports:*** basketball M(s)/W(s), ice hockey M(s)/W(s), rugby W(s), soccer M(s)/W(s), swimming and diving M(s)/W(s), track and field M(s)/W(s). ***Intramural sports:*** badminton M/W, basketball M/W, fencing M(c)/W(c), golf M/W, ice hockey M/W, lacrosse M/W, rock climbing M/W, rugby M(c)/W(c), soccer M/W, softball W, tennis M(c)/W(c), ultimate Frisbee M/W, volleyball M/W.

Campus security: 24-hour emergency response devices and patrols, student patrols, late-night transport/escort service, controlled dormitory access, video camera monitored entrances, hallways.

Student services: health clinic, personal/psychological counseling, women's center.

COSTS

Costs (2017–18) ***Tuition:*** province resident $4974 full-time; nonresident $4974 full-time; International tuition $17,527 full-time. Full-time tuition and fees vary according to course load. Part-time tuition and fees vary according to course load. ***Required fees:*** $1048 full-time. ***Room and board:*** Room and board charges vary according to board plan and housing facility. ***Waivers:*** senior citizens and employees or children of employees.

APPLYING

Options: electronic application, deferred entrance.

Application fee: $100 Canadian dollars.

Required: high school transcript, minimum 2.0 GPA. ***Required for some:*** minimum 3.0 GPA, interview.

Application deadlines: 6/30 (freshmen), 6/30 (transfers).

Notification: continuous (freshmen), continuous (transfers).

CONTACT

Registrar's Office, University of Lethbridge, 4401 University Drive, Lethbridge, AB T1K 3M4, Canada. *Phone:* 403-320-5700. *Fax:* 403-329-5159. *E-mail:* regoffice@uleth.ca.

University of Manitoba

Winnipeg, Manitoba, Canada

http://www.umanitoba.ca/

CONTACT

Mr. Peter Dueck, Director of Enrollment Services, University of Manitoba, Winnipeg, MB R3T 2N2, Canada. *Phone:* 204-474-6382.

University of New Brunswick Fredericton

Fredericton, New Brunswick, Canada

http://www.unb.ca/

- **Province-supported** university, founded 1785, part of Province of New Brunswick
- **Urban** 7100-acre campus
- **Endowment** $244.0 million
- **Coed**

FACULTY

Student/faculty ratio: 15:1.

ACADEMICS

Calendar: Canadian standard year. *Degrees:* bachelor's, master's, and doctoral.

Library: Harriet Irving Library plus 4 others.

STUDENT LIFE

Housing options: coed, men-only, women-only, special housing for students with disabilities. Campus housing is university owned. Freshman campus housing is guaranteed.

Activities and organizations: drama/theater group, student-run newspaper, radio station, choral group.

Athletics Member CIS.

Campus security: 24-hour emergency response devices and patrols, student patrols, late-night transport/escort service, controlled dormitory access.

Student services: health clinic, personal/psychological counseling, women's center, legal services.

COSTS & FINANCIAL AID

Costs (2016–17) ***Tuition:*** province resident $6187 Canadian dollars full-time, $619 Canadian dollars per course part-time; International tuition $13,905 Canadian dollars full-time. Full-time tuition and fees vary according to course load, location, and program. Part-time tuition and fees vary according to course load, location, and program. ***Required fees:*** $589 Canadian dollars full-time, $35 Canadian dollars per course part-time. ***Room and board:*** $9170 Canadian dollars. Room and board charges vary according to board plan and location. ***Payment plans:*** installment, deferred payment.

Financial Aid Of all full-time matriculated undergraduates who enrolled in 2007, 123 state and other part-time jobs (averaging $1264). ***Financial aid deadline:*** 5/15.

APPLYING

Standardized Tests *Required for some:* SAT (for admission).

Required: high school transcript. ***Required for some:*** essay or personal statement, letters of recommendation, interview, supplementary form and life sketch for nursing, resumé and cover letter for Renaissance College.

CONTACT

University of New Brunswick Fredericton, PO Box 4400, Fredericton, NB E3B 5A3, Canada. *Phone:* 506-453-4865.

University of New Brunswick Saint John

Saint John, New Brunswick, Canada

http://www.unb.ca/

- **Province-supported** comprehensive, founded 1964
- **Urban** 250-acre campus
- **Coed**
- **Moderately difficult** entrance level

ACADEMICS

Calendar: Canadian standard year. *Degrees:* certificates, diplomas, bachelor's, master's, doctoral, and postbachelor's certificates.

Library: Hans W. Klohn Commons. Students can reserve study rooms.

STUDENT LIFE

Housing options: coed. Campus housing is university owned.

Activities and organizations: drama/theater group, student-run newspaper, radio station, choral group, Business Administration Society, OPTAMUS, International Student Association, Chinese Cultural Association, Muslim Student Association.

Campus security: 24-hour emergency response devices and patrols, student patrols, late-night transport/escort service, controlled dormitory access.

Student services: health clinic, personal/psychological counseling, women's center.

FINANCIAL AID

Financial Aid Of all full-time matriculated undergraduates who enrolled in 2015, 140 state and other part-time jobs (averaging $500).

APPLYING

Standardized Tests *Required:* SAT (for admission).

Options: electronic application, early admission, deferred entrance.

Application fee: $55 Canadian dollars.

Required: high school transcript.

CONTACT

University of New Brunswick Saint John, PO Box 5050, Saint John, NB E2L 4L5, Canada.

University of Northern British Columbia

Prince George, British Columbia, Canada

http://www.unbc.ca/

CONTACT

Pamela Flagel, Associate Registrar Enrollment, University of Northern British Columbia, Office of the Registrar, 3333 University Way, Prince George, BC V2N 4Z9, Canada. *Phone:* 250-960-6300. *Fax:* 250-960-6330. *E-mail:* registrar-info@unbc.ca.

University of Ottawa

Ottawa, Ontario, Canada

http://www.uottawa.ca/

CONTACT
University of Ottawa, 550 Cumberland Street, Ottawa, ON K1N 6N5, Canada. *Phone:* 613-562-5800 Ext. 1594.

University of Prince Edward Island

Charlottetown, Prince Edward Island, Canada

http://home.upei.ca/

CONTACT
University of Prince Edward Island, 550 University Avenue, Charlottetown, PE C1A 4P3, Canada. *Phone:* 902-566-0634.

University of Regina

Regina, Saskatchewan, Canada

http://www.uregina.ca/

- **Province-supported** university, founded 1974, part of intentionally left blank
- **Urban** 76-hectare campus
- **Endowment** $41.7 million
- **Coed** 12,961 undergraduate students, 83% full-time, 62% women, 38% men
- **Minimally difficult** entrance level, 72% of applicants were admitted

UNDERGRAD STUDENTS
10,727 full-time, 2,234 part-time. Students come from 13 provinces and territories; 108 other countries; 18% are from out of state; 4% transferred in; 10% live on campus.

Freshmen:
Admission: 5,126 applied, 3,704 admitted, 2,035 enrolled. ***Average high school GPA:*** 3.7.
Retention: 83% of full-time freshmen returned.

FACULTY
Total: 417, 104% full-time, 75% with terminal degrees.
Student/faculty ratio: 23:1.

ACADEMICS
Calendar: semesters. *Degrees:* certificates, diplomas, bachelor's, master's, doctoral, and postbachelor's certificates.
Special study options: academic remediation for entering students, adult/continuing education programs, advanced placement credit, cooperative education, distance learning, double majors, English as a second language, honors programs, independent study, internships, off-campus study, part-time degree program, services for LD students, student-designed majors, study abroad, summer session for credit.
Computers: 412 computers/terminals are available on campus for general student use. Students can access the following: computer help desk, free student e-mail accounts, online (class) grades, online (class) registration, online (class) schedules. Campuswide network is available. 100% of college-owned or -operated housing units are wired for high-speed Internet access. Wireless service is available via entire campus.
Library: Dr. John Archer Library plus 5 others. *Books:* 839,614 (physical), 330,732 (digital/electronic); *Serial titles:* 163,120 (physical), 131,946 (digital/electronic); *Databases:* 535. Weekly public service hours: 105; students can reserve study rooms.

STUDENT LIFE
Housing options: special housing for students with disabilities. Campus housing is university owned. Freshman campus housing is guaranteed.
Activities and organizations: drama/theater group, student-run newspaper, University of Regina Students' Union, Biology Undergraduate and Graduate Society, Institute of Electrical and Electronics Engineers (IEEE) U of R Students Branch, UR Toastmasters, Inter-Varsity Christian Fellowship.
Athletics Member CIS. ***Intercollegiate sports:*** basketball M(s)/W(s), cross-country running M(s)/W(s), football M(s), ice hockey M(s)/W(s), soccer W(s), swimming and diving M(s)/W(s), track and field M(s)/W(s), volleyball M(s)/W(s), wrestling M(s)/W(s). ***Intramural sports:*** badminton M/W, basketball M/W, bowling M/W, cheerleading M(c)/W(c), fencing M(c)/W(c), football M/W, golf M(c)/W(c), rowing M(c)/W(c), rugby M(c)/W(c), soccer M/W, softball M/W(c), tennis M/W, ultimate Frisbee M/W, volleyball M/W.
Campus security: 24-hour emergency response devices and patrols, controlled dormitory access, CCTV, card access and some alarm monitoring.
Student services: health clinic, personal/psychological counseling, women's center.

COSTS
Costs (2016–17) ***Tuition:*** province resident $6195 Canadian dollars full-time, $207 Canadian dollars per credit hour part-time; International tuition $18,585 Canadian dollars full-time. Full-time tuition and fees vary according to course load and program. Part-time tuition and fees vary according to course load and program. ***Required fees:*** $798 Canadian dollars full-time. ***Room and board:*** $7480 Canadian dollars; room only: $6470 Canadian dollars. Room and board charges vary according to board plan and housing facility. ***Waivers:*** senior citizens and employees or children of employees.

APPLYING
Standardized Tests *Required for some:* SAT or ACT (for admission).
Options: electronic application, early admission, early action, deferred entrance.
Application fee: $100 Canadian dollars.
Required: high school transcript, minimum 2.3 GPA. ***Required for some:*** essay or personal statement, 2 letters of recommendation, interview, portfolio, audition, 2.3 minimum GPA.
Application deadlines: 8/15 (freshmen), 8/15 (transfers), 3/15 (early action).

CONTACT
University of Regina, 3737 Wascana Parkway, Regina, SK S4S 0A2, Canada. *Phone:* 306-585-5345. *Toll-free phone:* 800-644-4756.

University of Saskatchewan

Saskatoon, Saskatchewan, Canada

http://www.usask.ca/

- **Province-supported** university, founded 1907
- **Urban** 1865-acre campus
- **Coed** 17,327 undergraduate students
- 65% of applicants were admitted

UNDERGRAD STUDENTS
12% live on campus.

Freshmen:
Admission: 7,393 applied, 4,801 admitted.
Retention: 80% of full-time freshmen returned.

FACULTY
Total: 1,087.

ACADEMICS
Calendar: Canadian standard year. *Degrees:* certificates, diplomas, bachelor's, master's, doctoral, and postbachelor's certificates.
Special study options: accelerated degree program, advanced placement credit, cooperative education, distance learning, double majors, English as a second language, honors programs, independent study, internships, off-campus study, part-time degree program, services for LD students, study abroad, summer session for credit.
Computers: Students can access the following: computer help desk, free student e-mail accounts, online (class) grades, online (class) registration, online (class) schedules, student portal. 100% of college-owned or -operated housing units are wired for high-speed Internet access. Wireless service is available via entire campus.
Library: University of Saskatchewan Main Library plus 7 others.

STUDENT LIFE
Housing options: coed. Campus housing is university owned.
Activities and organizations: drama/theater group, student-run newspaper, choral group.

Athletics Member CIS. ***Intercollegiate sports:*** basketball M/W, cross-country running M/W, football M, ice hockey M/W, soccer M/W, track and field M/W, volleyball M/W, wrestling M/W. ***Intramural sports:*** badminton M/W, basketball M/W, football M/W, ice hockey M/W, soccer M/W, ultimate Frisbee M/W, volleyball M/W.

Campus security: 24-hour emergency response devices and patrols, student patrols, late-night transport/escort service, controlled dormitory access.

Student services: health clinic, personal/psychological counseling, women's center, legal services.

COSTS & FINANCIAL AID

Costs (2017–18) ***Tuition:*** province resident $6103 full-time; nonresident $6103 full-time; International tuition $15,868 full-time. Full-time tuition and fees vary according to course load and program. ***Required fees:*** $423 full-time. ***Room and board:*** Room and board charges vary according to board plan, housing facility, and location. ***Payment plan:*** installment. ***Waivers:*** senior citizens and employees or children of employees.

Financial Aid ***Financial aid deadline:*** 3/15.

APPLYING

Options: electronic application, early admission.

Application fee: $90 Canadian dollars.

Required: high school transcript. ***Required for some:*** essay or personal statement, interview.

Application deadlines: 5/1 (freshmen), 5/1 (transfers).

Notification: continuous (freshmen), continuous (transfers).

CONTACT

University of Saskatchewan, 105 Administration Place, Saskatoon, SK S7N 5A2, Canada. *Phone:* 306-966-5788.

University of the Fraser Valley

Abbotsford, British Columbia, Canada

http://www.ufv.ca/

- **Province-supported** comprehensive, founded 1974
- **Urban** 64-hectare campus with easy access to Vancouver
- **Endowment** $11.0 million
- **Coed** 8,499 undergraduate students, 44% full-time, 59% women, 41% men

UNDERGRAD STUDENTS

3,725 full-time, 4,774 part-time. Students come from 10 provinces and territories; 61 other countries; 5% American Indian or Alaska Native, non-Hispanic/Latino; 84% Race/ethnicity unknown; 11% international.

Freshmen:

Admission: 1,596 enrolled.

Retention: 78% of full-time freshmen returned.

FACULTY

Total: 700, 46% full-time, 30% with terminal degrees.

ACADEMICS

Calendar: semesters. *Degrees:* certificates, diplomas, associate, bachelor's, master's, and postbachelor's certificates.

Special study options: academic remediation for entering students, adult/continuing education programs, advanced placement credit, cooperative education, distance learning, double majors, English as a second language, honors programs, independent study, internships, off-campus study, part-time degree program, services for LD students, student-designed majors, study abroad, summer session for credit.

Computers: Students can access the following: computer help desk, free student e-mail accounts, online (class) grades, online (class) registration, online (class) schedules. Wireless service is available via entire campus.

Library: Peter Jones Library plus 3 others. *Books:* 180,000 (physical), 354,000 (digital/electronic). Students can reserve study rooms.

STUDENT LIFE

Housing options: coed. Campus housing is university owned. Freshman applicants given priority for college housing.

Activities and organizations: drama/theater group, student-run newspaper, radio station.

Athletics Member CIS. ***Intercollegiate sports:*** basketball M(s)/W(s), soccer M(s)/W(s), wrestling M(c)/W(c). ***Intramural sports:*** badminton M/W, basketball M/W, cross-country running M(c)/W(c), soccer M/W, volleyball M/W, wrestling M(c)/W(c).

Campus security: 24-hour emergency response devices and patrols, late-night transport/escort service, controlled dormitory access.

Student services: personal/psychological counseling.

COSTS

Costs (2017–18) ***Tuition:*** province resident $4778 full-time, $159 per credit hour part-time; nonresident $4778 full-time, $159 per credit hour part-time; International tuition $16,100 full-time. Full-time tuition and fees vary according to course load. Part-time tuition and fees vary according to course load. ***Required fees:*** $524 full-time, $154 per term part-time. ***Room and board:*** $7725; room only: $5725. Room and board charges vary according to board plan. ***Waivers:*** senior citizens and employees or children of employees.

APPLYING

Options: electronic application, early admission, deferred entrance.

Application fee: $45 Canadian dollars.

Required: high school transcript. ***Required for some:*** essay or personal statement, 2 letters of recommendation, interview, minimum GPA of 2.0 to 2.67.

Notification: continuous (freshmen), continuous (transfers).

CONTACT

Ms. Julie Croft, Admissions Assistant, University of the Fraser Valley, 33844 King Road, Abbotsford, BC V2S 7M8, Canada. *Phone:* 604-504-7441 Ext. 4450. *Toll-free phone:* 888-504-7441. *E-mail:* jjulie.croft@ufv.ca.

University of Toronto

Toronto, Ontario, Canada

http://www.utoronto.ca/

- **Province-supported** university, founded 1827
- **Urban** 714-hectare campus
- **Endowment** $2.1 billion
- **Coed** 70,592 undergraduate students
- **Very difficult** entrance level

UNDERGRAD STUDENTS

Students come from 12 provinces and territories; 165 other countries; 6% are from out of state; 15% live on campus.

FACULTY

Student/faculty ratio: 24:1.

ACADEMICS

Calendar: fall/winter terms and a summer session. *Degrees:* certificates, diplomas, bachelor's, master's, and doctoral.

Special study options: adult/continuing education programs, cooperative education, double majors, English as a second language, off-campus study, part-time degree program, services for LD students, study abroad, summer session for credit.

Computers: 2,000 computers/terminals are available on campus for general student use. Students can access the following: campus intranet, computer help desk, free student e-mail accounts, online (class) registration, online (class) schedules. Campuswide network is available. Wireless service is available via classrooms, computer centers, computer labs, dorm rooms, learning centers, libraries, student centers.

Library: Robarts Library plus 43 others. *Books:* 19 (physical), 6 (digital/electronic). Students can reserve study rooms.

STUDENT LIFE

Housing options: coed, women-only. Campus housing is university owned and leased by the school. Freshman campus housing is guaranteed.

Activities and organizations: drama/theater group, student-run newspaper, radio station, choral group, national fraternities, national sororities.

Athletics Member CIS. ***Intercollegiate sports:*** archery M/W, badminton M/W, basketball M/W, crew M, cross-country running M/W, fencing M/W, field hockey W, football M, golf M, gymnastics M/W, ice hockey M/W, rugby M, skiing (cross-country) M/W, skiing (downhill) M/W, soccer M/W, squash M/W, swimming and diving M/W, tennis M/W, track and field M/W, volleyball M/W, wrestling M. ***Intramural sports:*** archery M/W, badminton M/W, basketball M/W, crew M, fencing M/W, field hockey W, football M/W, gymnastics M/W, ice hockey M/W, lacrosse M/W, racquetball M, rugby M, skiing (downhill) M/W, soccer M/W, squash M/W, swimming and diving M/W, tennis M/W, track and field M/W, volleyball M/W, water polo M/W.

Campus security: 24-hour emergency response devices and patrols, student patrols, late-night transport/escort service.

Student services: health clinic, personal/psychological counseling, women's center, legal services.

COSTS

Costs (2017–18) ***Tuition:*** province resident $4883 full-time; nonresident $4883 full-time. Full-time tuition and fees vary according to course level, course load, program, and student level. Part-time tuition and fees vary according to course load, program, and student level. ***Required fees:*** $1000 full-time. ***Room and board:*** Room and board charges vary according to board plan, housing facility, location, and student level. ***Payment plan:*** installment. ***Waivers:*** senior citizens and employees or children of employees.

APPLYING

Standardized Tests *Required:* SAT and SAT Subject Tests or ACT (for admission).

Options: deferred entrance.

Application fee: $255 Canadian dollars.

Required: high school transcript. ***Required for some:*** interview.

Application deadlines: 3/1 (freshmen), 7/1 (transfers).

Notification: continuous (freshmen), continuous (transfers).

CONTACT

University of Toronto, 27 King's College Circle, Toronto, ON M5S 1A1, Canada. *Phone:* 416-978-2190. *Fax:* 416-978-7022.

University of Victoria

Victoria, British Columbia, Canada

http://www.uvic.ca/

CONTACT

Mr. Bruno Rocca, Student Recruitment Director, University of Victoria, PO Box 1700, STN CSC, Victoria, BC V8W 2Y2, Canada. *Phone:* 250-721-8121 Ext. 8109. *Fax:* 250-721-6225. *E-mail:* admit@uvic.ca.

University of Waterloo

Waterloo, Ontario, Canada

http://www.uwaterloo.ca/

- **Province-supported** university, founded 1957
- **Suburban** 1000-acre campus with easy access to Toronto
- **Coed** 31,238 undergraduate students, 97% full-time, 47% women, 53% men
- **Moderately difficult** entrance level

UNDERGRAD STUDENTS

30,430 full-time, 808 part-time.

Freshmen:

Admission: 7,885 enrolled.

FACULTY

Total: 1,211.

Student/faculty ratio: 25:1.

ACADEMICS

Calendar: trimesters. *Degrees:* bachelor's, master's, and doctoral.

Special study options: cooperative education, distance learning, double majors, English as a second language, honors programs, internships, off-campus study, part-time degree program, services for LD students, study abroad.

Computers: 6,000 computers/terminals are available on campus for general student use. Students can access the following: campus intranet, computer help desk, free student e-mail accounts, online (class) grades, online (class) registration, online (class) schedules. Campuswide network is available. Wireless service is available via entire campus.

Library: Dana Porter Library plus 11 others. Students can reserve study rooms.

STUDENT LIFE

Housing options: coed. Campus housing is university owned. Freshman campus housing is guaranteed.

Activities and organizations: drama/theater group, student-run newspaper, choral group, marching band, national fraternities, national sororities.

Athletics ***Intercollegiate sports:*** badminton M/W, baseball M, basketball M/W, cheerleading M/W, cross-country running M/W, field hockey W, football M, golf M/W, ice hockey M/W, rugby M/W, skiing (cross-country) M/W, soccer M/W, squash M/W, swimming and diving M/W, tennis M/W, track and field M/W, volleyball M/W. ***Intramural sports:*** archery M(c)/W(c), badminton M(c)/W(c), baseball M/W, basketball M/W, bowling M/W, crew M(c)/W(c), cross-country running M(c)/W(c), equestrian sports M(c)/W(c), fencing M(c)/W(c), football M/W, golf M(c)/W(c), ice hockey M/W, racquetball M(c)/W(c), rock climbing M(c)/W(c), sailing M(c)/W(c), skiing (cross-country) M(c)/W(c), skiing (downhill) M(c)/W(c), soccer M(c)/W(c), softball M/W, squash M(c)/W(c), swimming and diving M(c)/W(c), table tennis M(c)/W(c), tennis M/W, ultimate Frisbee M(c)/W(c), volleyball M/W, water polo M(c)/W(c), weight lifting M(c)/W(c).

Campus security: 24-hour emergency response devices and patrols, student patrols, late-night transport/escort service, controlled dormitory access.

Student services: health clinic, personal/psychological counseling, women's center, legal services.

COSTS

Costs (2017–18) ***Tuition:*** province resident $10,400 full-time, $716 per course part-time; International tuition $28,000 full-time. Full-time tuition and fees vary according to course load, degree level, program, and student level. Part-time tuition and fees vary according to course load, degree level, program, and student level. ***Required fees:*** $800 full-time, $65 per term part-time. ***Room and board:*** $10,734; room only: $5534. Room and board charges vary according to board plan, housing facility, and location. ***Payment plan:*** deferred payment. ***Waivers:*** senior citizens and employees or children of employees.

APPLYING

Options: electronic application, early admission, deferred entrance.

Application fee: $140 Canadian dollars.

Required: high school transcript. ***Required for some:*** essay or personal statement, interview. ***Recommended:*** essay or personal statement.

Notification: 5/26 (freshmen).

CONTACT

University of Waterloo, 200 University Avenue West, Waterloo, ON N2L 3G1, Canada. *Phone:* 519-888-4567. *E-mail:* myapplication@uwaterloo.ca.

The University of Western Ontario

London, Ontario, Canada

http://www.uwo.ca/

- **Province-supported** university, founded 1878
- **Suburban** 1200-acre campus
- **Coed**
- **Very difficult** entrance level

ACADEMICS

Calendar: Canadian standard year. *Degrees:* certificates, diplomas, bachelor's, master's, doctoral, and postbachelor's certificates.

Library: Western Libraries plus 7 others. Students can reserve study rooms.

STUDENT LIFE

Housing options: coed, special housing for students with disabilities. Campus housing is university owned. Freshman campus housing is guaranteed.

Activities and organizations: drama/theater group, student-run newspaper, radio and television station, choral group, marching band, Pre-

Medical Society, Western Investment Club, Purple Spur Society, Pre-Business Students' Network, Pre-Law Society, national fraternities, national sororities.

Athletics Member CIS.

Campus security: 24-hour emergency response devices and patrols, student patrols, late-night transport/escort service, controlled dormitory access, Campus Community Police, SERT: Student Emergency Response Team, Western Foot Patrol.

Student services: health clinic, personal/psychological counseling, legal services.

COSTS & FINANCIAL AID

Costs (2016–17) ***Tuition:*** province resident $6338 Canadian dollars full-time, $1267 Canadian dollars per course part-time; International tuition $24,643 Canadian dollars full-time. Full-time tuition and fees vary according to course level and program. Part-time tuition and fees vary according to course load, location, and program. ***Required fees:*** $1423 Canadian dollars full-time, $170 Canadian dollars per course part-time. ***Room and board:*** $12,815 Canadian dollars; room only: $8050 Canadian dollars. Room and board charges vary according to board plan, housing facility, and location.

Financial Aid Of all full-time matriculated undergraduates who enrolled in 2015, 1,561 state and other part-time jobs (averaging $2330).

APPLYING

Standardized Tests *Required:* SAT or ACT (for admission).

Options: electronic application, deferred entrance.

Application fee: $155 Canadian dollars.

Required: high school transcript, minimum 3.5 GPA. ***Required for some:*** supplemental profile, interview or audition.

CONTACT

Undergraduate Recruitment and Admissions, The University of Western Ontario, Western University, London, ON N6A 3K7, Canada. *Phone:* 519-661-2100. *Fax:* 519-661-3710. *E-mail:* reg-admissions@uwo.ca.

University of Windsor

Windsor, Ontario, Canada

http://www.uwindsor.ca/

- **Province-supported** university, founded 1857
- **Urban** 125-acre campus with easy access to Detroit
- **Endowment** $84.3 million
- **Coed** 12,426 undergraduate students, 85% full-time, 52% women, 48% men

UNDERGRAD STUDENTS

10,565 full-time, 1,861 part-time. Students come from 10 provinces and territories; 83 other countries; 2% transferred in; 45% live on campus.

Freshmen:

Admission: 2,229 enrolled.

Retention: 86% of full-time freshmen returned.

FACULTY

Total: 898, 64% full-time, 55% with terminal degrees.

Student/faculty ratio: 23:1.

ACADEMICS

Calendar: semesters. *Degrees:* certificates, bachelor's, master's, doctoral, and postbachelor's certificates.

Special study options: academic remediation for entering students, accelerated degree program, adult/continuing education programs, advanced placement credit, cooperative education, distance learning, double majors, English as a second language, external degree program, honors programs, internships, off-campus study, part-time degree program, services for LD students, student-designed majors, study abroad, summer session for credit.

Unusual degree programs: 3-2 computer science.

Computers: 1,225 computers/terminals are available on campus for general student use. Students can access the following: campus intranet, computer help desk, free student e-mail accounts, online (class) grades, online (class) registration, online (class) schedules, online transcripts, degree audits, bursaries, grants, online applications for graduation. Campuswide network is available. 100% of college-owned or -operated housing units are wired for high-speed Internet access. Wireless service is available via entire campus.

Library: Leddy Library plus 2 others. *Books:* 886,201 (physical), 673,676 (digital/electronic); *Serial titles:* 33,354 (physical), 85,907 (digital/electronic). Weekly public service hours: 108; students can reserve study rooms.

STUDENT LIFE

Housing options: coed, men-only, women-only, special housing for students with disabilities. Campus housing is university owned. Freshman campus housing is guaranteed.

Activities and organizations: drama/theater group, student-run newspaper, radio station, choral group, University of Windsor Student Alliance, Environmental Awareness Association, Social Science Society, Commerce Society, Science Society, national fraternities.

Athletics Member CIS. ***Intercollegiate sports:*** basketball M(s)/W(s), cross-country running M(s)/W(s), football M(s), golf M/W, ice hockey M(s)/W(s), soccer M(s)/W(s), track and field M(s)/W(s), volleyball M(s)/W(s). ***Intramural sports:*** badminton M/W, baseball M/W, basketball M/W, cheerleading M(c)/W(c), football M/W, ice hockey M/W, rugby M/W, soccer M/W, softball M/W, swimming and diving M/W, table tennis M/W, ultimate Frisbee M/W, volleyball M/W, water polo M/W, weight lifting M/W.

Campus security: 24-hour emergency response devices and patrols, student patrols, late-night transport/escort service, controlled dormitory access.

Student services: health clinic, personal/psychological counseling, women's center, legal services.

FINANCIAL AID

Financial Aid Of all full-time matriculated undergraduates who enrolled in 2010, 450 state and other part-time jobs (averaging $1166). ***Financial aid deadline:*** 6/15.

APPLYING

Standardized Tests *Required for some:* SAT or ACT (for admission), SAT and SAT Subject Tests or ACT (for admission), SAT Subject Tests (for admission).

Options: electronic application.

Required: high school transcript, minimum 3.0 GPA. ***Required for some:*** essay or personal statement, minimum 3.3 GPA, 1 letter of recommendation, interview.

CONTACT

Ms. Charlene Yates, Associate Registrar, University of Windsor, Office of the Registrar, 401 Sunset Avenue, Windsor, ON N9B 3P4, Canada. *Phone:* 519-253-3000 Ext. 3332. *Toll-free phone:* 800-864-2860. *Fax:* 519-971-3653. *E-mail:* registrar@uwindsor.ca.

The University of Winnipeg

Winnipeg, Manitoba, Canada

http://www.uwinnipeg.ca/

CONTACT

Mr. Colin Russell, Registrar, The University of Winnipeg, 515 Portage Avenue, Winnipeg, MB R3B 2E9, Canada. *Phone:* 204-786-9776. *Fax:* 204-786-8656. *E-mail:* admissions@uwinnipeg.ca.

Vancouver Island University

Nanaimo, British Columbia, Canada

http://www.viu.ca/

CONTACT

Mr. Andrew Amour, Associate Registrar, Admissions and Registration, Vancouver Island University, 900 Fifth Street, Nanaimo, BC V9R 5S5, Canada. *Phone:* 250-740-6355. *Fax:* 250-740-6479.

Vanguard College
Edmonton, Alberta, Canada
http://www.vanguardcollege.com/

CONTACT
Vanguard College, 12140 103rd Street, Edmonton, AB T5G 2J9, Canada. *Phone:* 780-452-0808 Ext. 231. *Toll-free phone:* 866-222-0808. *E-mail:* admissions@vanguardcollege.com.

Wilfrid Laurier University
Waterloo, Ontario, Canada
http://www.wlu.ca/

CONTACT
Wilfrid Laurier University, 75 University Avenue West, Waterloo, ON N2L 3C5, Canada. *Phone:* 519-884-0710 Ext. 6099.

York University
Toronto, Ontario, Canada
http://www.yorku.ca/

CONTACT
International Recruitment, York University, N301 Bennett Centre for Student Services, 4700 Keele Street, Toronto, ON M3J 1P3, Canada. *Phone:* 416-736-5825. *Fax:* 416-736-5741. *E-mail:* intlenq@yorku.ca.

INTERNATIONAL

BULGARIA

American University in Bulgaria
Blagoevgrad, Bulgaria
http://www.aubg.edu/

- **Independent** comprehensive, founded 1991
- **Small-town** 12-acre campus with easy access to Sofia, Bulgaria
- **Endowment** $23.9 million
- **Coed** 833 undergraduate students, 100% full-time, 51% women, 49% men
- **Very difficult** entrance level, 30% of applicants were admitted

UNDERGRAD STUDENTS
833 full-time. Students come from 37 other countries; 100% Race/ethnicity unknown; 85% live on campus.

Freshmen:
Admission: 1,491 applied, 445 admitted. ***Average high school GPA:*** 3.65. ***Test scores:*** SAT critical reading scores over 500: 57%; SAT math scores over 500: 88%; ACT scores over 18: 100%; SAT critical reading scores over 600: 21%; SAT math scores over 600: 70%; ACT scores over 24: 75%; SAT critical reading scores over 700: 3%; SAT math scores over 700: 9%; ACT scores over 30: 50%.

Retention: 98% of full-time freshmen returned.

FACULTY
Total: 77, 64% full-time, 71% with terminal degrees.

Student/faculty ratio: 15:1.

ACADEMICS
Calendar: semesters. *Degrees:* bachelor's and master's.

Special study options: advanced placement credit, double majors, honors programs, independent study, internships, services for LD students, student-designed majors, study abroad.

Computers: 363 computers/terminals and 8 ports are available on campus for general student use. Students can access the following: computer help desk, free student e-mail accounts, online (class) grades, online (class) registration, online (class) schedules. Campuswide network is available. 100% of college-owned or -operated housing units are wired for high-speed Internet access. Wireless service is available via entire campus.

Library: Panitza Library. *Books:* 119,597 (physical), 263,000 (digital/electronic); *Serial titles:* 1,216 (physical), 39,099 (digital/electronic); *Databases:* 34. Weekly public service hours: 56; study areas open 24 hours, 5-7 days a week; students can reserve study rooms.

STUDENT LIFE
Housing options: on-campus residence required through senior year; coed, special housing for students with disabilities. Campus housing is university owned. Freshman campus housing is guaranteed.

Activities and organizations: drama/theater group, student-run newspaper, radio station, choral group, Computer Science Student Union, AUBG Political Science Club, Better Community Club, AUBG Broadway Performance Club, Business Club.

Athletics *Intramural sports:* basketball M/W, cheerleading W(c), equestrian sports M(c)/W(c), football M(c), gymnastics W, soccer M(c), softball M/W, volleyball M/W.

Campus security: 24-hour patrols, controlled dormitory access.

Student services: health clinic, personal/psychological counseling.

COSTS
Costs (2017–18) *Comprehensive fee:* $13,890 includes full-time tuition ($11,700), mandatory fees ($580), and room and board ($1610). Part-time tuition: $975 per credit hour. ***College room only:*** $1410. Room and board charges vary according to housing facility. ***Waivers:*** employees or children of employees.

APPLYING
Standardized Tests *Required for some:* TOEFL, IELTS, or ESOL for students whose primary language is not English. *Recommended:* SAT (for admission), SAT or ACT (for admission).

Options: electronic application, early admission, deferred entrance.

Application fee: $25.

Required: essay or personal statement, high school transcript, minimum 3.0 GPA, 2 letters of recommendation.

Application deadlines: 6/1 (freshmen), 6/1 (transfers).

CONTACT
Ms. Svetlana Salovska, Enrollment Executive Director, American University in Bulgaria, 1 Izmirliev Square, 1st Floor, Blagoevgrad 2700, Bulgaria. *Phone:* 359-73 888 218. *Fax:* 359-73 883 227. *E-mail:* admissions@aubg.edu.

CAYMAN ISLANDS

International College of the Cayman Islands

Newlands, Cayman Islands

http://www.icci.edu.ky/

CONTACT

International College of the Cayman Islands, PO Box 136, Savannah Post Office, Newlands, Grand Cayman, Cayman Islands.
Phone: 345-325-6454.

EGYPT

The American University in Cairo

Cairo, Egypt

http://www.aucegypt.edu/

- **Independent** comprehensive, founded 1919
- **Suburban** 260-acre campus with easy access to Cairo
- **Endowment** $573.7 million
- **Coed** 5,585 undergraduate students, 90% full-time, 54% women, 46% men
- **Very difficult** entrance level, 48% of applicants were admitted

UNDERGRAD STUDENTS

5,043 full-time, 542 part-time. Students come from 31 other countries; 0.6% transferred in; 7% live on campus.

Freshmen:

Admission: 2,948 applied, 1,405 admitted, 942 enrolled. ***Test scores:*** SAT critical reading scores over 500: 47%; SAT math scores over 500: 94%; SAT critical reading scores over 600: 9%; SAT math scores over 600: 55%; SAT critical reading scores over 700: 1%; SAT math scores over 700: 14%.

Retention: 91% of full-time freshmen returned.

FACULTY

Total: 724, 55% full-time, 69% with terminal degrees.

Student/faculty ratio: 11:1.

ACADEMICS

Calendar: semesters. *Degrees:* diplomas, bachelor's, master's, and doctoral (majority of students are Egyptians; enrollment open to all nationalities).

Special study options: academic remediation for entering students, cooperative education, double majors, English as a second language, honors programs, independent study, internships, services for LD students, study abroad, summer session for credit.

Computers: 120 computers/terminals are available on campus for general student use. Students can access the following: campus intranet, computer help desk, free student e-mail accounts, online (class) grades, online (class) registration, online (class) schedules, learning management system, unofficial transcripts, ID creation. Campuswide network is available. 100% of college-owned or -operated housing units are wired for high-speed Internet access. Wireless service is available via entire campus.

Library: American University in Cairo Library plus 1 other. *Books:* 521,994 (physical), 255,462 (digital/electronic); *Databases:* 134. Weekly public service hours: 80; students can reserve study rooms.

STUDENT LIFE

Housing options: men-only, women-only, special housing for students with disabilities. Campus housing is university owned and leased by the school. Freshman applicants given priority for college housing.

Activities and organizations: drama/theater group, student-run newspaper, choral group, AIESEC, Theater and Film Club, VIA, ACT, Mashrou3 Kheir.

Athletics ***Intercollegiate sports:*** archery M, badminton M/W, basketball M/W, crew M/W, fencing M/W, gymnastics M/W, soccer M/W, squash M/W, swimming and diving M/W, table tennis M/W, tennis M/W, track and field M/W, volleyball M/W, water polo M. ***Intramural sports:*** basketball M/W, soccer M/W, squash M/W, table tennis M/W, tennis M/W, volleyball M/W, weight lifting M.

Campus security: 24-hour emergency response devices and patrols, controlled dormitory access.

Student services: health clinic, personal/psychological counseling.

FINANCIAL AID

Financial Aid ***Average financial aid package:*** $3548. ***Average need-based gift aid:*** $2781. ***Financial aid deadline:*** 9/15.

APPLYING

Standardized Tests *Required for some:* SAT (for admission), SAT or ACT (for admission), SAT Subject Tests (for admission).

Options: electronic application, early admission, early action, deferred entrance.

Application fee: $80.

Required: essay or personal statement, high school transcript, minimum 2.0 GPA.

Application deadlines: 3/1 (freshmen), 3/1 (transfers), 3/1 (early action).

Notification: continuous (freshmen), continuous (transfers).

CONTACT

Ms. Randa Kamel, Chief Enrollment Officer, The American University in Cairo, AUC Avenue, PO Box 74 New Cairo 11835, Cairo, Egypt.
Phone: 202-26154601. *E-mail:* randakamel@aucegypt.edu.

FRANCE

The American University of Paris

Paris, France

http://www.aup.edu/

- **Independent** comprehensive, founded 1962
- **Urban** campus with easy access to Paris, France
- **Endowment** $827,164
- **Coed** 917 undergraduate students, 92% full-time, 71% women, 29% men
- **Moderately difficult** entrance level, 73% of applicants were admitted

UNDERGRAD STUDENTS

843 full-time, 74 part-time. Students come from 47 states and territories; 100 other countries; 6% transferred in; 60% live on campus.

Freshmen:

Admission: 1,343 applied, 980 admitted, 174 enrolled.

Retention: 69% of full-time freshmen returned.

FACULTY

Total: 117, 54% full-time, 60% with terminal degrees.

Student/faculty ratio: 9:1.

ACADEMICS

Calendar: semesters. *Degrees:* bachelor's and master's.

Special study options: advanced placement credit, double majors, English as a second language, honors programs, independent study, internships, off-campus study, part-time degree program, student-designed majors, study abroad, summer session for credit.

Computers: 155 computers/terminals are available on campus for general student use. Students can access the following: campus intranet, computer help desk, free student e-mail accounts, online (class) grades, online (class) registration, online (class) schedules, free office software. Campuswide network is available. Wireless service is available via entire campus.

Library: AUP Library. *Books:* 41,927 (physical), 505,432 (digital/electronic); *Serial titles:* 28 (physical), 44,960 (digital/electronic); *Databases:* 32. Students can reserve study rooms.

STUDENT LIFE

Housing options: on-campus residence required for freshman yearCampus housing is provided by a third party.

Activities and organizations: drama/theater group, student-run newspaper, television station, choral group, AUP Student Media (ASM) - Print, Video, Audio, White Mask (Theatre), Student Government Association, Environmental and Community Services Committee, Sports Association.

Athletics ***Intercollegiate sports:*** equestrian sports M/W. ***Intramural sports:*** badminton M(c)/W(c), basketball M, cheerleading M(c)/W(c), equestrian sports M/W, volleyball W.

Campus security: 24-hour emergency response devices, valid student ID required for all building entries.

Student services: personal/psychological counseling.

COSTS & FINANCIAL AID

Costs (2017–18) ***Tuition:*** $32,288 full-time. Full-time tuition and fees vary according to degree level. Part-time tuition and fees vary according to course load and degree level. ***Required fees:*** $1443 full-time. ***Room only:*** Room and board charges vary according to housing facility. ***Payment plan:*** installment. ***Waivers:*** children of alumni and employees or children of employees.

Financial Aid Of all full-time matriculated undergraduates who enrolled in 2015, 132 applied for aid, 121 were judged to have need, 7 had their need fully met. In 2015, 11 non-need-based awards were made. ***Average percent of need met:*** 23. ***Average financial aid package:*** $13,184. ***Average need-based loan:*** $4188. ***Average need-based gift aid:*** $10,667. ***Average non-need-based aid:*** $3717.

APPLYING

Standardized Tests *Required for some:* TOEFL, TOEIC or IELTS for students whose primary language is not English. *Recommended:* SAT or ACT (for admission).

Options: electronic application, deferred entrance.

Application fee: $70.

Required: essay or personal statement, high school transcript, 2 letters of recommendation. ***Recommended:*** minimum 3.0 GPA, interview.

Application deadlines: 3/15 (freshmen), 3/15 (transfers).

Notification: continuous (freshmen), continuous (transfers).

CONTACT

International Admissions Office Counselors, The American University of Paris, 5 boulevard de la Tour Maubourg, Paris 75007, France. *Phone:* +33 1 40 62 07 20. *Fax:* +33 1 47 05 34 32. *E-mail:* admissions@aup.edu.

The New School–Parsons Paris

Paris, France

http://www.newschool.edu/parsons-paris/

- **Independent** comprehensive, founded 2013, part of The New School
- **Urban** campus with easy access to Paris
- **Endowment** $346.9 million
- **Coed** 108 undergraduate students, 97% full-time, 83% women, 17% men
- **Moderately difficult** entrance level, 75% of applicants were admitted

UNDERGRAD STUDENTS

105 full-time, 3 part-time. 2% Black or African American, non-Hispanic/Latino; 6% Hispanic/Latino; 5% Asian, non-Hispanic/Latino; 0.9% Two or more races, non-Hispanic/Latino; 5% Race/ethnicity unknown; 59% international; 11% transferred in; 25% live on campus.

Freshmen:

Admission: 136 applied, 102 admitted, 42 enrolled.

FACULTY

Total: 48, 10% full-time, 6% with terminal degrees.

Student/faculty ratio: 7:1.

ACADEMICS

Calendar: semesters. *Degrees:* bachelor's and master's.

Special study options: advanced placement credit, cooperative education, distance learning, English as a second language, independent study, internships, off-campus study, services for LD students, student-designed majors, study abroad, summer session for credit.

Computers: Students can access the following: campus intranet, computer help desk, free student e-mail accounts, online (class) grades, online (class) registration, online (class) schedules. Campuswide network is available. 100% of college-owned or -operated housing units are wired for high-speed Internet access. Wireless service is available via entire campus.

Library: ***Books:*** 718,102 (digital/electronic); *Serial titles:* 90,364 (digital/electronic); *Databases:* 529.

STUDENT LIFE

Housing options: Campus housing is provided by a third party.

Campus security: 24-hour emergency response devices and patrols.

APPLYING

Options: electronic application, early admission, early action, deferred entrance.

Application fee: $50.

Required: essay or personal statement, high school transcript, 1 letter of recommendation. ***Recommended:*** interview.

Application deadlines: rolling (freshmen), 3/15 (transfers), 11/1 (early action).

Notification: continuous (freshmen), continuous until 4/1 (transfers), 12/20 (early action).

CONTACT

Mr. Mike Fakih, Director of Admissions for Parsons Paris, The New School–Parsons Paris, 72 Fifth Avenue at 13th Street, New York, NY 10011. *Phone:* 212-229-5150. *Toll-free phone:* 800-292-3040. *E-mail:* fakihm@newschool.edu.

Paris College of Art

Paris, France

http://www.paris.edu/

- **Independent** comprehensive
- **Urban** campus
- **Coed**

ACADEMICS

Calendar: semesters. *Degrees:* certificates, bachelor's, and master's.

STUDENT LIFE

Housing options: college housing not available.

Student services: personal/psychological counseling.

COSTS & FINANCIAL AID

Costs (2016–17) ***Tuition:*** 27,200 euros full-time. Part-time tuition and fees vary according to course load.

Financial Aid Of all full-time matriculated undergraduates who enrolled in 2010, 46 applied for aid, 41 were judged to have need. 40 state and other part-time jobs (averaging $2300). In 2010, 14 non-need-based awards were made. ***Average percent of need met:*** 75. ***Average financial aid package:*** $11,500. ***Average need-based gift aid:*** $8600. ***Average non-need-based aid:*** $4200. ***Financial aid deadline:*** 8/1.

APPLYING

Standardized Tests *Required for some:* SAT or ACT (for admission).

Required: essay or personal statement, high school transcript, interview.

CONTACT

Paris College of Art, 15 rue Fénelon 75010 Paris, France.

Schiller International University

Paris, France

http://www.schiller.edu/

CONTACT

Schiller International University, 9 rue d'Yvart, F-75015 Paris, France. *Toll-free phone:* 800-261-9571 (in-state); 800-261-9751 (out-of-state).

GERMANY

Schiller International University

Heidelberg, Germany

http://www.schiller.edu/

CONTACT
Ms. Kamala Dontamsetti, Associate Director of Admissions, Schiller International University, 300 East Bay Drive, Largo, FL 33770. *Phone:* 727-736-5082 Ext. 234. *Toll-free phone:* 800-261-9571 (in-state); 800-261-9751 (out-of-state). *Fax:* 727-734-0359. *E-mail:* kamala_dontamsetti@schiller.edu.

GREECE

American College of Thessaloniki

Pylea, Greece

http://www.act.edu/

- **Independent** comprehensive, founded 1886
- **Suburban** 40-acre campus with easy access to Thessaloniki
- **Endowment** $5.4 million
- **Coed** 442 undergraduate students, 88% full-time, 55% women, 45% men
- **Minimally difficult** entrance level, 76% of applicants were admitted

UNDERGRAD STUDENTS
387 full-time, 55 part-time. Students come from 20 other countries; 1% transferred in; 51% live on campus.

Freshmen:
Admission: 109 applied, 83 admitted, 69 enrolled. ***Average high school** GPA:* 3.1.
Retention: 72% of full-time freshmen returned.

FACULTY
Total: 62, 24% full-time, 58% with terminal degrees.
Student/faculty ratio: 14:1.

ACADEMICS
Calendar: semesters. *Degrees:* certificates, bachelor's, and master's.
Special study options: academic remediation for entering students, accelerated degree program, advanced placement credit, double majors, English as a second language, honors programs, independent study, internships, part-time degree program, services for LD students, study abroad, summer session for credit.
Computers: 150 computers/terminals and 30 ports are available on campus for general student use. Students can access the following: campus intranet, computer help desk, free student e-mail accounts, online (class) grades, online (class) schedules. Campuswide network is available. 100% of college-owned or -operated housing units are wired for high-speed Internet access. Wireless service is available via entire campus.
Library: Bissell Library plus 1 other. *Books:* 43,424 (physical), 151,713 (digital/electronic); *Serial titles:* 17 (physical), 38,182 (digital/electronic); *Databases:* 48. Weekly public service hours: 56; students can reserve study rooms.

STUDENT LIFE
Housing options: coed. Campus housing is university owned, leased by the school and is provided by a third party. Freshman applicants given priority for college housing.
Activities and organizations: drama/theater group, student-run newspaper, radio station, ACT Radio Station, Tennis Club, The Geopolitical Circle, Painting Club, Drama Club.
Athletics ***Intercollegiate sports:*** basketball M, soccer M, table tennis M/W, tennis M/W, volleyball M/W. ***Intramural sports:*** basketball M, sailing M/W, sand volleyball M/W, soccer M/W, table tennis M/W, tennis M/W, volleyball M/W.
Campus security: 24-hour emergency response devices and patrols, controlled dormitory access.
Student services: health clinic, personal/psychological counseling.

COSTS
Costs (2017–18) ***Tuition:*** $8400 full-time, $280 per contact hour part-time. Part-time tuition and fees vary according to course load. ***Room only:*** Room and board charges vary according to housing facility. ***Payment plan:*** installment. ***Waivers:*** employees or children of employees.

APPLYING
Options: electronic application, deferred entrance.
Application fee: 75 euros.
Required: high school transcript, CV. ***Required for some:*** essay or personal statement, interview. ***Recommended:*** minimum 2.0 GPA.
Application deadlines: rolling (freshmen), rolling (transfers).
Notification: continuous (freshmen), continuous (transfers).

CONTACT
Mrs. Roula Lebetli, Director of Admissions, American College of Thessaloniki, PO Box 21021, Pylea, Thessaloniki 55510, Greece. *Phone:* +30-2310-398239. *Fax:* +30-2310-398389. *E-mail:* admissions@act.edu.

DEREE - The American College of Greece

Athens, Greece

http://www.acg.edu/

- **Independent** comprehensive, founded 1875
- **Suburban** 64-acre campus with easy access to Athens
- **Coed** 2,958 undergraduate students, 39% full-time, 52% women, 48% men
- **Moderately difficult** entrance level, 71% of applicants were admitted

UNDERGRAD STUDENTS
1,139 full-time, 1,819 part-time. Students come from 62 other countries; 0.5% transferred in; 4% live on campus.

Freshmen:
Admission: 606 applied, 430 admitted, 407 enrolled. ***Average high school** GPA:* 3.3.
Retention: 88% of full-time freshmen returned.

FACULTY
Total: 254, 50% full-time, 60% with terminal degrees.
Student/faculty ratio: 10:1.

ACADEMICS
Calendar: semesters 2 summer sessions. *Degrees:* bachelor's, master's, and postbachelor's certificates.
Special study options: academic remediation for entering students, accelerated degree program, adult/continuing education programs, advanced placement credit, double majors, English as a second language, honors programs, independent study, internships, part-time degree program, services for LD students, student-designed majors, study abroad, summer session for credit.
Computers: 306 computers/terminals are available on campus for general student use. Students can access the following: computer help desk, free student e-mail accounts, online (class) grades, online (class) registration, online (class) schedules, learning management system. Campuswide network is available. 100% of college-owned or -operated housing units are wired for high-speed Internet access. Wireless service is available via computer centers, computer labs, dorm rooms, learning centers, libraries.
Library: John S. Bailey Library plus 1 other. *Books:* 129,000 (physical), 308,000 (digital/electronic); *Serial titles:* 60 (physical), 13,000 (digital/electronic); *Databases:* 45. Weekly public service hours: 72; students can reserve study rooms.

STUDENT LIFE
Housing options: coed, special housing for students with disabilities. Campus housing is university owned. Freshman applicants given priority for college housing.
Activities and organizations: drama/theater group, student-run newspaper, choral group, DEREE Ambassadors, DEREE Orientation Leaders, Debate Club, DEREE SAB (Student Activities Board), Innovation and Entrepreneurship Clib.
Athletics ***Intercollegiate sports:*** basketball M(s)/W(s), rugby M, soccer M(s)/W, swimming and diving M/W, volleyball M/W(s), water polo M.

Intramural sports: archery M/W, basketball M/W, rock climbing M/W, soccer M/W, swimming and diving M/W, table tennis M/W, tennis M/W, track and field M/W, volleyball M/W.

Campus security: 24-hour emergency response devices and patrols, controlled dormitory access.

Student services: health clinic, personal/psychological counseling.

COSTS & FINANCIAL AID

Costs (2016–17) ***One-time required fee:*** 50 euros. ***Tuition:*** 9900 euros full-time, 330 euros per credit hour part-time. Full-time tuition and fees vary according to course load. Part-time tuition and fees vary according to course load. No tuition increase for student's term of enrollment. ***Room only:*** Room and board charges vary according to housing facility. ***Payment plan:*** installment. ***Waivers:*** employees or children of employees.

Financial Aid ***Financial aid deadline:*** 9/1.

APPLYING

Options: electronic application, deferred entrance.

Required: essay or personal statement, high school transcript, minimum 2.1 GPA, 1 letter of recommendation, interview.

Application deadlines: rolling (freshmen), rolling (transfers).

Notification: continuous until 6/15 (freshmen), 6/15 (transfers).

CONTACT

Ms. Loukia Kanatsouli, Dean of Enrollment and International Students, DEREE - The American College of Greece, 6 Gravias Street, Aghia Paraskevi, Athens 15342, Greece. *Phone:* +30-210-600-9800 Ext. 1474. *Fax:* +30-210-608-2344. *E-mail:* lkanatsouli@acg.edu.

IRELAND

Institute of Public Administration

Dublin, Ireland

http://www.ipa.ie/

CONTACT

Dr. Denis O'Brien, Registrar, Institute of Public Administration, 57-61 Lansdowne Road, Dublin 4, Ireland. *Phone:* 353-1-240-3600. *Fax:* 353-1-668-9135. *E-mail:* undergrad@ipa.ie.

ITALY

The American University of Rome

Rome, Italy

http://www.aur.edu/

- **Independent** comprehensive, founded 1969
- **Urban** 1-acre campus
- **Coed** 411 undergraduate students, 100% full-time, 70% women, 30% men
- **Moderately difficult** entrance level, 95% of applicants were admitted

UNDERGRAD STUDENTS

411 full-time. Students come from 41 states and territories; 60 other countries; 4% transferred in; 55% live on campus.

Freshmen:

Admission: 149 applied, 141 admitted, 48 enrolled. ***Average high school GPA:*** 3. ***Test scores:*** SAT critical reading scores over 500: 75%; SAT math scores over 500: 75%; SAT writing scores over 500: 50%; ACT scores over 18: 82%; SAT critical reading scores over 600: 25%; ACT scores over 24: 46%; ACT scores over 30: 28%.

Retention: 73% of full-time freshmen returned.

FACULTY

Total: 79, 14% full-time, 54% with terminal degrees.

Student/faculty ratio: 14:1.

ACADEMICS

Calendar: semesters. *Degrees:* associate, bachelor's, and master's.

Special study options: academic remediation for entering students, advanced placement credit, double majors, English as a second language, independent study, internships, off-campus study, part-time degree program, services for LD students, student-designed majors, study abroad, summer session for credit.

Computers: 68 computers/terminals and 80 ports are available on campus for general student use. Students can access the following: campus intranet, computer help desk, free student e-mail accounts, online (class) grades, online (class) registration, online (class) schedules, Learning Management System. Campuswide network is available. 100% of college-owned or -operated housing units are wired for high-speed Internet access. Wireless service is available via entire campus.

Library: The American University of Rome Library. *Books:* 13,489 (physical), 150,720 (digital/electronic). Weekly public service hours: 55; students can reserve study rooms.

STUDENT LIFE

Housing options: men-only, women-only. Campus housing is provided by a third party. Freshman applicants given priority for college housing.

Activities and organizations: drama/theater group, student-run newspaper, choral group, Student Government, Community Services, Men and Female soccer teams, Business Club, International Relations Club.

Athletics ***Intercollegiate sports:*** soccer M/W, volleyball M/W.
Intramural sports: basketball M, cross-country running M/W, gymnastics M/W, tennis M/W.

Campus security: 24-hour emergency response devices, security guards during opening hours and 24-hour surveillance cameras.

Student services: health clinic, personal/psychological counseling.

COSTS

Costs (2017–18) ***One-time required fee:*** $230. ***Comprehensive fee:*** $28,712 includes full-time tuition ($23,000), mandatory fees ($382), and room and board ($5330). Full-time tuition and fees vary according to course load and degree level. Part-time tuition: $2875 per course. Part-time tuition and fees vary according to course load and degree level. ***College room only:*** $4550. ***Payment plan:*** installment. ***Waivers:*** employees or children of employees.

APPLYING

Standardized Tests *Required for some:* TOEFL or IELTS for non-English high school students. *Recommended:* SAT or ACT (for admission).

Options: electronic application, deferred entrance.

Application fee: $75.

Required: essay or personal statement, high school transcript, minimum 2.5 GPA, 1 letter of recommendation, interview.

Application deadlines: rolling (freshmen), rolling (transfers).

Notification: continuous (freshmen), continuous (transfers).

CONTACT

Ms. Jessica York, Admissions Counselor, The American University of Rome, Via Pietro Roselli 4, Rome 00153, Italy. *Phone:* -+39 0658330919. *Toll-free phone:* 877-592-1287. *Fax:* +39 0658330992. *E-mail:* admissions@aur.edu.

★ John Cabot University

Rome, Italy

http://www.johncabot.edu/

- **Independent** 4-year, founded 1972
- **Urban** campus with easy access to Rome
- **Coed**

FACULTY

Student/faculty ratio: 9:1.

ACADEMICS

Calendar: semesters. *Degrees:* associate and bachelor's.

Library: Frohring Library plus 1 other. *Books:* 34,218 (physical); *Databases:* 39. Weekly public service hours: 86; students can reserve study rooms.

COLLEGES AT-A-GLANCE

STUDENT LIFE
Housing options: coed, men-only, women-only. Campus housing is leased by the school and is provided by a third party. Freshman campus housing is guaranteed.
Activities and organizations: drama/theater group, student-run newspaper, Business Club, Model United Nations, Student Government, Performing Arts Society, Student Newspaper.
Campus security: 24-hour emergency response devices and patrols, controlled dormitory access.
Student services: health clinic, personal/psychological counseling.

COSTS
Costs (2016–17) ***Comprehensive fee:*** $34,690 includes full-time tuition ($23,900) and room and board ($10,790). Full-time tuition and fees vary according to course load. Part-time tuition and fees vary according to course load. No tuition increase for student's term of enrollment. ***College room only:*** $9600. Room and board charges vary according to board plan and housing facility.

APPLYING
Standardized Tests *Required for some:* SAT or ACT (for admission).
Required: essay or personal statement, high school transcript, 2 letters of recommendation, interview. ***Recommended:*** minimum 2.7 GPA.

CONTACT
Ms. Nadia Spagnoli, Coordinator of US Admissions, John Cabot University, Via della Lungara 233, Roma 00165, Italy. *Phone:* 855-528-7662. *Toll-free phone:* 855-528-7662.
E-mail: admissions@johncabot.edu.

See below for display ad and page 1382 for the College Close-Up.

KENYA

United States International University–Africa

Nairobi, Kenya

http://www.usiu.ac.ke/

- **Independent** comprehensive, founded 1977, part of Alliant International University
- **Urban** 120-acre campus
- **Coed** 4,185 undergraduate students, 93% full-time, 54% women, 46% men
- **Moderately difficult** entrance level, 77% of applicants were admitted

UNDERGRAD STUDENTS
3,873 full-time, 312 part-time. 5% live on campus.

Freshmen:
Admission: 833 applied, 644 admitted, 518 enrolled. ***Average high school GPA:*** 2.79.

FACULTY
Student/faculty ratio: 30:1.

ACADEMICS
Calendar: trimesters. *Degrees:* bachelor's and master's.
Special study options: adult/continuing education programs, off-campus study, part-time degree program, summer session for credit.
Library: Library and Information Center.

STUDENT LIFE
Housing options: coed. Campus housing is university owned and is provided by a third party.
Activities and organizations: drama/theater group, student-run newspaper, radio station, choral group, Business club, Aiesec, Basket Ball, Hockey, Drama club.
Athletics ***Intercollegiate sports:*** basketball M(s)/W(s), field hockey M(s)/W(s), rugby M(s), soccer M(s), swimming and diving M(s)/W(s),

tennis M/W, track and field M(s)/W(s). ***Intramural sports:*** basketball M/W, field hockey M/W, rugby M, soccer M, softball M/W, swimming and diving M/W, table tennis M/W, tennis M/W, track and field M/W, weight lifting M/W.

Campus security: 24-hour emergency response devices and patrols, 24-hour Hostel reception security desk.

Student services: health clinic, personal/psychological counseling.

COSTS

Costs (2016–17) ***One-time required fee:*** 5000 Kenyan shillings. ***Comprehensive fee:*** 512,580 Kenyan shillings includes full-time tuition (261,000 Kenyan shillings), mandatory fees (23,400 Kenyan shillings), and room and board (228,180 Kenyan shillings). Full-time tuition and fees vary according to course load, degree level, program, and reciprocity agreements. Part-time tuition: 7250 Kenyan shillings per unit. Part-time tuition and fees vary according to course load, degree level, program, and reciprocity agreements. ***Required fees:*** 7800 Kenyan shillings per term part-time. ***College room only:*** 90,000 Kenyan shillings. Room and board charges vary according to board plan. ***Payment plan:*** installment. ***Waivers:*** children of alumni and employees or children of employees.

APPLYING

Standardized Tests *Required for some:* TOEFL for students whose high school language of instruction was not English.

Options: deferred entrance.

Application fee: 50 Kenyan shillings.

Required: high school transcript, minimum 2.5 GPA. ***Required for some:*** interview.

Application deadlines: rolling (freshmen), rolling (transfers).

Notification: continuous (freshmen), continuous (transfers).

CONTACT

United States International University–Africa, PO Box 14634, Thika Road Kasarani, Nairobi 00800, Kenya.

LEBANON

American University of Beirut

Beirut, Lebanon

http://www.aub.edu.lb/

- **Independent** university, founded 1866
- **Urban** 61-acre campus with easy access to Beirut
- **Endowment** $525.9 million
- **Coed** 7,072 undergraduate students, 95% full-time, 50% women, 50% men
- 68% of applicants were admitted

UNDERGRAD STUDENTS

6,697 full-time, 375 part-time. Students come from 76 other countries; 0.4% transferred in; 18% live on campus.

Freshmen:

Admission: 4,839 applied, 3,269 admitted, 1,719 enrolled. ***Test scores:*** SAT critical reading scores over 500: 46%; SAT math scores over 500: 94%; SAT writing scores over 500: 55%; SAT critical reading scores over 600: 10%; SAT math scores over 600: 67%; SAT writing scores over 600: 15%; SAT critical reading scores over 700: 1%; SAT math scores over 700: 23%; SAT writing scores over 700: 1%.

Retention: 93% of full-time freshmen returned.

FACULTY

Total: 1,182, 75% full-time, 73% with terminal degrees.

Student/faculty ratio: 11:1.

ACADEMICS

Calendar: semesters. *Degrees:* certificates, diplomas, bachelor's, master's, doctoral, and postbachelor's certificates.

Special study options: academic remediation for entering students, advanced placement credit, double majors, English as a second language, honors programs, independent study, internships, services for LD students, study abroad, summer session for credit.

Computers: 1,476 computers/terminals and 1,320 ports are available on campus for general student use. Students can access the following: campus intranet, computer help desk, free student e-mail accounts, online (class) grades, online (class) registration, online (class) schedules. Campuswide network is available. 100% of college-owned or -operated housing units are wired for high-speed Internet access. Wireless service is available via entire campus.

Library: Naami Jafet Memorial Library plus 3 others. *Books:* 425,000 (physical), 1.2 million (digital/electronic); *Serial titles:* 5,000 (physical), 191,998 (digital/electronic); *Databases:* 722. Weekly public service hours: 109.

STUDENT LIFE

Housing options: on-campus residence required for freshman year; men-only, women-only. Campus housing is university owned. Freshman campus housing is guaranteed.

Activities and organizations: drama/theater group, student-run newspaper, choral group, Red Cross Club, Biology Society, Business Society, Music Club, Palestinian Cultural Club.

Athletics ***Intercollegiate sports:*** badminton M/W, basketball M/W, cheerleading W, cross-country running M/W, football M, rugby M/W, skiing (downhill) M/W, soccer M/W, squash M/W, swimming and diving M/W, table tennis M/W, tennis M/W, track and field M/W, triathlon M/W, ultimate Frisbee M/W, volleyball M/W, water polo M. ***Intramural sports:*** archery M/W, basketball M/W, cross-country running M/W, fencing M/W, football M, rugby M/W, soccer M/W, squash M/W, swimming and diving M/W, table tennis M/W, tennis M/W, track and field M/W, ultimate Frisbee M/W, volleyball M/W, weight lifting M/W.

Campus security: 24-hour emergency response devices and patrols, late-night transport/escort service, controlled dormitory access, staff monitors entrance 24/7.

Student services: health clinic, personal/psychological counseling, legal services.

COSTS & FINANCIAL AID

Costs (2016–17) ***Tuition:*** $21,270 full-time, $689 per credit part-time. Full-time tuition and fees vary according to course load, degree level, program, and student level. Part-time tuition and fees vary according to course load, degree level, program, and student level. ***Required fees:*** $716 full-time. ***Room only:*** $2814. Room and board charges vary according to housing facility and location. ***Payment plan:*** deferred payment. ***Waivers:*** employees or children of employees.

Financial Aid Of all full-time matriculated undergraduates who enrolled in 2015, 4,025 applied for aid, 3,112 were judged to have need. 22 state and other part-time jobs (averaging $1350). In 2015, 33 non-need-based awards were made. ***Average financial aid package:*** $9718. ***Average need-based loan:*** $6262. ***Average need-based gift aid:*** $9362. ***Average non-need-based aid:*** $23,842. ***Average indebtedness upon graduation:*** $15,227. ***Financial aid deadline:*** 12/18.

APPLYING

Standardized Tests *Required:* SAT (for admission). *Required for some:* SAT Subject Tests (for admission), TOEFL for international applicants.

Options: electronic application, early admission, early action, deferred entrance.

Application fee: $80.

Required: high school transcript. ***Required for some:*** 2 letters of recommendation, interview. ***Recommended:*** essay or personal statement.

Application deadlines: 12/18 (freshmen), 4/30 (transfers), 11/30 (early action).

Notification: 3/30 (freshmen), continuous until 6/30 (transfers), 1/31 (early action).

CONTACT

Dr. Salim Kanaan, Director of Admissions Office, American University of Beirut, PO Box 11-0236, Riad El-Solh, 1107 2020, Lebanon. *Phone:* 961-1374374 Ext. 2592. *Fax:* 961-1750775. *E-mail:* admissions@aub.edu.lb.

Lebanese American University
Beirut, Lebanon
http://www.lau.edu.lb/

- **Private** comprehensive, founded 1835
- **Urban** 50-acre campus with easy access to Beirut, Byblos, Tripoli
- **Endowment** $422.3 million
- **Coed** 7,590 undergraduate students, 94% full-time, 49% women, 51% men
- **Moderately difficult** entrance level, 88% of applicants were admitted

UNDERGRAD STUDENTS
7,148 full-time, 442 part-time. Students come from 74 other countries; 19% are from out of state; 1% transferred in; 6% live on campus.

Freshmen:
Admission: 4,999 applied, 4,392 admitted, 1,788 enrolled. ***Average high school GPA:*** 2.97. ***Test scores:*** SAT critical reading scores over 500: 20%; SAT math scores over 500: 78%; SAT writing scores over 500: 32%; SAT critical reading scores over 600: 4%; SAT math scores over 600: 38%; SAT writing scores over 600: 7%; SAT math scores over 700: 7%; SAT writing scores over 700: 1%.
Retention: 90% of full-time freshmen returned.

FACULTY
Total: 797, 37% full-time, 45% with terminal degrees.
Student/faculty ratio: 17:1.

ACADEMICS
Calendar: semesters. *Degrees:* bachelor's, master's, doctoral, and postbachelor's certificates.
Special study options: academic remediation for entering students, advanced placement credit, double majors, honors programs, internships, part-time degree program, services for LD students, study abroad, summer session for credit.
Computers: 1,359 computers/terminals and 2,200 ports are available on campus for general student use. Students can access the following: campus intranet, computer help desk, free student e-mail accounts, online (class) grades, online (class) registration, online (class) schedules, online forms requests, online and mobile course management system. Campuswide network is available. 100% of college-owned or -operated housing units are wired for high-speed Internet access. Wireless service is available via entire campus.
Library: Riyad Nassar Library plus 3 others. *Books:* 552,500 (physical), 337,615 (digital/electronic); *Serial titles:* 604 (physical), 82,981 (digital/electronic); *Databases:* 160. Weekly public service hours: 98; students can reserve study rooms.

STUDENT LIFE
Housing options: coed, men-only, women-only, special housing for students with disabilities. Campus housing is university owned, leased by the school and is provided by a third party.
Activities and organizations: drama/theater group, student-run newspaper, choral group, Event Organization Club, Debate Club, UNESCO Club, International Affairs Club, Red Cross Club.
Athletics ***Intercollegiate sports:*** badminton M/W, basketball M(s)/W(s), cross-country running M/W, rugby M(s)/W, skiing (downhill) M/W, soccer M(s)/W(s), swimming and diving M(s)/W(s), table tennis M(s)/W(s), tennis M(s)/W(s), track and field M(s)/W(s), triathlon M(s), volleyball M(s)/W(s), water polo M(s). ***Intramural sports:*** basketball M/W, soccer M/W, swimming and diving M/W, table tennis M/W, tennis M/W, volleyball M/W.
Campus security: 24-hour emergency response devices and patrols, 24/7 security at residence halls.
Student services: health clinic, personal/psychological counseling, women's center.

COSTS
Costs (2016–17) ***Tuition:*** $16,220 full-time, $678 per credit part-time. Full-time tuition and fees vary according to course load, degree level, and program. Part-time tuition and fees vary according to course load, degree level, and program. ***Required fees:*** $528 full-time, $528 per year part-time. ***Room only:*** Room and board charges vary according to housing facility and location. ***Payment plans:*** installment, deferred payment. ***Waivers:*** employees or children of employees.

APPLYING
Standardized Tests *Required:* SAT or ACT (for admission). *Required for some:* SAT Subject Tests (for admission), Institutional English Test (English Entrance Exam EEE) or International TOFEL.
Options: electronic application, early admission, deferred entrance.
Application fee: $80.
Required: high school transcript, minimum 2.0 GPA.
Application deadlines: 7/15 (freshmen), 7/15 (transfers).
Notification: continuous until 3/1 (freshmen), continuous until 3/1 (transfers).

CONTACT
Miss Nada Hajj, University Director of Admissions, Lebanese American University, PO Box 13-5053 Chouran Beirut 1102 2801, Lebanon, Beirut, Lebanon. *Phone:* 961-1786456 Ext. 1111. *Fax:* 961-1786456. *E-mail:* nhajj@lau.edu.lb.

MEXICO

Instituto Tecnológico y de Estudios Superiores de Monterrey, Campus Central de Veracruz
Córdoba, Mexico
http://www.ver.itesm.mx/

CONTACT
Ing. Luis Pablo Villareal, Registrar, Instituto Tecnológico y de Estudios Superiores de Monterrey, Campus Central de Veracruz, Avenida Eugenio Garza Sada 1, Apartado Postal 314, 94500 Córdoba, Veracruz, Mexico. *Phone:* -27-13-23-40 Ext. 123.

Instituto Tecnológico y de Estudios Superiores de Monterrey, Campus Chiapas
Tuxtla Gutiérrez, Mexico
http://www.chs.itesm.mx/

CONTACT
Lic. Luis Enrique Cancino, Registrar, Instituto Tecnológico y de Estudios Superiores de Monterrey, Campus Chiapas, Carretera a Tapanatepec Km 149&746, Apartado Postal 312, 29000 Tuxtla Gutiérrez, Chiapas, Mexico. *Phone:* -96-15-1723.

Instituto Tecnológico y de Estudios Superiores de Monterrey, Campus Chihuahua
Chihuahua, Mexico
http://www.chi.itesm.mx/

CONTACT
Ing. Juan Manuel Fernandez, Registrar, Instituto Tecnológico y de Estudios Superiores de Monterrey, Campus Chihuahua, Colegio Militar 4700, Colonia Nombre de Dios, Apartado Postal 728, 31300 Chihuahua, Chihuahua, Mexico. *Phone:* -14-17-48-58 Ext. 117.

Instituto Tecnológico y de Estudios Superiores de Monterrey, Campus Ciudad de México

Ciudad de Mexico, Mexico

http://www.ccm.itesm.mx/

CONTACT

Admissions Office, Instituto Tecnológico y de Estudios Superiores de Monterrey, Campus Ciudad de México, Calle del Puente #222 esquina con Periférico, 14380 Colonia Huipulco, Tlalpan, MDF, Mexico. *Phone:* -5-673-6488.

Instituto Tecnológico y de Estudios Superiores de Monterrey, Campus Ciudad Juárez

Ciudad Juárez, Mexico

http://www.cdj.itesm.mx/

CONTACT

Lic. Alberto Trejo, Registrar, Instituto Tecnológico y de Estudios Superiores de Monterrey, Campus Ciudad Juárez, Boulevard Tomas Fernandez y Avenida A J Bermudez, Apartado Postal 3105-J, 32320 Ciudad Juárez, Chihuahua, Mexico. *Phone:* -16-17-88-07 Ext. 113.

Instituto Tecnológico y de Estudios Superiores de Monterrey, Campus Ciudad Obregón

Ciudad Obregón, Mexico

http://www.cob.itesm.mx/

CONTACT

Lic. Judith Almeida, Registrar, Instituto Tecnológico y de Estudios Superiores de Monterrey, Campus Ciudad Obregón, Dr Norman E Borlaug Km 14, Apartado Postal 662, 85000 Ciudad Obregón, Sonora, Mexico. *Phone:* -64-15-03-12.

Instituto Tecnológico y de Estudios Superiores de Monterrey, Campus Colima

Colima, Mexico

http://www.itesm.edu/wps/wcm/connect/Campus/COL/colima/

CONTACT

Lic. Manuel Perez Rivera, Registrar, Instituto Tecnológico y de Estudios Superiores de Monterrey, Campus Colima, Prolongacion Ignacio Sandoval s/n, Fraccionamiento Jardines de Vista Hermosa, Apartado Postal 190, 28010 Colima, Colima, Mexico. *Phone:* -33-12-53-39.

Instituto Tecnológico y de Estudios Superiores de Monterrey, Campus Cuernavaca

Temixco, Mexico

http://www.cva.itesm.mx/

CONTACT

Lic. Miguel Angel Machua, Registrar, Instituto Tecnológico y de Estudios Superiores de Monterrey, Campus Cuernavaca, Paseo de la Reforma 182-A, Colonia Lomas de Cuernavaca, 62000 Temixco, Morelos, Mexico. *Phone:* -73 18-49-57.

Instituto Tecnológico y de Estudios Superiores de Monterrey, Campus Estado de México

Estado de Mexico, Mexico

http://www.cem.itesm.mx/

CONTACT

Prof. Jose de Jesus Molina, Registrar, Instituto Tecnológico y de Estudios Superiores de Monterrey, Campus Estado de México, Carretera Lago de Guadalupe Km. 3.5, Atizapan de Zaragoza, Estado de Mexico 52926, Mexico. *Phone:* -5-873-3600.

Instituto Tecnológico y de Estudios Superiores de Monterrey, Campus Guadalajara

Zapopan, Mexico

http://www.gda.itesm.mx/

CONTACT

Ms. Janet Martell Sotomayor, Registration Director, Instituto Tecnológico y de Estudios Superiores de Monterrey, Campus Guadalajara, Avenida General Ramón Corona 2514, Colonia Nuevo Mexico, 45140 Zapopan, Jalisco, Mexico. *Phone:* -3-669-3006.

Instituto Tecnológico y de Estudios Superiores de Monterrey, Campus Hidalgo

Pachuca, Mexico

http://www.hgo.itesm.mx/

CONTACT

Lic. Lizbet Melo, Registrar, Instituto Tecnológico y de Estudios Superiores de Monterrey, Campus Hidalgo, Boulevard Felipe Angeles s/n al lado de la Unidad Deportiva, Apartado Postal 337, 42090 Pachuca, Hidalgo, Mexico. *Phone:* -714-25-00 Ext. 128.

Instituto Tecnológico y de Estudios Superiores de Monterrey, Campus Irapuato

Irapuato, Mexico

http://www.ira.itesm.mx/

CONTACT

Ing. Marcela Beltrán, Registrar, Instituto Tecnológico y de Estudios Superiores de Monterrey, Campus Irapuato, Paseo Mirador del Valle No. 445, Col. Villas de Irapuato, Apartado Postal 568, 36660 Irapuato, Guanajuato, Mexico. *Phone:* -46-230342.

Instituto Tecnológico y de Estudios Superiores de Monterrey, Campus Laguna

Torreón, Mexico

http://www.lag.itesm.mx/

CONTACT

Ing. Aroldo Camargo Soto, Registrar, Instituto Tecnológico y de Estudios Superiores de Monterrey, Campus Laguna, Paseo del Tecnologico s/n Ampliacion La Rosita, Apartado Postal 506, 27250 Torreón, Coahuila, Mexico. *Phone:* -17-20-66-61 Ext. 23.

Instituto Tecnológico y de Estudios Superiores de Monterrey, Campus León

León, Mexico

http://www.leo.itesm.mx/

CONTACT

Lic. Eddie Villegas, Registrar, Instituto Tecnológico y de Estudios Superiores de Monterrey, Campus León, Avenida Eugenio Garza Sada s/n Colonia Cerro Gordo, Apartado Postal 872, 37120 León, Guanajuato, Mexico. *Phone:* -47-17-10-00 Ext. 131.

Instituto Tecnológico y de Estudios Superiores de Monterrey, Campus Monterrey

Monterrey, Mexico

http://www.mty.itesm.mx/

CONTACT

Lic. Carlos Ordoñez, International Student Advisor, Instituto Tecnológico y de Estudios Superiores de Monterrey, Campus Monterrey, Avenida Eugenio Garza Sada 2501 Sur Colonia Tecnnologico, Sucursal de Correos J, 64849 Monterrey, Nuevo León, Mexico. *Phone:* -52 81 8328 4065 Ext. 3942.

Instituto Tecnológico y de Estudios Superiores de Monterrey, Campus Querétaro

Santiago de Querétaro, Mexico

http://www.qro.itesm.mx/

CONTACT

Lic. Marco Vinicio Lopez, Registrar, Instituto Tecnológico y de Estudios Superiores de Monterrey, Campus Querétaro, Avenida Epigmenio González #500, Apartado Postal 37, 76130 Querétaro, Querétaro, Mexico. *Phone:* -42-17-38-25 Ext. 156.

Instituto Tecnológico y de Estudios Superiores de Monterrey, Campus Saltillo

Saltillo, Mexico

http://www.sal.itesm.mx/

CONTACT

Lic. Esteban Ramos, Registrar, Instituto Tecnológico y de Estudios Superiores de Monterrey, Campus Saltillo, Prolongacion Juan de la Barrera 1241 Ote, Apartado Postal 539, 25270 Saltillo, Coahuila, Mexico. *Phone:* -84-15-06-90 Ext. 12.

Instituto Tecnológico y de Estudios Superiores de Monterrey, Campus San Luis Potosí

San Luis Potosí, Mexico

http://www.slp.itesm.mx/

CONTACT

Ing. Consuelo Gonzalez, Registrar, Instituto Tecnológico y de Estudios Superiores de Monterrey, Campus San Luis Potosí, Avenida Robles 600, Colonia Jacarandas, Apartado Postal 1473 Suc E, 78140 San Luis Potosí, SLP, Mexico. *Phone:* -48 13-3441 Ext. 14.

Instituto Tecnológico y de Estudios Superiores de Monterrey, Campus Sinaloa

Culiacán, Mexico

http://www.sin.itesm.mx/

CONTACT

Lic. Hugo Guerrero, Registrar, Instituto Tecnológico y de Estudios Superiores de Monterrey, Campus Sinaloa, Boulevard Culiacán 3773, Apartado Postal 69-F, 80800 Culiacán, Sinaloa, Mexico. *Phone:* -67-14-03-69.

Instituto Tecnológico y de Estudios Superiores de Monterrey, Campus Sonora Norte

Hermosillo, Mexico

http://www.her.itesm.mx/

CONTACT

Ing. Victor Eduardo Perez Orozco, Library and Admissions/Registration Director, Instituto Tecnológico y de Estudios Superiores de Monterrey, Campus Sonora Norte, Carretera Hermosillo-Nogales Km 9, Apartado Postal 216, 83000 Hermosillo, Sonora, Mexico. *Phone:* -62-15-52-05 Ext. 131.

Instituto Tecnológico y de Estudios Superiores de Monterrey, Campus Tampico

Altimira, Mexico

http://www.itesm.edu/wps/portal?WCM_GLOBAL_CONTEXT=/migration/TAM2/Tampico

CONTACT

Ing. Javier Ponce, Registrar, Instituto Tecnológico y de Estudios Superiores de Monterrey, Campus Tampico, Boulevard Petrocel Km 1.3, Corredor Industrial, Carretera Tampico-Mante, 89120 Altimira, Tamaulipas, Mexico. *Phone:* -126-4-19-79.

Instituto Tecnológico y de Estudios Superiores de Monterrey, Campus Toluca

Toluca, Mexico

http://www.tol.itesm.mx/

CONTACT

Ing. Victor M. Martinez Orta, Registrar, Instituto Tecnológico y de Estudios Superiores de Monterrey, Campus Toluca, Ex-hacienda La Pila, 100 metros al norte de San Antonio Buenavista, 50252 Toluca, Estado de Mexico, Mexico. *Phone:* -72-74-11-92.

Instituto Tecnológico y de Estudios Superiores de Monterrey, Campus Zacatecas

Zacatecas, Mexico

http://www.zac.itesm.mx/

CONTACT

Lic. de Lourdes Zorrilla, Business Affairs Director and Registrar, Instituto Tecnológico y de Estudios Superiores de Monterrey, Campus Zacatecas, Calzada Pedro Coronel #16, Frente al Club Bernades, Municipio de Guadalupe, 98000 Zacatecas, Zacatecas, Mexico. *Phone:* -49 23-00-40.

Universidad de las Americas, A.C.

Mexico City, Mexico

http://www.udladf.mx/

CONTACT
Universidad de las Americas, A.C., Calle de Puebla 223, Col. Roma, 06700 Mexico City, Mexico.

Universidad de las Américas Puebla

Puebla, Mexico

http://www.udlap.mx/

CONTACT
Miss Madet Ruisenor-Quintero, Director of Student Enrollment Office, Universidad de las Américas Puebla, Ex-Hacienda Santa Catarina Martir, Cholula, Puebla 72820, Mexico. *Phone:* -52 229-2024.

Universidad de Monterrey

San Pedro Garza Garcia, Mexico

http://www.udem.edu.mx/

CONTACT
Universidad de Monterrey, Av. Ignacio Morones Prieto 4500 Pte, 66238 San Pedro Garza Garcia, NL, Mexico. *Toll-free phone:* 800-801-UDEM.

MONACO

The International University of Monaco

Monte Carlo, Monaco

http://www.monaco.edu/

CONTACT
Dr. Gisele Dudognon, Director of Admissions, The International University of Monaco, 2, Avenue Albert II, MC-98000 Principality of Monaco, Monaco. *Phone:* 377-97-986-994. *Fax:* 377 92052 830. *E-mail:* gdudognon@monaco.edu.

SOUTH AFRICA

University of South Africa

Pretoria, South Africa

http://www.unisa.ac.za/

CONTACT
Contact Centre, University of South Africa, PO Box 392, Pretoria 0003, South Africa. *Phone:* 27-11 670-9000. *Fax:* 012 429 4150. *E-mail:* study-info@unisa.ac.za.

SPAIN

Saint Louis University–Madrid Campus

Madrid, Spain

http://www.slu.edu/madrid

- **Independent Roman Catholic (Jesuit)** comprehensive
- **Urban** 1-acre campus with easy access to Madrid, Spain
- **Coed** 659 undergraduate students, 12% full-time, 5% women, 6% men
- **Moderately difficult** entrance level, 43% of applicants were admitted

UNDERGRAD STUDENTS
76 full-time. Students come from 50 states and territories; 65 other countries; 75% are from out of state; 33% transferred in; 65% live on campus.

Freshmen:
Admission: 406 applied, 173 admitted, 76 enrolled. ***Test scores:*** SAT critical reading scores over 500: 95%; SAT math scores over 500: 95%; SAT critical reading scores over 600: 25%; SAT math scores over 600: 25%; SAT critical reading scores over 700: 10%; SAT math scores over 700: 10%.

FACULTY
Total: 94, 40% full-time, 57% with terminal degrees.

Student/faculty ratio: 14:1.

ACADEMICS
Calendar: semesters. *Degrees:* bachelor's and master's.

Special study options: advanced placement credit, cooperative education, double majors, English as a second language, honors programs, independent study, internships, services for LD students, study abroad, summer session for credit.

Computers: Students can access the following: computer help desk, free student e-mail accounts, online (class) grades, online (class) registration, online (class) schedules. Campuswide network is available. 100% of college-owned or -operated housing units are wired for high-speed Internet access. Wireless service is available via entire campus.

Library: Main Library plus 1 other.

STUDENT LIFE
Housing options: men-only, women-only. Campus housing is provided by a third party. Freshman campus housing is guaranteed.

Activities and organizations: drama/theater group, student-run newspaper, choral group, Student Government, Campus Ambassadors, Student Magazine, Theatre Club, Babel Language Exchange.

Athletics *Intramural sports:* baseball M/W, basketball M/W, cross-country running M/W, equestrian sports M/W, field hockey M/W, football M/W, golf M/W, lacrosse M/W, racquetball M/W, soccer M/W, squash M/W, swimming and diving M/W, tennis M/W, ultimate Frisbee M/W, volleyball M/W.

Campus security: 24-hour emergency response devices.

Student services: personal/psychological counseling.

COSTS
Costs (2017–18) *One-time required fee:* $200. ***Comprehensive fee:*** $28,736 includes full-time tuition ($21,076), mandatory fees ($180), and room and board ($7480). Part-time tuition and fees vary according to course load and degree level. ***College room only:*** $4400. Room and board charges vary according to housing facility. ***Payment plan:*** installment. ***Waivers:*** children of alumni and employees or children of employees.

APPLYING
Standardized Tests *Required for some:* SAT or ACT (for admission), IB, A-Levels, French Baccalaureate, Selectividad, Maturita, or Abitur.

Options: electronic application, deferred entrance.

Required: essay or personal statement, high school transcript, minimum 2.5 GPA. ***Recommended:*** 2 letters of recommendation.

Application deadlines: 5/31 (freshmen), 5/31 (transfers).

Notification: continuous (freshmen), continuous (transfers).

CONTACT
Ms. Heidi Buffington, Director of Admissions, Saint Louis University–Madrid Campus, Avenida del Valle, 34, Madrid 28003, Spain. *Phone:* -34 91-554-5858 Ext. 206. *Fax:* 34 91-554-6202. *E-mail:* hbuffin1@slu.edu.

Schiller International University

Madrid, Spain

http://www.schiller.edu/

CONTACT
Ms. Kamala Dontamsetti, Associate Director of Admissions, Schiller International University, 300 East Bay Drive, Largo, FL 33700. *Phone:* 727-736-5082 Ext. 234. *Toll-free phone:* 800-261-9571 (in-state); 800-261-9751 (out-of-state). *Fax:* 727-734-0359. *E-mail:* admissions@schiller.edu.

SWITZERLAND

Ecole Hôtelière de Lausanne

Lausanne, Switzerland

http://www.ehl.ch/

CONTACT

Ecole Hôtelière de Lausanne, Route de Cojonnex 18, Le Chalet-a-Gobet, CH-1000 Lausanne 25, Switzerland. *Phone:* -41 21 785 1111.

Franklin University Switzerland

Sorengo, Switzerland

http://www.fus.edu/

CONTACT

Peter Dorthe, Director of Admissions, Franklin University Switzerland, US Office, The Graybar Building, Suite 2746, 420 Lexington Avenue, New York, NY 10170. *Phone:* 212-922-9650. *Fax:* 212-922-9870. *E-mail:* info@fc.edu.

Glion Institute of Higher Education

Glion-sur-Montreux, Switzerland

http://www.glion.edu/

CONTACT

Admissions, Glion Institute of Higher Education, Route de Glion 111, CH-1823 Glion-sur-Montreux, Switzerland. *Phone:* 41-0 21 989 26 77. *Fax:* 41-0 21 989 26 78. *E-mail:* info@glion.edu.

International University in Geneva

Geneva, Switzerland

http://www.iun.ch/

CONTACT

Ms. Virginie Morel, Admissions Officer, International University in Geneva, Geneva 1215, Switzerland. *Phone:* -41 22710-7110. *Fax:* 41 22710-7111. *E-mail:* bachelor@iun.ch.

Les Roches International School of Hotel Management

Bluche, Switzerland

http://www.lesroches.edu/

CONTACT

Enrollment Management Department, Les Roches International School of Hotel Management, CH-3975 Bluche, Switzerland. *Phone:* 41-021 989 26 44. *Fax:* 41-021 989 26 45. *E-mail:* info@lesroches.edu.

TAIWAN

Christ's College

Taipei, Taiwan

http://www.christc.org.tw/

CONTACT

Ms. Lucy Li, Recruiter, Christ's College, No. 51, Ziqiang Road, Tamsui District, New Taipei City 251, Taiwan. *Phone:* -+886-2-2809-7661. *Fax:* +886-2-8809-1084. *E-mail:* lucyli@christs-college.org.

UNITED ARAB EMIRATES

The American University in Dubai

Dubai, United Arab Emirates

http://www.aud.edu/

- **Proprietary** comprehensive, founded 1995
- **Urban** campus
- **Coed** 2,350 undergraduate students, 88% full-time, 50% women, 50% men
- 38% of applicants were admitted

UNDERGRAD STUDENTS

2,074 full-time, 276 part-time. Students come from 105 other countries.

Freshmen:

Admission: 1,533 applied, 583 admitted, 449 enrolled.

FACULTY

Total: 189, 68% full-time.

ACADEMICS

Calendar: semesters. *Degrees:* certificates, bachelor's, and master's.

Special study options: accelerated degree program, advanced placement credit, double majors, English as a second language, honors programs, independent study, internships, part-time degree program, services for LD students, study abroad, summer session for credit.

Computers: 864 computers/terminals are available on campus for general student use. Students can access the following: computer help desk, free student e-mail accounts, online (class) grades, online (class) registration, online (class) schedules. Campuswide network is available. 100% of college-owned or -operated housing units are wired for high-speed Internet access.

Library: University Library.

STUDENT LIFE

Housing options: men-only, women-only. Campus housing is university owned. Freshman campus housing is guaranteed.

Activities and organizations: drama/theater group, student-run newspaper, Student Government Association, Community Service Club, Drama Club, Music Club, Debate Club.

Athletics ***Intercollegiate sports:*** basketball M/W, soccer M/W, tennis M/W, volleyball M/W. ***Intramural sports:*** basketball M/W, football M/W, soccer M/W, swimming and diving M/W, table tennis M/W, tennis M/W, track and field M/W, volleyball M/W.

Campus security: 24-hour patrols.

Student services: health clinic, personal/psychological counseling.

APPLYING

Standardized Tests *Required for some:* SAT or ACT (for admission), SAT Subject Tests (for admission).

Options: early admission.

Application fee: 55 United Arab Emirates dirhams.

Required: high school transcript, minimum 2.0 GPA, 2 letters of recommendation. ***Required for some:*** interview. ***Recommended:*** essay or personal statement.

CONTACT

Mrs. Carol Maalouf, Director of Admissions, The American University in Dubai, PO Box 28282, Dubai, United Arab Emirates. *Phone:* -971 4 399 9000 Ext. 170. *Fax:* 971 4 399 8899. *E-mail:* admissions@aud.edu.

American University of Sharjah
Sharjah, United Arab Emirates
http://www.aus.edu/

CONTACT
American University of Sharjah, PO Box 26666, Sharjah, United Arab Emirates. *Phone:* -971 6 515-5555.

UNITED KINGDOM

Hult International Business School
London, United Kingdom
http://www.hult.edu/

- **Independent** comprehensive, founded 1959
- **Urban** campus with easy access to San Francisco, London
- **Coed** 1,147 undergraduate students, 100% full-time, 38% women, 62% men
- **Moderately difficult** entrance level, 50% of applicants were admitted

UNDERGRAD STUDENTS
1,147 full-time. Students come from 24 states and territories; 153 other countries; 63% are from out of state; 0.1% Black or African American, non-Hispanic/Latino; 0.8% Hispanic/Latino; 0.9% Asian, non-Hispanic/Latino; 0.1% Native Hawaiian or other Pacific Islander, non-Hispanic/Latino; 0.4% Two or more races, non-Hispanic/Latino; 4% Race/ethnicity unknown; 92% international; 5% transferred in.

Freshmen:
Admission: 3,206 applied, 1,609 admitted, 378 enrolled. ***Average high school GPA:*** 3.03. ***Test scores:*** SAT critical reading scores over 500: 47%; SAT math scores over 500: 54%; SAT critical reading scores over 600: 18%; SAT math scores over 600: 30%; SAT critical reading scores over 700: 6%; SAT math scores over 700: 12%.

Retention: 85% of full-time freshmen returned.

FACULTY
Total: 131, 37% full-time, 37% with terminal degrees.

Student/faculty ratio: 15:1.

ACADEMICS
Calendar: 5-term academic calendar: required fall, winter, spring terms; optional Summer 1, Summer 2 terms. *Degrees:* bachelor's, master's, and doctoral.

Special study options: academic remediation for entering students, accelerated degree program, advanced placement credit, English as a second language, honors programs, independent study, internships, services for LD students, study abroad, summer session for credit.

Computers: 15 computers/terminals are available on campus for general student use. Students can access the following: campus intranet, computer help desk, free student e-mail accounts, online (class) grades, online (class) registration, online (class) schedules. Campuswide network is available. 100% of college-owned or -operated housing units are wired for high-speed Internet access. Wireless service is available via entire campus.
Library: Main Library plus 2 others. *Books:* 1,815 (physical).

STUDENT LIFE
Housing options: on-campus residence required through sophomore year; coed. Campus housing is leased by the school. Freshman applicants given priority for college housing.

Activities and organizations: drama/theater group, student-run newspaper, choral group, Language Cafe, Model United Nations, International Law Society, Hult RISE (charity club), Consultancy Club.

Athletics *Intercollegiate sports:* basketball M/W, soccer M/W. ***Intramural sports:*** badminton M/W, cheerleading W, golf M/W, rugby M, skiing (downhill) M/W, swimming and diving M/W, table tennis M/W.

Campus security: 24-hour emergency response devices and patrols, controlled dormitory access.

Student services: personal/psychological counseling.

COSTS
Costs (2017–18) *Tuition:* 24,900 British pounds full-time. Full-time tuition and fees vary according to course load and location. ***Room only:*** Room and board charges vary according to board plan, housing facility, location, and student level. ***Payment plan:*** installment. ***Waivers:*** children of alumni and employees or children of employees.

APPLYING
Standardized Tests *Required for some:* SAT or ACT (for admission), TOEFL, IELTS, or PTE for non-native English speakers.

Options: electronic application.

Application fee: 75 British pounds.

Required: essay or personal statement, high school transcript, 2 letters of recommendation. ***Required for some:*** interview.

Application deadlines: rolling (freshmen), rolling (transfers).

Notification: continuous (freshmen), continuous (transfers).

CONTACT
Hult International Business School, 35 Commercial Road, London E1 1LD, United Kingdom. *Phone:* -44 207 341 8555.
E-mail: bachelor@hult.edu.

London Metropolitan University
London, United Kingdom
http://www.londonmet.ac.uk/

CONTACT
London Metropolitan University, 166-220 Holloway Road, London N7 8DB, United Kingdom.

Open University
Milton Keynes, United Kingdom
http://www.open.ac.uk/

CONTACT
Open University, Walton Hall, Milton Keynes MK7 6AA, United Kingdom.

Regent's University London
London, United Kingdom
http://www.regents.ac.uk/

CONTACT
Admissions Director, Regent's University London, Inner Circle, Regent's Park, London NW1 4NS, United Kingdom. *Phone:* 44-0 207 487 7505. *Fax:* 44-0 207 487 7425. *E-mail:* bacl@regents.ac.uk.

★ Richmond, The American International University in London

Richmond, United Kingdom

http://www.richmond.ac.uk/

CONTACT

Mr. Nick Atkinson, Director of United States Admissions, Richmond, The American International University in London, 343 Congress Street, Suite 3100, Boston, MA 02210-1214. *Phone:* 617-450-5617. *Fax:* 617-450-5601. *E-mail:* us_admissions@richmond.ac.uk.

See below for display ad and page 1474 for the College Close-Up.

College Close-Ups

NOTICE: Certain portions of or information contained in this book have been submitted and paid for by the educational institution identified, and such institutions take full responsibility for the accuracy, timeliness, completeness and functionality of such content. Such portions or information include (i) each display ad in the "Profiles" section from pages 55 through 1272 that comprises a half or full page of information covering a single educational institution, and (ii) each two-page description in the "College Close-Up" section from pages 1274 through 1606.

A ★ indicates that the school has detailed information with a Premium Profile on Petersons.com.

ACADEMY OF ART UNIVERSITY

SAN FRANCISCO, CALIFORNIA

★ To read more about this school, visit http://petersons.to/academyofartuniversity

ACADEMY *of* ART UNIVERSITY®
FOUNDED IN SAN FRANCISCO 1929
BY ARTISTS FOR ARTISTS

The University

In 1929, Academy of Art University founder Richard S. Stephens, who was the advertising Creative Director of *Sunset* magazine, acted on his belief that "aspiring artists and designers, given proper instruction, hard work, and dedication, can learn the skills needed to become successful professionals." His new School of Advertising Art consisted of 46 students meeting in one room on San Francisco's Kearny Street.

The instructors, who were professional artists, brought real-world problems, situations, solutions, and practical experience to the students. Based on this idea, the school's philosophy was formulated: Hire established professionals to teach the art and design professionals of tomorrow. At that time, advertising consisted primarily of illustrations, photos, and copy. Consequently, it became necessary to teach beginning students the fundamentals of drawing, painting, color, light, and photography as well as layout and typography.

When Richard A. Stephens succeeded his father as President in 1951, the Foundations Department was added, ensuring all students mastered the basic principles of traditional art and design. Illustration soon expanded to include fine arts (drawing, painting, sculpture, and printmaking), and advertising design led to the School of Graphic Design. A Fashion School (design, knitwear, textiles, and merchandising) and an Interior Design School were also added. In 1966, the Academy officially became a college, and a decade later began offering the Master of Fine Arts degree. Later, five more buildings were purchased, and by 1992, the student body comprised more than 2,500 students.

The leadership of the Academy was then turned over to the third generation. Dr. Elisa Stephens, granddaughter of the school's founder, quickly determined that the school's small School of Web Design & New Media had enormous potential to prepare students for multimedia careers with such companies as Pixar, Adobe, and Walt Disney Productions. It is now one of the largest departments at the Academy. In 2004, the name of the school was changed from Academy of Art College to Academy of Art University, in recognition of its depth, scope, and quality.

Today, Academy of Art University is the largest accredited private art and design university in the nation. Nearly one third of the student body is made up of international students. The Academy has over 30 facilities that house classrooms, studios, galleries, and residence halls. The students, who are admitted through an open-enrollment policy, aspire to earn A.A., B.A., B.F.A., B.S., B.Arch., M.A., M.F.A., or M.Arch. degrees or an Art Teaching Credential. Students can study in San Francisco or through the Academy's flexible online programs.

The Academy maintains a system of courtesy shuttles to connect the different points of the campus, all of which are located within the city limits of San Francisco, one of the world's most vibrant and beautiful cities. The instructors, who are working art and design professionals from around the world, are drawn to the Academy and to the creative and intellectual center that is the Bay Area. Extensive senior-year internship programs allow students to gain valuable experience and develop strong portfolios in their chosen field prior to graduation.

Academy of Art University is an accredited member of the WASC Senior College and University Commission (WSCUC), National Association of Schools of Art and Design (NASAD), Council for Interior Design Accreditation (CIDA) for B.F.A.-IAD and M.F.A.-IAD, National Architectural Accrediting Board (NAAB) for B.Arch. and M.Arch., and California Commission on Teacher Credentialing (CTC).

Location

The city of San Francisco is one of the great cultural centers of the world; a melting pot of diversity, culture, and creativity that has spawned major museums and galleries, world-class opera and theaters, dance companies, film production and recording studios, technological innovation, performing artists ranging from classical to popular music, and numerous other cultural opportunities. The city's status as a tourist mecca located on the Pacific Rim ensures that one encounters people from all corners of the world.

The climate is moderate and offers kaleidoscopic blends of sunshine and fog most of the year. The Northpoint campus is located at the historic Cannery building near world-famous Pier 39, where students can view Alcatraz Island from their classroom windows. In addition, four campus buildings are located two blocks from historic Union Square, in the commercial heart of the city, and three others are located near the Financial District. Shop 657, a store in Union Square, opened in December 2014 to display AAU designs and provide merchandising students real-world experience.

The city offers myriad locations for field trips and studio visits. World-renowned artists display their creations in the Academy's five nonprofit art galleries, which are open to the public. The Academy is an urban institution that both draws upon and contributes to the cultural wealth of the community in which it resides.

Majors and Degrees

Academy of Art University offers A.A., B.A., B.F.A., B.S., B.Arch., M.A., M.F.A., and M.Arch. degrees and an Art Teaching Credential. Programs are available online and in San Francisco in the following: acting* (speech, improv, physical acting), advertising (creative strategy, art direction, copywriting, television commercials), animation & visual effects (background painting/layout design, character development, storyboard art, 3-D modeling, VFX/compositing), architecture (structures, materials and methods of construction, design process, structural and environmental systems), art education (learning to teach in museums, developmental psychology, teaching art in the community), art history (Renaissance art, American art history, ancient art history, looking at art, philosophy), art teaching credential (learning to teach both children and adults), communications & media technologies (journalism, editing, short-form documentary), costume design (design research, production bible, costume consistency, hair and makeup), fashion (design, knitwear, merchandising, textiles), fashion journalism (fashion writing, editorials for magazines, newspaper writing, fashion news, social media), fashion marketing (market research, analysis of business trends, digital and social media trends, effective branding, written communication), fashion merchandising (fashion business analysis, product selection, effective business plan), fashion product development (identify materials, manufacturing process, understanding of brand, consumer, and price point, technical drawings, knowledge of computer software), fashion styling (advanced skills for styling fashion products, photography, composition, lighting, hair styling, make-up artistry, art direction, production management), fashion textile design (design research, sketchbook, concept selection, original design production, trial and self-edit designs), fashion visual merchandising, research and concept development, visual presentation, creative merchandising concepts, verbal and written presentation), fine art (painting, printmaking, sculpture), game development (game engines, prototyping, level design, game art, 3-D modeling), game programming (engineering and programming techniques, math and object-oriented programming, complex algorithms, writing code), graphic design (corporate and brand identity, package design, print and collateral), illustration (children's books, editorial, comic books), industrial design (furniture design, product design, toy design, transportation design), interior architecture & design (commercial and residential design, furniture design), jewelry & metal arts (fashion jewelry design, enameling, stone setting, casting, welded and fabricated sculpture), landscape architecture (plant design, elements in landscape, grading and drainage, urban open spaces), motion pictures & television (cinematography, directing, editing, producing, production design, screenwriting), music production & sound design for visual media (harmony, arranging, orchestration, music production techniques, scoring for film), photography (architecture, advertising, digital documentary, editorial, fashion, fine art, landscape, photojournalism, portraiture), studio production for advertising & design, visual development (concept art for animation, film, and games; digital painting; character design; cinematic storytelling; Marquette sculpting; environment creation), web design & new media (user experience design, interactive design, new media, web design), and writing for film, television, & digital media. * Acting degree program is currently not available online.

Academic Programs

The Bachelor of Fine Arts degree requires foundations courses, major courses, art electives, and liberal arts courses. Fundamental courses are related specifically to students' majors to prepare them to begin intense focus courses in their field by the sophomore year. All major courses of study are structured so the student builds upon skills learned the previous semester and advances to the next level of technical or creative proficiency. Some related major courses may be taken concurrently.

Liberal arts courses teach practical applications for forging a professional career in art and design. International students who come from countries where English is not the primary language may take additional EAP (English for Art Purposes) classes, as determined by English language proficiency testing. Students are advised to meet with departmental directors at least once during the academic year to have their progress assessed. Portfolios are reviewed before the junior year to determine whether or not a student has progressed sufficiently to continue study at the Academy.

Academic Facilities

Academy of Art University's industry-standard facilities offer students the tools they need to prepare for professional careers in art and design. The Academy invests in top-notch equipment to ensure it remains on the cutting edge of technology. Learning on industry-standard equipment, students gain hands-on experience.

Academy of Art University students have access to an array of digital tools. The School of Game Development and the School of Animation & Visual Effects provide the latest equipment, as well as a video and Cintiq lab, green screen studio, and sound booth. The School of Web Design & New Media houses a usability lab with the most current software, while the School of Music Production & Sound Design for Visual Media offers the latest sound design and video editing tools and is proud to have a new flagship mixing console, the Avid S6. The Academy is the first university in California to offer this new console and the second organization in California other than Skywalker Sound to own the console.

The School of Advertising is designed to look, feel, and function like an ad agency. Located in the heart of San Francisco's Financial District, the School of Graphic Design has the latest industry tools that enable students to have a seamless transition into the world of work following graduation. And the School of Illustration is housed in a unique historic building in San Francisco's Union Square District. The original libraries, meeting rooms, theater, and a ballroom have been transformed into drawing/painting studios and classrooms.

Undergraduate and graduate students in Architecture, Interior Architecture & Design, and Landscape Architecture share an 800-square-foot materials library and plotting room, as well as a model shop. The School of Industrial Design offers multiple shop facilities and a 3-D computer lab. The School of Landscape Architecture benefits from being located in San Francisco, the hub of urban landscape design.

Fashion students have access to studio facilities for women's, men's and children's wear, as well as textile design, knitwear design, and fashion merchandising and marketing. Surrounded by world-renowned museums and galleries, the School of Fine Art and the School of Art History facilities include thousands of square feet of studio space with everything their students need to bring their individual visions to life.

The School of Motion Pictures & Television and the School of Acting facilities include a postproduction area, green screen studio, screenwriting lab, and several soundstage studios. Students of the School of Communications & Media Technologies have access to a cutting-edge radio studio and television studio, complete with robotic cameras, anchor desks and interview sets, teleprompters, and green screens. School of Photography facilities are equipped with both traditional and digital photographic technology.

The library provides advanced digital tools, making it possible for students to access extensive art and design image resources and information on demand. The Academy Resource Center offers all students free learning support services including study hall tutoring, academic coaching, English as second language support programs, a writing lab, and a multimedia language lab.

Costs

As of Fall 2016, undergraduate tuition is $873 per credit unit. Full-time students must carry at least 12 semester units per term. There is a nonrefundable $50 fee when applying. Lab fees run from $25 to $400 per semester, depending on the class. Tuition and fees are subject to change at any time. Art supplies can run from $250 to $1,500 per semester, depending on the major. The Academy has most of the expensive technical equipment available for students to borrow or use in a lab.

Academy of Art University operates many residence halls within the city. Several housing options are offered, and costs vary based on the building and room/unit assigned. For further information, students may contact the Department of Housing & Residence Life directly at 415-618-6335 or by e-mail at housing@academyart.edu.

Financial Aid

The Academy offers financial aid packages consisting of grants, loans, and work-study to eligible students with a demonstrated need. Low-interest loans are available to all eligible students, regardless of need. As financial aid programs, procedures, and eligibility requirements change frequently, applicants should contact the Financial Aid Office at financialaid@academyart.edu or 800-544-2787 (toll-free, U.S. only).

Faculty

The Academy averages 1,404 instructors in Fall/Spring semester, most of whom are full-time art and design professionals and part-time teachers. The student-teacher ratio for undergraduate classes averages 14:1.

Student Government

Although there is no formal student government, each department has between two and three student representatives who meet with the President as needed throughout the semester to discuss any student issues.

Admission Requirements

Applicants for the A.A., B.A., B.F.A., B.S., and B.Arch. programs must have a high school diploma or equivalent. There is no portfolio requirement. M.A., M.F.A., and M.Arch. Applicants must have a bachelor's degree and submit a portfolio and statement of intent. International students take written and speech tests to determine which EAP (English for Art Purposes) classes may have to be completed. Most EAP classes can be taken in conjunction with art and design classes. All foundations classes offer specialized EAP sections with instructors trained for language assistance. The application fee is $50 for undergraduates. A $1,000 tuition deposit applies to international applicants.

What Sets Academy of Art University Apart

The Academy is one of the few art and design schools that believes in nurturing the whole artist; this includes developing athletic ability along with artistic talent. Students can participate in intercollegiate, intramural, and club sports. With Pacific West honors and national championships, the Academy offers basketball, baseball, softball, cross country, track & field, soccer, golf, volleyball, and tennis for its students to partake in. Furthermore, the Academy is proud to be the only art school in the NCAA Division II. Students have gone on to compete in the Olympics and have been drafted by professional leagues to play their sport professionally.

Application and Information

Students may apply to enter the Academy at the beginning of the Spring, Fall, or Summer semesters. Information in this profile is subject to change. Students should contact Academy of Art University for current information or visit www.academyart.edu to learn about total costs, median student loan debt, potential occupations, and other information.

Academy of Art University
79 New Montgomery Street
San Francisco, California 94105
Phone: 415-274-2200
800-544-2787 (U.S. only)
Fax: 415-618-6287
E-mail: info@academyart.edu
Website: www.academyart.edu
https://www.facebook.com/AcademyofArtUniversity
https://twitter.com/academy_of_art
https://plus.google.com/+academyofartuniversity/posts
http://www.pinterest.com/academyofartuni
http://academyofartu.tumblr.com
http://instagram.com/academy_of_art
http://www.youtube.com/user/academyofartu
http://weheartit.com/AcademyofArtU

Academy of Art University's downtown campus.

COLLEGE CLOSE-UPS

ALLEGHENY COLLEGE

MEADVILLE, PENNSYLVANIA

★ To read more about this school, visit http://petersons.to/

The College

One of Loren Pope's forty "Colleges That Change Lives," Allegheny is cited as the premiere college in the country for students with "unusual combinations" of interests and talents. On its historic campus—where the liberal arts and sciences have been taught for almost 200 years—students develop combinations of majors and minors in areas that may, at first glance, seem unrelated: biology and economics, political science and music, history and psychology. Allegheny students share an abiding passion for learning and life, a spirit of camaraderie, and a respect for shared inquiry that spans all areas of study. Neuroscience majors play in the Civic Symphony and build houses during Alternative Spring Break. Students prepare for law school while playing basketball and interning in Washington, D.C. Computer science majors present work in philosophy at national conferences.

Building on a combination of academic disciplines and passions, every student completes the comprehensive Senior Project under the guidance of a faculty adviser in his or her major field. The project demonstrates the skills most prized by employers and graduate schools: the ability to complete a major assignment, work independently, analyze and synthesize information, and to write and speak persuasively.

Allegheny students are encouraged to explore all of their interests and to look at academic disciplines from multiple perspectives, which leads them to extraordinary outcomes. Biochemistry majors use the skills they learned in communication arts to start marketing careers with the Environmental Protection Agency. English majors collaborate with the College's pre-health advisers and enjoy acceptance rates to medical school between 80 and 100 percent—twice the national average. And over 95 percent of Allegheny's job-seeking graduates find employment within six months.

Leaders in business, government, medicine, education, and community service frequently declare that the future belongs to individuals who are innovators, inventors, and big-picture thinkers, those who think both analytically and creatively. It is this preparation for the global marketplace, and for life, that Allegheny, with its emphasis on "unusual combinations," is nationally known for providing.

Location

Central campus looks like a traditional college with a rich liberal arts heritage and tradition, with its 79 acres of rolling lawns and brick walkways, historic buildings, and century-old oaks and elms. A 203-acre recreational complex and a 283-acre nature reserve complement state-of-the-art classrooms, labs, theaters, studios and other facilities.

The campus overlooks the town of Meadville, a county seat that features a courthouse, hospital, a variety of industries, and more. Allegheny students connect with the community in many ways, from running after-school programs to taking in the latest movies, from creating art installations to checking out live music.

Allegheny students live in a section of the country that most people get to see only on vacation. Northwest Pennsylvania is a nature-lover's paradise of verdant, undisturbed forests and streams and lakes that are gems of biodiversity. It's no wonder that the College has one of the oldest Outing Clubs in the country.

Allegheny is ideally situated within 2 hours of the social and transportation hubs of Pittsburgh, Cleveland, and Buffalo. Being just close enough to major cities allows for frequent excursions to major sporting events, concerts, and other attractions.

Majors and Degrees

Allegheny students can earn the Bachelor of Arts (B.A.) or the Bachelor of Science (B.S.) degree in the following programs of study: applied computing; Arabic; art and technology; art and the environment; art (studio); art history; Asian studies; astronomy; biochemistry; biology; black studies; business economics; chemistry; Chinese studies; classical studies; communication arts; community and justice studies; computer science; creative writing; dance and movement studies; economics; education studies; English; environmental geology; environmental science; environmental studies; environmental writing; French; French studies; geology; German; German studies; global health studies; history; international studies; Jewish studies, journalism in the public interest; Latin; Latin American and Caribbean studies; mass communication/media studies; mathematics; medieval and Renaissance studies; Middle East and North African studies; music; music history; music performance; music theory; neuroscience; philosophy; physics; political science; pre-dental; pre-law; pre-medicine; pre-nursing; pre-pharmacy; pre-veterinary studies; psychology; religious studies; Spanish; theatre; women's, gender, and sexuality studies; writing; and self-designed majors.

Students may also take advantage of accelerated master's and doctoral degree programs, teacher certification programs, and engineering cooperative programs with other top institutions.

Academic Programs

Allegheny College believes so strongly in unusual combinations that they are built right into its curriculum; it is one of the few liberal arts colleges nationally that requires students to choose a minor as well as a major. In some ways, this may make school more difficult. But most students at Allegheny are individuals for whom the most difficult thing would be to give up some vital part of themselves. Some Allegheny students have majors and minors that complement each other in predictable ways—an international studies major with a minor in French, for example. But there are other students whose majors and minors represent very different aspects of themselves—an environmental studies major with a minor in creative writing or a chemistry major with a minor in history. Coupled with experiential learning and the distinctive Senior Project, seeing academic disciplines from multiple perspectives leads to extraordinary outcomes.

During the first two years, every Allegheny student participates in seminars that focus on written and oral communication as well as academic and career advising, and the faculty instructor serves as adviser for both years. This progressive course sequence, in addition to the Junior Seminar and Senior Project, helps students create a four-year experience to match all of their needs and goals.

Under the guidance of a faculty adviser in his or her major field, every student completes the Senior Project, a significant piece of original scholarly work with a creative, analytical, or experimental focus. The project mirrors a master's thesis and requires project management skills, independent work, writing and presentation skills, and the ability to analyze and synthesize information. Allegheny has required a senior capstone experience since the college's first commencement ceremony in 1821. The Council on Undergraduate Research recognized Allegheny as the top baccalaureate college in the nation for providing high-quality research experiences to undergraduates.

In the National Survey of Student Engagement, responses by college freshmen placed Allegheny within the top 10 percent in the United States for both a supportive campus environment and level of academic challenge.

Off-Campus Programs

Allegheny College recognizes the enormous academic, professional, and personal value of studying off-campus, nationally or internationally. Allegheny students can experience multiple off-campus adventures, learning with an eclectic group of students with diverse academic majors and interests. The Gateway facilitates a variety of opportunities through study abroad, career services, community service, and more.

The College sponsors semester and year-long study-away programs, some of which require skills in languages other than English, and others with no language requirements. More than 190 Allegheny students and faculty participate in forty Allegheny-sponsored study abroad programs in twenty countries.

In addition, faculty members lead students each year on intensive three-week experiential learning seminars. These for-credit, faculty-designed programs occur at the end of each spring semester. Recent excursions took students to Denmark and Germany, Greece, Italy, Turkey, and South Africa.

The Office of Career Education maintains a database of 2,500 internship and shadowing opportunities, including especially popular ones in Boston, New York City, Los Angeles, and Washington, D.C. Students at Allegheny can choose among several kinds of internships, including academic internships taken for credit that often take place during a spring or fall semester and noncredit internships throughout the summer.

Academic Facilities

Allegheny boasts the nationally acclaimed Steffee Hall of Life Sciences, which incorporates state-of-the-art labs located right next to classrooms and faculty offices. A new environmental science center features the best in sustainable practices with a living wall, aquaponics equipment, and solar panels. Students also benefit from the GIS learning lab, planetarium, and seismographic network station.

The multimillion-dollar Vukovich Center for Communication Arts, which meets LEED certification standards and has a rooftop garden, features a learning theater, scene and costume shops, and video production facilities. Language students enjoy a multimedia learning lab, and dancers work in bright, functional studio and performance spaces. The Bowman, Penelec, and Megahan art galleries display student and faculty work as well as visiting exhibits.

Allegheny's Learning Commons provides academic support to all students through professional guidance, peer mentors, training, and effective learning tools. The center is housed in Pelletier Library, which offers more than 900,000 volumes, as well as extensive digital resources, research tools, and unique meeting spaces.

Costs

For 2017–18, tuition and fees are $45,970. Room and board is $11,650.

Financial Aid

Through the generous support of its alumni, Allegheny is able to provide over $43 million in achievement-based scholarships; need-based grant assistance; and aid awarded to students from federal, state, and private sources. Allegheny's financial assistance allows many students the opportunity to make a college choice based on value and fit, rather than financial constraints.

Allegheny's Trustee Scholarships are awarded without regard to financial need to students who have balanced academic excellence with other distinctive activities while in high school. Awards range up to $112,000, distributed equally over four years of study at Allegheny (up to $28,000 per year), and renew automatically.

Faculty

Whether it's conducting research, teaching a First-Year Seminar, leading a three-week study tour, co-authoring an article or making an authentic French dinner, faculty work and learn alongside students every day. There's no graduate school buffer between undergraduates and faculty. Students don't have to wait behind graduate students for research positions on faculty-led projects or compete against hundreds of other students for the lead roles in plays or an editorship at the literary magazine.

Of the 173 full-time faculty members, 91 percent have earned the highest degree in their fields. The student to faculty ratio is 11:1, and introductory classes have an average of 19 students. Advanced classes have an average of 12 students, and some seminars have fewer than 10. Of all classes, 88 percent have fewer than 30 students.

Every student has a faculty adviser for the first two years and a faculty adviser in his/her major field for the final two years. Culminating with their work guiding students through the Senior Project, faculty members are not only supportive and engaging teachers but true leaders and mentors.

Student Government

The Allegheny Student Government is the official voice and administrative unit of the student body. This extremely active and influential organization concerns itself with the quality of the educational, cultural, and social aspects of the Allegheny community. Its members organize and coordinate programs of a cocurricular and extracurricular nature and sponsor more than 120 student-run clubs and organizations.

Students serve on every major college committee, including faculty searches, sustainability efforts, and strategic planning. Their presence exemplifies the importance placed on student participation and represents the influence students have on the institution.

Admission Requirements

From the time a prospective student first contacts Allegheny, the college's holistic approach is directed to addressing his or her unique character, needs, and aspirations. During the application process, primary attention is focused on those criteria that indicate academic promise, including difficulty of high school classes, GPA, and class rank. Careful consideration is also given to those personal qualities that are important in the total success of the college experience: school and community activities, recommendation letters, and the personal essay. Students are encouraged to share additional information through the college's application supplement and an interview and visit. Allegheny embraces the concept that standardized test scores do not exclusively reflect a student's full range of abilities or potential to succeed in college. As a result, Allegheny is now test optional. ACT and SAT I scores are optional for U.S. citizens and permanent residents.

The result is a highly personalized approach to the selection of students that remains consistent with the aims of the college, respects the individuality of each applicant, and ensures equal consideration of every candidate. The College encourages diversity and actively seeks students from all ethnic, religious, racial, political, geographic, and socioeconomic backgrounds.

Application and Information

Office of Admissions
Allegheny College
520 North Main Street
Meadville, Pennsylvania 16335
Phone: 814-332-4351
800-521-5293 (toll-free)
Fax: 814-337-0431
E-mail: admissions@allegheny.edu
Web site: http://www.allegheny.edu/unusualcombinations
http://www.allegheny.edu/distinctions
http://www.allegheny.edu/visit
http://www.allegheny.edu/apply

Recognized among Loren Pope's 40 *"Colleges That Change Lives,"* Allegheny College is one of the nation's most historic and innovative institutions of higher education. Allegheny is one of the only colleges in the country that requires students to choose both a major and minor, ensuring they develop the skills needed to be analytical and creative.

AMRIDGE UNIVERSITY
MONTGOMERY, ALABAMA

AMRIDGE
UNIVERSITY

COLLEGE CLOSE-UPS

The University

Founded in 1967, Amridge University has been a long-time leader in online education. Distance learning is the primary instructional delivery system for all its programs. Amridge's focus is on supporting students from their first point of inquiry all the way through completion of their academic degree program. Its goal is to help students obtain their degree through a variety of student support services and rigorous academic support.

Amridge University is accredited by the Southern Association of Colleges and Schools Commission on Colleges (SACS-COC), sacscoc.org, to award bachelor's, master's, and doctoral degree programs in business, counseling, Biblical studies, and many more. Amridge is one of the most affordable private universities in the United States. It offers scholarships and incentive discounts for military students, first-time freshmen, sister institution staff, ministers, and corporate alliances.

With over forty-five years in higher education, Amridge University has taught in the online education arena since 1993. Through the vision of the leadership of the institution, Amridge was chosen as one of the first fifteen participants in the nation selected by the U.S. Department of Education to pilot distance education on a broad level, resulting in a change to the federal law to allow more students access to distance education.

Location

Amridge University is located in Montgomery, Alabama, the capital city of the state. The University is strategically located in the central part of the state between Huntsville, and Mobile. The city is clean and modern, with beautiful residential areas, parks, and playgrounds, and fine schools and universities. Students and families can also enjoy its museums, zoo, and facilities of the capitol building. Montgomery has two major U.S. Air Force installations: Maxwell Air Force Base and Gunter Annex. Maxwell is where the Air War College is located and is a strategic center for education. The metropolitan area has a population of more than 350,000 citizens. There are many churches and educational institutions. The city has an abundance of good housing in addition to other advantages. The Montgomery Regional Airport is located six miles southwest of the capital city of Montgomery.

Majors and Degrees

Undergraduate degrees are awarded in Biblical studies, business administration, human development, human resource management, management, and criminal justice. These degrees promote biblical and Christian ministry skills, human development skills, knowledge in the arts, and management communication skills.

Amridge University students are fully matriculated students of Amridge University with full student privileges, rights, and responsibilities. A student must fulfill the required semester hours in a program as well as the basic requirements of the core curriculum. All core and general education requirements can be received from the University. Amridge University is a participating member of GoArmyEd and is Military Friendly Higher Education Institution.

Academic Programs

Amridge University operates on a 15-week semester basis and uses an academic calendar to articulate important guidelines for students during the academic year. The fall semester runs from September to December, during which a 10-week and 8-week selection of courses is offered; the spring semester runs from January to April, including a 10-week and 8-week selection of courses; and the summer semester runs from April to August, including a 10-week and 8-week selection of courses. Distance learning is the primary instructional delivery system for all degree programs offered at Amridge and the University focuses on supporting students in the online learning format.

Canvas LMS™ and RingCentral™: Amridge University uses Canvas for the delivery of all course materials and videos. The Canvas portal is monitored locally by the Network Operations Center of Amridge University and is available 24/7 for student access. Amridge University uses RingCentral as a course conferencing system and delivery technology for live-stream classes. This includes live-streamed seminars, live-streamed weekly classes, and live classes recorded as archives for later viewing. With RingCentral, a webcam, and a headset with microphone, students can see and hear their instructor, give class presentations, and engage in live discussions with classmates and instructors. Students can chat with classmates, raise their hand (virtually) to ask a question, and receive files from their instructor or classmates. RingCentral is accessible within each Canvas course. Setup and configuration support is provided by Amridge University technical support.

Amridge uses all.amridgeuniversity.edu, a mass communication system that allows the University to send messages, emergency alerts, and quick notifications. Students are added into the system on a semester basis. Because Amridge Connect is an alert system, students are not able to opt out.

Amridge Connect iPad Program: Amridge is committed to providing students with learning tools that give them access to course work and assignments from any location. As part of its commitment to embrace twenty-first century technology for education, the University has adopted the iPad as a technological tool for teaching and learning. During the course registration process, all students are given the opportunity to purchase a University-issued iPad to use as a resource for accessing courses when they are not seated in front of a desktop computer. Distance learners require a mobile and flexible style of learning and an iPad can be a valuable resource.

The policy of Amridge University is to provide reasonable accommodation for persons who are handicapped or disabled as designated in Section 504 of the Rehabilitation Act of 1973 and the Americans with Disabilities Act of 1990. Although the Morgan W. Brown building is not equipped with an elevator, the needs of the physically challenged can be met from the first floor. These include registration, counseling, library facilities, classroom facilities, restrooms, breakroom facilities, and others. Ample parking is provided.

Academic Facilities

Amridge University sits on a stately 9-acre campus adjoining Interstate 85. A beautiful building houses the administration offices, classrooms, and Library Resource Center.

Costs

Undergraduate tuition per semester hour is $375. First-time full-time students receive a reduced rate of $250 per semester hour. These rates are guaranteed through the student's degree program, as long as students maintain continuous full-time enrollment and are in good academic standing.

Financial Aid

More than 90 percent of all Amridge students receive financial aid in the form of grants, such as the Federal Pell Grant; scholarships from Amridge; and other sources. The amount of aid given is determined by the college's analysis of the Free Application for Federal Student Aid (FAFSA). All financial aid forms must be received by the Financial Aid department before a student can finalize enrollment.

Faculty

The instructional faculty members total approximately 100. Approximately 65 percent of the full-time faculty members hold doctoral degrees, 100 percent hold master's degrees, and 100 percent hold terminal degrees. Faculty members specialize in their areas and have exceptional training in distance learning delivery.

Student Government

Student volunteers serve as members of the Student Advisory Committee. Volunteers are appointed by the Student Services Team, with recommendations from the deans. The committee meets on a regular basis and is reorganized on an annual basis. Concerns, recommendations, and requests are presented directly from the committee to the appropriate University area.

Admission Requirements

Amridge University is open to all academically qualified persons. The University has developed a streamlined admissions process to help prospective students complete the process expeditiously so they can begin their studies. Students are strongly encouraged to work closely with University staff members to complete all steps to attain official (non-provisional) admission status for their respective degree program. Upon acceptance to the University, each student is assigned an academic adviser whose primary responsibility is to oversee the academic progress of each student and motivate them to succeed both inside and outside the classroom.

Application and Information

For further information, students may contact:
Admissions
Amridge University
1200 Taylor Road
Montgomery, Alabama 36117
Phone: 888-790-8080 (toll-free)
Fax: 334-387-3878
E-mail: cc@amridgeuniversity.edu
Website: http://www.amridgeuniversity.edu

Amridge University has been a leader in distance learning since 1993.

ANDERSON UNIVERSITY

ANDERSON, INDIANA

★ For more information, visit http://petersons.to/andersonu

The University

Anderson University integrates its Christian roots with academic excellence.

Students at Anderson University (AU) are encouraged to live out the values of responsibility, integrity, excellence, generosity, and servant leadership. At the same time, AU offers a rigorous academic program with more than 50 majors that has consistently placed the institution among America's top colleges by U.S. News & World Report, Colleges of Distinction, the Princeton Review, and Forbes.

Anderson University was founded in 1917 by the Church of God (Anderson, Indiana) movement with the purpose of training men and women to serve in ministry around the world. In 1950, AU opened its first graduate school—The School of Theology. Now marking its centennial year, Anderson University continues to train men and women for ministry but has also become known for its many other offerings, such as its undergraduate and graduate programs in the Falls School of Business; its highly competitive nursing and athletic training programs; and its popular social services majors, such as psychology, social work, and criminal justice.

Location

Anderson University is located 30 minutes northeast of Indianapolis, a short drive from the capital city of Indiana. Students are minutes away from professional sports arenas, cultural opportunities, and the Indianapolis International Airport. Being so close to Indianapolis means students benefit from internships, mentorships, and practicums.

Majors and Degrees

Anderson University offers the following bachelor's degrees:

Bachelor of Arts (B.A.): Majors in accounting, athletic training, Bible and religion, biochemistry, biology, chemistry, Christian ministries, cinema and media arts, computer science, criminal justice, dance business, dance performance, English, exercise science, family science, finance, general studies, global business, history, information security, international relations, management, marketing, mathematics, mathematics–decision making, mathematics–economics, mathematics–finance, music, music business, national security, physical science, political science, political science/philosophy/economics, psychology, public relations, social work, songwriting, Spanish, sport and recreational leadership, sport marketing, visual communication design, worship arts, and youth ministries.

Bachelor of Music (B.M.): Major in musical theatre.

Bachelor of Science (B.S.): Majors in computer science, computer engineering, electrical engineering, mechanical engineering, and physics.

Anderson also offers a Bachelor of Science in Nursing (B.S.N.) degree and an Associate of Arts in Criminal Justice program.

Academic Programs

As a Church of God academic institution, Anderson University is committed to the goals and ideals of liberal education as understood through a Christian faith perspective. The requirements for undergraduate degrees have been established with these commitments in mind. Anderson University's conception of liberally educated people involves the freeing and empowering of the total person—spiritually, intellectually, aesthetically, emotionally, and physically. The core liberal arts requirements range from 40–43 hours.

The academic year is broken down into two semesters and three 4-week and one 3-week summer sessions.

Anderson University is one of the few Christian colleges with an engineering program, with majors in mechanical, electrical, and computer engineering. Anderson University also owns its own solar race car, which students are preparing for its first competition in 2018.

Anderson University also offers degrees in national security studies and information security. These programs bring nationally recognized speakers (such as Robert Mueller, former director of the FBI) to campus to interact with students, as well as off-campus opportunities to work with the latest technology in the areas of national and information security.

Off-Campus Programs

Students at AU are serious about becoming the hands and feet of God. Through Campus Ministries, they reach out to the Anderson community by working with the homeless, becoming mentors to troubled teens, taking on work projects at local women's shelters, winterizing homes with the Madison County United Way, and visiting the elderly in nursing homes.

The university's Tri-S program allows students to travel the world on medical, work, cultural, and ministry teams. Students have traveled to India to work with Mother Teresa's home for the destitute and dying, to Hungary and Romania to work in orphanages, to Africa to work alongside Church of God missionaries, to Grand Cayman to teach Vacation Bible School, and to South America to improve facilities and worship with local communities. During the 50 years of the Tri-S program's existence, more than 21,000 students have traveled abroad, reaching 102 countries.

Students also have opportunities to study abroad during a semester, including student teaching overseas. Within the United States, students may also spend a semester of study at the Chicago Center, where they can focus on urban issues.

Academic Facilities

Anderson University's facilities include an engineering center, a newly constructed performance hall, dedicated dance studios, a renovated science building, a broadcasting center, a wellness center, an observatory, and an academic library housing the York Children's Literature Collection and the Gaither Hymnal Collection.

The Kardatzke Wellness Center, a 132,000-square-foot facility, houses programming for health, recreation, and wellness in all forms—spiritual, emotional, physical, and social. The Wellness Center is ADA accessible and connects the existing O. C. Lewis Gymnasium and Bennett Natatorium. The Wellness Center features a weight room, fitness area, and two indoor walking/running tracks open to all students. Students are also welcome to use any of the multiple basketball courts in the fieldhouse. The facility is the largest building project in the university's 100-year history and includes approximately $600,000 of instructional athletic equipment addressing various areas of fitness and development. The facility also houses the university's sports medicine center and a human performance center.

The newest building project on the university's campus is the York Performance Hall. The state-of-the-art 24,000 square-foot facility, with a cost of $5.5 million, adjoins the existing music wing of the Krannert Fine Arts building, bringing together classrooms, rehearsal rooms, and the new performance venue. The performance hall is designed to be a flexible performance space for ensembles, solo student performances, and visiting artists. The facility also houses the university's Warner Sallman collection. A selection of his paintings are continuously on display on the second floor of the building.

Genesys, a global leader of cloud services for customer engagement, communications, and collaboration, has opened a technology training center in partnership with Anderson University on the university's campus. It was launched to provide hands-on training for paid Interactive Intelligence interns enrolled in Anderson University's School of Science and Engineering. The program is ideal for students pursuing careers in computer science, information systems, or software engineering, with a specific interest in software testing.

Costs

For the 2017–18 academic year, full time tuition is $29,210 per year. Fees are $500 per year. Room costs are $6,120 and food service is $3,620 per year.

Books are estimated at $1,200 per year. Estimates for travel and personal expenses total $2,800 per year. Some expenses may vary.

Financial Aid

Anderson University is committed to promoting college affordability. More than 98 percent of students receive additional financial aid. Student Financial Services strives to make it financially possible for admitted students to enroll and for enrolled students to graduate.

On top of federal student aid (if eligible), students at AU benefit from scholarships. Some scholarships are based on need and others are based on academic performance. Among the scholarships offered is the Matching Church Scholarship. This fund matches a scholarship given to a student by his or her church up to $750 a semester. A list of scholarships offered at AU is available at anderson.edu/scholarships.

AU also works with the Federal Work Study program to offer job opportunities to students on campus.

Faculty

During the 2016–17 academic year, Anderson University had 118 full-time faculty and 16 part-time faculty members. The student-to-professor ratio is 12:1, with an average class size of 19 students. Eighty-three percent of the university's tenure/tenure-track faculty hold doctorates or other terminal degrees. No classes at Anderson University are taught by graduate assistants.

Student Life

AU promotes a community centered on student life, presenting opportunities with student government, theatre and music, athletics, and a variety of interest clubs.

The Campus Activities Board sponsors a robust intramural program, offering 15 different sports during the course of the academic year. The university's athletic department also offers 14 different intercollegiate sports competing in the Heartland Collegiate Athletic Conference (NCAA Div. III).

Students can also participate in social/service clubs and interest clubs, including sports-related interest clubs. The Anderson University Student Government Association serves as the governing body for interest clubs not associated with an institutional department or major. Interest clubs generally exist at the initiative of students.

Social and service clubs exist to enhance the quality of the social and spiritual life of the AU community by providing opportunities for involvement in service, social, and spiritual activities for students.

The Student Government Association (SGA) promotes student development spiritually, intellectually, socially, and physically. Its purpose is to help maintain intellectual honesty and academic freedom and to assure responsibility for furthering an effective, balanced, and healthy campus environment.

Anderson University academic departments also sponsor active honor societies. Admittance is based on academic achievement. The university also has a thriving Honors Program.

Admission Requirements

Prospective students can apply online at https://www.anderson.edu/apply. In order to be considered for admission, the prospective student will need to have high school transcripts, transcripts from other colleges attended (if applicable), and ACT or SAT scores to the Anderson University Office of Admissions. The Office of Admissions does not require an application fee and has a rolling application policy with no set application deadline.

For more information, prospective students may contact:
Anderson University
Office of Admissions
1100 East Fifth Street
Anderson, Indiana 46012
Phone: 800-428-6414 (toll-free)
765-641-4080
Fax: 765-641-4091
E-mail: info@anderson.edu
Website: https://www.anderson.edu/

ANNA MARIA COLLEGE

PAXTON, MASSACHUSETTS

★ To read more about this school, visit http://petersons.to/annamariacollege

The College

Anna Maria College is a private, four-year, Catholic coeducational institution that was founded in 1946 by the Sisters of Saint Anne in Marlboro, Massachusetts. In 1952, AMC moved to its current 192-acre campus in Paxton, Massachusetts. Originally a women's college, AMC has been coeducational since 1973. The College has grown significantly over the last seventy years. Currently, a total of 1,500 students are enrolled, of whom approximately 1,000 are undergraduates.

Anna Maria College is a close-knit community of teachers and learners. Small class sizes allow for mentor relationships to develop between faculty members and students. Freshman and sophomore classes generally have between 15 and 20 students; some upper-level classes have as few as 10 students. Faculty members teach and advise students, recognizing the unique skills, abilities, and identity of each person as an individual. Students are supported when necessary and challenged at all times. Classes are never taught by graduate assistants.

In recent years the College has undergone significant change. Offerings have been enhanced, general education requirements have been revised, and extracurricular and athletic opportunities have grown, to ensure that students have access to the programs and services that will help develop their mind, body, and spirit. All majors are now organized under a school structure with six different schools: Business, Education, Fire and Health Sciences, Humanities, Justice and Social Sciences, and Visual and Performing Arts. An honors program with a unique international experience has become extremely popular. The recent addition of new programs in forensic criminology, health and community services, emergency management, and marketing communications has added greatly to the wide range of professional offerings available to students.

As part of the master plan, AMC has already enhanced and revitalized the campus with an all-purpose athletic field and stadium; three new residence halls, one of which offers suite-style housing; a fitness center; and a high-tech learning setting known as the Information Commons, which features computer stations and study areas for students. The College has also established the Student Success Center that brings tutoring, counseling, and support services together under one roof.

Anna Maria College is accredited by the New England Association of Schools and Colleges, the Council on Social Work Education, the American Music Therapy Association, and the Accreditation Commission for Education in Nursing, Inc. AMC is approved by the Board of Registration in Nursing in Massachusetts and the Massachusetts Department of Education.

Approximately 70 percent of Anna Maria College's undergraduates reside in on-campus residence halls. Students enjoy a full social life both on campus and within the college-city atmosphere of nearby Worcester, Massachusetts.

Anna Maria College's NCAA Division III athletic programs offer intercollegiate competition for men (baseball, basketball, cross-country, football, lacrosse, and soccer,) and women (basketball, cross-country, field hockey, soccer, softball, tennis, and volleyball). Intramural and recreational offerings are also available to students who do not wish to participate on competitive sports teams.

Anna Maria College provides a wireless campus, with more than 500 computers linking classrooms, offices, the Student Success Center, labs, the Information Commons, and all residence hall rooms. In addition to College-owned computers, students have the opportunity to access the College network to gain access to the Internet from any location on campus via the College's wireless network and their own computers.

Location

Anna Maria College is located on a 192-acre campus in Paxton, Massachusetts, 8 miles from Worcester's vibrant downtown. The city offers numerous professional, cultural, and entertainment opportunities, and Boston, Providence, and Hartford are only an hour away.

Local attractions include big-name entertainment and minor league sports teams at the DCU Center; art, history, and science museums; classical and contemporary music performances and theatrical performances at the Hanover Theater and Mechanics Hall; and day and night skiing at Wachusett Mountain.

Majors and Degrees

Anna Maria College offers a four-year curriculum of undergraduate instruction leading to bachelor's degrees in the following areas: art; art therapy; business administration; Catholic studies; criminal justice; early childhood education; elementary education; emergency management, English; fire science; forensic criminology; graphic design; health and community services; health science; history; human development/human services; law and society; liberal studies; music; music education; music therapy; nursing; paramedic science; psychology; social work; sport management; and studio art.

Art and music therapy, business, criminal justice, fire science, education, nursing, social work, and sport management are the most popular majors. The Fifth Year Option allows undergraduate students in good academic standing a unique opportunity to earn both their undergraduate and graduate degrees in five years. Fifth-year master's options are available in business administration, counseling psychology, criminal justice, education, social work, and fire science.

Academic Programs

When the Sisters of Saint Anne founded Anna Maria College in 1946, their mission was to increase access to high-quality education, educational innovation, and respect for service to others through the development of the total human being. That mission has not changed in over seventy years. As a Catholic college, the relationship between faith and reason is looked at closely. An AMC education is distinct because of its integration of rich tradition, diversity of knowledge, and the understanding of human history, institutions, and societies with Catholic teachings and traditions. The foundation of Anna Maria College's academic programs is the general education curriculum, which integrates the Catholic character with a commitment to liberal arts education.

Students are encouraged to go beyond their immediate interests to disciplines that may be connected by similar methods, history, theory, or application. The end result is a strong liberal arts foundation with a focused knowledge and professional preparation in a chosen area of concentration. Anna Maria also encourages students to explore their own areas of interest and design their own majors.

While at Anna Maria, students can gain practical experience and explore career options through internship programs, fieldwork, academic seminars, and summer programs. They also learn through practicums, part-time work, and community service.

Off-Campus Programs

Anna Maria College is a member of the Higher Education Consortium of Central Massachusetts (HECCMA), a group of twelve area colleges (Anna Maria College, Assumption College, Becker College, Clark University, College of the Holy Cross, Massachusetts College of Pharmacy and Allied Health, Nichols College, Quinsigamond Community College, Tufts University School of Veterinary Medicine, University of Massachusetts Medical School, Worcester Polytechnic Institute, and Worcester State College). Students may enroll in non-major courses at any of the member institutions and have credits transferred at no additional cost.

Anna Maria offers several off-campus opportunities for which academic credits are awarded. There are opportunities for study abroad, as well as an Urban Seminar course with travel to various locations worldwide. Students are also eligible to apply for Army and Air Force ROTC programs, available through HECCMA. A Washington, D.C. internship is offered for students in all majors, and a Disney internship is also available.

Academic Facilities

The Information Commons offers students a high-tech learning environment where they have access to the latest technologies in a setting that supports academic success. The traditional library is located in the lower level of the Information Commons. The Mondor-Eagan Library houses Anna Maria College's literary collection and archives. The library also links the combined material resources of central and western Massachusetts' libraries, making more than 4 million books and periodicals accessible to students.

Classrooms are located in Trinity Hall, Cardinal Cushing Hall, and Foundress Hall, which also houses the Zecco Performing Arts Center. Trinity Hall houses the Student Success Center. Other facilities include Madore Chapel, St. Joseph Hall for Sciences, and Miriam Hall for music, performance, and art.

Costs

Costs for the 2017–18 academic year include tuition, $34,855; fees, $2,270; and room and board, $13,915.

Financial Aid

Ninety-nine percent of the most recent freshman class received financial aid in the form of scholarships, grants, loans, and work-study program awards. Some available sources of funds are the Federal Pell Grant, Federal Supplemental Educational Opportunity Grant, and Federal Perkins Loan programs. To apply for aid, students should submit the Free Application for Federal Student Aid (FAFSA), which can be found at http://www.fafsa.ed.gov. Aid is awarded on the basis of need. Non-need-based scholarships ranging in amount from $15,000 to $20,000 are also available. For further information, students should call 508-849-3366.

Faculty

Anna Maria College has 150 full- and part-time faculty members. Faculty members have a deep respect for scholarship and research and are dedicated to teaching and to the success of the student. The Center for Teaching Excellence provides opportunities for faculty to hone new skills and pursue their research.

Student Government

The Student Government Association (SGA) is the official representative of the student body, serving as the link between students and the administration. There are more than twenty clubs and organizations under the SGA, offering many activities and opportunities to participate in the extracurricular life of AMC.

Admission Requirements

At Anna Maria College, every application is considered individually and weighed on its own merits. Emphasis is placed on the applicant's transcript and recommendations. SAT and ACT scores are optional. Extracurricular activities and leadership positions are also important. Successful completion of a four-year college-preparatory program is required. Application for admission to Anna Maria is encouraged for all academically qualified candidates regardless of race, religion, age, gender, or creed.

Application and Information

To apply, students should submit a completed application form (Anna Maria is a member of the Common Application). An official high school transcript should be sent to the Office of Admission along with an essay and letter of recommendation. Prospective students can schedule a campus visit via the AMC website (www.annamaria.edu) or by calling 508-849-3360. AMC is on rolling admissions; however, the application priority deadline for financial aid is March 1. Transfer students must submit official transcripts of all postsecondary courses.

Anna Maria College invites students to learn more about AMC's community by visiting the campus. Students should call the Undergraduate Office of Admission to schedule an appointment. For detailed information about Anna Maria College's distinctive programs and campus community, prospective students should contact:

Dean of Admission and Financial Aid
Anna Maria College
50 Sunset Lane
Paxton, Massachusetts 01612-1198
Phone: 508-849-3360
Fax: 508-849-3362
E-mail: admission@annamaria.edu
Website: http://www.annamaria.edu

AMC students enjoy the beautiful New England Campus at Anna Maria College.

AQUINAS COLLEGE
GRAND RAPIDS, MICHIGAN

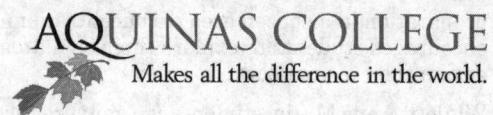

AQUINAS COLLEGE
Makes all the difference in the world.

★ To read more about this school, visit http://petersons.to/aquinascollege

The College

Recently named a Top 50 Catholic college, Aquinas is located on the eastern edge of the city of Grand Rapids. Aquinas enjoys all of the advantages of Michigan's second-largest city and is just a 3-hour drive from Detroit or Chicago. The Aquinas College campus is an interesting blend of early-nineteenth century architecture coupled with modern-day structures. The campus abounds with natural beauty; it has been called the most beautiful small campus in Michigan. Its 90 species of trees, winding woodland paths, and inviting creeks and ponds create a peaceful 117-acre environment that students of all ages find welcoming.

Founded by the Dominican Sisters of Grand Rapids in 1886, Aquinas has a Catholic heritage and a Christian tradition. For more than 130 years, Aquinas College has inspired students to transform the world by providing a liberal arts education infused with the Catholic Dominican values of prayer, study, service, and community. It is lived out by Aquinas students who volunteer their time and talents in the Grand Rapids community and by those who travel to places such as the Dominican Republic; Appalachia, Kentucky; or any of a dozen other service-learning project sites. An ability to see the world from different perspectives is the hallmark of an Aquinas-educated student.

An Aquinas education makes graduates more employable. Each year, hundreds of Aquinas students find businesses, government agencies, and other organizations eager to offer field experience and internship opportunities. Students can find employment and internships with organizations such as the American Cancer Society, Detroit Red Wings, Grand Rapids Art Museum, Meijer, Mercy Health, Steelcase, United States Senate, Van Andel Institute, and Walt Disney World, to name a few. Over 90 percent of Aquinas seniors find jobs or enroll in graduate school within six months after graduation.

Aquinas sees a liberal arts education as career preparation. The Aquinas general education plan exposes students to the necessary skills that enable them to become critical thinkers, articulate speakers, strong writers, and effective problem solvers. Aquinas faculty members insist that students carry values as well as skills into the workplace. The College's curriculum, with its more than 60 majors, is designed to provide students with both breadth and depth and to foster a thirst for knowledge and truth and a spirit of intellectual dialogue and inquiry. Coupled with nationally recognized internship programs, it prepares students to both live and work in the rapidly changing world of today and tomorrow.

Arriving from places as near as Grand Rapids, Chicago, and Detroit and as far as China and South America, the approximately 2,000 students include 1,400 full-time, 250 part-time, 150 graduate students, and almost 200 students in nursing, which is a collaborative program with Detroit Mercy. The Insignis program at Aquinas encourages students of exceptional academic ability to participate in social and intellectual activities such as lectures and receptions for visiting scholars and trips to places of cultural interest. Aquinas offers more than 70 student organizations, ranging from intramural teams and departmental clubs to a wide variety of musical groups, student publications, and service organizations.

In addition to its undergraduate degrees, Aquinas also offers Master in the Art of Teaching, Master of Art in Counseling, Master in Education, Master of Management, and Master of Clinical Psychology degrees.

Location

Aquinas' location in Grand Rapids allows students to reap the benefits of west Michigan's economic, educational, and cultural center. The city was recently recognized as one of the "Top 52 Places to Go in the World" by the *New York Times*. Grand Rapids combines big-city excitement and small-town charm. There are cosmopolitan amenities ranging from four-star hotels and restaurants to top-notch cultural facilities and entertainment venues. Established attractions include ArtPrize, Laughfest, the Gerald R. Ford Presidential Museum, the Van Andel Public Museum, the 10,000-seat Fifth Third Park for Whitecaps minor-league baseball, the 70-acre Fredrik Meijer Gardens, and the 12,000-seat Van Andel Arena, home to the Grand Rapids Griffins AHL hockey team and a venue for nationally known music concerts and performances. With nearly half a million area residents, there are abundant recreation, arts, and cultural opportunities available.

Majors and Degrees

Aquinas College offers the following undergraduate degree programs: Bachelor of Arts, Bachelor of Fine Arts, Bachelor of Arts in general education, Bachelor of Music Education, Bachelor of Science, Bachelor of Science in Business Administration, Bachelor of Science in sustainable business, and Bachelor of Science in International Business. A Bachelor of Science in Nursing degree program is offered in collaboration with the University of Detroit Mercy and Mercy Health St. Mary's.

Majors and programs of study are offered in:

- accounting
- accounting/business administration
- art
- art/business administration
- art history
- biology
- business administration
- business administration/chemistry
- business administration/communication
- business administration/music
- business administration/sport management
- chemical physics
- chemistry
- child life specialist
- communication
- community leadership
- computer information systems
- data analytics
- drawing
- economics
- education
- engineering
- English
- environmental studies
- exercise science
- French
- geography
- German
- health
- health science
- history
- international studies
- Irish studies
- Japanese
- journalism/publications
- learning disabilities
- management information systems
- marketing
- mathematics
- music
- organizational communication
- painting
- philosophy
- photography
- physical education and recreation
- physics
- political science
- printmaking
- psychology
- sculpture
- social science
- sociology
- Spanish
- studio art
- sustainable business
- theatre
- theatre for social change
- theology
- translation and interpretation
- urban studies
- visual arts administration
- women's studies
- world languages

Associate degrees are also available, including the Associate of Arts and the Associate of Science.

Pre-professional programs include dentistry, law, medicine, occupational therapy, physical therapy, physician's assistant studies, and veterinary science.

Academic Programs

In addition to their major and minor fields of study, students take a First Year Experience Course and an integrated skills course called Inquiry and Expression. This course spans the first semester of the freshman year and has an emphasis on writing integrated with reading critically, oral communication skills, critical thinking, library/electronic research methods, computer utilization, and basic quantitative reasoning. The thematic content is American Pluralism: The Individual in a Diverse America. As juniors, they are required to take 3 hours in Theological Foundation. Students are also required to be proficient in a second language through the 102 level. There also is a distribution plan in the general education plan covering social science, history/philosophy, natural world, artistic and creative studies, and mathematics. The Aquinas Advantage Center expands learning beyond the classroom by housing co-curricular opportunities for study away, internships, and faculty guided research in one central department. The College follows a two-semester calendar with a summer session. Aquinas also accepts credit through CLEP, Advanced Placement, and International Baccalaureate.

Off-Campus Programs

Students have the option of participating in the Dominican College Campus Interchange Program. Cooperating colleges are Barry University in Miami, Florida; Dominican College in San Rafael, California; and St. Thomas Aquinas College in Sparkill, New York. Students can increase their language skills through cultural-immersion programs in Costa Rica, France, Italy, Japan, Spain, or Germany. An Aquinas faculty member accompanies approximately 30 students to Aquinas' study center in Tully Cross, Ireland. Students have the opportunity to earn a full semester of credit while traveling abroad, and living in a rural Irish community. The curriculum is centered on several aspects of Irish studies.

Academic Facilities

The Grace Hauenstein Library is a $6-million facility with resources that include a public access catalog, audiovisual materials, circulation and course reserve materials, reference services, and interlibrary loan services (free access to more than 60 million books and documents from libraries across the country). Albertus Magnus Hall of Science features the handicapped-accessible Baldwin Observatory and a greenhouse. Other facilities include the Cook Carriage House student center and the Art and Music Center, featuring a 200-seat recital hall, an art gallery, and a sculpture studio. The Aquinas Performing Arts Center is a $7-million facility providing a state-of-the-art theater venue. Five apartment buildings also provide great housing options for upperclassmen.

AQnet allows residents and commuters to wirelessly connect their personal computers or other devices to the Internet while on campus. Students will find centrally located kiosks and computer labs on campus in classrooms, residence halls, the Grace Hauenstein Library, and common areas.

Costs

For 2017–18, tuition is $30,746 and room and board are $9,708 for a total of $39,816. Annual fees are $498 per year. Other expenses, including books, travel, and personal supplies, average $2,000.

Financial Aid

Aquinas College awards both merit-based financial assistance and traditional need-based assistance to qualified students. The Spectrum Scholarship Program was developed to recognize students' achievements in academics, leadership, and service. More than 95 percent of entering freshmen receive some form of financial assistance. The College administers the traditional grant and loan programs, including Ford Federal Direct Loans and Federal PLUS loans. Athletic grants are also available. The College participates in an automatic payment program. This plan assists students in paying costs over a period of time. To apply for financial assistance, students must complete the Free Application for Federal Student Aid (FAFSA).

Faculty

Aquinas faculty members are teachers first: while research plays an important part in the Aquinas faculty's development, teaching remains the number-one priority. In addition to teaching, faculty members serve as academic advisers, mentors, and advisers to various clubs and organizations on campus. With a student-professor ratio of 11:1, faculty members give individual attention and assistance to students. All classes and labs are taught by faculty members, not graduate assistants. More than 80 percent of Aquinas faculty members have doctoral or terminal degrees.

Student Government

The Student Senate is the governing body of Aquinas students. Senators are chosen by securing twenty-five signatures of students in support of their involvement. These students have both voice and vote on issues facing the College's Academic Assembly. The Senate is responsible for many of the academic, social, recreational, and cultural activities on the campus.

Admission Requirements

Freshman and transfer applications are received on a rolling basis. A candidate for admission to Aquinas is considered on the basis of academic preparation, scholarship, and character. Admission depends on a number of factors, including academic records and ACT or SAT test scores. The online application for admission does not require a fee. The admissions office reserves the right to review applications on a case-by-case basis. Curriculum, extracurricular activities, and any extenuating circumstances are considered in the decision. Letters of recommendation are encouraged but not required.

Application and Information

Prospective students may submit a free application for admission at https://www.aquinas.edu/undergraduate.

For further information, interested students should contact:

Angie Schlosser-Bacon
Director of Admissions
Aquinas College
1700 Fulton E
Grand Rapids, Michigan 49506-1801
Phone: 616-632-2900
800-678-9593 (toll-free)
E-mail: admissions@aquinas.edu
Website: aquinas.edu

ASSUMPTION COLLEGE

WORCESTER, MASSACHUSETTS

★ To read more about this school, visit http://petersons.to/assumptioncollege

The College

Assumption College, established in 1904 by the Augustinians of the Assumption, is a coeducational institution known for its classic liberal arts curriculum and strong academic programs in business and professional studies. The College's 2,000 undergraduates choose among 41 majors and 48 minors, gaining a depth and breadth of knowledge that serves as a foundation for personal fulfillment and lifelong success. Students' educational experience is grounded in the rich Catholic intellectual tradition, which cultivates both the mind and the personal values students require to meet the demands of a constantly changing world. Undergraduate and graduate students are guided by faculty and staff members in a thriving community that develops individuals known for critical intelligence, thoughtful citizenship, and compassionate service.

The academic journey is characterized by individual attention and the quest for personal excellence. With a student-faculty ratio of just 12:1, Assumption's professors serve as mentors who challenge students to ask questions, find their own answers, and grow—intellectually, socially, and spiritually. Students are encouraged to pursue hands-on experience at internships and to participate in individual research projects. The result? Ninety-six percent of the graduates who responded to a survey six months after graduation are either employed or enrolled in graduate school.

At Assumption, 90 percent of the undergraduates live on campus and housing is guaranteed for all four years. The campus is lively seven days a week with academic programming, activities sponsored by student clubs and organizations, community service opportunities, campus ministry programs, and intercollegiate, intramural, and club sports. The College's state-of-the-art recreation center offers a number of opportunities for students to exercise or participate in intramural sports.

Location

The College's 185-acre campus is situated in a beautiful, residential neighborhood just minutes from downtown Worcester, Massachusetts. Worcester, the second-largest city in New England, is a vibrant college town, home to 35,000 students. The city offers extensive opportunities for internships in virtually every field, as well as numerous entertainment and community service options. Great restaurants, cultural venues and programs, and retail shops provide students with an array of off-campus activities. Worcester is also centrally located to exciting urban areas such as Boston; Providence, Rhode Island; and Hartford, Connecticut only an hour's drive away. The mountains of Vermont and New Hampshire provide skiing, hiking, and sightseeing opportunities. There are numerous daily commuter trains to Boston as well as other transportation options.

Majors and Degrees

Assumption offers undergraduate and graduate degrees.

Undergraduates pursue Bachelor of Arts degrees. The most popular majors include English (concentrations in literature or writing and mass communications), history, political science, psychology, the natural sciences (biology, biotechnology and molecular biology, neuroscience, chemistry, and environmental science), education, human services and rehabilitation studies, and business disciplines such as accounting, international business, management, marketing, and organizational communication. Minors are offered in 48 areas. Pre-professional advising programs are available for medicine, law, and dentistry.

The College has also developed partnerships with a number of highly regarded institutions to provide students with additional options, including engineering with the University of Notre Dame and Washington University in St. Louis, environmental science with Duke University, and law (3+3 programs with Duquesne, Vermont, and Western New England law schools). There are agreements for numerous medical professions as well, and joint seven-year programs are also available for those interested in podiatry or optometry.

Assumption College offers graduate degrees in applied behavior analysis, business, special education, school counseling, clinical counseling psychology, health advocacy, and rehabilitation counseling. An accelerated 6-in-5 combined bachelor's and master's degree is offered in several programs.

Academic Programs

The College's classic liberal arts curriculum promotes lively discussion of the books, ideas, people, and events that have shaped civilization. Faculty members and students explore the rich Catholic intellectual tradition together as they seek truth and the nature of the world.

Assumption also offers academic programs and courses that help students achieve their full potential. The College's Honors Program encourages students to challenge themselves intellectually through intensive study and independent research. The SOPHIA (SOPHomore Initiative at Assumption) program is designed to help students discover a deeper connection between their spiritual, personal, and professional lives. Air Force and Army ROTC are also available at a neighboring institution.

Assumption College follows a traditional two-semester calendar, from late August to mid-May, as well as an optional January intersession. The Graduate Studies programs and the Center for Continuing and Career Education also offer two summer sessions for students.

Undergraduates complete a core curriculum that provides a strong foundation in the liberal arts, in addition to developing the skills and knowledge necessary for their professional career. Students must complete 120 credit hours in all academic programs to earn a degree.

Off-Campus Programs

The College and eleven other institutions of higher learning compose the Colleges of Worcester Consortium, which combines resources to offer the 35,000 college students in the area even greater academic and social opportunities. Assumption students may cross-register for academic credit at any of the participating colleges and enjoy their social and cultural events. Free transportation to and from other participating institutions is available.

Eligible students may choose to spend a semester or a year abroad. Assumption opened a campus in Rome in February 2013. The campus provides the opportunity for a close learning community where students live, study, and travel together in the city that forged the foundations of Western Civilization. The College's students have studied abroad in Australia, Austria, Chile, China, Costa Rica, the Czech Republic, England, France, Germany, Greece, Ireland, Italy, Japan, the Netherlands, Spain, and other locations. There are also numerous one- and two-week international experiences led by Assumption faculty.

Seventy-nine percent of Assumption students have undertaken at least one internship, where they explore their professional choices and broaden their workplace skills at local, regional, national, and international sites. In recent years, they have interned at PBS, the U.S. House of Representatives, Ralph Lauren, the Hungarian Embassy, Smith Barney, Fidelity, *The Rachel Ray Show, The Daily Show with Jon Stewart*, ABC News, PricewaterhouseCoopers, AT&T, Sony Japan, and countless other organizations.

Campus Facilities

The College has invested more than $80 million to enhance campus facilities.

The Testa Science Center houses the Department of Natural Sciences and features multiuse classrooms with state-of-the-art technology, ten teaching laboratories, seven laboratories dedicated to faculty and student research, a greenhouse, and student lounge areas.

The Information Technology Center houses computer labs, technology-rich classrooms, and an experienced support staff. Students can learn Web authoring, graphics and animation, digital video, and multimedia production. The digital audio studio is available to all students and faculty members.

Assumption offers a variety of housing options to accommodate the 90 percent of students who choose to live on campus. There are traditional residence halls, suites, a living and learning residence, and apartments with full kitchens. All resident students have individual hard-wired and wireless Internet access in their rooms. The College's stadium and athletic facilities support Assumption's 24 NCAA Division II intercollegiate teams, recreational programs, and the physical well-being of the campus community.

Costs

For 2016–17, tuition was $35,510, room and board were $11,660, and student fees were $750. The board plan is required for all first-year students.

Financial Aid

The College offers financial aid based on demonstrated need and scholastic achievement. The College requires that students submit the Free Application for Federal Student Aid (FAFSA). This form should be filed by February 15, so that the College may consider the information as it makes financial aid awards.

All applicants for admission are considered for merit awards of up to $20,000 per year. Funds awarded through this program reflect the College's commitment to academic excellence and student leadership.

Faculty

More than 94 percent of the Assumption College faculty members hold the highest degree in their field. They are active scholars presenting their ideas and research at professional conferences, writing books and articles, and publishing in journals. With a student-to-faculty ratio of 12:1, professors work closely with students and challenge them to explore new paths of knowledge and make their own discoveries. All of Assumption's academic advisors are full-time faculty members.

Student Organizations and Government

There are more than 60 clubs and organizations on campus, offering students many opportunities in community service, sports, academics, leadership, and special interests. The Student Government Association (SGA), the elected representatives of the student body, coordinates official communication between the student community and the College administration and officially recognizes student clubs and activities.

Admission Requirements

All applicants must graduate from an accredited secondary school with a minimum of 18 academic units. These units should include 4 years of English, 3 years of mathematics, 2 years of a foreign language, 2 years of history, 2 years of science, and 5 additional academic units.

Admission to Assumption is test-score optional. When submitting an application, an essay and recommendations are required. Interviews are recommended, but not required.

The number of solid academic courses, including the number of honors-level or Advanced Placement–level courses, is considered during the application review process.

The Admissions Committee understands that grading standards vary from school to school and from one course to another. Class rank provides some context within which to place the grades of students applying from a given school, but is not the only factor weighed when considering a student for admission. Some schools also provide grade distribution charts. The Committee also considers whether the applicant's grade point average or rank in class is weighted or unweighted.

Application and Information

Campus visits are strongly recommended. Appointments can be scheduled Monday through Friday. Group Information Sessions are held most Saturdays in the fall.

Applicants must submit a completed application, a $50 application fee, official transcripts, a recommendation letter, and an essay. Applications for early action admission must be received by November 1. There is a second early action admission deadline of December 15. The deadline for regular admission is February 15. Students may complete the Common Application and Supplement at www.commonapp.org.

For more information, students should contact:
Office of Admissions
Assumption College
500 Salisbury Street
P.O. Box 15005
Worcester, Massachusetts 01609-1296
Phone: 508-767-7285
866-477-7776 (toll-free)
E-mail: admissions@assumption.edu
Website: www.assumption.edu
twitter.com/AssumptionNews
facebook.com/assumptioncollege

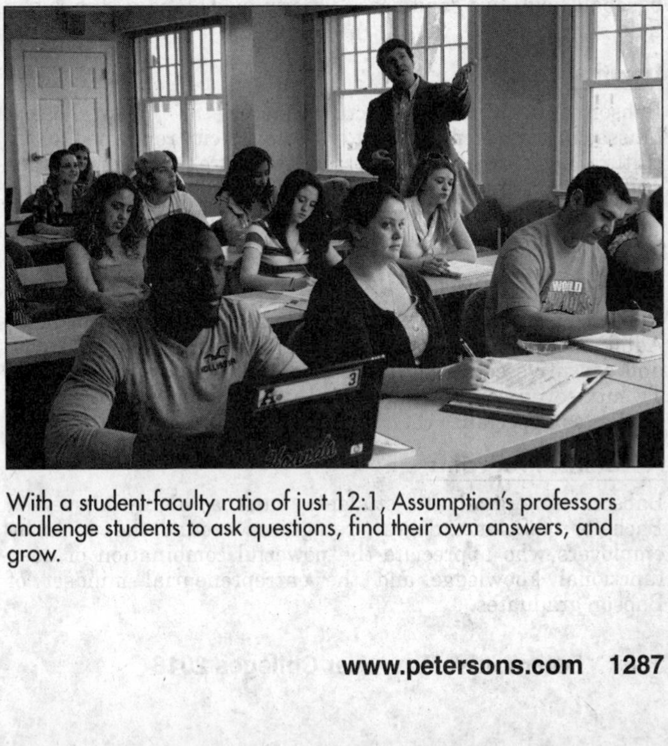

With a student-faculty ratio of just 12:1, Assumption's professors challenge students to ask questions, find their own answers, and grow.

COLLEGE CLOSE-UPS

BABSON COLLEGE

WELLESLEY, MASSACHUSETTS

★ To read more about this school, visit http://petersons.to/babsoncollege

BABSON

The College

Babson College is the educator, convener, and thought leader for Entrepreneurship of All Kinds™. As the only school to teach Entrepreneurial Thought and Action®, Babson shapes the leaders the world needs: those with strong functional knowledge and the skills and vision to navigate change, accommodate ambiguity, solve problems, and motivate teams in a common purpose. Every day, Babson students, faculty, and alumni address real-world business and societal problems, creating sustainable economic and social value in today's fast-paced global economy. Babson is accredited by the International Association for Management Education, AACSB International–The Association to Advance Collegiate Schools of Business, the New England Association of Schools and Colleges, and the European Quality Improvement System (EQUIS).

The 2016–17 undergraduate enrollment was just over 2,200 students with 48 percent women and 52 percent men. Babson is a residential college and is a fast-paced community alive with intellectual, cultural, athletic, and social activities. Approximately 85 percent of the undergraduate student body lives on campus all four years in fourteen residence halls. Housing options include fraternity and sorority housing, and entrepreneurial, service-oriented, and other specialty-themed housing.

Babson College is an NCAA Division III school. Most of the College's intercollegiate teams compete in the New England Women's and Men's Athletic Conference (NEWMAC). There are twenty-two men's and women's varsity sports teams, with additional club and intramural sports available to all students. More information is available at www.babsonathletics.com.

The Webster Center features an indoor, 200-meter, six-lane track; a field house; a gymnasium with three basketball courts; a racquetball court; a 25-yard, six-lane pool with 1- and 3-meter diving boards; a fitness center; squash courts; and a dance/aerobics studio. The Babson Skating Center features a 600-seat skating arena. Outdoor facilities include eight tennis courts, an AstroTurf field, a game field, a renovated softball diamond, a baseball field, two sand-based varsity fields, and a club rugby field.

Location

Babson's beautiful 370-acre campus is in Wellesley, Massachusetts, 14 miles west of Boston, a city renowned for its cultural and recreational opportunities. More than sixty colleges and universities bring more than 250,000 college students to the Boston area, making it one of the world's best college towns for cultural exchange and research.

Majors and Degrees

Babson offers a Bachelor of Science degree, a Master of Business Administration degree, two Master of Science degree programs, and executive education programs for business professionals. Twenty-seven concentrations are available for undergraduate students to specialize their studies.

Academic Programs

Babson undergraduate students earn a highly respected Bachelor of Science degree, recognized around the world by employers who appreciate the powerful combination of deep functional knowledge and the entrepreneurial mindset of Babson graduates.

First-year courses at Babson lay the groundwork for students' future courses—and careers—starting with the Foundations of Management and Entrepreneurship (FME) course, a yearlong immersion into the business world. A team of 10–15 students develops and manages an actual business or service organization, studying organizational behavior, marketing, entrepreneurship, and operations, while emphasizing the integrated role these functions have in a business. Students will have the chance to dabble in all areas of the organization, testing what disciplines and possible careers they would like to pursue further.

Students will also take integrated liberal arts foundation courses providing them with valuable analytic and communication skills and an appreciation for the arts and humanities. Throughout the year, students will develop a deeper understanding (and appreciation) of themselves and their goals, as they continue to prepare to excel in business and in life.

A weekly First-Year Seminar will ease each student's transition to college life by helping them develop an awareness of campus resources, providing a support group for challenges that arise, and teaching communication and study skills. Members of the Babson community—including alumni, faculty, staff members, and peer mentors—provide personal and professional support throughout all four years.

Second-year students take an integrated series of courses in finance, economics, marketing, information technology, management accounting, and operations management. These courses offer functional knowledge of each discipline, and because they are thematically linked, they also provide the broad perspective of a CEO.

Students look at actual business problems via case studies and get real-world experience by studying, touring, interacting with, and presenting to local companies. Pursuing topics more intensively allows students to focus on certain areas of concentration and begin to formulate ideas on what to pursue in life after college.

Throughout the third and fourth years at Babson, students begin to think about issues with increased confidence, independence, and creativity. There is flexibility to reflect on career options and to pursue courses that align with personal and professional goals. In addition to management and liberal arts electives, students gain field experience via internships or consulting programs. Students may also opt to take their education abroad for a semester or short elective during schools breaks and apply it to real-life situations in countries around the world.

Babson offers twenty-seven optional concentrations in both business and liberal arts disciplines; descriptions can be found at www.babson.edu/concentrations. Students may focus their course of study by choosing a concentration in their areas of interest. Special programs, such as the Weissman Scholarship program, the Honors Program, the Center for Women's Entrepreneurial Leadership Scholars Program, the Management Consulting Field Experience, the Babson College Fund (student-managed endowment), Master of Science in Accounting (MSA), and independent research allow students to take advantage of customized learning opportunities at Babson.

Entering students may be granted credit or advanced course placement for successful scores on Advanced Placement (AP) examinations administered by the College Board as well as some courses in the International Baccalaureate (I.B.) curriculum.

Babson operates on a two-semester academic calendar. Semesters run from September to December and from late January through May. An optional credit-bearing three-week winter session is offered in January, and two summer sessions are offered—one from late May to early July and one from mid-July to mid-August.

Faculty

Because of Babson's close-knit community, students are able to form close relationships with the faculty. Of the 254 faculty members, 169 are full-time, and 88 percent of the full-time faculty members hold a doctoral degree or its equivalent. Faculty members are accomplished entrepreneurs, executives, scholars, authors, researchers, poets, and artists who bring an intellectual diversity that adds depth to Babson's educational programs and offers students a rich, challenging experience. Babson's student-faculty ratio is 14:1 and faculty members teach 100 percent of the courses. More information can be found at www.babson.edu/faculty.

Student Government

Students are encouraged to take an active role in campus activities and student government. The Student Government Association promotes students' interests; allocates funds to campus organizations for academic, social, and recreational activities; licenses student-run businesses; and helps formulate and maintain student regulations. There are over 115 student clubs and organizations currently on campus.

Off-Campus Programs

Babson has a partnership with Wellesley College and the Franklin W. Olin College of Engineering, an independent institution located on a 70-acre site adjacent to Babson. Babson, Olin, and Wellesley are collaborating inside and outside the classroom in order to provide extraordinary opportunities in all aspects of the student experience, including joint academic and research programming, student life programming, and lecture series.

Babson's vibrant education abroad programs enable students to spend a summer, semester, or school break abroad. Currently, 108 programs are offered in thirty-five countries, and full academic credit is given for approved management and liberal arts courses.

Academic Facilities

Horn Library houses an extensive business collection of print, media, and online information resources. Students have campus-wide access to library resources. Wireless access is available throughout the campus. Every incoming Babson undergraduate student receives a leased laptop computer, which is replaced after the sophomore year.

Other facilities are the Donald W. Reynolds Campus Center, the Richard W. Sorenson Family Visual Arts Center, the Stephen D. Cutler Center for Investments and Finance, the Glavin Family Chapel, and the Arthur M. Blank Center for Entrepreneurship.

Costs

For 2015–16, tuition was $46,784.

Financial Aid

Babson is committed to educating students from diverse backgrounds. Applying for financial aid does not affect a student's chances of being admitted to Babson College. Financial assistance is awarded on merit and demonstrated financial need.

Half of Babson students receive some form of financial assistance. Need-based financial assistance is available to U.S. citizens and permanent residents of the United States. A small number of need-based scholarships are awarded each year to international students as part of the Global Scholars Program. Babson's merit scholarships include Weissman Scholarships, Presidential Scholarships, The Center for Women's Entrepreneurial Leadership Scholarship, and the Diversity Leadership Awards. Application for aid is made by submitting the Free Application for Federal Student Aid (FAFSA) and the Financial Aid PROFILE of the College Scholarship Service. The application deadline for first-year undergraduate students is February 1. For transfer students the deadline is April 1 for September enrollment, and November 1 for January enrollment.

Admission Requirements

In selecting new students, the admission office considers each candidate based on academic factors such as high school record, recommendations, standardized test scores, and essays. Nonacademic factors are also considered, including extracurricular activities, demonstrated leadership abilities, character/personal qualities, volunteer work, work experience, creativity and enthusiasm, and a willingness to contribute to the Babson community in meaningful ways. Evaluation is based upon comparisons of the qualifications of those who apply. The degree of competition is set by the caliber of the applicants themselves. Consideration is given to the depth and rigor of each candidate's academic program, academic motivation and achievement, and progress from one year to the next. Prospective students are strongly encouraged to have completed or be currently enrolled in a pre-calculus math class.

Babson College offers three application plans: early decision, early action, and regular decision. For more information about these plans and their deadlines, prospective students should visit Babson's website at www.babson.edu/ugrad. Campus visits and group information sessions with an admission counselor are strongly recommended.

Application and Information

For further information or application forms, students should contact:

Lunder Undergraduate Admission Center
Babson College
Babson Park, Massachusetts 02457-0310
Phone: 781-239-5522
800-488-3696 (toll-free)
Fax: 781-239-4006
E-mail: ugradadmission@babson.edu
Website: www.babson.edu/ugrad
www.facebook.com/babsonadmission
www.twitter.com/BabsonAdmission

Tomasso Hall

COLLEGE CLOSE-UPS

BALDWIN WALLACE UNIVERSITY

BEREA, OHIO

★ To read more about this school, visit http://petersons.to/baldwinwallaceuniversity

The University

Founded in 1845, Baldwin Wallace University (BW) in Berea, Ohio, is an accredited institution affiliated with the United Methodist Church that blends the hallmarks of a traditional liberal arts education with an emphasis on professional preparation. Baldwin Wallace has a long history of diversity, as it was one of the first institutions of higher learning in the nation to admit students without regard to race or gender. That spirit of inclusiveness has flourished and evolved into a personalized approach to education, one that stresses individual growth as students learn to learn, respond to new ideas, adapt to new situations, and prepare for the certainty of change.

With an enrollment of approximately 3,000 full-time undergraduate students and a total campus population of 4,000 students, BW offers unique opportunities for engaged, transformative learning. There are 28 states represented at BW with 26 percent of first-year students coming from outside of Ohio, 24 percent of first-year students are students of color, and 34 percent of students would be the first in their families to earn a four-year college degree. First-year students have an average high school GPA of 3.46, a composite ACT score of 24, and a combined SAT (verbal + math) score of 1069.

Experiential learning is key to a BW education and is a requirement for all undergraduates. BW maintains a proven commitment to the liberal arts and sciences—characterized by excellence in teaching and learning that provides a strong foundation for internships, faculty-directed research, performance, and service-learning programs. Students work with faculty and staff to combine these opportunities in a way that prepares graduates for success after college.

In a recent post-graduation alumni survey, 92 percent of respondents found rewarding jobs or entered the graduate or professional school of their choice within one year of graduation. Some programs—including athletic training, communication disorders, music therapy, and neuroscience—have graduate school acceptance rates at or near 100 percent.

BW offers many distinctive academic programs. BW's neuroscience program has been recognized as the Undergraduate Program of the Year by the *Society for Neuroscience*.

BW is also home to a world-renowned Conservatory of Music. The undergraduate-only nature of the Conservatory offers collaborative mentoring opportunities with a faculty of accomplished artists plus extraordinary opportunities for performance in a variety of ensembles. The University hosts the country's oldest collegiate Bach Festival.

BW has an early medical school acceptance agreement with Ohio University's Heritage College of Osteopathic Medicine, Lake Erie College of Osteopathic Medicine, and Northeast Ohio Medical University, aimed at developing a pipeline of pre-med students committed to primary care.

Location

Baldwin Wallace students enjoy the best of both worlds. Berea, Ohio, with its tree-lined streets, picturesque homes, and population of 19,000, is an ideal suburban college town. At the same time, students are only 20 minutes from the heart of Cleveland (known as the CLE), which is home to many *Fortune 500* companies and burgeoning tech and healthcare sectors. As such, Northeast Ohio provides students with outstanding internship and field experience opportunities that maximize real-world preparation and the value of a BW degree. Each year, approximately 450 BW students complete internships at business, nonprofit, and government sites in the area. Cleveland is also known for first-rate museums and galleries, professional sporting events, a world-class orchestra, exciting nightlife, an extensive park system with access to Lake Erie, and Playhouse Square—Cleveland's Theater District—the largest performing arts center in the United States outside of New York.

Approximately 85 percent of first-year students live on campus in a variety of settings, including residential learning communities. Students 21 years or older also have access to University-owned apartments. A renovated residential complex featuring suite-style living is also available. All full-time students are required to live on campus during their first and second years, with residency exemptions available for commuting students who live with their families.

Majors and Degrees

Baldwin Wallace offers the Bachelor of Arts (B.A.), Bachelor of Science (B.S.), Bachelor of Science in Education (B.S.E.), Bachelor of Music (B.M.), Bachelor of Fine Arts (B.F.A.) and Bachelor of Music in Education (B.M.E.) degrees. A Bachelor of Science in Nursing (B.S.N.) degree is offered in an accelerated format to students who have previously completed a bachelor's degree. Majors and programs include accounting, acting (B.F.A), art (studio), arts management & entrepreneurship, athletic training, biology, broadcasting & mass communication, business administration, chemistry, communication sciences & disorders, communication studies, computer information systems, computer network security, computer science, creative writing, criminal justice, digital media & design: graphic design or interactive design, economics, education, engineering (general), English, exercise science, film studies, finance, French, German, healthcare management, health coaching & health promotion, health & physical education, history, human resource management, industrial & organizational psychology, innovation & entrepreneurship, international business, international studies, management, marketing, mathematics (applied), mathematics (pure), national security, neuroscience, philosophy, physics, political science, pre–physical therapy, pre–social work, primary healthcare advancement, psychology, public health, public history, public & nonprofit management, public relations, religion, sociology, software engineering, Spanish, sport management, sustainability, and theatre: acting & directing, dance & movement, design & technical, or stage management. Sixty-seven liberal arts minors are offered. The BW Conservatory of Music offers majors in music composition, music education, music history & literature, music performance: keyboard, strings, voice, or woodwinds/brass/percussion, music theatre, music theory, music therapy, as well as two liberal arts in music (B.A.) majors, one with an academic emphasis and the other with an applied emphasis.

Academic Programs

Eighty majors and several 3-2 cooperative and pre-professional programs are available to traditional Baldwin Wallace undergraduates. The Honors Program offers innovative coursework and rigorous student-focused initiatives centered on fostering critical thinking, problem-solving and communication skills for approximately 250 high-achieving students.

International Programs

Baldwin Wallace sends over 30 percent of its full-time undergraduate student body abroad each year in over thirty different programs. BW offers long-term and short-term programs in Africa, Asia, Australia, Europe, and Latin and South America. BW has institutional (exchange) partnerships with institutions around the globe, where students can study for a semester, summer, or academic year. International options include Australia, China, Ecuador, England, France, Germany, Ghana, India, Ireland, Japan, Morocco, South Korea, Sweden and Spain.

In addition to traditional exchange programs, BW features a series of focused full-semester seminars that are led by BW faculty and staff members and examine specific topics or geographic regions. Quite literally, students learn while on the road. Full-semester seminars are offered in alternating academic years. One example of a full-semester seminar is Seminar in Europe. Students travel through Europe experiencing different cultures across the continent.

BW also sponsors faculty-led two- to three-week seminars for credit in May, which are ideal for students who seek an international experience but do not want to be away for extended periods of time. BW has many short-term opportunities including a two-week immersion course in British theatre that includes a nine-day trip to London or a three-week program to Brazil to understand the process of economic and political development in Brazil. Past and current programs include travel to China, Germany, Guatemala, Ghana, England, Ireland, and India.

Academic Facilities

Baldwin Wallace continues to invest in facilities for student learning, including the Thomas Family Center for Science and Innovation, a facility featuring a combined 100,000 square-feet of comprehensive laboratory, research, and study space. This complex includes the Center for Innovation and Growth, a facility that prepares tomorrow's leaders to change their world as students learn—and practice—skills in creativity, innovation, and entrepreneurship.

The BW Conservatory of Music is housed within the Boesel Musical Arts Center, which provides students with world-class rehearsal and performance spaces. The BW Conservatory of Music is now designated as an All-Steinway School, ensuring students have access to the finest pianos in the world and best tools for success. The BW Conservatory of Music is also home to the Jones Music Library and the Riemenschneider Bach Institute, where priceless Bach-related manuscripts and first editions are stored.

These facilities complement the extensive offerings already available to students, including twenty campus computer labs; a campus TV station and 4,000-watt radio station; recently renovated recreation and athletic facilities; an on-campus gallery showcasing the work of student, faculty, and area artists; and the Burrell Memorial Observatory. A new campus master plan, already being implemented, will enhance facilities to support BW's mission and create an even more pedestrian-friendly, environmentally responsible campus with inviting green spaces.

Costs

Baldwin Wallace's tuition ranks among the lowest and most affordable of private colleges in Ohio. In 2017–18, full-time (12–18 credit hours) liberal arts student tuition is $31,668 per academic year and $10,796 for room and board (BW does not have fees). Conservatory student tuition is $34,308 for the 2017–18 academic year.

Baldwin Wallace offers a four-year graduation guarantee—a promise that academically prepared students who meet specified benchmarks during their study at BW will earn their bachelor's degrees in four years or fewer. If a student who follows the agreement does not graduate in four years, BW will pay up to one year's additional tuition for the additional course work needed to graduate.

Financial Aid

To help students and their families meet the cost of a high-quality education, Baldwin Wallace awards nearly $50 million annually to students in the form of scholarships, grants, loans, and work-study opportunities. About 82 percent of all BW full-time undergraduates have financial need. One hundred percent of all full-time undergraduate students with financial need received financial support from BW in 2016–17.

Renewable merit scholarships ranging from $12,000 to $16,000 are awarded to incoming first-year students who have demonstrated a commitment to academic preparation and achievement. The University also offers talent scholarships and special awards, as well as scholarships for transfer students.

Faculty

Close relationships are at the heart of the Baldwin Wallace experience. The student-faculty ratio is 12:1, allowing for a more personalized and collaborative academic environment. Professors share their wisdom and experience on a one-to-one basis, helping students choose classes or assisting students in their search for the perfect internship. From corporate executives and lifelong educators to environmentalists and practicing professionals, BW's 469 full-time and part-time faculty members bring impressive credentials from their fields and are dedicated and talented teachers who want to provide an educational experience that goes well beyond the textbook.

Student Clubs and Organizations

Baldwin Wallace students participate in more than 120 clubs, professional organizations, and honor societies, ranging from community service and political action groups to student government and student-run media to marching band to fraternities and sororities. Almost one in five undergraduate students competes in one of 23 NCAA Division III varsity sports in the competitive Ohio Athletic Conference (OAC), and many others participate in club sports, intramurals, and recreational activities.

Admission Requirements

When it comes to GPA, class rank or standardized test score requirements, Baldwin Wallace believes in giving balanced consideration to all aspects of a student's college preparation. BW reviews the following information for each applicant: completed application for admission (BW is a member of the Common Application and does not have an application fee for students submitting materials online), high school transcript, SAT/ACT test results (or a recently graded writing sample if student has a 3.0+ GPA and is eligible to be test-optional), and school report form. Applicants to the BW Conservatory of Music have additional requirements, as do applicants to the B.F.A. in acting program, including an audition.

Application and Information

Students may begin applying to BW for the following fall term as of August 1, though the first notifications for admission will not be sent until early October. Beginning in October, applicants are notified of admission decisions on a rolling basis within two to four weeks upon the completion of their application to BW. The priority application deadlines are November 1 and February 1. Applicants to the BW Conservatory of Music and/or to the B.F.A. in acting program may have separate deadlines to consider and should consult the BW website. Although students are encouraged to apply before May 1 so they are in a position to meet the priority student deposit deadline, applications will continue to be accepted on a space available basis until the start of the fall semester.

Baldwin Wallace University
275 Eastland Road
Berea, Ohio 44017-2088
Phone: 440-826-2222
877-BW-APPLY (toll-free)
Fax: 440-826-3830
E-mail: admission@bw.edu
Website: http://www.bw.edu/admission
Social Media: @BWadmission

Baldwin Wallace Class of 2020

COLLEGE CLOSE-UPS

BARD COLLEGE AT SIMON'S ROCK
GREAT BARRINGTON, MASSACHUSETTS

Bard College at SIMON'S ROCK *the Early College*

The College

Bard College at Simon's Rock, The Early College is the country's only four-year residential college of the liberal arts and sciences specifically designed to provide bright, highly motivated students with the opportunity to begin college after the 10th or 11th grade. Students can earn an Associate of Arts (A.A.) degree after two years of study and a Bachelor of Arts (B.A.) degree after four. Merit scholarships and need-based aid are available. The average age of entering students is 16.

Founded in 1964 by Elizabeth Blodgett Hall, Simon's Rock welcomed its first entering class in 1966 and in 1979 became a part of Bard College, located 50 miles away at Annandale-on-Hudson, New York.

For fifty years, Simon's Rock has demonstrated that high school–age students are fully capable of college work; that they thrive intellectually and socially in a small-college environment; that serving these students well requires a faculty committed to distinction in teaching and scholarship, as well as active participation in the students' social and personal development; and that a coherent general education in the liberal arts and sciences should be the foundation for early college students. Based on the success of the College and its graduates, Simon's Rock serves as a model for the growing U.S. early college movement.

Location

Bard College at Simon's Rock is located in Great Barrington, Massachusetts (population 7,500), named "Best Small Town" in America by *Smithsonian* magazine in 2012. Built on 275 rolling and wooded acres in the Berkshire Hills of western Massachusetts, Simon's Rock is just 2½ hours from Boston and New York City. The Berkshires' natural beauty and variety of cultural attractions make the area an unusually appealing place in which to live. The terrain is excellent for hiking, bicycling, cross-country and Alpine skiing, canoeing, and climbing. Nationally renowned arts organizations, including the Tanglewood Music Festival, Jacob's Pillow Dance Festival, and Shakespeare and Company are located nearby. Great Barrington is a thriving business community with shops, restaurants, and a variety of schools and service agencies in which Simon's Rock students work and volunteer.

Majors and Degrees

The College offers programs leading to the A.A. and B.A. degrees in the liberal arts and sciences. Students may complete their B.A. studies in one of 35 different concentrations reflecting most traditional disciplines, choose one of several interdisciplinary concentrations, and may design their own second concentration. Many Simon's Rock B.A. students study more than one discipline.

Academic Programs

The academic program at Simon's Rock combines a core curriculum in the liberal arts and sciences with extensive opportunities for students to pursue their own interests through electives, tutorials, independent studies, internships, and study abroad.

The core curriculum comprises approximately half of students' total course load during their first two years. Requirements include the Writing and Thinking workshop, held the week before the regular semester begins; first-year, sophomore, and cultural perspectives seminars; and courses in the arts, mathematics, natural sciences, and foreign languages. The College also requires that students participate in the campus Active Community Engagement program, which involves them in athletics, health and wellness education, and community service opportunities on and off campus.

All new students are assigned a faculty adviser, who meets with them weekly during their first semester and regularly throughout the rest of their time at Simon's Rock. Classes are small, faculty members are accessible, and opportunities to pursue individual interests are extensive.

After earning the A.A., about 50 percent of students stay to complete their B.A. The rest transfer, usually to highly competitive colleges and universities in the U.S. and abroad. Through the sophomore planning process, students receive individualized guidance from advisers and faculty as they explore options for their last two years of undergraduate study.

Students who stay for a B.A. apply for admission to a concentration through a process called Moderation. Students meet with a group of faculty in their area(s) of interest to review their accomplishments and plan the remainder of their education at Simon's Rock. Options include advanced course work at Simon's Rock, junior year study-away programs, independent study, involvement in faculty research projects, specialized tutorials, internships, and courses at Bard College's main campus, which offers more than 800 classes each year. In addition, students may draw on the expertise of Bard faculty in the Moderation and Thesis processes, or arrange to spend a semester in residence at Bard.

The senior thesis is the focus of each B.A. student's final year. Drawing on the skills in analysis and synthesis acquired during the preceding three years, students devote themselves wholeheartedly to the project, which is defined and developed under the guidance of two or more faculty members. Recent theses have taken many forms: critical studies in literature, psychological research, musical compositions, creative fiction, translations, scientific experiments, mathematical problem solving, artistic exhibitions and performances, and various combinations of these forms.

The regular academic program is supplemented by a number of signature programs. The Simon's Rock/Columbia University Engineering Program offers three years at Simon's Rock and two years at Columbia's School of Engineering and Applied Science, after which students receive both a B.A. from Simon's Rock and a B.S. from Columbia University. A similar arrangement exists with the engineering school at Dartmouth University. A partnership with Vermont Law School offers two accelerated degree programs through which students earn a B.A. from Simon's Rock and a master's degree in either Environmental Law and Policy or Energy Regulation and Law from Vermont Law in a total of four years.

Through Simon's Rock Scholars at Oxford, a select group of students is admitted to spend their junior year at Lincoln College or St Catherine's College of the University of Oxford in England each year. The College also offers a half- or full-year program in creative writing at the Centre for New Writing at the University of Manchester in the UK and the opportunity to pursue Chinese language immersion study at Qingdao University in China. Students interested in theater can spend a year at London Dramatic Academy; those interested in photography can study at the International Center of Photography in New York City.

Off-Campus Programs

Students work with the Office of Academic Affairs and the Win Student Resource Commons to find study-abroad and internship opportunities suited to their goals and interests. Established independent programs (the School for Field Studies, SEA Semester, Global Routes), programs through other schools (Oxford University, the Sorbonne), and special Simon's Rock programs (fieldwork in geography in China) provide immersive in-depth learning. Students have recently taken intensive math instruction at Central European University in Budapest, Hungary; helped build a school in a remote village in northern Thailand; and served as apprentices to dancers, drummers, mask carvers, and batik artists in Bali. Students can also take advantage of Bard College's study-abroad and international programs, including special arrangements with universities in Germany, Russia, and South Africa, and intensive language immersion programs in China, France, Germany, Italy, Japan, Morocco, Mexico, and Russia. Programs can last for a semester, a full academic year, or shorter periods during breaks.

Academic Facilities

The Fisher Science and Academic Center houses the College's biology, chemistry, ecology, and physics laboratories; research labs for faculty members and students; classrooms and tutorial rooms; a sixty-seat lecture center; and faculty offices. The Daniel Arts Center incorporates a 350-seat theater and concert hall, a black box theater, and a dance studio and rehearsal facilities; painting, drawing, photography, ceramics, metalworking, printmaking, 3-D, video production, and digital arts studios; exhibition areas; and spaces for large-scale art and set construction. A music hall, a recording studio, and music practice rooms are also available to students in the arts. The Liebowitz International Center, which opened in 2011, houses faculty and programs focused on global issues, as well as state-of-the-art classrooms. The campus library is a unique space, one that combines both academic and social aspects, playing an important role in students' lives. The library provides a comfortable, welcoming place for reading, research, and reflection, as well as room to collaborate and engage with a like-minded community. Simon's Rock students also have access to the Bard College library. An interlibrary loan system provides access to other college and university collections. The Kilpatrick Athletic Center includes squash courts, a basketball court, an elevated track, a swimming pool, a rock-climbing wall, and a full-service fitness center.

Costs

For 2016–17, tuition and fees were $50,600, and room and board were $14,060. Other fees included health services fees of $997, a student activity fee of $200, and a $650 orientation fee for first-year students.

Financial Aid

Simon's Rock is committed to making an early college education available to a diverse group of highly motivated, academically qualified students. U.S. citizens and permanent residents are eligible for federal and state grant and loan aid, as well as institutional scholarships and grants. International students are eligible to receive Simon's Rock scholarships and grants. Approximately 85 percent of students receive some form of financial aid. Applications for admission and financial aid are considered on a rolling basis as long as space remains available; early application is encouraged. All applicants will be considered for any merit scholarships for which they are eligible; no additional application is required. Applicants typically hear a decision within six to eight weeks of completing their application.

Faculty

The College has approximately 50 full-time faculty members, 95 percent of whom holds either a doctorate or a terminal degree in their field. Simon's Rock supplements this full-time faculty with visiting scholars, regular adjunct faculty members in music and studio arts, and part-time faculty members in other areas as needed. Faculty members are distinguished not only by their excellence in teaching and advising but also by their sensitivity to the particular developmental needs of the College's younger students. Faculty work together to ensure that all students develop strong analytical abilities, skills in written and verbal expression, and knowledge across disciplines.

Student Government

Students at Simon's Rock participate in the governance of the community through elected and appointed positions on College committees that oversee academic and social life. The campus is characterized by respect for individual rights and a strong sense of community.

Admission Requirements

Simon's Rock seeks students who are smart, independent-minded, self-directed, creative, and passionate about learning. The admission staff works closely with prospective students and their parents to ensure that the decision to enter Simon's Rock is the right one. The College understands that students are not defined solely by grades and test scores. For this reason, two essays and a personal interview are required of each applicant. The application also requires an official high school transcript, three letters of recommendation, and parent statement. Standardized test scores are optional for most applicants; international students for whom English is not a first language, or who have not studied for at least two years in a school in which English is the primary language of instruction, must submit TOEFL scores.

Application and Information

Candidates should submit their materials by one of a series of submission dates listed on the Simon's Rock website (www.simons-rock.edu) and will receive a decision by the corresponding notification date, which is typically within six weeks. Applying by one of the earlier dates is strongly encouraged. There is no application fee.

Bard College at Simon's Rock is on Facebook (http://www.facebook.com/simonsrock) and Twitter (http://twitter.com/SimonsRock).

To schedule an interview or request further information, students should contact:

Office of Admission
Bard College at Simon's Rock
84 Alford Road
Great Barrington, Massachusetts 01230-1978
Phone: 413-528-7228
800-235-7186 (toll-free)
Fax: 413-541-0081
E-mail: startnow@simons-rock.edu
Website: simons-rock.edu

Simon's Rock students can explore their academic interests in a community of peers and start college early with others who share their love of learning.

COLLEGE CLOSE-UPS

BARNARD COLLEGE

NEW YORK, NEW YORK

★ To read more about this school, visit http://petersons.to/barnardcollege

The College

The founders of Barnard College were among the stalwart pioneers in the late nineteenth-century crusade who sought to make access to higher education available to women. Founded in 1889 and formally partnered with Columbia University since 1900, today Barnard serves more than 2,500 students from almost every state and more than fifty countries. It remains a partner of Columbia, with students at both schools regularly cross-registering for courses taught at either institution. Barnard students have access to the University's resources and graduates receive their degree from Columbia. Despite this close connection, Barnard College remains a small, independent liberal arts college, devoted solely to the undergraduate education of women. The College maintains its own Board of Trustees, faculty, administrative staff, endowment, admissions process, and sole ownership of its property and physical plant. It offers the intimacy of a small college with the added advantages of a large research university.

The self-contained Barnard campus occupies 4+ acres of urban property along Broadway between 116th and 120th streets and serves as an oasis from the hustle and bustle of New York City. An amalgam of styles comprise Barnard's architectural influences; the result is a blending of classic and modern. Barnard Hall, home of the Ethel S. LeFrak '41 and Samuel J. LeFrak Center; the Barnard Center for Research on Women; a portion of the library, including reserves, zines, and circulating media collection, along with study spaces; the empirical reasoning lab; and the Julius S. Held Lecture Hall, stands opposite the main gates of the College. The south end of the campus, referred to as the Quad, contains the Brooks, Reid, Hewitt, and Sulzberger residence halls; first-year students are housed in three of the four buildings in the Quad. Additional housing (twelve residence halls in total) provides those entering as first-years guaranteed housing for four years of continuous enrollment at Barnard. The latest campus addition, the Diana Center, a 70,000-square-foot student center, added a new element of design in 2010. Its seven-story glass structure stretches across campus, linking the historic gates of the entrance at the south end of campus, to one of the original campus buildings, Milbank Hall, on the north. Construction is currently underway for a new teaching and learning center, The Milstein Center, slated to open in fall 2018.

Location

Barnard is located north of Central Park on the upper west side of Manhattan, in the safe and student-friendly Morningside Heights neighborhood. The campus is directly across from Columbia University, and has six additional educational institutions as neighbors. Abounding with cultural, educational, internship, and professional opportunities and more than 500,000 college students, New York is Barnard's laboratory.

Majors and Degrees

Students can earn a Bachelor of Arts in the following subjects: Africana studies, American studies, ancient studies, anthropology, architecture, art history, Asian and Middle Eastern cultures, astronomy, biochemistry, biological sciences, chemistry, classics (Greek and Latin), comparative literature, computer science, dance, economics, education, English, environmental biology-science or studies, European studies, film studies, French, German, history, human rights, Italian, Jewish studies, mathematics and applied mathematics, medieval and Renaissance studies, music, neuroscience, philosophy, physics, political science, psychology, religion, Russian and Slavic studies, sociology, Spanish and Latin American cultures, statistics, theater, urban studies, and women's, gender, and sexuality studies. The College provides an excellent education program, leading to teaching certification with a specific urban studies track, and prepares students for programs in health and medicine, law, and business, as well as further study in a variety of graduate programs.

Barnard College also offers double- and joint-degree programs in cooperation with other schools within the Columbia community. These include a five-year M.P.A./M.I.A. (3-2) program offered in conjunction with the School of International and Public Affairs. In cooperation with the School of Law, Barnard offers an accelerated program in interdisciplinary legal education, where select students can begin their legal studies after three years. Through the School of Engineering and Applied Science, Barnard students can pursue a five-year (3-2) program in all branches of engineering, leading to both an A.B. and a B.S. degree. Through an agreement with List College of the Jewish Theological Seminary, students can earn an A.B. degree from Barnard and a B.A. in Jewish Studies.

Academic Programs

Two required courses, First-Year Seminar and First-Year Writing, set the foundation for a Barnard education with small seminar classes, limited to 16 and 12 students, respectively. In addition to these First Year Experience courses, Barnard's flexible general education requirements are organized around Foundation Requirements in four subject areas and Modes of Thinking that connect to six themes. A generous list of courses allows for students to choose which options interest them most. Barnard students shape their educational experience by choosing courses that enhance the way they view the world.

Advanced placement and I.B. credit are available. Barnard operates on a two-semester calendar, with classes beginning in early September. The fall semester ends in mid-December; classes resume for the spring semester in mid-January and end in mid-May.

Off-Campus Programs

As an independent partner of Columbia University, Barnard offers students open access to courses, libraries, and other facilities of the University. With special permission, students may also register for selected classes in Columbia's graduate and professional schools. In addition, two highly selective lesson exchange programs with the Juilliard School and the nearby Manhattan School of Music allow qualified Barnard students to take music lessons in a conservatory setting.

Barnard has a rich history and tradition of study abroad dating back to the 1930s. Today, qualified students are eligible to study in nearly 100 programs in more than fifty countries worldwide and nearly forty percent of Barnard students spend a semester or year abroad. Students are currently studying in Argentina, Australia, Austria, Bolivia, Brazil, Chile, China, Costa Rica, Czech Republic, Denmark, Ecuador, England, France, Germany, Greece, Hungary, Ireland, Israel, Italy, Japan, Jordan, Kenya, Madagascar, Netherlands, New Zealand, Panama, Peru, Russia, Scotland, Senegal, South Africa, Spain, Switzerland, and other locations. Students may also participate in a domestic exchange with Spelman College in Atlanta or Howard University in Washington, D.C.

Barnard's location offers its students a variety of work experiences through more than 2,500 internships. More than two thirds of Barnard students participate in internships throughout the academic year and/or summer.

Academic Facilities

Historic Milbank Hall anchors the north end of campus, topped by the 2,500-square-foot Arthur Ross Greenhouse, housing administrative and faculty offices in addition to the Minor Latham Playhouse. Sulzberger Tower and the residential quadrangle secure the south end of campus where most Barnard students reside. There are more than 400,000 volumes in the library, both off-site and in its temporary home in LeFrak Center (there are nearly 12 million volumes in the University library system, the sixth-largest in North America) with a zine collection focused on feminism and femme identity by people of all genders with an emphasis on zines by women of color; dance studios and classrooms in Barnard Hall and its Annex; state-of-the-art science labs in the fourteen-story Altschul Hall; and architecture classrooms with a view in the multipurpose Diana Center, with its terra-cotta glass façade, black box theatre, and art gallery, among other remarkable features.

Costs

Tuition and fees for 2016–17 were $47,631. Room and board costs are an additional $15,110.

Financial Aid

Financial aid at Barnard is awarded based upon demonstrated need. Federal funds and institutional grants are administered as determined by federal and institutional methodology, assuming College aid is supplementary to family resources. Barnard gives no merit or athletic scholarships. Once need has been established, Barnard covers 100 percent of demonstrated need with a combination of grants, loans, and work-study or student employment. Approximately 50 percent of the students at Barnard receive some form of financial aid.

Barnard College has a need-blind admission policy in which all applications from first-years who are U.S. citizens or permanent residents are judged solely on merit without reference to financial circumstances. International and transfer students are considered for need-based aid from a limited pool of funding.

Faculty

Barnard College employs more than 300 teaching faculty members with a student-faculty ratio of 8:1 (10:1 FTE). Barnard's faculty includes editors of leading scholarly journals, prize-winning novelists and translators, and frequent winners of awards from respected foundations, corporations, and government agencies. They are actively engaged in research and publication in their respective fields, but they regard teaching as their primary commitment. From the start of their time at the College, all students have faculty advisers who assist them in selecting courses and designing individual academic programs, in addition to a vast network of decanal, staff, and peer advising.

Student Government

Barnard women have access to more than eighty clubs and organizations on the College campus alone. Add to this list the hundreds of additional dually recognized clubs with members from both Barnard and Columbia, provided for through Barnard's long-standing partnership with the University, and strong friendships develop among students from both sides of Broadway. Student groups include performance groups, academic and pre-professional, ethnic and cultural, language, community service, and publications. Social interaction and cooperation between Barnard and Columbia groups is virtually seamless, with Barnard women regularly joining and leading a variety of Columbia organizations. Students, faculty members, and administrators also serve on tripartite committees and share responsibility for policy on curriculum, housing, financial aid, orientation, and the library.

Admission Requirements

The Committee on Admissions selects women of proven academic strength who exhibit the potential for further intellectual growth. Careful consideration is given to candidates' high school records, recommendations, writing skills, standardized test scores, special abilities and interests, and personal and educational context.

Admission to Barnard is highly selective and candidates for admission to the first-year class are expected to have taken a highly rigorous college-preparatory program. Students educated in a non-English-speaking setting or who have studied in English for less than four years must also take the TOEFL or IELTS exam. Interview opportunities are available for first-year students, but are not required. Interviews are not part of the transfer admission process.

Application and Information

Applicants for first-year admission should apply in the fall of their senior year of high school. Applications must be received by January 1 and must include the nonrefundable application fee. Students are notified in late March. Well-qualified high school seniors who have selected Barnard as their first-choice college may instead apply under the binding early decision plan. Early decision applications must be submitted by November 1. Barnard accepts sophomore and junior transfer students. Transfer applications must be submitted by March 15 for consideration for September entrance and by November 1 for consideration for January.

For more information about Barnard College, students should contact:

Jennifer Fondiller
Dean of Enrollment Management
Barnard College, Office of Admissions
3009 Broadway
New York, New York 10027
Phone: 212-854-2014
Fax: 212-280-8797
E-mail: admissions@barnard.edu
Website: http://www.admissions.barnard.edu

A view of Milbank Hall from the Diana, Barnard's multipurpose student center.

BAY STATE COLLEGE

BOSTON, MASSACHUSETTS

★ To read more about this school, visit http://petersons.to/baystatecollege

Bay State College
Where Your Success Matters.

The College

Founded in 1946, Bay State College is a private, independent coeducational institution located in Boston's historic Back Bay. Since its founding, Bay State College has been preparing graduates for outstanding careers and continued education.

The College offers associate degrees, bachelor's degrees, and one certificate program. The educational experience offered through the variety of associate and bachelor's degree programs prepares students to excel in the career of their choice. The College gives students constant access to the people, places, and knowledge they need to succeed. Through the transformative power of its core values of quality, respect, and support, Bay State College has been able to assist students with setting and achieving goals that prepare them for careers and continued education.

Recognizing that one of the most important aspects of college is life outside the classroom, the Office of Student Affairs seeks to provide services to Bay State College students from orientation through graduation and beyond. There are many clubs and organizations on campus, such as the Criminal Justice Society, the Student Government Association, and the Entertainment Management Association. Bay State College students enjoy the opportunity to create clubs and organizations that meet their interests. Special events throughout the year include a fashion show and a host of events produced by the Entertainment Management Association. Students also enjoy professional sports teams such as the Boston Celtics and the Boston Red Sox.

One of the unique aspects of living at Bay State College is the residence halls. With their location in the historic Back Bay, the buildings are original Victorian town houses and brownstones. Each building has its own character and charm, making living on campus a distinctive experience. Each building has a computer lab with free Internet access, coin-operated laundry, vending machines, a house phone with free local calling, and a social lounge that includes cable television and a microwave oven. Each student room has basic cable service and wireless Internet access.

The Career Services office offers career assistance to both current students and alumni, continuing to provide assistance and support to them throughout their careers, with career-management counseling, workshops, career panels, guest speakers, resume and cover letter reviews, interview preparation, and job listings.

Bay State College is accredited by the New England Association of Schools and Colleges; is authorized to award the Associate in Science, Associate in Applied Science, and three Bachelor of Science degrees by the commonwealth of Massachusetts; and is a member of several professional educational associations. The College's medical assisting program is accredited by the Accrediting Bureau of Health Education Schools (ABHES). The College's nursing program is accredited by the Accreditation Commission for Education in Nursing. The physical therapist assistant studies program is accredited by the Commission on Accreditation in Physical Therapy Education (CAPTE) of the American Physical Therapy Association (APTA).

Location

Located in the historic city of Boston, Massachusetts, and surrounded by dozens of colleges and universities, Bay State College is an ideal setting in which to pursue a college degree. Tree-lined streets around the school are mirrored in the skyscrapers of the Back Bay. The College is located within walking distance of several major-league sports franchises, concert halls, museums, the Freedom Trail, Boston Symphony Hall, the Boston Public Library, and the Boston Public Garden. World-class shopping and major cultural and sporting events help make college life an experience that students will always remember. The College is accessible by the MBTA, commuter rail, and bus and is near Boston Logan International Airport.

Majors and Degrees

Bay State College is continually reviewing, enhancing, and adding new programs to help graduates remain industry-current in their respective fields.

Bachelor's degrees are offered in criminal justice, fashion industry, information technology, management, music industry, and nursing (RN to B.S.N.).

Associate degrees are offered in accounting, business administration, criminal justice, health studies, information technology, medical assisting, nursing, physical therapist assistant studies, and retail business management.

A certificate in medical assisting is also offered.

Academic Programs

Bay State College operates on a semester calendar. The fall semester runs from early September to late December. The spring semester runs from late January to mid-May. A second campus is located in Taunton, Massachusetts.

Bay State College also offers courses on-ground and online to working adults in its Evening and Online Division. The courses, offered in eight-week sessions, allow more flexibility for students who must balance work and family commitments while pursuing their education.

Off-Campus Programs

The internship program, available in all major areas of study, provides students with practical field experience, enabling them to hone their skills and gain insight into the various technologies employed in their respective fields. Fieldwork is a requirement for many majors and is a great opportunity for students to build resumes, apply what they have learned in the classroom, and gain a competitive advantage in the job market.

Students from Bay State College are among the 250 students participating in the Walt Disney World College Program. During their stay at Walt Disney World, students receive on-the-job training and classroom experience. This is just one of the many internship possibilities for students each year at Bay State College.

Academic Facilities

The library has a combined book collection of approximately 5,300 books. In addition, Bay State College has 100 periodicals and 200 audiovisual titles. The College's sixty computers have access to the Internet and several databases for magazine and journal articles, including ProQuest Academic, LexisNexis Academic, JSTOR, Infotrac, Newsbank, EBSCO, the Internet Public Library, and the Library of Congress Research Tools. The library also participates in an interlibrary-loan program with the Boston Regional Library System.

Costs

Tuition for 2017–18 for full-time students is $27,150 per year (some costs vary by program). Room and board are $13,000 per year; student services fee, $400; and student activity fee, $50. The cost of books and additional fees varies by major. A residence hall security deposit of $300 and a technology fee of $300 are required of all resident students. Tuition for evening and online students is $380 per credit hour, with the exception of information technology, medical assisting, and health studies programs which are charged at the rate of $550 per credit hour.

Financial Aid

Financial aid is available to those who qualify. The College's financial aid staff works one-on-one with every student to help them find what is best for their specific situation: scholarships, grants, loans, payment plans, or a combination of those. The College also offers numerous part-time employment and work-study opportunities during the academic year.

Faculty

There are 99 faculty members, with the majority holding advanced degrees. The student-faculty ratio is 18:1.

Student Government

The Student Association serves as the voice of the Bay State College student body. It consists of a group of elected student representatives from the various academic programs. Roles and responsibilities of Student Association members include providing input on College policies and procedures, assuming leadership roles on campus, acting as a voice of the student body, and planning activities and events.

Elections are held every fall, and all students are encouraged to vote. The group comprises representatives from each College department, club, and organization, and membership spans all four class years.

Admission Requirements

An applicant to Bay State College must be a high school graduate, a current high school student working toward graduation, or a recipient of a GED certificate. The Office of Admissions recommends that applicants to the associate degree programs have a minimum 2.0 GPA on a 4.0 scale; if available, applicants may submit SAT or ACT scores. Applicants must receive the recommendation of a Bay State College admissions officer. Applicants to the bachelor's degree programs must have a minimum 2.3 GPA on a 4.0 scale and must also submit SAT or ACT scores. A personal interview is highly recommended for all students, and parents are encouraged to attend. Students are responsible for arranging for their official high school transcripts, test scores, and letters of recommendation to be submitted to Bay State College. International applicants must also submit high school transcripts translated into English with an explanation of the grading system, a TOEFL score of at least 500 on the paper-based exam or 173 on the computer-based exam if English is not the native language, and financial documentation. The nursing, physical therapist assistant studies program, and Evening and Online Divisions have different or additional admission requirements. For more information about these programs, students should visit the website at http://www.baystate.edu.

The Bay State College Admissions Office notifies applicants of a decision within three weeks of receipt of the transcript and other required documents. When a student is accepted to Bay State College, there is a $100 nonrefundable tuition deposit required to ensure a place in the class, which is credited toward the tuition fee. Deposits are due within thirty days of acceptance. Once a student is accepted, a Bay State College representative creates a personalized financial plan that provides payment options for a Bay State College education.

Application and Information

Applications are accepted on a rolling basis. The fall tuition payment due date is July 1; the spring tuition payment due date is December 1.

Applications should be submitted to:

Admissions Office
Bay State College
122 Commonwealth Avenue
Boston, Massachusetts 02116
Phone: 800-81-LEARN (toll-free)
Fax: 617-249-0400
E-mail: admissions@baystate.edu
Website: http://www.baystate.edu
http://www.facebook.com/baystatecollege
http://twitter.com/baystatecollege

Giving students access is an essential part of a Bay State College education. Students have access to a community of support, experiential learning, faculty with real-world experience, and a dynamic location in the heart of the city.

BENTLEY UNIVERSITY

WALTHAM, MASSACHUSETTS

★ To read more about this school, visit http://petersons.to/bentleyuniversity

BENTLEY UNIVERSITY

The University

Bentley University believes that education should prepare students for whatever the world sends their way. That's why Bentley's one-of-a-kind curriculum starts with a core business foundation, infused with the kind of critical thinking and cultural understanding that comes from the study of the arts and sciences. As a result, Bentley students are highly sought after by today's leading organizations because of their professionalism, exposure to state-of-the-art research tools, and diverse, real-world experience. In its 2016 "Best Undergraduate Business Schools" issue, *Bloomberg Businessweek* ranked Bentley 10th among the country's top undergraduate business programs.

Located on a classic New England campus minutes from Boston, Bentley offers a wide variety of majors and minors, as well as optional liberal studies and business studies majors designed to create a modern intersection of the arts and sciences and business that's unique in higher education. This fusion of business fundamentals and liberal arts enables Bentley students to think outside of the box when faced with critical decisions in the workplace.

Bentley's career services office was recently ranked first in the country by the Princeton Review. The Miller Center for Career Services offers resources including an on-campus recruiting program involving 1,000 national and international companies; an online job and internship database; career fairs; workshops on topics such as interviewing and networking; and a Career Development Seminar (CDI 1901) for first-year students.

This approach works: In 2016, more than 95 percent of students found employment or enrolled in graduate school within six months of graduation. Their median annual salary was $55,000.

Approximately 98 percent of freshmen live on campus. Twenty-three residence halls provide a range of housing options: dorms, suites, and apartments. Housing is provided for all four years; all residence halls are air-conditioned and typically include study lounges, exercise facilities, TV lounges, and game rooms. Bentley has a variety of meal plans for students to choose from as they move into suites and apartments with kitchens. There are eleven places on campus to dine, offering an array of food options from buffet-style cafeterias to a Currito to Dunkin' Donuts.

Students live and learn in a multicultural environment that prepares them to thrive in today's diverse world. International students representing nearly 100 countries make up 16 percent of the student body and bring valuable perspectives to the Bentley community.

Supporting Bentley's commitment to diversity are offices such as the Multicultural Center, Spiritual Life Center, Center for International Students and Scholars, Center for Women in Business, and the Women's Center.

The newly renovated Student Center is the hub of campus activity and is home to the main dining room, the pub, eateries, student services, and more than 100 student organizations. These groups represent academics, the arts and media, religions, fraternity and sorority life, and cultural interests.

Athletic programs are a Bentley hallmark and include intramurals, recreational sports, and more than 20 varsity teams in NCAA Divisions I and II. The Dana Athletic Center houses a weight and fitness complex, food court, locker rooms, a gym, a basketball court, volleyball and racquetball courts, a competition-size pool with a diving tank, and saunas. Outdoor facilities include soccer and baseball fields, a track, and tennis courts.

Location

Bentley's location in Waltham, Massachusetts—just minutes west of Boston—puts the city within easy reach. As the country's ultimate university town, Boston's options range from theater to art exhibits, dance clubs to concerts, and championship sports to world-class shopping. Bentley's free shuttle makes regular trips to Harvard Square in Cambridge, just a subway ride from Boston. Boston also offers many opportunities for internships and jobs after graduation.

Majors and Degrees

The Bentley curriculum is a ground-breaking integration of business and the arts and sciences that has been featured in the *Wall Street Journal*.

To that end, Bachelor of Science (B.S.) degree programs enable students to gain in-depth knowledge and skills in specific business disciplines: accountancy, actuarial science, computer information systems, corporate finance and accounting, creative industries, economics–finance, finance, information design and corporate communication, information systems audit and control, management, managerial economics, marketing, mathematical sciences, and professional sales.

Bentley also offers Bachelor of Arts (B.A.) degree programs with majors in English, global studies, health sciences, history, liberal arts, media and culture, philosophy, public policy, Spanish studies, and sustainability science. All Bachelor of Arts students gain business experience through either the Business Studies Major (BSM) or minor. All students can also choose from one of 35 minors, including entrepreneurial studies, law, and sports management.

The Liberal Studies Major (LSM), an optional double major, can be combined with any business program. It provides students with a competitive edge by building meaningful connections across and within disciplines. To complete the LSM, students do not need to take any extra courses beyond those normally required. It allows students to add another credential to their degree, helping them stand out to employers. LSM concentrations include American studies; diversity and society; earth, environment, and global sustainability; ethics and social responsibility; global perspectives; health and industry; media arts and society; and quantitative perspectives.

Academic Programs

The Honors Program allows students in the top 10 percent of their class to select honors-level courses each semester that provide extra intellectual challenge in a seminar atmosphere.

The Women's Leadership Program is sponsored by Bentley's Center for Women and Business, and gives participants the opportunity to participate in workshops, roundtables, and special events that explore critical gender equity issues on a deeper level, while developing effective leadership and communications skills. The program also includes a $10,000 annual award toward tuition, totaling $40,000 over four years.

The Falcon Fast-Track Program is a streamlined graduate school enrollment option for top-tier Bentley graduates with a GPA of 3.2 or higher. This new program allows qualified Bentley graduates to obtain a master's degree after completing a bachelor's degree (up to five years after graduation) without going through the traditional application process, including waiver of the GMAT or GRE, and no application fee.

Off-Campus Programs

Hands-on experience is emphasized across the curriculum. Internships, study abroad, service-learning, and corporate partnerships allow students to apply classroom theory in the community.

Each year, more than 90 percent of students complete at least one internship, building valuable work experience and networking connections. Some of the top internship employers include Fidelity Investments, the TJX Companies, Liberty Mutual, Bain & Company, and all of the Big Four accounting firms.

Bentley students can gain insight into different cultures by studying abroad. Programs take place in more than 25 countries and vary in length from one week to a full academic year.

Through Bentley's Service-Learning Center, students build skills in business, communication, and teamwork while assisting nonprofit and community-based organizations both locally and internationally.

Academic Facilities

Concepts taught in the classroom are put to use in several high-tech learning laboratories.

Bentley's financial Trading Room combines state-of-the-art technology and real-time data to offer first-hand exposure to financial concepts in simulated trading sessions. Resources include Bloomberg, Capital IQ, Datastream, FactSet, Thomson One Analytics, Portfolio Analysis, MATLAB, S&P Compustat, and Worldscope.

The Center for Marketing Technology plays an integral role in marketing programs. Students gain a full grasp of software options, familiarity with research tools and techniques, and knowledge of new digital marketing frameworks.

The Accounting Center for Electronic Learning and Business Management (ACELAB) introduces cutting-edge technologies that are reshaping the accounting profession. Students have access to auditing and tax preparation software as well as other professional applications from industry leaders such as SAP and Oracle.

The Center for Languages and International Collaboration (CLIC) is a key resource for language courses, international studies majors, and students with an interest in global issues. The center promotes collaboration among Bentley students and their counterparts overseas.

The Media and Culture Labs and Studio feature resources for video production and editing as well as digital photography. The lab provides students with industry-standard software programs for screenwriting, sound mixing, graphic design, and DVD authoring.

The User Experience Center (UXC) features labs ideal for usability testing. Students use the applications employed by technical communicators, web developers, user-interface designers, and usability specialists.

The CIS Learning and Technology Sandbox is a collaborative space for learning new technologies. Its resources include Google TVs, Xbox 360 with Kinect, study spaces, large-screen TVs, a smart board, specialized networking equipment, and the latest in Windows, Linux, and Android development software.

The Bentley Library is outfitted with computer workstations, group study rooms, and wireless network access. It also has an exceptional number of online database resources, research guides, and consultation appointments are available to assist students with their projects.

Costs

Tuition for resident and nonresident students during the 2017–18 academic year is $46,370. Room and board (double room, meal plan) costs are $15,720. Additional expenses include books, supplies, technology fee, and personal and travel expenses.

Financial Aid

Bentley's financial aid program includes both scholarships based on academic achievement, which are awarded through the admission process, as well as grants based on financial need. Bentley administered nearly $100 million in aid to undergraduate students last year. Well over half of that amount came in the form of grants and scholarships directly from Bentley. Significant institutional resources are committed each year so that all academically qualified students have access to a Bentley education regardless of their financial resources. Currently, more than 70 percent of undergraduates receive some type of financial assistance—either grants, scholarships, loans, and/or work study.

Faculty

Bentley faculty members are teacher-scholars known for their classroom skills and cutting-edge research. They bring practical, real-world experience to the classroom, based on years of professional involvement in their fields. Faculty research focuses on issues of prime importance to current business practice. Much of the research is conducted in partnership with leading organizations. A student-faculty ratio of 12:1 and average class size of 26 ensure a personal experience for students. All courses are taught by professors; there are no teaching assistants. Students often note that professors are accessible to them outside of the classroom.

Student Government

Bentley has a number of student governing groups, including the Student Government Association, Residence Hall Association, and the Graduate Student Association.

Admission Requirements

Applicants are encouraged to complete a competitive university preparatory program. Recommendations include four years of English, four years of mathematics (preferably algebra I and II, geometry, and pre-calculus or its equivalent), and three to four years each of history, laboratory science, and a foreign language.

Along with the application, students must submit a secondary school transcript, letters of recommendation from a teacher and a counselor, and official scores of either the SAT or ACT. Bentley has a separate application for transfer students. Applicants who are nonnative speakers of English must also submit official scores of the Test of English as a Foreign Language (TOEFL).

Application and Information

Bentley University accepts the Common Application. Candidates for the fall semester are notified in late March; spring semester candidates and transfers are notified on a rolling basis.

Prospective students can visit bentley.edu/undergraduate/applying for application information and deadlines.

For more information, students should contact:

Office of Undergraduate Admission
Bentley University
175 Forest Street
Waltham, Massachusetts 02452-4705
Phone: 781-891-2244
800-523-2354 (toll-free)
Fax: 781-891-3414
E-mail: ugadmission@bentley.edu
Website: bentley.edu/undergraduate
facebook.com/bentleyadmission
twitter.com/ugabentley

Bentley students have access to professional research tools, cutting-edge software, and other valuable resources in seven high-tech learning labs and a state-of-the-art library.

BERKLEE COLLEGE OF MUSIC

BOSTON, MASSACHUSETTS

Berklee

★ To read more about this school, visit http://petersons.to/berkleecollegeofmusic

COLLEGE CLOSE-UPS

The College

Berklee College of Music was founded on the revolutionary principle that the best way to prepare students for careers in music is through the study and practice of contemporary music. For over 70 years, the college has evolved to reflect the state of the art in music and the music business, leading the way with the world's first baccalaureate studies in jazz, rock, electric guitar, film scoring, songwriting, turntables, electronic production, and more than a dozen other genres and fields of study. Berklee serves distance learners worldwide through its award-winning online school, Berklee Online. The college's national after-school music program for underserved teens, the Berklee City Music Network, is in 41 cities and counting. Berklee's campus in Valencia, Spain, hosts the college's first graduate programs in contemporary performance; global entertainment and music business; scoring for film, television, and video games; and music technology innovation. With a diverse and talented student body representing nearly 100 countries, and alumni who have collectively won more than 310 Grammys and Latin Grammys, Berklee is the world's premier learning lab for the music of today—and tomorrow.

Berklee has proven its commitment to this approach by wholeheartedly embracing change. The musical landscape looks nothing like it did when Berklee was founded in 1945, but the college has remained current by supplementing its core curriculum with studies in emerging musical genres and indispensable new technology. Berklee also has responded to important developments in music education and music therapy, making good on its promise to improve society through music.

At Berklee, students acquire a strong foundation of contemporary music theory and technique, then build upon that foundation by learning the practical, professional skills needed to sustain a career in music. Students can earn either a fully accredited four-year baccalaureate degree or a professional diploma in music production and engineering, film scoring, music business/management, electronic production and design, songwriting, and music therapy, as well as the traditional mainstays of performance and composition. Perhaps more importantly, these disciplines prepare students for employment in the music industry.

Berklee attracts a diverse range of students who reflect the multiplicity of influences in today's music, including jazz, rock, hip-hop, country, gospel, electronica, Latin, and funk. The college is a magnet for aspiring musicians from every corner of the earth, which gives the school a uniquely international flavor. Of all U.S. colleges and universities, Berklee has one of the largest percentages of undergraduates from outside the United States—more than 30 percent. Reflecting the interplay between music and culture, Berklee creates an environment where aspiring music professionals learn how to integrate new ideas and showcase their distinctive skills in an evolving community.

The college's alumni form a wide network of industry professionals who use their openness, virtuosity, and versatility to take music in new directions. Notable alumni include Jeff Bhasker, Gary Burton, Terri Lyne Carrington, Bruce Cockburn, Juan Luis Guerra, Roy Hargrove, Amy Heidemann (Karmin), Quincy Jones, Diana Krall, Aimee Mann, Arif Mardin, Branford Marsalis, Danilo Pérez, John Scofield, Howard Shore, Alan Silvestri, Esperanza Spalding, Susan Tedeschi, and Gillian Welch.

Location

Berklee College of Music is located in Boston's Fenway Cultural District. An international hub of intellectual and creative exploration, the neighborhood includes many of the world's other great colleges and universities, treasure-filled museums and galleries, and world-class performing arts centers such as Symphony Hall and the Wang Center. Great performers appear at the Berklee Performance Center, and the college's all-ages venue, Cafe 939, highlights up-and-coming international performers in all genres. In addition to the music made at Berklee, there is a lively club and concert scene in the area with coffeehouses featuring folk and bluegrass music; neighborhood clubs offering jazz, reggae, and world music; and clubs specializing in rock, blues, dance, urban, and country music.

Berklee students participate in intramural sports and fitness programs at Berklee and at other ProArts Consortium member institutions; enjoy professional sporting events like baseball with the Boston Red Sox at Fenway Park, hockey with the Boston Bruins, basketball with the Boston Celtics, and football with the New England Patriots; attend theater, club, and concert hall events year-round throughout the city; and walk and bike through the city's many parks and public gardens. The college is on Boston's public transportation system, allowing students to take advantage of all that Boston has to offer.

In 2011, Berklee launched an international campus offering master's of music and art degrees in Valencia, Spain, in the heart of the City of Arts and Sciences complex in the Palau de les Arts. Valencia boasts the highest number of musicians per capita in Spain, and thousands of Valencians of all ages are involved in musical activities. With more than 500 symphonic bands throughout the region and representing countless music styles, including classical, rock, pop, and jazz, the Berklee campus in Valencia aims to be a main hub for the study, evolution, and global proliferation of many musical genres, including flamenco, in Europe, Latin America, the Middle East, and all over the world.

Majors and Degrees

Berklee offers a Bachelor of Music (B.M.) degree program and a four-year program leading to a professional diploma. Students may choose to major in composition, contemporary writing and production, electronic production and design, film scoring, jazz composition, music business/management, music education, music production and engineering, music therapy, performance, professional music, or songwriting. In addition, students may choose from 19 minors: acoustics and electronics, American roots music, audio design for video games, commercial record production, conducting, drama, English, history, instrument repair, music and society, music technology, performance studies in Latin music, philosophy, psychology, recording and production for musicians, theory of jazz and popular song, video game scoring, visual culture and new media studies, and writing for TV and new media. The college also offers a five-year, dual-major option in which students graduate with an even more marketable education that expands their career options in the music industry.

Academic Programs

The Bachelor of Music program offers a complete music curriculum combined with liberal arts courses in English, history, languages, mathematics, philosophy, and physical and social sciences. Intensive concentration in music subjects provides students with the necessary tools for developing their musical talents to the fullest and prepares them for the multifaceted and ever-changing demands of today's professional music. The degree program is especially appropriate for students who wish to earn a formal degree; are interested in pursuing a career in music education, music therapy, or music business/management; or want to continue their studies at the graduate level.

The diploma is designed for students who want to focus exclusively on contemporary music studies and still get the benefits of a Berklee experience, as well as students who have already earned a bachelor's degree at another institution.

All students must complete the core music curriculum, which consists of harmony, arranging, ear training, and introduction to music technology; instrumental studies; ensembles and instrumental labs; and the concentrate courses designated for each major. All degree candidates must complete the general education curriculum and traditional music studies courses.

Off-Campus Programs

Through the Professional Arts Consortium (ProArts), an association of six area institutions dedicated to the performing and visual arts, Berklee students can take courses at leading Boston arts institutions in communications, modern dance, visual arts, ballet, architectural and graphic design, theater arts, and liberal arts. The other members of the consortium are Boston Architectural Center, the Boston Conservatory, Emerson College, Massachusetts College of Art, and the School of the Museum of Fine Arts.

Students who major in music business/management may be eligible to receive credit for their Berklee course work toward an M.B.A. from Suffolk University.

The Berklee International Network is a shared endeavor designed to promote the effectiveness of contemporary music education among members and to advance the value of contemporary music education internationally. Berklee faculty and staff members visit network member schools annually to conduct workshops and clinics and to audition students for scholarships for full-time study at Berklee. There are currently 19 members of the network in Argentina, Australia, Brazil, Canada, Colombia, Ecuador, Finland, France, Germany, Greece, Hong Kong, Ireland, Israel, Japan, Korea, Malaysia, Puerto Rico, and Spain.

The college has a robust internship program, with students learning in music companies in Los Angeles, New York, Nashville, London, and beyond, as well as a semester-long global studies program at Berklee's campus in Valencia, Spain.

Academic Facilities

Berklee students have the opportunity to work in the college's state-of-the-art music technology facilities, using some of the most sophisticated recording and synthesis equipment currently available, in addition to facilities specifically designed for the areas of composition, arranging, and film scoring. The facilities at Berklee are furnished with the instruments and equipment that are being used in the world beyond the classroom. Berklee's performance facilities include the Berklee Performance Center, a 1,200-seat concert hall hosting more than 300 student, faculty, and other concerts each year; Cafe 939, a state-of-the-art, all-ages, student-run music venue and coffeehouse; four recital halls equipped with a variety of sound reinforcement systems; more than 40 ensemble rooms; over 80 private instruction studios; about 300 private practice rooms; and an outdoor concert pavilion.

Technological facilities include the Recording Studio Complex, consisting of 13 studio facilities that offer multitrack digital and analog recording capability, automated mix-down, digital audio editing, video postproduction, 5.1 multichannel surround mixing, and comprehensive signal processing equipment; electronic production and design labs, with nine facilities featuring hundreds of synthesizers, standard and alternate controllers, effects processors, recorders, mixers, computers, and software representing many of the industry's most progressive manufacturers; the Learning Center, a networked, computer-based training facility; the Professional Writing Division MIDI lab and advanced classroom, with 28 digital audio/MIDI work-stations; and film-scoring classroom, labs, and scoring studio complex, offering students the opportunity for hands-on study in the areas of film music composition, conducting, MIDI sequencing, and digital music editing. In January 2013, the college opened its state-of-the-art 160 Massachusetts Avenue Building, a 16-story tower that houses over 350 students and includes a ten-studio recording complex.

Costs

Information on costs is available online at berklee.edu/financial-aid/cost-of-attendance.

Financial Aid

A very large percentage of the student body receives some form of financial aid, so no student should allow financial barriers to stop him or her from applying to the college. Funds are available from many different sources, including Berklee and federal and state programs. Students are eligible for merit-based scholarships and, in cases of demonstrated need, federal assistance is provided. Subsidized loans, a tuition-installment plan, and campus employment are also available. Financial aid counselors are available to students and their families to discuss the various options available to them. Students should be aware that there are specific deadlines for federal and state fund applications and for scholarships. Berklee awards more than $35 million in scholarships each year to students from all over the world who demonstrate the potential to succeed in today's music industry.

Berklee's Office of Scholarships and Student Employment provides extensive opportunities for both domestic and international students to apply for merit-based scholarships via audition (entering students) or submission of an achievement portfolio (continuing and returning students who have successfully completed a minimum of two semesters).

Faculty

The personal attention students receive from teachers at Berklee guides them beyond the theoretical so that they can apply what they've learned in their next ensemble rehearsal, evening jam session, or gig. All instruction is administered by Berklee faculty members, the 600 teachers and talented artists who demonstrate their commitment to music education in the classroom and beyond. Most faculty members also write and arrange music, perform in concert halls and clubs, make recordings, or perform on television and radio, and some do it all. All faculty members bring to the classroom knowledge of music and the wisdom that comes from professional music experience.

Student Government

Berklee's broad-based system of governance relies on participation from all areas of the college community. The Council of Students represents the voice and perspectives of students regarding all of the issues reviewed by the college. Students are also asked to serve on a wide variety of college committees that advise administrators on such topics as the college's master plan, honorary degree recipients, the website, and academic and student policies. And many of Berklee's student leaders have the opportunity to meet with the president, vice presidents, and trustees during the academic year to discuss current issues, concerns, and institutional activities.

Admission Requirements

Berklee's board of admissions seeks students who show high potential—who are creative, collaborative, and who have something extra that sets them apart. The college considers every aspect of an applicant's strengths and looks for candidates who reflect the rich diversity of Berklee's curriculum, with high musical aptitude as players or writers; or in business, production, music therapy, or music education.

The college takes academics into consideration as well as musical aptitude. Berklee does not have specific GPA or test score requirements, nor does it have specific class rank requirements. The audition and interview process, along with a comprehensive and holistic evaluation of each applicant, provides a wealth of information to assess students' ability to succeed at Berklee.

Application and Information

Berklee uses fixed application deadlines for each semester of entry. Applying to the college is a three-step process. All applicants must submit an online application, participate in a live audition and interview, and mail in the appropriate transcripts to be considered for full-time enrollment at the college.

The online application asks that students provide their personal contact information, indicate whether they are a vocalist or instrumentalist; and name their preferred audition and interview location. A live audition and interview is required as part of the application. A complete listing of audition dates, deadlines, and locations throughout the world is available on Berklee's website.

The college also asks that students provide information about their musical and academic background. All supporting materials must be postmarked by the posted deadline date. To learn more about how to apply to the college, and information about the audition and interview experience, students should visit http://www.berklee.edu/admissions.

For further information, students should contact:

Office of Admissions
Berklee College of Music
1140 Boylston Street
Boston, Massachusetts 02215
Phone: 617-747-2221 (worldwide)
800-BERKLEE (toll-free in the U.S. and Canada)
Fax: 617-747-2047
E-mail: admissions@berklee.edu
Website: http://www.berklee.edu
http://www.facebook.com/berkleecollege
http://twitter.com/BerkleeCollege
http://www.youtube.com/berkleecollege

Berklee College of Music students using state-of-the-art music technology.

COLLEGE CLOSE-UPS

BETHEL COLLEGE

MISHAWAKA, INDIANA

★ For more information, visit http://petersons.to/bethelcollege

The College

Going to college is about much more than earning a degree. Bethel wants students to become completely connected: to understand, with depth and insight, the world and students' place in it. It can be challenging, but Bethel offers the resources students need to succeed.

Bethel is an evangelical Christian college affiliated with the Missionary Church. Its 1,650 students represent more than 20 denominational affiliations and come from 27 states and 41 different countries Twenty-three percent of the student body is multicultural.

As a college of the arts and sciences, Bethel provides students with skills they will use throughout their lifetime: effective communication, resourceful problem solving, teamwork, and critical thinking. This solid preparation means that students enjoy success as they pursue their careers or graduate school. With more than 50 areas of study, students are able to learn what they love and put it to use in the real world.

The solid preparation built into a Bethel education means their graduates in every program enjoy exceptional success. Consider these facts:

- Bethel graduates have been admitted to top-ranking graduate and professional schools, including those at Indiana University, University of Notre Dame, Stanford University, the Peabody Institute of The Johns Hopkins University, Gordon-Conwell Seminary, Cornell University, and many others
- Bethel has the highest percentage of alumni rated as "highly effective teachers" in the classroom of any other college in Indiana, according to a report by the Indiana Department of Education.
- 92 percent of Bethel students who have applied to medical school have been accepted, more than twice the national average of 45 percent.
- Sign language interpreting students achieved a 100 percent pass rate for the National Interpreter Certification (NIC) written exam.

Connection after connection, the people at Bethel—students, faculty, and staff—are a community. Individuals connect their faith with learning, science with scripture, revelation with research, and competition with compassion. Bethel College is the ground for spirited connections.

Location

Bethel is urban-situated, in a vibrant location, rich with opportunity. The Mishawaka/South Bend area of Northern Indiana is home to 250,000 residents, five colleges, the second largest shopping district in the state, and 50 parks. Several local attractions, like the Potawatomi Zoo, South Bend Chocolate Café, The Morris Performing Arts Center, and the South Bend Cubs, are within minutes of campus. Students enjoy the serenity of a suburban campus setting, but they can also stand on the sandy beaches of Lake Michigan, which is less than an hour away, or visit the city of Chicago only 90 miles from campus. With more than 16,000 organizations in the region, students can pursue an internship or job at a major business, health care facility, church, social service agency, or governmental office.

Majors and Degrees

Bethel offers more than 50 different programs of study at the undergraduate, pre-professional and graduate level.

Undergraduate degree programs include: Accounting, American Sign Language–Deaf Studies*, American Sign Language–Interpreter Training, Applied Politics, Art–Graphic Design, Art–Studio Arts, Biblical Languages*, Biblical Studies*, Biochemistry and Molecular Biology, Biology, Business Administration, Business Management*, Chemistry, Christian Ministries, Biblical Studies Track, Children's Ministries Track, Christian Ministries Track, Sports Ministries Track, TESOL Track, Youth Ministries Track, Communication, Computer Science*, Criminal Justice, Cross-Cultural Communication*, Design*, Economics*, Economics and Finance, Education, Art, Early Childhood, Elementary, English, Health/Physical Education, Mathematics, Music, Science–Biology, Science–Chemistry, Social Studies, Special Education, Engineering and Management, English & Writing, Exercise Science, Family Studies*, Financial Services Professional, History, Humanities, Intercultural Studies, International Health, Leadership*, Liberal Studies, Marketing*, Mathematics, Mathematics/Physics (Engineering 3-2), Music (General), Music/Church Music*, Music Performance, Musical Theatre*, Nursing, Pastoral Ministries, Philosophy, Physics*, Psychology, Sociology, Spanish*, Sport Management, Sport Studies, Teaching English to Students of Other Languages (TESOL), Theatre Arts, Undecided/Exploratory Studies, Worship Arts, and Youth Ministry*.

** Associate degree, minor, or concentration*

Pre-professional programs are available in the following fields: Dentistry, Law, Medicine, Optometry, Pharmacy, Physical Therapy, Seminary, and Veterinary Medicine.

Bethel also offers several graduate degree programs, including the Master of Arts in Business Administration (MBA), Master of Arts in Counseling, Master of Arts in Education, Master of Arts in Ministry, Master of Arts in Pastoral Ministries, Master of Arts in School Administration, Master of Arts in Special Education, Master of Arts in Teaching, Master of Arts in Theological Studies, Master of Science in Nursing, and Transition to Teaching program. Additional information is available at BethelCollege.edu/Academics.

Academic Programs

Students who have not made a decision about their major and want to explore the wide range of options available to them can do so through Bethel's unique exploratory studies program. The program offers time to exercise intellectual curiosity and define long-term academic and career goals. Students can start by taking The Bethel Core, 54 credit hours in liberal arts courses that are required for almost all majors.

Bethel's Center for Academic Success provides a range of student support services: tutoring, study spaces, the Disability Services office, and more.

Bethel College is accredited by the Higher Learning Commission, Indiana Division of Professional Standards, National Association of Schools of Music, National Council for Accreditation of Teacher Education, Accreditation Commission for Education in Nursing, and Indiana Professional Licensing Agency.

Off-Campus Programs

Students aren't limited to the four walls of the classroom. Bethel College has a global vision for its students to not only learn about the world, but also to go abroad, experience new cultures, and serve others. The Global Engagement Office exists to enable students to move beyond their current cultural, spiritual, academic and relational contexts. Through short-term and semester-length trips, students encounter fresh cultural experiences and service opportunities designed to challenge them academically, stretch their global outlook, and spur them on spiritually, all while growing in Christian community. Bethel offers educational opportunities across the country and around the world, with semester-abroad programs in Australia, Costa Rica, Jordan, Oxford, South Africa, and Uganda. There are also opportunities to travel during the summer to places like Spain or Indonesia or to go on week-long trips called Task Force Teams to places like Guatemala, Thailand, Alaska, or California. Additional information can be found at BethelCollege.edu/MoveBeyond.

Preparing servant leaders is central to Bethel's mission, so it shouldn't surprise one to learn the campus is home to a variety of community-focused ministries and missions. Students can act on their faith through service learning, which provides opportunities to tutor children, build houses, feed the hungry, and clean parks and neighborhoods. Students take part in an annual service workday, when classes are cancelled and Bethel students, faculty, and staff pitch in to serve the community. In addition, each dorm is matched to an organization in the community where they serve in a variety of ways.

Academic Facilities

Always a small but solid college of the arts and sciences, Bethel is emerging as a strong, progressive and dynamic regional campus. Since 2000, more than 20 buildings have been added to Bethel's campus including Bridges Hall, a women's residence hall; Sufficient Grounds Café and Campus Store; Jenkins baseball stadium, an addition to Science Hall, Logan Village, and a ceramics studio.

The Otis Bowen Library is an integral part of Bethel and its educational systems. The library supports the various divisions within the undergraduate college, the graduate programs, and the professional growth of the professors and the recreational and general interest of the college. Special collections include the Education Resource Center, the Archives of Bethel College, the Missionary Church Archives and Historical Collection, and the Dr. Otis R. Bowen Museum and Archives.

Costs

In the 2017–18 academic year, tuition is $27,580. Room and board (14 meal/week plan) costs total $8,420 and there is also a $350 service fee. Actual direct costs may vary based on meal plan selection and housing assignment.

Financial Aid

More than 97 percent of Bethel students receive financial assistance. Merit awards range from $2,000 to $16,000 and are available for traditional undergraduate students. There are also awards based on talent and ability through art, athletics, music, and theater. More details can be found at BethelCollege.edu/FinancialAid.

Faculty

Eighty-two percent of the full-time, tenured Bethel faculty hold a terminal degree in their field. They consider their primary role to be teachers and mentors to Bethel students. The student-faculty ratio is 12:1 and the average class has 16 students, which allows students more opportunity to receive personal attention from professors.

Student Life

More than 30 active student organizations provide ample opportunities for Bethel students to get involved. Students can stay active via intramural sports like powder-puff and flag football, indoor and sand volleyball, League of Legends, 3 versus 3 and 5 versus 5 basketball, futsal, dodgeball, and softball. They can connect with others who have similar interests by joining a club: American Sign Language Club, Black Student Fellowship, Enactus (business club), International Student Fellowship, Mu Alpha Theta (math club), Psychology Club, Student Council, Students for Life, and The Company (theater arts). Additional information is available at BethelCollege.edu/StudentLife.

The Bethel Pilots are perennial powerhouses, competing in the Crossroads League of the NAIA and in the National Christian College Athletic Association (NCCAA). The Pilots have won more than 35 national team championships since 1990. A broad spectrum of athletic teams for both men and women compete at Bethel: baseball (m), basketball (m/w), cheerleading (m/w), cross-country (m/w), drumline (m/w), golf (m/w), lacrosse (w), rugby (m), soccer (m/w), softball (w), tennis (m/w), track and field (m/w), and volleyball (w).

Application and Information

Application priority dates are December 1 and March 1. Prospective students must submit a completed online application, official SAT or ACT sores, and an official high school transcript including at least six semesters (sent directly to Bethel). Transfer students need not submit test scores if they have passed college-level courses in both math and English, however official college transcripts from all colleges or universities attended are required. Bethel is recognized as a home-school-friendly college; a template for home school students' high school transcripts is available from the Bethel Admission Office. Further details are online at BethelCollege.edu/Apply.

Office of Admission
1001 Bethel Circle
Mishawaka, Indiana 46545
United States
Phone: 800-422-4101
E-mail: Admissions@BethelCollege.edu
Website: BethelCollege.edu/Info

BOSTON COLLEGE
CHESTNUT HILL, MASSACHUSETTS

The University

Boston College (BC) was founded in 1863 by the Jesuits to serve the sons of Boston's Irish immigrants. Today a coeducational university on more than 239 acres in Chestnut Hill, BC may seem a world apart from the small school in the crowded heart of Boston that was its first home. Through more than fifteen decades of growth and change, however, BC has held fast to the Jesuit ideals that inspired its founders. A Jesuit education today, as a century ago, is grounded in the liberal arts and in a commitment to the service of others.

Undergraduates may enroll in the College of Arts and Sciences, the Wallace E. Carroll School of Management, the Connell School of Nursing, or the Lynch School of Education.

BC's approximately 9,000 undergraduates come from many backgrounds. The university draws from nearly all fifty states and more than fifty-five countries. Students' religious and cultural backgrounds are similarly diverse. Today, the university's AHANA (African American, Hispanic, Asian, and Native American) and international students make up approximately 30 percent of the undergraduate student body.

In today's complex and increasingly diverse world, the university believes that the best education is one that broadens a student's capacity to reason, think, and make critical judgments in a wide range of areas. Thus, each BC student fulfills a core of liberal arts courses from which he or she can pursue degrees in more than fifty areas of study and choose from more than 1,400 course offerings throughout the university.

According to several recent national publications, BC is in the top tier of the nation's colleges and universities. The foundation for that achievement is the university's scholars and researchers—805 full-time professionals who make up the faculty. The kinship between teachers and students is one of the hallmarks of a BC education; that relationship is nurtured by a student-teacher ratio of 11.9:1. The median class size at the university is 20 students.

At BC, learning continues beyond the classroom in more than 225 student-run organizations. These include student government, honor societies, language and cultural organizations, performance ensembles, political groups, preprofessional clubs, publications, and service organizations. BC also sponsors thirteen varsity teams for men and sixteen for women, all of which compete at the NCAA Division I level. The College also supports over sixty club and intramural sports.

Boston College's public affairs office maintains university profiles on five of the major social networking sites, including Twitter (http://twitter.com/BostonCollege), Facebook (http://www.facebook.com/BostonCollege), YouTube (http://www.youtube.com/bostoncollege), Instagram (http://instagram.com/BostonCollege), and Google+ (https://plus.google.com/+bostoncollege).

Location

Located in the Chestnut Hill section of Newton, BC sits on the doorstep of one of America's great cities, a center of culture and education for more than three centuries. It is an energetic, cosmopolitan city that draws life and enthusiasm from the more than 200,000 college students in residence during the academic year. Located just 6 miles from downtown Boston and with easy access to the city via the trolley system that stops at the foot of the campus, BC offers the best of both worlds: a scenic suburban setting neighboring an exciting metropolitan center.

Majors and Degrees

The College of Arts and Sciences (A&S) is the oldest and largest of the four undergraduate schools at BC. A&S students must complete thirty-eight 1-semester courses, thirty-two of which are in A&S departments. The normal course load is five courses per semester for the first three years and four courses per semester during the senior year. The undergraduate curriculum includes the university core curriculum and ten to twelve courses in the major field, with the remainder of courses chosen as electives. A&S offers degrees in the following areas: art history, biochemistry, biology, chemistry, classical studies, communication, computer science, economics, English, environmental geosciences, environmental studies, film studies, French, geology, geological studies, geophysics, German studies, Hispanic studies, history, independent major, international studies, Islamic civilizations and societies, Italian, linguistics, mathematics, music, philosophy, physics, political science, psychology, Russian, Slavic studies, sociology, studio art, theater, and theology. Preprofessional advisement is also available in medical, dental, veterinary, and legal programs. Students can also select from twenty-one departmental minors, or seventeen interdisciplinary minors.

The Carroll School of Management educates students to be leaders in business and industry and in public agencies, educational institutions, and service organizations. The Carroll School offers concentrations in accounting, accounting information systems, computer science, corporate reporting and analysis, economics, finance, general management, human resource management, information systems, management and leadership, marketing, and operations and strategic management.

The Lynch School of Education prepares students for education and human services professions. Programs provide a general education, professional preparation, and specialized education in the major field. Fieldwork in area schools is closely linked to course work in each specialization. The Lynch School awards degrees upon completion of thirty-eight courses, including the university core curriculum, a major field of study in education, and a second major in a subject field or an interdisciplinary area in A&S that complements the student's program. Areas of specialization include applied psychology and human development, elementary education, and secondary education. The Lynch School also offers interdisciplinary majors in American heritages, general science, mathematics/computer science, and perspectives on Spanish America.

The Connell School of Nursing offers a four-year program of study leading to a Bachelor of Science degree. The three major components to the curriculum are nursing major courses, electives, and the required university core curriculum. In all courses, principles of wellness, illness, rehabilitation, and health maintenance serve as a theoretical basis in preparing students for professional nursing practice. Nursing courses include traditional classes, simulated and audiovisual laboratory activities on campus, and clinical learning activities in health-care settings.

Academic Programs

Every BC education is centered on a core curriculum—a set of required courses. BC offers a core curriculum because it believes in the unity of knowledge. While the core, which is continually reviewed by a committee of faculty members, varies somewhat by school, its common elements include literature, natural science, writing, philosophy, theology, social science, history, mathematics, fine arts, and cultural diversity.

There are a wide variety of extraordinary academic programs available to BC students to enhance their educational experience. They include, among others, honors programs within each of the university's four undergraduate schools, Undergraduate Faculty Research Fellows, the Scholar of the College, PULSE, and Perspectives on Western Culture.

Off-Campus Programs

BC encourages all students to take part in internship programs. More than 80 percent of BC undergraduates participate in at least one internship or prepracticum placement during their college years. Internships can be paid or unpaid and may take place during the academic year or the summer; some carry academic credit.

BC students may take on the challenge of international study in more than sixty programs administered by BC at universities in more than forty countries. BC students who study abroad typically do so in their junior year, but there is also a range of full-year and summer-abroad opportunities. The Office of International Programs helps students with program selection and applications and maintains a library of reference books and professional evaluations of international study programs.

Academic Facilities

BC's eight libraries contain more than 3 million printed volumes, over 4 million items in microform, 623,286 e-books, 455,651 government documents, 44,891 serial subscriptions, and a wide collection of films and archival items. The resources of the library system range from some of Europe's earliest printed books to hundreds of computerized databases. Students with personal computers have dorm-room access to these databases as well as to Quest and other library information sources through Agora, the campus information network. BC also offers a 24/7 "Ask a Librarian" e-mail service and the capability to text questions to a librarian. In addition, all of BC's libraries and classrooms offer a wireless network that provides access to these resources and the Internet.

Research laboratories in the state-of-the-art science facilities have been specially designed to accommodate the advanced instrumentation required for modern science and to provide flexibility for accommodating new equipment. The $85-million expansion to the Higgins Biology and Physics Center was carefully designed to place classrooms, laboratories, computer facilities, and office space in proximity and to facilitate interaction among faculty members, researchers, and students. In addition to the Center's seventeen new teaching laboratories, special working labs are designed and outfitted for research and teaching in the fields of biology and physics.

Boston College opened Stokes Hall in January 2013. This $78-million facility was strategically designed to foster interdisciplinary collaboration among BC's humanities departments and enhanced student-faculty interaction, with thirty-six state-of-the-art classrooms and 200 faculty offices for the Classical Studies, English, History, Philosophy, and Theology departments. Stokes Hall also houses the Academic Advising Center, College of Arts and Sciences Honors Department, and Office of First Year Experience, as well as common areas, conference rooms, a coffee shop, and an outdoor garden and plaza that provide multiple meeting spaces to connect students and faculty.

In 2016, Boston College opened a new residence hall with 460 beds, as well as a new museum of art which hosts modern architecture with larger space for exhibits, functions, and meetings.

Costs

Tuition for the 2016–17 academic year was $50,480, which included a student activity fee and campus health fee of $816. The total for room and board was $13,818, which included the board plan. Freshman mandatory fees include a one-time required charge of $486 for first-year orientation and student identification.

Financial Aid

BC maintains a financial aid program to assist deserving and qualified students who might otherwise not be able to attend the university. Boston College is committed to providing funds to meet the full demonstrated need of every admitted student who applies for financial aid. Overall, 67 percent of students receive some form of financial aid with the University awarding over $110 million annually in need-based scholarships and grants. Assistance for freshmen alone included more than $20 million in need-based grants. The university offers financial aid to students based on need as demonstrated by completion of the College Scholarship Service's Financial Aid PROFILE and the Free Application for Federal Student Aid (FAFSA). All requirements and deadlines and complete instructions are available in BC admission literature. An application for financial aid in no way affects a decision on admission.

Each year, BC chooses 15 incoming freshmen as Presidential Scholars to receive merit-based, full-tuition scholarships. Students are selected from all candidates who apply through the early action program.

Faculty

BC has 805 full-time faculty members. Of these faculty members, 98 percent hold doctoral degrees. Over 50 Jesuits live on BC-owned property and make up one of the largest Apostolic Jesuit communities in the world. Approximately half of these members are active in the College's administration and teaching.

Student Government

The Undergraduate Government of Boston College (UGBC), formed in 1968, is led by the president and vice president, who are elected in the spring of each year by the entire student body. UGBC's goal is to serve the students by providing services and opportunities and by representing them in the best manner possible to the university community. To accomplish this goal, UGBC provides many educational, social, and cultural programs, such as concerts, lectures, roundtables, and more.

Admission Requirements

The undergraduate admission staff pays particular attention to students who have done well in a demanding college-preparatory curriculum, including Advanced Placement (AP) and honors courses when available. For the class of 2020, there were 28,956 applications for 2,359 places. The majority of incoming freshmen ranked comfortably in the top 10 percent of their high school class. The SAT scores of the middle half of admitted freshmen were 1900–2190. On the ACT, scores of the middle half were between 30 and 33.

Application and Information

Students applying to Boston College for a place in the freshman class must complete both the Common Application and the Boston College Supplemental Application. All applicants should submit the BC Supplemental Application as soon as they have decided to apply to Boston College. Students are encouraged to review the electronic application instructions on BC's website at http://www.bc.edu/content/bc/admission/undergrad/process.html and then apply at http://www.commonapp.org.

Students applying through the regular admission program must submit the Common Application and all other required forms, along with the $75 application fee, by January 1. Candidates are notified of action taken on their application in early April. Admitted students intending to matriculate are required to forward a confirmation fee to the Admission Office postmarked by May 1.

Students with superior academic credentials who view Boston College as a top choice may apply through the nonbinding early action program. These applicants must submit both application forms, along with the $75 application fee, by November 1. Candidates learn of their admission decision before December 25 but have the standard deadline (May 1) to reserve their places as freshmen. Boston College does permit students to apply under early action if they have applied to an early decision college.

BC accepts approximately 150 transfer students each year. Transfer candidates should request applications for transfer admission from the Office of Undergraduate Admission or via the website at http://www.bc.edu/transfer. In addition to high school records and standardized test results, transfer applicants must furnish transcripts from all postsecondary institutions they have attended.

For more information, students should contact:

Office of Undergraduate Admission
Devlin Hall 208
Boston College
Chestnut Hill, Massachusetts 02467
Phone: 617-552-3100
800-360-2522 (toll-free)
Fax: 617-552-0798
Website: http://www.bc.edu

COLLEGE CLOSE-UPS

BOSTON UNIVERSITY

BOSTON, MASSACHUSETTS

BOSTON UNIVERSITY

The University

Boston University (BU) is a private teaching and research university ranked #39 in the nation and #32 in the world by *U.S. News & World Report*. Students study with world-renowned faculty, including Fulbright Scholars, Pulitzer Prize winners, a MacArthur Fellow, Nobel Prize winners, and a former Poet Laureate. With an average class size of 27 and a 12:1 student-to-faculty ratio, these amazing professors become more than just a face students see in class. There are hundreds of research projects that allow undergraduates to work directly with faculty as early as freshman year through the Undergraduate Research Opportunities Program (UROP). With ten undergraduate schools and colleges; over 250 majors and minors, more than 600 in-depth, global courses; and one of the top 20 study-abroad programs in the country, the challenges at BU are vast and varied.

Among the academic opportunities at BU are several top-ranked programs such as biomedical engineering, occupational therapy, archaeology, business, and deaf studies. High-achieving students can also pursue dual degrees, combined B.A./M.A. programs, or be admitted to the prestigious Arvind and Chandan Nandlal Kilachand Honors College. BU students come from all fifty states and more than 100 countries; they are bright, driven, and inquisitive.

Located in the heart of Boston, students experience the city as an extension of the campus for study, internships, employment, and cultural and recreational activities. With four years of guaranteed campus housing, and 80 percent of undergraduates living on campus all four years, the campus feels like a true residential community in the heart of Boston.

Location

Boston provides an environment rich in intellectual and cultural stimuli; no other city in the world can compete with Boston's remarkable concentration of higher education institutions, world-renowned medical centers, and historic and cultural attractions. Students make up 20 percent of Boston's population during the academic year, enhancing the atmosphere of learning and excitement. The city provides many opportunities for impressive internship and research positions and is a world-class center for attractions including the Museum of Fine Arts, Fenway Park, the Boston Symphony Orchestra, and a thriving theater district.

Majors and Degrees

Boston University grants the B.A., B.S., B.S.B.A., B.L.S., Mus.B., and B.F.A. degrees. Of the University's seventeen schools and colleges, ten offer opportunities for undergraduate study.

As BU's largest academic division, the College of Arts and Sciences (CAS) offers a diverse learning community with world-class research faculty. Students may major in American studies; ancient Greek; ancient Greek and Latin; anthropology; anthropology and religion; archaeology; architectural studies; astronomy; astronomy and physics; biochemistry and molecular biology; biology; biology with a specialization in behavioral biology; biology with a specialization in cell biology, molecular biology, and genetics; biology with a specialization in ecology and conservation biology; biology with a specialization in neurobiology; chemistry; chemistry with specialization in biochemistry; chemistry with specialization in teaching; Chinese language and literature; cinema and media studies (also offered in COM); classical civilization; classics and philosophy; classics and religion; comparative literature; computer science; earth and environmental sciences; economics; economics and mathematics; English; environmental analysis and policy; French and linguistics; French studies; geophysics and planetary sciences; German language and literature; history; history of art and architecture; Italian studies; Japanese and linguistics; Japanese language and literature; Latin; linguistics; linguistics and philosophy; linguistics and speech, language, and hearing sciences; marine science; mathematics (includes statistics); mathematics and computer science; mathematics and mathematics education; mathematics and philosophy; music (nonperformance); neuroscience; philosophy; philosophy and physics; philosophy and political science; philosophy and psychology; philosophy and religion; physics; political science; pre-dentistry; pre-law; pre-medicine; pre–veterinary medicine; psychology; religion; Russian language and literature; sociology; Spanish; and Spanish and linguistics. Special curricula include seven-year accelerated programs in liberal arts medicine or liberal arts dentistry; the Modular Medical Integrated Curriculum (MMEDIC); the BU dual-degree program; the CFA/CAS double-degree program; the SED/CAS double-degree program; and various combined B.A./M.A. degree programs.

The College of Fine Arts (CFA) offers programs in the School of Music (composition and theory, music education, musicology, and performance), the School of Theatre (acting, design, stage management, production, and theater arts/performing), and the School of Visual Arts (art education, graphic design, painting, printmaking, and sculpture). There is also a double-degree program that allows students to earn two bachelor's degrees simultaneously in the CFA and the CAS.

The College of General Studies (CGS) offers a demanding, two-year program in the liberal arts and sciences that features an integrated core curriculum. It stresses an interdisciplinary approach to teaching. After two years, students continue into one of BU's degree-granting schools or colleges to complete their studies.

Located in one of the largest media markets in the nation, the College of Communication (COM) offers majors in cinema and media studies (also offered in CAS); communication (advertising, public relations, communication); film and television (production, writing, management); and journalism (with specialization available in broadcast, magazine, news-editorial, online, and photojournalism).

Majors in the College of Engineering (ENG) include biomedical engineering (a program ranked twelfth in the country by *U.S. News & World Report*), computer engineering, electrical engineering, mechanical engineering, and mechanical engineering with specialization in aerospace.

The College of Health and Rehabilitation Sciences: Sargent College (SAR) is one of the oldest and top-ranked health sciences schools in the country. It offers programs in behavior and health; health science; human physiology; nutrition; and speech, language, and hearing sciences. Also offered is a six-year B.S./D.P.T. program.

The Frederick S. Pardee School of Global Studies is housed within the College of Arts & Sciences and is dedicated to advancing human progress and improving the human condition. The School's education, research, and initiatives aim to produce globally competent citizens and leaders. Consisting of two divisions—international studies and regional studies—the School offers programs in Asian studies, European studies, international relations, Latin American studies, and Middle East and North Africa studies.

Areas of concentration in the School of Education (SED) include bilingual education (includes TESOL), deaf studies, early childhood education, elementary education, English education, mathematics education, modern foreign languages education, science education, social studies education, and special education. The SED/CAS double-degree program is also offered.

Located in one of the hospitality and tourism capitals of the world, the School of Hospitality Administration (SHA) offers a rigorous program in the management of hotels, restaurants, food and beverage service, travel and tourism, and entertainment. Concentrations in event management, hospitality marketing, and hospitality real estate development are also offered.

With a unique global curriculum, the Questrom School of Business (Questrom) offers concentrations in accounting, entrepreneurship, finance, general management (business), health and life sciences, international management, law, management information systems, marketing, operations and technology management, organizational behavior, real estate, and strategy and innovation.

Academic Programs

A Boston University education combines the elements of a traditional liberal arts education with training for the professions. There are 250 programs of study to choose from, including BU's top-ranked biomedical engineering, occupational therapy, deaf studies, economics, international relations, management information systems, journalism, theatre, and archeology programs. Highly qualified freshmen may also be invited to participate in the prestigious Arvind and Chandan Nandlal Kilachand Honors College.

Boston University has more than 100 study-abroad opportunities that take students around the world for courses, internships, and fieldwork. Opportunities are offered on six continents, in over thirty countries, and in cities such as Auckland, Beijing, Dresden, London, Los Angeles, Madrid, Paris, Sydney, and Washington, D.C. Programs offered include studies in art/architecture, business/economics, engineering, health and human services, journalism/communications, visual/performing arts, and many more. Fieldwork programs may be found in locations that include Ecuador and Spain, with study-abroad options that include programs in Grenoble, Padova, Quito, and Venice. Summer study programs are available in Argentina, Australia, China, England, France, Ireland, Italy, Spain, and the United States.

BU's Center for Career Development provides students the resources they need to select a major or get internships or part-time jobs in any number of fields.

Boston University operates on a calendar of two semesters and two summer terms. Students generally take four courses each semester; thirty-two courses are required for graduation. Most degree programs are built around a core of humanities and social and natural sciences. Concentrations require eight to thirteen courses. Electives generally total 30–40 percent of the courses taken, allowing for interdisciplinary study.

Academic Facilities

The new Yawkey Center for Student Services is home to BU's Center for Career Development, Educational Resource Center, Pre-professional Advising Center with pre-med and pre-law advising services, and the two-story Marciano Commons dining hall. The Engineering Product Innovation Center (EPIC) is a 15,000-square-foot facility where undergraduates can experiment with developing new products, from design to manufacturing. West campus features the modern Student Village, including Agganis Arena; the Fitness and Recreation Center, complete with a 35-foot rock-climbing wall; and high-rise, apartment-style dorms. BU also has a life science and engineering facility with 187,000-square-feet of laboratory and research space for the biology, bioinformatics, chemistry, and bioengineering departments. The state-of-the-art Photonics Center features classroom and laboratory space for the College of Engineering as well as labs designed to support industry partners who seek to develop new photonics-based products. The Questrom School of Business building also offers technologically advanced educational facilities, with a dedicated career center and management library.

Through Boston University Information Services and Technology, students have access to public computing facilities equipped with workstations, terminals, and laser printers as well as a high-speed campus network. An 890-seat proscenium theater, studio space for visual arts students, practice rooms for music, and a 575-seat music performance center are indicative of BU's support for the arts. More than 2.8 million library volumes and over 4.7 million microform units are contained in Mugar Memorial Library, where the Twentieth-Century Archives are held, including the papers of Dr. Martin Luther King, Jr., Theodore Roosevelt, Robert Frost, and Bette Davis.

Costs

Tuition for 2017–18 is $50,980, estimated room and board costs are $15,270, and University and college fees are $1,102. These costs are exclusive of books, supplies, transportation, and personal expenses.

Financial Assistance

Boston University helps students realize their dreams with several different kinds of financial aid: BU scholarships, federal and state grants, federal loans, federal work-study awards, and financing and payment plan options. Financial aid is offered on the basis of calculated financial eligibility, and two or more types of aid are often combined in award packages. Approximately 83 percent of students who apply for aid and enroll at BU receive assistance. Students must submit the FAFSA and the CSS PROFILE by established deadlines to be considered. In addition, the Trustee Scholarship (full tuition) and the Presidential Scholarship ($20,000) are offered to the highest achieving students who apply for admission.

The University makes every effort to assist students with calculated financial eligibility, however funds are limited. All applicants who anticipate the need for financial aid are encouraged to apply.

Faculty

Seventy-eight percent of BU faculty members have a Ph.D. or equivalent and include Nobel Prize winners, Guggenheim scholars, Emmy Award winners, and Sloan Research Fellows. In addition to fulfilling their classroom responsibilities, faculty members are accessible as academic and career advisers who assist students in obtaining internships as well research opportunities.

Admission Requirements

The Board of Admissions considers each candidate individually. Primary emphasis is placed on the strength of the secondary school record, but required test scores, character, breadth of interest, school recommendations, and other personal qualifications are also carefully evaluated. Students are required to submit the SAT or the ACT, with the exception of those applying to the College of Fine Arts. SAT Subject Tests are recommended, but not required, for students submitting the SAT. A full listing of the standardized testing requirements can be found in the requirements and standards chart at www.bu.edu/admissions/apply/freshman/program-requirements. Secondary school graduation or an equivalency diploma is required of all candidates; for the College of Fine Arts a prescreening, audition, or a portfolio may be required, depending on the program of interest. For certain programs, interviews and SAT Subject Test scores are required. Boston University offers programs of early decision (binding agreement), early decision 2 (binding agreement), and deferred admission.

Transfer applicants are considered for September or January admission. Transfer students are not eligible for admission to the accelerated liberal arts medical or dental programs or the six-year, combined Bachelor of Science in Health Studies/Doctor of Physical Therapy program. January admission to the College of Fine Arts School of Theatre is also not available to transfer students.

Boston University admits qualified students to all its programs and activities regardless of their race, color, national origin, religion, sex, age, or disability.

Application and Information

Boston University requires the Common Application. Information on applying is available online at www.bu.edu/admissions/apply. The deadline for regular decision applications is January 2. Applicants for early decision must apply by November 1. Accelerated medical and dental program applications are due November 15. The deadline for the Trustee Scholarship (full tuition) and the Presidential Scholarship ($20,000) is December 1. Students must submit the College Scholarship Service (CSS) Financial Aid PROFILE and the Free Application for Federal Student Aid (FAFSA) by February 1.

Transfer students applying for September admission should submit their applications, CSS PROFILE and FAFSA forms by March 1 or by November 1 for January admission.

Boston University Admissions
233 Bay State Road
Boston, Massachusetts 02215
Phone: 617-353-2300
E-mail: admissions@bu.edu
Website: http://www.bu.edu/admissions
http://www.facebook.com/BUadmissions
https://twitter.com/ApplyToBU

Students at Boston University find that nothing separates them from Boston's world-class museums, vibrant culture, legendary sports teams, rich history, or world-renowned scientific and medical communities.

BRYN MAWR COLLEGE

BRYN MAWR, PENNSYLVANIA

★ To read more about this school, visit http://petersons.to/brynmawrcollege

BRYN MAWR COLLEGE

The College

Every year 1,300 undergraduate women and 400 graduate students from around the world gather on Bryn Mawr College's historic campus to study with leading scholars, conduct advanced research, and expand the boundaries of what's possible.

The undergraduate college is known as one of the most academically rigorous liberal-arts colleges in the nation and consistently ranks among the top feeder schools to the world's premier graduate programs and professional schools.

Bryn Mawr's, Leadership, Innovation and Liberal Arts Center (LILAC), Office of Civic Engagement, and the Praxis Program, which integrates fieldwork with theoretical study, provide students with extensive opportunities for internships in nearby Philadelphia and beyond, where they may apply their knowledge outside the classroom. Many students pursue independent and interdepartmental majors with faculty permission. Joint academic programs also exist with Haverford, Swarthmore, and the University of Pennsylvania.

Through advanced research projects, summer internships, and collaborative research with faculty members, students are involved in the local, national, and global communities.

Bryn Mawr offers a unique interdisciplinary experience, 360°, in which a cohort of students takes several courses together to engage multiple aspects of a topic or theme, giving students an opportunity to investigate thoroughly and thoughtfully a multitude of perspectives. Typical 360°s focus on the history, economic concerns, cultural intersections, and political impact of an era, decision, event, policy, or important scientific innovation. 360° participants hone their arguments and insights through writing and research, develop strategies for teamwork that push the limits of their talents and creativity, and work with professors and scholars to promote big-picture thinking.

Bryn Mawr's prestigious alumnae include the first woman to be president of Harvard University, one of the first women to receive the Nobel Peace Prize, the first woman neurosurgeon, and the first and only woman to receive four Academy Awards.

Diversity is central to Bryn Mawr's mission as an extraordinary liberal-arts college, improving the academic experience and enriching the campus community. Students of color and international students make up 56 percent of the undergraduate enrollment. Bryn Mawr's student body is composed of women from fifty U.S. states, districts, and territories and sixty other countries.

Above all else, Bryn Mawr women share a tremendous respect for individual differences, not merely a passive tolerance of other lifestyles and points of view. The result is a community that resounds with the energy, healthy friction, and range of perspectives that can only come from true cultural and ideological diversity.

The diversity that Bryn Mawr students experience, in and out of the classroom, helps prepare them to be confident global citizens and leaders.

Bryn Mawr women share a commitment to a community that is based on inclusion and support, reinforced by the College's Honor Code, a set of principles stressing personal integrity and mutual respect. In the words of one graduating senior, "This is a place where being yourself makes you feel part of something larger than yourself. A strong sense of self is what we all have in common."

Bryn Mawr is a charter member of the Centennial Conference and is home to twelve NCAA varsity athletic teams. Students may compete in badminton, basketball, crew, cross-country, field hockey, lacrosse, soccer, swimming, tennis, indoor track and field, outdoor track and field, and volleyball. The Bern Schwartz Fitness and Athletic Center offers enhanced spaces for training, fitness, and aquatics.

Goodhart Hall serves as a hub for the College's performing arts scene and boasts a theater for 500+, a teaching theater, scene shop, music rooms, and several performance spaces. Other performance spaces include the Pembroke Dance Studio and the Denbigh Studio.

Bryn Mawr students participate in more than 100 active student organizations. The tricollege community of Haverford, Swarthmore, and Bryn Mawr also sponsors many student groups and activities.

Location

Students at Bryn Mawr have the best of it all in terms of location. The campus itself is such a picture-perfect example of Collegiate Gothic that it has been used as the backdrop for many motion pictures. A quick 5-minute walk into the suburban town of Bryn Mawr finds an eclectic mix of funky independent and favorite franchise coffee shops, eateries, and retailers; an historic movie theater; and a commuter train that can take students to the heart of Philadelphia in less than 20 minutes.

Philadelphia has a bustling arts scene and nightlife and is home to more than 250,000 college students. Bryn Mawr women enjoy a rich academic and social life on their own campus and at neighboring tricollege partners, Haverford and Swarthmore Colleges, as well as the University of Pennsylvania.

Bryn Mawr's relationship with Haverford College is particularly close and students participate in many bicollege extracurricular activities, including the orchestra, the chorus, the drama program, and a bicollege newspaper. A 20-minute walk or a 5-minute ride on the bicollege Blue Bus brings students from one campus to the other.

Almost all students live on campus in one of thirteen main residence halls. Two of the buildings are listed on the National Register of Historic Places, and one is also a National Historic Landmark.

Majors and Degrees

Bryn Mawr College grants the Bachelor of Arts (A.B.) degree with majors, minors, and concentrations in more than forty areas: Africana studies; anthropology; astronomy; biochemistry; biology; chemistry; child and family studies; Chinese; classical and Near Eastern archaeology; classical culture and society; classical languages; comparative literature; computational methods; computer science; creative writing; dance; East Asian languages and cultures; economics; education; English; environmental studies; film studies; fine arts; French and Francophone studies; gender and sexuality; geoarchaeology; geology; German and German studies; Greek; growth and structure of cities; Hebrew and Judaic studies; health studies; history; history of art; international studies; Italian studies; Japanese; Latin; Latin American, Iberian, and Latina/o studies; linguistics; mathematics; Middle East studies; music; neurosciences; peace, conflict, and social justice studies; philosophy; physics; political science; psychology; religion; Romance languages; Russian; sociology; Spanish; and theater studies. In consultation with faculty and academic advisers, students may apply to the following partnership degree programs: a 3-2 engineering degree through the California Institute of Technology; a 4+1 engineering degree via the University of Pennsylvania; or a 3-2 City and Regional Planning degree, also from the University of Pennsylvania.

There are nearly 3,000 course exchanges between Bryn Mawr and Haverford each year, selected from a jointly published course list. Bryn Mawr students may major in any of Haverford's coordinate departments or in astronomy, classics, fine arts, music, or religion while earning a Bachelor of Arts degree from Bryn Mawr. Students may also apply to obtain their master's through the combined A.B./M.A. program in chemistry, classical and Near Eastern archaeology, French, Greek studies, Latin language and Roman studies, classical studies, history of art, mathematics, and physics.

Academic Programs

The Bryn Mawr curriculum is designed to encourage breadth of learning and training in the fundamentals of scholarship. At some point during their first three years at Bryn Mawr, students are required to complete Approaches to Inquiry, a curriculum designed to introduce possibilities and problems in scientific investigation, critical interpretation, cross-cultural analysis, and inquiry into the past. Many options are available to fulfill these requirements and students are encouraged to explore. Innovative curricular options include the growth and structure of cities program; the Middle East Studies program; 360°; and Focus Courses, which are demanding, half-semester courses that may ignite a new intellectual passion. Mature, sophisticated, in-depth study in a major program during the last two years is designed to prepare students for the lifelong pleasure and responsibility of educating themselves and playing an active role in contemporary society. The curriculum encourages independence within a rigorous but flexible framework. Each student chooses and plans her major in consultation with her dean and faculty adviser. Some students take advantage of this freedom to design an independent major, while others fashion their own intellectual perspectives by enrolling in courses that span academic fields or assisting with a faculty member's research project.

With certain restrictions, full-time Bryn Mawr students may also take courses at Swarthmore College, the University of Pennsylvania, and Villanova University during the academic year without paying additional fees.

Off-Campus Programs

Bryn Mawr is only 20 minutes by car or seven short stops by train from the vast cultural and professional resources of Philadelphia, the nation's sixth-largest city. Philadelphia is an incredible resource for Bryn Mawr—a truly accessible city, rich with cultural and professional opportunities, including the Philadelphia Museum of Art, the Philadelphia Orchestra, the Pennsylvania Ballet, numerous theaters, professional sports teams, and some of the nation's most important historic sites. Students may also take advantage of internship opportunities in Center City law firms, art galleries, government agencies, hospitals, TV studios, banks, and schools. When Philadelphia seems too small, 1 in 3 Bryn Mawr students take advantage of one of Bryn Mawr's many study-abroad options.

Academic Facilities

Bryn Mawr ranks among the top 25 of all U.S. colleges and universities in the percentage of female graduates going on to earn a Ph.D. Bryn Mawr students have unlimited access to libraries and laboratories equal to those of many graduate programs, allowing students to pursue independent research at a level unavailable at most undergraduate institutions. These resources include an extensive array of laboratory equipment for the study of science, such as a robotics lab, laser with rangefinder, DNA analyzers, and a geological subsurface profiling system. More than 1 million volumes in a network of open-stack libraries are available to Bryn Mawr students, as well as access to the libraries of both Haverford and Swarthmore Colleges via the Tripod Library System.

In addition, the College has recently enhanced several of its buildings to support student inquiry in all of the liberal arts, including a $19-million renovation of the Marjorie Goodhart Theater which consists of a new state-of-the-art theater, practice rooms, a teaching theater, and scene shop; the upgrade of Dalton Hall, home to Bryn Mawr's social science labs and classrooms; and Bettws-y-Coed, a center for the study of psychology complete with new labs, faculty offices, and meeting rooms. Four former faculty residences have also been renovated to house the student activities village, Cambrian Row.

Costs

In 2017–18, Bryn Mawr tuition, room and board, and fees total $66,410.

Financial Aid

To apply for financial aid, students must submit the Free Application for Federal Student Aid (FAFSA), the College Scholarship Service (CSS) PROFILE form, and if applicable, the CSS Noncustodial Parent PROFILE. The College also requires a signed copy of the custodial and noncustodial parents' prior year federal income tax returns, including W-2 forms, and all schedules and attachments. The student's federal income tax return is only required if the student is selected for verification. Tax returns must be submitted to The College Board's Institutional Documentation Service (IDOC). Applicants who are not citizens of the U.S. may file the (CSS) PROFILE. Non–U.S. citizens must also submit letters (in English) from their parents' employers stating gross income and the value of any perquisites, subsidies, and benefits directly to the Office of Financial Aid. Prospective freshmen are notified of admission and financial aid decisions simultaneously.

Faculty

The Bryn Mawr faculty has 153 full-time members, of whom 56 percent are women and 20 percent are professors of color. The College's student-faculty ratio is 8:1. Few colleges or universities can genuinely claim the intellectual curiosity, intensity, and passion found at Bryn Mawr. Classes are small (many have fewer than 15 students), and faculty members come to know their students as individuals. That means more than just being on a first-name basis. In fact, Bryn Mawr faculty members, world-renowned leaders in their fields, regard their students as junior colleagues, fully capable of working at a high level, developing their own ideas, and making important contributions. It is in this way that, perhaps more than at any other school, Bryn Mawr feels like a graduate school on an undergraduate level.

Student Government

Bryn Mawr's culture of innovative leadership dates back to 1892 and the founding of the Student Self-Government Association (SGA), the oldest undergraduate governing body in the country. SGA gives Bryn Mawr students the responsibility of running many campus organizations and activities and participating in discussions and resolutions of important issues, such as curriculum and faculty appointments.

Admission Requirements

Every year, Bryn Mawr receives many more outstanding applications for admission than can be admitted into the first-year class of about 360 students. As members of the Common Application, Bryn Mawr practices holistic review, with admission decisions based on a number of factors. Strength of the applicant's high school curriculum within the context of the high school and academic performance are of significant importance. Other factors considered are a student's writing, recommendations from the high school counselor and academic teachers, test scores (optional), involvement in school and community, and diverse or unique perspectives and talents a student might bring to the Bryn Mawr community.

Basic high school academic requirements include 4 years of English, 3 years of mathematics, at least 1 year each of a laboratory science and history, and a solid foundation in at least one foreign language. However, most applicants are well prepared for the academic rigor of Bryn Mawr and have taken at least three lab science courses as well as mathematics courses that include trigonometry. Standardized test scores for U.S. applicants or U.S. permanent residents are not required. Non-U.S. citizens and non-U.S. permanent residents are required to submit standardized test scores (SAT I or ACT) as well as either the TOEFL or IELTS if their primary language is not English and/or their language of instruction over the past four years has not been English. Complete details may be found on the Bryn Mawr website.

An interview, either at the College or with a local alumnae representative, is also strongly recommended.

Bryn Mawr exclusively accepts the Common Application and waives the $50 application fee when students apply online. Application forms should be submitted by November 15 for fall early decision applicants, by January 1 for winter early decision applicants, and by January 15 for regular decision applicants.

Transfer students must complete a minimum of two years of work at Bryn Mawr to qualify for the A.B. degree.

Application and Information

The Office of Admissions is open from 9 a.m. to 5 p.m. on weekdays and some Saturdays throughout the year. Please visit the College website http://www.brynmawr.edu/admissions to plan a visit. Bryn Mawr accepts the Common Application, which can be found online (http://www.commonapplication.org). For additional information, prospective students should contact:

Bryn Mawr College Office of Admissions
101 North Merion Avenue
Bryn Mawr, Pennsylvania 19010-2899
Phone: 610-526-5152
Fax: 610-526-7471
E-mail: admissions@brynmawr.edu
Websites: http://www.brynmawr.edu
http://www.brynmawr.edu/admissions/
http://www.facebook.com/BrynMawrCollege
http://twitter.com/BrynMawrCollege

COLLEGE CLOSE-UPS

CALIFORNIA UNIVERSITY OF PENNSYLVANIA

CALIFORNIA, PENNSYLVANIA

CAL U

★ For more information, visit http://petersons.to/calupenn

The University

Guided by a special mission in science and technology, California University of Pennsylvania (Cal U) offers professional, career-focused programs in the arts and sciences, technologies, and education that engage students in applied and active learning. At Cal U, highly trained faculty members, caring staff and exceptional facilities combine to help every student prepare for a meaningful career. A proud member of Pennsylvania's State System of Higher Education, Cal U serves more than 7,500 undergraduate and graduate students.

Location

The University is located on 294 acres in the borough of California, Pennsylvania, about 35 miles south of Pittsburgh on the banks of the Monongahela River.

Cal U's location in rural southwestern Pennsylvania makes it easy to enjoy camping, hiking, fishing, skiing, and other outdoor activities. The University is also within easy driving distance of architect Frank Lloyd Wright's Fallingwater, one of America's foremost architectural treasures.

For those who prefer city life, the campus offers ready access to the Pittsburgh metropolitan area and its many cultural attractions and sporting events. Shopping, concerts, museums, theater, and more are all just a short drive away. The University organizes regular trips to Pittsburgh and other locations, so students can experience a wide variety of performances and activities.

Majors and Degrees

California University of Pennsylvania offers more than 100 undergraduate majors and concentrations and 95 graduate and professional programs, on campus and 100 percent online. Academic programs are offered through Cal U's three Colleges and its School of Graduate Studies and Research.

Cal U's **Eberly College of Science and Technology** offers scientific, technological, and career-oriented degree programs to prepare students for the complex and evolving demands of the industrial, business, and healthcare fields, as well as for further study in graduate and professional schools.

To help students develop personally and professionally, the College has designed an enriching curriculum built around two education components. The general education component provides a well-rounded education to maximize effectiveness in the workplace and as socially responsible citizens. The professional component includes the critical technical, scientific, business, and support courses that form the foundation for immediate employment or advanced study in each student's chosen field.

Laboratory and workshop experiences supplement a foundation in theory, and many of Cal U's programs provide active learning and internship opportunities that integrate real-world experience with classroom learning.

The Eberly College of Science and Technology includes the following departments: Applied Engineering and Technology; Biological and Environmental Sciences; Business and Economics; Chemistry and Physics; Earth Science; Math, Computer Science, and Information Systems; Nursing; and Professional Studies.

Cal U's **College of Education and Human Services** offers career-oriented degree programs to prepare students for the complex demands of the education and human services fields, or for advanced-level study.

Teacher education is the historical mission of California University of Pennsylvania, and the university offers professional certification and degree programs in a variety of fields, including early childhood/elementary, middle level and secondary education, special education, and technology education.

In addition, the departments of TRIO and Academic Services, Communication Disorders, Counselor Education, Health Science, Exercise Science and Sport Studies, and Social Work provide professional degrees, certifications, and certificate programs.

By combining classroom learning and field experiences, the College of Education and Human Services helps to create a dynamic community of learners and self-assured graduates who are ready to make an impact on their chosen professions. All programs leading to licensure are accredited by their appropriate national organizations.

Cal U's **College of Liberal Arts** furthers intellectual development in the arts, humanities, and social sciences through the departments of Art and Languages; Communications, Design and Culture; Criminal Justice; English; History, Politics and Society; Music and Theatre; and Psychology.

In addition, the College houses the University Honors Program and offers a degree program in liberal studies, an interdisciplinary minor in leadership studies, and a minor in women's studies.

Liberal arts programs at Cal U give students a solid academic foundation in their chosen discipline while fostering skills that employers find essential in any field: critical and analytical thinking, problem solving, communication skills, teamwork, and individual initiative. These programs foster creativity and self-expression as they help students see connections—between the past and the present, the world we know and the ones we imagine, and the local community and the global society.

Cal U's **School of Graduate Studies and Research** offers professional doctorates, master's degrees, certifications, and certificate programs. Both on-campus and online options are available to students who want to add to their knowledge, enhance their resumes, or advance their careers.

Evening classes, accelerated programs, and Cal U Global Online, the University's 100 percent online learning community, make it easier for students to balance earning a degree or other credential with career and family demands. Dual-degree and certificate programs, as well as Cal U's professional doctorates, help students target advanced learning to meet their professional needs.

Highly qualified faculty in Cal U's School of Graduate Studies lead programs that combine rigorous coursework with practical, career-focused experience. Caring staff in the Graduate Admissions and Global Online offices work with students step by step to help them achieve their educational goals as quickly and affordably as possible.

Costs

In 2016–17, undergraduate tuition at Cal U was $7,238 for Pennsylvania residents and $10,858 for out-of-state residents. The average cost of room and board for an incoming freshman was $10,086, and fees were $2,908. Books, travel expenses, and other supplies are additional.

Financial Aid

More than 90 percent of all students attending Cal U receive some type of financial aid. The federal Free Application for Federal Student Aid (FAFSA), along with the cost of education, determines whether a student is eligible for need-based assistance. A variety of merit-based scholarships also are available. Cal U works individually with students to build a financial aid package customized to meet their needs.

Faculty

Cal U is a student-centered university that is committed above all to academic excellence and intellectual rigor. All courses are taught by faculty members, not teaching assistants or graduate students.

Stellar faculty are dedicated to helping students take important steps toward achieving their career goals. Among Cal U's professors are Fulbright Specialists, Frederick Douglass Scholars, and recipients of grants from prestigious organizations such as the National Science Foundation and the National Endowment for the Humanities. But at the end of the day, faculty members say that teaching, motivating, and inspiring students is what they do best.

Student Research

Cal U's Center for Undergraduate Research facilitates faculty-led research experiences for students in all majors, providing financial support for student proposals and a student travel fund to support presentations at local, regional, and national events.

Students and faculty showcase their research, scholarship, creative activity, and application at the annual Strike a Spark Conference, an opportunity to hone presentation skills and share their work with the entire campus community.

The SAI Farm, owned and operated by Cal U students, provides an outdoor setting for research projects just over a mile from campus. At community sites throughout western Pennsylvania, students put classroom skills into practice. And opportunities such as the Madagascar Field School give inquisitive scholars a global perspective—and an experience they never forget.

University Honors Program

The University Honors Program at Cal U gives a select group of students a safe, supportive community in which to excel academically, socially, and professionally.

Honors Program students pursue innovative research projects and join other ambitious students in classes taught by Cal U's most distinguished faculty. They have opportunities to make the most of their Cal U education and to position themselves to excel after graduation, whether they choose to begin a career or enter graduate or professional school.

Each semester the Honors Program organizes three- to five-day excursions that allow students to conduct hands-on research; visit libraries, archives, and museums related to their research and coursework; and visit important cultural and historical sites. Many students use an excursion to begin their Honors Program thesis.

In addition, Cal U students in the University Honors Program can receive a scholarship to travel abroad with other honors students from Pennsylvania's State System of Higher Education.

Four-Year Graduation Plan

Cal U's Four-Year Graduation Plan helps students stay on track to complete a bachelor's degree in four years. First-year students agree to stick to one major, take a full course load, and maintain an acceptable grade-point average. In turn, the University provides advising and counseling services every semester, and the Academic Scheduling Center helps students develop an academic plan and keep track of their progress.

Students who follow the Four-Year Graduation Plan do more than graduate on time—they save money by finishing their studies on schedule and getting started on a career.

Career Services

Cal U's Career and Professional Development Center helps students prepare for the future. The Career Advantage program guides students as they make choices about academic majors, explore career options, gain experience, and transition into the workforce. The Career Center staff maintain connections with the region's employers, who regularly visit campus for networking events, job fairs and career training programs.

The Internship Center links Cal U students with employers for a mutually beneficial experience. High-quality, supervised internships allow Cal U students to test-drive their future careers, hone professional skills, build resumes, network, and gain an edge in the job market.

Leadership Training

Cal U's prepares students to take the lead, no matter what field of study they choose to pursue. Students can add a leadership minor that teaches them to think critically about global issues and learn to become leaders in education, business, science, or the arts.

And when students practice effective leadership in class, through community service, and as members of clubs and organizations, the results are documented on an official Activities Transcript.

Student Government

Cal U's Student Government is the official governing body for students. The forum establishes channels of communication between students and administrators/faculty, and it sponsors programs and activities to enrich campus life.

Student Government is part of the Student Association Inc. (SAI), the nonprofit corporation owned and operated by students of Cal U. Along with serving the student body, SAI and Student Government provide opportunities for students to develop leadership and community service skills.

Admissions Requirements

Prospective freshmen students who want to be considered for admission to Cal U as a degree-seeking student must submit an application or admission with a $25 application fee, official high school transcripts or GED credential, and official SAT or ACT scores.

Applicants will be considered for admission to Cal U after careful review of high school record, class rank, academic coursework, and SAT/ACT scores. Attention is given to personal essays, extracurricular activities, and letters of recommendation, if submitted.

Graduate admission varies by program. Information is available at calu.edu.

Application and Information

Applicants may apply online at calu.edu or may contact the Office of Admissions.

California University of Pennsylvania
c/o Undergraduate Admissions–Box 94
250 University Ave.
California, Pennsylvania 15419
Phone: 888-412-0479 (toll-free)
E-mail: admissions@calu.edu
Website: www.calu.edu

COLLEGE CLOSE-UPS

CASTLETON UNIVERSITY

CASTLETON, VERMONT

Castleton
UNIVERSITY

The University

Since Castleton University first opened its doors in 1787, it has been dedicated to providing a quality level of higher education to those eager to learn. Vermont's first institution of higher education, and the eighteenth oldest in the United States, the 165-acre campus is located in Castleton, a historic Vermont village. Sixty-five percent of the 1,900 full-time undergraduate students at the University are Vermonters with the balance of the student population coming across the United States and thirty-seven countries, while New England and the Middle Atlantic states make up a majority of the out-of-state population.

Castleton is committed to providing an undergraduate education in which the liberal arts and career preparation complement each other. A commitment to community engagement, and experiential learning through civic-mindedness and internship has become central to the Castleton mission, providing students with a unique experience. Through an innovative program called Soundings, first-year students earn academic credit by attending a series of special events that include theater, music, dance, film, debate, and opinion from influential people. New students also participate in the First-Year Seminar, giving them the opportunity to develop the skills of a successful college student. First-year students may apply for the University's honors program.

There are eleven major residence halls which are communities where students are challenged to interact with others, learn respect and appreciation for differences, become involved in community governance, and receive support for their academic endeavors. Together, the residences accommodate nearly 1,100 students. Each residence hall room is equipped with at least two wired broadband Internet hookups and wireless access. There is no additional charge for this service. Off-campus housing is available in the Castleton, Fair Haven, and Rutland areas through private landlords. All students have access to three dining options on campus: Huden Dining Hall, Fireside Café, and the Coffee Cottage. All students are allowed to have automobiles on campus and parking is free.

More than fifty clubs and organizations provide a wide variety of student activities that include club sports, an FM radio station, the student newspaper, and an active outing club. Other clubs relate to University majors and future careers; still others serve the University or local community. At the varsity level, men compete in baseball, basketball, cross-country, football, golf, ice hockey, lacrosse, alpine skiing, Nordic skiing, soccer, tennis, track and field, and wrestling. Women compete in basketball, cross-country, field hockey, golf, ice hockey, lacrosse, alpine skiing, Nordic skiing, soccer, softball, tennis, track and field, and volleyball. Nearly 700 students compete for Castleton on a varsity sports team at the NCAA Division III level, while countless others take advantage of the robust intramural and recreational sports programs offered.

Since 2002 Castleton has invested nearly $75 million in infrastructure improvements including a $25.7-million project that included the construction of Spartan Stadium, renovation and expansion of the Campus Center and the Spartan Athletic Complex, and improvements to the baseball and softball fields. In 2012, Castleton debuted new lighted tennis courts, a facilities barn, the renovation of Huden Dining Hall, the construction of Hoff Hall, a LEED Gold-certified residence hall with room for more than 160 students, and the impressive Castleton Pavilion, the largest indoor-outdoor venue of its kind in the state of Vermont.

The 2013–14 academic year saw the inauguration of "Castleton on the Move," a strategic plan and blueprint for the University's next ten years. Highlighted by new and enhanced graduate programs and a vision to become Vermont's public master's institution, the plan also includes incremental enrollment growth; a focus on international enrollment; and increased opportunities for students in nearby Rutland through entrepreneurial ventures such as the Castleton Downtown Gallery, the Castleton Polling Institute, and Castleton Downtown, which is home to the Center for Community Engagement, Center for Entrepreneurial Programs, and Center for Schools.

Location

The campus is 12 miles west of Rutland, one of Vermont's largest cities. Montreal, Boston, Hartford, Albany, and New York City are all within easy driving distance. Amtrak passenger trains to and from New York City stop in the village of Castleton. Killington and Pico ski areas, Lake Bomoseen, and the Green Mountains provide excellent recreational opportunities and an exceptional living and learning environment.

Majors and Degrees

Castleton University offers more than 75 programs of study for undergraduate and grade students, with B.A. or B.S. degrees in: accounting, American literature, art, athletic training, biology, chemistry, children's literature, computer information systems, communication, criminal justice, digital media, elementary education, environmental science, exercise science, forensic psychology, geology, graphic design, health education, health science, history, journalism, management, marketing, mass media, mathematics, music, music education, nursing, physical education, psychology, public relations, secondary education, social work, sociology, Spanish, special education, sports administration, theater arts, and world literature. Associate degrees can be earned in business, communication, computer programming, criminal justice, or general studies.

Academic Programs

The Castleton curriculum is designed to provide the student with a strong liberal arts background plus the opportunity for career preparation in a specific area. Students receive individual attention from faculty, with an average class size of 17. Castleton's curriculum is based on the belief that a well-rounded education that expands students' horizons and teaches them how to write and to solve problems creatively is critical in preparation for all careers. All four-year students are required to complete a core of general education requirements during the four-year degree program. The first year of study can be used by the undecided student to explore various areas of interest. The student with a specific career interest may begin study in the major field as a first-year student, although four-year students are not required to formally declare their major until the end of the sophomore year.

Castleton students typically enroll in five courses each semester. The academic calendar consists of two 15-week semesters and three 4-week summer sessions. Grading is traditional, and a pass/no-pass option is available. Internships and field experiences complement the academic programs at Castleton and are a requirement for graduation in many.

Students may transfer internally from two-year to four-year programs in business, communication, computer information systems, criminal justice, and general studies. Students who transfer to Castleton after graduating from an accredited two-year college are granted full transfer credit for all academic work up to 64 credits or the number required for the associate degree.

First-year students achieving at least a 3.5 grade point average in their first year at Castleton are recognized by the Castleton Chapter of Phi Eta Sigma, a national honor society that recognizes first-year scholastic achievement in colleges and universities throughout the country. Outstanding junior and senior scholars are recognized by the Castleton Chapter of Alpha Chi. Pinnacle, the honor society for nontraditional students, honors qualified candidates. There are honor societies in business administration, women's studies, history, science and mathematics, theater arts, education, psychology, and Spanish. Students who have achieved a 4.0 grade point average are named to the President's List and those with a 3.5 grade point average or better to the Dean's List.

Academic Facilities

The Calvin Coolidge Library houses a collection of more than 500,000 books, periodicals, microforms, and nonprint media. Access to Castleton's library resources and outside scholarly sources is made possible through numerous online and CD databases; a sophisticated, networked electronic library system; the Internet; and strong consortial relationships within the state of Vermont. An audiovisual media facility provides a wide range of audiovisual equipment, including digital video editing, digital cameras, and presentation equipment.

Castleton's Stafford Academic Center houses the Academic Computing Center, a high-tech multimedia lecture hall, and the departments of education, mathematics, and nursing.

The Spartan Athletic Complex houses Glenbrook Gymnasium, two athletic training rooms, a swimming pool, two racquetball courts, two fitness centers, and a large indoor activity area. Spartan Arena, the home of the men's and women's ice hockey teams, as well as a fitness center, is a short drive away in Rutland Town.

The Fine Arts Center houses the 500-seat Casella Theater; black box theater; and facilities for art, drama, dance, and music. A television studio opened in 2010 as part of an addition to Leavenworth Hall.

The Jeffords Center houses science classrooms and laboratories, a state-of-the-art auditorium, laboratories for faculty and student research projects, and a greenhouse. An astronomical observatory is a short walk away.

Costs

Costs for 2017–18 are as follows: tuition for Vermont residents, $10,872, and for nonresidents, $26,424. Room and board expenses total $10,290. Annual fees are $1,328.

Financial Aid

Eighty percent of Castleton's full-time undergraduate students receive financial assistance from federal, state, the University, or other sources. Grants, loans, and work-study jobs are available for qualified students. Applicants for financial aid should file the Free Application for Federal Student Aid (FAFSA) form by April 1 of the senior year in high school. All financial aid awards are based on need.

Castleton offers an array of scholarships for first-year, transfer, international, and returning students.

For new students, Castleton Admissions reviews each applicant holistically; all application materials submitted are taken into consideration for initial acceptance. New Student Scholarships further recognize students' commitment to and success in academic and extra-curricular involvement.

Amounts range from $1,000 to $10,000 per year. Any individual who can provide proof of valedictorian status from a regionally accredited or state-approved public or independent high school will be eligible for the full tuition Valedictorian Scholarship and may be invited to participate in honors programming. There are also special scholarships for students wishing to study music or Spanish.

Faculty

The full-time faculty at Castleton consists of 103 men and women, 96 percent of whom hold terminal degrees in their field. Adjunct faculty members, many of them local businesspeople and members of the professions, complement the efforts of the full-time faculty. The student-faculty ratio is 14:1. Each student has a faculty member as an adviser.

Student Government

The Student Government Association (SGA) at Castleton operates with three branches, which are the Congress, the University Court, and the Campus Activities Board (CAB). All students participating in any facet of these groups are automatically members of the SGA.

As the student government of Castleton, the SGA represents the interests of Castleton students and administers the Student Activity Fee. This fee is assessed to all students and is used to fund activities on campus as well as numerous clubs and organizations.

Admission Requirements

Applicants are evaluated on the basis of their secondary school records, standardized test scores, and recommendations. Admission is granted to those applicants who have demonstrated their ability and potential to meet the challenges of a postsecondary learning experience.

Application and Information

Students may apply for admission through the Common Application. Under Castleton's rolling admission policy, applications are processed throughout the year, and candidates are notified of the admission decision as soon as their files are complete. Students are admitted in the fall and spring semesters.

For more information about Castleton University or to arrange a campus visit, students should contact:

Office of Admissions
Castleton University
Castleton, Vermont 05735
Phone: 802-468-1213
800-639-8521 (toll-free)
Fax: 802-468-1476
E-mail: info@castleton.edu
Website: http://www.castleton.edu

The Castleton campus is nestled at the base of the Green Mountains, and has a panoramic view of every season.

THE CATHOLIC UNIVERSITY OF AMERICA

WASHINGTON, D.C.

★ To read more about this school, visit http://petersons.to/catholicuniversity

The University

The Catholic University of America, located in Washington, D.C., combines the resources of a major research university with the comfortable feel of a liberal arts college comprising roughly 3,250 undergraduates.

The Catholic University of America brings together a rich tradition of Catholic spirituality with a proven record of academic excellence. Catholic University is a place where students and faculty work together, and, with more than 70 majors and over 100 clubs, there is always a way for students to explore all of their interests.

At Catholic University, life is more than course work. The family-like atmosphere will have students laughing with friends over exam week's Midnight Breakfast, volunteering their skills to help families through Habitat for Humanity, museum-hopping with their roommates, and exceeding their own expectations throughout their college careers.

While proudly a Catholic university, the spirit of inquiry and academic freedom is embraced, and students of all faith backgrounds are welcomed. Students find an inviting Catholic presence on campus—the door is always open for students who want the opportunity to pray, attend services, go on a retreat, or talk to a spiritual adviser.

Location

The excitement of the nation's capital is just a Metrorail ride away from the University's residential college campus, the largest and greenest campus in the District of Columbia.

Washington, D.C., is one of the nation's largest college towns, with more than 100,000 students at colleges and universities in the region. The University participates in the Consortium of Universities of the Washington Metropolitan Area, so students have access to courses at other universities, including American, Georgetown, George Washington, Howard, and the University of Maryland College Park. With 91 stations throughout the city and surrounding areas, including Catholic University's own stop, the Metrorail system is safe, fast, and convenient.

Majors and Degrees

With more than 70 undergraduate majors, 10 academic schools that grant undergraduate degrees, and small class sizes, Catholic University offers remarkably diverse areas of study. Students can delve deeply into their major interests while rooting their studies in the enduring liberal arts.

Degree programs are offered in the following majors: accounting, anthropology, architecture, architecture and civil engineering, art history, art–studio art, biochemistry, biology, biomedical engineering, chemical physics, chemistry, city and regional studies, civil engineering, classical civilization, classical humanities, classics–Greek and Latin, computer science, construction engineering and management, drama, economics, education studies (non-teaching), education, electrical engineering, English language and literature, environmental chemistry, environmental engineering, environmental studies, finance, French and Francophone studies, German studies, Hispanic studies, history, instrumental performance, international business, international economics and finance, Italian studies, management, marketing, mathematics, mathematics and physics, mechanical engineering, media and communication studies, medieval and Byzantine studies, music composition, music education, music–general, music–instrumental performance, music–organ, music–piano, music–voice performance, musical theatre, nursing, organ, philosophy, physics, piano, politics, psychology, social work, sociology, Spanish, structural/geotechnical engineering, studio art, theology and religious studies, and voice performance.

Additional information on undergraduate majors can be found online at www.cua.edu/undergraduateprograms.

Academic Programs

Catholic University offers all of the benefits of a major research university within a nurturing educational community.

All undergraduates participate in the First-Year Experience (FYE), an introduction to the life of the mind through coursework and activities rooted in the liberal arts and the Catholic intellectual tradition. Within Learning Communities, students take a sequence of four core classes in philosophy, theology, and English. The FYE also goes beyond the classroom with service learning activities, class-based excursions into Washington, D.C., an annual Speaker Series, and one-on-one academic advising.

The Undergraduate Advising Center provides dynamic advising resources for all students. The Center for Academic Success offers a wide range of academic services designed to help students of all abilities strengthen their skills and take an active role in their education.

The University Honors Program offers a challenging and inspiring liberal arts program to motivated students with outstanding academic promise. Through the give and take of intimate, seminar-style classes, UHP students find themselves pushed to be more broad-minded and rigorous, more thoughtful, quicker on their feet, more keenly critical, and more humane in their pursuit of the truth. In addition to an outstanding academic program, the UHP offers a variety of excellent social and cultural opportunities. Those who choose to live in the Centennial Village Honors Community enjoy even more opportunities for enrichment.

There are over 2,000 internship opportunities for students. On average, 67 percent of student internships are paid while the other 33 percent are done for class credit during the semester or summer. Students have recently had the advantage of internships with the FBI, Congress, JP Morgan, and Community Family Life Services, to name a few of the exciting opportunities for students from all schools and majors to develop skills in their chosen field. The Office of Career Services works with students throughout the job/internship process from resume workshops to mock interviews while connecting students with Catholic University alumni throughout the country and around the world. Catholic University students studying abroad in Brussels, Dublin, and London also have the opportunities to intern with the European Union, Irish Parliament, and British Parliament, respectively.

Off-Campus Programs

International outreach has been a central part of the University's mission since its founding. The Education Abroad Program continues that tradition. Any financial aid received on campus can be applied to an education abroad program. Students can choose to study and live in countries such as Australia, Belgium, Chile, China, England, France, Germany, Greece, Guatemala, Ireland, Italy, Mexico, Poland, and Spain, to name a few. With opportunities in more than 50 cities worldwide, students of any major can spend a summer, a semester, or a year abroad, immersed in a new culture.

The Rome Center of The Catholic University of America and Australian Catholic University offers semester-long programs, primarily for students enrolled in the schools of arts and sciences, business and economics, music, and architecture; a month-long Summer Experience Abroad for architecture majors; short courses in law, canon law, business and economics, and theology and religious studies; and a summer program for the First-Year Experience.

Costs

For the 2016–17 academic year, tuition was $41,800, room and board was $13,820, and fees totaled $736. Costs for books, transportation, and personal expenses are estimated at $4,106 for a total annual estimated cost of attendance of $60,462.

Financial Aid

The Catholic University of America offers several forms of financial assistance to qualifying students. The University's focus is on helping as many eligible students as possible achieve their goal of obtaining a high quality academic and values-based education. Nine out of every 10 full-time students at Catholic University receive some level of financial aid, based on both need and academic potential.

Faculty

Professors at The Catholic University of America research compelling issues in their fields, connecting knowledge of the past to the promise of the future. The University's notable academic leadership has produced dozens of Fulbright, Guggenheim, Wilson, Mellon, and Oxford scholars. Catholic University stands out among research universities because undergraduate studies are a vital part of the faculty's interests. Four of every five professors teach at the undergraduate level.

Student Activities

Students are involved on campus and in the community in a wide array of activities. With more than 100 student organizations, Catholic University makes it easy for students to pursue their interests in virtually every field and activity imaginable. All activities are open to all students regardless of major or year in college. There are activities and organizations that emphasize academics, professions, community service, multiculturalism, politics, spiritual life, recreation, singing, dancing, student government, media, and more.

Admission Requirements

Prospective students are expected to have a rigorous and well-rounded academic background including 4 years of English, 4 years of social studies, 3 years of mathematics, 3 years of science (including at least 1 laboratory science), at least 2 years of a foreign language, and 1 year of fine arts or humanities.

The Catholic University of America is now test-optional for undergraduate admission. Submission of standardized test scores is optional for students applying for undergraduate admission. First-year and transfer applicants will receive full consideration for admission and merit-based scholarships regardless of whether they submit the results from the SAT or the ACT.

Application and Information

The Catholic University of America utilizes the Common Application. The Early Action application deadline is November 1 and the Early Decision application deadline is November 15; both Early Action and Early Decisions will receive notification on or around January 1. The regular decision application deadline is January 15, with notification on or around March 20.

The Catholic University of America invites prospective students and their families to visit the campus, meet admissions staff and current students, and learn about the many opportunities the University offers.

For more information, prospective students should contact:

Office of Undergraduate Admissions
The Catholic University of America
620 Michigan Avenue, N.E.
Washington, D.C. 20064
United States
Phone: 202-319-5305
800-673-2772 (toll-free)
Fax: 202-319-6533
E-mail: cua-admissions@cua.edu
Website: http://admissions.cua.edu

Catholic University's 176-acre campus is the largest in Washington, D.C. The Basilica of the National Shrine of the Immaculate Conception is located adjacent to the University Mall.

CHAMPLAIN COLLEGE

BURLINGTON, VERMONT

★ To read more about this school, visit http://petersons.to/brynmawrcollege

The College

Champlain College—a pioneer of innovation in higher education since 1878—is a national leader in preparing students for rewarding careers and successful lives. A private, nonprofit college with 2,200 full-time residential undergraduate students, as well as online adult undergraduate and master's degree students, Champlain's enlightened academic model is what sets the Burlington, Vermont, school apart. Its distinctive, career-driven, interdisciplinary programs equip students with the professional and intellectual knowledge and life-management skills to provide the greatest potential for future opportunity.

In addition to its main campus in Vermont, Champlain College has two international campuses: one in Montreal, Canada, and the other in Dublin, Ireland (champlain.edu/champlain-abroad). Champlain College is accredited by the New England Association of Schools and Colleges.

The undergraduate student body represents 46 states and 17 countries. Small class sizes average 16 students, with an overall student-to-faculty ratio of 14:1. More than 50 student clubs and organizations—ranging from the Ski & Ride and Equestrian Clubs to the Quidditch and Dance Teams—keep students involved and engaged in campus life (champlain.edu/activities-clubs).

Champlain's 22-acre campus is situated in the heart of Burlington's historic Hill Section neighborhood, which overlooks Lake Champlain and the Adirondack Mountains. All first-year students live in one of 19 restored Victorian-era mansion residence halls—a unique atmosphere in which to learn and live—and sophomores, juniors, and seniors have the option to live in contemporary suite- and apartment-style residence halls.

Champlain's radically pragmatic education is underscored by its 29 career-focused majors, 28 minors, and 27 specializations in the Robert P. Stiller School of Business, the Division of Communication & Creative Media, the Division of Education & Human Studies, and the Division of Information Technology & Sciences. Champlain also offers 9 master's degree programs as well as online graduate certificate programs.

In addition to a professionally focused curriculum, Champlain students gain invaluable hands-on career experience through the College's Centers of Excellence—on-campus learning centers (champlain.edu/centers).

Champlain's Upside-Down Curriculum allows students to begin their major courses in the first semester and participate in internships as early as the summer after their first year. A full 90 percent of Champlain students complete one or more internships or professional work experiences by graduation. Champlain students are the interns of choice at numerous businesses throughout Vermont and beyond; many students are offered full-time employment after graduation (champlain.edu/internships).

Providing students with a career-focused and relevant education is Champlain College's primary mission. Outcome data demonstrates that Champlain's approach is highly effective. Based on data collected from 91 percent of the Class of 2015, 96 percent are employed or continuing their education within one year of graduating. Of the 93 percent who are employed, 88 percent are already in career-relevant positions (champlain.edu/career-success).

Champlain appears regularly on the nation's premier Best Colleges rankings. The College was named a "Most Innovative School" in the North for the second year in a row by *U.S. News & World Report's* 2017 America's Best Colleges. Fisk *Guide to Colleges 2017* recognized Champlain as one of the "best and most interesting schools in the United States, Canada, and Great Britain." Champlain was also featured in The Princeton Review's *The Best 381 Colleges: 2017 Edition*, and *SC Magazine* named Champlain as having the Best Cyber Security Higher Education Program in the nation.

Location

Champlain's residential campus is in the center of Burlington, Vermont's largest city, and is located on the eastern shore of Lake Champlain, with New York's Adirondack Mountains to the west and Vermont's Green Mountains to the east. Burlington is home to 43,000 residents (in a metro area of 211,000), including nearly 15,000 college students. The Church Street Marketplace, the commercial heart of the city located just a few blocks from the campus, attracts both locals and tourists to its numerous shops, coffee bars, and restaurants. Montreal, Canada, is 94 miles to the north; Boston is 220 miles to the southeast; and New York City is 285 miles to the south.

Burlington is frequently cited in national media as one of the nation's best college towns and best places to live and work (champlain.edu/burlington). The area is home to five colleges, as well as the UVM Medical Center, one of the leading medical centers in the East. There is an international airport; an Amtrak passenger train route with connections to Montreal, New York City, and Washington, D.C.; and long-distance bus service to Boston, Hartford, and New York City.

Majors and Degrees

Champlain College offers Bachelor of Science (B.S.), Bachelor of Arts (B.A.), Bachelor of Fine Arts (B.F.A.), Bachelor of Social Work (B.S.W.), and Bachelor of Science in Business Administration (B.S.B.A.) degree programs. In addition to majors in high-growth, traditional fields like accounting, law and communication, students can find cutting-edge programs like Game Production Management, Computer & Digital Forensics, and Environmental Studies & Policy. Students who are undecided about a major may apply as undeclared in a particular division. The undergraduate curriculum also offers specialization options within majors, as well as career-focused minors, which are open to all students.

Academic Programs

Champlain's Upside-Down Curriculum allows students to take courses in their major starting in their first semester. Beyond the Upside-Down Curriculum, Champlain takes a multidimensional academic approach that encompasses the professional, academic, and practical knowledge students need to grow and thrive in an ever-changing world. The Major Dimension gives students career-focused majors and prepares them for their lifelong professional success; it also includes extensive experiential learning, internships, and field study. The Core Dimension is the College's four-year, innovative liberal arts curriculum, offering courses that form the foundation of critical thinking and intellectual leadership. The Life Experience & Action Dimension (LEAD) program teaches lifelong career management skills, as well as financial and interpersonal understanding, that prepare students for a well-managed and meaningful life.

Champlain's comprehensive approach to professional readiness is further exemplified through the College's Career Collaborative. Extending far beyond the College itself, Career Collaborative leverages all of the career-focused academic programs and connects students with practical, hands-on, relevant, experiential learning opportunities. Career Collaborative also provides students with immersive programs in professional development that include career preparation activities, such as portfolio development, hands-on learning, and on-campus recruitment events.

Off-Campus Programs

The Office of International Education ensures that students graduate prepared to be engaged citizens with international experience and a global perspective. In addition to Champlain's international campuses in Montreal, Canada, and Dublin, Ireland, the College also has global partners in Argentina, China, Italy, Morocco, and New Zealand. Students can also study abroad through approved third-party providers at other locations. More than 53 percent of Champlain students study abroad.

Academic Facilities

Champlain's main academic facilities continue to expand and evolve, incorporating the latest equipment and technology to match the nature and requirements of the College's career-focused majors. All students have full access to all campus computer labs, 3-D animation and game production labs, multimedia classrooms, digital and traditional photography labs, and the Emergent Media Center® and MakerLab, among other lab spaces.

The Center for Communication & Creative Media is home to the largest academic division at the College. The state-of-the-art space features game and graphic design labs, sound studios, a filmmaking and broadcast media production stage, art gallery, and drawing studio. The S. D. Ireland Family Center for Global Business & Technology is home to the Robert P. Stiller School of Business as well as the David L. Cooperrider Center for Appreciative Inquiry.

The Holly D. and Robert E. Miller Information Commons is a recipient of the Excellence in Academic Libraries Award from the Association of College and Research Libraries (ACRL). It combines the features of a traditional library with advanced technologies such as multimedia laboratories, specialized electronic classrooms, and online distance-learning systems.

Costs

Tuition for 2017–18 is $39,718; room and board is $14,906. Total standard cost of attendance including tuition, fees, and room and board, is $54,724.

Financial Aid

Champlain invests in its students and recognizes academic achievement each year through need- and merit-based scholarships and financial aid. Each year, Champlain students receive more than $32 million in scholarships. More than 90 percent of students received scholarship funds to help pay their educational costs.

Special efforts are made to include support for new Americans, U.S. veterans, single parents, Vermont students who are the first in their family to attend college, women interested in studying in technology fields, and student entrepreneurs.

Students interested in receiving need-based financial aid must complete the Free Application for Federal Student Aid (FAFSA).

Faculty

Champlain's faculty members bring outstanding academic credentials to the classroom; they have also built their careers in the workplace and bring their practical, professional expertise to the educational experience. Champlain College employs 116 full-time professors as well as adjunct professors who, in addition to their academic credentials, have ongoing professional experience in the fields in which they teach. Faculty members teach all classes; students will never have a class taught by a teaching assistant.

Admission Requirements

For first-year applicants, the College requires an official high school transcript (or GED), SAT or ACT scores, two letters of recommendation, a short essay, and an application for admission. Personal interviews are not required but a campus visit is strongly recommended. Students applying to majors in Game Design, Game Art & Animation, Graphic Design & Digital Media, Filmmaking, and Creative Media, must also submit a portfolio. Students may earn advanced standing by submitting appropriate scores on Advanced Placement or International Baccalaureate examinations. International applicants whose native language is not English also must submit TOEFL, IELTS, or PTE results. Transfer applicants must submit official transcripts from all post-secondary institutions they attended, and SAT or ACT scores are recommended.

Champlain College uses the Common Application as well as the Champlain College Application for enrollment in fall or spring semesters. Transfer applicants can apply on a rolling basis. Links to applications can be found at champlain.edu/apply.

Students can apply either through the Early or Regular Decision program. Early Decision is a binding agreement, and students are encouraged to apply through this program only if Champlain College is their first choice. Additional details regarding application options and deadlines are available at champlain.edu/deadlines.

Champlain College admits students without regard to race, creed, color, national and ethnic origin, religion, age, gender, sexual orientation, or qualified disability and does not discriminate in the administration of its educational and admission policies, scholarships and loan programs, or other College-administered programs. Champlain College makes reasonable accommodations to the disabilities of otherwise qualified students, applicants or employees.

Application Information

Director of Admissions
Champlain College
163 South Willard Street
P.O. Box 670
Burlington, Vermont 05402-0670
Phone: 802-860-2727
800-570-5858 (toll-free)
Fax: 802-860-2767
E-mail: admission@champlain.edu
Website: champlain.edu

The Champlain College campus, home to 2,200 career-focused undergraduates, combines renovated historic buildings and modern facilities in a pedestrian-friendly campus overlooking Lake Champlain and the top college town of Burlington, Vermont.

CLEMSON UNIVERSITY

CLEMSON, SOUTH CAROLINA

★ To read more about this school, visit http://petersons.to/clemsonuniversity

The University

A top-23 public university with a reputation for excellence that's known worldwide, Clemson University leads the way in providing a hands-on education—in the lab, in the arts, and in the field. Clemson was founded in 1889 with a mission to be a "high seminary of learning" dedicated to teaching, research, and service. Today, Clemson is one of the country's most selective public research universities, and these three concepts remain prevalent, providing the framework for an exceptional educational experience.

At Clemson University, professors take the time to get to know students and explore innovative ways of teaching. Exceptional teaching is one reason Clemson's retention and graduation rates rank among the highest in the country for public universities.

Exceptional teaching is also why Clemson continues to attract an increasingly talented student body. In 2016, more than half of the entering freshmen were ranked in the top 10 percent of their high school classes, and the freshman class averaged 29 on the ACT, placing Clemson in the top seven public universities in the nation, as ranked by freshman ACT scores (*U.S. News & World Report*, 2017).

Clemson is committed to world-class research and is ranked in the highest research university category by the Carnegie Classification of Institutions of Higher Education. The University is also invested in the success of its students. Student retention at Clemson is consistently more than 90 percent. Much of this is due to the Academic Success Center (ASC). Established in 2001, the ASC has been recognized nationally and internationally by organizations related to tutoring, supplemental instruction, and collegiate learning. The ASC moved into a new, 35,000 square-foot facility in 2012 where it offers free one-on-one tutoring services for more than 80 courses and provides tutoring for additional courses as the need arises. Peer-assisted learning, academic skills workshops, and academic counseling are also available—free to all Clemson students. It is estimated that more than 50 percent of freshmen use ASC services during their first semester.

Clemson has also received national recognition for its innovative Communication Across the Curriculum (CAC) program. At Clemson, CAC is a standard teaching method used in nearly every department. Professors use CAC to focus on providing real-life challenges that require students to think and communicate effectively.

From cheering on the Tigers at a football game to socializing in the Hendrix Student Center, Clemson students can participate in a wide variety of activities outside the classroom. The more than 400 campus clubs and organizations include fraternities and sororities, as well as honorary, international, military, performing arts, political, professional, religious, service, social interest, special interest, sports and fitness, and student media programs and activities.

With 19 intercollegiate sports, Clemson offers exciting spectator sports year-round. Clemson is a charter member of the Atlantic Coast Conference (ACC) and is an NCAA Division I school. Admission to most regular-season home events is included in University fees for full-time students.

Clemson University is accredited by the Commission on Colleges of the Southern Association of Colleges and Schools to award bachelor's, master's, specialist, and doctoral degrees. Questions about the accreditation of Clemson University can be directed to the Commission on Colleges at 1866 Southern Lane, Decatur, Georgia 30033-4097; phone: 404-679-4500.

Location

Approximately midway between Charlotte, North Carolina, and Atlanta, Georgia, Clemson University is located on 1,400 acres in the foothills of the Blue Ridge Mountains and along the shores of Hartwell Lake. Great weather and proximity to natural wonders and large cities offer year-round recreational opportunities.

The University's enrollment of more than 23,000 undergraduate and graduate students makes it a defining presence in Clemson, South Carolina, a town of about 14,000. Students may live on campus in one of the 21 residence halls and four apartment complexes, most of which are within a 15-minute walk to class or downtown. More than 99 percent of students live on campus their freshman year.

CLEMSON UNIVERSITY 1889

Majors and Degrees

Clemson offers more than 80 undergraduate and 119 graduate degree programs through seven academic colleges: Agriculture, Forestry, and Life Sciences; Architecture, Arts, and Humanities; Behavioral, Social and Health Sciences; Business; Engineering, Computing and Applied Sciences; Education; and Science. Undergraduate students can earn B.A., B.S., or preprofessional degrees in accounting; agribusiness; agricultural education; agricultural mechanization and business; animal and veterinary sciences; anthropology; architecture; art; biochemistry; bioengineering; biological sciences; biosystems engineering; chemical engineering; chemistry; civil engineering; communication; computer engineering; computer information systems; computer science; construction science and management; early childhood education; economics; electrical engineering; elementary education; English; environmental and natural resources; environmental engineering; financial management; food science and human nutrition; forest resource management; genetics; geology; graphic communications; health science; history; horticulture; industrial engineering; justice studies; landscape architecture; language and international health; language and international trade; management; marketing; materials science and engineering; mathematical sciences; mathematics teaching; mechanical engineering; microbiology; modern languages (American Sign Language, Chinese, French, German, Italian, Japanese, and Spanish); nursing; packaging science; Pan African studies; parks, recreation, and tourism management; philosophy; physics; plant and environmental sciences; political science; prepharmacy; preprofessional health studies; prerehabilitation sciences; preveterinary medicine; production studies in performing arts; psychology; religious studies; science teaching; secondary education; sociology; special education; sports communication; turfgrass; wildlife and fisheries biology; women's leadership; world cinema; and youth development studies.

Academic Programs

Clemson's academic year is divided into two semesters. The fall semester begins in mid-August and the spring semester starts in early January. Three summer sessions and four mini-semesters are also available. Students average 16 credit hours per semester, and Clemson requires all students to complete some general education classes specified by the University before graduation. The number of completed credit hours required for graduation varies, depending on the major.

Calhoun Honors College is a University-wide program that combines the strengths of a public, land-grant university with those of a highly selective small college. Calhoun scholars may choose to pursue departmental honors within their specific academic discipline. In addition, EUREKA! (Experiences in Undergraduate Research, Exploration, and Knowledge Advancement) is a unique and exciting program that enables honors students to pursue research and scholarly activities with faculty members across all disciplines. The advantages of membership in the Honors College include priority registration, extended library loan privileges, honors research grants, and a special living-learning community.

The National Scholars Program is a highly selective program for exceptional students who strive to meet their highest intellectual potential. One of its goals is to develop the interests and talents students need to compete for Rhodes, Marshall, and Truman scholarships; Fulbright Grants; National Science Foundation Graduate Fellowships; and other prestigious international fellowships. In 2014–15, five Clemson students received National Science Foundation Graduate Fellowships. Two Clemson graduates received Fulbright grants to conduct research or teach abroad, and four students were named Goldwater Scholars.

Clemson's Creative Inquiry (CI) program allows undergraduate students to engage in research about problems that spring from their own curiosity, from a professor's challenge, or from the pressing needs of the world around them. Team-based investigations are led by a faculty mentor and typically span two to four semesters. Students take ownership of their projects and take the risks necessary to solve problems and get answers. This invaluable experience produces exceptional graduates, capable of thinking critically, solving problems as a team, and communicating and presenting their ideas to others. In 2015–16, 4,917 students participated in 421 CI teams.

Clemson's nationally recognized Programs for Educational Enrichment and Retention (PEER) is committed to improving the academic performance of underrepresented students in engineering and science.

Off-Campus Programs

Clemson's students are strongly encouraged to incorporate a study-abroad experience in their overall Clemson journey. Programs are available on six continents for all disciplines and interests. These include faculty-led programs, exchange programs, and programs available through Clemson's partnerships with study-abroad providers and institutions.

Students in a variety of majors also have opportunities at other Clemson campuses around the world, including the Archbold Center in Dominica; the Daniel Center in Genoa, Italy; and the Clemson University Brussels Center in Belgium. There are other campuses around South Carolina, including Greenville, Greenwood, and Charleston.

The Cooperative Education program provides an opportunity for students to alternate periods of academic study with semesters of paid, career-related, engaged-learning experiences to bridge the gap between academic study and its application in professional practice. Clemson's Center for Career and Professional Development helps to pair students with companies seeking interns or co-op students. The Princeton Review ranks Clemson's career services program as the number-five career office in the nation, and with help from the career center, about 2,200 students participate in academic internships and co-ops annually. Because co-op experiences have been proven to enhance academic performance and provide a competitive edge when seeking full-time employment, Clemson students can now add on-campus internship experiences to their resumes. Students can work part- or full-time, with many in full-time positions having the option of earning credit. The University has made an investment to fund a portion of these experiences, so these on-campus jobs are paid positions.

Academic Facilities

The Clemson campus is a blend of historic buildings and advanced research facilities surrounded by stately trees and lush greenery.

Clemson's main library, the Robert M. Cooper Library, is located at the center of campus and provides a variety of services and up-to-date collections. The University's wireless networking capability lets students communicate with professors and classmates, read online course materials, check email, and conduct research—all from their own laptops.

The campus offers an array of facilities and programs designed to enhance a student's entire educational experience. These include the Pearce Center for Professional Communication, Class of 1941 Studio for Student Communication, Rutland Institute for Ethics, and the Academic Success Center.

Clemson real estate holdings also include more than 32,000 acres of forestry and agricultural lands throughout the state, most of which are dedicated to the University's research and service missions.

Costs

For the 2016–17 academic year, undergraduate tuition and fees were $14,708 for South Carolina residents and $34,590 for out-of-state residents. Room and board costs were approximately $9,144, and books and supplies were around $1,308. Estimated personal and transportation expenses were $3,502, and the one-time laptop computer cost was about $1,800.

Financial Aid

Financial aid is usually awarded based on need to supplement the amount students and their parents can contribute to college expenses. The University also awards some scholarships based entirely on academic merit. Clemson offers financial aid in the form of grants, scholarships, loans, and part-time employment, and 84 percent of all students receive financial aid at Clemson.

Entering freshmen are evaluated on a competitive basis for scholarships using the admission application. There is no separate scholarship application. For academic recruiting scholarships, selection of domestic students is based on test scores, high school class rank, and other academic factors. Stipends for in-state residents range from $500 per year to the full cost of attendance. Merit scholarships for out-of-state students range from $7,500 per year to the full cost of attendance. Academic recruiting scholarships are available only to entering freshmen and are renewable for three additional years if the minimum standards are maintained. The application for admission is the first step for prospective freshmen to be considered for merit awards.

General scholarships are awarded to both entering freshmen and upperclassmen. These may have special criteria set up by the donor, such as a certain residency, major, or career interest. Because of the restrictions on many of these scholarships, it is impossible to predict the recipients. The scholarship selection process is very competitive. Stipends range from $250 to $7,500.

Faculty

Clemson has more than 1,000 full-time faculty members, with around 88 percent holding a Ph.D. or terminal degree in their fields. In addition, the University has more than 100 part-time faculty members. Faculty honors include the Fulbright Scholarship, Guggenheim Fellowship, National Science Foundation CAREER Award, National Institutes of Health Senior Scientist Award, and membership in the American Academy of Arts and Sciences. The average class size is 31, and the student-to-faculty ratio is 18:1.

Admission Requirements

In 2016, the University received about 22,506 applications for a fall freshman class of 3,685. Transfer applications were received from 2,964 students, 1,361 of whom enrolled. Undergraduate applications are available online at clemson.edu/admissions.

For freshman applicants, the following factors are considered: class standing, standardized test scores (SAT or ACT), high school curriculum, grades, and choice of major. Entering freshmen must have completed 4 credits of English, 3 credits of mathematics, 3 credits of laboratory science, 3 credits of a foreign language (in the same language), 3 credits of social sciences, 1 credit of U.S. history, 1 credit of physical education or ROTC, and 1 credit of fine arts.

To be considered for transfer admission, candidates must have completed a full year of college study (a minimum of 30 semester hours or 45 quarter hours of transferable work completed after secondary school conclusion), earned a minimum cumulative GPA of at least 2.5 on a 4.0 scale (3.0 preferred), and completed freshman-level courses in English, science, and mathematics for their intended major at Clemson. Students may also transfer into Clemson after successful completion of their freshman year through the Bridge to Clemson program, a collaborative first-year academic and residential life partnership between Clemson University and Tri-County Technical College. Bridge is available by invitation only to qualified Clemson freshman applicants who have the potential to be successful at Clemson but, due to its competitive admissions landscape, could not be admitted directly into the University for their freshman year.

Application and Information

Application deadlines for freshman admissions are December 1 (priority date for fall semester), May 1 (fall semester), and December 15 (spring semester). For transfer admissions, the application deadlines are July 1 (fall semester) and December 15 (spring semester).

Office of Admissions
Clemson University
105 Sikes Hall, Box 345124
Clemson, South Carolina 29634-5124
Phone: 864-656-2287
Fax: 864-656-2464
E-mail: cuadmissions@clemson.edu
Website: http://www.clemson.edu/admissions

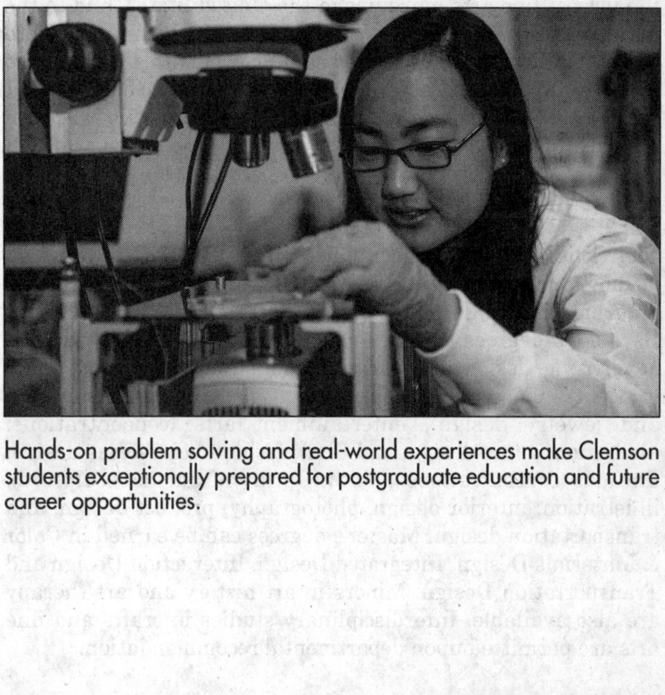

Hands-on problem solving and real-world experiences make Clemson students exceptionally prepared for postgraduate education and future career opportunities.

COLLEGE FOR CREATIVE STUDIES

DETROIT, MICHIGAN

COLLEGE *for* Creative STUDIES

The College

The College for Creative Studies (CCS) is one of the nation's leading art and design education institutions. A private, fully accredited, four-year college located in Detroit, CCS offers Bachelor of Fine Arts degrees in eleven majors and Master of Fine Arts degrees in four majors. The College provides a dynamic learning environment in which students explore issues of art and design and the culture in which they exist while preparing for careers in the professional world. CCS is credited with having one of the world's most recognized programs in transportation design and for placing more graduates in automotive design careers than any other school.

The College is dedicated to providing an educational environment most conducive to the development of outstanding artists and designers. The teaching is directed not only toward developing technical excellence but also toward stimulating intellectual potential. Graduates are well prepared to join the professional world, have the overall ability to carry on their education as desired, are able to communicate effectively, and have a basic understanding of today's artistic, social, and intellectual world and its traditions. The current enrollment is more than 1,400 men and women.

Location

CCS' world-class facilities are located on two sites—the Walter and Josephine Ford Campus and the A. Alfred Taubman Center for Design Education, just a mile apart. At each site, students have access to the latest equipment and workspaces found in the leading creative companies. Twenty-eight major cultural and educational institutions are within easy walking distance. Students have full access to the Detroit Institute of Arts, one of the largest fine arts museums in the United States, and to the main branch of the Detroit Public Library, which offers more than 2 million volumes. Other available facilities include the New Detroit Science Center, Detroit Children's Museum, Detroit Historical Museum, and the Charles H. Wright Museum of African American History.

Majors and Degrees

The College for Creative Studies offers a four-year program leading to the Bachelor of Fine Arts (B.F.A.) degree and a two-year program granting a Master of Fine Arts (M.F.A.) degree. Bachelor's degrees can be earned in advertising–copywriting, advertising–design, art education, communication design, crafts (concentrations: ceramics, fiber design, glass, and metalsmithing and jewelry design), entertainment arts (concentrations: animation, game design, and film), fashion accessories design, fine arts (concentrations: painting, print media, and sculpture), illustration, interior design, photography, product design, and transportation design. Master's degrees can be earned in Color & Materials Design, Integrated Design, Interaction Design and Transportation Design. Minors in art history and art therapy are also available. Interdisciplinary studies in crafts and fine arts are permitted upon departmental recommendation.

Academic Programs

The B.F.A. degree requires completion of 126–127 credit hours: 78 in studio areas and 42–43 in general studies courses and 6 in general elective classes. In addition to course work in their chosen major, first-year students take courses in the Foundation Department, where they study drawing, color theory, and basic design. Students in all majors also take courses in the Liberal Arts Department, designed to provide them with an understanding of the larger social and cultural context in which they live. Typical weekly schedules for full-time students comprise 24 studio hours and six academic hours.

The M.F.A. degree requires completion of 60 credit hours and focuses on fostering critical thinking in a design context while keeping contemporary business reality in mind. CCS graduate classes are taught by industry leaders and an internationally recognized roster of visiting designers and artists with experience in design strategy, user-centric research, design execution and presentation, as well as entrepreneurial practices.

CCS' Continuing Education division offers a rich variety of high-quality art and design programs year-round to students of all ages and artistic backgrounds. High school sophomores, juniors, and seniors can earn college credit in CCS' Summer Experience Pre-College Program. Also available are portfolio preparation courses and professional development programs for teachers.

Off-Campus Programs

Independent study, internships, and study-abroad programs are available. Mobility programs, offered in cooperation with thirty-one other colleges in the Association of Independent Colleges of Art and Design (AICAD), allow students to take advantage of course offerings at other institutions while pursuing a degree at the College. In addition, seniors may study in a studio space in New York City to which CCS has access. Juniors and seniors also have the opportunity to spend a full year of study at an accredited institution abroad.

Academic Facilities

The CCS campus totals 16 acres, with approximately 1.5 million square feet of space. Located in midtown Detroit, the College is made up to two sites, the Walter and Josephine Ford Campus and the A. Alfred Taubman Center for Design Education.

The Walter and Josephine Ford Campus consists of the Kresge-Ford Building, Walter B. Ford II Building, the Manoogian Visual Resource Center, Yamasaki Building, and the Art Centre Building.

The Kresge-Ford Building was completed in 1975 and was a major addition to the College's classroom, studio, and office space. Currently the building houses the Art Education, Crafts, Fine Arts, Liberal Arts, and Photography departments. The Arts & Crafts Cafe, two student lounges and the Student Success Center are also located here.

The Walter B. Ford II Building, is a state-of-the art facility wired with a single digital network to carry voice, data, and video. The building houses the Entertainment Arts, Illustration, and Foundation departments and incorporates high-tech flexible classrooms with both traditional and computer workstations and a 250-seat auditorium equipped with LCD and HD projectors, VHS/DVD/Blu-ray technology, and 7.1 surround sound. In addition, the building also provides space on each floor for the exhibition of student work and includes numerous traditional animation labs, "The Stage"—a large production studio, a recording room and sound studios, figure and anatomy dry studios, and an Oxberry.

The Taubman Center is home to the College's six undergraduate design departments; graduate-degree programs in color and materials design, integrated design, interaction design, and transportation design; and the Henry Ford Academy: School for Creative Studies, an art and design charter school for middle and high school students. This second campus site has enabled CCS to expand its curriculum to include new areas of the creative industries, improve facilities for all of its departments, and connect with the local community through the Detroit Creative Corridor Center. It represents the College's commitment toward accelerating metro Detroit's transition to an innovation-based economy by renewing the infrastructure of an important urban neighborhood; attracting, developing, and retaining talent in the creative industries; spurring research in sustainable product development; and creating jobs and new business opportunities.

Costs

For the 2016–17 academic year, tuition was $1,315 per credit hour or $19,725 per semester for full-time enrollment (12 to 18 credits). Housing costs range from $2,610 or $2,875 per semester. The estimated cost of materials and supplies is $2,500 in most fields of study.

Financial Aid

The College participates in the Federal Pell Grant, Federal Supplemental Educational Opportunity Grant, Federal Work-Study, Federal Stafford Student Loan, Federal PLUS loan, Michigan Tuition Grant, Michigan Competitive Scholarship, Michigan Work Study, Michigan Merit Award, Michigan Educational Trust, and Michigan Educational Savings Plan programs. The College also awards scholarships, based on artistic ability and academic excellence, to currently enrolled and prospective students.

The College attempts to financially assist qualified students who apply, contingent upon the availability of funds.

Faculty

The College has 425 faculty members. All members of the studio art faculty are professionals in their individual fields who bring diverse backgrounds and experiences to the classroom.

Student Government

Students participate in the leadership of the school in several ways. The Student Coalition is composed of representatives from each department and takes an active role in areas affecting student life. The coalition works with the Student Programming Coordinator to organize dances and other events during the year. The coalition was active in the founding of U245, the student-run gallery, and continues to support its activities.

Admission Requirements

The Office of Admissions at the College for Creative Studies is dedicated to assisting students in evaluating educational alternatives and career possibilities in the visual arts.

Applicants must have maintained a GPA of at least 2.5 in high school or successfully passed a high school equivalency examination and must submit SAT or ACT scores and a portfolio of representative work. Applicants who have had previous college experience are required to submit an official transcript from each institution attended. Personal interviews are available.

Application and Information

Applications for the fall term are accepted through August 1. Applications for the second semester should be submitted prior to December 1.

For application forms, catalogs, and additional information, students should contact:

Office of Admissions
College for Creative Studies
201 East Kirby
Detroit, Michigan 48202-4034
United States
Phone: 313-664-7425
800-952-ARTS (toll-free)
Website: http://www.collegeforcreativestudies.edu

Aki Choklat, Chair of Fashion Accessories Design, works with students on the design of a new shoe.

THE COLLEGE OF NEW JERSEY

EWING TOWNSHIP, NEW JERSEY

★ To read more about this school, visit http://petersons.to/tcnj

TCNJ THE COLLEGE OF NEW JERSEY

The College

The College of New Jersey (TCNJ) welcomes students who have the talent and motivation to succeed in a highly rigorous academic environment. Founded in 1855, the College enrolls about 6,500 full-time undergraduates, two thirds of whom reside on campus. Today it is heralded by *U.S. News & World Report* as well as *Barron's* as one of the most competitive schools in the nation, public or private. TCNJ serves a diverse student body, preparing graduates to excel as leaders in their chosen fields.

TCNJ has set the standard for public higher education. Students appreciate the atmosphere they find at TCNJ, a school large enough to provide a full range of academic and extracurricular choices, yet small enough to be a genuine residential community of friends and fellow learners. With professors committed to collaboration in and out of the classroom and facilities of enviable quality, TCNJ represents an exceptional value in higher education.

In order to enhance student development and empowerment, TCNJ's curriculum is built around five key experiences which permeate every major in the seven academic schools. Small classes prioritizing discussion and inquiry create a Personalized, Rigorous, and Collaborative Learning Environment where students and faculty work side by side in developing skills and applying concepts. Undergraduate Research, Mentored Internships, and Field Experiences give TCNJ students opportunities to get out of the classroom, develop their professional skill sets, and discover exciting career paths and academic endeavors. Passion for civic responsibility and a commitment to Community-Engaged Learning ensures that TCNJ graduates enter the professional world as top-notch scholars and citizens. Opportunities for Global Engagement found on the TCNJ campus and facilitated through internationally recognized study-abroad programs allow students to expand their internal scope and frame their academic goals and achievements in a truly global context. Finally, academic and extracurricular programs designed to foster Leadership Development help students build confidence and decision-making skills that they will need to solve the problems of tomorrow and build a brighter future.

All first- and second-year students at TCNJ are guaranteed on-campus housing, and most juniors and seniors continue to live on campus. Rooming arrangements are quite flexible, from doubles in freshman residence halls to suites and single rooms and on-campus town houses or apartments for upper class students. Over 200 student organizations on campus offer numerous opportunities for leadership development, community engagement, and the cultivation of lifelong friendships. Engaged and motivated within and beyond the classroom, an exceptional 96 percent of first-year students return for their sophomore year.

The arts flourish in two theaters, a recital hall, an art gallery, and numerous other campus venues. Student performances, professional groups on tour, and a large variety of films, lectures, local bands, and solo entertainers fill the academic year with opportunities for cultural enrichment.

Student wellness is given high priority at the College, with many facilities for recreation and physical conditioning. In fall 2015, TCNJ opened a brand-new student fitness center as part of the Campus Town project. This facility complements the workout spaces, 25-meter swimming and diving pool, and basketball court housed in Packer Hall; the weight room and indoor track in the Student Recreation Center; and the numerous, well-lit athletic fields across campus. In addition to these recreational resources, TCNJ employs dieticians, nutritionists, and other specialists committed to promoting healthy lifestyles and overall wellness in the realms of mind, body, and spirit.

As one of the top-ranked Division III members of the National Collegiate Athletic Association, TCNJ offers twenty sports: ten for men and ten for women. Since 1979, TCNJ student-athletes have amassed more than forty national championships and over thirty runner-up awards, giving the College an aggregate of more than seventy first- and second-place finishes. TCNJ has produced over 40 individual national champions and more than 50 CoSIDA Academic All-Americans. In the past two decades, TCNJ has finished in the top ten of the Learfield Sports Director's Cup races more than fifteen times.

In addition to its NCAA athletics, TCNJ offers a wide variety of recreation programs for intramural competition and self-governing sports clubs. Each year, more than 3,500 students play with these less demanding, but still spirited and competitive teams.

Location

Students at The College of New Jersey live and learn on a picturesque, 289-acre campus located in suburban Ewing Township, approximately 15 minutes from downtown Princeton; 10 minutes from Bucks County, Pennsylvania; and 5 miles from the state capital of Trenton. Woodlands and lakes surround major academic and residential buildings, which bear a distinctive Neoclassical Georgian Colonial aesthetic. The campus is 30 miles from the theaters and museums of Philadelphia and 60 miles from those in New York City, and public and mass transit services are easily accessible. In 2015, TCNJ completed the first phase of the Campus Town project. Adding an attractive downtown component to an already appealing campus, Campus Town offers students brand new residential opportunities, a pristine Barnes and Noble bookstore and café, and a comprehensive fitness center. Retail and dining establishments have been incorporated as well, with additional businesses scheduled to open throughout 2017 and into 2018.

Majors and Degrees

The College of New Jersey offers rigorous, personalized programs culminating in the Bachelor of Arts, Bachelor of Fine Arts, Bachelor of Music, Bachelor of Science, Bachelor of Science in Engineering, and Bachelor of Science in Nursing degrees.

TCNJ grants degrees in the following majors: Accountancy, African American Studies, Art Teacher Preparation (K–12); Art History; Biomedical Engineering; Biology*; Business Administration (specializations in finance, interdisciplinary business, management, and marketing); Chemistry*; Civil Engineering; Communication Studies; Computer Engineering; Computer Science; Criminology; Early Childhood Education; Education of the Deaf and Hard of Hearing; Economics*; Electrical Engineering; Elementary Education; Engineering Science (students may specialize in engineering management or policy and society); English*; Global Business; Health and Exercise Science; Health and Physical Education (teacher preparation K–12); History*; Interactive Multimedia; International Studies; i-STEM (integrative science, technology, engineering, and mathematics); Journalism and Professional Writing; Mathematics*; Mechanical Engineering; Music (options in performance and K–12 teacher preparation); Nursing; Philosophy; Physics*; Political Science; Psychology; Public Health; Sociology and Anthropology; Special Education; Spanish*; Technology Education /Pre-Engineering (K–12); Urban Education; Visual Arts (options in fine arts, graphic design, and lens-based art); and Women, Gender, and Sexuality Studies.
**Programs in which students may prepare for teacher certification*

Specialized Programs: TCNJ offers a number of 5-year combined Master of Arts in Teaching degrees with dual certification in Elementary Education, and either Special Education, Urban Education, or Deaf and Hard-of-Hearing Education. Students may also enroll in a 7-year B.S./M.D. degree program with the New Jersey Medical School (Newark) or a 7-year B.S./O.D. degree program with the State University of New York College of Optometry. The College also offers a Medical Careers Advisory Committee for premed students and a Pre-Law Advisement Committee for students planning a career in law. Sixty-four percent of TCNJ undergraduates seeking admission to medical school and 88 percent seeking admission to law school are accepted into their top choice programs. Both of these figures significantly exceed national averages.

Academic Programs

All academic courses contain significant out-of-class requirements, which foster deeper student-faculty collaboration. All baccalaureate degrees require at least thirty-two courses, including a core curriculum in the traditional arts and sciences. The average class size is 23 students for upper-division lectures.

The thirty-week year is divided into fall and spring semesters; during the summer, courses are offered in two 5-week sessions and one 6-week session. Winter Session guarantees all of the benefits of full-time TCNJ courses in a more compact time frame, in addition to study-abroad opportunities. For those students who find that they cannot fit study abroad into their standard semester, Winter and Summer Session students travel everywhere from New Orleans to London.

Seminars, independent studies, and capstone courses give many students the opportunity for challenging advanced study in close collaboration with faculty mentors. Many TCNJ students publish the results of these endeavors or present them at national and regional conferences.

The Honors Program offers students highly intensive academic experiences without adding extra obstructions on the path toward degree completion. Honors courses promote an interdisciplinary perspective and curriculum, concentrating on central themes relevant to cultural development. All honors classes are small, personalized, and stimulating.

Off-Campus Programs

TCNJ offers students a variety of full-year and one-semester programs of study abroad as well as study at other colleges and universities within the United States. Exchange programs are available in 80 cities in Australia, Austria, Canada, Denmark, France, Germany, Greece, Israel, Japan, Mexico, the United Kingdom, and numerous other countries. National exchanges are available at more than 130 participating institutions in the United States, the U.S. Virgin Islands, Puerto Rico, and Guam. The College of New Jersey is proud to host the New Jersey State Consortium for International Studies.

Academic Facilities

TCNJ has been nationally recognized as one of the most beautiful campuses in the nation. Within the past several years, TCNJ has built and opened a Science Complex, Biology Building, Social Science Building, College Spiritual Center, Art and Interactive Media Building, Education Building, student apartments, and a state-of-the-art library, which serves as the intellectual and social hub of campus. The College is also in the construction stages for a new, comprehensive STEM (science, technology, engineering, and mathematics) building, with completion scheduled for 2017. Campuswide networking provides full Internet accessibility from all residence hall rooms and more than twenty student computing laboratories.

Costs

For up-to-date information on in-state and out-of-state tuition and fees costs, as well as room and board figures, prospective students should head online and visit http://www.tcnj.edu/~sfs/tuition/index.html.

Financial Aid

Over 50 percent of full-time undergraduates receive some form of financial aid, such as federal, state, and institutional grants; merit scholarships; student employment; and loan assistance. The Free Application for Federal Student Aid (FAFSA) or Renewal FAFSA is used to apply for need-based aid at the federal and state levels.

Scholarships and grants include The College of New Jersey Merit Scholars Program, Founders Scholars, Provost Scholars, Bonner Scholars, Chairman of the Board Merit Scholars, the New Jersey Tuition Aid Grant, Federal Pell Grants, Federal Supplemental Educational Opportunity Grants (FSEOG), Educational Opportunity Fund (EOF) Promise Award, and Army and Air Force ROTC Scholarships, as well as other institutional scholarships. Loans include the Federal Subsidized and Unsubsidized Stafford Loans, the Federal Perkins Loan, the Federal Parent Loan for Undergraduate Students (PLUS), the New Jersey CLASS Loan, private/alternative loans, nursing loans, and short-term emergency loan funds. Student employment options include the need-based Federal Work-Study Program (on- and off-campus positions) as well as institutionally supported campus jobs.

Faculty

The approximately 335 full-time members of the College of New Jersey faculty are teachers and scholars possessing terminal degrees in their respective fields. They are also active researchers, authors, artists, performers, and regular contributors in their academic disciplines. All classes are led by full-time faculty members; there are no classes taught by graduate assistants. TCNJ boasts a student-faculty ratio of 13:1. From their first day, students work closely with faculty mentors, contributing to a wide array of projects. Members of the faculty have attracted many significant grants, fellowships, and awards, including the Bancroft Prize in History, Fulbright Scholarships, and grants from the National Science Foundation, the National Institute for Advanced Study, the Guggenheim Foundation, and the National Endowment for the Humanities. Faculty members mentor their students, preparing them for careers, graduate and professional schools, and prestigious fellowships such as the Fulbright, Truman, and Marshall Fellowships.

Student Governance and Programming

The Student Government Association at the College, is governed by elected representatives and works to support and empower all undergraduate students. Members of the Student Finance Board oversee and administer approximately $500,000 in student funds. The College Union Board sponsors a wide range of special events, including recent visits by Seth Meyers, Soledad O'Brien, Nick Offerman, and John Oliver.

Admission Requirements

The College of New Jersey seeks students who show intellectual curiosity, academic talent, and the potential to contribute to TCNJ's vibrant community. The College is committed to attracting students from diverse economic, racial, social, and geographic backgrounds. A high school record of college-preparatory credits, rigorous honors and Advanced Placement courses, high school class rank, SAT scores, and special interests, skills, and qualities can be influential in application review. Certain departments, such as Art and Music, waive the SAT/ACT submission requirement and use additional criteria such as portfolio submissions and auditions to evaluate candidates seeking admission. The College of New Jersey reviews candidates holistically and takes into consideration the variations in high schools and communities in which the applicants reside.

Application and Information

The College of New Jersey is a member of the Common Application. The deadline for applications for Spring enrollment is November 1. The Regular Decision application deadline for Fall enrollment is February 1. There is a $75 application fee. Candidates who apply only to The College of New Jersey under the Early Decision agreement may apply before November 1 and will be notified on or before December 1. Early Decision applicants unable to complete and submit their application prior to November 1 may apply up until January 1 and receive notification on or before February 1. Students applying to the seven-year Accelerated Medical program must apply by December 1. For Fall enrollment, the College requires incoming students to pay an enrollment deposit of $600 no later than May 1.

For more information, students should contact:

The College of New Jersey
P.O. Box 7718
Ewing, New Jersey 08628-0718
United States
Phone: 609-771-2131
Website: http://www.tcnj.edu

The College of New Jersey, a marvel of Neoclassical Georgian Colonial architecture, welcomes students to one of the most beautiful campuses in the United States.

COLLEGE CLOSE-UPS

COLLEGE OF STATEN ISLAND OF THE CITY UNIVERSITY OF NEW YORK

THE CITY UNIVERSITY OF NEW YORK
College of Staten Island

STATEN ISLAND, NEW YORK

★ To read more about this school, visit http://petersons.to/collegeofstatenisland

The College and the University

The College of Staten Island (CSI) is a four-year senior college within the City University of New York (CUNY) and is Staten Island's only public institution of higher learning. CSI is dedicated to access and excellence and currently serves over 14,300 students.

Offering over eighty programs and areas of study, the College ensures that students receive a thorough liberal arts education through core requirements that include classes in the arts and humanities, mathematics, sciences, and social sciences.

In addition to the exciting array of undergraduate degrees and majors available, CSI also awards master's degrees in the following disciplines: Accounting; Biology; Biology: Biotechnology Track; Business Management; Cinema and Media Studies; Clinical Mental Health Counseling; Computer Science; Education; Electrical Engineering; English; Environmental Science; History; Liberal Studies; Neuroscience; Nursing: Adult-Gerontological Health; Social Work; and Teaching of English to Speakers of Other Languages. CSI also offers the following post-master's and advanced certificates: Adult-Gerontological Health Nursing, Autism Spectrum Disorders, Business Analytics of Large-Scale Data, Cultural Competence, Leadership in Education, and Teaching of English to Speakers of Other Languages. CSI proudly confers the Clinical Doctorate of Physical Therapy (D.P.T.) and the Doctorate of Nursing Practice (D.N.P.).

Housing: CSI offers students an opportunity to live on campus in luxury apartment-style housing. Located in two brand-new buildings, Dolphin Cove North and South contain 133 furnished apartments housing 454 residents. The buildings offer both private and semi-private bedroom accommodations with semi-private bathrooms and full kitchens. Other amenities include a study lounge, fitness center, and convenient parking. Housing is filled on a first-come, first-served basis.

Location

Conveniently located in the heart of Staten Island, CSI's park-like 204-acre property is the largest single college campus, public or private, in New York City. Classrooms and academic offices are located in fourteen neo-Georgian buildings that form two quadrangles connected by the campus walk, which extends between the Library and the Campus Center. The Library, Dolphin Cove North and South, the Campus Center, the Biological Sciences/Chemical Sciences building, the Center for the Arts, and the Sports and Recreation Center provide outstanding facilities for scholastic and community activities.

CSI St. George, an extension of the CSI Willowbrook campus, located at 120 Stuyvesant Place, is home to a dynamic 16,000 square-foot facility that is centrally located at the Island's transportation hub, with convenient access for full- and part-time students from the thriving and diverse community of St. George, as well as commuters from Manhattan, Brooklyn, and the Bronx.

CSI's location offers students the better of two worlds, with Staten Island providing a suburban environment with some of the most interesting landscapes in the metropolitan area, and Manhattan, the center of cultural and social life in the city, being only 25 minutes from the Island by ferry. In addition, the Verrazano-Narrows Bridge provides direct access between Staten Island and Brooklyn.

Majors and Degrees

CSI offers the following associate degrees: Business (A.A.S.): Accounting, Finance, Information Systems, International Business, Management, and Marketing specializations; Computer Technology (A.A.S.): Programming and Information Science sequences; Engineering Science (A.S.); Liberal Arts and Sciences (A.A./A.S.); and Nursing (A.A.S.).

CSI offers the following bachelor's degree programs: Accounting (B.S.); African and African Diaspora Studies (B.A.); American Studies (B.A.); Art (B.A./B.F.A.): Studio Art and Photography concentrations; Biochemistry (B.S.); Biology* (B.S.): Bioinformatics, Ecology, Evolution, and Behavioral Biology, Molecular, Cellular, and Developmental Biology, Neuroscience, and Health Science options; Business (B.S.): Finance, International Business, Management, and Marketing concentrations; Chemistry* (B.S.); Cinema Studies (B.A.): Critical Studies and Production concentrations; Communications (B.S.): Journalism, Media Studies, Design and Digital Media, and Corporate Communications concentrations; Computer Science (B.S.); Computer Science/Mathematics (B.S.); Drama (B.S.); Earth and Environmental Science (B.S.); Earth Science* (B.S.); Economics (B.A./B.S.): Business and Finance specializations; Education: Early Childhood, Childhood, and Adolescence programs; Electrical Engineering (B.S.); Engineering Science (B.S.): Computer and Mechanical specializations; English* (B.A.): Writing, Linguistics, Literature, and Dramatic Literature concentrations; Geography (B.A.); History* (B.A.); Information Systems and Informatics (B.S.); International Studies (B.A.); Italian Studies* (B.A.); Mathematics* (B.S.): Pure and Applied Mathematics emphases; Medical Technology (B.S.); Music (B.A./B.S.): Classical Performance, Literature and Theory, Music Technology, Jazz Studies, and Performance concentrations; Nursing (B.S.); Philosophy (B.A.); Philosophy and Political Science (B.A., dual major); Physics* (B.S.); Political Science (B.A.); Pre-Professional Preparation: Dentistry, Law, Medicine, Optometry, Physical Therapy, Chiropractic, and Podiatry programs; Psychology (B.A./B.S.); Science Letters and Society (B.A.): Early Childhood sequence (Birth–2) and Childhood sequence (1–6); Social Work (B.S.S.W.); Sociology–Anthropology (B.A.); Spanish* (B.A.); and Women's, Gender, and Sexuality Studies (B.A.).

**Adolescence Education track (grades 7–12) available.*

Academic Programs

CSI offers two-year programs in career areas and in liberal arts and sciences, and four-year programs with majors in the traditional fields of study. General education requirements have been established for all degrees. Credit may be awarded for internships, research, and experiential learning. Students may graduate with honors in most bachelor's degree majors.

The College offers classes scheduled during both the day and evening, seven days a week, with a variety of course combinations leading to associate and bachelor's degrees, providing opportunities for nontraditional students to pursue a college education at more convenient times. CSI also offers intensive summer and winter sessions.

Honors Programs: The College offers several honors programs. Programs include Macaulay Honors College at CSI (MHC), the College's most selective full scholarship program*; The Verrazano School, a local honors program that creates learning communities and provides scholarships for study abroad; and Teacher Education Honors Academy at CSI (TEHA), a scholarship program designed to highly train select students to teach mathematics and science in New York City Department of Education middle and high schools.

**Scholarship receipt subject to eligibility requirements.*

Off-Campus Programs

CSI students may use the resources of and receive credit for courses taken at other CUNY colleges to support their education. The College also gives a number of courses for credit at off-campus locations throughout the city through internships at major corporations and other sites. Exceptional study-abroad opportunities are available through CSI's Center for Global Engagement, which offers students the option of earning academic credit for study in Australia, Belgium, China, Costa Rica, Denmark, Ecuador, England, France, Greece,

Hong Kong, Ireland, Italy, Japan, Northern Ireland, Scotland, Spain, Sweden, or St. John, U.S. Virgin Islands. Students may also pursue study-abroad programs in additional countries through the College Consortium for International Studies (CCIS).

Academic Facilities

The academic buildings are designed to house approximately 300 state-of-the-art laboratories and classrooms; each has its own computer lab, study lounge for students, and faculty offices.

The Campus Center is where students can relax, dine, and be entertained. The two-story rotunda at the heart of the structure contains the main dining facilities, the College's health services, a bookstore, offices for student organizations, study lounges, a small performance/café space, game rooms with the latest game consoles, and the state-of-the-art student-operated studios of WSIA 88.9, the only FM radio station on Staten Island.

The Center for the Arts complex provides facilities for teaching in the instructional wing and performance spaces in the public wing. The complex of public facilities includes a 911-seat auditorium, a 442-seat fully equipped theater, a 156-seat recital hall, a 143-seat lecture hall, an experimental Black Box Theater, art galleries, and a conference center. Classrooms, lecture halls, studios, screening rooms, and offices for faculty members are located in the instructional wing.

The CSI Library is staffed with librarians trained in every discipline offered at the College, who also hold faculty status and rank. The Library's total collection consists of approximately 532,189 books and ebooks, 77,283 electronic journals, 220 electronic resources, 19,800 streaming video titles, and 5,000 sound recordings. The Library's online catalog provides complete access to the collections, including access to holdings of other CUNY libraries. Students also have electronic access to database and research tools 24 hours a day via the Internet. In addition, the Library maintains a collection of current textbooks donated by the CSI Student Government. These and other course materials are available at the Reserve Desk. Wireless laptops are loaned to students for use throughout the Library. The Library building also houses the Office of Academic Support and the Cybercafé, which offers Starbucks® coffee.

The laboratory science building provides facilities for teaching and for two research centers: the Center for Environmental Science and the Center for Developmental Neuroscience and Developmental Disabilities. It consists of a research wing and an instructional wing. State-of-the-art laboratories serve students and faculty members in their teaching and research.

The CSI Astrophysical Observatory is a world-class resource that has been recognized by the International Astronomical Union as an official asteroid-tracking station.

CSI is dedicated to keeping its campus up-to-date during these technology-centric times. Planned updates include the highly innovative Interdisciplinary High-Performance Computational Center and expansions to the Library and Campus Center.

Costs

For 2017–18, undergraduate tuition for New York State (NYS) residents is $275 per credit for resident part-time matriculated students, $3,165 per semester for resident full-time matriculated students, and $400 per credit for resident non-degree students. Nonresident full- and part-time students are charged $560 per credit, and nonresident non-degree students are charged $840 per credit. Graduate NYS resident tuition is $5,065 per semester for students attending the College full-time and $425 per credit for resident part-time students. Nonresidents are charged $780 per credit for full- and part-time attendance.

Financial Aid

Financial aid is available through state and federal programs and includes the New York State Tuition Assistance Program (TAP) awards, Federal Pell Grants, Supplemental Educational Opportunity Grants (SEOG), Search for Elevation and Education through Knowledge (SEEK) awards, the Accelerated Study in Associate Programs (ASAP) awards, Federal Work-Study Program awards, and student loan programs. Information about programs, application procedures, and deadlines is available from the Financial Aid Office.

The CSI Scholarship is awarded annually to incoming freshmen, transfer, and current students with a 90.00 or 3.25 (or higher) GPA. Further information about scholarships is available from the Career and Scholarship Center.

Faculty

The College has a full-time faculty of 395, of whom approximately 90 percent hold a doctoral degree or the highest attainable degree in their field. Numerous faculty members have made significant contributions in many areas of scholarship, creativity, and public service and have received prestigious grants and awards.

Student Government

A single body, the Senate, is composed of 25 elected students and represents the interests of the College's students, serving as liaison to faculty and administrators. The Senate derives funding from the Student Activity Fee and sponsors many academic and nonacademic programs benefiting students.

Admission Requirements

A freshman applicant seeking admission to a bachelor's degree program must pass the CUNY Assessment Tests (CATs) in reading, writing, and mathematics unless he or she qualifies for exemption based on their high SAT, ACT, or Regents Examination scores. Admission to a bachelor's degree program is determined by the applicant's high school courses, academic average, and the combined verbal and mathematics SAT scores. The College accepts applicants whose scores reach or exceed the College's minimum bachelor's degree program requirements. A faculty admissions committee may consider admitting applicants whose scores approach the College's minimum requirements. Entering first-year students may be admitted to associate-level programs if they have graduated from an accredited high school or have earned a high school equivalency diploma. A transfer applicant with 30 or more credits completed at the time of application must have a minimum cumulative GPA of 2.00. Applicants with fewer than 30 credits must have a GPA of at least 2.00 and must meet freshman entrance criteria.

Application and Information

Requests for further information and application materials should be directed to:

College of Staten Island/The City University of New York
Office of Recruitment and Admissions, Building 2A, Room 103
Staten Island, New York 10314
Phone: 718-982-2010
E-mail: admissions@csi.cuny.edu
Website: www.csi.cuny.edu

The CSI Library offers access to over 532,000 books and 77,000 electronic journals. All CSI students may also use the libraries and databases of other CUNY schools, allowing them access to millions of resources.

COLUMBIA UNIVERSITY

Columbia College/The Fu Foundation School of Engineering and Applied Science

NEW YORK, NEW YORK

The University

Columbia College and The Fu Foundation School of Engineering and Applied Science (Columbia Engineering) offer their students unique advantages; they are at the same time small, selective colleges and integral components of a major research university. Students benefit from over 250 years of rich history and distinction, easy access to the immense resources of New York City and a dynamic residential community where "Columbia Blue" is worn with pride at events ranging from Lions' basketball games to the World Leaders Forum, from the Varsity Show to late-night study sessions in the residence halls.

The Columbia College student body is composed of approximately 4,500 students; the Columbia Engineering student body has roughly 1,500. Students come from all fifty states and over ninety countries. They represent a dazzling array of ethnic, social, economic, cultural, religious, and geographic backgrounds. The diversity of Columbia's student body reflects the diversity of New York City, the world's most international city.

Columbia guarantees four years of on-campus housing to all entering first-year students. Nearly all undergraduates remain in University residence halls for all four years.

Columbia students take part in extracurricular groups of all kinds: artistic (theater, music, dance, film, and visual arts), athletic (thirty-one Division I varsity sports and dozens of club and intramural sports), communications (the *Columbia Daily Spectator*, the *Columbia Journal of Literary Criticism*, WKCR-FM, and many others), community service (Amnesty International, Big Brother/Big Sister programs, after-hours tutoring programs, a volunteer ambulance squad, and partnerships with dozens of hospitals, soup kitchens, and homeless shelters), and preprofessional (the Charles Drew Pre-Medical Society, the National Society of Black Engineers, and more). Other groups represent students' ethnic, religious, political, and gender identities. There are thirty fraternities and sororities. Alfred Lerner Hall houses office and meeting space for student organizations, a black box theatre, a cinema, the James H. and Christine Turk Berick Center for Student Advising, and many dining options.

Location

Columbia shares its Manhattan neighborhood, Morningside Heights, with a number of other notable institutions: Barnard College, the Cathedral of St. John the Divine, Union Theological Seminary, Jewish Theological Seminary, and the Manhattan School of Music, to name a few. Many faculty members from Columbia and the other surrounding schools make their homes in the neighborhood. Morningside Heights is an area known for bookstores, wonderfully varied restaurants, and merchants that cater to student tastes, student budgets, and student hours.

Students are encouraged to and assisted in making full use of New York's breathtaking variety of cultural, recreational, and professional resources. Through the Columbia Arts Initiative, students can receive discounted tickets to Broadway shows, film screenings, art galleries, and a multitude of cultural events in New York City. Passport to NYC offers students free access to over thirty museums throughout the city. Columbia students can be found any day of the week exploring the Metropolitan Museum of Art, the Museum of Modern Art, the Guggenheim Museum, the Museum of African Art, the Museo del Barrio, or the Asia Society. They might be discovering the theatrical offerings on, off, or "off-off" Broadway (or on campus); attending the opera, ballet, or symphony at Lincoln Center; enjoying jazz in Greenwich Village or blues at the Apollo; sampling *pai gwat* in Chinatown; or biking or jogging in Central Park. Columbia's Center for Career Education offers students opportunities to explore career pathways in depth; nowhere else in the world does the concentration of industries allow such a range of possibilities for internships and post-graduate employment. New York's public transportation system puts the entire city within easy reach of Columbia students; the campus is directly served by a subway line and five bus routes.

Majors and Degrees

Columbia College grants the B.A. degree in more than eighty programs of study in the humanities, social sciences, and pure sciences, including many interdisciplinary majors. Columbia Engineering grants the B.S. degree in sixteen engineering fields. A five-year program that begins in either school allows students to receive both a B.A. from Columbia College and a B.S. from Columbia Engineering.

Joint degree programs offer selected students the opportunity to combine their undergraduate work with study in Columbia University's schools of law and international affairs and with the Juilliard School.

Academic Programs

Columbia College is known for its Core Curriculum, a set of common courses required of all undergraduates and considered the necessary general education for students, irrespective of their choice in major. The communal learning—with all students encountering the same texts and issues at the same time—and the critical dialogue experienced in small seminars are the distinctive features of the Core. Begun in 1919, the Core Curriculum is one of the founding experiments in liberal higher education in the United States, and it remains vibrant nearly a century later. One of the signature courses in the Core is Contemporary Civilization, a year-long historical survey of Western civilization's religious, political, and moral philosophies; another is Literature Humanities, a year-long introduction to Western culture's most seminal and meaningful literary works. A second year of humanities offers a semester each of music and art appreciation, encouraging students to experience the cultural treasures of New York City. The Global Core requirement enlarges the scope of inquiry beyond the Western focus in order to promote learning and thought about the variety of cultures and the diversity of traditions that interact in the United States and the world today. Frontiers of Science outlines the approaches that scientists take to answer compelling problems in the natural world and introduces students to scientific research methods. University Writing equips students with the ability and thoughtfulness to read and write essays in order to participate in the academic conversations that form Columbia's intellectual community. The Core Curriculum exposes Columbia's multicultural student body to a variety of disciplines, preparing them for the complex questions and issues of modern society.

The strength of Columbia Engineering's education is in its uniquely broad curriculum, preparing students not only to be world-class engineers but also to be global leaders across industries who are equipped and motivated to address the most pressing global challenges. In addition to taking rigorous math and science courses typically offered at top undergraduate programs, Columbia Engineering students benefit from programming that fosters innovation and entrepreneurship, and are also required to take courses in the liberal arts alongside their College counterparts, providing them with interdisciplinary tools for real-world problem solving. This type of broad academic exposure is what alumni often cite as the foundation of their later academic and professional success. Another hallmark of the Columbia Engineering education is the Art of Engineering, where students are introduced to the field through interactive lectures, group projects, and guest speakers. A key component of the course is a semester-long, hands-on group project. Past examples of projects include mathematically modeling the U.S. elections, designing vital signs monitors, and modifying a laser pointer to transmit digital data over long distances. In addition to the technical issues discussed in the course, other key issues of importance in professional engineering such as ethics, project management, and societal impact are addressed.

Off-Campus Programs

Columbia maintains a network of global centers, developing opportunities for research, scholarship, teaching, and service across borders. With eight international locations ranging from Turkey to Chile and from Kenya to China, undergraduate options include summer Arabic language programs in Amman, Jordan or a semester-long French literature program in Paris at Columbia's Reid Hall. Columbia also has direct enrollment agreements with many partner institutions abroad, as well as a growing number of exchange programs with universities abroad.

Columbia was the first U.S. college to offer an integrated year-abroad program with the Universities of Oxford and Cambridge. Other programs allow students to work at the University of Kyoto in Japan or at the Free University of Berlin in Germany.

Altogether, Columbia students, with the help of advisers from the Office of Global Programs, may choose from over 150 study-abroad programs on nearly every continent.

Academic Facilities

Columbia has the fifth-largest research library system in the world, consisting of 12 million volumes and 26 million manuscripts within 3,000 collections. Included in the twenty-two libraries are the collections of the Avery Architectural and Fine Arts Library, the Starr East Asian Library, the Rare Book and Manuscript Library, and the Burke Library of Union Theological Seminary. All divisions are open to Columbia undergraduates. The LEED Gold–certified Northwest Corner Building houses cutting-edge labs that bring together researchers in biology, chemistry, physics, and engineering, as well as a science library, lecture hall, and café. Students may also make use of an electronic music lab, a cyclotron, an oral history collection, the facilities and programs of the Lamont-Doherty Earth Observatory, and oceanographic research ships.

Costs

Tuition for the 2016–17 academic year was $55,056. Room and board for all first-year students were $13,244. With typical fees, books, and supplies, the total cost of a year at Columbia was approximately $71,585.

Financial Aid

The Office of Financial Aid and Educational Financing believes that cost should not be a barrier to students pursuing their educational dreams. All first-year candidates who are U.S. citizens, have U.S. permanent resident or political refugee status, or are undocumented students who reside in the U.S. are considered for admission without regard to their financial need. International students who do not fit into the above categories should be aware that their admissions process is not need-blind; their financial need is taken into account at the time of admission. Regardless of citizenship, Columbia meets the full demonstrated need of every student admitted as a first-year or transfer student. All financial aid at Columbia is based on need, in the form of grants and student work only, not loans. Parental contributions are significantly reduced for a large portion of students receiving financial aid. Prospective students should go to http://cc-seas.financialaid.columbia.edu/ for information on specific requirements and deadlines.

Faculty

The student-to-faculty ratio is 6:1. Core Curriculum classes are capped at 22 students, and 80 percent of classes have 20 students or fewer. The Columbia faculty is committed to both teaching and research, and all faculty members, including the president of the University, teach undergraduates. All faculty members maintain office hours, and each student receives a faculty adviser from the department that he or she chooses as a major.

Admission Requirements

The Columbia first-year class of 1,400 students is selected from a much larger pool of applicants through a holistic, committee-based review process. There are no specific course requirements for admission, but applicants must present evidence that they are prepared for college work in a variety of disciplines as required for the Columbia degree. Accordingly, the following preparation is strongly recommended: 4 years of English, including meaningful work in literature and writing; 3 (preferably 4) years of mathematics, including precalculus and calculus where offered; 3 (preferably 4) years of history and social studies; 3 or more years of the same foreign language; and 3 (preferably 4) years of laboratory science (including chemistry and physics where available). Modifying the preparatory program just outlined—by taking more work in some subjects and less in others—is not only acceptable but may be desirable in individual cases.

Standardized tests are required for admission, according to the following guidelines. Students must take *either* the SAT *or* the ACT. Students who take the SAT more than once are evaluated on the highest score they receive in any individual section. Applicants taking the ACT more than once are evaluated on the highest score received in any individual section. The writing component of both exams is optional. For applicants applying to enter in fall of 2018, Columbia will continue to accept the 2400-point SAT (discontinued in March 2016) or the 1600-point SAT.

While Columbia does not require SAT or ACT writing tests or SAT Subject Tests, students who have taken these exams may submit their results if they wish them to be considered.

Applicants to either Columbia College or Columbia Engineering should have the testing service report their standardized test scores directly to the Office of Undergraduate Admissions (SAT code 2116, ACT code 2717).

Transfer students may enter Columbia in the fall term only.

Columbia College and Columbia Engineering each have a Visiting Students Program, which allow students to attend for one or both semesters of their sophomore, junior, or senior year.

Application and Information

Students may apply via the Common Application or the Coalition Application. Students for whom Columbia is their definite first choice are encouraged to apply early decision. The early decision deadline is November 1, and candidates are notified by mid-December. Students admitted to Columbia under early decision are required to matriculate at Columbia and withdraw their applications to other colleges. The regular decision deadline is January 1, and candidates are notified by April 1. Admitted students must respond to Columbia's offer of admission by May 1.

For further information, interested students should contact:

Office of Undergraduate Admissions
Columbia University
1130 Amsterdam Avenue, MC 2807
New York, New York 10027
Phone: 212-854-2522
Fax: 212-854-1209
E-mail: ugrad-ask@columbia.edu
Website: http://undergrad.admissions.columbia.edu/
http://www.facebook.com/columbiaadmissions
http://www.twitter.com/hamiltonhall
http://www.instagram.com/columbiaadmissions

COLLEGE CLOSE-UPS

COLUMBIA UNIVERSITY SCHOOL OF GENERAL STUDIES

NEW YORK, NEW YORK

★ To read more about this school, visit http://petersons.to/columbiauniversitygs

The University and the School

The Columbia University School of General Studies (GS), founded in 1947, is the finest liberal arts college in the United States created specifically for returning and nontraditional students seeking a rigorous, traditional, Ivy League undergraduate education full or part time. Students come from a variety of backgrounds and, for personal or professional reasons, most have interrupted their educations, never attended college, or are only able to attend part time. GS is unique among colleges of its type, because its students are fully integrated into the Columbia undergraduate curriculum: they take the same courses, with the same faculty members, and earn the same degree as all other undergraduates at the University.

In the classroom, the diversity and varied personal experiences of the student body promote discussion and debate that is unparalleled in the Ivy League, fostering an environment of academic rigor and intellectual development. GS has more than 2,000 undergraduate degree candidates and more than 400 Postbac Premed students. The average age of the GS student body is 27, and more than 70 percent of GS students attend classes full time.

In addition to its bachelor's degree programs and the Columbia University Postbaccalaureate Premedical Program, GS offers combined undergraduate/graduate degree programs with Columbia's Schools of Engineering and Applied Science, Social Work, International and Public Affairs, Law, Business, Dental Medicine, and Public Health, as well as Teachers College and the College of Physicians and Surgeons. More than 70 percent of GS students go on to earn advanced degrees after graduation.

Location

Columbia University is located in Morningside Heights, on the Upper West Side of Manhattan. The University's neighbors include the Union Theological Seminary, the Jewish Theological Seminary, the Manhattan School of Music, Mount Sinai St. Luke's Hospital, Riverside Church, and the historic Cathedral of St. John the Divine, the largest cathedral in the world. The diversity of intellectual and social activities offered by these institutions is one of Columbia's great assets; another is New York City itself, which offers Columbia students a rich and almost boundless variety of social, cultural, and recreational opportunities that are themselves an education.

Majors and Degrees

The School of General Studies grants a B.A. degree and offers more than eighty majors and concentrations, including African American studies; American studies; ancient studies; anthropology; applied mathematics; archaeology; architecture; art history; astronomy; astrophysics; biochemistry; biology; biophysics; business management; chemical physics; chemistry; classics; comparative literature and society; computer science; creative writing; dance; data science; drama and theater arts; earth and environmental science; East Asian studies; economics; education; English; environmental biology; environmental chemistry; environmental science; ethnicity and race studies; evolutionary biology of the human species; film and media studies; financial economics; French; German literature and cultural history; Hispanic studies; history; human rights; information science, Italian cultural studies; Italian language and literature; jazz studies; Jewish studies; Latin American and Caribbean studies; Latin American and Iberian cultures; linguistics; mathematics; medieval and renaissance studies; Middle Eastern, South Asian, and African studies; modern Greek studies; music; neuroscience and behavior; philosophy; physics; political science; Portuguese studies; psychology; regional studies; religion; Russian language and culture; Russian literature and culture; Slavic studies; sociology; statistics; sustainable development; urban studies; visual arts; women's and gender studies; and Yiddish studies.

GS is home to the Columbia University Postbaccalaureate Premedical Program, the oldest and largest of its kind in the United States, as well as undergraduate dual-degree programs with the French University Sciences Po, City University of Hong Kong, and List College of the Jewish Theological Seminary.

The Dual BA Program between Columbia University and Sciences Po is an intensive, transatlantic course of study in which undergraduate students earn two bachelor's degrees in four years, once each from Sciences Po and Columbia University. Students begin by spending two years at one of three Sciences Po campuses, each of which is devoted to a particular region of the world and offers a heavy linguistic and cultural focus. After completing Sciences Po's interdisciplinary social sciences curriculum, students matriculate at GS to complete core and major requirements. Upon graduation, students are eligible for guaranteed admission to a graduate program at Sciences Po. Admission to the Dual BA Program is highly competitive, and high school seniors are eligible to apply.

The Joint Bachelor's Degree Program between City University of Hong Kong and Columbia University offers students an international undergraduate educational experience—a program spanning two continents, in cosmopolitan cities that allow students to engage directly with the world around them. Joint Bachelor's Degree Program students earn two bachelor's degrees in four years, one each from City University of Hong Kong and Columbia University. Students who wish to be considered for admission to the Joint Bachelor's Degree Program must first apply and be accepted to the City University of Hong Kong, at which time they will be eligible for consideration.

Academic Programs

The School of General Studies offers a traditional liberal arts education designed to provide students with the broad knowledge and intellectual skills that foster continued education and growth in the years after college as well as providing a sound foundation for positions of responsibility in the professional world.

Requirements for the bachelor's degree comprise three elements: (1) core requirements, intended to develop critical skills in writing and quantitative reasoning while providing exposure to a range of knowledge and disciplines; (2) major requirements, designed to provide students sustained and coherent exposure to a particular discipline in an area of strong intellectual interest; and (3) elective courses. Students are required to complete a minimum of 124 points for the bachelor's degree; 60 of these may be in transfer credit, but at least 64 points (including the last 30 points) must be completed at Columbia.

Off-Campus Programs

Columbia students are encouraged to enhance their academic experiences through the more than 150 study-abroad programs offered in more than 100 cities around the world. Options include studying in Paris at the Columbia University Global Center, in Kyoto at the Consortium for Japanese Studies, in Kenya completing the Tropical Biology and Sustainability Program, or in Cuba taking courses at the University of Havana, to name a few.

Academic Facilities

The Columbia University Libraries constitute the nation's fifth-largest academic library system, with a collection of more than 13 million volumes, more than 160,000 journals and serials, and an extensive array of additional resources. Of the twenty-two libraries in the system, five are designated Distinctive Collections because of their unusual depth and nationally recognized excellence. The Fairchild Life Sciences Building houses research facilities, laboratories, electron microscopes, and a vast amount of biochemical equipment used for teaching and research. The University's physics building has been the scene of many important developments in the recent history of physics, including the invention of the laser and the first U.S. demonstration of nuclear fission.

Costs

For the 2016–17 academic year, tuition was $1,692 per point (credit), and annual living (room and board) and personal expenses (books, local commuting costs, and other expenses) were $23,270.

Financial Aid

The School of General Studies awards financial aid based upon need and academic ability. Approximately 70 percent of GS degree candidates receive some form of financial aid, including federal Pell grants, New York State grants, federal unsubsidized and subsidized Stafford loans, institutional scholarships, and Federal Work-Study Program awards. The average scholarship award ranges from $8,000 to $10,000 for first-year students.

Faculty

All undergraduate liberal arts courses at Columbia University are taught by members of the Columbia University Faculty of Arts and Sciences. These distinguished scholars in virtually every discipline also teach students in Columbia College, the Graduate School of Arts and Sciences, the School of the Arts, and the School of Professional Studies. The student-faculty ratio is 6:1, and GS students have many opportunities to work closely with faculty members, both in small classes and research projects. Faculty members also serve as departmental advisors to students majoring in their area of study and maintain regular office hours.

Student Government

One student represents GS in the University Senate, a decision-making body comprising students, faculty members, and administrative staff members from each division of the University. In addition, two GS students sit as voting members on the Committee on Instruction, which oversees the curriculum of the School. The General Studies Student Council elects officers each year and sponsors activities for students and the Premedical Association sponsors events related to the medical school admissions process.

Admission Requirements

The GS admission policy is geared to the maturity and varied backgrounds of its students. Aptitude and motivation are considered along with past academic performance, standardized test scores, and employment history. The School's admission decisions are based on a careful review of each application and reflect the Admissions Committee's considered judgment of the applicant's maturity, academic potential, and present ability to undertake course work at Columbia.

Admission requirements include a completed application form; an autobiographical statement; two letters of recommendation from academic or professional evaluators; official transcripts from all high schools, colleges, and universities attended; official SAT or ACT scores (some applicants may also take the General Studies Admissions Examination); and a nonrefundable application fee of $80.

Students from outside the United States may apply to the School of General Studies to start or complete a baccalaureate degree. In addition to the materials previously described, international applicants must submit official scores from the Duolingo English Test, TOEFL, or IELTS.

Application and Information

Fall early action applications completed by January 15 will receive a March 1 decision; applications completed by March 1 will receive a decision by May 1. Spring early action applications completed by September 1 will receive an October 1 decision; applications completed by October 1 will receive a decision by November 15.

For more information, students should contact:

Curtis M. Rodgers, Vice Dean
Office of Admissions and Educational Financing
School of General Studies
408 Lewisohn Hall
2970 Broadway
Columbia University, Mail Code 4101
New York, New York 10027
Phone: 212-854-2772
E-mail: gsdegree@columbia.edu
Website: http://gs.columbia.edu
http://facebook.com/ColumbiaGS
http://twitter.com/ColumbiaGS
http://youtube.com/GSColumbia

Morningside Campus, Columbia University.

DAEMEN COLLEGE

AMHERST, NEW YORK

★ To read more about this school, visit http://petersons.to/daemencollege

DAEMEN COLLEGE
A World of Opportunity

The College

Daemen College prepares students to achieve their personal best, pursue meaningful careers, and embrace the joy of life-long learning. Students work closely with faculty on original work, whether it is a research study or an art project. They learn to approach a problem from multiple perspectives and how to learn to succeed. The mission of Daemen College is to prepare students for life and leadership in an increasingly complex world. Founded on the principle that education should elevate human dignity and foster civic responsibility and compassion, the College seeks to integrate the intellectual qualities acquired through study of the liberal arts with the education necessary for professional accomplishment. This integration aims at preparing graduates who are dedicated to the health and well-being of both their local and global communities.

Founded in 1947, Daemen College is a private, nonsectarian, co-educational, comprehensive college. With approximately 2,000 undergraduate and 1,000 graduate students, Daemen's students come from all over New York and the United States, as well as from many other countries. Student organizations, themed dinners, movie nights, internationally famous speakers, and more contribute to a dynamic campus life. In addition, Daemen has been designated a Military Friendly School and provides a comprehensive support system for veterans and their families.

Daemen is an NCAA Division II member of the East Coast Conference. Wildcat Athletics is committed to building everyday champions for men's and women's basketball, soccer, tennis, cross-country, track and field, men's golf, women's volleyball, bowling, and triathlon. Students who wish to be involved can now personalize what being a Wildcat means to them—ranging from an expanded recreation and intramurals program to competitive club sports.

Location

Daemen's beautiful, 39-acre suburban campus is located in Amherst, New York, just minutes from Buffalo. Daemen offers convenient access to one of the country's most vibrant regions, spanning Buffalo-Niagara, the Great Lakes, and a cross-border corridor with Ontario, Canada, less than a two-hour drive from cosmopolitan Toronto. Renowned for the arts, Buffalo offers exceptional theater, music, art, restaurants, and major league sports. The campus is easily accessible by major rail, plane, and motor routes which service the city of Buffalo.

Majors and Degrees

Daemen College offers a liberal arts education with a variety of available majors, minors, and programs. Daemen's core curriculum provides an innovative competency-based foundation for all majors that focuses on seven core elements: critical thinking and creative problem solving, information literacy, communication skills, affective awareness, moral and ethical discernment, contextual integration, and civic responsibility. In today's rapidly changing world, the competencies developed in the core curriculum will have lasting value and provides students with a strong basis for life-long learning.

The core is designed to strengthen students' abilities to become intellectually curious, acquire professional rewards, become responsible citizens, and deal with change. The seven core competencies are introduced at the freshman level, and are emphasized across the entire curriculum so that students develop a greater understanding of, appreciation of, and practice of these important life skills through their academic work.

Daemen offers a unique value-added opportunity to students who wish to enhance their liberal arts degree. Known as +Plus Pathways, students can focus their core and free electives in areas such as community development, community health, global business, health policy, and human resource administration.

Daemen's degree programs are known for preparing students to pursue a higher level of achievement. Athletic Training graduates have achieved a 100 percent first-time pass rate on the National Athletic Trainers' Association Board of Certification exam, a rate that significantly surpasses the national average of 82.7 percent. Daemen College has been ranked among the top schools in the nation on the "50 Best Value Small Colleges for Biology and Business Administration Degrees" list released by Best Value Schools. Daemen's hands-on approach, combined with small classes and exceptional instruction in the Education Department, has led to combined pass rates on the annual New York State Teacher Certification Examinations that consistently exceed 90 percent. Daemen's Physical Therapy program has first-time pass rates on the National Physical Therapy Examination (NPTE) at or above both New York state and national averages, and a current three-year average ultimate pass rate of 100 percent. Physician Assistant students have a 98 percent first-attempt pass rate on the NCCPA Certification Exam. Those are just a few examples highlighting the successes of Daemen students.

Undergraduate majors at Daemen include:

- Accounting (B.S./M.S.)
- Animation
- Applied Theater
- Art: Drawing, Illustration, Painting, Sculpture, Visual Arts Education K–12
- Arts Administration (B.S./M.S.): Comprehensive Arts, Fine Arts, or Theater
- Athletic Training (B.S./M.S.)
- Biology: Adolescence Education 7–12, Environmental Studies
- Biology/Cytotechnology (B.S./M.S.)
- Biochemistry
- Business Administration: Human Resource Management, International Business, Marketing, Sport Management
- Business Administration/International Business (B.S./M.S.)
- Education: Adolescence Special Education 7–12, Childhood Education 1–6, Childhood Education/Special Education 1–6, Early Childhood Education/Special Education B–2
- English: Adolescence Education 7–12, Professional Writing and Rhetoric Specialization
- French: Adolescence Education 7–12
- Graphic Design
- Health Promotion: Community Health, Complementary and Alternative Health Care Practices, Health and Fitness
- History
- History and Political Science: Adolescence Education 7–12, Environmental Studies
- Mathematics: Adolescence Education 7–12

- Natural Sciences: Environmental Studies, Forensic Science, Health Science
- Nursing (1+2+1 Partner Program), R.N.–B.S.
- Paralegal Studies
- Physical Therapy (B.S, .N.S./D.P.T.)
- Physician Assistant Studies (B.S./M.S.)
- Political Science
- Psychology
- Religious Studies
- Social Work
- Spanish: Adolescence Education 7–12
- Sustainability (Global and Local)
- Pre-professional Programs: Pre-Dentistry, Pre-Law, Pre-Medicine, Pre-Pharmacy, Pre-Veterinary

Academic Programs

Daemen has been named a College of Distinction for its exemplary commitment to engaged students, great teaching, vibrant communities, and successful outcomes. Intellectual and civic leadership at Daemen College is a valued life skill that's woven into the fabric of the academic culture. Daemen takes pride in offering an impressive range of leadership opportunities to students—from Student Alumni Ambassadors to Peer Mentors, Learning Center Coaches to Admissions Tour Guides, and Career Peer Coaches. These and other opportunities help students gain practical exposure to program planning, delegation, motivation of personnel, problem-solving, critical thinking, and other characteristics of effective leadership.

Research is carried out on a host of different fronts, from an innovative student/faculty think tank, to a high-profile wound therapy initiative. General research projects that include an enormous diversity of interests are showcased annually at the College's popular Academic Festival, held each spring.

Daemen's Honors program meets the intellectual needs of the best students, ensuring that the college experience challenges their minds and fosters their potential to contribute both to the community and to society at large. Students who have demonstrated excellence in learning can benefit from honors courses, which examine complex issues from multiple perspectives, use primary sources rather than textbooks, and present special opportunities for research.

Off-Campus Programs

Career Services works with students to create a personalized Individual Career Action Plan (iCAP) and helps students to find internships or co-op positions to gain real-world experience. These experiences give students the chance to gain more insight into their fields and prepares them for employment after graduation. Internships are available in a wide range of fields and can be local, national, or international, including excellent opportunities with the Washington Internship Institute.

Daemen's Office of Global Programs coordinates distinctive international programs. In today's global economy, it is vital that students learn about different cultures, political systems, and histories. International study is a staple of the Daemen experience. Students choose from semesters abroad, summer programs, and accelerated January term trips.

Daemen believes strongly in learning through service. All undergraduate students at Daemen engage in various service learning activities. Students participate as individuals or groups in short- and long-term projects or assignments that benefit the local, national, or global communities.

Academic Facilities

Daemen College has an outstanding campus supported by facilities that range from the state-of-the-art Academic and Wellness Center and modern Visual and Performing Art Center to the LEED award-winning Research and Information Commons.

Costs

For the 2016–17 academic year, tuition and fees were $26,940, and room and board were $12,125.

Financial Aid

Daemen creates individualized financial aid packages. Generous scholarships make attending the College affordable. Ninety-five percent of full-time undergraduates received some kind of financial assistance. Daemen awards merit scholarships based on academic and leadership achievement.

Faculty

At the heart of Daemen's integrated learning experience is the relationship that can develop between the college's faculty and its students. Small class sizes and a 12:1 student-faculty ratio ensure that students will have an engaging and interactive classroom experience. Daemen prides itself on maintaining a student-centered atmosphere and a close professional and collaborative association among all members of the college community. Assisted by a supportive faculty, Daemen students are encouraged to pursue goals beyond their initial expectations, to respond to academic challenges, and to develop habits of mind that enrich their lives and their community.

Admission Requirements

Daemen offers a rolling admissions policy. The average student enrolled has a 91 GPA and an SAT score of 1060 (old) or 1130 (new). The admissions staff helps guide students through the process from start to finish.

Application and Information

Prospective students can apply for free online at daemen.edu/apply or commonapp.org.

Daemen College
4380 Main Street
Amherst, New York 14226
Phone: 716-839-8225
800-462-7652 (toll-free)
716-218-8830 (text)
E-mail: admissions@daemen.edu
Website: daemen.edu

Visit Daemen—that's the best way to really get a feel for what the College has to offer.

No person shall, on the basis of sex, race, color, ethnic and national origin, handicap, religion, or age, be denied admission or be subjected to discrimination in admission to Daemen College.

COLLEGE CLOSE-UPS

DEAN COLLEGE

FRANKLIN, MASSACHUSETTS

The College

Founded in 1865, Dean is a unique New England college awarding both four-year baccalaureate and two-year associate degrees. Students may choose from nearly two-dozen academic programs supported by state-of-the-art facilities, a dedicated teaching faculty, and professional advising known for exceptional personalized academic support.

Located 45 minutes outside Boston in the town of Franklin, Massachusetts, Dean's attractive 100-acre campus is home to WGAO-FM, the Joan Phelps Palladino School of Dance, and several buildings listed on the National Register of Historic Places. There are two fitness centers, a gymnasium, and athletic fields, as well as a library learning commons, an advising center, a 214-seat theater, and numerous dance studios.

Nearly all of Dean's 1,200 full-time students live on campus, and housing is available for all four years. The student body is impressively diverse with more than 30 states and 25 countries represented (and an additional 500 part-time students). The College sponsors 14 championship-caliber athletic teams, an Honors Program, internship and study abroad opportunities, an executive lecture series, and dozens of clubs, performance groups, and student organizations.

Dean College graduates are very successful. Of those receiving a bachelor's degree last year, 95 percent were employed or attending graduate school within a year. Among associate degree graduates, 98 percent were accepted as transfers to highly selective universities across the United States or had plans to continue their bachelor's degree at Dean.

Location

Dean's home town, Franklin, is a charming, historic Massachusetts community. The suburban setting is safe and convenient to downtown Boston with many local stores and restaurants to support an active college campus. The Commuter Rail—just three blocks from Dean—provides frequent train service to the city center, and students can reach popular destinations such as baseball's Fenway Park, the TD Garden, Museum of Fine Arts, and Harvard Square in less than an hour. Providence, Rhode Island, is even closer (40 minutes) where students can shop at Providence Place or see events at the Dunkin' Donuts Center and Rhode Island Center for the Performing Arts.

The area's biggest attractions are only minutes from Dean: Patriot Place and Gillette Stadium (home of the New England Patriots), the fashionable Wrentham Outlets, and Comcast Center outdoor amphitheater. For day trips, students can easily get to the beaches on Cape Cod, see Newport's mansions, or reach the mountains in nearby New Hampshire and Vermont.

Majors and Degrees

Dean College provides a wide range of programs across four academic schools: the School of Liberal Arts & Sciences, School of the Arts, School of Business, and the Joan Phelps Palladino School of Dance.

Bachelor's degrees are available in arts and entertainment management; business management; communications; criminal justice and homeland security management; dance; English; history; liberal arts and studies; psychology; sociology; sports fitness, recreation, and coaching; sport management; and theatre.

Dean also offers associate degree programs in pre-athletic training, business management, coaching, communications, criminal justice, dance, early childhood education, English, environmental studies, exercise science, general studies, health sciences, history, mathematics, physical education, pre-nursing, psychology, science, sociology, sport management, and theatre/musical theatre.

Academic Programs

Dean is accredited by the New England Association of Schools and Colleges. Graduation requirements include a 2.0 cumulative grade point average (GPA) and demonstrate competency in reading/writing, mathematics, and computers. Bachelor's degree candidates must complete a required internship or other experiential learning opportunity related to their major.

The Honors Program at Dean offers academically talented students an opportunity to engage in stimulating and challenging courses, seminars, and colloquia. Students who meet the honors entrance criteria enroll in special course sections reserved for honors students or may enhance non-honors courses with additional intensive readings and analysis approved by the instructors. The Honors Program also offers exciting academic and cultural activities outside the traditional classroom environment.

Study-abroad and study-away opportunities are increasingly popular at Dean. Students may choose programs across the globe through cooperative arrangements facilitated by the College or take advantage of Dean's relationship with the Washington Center Program for study and internships in Washington, D.C.

The Dean Leadership Institute sponsors an Executive Lecture Series that brings leaders in business, media, and the arts to campus. Featured speakers share their insights into post-graduate opportunities and help build each student's career network. Recent guests include Bert Jacobs (Life is Good), Bob Kraft (Kraft Group/New England Patriots), Anne Finucane (Bank of America), and James Roosevelt (Tufts Health Plan).

The Arch Learning Community provides comprehensive support for students with diagnosed learning differences. Arch students receive dedicated academic advising and a cohort educational model specially designed to help LD students maximize their academic and personal potential and find success within the rigors of a traditional college curriculum.

Academic Facilities

Students have access to a wide range of facilities, including the Green Family Library-Learning Commons and E. Ross Anderson Library, Berenson Writing Center, and Morton Family Learning Center—all housed under one roof. Together, these form the hub of Dean's academic support efforts. There are print and online resources for class projects, academic coaches to provide professional one-on-one mentoring, peer tutoring services, the Technology Service Center, and space for weekly faculty drop-in sessions where students can participate in group or individual advising.

Other academic facilities include the A.W. Pierce Technology and Science Center, which houses science and computer labs as well as the Alden Center high-tech master classroom; the Dean College Children's Center, an on-campus pre-school, which doubles as a learning laboratory for student teachers; and Campus Center, where students can find the Advising Center, Main Stage Theater, Guidrey Center, student activities office, and newly renovated classrooms featuring SmartBoard technology.

Costs

The basic costs related to attending Dean College for 2017–18 are $38,090 for tuition and fees and $16,346 for room and board.

Financial Aid

Last year, the College provided more than $20 million of merit-based financial aid; 90 percent of Dean students receive some form of merit-based aid with an average award of $17,000 per year. These awards are based solely on the information students provide in their application for admission—not financial need—and help to reduce the average cost of attendance by over 30 percent. In addition, most students apply for—and receive—federal and state financial aid, which is separate from (and can be added to) Dean's scholarship awards.

Student financial aid packages are generally a combination of grants, loans, and work-study, contingent upon demonstrated financial need and the availability of funds. The College participates in all Federal Title IV and Federal Family Education Loan Programs. Students must submit the Free Application for Federal Student Aid (FAFSA) in order to be considered for need-based aid. Upon receipt of a valid FAFSA, full-time students are considered for all of the financial aid programs that Dean administers. Residents of Massachusetts and other reciprocal states may also be eligible for state scholarships, grants, or loans.

Faculty

Dean's dedicated faculty members, advisers, and educational specialists—some of the best in their respective fields—offer direct, personal involvement to help students obtain the full value of their college experience. The average class size is 18 students.

Student Government

The Student Government Association serves as a liaison between the student body and Dean College administration. It disseminates information about College policies, seeks out student opinion, allocates funds collected from the activities fee to clubs and organizations through a budget request process, and coordinates the activities of various clubs, groups, and organizations campus wide.

Admission Requirements

Every application to Dean is carefully reviewed by the Admission Committee. In addition to the application form, students must submit an official high school transcript. A letter of recommendation from a guidance counselor or teacher, a personal statement or essay, and SAT or ACT scores are all optional. Interviews are not required but are strongly recommended. Students applying for the dance and theatre programs must audition.

Application and Information

Students who identify Dean as a top choice may choose to apply under the early action plan, with an application deadline of December 1. The College accepts applications on a rolling basis thereafter, though it is recommended that applications be submitted by March 15 to ensure access to the highest level of financial aid and priority in housing and class registration. Once an application is complete, an admissions decision is typically made within four weeks.

For more information, contact:

Office of Admissions
Dean College
99 Main Street
Franklin, Massachusetts 02038
Phone: 508-541-1508
877-TRY-DEAN (toll-free)
E-mail: admissions@dean.edu
Website: http://www.dean.edu

Dean Hall, built in 1865 when Dean College was established.

DOMINICAN UNIVERSITY OF CALIFORNIA

SAN RAFAEL, CALIFORNIA

The University

Located only 12 miles from the Golden Gate Bridge in San Rafael, California, Dominican University of California's commitment to integrating the liberal arts and the professions prepares students for lives of purpose. The University, founded in 1890, balances academics with extensive practical, hands-on experiences, including service-learning, research, and internships with some of the Bay Area's largest and fastest-growing companies. Upon graduation, students are well-prepared to enter professional life or continue their studies in medical or graduate school.

Dominican has approximately 2,000 students, including 1,480 undergraduates and 528 graduate students. Dominican's 80-acre, parklike setting contains towering redwood trees, state-of-the-art facilities, and historic, ivy-clad buildings. With over 357 full- and part-time faculty members and a 10:1 student-faculty ratio, Dominican provides students with an exceptional level of support and mentorship. The University enjoys a century-long reputation for excellence in scholarship, research, and community outreach, and was named to the President's Higher Education Community Service Honor Roll. It was also cited as a Community Engagement institution by the Carnegie Foundation for the Advancement of Teaching, and has been recognized as a "College of Distinction."

Dominican supports eleven intercollegiate teams that compete in the NCAA Pacific Western Conference: men's and women's basketball, golf, cross-country, and soccer; and women's softball, tennis, and volleyball. The men's lacrosse team is a member of the Western Collegiate Lacrosse League (WCLL), competing against UC Berkeley, Stanford, UC Santa Clara, and other top West Coast programs. In addition to being fierce competitors, Dominican Penguins are dedicated student athletes. The school's teams have earned the Pacific West Conference Academic Achievement Award for the last six years.

Activities: Students can be involved in Student Government (ASDU), the Honors Program, recreational sports, Campus Ministry, and/or many other clubs and organizations on campus. The Conlan Recreation Center offers regulation basketball and volleyball courts, a weight-training and fitness room, a multipurpose room (great for aerobic, self-defense, and yoga classes), and a swimming pool surrounded by picturesque gardens. The John F. Allen Athletics Complex was built in 2012 and features Kennelly Field, a new multipurpose artificial turf field; Penguin Field for women's softball; and the Castellucci Family Tennis Center, featuring six brand-new regulation tennis courts. For a more academic experience, students can attend one of the many lectures Dominican hosts featuring prominent speakers. Recent speakers include actress Kate Hudson, Huffington Post co-founder Arianna Huffington, world renowned CEO Jack Welch, and Emmy-winning personality Giada De Laurentiis.

Dominican's residence halls offer a variety of living accommodations, from single to triple rooms, to apartment-style housing in the Edgehill Complex. Caleruega Hall is the main dining facility of the University; it offers a variety of dining options, from a choice of sustainable local farm fresh foods, and vegan and vegetarian options. Chilly's Café offers fresh salads and sandwiches, as well as a full selection of coffee and espresso drinks, smoothies, pastries, ice cream treats, and snacks. The café (open Monday thru Thursdays until 10 p.m. and Fridays until 2 p.m.) is a great place to relax, meet classmates, or study. Caleruega Hall also serves as an entertainment venue on campus, and is host to student dances, live music performances, and various student events.

Location

San Francisco, the mountains, the ocean—everything is within reach. Located in San Rafael, California, 12 miles north of the Golden Gate Bridge, Dominican's proximity to San Francisco offers students immediate access to a wide range of internship, service, employment, cultural, and recreational opportunities. In walking distance from campus, San Rafael features sidewalk cafes, a seasonal farmer's market, nightclubs and theaters, and numerous shops and boutiques. Dominican borders thousands of acres of beautiful hiking trails and Muir Woods and the stunning Point Reyes National Seashore are both just a short drive away.

Majors and Degrees

Dominican offers students twenty-four majors and thirty minors. There are four schools within the University: the School of Arts, Humanities, and Social Sciences; the Barowsky School of Business; the School of Education and Counseling Psychology; and the School of Health and Natural Sciences.

Undergraduate degrees (B.A., B.S., B.S.N., and B.F.A.) are awarded, and there are several specialty degree programs offered. Some of these include the B.F.A. in dance, a nursing program, a five-year program leading to the Bachelor of Science in health science combined with a Master of Science in occupational therapy, the 4+1 Bachelor's/M.B.A. program, and the Dual Degree/Dual Credential Program.

In addition to its undergraduate programs, Dominican also offers graduate programs in biological sciences (M.S.), business administration (M.B.A.) with three concentrations, counseling psychology (M.S., M.F.T.), education (M.S.), humanities (M.A.), and occupational therapy (M.S.O.T.).

Academic Programs

The General Education Program offers exposure to the major areas of knowledge in the humanities, arts, and natural and social sciences. It is designed to provide a sequence of courses with a thematic focus that integrates the wisdom and perspectives of several disciplines. The focus assists students in discovering relationships between areas of knowledge, beliefs, cultures, and peoples that differ globally and historically, as well as in acquiring an awareness of tradition, a love of discovery, a respect for the diversity of the human condition, and a realization of human interdependence. Courses within the General Education Program also expose students to a variety of learning experiences, including discussion, lectures, seminars, simulations, and practicums.

Dominican University of California's incoming first-year students explore the origins and evolution of the universe in an interactive, multidisciplinary course based on Big History. Throughout the year, students gain a greater understanding of today's issues by studying the many links between nature and humankind. Big History is an emerging academic discipline that provides a unifying overview of the 14 billion-year history of the universe, from the big bang to the present day. Big History synthesizes history, astronomy, chemistry, biology, geology, sociology, and other fields to provide a cohesive picture, to scale, of the history of the human race and its relationship to the planet.

Opportunities to Engage the World

England, Japan, Australia, Spain, Sweden, Indonesia, South Africa—the world is at Dominican students' fingertips. Fostering an appreciation of cultural diversity and global interdependence is a fundamental part of a Dominican education. The University encourages students to develop a rich understanding of different cultural perspectives and experiences, and there is no better way to do that than by spending time living, learning, and working in another country.

Dominican encourages students to study abroad for two reasons: personal growth and professional development. There is a growing demand, across industries and geographic locations, for professionals who are multilingual and multicultural. Studying abroad and learning a new language can give students the competitive edge that they will need once they graduate. In 2015, Dominican launched the Thomas and Joanne Peterson Endowed Scholarship for Dominican Scholars at Oxford. The program supports Dominican students selected to study at the University of Oxford as part of a new agreement between Dominican and St. Catherine's College, one of Oxford's 44 autonomous colleges and permanent private halls.

A hallmark of a Dominican education is the belief that the most important aspect of a quality education is the personal interaction between professor and student. A program of engaged learning builds on this premise, incorporating active, collaborative learning in the classroom with enriching educational experiences beyond the physical classroom. Engaged learning at Dominican includes study abroad, internships, leadership, undergraduate research programs, and service learning initiatives. These experiences are interwoven with Dominican's distinctive programs, offering students a multitude of outlets to better understand themselves and the world around them.

Costs

Undergraduate full-time tuition (12–17 units per semester) was $42,950 per year for the 2016–17 year. Fees were $450; room and board (including a fourteen-meal-per-week plan) were approximately $13,650 for the year.

Financial Aid

Financial aid is awarded on the basis of need and merit. Merit awards are available for both first-year and transfer students based on academic achievement. Dominican participates in various federal and state need-based financial aid programs and also has its own financial aid funds available, donated by generous alumni and friends, to help meet University costs.

Need-based financial aid comes in the form of scholarships, grants, part-time employment, and loans. The federal and state financial aid programs are the Federal Supplemental Educational Opportunity Grant, Teacher Education Assistance for College and Higher Education (TEACH) Grant, Federal Pell Grant, Federal Work-Study Program, Federal Direct Stafford Student Loans, Federal Direct PLUS loans, and Cal Grants A and B. Eligibility for need-based aid is determined after the student, who must be a citizen or permanent resident of the United States, files the Free Application for Federal Student Aid (FAFSA). The need-based financial aid deadline for first-priority consideration is March 2, although late applications are accepted. (Residents of California must file by March 2 to be eligible for Cal Grant consideration.)

Faculty

Students find themselves intellectually challenged by faculty members who hold degrees from colleges and universities throughout the world. The faculty is committed to individualized teaching and careful supervision of students' development. Seventy-three percent of Dominican's full-time faculty members hold doctorates or other terminal degrees.

Student Government

The primary group that helps students plan and provide campus activities, distributes activity funds, initiates changes in policy, and represents themselves to the University's administration and the broader community is the Associated Students of Dominican University (ASDU). This group of elected student representatives serves both as the student activities association and the student government board. The members of the ASDU Senate are representatives from all four class levels of regular day-program students.

Admission Requirements

Dominican University of California welcomes applications from prospective students of all ages, religions, races, and national origins. The University believes that academic potential is measured by more than grades alone. Each candidate for admission is given individual consideration and is evaluated by the Office of Admissions on the basis of the student's past scholastic record, present motivation, and potential intellectual development, as indicated by all of the admission materials submitted.

The application materials for first-year students include the following: a completed application; an official high school transcript to date; one letter of recommendation from a teacher, administrator, or counselor; scores from either the SAT or ACT; and a personal essay, as described in the application. Transfer students should submit a completed application and official transcripts of all college course work completed to date. Transfer applicants with fewer than 24 units will also be asked to provide a high school transcript and test scores. In addition, they must submit an essay on one of the topics listed in the application and one letter of recommendation from a teacher, counselor, or professional colleague. Applications for admission are reviewed on a rolling basis; the priority deadline for the fall semester is February 1, and for the spring semester the priority deadline is September 1. Nurses and occupational therapy applicants need a separate essay describing why they want to be in their profession.

Application and Information

Students may apply online at the University's website (www.dominican.edu), or by using the Common Application. Students may also obtain admissions information by contacting:

Dominican University of California
Office of Admissions
50 Acacia Avenue
San Rafael, California 94901-2298
Phone: 415-485-3204
888-323-6763 (toll-free)
Fax: 415-485-3214
E-mail: enroll@dominican.edu
Website: dominican.edu

COLLEGE CLOSE-UPS

DREXEL UNIVERSITY

PHILADELPHIA, PENNSYLVANIA

★ To read more about this school, visit http://petersons.to/drexeluniversity

Drexel UNIVERSITY

The University

Drexel University is a comprehensive global research university that has maintained a reputation for academic excellence since its founding in 1891. The University's use-inspired focused approach to learning prepares undergraduates for a variety of careers and graduate school. Cooperative education is a vital part of a Drexel education. Students gain professional experience in jobs related to their career interests by alternating classroom study with periods of full-time employment. The 2016 undergraduate enrollment numbered 13,296 full-time students representing 48 states (and 3 U.S. territories) and 118 other countries. All international students compose about 17.5 percent of the undergraduate population. Drexel University grants bachelor's, master's, and doctoral degrees—as well as certificates—in a variety of programs.

Drexel offers 18 Division I varsity athletic programs and competes in the Colonial Athletic Association Conference. The University also sponsors intramural and club sports.

There is always something to do on campus, including events such as dances, lectures, excursions, community service projects, and free movie screenings from the Campus Activities Board (CAB), and other activities related to Drexel's more than 30 active fraternities and sororities. Students can also take part in performing arts groups in dance, theater, and music; a variety of extracurricular activities; and over 400 student organizations.

Location

Drexel is located in the heart of Philadelphia, the nation's fifth-largest city, and shares its University City neighborhood with five other universities. With thousands of college student residents, University City is a great place for students to spend their college years in an urban campus setting, surrounded by the amenities of the city and the diversity of their peers. Philadelphia is home to some of the nation's best historical and cultural attractions and offers a vibrant social and cultural scene, dynamic arts, and major league athletics of a first-class city. Drexel's location offers easy access to public transportation and the Drexel shuttle provides convenient, free transportation between campuses for Drexel students. Adjacent to Drexel's University City Campus, Amtrak's 30th Street Station is a hub for trains and buses to the Philadelphia suburbs, New York City, Washington, D.C., and the Philadelphia International Airport.

Academic Disciplines

Whatever their interests, students at Drexel are at the forefront of their fields. Drexel offers more than 90 undergraduate majors and over 20 accelerated degree programs. Academic majors include fields include such as business, computing and informatics, design and art, education, engineering, entrepreneurship, health professions, hospitality, humanities and social sciences, nursing, public health, sciences, and undeclared.

Accelerated degree programs allow students to earn both a bachelor's and an advanced degree in a shortened period of time. Drexel's accelerated degree options include the BA/BS/JD in law; BA/BS/MD in medicine; BS/DPT in physical therapy; BS/MHS in physician assistant studies; BS/MPH in public health; BS/MBA programs in business, culinary arts and science, computing and security technology, design and merchandising, entertainment and arts management, hospitality management, information systems, and music industry; BS/MS programs in accounting, biomedical engineering, communication, computing and informatics, education, engineering, and psychology; BS/MA in creative arts in therapy, dance/movement therapy; BA/BS/MS in science, technology, and security; and BA/BS in history/MS in library and information sciences.

Academic Enhancement Programs

Qualified students can apply to the Honors Program, one of many exciting opportunities offered by the Pennoni Honors College. The Honors Program offers enhanced academic and extracurricular options to talented students through course work, speakers, social activities, and travel. Honors students receive benefits such as small Honors classes, Honors housing, free tickets to cultural events in Philadelphia, Honors-specific advising and mentoring, and priority registration for classes. Students in the Honors Program who satisfy the requirements are eligible for Graduation with Honors, or for the most accomplished students, Graduation with Distinction.

Drexel is a world-class comprehensive research institution committed to use-inspired research with real-world applications. Research at Drexel is driven by faculty from all disciplines and students are encouraged to seek opportunities to partner with world-renowned faculty or develop independent research projects. The STAR (Students Tackling Advanced Research) Scholars program invites qualified students to participate in faculty-mentored research projects in their chosen fields as early as freshman year. Students who take part in research may be eligible for stipends or academic credit.

Opportunities for Enrichment

Drexel's experiential learning model recognizes the importance of both academic and professional preparation. Drexel's cooperative education program (Drexel Co-op), provides professional employment experiences for students, giving them the opportunity to test-drive a career before they enter the workforce. The benefits are obvious — during their time at Drexel, students experience up to three different co-ops (up to 18 months). Drexel Co-op connects them with industry leaders and brings their cooperative education experiences back into the classroom. Because of this, Drexel students graduate having already built a professional network, and they typically receive higher starting salaries than their counterparts from other schools.

Drexel brings an international dimension to University life through its academic programs, study and cooperative education abroad, major research projects, global classrooms, conferences, and cultural events. Last year, more than 900 Drexel students had an international experience studying, doing research, and participating in service-learning abroad. These students represented every major and took advantage of more than 80 program opportunities. With programs in Africa, Asia, Europe, Latin America, and the Pacific, locations are as varied as the interests of Drexel students.

Students can also become civically engaged and fulfill public service and leadership at Drexel's Lindy Center for Civic Engagement.

Academic Facilities

Drexel has three campus locations: University City Campus, Center City Campus, and Queen Lane Campus. The University's library system comprises the W. W. Hagerty Library, the Library Learning Terrace, the Legal Research Center, and three health sciences libraries. The W. W. Hagerty Library, the University's central library located on the University City campus, maintains subscriptions to nearly 12,000 electronic journals, which are accessed via the library website, along with academic journals and 200 databases. Students may borrow laptops for use in the library. The Library Learning Terrace, a 3,000-square-foot flexible learning space located in a residence hall and staffed by librarians, enables students to learn and research collaboratively through a variety of technologies. The Legal Research Center on the third floor of the Kline School of Law shares University databases while continuing to acquire new material. The additional libraries on the health sciences campuses provide study space, 75,000 books, and network access to the same set of online journals and databases.

The University comprises many state-of-the-art spaces for students. One popular student location is the twelve-story, 177,500-square-foot Gerri C. LeBow Hall, which houses the LeBow College of Business, along with the Chestnut Square complex, which features mixed-use housing and retail, including a Shake Shack. The URBN Center houses the Westphal College of Media Arts & Design and provides space for exhibitions, labs, studios, and a black box theater. The five-story, 130,000-square-foot Papadakis Integrated Sciences Building features classrooms and North America's largest biowall. In addition, The Summit at University City provides more student housing and mixed-use commercial space.

Costs

For the 2017–18 academic year, Drexel's estimated cost of attendance for a full-time undergraduate student starting as a freshman includes includes $49,362 in tuition, $2,405 in fees, and $13,890 in room and board. Students also incur additional costs for books (which vary by program), a computer for personal use, transportation, and miscellaneous personal costs.

Financial Aid

Freshmen eligible for merit and/or need-based funds were awarded financial aid in the 2016–17 academic year. The average financial aid awards for full-time degree-seeking undergraduates in the 2016–17 academic year, including all grant and scholarship sources, was $28,744. All incoming students are encouraged to submit both the CSS PROFILE and the Free Application for Federal Student Aid (FAFSA) by specific deadlines. Financial aid notifications to students begin mid-December for students accepted during Early Action and Early Decision. The Drexel Liberty Scholars Program also provides 50 full-tuition and fees scholarships to low-income students who live in Philadelphia. The Drexel Global Scholar program grants full-tuition scholarships to exceptional international students who are also committed to global leadership..

Faculty

The University requires faculty members engaged in research and graduate-level teaching to also teach at the undergraduate level, allowing all students to benefit from the research activities of the faculty. Specially selected faculty members serve as advisors for freshmen. The student–faculty ratio is 10:1.

Admission Requirements

All colleges within the University require completion of a college-preparatory program in high school that includes at least 3 years of mathematics and 1 year of laboratory science. Students applying to a major in the sciences or business and engineering are required to take 4 years of mathematics (through trigonometry) and 2 years of laboratory science. Engineering requires 4 years of mathematics (through trigonometry and precalculus), chemistry, and physics. Biomedical engineering requires 1 year of calculus and 1 year of physics. Computer science and software engineering require 4 years of math (including trigonometry and calculus) and 2 years of lab science. The quality of academic performance is more important than merely meeting minimum requirements. The strength of preparation is judged primarily by rigor of course work and rank in class or relative grade point average (GPA), by the degree of improvement in the quality of the academic record, and by the comments and recommendations from principals, school counselors, or teachers. Freshman applicants are required to submit standardized test scores—including the SAT, ACT, SAT Subject, AP, or IB—and can also utilize Drexel's flexible testing form of submission. Students who were accepted and enrolled in the fall of 2016 had an average unweighted GPA of 3.55 on a 4.0 scale, an average SAT math score (25th–75th percentiles) of 560–670, and an average SAT critical reading score (25th–75th percentiles) of 520–620. The essay from the Common Application or personal statement is required. Design and Media majors may also be required to submit a writing supplement or portfolio. Transfer applicants should complete a minimum of 24 college credits from a regionally accredited institution. Transfer applicants who have fewer than 24 college credits and graduated from high school less than two years prior to their application will also need to submit their high school transcript and SAT or ACT scores.

Application and Information

Applications are accepted through the Common Application only. The application fee is $50, and all Common App waivers are honored. Students may choose to apply under the Early Action, Early Decision, or Regular Decision options. Early Action means that students can apply by an earlier deadline to receive an admission decision earlier than students who apply Regular Decision. Early Action admission is not binding. Early Decision is a binding application plan and, if accepted, students must withdraw all other active applications and commit to enrolling at Drexel. The Early Action and Early Decision deadlines are November 1, with admission decisions rendered in mid-December. Applications for Regular Decision full-time undergraduate status are due January 15, with admission decisions rendered no later than April 1. Applications for the BA/BS/MD accelerated degree program are due November 1. Drexel subscribes to the College Board candidates reply date of May 1. Transfer student deadlines vary by major and term of entry. For transfer application deadlines, please visit drexel.edu/undergrad/apply/deadlines.

Undergraduate Admissions
Drexel University
3141 Chestnut Street
Philadelphia, Pennsylvania 19104-2876
Phone: 215-895-2400
800-2-DREXEL (toll-free)
Fax: 215-895-1285
E-mail: enroll@drexel.edu
Website: drexel.edu/admissions (admissions)
drexel.edu/undergrad/apply (application)
facebook.com/DrexelAdmission (Facebook)
twitter.com/DrexelAdmission (Twitter)

Drexel students on Chestnut St. in University City, Philadephia, Pennsylvania.

COLLEGE CLOSE-UPS

ELIZABETHTOWN COLLEGE

ELIZABETHTOWN, PENNSYLVANIA

★ To read more about this school, visit http://petersons.to/elizabethtowncollege

Elizabethtown College

The College

Founded in 1899, and located in historic Lancaster County, Pennsylvania, Elizabethtown College offers students more than fifty academic programs in liberal arts, sciences, and professional studies. A selective, private institution, the College is driven by its motto, "Educate for Service," and links classroom instruction with experiential learning through Signature Learning Experiences (SLEs), which supplement classroom learning and include choices in supervised research, cross-cultural experiences, community-based learning, internships, and capstone courses. SLEs prepare students for lives of purpose and are the hallmarks of the Elizabethtown experience.

Home to about 1,800 traditional students from twenty-seven states and twenty-three countries, 85 percent live on the 203-acre campus in residence halls, townhouses and apartments, and college-owned houses called student-directed learning communities, where students commit to community-focused service work. Wi-Fi is available in all campus buildings.

In addition to an active intramural and club sports program, Blue Jay Athletics fields 23 NCAA Division III teams for men (baseball, basketball, cross-country, golf, lacrosse, soccer, swimming, tennis, track and field [indoor/outdoor], and wrestling) and women (basketball, cross-country, field hockey, golf, lacrosse, soccer, softball, swimming, tennis, track and field [indoor/outdoor], and volleyball).

The Center for Student Success offers academic advising, personal counseling, and health and wellness programming. Career Services provides students of all class years and alumni, with professional and career development services. The Center for Student Involvement includes: Student Activities (OSA), International Student Services, Diversity, and Chaplain/Religious Life.

The campus offers four dining venues: The Marketplace (traditional dining space); The Jay's Nest (deli/quick-serve/convenience store); The Blue Bean (coffee shop); and The Jay's Truck (food truck). Recreational spaces and offerings include The Body Shop, Thompson Gymnasium, fitness classes, an outdoor track, a pool, and lots of paths and green space. Koon's Activity Venue is a multipurpose entertainment and educational space. Leffler Chapel and Performance Center features an 840-seat auditorium. The campus events calendar boasts more than 125 arts and cultural happenings each academic year, not including student-run programming from OSA and the 80+ campus clubs.

Elizabethtown holds accreditations from the Middle States Commission for Higher Education, American Chemical Society for Clinical Lab Services, National Association of Schools of Music, National Council on Social Work Education, Accreditation Council for Occupational Therapy Education, Association of Collegiate Business Schools and Programs (ACBSP), and the Accreditation Board for Engineering and Technology Inc. (ABET).

In addition to its traditional undergraduate programs, Elizabethtown also offers a Master of Science degree in occupational therapy; a master's degree in public policy; a Master of Special Education (4+1); a Master of Education in Curriculum and Instruction in Peace Education; and, through its School of Continuing and Professional Studies, Master of Business Administration (M.B.A.) and Master of Strategic Leadership degrees.

Location

Elizabethtown borough is a community of 20,000 people located in historic Lancaster County in south-central Pennsylvania, 20 minutes from Harrisburg (state capital), Hershey, and Lancaster; 90 minutes from Philadelphia and Baltimore; and a few hours from New York and Washington, D.C. The Amtrak station in Elizabethtown offers train service to and from New York, Philadelphia, and Pittsburgh. The Harrisburg International Airport is 15 minutes away.

Majors and Degrees

Bachelor of Arts degrees are awarded in communications, economics, English, fine arts, French, German, history, interfaith leadership studies, Japanese, legal studies, music, philosophy, political science, psychology, religious studies, social work, sociology-anthropology, Spanish, Spanish education, and theatre.

Bachelor of Science degrees are offered in accounting, actuarial science, biochemistry, biology, biotechnology, business administration, chemistry, computer engineering, computer science, early childhood education, elementary/middle-level education, engineering, environmental science, forestry and environmental management, general science education, health sciences, international business, information systems, mathematical business, mathematics, physics, and social studies secondary education.

Bachelor of Music degrees are offered in music education and music therapy.

More than ninety minors and concentrations are offered, including Asian studies, data analytics, women and gender studies, peace and conflict studies, and engineering concentrations in electrical, industrial and systems, mechanical, and environmental, as well as seven secondary education certification programs.

The College offers a variety of cooperative programs that allow qualified students to combine undergraduate studies with direct admission into graduate school. These include the Doctor of Physical Therapy programs at Thomas Jefferson University and Widener University, the Doctor of Osteopathic Medicine program at Philadelphia College of Osteopathic Medicine and Lake Erie College of Osteopathic Medicine, Temple University's School of Dentistry, and the Master of Molecular Medicine program with Drexel University College of Medicine.

The Primary Care Pre-Admissions Program through the Pennsylvania State University College of Medicine at the Milton S. Hershey Medical Center provides options for Elizabethtown students who are Pennsylvania residents and are pursuing careers in internal medicine, family practice, and pediatrics.

The College also offers a Law Early Admissions program (LEAP) with Drexel University Earle Mack School of Law and Widener University School of Law.

Academic Programs

An interdisciplinary first-year seminar and a strong core curriculum create a solid foundation for a student's chosen area of study. The core develops critical analysis and communication skills that ensure adaptability in the ever-changing global marketplace. Independent and directed studies, undergraduate research, and internships are available.

The Elizabethtown College Honors Program offers top students a highly selective program of study with the opportunity for a stipend to fund professional development, research, or travel-related study.

Called to Lead is a leadership-building program that helps students aspire to lead purposeful lives. Scholarship and Creative Arts Day, held each spring, gives students of all majors and class years the opportunity to showcase their research or creative works. The Center for Global Understanding and Peacemaking, Bowers Writers House, and The Young Center for Anabaptist and Pietist Studies all offer a variety of academic programming that further reinforce classroom experiences. The Social Enterprise Institute offers students the opportunity to collaborate with faculty and industry fellows to create sustainable social and economic value both domestically and internationally. The Momentum program, a pre-orientation program helps first-generation college students prepare for the academic expectations of Elizabethtown.

Off-Campus Programs

During their time at Elizabethtown, each student is guaranteed to experience at least two of the following Signature Learning Experiences: undergraduate research, study abroad, community-based learning, internships/fieldwork, and capstone course work.

Students may study abroad for a semester in twenty-six different locations on six continents through the College's affiliate programs. Short-term academic study tours or service-learning trips are offered. The Center for Community and Civic Engagement offers numerous community-based learning experiences locally, regionally, and nationally.

Academic Facilities

The High Library contains more than 250,000 volumes and an extensive collection of journals and other research materials; computers and printers; conference rooms; and private, individual, and group study areas. Librarians help students with research projects and using library resources effectively.

The campus features numerous academic buildings, including the James B. Hoover Center for Business, The Masters Center for Science, Mathematics, and Engineering. The student center, Brossman Commons, is home to the Tempest Theatre and a dance studio, and Zug Memorial Hall houses a recital hall and private and group practice rooms. Steinman Center for Communications and Arts features a television studio, radio station, and office space for the College newspaper. The College houses three art galleries and the Masters Mineral Gallery.

Elizabethtown is home to The Young Center for Anabaptist and Pietist Studies, a world-renowned research center focusing on the Amish and other similar religions. The S. Dale High Center for Family Business, a local research and resource center for family-owned businesses, partners with academic departments for events and programs.

Costs

For 2017–18, tuition is $45,350 and room and meals are $10,990, for a total comprehensive fee of $56,340. Students should also plan for an additional $2,000 for books, transportation, and personal expenses, for a total cost of $58,340. Financial aid is based on this figure.

Financial Aid

Elizabethtown College works with students and their families to make education affordable. Ninety-five percent of students receive some form of aid; packages typically combine scholarships, grants, loans, and student employment. More than half of Elizabethtown's first-year students receive renewable merit-based scholarships, which are awarded on a competitive basis and without regard to need.

To apply for aid, students must file the Free Application for Federal Student Aid (FAFSA). Students are assigned a personal financial aid counselor to help them throughout their years at the College. Elizabethtown's deadline for financial consideration is March 15.

Faculty

Elizabethtown has a teaching faculty of 129 full-time professors. The student-faculty ratio is 12:1. Ninety-four percent of the full-time faculty members hold a Ph.D. or the highest earned degree in their field. In addition to being assigned a faculty adviser for the First-Year Seminar program, when students declare a major, they are also assigned a new faculty adviser within the academic department of their declared major.

Student Government

Students play an active role in campus governance through Student Senate, the Campus Residence Association, and other organizations. Representative members of Student Senate are elected from each class. They advocate for students, coordinate special events, and allocate funds for student activities and the more than eighty student-run clubs and organizations. Students Working to Entertain E-town (S.W.E.E.T.) allocates funding for weekend programs, campus social activities, and entertainment for the College community.

Admission Requirements

Elizabethtown believes the right fit is more than just SAT scores and GPA; other admission factors considered at the College are academic fit, co-curricular fit, and social fit. Admissions decisions are made without regard to sex, sexual orientation, race, religion, physical handicap, or place of residence. On average, 71 percent of all applicants are accepted. The middle 50 percent of enrolled students scored between 990 and 1220 on the critical reading and mathematics sections of the SAT, and 30 percent were in the top 10 percent of their high school class.

The College is a diverse and exciting community, one that is composed of students who display leadership abilities and special talents. Campus interviews are highly recommended but not required for most students, although the College reserves the right to require interviews in special cases. Applicants to the Honors Program and occupational therapy program are required to interview. Auditions are required for music students.

Early admission is available for highly qualified high school juniors.

Application and Information

The College operates on a rolling admission basis—applications are processed as they are received—and the application deadline is March 1. Students can apply using the Common Application or online at the College's website. Applicants must submit a high school transcript, SAT or ACT scores, and a personal statement, essay, or graded paper. Early application is strongly recommended. Accepted students should notify the College of their decision to attend by May 1. Students who are interested in the Elizabethtown College Honors Program must submit a completed application by January 15.

For more information, students should contact:

Lauren Deibler, Director of Admissions
Elizabethtown College
One Alpha Drive
Elizabethtown, Pennsylvania 17022-2298
Phone: 717-361-1400
Fax: 717-361-1365
E-mail: admissions@etown.edu
Website: http://www.etown.edu

Elizabethtown College, home to about 1,800 students, offers more than fifty majors and ninety minors and concentrations.

COLLEGE CLOSE-UPS

ELMHURST COLLEGE

ELMHURST, ILLINOIS

★ To read more about this school, visit http://petersons.to/elmhurstcollege

COLLEGE CLOSE-UPS

The College

A private college in the heart of the Chicago metropolitan area, Elmhurst College is committed to helping students reach their full potential—in college and in the world beyond. An Elmhurst education is about more than courses and credits; it's about defining values, exploring the world, and preparing for a life of service, meaning, and achievement.

Elmhurst is one of the top 10 colleges in the Midwest, according to *U.S. News & World Report*, and it also ranks among the best values in the region. With more than 60 undergraduate majors and more than 17 graduate programs, Elmhurst boasts a student-to-faculty ratio of just 14 to 1. In small classes, professors get to know their students as individuals.

Beyond the classroom, students get plenty of opportunities to put their passions and talents into action in more than 100 campus activities. Elmhurst's 20 athletic teams compete in NCAA Division III and have won conference championships in five sports over the past decade.

More than 80 percent of Elmhurst undergraduates gain on-the-job experience through internships or service work, and nearly 94 percent of Elmhurst graduates find full-time employment or enter graduate school within a year of graduation. The College's robust career programs include more than 2,000 options for internships and other professional experiences.

Students come to Elmhurst from many states and countries, and from nearly every religious, racial and ethnic background. The student body comprises about 2,800 full-time undergraduate students, 150 adults pursuing an undergraduate degree and 550 graduate students.

Elmhurst College is accredited by the Department of Education of the State of Illinois, and by the Higher Learning Commission, a member of the North Central Association of Colleges and Schools. The baccalaureate degree in nursing and master's degree in nursing at Elmhurst College are accredited by the Commission on Collegiate Nursing Education (http://www.aacn.nche.edu/ccne-accreditation).

Location

Elmhurst's 48-acre grounds are an arboretum, with more than 120 varieties of trees, shrubs and other woody plants. The gorgeous campus is a green oasis in the heart of a quiet, safe suburb—but it's also just a few blocks from the Elmhurst Metra station, where students can catch the train for a 30-minute ride to downtown Chicago, providing easy access to world-class cultural, entertainment, and professional opportunities.

Academics

With more than 60 undergraduate majors and 17 pre-professional programs, Elmhurst boasts a student-to-faculty ratio of just 14 to 1. In small classes, students work closely with faculty members who are experts in their fields—and whose primary mission is teaching.

Many students collaborate with faculty on high-level research projects, studying subjects ranging from metastatic breast cancer to the effect of acting lessons on aging brains. An Honors Program offers special opportunities for students who are especially motivated by academic challenges.

Beyond the classroom, Elmhurst offers study-abroad opportunities in 44 countries. A special January Term offers undergraduate students the chance to undertake courses and field projects off campus.

Career Development

Elmhurst students gain real-world experience starting their first year. Internships, professional mentors, and shadowing experiences help them define their future and provide them the skills to succeed. Nearly 94 percent of Elmhurst College graduates are employed or in graduate school within a year of graduating.

Facilities

The Elmhurst campus combines the high-tech necessities of a modern education with the charm of a classic college campus. Its classic red-brick buildings boast wireless Internet access, smart classrooms, and more. In addition, the College has a long tradition of responsible stewardship of the environment. From low-impact lighting and permeable paving to a LEED-certified residence hall, Elmhurst incorporates green principles throughout campus life.

Costs

Full-time undergraduate tuition for 2017–18 is $36,070; basic room and board is $10,144.

Financial Aid

Elmhurst College is committed to making college affordable; 100 percent of new students receive financial aid in the form of grants, scholarships, loans, and work-study. Last year, the average financial aid package was $25,830.

Campus Life

Students at Elmhurst find plenty of opportunities to put their passions and talents into action. The College offers more than 100 student organizations, including everything from Habitat for Humanity to the Black Student Union to religious groups and Greek life.

Many Elmhurst students live on campus, where they find all the amenities of home—plus the convenience of close proximity to classes, the library, the gym and all your favorite student activities. The College's six residence halls are equipped with full kitchens, cozy gathering spots, Internet access, voice mail, and free cable TV. Each hall sponsors a variety of events—like movies, workshops, and barbecues—and has the support of an expert residence life staff.

Elmhurst also offers an array of services and resources designed to help students navigate the pressures of college life. Services in the Division of Student Affairs include individual counseling, support with housing issues, comprehensive health care services, transition assistance, and diversity education.

Admission Requirements

Elmhurst gives preference to students who have completed 16 academic units, including 3 units of English; 2 units each of mathematics, laboratory science, and social studies; and 7 units in additional college preparatory subjects.

Application and Information

To apply, prospective students should submit the following:

- **The application for admission.** Students may apply online at https://connect.elmhurst.edu/apply.
- **High school transcript** or GED test results.
- **Scores from the ACT or SAT,** sent directly from the testing corporation to Elmhurst. (Elmhurst's ACT code is 1020 and its SAT code is 1204).
- **A recommendation** from a high school faculty member (encouraged, but not required).

Elmhurst has an Early Action deadline (nonbinding) of November 1 with a December 1 notification. Rolling admission notifications begin mid-December.

Prospective students are encouraged to visit the campus, either individually or as part of a scheduled event. Admission events range from campus tours and open houses to information sessions and overnight visits.

The Office of Admission at Elmhurst College welcomes students' questions and comments.

For more information, please contact:

Office of Admission
Elmhurst College
190 Prospect Avenue
Elmhurst, Illinois 60126-3296
United States
Phone: 630-617-3400
800-697-1871 (toll-free)
E-mail: admit@elmhurst.edu
Website: http://www.elmhurst.edu/admission

The Elmhurst College campus is a 48-acre arboretum within easy access of the limitless opportunities of downtown Chicago.

EMBRY-RIDDLE AERONAUTICAL UNIVERSITY

DAYTONA BEACH, FLORIDA

EMBRY-RIDDLE Aeronautical University™
FLORIDA | ARIZONA | WORLDWIDE

★ To read more about this school, visit http://petersons.to/erau

The University

Embry-Riddle Aeronautical University's reputation as the leader in aviation and aerospace education is recognized worldwide. The University's history and legacy date back almost to the time of the Wright brothers. Embry-Riddle is an independent, nonsectarian, not-for-profit, coeducational university serving culturally diverse students seeking careers in aviation, aerospace, engineering, business, security and intelligence, and related fields. Residential campuses in Daytona Beach, Florida, and Prescott, Arizona, provide education in a traditional setting, while the Worldwide campus provides instruction through more than 130 centers in the United States, Europe, Asia, and the Middle East and through online learning.

Approximately 5,400 undergraduate students and 600 graduate students are currently enrolled at the 185-acre Daytona Beach residential campus. Students come from all fifty states, and nearly 100 countries are represented, making Embry-Riddle a truly international university.

Currently 28 undergraduate degree programs, 15 graduate programs, and 7 doctoral programs are offered at the Daytona Beach campus. Embry-Riddle's premier aeronautical science (professional pilot) program and nationally ranked aerospace engineering program are the largest on campus and among the largest of their type in the nation.

Embry-Riddle conducts applied research and is leading the development of the Next Generation Air Transportation System along with the Federal Aviation Administration, Lockheed Martin, Boeing, and other high-tech organizations. Student research projects include development of green technologies like Embry-Riddle's EcoCAR and the world's first-of-its-kind hybrid aircraft. Alumni are leaders in every facet of the aviation and aerospace industries and serve as a strong network and resource for students.

Students at the Daytona Beach campus enjoy a wide array of activities and clubs, many focused on aviation and aerospace, as well as fraternities, sororities, and athletic opportunities. Thirty-four percent of students live on campus.

Embry-Riddle's award-winning precision flight demonstration teams offer students the opportunity to compete nationally in air and ground events. Embry-Riddle also has the largest all-volunteer Air Force ROTC detachment in the country and a prominent Naval ROTC unit and Army ROTC battalion. Embry-Riddle athletes compete in intercollegiate and intramural sports, including baseball, basketball, crew, cross-country, golf, lacrosse, rowing, soccer, tennis, track, volleyball, and ice hockey.

The 68,000-square-foot ICI Center contains two full-size NCAA basketball courts, a fitness center, and a weight room. The ICI Center provides a place to host sporting events and assemblies. The University sports complex also includes two soccer fields, the Sliwa Stadium ballpark, the Crotty Tennis Center, and the Track and Field Complex. The Tine Davis Fitness Center is adjacent to the pool and features comprehensive fitness services and wellness programs. Recent expansions to athletic facilities include a softball complex for women's fast-pitch softball, as well as two artificial turf fields for intramural competition.

The Center for Faith and Spirituality accommodates the variety of faiths represented by the student body of Embry-Riddle. It consists of a 140-seat nondenominational worship area and four prayer rooms (Catholic, Jewish, Muslim, and Protestant).

Location

The year-round clear flying weather and the resort communities surrounding Embry-Riddle's residential campus in Daytona Beach, Florida, offer students an excellent environment in which to study, fly, and enjoy recreational activities. The campus, which is located adjacent to the Daytona Beach International Airport, is only 3 miles from what is labeled the world's most famous beach. The high-technology industries located in nearby Orlando and Kennedy Space Center provide the University with an outstanding support base. In addition, Walt Disney World and other theme parks are about an hour's drive from campus.

Majors and Degrees

The Daytona Beach campus of Embry-Riddle awards undergraduate degrees at the baccalaureate and associate level. Bachelor of Science degrees are offered in a variety of areas, each with a focus on the aviation, aerospace, security, and related industries. A growing major in unmanned aircraft systems science (open only to U.S. citizens) combines Embry-Riddle's expertise in flight, air traffic management, safety and engineering. The College of Engineering offers majors in aerospace engineering, civil engineering, computer engineering, electrical engineering, mechanical engineering, and software engineering. All engineering programs, including Engineering Physics, are ABET accredited.

Students who are interested in business administration may elect to major in management, accounting and finance, or marketing. An aviation business administration major is also available with majors in air transportation and supply chain management.

The College of Aviation awards degrees in aeronautical science (professional piloting), air traffic management, aviation maintenance science, aerospace and occupational safety, spaceflight operations, and meteorology. Other majors include astronomy and astrophysics, interdisciplinary studies (design your own major), communication, computational mathematics, global conflict studies, homeland security, human factors psychology, and space physics, all housed in the College of Arts & Sciences. The College's newest major, and the only one of its kind in the nation, is aerospace physiology, a pre-med program open to students in the fall of 2017. Students entering Embry-Riddle with an undecided major have the opportunity to explore a variety of academic pursuits before making a commitment to a specific track.

Academic Programs

Even a field as specialized as aviation requires a broad educational background. General education courses required of all students who are pursuing a baccalaureate program include communication skills, such as English composition, literature, and technical report writing; humanities; social sciences; mathematics; physical sciences; economics; and computer science. To ensure academic success, Embry-Riddle provides free tutorial services.

The academic year is divided into two semesters of fifteen weeks each, with the summer session divided into two terms. The average course load for each fall or spring semester is 15 credit hours.

Study abroad offers students the opportunity to better understand the global nature of the aviation and aerospace industries. The Cooperative Education and Internship program adds value to the educational experience and allows students to gain real-world professional and networking skills.

Academic Facilities

The College of Aviation building at the Daytona Beach campus provides an unsurpassed environment for aviation education and research. The multimillion-dollar simulation laboratories duplicate the components and functions in the national airspace system, including capabilities to replicate actual weather reporting, airports, airways, air traffic control, flow control, and pilot and aircraft performance as found in the national air transportation system. Flight instruction is provided in the Embry-Riddle fleet of sixty-plus aircraft and a wide array of flight training devices. Aircraft are equipped with Automatic Dependent Surveillance-Broadcast (ADS-B) technology that decreases hazards associated with traffic, weather, and terrain. The High-Altitude Normobaric Lab allows students to experience the symptoms of high-altitude hypoxia to better enable them to recognize and recover from this threat. Embry-Riddle is the first university in the nation to acquire this technology.

The Advanced Flight Simulation Center gives Embry-Riddle students the opportunity to train in world-class simulators. The center, with more than 20,000 square feet of space and four high bays, currently houses two advanced aviation training devices (AATDs), eight Cessna 172S NAVIIIs (Skyhawk), two Diamond DA42 TAE Twin Stars, two Diamond DA42 L360s, and one Canadair Regional Jet (CRJ-200). These devices duplicate the actual cockpit, adverse weather conditions, a full range of emergency situations, and virtually any flight pattern and complement flight training done in actual aircraft. Flight simulation enables students to learn aircraft performance, experience aerodynamic effects, and perform flight maneuvers immediately and without risk. Qualified to Level 6, the University's devices faithfully reproduce Embry-Riddle's fleet of single-engine and multiengine aircraft and are equipped with 220-degree panoramic visual theaters. In addition, the Aviation Building houses air traffic control and tower simulators, one motion-based disorientation trainer, and six basic aviation training devices (BATDs).

The James Hagedorn Aviation Complex includes 96,000 square feet in a three-building facility and is home to flight training operations, aircraft maintenance training, and a fleet maintenance hangar. The Emil Buehler Aviation Maintenance Science building's cutting-edge labs dedicated to aircraft systems, turbine engines, metallic and composite materials, and avionics electronics prepare students to become maintenance professionals. The facility includes classrooms, a licensed engine-repair station, a machine shop, and a third-floor observation deck overlooking the flight line and Daytona Beach International Airport runways.

The Lehman Engineering and Technology Center is home to the College of Engineering. Labs include the advanced vehicles green garage, wind tunnel lab, materials testing lab, clean energy systems lab, cybersecurity engineering lab, nanomaterials and composites labs, rocket lab, spacecraft development lab, and many more. Students use the labs to work in teams to develop hands-on projects. Research is conducted by faculty members and graduate and undergraduate students.

The newest academic facility is the 140,000 square-foot College of Arts & Sciences building, the largest structure on campus and home to the largest university-based telescope in the state of Florida. The building contains twenty-five labs dedicated to astronomy, astrophysics, atmospheric and space physics, control theory, and engineering physics.

The College of Business academic building features the aviation operations simulation lab, which is used to develop and evaluate aviation/airline operational strategies and processes. In addition, the College's Teaching Airport, a partnership between Embry-Riddle and Daytona Beach International Airport, is focused on teaching, research, and public outreach.

The Capt. Willie Miller Instructional Center, a lecture auditorium and classroom complex, provides space for large audience events, including presentations by distinguished lecturers and speakers.

A new Student Union is scheduled to be completed in 2018 and will house the Jack R. Hunt Memorial Library and serve as the community hub with retail, food, and entertainment options. Not only will it be the largest building on campus, it will encompass numerous university and campus departments, facilities, and services.

Costs

For the 2017–18 academic year, tuition and fees are $17,486 per semester. Flight fees are charged in addition to tuition. On-campus room and board costs are approximately $5,550 per semester. Personal expenses, books, and fees are in addition to the above. Students who graduate from a Florida high school receive a 5 percent discount. Costs are subject to change.

Financial Aid

Applicants for financial aid are required to complete the Department of Education's Free Application for Federal Student Aid (FAFSA) and any other documents requested by the University. Students are encouraged to apply early if they wish to be considered for all types of programs. All applicants are automatically reviewed for merit scholarship eligibility.

Faculty

The faculty members provide an excellent balance of professional experience and academic achievement. Many faculty members who teach in the specialized and major programs have had professional experience in their areas of instruction. The student-faculty ratio is 17:1, and the average class size is 26. The primary concern of each faculty member is research, personalized teaching in classrooms and laboratories, on the flight line, and in student advising.

Student Government

The University places great emphasis on student self-government. The Student Government Association supports publication of the weekly newspaper and oversees the Touch-N-Go Office that organizes campus entertainment and broadcast of the student radio station, WIKD-FM.

Admission Requirements

Admission is open to any qualified applicant, regardless of creed, sex, race, national origin, handicap, or geographical location. When evaluating an applicant for admission, Embry-Riddle takes into consideration a student's high school academic record (both courses taken and overall grade point average), rank in class, and activities. Embry-Riddle values individual academic achievement, initiative, talent, and character above standardized testing. Therefore, submission of standardized test scores (SAT or ACT) is optional for admission. If scores are submitted, they will be treated as supplemental information through the evaluation process. Students who do not feel that their scores accurately reflect their abilities do not need to submit them. Scores are not used for placement in freshman classes. Transfer students are required to submit official transcripts from all colleges and universities attended. High school transcripts are not required if the student has earned 30 college credits or more.

Application and Information

Embry-Riddle requires each applicant to submit an application form and fee, two letters of recommendation, and an official high school/college transcript. Flight students must provide an FAA Class I or Class II medical certificate. When a student is accepted for admission, tuition and housing deposits are required by May 1 for a fall start date. Embry-Riddle operates on a rolling admissions basis, and admission decisions are rendered throughout the year.

University Admissions
Embry-Riddle Aeronautical University
P.O. Box 11767
Daytona Beach, Florida 32120-1767
Phone: 386-226-6100
800-862-2416 (toll-free nationwide)
E-mail: daytonabeach@erau.edu
Website: http://www.daytonabeach.erau.edu
http://www.facebook.com/eraudb
http://twitter.com/ERAU_Daytona
http://www.youtube.com/EmbryRiddleUniv
https://www.instagram.com/embryriddledaytona

Embry-Riddle Aeronautical University, Daytona Beach, Florida, campus.

COLLEGE CLOSE-UPS

EMBRY-RIDDLE AERONAUTICAL UNIVERSITY

PRESCOTT, ARIZONA

EMBRY-RIDDLE
Aeronautical University
PRESCOTT, ARIZONA

★ To read more about this school, visit http://petersons.to/eraprescott

The University

Embry-Riddle Aeronautical University's Prescott, Arizona campus is recognized and respected worldwide for cutting-edge instruction and training for tomorrow's aviation, aerospace, security and intelligence leaders.

Embry-Riddle is a private, four-year university accredited by SACS. The coed student population of just over 2,450 undergraduates comes from all fifty states and over thirty nations.

There are more than 100 student clubs and organizations including professional associations, fraternities, sororities, specialty clubs, and intramural sports. The National Association of Intercollegiate Athletics (NAIA) teams compete regionally and nationally as members of the CalPac Conference. Men's and women's teams include basketball, cross-country, golf, and soccer, along with men's wrestling, women's volleyball, and women's softball. The Golden Eagles flight team has consistently ranked among the top in the country in Safety and Flight Evaluation Conference (SAFECON) competitions, capturing the national championship title ten times.

Within a year of graduation, 96 percent of graduates are either employed within their discipline or continuing their education.

Location

Prescott is a mile-high city and its climate reflects seasonable weather excellent for flying. Daytime averages are 80°F in the summer and 45°F in the winter. The local mountains reflect the spirit of the West, where students enjoy skiing, hiking, mountain biking, kayaking, rock climbing, and tours of the Grand Canyon.

Majors and Degrees

Twenty-four majors are offered through four different colleges: Arts and Sciences, Aviation, Engineering, and the nation's first College of Security and Intelligence.

Aeronautical Science, the professional pilot program, offers fixed-wing or rotary-wing flight options. The program emphasizes hands-on training to prepare students for a career in the aviation industry with airlines, corporate and commercial aviation, or the military.

Aeronautics builds upon pre-existing experience and training in aviation, or other technical fields. It also allows the flexibility to build a major with an aviation focus and a professional outcome.

Aerospace Engineering instructs the scientific principles that govern the design of airplanes, spacecraft, and jet engines. The program focuses primarily on the engineering of mission-oriented vehicles for atmospheric or space flight.

Air Traffic Management blends simulation training with rigorous academic study. Hands-on air traffic training prepares students for a career as an air traffic controller with the Federal Aviation Administration (FAA).

Applied Meteorology provides a practical understanding of the physics and dynamics of the atmosphere to forecast complex phenomena. This program offers areas of concentration in flight, meteorology for aviation operations, military meteorology, and research.

Astronomy emphasizes both a hands-on and theoretical education in the study of celestial objects and astrophysics. The Campus Observatory Complex, as well as Prescott's excellent viewing conditions, enhance education beyond the classroom.

Aviation Business Administration integrates in-depth studies of aviation, transportation, and government interface with a strong business foundation, and is approved by the Aviation Accreditation Board International (AABI).

Business Administration students experience a unique hands-on learning approach by taking their education outside the classroom and consulting with actual clients through a faculty-led student team. Students produce start-up business plans, strategic management plans, and conduct fraud-risk analysis.

Computer Engineering provides a background in the design of digital hardware and software systems including communications systems, computers, and devices that contain computers. A senior design project will closely follow the development of an engineering project in the industry.

Cyber Intelligence and Security empowers students to lead, manage, administer, and create organizations in cyber security. Students study computer forensics, information warfare, and technical intelligence while utilizing the University's state-of-the-art *Cyber Security Lab.*

Electrical Engineering is a systems-oriented program that includes analog and digital circuits, communication systems, computers, control systems, electromagnetic fields, energy sources and systems, and electronic materials and devices.

Forensic Accounting and Fraud Examination is where law enforcement meets the accounting world. Graduation prepares students for the Certified Fraud Examiner (CFE) exam and Certification, and incorporates criminal investigative skills with areas of accounting, including financial, managerial, information systems, governmental, auditing, tax accounting, and psychology.

Forensic Biology combines biology, chemistry, and law to give students experience in forensic science laboratories, law enforcement, and legal contexts. Hands-on activities include evidence collection, crime scene investigation, tissue sampling and analysis, and emphasis on DNA techniques. This major also fulfills pre-med requirements.

Forensic Psychology is the science of human behavior and prepares students to work in civil, legal, and criminal environments as experts in understanding, evaluating, and predicting human behavior. Training combines the study of global and cyber security, forensic science, the U.S. legal system and international affairs.

Global Business prepares students for international management. Classroom topics include global events and issues related to transportation, trade, public policy, technology, resources, energy, and the environment. Students study international cultures with a focus on emerging markets.

Global Security and Intelligence Studies gives graduates an expertise in terrorism, asymmetrical warfare, transportation security, threats to manufacturing facilities, corporate offices, computer systems, and telecommunications infrastructure. Students prepare for careers with the FBI, CIA, State Department, military intelligence, and private sectors. Options include Mandarin Chinese, Arabic, Spanish, and Russian.

Industrial Psychology and Safety explores the disciplines of aviation safety, occupational safety, industrial hygiene, ergonomics, and quantitative methods. The program delivers a foundation in human behavior and cognition as it relates to safety and organizational effectiveness.

Interdisciplinary Studies is a unique option allowing students to customize their undergraduate curriculum to match specific career goals by choosing three major areas of study to create their own major.

Mechanical Engineering focuses on the design of robotic, propulsion, and energy systems. The program prepares students for the vast career applications in this field including aerospace, automotive, robotics, thermal environmental control, recreational products, medicine, and manufacturing.

Simulation Science, Games and Animation instructs students to design and build technologies underlying aviation simulators, computer aided design (CAD) systems, computer animation software, streaming video networks, and computer games.

Software Engineering prepares students to work as programmers and software engineers, constructing software systems and developing system requirements. A unique cyber security track allows graduates to support the nation's need for cyber security to protect a company's proprietary information.

Space Physics is an applied physics program designed to prepare students for graduate studies in physics, astrophysics, and exotic propulsion systems, as well as for work in space and aerospace related industries.

Unmanned Aerial Systems focuses on the design, operation, and business components of the emerging unmanned aerial vehicles industry. This program emphasizes practical applications such as search and rescue, first responder, hazardous surveillance, or evaluation of emergencies.

Wildlife Science is the only undergraduate environmental science program in the country with a focus on the aviation and aerospace industries. Students with interest in wildlife biology, environmental science, and working in the outdoors should explore this growing and rewarding career field.

Academic Programs

Education at Embry-Riddle goes beyond the classroom. Through participation in internships and cooperative education arrangements, students in all fields of study gain valuable work experience with companies such as Delta Air Lines, the Federal Aviation Administration, Honeywell, Gulfstream, Lockheed Martin, NASA, the CIA, SpaceX, and more.

Army and Air Force Reserve Officer Training Corps (ROTC) courses are also available to all students. Embry-Riddle produces more Air Force officers and aviators than any institution except the Air Force Academy.

Faculty

Faculty, not graduate students, teach all classes. The average class size is 25, with a student-faculty ratio of 16:1. Faculty bring teaching and industry backgrounds to the classroom; most have extensive practical experience in their field and outstanding academic credentials.

Academic Facilities

Numerous laboratories and state-of-the-art equipment provide students many opportunities to explore, investigate, experiment, build, and participate in undergraduate research.

The Robertson Aviation Safety Center houses the nation's only university-level accident investigation laboratory. This outdoor facility allows for studying wreckage sites of actual aircraft accidents.

The Glen Doherty Center for Security and Intelligence serves as a laboratory for students of the nation's first College of Security and Intelligence to simulate exercises in emergency management and homeland security. Labs include Computer Security and Forensic Science, where students run forensic tests on cyber threats and crime scene evidence.

The recently completed STEM Education Center includes particle physics, exotic propulsion, optics, and remote sensing labs for space physics and astronomy majors, as well as advanced forensic, biology, chemistry, and robotics labs. It also contains an IMAX planetarium for use by all majors and the community. There is also a campus observatory housing a CCD (charged coupled device) debris telescope.

In the Aerospace Experimentation and Fabrication Building (AXFAB), students have access to a two-axis electromagnetic shaker, vacuum chambers to simulate space environment, and 3-D printers. Additionally, there is the Aerial Robotics Laboratory for research and development of unmanned systems; the Aerodynamics Laboratory which houses five wind tunnels; and the Propulsion Laboratory providing a micro-turbojet.

The King Engineering and Technology Center is home for the computer, electrical, and software engineering students. There is a design suite for autonomous vehicles as well as labs for communications, control theory, power, digital circuits, and linear circuits.

The Flight Training Center is located at the Prescott Municipal Airport 2 miles from campus. The fleet includes Cessna 172s, Diamond DA42 NGs, an American Champion Super Decathlon for extreme attitude recovery, and two Cessna 150s, furnished with Garmin G1000 navigation systems, for the flight team. All aircraft are ADS-b equipped. Also at the flight line are three Frasca 172 level 6 flight-training devices with 220° visual displays.

Additional College of Aviation facilities include an Air Traffic Control Lab, Student Innovation Lab for unmanned aerial systems research and development, and a Weather Center, which has radar and weather balloon launch capabilities.

Athletic facilities include indoor volleyball and basketball courts, fitness center, multipurpose gym, and matted wrestling room. Other facilities include a softball field, intercollegiate soccer field, tennis courts, sand volleyball courts, 25-yard swimming pool, racquetball courts, climbing wall, running track, and multisport recreation field. All facilities are available free of charge to all students.

Costs

The 2015–16 academic year tuition for all programs was $16,913 per semester for full-time students. Flight fees are charged in addition to tuition. The average on-campus housing rate for first-year students is $2,700 per semester; the required meal plan for freshmen is $2,195 per semester. Students also need to account for the cost of books, transportation, and personal expenses.

Financial Aid

Students can find many sources to assist with funding their education. Filing the FAFSA is important. Embry-Riddle also provides assistance in the form of academic scholarships, need-based grants, on-campus jobs, veterans' educational benefits (Embry-Riddle is a Yellow Ribbon school), and ROTC incentives.

Admission Requirements

Each student receives individual consideration for admission based on a variety of factors and circumstances. Completion of the application for admission begins this process; students also need to submit official transcripts, score reports for either the SAT or ACT (not required but highly recommended), and two letters of recommendation.

Application and Information

For additional information, students should contact:
Embry-Riddle Aeronautical University Admissions
3700 Willow Creek Road
Prescott, Arizona 86301
United States
Phone: 928-777-6600
800-888-3728 (toll-free)
E-mail: prescott@erau.edu
Website: http://prescott.erau.edu

The beautiful Prescott, Arizona campus glows in front of its dramatic, picturesque Granite Mountain backdrop.

EMERSON COLLEGE
BOSTON, MASSACHUSETTS

★ For more information, visit http://petersons.to/emersoncollege

The College

Founded in 1880 and located in the heart of Boston, Massachusetts, Emerson College is the nation's premier institution for the study of communication and the arts. Students may choose from nearly 30 undergraduate programs supported by state-of-the-art facilities and a nationally renowned faculty. Emerson's campus is home to WERS-FM, the oldest noncommercial radio station in Boston; the historic 1,200-seat Cutler Majestic Theatre; and *Ploughshares*, the award-winning literary journal for new writing.

Emerson College offers educational programs that prepare undergraduate and graduate men and women to assume positions of responsibility and leadership in communication and the arts and to pursue scholarship and work that brings innovation to these disciplines.

Originally a small, regional school of oratory, Emerson has evolved into a diverse, coeducational, and multifaceted degree-granting institution with a liberal arts rather than conservatory orientation. But its mission and focus remains largely the same: to explore and push the boundaries of communication, art, and culture and, thereby, to contribute to the advancement of society.

Many of the College's 37,000+ alumni remain active participants in the life of Emerson. Although concentrated in Massachusetts, California, and New York, Emersonians can be found working in virtually every major media, entertainment, or arts enterprise across the country.

The College's 3,790 undergraduate and 682 graduate students come from across the United States and fifty-seven countries. Many undergraduate students live on campus, some in special learning communities, such as the Writers' Block, Film Immersion Community, and Digital Culture Floor. There is a fitness center, athletic field, and several residence halls, including a fourteen-story campus center and residence hall that houses a gymnasium and student-services offices. Emerson is slated to open a new 18-story residence hall and a new 18,000 square-foot Dining Center in fall 2017.

Emerson is fully accredited by the New England Association of Schools and Colleges as authorized by the Commission on Institutions of Higher Education. Emerson is also accredited by the Council on Academic Accreditation of the American Speech-Language-Hearing Association and the Massachusetts Department of Education.

Location

Emerson College is located in Boston, Massachusetts, the most popular college city in the U.S. Emerson's campus is in the heart of downtown Boston and the city's Theatre District, just steps from the Massachusetts State House, Boston Common, the historic Freedom Trail, Boston Public Garden, Chinatown, and countless restaurants and museums.

Emerson College's Boston campus is located at the gateway to the city's bustling Theatre District, in close proximity to cultural resources, media outlets, and public transportation. It comprises a cluster of nine buildings near the intersection of Boylston and Tremont Streets (adjacent to historic Boston Common) plus the magnificent Paramount Center, a performing arts and residence center on nearby Washington Street. The College also has facilities in Los Angeles and the Netherlands.

The Boston campus has been assembled during the past 30 years as the College moved to the Theatre District from the Back Bay. Since 1993, Emerson has invested more than $500 million in preserving and restoring historic spaces and also creating new facilities. Emerson's decision to create the "Campus on the Common" is widely credited with reviving and revitalizing this section of Boston, attracting the development of private residences, hotels, restaurants, and other retail spaces. Emerson is continuing its legacy of preservation and restoration through its plans to renovate the Little Building, the Colonial Theatre, and create a new residence hall in Boylston Place. When these projects are completed, the College will be able to house nearly 70 percent of its students and will have preserved several additional historic spaces for future generations.

Majors and Degrees

Boston's Emerson College offers Bachelor of Arts, Bachelor of Fine Arts, and Bachelor of Science degrees. Undergraduates can major in acting; business of creative enterprises; comedic arts; communication disorders; communication studies; creative writing; journalism; marketing communication; media arts production; media studies; musical theatre; political communication; production; sports communication; stage and production management; stage and screen design/technology; theatre; theatre design/technology; theatre education; theatre education and performance; theatre and performance; or writing, literature, and publishing. The individually-designed interdisciplinary program also allows students to create their own major from the multitude of programs offered in communication, arts, and the liberal arts with faculty approval.

In addition to Emerson's established majors, Emerson's Interdisciplinary Studies program allows students to design their own major.

Academic Programs

The Institute for Liberal Arts and Interdisciplinary Studies is also home to Emerson's highly competitive Honors Program. Emerson offers a wide range of student support services including the Academic Advising Center, Career Services, disability services, and the Lacerte Family Writing and Academic Resource Center.

Emerson College is committed to creating a campus environment that supports and promotes superior research, premier creative activities, and innovative scholarly pursuits. The mission of the Office of Research and Creative Scholarship (ORCS) is to serve the Emerson community by providing information, personal assistance, services, and programs to those who seek financial support for scholarly endeavors. The Office will also provide college-wide leadership in the development of research and sponsored program activities, and work closely with faculty, staff and senior administrators in shaping the effort to build a more robust program of grants and sponsored research.

Off-Campus Programs

Hundreds of internship placements exist throughout Boston and in major cities across the country, including Emerson College's Los Angeles center—a state-of-the-art facility home to a residential study and internship program in the hub of the global entertainment industry. Emerson also offers a semester-long program in Washington, D.C. Students also have the option to register for courses with six other arts colleges in Boston through the ProArts Consortium.

The Office of Internationalization and Global Engagement (IGE) seeks to enhance global engagement by utilizing Emerson's collective talent, energy, human and financial resources to support compelling transformation and change in international education across disciplines and around the world. Students can study abroad at the college's castle in the Netherlands; additional study abroad opportunities in China, the Czech Republic, Spain, and more.

Academic Facilities

Nearly half of Emerson's facilities are new or renovated since 2002. Students have access to the highest quality equipment, clinical facilities devoted to communication disorders research and treatment, and an integrated digital newsroom for aspiring journalists.

The College also owns more performance space than any other institution in Boston. The eleven-story Tufte Performance and Production Center has rehearsal space, a theatre design/technology center, makeup lab, and costume shop. Emerson's Paramount Center performance facility houses a sound stage, black box theater, scene shop, film screening room, and residence hall. Other performance facilities include the Cutler Majestic Theatre, a 1,200-seat Broadway-style theatre, renovated in 2002, and the Bill Bordy Auditorium and Theater.

Emerson has one of the largest installations of film, video, and audio post-production facilities of any college in the country. Digital production labs contain workstations with multimedia production and digital video/audio applications. Emerson has been designated a New Media Center since 1995. Emerson also has numerous radio, television, and film outlets and facilities:

Clinical facilities include the Robbins Speech, Language and Hearing Center in the Department of Communication Sciences and Disorders. Graduate students work with patients and participate in a variety of Emerson-run clinics that are widely recognized in the field.

In addition, the Iwasaki Library houses more than 180,000 volumes and serial subscriptions, 10,000 microforms, 11,000 audiovisual materials, and 8,000 e-books. Students can access the resources of a dozen cooperating libraries through Emerson College's membership in the Fenway Library Consortium.

Costs

In the 2017–18 academic year, full-time undergraduate student tuition is $44,032, room and board (for a double room) is $16,992, and the student services fee is $800.

Financial Aid

Emerson offers a variety of financial assistance programs. Approximately 75 percent of Emerson's student body receives financial assistance to help pay for their education. Sources of support may include institutional gift aid, academic scholarships, need-based grants, loan programs, work-study, and payment plans. There are also merit scholarships available through the Office of Undergraduate Admission. All applicants are automatically reviewed for eligibility for these merit scholarships once they have submitted their application.

Faculty

With a student-faculty ratio of 15:1, students at Emerson College develop close relationships with remarkably talented and active instructors who are experts in their fields. Emerson's 456 full- and part-time faculty members are nationally recognized and award-winning authors, directors, researchers, producers, journalists, playwrights, actors, and more. The majority of the faculty has earned doctorates or the highest degree obtainable in their field.

Student Life

Emerson students are doers and learners, creating and collaborating even after class is over for the day. The college offers more than 80 student organizations and performance groups, student publications, and honor societies. Emerson also supports 14 NCAA Division III men's and women's athletic teams.

The College has four residence halls, three of which are newly renovated or brand new within the last five years. Students use the nearby Boston Common for relaxation and recreational activities such as tennis, softball, running, Quidditch, and ice-skating. The Field at Rotch Playground, located a mile from campus, serves as a practice and playing field while the Bobbi Brown and Steven Plofker Gym is the site for men's and women's basketball and volleyball games and other events.

Admission Requirements

Admission is competitive; each year, more than 9,100 applications are received for a class of approximately 890. Selection is based on academic promise as indicated by secondary school performance, recommendations, writing competency, and SAT or ACT scores (or TOEFL if English is not the first language). Emerson also considers personal qualities as seen in extracurricular activities, community involvement, and demonstrated leadership.

Application and Information

Emerson College accepts the Common Application and the Emerson Application. Students are required to complete all parts of their chosen application, including the Emerson-specific questions and writing supplement. There are additional requirements for students applying to Performing Arts programs, Comedic Arts, or Media Arts Production.

The deadline for fall admission for first-year students is January 15 (Early Action is November 1), and for transfer students, the deadline is March 15. The spring admission deadline is November 1 for first-year students and transfer students.

Emerson College Admissions
120 Boylston Street
Boston, Massachusetts 02116
United States
Phone: 617-824-8500
E-mail:
Website: www.emerson.edu

EMMANUEL COLLEGE

BOSTON, MASSACHUSETTS

★ To read more about this school, visit http://petersons.to/emmanuelcollege

EMMANUEL COLLEGE

COLLEGE CLOSE-UPS

The College

Emmanuel is a dynamic Catholic liberal arts and sciences college in the heart of Boston. Founded in 1919 by the Sisters of Notre Dame de Namur as the first Catholic college for women in New England, Emmanuel today is a private, coeducational, residential college with a 17-acre campus in the center of Boston's educational, scientific, cultural, and medical communities. The College enrolls 1,800 traditional undergraduate students from 28 states and 52 countries.

At Emmanuel, excellence in the liberal arts and sciences intersects with experiential learning opportunities and scores of co-curricular activities that promote engagement and leadership. The College offers more than 50 majors, minors, and areas of study for undergraduates, along with graduate programs in education, nursing, and management.

Emmanuel and five neighboring colleges comprise the Colleges of the Fenway (COF) consortium, a collaboration that offers cross-registration and joint student life activities at no additional cost. Students benefit from the best of both worlds: living and learning in a small-college setting while enjoying the resources of a larger academic environment. Collectively, the COF represents 12,000 undergraduate students, more than 700 full-time faculty members, and 2,300 course offerings.

Students at Emmanuel College receive personalized attention from orientation to graduation and beyond. The Office of Academic Advising assists in the academic transition from high school to college. Each incoming student is assigned an academic adviser with whom they will explore majors, select courses for each semester, and create a four-year academic plan.

The Career Center supports and guides students in identifying and achieving their career goals, while striving to educate, encourage, and empower students to take an active role in their professional development. The Career Center partners with students and alumni in their internship and job searches and provides career assessments, resume and cover letter review, mock interviews, and more.

Emmanuel College is accredited by the New England Association of Schools and Colleges, Inc. (NEASC) through its Commission on Institutions of Higher Education.

Location

Emmanuel's campus is located in the heart of the Fenway neighborhood, and the area offers much more than the famous ballpark that bears its name.

As a part of the Longwood Medical and Academic Area, Emmanuel is located within a hub of hospitals, colleges, and research institutes, including Dana-Farber Cancer Institute, Harvard Medical School, and Boston Children's Hospital, offering students interested in health care, science, and technology an established network for internships and a head start in developing valuable skills for future careers. Beyond medicine and research, the Fenway is also home to Boston art institutions such as the Museum of Fine Arts and the Isabella Stewart Gardner Museum.

Across the street from campus, the Muddy River offers a front-row seat to Boston's Emerald Necklace, a series of six parks and waterways stretching throughout the city that includes miles of green spaces, bike and running trails, rivers, and ponds.

Majors and Degrees

Emmanuel College offers the following majors and degree programs:

Bachelor of Arts: accounting, American studies (concentrations in cultural studies and American politics and society), art therapy (pre-professional program), economics, education (elementary and secondary), English (concentrations in communication & media studies, literature, and writing & literature), history, international studies (concentrations in diplomacy & security and sustainability & global justice), management (concentrations in marketing and sport management), mathematics, philosophy, political science (concentrations in international relations & comparative politics and American politics & government), psychology (concentrations in counseling & health and developmental psychology), secondary education, Spanish, sociology (concentrations in criminology, human services, and social inequality & social justice), studio art, and theology & religious studies.

Bachelor of Science: biology (concentrations in biochemistry, health sciences, neuroscience, and physiology), biostatistics, chemistry (concentrations in biochemistry and forensic science), and psychology neuroscience.

A **Bachelor of Fine Arts** degree is offered in graphic design.

The **Education** program is a licensure program that prepares students for teaching in the elementary and secondary grade levels. The program complies with licensure requirements established by the Massachusetts Department of Elementary and Secondary Education.

The individualized major is designed for highly motivated and self-directed students whose career goals and intellectual interest can be best served through a carefully constructed program. Students who choose an individualized major work closely with a faculty adviser throughout their program.

Academic Programs

The Arts and Sciences undergraduate program requires a minimum of 128 credit hours and a minimum cumulative grade point average of 2.0 earned through a combination of degree requirements and electives. The degree requirements consist of five components, including proven competency in mathematics, writing communication, and a second language; completion of the Academic Connections for Excellence (ACE) seminar for first-year students; completion of the domains of knowledge program; completion of a major program; and completion of a capstone experience through the major.

Emmanuel College's Honors Program invites talented and motivated students to make the most of their time in college by participating in a rigorous academic and co-curricular experience. While honors students are closely mentored by faculty and staff members, students in the program are encouraged to think creatively, learn independently, and develop their leadership skills across campus. The Honors Program combines reading- and writing-intensive coursework with complementary opportunities that highlight Boston's outstanding music, lectures, arts, theaters, and museums—all of which culminates in a distinction project in each student's individual major.

Off-Campus Programs

In partnership with the Colleges of the Fenway's Global Education Opportunities (GEO) Center, Emmanuel's Office of International Programs offers access to more than 500 study-abroad programs in over 70 countries—from a week at spring break to a summer, a semester, or a year.

Emmanuel faculty also lead academic courses with travel components to countries like Italy, France, Ireland, South Africa and India, among others.

Facilities

The Administration Building, built in 1914, is Emmanuel's oldest and largest building. Recent renovations have ensured it will continue to serve as a bridge from the groundbreaking Emmanuel of the past to the vibrant and dynamic learning environment of the present, from the historic Chapel to high-tech classrooms, which feature dual 80-inch, high-definition LED displays.

The Maureen Murphy Wilkens Science Center is a world-class science center designed to foster interactive learning and community building. The building's four floors include 14 laboratories for biology, chemistry, physics, biochemistry, and neuroscience; multi-purpose classrooms; meeting spaces; and common areas.

Emmanuel's 16 Division III men's and women's varsity athletic teams practice and compete in state-of-the-art facilities including the Jean Yawkey Center Gymnasium, which includes one NCAA regulation court or two full-size practice courts, with bleacher seating for 1,200–1,400. Just steps from campus, city-owned Roberto Clemente Field in the Back Bay Fens serves as home field for Emmanuel softball, soccer, and lacrosse teams, as well as the practice facility for track and field.

The Jean Yawkey Center is the living room of campus, home to the Marian Hall Dining Room, Atrium Café, gymnasium, fitness center, bookstore, and a sunny atrium where students relax between classes and get in some solo or group study time.

The Cardinal Cushing Library offers extensive study space, with individual study carrels and computer stations, as well as large tables for group projects and meetings. The library contains an extensive collection of more than 165,000 volumes in the electronic, circulating, and reference collections; 2,000+ active journal subscriptions in print and online; and more than 60 online database resources. The library is also home to the Academic Resource Center, which offers a variety of services to assist students in their quest for academic excellence.

Costs

Costs for the 2017–18 academic year are $38,584 for tuition, $14,628 for room and board (double occupancy), and $260 in additional fees. Some science lab and studio art classes have additional costs.

Financial Aid

Emmanuel College is committed to making education affordable. Emmanuel supports students by offering merit-based scholarships and need-based grants and by participating in all federal and state grant, scholarship, and loan options. Students applying for financial aid must submit the Free Application for Federal Student Aid (FAFSA) each year by the priority filing date of February 15.

Emmanuel also strives to assist students with educational costs through a robust student employment program. On-campus positions are open to all students eligible for work in the United States, regardless of financial need.

Faculty

Every Emmanuel College class is taught by a professor, not a teaching assistant. Faculty members are also working scholars who publish, present, and secure federal grants, and their accomplishments constantly inform and inspire the curriculum. With a student-faculty ratio of 13:1, Emmanuel undergraduates receive personal attention and have the opportunity to dive into advanced research and explore the depths of their disciplines side-by-side with faculty as early as their freshman year.

Student Clubs and Organizations

Emmanuel offers over 90 clubs and organizations representing academic, political, multicultural, campus and community outreach, creative, artistic, and religious interests, as well as club sports and other special-interest groups. The College's Office of Multicultural Programs strives to offer programs, events, and services that strengthen cultural awareness, promote inclusivity, and affirm identity.

The College also has a long tradition of community service and a commitment to social justice, with many opportunities available through the Office of Mission and Ministry. Opportunities include annual college-wide days of service, weekend service programs, the Four-Year Service Program, Alternative Spring Break, charity events and awareness, and more.

Admission Requirements

Emmanuel College welcomes applications from students across the country and around the world to join a diverse student body that brings a wealth of experience and knowledge to share with the College community. The Office of Admissions considers all aspects of students' records and experience as part of the admissions decision. In addition to a strong secondary school academic program, the College carefully considers what it learns about students through recommendation letters, essays, activities, standardized test scores, and other information.

Required application materials for domestic first-year students includes an application form through the Common Application, an official high school transcript, an essay, and two letters of recommendation. Standardized test scores are optional, and an interview with an admissions counselor, while not required, is recommended.

Application and Information

Emmanuel College uses the Common Application. There are three admissions deadlines for incoming first-year students: Early Action 1 (November 1), Early Action 2 (December 1) or Regular Decision (February 15). Transfer students applying for the fall semester should have all application materials postmarked or submitted electronically by April 1. For first-year or transfer students applying for January admission, applications are due by December 1. For more information, students should contact:

Office of Admissions
Emmanuel College
400 The Fenway
Boston, Massachusetts 02115
Phone: 617-735-9715
Fax: 617-735-9801
E-mail: enroll@emmanuel.edu
Websites: www.emmanuel.edu
www.facebook.com/emmanuelcollege
Twitter: @emmanuelcollege
Instagram: emmanuelcollege

The Emmanuel College quad.

COLLEGE CLOSE-UPS

EMORY & HENRY COLLEGE

EMORY, VIRGINIA

★ For more information, visit http://petersons.to/emoryhenry

The College

Increasing student excellence since 1836, Emory & Henry is a coeducational, private, Methodist-affiliated, liberal arts college in the highlands of southwest Virginia. Emory & Henry (E&H) is accredited by the Southern Association of Colleges and Schools Commission on Colleges to award bachelor's, master's, and doctoral degrees. The College derives its name from John Emory, an eminent Methodist bishop of the era when the College was founded, and Patrick Henry, a renowned Virginian and patriot of the American Revolution. The names represent principles that guide the College yet to this day: the vitality of faith and civic virtue.

Emory & Henry College has distinguished itself in its support of a strong research program in the arts and sciences, explicitly designed to encourage student collaboration and initiative towards academic and personal growth to affect positive social change. A hallmark of the College's civic engagement is its leadership in advancing a pragmatic understanding of sustainable communities and practices.

The College's exceptional faculty is committed to teaching as a transformative practice—an opportunity to inspire students to re-imagine the nature and purpose of their education in order to contribute positive results to our world. The ampersand (&) in the College's name reflects the integrative learning experience at Emory & Henry where students connect what they're passionate about to what they're learning via project-based, hands-on work and critical reflection. E&H students showcase their work to the campus, local, and broader community.

The E&H academic program excels in a broad-based liberal arts education, including pre-professional programs in health services, international studies, the arts, business programs, and teacher education. The E&H School of Health Sciences offers professional programs in health sciences including Doctor of Physical Therapy, Master of Occupational Therapy, and Master of Physician Assistant Studies. The College has developed master's degree programs in Community & Organizational Leadership, American History, Professional Studies, and Reading Specialist.

Emory & Henry College enrolls 1,024 students in the undergraduate population, including students from 8 countries and 30 states with 20 percent diversity.

Emory & Henry's reputation is supported by its numerous accolades, including many that distinguish it from other Virginia colleges. It is one of only 40 institutions recognized in the best-selling guidebook, *Colleges That Change Lives*. The book praises the historic college for the difference it makes in the lives of students. "Virginia has no shortage of familiar schools with robust reputations. But Emory & Henry does the finest job of them all of producing contributors to society," according to the book's author, Hilary Masell Oswald.

Washington Monthly has ranked the College among the top 50 liberal arts colleges and universities in the nation and Forbes magazine ranks its faculty in the top 25 in the nation. *Newsweek* ranks Emory & Henry among the top 5 institutions nationwide in providing service learning. The Corporation for National and Community Service has recognized Emory & Henry College as one of the top service-minded educational institutions in the nation in 2016 in general community service and education community service. In addition, Emory & Henry is named one of six colleges and universities nationwide to receive the President's Award, the highest national recognition for service learning in 2010.

Location

Emory & Henry College's main campus, located in scenic Emory, Virginia, is listed on the National Register of Historic Places and is nestled seven miles north of the historic town of Abingdon, Virginia—home of Barter Theatre, the State Theatre of Virginia. Emory & Henry partners with Barter Theatre to provide theatre students with professional internships, workshops, and master classes throughout the academic year. Some 15 miles further south is Bristol, home to the E&H Equestrian Center and the birthplace of country music—offering a rich downtown experience. Nineteen miles north of Emory is Marion, Virginia., home of the E&H School of Health Sciences, the Lincoln Theatre, and Hungry Mother State Park. The scenic beauty of Emory & Henry College is outstanding among all colleges, as evidenced by the recent Top Outdoor Adventure School award by *Blue Ridge Outdoors* magazine. The area offers an outdoor wonderland with access to the Appalachian Trail and other recreational opportunities including paddling, hiking, climbing, snow skiing, waterskiing, and horseback riding. A virtual tour of campus is available at www.ehc.edu/tour and personalized campus visits are available at www.ehc.edu/visit.

Majors & Degrees

Emory & Henry College excels in liberal arts education and offers a wide range of degree programs including pre-professional programs in health sciences, international studies, the arts, business, and education. Links with additional details about each program can be found at www.ehc.edu/academics.

Academic Facilities

The Ampersand Center offers students access to grants and guidance, with academic research empowered by the extensive collection of knowledge and databases housed at Kelly Library, where students access the technology and research tools that resource hands-on project work. Classrooms are equipped with smart technology with both PC and Mac labs available for student work. Students engage in research and a wide range of projects including internships in conjunction with career services, receiving academic credit for off-campus work in community agencies and businesses. Many Emory & Henry students have completed internships in surrounding communities, while others pursue national internships.

Costs

Tuition for new full-time, resident undergraduate students is fixed for each entering class cohort group. Tuition for the 2017–18 academic year is $34,500, $550 for general residential fees, $200 for the student activity fee, $6,200 for average room, and $5,620 for average board.

Financial Aid

At Emory &Henry, 99 percent of students receive financial aid with 84 percent receiving need-based aid. The average first-year student's scholarship is $27,924.

Faculty

Emory & Henry College professors are among the best in the nation, having been honored by state and national teaching awards nineteen times in the last 29 years. When adjusted for the size of the institution, this record is unmatched by any other Virginia college and is a distinction shared by only a handful of institutions in the nation.

The College has 85 full-time and 63 part-time faculty members; 86 percent of the faculty members hold terminal degrees. The current student-faculty ratio is 11:1. Every student is provided with a faculty advisor who assists in the best selection of courses and offers professional guidance throughout their academic career and beyond.

While faculty members are encouraged to continue study and research, their primary function is teaching. Many professors mentor unique interest groups on campus and live near the campus—making their homes open to students for special events, informal class meetings, or other activities.

Student Life

Emory & Henry College students are actively engaged in making a difference in communities, applying their knowledge and their energy to making positive change. These efforts not only benefit communities, but they also transform the lives of students, helping them see their impact on the world and helping them gain experience that benefits both their careers and their communities well into the future.

Students at Emory & Henry actively run and participate in more than 40 student organizations including the Student Government Association, local Greek chapters, honor societies, the Outdoor Program, spiritual life, highly celebrated musical groups, marching band, student media, service clubs, and multi-cultural organizations.

Emory & Henry offers comfortable, modern, on-campus housing options, including newly constructed or renovated residence halls. Students enjoy a variety of dining options from the main Van Dyke Center Dining Hall to the relaxed atmosphere of the Wow Cafe at the Hut, Stinger's Café, and Macados. Room assignments are based on compatibility information provided on the housing form.

Special student services include the Appalachian Center for Civic Life focused on service and community engagement, and the Powell Resource Center, which offers counseling and disability support and serves as the hub for all student support services to help students through the journey of college life. Other areas of support consist of the Inclusion & Dialogue Center, Writing Center, and Quantitative Literacy Center.

Emory & Henry students participate in a wide variety of study-abroad programs. From Rome to Beijing, students experience cultures and people in a way that enriches their perspectives on their studies and their lives. The College helps students prepare for these experiences through language study and courses offered through a comprehensive international studies program.

Emory & Henry College competes with other U.S. and Virginia colleges, participating in NCAA Division III athletics. It is a member of the respected Old Dominion Athletic Conference (ODAC). Emory & Henry offers 20 men's and women's intercollegiate sports and 22 intramural sports. Men's sports include baseball, basketball, cross-country, equestrian, football, golf, soccer, swimming, track and field, and tennis. Women's sports include basketball, cross-country, equestrian, golf, soccer, softball, swimming, tennis, track and field, and volleyball. The College also offers a coed, competitive cheer and dance team. More information is available at GoWasps.com.

Application and Information

Emory & Henry applicants are encouraged to apply to the College as early as possible to be eligible for the maximum amount of merit scholarships, interest program, and performance awards. Scholarship interviews or audition days are held in the fall semester for students to apply based on specific criteria. Prospective undergraduate students may apply online using the College's online application at www.ehc.edu/apply, or by submitting the Common Application.

Emory & Henry offers early decision options for students desiring to be committed to Emory & Henry as their college choice with Early Action I deadline on November 15, Early Action II Deadline on January 15, and Regular Decision Deadline on April 1. To apply for admission, students should submit the basic application form, their high school transcripts, scores from either the SAT or ACT, and an essay. Students have the option to include a letter of recommendation. Transfer applicants should submit a transcript from any college previously attended and a Dean's Certificate from the last college they were enrolled. The rolling admissions policy allows notification of a decision within two weeks after a file has been completed should students fall outside the application deadlines.

For more information, interested students should contact:

Emory & Henry College
Office of Admissions
P.O. Box 947
Emory, Virginia 24327
Phone: 276-944-6133
800-848-5493 (admissions)
E-mail: admission@ehc.edu
Website: www.ehc.edu

Emory & Henry College is located in beautiful Southwest Virginia boasting access to the region's best outdoor adventure.

THE EVERGREEN STATE COLLEGE

OLYMPIA, WASHINGTON

★ To learn more about this school, visit http://petersons.to/evergreenstate

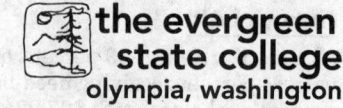

the evergreen state college olympia, washington

The College

The Evergreen State College is a progressive, public liberal arts college located in Olympia, Washington, in the beautiful Pacific Northwest.

Since opening its doors in 1971, Evergreen has established a national reputation for leadership in developing innovative interdisciplinary, collaborative, and team-taught academic programs. The College offers a vibrant undergraduate program, three graduate programs, and public service centers that constitute a unique academic setting.

Evergreen has been a leader in environmental education from the beginning. In recent years, the school has stepped up its commitment to sustainability to reach beyond the classroom and even the campus.

Evergreen values a student-centered learning environment, a link between theory and practice, and a multicultural community of diverse faculty, students, and staff working together. Current enrollment is approximately 4,000.

Location

Evergreen is located in Olympia, Washington, at a cultural crossroad. In one direction lies urban excitement. In another lies outdoor adventure. In yet another there are many homegrown amenities. Its students—known as "Greeners"—have easy access to oceans, mountains, rainforests, and some of America's hippest cities.

Olympia's diverse offerings include a farmer's market and food co-op, the Olympia Film Society and Arts Walk, a rich music scene, the annual Procession of the Species event, and of course, a thriving coffee culture. Local parks provide trails, sports fields, beaches, a skate park, lakes, rivers, waterfalls, and forests.

The cities of Seattle and Portland are a short distance away, as are the Pacific Coast, skiing and snowboarding opportunities, state forests, nature preserves, and three national parks.

Majors and Degrees

Students at Evergreen are challenged to think beyond formal majors and instead can mix a variety of interests to develop their own area of emphasis based on their unique goals. The College offers programs and courses in more than 60 fields of study, including: anthropology; biology and life sciences (biology, botany, health, zoology); business and management; chemistry; cultural and ethnic studies (African American studies, gender and women's studies, international studies, queer studies); economics; education (outdoor leadership and education); environmental studies (agriculture, ecology, field studies, geology, marine science, natural history); geography; history (American studies, classics); language studies (linguistics); literature; mathematics; Native American and indigenous studies; performing arts (dance, music, theater); philosophy (aesthetics, philosophy of science, religious studies); physics (astronomy); political economy and political science (government, law and government policy, law and public policy, political economy, political science); psychology (consciousness studies); sociology; somatic studies; study abroad; sustainability studies; visual and media arts (art history, media arts, media studies, moving image, visual arts); and writing.

Academic Programs

At Evergreen, students experience a different way of learning, with programs that explore the many sides of a theme or topic, and fewer prerequisites. Narrative evaluations from faculty replace competitive grades with meaningful feedback. Students write summative, Academic Statements every year to review and connect common themes in their education each year. When students are ready to graduate, the final statement will act as a cover letter for the narrative evaluations from the faculty in their official transcript.

Evergreen's interdisciplinary programs reflect the real world. Most Evergreen classes, called programs, cover more than just one subject. Full-time programs combine subjects taught by several faculty members from different fields. A program connects these fields with an overarching theme, reflecting the interconnectedness of the real world.

Freshmen students can access top-tier equipment like nuclear magnetic resonance spectroscopes, 3-D printers, and studio cameras, right out of the gate, unlike other colleges that require upper-level experience or research clearance.

Upper-level students create their own program—with the help of a faculty sponsor they set goals, and develop a syllabus as part of their individual learning contract. They also have the opportunity to do research or internships. In addition, focused courses (2–6 credits) are available to complement their course of study. Students learn how to be an active, engaged citizen no matter which career they choose.

Eighty-eight percent of Evergreen graduates are employed or pursuing graduate or professional studies within one year of graduation. The school's three graduate programs—Master's in Environmental Studies, Master's in Public Administration, and Master's in Teaching—ground students in values of service, community, social justice, and stewardship.

Costs

Evergreen's great education comes at a modest price. Greeners benefit from having the fastest time to degree completion among Washington's public four-year institutions. That means less in total costs for students. Those who borrow while attending Evergreen typically borrow below state and national averages (source: State of Washington Education Research and Data Center).

Estimated cost of attendance for the 2016–17 academic year included tuition ($6,534 for Washington residents and $23,007 for nonresidents); room and board, $9,360; books and supplies, $750; transportation, $1,125; and miscellaneous, $2,055; for a total of $19,824 (resident) or $36,297 (nonresident).

Financial Aid

Sixty-four percent of Greeners receive financial aid. The average award is $12,714. The Financial Aid Counselors encourage all students to use the Free Application for Federal Student Aid (FAFSA) to apply for federal and state aid. Evergreen's priority deadline to receive complete and valid information from the federal processor is February 1. Evergreen's school code is 008155. Undocumented Washington resident students can apply through the Washington Application for State Financial Aid (WASFA). The priority deadline for the WASFA is also February 1.

Evergreen offers a variety of scholarships every year to new and continuing students. Some awards are based upon academic fields of study: the arts, computer studies, environmental studies, laboratory sciences and writing, for example. Students should review the scholarship application process and be prepared to submit their applications by the February 1 deadline.

Faculty

Evergreen's instructional faculty numbers 224, with 157 of those being full time. Of those, 80.8 percent have a Ph.D. or terminal degree in their field. The undergraduate student to faculty ratio is 22:1.

Campus Culture

The Evergreen experience is unique. Whether it's through athletics, recreation, or the arts, Greeners do things a little bit better, or smarter, or just differently. Through the Geoduck Student Union, students are empowered to get involved in positive social and political change, shape campus culture, and make college life better, year after year.

When it comes to campus housing, students can choose what's right for their lifestyle. Whether students prefer same-gender living arrangements or vegan eating, Evergreen can accommodate most lifestyle pursuits. First-year students will live in the residence halls. Apartments and modular housing become available after that.

Campus dining offers the community opportunities to spend quality time together. The Greenery, The Marketplace, The Flaming Eggplant, and other venues are ready to serve the dining needs of students.

Admission Requirements

Applicants must be high school graduates who have met basic college-preparatory standards (4 credits English, 3 credits mathematics, 3 credits social studies, 2 credits of a single foreign language, and 2 credits of science) and taken challenging electives beyond that. Grade point average and test scores will be used in the comprehensive admission review process. The average GPA for freshmen admitted in 2015 was 3.15. The average SAT composite (critical reading and math) score was 1084 and the average ACT composite test score was 24. The SAT writing test and subject tests are not required. Good standing in any college-level work attempted while in high school or after high school graduation is also required. The quality of the college work will be taken into consideration as well.

Requirements for home-school students, GED applicants, applicants with a high school proficiency exam, or who are 25 or older can be found on the College's website (http://evergreen.edu/admissions/requirements/freshman.htm).

Application and Information

Potential students can apply online or via mail. There is a $50 nonrefundable application fee. Evergreen accepts e-transcripts from other schools and colleges that are registered members with Docufide, National Student Clearinghouse, Naviance, Parchment, and Scrip-Safe International. Please make sure that the school or college is a registered member before requesting the e-transcript. Official transcripts sent through the mail must arrive in a sealed envelope from the issuing school/college registrar. ACT or SAT scores for incoming freshmen should be sent by the testing agency. Evergreen's ACT school code is 4457 and the SAT school code is 4292.

The priority admission application deadline is February 1 for the fall quarter, October 1 for the winter quarter, and December 1 for the spring quarter.

In most cases, admission decision letters are sent within 10 working days after the application file is complete and/or has been reviewed by the Admissions Committee.

For more information, students should contact:

The Evergreen State College
Office of Admissions
2700 Evergreen Pkwy NW
Olympia, Washington 98505
Phone: 360-867-6170
Fax: 360-867-5114
E-mail: admissions@evergreen.edu
Website: http://evergreen.edu/home

FASHION INSTITUTE OF TECHNOLOGY
State University of New York

FIT Fashion Institute of Technology
State University of New York

NEW YORK, NEW YORK

★ To read more about this school, visit http://petersons.to/fit

The College

The Fashion Institute of Technology (F.I.T.), a college of the State University of New York, has been a leader in career education in art, design, business, and technology for more than 70 years. FIT infuses its nearly 50 majors with a comprehensive liberal arts education, providing students with a singular blend of hands-on, practical experience and a pioneering curriculum that prepares them for success and leadership in the intensely competitive global marketplace. FIT offers a wide range of outstanding programs that are affordable and relevant to today's rapidly changing industries. Internationally renowned, FIT draws on its New York City location to provide a vibrant, creative community in which to learn. The schools of Art and Design, Business and Technology, and Liberal Arts offer programs leading to Associate in Applied Science (A.A.S.), Bachelor of Fine Arts (B.F.A.), and Bachelor of Science (B.S.) degrees. The School of Graduate Studies offers seven programs leading to Master of Arts (M.A.), Master of Fine Arts (M.F.A.), and Master of Professional Studies (M.P.S.) degrees. The college is accredited by the Middle States Commission on Higher Education, the National Association of Schools of Art and Design, and the Council for Interior Design Accreditation. FIT serves approximately 10,000 students from the greater metropolitan area, New York State, across the country, and around the world, providing full- and part-time study, evening/weekend degree programs, and online studies. Job placement rates for bachelor's and associate degree graduates who responded to a recent survey were 90 and 70 percent respectively.

FIT's faculty members bring high-level industry experience to the classroom, working as corporate executives, entrepreneurs, consultants, designers, artists, and authors. Both practitioners and scholars, they connect students with real-world practice in their fields, fostering collaboration, innovation, and a global perspective. Academic departments consult with industry leaders to ensure that the curriculum and classroom technology remain current with evolving professional practices.

FIT offers a complete college experience, with a vibrant campus life. Four residence halls house 2,300 students. Residential counselors and student staff members live in the residence halls, helping students adjust to college life and New York City.

The college hosts more than sixty student organizations and clubs, related to academics, athletics, special interests, and publications, including a campus newspaper, a fashion and beauty magazine, and an art and literary magazine. Intercollegiate teams and individual sports include cross-country, track and field, tennis, women's soccer, swimming and diving, and women's volleyball. Students take part in an array of fitness classes, including aerobics, dance, spin, and yoga, and they can work out in a 5,000 square-foot fitness center.

The David Dubinsky Student Center houses a dining hall and Starbucks café, game room, radio station, student-run boutique, student government and club offices, dance studio, health services, disability services, and counseling center.

Location

Occupying an entire block in Manhattan's Chelsea neighborhood, FIT's campus offers a vibrant urban experience. This location, at the heart of the fashion, advertising, visual arts, design, business, and communications industries, provides students unparalleled exposure to their fields through internships, field trips, mentorships, and industry-sponsored research and competitions. A wide range of cultural resources and entertainment options—from dining to museums to theater—are available within walking distance from campus, which is also convenient to subway and bus lines and major rail and bus transportation hubs.

Majors and Degrees

FIT offers fifteen Associate in Applied Science (A.A.S.) and twenty-six baccalaureate programs. All first-time students complete a two-year A.A.S. program in their major area of study and then typically continue in a related, two-year Bachelor of Fine Arts (B.F.A.) or Bachelor of Science (B.S.) program. Some students choose to begin their careers after earning the A.A.S., which qualifies them for entry-level positions in their chosen field. All programs include a required liberal arts component. In addition, FIT offers a variety of minors that students may elect to complete.

The School of Art and Design offers ten A.A.S. and fourteen B.F.A. programs and two minors; the Jay and Patty Baker School of Business and Technology offers four A.A.S. and ten B.S. programs and one minor; and the School of Liberal Arts offers one A.A.S. and two B.S. programs and twenty-two minors. There is one interdisciplinary minor shared by all three undergraduate schools.

The fifteen A.A.S. programs, all of which provide the foundation for one or more corresponding baccalaureate-level programs, are accessories design*, advertising and marketing communications*, communication design foundation*, fashion design*, fashion business management* (with an online option), film and media, fine arts, illustration, interior design, jewelry design, menswear, photography and related media, production management: fashion and related industries, textile development and marketing*, and textile/surface design*. Programs with an * are also available as a one-year option for students with transfer credits, and the one-year fashion business management A.A.S. program is offered fully online.

The fourteen B.F.A. programs are accessories design, advertising design, computer animation and interactive media, fabric styling, fashion design (specializations in children's wear, intimate apparel, knitwear, special occasion, and sportswear), fine arts, graphic design, illustration, interior design, packaging design, photography and related media, textile/surface design, toy design, and visual presentation and exhibition design.

The twelve B.S. programs are advertising and marketing communications, art history and museum professions, cosmetics and fragrance marketing, direct and interactive marketing, entrepreneurship for the fashion and design industries, fashion business management, film and media, home products development, international trade and marketing for the fashion industries, production management: fashion and related industries, technical design, and textile development and marketing.

Nine of the degree programs are also available through evening/weekend study: advertising and marketing communications (A.A.S. and B.S.), communication design foundation (A.A.S.), fashion design (A.A.S.), fashion business management (A.A.S. and B.S.), graphic design (B.F.A.), illustration (B.F.A.), and international trade and marketing for the fashion industries (B.S.). The international trade and marketing program (B.S.) and the fashion business management program (A.A.S. only) are also available fully online.

Academic Programs

FIT's liberal arts courses hone critical thinking and communication skills, foster understanding of world cultures, and encourage students to become global citizens. Liberal arts courses are a key component of every major, and are adapted to the needs of each program. FIT's curriculum offers a range of subject-based and interdisciplinary minors that let students expand and deepen their major studies or explore additional interests. Liberal Arts minors include communication studies, dance, film and media, economics, international politics, Latin American studies, Mandarin Chinese, and women and gender studies; Art and Design minors are creative technology and design thinking; the Business and Technology minor is international trade and marketing; the ethics and sustainability minor is offered jointly through all three schools.

The Career and Internship Center offers lifetime placement services to graduates. Internships are a required element of many programs and are available to all students. Nearly one-third of FIT student interns are offered employment on completion of their internships.

The Presidential Scholars honors program, available to academically exceptional students in all disciplines, offers special liberal arts courses, projects, colloquiums, extracurricular activities, and off-campus visits designed to broaden horizons and stimulate discourse. Presidential Scholars are also awarded priority course registration and an annual merit stipend.

Precollege programs (fitnyc.edu/precollege) are available to middle and high school students during the fall, spring, and summer. More than 100 courses provide the chance to learn in an innovative environment, to develop art and design portfolios, to explore the business and technological sides of a wide range of creative careers, and to discover natural talents and abilities.

The Center for Continuing and Professional Studies (fitnyc.edu/ccps) provides courses for students and working professionals to pursue a certificate or further their knowledge in a particular area.

Off-Campus Programs

FIT has two campuses in Italy—one in Milan, one in Florence—where students study fashion design or fashion business management and gain firsthand experience in the dynamics of European fashion. The study-abroad experience allows students to immerse themselves in diverse cultures and prepares them to live and work in a global community. Australia, China, England, France, and Mexico are some of the other countries where FIT offers study-abroad courses. Students can study abroad during the winter or summer sessions, or for a semester or a full academic year.

Academic Facilities

FIT provides its students with an urban campus of classrooms, laboratories, and studios that reflect the most advanced educational and professional practices. The Fred P. Pomerantz Art and Design Center houses studios, a printmaking room, display and exhibition design rooms, a model-making workshop, and a graphics printing service bureau. The Peter G. Scotese Computer-Aided Design and Communications Center allows students to explore the latest advancements in technology and their integration in design, photography, and computer graphics and animation. The fragrance studio, a professionally equipped fragrance development laboratory, is the only one of its kind on a U.S. college campus. Cutting and sewing laboratories offer the most advanced design and cutting machinery among educational facilities in the United States. The lighting laboratory, an educational and professional development facility, features more than 400 commercially available lighting fixtures. Other college facilities include a broadcasting studio, knitting and weaving labs, a multimedia foreign language laboratory, forty-six computer labs, and several additional labs with computers reserved for students in specific programs.

The Museum at FIT is New York City's only museum dedicated to fashion. Students, designers, and historians use it for research and inspiration. The museum, which is accredited by the American Alliance of Museums, operates year-round, and its exhibitions are free and open to the public. The Gladys Marcus Library provides more than 300,000 volumes of print, nonprint, and electronic materials. Students also have access to the library's Special Collections, a highly specialized repository of primary source research materials related to the fields of fashion and design. The library also offers specialized resources, such as clipping files, fashion and trend forecasting services, and sketch collections.

Costs

For 2016–17, the associate-level tuition per semester was $2,295 for in-state residents and $6,885 for nonresidents. Baccalaureate-level tuition per semester was $3,235 for in-state residents and $9,796 for nonresidents. Undergraduate housing costs ranged from $6,693 to $6,892 per semester for traditional residence hall accommodations with mandatory meal plan and from $6,175 to $10,289 for apartment-style accommodations. Meal plans varied from $1,851 to $2,369 per semester. Textbook costs and other nominal fees, such as locker rental or laboratory use, vary per program. Costs are subject to change.

Financial Aid

FIT attempts to remove financial barriers to college entrance by providing scholarships, grants, loans, and work-study employment for students in financial need. Over two-thirds of full-time, matriculated undergraduate students who complete the Free Application for Federal Student Aid (FAFSA) process receive some type of assistance through loans and/or grants. The college directly administers its own institutional grants and scholarships, which are provided by the FIT Foundation.

College-administered federal funding includes Federal Pell Grants, Federal Perkins Loans, Federal Supplemental Educational Opportunity Grants, Federal Work-Study, and Federal Family Educational Loans, which include student and parent loans. New York State residents who meet state guidelines for eligibility may also receive Tuition Assistance Program (TAP) and/or Educational Opportunity Program (EOP) grants.

Financial aid applicants must file the FAFSA. Students are also encouraged to apply for all available outside sources of aid. Additional documentation may be requested by the Financial Aid Services office. The FAFSA should be completed prior to February 15 for fall applicants or prior to November 1 for spring applicants.

Faculty

FIT's faculty is drawn from top professionals who bring their industry experience to the classroom and introduce students to the real-world opportunities and challenges of their disciplines through field trips, guest lectures, and sponsored competitions. Student-instructor interaction is encouraged, with no class larger than 25 and more often smaller, and courses are structured to foster participation, independent thinking, and self-expression.

Student Government

The FIT Student Government Association gives all students the privileges and responsibilities of citizens in a self-governing college community. Many faculty committees include student representatives, and the president of the student government sits on FIT's Board of Trustees.

Admission Requirements

Applicants for undergraduate admission must be either candidates for or recipients of a high school diploma or a General Educational Development (GED) certificate. Admission is based on strength and performance in college-preparatory course work and the student essay. A portfolio evaluation is required for art and design majors. Specific portfolio requirements are explained on FIT's website. SAT and ACT scores are required for placement in math and English classes and for students applying to the Presidential Scholars honors program. International applicants whose native language is not English must submit scores from either the TOEFL, IELTS, or PTE examinations.

Transfer applicants must submit official transcripts from all post-secondary institutions attended for both admission and credit evaluation. Transfers students may qualify for the one-year A.A.S. option if they hold a baccalaureate degree from an accredited college or if they have a minimum of 30 transferable credits from an accredited college, including 24 credits that are equivalent to FIT's liberal arts requirements.

Students seeking admission to a B.F.A. or B.S. program must hold an A.A.S. degree from FIT or an equivalent degree from an accredited college. They must also meet the appropriate prerequisites for the specific major and must have completed FIT's liberal arts requirements. Further requirements may include an individual interview with a department committee, review of academic standing, and a portfolio review (for applicants to B.F.A. programs). Any student who applies for transfer to FIT from a four-year program must have completed a minimum of 60 credits, including the requisite art or technical courses and the liberal arts requirements.

Application and Information

Students interested in FIT's undergraduate programs are encouraged to attend an information session and take a student-led tour of the campus. The visit schedule is available online at fitnyc.edu/visitfit. A virtual tour of the campus can be found online at fitnyc.edu/virtualtour. Interested candidates may apply online at fitnyc.edu/admissions.

For more information, students should contact:

Undergraduate Admissions
Fashion Institute of Technology
227 West 27th Street, Room C139
New York, NY 10001-5992
Phone: 212-217-3760
E-mail: fitinfo@fitnyc.edu
Website: fitnyc.edu/admissions
facebook.com/FashionInstituteofTechnology
instagram.com/fitnyc
twitter.com/fit

FLORIDA SOUTHERN COLLEGE

LAKELAND, FLORIDA

★ To read more about this school, visit http://petersons.to/floridasoutherncollege

The College

The oldest private college in the state, Florida Southern College (FSC) was chartered in 1883 and settled on the shores of the spectacular Lake Hollingsworth in Lakeland in 1922.

Today, Florida Southern is a nationally ranked residential, coeducational, and comprehensive college recognized for its commitment to providing engaged learning experiences to its students. Florida Southern's 2,500 students represent nearly every state and fifty countries. Students choose Florida Southern because of its national reputation for dynamic, hands-on learning in an atmosphere that is friendly and personal.

Experiencing the world beyond the classroom is an essential part of a Florida Southern education. Along with providing ample opportunities to conduct lab and field research, become involved in community service, and perform, Florida Southern guarantees each student an internship and study abroad experience. Florida Southern also guarantees its students will graduate in four years.

Members of the community take great pride in the beautiful campus, a historic landmark and home to the world's largest single-site collection of buildings designed by renowned architect Frank Lloyd Wright.

As a residential community, Florida Southern provides its students with a wide range of housing options, including all-female and all-male halls, coed halls, suite-style living arrangements, and off-campus apartments. The College also dedicates spaces to various majors, honors students, and fraternity and sorority life. Accommodations are well equipped and feature stunning views of the lake, contemporary student lounges, modern kitchens and bathrooms, and wireless Internet access.

Athletic facilities are first rate. The George Jenkins Field House includes a three-court gymnasium, a weight room, and an athletic training room. The College recently began a multi-million dollar renovation to the Barnett Athletic Complex providing state-of-the-art facilities for softball, soccer, and lacrosse. The popular Nina B. Hollis Wellness Center, the hub of student life, offers a fully equipped fitness center, an aerobics/dance studio, an intramural gymnasium, racquetball courts, and a competition-sized swimming pool. Directly across from the Wellness Center is Lake Hollingsworth, which offers kayaks, paddleboards, and water-skiing.

The student body is extremely involved. With more than eighty clubs, Florida Southern offers countless ways for students to pursue their interests while making lasting connections. Florida Southern is also home to 14 national fraternities and sororities. FSC's Moccasins are members of NCAA Division II. The nineteen varsity programs, including men's and women's lacrosse teams and a nationally ranked water-skiing team and equestrian club, have won 29 national championship titles. Other popular student activities are intramural sports, drama and music groups, publications, and organizations related to academic and political, religious, and social interests. A high percentage of students are involved in volunteer programs in the community, state, and internationally.

Location

Florida Southern's campus consists of approximately 113 acres on the shore of Lake Hollingsworth in Lakeland, Florida, a dynamic suburban community of about 120,000 residents in the heart of Florida's High-Tech Corridor. The campus is within walking distance of Lakeland's historic downtown, and Lakeland is 40 miles east of Tampa and 50 miles west of Orlando. Within an hour's drive of the state's major recreational attractions, including Walt Disney World and award-winning beaches, the College is ideally situated for internships and job opportunities with leading corporations that tap into one of the largest markets in the United States. Students enjoy Festival of Fine Arts series performances in music, dance, and drama, distinguished speakers, and business symposiums. The local Lakeland Center also offers many cultural and entertainment opportunities.

Majors and Degrees

Florida Southern College offers Bachelor of Arts, Bachelor of Fine Arts, Bachelor of Music, Bachelor of Music Education, Bachelor of Science, and Bachelor of Science in Nursing degrees in more than fifty majors including accounting, art (art education, art history, graphic design, and studio art), biochemistry and molecular biology, biology, biotechnology, business administration (career tracks in finance, international business, management, and marketing), business and free enterprise, chemistry, citrus, communication (advertising and public relations, digital media, film studies, multimedia journalism, interpersonal and organizational communication, political communication, and sports communication), computer science, criminology, dance, economics and finance, education (elementary, music, and secondary), English, exercise science, history, healthcare administration, humanities, marine biology, mathematics, music (music education, music management, and music performance), nursing, philosophy, political economy, political science, psychology, religion, social science, Spanish, sports management, theater arts (musical theater, theater performance, and technical theater/design), and youth ministry.

Outstanding pre-professional programs are offered in dentistry, engineering, law, medicine, pharmacy, physical therapy, theology, and veterinary medicine. Florida Southern's pre-law program boasts a 100 percent acceptance rate into law school, with similar results for pre-med students. One hundred percent of accounting majors pass the CPA exam and go on to find jobs. The School of Education and School of Health Sciences also have 100 percent placement rates for their education and nursing majors, respectively.

An honors program provides special opportunities for a select group of entering first-year students to explore topics of common interest in an integrated and interdisciplinary fashion.

Academic Programs

Florida Southern's rigorous degree programs require the satisfactory completion of a minimum of 124 semester hours with a minimum grade point average of 2.0. Students and professors work together in discussion-based classes featuring debate, collaborative projects, and other forms of engaged learning. The College operates on the semester system, with two 15-week semesters, and summer sessions. The average course load is 16 hours per semester. Along with course work in their major, students are required to complete a general education curriculum designed to help develop knowledge, communication, and critical-thinking skills, as well as attitudes for lifelong success.

As part of FSC's engaged-learning model, students work collaboratively with faculty on research, fieldwork, and service projects. For example, business students have established strategic plans and operational reports for corporate and nonprofit organizations. Nursing students have delivered babies in Tanzania, and chemistry students have collaborated with faculty members to become published in national academic journals, such as *The Journal of Physical Chemistry*. Fine arts students have performed alongside talented faculty and visiting performers. Regardless of their course of study, Florida Southern students graduate with the real-world experience employers seek.

The FSC experience is career focused from day one. The College's career counselors help students explore their strengths and provide continual evaluation of career options with personalized guidance on resume building, interviewing, and landing the ideal first post-college job.

An honors program provides special opportunities for a select group of entering first-year students to explore topics of common interest in an integrated and interdisciplinary fashion.

Off-campus Programs

Entering first-year students are guaranteed a travel-study opportunity during their junior or senior year at Florida Southern. Students have traveled to Africa, the Caribbean, China, Costa Rica, England, France, Italy, Mexico, Washington, D.C., and other exciting destinations.

Florida Southern College is also affiliated with The Washington Center (TWC), a highly regarded, nonpartisan internship provider with international scope. As the only private institution of higher education in the state to affiliate with TWC, FSC students have access to prestigious and valuable field experiences. Programs include tailored academic seminars and internships with governmental, international, corporate, and nonprofit organizations.

Academic Facilities

The FSC campus combines beautiful landscape with modern buildings designed by world-famous architects.

The campus's newest addition is the 40,000-square-foot Becker Business Building, designed by renowned architect Robert A. M. Stern. This premiere business education center features high-tech classrooms equipped with the latest educational technology. It also houses a simulated trading floor that functions as a laboratory in which students learn firsthand about investment analysis and trading strategies. The technologically advanced Joe K. and Alberta Blanton Nursing Building, home to the College's growing School of Nursing, features patient simulators in the state-of-the art treatment simulation laboratory. The Dr. Marcene H. and Robert E. Christoverson Humanities Building comprises contemporary classrooms along with language labs and the film studies center. The recently renovated, Frank Lloyd Wright's Polk Science Building is home to FSC's natural science and pre-medical programs and is outfitted with a wide range of cutting-edge instrumentation, such as a nuclear magnetic resonance spectrometer, the preeminent device in determining the structure of chemical compounds. The building also features the world's only Wright-designed planetarium.

The Marshall and Vera Lea Rinker Technology Center is the nucleus for learning on campus. It houses the College's main computer lab, classrooms, and small group study areas and provides students with the latest technologies.

An integral part of the intellectual life of the College, FSC's E. T. Roux Library provides access to a rich collection of materials, including print and digital books; periodicals; electronic databases; a media collection that includes CDs, DVDs, and CD-ROMs; a substantial microforms collection; and seating for almost 500 students. The Library is also home to TûTû's Cyber Café, a comfortable venue for club meetings as well as late-night study groups. Adjacent is the Sarah D. and L. Kirk McKay, Jr., Archives Center that houses the archival materials of the Florida Conference of the United Methodist Church, the Center for Florida History collection, the Florida Citrus Archives, along with the College's collection of Frank Lloyd Wright memorabilia.

The campus also boasts a fine arts complex that includes Branscomb Memorial Auditorium (seating 1,800 and nationally known for its perfect acoustics), the Marjorie M. McKinley Music Building, the Melvin Art Gallery, and the Loca Lee Buckner Theater.

Florida Southern is also home to a preschool lab and the Roberts Academy, the first transitional school for children with dyslexia in the state of Florida, each providing an opportunity for students majoring in elementary education to observe and teach.

Costs

The comprehensive cost for 2017–18 is $45,978 per year ($34,774 for tuition and standard fees and $11,204 for room and board). FSC estimates that $1,150 is adequate for books and supplies, and $1,500 should cover personal expenses, exclusive of travel to and from home.

Financial Aid

Consistently rated as a best value, 98 percent of all FSC students receive financial assistance. Each year, Florida Southern offers more than $20 million in college aid on the basis of academic merit; talent in athletics (baseball, basketball, cross-country, golf, soccer, softball, swimming, tennis, volleyball, or lacrosse), fine arts, theater, leadership, or community service; or student need. The College's most talented applicants are invited to apply for several of the College's Prestige Scholarships, which cover up to the full cost of tuition and fees, as well as additional stipends for study abroad.

Florida Southern understands that everyone's financial situation is different and offers students assistance in meeting their educational expenses through scholarships, grants, loans, and campus employment. To demonstrate need, an applicant is required to file the Free Application for Federal Student Aid (FAFSA). Applicants for aid must reapply each year. Florida Southern participates in the Federal Perkins Loan, Federal Supplemental Educational Opportunity Grant, and Federal Work-Study college-based programs. All applicants are expected to apply for any entitlement grant for which they are eligible, such as a Federal Pell Grant and, for Florida residents, the Florida Student Assistance Grant. The Federal Stafford Direct Student Loan Program is also available. To be considered for these aid programs, a completed FAFSA must be filed; the priority-filing deadline is March 1.

Faculty

FSC faculty members are more than professors—they also function as advisers, mentors, and a true partner in a student's learning. The student-faculty ratio is 13:1 and 86 percent of Florida Southern's faculty members have doctoral or other terminal degrees. Not only are they top scholars in their fields, but they are also devoted to providing students with personalized attention and a truly outstanding education. Faculty members are selected for their teaching abilities and their ability to relate to the needs and concerns of their students.

Admission Requirements

Florida Southern looks for two things in applicants: performance and promise. The majority of students who have been accepted have a weighted GPA of 3.7 or better in college-preparatory courses (including four courses in English, three in mathematics, and the balance divided among science, foreign language, and social science), and have earned an average SAT score of 1138 (combined reading and math scores) or a composite score of 26 on the ACT. All applicants must graduate from an accredited high school.

The Admissions Office is committed to reviewing individual applicants on their own merits based on the level of challenge attempted, patterns of grades over time, recommendations from references, and an applicant's own assessment of the learning environment best suited to his or her needs. Evidence of leadership and community service also are typical attributes of a successful applicant. Applicants are encouraged to visit campus and meet with an Admissions Counselor. (Qualified high school juniors may apply for early admission if they have the recommendation of their secondary school and have had a personal interview with the Director of Admissions.)

Florida Southern welcomes applications from students resuming their education and from older students who have delayed their entrance into college. The College typically enrolls 100 transfer students annually. Transfer applicants should have a minimum 2.5 grade point average and eligible to return to or be graduates of their former institutions. Transfer students with fewer than 25 semester hours must submit high school transcripts and standardized test scores. Applicants who hold Associate of Arts degrees from regionally accredited two-year institutions are typically granted junior standing. All applicants are encouraged to interview; an interview may be required for some candidates.

Credit by examination is awarded on the basis of successful scores on Advanced Placement tests, the International Baccalaureate (I.B.), Advanced International Certificate of Education (AICE), and College-Level Examination Program (CLEP) tests.

Application and Information

An application is considered by the Admissions Committee when it has been received with required test scores, references, and transcripts from each school attended. Because all students are required to live on campus unless they are seniors, married, or living with their parents, early application is desirable to ensure that housing is available. The freshman application priority date is March 1. The deadline for early decision applicants is December 1.

For more information about Florida Southern College, prospective students should contact:

Office of Admissions
Florida Southern College
111 Lake Hollingsworth Drive
Lakeland, Florida 33801-5698
Phone: 800-274-4131 (toll-free)
E-mail: fscadm@flsouthern.edu
Website: http://www.flsouthern.edu

Florida Southern College is a comprehensive, selective, residential college ideally located in historic Lakeland, midway between Tampa and Orlando.

GANNON UNIVERSITY

ERIE, PENNSYLVANIA

★ To read more about this school, visit http://petersons.to/gannonuniversity

Believe in the possibilities.

The University

Gannon University is a Catholic, diocesan university founded in 1925 and dedicated to excellence in teaching, scholarship and service. The faculty and staff prepare students to be global citizens through programs grounded in the liberal arts, sciences and professional specializations. Inspired by the Catholic Intellectual Tradition, Gannon offers a comprehensive, values-centered learning experience that emphasizes faith, leadership, inclusiveness, and social responsibility.

Gannon consistently receives high marks from *U.S. News & World Report*; the 2017 edition of *America's Best Colleges* recognized Gannon as one of the top ten "Best Value Schools" among regional universities in the north region. Gannon University also earned national recognition as a 2016–17 Catholic College of Distinction, one of 74 across the nation to have been selected.

Located in downtown Erie, Pennsylvania, Gannon is close to businesses, organizations and government agencies that are active partners in helping students receive hands-on learning. The campus includes the Recreation and Wellness Center, which recently underwent an expansion project that included a complete interior renovation, new cardio equipment and new locker rooms. Gannon's residence halls, apartments, academic buildings, administrative offices and chapel are centered around the Waldron Campus Center—the heart of Gannon's campus—where members of the University's close-knit community meet, dine, study and socialize.

Student-athletes excel at Gannon in NCAA Division II intercollegiate athletics. Men's teams include baseball, basketball, cross-country, football, golf, soccer, swimming and diving, water polo and wrestling. Women's teams include acrobatics and tumbling, basketball, competitive cheer, cross-country, golf, lacrosse, soccer, softball, swimming and diving, volleyball and water polo. Many of Gannon's athletes compete at the McConnell Family Stadium, a multipurpose athletic field that is conveniently located on campus. New to the Recreation and Wellness Center is a 51,300 square-foot, indoor field house that features an 80-yard practice facility for all teams and students to use. Gannon also offers students a year-round intramural and club sports program.

The student body consists of more than 4,400 students, 2,672 of whom are undergraduates. The Student Success Center provides students with internship placement, career development, employment assistance and tutoring services.

Location

Gannon is located in Pennsylvania's fourth-largest city, within walking distance of shops, restaurants, theaters and professional sports venues. Gannon's urban campus is within a two-hour drive of Cleveland, Buffalo and Pittsburgh. Its unique location and facilities create a special atmosphere conducive to learning, scholarship, research, service and personal growth. The campus is within five miles of Interstates 79 and 90, and five miles from Erie International Airport. Erie is also serviced by rail and bus transportation.

Majors and Degrees

In the College of Humanities, Education and Social Sciences, areas of study are: advertising communication, communication arts, criminalistics, criminal justice, English (with concentrations in applied communications, literature, and writing), foreign language and international studies, foreign language and literature, history, interdisciplinary studies, international studies, journalism communications, legal studies, mortuary science, performance for media and stage, philosophy, political science, prelaw, a 3+3 prelaw program that includes early admission to Duquesne University, psychology, social work, theatre and communication arts, theatre technologies and design and theology.

In the School of Education, the areas of study are early childhood education PreK–4, early childhood education PreK–4/special education PreK–8, middle level education 4–8 and secondary education (in biology, English, mathematics and social studies).

The Morosky College of Health Professions and Sciences offers degrees including: athletic training (master's), medical laboratory science, nursing, nutrition and human performance, occupational therapy (five-year direct-entry master's and a doctorate offered at the Ruskin, Florida campus), physical therapy (direct-entry doctorate), physician assistant (five-year direct-entry master's), public health, radiologic sciences, respiratory care, sport and exercise science, and undecided health science. Also offered are 14 pre-professional programs for students who wish to enter chiropractic, dental, medical, optometry, pharmacy, podiatry or veterinary school, as well as accelerated and cooperative programs for all options.

Degrees are also offered in biochemistry, biology, chemical engineering (cooperative program), chemistry, environmental science, forensic science, freshwater and marine biology, mathematics and science.

The College of Engineering and Business offers degrees in biomedical engineering, computer science, electrical engineering (including a five-year co-op program), environmental engineering, environmental science, industrial engineering, information systems, mechanical engineering (including a five-year co-op program) and software engineering.

Programs in the Dahlkemper School of Business include accounting, entrepreneurship, finance, healthcare management, international management, management, marketing, risk management and insurance, sport management and marketing, and supply chain management. All business students are encouraged to participate in an internship before graduation.

Academic Programs

A faculty adviser is assigned to each student to assist with academic planning. A department chairperson and faculty adviser also assist in selecting courses that fulfill requirements and meet the student's desired career objectives. The basic graduation requirements for bachelor's degree candidates are 128 credit hours, including completion of requirements for the major and the liberal studies program. Associate degree students must complete 60 to 68 credit hours, depending on the program. Students may receive credit through the Advanced Placement program.

Gannon offers a program for students with learning disabilities (PSLD) and an Army ROTC program.

Gannon's academic calendar consists of two full semesters, running from August to December and from January to May. There are also optional summer classes.

Academic Facilities

Beyer Hall reopened this year, after a 40,000 square-foot expansion project created a collaborative space where students from around the world can come together to learn, participate in campus life and organizations, and discover ways to engage the world.

Programs such as advertising communication, communication arts, journalism, and theatre are housed in the Center for Communication and the Arts. This building provides state-of-the-art technology and houses Gannon's award-winning radio station, 90.5 WERG, and its student newspaper, *The Gannon Knight*.

All business courses are now held in the Center for Business Ingenuity, which is also home to Gannon's Small Business Development Center and the Erie Technology Incubator. The co-location of these entities and the hands-on opportunities they offer have a tremendous impact on the student experience. In addition, the business curriculum now incorporates the SAP software used by many global enterprises.

The Center for Advanced Engineering houses Gannon's mechanical, biomedical and industrial engineering programs. Students receive hands-on learning opportunities in the Industrial Engineering Laboratory and in the region's only Biomedical Engineering Motion-Capture Center to solve biological and medical challenges and enhance quality of life.

Students in Gannon's criminal justice program utilize the Forensic Investigation Center that features classroom space, a forensic laboratory, a firearms training simulator, and spaces to create simulated crime scenes.

The Zurn Science Center has laboratories for research in biology, anatomy, physics, chemistry and engineering. The building also houses innovative technology, such as several 3-D printers, an open engineering computer lab and additional computer labs for student use. There are numerous classrooms and two auditoriums in the building.

The Morosky College of Health Professions and Sciences is located in the Robert H. Morosky Academic Center. This 99,000-square-foot facility includes classrooms, labs and faculty offices. It also includes a 5,800-square-foot, state-of-the-art Patient Simulation Center.

The A. J. Palumbo Academic Center houses the College of Humanities, Education and Social Sciences. The University's honors program as well as academic support services are also located in Palumbo.

Renovations began on Nash Library in summer 2016, with completion expected in spring 2018. This modernization project includes the creation of a research and learning commons that will foster collaboration and provide resources, services and equipment to support students' academic work.

Other academic buildings include Scottino Hall, home of the Schuster Theatre; and the Nash Library, the hub of academic life at Gannon.

Costs

For 2016–17, full-time tuition was $14,650 per semester ($15,535 for engineering and health sciences), or $29,300 per academic year ($31,070 for engineering and health sciences). Tuition for part-time students was $710 to $760 per credit hour. Room and board range from $5,260 to $6,945 per semester. The total cost for the academic year at Gannon was between $30,042 for commuting students and between $40,892 and $46,032 for resident students, depending on the program of study.

Financial Aid

The University offers an integrated financial aid program of scholarships, grants, loans, and employment. Over $27 million in student scholarship and financial aid is provided to 94 percent of undergraduate students. Gannon's financial aid program is open to all full-time students attending classes during the period from August to May. Students seeking financial aid can file the admissions and financial aid applications as early as October 1 and should file by the preferred deadline of March 15. Numerous scholarship opportunities are available to qualified students. Each year the University offers its top incoming freshmen the ability to compete for full-tuition scholarships. Application deadline for this competition is December 15 with an on-campus competition in late January or early February.

Faculty

Gannon's faculty numbers more than 400 and 69 percent of the full-time faculty members have either doctoral or terminal degrees. The student-to-faculty ratio is 13:1, and average class size is approximately 25 students.

Admission Requirements

Gannon University actively recruits students of all races, faith traditions, and ages from all geographic regions of North America and abroad. Applicants must submit scores (including senior-year scores) on either the SAT or ACT, an up-to-date official transcript of the high school record (plus official college transcripts for transfer applicants), and a completed application form. Applications can be completed online at www.gannon.edu/apply or via the Common Application.

Admission decisions are based upon numerous factors, most importantly the high school record as demonstrated through grades and SAT and/or ACT scores and other test scores that may be available. Recommendations and personal statements also affect admission decisions. Transfer and international students should check with the admissions office for special application procedures.

Application and Information

Gannon operates on a rolling admissions basis; there is no deadline for filing applications with the exceptions of the physician assistant program, which has a deadline of November 1 for the fall semester. Due to the competitiveness of some programs, students interested in the nursing or occupational therapy programs are strongly encouraged to file applications in September. Early applications are recommended, as are enrollment deposits.

To find out more, contact:

Office of Admissions
Gannon University
109 University Square
Erie, Pennsylvania 16541
Phone: 814-871-7240
800-GANNON-U (426-6668, toll-free)
Fax: 814-871-5803
E-mail: admissions@gannon.edu
Website: http://www.gannon.edu

GEORGIAN COURT UNIVERSITY

LAKEWOOD, NEW JERSEY

★ To read more about this school, visit http://petersons.to/georgiancourtuniversity

GEORGIAN COURT UNIVERSITY

THE MERCY UNIVERSITY OF NEW JERSEY

COLLEGE CLOSE-UPS

The University

Georgian Court University (GCU) is a place where heart and intellect meet. GCU students learn to expand their possibilities while fostering their unique gifts and becoming more engaged citizens of the world. The historic 156-acre campus is home to over 2,000 students, creating a community of scholarship, empowerment, and professional relationships.

Georgian Court University is a four-year, private coeducational university located in Lakewood, New Jersey. GCU is set on a magnificent 156-acre estate formerly belonging to financier George Jay Gould; the campus is conveniently situated 60 miles from New York and Philadelphia, and only 10 miles from the Jersey Shore. Bordering Lake Carasaljo, the site is a National Historic Landmark with alluring statuary, beautiful architecture and lush gardens.

The current GCU campus was sold to the Sisters of Mercy in 1924 from the heirs of George Jay Gould. The original estate featured an indoor swimming pool, tennis court, and bowling alley, all housed in what is now called the Casino, which has been completely restored. Gould's estate also boasted a Japanese Garden, Formal Garden, and classical Italian Gardens, which still grace the campus with their natural and sculptural beauty.

As a forward-thinking university that supports diversity and academic excellence, GCU welcomes students of all faiths and backgrounds. The university offers a curriculum that is broad enough to be truly liberal, yet specialized enough to provide in-depth preparation for careers or further study.

As a coeducational institution, GCU continues to grow while maintaining a small-scale setting that provides a big value: a community based on the Mercy core values, including respect, integrity, justice, compassion, and service. Each GCU student shapes the experiential academic environment, which makes for a vibrant environment of teachers and learners.

GCU works to make its educational program available to all qualified students, regardless of financial need; in 2016–17, 97 percent of students received financial aid.

GCU has many points of pride and is ranked by the following: 2016 *Washington Monthly* "Best Bang for the Buck;" 2016 *U.S. News & World Report* "Best Colleges & Universities;" 2016 Catholic College of Distinction; 2016 College of Distinction; and *Victory Media* declared GCU a 2017 Military-Friendly School.

Georgian Court University is accredited by the Middle States Commission on Higher Education.

Location

Set on a magnificent 156-acre estate that formerly belonged to financier George Jay Gould, the campus is conveniently situated 60 miles from New York and Philadelphia, and only 10 miles from the Jersey Shore. Bordering Lake Carasaljo, the site is a National Historic Landmark with alluring statuary, beautiful architecture, and lush gardens.

The campus is easily accessible from Route 9, the Garden State Parkway, and Interstate 195. New Jersey Transit bus access is within walking distance, giving students quick, inexpensive transportation to points of interest throughout the tristate area.

Majors and Degrees

Georgian Court University offers degree programs in the following disciplines: Accounting; Applied Arts & Sciences; Art & Visual Studies; Biochemistry; Biology; Business Administration; Chemistry; Clinical Laboratory Sciences; Criminal Justice; Dance; Digital Communication; Digital Design; Education; English; Exercise Science, Wellness, & Sports; Graphic Design & Multimedia; Health Information Management; History; Interdisciplinary Studies; Latino Business Studies; Management; Marketing; Mathematics; Medical Imaging Sciences; Natural Sciences; Nursing; Pre-Professional Career Preparation (preparation for medical careers); Psychiatric Rehabilitation & Psychology; Psychology; Religious Studies; Social Work; Spanish; and Visual Art.

Minors are offered in: Accounting; American Studies; Anthropology; Biology; Business Administration; Chemistry; Coaching; Computer Information Systems; Dance; Dance Therapy; Digital Communication; Economics; English; Exercise Science, Wellness, & Sports; Finance; Gerontology; Global Justice & Society; Graphic Design; History; Homeland Security; Integrative Health; International Area Studies; Latino/a and Caribbean Studies; Law Enforcement & Corrections; Management; Marketing; Mathematics; Politics, Law, and History; Psychology; Religious Studies; Social Media Marketing; Social Work; Sociology; Spanish; Sports Management; Studio Art; Sustainability; The USA and the World; Women's Studies; and Writing.

Academic Programs

GCU works to help students develop their academic skills in a supportive, caring environment. The Academic Development & Support Center (ADSC) offers tutoring and other academic support services so students can get the most out of their education. Disabilities Services, Peer Tutoring, and a fee-based support program for students with learning differences are also available.

Georgian Court University's Honors Program allows students to pursue academic honors and collaborate with faculty members in a variety of special courses. Honors students can benefit from courses that emphasize primary texts and sources, rigorous scholarly writing assignments and oral presentations, belonging to a committed community of scholars, preference in academic advisement and course registration, assistance with funding to present at regional and national conferences, and special advising regarding graduate and professional school applications and prestigious fellowship opportunities.

The Office of Career Services, Corporate Engagement and Continuing Education helps bridge the gap from being a student to becoming a professional and progressing through a career. The office has a wide array of tools and resources to help students find jobs and internships, identify and market their skill set, network, compile a resume, and prepare for interviews. These life-long, free services are available to both students and alumni.

Off-Campus Programs

The Office of Global Education Programs manages study abroad and travel abroad experiences. Study abroad trips last from a week to a year outside the United States, and students can earn credit. Georgian Court has formalized arrangements and discount agreements with several international universities. Travel abroad opportunities can satisfy an experiential learning or service requirement.

In addition to offering students opportunities to study abroad, Georgian Court University offers joint-degree programs allowing students to take courses at GCU and at a partner institution.

Academic Facilities

Jeffries Hall is Georgian Court's largest academic building, providing classrooms, seminar rooms, offices, art studios, and computer labs. The state-of-the-art Audrey Birish George Science Center offers the latest laboratory and instruction space for scientific study.

The Sister Mary Joseph Cunningham Library offers a wealth of resources to assist students in their studies and research pursuits. The library offers extensive online resources, special collections and archives, and spacious facilities for meetings and presentations.

Other campus buildings include the Raymond Hall Complex, which houses the School of Education, the Raymond Hall Computer Center, and the GCU Dining Hall. The School of Business and the Department of Psychology are based in Farley Center, which includes a computer lab, student lounge, and an International Collaboration Center.

Costs

For the 2016–17 academic year, tuition was $15,079 per semester for full-time students (12–18 credits); the nursing program tuition was $16,147. Part-time tuition (11 credits or fewer) was $690. Room and board was $5,404 per semester, with a $1,293 single room supplement. Fees included a full-time comprehensive fee of $730, a part-time comprehensive fee of $365, and a full-year parking fee of $193 (plus $13.51 New Jersey sales tax). Other small miscellaneous fees may be applicable.

Financial Aid

Georgian Court University is proud to meet the financial aid needs of its students with an annual budget of $20,000,000 in institutional aid. The University believes that a good education is a right—not a privilege. Through internal scholarships and outside scholarships, Georgian Court strives to make education attainable for all students.

In addition, there are GCU institutional, Federal, and State grants available for students who meet specific criteria. Students can also take advantage of the loan programs that are explained in further detail in the student loan section of the University's website.

Faculty

At GCU, 90 percent of the full-time faculty members hold doctoral degrees. From the freshman year on, students have the opportunity to take classes taught by department chairs, even school deans. Georgian Court features an average class size of 13, which promotes individual attention and open, thoughtful discourse among students and professors. All students receive individual counseling by a faculty adviser.

Student Government

The Student Government Association (SGA) of Georgian Court University is the official representative voice of the GCU student body. The SGA advocates on behalf of the students' interests and concerns. Through representation on University committees and other special meetings, the Student Government Association continues to play a vital role in fostering community and providing a direct link between students, faculty, and administration. The University also boasts several programs to help engage and develop students' leadership abilities, as well as a plethora of other clubs and organizations catering to a broad range of interests and lifestyles.

Admission Requirements

Georgian Court University welcomes applications from qualified students of all faiths and backgrounds who desire a liberal arts education. The University strives to enroll students who can benefit most from its academic program. In 2016, 45 percent of GCU's student population were first-generation college students. Entrance is based on individual merit. The high school record of achievement is of primary importance and must reflect solid performance. The majority of students at Georgian Court ranked in the upper half of their senior high school class. Transfer students are accepted into the freshman, sophomore, and junior classes for fall and spring semesters. All transfer applicants must be in good standing at their previous college. Applicants with fewer than 24 credits must fulfill all requirements for admission to the freshman class.

Further consideration is given to the applicant's extracurricular activities and the letters of recommendation submitted by teachers, counselors, employers, or similarly qualified people.

Application and Information

Applicants must submit their completed application (online via the Common Application or print and complete a paper application), a $40 application fee, their official high school transcript, SAT (GCU code: 2274) or ACT (GCU code: 2562) scores, two letters of recommendation, and an optional essay. Georgian Court has rolling deadlines for first-year students, so applications can be accepted throughout the year.

A campus interview is encouraged but not necessary. A guided tour of the campus is available at the interview.

For further information, prospective students should contact:

Office of Admissions
Georgian Court University
900 Lakewood Avenue
Lakewood, New Jersey 08701-2697
United States
Phone: 732-987-2700
800-458-8422 Ext. 2700 (toll-free)
Fax: 732-987-2084
E-mail: admissions@georgian.edu
Website: http://www.georgian.edu/admissions

Georgian Court University's 67,000 square-foot, state-of-the-art Wellness Center.

GODDARD COLLEGE

PLAINFIELD, VERMONT

★ To read more about this school, visit http://petersons.to/goddardcollege

Goddard College

The College

With its main campus nestled in rural Vermont, Goddard College is recognized for innovation in education. Its mission is to advance the theory and practice of learning by undertaking new experiments based upon the ideals of democracy and the principles of progressive education asserted by John Dewey. At Goddard, students are regarded as unique individuals who will take charge of their learning and collaborate with other students, staff, and faculty to build a strong community. Goddard encourages students to become creative, passionate, lifelong learners, working and living with an earnest concern for others and the welfare of the Earth.

Goddard's semester format comprises an intensive eight-day residency on campus followed by 16 weeks of independent work and self-reflection in close collaboration with a faculty adviser. A student's semester studies are carried out where the student is, be that in their home community, engaged in a service project, traveling, and so on. Faculty evaluations form the basis of the narrative transcript, which—in place of letter grades—provides external readers with a precise, detailed synopsis of the student's learning.

Goddard offers Bachelor of Arts (B.A.) degree programs in education, health arts and sciences, individualized (self-designed) studies, psychology, and sustainability, as well as a Bachelor of Fine Arts (B.F.A.) degree in creative writing. The College also offers graduate study options in community education, clinical mental health counseling, consciousness studies, creative writing, dual language early childhood education, health arts and sciences, psychology, social innovation and sustainability, teacher licensure, transformative language arts, and individualized (self-designed) studies.

Goddard College is accredited by the New England Association of Schools and Colleges, through its Commission on Institutions of Higher Education, to offer bachelor's and master's degrees.

Location

Goddard College is located on the grounds of a late-nineteenth-century model farm in Plainfield, Vermont, just outside Montpelier. The Greatwood Farm and Estate consists of shingle-style buildings and gardens designed by noted American architect Arthur Shurcliff. The campus buildings were added to the National Register of Historic Places in 1996.

Goddard also has satellite campuses in Seattle, Washington, and at the Fort Worden State Park in Port Townsend, Washington.

Majors and Degrees

Goddard offers the Bachelor of Arts in community education, dual language early childhood education, health arts and sciences, psychology, sustainability, teacher licensure, and individualized (self-designed) studies. The college offers the nation's only low-residency Bachelor of Fine Arts in Creative Writing degree program.

Academic Programs

Students must accumulate 120 semester-hour credits to earn the Bachelor of Arts or Bachelor of Fine Arts degree from Goddard College.

Students may apply to transfer up to 75 semester hour credits toward a Goddard undergraduate degree. This can be a combination of credit from regionally accredited colleges and universities, Advanced Placement (AP) examinations, and College Level Examination Program (CLEP) examinations.

Instead of taking traditional classes in a given set of academic areas, students demonstrate progression toward meeting degree requirements through the submission of Progress Review Portfolios following the first year and prior to the final year of study.

All students produce a senior study, or thesis, prior to earning the baccalaureate degree.

B.F.A. in Creative Writing: Students study fiction, poetry, memoir and nonfiction, and hybrid forms in the first low-residency B.F.A. degree program in the country. Students may seek sole vocations in writing, or integrate their creative writing into professions such as psychology, social work, library science, or education. With the B.F.A. in Creative Writing degree program, students may also go on to pursue graduate work in creative writing, literature, or professional writing.

Goddard's creative writing program is a 120-credit degree program open to transfer students who have already completed approximately 60 liberal arts credits. Students may be eligible to bring a combination of transfer credits and/or credits awarded for prior learning and experience into the degree program. Students wishing to enter the degree program without 60 credits may enter Goddard's individualized studies program to gain credits.

The senior project is completed at the end of the program. Students prepare their manuscripts, study papers on the topics of their choosing, annotated bibliographies, and readings of their works to the residents of the college. All students leave the program with complete drafts of finished manuscripts.

B.A. in Education: The Bachelor of Arts in Education degree program is of special interest to educators, parents, or community/cultural workers who seek knowledge in the field of educational pedagogy and progressive education. Students may pursue an individualized focus in education, teacher licensure, dual language early childhood education, or community education. Goddard College's B.A. in Education program licensure degree option is approved by the Vermont Agency of Education to offer initial Vermont teacher licensure in the following endorsement areas: early childhood (birth to age 6, K to grade 3 or both); elementary (K–6); art (pre-K to 6, 7 to 12, or pre-K to 12); middle grades (5–9); secondary English; and secondary social studies.

The low-residency B.A. in Education degree program is a 120-credit program open to transfer students who have already completed approximately 60 liberal arts credits and who wish to extend their knowledge in the field of education to meet personal or professional goals. Students may be eligible to bring a combination of transfer credits and/or credits awarded for prior learning and experience into the degree program.

The B.A. in Education degree program is available as a licensure program (on the Vermont campus only) or as a non-licensure option (on both the Vermont and Seattle, Washington campuses).

B.A. in Health Arts and Sciences: Student work in health arts combines integrative health studies, holistic sciences, health philosophy, multicultural perspectives, social change, self-awareness, and self-care practices to bridge nature, culture, and healing. Potential course subjects include community and environmental health, women's health and midwifery, men's health, botanical medicine and ethnobotany, nutritional health, expressive arts, body and movement therapies, integrative health, integrative nursing, mind-body health, ecopsychology, and cross-cultural healing.

The low-residency B.A. in Health Arts and Sciences degree program is a 120-credit degree program open to transfer students who have already completed approximately 60 liberal arts credits.

Individualized B.A. degree program: The individualized studies degree program at Goddard emphasizes personal and social transformation, meditative action, positive self-development, and a wide breadth of knowledge. Students may bring up to 75 approved credits into the program through a combination of transfer or credits earned through an assessment of prior learning.

B.A. in Sustainability: Working closely with faculty advisers, students design courses of study that are individualized and interdisciplinary, practical as well as visionary. Students understand that the earth and its people face unprecedented environmental and social challenges, as well as unparalleled opportunities to build a sustainable future. Goddard welcomes students who are determined to create just lives and livelihoods as partners with the earth and its peoples. Topics of study include alternative energy, soil science, local food systems, waste management, and the ethical dimensions of international trade.

The low-residency B.A. in Sustainability degree program is a 120-credit degree program open to transfer students who have already completed approximately 60 liberal arts credits.

B.A. in Psychology: Goddard's B.A./M.A. fast-track degree program in psychology and counseling is a low-residency accelerated degree program that affords learners a seamless path to obtain their bachelor's and master's degrees over a shorter period of time. Students pursue standard undergraduate degrees in psychology with the final semester counting for both the B.A. degree program and as the first 15 hours of the M.A. degree program.

The low-residency B.A. in Psychology is a 120-credit degree program open to transfer students who have already completed approximately 60 liberal arts credits.

Academic Facilities

Goddard's campus includes a library, dormitories, and meeting spaces. Students and faculty are dispersed, but students enjoy intense relationships with their faculty advisors, which both students and faculty experience as rewarding and intimate, in the best sense of that word. The college relies on web-based communications to connect the dispersed Goddard community. Each student has a completely individualized curriculum, with as many curricula as we have students.

Costs

Tuition varies by degree. For the most up-to-date information, prospective students should visit www.goddard.edu/admissions/tuition-and-fees.

Financial Aid

Eighty-five percent of all Goddard students receive federal financial aid. Among undergraduate students, 63 percent receive the Pell Grant. The highest level of aid comes in the form of subsidized and unsubsidized federal loans, though Goddard awarded $454,000 in institutional aid in 2013–14 academic year.

Faculty

Goddard maintains a low 8:1 student-faculty ratio. Faculty serve as mentors and collaborators in student's individualized curriculum. The Goddard faculty members have longstanding presence in the College and bring to their work a host of professional skills, expertise, and interests.

Student Government

The Student Council acts as a conduit for the student voice by responding to, and advocating for, the needs of students, as individuals or groups, along with serving as liaisons to the greater Goddard community, including prospective students, staff, faculty, administration, and the Board of Trustees. Students elect Student Council members as representatives from their unique programs.

Admission Requirements

Applications receive a holistic review. Goddard does not require a minimum GPA or standardized test scores. Applications should demonstrate an understanding of Goddard's student-driven, low-residency model. The application essay should articulate why Goddard is the right fit. The College also seeks students who are willing to think critically about their personal and academic experiences, who express a willingness to take responsibility for their learning, and whose academic record demonstrates sufficient preparation for writing-intensive, independent, and critical work in the liberal arts and sciences.

Application and Information

Goddard's rolling admission process allows students to apply and receive notification at any time in the year before the semester in which they would like to enter. Application deadlines are thirty days before the semester begins.

For further information, prospective students should contact:

Admissions Office
Goddard College
123 Pitkin Road
Plainfield, Vermont 05667
United States
Phone: 800-906-8312 (admissions)
E-mail: admissions@godddard.edu
Website: http://www.goddard.edu

All of Goddard's degree programs are highly individualized, guided by students' particular learning needs and professional goals.

GOSHEN COLLEGE

GOSHEN, INDIANA

★ To read more about this school, visit http://petersons.goshencollege

The College

Goshen College (GC) is an affordable, nationally-recognized, liberal arts college in Northern Indiana known for leadership in intercultural and international education, sustainability, and social justice. The College offers bachelor's degrees in more than 65 areas of study, as well as select master's degrees. Goshen enrolls approximately 850 students from 31 states and 26 countries and is recognized for its innovative, life-changing study abroad program (Study-Service Term), and exceptional educational value. The 135-acre tree-filled campus features a world-class Music Center and a Rec-Fitness Center for 13 intercollegiate athletic teams. The extended campus includes a 1,189-acre natural sanctuary (the Merry Lea Environmental Learning Center near Wolf Lake, Indiana) and a marine biology lab in the Florida Keys. Rooted in the historically peaceful Mennonite church and established in 1894, the College's Christ-centered mission produces passionate learners, compassionate peacemakers, global citizens, and servant leaders. The College's doors are open to all, with students from 40 different Christian denominations and several world religions. Experiential learning, faculty mentors, and strong friendships are significant community strengths for students.

Goshen College was ranked #5 in *U.S. News & World Report*'s 2017 "Best National Regional Colleges in the Midwest," and also received recognition for enrolling a high percentage of international students, its unique study abroad program, having a high graduation rate, for campus ethnic diversity, and for having least debt among graduates. Goshen's record of sustained excellence has attracted other national attention as well. In 2015, Kiplinger's listed Goshen among the top 5 percent of all four-year colleges and universities in the United States for best value. *Washington Monthly* ranked Goshen College #3 among the "Top 100 National Baccalaureate Colleges." The *Christian Science Monitor* ranked Goshen fifth on their list of "Top Ten Most Globally Minded Colleges." Goshen College is included in the discriminating "Colleges of Distinction" listing and was named by the Women's Choice Award as a top college for women.

In a highly energetic, Christ-centered environment, students have plenty of opportunities to cultivate leadership skills and assume responsibility. Goshen belongs to the National Association of Intercollegiate Athletics as part of the competitive Crossroads League, with intercollegiate men's and women's basketball, cross-country, golf, soccer, tennis, track and field, and volleyball; men's baseball; and women's softball. More than half of Goshen students participate in intramural athletics. All students have free access to the Roman Gingerich Recreation-Fitness Center.

Students edit a weekly newspaper and a yearbook, operate a state and national award-winning radio station, produce a campus television news program, serve on campus publishing editorial boards, and perform in mainstage theater and opera productions or in the six instrumental and vocal ensembles. Representatives of the student body are elected to serve on the Student Senate and Campus Activities Council. Campus groups also include the Student Women's Association, Black Student Union, Campus Ministries Team and Traveling Worship Team, PAX, Latino Student Union, Nursing Students Association, Eco-PAX, Social Work Action Association, International Students Club, and Pre-Med Club.

Most Goshen students live in one of the College's six residence halls. In addition, the residence halls offer lounges and a student-run coffee bar. Small-group housing is a popular option for upper-level students. The campus also offers a hall for juniors and seniors with apartment-style units. College-owned houses are available for married students and families.

With a longtime emphasis on experiential learning, Goshen's programs encourage partnerships between the College and the community by placing students in practicum, internship, and service experiences. In addition, the College holds an annual Community Engagement Day for all first-year students; classes are suspended so that students and faculty can participate in community service projects. Students also benefit from the Center for Intercultural and International Education, which equips students, community leaders, and educators with the intercultural skills they need to create opportunities for justice, mutuality, respect, equality, equity, and peacemaking.

Location

The campus is on the south side of Goshen, a culturally and economically diverse city of 30,000 in north-central Indiana, by car 2 hours east of Chicago and 45 minutes east of South Bend. Known as the Maple City for its shady avenues, Goshen offers many diverse cultural, educational, employment, and recreational opportunities. Most notably, Goshen maintains its small-town charm while offering a multitude of activities and experiences often found in larger cities.

Majors and Degrees

Goshen College offers more than 65 programs of study. The Bachelor of Arts is awarded in accounting; American Sign Language education; art; Bible and religion; biology; broadcasting; business; chemistry; communication; computer science; elementary education; elementary education/special education; elementary education/English learners; engineering physics; English; environmental and marine science; exercise science; film production; history; informatics; information technology; interdisciplinary studies; journalism; marketing; mathematics; molecular biology and biochemistry; music; nursing; peace, justice, and conflict studies; physical education; physics; psychology; public relations; secondary education; sign language interpreting; social work; sociology; Spanish; sustainability management; sustainability studies; sustainable food systems; Teaching English as a Second Language (TESOL); theater; and writing. In addition, a Bachelor of Science in Nursing (B.S.N.) is awarded.

The College also offers minors in more than 30 areas. Unique programs of study include agroecology, American Sign Language, Anabaptist-Mennonite studies, conflict transformation studies, entrepreneurship, global economics, graphic design, health, international studies, music for social change, musical theater, peace and justice studies, philosophy, piano pedagogy, political studies, recreation and sport, sport management, social policy, sustainability, theological studies and Christian ministries, and women and gender studies. Interdisciplinary majors usually combine work in three different departments and allow students to tailor their studies to individual interests. Pre-professional programs in architecture, dentistry, engineering, law, medicine, pharmacy, physical therapy, seminary, and veterinary medicine are available as well.

At the graduate level, a Master of Science (M.S.) degree in nursing, a Master of Business Administration (M.B.A.), and a Master of Arts in environmental education are awarded.

Academic Programs

The College calendar consists of two 15-week semesters and a 3½-week May term. A total of 120 semester hours (124 for elementary education majors) is required for graduation. The Goshen Core (sometimes called "general education" at other schools) is the set of courses and requirements that applies to all traditional undergraduate students, no matter what major they choose. In Goshen's uniquely designed program, students learn how to think critically, communicate clearly, and solve complex problems in a global context—skills they will need to craft tomorrow's solutions. Most majors require a practicum for graduation.

Off-Campus Programs

Goshen is one of the few U.S. colleges—and was one of the first—to require international education. Most students (nearly 80 percent)

choose to fulfill this through the Study-Service Term (SST) program, a semester abroad, including course work and field experience in a service assignment, in a significantly different culture. Students also can fulfill the requirement by taking courses on campus or by participating in other study abroad programs.

Goshen's international education program ranks number four in the country by Best College Reviews. Since the SST program began in 1968, more than 7,500 Goshen students have benefited from it tremendously, both academically and personally. The program has served as the model for international education programs across the country. In the SST program, students spend six weeks together focusing on the study of one country while immersed in its language and culture. The six-week SST field experience gives students a chance to develop interpersonal skills and to work alongside local residents in service to others. The field experience often relates to the students' major areas of study. During both parts of the program, students typically live with host families. Most SST units cost the same as a semester on campus. Goshen students earn 13–14 hours of credit for SST; however, the benefits continue for a lifetime. SST gives students a broader context for living their lives while helping them set an appropriate individual direction. The growing internationalization of U.S. business and culture amplifies SST's benefits; now, more than ever, foreign language skills and knowledge of other cultures are advantages in the job market.

Other off-campus programs include courses in marine biology at the College's center in the Florida Keys; a Sustainability Leadership Semester at the College's Merry Lea Environmental Learning Center—a 1,189-acre natural sanctuary; and courses during May term, including Arts in London, Business in China or Spain, Ecology and Economics in Ecuador, Public Relations in Kenya, Sustainability in India, Nursing in Nepal, and Sports in Nicaragua.

Academic Facilities

On its 135-acre campus, Goshen College has nineteen major buildings and laboratories. The Roman Gingerich Recreation-Fitness Center features a 200-meter indoor running track, weight room, three full-size gymnasium courts, racquetball and squash courts, climbing wall, a turf training facility, and sports medicine training room and exercise science lab. In addition, it houses the physical education department, student health center, and intramural and intercollegiate athletics. The campus is home to a 68,000-square-foot Music Center, which features 1,000- and 300-seat performance halls with some of the best acoustics in the nation. The building also houses an art gallery, rehearsal space, studios, and the Community School of the Arts, which serves hundreds of community students (children through adults) each year.

The Science Building features the Turner Precision X-Ray Measurements Laboratory and the Biological Research Laboratory. The Turner Laboratory gives physics majors a rare opportunity to assist in basic research on crystals; the Biological Research Laboratory is equipped with an electron microscope, Geiger system, climate chambers, incubators, and microtechnique systems. Each summer, students from any discipline may apply to the Maple Scholars Program for undergraduate research, which pays a stipend and pairs students with a faculty member for significant research exploration in an area of their interest, such as holography, poetry, genetics, nonviolence, painting, and more. The College regularly does research for larger universities and major industries.

The Harold and Wilma Good Library houses a collection of 130,000 volumes and 800 periodicals as well as the Mennonite Historical Library.

The Merry Lea Environmental Learning Center of Goshen College, an 1,189-acre nature preserve 40 miles southeast of the campus, offers internships in environmental and elementary education and is a key site for the College's environmental science major and minors, the Sustainability Leadership Semester, the Agroecology Summer Intensive, and the graduate program in environmental education.

The John S. Umble Center for the Performing Arts is recognized internationally for its exceptional theater acoustics and design.

Costs

Tuition for 2017–18 is $33,200 and room and board are $10,500. Costs include two 15-week semesters and one 3½-week May term.

Financial Aid

In 2016, 99 percent of the College's students received some type of financial assistance through federal, state, and Goshen College programs and work-study opportunities. The average award was $23,800. Goshen offers more than 130 different scholarships. College aid (if applying before December 15) includes the President's Leadership Award, $20,000; Dean's Academic scholarship, $15,000; High Honors Academic Scholarship, $13,000; Honors Academic Scholarship, $11,000; Academic Excellence Scholarship, $8,000; and the Academic Scholarship, $6,000. Applications for financial aid received after December 15 receive a slight reduction in scholarship award amount. About 87 percent of incoming students receive academic scholarships. Work-study and other on-campus jobs are available.

Faculty

The faculty includes about 70 full-time and 40 part-time members. Most have lived, served, or worked abroad. The student-faculty ratio is 10:1.

Student Government

The Student Senate acts as an advocate of student concerns and corresponding policy changes and works with the administration, including making significant appointments to campus committees. The Campus Activity Council plans regular and engaging student activities.

Admission Requirements

Applicants should rank in the upper half of their high school graduating class and may apply for admission at any time after their junior year and up to one month before they wish to begin their studies at the College. ACT or SAT scores are required.

Recommended high school work includes 4 years of English, 2 years of science, 2 years of social science, 2 years of mathematics, and 2 to 4 years of a foreign language. Prospective students are encouraged to visit the campus and meet with faculty members and students. Special campus open houses scheduled throughout the year provide excellent opportunities for visits.

Application and Information

Admissions Office
Goshen College
1700 South Main Street
Goshen, Indiana 46526
Phone: 844-704-3400 (toll-free)
Fax: 574-535-7609
E-mail: admissions@goshen.edu
Website:www.goshen.edu
www.facebook.com/goshencollege (Facebook)
www.twitter.com/goshencollege (Twitter)
www.instagram.com/goshencollege (Instagram)
www.youtube.com/goshencollege (YouTube)

Goshen College is nationally recognized for leadership in intercultural and international education, sustainability, and social justice.

GRAND VIEW UNIVERSITY

DES MOINES, IOWA

GRAND VIEW UNIVERSITY

★ To read more about this school, visit http://petersons.to/grandviewuniversity

The University

Grand View University is a liberal arts institution that offers a high-quality education to a diverse student body in a career-oriented, liberal arts–grounded curriculum at its campus in Iowa. Founded in 1896, Grand View (GV) welcomes traditional students, adult learners, and graduate students representing a wide range of ethnic, religious, and cultural backgrounds.

At Grand View, students find a winning combination of high-quality programs, experienced professors, and caring individuals. With 2,000 students and an average class size of 16, students get to know their professors and other students well. Learning is an interactive process at Grand View—students engage in lively discussions, work on real-world projects, and participate in career-related work experiences.

Grand View stands out from other universities because of its partnerships with leading businesses and organizations in Des Moines, which has led to challenging internships and stellar job placement—for more than two decades nearly 100 percent of GV graduates have found jobs right after graduation or continued their education.

Students are encouraged to develop leadership and team skills through involvement in campus organizations, which include intercollegiate and intramural athletics, speech and theater groups, major department clubs, student government, musical ensembles, and honor societies. Grand View's student leadership program provides opportunities for students with or without leadership experience to seek and develop critical thinking, interpersonal, and networking skills.

Student athletes compete in men's baseball, basketball, bowling, competitive cheer (coed), cross-country, football, golf, soccer, tennis, track and field, volleyball, and wrestling, and women's basketball, bowling, competitive cheer (coed), competitive dance, cross-country, golf, soccer, softball, tennis, track and field, and volleyball. Grand View is a member of the Heart of America Conference of the National Association of Intercollegiate Athletics. Athletic scholarships are available.

Location

Grand View is located in Des Moines, a metropolitan area of more than half a million people in central Iowa. Des Moines is the seat of state government and serves as the communications hub for Iowa. Nationally recognized organizations that have their corporate offices in Des Moines include DuPont/Pioneer, the Principal Financial Group, Meredith Corporation, Wells Fargo Home Mortgage, and the *Des Moines Register*.

In essence, Grand View's campus is the entire city of Des Moines because students aren't limited by the confines of a small campus or small town. In a given day, students can catch an Iowa Cubs professional baseball doubleheader, head down to the Court Avenue district for great food and nightlife, or take in a concert at Wells Fargo Arena.

A thriving arts program in Des Moines features the Des Moines Metro Opera, Ballet Iowa, the Des Moines Symphony, the Des Moines Art Center, the Des Moines Playhouse, and many others. The summer Des Moines Arts Festival is ranked third in the nation.

Majors and Degrees

Grand View University offers forty majors in areas such as accounting, applied mathematics, art education, biology, biochemistry, biotechnology, business administration (with concentrations in areas such as finance, game design, human resource management, management, and marketing), church music, computer science, criminal justice, digital media production, elementary education, English, graphic design, graphic journalism, health promotion and kinesiology, history, human services, individualized major, journalism and public relations, liberal arts, management information systems, multimedia communication, music, music education, organizational studies, paralegal studies, physical education, political studies (prelaw or public administration), psychology, secondary education, Spanish for careers and professionals, studio arts, theater arts, and theology. Grand View also offers a Bachelor of Science degree in nursing, as well as an RN to B.S.N. program.

The university also offers five master's degree programs: the Master of Science in Organizational Leadership, the Master of Science in Nursing (clinical nurse leadership and nursing education), the Master of Education, Master of Science in Sport Management and Master of Science in Athletic Training.

Academic Programs

Grand View operates on a 4-4-1 academic calendar. The first semester runs from late August to December. The second semester begins in early January and ends in late April. Three one-month summer sessions are offered in May, June, and July, as is a summer trimester evening program.

Grand View's general education core takes an innovative, integrated approach to developing essential abilities employers seek in graduates, such as writing, speaking, analysis, problem-solving, and critical thinking. Through their coursework, students can gain the personal and intellectual depth that will help them thrive in today's knowledge-based economy and in their communities.

The Logos honors program augments the general education core. By invitation, freshmen and sophomores enrolled in this

COLLEGE CLOSE-UPS

program complete a series of courses designed to challenge exceptional students.

An active study-abroad program gives students opportunities to learn in an international setting, particularly through a partnership with the Danish Institute for Study Abroad, IBA, and China's Tianfu University.

The Grand View academic mission is to provide a diverse student body with an academically rigorous education. In order to meet this commitment, Grand View provides a variety of learning environments and teaching techniques. Grand View's results on the 2015 National Survey of Student Engagement, a measure of educational quality used by 1,000 colleges and universities, ranked GV comparable to the top 10 percent of all NSSE schools on five out of the ten benchmarks for first-year students and in the top 50 percent on the remaining five.

Costs

For 2017–18, the comprehensive cost for freshmen living on campus is approximately $35,000, which includes tuition, an activity fee, a technology fee, a parking fee, and room and board. Students have several residential and meal plan options that affect cost. Health services and Internet access are also included in the comprehensive fee.

Financial Aid and Affordability

All incoming Grand View freshmen are automatically enrolled in GV COMPLETE, a new program that allows students to plan and finance their entire degree right from the beginning, with a four-year financing plan and a four-year academic plan. GV COMPLETE is designed to help make a Grand View education more affordable by limiting increases in tuition, room, and board over students' four years; to support students in making the most out of the scholarships, grants, and loans that will become key parts of their financing; and to encourage four-year graduation.

Most full-time Grand View students receive financial assistance. The average freshman full-time award package is usually around $26,500 with about $19,000 in grants and scholarships, and the remainder in work-study and student loans. The amount of aid is determined through a combination of merit and analysis of need as determined through the Free Application for Federal Student Aid. The priority deadline for financial aid is March 1. Students receive notification of financial aid packages following acceptance of admission to the university and receipt of their financial aid analysis of need.

Faculty

There are approximately 94 full-time faculty members and 120 part-time faculty members. More than 70 percent of full-time faculty members hold terminal degrees. All classes are taught by professors; no graduate or teaching assistants instruct Grand View classes.

Student Government

Students participate in Grand View governance. The Student Activities Council and Viking Council plan student activities that promote educational, social, cultural, and recreational aspects of student life. Students serve as representatives on faculty and staff search committees, programming committees, and student life committees.

Admission Requirements

Applicants' files are reviewed to determine their preparation for a Grand View education. Official high school transcripts and submission of ACT or SAT scores are required for applicants with less than 24 semester hours of college credit. Applicants transferring from another college are required to submit official transcripts from all colleges previously attended.

Application and Information

For more information about Grand View, students should contact:
Admissions Office
Grand View University
1200 Grandview Avenue
Des Moines, Iowa 50316
Phone: 515-263-2810
800-444-6083 (toll-free)
Fax: 515-263-2974
E-mail: admissions@grandview.edu
Website: http://www.admissions.grandview.edu
http://www.facebook.com/pages/Grand-View-University/315068091675 (Facebook)

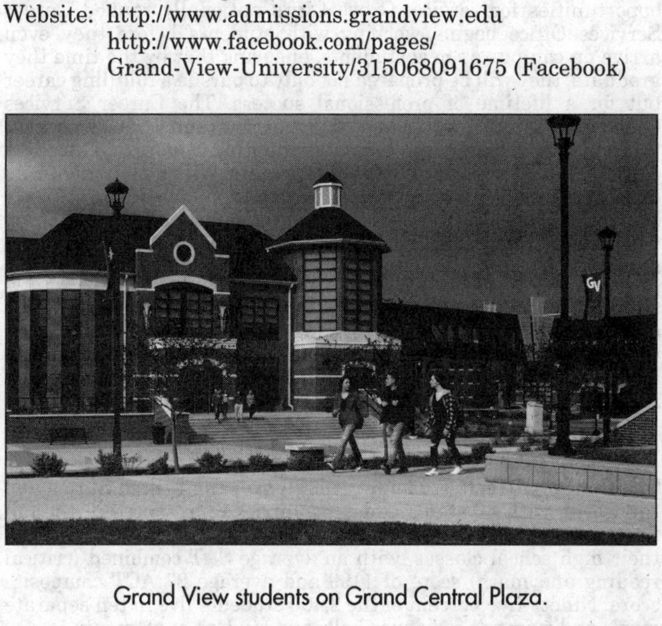

Grand View students on Grand Central Plaza.

GROVE CITY COLLEGE

GROVE CITY, PENNSYLVANIA

★ To read more about this school, visit http://petersons.to/grovecitycollege

The College

Building a strong and faithful future

Students flourish at Grove City College because faith is the foundation of everything they do. From the classroom to the practice fields, from the dining halls to the dormitories, Grove City students and faculty seek to understand how they might bring God glory in all of their daily activities and ultimately how they might use their unique gifts and abilities to serve others. The College equips students to discover and pursue their unique callings through an academically excellent and Christ-centered learning and living experience.

The cornerstone of its excellent education is the incredible community of learners—students, faculty, and staff who are committed to pursuing knowledge and truth for the advancement of the common good. Surrounded by peers and mentors who sharpen them, students develop into leaders of the highest proficiency guided by these core values: faithfulness, excellence, community, stewardship, and independence. Grove City College students and graduates see extraordinary outcomes, including: a 94 percent freshman retention rate; a 13:1 student-faculty ratio; an 80 percent four-year graduation rate; a 97 percent job and graduate school placement rate; 14 to 19 percent higher starting and midcareer salaries; and a $453,000 return on investment.

Grove City College offers students and families an amazing value. Tuition and costs run about half the national average before scholarships and financial aid. Unlike the vast majority of colleges and universities, the College does not practice tuition discounting—tuition price is the same for every student and no student unwittingly subsidizes another student's tuition through artificial scholarships.

Faith and freedom are the College's guiding principles. Founded in 1876, it is nationally known as a beacon of individual, academic and religious freedom. The Princeton Review, *U.S. News & World Report*, and others place the College in the top tier of private liberal arts colleges in national rankings for educational quality, value, and return on investment. It is accredited by the Middle States Commission on Higher Education.

Students have access to exclusive internships and have amazing opportunities for service. Grove City's nationally ranked Career Services Office begins working with students before they even arrive on campus as new students, ensuring that by the time they graduate, they will be prepared not only to pursue a fulfilling career but for a lifetime of professional success. The Career Services Office also works with scores of prospective employers who visit the campus annually to interview graduating seniors and attend a career fair that draws hundreds of recruiters. With a placement rate of 96 percent within six months of graduation, one of Grove City's strengths is placing students in business, industrial, and teaching positions, as well as in professional institutions such as medical schools.

Grove City College offers degrees in the arts and sciences across 60 programs of study while providing a solid liberal arts education that equips students with an understanding of the ideas, literature, and history upon which civilization rests. The College values its independence as a private institution and does not accept any federal aid, allowing it to remain free from government regulation and focused on academic excellence and scholarship.

The College attracts students from all over the United States and the world, with 46 states and 11 countries represented in the fall 2016 term. Students are overwhelmingly among the top fifth of their high school classes, with an average SAT combined (critical reading and math) score of 1199 and average 27 ACT composite score. Ninety-five percent of the 2,400 students live in ten separate men's and women's residence halls and student apartments.

There are more than 150 student organizations and special interest groups, including local fraternities and sororities. Grove City College maintains one of the most active intramural programs in the country, along with club and varsity sports programs that include twenty-one NCAA Division III intercollegiate teams.

Prospective students may learn more about Grove City College at www.gcc.edu.

Location

Grove City, a town of 8,000 people, is 60 miles north of Pittsburgh and is located 4 miles from restaurants, hotels, and a 140-store outlet mall. Convenient to I-79 and I-80, Grove City is only a day's drive from Chicago, New York City, Toronto, and Washington, D.C. The municipal airport has a 4,500-foot runway, and there is bus service to the bus and train stations and airport located in Pittsburgh.

Majors and Degrees

Grove City College offers undergraduate degrees in liberal arts, sciences, engineering, and music. The Bachelor of Arts (B.A.) is offered with majors in communication studies, economics, English, history, modern language, political science, psychology, philosophy and Biblical and religious studies, and sociology. Pre-professional students in law or theology usually earn the B.A. degree. Interdisciplinary major programs are also available for qualified students.

The Bachelor of Science (B.S.) is granted with majors in accounting, biochemistry, biology, business economics, business management, chemistry, chemistry secondary education, chemistry/general science education, computer information systems, computer science, PreK–4 elementary education, PreK–8 special education, entrepreneurship, exercise science, finance, industrial management, international business, marketing management, mathematics, middle level education, physics, physics/computer, physics/general science secondary education, and psychology. Pre-professional students often select one of these majors for dentistry, medicine, or other health fields.

The Bachelor of Science in Mechanical Engineering (B.S.M.E.) degree is also offered. The Bachelor of Science in Electrical Engineering (B.S.E.E.) degree provides for concentration areas in either electrical or computer engineering. Both engineering degree programs are accredited by the Engineering Accreditation Commission of the Accreditation Board for Engineering and Technology, Inc. (ABET).

The Bachelor of Music (B.M.) degree is awarded to those who major in music, music/business, music/performing arts, music/religion, and music education.

In addition to the majors listed above, secondary education (grades 7–12) certification is also available in biology/general science, English, English/communication, math, physics, and social science. Grades 7–12 certification is available in biology/general science/environmental science, French, and Spanish.

Academic Programs

Grove City College's goal is to educate young men and women and assist them in developing as complete individuals—academically, spiritually, and physically. The general education requirements provide all students with a high level of cultural literacy and communication skills. They include 46 semester hours of courses with emphases in the humanities, social sciences, and natural sciences; in quantitative and logical reasoning; physical education; and in science, faith, and technology, as well as a language requirement for all majors except engineering and science. Degree candidates must also complete the requirements in their field of concentration and electives. To graduate, a student must have completed a minimum 128 semester hours as well as the chapel attendance requirement. On average, 78 percent of those entering as freshmen stay and receive a diploma in four years and 83 percent in six years.

A distinctive liberal arts–engineering program includes engineering courses plus courses in the humanities to provide students with a well-grounded preparation for entering the engineering field, as well as the civic and cultural life of society. The economics program exposes students to all economic philosophies, yet it strongly advocates economic freedoms and free markets.

Grove City follows the semester calendar plan. Academic credit may be granted to incoming freshmen on the basis of scores on appropriate Advanced Placement tests, International Baccalaureate tests, or College-Level Examination Program tests. Honors courses, independent study, seminars, and the opportunity for students to study abroad for credit are also offered.

Academic Facilities

The Hall of Arts and Letters features a 200-seat lecture hall, forty classrooms (including multimedia-equipped rooms and tiered "case study" rooms), eighty faculty offices, the Early Education Center, the Curriculum Library, and language, computer, and video production labs.

STEM Hall, completed in 2013, features state-of-the-art laboratory and classroom space dedicated to teaching science, technology, engineering and math. Four of its labs employ an innovative science-in-sight design. STEM, Hoyt Hall and Rockwell Hall provide ample space for biology, chemistry, engineering, and physics education. The College owns an observatory, and the remote structure is utilized for astronomy classes as well as faculty and student research.

The College library houses 162,000 books and serials; 3,600 audio/video tapes, CDs, and DVDs; and 112 current serial subscriptions. In addition, the College has access to 58,885 journal titles through its collection of full-text journal databases.

The Weir C. Ketler Technological Learning Center houses PC and Mac labs, a lecture hall, video production lab, the College's FM radio station, and the campus print shop. It also houses the computer help desk and repair center for the laptop computers that all freshmen receive along with a color printer/scanner/copier.

The J. Howard Pew Fine Arts Center has art, photography, and music studios; a rehearsal hall; a small theater; a museum; an art gallery; music practice rooms; and a 675-seat, acoustically tunable auditorium and stage large enough to accommodate the most elaborate drama productions and concerts. An addition contains additional classrooms, practice rooms, and a 180-seat recital hall.

Costs

As a relatively small, financially sound college, Grove City College is able to charge an unusually low tuition in comparison to other independent institutions of similar quality. The 2016–17 annual tuition charge was $16,630 for all degrees. The cost of a tablet PC for all freshmen is included in the tuition fees. There is no comprehensive fee. Part-time tuition was $524 per credit. Room and board were $9,062. Expenses for books, laundry, transportation, and personal needs vary considerably with the lifestyle of the individual.

Financial Aid

Because the College's tuition charges are low and it doesn't participate in tuition discounting, every student, in effect, receives significant financial assistance. Seventy percent of the freshmen received some form of financial aid for the 2015–16 school year. Students applying for financial assistance must complete Grove City College's financial aid form. The College employs over 1,000 of the 2,500 students on campus, so there is plenty of opportunity for employment, both on and off campus.

Faculty

Grove City College faculty members are primarily focused on teaching students, although many members are involved with research and writing, Eighty percent of the full-time faculty members hold doctoral or other terminal degrees. Many of the administrative staff members also teach part-time in various departments. The student-faculty ratio is approximately 13:1. Faculty members emphasize teaching and attention to the students' individual needs; they also participate extensively in the College's extracurricular programs.

Student Government

The Student Government Association provides an opportunity for direct student interaction with the faculty members and administration in matters relating to campus activities. Students serve on regular College committees (library, publications, religious activities, and student activities) and also on the Men's and Women's Governing Board and the Discipline Committee.

Admission Requirements

The College seeks academically qualified students without regard to age, race, color, creed, sex, marital status, disability, or national/ethnic origin. An applicant for admission should be a high school graduate with the following recommended units: English, 4; foreign language, 3; mathematics, 3; history, 2; and science, 3. Engineering, science, and mathematics majors should have 4 units each in both mathematics and science. An interview is highly recommended, especially for those who live within a day's drive (400 miles). Auditions are required for music majors.

Transfer students may receive advanced standing if they have maintained good academic standing at their previous institution(s).

Application and Information

An Early Decision applicant should take the SAT, ACT, and/or CLT in the eleventh grade, visit the College for an interview, and submit the application by November 15; notification of the admission decision is mailed on December 15. The application should include scores on the SAT, ACT, or CLT; a high school transcript; two letters of recommendation (one academic and one character or spiritual reference); and a nonrefundable application fee of $50. Admitted Early Decision applicants must accept by January 15 and submit a nonrefundable deposit of $250.

A Regular Decision applicant should take the SAT, ACT, and/or CLT by October or November of the senior year in high school. Applicants seeking Regular Decision must submit the completed application and supporting documents by February 1 of their senior year. Notification of the admission decision is mailed on March 1. Students who are offered admission should reply as soon as possible, but no later than May 1, and include a nonrefundable deposit of $250. Applications received after February 1 are considered as space permits.

Additional information may be obtained from:

Sarah E. Gibbs
Director of Admissions
Grove City College
100 Campus Drive
Grove City, Pennsylvania 16127-2104
Phone: 724-458-2100
Fax: 724-458-3395
E-mail: admissions@gcc.edu
Website: http://www.gcc.edu
www.facebook.com/GCCAdmissions (Facebook)
http://twitter.com/GroveCtyCollege (Twitter)
instagram.com/GroveCityAdmissions (Instagram)
http://www.youvisit.com/tour/grovecitycollege?pl=v
(YouVisit virtual tour)

Harbison Chapel is a center of the Christian community at Grove City College.

COLLEGE CLOSE-UPS

GWYNEDD MERCY UNIVERSITY

GWYNEDD VALLEY, PENNSYLVANIA

★ To read more about this school, visit http://petersons.to/gwyneddmercyuniversity

Gwynedd Mercy University

The University

Gwynedd Mercy University (GMercyU) is a Catholic university with a strong foundation in the liberal arts and a deep commitment to the Mercy tradition of service to society. GMercyU believes that each person has the power to be a hero—to another individual, to a community, to the world. The University supports students in their quest to find their superpower with a dedicated team of professors who take an interest in who they are, and who they aspire to be. Students are encouraged to join a growing team of distinctive Mercy graduates who are doing more than launching successful careers; they're living productive and meaningful lives. With excellent programs in nursing, allied health, arts and sciences, education, and business, GMercyU supports students in making a difference in their own lives and in the lives of others.

GMercyU is set on 160 beautiful acres in southeastern Pennsylvania and is home to nearly 2,000 undergraduate students, 19 NCAA Division III athletic teams, and dozens of clubs and organizations. The University is large enough to offer a vibrant campus life but small enough that students get the personal attention they need to find their superpower.

In addition to taking classes toward graduation, students can join the University's nationally-renowned choir, join the student leadership program, improve the lives of others through Alternative Spring Break and Mercy Works programs, be part of a winning athletic team, hang out in the Late Nite Lounge, or choose from many other options. Student also can enjoy several on-campus dining choices or take a free shuttle to nearby restaurants when they're looking for a change of scene. Campus also is just 30 minutes from Philadelphia, providing easy access to a wide array of cultural, entertainment, internship, career, and volunteer opportunities in one of the nation's most exciting cities.

With more than 20,000 alumni, Gwynedd Mercy University has a strong reputation for preparing distinctive graduates who make a difference in the world. Payscale named Gwynedd Mercy University as one of the "Top Colleges for Producing Graduates Who Make the World a Better Place" in 2014. In 2016, Payscale also ranked GMercyU as a Top 20 School in Pennsylvania for Return on Investment, and the *Wall Street Journal/Times Higher Education* College Rankings placed Gwynedd Mercy University among the top schools in the nation for the things that matter most, including student outcomes. Gwynedd Mercy University also is considered a College of Distinction, and is part of the U.S. President's Community Service Honor Roll.

Location

Gwynedd Mercy University's idyllic 160-acre campus is located in Gwynedd Valley, Pennsylvania, a suburb 30 miles from downtown Philadelphia. While on campus, students can enjoy beautiful outdoor spaces perfect for a long run, a friendly game of Frisbee, or a quiet lunch with friends under a tree. Philadelphia's Old City, South Street, sports arenas, and some of the best restaurants and concert venues around are just a 30-minute car or train ride from campus. The University also is just minutes from several major highways, including the Pennsylvania Turnpike and Interstate 95. In addition to the vibrant city life of Philadelphia, New Jersey beaches, the Pocono Mountains, Washington D.C., and New York City are just about two hours from campus. Students can take advantage of free shuttle service to the local train station or to the many shops, restaurants, and entertainment areas nearby.

Majors and Degrees

Gwynedd Mercy University offers baccalaureate degrees in accounting, behavioral/social gerontology, biology, communication, computer information science, criminal justice, education/special education, English, finance, history, human resource management, human services, management, marketing, mathematics, medical laboratory science, nursing, occupational science/pre-OT, philosophy, psychology, radiologic technology, radiation therapy, respiratory care, social work, and sports management.

Associate degrees are awarded in liberal studies, natural science, and respiratory care. GMercyU also offers a number of master's degrees in business, education, and nursing, including a 4+1 MBA program on campus. Students who want to earn their doctorate degrees can choose from programs in education and nursing. Many graduate programs are offered in accelerated and/or online formats.

Academic Programs

The academic year is divided into two semesters, and most baccalaureate degree programs require the completion of a minimum of 125 credit hours. All of Gwynedd Mercy University's undergraduate programs include a strong focus on the liberal arts to ensure students develop some of today's most in-demand skills, including communication, critical thinking, and problem-solving. Liberal arts courses include language; literature and the fine arts; humanities; and behavioral, social, and natural sciences. Students have access to the Academic Resource Center for tutoring and writing assistance at no additional charge.

Individualized credit-bearing internships and work experience programs are available and recommended in all majors to give students firsthand experience in their chosen field before they graduate. Nearby Fortune 500 companies offer a variety of experiences to students in business and accounting, for example. TAP, the Teacher Apprentice Program, places every education major in the classroom one day a week beginning in their first year. All allied health and nursing programs require clinical experience. Students also have the opportunity to conduct research and present at academic and industry conferences, depending on their major. Students are encouraged to develop a global perspective through various study abroad and alternative spring break service opportunities.

Off-Campus Programs

The excellent on-campus laboratory facilities are extended by affiliations with more than 200 hospitals and health care agencies in Pennsylvania, New Jersey, and Delaware, where students may complete their clinical experiences. Merck provides a one-semester industrial laboratory experience for qualified biology majors. Gwynedd Mercy University also maintains a close relationship with nearby universities and companies, including Johnson & Johnson, McNeil, Sun Company, and Jefferson University, just to name a few.

Academic Facilities

Gwynedd Mercy University has expanded its physical facilities as its student enrollment has increased. Frances M. Maguire Hall is home to the Frances M. Maguire School of Nursing and Health Professions as well as the division of natural sciences. This 50,000 square-foot state-of-the-art facility offers laboratories for areas such as nursing skills, respiratory care, radiation therapy, organic chemistry, and microbiology. The University's SIM® family includes newborn, infant, child, and adult simulation mannequins that allow students to practice techniques before performing them on real patients in clinical settings. An advanced video system also gives students real-time feedback on care techniques.

Gwynedd Mercy University continues to "discover the Next" with the addition of the newest academic building on campus, University Hall, which opened in the spring of 2014. The building is the home of the School of Business and Education. University Hall is equipped with state-of-the-art technology to further enhance educational opportunities, including a Financial Trading Room, equipped with a real-time stock ticker.

The Griffin Complex houses the University's recreation facilities, including a full gymnasium and track, racquetball court, and weight room. The University's Julia Ball Auditorium is a 400-seat space for theatrical productions, musical events, and other cultural and academic programs. The Student Technology Center is equipped with personal computers and printers and the latest software for student use. The Valie Genuardi Hobbit House is a fully licensed academic lab school located right on campus. It is home to nursery and pre-kindergarten students, and also provides a place for students in the School of Business and Education to gain valuable hands-on experience.

The Keiss Hall Library and Learning Commons links academic support services, library services, and career development services, providing a one-stop academic center that facilitates student success.

Costs

The published 2017–18 academic year tuition for full-time students (12 to 18 credits per semester) is $32,820. The published tuition for allied health and nursing students is $34,820. Room and board costs average $12,070. Professional liability fees for students enrolled in clinical components and lab fees are extra. The University offers generous scholarships ranging from $11,000 to full tuition, and other financial aid to qualified students.

Financial Aid

Gwynedd Mercy University's financial aid program is designed to provide financial assistance to academically qualified students whose resources are inadequate to meet the costs of attending the University. The student Financial Aid Committee endeavors to assist as many students as possible, using Gwynedd Mercy University funds as well as federal, state, and other available funds. Aid is awarded on the basis of demonstrated financial need, academic proficiency, and responsible campus citizenship. In 2015–16, 100 percent of the University's first-time full-time students received some form of financial aid.

Faculty

The University's student-faculty ratio is 11:1, allowing for personal contact, advising, and after-class instruction. This is a widely acknowledged strength of the Gwynedd Mercy University experience. For nursing students in the clinical setting, there are never more than 8 students to 1 clinical adviser; in the allied health programs, there often is one-to-one instruction. The quality of teaching is enhanced by the diversified interests of the faculty. Faculty members teach both day and evening classes, allowing students the greatest flexibility in scheduling. Tutoring is available in all disciplines at no additional charge.

Student Government

All students are encouraged to take part in the responsibilities of student government. Student participation and shared responsibility for the welfare of the University are promoted through a framework of committees.

Admission Requirements

Admission to Gwynedd Mercy University is based on a student's high school record, rank in class, SAT or ACT scores, counselor's recommendation, and choice of major. Entrance requirements vary with the program. The rolling admission policy allows students to be informed of an admission decision within two to three weeks of submitting their completed application.

Gwynedd Mercy University awards credit for satisfactory completion of Advanced Placement courses, provided students receive an AP exam score of 3 or higher.

A minimum 2.0 grade point average (on a 4.0 scale) is generally required to transfer from another institution. Gwynedd Mercy University does, however, retain the right to require a higher GPA for admission to some programs.

Gwynedd Mercy University does not discriminate against any applicant for admission to or employment at the University because of race, religion, age, gender, sexual orientation, gender identity, national origin, disability, color, marital status, veteran status, genetic characteristics, or any other characteristic protected by federal, state, or local law in the administration of its educational, admission, scholarship, or loan policies.

Application and Information

All prospective applicants are urged to visit the campus to meet with an admission counselor, dean, or program director. To apply for admission, applicants should complete the online application available at gmercyu.edu. First-time freshmen must also submit an official high school transcript or equivalency certificate; a written recommendation from a principal, teacher, guidance counselor, or employer; and results of the SAT or ACT (for recent high school graduates). All applicants should verify that they meet the specific requirements and have the necessary high school prerequisites for admission.

Students who wish to transfer to Gwynedd Mercy University should submit the same online application, high school and college transcripts, and a letter of recommendation.

For additional information or to schedule campus tours and visits, students are encouraged to register with the Enrollment Support Services Office at admissions@gmercyu.edu or contact the office at 800-342-5462.

For more information, contact:

Office of Admissions
Gwynedd Mercy University
1325 Sumneytown Pike
P.O. Box 901
Gwynedd Valley, Pennsylvania 19437-0901
Phone: 800-342-5462 (toll-free)
E-mail: admissions@gmercycu.edu
Website: http://www.gmercyu.edu/admissions-aid/undergraduate-admissions
https://twitter.com/GMercyU
https://www.facebook.com/GMercyU

Students walk to and from classes in University Hall, the newest academic building on campus.

HARDING UNIVERSITY

SEARCY, ARKANSAS

★ To read more about this school, visit http://petersons.to/hardinguniversity

HARDING UNIVERSITY

The University

Harding University was founded on Christian principles and a liberal arts tradition. Since 1924, Harding has challenged its students to pursue scholarship, service, teamwork, excellence, and commitment. The largest private university in Arkansas, it is ranked by *U.S. News and World Report* and Princeton Review as one of the top liberal arts universities in the South and attracts exceptional high school students representing every U.S. state and more than 54 nations and territories.

Harding University is accredited by the Higher Learning Commission and maintains specialized accreditation for its programs as appropriate to its educational purpose. Students have opportunities for hands-on learning whether it be engineering majors developing concept, design, and construction of an off-road vehicle; journalism majors managing, writing and editing for the student newspaper; or nursing majors conducting exam simulations on high-fidelity mannequins. With a student-teacher ratio of 17 to 1, strong relationships are built in and out of the classroom.

Students can cultivate friendships and interests with 120 academic and professional organizations and 31 social clubs. Ranging from the arts, music, politics, business, diversity, children, missions, service, and the environment, the clubs on campus offer a variety of interests to explore.

Provided with a Christian perspective through which to appreciate various disciplines, students excel as scholars and develop leadership skills. As a result, Harding alumni display character, conviction, and a competitive edge and are prepared for success at prestigious graduate schools and companies throughout the nation.

Location

Harding is located in Searcy, Arkansas, and offers students a hometown feeling with easy access to major cities. The University is about an hour away from Little Rock, Arkansas, and the Bill and Hillary Clinton National Airport and is about 2 hours away from Memphis, Tennessee. Located in The Natural State, University students have several nearby options such as the Little Red River, Pinnacle Mountain, and Petit Jean State Parks for fishing, camping, hiking, and other outdoor activities. Arkansas is home to 52 state parks.

Majors and Degrees

Housed within nine colleges, the University offers more than 100 academic majors, including 14 preprofessional programs, taught by top instructors.

Within the College of Allied Health, students may earn a Bachelor of Arts degree in communication sciences and disorders, a Master of Science degree in speech-language pathology, a Master of Science degree in physician assistant studies, and a Doctor of Physical Therapy degree.

The College of Arts and Humanities offers a wide range of degrees in the humanities, arts, English language and literature, foreign language and international studies, history and social science, mass communication, music, oral communication, and theater.

In the College of Bible and Ministry, there are degrees in Bible and religion, biblical languages, Christian education, missions, preaching, and youth and family ministry.

Students in the Paul R. Carter College of Business Administration may receive degrees in accounting, economics, finance, global economic development, health care management, international business management, management information systems, marketing, and professional sales.

Those interested in teaching may earn degrees in early childhood P–4, middle childhood/early adolescence English/language arts/social science 4–8, middle childhood/early adolescence math/science 4–8, secondary education, and special education endorsement (P–3) in the Cannon-Clary College of Education.

The Carr College of Nursing offers a Bachelor of Science in Nursing, enabling students to take the NCLEX-RN exam after graduation. There also is a Master of Science in Nursing degree program, preparing students to be family nurse practitioners.

Students can earn a Doctor of Pharmacy degree through the University's four-year program in the College of Pharmacy.

The College of Sciences allows students to study health sciences, behavioral sciences, biology, chemistry, computer science, engineering and physics, exercise and sport sciences, family and consumer sciences, kinesiology, and mathematics.

Academic Programs

For the basic requirements necessary for each degree, prospective students should visit the Harding University online catalog at www.harding.edu/catalog.

Students may apply and participate in the Honors College with acceptance based on acceptance to the University and an ACT score of 27 or higher or an SAT score of 1220 or higher. These students may take honors-level courses and graduate with honors.

In addition, various majors may allow students to receive their teaching licensure in the process.

Off-Campus Programs

Harding offers multiple study abroad programs in locations such as Australia, Chile, England, France, Greece, Italy, and Zambia that will help expand cultural awareness and understanding. Nearly 50 percent of each graduating class takes advantage of one of Harding's international experiences. At each location, students are accompanied and taught by University faculty. Costs are based on 16 tuition hours and include housing and meals.

Academic Facilities

Harding's campus consists of 13 academic buildings, cafeteria, two auditoriums, a world-class recreation center, a library, a performing arts center, a student center, student health services, 14 residence halls, and six apartment complexes.

Costs

The basic undergraduate, on-campus cost for 2016–17 for 15 hours of enrollment per semester was $8,970 for a semester and $17,940 for the year. Tuition was $598 per course hour. Students paid $500 a year for a required technology fee, $3,398 for a standard dorm room, and $3,490 for a standard meal plan of 190 meals plus a $225 declining cash balance. The overall total came to $25,395.

Financial Aid

On average, 90 percent of Harding University freshman students receive financial assistance. In 2015–16, Harding awarded students more than $13 million in institutional need-based grants and more than $24 million in institutional scholarships. In addition, students received nearly $9 million in federal, state, and externally funded scholarships and grants.

Admission Requirements

Students wishing to apply to Harding must have a 19 ACT or 900 SAT and 3.0 high school GPA (on a 4.0 scale). In addition, high school graduates should have completed at least 15 units in academic subjects. Specifically, an applicant should have completed 4 units of English, 3 units of mathematics (taken from general math, geometry, algebra, trigonometry, precalculus, or calculus), 3 units of social studies (taken from civics, American history, world history, or geography), and 2 units of natural science (taken from physical science, biology, physics, or chemistry). Students planning to major in any area of health care are strongly encouraged to take one or more chemistry courses while in high school. Although not required for admission, two years of foreign language is recommended. The additional units may come from any academic area.

Application and Information

Prospective students may apply online at www.harding.edu/apply/.

Because Harding receives so many applications, it recommends that students apply before fall of their senior year of high school—even if they haven't taken the ACT or SAT. Admissions advisers are glad to help students through this process.

For more information, prospective students should contact:

Harding University
Box 12255
Searcy, Arkansas 72149-5615
Phone: 501-279-4407
Website: http://www.harding.edu
http://www.facebook.com/HardingU
http://www.twitter.com/HardingU

Harding University's student population represents all 50 states and 54 nations and territories. With more than 5,900 students, Harding is the largest private college or university in Arkansas.

HIGH POINT UNIVERSITY

HIGH POINT, NORTH CAROLINA

★ For more information, visit http://petersons.to/highpoint

HIGH POINT UNIVERSITY

The University

At High Point University, every student receives an extraordinary education in an inspiring environment with caring people.®

U.S. News & World Report ranked High Point University #1 among Regional Colleges in the South, the Most Innovative Regional College in the South, and #1 for Best Undergraduate Teaching in Regional Colleges in the South. The environment of excellence transforms high school students into distinguished scholars who are prepared to tackle the challenges of the 21st century and thrive in an ever-changing global marketplace.

With more than 4,600 undergraduate students, High Point University (HPU) is a small liberal arts school with big-school facilities. Its 16 varsity teams play at the NCAA Division I level. Students come to HPU from 48 states and 37 countries, providing the school with great diversity in student history and experience. Yet, High Point University offers its students a safe community that feels like home, where the average class size is 17 and professors don't just know students' names—they know who they are and who they want to become.

The array of majors is vast and each has been uniquely designed to challenge, inspire and transform. The academic program includes 47 undergraduate majors, 51 undergraduate minors, 12 preprofessional programs, and 13 graduate programs.

The curriculum emphasizes the study of the liberal arts in the belief that there is no better way to encourage communication skills, critical thinking, and personal integrity. The goal is to feed students' appetites for academic achievement and equip them for further education, the job market, or lives of service. Within the classroom environment, students find High Point University professors to be engaging mentors, eager to share their own research and scholarly interests; and beyond the classroom, students are constantly met with opportunities to learn in a very practical and innovative way. HPU's signature experiential learning program differentiates this collegiate experience from others, and reinforces what is taught in the classroom while providing students with resources for professional networking and deep, practical knowledge of their fields.

Founded in 1924, High Point University has a strong academic history and is committed to building character, modeling values, and ensuring that students graduate with both expertise in their disciplines and the skills necessary to be successful in life.

Location

The cities of High Point, Greensboro, and Winston-Salem in North Carolina form the Piedmont Triad, with High Point University located in the center of the state. The Appalachian Mountains are 2 hours away and the Atlantic coast is 3-1/2 hours away.

Majors and Degrees

High Point University offers Bachelor of Arts (B.A.) and Bachelor of Science (B.S.) degrees. Students may choose from the following majors and concentrations through the colleges listed below.

The School of Art and Design: Graphic Design and Digital Imaging, Interior Design, Studio Art, and Visual Merchandising Design.

The Earl N. Phillips School of Business: Accounting, International Business, Business Administration with an optional concentration in entrepreneurship; Marketing; and Sales, with an optional concentration in the furniture industry.

The Nido R. Qubein School of Communication: Documentary Media, Electronic Media Production, Game and Interactive Media Design, Journalism, Media and Popular Culture Studies, and Strategic Communication.

The School of Education: Elementary Education; Health and Physical Education; Secondary Education (9–12 licensure), with sub areas in biology, comprehensive science, English, history, and mathematics; Special Education (K–12 Licensure); and Special Subjects (K–12 Licensure), with sub areas in art education and Spanish.

The School of Health Sciences: Athletic training, Exercise Science, Physical Therapy, and Physician Assistant Studies..

The David R. Hayworth College of Arts and Sciences: Actuarial Science; Biochemistry; Biology; Chemistry; Computer Science; Criminal Justice; English with sub areas in literature and writing; History; Human Relations; International Relations; Mathematical Economics; Mathematics; French and Francophone Studies; Spanish; Music with sub areas in instrumental studies, piano/organ, and voice; Nonprofit Leadership and Management; Philosophy; Physics; Political Science; Psychology; Religion; Sociology; and Theatre with sub areas in performance, technical, dramatic writing, and collaborative theater.

The High Point University Graduate School offers the following programs: Strategic Communication (M.A.); Doctor of Education in Educational Leadership (Ed.D.); Educational Leadership (M.Ed.); Elementary Education (M.Ed.); Secondary Math (M.Ed.); Special Education (M.E.); Teaching Elementary Education K–6 (M.A.T.); Teaching Secondary Mathematics 9–12 (M.A.T.); Educational Administration (add-on license); History (M.A.); Master of Business Administration (M.B.A.); Nonprofit Management (M.A.); Master of Physician Assistant Studies (M.P.A.S.); and Doctor of Pharmacy (Pharm.D.).

Academic Programs

High Point University is committed to academic excellence. With small classes, caring professors and a myriad of student success stories, HPU has positioned itself as a place for scholars to thrive. A vibrant and engaging Honors Scholars Program recognizes and encourages creativity and academic achievement in top academic students.

Throughout their time at HPU, students are given real-world practical learning opportunities. The Office of Career and Professional Development helps students secure internships and jobs with companies as NASA, MTV, Disney, Krispy Kreme, NBC, the Democratic and Republican National Conventions, and Merrill Lynch. The connections that students are exposed to during internships can often help lead them to full-time positions.

Off-Campus Programs

With a variety of extraordinary options at some of the most prestigious universities in the world, students at High Point University are encouraged to travel abroad as early as the summer after their freshman year. The university has partnerships with 25 different universities in 29 different countries including Argentina, Australia, Austria, the Czech Republic, Ecuador, Fiji, France, Germany, India, Italy, Japan, Russia, South Africa, Spain, and the United Kingdom.

An expanding Service Learning Program also provides more than a dozen courses with an off-campus service-learning component. These courses put students in community agencies committed to furthering the common good, where they can see and experience first-hand the issues they discuss in class.

Academic Facilities

Cottrell Hall, home to the Flanagan Center for Student Success is a 40,000 square-foot facility that is the central hub of activity for students preparing for job interviews, seeking career development opportunities, and looking for ways to diversify their career skills. It houses the Office of Career and Professional Development, the Office of Study Abroad, the Office of Undergraduate Research and Creative Works, the Center for Entrepreneurship, Service Learning, the Freshman Success Program, and more.

HPU's Human Biomechanics and Physiology Lab is one of the most advanced of its kind. With state-of-the-art equipment and 13,150 square-feet of learning space, the lab is capturing national attention.

The Nido R. Qubein School of Communication features two high-definition TV studios, audio recording studios, a screening theater, editing labs, a student-operated radio station, a nationally-cited survey and research center, an interactive media and game design facility, and various computer labs. The school's Board of Advisers includes leaders in radio, television, newspaper, and magazine companies across the nation.

HPU's School of Art and Design emphasizes the importance of hand skills combined with technological proficiency in profession-specific software. Students studying in the School of Art and Design have access to cutting-edge equipment including a technology lab and several design-specific computer labs.

The 31,000 square-foot, LEED-Certified School of Education building houses the psychology department and the NCATE-accredited education school. It is equipped with simulated classrooms and clinical labs where psychology majors and conduct hands-on testing and experiments.

The Plato S. Wilson School of Commerce houses the Center for Financial Research, which serves as a trading room and allows students to receive real-world, practical learning opportunities. The Center includes teaching and research technology, including financial databases, investment software, a stock ticker, and more.

Costs

For the 2017–18 academic year, High Point University's tuition and fees (including tuition, parking, laundry, entrance to athletic and cultural events, intramurals, Campus Concierge service, academic tutoring, library and media services, etc.) for full-time students is $34,005; room and board are $13,350.

Financial Aid

The Office of Student Financial Planning works diligently to assist students in their pursuit of postsecondary education at High Point University. Although the financial aid process can be complex, High Point's Financial Planning staff is well-trained and highly qualified to make students' experiences positive and rewarding.

Interested students should submit the Free Application for Federal Student Aid (FAFSA) electronically via www.fafsa.ed.gov. The earliest that students may begin filing the FAFSA is January 1 of the senior year prior to the semester of entrance to HPU. The HPU school code is 002933.

The results from filing the FAFSA will be electronically transmitted to HPU for review. This form will produce an expected family contribution based on the family's financial data and will determine students' eligibility for HPU's need-based programs.

HPU will not be able to estimate students' eligibility for need-based aid until the FAFSA is filed. While there is not a deadline date to the FAFSA, it is important to file as early as possible; HPU will begin developing financial aid packages for students by March 1.

All major High Point University academic scholarships are awarded through the Presidential Scholarship Program. Each undergraduate admissions application also serves as an application for the scholarships.

Faculty

High Point University has a student-faculty ratio of 15:1 and an average class size of fewer than 17 students. More than 80 percent of faculty members have earned either the Ph.D. or other terminal degrees. Faculty members teach all classes; HPU does not use any graduate students or assistants to teach class. The Student Success Coaches are responsible for providing appropriate academic and transitional support to first-year students applicable to all aspects of the student's life tasks: academic, personal, social, and career. The coaches assist in this transition to college life and serve as the academic adviser for the first year. Students are assigned to success coaches based on their academic major.

Student Activities

With more than 100 student-led clubs and organizations represented on campus, HPU intentionally seeks to involve students in campus life through a diverse variety of platforms, including professional development associations, fine arts clubs, fraternities and sororities, honors societies, an active student government organization, religious life clubs, service organizations, special-interest groups, and more. In addition, HPU students annually provide more than 110,000 hours of voluntary service to the local community.

Admission Requirements

Freshman applicants must be graduates of accredited secondary schools and must meet the minimum course requirements which are as follows: 4 English units, 4 mathematics units, 3 science units, 3 social studies units, and 2 foreign language units. Freshman applicants must submit their scores on the SAT or the ACT. International applicants should submit both TOEFL and SAT or ACT scores. Campus visits and personal interviews are strongly recommended.

Students who have completed Advanced Placement courses in high school and who have achieved scores of 4 or 5 on the Advanced Placement test administered by the College Board may receive credit at High Point University. Applicants may also receive credit for university-parallel courses successfully completed prior to enrollment at High Point University, including courses completed while in high school through dual-enrollment or International Baccalaureate programs.

Application and Information

The Office of Undergraduate Admissions accepts online applications for enrollment on a competitive basis using the Common Application. Freshmen deadlines are as follows:

- Early Decision (binding) application deadline: November 1
  Admissions notification date: November 27
- Early Action (nonbinding) application deadline: November 15
  Admissions notification date: December 15
- Early Decision II (binding) application deadline: February 1
  Admissions notification is rolling
- Regular Decision application deadline: March 15
  Admissions notification is rolling past February 1

Over 85 percent of enrolled students each year will apply using one of the two early November application plans.

Official transcripts (high school and college, where applicable), one letter of recommendation, and a Counselor Report Form must be sent directly to the university by the appropriate school official. Students should request that copies of their SAT, ACT, or TOEFL scores be sent to the Office of Admissions at High Point University by the testing agency. All requests for application materials and information should be directed to:

Office of Undergraduate Admissions
High Point University
One University Parkway
High Point, North Carolina 27268-3598
United States of America
Phone: 336-841-9216
800-345-6993 (toll-free)
E-mail: admiss@highpoint.edu
Website: http://www.highpoint.edu

HILLSDALE COLLEGE
HILLSDALE, MICHIGAN

★ For more information, visit http://petersons.to/hillsdalecollege

HILLSDALE COLLEGE
PURSUING TRUTH · DEFENDING LIBERTY SINCE 1844

COLLEGE CLOSE-UPS

The College

Hillsdale College is a private, independent, nonsectarian institution of higher learning founded in 1844 by men and women who described themselves as "grateful to God for the inestimable blessings" resulting from civil and religious liberty and as "believing that the diffusion of sound learning is essential to the perpetuity of those blessings." The College has maintained institutional independence since its founding by refusing to accept aid from or control by federal authorities. Far-reaching private support from a national constituency has enabled Hillsdale to continue its trusteeship of the intellectual and spiritual inheritance tracing to Athens and Jerusalem, a heritage finding its clearest expression in the American experiment of self-government under law.

The undergraduate enrollment for fall 2016 was 1,440, of whom 50 percent were men and 50 percent were women. The College draws students from forty-eight states and twelve other countries. Approximately 35 percent of students are from Michigan. The entering freshman class in 2016 had the following mid-range scores: high school grade-point average of 3.67–4.0, ACT of 28–32, and SAT of 1830–2150 (old)/1310–1490 (new). These scores are all well above national averages.

Location

Hillsdale College is located amidst the hills, dales, and lakes of south-central Michigan. The Indiana and Ohio turnpikes are each 30 minutes away, and the College is within close reach of such metropolitan areas as Detroit, Chicago, Cleveland, Toledo, Ft. Wayne, and Indianapolis. The town of Hillsdale is a county seat with a population of 10,000. Stores, churches, restaurants, and movie theaters are all within walking distance of the campus.

Majors and Degrees

Hillsdale awards Bachelor of Arts and Bachelor of Science degrees in accounting, applied mathematics, art, biochemistry, biology, chemistry, classics, economics, English, exercise science, financial management, French, German, Greek, history, Latin, marketing/management, mathematics, music, philosophy, physical education, physics, politics, psychology, religion, rhetoric and public address, Spanish, speech, sport management, sport psychology, and theater. Interdisciplinary majors are available in American studies, Christian studies, comparative literature, European studies, international studies in business and foreign language, political economy, and sociology and social thought. Preprofessional programs are offered in allied health sciences (including optometry, pharmacy, and physical therapy), dentistry, education, engineering, environmental sciences, journalism, law, medicine and osteopathy, theology, and veterinary medicine.

The Academic Program

Hillsdale operates on a two-semester schedule, with the fall term beginning in late August and ending in mid-December and the spring term beginning in mid-January and ending in mid-May. Two 3-week summer sessions are also offered.

The College maintains its defense of the traditional liberal arts curriculum, convinced that it is the best preparation for meeting the challenges of modern life, and that it offers to people of all backgrounds not only an important body of knowledge, but also timeless truths about the human condition. The liberal arts are dedicated to stimulating students' intellectual curiosity, to encouraging the critical, well-disciplined mind, and to fostering personal growth through academic challenge. Every Hillsdale College student is required to complete a structured core of courses in the humanities, natural sciences, and social sciences, including Great Books courses and a course on the U.S. Constitution. All students declare a major by the end of the sophomore year. To graduate, students must complete a minimum 124 hours of course work and fulfill the requirements of at least one major field. The B.A. program includes a foreign language proficiency requirement. The B.S. program requires additional studies in mathematics and the natural sciences.

The Center for Constructive Alternatives conducts four weeklong symposia during the academic year and is one of the largest college lecture series in America. These programs, with themes ranging from historical to political, business, science, and the arts, bring to the campus distinguished scholars and public figures of national and international renown. All students are required to enroll in one seminar for credit.

Off-Campus Programs

For forty years, the Washington Hillsdale Internship Program (WHIP) has provided students the opportunity to participate in full-time, academically intensive internships in the nation's capital. The program has been significantly bolstered with the 2008 establishment of the Hillsdale College Allan P. Kirby, Jr. Center for Constitutional Studies and Citizenship in Washington, D.C. Past interns and fellows have been placed in locations as challenging and rewarding as the U.S. House of Representatives, the U.S. Senate, the White House, various think tanks including the Heritage Foundation, news and media outlets, national security agencies, lobbying firms, international trade and relations organizations, and private sector companies.

Through the College's affiliations with the Center for Medieval and Renaissance Studies and the Oxford Study Abroad Program, Hillsdale students are able to study abroad for a summer or a year at one of the more than thirty colleges of Oxford University. Hillsdale offers a summer business program in cooperation with Regent's College in London, England, and the opportunity to study at the University of St. Andrews in St. Andrews, Scotland. Science students benefit from Hillsdale's 685-acre field research laboratory in northern Michigan, a marine biology program in the Florida Keys, and internship opportunities with the Omaha Zoo. Foreign language students frequently study abroad in Argentina, France, Germany, and Spain. Qualified individual students who wish to study in another country for a semester or a year are assisted by their faculty advisor and the registrar in planning a program that enables them to gain academic credit as well as take full advantage of their experience.

Academic Facilities

The Hillsdale College Mossey Library is a three-floor facility with a collection of more than 1,000,000 volumes. In addition to the main study and research collections, the Library also contains a number of rare and special holdings, including the Ludwig von Mises, Russell Kirk, Richardson Heritage, and Richard Weaver collections. Connected to other Michigan libraries through MelCat, and with college libraries nationwide via interlibrary loan, students have access to most any material necessary for on-campus research. Numerous individual study areas and group study rooms are available for students, as well as computer research terminals.

Lane and Kendall Halls at the front of campus serve as the primary academic facilities in the social sciences and humanities and contain classroom space and faculty offices, as well as a special laboratory for experimental psychology. The Strosacker Science Center houses the departments of biology, chemistry, and physics. The Joseph H. Moss Family Laboratory Wing, completed in 2008, is a 17,000-square-foot addition that includes a microbiology/cell biology lab, anatomy/physiology lab with human cadaver access, conservation genetics lab, water lab, greenhouse, and organic/general chemistry labs. The 32,000-square-foot Herbert Henry Dow Science Building provides additional classrooms, research laboratories, animal rooms, and a computer lab. The Mary Randall Preschool is a circular laboratory school in which nursery school children are taught by students specializing in early childhood education and psychology. Experts in the field have called this building "a model for the nation." The Hillsdale Academy, a K–12 private model school, provides additional opportunities for classroom observation.

The Roche Sports Complex is a facility available to varsity athletes and the general student body alike. The building houses the

60,000-square-foot Dawn Tibbetts Potter Arena, which features a student fitness center and basketball/volleyball courts. The building also houses the John "Jack" McAvoy Natatorium for swimming and diving, an exercise physiology and sports medicine facility, four racquetball courts, extensive locker room space, and a weight/fitness room. Adjacent is the 7,000-seat capacity Frank "Muddy" Waters Stadium, which features an artificial surface football field; all-weather, Olympic-quality eight-lane running track; outdoor tennis courts; and fields for soccer, baseball, and women's softball. The new Margot V. Biermann Athletic Center houses a six-lane track and four tennis courts.

The Sage Center for the Arts is home to the departments of art, theater, and speech. This 47,000-square-foot facility contains studios, classroom space, an exhibition gallery, a prop- and scene-construction shop, a sound studio, graphics lab, black box theatre, and the Markel Auditorium, a 353-seat performance hall (with orchestra pit). Completed in 2003, the 32,809-square-foot Howard Music Hall houses office, studio, classroom, rehearsal, and performance space for the John E. N. and Dede Howard Department of Music. Notable features include the McNamara Rehearsal Hall, Conrad Recital Hall, and studio space for percussion and jazz studies. Lower-level practice rooms are available to students during business hours without reservation.

Dedicated in January 2008, the 53,000-square-foot Grewcock Student Union is the center of student life. The two-story structure houses the cafeteria, bookstore, student mail center, offices for student activities and publications, a lounge with a 100-inch flat screen television, a formal lounge and conference room, AJ's Café, and a game area. The entire building is wireless, and any Hillsdale student can check out a laptop at the main desk.

Faculty

The faculty consists of 127 full-time members with a 10:1 student-teacher ratio and average class sizes of 15. No classes are taught by graduate students. The size and closeness of the College community enable personal attention and faculty mentorship inside the classroom and during office visits after class. Each student has a faculty advisor for core and major coursework who directs the program of study and provides academic and career counseling. Hillsdale's faculty considers teaching their first priority. Many faculty members also engage in research and scholarly writing, supported by summer and sabbatical leaves funded by the College, and are often invited to comment on the national scene in lecture programs and media outlets.

Athletics

Hillsdale's Charger athletes compete in 14 intercollegiate NCAA Division II varsity sports as part of the Great Lakes Intercollegiate Athletic Conference (Great Midwest Athletic Conference, effective July 2017). Hillsdale College sponsors varsity basketball, cross-country, swimming and diving, softball, tennis, indoor and outdoor track and field, and volleyball for women, and varsity baseball, basketball, cross-country, golf, football, tennis, and indoor and outdoor track and field for men. Since 1998, the College has produced 107 athletic All-Americans and 28 conference champions, and Hillsdale teams have qualified for national tournaments nineteen times. Thirty-four athletes have earned national academic honors in their respective sports as well.

Hillsdale also enthusiastically supports men's and women's intramural sports programs, which include flag football, volleyball, basketball, table tennis, racquetball, dodgeball, sand volleyball, and special events like Intramural Games. Hillsdale encourages and supports club sports too, and currently has 12 recognized groups—men's baseball, men's rugby, men's soccer, women's soccer, co-ed firearms club, men's golf, women's volleyball, men's volleyball, co-ed crew, co-ed equestrian club, women's cheerleading, and co-ed tennis. The College also sponsors a competitive shotgun team.

Student Life

Four national fraternities, three national sororities, and more than 100 other social, academic, spiritual, and service organizations provide Hillsdale students with a diverse array of cocurricular opportunities. A resident drama troupe and dance company, a concert choir and chamber chorale, a jazz program with big band and combos, instrumental chamber ensembles from string quartets to percussion ensemble, and a symphony orchestra and band constitute the College's performing arts organizations.

Hillsdale students are housed in dormitories, fraternity and sorority houses, and various off-campus dwellings. Single and double rooms are available on campus; there are no coed dormitories. Each College-owned residence hall is supervised by a resident director and resident advisers. All freshmen (except commuters) are required to live on campus; upperclass students seeking to live off campus must apply to the dean of men or dean of women for this privilege.

Special student services provided by the College include career planning and placement counseling, academic advising and tutoring, and a health service staffed by a physician and a resident nurse.

Student Government

Hillsdale's student government and campus organizations offer students special opportunities to develop leadership skills that enrich both their collegiate experience and lives after graduation. The governing organization of the student body is the Student Federation, which is composed of 18 elected representatives. This group funds student organizations, sponsors all-College entertainment, and acts upon matters of concern to the student community.

Costs

Annual tuition for the 2016–17 academic year was $24,670, room was $5,040, board was $5,160, and mandatory fees were $852. Books, supplies, and personal expenses (including travel, recreation, and clothing) are estimated at $3,000 per year.

Financial Aid

Hillsdale College is an institution of national prominence, a reputation due in large part to its complete independence from government funds. Hillsdale College does not accept, nor are its students permitted to receive, any federal or state financial aid, either directly or indirectly. Through the support of generous donors, Hillsdale provides alternative, privately-funded aid sources. Ninety-six percent of new Hillsdale College students receive financial aid in the form of scholarships, grants, loans, and employment, with average aid packages around $18,000. An application for admission to Hillsdale College also serves as an application for scholarships; need-based aid consideration requires the Confidential Family Financial Statement (available online). The FAFSA is non-applicable.

Admission Requirements

Admission to Hillsdale College is a privilege extended to students who are able to benefit by, and contribute to, the academic and social environment of the College. A formal application to Hillsdale College includes (1) a completed application form, (2) the scores from either the Scholastic Aptitude Test (SAT), the American College Test (ACT), or the Classic Learning Test, (3) an official transcript of high school grades (and post-secondary grades, if available), (4) thoughtful essay and short answer responses, (5) two academic letters of recommendation, and (6) a résumé of extracurricular activities, volunteerism, leadership, and work experience. An interview is recommended, but not required. Transfer students must include a Dean of Students Transfer Form and official college transcript(s). International students must submit all required documents in English; the ACT or SAT is required, the TOEFL is optional.

Application and Information

Students may apply to Hillsdale College any time after the completion of the junior year of high school. A formal application includes a completed application form accompanied by a nonrefundable fee of $35 (free if submitted online) and all required credentials. Application plans include early decision (November 1), priority scholarship (January 1), and regular decision (April 1). Hillsdale College has been distinguished since its founding in 1844 by voluntarily adhering to a nondiscriminatory policy regarding race, religion, sex, and national or ethnic origin—long before the government began regulating such matters. All records and forms should be mailed to:

Admissions Office
Hillsdale College
33 East College Street
Hillsdale, Michigan 49242-1298
Phone: 517-607-2327
Fax: 517-607-2223
E-mail: admissions@hillsdale.edu
Website: http://www.hillsdale.edu

HOFSTRA UNIVERSITY

HEMPSTEAD, NEW YORK

★ To read more about this school, visit http://petersons.to/hofstrauniversity

HOFSTRA UNIVERSITY®
prideandpurpose

The University

Hofstra University is a dynamic private university located in the heart of Nassau County, just 25 miles east of New York City—the business, cultural and entertainment capital of the world. Since its founding in 1935, Hofstra has evolved into an internationally renowned university that continues to achieve recognition as an institution of academic excellence. Hofstra has 24 academic accreditations and 27 total accreditations, including consistent recognition on the Best College lists of *U.S. News & World Report*, The Princeton Review, *Fiske Guide to Colleges*, *Washington Monthly*, and *Forbes* magazine.

Hofstra University is one of only three universities in the New York metropolitan area with schools of engineering, medicine, and law. In the fall of 2016, Hofstra renamed its School of Engineering and Applied Science to the Fred DeMatteis School of Engineering and Applied Science, to honor Fred DeMatteis, a visionary builder, leader, philanthropist, and a contributor to construction and real estate development in the New York Metropolitan area. The Hofstra Northwell School of Medicine at Hofstra University graduated its charter class in May 2015, shortly after the grand opening of the school's new, 63,000 square-foot addition, which more than doubled the size of the school. In fall 2015, Hofstra welcomed its inaugural class of nursing students into the new Hofstra Northwell School of Graduate Nursing and Physician Assistant Studies. Also in fall 2015, Hofstra received a multimillion dollar gift from alum and trustee Peter S. Kalikow to create a new school devoted to training the next generation of public policy leaders: the Peter S. Kalikow School of Government, Public Policy and International Affairs.

Hofstra's diverse and driven student body of nearly 11,000 can choose from more than 160 undergraduate and 165 graduate program options in government, liberal arts and sciences, business, engineering, communication, teacher education, law, health professions and human services, and honors studies. Hofstra offers more than 100 dual-degree programs that allow students to earn both an undergraduate and graduate degree in less time than if each degree was pursued separately. More information is available at hofstra.edu/academics and hofstra.edu/dualdegree.

Hofstra hosts hundreds of social, academic, and cultural events each year. Notably, Hofstra is the only university chosen to host three consecutive U.S. Presidential debates, in 2008, 2012, and 2016. Hofstra also hosted the New York state gubernatorial debate in 2010. Those events help foster a connection between classroom work and extracurricular interests, as well as encourage civic engagement among Hofstra's students.

In addition, Hofstra offers 17 intercollegiate athletic programs that compete at the NCAA Division I level and more than 200 academic, fraternal/sororal, media, multicultural, performance, pre-professional, religious, social, social/political, and sports clubs and organizations. The David S. Mack Sports and Exhibition Complex, a 93,000 square-foot facility that includes an Olympic-sized swimming pool, is home to the Hofstra Pride men's and women's basketball teams and wrestling, and is also the site for events such as commencements, exhibitions, trade shows, televised political events, and concerts.

Each year, more than 2,500 organizations recruit Hofstra students for employment through on-campus and online methods. In addition, nearly 80 percent of students complete at least one internship at a top company before they graduate, thus gaining critical work experience that gives them an edge in a competitive job market.

Hofstra, students join a network of more than 131,000 alumni, including outstanding alumni such as Academy Award–winning film director and producer Francis Ford Coppola; best-selling author Nelson DeMille; vascular surgeon Dr. Donna Mendes; president of the New York Yankees Randy Levine; creator, executive producer, and writer Philip Rosenthal and actress Monica Horan from *Everybody Loves Raymond*; Lawrence Herbert, inventor of the Pantone Matching System; and New York State Comptroller Thomas P. DiNapoli.

At Hofstra, it's all about choice. Students can live in one of the 35 residence halls, each with a unique flair and life of its own. Hofstra students also have access to 18 on-campus dining facilities.

Location

Hofstra's 244-acre suburban campus is a short train ride from all the cultural, recreational, internship, and career opportunities New York City has to offer—and only minutes from beautiful beaches, shopping malls, restaurants, and two airports.

Majors and Degrees

The Bachelor of Arts (B.A.) is awarded in African studies; American studies; anthropology; art history; Asian studies; biology; chemistry; Chinese; Chinese studies; classics; comparative literature and languages; computer science; criminology; dance; drama; early childhood and childhood education (with dual major in another discipline); early childhood education (with dual major in another discipline); economics; elementary education (with dual major in another discipline); engineering science; English; English education; film studies and production; fine arts; foreign language education (French, German, Italian, Russian, Spanish); French; geography; geology; German; global studies; Hebrew; history; individually designed B.A. major in humanities, natural sciences, or social sciences;, Italian; Japanese and Japanese studies; Jewish studies; journalism; labor studies; Latin; Latin American and Caribbean studies; liberal arts; linguistics; mass media studies; math education (with a dual major in another discipline); mathematical economics; mathematics; music; philosophy; physics; political science; pre-health with a concentration in humanities and social sciences; psychology; public relations; public policy and public service; radio production and studies; religion; rhetorical studies; Russian; science education (biology, chemistry, earth science, physics); science technology, engineering and mathematics (STEM); social studies education (with a dual major in another discipline); sociology; Spanish; speech-language-hearing sciences; sustainability studies; television production and studies; urban ecology; and women's studies.

The Bachelor of Business Administration (B.B.A.) is awarded in accounting, entrepreneurship, finance, information systems, international business, legal studies in business, management, marketing, and supply chain management.

The Bachelor of Science (B.S.) is offered in applied physics, athletic training, biochemistry, biology, business economics, chemistry, community health, computer engineering, computer science, computer science and mathematics (dual major), economics, electrical engineering, environmental resources, exercise science, fine arts, forensic science, geology, health education, health science, industrial engineering, mathematical business economics, mathematical finance, mathematics, mechanical engineering, music, philosophy, physics, pre-medical, psychology, sustainability studies, urban ecology, video/television, video/television and business, and video/television and film.

The Bachelor of Science in Education (B.S.Ed.) is offered with specializations in dance, fine arts, music, and physical education.

The Bachelor of Engineering (B.E.) is offered in engineering science with specializations in biomedical engineering and civil engineering.

The Bachelor of Fine Arts (B.F.A.) is awarded in theater arts and dance.

Combined (dual) degrees offered include Bachelor of Arts/Juris Doctor (B.A./J.D.) in collaboration with the Maurice A. Deane School of Law at Hofstra University; Juris Doctor/Master of Business Administration (J.D./M.B.A.) in collaboration with the Maurice A. Deane School of Law and the Frank G. Zarb School of Business; Juris Doctor/Master of Public Health in collaboration with the Maurice A. Dean School of Law and the School of Health Professions and Human Sciences; B.S./M.S. in physician assistant studies; B.S./M.D. and B.A./M.D., through the Hofstra Northwell School of Medicine at Hofstra University; and various majors and concentrations leading to the B.A./M.B.A., B.S./M.B.A., B.A./M.S.Ed., B.A./M.A., B.A./M.S., B.S./M.S., B.B.A./M.S.Ed., B.B.A./M.S., and B.B.A./M.B.A.

Academic Programs

Requirements for graduation vary among schools and majors. A liberal arts core curriculum is an integral part of all areas of concentration. The University calendar is organized on a traditional fall and spring semester system, and offers an optional January session and three optional Summer sessions (between May and August).

Hofstra offers innovative programs designed to meet the needs of its diverse student body. These include Hofstra University Honors College, Legal Education Accelerated Program (LEAP), Hofstra 4+4 Program, First-Year Connections, and living/learning communities.

Hofstra University Honors College students can elect to study in any of the University's undergraduate programs and are involved in all fields of advanced study.

The Legal Education Accelerated Program allows students to earn both a B.A. and a J.D. in just six years.

The Hofstra 4+4 Program allows students to earn both a bachelor's degree (B.A. or B.S.) and M.D. in eight years in collaboration with the Hofstra Northwell School of Medicine.

First-Year Connections, an optional integrated academic and social program, helps first-year students connect with one another as well as with all the resources and opportunities offered at the University. The program offers seminars and course clusters, which satisfy the general education requirements for all majors, and features small classes taught by distinguished faculty.

Through Hofstra's living/learning communities, students are exposed to environments that are intellectually stimulating, supportive, and conducive to building lasting friendships and a memorable first-year experience. These communities are associated with several first-year clusters and seminars, giving students the opportunity to live with many students who are in their classes and who share their interests.

Off-Campus Programs

Hofstra extends learning beyond the classroom through varied internship programs and study-abroad opportunities. The internship programs take advantage of Hofstra's proximity to New York City, allowing students to gain real-life experience in areas such as finance, business, media, advertising, and entertainment. Through study-abroad programs in Europe, Asia, South America, and other locations, students can explore the world while earning college credits. More information is available at hofstra.edu/studyabroad.

Academic Facilities

Hofstra students have endless opportunities for experiential learning in cutting-edge campus facilities. Students can work in the Martin B. Greenberg Trading Room (which is equipped with 34 Bloomberg terminals and is among the largest academic training facilities in the world) or conduct research with a distinguished professor in innovative labs on campus, including a big data lab, a robotics and advanced manufacturing lab, and a cell and tissue engineering lab.

The Lawrence Herbert School of Communication contains one of the largest broadcast facilities in the northeastern United States, as well as a converged newsroom and multimedia classroom. Plus, Hofstra students benefit from real-world experience at the award-winning on-campus radio station, WRHU 88.7 FM (Radio Hofstra University), which is the only college radio station in the nation that is the flagship for a professional sports franchise, the NHL's New York Islanders.

Costs

The 2016–17 annual tuition and fees for a full-time undergraduate student were $42,160. The cost of a housing and dining plan was approximately $14,460. Books and supplies cost approximately $1,000; personal expenses and transportation generally amount to $3,245. For the full tuition and fees schedule, visit hofstra.edu/tuition.

Financial Aid

Hofstra University works hard to make a private college education affordable for students and families, and offers several financial aid options for new undergraduates, including interest-free payment plans and a money-saving four-year locked-in rate for tuition and fees (hofstra.edu/lockedintuitionrate) that can help students manage costs from admission through graduation. For detailed information, students should visit hofstra.edu/FinancialAid.

Faculty

More than 92 percent of Hofstra faculty members hold terminal degrees in their field. Hofstra professors are Guggenheim Fellows and Fulbright scholars; Emmy Award recipients; prize-winning scientists; leaders in business, education, and health professions; and knowledgeable and insightful thinkers. With an average undergraduate class size of 21 and a student-to-faculty ratio of 13:1, students are challenged and encouraged to think critically in an open and diverse learning environment.

Student Government

The Student Government Association (SGA) is Hofstra University's student-run governing body and is comprised of full-time undergraduate students that act as a liaison between Hofstra students and the University's faculty, administration, and Board of Trustees. In addition, SGA plans and executes multiple programs and initiatives throughout the academic year, and oversees and finances of over 180 clubs and organizations.

Admission Requirements

Hofstra is a competitive institution that seeks to enroll students who demonstrate academic ability, intellectual curiosity, and the motivation to succeed and contribute to the campus community. Careful consideration is given to a student's high school record, types of courses taken, SAT or ACT scores (if applicable), letters of recommendation, extracurricular involvement, and the personal essay. Submitting test scores to Hofstra is optional. Prospective students should visit hofstra.edu/testing policy for more information. The most competitive applicants will have followed a rigorous college preparatory curriculum and will have taken advantage of honors and advanced placement–level courses where appropriate. The Office of Admission prefers a high school curriculum that includes 4 years of English, 3 to 4 years of social studies, 2 to 3 years of foreign language, 3 years of mathematics (4 years for engineering applicants), and 3 years of science (4 years for engineering applicants). Campus visits are strongly recommended. Hofstra accepts applications from first-year, transfer, and international students.

Application and Information

For students whose first choice is Hofstra, there are two early action periods: when an application is submitted by November 15, notification is made to the student by December 15; when an application is submitted by December 15, notification is made to the student by January 15. Students applying for regular decision are considered on a rolling basis.

First-year applicants must submit an application, $70 application fee, high school transcript, SAT or ACT scores, essay, and letter of recommendation. Hofstra accepts applications via mail or online and participates in the Common Application.

For more information, students should contact:
Hofstra University
Office of Undergraduate Admission
100 Hofstra University
Hempstead, New York 11549-1000
Phone: 516-463-6700
Fax: 516-463-5100
E-mail: admission@hofstra.edu
Website: http://www.hofstra.edu/admission

Hofstra students live and learn in the best of both worlds. Professors teach in traditional classroom settings, but lectures expand into the world beyond. With NYC only a 45-minute train ride away, students can immerse themselves in diverse cultural and entertainment activities, while applying what they learn in the classroom at internships and co-op programs. .

COLLEGE CLOSE-UPS

HOLY NAMES UNIVERSITY

OAKLAND, CALIFORNIA

★ For more information, visit http://petersons.to/holynamesu

The University

Founded in 1868, Holy Names University (HNU) provides liberal arts education in the Catholic tradition. It consistently ranks as one of the most diverse universities in the nation, and it receives the highest accreditation from the Western Association of Schools and Colleges.

Nearly 1,200 students have access to 19 bachelor degrees, seven master degrees, and four degree-completion programs. These rigorous programs along with small class sizes, dedicated teachers, personal attention, and focus on social justice prepare students for leadership and service roles.

Holy Names University's rigorous academic programs ensure that students graduate with the intelligence, experience, and confidence to obtain rewarding positions in many fields. The U.S. Bureau of Labor Statistics projected growth through 2024 for occupations that Holy Names' graduates are qualified to obtain including the following: accountants and auditors: 11 percent (faster than average); biological technicians: 5 percent (as fast as average); financial analysts: 12 percent (faster than average); kindergarten and elementary school teachers: 6 percent (as fast as average); personal financial advisors: 30 percent (much faster than average); public relations specialists: 6 percent (as fast as average); and technical writers: 10 percent (faster than average).

Location

Holy Names University is situated on 60 wooded acres in the hills of Oakland, California. Its location offers a spectacular view of Oakland, San Francisco, and the Bay. The area's coastal climate provides temperate winters; clear, sunny fall and spring days; and sunny, breezy summers. The university's location amongst the hills provides a safe, beautiful, tranquil place to learn. Parks that surround the campus provide outdoor recreation like bicycling, hiking, and horseback riding.

HNU's close proximity to San Francisco provides easy access to urban amenities like museums, performing arts, and professional sporting events. Attractions like Carmel, Lake Tahoe, Monterey Bay, and Yosemite National Park are within driving distance

Major and Degrees

Business programs: Students interested in business can pursue Bachelor of Science (B.S.) in Accounting or Bachelor of Arts (B.A.) in Business degrees. The B.A. in Business has six concentrations: business communication, finance, international business, management marketing, or sports management.

Programs in the Humanities: Students who want to study disciplines that relate to human culture can earn B.A. degrees in the following areas: Communication Studies, English, History, Philosophy, or Religious Studies.

Programs in the Social Sciences: Students with an interest in how people develop societies and behave and interact in those societies can choose from the following A.A. programs: Criminology, International Relations, Intercultural Peace and Justice, Latin American and Latino/a Studies, Psychology, or Sociology.

Art Programs: Students whose goal is to strengthen their creativity as well as their performing or visual arts skills can earn these degrees: Multimedia Arts and Communication (B.A.), Music (B.A.), or Bachelor of Music (B.M.) in piano, vocal, or instrumental.

Life Science Programs: Students who enjoy studying living organisms or the relationship between behavior and physiological processes among humans and other animals have three options: Biological Science (B.A.), Biological Science (B.S.), or Psychobiology (B.S.).

Liberal Studies: Students who'd like to take a diverse range of courses in all of the university's divisions can pursue the B.A. in Liberal Studies.

Academic Programs

The Connections Project First-Year Experience (CP FYE) program is designed to help first-year students connect with the HNU community in meaningful ways that will support their social and academic transition into college life, including learning how to learn; learning how to serve; and learning how to lead.

Providing students with comprehensive support, the staff and departments in the Advising and Learning Resources area offer assistance with academic planning, tutoring and other learning supports, and disability services. The university strives to provide a wide range of resources for academic success and to work with students to identity and achieve their academic goals.

HNU's Center for Social Justice and Civic Engagement has increasingly been acknowledged as a model for aligning educational actions with institutional mission. The work of the Center has been recognized as enriching the understanding of social issues through personal exploration and socially responsible leadership at the University and within the local and global community.

Off-Campus Programs

In order to fully prepare students for today's global marketplace, Holy Names University encourages students to have at least one international experience during their college years. That philosophy has guided HNU in its vision to create unique, affordable, service-oriented study abroad opportunities. Students may participate in either a semester or a year of study in a foreign country through HNU's affiliation with Central College Abroad.

Students may also take courses that provide Study Trip Immersion Experiences. These opportunities are part of coursework within the Latin American & Latino/a Studies and the Religious Studies programs. The Study Trip Immersion Experience travels in alternate years to Oaxaca, Mexico, and to El Salvador, Central America. The Study Trip participants also do service learning each semester in the local community.

Costs

For the 2017–18 academic year, full-time undergraduate tuition totals $37,672 with a campus fee of $516 per year. Residence hall room rates range from $6,444 to $9,618 per year and meal plans range from $5,770 to $6,194 per year, depending on the options selected.

Financial Aid

Holy Names University is one of the most affordable private universities in the San Francisco Bay Area. In fact, all incoming freshman and day transfer students receive university grants and/or scholarships like the following: Holy Names University Grants, athletic scholarships, Catholic High Schools scholarship, merit scholarships, music scholarships, and the Sister Marie Rose Durocher Scholarship.

Many undergraduate students also qualify for one or more of these financial aid resources: Cal Grant A & B (California state grants), Federal Pell Grant, Federal Direct Subsidized Stafford Loans, Federal Direct Unsubsidized Stafford Loans, Federal Parent Plus Loans, Federal Perkins Loans, private loans, and student employment.

Faculty

Holy Names University's faculty is highly qualified; 90 percent of full-time faculty members have the highest possible degree in their field. A low 13:1 student-faculty ratio facilitates interaction and involvement with students.

Faculty members bring unique experienwces and perspectives to their classrooms. For example, students learn about Central America's history from a professor who grew up in El Salvador. They learn accounting and marketing strategies from a professor who's also a Certified Public Accountant and former entrepreneur.

As a licensed architect with more than 25 years of experience, Associate Professor of Management James Stryker, Ph.D. brings his own unique experiences to the classroom. His professional expertise includes starting and managing a design practice and working as the director of facility design and management for a Fortune 100 pharmaceutical company.

Student Life

Holy Names is a close-knit community where students build meaningful partnerships with faculty members. On-campus housing gives them the opportunity to create friendships and build strong ties with fellow students from diverse backgrounds and origins.

Residential living also provides easy access to opportunities that enable students to express their creativity, have fun, help others, and take on leadership roles. Students can enjoy a wide range of activities—here are just a few options::

- attend events like carnivals, dances, and NCAA intercollegiate athletic games
- become peer mentors
- engage in spiritual growth through the Campus Ministry
- join student clubs and organizations
- participate in student government
- pursue social justice work through the Center for Social Justice and Civic Engagement

Admission Requirements

Faculty Freshman applicants are considered for admission based on the overall strength of their high school preparation, SAT or ACT scores (SAT code is 4059 and ACT code is 0230), personal essay, letter of recommendation, extracurricular activities, and individual talents and achievements.

Application and Information

Holy Applications are accepted on a rolling basis from October 1 to August 1. Eligible incoming freshman students who complete the Application for Admission by the March 2 priority deadline will be automatically awarded scholarships based on academic merit.

All applicants are strongly encouraged to complete the Free Application for Federal Student Aid (FAFSA) by the March 2 priority deadline. In addition, California residents should submit a GPA Verification Form to the California Student Aid Commission by March 2, the deadline for Cal Grant eligibility.

Online applications are free. Undergraduate paper applications are $20. Undergraduate applicants can also apply through The Common Application. Application forms and instructions and requirements for transfer and international students are available at https://www.hnu.edu/admissions/undergraduate/application-information:

For additional information, prospective students should contact:
Holy Names University
Office of Undergraduate Admission
3500 Mountain Boulevard
Oakland, California 94619
Phone: 510-436-1351
Fax: 510-436-1325
E-mail: admissions@hnu.edu
Website: https://www.hnu.edu

Holy Names University's location in the Oakland Hills provides wonderful views of the San Francisco Bay and many great opportunities in the Bay Area.

COLLEGE CLOSE-UPS

JOHN CABOT UNIVERSITY

ROME, ITALY

★ To read more about this school, visit http://petersons.to/johncabotuniversity

The University

John Cabot University (JCU) was founded in 1972 and is the first overseas American university in Italy with regional accreditation by the Middle States Commission on Higher Education. JCU is a liberal arts college following the American system of education but with a distinctive European and international character. Located in the historic center of Rome, the University has unparalleled access to history, culture, and the active international communities associated with the United Nations organizations and embassies. With a commitment to a serious liberal arts education and a unique relationship with leading multinational corporations, media, and other cultural and international organizations, JCU provides degree-seeking students the academic training and opportunities to participate in exclusive internships that will allow them to enter directly into challenging careers after graduation, or to continue their studies at prestigious graduate programs.

The University has a diverse and unique student body, comprised of American, Italian, and international degree-seeking students from more than seventy countries. This group is complemented by visiting American students from universities across the United States. The visiting students bring their own regional diversity, which enhances the international diversity at JCU, resulting in a dynamic and engaging student body. JCU's commitment to creating a student community of both degree-seeking and visiting students results in the friendly, close community of a small campus, with the wide-ranging networks that come from studying with a large pool of students from across the United States.

The average class size is 15 students, and there are approximately 100 full- and part-time faculty members with advanced degrees from universities all over the world. Students work closely with professors and receive the individual attention needed to develop their academic abilities. JCU graduates are accepted into acclaimed graduate programs in the United States, the United Kingdom, and Europe, such as Columbia University, Johns Hopkins University, London School of Economics, and Università Bocconi.

The University is licensed by the Delaware Department of Education to award its degrees and is authorized by the Italian Ministry of Research and Instruction to operate as an institution of American higher education in Rome. John Cabot University was accredited in 2003 by the Middle States Commission on Higher Education (http://www.msche.org).

Location

John Cabot University is located in Rome, Italy, in the picturesque Trastevere neighborhood, just down the river from St. Peter's Basilica and the Vatican and a short walk from the Colosseum and Roman Forum. The University has two campuses within a 5-minute walk of each other and a student residence with 24/7 security, also a 5-minute walk away. The Frank J. Guarini Campus consists of a main building with three floors and an adjacent wing connected by terraces and courtyards. The property offers students a quiet atmosphere in which to study and interact, while historic, bustling Rome is just a few steps away. Surrounded by the gardens of the Accademia dei Lincei (the National Academy of Sciences, of which Galileo was an early member) and the Villa Farnesina of Raphael's famous frescoes, the Guarini Campus is buttressed by the Aurelian Wall of the Roman Empire. The Guarini Campus is approached through the Porta Settimiana, which was built in the third century and later rebuilt by Pope Alexander VI Borgia in 1498. JCU also has spacious classrooms and a cafeteria in the Tiber Campus, which is located along the banks of the famous Tiber River. Both campuses are equipped with WiFi, and classrooms are furnished with multimedia equipment. JCU's fine arts and art history classes often meet at famous monuments such as the Colosseum and the Forum. In essence, all of Rome is John Cabot University's campus, and students take advantage of JCU's urban setting, meeting with friends and faculty at local cafés as well as in many of the piazzas that are tucked away within the streets of Rome's historic center.

Majors and Degrees

John Cabot University offers the Bachelor of Arts degree in thirteen majors: art history, business administration, classical studies, communications, economics and finance, English literature, history, humanistic studies, international affairs, international business, Italian studies, marketing, and political science. JCU also offers a joint degree in communications with the University of Milan, allowing students to simultaneously earn an American and European Bachelor of Arts degree. Students may select minors in all of the major areas, as well as in creative writing, entrepreneurship, philosophy, and psychology. John Cabot also offers the Associate of Arts degree in all major fields of study. Each of these programs is designed to offer a unique learning and living experience in a setting rich in history, culture, and geopolitical interaction. All majors are complemented by internship opportunities at the United Nations, museums, and international firms in Rome. JCU's Career Services Center offers support for students' preparation and transition into post-graduate activities, offering over 300 internship and job opportunities each year. JCU's 10,000-member alumni network spans 110 countries and includes business leaders, politicians, diplomats, artists, scholars, and entrepreneurs, providing additional opportunities for graduates to continue their career development through international connections.

Academic Programs

The American higher education system encourages experimentation and breadth, particularly during the first two years of the university experience. The curricula of the University's programs are divided into two basic categories: the general distribution requirements of the first two years of study, which give the student a broad exposure to the basic disciplines of the liberal arts educational experience, and the specific requirements of each degree awarded by the University.

The general distribution requirements and other introductory courses equip the student to select an area of specialization as a degree candidate. The degree requirements include ten to twelve core courses deemed by faculty members to be essential to the discipline of the degree. Other requisites include electives that support the core program and allow students to take courses in other discipline areas of particular interest.

The academic year is divided into two semesters of fifteen weeks each, beginning in late August and mid-January. In one semester, a student normally takes five courses, earning 15 credits in the semester and 30 credits in the year. Two 5-week summer sessions allow students to take one or two additional courses per summer session. To earn the Bachelor of Arts degree, a student must complete 120 credits (forty courses); to earn the Associate of Arts degree, a student must complete 60 credits (twenty courses).

JCU accepts up to 60 transfer credits, including the IB diploma, AP exams, UK A-Levels, and other college-level courses.

Special programs include English language preparation for university study (ENLUS) for non-native English speakers, after which students who successfully complete the program may transfer directly into one of JCU's degree programs.

Off-Campus Programs

The Go Global program at JCU offers degree-seeking students the opportunity to study at partner universities in the United States, Europe, Africa, Asia, and the Americas. This opportunity contributes to educational growth and cultural awareness, and helps prepare students for careers in international fields.

Academic Facilities

The Frohring Library provides the latest in online access to academic journals and indexes, and is the University center for research in support of the academic programs as well as a quiet place for study and pleasure reading. The University's four computer laboratories contain desktop computers (Macs and PCs) equipped with the latest software as well as printers and a full-color scanner. The University is equipped with high-speed WiFi across campus, a studio art facility, a fitness center, a cafeteria, and a digital media lab.

Costs

Tuition for 2017–18 is $23,900 and housing costs begin at $4,800 per semester.

Financial Aid

U.S. citizens attending a college or university outside the United States are eligible to apply for Title IV Federal Financial Aid, including the Parent Loan for Undergraduate Students (PLUS), the Stafford Loan programs, and the U.S. Department of Education's Direct Lending Program. Academic scholarships are awarded by the University each year, based on merit and need; they include the Presidential Scholarship, the Financial Assistance Grant, the Dean's List Scholarship, the Italian Merit Scholarship, and the Expansion Scholarship for Latin American students. A number of work-study assistantships are available for students who are interested in and capable of assisting the administrative offices and academic departments of the University.

Faculty

The University has a distinguished faculty of professors from around the world who are actively engaged in research. In addition to teaching, faculty members take part in academic advising and co-curricular activities, such as field trips, lectures, and seminars.

Student Government

Student government at JCU contributes significantly to the quality of student life. A Student Senate is elected each year to coordinate activities. During the year, the Student Government sponsors a number of programs, such as the International Student Government Conference, which brings together student leaders from Italy, Europe, and the Middle East. The Student Government works with a faculty adviser and staff adviser in planning social, cultural, intellectual, and sports activities to respond to students' interests and needs.

Admission Requirements

Successful applicants must have a scholastic record demonstrating a commitment to their studies and the ability to succeed at college-level work.

The previous school's documentation of the applicant's academic ability, motivation, character, and contribution to school life is very important. The University does not prescribe a fixed secondary school course of study but considers both the quality and breadth of the student's record. Results of the SAT or the ACT are required for high school students graduating from an American secondary school.

The University is open to all applicants without regard to race, national origin, religion, or gender.

For applicants coming from the U.S. secondary school system, a standard college-preparatory program is expected. For applicants from other national systems, an essential requirement is successful completion of a secondary school program permitting university admission in the respective system. Students holding the Italian Diploma di Maturità, the International Baccalaureate, or other equivalent academic credentials may be granted advanced standing.

Applicants who did not attend an English-language secondary school or university for at least two years must demonstrate sufficient preparation in the English language. Standardized test scores, such as the Test of English as a Foreign Language (TOEFL) or the International English Language Testing System (IELTS), are required.

Application and Information

Admissions decisions are based on the review of official transcripts, results of standardized tests, the student's GPA, final examination results, a personal statement, an interview, and letters of recommendation from teachers or school counselors. A completed application must be accompanied by a nonrefundable application fee of $50/€50. Students may complete the application online or apply through the Common Application. The University has three application deadlines for fall: November 15 (Early Action), March 1 (Regular Decision), and June 1 (Late Decision). The spring application deadline is October 15. Candidates are urged to submit their application and supporting documents as early as possible, as greater scholarship funds may be available.

Students may apply online at https://netcommunity.johncabot.edu/application#.

For additional information, prospective students should contact:

Admissions Office
John Cabot University
Via della Lungara, 233
00165 Rome
Italy
Phone: 855-JCU ROMA
E-mail: admissions@johncabot.edu
Website: http://www.johncabot.edu
https://www.facebook.com/JohnCabotUniversity
http://twitter.com/#!/JohnCabotRome
http://instagram.com/johncabotuniversity

John Cabot University is located in the picturesque Trastevere neighborhood, just down the river from St. Peter's Basilica and the Vatican, and a short walk from the Colosseum and Roman Forum.

COLLEGE CLOSE-UPS

JOHNS HOPKINS UNIVERSITY
Krieger School of Arts and Sciences and Whiting School of Engineering

BALTIMORE, MARYLAND

★ To read more about this school, visit http://petersons.to/johnshopkins

The University

As America's first research institution, Johns Hopkins University is well known for innovative advances in everything from technology to history. The university emphasizes the importance of exploration and discovery in the undergraduate experience. Learning occurs through hands-on experiences across all academic disciplines and within every subject imaginable. The lack of a core curriculum fosters academic freedom, which allows students to create their own unique interdisciplinary paths. They choose classes they are genuinely interested in, not just required to take, so there's a real sense of curiosity around learning that extends beyond the classroom setting.

Collaborative learning is fundamental to the academic environment and cross-disciplinary partnerships occur between students of all academic areas. Hopkins professors, another invaluable resource, are enthusiastic about teaching and often include undergraduates in their own ground-breaking research. Students get to know their professors and classmates the way they would at a small liberal arts college but have all of the opportunities of a major research institution with a global reach. As a part of this community, undergraduates not only work alongside experts who share their interests but they run with projects of their own design. In fact, the university remains a national leader of research funding and students in all programs within the Krieger School of Arts & Sciences and Whiting School of Engineering gain practical experiences through research conducted both on and off campus.

The Homewood campus brings together students with diverse interests. Diversity of thought, culture, and interests cultivates a dynamic, open-minded environment. With over 300 student-run organizations, students find leadership opportunities and the chance to get involved on campus and beyond.

Location

Located in Baltimore, Maryland, the undergraduate Homewood campus is a traditional college campus with all the advantages of a major city just beyond its front gates. The 140-acre campus, featuring grassy quads and brick buildings, is surrounded by residential areas and neighborhoods that boast one-of-a-kind boutiques, restaurants, historic theaters, and an arts and entertainment district. Baltimore's resources make it an extension of the classroom and an integral part of a Hopkins education. The experiences Hopkins students find in Baltimore create lasting memories and offer preparation for future success in a wide variety of industries. Hopkins students also embrace the University's long-standing commitment to the city and use their skills to make an impact on the city that becomes their second home.

Majors and Degrees

Academics at Hopkins are interdisciplinary and collaboration is encouraged—between students and across disciplines. The majority of programs combine different areas of study to help students think more comprehensively about issues. This establishes a dynamic, engaging learning environment where students from various backgrounds bring an array of perspectives to class discussions. More than 60 percent of Hopkins students pursue a double major or minor, often creating unique combinations like electrical engineering and romance languages or biomedical engineering and business. The full list of majors and minors can be found online at apply.jhu.edu/discover/majors-minors.

Academic Programs

Undergraduates in all programs in the Krieger School of Arts & Sciences and Whiting School of Engineering gain practical experience through research conducted both on and off campus. Several funded programs, such as the Provost's Undergraduate Research Awards and the Woodrow Wilson Undergraduate Research Fellowship, are available to give participants the chance to complete projects of their own design. Students also encounter real-world experiences—like implementing marketing plans for local companies and heading startup businesses on campus—through the Center for Leadership Education—and classes in business, marketing, and communications, accounting and financial management, and entrepreneurship and management. Students can pursue their creative interests through the Center for Visual Arts, which offers an array of programs and almost 40 studio courses.

Students interested in pursuing law or medicine choose any major/minor combination but follow a pre-law or pre-med advising track offered through the Office of Pre-Professional Advising. The biomedical engineering (BME) program at Johns Hopkins, widely regarded as one of the best in the world, is the only undergraduate limited-enrollment major.

Several combined programs are available for undergraduates who want to broaden their educational experience. The Peabody Double Degree Program allows qualified students to simultaneously earn a bachelor of music from the Johns Hopkins Peabody Institute and a B.A or B.S. from Johns Hopkins University. The Direct Matriculation Programs: Master's in International Studies and Master's in Global Health Studies, allow qualified students displaying a strong interest in either area to pursue a combined bachelor's/master's degree with the Johns Hopkins School of Advanced International Studies (SAIS) or the Johns Hopkins Bloomberg School of Public Health. The University also offers the Army ROTC program on campus and the Air Force ROTC program in cooperation with the University of Maryland, College Park.

Off-Campus Programs

Off campus, the city of Baltimore provides unique academic, cultural, and pre-professional experiences. Some classes partner with local organizations to give students practical experiences that complement classroom lectures—like engineering a "fish ladder" at Maryland's Bloede Dam or replicating ancient Greek pottery work at Baltimore Clayworks. Due to the vast network of Hopkins schools and facilities that extends throughout Baltimore (and abroad), undergraduates have the chance to take courses and participate in research at the other divisions of Johns Hopkins University, including the Peabody Conservatory, the School of Nursing, the Bloomberg School of Public Health, the Nitze School of Advanced International Studies, the School of Education, the Carey Business School, and the School of Medicine. In addition to local programs and opportunities, each year more than 500 students study abroad in nearly 30 countries all over the globe. The University also participates in a cooperative program with other colleges in the Baltimore area.

Academic Facilities

Collaborative learning is fundamental to the academic environment and many of the newest buildings were designed to foster collaboration across disciplines. The Brody Learning Commons (BLC) is one of the most popular places for students to gather, study, and work together. Designed with student input, the building is directly connected to the library and contains the latest learning technology—like interactive projectors that allow students to write on walls and video teleconferencing capabilities. The Undergraduate Teaching Labs (UTL) is another recently constructed building, a 105,000-square-foot facility equipped with the latest lab technology that enables synergistic, cross-disciplinary partnerships and research opportunities. Malone Hall was built in 2014 and is a hub for the computer science department, where faculty and students work on innovative projects. The Milton S. Eisenhower Library on the Homewood campus is part of the University's Sheridan Libraries, which comprise the Milton S. Eisenhower Library, the John Work Garrett Library, the Albert D. Hutzler Undergraduate Reading Room, and the George Peabody Library. Together, these libraries provide one of the most comprehensive learning resources in the world. Two on-campus creative centers provide resources for students in the arts: the Mattin Student Arts Center contains theaters, a dance studio, music practice rooms, film and digital labs, darkrooms, and art studios; the Brown Foundation Digital Media Center offers digital tools like high-end computers and cameras that enable digital and audio composition and editing, animation, virtual painting, 3-D modeling, and workshops for programs like Adobe After Effects. Off campus, just a short shuttle ride away, the Johns Hopkins–MICA Film Center gives students access to state-of-the-art production facilities.

Costs

Costs for 2016–17 were $50,410 for tuition and $14,976 for room and board, plus personal expenses like books and travel. (Expenses such as travel and room and board vary based on choices.)

Financial Aid

Johns Hopkins is dedicated to enrolling the strongest students each year regardless of financial need, and does so by offering a variety of financial support programs for all types of families as well as personalized guidance through the process of finding the right path for them. The University will meet 100 percent of calculated need and also offers a broad range of grants and support. Last year, students received over $80 million in grant money towards their Hopkins education, with an average need-based grant for first-year students of over $38,000. More details, including financial aid application requirements and deadlines, are available online at apply.jhu.edu/financial-aid.

Faculty

As a global research university, Johns Hopkins attracts esteemed faculty. Hopkins professors are experts in their fields who are constantly making important contributions to their industries and academia at large. They've accomplished impressive accolades such as placing 100 percent of their class in finance jobs, winning the Nobel Peace Prize, and being granted awards for decades-long research studies. They're enthusiastic about teaching, often including undergraduates in their own ground-breaking research, and are always accessible to advise and assist students. Several University-sponsored programs bring students and faculty together in nonacademic settings and it's not unusual to brainstorm research ideas over coffee or debate philosophical theories during office hours.

Admission Requirements

Johns Hopkins looks for students who are eager to take advantage of the resources and opportunities at the University and who will contribute to the campus community. The student's academic character, intellectual curiosity, impact and initiative, and extracurricular involvement play a significant role in application review. A student's intellectual interests and accomplishments are of primary importance, and the admissions committee considers each applicant's scholastic record, standardized test results, essays, and recommendations from secondary school officials. In addition to the application and the Hopkins supplement, including a school-specific essay, other required documents include: two teacher recommendations, the secondary school report, and scores on the SAT or the ACT. The University enrolls a first-year class of approximately 1,300 men and women from across the globe. In addition, transfer students from other colleges and universities are admitted to the sophomore and junior classes. Prospective students should refer to apply.jhu.edu/apply for more information about the application process.

Application and Information

Johns Hopkins accepts the Coalition Application, the Common Application, and the Universal College Application, all with a Johns Hopkins supplement. Students who are certain Johns Hopkins is the place for them should consider applying under the Early Decision plan. This requires that the application be submitted by November 1. The deadline for the Regular Decision application is usually January 1. (Note: Deadlines can vary slightly from year to year; see apply.jhu.edu/apply for specific dates.) Notification is given by April 1 for Regular Decision students and by December 15 for those applying under the Early Decision plan. Students wishing to enroll in the biomedical engineering (BME) program must indicate BME as their first choice major on their application. Students applying to the Direct Matriculation Program: Master's in International Studies (DMP) or Direct Matriculation Program: Master's in Global Health Studies must submit an additional application and essay to be considered. First-year students who apply to the BME major or Direct Matriculation Program receive notification at the time of their admission to Johns Hopkins University.

Office of Undergraduate Admissions
Johns Hopkins University
Mason Hall
3400 North Charles Street
Baltimore, Maryland 21218-2683
Phone: 410-516-8171
Fax: 410-516-6025
E-mail: gotojhu@jhu.edu
Website: http://apply.jhu.edu

Johns Hopkins undergrads walking to class on the Homewood campus.

KETTERING UNIVERSITY

FLINT, MICHIGAN

Kettering UNIVERSITY

★ To read more about this school, visit http://petersons.to/ketteringuniversity

The University

Founded in 1919, Kettering University is a private university specializing in science, technology, engineering, math (STEM), and business degrees. The university enrolls about 2,500 undergraduate students and offers a 14:1 student-faculty ratio. Most classes have fewer than 20 students and are taught by Ph.D.-level professors, not teaching assistants. This combination of small class size and highly qualified teaching staff ensures students a much more personalized learning experience.

Kettering is a highly acclaimed university with the one of the country's most modern cooperative education and experiential learning programs. Students in all majors alternate between study terms and full-time work terms. During study terms, students learn material in small, intense classes and labs. During work terms, students work as paid professionals for major companies in industries related to their fields of study. Kettering students have done everything from testing ballistic systems for the U.S. government to reengineering crowd management at Disney World. Kettering has the only cooperative education and experiential learning program of its kind in the country, with students beginning to work in co-op positions as early as their freshman year. Students graduate from Kettering with 2½ years of professional experience and impressive resumes.

Kettering University's cooperative education and experiential learning program pairs hands-on education with real-world experience. This unique system of education prepares students to be business and industry leaders, innovators, and thinkers, with cutting-edge skills who are ready to compete in the global marketplace.

Kettering University is accredited by the North Central Association of Colleges and Schools, the Accreditation Board for Engineering and Technology (ABET), and the Association of Collegiate Business Schools and Programs (ACBSP). Kettering is also a member of the National Commission of Cooperative Education (NCCE) and the Association of Independent Technological Universities.

Along with their academic talents, Kettering students bring a wide range of skills and interests with them to campus. The university offers more than 50 student organizations, including 12 fraternities and 5 sororities, an active student government, a state-of-the-art recreation and fitness facility, and very competitive intramural sports, all aimed at nurturing all aspects of students' experience on campus. Recreation facilities include athletic fields, tennis courts, and a recreation center with an Olympic-size, six-lane swimming pool; aerobic fitness rooms; a full line of Nautilus equipment; and basketball, tennis, and racquetball courts.

Kettering also offers a number of in-demand Master of Science degree programs, including an M.B.A., which are available both on-campus and online.

Professional counseling, support services, and healthcare services are available. More information about Kettering can be found on Facebook (facebook.com/ketteringu), Twitter at (@ketteringU), or Instagram (@KetteringU1919).

Location

Kettering University is located in Flint, Michigan, which is 60 miles west of Lake Huron and 60 miles north of Detroit. Flint has approximately 100,000 residents and a metropolitan area population of 420,000.

Flint is particularly proud of its Cultural Center, which is only 10 minutes from Kettering's campus. Built and endowed entirely by the gifts of private citizens, the Cultural Center includes the Alfred P. Sloan Museum, the Whiting Auditorium (home of the Flint Symphony and host to leading stage shows and entertainers), the Robert T. Longway Planetarium (Michigan's largest and best-equipped sky show facility), the Flint Institute of Arts, the F. A. Bower Theater, the Dort Institute of Music, Mott Community College, and the Flint Public Library. Nearby is the University of Michigan–Flint campus.

The area also offers numerous outdoor and indoor recreational opportunities, including access to county wide trail systems that pass through Kettering's campus. Within a few minutes' drive are downhill and cross-country skiing facilities, lakes for the entire range of water sports, a wide selection of good public golf courses, excellent indoor and outdoor skating rinks, and plentiful shopping facilities and restaurants

Majors and Degrees

Kettering University offers a 4½-year, professional cooperative education and experiential learning program with Bachelor of Science degrees in applied biology, applied mathematics, applied physics, biochemistry, business administration, chemical engineering, chemistry, computer engineering, computer science, electrical engineering, engineering physics, industrial engineering, and mechanical engineering.

Kettering also offers a variety of dual-degree programs and more than 50 minors, specialties, and concentrations, to ensure that students' degrees are tailored to their interests and career goals. Examples include computer gaming, acoustics, medical physics, alternative energy, and a premed course of study.

Academic Programs

Although each program at Kettering University has its own requirements, 160 credit hours are generally required for graduation. The program involves nine academic terms and nine work terms, two of which are centered on the Cumulative Undergraduate Experience (CUE), which is a focused, major work project which displays tangible proof of the student's growth, knowledge, and mastery of real-world skills necessary for success. Students alternate between 11-week periods of academic study on the campus in Flint and twelve-week periods of related work experience with their corporate employer. The academic year consists of two 3-month academic terms on campus and two 3-month terms of paid work experience.

Academic Facilities

Kettering University offers innovative facilities, labs, and educational resources, and students start using them as early as their freshman year. The Crash Safety Center, for example, is the only facility of its kind in the nation used in an undergraduate program. The University also offers labs in areas such as fuel-cell research, polymer optimization, machining, acoustics, and more.

Kettering is fully networked and allows 24-hour access to computer resources and the Internet from dorms and labs. A 445-student residence hall and an apartment complex are located on the campus for student housing. The library offers more than 100,000 cataloged volumes and 540 periodicals. And through online resources like Kettering Connect and Blackboard, students can always be in touch with professors and university staff members.

Costs

For 2016–17, tuition costs were $39,790 and room and board cost $7,780.

Kettering offers fixed-rate tuition, and was the first STEM university in Michigan to do so. For students making normal progress towards their degrees, tuition rates will not change during their course of study, removing some of the guesswork associated with budgeting for college costs.

Financial Aid

Kettering University invests in the academic success of its students through generous financial aid packages that include scholarships, loans, and work-study opportunities. Approximately 99 percent of Kettering students receive some sort of financial aid. Factor in co-op earnings—between $40,000 and $65,000 over the course of the college career—and the fixed-rate tuition guarantee, and students are able to take advantage of one of the best values in education today. In addition, Kettering's Merit Scholarship program awards students with extremely generous scholarship packages. Students should fill out the Free Application for Federal Student Aid (FAFSA) and request a copy of the analysis to be sent to Kettering University. The university works to create a financial aid package for based on those results.

Faculty

Kettering University's faculty members balance a commitment to teaching with focused applied research interests, many of which undergraduate students participate in. Most professors have industrial experience in addition to academic credentials and maintain contact with industry through consulting, sponsored research, and advising on student thesis projects. More than 84 percent of faculty members hold a Ph.D. Because only half of the students are on campus at any one time, class sizes are small, and opportunities for enrichment and extra help from faculty are readily available.

Admission Requirements

Admission to Kettering University is competitive and based on scholastic achievement and extracurricular interests, activities, and achievements. Applicants are required to have earned the following: 3 years of English, 2 years algebra, 1 year of geometry, 1 semester of trigonometry, 2 years of lab science (1 must be physics or chemistry; both are recommended). Applicants must submit results of the SAT or ACT (Kettering's ACT code number is 1998 and the SAT code number is 1246). Most Kettering University students are in the top 10 percent of their graduating class. Kettering University also welcomes students wishing to transfer from other colleges and universities. The transfer alternative is an excellent way to gain admission for students who do not enroll as freshmen.

Application and Information

Students can apply online at http://www.kettering.edu/apply or through the Common Application. Students should call 800-955-4464 ext. 7865 for assistance.

Kettering officials review applications and let students know if they have been accepted. Although Kettering accepts and processes applications throughout the year, it is best to apply as early as possible. Once accepted, students receive information on programs and the professional co-op program, which are only available to admitted students. Students should complete the co-op registration (resume) online and pay a $300 tuition deposit (to be credited to the first-semester tuition). The deposit shows that a student is as serious about Kettering as Kettering is about the student and ensures a place in the entering class and eligibility to begin the co-op employment search process.

For more information, prospective students should contact:

Admissions Office
Kettering University
1700 University Avenue
Flint, Michigan 48504
United States
Phone: 810-762-7865
800-955-4464 Ext. 7865 (toll-free in the United States and Canada)
E-mail: admissions@kettering.edu
Website: https://www.kettering.edu
https://www.facebook.com/KetteringUniversity
https://www.twitter.com/KetteringU
https://www.instagram.com/ketteringu1919

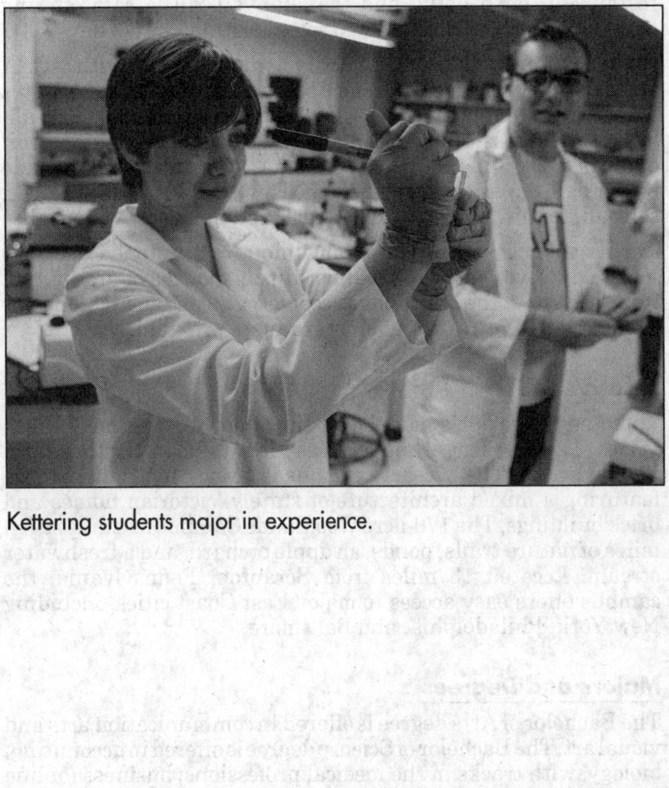

Kettering students major in experience.

COLLEGE CLOSE-UPS

KEYSTONE COLLEGE

LA PLUME, PENNSYLVANIA

★ To read more about this school, visit http://petersons.to/keystonecollege

Keystone College

The College

Founded in 1868, Keystone College is a leading, comprehensive, student-centered college educating students in the liberal arts and sciences tradition. An independent, coeducational college, Keystone College provides distinctive undergraduate and graduate programs grounded in a competitive learning environment. Students receive a comprehensive education with active and engaged learning opportunities that stimulate interests, improve skills, and ensure career readiness. The College currently enrolls nearly 1,400 students from fourteen states and six countries, including students enrolled in some of Keystone's fully online programs. Students can choose from over forty programs of study and earn associate, bachelor's, and master's degrees. Keystone College is accredited by the Middle States Association of Colleges and Secondary Schools.

For the ninth consecutive year, Keystone College has been ranked by *U.S. News & World Report* as one of the nation's best colleges and also ranked in the top tier for highest proportion of classes under 20 students. Over 70 percent of classes at Keystone College have fewer than 20 students, providing an individualized learning environment for all. Keystone is also nationally recognized as one of the best schools for soldiers and veterans.

On-campus housing is available to all full-time students in good standing. A variety of arrangements and room options are available in eight different residence halls. Keystone also offers residential Living–Learning Communities that allow students in similar phases of development or with similar interests and goals to live and study together. Both commuter and resident students have meal plan options and can choose between two different dining facilities: an "all you care to eat" student restaurant, open daily; and the Giant's Grill, a café offering made-to-order and grab-and-go selections, open weekdays.

Keystone College boasts 21 varsity athletic teams, with NCAA Division III affiliation. All teams compete in the Colonial States Athletic Conference (CSAC). Men's teams include baseball, basketball, cross-country, golf, lacrosse, soccer, tennis, indoor/outdoor track and field, and wrestling. Women's teams include basketball, cross-country, field hockey, golf, lacrosse, soccer, softball, tennis, indoor/outdoor track and field, and volleyball.

The Keystone Promise, a program unique to Keystone College, is a pledge to every student that within six months of graduating from Keystone they will have received at least one job offer or been accepted into a transfer or graduate program.

Location

Voted as the region's most beautiful campus, Keystone College is located at the foot of the Endless Mountains in Northeastern Pennsylvania. The 276-acre campus is both scenic and historic, featuring a mixed architecture of stately Victorian homes and brick buildings. The 170-acre Woodlands Campus features seven miles of nature trails, ponds, an apple orchard, and a freshwater stream. Located 13 miles from Scranton, Pennsylvania, the campus offers easy access to major East Coast cities, including New York, Philadelphia, and Baltimore.

Majors and Degrees

The Bachelor of Arts degree is offered in communication arts and visual art. The Bachelor of Science degree is offered in accounting; biology, with tracks in the medical professions; business (online or traditional); criminal justice, with a track in prelaw; criminal justice/psychology double major; early childhood education, with a special education certification option; environmental biology; environmental resource management; forensic biology; geology; hospitality business management; information technology; public health; social sciences; psychology; sport and recreation management; teaching: art education; teaching: child and society (noncertification program); teaching: social studies education (4–8); teaching: language arts (4–8); teaching: math education (7–12); teaching: social studies education (7–12); and wildlife biology.

Accelerated certification programs are available in teaching: art education (K–12), teaching: early childhood education, teaching: early childhood education/special education, teaching: math education (7–12), and teaching: social studies education (7–12).

The Associate of Applied Science degree is offered in information technology. The Associate in Fine Arts is offered in art. The Associate in Arts is offered in communications, environmental studies, liberal studies, and wildlife biology. The Associate in Science is offered in business (online and traditional); criminal justice; early childhood education; and health sciences with emphasis in medical technology, nursing/cytotechnology, occupational therapy/respiratory care, and radiotherapy/medical imaging/cardiac perfusion.

Academic Programs

The College runs on a two-semester schedule (fall and spring) and has evening, online, and weekend classes available, as well as additional course options during winter and spring intercessions and summer sessions. The number of credit hours required to earn a degree is dependent upon the field of study chosen, and students must have attained a minimum cumulative GPA of 2.0. Every student must complete a set of general education core requirements in addition to the courses specific to his or her major course of study, plus free electives. Depending on their course of study, students may also be required to complete an internship or co-op before graduation.

There are opportunities for double majors as well as minors and concentrations in various fields of study.

The College offers an Honors Program to which students can be invited if they meet the 3.50 minimum GPA requirement. This program provides honors-designated courses, an enriched writing course, membership in the President's Book Club, access to a private study lounge, priority course registration, and honors designation at graduation. In addition, the Honors Program provides co-curricular activities, service opportunities, and intellectual and social support.

Academic Facilities

Keystone's campus includes thirty-two academic and administrative buildings and eight residence halls, as well as state-of-the-art athletic facilities including a new field and track complex. The Harry K. Miller Library is available on campus to all students. This facility offers standard print and online research opportunities. The Hibbard Campus Center is the setting for the campus bookstore, the student restaurant and Giant's Grill café, as well as a U.S. post office, a student-run radio station (WKCV), and reception halls. The campus also boasts an art gallery, a celestial observatory, early childhood center, career development center, advising center, theater, and 3-D printer. Fine Arts students benefit from distinct studio facilities such as those for glass blowing, sculpture, graphic arts, photography, and 3-D printing. Keystone College also serves as the home for the Keystone College Environmental Education Institute and the Countryside Conservancy.

Costs

Tuition and fees for Keystone College for the 2017–18 academic year are $25,920, while room and board costs are $10,700. All textbooks, whether hard copy or digital, and course materials are included in the cost of tuition. All performance music and choral group activities, including instrument rentals, and private lessons, are also included in the cost of tuition. Additional expenses, such as supplies, course fees, and travel, vary according to major and housing status.

Financial Aid

The Financial Aid Office provides adequate funds and resources to meet the financial needs of students from all income categories. In fact, 97 percent of incoming freshmen receive financial aid. Scholarships are awarded based on merit, academic performance, and extracurricular involvement. Keystone College also participates in the following federally sponsored programs: Federal Pell Grant, Federal Supplemental Educational Opportunity Grant (FSEOG), Federal Direct PLUS Loan, and Federal Direct Student Loan. Keystone also offers College employment programs to students and alternative loans as well as state grants and Keystone grants. In order to be considered for financial aid, students must complete the Free Application for Federal Student Aid (FAFSA). Keystone's financial aid code is 003280.

The Keystone Commitment Loan Repayment Assistance Program is provided to all first-time, full-time freshmen, starting in fall 2017, who are pursuing a bachelor's degree. Through this program, once a student graduates and is employed full-time, if they don't earn $40,000 per year Keystone College will help them repay their student (and Parent PLUS) loans until they do. This program eases some of the fear of student loan debt and allows graduates to pursue the career of their choice.

Faculty

The student-faculty ratio is 11:1, and the average class size is 13 students. Keystone College is supported by strong interpersonal relationships among its students and faculty and staff members. All faculty members post regular office hours and are generally available outside of these hours for any student when necessary.

Student Government

Student Government is the central governing body of all student government organizations on the campus. It serves as the liaison between the student body and the College administration. Members are chosen by their peers and are responsible for improving and maintaining student life both on and off campus. Students may choose from more than thirty different clubs and organizations, including those with academic, service-oriented, and social interests. The College also boasts an active performance music program including bands, ensembles, and a chorale.

Admission Requirements

Keystone accepts qualified students regardless of race, religion, disability, or national origin, and admissions are on a rolling basis. Admission is based on prior academic performance and the ability of the applicant to profit from and contribute to the academic, interpersonal, and extracurricular life of the College. Applicants must submit official high school transcripts in order to be considered for admission. Letters of recommendation and/or a personal statement are also recommended, but not required. Keystone College has a test-optional policy. Students are encouraged to submit SAT or ACT scores if they believe the results are a positive reflection of their academic ability, but students who choose to withhold scores will not be at a disadvantage in the application review process. The College does reserve the right to request test scores in some cases. All students are strongly encouraged to visit the campus for a personal interview with the admissions staff and a member of the faculty from the student's area of interest. Students applying to the art and teaching–art education programs are required to participate in a portfolio interview in order to be considered for formal admission into the program.

Transfer students in good academic and financial standing at their current institution are also encouraged to apply to Keystone. Transfer students should contact the Office of Admissions and are required to submit transcripts from each college attended, and may also be required to submit high school transcripts.

Admission and scholarship decisions are usually made within two days from the time all required materials are received in the Office of Admissions.

Application and Information

Students wishing to be considered for admission must submit an application, along with official high school transcripts and college transcripts (if applicable), any letters of recommendation, personal statement, and scores from the SAT or ACT if they choose (Keystone's CEEB code numbers are 2351 for the SAT, 3602 for the ACT).

Applications and any additional information about Keystone College may be obtained by contacting:

Office of Admissions
Keystone College
One College Green
P.O. Box 50
La Plume, Pennsylvania 18440
United States
Phone: 570-945-8111
800-824-2764 (toll-free), Option 1
E-mail: admissions@keystone.edu
Website: http://www.keystone.edu

Keystone students enjoying the scenic campus in fall.

KING'S COLLEGE

WILKES-BARRE, PENNSYLVANIA

★ To read more about this school, visit http://petersons.to/kingscollege

The College

King's College is an independent, coed, four-year Catholic college with 2,400 students. Founded in 1946 by the Holy Cross Priests and Brothers from the University of Notre Dame, King's prepares students for a purposeful life with an education that integrates the human values inherent in a broadly based liberal arts curriculum. The College encourages the religious, moral, personal, and social development of its students.

In addition to the undergraduate degrees, King's College offers a Master of Science (M.S.) degree in health-care administration, a Master of Education (M.Ed.) degree in reading or curriculum and instruction, and a five-year physician assistant studies program leading to a master's degree.

Academic advising begins before students enroll and continues with an innovative program of career development across the curriculum. King's Academic Skills Center includes a nationally certified tutoring program and a faculty-staffed writing center. More than 70 percent of students who attend King's graduate from the College, which is well above the national average, and 99 percent are employed or attend graduate school within six months of graduation.

The charming urban campus comprises eight city blocks and features many buildings and centers that house King's numerous academic programs, including the Charles E. and Mary Parente Life Sciences Center, the Mulligan Physical Sciences Center, and the William G. McGowan School of Business. The 15-acre campus also includes Monarch Court; the Sheehy-Farmer Campus Center, which offers an art gallery, an outdoor waterfall and patio, a student restaurant, and marketplace dining; the J. Carroll McCormick Campus Ministry Center; and the William S. Scandlon Physical Education Center, which features a 3,200-seat basketball arena, wrestling facilities, racquetball and handball courts, an Olympic-size swimming pool, a wellness center, and a state-of-the-art sports medicine facility. In addition, an expansion of the Scandlon Center was recently completed, which includes three multipurpose courts as well as new offices, meeting rooms, and additional sports medicine facilities.

The new King's on the Square facility is a vibrant and dynamic center for learning and living in the heart of downtown Wilkes-Barre. King's on the Square is home to a number of professional programs, including physician assistant studies, athletic training, and exercise science. The new center also includes attractive and safe student residences that bring students in direct contact with the downtown environment; a community-centered art and cultural display center; and a Chick-fil-A restaurant for students, faculty, staff, and the downtown community. King's on the Square has quickly established itself as a safe, productive, and bustling downtown anchor.

The six-story administration and science buildings form a unit that houses the College's newly renovated theater, the Susquehanna Place dining hall and coffee bar, administrative offices, science laboratories, and classrooms. Residence halls have cable television, wireless Internet access, and 24-hour computer labs. Many of King's athletic teams train and compete just two miles from campus at the Robert L. Betzler Athletic Complex, a 33.5-acre athletic facility that includes McCarthy Stadium; a field house; and fields for baseball, softball, men's and women's soccer, football, and field hockey.

More than fifty student organizations provide King's students with a wide range of opportunities to explore interests outside of the classroom. King's has 25 NCAA Division III teams including men's baseball, basketball, football, golf, ice hockey, lacrosse, soccer, swimming, tennis, and wrestling; women's basketball, field hockey, ice hockey, lacrosse, soccer, softball, swimming, tennis, and volleyball; and coed cross-country.

The College offers cheerleading, ice hockey, and track and field as club sports. Intramural sports include basketball, flag football, indoor soccer, racquetball, and dodgeball. Other co-curricular activities include: academic clubs in almost every department, the King's Players (theater), Cantores Christi Regis (choir), Campus Ministry, the Experiencing the Arts Series, *The Crown* (student newspaper), the *Regis* (yearbook), and the *SCOP* (literary magazine).

Location

The King's campus is located in a residential area near downtown Wilkes-Barre, Pennsylvania, a city of approximately 50,000 on the banks of the Susquehanna River. A growing city, Wilkes-Barre has developed both economically and culturally, yet it has avoided many typical urban problems. Shopping malls, multiplex theaters, a brand new riverfront park, art galleries, and restaurants are nearby. Two blocks from King's is the F. M. Kirby Center, which has hosted national performances, music groups, traveling theater, and more. National recording acts regularly perform in nearby venues.

King's is a short drive from several ski resorts, state parks, and major lakes where students can participate in many seasonal outdoor activities. Students can also enjoy professional sports action including the New York Yankees' AAA baseball team, the Pocono International Raceway which hosts two NASCAR races each season, and the Pittsburgh Penguins' minor-league ice hockey team. The Mohegan Sun Arena is the host to many concerts and events, and is the site of the King's commencement. The campus is close to major metropolitan areas including New York City and Philadelphia (each a 2½-hour drive); Washington, D.C., and the attractions of New England are within a 4-hour drive.

Majors and Degrees

King's awards the Master of Science, Master of Education, Bachelor of Arts, Bachelor of Science, Associate of Arts, and Associate of Science degrees. The College's thirty-six major programs are offered in the arts and sciences and the William G. McGowan School of Business, which is accredited by AACSB International—The Association to Advance Collegiate Schools of Business.

Arts and sciences include the humanities and social sciences division (computers and information systems, criminal justice, economics, English–literature, English–professional writing, French, history, mass communications, philosophy, political science, psychology, sociology, Spanish, theater, and theology); the education division, which is accredited by NCATE (preschool–grade 4, secondary certification, and special education); the science division (biology, chemistry, computer science, engineering, environmental science, environmental studies, general science, mathematics, neuroscience, and physics); and the allied health division (clinical lab science, physician assistant studies, exercise science, and athletics training education/sports medicine accredited by CAAHEP). Beginning in the fall of 2018, the College also will offer a Bachelor of Science degree in nursing. Available majors in the William G. McGowan School of Business are accounting, finance, human resources management, international business, management, and marketing. King's offers pre-professional programs in chiropractic, dentistry, law, medicine, optometry, pharmacy, and veterinary science. The engineering program is a 3+2 dual-degree program with the University of Notre Dame, in which students spend three years at King's and then two years at Notre Dame.

Academic Programs

The general education program at King's is recognized nationwide by its peers. King's is included in *Barron's Best Buys in College Education* and has been honored in nineteen consecutive issues of *U.S. News & World Report's Best Colleges Guide*. The College was also recognized by the John Templeton Foundation Honor Roll for Character-Building Colleges, the Forbes/CCAP list of America's best colleges, and is one of sixteen institutions nationwide named to the Greater Expectations initiative.

The honors program offers highly motivated students the challenge of learning in discussion-centered courses that explore distinctive subject matter with exciting and innovative approaches. Twenty honor societies encourage students to excel in their chosen fields and recognize students for their academic distinction; members are honored each year at the All-College Honors Convocation. Science students receive hands-on lab training much earlier than students at other institutions and work together with faculty members on real-world research projects.

Off-Campus Programs

Experiential learning (via internships) is available in conjunction with almost every major. King's students have interned at CNN, the New York Stock Exchange, PricewaterhouseCoopers, the U.S. House of Representatives, U.S. Senators' offices, the U.S. Department of Energy, Walt Disney World, and Xerox Corporation, among other places. Every year, students are placed with local, regional, and national companies around the globe.

Through the study-abroad program many of King's students have studied on campuses throughout Europe, Thailand, China, Australia, and various other countries.

Academic Facilities

King's facilities include the 51,000-square-foot, three-story D. Leonard Corgan Library, which contains several study rooms, a 160,000-volume collection, and a computerized catalog, which students can access from their home or residence hall. The library provides full-text databases from every computer on campus, and access to college and research libraries throughout the United States. Students and faculty members also have direct access to more than 1 million volumes through the local library cooperative (NEPBC).

King's features computer labs with more than 440 PCs, 24-hour labs in residence halls, e-mail accounts for all students, computerized library databases, multimedia classrooms with a variety of instructional aids, course discussions on Moodle, distance-learning facilities for teleconferencing, and cross-registration with area colleges that enables students to take courses complementary to their majors.

The Charles E. and Mary Parente Life Sciences Center, which contains a molecular biology laboratory and a genomics center, includes computer facilities, instrumentation rooms, a rooftop greenhouse, and environmental chambers. The Mulligan Physical Sciences Center includes modern research laboratories, computer facilities, and state-of-the-art instrumentation used for molecular identification. The five-year physician assistant studies program (master's degree) is located in the new King's on the Square facility, which includes a state-of-the-art gross anatomy lab, four clinical practice labs, and ten examination rooms.

Costs

For the 2017–18 academic year, tuition for full-time students is $35,830; average room and board total $12,408.

Financial Aid

King's assists all qualified students through its financial aid programs. Currently, more than 99 percent of King's students receive financial aid in the form of scholarships, grants, work-study, or loans. For 2017, the average financial aid award was $26,283, removing a significant amount of the financial obligation from students and their families. Aid is awarded on the basis of demonstrated financial need (the difference between the total cost of education and the expected family contribution).

In addition to financial aid programs, installment payment plans are available, offering students and/or their families the ability to make monthly payments throughout the academic year. Students who wish to be considered for financial aid must fill out the Free Application for Federal Student Aid (FAFSA) and the King's College Financial Aid Application. The preferred FAFSA filing deadline for first-year students is February 15.

Faculty

King's College has 131 full-time and 96 part-time faculty members. Eighty-five percent of the full-time faculty members have a Ph.D. or an equivalent terminal degree. Graduate assistants do not teach courses. The student-faculty ratio is 12.9:1.

Student Government

The student government coordinates and participates in numerous activities for both the student body and the surrounding community. It regularly holds open forums for students and senior administrators at the College, coordinates informal socials for the students with the College president, and makes presentations at each meeting of the Board of Directors. In addition, the student government sponsors events that foster awareness for social and justice issues and a celebration of cultural diversity.

Admission Requirements

King's encourages applications from qualified high school students and those who wish to transfer from another institution. To be considered for admission, students must be prepared to successfully pursue a program of study at the College, as evidenced by the quality of previous academic and extracurricular performance, the recommendation of school officials and character references, and the student's display of personal promise, maturity, and motivation. King's admits students of any race, sex, color, creed, or national or ethnic origin.

Admission decisions are made for both high school students and transfer students with the understanding that all current courses and examinations will be completed satisfactorily. Candidates should complete 4 years of mathematics (through trigonometry or pre-calculus). One year each of high school chemistry, biology, and physics is also strongly recommended.

The Office of Admission offers two methods for candidates to apply for admission: the SAT/ACT Traditional Choice and the Test Optional Choice. Applicants are required to state their preference prior to the application review, and the decision is nonreversible. Students who select the SAT/ACT Traditional Choice must submit a completed application, official high school transcripts, SAT or ACT scores, guidance counselor recommendation, an essay, and the $30 application fee, which is waived if students apply online. Students who choose the Test Optional Choice must submit a completed application, official high school transcripts, an official graded writing sample from either their junior or senior year—submitted and notarized by the high school guidance office, guidance counselor recommendation, an essay, and the $30 application fee, which is waived if students apply online.

Application and Information

Applicants should forward a completed application and the $30 fee to the Office of Admission or apply online at www.kings.edu in order to waive the application fee. Secondary and postsecondary (if applicable) transcripts must be sent. Admission decisions are not made until all credentials are received. King's subscribes to a rolling admission policy. Decisions are announced within two weeks from the date of application. Upon notification of acceptance, a $200 nonrefundable deposit is requested to reserve a place in the class. The deposit deadline is May 1 but may be extended upon request. To schedule an interview, obtain an application form, or for more information, students should contact:

Office of Admission
King's College
133 North River Street
Wilkes-Barre, Pennsylvania 18711
Phone: 570-208-5858
888-KINGS-PA (toll-free)
E-mail: admissions@kings.edu
Website: http://www.kings.edu
http://www.facebook.com/kingscollegepa
http://twitter.com/KingsCollege_PA

KUTZTOWN UNIVERSITY OF PENNSYLVANIA

KUTZTOWN, PENNSYLVANIA

★ To read more about this school, visit http://petersons.to/kutztownuniversity

The University

For the last 150 years, students who choose Kutztown University choose to become part of a community defined by bright, ambitious students; brilliant, dedicated faculty; and a diverse, vibrant learning atmosphere.

Kutztown University (KU) is a four-year public institution located 30 minutes from Allentown and Reading, 90 minutes from Philadelphia, and 2 hours from New York City. Founded in 1866, KU has nearly 9,000 undergraduate and graduate students, more than 100 areas of study, 200 student organizations, and 21 NCAA Division II athletic programs—all housed on a beautiful 289-acre campus.

Location

Kutztown offers the benefits of a safe, quaint, walkable community with access to the Northeast's best cities. The campus is a hub for public transportation with daily routes to Philadelphia and New York City. Students can check out the Philadelphia Zoo or Adventure Aquarium, catch the Art Bus to New York City to explore the Museum of Modern Art, or take a trip to Washington, D.C. to visit the Smithsonian. In addition to the opportunities for arts and entertainment, great opportunities for internships and career exploration and also within easy reach.

Locally, the beauty of the eastern Pennsylvania countryside offers easy access to hiking, biking, skiing, and other outdoor activities. Students can sample Pennsylvania Dutch culture both on and off campus, but when the conveniences of a major city are needed, Allentown and Reading are just a short drive away.

Majors and Degrees

When it comes to areas of study, there is a lot to choose from, including KU's Programs of Distinction, which prepare students to enter today's fastest-growing fields. From cinema, television, and media production, biochemistry, education, and marketing to communication design, criminal justice, marine science, and software development, KU has what today's students are seeking. They can choose from recognized Programs of Distinction in Education, Sciences, Computer Science, and the Visual and Performing Arts.

College of Business: Students learn the skills necessary and prepare to take on the global challenges of today's business environment through programs in accounting, finance, management, marketing, sports management, and leadership development. KU's Business Administration programs have earned the prestigious Association to Advance Collegiate Schools of Business (AACSB) International. AACSB accreditation is the hallmark of excellence in business education and positions KU's programs among the top 5 percent of business schools internationally. The Leisure and Sport Studies program, one of the largest and fastest growing at KU, received its Commission on Sport Management Accreditation (COSMA) in fall of 2015, placing it among the few accredited programs in the United States.

College of Education: Students can study and prepare for a career as a lifelong learner and teacher in elementary education (grades Pre-K–4 or 4–8), secondary education, special education, library science, instructional technology, and school counseling. KU has one of only four programs in the U.S. that offer a major in special education with a focus on visual impairment. It also boasts one of the few clinically-based reading specialist programs as well as a brand new autism endorsement certification. Teacher education programs at Kutztown University are nationally accredited by the Council for the Accreditation of Educator Preparation (CAEP, formerly NCATE).

College of Liberal Arts and Sciences: From ancient civilizations to today's cultural norms, living things to fossilized remains, students can research and apply their natural curiosity to learn how and why people, languages, and processes exist as they do and what tomorrow may bring.

KU offers a wide variety of programs: anthropology, biological sciences, chemistry, computer science, criminal justice, English, environmental science, geography, geology, German studies, history, marine science, mathematics, paralegal studies, philosophy, physics, political science, psychology, public administration, professional writing, sociology, social work, or Spanish. A traditional liberal arts education has proven valuable to employers. Students develop the communication, writing, research, teamwork, and critical-thinking skills that are marketable in a wide range of fields. KU's commitment to undergraduate research ensures students have opportunities to present their findings at local and national meetings, and they may even be published in an academic journal alongside the professor's work. Internships are another opportunity to gain further work experience.

College of Visual and Performing Arts: Students can unleash their creativity as KU pushes them to their limits and beyond, whether craft the best piece for a portfolio or the soundtrack of their life.

The College of Visual and Performing Arts awards degrees in art history; music; music: commercial emphasis; communication studies; and cinema, television, and media production; as well as art education and music education. Fine Arts degrees are offered in applied digital arts, communication design (graphic design), crafts, and studio art with concentrations in digital media, drawing, painting, photography, print making, and sculpture. Minors offered in audio engineering, digital communication and new media, entrepreneurship, and jazz offer an eclectic opportunity to students pursuing the arts.

Academic Programs

Kutztown students can take advantage of a long list of unique academic opportunities such as undergraduate research, living and learning communities, experiential learning options, and practical application through student leadership and organizations. KU offers expert faculty and small, personalized learning opportunities both in class and in the field.

For students seeking a challenge, the Honors Program at KU provides challenges in new and exciting ways, while offering many perks and privileges. Honors students access specialized courses, internships, conferences, committees, and independent study programs. The Honors Program also offers a summer Honors Study Abroad program and a number of merit-based scholarships.

KU's Career Development Center is available to all students and alumni and offer superior assistance with everything from choosing a major to finding an internship, or landing jobs after graduation and beyond.

Off-Campus Programs

KU students can make the world their classroom, by choosing to study away from campus, nationally or internationally, through more than 150 student exchange programs. KU participates in international studies programs where students can immerse themselves in the history and culture of England, Spain, Austria, China, Ecuador, or South Africa, just to name a few, all while maintaining a focused area of study and earning credits toward graduation.

Costs

Kutztown University offers an excellent value to students via affordable tuition; numerous scholarship, grant, loan, and campus employment opportunities; and highly successful student outcomes. For the 2016–17 school year, tuition (up to 18 credits), fees, and on-campus room and meals for Pennsylvania residents was $19,826; for out-of-state students, the cost was $23,680.

Out-of-state students who are admitted to the university now receive a 40 percent reduction in the cost to attend, saving families more than $7,000 per academic year.

Financial Aid

The goal of financial aid is to place a quality education within reach. The goal of a college education is to get a great job and establish a career. And KU grads do just that. The best part of investing in education is that its value will only increase. On average, with a bachelor's degree, lifetime earning potential increases by $1 million.

More than 80 percent of Kutztown University students finance their education with some form of financial aid. With numerous scholarship, grant, loan, and campus employment opportunities; affordable tuition; and highly successful student outcomes, Kutztown University offers a tremendous value.

Students seeking scholarships are encouraged to apply early. The only form needed to apply for financial aid is the FAFSA. KU must receive the completed and processed FAFSA by February 15 for applicants to be considered for scholarships or other awards.

Faculty

Although many professors at KU are involved in important research and are leaders in their fields, their primary interest is in the classroom. The University has more than 350 full-time instructors and the average class size is 25. Approximately 90 percent of the faculty members hold terminal degrees in their field of study. Upon enrollment in the University, each student is assigned a faculty adviser to help plan his or her academic career.

Campus Life

KU offers an array of living choices: traditional or suite-style residence halls, apartments, and townhouses for approximately 4,400 students on campus. Students live on campus the first two years.

Involvement on campus is the key to having an enjoyable, fulfilling experience at KU. Students are encouraged to join a club, volunteer, cheer on the Golden Bears, and more during their four years at KU.

Admission Requirements

Kutztown University operates on a rolling admissions basis, meaning applications are accepted throughout the year. Admission requirements are outlined on the application page of the University's website. Admission decisions are based on grade point average and standardized test scores (both SAT and ACT scores are accepted). Certain academic programs have other admission requirements; those details are outlined on the website.

Application and Information

The completed application, $35 nonrefundable application fee, test scores, official final transcripts, and other required materials must be submitted to the Office of Admissions. To learn more, prospecitve students can visit www.kutztown.edu/apply. To speak with an admissions representative, contact:

Office of Admissions
Kutztown University of Pennsylvania
Kutztown, Pennsylvania 19530
United States
Phone: 610-683-4060
E-mail: admissions@kutztown.edu
Website: http://www.kutztown.edu/admissions

Old Main Clock Tower at Kutztown University.

COLLEGE CLOSE-UPS

LE MOYNE COLLEGE

SYRACUSE, NEW YORK

LE MOYNE
Greatness meets Goodness

★ To read more about this school, visit http://petersons.to/lemoynecollege

The College

Le Moyne College is a four-year, coeducational Jesuit college of approximately 2,800 undergraduate students that uniquely balances a comprehensive liberal arts education with preparation for specific career paths or graduate study. Founded by the Society of Jesus in 1946, Le Moyne is the second youngest of the twenty-eight Jesuit colleges and universities in the United States. Its emphasis is on the education of the whole person and on the search for meaning and value as integral parts of an intellectual life. Le Moyne's personal approach to education is reflected in the quality of contact between students and faculty members.

A wide range of student-directed activities, athletics, clubs, and service organizations complement the academic experience. Intramural sports are very popular with Le Moyne students; nearly 85 percent of the students participate. Le Moyne also has twenty-one NCAA intercollegiate teams (ten for men and eleven for women). Athletic facilities include a new soccer/lacrosse turf field, softball and baseball fields; basketball, and racquetball courts; a weight-training and fitness center; practice fields; and two gymnasiums. A recreation center houses an Olympic-size indoor swimming pool, jogging track, indoor tennis and volleyball courts, and additional basketball, racquetball, and fitness areas.

Around 85 percent of students live in residence halls, apartments, and town houses on campus. The Residence Hall Councils and the Le Moyne Student Programming Board organize a variety of campus activities, including concerts, dances, a weekly film series, student talent programs, and special lectures as well as off-campus trips and skiing excursions. The College also has a plaza, which houses its bookstore, a café, and a pizzeria. The new Dolphin Den, which features a food court and a convenience store, is a popular space for students to meet, have a bite to eat, or just spend a quiet moment relaxing by the fireplace.

Location

Le Moyne's 160-plus acre, tree-lined campus is located in a residential setting 10 minutes from downtown Syracuse, the heart of New York state, whose metropolitan population is about 700,000. Syracuse is convenient to most major cities throughout the Northeast, New England, and Canada and offers a wide array of shopping centers and restaurants, many near Le Moyne. Syracuse offers year-round entertainment in the form of rock concerts at the Landmark Theatre, professional baseball and hockey, Bristol Omnitheatre, Syracuse Stage, Everson Museum of Art, and the Armory Square district downtown, which offers one-of-a-kind eateries, pubs, and coffeehouses in addition to a wide variety of social and cultural events. All are easily accessible via the excellent public transportation service, which schedules regular stops on Le Moyne's campus. Just a few miles outside the city are the rolling hills, picturesque lakes, and miles of open country for which central New York is renowned. An extensive network of state and county parks, recreational areas, and other facilities offers an abundance of recreational opportunities, including swimming, boating, hiking, downhill and cross-country skiing, snowboarding, and golf.

Majors and Degrees

Le Moyne College awards the Bachelor of Arts degree in biological sciences, communication (advertising, filmmaking, journalism, media studies, music and culture, music industry, music journalism, public relations, television/radio), computer science, criminology (human services, international affairs, law enforcement, research), economics, English (creative writing, literature), French, history, mathematics (actuarial science, pure mathematics, statistics), peace and global studies, philosophy, physics, political science, psychology, religious studies, sociology (anthropology, criminology, human services, research and theory), software applications and system development, Spanish, and theatre arts. The Bachelor of Science degree is awarded in biochemistry, biological sciences (health professions, molecular biology, neurobiology), chemistry, economics, environmental science systems, environmental studies, general science, physics, and psychology. The Bachelor of Science is also awarded in accounting, business analytics, finance, human resource management, information systems, management and leadership, and marketing. A Bachelor of Science in nursing is offered as well.

Students may minor in advanced writing, arts administration, business administration, classical humanities, film, gender and women's studies, Irish literature, Italian, Latin, legal studies, health information systems, medieval studies, music, urban and regional studies, or visual arts, as well as most of the major fields of study offered. Preprofessional programs are offered in dentistry, law, medicine, occupational therapy, optometry, physical therapy, direct-entry physician assistant studies, podiatry, and veterinary science. Students may prepare for teaching careers through certification programs in adolescent education, dual adolescent/special education, dual childhood/special education, and TESOL.

Le Moyne College and the L. C. Smith College of Engineering and Computer Science at Syracuse University offer a dual-degree program in which students may earn a bachelor's degree from Le Moyne and a master's degree in engineering from Syracuse University. Concentrations include aerospace; chemical, electrical, and mechanical engineering; computer science; and other fields of engineering.

Formal accelerated 3-4 programs are offered in dentistry, optometry, and podiatry in cooperation with the State University of New York at Buffalo School of Dental Medicine, Pennsylvania College of Optometry at Salus University, and the New York College of Podiatric Medicine. Predental students may also participate in an early assurance program with the State University of New York at Buffalo School of Dental Medicine. Cooperative 3-2 dual-degree programs in engineering are available with Clarkson University, Manhattan College, and University of Detroit Mercy.

SUNY Upstate Medical University in Syracuse offers students pursuing careers in the health-related professions an accelerated 3-3 doctoral-level transfer program in physical therapy as well as two-year cooperative transfer programs in medical technology, and respiratory care. Premedical students at Le Moyne are also offered the opportunity to participate in a medical school early assurance program. An early assurance program for premedical students is also available through the State University of New York at Buffalo School of Medicine and formal agreements also exist with Fordham's School of Law and Syracuse University School of Law.

Academic Programs

While each major department has its own sequence requirements for the minimum 120 credit hours needed for the Le Moyne degree, the College is convinced that there is a fundamental intellectual discipline that should characterize the graduate of a superior liberal arts college. Le Moyne's core curriculum provides this foundation by including studies of English language and literature, philosophy, history, religious studies, natural sciences, and social sciences.

For exceptional students, Le Moyne offers an integral honors program that includes an interdisciplinary humanities sequence as well as departmental honors courses. Le Moyne also offers a part-time course of study during evening hours through its Center for Continuing Education.

Le Moyne students may enroll in Army and Air Force ROTC programs in conjunction with Syracuse University.

Off-Campus Programs

The study-abroad program allows qualified students to spend a semester or year in almost any country throughout the world. Le Moyne College has study-abroad programs or affiliations in the Czech Republic, Dominican Republic, England, Germany, Ireland, Scotland, and Spain. Students can also use partner programs to study in locations such as Australia, Costa Rica, Egypt, France, Italy, Japan, and South Africa. Le Moyne is a participant in the sixty-member New York State Visiting Student Program. As part of the mission of preparing future leaders, Le Moyne College places a strong emphasis on career preparation through internships and other forms of experiential education. Academic departments and the Office of Career Advising and Development both provide programs and services for students interested in interning part time and full time, both locally and in major cities such as New York and Washington, D.C. The Offices of Service Learning and the Academic Deans are also involved in experiential education to promote learning outside the classroom. In the sciences, students take part in campus research with mentor faculty members. Others receive assistance in pursuing outstanding opportunities off campus in leading research laboratories and health-care settings. The College has maintained a long-standing relationship with the Washington Center internship programs, where students from all majors complete full-time semester-long internships in Washington, D.C., with government, business, or major nonprofit organizations. Faculty members in the Political Science Department assist students interested in opportunities in Albany, the state's seat of government, with either the New York State Senate or Assembly. Finally, the education programs at Le Moyne put students into school classrooms starting immediately as freshmen and continuing each year until graduation.

Academic Facilities

Le Moyne students benefit from an ongoing commitment to technological excellence. The College's forty-two buildings are equipped with accounting, biology, chemistry, computer science, physics, psychology, and statistics laboratories. The W. Carroll Coyne Center for the Performing Arts houses generous production, performance, and classroom space; the latest light and sound technology; scene and costume shops; an aerobics and dance studio; and rehearsal rooms for instrumental and choral music. Academic facilities also include an extensively renovated color television studio; a radio/recording studio; a receiver-antenna satellite dish; transmission and scanning electron microscopes; a nuclear magnetic resonance spectrometer; a gas chromatograph/mass spectrophotometer; a 240,000-volume, open-stack library; and extensive on-site computer facilities. A fiber-optic network enables students to access the library system, the campus network, and the Internet from several computer labs around the campus or from their personal computers in their rooms. All classrooms are smart classrooms, with multimedia capabilities that expand and enrich the learning process. Le Moyne students have access to other libraries through the Central New York Library Resources Council, and the campus Academic Support Center is available to students for instructional support. In addition, Le Moyne recently opened a 48,000-square-foot addition to its existing science complex, and the Madden School of Business, featuring a state-of-the-art trading floor and analytics lab.

Costs

For 2017–18, Le Moyne's tuition is $32,840. Room and board charges are $13,400. Additional fees amount to approximately $1,065.

Financial Aid

Financial aid is offered to a large percentage of Le Moyne's students through scholarships, grants, loans, and work-study assignments. Le Moyne offers a generous program of merit-based academic and athletic scholarships as well as financial aid based on a student's need and academic promise. Federal funds are available through the Federal Pell Grant, Federal Work-Study, Federal Supplemental Educational Opportunity Grant, and Federal Perkins Loan programs. A student's eligibility for need-based financial aid is determined from the Free Application for Federal Student Aid (FAFSA). It is recommended that the FAFSA be submitted by February 1.

Faculty

The Le Moyne full-time faculty numbers 150 men and women; 94 percent have earned the highest degree in their field. With an average class size of 20, a student-faculty ratio of 13:1, and private offices for all full-time faculty members, the College promotes a personal as well as an academic relationship between students and faculty members. All classroom instruction is done by faculty members, and they are happy to assist and encourage students who wish to pursue undergraduate research through tutorials or senior research projects. These projects are carried out in an atmosphere free of competition from graduate students for books, laboratories, or professors' time. Le Moyne emphasizes advising and academic counseling for students throughout their four years.

Student Government

The College encourages student leadership in all activities. Positions of leadership are open to students in all class years. Students are represented by a Student Senate and have formal representation through the senate on most College-wide committees involved in decision making and policy formation.

Admission Requirements

Le Moyne seeks qualified students who are well prepared for serious academic study. Secondary school preparation must have included at least 17 college-preparatory high school units, 4 of which must be in English, 4 in social studies, 3–4 in mathematics, 3–4 in foreign language, and 3–4 in science. It is also recommended that prospective science and mathematics majors complete 4 units of mathematics and science. Students applying to Le Moyne College have the option of submitting their SAT and ACT test scores or withholding them for consideration as part of the admission process. However, for those wishing to be considered for top academic scholarships, the SAT or ACT is required and should be taken no later than December or January of the senior year in high school. Campus visits are strongly recommended, as the admission process is a personal one. As bases for selection, academic achievement and secondary school recommendations are of primary importance. Out-of-state and international students are encouraged to apply.

Application and Information

Le Moyne offers students the opportunity to apply in two ways: early action or regular admission. The early action program is nonbinding and provides high school students the opportunity to receive an admission decision by December 15 of their senior year. The early action application deadline is November 15. Regular admission applications are reviewed and admission decisions are made on a rolling basis beginning January 1. The priority deadline for applications is February 1; all students who wish to be considered for academic merit scholarships should have a completed application on file in the Office of Admission before this date. All students are encouraged to include Le Moyne (002748) on their FAFSA submission. Transfer students are encouraged to apply before August 1 for the fall semester and December 1 for the spring semester. Orientation programs for incoming first-year students take place in June and early July. Transfer student orientation programs are offered throughout the summer.

Mary Chandler
Senior Director of Admission
Le Moyne College
Syracuse, New York 13214-1399
Phone: 315-445-4300
800-333-4733 (toll-free)
E-mail: admission@lemoyne.edu
Website: http://www.lemoyne.edu
facebook.com/lemoyne
twitter.com/lemoynecollege
instagram.com/lemoyne_college
youtube.com/lemoynecollege

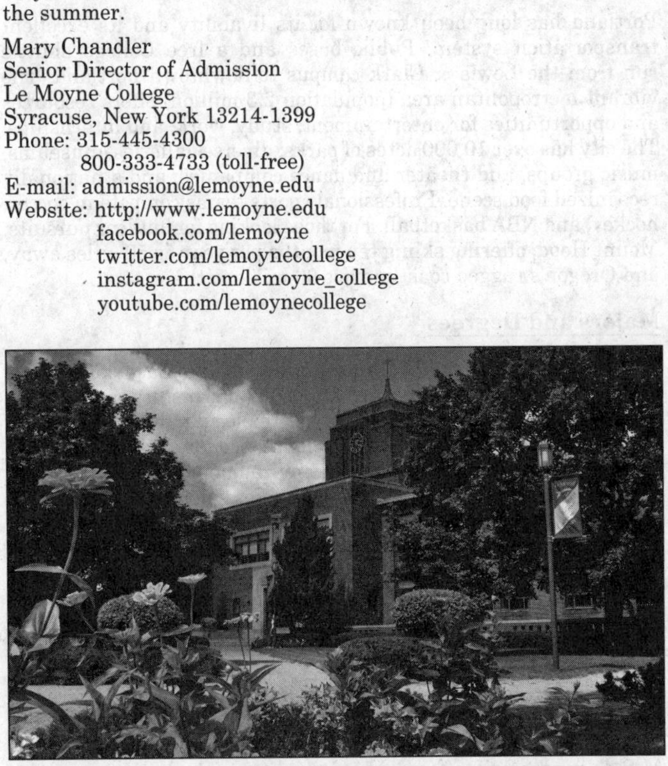

Grewen Hall, the College's oldest building, overlooks Le Moyne's beautiful 160-plus acre campus.

COLLEGE CLOSE-UPS

LEWIS & CLARK COLLEGE

PORTLAND, OREGON

The College

A private college with a public conscience, Lewis & Clark College has a global reach that extends well beyond its location in Portland, Oregon. Located on a 137-acre campus in a wooded residential area six miles from downtown, the College is a starting point for students to explore the wider world and find their place in it.

The student body is known for its geographic diversity. In fall 2016, of the 2,033 undergraduates, 11 percent were from Oregon, and 84 percent came from 45 other states plus the District of Columbia. Five percent of the students are international, representing 75 countries. Approximately 69 percent live in housing on campus, most of which is coed (91 percent). There are no fraternities or sororities.

The College offers over 120 student-run clubs and activity groups, including social justice and service organizations; international, cultural, and diversity clubs; media groups, including a radio station and weekly newspaper; and religious and spiritual life organizations. Cultural events such as lectures, student-run symposia, art exhibits, theater productions, concerts, recitals, and dance performances occur on a regular basis. Currently, there are 19 NCAA Division III varsity athletic teams, 7 club teams, and numerous intramural sports. The renowned College Outdoors Program offers adventures such as backpacking, rafting, snowshoeing, caving, sea kayaking, and environmental service projects in Oregon's and Washington's nearby wilderness areas.

Location

Portland has long been known for its livability and its excellent transportation system. Public buses and a free College shuttle run from the Lewis & Clark campus to downtown Portland. The vibrant metropolitan area (population 2.3 million) offers resources and opportunities for entertainment, study, work, and internships. The city has over 10,000 acres of parks; diverse galleries, museums, music groups, and theater and dance companies; and a nationally recognized food scene. Professional sports teams compete in soccer, hockey, and NBA basketball. For those looking for outdoor pursuits, Mount Hood, offering skiing ten months per year, is 50 miles away, and Oregon's rugged coastline lies 90 miles to the west.

Majors and Degrees

Lewis & Clark offers programs leading to the Bachelor of Arts degree. Academic majors include art (art history and studio art), Asian studies, biochemistry and molecular biology, biology, chemistry, classics, computer science, computer science and mathematics, economics, English, environmental studies, French studies, German studies, Hispanic studies, history, international affairs, mathematics, music, philosophy, physics, political science, psychology, religious studies, rhetoric and media studies, sociology/anthropology, theater, and world languages and literature. Students may also design a major or pursue a double major and numerous minors. Pre-professional preparation is available in the fields of law, medicine, business, entrepreneurship, and education.

Dual-degree (3-2 and 4-2) programs in engineering are offered in cooperation with Columbia University, Washington University (St. Louis), and the University of Southern California. A 4-2 B.A./M.B.A. program is offered in cooperation with the University of Rochester's Simon Graduate School of Business. A 4-1 B.A./M.A.T. program is offered through Lewis & Clark's Graduate School of Education and Counseling. In addition, there is a guaranteed admission agreement with Lewis & Clark's Law School for students meeting certain criteria.

Academic Programs

The liberal arts curriculum offers sufficient structure to ensure depth and breadth of study, but it also incorporates a high degree of freedom. In the four-year plan of study, approximately one-third of a student's time is devoted to general education, one-third to a major program, and one-third to elective courses. Students are also encouraged to participate in departmental honors programs, undergraduate research, independent study, and internships.

The academic calendar consists of two 15-week semesters. A normal load is four 4 semester-hour academic courses, plus one or more activity courses. The fall semester begins early in September and ends in mid-December, and the spring semester begins in mid-January and ends in early May. A limited number of courses are offered during two summer sessions.

The community of scholars at Lewis & Clark College is dedicated to personal and academic excellence. Joining the Lewis & Clark community obligates each member to observe the principles of mutual respect, academic integrity, civil discourse, and responsible decision-making.

Off-Campus Programs

Lewis & Clark offers nationally recognized international and off-campus study opportunities. Usually, 20 to 24 students plus a faculty leader participate in each program. More than half of the College's graduates have taken advantage of these outstanding programs, often satisfying General Education or major requirements at the same time.

Overseas study may have either a general-culture focus or a specialized academic focus. Sites for overseas study programs from 2017 through 2020 are Australia, Chile, China, Cuba, Dominican Republic, East Africa, Ecuador, England, France, Germany, Greece, India, Ireland, Italy, Japan, Morocco, New Zealand, Russia, Senegal, South Korea, Spain, and Vietnam. Domestic programs are available in the Arizona borderlands, New York, and Washington, D.C.

Academic Facilities

The Aubrey R. Watzek Library is open 24 hours per day when school is in session and offers individualized reference assistance for students. The library houses more than 740,000 items and its website provides access to its catalog as well as to a full range of electronic resources. The library is a member of Summit, a consortium of 39 academic libraries that have a unified catalog that enables students to request and receive materials from member libraries within two days.

Music department facilities include a 410-seat recital hall equipped with an orchestra pit and stage elevator; an extensive collection of more than 4,000 recordings; 22 practice rooms; 43 pianos; two harpsichords; a Baroque organ; an electronic music studio; Zimbabwe marimbas; and an Indonesian gamelan orchestra. The 600-seat chapel houses an 85-rank Casavant organ.

The visual arts center is equipped with studio space for painting, drawing, ceramics, sculpture, design, and printmaking as well as a photography lab. The department also has a Visual Resources Collection of 50,000 slides and several thousand digital images representing artwork from a wide range of media, time periods, world regions, and cultures. The humanities and social sciences also enjoy state-of-the-art classrooms and lab facilities.

The natural science buildings are equipped with modern instrumentation to support collaborative student-faculty research. Among the notable facilities are laboratories for the study of astrophysics, the biomechanics of animal locomotion, human-computer interactions, molecular modeling and parallel computing, a scanning electron microscope, a modern greenhouse, and an astronomical observatory with Newtonian and solar telescopes. Ecological investigations and studies of the environmental impacts of human activity are conducted both on the College's heavily wooded campus and at the nearby Tryon Creek State Park.

Computer labs house more than 130 computers, along with peripherals such as scanners, printers, and digital video editing equipment. Digital, still and video cameras, digital audio recorders, and more are available for checkout. All residence halls have wireless networks. The institution has a 1000 Mbps connection to the Internet.

Costs

Tuition and fees for 2017–18 are $48,988. The room and board charge is $11,996 for 14 (flex) meals per week; other meal plans are also available. The estimate for books and personal expenses is $2,112.

Financial Aid

In 2015–16, 91 percent of the College's students received some form of financial assistance. A financial aid package may include institutional, state, and/or federal resources. Lewis & Clark College participates in a variety of federal aid programs that may include Federal Pell and Supplemental Educational Opportunity Grants, Federal Direct and Perkins loans, as well as Federal Work-Study. To receive priority consideration for need-based financial aid, students must meet appropriate deadlines for admission and should submit the Free Application for Federal Student Aid (FAFSA) and the CSS/Financial Aid PROFILE application by the date appropriate for their admissions plan as noted at go.lclark.edu/fao.

Lewis & Clark offers renewable merit-based scholarships and participation awards to students who demonstrate the qualities of mind, self-discipline, and commitment to learning that characterize the best in Lewis & Clark students. These awards range from $1,000 to full tuition. Many of these scholarships are awarded through the admissions process and don't require a separate application. Others require additional paper work. Details on merit-based scholarship opportunities can be found at go.lclark.edu/fao.

Faculty

The 163 full-time members of the faculty are committed to undergraduate teaching and advising and are also active in research, writing, and publishing. Involving students in the research process is of high priority. Ninety percent of the full-time faculty members hold a Ph.D. or the highest advanced degree in their discipline. The student-faculty ratio is 12:1. The average class size is 18, with 88 percent of classes having 29 or fewer students.

Student Government

The Associated Students of Lewis & Clark (ASLC) consists of a Student Senate, governing boards, and appointed students who serve on faculty constitutional, standing, and special committees. The 30 members of the Student Academic Affairs Board (SAAB) are appointed on a departmental basis to represent the student body in discussions concerning academics at the College and to support student academic initiatives through a grant program. Students may apply for one of four different types of grants: student-initiated research, academic conference attendance, visiting scholars program, and Arts and Expression.

Admission Requirements

Lewis & Clark College seeks first-year and transfer applicants who are committed to academic excellence and personal growth. Admission is competitive. Applications are carefully reviewed and examined for degree of academic preparation, ability to express ideas in essay form, participation in activities, citizenship and community service, and support given by the school through recommendations. Campus visits are encouraged. Interviews are available but not required. Recommended high school preparation includes 4 years of English, 3 to 4 years of history or social science, 4 years of mathematics, 3 years of laboratory science, 2 to 3 years of foreign language, and 1 year of fine arts. The SAT or ACT is required, unless the student is applying via the Test-Optional Portfolio Path.

Application and Information

First-year applicants should submit the Common Application with the personal essay and supplemental questions; an official high school transcript, including senior grades from the first marking period; a record of SAT or ACT scores (unless applying via the Test-Optional Portfolio Path); the Common Application's School Report form; and at least one recommendation from an academic teacher. Application deadlines for the fall semester are November 1 for binding early decision (notification by December 15), November 1 for nonbinding early action (notification by January 1) and January 15 for regular decision (notification by April 1).

Transfer applicants are evaluated on a rolling basis. To ensure full consideration, the College strongly recommends that transfer students submit all credentials before the end of March.

The application deadline for first-year and transfer students for the spring semester is November 1 (notification within three weeks of file completion).

The Test-Optional Portfolio Path admissions program provides an opportunity for applicants who have shown exceptional academic initiative to demonstrate the full extent of their pursuits by presenting a portfolio of their academic work. Under this plan, SAT or ACT scores are optional. More details about the Portfolio Path can be found online at go.lclark.edu/portfolio_path.

For more information about Lewis & Clark College or to arrange a visit, students should contact:

Office of Admissions
Lewis & Clark College
0615 SW Palatine Hill Road
Portland, Oregon 97219-7899
Phone: 503-768-7040
800-444-4111 (toll-free)
Fax: 503-768-7055
E-mail: admissions@lclark.edu
Website: www.lclark.edu

Lewis & Clark students learn through a rigorous curriculum that builds intellectual depth and breadth, creativity, and critical thinking skills in its graduates.

LINCOLN UNIVERSITY

LINCOLN UNIVERSITY, PENNSYLVANIA

★ For more information, visit http://petersons.to/lincolnuniversity

The University

Founded in 1854, Lincoln University is the country's first degree-granting HBCU (Historically Black College and University). Since its beginning, the university has attracted an international and interracial student body from surrounding communities, the region, and other nations. Its most notable alumni include Poet Langston Hughes ('29) and former Associate Justice of the Supreme Court of the United States Thurgood Marshall ('30).

The university continues to cultivate leaders and achievers. It offers approximately 2,000 students more than 35 liberal arts and science-based undergraduate programs; graduate programs in business, counseling, education, and human services.

Its learning environment emphasizes concern for each student, quality education, and small classes. As a result, students graduate prepared to create successful careers in today's fast-paced, technology-based, global environment.

Lincoln University is accredited by the Middle States Commission on Higher Education.

Location

The main campus is in Lincoln University, Pennsylvania, which is in the northeastern region of the United States. The beautiful campus is situated amid wooded hilltops and rolling farmlands. Located on 422 acres in southern Chester County, the campus marries tradition and modern facilities, with sweeping pathways that encourage walking and contemplation within a safe and scenic landscape.

Lincoln's close proximity to several major cities provides the tranquility of a rural setting and the excitement of the metropolis. The campus is 45 miles from Philadelphia, Pennsylvania; 55 miles from Baltimore, Maryland; 25 miles from Wilmington, Delaware; and 15 miles from Newark, New Jersey.

Majors and Degrees

Lincoln University's academic programs fall under one of three colleges: the College of Arts, Humanities, and Social Sciences; the College of Professional, Graduate, and Extended Studies; and the College of Science and Technology.

Programs of study available include: accounting, anthropology, biochemistry and molecular biology, biology, black studies (minor), business and entrepreneurial studies for non-business majors (minor), chemistry, computer science, criminal justice, economics (minor), engineering science, English liberal arts, entrepreneurship (minor), finance, foreign languages, general science, health science, history, human services, information technology, international relations (minor), liberal studies, management, mass communications, mathematics, music, nursing pre-licensure B.S.N., nursing RN to B.S.N., Pan-Africana studies, philosophy, physics, political science, pre-law certificate program, psychology, religion, sociology, and visual arts.

Some of Lincoln University's most popular areas of study are the following:

The **Registered Nurse (RN) to Bachelor of Science in Nursing (B.S.N.)** program develops nurse leaders skilled at providing high quality, holistic, patient-centered nursing care. Areas of study include leadership, population health, professional roles and values, and research. The program is offered part-time either online or on-campus.

The **Bachelor of Science (B.S.) in Accounting** prepares students for careers as Certified Public Accountants (CPAs). Its curriculum provides professional and technical knowledge of accounting theory and practice. It also exposes students to specific areas of accounting including accounting information systems, audit, financial and managerial accounting, international accounting, and taxation.

The **Bachelor of Science (B.S.) in Biology** strengthens students' knowledge of foundational areas in biology at the molecular, cellular, organismal, and ecosystem levels. It also trains students to conduct original scientific investigations and communicate their research and findings to interested parties.

The **Bachelor of Science (B.S.) in Computer Science** trains students to design, develop, and test computer programs in languages like Assembly, C++, Java, and Visual BASIC. It also trains students to read, analyze, organize, store, and utilize data by creating graphical user interface forms, developing database design and modeling, and using data structures.

The **Bachelor of Science (B.S.) in Criminal Justice** provides students with in-depth information about how the criminal justice system works at the local, state, and federal levels. It explains how interactions between criminal justice institutions and the people in these settings change over time. It also provides awareness about how different social forces impact the types and rates of criminal behavior.

The **Bachelor of Science (B.S.) in Engineering Science** includes course work in civil, computer, electrical, and environmental engineering. It trains students to use engineering, mathematics, and science principles to solve problems. It also prepares them to design and conduct experiments as well as analyze and interpret data.

The **Bachelor of Arts (B.A.) in Music Performance** provides a creative and broad music curriculum that emphasizes band instrument, orchestral instrument, piano, and voice. Through research, lectures, and rigorous practice, students gain the performance skills and knowledge to pursue careers as educators and/or performers.

Academic Programs

Lincoln University offers undergraduate courses during two 15-week semesters and one or two six-week summer sessions each year.

Students have access to a broad range of academic, professional, and social resources including the following: Career Services, Center for Advising and Student Achievement, Horace Mann Bond Honors Program, international programs and services, Math Learning Center, placement assessment, Women's Center, Writing and Reading Center, and a writing proficiency program.

Costs

For the 2017–18 academic year, first-year tuition and fees total $12,240 for Pennsylvania residents and $18,012 for out-of-state students. Housing costs for the year are $5,135 and the most popular meal plan is $4,364. Costs for books and other supplies are estimated at about $2,000 per year.

Financial Aid

A college education is an important investment in the future. There are many options available for financial assistance, and more than 90 percent of students at Lincoln make use of these resources to meet their obligations. Lincoln University provides scholarships and participates in the following grant and loan programs: Federal Pell Grant, Federal Supplemental Educational Opportunity Grant, Federal Subsidized Direct Loan, Federal Unsubsidized Direct Loan, Federal PLUS Loan, and Pennsylvania State Grant.

The university also participates in financial assistance programs for veterans. Plus, it allows students who reside in the following states (and the District of Columbia) to use grants from their states to cover expenses: Connecticut, Delaware, Maine, Massachusetts, Ohio, Rhode Island, and West Virginia.

To be eligible for all forms of financial aid, including work-study and most university-funded scholarships, prospective students first need to complete the Free Application for Federal Student Aid (FAFSA). All FAFSA applications should be filed by April 1 for the following academic year to receive priority consideration for most types of financial assistance.

Faculty

Lincoln has 96 full-time faculty members; 79 percent of those hold a doctoral or highest academic degree in their field. The student-faculty ratio is 12:1 and 79 percent of all classes have fewer than 30 students.

The university's faculty members help students connect classroom experiences to industry. As leaders in their fields, they bring an extensive range of theoretical and practical experience to their teaching. They're also dedicated to helping students achieve both their academic and career goals.

Marilyn Button serves as chair of the Department of Languages and Literature, Professor Nancy Norman-Marzella whose credentials include an M.S.N., N.P., and C.N.E.; associate professor, and Professor Tondalaya Carroll chair of Business and Entrepreneurial Studies are among the university's dedicated faculty.

Student Life

Students at Lincoln University enjoy countless opportunities to form supportive and lasting friendships with fellow students. Most of them live on campus, which makes socializing, studying, and working more convenient. They have access to more than 60 student clubs, organizations, fraternities, and sororities; community service projects; activities and events; intramural sports; and bands. There is also a recreation center, Wellness Center, health services, and counseling services.

The Lincoln Lions athletic teams compete in NCAA Division II and the Central Intercollegiate Athletic Association. Men's sports include baseball, basketball, cross-country, football, and track and field; women's sports are basketball, cross-country, softball, soccer, track and field, and volleyball.

Admission Requirements

Applicants to Lincoln University must submit: a completed application for admission; an official high school transcript or GED test results and certificate along with a high school transcript; scores from either the Scholastic Aptitude Test (SAT) or American College Test (ACT); and a $20 application fee. Recommended, but not required are two letters of recommendation and an application essay that the applicant writes about themselves and events in their life that have made a difference in the way they view themselves and others (minimum 250 words).

Application and Information

Freshman and transfer students may apply online via the university's website, or applications can be downloaded and mailed. When the application is received, the student will be notified by postcard. After all test scores, transcripts, application fee, recommendations, and other supporting documents have been received, the Admissions Office will review the application. It usually takes at least 14 business days to complete the evaluation process. Lincoln University has a rolling admission system; however, in order to obtain on-campus housing and a better financial aid package, students are advised to apply as quickly as possible. Priority deadlines are April 15 for the fall semester and December 15 for the spring semester.

For more information, prospective students should contact:

Lincoln University
Office of Undergraduate Admissions
Cannon House 103
1570 Baltimore Pike
Lincoln University, Pennsylvania 19352
Phone: 484-365-8000
800-790-0191 (toll-free)
Fax: 484-365-8109
E-mail: admissions@lincoln.edu
Website: http://www.lincoln.edu

The Student Union Building at Lincoln University in Pennsylvania.

LINFIELD COLLEGE

McMINNVILLE, OREGON

★ To read more about this school, visit http://petersons.to/linfieldcollege

Linfield College

The College

Linfield College (1858) is an independent, coeducational, residential, comprehensive liberal arts and sciences college dedicated to providing an educational environment conducive to learning and participation. There are 1,700 full-time students on the McMinnville campus. These students come primarily from the thirteen Western states (twenty-five states overall) but also from twenty-six other countries. Students of color make up 33 percent of the student body, and 6 percent of students are international. Most students are between 18 and 22. Linfield is primarily residential, with seventeen residence halls, each accommodating between 10 and 100 residents. Each hall establishes its own calendar of social, educational, and recreational events throughout the year. Students who reside on campus eat their meals in the College dining hall. Houses and apartments are available for upper-division students. Social clubs, professional organizations, four sororities and four fraternities, service clubs, and almost forty other organizations play an important role in the daily life of a Linfield student. Linfield's winning athletics tradition fosters participation at all levels of competition. Women compete in intercollegiate basketball, cross-country, golf, lacrosse, soccer, softball, swimming, tennis, track and field, and volleyball. Men compete in intercollegiate baseball, basketball, cross-country, football, golf, soccer, swimming, tennis, and track and field. Linfield also has an extensive and active year-round intramural program.

Linfield hosts the Oregon Nobel Laureate Symposium, one of five such symposiums worldwide. At each symposium, several Nobel laureates come to share their backgrounds and expertise within the context of a basic theme.

The Linfield–Good Samaritan School of Nursing, an academic unit of the College at its Portland campus, prepares students for careers in nursing. This campus, at the Good Samaritan Hospital and Medical Center, has residence facilities, food service options, and a residence life program. In 2006, the Portland campus programs became open only to transfer admission.

Location

Located in McMinnville, 40 miles southwest of Portland, Linfield College is a leader in the cultural, educational, and recreational events of the fast-growing community of 35,000. Linfield is situated on 189 acres with most classrooms no more than a 10-minute walk from any of the twenty-four on-campus apartment buildings and residence halls. With most students living on campus, Linfield offers a welcoming and lively community.

Coffeehouses, cinemas, boutiques, a community theater, the Evergreen Air and Space Museum (including an IMAX theater and water park), bowling alleys, and a wide variety of restaurants are within walking distance for Linfield students. The central Oregon coast is an hour to the west, and the outdoor activity areas of the Oregon Cascade Range, including year-round skiing at Mount Hood, are two hours to the east. Salem, the state capital of Oregon, is 25 miles to the southeast, and Eugene is 80 miles south. Rainfall in western Oregon averages 42 inches annually and the winter temperature averages 41°F.

Majors and Degrees

Linfield offers the Bachelor of Arts degree in communication arts, creative writing, electronic arts, Francophone African Studies, French studies, German, German studies, history, intercultural communication, international relations, Japanese, Japanese studies, Latin American/Latino studies, literature, mass communication, music, philosophy, political science, religious studies, sociology, Spanish, studio art, and theater arts. The Bachelor of Arts or Bachelor of Science degree is offered in accounting, anthropology, applied physics, athletic training, biochemistry and molecular biology, biology, business, chemistry, computing science, economics, elementary education, environmental studies, exercise science, finance, international business, marketing, management, mathematics, physical activity and fitness studies, physical education, physics, and psychology. A Bachelor of Science in Nursing (B.S.N.) is also available. The College has programs to prepare students for advanced study in any health profession, including medicine, as well as law. The education department offers a strong program of teacher certification at the secondary and elementary levels.

Academic Programs

The academic year is divided into two 15-week semesters (fall and spring) and a four-week winter term in January. The January Term, required for first-year students, but optional for students in subsequent years, offers regular departmental courses and off-campus and international study. Academic courses are assigned 1–5 semester credit hours each; 125 credits are required for a B.A. or a B.S. degree. Students divide their time equally among required general education courses, a major area of study, and elective subjects. The Linfield Curriculum courses, selected to provide a solid foundation in the liberal arts, require students to take 3 semester hours in each of the six Modes of Inquiry as well as one upper-division course in one of these areas. These Modes of Inquiry are as follows: Vital Past; Ultimate Questions; Individuals, Systems, and Societies; Natural World; Creative Studies; and Quantitative Reasoning. In addition, students are required to take a writing-intensive course, a course addressing global pluralisms, and a course dealing with United States pluralism. Individually designed majors are available with faculty approval. Students majoring in a foreign language spend an academic year in a country in which the language being studied is the native tongue.

The College offers courses in English through the English Language and Culture Program. These courses are designed to help international students whose native language is not English to achieve competence in academic and social English skills, so that they may work effectively in their undergraduate classes at Linfield.

Off-Campus Programs

Off-campus educational experiences include the Semester Abroad program, involving four months of study in Australia, Austria, China, Ecuador, England, France, Germany, Ireland, Japan, New Zealand, Norway, Senegal, South Korea, and Spain. Transportation for the first round-trip is included in the cost of tuition, and most of these study programs cost the same as a semester on campus. January Term study-abroad programs for four weeks are also offered. Recent offerings included Health Care in Kenya; China's Solutions to Energy Issues in the Twenty-first Century; Art and Visual Culture of Catalonia, Spain; and Australia: From Colony to Asian Power.

Academic Facilities

In recent years, the College has opened two residence halls, six apartment buildings, the James F. Miller Fine Arts Center, the Marshall Theatre and communication arts facility, the Vivian A. Bull Center for Music, and the Nicholson Library. The library covers 56,000 square feet and combines traditional collections of books and journals with the new and changing digital and electronic technology to provide access to the web and web-based designs. The studio theater has an audience seating capacity of up to 140 and includes space for set construction and design.

In 2011, Linfield reopened the former library to provide new classroom and office space for the departments of business, economics, English, and philosophy. This state-of-the-art facility, T. J. Day Hall, includes the College's writing center and the Linfield Center for the Northwest (LCN). The LCN cultivates regionally relevant partnerships for training, research, service learning, and cultural or artistic exchanges. These opportunities promote student engagement in regional issues and produce real-world change. T. J. Day Hall is Linfield's first LEED-certified Gold building, underscoring the College's commitment to sustainability and conservation.

Murdock and Graf Halls house the biology, chemistry, and physics departments and up-to-date laboratories and equipment. Other facilities include art galleries and studios, a 250-watt FM radio station, an experimental psychology lab, dance and music studios, a preschool, and a 425-seat auditorium that houses a three-manual, 48-rank Casavant pipe organ.

Linfield students benefit from a communications and technology network that includes phone service, voice mail, e-mail, and wireless Internet connections in each residence hall room. In addition, there is wireless access in the library and all other areas of the campus.

The Health and Physical Education/Recreation Complex houses three gymnasiums; weight rooms; fitness laboratories with a hydrostatic weighing tank, a metabolic and pulmonary measuring system, and an electrocardiovascular exercise ECG system; an eight-lane, 25-yard indoor pool; handball and racquetball courts; classrooms; offices; and a 28,000-square-foot field house.

Costs

For 2016–17, tuition and fees were $39,700 per two-semester year, board was $5,160, and a double room was $6,160. There was a $235 per-credit fee for on-campus January Term classes, which is waived for first-year students.

Financial Aid

Eligibility for most of Linfield's assistance programs is based on need as determined by a federally approved needs analysis processor. The only form required for need-based programs is the Free Application for Federal Student Aid (FAFSA). Linfield participates in the federal grant, loan, and work programs, and other forms of financial assistance on the basis of demonstrated need.

The College awards scholarships to full-time students based on scholastic achievement, independent of financial need. These academic scholarships vary from 30 to 60 percent of tuition. A number of criteria are used when determining scholarships, including grade point average, strength of curriculum, and standardized test scores. Linfield sponsors special scholarships for National Merit finalists. The College also sponsors an annual Competitive Scholarship Day in February. Participation is limited to high school seniors who meet particular academic requirements and apply by December 1. Each academic department offers prizes ranging from $12,000 to $20,000, divided over the student's four years at Linfield. Scholarships are also available to students from the departments of music, theater, and communication who demonstrate outstanding leadership and community service. Financial assistance for non–U.S. citizens is limited to partial-tuition scholarships and the opportunity to work part-time on campus.

Faculty

There are 129 faculty members, each of whom is committed to undergraduate teaching and scholarship. Ninety-two percent have doctoral or other terminal degrees within their field. The student-faculty ratio is 11:1, and faculty members serve as academic advisers. There are no teaching assistants.

Student Government

Students have a significant voice in establishing and changing College policies and regulations. The Student Senate, chosen through campus elections, is the focus of student opinion and debate. Students are represented on most College governing councils and committees with faculty members and trustees, and they are encouraged to express and implement their ideas on academic or extracurricular matters.

Admission Requirements

Admission to Linfield College is selective. Admission is granted to students who are likely to grow and succeed in a personal and challenging liberal arts environment. Each applicant is judged on individual merit, based on high school performance, a writing sample, recommendations from teachers and counselors, precollege standardized test results (ACT or SAT), and the depth and quality of an applicant's involvement in community and school activities. Linfield is a member of the Common Application Association.

International students whose education has been in a language other than English must submit certified English translations of their academic work. Proficiency in English is required, as demonstrated by an official TOEFL score report or other English proficiency exam.

Application and Information

The early action deadline is November 1 (with notification by January 15) and the regular decision priority deadline is February 1 (with notification by April 1).

Interviews are not required, but students are encouraged to visit. Appointments should be made in advance and can be requested online at http://www.linfield.edu/stopby. The Linfield website provides students with information on academic programs, student life, and athletics.

Interested students are encouraged to contact:

Office of Admission
Linfield College
900 SE Baker Street
McMinnville, Oregon 97128
Phone: 503-883-2213
800-640-2287 (toll-free)
Fax: 503-883-2472
E-mail: admission@linfield.edu
Website: http://www.linfield.edu/admission
https://www.facebook.com/LinfieldCollege/
https://twitter.com/linfieldcollege
https://www.instagram.com/linfieldcollege/

Linfield College is located 1 hour southwest of Portland, Oregon's largest city, on nearly 200 acres. Nearly sixty buildings, many built in Georgian colonial style, house forty academic departments among a grove of oak trees.

LOYOLA UNIVERSITY MARYLAND

BALTIMORE, MARYLAND

★ To read more about this school, visit http://petersons.to/loyolauniversityinmaryland

LOYOLA
UNIVERSITY MARYLAND

The University

Loyola University Maryland is a Jesuit, Catholic comprehensive university committed to the educational and spiritual traditions of the Society of Jesus and the development of the whole person. Accordingly, the University inspires students to learn, lead, and serve in a diverse and changing world.

Loyola's current full-time undergraduate enrollment is 4,104; 82 percent of the student body lives on campus, with all first-year students participating in Messina, Loyola's living learning program. The University encourages co-curricular activities that contribute to the academic, social, and spiritual growth of the student. These include social and cultural organizations, student government activities, an ROTC program, national honor societies, and Patriot League Division I athletic programs such as basketball, cross-country, golf, lacrosse, rowing, soccer, swimming and diving, tennis, track, and volleyball. The majority of the student body participates in the wide variety of club and intramural sports offered.

In recent years, Loyola's campus has undergone significant expansion. Thirteen apartment complexes and four first-year residence halls provide Loyola students with on-campus housing. In 2011, the Donnelly Science Center was expanded, making it the largest academic building on the Evergreen campus. The Andrew White Student Center offers several dining choices, as well as spacious meeting and recreational space. The Student Center also provides facilities for athletics, the communication department, and the fine arts, including the McManus Theatre and Reitz Arena, which holds as many as 3,000 people for various events. The Student Center also has an art gallery, classrooms, black box theatre, and music, photography, and studio art labs. Loyola's recreational sports facility is the Fitness and Aquatic Center. This state-of-the-art 115,000 square-foot athletic facility provides an indoor pool, basketball courts, squash courts, a climbing wall, fitness equipment, tracks, and outdoor playing fields. The Ridley Athletic Complex, completed in spring 2010, is a 6,000-seat grandstand stadium that hosts lacrosse, soccer, and rugby games. The adjacent McClure Tennis Center features eight lighted courts and a locker room facility.

Location

The Loyola campus is located in a residential area of north Baltimore, five miles from the city's Inner Harbor area. This location offers students the advantage of quiet residential living with the attractions and amenities of city life. Other colleges and universities in the vicinity help to expand the social calendar and academic life. The fourth-largest metropolitan area in the United States, Baltimore/Washington D.C. has a wide variety of theaters, museums, professional and intercollegiate sports events, and historical points of interest.

Majors and Degrees

Loyola offers more than 30 majors and more than 45 minors. The Bachelor of Arts degree is awarded in art history, classical civilization, classics, communication, comparative cultures and literary studies, computer science, economics, elementary education, English, fine arts, French, German, global studies, history, philosophy, political science, psychology, sociology, Spanish, speech-language-hearing sciences, theology, and writing. The Bachelor of Business Administration degree is awarded in accounting, business economics, finance, information systems, international business, management, and marketing. The Bachelor of Science degree is awarded in biology, chemistry, computer science, engineering (with concentrations in mechanical, computer, electrical, and materials), mathematics, statistics, and physics.

Academic Programs

The curriculum at Loyola is divided into three parts: the core, the major, and electives. The core contains those courses that Loyola considers essential to the liberal arts curriculum. These courses, which are required of all students regardless of major, are completed throughout the four years. The core consists of a classical or modern language, English literature, writing, mathematics and natural science, social science, fine arts, history, philosophy, ethics, and theology. Majors enable students to pursue their specialized area of study in depth. Electives give students the opportunity to broaden their intellectual and cultural background in areas of special interest. To prepare for graduate study, students may enroll in one of three pre-professional programs: pre-health, pre-medical, or pre-law.

Messina, Loyola's first-year experience, is designed to help students adjust quickly to college-level work and forge a clear path to success at Loyola and in the life and career that will follow. Messina offers a similarly distinctive and powerful beginning, an opportunity to explore a wide range of academic disciplines, appreciate their interconnectedness, and take to heart the importance of learning in a student's personal and intellectual growth.

Off-Campus Programs

Loyola University Maryland participates in a cooperative program with Notre Dame of Maryland University, Johns Hopkins University, Goucher College, Morgan State University, Towson University, the Peabody Conservatory of Music, Stevenson University, University of Maryland (Baltimore County), and the Maryland Institute College of Art. Loyola students may cross-register at any of these area colleges and universities.

Students in good academic standing may pursue studies abroad through Loyola's programs in Accra, Ghana; Alcalá, Spain; Athens, Greece; Auckland, New Zealand; Bangkok, Thailand; Beijing, China; Berlin, Germany; Cape Town, South Africa; Copenhagen, Denmark; Cork, Ireland; Dubai, United Arab Emirates; Glasgow, Scotland; Leuven, Belgium; Lyon, France; Melbourne, Australia; Newcastle, England; Paris, France; Rome, Italy; and San Salvador, El Salvador. Loyola also participates in exchange programs with eight other countries, offers summer and winter study tours, and assists students in applying to a variety of non-Loyola affiliated international study programs each year.

Academic Facilities

The Donnelly Science Center houses class laboratory spaces, research laboratories, offices, a conference room for the natural sciences, storage, a vivarium, a microscopy center, and a robotics laboratory. Spacious hallways connecting the building's wings on all levels include spaces for science displays and gathering areas for students and faculty in biology, chemistry, physics, computer science, and engineering.

The Sellinger School of Business and Management is Loyola's AACSB-accredited business school. Highlights of this school include experiential learning requirements, the Sellinger Scholars honors program, many student associations, and the Student Experiential Learning Lab, a state-of-the-art trading room that allows students access to the three most widely used databases in the finance industry—Reuters, Morningstar, and Bloomberg—and features a six-screen video display for breaking news and real-time market updates and a scrolling price ticker.

Costs

For 2017–18, tuition for all undergraduate students is $46,160 per year. Housing costs are $10,070 or $11,340, depending upon the specific residence hall in which the student lives. The base meal plan for first-year residential students is $5,570 per year and student fees are estimated at $1,400.

Financial Aid

The University strives to make a Loyola education accessible for qualified students of all socioeconomic backgrounds. Financial aid is awarded based on academic ability and financial need. Seventy-two percent of the student body receives financial assistance in the forms of Loyola University Maryland grants and scholarships, state scholarships, Federal Supplemental Educational Opportunity Grants, Federal Pell Grants, Federal Perkins Loans, and Federal Work-Study Program opportunities. To apply for financial assistance, students must submit the Free Application for Federal Student Aid (FAFSA) and the CSS/Financial Aid PROFILE through the College Scholarship Service. The financial aid application deadline is January 15.

Faculty

Loyola intends to maintain its faculty-student ratio of approximately 12:1 and an average class size of 20 students to ensure its continued focus on students as individuals. Of the 369 full-time faculty members, 73 percent are tenured or on the tenure track. Zero classes are taught by graduate students or teaching assistants.

Student Government

The Student Government serves three chief functions, which make its existence not only valuable but also necessary. These functions are to represent the student body outside the University, to provide leadership within the student body, and to perform services, both social and academic, for the students. Responsibility for budgeting activities also rests with the Student Government. The president of the Student Government is a member of the College Academic Council.

Admission Requirements

The admission evaluation at Loyola combines an analysis of academic information submitted along with a review of recommendations, the record of extracurricular involvement, and evidence of special talent, leadership, and service. The admission committee does not use a formula or have strict cutoffs. Instead, the admission office's goal is to conduct a balanced and holistic review, taking a number of factors into account. Submission of SAT and ACT scores is optional for all first-year applicants, excluding home-school students. Students who choose not to submit standardized test scores must submit an additional teacher letter of recommendation or personal essay. Students may apply early decision (binding), early action (nonbinding), or regular decision (nonbinding). The University welcomes applications from students of character, intelligence, and motivation, without discrimination on the grounds of race or religious belief.

Application and Information

Interested students seeking to enroll at Loyola may apply online using the Common Application. Each applicant must submit a school counselor letter of recommendation, a teacher letter of recommendation, and a personal statement. Applicants for financial aid must file the Free Application for Federal Student Aid (FAFSA) to be considered for federal student aid and also file the CSS Profile application to be considered for all forms of institutionally funded need-based aid. A $60 application fee must accompany the application for admission.

For additional information, students are encouraged to contact:

Undergraduate Admission Office
Loyola University Maryland
4501 North Charles Street
Baltimore, Maryland 21210-2699
Phone: 410-617-5012
800-221-9107 (toll-free)
Website: http://www.loyola.edu/undergraduate
http://www.facebook.com/LoyolaMarylandAdmission
https://twitter.com/LOYOLAdmission
https://instagram.com/LOYOLAdmission

Loyola University Maryland is located in residential Baltimore, five miles from the Inner Harbor and less than an hour from Washington, D.C., affording students access to an array of cultural events, internship opportunities, and field experiences.

LUTHER COLLEGE

DECORAH, IOWA

★ To read more about this school, visit http://petersons.to/luthercollege

LUTHER COLLEGE

The College

Luther College, founded in 1861 by Norwegian immigrants, is a four-year residential liberal arts college of the Lutheran church (ELCA). The College is an academic community of faith and learning where students of promise from all beliefs and backgrounds have the freedom to learn, to express themselves, to perform, to compete, and to grow. Located in Decorah, Iowa, the College is home to nearly 2,150 students from forty-three states and sixty-five countries. Thirty percent of the students are from Iowa; 84 percent come from the four-state area of Iowa, Minnesota, Wisconsin, and Illinois. In 2016–17, 143 international students choose to study at Luther.

In keeping with its liberal arts tradition, the College requires students to develop a depth of knowledge in their chosen major and a breadth of knowledge through exposure to a wide range of subjects and intellectual approaches (general requirements). Learning at Luther is about engagement: faculty members who are passionate in their teaching and scholarship; students who are bright, active, and involved; and a College community characterized by personal attention, hands-on experiences, academic challenge, and community support. At Luther, all students become immersed in the liberal arts through the College's Paideia program. This program, which is uncommon in its approach, helps train students' minds and develop their research and writing skills as they explore human cultures and history. In addition, Luther offers a Phi Beta Kappa chapter and departmental honor societies, evidence of the quality of teaching and learning on campus.

At Luther, students are encouraged to seek out connections between their lives in the classroom and their lives outside the classroom. The College provides a stimulating cultural and educational atmosphere by bringing distinguished public figures, theater groups, musicians, and educators to the campus. Cocurricular activities are an important part of college life. The College sponsors six choirs, three orchestras, three bands, two jazz bands, and a full theater and dance program. Numerous student organizations and societies provide ample opportunities for student involvement in meaningful activities. As a community of faith, students can participate in chapel, weekly Sunday worship, and outreach teams.

Nineteen intercollegiate sports are offered. Men may participate in ten sports: baseball, basketball, cross-country, football, golf, soccer, swimming, tennis, track and field, and wrestling. Women compete in nine intercollegiate sports: basketball, cross-country, golf, soccer, softball, swimming, tennis, track and field, and volleyball. Club sports include Ultimate (Frisbee) and rugby. Seventy percent of the student body is involved in an extensive intramural and recreational sports program. Available for recreational use are twelve outdoor tennis courts, an eight-lane polyurethane 400-meter track, numerous cross-country running and ski trails, and 15 acres of intramural fields. The well-equipped Regents Center houses four hardwood basketball courts, a wrestling complex, three racquetball courts, and a 3,000-seat gymnasium. A sports forum accommodates a six-lane, 200-meter indoor track; six indoor tennis courts; locker rooms; and athletic training facilities. The Legends Fitness for Life Center provides the latest fitness equipment and a 30-foot-high rock-climbing wall. A new aquatic center opened in the fall of 2013 that features an eight-lane stainless steel pool complete with diving well.

Location

The College is located in Decorah, a city of 8,100 people in the scenic bluff country of northeast Iowa. The Upper Iowa River, which runs through the campus, is designated as a National Scenic and Recreational River. Rich in Scandinavian heritage, Decorah is a popular recreation area, providing opportunities for canoeing, kayaking, fishing, hunting, cross-country skiing, camping, hiking, biking, and spelunking. Three airports are located within a 75-mile radius of Decorah: in Rochester, Minnesota; Waterloo, Iowa; and La Crosse, Wisconsin.

Majors and Degrees

Luther College grants the Bachelor of Arts (B.A.) degree and offers majors in accounting, Africana studies, anthropology, art, athletic training, Biblical languages, biology, business (management), chemistry, classics, communication studies, computer science, dance, data science, economics, elementary education, English, environmental studies, French, German, health and fitness promotion, health education–teaching, history, international studies, management, mathematics, mathematics/statistics, music, neuroscience, Nordic studies, nursing, philosophy, physical education–exercise physiology, physical education–teaching, physics, political science, psychology, religion, Russian studies, secondary education, social work, sociology, Spanish, theatre, and women and gender studies. Preprofessional preparation is offered in dentistry, engineering, law, medicine, optometry, pharmacy, physical therapy, seminary, and veterinary medicine.

Academic Programs

Luther operates on a 4-1-4 academic calendar. The first semester runs from September to December, followed by a three-week January Term and the second semester, which runs from February to May. Two four-week summer sessions are offered in June and July. All students must complete at least thirty regular courses and two January-term courses in order to graduate from Luther. Other requirements for graduation include four common foundational courses: Paideia (111 and 112); foreign language (typically one or two courses); religion (two courses, one of which must be in biblical studies); and wellness (two 1-credit courses). In addition to a focused area of study (the major, which usually requires eight to ten courses), Luther requires all students to take courses in three general fields of inquiry: the natural world (two courses); human behavior (two courses); and human expression (two courses). Before graduating, students are required to bring together all they have learned in two culminating experiences: senior project (one course); and Paideia 450. Luther students also develop the perspectives and skills they will utilize in their lives as citizens and professionals equipped for distinguished service. Qualified students may develop interdisciplinary majors with faculty advisers.

Off-Campus Programs

Luther operates under the belief that the best education connects students with global issues and helps them engage with the larger world. Luther is consistently ranked among the top baccalaureate colleges in the nation for the number of students studying abroad prior to graduation.

Luther's off-campus programs not only span the globe, but also offer in-depth and immersive study in a wide variety of subjects. Students may participate in programs during fall and spring semesters, the January Term, and summer sessions.

The College's signature off-campus programs include an academic-year program in Nottingham, England; a semester program in Sliema, Malta; a semester program in Münster, Germany; and a semester program in Coldigioco, Italy. In addition, Luther is part of a thirteen-college consortium which runs a successful Washington Semester in Washington, D.C. Students also have options for urban study at several centers in Chicago.

Each January Term, 300–400 Luther students study on eighteen to twenty-five faculty-led domestic and international programs.

Finally, Luther students have a wide variety of off-campus options through Luther-affiliated programs, such as those sponsored by the Associated Colleges of the Midwest, Institute for Study Abroad–Butler

COLLEGE CLOSE-UPS

University, the Institute for the International Education of Students (IES), and International Studies Abroad (ISA), among others.

Academic Facilities

The 1,000-acre campus includes the Preus Library, housing 340,812 volumes, over 800 print periodicals, 200,000 electronic books, and the College art collection. The library's circulation desk, Research Help Desk, Technology Help Desk, and Digital Media Center connect students with the resources they need. Two science teaching facilities, Sampson Hoffland Laboratories and Valders Hall of Science, feature modern, well-equipped labs as well as a planetarium, a greenhouse, a herbarium, a live-animal center, a human anatomy laboratory, a natural history museum, and a psychology sleep laboratory. Within easy walking distance of the campus, the field study area offers an ideal setting for studies in aquatic biology, ecology, and field biology. Five ponds, two reestablished prairies, marshes, wooded areas, and agricultural lands are available for classwork and independent study. The College has wired and wireless networking support throughout the campus. Residence halls, classrooms, and labs are outfitted with computers, printers, and academic software. Multiple connections to the Internet provide high bandwidth and reliable connectivity.

Luther College maintains radio station KWLC-AM, and the College's affiliate station, KLSE-FM, is part of the Minnesota Public Radio network. Luther is also home to one of the largest archaeological research centers in Iowa. In addition to computer facilities and video screening rooms, the Language Learning Center houses a foreign language media library with over 800 foreign language films, audio books, and print books for language learners.

The economics and business, mathematics, and computer science departments are located in the impressive F. W. Olin Building.

The award-winning Jenson-Noble Hall of Music contains 32,000 square feet of classrooms, studios, practice rooms, and rehearsal rooms for keyboard, vocal, and instrumental music. The Center for Faith and Life (CFL) houses a 42-stop/62-rank organ in the 1,600-seat auditorium for the performing arts. A 200-seat recital hall, a 24-hour meditation chapel, and one of four campus art galleries are located in the CFL as well. The Center for the Arts serves as the home for theater, dance, and the visual arts.

Costs

For 2017–18, the comprehensive fee is $49,900, which includes tuition, room, board, a technology fee, subscription to student publications, and admission to College-supported concerts, lectures, and other events. A room telephone, cable TV, computer access from residence hall rooms, and a health-service program were also included. Private music lessons are $495 per semester. It is estimated that an additional $3,015 is adequate for books, clothing, entertainment, and other personal expenses.

Financial Aid

More than 98 percent of all Luther students receive financial aid in the form of grants, scholarships, low-interest loans, and work-study jobs on campus. Luther awards Founders, President's, and Dean's Scholarships to students demonstrating superior academic achievement. The amount of aid given is determined by an analysis of the Free Application for Federal Student Aid (FAFSA).

Faculty

There are 175 full-time faculty members; 95 percent hold a Ph.D., first professional, or other terminal degree. The student-faculty ratio is 11:1.

Student Government

Students share in the governance of the College and participate in social and cultural programming. They have full membership on most College committees, majority representation in the Community Assembly, and nonvoting representation on the Board of Regents.

Admission Requirements

Admission is selective. An applicant must be a graduate of an accredited high school and have completed at least 4 units of English, 3 units of mathematics, 3 units of social science, and 2 units of natural science. It is strongly recommended that the applicant have at least two years of a foreign language. Sixty-three percent of entering students rank in the top quarter of their high school class. Transfer students may enroll at the beginning of the fall or spring semester or the January term.

Application and Information

An application, SAT or ACT scores, an educator's reference, and a transcript of previous academic work are required for admission. On-campus interviews are recommended but not required. For more information about Luther, students should contact:

Admissions Office
Luther College
700 College Drive
Decorah, Iowa 52101-1042
Phone: 563-387-1287
800-458-8437 (toll-free)
Fax: 563-387-2159
E-mail: admissions@luther.edu (admissions)
finaid@luther.edu (financial aid)
global@luther.edu (international)
Website: http://admissions.luther.edu
http://www.facebook.com/luthercollege1861
http://twitter.com/luthercollege

Luther College students learn in a community that emphasizes rigorous academics, a world-class music program, competitive athletics, and opportunities to put their classroom learning to the test through internships, independent research, and study abroad. Typically, 98–99 percent of Luther graduates are employed, attending graduate school, or engaged in an internship or volunteer work within eight months of graduation.

COLLEGE CLOSE-UPS

LYNDON STATE COLLEGE

LYNDONVILLE, VERMONT

★ For more information, visit http://petersons.to/lyndonstatecollege

The College

This small college shines a bright light. For the 1,200 students who come here from Vermont, New England, and around the world, Lyndon State College (LSC) offers a hands-on, experiential education, nationally recognized professional programs, and an incredibly friendly atmosphere—all leading directly to rewarding careers or graduate study. Recent grads enjoy a 95 percent job or graduate school placement rate within twelve months of graduation.

The hallmark of a Lyndon education is experiential learning, with hands-on activities in the first years of school. New students can be confident that they are pursuing the right field of study while rubbing shoulders with faculty members and other students in their department.

A Lyndon education can take students anywhere. There are more than 30 LSC alumni at ESPN. Lyndon's meteorology grads are famously found everywhere there's weather; The Weather Channel's Jim Cantore is a graduate and returns to campus every fall to teach the next generation of LSC broadcast meteorologists. Graduates of Lyndon's Mountain Recreation Management program—the first program of its kind in the country—are national leaders in the winter resort and recreation industry. And Lyndon stays on the cutting edge; the new climate change science degree is one of the just a few of its kind in the country.

This is all a result of the real-world experiences students can immerse themselves in at Lyndon. Music business and industry interns can be found working on concert tours for world-famous musician. Lyndon atmospheric sciences students regularly take first place in national forecasting competitions. Electronic journalism arts students routinely win national awards for their daily live news broadcasts—including a coveted Emmy™ award for the nation's best college newscast.

Campus events range from the intellectual to the physical, with abundant opportunities for learning and fun. A rich mix of comedy, music, speakers, theater, performing arts, film, off-campus travel, adventure programming, and community service is offered by the College to enrich life outside the classroom. The College's popular music business and industry program guarantees a lively live music scene. Films are shown in the campus theater throughout the semester. Traditions from far to near—from Guatemala, India, and Russia to Vermont sugar-on-snow parties—are part of Lyndon's diverse campus culture.

There are more than thirty student organizations including the campus radio station (91.5 FM The Impulse); theater group (Twilight Players); and numerous sports, social, service, and academic clubs.

Lyndon competes in NCAA Division III athletics in baseball, basketball, cross-country, lacrosse, soccer, softball, tennis, track and field, and volleyball. LSC's cross-country squads are perennial champs. Intercollege club sports include hockey and rugby. The USA Sevens named Lyndon's pitch among the best in the world. And Lyndon's students participate in an intramural sport. More sports information can be found online at http://www.lyndonhornets.com.

Lyndon is Vermont's adventure recreation campus. On campus there's an indoor climbing center, ice climbing on "Fountain Mountain," eighteen holes of disc golf, two ropes courses, a terrain park, biking and hiking trails, and a new skate park. Students canoe, kayak, paddleboard, skate, play hockey, fish, and "spring dip" in and on the College's three ponds. Nearby there's skiing and snowboarding at Burke and Jay Peak. Kingdom Trails, a 100-mile network consistently rated as the finest bike trail system in the Eastern United States, is just 10 minutes from campus (and was created by alums of LSC's recreation department).

There are ten residence halls, including a 132-unit, apartment-style hall for juniors and seniors. Each room is equipped with Internet, cable TV, and telephone. Students who live on campus eat at the Stevens Dining Hall and the Hornet's Nest Snack Bar. All students are allowed to have vehicles on campus.

In July 2018, Lyndon State College will join with Johnson State College to become Northern Vermont University.

Location

The modern 174-acre campus is located in Lyndonville, Vermont, high on a hillside overlooking Burke Mountain in the heart of Vermont's scenic Northeast Kingdom, a *National Geographic*–designated geotourism area. It is easily accessible from all points by Interstate 91, a 3-hour drive from Boston and Springfield, Massachusetts, and 2.5 hours from Montreal. Additional information on the area can be found at http://www.nekchamber.com.

Majors and Degrees

Lyndon offers bachelor's degrees in accounting, animation and illustration, applied psychology/human services, atmospheric sciences/meteorology, business administration, cinema/video production, climate change science, computer information systems, criminal justice, early childhood education, elementary education, electronic journalism arts/television studies, English, environmental science, exercise science, global studies, graphic design, liberal studies, mathematics, mountain recreation management, music business and industry, natural science, philosophy, professional media communications, secondary education (English, mathematics, natural sciences, and social sciences), sport management, social sciences, sustainability studies, and visual communications.

Associate degrees are offered in applied science, business administration, computing, electronic journalism arts/television studies, general studies, human services, music business and industry, professional media communications, special education, visual arts, and visual communications.

There are graduate programs in education, liberal studies, and mental health counseling.

Academics

Lyndon was established in 1911 as a one-room teacher-training college with 3 students. Teacher training is still a big part of the picture, but today, LSC is best known for innovative professional programs that combine real-world experience and career-ready skills, with a traditional education in the liberal arts.

Lyndon operates on a two-semester calendar plus a six-week summer session and a two-week winter term. To graduate with a bachelor's degree, students must complete 122 hours of credit and meet College and program requirements. Sixty-two semester hours are required for associate degrees. Incoming students are tested for competence in writing and mathematics; deficiencies must be made up in noncredit classes during the first two semesters.

Lyndon's Academic Support Center, Career Planning and Placement Office, Financial Aid Office, Student Life, and Health Services are just some of the entities that serve the needs and promote the well-being of students. Complete information can be found at www.lyndonstate.edu/degree-programs.

Off-Campus Programs

Off-campus study is part of the curriculum in all majors in the form of paid and unpaid internships, site visits, hands-on projects, research, independent study, and/or field trips.

Lyndon grants credit for study in other countries through an approved program such as the Experiment in International Living or the American Institute for Foreign Study. Lyndon offers faculty- and staff-accompanied trips each semester to places such as Greece, Russia, Ecuador, England, China, Guatemala, Kenya, and many other countries of personal and academic interest.

Academic Facilities

Lyndon State College offers a modern, well-equipped campus. There are smart classrooms, two lecture halls, six computer classrooms, six science labs, and two general computer labs. There is a digital media, graphic design, video editing, and photo lab; a GIS-mapping lab; comprehensive weather center, atmospheric science lab, and observation deck; two exercise science labs; a recording studio/music business and industry lab; an instructional materials center for education majors; a psychology lab and reading lab; and LSC TV's News7 broadcast production studio. The Alexander Twilight Theatre and Moore Community Room provide flexible space for gatherings, activities, and performances of all kinds.

The library maintains a collection of more than 110,000 circulating volumes as well as periodicals, audio and video materials, and microfiche collections.

Costs

The 2016–17 tuition for Vermont residents is $10,224 per year; for nonresidents, it is $21,912. The NEBHE regional program allows for a $6,576 discount for New England students in eligible programs (program eligibility by state can be found at www.lyndonstate.edu/NEBHE); $5,500 discount for eligible New Hampshire and many New York students regardless of program. Room and board (21-meal plan) for one academic year is $9,988. Required College fees, not including health and accident insurance, total $1,066. Total expenses for a Vermont resident living on campus are $22,278; for a nonresident, $32,966. Miscellaneous expenses are estimated at $1,100. Complete information on costs can be found at www.lyndonstate.edu/tuition.

Financial Aid

Financial aid is available in the form of loans, grants, and campus employment under the Federal Work-Study Program. Approximately 89 percent of the student population receives some type of financial aid from institutional and outside sources. Approximately 35 percent of students are employed by either the Federal Work-Study Program or the Lyndon dining hall.

Applicants for aid are required to complete the Free Application for Federal Student Aid (FAFSA). In addition to filing the FAFSA, transfer students are required to have a financial aid transcript completed by the financial aid officer of each college they attended.

Faculty

Lyndon's faculty consists of 118 members, 95 percent of whom hold the highest degree in their field from research institutions such as Harvard, Columbia, Yale, and USC. Many of Lyndon's professors have come to Lyndon to teach following prestigious careers at corporations and organizations such as CNN, National Public Radio, and Hewlett-Packard. Some are successful entrepreneurs, offering real world expertise to back up their classroom teaching.

Faculty members serve as academic advisers and mentors to students and student organizations. Student evaluation of teaching is a formal process and is used in personnel decisions.

Student Government

Students actively represent Lyndon on the Vermont State Colleges' Board of Trustees, in the Vermont State Colleges' Student Association, and on many campus committees. The Student Senate heads the student organizations.

Admission Requirements

Lyndon emphasizes academic success as reflected on high school or college transcripts, and social and academic potential as reflected in letters of recommendation. Lyndon seeks applicants whose academic record reveals maturity and motivation as well as a sense of responsibility and leadership.

Entrance requirements include 4 years of English and 2 to 3 years each of mathematics, science, and history. Foreign language is desired. International students seeking to attend Lyndon can find detailed information on the College's website. The SAT is optional. Complete information about admissions requirements is available at www.LyndonState.edu/apply.

Admission requirements for transfer students are the same as those for first-year applicants, but an official transcript must also be obtained from each college-level institution that the applicant has attended. Transcripts are required even if no credit is being transferred from a particular institution. Transfer credit may be given at Lyndon for all courses completed with the equivalent of a grade of C or higher at accredited or officially approved institutions.

Application and Information

Interested prospective students can apply online at www.LyndonState.edu/apply. A nonrefundable $49 fee must accompany each application. First-year applicants who are unable to afford the application fee should complete the paper application and ask their guidance counselor to sign a College Board fee waiver, or print a copy of the NACAC application fee waiver and ask their counselor to complete it. When these forms are ready, prospective students should mail them to Lyndon, along with their application, all transcripts of academic work completed, and their board scores. Lyndon State College accepts the Common Application.

For further information, students should contact:

Office of Admissions
Lyndon State College
P.O. Box 919
Lyndonville, Vermont 05851
Phone: 800-225-1998 (toll-free)
Fax: 802-626-6335
E-mail: admissions@lyndonstate.edu
Website: http://www.lyndonstate.edu

Students on the set of Lyndon's News7. Since 2004, the student-produced daily newscasts have garnered over 80 regional and national awards.

MANHATTAN COLLEGE

RIVERDALE, NEW YORK

★ To read more about this school, visit http://petersons.to/manhattancollege

MANHATTAN COLLEGE

The College

Manhattan College has more than sixty programs that build upon a strong liberal arts foundation and offer professional preparation in liberal arts, business, education and health, science, and engineering. Learning extends beyond the classroom through internships in New York City and beyond.

The College is one of only a few U.S. colleges to have chapters of all five of these distinguished national honor societies: Phi Beta Kappa, Beta Gamma Sigma, Kappa Delta Pi, Sigma Xi, and Beta Pi.

Payscale rated Manhattan College as the top Catholic college on its 2016 College Return on Investment (ROI) Report.

Following in the Lasallian Catholic tradition, many Manhattan College students actively define their commitment to social justice by balancing their traditional lifestyles with immersion and service experiences around the city, country, and world.

Each year, Campus Ministry and Social Action (CMSA) organizes several L.O.V.E. programs (Lasallian Outreach Volunteer Experience), which give students the opportunity to travel to some of the world's poorest areas in New Orleans, West Virginia, Kenya, Ecuador, and the Dominican Republic to volunteer with people of very different socioeconomic backgrounds.

Closer to home, the Lasallian Collegians volunteer on campus and in New York City by arranging school blood drives, toy drives, soup kitchen trips, and food runs. In addition, the Arches, a learning-living resident program, offers first-year students the opportunity to live in community, attend two classes together, and experience New York City through service projects in the city.

The tight-knit College community is comprised of 3,927 students. With a 12:1 student-to-faculty ratio, professors know students personally and care about their success. The majority of students live on the traditional collegiate campus, just a subway ride from midtown Manhattan.

Location

Manhattan College's 23-acre campus is located 10 miles north of midtown Manhattan in the suburban Riverdale section of the Bronx, about a mile from Westchester County. The College is located in the world's greatest cultural hub, where renowned museums and landmarks serve as off-campus classrooms. Students have access to internship and job opportunities at some of the country's most prestigious companies.

Majors and Degrees

Liberal Arts: The curriculum of the School of Liberal Arts provides programs that lead to a Bachelor of Arts or Bachelor of Science degree with majors in the humanities and the social sciences, including art history, communication, economics, English, fine arts, government, history, labor studies, modern foreign languages, philosophy, psychology, religious studies, and sociology. Interdisciplinary majors include international studies, peace studies, and urban studies.

Science: In the School of Science, programs lead to a Bachelor of Science or Bachelor of Arts degree with majors in biochemistry, biology, chemistry, computer science, environmental science, mathematics, and physics. Pre-medical, pre-dental, and pre–veterinary studies programs are also available.

Engineering: The School of Engineering has a well-deserved reputation as one of the best college engineering schools in the nation and offers programs leading to a Bachelor of Science degree in chemical, civil, computer, electrical, and mechanical engineering. The program is fully accredited by the Educational Accreditation Commission of ABET. Graduate programs are also available in chemical, civil, computer, electrical, environmental, and mechanical engineering.

Business: The School of Business, accredited by AACSB International, has programs leading to a Bachelor of Science in Business Administration degree with majors in accounting, business analytics, computer information systems, economics, finance, global business studies, management, and marketing. In addition, Manhattan College also offers the following graduate programs: the Bachelor of Science in Professional Accounting/Master of Business Administration and the Bachelor of Science in Business/Master of Business Administration, which offer students the opportunity to complete a five-year multiple award program.

Education and Health: The School of Education and Health offers a curriculum leading to a Bachelor of Arts degree in childhood education, childhood/special education (dual program), and adolescent education. The kinesiology curriculum leads to a Bachelor of Science degree in physical education and exercise science. The health curriculum leads to a Bachelor of Science degree in allied health, with a concentration in health-care administration, health counseling, or scientific foundations. Curricula in radiological and health sciences lead to a Bachelor of Science in radiation therapy, radiologic technology, or nuclear medicine technology. In addition, the School of Education and Health offers the five-year childhood/special education program, which allows the student to receive a bachelor's and master's degree with eligibility to pursue certification for grades 1–6 in regular and special education. The School of Education and Health also offers master's degrees and professional diplomas in school counseling, mental health counseling, special education, and school building leadership. All programs are approved by the New York State Education Department and accredited by the Teacher Education Accreditation Council (TEAC).

Academic Programs

The core curriculum shared by the Schools of Liberal Arts and Science studies some of the vital works of humankind, explores new ideas, examines the meaning of scientific experimentation, and encourages a student to develop his or her thinking and leadership abilities. The major programs offer advanced work in specific humanistic and scientific disciplines and opportunities to work on research projects in collaboration with faculty scholars.

In the School of Engineering, all engineering students follow a common core curriculum during the first two years and choose a major at the beginning of the junior year. Each curriculum includes a generous selection of courses in basic sciences, the engineering sciences, humanistic studies, and mathematics.

The School of Business prepares students for positions of executive responsibility in business, government, and nonprofit organizations. The business curriculum is based on a strong commitment to liberal education and is well balanced between professional business courses, humanities, sciences, and social sciences. This is a reflection of the school's belief that executives should be broadly educated and should involve themselves, as well as their organizations, in efforts to solve social problems.

The School of Education and Health prepares students for teaching, counseling, and health professions. Students complete the College's core curriculum in liberal arts and sciences and then complete a major in various programs in the school's three departments: education, kinesiology, and radiological and health professions. All programs include internships/practicums in schools, hospitals, or other institutions. Graduates of the school's teacher-preparation programs receive New York State provisional teaching certification. The school also offers a five-year B.A./M.S. program in childhood/special education and special education.

Off-Campus Programs

Manhattan College also offers study-abroad programs in many countries; arrangements can be made to study in a country of choice. Students in the School of Business may participate in the International Field Studies Seminar. As participants, they spend time in another country studying the effect of that environment on international firms. Career services and co-op education integrate classroom theory with the practical experience of a job in industry, business, the social services, the arts, or government. Portions of the education courses are conducted in New York City schools, so that student teachers may gain experience in urban education at an early stage.

Academic Facilities

There are more than forty scientific and engineering laboratories at Manhattan, including the Research and Learning Center, as well as a modern language laboratory and a computer information systems laboratory. Manhattan's O'Malley Library is a state-of-the-art facility featuring modern accommodations for study and research.

The Raymond W. Kelly ('63) Student Commons, which opened in the fall of 2014, is a 70,000-square-foot building, which has quickly become a focal point on campus. It enhances the College's ability to integrate academics and student life, and provides space for fitness and wellness programming, cultural and community events, dining, student activities, and student collaboration.

Costs

For 2017–18, the tuition for Manhattan College is $38,200 per year plus program fee. Room and board for the year is $15,600.

Financial Aid

Manhattan grants or administers financial assistance in the form of tuition awards to students on the basis of need and/or ability. Need is evaluated by submitting the FAFSA. In addition to a merit scholarship fund, Manhattan offers endowed scholarships, special category scholarships and student athletic grants, Federal Pell Grants, Federal Supplemental Educational Opportunity Grants, student loans, Federal Work-Study Program awards, and New York State financial assistance are also available to students who qualify. Forty-eight percent of all students receive merit aid with 94 percent of the students receiving aid.

Faculty

Manhattan's faculty has 219 full-time faculty members. Ninety-three percent of the faculty members hold doctorates. They are available to students for informal guidance and counseling and serve as official moderators of many campus organizations.

Admission Requirements and Application Information

An application for admission to Manhattan College may be submitted using the Common Application or a Manhattan College Application. An application fee of $75 is required.

In reviewing applications for admission, the most emphasis is placed upon student course selection and the rigor of the course curriculum as well as on cumulative grade point average. All applicants must have completed a minimum of 16 units in academic subjects to be qualified for admission.

Applicants for freshman admission need to submit SAT or ACT scores. Only a student's highest scores are considered for admission and scholarship eligibility.

Grades and examination scores alone do not adequately evaluate a student's ability to be successful in college. Therefore, appropriate character references are considered important when reviewing candidates for admission. One letter of recommendation from a teacher or guidance counselor is required. Applicants must also submit a brief personal statement or college essay.

Interviews are recommended but not required as part of the admissions process.

Applications are reviewed on a rolling admission basis. Manhattan will consider for admission any qualified student upon completion of the junior year. Students must continue to demonstrate progress at the same academic level in their senior year and that all secondary school graduation requirements must be met, and a diploma issued, in order to enroll. Junior college or other transfer students are welcome. Manhattan College requires applicants whose native language is not English to take the Test of English as a Foreign Language (TOEFL), IELTS, the SAT, or ACT exam. The average SAT score is 1100–1240.

The high school report, recommendation letters, and transcript must be submitted by the high school guidance counselor. There is a rolling admissions policy and a March 1 deadline for financial aid applications.

For more information, contact:

William J. Bisset, Ph.D.
Vice President for Enrollment Management
Manhattan College
Riverdale, New York 10471
United States
Phone: 718-862-7200
800-MC2-XCEL (toll-free)
E-mail: admit@manhattan.edu
Website: http://www.manhattan.edu

Manhattan College centers a great deal of its campus activity around the main quadrangle.

COLLEGE CLOSE-UPS

MANHATTANVILLE COLLEGE

PURCHASE, NEW YORK

Manhattanville COLLEGE®

The College

While the 100 beautiful acres that make up Manhattanville are located in a quiet suburban setting, the culture, entertainment, and excitement of New York City are only 30 minutes away. The private coeducational college founded in 1841 draws its 1,800 students from more than fifty countries and thirty-five states. Manhattanville College is ranked in the Princeton Review and *Newsweek* as one of the best colleges for undergraduate study. Manhattanville College has created a small global village. This richly diverse community embodies the College's mission: to educate students to be ethical and socially responsible leaders in a global community.

Learning is at the heart of Manhattanville, and the College's proximity to New York City creates a constant flow of opportunity that brings learning to life. Manhattanville students know how to have fun, but they also have a sense of purpose. The College's social conscience is informed by a commitment to serving the community. The Corporation for National and Community Service named Manhattanville College in the 2013 President's Higher Education Community Service Honor Roll for excellent services. The Duchesne Center serves as the coordinator and catalyst for service learning, community outreach, culture, and leadership across the College campus and around the world. Last year, students participated in over 30,000 hours of community service. Manhattanville students actively seek opportunities to serve humanitarian causes in the developing world.

The College's global perspective is enriched by its role as a Non-Governmental Organization of the United Nations. Select students have an opportunity to intern at the UN and to study with an ambassador.

Location

Manhattanville's campus lies in the heart of Westchester County, bordered on the east by Long Island Sound and on the west by the Hudson River. From the roof of Reid Castle, which serves as the campus's main hall, the skyline of Manhattan is visible. This proximity to the city that calls itself the "Capital of the World" is one of Manhattanville's many assets. The College provides free transportation to the city on Saturdays and to Manhattan-bound commuter trains seven days a week so students can take advantage of all New York City has to offer.

Majors and Degrees

Manhattanville College offers undergraduate degrees in more than fifty academic concentrations in the arts and sciences, including Bachelor of Arts (B.A.), Bachelor of Science (B.S.), Bachelor of Fine Arts (B.F.A.), and Bachelor of Music (B.Mus.) degrees; a self-designed major; a double major with teacher certification; and preparation for professional and graduate study (pre-law, pre-medical, pre–physical therapy, and pre–speech language pathology).

Students may choose from the following areas of study: accounting, African studies, American studies, art history, art (studio), biochemistry, biology, business management, chemistry, classical civilizations, communications studies, computer science, creative writing, criminal justice, criminal law, dance and theatre, dance therapy, digital media production, economics, education, English, environmental studies, film studies, finance, French, German, history, Holocaust and genocide studies, human resource management, international management, international studies, Irish studies, Italian, Latin American studies, legal studies, marketing, mathematics, museum studies, music, music education, music business, musical theatre, music technology, neuroscience, philosophy, political science, pre-dental, pre-health, pre-law, pre-medical, pre–physical therapy, pre–speech language pathology, psychology, self-designed major, social justice, sociology and anthropology, Spanish, sport studies, women's studies, world literature, and world religions.

This listing can be found online at http://www.mville.edu/academics.

Academic Programs

Manhattanville College offers full-time, part-time, and accelerated opportunities for study as well as dual-degree programs. The Manhattanville curriculum nurtures intellectual curiosity and independent thinking. Students and professors form close collaborative relationships beginning with the first year program, an interdisciplinary survey of the liberal arts that is required of all freshmen.

Under the guidance of a faculty adviser, the student maps an academic and co-curricular program, establishing a major from different branches of the liberal arts. The student may begin studies in the chosen field as early as the freshman year. Over the course of four years of study, the student assembles a portfolio consisting of study plans, evidence of academic proficiency in written critical analysis and qualitative research, annual evaluations, transcripts, and examples of the student's best work.

A special option for B.A. candidates is the self-designed major. If a student's interests direct them beyond existing departmental majors, they may propose a program of study to the Board of Academic Standards. Manhattanville students also have the opportunity to earn academic credit for internships in New York City.

Manhattanville College offers college credit for A-level exams, International Baccalaureate, and Advanced Placement examinations.

Off-Campus Programs

Manhattanville offers more than 100 study-abroad opportunities through either direct exchange programs or study-abroad providers at various levels of language proficiency, including Argentina, Belgium (internship at the European Union), Chile, England, France, Germany, Ireland, Italy, Japan, South Africa, Mexico, and Spain, among others. There is also a world of over 650 domestic and international internship possibilities with leading groups such as Apple, Condé Nast, IBM, and MasterCard.

Academic Facilities

Manhattanville is one of the first colleges in the U.S. to outsource a service that enables students to interact online with experienced reference librarians at any time of the day or night from anywhere in the world. The virtual research service, "Ask a Librarian 24/7," uses co-browsing to connect students with professional librarians who can answer questions about research and help students navigate the College's extensive array of subscription databases and other library resources. Manhattanville's teaching library, which supports the School of Education, ranks among the foremost undergraduate teaching libraries in the country. The Menendez Language Laboratory includes videos and record libraries that provide materials for class instruction and individual practice in French, Spanish, Russian, Italian, German, Chinese, Japanese, Hindi, Marathi, Modern Hebrew, and English as a second language. The College provides a writing clinic, a reading clinic, audiovisual facilities, and a bibliographic instruction program. The library building is open 24 hours a day, seven days a week through most of the fall and spring semesters, and it has computer labs, quiet study areas, group-study rooms, and a café where students and faculty members can meet informally.

Among the College's other academic facilities and resources are the art studio, science laboratories, the performing arts facilities, and student media facilities.

The College has state-of-the-art computers, computer labs, and campus networking for student use and instruction. In addition, advanced music technology systems offer performing arts students limitless opportunities for creativity.

Costs

For the 2017–18 academic year, tuition is $37,910 and the average room and board costs are $14,520.

Financial Aid

Manhattanville College offers both merit scholarships and need-based financial aid. Over 90 percent of students receive financial awards. The Free Application for Federal Student Aid (FAFSA) is required. The types of awards available are honors, merit, arts, and community service scholarships; Manhattanville grants and scholarships; Federal Perkins Loans; Federal Stafford Student Loans; Federal Pell Grants; Federal Supplemental Educational Opportunity Grants; Federal Work-Study Program awards; and Tuition Assistance Program awards.

For scholarship information and advice about financial aid eligibility, prospective students should visit www.mville.edu/financialaid.

Faculty

Nearly 90 percent of faculty members have Ph.D. or terminal degrees in their fields. Many faculty members live on the campus. The Manhattanville curriculum nurtures intellectual curiosity and independent thinking. The student-faculty ratio of 12:1 promotes close and collaborative relationships between faculty members and students, aided by the structure of the curriculum and the Portfolio System, which fosters collaboration between student and faculty adviser. Faculty members, not teaching assistants, teach all Manhattanville classes, and 80 percent of the classes have 20 or fewer students.

Student Government

Students in large measure shape the quality of life on the Manhattanville campus. Elected representatives of the student body run the student government, which serves as a principal means of communication among the administration, faculty members, and students. Its board of directors is responsible for formulating policy on student life and for implementing this policy through various committees. Student government members also serve on the College's policymaking and ad hoc committees.

Admission Requirements

Manhattanville College admits candidates for undergraduate degrees if their academic records indicate a competence to engage in a challenging liberal arts curriculum. Admission to the College is selective, and the most important consideration is the student's secondary school performance. When weighing this aspect, the admissions committee evaluates the quality of the school, the strength of the student's program, and success in those studies. Next, the committee considers the various recommendations that are submitted on behalf of the student, along with standardized test scores if submitted (Manhattanville is a test-optional institution) and the student's personal statement. A campus interview is strongly recommended. Applicants for all performing arts programs are required to either upload a recording via GetAcceptd.com or attend a live audition on campus. Students who plan to apply for the B.F.A. degree program should present portfolios to the art department for evaluation. Students who plan to study in these areas may audition for scholarships.

Application and Information

Applying is straightforward—submit the completed application, official high school transcript, letters of recommendation, a personal statement, and optional SAT or ACT scores. Transfer applicants should submit an official transcript from each school attended. Admission is rolling with a priority deadline of March 1 for all enrollment. Early action deadline is December 1. For details, students should visit www.Mville.edu or contact the College via e-mail at admissions@mville.edu or by phone at 914-323-5464.

The College subscribes to the Candidates Reply Date. Applications should be submitted as early in the senior year as possible. Candidates may apply online at www.mville.edu/apply.

Manhattanville College is committed to equality of educational opportunity, and is an equal opportunity employer. The College does not discriminate against current or prospective students and employees on the basis of race, color, sex, national and ethnic origin, religion, age, disability, or any other legally protected characteristic. This College policy is implemented in educational and admissions policies, scholarship and loan programs, athletic and other school-administered programs, and in employee-related programs.

For further information, students should contact:

Office of Undergraduate Admissions
Manhattanville College
2900 Purchase Street
Purchase, New York 10577
United States
Phone: 914-323-5464
E-mail: admissions@mville.edu
Website: http://www.mville.edu
http://www.facebook.com/Manhattanville
http://www.twitter.com/Mville_College
https://www.youtube.com/user/ManhattanvilleVideo
https://www.instagram.com/mville_admissions/

Reid Hall (The Castle) is the centerpiece of the Manhattanville College campus.

COLLEGE CLOSE-UPS

MARLBORO COLLEGE

MARLBORO, VERMONT

★ To read more about this school, visit http://petersons.to/marlborocollege

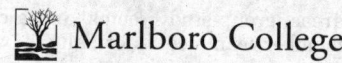

Marlboro College

The College

Marlboro College is an intentionally small, intellectually demanding liberal arts college, where students with a passion for learning pursue their deepest interests. An exceptionally close-knit learning environment in the inspiring natural setting of Vermont's Green Mountains, Marlboro offers student-designed study through small classes and advanced individualized study. Rather than follow a prescribed academic program, Marlboro students work closely with faculty advisers to map out an individualized course of study based on their intellectual interests. Marlboro's goal is to teach students to think clearly and learn independently, develop a command of clear writing, and aspire to making a difference in the world, all while participating responsibly in a self-governing community.

Marlboro was founded in 1946, and the college's rural, 300-plus-acre campus includes the original cluster of barns and other farm buildings that were converted by the first students and faculty members into classrooms and dormitories. The campus also features 17 miles of trails, and the Outdoor Program offers instruction and equipment for backpacking, cross-country skiing, kayaking, rock climbing, snow-shoeing, and other outdoor recreational opportunities that bring students in touch with the surrounding environment. The soccer team competes with other colleges, and more impromptu gatherings of students play volleyball, basketball, softball, and Ultimate (Frisbee) on an informal basis. In addition, Marlboro's much-anticipated broomball tournament (a game akin to hockey, but with less skill and grace) takes place each winter, with prizes for the winning teams and those with the best costumes. Campus committees organize many events both on and off campus, including concerts, lectures, poetry and fiction readings, art shows, and trips to Boston, Montreal, and New York for museum visits, shopping, and baseball games. Other activities that enrich campus life include parties, dances, plays, and film screenings.

Marlboro is—and intends to remain—one of the nation's smallest liberal arts colleges, with some 300 students on average. They come from all across the United States and several other countries and represent a rich diversity of socioeconomic backgrounds, perspectives, and interests. Transfer students—who make up one quarter of each incoming class—bring an important wealth of perspective to the campus community. More than 80 percent of all students live in campus housing, which consists of small dormitories and several four-bedroom cottages.

Location

The center of Marlboro, just 2 miles from the college, is a quintessential Vermont village, with a post office, a town clerk's office, and an inn. The total population of the town is 1,200 residents, more in the summer during the famous Marlboro Music Festival. The town of Brattleboro, 12 miles away, is a lively cultural and commercial center with bookstores, restaurants, coffee shops, a community food cooperative, music venues, and a movie theater. The college is 2 hours by car from Boston and 4 hours from New York City and Montreal.

Areas of Study and Degrees

Marlboro confers Bachelor of Arts and Bachelor of Science degrees in 34 fields. Areas of study offered include American studies, anthropology, art history, Asian studies, biology, ceramics, chemistry and biochemistry, classics, computer science, cultural history, dance, economics, environmental studies, film/video studies, gender studies, history, languages, liberal studies, literature, mathematics, music, painting, philosophy, photography, physics and astronomy, politics, psychology, religion, sculpture, sociology, theater, visual arts, world studies, and writing.

Students at Marlboro have the freedom to design their own course of study based on these degree fields, with the support and guidance of inspiring faculty members, and are encouraged to make interdisciplinary connections and pursue individualized research. The college also offers Bachelor of Arts and Bachelor of Science degrees in international studies through its World Studies Program, which includes a six-to-eight month internship in another country. Marlboro confers master's degrees and related certificates in management and teaching through programs offered at its graduate center in nearby Brattleboro, which provides a practical and seamless next step for many undergraduate students.

Academic Programs

In the first two years, Marlboro students study broadly, discover new interests, and begin to see the connections that lead many to pursue interdisciplinary work. Each new student is paired with a faculty adviser and joins an advising group of students with similar interests that meets each week. Students learn from each other, as well as from their engaging professors, in seminar-style classes.

Marlboro believes that clear writing both reflects and engenders clear thinking. Whether their academic interests lean toward Russian literature or contemporary dance, students write prodigiously over the course of their time at Marlboro. The college requires each new student to pass a Clear Writing Requirement within three semesters of enrolling. Designated writing courses, faculty advisers, and student writing tutors all help new students meet the requirement. Whatever career paths Marlboro students forge, they all benefit from the ability to process complex information and effectively communicate their ideas to others.

More than any other academic component, Marlboro's Plan of Concentration sets the college apart from other undergraduate programs. Undertaken by all Marlboro students in their junior and senior years, the Plan is the collection of related projects and papers that form the final product of the student's academic work at Marlboro. It is an individualized program of classes, research, experiences, one-to-one study, and original thought, driven by the student's interests and academic goals and designed in close collaboration with faculty sponsors. Final evaluation of the student's Plan is conducted by her or his faculty advisers and an outside examiner who is a recognized expert in the student's field.

Off-Campus Programs

Marlboro College sponsors multiple academic adventures and service-learning trips each year, ranging from community work in South Carolina and Cambodia to interdisciplinary research in Cuba, China, Kenya, and Vietnam. Whether they are in the World Studies Program or not, students working on their Plan of Concentration often travel abroad or attend other institutions for a period of time to complement their academic work. Marlboro faculty members may help plan these pursuits and frequently aid students in securing internships in their academic fields.

Academic Facilities

Marlboro's academic facilities offer small classrooms and inviting faculty offices for students to meet in small groups and individually with their professors. Facilities are open 24 hours a day, supporting student research and creative explorations in a DNA lab, a black-and-white darkroom, a digital film-editing studio, art and pottery studios, and an astronomical observatory. The Rudolf and Irene Serkin Performing Arts Center offers more than 10,000 square feet for music, dance, and drama rehearsals and performances. Marlboro's Total Health Center provides additional space for medical and psychological counseling services as well as a fitness room. The new Snyder Center for the Visual Arts, which opened in 2016, includes studios, classrooms, gallery space, and a digital media lab.

Costs

Tuition and fees at Marlboro were $39,086 for the 2016–17 academic year. Room and board costs were $10,802.

Financial Aid

More than 90 percent of all full-time Marlboro students receive some form of financial help. The college is committed to helping any student who qualifies for admission assemble the financial resources necessary to attend, and need is not a factor in the admission decision. Merit scholarships and grants are also available.

Faculty

Marlboro's 40 full-time faculty members are committed first and foremost to teaching. The lively exchange of ideas between teachers and students is the cornerstone of the Marlboro curriculum. The college's 6:1 student-faculty ratio sparks dynamic exchanges between students and their teachers both in and out of the classroom, and fosters a close-knit community in which asking questions is more important than knowing the right answers.

Student Government

All students, faculty, and staff members are equal members of the college Town Meeting, when the community comes together each month to debate and decide budget initiatives, college policies, and other issues that affect daily life. A board of selectpersons, elected by the college community, serves the college's interests and is responsible for drafting the Town Meeting agenda. Students serve with faculty and staff members on more than 30 college committees, including those that make decisions on hiring faculty, housing policies, and special scholarships. Other important committees include the social committee and the Community Court, which is responsible for enforcing campus standards of conduct.

Admission Requirements

The Admissions Committee seeks students with intellectual promise; a high degree of motivation, self-discipline, personal stability, and social concern; and the ability and desire to contribute to the college community. All applicants are considered without regard to race, creed, sex, sexual orientation, gender identity or its expression, national or ethnic origin, age, or disability. Homeschoolers, transfers, veterans, and older or returning students are encouraged to apply.

Like most colleges, Marlboro requires students to submit several forms of documentation, from high school transcripts to teacher recommendations. SAT or ACT scores are optional, and whether they are submitted or not, the admissions office evaluates each applicant as a unique individual who possesses qualities that are not necessarily quantifiable.

A campus visit is strongly recommended for all applicants, and interviews are required. Marlboro does not use a formulaic approach in making admission decisions. Applicants are encouraged to demonstrate their particular strengths; the goal is a successful match between the student and the college.

Application and Information

New students and transfers are admitted for either the spring or the fall semester. Applicants for the fall semester have a choice of three admission plans. The early decision plan is for those students who have thoroughly researched Marlboro and for whom Marlboro is the first choice. Applicants should be aware that early decision is binding. The early decision deadline for first-year students to submit application materials is November 15, and applicants are notified by December 1. Early action, a nonbinding plan, has a deadline of January 15. These applicants are notified of a decision on February 1. The regular admission deadline is March 15. The deadline for transfer students to submit applications materials for the fall semester is rolling.

Students can apply to Marlboro through the Common Application or directly through Marlboro College's own application, found on the college website. All applications should include the Marlboro College supplement form with a "Why Marlboro" personal statement, a $50 application fee, complete transcripts from all secondary schools and colleges currently or previously attended, an analytical writing sample, and two letters of recommendation. SAT or ACT test scores are not required, but will be taken into consideration if submitted by the prospective student. In lieu of a high school transcript, homeschooled students must submit a detailed description of their curriculum (including reading lists and academic study areas).

Office of Admissions
Marlboro College, 2582 South Road
Marlboro, Vermont 05344-0300
United States
Phone: 802-257-4333
800-343-0049 (toll-free)
Fax: 802-451-7555
E-mail: admissions@marlboro.edu
Website: http://www.marlboro.edu

Classes at Marlboro College are small and informal, enabling faculty members to bring an extraordinary degree of commitment, passion, and mentoring to their teaching.

MARYWOOD UNIVERSITY

SCRANTON, PENNSYLVANIA

Marywood UNIVERSITY

★ To read more about this school, visit http://petersons.to/marywooduniversity

The University

Marywood University enrolls more than 2,800 students in its undergraduate, graduate, and doctoral programs. Founded in 1915 by the Sisters, Servants of the Immaculate Heart of Mary, the University provides a framework for educational excellence that enables students to develop fully as persons and to master professional and leadership skills necessary for meeting human needs.

Students at Marywood have the opportunity to build on their academic interests and proactively shape their educational experience. Marywood believes in the power of the individual and in the premise that education is the most empowering tool.

Marywood is fully accredited by the Commission on Higher Education of the Middle States Association of Colleges and Schools. Program-specific accreditations are available to review online at www.marywood.edu/academics.

Marywood's athletic programs provide students with opportunities to play on competitive intercollegiate, club, and intramural teams. Students compete on an intercollegiate basis in baseball, basketball, cross-country, field hockey, golf, lacrosse, rugby (new in 2018), soccer, softball, swimming/diving, tennis, track and field, and volleyball. Marywood is a member of NCAA Division III, the Colonial States Athletic Conference (CSAC), and the Eastern College Athletic Conference.

Prospective students can connect with Marywood through social networks including Facebook (facebook.com/marywoodu), Twitter (twitter.com/marywoodu), and YouTube (youtube.com/marywoodu).

Location

Marywood's campus is part of an attractive residential area of Scranton, in northeastern Pennsylvania. With a population of 78,000, Scranton is the fifth-largest city in Pennsylvania. Marywood is close to many major cities of the Northeast; traveling by car, it is 2½ hours to New York and Philadelphia, 4 hours to Washington, D.C., and 5½ hours to Boston. Several airlines serve the Wilkes-Barre/Scranton International Airport, which is 20 minutes from the campus. The Pocono Mountains, offering spectacular scenery and an abundance of outdoor recreational opportunities, including downhill skiing, are a short distance from campus.

Academic Programs

All students are required to complete a core curriculum in the liberal arts in addition to the courses in their major. Opportunities for undergraduates abound through double majors, honors and independent-study programs, practicums, internships, and study abroad. Army and Air Force ROTC programs are available.

Majors and Degrees

At the undergraduate level, Marywood awards the Bachelor of Arts (B.A.), Bachelor of Architecture (B.Arch.), Bachelor of Business Administration (B.B.A.), Bachelor of Environmental Design in Architecture (B.E.D.A.), Bachelor of Fine Arts (B.F.A.), Bachelor of Music (B.M.), Bachelor of Science (B.S.), Bachelor of Science in Nursing (B.S.N.), and Bachelor of Social Work (B.S.W.).

Marywood offers majors in the following areas of study: accounting, ad hoc (self-designed), advertising and public relations, architecture and interior architecture/design, art (studio: ceramics, painting, sculpture, illustration; design: graphic design, photography), art therapy, arts administration (art, music, theater), athletic training, aviation management, biology, biology secondary education, biotechnology, communication sciences and disorders (speech-language pathology), computer science, criminal justice, cyber security (information security), digital media and broadcast production (broadcast, corporate), early childhood education, English (literature and writing), environmental science, exercise science, financial planning, English secondary education, health services administration, history, history/pre-law, history secondary education, hospitality management, industrial/organizational psychology, international business, journalism, management, marketing, mathematics, mathematics secondary education, medical laboratory science, music education, music performance, music therapy, nursing, nutrition and dietetics, philosophy, pre-physician assistant studies, psychology, psychology/clinical practice, religious studies, retail business management, science, sociology, social work, Spanish, Spanish secondary education, special education/elementary education (dual certification), and theater.

Marywood offers bachelor's to master's degree programs in accounting, art therapy, biotechnology, communication arts, criminal justice, cyber security (information security), education, financial information services, health services administration, physician assistant studies, social work, and speech language pathology.

Off-Campus Programs

Study-abroad opportunities are available in countries such as Australia, Canada, England, France, Mexico, and Spain. Through Studio Art Centers International (SACI), art students may study in Florence, Italy.

Academic Facilities

In recent years, the University has made major improvements to campus, including new athletic, residence, and dining facilities, and one of the finest studio arts facilities in the northeast. The Learning Commons, opened in fall 2015, is a 21st century–style library featuring four levels of open, accessible, and technologically advanced facilities. The Insalaco Center for Studio Arts features 60,000 square feet of fully equipped studios, labs, and classroom spaces for a broad variety of artistic disciplines. The Center for Architectural Studies offers students two levels of studio space in a spacious, adaptive re-use of Marywood's former gymnasium and pool space. A new Center for Communication Arts offers a wide range of media tools, including a soundstage for television production and audio recording, a radio station, video and editing rooms, an animation studio, and print journalism facilities.

Costs

Tuition for full-time students (12–18 credits per semester) for the 2017–18 academic year is a flat fee of $32,190. There is also a general fee of $1,500 for full-time students. Costs for room and board for a full academic year are approximately $13,900, depending on which meal plan is selected and the desired room occupancy.

Financial Aid

Marywood offers a comprehensive program of financial aid to assist students in meeting educational costs. Eligibility for federal and state programs is based on demonstrated financial need, as determined by a federal eligibility formula that analyzes family income and assets. In addition, approximately $29 million in institutional aid is awarded annually to Marywood students. Applicants to Marywood are considered for all financial assistance programs for which they qualify. Candidates are required to submit the Free Application for Federal Student Aid (FAFSA) and the Marywood application form.

Faculty

Among faculty members at Marywood, 152 are full-time, and 87 percent of these hold the Ph.D. or the highest degree in their field. The student-faculty ratio is 12:1. Faculty members are evaluated on their teaching and on their scholarly and artistic activities.

Student Government

All matriculated students in the undergraduate school are members of the Student Government Association (SGA). The SGA operates with a number of committees, including the Student Council, the Resident Committee, and the Commuter Committee. The association plays a key role in establishing a positive campus environment.

Admission Requirements

Candidates for admission should demonstrate reasonable progress toward graduation in an accredited secondary school, have graduated from a secondary school, or offer evidence of an equivalent secondary education. Each candidate should show satisfactory academic preparation in 16 units of subject matter, including 4 units of English, 3 units of social studies, 2 units of mathematics, 1 unit of science with laboratory, and 6 additional units. Prospective students should check with the Office of University Admissions regarding current standardized test requirements.

In addition to fulfilling general admission requirements, candidates for admission to a degree program in architecture, art, education, music, nursing, pre–physician assistant studies, and speech language pathology must meet special standards established by the department. Prior to enrollment, music, theater, and art candidates are required to audition or to present an art portfolio.

For certain programs, candidates without the recommended distribution of units may be eligible for admission if their course work as a whole and the results of their tests offer evidence of a strong foundation for college work. Candidates who are deficient in required course work may complete the appropriate work during the summer or first year in college.

A student who demonstrates satisfactory academic performance at another college may apply for admission as a transfer student. Academic courses presented for transfer should be equivalents of courses required by the programs of study at Marywood. Students should have earned a grade of C or higher in their course work; C– will not transfer. A student should expect to earn a minimum of 42 credits at Marywood; ordinarily, at least one half of the credits required for a major must also be earned at Marywood.

International candidates are required to meet the academic standards for admission, demonstrate proficiency in the use of the English language, and submit documentation of having sufficient funds to cover educational and living expenses for the duration of study. To certify proficiency in the use of English, international applicants whose primary language is not English must submit scores from the Test of English as a Foreign Language (TOEFL) or the IELTS.

Application and Information

Applications for admission are considered on a rolling basis; however, candidates are strongly encouraged to submit applications by March 1. Applications received after March 1 are considered on the basis of available space in particular programs. To be considered for admission, freshman applicants must submit to the Office of Admissions a completed application (paper or online), a nonrefundable $35 application fee (waived if applying online), an official high school transcript, an official report of scores from the SAT or ACT, and at least one letter of recommendation. Students can apply online at www.marywood.edu/admissions/applying.

Transfer students must submit a completed application, a nonrefundable $35 application fee (waived if applying online), an official high school transcript, official academic transcript(s) reflecting all college course work for which the candidate has enrolled, and at least one letter of recommendation.

All submitted credentials become the property of Marywood and are not returnable to the applicant. Admission standards and policies are free of discrimination on grounds of race, color, national origin, sex, age, or disability.

For further information, interested students should contact:

Christian DiGregorio, Senior Director
University Admissions
Marywood University
2300 Adams Avenue
Scranton, Pennsylvania 18509
Phone: 866-279-9663
Fax: 570-961-4763
E-mail: yourfuture@marywood.edu
Website: http://www.marywood.edu/admissions
www.facebook.com/marywoodu
www.twitter.com/marywoodu
www.youtube.com/marywoodu

The majestic Rotunda located in the Liberal Arts Center on Marywood's campus.

MASSACHUSETTS COLLEGE OF ART AND DESIGN

BOSTON, MASSACHUSSETTS

★ To read more about this school, visit http://petersons.to/mcad

MASSART
MASSACHUSETTS COLLEGE OF ART AND DESIGN

The College

Founded in 1873, Massachusetts College of Art and Design (MassArt) is the nation's first and only freestanding, publicly supported college of art and design, and the first to grant a degree. The college educates more than 2,000 students each year in a variety of disciplines including architecture, industrial design, painting, fashion design, and art education, offering undergraduate and graduate programs that prepare them to participate in the creative economy as fine artists, designers, and art educators.

MassArt is accredited by the New England Association of Schools and Colleges (NEASC) and the National Association of Schools of Art and Design (NASAD). The college is a member of the Association of Independent Colleges of Art and Design (AICAD).

Located in Boston's hub of arts and culture along the Avenue of the Arts (Huntington Avenue), MassArt is a member of several academic consortia and neighborhood associations that seek to expand educational resources available to students and enhance the economic vitality of the area. Boston also serves as an extended classroom for students. In addition to visiting many local museums, galleries, and artists' studios, students can expand their knowledge of revolutionary history by walking the Freedom Trail, discover world-class landscape architecture in one of the many public parks or gardens, or relax in one of the city's many entertainment or shopping districts. As a world leader in innovation, Greater Boston serves as headquarters for many companies, including Converse, TJX Corporation, and Fidelity Investments—all of which employ MassArt graduates. MassArt alumni also have a long history of entrepreneurship, as evidenced by the founding of companies such as CloudKid, Moth Design, and Aviary Gallery. In keeping with its longstanding public mission, MassArt's doors are always open to community members. Each year, thousands of visitors come to MassArt for a first-hand experience with art and design. The college's professional and student exhibitions, educational programs for young people, creative careers conferences, visiting artist and lecture programs, and other community-minded events provide students with a unique experience of connecting with their neighbors as well as professional artists, designers, and educators.

Majors and Degrees

MassArt awards the Bachelor of Fine Arts (B.F.A.) degree in 18 disciplines: animation, architectural design, art education, ceramics, fashion design, fibers, film/video, glass, graphic design, history of art, illustration, industrial design, jewelry and metalsmithing, painting, photography, printmaking, sculpture, and the interdisciplinary Studio for Interrelated Media.

Academic Programs

The undergraduate degree curriculum is sequential, and all students must complete the first-year foundation program, which provides compulsory exposure to the basics of 2-D and 3-D art and design. Graduation requirements include an elective studio and multiple critical studies courses. Fully one-third of the course requirements for the B.F.A. degree program are in liberal arts. B.F.A. students have specific course and distribution requirements in social sciences, writing and literature, and science and mathematics. Students must complete a total of 120 credits to earn the B.F.A. degree from MassArt.

Each year of study requires satisfaction of 30 credits, as follows:

Freshman year (foundation year): two semesters of Drawing—figurative and breadth (6 credits); Visual Language 2-D (3 credits); Time 4-D (3 credits); Form Study 3-D (3 credits); Studio Elective (3 credits); Written Communication (3 credits); Freshman Seminar (3 credits); Introduction to Western Art (3 credits); and History of Art Elective (3 credits).

Sophomore, junior, and senor years comprise select major requirements (12 credits); Studio/Open Elective (6 credits); and Liberal Arts/History of Art Electives (12 credits).

Off-Campus Programs

Students can enhance their artistic perspective through a MassArt International Exchange, AICAD Mobility, or a third-party study-abroad program. Qualified undergraduate students may participate in these programs during one semester of their junior year. Students may also consider a range of summer courses abroad. A wide range of programs is available to MassArt students.

For over 20 years, MassArt faculty members have also offered international travel courses across disciplines and to destinations all over the globe. The International Education Center supports both faculty and students in these courses, from conception to the flight home. By participating in a travel course, students join a group of globally inspired artists and designers led by MassArt faculty experts on an once-in-a-lifetime travel experience.

Academic Facilities & Housing

The MassArt campus spans an entire city block, offering students access to 1 million square feet of studio, classroom, living, and exhibition space. The entrance to the college is through the Design and Media Center, a 70,000-square-foot, $45 million space designed for interdisciplinary collaboration, opened in January 2016. The college offers state-of-the-art facilities and studios housed in nine buildings along Huntington Avenue in the Fenway neighborhood of Boston, with renowned museums such as the Museum of Fine Arts and the Isabella Stewart Gardner Museum just steps away from campus. About 89 percent of MassArt freshmen live on campus in residence halls designed to create a convenient, safe, and comfortable environment and offer unique facilities designed to address the needs of MassArt's student-artists. Public transportation makes MassArt easily accessible, with bus and subway routes that stop at or near the college.

Tuition and Fees

MassArt offers three different levels of tuition based on in-state, New England, or out-of-state residency. For the 2017–18 academic year, in-state tuition and fees are set at $12,700; New England tuition and fees are $25,600; and out-of-state tuition and fees are $34,400. The average coast of room and board is $13,000, and non-billed expenses for a student average $3,600.

Financial Aid

The Office of Student Financial Assistance at MassArt is committed to helping students and their families get the resources needed to fund each student's education, ensuring that access to a chosen field is not limited by the cost of attendance. The college offers a wide range of options for financial assistance so that all students interested in attending MassArt may do so regardless of their

COLLEGE CLOSE-UPS

financial means. MassArt provides financial assistance to students in the form of loans, grants, scholarships, and work-study.

Students must file the FAFSA by the posted date on the college's website in order to meet MassArt's priority deadline and to be considered for all aid opportunities. The FAFSA can be completed as early as October 1.

Faculty

With 115 full-time and 152 part-time faculty members, the MassArt undergraduate student to teacher ratio is 10:1. MassArt faculty members are accomplished working artists, designers, and educators who bring their expertise into the studios and classrooms, providing real-world learning opportunities and industry connections for their students. Notable faculty include Barbara Bosworth, who received a Pollock-Krasner Award in 2015 to support her book *The Meadow;* and Flip Johnson, an award-winning animator whose work has been screened at major international film festivals. In December 2015, MassArt faculty and staff embarked on a collaboration with the City of Boston to establish Boston AIR, an Artist-In-Residence program.

Students are also exposed to working designers and artists through the Visiting Artist Program, which features lectures, seminars, workshops, and classroom interaction. Recent visiting artists include Janette Brossard, Dan Clayman, Andre Dubus, and Maya Hayuk.

Alumni

Notable of the college include Arne Glimcher, founder/owner of Pace Gallery; conceptual multimedia artist William Wegman, designer Brian Collins, time-based artist Christian Marclay, interior designer Kelly Wearstler, Oscar-winning set designer Nancy Haigh, and MIT Media Lab co-founder Muriel Cooper.

Student Profile and Opportunities

The MassArt community attracts students from more than 42 states and territories and 50 countries. Among the undergraduate students entering MassArt in Fall 2016, 67 percent came from Massachusetts, 16 percent from other New England states, and 17 percent from other U.S. and international locations. Twenty-six percent of B.F.A. students self-identify as ALANA (African American, Latino, Asian, and Native American). MassArt maintains consortium arrangements with thirteen other colleges and art schools within a one-mile radius of campus, all of which provide cross-registration, performing arts, athletic, and social opportunities for students.

Three student galleries on campus offer students a variety of opportunities to share their work with the MassArt community and the public. MassArt is also home to the Bakalar & Paine Galleries, the largest free contemporary art space in New England, which showcases at least four professional exhibitions by emerging and established artists yearly, and exhibits student work twice a year.

The annual All-School Show highlights student work from every department over a three-week period, and students are invited to show their work for consideration alongside professional artists and alumni at the MassArt Annual Auction. The biannual MassArt Made Sale gives students experience in a professional jury process and an opportunity to sell their work.

Admission Requirements

Academic admission standards have been established by MassArt to assess applicants' preparation for college-level work in the B.F.A. degree program. Meeting these standards does not guarantee admission to the college; many other elements are considered in the evaluation of an application, and admission is very competitive.

A high school GPA, based on college-preparatory courses, and weighted for honors and advanced placement courses, is calculated at the end of the applicant's seventh semester. The minimum GPA for admission is 3.0 (on a 4.0 scale). If a student's GPA falls below 3.0, MassArt reserves the right to contact the student and/or guidance counselor during the admissions process to further determine a student's college readiness.

Students must submit the following in order to be reviewed by Admissions:

- Application form and $70 application fee
- Statement of purpose
- Portfolio submission of 15–20 examples of a student's strongest and most recent artwork, reflecting their interests, skills, and willingness to explore, experiment, and express themselves
- Official high school transcript
- Two letters of recommendation
- Resume/list of activities
- Copy of alien registration card (legal permanent residents only)

Application and Information

First-year student deadlines are December 1 for Early Action and February 1 for Regular Decision. The transfer deadline is February 1. Applicants are informed of their admission decision on a rolling basis.

Contact Information

Lauren Wilshusen, Director of Admissions
Massachusetts College of Art and Design
621 Huntington Avenue
Boston, Massachusetts 02115
Phone: 617-879-7222
E-mail: admissions@massart.edu
Website: www.massart.edu
www.facebook.com/MassArtBoston/
www.twitter.com/MassArt

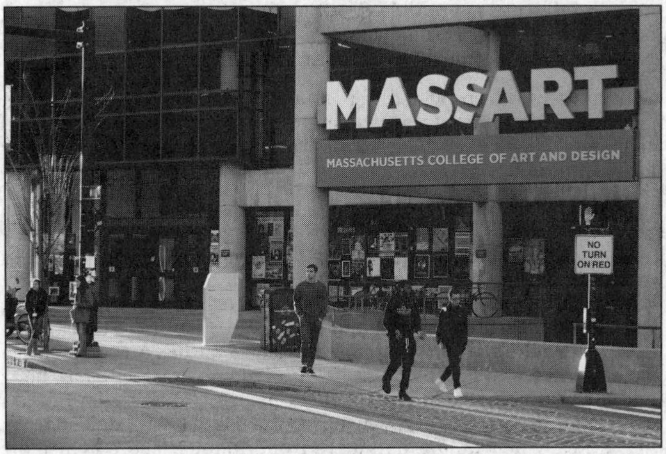

The Tower Building on the campus of MassArt.

COLLEGE CLOSE-UPS

MILLERSVILLE UNIVERSITY OF PENNSYLVANIA

Millersville University

MILLERSVILLE, PENNSYLVANIA

★ To read more about this school, visit http://petersons.to/millersvilleuniversityofpennsylvania

The University

Millersville University of Pennsylvania, nestled in the hills of Amish country, offers a wide range of programs and a commitment to high-quality undergraduate and graduate instruction. Millersville's student body of approximately 8,100, including 7,200 undergraduates, is large enough for the University to offer over 100 academic programs, plus master's and doctoral degree programs. The University is also small enough to provide friendly service and individual attention. Students report that the relaxed, friendly campus atmosphere is one component of their superior collegiate experience at Millersville. The campus features a beautiful green and flowered landscape, a pond with resident swans, and clean, well-maintained facilities.

Millersville University was established more than 150 years ago, in 1855, as a normal school, the first one in Pennsylvania. It remained a teachers college until 1962 when it was authorized to offer liberal arts degrees. It has been Millersville University of Pennsylvania since 1983.

Students most frequently cite Millersville's excellent academic reputation and affordable tuition as the top two reasons why they chose the University. Education, business administration, psychology, biology, English, speech communications, and sociology are among the most popular majors offered. Millersville's undergraduates are diverse; one in nine students attends part-time, 23 percent are members of a racial/ethnic minority group, and 10 percent are more than 25 years old. Thirty-three percent of Millersville undergraduates are from Lancaster County, 63 percent from elsewhere in Pennsylvania, 5 percent from out of state, and 2 percent from other countries.

The University offers 19 intercollegiate varsity sports in NCAA Division II as well as intramural and club sports. There are a wide range of special interest clubs, fraternities and sororities, musical organizations, publications, and broad cultural programs available.

Thirty-one percent of undergraduates live on campus in residence halls, with the rest commuting from home or living nearby. Coed dormitories and apartments are available for students. Freshmen and sophomores not commuting from home are required to live on campus. The possession, use, or sale of alcoholic beverages and illegal drugs is prohibited on the University campus. Smoking is prohibited in all academic and residential buildings on campus. Freshmen are permitted to have cars on campus.

Special services provided for students include free tutoring, academic advisement, career planning and placement, personal counseling, health services, wellness activities, and special facilities for commuters.

Location

Millersville is three miles from Lancaster city, a growing metropolitan area. Lancaster County is an exceptionally friendly and beautiful area with a large number of art galleries, stores, restaurants, theaters, parks, and tourist attractions. The campus is served by the area bus system, and Lancaster has Amtrak service for easy access to nearby cities like Philadelphia, which is an hour and a half away; Washington, D.C., which is two and a half hours away; and New York City, which is three hours away. Baltimore is also an easy hour and a half drive from campus. There is also air service nearby.

Lancaster County is one of the fastest-growing counties in Pennsylvania and has one of the lowest unemployment rates in the state. The local economy is sound and diverse. Sixty percent of Millersville graduates choose to settle within the county.

Majors and Degrees

Millersville offers the Bachelor of Arts degree in anthropology, art, biology, chemistry, earth sciences, economics, English, environmental geology, French, geography, German, government and political affairs, history, international studies, mathematics, music, philosophy, physics, psychology, social work, sociology, and Spanish.

The Bachelor of Science degree is offered in allied health technology; applied engineering, safety and technology; biology; business administration; chemistry; communications and theatre; computer science; geology; mathematics; meteorology; occupational safety and environmental health; ocean sciences and coastal sciences; and physics.

The Bachelor of Science in Education degree with teaching certification is offered in art education, biology, chemistry, earth sciences, Pre-K–4 education, English, French, German, mathematics, middle level education, music education, physics, social studies, Spanish, special education, and technology education. Millersville now offers degree programs in inclusive education, allowing students to specialize in an age group and subject area while also learning how to teach students with special needs.

The University also offers the Bachelor of Fine Arts degree in art; the Bachelor of Science in nursing degree for RNs only (a fully online and on-campus modalities are available); and the Associate of Technology degree in applied engineering, safety and technology.

Other new academic programs have been added to Millersville's offerings to better serve the student body with specialized degrees. The multidisciplinary studies major allows students to work with a faculty advisor to combine their unique areas of interest and create a custom degree focus. The Paul H. Slaugh Jr. entrepreneurship minor allows students to combine entrepreneurship with a major of their choosing. Millersville now also offers degree programs in entertainment technology, sports journalism, and environmental hazards and emergency management. Students should refer to the website for a complete listing. More than 65 minors are offered along with engineering programs for chemistry majors. Special advisement is available for students interested in pre-medicine and pre-law.

Academic Programs

Millersville University places a strong emphasis on the liberal arts. Nearly half of the courses required for all its undergraduate degrees, including those with technical or professional majors, are in the liberal arts. This prepares students for a lifetime of learning and gives them a background in writing, speaking, analysis, and critical thinking across a broad range of subjects.

Millersville's baccalaureate degree programs have four common curricular elements: proficiency requirements in English composition and speech; the general education program, which constitutes about half the curriculum; the major field of study; and elective courses, if needed, to meet the minimum of 120 credits required for graduation. Within this framework, students have many choices in developing programs of study.

The general education program has requirements in writing, speaking, humanities, natural sciences and mathematics, social sciences, and interdisciplinary and/or multicultural study. There is also a health and physical education requirement.

Millersville offers a University Honors College, departmental honors programs, independent study, a pass/fail option, and special advisement to students who are undecided about a major.

The University operates on a 4-1-4 academic calendar with summer sessions.

Off-Campus Programs

An exchange agreement with Franklin & Marshall College allows Millersville students to take select Franklin & Marshall courses not offered at Millersville. Cooperative education internships are available to students in most majors, and some majors offer or require specialized internships. Millersville has study-abroad programs in Australia, Chile, China, England, France, Germany, Ireland, Japan, Peru, Scotland, South Africa, Spain, and other countries. Qualified students who wish to study abroad elsewhere may do so through the University's cooperative arrangements with other colleges and universities. Students may also choose to student teach or participate in an internship abroad.

Academic Facilities

With numerous study areas, classrooms, and even a café, the new Dr. Francine G. McNairy Library and Learning Forum is a relaxing and visually pleasing place where students can study and work. Materials from other libraries are available through interlibrary loan.

The University's computing facilities support both PC and Apple platforms. There are more than 400 terminals and computer stations available in multiple computer labs across campus. On-campus access to the Internet is available for all faculty members and students. Wireless access is available in all buildings, residence halls, classrooms, and offices.

Other University facilities include an extensive scientific instrumentation inventory, industry and technology laboratories, a variety of art studios and galleries, two visual and performing arts centers, a state-of-the-art sound studio, three gymnasiums, two swimming pools, radio and television production facilities, soundproof music practice modules, and a language laboratory.

Costs

Annual tuition and fees in 2016–17 were $11,494 (based on 15 credits per semester) for Pennsylvania residents and $20,854 for out-of-state students. Annual room and board charges for 2016–17 were $13,484.

Financial Aid

Approximately 82 percent of Millersville undergraduates receive financial aid through grants, scholarships, employment, and loans. Scholarships are available on the basis of academic performance. Federal Pell, Federal Supplemental Educational Opportunity grants, and Pennsylvania Higher Education Assistance Agency (PHEAA) grants are awarded on the basis of need. Students may also qualify for Federal Perkins Loans and Federal Stafford Student Loans. On-campus and off-campus job opportunities are plentiful, with nearly one-third of students holding an on-campus job.

Students applying for a federal or state grant, Federal Work-Study, or a Federal Perkins Loan must complete the Free Application for Federal Student Aid. The forms are available from high school guidance offices, from the Financial Aid Office, or online at http://www.fafsa.ed.gov. Deadlines are given in the forms' instructions.

Faculty

Millersville University faculty members are dedicated to teaching and to offering individual attention. In 2015–16 the University employed 475 full and part-time faculty. Ninety-eight percent of the full-time faculty members hold a doctorate or the terminal degree in their field. The University keeps a relatively low student-faculty ratio of 22:1 and an average class size of approximately 25. No classes are taught by graduate or teaching assistants.

Student Government

Millersville University students participate in University governance through the Student Senate, faculty-student committees, and representation on the Faculty Senate, the Council of Trustees, and the Millersville Borough Council. The Student Senate works with faculty members and the administration on major University policies.

Admission Requirements

Millersville University admits approximately 60 percent of its applicants. More than 80 percent of its full-time freshmen rank in the top 40 percent of their high school class. Academic records are the most important factor in admission decisions. Applicants must have successfully completed at least 4 years of high school English, 3 years of social studies, 3 years of mathematics, and 3 years of science (1 unit must be a lab). In addition, 2 years of foreign language is strongly recommended.

Since meeting people with different backgrounds and interests is an important part of the college experience, Millersville University is committed to recruiting a diversified student body. SAT or ACT scores are required. Letters of recommendations are encouraged. Out-of-state, international, nontraditional, and transfer applicants are welcome. Exceptional high school students may apply for early admission at the end of their junior year. Admitted applicants may request to defer their admission for up to two semesters. Advanced standing is offered through CLEP and AP examinations.

Application and Information

To apply, students should submit an online application with a $40 processing fee and official copies of the high school record and SAT or ACT scores (freshman applicants only, transfer students must submit official transcripts from all previous institutions). The paper application fee is $50. The University has a rolling admission policy, and students are encouraged to apply early (by mid-November) in their senior year for fall admission. Applicants are usually notified of a decision within a month after a completed application and required materials are received. Students can apply to Millersville via the Pennsylvania State System of Higher Education App or the Common App.

For application forms and additional information, students should contact:

Office of Admissions
Millersville University of Pennsylvania
P.O. Box 1002
Millersville, Pennsylvania 17551-0302
Phone: 717-871-4625
800-MU-ADMIT (toll-free)
E-mail: admissions@millersville.edu
Website: www.millersville.edu
YouTube: www.youtube.com/millersvilleu
Facebook: www.facebook.com/villeadmissions
Twitter: https://twitter.com/VilleAdmissions
Virtual tour: www.youvisit.com/millersville

Millersville University offers a beautiful campus located in Lancaster County, Pennsylvania, with easy access to major metropolitan centers, such as New York, Philadelphia, and Washington, D.C.

MILLS COLLEGE

OAKLAND, CALIFORNIA

MILLS

★ To read more about this school, visit http://petersons.to/millscollege

The College

Located in the heart of the San Francisco Bay Area, Mills College helps students tap into their boldness and determination, creativity and conviction, with an education that changes lives. In an inclusive community of inspiring women, Mills students gain the skills, the confidence, and the power to make a statement in their careers and in the world.

The 10:1 student-faculty ratio enables students to work closely with Mills professors, who are fiercely dedicated to teaching and mentoring independent thinkers. Students delve into their studies in interactive classes (16 is the average class size) that spark debate and engaged learning. The College encourages students to cross boundaries and explore how different fields inform and enhance each other, creating eclectic areas of interdisciplinary study such as dance and sociology or math and philosophy.

Outside of the classroom, the 135-acre Mills campus has something for everyone. Students can join a wide range of clubs, write for the student newspaper, attend experimental music concerts, volunteer in the local community, take Zumba or karate classes, and just hang out at the outdoor pool. Many also become teammates as part of the College's six National Collegiate Athletic Association (NCAA) Division III sports teams, competing against other schools in cross-country, rowing, soccer, swimming, tennis, or volleyball. While the students and their interests are diverse in every way, the one constant is a commitment to supporting each other's success and improving the world around them.

Mills has been educating women since 1852, and in 1920, added innovative graduate programs for women and men to its academic offerings. Always a college of firsts, among women's colleges Mills was: the first west of the Rockies, the first to create a computer science major, one of the first to offer a modern dance major, and the first to enact an admission policy for transgender students. *U.S. News & World Report* ranks Mills among the top colleges in the West and #1 in Best Value Colleges. Mills is also ranked as one of the best colleges in the nation by The Princeton Review. The College has been home to alumnae who have gone on to excel as authors, composers, lawyers, professors, ambassadors, scientists, news anchors, governors, congresswomen, and activists.

Location

Mills students live and study in Oakland, California, one of the most ethnically diverse cities in the United States. Major media outlets, including the *New York Times* and *Forbes*, have ranked Oakland among the best cities in America. Students take full advantage of the area, enjoying the First Friday gallery crawls, hiking through Redwood Regional Park, and getting involved in the community through service learning.

Beyond Oakland, students explore all the Bay Area has to offer, including Ocean Beach, the Golden Gate Bridge, the San Francisco Museum of Modern Art, and the California Academy of Sciences. Arts organizations, healthcare providers, tech giants, and nonprofits also call the Bay Area home, and the career services office at Mills keeps tabs on internships and job openings as one of the many ways it helps prepare students for future careers. Students have gained hands-on experience at organizations such as the American Civil Liberties Union, Children's Hospital Oakland, Google, and the Office of Congresswoman Barbara Lee, a proud Mills alumna.

Majors and Degrees

Mills offers a Bachelor of Arts or Bachelor of Science degree in a variety of majors that enable students to discover and dive deeply into the academic programs that most inspire them. Whatever their area of interest, Mills students will find themselves asking tough questions, challenging preconceived ideas, thinking critically, and creating solutions for social issues with support from their professors and classmates.

Mills offers the Bachelor of Arts (B.A.) degree in art and technology; art (history and studio); biochemistry and molecular biology; biology; biopsychology; business administration; business economics; chemistry; child development; computer science; dance; data science; economics; English; environmental science; environmental studies; ethnic studies; global humanities and critical thought; history; international relations; Latin American studies; mathematics; music; philosophy; politics, economics, policy, and law; psychology; public health and health equity; sociology; theater studies; and women's, gender and sexuality studies. The major in child development meets the requirements for a state child development permit for teaching in preschool and day-care centers and provides a strong basis for graduate school and for many other careers. Special pre-medical advising is available.

Mills offers the Bachelor of Science (B.S.) degree in biochemistry and molecular biology, biology, biopsychology, chemistry, environmental science, mathematics, and public health and health equity. Mills also provides the first two years of courses leading to a Bachelor of Science in Nursing degree. Upon successful completion of the two-year program at Mills, students are guaranteed admission into a prestigious nursing school to pursue their professional training.

Students can also choose to create their own major, working with three faculty advisers to plan an individual program that draws together courses from across the curriculum and creates an integrated educational experience.

Mills offers ten unique programs that enable students to earn both a bachelor's and a master's degree in less time—increasing their career options after college. The bachelor's-to-master's accelerated degree programs are: B.A./M.A. applied economics, B.A./M.B.A. business administration, B.A./M.A. computer science, B.A./M.A. early childhood education, B.A./M.A. early childhood special education, B.A./M.A. education/teaching credential, B.A./M.A. infant mental health, B.A./M.A. mathematics, B.A./M.P.P. public policy, and B.A./Joint M.P.P./M.B.A.

Academic Programs

To earn a Mills bachelor's degree, students complete 120 semester credits (usually 15 credits each semester). Grading is traditional, and a pass-fail option is available outside the major.

The core curriculum at Mills prepares students to successfully pursue any career and educational opportunities that they choose throughout their lives. The principal goal is for students to graduate as fully engaged global citizens who combine confidence, the ability to think independently, and a sense of responsibility for the wider community and world. The core curriculum emphasizes the value of diverse perspectives, critical analysis, and knowledge as being essential to social change. The requirements fall into three outcome categories: foundational skills (critical analysis, information literacy, written and oral communication, and quantitative literacy), modes of inquiry (race, gender, and power; scientific inquiry; language other than English; and international perspectives), and contributions to knowledge and society (community engagement and creativity, innovation, and experimentation).

Faculty

Great professors don't lecture—they inspire. At Mills, students learn through lively discussions and hands-on exploration led by accomplished faculty who are dedicated to teaching and passionately engaged in research and creative endeavors. Nearly 80 percent of Mills faculty hold the highest degrees in their field; approximately 70 percent are women, and over one-third are faculty of color. The excellent student-faculty ratio gives students opportunities to work alongside these diverse, expert scholars to present at conferences, stage performances, contribute to original research, curate exhibitions, and coauthor journal articles. No matter what students are interested in, Mills professors encourage them to pursue their unique paths thoughtfully and enthusiastically.

Off-Campus Programs

Students can expand their learning off campus by signing up for the College's cross-registration program, which enables students to expand their perspective and their learning by taking a course at local schools such as California College of the Arts; California State University, East Bay; Saint Mary's College of California; or UC Berkeley. For an academic adventure within the United States, students can take advantage of the College's domestic study program. They may participate in exchange or visiting programs at schools including Barnard, Manhattanville, Mount Holyoke, Simmons, Spelman, and Wellesley.

The College's international study-abroad opportunities help students discover fresh ways of thinking, learn a new language, or explore a subject in its native land. With access to more than 20 institutions across the globe, recent Mills students have studied abroad in countries including Argentina, France, India, Ireland, New Zealand, and Scotland.

Student Clubs and Organizations

At Mills, students are part of an energetic campus community that strives for inclusion, growth, and cultural diversity through a variety of groups, clubs, and activities to explore throughout the year. The many clubs reflect social or political interests; celebrate shared identities; and explore academic interests, hobbies, or entertainment. The roster of student-led organizations includes the Black Student Collective, Earth CORPS, El Club de Español, Feminist Democrats, Hip Hop Dance Club, and the Mills Computer Club.

Academic Facilities

The facilities at Mills reflect and support the many passions, interests, and academic pursuits of its students. They can view the latest exhibition at the on-campus art museum, create experimental music in Littlefield Concert Hall, build an aquaponics system in the Botanic Garden, or create new forms of dance in Lisser Hall.

Students in STEM fields benefit from the state-of-the-art learning environment in the Betty Irene Moore Natural Sciences Building. In addition to high-tech classrooms, multiple teaching laboratories, and a research lab, the LEED-certified Platinum facility is a model of green construction. Next door, the Botanic Garden provides a living laboratory for ecological restoration and biology research.

The Jeannik Méquet Littlefield Concert Hall hosts a cutting-edge concert series, student-led fine arts performances, College ceremonies, and special community events. It features an expanded stage area and enhanced acoustic features for performances and recording. Nearby Lisser Hall contains a flexible proscenium stage and an experimental theater; it also is home to the annual "Mills Got Talent" student showcases.

The highly regarded Children's School at Mills College provides an opportunity to engage in hands-on learning for students seeking careers in early childhood education. Students can also conduct research in the Early Childhood and Family Research Lab, Center for Play Research, and Language Development Lab on campus.

The Mills College Art Museum houses the largest permanent collection of any liberal arts college on the West Coast and attracts a wide array of innovative exhibitions, with an emphasis on female artists. Students also have the rare opportunity to work behind the scenes, documenting and digitizing priceless artwork, curating exhibitions, and leading the senior thesis art show.

The Special Collections at the F. W. Olin Library include historical and literary treasures such as a copy of Shakespeare's First Folio, a Mozart manuscript, and a leaf from a Gutenberg Bible. The library is also home to the Center for the Book, a forum for celebrating the powerful cultural impact of the book, in all of its forms.

Costs

Mills offers students a life-changing education with one-on-one attention from outstanding faculty, top-notch facilities, and an inspiring community of innovative thinkers—all in a beautiful and intimate setting. In 2017–18, tuition is $44,765 and room and board are $13,528. As a top-ranked private college, Mills' costs are competitive with other colleges of its caliber. The College also offers a range of scholarships and financial aid packages to ensure that a Mills education is within reach for smart, creative individuals who want to make an impact on the world.

Financial Aid

More than 80 percent of incoming Mills students receive some form of financial aid. The College offers a variety of merit- and need-based scholarships that can total up to $26,000 for first-year students and up to $17,000 for transfer students. Additional aid is available through federal and state grants, private scholarships, loans, and work-study opportunities.

To be considered for government aid and need-based Mills scholarships, first-year and transfer students must file the Free Application for Federal Student Aid (FAFSA) by the appropriate deadline. California residents must also file the Cal Grant GPA Verification Form to be considered for a Cal Grant.

Mills recognizes students' academic achievements, demonstrated leadership skills, contributions to the community, and special talents through a wide variety of merit scholarships. All entering fall-term, full-time applicants who meet certain academic or talent eligibility requirements are considered for Mills scholarships, with no additional application form needed.

Admission Requirements

Admission to Mills is selective, yet holistic. The admission process is designed to allow students to share a complete picture of their experiences, passions, activities, and what they hope to achieve, in addition to their academic accomplishments.

Most first-year students admitted to Mills have a B+ average and have followed a full college-preparatory course in their secondary school, including 4 years of English, 3 to 4 years of mathematics, 2 to 4 years of foreign languages, 2 to 4 years of social sciences, and 2 to 4 years of a laboratory science. Additional course work in fine arts is given positive consideration, as are special talents or interests. Submission of SAT or ACT scores is not required. Course credit may be awarded for the College Board Advanced Placement tests and the International Baccalaureate program's higher-level examinations.

Mills welcomes applications from transfer students and women who have delayed their entrance to college or who wish to continue work on their bachelor's degrees. The high school transcript requirement is waived if 24 or more transferable semester units have been completed. For international students, TOEFL, IELTS, or ELS are required to satisfy English language proficiency requirements. Applications should be accompanied by transcripts, a letter of recommendation, and, for international students, language test scores. An interview, either on campus or online through Skype or FaceTime, is strongly recommended for all applicants.

Application and Contact Information

First-year students: Fall admission application deadlines are November 15 for early action and January 15 for regular decision. All required materials are due by January 15.

Transfer students: Fall admission application deadlines are March 1 for priority scholarship consideration and April 1 for regular decision.

Spring admission application deadline: November 1 for both first-year and transfer students. Admission decisions are mailed on a rolling basis.

For more information, students are invited to contact:

Office of Undergraduate Admissions
Mills College
5000 MacArthur Boulevard
Oakland, California 94613
Phone: 510-430-2135
800-87-MILLS (toll-free)
Fax: 510-430-3298
E-mail: admission@mills.edu
Website: http://www.mills.edu/undergrad
http://www.facebook.com/millscollege (Facebook)
http://twitter.com/millscollege (Twitter)
http://youtube.com/millscollege (YouTube)

At Mills, students are encouraged to stand out, emboldened to think big, and empowered to make a statement.

MISERICORDIA UNIVERSITY

DALLAS, PENNSYLVANIA

MISERICORDIA UNIVERSITY

★ To read more about this school, visit http://petersons.to/misericordiauniversity

The University

Misericordia University is a high-quality liberal arts and professional studies institution rooted in service to others and committed to challenging academics and the personal attention students deserve. Founded by the Religious Sisters of Mercy in 1924, Misericordia offers undergraduate and graduate programs to resident and commuter students, as well as adult students. Current enrollment is more than 2,800 men and women.

The University cultivates a spirit of community service and a lifelong love of learning in its students through extracurricular activities, experiential learning, and challenging academic programs. In the National Survey of Student Engagement, Misericordia students say they are more involved in learning and have better relationships with faculty members and peers than students at other similar institutions. Misericordia is also ranked in the top tier of *U.S. News & World Report's* America's Best Regional Universities–North Category 2017.

Misericordia operates twelve residential facilities, including five residence halls, a town house complex, and off-campus housing, with a total capacity of more than 1,100 students. This includes three nearby homes are reserved for upper-level students. Residents have a number of options, including single rooms and wellness housing. Each residence hall offers study rooms, laundry facilities, and recreational lounges. The Metz Dining Hall is located in the Banks Student Life Center, which also houses a "We Proudly Brew Starbucks" coffee shop, a Chick-fil-A Express, and the Chopping Block restaurant, and the renovated Student Union that features flat-screen televisions as well as pool and foosball tables.

There are numerous campus activities. Besides Student Government, there are over 40 chartered student clubs and organizations. Cultural events, Campus Ministry, intramural and intercollegiate athletic programs, performing arts shows, art exhibits, and many other social activities complement the academic experience. The Metz Field House provides enhanced facilities for student athletes. In keeping with the University's tradition of Mercy, Service, Justice, and Hospitality, students have opportunities to develop leadership potential through service projects. Misericordia earned a spot on the President's National Community Service Honor Roll for the past several years.

On spring break, students have served the needy in rural Appalachia, the Gulf Coast, Texas, California, Philadelphia, and the South Bronx. Students have volunteered abroad in Jamaica, Guyana, and Romania.

Personalized attention is the key to the support available in the Student Success Center. A psychologist, counselors, therapists, and peer counselors conduct workshops each semester on a variety of topics, including test anxiety, stress management, time management, and goal setting. Many services are free of charge to students and contacts are confidential.

First-year students may join the Guaranteed Placement Program (GPP) through the Insalaco Center for Career Development. The GPP program includes academic standards, cocurricular activities (such as leadership and service projects), internships, resume development, etiquette development, and interviewing skills. If a student fulfills the program's requirements and is not employed in his or her field or enrolled in graduate or professional school within six months of graduation, a paid internship is assured. The center also co-presents the Choice Program, which offers special guidance for students who have not declared a major. Opportunities for career exploration, cooperative education, and internships help students develop the skills they need to be successful when they enter the working world.

Student Health Services staff members provide first aid, assessment and treatment of common illnesses, and referrals for more serious health conditions. Health center activities are directed by a nurse practitioner. A self-care room offers reference materials and up-to-date information on personal health concerns. All services are confidential.

A rapidly evolving world has increased the number of adults who seek higher education. Misericordia offers bachelor's, master's, and doctoral programs for adult learners in several formats. The Ruth Matthews Bourger Women with Children program provides housing and support services for single women with children who are working toward their undergraduate degree. Convenient evening, online, and weekend formats also are available for people with families and full-time jobs.

Master's degrees are available in education, nurse practitioner studies, occupational therapy, speech/language pathology, business administration, and organizational management. A doctoral program in physical therapy is available to students entering in a full-time format, and doctoral programs in occupational therapy and nursing practice are available for graduate students via part-time study, including online and in-class components.

The University is fully accredited by the Middle States Association of Colleges and Schools. The medical imaging, nursing, occupational therapy, physical therapy, social work, and speech-language pathology programs are accredited by the National League for Nursing Accrediting Commission, the Council on Social Work Education, the Joint Review Committee on Education in Radiologic Technology, the American Occupational Therapy Association, the American Physical Therapy Association, and the American Speech-Language and Hearing Association.

Location

Located in northeastern Pennsylvania, Misericordia University is the oldest four-year institution of higher education in Luzerne County. Expansive lawns and thick stands of trees dominate the 124-acre upper and expanding lower campuses. It is 9 miles from the city of Wilkes-Barre. The area offers shopping centers, malls, cinemas, skiing, professional sporting events, and a variety of cultural activities. Pennsylvania's largest natural lake and two state parks are nearby, as are Pocono ski resorts. Metropolitan New York and Philadelphia are each within a 3-hour drive. Public and university-sponsored transportation serves the campus.

Majors and Degrees

Misericordia University awards the Bachelor of Arts (B.A.) degree in English, history, government, law and national security, and philosophy. The Bachelor of Science (B.S.) degree is awarded in accounting, applied behavioral science, biochemistry, biology, business administration, chemistry, clinical laboratory science, mass communications and design, computer science, diagnostic medical sonography, elementary education, health care management, information technology, management, mathematics, medical imaging, medical science, professional studies, psychology, secondary education, special education, sport management, and statistics. A Bachelor of Health Science (B.H.S.) with a specialization in patient navigation is awarded to health science: patient navigation students; the Bachelor of Science in Nursing (B.S.N.) is awarded to nursing majors, and a Bachelor of Science in Social Work (B.S.W.) is awarded to social work majors. Specializations in accounting, early childhood education, prelaw, special education, and preprofessional occupations are also available. Certification programs include addictions counseling, picture archiving and communications administrator, diagnostic medical sonography, geriatric care management, gerontology, health-care informatics, post-professional pediatrics certificate for occupational therapists and physical therapists, and secondary education. These may be taken in support of several degrees offered by Misericordia or as stand-alone programs.

The University also offers five-year entry-level graduate majors in occupational therapy and speech-language pathology. Students graduate with a master's degree in speech-language pathology or occupational therapy and a bachelor's degree in health sciences. The physical therapy program is a 6½-year doctoral program. Students graduate with a bachelor's degree in one of several areas and a Doctor of Physical Therapy (D.P.T.) degree.

Academic Programs

Candidates for the B.A., B.S., B.S.N., or B.S.W. must fulfill a 48-credit liberal arts core curriculum in addition to the requirements of their chosen major to graduate. They must earn at least 36 credit hours in a chosen field. For regularly enrolled students, the average requirement for a baccalaureate degree is a total of 126 credits. Other options include minors, specializations, certifications, and electives. Other degrees have specialized requirements. Interested students should consult the academic catalog for the most current information.

Courses are offered on a semester basis, beginning in August and January and ending in December and May. Summer, weekend, online, and accelerated courses are also available.

Academic Facilities

The chemistry, physics, and biology departments all have fully equipped research laboratories available to students in these fields. State-of-the-art equipment includes high-performance liquid chromatography (HPLC), a rotary evaporator, and a new gas chromatograph mass spectrometer. The science building contains a gross anatomy laboratory, a rare asset for a university of this size. The University also houses an energized radiation laboratory for the medical imaging program. The Passan Hall–College of Health Sciences provides classrooms and high-tech laboratories for the occupational therapy, physical therapy, speech-language pathology, and nursing programs in a facility devoted to these majors.

In addition to the four main computer labs, most other campus buildings and common areas offer wireless Internet access. The University operates MyMU, a secure online portal where students can access e-mail, course schedules, class registration tools, and student account and registration information from a single sign-on.

Mercy Hall, the original administrative building, offers multi-purpose academic classrooms and facilities. Many key student service departments, including the registrar, student accounts, and financial aid are centralized in one area in Mercy Hall. Sandy and Marlene Insalaco Hall houses the Pauly Friedman Art Gallery, café, computer labs, an ensemble room, fine arts classroom, music teaching and practice areas, and the Assistive Technology Research Institute.

The new Michael and Tina MacDowell Residence Hall hosts three ultramodern classrooms on the first floor.

The three-story Mark Kintz Bevevino Library covers 37,500 square feet and houses stacks for 90,000 volumes. Materials include information and communication technology and a reference section that offers books, serials, and a variety of periodicals as well as reference search tools.

Costs

Full-time undergraduate tuition for 2016–17 was $29,150 per year. The general fee was $1,590. Housing options include traditional rooms, suites, town houses, and lower-campus housing. The median room cost was $7,280. All resident students must participate in a 9-, 12-, or 14-meal plan. In addition, town house residents are eligible to choose a five-meal plan. The median board cost is $4,570.

Financial Aid

All students applying for financial aid must complete the Free Application for Federal Student Aid (FAFSA) by May 1, but it can be completed as early as October 1 of senior year. This is used for Federal Pell Grants, Federal Supplemental Educational Opportunity Grants (FSEOG), subsidized and unsubsidized Federal Direct Student Loans, Federal Perkins Loans, nursing loans, and the Federal Work-Study Program. This application is also the basis upon which state and institutional aid is awarded. The University also offers a no-interest monthly payment plan. Many scholarships are available including $20 million in presidential scholarships based on academic ability and $4.6 million in McAuley Awards for students who have experience in leadership roles and volunteer service.

Faculty

There are 136 full-time faculty members. A student-faculty ratio of 11.3:1 results in students receiving a great deal of individual attention from a highly qualified faculty; 77 percent of the faculty members hold doctorates. Besides student academic advising, the faculty members also serve as advisers to clubs.

Student Government

An active student government organization serves as a liaison between the students and the faculty and staff members. The administration enables students to become involved by serving as student representatives on various University committees.

Admission Requirements

Misericordia University admits applicants based on their secondary school record, high school recommendation, extracurricular activities, and personal promise. The University requires SAT or ACT scores.

Transfer students with a cumulative average of at least 2.0 (4.0 scale) may be considered for admission and may receive advanced standing. Some majors require a 2.5 or higher cumulative average. Transfer students must submit official high school transcripts and a transcript of work completed at other colleges and universities.

Application and Information

Applicants must submit an official application form (available upon request), transcripts, and SAT or ACT scores. Applicants may also apply through the University's website. There is a nonrefundable application fee of $35, which is waived for students who visit the campus or apply online.

The University considers applications on a rolling basis. Usually, candidates are notified of the admission decision within three weeks of receipt of all required materials.

For more information, students should contact:

Office of Admissions
Misericordia University
301 Lake Street
Dallas, Pennsylvania 18612-1090
Phone: 570-674-6461
866-262-6363 (toll free)
Fax: 570-675-2441
E-mail: admiss@misericordia.edu
Website: http://admissions.misericordia.edu
www.twitter.com/misericordiaUAD
www.facebook.com/misericordiauniversity
www.facebook.com/misericoridau

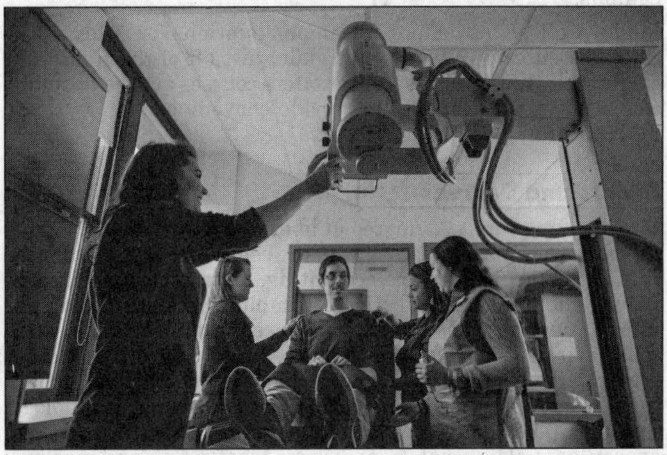

Misericordia University offers multiple medical and health science degree options on the undergraduate and graduate levels.

COLLEGE CLOSE-UPS

MOLLOY COLLEGE

ROCKVILLE CENTRE, NEW YORK

★ To read more about this school, visit http://petersons.to/molloycollege

The College

What college offers a great education with small classes, wonderful internships, community service projects, and international trips, plus an amazing campus life program to round out the college experience? Welcome to Molloy College.

Molloy, an independent, private Catholic college based in Rockville Centre, was founded in 1955 by the Sisters of Saint Dominic in Amityville, New York. The College serves a student population of more than 4,900 undergraduate and graduate students. Molloy students can earn degrees in a variety of outstanding academic programs, including nursing, business, education, social work, music therapy, and many more.

Prospective students are always looking for an academic environment that offers the best fit for the student and the best value for their tuition dollar. Molloy was recently named the #1 Value All-Star in the nation by *Money* magazine. This recognition was part of the magazine's annual college rankings, which acknowledge the best of the country's institutions in a variety of categories. Molloy's top ranking was based on a variety of factors, including graduation rates and earnings of graduates.

Molloy continues to earn recognition in many areas. College Factual recently named Molloy the #1 college for health professions, as well as naming Molloy's undergraduate nursing program the best in the nation. In addition, the College's residence halls were voted Best in New York by Niche.com, and these rankings also referenced Molloy's freshmen retention rate, which is among the highest in the country (85 percent). Also of note, Molloy graduates' starting salaries have ranked among the highest in the U.S. in surveys conducted by Georgetown University and PayScale.com.

Location and Environment

Molloy is located on the South Shore of Long Island in Rockville Centre. Its proximity to New York City allows students to benefit from the cultural and social opportunities that Manhattan has to offer, and it's just a short train ride away from the 30-acre campus.

Molloy College also offers off-campus locations for study at the Suffolk Center in East Farmingdale, just off of the Route 110 corridor. In addition, the College offers courses at area hospitals and schools, all designed to provide convenience for graduate and continuing education students.

Majors and Degrees

Molloy offers the A.A. degree in liberal arts; the A.A.S. degree in cardiovascular technology and respiratory care; and the B.A. or B.S. degree in accounting, art, biology, business management, communications, computer science, computer information systems, criminal justice, education, English, earth and environmental studies, finance, history, interdisciplinary studies, marketing, mathematics, modern languages, music, music therapy, new media, nuclear medicine technology, nursing, philosophy, political science, psychology, sociology, speech language pathology/audiology, theatre arts, and theology; the B.S.W. degree in Social Work; and the B.F.A. in art, music, and theatre arts. Teacher certification programs are available in childhood (1–6), adolescence (7–12), special education, and birth–grade 2 childhood special education.

On the graduate level, Molloy offers a Master of Science degree as well as post-master's certification in nursing and education M.B.A. programs are available in business, accounting, healthcare, marketing, and personal financial planning; a master's program in clinical mental health counseling was recently launched as well. A master's in social work is offered through Molloy's partnership with Fordham University. Molloy also offers graduate degrees in criminal justice, music therapy, and speech-language pathology. The College offers three doctoral programs: a Ph.D. in nursing and a Doctor of Nursing Practice (D.N.P.), as well as an Ed.D. in Education.

Students interested in pre-dental, pre-law, pre-medical, or pre-veterinary programs are offered special advisement.

Articulation agreements with community colleges and established transfer credit policies ensure ease of transferability. Experienced admissions counselors will evaluate transfer applicants' credits and help plan toward a path toward degree completion.

Academic Programs

At Molloy, small class size, engaging and experienced faculty, and renowned academic programs help ensure student success, both in the classroom and beyond.

Molloy strives to make the college experience convenient for all students. The College offers evening and weekend classes, many in online and hybrid formats, with accelerated schedules designed to accommodate students' busy schedules.

A minimum of 128 credit hours is required for a baccalaureate degree; these courses include a strong liberal arts general education curriculum for every major field of study. Students may choose a double major, and many minors are available. Molloy has a 4-1-4 academic calendar.

Students may earn CLEP and CPE credit, and advanced placement credit is granted for a score of 3 or better on the AP exam. Qualified full-time students may participate in the Army ROTC program at Hofstra University or St. John's University on a cross-enrolled basis. Molloy students may also elect Air Force ROTC on a cross-enrolled basis with New York Institute of Technology.

Off-Campus Programs

The vast majority of students at Molloy enjoy an internship at some point in their academic careers. These real-world experiences are a crucial part of the learning process and ensure that students enter their chosen field ready to make strong contributions.

Molloy students are also instilled with the belief that they can make a difference beyond the classroom. As part of Molloy's tradition of service, students become involved in projects that help underserved populations in New York City, New Orleans, Puerto Rico and Haiti, to name but a few locations. Through the College's international education program, students seek enrichment and greater understanding of the world by participating in trips to Europe, Japan, South America, and other locales around the globe.

Facilities

In recent years Molloy has added a number of new facilities, including two residence halls, a student center, and a performing arts theatre, all of which enhance the student experience. In additon, Molloy recently opened the Barbara H. Hagan School of Nursing to support its nationally ranked nursing programs.

Molloy is a wireless campus and its computer labs house more than 325 PCs. Many departments have their own computer labs with state-of-the-art equipment.

The James E. Tobin (JET) Library is the center of academic research on the Molloy College campus. Beyond the library's physical collection of books, media, and periodicals, it also provides 24/7 access to over 250,000 ebooks as well as full text to over 170 million articles contained within its 80+ subscription databases. The facility itself contains reference computers, three classrooms, a media center, and designated areas for both group and private study. The Information Commons, located in the Public Square, offers an additional 40 computers as well as four study rooms that can be reserved in advance. Reference services are available to both on-campus and remote researchers in a variety of ways, including a chat service that is available all of the hours the library is open.

The Wilbur Arts Center features numerous art and music studios, a cable television studio, and the Lucille B. Hays Theatre. The school also has six science labs, a language lab, the education resource center, new state-of-the-art nursing labs, and a behavioral sciences research facility.

Costs

For 2016–17, tuition was $28,000 and required fees were $1,190. Students can expect to spend about $1,400 on books.

Financial Aid

Financial aid, which is based on academic achievement and financial need, is awarded to more than 85 percent of the student body. Aid is awarded in the form of scholarships, grants, loans, and Federal Work-Study Program employment. Merit-based scholarships and grants are also available.

Students are required to complete the FAFSA application every year. Full- and partial-tuition scholarships are available through the following: Molloy Scholars, Dominican Scholarships, Fine Arts Scholarships, Community Service Awards, and other funded scholarships. The Transfer Scholarship Program awards partial-tuition scholarships to students transferring into Molloy College with at least a 3.0 cumulative GPA. Nursing transfers are required to have a 3.3 GPA to be eligible for a transfer scholarship. Athletic grants (Division II only) are awarded to full-time students who show superior athletic ability in baseball, basketball, cross-country, equestrian, lacrosse, soccer, softball, tennis, or volleyball.

Faculty

Molloy's 10:1 undergraduate student-faculty ratio reflects the College's commitment to its students. In addition, the College has increased the number of faculty members by more than 10 percent in recent years. Of those faculty members, more than 77 percent have doctoral degrees.

Student Organizations and Activities

Molloy offers plenty of opportunities for its 4,900+ undergraduate and graduate students.

There are more than 50 academic programs, approximately 60 clubs and honor societies, various service opportunities, and NCAA Division II athletics, providing abundant opportunities for each student to not only strive for academic excellence, but also explore new interests, pursue athletics, and enrich the community.

Admission Requirements

While Molloy is a selective college, admissions counselors respect each individual applicant and consider the whole student—not just test scores—when making admissions decision. Prospective freshmen must submit their high school credentials, SAT or ACT scores, the Molloy application, and a $40 nonrefundable application fee. While not required, a personal interview is strongly suggested.

Entrance requirements include graduation from high school or equivalent with 20.5 units, including the following: 4 units of English, 3 units of a foreign language, 3 units of mathematics, 4 units of social studies, and 3 units of science. Those who plan to major in mathematics must have 4 units of high school mathematics and 2 units of science, including either chemistry or physics. Biology majors must have biology, chemistry, physics, and 4 units of mathematics. Nursing majors must have biology and chemistry. Cardio-respiratory science majors must have biology, chemistry, and mathematics. Nuclear medicine majors must have high school algebra and biology. Applicants lacking above requirements are reviewed on an individual basis.

Application Information

Molloy College offers rolling admissions at the undergraduate level. Early action on admission will be made promptly on applications received by December 1 of the senior year from well-qualified students who have filed all their credentials with the admissions office.

Prospective students are invited to visit the campus. Questions or requests for more information can be directed to:

Undergraduate Admissions
Molloy College
1000 Hempstead Avenue
Rockville Centre, New York 11571
Phone: 516-323-4000
888-4-MOLLOY (toll-free)
E-mail: admissions@molloy.edu
Website: http://www.molloy.edu
http://www.facebook.com/GoMolloy
http://www.twitter.com/MolloyCollege

MONMOUTH UNIVERSITY

WEST LONG BRANCH, NEW JERSEY

★ To read more about this school, visit http://petersons.to/monmouth

MONMOUTH UNIVERSITY

The College

Monmouth University is a first-tier, private university located along New Jersey's northern coastline that offers a welcoming and dynamic setting for student development. Innovative academic programs, individual faculty attention, and nationally ranked Division I athletics make this private university a great place for students to prepare for their futures.

Monmouth's beautiful coastal campus sits at the heart of a vibrant culture rich in history, the arts, technology, and entrepreneurship. Just an hour from New York and Philadelphia, the University provides a welcoming and dynamic setting that prepares students to succeed in life after graduation. Renowned faculty are actively involved in advancing academic research nationwide while encouraging meaningful community involvement and critical thinking for self-fulfillment.

A comprehensive selection of in-demand degree programs are led by innovative faculty in a small class setting, where students are active participants in their education.

Monmouth has a diverse student body comprising approximately 6,400 undergraduate and graduate students. While many are from the Northeast, students come from all across the United States, as well as nations around the world. Monmouth offers traditional residence halls and garden-style apartments. Some University-sponsored beachfront campus housing is also offered to students who meet certain requirements.

Students at Monmouth have an assortment of extracurricular activities to choose from, including more than 120 student-run clubs and organizations, such as the Student Government Association, the campus newspaper (The Outlook), the FM radio station (WMCX), the television station (Hawk TV), the online news portal (The Verge), the yearbook (Shadows), the literary magazine (Monmouth Review), and various sororities and fraternities. Special events are held throughout the year, including art exhibits, concerts, lectures, and sightseeing trips. Monmouth's Alternative Spring Break provides students with the opportunity to travel globally to take part in service projects and community building.

Students can also cheer on Monmouth's 23 NCAA Division I men's and women's athletic programs. The teams compete primarily in the Metro Atlantic Athletic Conference (MAAC), with the exception of football, which competes in the full-scholarship Big South Conference, and bowling, a member of the Southland Bowling League. The University's basketball and track and field teams compete in the 153,200-square-foot OceanFirst Bank Center, a 4,200-seat venue that opened in 2009. All Monmouth students have access to the arena, which also houses a 200-meter, six-lane indoor track; fitness center; conference space; the University Store; and luxury suites. The University's football, lacrosse, and outdoor track and field programs open their new home in fall 2017, with the debut of Monmouth Stadium. The new stadium will accommodate 4,200 fans and feature state-of-the-art media facilities and end zone to end zone seating.

Monmouth offers something for everyone, and it strives to ensure that students have the resources and support to pursue their goals. The Center for Student Success (CSS) assists students through a variety of academic and career counseling services and programs. Graduates benefit from continued relationships with the Monmouth family. Many return to campus to visit friends, discuss projects with faculty members, and even recruit the next generation of alumni.

Location

Monmouth's coastal campus provides a safe, suburban setting in one of the world's largest metropolitan regions, ideally positioned to help students develop and pursue their career interests while enjoying rich cultural opportunities. Approximately one hour from both New York City and Philadelphia, and one mile from the coastal beaches of the Atlantic Ocean, the University is also at the heart of the coast's vibrant tri-city region.

Economic and political centers of the country and the world are made real and accessible through fascinating internships, a robust study-abroad program, and multiple field experience opportunities. Corporate global headquarters, world-class museums, Madison Square Garden, the Barclays Center, and other sports hubs, shops, restaurants, and theaters are all within reach of the campus.

Majors and Degrees

Monmouth University offers 32 baccalaureate degree programs in six academic schools that share the University's commitment to providing a rigorous academic experience grounded in the liberal arts. The Leon Hess Business School awards bachelor's degrees in business administration with concentrations in accounting; economics; finance; economics and finance; international business; management and decision sciences; marketing; marketing, management, and decision sciences; and real estate. The School of Education awards bachelor's degrees that allow students to earn certification as elementary and secondary school teachers; the school also offers various endorsements, such as English as a second language and teacher of students with disabilities. The Wayne D. McMurray School of Humanities and Social Sciences awards bachelor's degrees in anthropology, art, communication, criminal justice, English, fine arts, foreign language, history, homeland security, music, political science, psychology, and sociology. A Spanish and international business B.A. degree is awarded jointly through the Leon Hess Business School and the School of Humanities and Social Sciences. The School of Science awards bachelor's degrees in biology, chemistry, clinical laboratory sciences, computer science, marine and environmental biology and policy, mathematics, medical laboratory science, and software engineering. The School of Social Work awards the Bachelor of Social Work degree. The Marjorie K. Unterberg School of Nursing and Health Studies awards bachelor's degrees in health studies and health and physical education, as well as the Bachelor of Science in Nursing. A pre-professional advising program is available for students who intend to pursue careers in medicine, dentistry, or other healthcare fields. Monmouth also offers a number of Five-Year Baccalaureate/Master's programs, which enable qualified students to earn a bachelor's and a master's degree in five years in business, computer science, criminal justice, education (select programs), English, history, social work, or software engineering.

Academic Programs

The curriculum at Monmouth University is focused on learning experiences that are both high impact and immersive, extending beyond the classroom, and designed to prepare students for life after college.

Monmouth challenges students in a demanding college environment built on a regimen of reading, deliberating, writing, experimenting, and discussion that ignites curiosity, helps uncover latent passions, and discover a greater sense of purpose.

Transformative learning extends beyond the lecture hall, through a campus-wide culture of teaching excellence that includes linked-learning communities, first-year and senior seminars, study abroad, common readings, experiential education opportunities, community-based participatory research and service-learning courses. Students study abroad in Australia, England, Italy, Spain, and more. Additionally, Monmouth's alternative break allows students to take part in service projects and community building activities in locales around the globe including Guatemala, Haiti, and Nicaragua.

Monmouth students have access to internships, practicums, and even employment opportunities during their course of study. Many students have internships in New York City and Philadelphia, with industry leaders including JPMorgan Chase, NBCUniversal, L'Oreal, and others. The University also partners with the Washington Center, allowing students to earn credit for experiential learning gained through internships and symposia in the nation's capital.

Monmouth's location and network provide tremendous academic opportunities to students. For example, students in Monmouth's music industry program interface with industry professionals in and beyond the classroom, managing their own record label, Blue Hawk Records. There is a real spirit of entrepreneurship on campus that comes to life through student activities like the student-managed investment fund Hawk Capital. Marine and environmental biology and policy students benefit from the University's proximity to coastal waterways.

Qualified students accepted to the University's Honors School participate in an educational environment that encourages and supports intellectual and personal excellence. First-year courses are clustered to enhance interactive learning, with professors who develop common themes and assignments. Honors classes are distinguished by in-depth coverage of material through discussion and writing, smaller class sizes, and a heightened student-faculty rapport. In their final year, each Honors School student researches, writes, and publicly presents an honors thesis, guided by a faculty member who serves as their academic mentor.

Academic Facilities

Monmouth's 55 buildings provide a synthesis of historical architecture and modern aesthetics. The campus' signature building is Woodrow Wilson Hall, a National Historic Landmark, which served as Daddy Warbucks' mansion in the 1982 film *Annie*. The library, the former mansion of Murry and Leonie Guggenheim, is listed on the National Register of History Places and holds 290,000 print and online monographs, 180 databases (abstracts and full-text, e-books, motion picture, image, tools), over 74,000 electronic and print journal subscriptions, and over 1,200 media items. The Lauren K. Woods Theatre, once the Guggenheim carriage house, is a showcase for professional and student performances and that offer students direct experience with all phases of the theater arts.

The Jules L. Plangere Jr. Center for Communication, which is home to the Department of Communication, provides state-of-the-art studios and editing facilities. Joan and Robert Rechnitz Hall houses the Department of Art and Design and features an art gallery, Mac labs, a reception area, and an animation and editing studio. The newest facility is Pozycki Hall, a two-story addition to the Samuel E. and Mollie Bey Hall and home to the Kislak Real Estate Institute. It includes a 150-seat lecture hall, student lounge, general and computer classrooms, and spacious meeting rooms.

Costs

For 2017–18, tuition and fees are approximately $36,733 per year. Annual room and board costs are approximately $13,451; actual costs are determined by the room and meal plan selected.

Financial Aid

At Monmouth, 99 percent of first-year students receive some form of financial aid; about 96 percent receive a scholarship or grant (federal, state, or University); the average scholarship/grant package is $22,521; and the average financial aid package, including student loans and work study, is approximately $26,944. All this, combined with the fact that Monmouth awards more than $59 million in institutional aid to students each year, makes Monmouth an affordable option for many families.

A wide range of University scholarships and grants are offered to all prospective full-time, first-year, and transfer students on the basis of academic performance.

The University participates in all federal and state grant and loan programs. To establish eligibility and to capitalize on available assistance, students should complete the Free Application for Federal Student Aid (FAFSA), which is available after October 1. Students and their families may call 732-571-3463, e-mail finaid@monmouth.edu, or visit the Financial Aid Office for assistance.

Students interested in attending Monmouth can get an estimate of their eligibility for federal, state, and institutional aid, even before submitting their application. To complete the University's Scholarship Inquiry Form and Net Price Calculator, visit www.monmouth.edu/scholarship and www.monmouth.edu/netpricecalculator

Faculty

The University's professors are leaders in their fields and contribute through research, publishing, and consulting services to their respective academic areas. There are 302 full-time and 385 part-time faculty members. Approximately 75 percent of full-time faculty members have doctorates or terminal degrees in their fields. The average class size is 21, and the student-faculty ratio is 13:1.

Student Government

The Student Government Association (SGA) is an important and necessary voice in the University community; its views are recognized and respected. Monmouth students who wish to get involved with SGA can also do so as general members. This flexible form of involvement does not require a student to run for a position or participate in any one of the elections that are sponsored by SGA. More information is available at www.monmouth.edu/sga.

Admission Requirements

Many factors are considered in an admission application. For first-year applicants, a committee evaluates the high school transcripts and SAT or ACT scores, one letter of recommendation, and a personal essay. A resume of activities including leadership positions held and other information supporting the application are also welcome. Campus tours and information sessions with admission counselors are available. Transfer students must submit official transcripts from all colleges attended. If transfer students have earned fewer than 24 transferable credits, they must fulfill first-year admission requirements as well. Nursing applicants must apply by December 1 and submit a nursing-specific essay.

Application and Information

Early action is a nonbinding option for students who wish to receive an early response from Monmouth. December 1 is the deadline for early action and nursing applicants, and admission decisions are mailed by January 15. The application deadline for regular decision is March 1, with an admission decision notification date prior to April 1. Applications received after March 1 are considered on a space-available basis. First-year housing is guaranteed for students who submit the required enrollment deposit, housing deposit, and housing contract by May 1. Students who submit their deposits and housing contract after May 1 may be placed on a wait list for admission and/or housing.

For further information, students should contact:

Office of Undergraduate Admissions
Monmouth University
400 Cedar Avenue
West Long Branch, New Jersey 0774-1898
Phone: 732-571-3456
800-543-9671 (toll-free)
Fax: 732-263-5166
E-mail: admission@monmouth.edu
Website: http://www.monmouth.edu
http://www.facebook.com/monmouthuniversity
http://www.twitter.com/monmouthu
http://www.youtube.com/monmouthuniversity

Monmouth University's Woodrow Wilson Hall is designated as a National Historic Landmark.

COLLEGE CLOSE-UPS

MORAVIAN COLLEGE

BETHLEHEM, PENNSYLVANIA

MORAVIAN COLLEGE

★ For more information, visit http://petersons.to/moraviancollege

The College

Moravian College is a private liberal arts college in Bethlehem, Pennsylvania. America's sixth-oldest college and the first to educate women, Moravian delivers a values-based liberal arts education in a caring environment, through which it nurtures in students the capacities for leadership, lifelong learning, and positive societal contributions.

The College was founded in 1742 by followers of John Amos Comenius, the 17th-century Moravian bishop whose humanistic ideals helped to shape modern education. Those ideals—that learning should be available to all, that teaching should be in accord with human nature, and that education should be applied to practical uses—are very much alive some 275 years later. Today, the College enrolls students from a great variety of socioeconomic, religious, racial, and ethnic backgrounds; provides for highly personalized learning experiences; and offers many opportunities for students to direct their education toward individual and professional goals. They, too, can turn something seemingly small into something amazing, unimaginable, and bigger than themselves—just like its founders.

Moravian College emphasizes the deliberate integration of a broad-based liberal arts curriculum with hands-on learning experiences to prepare its students not just for employment, but for successful careers. The College excels at transforming good students into highly competent graduates who can put theory into practice, helping them enter the workplace with confidence or shine in graduate school.

Students benefit from Moravian College's strong academic majors, opportunities for internships and co-ops, undergraduate research alongside faculty mentors, and programs that foster a drive and curiosity to pursue their passions. The 12:1 student-faculty ratio means students get personal attention from a dedicated faculty to ensure their success. The proof is in the results: 97 percent of students who earn a bachelor's degree do so in four years.

In a recent survey of graduates, more than 91 percent felt their Moravian education fully prepared them for work and/or graduate school; in fact, 92 percent of graduates are either employed full-time or attending graduate school within ten months of graduating. In the same survey, more than 90 percent cited full confidence in the leadership abilities and critical-thinking skills acquired during their four years at Moravian.

Moravian College's value and leadership in the liberal arts continues to be recognized by its community and respected national boards. The Princeton Review named Moravian College to its "381 Best Colleges" and "361 Green Colleges" lists in 2016, and the College is also consistently included in "Barron's Best Buys in College Education." In addition, Moravian College is among the top liberal arts colleges in the *U.S. News & World Report* ranking of colleges and universities, and *Bloomberg Businessweek* named the College among the top 25 percent of schools providing a high return on investment. In 2016, Educate to Career ranked the College in the top 3 percent nationally for graduate outcomes—the best in its area and number two in Pennsylvania. Locally, members of the greater Lehigh Valley community named Moravian College "Best Local College" two years in a row.

Location

Moravian College is located in historic Bethlehem, Pennsylvania, and the Lehigh Valley. The College's two campuses are located at either end of a busy retail section of Main Street, on an area known as "the Moravian Mile." The area offers students an environment rich in history, culture, and outdoor recreation. Students may take frequent trips to Philadelphia, New York City, Washington DC, and the Pocono Mountains, all located within 75 minutes of campus.

The lively city of Bethlehem is known for its historic sites, which date back to before the Revolutionary War; art; craftsmanship; and music events. The annual nine-day Musikfest attracts over a million visitors each August. *Money* magazine has ranked Bethlehem as one of the Top 100 Best Places to Live.

Majors and Degrees

Moravian College offers more than 55 majors and programs. The Bachelor of Arts (B.A.) degree is available in 13 majors: art, economics and business, education, English, environmental policy and economics, foreign languages, history, music, philosophy, political science, psychology, religion, and sociology.

The Bachelor of Science (B.S.) degree is available in 9 majors: biochemistry, biological science, chemistry, education, environmental science, mathematics and computer science, neuroscience, nursing, and physics and earth science.

Moravian also offers several concentrated Bachelor of Music (B.Mus.) programs through the departments of education and music. The College achieved the designation as an "All-Steinway School" in 2013.

Minor fields of study are available in Africana studies; international studies; ethics; peace and justice; writing arts; medieval studies; and women's, gender, and sexuality studies.

Academic Programs

The philosophical basis of Moravian's curriculum is to provide students with the skills they will need most to compete in the global economic and cultural climate of the new century. The curriculum includes courses intended to sharpen students' critical skills such as writing, computer competence, and the ability to approach academic subjects from a variety of disciplines. The Learning in Common component of the general education curriculum presents students with sets of courses in multidisciplinary clusters designed to complement each other and build connections among fields.

Off-Campus Programs

Hands-on learning opportunities such as field studies, co-ops, and internships also help students develop professional skills and build a network of professional contacts while still in school. Moravian College students have completed field study placements at such prestigious organizations as AT&T Microelectronics, Merrill Lynch, Johnson & Johnson, Tiffany & Co., and St. Luke's Hospital. The College has a unique partnership with Merck & Co., which allows computer science students to hone their technical skills and deepen their understanding of how to use and manipulate data appropriately. They do this through paid summer research opportunities, internships, capstone projects, and co-ops, all the while working on real Merck and open source projects. These connections and the exceptional work of the College's Career and Civic Engagement Office allows more than 92 percent of Moravian graduates to be employed full-time or attending graduate or professional school within 10 months of graduation.

Student Opportunities for Academic Research (SOAR) provides an undergraduate student research experience in collaboration with a faculty mentor. SOAR students receive stipends, travel allowances, and research expenses to support research in a variety of areas. Many students have presented their works at academic conferences across the region.

In addition, independent study and honors research programs allow students to delve deeply into areas of personal interest. These opportunities also allow students to work closely with senior faculty members on research projects—an unusual opportunity at the undergraduate level.

Moravian students have the opportunity to study in one or more of 20 countries. Undergraduates are also eligible to take courses at five neighboring schools including Lafayette College, Lehigh University, Cedar Crest College, DeSales University, and Muhlenberg College. The five schools and Moravian College are members of L.V.A.I.C., the Lehigh Valley Association of Independent Colleges.

Academic Facilities

The College's two campuses—the Main Street Campus and the Priscilla Payne Hurd Campus—are located within 8 blocks of each other and represent the school's past and state-of-the-art future.

Comenius Hall, home to the social science departments and the visual historic landmark for the College, was remodeled to improve classroom spaces and add more student study space. In 2013, Moravian completed phase two of its $13.2 million renovation of the Collier Hall of Science; major upgrades were made to the building infrastructure and student study spaces were added. The new GIS and computational modeling lab allows for high-end computing and sophisticated analysis of scientific data. Just last year, Moravian College opened its Sports Medicine and Rehabilitation Center, a 43,000 square-foot state-of-the-art home to the new Master of Science in Athletic Training program and future Occupational Therapy and Physical Therapy programs. The building also provides facilities for real athletic trainers from St. Luke's University Health Network, from whom students will gain real-world experience. In the fall of 2017, the Sally Breidegam Miksiewicz Center for Health Sciences is slated to open to nursing, informatics, public health, and health sciences students. The $23 million building will feature leading-edge technology, enhanced classrooms and research labs, a health informatics computer lab, a virtual cadaver lab, and creative spaces for student and faculty interaction.

The College is dedicated to updating its amenities, including the renovation of several residence halls and a 10,000 square-foot modern fitness/wellness area. The student union (or HUB) was renovated to add new student dining and meeting spaces, and an outdoor patio with fire pit. A residence hall called the HILL, containing only single rooms in suite-style living, was opened in 2009.

Moravian College issues a MacBook Pro laptop and an iPad to all incoming freshmen. Equipping students with the latest ensures students gain the 21st-century knowledge and skills that will be transferrable to numerous careers.

Costs

In the 2016–17 academic year, tuition totaled $38,556 with fees of approximately $1,731. Residential fees ranged from $6,792 to $8,084 per year (depending on style of accommodation) and meal plans ranged from $4,098 to $5,898 per year for resident students and $278 to $1,658 for commuter students (optional). Health and accident insurance is required for all Moravian students.

Financial Aid

Moravian College is committed to making education financially possible for all students. In fact, over 95 percent of students receive some form of financial aid through grants, scholarships, loans, and part-time employment. Moravian College commits over $30 million annually to assisting students with the cost of tuition.

Moravian offers merit scholarships to students who demonstrate strong academic achievement, citizenship, and leadership skills. Scholarships are awarded at time of admission and every student who applies for admission is considered for a merit award. Generally, students should have academic and personal credentials that place them well above College averages in both GPA and SAT scores. The Moravian College Heritage Grant is presented to first-generation college students, particularly those from diverse or underrepresented groups. Mo's Fund has been established to provide one-time financial support to Moravian College students who are experiencing a financial hardship, and U.S. military personnel (and their dependents) who have served or are currently serving can take advantage of education benefits at Moravian College.

Thanks to a network of alumni and friends who support the scholarship funds, capital campaigns, and endowment, students receive direct and indirect financial support that makes Moravian College affordable.

Faculty

The College boasts a student-faculty member ratio of 12 to 1. Faculty and staff members provide personal attention and mentorship to students to help each student identify and prepare for the most appropriate career or post-graduate path for that student.

Student Activities

Campus life opportunities at Moravian College are designed to educate the whole person by promoting personal development, leadership skills, and global responsibility. Though the college is spread across two campuses, Moravian prides itself on having a close-knit community. On-campus housing is guaranteed for all four years of study, and fraternity and sorority housing is also available.

Student activities and campus cultural events provide opportunities to explore new interests. The campus is home to more than 80 student-led programs and Greek organizations, including the Equestrian Team, Beta Beta Beta, Moravian College Community Orchestra, and WRMC radio station. Long-held traditions like Christmas Vespers enliven the student experience.

Admission Requirements

Moravian College is a member of the Common Application group. Students may apply to Moravian by submitting the Common Application or by submitting the Moravian College Online Application. In addition to the completed application form, a high school transcript SAT/ACT scores, letters of recommendation, and an essay are required for admission. Candidates for admission should be enrolled in a high school college-preparatory curriculum to prepare for successful study in a liberal arts program.

Moravian College awards credit to students who have passed at an acceptable level certain Advanced Placement Examinations taken prior to admission.

Interested students should submit an application for admission during the fall or winter of their senior year in high school. The deadline for Early Decision is January 15. Although an interview is not required, candidates should make every effort to visit the campus to discuss their enrollment plans with an admissions counselor.

Application and Information

For more information about Moravian College, prospective students should contact:

Admissions Director
1200 Main Street
Bethlehem, Pennsylvania 18018
Phone: 800-441-3191
610-861-1320
Fax: 610-625-7930
E-mail:
Website: www.moravian.edu

Historic Comenius Hall at Moravian College

COLLEGE CLOSE-UPS

MOUNT ALOYSIUS COLLEGE

CRESSON, PENNSYLVANIA

★ To read more about this school, visit http://petersons.to/mountaloysiuscollege

The College

Mount Aloysius College is a private, comprehensive, Catholic liberal arts college sponsored by the Sisters of Mercy. The College welcomes people of all faith traditions. Established in 1853, Mount Aloysius College offers both undergraduate and graduate education. Since the founding of the College, nearly 16,000 students have become proud Mount Aloysius alumni. The College is committed to providing small class sizes, and students benefit from accessible faculty and staff. Mount Aloysius students come mostly from throughout Pennsylvania and the mid-Atlantic Region. There are over 2,500 students enrolled (unduplicated headcount).

Mount Aloysius College is one of 18 Mercy Colleges nationwide. Students are encouraged to synthesize faith with learning, to develop competence with compassion, to apply their talents and gifts to the service of others, and to assume leadership in their community.

Student activities play a distinctive role in personal growth. At Mount Aloysius College, there are approximately 100 organized clubs, groups, honor societies, and an intramural sports program. Activities include a student newspaper, residence hall associations, student government, cheerleading, dance team, scholarship-funded theater and choir programs, and a student activities planning board. Mount Aloysius fun includes social events, intramural sports, athletic events, comedians, live music, theater, educational events, campus forums, and awesome guest lectures.

Mount Aloysius College is a member of NCAA Division III. Athletic programs involve both women and men and include basketball, cross-country, golf, soccer, and tennis. Men's baseball and women's bowling, softball, and volleyball are also offered. Athletes benefit from the Ray S. and Louise S. Walker Athletic Field Complex, which includes a softball field, one of the finest soccer fields in the area, and the Calandra-Smith baseball complex. Recently the Mountie Stables were opened to the College and to the community. The Stables add dugouts, lockers, showers, storage, and concession facilities to the school's athletic infrastructure.

Opened in autumn 2013, the new Athletic Convocation and Wellness Center is a spectacular 87,400 square-foot multipurpose facility on the western edge of the beautiful and expansive 193-acre campus. This facility takes Mount Aloysius athletics to a new level and adds a welcomed special events venue to the southern Allegheny Mountains. The Center houses a main gymnasium and events venue with seating for over 2,500, home and visitor locker rooms, and trainer facilities. There is also a full-size auxiliary gymnasium. Athletic offices, Institutional Advancement, Student Affairs, Business faculty offices, and fully integrated smart classrooms and conferencing facilities are also located in the building. On the ground floor, a new state-of-the-art wellness center offers both cardio and resistance training in a spacious, modern environment.

In spring 2014, an anonymous donor memorialized the late Sr. Virginia Bertschi, RSM by repurposing the former Health and Fitness Center. The new Bertschi Center and Technology Commons—with open architecture, vivid colors, and glass walls offering great views of the campus and surrounding mountains—is an additional social, technology, and special events venue that serves both commuter and resident students.

The main campus building is a picturesque structure dating to 1897. It houses the admissions, financial aid, security, health, and academic offices, along with the Office of the President, classrooms, the region's premiere nursing simulation center, and the Wolf-Kuhn Art Gallery. Cosgrave Center is the hub of campus life. The building contains the dining hall, snack bar, bookstore, child-care center (part of the elementary education/early childhood program at the College), lounges, recreational rooms, student affairs offices, and meeting rooms. Ihmsen Halls are key housing facilities for residential students. Misciagna Residence is a state-of-the-art residence hall, providing 25 suites and private bathrooms. McAuley Hall features both double and single rooms and a large multipurpose room and study lounges on all three floors. Alumni Hall is a historic, multipurpose facility used for College drama, musicals, lectures, and performing arts events. The College operates 12 months per year and opens its facilities to the Southern Allegheny community.

The College is 100 percent wireless, and smart classrooms are located throughout the campus.

Mount Aloysius is fully accredited by the Middle States Association of Colleges and Schools and approved by the Pennsylvania Department of Education. All nursing and health studies programs are fully accredited by their professional accrediting bodies, including the National League for Nursing Accrediting Commission, the Commission on Accreditation for Programs of Diagnostic Medical Sonography, the Commission on Accreditation in Physical Therapy Education, the American Association of Medical Assistants, and the Joint Commission on Accreditation for Programs of Surgical Technology.

In addition to its undergraduate programs—both associate and bachelor's degrees—Mount Aloysius offers master's degree programs in business administration, behavioral specialist consulting, community counseling, and psychology.

Location

Mount Aloysius College is located in the scenic Southern Allegheny Mountains of west-central Pennsylvania, in the town of Cresson. Convenient and accessible from U.S. Route 22, the College's setting is rural but mere minutes from State College, Altoona, Johnstown, and Pittsburgh, Pennsylvania. The area has warm, beautiful summers; brisk, breathtaking autumns; invigorating winters; and cool, blooming springs. Facilities are available for biking, golfing, swimming, horseback riding, waterskiing, boating, hiking, spelunking, cross-country and downhill skiing, picnicking, and amusement parks. A well-kept system of State Parks is convenient to the College as are shopping malls, golf courses, and numerous historical sites.

Majors and Degrees

Mount Aloysius College awards bachelor's and associate degrees in the arts, sciences, and health studies fields in both career-oriented and traditional liberal arts programs. Baccalaureate degrees are available in accounting, American Sign Language/English interpreter education, behavioral and social science, biology and general science, business administration (includes a fifth-year MBA option), computer science, criminology, dentistry (4-4), elementary/early childhood education and secondary education (with certifications), English, general science, history/political science, humanities, information technology, math/science, medical imaging, nursing (RN-BSN program), nursing (2+2), occupational therapy (3-2), osteopathic medicine (3-4), pharmacy (3-3), physical therapy (4-3), physician assistant studies (3-2), prelaw, psychology, and undecided/exploratory. Associate degrees are offered in applied technology, business administration, criminology, early childhood studies, general studies, legal studies, liberal arts, medical assistant studies, nursing, physical therapist assistant studies, radiography/medical imaging, sign language/deaf studies, and surgical technology.

Academic Programs

Whether preparing students for careers upon graduation or for graduate school, Mount Aloysius recognizes the importance of a broad and liberal education. Thus, in addition to receiving solid preparation for a chosen career, every student at the College receives a foundation in the arts, sciences, and humanities through an outstanding core curriculum. Strong emphasis is placed on the specialized courses within each program of study, and many academic programs combine classroom experience with internships and related training at area clinical sites, agencies, and institutions. In addition to its regular academic programs, Mount Aloysius offers independent and directed study with a commitment to service, a central component of a Mercy education. The College has an excellent honors program and academic services area. The academic calendar has two traditional semesters and optional summer sessions.

Off-Campus Programs

An important feature of many academic programs is off-campus training. The majority of the College's programs of study require credit-yielding practicums at partnering hospitals, public and private schools, or health or human service agencies. Students in all health programs benefit from required clinical training during their time at the College.

Academic Facilities

In 1995, Mount Aloysius College opened both a new Library and a new era, signifying greater access to information for the College community. This state-of-the-art Library is the campus hub for technology and study. With a Buhl Electronic Classroom and more than 80,000 print and nonprint titles, the Library is an impressive, 31,000 square-foot facility with ample seating space, four group-study rooms, a reading lounge, a law library and classroom, an unparalleled 18,000-volume Ecumenical Collection donated by Pastor Gerald Myers, and ample room for expansion. This facility is completely automated, with an online catalog and access to remote libraries and the Internet through more than 30 workstations. The Library also houses the Information Technology Center, home to 15 multimedia workstations and the latest educational software.

Pierce Hall serves as the campus science center. A state-of-the-art, 31,000 square-foot facility, it was completed in 1997. Pierce Hall houses all science labs, health science centers, and the offices of science faculty. Academic Hall is home to the College Honors Program. It houses classrooms, labs, seminar rooms, faculty offices, and electronic classrooms. The College is proud of its bridge to the past and its progress in providing 21st century learning facilities.

Costs

Annual tuition and fees for the 2016–17 academic year for full-time students were $20,710; room and board were $9,500. Up-to-date cost information is available online at http://www.mtaloy.edu/tuition-fees/tuition-and-fees.

Financial Aid

Mount Aloysius prides itself on affordability. Many MAC students hail from proud families of modest means and many are first-generation students. The College understands the expense involved in acquiring a quality education and encourages all students to apply for all available aid. Through the Office of Financial Aid, the College assists students in applying for state and federal grants, loans, work-study awards, merit scholarships and more. The College awards academic monies based on GPA and SAT or ACT scores. These awards are renewable over a four-year period and range from $3,000 to $14,000 per year. Mount Aloysius College participates in all federal and state programs; fully 94 percent of Mount Aloysius College students receive some form of financial aid. *U.S. News & World Report* has ranked Mount Aloysius College as one of the best-priced private liberal arts colleges in the United States.

Faculty

The Mount Aloysius faculty consists of approximately 175 members, whose primary responsibility is teaching and advising students. Many faculty members hold advanced or terminal degrees and are expected to maintain close instructional ties with students. Many professors hold national, professional certificates in such disciplines as criminology, education, law, and nursing. The Mount Aloysius student-faculty ratio of 12:1 allows close contact between students and faculty members, providing personal attention in a highly structured environment—a key ingredient in the College's academic philosophy.

Student Government

The Student Government Association (SGA) represents students on all issues that concern the College. The SGA appoints student representatives to all student-oriented College committees. The College encourages student participation in the general governance structure and other matters concerning the development and implementation of policies on residential student life.

Admission Requirements

The College enrolls a freshman class of approximately 350 students. The total class of 550 includes transfer students. Admission is selective, based on academic promise, as indicated by a student's secondary school performance and activities, standardized test scores, and special experience and talents. Applicants are required to have or expected to earn a diploma from an approved secondary school or a GED diploma. Submission of official transcripts and SAT or ACT scores is required. In addition to the general admission requirements, specific admission requirements exist for the health programs.

For further information, students should visit the College's website at http://www.mtaloy.edu. Prospective students are encouraged to visit the scenic 193-acre campus. The College is open Monday to Friday from 8:30 a.m. to 5 p.m. and on select Saturdays.

Application and Information

To apply for admission to Mount Aloysius College, candidates are encouraged to submit their application and $30 application fee to the Office of Undergraduate and Graduate Admissions. In addition, students may apply online.

For further information, students should contact:

Office of Undergraduate and Graduate Admissions
Mount Aloysius College
7373 Admiral Peary Highway
Cresson, Pennsylvania 16630
Phone: 814-886-6383
888-823-2220 (toll-free)
Fax: 814-886-6441
E-mail: admissions@mtaloy.edu
Website: http://www.mtaloy.edu

Mount Aloysius College, located on a beautiful 193-acre campus in Cresson, Pennsylvania provides a safe, vibrant learning community. Nestled in the southern Allegheny Mountains, Mount Aloysius is one of 18 U.S. Mercy colleges and universities. Mount Aloysius offers year-round recreational and cultural opportunities. Students enjoy both the security of the campus and the proximity to State College to the east and Pittsburgh to the west. Mount Aloysius College is minutes away from all the amenities of Altoona and Johnstown, Pennsylvania. Interstate highways, the Pennsylvania Turnpike, AMTRAK train service, bus service, and several airports make Mount Aloysius College convenient from anywhere.

MUHLENBERG COLLEGE

ALLENTOWN, PENNSYLVANIA

★ To read more about this school, visit http://petersons.to/muhlenbergcollege

The College

Founded in 1848, Muhlenberg College aims to develop independent critical thinkers who are intellectually agile, characterized by a zeal for reasoned and civil debate, knowledgeable about the achievements and traditions of diverse civilizations and cultures, able to express ideas with clarity and grace, committed to lifelong learning, equipped with ethical values, and prepared for lives of leadership and service.

Muhlenberg students achieve the College's goals by assuming strong individual responsibility for intense involvement in rigorous academic work and for personal involvement within the College community. The more than 110 student organizations provide outlets for the diversified cultural, athletic, religious, social, leadership, and service interests of the students. The campus is primarily residential; more than 90 percent of the 2,200 students live on campus. A close sense of community develops naturally, one in which their diversified academic and personal interests enable students to contribute positively to the intellectual and personal growth of their peers.

Students are aided by an active Career Center in relating academic and personal knowledge and skills to appropriate career goals and in obtaining positions upon graduation. About one third of a typical graduating class proceeds immediately to graduate or professional school, while two thirds pursue a career immediately upon graduation.

Location

Muhlenberg College is located on a campus of 82 acres in suburban west Allentown, an area made up primarily of attractive family homes and parks. The downtown area of Allentown, a city of approximately 105,000 people, is a 10-minute ride from the campus. The College is located 90 miles west of New York City and 60 miles north of Philadelphia.

Majors and Degrees

Muhlenberg offers the Bachelor of Arts (A.B.) degree in the following fields: accounting, American studies, anthropology, art history, business administration, dance, economics, English, film studies, finance, French, history, international studies, Jewish studies, media and communication, music, philosophy, philosophy/political thought, political economy, political science, psychology, religious studies, Russian studies, sociology, Spanish, studio art, and theater. The Bachelor of Science (B.S.) degree is offered in the following fields: biochemistry, biology, chemistry, computer science, environmental science, mathematics, natural sciences, neuroscience, physical science, physics, and public health. Students may also design their own major. Minors are offered in most of the major fields, as well as in Africana studies, creative writing, documentary storytelling, German studies, innovation and entrepreneurship, Italian studies, Latin American and Caribbean studies, women's and gender studies, public health, sustainability studies, and Asian traditions.

In addition, students may receive certification to teach at the elementary and secondary levels. Other opportunities include a 3-4 dental program with the University of Pennsylvania; a 3-3 B.S./Ph.D. program in physical therapy with Thomas Jefferson University; a 3-2 B.S./M.S. program in occupational therapy with Thomas Jefferson University; a 3-2/4-2 combined program in engineering, offered in cooperation with Columbia University; a 3-2 combined program in forestry, offered in cooperation with Duke University; and a 4-4 dual-admission program with SUNY College of Optometry.

Academic Programs

The A.B. and B.S. programs emphasize breadth of study in the liberal arts as well as in-depth study of a particular academic major. All students must fulfill requirements in the arts, foreign culture, the humanities, social sciences, and natural sciences. Strong achievement on Advanced Placement examinations may enable a student to receive advanced placement, possibly with credit. Scores of 4 or 5 earn automatic credit. Scores of 3 are evaluated by the appropriate department.

Students work closely with academic advisers to formulate programs well suited to their individual interests, abilities, needs, and goals. Generally, students are expected to declare their major at the end of the freshman year; however, many students later change their academic major with no difficulty. A double major is possible, and about a third of Muhlenberg students graduate with a double major. The College also enriches the freshman-year experience through more than thirty-five special-focus First-Year Seminars. Seniors have the opportunity to synthesize and integrate their academic experience through a Culminating Undergraduate Experience (CUE).

Off-Campus Programs

Study abroad is available through Muhlenberg's Semester-in-London Program, Netherlands semester, Dublin semester, or more than 160 affiliate agreements with international universities all over the world. In addition, the Lehigh Valley Association of Independent Colleges sponsors summer study-abroad options in a variety of foreign countries. Credit for study-abroad programs sponsored by other institutions or by private agencies may also be transferred to Muhlenberg by special arrangement.

Students may participate in a variety of internships in local businesses, health-care facilities, schools, public agencies, theaters, broadcasting stations, and magazines. Government internships in Harrisburg, Pennsylvania, and Washington, D.C., and an Ethics and Public Affairs semester in Washington, D.C., as well as a New York City semester at Jewish Theological Seminary also are available.

Students may enroll in courses offered at any of the five other member institutions of the Lehigh Valley Association of

Independent Colleges: Lafayette College, Lehigh University, Cedar Crest College, DeSales University, and Moravian College.

Academic Facilities

Muhlenberg's library collection contains more than 200,000 volumes as well as numerous government documents, periodicals, and electronic and online resources. The $12-million Harry C. Trexler Library, a state-of-the-art library facility, opened in 1988. Students may also use library materials owned by the other institutions participating in the Lehigh Valley Association of Independent Colleges.

The Baker Center for the Arts was designed for Muhlenberg by the well-known architect Philip Johnson. It houses a modern theater complex, a recital hall, classrooms, art studios, and a fine arts gallery. The Trexler Pavilion for Theater and Dance opened in 2000 and provides dance performance and studio space, a new theater, a Black Box, and additional arts spaces. The College augmented its arts facilities with the Rehearsal House in 2011.

Life science facilities include numerous laboratories, classrooms, two electron microscopes, a DNA sequencer, an isolation room used for growing and studying viruses, and a museum of natural history. Facilities supporting students in the physical sciences include equipment for optics, electronics, and atomic, nuclear, and solid-state physics. A new 40,000-square-foot addition to the science facilities opened in fall 2006. The College supports both Microsoft and Apple applications throughout campus.

Costs

The comprehensive tuition and fees for the 2016–17 academic year was $48,310. The room and board fee averaged $10,985. The total cost for a resident student was approximately $59,295.

Financial Aid

Muhlenberg College endeavors to make its educational opportunities available to all qualified students regardless of their financial circumstances. While most financial aid at Muhlenberg is based on financial need as demonstrated by the College Scholarship Service Financial Aid PROFILE and FAFSA, there is also significant merit aid available. Typically, about 85 percent of Muhlenberg's students qualify for and receive aid from all sources (institutional, federal, state, and private).

Faculty

The Muhlenberg faculty consists of 177 full-time and 125 part-time members. Eighty-five percent of full-time faculty members hold doctoral or terminal degrees. While many faculty members are distinguished for their scholarly research, teaching is the main emphasis of their work. Professors at all levels work closely with students both inside and outside of the classroom. Many department heads teach introductory courses, and no courses are taught by graduate students or teaching assistants.

Student Government

Muhlenberg students are expected to demonstrate a high level of responsibility with regard to their own governance and to participate extensively in internal decision-making and communication processes throughout the campus. These responsibilities are coordinated by the United Student Government, which transacts all business pertaining to the student body. This organization is in charge of a student activities budget of more than $350,000. In addition, 2 students serve as representatives to the Board of Trustees, and students hold membership on many faculty committees.

Admission Requirements

The College selects students who give evidence of ability and scholastic achievement, seriousness of purpose, and the capacity to make constructive contributions to the College community and the world. Approximately 70 percent of a typical first-year class ranked in the top fifth of their secondary school class. SAT scores for entering freshmen average approximately 610 verbal, 615 math, and 610 writing. The ACT Composite average is 28.

Submission of SAT or ACT scores is optional. An on-campus interview is strongly recommended for all applicants and required for students who choose not to submit standardized test scores.

Application and Information

Students who wish to be considered for admission should submit a completed application form as early as possible during their senior year of secondary school and no later than February 15. Regular decision candidates receive notice of admission decisions in late March. Early decision plans are available, and the College fills approximately half of its freshman class via early decision. Transfer admission is also possible.

For further information, interested students should contact:

Christopher Hooker-Haring
Vice President of Enrollment Management
Muhlenberg College
Allentown, Pennsylvania 18104-5586
Phone: 484-664-3200
E-mail: admissions@muhlenberg.edu
Website: http://www.muhlenberg.edu

The Bell Tower of the Haas College Center stands as the focal point of the Muhlenberg College campus.

NEUMANN UNIVERSITY
ASTON, PENNSYLVANIA

★ To read more about this school, visit http://petersons.to/neumannuniversity

The University

Neumann University (http://www.neumann.edu), a Catholic co-educational institution in the Franciscan tradition, recognizes the value of developing intellectual excellence, professional competence, and strong community life. As a university that balances the liberal arts with the professions, Neumann was founded to meet and expand the educational and professional horizons of men and women through instruction that is based on values, ethical behavior, and service to others. With its Living and Learning Center residence halls, Neumann University is able to serve a diverse geographic and demographic population.

Founded and sponsored by the Sisters of St. Francis of Philadelphia, the University is committed to a varied student body and welcomes students of all denominations. Enrollment is around 2,900.

The Life Center houses the Meagher Theatre, the Bruder Athletic Center, and the Crossroads Cafe dining facility. Intercollegiate sports include women's basketball, cross-country, field hockey, golf, ice hockey, indoor track, lacrosse, soccer, softball, swimming, tennis, track, and volleyball; and men's baseball, basketball, cross-country, golf, ice hockey, indoor track, lacrosse, soccer, tennis, track, and volleyball. Neumann University competes as a member of the National Collegiate Athletic Association (NCAA) Division III, the Colonial States Athletic Conference, and the Eastern Collegiate Athletic Conference (ECAC). Intramural sports and club teams are available to all members of the campus community.

The Living and Learning Center is designed to provide a state-of-the-art residential experience, with a focus on education within a real-world living environment. Technologically smart, the center connects students to both faculty members and friends via wireless Internet, which is available in every suite and apartment. The center also houses a separate computer lab, a fitness center, a reflection room, various study rooms with warming kitchens for group study or meetings, and a laundry.

The University provides a full range of services to students, including career placement, career and personal counseling, a tutoring program, and health services.

Neumann students are involved in a wide variety of campus and community activities. Major and special interest clubs are available for student participation. Clubs bring together students who share common interests and help foster new friendships.

At Neumann, the spiritual dimension of one's life is recognized as integral to total human development. The Ministry Team provides a pastoral presence on campus and promotes a sense of community. The entire University community is invited to serve the needs of the poor and neglected in society through various outreach programs, with special attention to the need for peace and justice in the world today.

Neumann is well positioned to respond to the academic and extracurricular needs of students who are of traditional or nontraditional age, commuters or residents, and full-time or part-time.

In addition to undergraduate programs, Neumann confers master's degrees in accounting, education, nursing, organizational and strategic leadership, pastoral counseling, and sport business as well as doctoral degrees in education (Ed.D.), pastoral counseling (Ph.D.), and physical therapy (D.P.T.).

Location

Neumann, with a beautiful 68-acre suburban campus in Aston, Delaware County, Pennsylvania, is a short distance from Philadelphia; Wilmington, Delaware; southern New Jersey; and Maryland. It is easily accessible from major arteries such as I-95, Route 476, Route 1, and the Pennsylvania Turnpike.

Majors and Degrees

Neumann offers strong academic majors leading to a Bachelor of Arts degree or a Bachelor of Science degree in accounting, arts production and performance, biology, business administration, communication and digital media, computer information systems, criminal justice, education, English, health sciences, liberal arts, marketing, nursing, political science, psychology, public safety administration, social work, and sport management. The education programs lead to teacher certification in early elementary (PK–4), special education (PK–8) or secondary education. Pre-professional programs in engineering, law, medicine, pharmacy, and physical therapy are also available. An accelerated evening program for adults leads to an Associate of Arts, Bachelor of Arts, or Bachelor of Science degree in liberal studies or professional studies.

Academic Programs

The academic program at Neumann University is composed of a core curriculum (required of all students), a major area of study (chosen by each student), and a wide range of elective offerings. Students may also choose a minor area of study. The University's broad base of liberal arts offerings prepares students for the intellectual and social challenges they will face in the employment marketplace and throughout their lives. The core is intended to provide basic knowledge of the liberal arts and sciences; develop verbal, written, and symbolic communication skills; and stimulate interest in a broad range of topics for the purpose of enhancing the individual's contributions to society, thereby enabling the individual to realize full human potential.

Classroom instruction is supplemented by field experience and internships, through which students can earn credit and gain experience by working in a job related to their career interest. Fieldwork and student teaching are required of all education majors. Clinical practice for the nursing major occurs in a variety of health-care facilities in the tri-state area.

The honors program is an opportunity for academically talented students to explore imaginative and innovative perspectives on learning. It is also an opportunity to stimulate and motivate students to expand their knowledge and interest and to strive for greater excellence. Moreover, it is a reward for prior perseverance and dedication as well as an obligation to use skills and abilities in service to others. Admission to the honors program is by invitation.

Neumann University has transfer articulation agreements with numerous schools throughout the area.

Academic Facilities

The Child Development Center is a state-of-the-art, octagonal-shaped building, specifically designed to house an educational program for preschoolers. As a state-licensed day-care facility, it enrolls children of Neumann students, the faculty, and the community. The Child Development Center is part of the Division of Education and Human Services. Students enrolled in education courses use the center for observation, practical experience, and student teaching.

The Academic Computing Center is located on the ground floor of the University. The computers are viewed as tools to support all fields of study and all students and faculty members. Neumann University provides wireless access across campus. Computers are available to all students, as is software related to various academic disciplines.

The University library contains a balanced collection of more than 55,000 physical volumes and films, 20,000 e-books, and nearly 100,000 electronic journals. E-books and journals can be accessed from anywhere with an Internet connection. Collaboration with faculty and membership in local consortia (TCLC, SEPCHE) ensures access to the most relevant resources for academic success. Professional librarians provide in-person research support seven days a week and also create online Research Guides and video tutorials for around-the-clock assistance. Librarians also provide cutting-edge instruction to help develop essential 21st-century skills like critical thinking, technological literacy, and information management. Quiet study rooms, collaborative group spaces, and an open computer lab and Wi-Fi collectively support student study needs.

Costs

Tuition and fees for full-time students (12 to 19 credits per semester) in 2016–17 is $28,710. Room and board were $12,520.

Financial Aid

Typically, about 95 percent of Neumann undergraduate students receive some form of financial aid (scholarships, grants, and student loans).

Neumann offers a variety of renewable scholarships each year to entering full-time freshmen and transfer students. Interested applicants should contact the Office of Admissions and Financial Aid as soon as possible to determine eligibility.

In addition to Neumann scholarships, funds are available through the Federal Pell Grant, Federal Supplemental Educational Opportunity Grant, and Federal Work-Study Programs. Many states provide grant money to attend Neumann (non-Pennsylvania residents should check with their state's higher education agency for details). Veterans Administration benefits can be received by qualified veterans or their dependents. Federal Stafford Student Loans and Federal PLUS Program loans are available and can be applied for through Neumann's preferred lender or any participating bank. Neumann also offers institutional need-based grants. All students requesting financial aid must complete the Free Application for Federal Student Aid (FAFSA) each year to determine eligibility. In order to expedite processing, the FAFSA should be submitted by March 15 for the following school year. Financial aid funds are renewable annually based on need, as determined by the FAFSA results.

Faculty

Neumann students describe faculty members as sincere, hard-working, determined, and energetic. Faculty members view themselves, first, as teachers and are proud partners in their students' journeys toward professional careers. Each student has a faculty adviser, who assists in arranging a program designed to meet the student's educational goals. Many faculty members serve as moderators of student clubs. The student-faculty ratio is 13:1.

Student Government

The Student Government Association (SGA) is the representative body for all students. Its function is to implement the aims and purposes of the University, foster cooperation in student relationships, assist the University in being responsive to the needs of the student body, and encourage personal responsibility for an intelligent system of student self-government. Through the Student Activities Board, social functions are planned throughout the year. Students serve on various University committees, including the Student Affairs Committee of the Board, Academic Advising Committee, Honors Program Committee, Registration/Orientation Task Force, and Student Judicial Board. For full-time students, a Student Government Association fee of $85 per semester is required.

Admission Requirements

Neumann has a rolling admission policy and accepts applications throughout the year. Applicants are considered on the basis of high school record, SAT or ACT scores, recommendations, class rank, and other indicators of potential to succeed in university-level studies. Applications for admission are reviewed without regard to sex, race, creed, color, national origin, age, sexual orientation, pregnancy, military status, religion, or disability. Applicants should be graduates of an accredited high school (or present equivalent credentials) and have a recommended curriculum of 16 units of high school course work, distributed as follows: 4 in English, 2 to 3 in science, 2 in mathematics, 2 in social studies, 2 in foreign language, and 4 in electives. Students intending to pursue a major in biology or clinical laboratory science must have at least 1 year of high school biology and chemistry, and high school physics is highly recommended.

Neumann participates in the Advanced Placement (AP) Program and the College-Level Examination Program (CLEP).

An interview and tour of the campus are highly recommended for all prospective students and parents. Visits can be arranged by contacting the Office of Admissions.

Application and Information

Applicants for freshman admission are requested to have SAT or ACT scores and high school transcripts sent to the Office of Admissions. A nonrefundable $35 application fee should accompany the completed application. A free application is available online at http://www.neumann.edu.

Neumann University welcomes applications from students who have attended or are currently attending either two-year or four-year regionally accredited institutions of higher learning.

For further information, students should contact:

Office of Admissions
Neumann University
One Neumann Drive
Aston, Pennsylvania 19014-1298
United States
Phone: 610-558-5616
800-9NEUMANN (toll-free)
E-mail: neumann@neumann.edu
Website: http://www.neumann.edu

Students love the newest building on campus, the Mirenda Center for Sport, Spirituality, and Character Development.

NEUMONT UNIVERSITY

SALT LAKE CITY, UTAH

★ To read more about this school, visit http://petersons.to/neumontuniversity

The University

Neumont University is different by design. To address shortcomings in traditional higher education, Neumont's founders met with educators and leading employers from around the country to design an innovative computer science curriculum that better prepares students to meet the needs of the rapidly evolving technology industry. The result is a computer science education that merges academic rigor, exposure to cutting-edge technologies, and relevant professional knowledge through a real-world project-based curriculum.

Neumont's mission is to provide a professional education that is rich in ideas, current in industry best practices, and deep in technological insight from the input of industry-leading partners. The University is committed to a collaborative learning process, a high-quality learning environment, contributing broadly to students' lives, and bringing value to the enterprises with its business partners. Neumont graduates are known for their technology expertise and business acumen, their capacity to innovate, and their motivation to succeed. Ninety-seven percent of graduates are employed within six months of graduation, with an average starting salary of $63,000 per year.

Neumont's original approach to computer science education has been recognized and cited by major news outlets from around the country and the U.S. Department of Education for innovation in higher education. Neumont's unique curriculum combines classroom instruction and labs with a collaborative learning environment and real-world project experiences for companies like IBM, Nike, and Bosch. The campus was custom-designed to fit the University's needs with a focus on interactive classrooms, study areas, project rooms, and labs.

Neumont's students come from all across the United States. In the fall of 2016, 85 percent of all current students came from outside the state of Utah. The student body is 88 percent male and 12 percent female, and the student-to-faculty ratio is 21:1.

The Office of Student Affairs assists students in creating groups that meet regularly for different activities and events. Clubs and organizations may focus on a single game (i.e., Magic the Gathering, Pathfinder, or billiards) or they may focus on a specific issue like fitness, women in technology, or equality.

Freshmen are required to live in Neumont-sponsored housing for their first four quarters. Students are housed in buildings near the campus in downtown Salt Lake City. Every apartment comes with furnished bedrooms, kitchens, and living spaces. All utilities are included, as well as high-speed internet, on-site laundry, and access to fitness facilities.

Location

Neumont's convenient location offers a chance for our students to enjoy a little bit of everything. Salt Lake City offers a vibrant local scene where art, food, and music converge daily. Plus, it's just minutes away from world-class hiking, camping, skiing, and snowboarding.

The downtown campus is conveniently located on public transit lines, including TRAX, which offers service to the Salt Lake International Airport (SLC) and other points of interest. TRAX is Utah's light rail system that connects Eastside Apartments, 644 City Station, and The Mercer with the academic center. Students are encouraged to walk, use TRAX, bike, or make use of Salt Lake's bike share programs. All apartment complexes are conveniently located near grocery stores, entertainment venues, and restaurants. In addition, Neumont offers a weekly van service to big box retailers.

Majors and Degrees

Neumont offers 180-credit Bachelor of Science degrees which can be completed in three years. Students attend classes year-round with a three-week break between each ten-week quarter. Students major in one of five areas of technology:

- B.S.C.S.: Bachelor of Science in Computer Science
- B.S.G.D.: Bachelor of Science in Software & Game Development
- B.S.I.S.: Bachelor of Science in Computer Information Systems
- B.S.T.M.: Bachelor of Science in Technology Management
- B.S.W.D.: Bachelor of Science in Web Design & Development

Academic Programs

The Neumont academic model is simple: students learn to master technology in a project-based environment. In the tech industry, nearly all software is developed in a team, so students learn how to fill different roles, meet deadlines, manage requirements, and resolve conflicts.

The curriculum sequentially weaves increasingly complex projects and faculty mentoring into every aspect of a student's education. During their final quarters at Neumont, students participate in Enterprise Projects and develop real-world solutions for real companies.

Each degree program follows a project-based learning model that requires students to work in small teams to complete projects. Students in undergraduate programs are required to attend courses full-time and can earn a bachelor's degree in three years by attending class year-round.

Every student is assigned an Advocate to help them make decisions regarding their career goals and degree choice and to ensure they are on track for graduation.

Costs

For the 2016–17 academic year, tuition was $7,650 per quarter, housing was $1,890 per quarter, and books and supplies were $400 per quarter. There is a one-time $2,500 charge for a laptop computer. The activities fee was $150 per quarter and the technology fee was $350 per quarter. Once students progress beyond the fourth quarter of study there are also some program-specific fees of up to $210 per quarter.

Financial Aid

Neumont's Office of Financial Aid works with each student to create a customized package of grants, loans, and scholarships to fund tuition, fees, housing, books, and living expenses. Every student is encouraged to submit the Free Application for Federal Student Aid (FAFSA). In addition to offering several scholarships and grants, Neumont participates in federal grant programs and federal and private loan programs.

There are also a variety of opportunities for student employment on and off campus. Students interested in pursuing Neumont-sponsored employment opportunities must be in good academic standing. All student employment is based on approval from the student's Advocate and the Dean of Students.

Faculty

Each member of Neumont's faculty is hired specifically for their professional experience and expertise in the computer science industry. Professors are required to teach designated learning outcomes that allow students to work in a real-world, professional environment. All core computer science classes are taught by faculty members with experience in software engineering and a passion for teaching.

Admissions

The Admissions Committee evaluates applicants to determine if they have the qualifications and commitment needed to succeed in Neumont's rigorous academic environment. With an average acceptance rate of 80 percent, Neumont students are dedicated and driven tech-geeks. The committee relies heavily on academic achievements, such as standardized test score (ACT and/or SAT) and cumulative high school GPA, to assess an applicant. On average, students who enrolled in the fall of 2016 had a cumulative high school GPA of 3.15, an average composite ACT score of 25, or an average combined math and reading SAT score of 1090.

Because not all of an applicant's strengths can be shown through a test score, the committee also evaluates life experience, personal essays, technology expertise, interest in technology, and proven work ethic. Applicants are invited to contact the Office of Admissions if there is something about their background beyond test scores and GPA that should be evaluated.

Neumont accepts applications for admission three times a year. Applications, including transcripts and test scores, must be submitted by the early, general, or late admission application deadlines. In addition to academic achievement, applicants will be evaluated based on their passion for technology and work ethic.

Neumont welcomes international applicants. If the applicant is not a U.S. Citizen or permanent resident, visit the University's International Students page on the website for application information or contact the Director of Enrollment.

Interested students are invited to visit the campus or take a virtual tour at http://www.neumont.edu/campustour.

For more information, prospective students should contact:

Karick Heaton, Director of Enrollment
Neumont University
143 South Main Street
Salt Lake City, Utah 84111
Phone: 888-638-6668
801-302-2800
E-mail: admissions@neumont.edu
Website: www.neumont.edu
www.facebook.com/neumontuniversity
www.twitter.com/neumontU
www.instagram.com/neumontu
www.youtube.com/user/neumontuniversity

NEW COLLEGE OF FLORIDA

SARASOTA, FLORIDA

New College
THE HONORS COLLEGE of Florida

The College

New College of Florida offers serious students the opportunity to pursue rigorous academic study in an environment designed to promote depth in thinking, free exchange of ideas, and highly individualized interaction with faculty members. The College was founded as a private institution in 1960 with a devotion to the values implicit in a liberal arts and sciences education, and a dedication to creating an innovative academic program where talented students and outstanding faculty members could come together and pursue learning through small classes, seminars, and independent study to pursue advanced undergraduate research.

In 2001, New College was designated as the official Honors College in the liberal arts and sciences for the State University System of Florida. New College is regularly featured in guidebooks as being among the nation's leading educational values and as one of the country's top small, public colleges. The College is also known as one of the nation's top producers of Fulbright scholarship recipients, with 21 in the last five years alone, a better per-capita performance than almost all U.S. colleges and universities.

About 80 percent of New College graduates go on to pursue graduate or professional study at leading institutions, in recent years attending Harvard, Yale, MIT, Georgetown and Berkeley.

New College's student population is 861, of whom approximately 61 percent are women. Approximately 20 percent of students are out-of-state or overseas residents.

The College's 110-acre bayfront location on the Gulf of Mexico includes basketball, racquetball, tennis, and volleyball courts; a multipurpose soccer, softball, and athletic field; a running trail; a 25-meter swimming pool; and a comprehensive fitness center. The New College sailing team is part of the Inter-Collegiate Sailing Association of North America (ICSA). Students also compete in recreational and intramural sports including soccer, tennis, fencing, flag football, softball, and swimming. Sailboats, kayaks, and canoes are also available free of charge.

Location

On the coastline of the Gulf of Mexico in southwest Florida, New College serves as the northern gateway to Sarasota, a bustling city 50 miles south of Tampa. Sarasota is noted for its recreational, cultural, and artistic attractions, including beautiful white-sand beaches and an abundance of professional theater, art, and music venues. Notably, New College sits adjacent to the world-famous John and Mable Ringling Museum of Art, which offers students free entry to view its Baroque and Renaissance art collections.

Many major airlines serve Sarasota-Bradenton International Airport, which is near the College. Buses link the campus to downtown, shopping malls, parks, and beaches, though bicycling is the favored means of transportation among students.

Majors and Degrees

New College awards the Bachelor of Arts degree in liberal arts and sciences. Each of the College's nearly forty different areas of concentration (majors) is an individualized program that students design in consultation with faculty members. These include anthropology; applied mathematics; art; art history; biochemistry; biology; biopsychology; chemistry; Chinese language and culture; classics; computer science; economics; English; environmental studies; European studies; French; gender studies; German studies/German language and literature; history; humanities; international and area studies; literature; marine biology; mathematics; medieval and Renaissance studies; music; natural sciences; neurobiology; philosophy; physics; political science; psychology; public policy; religion; Russian language and literature; social sciences; sociology; Spanish language, literature, and culture; and urban studies. Partial areas of concentration include theater. Students may also pursue special program areas of concentration with faculty approval. Pre-medical, pre-law, pre-M.B.A., pre-veterinary, and other advanced-degree program advising and guidelines are provided by faculty members and by the Center for Engagement and Opportunity.

Academic Programs

New College's distinctive curriculum enables students, in close consultation with faculty members, to develop programs of seminars, tutorials, independent research, internships, and off-campus experiences that meet each student's personal academic interests and goals.

At the end of each semester, rather than grades, students receive detailed narrative evaluations as well as satisfactory/unsatisfactory assessments of their work from individual faculty members. Graduation requirements include satisfactory completion of seven academic contracts (a set of academic courses and other goals for the semester, planned by the student and faculty adviser), three independent-study projects, a senior thesis or project, and an oral baccalaureate examination. In addition to the requirements for individual majors, students must complete eight courses within the liberal arts curriculum, with at least one course each in the humanities, social sciences, natural sciences, and diverse perspectives. Students must also meet basic proficiency in mathematics and English language and advanced proficiency in written and oral English language.

The College operates on a 4-1-4 calendar year, including a January interterm when students undertake independent study projects, such as library, laboratory, or field research; internships; and performing arts projects, all of which they design and complete under faculty sponsorship.

Off-Campus Programs

New College believes that internships, fieldwork, and independent research can make a major contribution to an undergraduate education, and facilitates such study through its flexible, individualized curriculum and special support services. New College is a member of the National Student Exchange, which provides access to nearly 200 universities with programs in the U.S. and abroad (many with comparable tuition costs) and the Consortium for Innovative Environments in Learning.

Academic Facilities

New College's Jane Bancroft Cook Library is befitting of one of the country's leading colleges for the liberal arts and sciences and has an open stack arrangement that allows free access to most materials. With a resident collection of more than 285,000 items, and unmediated access to more than 11 million items from the State University System of Florida Libraries, Cook Library provides research-level collections to students and faculty. The library also boasts access to the University of South Florida electronic collections. In total, the library has access to more than 10,000 electronic serial titles, including scholarly journals, newspapers, digital images and videos, and datasets. Through a comprehensive online interlibrary loan system, New College students have convenient access to holdings of libraries throughout the world. In addition, the library offers research instruction; digital services; data management and grant compliance services; and numerous workshops, lectures, seminars, and other offerings. Robust wireless network access is available to all users.

The Harry Sudakoff Conference Center hosts visiting lecturers, meetings of campus and community organizations, and special events. The Caples Fine Arts Complex includes the 264-seat Mildred Sainer Music and Arts Pavilion, which features student, local, and national performances; the Lota Mundy Music Building, which houses eight music practice rooms and the Benjamin and Barbara Slavin Electronic Music Studio; the Christianne Felsmann Fine Arts Building; the Betty Isermann Fine Arts Gallery and Studio; and a sculpture studio.

The R. V. Heiser Natural Sciences Complex houses laboratories, classrooms, offices, a state-of-the-art optical spectroscopy and nanomaterials laboratory, a research greenhouse, herbarium, a computer lab, two electron microscopes, and an auditorium. An $8 million addition, which will expand Heiser by 50 percent, is scheduled to open in fall 2017. The Rhoda and Jack Pritzker Marine Biology Research Center, one of the leading marine research centers in southwest Florida, features culture rooms, laboratories, and aquariums with water drawn from Sarasota Bay.

The College's 35,000 square-foot Academic Center, which opened in 2011, was awarded LEED Gold certification by the U.S. Green Building Council. It includes a state-of-the-art computer lab, classrooms, faculty offices, and a student lounge.

Costs

For the 2017–18 academic year, the estimated in-state tuition and fees at New College of Florida are $6,916 and out-of-state tuition and fees is $29,944. Room and board costs were $9,264.

Financial Aid

Most students receive scholarship funding from either New College of Florida or the New College Foundation. Approximately 96 percent of New College students receive some form of financial assistance, including academic scholarships and need-based financial aid. To apply for federal and need-based financial aid, students should file the Free Application for Federal Student Aid (FAFSA). November 1 is the priority date for need-based financial aid. No additional forms are required for most of the College's scholarship programs. New College of Florida guarantees an offer of scholarship funding to all admitted applicants with admission files completed by April 15, so long as they are US citizens or eligible non-citizens, and have not yet earned a bachelor's or advanced degree. The same deadline applies to freshmen, transfers, and internationals.

Faculty

Of New College's regular, full-time faculty members, 97 percent hold the highest degree awarded in their field of study, usually the doctorate. They come to New College from the finest universities nationally and abroad, drawn to an environment that emphasizes excellence in teaching and fosters a close-knit community of scholars. Faculty members sponsor individual students in the formulation of their academic programs, gradually moving toward a form of mentorship through which joint research is sometimes pursued. A 10:1 student-faculty ratio is a key factor in the College's individualized approach to education. At New College, all classes are taught by faculty, not by teaching assistants.

Student Government

Student input is a decisive factor in campus governance. Elected student representatives serve on the Board of Trustees and most major policymaking committees, and are voting participants in divisional and campuswide faculty meetings. The New College Student Alliance, the College's student government, has authority over funding for recreational events, social events, student clubs and organizations on campus, and allocation of the Green Fee for environmentally friendly projects.

Admission Requirements

New College of Florida seeks highly capable students eager to take responsibility for their own education. The admissions staff reviews each candidate individually, assessing his or her potential for success within, and contribution to, the College's unique environment. Course selection, academic record, and writing ability are focal points of the committee's review. Almost two-thirds (63 percent) of the first-year students entering in fall 2016 ranked in the top 20 percent of their high school class. The middle 50 percent of SAT takers had a combined score of 1150–1340 on the critical reading and math sections. The middle 50 percent of ACT takers had a composite score of 26–31.

All prospective students may apply for entrance to either the fall or the spring term. However, the College reserves the right to modify or cancel the spring admission cycle if its enrollment goals have been met. Candidates must submit an admission application, fee or fee waiver, official transcript(s), SAT or ACT scores, and a letter of recommendation. A campus visit and demonstrated interest are also recommended for all those with serious interest in applying.

Application and Information

Admissions application materials and descriptive literature are available through the New College Office of Admissions and Financial Aid. The deadline for priority admission is November 1. All students who meet this deadline will receive a decision by April 1, however some students will receive their decisions sooner. Applications will continue to be accepted on a rolling basis November 2 through April 15. Those students who apply during that time will receive their decisions on a rolling basis. A completed application and all supporting documents must be submitted to the Office of Admissions and Financial Aid before a candidate is considered for admission.

Inquiries and application requests should be directed to:

Kathleen M. Killion
Dean of Enrollment Services
New College of Florida
5800 Bay Shore Road
Sarasota, Florida 34243-2109
United States
Phone: 941-487-5000
Fax: 941-487-5001
E-mail: admissions@ncf.edu
Website: http://www.ncf.edu
http://www.facebook.com/newcollegeofflorida
http://twitter.com/NewCollegeofFL
http://www.youtube.com/user/NewCollegeofFL

New College of Florida's historic waterfront campus features spectacular sunsets, wetlands, an intertidal lagoon, and boat access.

NIAGARA UNIVERSITY

NIAGARA UNIVERSITY, NEW YORK

★ To read more about this school, visit http://petersons.to/niagarauniversity

Education That Makes a Difference

The University

Niagara University (NU), founded in 1856, is a private, comprehensive university rooted in a Catholic and Vincentian tradition. The suburban campus combines the old and new; both ivy-covered buildings and modern architectural structures line its picturesque landscape. The University is easily accessible via the New York State Thruway, both the Buffalo and Niagara Falls international airports, and rail and bus service.

There are approximately 3,200 undergraduate and 825 graduate students enrolled at Niagara. A large percentage of these students take advantage of the more than 100 extracurricular and cocurricular activities offered. Volunteer work in the community is popular among the students and enhances learning and community relations.

University sports teams compete on the Division I level and are members of the NCAA, the Metro Atlantic Athletic Conference and the Atlantic Hockey Association. Intercollegiate sports for men include baseball, basketball, cross-country, golf, ice hockey, soccer, swimming and diving, and tennis. Intercollegiate sports for women include basketball, cross-country, golf, lacrosse, outdoor track and field, soccer, softball, swimming and diving, tennis, and volleyball. Club sports include cheerleading, danceline, hockey, rugby, skiing, wrestling, and many others. The Kiernan Recreation Center offers a variety of sports and recreational facilities, including a multipurpose gymnasium, a swimming and diving pool, an indoor track, racquetball courts, free weight and Nautilus rooms, and aerobics rooms. There are several outdoor athletic fields as well as basketball and tennis courts.

Additional student services include the Student Health Center; the Office of Academic Support, which provides free tutoring services; and the Office of Career Services, which offers professional and career counseling. Other services include counseling, new student orientation, academic support, and veterans' affairs.

Niagara University's housing accommodations include five residence halls, a grouping of five small cottages, and a student apartment complex.

The University offers graduate studies in business, counseling, criminal justice, education, finance, interdisciplinary studies, sport management and a Ph.D. in leadership and policy.

Location

Niagara University's picturesque 160-acre campus is located in the town of Lewiston, New York, two minutes off the I-190 on Route 104. The campus is situated on Monteagle Ridge overlooking the lower Niagara River, which connects the two Great Lakes of Erie and Ontario. The University's suburban campus setting is just a few miles from the world-famous Niagara Falls, 20 minutes from Buffalo, which offers a variety of cultural events, sports, and entertainment opportunities, and just 90 minutes from Rochester and Toronto, Canada's largest metropolitan area. In addition, the University is minutes away from the quaint village of Lewiston, New York, and the city of Niagara Falls, New York.

Majors and Degrees

The **College of Arts and Sciences** offers the Bachelor of Arts degree in art history with museum studies, chemistry (with a concentration in environmental studies), communication studies, English, French, gerontology, history, international studies, liberal arts, life sciences, mathematics, philosophy, political science (with a concentration in environmental studies), psychology, religious studies, social sciences, sociology, and Spanish. The Bachelor of Science degree is awarded in actuarial science, biochemistry (with a concentration in bioinformatics), biology (with concentrations in bioinformatics, biotechnology, and environmental studies), chemistry (with concentrations in computational chemistry and environmental studies), computer and information sciences, criminology and criminal justice, mathematics, nursing, and social work. This division also offers the Bachelor of Fine Arts degree in theatre studies (with concentrations in performance, design and production, and theatre specializations). Preprofessional programs are offered in dentistry, law, medicine, pharmacy, veterinary medicine, and Army ROTC. An Associate of Arts degree is available in general studies. Enrichment courses in fine arts and languages are also available. A combination five-year B.S./M.S. program is available to students in the criminal justice administration program; psychology majors can engage in a six-year B.A./M.S. program in clinical mental health counseling; and an accelerated nursing program and an R.N.-to-B.S.N. program is offered for students who already have their R.N.

Preprofessional Partnerships: NU offers a number of preprofessional partnerships. These include a 3+4 partnership in pharmacy with the State University of New York at Buffalo (SUNY), a 2+3 partnership in pharmacy with Lake Erie College of Osteopathic Medicine (LECOM), a 3+4 partnership in medicine with LECOM, and a 3+4 partnership in dentistry with SUNY at Buffalo. Qualified premedical Niagara students are eligible to apply for the early assurance program sponsored by the SUNY at Buffalo.

Niagara University's **College of Business Administration** is accredited by AACSB International—The Association to Advance Collegiate Schools of Business and offers a B.B.A. and a combination B.B.A./M.B.A. degree (five-year program) in accounting. This division offers B.S. degrees in economics, finance, management (with concentrations in human resources, international business, and supply chain management), and marketing (with a concentration in food marketing), as well as a B.A. in economics. In addition, an A.A.S. degree can be earned in business. Students gain real-world experiences through internships, study abroad, and via cooperative education programs as well as research being conducted in several business-focused campus centers.

Holding the highest accreditations possible in both the United States and Canada—the United States Council for the Accreditation of Educator Preparation (CAEP) and Canada's Ontario College of Teachers—Niagara University's **College of Education** provides students with an option of earning dual certification to teach in both countries. The College of Education offers bachelor's degree programs leading to New York state initial certification in early childhood and childhood (birth–grade 6), childhood (grades 1–6), childhood and middle childhood (grades 1–9), middle childhood and adolescence (grades 5–12), adolescence (grades 7–12), special education and childhood (grades 1–6), special education and adolescence (grades 7–12), and in Teaching English to Speakers of Other Languages (TESOL). All education majors pursue an academic concentration to establish expertise in one of the following subject areas: business, English, French, liberal arts, mathematics, social studies, and Spanish. Business education is offered only for grades 5–12. The academic concentrations in biology, chemistry, or liberal arts can only be pursued in the early childhood and childhood (birth–grade 6), and special education and childhood (grades 1–6). Most other states, and Puerto Rico, have reciprocity agreements with New York, so an NU education would qualify education majors to teach in those states as well.

The **College of Hospitality and Tourism Management** provides a career-oriented curriculum leading to a B.S. degree in three specific areas: hotel and restaurant management (with concentrations in food and beverage management; luxury hospitality operations; and hotel planning, development, and operations), sport management (with concentrations in sport operations and revenue management), and tourism and recreation management (with concentrations in event and meeting management and tourism destination management). The College of Hospitality and Tourism Management offered the world's first bachelor's degree in tourism. NU's hotel and restaurant program, the second oldest in New York state, was the seventh program nationally to be accredited by the Accreditation Commission for Programs in Hospitality Administration by the Council of Hotel, Restaurant, and Institutional Education. The College introduces students to a comprehensive body of knowledge about the hotel, restaurant, tourism, and recreational areas and applies this knowledge to current industry challenges. The College requires that its students accumulate 800 hours of industry-related experience. These and other practical experiences offer NU students the knowledge necessary to advance in the field. Students work with industry leaders in classroom projects, join academic clubs and professional organizations, and participate in special trips to trade shows and conventions and specially designed study-abroad experiences, making NU a national leader in the area.

For students who are undecided about which major to choose, Niagara University offers its award-winning **Academic Exploration Program (AEP).** AEP provides a structured opportunity for students to participate in a thorough, organized process of selecting a major that meets their academic talents and career goals while fulfilling requirements to graduate with classmates on time.

Academic Programs

Niagara University's curricula enable students to pursue their academic preferences and to complete courses that lead to proficiency in other academic areas. Courses that have been considered upper-division courses are available to all students. This provides students with the opportunity to take more challenging courses early in their collegiate career. The Honors program provides special academic opportunities that stimulate, encourage, and challenge participants. In addition, an accelerated three-year degree program is offered to qualified students.

Niagara grants credit for successful scores on the Advanced Placement, College-Level Examination Program, and the International Baccalaureate tests.

Internships, research, independent study, and cooperative education are available in many academic programs. An Army ROTC program is also offered.

The University operates on a two-semester plan (fall and spring). A comprehensive summer session offers a variety of courses.

NU is fully accredited by the Middle States Association of Colleges and Schools. The University's programs in the respective areas are accredited by the Council for the Accreditation of Educator Preparation, AACSB International–The Association to Advance Collegiate Schools of Business, and the Council on Social Work Education. The chemistry department has the approval of the American Chemical Society. The travel, hotel, and restaurant administration program is accredited by the Commission for Programs in Hospitality Administration.

Off-Campus Programs

For those students who wish to study abroad, the University offers programs in Argentina, Australia, Chile, China, England, France, Ireland, Italy, Japan, Spain, Thailand, and many other countries. Students may choose from more than 200 programs in more than 30 countries available through the University's membership in the American Institute for Foreign Studies, Center for Cross-Cultural Study, College Consortium for International Studies, Global Learning Semesters, and Semester at Sea.

Academic Facilities

In recent years, Niagara University has experienced a process of transformation that has significantly developed the physical character of the University's campus and its 21st-century approach to teaching and learning.

The $33 million B. Thomas Golisano Center for Integrated Sciences offers 50,000 square-feet of learning space and cutting-edge equipment that encourages collaboration among scientific disciplines. The Academic Complex, the home to the College of Education and the College of Business Administration (Bisgrove Hall), is a state-of-the-art learning facility, with a simulated trading floor. A newly renovated and expanded Dining Commons features presentation-style cooking, a variety of comfortable seating options, and bold colors and design elements that create an inviting environment for NU students to gather and enjoy meals.

Dunleavy Hall includes a computerized lecture hall and TV production rooms. The University's facilities also include the Gallagher Center, NU's student union and home court of Purple Eagles D-I athletics; the Computer Center; St. Vincent's Hall; the Kiernan Center, NU's athletic and recreation center; the Elizabeth Ann Clune Center for Theatre; the Castellani Art Museum; and Dwyer Arena, a dual-rink ice hockey complex.

The University's library supports student learning and knowledge creation by providing assistance and access to online and print information resources, technology, and individual and collaborative work and study space. Assistance is available in person and via online chat, text, email, and phone. The library's main floor is open 24 hours a day during the school year.

Costs

Tuition for 2016–17 was $29,500. Room and board (with a choice of meal plans) cost an additional $12,700 per year. Fees were estimated at $1,450 per year. Niagara estimates that an additional $2,500 to $3,050 per year is adequate for books, laundry, and other essentials, such as travel to and from home.

Financial Aid

Ninety-nine percent of the entering freshmen and transfer students received a financial aid package which may include merit-based scholarships, loans, grants, or campus employment. Students seeking financial aid should file the Free Application for Federal Student Aid (FAFSA). New York state residents should also file a Tuition Assistance Program (TAP) application.

Faculty

Niagara University has a dedicated, accessible faculty that genuinely cares about the academic and personal growth of their students. Their commitment to teaching is their primary concern. A student-to-faculty ratio of 13:1 and an average class size of approximately 19 allow personal attention and classroom interaction.

Admission Requirements

The University welcomes men and women who have demonstrated aptitude and academic achievement at the high school level. Either SAT or ACT test scores are required. International students are required to submit the results of their TOEFL examination and a translation of their academic documentation. Interviews are recommended. Transfer students are accepted in any semester. (Transfer credit is evaluated individually by the dean of each division.) Students who complete high school in less than four years are eligible for early admission. Students may also apply under an early action program. Economically and educationally disadvantaged students from New York State are eligible to apply for admission through the Higher Educational Opportunity Program (HEOP).

Application and Information

Niagara operates on a rolling admission basis and adheres to the College Board Candidates Reply Date. Nursing and theatre applicants are encouraged to apply by mid-December of their senior year. A visit to the campus is recommended, and overnight accommodations in a residence hall are available through the Niagara Nights program.

Information on all aspects of the University can be obtained by contacting the Office of Admissions or by visiting www.niagara.edu.

Mark Wojnowski
Director of Admissions
Niagara University
Niagara University, New York 14109-2011
Phone: 716-286-8700
800-462-2111 (toll-free)
Fax: 716-286-8710
E-mail: admissions@niagara.edu
Website: http://www.niagara.edu
http://www.facebook.com/niagarau
http://twitter.com/niagarauniv
http://instagram.com/NiagaraUniversity

Adjacent to the international border between the United States and Canada, Niagara University's 160-acre campus runs along the top of picturesque Monteagle Ridge, overlooking the Niagara River gorge just 4 miles north of the world-famous waterfalls.

NORTHEASTERN UNIVERSITY

Northeastern University

BOSTON, MASSACHUSETTS

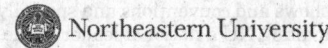

★ To read more about this school, visit http://petersons.to/northeasternuniv

The University

There's a certain energy about Northeastern University. It comes from the bright, ambitious students, exhibiting a strong sense of purpose in the classroom and while working or studying abroad. In the city of Boston—the ultimate college town—and across the globe, Northeastern students challenge themselves intellectually, investigate career options, participate in community service, and graduate both personally and professionally prepared for their future careers and graduate school.

Northeastern is a leader in interdisciplinary research, urban engagement, and the seamless integration of classroom learning with real-world experiences. The academic curriculum is enhanced by experiential learning opportunities including undergraduate research, professional work experience, global programs, and service learning options. Anchored by the world's largest, most innovative cooperative education program, Northeastern prepares students for a lifetime of achievement.

The current undergraduate enrollment of 17,923 is made up of students of all backgrounds and interests, giving Northeastern its distinctive culture. Students can join a cultural club, participate in cutting-edge research with faculty from various disciplines, or perform with an award winning a capella group. They can travel to nearby New Hampshire or Vermont for a ski club trip, play varsity or club basketball, tutor children in the community, volunteer at a local soup kitchen, and more. Students have countless opportunities to make lifelong friendships, to try something brand new—a class, a sport, or a career path—to hone their leadership skills, and have fun. Quiet corners of the campus feel far from city streets and give students a secluded haven to read, write, or relax in and around the 73-acre campus, a dynamic and welcoming stretch of leafy green in the heart of Boston.

Location

Northeastern's residential campus is located in the center of Boston, where the distinctive neighborhoods of the Back Bay, South End, Fenway, and Roxbury meet. Over half of the student body lives on campus and many of the residence halls have amazing views of the Boston skyline.

The Back Bay area, known for its many cultural and educational institutions, is just steps away from Symphony Hall, the New England Conservatory of Music, the Museum of Fine Arts, and the Isabella Stewart Gardner Museum. The South End is home to elegant Victorian row houses, a vibrant arts scene, hidden gardens, and some of the finest dining in Boston. The Fenway area, with its beautiful rose garden, bicycle and jogging paths, and Fenway Park (home of the Boston Red Sox) is also just a few blocks away.

Majors and Degrees

Northeastern's undergraduate programs are divided among eight colleges.

The College of Arts, Media and Design awards degrees in architecture; arts, media arts and design; communication studies; game design; journalism; media and screen studies; as well as music/music industry; music composition and technology; studio art; and theatre.

The D'Amore-McKim School of Business offers two degree options: the Bachelor of Science in Business Administration (B.S.B.A.) and the Bachelor of Science in International Business (B.S.I.B.), which includes language instruction as well as international study and work. D'Amore-McKim offers concentrations in accounting; entrepreneurship and innovation; finance; international business, with six concentrations; management; management information systems; marketing; and supply chain management.

The College of Computer and Information Science awards degrees in computer science and information science and also offers combined majors that pair computer science with biology; business; cognitive psychology; communication studies; computer engineering; cyber operations; digital art; environmental science; game design; interactive media; journalism; mathematics; music; music composition and technology; and physics; and pair information science with business; cognitive psychology; environmental science; and journalism.

The College of Engineering offers degrees in bioengineering; chemical; civil; computer; electrical; industrial; and mechanical engineering.

The Bouvé College of Health Sciences awards degrees in health science; nursing; pharmacy; and physical therapy. The college also offers a six-year Doctor of Pharmacy degree and a six-year program leading to a Doctor of Physical Therapy.

The College of Science awards degrees in applied physics; behavioral neuroscience; biochemistry; biology; biomedical physics; chemistry; environmental science; environmental studies; linguistics; marine biology; mathematics; physics; and psychology.

The College of Social Sciences and Humanities awards undergraduate degrees in African American studies; American Sign Language; Asian studies; criminal justice; cultural anthropology; economics; English; history; human services; international affairs; Jewish studies (combined major only); philosophy; political science; religious studies; sociology; and Spanish.

The Explore Program for undeclared students offers a wide array of academic opportunities designed to help students who want to explore their options before committing to any major(s). The program provides the support and guidance students need to discover and eventually choose one of Northeastern's undergraduate programs.

Academic Programs

Award-winning faculty mentors are at the heart of a Northeastern education, as well as a rigorous and innovative curriculum, undergraduate research opportunities, and global and professional experiences that challenge and transform. Northeastern's innovative programs encompass a wide range of majors, concentrations, and interdisciplinary studies along with honors, preprofessional, and study-abroad programs.

Northeastern's approach to educating its students is to integrate a challenging academic curriculum with experiential learning opportunities including research, global experiences, service learning, and the university's signature cooperative education program (co-op), enabling students to make deep connections between their field of study and the world around them. At Northeastern, Rigorous Academics + Immersive Experiences = Experiential Learning.

After completing their first year, Northeastern students integrate classroom learning with immersive six-month periods of full-time professional work, global study, service, or research experiences related to their major or interests. Northeastern's flexibility enables students to choose a four- or five-year path with up to eighteen months of experience, strengthening their professional network and giving them confidence—and a significant edge in the job market. Students learn what career is a good fit for them—and what careers are not—all before graduating. In addition, half the students are offered full-time jobs from co-op employers.

Northeastern partners with over 3,350 co-op employers around the globe, including some of the world's largest and most reputable companies: Pfizer, John Hancock, Google, Fidelity Investments, ESPN, IBM, General Electric, Massachusetts General Hospital, Microsoft, NASA, Disney, and the Boston Globe, just to name a few.

Experiential learning opportunities have been available in 134 countries around the world since 2006.

The University Honors Program allows a select group of students to participate in enriched opportunities and offers experiences that include honors sections of academic courses, seminars, independent research, and specialized study abroad programs.

The University Scholars Program is Northeastern's most prestigious scholarship program. Every scholar is provided with broad access to the university and the opportunity to design a tailored program that potentially spans colleges, departments, and global partner institutions to address each scholar's unique academic goals and career aspirations, as well as to advance their entrepreneurial ideas.

Academic Facilities

Northeastern is home to over 50 research centers and undergraduates have ample opportunities to work alongside their professors to aid and conduct research on a variety of topics. The new 220,000 square-foot Interdisciplinary Science and Engineering Complex will further evolve Northeastern's research enterprise by providing state-of-the-art infrastructure and fostering collaboration across disciplines.

The university library system is comprised of Snell Library, a 240,000 square-foot central library on the Boston campus, the School of Law Library, and a small supplemental collection at the Nahant Marine Science Center. Snell Library houses 780,669 print volumes, 548,806 e-books, 1,163,735 microform units, and access to 83,511 licensed electronic journals, as well as 23,437 audio, video, and computer software items, and 5,712 linear feet of archival material as of June 2014.

Northeastern University provides a broad range of academic and administrative computer resources to students, faculty, and staff members. Many computing resources are available, including an extensive wireless network, technology-assisted classrooms, computer labs, and the myNEU Admitted Student Portal, which allows students to access many administrative and academic functions online.

Costs

For 2016–17, tuition was $46,720, and room and board fees were $15,050. Regardless of time to degree, tuition is charged only while students are earning course credit.

Financial Aid

The university operates a substantial aid program designed to make attendance feasible for all qualified students. By coordinating the resources of the university and various public and private scholarship programs, the Office of Student Financial Services was able to provide more than $253.8 million in grant and scholarship assistance this past year. More than 75 percent of students receive some form of financial aid. Northeastern participates in all federal aid programs. Financial aid is based on need and academic merit and may consist of grants, loans, work-study employment, or any combination of the three. To apply, students must file the Free Application for Federal Student Aid (FAFSA) and a CSS PROFILE form with the College Scholarship Service by the priority filing date of February 15.

Faculty

The university has more than 1,200 full-time faculty members with a wide variety of research and teaching interests and specialties. Academic advisers in each college work closely with students to assist them in developing programs suited to their interests and abilities. Co-op advisers assist students in resume-building, honing interview skills and tactics, and developing contacts with businesses and employers to support networking and professional opportunities.

Admission Requirements

Students may enter the university with advanced credit on the basis of test scores on Advanced Placement (AP) examinations, the International Baccalaureate (I.B.) examinations, or with successful completion of accredited college-level courses. In addition to the application for admission, prospective freshmen must submit official high school transcript(s) (or official GED score reports); official transcripts for any college-level coursework taken while a secondary-school student; written recommendations from their secondary school counselor and a teacher; and scores from the SAT (Northeastern's College Board code is 3667) or ACT, including the writing section. Please visit the university's website for additional admission details for specific student populations and transfer admissions requirements (northeastern.edu/admissions).

Application and Information

Admission to Northeastern is selective and competitive. For the freshman class entering in Fall 2016, the university received approximately 51,000 applications for 2,800 seats in the freshman class. Students are reviewed in the context of their environment, with attention paid to their academic course selection and rigor, academic achievement, extracurricular involvement and impact, and their potential fit with Northeastern, including the demonstration of personal traits like leadership, adaptability, a global perspective, or an entrepreneurial spirit.

November 1 is the deadline for both the Early Action admission program and the binding Early Decision program. Students who have carefully explored their college options and have decided that Northeastern is where they want to enroll may choose to apply under the Early Decision program. Admitted Early Decision students are required to pay a deposit by January 15. The deadline for the regular admission program is January 1. Admitted students are required to pay a deposit by May 1 to secure a place in the class. For transfer students, the admission deadlines are April 1 for fall and October 1 for spring admission. Fall transfer and spring admission decisions are made on a space-available basis and are released online by June 15.

Northeastern offers a variety of visit options including information sessions and campus tours. For more information, or to register, visit northeastern.edu/admissions/connect/visit.

For more information, students should contact:

Office of Undergraduate Admissions
240 West Village F
Northeastern University
360 Huntington Avenue
Boston, Massachusetts 02115
Phone: 617-373-2200
E-mail: admissions@northeastern.edu
Website: northeastern.edu/admissions

Northeastern's campus skyline and Centennial Common, a typical quad where students relax, study, and hang out with friends.

NORTHERN ARIZONA UNIVERSITY

FLAGSTAFF, ARIZONA

★ To read more about this school, visit http://petersons.to/nau

The University

Founded in 1899, Northern Arizona University (NAU) is a fully accredited four-year public university centered on students. For those interested in a collaborative community with a breadth of stellar programs and a dedicated research agenda, NAU offers a comfortable university environment ideal for academic achievement, personal growth, professional outcomes, and adventure.

The university's Flagstaff campus offers the amenities of a big-campus environment with a small-campus feel—all in a beautiful mountain location that ranks among the best college towns in the nation. NAU also has innovative partnerships with dozens of Arizona community colleges, which gives students affordable and convenient options for transferring into an NAU bachelor's degree program.

NAU offers a comprehensive range of nearly 100 majors to choose from and many nationally ranked programs, taught by professors who recognize potential and will help students realize theirs. Students have an abundance of opportunities to participate in important research and creative and scholarly projects alongside faculty who bring their focus to their labs and their passion to the classrooms. Nearly 3,000 undergraduates participate in research and professional internships each year, placing them shoulder-to-shoulder at the brink of discovery. High-achieving students can even work simultaneously on select master's degrees and graduate in as few as five years with both a bachelor's and a master's degree. And students can find everything they need to accomplish their goals, including programs and support services—from enrollment to graduation and beyond.

NAU also delivers a predictable price tag through its fixed tuition rate, known as The Pledge. Students who attend the Flagstaff campus will pay the same fixed tuition rate for up to four years with a no-increases guarantee. Students who live in one of 14 Western states can save nearly 40 percent on the out-of-state tuition rate through the Western Undergraduate Exchange (WUE). Every major is eligible for the WUE rate.

Location

With a population of around 70,000, Flagstaff is a vibrant high-elevation mountain town that breaks the Arizona stereotype. Temperatures rarely exceed 90 degrees in the summer, fall brings a brilliant change of color, winter snowfall averages more than 100 inches, and spring bursts with blossoms. The region's unparalleled natural scenery is enhanced by hundreds of great restaurants and a robust arts and entertainment scene. The four-season climate provides recreational opportunities that range from scenic hiking and biking to skiing and snowboarding. The campus sits just 75 miles south of the Grand Canyon—close enough that studies might bring students there to collect water samples from the Colorado River, discuss issues related to Native populations, participate in interactive painting workshops, or explore the art and culture of the region.

Flagstaff's charm, location, and recreational opportunities consistently pull in top honors and distinctions from national publications. Time.com named it one of the nation's happiest cities, and the American Institute for Economic Research's 2017 College Destinations Index named Flagstaff the No. 1 Best College Town in Arizona and No. 3 in the nation. *Outside Magazine* also has named Flagstaff among the best places to live in the United States. Prospective students can explore some of the most popular local sights through NAU's new, fully immersive online regional tour: nau.edu/explore.

In addition to Northern Arizona University's Flagstaff campus, NAU also has dozens of statewide locations, providing a convenient way for students to complete an NAU degree at an Arizona community college. Online options also allow students to take classes that work with their schedule.

Academics

NAU offers nearly 100 bachelor's degrees, about 50 master's degrees, 14 doctoral degrees, and a wide range of minors, certificates, and emphases, so students are sure to find a program that's right for them. Majors and programs are organized by academic discipline under eight colleges: the College of Arts and Letters; the College of Education; the College of Engineering, Forestry, and Natural Sciences; the College of Health and Human Services; the College of Social and Behavioral Sciences; The W. A. Franke College of Business; the Honors College; and the Graduate College. Some of the university's most popular majors include criminology and criminal justice, biomedical science, nursing, and mechanical engineering.

Through the Honors College, students can pursue a rewarding and enriching academic path that emphasizes small, interactive classes where students gain critical-thinking skills that appeal to employers and graduate schools. Academically motivated students are inspired by the meaningful engagement found by living and working among a group of motivated students who share a passion for learning.

To complete a bachelor's degree at NAU, students must complete 120 units of credit, including all liberal studies and capstone requirements, and all requirements for a student's specific academic plan. Other requirements, such as transfer credit restrictions and minimum GPA, also apply. Detailed information can be found at nau.edu/academics.

Beyond the Classroom

A degree from NAU represents a quality educational experience—one that incorporates a practical learning approach beyond any textbook. Nearly 600 NAU students each year travel to partner institutions in one of 61 foreign countries for a study-abroad experience. Those wishing to stay closer to home can study at one of 200 U.S. institutions through the National Student Exchange program. An internationalization strategy at NAU incorporates global cultures into every discipline. And the Interdisciplinary Global Programs in Business, Engineering, and International Affairs infuse language, culture, and a year abroad into students' studies—participants graduate with two degrees: one in their field of study and one in their chosen foreign language.

A signature of the NAU undergraduate experience is a focus on engaged and active learning. Nearly 3,000 undergraduates each year work alongside skilled faculty and mentors who provide practical research opportunities. More than 1,000 students convene each spring for the Undergraduate Symposium, a large-scale event where students share their research and discoveries and present scholarly and creative work to their peers, professors, and the Flagstaff community.

NAU also takes advantage of its prime location with world-class outdoor education opportunities. An interdisciplinary Grand Canyon semester offers students immersion in the science, culture, and politics of one of the truly unique regions of the U.S. Flagstaff is the world's first International Dark Sky City and offers unparalleled night skies and stargazing facilities for astronomical research, including the Discovery Channel Telescope, the world's fifth-largest. And the 50,000-acre Centennial Forest offers forestry majors and students in other environmental studies programs the chance to conduct research and practice maintenance of a variety of ecosystems.

Facilities

With nearly 90 percent of freshmen choosing to live on campus, students begin to build their community the moment they arrive at NAU. They can even choose to live in one of 30 on-campus Learning Communities with others who share their interests or academic major. Multiple Academic Success Centers on campus provide distinct types of tutoring, most at no cost. And the 225,000-square-foot Cline Library offers an array of services, research materials, and study spaces, and students can reserve rooms, check out laptops, and get help with technology or writing.

The visually striking, five-story Science and Health Building serves as a symbol of the university's rise to scientific and research prominence. This is where students interested in medicine, dentistry, research, or science education will take some of their first steps toward a professional career. The university's one-of-a-kind Native American Cultural Center was built with input from 22 tribes and reflects NAU's commitment to Native American students and to helping others learn more about these cultures.

NAU's new Aquatic and Tennis Complex attracts international athletes and Olympic teams for high-altitude training, and a world-class recreation facility at the Health and Learning Center offers a 38-foot climbing wall, an indoor jogging track, a fully equipped weight room, cardio, and much more.

A visit to campus is the best way to learn more about the university's impressive facilities; for those who can't make it to Flagstaff in person, NAU's online virtual tour is the next best thing: nau.edu/virtualtour.

Costs

NAU tuition and fees for 2017–18 are $11,059 per academic year for Arizona residents and $24,841 for nonresidents. Under the Western Undergraduate Exchange (WUE) program, students from 14 qualifying states pay a tuition rate nearly 40 percent lower than the out-of-state rate. The 2017–18 WUE tuition and fee rate is $16,078 per academic year. Tuition rates are set each spring by the Arizona Board of Regents. Room, board, books, transportation, and personal expenses vary by student and are not included in the tuition costs.

NAU makes financial planning for college easier with The Pledge, a four-year fixed-tuition guarantee. Students who attend on the Flagstaff campus will pay the same fixed-tuition rate for up to four years. In addition, students with a meal plan will have the same rates for up to two years. More details of The Pledge can be found at nau.edu/pledge.

Financial Aid

Students are automatically considered for merit scholarships when they apply and have submitted their test scores. Arizona residents might be eligible for the Lumberjack Scholars Award, which covers up to 100 percent of the cost of in-state tuition. Nonresidents might be eligible for a number of awards including the President's Excellence Scholarship, valued at $36,000 over four years. NAU's friendly financial aid staff is available to help students explore other opportunities such as private scholarships, grants, and loans in order to make their education as affordable as possible. More details regarding financial aid can be found at nau.edu/finaid.

Faculty

Northern Arizona University is designed for discovery. The faculty and staff care about student success and encourage students to push past their limits and develop new strengths. From biology to social sciences, professors weave interactive learning into NAU's curriculum, providing students with the hands-on experience they need to succeed and opportunities to make original contributions to a field of study.

NAU professors from a variety of disciplines are among the leading experts in their fields, such as astronomy professor David Trilling, who is one of the world's foremost asteroid researchers and works on several NASA-funded projects investigating hundreds of asteroids, including those that could strike Earth. Biology professor Kiisa Nishikawa's muscle function theory is improving prosthetic devices and neuromuscular disease treatment. And entomology professor Rich Hofstetter studies how loud rock music might slow the infestation of bark beetles, which destroy pine trees and increase wildfire danger in Southwestern forests.

Student Clubs and Organizations

Getting involved in campus life is one of the best ways students can gain leadership skills and define their own NAU experience. Northern Arizona University offers more than 350 clubs and organizations ranging from sport clubs and intramurals to sororities and fraternities. There is also a wide range of leadership, academic, and service organizations related to almost every hobby, passion, or academic interest students might have.

Studies have shown that students who are involved in campus activities are more likely to be successful; it's also a great way to meet new friends. NAU students can join organizations such as First Jacks, which empowers first-generation college students toward personal and academic success; or find a sense of *Ohana*, or family, with the HAPA Hawaiian Club. The university's thriving intramural sports program ranges from favorites such as basketball and soccer to unique sports such as Canoe Battleship and even Quidditch. NAU's ultra-competitive ice hockey team, the IceJacks, is one of nearly 40 club sports and ranks among the top teams in the American Collegiate Hockey Association's Western region. Whatever a student's interest, pursuits, or background, there is a club or organization offering a sense of community and a chance to get involved.

Admission Requirements and Application Information

NAU applicants will be offered admission if they demonstrate a 3.0 high school core GPA and have no deficiencies in the 16 required college preparatory courses. Students will be considered for admission if they have a 2.5 high school core GPA and no more than one deficiency in any two areas of the college preparatory courses.

Students can apply online. They are required to access their high school transcripts and self-report them on the online application. A $25 application fee is required, and NAU also requests that students send ACT and/or SAT scores in order to be considered for scholarships. Deadlines and additional details are available online at nau.edu/admissions.

Northern Arizona University
Undergraduate Admissions and Orientation
P.O. Box 4084
Student and Academic Services Building (#60)
Flagstaff, Arizona 86011-4084
Phone: 888-628-2968 (toll-free)
Fax: 928-523-6023
E-mail: admissions@nau.edu
Website: nau.edu

Students enjoy the sights and seclusion of the scenic third-floor study lounge at NAU's Health and Learning Center.

NORTHERN KENTUCKY UNIVERSITY

HIGHLAND HEIGHTS, KENTUCKY

NKU NORTHERN KENTUCKY UNIVERSITY

COLLEGE CLOSE-UPS

The University

Northern Kentucky University (NKU) was founded in 1968 and is the newest of Kentucky's eight state universities. Nestled in a quiet suburb, NKU is just minutes from the entertainment and career opportunities of downtown Cincinnati. NKU has an enrollment of more than 14,500 students from forty-five states and fifty-nine countries and is accredited by the Southern Association of Colleges and Schools. The Salmon P. Chase College of Law is accredited by both the American Bar Association and the Association of American Law Schools.

There are more than 220 student organizations and NKU's athletic teams compete in the NCAA Division I Horizon League Conference. Intercollegiate sports are offered for men and women in basketball, cross-country, track, golf, soccer, and tennis; for men in baseball; and for women in fast-pitch softball and volleyball. Intramural activities vary by semester, but include basketball, dodgeball, field hockey, flag football, ice hockey, racquetball, soccer, softball, taekwando, volleyball, and many others. A complete list can be found online at http://campusrec.nku.edu.

Majors and Degrees

NKU offers 72 bachelor's degrees; 6 associate degrees; 24 graduate programs; and the Juris Doctor, the Doctor of Education in Educational Leadership, and the Doctor of Nursing Practice degree, as well as 28 graduate certificates.

Academic Programs

NKU operates on a semester calendar. To receive a bachelor's degree, students must complete a minimum of 120 credit hours. At least 60 credit hours are required for the associate degree.

The University offers a variety of career planning and placement, internship, independent study, work-study, and cooperative-education programs. There is also an advising, counseling, and testing Center available. Other programs include an honors program, a program that allows for the dual enrollment of high school students, a program where students can combine their career interests in the liberal arts and engineering fields, and University 101, an orientation program for freshmen and transfer students.

NKU recognizes credit earned through the Advanced Placement (AP) Program and the general, subject, and institutional tests of specific College-Level Examination Program (CLEP). A maximum of 45 credit hours may be applied toward the bachelor's degree from the AP and CLEP examinations. The International Baccalaureate program allows students to earn credit in science, mathematics, psychology, and languages.

Off-Campus Programs

More than 330 students participated in study-abroad programs in twenty-six countries worldwide.

Academic Facilities

Among the academic facilities at NKU are an anthropology museum, a biology museum, and an art gallery with rotating exhibits. NKU also has a laser projection planetarium; laboratories for nursing, respiratory care, and radiologic technology; the 9,000-seat BB&T Arena; and the James C. and Rachel M. Votruba Student Union, a student-centered facility, and focal point for campus programs and student organizations.

NKU's Griffin Hall, the home of the College of Informatics, is designed to help students interested in communication and media, computer science, information technology, or management information systems become the new generation of professionals who will build the region's information economy. The W. Frank Steely Library contains 311,155 book titles and maintains 1,729 paper periodical subscriptions (additional periodicals are available in electronic format). Computer laboratories offer students opportunities to learn and utilize a variety of software programs. The Computer Science Department and Criminal Justice Department have collaborated to offer students a computer forensics minor to teach students how to handle digital evidence and how to present such evidence in court.

Costs

Tuition and fees for 2016-2017 were $9,000 for Kentucky students, $13,608 for metro students, and $18,000 for nonresidents. Other costs included $7,500–$9,500 for room and meals, about $850 for books and supplies, and $3,000 for miscellaneous expenses.

Financial Aid

Northern Kentucky University awards more than $6 million in academic scholarships each year to the incoming freshman class. The University awards scholarships to highly motivated students who demonstrate strong academic performance. Students who achieve a 2.5 GPA and a 21 ACT or 1060

SAT are considered for academic awards. The University offers numerous scholarship levels. Each scholarship level has merit guidelines that students must meet to qualify. To be considered to academic scholarships, interested students need to apply for admission by February 15 (based on availability of funds). For fall 2017, there is no separate scholarship application for general Northern Kentucky University academic scholarships. Students who qualify for a scholarship receive an award letter upon acceptance to NKU. Prospective students can visit scholarships.nku.edu for information on additional scholarship opportunities that require an application, letters of recommendation, or an essay. There is no deadline for the University's financial aid application; however, students who wish to receive institutional aid must apply by February 1 for priority consideration. Applicants are notified of acceptance on a rolling basis.

Faculty

More than 82 percent of the faculty members at NKU hold a doctoral degree or the terminal degree in their field. Classes are small, with an average class size of 24 and a student-faculty ratio of 17:1. All classes are taught by faculty members; no classes are taught by graduate assistants.

Student Government

Student Government (SG) is the elected student assembly at Northern Kentucky University. It is the official student voice on campus and represents the student viewpoint on University committees. All SG meetings are open, and students are encouraged to attend.

Admission Requirements

Incoming freshmen must submit an application for admission; arrange for the official ACT, SAT, or COMPASS score report to be sent; and request that the high school send an official transcript. In order to be considered for regular admission, a student must meet precollege curriculum requirements for Kentucky and institutional admission standards. Out-of-state applicants must also meet the Kentucky precollege curriculum requirements.

Based on the review of official test results and the precollege curriculum, students are admitted into one of two categories: regular admission or admission with conditions. Students who have two or more deficiencies are encouraged to retake the ACT or SAT so an additional review can be completed. Students with two or more deficiencies may be asked to submit an essay, letters of recommendation, and an activities portfolio before an admission decision can be rendered. Students with two or more deficiencies who are offered admission will be required to participate in the Pathfinders Program, which is designed to enhance student engagement and provide tools needed for future academic achievement. The program includes: mandatory advising, completion of University 101 (Introduction to College) course, participation in study tables, tutoring, and college success workshops. Some degree programs require that students meet additional criteria; more information is available in the current catalog (http://www.nku.edu).

Application and Information

The $40 paper application fee may be waived for applicants with demonstrated need. The fall semester early action and scholarship deadline is February 15, assured consideration deadline is February 15, enrollment confirmation deadline is May 1, and the final deadline is July 1. The priority application deadline for the nursing program is January 31. The priority application deadline for the respiratory care program is February 15.

For more information, students should contact:
Office of Admissions
Northern Kentucky University
Highland Heights, Kentucky 41099
Phone: 859-572-5220
800-637-9948 (toll-free)
E-mail: admitnku@nku.edu
Website: http://admissions.nku.edu
http://www.facebook.com/nkuedu
http://twitter.com.nkuedu

Northern Kentucky University's modern campus is set in Highland Heights, just minutes from downtown Cincinnati.

NOTRE DAME COLLEGE

SOUTH EUCLID, OHIO

★ To read more about this school, visit http://petersons.to/notredamecollege

NOTRE DAME COLLEGE

The College

Notre Dame College (NDC) provides a career-focused liberal arts education, so students are prepared to be successful in their chosen fields; service learning and a values-based curriculum, so students get real-world work experience; and caring personal attention in the classroom and in extracurricular activities, so students develop as innovative spirits.

Founded as an all-women's school in 1922 by the Sisters of Notre Dame, the College has grown strategically to keep pace with the changing needs of students and the dramatic changes in higher education. Notre Dame became coeducational in 2001 and since then, total enrollment has since grown from 875 to 2,100. But it has never lost sight its focus on helping students succeed in school, contribute to their communities, deepen their respect for others, and become good citizens for life.

With a strong foundation in the liberal arts, Notre Dame offers a wide variety of majors and programs delivered in ways that meet the needs for flexibility and convenience of today's students. From the traditional on-campus course offerings and the rich student life experiences they provide, to online and evening classes for adults, veterans, part-time and degree-completion students, the needs of the student in a complex work, study, and family environment are supported with the same personal attention for which the College has always been known.

Today, Notre Dame College offers stimulating academics, personalized attention, small class sizes, NCAA Division II intercollegiate athletics and active student life programs. A snapshot of the fall 2016 traditional NDC student population shows: 45 percent female, 55 percent male; 55 percent Catholic; 28 percent minority; 55 percent student-athletes; 81 percent of freshmen applicants are accepted for admission. The student body represents 35 states and 21 foreign countries.

Notre Dame College is fully accredited by the Higher Learning Commission, the National Association of Independent Colleges and Universities (NAICU), the American Association of Colleges for Teacher Education, the National Council for Accreditation of Teacher Education (NCATE), and the Ohio Board of Regents.

Location

Located in South Euclid, Ohio, the 48-acre campus is in a residential neighborhood just 25 minutes from downtown Cleveland and all the excitement and cultural wealth of the city, such as the Rock and Roll Hall of Fame and Museum, the Cleveland Metroparks, several professional sports teams, and University Circle, one of the richest cultural, theatrical, entertainment, healthcare, and employment regions in the nation. Only five minutes from Legacy Village and Beachwood Place, Cleveland's lifestyle retail centers, the area combines all the opportunities of a major urban and educational center with the relaxed atmosphere of a suburb.

The beautiful campus provides the perfect setting for the Clara Fritzsche Library; the historic Administration Building; the Regina Complex, which houses classrooms, offices, a gym, and an auditorium; Connelly Center, the dining hall and student center; Keller Center, the recreational and fitness facility; and five residence halls that house 655 students, including two newer apartment-style facilities for upperclass students.

Majors and Degrees

The College offers majors in 30 disciplines and confers associate, bachelor's, and master's degrees in arts and humanities, business administration, education, nursing and science and mathematics. The full list of academic majors and programs is online at NotreDameCollege.edu/academics.

Academic Programs

A signature program at Notre Dame is the Academic Support Center for Students with Learning Differences (ASC), an advocacy program for students diagnosed with ADD, ADHD, or dyslexia, a group traditionally underserved in postsecondary education. Through the ASC, students have access to quality educational opportunities and support services necessary to be successful in the collegiate environment. The ASC has been recognized nationally by Milestones Autism Organization, the International Dyslexia Association (IDA), and the Learning Disabilities Foundation of America. In addition, the College's Division of Education is endorsed by the IDA for its curriculum that prepares educators to teach reading to students who are dyslexic.

Notre Dame College launched The FirstGen Center in 2015, an innovative mentoring initiative designed to provide support to undergraduates who are the first in their families to attend college. Nationwide, this represents a large number of students whose likelihood of making it to graduation is very low. The FirstGen Center's comprehensive mentoring program aims to significantly boost graduation rates by providing resources, support services and a network of 'first responders' to help students persist to graduation and successfully transition from college to career.

The Enterprise Development Center, also established in 2015, creates paid on-campus internship experiences for Notre Dame students in all majors and off-campus internship experiences working with local high- and low-tech startups and small businesses.

For the bachelor's degree, students must earn between 120 and 128 semester hours of credit, depending on the program of study, with a minimum cumulative grade point average of 2.0. From 36 to 68 semester hours of credit are required in the major field of study. Through a cooperative education program, students can earn a maximum of 6 credit hours for paid or volunteer work experience related to their academic field of study. All students are required to complete a coop or internship experience.

Advanced Placement credit is awarded to students who have demonstrated the ability to pursue coursework beyond the level of entering freshmen, as indicated by their scores on the Advanced Placement (AP) or College-Level Examination Program (CLEP) tests of the College Board. College credit is given on the basis of a decision made jointly by the academic dean and the department involved.

Academic Facilities

The Career Services Center coordinates jobs and internships for students and interacts with faculty to create meaningful programs that link academics to the workplace. It further offers graduate school advising, resume preparation assistance, interviewing and job search coaching, posting of positions available, and a resource library. On-campus recruiting opportunities attract scores of employers to the College to meet students firsthand.

The Clara Fritzsche Library houses a modern media center and has a capacity for 100,000 volumes. As a member of OhioLINK, the College also has online access to members throughout the state, with access to more than 31 million library items and more than 90 research databases.

The Dwyer Success Center consists of an electronic classroom, a student computer lab, a writing lab, a test proctoring room and a tutoring room. The writing lab is staffed by English faculty who provide professional writing assistance to students free of charge. The tutoring room is staffed with graduate assistants and upperclass peer tutors for one-on-one study skills and subject specific assistance.

The multimedia lab for graphic design majors offers PC and Macintosh technology for advanced multimedia production capabilities.

The Finn Center for Adult, Graduate, Online, and Professional Programs unifies all aspects of adult education at NDC, providing convenient, flexible programs for educational advancement on days, nights, weekends, and the Web.

Costs

For the 2016–17 academic year tuition and fee charges were $28,300. Room and board costs were $9,550 for double occupancy and a full meal plan.

Financial Aid

A comprehensive financial assistance program of more than $25 million assists more than 95 percent of all full-time students and includes: federal grants, federal work-study, federal Perkins loans, federal student loan programs; the State of Ohio's College Opportunity Grant (OCOG); and Notre Dame College grants and scholarships.

Faculty

The College has 59 full-time faculty members, augmented by highly qualified instructors. Faculty members hold advanced degrees from more than thirty universities in the United States, Canada, and Europe. The student-faculty ratio is 16:1.

Student Life

The College is a living community with a variety of clubs and organizations that enrich the overall student experience and offer leadership development and experience. Performing arts programs, social activities, intramurals and fitness, and cultural and intellectual pursuits ensure every student has many opportunities to get involved.

Campus Ministry promotes the spiritual growth of the College community and facilitates community service and programs that provide students many opportunities to serve at local charities and national programs such as Habitat for Humanity.

The Notre Dame College Falcon athletic program offers 25 scholarship sports for men and women; 21 of these sports compete in the NCAA Division II Mountain East Conference. Among many athletic accolades of note, just since 2014, the College's wrestling team won the 2014 and 2016 NCAA Division II National Championship; the women's golf team won the 2014 MEC Tournament for the first time in program history; the women's soccer team won the 2014 MEC Tournament and advanced to the NCAA Tournament for the first time in program history; the men's soccer team advanced to the NCAA Tournament for the second time in as many years; and both the men's and women's rugby teams qualified for the Final Four of the ACRA National Tournament, with the women's team winning the National Championship in 2015 and men's team in 2016.

Admission Requirements

A Notre Dame looks for a diversity of students, ranging in religious, racial, educational and socioeconomic backgrounds. The college welcomes undergraduates and graduates, adult and high school dual-enrollment students, residents of Ohio and residents of other states and countries, and those with interests ranging from academics to athletics to campus clubs and more.

Candidates for admission as first-time, full-time freshmen are reviewed on an individual basis, and decisions are based on a broad range of criteria. The most important considerations are the candidate's high school performance; aptitude for verbal and mathematical reasoning, as measured by performance on standardized tests; and counselor and teacher recommendations.

A student planning to attend Notre Dame College should take the strongest possible college preparatory program available. The following distribution of courses is considered to be standard academic preparation: English, 4; mathematics, 3 (to include algebra I, geometry, and algebra II); science, 3 (with laboratory experience); social studies, 3; foreign language, 2 (from the same language); and fine arts, 1. Applicants should generally rank in the upper half of their high school graduating class and have a minimum cumulative grade point average of 2.5 (unweighted): 2.5; a minimum ACT composite score of 19; and a minimum SAT score of 900 (Critical Reading and Math).

Students who want to transfer from other regionally accredited colleges and universities are admitted to advanced standing upon presentation of evidence of scholarship and character.

Notre Dame College strongly recommends that prospective students schedule an appointment to visit the campus and talk with an admissions counselor.

Application and Information

A free application is available online at NotreDameCollege.edu.

The College maintains a rolling admission policy. To apply, students should submit the completed application for undergraduate admission, an official transcript of their high school record, and results of the ACT or SAT to:

Office of Admissions
Notre Dame College
4545 College Road
South Euclid, Ohio 44121
Phone: 216-373-5355
877-NDC-OHIO Ext. 5355 (toll-free)
Fax: 216-373-5278
E-mail: admissions@ndc.edu
Website: http://NotreDameCollege.edu
http://www.facebook.com/NotreDameCollege
http://twitter.com/NotreDameOhio
http://www.youtube/notredamecollege

OHIO NORTHERN UNIVERSITY

ADA, OHIO

OHIO NORTHERN UNIVERSITY

The University

Ohio Northern University (ONU) has a 94 percent job and graduate school placement rate. Its long-standing success is partly because of excellent professors, partly because of ambitious students, and partly because the University has always been rooted in the future. At ONU, students move toward a career long before they graduate—and ONU's alumni successes prove it. With top-ranked programs and opportunities outside the classroom, any path a student chooses at ONU will be grounded in concrete applications for the future. Established in 1871 and comprised of five colleges (Arts & Sciences, Business Administration, Engineering, Pharmacy, and Law), ONU's beautiful residential campus is made up of more than sixty modern residences and academic buildings and provides a vibrant campus experience.

Students can choose from a variety of campus activities including more than 200 student organizations; four national sororities and five national fraternities; fine arts, music, and theatrical events; and intramural and club sports. Residence hall living is an integral part of the educational program, contributing to a student's personal development. There are nine residence halls on campus as well as eight campus apartment complexes and an Affinity Housing complex.

The ONU Polar Bears compete successfully at the NCAA Division III level in twenty-three varsity sports as part of the highly respected Ohio Athletic Conference. ONU has twelve men's teams (baseball, basketball, cross-country, football, golf, lacrosse, soccer, swimming and diving, tennis, indoor and outdoor track, and wrestling) and eleven women's teams (basketball, cross-country, fast-pitch softball, golf, lacrosse, soccer, swimming and diving, tennis, indoor and outdoor track, and volleyball).

Location

Ohio Northern University's campus is situated on 342 beautiful acres in the village of Ada (population 5,500). Located in northwestern Ohio, ONU is easily accessible by major highways and conveniently located near major cities such as Columbus, Dayton, Toledo, and Fort Wayne, Indiana.

Majors and Degrees

Ohio Northern University offers the undergraduate degrees: Bachelor of Arts, Bachelor of Fine Arts, Bachelor of Music, Bachelor of Science, Bachelor of Science in Business Administration, Bachelor of Science in Civil Engineering, Bachelor of Science in Medical Laboratory Science, Bachelor of Science in Computer Engineering, Bachelor of Science in Electrical Engineering, Bachelor of Science in Mechanical Engineering, and Bachelor of Science in Nursing. In addition to the undergraduate programs, ONU offers a Master of Science in Accounting; Juris Doctor; Doctor of Pharmacy (Pharm.D.), which is a 0-6, direct entry program; and the Master of Laws (LL.M.) in Democratic Governance and Rule of Law. The 3+3 Law Admissions Program leads to an approved bachelor's degree plus a juris doctorate degree. Majors considered for the 3+3 Admissions Program include business administration; chemistry; English; history; philosophy; philosophy, politics, and economics (PPE); political science; religion; and sociology.

Majors are offered in accounting; advertising design; applied mathematics; art education; athletic training; biochemistry; biology; chemistry; civil engineering; communication studies; computer engineering; computer science; construction management; creative writing; criminal justice; early childhood education; electrical engineering; engineering education; engineering exploratory; environmental and field biology; exercise physiology; forensic biology; French; German; graphic design; history; international theatre and production; language arts education; literature; management; manufacturing technology; marketing; mathematical statistics; mathematics; mechanical engineering; medical laboratory science; middle childhood education; molecular biology; multimedia journalism; music; music education; musical theatre; music performance; nursing; pharmaceutical and healthcare business; pharmacy; philosophy; philosophy, politics, and economics; physics; political science; professional writing; psychology; public health; public relations; religion; risk management and insurance; social studies; sociology; Spanish; sport management; studio arts; technology education; theatre; youth ministry; undecided business; undecided general studies; and undecided sciences.

Special preprofessional programs are available in dentistry, law, medicine, occupational therapy, physical therapy, physician assistant, seminary, and veterinary medicine. Teacher licensure programs are offered at the early childhood, middle childhood, adolescent/young adult, and multiage levels within 16 programs and two endorsement areas. Changes in programs of study are updated at www.onu.edu.

Academic Programs

The Getty College of Arts & Sciences creatively combines a traditional liberal arts education with cutting-edge preprofessional studies. The college offers more than 50 majors in 17 academic departments, and students can earn a Bachelor of Arts, Bachelor of Fine Arts, Bachelor of Music, Bachelor of Science, Bachelor of Science in Medical Laboratory Science, or Bachelor of Science in Nursing.

Students in the sciences have been honored by the Barry M. Goldwater Scholarship and Excellence in Education Foundation for eleven consecutive years. The college has also been recognized as one of the top 200 programs in the nation for creative students in *Creative Colleges: A Guide for Student Actors, Artists, Dancers, Musicians and Writers*.

Working closely with dedicated faculty members, students complete the general education requirements, delve deeply into advanced courses, and engage in high-impact learning through research, internships, practicum experiences, study abroad, and more.

The Dicke College of Business Administration focuses on creating ethical, entrepreneurial, and professional business and civic leaders. The college offers a rigorous academic curriculum with signature programs in pharmaceutical and healthcare business, and risk management and insurance. Internships are required by the college and are available year-round. There are international programs, including study abroad, work abroad, and study tours. An office of experiential learning supports students looking for these opportunities. The course of study for the Bachelor of Science in Business Administration includes a four-year business core experience themed around strategic business planning. Personal attention and mentoring from faculty members, small intimate classes, and active student organizations combine with an emphasis on experiential learning, global awareness, and the entrepreneurial spirit. The college is accredited by the AACSB International—The Association to Advance Collegiate Schools of Business. The Dicke College of Business Administration is ranked by *Bloomberg Businessweek* among the top 50 undergraduate business programs in the United States and the top private school business program in Ohio.

The T. J. Smull College of Engineering is noted for its hands-on learning; small, intimate classes; dedicated, accessible professors; and world-class, top-ranked instruction. Ranked thirty-first in the nation for undergraduate engineering programs by *U.S. News & World Report*, ONU's engineering and computer science programs prepare graduates who think critically, lead confidently, and have solid technical foundations upon which to build successful long-term careers. From strong lab components to a host of experiential learning opportunities, ONU's faculty is committed to helping its students achieve their educational goals and realize their dreams. The college features six accredited, disciplinary majors in civil, computer, electrical, and mechanical engineering; computer science; and engineering education, a degree option supporting the demand for high school math teachers with engineering degrees.

The courses for the first academic year are essentially the same for each degree program, offering students an easy track to move from one program to another if initially uncertain which disciplines they prefer to study.

An optional five-year co-op program is available for students in each program, provided they maintain a minimum 2.5 GPA. The college focuses on high-impact learning as an essential part of an engineering education; thus, in addition to a co-op program, students apply their classroom learning in freshman design projects, senior capstone projects, national design competitions, and numerous engineering projects in community services (EPICS). Further, many opportunities are available for valuable work experience through the co-op and internship programs, with a historically high job-placement rate for graduates.

For more than 130 years, the Raabe College of Pharmacy has offered distinctive, challenging, and comprehensive training for some of the nation's most talented pharmacists. This University signature program features a six-year Doctor of Pharmacy (Pharm.D.) degree accredited by the American Council on Pharmaceutical Education. This program is direct-entry, admitting students immediately from high school into the college's professional program. This approach enables students to take pharmacy courses from the very first day. A rigorous curriculum utilizes an innovative modular format to organize learning around the human body systems and patient care implementation.

Cutting-edge clinical facilities include the Pharmacy Skills Center, where students access state-of-the-art compounding/counseling pods with portable OTC simulation stations. Students gain considerable experience through a strong undergraduate research program and may pursue minors or dual majors in other areas. Faculty members are teaching-focused but remain current in their research disciplines. Upon graduation, students are well schooled in every aspect of pharmacy and have a high placement rate.

Off-Campus Programs

Many majors may take part in study-abroad programs developed in consultation with faculty members. Field experiences and internships are available to most majors. Externships are required of all pharmacy majors and place students in retail and clinical experiences. Teacher licensure requires one semester of primary or secondary classroom teaching experience under the supervision of practicing teachers. Additional opportunities include computer science and mathematics co-op programs (professional practice), engineering co-op programs (professional practice, domestic and international), and an honors program. All off-campus learning experiences carry credit.

Academic Facilities

Among the nineteen modern academic buildings on campus, the newest is the Mathile Center for the Natural Sciences, which expands the science-learning environment. This 95,145-square-foot student-centered academic research and learning facility blends hands-on teaching excellence with advanced technology in a functional modern environment.

The College of Business Administration's Dicke Hall offers students a modern setting for high-tech classrooms, meeting rooms and a 150-seat lecture forum.

ONU's Heterick Memorial Library and the Taggart Law Library provide information resources and services to support course offerings and foster independent study.

The Freed Center for the Performing Arts houses Communications and Theatre Arts classrooms and features a 550-seat theater/concert hall, a 120-seat studio theater, and television and radio production facilities. WONB-FM is the commercial-free voice of ONU.

Costs

Tuition and fees charges for the 2017–18 year are $30,990 for the colleges of Arts & Sciences and Business Administration; $35,370 for the College of Engineering; and $36,500 for the College of Pharmacy. These totals do not include room and board.

Financial Aid

Even with one of the highest returns on investment in the nation, ONU invests more than $45 million toward merit-based scholarships and need-based resources. To be considered, the student should submit the FAFSA to the University along with the admission application.

Faculty

More than 210 full-time faculty members bring extensive academic, work, travel, and life experience to their classrooms. Ohio Northern values excellence, innovation, technology, diversity, and its people. With an 11:1 student-faculty ratio, students get lots of personal attention from professors who are passionate about teaching and mentoring.

Student Government

The Student Senate provides self-government in many areas of student life and seeks to further ideals of character and service to the University. The Student Senate serves as the official representative group of the student body to the University administration and agencies in matters pertaining to the student body.

Admission Requirements

High school students applying for admission to the University should present an official transcript indicating at least 16 total units of study, including work in specific academic areas as indicated by each college. Applicants are also required to submit scores on the ACT and/or SAT. For scholarship purposes, the traditional sections of the ACT and the SAT are considered. An on-campus interview is also recommended.

Application and Information

In the colleges of Arts & Sciences, Business Administration, and Engineering, a student's file is considered complete when it contains the application, official high school transcript, and ACT and/or SAT scores. The College of Pharmacy requires a personal statement and a recommendation in addition to the previous items.

The College of Pharmacy's application deadline is December 1 for entering freshmen. A campus visit is strongly encouraged for consideration for admittance into this college.

Requests for catalogs or additional information should be directed to:

Office of Admissions
Ohio Northern University
525 South Main Street
Ada, Ohio 45810
Phone: 888-408-4668 (toll-free)
Fax: 419-772-2821
E-mail: admissions-ug@onu.edu
Website: www.onu.edu
www.facebook.com/ohionorthern
www.twitter.com/ohionorthern

Fifth-year pharmacy students (from left) Ruth Aminu, Emily Somerfield, Alicia Sawmiller, and Caleb VonStein work in the Pharmacy Skills Center of the Ohio Northern University College of Pharmacy. An Ohio Northern University education is based on experiential, hands-on learning and students are guided by professors who know them personally and care about their lifelong success.

OHIO WESLEYAN UNIVERSITY

DELAWARE, OHIO

★ For more information, visit http://petersons.to/ohiowesleyanu

Ohio Wesleyan University

COLLEGE CLOSE-UPS

The University

Ohio Wesleyan University (OWU) offers a liberal arts education that nourishes students' minds and spirits. OWU provides the adventure, knowledge, and meaning that enable students to reach their full potential. Collaborating with professors on research projects, obtaining grants to explore new academic terrain, gaining practical experience from internships, and participating in sports and clubs are just some of the opportunities available at the university.

Students, who represent 47 states and territories and 32 countries, are invited to choose from more than 90 majors or even create their own. Over one-fourth pursue double majors. Through The OWU Connection, students learn to think creatively and critically, communicate their ideas, solve complex problems, and apply their knowledge in real-world settings.

Because of its commitment to excellence in liberal arts education, Ohio Wesleyan University is ranked among the top universities in the nation. *U.S. News & World Report* ranked it one of the best liberal arts colleges in its 2017 edition of America's Best Colleges. *The Princeton Review* listed it among the Best 381 Colleges and Best Midwestern colleges. *Money* magazine named it one of the country's Best Colleges for Your Money.

Ohio Wesleyan University's focus on providing rigorous academics and transforming theory into practice ensures that students graduate with the skills and experience that impress employers and graduate schools. Upon graduation, students join a network of successful alumni and obtain positions with employers in many industries, which recently have included JPMorgan Chase, Nationwide Financial, Orlando Repertory Theatre, Teach for America, Audubon Zoo, Democratic Party of Virginia, Cincinnati Children's Hospital, Cardinal Health, Battelle, Boehringer Ingelheim, M.D. Anderson Cancer Center, AmeriCorps, Philadelphia Eagles, and others.

Location

Ohio Wesleyan University is located in Delaware, Ohio, in the Midwestern region of the United States. Its beautiful 200-acre campus has 61 buildings and 11 locations on the National Register of Historic Places.

It takes just 5 minutes for students to walk to downtown Delaware, where they'll find a variety of coffee shops, restaurants, and shopping venues. Attractions include the Strand Theatre and Whit's Frozen Custard, and events such as monthly First Friday celebrations and Farmers' Market Saturdays.

The campus is only 30 minutes from Columbus, Ohio. This thriving metropolis offers many recreational options including professional sports, restaurants, shopping, major concerts, and art galleries. It also has outstanding work and internships opportunities.

Majors and Degrees

OWU's academic majors combine focused study with expert faculty, real-world internship and research opportunities, and the expansive understanding that comes from studying the liberal arts. More than 25 percent of OWU students pursue at least two majors, one of the highest percentages in the country.

Available majors include: accounting; ancient studies; anthropology and sociology; astrophysics (B.S. and B.A.); biochemistry; general or ACS certified; biology; black world studies; botany; business administration; chemistry: general or ACS certified; classics; communication; comparative literature; computer science; dance; data analytics; earth science; East Asian studies; economics; education: early childhood or middle childhood, English: creative writing or literature; environmental science; environmental studies; finance; economics; film studies; fine arts: art education, art history, studio art (B.A.), or studio art (B.F.A.); French; genetics; geography; geology (B.S. and B.A.); German; health and human kinetics: general, exercise science, health promotion, sports and exercise management; history: general or education; interdisciplinary (self-designed); international business; international studies: general, developing countries, or Europe; journalism, Latin American studies; management economics, mathematics; general or statistics; medieval studies, microbiology (B.S. and B.A.); Middle Eastern studies; music: B.A., composition, education, or performance; neuroscience, nutrition, philosophy, physics (B.S. and B.A.); planetary science, politics and government, pre-law; pre-medicine/pre-dentistry; pre-optometry; pre–public administration; pre-theology; pre–veterinary medicine; psychology; religion; renaissance studies; social justice; sociology/anthropology; Spanish; theatre; urban studies; women's and gender studies; and zoology: general or pre-professional.

Academic Programs

The OWU Connection, Ohio Wesleyan's unique academic program, connects traditional liberal arts with real-world experience. Interdisciplinary classes and programs explore areas where different fields blend; travel-learning courses augment classroom learning with international travel and study; Theory-to-Practice Grants allow students to conduct research and gain experience in settings around the globe; and meaningful internships and signature projects help students coalesce four years of learning.

Ohio Wesleyan's Leland F. and Helen Schubert Honors Program offers students the opportunity to tailor their education to specific needs and interests, pursue advanced topics, master complex analytical and research skills, work independently, and widen career options.

Off-Campus Programs

More than half of all OWU students enrich their campus experience with travel-learning to more than 30 countries. OWU offers semester-long programs in Salamanca, Spain;

Tanzania; and more. Internship programs include New York Arts and Wesleyan in Washington. Travel-Learning Courses go to Argentina, Ireland, Germany, Japan, Costa Rica, and more. Theory-to-Practice Grants fund student projects around the world.

Costs

The general fees at Ohio Wesleyan are comparable to those at institutions of similar size and reputation. For the 2017–18 academic year, residential tuition is $44,430; standard room is $6,450; average board is $5,500; and the activity fee is $260 for a total of $56,640. Fees vary for international and commuter students.

Financial Aid

Ohio Wesleyan University makes every effort to make earning a degree from a top-tier university affordable. More than 95 percent of students receive financial aid from one or more of the following sources: need-based grants, government-sponsored student loans, merit scholarships and awards, and/or student employment through the Federal Work-Study and OWU Institutional Student Employment programs.

To be considered for all merit scholarships, the admission application must be received by the Regular Decision deadline of March 1. Priority consideration is given to applications received by the Early Action deadline of January 15. To be considered for all available need-based financial aid, the Free Application for Federal Student Aid (FAFSA) should be submitted.

Faculty

Students learn in small classes from faculty members who are accomplished teachers, excellent researchers, and skilled practitioners. There are no graduate teaching assistants at OWU. Ohio Wesleyan students consistently rate the faculty highly for quality of teaching, excitement about their academic disciplines, mentoring, commitment, and accessibility. There are 146 full-time faculty members. The average class size is 17 students and the student-faculty ratio is 11:1. Every year students select 10 favorite professors to deliver 3-minute i^3 lectures, which can be seen on the OWU website.

Student Life

Ohio Wesleyan University provides a diverse community where 25 percent of students are multicultural or come from other countries. Nearly every student lives on campus all four years, creating a close-knit community. Housing options include residence halls, Greek houses, and small living units (SLUs) that allow students passionate about a topic to live and learn together.

OWU offers 23 varsity sports (expanding to 25 in fall 2018)and is a competitive member of the NCAA Division III and North Coast Athletic Conference.

A myriad of resources ensure that students can create a rewarding and memorable college experience. OWU is proud to offer its students more than 150 clubs and organizations; fraternities and sororities; fine, performing, and visual arts opportunities; spirituality and religious programs; community and global service opportunities; diversity and multicultural programs; and campus events and celebrations throughout the school year.

Admission Requirements

Ohio Wesleyan accepts the Common Application and the OWU Online Application. The application fee of $35 is waived for online applications. In addition to the application, OWU requires a secondary school report and counselor recommendation; official high school transcript; optional SAT or ACT scores (SAT code: 1594; ACT code: 3316), and an admission essay. A teacher evaluation form is also strongly encouraged.

Ohio Wesleyan no longer requires high school students who have a cumulative GPA of 3.0 or higher by the end of the junior year to submit SAT or ACT scores for admission consideration. OWU believes that mastery of a rigorous college preparatory curriculum is a more significant predictor of college success than a single test on a single day. The university's holistic review process also considers recommendations from teachers and the quality of extracurricular involvement.

However, to be considered for a Schubert Scholarship, or for invitation into the Honors Program, applicants may want to include test scores if they are above Ohio Wesleyan's average test scores.

Application and Information

The Early Decision application deadline is November 15, with notification November 30. Applicants must also complete and submit the Early Decision form with their application. The deadline for Early Action I is December 1, with notification December 15. The Early Action II deadline is January 15, with notification January 30. The regular decision application is March 1, with notification March 15.

For more information, prospective students should contact:
Ohio Wesleyan University
61 South Sandusky Street
Delaware, Ohio 43015
Phone: 800-922-8953
Fax: 740-368-3314
E-mail: owuadmit@owu.edu
Website: www.owu.edu

Ohio Wesleyan University's 200-acre campus offers endless opportunities for students to fully experience the richness and connectedness of a liberal arts education.

COLLEGE CLOSE-UPS

OLIVET NAZARENE UNIVERSITY

BOURBONNAIS, ILLINOIS

★ To read more about this school, visit http://petersons.to/olivetnazareneuniversity

OLIVET
NAZARENE UNIVERSITY

The University

Olivet Nazarene University (ONU) is a private, Christian liberal arts university with a strong emphasis on academic excellence and Christ-centered living. Olivet's 275-acre Bourbonnais campus offers world-class facilities for learning, personal development, entertainment, and all aspects of student life. The atmosphere promotes academic rigor, fun, relationship building, career preparation, and spiritual growth.

The student body of 4,900—including 2,900 undergraduates—represents more than 40 denominations, most U.S. states, and more than 20 countries. Olivet operates on a two-semester schedule from August to May, and two summer sessions are available.

Faculty, staff, and administration are dedicated to teaching, encouraging, and mentoring each student as a whole person—academically, socially, and spiritually. Olivet's high retention, graduation, and employment/placement rates demonstrate the University's commitment to student success.

Outside the classroom, Olivet students participate in more than 90 clubs, ministries, honor societies, and organizations, including 20 intramural sports, the 195-member marching band, two orchestras, 21 musical ensembles, and theater groups.

ONU competes in 21 intercollegiate men's and women's sports as a member of the National Association of Intercollegiate Athletics (NAIA), the National Christian College Athletic Association (NCCAA), and the Chicagoland Collegiate Athletic Conference (CCAC).

A signature structure on the Olivet campus is the 3,046-seat Betty and Kenneth Hawkins Centennial Chapel, the venue for chapel services, concerts, and campus events, and home to the Kankakee Valley Symphony Orchestra.

Facilities also include the 168,000 square-foot Douglas E. Perry Student Life and Recreation Center, featuring an eight-lane running track, two swimming pools, a four-story rock climbing wall, basketball courts, and other amenities that include workout facilities used by the Chicago Bears of the National Football League. The ONU campus is home to the Chicago Bears' summer training camp, which annually draws national and local media coverage as well as thousands of fans to Olivet's campus.

In addition to traditional undergraduate programs, Olivet offers 11 master's degree programs, a Doctor of Education in ethical leadership, and degree-completion continuing studies programs through the School of Graduate and Continuing Studies (SGCS). Programs are designed to facilitate a seamless transition from undergraduate to master's programs. As it strives to meet the needs of adults returning to school, the SGCS also helps working adults complete degree requirements without interrupting their employment. Courses and programs also provide resources to help enhance students' personal and professional lives.

The SGCS offers courses on the main campus in Bourbonnais and at more than 100 learning locations throughout Chicagoland and the Midwest. Students benefit from robust online programming, as well as courses offered in more than 150 churches, schools, hospitals, and other locations convenient to their homes or workplaces.

The University is also home to Shine.FM, a top-rated contemporary Christian radio network. Olivet-owned Shine.FM broadcasts over the air in the Chicago area, Indianapolis, Northwest Indiana, and Lansing, Michigan; online at Station.Shine.FM; and via the Shine.FM app. Olivet students studying multimedia communication work alongside seasoned professionals in operating the station.

Location

Olivet's main campus is located just 50 miles south of Chicago's Loop, in the historic village of Bourbonnais, Illinois. The area offers shopping, restaurants, entertainment, and outdoor recreation through the Kankakee River State Park system.

Students benefit from ONU's proximity to Chicago's cultural, sports, and entertainment attractions. Plentiful professional internships and employment opportunities are additional advantages.

Other ONU locations include Rolling Meadows and Oak Brook, Illinois; Indianapolis, Indiana; Grand Rapids and Grand Ledge, Michigan; and Hong Kong.

Majors and Degrees

Olivet confers Bachelor of Arts (B.A.) and/or Bachelor of Science (B.S.) degrees in more than 140 areas of study (majors, minors, and concentrations), including accounting, actuarial Science, art, art–drawing/illustration, art–digital graphics, art–painting, art–photography, art education, athletic coaching, athletic/training, biblical languages, biology, biology teaching, business administration, business–healthcare, management, business–human resource management, business–management, business–not-for-profit/philanthropy, business–operations management, business–public administration, chemistry, chemistry–biochemistry, chemistry–forensics, chemistry teaching, child development, children's ministry, Christian education, communication studies, communication teaching, computer science, corporate communication, criminal justice, criminal justice–law enforcement, dietetics, early childhood education, earth and space science teaching, economics, economics and finance–applied economics, economics and finance–Certified Financial Planning, economics and finance–corporate finance, elementary education, engineering–architectural, engineering–chemical, engineering–civil, engineering–computer, engineering–electrical, engineering–environmental, engineering–industrial, engineering–mechanical, engineering–software, English, English as a Second Language, English as a Second Language teaching, English education, environmental science, exercise science, family and consumer sciences, family and consumer sciences–family studies, family and consumer sciences–hospitality, family and consumer sciences–education, fashion merchandising, finance, French, general studies, geography, geological science, Greek, health education, Hebrew, history, history teaching, information systems, information technology, intercultural studies, interior design, international business, leadership studies, legal studies, literature, management information systems, marketing, marketing–commercial graphics, marketing–international, marketing–management, marketing–public relations, mass communications, mathematics, mathematics education, military affairs, military science, ministerial missions, multimedia communication, multimedia communication–film studies, multimedia communication–journalism, multimedia communication–live event media, management, multimedia communication–ministry media, multimedia communication–radio/record industry, multimedia communication–TV/video production, music, music composition, music education, music ministry, music performance, musical theatre, nursing, pastoral ministry, philosophy, physical education and health teaching, physical sciences, political science, pre-art therapy, pre-dental, pre-law, pre-medicine, pre-optometry, pre-pharmacy, pre-physical therapy, pre-physician's assistant, pre-seminary, pre-veterinary, psychology, psychology teaching, public policy–domestic, public policy–foreign, public relations and strategic communication, recreation, recreation/sport/fitness, religion, religion–biblical studies, religion–philosophy, religion–theology, religious studies, social science, social science education, social work, sociology, Spanish, Spanish education, special education, sport management–administration, sport management–marketing, theatre, writing, youth ministry, and zoology.

Academic Programs

Olivet is dedicated to "An Education with a Christian Purpose." This commitment to Christ-centered learning mandates nothing less than the highest quality academic programs. Olivet's liberal arts curriculum requires that students complete 45 to 58 hours of general education courses. With the addition of major and minor programs of study, students must complete a minimum of 128 credit hours to earn a bachelor's degree. Credit may be earned through advanced placement (AP) and College Level Examination Program (CLEP) tests. Students may also participate in the on-campus U.S. Military Reserve Officers' Training Corps (ROTC).

Olivet offers 10 distinct accelerated bachelor's/master's (4+1 style) programs, in which students can obtain a bachelor's and a master's degree in approximately five years. These programs include majors in accounting; business administration; management information systems; economics/finance (with concentrations in certified financial planning, corporate finance, or public economics); international business or marketing leading to a Master of Business Administration; a major in business administration or a minor in business leading to a Master of Organizational Leadership; or a Master of Arts in Pastoral Ministry, Family Ministry, or Urban Ministry.

In fine arts, Olivet's School of Music earned the Apple Distinguished Program designation for 2014 through 2016 for its iLearn@Olivet initiative, which provides an iPad to every member of the Tiger marching band and all music majors, as well as faculty and staff members. The Department of Art and Digital Design also utilizes iPad and Apple technology for instruction and student projects.

Off-Campus Programs

Each semester, ONU offers off-campus study programs, including the Council for Christian Colleges and Universities BestSemester programs, such as American Studies Program in Washington, D.C.; Australia Studies Centre; Contemporary Music Center; Latin American Studies Program; Los Angeles Film Studies Center; Middle East Studies Program; Oxford Summer Programme; and Uganda Studies Program.

Other study programs include AuSable Institute of Environmental Studies, International Business Institute, ISA Spain (Barcelona), Nazarene International Language Institute, Oxford Summer Program, Quetzal Education Research Center (QERC), Environmental Studies (Costa Rica), and Tokyo Christian University. Costs are usually comparable to a semester at Olivet, and students earn academic credit for these programs. Some financial aid is available.

Numerous short-term educational and mission-oriented trips are available to ONU students during the Christmas, spring, and summer breaks. More than 250 Olivet students participate in mission trips each year.

Academic Facilities

ONU continues to expand and refine its main campus facilities to anticipate the needs of the steadily increasing student population.

In 2014, to accommodate the growing engineering program, the University completed an expansion and renovation of Reed Hall of Science. The building now has a three-story wing dedicated to studying technology and innovation, as well as state-of-the-art engineering design labs for students in the Walker School of Engineering. Plans call for another Reed expansion—for the natural sciences program—as well as expansion and renovation of Larsen Fine Arts Center and Wisner Hall of Nursing and Health Sciences.

State-of-the-art academic facilities include Benner Library and Resource Center, information hub for digital and print research and communication; and Strickler Planetarium, renovated in 2008 with the same technology as Chicago's Adler Planetarium (one of the Midwest's few all-digital planetariums).

Costs

The cost of an Olivet education continues to be competitive for private colleges nationwide. A full year's tuition for 2016–17 is $32,950, based on 12 to 18 credit hours. Room and board are estimated at $7,900 for the year, based on double occupancy and a meal plan. Additional fees are $990 for the year. Olivet offers an interest-free payment plan with four equal payments per semester.

Financial Aid

Olivet participates in all federal and state financial aid programs while also offering institutional need-based assistance and various academic and extracurricular scholarships. For school year 2015–16, Olivet awarded more than $110 million in financial aid, with 99 percent of ONU's traditional undergraduates receiving a collective total of $60.9 million in federal and state grants and institutional grants and scholarships. The University participates in all federal and state financial aid programs. To apply for aid, students must fill out the Free Application for Federal Student Aid (FAFSA). Priority deadline for FAFSA filing is December 15. The University creates a financial aid package once a student is an accepted ONU applicant.

Faculty

For more than 130 full-time ONU faculty members, teaching is a ministry. These dedicated Christian leaders are the key to excellent education inside and outside the classroom. Olivet's 17:1 student-faculty ratio gives faculty the opportunity to teach, mentor, and encourage students with personal attention. Faculty members are deeply committed and involved in campus life, whether sponsoring social organizations and clubs, participating in talent shows, tutoring in their offices, or talking with students over lunch in the dining room. Faculty and ONU staff members also work side-by-side with students in local and regional ministry projects. Beyond spiritual modeling, course instruction, and service roles, faculty members maintain an agenda for professional growth through staying current in their respective fields of study, professional leadership, and published scholarship projects.

Student Government

The Associated Student Council (ASC) is the ONU student government organization on campus. The executive council consists of a president, vice president of finance, vice president of spiritual life, vice president of social affairs, vice president of publicity, vice president of women's residential life, vice president of men's residential life, and vice president of office management, as well as the editors of *The GlimmerGlass* student newspaper and *Aurora* yearbook. These students work alongside the University's administrative team to ensure the welfare and promotion of campus activities and organizations.

Admission Requirements

Admission to Olivet is moderately difficult. Students are considered for admission on the basis of high school GPA and ACT or SAT scores. For international students, TOEFL results are also considered. Students with low test scores and/or GPA may be admitted on a provisional basis. A campus visit and interview are strongly recommended for all prospective students.

Application and Information

Applications are processed on a rolling basis. Application deadline is May 1. For some scholarships, an early decision is required. Students may apply through Olivet's website or by mail. The process includes the written or electronic application, high school transcripts, and ACT or SAT scores. An enrollment deposit is collected to prioritize student housing and class registration.

For more information or to arrange a campus visit, contact:

Office of Admissions
Olivet Nazarene University
One University Avenue
Bourbonnais, Illinois 60914
Phone: 800-648-1463 (toll-free)
E-mail: admissions@olivet.edu
Website: http://www.olivet.edu
http://www.facebook.com/olivetnazareneuniversity
http://twitter.com/OlivetNazareneU and
http://twitter.com/ONUInsider
http://www.youtube.com/olivetnazareneu
http://instagram.com/olivetnazarene

Olivet Nazarene University is a place where top-tier academic instruction, social connection, and spiritual development intersect to prepare students for their careers, futures, and lives of service to God and humanity.

COLLEGE CLOSE-UPS

PACIFIC UNIVERSITY

FOREST GROVE, OREGON

★ To read more about this school, visit http://petersons.to/pacificuniversity

The University

Pacific University is a private, fully accredited university with more than sixty undergraduate fields of study and sixteen graduate and professional programs. With colleges in the Arts and Sciences, Business, Education, Health Professions, and Optometry, the University's four Oregon campuses draw more than 3,800 students.

Students come from around the United States and abroad for a wide variety of programs, but they share a common Pacific University experience: small classes, a nurturing environment, and personal attention. Students learn from the university's full-time faculty members, who are devoted to teaching and to forming close mentoring relationships with their students. Recent graduates at both the undergraduate and graduate level say that access to the high-quality faculty is a hallmark of the University.

As the first chartered university west of the Mississippi, Pacific University has a long history of excellence. At every level, its curriculum emphasizes real-world experience, service learning, and preparation to contribute to a global community.

The Forest Grove Campus is Pacific University's residential campus, where most undergraduate students study.

The campus is home to six residence halls and a student apartment complex; the newest residence hall opened in fall 2014. Many of the newer buildings feature double-occupancy rooms or suites, as well as shared study spaces, kitchens, and game rooms. The residential nature of the campus creates a vibrant living environment, where students develop close, lifelong friendships.

There are more than sixty student interest groups at Pacific University, including student media, academic societies, religious and political organizations, and service clubs. One of the largest student organizations, Na Haumana O Hawai'i, unites Pacific's significant population of students from Hawai'i and presents an authentic lu'au each year. Pacific University also is home to an active Greek system.

Pacific University also is a member of the NCAA Division III Northwest Conference. The campus athletic center houses a gymnasium, fitness center, state-of-the-art indoor field house featuring FieldTurf, handball/racquetball courts, wrestling room, and a sports medicine training facility. The Lincoln Park Athletic Complex, a partnership with the City of Forest Grove, features a 1,100-seat stadium with a nine-lane, 400-meter track, a FieldTurf soccer/football/lacrosse field, a Bond baseball field, and a varsity softball field.

Almost a third of undergraduate students participate in varsity athletics. Men's sports include baseball, basketball, cross-country, football, golf, soccer, swimming, tennis, track and field, and wrestling. Women compete in basketball, cross-country, golf, lacrosse, rowing, soccer, softball, swimming, tennis, track and field, volleyball, and wrestling. Students also participate in junior varsity and club sports.

Informal sports also are a highlight of the Pacific University student experience. Students compete in intramural sports, and they also enjoy outdoor recreation opportunities through Outdoor Pursuits, which offers training, equipment, and organized trips for snowboarding and skiing, rock climbing, camping, kayaking, and much more. Students also can rent bicycles for a semester or for the year from Outdoor Pursuits to get around the bike-friendly Forest Grove area.

Locations

Pacific University was founded in Forest Grove, Oregon, in 1849. The historic college town, population 22,000, is now home to the 55-acre oak-covered campus on the west side of the Portland Metro Area. About 25 miles from downtown Portland and an hour from the Oregon Coast or Mount Hood, Forest Grove is the perfect home base for exploring the best of Oregon's urban and outdoor adventures.

Pacific University also offers health professions and graduate business programs on its growing campus in Hillsboro, Oregon, the fifth-largest city in the state. Located on the regional light-rail line in the Hillsboro Health and Education District, the Hillsboro Campus connects students with world-class learning opportunities and real-world experience as they connect with local businesses, hospitals, and nonprofit organizations.

Undergraduate and graduate teaching programs, as well as a Master of Social Work program, are offered at Pacific University's campus in Eugene.

Pacific University's newest campus is in Woodburn, one of the most diverse and fastest-growing communities in Oregon. The College of Education has a science, technology, engineering, and math teaching program embedded in the local school district and also offers a degree track in elementary education and English language learning at the Woodburn Campus.

Majors and Degrees

Pacific University is known for its excellent liberal arts foundation, as well as the superior preparation its students receive to go on to careers and advanced study. In particular, the University is heralded for its graduate programs in health professions, as well as its undergraduate preparation for healthcare fields and medical school.

Pacific emphasizes the education benefits of research projects, internships, study-abroad experiences, and service learning. Most freshmen participate in a semester-long first-year seminar program designed to introduce students to college-level writing and research expectations. The core curriculum emphasizes writing, reasoning, and communication skills, as well as global perspectives and service. Pacific University also requires most students to complete a senior capstone, a year-long research project designed and implemented by students and culminating in a presentation to the University community.

Most undergraduate programs operate on a two-semester calendar with an optional January term and limited summer courses. Many graduate and professional programs have year-round calendars.

The Pacific University College of Arts and Sciences offers most undergraduate majors, including programs in anthropology/sociology, applied science, art, bioinformatics, biology, chemistry, computer science, criminal justice, dance, economics, English, environmental science, exercise science, history, international studies, mathematics, media arts, modern languages, music, philosophy, physics, politics and government, psychology, public health, social work, and theatre. The College of Arts and Sciences also offers a nationally recognized, low-residency Master of Fine Arts in writing program, and a new Master of Social Work program.

The College of Business offers undergraduate tracks in accounting, finance, international business, marketing, and business administration, as well as a one-year MBA program.

The College of Health Professions provides an undergraduate program in dental hygiene studies and an online bachelor of health science program, as well as graduate programs in athletic training, audiology, healthcare administration, occupational therapy, pharmacy, physical therapy, physician assistant studies, and professional psychology as well as a graduate-level certificate program in gerontology.

The College of Education offers an undergraduate major in education and learning, as well as a Bachelor of Education in elementary education and English language learning. Graduate programs in the College of Education include a fifth-year Master of Arts in Teaching, a Master of Arts in teaching special education, a Master of Education, and several endorsement options. Also available is a master's degree in speech-language pathology, as well as an undergraduate minor in communication sciences and disorders that prepares students for the speech-language pathology program.

The College of Optometry offers a Doctor of Optometry program, as well as master's and Ph.D. programs in vision science.

Costs

Tuition and fees for the 2016–17 school year were $41,054 for undergraduates in the College of Arts and Sciences. Room and board were $11,822 for a double room and a University meal plan. Pacific University was named a Best Value School by *U.S. News & World Report*.

Financial Aid

Financial assistance at Pacific is awarded on the basis of demonstrated need, academic merit, and talent. The Free Application for Federal Student Aid (FAFSA) is used in evaluating need. Prospective students are encouraged to apply for financial assistance by submitting the FAFSA to the federal processor as soon after October 1 as possible. Pacific provides financial assistance through grants, scholarships, loans, and part-time employment. For more information prospective students can e-mail financialaid@pacificu.edu.

Faculty

Pacific's outstanding faculty members provide the foundation for the University's academic program. A student-faculty ratio of 10:1 and an average class size of 19 students in undergraduate courses allows for personal attention from the professors. Pacific University does not use graduate or teaching assistants; all faculty members teach their own courses.

Admission Requirements

Pacific University is selective in considering new students. Primary consideration is given to a candidate's academic preparation and potential for successful study at the college level, as assessed by evaluating the student's transcripts of college-preparatory work, counselor and teacher recommendations, personal essay, SAT and/or ACT scores, and other student-submitted information. Transfer students must submit high school records and test scores if they have completed less than 30 semester hours, plus official transcripts from any institution previously attended.

Application and Information

Students may apply early and may be notified early through the modified rolling admissions plan. Pacific University is an exclusive member of the Common Application. For additional information, interested students should contact:

Office of Admissions
Pacific University
2043 College Way
Forest Grove, Oregon 97116
Phone: 503-352-2218
800-677-6712 (toll-free)
E-mail: admissions@pacificu.edu
Website: http://www.pacificu.edu
http://www.facebook.com/pacificu
http://www.twitter.com/pacificu

PEPPERDINE UNIVERSITY
Seaver College
MALIBU, CALIFORNIA

PEPPERDINE

The University and The College

Pepperdine University is a private, faith-based university committed to the highest standards of academic excellence and Christian values, where students are strengthened for lives of purpose, service, and leadership.

Seaver College, Pepperdine's undergraduate liberal arts college, is comprised of approximately 3,300 students, 55 percent of which come from California. Thirty-five percent hail from the other forty-nine states, and 10 percent are international. The 2016–17 freshmen class had an average high school GPA of 3.76. It's this diversity of backgrounds and worldviews that helps contribute to Pepperdine's unique educational experience.

Nestled between the Santa Monica Mountains and the Pacific Ocean, Pepperdine's Malibu campus provides fantastic on-campus housing options for all students. Students are required to live on campus during their first and second years, and also have premium residence halls available as upperclassmen.

Students have a wide range of extracurricular activities and organizations to choose from, including social, honor, service, spiritual, professional, divisional, and special interest clubs. Pepperdine provides students with interests in communications and media the chance to be involved with the campus radio station, weekly student newspaper and television broadcast.

Pepperdine has 17 Division One men's and women's athletic programs that have won an impressive 13 national team championships and 12 individual national championships. As a member of the West Coast Conference, the University houses a 3,500-seat gymnasium, an Olympic-size swimming pool, a tennis pavilion and sixteen additional tennis courts, an intramural field, and a 2,000-seat baseball stadium.

Pepperdine's graduate schools include the School of Law, School of Public Policy, School of Education and Psychology, and the George L. Graziado School of Business and Management. These distinguished programs offer master's degrees in law, dispute resolution, public policy, business, and more.

Location

Overlooking the Pacific Ocean in scenic Malibu, California, and less than an hour from downtown Los Angeles, Seaver's Malibu campus offers both the benefits of a small coastal community and the advantages of proximity to a major metropolitan area.

Malibu is a pristine beach community with excellent restaurants, a movie theater, and shopping centers complete with banking facilities and industry-leading brands. The winding seashore and rugged beauty of Malibu connects students to a litany of nightlife options in Santa Monica, Hollywood, and Los Angeles. Malibu's clean air provides an environment conducive to study, while the moderate climate permits year-round outdoor recreation. In addition to making use of the physical education facilities on campus, students can enjoy swimming, surfing, horseback riding, fishing, hiking, boating, kayaking, and other activities in the vicinity. As an international epicenter of culture, industry, and trade, Los Angeles provides students with a one-of-a-kind living experience.

Majors and Degrees

Students can choose from forty-five majors and thirty-seven minors. Seaver College awards the Bachelor of Arts in advertising, art, art history, biology, chemistry, communication, creative writing, economics, English, film studies, French, German, Hispanic studies (Spanish), history, integrated marketing communication, international studies, Italian, journalism, liberal arts, math education, media production, music, natural science, philosophy, political science, psychology, public relations, religion, sociology, sport administration, sports medicine, theater and music, theater and media production, and theater arts.

The Bachelor of Science is awarded in accounting, biology, business administration, chemistry, computer science and mathematics, international business, mathematics, nutritional science, physics, and sports medicine. A teacher education program offers credentials in single or multiple subjects.

Academic Programs

The academic programs at Seaver College provide students with a liberal arts education in a Christian atmosphere that sharpens critical thinking, improves information literacy, and builds a learning community. Students must complete 128 units for the B.A. or B.S. degree, including 64 units in general education requirements and 40 or more in upper-division studies.

Major requirements may be fulfilled through three basic arrangements. Students who specialize in a discipline must complete at least 24 units of upper-division work in their chosen discipline. Students may choose an interdisciplinary major, entailing at least 40 units of upper-division work, with courses ranging broadly across disciplinary lines within a division and on occasion crossing divisional lines, in one of the following fields of study: communication, English, humanities, international studies, liberal arts, or religion. Alternatively, students may initiate a contract major by presenting an application for specific upper-division courses to the Dean of Seaver College.

Seaver College functions on a semester plan; the regular academic year consists of two semesters from late August to April. In addition to the regular academic year, summer sessions run from early May to August.

At Seaver, instruction and study are adapted both to students' abilities and to the nature of the course content, instead of utilizing only the traditional lecture method. Programs involve several types of learning experiences: seminars, integrated lectures, individual study, fieldwork, and laboratories. Students are never taught by a teacher's assistant at Pepperdine; the average class size is 19 students and a student-to-faculty ratio of 13:1 fosters an environment where professors are invested in the growth and success of their students.

The Dean's List of undergraduate students is published each semester, comprised of the top 10 percent of the class with a grade point index no lower than 3.5. Other honors include cum laude for students graduating with a scholastic level of at least 3.5, magna cum laude for 3.7, and summa cum laude for 3.9.

Off-Campus Programs

At Seaver, students have the opportunity to study abroad in Buenos Aires, Argentina; Florence, Italy; Heidelberg, Germany; Lausanne, Switzerland; London, England; and Shanghai, China. The academic programs emphasize European, Latin American, or Asian history and culture. Seaver also offers an internship-based program in Washington, D.C. and summer special interest programs in Spain, Thailand, East Africa, and the Middle East. Classes are taught by Seaver faculty members. Serious study and the daily experiences of living in another country give students a special depth of understanding of other cultures and a broader world perspective.

The Buenos Aires program accommodates approximately 60 students who live in the homes of carefully selected host families. The Florence program houses approximately 55 students who live in a Florentine villa and residential complex with classrooms, a library, a computer facility, and recreational facilities. The Heidelberg program has space for approximately 50 students at the Moore Haus, located near the city's famous castle. Classes are held in modern facilities in downtown Heidelberg. The Lausanne program accommodates about 70 students. The Pepperdine facility is located in La Croisée near the center of Lausanne, which has a picturesque view of Lake Geneva and the French Alps. The London program has space for approximately 40 students in the Knightsbridge area. In addition to living quarters, the facility includes classrooms, a library, a computer room, offices, and a student center. The Shanghai program accommodates approximately 40 students who live in the Pepperdine-owned jia, meaning "house," which is located in the French Concession area near the American Consulate. The majority of the international program facilities are University-owned.

Academic Facilities

The Malibu campus is home to academic complexes containing seminar and lecture rooms, art studios, communication facilities, science and computer laboratories, mini-theaters, a recital hall, and administrative offices. The newly renovated Payson Library is the global gateway to knowledge and provides students access to thousands of online journals, articles, and periodicals through various databases. Payson Library serves as a sanctuary for study, learning, and research by encouraging discovery, contemplation, social discourse, and creative expression.

The 300-seat George Elkins Auditorium is used for public presentations and lectures. The Center for the Arts facility includes the renowned Frederick R. Weisman Museum of Art and the Smothers Theatre, which seats 450 people and is used for dance, music, and theater performances. The Center for Communication and Business building houses a state-of-the-art radio and television production center where students have the opportunity to work on Pepperdine's cable television and radio stations.

Costs

Costs for the 2016–17 academic year were $49,770 for tuition, $14,330 for room and board, and $252 for additional fees.

Financial Aid

Approximately 79 percent of Seaver's students receive some form of financial assistance through scholarships, loans, grants, work-study programs, or jobs within the University. To be eligible for financial assistance from institutional resources, an undergraduate student must be enrolled in at least 12 units. To ensure full consideration, the Free Application for Federal Student Aid (FAFSA) should be submitted by the priority deadlines of February 15 for the fall semester and October 15 for the spring semester. Students who qualify should also apply for the Cal Grant (California residents only). Prospective students will receive their estimated financial assistance award after admission to the University but prior to the enrollment deadline.

Faculty

Seaver College's faculty includes men and women of high academic distinction whose primary focus is instruction with a secondary focus on research. Fifty-four percent of faculty members are full-time, and 88 percent of full-time faculty members hold a doctorate or terminal degree in their field. Upon enrollment, each student is assigned an academic adviser from among the faculty members. A qualified counseling staff is also available to assist with personal, professional, and academic needs.

Student Government

The Student Government Association (SGA) is composed of student leaders dedicated to providing Pepperdine's students with quality representation through innovative advocacy programs. SGA serves as the voice of the students to the Seaver administration and works in coordination with the Student Activities Office in establishing activities and maintaining school policies. Seaver has more than 1,000 programmed on-campus events each year including movies, sightseeing trips, guest performances, dances, speakers, and more. Pepperdine has eight nationally recognized sororities and five fraternities and there are over 110 different student clubs and organizations on campus that focus on a range of interests, including academic, language, art, music, dance, drama, sports, and politics.

Admission Requirements

Applicants are admitted on the basis of their academic record, SAT or ACT scores, and personal information and references. Transfer applicants are high school graduates who have taken any transferable college units after graduating high school. Students who took colleges courses prior to graduating high school are not considered transfer students and should apply as a first-year student. To ensure full consideration for the fall semester, students should apply by the January 5 deadline. October 15 is the regular deadline for the spring semester. Decision letter dates are announced in the current application form.

Seaver College seeks to enroll a diverse student body. As such, Pepperdine University does not unlawfully discriminate on the basis of any status or condition protected by applicable federal or state law in the administration of its educational policies, admission, financial assistance, employment, educational programs, or activities.

Application and Information

To request information, students should contact:

Office of Admission
Seaver College
Pepperdine University
Malibu, California 90263-4392
Phone: 310-506-4392
E-mail: admission-seaver@pepperdine.edu
Website: http://seaver.pepperdine.edu/admission
https://seaver.pepperdine.edu/admission/risingtide (Docuseries)
http://on.fb.me/Seaver_Admission (Facebook)
http://twitter.com/#!/SeaverAdmission (Twitter)
http://instagram.com/seaveradmission# (Instagram)
http://bit.ly/YouTube_Pepperdine (YouTube)
http://pinterest.com/seaveradmission/ (Pinterest)

The 830-acre Malibu campus of Pepperdine University, Seaver College, overlooks the Pacific Ocean, 30 miles west of Los Angeles, California.

COLLEGE CLOSE-UPS

PHILADELPHIA UNIVERSITY

PHILADELPHIA, PENNSYLVANIA

★ To read more about this school, visit http://petersons.to/philadelphiauniversity

PHILADELPHIA UNIVERSITY

The University

Since the late 19th century, Philadelphia University has been a leader in professional education, helping individuals meet the challenge of achieving their goals. The University is committed to providing an experiential education and is recognized as a leader in the architecture, design, business, engineering, liberal arts, textiles, fashion, science, and health fields.

At Philadelphia University, personal attention and ongoing advisement are cornerstones. From the moment students enroll, they have a network of resources to help them transition to a university environment, find academic support, and facilitate their personal and professional development. These benefits, together with an emphasis on quality education, are the reasons why the school brings out the best in every student.

The Philadelphia University student body is academically, geographically, culturally, and economically diverse. The University has 3,500 full- and part-time students from 40 states and 25 countries. More than 90 percent of Philadelphia University freshmen live in one of its residence halls. Class sizes average 18 students, allowing for lively discussions and fostering relationships between and among its students and its experienced and dedicated faculty. Often, students can partner with faculty members to pursue joint research interests and gain career experience.

Philadelphia University has established a phenomenal record of career success for its graduates; its career placement rate in major-related jobs has consistently been above 90 percent, within a few months of graduation, for more than twenty years. Ninety-five percent of Philadelphia University's 2015 graduates are working in their disciplines or have been accepted to the graduate school of their choice.

Philadelphia University offers many chances for its students to get involved outside of the classroom—from clubs and student-run organizations to campus-wide community service projects, from Open Mic nights to resume writing workshops—learning is integrated in all the University does.

In addition, Philadelphia University is a member of the CACC conference at the NCAA Division II level for the following sports: men's baseball, basketball, cross-country/track, golf, soccer, and tennis, and women's basketball, cross-country/track, golf, lacrosse, rowing, soccer, softball, tennis, and volleyball. An extensive intramural sports program is also available to all students.

Founded in 1884, Philadelphia University is a private institution of higher learning, fully accredited by the Middle States Association of Colleges and Schools.

Location

Philadelphia University is located 15 minutes northwest of Center City Philadelphia, a rich and vibrant city in Pennsylvania. The 52 buildings on the University's 100-acre campus range from historic Victorian mansions to contemporary classroom, library, and residential facilities. Philadelphia University offers the best of both worlds: a beautiful campus with tree-lined walkways, spacious lawns, and classical architecture, just minutes away from its extended classroom—one the nation's most exciting and lively cities, filled with entertainment, cultural events, and more than 300 years of American history.

Majors and Degrees

Philadelphia University offers more than 50 undergraduate and graduate degree programs leading to the Bachelor of Science, Bachelor of Architecture, Bachelor of Science in Engineering, Bachelor of Landscape Architecture, master's degrees, and a doctoral degree in textile engineering and science.

Philadelphia University's most popular degrees include fashion, architecture, engineering, landscape architecture, textiles, digital media, liberal arts, merchandising, marketing, business, psychology, chemistry, and biology.

Academic Programs

Through a unique blend of liberal and specialized education with an interdisciplinary focus, the University prepares students for today's complex, global workplace. The University achieves this by focusing on innovation, innovative thinking and an award-winning Nexus Learning approach—active, collaborative learning that is connected to the real world and infused with the liberal arts.

Study-abroad and internship opportunities are available for fall, spring, and summer semesters at locations all around the world. Along with an exciting and memorable experience, students may receive credit for courses and positions that apply directly to their challenging, professional-oriented curricula.

Costs

For the 2017–18 academic year, tuition totals $38,160 and the general fee is $970. Room rates range from $6,080 to $9,470, depending on style of accommodations; meal plans range from $2,340 to $6,925. Books and supplies are estimated at $1,000. Costs are subject to change.

Financial Aid

Philadelphia University is committed to making a high-quality, professional education affordable for every qualified student. If meeting educational costs is a concern, applicants are encouraged to apply for financial aid, regardless of family financial circumstances. Over 90 percent of students receive aid in the form of grants, loans, campus employment and/or scholarships. Merit, need-based, and athletic scholarships are available. More information on scholarship opportunities is available on the University's website at http://www.philau.edu/financialaid/undergraduate/scholarships/.

Admission Requirements

To be considered for admission to Philadelphia University, first-year applicants must submit:

- $40 nonrefundable application fee
- Official high school transcript(s)
- SAT and/or ACT scores. The PhilaU code for the SAT is 2666 and the ACT is 3668.
- Letter of recommendation from a teacher or counselor who can speak to academic preparation and college readiness. An academic recommendation form is available to download from the University's website.
- Essay of at least 250 words.

Philadelphia University does not require a portfolio review for first-year applicants. If an applicant has some college-level coursework, a portfolio review may be required to assess transferable credit.

Application and Information

Philadelphia University offers a rolling admissions policy without an application deadline (with the exception of a December 15 deadline for the Physician Assistant Studies program). The Admissions Committee begins reviewing applications for fall terms in October and for spring terms in June. The Admissions Committee will review applications for a given term until all programs are filled. Some academic programs, as well as on-campus housing, may have limited capacity and may close earlier than others. For this reason, students are encouraged to apply early in the academic year prior to their desired enrollment term. After submitting all required application materials, applicants can expect to receive their admissions decision within 4 to 6 weeks.

The Admissions Committee reviews each candidate's application by examining a variety of factors, including high school and/or college academic performance, standardized test scores (SAT and/or ACT), counselor or teacher recommendation, and application essay. Involvement in extracurricular activities, volunteer or work experience relevant to a candidate's chosen major, and the level of the candidate's academic curriculum are also considered. Philadelphia University has a customized admissions application and also accepts the Common Application. To apply online to Philadelphia University as an undergraduate student, complete the PhilaU Online Application or Common Application.

Prospective students are encouraged to visit Philadelphia University. There are several types of visit opportunities available.

For more information, contact:

Office of Admissions
Philadelphia University
4201 Henry Avenue
Philadelphia, Pennsylvania 19144
Phone: 215-951-2800
E-mail: admissions@PhilaU.edu
Website: http://www.philau.edu/undergrad

PLATT COLLEGE SAN DIEGO

SAN DIEGO, CALIFORNIA

★ For more information, visit http://petersons.to/platt-college-sandiego

PLATT COLLEGE
DIGITAL ■ MEDIA ■ DESIGN

The College

Built on the historic site of the original Jack in the Box, Platt College San Diego (PCSD), is the first and only accredited, degree-granting college that solely specializes in Graphic Design, Web Development, 3-D Modeling/Assets, and Digital Filmmaking/VFX within the greater San Diego area. With small class sizes, inverted curriculum, and project-based instruction, Platt College San Diego offers educational programs that are designed to empower and generate an atmosphere of creative learning and development.

Why Platt College San Diego?

- Small class sizes
- Complete design classes first to become marketable quickly
- One design class at a time
- Day or evening classes available
- No application, parking or monthly material fees
- Books and supplies included
- Locked tuition cost with no hidden fees
- Easy transfer credit evaluation
- VA approved

Majors and Degrees

The Bachelor of Science degree in Media Arts with an emphasis on Web Design and Development, prepares students for careers in the web world. This program is structured to compliment the revolutionary changes in interactive design that have catapulted the primarily print media area of graphic design into new arenas that combine audio, video, text, graphics, animation, and commerce.

The Bachelor of Science degree in Media Arts with an emphasis in 3D Modeling and Design prepares students for a broad range of design and technology skills. Mastering these skills results in artist's/designer's ability to express visual creativity through technology and the creative process.

The Bachelor of Science Degree in Media Arts with an emphasis in Digital Video Production offers solid knowledge enabling them to solve complex video production problems and create professional artistically unique products.

PCSD also offers an Associate of Applied Science: Graphic Design degree program and an Associate of Applied Science: Graphic Design degree program.

Facilities and Equipment

The 18,500 square-foot campus of classrooms, computer labs, library, and administrative offices is located in the metropolitan area of San Diego. The facilities for core curriculum courses (taught in computer labs) in terms 1–4 accommodate a maximum of 30 students. The core curriculum courses in terms 5 and 6 (upper division) accommodate a maximum of 12 students (in the computer labs). The general education lecture classrooms accommodate a maximum of 30 students. In all cases, class sizes are carefully controlled to provide individualized assistance, which is PCSD's hallmark.

The campus is accessible to the physically challenged with designated parking and an elevator. The facilities and equipment comply with all federal, state, and local ordinances relating to fire, building, and health and safety codes. Equipment typical of that used in today's industry is in place in the classrooms and is available for student use. A specific list of equipment utilized in each classroom can be requested from the admissions department. Internet access is available throughout the facilities.

Admission Requirements

Prior to the start date, candidates for enrollment in PCSD must provide evidence of high school completion in the form of an original diploma from a regionally accredited high school or the recognized equivalent (i.e. an original GED certificate or score report or California High School Proficiency Exam certificate or score report), or in the form of an official transcript.

All applicants must interview with an admissions representative prior to enrollment. Those interviewing in person will be given a tour of the facility to view classrooms, equipment, explore financial aid options (for those who qualify), and see examples of student work. Those unable to interview in person must have an admissions interview by phone.

PCSD uses an aptitude test to measure the candidate's academic preparedness to undertake college-level course work in English and mathematics. Other nationally based exams, such as the SAT or ACT exam, will be considered. In addition, the applicant's past academic performance and work experience may be reviewed to determine if the individual can benefit from training at PCSD.

Transfer of Credit to Platt College

The PCSD will consider the transfer of credits for completed coursework from other accredited institutions. Transcripts from all previously attended institutions, military transcripts, and AP/CLEP/DSST scores must be submitted to the College from the institution granting the credit and must be officially signed and sealed.

To be eligible for transfer of general education credit to PCSD, a minimum grade of "C" or a 2.0 in the transfer course must have been achieved, and the credit must be considered comparable to the level of coursework of the PCSD's program and non-remedial in nature. The College utilizes American Council on Education (ACE) recommended scores for CLEP and DSST.

Career Services

The ultimate goal of PCSD is for graduates to be employed in their field of training. The school maintains a career services program designed to assist qualified students and graduates in obtaining career goals. Leads for full or part-time job opportunities are solicited or contacted from a variety of industry sources and networking opportunities. Graduates and students are encouraged to utilize these employment opportunities as they become available.

The career services department advises students on interviewing skills, resume writing, and job search techniques.

Although the College cannot guarantee employment, many graduates who actively seek employment with the assistance of the career services department secure jobs in their field of training. A statistical report indicating placement percentages for each program is provided to each prospective student by the admissions department prior to enrollment.

Many companies have benefited from hiring PCSD Alumni, such as: Activision/Blizzard, Apple, DC Comics, Digital Domain, Disney, Google, ILM, Infinity Ward and Nike to name a few.

Costs

Platt College San Diego offers a locked tuition with no hidden fees. Books and supplies are included and there are no application, parking, or monthly material fees. Costs vary by program. The most up-to-date tuition information is available online at https://platt.edu/downloads/pcsd_tuition.pdf.

Financial Aid

Students applying for financial aid must submit the Free Application for Federal Student Aid (FAFSA). Students must meet the eligibility requirements of the program to qualify. PCSD participates in a variety of financial aid programs: the Federal Pell Grant, Federal Supplemental Educational Opportunity Grant (FSEOG), Veterans' Education Programs (Post911, the GI Bill, and the Yellow Ribbon Program), the Iraq and Afghanistan Service Grant, Cal Grants, the Federal Work-Study Program, the Stafford Loan Program, and the PLUS Loan Program.

The Platt College San Diego Academic Scholarship and PCSD Extended Opportunity Scholarship are also available to help qualified students pay for their education.

Student Life

Platt strives to balance the serious business in the classroom with fun outside of it. Often live media demonstrations, music, poetry, dance, raffle prizes, refreshments and spontaneous opportunities to be creative can be enjoyed in the Platt Courtyard. Students, faculty, and staff gather often in the courtyard to celebrate holidays or bring awareness to cultural events.

Students are encouraged to showcase their artwork at galleries and exhibits throughout the San Diego area. Extracurricular activities, such as field trips, competitions, and cultural events, provide a variety of opportunities to become inspired outside of the classroom. Students have access to a master list of numerous community service opportunities and are encouraged to take part in charitable and community service throughout the year.

Accreditation and Approvals

The College is accredited by the Accrediting Commission of Career Schools and Colleges (ACCSC) is listed by the U.S. Department of Education as a nationally recognized accrediting agency.

Platt College San Diego is a private institution approved by the Bureau of Private Postsecondary Education (BPPE).

How to Get Started

Potential students can take their first step toward being part of the Platt College San Diego experience by calling 866-PLATTCOLLEGE or 866-752-8826 or going online at platt.edu to schedule a visit.

For more information, contact:
Steve Gallup, Director of Admissions/Marketing
Platt College San Diego—Digital Media Design
6250 El Cajon Boulevard
San Diego, California 92115
United States
Phone: 866-752-8826
Fax: 619-308-0570
E-mail: sgallup@platt.edu
Website: https://platt.edu

COLLEGE CLOSE-UPS

PRATT INSTITUTE

BROOKLYN, NEW YORK

★ To read more about this school, visit http://petersons.to/prattinstitute

Pratt

The Institute

Industrialist and philanthropist Charles Pratt founded Pratt Institute in 1887 to educate students for various professions on a non-degree level. As the educational preparation necessary for various professions expanded, Pratt Institute moved to offer baccalaureate degrees with its first granted in 1938 and its first graduate degree granted in 1950. Now, with twenty-seven undergraduate majors and concentrations, Pratt offers students a wide variety of programs in which to major or take elective courses.

With its undergraduate ranked programs in art, design, and architecture ranked among the top five or ten in the country, Pratt has been ranked among the top design schools in the United States by *Business Week*. Pratt was also ranked number one in the country for its fine arts and studio programs by *USA Today*.

In addition to the four-year programs on its Brooklyn campus, Pratt offers students several additional locations to pursue their education: a two-year program in Utica, New York, at PrattMWP; and an associate degree program in fine art, graphic design, illustration, and gaming as well as a two- and four-year degree in construction management in Manhattan.

Although the characteristics and educational requirements of the professions for which Pratt prepares students have changed over the course of a century, the Institute has succeeded in pursuing its abiding purpose—to blend theoretical learning with professional and humanistic development—and has kept its curricula current by hiring practicing professionals to teach. Standards are high, modeled after the professional world. Faculty members connect students with internships and eventually jobs after graduation. Industry projects and internships provide students with real-world experience. Eighty-seven percent of Pratt's graduates are working within the first year after graduation.

Pratt Institute offers four-year bachelor's, two-year associate's, and master's degrees. Pratt's national and international reputation attracts undergraduate and graduate students from forty-eight U.S. states and over eighty countries. Students who choose Pratt are committed to the study of art, design, architecture, or creative writing and to their career objectives.

A short subway or bus ride from the museums, galleries, and design centers of both Manhattan and Brooklyn, Pratt Institute's main campus in Brooklyn, New York features twenty-five buildings of differing architectural styles spread throughout a beautifully landscaped 25-acre campus. The campus was ranked by *Architectural Digest* as one of the top ten campuses nationwide with the best architecture. It includes a contemporary sculpture garden (ranked among the top ten campus art collections by *Public Art Review*), an athletic center, residence halls, dining halls, outstanding studio facilities, and historic buildings. Nineteen of the buildings house studios, classrooms, laboratories, administrative offices, auditoria, sports facilities, food services, and student centers. A new green LEED gold-certified building houses student administrative services including admissions, undergraduate and graduate digital arts programs, and various administrative offices, including student financial services and the registrar's offices. Six buildings are student residences, including the Stabile Hall freshman residence, which provides studio space on each floor; a new freshman residence hall is scheduled to be completed by fall 2018. There is adequate parking for residents and commuters. Student services include career planning and placement, health and counseling, a disabilities office, a HEOP program, and student development. More than sixty student organizations are available including fraternities and sororities, honorary societies, professional societies, and clubs.

Location

Pratt Institute, the country's premier college of art, design, writing, and architecture, has its main campus in the Clinton Hill neighborhood of Brooklyn, just minutes from downtown Manhattan. Ninety percent of Pratt's freshmen and over half of its undergraduates live on the tree-lined Brooklyn campus. Minutes from the Brooklyn Museum and the Brooklyn Academy of Music, Pratt is ideally located, providing students with a green oasis just minutes from the art capital of the world, Manhattan. The Manhattan campus is located in Chelsea. The Utica campus, home to the first two years of Pratt's programs in fine art, communications design, photography, and art and design education (teacher certification) with automatic relocation to the Brooklyn campus for the junior year,, is located in upstate New York.

Majors and Degrees

Pratt Institute offers the Bachelor of Architecture, Bachelor of Fine Arts, Bachelor of Art, Bachelor of Industrial Design, Bachelor of Professional Studies, Bachelor of Science, Associate of Occupational Studies, and Associate of Applied Science degrees.

The Bachelor of Architecture degree program is a five-year, accredited program. For the Bachelor of Fine Arts degree, a candidate may choose to major in art and design education (art teacher certification), history of art and design, communications design (branding and art direction, graphic design, illustration), digital arts (3-D animation, 2-D animation, and interactive arts), fashion design, film, fine arts (ceramics, drawing, jewelry, painting, printmaking, sculpture), interior design, photography, or writing. The Bachelor of Arts is offered in critical and visual studies and art history. The Bachelor of Industrial Design is offered for students interested in product and furniture design. In the Bachelor of Professional Studies degree program, the major is in construction management. Students seeking the Bachelor of Science degree can major in construction management or professional services management.

The two-year Associate of Occupational Studies degree is offered in game design and interactive media, graphic design, and illustration. The Associate of Applied Science is offered in painting/drawing and graphic design/illustration. The two-year Associate of Applied Science degree is transferable to a four-year program.

Students may also earn combined bachelor's/master's degrees. Programs include the B.F.A./M.S. in art and design education as well as art history.

Academic Programs

Educating artists and creative professionals to be responsible contributors to society has been the mission of Pratt Institute since it assembled its first group of students in 1887. Within the structure of that professional education, Pratt students are encouraged to acquire the diverse knowledge that is necessary for them to succeed in their chosen fields including sustainability. In addition to the professional studies, the curriculum in each of Pratt's schools includes a broad range of liberal arts courses. Students from all schools take these courses together and have the opportunity to examine the interrelationships of art, science, technology, and human need.

At the time of graduation, students in the associate degree programs have completed 67 credit hours of course work. In the bachelor's programs, credit-hour requirements are 126 credits with opportunities to take electives in other disciplines or minors, depending on the particular program. For the Bachelor of Architecture degree, 170 credits are required.

Pratt's academic calendar consists of two semesters plus optional summer terms that allow students to choose alternative courses or various options usually not offered during the fall or spring semester.

Off-Campus Programs

Pratt Institute offers credit for a wide variety of off-campus study programs. The internship program offers qualified students challenging on-the-job experience related to their major fields of interest; this extension of the classroom and laboratory into the professional world adds a practical dimension to periods of on-campus study.

International programs, available during all academic sessions, have included art and design offerings in the cities of Copenhagen and Rome and in the countries of England, France, Italy, and South Africa. Architecture programs have been held in Italy, Finland, and Japan. New programs are developed regularly in these and other countries. A semester-long program is offered in Rome each year.

Academic Facilities

Founded as the first free library in Brooklyn, the Pratt Institute Library has more than 176,674 bound volumes, 84,604 art books, 237 print and online art and art history journals, a rare book collection, and subscriptions to journals online through JSTOR, EBSCO, and others. The library also has serial backfiles and other material, including government documents; 251,603 audiovisual materials; and 3,996 microforms and subscribes to 925 periodicals—the largest collection of any independent art school. With their ID cards, Pratt students also have access to numerous college libraries in the metropolitan area.

Extensive studio and state-of-the-art computer lab facilities are provided for all Pratt students. In the School of Art and Design, these include studio, shop, and technical facilities for work in all media, from the traditional to the most experimental. Gallery space, both on campus and at Pratt Manhattan, is extensive, showing the work of students, alumni, faculty members, staff members, and other well-known artists, architects, and designers.

Costs

Tuition for the 2017–18 academic year is $47,986. Room charges are $8,400 per academic year. A meal plan is available, and costs about $3,620 for the year. The fees are approximately $2,052. The estimated cost of books and supplies is $1,750 per academic year. Students should allow an additional $3,000 for transportation and personal expenses. For an updated list of tuition and fees, prospective students should visit www.pratt.edu/admissions/financing-your-education/financing-undergraduate/cost-of-attendance.

Financial Aid

Pratt Institute offers an extensive program of merit-based scholarships, need-based grants, loans, and awards based on academic achievement, talent, financial need, or all three. More than 75 percent of Pratt students receive financial assistance through one or more of these kinds of aid.

Faculty

The faculty at Pratt Institute is exceptional in that a large number of practicing professionals augment the regular full-time faculty. There are 149 full-time and 983 part-time faculty members. In small classes and studios, students have easy access to professors whose natural environment is the design studio, the architectural office, or the industrial research department. Faculty members often connect students with internships and eventually jobs.

Student Government

The Student Government Association (SGA) maintains primary responsibility for all student interests and involvement at Pratt. All undergraduate students are encouraged to become involved in the SGA, whose main functions are allocating and administering funds collected through the student activities fee, scheduling student activities, and representing the student viewpoint to the rest of the Pratt community.

Admission Requirements

Pratt Institute attracts and enrolls highly motivated and talented students from diverse backgrounds. Applications are welcome from all qualified students, regardless of age, sex, race, color, religion, national origin, or handicap. Admission standards at Pratt are high. One of the major components for admission consideration in art, design, or architecture is the evaluation of a student's art or writing portfolio, which must be submitted along with the other required documents.

All applicants to four-year programs must submit official transcripts, test scores, and a visual or writing portfolio with the exception of construction management applicants who are not required to submit a portfolio. Instructions may be found at www.pratt.edu/apply.

The admission committee bases its decisions on careful reviews of all credentials submitted by applicants in relation to the requirements of the program to which students seek admission. International students must submit TOEFL or IELTS scores or SAT scores, but not both. In certain cases, extraordinary talent may offset a low grade or a test score.

Application and Information

Pratt has two admissions deadlines: November 1 for early action and January 5 for regular admissions. To receive full consideration, students must submit their applications by January 5 for anticipated entrance in the fall semester and by October 1 for anticipated entrance in the spring semester. Additional details regarding application deadlines can be found on Pratt's website: https://www.pratt.edu/admissions/applying/applying-undergraduate/ug-application-requirements/.

For more information about Pratt Institute, students should contact:

Office of Admissions
Pratt Institute
200 Willoughby Avenue
Brooklyn, New York 11205
Phone: 718-636-3514
800-331-0834 (toll-free)
E-mail: admissions@pratt.edu
Website: www.pratt.edu
www.pratt.edu/request (Catalog request)
www.pratt.edu/visit (Visit information and online campus tour registration)
http://on.fb.me/pratt_admissions (Facebook)

Pratt's campus in the spring. © 2014 Bob Handelman

QUINNIPIAC UNIVERSITY

HAMDEN, CONNECTICUT

★ To read more about this school, visit http://petersons.to/quinnipiac

Quinnipiac UNIVERSITY

The University

Quinnipiac University offers four-year and graduate-level degree programs leading to careers in health sciences, nursing, business, communications, engineering, natural sciences, education, liberal arts, law, and medicine. A curriculum that combines a career focus with a globally oriented liberal arts background prepares graduates for the future, whether they start their careers right after commencement or opt to pursue advanced study.

Quinnipiac is coeducational and nonsectarian and currently enrolls 6,780 full-time undergraduates, 1,445 full-time graduate law and medical students, and 1,675 part-time students in its undergraduate, graduate, and professional programs. Twenty-five percent of the students are residents of Connecticut; the rest represent primarily the northeast corridor, in all thirty-one states including Alaska, California, and Texas, and thirty countries. Quinnipiac is big enough to sustain a wide variety of people and programs but small enough to keep students from getting lost in the shuffle. Life on campus emphasizes students' personal, as well as academic, growth. The approximately 120 student organizations, 16 Greek chapters, and extracurricular activities, including intramural and intercollegiate (NCAA Division I) athletics, give students a chance to exercise their talents, muscles, and leadership skills. The University has a student newspaper, TV station, and an FM radio station (WQAQ) and twenty-one intercollegiate teams in men's baseball, basketball, cross-country, ice hockey, lacrosse, soccer, and tennis, and in women's acrobatics and tumbling, basketball, cross-country, field hockey, golf, ice hockey, lacrosse, rugby, soccer, softball, tennis, track (indoor and outdoor), and volleyball. Teams compete in the MAAC conference; men's and women's ice hockey teams in the ECAC; and women's field hockey in the Big East.

The University has three distinct campus settings. The 250-acre Mount Carmel campus has fifty buildings including the Arnold Bernhard Library, academic facilities, an athletic and recreation center, and twenty-five residence halls of different styles, mainly for freshmen and sophomores, with traditional double and quad (4-person) rooms, suites, and multilevel suites and apartments with kitchens. About 95 percent of all freshmen and 75 percent of the total undergraduate population live in Quinnipiac housing. The nearby 250-acre York Hill campus includes the TD Bank Sports Center with twin 3,500-seat arenas for ice hockey and basketball; a suite-style with single and double rooms 1,500-bed residence halls and townhouses for juniors and seniors; "Rocky Top," a lodge-like student center; spectacular views; and a multilevel parking garage for 2,000 vehicles. Seniors may also live in University-owned houses or apartments. Senior-year housing is on a space-available basis. A free shuttle takes students between all three campuses. The 104-acre North Haven campus is just 4 miles away and provides state-of-the-art facilities for graduate and upper division offerings in several programs in the Schools of Health Sciences, Nursing, Education, Law, and Medicine. The Center for Medicine, Nursing, and Health Sciences offers a cooperative learning environment geared to educate the health-care team.

Career planning takes place in each of the schools with assistance from the deans' offices. It begins with faculty advisement, along with career exploration, a strong focus on internships and clinical placements, consideration of various major and job fields, and exposure to prospective employers and job preparation. Approximately 30 percent of the undergraduate student population remains at Quinnipiac for their graduate degree in combined or direct entry majors, particularly in education, business, communications, physical and occupational therapy, physician assistant, and social work programs. A particularly innovative Business 4-year (3+1) program offers academically talented applicants to the School of Business the opportunity to complete both a B.S. and an M.B.A. in just four years. A similar 4-year (3+1) program in the School of Communications offers students an undergraduate B.A. or B.F.A. and a graduate M.S. in 4 years. And academically strong students can combine an undergraduate B.A. with a J.D. degree in the School of Law in just 6 instead of the traditional 7 years.

Graduate programs lead to the Master of Science (M.S.) degree in accounting, information technology, interactive media, journalism, molecular and cell biology, organizational leadership, public relations, and teacher leadership; the Master of Health Science in anesthesiologist assistant, medical lab sciences, cardiovascular perfusion, pathologist assistant, and physician assistant; a Master of Science in Nursing plus the Doctor of Nursing Practice in adult and family nursing and nurse anesthesia; the Doctor of Physical Therapy; a Master of Health Sciences in Advanced Medical Imaging and Leadership; the Master of Business Administration; the Master of Business Administration in Health Care Management; the Master of Business Administration–Chartered Financial Analyst; the Master of Arts in Teaching; and the Master of Social Work. The Quinnipiac University School of Law offers full- and part-time programs leading to a J.D. degree or J.D./M.B.A. degree in combination with the School of Business. Several of the graduate degree programs are offered online or in a hybrid format. The Frank H. Netter MD School of Medicine focuses on developing doctors as part of a health-care team with a focus on primary care, rehabilitative medicine, and global health.

Location

Situated at the foot of Sleeping Giant Mountain in Hamden, Connecticut, Quinnipiac provides the best of the suburbs and the city. The University is only 8 miles from New Haven, 30 minutes from Hartford (the state capital), and less than 2 hours from New York City and Boston. Bordering the campus is the 1,700-acre Sleeping Giant State Park, for walking and hiking. The free campus shuttle takes students to nearby shopping and restaurants, as well as to New Haven, where they can visit various art and science museums, attend a performance at Yale Rep or the Shubert Theater, find great restaurants, and have easy access to Metro North and Amtrak at the New Haven train station.

Majors and Degrees

The Schools of Health Sciences and Nursing grant bachelor's degrees in athletic training, biomedical science, health and science studies, microbiology/immunology, and nursing. Combined B.S./graduate degree programs include occupational therapy (5½-year entry-level master's), physical therapy (6- or 7-year entry-level doctorate), physician assistant studies (6-year freshman entry-level master's), and radiologic science and diagnostic medical sonography (both can be a 3-year accelerated B.S.). Students who wish to prepare for entry into medical, dental, chiropractic, veterinary, or other medical schools work with a premed adviser and the pre-health advisory committee.

The School of Business (accredited by AACSB International and ranked in the top 100 Best Undergraduate Business Schools in 2014 *Bloomberg BusinessWeek*) offers bachelor's degree programs in accounting, biomedical marketing, entrepreneurship, finance, computer information systems, international business, management, and marketing. The school offers an innovative Business 4-year (3+1) B.S./M.B.A. program to highly qualified business students, also a fast-track, five-year combined-degree program in which students from all majors may gain preadmission to the M.B.A. program, allowing them to fast-track through their M.B.A. in 12–14 months after earning their bachelor's degree by taking several undergraduate and graduate business courses while undergraduates. Students, are awarded a B.A. in the College of Arts and Sciences or Communications or the B.S. degree in Health Sciences, Engineering, or Business and then complete their graduate degree in accounting, business administration, or computer information systems (M.S. or M.B.A.).

The School of Engineering offers degrees in computer sciences and in mechanical, industrial, civil, and software engineering.

The College of Arts and Sciences offers bachelor's degree programs in behavioral neuroscience, biochemistry, biology, chemistry, criminal justice, economics, English, gerontology, history, interdisciplinary studies, independent study, law in society, mathematics, philosophy, political science, psychology, sociology, Spanish, and theater. Qualified students can go on to the Master of Science in molecular and cell biology program or pursue graduate programs in education, business, law, health sciences, journalism, interactive media, medicine, and social work.

The School of Communications offers undergraduate majors in advertising and integrated communications, communications/media studies; film, television, and media arts; graphic and interactive design; journalism; and public relations, plus a B.F.A. in film and graduate programs in journalism, public relations, sports journalism, and interactive media. One highlight is "QU in LA," a Los Angeles location for summer/fall/spring internships for communications and business students in particular, but open to all undergraduate and graduate Quinnipiac students.

The School of Education's five-year program for undergraduates provides certification for teaching elementary and secondary grades through a B.A./Master of Arts in Teaching (M.A.T.) program (accredited by CAEP the Council for the Accreditation of Education Preparation). Students complete a B.A. or B.S. in a subject area or in Interdisciplinary Studies in the College of Arts and Sciences; take the freshman course, Introduction to the Teaching Profession; and then continue the M.A.T. course work in their junior and senior years and complete the degree in a final graduate year.

Academic Programs

The Quinnipiac Learning Paradigm begins at orientation, involving students in identifying their strengths and goals, and follows through to graduation. Students begin their electronic portfolio to track their accomplishments and learning. The foundation of the University Curriculum encourages students to explore a variety of options when selecting a major, double major, major and minor, or combined undergraduate/graduate degrees. The Writing Across the Curriculum initiative (WAC) stresses the improvement in writing skills in all subject areas. The University honors program addresses the needs and interests of the most academically talented and committed students. Advanced placement, credit, or both are given for appropriate scores on Advanced Placement tests and CLEP general and subject examinations as well as for scores of 4 or higher in the International Baccalaureate higher-level subjects.

Off-Campus Programs

Students can study abroad in a variety of countries. Most students choose a study-abroad option in their sophomore year, many at Quinnipiac's affiliated program in Ireland. Students in any of the six undergraduate schools can also get hands-on experience in their field through off-campus internships and clinical placements in the health sciences. Academic credit is available for internships and affiliations, which are often part of degree requirements.

Academic Facilities

Academic life focuses on the Bernhard Library. This attractive facility provides individual carrels and small rooms for group study and is open 24/7 during the fall and spring semesters. A wireless network provides access to automated library systems and extensive Web-based resources. The Learning Commons, located in the north wing, offers individual tutoring assistance along with helpful learning workshops.

The School of Communications provides 4K (ultra-high-definition) cameras and editing rooms; multimedia and digital design labs; a high-definition TV production studio; audio production; print journalism; a news innovation center; and all the latest software for film, video, interactive media, websites, graphics, and animation. The computer cluster in the Financial Technology Center at the School of Business is a high-tech, simulated trading floor providing students with the opportunity to access real-time financial data, conduct interactive trading simulations, and develop financial models in preparation for careers in finance. The Center for Innovation and Entrepreneurship and the App Lab encourage students in all majors to think creatively.

Engineering uses a long list of workshops for hands-on learning: computer-aided engineering, biomedical, circuits and controls, environmental, fluids, geotechnical, hydraulics, rapid prototyping and performance optimization.

The Center for Medicine, Nursing, and Health Sciences on the North Haven campus provides state-of-the-art facilities for the Schools of Medicine, Nursing, Health Sciences, Law, and Education. In addition to a breathtaking location and expansive exterior and interior spaces, there are specialized facilities and equipment for each program, such as movement study/motion analysis and biomechanics labs; the ergonomics and assistive technology lab; a model adaptive apartment; an orthopedics lab; several rehabilitative sciences labs; CT scan, MRI, radiography, ultrasound, and mammography facilities; and the latest clinical skills simulation labs for adults and pediatric/neonatal patients including an intensive care unit, physical diagnosis lab, physical exam suite, health assessment labs, human anatomy lab, and two operating suites. Medical and health science and nursing students are educated in an inter-professional atmosphere.

Costs

The 2017–18 total direct costs are $60,970, of which tuition and fees total $46,100 (for students taking 12–16 credits per semester). Room and board average $14,190 (and includes $3,200 allocated to the meal plan). There is also a $680 technology fee. Indirect expenses, estimated at $2,800 per year, include books, personal, and travel expenses.

Financial Aid and Scholarships

Quinnipiac designs financial aid packages to include need-based grants and merit-based scholarships that do not have to be repaid, plus self-help financial aid programs such as federal and University-based work study, and loans. Students and families seeking need-based aid will file the Free Application for Federal Student Aid (FAFSA) to determine need. Transfer students are eligible for the same need-based financial aid consideration as first-time freshmen.

Faculty

The faculty is characterized by its teaching competence and outstanding academic qualifications. Of the 369 full-time faculty members, 85 percent have earned a Ph.D. or the appropriate terminal degree in their field. The faculty also includes a number of part-time teachers who are practicing professionals and experts in their fields. Classes are taught by these scholars and professionals and not by student instructors, and a low student-faculty ratio promotes close associations among faculty members and students.

Student Government

The Student Government is the student legislative body of Quinnipiac. It represents student opinion, promotes student welfare, supervises student organizations, appropriates funds for student groups, and provides voting student representation on the Board of Trustees.

Admission Requirements

Quinnipiac seeks students from a broad range of backgrounds. On average, freshman students have a 3.4 GPA or better average in college-preparatory courses (transfer students generally have a 2.5 GPA or better), rank in the top 25 percent of their high school class, and have an average combined score of 1100 on the SAT (critical reading plus math) or an ACT composite of 25. Visits to the campus for an interview, open house, group information session, or a campus tour are strongly encouraged and can be arranged at www.quinnipiac.edu/visit. Transfer students are welcome to make an appointment to discuss requirements and the transfer of credit from previous institutions. Quinnipiac sponsors six open house programs during the year and several Saturday morning information sessions followed by a campus tour.

Application and Information

Quinnipiac generally receives about 23,000 applications for admission and admits about 65 percent, to enroll an incoming class of 1,900 freshmen and 200 transfer students. Quinnipiac has a rolling admission policy for its undergraduate programs and therefore recommends that freshman applicants submit the application fairly early in the fall of their senior year, followed by their transcript, first marking period grades, and test scores (if required—see website for details) well before the deadline of February 1. Students applying to the 6-year physician assistant program should submit the application by October 15, and those applying to physical therapy, nursing, and occupational therapy programs should submit the application by November 15. An early decision (binding) option is available in all majors with an application deadline of November 1. Applications are reviewed as soon as they are complete, and the University begins notifying students of decisions in November. Quinnipiac is a member of the Common Application. Students placed on a waiting list are notified of any openings by June 1. Quinnipiac subscribes to the May 1 Candidates Reply Date Agreement. For information about full-time undergraduate study, students should contact:

Office of Undergraduate Admissions
Quinnipiac University
Hamden, Connecticut 06518-1940
Phone: 203-582-8600
800-462-1944 (toll-free)
Fax: 203-582-8906
E-mail: admissions@qu.edu
Website: www.quinnipiac.edu
www.facebook.com/QuinnipiacUniversity
twitter.com/QU_Admissions
quadmissions-blogspot.com/
www.youtube.com/quinnipiacuniversity

For information regarding transfer and part-time study:

Office of Transfer and Part-time Admissions
Quinnipiac University
Hamden, Connecticut 06518-1940
Phone: 203-582-8612
Fax: 203-582-8906
E-mail: transferadmission@qu.edu

COLLEGE CLOSE-UPS

REED COLLEGE

PORTLAND, OREGON

★ To read more about this school, visit http://petersons.to/reedcollege

The College

Referred to as one of the most intellectual colleges in the country, Reed is known for its high standards of scholarly practice, creative thinking, and engaged citizenship. Self-discipline and a genuine enthusiasm for academic work and intellectual exchange are valued, and the Honor Principle, Reed's ethos that guides both academic and campus life, ensures personal responsibility and mutual respect for its small community of 1,410 students and 161 faculty members. More than four-fifths of Reed's students come from outside the Northwest, with one-fifth from the Northeast and one-tenth from outside of the United States. Over 30 percent of Reed's students identify with historically underrepresented racial and ethnic backgrounds. Reed's twenty-three residence halls enable approximately 70 percent of students to live on campus.

At its founding, Reed rejected fraternal societies and varsity sports. The goal was to foster a climate of inclusivity and collaboration focused on academics. This atmosphere persists, with student groups—social, religious, and cultural—open to all and fitness and the development of athletic skills taking precedence over competition.

Location

Reed's 116-acre wooded campus is located in a residential section of southeast Portland. The city, a welcoming metropolis, offers a thriving local music scene, diverse restaurants and food carts, tranquil Japanese and Chinese gardens, noisy downtown clubs, a plethora of bridges and bike paths, and the largest independent bookstore in the world. Just 90 minutes west of Portland are the wild beaches of the Pacific Ocean; 90 minutes east are the ski slopes of Mount Hood where Reed owns a ski cabin for use by the college community.

Majors and Degrees

Reed College awards the Bachelor of Arts degree in a variety of traditional fields, as well as in interdisciplinary combinations. Students may select from the following majors: American studies, anthropology, art, biochemistry and molecular biology, biology, chemistry, chemistry-physics, Chinese literature, Chinese studies, classics, classics-religion, comparative literature, computer science, dance, dance-theater, economics, English literature, environmental studies, French literature, German literature, history, history-literature, international and comparative policy studies, linguistics, literature-theater, mathematics, mathematics with concentrations in either computer science or statistics, mathematics-economics, mathematics-physics, music, philosophy, physics, political science, psychology, religion, Russian literature, sociology, Spanish literature, and theatre.

Students may also design their own interdisciplinary majors. The approval of such special programs, which link two or more disciplines, is reviewed by the student's adviser and the departments concerned.

Reed offers several combined 3-2 programs, which allow the student to earn both a bachelor's degree from Reed and a professional degree from the cooperating institution. Science programs and institutions include engineering, computer science (California Institute of Technology, Columbia University, and Rensselaer Polytechnic Institute), and forestry-environmental sciences (Duke University). The college also has a combined program in visual arts (Pacific Northwest College of Art).

Academic Programs

Hallmarks of academic life at Reed include the small-group conference method of teaching and its reliance on active student participation; a de-emphasizing of grades coupled with comprehensive narrative feedback; a yearlong interdisciplinary humanities program; and distribution requirements that balance breadth of learning with the depth of designing an in-depth senior thesis. In addition to fulfilling the requirements for the major, taking the humanities course, and writing the senior thesis, students must satisfy a distributional requirement, consisting of two core classes from each of the following academic groups: literature, philosophy, and the arts; history, social sciences, and psychology; the natural sciences; and math, foreign language, logic, and linguistics. Students must also take two classes from one other department outside their major course of study.

Off-Campus Programs

Reed participates in domestic exchange programs with Howard University in Washington, D.C.; Sarah Lawrence College in New York; and Sea Education Association in Massachusetts. In addition, Reed provides study-abroad opportunities for students in Australia, Argentina, China, Costa Rica, Cuba, Ecuador, Egypt, France, Germany, Greece, Hungary, Ireland, Israel, Italy, Kenya, Lebanon, Morocco, Palestine, Russia, South Africa, Spain, Turkey, Turks and Caicos, and the United Kingdom. Students may also arrange independent study plans in consultation with appropriate faculty members, the director for off-campus studies, and the registrar.

Academic Facilities

Students have access to Reed's substantial library collection by searching the online catalog in the library or from any computer on the campus network. Through its participation in Summit, a union catalog of Oregon and Washington academic libraries, Reed provides online access to other library catalogs and databases. Students may borrow materials directly from academic libraries in the Portland area, as well as from collections worldwide through interlibrary loan. In addition, the Reed library accommodates a first-rate art gallery, a language lab, and a multimedia resource facility. The Reed library is open 18 hours most days and 24 hours a day during examinations.

The science laboratories at Reed are among the best equipped of any undergraduate college in the United States. These include the A. A. Knowlton Laboratory of Physics, the Arthur F. Scott Laboratory of Chemistry, and the L. E. Griffin Memorial Biology Building. Reed's nuclear research reactor (the only such reactor in the country that is staffed primarily by undergraduates) and radiochemistry lab are actively used for student research, instruction, and training. For those interested in the arts, the campus houses studio art facilities that recently saw a $2-million expansion, performing arts facilities, twenty instrumental practice rooms, a computer music laboratory, a recording system, and an 800-seat auditorium. In fall 2013, Reed opened a new $28-million Performing Arts Building, representing a major step forward in the college's commitment to the important role the arts play at Reed. Other popular facilities include a radio station and Reed's newly expanded sports center, which offers a climbing wall and a nationally recognized outdoor program.

Costs

Tuition for 2016–17 was $51,850, and room and board was $13,150. The student body fee was $300, bringing the yearly total cost to approximately $65,030. The cost of books and incidental expenses averages approximately $2,000.

Financial Aid

Over half of the Reed student body receives financial assistance from the college. A full need-based financial aid program makes Reed accessible to students from a wide range of economic backgrounds. The college guarantees to meet the full demonstrated need of all continuing students in good academic standing who complete their financial aid applications on time. Reed's own funds are the primary source of grants to students, making up 84 percent of the average financial aid package in 2016–17. Reed also administers federal and state grants as well as federally subsidized loan programs. Campus employment and work-study programs are available. The size of a financial aid award is based solely upon analysis of the student's need. The average amount awarded to students receiving financial aid in 2016–17 was $44,915, which includes grants, loans, and work opportunities. Reed students' average graduating loan debt for all four years is $19,528, well below the national average.

Faculty

All classes at Reed are taught by professors rather than by teaching assistants. Classes are small, averaging about 15 students. The opportunity to work closely with faculty members is noted by students as one of the great benefits of a Reed education. Reed faculty members point to the opportunity to work with students who are serious scholars as one of the great benefits of teaching at Reed. Faculty members commit themselves primarily to teaching, with scholarly and scientific research furthering this primary goal; they view students as partners in learning, often serving as coauthors and co-investigators on professional papers and research projects. This close association is due, in large part, to a 9:1 student-faculty ratio and the one-on-one relationship between thesis adviser (a professor) and student during the senior year.

Student Government

The Student Senate is the central body in student governance. The Senate consists of the student body president, vice president, and 8 student representatives, all elected by the students. Its two primary functions are to allocate student body funds and to represent student interests and concerns to the faculty, administration, and Reed College Board of Trustees. The Senate distributes approximately $40,000 each semester to the many student organizations on campus. As agreed under the community constitution, students participate fully in discussions and decisions on a wide variety of issues. The Student Committee on Academic Policy and Planning participates in debate about the curriculum at Reed; many other committees, from the Library Board to the Reactor Committee, have substantial student input. The Senate and student body president make all student appointments to such committees.

Admission Requirements

Reed welcomes applications from freshman and transfer candidates who are genuinely committed to the pursuit of a liberal arts education and a rigorous academic program. Those applicants are admitted who, in the view of the Admission Committee, are most likely to become successful members of and contribute significantly and honorably to the Reed community. The college is committed to maintaining a student body distinguished by its intellectual passion and its diverse range of backgrounds, interests, and talents.

Admission decisions are based on many integrated factors, but academic accomplishments and talents are given the greatest weight in the selection process. A strong secondary school preparation, including honors and advanced courses where available, improves a student's chances for admission. Such a program usually includes: 4 years of English and 3 to 4 years of mathematics (through pre-calculus), science, foreign language, and history or social studies. Given the wide variation in high school programs and quality, however, there are no fixed requirements for secondary school courses. Applicants are expected to have obtained a secondary school diploma prior to enrollment, although exceptions are occasionally made. There are no cutoff points for high school or college grades or for test scores.

Reed recognizes the qualities of character—in particular, motivation, intellectual curiosity, individual responsibility, and community and social consciousness—as important considerations in the selection process, beyond a demonstrated commitment to academic excellence. Thus, the Admission Committee looks for students whose accomplishments and interests in various fields of endeavor will contribute to the overall liveliness of the Reed community. Personal interviews, either on or off campus, are not a requirement in the admission process but are recommended whenever possible. Applications for early decision should be submitted by November 15 (Option I) or December 20 (Option II), early action applications should be submitted by November 15, regular freshman admission by January 1, and transfer candidates by March 1.

Application and Information

The Office of Admission is open Monday through Friday from 8:30 a.m. until 5 p.m. (Pacific time) all year, except for major holidays. The Admission Office is also open on select Saturdays in the spring and fall. Reed College uses both the Coalition Application and the Common Application; students can find a complete list of application requirements online at reed.edu/apply/guide-to-applying.

For further information or to arrange a campus tour, overnight stay, information session, or interview, students should contact:

Office of Admission
Reed College
3203 Southeast Woodstock Boulevard
Portland, Oregon 97202-8199
Phone: 503-777-7511
800-547-4750 (toll-free)
Fax: 503-777-7553
E-mail: admission@reed.edu
Website: reed.edu

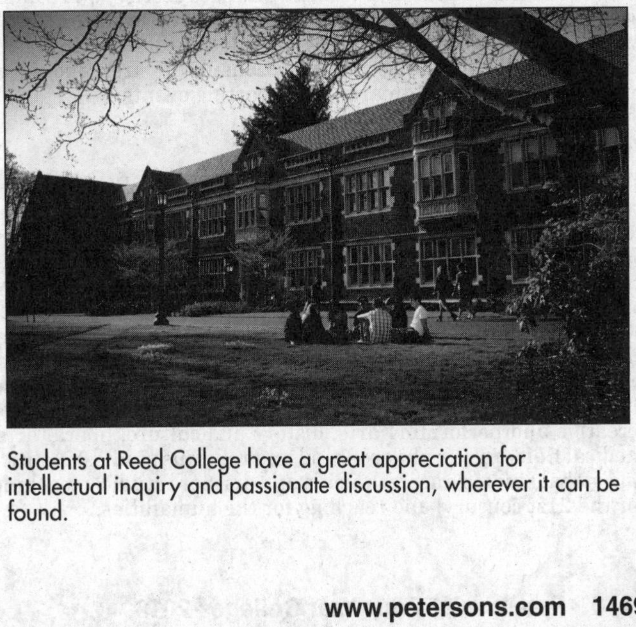

Students at Reed College have a great appreciation for intellectual inquiry and passionate discussion, wherever it can be found.

COLLEGE CLOSE-UPS

REGIS COLLEGE

WESTON, MASSACHUSETTS

REGIS
A CATHOLIC UNIVERSITY IN GREATER BOSTON

★ For more information, visit http://petersons.to/regiscollege

The College

Regis is a leading Catholic university in Greater Boston with 2,000 undergraduate, graduate, and doctoral students in the arts, sciences, and health professions devoted to engagement, service, and advancement in a global community.

The Princeton Review has named Regis among the top Northeast colleges in the nation for academic excellence. The university provides Apple iPads to all full-time students and faculty, and is recognized as a leader in interactive digital education. Regis was also named a "hidden gem" school by Colleges of Distinction for its excellence in providing outstanding teaching and an engaging, vibrant community for students.

Regis offers more than 30 academic majors, minors, and preprofessional programs that provide firm foundations in the liberal arts, sciences, and social sciences. These programs prepare students for careers in high-demand fields, including business, education, health, and public service. Internships, clinical placements, student-teaching, and research opportunities allow students to integrate their skills and knowledge developed over the course of their studies into real-world experiences.

Regis partners with affiliate colleges across the world to provide study abroad opportunities from the United Kingdom and Ireland to Italy and Japan.

Regis is a student-centered environment. The diversity of its students, clubs, and organizations is of utmost importance and the university seeks to provide the highest quality of support and education for all students. More than twenty-six states and thirty countries are represented in the student body; 30 percent of the student population consists of minority and international students and over 40 percent of degree-seeking undergraduates are first-generation college students.

Regis is one of only three schools in New England to be named a Center of Excellence in Nursing Education by the National League of Nursing. Regis has been recognized for creating environments that enhance student learning and professional development. Regis is accredited by the New England Association of Schools and Colleges.

Location

Regis's campus is located in Weston, Massachusetts, just 12 miles west of Boston. Regis operates a regular shuttle to the area's MBTA rapid-transit system so students can take advantage of the many cultural and social attractions in the area, including museums, historic landmarks, and sporting events.

Majors and Degrees

The School of Arts and Sciences at Regis offers bachelor's degree programs in a wide range of career-focused tracks. Programs combine a strong core curriculum with practical experience opportunities to help students develop knowledge, values, and professional skills. Bachelor's degrees are offered in biology; biomedical engineering; communication; criminal justice studies; education with licensure in early childhood education, elementary education, middle school education, and secondary school education; English; environmental sustainability; global business management; interdisciplinary studies in the humanities (creative and performing arts, history and culture, liberal arts, medical humanities, philosophical and religious studies); politics and global studies; race, ethnicity, and diaspora studies; teaching for the 21st century; and teaching for the humanities.

A 3+3 partnership has been established with Western New England Law School (WNELS) to provide students with the opportunity to earn both a bachelor's degree and a law degree in six years as opposed to seven. Students attend Regis for three years and then transition to WNELS to complete the remaining three years of law school. After the first year of law school has been successfully completed at WNELS, students receive their bachelor's degree from Regis. A pre-law track of study is also available.

The School of Health Sciences offers interdisciplinary, cutting-edge programs designed to prepare students for successful careers in ever-changing fields. Bachelor's degrees are offered in diagnostic medical sonography, exercise science, neuroscience, nuclear medicine, nutrition, psychology, public health, social work, and sports management.

A 3+4 partnership has been established with St. George's University in Grenada. Regis and St. George's University School of Medicine and School of Veterinary Medicine offer direct and guaranteed acceptance into medical school or veterinary school for qualified students. Participants will complete seven years of study—three years at Regis (from which they ultimately earn a bachelor's degree), then four years of medical or veterinary school at St. George's University in Grenada, West Indies. St. George's University offers residency and clinical rotations at affiliated hospitals in the United States. To be eligible for admission into this accelerated program, students must complete the requirements of their major and the Core Curriculum requirements of Regis in their first three years of study and meet the admission criteria set forth by St. George's University for medical school or veterinary school.

Preprofessional programs with the School of Health Sciences include pre-dental, pre-medical, and pre-veterinary.

The Regis School of Nursing was the first in New England to be designated as a Center for Excellence in Nursing Education by the National League of Nursing (NLN). Students in the nursing major receive individualized attention from professors and use the latest technology in both their classrooms and labs. Students are also able to bring their classroom knowledge to life during clinical rotations, where they are exposed to various areas of nursing including medical, surgical, psychiatric, pediatric, maternity, and community health.

Academic Programs

The Academic Advising Department at Regis supports throughout their academic experience. This includes assistance in making class choices and reaching their academic goals and defining their career goals.

The Center for Internships and Career Placement actively reaches out to the community to provide part-time jobs, internships, and professional job opportunities. Using a curriculum that's unique to Regis, students are taught how to identify and land the job that's right for them. Other career assistance includes online tools and required courses, workshops, one-on-one counseling, and career development and recruitment events.

The Regis Honors Program provides qualified students with intellectually and personally stimulating experiences, including academically rigorous courses; participation in community leadership, service learning, and service; and personal enrichment opportunities. Honors students explore complex issues of civic responsibility and global citizenship, and develop skills in contributing to the betterment of society, a central goal of Regis' mission.

The Regis Undergraduate Writing Program offers students the opportunity to hone their professional and creative writing skills and effectively communicate their ideas, opinions, and research in a wide variety of genres and disciplines. The first-year writing program and upper-level writing-intensive courses strengthen students' ability to develop, draft, revise, and edit writing projects for diverse audiences and purposes.

Academic Facilities

The Regis campus, 132 acres on the grounds of a former estate, is beautiful and historic with modern updates. In 2015, the first phase of a sweeping Master Plan for the campus was completed: a transformed campus quadrangle, a new residence and activities wing to Maria Hall, and a reimagined Library featuring the Lorraine Tegan Learning Commons. Also among the college's newest facilities are synthetic turf playing fields, an eight-lane track, tennis courts, and softball complex.

RegisNet, the campus-wide fiber-optic network, provides access to high-speed Internet connections, email, common calendars, and the Minuteman Library Network, the Regis Library's 24/7 online network. There are active ports throughout campus, twelve computer labs (two with 24/7 availability), ITS Help Desk, and the Moodle online learning tool used by over 40 percent of faculty. Wireless coverage is provided across campus to over 621,000 square feet of campus building space. Exterior wireless service is provided to enhance the "classroom without walls."

Costs

For the 2017–18 academic year, tuition is $39,820 and room and board is $14,740. All charges and fees are determined by the Board of Trustees and are subject to change.

Financial Aid

More than 90 percent of students at Regis receive financial assistance in the form of merit scholarships or need-based institutional grants, state and federal grants, loans, and work-study jobs. Students who are not eligible Federal Work-Study funding may apply for employment on campus.

Merit scholarships are available for up to four years, as long as students maintain their renewal requirements. Scholarships include the S. Therese Higgins CSJ Scholarship, S. Jeanne D'Arc O'Hare Merit Award, Tower Scholarship, and Anniversary Scholarship. The Alumni Scholarship is available to both first-year and transfer students, and the Phi Theta Kappa Scholarship is designated specifically for transfer students.

Faculty

The qualified and dedicated faculty at Regis includes 96 full-time and 114 part-time instructors. Seventy percent of the full-time faculty members hold a doctoral or other terminal degree. The student-faculty ratio is 11:1.

Student Life

Regis prides itself on a strong, caring community, with the right mix of challenge and support, and personalized attention. The comfortable campus provide a setting where it's easy to make friends and get to know professors. To promote community, Regis guarantees four-year on-campus housing. That sense of community extends from classrooms to residence halls, clubs and activities, campus ministry, athletics, and career planning.

The student affairs division at Regis provides on-campus activities, including nearly 30 student clubs and activities, campus ministry, and 18 NCAA Division III athletics teams.

Admission Requirements

Regis considers each application holistically and thoroughly evaluates the credentials and reviews all aspects of every candidate's application. Many factors are considered, including academic performance in a college preparatory curriculum and grades received; leadership qualities and participation in extracurricular activities; the required essay, demonstrating a student's ability to think critically and communicate effectively; letters of recommendation; SAT/ACT scores (optional for all academic programs except nursing); and an interview with an admission representative (highly recommended, but not required).

The following college preparatory credentials are recommended: English, 4 years; mathematics, 3 years (algebra I and II, geometry), natural science, 3 years (2 with a lab); social science, 3 years; foreign language, 2 years (same language); and electives, 3 or 4 years.

Regis welcomes applicants for admission without regard to race, color, religious affiliation, national or ethnic origin, or learning or physical disability.

Application and Information

Regis accepts the Common Application. In addition to that form, applicants must also submit their official secondary school transcript, a personal essay, at least one signed letter of recommendation from a secondary school counselor or teacher, and a nonrefundable $50 application fee. Regis is a test-optional institution, with the exception of home-schooled students, those interested in applying to the nursing major, and those interested in the St. George's University Accelerated Medical/Veterinary School Program. TOEFL scores may be requested if the student's native language is not English.

Students who wish to be considered for Early Action must apply by December 1. Regis accepts applications on a rolling basis, with priority given to those students who apply before February 1.

Admitted students should submit a nonrefundable enrollment deposit by the candidate's reply date of May 1. Deposits received after May 1 will be accepted on a space-available basis. Admitted students applying for the spring semester (January) should submit a nonrefundable enrollment deposit by January 1.

A final high school transcript and an official indication of graduation must be received by the Office of Admission no later than July 15. Failure to submit these documents may result in the student's acceptance being rescinded and cancellation of the Financial Aid Award letter.

Office of Undergraduate Admission
Regis College
235 Wellesley Street
Weston, Massachusetts 02493
Phone: 866-438-7344
E-mail: admission@regiscollege.edu
Website: http://www.regiscollege.edu

COLLEGE CLOSE-UPS

RICHMOND, THE AMERICAN INTERNATIONAL UNIVERSITY IN LONDON

LONDON, ENGLAND

RICHMOND
THE AMERICAN INTERNATIONAL
UNIVERSITY
IN LONDON

★ To read more about this school, visit http://petersons.to/richmond

The University

Richmond, The American International University in London, prepares men and women to serve with purpose and generosity in an interdependent and multicultural world. Richmond offers a strong academic program with many choices of fields of study, an exceptional faculty, superb campus life, and fellow students from all over the world. In the United States, Richmond is accredited by the Commission on Higher Education of the Middle States Association of Colleges and Schools, a regional accrediting body recognized by the U.S. Department of Education. Richmond is accredited in the United Kingdom by the Open University and holds related degree validation. The University's undergraduate and graduate degrees are designated by the United Kingdom's Department of Education and Employment. The University is a comprehensive American liberal arts and professional university. In addition to the undergraduate degree programs described below, Richmond offers M.A. and M.B.A. degrees in a range of different subjects.

Freshmen and sophomores study and live at the Richmond campus, 7 miles from central London. Junior and senior years are spent at the Kensington campus in one of London's most beautiful residential and historic districts. As part of their four-year B.A. degree program, students may spend a semester or a year studying at one of the University's two international study centers in Florence and Rome, Italy. Richmond currently enrolls over 1,000 students from more than 100 countries. Approximately 48 percent of the degree students are from Europe and the United Kingdom, 4 percent are from Asia, 6 percent are from the Middle East, 6 percent of the student body represents the continent of Africa, and 1 percent is from South America. The remaining 35 percent of the degree students are from North America. About 350 study-abroad students from various universities are enrolled for a semester or a year at Richmond.

Small classes, averaging 15–20 students, enable students to receive personal attention from professors in a supportive environment. The curriculum and academic advising system are structured to enable students to choose courses that provide broad knowledge, relevant skills, and an understanding of the world's many cultures and nations.

Richmond students supplement academic programs with activities that complement and balance the classroom experience. Many extracurricular and cocurricular programs are available to students, including student government, the Green Project, Model United Nations, Amnesty International, Richmond Free Press, Top of the Hill music club, and sports and business clubs.

Location

The Richmond Hill campus in the London suburb of Richmond offers a variety of entertainment, shopping, cultural, and recreational opportunities. Only yards from the University campus is Richmond Park, more than 2,200 acres of rolling hills and lush woodland, where one can ride horses, play tennis, jog, or simply relax. The journey from Richmond into Central London takes approximately 30 minutes using public transportation.

The Kensington campus is located in the heart of London's Borough of Kensington, which has fine museums, libraries, theatres, concert halls, historic buildings, and well-known cultural and educational resources. The University takes full advantage of London's cultural and social resources through selected academic courses, work experience placements with multinational corporations, and special visits to museums, art galleries, theatres, and concert halls.

Majors and Degrees

Richmond operates its academic program on the American system. The University offers the four-year Bachelor of Arts (B.A.) degree in more than twenty majors, with a further choice of twenty minors. Majors offered by the University include: accounting and finance; art history and visual culture; business management (entrepreneurship, finance, international business); communications; development economics, development studies; economics; fashion management and marketing; film studies; financial economics; history; international journalism and media; international relations; marketing; performance and theatre arts; political science; and psychology.

Academic Programs

In order to graduate with the dual-validated U.S. and U.K. degree [B.A./B.A. (Honors)], students must earn a minimum of 120 credits. Usually, this means taking a full load for four years, or eight semesters. Within these 120 credits, students must complete all course requirements for their majors. Students must also meet the University's Language Proficiency and General Education requirements. In addition, valuable work experience for credit is offered through the International Internship program. Placements have been at the International Herald Tribune, General Electric, The House of Commons, CNN, the United Nations, Lloyds Bank, the Museum of London, and Sony Music Corporation.

Credit is also awarded for Advanced Placement tests (6 credits for each subject grade of 3, 4, or 5); a grade of A, B, or C on the A Level exams is awarded 9 credits (6 for D or E). Credit is also awarded for the International Baccalaureate, the Baccalauréat de l'Enseignement du Second Degré (France), the Abitur/Reifzuegnis (Germany), the Diploma di Maturità (Italy), and the School Leaving Diploma (Denmark, Finland, Norway, and Sweden).

The fall semester begins in early September and ends in mid-December. The spring semester begins in mid-January and runs through mid-May. A session of summer school runs from mid-May to late June.

Off-Campus Programs

Students may complement their studies in London with a semester, year, or summer at one of two international study centers. The centers are located in Florence and Rome, Italy, and each offer an intensive study of the language and culture of the country. The Florence Study Center emphasizes studio and fine arts. The Rome Study Center offers courses in Italian language and culture, art history, economics, and political science.

Academic Facilities

Information technology is integrated into the curriculum in ways that are natural to the discipline under study. Supporting this are eight student computer laboratories with more than 140 current-specification computers, which connect to the Internet and are networked for student, faculty, and administrative use. Wireless network access is also available on campus.

Richmond's libraries support the courses taught at each campus. Students may use either campus library. The libraries house over 95,000 items including books, DVDs, music CDs, company annual reports, and student theses. In addition, the libraries have subscriptions to a number of journal and magazine titles, along with a variety of national and international newspapers. Richmond students also have access to the many specialized libraries within the London area.

Costs

Tuition for the 2017–18 academic year is $38,000. Room and board costs start at $12,100. Personal expenses, books and supplies, clothing, recreation, and travel costs also need to be factored in as these are not included in tuition and room and board fees.

Financial Aid

Merit-based scholarships are awarded annually to students of high academic ability. Financial aid for U.S. citizens includes Federal Direct Stafford Student Loans and Federal PLUS loans. All U.S. citizens must file the Free Application for Federal Student Aid (FAFSA) to qualify for federal loans. The FAFSA school code for Richmond is G10594. Need-based Richmond scholarships are also available. Students should contact the admissions office for details regarding application procedures for scholarships and financial aid.

Faculty

The student-faculty ratio of 10:1 enables optimum interaction and individualized instructional assistance. The 118 faculty members (50 full-time, 68 part-time) have professional degrees from top European and American universities such as Harvard, the University of California (Berkeley), the University of Michigan, Cambridge, Oxford, the London School of Economics, the Royal College of Art, and the University of Bonn.

Student Government

The Richmond Student Union acts as a resource for all students, student organizations, and clubs to voice their opinions and ideas. The Student Union functions as a network between the student body and the administration. Using student ideas, it holds events and seeks to feature student talent while enhancing the overall University experience. The Student Union is ongoing in its development and thus offers possibilities for students to shape and change it. It is an organization directed by students for students and is structured to provide flexibility as well as the opportunity for all students to become involved.

Admission Requirements

Applicants are admitted on the basis of academic performance, references, intended major, and career interests. The required essay is of paramount importance. Applicants to Richmond have usually completed a total of twelve years of primary and secondary school with a minimum grade of C+ (2.5 out of 4.0) in the American high school grading system, or its equivalent. British system students should have attained a minimum of three A levels (grades BBC) in acceptable academic subjects. Equivalent qualifications gained under other educational systems are also considered for the purpose of admission.

Students must submit a completed application form and application fee, an essay, transcripts of all secondary and postsecondary school work, and one confidential letter of academic recommendation. SAT or ACT scores are optional. The SAT code for Richmond is 0823L. The ACT code is 5244. Evidence of proficiency in the English language is required from students whose first language is not English or who did not attend English-speaking schools. Standardized test scores, such as the IELTS are considered in assessing students' language capability.

Richmond admits students on a rolling basis, and applicants are encouraged to submit their application at the earliest opportunity. All documents in languages other than English must be accompanied by official translations. Applicants are usually notified of a decision within three to four weeks.

Application and Information

An application for admission and further information may be submitted online at www.richmond.ac.uk using either the Richmond Direct Application or the Common Application.

Applicants residing in North America should contact:

Office of Admissions
Richmond, The American International University in London
343 Congress Street, Suite 3100
Boston, Massachusetts 02210-1214
Phone: 617-450-5617
Fax: 617-450-5601
E-mail: usadmissions@richmond.ac.uk
Website: http://www.richmond.ac.uk

Students outside Richmond University in London.

RIDER UNIVERSITY

LAWRENCEVILLE, NEW JERSEY

★ To read more about this school, visit http://petersons.to/rideruniversity

COLLEGE CLOSE-UPS

1865

The University

When students join Rider University's vibrant living-and-learning community, life—and learning—is never the same. Guided by Rider's gifted faculty and supported by its staff, Rider students discover powerful new ways to connect learning to the world around them.

The University is located in central New Jersey, easily accessible to New York City and Philadelphia, offering students great opportunities for exploration, culture, leadership development, internships, and jobs.

Students are at the heart of everything that happens at Rider. The University's student-centered commitment begins with professors who are focused on teaching and mentoring students. That commitment is shared by the entire University community, where every staff member is available to support students and their goals. It's a unique environment dedicated to giving students the self-confidence, skills and strong foundation essential for professional and personal success.

Students come to Rider from 38 states, three U.S. territories, and 68 countries. Each year, Rider enrolls 3,800 undergraduate and 1,000 graduate students.

The greatest legacy of a Rider education is measured by the success of its alumni. Rider alumni have gone on to great success at many of the country's top-ranked graduate and professional schools. They have competed for and won prestigious internships, research grants, scholarships, and fellowships—including numerous Fulbright Scholars.

The outcomes of a Rider education are clear: over 90 percent of Rider graduates are employed full- or part-time, pursuing graduate study, or involved in a volunteer or fellowship position within six months of graduating. And, 273 Rider alumni are presidents, CEOs, and leaders of national or international corporations or organizations.

Location

Rider's central location between two vibrant metropolitan centers—New York and Philadelphia—offers great opportunities for adventure, exploration, culture and shopping, plus internships and jobs. Rider is just minutes away from historic downtown Princeton, incredible nature trails, shopping malls, and more. Students can head an hour in any direction to laze at the beach, downhill ski, or enjoy the sights and sounds of the big city. Whether it's for sightseeing or shows, auditions or internships, Rider is only 90 minutes by train to the heart of Manhattan or an hour to downtown Philadelphia.

Majors and Degrees

At Rider, students can choose from nearly 70 undergraduate and 35 graduate programs through five colleges/schools: College of Business Administration; College of Liberal Arts and Sciences; School of Education; School of Fine and Performing Arts; and College of Continuing Studies. Interdisciplinary majors are plentiful, and dual majors are encouraged.

Academic Programs

Lessons learned in the classroom at Rider are complemented and reinforced with rich hands-on experiences. Students have the opportunity to participate in impressive professional internships, student-faculty research, honors and study-abroad programs, and volunteer experiences.

Rider students do lab work, perform on stage, hold leadership roles on campus, and work at the TV station as early as freshman year. Education majors are guaranteed 700 hours of classroom experience through field placements that begin in the sophomore year. Each year, Rider students complete more than 1,000 internships, co-ops, and field placements as part of their degree studies. Rider's award-winning Model UN program, innovative Global Village class, and a wealth of study-abroad and international partnership programs provide opportunities for students to experience the world in a new way.

Learning is enhanced by course work that reflects the latest best practices and technology, and guest lectures by leading experts. With plenty of real-world opportunities in nearby New York and Philadelphia, these great cities are true learning laboratories for students.

By building on these experiences, achievements, credentials, and contacts, Rider students discover what they love to do most—and stand out from the competition when they graduate.

Each of Rider's colleges has a career adviser who specializes in providing the support and preparation needed to move students from their majors to relevant careers. Students begin planning for the future in their first semester, using the expert resources of the Career Development and Success Center to create a compelling professional portfolio and a targeted resume. More information is available online at www.rider.edu/careers.

Students also have opportunities to develop polished interview skills through interactive workshops and alumni videos, launch their job search through the Rider career "handshake" site, and shadow and network with Rider alumni. Rider also hosts career fairs attended each year by hundreds of employers who come to campus to recruit candidates.

Costs

Rider is proud to be private and affordable. Students benefit from the many advantages of Rider's private university experience, and generous scholarship and financial aid programs that focus on making its bottom-line costs extremely competitive with most public colleges and universities.

For the 2017–18 academic year, tuition will be $40,570 for full-time students. There is a student activities fee of $145 per semester and a technology fee of $225 per semester. There may be additional fees associated with certain academic programs.

Housing options ranged from $4,820 to $6,380 per semester, depending on the type of residence selected. Meal plans ranged from $2,530 to $2,610 per semester. Additional details can be found online at http://www.rider.edu/offices-services/financial-aid-scholarships/tuition-fees/housing-and-dining-rates.

Financial Aid

Financial aid is personal and tailored to each student's needs and circumstances, starting with the assigning of a personal financial aid advisor to each student. Ninety-nine percent of Rider students receive various forms of financial aid and 98 percent receive Rider-funded scholarships and gift aid. The average annual student assistance package at Rider is more than $33,000. More information on financial aid and scholarship availability can be found at http://www.rider.edu/offices-services/financial-aid-scholarships.

Faculty

Rider's professors are passionate about their disciplines, but teaching is their top priority. They are distinguished authors, educators, scholars, scientists, performing artists, and researchers; an impressive 97 percent hold a doctorate or the highest degree in their field. With an average class size of 22 and a 12:1 student/faculty ratio, classes at Rider are small and collegial.

Student Life

Rider's focus on engaged learning helps students grow, professionally and personally, through abundant global and cultural experiences, honors and leadership development programs, service-learning opportunities, and exposure to the arts.

Rider's vibrant and active campus community includes student government, more than 150 student organizations, fraternities and sororities, plus 20 NCAA Division I men's and women's teams, and 28 club and intramural sports. Getting involved offers students the chance to inspire and lead others, manage budgets, plan successful events, and engage in big-picture thinking.

Admission Requirements

Rider University welcomes students with a variety of academic backgrounds. When reviewing an application for admission, the Undergraduate Admission Office takes a holistic approach by assessing academic performance, letters of recommendation, and admission essay. Once the committee has reviewed the entirety of the student's academic experience, an admission decision will be made.

Potential students must submit official transcripts from their high school or for any college work they may have completed while in high school, a letter of recommendation, scores from SAT or ACT test (writing section is not required), and a $50 nonrefundable application fee.

Application and Information

The application deadlines for the fall semester are the following: Early Action (nonbinding), November 15; musical theatre, January 1; and scholarship deadline, January 15. For spring admission, the scholarship deadline is December 15.

Campus tours are offered Monday through Friday at 10 a.m. and 1 p.m. and select Saturdays at 10 a.m. or 1 p.m. To register for a tour online, visit http://rider.edu/visit.

For details on application dates and more, visit http://www.rider.edu/applynow.

Office of Admission
Rider University
2083 Lawrenceville Road
Lawrenceville, New Jersey 08648
Phone: 609-896-5000 (Main)
800-257-9026 (Admission)
E-mail: admissions@rider.edu
Website: http://www.rider.edu

Rider University's vibrant and engaged learning community brings together people from diverse backgrounds, talents, and perspectives to explore subjects, tackle problems, share ideas, embark on adventures, and create solutions.

RIPON COLLEGE

RIPON, WISCONSIN

The College

Established in 1851, Ripon College is Wisconsin's best-value private college and a national leader in liberal arts education, devoted to ensuring every student realizes his or her unique potential. Ripon's five-course Catalyst curriculum rigorously develops the 21st-century skills employers seek while streamlining the path to graduation. Students enjoy extensive freedom to pursue their passions and craft their own academic program of study. Students are overwhelmingly satisfied with the amount of personalized attention they receive from devoted faculty and staff. Within six months of graduation, 96 percent of alumni are employed, in graduate school or student-teaching.

Ripon is a member of the prestigious Associated Colleges of the Midwest (ACM). The College competes athletically as part of the Midwest Conference and offers 21 NCAA Division III varsity teams. Ripon has a student-to-faculty ratio of 11:1, and the average class size is fewer than 20 students.

Location

The College is in the historic city of Ripon, Wisconsin—a friendly, safe community of just under 8,000 people, 80 miles northwest of Milwaukee, 70 miles southwest of Green Bay, 73 miles northeast of Madison, 180 miles northwest of Chicago, and 255 miles southeast of the Twin Cities in Minnesota. The nearest airport is 40 minutes away in Appleton, Wisconsin.

The campus comprises 250 tree-lined acres and 27 buildings, 10 of which are listed on the National Register of Historic Places. A sustainable campus, Ripon is home to the Ceresco Prairie Conservancy with 130 acres of native prairie, oak savanna, and wetland habitat in the making.

Majors and Degrees

Ripon College offers a four-year graduation guarantee with 30 majors and 42 minors, including a variety of fast-track pre-professional programs. Every student graduates with a concentration in Applied Innovation upon completing the five-course Catalyst curriculum.

Majors include Anthropology, Art History, Biology, Business Management, Chemistry, Chemistry–Biology, Communication, Economics, Educational Studies, English, Environmental Studies, Exercise Science/Athletic Training Track, Foreign Languages, Global Studies, History, Mathematics, Music, Philosophy, Physical Education, Physical Science, Politics and Government, Psychobiology, Psychology, Recreation Physical Education, Religion, Sociology, Spanish, Sport Management, Studio Art, and Theatre.

Minors include American Studies, ARMS (Ancient, Renaissance, and Medieval Studies), Anthropology, Art History, Astronomy, Biology, Business Management, Chemistry, Classical Studies, Coaching, Communication, Criminal Justice, Dramatic Literature, Economics, Educational Studies, English, Entrepreneurship, Environmental Biology, Francophone Studies, French, Health, History, Latin American and Caribbean Studies, Law and Society, Mathematics, Military Leadership, Music, National Security Studies, Nonprofit Management, Philosophy, Physics, Politics and Government, Psychology, Religion, Socially Responsible Leadership, Sociology, Spanish, Studio Art, Theatre Production, and Women's and Gender Studies.

Pre-professional programs include Government Service, Journalism, Library and Information Science, Military Leadership, Ministry, Pre-Engineering, Pre-Law, Pre-Med and Health Sciences (medicine, dentistry, veterinary medicine, optometry, podiatry, physical therapy, pharmacy, nursing, chiropractic medicine, sports medicine), and Social Work.

Teacher certification is offered in Early Childhood, Elementary, Middle/Junior High, Secondary, and Bilingual/ESL. In addition, Ripon offers licensure in 26 subject areas. Teacher certification programs approved by the Wisconsin Department of Public Instruction prepare students for licensure at the early childhood/middle childhood level (grades PK through 5), the middle childhood/early adolescence level (grades 1 through 8), the early adolescence/adolescence level (grades 6 through 12), and cross categorical special education (MC-EA). The educational studies department also offers PK–12 certification programs in Art, Foreign Languages (French and Spanish), Music, Physical Education, Physical Education and Health, and Theatre (pending program approval).

Academic Programs

Ripon's innovative new curriculum, Catalyst, was rolled out to the first-year class during the fall semester of 2016. Ripon's liberal arts curriculum introduces students to a wide variety of disciplines. About 40 percent of students complete double or triple majors, while some create special self-designed majors. Hallmarks of a Ripon education are excellent communication skills, both written and oral; critical-thinking and problem-solving skills; and the opportunity to explore serious research pursuits alongside faculty as an undergraduate, no matter what the student's major may be.

A Ripon education can take students anywhere, as demonstrated by the College's talented and well-known alumni. One student studied psychology and played basketball at Ripon, then become a seven-time Grammy winner: jazz singer Al Jarreau (1962). Another, Oliver Williamson (1954) earned a Nobel Prize in economics. Jeff Bantle (1980), a chief flight director with NASA, helped guide the space shuttle into orbit, and Gail Dobish (1976) is an international opera star. Neonatologist Dr. Jonathan Muraskas (1978) is credited with saving the world's smallest premature baby, and Richard Threlkeld (1959) covered the world as former Moscow correspondent for CBS News. Other entertainment notables include Harrison Ford (1964), Spencer Tracy (1924), and Justin Neibank (1978). Recent alumni Zach Morris (2002) studied at Oxford University as a Rhodes Scholar and also found time to play touch football with former President Bill Clinton and spend an evening at Buckingham Palace with Queen Elizabeth.

Off-Campus Programs

United States or abroad? Three weeks, one semester, two semesters? Students can choose from more than 40 programs, each officially sanctioned by and affiliated with Ripon. Although most programs are connected with a major or minor program, all are open to every Ripon student, regardless of major. Scholarships are available to pursue off-campus study.

Programs are offered throughout the United States, including Chicago; Knoxville, Tennessee; Nashville, Tennessee; a southwest Indian reservation; Washington, D.C.; Woods Hole, Massachusetts; and experiences at sea. International programs are offered in Europe, Africa, South America, Central America, India, and Asia.

Ripon College offers three-week Liberal Arts In Focus courses in May. Taught in short, intensive blocks, In Focus courses are designed as immersion experiences to provide a bridge between the theory and content of disciplines. Recent courses have included history lessons in Italy; intensive biology field studies in

Costa Rica and the Wilderness Field Station near Ely, Minnesota; and a unique English course in Great Britain covering children's fantasy literature from Beatrix Potter to Harry Potter.

Academic Facilities

The 27 buildings on the Ripon campus include historic limestone structures and more modern facilities. Recent updates include an apartment-style residence hall; the multimillion dollar renovation of a main classroom building; and enhancements to the student union, dining facilities, and student activity spaces.

The athletics, health, and wellness facilities are undergoing a $22-million renovation and expansion that will feature new classrooms, an atrium, state-of-the-art fitness center, an NCAA indoor track, performance courts, fitness studios, athletic training center, and other upgrades that are set to be completed in August 2017.

C. J. Rodman Center for the Arts is home to a theater with a state-of-the-art computerized lighting system, a recital hall with one of only 50 existing Bedient organs, an art gallery, a high-tech lab, and a sculpture garden.

Bovay's Study Bar & Mercantile opened in March 2017 in a historic building in downtown Ripon. This unique venue features a 30-student high-tech classroom, office space, a study bar with barista coffee service, a mercantile with official Ripon College apparel and gifts, and flexible meeting space. Bovay's is open late into the evening and features barista coffee service during peak study hours. Student interns working in the space will benefit from hands-on experiential training in marketing, merchandising, and small-business management.

Ripon College provides a secure, high-speed (802.11ac) Wi-Fi network in every building on campus. In addition, a state-of-the-art fiber optic network (10 Gb/s) connects all academic buildings, administrative buildings, and residence halls. Connectivity to the Internet and Internet2 is provided by WiscNet at a speed of 1 Gb/s.

Student, faculty, and staff are issued a G Suite account that offers a variety of productivity tools (Gmail, Calendar, Drive, Docs, Hangouts) to enhance campus collaboration and communication. Multi-functional devices (MFDs) are located in every academic and administrative building to service the campus printing, copying and scanning needs. The College also has a 3-D printer that several faculty have incorporated into their course curricula.

Open-use computer labs are located across campus, offering both Windows and Mac OS devices, projectors, and MFDs.

Ripon College has partnered with Apogee to provide a cutting-edge cable TV/video solution. With the revolutionary IPTV service, Stream2, students can view HD content live, on-demand, or recorded (20 hours of DVR storage per user) on their laptops, tablets, and smartphones.

Library staff provide friendly and efficient circulation, reference, instruction, and interlibrary loan services that aid in research. The library also houses the College archives, a computer lab, digital media stations, and more than 25 online databases. Library holdings include access to more than 300,000 physical and electronic books and 55,000 periodicals.

Costs

Tuition for the 2017–18 academic year is $41,535, room and board is $8,156, and fees are $300, for a total cost of $49,091.

Financial Aid

Pursuing a college degree is an important investment, so financial circumstances will never affect Ripon's admission decision. The College provides 100 percent of students with the financial assistance necessary to graduate and works to ensure a great economic value per every dollar spent.

Ripon offers its students competitive packages with funding from many sources: merit-based scholarships, need-based grants, educational loans, work-study, and scholarships from outside organizations. Academic scholarships range from $16,000 to $32,000 per year.

Student Organizations and Activities

From pre-professional programs to paintballing, Ripon College hosts more than 60 student-run clubs and organizations. Students are encouraged to lead the programs, supported by the Student Senate's activity fee. This allows students to collaborate on conceiving, organizing, marketing, and developing unique activities.

Ripon's NCAA Division III Intercollegiate Teams compete in the Midwest Conference. Men's varsity sports include: baseball, basketball, cross-country, cycling, football, soccer, swimming and diving, tennis, and indoor and outdoor track and field. Women's varsity sports include: basketball, cross-country, cycling, dance, soccer, softball, swimming and diving, tennis, indoor and outdoor track and field, and volleyball.

In addition, Ripon offers a variety of intramural sports throughout the year, including kickball, dodgeball, flag football, indoor soccer, inner-tube water polo, basketball, bowling, volleyball, and aerobics.

Admission Requirements

The faculty committee on academic standards establishes the criteria for admission. The school considers a variety of factors. An admission application and secondary school record are required for admission while standardized test scores (SAT or ACT), recommendations, a written essay, and extracurricular or community service activities may also be considered. Ripon's admission process reflects the personal attention students can expect to receive during their college careers, and applicants are encouraged to provide any additional information that they consider helpful.

Ripon encourages applications from those students who are best prepared to benefit from and contribute to the academic and extracurricular programs that it offers. In evaluating applications, attention is paid to evidence of academic achievement, as indicated both by the distribution of courses taken in secondary school and by performance in those courses.

For further information, students should contact:

Leigh D. Mlodzik
Dean of Admission
Ripon College
300 Seward Street
P.O. Box 248
Ripon, Wisconsin 54971-0248
Phone: 800-947-4766 (toll-free)
E-mail: adminfo@ripon.edu
Website: http://www.ripon.edu

Ripon's 11:1 student-to-faculty ratio means students regularly experience one-on-one interactions with their professors.

RIVIER UNIVERSITY

NASHUA, NEW HAMPSHIRE

★ For more information, visit http://petersons.to/rivieruniversity

The University

Rivier University, a private Catholic university founded in 1933 by the Sisters of the Presentation of Mary, has earned a reputation for excellence with distinguished academic programs. Rivier offers many of the region's leading programs at the undergraduate, graduate, postgraduate, and doctoral levels.

Rivier's School of Undergraduate Studies enrolls approximately 1,400 students, including more than 780 full-time day students. With a 15:1 student-faculty ratio, day students have plenty of opportunities to connect with faculty and become active members of the academic community.

The majority of undergraduate students enroll from the six New England states. Rivier also attracts students from all over the United States as well as international students representing countries in Africa, Asia, Europe, and the Middle East. Students who live on campus reside in four modern residence halls, some with suite-style options. Rivier also provides substance-free housing and honors housing. The Dion Center features the University's student center and the newly renovated Dining Center which offers a healthy, upscale dining experience. The commuter lounge, a campus store, student development offices, and meeting rooms are also available in the Dion Center.

The Office of Student Affairs, the Student Government Association, and more than 17 student clubs and organizations provide a calendar of social, cultural, and recreational activities, including concerts, live entertainment, films, and sporting events. The University and student organizations frequently organize outings, including trips to locations such as Boston and New York. Students also enjoy performances by the Rivier Theater Company.

Rivier's orientation for new students introduces them to the University's wide array of services, such as academic advisers, the Writing and Resource Center, and peer tutors. The Health Services Center and the Wellness and Counseling Center ensure students' physical and emotional well-being. A full-time chaplain and Campus Ministry staff coordinate spiritual activities and service opportunities.

Be Remarkable

University programs feature a strong liberal arts foundation and proactive professional preparation. Students are encouraged to "Be Remarkable" through Rivier's unique combination of classroom learning, real-world experiences, and career preparation. Vocational exploration begins in the first year, and a personal, four-year academic and professional action plan is offered to each student, charting a path to achieving their goals. Close collaboration between academics, Student Advising, faculty, and the Career Development Center facilitates students' achievement and tracks progress on their plans.

Employment Promise Program

Rivier University has instituted an innovative Employment Promise Program to enhance career preparation and employability of students in all academic disciplines. The program demonstrates the University's confidence in its educational experience marked by distinctive academic programs, committed faculty, and active learning. Through this initiative, the University promises invested students that they will secure a job within nine months of graduation. If they do not, they will receive additional support in the form of payment of monthly federal subsidized student loans for up to one year or enrollment in up to six Rivier master's degree courses tuition-free. Rivier is the only institution in New Hampshire to offer this program.

Athletics

Rivier is a Division III member of the NCAA and sponsors 13 intercollegiate sports. Rivier Raiders compete in men's and women's soccer, volleyball, cross-country, basketball, and lacrosse; men's baseball; and women's field hockey and softball. The men's volleyball team has been nationally ranked every year since 2001. The Muldoon Health and Fitness Center is home to Rivier's varsity athletics, fitness activities, and recreation programs including volleyball, floor hockey, basketball, weight training, indoor soccer, and more. The campus also has a turf rectangular field and a natural grass softball field, as well as a beach volleyball court and cross-country trail. Student athletes can take advantage of an on-campus athletic training clinic for injury assessment and rehabilitation.

Location

Nashua (population approximately 87,000) is located in southern New Hampshire. The city of Boston lies within easy access 40 miles to the south. Local access to public transportation provides for easy travel to and from the campus. Recreational activities abound year-round at nearby lakes and ski areas, in the White Mountains to the north, and at the seacoast, just an hour's drive to the east. The Manchester airport is a 15-minute drive from campus, convenient for students who must access air travel.

Majors and Degrees

Rivier University awards Bachelor of Arts and Bachelor of Science degrees in the following areas: biology, biology education, biotechnology, business, criminal justice, early childhood education, education and community leadership, elementary education, English, English education, finance, global studies, history, homeland and international security, human development, liberal studies, marketing, mathematics, mathematics education, nursing, political science, psychology, public health, secondary education, social studies education, sociology, and special education. The University offers preprofessional programs in law, dentistry, medicine, and veterinary medicine.

Academic Programs

Professional studies and liberal arts programs prepare students for a rapidly changing, highly technological, and global society. The broad-based curriculum focuses on preparing students for rewarding careers and furthering their personal growth. The University launched a new core curriculum, offering opportunities for service learning, servant leadership, civic engagement, and community service to support the intellectual growth of students and enhance student leadership. Students choose from courses in three areas: humanities and social sciences, mathematics and natural sciences, and languages in the core complement. The new core is aligned with the Association of American Colleges and Universities' (AAC&U) essential learning outcomes, which provide Rivier graduates with the strong intellectual and practical skills that are in demand in the workplace. A bachelor's degree requires a minimum of 120 credits with a grade point average of at least 2.0. For an associate degree, the student must complete a minimum of 60 credits with a grade point average of at least 2.0.

All departments encourage qualified students to pursue internships in their field of study. Students in Rivier's public health major will work alongside public health professionals at local agencies, and a study-abroad component offers first-hand global perspective and experience. Education majors student teach in local schools. Nursing majors complete clinical rotations in healthcare facilities throughout southern New Hampshire and northern Massachusetts. History, law, and political science majors may work in a law office, business, legal-assistance agency, or government agency. Sociology and psychology majors work with local social service agencies. English and marketing majors work in public relations, broadcasting, or corporate communications positions. Business majors work in advertising, management, and technology.

Honors and awards for students include placement on the dean's list, membership in Kappa Gamma Pi or Psi Chi, listing in *Who's Who Among Students in American Universities and Colleges*, listing in *The National Dean's List*, and degrees with honors. Academically talented students may also apply to the four-year Global Scholars Honors Program.

The academic year is divided into two 14-week semesters. Students usually take five courses each semester. Additional courses are offered during the summer. Academic credit may be granted to incoming freshmen on the basis of Advanced Placement test and CLEP examination scores. Students may also "challenge" courses and receive credit by special examination.

Off-Campus Programs

Through Rivier University's membership in the New Hampshire College and University Council, a sixteen-member consortium of senior and two-year colleges, Rivier students may register for courses at any of the member colleges and receive transfer credits.

Academic Facilities

Academic facilities include Memorial Hall, which houses 14 classrooms, the Office of Global Engagement, faculty offices, a lecture hall, a behavioral science lab, and Rivier's art gallery. The Academic Computer Center features up to 68 workstations with a full range of cutting-edge software and Internet/email access. Regina Library provides access to more than 150,000 e-books and over 80 research databases, as well as more than 3 million volumes in 12 area libraries on virtually every academic subject. The Writing and Resource Center offers assistance from professional writing consultants as well as peer tutors. Other academic facilities include nursing and science laboratories; a physical assessment lab and nursing skills simulation lab, which provide nursing students with practical experience using blood pressure cuffs, ophthalmoscopes, IV pumps, high-fidelity patient simulators, and more; the McLean Center for Finance and Economics; the BAE Student Research Lab; a clinical psychology lab; electronic classrooms offering multimedia learning tools; and the Benoit Education Center, which houses the eight-classroom Landry Early Childhood Center, observation rooms, and an educational resource center.

Costs

Tuition and fees for the academic year 2017–18 are $29,990; room and board, $12,168; and books and supplies, approximately $1,400.

Financial Aid

Financial aid is awarded on the basis of the financial need of the student and family. Approximately 98 percent of Rivier's full-time undergraduate students receive financial aid from the University or from government or private sources. Federal aid includes Federal Pell Grants, Federal Supplemental Educational Opportunity Grants, Federal Perkins Loans, Federal Direct Stafford Student Loans, the Federal Direct PLUS loan program, and the Federal Work-Study Program. To be considered for financial aid, a student must file the Free Application for Federal Student Aid (FAFSA) with the federal government as soon as possible after October 1 for the coming year. FAFSA results should be on file with the University Financial Aid Office prior to March 1 for the following academic year. Each applicant is assessed individually to determine the best combination of grant, work, scholarship, and loan amounts to meet the need of the student. The University awards more than $10 million in institutional merit-based scholarships and grants annually. For more information, students should contact the Office of Financial Aid.

Faculty

The University employs 69 full-time faculty members. Part-time instructors in specialized areas are working professionals who bring current knowledge and expertise in their field to their classes. All classes are taught by faculty members, and department chairs serve as academic advisers to students in their major programs.

Student Government

Every full-time day student automatically becomes a member of the Student Government Association (SGA) upon registration and payment of the student activity fee. The SGA's main goals are to stimulate active participation in all University functions; to establish and maintain effective channels of communication among members of the University community and the community at large; to foster a mutual trust; to encourage a spirit of cooperation; and to initiate new endeavors. The SGA also supervises student clubs and organizations and oversees their finances. The SGA Executive Board serves as the channel of communication through which the views of the students on institutional policies reach the University administration.

Admission Requirements

Applicants for admission should ordinarily have completed, in an accredited high school, a minimum of 16 academic units, including 4 of English, 2 of a modern foreign language, 3 of mathematics, 2 of social science, 1 of laboratory science, and 3 of electives. The most successful candidates are in the upper half of their class, with at least a B average. The University does not require SAT or ACT scores as part of a student's overall admissions file, except for nursing students. While nursing students are required to provide SAT or ACT scores, all other students have the option to submit their scores. A personal interview is strongly recommended but not required.

Rivier welcomes applications from qualified transfer candidates from accredited institutions, as well as applications from international students. Transfer students must forward transcripts of all previous college work and a high school transcript. International students must fulfill the requirements for general admission; they may also be required to submit Test of English as a Foreign Language (TOEFL) scores. Deferred admission may be granted to students who wish to postpone entrance for up to one year, provided they have not been enrolled full-time at another postsecondary institution.

Application and Information

Applications must be accompanied by an essay, one letter of recommendation, and a high school transcript. The School of Undergraduate Studies employs a system of rolling admission that allows qualified students to be admitted approximately one month after their application is completed. Transfers should apply by June 1 for fall admission and by December 1 for spring admission. Those applying for financial aid should observe the March 1 deadline. Interviews are arranged through the Admissions Office. Students may apply online using the Common Application or the application on the University's website.

For an application or additional information, please contact:

Office of Undergraduate Admissions
Rivier University
420 South Main Street
Nashua, New Hampshire 03060
Phone: 603-897-8507
Fax: 603-891-1799
E-mail: admissions@rivier.edu
Website: http://www.rivier.edu

Students enjoy Rivier's great location in the heart of New England—approximately an hour's drive from Boston, the mountains, and the seacoast.

ROBERT MORRIS UNIVERSITY

MOON TOWNSHIP, PENNSYLVANIA

★ To read more about this school, visit http://petersons.to/robertmorrisuniversity

The University

A private university in Pittsburgh's suburban hills, Robert Morris University (RMU) is a nationally ranked doctoral degree-granting university set on a 230-acre former estate that is a short drive from the cultural and commercial opportunities of a major city. Founded in 1921, RMU offers more than 80 undergraduate and graduate degree programs, including many online options, providing more than 5,000 students academic excellence with a professional focus.

The University built its reputation in the business fields of accounting, finance, marketing, and management. It has grown to include programs in communications, information systems, engineering, mathematics, science, education, social sciences, nursing, and health sciences. RMU uses a student engagement transcript to document internships, service-learning activities, study abroad, leadership roles, and other learning outside the classroom.

RMU is a teaching-centered institution featuring small classes taught by professors and a student-faculty ratio of 15:1. Recent years have seen the construction of new buildings for the School of Business, the School of Communications and Information Systems, and the School of Nursing and Health Sciences, along with major expansion and renovation of the School of Engineering, Mathematics, and Science, and the School of Education and Social Sciences. New residence halls accommodate a growing student population on a campus that has evolved from commuter to residential, with more than 85 percent of freshmen living in campus housing.

Visiting international scholars and a variety of opportunities to study abroad—for a semester or just a few weeks—enrich students' global perspectives. Students can participate in any of nearly 100 clubs and organizations. The Student Life Office organizes dances, parties, movie screenings, comedy acts, health and wellness fairs, educational programs, and day trips. Business organizations, professional clubs, and honor societies provide students with career preparation opportunities.

The University's competitive athletics program fields sixteen NCAA Division I teams, and the Colonials have won numerous titles and championships. The University is building the new UPMC Events Center on campus, opening in 2019, for its men's and women's basketball programs—the women have won the Northeast Conference title three of the last four years, while the men have the most conference titles in the NEC and won most recently in 2015. Nationally ranked Division I men's and women's ice hockey teams play at the RMU Island Sports Center, a 32-acre sports and recreation complex. Students can also participate in a number of club and intramural sports on campus.

Location

The 230-acre main campus is located in Moon Township, Pennsylvania, just 15 minutes from Pittsburgh International Airport and 17 miles from downtown Pittsburgh. The RMU Island Sports Center is 15 minutes from campus on Neville Island.

Majors and Degrees

Robert Morris University offers 51 undergraduate programs of study: accounting, actuarial science, advertising, biology, biomedical engineering, business, communication, competitive intelligence systems, computer information systems, corporate communication, criminal justice, cyber forensics and information security, economics, education (early childhood, special education, middle level, and business education), engineering, English, environmental science, finance, graphic design, health services administration, history, hospitality and tourism management, industrial engineering, information sciences, intelligence systems, journalism, management, manufacturing engineering, marketing, mathematics, mechanical engineering, media arts, nuclear medicine technology, nursing, organizational leadership, photography, political science, pre-medicine, professional communications/information systems, psychology, public relations, social science, sociology, software development, software engineering, special education, sport management, sport psychology, theater, TV/video production, web design, and writing.

Fully online bachelor's degree programs are available in business, criminal justice, cyber forensics and information security, English, health services administration, hospitality and tourism management, organizational leadership, psychology, and RN–M.S.N.

The University offers five-year integrated bachelor's/master's degree programs, medical school affiliation, cooperative education programs, an integrated 3+3 J.D. program with Duquesne University School of Law, and an honors program.

Academic Programs

Robert Morris operates on a two-semester schedule with various summer sessions. A total of 120 credits are required for most bachelor's degrees. Internship or co-op credits of 3 to 12 hours may be used toward degree requirements. The University participates in a cross-registration program with nine local colleges through the Pittsburgh Council on Higher Education consortium.

Academic Facilities

The 2016 completion of Scaife Hall, which includes a new nursing simulation center, means that each of the University's five schools has its own home, each fully equipped with learning technology, including state-of-the-art laboratories and studios, simulation equipment, and videoconferencing. Learning resources include a traditional library with more than 137,000 bound volumes, 80 reference databases, and 600 periodical subscriptions.

Costs

Annual tuition for the 2017–18 year is a $28,210 flat rate, based on a 24- to 36-credit, two-semester schedule. Annual room and board is $11,180 based on double occupancy and the Patriot meal plan.

Financial Aid

Ninety percent of RMU undergraduates who request it receive some sort of financial aid, including scholarships, grants, loans, and work-study programs. Both need-based and achievement-based awards are available. All applicants must complete the admissions application, the Free Application for Federal Student Aid, and the grant forms from their own state.

Faculty

The University has more than 480 full- and part-time faculty members; 87 percent of full-time faculty members hold terminal degrees. The student-faculty ratio is 15:1 and the average class size is 22. Students may take advantage of the expertise offered by the faculty in academic advisement and counseling, as well as counseling from the staff at the Center for Student Success.

Student Government

The Student Government Association represents all student organizations, including fraternities and sororities. Members participate in the planning of all social and cultural events on campus.

Admission Requirements

First-time freshmen must submit an application for admission with a $30 application fee (waived for online applicants), official high school transcripts or GED credential, and official SAT or ACT scores. Preference is given to applicants with a minimum 3.0 high school GPA and a combined SAT score of 1000 (Reading + Math) or a composite ACT score of 22.

Transfer students who have earned credits from another regionally accredited institution must submit transcripts from all postsecondary institutions attended and must have a minimum 2.0 GPA. Students with less than 30 college credits must also submit high school transcripts or GED credential.

Certain select academic programs have higher admissions criteria. Students are encouraged to arrange for a campus visit with an admissions counselor.

Application and Information

Students are encouraged to submit applications in the fall of their senior year of high school. Official transcripts and counselor recommendations should accompany the application; there is a $30 application processing fee that is waived for online applicants.

Robert Morris uses a rolling admission system; students are considered for acceptance as soon as all application materials have been received and evaluated.

For additional information and application materials, students should contact:

Kellie Laurenzi
Dean of Admissions
Robert Morris University
6001 University Boulevard
Moon Township, Pennsylvania 15108
Phone: 800-762-0097 (toll-free)
Website: http://www.rmu.edu
http://www.facebook.com/RMUpgh
http://twitter.com/rmu
http://www.youtube.com/RMUNewsTube

RMU students engage in a campus tradition: taking selfies with "Bronze Bob," a statue of university namesake Robert Morris.

COLLEGE CLOSE-UPS

ROCHESTER INSTITUTE OF TECHNOLOGY

R·I·T

ROCHESTER, NEW YORK

COLLEGE CLOSE-UPS

The University

Rochester Institute of Technology (RIT) is among the world's leading career-oriented, technological universities. RIT offers more than ninety undergraduate programs in areas such as engineering, computing and information sciences, engineering technology, business, hospitality, science, art, design, photography, biomedical sciences, game design and development, and the liberal arts including psychology, advertising and public relations, and public policy. Students may choose from more than eighty different minors to develop personal and professional interests that complement their academic program. RIT is a world leader in experiential education, which includes cooperative education, internships, study abroad, and undergraduate research. As home to the National Technical Institute for the Deaf (NTID), RIT is a world leader in providing access services for deaf and hard-of-hearing students. RIT enrolls students from every state and more than 100 countries.

Close to 70 percent of RIT's approximately 15,400 full-time undergraduate students live on the campus in residence halls or campus apartments.

Each year, RIT's more than 300 student organizations sponsor over 1,300 on-campus activities. RIT offers 23 varsity sports, including Division I men's and women's hockey. Recreational facilities are exceptional and include two ice rinks, an aquatics center, a field house with an indoor track, and fitness facilities.

Location

The greater Rochester area has a population of about 800,000. Per-capita income is among the highest in the nation for metropolitan centers. The area's many internationally known industries employ a high proportion of scientists, technologists, and skilled workers. Rochester's industries have always been closely associated with RIT's programs and progress. Rochester is also a hub for higher education with twelve colleges and universities in the area.

Majors and Degrees

The College of Applied Science and Technology offers the Bachelor of Science (B.S.) degree in applied technical leadership (upper-division, online only), civil engineering technology, computer engineering technology, electrical engineering technology, electrical/mechanical engineering technology, manufacturing engineering technology, and mechanical engineering technology. It also grants the Bachelor of Science in environmental sustainability, health and safety, international hospitality and service management, and packaging science. An undeclared option allowing freshmen to delay selecting a major for up to a year is available in the School of Engineering Technology.

The E. Philip Saunders College of Business offers the B.S. in accounting, finance, new media marketing, international business, management, management information systems, and marketing. A 4+1 M.B.A. option is available, as are several minors, including entrepreneurship, digital business, and supply chain management. An undeclared option allowing freshmen to delay the selection of their major for up to one year is available.

The B. Thomas Golisano College of Computing and Information Sciences offers the B.S. in computer science, computing security, computing and information technologies, game design and development, human-centered computing, new media interactive development, software engineering, and web and mobile computing. The college also offers a computing exploration option for undeclared freshman students.

The Kate Gleason College of Engineering grants the B.S. in biomedical engineering, chemical engineering, computer engineering, electrical engineering, industrial and systems engineering, mechanical engineering, and microelectronic engineering. Degree options in aerospace, automotive, bio-engineering, biomedical, energy and environment, ergonomics, information systems, manufacturing, and software engineering are also offered within the college. Accelerated B.S./M.S. options are available. The Engineering Exploration Program, which allows freshmen to delay the selection of their major for up to one year, is available.

The College of Health Sciences and Technology offers B.S. programs in biomedical sciences, diagnostic medical sonography, exercise science, nutrition management, and a five-year physician assistant B.S./M.S. program.

The College of Imaging Arts and Sciences offers the Bachelor of Fine Arts in advertising photography, ceramics and ceramic sculpture, film and animation, fine art photography, fine arts studio, glass, graphic design, illustration, industrial design, interior design, medical illustration, metals and jewelry design, new media design and imaging, photojournalism, 3-D digital graphics, visual media, and woodworking. The college also offers B.S. programs in biomedical photographic communications, digital media, graphic media, imaging and photographic technology, motion picture science, and new media/publishing. An undeclared option allowing freshmen to delay the selection of their major for up to one year is available in the School of Art, the School of Design, the School for American Crafts, and the School of Photographic Arts and Sciences.

The College of Liberal Arts offers B.S. programs in advertising and public relations, communication, criminal justice, digital humanities and social sciences, economics, journalism, international and global studies, museum studies, philosophy, psychology, public policy, and sociology and anthropology. The Liberal Arts Exploration Program is designed to help undecided students formulate education and career plans.

The College of Science offers B.S. programs in applied mathematics, applied statistics and actuarial sciences, biology, biochemistry, bioinformatics, biotechnology and molecular bioscience, chemistry, computational mathematics, environmental science, imaging science, and physics. Special options are available in premedical studies (medicine, dentistry, veterinary medicine). Minors are available in astronomy, exercise science, imaging science, mathematics, physics, and statistics. Accelerated B.S./M.S. and B.S./M.B.A. programs are available. General Science Exploration allows freshmen to delay the selection of their major for up to one year.

Home of the National Technical Institute for the Deaf, RIT is a world leader in providing educational opportunities and access services for deaf and hard-of-hearing students. NTID awards associate degree programs and offers pre-baccalaureate studies for deaf and hard-of-hearing students. The associate degree programs prepare students for immediate employment after graduation or transfer into one of RIT's bachelor's degree programs. The pre-baccalaureate studies program prepares students for entry into RIT's bachelor's degree programs. Nearly 600 of the 1,150 deaf and hard-of-hearing students at RIT are enrolled in bachelor's degree programs in the other eight colleges.

Academic Programs

Most students entering as freshmen enroll directly in the academic program of their choice. Options for undeclared students are offered by most colleges as described above. A University Studies program is available for entering freshmen who wish to explore programs in two or more colleges. Students interested in pre-law, pre-medical, and other pre-health professions may enroll in any major at RIT and take advantage of pre-professional advising programs that provide the guidance necessary to complete the admission requirements for graduate programs in law, medicine, and other health professions. Undergraduates may choose from more than eighty different minors. Double-majors and accelerated dual-degree (combined bachelor's/masters) options are available. The RIT honors program admits approximately 150 freshmen annually. Air Force and Army ROTC programs are available on the campus. A Naval ROTC program is offered jointly with the University of Rochester.

Every academic program at RIT offers some form of experiential education opportunity, including cooperative education, internships, study abroad, undergraduate research, and industry-sponsored projects. Co-op students alternate periods of full-time study with periods of full-time paid work experience directly related to their field of study and career interests. Last year, more than 4,300 students completed approximately 5,700 co-op assignments with nearly 2,100 employers, earning collectively in excess of $45 million.

Off-Campus Programs

RIT has four international locations. RIT Croatia is located in Dubrovnik and Zagreb, Croatia and offers undergraduate degree programs in hospitality and service management, information technology, and international business. The American University of Kosovo in Pristina provides career-oriented programs that foster links between the university, industry, and government in support of workforce development. RIT Dubai offers graduate and undergraduate programs in business, engineering, service leadership, and information sciences.

Academic Facilities

Excellent facilities add to the quality of academic life. Students have access to some of the most up-to-date microelectronic, telecommunications, and computer engineering facilities in the U.S. RIT's Wallace Library is a true multimedia learning center. Its collections are exceptionally extensive in the areas of art and design, education for the deaf, photography, and printing.

Students use state-of-the-art computer equipment regardless of their major. Central computer systems can be accessed via a high-speed data network connecting the library, academic facilities, residence hall rooms, and on-campus apartments. There are more than sixty locations campuswide, with wireless networking connectivity utilizing 802.11b technology. The RIT campus network is served by two OC3 connections, each operating at a data rate of 155 Mbps, and one T3 connection operating at 45 Mbps. RIT is among a select group of institutions with access to the Internet2 research network, a collaborative research and development effort led by more than 170 U.S. universities working in partnership with industry and government.

Costs

For 2016–17, undergraduate tuition for the academic year (two semesters) was $38,024. Fees, including the activities and health fees, are $544. Room and board (twenty meals per week) cost $12,500.

Financial Aid

Approximately 77 percent of RIT's full-time undergraduates receive some form of financial aid that includes RIT scholarships, alumni or industry-supported scholarships, and state and federal government grants. A variety of loans and part-time work positions are available. The FAFSA must be submitted by March 1. Giving full recognition to scholarship apart from financial need, RIT awards a number of academic scholarships based on grades, test scores, and activities. Freshmen applying by January 15 and transfers applying by March 1 are considered for these scholarships.

Faculty

There are 1,023 full-time faculty members, 441 part-time faculty members, and an administrative and supporting staff of more than 2,200. Approximately 71 percent of the faculty members have earned a Ph.D. or the terminal degree in their field.

Student Government

The Student Government is the representative body for students. It works with RIT administration, faculty, and staff members to communicate the needs and desires of the student body and to communicate decisions of the administration to students. Fraternity and sorority members, off-campus and hearing-impaired students, and students from minority groups elect special representative bodies. All full-time and part-time undergraduate and graduate students are represented in Student Government.

Admission Requirements

Admission to RIT is competitive and varies from selective to highly selective depending on the desired program of study. The major factors determining freshman admission are strength of academic program, high school performance, and ACT or SAT test results. College performance is the main factor for transfer candidates. Students applying for programs in art, design, and crafts must submit a portfolio as part of the application process.

RIT promotes and values diversity and admits qualified men and women of any race, color, national or ethnic origin, religion, sexual orientation, gender identity, gender expression, or marital status. RIT does not discriminate on the basis of handicap in the recruitment or admission of students or in the operation of any of its programs or activities, as specified by federal laws and regulations.

Application and Information

An application, a nonrefundable processing fee of $60, official transcripts of all secondary school or college records, and SAT or ACT scores (for prospective freshmen) should be forwarded to RIT. Freshman applicants who provide all required materials for fall entry by January 15 receive admission notification by March 15. Prospective freshmen who apply after February 1 are considered on a space-available basis. A binding early decision plan is offered to prospective freshmen who have completed applications and filed credentials by November 15 to receive notification by January 1. Transfer applicants are strongly recommend to file their materials on or before March 1 for fall or summer admission and November 1 for spring admission. Fall applicants to the physician assistant program must have all application materials in by December 1.

For application forms, students should contact:

Director of Undergraduate Admissions
Rochester Institute of Technology
60 Lomb Memorial Drive
Rochester, New York 14623-5604
Phone: 585-475-6631
Fax: 585-475-7424
E-mail: admissions@rit.edu
Website: http://www.rit.edu
http://www.facebook.com/RITfb
http://twitter.com/RITAdmissions

A view of the campus.

SAINT ANSELM COLLEGE
MANCHESTER, NEW HAMPSHIRE

★ To read more about this school, visit http://petersons.to/saintanselmcollege

The College

Saint Anselm College is a nationally-ranked private, Catholic, undergraduate institution with approximately 2,000 students. Founded in 1889 by the world's oldest religious order, the Benedictines—a Catholic order that has endured and thrived for more than 1,500 years—Saint Anselm is accredited by the New England Association of Schools and Colleges and holds membership in the Association of American Colleges, The American Council on Education, the National Catholic Educational Association, and the National Association of Independent Colleges and Universities. It is the third-oldest Catholic college in New England.

Saint Anselm College prepares students for life. With a liberal arts education, graduates are ready for real career experience, and for the challenges that lie ahead. They take their Saint Anselm experience with them to think critically, communicate effectively, and solve problems creatively.

Saint Anselm graduates are CEOs, doctors, lawyers, nurses, engineers, teachers, marketers, and researchers. They are humanitarians, healers, and philanthropists. They graduate Saint Anselm with the drive to achieve, empowered to make the world a better place. In fact, 98 percent of the class of 2015 was employed, in graduate school, or engaged in service within six months of graduation.

There's much to see and do on campus from open skate nights at Sullivan Arena to spring concerts on the quad. Academic buildings, such as the Goulet Science Center and Gadbois Hall, house innovative labs where remarkable research happens every day. There are cell culture labs, climate-controlled environmental chambers, a greenhouse, a sleep lab, SimMan labs, and more. In the library, students have access to the latest technological advances and a range of workspaces for individuals and groups.

Recreational facilities include the Carr Center with basketball courts and the 9,000 square-foot, three-level fitness center. Saint Anselm College boasts some of the top athletic facilities in the Northeast-10 Conference. The College's twenty intercollegiate athletic teams play all of their home contests on campus (with the exception of the golf team and the ski team) at Grappone Stadium, Sullivan Arena, or Melucci Field.

Ninety-two percent of Saint Anselm students live on campus in traditional residence halls, suites, townhouses, or apartments. A new 47,000-square-foot, 150-bed residence hall was completed in August 2014 offering students an innovative, living-learning community. Whether students live on campus or commute, everyone has access to Saint Anselm College's amazing food, ranked eighth in the nation by the Princeton Review.

New Hampshire Institute of Politics: Saint Anselm is home to the New Hampshire Institute of Politics & Political Library (NHIOP), which offers unparalleled opportunities for students to be in the front row of the democratic process. Its auditorium, West Wing, TV studio, and classrooms are where students meet today's prominent political policy thinkers and researchers, journalists and authors, scientists, industry executives, global leaders, and presidential candidates. The Institute, nationally known to political scholars and strategists, is an essential campaign stop for presidential candidates. All of the U.S. presidents in the last fifty years have visited Saint Anselm.

Location

Saint Anselm College is located on 380 acres in Manchester, New Hampshire and is an hour drive from Boston, the Atlantic Ocean and New Hampshire seacoast, and the White Mountains. Just minutes from downtown Manchester, students can find all the venues a small city has to offer: great restaurants and coffee shops, a theater, museum, minor league baseball and hockey teams, and a concert and sports arena to name a few. The Manchester-Boston Regional Airport is also just minutes from the College.

Majors and Degrees

At Saint Anselm College, students may earn a Bachelor of Arts degree in the following academic programs and majors: accounting, American studies, applied physics, archaeology, biochemistry, biology, business, chemistry, classics, communication, computer science, computer science with business, computer science with mathematics, criminal justice, economics, education studies: elementary and secondary, engineering physics (3-2 program), English, environmental science, environmental studies, finance, fine arts (art history, music, and studio art), forensic science, French, German studies, great books, history, international business, international relations, marketing, mathematics, mathematics with economics, natural science, peace and justice studies, philosophy, physics, politics, psychology, social work, sociology, Spanish, and theology. The College also offers a Bachelor of Science in Nursing (B.S.N.) through a traditional, undergraduate nursing program and a hybrid RN-to-B.S.N. program.

Saint Anselm students may pursue preprofessional programs in dentistry, law, medicine, theology, and veterinary medicine.

The engineering physics (3-2) program partners with the University of Notre Dame, University of Massachusetts-Lowell, Catholic University of America, and Manhattan College. More information is available online at www.anselm.edu/engineering.

Off-Campus Programs

At Saint Anselm College, a liberal arts education gives students a solid foundation for any career, but opportunities outside the classroom give students a competitive edge and real job experience.

Students find all kinds of experiential learning opportunities at Saint Anselm including internships, research, study abroad, and volunteering. Students of all majors and interests can find opportunities for internships through the Career Development Center, which also brings employers to campus and advises students throughout their job search.

Internships are offered in Boston, New York City, Washington, D.C., Manchester, and beyond. Some recent internships opportunities have included: the Boston Bruins, United States Secret Service, Fidelity Investments, the United States Senate, Fox News, and the American Cancer Society.

Many students work closely on research projects with faculty members on campus to gain valuable lab skills, but there are also opportunities at local hospitals and businesses.

Students interested in study abroad can travel the world visiting such places as Thailand, Morocco, and South Africa. In recent years, students have studied marine biology on Australia's Great

Barrier Reef, art history in the museums of Florence, finance in London, language in Spain and France, the culture of peace in Peru, and political history in Ireland. Saint Anselm College offers a semester abroad in Orvieto, Italy, with classes taught by Saint Anselm College faculty. If studying abroad for an entire semester seems too long, Saint Anselm students have traveled with faculty members on week-long trips to places such as China, Panama, and Vietnam.

Saint Anselm students have gained essential leadership and organizational skills through volunteering, doing everything from teaching English to new Americans to working the crisis hotline at the YWCA. In addition, every winter and spring break, Saint Anselm students travel to organizations around the country to volunteer at service sites through Service & Solidarity Mission trips. These service trips challenge students, giving them valuable perspectives and changing their views on the world.

Costs

For the 2017–18 academic year, tuition is $38,960, room and board is $14,146, and fees are $1,030.

Financial Aid

Saint Anselm provides students with financial aid opportunities through both private and federal aid programs. The College provides financial aid to offset the reasonable monetary investment that the student and family are expected to contribute. Ninety-seven percent of the College's undergraduates receive some degree of financial aid. Saint Anselm's financial aid opportunities include grants, loans, scholarships, and employment positions.

Merit scholarships are awarded to outstanding students. Two forms are required in applying for aid; the student must submit the CSS/Financial Aid PROFILE and the Free Application for Federal Student Aid (FAFSA).

Faculty

With an average class size of 18 and a student-faculty ratio of 10 to 1, students receive individual attention in small classes. With 200 professors and no teaching assistants, Saint Anselm faculty members are committed to the success of their students.

Student Clubs

With more than sixty-five clubs and organizations, twenty varsity athletic teams, a performing arts center, and an art gallery, Saint Anselm students have plenty of activities to explore. From the soccer club to the mock trial team to the Muslim Student Association, there is a club for every interest, cultural to academic.

Students interested in service will be right at home volunteering through the Meelia Center for Community Engagement or through Campus Ministry. Saint Anselm students volunteered more than 20,000 hours last year. Service & Solidarity Mission trips, held during each winter and spring break, allow Saint Anselm students to volunteer at locations around the country.

Saint Anselm College is part of the Division II Northeast-10 and ECAC Conferences and offers men's intercollegiate baseball, basketball, cross-country, football, golf, ice hockey, lacrosse, skiing, soccer, and tennis; and women's basketball, cross-country, field hockey, ice hockey, lacrosse, skiing, soccer, softball, tennis, and volleyball. Saint Anselm also has a variety of club, recreational, and intramural sports teams.

Admission Requirements

In reviewing applicants for the first-year class, admission considers each prospective student carefully. Counselors assess each applicant's secondary school performance, SAT or ACT scores (optional for non-nursing majors, nursing majors must submit scores), recommendation letters, and the written essay. Of highest priority is the applicant's secondary school transcript, with a specific focus on both the rigor of course study and the marks received. Saint Anselm invites transfer and international students to apply.

Saint Anselm College has the following admission deadlines:

- Early action—November 15
- Early decision—December 1
- Nursing majors—must apply by one of the early deadlines
- Regular decision—February 1

Saint Anselm College invites students and families to visit campus for a tour, information session, and/or interview.

For more information, prospective students should contact:

Office of Admission
Saint Anselm College
100 Saint Anselm Drive
Manchester, New Hampshire 03102
Phone: 603-641-7500
888-426-7356 (toll-free)
E-mail: admission@anselm.edu
Website: http://www.anselm.edu

Saint Anselm's campus is home to students, instructors, researchers, and administrators, all striving to create a community where learning shapes living and where the search for knowledge takes place in an environment that values critical thinking, multicultural exchange, and service to humanity.

COLLEGE CLOSE-UPS

SAINT FRANCIS UNIVERSITY

LORETTO, PENNSYLVANIA

★ To read more about this school, visit http://petersons.to/saintfrancisuniversity

SAINT FRANCIS UNIVERSITY
FOUNDED 1847

The University

As the first Franciscan university in the nation, Saint Francis University has been has educating competent, caring professionals for 170 years. The private, Catholic, coeducational institution founded by the Franciscan Friars of the Third Order Regular, welcomes students of all faiths and currently enrolls more than 2,600 students from more than 20 countries.

The University offers highly targeted, career-focused programs grounded in the liberal arts tradition of inquiry and self-discovery. The values of respect, drive, generosity, and joy run deep in the University culture and help to prepare ethical, knowledgeable professionals with a passion to shape the world. This holistic approach to career preparation is supported by respected faculty who work closely with students in small settings to meet individual goals.

Saint Francis students are encouraged to make a difference through research and service projects, and many start as early as their freshman year. Undergraduate students work alongside Ph.D. faculty members conducting research and service projects as part of classes and through specialized learning centers such as the Center for Watershed Research and Service, The Keirn Family World War II Museum, the Center for the Study of Occupational Regulation, and the Center for Rural Cancer Survivorship.

Every student is encouraged to look beyond the classroom for career and personal growth through service leadership, undergraduate research, internships, and global opportunities. Saint Francis students graduate with a custom transcript in addition to their academic transcript known as their L.I.S.T. (Leadership, Involvement, Service Transcript) that quantifies these co-curricular accomplishments for employers.

The University is home to a vibrant campus life experience which capitalizes on its natural, rural setting as well as activities organized through student leaders. There are more than 50 official clubs and organizations including Campus Ministry, club sports, Greek Life, the Literary Guild, and marching band. Athletics also plays a major role in the student life with twenty-three NCAA Division I sports for men and women ranging from football to water polo.

Location

Saint Francis University's picturesque campus is situated on 600 acres in the heart of the Allegheny Mountains. The campus is located in the borough of Loretto, which has a population of approximately 1,400. The campus is 6 miles from the county seat of Ebensburg, which has a population of 4,000. The cities of Johnstown and Altoona are within 25 miles of Loretto and have populations of 35,000 and 55,000, respectively. The University is a 90-minute drive east of Pittsburgh.

Majors and Degrees

Saint Francis University offers more than 60 undergraduate majors and concentrations through four distinct academic schools. Each school couples classroom curriculum with embedded research and outreach centers for in-depth experiences.

School of Arts and Letters: Arts and Letters, Criminal Justice, Early Childhood Education, English, Environmental Studies, Fermentation, History, International Studies, Middle Childhood Education, Philosophy, Political Sciences, Pre-Law, Public Administration/Government Services, Religious Studies, Social Work, Sociology, Spanish, and Women's Studies.

School of Business: Accounting, Economics, Entrepreneurship Concentration, Finance, Healthcare Management, Management, Management Information Systems (M.I.S.), Marketing, and MBA (5-year, undergraduate entry).

School of Health Sciences: Exercise Physiology, Healthcare Studies (pre–allied health, pre-Occupational Therapy, Pre-Physician Assistant), Nursing, Occupational Therapy (5-year master's degree), Physical Therapy (6-year doctorate program), and Physician Assistant Sciences (5-year master's degree).

School of Sciences: Aquarium and Zoo Sciences, Biology, Biochemistry, Chemistry, Computer Science, Engineering, Environmental Engineering, Mathematics, Petroleum and Natural Gas Engineering, and Pre-Professional (dentistry, optometry, pharmacy, veterinary).

The University is accredited by the Middle States Association of Colleges and Schools. Many departmental programs also hold program-level accreditations. A complete list of accreditations may be found in the University catalog or online at www.francis.edu.

Academic Programs

The program of study leading to a bachelor's degree is usually completed in eight semesters. To qualify for graduation, a student must follow a program of study approved by the Office of the Provost that totals at least 128 credits distributed among liberal arts courses, major requirements, collateral requirements, and general electives. All students, regardless of major, are required to complete the University's general education program of 58 credits. A majority of academic programs integrate hands-on learning opportunities using undergraduate research, clinical fieldwork experiences, study abroad, or independent study.

Off-Campus Programs

Students at Saint Francis University may, with permission of the University's administration, spend their junior year of study abroad or may earn credit for participation in summer programs conducted in Canada, France, Germany, Spain, and other countries by accredited American colleges and universities.

Students are encouraged to take advantage of the University's study abroad facility in Ambialet, France anytime throughout their academic career. The Semester in France program offers study for students within any major for the same tuition costs as studying on campus.

A number of departments offer students the opportunity for off-campus study. For some majors, such as nursing, occupational therapy, physical therapy, physician assistant science, education, medical technology, and social work, internships and/or clinical rotations are required. Saint Francis

University strongly encourages students in all other academic majors to complement their field of study with an internship, study abroad, a community service experience, or academic research with a faculty member.

Academic Facilities

The Campus Mall is flanked by academic buildings dedicated to each of the four academic schools. The newest construction projects include a re-imagined space for The Shields School of Business and a state-of-the art 70,000 square-foot science center. These projects complement the DiSepio Institute for Rural Health and Wellness Center which provides a clinical training area for health sciences. The University's Capital Campaign includes additional enhancements for health sciences. Students in the Arts and Letters conduct archival research in the newly opened Keirn Family World War II Museum.

Costs

For 2016–17, tuition was $32,244. In addition, there were fees for expenses associated with lodging, food, insurance, facilities, technology, orientation, and travel. The estimated total per student ranged from $43,563 to $46,825. Detailed cost breakdowns are available on the University website

Financial Aid

Approximately 98 percent of the Saint Francis University student body receives financial aid. In addition to participating in federal and state need-based student aid programs, Saint Francis University offers its own substantial grant program and a generous scholarship program that is based on SAT or ACT scores, high school average, and class rank. Academic awards range from $1,000 to $16,000 annually.

Faculty

Faculty members are chosen for their knowledge of subject matter, as well as for their ability to communicate. Of the teaching faculty at Saint Francis University, 90 percent hold a doctorate or the highest degree attainable in their specific field of expertise. No teaching assistants or graduate students teach classes at Saint Francis University.

Student Clubs and Organizations

Saint Francis University offers an extensive list of co-curricular organizations for students. Over 60 clubs and organizations allow students to choose to become involved in areas of interest. A Greek life community, Student Government Association, and Student Activities Organization provide students additional leadership and involvement opportunities. Several club sport teams are available for students.

Admission Requirements

The admission committee considers applicants and renders decisions on the basis of the secondary school record, the recommendation of the secondary school principal or counselor, and the results of the SAT or ACT. Applicants to the School of Health Science should be aware of specified application requirements and deadlines. Applicants should have a minimum of 16 academic units and are strongly encouraged to visit the University campus for an admission interview and tour. Interviews and campus tours are available Monday through Friday throughout the year and select Saturday mornings while classes are in session.

Transfer students must submit a formal transfer application and a college clearance form in addition to official transcripts from each high school and college previously attended. Transfer students receive an advanced standing evaluation after an offer of admission has been made.

Saint Francis University, an equal opportunity/affirmative action employer, complies with applicable federal and state laws regarding nondiscrimination and affirmative action, including Title IX of the Educational Amendments of 1972, Titles VI and VII of the Civil Rights Act of 1964, and Section 504 of the Rehabilitation Act of 1973. Saint Francis University is committed to a policy of non-discrimination and equal opportunity in employment, education programs and activities, and admissions that includes all persons regardless of race, gender, color, religion, national origin or ancestry, age, marital status, disability, or Vietnam-era veteran status. Inquiries or complaints may be addressed to the University's Director of Human Resources/Affirmative Action/Title IX Coordinator, Saint Francis University, Loretto, Pennsylvania 15940; telephone: 814-472-3264.

For other University information, students should call 814-472-3000 or visit the website at www.francis.edu.

Application and Information

The University operates under a rolling admission policy. The occupational therapy and physical therapy programs have a January 15 priority application deadline. The Physician Assistant Sciences program has a November 15 priority application deadline. For more information about Saint Francis University, students should contact:

Vice President for Enrollment Management
Saint Francis University
P.O. Box 600
Loretto, Pennsylvania 15940
Phone: 814-472-3100
866-342-5738 (toll-free)
E-mail: admissions@francis.edu
Website: http://www.francis.edu
http://www.facebook.com/SaintFrancisUniversity
http://twitter.com/SaintFrancisPA

In the fall of 2016, following a year-long $7 million renovation and expansion project, Schwab Hall welcomed students once more, this time re-imagined as home to The Shields School of Business. The project was funded entirely by donations from alumni and friends of the University.

SAINT JOSEPH'S UNIVERSITY

PHILADELPHIA, PENNSYLVANIA

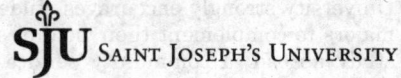

SJU Saint Joseph's University

★ For more information, visit http://petersons.to/saintjosephsu

The University

Saint Joseph's University (SJU) is a nationally recognized, Catholic, Jesuit university. For 160 years, Saint Joseph's has advanced the professional and personal ambitions of men and women by providing a rigorous Jesuit education—one that demands high achievement, expands knowledge, deepens understanding, stresses effective reasoning and communication, develops moral and spiritual character, and imparts enduring pride. SJU's Haub School of Business is AACSB accredited, recognized by the National Honor Society Phi Beta Kappa chapter, and listed on the President's Higher Education Community Service Honor Roll. Saint Joseph's is the home to almost 5,000 undergraduate students and over 3,500 graduate and doctoral students.

As a Jesuit university, Saint Joseph's believes each student realizes his or her fullest potential through challenging classroom study, applied learning opportunities, and a commitment to excellence in all endeavors. The University also reinforces the individual's lifelong engagement with the greater world. Graduates of Saint Joseph's attain success in their careers with the help of an extensive network of alumni who have become leading figures in business, law, medicine, education, the arts, technology, government, and public service.

A Saint Joseph's education encompasses all aspects of personal growth and development, reflecting the Ignatian credo of *cura personalis*. Guided by faculty members who are committed to both teaching and scholarship, students develop intellectually through an intense liberal arts curriculum and advanced study in a chosen discipline. Students mature socially by participating in the University's campus life, noted for its rich variety of activities, infectious enthusiasm, and mutual respect. Students grow ethically and spiritually by living the Jesuit ideal of *magis* both in the classroom and in the larger society beyond the campus.

Steeped in the Jesuit, Catholic tradition, Saint Joseph's provides a rigorous, intensive education that both disciplines and expands the mind. Student's develop a lifelong desire to learn and grow while also acquiring the skills and knowledge necessary for success in their professional lives. At the core of this education is a general education program, which exposes students to primary fields of inquiry and the cultural values that shape their world. A Jesuit emphasis on engaged teaching and mentoring permeates the university. Faculty members at Saint Joseph's, many of whom are leading scholars in their disciplines, expect students to perform at the highest level and set demanding standards within the curriculum.

Saint Joseph's is at the forefront of utilizing innovative technologies to enhance and promote learning. These technologies are widely integrated into the educational process both in class and beyond, where they are also used for individual and collaborative research projects. By mastering these tools and achieving technological fluency, Saint Joseph's students gain a valuable edge in their careers.

Saint Joseph's students engage enthusiastically in all facets of campus life—academic, social, athletic, ethical, and spiritual. Their active participation creates a vibrant, dynamic campus community, one that embraces a "not for spectators" attitude. In all their activities, students emphasize personal integrity as well as a respect and care for others. This produces a mutually supportive, humane, and tolerant environment for individual success and service to others.

Location

Located on the edge of metropolitan Philadelphia, Saint Joseph's provides ready access to the vast career opportunities and cultural resources of America's fifth-largest city, while affording students a cohesive and intimate campus experience.

Because of its location, Saint Joseph's has close ties to the professional opportunities and cultural life of Philadelphia. Students enjoy direct access to internships and cooperative education programs. Philadelphia also offers ample outlets for community involvement and service, and students can easily take advantage of Philadelphia's professional sports, entertainment, and cultural events. Philly is great for students.

Majors and Degrees

Saint Joseph's offers full-time baccalaureate degree programs in over fifty major fields of study and numerous specialty programs, which are administered by two separate colleges.

The College of Arts and Sciences awards bachelor's degrees in actuarial science, ancient studies, art, art education, Asian studies, autism behavioral studies, biology, chemical biology, chemistry, communication studies, computer science, criminal justice, economics, education (early childhood/elementary PreK–4; early childhood/elementary PreK–4 + special education K–8 [double major]; elementary/middle years 4–8), English, environmental science, European studies, French, German, history, interdisciplinary health services, international relations, Italian, mathematics, music, philosophy, physics, political science, psychology, religious studies, sociology, Spanish, theater and film, and theology.

The Erivan K. Haub School of Business awards bachelor's degrees in accounting; business administration; business intelligence and analytics; entertainment marketing; family business and entrepreneurship; finance; food marketing; international business; leadership, ethics, and organizational sustainability; managing human capital; marketing; pharmaceutical and healthcare marketing; risk management and insurance; and sports marketing. A co-op program is available for all business majors.

Five-year B.S./M.S. programs are offered in education, international marketing, psychology, and writing studies. The University also offers special academic minors in advertising and public relations; Africana studies; American studies; animal studies; art history; behavioral neuroscience; business; Chinese language and culture; environmental and sustainability studies; faith-justice studies; gender studies; interdisciplinary health care ethics; Italian studies; journalism; justice and ethics in the law; Latin American studies; Medieval, renaissance, and reformation studies; music industry; real estate finance; special education; secondary education; and TESOL (teaching English to speakers of other languages). SJU works in partnership with Thomas Jefferson University on joint-degree programs in bioscience technologies, nursing, occupational therapy, physical therapy, and radiologic science.

Academic Programs

At Saint Joseph's University, the aim of providing the student with the qualities of a liberally educated individual is pursued through a threefold plan encompassing forty courses. The major concentration (ten to sixteen courses) is intended to provide students with depth in a given field in order to prepare them for effective work in that field or graduate study. The general education program (fifteen to eighteen courses) is intended to ensure that students have mastered basic skills necessary for further work, have been exposed to the main divisions of learning, have been introduced to several new fields of study, and have acquired an appreciation for diversity and an ethically-informed perspective. Art and literature, non-native languages, mathematics, natural sciences, history, social sciences, philosophy, and theology are among the areas of study included in the general education program. Electives (six to fifteen courses) are intended to provide flexibility by encouraging students to pursue studies in areas they have found interesting, to test their interest in an unexplored area, or to deepen their knowledge in the major field.

Within the Saint Joseph's honors program, the curriculum will challenge students' intellect, creativity, and time-management skills. Honors students attend special events, receptions, concerts, and lectures, and have opportunities to present research and creative work at national conferences and seminars.

Off-Campus Programs

Saint Joseph's encourages an internship or co-op experience and provides hundreds of ways for students to connect with the nation's top employers. SJU Summer Scholars gives students the opportunity to dive into a special research or creative project while working closely with a faculty mentor. Students may study abroad in places like China, Ireland, Italy, South Africa, and more. There are also many opportunities to gain a real-world understanding of human and social issues while taking part in the well-known service-learning programs.

Academic Facilities

The facilities at Saint Joseph's are a blend of the old and the new. Barbelin/Lonergan Hall is a fine example of collegiate Gothic architecture. Its spire carillon tower rises above the campus and is easily the most recognizable landmark at Saint Joseph's. Mandeville Hall, a modern international academic center, is the home of the Erivan K. Haub School of Business. Mandeville Hall offers classrooms with state-of-the-art technology, and a Wall Street trading room, with access to electronic sources of financial and investment data. The new Post Learning Commons has become a hub for students seeking space for collaboration, studying, and relaxation, with its floor-to-ceiling windows for spectacular views of the campus, expanded and varied study spaces, plush lounges, and a café. Villiger, the University's newest residence hall, and three other on-campus residence halls house the entire freshman class.

Costs

Current tuition for one academic year is $43,880. The average cost for room and board is $14,840. These costs do not include student fees associated with specific majors or residence halls.

Financial Aid

Many of Saint Joseph's students receive merit and/or federal financial assistance. More than 90 percent of the University's student body receives assistance in the form of academic and athletic scholarships, grants, loans, and work-study funds. In 2016, 97 percent of new freshmen were awarded grants and scholarships over the last five years combined.

Students are automatically considered for merit scholarships upon application to the University. Students who wish to be considered for federal financial assistance should submit the Free Application for Federal Student Aid (FAFSA). Residents from states other than Pennsylvania should file the FAFSA and the proper state grant application from the Education Assistance Agency of their resident state.

Faculty

Saint Joseph's esteemed research faculty is committed to undergraduate teaching. A student-faculty ratio of 14:1 and an average class size of 23 offer excellent opportunities for students and faculty members to interact, both inside and outside the classroom. One hundred percent of the full-time, tenure-track faculty members hold a doctorate or terminal degree in their field.

Student Leadership and Activities

The Office of Student Leadership and Activities is dedicated to enhancing the educational development of students by providing opportunities for involvement in co-curricular programs and services. These include athletics, leadership programs, student clubs and organizations, Greek life, event programming and planning, and the University Student Senate.

More than 97 percent of the Class of 2016 completed an experiential learning opportunity, from a co-op at Estée Lauder to an internship at IBM to a semester abroad in Spain.

SJU students are leaders. They assist in academic departments, participate in student government and are responsible for running Mass, large fundraising campaigns and events, and sometimes leading over 500 students on a service immersion trip to Appalachia each year.

Admission Requirements

Candidates for admission to the freshman class must submit evidence of academic achievement in a college-preparatory program. In addition to the application students must submit an official high school transcript, letter of recommendation, a $50 application fee, and a personal essay.

Application and Information

Merit scholarships are awarded within the context of a deadline admissions policy with an early action application deadline of November 15 and a regular decision deadline of February 1.

More information is available online at sju.edu/apply.

Office of Undergraduate Admissions
Saint Joseph's University
5600 City Avenue
Philadelphia, Pennsylvania 19131-1395
Phone: 610-660-1300
E-mail: admit@sju.edu
Website: sju.edu
facebook.com/sjuadmissions
twitter.com/sjuadmissions

The Post Learning Commons Building at Saint Joseph's University is a hub of social and studious activity in the center of campus.
(Photo credit: Melissa Kelly)

COLLEGE CLOSE-UPS

ST. LAWRENCE UNIVERSITY

CANTON, NEW YORK

★ To read more about this school, visit http://petersons.to/stlawrenceuniversity

The University

St. Lawrence University invites students to learn new ways of seeing the world, voicing ideas, and connecting with others. Graduates have the tools with which to think clearly, express themselves persuasively, and step into the global community with an understanding of their responsibility to all people and to the planet. These tools have helped St. Lawrence graduates find success; nearly 97 percent of the most recent graduating class was employed or enrolled in graduate school less than a year after graduation.

Founded in 1856, St. Lawrence is the oldest continuously coeducational degree-granting institution of higher learning in New York State. Initially established as a theology school for the Universalist Church, it quickly evolved into the liberal arts college that it is today. St. Lawrence is a private, nonsectarian university of approximately 2,500 undergraduate men and women, with a small graduate program in education. St. Lawrence is known for its residential/academic First-Year Program, its international study opportunities and area studies programs, its students' strong interest in the environment and the outdoors, and its strong sense of community.

St. Lawrence students are self-starters. The self-designed major is popular, intramural sports leagues are always full, and more than 170 student clubs and organizations serve broad interests, from communication to community service and creativity to social action. The University routinely hosts well-known speakers, while concerts, plays, and films are regulars on the weekly events calendar.

St. Lawrence students have historically placed high value on athletic activity, and a large number participate in varsity, intramural, or club sports. Most of the 34 varsity men's and women's teams compete at the NCAA Division III level, with the exception of men's and women's ice hockey, which compete in Division I, and riding, Alpine skiing, Nordic skiing, squash, and men's crew. Recreational facilities include cross-country ski and running trails; indoor and outdoor tennis courts; an athletic complex with a gymnasium, two field houses, a 133-station fitness center, a three-story climbing wall, and a pool; an ice rink; an equestrian center; a boathouse; a golf course; a nine-lane all-weather track; an artificial-turf field for lacrosse and field hockey; ten squash courts; and performance fields for soccer, football, baseball, and softball.

Residential life is an important aspect of the St. Lawrence experience. The University's innovative and highly regarded First-Year Program creates communities in which groups of approximately 30–35 first-year students live and learn together. In the upperclass years, students can choose from traditional residence halls, Greek chapter houses, suites, and theme cottages that focus on student interests such as low-impact living and community service. Seniors may also choose townhouses. St. Lawrence sponsors a full range of student services, from counseling to career planning.

Location

St. Lawrence is situated on a 1,000-acre campus in the village of Canton, New York (population 6,400), the seat of St. Lawrence County. Canton, with its Victorian homes, tree-lined streets, village green, farmer's market, restaurants, and small shops, is typical of college towns throughout the Northeast. Students and residents often mix in stores, at athletic events, and in community projects. Ottawa, Canada's capital, is 75 minutes to the north, while Lake Placid, one of America's hiking and skiing meccas, is 90 minutes to the southeast.

Majors and Degrees

St. Lawrence offers the Bachelor of Arts and Bachelor of Science degrees; students can choose from 69 majors and have the option of picking one of 40 minors. Combined five-year programs with other institutions are in place in engineering and management, and specialized advising is offered in preparation for postgraduate work in dentistry, law, medicine, nursing, physical therapy, and veterinary medicine.

Academic Programs

St. Lawrence's foremost mission is to provide its students with a liberal arts education. Students complete requirements in six areas and concentrated work in a major field as well as demonstrating competence in writing. Close faculty-student interaction is a hallmark of a St. Lawrence education. Every semester, many students engage in independent or honors projects, often working with professors on joint research projects that lead to publication in leading scholarly journals. A senior project is required in most majors.

Off-Campus Programs

St. Lawrence University supports a variety of off-campus programs on six continents that allow students to enrich their majors, expand their world, gain cross-cultural skills, and prepare to be responsible global citizens. Nearly 70 percent of St. Lawrence students study off campus during their collegiate careers. St. Lawrence operates programs in Australia, Austria, Canada, China, Costa Rica, the Czech Republic, Denmark, England, France, India, Italy, Japan, Jordan, Kenya, New Zealand, Spain, Thailand, and Trinidad and Tobago. The Kenya program is based at the University-owned and operated campus in the suburbs of Nairobi. The program strives to provide students with a unique study-abroad experience. In addition, the University's membership in the International Student Exchange Program (ISEP) permits students to directly enroll in universities in more than 50 additional countries. St. Lawrence also operates a program at Fisk University in Nashville, Tennessee, and administers its own Adirondack Semester Program, Sustainability Semester Program, and the Liberal Arts in New York City Semester Program. The University also enrolls students in The Washington Center internship program, located in Washington, D.C.

Academic Facilities

Owen D. Young Library and Launders Science Library contain more than a million volumes as well as electronic resources and ample space for reading and research. Griffiths Arts Center is the home of the University's art and art history, performance, and communication studies academic programs as well as two theaters; an art gallery in which selections from St. Lawrence's 7,000-piece permanent collection are frequently shown; and the Peterson-Kermani Performance Hall, a 19,000-square-foot space for the performing arts. A unified science complex houses the departments of Biology, Chemistry, Physics, Psychology, Geology, and Mathematics, Computer Science and Statistics and is connected via a covered hallway to the science library and computing center. The 130,000-square-foot Johnson Hall of Science was the first LEED-certified gold science building in New York State. Richardson Hall, St. Lawrence's oldest building and on the National Register of Historic Places, is home to the English and religious studies departments. Other departments can be found in academic buildings clustered on one part of the campus, so classrooms are not far apart.

Costs

The comprehensive fee for 2017–18 is $66,642, including tuition, fees, room, and board.

Financial Aid

St. Lawrence awards both merit scholarships and need-based financial aid. More than 97 percent of the University's students receive some form of financial assistance, including scholarships, grants, student loans, and campus jobs. St. Lawrence is committed to assisting as many students as possible and recognizes academic and personal achievement in making financial aid decisions. To apply for need-based financial aid, students must file the Free Application for Federal Student Aid (FAFSA) between October 1 and February 1 and request that the results be sent directly to St. Lawrence.

Faculty

The 210 members of St. Lawrence's faculty are teachers and scholars who pride themselves on not just knowing student names, but knowing students. While teaching and advising are their primary responsibilities, they are also active researchers, artists, performers, and regular contributors in their academic disciplines. Faculty members teach all courses at St. Lawrence; no undergraduate courses are taught by graduate students. Active teaching assistants and tutoring programs, involving qualified upperclass students, are closely supervised by faculty members. The student-faculty ratio is about 11:1. Faculty members hold regular office hours, serve as academic advisers to students, and frequently take part in extracurricular activities on campus.

Student Government

The Thelomathesian Society, comprised of all students on campus, is governed by a senate of elected representatives. The senate distributes funds in support of student activities and provides two student delegates to the University's Board of Trustees.

Admission Requirements

St. Lawrence seeks students who can be successful in a demanding academic program and who can contribute to the quality of life of the community. The University is committed to enrolling students who represent the widest possible diversity of economic, social, ethnic, and geographic backgrounds. Academic preparation and ability are the most important criteria, but demonstrated ability in the creative arts, athletics, and/or social service is also a measure of a student's potential to benefit the St. Lawrence community. Candidates may choose whether or not to submit standardized test scores (SAT or ACT); University admissions are test-optional for domestic students. International students are required to submit SAT scores. A campus visit is strongly encouraged, and interviews may be scheduled on campus or off campus in certain areas.

Although there is no set distribution of required high school courses, successful applicants typically show strong preparation in the humanities, social sciences, mathematics, and natural sciences. Honors, Advanced Placement, and International Baccalaureate courses are opportunities for applicants to demonstrate intellectual maturity and curiosity, qualities highly valued in the admission process.

Application and Information

St. Lawrence uses the Common Application as its sole application form. The application processing fee is $60, which is waived if candidates have made an official visit to campus. Regular decision applications should be submitted by February 1, with notification in mid-March. Students who decide that St. Lawrence is their first choice may apply early decision. The priority deadline for early decision begins November 1; students may commit to early decision up until February 1. Early decision candidates will generally be notified within two weeks of receipt of a completed application.

Transfer candidates should submit applications no later than November 1 for the spring semester or March 1 for the fall semester.

For additional information, students should contact:

Office of Admissions and Financial Aid
St. Lawrence University
23 Romoda Drive
Canton, New York 13617
Phone: 315-229-5261 (admissions)
800-285-1856 (admissions, toll-free)
315-229-5265 (financial aid)
800-355-0863 (financial aid, toll-free)
E-mail: admissions@stlawu.edu or finaid@stlawu.edu
Website: http://www.stlawu.edu
http://www.facebook.com/StLawrenceU
http://twitter.com/StLawrenceU
http://instagram.com/StLawrenceU
http://www.youtube.com/StLawrenceU
https://www.snapchat.com/add/stlawrenceu

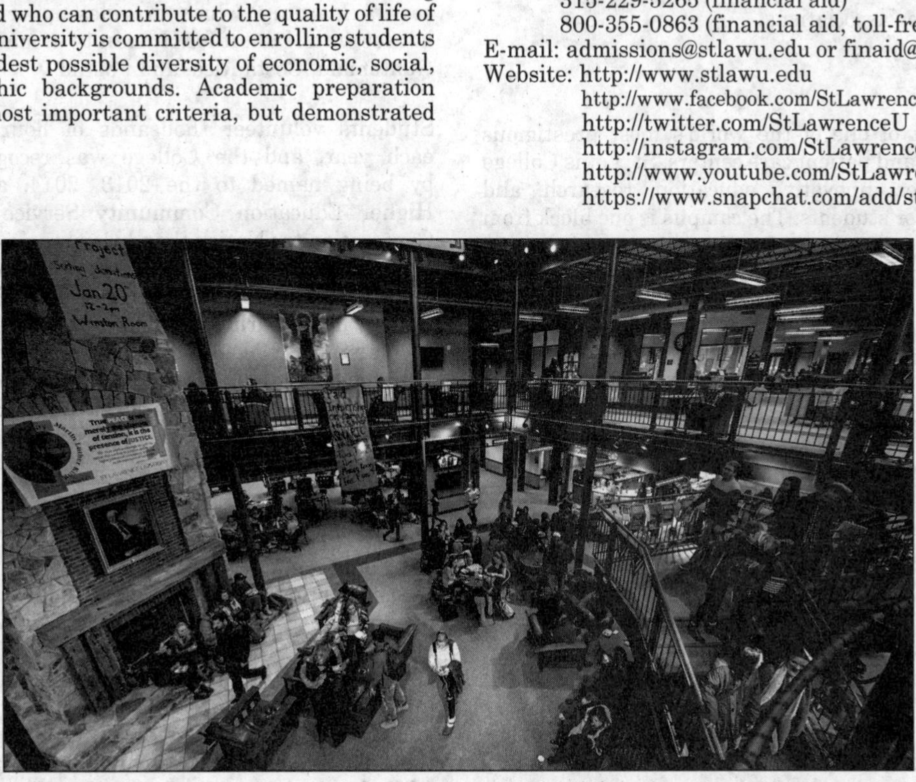

Located in the center of campus, the Sullivan Student Center is home to the Northstar Café, Career Services, the Campus Mailroom, Student Activities, Volunteer Services, Residence Life, and plenty of comfortable student study and meeting spaces.

ST. LOUIS COLLEGE OF PHARMACY

ST. LOUIS, MISSOURI

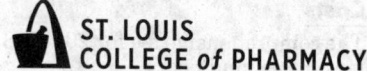

ST. LOUIS COLLEGE *of* PHARMACY

★ To read more about this school, visit http://petersons.to/stlouiscollegeofpharmacy

The College

Founded in 1864, St. Louis College of Pharmacy is the third-oldest continuously operating college of pharmacy in the nation. Members of the first board of trustees included pharmacists, physicians, and business leaders, such as Henry Shaw, founder of the Missouri Botanical Garden, and John O'Fallon, nephew of explorer William Clark. *U.S. News & World Report* ranked the College as one of the top four private colleges of pharmacy in the country in 2016. Nearly 1,400 students from 32 states are currently enrolled at the College.

St. Louis College of Pharmacy is an independent college that offers both undergraduate and professional degrees. Undergraduate degrees from the College prepare students for health professions careers, and they can serve as a strong foundation for graduate or professional study.

The College's four-year Doctor of Pharmacy program prepares students to be leaders and innovators locally, nationally, and internationally. Its more than 7,000 alumni practice in 48 states and 12 different countries. Locally, more than 70 percent of practicing pharmacists in the St. Louis metropolitan area are graduates of the College and practice in a variety of areas: community or hospital pharmacies, drug development, managed care, consultant pharmacies, pharmaceutical industry, military, academia, or pharmacy associations.

Location

Located in the heart of one of the world's most prestigious biomedical, research, and patient care centers, St. Louis College of Pharmacy provides innovative education, research, and career opportunities for students. The campus is one block from Forest Park, with its 1,300 acres of green space, tennis courts, ice skating rink, golf course, world-class museums, zoo, outdoor opera theater, and science center. Students at the College are near the cultural and entertainment scene of St. Louis on a safe, nearly nine-acre campus within a block of public transportation.

Academic Programs

St. Louis College of Pharmacy is an excellent place for students to prepare for a health professions career. The College offers undergraduate degrees including a Bachelor of Science in Health Humanities and Bachelor of Science in Health Sciences, as well as a Doctor of Pharmacy (Pharm.D.).

Many students pursue a Doctor of Pharmacy (Pharm.D.) with an integrated Bachelor of Science (B.S.). After completing their undergraduate requirements and first professional year in the program, students earn a Bachelor of Science that recognizes their strong preparation in math, science, and liberal arts. As long as requirements are met, many students in the undergraduate program may progress into the Doctor of Pharmacy (Pharm.D.) program without additional testing.

The undergraduate program provides an innovative teaching model, which integrates coursework across foundational subject areas to improve learning and advance health care. Students also are able to identify and incorporate specialty areas into their studies to prepare them for the wide variety of health care professions. Offerings include professional elective tracks and a graduate certificate in business administration or an Master of Business Administration degree through a collaborative agreement with the University of Missouri-St. Louis.

The College's Doctor of Pharmacy (Pharm.D.) and integrated Bachelor of Science (B.S.) are accredited by the Higher Learning Commission of the North Central Association of Colleges and Schools. The Pharm.D. is also accredited by the Accreditation Council for Pharmacy Education.

Off-Campus Programs

St. Louis College of Pharmacy offers Advanced Pharmacy Practice Experiences (APPEs) and international experiences in Bangladesh, China, Costa Rica, England, Ethiopia, Ghana, India, Ireland, Israel, Mexico, Portugal, Saudi Arabia, Singapore, South Africa, and Swaziland. Students make an impact on health care worldwide, working in hospital and outpatient HIV/AIDS clinics, developing pharmacy assistant programs, and participating in student exchange programs. Students also are able to enroll in courses such as international service learning, which provides opportunities to help build houses with Habitat for Humanity in many locations, including Guatemala, Costa Rica, and Poland.

Students volunteer thousands of hours in the community each year, and the College was recognized for its efforts by being named to the 2013, 2014, and 2015 President's Higher Education Community Service Honor Roll by the Corporation for National and Community Service—the highest honor a college or university can receive for its commitment to volunteering, service learning, and civic engagement. The College has spearheaded numerous off-campus service events, such as STLCOP C.A.R.E.S. (Community Awareness Reaching Everyone in St. Louis), St. Louis Medication Disposal Initiative, the Asthma-Friendly Pharmacies program, and Boo Fest, a sugar-free Halloween event for children with Type 1 diabetes and their families.

Facilities

St. Louis College of Pharmacy is wrapping up a physical transformation of campus to better meet the needs of students, faculty, and staff. In fall 2017, the new, seven-story Recreation and Student Center (RAS), is scheduled to open. It will house North Residence Hall, dining hall, competition and intramural gymnasiums, indoor track, and student support and development resources. In summer 2015, the state-of-the-art Academic and Research Building (ARB) opened. The ARB features a welcome center, classrooms, teaching and research labs, auditorium, library, and study spaces accessible to students 24/7.

Jones Hall has been a part of the College's campus since it was constructed in 1927. Since then, there have been several major renovations, including 2003 and 2015. Jones Hall is home to several large classrooms, basic science laboratories, and offices for faculty and staff.

South Residence Hall is at the center of campus and houses students and resident assistants. Students are part of a small, supportive environment that emphasizes community and personal development. Social and educational activities help students be successful both inside and outside the classroom. Support is offered in many ways, including individual counseling, tutoring, individual coaching, student-to-student mentoring, and disability accommodations.

Costs

For the 2016–17 academic year, undergraduate tuition and fees were $28,620 and the professional program tuition and fees were $33,027. A computer (issued to all new students) and lab fees are included in the total costs. Room and board costs for the academic year were $10,901 for shared units and $11,701 for suites. Additional costs, including books, student activity fees, student health fees, professional program fees, and new student program fees vary each year but average $900 per semester.

Financial Aid

The College offers merit- and need-based scholarships to new students by performing a holistic evaluation of each student's academic achievement, financial need, community service, and leadership experience. Most scholarships awarded to new students are renewable. The average institutional financial aid received by freshmen in 2016 was $11,437.

The College participates in all applicable federal and state financial aid programs. Scholarships, grants, loans, and student employment are offered to help qualified students pay for college expenses.

Students planning to attend the College in the fall semester should submit the Free Application for Federal Student Aid (FAFSA).

Student Government, Clubs, and Organizations

St. Louis College of Pharmacy provides a full student life experience, including more than 60 professional and social fraternities, intramurals, club sports, pharmacy organizations, and special interest groups. The College participates in 12 NAIA Division I sports: men's and women's cross-country, men's and women's basketball, women's softball, men's and women's track and field, men's and women's tennis, men's and women's soccer, and women's volleyball.

Some campus organizations include: Adventure Club, Campus Crusade for Christ (CRU), ConjuRxings (literary magazine), Euts Dance Team, Gay/Straight Alliance (GSA), GEARS (Gaming, Electronics, Anime, Rec, Sci-Fi), International Student Organization (ISO), Pharmakon (school newspaper), Prescripto (yearbook), Roller Hockey, STLCOP Book Club ("Booksies"), Student Alumni Association (SAA), Student Government Association (SGA), Student Organization for Drug and Alcohol Awareness (SODAA), Students of Service, and theater.

Admission Requirements

All students applying for admission to St. Louis College of Pharmacy must present evidence of the satisfactory completion of a four-year course of study in, and graduation from, a high school approved by a recognized accrediting body. It is recommended that the high school course of study include 4 units of English; 4 units of math, including pre-calculus or calculus; and at least 3 units of science, including biology and chemistry.

Required application materials include the following: completed application and $55 nonrefundable application fee, high school transcripts, official ACT or SAT score reports, academic reference form, science reference form, math reference form, and personal essay.

Application and Information

Application deadlines can be found online at stlcop.edu.

For additional information or to apply, students should contact:

Office of Admissions
St. Louis College of Pharmacy
4588 Parkview Place
St. Louis, Missouri 63110-1088
Phone: 314-446-8328
800-278-5267 Ext. 8328 (toll-free)
E-mail: admissions@stlcop.edu
Website: stlcop.edu
facebook.com/stlcop
twitter.com/stlcopedu

Located in the heart of one of the world's finest biomedical research and patient care centers, St. Louis College of Pharmacy provides innovative education, research, and career opportunities for students.

SAINT MARY'S COLLEGE

NOTRE DAME, INDIANA

SAINT MARY'S COLLEGE NOTRE DAME, IN

The College

Saint Mary's College is a Catholic undergraduate women's college located in Notre Dame, Indiana, offering graduate programs for women and men. The Sisters of the Holy Cross founded the College in 1844.

The undergraduate community is made up of bright, talented women who are on the path to self-discovery. Saint Mary's curriculum is challenging, not only in the student's chosen area of study, but also within the liberal arts. The Saint Mary's College experience includes its unique general education program (the Sophia Program), writing proficiency standards, senior comprehensive programs, and the development of exceptional critical thinking skills. Ninety-three percent of the school's graduates complete their degrees in four years, and whether they choose new careers, graduate school, or postgraduate service, Saint Mary's alumnae are prepared for life.

With more than 1,500 undergraduate students from approximately 40 states and about 15 countries, Saint Mary's brings together women from a wide range of backgrounds and experiences. International and diverse students compose 19 percent of the student body. Thirty-five women and men were enrolled in the graduate programs in 2015–16.

Saint Mary's unique relationship with the University of Notre Dame provides access to the exciting atmosphere of a large university—just across the street. Students at both schools can take courses at either institution. Saint Mary's students can audition for Notre Dame's legendary marching band or work for *The Observer*, the student newspaper for Saint Mary's and Notre Dame. In addition, students participate in dances, concerts, lectures, and social organizations on both campuses. Holy Cross College is also just next door to Saint Mary's College. Holy Cross congregations founded all three campuses.

Saint Mary's residential campus becomes the students' second home. Saint Mary's five residence halls include Opus Hall, which offers apartment-style living for seniors on campus. Residence halls host events and compete with each other in intramural athletics. Each hall also sponsors a local nonprofit organization that provides students with service opportunities. All residence halls have chapels, and the Church of Our Lady of Loretto, the main worship space, offers daily Mass on campus.

As an NCAA Division III school and a member of the Michigan Intercollegiate Athletic Association (MIAA), Saint Mary's sponsors varsity teams in basketball, cross-country, golf, lacrosse, soccer, softball, tennis, and volleyball. Club sports, co-sponsored with Notre Dame, include gymnastics and figure skating. In addition, Saint Mary's offers many intramural sports. The new Angela Athletic and Wellness complex is scheduled to open in spring of 2018, complete with a training and fitness center with weight and cardio machines, an indoor track, fitness classes for every level, a cafe, and study spaces.

Location

Saint Mary's beautiful 100-acre campus, set alongside the Saint Joseph River, is across the street from the University of Notre Dame, next door to Holy Cross College, minutes north of the city of South Bend (population 101,000), 90 miles from Chicago and 140 miles from Indianapolis. The South Bend community provides opportunities for internships, field practicums, and volunteer service. Eighty percent of Saint Mary's students engage in service by the time they graduate (the national average is approximately 55 percent).

Majors and Degrees

Saint Mary's College offers five undergraduate degree programs: Bachelor of Arts, Bachelor of Science, Bachelor of Business Administration, Bachelor of Fine Arts, and Bachelor of Music, and more than 30 major areas of study, such as business, nursing, art, chemistry, and social work. The College offers more than 40 minors, including American history, anthropology, computer science, environmental studies, justice studies, Latin American studies, and women's studies.

Saint Mary's also offers two graduate degrees: a Master of Science and a Doctorate. All programs that fall under these degrees are coeducational and include a Master of Science in Data Science, a Master of Science in Speech Language Pathology, and a Doctorate of Nursing Practice.

In addition, a five-year, dual-degree engineering program is offered in cooperation with the University of Notre Dame and leads to a bachelor's degree from Saint Mary's College and a Bachelor of Science in Engineering degree from Notre Dame in aerospace, chemical, civil, computer, electrical, environmental, or mechanical engineering.

Saint Mary's education department, accredited by the National Council for Accreditation of Teacher Education, offers an elementary education major (grades K–6) and a secondary education minor (grades 5–12). With an elementary education major, students can also receive mild intervention licensure (K–6) and an Indiana reading licensure (P–12). Saint Mary's also offers minors in English as a second language and early childhood education. In addition, the department offers programs for those interested in teaching the visual arts or music. Secondary education requires a major in one of the following: English, Spanish, mathematics, science (science majors must complete licensing requirements in chemistry or life science), history (history majors must complete additional course work in political science and one of the following: sociology, psychology, economics), and political science (political science majors must complete additional course work in history and one of the following: sociology, psychology, economics).

Academic Programs

In addition to completing the required credit hours in her chosen field, every undergraduate student completes a senior comprehensive in her major (a thesis, a research or creative project, or a written or oral examination). All undergraduate students must also complete a writing-intensive "W" course, usually in the first year, and an advanced portfolio of writing in the major discipline, usually in the senior year.

Off-Campus Programs

Intercultural competence is a cornerstone of the liberal arts education. Saint Mary's combines that with travel and adventure through study-abroad experiences in at least 17 locations: Argentina, Australia, Austria, China, Ecuador, England, France, Greece, Honduras, Ireland, Italy, Jamaica, Morocco, South Africa, South Korea, Spain, and Uganda. Saint Mary's students may also study in other countries through a cooperative program with the University of Notre Dame. Domestic programs include a semester at American University in Washington, D.C. for political science majors, opportunities for student teachers in Native American communities, and the Catalyst Trip, a journey to sites significant to the history of social justice.

Academic Facilities

Several buildings have computer labs in addition to computer "collaboratories," where students and faculty members can conduct online research in classroom settings.

The Cushwa-Leighton Library houses a collection of more than 228,000 volumes. Also located in the library are the Trumper Computer Center, the Instructional Technology Resource Center, and a rare-book room.

Laboratory facilities are available for biology, chemistry, physics, psychology, and foreign language students. Art studios, music practice rooms, O'Laughlin Auditorium, and Little Theatre provide space for fine arts creation, practice, and performance. Spes Unica Hall, an academic building, provides students with technology-equipped classrooms, group and individual study spaces, and presentation spaces.

The Early Childhood Development Center provides education and psychology majors with a unique opportunity to work with young children on campus.

Costs

Expenses for the 2017–18 academic year include tuition and fees, $40,800; room and board, $12,100 (average); and miscellaneous expenses (approximate cost of books, transportation, and living costs), $2,300.

Financial Aid

The College strives to make a Saint Mary's education available for every admitted student by offering financial aid packages that might include institutional need-based assistance, merit scholarships, and work-study opportunities in addition to state and federal grants and loans. One-hundred percent of admitted students receive some sort of financial aid in College grants and scholarships.

All applicants for financial aid must complete the Free Application for Federal Student Aid (FAFSA) by March 1 for each year that they desire assistance.

Faculty

Saint Mary's professors are experts in their fields of study and mentors to their students inside and outside the classroom. Of the full-time faculty members, 83 percent hold earned doctorates or other terminal degrees. Saint Mary's also has 73 part-time faculty members.

Student Government

The Student Government Association (SGA) is a dynamic student-led organization that sponsors extracurricular and co-curricular activities including service projects, social events, and learning experiences. It provides student participants with leadership opportunities that often include leadership training. SGA has voting representatives on the president's two highest advisory boards, the Student Affairs Council and the Academic Affairs Council. A student is also a voting member of the College's Board of Trustees.

Admission Requirements

Applicants for undergraduate admission to Saint Mary's College should be impending graduates of an accredited high school. Home-schooled students are also encouraged to apply. All applicants must complete a four-year, college-preparatory curriculum that consists of a minimum of 16 academic (Carnegie) units where one unit represents one full year of study. The minimum requirements are: 4 units of English, 2 units of the same foreign language, 3 units of college-preparatory mathematics (beginning with algebra I), 2 units of laboratory science, and 2 units of history or social science. The remaining required units should consist of three additional units in the above listed subjects.

Applications must include an academic transcript showing current rank and senior-year courses (if available), a secondary school report, SAT or ACT scores, and an essay. There is no application fee, and Saint Mary's is a member of the Common Application.

Saint Mary's encourages students to visit the campus for a tour and informational meeting with an admission counselor. Arrangements to attend classes, meet with coaches, stay overnight, or have an admission meeting via phone (for students who do not visit campus) can be made by contacting the Office of Admission.

Application and Information

Saint Mary's has two application and notification programs: early decision and modified rolling regular admission. Highly qualified students who have selected Saint Mary's as their first choice for admission may apply under the early decision program. The application deadline is November 15, and the notification date is December 15. Students who apply for modified rolling admission, and those whose application files are complete on or before December 1 are notified of the admission decision by mid-January. Applications received after December 1 are reviewed in the order in which they become complete. The priority application deadline for regular admission is February 15. Applications are accepted, however, as long as space is available.

Interested students are encouraged to contact:

Office of Admission
Saint Mary's College
Notre Dame, Indiana 46556-5001
Phone: 574-284-4587
800-551-7621 (toll-free)
Fax: 574-284-4841
E-mail: admission@saintmarys.edu
Website: www.saintmarys.edu
facebook.com/saintmaryscollegeadmission

We promise you discovery. Discovery of yourselves, discovery of the universe, and your place in it.
—Sister Madeleva Wolfe, CSC,
President of Saint Mary's College from 1934–1961

ST. NORBERT COLLEGE

DE PERE, WISCONSIN

The College

With more than $100 million in new construction and renovations over the past nine years, and record-setting enrollments, St. Norbert College is ascending at a pace unprecedented in its history. The riverfront campus is part of the thriving corporate, entertainment, educational, arts, and cultural environment of northeastern Wisconsin, and the college's influence is increasingly felt regionally, nationally, and globally.

The St. Norbert learning community helps students become critical thinkers, strong writers, and able communicators, in a setting that encourages student-faculty collaborations. The graduate-level work done by St. Norbert undergraduates, even as first-year students, is notable and puts them ahead of their peers when heading to graduate school or the workforce.

St. Norbert seeks to challenge student viewpoints and encourage exploration of new or different ideas, in an environment where students from around the world come together in exploration of local and global perspectives.

Faculty members at St. Norbert are active researchers and creators who make ongoing and exceptional contributions to their fields. They're also compassionate individuals who care not only about their students' grades, but also about their growth, making time for one-on-one conversations with them on a daily basis. Student success is the faculty's top priority, and their commitment to that goal extends far beyond the classroom.

St. Norbert offers more than 40 programs of study, including several pre-professional programs. Students can also design their own major. Study-abroad options abound, as do numerous service opportunities for students locally, nationally, and internationally.

Each St. Norbert student is paired with an advisor who helps ensure that the student is on track with classes and will graduate in four years. St. Norbert's innovative career and professional development office helps students transition to graduate school and the workforce with great success: when students are surveyed nine months after graduation, more than 93 percent are employed or attending graduate school.

Student life offers a blend of learning and fun. Students flourish within the academically challenging environment, but with more than 80 clubs and organizations on campus, there's no shortage of ways to become involved outside the classroom. The 20 Division III athletics teams produce conference champions, national champions, and more Academic All-Americans than any school in the Midwest Conference.

Students frequently comment on the sense of community and worldwide opportunities available at St. Norbert. They talk about the challenges of the classroom and the heartfelt rewards of service opportunities. Graduates value the friendships with peers and faculty members that started at St. Norbert and often last a lifetime.

Location

The St. Norbert campus, approximately 108 acres, is located on the banks of the Fox River in De Pere, Wisconsin, just minutes south of Green Bay, a metropolitan area of about 300,000 people. Rich in culture, arts, and entertainment, historic De Pere and the greater Green Bay area are recognized among the 100 best communities for young people by America's Promise Alliance. The campus is part of a vibrant 18-county region of 1.2 million people, home to Fortune 500 companies, hospitals, schools, and service organizations, many of which eagerly offer St. Norbert students internships.

Majors and Degrees

St. Norbert offers programs leading to the Bachelor of Arts, Bachelor of Science, Bachelor of Music, and Bachelor of Business Administration degrees.

Programs of study at St. Norbert include: accounting, American studies, art–fine arts, art–graphic design, biology–biomedical, biology–organismal, business administration, chemistry, chemistry–biochemistry, classical studies, communication and media studies, computer science, computer science–business information systems, computer science–graphic design and implementation, economics, education, English, English–creative writing, environmental science, French, geography, geology, German, history, human services (social work), international business and language area studies, international studies, Japanese, leadership studies, mathematics, military science/ROTC, music, natural sciences, peace and justice, philosophy, physics, political science, pre-dental, pre-engineering, pre-law, pre-medical, pre-nursing, pre-pharmacy, pre-veterinary, psychology, religious studies, religious studies–youth ministry, sociology, Spanish, teacher education, theatre studies, and women's and gender studies.

Graduate Programs: Through the college's Donald J. Schneider School of Business & Economics, founded in 2014, St. Norbert offers both undergraduate studies and an M.B.A. program. The Schneider School is also fast becoming the region's center for the study of sound business practices, championing principles and methods that will contribute to a thriving northeast Wisconsin.

In addition, St. Norbert College offers Master of Arts in Liberal Studies and Master of Theological Studies degrees.

Academic Programs

As a liberal arts institution, the college prepares students for a lifetime of challenges and opportunities by equipping them with exceptional communication abilities, as well as critical-thinking, problem-solving, and leadership skills. An honors program offers additional challenge in areas of general education to those of superior ability. St. Norbert holds one of the highest four-year graduation rates in the Midwest, backed by a four-year graduation guarantee.

Several St. Norbert students are recipients of full Army ROTC scholarships each year. Among the college's alumni are an impressive 12 Army generals who completed ROTC at St. Norbert.

Off-Campus Programs

St. Norbert students, regardless of major, can spend a summer, a semester, or a year abroad. In fact, 30 percent of St. Norbert students spend at least one semester abroad during their four years compared to less than 4 percent nationally. The college has more than 75 study-abroad program sites in 29 countries on six continents. An international study component is a part of majors in French, Spanish, and German, as well as both the international business program and the international studies major. All approved international study carries regular academic credit. St. Norbert scholarship assistance and other financial aid carry over to overseas study.

St. Norbert considers international experience vital to today's graduates and it is a key component of the college's educational mission. St. Norbert's international curriculum, taught by a faculty committed to global learning, prepares students to live in a global society. A Washington semester is also available through American University in Washington, D.C.

Additional service-learning opportunities are available throughout the year. Students can participate in the TRIPS (Turning Responsibility Into Powerful Service) program in local, national, and international locations, or take part in a variety of other off-campus service opportunities.

Academic Facilities

A state-of-the-art library houses more than 250,000 volumes. The 80,000-square-foot library features enhanced technology, flexible study and classroom spaces, and a 24-hour computer study area. A high-tech studio on the lower level of the library opened in 2013 and has become a favorite place for students to collaborate.

The F. K. Bemis International Center provides students with opportunities to prepare for careers with greater international emphasis. Students from nearly 20 countries attend St. Norbert College annually. The center also serves as a resource for K–12 schools and Wisconsin businesses for language instruction, translation, and interpretation.

The stunning, $40 million Gehl-Mulva Science Center was completed in 2015 and houses the science programs as well as the Medical College of Wisconsin's northeast Wisconsin campus. The 160,000 square-foot facility features state-of-the-art equipment and classrooms equipped with the latest technology. The science center has been awarded LEED Gold certification for its environmental sustainability and energy efficiency.

The recently completed Cassandra Voss Center offers innovative, holistic programming about gender, identity, and diversity, attracting leading figures in the field as speakers.

Fifteen residence halls provide the link between living and learning at St. Norbert. Some residence halls focus on community service or feature campus programs, such as the honors program. An apartment-style residence hall offers upperclassmen a transitional experience to living on their own. Many halls have chapels for students.

An enviable outdoor athletics complex provides the practice and competition venue for football, soccer, and track and field. A signature addition to the campus, the brand-new Mulva Family Fitness Center, is home to the college's indoor sports, health facilities, and much-anticipated aquatics center.

Michels Commons, completed in 2012, is where students eat their meals and gather in Dale's Sports Lounge on evenings and weekends. Chefs prepare meals in front of the students and are able to get immediate feedback on favorite recipes. The college ranks in the top 3 percent in the nation for its food.

Costs

For 2017–18, tuition and required fees for full-time students total $36,593 for the year. Room and board costs average $9,467 per year.

Financial Aid

Students share in more than $50 million of financial aid each year, including scholarships and grants, campus jobs, and educational loans. More than 97 percent of St. Norbert students receive financial aid, with the average aid amount of more than $24,000 per year. There are both need-based and merit-based awards.

Need-based awards are made on the basis of the Free Application for Federal Student Aid (FAFSA; St. Norbert College's code is 003892) and the St. Norbert College institutional application for financial aid. First-year applicants should submit their FAFSA by January 1 of their senior year of high school.

A multitude of work-study positions exist on campus as well as paid community internships. St. Norbert students graduate with an average indebtedness of about $34,441.

Faculty

The St. Norbert faculty is composed of roughly 200 men and women, with 90 percent of the full-time faculty members holding the doctoral or other terminal degree in their field. The student-to-faculty ratio is 14:1, and student success is the top priority of the faculty. They work closely with students in their major area of study, help students prepare for graduate school, write letters of recommendation, and work with those who seek independent study and research opportunities. Research fellowships and collaborations with faculty members are available to all students—as early as their first year—who may ultimately have the opportunity to present their research findings collaboratively with faculty members at national conferences. Faculty members also work with the career and professional development office in its professional practice program.

Student Government

The college's Student Government Association (SGA) is active on campus, with representation extending as far as the college's board of trustees. The president of the college and his cabinet respect the voice of the student body, and openly discuss issues that impact students and the college community. There are more than 80 organizations for students to get involved in.

Admission Requirements

St. Norbert College welcomes enrollment from a diverse group of students who are prepared academically and who will make a contribution to the college's living and learning community. The whole student is considered, not just their grades and test scores. Students who are likely to succeed in this environment are accepted. The average GPA of admitted students was 3.5, and the average ACT composite score was 25. Students with superior scores and grades are invited to enroll in the honors program. The college encourages and welcomes applications from international, transfer, and diversity students.

Application and Information

Because the college gives preference to students according to the date of admission and enrollment deposit, it benefits students to apply as early as possible in their senior year. Notification of the admission decision is made on a rolling basis beginning in late September. A $350 nonrefundable deposit is required to confirm enrollment.

For more information about St. Norbert College, students should contact:

Edward Lamm
Vice President for Enrollment Management and Communications
St. Norbert College
100 Grant Street
De Pere, Wisconsin 54115
Phone: 920-403-3005
800-236-4878 (toll-free)
E-mail: admit@snc.edu
Website: http://www.snc.edu
http://www.snc.edu/go/socialmedia

A welcoming, supportive community greets first-year students at Convocation.

ST. THOMAS AQUINAS COLLEGE

SPARKILL, NEW YORK

★ To read more about this school, visit http://petersons.to/stthomasaquinascollege

The College

St. Thomas Aquinas College (STAC) was founded in 1952 as a three-year teacher-training college with 30 students. Today, the College offers more than 100 different majors, minors, specializations, and dual degree programs and has a total student body of 2,800 in all programs, on and off campus. Much growth and development has taken place over the College's history. The College offers a Master of Science in Education, with concentrations in autism, literacy, special education, and educational leadership as well as postgraduate certificate programs in autism (online), literacy, special education, and teacher leadership (online). The College also offers a Master of Business Administration (M.B.A.) program with concentrations in finance, management, and marketing; and an online M.B.A. in general studies. St. Thomas offers a Master of Science in Teaching program for individuals without a background in teacher education who are seeking a career change. The College is home to New York University's Master in Social Work program.

The suburban campus includes two residential complexes: Aquinas Village, which consists of self-contained townhouse units that house 300 students, and the McNelis Commons, which consists of townhouse residential units that house 375 students and a common dining hall and laundry building. Approximately 40 percent of the College's full-time student population resides on campus.

Extracurricular activities are provided through forty different organizations, including the Spartan Volunteers, a community service program; a student-run radio station (WSTK); the Laetare Players dramatic and musical club; and the student-edited campus newspaper and yearbook. The College has 18 NCAA Division II teams in men's and women's cross-country, indoor and outdoor track and field, basketball, soccer, lacrosse, and tennis; women's field hockey and softball; and men's baseball and golf. There are a number of club sports including ice hockey, cheerleading and dance, bowling, and ski and snowboarding, as well as intramural athletics.

The College has a campus ministry office, a health office, and residence life, career development, and counseling services.

Location

The College is located in Rockland County, just 15 miles north of New York City, giving students quick access to learning, cultural, internship, and career opportunities in one of the world's most exciting cities.

Majors and Degrees

St. Thomas Aquinas College's School of Business offers accounting (and accounting as a dual degree with an M.B.A. degree), finance, hospitality management, management, marketing, and sport management. Minors are offered in business management, marketing, economics, human resource management, international business, sport management, and management information systems. Specializations are in management relations/industrial and organizational psychology.

The School of Arts & Sciences offers degrees in the humanities, mathematics, natural sciences, and social sciences. Programs are available in art therapy, art and visual communications in graphic design or media art, communication arts, creative writing, English, journalism, philosophy and religious studies, Romance languages, Spanish, mathematics, computer sciences, biochemistry, biology, exercise science, forensic science, medical technology, natural sciences, criminal justice, psychology, therapeutic recreation, social science, and history. There are specializations in biology, chemistry, and physics. Minors include art therapy, biology, chemistry, communication arts, computer information science, criminal justice, English, fine arts, history, journalism, mathematics, performing arts, physics, public relations, religious studies, social media, sociology, Spanish, therapeutic recreation, and creative writing. A full listing of all programs can be found online at www.stac.edu.

The School of Education offers programs in grades 1–6 childhood education, the same plus special education, birth–6 early childhood and childhood education, and grades 7–12 adolescence education. An art education program with certifications in grades K–12 is offered as well as a middle school extension that adds to either the elementary or secondary degree, enabling the student to certify for all middle school grades. The School of Education also offers several dual-degree programs: B.S./B.A. and M.S.Ed. in childhood (B.S.) and special education (M.S.Ed.), grades 1–6; mathematics (B.S.) and special education (M.S.Ed.), grades 7–12; social sciences (B.S.) and special education (M.S.Ed.), grades 7–12; and Spanish (B.A.) and special education (M.S.Ed.), grades 7–12.

The College offers a five-year dual-degree program in mathematics/engineering with The George Washington University (GWU) or Manhattan College. Students study at St. Thomas for three years. After completion of their final two years at either GWU or Manhattan, they earn a B.S. in mathematics from STAC and a B.S. in engineering from one of the other two institutions. The College also offers several dual-degree options in biology: a dual degree in biology (B.S. from STAC) and biomedical engineering (M.S. from Polytechnic University), a dual degree in biology (B.S. from STAC) and physical therapy (D.P.T. from New York Medical College), a dual degree in biology (B.S. from STAC) and chiropractic (D.C. from New York Chiropractic College), and a dual degree in biology (B.S. from STAC) and podiatry (D.P.M. from New York College of Podiatric Medicine). There are several other strategic alliances, such as preferred admission to St. John's University School of Law in New York and a similar program with Barry University School of Law in Florida that includes scholarship funds. St. Thomas also has strategic agreements with St. John's University for an M.P.S. in sport management and a Master of Public Health.

Academic Programs

The College strives to develop students who are not only generally educated but also possess advanced knowledge in specialized areas, are prepared for further study, and have the background to undertake fulfilling careers. To earn a bachelor's degree, students must complete a total of 120 semester hours, including a minimum of 51 credits in a core curriculum; complete all requirements for the specific major; and complete the final 30 hours at St. Thomas. The College awards up to 30 credits for life experience and up to 30 credits for achievement on the College-Level Examination Program (CLEP). The College operates on a semester calendar (quarterly on the M.B.A. level). Students may enroll in classes in the fall, winter (a one-month session), spring, and summer (three separate sessions). Undergraduate students can apply for the fall and spring semesters. Graduate education students can apply for the fall, spring, and summer semesters. Classes are scheduled during the day and evening, and students are permitted considerable academic flexibility in planning their programs.

Students can pursue independent study and internships, and many majors require a field practicum. The College maintains an active Center for Academic Excellence as a resource for enhancing academic performance, and students are encouraged to meet regularly with faculty advisers for academic guidance and career direction.

The College has a widely recognized program for college-age learning-disabled students, called the Pathways Program (at an additional cost). The College also participates in the New York State Higher Education Opportunity Program and provides an honors program (freshman applicants only) for exceptionally qualified students with a limited number of 70 percent scholarships. The honors program includes summer study at Oxford University. The Aquinas Leaders Work Scholarship program is for qualified students (freshmen applicants only) with strong academic abilities and a desire to gain work experience each semester that can be related to academic pursuits. Aquinas Leaders receive financial awards that cover approximately 60 percent of tuition costs over four years.

Off-Campus Programs

The College offers a variety of degree programs to active-duty military personnel, spouses, and dependants at the United States Military Academy at West Point. Associate and bachelor's degree are offered in a variety of areas at a discounted tuition rate.

Through articulation agreements with high schools, students can take college-level courses for credit at their own high schools at a very discounted tuition rate. This program provides high school students an opportunity to get a jump-start on their college careers by immersing them in college-level coursework and providing them with transferrable college credits for it.

The College offers a campus interchange program involving other fully accredited colleges (Barry University in Miami Shores, Florida; Dominican College of San Rafael in San Rafael, California; Aquinas College in Grand Rapids, Michigan; and Kyung Hee University, Korea) through which a student may enroll in courses at one of the participating colleges for a semester or set time frame. The College also offers a number of study-abroad opportunities for students throughout the entire year with as short a period as one week for a communication arts class in London.

The study-abroad program provides opportunities at colleges and universities in such places as Brazil, Canada, England, France, Hungary, Ireland, Italy, Morocco, and Spain. Several other locations are also available.

Academic Facilities

Borelli Hall, a green-designed, LEED-certified Silver building, features new classrooms with interactive board technologies. Costello Hall houses the science laboratories, technology theaters, and Azarian-McCullough Art Gallery. Spellman Hall houses a multiroom technology corridor, with a state-of-the-art communication studio where students produce their own news show, and technology and language labs. Lougheed Library provides a variety of online research opportunities for students. The Bloomberg Professional Laboratory provides students with the same platform for news, data, analytics, and research used by the world's leading banks, corporations, government agencies and public policy makers, law firms, libraries, energy companies, and media outlets. Aquinas Hall houses athletic facilities and a fitness center. Maguire Hall is home to classrooms, art studios, and the Sullivan Theater. Additional meeting areas are provided in the Romano Student-Alumni Center and in the two residence complexes, McNelis Commons and Aquinas Village. There is an after-hours club in the McNelis Commons dining hall for student activities.

Costs

For 2016–17, the tuition for full-time study (12 to 16 credits per semester) was $28,800; annual fees were $800. Room and board at the College Commons were $12,390. Certain studio, laboratory, and computer courses carry fees.

Financial Aid

In 2016–17, 85 percent of the student body received financial aid. The College is committed to providing students with the resources necessary to continue their education. Students must submit the Free Application for Federal Student Aid (FAFSA) each year. The College awards academic and merit scholarships from $5,000 up to 70 percent scholarships and provides need-based aid from the College as well as athletic grants and all federal and New York State aid programs.

St. Thomas strives to partner with the student to make college education affordable. The College has one of the lowest private college tuition rates in New York State, and scholarships make it even more affordable. The College is also a member of the Yellow Ribbon program for veterans enabling a qualified veteran to study with a full tuition scholarship.

Faculty

The faculty has 70 full-time and 55 part-time members; 80 percent have terminal degrees. The student-faculty ratio is 18:1. All faculty members participate in the academic advising of students and serve on College committees. Many serve as advisers to extracurricular activities.

Student Government

The Student Government consists of elected members who officially represent the student body, are responsible for planning and implementing student-originated programs, and coordinate and oversee all extracurricular organizations. Through its various offices, students play a vital part in offering consultation on new policies, planning social and cultural events, managing student funds, and operating the judicial system. In addition, the College Forum, which is composed of elected students, faculty members, alumni, administrators, and trustees, meets regularly to discuss policies, procedures, long-range plans, and any problems affecting the College.

Admission Requirements

All applicants must have successfully completed an approved secondary school program or the equivalent, including 4 years in English, 3 years in mathematics, 3 years in science, 2 years of foreign language, and 4 years of social studies. Applicants whose high school background varies from the recommended pattern are considered. Freshman applicants must submit the application for admission, including an essay, high school transcripts, SAT and/or ACT scores, and a letter of recommendation. Transfer students must submit the application and official transcripts of all previous college work. An academic evaluation is prepared for every matriculant. The College is a member of the Common Application and students are strongly encouraged to apply online through that service.

Application and Information

Candidates should submit completed application forms to the Admissions and Financial Aid Office and must request that their official transcripts be sent to the Admissions Office from their school. Students are notified of the admission decision on a rolling basis upon receipt of all the necessary credentials. The College is a member of the Common Application and students can find the link to apply on its website, http://www.stac.edu/apply.

St. Thomas Aquinas College does not discriminate in its educational programs, activities or employment practices based on race, color, national origin, sex, sexual orientation or expression, disability, age, religion, ancestry, genetic information, marital status, veteran status or any other legally-protected category. Announcement of this policy is in accordance with State and with Federal law, including Title VI and Title VII of the Civil Rights Act of 1964, Title IX of the Education Amendments of 1972, Section 504 of the Rehabilitation Act of 1973, the Age Discrimination in Employment Act of 1967 and the Americans with Disabilities Act of 1990. For more information, please contact: EEO, Section 504/ADA and Title IX Compliance Officer, 125 Route 340, Sparkill, New York 10976; phone: 845-398-4044.

For more information or an application, students should contact:
Admissions and Financial Aid Office
St. Thomas Aquinas College
125 Route 340
Sparkill, New York 10976-1050
Phone: 845-398-4100
E-mail: admissions@stac.edu
Website: http://www.stac.edu

St. Thomas Aquinas College's Costello Hall in the fall.

SAINT VINCENT COLLEGE

LATROBE, PENNSYLVANIA

★ To read more about this school, visit http://petersons.to/saintvincentcollege

The College

Founded in 1846, Saint Vincent College is the first Benedictine college in the United States. It is an educational community rooted in the tradition of the Catholic faith, the heritage of Benedictine monasticism, and the love of values inherent in the liberal approach to life and learning. There are 1,590 full-time undergraduate students and 62 part-time students, of whom 73 percent reside on campus. The College welcomes students from twenty-six states and eight other countries. In addition to more than fifty programs in the liberal arts and sciences, the College offers the Master of Science degrees in education: in counselor education, curriculum and instruction, instructional design and technology, science education, special education, and school administration and supervision. The College also offers postbaccalaureate and certification programs in special education, instructional technology specialist, principal, early childhood director, English as a second language, and online teaching. Other graduate and professional programs include a Master of Science in management: operational excellence, a Master of Science in criminology, and a Doctor of Nurse Anesthesia Practice.

Student services include advising, athletics, career placement and planning, computer assistance, and a wellness center. Students choose from more than fifty social, political, cultural, service, recreational, and religious student organizations. Saint Vincent College is accredited by the Department of Education of the Commonwealth of Pennsylvania, the Middle States Association of Colleges and Schools, and the Association of Collegiate Business Schools and Programs.

Location

Saint Vincent College is located on 200 acres in the Laurel Highlands of southwestern Pennsylvania. Noted for its beautiful countryside, the region offers abundant opportunities for outdoor recreation and adventure. Excellent sites for hiking, mountain biking, skiing, camping, and white-water rafting are less than half an hour from the campus in ten state forests. Pittsburgh, a regional center of culture and the arts, is only 35 miles to the west. The city offers music, museums, theater, shopping, nightlife, and sports.

Majors and Degrees

The College offers more than fifty degree programs; the most popular majors are biology, psychology, criminology, law and society, management, and accounting. The College is organized into four schools: the Alex G. McKenna School of Business, Economics, and Government; the Herbert W. Boyer School of Natural Sciences, Mathematics, and Computing; the School of Humanities and Fine Arts; and the School of Social Sciences, Communication, and Education.

The McKenna School includes majors in the areas of accounting, business education information technology, economics, finance, international business, joint economics and mathematics, management, marketing, politics, political science, and public policy. The School of Natural Sciences, Mathematics, and Computing offers degrees in biochemistry, bioinformatics, biology, chemistry, computer science, cybersecurity, engineering science, environmental chemistry, environmental science, information technology, integrated science, mathematics, mathematics/engineering, and physics/physics education. The School of Humanities and Fine Arts offers majors in arts administration (performing arts), art education, art history, English, graphic design, history, liberal arts, music, music performance, philosophy, philosophy/politics, philosophy/theology, Spanish, studio arts, and theology. The School of Social Sciences, Communication, and Education offers degrees in anthropology, communication, criminology, law and society, education (early childhood or middle grades), pre-law, psychology and sociology. Middle grade certification is offered in language arts, mathematics, science, and social studies, while minors in K–12 and secondary education include art, biology, business/computing and information technology, chemistry, Chinese, English, French, mathematics, physics, social studies, and Spanish.

The College offers a law school 3+3 program in cooperation with Duquesne University. Students complete their requirements in English, history, political science, public policy analysis, and sociology at Saint Vincent College. In addition, in conjunction with university schools of engineering, the College offers a five-year cooperative liberal arts and engineering program, as well as a four-year degree in engineering science.

Saint Vincent offers pre–health training in accelerated osteopathic medicine, accelerated podiatric medicine, allopathic medicine, chiropractic medicine, dental medicine, occupational therapy, optometry, pharmacy, physician assistant studies, physical therapy, and veterinary medicine in cooperation with various professional schools.

Students may select minor areas of study in accounting, anthropology, art history, arts administration, biochemistry, biology, biotechnology, chemistry, children's literature, children's studies, Chinese language and culture, communication, computing and information science, economics, education, English, environmental chemistry, environmental science, finance, fine arts, forensic science (computer security, financial investigations, or natural science), French, German, graphic arts, history, international business, international studies, Italian, Latin, liberal arts, management: operational excellence, marketing, mathematics, music, music history, peace and justice, philosophy, physics, political science, public administration, psychology, sociology, Spanish, studio arts, and theology.

Academic Programs

An academic year consists of two semesters, fall and spring, with the opportunity to earn credits in the summer. Saint Vincent College requires each student to complete a minimum of 124 credits, satisfy the requirements for the major(s) as specified by the department(s) or school(s), achieve an overall grade point average of at least 2.0 as well as a grade point average of at least 2.0 in the major, and satisfy the capstone requirement as specified by the major department(s) or school(s). Each student must complete a core curriculum. The core curriculum provides all students with a broadly based education that provides a general body of knowledge in the humanities, social sciences, natural sciences, and mathematics; an interdisciplinary view of that knowledge base; and the skills to increase that general body of knowledge throughout their lives. Special programs include national and international academic honor societies, a cooperative education and internship program, an interdisciplinary writing program, and an honors program. An annual Academic Conference allows students to showcase their work across a variety of disciplines.

Off-Campus Programs

Saint Vincent students may choose to learn in surrounding communities, those across the country, or around the world.

Service plays a prominent role in the life of the campus—nearly two-thirds of seniors take part in a service project, and every student organization completes at least one service project each year. There are numerous local service opportunities, as well as service trips to Alaska, Appalachia, New Jersey, and abroad in Brazil, China, Guatemala, Haiti, Italy, and Taiwan.

Students can study abroad for a semester, an academic year, summer, or spring break in places as diverse as Argentina, Australia, China, Egypt, Great Britain, France, India, Italy, Japan, Poland, Russia, South Africa, Taiwan, and Turkey. In addition to options in dozens of other countries, the College has affiliations with nine Chinese colleges and universities.

From the breadth of the liberal arts curriculum to the excitement of hands-on learning, Saint Vincent's goal is to encourage a love for learning that endures.

Academic Facilities

Saint Vincent College has invested more than $100 million in campus facilities during the past ten years, including the $44-million Dupré Science Pavilion, where every student takes at least two laboratory classes. Its James F. Will Engineering and Biomedical Sciences, Hall, slated to open in 2017, is specifically designed for collaborative, interdisciplinary learning.

The result is a modern, student-friendly campus that features accessible computer laboratories and workstations; fiber-optic cabling between buildings; Wi-Fi across campus and specialized laboratories for the study of astronomy, ecology, genetics, geology, human anatomy, life sciences, microbiology, optics, organic chemistry, physiology, and other subjects. From the multimedia computer lab to the nature reserve (created by the late golfing legend and College supporter Arnold Palmer) to the $14-million Fred Rogers Center for Early Learning and Children's Media, Saint Vincent offers many resources to help students intensify their learning.

Traditionally, Benedictine institutions have granted a place of honor to the library. Open 89 hours a week, the Latimer Family Library offers access to more than 250,000 printed volumes; 99,000 microforms such as microfilm, microfiche, and cards; 3,000 musical scores; 400 periodical subscriptions; and online access to electronic journals through 19 different databases. The library also houses a collection of rare books and incunabula (pre-1500 imprints). It also provides plentiful space for quiet studying.

The Robert S. Carey Student Center, covering more than 2 acres, contains the Frank and Elizabeth Resnik Swimming Pool, a gymnasium, performing arts center, wellness center, bookstore, fitness center, locker rooms and training rooms, snack bar, student lounge, chapel, billiards room, art gallery, art studios, and music practice rooms.

Costs

Tuition and fees at Saint Vincent for 2016–17 were $16,907 per semester, and room and board costs average $5,406 per semester, depending on accommodations and meal plan. Books and supplies cost $1,000–$1,500 per year. Costs are subject to change.

Financial Aid

Saint Vincent College offers a comprehensive program of financial aid in the form of scholarships, grants, loans, part-time employment, and deferred-payment schedules and coordinates programs from the federal and state financial aid program. In 2016–17, 100 percent of first-year students who applied for financial aid were offered assistance. The College annually awards qualified freshmen academic scholarships of up to $20,500 per year, renewable for up to four years, for excellence in academic achievement. In addition, the College offers first-generation grants, out-of-state grants, and grants to graduates of Catholic high schools and Benedictine parishes, among others. Other financial aid opportunities include Federal Direct Student Loans and Federal PLUS loans. Residents of Pennsylvania may be eligible for the Pennsylvania Higher Education Assistance Agency Grant program. In order to be considered for financial aid, students must complete the Free Application for Federal Student Aid (FAFSA).

Faculty

The faculty numbers 102 members, of whom 91 percent hold terminal degrees. Members of the faculty have earned doctorates or terminal degrees at such schools as Catholic University of America, Cornell, Duke, Fordham, Northwestern, Notre Dame, NYU, Stanford, Yale, and the Universities of California, Chicago, and Pennsylvania. Faculty members are engaged as principal investigators in research and other projects funded through government agencies such as the National Science Foundation and the U.S. Department of Education and private foundations. The student-faculty ratio is 12:1, and no classes are taught by teaching assistants. Faculty members have chosen to teach at Saint Vincent in part because they value the quality of student-teacher interaction, specifically the emphasis on high standards, personalized learning, fieldwork, hands-on experience, and the high level of classroom participation.

Student Government and Student Activities

The Student Government Association (SGA) builds community at the College by providing opportunities for the students, faculty members, and administrators to share in their common interests. All class officers, senators, and representatives can vote in the unicameral senate that makes up the student government.

The sense of community that Saint Vincent is known for is fostered from the day students arrive on campus. Orientation lasts five weeks and involves more than 150 upperclassmen whose mission is to make freshmen feel at home. Every student is matched with an upperclassman who serves as a big brother or big sister throughout the first year. In the residence halls (where more than 70 percent of students live), trained prefects foster a safe living environment and provide guidance and advice, along with activities and educational programs.

The College community is proud of the Catholic, Benedictine tradition that has shaped life on the campus for nearly 170 years. In keeping with the tradition of hospitality, Saint Vincent welcomes students of all faiths or of no faith. The campus includes places for prayer, as it is an important part of life for many of our administrators, faculty members, and students—no matter their faith traditions.

Admission Requirements

Saint Vincent College has a rolling admission policy. Adequate preparation for college is an important determinant for a successful college education. Fifteen secondary school academic units are required for admission to Saint Vincent College. These 15 units must include 4 units of English, 3 or more units of college-preparatory mathematics, 1 unit of laboratory science, and 3 units of social science; 2 units of a foreign language are preferred among 5 elective units. Engineering students must have 1 unit in plane geometry, 1 unit in intermediate algebra, 1 unit in physics, and ½ unit in trigonometry in addition to those listed above. Art education, art studio, and graphic design majors must submit a portfolio for acceptance to the Fine Arts Department, and music and music performance students must audition for acceptance.

Transfer students are invited to apply to Saint Vincent College, which awards generous scholarships to academically capable transfer students. The applicant's academic achievement and personal history at the postsecondary schools previously attended are of primary importance in the decision for admission.

Application and Information

To be considered for admission, a freshman applicant must submit a completed application form with the nonrefundable $25 application fee, an official transcript sent directly to Saint Vincent College from the guidance office at the secondary school of graduation, and an official copy of the test results from the SAT or ACT.

An application and additional information may be obtained by contacting:

Office of Admission and Financial Aid
Saint Vincent College
300 Fraser Purchase Road
Latrobe, Pennsylvania 15650-2690
Phone: 800-782-5549 (toll-free)
E-mail: admission@stvincent.edu
Website: http://www.stvincent.edu
https://www.facebook.com/saintvincentcollege (Facebook)
https://twitter.com/MySaintVincent (Twitter)
https://www.youtube.com/user/saintvincentcollege (YouTube)
https://instagram.com/SaintVincentCollege (Instagram)

Saint Vincent College offers a warm and welcoming atmosphere combined with technologically advanced facilities including the $44-million Sis and Herman Dupré Science Pavilion, dedicated in 2013 and expanded in 2017.

COLLEGE CLOSE-UPS

SETON HALL UNIVERSITY

SOUTH ORANGE, NEW JERSEY

★ To read more about this school, visit http://petersons.to/setonhalluniversity

The University

As one of the nation's leading Catholic universities, Seton Hall provides over ninety rigorous academic programs that are highly ranked by the Princeton Review, *U.S. News & World Report,* and *Bloomberg Businessweek.* Seton Hall offers all the advantages of a large research university—national reputation; challenging academic programs; notable alumni; state-of-the-art facilities; renowned faculty; and extensive opportunities for internships, research, and scholarship—with all the benefits of a small, supportive, and nurturing environment. The 14:1 student-to-faculty ratio and average class size of 21 students means faculty members know more about each student than just their name.

The University's accomplished faculty members include Fulbright Scholars, prominent researchers, authors, artists, filmmakers, former school superintendents and principals, leaders in nursing, former ambassadors, analysts, and lawmakers—all of whom are dedicated to their fields and their students. They have graduated from some of the nation's leading institutions, including Seton Hall, Harvard, Columbia, Yale, Princeton, and Dartmouth. While faculty members shine in the lecture halls and on the national stage every day, they also meet regularly with students outside the classroom and help them learn to think critically.

Seton Hall offers more than 17,000 internship opportunities, and over 81 percent of students have an internship—or two—on their resume before graduation. This is just one of the reasons Seton Hall graduates have an employment rate almost 25 percent higher than the national average and mid-career earnings 50 percent higher than the national average. Seton Hall was recently ranked in the top 5 in the nation for providing internship opportunities. This national reputation coupled with the University's stellar academic programs draws over 550 employers to campus each year to recruit graduates.

Seton Hall is a Catholic university with a 160-year tradition of educational excellence. A welcoming community, Seton Hall embraces students of all faiths and inspires them to become servant-leaders who make a difference in the world. The University community performs over 40,000 hours of community service annually.

Location

Nestled in the suburban village of South Orange, New Jersey, Seton Hall provides small-town charm combined with big-city opportunities. The University's 58-acre, suburban, park-like campus sits proudly in this picturesque town with tree-lined streets; historic, gracious homes; and quaint shops just 14 miles from New York City—close to all the action, but not engulfed by it.

The bustling town center—with diners, pizzerias, banks, pharmacies, Starbucks, Cold Stone Creamery, a gourmet marketplace, South Orange Performing Arts Center, a movie theater, and more—is just a 5-minute walk from campus. The train station, right in the center of town, provides a direct link to NYC's Penn Station, just 30 minutes away.

The University takes full advantage of all the Big Apple has to offer; after all, it's where the worlds of entertainment, art, publishing, global finance, international diplomacy, and fashion collide. NYC is also one of the world's largest job markets, brimming with internship and job placement opportunities in a variety of companies. Seton Hall students have interned at leading companies like Goldman Sachs, American Express, CNN, the U.S. Secret Service, the United Nations, The *New York Times*, Prudential, The Museum of Natural History, Lockheed Martin, NBC, Sony Music, JPMorgan Chase, Lincoln Center and more.

One of the wealthiest states in the nation, New Jersey is brimming with opportunity. Seton Hall's backyard boasts a powerhouse corporate corridor of more than fifty Fortune 500 companies, pharmaceutical giants, and major corporations. For students, this means networking, internships, and career opportunities.

Academic Programs

Seton Hall is a place where great minds are exposed to even greater opportunities. This is evident in the dozens of student and alumni national scholars and fellows, including nearly 20 prestigious Fulbright Scholars since 2009, as well as Rhodes, Udall, Pickering, Marshall, Critical Language, and Truman Scholars and more than 100,000 alumni who are now successful as CEOs, judges, doctors, principals, CFOs, journalists, nurses, diplomats, and more. About 1,000 Seton Hall graduates have served in executive positions at firms like Oppenheimer, Visiting Nurse Service of New York, American Express, and Merrill Lynch. They have served as elected officials in Washington, D.C., and in hundreds of state capitals and town halls throughout the country. In New Jersey alone, almost 20 percent of the state legislators holds a Seton Hall degree.

Seton Hall's commitment to academic excellence is evident in the more than ninety academic programs offered through six undergraduate schools and colleges. In addition, the University has recently announced plans to form a medical school in partnership with Hackensack University Medical Center; the first class is scheduled to begin in the fall of 2018. A joint degree program for direct admission as a freshman applicant is also planned.

Majors and Degrees

Accounting•
Accounting (5-year B.S./M.S. dual-degree∞)
Africana Studies•
American Humanics√
Ancient Greek†
Anthropology•
Applied Scientific Mathematics†
Arabic†
Archaeology†
Art (Art History•, Fine Arts•, Graphic Interactive and Advertising Design•)
Asian Studies•
Athletic Training (5-year B.S./M.S. or B.A./M.S. dual-degree)∞
Biochemistry
Biology (B.A. or B.S.)
Broadcasting, Visual and Interactive Media•
Business Administration•‡
Catholic Studies•‡
Catholic Theology•
Chemistry•
Classical Culture†
Classical Languages†
Classical Studies•
Communication•
Computer Graphics√
Computer Science•
Creative Writing
Criminal Justice•
Data Visualization and Analysis√
Digital Media and Video√
Digital Media Production for the Web√
Diplomacy and International Relations•
Early Childhood (integrated with elementary and special education)
Elementary Education (integrated with early childhood and special education)
Education with Speech Language Pathology (6-year B.S.E./M.S. dual- degree)∞
Economics (B.A. or B.S.)
Engineering (Biomedical, Chemical, Civil, Computer, Electrical, Industrial, Mechanical)§
English•
Entrepreneurial Studies√
Environmental Sciences†
Environmental Studies•
Ethics and Applied Ethics†
Finance
French•
Gerontology√
Graphic, Interactive, and Advertising Design
History•
Information Technologies√
Information Technology Management‡
International Business
International Relations
Italian•
Italian Studies†
Journalism•
Latin†
Latin America and Latino/Latina Studies•
Law (3+3 program)∞
Legal Studies in Business†
Liberal Studies
Management
Marketing
Mathematical Finance
Mathematics•
M.B.A. (5-year B.S./M.B.A. or B.A./ M.B.A. dual-degree)∞
Modern Languages

Music (Comprehensive Music/ Music Education, Music Performance•)
Musical Theatre†
Nonprofit Studies†
Nursing
Occupational Therapy (6-year B.A./M.S. dual-degree)∞
Online Course Development and Management√
Philosophical Theology√
Philosophy•
Physical Therapy (6-year B.S./D.P.T. dual-degree)∞
Physician Assistant (6-year B.S./M.S. dual-degree)∞
Physics (B.A. or B.S.)•
Political Science•
Pre-Dental*
Pre-Law*
Pre-Medical*
Pre-Optometry*
Pre-Veterinary*
Psychology (B.A. or B.S.)•
Public Relations
Religion•
Russian†
Russian and East European Studies†√
Secondary Education (optional integration with special education)
Social and Behavioral Sciences
Social Work•
Sociology•
Spanish•
Special Education (integrated with early childhood, elementary, and secondary education)
Speech Language Pathology (6-year B.S.E./M.S. dual- degree)∞
Sport Management•
Supply Chain Management√
Theatre and Performance•
Web Design√
Women and Gender Studies†
Writing†
Undecided

• Minor also available
† Minor only
√ Certificate program only
‡ Certificate program also available
§ Dual-degree program with New Jersey Institute of Technology
∞ Seton Hall dual-degree program
* Pre-professional programs (students must also select a major)

Campus Facilities

Seton Hall places a strong emphasis on the use of state-of-the-art technology, facilities, and support services to aid in its students' development. Many investments have been made to the campus infrastructure, including the recent construction of a new academic classroom building, new residence hall space, a new parking deck, a Dunkin' Donuts, and a new recreation and fitness center. In addition, the campus boasts a state-of-the-art research library complete with a computerized catalog and 200 computer terminals. The Science and Technology Center is home to state-of-the-future biology and chemistry labs, an atrium, and auditorium, as well as an observatory and greenhouse.

The campus also offers many unique learning labs, such as a Mock Trading Room, Patient Simulation Laboratory, Market Research Center, a student-run radio station (ranked the number-one noncommercial radio station by the National Association of Broadcasters), and Sport Polling Center. All incoming students are provided a new, fully loaded laptop computer.

Costs

Seton Hall offers a flat-tuition rate for students taking between 12 and 18 credit hours. The 2016–17 tuition and fees were $39,558. Room and board costs vary depending on meal plans; however, the average rate is $13,108.

Financial Aid

Paying for college is a major investment. Seton Hall University has been rated as one of the best schools in the nation for return on investment and is committed to providing students with the resources needed to make their dreams a reality. The University gives over $83 million in aid each year; 98 percent of students receive some form of financial aid, and 97 percent receive scholarships or grants directly from the University. Most scholarships are automatically awarded upon admission and do not require separate applications. However, there are also several special scholarships for which students can apply; more information on those is available online at www.shu.edu/go/scholarships. Seton Hall also provides need-based aid to eligible students who complete the Free Application for Federal Student Aid (FAFSA) form by December 1.

Student Organizations and Activities

On campus, Seton Hall leaders learn to put their ideas into action; discover something new; become part of a community; and build trust, spirit, and lasting friendships. Extracurricular activities abound, with over 130 clubs and organizations, twenty-two Greek societies, fourteen Division 1 Big East athletic teams, and extensive club and intramural sports. Students can audition for one of the many theater productions each year; broadcast at the award-winning, student-run radio station, WSOU-FM, which attracts more than 120,000 listeners a week from the NYC area; be part of the Brownson Speech and Debate team, which has been ranked among the top 20 college and university forensic teams for years; or write for one of three student newspapers. More than two thirds of Seton Hall students participate in clubs and organizations and over 50 percent participate in club or intramural sports.

Admissions Process

Seton Hall takes a holistic approach to reviewing applications for admission, considering academic performance in high school, grades and the rigor of the curriculum, and SAT and/or ACT scores. These are essential indicators of a potential student's ability to succeed at Seton Hall. A personal essay, recommendations, extracurricular activities, and interest in the University are also considerations. Students can apply using the Common Application or the Seton Hall application, located on the admission.shu.edu website.

The typical student who entered Seton Hall last year had an average GPA of 3.6 (B+), an average SAT score of 1150 (old SAT) or 1220 (new SAT), and/or an average ACT score of 25.

Application and Information

Potential students are encouraged to visit Seton Hall in person. Tours are offered Mondays through Fridays at 10 a.m. and 2 p.m. and on Saturdays at 10 a.m., noon, and 2 p.m. Open houses are offered in mid-October, mid-November, mid-February, and late April. Visits can be scheduled online at www.shu.edu/visiting

For more information, prospective students should contact:

Office of Undergraduate Admissions
Seton Hall University
400 South Orange Avenue
South Orange, New Jersey 07079
Phone: 800-THE-HALL (843-4255; toll-free)
E-mail: thehall@shu.edu
Website: http://www.admissions.shu.edu

Students enjoy a spring day on the University Green, the scenic pathway located at the heart of Seton Hall's campus.

SIMPSON COLLEGE

INDIANOLA, IOWA

★ To read more about this school, visit http://petersons.to/simpsoncollege

The College

Founded in 1860, Simpson College is a private liberal arts college affiliated with the United Methodist Church. Simpson produces successful students by combining the best of a liberal arts education with outstanding career preparation and extracurricular programs. With 1,400 full-time students and a student to faculty ratio of 13:1, students have the opportunity to work closely with their professors. Simpson's faculty members are as dedicated to their fields of study as they are to teaching—and it shows in the classroom. When this type of dedication and passion is combined with well-prepared and motivated students, the potential for success is unlimited.

The campus is located just minutes from Iowa's capital city, Des Moines, which was recently ranked as the top city for business and careers. The proximity to Des Moines allows Simpson students to take advantage of an abundance of internship opportunities. Whether working with Fortune 500 companies, spending time in an elementary school, or gaining resume-building experiences in a medical field, students learn to push their own boundaries. Simpson's excellent internship program gives students an advantage in today's competitive job market.

Simpson's beautiful, tree-lined campus in Indianola provides small-town friendliness and safety, while the campus facilities are continually enhanced and updated for academic and recreational opportunities. Recent multimillion-dollar projects include the renovation and expansion of Blank Performing Arts Center (2011), renovation of outdoor athletic facilities (2011), and the addition of a stunning new student center (2012). A $6-million expansion and renovation of the Simpson Athletic Complex and Steven Johnson Fitness Center was completed in January 2014.

Simpson's 4-4-1 academic calendar includes a May Term that provides students with unique learning opportunities in the classroom, an internship setting, or while studying abroad. Throughout the year, students take advantage of Simpson's innovative Engaged Citizenship Curriculum. The curriculum allows students to gain skills and experiences valued most by employers while choosing classes that interest them.

Extracurricular activities at Simpson are designed to supplement and reinforce the academic programs and contribute to a total learning experience. Activities range from an award-winning music program to nationally recognized NCAA Division III athletic teams. Students have the opportunity to participate in student government, campus publications, religious life, music, theater, departmental clubs, and various other organizations. Simpson competes in 19 intercollegiate sports and has an extensive intramural program. Simpson has eight Greek chapters on campus, including three national fraternities, one local fraternity, one local sorority, and three national sororities; each with their own house.

Location

Simpson is located in Indianola, a residential community with a population of 14,400. Indianola is 12 miles south of Des Moines, with easy access to Interstates 35 and 80. The Des Moines International Airport is 20 minutes from campus. Indianola is host to nationally known events including the Des Moines Metropolitan Opera and the National Balloon Classic. The vibrant, small-town community has many choices for entertainment and recreation including Lake Ahquabi State Park, Summerset Trail, and unique restaurants and shops within walking distance of campus. Indianola's proximity to Des Moines gives students plenty of distinct advantages. Within minutes, students are right in the heart of some of the best entertainment and employment options Iowa and the Midwest have to offer.

Majors and Degrees

Simpson College grants Bachelor of Arts and Bachelor of Music degrees. Majors include accounting, actuarial science, applied philosophy, art, biochemistry, biology, business management, chemistry, clinical health science, computer information systems, computer science, criminal justice, economics, education (elementary and secondary), English, environmental science, exercise science, forensic science/biochemistry, French, German, graphic design, health services leadership, history, human services, interactive media, interdisciplinary studies, international management, international relations, management information systems, mathematics, multimedia journalism, music, music education, music performance, neuroscience, philosophy, physical education, physics, political science, psychology, public relations, religion, sociology, Spanish, sports administration, sports communication, studio art, and theater arts.

Simpson also offers pre-professional programs in athletic training, chiropractic, dentistry, engineering, law, medicine, nursing, optometry, pharmacy, physical therapy, theology/ministry, and veterinary medicine. Concentration areas such as early childhood education and ethics are available, as well as many additional minors, including women's studies, human resources management, Latin American studies, and coaching endorsements.

Academic Programs

Simpson College operates on a 4-4-1 academic calendar. The first semester starts in late August and ends in mid-December; the second semester starts in mid-January and ends in late April. A three-week session takes place during the month of May. During this period, students participate in a field experience/internship, study abroad, or take a course on campus with a hands-on focus.

The First-Year Program is an extensive program of orientation, team building, mentoring, community service, advising, and course work structured to help new students adapt to their first year of college. The program begins with summer orientation and continues throughout the academic year. The academic component of the First-Year Program is the Simpson Colloquium, a joint classroom and advising concept that is unique among first-year programs. These courses are small in size—no more than 18 first-year students each—and all are taught by each student's faculty adviser.

With Simpson's Engaged Citizenship Curriculum, students delve deeper in their courses and focus more on projects that provide hands-on understanding of the subject matter. These courses allow students to work closely and build strong relationships with faculty members, one of the hallmarks of a Simpson education. The curriculum encourages students to take advantage of Simpson's community partnerships, hold internships, study abroad, or conduct independent research. It was developed in response to research that indicates future employers are looking for effective communicators, innovators, and problem solvers. Simpson is on the forefront of providing the kind of experiential, liberal arts education that college graduates need to succeed in their careers and achieve fulfillment in their lives.

Off-Campus Programs

Simpson provides many opportunities for studying abroad, with the choice of a semester-long program or a three-week May Term. Simpson's semester-long, faculty-led study abroad programs include England, Germany, Thailand, Tahiti, Australia, and Chile. Students also have the opportunity for semester study-abroad programs in France, Spain, Italy, and more locations.

In addition, 10 to 15 travel courses are offered each May Term. Recent destinations include Africa, Central America, Great Britain, France, Greece, Ireland, New Zealand, the Galapagos Islands, Brazil, Argentina, and Scandinavia. May Term study abroad courses are led by Simpson faculty members and give students the opportunity to experience a different culture while gaining a stronger global perspective. Simpson has been recognized as one of the top colleges in the nation for its percentage of students who study abroad.

The Capitol Hill Internship Program (CHIP) provides students with the opportunity to spend either the fall or spring semester in Washington, D.C. Past participants have had various experiences including interning for members of Congress, the Smithsonian Institution, the Republican National Committee, the Justice Department, CNN, the Australian Embassy, and FOX News.

Academic Facilities

Simpson has a wireless campus network with high-speed Internet access. There are numerous computer labs throughout campus where students can use standard office suite applications or specialized, discipline-specific applications.

The Carver Science Center, named after Simpson's most distinguished alumnus George Washington Carver, provides state-of-the-art research facilities, computer labs, a cadaver lab, and classrooms.

The Henry H. and Thomas H. McNeill Hall houses classrooms for business management, accounting, health services leadership, and economics. In addition, the hall houses a seminar room and the Pioneer Hi-Bred International Conference Center.

The Amy Robertson Music Center is home to Simpson's acclaimed music department and contains the Sven and Mildred Lekberg Recital Hall, ten studios, twenty-two practice rooms, a music computer lab, and the band rehearsal room. The Salsbury Wing includes a choral rehearsal room, a classroom, and studios.

Dunn Library, a modern academic learning resource center, contains over 175,000 books, periodicals, videos/DVDs, and CDs. Many resources (print and online) can be located from the library website. Additional materials for research can be obtained through a national interlibrary loan network. The Center for Academic Resources is also located in Dunn Library, which provides free academic support services to all students.

The A. H. and Theo Blank Performing Arts Center underwent a multimillion-dollar expansion and renovation in 2011. The center accommodates Simpson's well-known programs in theater arts and opera. It includes the magnificent 500-seat Pote Theatre, with both proscenium and hydraulically controlled thrust stages, a studio theater, the Barborka Gallery, technical facilities, and shops and classrooms.

Wallace Hall, named to the National Register of Historic Places, contains facilities for education, sociology, and applied social science.

Mary Berry Hall houses the psychology department which includes six labs, a control room for observation and data processing, and an animal care space. In addition, the building is home to humanities classrooms, a language lab, faculty offices, and the Farnham Art Galleries.

The Gaumer Center contains offices for multimedia communication and art and provides space for the college newspaper, *The Simpsonian*, and radio station KSTM.

Faculty

Simpson offers one professor for every 13 students. Simpson's faculty members serve as academic advisers as well as teachers. Their commitment goes beyond the classroom as they often attend college plays, operas, and athletic events, reinforcing their sincere interest in the lives of the students and their ultimate success.

Costs

Tuition and fees for 2017–18 are $37,663; room charges are $3,860; and board is $4,103. These figures do not include books, music fees, or personal expenses.

Financial Aid

Simpson College is dedicated to making it financially feasible for qualified students to experience the advantages of a Simpson education. In fact, 100 percent of full-time Simpson students receive some form of financial assistance. Generous gifts from alumni, trustees, and friends of the College—in addition to state and federal student aid programs—make this opportunity possible. Simpson offers financial assistance on both a need and non-need basis. Need is determined by filing the Free Application for Federal Student Aid.

Financial assistance granted on a non-need basis includes generous academic scholarships (awarded on the basis of prior academic records) and talent scholarships (available in theater, music, art, and speech/debate). The talent scholarships are determined by audition/portfolio or application.

Also, specific scholarships such as the John C. Culver Fellowship, the Iowa History Center Scholarship, and the Wesley Service Scholarship can be obtained through application.

Admission Requirements

A strong academic record is essential. Applications are acted upon by an admissions committee, which is elected by the faculty. These faculty members consider the college-preparatory courses taken and the grades received in those courses (transcripts and cumulative GPA), and standardized test scores (ACT and/or SAT), including test sub scores, as well as a high school report form/guidance counselor recommendation.

Transfer applicants are accepted on the basis of successful completion of academic work at an accredited college or university.

Application and Information

Applications are accepted on a rolling basis beginning in early fall and continuing on a space-available basis. Simpson's rolling admission policy allows flexibility; however, early application is recommended.

Application information can be found at www.simpson.edu/apply.

For additional information or to obtain application materials, students should contact:

Office of Admissions
Simpson College
701 North C Street
Indianola, Iowa 50125
Phone: 515-961-1624
800-362-2454 Ext. 1624
E-mail: admiss@simpson.edu
Website: http://www.simpson.edu
http://www.facebook.com/simpsoncollege
http://twitter.com/simpsoncollege
http://www.youtube.com/simpsonweb
http://instagram.com/simpsoncollege

Simpson's $14-million Kent Campus Center opened in fall 2012 and is the hub for student activities and events.

SKIDMORE COLLEGE

SARATOGA SPRINGS, NEW YORK

SKIDMORE COLLEGE

★ To read more about this school, visit http://petersons.to/skidmorecollege

The College

Skidmore College is an independent liberal arts college of 2,500 students from 44 states and more than 60 countries that prides itself on its creative approaches to just about everything. Hence the College's belief that "Creative Thought Matters." About 60 percent of the student body is female and 40 percent male, with 22 percent being domestic students of color, 11 percent international students, and 13 percent first-generation students.

Students enjoy a full schedule of intellectual, cultural, and social activities, such as lectures, visiting scholars in residence, art exhibits, concerts, and dance and theater performances. There are approximately 130 student organizations, including a newspaper, radio and TV stations, ethnic and cultural associations, art and literary journals, and a volunteer network. There are no fraternities or sororities. A strong NCAA Division III intercollegiate sports program for men and women—19 teams in all—includes baseball, basketball, field hockey, golf, ice hockey, lacrosse, riding, rowing, soccer, softball, swimming and diving, tennis, and volleyball. Skidmore competes in the Liberty League, which also includes Bard, Clarkson, Hobart and William Smith, Rensselaer Polytechnic Institute, Rochester Institute of Technology, St. Lawrence, Union, and Vassar. The College has programs in intramural and club sports, health, fitness, and wellness.

Skidmore's campus includes more than 50 buildings. The Williamson Sports and Recreation Complex has a pool and diving well, racquet-sport courts, basketball and volleyball courts, several intramural gyms, three dance studios, a weight room, a fitness center, and a human performance laboratory. Adjacent to the complex are Wachenheim Field, a small stadium with an artificial turf field for soccer, lacrosse, and intramurals, and a 400-meter all-weather track; softball and field hockey turf fields; and the lighted Wenger Tennis Courts. The Frances Young Tang Teaching Museum and Art Gallery, unique in its interdisciplinary approach to exhibits and programming, opened in 2000.

The 950-acre campus, 300 acres of which consists of the recreation and research-rich North Woods, has been recently upgraded with renovations to science, athletics, dining, and residential facilities. Skidmore's newest academic building, opened in 2010, is the Zankel Music Center, featuring a spectacular 600-seat recital hall and state-of-the art recording studio. In addition, the Northwoods Apartments, opened in 2007 for upperclassmen, feature "green" apartments that use geothermal heating and cooling systems. The similar Sussman Village Apartments were completed in 2013. Some 40 percent of Skidmore's buildings are heated and cooled geothermally.

Location

Saratoga Springs, 30 miles north of Albany, New York's state capital, is perennially short-listed as one of the most interesting and vibrant small cities in the U.S. Famed for health, history, and horses—its mineral waters, Revolutionary War battlefield, and the nation's oldest thoroughbred racetrack—Saratoga is renowned as an arts and cultural destination. In 2015, *Travel + Leisure* named Saratoga Springs one of America's Top 10 College Towns. The Saratoga Performing Arts Center is summer home to the New York City Ballet, Philadelphia Orchestra, and Opera Saratoga, and is a performing venue for top rock and jazz musicians. The city's downtown is just a 10-minute walk from Skidmore and is brimming with galleries, clubs, shops, coffeehouses, and restaurants. The city's location near the foothills of the Adirondack Mountains puts an abundance of outdoor recreational opportunities—ski areas, state parks, lakes, and mountainous regions of New York, Vermont, and Massachusetts—within an hour's drive. Boston, New York City, and Montreal are each approximately 180 miles from the campus.

Majors and Degrees

Skidmore College grants degrees in 43 academic disciplines, including a Bachelor of Arts degree in the following liberal arts subjects: American studies, anthropology, art history, Asian studies, biology, chemistry, classics, computer science, economics, English, environmental science, environmental studies, gender studies, geosciences, history, international affairs, mathematics, music, neuroscience, philosophy, physics, political science, psychology, religious studies, sociology, and world languages and literatures (French, German, and Spanish). The Bachelor of Science degree is granted in areas of a more professional nature, including business, dance, education studies, exercise science, social work, studio art, and theater. There are seven interdepartmental majors, business-French and political-Spanish being just two examples. Self-determined majors, double majors, and minors are also available. Most majors have corresponding minors. Minors are also available in arts administration, Chinese, intergroup relations, Italian, Japanese, Latin American studies, and media and film studies. In keeping with the College's creative spirit and the realities of the marketplace, about half of Skidmore students choose a second major or minor.

Through partnerships with other institutions, Skidmore offers enhanced program/degree offerings in business, education, engineering, nursing, and physical and occupational therapy. These include 4+1 M.B.A. programs with Rochester Institute of Technology, and Clarkson University Graduate School; the Whitman MBA Advantage program with Syracuse University; 4+1 M.S.A. and M.S.F. programs with Syracuse; dual-degree programs in engineering with Clarkson, Dartmouth College, and Rensselaer Polytechnic Institute; an M.S. in accountancy with Wake Forest University; dual-degree programs in physical therapy and occupational therapy with Sage Graduate School; an M.S. in Teaching with Clarkson; and a 4+1 nursing program (New York University School of Nursing). Skidmore also has certification programs in teaching and social work and preprofessional programs in law and medicine/health professions.

Academic Programs

The Skidmore journey begins with the College's First-Year Experience, which introduces students to the interdisciplinary academic program and overall approach to learning and connects them with a faculty adviser/mentor. Talented but economically disadvantaged students accepted into the Opportunity Program (Higher Education Opportunity Program and Academic Opportunity Program) participate in a month-long summer program. Some 250 students opt to apply for entry into Skidmore's Periclean Honors Forum on the basis of academic achievement and aspirations, leadership qualities, and civic commitment.

Generally, students choose a major by the end of sophomore year. They are also expected to take one to two courses in both quantitative reasoning and expository writing, and at least one course of the following: natural science, social science, arts, humanities, and culture-centered inquiry. There is plenty of academic support through Student Academic Services. In their junior and senior years, students often add value to their courses of study through faculty-student collaborative research (academic year and summer program), internships (many funded and for credit), volunteerism, service learning, and off-campus study.

Off-Campus Programs

About 60 percent of Skidmore's students spend a semester or year off campus. In addition to Skidmore programs in England, France, and Spain, students can access approximately 120 international programs through the College's Approved Programs structure, including programs in Africa, Asia, Europe, Latin America, and Australia. All academic majors and minors can be accommodated and transfer credits are guaranteed for students studying on an Approved Program. Financial aid is transferable to most off-campus study programs. Annually, nearly 25 percent of the student body members engage in research with a faculty mentor, including more than 80 in the Summer Student-Faculty Research program. The College also offers a Washington Semester (internship in conjunction with American University) and a semester at the Marine Biological Laboratory in Woods Hole, Massachusetts.

Academic Facilities

Skidmore's 950-acre campus is comprised of more than 50 buildings. The newest academic building, the Arthur Zankel Music Center, features a spectacular 600-seat recital hall and a state-of-the-art recording studio. Skidmore's visual and performing arts space includes the Saisselin Art Center, with studios and the Schick Art Gallery; the Janet Kinghorn Bernhard Theater, with a seating capacity of 350, and an experimental black box theater; and the Dance Center. The Frances Young Tang Teaching Museum and Art Gallery provides a focal point for cross-disciplinary study through the visual arts. The Dana Science Center offers state-of-the-art teaching and research space, including a microscopy center. Dana links the College's science departments to the Mathematics and Computer Science departments in neighboring Harder Hall, which features a Linux lab with more than 20 workstations for advanced computer science projects.

Costs

In 2016–17, tuition and fees were $50,684, a double dorm room was $7,998, and board was $5,532.

Financial Aid

Skidmore annually provides approximately $42 million in financial aid. The average 2016–17 first-year aid package was $39,900 and ranged from $2,000 to $65,000; 42 percent of students receive need-based grants; 50 percent receive some form of financial aid; and 50 percent are given the opportunity to work on campus. Average postcollege student debt (just under $23,000) is well below the national average. Students interested in applying for admission are encouraged to do so regardless of their intention to seek financial aid. The FAFSA, a copy of the federal income tax form, and the CSS Profile must be filed each year. The College hosts an annual Filene Music Scholarship Competition to award four to six $48,000 ($12,000 per year) scholarships on the basis of musical ability without regard to financial need. Five to seven $15,000 scholarships ($60,000 over four years) in math and science are also awarded annually. The Skidmore Scholars in Science and Mathematics program provides up to eight S3M scholars with demonstrated financial need annual financial-aid packages with no loan component in the first two years and with reduced loans in years three and four.

Faculty

Skidmore College has more than 300 full-time faculty members, 87 percent of whom hold a doctorate or the highest degree in their field. The student-to-faculty ratio is about 8:1 and the average class size is 16. Although actively engaged in research and publication in their individual fields, Skidmore faculty members regard teaching as their primary commitment. All students have faculty advisers who assist them in selecting courses and in designing individual academic programs.

Student Government

Students at Skidmore play an active role in College governance. Through the Student Government Association (SGA) and membership on a number of major College committees, they participate in academic and social life. The SGA operates under the authority granted by the Board of Trustees and is dedicated to democratic self-government and responsible citizenship. Elected faculty members and student representatives serve on the All-College Council, the Academic Integrity Board, and the Social Integrity Board. Broad concerns of the SGA include educational policy, elections, social and student events, first-year orientation, student publications, and student clubs and organizations.

Admission Requirements

Those seeking admission to Skidmore's first-year class should complete a secondary school curriculum that includes at least 16 credits in college-preparatory courses. The Admissions Committee is also pleased to consider applications from qualified high school juniors who plan to accelerate and enter college early. Applicants typically have completed 4 years of English, 4 years of a foreign language, 4 years of mathematics, 4 years of social studies, and 3 to 4 years of laboratory science. Applicants must provide a secondary school transcript, letters of recommendation from two teachers of academic subjects, and a report from their guidance counselor. Although Skidmore is test optional (some exceptions for international and home-schooled students), students who wish to can submit their standardized test scores (SAT with writing or ACT with writing). A campus visit and interview is also recommended. (It is recommended that applicants check with Admissions prior to submitting standardized test scores as there may be changes.)

Through its participation in the Higher Education Opportunity Program, Skidmore enrolls capable, energetic, and ambitious New York state residents who, because of their academic and financial situations, would not otherwise gain admission to the College under traditional requirements. Skidmore's Academic Opportunity Program (AOP) recruits similar students who reside outside of New York. The programs are collectively referred to as the Opportunity Program.

Application and Information

Applicants for admission are requested to complete the Common Application—online at www.commonapp.org—and submit it with a $65 fee or request a fee waiver from their adviser. They may also apply through the Coalition for Access, Affordability, and Success, online at www.coalitionforcollegeaccess.org. All information should be postmarked by January 15. Applications from early decision candidates should be submitted by November 15 for the Round I early decision plan or by January 15 for the Round II early decision plan. Transfer candidates are urged to apply by April 1 for the next fall term and by November 1 for the next spring term. In addition to a high school transcript, transfer candidates are required to submit, by the appropriate deadlines, an official transcript of all college-level work completed, recommendations from two professors, and a statement regarding personal and academic standing from the dean of students at the current college. International students are given special attention throughout the admissions process. Applicants whose first language is not English are encouraged to submit the results of the Test of English as a Foreign Language (TOEFL). There are a limited number of need-based financial aid awards available for outstanding international students.

Mary Lou W. Bates
Vice President and Dean of Admissions and Financial Aid
Skidmore College
815 North Broadway
Saratoga Springs, New York 12866
Phone: 518-580-5570
800-867-6007 (toll-free)
E-mail: admissions@skidmore.edu
Website: www.skidmore.edu
www.facebook.com/SkidmoreCollege
http://twitter.com/skidmorecollege
https://www.instagram.com/skidmorecollege
https://www.pinterest.com/skidmorecollege
www.skidmore.edu/admissions/visit/youvisit.php#virtualtour
www.skidmore.edu/videos/ www.youtube.com/skidmorecollege

Autumn view of Skidmore's campus: Haupt Pond in the foreground, Case Center at left, and Scribner Library at right.

SOUTHERN ILLINOIS UNIVERSITY CARBONDALE

CARBONDALE, ILLINOIS

★ To read more about this school, visit http://petersons.to/southernillinoisuniversitycarbondale

SIU Southern Illinois University CARBONDALE

The University

Southern Illinois University Carbondale (SIU), chartered in 1869, is a comprehensive, state-supported institution with nationally and internationally recognized instructional, research, and service programs. SIU is fully accredited by the North Central Association of Colleges and Schools.

SIU offers more than 200 undergraduate majors, minors, and specializations; three associate degree programs; 95 baccalaureate degree programs; 80 master's degree programs; 34 doctoral programs; and professional degrees in law and medicine. SIU is a multicampus university that includes the Carbondale campus as well as the SIU School of Medicine at Springfield.

During the 2016 academic year, SIU's enrollment was 15,987, which included 12,182 undergraduate students, 3,183 graduate students, and 622 professional students. The average age of undergraduates is 23. International students account for 8.49 percent of SIU's total enrollment. Of U.S. undergraduate students, 17.91 percent are African-American, 0.21 percent are American Indian/Alaskan, 1.9 percent are Asian or Pacific Islander, and 9.19 percent are Hispanic.

Students who are ready to start college but not ready to commit to a specific major can enroll in SIU's Exploratory Student Advisement-Undeclared (EXPU) program. Advisers and career counselors help these students plan their education and careers. SIU faculty members, staff members, and alumni help students arrange internships, cooperative education programs, and work-study programs.

All single students under the age of 21 not residing with their parents or legal guardians, and with fewer than 26 credit hours earned after high school, are required to live in university-owned and operated residence halls. SIU offers three on-campus residential areas for single students, each with a dining hall, a post office, and laundry facilities. Learning Resource Centers, available on both sides of campus, offer writing centers, computer labs, and student lounges. University Housing Residence Hall Dining provides all-you-care-to-eat meals and late-night dining. Residence Hall Dining offers a variety of menus, vegetarian and light entrees, display cooking, and a full-time dietitian to help students with special dietary needs. Apartment housing is available for sophomore-, junior- and senior-level undergraduates, graduate students, and students with families.

SIU intercollegiate sports teams compete at the NCAA Division I level (football is Division I-FCS). Conference affiliations include the Missouri Valley Conference and the Missouri Valley Football Conference. Intercollegiate sports teams include men's and women's basketball, cross-country, diving, golf, swimming, and track and field; men's baseball and football; and women's softball and volleyball. The campus has various playing fields, several tennis courts, and a campus lake with a beach and boat dock. SIU's Student Recreation Center offers an Olympic-size pool; indoor tracks; handball/racquetball and squash courts; a climbing wall; weight rooms; basketball, volleyball, and tennis courts; outdoor equipment rental; an aerobic area; wallyball; martial arts; and dance and cardio studios.

The Student Center is one of the largest in the United States without a hotel. It holds a bookstore, several restaurants, a craft shop, facilities for bowling and billiards, headquarters for more than 275 student organizations and the student government office, four ballrooms, and an auditorium. On-campus events throughout the year include concerts, plays, festivals, guest speakers, and musicals.

Location

Carbondale is six hours south of Chicago, two hours southeast of St. Louis, and three hours north of Nashville, Tennessee. Four large recreational lakes, two great rivers (the Mississippi and the Ohio), and the 270,000-acre Shawnee National Forest are within reach of the campus. The mid-South climate is ideal for year-round outdoor activities.

Carbondale is a city of 26,000 that supports one large enclosed mall, several mini-malls, and theaters and restaurants. Students frequent the shops and restaurants that line Illinois Avenue and Grand Avenue.

Majors and Degrees

The university offers three Associate in Applied Science degree programs (aviation flight, physical therapist assistant, and radiologic sciences) at the College of Applied Sciences and Arts.

The College of Applied Sciences and Arts offers bachelor's degree programs in architectural studies; automotive technology; aviation management; aviation technologies; dental hygiene; electronic systems technologies; fashion design and merchandising; health care management; information systems technologies; interior design; mortuary science and funeral service; public safety management (off-campus only); radiologic sciences; and technical resource management.

The College of Agricultural Sciences offers bachelor's degree programs in agribusiness economics; agricultural systems and education*; animal science; crop, soil, and environmental management; forestry; horticulture; hospitality and tourism administration; and human nutrition and dietetics.

The College of Business offers bachelor's degree programs in accounting; business and administration (online only); business economics; finance; management; and marketing.

The College of Education and Human Services offers bachelor's degree programs in several undergraduate programs, many in conjunction with other colleges on campus. The programs include: art education*; behavior analysis and therapy; biological science education*; communication disorders and sciences; early childhood*; elementary education*; English teacher education*; exercise science; foreign languages (French, German, and Spanish)*; history education*; math education*; physical education teacher education*; public health; recreation; rehabilitation services; social science education*; social work; special education*; sport administration; and workforce education and development (** denotes educator licensure required through the university's Teacher Education program*).

The College of Engineering offers bachelor's degree programs in civil engineering; computer engineering; electrical engineering; electrical engineering technology; industrial technology; mechanical engineering; and mining engineering.

The College of Liberal Arts offers bachelor's degrees in Africana studies; anthropology; art; classics; communication studies; criminology and criminal justice; design; economics; English; geography and environmental resources; history; languages, cultures, and international studies; linguistics; mathematics; music; musical theater; paralegal studies; philosophy; political science; psychology; sociology; theater; and university studies.

The College of Mass Communication and Media Arts offers bachelor's degrees in cinema and photography; journalism; and radio, television, and digital media.

The College of Science offers bachelor's degree programs in biological sciences; chemistry; computer science; geology; mathematics; microbiology; physics; physiology; plant biology; zoology; and pre-professional programs and advisement in the following areas: chiropractic; dental; medical; nursing; occupational therapy; optometry; osteopathic medicine; pharmacy; physical therapy; physician assistant; podiatry; and veterinary medicine.

In addition to the many majors offered at SIU, specializations are offered in all colleges in many areas.

Academic Programs

Each bachelor's degree candidate must earn a minimum of 120 semester hours of credit, including at least 42 at the 300–400 level at a 4-year institution and the last 30 at SIU. Each student must maintain at least a "C" average in all course work at SIU and must fulfill the university core curriculum and the specific requirements of their degree programs. SIU awards credit through qualifying extension and correspondence programs, military experience, the High School Advanced Placement program, the College-Level Examination Program (CLEP), SIU's proficiency examination program, and work experience.

SIU offers honors coursework and special recognition for students who demonstrate exceptional academic achievement. The Air Force and Army offer ROTC programs at SIU. SIU offers fall and spring semesters, as well as a summer term.

Off-Campus Programs

Southern Illinois University Carbondale is committed to serving statewide, national, and international needs. This commitment is reflected in SIU Extended Campus, which offers educational opportunities located off campus. SIU Extended Campus is present at 20 military installations and 17 nonmilitary locations across 14 states, offering 24 online degree programs, 15 off-campus programs, and five military programs.

Off-campus credit programs are designed to meet the educational needs of adults wishing to pursue a degree but who are unable to travel to the Carbondale campus.

Additional information can be found at extendedcampus.siu.edu.

Academic Facilities

In addition to the 2.6 million volumes, 3.6 million microfilms, and more than 43,000 current periodicals and serials available in Morris Library, students and faculty members have access to more than 200,000 e-books. More details are available online at lib.siu.edu.

Students learn and practice in the Transportation Education Center based at the Southern Illinois Airport, outdoor laboratories, the student-run *Daily Egyptian* newspaper, WSIU-TV, WSIU-FM, art and natural history museums, a literary magazine, McLeod Theater, Memorial Hospital, a vivarium, plant biology greenhouses, University Farms, and Touch of Nature Environmental Center.

Costs

Tuition and fee charges for the 2016–17 academic year (fall and spring) for students enrolled in 15 or more semester hours were $13,481 for Illinois residents and $27,130 for out-of-state residents, including international students. Room and board totaled $10,186. (All costs are subject to change.) New freshman and transfer students from Arkansas, Indiana, Iowa, Kentucky, Missouri, Tennessee, and Wisconsin qualify for a reduced tuition rate equal to the Illinois in-state rate. The cost of books and school supplies varies among programs. The average cost is $1,100 per academic year. Beginning Fall 2017, SIU Carbondale is eliminating out-of-state tuition for undergraduate students and moving to an international/domestic rate structure.

Financial Aid

More than $284 million in financial aid was distributed to 16,631 SIU students in fiscal year 2016 through federal, state, and institutionally funded financial aid programs.

To apply for financial aid at SIU, students should complete the Free Application for Federal Student Aid (FAFSA). Applications that are filed before December 1 receive priority consideration for campus-based aid. The FAFSA can be completed online at fafsa.ed.gov, and students should list Southern Illinois University Carbondale (Federal School Code 001758) as a school of choice.

SIU has a large student employment program, with about 4,200 students employed each year in a variety of job classifications.

Faculty

Faculty members are dedicated to excellence in teaching and to their advancement of knowledge in a variety of disciplines and professions. Many faculty members are well-known nationally and internationally for their research contributions. The student-faculty ratio is 14.83:1. There are 762 full-time and 89 part-time instructional faculty members.

Teaching assistants at SIU are graduate students who assist faculty members in teaching.

Student Government

The Undergraduate Student Government (USG) represents the undergraduate student body at Southern Illinois University Carbondale in all matters pertaining to student welfare, student activities, and student participation in University planning and administration. The Undergraduate Student Government is composed of three separate branches: Judicial, Legislative, and Executive. The Executive branch consists of a president, vice president(s), chief of staff, and treasurer. The Legislative branch consists of 51 senators. Senators serve on various committees within USG including Internal Affairs, External Affairs, and the Funding Board. Senators also may serve on external campus advisory committees, representing the interests of the student body. The Judicial Board consists of five justices

Admission Requirements

Freshman applicants whose ACT composite score is at or above 23 (SAT score at or above 1130) and whose high school grade point average is at or above 2.0 (on a 4.0 scale) are admitted to the university. Applicants also can be admitted with an ACT composite score at or above 18 (SAT score at or above 940) and a high school GPA at or above 3.0 (on a 4.0 scale). All other applicants who meet the course subject pattern requirements will undergo a holistic review to determine potential admissibility. Admission of students who do not meet automatic admission requirements may be subject to conditions. Freshman applicants must meet course pattern requirements: 4 years of English, 3 years of mathematics, 3 years of laboratory science, 3 years of social science, and 2 years of electives.

Transfer applicants must have an overall grade point average of at least 2.0 on a 4.0 scale, based on work attempted at all institutions and calculated by SIU grading policies. Transfer applicants must also be eligible to continue at the last institution attended.

Some programs have higher admission requirements or require additional screening for admission. Undergraduates can apply online at admissions.siu.edu.

Application and Information

Admission is granted on a rolling basis. Application priority deadlines for freshmen and transfer students are May 1 for the summer term and fall semester, and Dec. 1 for the spring semester. The application fee is $40.

For more information, prospective students should contact:

Undergraduate Admissions
Mail Code 4710
1263 Lincoln Drive
Southern Illinois University Carbondale
Carbondale, Illinois 62901
Phone: 618-536-4405
E-mail: admissions@siu.edu
Website: http://www.siu.edu
http://www.facebook.com/SouthernIllinoisUniversityCarbondale
http://twitter.com/siuc

SIU Carbondale, ranked among the top 5 percent of the nation's public research institutions, offers more than 200 degree and certificate programs. Centrally located, diverse, and featuring remarkable amenities and hands-on learning opportunities, SIU provides 8,474 acres of possibilities.

COLLEGE CLOSE-UPS

SOUTHERN METHODIST UNIVERSITY
DALLAS, TEXAS

SMU.

★ For more information, visit http://petersons.to/smu

The University

Southern Methodist University (SMU) is a nationally ranked global research university in the dynamic city of Dallas. SMU's alumni, faculty, and 11,000-plus students in seven degree-granting schools demonstrate an entrepreneurial spirit as they lead change in their professions, communities, and the world.

SMU celebrates diversity, with students from all 50 states and more than 90 nations, as well as a variety of ethnic, socioeconomic, and religious backgrounds. Fifty-five percent of SMU first-year students come from outside Texas. Fall 2016 undergraduate enrollment included nearly 35 percent of students from diverse ethnic backgrounds.

Students can choose from more than 100 majors and 85 minors. One in five SMU students opts to pursue a double major. Students can customize their education by combining a major in the humanities or sciences with another in engineering, business or the arts for a dual degree.

SMU hosts more than 400 performances, concerts, and exhibits on campus during the school year. The Tate Lecture Series brings world-changers and experts to campus. Recent speakers have included Condoleezza Rice, Robert Edsel, Scott Kelly, and Brandon Stanton.

Location

SMU students benefit from the University's proximity to the heart of Dallas, which is home to amazing restaurants, a world-renowned arts district, exciting nightlife, and professional sports.

SMU's location in Dallas—and in a state that ranks No. 2 for Fortune 500 companies—offers students abundant internship opportunities. The Princeton Review 2017 ranks SMU No. 6 nationwide for internships. The Dallas area is home to companies such as American Airlines, AT&T, Texas Instruments, Toyota, Southwest Airlines, and ExxonMobil.

Dallas-Fort Worth is the nation's fourth-largest metropolitan area and home to about 7 million residents. Dallas offers top-tier museums and performance facilities, including the AT&T Performing Arts Center, Meyerson Symphony Center, Dallas Museum of Art, Nasher Sculpture Center, Perot Museum of Nature and Science, and SMU's Meadows Museum. The Dallas area is home to the Dallas Cowboys, Dallas Mavericks, Dallas Stars, Texas Rangers, FC Dallas, Lone Star Park, Texas Motor Speedway and professional golf tournaments.

Dallas-Fort Worth International Airport offers service to 149 domestic destinations—including access to every major city in the continental U.S. within four hours—and 57 international destinations out of 165 gates. Dallas Love Field, home to Southwest Airlines, serves more than 42,000 passengers daily.

SMU is a major contributor to the Dallas economy, and spending by its graduates living and working in the North Texas area generates about $6.18 billion in local economic activity.

Majors and Degrees

SMU offers strong undergraduate, graduate, and professional programs through seven schools.

The **Dedman College of Humanities and Sciences** is SMU's largest and most diverse academic unit. It is home to the humanities and social, natural, and mathematical sciences—disciplines that are the core of higher education. Undergraduate students in Dedman College may major and minor in more than 50 programs. Dedman College offers 18 graduate programs leading to a master's degree and 13 programs leading to a Ph.D. degree, plus numerous interdisciplinary programs.

The **Cox School of Business** equips students with the knowledge, skills, and experience needed to become business leaders. Major publications, including *Bloomberg Businessweek*, *The Economist*, and *Forbes*, rank SMU Cox among the top business schools nationally and globally. Degrees offered by the Cox School include: Bachelor of Business Administration with majors in accounting, finance; financial consulting, general business, management, marketing, real estate, finance, and risk management, and insurance; Full-Time, Fast Track Executive and Professional (part-time) Master of Business Administration; and master's degrees in accounting, business analytics, entrepreneurship, finance, management, and sport management (in partnership with the Simmons School).

The **Lyle School of Engineering**, ranked among the top 20 schools for highest-paid engineering graduates by College Factual 2017, prepares today's engineering students to be tomorrow's innovators equipped with both technical and leadership skills. Degree programs offered include bachelor's, master's, and doctoral degrees through the departments of Civil and Environmental Engineering; Computer Science and Engineering; Electrical Engineering; Engineering Management, Information and Systems; Mechanical Engineering; Multidisciplinary Studies; and dual- and joint-degree programs with other schools on campus, such as the Cox School of Business.

The **Meadows School of the Arts** prepares students to lead professional careers in the arts and communications and provides opportunities for all SMU students to grow in appreciation of the arts. A leader in innovative community engagement programs, Meadows challenges students to make a difference locally and globally by developing connections between arts entrepreneurship and social change. The School offers minors and bachelor's and master's degrees through 11 divisions: Temerlin Advertising Institute, Art, Art History (also offering a Ph.D.), Arts Management and Arts Entrepreneurship, Corporate Communication and Public Affairs, Creative Computation, Dance, Film and Media Arts, Journalism, Music, and Theatre.

The **Annette Caldwell Simmons School of Education and Human Development** prepares exemplary professionals and advances knowledge through evidence-based research. Undergraduate programs include a major and three minors in applied physiology and sport management and a major and a minor in educational studies. The school offers three doctoral programs, about 10 master's degrees, and a number of graduate professional-preparation programs. Its academic departments include Teaching and Learning, Applied Physiology and Wellness, Dispute Resolution and Counseling, Education Policy and Leadership, and Lifelong Learning.

Students at SMU can also opt to focus on specialized studies through degree-track programs such as pre-law, pre-health, physical therapy, and biomedical research.

SMU's undergraduate curriculum is complemented by the nationally recognized **Dedman School of Law**, offering a personalized legal education in a community of distinguished scholars, and **Perkins School of Theology**, which prepares women and men for faithful leadership in vital Christian ministry.

Academic Programs

Students benefit from small classes and opportunities for research, leadership development, and unique learning experiences on campus and around the world. Undergraduate students participate in scholarly research, civic engagement, professional internships, and creative activity related to education goals.

SMU faculty and students conduct research in the U.S. and worldwide in the sciences, engineering, education, arts, humanities, and business. Examples include natural hazards, water quality, cyber security, data analytics, learning disabilities, human performance, immigration, and the search for dark matter, as well as treatments for cancer, neurodegenerative diseases, diabetes, anxiety, and depression.

SMU received $26 million in external funding for projects during 2014–15. Sources include the National Science Foundation; National Institutes of Health; departments of Defense, Education, and Energy; foundations; and private industry. Research facilities include one of the nation's most powerful academic supercomputers, ManeFrame.

Off-Campus Programs

Students can expand their horizons with SMU Abroad's 150 programs in 50 countries to study for a semester, a summer, or a year. The unique SMU-in-Taos program brings history, science, and art to life at SMU's spectacular campus in Northern New Mexico.

Academic Facilities

SMU's campus includes 131 buildings featuring state-of-the-art teaching and learning facilities and equipment.

SMU's eight libraries house the largest private collection of research materials in the Southwest, with more than four million volumes.

The Meadows Museum houses one of the largest and most comprehensive collections of Spanish art outside Spain. A partnership with Madrid's Prado Museum includes the loan of major paintings from the Prado and an internship exchange.

SMU is also home to the George W. Bush Presidential Library and Museum. This is the first presidential library to share the campus of a private university.

Estimated Costs

For the 2017–18 academic year, undergraduate tuition and fees is $52,498; average housing and dining is $16,510.

Financial Aid

In addition to providing a valuable education with lifelong benefits, SMU partners with families to manage the cost of that education. Besides academic scholarships and customized financial aid packages for eligible students, SMU offers several payment plans. Three out of four SMU undergraduate students receive some form of financial assistance from the University, including academic or need-based aid. Kiplinger named SMU among its best values in private colleges. Competitive academic scholarships include the President's Scholars Program, the Nancy Ann and Ray L. Hunt Leadership Scholars Program, and scholarships offered by SMU's individual schools.

Faculty

SMU has 1,190 full- and part-time faculty members, and more than 80 percent of full-time faculty hold a Ph.D. or the highest degree in their field. The undergraduate student-to-faculty ratio is 11-to-1. About three out of four classes contain 30 students or fewer.

Student Life

Approximately 3,200 undergraduate and graduate students live on campus in 11 Residential Commons and six upperclass/graduate communities. The Residential Commons enable all first- and second-year students to live on campus and include on-site classes, social activities, and Faculty in Residence.

Students can make their mark, meet new people, and develop leadership skills through nearly 200 clubs and organizations spanning a variety of activities. They can also get involved in student government, campus programming, or community service. Annually, nearly 2,500 undergraduate volunteers make a difference through approximately 70 nonprofit agencies. Students also participate in Alternative Breaks national service projects. Other options for students include joining a religious or multicultural group, or getting involved in Greek life.

SMU has 17 NCAA Division I athletics programs, including the Mustang football team, which has played in three consecutive bowl games. Mustang spirit and traditions make for memories that will last a lifetime.

Students can stay in shape at the Dedman Center for Lifetime Sports with the latest health and fitness equipment. Students interested in sports can opt to participate in one or more of the 18 intramurals, such as flag football, basketball, and softball, and 15 club sports, such as lacrosse, baseball, and hockey.

Admission Requirements

SMU carefully considers each application with the goal of adding dimension to its diverse, ambitious community of scholars. The strongest applications are not always those with the greatest number of accomplishments, but those that resonate with authenticity and passion.

Prospective students need to submit a completed application (either SMU's online application; The Common Application; ApplyTexas; or Coalition Application for first-year undergraduate applicants), the completed Early Decision agreement form (if applying Early Decision), a $60 nonrefundable application fee, an official high school transcript, official SAT or ACT scores—SMU does not require the SAT optional essay or the ACT writing test (non-U.S. citizens and music, theatre, dance, studio art, and film B.F.A. applicants are not required to submit test scores), a personal essay, a counselor recommendation (required), a teacher recommendation (optional), an extracurricular resume (optional), and a Home School supplement (if applicable). Students applying for dance, music, theatre, art, or film programs should also review audition and portfolio requirements.

The Early Action (nonbinding) and Early Decision I (binding) deadline is November 1. The Regular Decision (nonbinding) and Early Decision II (binding) deadline is January 15.

Application and Information

The best way for students to get a feel for SMU is to visit. SMU offers many structured visits, such as Mustang Days, where prospective students can meet current students, talk with academic representatives, and tour campus. Prospective students can also attend an information session, speak with an admission counselor, and tour on a weekday or selected Saturday.

For more information, prospective students should contact:
SMU Undergraduate Admission
Southern Methodist University
6425 Boaz Lane
P.O. Box 750100
Dallas, Texas 75275
Phone: 214-768-2058
800-323-0672 (toll-free)
E-mail: ugadmission@smu.edu
Website: smu.edu/admission

COLLEGE CLOSE-UPS

SOUTHERN NEW HAMPSHIRE UNIVERSITY

MANCHESTER, NEW HAMPSHIRE

★ To read more about this school, visit http://petersons.to/snhu

The University

At Southern New Hampshire University (SNHU), there are no limits to what a student can do, be, or achieve. That same sense of limitless potential applies to SNHU as an institution, as well.

U.S. News and World Report has consistently ranked SNHU among the country's most innovative universities. This year, the publication ranked SNHU as the most innovative regional Tier 1 university in the northern United States—an impressive achievement for a school that is committed to consistently reinventing the way that education is delivered and received.

Academic programs are created with the real world in mind, so students are prepared to launch successful careers when they graduate. Classes are taught by highly credentialed faculty who have professional experience and remain current in their fields. Academic and personal support is readily available, both inside and outside the classroom. With small class sizes, students never feel like just a name or a number, and are able to get to know their professors. Students in need of help will find that faculty and staff are quick to rally around them and work toward furthering their understanding and success. With more than 50 undergraduate programs (in addition to more than 60 graduate programs), students can have meaningful experiences inside and outside of the classroom that will better prepare them for the real world.

A private university education can and should be affordable, and SNHU operates on the belief that college should change students' lives—not break the bank. That's why students with high school GPAs of 2.5 and higher can earn up to $20,000 in academic scholarships in addition to generous financial aid packages. More than 90 percent of the students at SNHU receive some type of financial aid.

SNHU is always looking to improve and provide innovative facilities that enhance and improve the student experience. A new Library Learning Commons opened in the fall of 2014, which features an IT help desk, the university Learning Center, a cozy café, and the Innovation Lab and Makerspace. In the fall of 2013, a new 300-bed freshman residence hall opened, offering a sustainable design, high-efficiency lighting systems, and individual temperature controls in every room. Additional campus features include a state-of-the-art academic center, a 47,700 square-foot dining center, a completely renovated student center, and more.

Students can get involved with over 65 student-run clubs and organizations at SNHU or even start their own. Intercollegiate teams compete in the Northeast-10 Conference of the NCAA's Division II, and available sports include baseball, men's and women's basketball, cheerleading, men's and women's cross-country, men's golf, ice hockey, men's and women's lacrosse, men's and women's soccer, softball, men's and women's tennis, women's track and field, and women's volleyball. Intramural sports are also extremely popular. SNHU's powerful athletic teams have earned honors from the NCAA and *USA Today* for high grades and 100 percent graduation rates.

Athletic facilities include an indoor, 25-meter competition-size swimming pool, a racquetball court, an aerobic studio, and more. A new athletics complex will be completed in the fall of 2017.

The Wellness Center provides short-term health care, health education, and counseling services for students, and develops a robust schedule of events around issues ranging from bullying and domestic violence prevention to nutrition and physical fitness. In addition, students with disabilities will find that SNHU ensures that all buildings and facilities on campus are handicapped-accessible.

The Career Development Center provides assistance with resume development, letter writing, company research, networking, and informational interviewing, in addition to facilitating internships and job opportunities. Lifetime counseling and career services are available to both current students and alumni.

Location

SNHU is conveniently located just 5 minutes from downtown Manchester, New Hampshire's largest city, and has been named one of the top college towns in the country. Public transportation is available, and students may keep cars on campus beginning in their freshman year. The mountains, beaches, and Boston are all just an hour away. CQ Press has repeatedly named New Hampshire one of the nation's most livable states.

Majors and Degrees

SNHU has three schools: the School of Arts and Sciences, the School of Business, and the School of Education. The university offers associate, bachelor's, master's, and doctoral degrees. Undergraduate programs provide students with a strong general education foundation and the knowledge and skills they need to succeed in their careers.

With the increased demand for graduates in the STEM fields, the University will add seven new majors in the field of aeronautics, engineering, and computer science and will be breaking ground on a new science and technology building in 2018 to support these programs. These new programs are aeronautical engineering, air traffic management, aviation management, computer science, construction management, electrical and computer engineering, and mechanical engineering

The School of Arts and Sciences offers degrees in communication, creative writing and English, English language and literature, environmental science, game art and development, game programming and development, graphic design and media arts, history, justice studies, law and politics (pre-J.D. option), liberal arts, mathematics, psychology, public service, and sociology.

The School of Business majors include accounting, accounting/finance, baking & pastry arts (A.S.), business administration, business analytics, business studies, computer information technology (B.S. option), culinary arts (A.S.), culinary management (B.S.), economics and finance, economics and math, fashion merchandising (A.S.), fashion merchandising and management (B.S.), hospitality business, hospitality management, international business, marketing, operations and project management, sport management, and technical management. SNHU also offers a unique Degree in Three program—offered in accounting and finance, business administration, computer information technology, economics and finance, fashion merchandising, hospitality business, international business, marketing, operations and project management, and sport management. Through Degree in Three, students are able to earn a Bachelor of Science degree in three years through a blend of traditional academics and real-world experience. The goal of the program is to foster and enhance effective communication, critical thinking, and teamwork. The program enables students to save more than $40,000 in tuition and room and board; take a traditional course load of five classes per semester; graduate in six semesters with no night, weekend, or summer courses; secure internships and participate in community events; and pursue interests—graduate school, employment, study abroad, etc.—instead of their fourth year.

The School of Education majors include early childhood education; elementary education; elementary education, with certification in general special education, history, and social studies education; middle school mathematics education; middle school science education; secondary mathematics education; and special education.

SNHU also offers an honors program, a prelaw program, and a pre-M.B.A. program for students seeking additional academic challenges.

Academic Programs

At Southern New Hampshire University, undergraduate students receive a broad education in the liberal arts and intense practice in oral and written communication, coupled with the specific knowledge and skills they need to succeed in their chosen fields.

Recognizing that successful leaders must be able to view problems from a variety of perspectives, the university mandates that all students complete courses in writing, fine arts, social sciences, mathematics, science, and public speaking. Students also have the opportunity to take elective courses in whatever areas capture their curiosity and may elect to concentrate their electives to earn a minor. The university curriculum offers both structure and flexibility so students can direct their own education.

One component of the core curriculum is the SNHU Experience sequence. This three-year, three-course curriculum introduces students to college and college-level work, prepares them for life after college (including resume and cover-letter writing preparation), and helps them demonstrate their academic, personal, and professional development throughout their SNHU experience.

Off-Campus Programs

Southern New Hampshire University excels at mixing academic theory with practical experience inside and outside the classroom. Undergraduates participate in off-campus cooperative education experiences and internships, which can earn them up to 12 academic credits. Such opportunities are based on a student's major and career goals and are typically undertaken during a student's junior or senior year. Students can work with faculty members and the Career and Professional Development Center to find appropriate assignments.

SNHU has established relationships with many respected, high-profile employers who provide internship and job opportunities, including Fidelity Investments, Google, IBM, New York Life, Walt Disney World, LEGO Systems, Marriott International, and even prominent sports organizations such as Major League Soccer, the Boston Celtics, the Boston Red Sox, and the New England Patriots.

Students also work with real-world off-campus partners in their courses. For example, marketing students have created media campaigns for area businesses, while education students assist local teachers in their classrooms. SNHU graduates are always in demand because businesses know they have been prepared to contribute both on the job and in their communities.

At SNHU, students are able to go beyond the campus and enjoy opportunities for studying abroad at a number of partnering institutions in countries around the world. In terms of tuition and room and board, studying abroad costs no more than living on campus and SNHU will even pick up the tab for a student's flight (up to $1,000) and the full cost of travel health insurance. All of the credits and grades earned overseas at a partner university will apply directly towards an SNHU degree.

Costs

For the 2017–18 academic year, undergraduate costs average $43,414 ($31,136 for tuition and fees and $12,278 for room and board). Students should plan to budget funds for books, supplies, travel, and personal expenses. Culinary arts students will also need to purchase uniforms and knife sets. In an effort to continue to remain an affordable private university option for as many students as possible, SNHU has frozen tuition for the 2017–18 academic year. Many families are surprised to learn that attending SNHU is often less expensive than seemingly lower-cost institutions.

Financial Aid

More than 90 percent of the SNHU students receive some form of financial aid, which may include need-based grants, academic and merit scholarships, work-study funds, and loans. SNHU also participates in the Federal Work-Study Program and the Federal Supplemental Educational Opportunity Grant Program. The school is also eligible under the Federal Stafford Student Loan Program and the Federal Pell Grant Program. Aid applicants should complete the Free Application for Federal Student Aid (FAFSA) by the priority deadline of March 15. Student Financial Services can provide the appropriate forms, or students can go online to http://www.fafsa.ed.gov. Academic, athletic, and leadership scholarships are also available for students who qualify.

Faculty

SNHU has more than 128 full-time faculty members and over 200 part-time instructors, with a student-faculty ratio of 15:1. A majority of the full-time faculty members at the university hold a Ph.D. or the equivalent degree in their area of expertise.

Programs at SNHU blend theory with practice to stimulate students' professional development and personal growth. Faculty members bring extensive academic, work, travel, and life experiences to their classrooms. Although their primary goal is teaching, faculty members remain current in their disciplines. Outside the classroom, faculty members are management consultants, CPAs, analysts, small-business owners, economists, accountants, marketing professionals, entrepreneurs, innkeepers, chefs, world travelers, artists, poets, novelists, psychologists, and much more.

Student Government

The Student Government Association is led by 25 students, including 5 officers, who represent all the students at SNHU. Its primary function is to represent the student body in campus affairs and to distribute student activity funds. One student is appointed to represent the student body on the Board of Trustees. Students are also appointed to most other standing committees, including the Dining Services Committee, Residence Life Committee, Public Safety Committee, the Curriculum Advisory Committee, and the Library Committee.

Admission Requirements

Applicants for admission are evaluated individually on the basis of academic credentials and personal characteristics. When reviewing applicants, primary emphasis is placed on a student's academic record, as demonstrated by the quality and level of college-preparatory course work and achievement attained. Most successful candidates admitted to SNHU present a program of study consisting of 16 college-preparatory courses, including 4 years of English, 3 or more years of mathematics (up through successful completion of algebra II), 2 or more years of science, and 2 or more years of social science. Separate consideration is given to admission decisions for transfer, nontraditional, international, and Bradley Three-Year Honors Program in Business applicants.

Application and Information

Applicants for undergraduate day programs must submit an application (via the Common Application), college essay, $40 application fee, official high school transcript, and one letter of recommendation from a school counselor or teacher. SNHU is a test-optional institution and SAT/ACT scores are not required.

Freshman applicants can apply before November 15 to be considered for the early action deadline. SNHU operates on a rolling admission basis; however, there is a priority application deadline of February 1. Admission and scholarship decisions are made within 30 days of receiving all required admission materials.

For more information about Southern New Hampshire University, students should contact:

Office of Admission
Southern New Hampshire University
2500 North River Road
Manchester, New Hampshire 03106-1045
Phone: 603-645-9611
Fax: 603-645-9693
Website: http://www.snhu.edu
http://www.facebook.com/snhuoncampus
http://www.twitter.com/snhuoncampus

SOUTHWESTERN ASSEMBLIES OF GOD UNIVERSITY

WAXAHACHIE, TEXAS

★ For more information, visit http://petersons.to/swassembliesofgodu

The University

Southwestern Assemblies of God University (SAGU) seeks creators, dreamers, and change-makers—students who long to be uncommon. SAGU Lions are pioneers. They look for opportunity in surprising places. They take common ideas and moments and create something uncommon.

The beauty of college is that learning takes place inside and outside of the classroom. Students at SAGU do far more than just learn from professors in class—they share knowledge with new friends, grow their soft skills through volunteerism and service, visit new places for field experience, take part in internships, and even travel to the other side of the globe. It's more than intercultural studies majors who travel the world. Business majors start small businesses in India. Ancient Studies majors excavate in Israel. And Education majors travel the world to teach English as a second language.

Lions are pioneers who find opportunity to live their Christian faith in diverse careers.

Southwestern Assemblies of God University is a Bible-based institution for theological and professional studies. It is rooted in the great commission of Jesus Christ to "Go into all the world and preach the good news to all creation" and to "make disciples of all nations... teaching them to obey everything I have commanded you" (Mark 16:15a; Matthew 28:19, 20).

The purpose of Southwestern Assemblies of God University is to prepare undergraduate and graduate students spiritually, academically, professionally, and cross culturally so as to successfully fill evangelistic, missionary, and church ministry roles and to provide quality educational and professional Christian service wherever needed throughout the world. The university also offers a number of fast-track programs in church leadership, child and family ministry, pastoral leadership, and youth and student ministry for those who want to earn a bachelor's and master's degree in 5 years.

Whether students are looking to pursue a career in ministry or in the workforce, SAGU holds to a high standard of academic excellence in curriculum and in the classroom.

SAGU's education program boasts a certification passing rate of 99 percent. Many Lions have teaching job offers when they graduate, as they are equipped with hands-on training and access to technology in the classroom. Business courses are taught by passionate professors who have experience in the field.

Here are just a few examples of jobs earned by recent SAGU graduates: producer, Warner Bros.; producer, Corporate ABC Entertainment; cabin services coordinator, Southwest Airlines; trooper, Texas Highway Patrol; licensed professional counselor, LakePointe Counseling Center; promotional developer, IPHC Ministries; customer account analyst, 3M; unit supervisor, Child Welfare Services; agent, Personal Economics Group; senior messaging architect, Zachry Holdings, Inc.; pastors, media pastors, worship pastors, and missionaries worldwide; and elementary, middle and secondary school teachers, nationwide

Southwestern Assemblies of God University is accredited by the Southern Association of Colleges and Schools Commission on Colleges (SACSCOC) to award associate, baccalaureate, master's, and doctoral degrees. Questions about the accreditation of Southwestern Assemblies of God University can be directed to the Commission on Colleges at 1866 Southern Lane, Decatur, Georgia 30033-4097; phone: 404-679-4500.

Location

The SAGU campus is located in Waxahachie, Texas, a cozy town full of history and culture. There's plenty of local shopping, restaurants, parks and coffee shops. SAGU's location provides the feel of a small town with the proximity to a big city. Just 30 minutes north is the greater Dallas/Fort Worth metroplex. Students enjoy professional sporting events, theme parks, museums, and some of the best restaurants in the state. Students have access to thousands of stores, theaters, restaurants, museums, theme parks, professional sports arenas, and more.

Majors and Degrees

SAGU is comprised of three colleges: the College of Bible and Church Ministries, the College of Music and Communication Arts, and the College of Business and Education.

Degree programs available include: Accounting, Ancient Studies, Bible and Theology, Biblical Studies, Business Administration, Child and Family Studies, Children and Family Ministries, Church Leadership, Communication Studies, Community Care and Counseling, Counseling, Criminal Justice, Digital Media Arts, Education (elementary, English language arts and reading middle and secondary, social studies/history middle and secondary, math education middle and secondary, music education, physical education, or theatre education), English, General Ministries, Human Resource Management, Human Services (counseling, criminal justice, psychology, or social work), Intercultural Studies, Interdisciplinary Studies, Management, Marketing, Mathematics, Music Occupational Leadership, Performance/Instrumental Performance, Pastoral Leadership, Psychology, Social Work, Sports Management, Theatre, Theological Studies, Worship Arts, and Youth and Student Ministries.

Academic Program

SAGU's academics will challenge and stretch students intellectually and spiritually as they learn how their chosen field relates to their Christian purpose. As the professor's utmost priority, students receive personalized instruction in a small-class environment.

Technology can serve a valuable role in education. SAGU allows ample opportunities to use educational technology within the context of the classroom. SAGU Digital Media Arts students take the lead and showcase their skills during student summer film projects. These projects have repeatedly won awards in film competitions and have been featured in national broadcasts. Students also produce SAGU Sports Network and entertainment broadcasts using industry-level equipment and the professional studio in the Hagee Communication Center.

Stage performances, blackbox theatrical performances and musical productions are performed twice each semester, offering opportunities for students to perform, design sets, and write. SAGU is one of the elite few schools to be officially recognized as an All-Steinway music program.

Off-Campus Programs

It's more than intercultural studies majors who travel abroad. Travel opportunities abound. SAGU is the only college sending students for outreach in every country in the world in just ten years. Students have already served in more than 120 countries in just six years.

Costs

For the 2017–18 academic year, tuition for full-time on-campus students is $9,725, plus a general fee of $480. Room fees range from $1,385 to $2,170 per year and the meal plan for on-campus students is $1,780 per year.

Financial Aid

Attending SAGU is an investment that will impacting the rest of our students' lives. Tuition, fees, room, and board are 20 percent lower than the average 4-year private, Christian university. Financial aid options including scholarships, grants, and loans, are available, making paying for college simple and affordable.

Student Life

One of the best reasons to attend a Christian university is the on-campus experience. There is a spiritual dynamic that can only be experienced by setting foot on campus. Surrounded by Christian faculty, caring dorm pastors, and Godly leaders, you will find yourself immersed in an environment that emphasizes your spiritual growth. You can make the most of daily chapel services, academic programs from a Christian world-view, and hands-on ministry opportunities. The relationships students form with their Christian roommates and peers will provide a network of support and a family of friends that last beyond college. During college, Lions are there to help, encourage, and pray for one another.

SAGU offers many student-run organizations for students to broaden their knowledge base, understand other cultures, challenge themselves, expand their network of connections, develop leadership qualities, and have fun!

Faith

An education at SAGU is based around seven core values:

Bible-based Education: God is the ultimate source of all knowledge and truth and has revealed Himself in Scripture; therefore, SAGU is committed to the authority of the Bible and the integration of biblical values in all academic disciplines. The pursuit of truth and its application in every area of life comes through understanding the Word of God, and knowing Christ.

Pentecostal Distinction: SAGU is committed to an environment that encourages students to experience Spirit baptism according to Pentecostal theology to obtain additional power for witness, personal edification through speaking in tongues in private prayer, and additional enablement through spiritual gifts, while continually pursuing spiritual formation and a Spirit-formed character. The university also encourages the operation of the gifts of the Spirit in worship services according to the scriptural directive.

Spiritual Formation: SAGU is committed to fostering spiritual formation among students that produces life-long spiritual growth and character development. Students are encouraged to develop their understanding of biblical faith, increase their desire to know and serve God, and develop personal integrity and character by applying biblical values to their lives. Chapel and local church participation is emphasized because worship is an important element in the university's strategy for spiritual formation.

Academic Excellence: SAGU is a university devoted, under God, to the pursuit of truth through the use of the mind. Students, therefore, are encouraged to bring their minds in submission to Christ and fulfill their responsibilities as stewards, and work for the integration of thinking and learning in the framework of a Christian worldview. Students are encouraged to develop their minds and intellects in the pursuit of knowing Christ and his creation, and seeking God's direction as they choose a vocation or career path.

Missions Mindedness: SAGU is founded on the belief that every believer has a personal responsibility for the Great Commission. SAGU intends that students will embrace missions-mindedness as evidenced by life-long personal involvement in world evangelism, a life of intercessory prayer for the lost, personal witness, contributing resources to world evangelism, and a willingness to go into full-time missionary work (if called by God) or, at a minimum, participate in a short-term mission trip.

Servant Leadership: SAGU's mission is founded on the belief that God intends every believer be actively involved in ministry that reflects service and servanthood.

Community and Personal Wellness: SAGU is committed to the understanding that discipleship occurs in community and in relationship, therefore students are encouraged to develop the social and relational skills needed to contribute to an affirming, loving, and giving community of believers.

Admission Requirements

SAGU allows rolling enrollment, so prospective students can complete and submit their applications anytime.

Students need to submit a completed application (available at http://www.sagu.edu/admissions/on-campus-admissions), faith and lifestyle statement, composite ACT or SAT scores, high school transcript showing date of graduation and minimum GPA of 2.0*, and the application fee.

For more information, students may contact:

Southwestern Assemblies of God University
Admissions Department
1200 Sycamore Street
Waxahachie, Texas 75165
Phone: 888-937-7248 (toll-free)
Fax: 972-923-8134
E-mail: admissions@sagu.eud
Website: www.sagu.edu
https://twitter.com/sagu
https://www.facebook.com/saguedu
https://www.instagram.com/saguedu

COLLEGE CLOSE-UPS

SPRINGFIELD COLLEGE

SPRINGFIELD, MASSACHUSETTS

★ To read more about this school, visit http://petersons.to/springfieldcollege

The College

Real-world experience through fieldwork and internships, combined with outstanding academic preparation, gives Springfield College graduates a competitive advantage when they move on to careers or graduate education. Students perform fieldwork, internships, or service learning as early as their first semester, gaining valuable experience while following the College's mission of leadership in service to others.

Internationally renowned for educating leaders in health sciences, human and social services, sports and movement studies, education, business, and the arts and sciences, Springfield College offers bachelor's, master's, and doctorate degree programs, and it is accredited by the New England Association of Schools and Colleges (NEASC) and numerous other disciplinary accrediting bodies. Springfield College is recognized in the top tier of Best Regional Universities—North Region, in the 2016 edition of *U.S. News & World Report*'s "Best Colleges."

The Mission: Springfield College is a private, coeducational institution that was founded in 1885 with its Humanics philosophy: "to educate students, in spirit, mind, and body for leadership in service to others." Humanics has remained the College mission to this day, and students, faculty members, and administration are committed to that mission.

The College has been named to the President's Higher Education Community Service Honor Roll, has received Carnegie Foundation Community Engagement Classification, and has won the Jostens/NADIIIAA Award of Merit for community service by student athletes. The Institute for International Sport named it one of the fifteen most influential educators through sport in America. Springfield College is designated by the YMCA of the USA as a premier leadership development center.

Student Population: A diverse student body of 3,286 undergraduate and graduate students at the main campus comes from across the country and around the world.

Cocurricular Activities: Enriching the undergraduate experience is an array of cocurricular activities, health and wellness programs, arts and cultural events; an extensive campus recreation program; and one of the nation's largest athletics programs for a midsized college. There are more than 100 organizations and opportunities for involvement. More than 80 percent of undergraduates participate in some form of athletics, including varsity teams, intramurals, or club sports. Approximately 44 percent of males and 32 percent of females enrolled in the traditional undergraduate programs on the Springfield College campus participate in intercollegiate athletics. There are men's and women's teams in basketball, cross-country, gymnastics, lacrosse, soccer, swimming, diving, tennis, track and volleyball; women's teams in field hockey and softball; and men's teams in baseball, football, golf, and wrestling. Approximately 90 percent of the student body uses the Wellness Center and 35 to 40 percent of students participate in intramurals or clubs specifically.

Campus Facilities: Ten campus residence halls provide guaranteed on-campus housing. Options include traditional residence halls and suite-style accommodations with private rooms for 2 to 4 students along with a shared lounge, kitchen, and bathrooms. There are single-gender and coeducational residences. Seniors may choose to live off campus. The main student dining facility features a range of fresh food options. There are snack and other light-fare services around the campus, including a food court in a two-story atrium.

Recreational Facilities: The award-winning Wellness & Recreation Complex facilities represent the best in collegiate recreational centers. The complex includes the Wellness Center, Field House, and Athletic Training/Exercise Science Complex with 160,560 square feet of instructional, athletic, and recreational space adjoining the Physical Education Complex and Art Linkletter Natatorium. The buildings support the College's degree programs in athletic training, physical education, exercise science, sport management, and related areas. They also contain and support the center for campus recreation and wellness with its comprehensive programming serving the entire campus community.

Location

Springfield College's picturesque, 182-acre campus includes several new and newly renovated state-of-the-art facilities that blend with traditional campus architecture. On the shores of Lake Massasoit in the Pioneer Valley, Springfield College is located in Springfield, the third-largest city in Massachusetts and fourth-largest in New England (Boston, Worcester, and Providence are larger). A wide range of social, cultural, and athletic activities enhance the valley, as well as twelve other colleges and universities. For example, Springfield Symphony Hall is the site of concerts, plays, musicals, and dance performances; the MassMutual Center in Springfield is home to the American Hockey League's Springfield Falcons; and the Naismith Memorial Basketball Hall of Fame is an international attraction.

Nearby cities and towns offer many additional attractions. Northampton bustles with trendy shops, coffee houses, galleries, theater productions, health food stores, nightclubs, and restaurants. The Berkshire Hills offer hiking, skiing, biking, and other outdoor activities. Boston lies 90 miles to the east, New York City is less than a 3-hour drive away, Vermont is 1 hour away, and Bradley International Airport is 20 miles south.

Majors and Degrees

Springfield College offers Bachelor of Science or Bachelor of Arts degrees in the following: accounting, American studies, applied exercise science, art, art therapy, athletic training/Doctor of Physical Therapy (seven-year dual-degree program), biology, communications/sports journalism, communication sciences and disorders, computer and information sciences, computer graphics/digital arts, criminal justice, dance, early childhood education, elementary education, emergency medical services management, English, finance, general business (opportunity for a unique 4 + 1 program culminating in an M.B.A.), general studies, health care management, health science/general studies, health services administration, health education (health studies), history, management, marketing, mathematics, mathematics and computer technology, nutritional sciences, occupational therapy, physical education (movement and sport studies), physical therapy (entry-level 6½-year program culminating in a Doctor of Physical Therapy degree), physician assistant (entry-level six-year program culminating in a Master of Science degree), psychology, recreation management, rehabilitation and disability studies, secondary education, sociology, special education, sport management, sports biology, and youth development. Undeclared majors receive help in determining their path in First-Year Seminar.

Academic Program

Consistent with the unique Springfield College Humanics philosophy, undergraduate education takes a holistic approach and prepares the student—in spirit, mind, and body—for a life of leadership in fields that help others.

The College has a two-semester academic calendar. To graduate, students must complete 120 credits including required courses for the major field of study, electives, and required courses for all students (writing, computer applications, arts and humanities, analytical and natural sciences, social sciences, international/multicultural studies, social justice, and physical education). Students may also earn credit for successful completion of Advanced Placement (AP) high school courses, and through the DANTES subject standard test and the College-Level Examination Program (CLEP) administered by the College Board.

Springfield College has agreements with several medical schools, which guarantee acceptance of its qualified students. In addition, many Springfield College programs allow undergraduates to take graduate-level courses.

There are campus chapters of the following honor societies: Beta Beta Beta (biology), Kappa Delta Pi (education), Phi Alpha (social work), Phi Epsilon Kappa (health, physical education, recreation or safety), and Psi Chi (psychology).

Off-Campus Programs

From their very first semester, Springfield students benefit from fieldwork, internships, and service learning. The College maintains relationships with businesses, nonprofits, public and private agencies, and schools, and students benefit from real-world experience early and often. Sites have included the Naismith Memorial Basketball Hall of Fame, American Hockey League, *The Boston Globe,* YMCAs, American Heart Association, MassMutual, Hilton Head Crowne Plaza, Reebok Health and Fitness Center, Baystate Medical Center, children's hospitals, parks and recreation departments, and more. The Springfield College Career Center assists students and alumni with exploring career options, identifying career-related experiential learning, refining job search skills, identifying employment opportunities, preparing for admission to graduate and professional schools, and networking with alumni.

Extensive study-abroad programs are available. Students may also enroll in courses at some of the other colleges in the Springfield area.

Academic Facilities

Technologically up-to-date, the campus is wireless and has smart classrooms, computer labs, a videoconferencing facility, a conference center, a language laboratory, a television studio, a journalism lab, a radio station, and more.

Science facilities include the Schoo-Bemis Science Center with state-of-the-art equipment; the Athletic Training/Exercise Science Complex, cited as one of the most outstanding in the nation; and the Health Sciences Center, with a human anatomy laboratory and sophisticated equipment for physical testing, analysis, and treatment. Herbert P. Blake Hall contains labs, testing, and treatment facilities, including the medical simulation laboratory, or sim lab, that features high-fidelity 3G adult and baby patient-simulator mannequins that respond like humans, allowing students to experience realistic, hands-on training and complicated medical techniques. Locklin Hall contains a well-equipped rehabilitation assessment and counseling services center.

For arts studies and programs, the renovated Fuller Arts Center and Appleton Auditorium is the site of performances, and the Visual Arts Center contains studio workspace and a public exhibition center.

The East Campus comprises an 82-acre forest ecosystem with camping facilities and lake shoreline. It supports the programs of Springfield College through purposefully designed, outdoor experiential-learning opportunities. The Springfield College Child Development Center is an exceptional fieldwork facility for students of education and psychology.

Babson Library, well known for its resources in physical education, psychology, education, and health and human services, contains a rich collection of full-text print and digital materials. Library staff members assist, and students have access to a full range of information sources.

Costs

For the 2016–17 academic year, tuition and fees were $34,980. Room and board costs were $11,940.

Financial Aid

Students are encouraged to apply for grants, loans, and student employment. Springfield College financial aid is awarded based on need and academic achievement. The College gives full consideration to students who submit the Free Application for Federal Student Aid (FAFSA) and the Springfield College Financial Aid Application by March 15 for first-year students and May 1 for transfer students. Students not eligible for financial aid may be considered for campus employment.

Faculty

Most of the 208 faculty members hold doctorates or other terminal degrees. The student-teacher ratio is 13:1.

Student Government

The Student Government Association, managed by elected students, promotes students' interests and welfare. It guides and finances more than 30 student organizations, adopts policies affecting students, and is a liaison between students and the College administration.

Admission Requirements

Springfield College evaluates applicants on the basis of academic and personal factors. Applications for regular admission or early decision must be submitted to the Office of Undergraduate Admissions and include a completed application form, a high school transcript, one personal reference, and SAT or ACT scores. Transfer students must also submit a transcript and a dean's report from each college attended.

Application due dates are as follows: undergraduate applicants, April 1; transfer students, August 1; athletic training and physical therapy programs, December 1; and physician assistant and occupational therapy programs, January 15.

Members of the Springfield College faculty and staff are interested in meeting each applicant and encourage candidates to visit the College and experience campus life. The College offers personal interviews, campus tours, and open-house programs and also facilitates contact with alumni and current students.

Application and Information

Springfield College accepts the Common Application. The Springfield College Admissions Committee reviews applications upon receiving them.

Application forms and information may be obtained from:

Office of Admissions
Springfield College
263 Alden Street
Springfield, Massachusetts 01109
Phone: 413-748-3136
800-343-1257 (toll-free)
E-mail: admissions@springfieldcollege.edu
Website: springfieldcollege.edu

Faculty members make time so students make the grade. The student-to-faculty ratio is 13:1, so faculty members get to know their students, and can provide assistance and guidance throughout their studies at Springfield College.

STATE UNIVERSITY OF NEW YORK COLLEGE OF ENVIRONMENTAL SCIENCE AND FORESTRY

SYRACUSE, NEW YORK

★ To read more about this school, visit http://petersons.to/sunyesf

The College

The SUNY College of Environmental Science and Forestry (ESF) is one of the nation's largest and most widely recognized environmental colleges. Founded in 1911, the College has grown beyond its original emphasis on forestry to include professional education in environmental science, landscape architecture, environmental studies, and engineering in addition to distinguished programs in the biological and physical sciences. Throughout its history, the College has focused on addressing the environmental issues of the time in its three mission areas—instruction, research, and public service. ESF graduates are well-prepared for environmental careers through specialized academic programs and a holistic approach to solving today's environmental and resource problems.

A leader in its field, ESF is one of the specialized doctoral degree–granting colleges within the State University of New York System. The College currently supports undergraduate and graduate degree programs in more than thirty environmentally-related disciplines. Graduate programs lead to the Master of Science (M.S.), Master of Landscape Architecture (M.L.A.), Master of Professional Studies (M.P.S.), and Doctor of Philosophy (Ph.D.) degrees. ESF's research program is conducted throughout the world and research funding totals more than $15 million per year.

ESF's main campus is located on 12 acres adjacent to Syracuse University and SUNY Upstate Medical University in an urban residential setting. There are 1,750 undergraduate and 550 graduate students enrolled at ESF. The College's unique partnership with Syracuse University offers ESF students the opportunity to take additional classes there for academic diversity and depth, and to participate in cultural events, student clubs, fraternities and sororities, and professional organizations.

ESF recently opened two new buildings on campus. Centennial Hall, is an environmentally friendly residence hall that houses more than 500 ESF students in a combination of double rooms and student apartments and the Gateway Center is a hub for campus events that serves as a showcase for the College's sustainability efforts. The center features a wood pellet–fueled heat-and-power plant designed to generate enough energy for five campus buildings.

Location

Syracuse, a metropolitan area of more than 730,000 people, is a leader in the health care and education industries and is recognized as one of the nation's emerging centers for the development of green technologies. It offers many cultural, recreational, and educational opportunities, including museums, live theater, college and professional sports, and historic points of interest. Syracuse is centrally located at the crossing point of two Northeast superhighways. The driving time to Syracuse from New York City, Philadelphia, Boston, Toronto, and Montreal is about 5 hours; from Buffalo and Albany, about 3 hours. The city is served by a modern international airport and major bus and rail lines.

Majors and Degrees

The SUNY College of Environmental Science and Forestry offers three undergraduate degrees: the Bachelor of Science (B.S.), the Bachelor of Landscape Architecture (B.L.A.), and the Associate in Applied Science (A.A.S.). The B.S. degree is awarded in aquatic and fisheries science, bioprocess engineering, biotechnology, chemistry, conservation biology, construction management, environmental biology, environmental education and interpretation, environmental health, environmental resources engineering, environmental science, environmental studies, forest ecosystem science, forest health, forest resources management, natural resources management, paper engineering, paper science, sustainable energy management, and wildlife science. A number of options and concentrations are offered within specific curricula. The B.L.A. degree, which requires a semester of off-campus study, is awarded in landscape architecture. Two-year A.A.S. degrees are awarded in forest technology, land surveying technology, and environmental and natural resources conservation at ESF's Ranger School campus in Wanakena, New York.

Academic Programs

All students at ESF have opportunities for specialized study as well as research and field experience. The Department of Environmental and Forest Biology is the largest department on campus and encompasses seven different majors, including biotechnology, conservation biology, wildlife science, aquatic and fisheries science, forest health, and environmental education and interpretation. Biology students are required to complete a four-week period of summer field study, usually at ESF's Cranberry Lake Biological Station, following their sophomore or junior year. Options for specialization within the chemistry program include biochemistry, environmental chemistry, and natural and synthetic polymer chemistry.

The construction management program teaches management, analysis, and design skills used in today's green construction process, with an emphasis on environmental and engineering issues.

Environmental resources engineering students learn skills in such areas as biological, environmental, and water resources engineering; mapping science; and geographic information systems.

The closely related environmental science program also deals with engineering science, along with areas of focus in watershed science, health and the environment, earth and atmospheric systems science, environmental analysis, and renewable energy. The new environmental health program focuses on the study of the intersection of human health and the physical environment. Analysis, prevention, and mitigation of potential environmental hazards are also studied.

Bioprocess engineering students focus on the engineering, biology, and chemistry of ecologically sound industrial technologies and processes, giving students career opportunities in areas such as chemical engineering and bioengineering, pharmaceuticals, and renewable energy.

The forest resources management curriculum offers areas of focus in forest management, measurement, and policy, along with forest ecology and biology. The program includes a minor in management offered in conjunction with Syracuse University. Natural resources management students can concentrate in specialized areas such as recreation or water resources management. Students in sustainable energy management focus on energy resources management, markets and policies, energy systems and sustainability, and renewable energy technologies. Forest and natural resources management students are required to complete a four-week period of summer field study at ESF's Wanakena campus prior to the junior year.

The environmental studies major offers specializations in environmental communication and society; biological science applications; and environmental policy, planning, and law.

The landscape architecture program is a five-year bachelor's degree that is accredited by the ASLA to provide preparation to enter this licensed profession. Students study site design, urban and regional planning, historic preservation, community and environmental design, and computer applications. During the first semester of the fifth year, the landscape architecture curriculum requires participation in off-campus independent study. Paper engineering students can study process and product design and environmental engineering applied to the pulp, paper, and related chemical industries, while paper science students focus on a variety of industry-specific research and management areas. In addition, ESF offers excellent preparation for graduate study in health professions, law, veterinary science, and medicine; the College has a joint admission agreement with the College of Medicine at nearby SUNY Upstate Medical University.

Academic Facilities

Specialized facilities and equipment include electron microscopes, plant-growth chambers, climate-controlled greenhouses, an animal environmental simulation chamber, a bioacoustical laboratory, a radioisotope laboratory, numerous computer labs, nuclear magnetic resonance spectrometers, gas chromatography apparatus, a mass spectrometer, ultracentrifuges, and X-ray and infrared spectrophotometers. The photogrammetric and geodetic facilities of the environmental resources engineering department are among the most extensive available in the United States. The paper science and engineering laboratory has a semi-commercial paper mill with accessory equipment. The sustainable construction management and engineering department has a strength-of-materials laboratory, a pilot-scale plywood laboratory, and a machining laboratory. The landscape architecture faculty has a one-of-a-kind environmental simulation laboratory. The greenhouses and forest insectary in Illick Hall are used to produce plant and insect materials for the classroom and laboratory. Extensive collections are available, including wood samples from all over the world, botanical materials, insects, birds, mammals, and fishes. The Roosevelt Wildlife Collection contains more than 10,000 species of well-preserved vertebrate and invertebrate animals and also recognizes the environmental interests and contributions of U.S. president Theodore Roosevelt.

The F. Franklin Moon Library includes the Academic Success Center for tutorial support in mathematics, writing, and other courses. Moon Library contains more than 100,000 specialized catalog items, including more than 1,800 research journals. The library also provides comprehensive abstract and indexing services relevant to the College's programs. Library facilities and services are supplemented by the collections at Syracuse University and the SUNY Upstate Medical University, both within walking distance.

ESF's regional campuses in Tully, Warrensburg, Cranberry Lake, Newcomb, and Wanakena, New York, offer a great diversity of forest sites that are used as outdoor teaching laboratories and for intensive research. ESF operates numerous field stations and provides students and faculty with access to over 25,000 acres of College-owned forest properties to support its instruction, research, and public service programs. These special properties make ESF one of the largest college campuses in the world.

Costs

Estimated costs for the 2016–17 academic year included resident tuition and fees of $8,240 and out-of-state tuition and fees of $18,090. Room and board expenses were $15,400. Books, personal expenses, and travel are estimated at $2,450.

Financial Aid

A wide variety of financial aid is available for ESF students, and more than 85 percent of the students receive some type of support. The forms of financial aid include merit- and need-based scholarships, grants, low-interest student loans, and student employment programs. All students are encouraged to apply for financial aid by completing the Free Application for Federal Student Aid (FAFSA).

Faculty

Faculty members at ESF are highly trained and dedicated to the College's teaching, research, and public-service missions. There are close to 140 full-time and 46 adjunct faculty members. Many are nationally and internationally recognized for their expertise in specialized fields. Nearly all regular faculty members hold twelve-month appointments. Just over 80 percent are tenured, and more than half are full professors, of whom 93 percent have earned doctorates. There is no distinction between the undergraduate and graduate faculty. Faculty members teach at both levels, and no courses are taught by teaching assistants. Faculty members serve as advisors to students and student groups and encourage excellence in scholarship and research. The student-faculty ratio is about 12:1.

Student Government

The College has a representative Undergraduate Student Association, and student representatives also participate in a counterpart association at Syracuse University. The ESF student government organizes and presents social activities, and its representatives attend College administrative meetings, communicate students' concerns and ideas to the administration, and serve as a conduit of information back to the student body. ESF students are obligated to abide by Syracuse University's rules and regulations when accessing classes or student services there.

Admission Requirements

Students who are interested in ESF have four enrollment options: early decision, regular freshman admission, guaranteed transfer admission, and regular transfer admission.

Outstanding high school seniors who have selected SUNY-ESF as their top choice may apply for early decision, a binding, first-choice application/early notification program for fall-entry freshmen. Students considering early decision admission must file an application and provide all supporting credentials to SUNY-ESF by the December 1 deadline. Students applying for early decision are notified by January 15.

Regular freshman admission is a second option for applicants who want to enroll immediately following high school. These candidates should demonstrate strong academic performance in a college-preparatory program, with emphasis on mathematics and science preparation. Students applying for regular freshmen entry are notified by March 1. All freshman candidates apply for admission to their intended programs of study.

Guaranteed transfer admission (GTA) candidates apply to ESF as high school seniors but are offered admission for either their sophomore or junior year. Students who plan to attend another college prior to transferring to ESF select this option to ensure a place at ESF for their chosen entry date. This option may also be offered to students who do not meet the freshman admission criteria. Those who are accepted for guaranteed transfer admission receive a letter of acceptance, contingent upon the successful completion of all the prerequisite courses required for the curriculum they have selected. The prerequisite courses are outlined and described in an enclosure with the student's acceptance letter and can also be found on the College's website at http://www.esf.edu.

Students are considered for admission to ESF on the basis of their previous college course work, overall academic aptitude, and interest in the College's programs. Consideration is given to both the quality and the appropriateness of each student's prior academic experience. The College has developed cooperative transfer programs with two-year colleges in New York, Connecticut, Massachusetts, New Jersey, and Pennsylvania.

Application and Information

Students may apply for fall or spring admission. Admission decisions are made on a rolling basis until the class is filled. ESF accepts either the State University of New York Application form or the Common Application. Links to both applications can be found online at http://www.esf.edu/admissions/freshman/apply.htm. Requests for more information should be directed to:

Office of Undergraduate Admissions
SUNY College of Environmental Science and Forestry
1 Forestry Drive
Syracuse, New York 13210-2779
Phone: 315-470-6600
Fax: 315-470-6933
E-mail: esfinfo@esf.edu
Website: http://www.esf.edu
http://www.facebook.com/sunyesf
http://twitter.com/sunyesf/
http://www.youtube.com/user/SUNYESFVIDEO

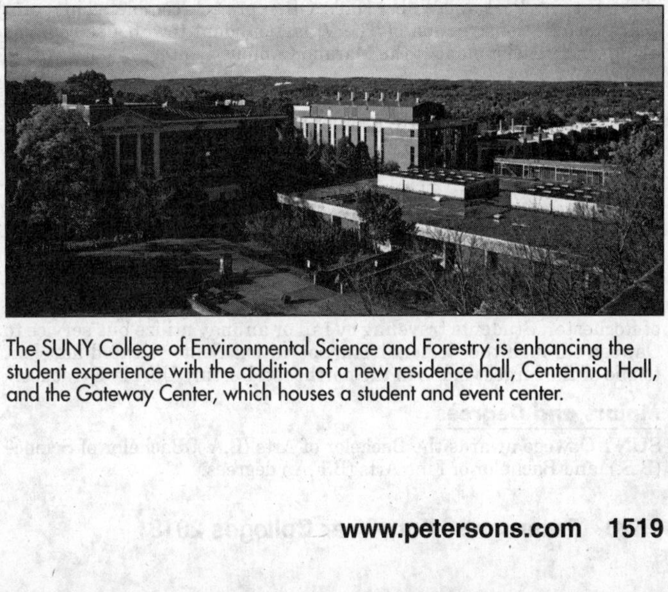

The SUNY College of Environmental Science and Forestry is enhancing the student experience with the addition of a new residence hall, Centennial Hall, and the Gateway Center, which houses a student and event center.

COLLEGE CLOSE-UPS

STATE UNIVERSITY OF NEW YORK AT OSWEGO

OSWEGO, NEW YORK

★ To read more about this school, visit http://petersons.to/sunyoswego

The University

Founded in 1861, SUNY Oswego is a comprehensive college with an excellent academic reputation and commitment to teaching, learning, research, and service. Total enrollment, including part-time and graduate students, is approximately 8,000 students. Approximately 6,800 students are currently enrolled as full-time undergraduates. More than 110 liberal arts and career-oriented programs are offered through the College of Liberal Arts and Sciences; School of Business; School of Communication, Media, and the Arts; and School of Education. The School of Education is nationally accredited by the National Council for the Accreditation of Teacher Education (NCATE), and the School of Business is internationally accredited by AACSB–The Association to Advance Collegiate Schools of Business. Other individual programs within the College of Liberal Arts and Sciences and the School of Communication, Media, and the Arts are accredited by specific discipline-oriented accrediting organizations.

Located on 696 acres on the southern shore of Lake Ontario, the spacious tree-lined campus consists of over fifty academic and residential buildings. Twelve residence halls and The Village townhouse complex offer a variety of on-campus housing opportunities to all degree-seeking students. More than 180 registered extracurricular organizations cover a wide range of social, academic, cultural, and intellectual interests. Theater, art, film, music, dance, and discussion events fill the campus cultural calendar throughout the school year as well. There is a full slate of twenty-four NCAA Division III intercollegiate sports for men and women, along with a full complement of competitive club sports and intramural athletics.

Oswego, a selective college, receives over 14,000 applications for some 2,000 freshman and transfer openings each fall. Accredited by the Middle States Association of Colleges and Schools, Oswego has been recognized by a number of authoritative guides for its outstanding academic opportunities and high academic standards. In recent years, SUNY Oswego has been cited for excellence and selectivity in *U.S. News & World Report's Best Colleges Guide, Colleges of Distinction,* and in both the Princeton Review's *Best Northeastern Colleges* and their *Best Value Colleges* for 2016. The Princeton Review ranks Oswego among the "Best in the Northeast." In 2016, for the fifth consecutive year, the Princeton Review and *USA Today* named SUNY Oswego to their "Best Value" listing of colleges and universities in the nation. Oswego is also included on *Kiplinger's Personal Finance* magazine's list of 100 best values in public colleges for 2015. The ranking cites four-year schools that combine outstanding academics with affordable cost.

The Oswego campus is undergoing a facilities renaissance with over $800 million invested in campus construction and renovations in recent years. Recently completed projects include the $118-million Richard S. Shineman Center for Science, Engineering, and Innovation; a new Biological Field Station lab facility; renovation and conversion of Romney Field House; and major renovations and additions to the School of Education's Park and Wilber Halls. Other projects completed in recent years include construction of The Village student townhouse complex along with development of the Marano Campus Center.

Location

With a population of nearly 20,000, the city of Oswego is a modest-sized, friendly upstate New York community. It is the country's oldest freshwater port and one of the leading ports on the Great Lakes and St. Lawrence Seaway. The city and its surrounding area are known for summer and winter recreation, including camping, boating, sailing, fishing, tennis, golf, ice skating, alpine and cross-country skiing, snowboarding, and sledding. It is at the heart of the booming sports fishing industry, with a thriving tourism scene. The campus is conveniently located 35 miles northwest of Syracuse and 65 miles east of Rochester. Students traveling by rail or air may utilize bus service to Oswego through the Regional Transportation Center located adjacent to one of the largest malls in the northeast, Destiny USA in Syracuse.

Majors and Degrees

SUNY Oswego awards the Bachelor of Arts (B.A.), Bachelor of Science (B.S.), and Bachelor of Fine Arts (B.F.A.) degrees.

Through the College of Liberal Arts and Sciences, students can earn a baccalaureate degree in American studies, anthropology, applied mathematics, applied mathematical economics, biochemistry, biology, chemistry, cinema and screen studies, cognitive science, computer science, creative writing, economics, electrical and computer engineering, English, French, gender and women's studies, geochemistry, geology, German, global and international studies, history, human development, information science, language and international trade, linguistics, mathematics, meteorology, philosophy, philosophy-psychology, physics, political science, psychology, public justice, sociology, software engineering, Spanish, and zoology.

The School of Business offers B.S. degree programs in accounting, business administration, finance, human resource management, marketing, operations management and information systems, and risk management and insurance.

The School of Communication, Media, and the Arts offers baccalaureate degree programs in art, broadcasting and mass communication, communication and social interaction, graphic design, journalism, music, public relations, and theater.

The School of Education offers B.S. degree programs in adolescence education, childhood education, teaching English to speakers of other languages (TESOL), technology education, technology management, vocational-teacher preparation, and wellness management.

In addition, three innovative five-year combined bachelor's and master's programs are available: a bachelor's degree in accounting with an M.B.A., a bachelor's in psychology with an M.B.A., and a bachelor's in psychology with a master's in human computer interaction.

Cooperative programs include a 2+2 program leading to a B.S. in medical imaging sciences, as well as a 3+3 program leading to a B.S./D.P.T. in physical therapy from SUNY Upstate Medical University; and a 3+4 pre-optometry program leading to a bachelor's in chemistry from Oswego and an O.D. in optometry from SUNY College of Optometry.

Academic Programs

Oswego offers students a broad range of courses in the liberal arts and in preprofessional and professional studies. In addition to core courses within a major, all students must satisfy general education requirements designed to strengthen basic writing and analytical proficiency, give students awareness of their cultural heritage, and provide a level of literacy in the social and behavioral sciences, natural sciences, and humanities. By completing these general education requirements during their first two years of study, students are able to select a major with a sense of confidence and purpose. Students who are certain of their academic interest may begin working on their major program in their first year.

Before arriving on campus, students are assigned an adviser from either their major area or the college's Student Advisement Center. Advisers assist students who have not declared a major; help with academic, personal, and career concerns; and collaborate in scheduling courses needed for graduation. In addition, most students are matched with a first-year peer adviser, an older student, to help them face the challenges of their first year. The college has more than 500 undeclared students; many drawn by Oswego's reputation for helping learners find their way in education and life.

Students may be selected for the college's honors program, which provides a challenging academic experience for high achievers regardless of major. Students also have the option of receiving credit through proficiency CLEP and Advanced Placement examinations while still in high school.

Off-Campus Programs

Opportunities exist for students to broaden their knowledge of other countries by participating in one of eighty different summer or semester overseas academic programs offered. Programs are available throughout the world, and costs are held as close as possible to the cost of an average semester on the Oswego campus. A newer option is short study-abroad quarter courses offering an intensive curriculum followed by a one-to-two-week experience in a foreign country. Through cooperative arrangements, Oswego also participates in semester programs in Albany and Washington D.C.

Internships and other field experiences are available for students from all disciplines through the Center for Experiential Learning. In addition, a formalized cooperative education program (co-op) is available to students from over twenty-five major areas. Each year, more than 1,000 Oswego students participate in internships, co-ops, and other career-awareness activities on campus, in the local area, and throughout the Northeast, the country, and the world.

Academic Facilities

Penfield Library is a high-tech information center supporting the curriculum, teaching, and research of SUNY Oswego. The library houses a collection of over 450,000 bound volumes, including partial U.S. and New York State government documents depositories, and provides access to nearly 26,000 print and/or electronic journals, magazines, and newspapers. Through Interlibrary Loan, Penfield can provide additional materials from libraries all over the world. The library's listening area has more than 12,000 recordings, cassettes, and CDs. Additional facilities include the Lake Effect Café, an online catalog, a 24-hour study room with computers, study carrels, wireless Internet access, and computer labs.

Campuswide computer technology services support students in their classroom, residence, and Internet activities. Students receive an account at the time of enrollment that can be activated online to access e-mail and other web services. High-speed Internet service is available from all residence hall rooms via Ethernet and wireless networks. Wireless access is also available throughout the campus. Other services include technology training workshops, Internet troubleshooting via an active help desk, web support for student clubs and organizations, free antivirus software and campuswide Gmail. The campus maintains hundreds of Macintosh and Windows-based computers in ten public-access labs. Students also have access to more than 500 computers and numerous Sun workstations in forty specialized departmental labs.

Adjacent to the campus, the college maintains the 330-acre Rice Creek Field Station, with its $5.5-million, 7,200-square-foot lab facility which opened its doors in the fall of 2013. The facility has two lab/classrooms, a lecture room, and exhibit areas with an indoor viewing gallery, providing a unique vista of the creek and pond. College classes and community education programs are regularly held at the field station, which ranks among the five most extensively used facilities of its kind in the country.

Tyler Hall, Oswego's fine arts center, has two art galleries that feature annual traveling exhibitions, locally produced theme exhibitions, and the best work of students and faculty members. Tyler Hall's Waterman Theatre hosts student plays, musical performances, and productions by internationally renowned traveling artists. The building recently underwent a $22.2-million rejuvenation, completed in 2016, to provide students with a more approachable, flexible and high-tech home for the performing fine arts.

The WRVO Stations, the college's 50,000-watt public radio outlet, provides outstanding on-campus internship opportunities. Communication Department facilities also include two new all-digital television studios, a modern radio lab, and two new journalism labs in Lanigan Hall. Student-run TV and radio stations and the college newspaper are located in the new Campus Center facilities.

Costs

Tuition for 2016–17 was $3,235 per semester for New York State residents and $8,160 per semester for nonresidents. Room and board charges were approximately $6,839 per semester for entering students, depending on the meal plan, and additional fees totaled approximately $1,475 per semester. SUNY Oswego guarantees that a student's initial first-year costs for room and board will be frozen for up to four consecutive years. Although many activities on campus are free of charge, students need to budget for personal expenses.

Financial Aid

Need-based financial assistance consists of grants, loans, and part-time employment. Oswego offers approximately $80 million in aid to its students annually. Students interested in financial aid must file a Free Application for Federal Student Aid (FAFSA). New York State residents also need to file an application for the state's Tuition Assistance Program (TAP). Priority is given to applications on file by March 1 for the fall term and November 15 for the spring term.

Oswego offers a very generous merit scholarship program. Students receive over $5 million annually in merit scholarships and approximately 35 percent of the entering freshman class receives one. The average four-year renewable scholarship is more than $2,800 per year. For scholarship qualifications and details, students should visit http://www.oswego.edu/admissions/scholarships.

Faculty

Consisting of more than 300 full-time members, Oswego's faculty is dedicated to undergraduate students. With approximately 88 percent of them holding doctoral or other terminal degrees from many of the finest institutions in the country, students can be assured of the opportunity for an outstanding undergraduate education. The student-faculty ratio is approximately 18:1. While dedicated to teaching first and foremost, Oswego's faculty members are also actively engaged in research—often in partnership with undergraduate students—as well as publications and public service.

Student Government

Students at SUNY Oswego are represented by the Student Association, which has as its aim the efficient and intelligent governance of a democratic student body. The functions of the Student Association are divided among various committees that allocate funds to student organizations, intercollegiate and intramural athletics, the student newspaper, literary magazine, TV studios, and radio station, as well as various social, cultural, and intellectual activities on campus.

Admission Requirements

Admission to Oswego is competitive, with high school average, academic program, and standardized test scores being the most important criteria for applicants. Special talents such as artistic, musical, athletic, and creative writing skills are also considered. The Committee on Admissions accepts results of either the ACT or the SAT. A campus admissions visit is encouraged.

Transfer students in good standing are encouraged to apply for admission. The average GPA for entering transfer students is 3.0.

Application and Information

Oswego accepts both The Common Application and the SUNY Application for admission. Both applications are available online at http://www.oswego.edu/apply. Oswego evaluates applications as they are completed and as space remains available. Applications completed by January 15 for the fall term or October 15 for the spring term are ensured equal consideration. Applications received after those dates are welcomed, although considered as space remains available.

Prospective students and their parents are encouraged to visit the campus to participate in a student-guided tour and speak with an admissions counselor. Visits can be scheduled online at www.oswego.edu/admissions. Interested candidates can also call the Office of Admissions in advance to schedule a visit.

For further information, students should contact:

Office of Admissions
229 Sheldon Hall
SUNY Oswego
Oswego, New York 13126
Phone: 315-312-2250
Fax: 315-312-3260
E-mail: admiss@oswego.edu
Website: http://www.oswego.edu

SUNY Oswego is located on 696 acres on the southern shore of Lake Ontario.

COLLEGE CLOSE-UPS

STERLING COLLEGE
CRAFTSBURY COMMON, VERMONT

Sterling College
Working Hands. Working Minds.

The College

Sterling College is *the* leading voice in environmental stewardship education. Environmental stewardship means working in harmony with the natural world—making sustainable choices that protect the climate, water, soil, and wilderness while ensuring that the world's food system is healthful and just. It also means fostering those ideals in other people of all ages and backgrounds.

Sterling College's essential enterprise is to create with its students an innovative education that inspires, challenges, and pushes them to discover their environmental stewardship vision, whether conducting research in the Arctic, growing food for themselves and others, drafting clean water legislation, or leading a youth group on a wilderness canoe trip.

Sterling believes this can't be done in a classroom alone, but needs to happen at the junctures where humanity and nature meet. Students need to be ready to get their hands dirty, both literally and figuratively.

Sterling College removes the barriers between living one's life and learning. It is for the student who wants to commit to becoming an environmental steward and looks forward to the rigor and challenge of working with both hands and mind.

"At Sterling, there's a real history of being able to see where you've been, where you are now, and where you're going. Sterling is a really experiential place. Here, you can get a feel for the kind of world you want to live in, and what kind of world we can create."
—Brighde Moffat '15

Academics: Sterling students are invested in solving the biggest issues of the 21st century: food, water, air, soil, energy, and climate. Working with faculty and staff, the College's students are tackling how to rethink humanity's relationship with the natural world.

Sterling College offers Bachelor of Arts degrees in Ecology, Environmental Humanities, Outdoor Education, Sustainable Agriculture, and Sustainable Food Systems. Students can also choose to design their own majors—some examples include Agroecology, Environmental Justice, Conservation Education, and International Agriculture and Business. Curriculum at Sterling is strongly interdisciplinary and grounded in the liberal arts, with interrelated coursework drawn from all five majors. Core requirements include Ecology, A Sense of Place, Tools and their Applications, and a series of experiences focused on wilderness survival and group dynamics. All new students, accompanied by faculty members, take part in Winter Expedition, a four-day, three-night trek along the ridge of the nearby Lowell Mountain Range. Expedition has been a tradition at Sterling College for over 50 years.

Students spend about 40 percent of their class time outside the traditional classroom setting.

Whether offered on campus in a laboratory or seminar room, on the side of a mountain, or in a barn or pasture, classes at Sterling are small and foster experiential learning and deep inquiry through close relationships between faculty members and students. The typical class size at Sterling is 10, and the student-to-faculty ratio is 7:1.

A highlight of a Sterling education is a ten-week, 6-credit internship anywhere in the world. Internships in agriculture, cross-cultural education, ecotourism, environmental education, hydrology, land and resource management, outdoor education, and wildlife rehabilitation and research are popular options.

Sterling's faculty is composed of 17 full-time members and 17 part-time members; 85 percent of the faculty have advanced degrees. Sterling is a destination for speakers, activists, and professionals who come to campus to share knowledge about sustainable systems and environmental stewardship.

Authentic Sustainability: Sterling was among the very first colleges in the United States to link the liberal arts to ecology, outdoor education, environmental humanities, and sustainable agriculture. Sterling believes that the wellbeing of humanity depends on small, interconnected communities committed to conscientious practices in agriculture and energy use, and in stewardship of the air, soil, and water.

In 2013, Sterling College became the third college in the United States, and the first college in Vermont, to announce its intention to divest its endowment from fossil fuels. For three consecutive years, the Real Food Challenge has ranked Sterling as the top college in the United States serving food on campus that is local, sustainable, organic, humane, and fair trade, with the Sterling Farm producing 35 percent of the College's food. In 2016, Sterling was in the top 25 of *Sierra* magazine's Greenest Schools in America, with a rank of #23 overall. Sterling was also ranked #1 for sustainable food and dining, #3 for academics, and #6 for investments by *Sierra*. In 2017, Sterling received an updated STARS Gold rating from the Association for the Advancement of Sustainability in Higher Education, ranking first in sustainability performance in Vermont and third in all of North America.

Work: Sterling College is one of only nine colleges recognized by the federal government as a Work College and the only Work College in the Northeast. It doesn't matter what a student's financial aid award is—every student puts his or her shoulder to the wheel and does the essential work to keep the campus going.

Through work experiences, students learn about group dynamics, the needs of a community, and the intentional use of resources. At Sterling, the community depends on the work of students, and the campus is a laboratory for gaining insight into the role of the individual in the health and welfare of the community.

Students are paid for their work, earning a minimum of $1,650 toward their tuition. And it's possible to earn more: as students build skills, there are higher-paying leadership positions available on campus. That money goes farther at Sterling—Work Colleges have reduced overhead and Sterling's tuition is 20 percent less than other private New England colleges.

"I was drawn to Sterling because of the Work Program. I know that at the end of four years I will walk away from Sterling with a resume full of work and life experiences that any employer would find of interest. Returning to a sense of place, community, and local resilience is the next step in the environmental movement. Sterling is at the forefront of this movement; a college education here trains you to be a leader through engaged practice in community living."
—Allyson Makuch '15

Community: At Sterling, students, faculty members, and staff members work to create community together. Sterling College strives to be an educational community in which people of all backgrounds and experiences feel at home, where differences are embraced, and where individuals take responsibility for furthering the dignity of all.

Sterling is small, and will remain so by design. It is the only college in the nation where the entire community of students and faculty members sit together each week for Community Meeting. Everyone is on a first-name basis, including the President, Deans, and faculty members.

Sterling College currently has three athletic teams on campus: Nordic skiing, shooting sports, and the nation's first collegiate mountain and trail running team, the Skyrunners.

Community life is informal. Sterling students are likely to enjoy a long weekend of hiking, a lively evening of contra dancing, caring for beehives with friends, snowshoeing at the Craftsbury Outdoor Center, or sitting by a bonfire at the College's woodland lean-tos above the Black River.

Location

Sterling's rural location is one of the College's most prized characteristics. The campus boasts 130 acres, with an additional 300 acres of boreal research forest.

This region of Vermont is known as the "Northeast Kingdom," and is an international destination for outdoor sports and adventure. There are four ski areas within 45 minutes of the College. When city life beckons, however, Burlington is about an hour or so away, and Montreal is only 2 hours from campus.

Majors and Degrees

Sterling College offers Bachelor of Arts degrees in Ecology, Environmental Humanities, Outdoor Education, Sustainable Agriculture, and Sustainable Food Systems. Students can also choose to design their own major.

Off-Campus Programs

Faculty-led, immersive, and environmentally focused, the Sterling College Global Field Studies program offers students the chance to discover the diversity of the planet's landscapes and cultures, as well as explore the complex, ever-changing co-evolutionary relationships among people and place. Students take the methods for learning a local ecology they have practiced on campus and apply these methods to new places. Global Field Studies are included as part of a student's fees at Sterling; there is no additional cost to participate. Recent Global Field Studies classes have been held in Belize, the Bahamas, Canada, Great Britain, the Hudson River watershed, Mexico, Scandinavia, and the Sierra Nevada.

Academic Facilities

The campus has 18 residential, administrative, and classroom buildings. Facilities include a woodshop, four computer labs, a draft horse barn, a blacksmithing and farrier shop, two greenhouses, a teaching kitchen, and the Brown Library.

Outdoor teaching facilities include a challenge course with a climbing wall, a managed wood lot and sugar bush, recreation and nature trails, large organic gardens, a sugarhouse, and the diversified Sterling Farm, powered by both tractor and draft animals.

Costs

Tuition for the 2016–17 academic year was $32,592, room and board was $9,560, and fees were $4,000.

Financial Aid

Choosing to go to college is one of the most important events in a student's life. Sterling College is committed to make this transformative education accessible and does everything it can to work with students and their families to plan an affordable path to graduation.

Every year, Sterling commits more than $2 million to support student financial aid. From small semester grants to full scholarships, Sterling College works diligently to create an affordable academic experience.

The average Sterling grant for 2015–16 was $20,229. The average student load debt for a graduate of Sterling College is $18,680—53 percent less than the national average of $35,051. Ninety-eight percent of Sterling students receive some form of financial aid.

"I know that financial aid is crucial to the strength of Sterling. Over my years here, I have seen that sound financial aid allows us to enroll the right students in the College—students who care about the environment and community and who want to make a difference in the world we live in."—*Ned Houston, Distinguished Professor and former Director of Financial Aid*

Admission Requirements

Admission to Sterling College opens the door to a transformative and affordable education, valuable work experience, and an eclectic, diverse, and socially conscious community.

Sterling College offers admission to both first-time college applicants and transfer applicants. There is also a significant population of student veterans and adult learners. Application review at Sterling is a highly individualized process, characterized by a personal approach.

Sterling practices test-blind admission. Standardized test scores are not considered during application review. An applicant's academic record is given equal weight with an applicant's work ethic, character, and passion for environmental stewardship.

Sterling requires an online application, a personal essay, two letters of recommendation, and a high school transcript or the equivalent. No student is granted admission to Sterling College until they have completed an interview—be it in person, over the phone, or via Skype.

Application and Information

High school seniors who wish to receive an early response to their application may apply for Early Decision or Early Action. For Early Decision, a completed application must be on file by November 15 to be notified of a decision on or before December 1. For Early Action, a completed application must be on file on or before December 15 to be notified of a decision on or before January 1. All other applicants are encouraged to submit applications before June 1 for fall enrollment, January 1 for spring enrollment, and April 1 for summer enrollment. Once completed, an application is reviewed for admission within two weeks.

Students should contact:

Tim Patterson, Director of Admission
Sterling College
P.O. Box 72
Craftsbury Common, Vermont 05827
United States
Phone: 802-586-7711
800-648-3591 (toll-free)
Fax: 802-586-2596
E-mail: admission@sterlingcollege.edu
Website:http://www.sterlingcollege.edu
www.facebook.com/SterlingCollegeVT
www.twitter.com/SterlingCollegeVT
www.instagram.com/sterlingcollegevt

Sterling College is the leading voice in higher education for environmental stewardship. It was among the first colleges to focus on sustainability. Sterling College students are invested in solving the biggest issues of the 21st century: food, water, air, soil, energy, and climate, as well as reshaping humanity's relationship with the natural world.

COLLEGE CLOSE-UPS

STEVENSON UNIVERSITY

STEVENSON AND OWINGS MILLS, MARYLAND

★ To read more about this school, visit http://petersons.to/stevensonuniversity

STEVENSON UNIVERSITY
Imagine your future. Design your career.®

The University

Stevenson University is a coeducational, independent institution dedicated to providing its 4,300 undergraduate and graduate students with a career-focused liberal arts education. Individual attention from faculty members, extensive career preparation gained through real-world training, and two ideal locations just north of Baltimore, Maryland, in Stevenson and Owings Mills, make the University truly unique. Stevenson University (SU) was formerly Villa Julie College.

At SU, academic quality is viewed as a personalized education that fosters intellectual growth and prepares students to thrive in work and life after graduation. With a student-faculty ratio of 15:1, it is easy to understand why students often cite the congenial rapport with faculty members as one of the University's strong points.

Through Stevenson University's concept of Learning Beyond, students step outside of the classroom to take their learning to the next level. Experiential learning opportunities include study abroad, service learning, field placements, internships, and independent research. In addition, through an approach known as Career Architecture℠, each student develops a professional career plan based on their values, skills, and strengths.

Stevenson's graduates maintain a strong placement rate—93 percent in the most recent poll, with students acquiring jobs or going on to further their education within six months of graduation.

At SU, students enjoy more than fifty clubs and organizations, multiple honor societies, and NCAA Division III athletics. The following sports are offered: men's and women's basketball, cross-country, golf, ice hockey, lacrosse, soccer, swimming, tennis, track and field, and volleyball; men's baseball and football; and women's field hockey, beach volleyball, and softball. Cheerleading, dance, club sports, and intramural sports are also extremely popular.

In addition to its undergraduate programs, the University offers a Master of Science degree in the following programs: business and technology management, communication studies, forensic science, cyber forensics, forensic studies, healthcare management, and nursing; and a Master of Arts degree in teaching.

Location

Stevenson University has two beautiful campuses in the heart of Maryland, in Stevenson and Owings Mills. SU students truly appreciate the beauty of a rural campus as well as the convenience and appeal of a more urban setting.

The original 60-acre Greenspring Campus is nestled among the rolling hills of Stevenson, Maryland. The Owings Mills Campus is a thriving center of student activity and offers both academic and residential facilities. Classes are held on both campuses, and the University provides a free shuttle service that runs between these locations.

In fall 2013, Stevenson expanded its Owings Mills campus with the addition of 28-acres on the north side of campus, which is the current home of the School of Design, the Fine School of the Sciences, and the Berman School of Nursing and Health Professions.

Majors and Degrees

Stevenson University offers the following bachelor's degree programs: accounting; applied mathematics; biochemistry; biology; business administration; business communication; business information systems; chemistry; computer information systems; criminal justice; digital marketing; early childhood education: liberal arts and technology; elementary education: liberal arts and technology; English language and literature; environmental science; fashion design; fashion merchandising; film and moving image; human services; interdisciplinary studies; legal studies; medical laboratory science; middle school education; nursing; nursing: RN to B.S. (adult accelerated only); psychology; public history; theatre and media performance; and visual communication design.

Stevenson's B.S. to M.S. option allows students to earn both a bachelor's and a master's degree in as few as five years. Graduate study begins in the spring semester of the junior year and runs concurrently with undergraduate work until the end of the spring semester of the senior year. All subsequent course work is at the graduate level.

Academic Programs

At SU, academic quality is regarded as a personalized curriculum that prepares students to enter the working world with the knowledge and skills that employers value, and the leadership and motivation for success that lasts a lifetime. SU infuses the traditional liberal arts education with a distinct career focus. The University's goal is to prepare students for career, graduate study, and productive involvement in today's world.

Academic Facilities

The University provides modern facilities that serve the needs of all students.

The University's Greenspring Campus includes a 350-seat theater, multiple computer labs and classrooms, video and graphic studios, science laboratories, a student union, and athletic facilities. Each classroom and laboratory on the campus is capable of multimedia projection and computer-assisted learning.

The Owings Mills Campus hosts the University's newest facilities, including an expansive student center and dining hall, a 10,000-square-foot community center, an expansive athletic complex with a new gymnasium, multiple classrooms and study spaces, a fitness center, and additional athletic fields. The state-of-the art 3,500-seat Mustang Stadium opened in 2011.

The Howard S. Brown School of Business and Leadership offers twelve traditional classrooms and seven seminar halls. The facility also includes two distance-learning labs where students are able to interact with other learners worldwide, six computer labs utilizing the most up-to-date equipment, a student lounge, a law library, and a high-tech digital mock trial courtroom.

In 2013, campus facilities grew with the north expansion, a 28-acre addition which houses the state-of-the-art School of Design, including 3-D printers, studio space equipped with a green screen, twelve private edit bays, a soundstage, and a prop room. In fall 2016, the Manning Academic Center opened, providing a home for the Fine School of the Sciences and Berman School of Nursing and Health Professions. The 200,000 square-foot former pharmaceutical facility features state-of-the-art laboratories, classrooms, offices, a terraria/aquaria room, a nursing simulation room, a printmaking studio, two 50-seat theaters, and more.

Costs

For the 2016–17 academic year, tuition and fees for full-time students were $33,168; room and board were $12,490.

Financial Aid

Stevenson University offers financial assistance to qualified students in the form of grants, scholarships, loans, student employment, and a special payment plan. On average, approximately 95 percent of the University's students receive some form of financial assistance. The University has a generous scholarship program and reviews all applicants for five levels of awards based on academic merit. SU participates in all major federal aid programs as well as all Maryland state programs. Applicants are required to file the Free Application for Federal Student Aid (FAFSA). The priority deadline for filing is February 15.

In addition to merit-based awards, specialty scholarships are available. The Founders' Scholarship, along with the Leadership Scholars' Program and the Service Scholars Program offered enhanced opportunities for qualified students. Stevenson also offers the Presidential Fellowship, a full-tuition scholarship, to students who have the potential to make a lasting impact on the Stevenson community as shown by their commitment to academic excellence along with proven leadership in school-based achievements, community service, and/or athletics. A separate application is required. The deadline to apply for the Presidential Fellowship is November 1.

Faculty

The faculty at Stevenson University is primarily a teaching faculty. The University's 15:1 student-teacher ratio demonstrates the institution's dedication to personalized education. A majority of the full-time faculty members have the doctoral or terminal degree offered in their field, and a significant number are widely published. In addition, many are concurrently employed as professional specialists in their fields.

Student Government

The Student Government Association (SGA) facilitates an environment that encourages students to express their thoughts and opinions concerning Stevenson University, its policies, and sponsored activities. The SGA serves as the principal governing body of all campus clubs and activities. In conjunction with the Office of Student Affairs, the SGA organizes an array of campuswide events that promote the social aspects of college life. Each student at Stevenson is welcome and encouraged to participate in all SGA functions.

Admission Requirements

Applications for admission to Stevenson University are reviewed on a rolling basis. In evaluating each applicant, the University considers the applicant's high school academic record, SAT or ACT scores, recommendations, writing sample, and any other special talents or personal interests. Admission to the University is determined without regard for race, color, sex, religion, national or ethnic origin, or handicap. SU complies with all applicable laws and federal regulations regarding discrimination and accessibility on the condition of handicap, age, veteran status, or otherwise.

Application and Information

Applications for admission to undergraduate programs should be received by March 1 for fall-semester entry and October 1 for spring-semester entry. Scholarship consideration adheres to earlier deadlines. Applications received after these dates are reviewed on a space-available basis. Students applying to the University as freshmen must submit official high school transcripts, standardized test scores, the Counselor Recommendation Form, typed responses to the essay questions listed on the application, and a $40 nonrefundable application fee. The application fee is waived for all students who apply online at www.stevenson.edu/apply or via the Common Application. Transfer students must submit official transcripts from all colleges or universities they have attended and should contact the Transfer Admissions Counselor to discuss additional credential requirements.

For further information and application forms, students should contact:

Admissions Office
Garrison Hall, Suite 200
Stevenson University
100 Campus Circle
Owings Mills, Maryland 21117-7804
Phone: 410-486-7001
877-468-6852 (toll-free)
Fax: 443-352-4440
E-mail: admissions@stevenson.edu
Website: http://www.stevenson.edu

The residences at Stevenson University offer spacious apartments and suites with extensive amenities.

STOCKTON UNIVERSITY

GALLOWAY, NEW JERSEY

★ To read more about this school, visit http://petersons.to/stocktonuniversity

STOCKTON UNIVERSITY

The University

Thinking translates into doing at Stockton. Students can get hands-on experience in nursing, public health, occupational therapy, or physical therapy at the two hospitals on campus; "live" a hospitality and tourism internship 24/7 at the Seaview, Stockton's world-class resort; use cutting-edge technology to preserve historic underwater wreck sites or analyze the seafloor's ecosystems at Stockton's Marine Science & Environmental Field Station; study artistic techniques firsthand through a partnership with the nearby Noyes Museum of Art or at the Philadelphia Museum of Art; or bask in the beautiful, 2,000-acre campus in the Pinelands National Reserve just minutes from the ocean, a perfect setting for Stockton's nationally renowned academic programs.

Stockton students engage fully with faculty, including Fulbright Scholars, a Guggenheim Fellow, and a Pulitzer-awarded author. Small classes are guided by professors who care as much about teaching as research, allowing for discussion, debate, and discovery in the classroom and beyond.

Rooted in a deep social and environmental consciousness, Stockton offers extensive service learning opportunities and has become an international leader in alternative energy research and conservation efforts.

Founded in 1969, The Richard Stockton College of New Jersey was named for one of the signers of the Declaration of Independence. In February 2015, Stockton celebrated a new designation and name change to Stockton University. This change highlights Stockton's tremendous overall growth, honoring a tradition of forward thinking and proven progression. The University offers bachelor's, master's, and doctoral degree programs designed to challenge the brightest students, providing many of the academic, technological, and cultural advantages of a large university, but with the communal spirit typical of smaller colleges.

Stockton enrolls over 8,600 students from New Jersey, the Mid-Atlantic states, and foreign countries, providing distinctive educational programs with a curriculum focused on developing the students' analytic and creative capabilities through the encouragement of individually planned courses of study.

The Stockton experience is enhanced by more than 130 clubs and organizations, an active Greek life, honor societies, and athletics. In addition to extensive intramural and club sports, NCAA Division III sports teams offered include men's baseball, basketball, lacrosse, and soccer, women's basketball, crew, field hockey, lacrosse, soccer, softball, tennis, and volleyball, and men's and women's cross-country and track and field. Students who participate in cocurricular activities have their experiences documented through the ULTRA (Undergraduate Learning, Training, and Awareness) program, culminating in a co-curricular transcript.

Stockton provides on-campus housing for more than 4,000 students in traditional residence halls, apartments, and at Stockton Seaview. All complexes are furnished and air conditioned, with cable TV and Internet access. Other students choose to live off campus in nearby townhouse and apartment complexes or winter rentals in one of the local shore towns.

Beyond its undergraduate programs, Stockton offers the following graduate degrees: Doctor of Physical Therapy, and Doctor of Education in organizational leadership; Master of Arts in American studies, criminal justice, Holocaust and genocide studies, education, educational leadership, and instructional technology; Master of Business Administration; Master of Science in communication disorders, computational science, nursing, and occupational therapy; Master of Social Work; and a Professional Science Master's in environmental science. Certificate and endorsement programs are offered in bilingual/bicultural education, ESL (English as a second language), family nurse practitioner, forensic psychology, health professions prep, homeland security, learning disabilities teacher consultant, middle school endorsement, New Jersey standard supervisor endorsement, preschool–grade 3 endorsement, reading specialist, special education, and student assistance coordinator.

Stockton University is accredited by the Commission on Higher Education of the Middle States Association of Colleges and Schools. In addition, the social work program is accredited by the Council on Social Work Education; teacher education is approved by the New Jersey Department of Education, the National Association of State Directors of Teacher Education and Certification, and the Teacher Education Accreditation Council; nursing is accredited by the New Jersey Board of Nursing and the Commission on Collegiate Nursing Education; chemistry is accredited by the American Chemical Society; physical therapy is accredited by the Commission on Accreditation in Physical Therapy Education of the American Physical Therapy Association; environmental health is accredited by the National Environmental Health Sciences and Protection Accreditation Council; health administration is accredited by the Association of University Programs in Health Administration; occupational therapy is accredited by the Accreditation Council for Occupational Therapy Education of the American Occupational Therapy Association; communication disorders is accredited by the American Speech-Language-Hearing Association and Council on Academic Accreditation in Audiology and Speech-Language Pathology; criminal justice is accredited by the Academy of Criminal Justice Sciences; and business is accredited by the Association to Advance Collegiate Schools of Business.

Location

Stockton's main campus is located in Galloway, New Jersey, nestled in the environmentally protected Pinelands National Reserve, just minutes west of Atlantic City and several beaches, an hour from Philadelphia, and 2 hours from New York City. Courses are also offered online and at the Atlantic City, Hammonton, Manahawkin, and Woodbine Instructional Sites. The Stockton Seaview Resort and its two championship golf courses allow for the expansion of the hospitality and tourism management program while preserving an iconic landmark in the region. Collaboration with the Sam Azeez Museum of Woodbine Heritage and the Noyes Museum of Art provides enriching exhibitions and educational programs. In addition, an expansion project has begun in Atlantic City, with construction underway on an academic building, parking garage, and residential facilities that overlook the Boardwalk; this campus will allow for Stockton's continued growth and support of its surrounding communities. The University plans to open its Atlantic City campus in 2018.

Majors and Degrees

The Bachelor of Arts, Bachelor of Fine Arts, and Bachelor of Science degrees are offered in studies in the arts (visual and performing), biochemistry/molecular biology, biology, business (accounting, finance, financial planning, management, marketing), chemistry, communications, computer science and information systems, criminal justice (forensic psychology/investigation, homeland security), economics, education, environmental science, exercise science, geology, health sciences, historical studies, hospitality and tourism management, languages and culture studies, liberal studies, literature, marine science, mathematics, nursing, philosophy and religion, physics, political science, psychology, sociology and anthropology, social work, and sustainability.

Stockton also offers preprofessional preparation in dentistry, law, medicine, pharmacy, veterinary medicine, communication disorders (speech therapy), occupational therapy, physical therapy, and physician assistant studies, with the master's in occupational therapy, communication disorders, and doctorate in physical therapy completed at Stockton. The University also has accelerated seven-year dual-degree articulation agreements with Rowan School of Osteopathic Medicine, Rutgers School of Dental Medicine, and Temple School of Podiatry; an accelerated dual-degree program in pharmaceutical engineering with New Jersey Institute of Technology; and five-year, dual-degree programs with New Jersey Institute of Technology, Rowan University, and Rutgers University for engineering. In addition, students can graduate from Stockton with a Bachelor of Science degree in biochemistry/molecular biology or biology and finish their Doctor of Pharmacy degree through the Ernest Mario School of Pharmacy at Rutgers University.

Academic Programs

To earn a baccalaureate degree from Stockton, a student must satisfactorily complete a minimum of 128 semester credits. Degree programs include a combination of general studies and program (major) studies. Bachelor of Arts students must earn 64 credits in general studies; Bachelor of Science students must earn 48. General studies courses are cross-disciplinary courses designed to introduce students to all major areas of the curriculum and to the intellectual skills necessary for success in college. Students must select courses from each major curricular area. The only required courses within general studies are basic studies (up to three); students may be exempt from these courses based on testing. Bachelor of Arts students must earn 64 credits in major studies; Bachelor of Science students must earn 80. Requirements are carefully structured and emphasize sequences of specific courses.

Stockton students have the opportunity to influence what and how they learn. The preceptorial system enables students to work closely with a faculty-staff preceptor in planning and evaluating courses and in exploring various career paths.

Off-Campus Programs

Off-campus experiences for credit are a requirement for most programs, namely in the form of internships, research projects, and field studies. Stockton sends more students to the Washington Internship Program than any other college or university outside the Washington, D.C., area.

Additional opportunities such as study abroad, Semester at Sea, and an honors program are also available.

Coordination of off-campus internship programs is provided by academic offices as well as the Career Center; coordination of foreign study is provided by the Office of Global Engagement.

Academic Facilities

Stockton's campus serves as a living-learning center, with academic, recreational, and living spaces mixed to promote interaction among students, faculty, and staff. Facilities include numerous interactive and electronic classrooms, an extensive library containing the Sara and Sam Schoffer Holocaust Resource Center, auditoriums, an art gallery, and performing arts center. An academic expansion project is underway on the Galloway campus, which will include a 58,000 square-foot addition to the current Unified Science Center as well as a new 38,000 square-foot structure for classroom and office space. The project has a scheduled opening date of spring 2018.

Costs

Costs for the 2016–17 academic year were $13,077 for in-state students and $19,861 for out-of-state students (flat-rate tuition up to 40 credits per year, fees); on-campus housing and board were $11,982 (double-occupancy residence room, Ultimate meal plan). Books, supplies, transportation, and personal items are extra. Costs are subject to change.

Financial Aid

Financial aid is available as scholarships, grants, loans, and work-study. Need-based financial aid is awarded according to student and family need. Students seeking financial aid should file the Free Application for Federal Student Aid (FAFSA) by March 1. Stockton offers aggressive and generous merit-based aid awards to academically talented freshman and transfer students based on standardized test scores, grade point average, high school class rank, and college-level performance.

Faculty

Stockton's faculty represent highly diverse academic, training, and social backgrounds, with 96 percent holding terminal degrees in their field. Faculty members work closely with students through small class sizes and individualized research opportunities, and share in social, recreational, and cultural programs with students and staff. This arrangement supports the exceptional rapport and learning relationships among students and faculty members.

Student Government

The Stockton University Student Senate consists of 25 student members. The advisory council is made up of 1 faculty member and 2 staff members. Student senators hold office for one year. The Student Senate reviews and makes recommendations on budgets of funded student organizations and acts as the official representative of the student body.

Admission Requirements

Stockton operates on rolling admission. Fall admission deadline is May 1 for most freshmen. Students should check the website for special program deadlines. Transfer deadline for fall admission is August 1. Spring (January) admission deadline for all students is December 1. Students may apply for admission to the fall or spring term and are notified of the admission decision as soon as their application file has been completed and reviewed. Freshman applicants must submit ACT and/or SAT scores. All students must submit official transcripts from all educational institutions attended. Admission is selective.

Armed Services veterans and those who have been away from formal education for some time are also invited to apply for admission. Stockton makes no distinction between part- and full-time students in offering admission.

Stockton offers special admission to a limited number of New Jersey students from educationally and financially disadvantaged backgrounds. Students wishing to explore this opportunity should contact the Admissions Office.

Application and Information

For more information, prospective students should contact:

Dean of Enrollment Management
Stockton University
101 Vera King Farris Drive
Galloway, New Jersey 08205-9441
Phone: 609-652-4261
866-772-2885 (toll-free)
Fax: 609-626-5541
E-mail: admissions@stockton.edu
Website: Stockton.edu
Facebook.com/StocktonUniversity
Twitter.com/@Stockton_edu

Stockton University offers quality, value, distinction, and location. The personal attention of a private, liberal arts institution and the value of a public education are combined at Stockton, New Jersey's distinctive public university.

COLLEGE CLOSE-UPS

STONEHILL COLLEGE

EASTON, MASSACHUSETTS

LUX ET SPES

STONEHILL COLLEGE

The College

Stonehill College provides the knowledge and experience students need to succeed in their chosen field along with a liberal arts foundation that fosters the kind of well-rounded and adaptable thinkers that today's leading organizations demand. Stonehill is a coed Catholic college with a welcoming, academically challenging community of more than 2,500 students on a beautiful, active campus 22 miles south of Boston. The College offers forty-three majors and fifty-three minors in its School of Business and School of Arts & Science, where students can pursue the humanities, natural and social sciences, education, and pre-professional advising programs. Stonehill graduates go on to successful careers and lead lives of purposeful learning, leadership, and responsible citizenship.

Stonehill is an engaged and active campus. More than 90 percent of students complete an internship, practicum, field experience, or study abroad by the time they graduate and more than 80 percent of Stonehill students participate in at least one sport at the varsity, club, or recreational level. Stonehill competes in the Northeast-10 Conference, the largest NCAA Division II conference in the U.S., and offers twenty-one varsity sports, including baseball, lacrosse, football, basketball, golf, and soccer. There are seventeen sports in the intramural program, including basketball, flag football, floor hockey, and softball, as well as indoor and outdoor soccer. Fourteen club sports such as rugby and volleyball are yet another option, offering a spirited, fun experience without the demands of NCAA conference-sanctioned athletics.

Founded by the Congregation of Holy Cross in 1948, Stonehill's mission is "to educate the whole person so that each graduate thinks, acts, and leads with courage toward the creation of a more just and compassionate world." Each year, more than 2,000 Stonehill students participate in community service, providing more than 95,000 hours of service.

Stonehill consistently receives national recognition as one of the country's top colleges. The Princeton Review has singled out Stonehill as one of the best in the nation for career services, most accessible professors, intramural sports, and study abroad. *Bloomberg Businessweek* recently ranked Stonehill's business program as among the best in the nation.

Location

Stonehill is in Easton, Massachusetts, a friendly residential community nestled between New England's largest capital cities. Just 22 miles from Boston, America's No. 1 college town, and 37 miles from Providence, it is perfectly situated for internships, service opportunities, and job prospects, as well as enjoying museums, professional sports, cultural events, and more.

Whether the abundant trees are in full bloom in the spring or the leaves are bursting into reds and golds in New England's colorful fall, Stonehill is beautiful every season of the year. Encompassing 384 acres, the campus features traditional landscaping, ponds, wooded trails, and Georgian-style architecture.

Majors and Degrees

Students may receive Bachelor of Arts degrees in American studies, art history, arts administration (museum studies, dance, music, and theater concentrations), astronomy, biology, Catholic studies, chemistry, communication (communication studies and mediated communication concentrations), criminology, economics, education (early childhood/elementary and secondary education minor), English, environmental studies, foreign languages, French, gender and sexuality studies, graphic design, health science, healthcare administration, history, interdisciplinary studies, mathematics, philosophy, physics, political science and international studies (government and politics, international relations, and public administration and public policy concentrations), psychology, religious studies, sociology, Spanish, studio arts, as well as visual and performing arts (generalist and music concentrations).

Bachelor of Science degrees are offered in astronomy, biochemistry, biology, chemistry, computer science, earth and planetary science, environmental science, mathematics, neuroscience, and physics. Bachelor of Science in Business Administration degrees are offered in accounting, finance, international business, management, and marketing. Stonehill's business department is accredited by the AACSB. The College partners with its sister school, the University of Notre Dame, to offer advanced degrees in management, accountancy, and entrepreneurship, in addition to a 3+2 program in engineering with concentrations in aerospace, chemical, civil, computer, electrical, environmental engineering, environmental earth sciences, and mechanical engineering.

Pre-professional advising programs are offered in dentistry, education, law, medicine, veterinary science, and medical technology. Students interested in the field of education can pursue programs in early childhood education, elementary education, and secondary education, which lead to initial teacher licensure from the Commonwealth of Massachusetts. Students may also design their own major by combining various departmental courses into a comprehensive multidisciplinary program.

Academic Programs

The core of Stonehill's liberal arts curriculum is the Cornerstone Program, which leads students to examine themselves, society, culture, and the natural world through courses in ethics, sciences, language, and more.

Stonehill's students and alumni succeed because the entire college community collaborates to help them develop the knowledge, skills, and character to meet their professional goals and to live lives of purpose and integrity. Graduates can be found around the world enrolled in top graduate programs, enjoying meaningful careers, and working to improve their communities.

Within one year of graduation, 94 percent of Stonehill graduates over the last five years were employed, doing service work, or in graduate school. Nearly 55 percent of the class of 2015 had secured jobs by graduation (the national average for colleges is 30 percent) at organizations such as Goldman Sachs, the New England Patriots, and Brigham and Women's Hospital. Others joined or applied for yearlong volunteer service programs such as the Peace Corps, Teach for America, AmeriCorps, and World Teach.

On average, Stonehill students graduate at a higher rate and in less time than students at many other colleges and universities. About 80 percent of Stonehill students graduate within four years, double the national average, which put Stonehill in eighth place on Best Choice School's "Most Affordable Colleges with High Four-Year Graduation Rates."

Off-Campus Programs

At Stonehill, students are given experiential learning opportunities that allow in-depth exploration of what they learn in the classroom and the opportunity to apply that knowledge in the real world. The National Survey of Student Engagement has ranked Stonehill in the top 10 percent of colleges nationwide for its enriching educational experiences such as competitive internships, nationally ranked study-abroad opportunities, and cocurricular programs.

Students also take part in interdisciplinary Learning Communities (LCs), which combine two academic courses from different disciplines with a team-taught seminar that explores an interrelated topic. Some LCs even incorporate travel to places such as Ireland, Italy, and the deserts of the Southwest.

In addition, Stonehill has frequently been ranked among the top twenty baccalaureate institutions in the nation for student participation in semester-long study abroad programs, according to the Institute of International Education's Open Doors Survey. Nearly 40 percent of Stonehill students study abroad before graduation in dozens of countries, including Argentina, Australia, China, Denmark, England, Ireland, Italy, Morocco, New Zealand, Spain, and South Africa.

Academic Facilities

Stonehill is dedicated to developing programs and projects that will continually improve quality of life for everyone on campus. Its $34 million science center, opened in 2009, provides state-of-the-art labs, observation rooms, and research areas, as well as a café and atrium (a popular meeting place for faculty, staff, and students).

More than 90 percent of Stonehill's students live on campus and very few leave on the weekends. In addition, all resident students are guaranteed housing for all four years. Students can choose from a variety of living options, including suites, townhouses, and double- and triple-occupancy rooms, and take advantage of amenities such as communal TV lounges, kitchen and laundry facilities, recreation rooms, pool tables, basketball courts, beach volleyball courts, and outdoor grills for barbecues.

Costs

For the 2016–17 academic year, Stonehill's costs were $39,900 for tuition and $15,230 for room and board.

Financial Aid

Stonehill is committed to helping each qualified student find the resources to make the dream of a Stonehill education become reality. Stonehill offers loans, grants, scholarships, employment programs, and tuition payment plans to help students become a part of the community here. In the 2016–17 academic year, 95 percent of full-time students received some form of aid. On average, students received $29,555 each in scholarships, grants, loans, and work-study. A wide range of competitive merit-based scholarships are also available to outstanding students who do not demonstrate a financial need.

To file for Stonehill scholarships and/or financial aid consideration, students should complete the online CSS PROFILE form at https://profileonline.collegeboard.com. Stonehill's CSS PROFILE code is 3770. In addition, students must file the Free Application for Federal Student Aid (FAFSA) online at http://www.fafsa.ed.gov to be considered for government funds. Stonehill's FAFSA code is 002217.

Faculty

With a student-faculty ratio of 12:1 and an average class size of 19, Stonehill sees individual attention as a key component of our academic programs. Stonehill's accomplished faculty champions its students throughout all four years and is dedicated to teaching and conducting publishable research with students to help develop their professional portfolio. Students benefit from graduate-level access to high-tech equipment, attend professional academic conferences, and coauthor in-depth papers, while guided by faculty mentors. Stonehill students take advantage of collaborating one-on-one with their professors on a regular basis and they are always taught by a faculty member, not a teaching assistant or graduate student.

Student Government

From enjoying on-campus activities to just hanging out with friends, students have plenty of opportunities for fun at Stonehill. The Student Government Association (SGA) is one of the country's most active—its programming won an award from the National Association of Campus Activities—so there's always something happening, from concerts and guest speakers to contests and game shows. Eighty clubs and organizations are available, including the College's arts and entertainment magazine *Rolling Stonehill*, the Ski/Snowboard Club, and the Neuroscience Society.

Stonehill also offers free transportation to Boston's public subway system, allowing easy access to the excitement of the city. And Stonehill's Fun Fund allows students to apply for SGA funds to go to off-campus events such as movies, plays, professional sport, and other events.

Admission Requirements

Last year, Stonehill enrolled 734 students into the class of 2020. The College actively seeks an academically strong and geographically, culturally, and ethnically diverse student body. In the admission process, all information on each applicant is carefully considered, but academic performance and high school curriculum are given the greatest weight. The Admission Committee evaluates the depth and strength of each applicant's course selection and the consistency of their grades. Competitive students should have completed a strong academic program from among their high school's most challenging offerings. Stonehill admission is test optional, but students may choose to submit scores from either the SAT or ACT. The Admission Committee also evaluates extracurricular activities, work, volunteer and community activities, recommendations, and writing samples. Stonehill awards credit for strong scores on AP, CLEP, and higher-level International Baccalaureate exams.

Application and Information

Aspirants for Stonehill, as first-year, transfer, or international students may apply online at https://www.commonapp.org. The Common Application is also available in paper form at high school guidance offices.

Stonehill offers three admission plans for first-year candidates: early decision (binding), early action (nonbinding), and regular decision. November 1 is the deadline for early action, December 1 is the deadline for early decision, and January 15 is the deadline for regular decision.

Office of Admission
Stonehill College
320 Washington Street
Easton, Massachusetts 02357-5610
United States
Phone: 888-694-4554
Fax: 508-565-1545
E-mail: admission@stonehill.edu
Website: http://www.stonehill.edu/admission/ (Admission)

Stonehill College is set on 384 acres of stately buildings and beautifully landscaped grounds, minutes from Boston and Providence.

TEMPLE UNIVERSITY

PHILADELPHIA, PENNSYLVANIA

TEMPLE UNIVERSITY

★ To read more about this school, visit http://petersons.to/templeuniversity

The University

With a reputation for providing an affordable, high-quality education, Temple University prepares students to be successful in everything that they do. At this vibrant, urban, public research university, passionate students turn opportunities into accomplishments: World-class labs are the proving grounds for innovative ideas. A classroom doubles as the boardroom of a tech startup. Professors do more than teach, they become longtime mentors. Temple students are driven to take action, and at Temple they have everything they need to achieve their goals.

Cutting-edge facilities—including a 247,000 square-foot Science Education and Research Center, more than 3,500 engaged faculty members, and top-ranked programs combine to create a dynamic academic environment that attracts students from across the country and around the world. With seventeen schools and colleges, eight campuses, and more than 38,000 students, Temple is the thirty-eighth largest university in the United States.

Living on campus puts students in the heart of the action. About 80 percent of freshmen live on campus, where they are a short walk from class, fitness facilities, Temple's famous food trucks, and the many events that take place every day at Temple. The University boasts a 10,200-seat entertainment complex that hosts NCAA Division I basketball games as well as concerts—Fetty Wap, Sam Smith, and Bob Dylan have all performed there. With more than 300 clubs, activities, and student organizations to choose from, Temple students are never bored. From activism to student-powered media to yoga, campus life is always exciting.

But a Temple education goes far beyond campus. The city is an extension of the classroom, and opportunities for hands-on learning are everywhere, from museums and technology meet-ups to internships in business, healthcare, media and the arts. Learning from experts first-hand means students are ready for anything when they graduate, and the University's nearly 320,000 alumni form a powerful support network.

Location

Each of Temple's distinct campuses has its own personality and environment, from urban to suburban to international. Temple's Main Campus is located just 1.5 miles from the center of Philadelphia, the second-largest city on the East Coast. By subway or on foot, Philadelphia is among the most walkable cities in the U.S.—students can explore all the city has to offer, including more than 100 museums, a thriving restaurant scene, numerous sports teams, and the largest urban landscaped park in the country. The professional world is also right outside Temple's door: There are thousands of opportunities for hands-on learning and internships in the Philadelphia area, and the University's more than 100,000 alumni in the region love to hire Temple students.

Temple's other seven campuses include a location in Tokyo—the largest and oldest American university in Japan—and another in Rome, Italy. Temple University Harrisburg is located in the heart of Pennsylvania's capital city. The University's campus in Ambler, Pennsylvania, is the hub of the University's environmental programs and home to a 187-acre arboretum that serves as a living laboratory. In addition to Main Campus, Temple's Philadelphia campuses are the Health Sciences Center just north of Main Campus, and the Center City and Podiatric Medicine campuses, both a short subway ride away in downtown Philadelphia.

Majors and Degrees

Temple offers 153 undergraduate degree programs, making it easy for students to follow, or discover, their passion. Students who need time to decide on a major can explore their interests through the University Studies program. Those who would like to accelerate their education can apply to one of Temple's many dual-degree programs.

The **Tyler School of Art** offers a B.F.A. with concentrations in ceramics/glass, fibers and materials, graphic and interactive design, metals/jewelry/CAD-CAM, painting, photography, printmaking, and sculpture; a B.A. in art history and visual studies; and a B.S. in art education. Tyler's Architecture Program confers a B.S. in architectural preservation, architecture (preprofessional), and facilities management. B.S. programs are offered in community and regional planning and in horticulture and landscape architecture.

The **Fox School of Business** offers a B.B.A. in accounting, actuarial science, business management, economics, entrepreneurship and innovation, finance, financial planning, human resource management, international business administration, legal studies, management information systems, marketing, real estate, risk management and insurance, and supply chain management.

The **College of Education** offers a B.A. in adult and organizational development and a B.S. in career and technical education, early childhood education, human development and community engagement, middle-grades education, and secondary education.

The **College of Engineering** offers a B.S. in engineering in civil engineering, electrical engineering, engineering (general program), and mechanical engineering. A B.S. is also offered in bioengineering, construction management technology, and general engineering technology.

The **College of Liberal Arts** offers a B.A. in Africology and African-American studies; American studies; anthropology; Asian studies; classics; criminal justice; economics; English; environmental studies; French; gender, sexuality, and women's studies; geography and urban studies; German; history; Italian; Jewish studies; Latin American studies; mathematical economics; neuroscience; philosophy; political science; psychology; religion; sociology; and Spanish.

The **Klein College of Media and Communication** offers a B.A. in advertising, communication studies, journalism, media studies and production, and strategic communication.

The **Boyer College of Music and Dance** offers a B.M. in composition, dance, jazz studies, music education, music history, music therapy, performance (specific instrument or voice), and theory; a B.F.A. is offered in dance.

The **College of Public Health** offers a B.S. in health information management; kinesiology; nursing; public health; speech, language, and hearing; and therapeutic recreation; a B.A. in linguistics is also offered.

The **College of Science and Technology** offers a B.S. in applied mathematics, biology, biophysics, chemistry, computer science, environmental science, geology, information science and technology, mathematical economics, mathematics, neuroscience (cell and molecular), physics, and pharmaceutical sciences.

The **School of Social Work** offers the B.S.W. degree.

The **School of Theater, Film, and Media Arts** offers a B.A. and a B.F.A. in theater and in film and media arts, as well as a B.F.A. in musical theater.

The **School of Tourism and Hospitality Management** offers a B.S. in sport and recreation management and in tourism and hospitality management.

Academic Programs

Students passionate about learning are attracted to Temple because of its variety of academic programs: More than 540 are offered, including 153 bachelor's degree programs. The University provides all of the resources and opportunities of a large, world-class research institution and the individual attention of a small college—average class size is only 26 students, with a 15:1 student-to-faculty ratio.

All students complete the General Education curriculum, a cross-section of courses that forms the intellectual foundation of a Temple education. But every student's experience at Temple is a unique and transformative one.

Some students pursue common interests in Living and Learning Communities. Academically qualified students gain extra intellectual challenges through the Honors Program. Temple's study-abroad programs offer opportunities to take learning around the world. Students might find their niche earning course credit while running Temple's cooperative, locavore café. The Hatchery is the Tyler School of Art's design incubator, where entrepreneurial students transform projects into real products.

Students have opportunities to work directly with renowned faculty on research and creative projects and present at professional conferences, publish in peer-reviewed journals, and premiere music and dance at venues around the globe.

A degree from Temple doesn't simply fill a transcript or create lines on a resume. Temple empowers students to spark change in themselves and prepares them to charge forward into the world.

Academic Facilities

Whether in a high-tech classroom or the University's Science Education and Research Center (SERC), Temple students learn in world-class facilities. At SERC, which is home to sixty-eight research and teaching labs and leading-edge technologies, students work with faculty on real-world projects, making the connection between understanding science and putting advanced research techniques into practice.

At the TECH Center—among the largest student computing labs in the country—students can collaborate in breakout rooms, edit video in a specialized lab, get assistance from the 24-hour help desk, or work on one of 700 computers. There are more than 100 other computer labs on campus, 3,600 student workstations, and 450 technology-enabled classrooms.

With the equivalent of more than 4 million bound volumes and an extensive special collection of rare books and archives, Temple's libraries rank among the top research libraries in North America. In spring 2016, the University broke ground for a new, state-of-the-art library that will feature a robotic book retrieval system and spaces devoted to traditional library activities, such as study and reading, as well as to technology-mediated activities, including data visualization and 3-D printing.

Costs

Tuition and fees for the 2016–17 academic year were $15,384 for Pennsylvania residents and $26,376 for out-of-state residents (tuition rates vary by major). Room and board for the academic year were about $11,298.

Financial Aid

Temple offers a multitude of options to help make college more affordable. A variety of scholarships, grants, loans, and work-study programs are available; 71 percent of first-year students receive need-based financial aid, and 43 percent receive academic scholarships. Four-year academic merit scholarships for talented freshmen range from $3,000 to full tuition, and several include summer stipends for research, internships, and study abroad.

More than 93 percent of the class of 2020 committed to Temple's Fly in 4 program, an innovative plan which helps students limit their debt and enter the workforce sooner by graduating in four years.

Faculty

Starting in their first semester, students at Temple have contact with faculty at the forefront of their fields—winners of prestigious teaching and research awards, scientists doing groundbreaking research, and working artists who exhibit all over the world.

Temple faculty members are also known for their practical experience—a marketing class may be led by a successful entrepreneur or music lessons given by a member of the Philadelphia Orchestra. Marine biologists, newspaper editors, published authors, practicing architects, and healthcare professionals all bring their expertise to the classroom.

And the roster of outstanding faculty members is growing. On average, Temple has hired 57 new faculty members per year for the past decade, from leading universities and research centers including Princeton University, MIT, and the Cleveland Clinic.

Admission Requirements

The Temple Option is an admissions path for determined and tenacious students who have the ability to succeed in college but may not perform well on standardized tests. Students can opt to submit SAT or ACT scores, or they can choose the Temple Option and respond to short-answer questions.

For freshman admissions, high-school grades (quality of courses and grade trends), standardized test scores or the Temple Option responses, and other factors are considered. Temple uses a sliding scale rather than absolute cutoffs. SAT subject tests and personal interviews are not required. Official copies of high-school transcripts and standardized test scores must be sent directly to the admissions office.

The deadline for spring admission is November 1. Temple offers rolling admissions and early action decision plans for the fall semester. Those interested in early action must submit a completed application by November 1 and will receive notification by mid-January. The rolling admissions deadline is February 1; freshman decisions begin in early fall. Temple's admissions process is holistic; every aspect of the student's academic history is considered. Typically, students with a B+ average or better in a strong college-prep curriculum in grades 9–12 and in the top 30 percent of their graduating classes are accepted. For students submitting test scores, the average SAT score in 2016 was 1240, and the average ACT composite was 27.

The application fee is $55; most students apply online through Temple or the Common Application.

Applicants are considered transfer students if they have attempted 15 or more college-level credits after high school. If this is not the case, they should apply as freshman students. In admissions decisions, careful consideration is given to the quality of a student's program, number of credits earned, and GPA. The average GPA for new transfer students is 3.13 (on a 4.0 scale). The architecture, nursing, and pharmacy programs have higher minimum GPA requirements. For most programs, transfer students must complete the application process by June 1 for the fall semester or by November 1 for the spring semester. The fall priority deadline for the health information management and nursing programs is February 1. SAT or ACT scores are not required if an applicant has earned at least 15 college-level credits.

Application and Information

A completed file contains an application form accompanied by a nonrefundable application fee, a secondary-school transcript (sent by the student's school), and SAT or ACT scores or responses to the Temple Option questions.

For additional information, students may contact:

Office of Undergraduate Admissions
Temple University
Philadelphia, Pennsylvania 19122-6096
United States
Phone: 215-204-7200
888-340-2222 (toll-free)
E-mail: askanowl@temple.edu
Website: nextstop.temple.edu
Facebook: facebook.com/TempleU
Twitter: @admissionsTU
Instagram: @admissionsTU
Snapchat: @admissionsTU

At Temple University, students share an uncommon drive.

TRINE UNIVERSITY

ANGOLA, INDIANA

★ To read more about this school, visit http://petersons.to/trineuniversity

TRINE UNIVERSITY

The University

Trine University has a reputation for producing work-ready graduates who are in demand, as proven by Trine's 99.3 percent job placement rate. The placement rate, along with the well-maintained campus, welcoming community, and opportunities to excel in and out of the classroom are just some of the reasons many students choose Trine.

Students can expect a well-rounded college experience with challenging courses taught by engaged, experienced faculty members, eager to help students excel. Small class size and a 14:1 student to faculty ratio are conducive to personalized attention and optimal classroom performance.

Trine is private, independent, and coeducational, offering associate, baccalaureate, and doctoral degrees to students in more than 35 programs, including engineering, mathematics, forensic science, pre–physical therapy, business, education, psychology, exercise science, criminal justice, and sport management.

Trine has invested more than $155 million in campus upgrades since 2000. In fall 2017, the university will open the new Thunder Ice Arena, which will be the home to its new men's and women's hockey teams as well as student and community activities. The new MTI Center, including basketball courts, a six-lane bowling alley, and esports arena, will begin hosting athletic, student and entertainment events in January 2018.

In fall 2016, Trine set an institutional record for enrollment for the third straight year. Trine has 4,998 students with more than 2,000 on the main campus.

The student body at Trine breaks down as follows:

- Academic averages for the freshmen class include a 3.45 GPA, 1055 SAT, and 23 ACT. Fifteen percent were in the top 10 percent of their high school graduating class and 46 percent were in the top 25 percent.
- Students represent 33 states and 20 countries.
- Engineering is the most popular program with 47 percent of students enrolled in the major.
- More than 600 students are involved in NCAA Division III athletics.

The 450-acre campus offers an inviting, safe, and vibrant atmosphere that complements the seriousness and determination with which Trine students pursue their academic goals. Trine has more than 60 academic, cultural, service, and Greek organizations and will have 24 varsity athletic teams for men and women in 2017.

Trine is a member of National Collegiate Athletic Association (NCAA) Division III and the Michigan Intercollegiate Athletic Association (MIAA), the nation's oldest athletic conference. Men's sports include baseball, basketball, cross-country, football, golf, lacrosse, soccer, tennis, track, and wrestling. Women's sports include basketball, cross-country, golf, lacrosse, soccer, softball, tennis, track, and volleyball. In fall 2017, the university will add men's and women's hockey teams as well as esports, women's triathlon, and bowling. Many students also participate on intramural sports teams.

Trine students excel on the field and in and out of the classroom.

- Chemical engineering seniors have won the American Institute of Chemical Engineers national individual design competition five times and have won the national design safety award numerous times.
- Trine's Tau Alpha Omicron chapter of the American Criminal Justice Association annually wins regional and national awards for marksmanship, crime scene investigation, and physical agility.
- In 2014, Trine's softball team made history by earning its first trip to the NCAA Division III National Championships. The team has appeared in the NCAA postseason every year since 2008 and hosted its first Super Regional championship in 2016.
- In 2015–16, Trine's Jared Holmquist was named the CoSIDA Academic All-American of the Year for Division III men's basketball, one of the highest scholar-athlete honors in the nation.
- Trine's track and field program has sent at least two participants to national championship meets since the beginning of the 2013–14 season, with an All-American honoree in every indoor and outdoor season since that date.
- During the 2015–16 school year, 47 Thunder student-athletes were recognized on all-conference teams. Trine boasted 132 student-athletes on the Michigan Intercollegiate Athletic Association honor roll for having above a 3.5 grade-point average and lettering in a varsity sport.

Location

Trine is in Angola, Indiana, the heart of northeast Indiana's scenic lake resort region, halfway between Chicago and Cleveland. Just a 45-minute drive from Indiana's second-largest city, Fort Wayne, Trine offers the safety and ease of a small-town environment, near some of the nation's most vital cities.

Majors and Degrees

The Allen School of Engineering & Technology awards Bachelor of Science degrees in biomedical, chemical and bioprocess, civil, computer, electrical, mechanical, and software engineering and design engineering technology. Minors are offered in aeronautical, biomedical, bioprocess, energy, environmental, metallurgical, plastics, software, and structural engineering.

The Ketner School of Business awards Bachelor of Science in business administration degrees with majors in accounting, business administration, golf management, management, marketing, and sport management.

The Franks School of Education awards Bachelor of Science degrees in elementary, health and physical, mathematics, science, and social studies education. In fall 2015 the school began offering a dual licensure in elementary education and special education/mild intervention K–6, and in 2016 the school added English education.

The Jannen School of Arts and Sciences awards Bachelor of Arts degrees with majors in communication, criminal justice, English, general studies (pre-legal and self-designated), informatics, mathematics, and psychology.

The Rinker-Ross School of Health Sciences offers a Bachelor of Science degree in biochemistry, biology, chemistry, exercise science, forensic science, and pre–physical therapy and pre-medical professional tracks, and a doctoral degree in physical therapy. The school plans to begin offering a Master of Science in physician assistant studies program beginning in August 2018.

The College of Graduate and Professional Studies, with eight education centers in Indiana and Michigan, awards associate, bachelor's, and master's degrees in 10 programs. Graduate programs include a Master of Business Administration and Master of Science degrees in leadership, criminal justice, engineering management, and information studies.

Academic Programs

Students learn from professionals with advanced degrees and industry expertise, and get hands-on experience in laboratories stocked with state-of-the-art equipment through internships and co-ops. About 90 percent of Trine students complete an internship, co-op, or other experiential learning.

Trine University is accredited by the Higher Learning Commission and a member of the North Central Association (www.hlcommission.org; phone: 312-263-0456). Trine's programs in chemical engineering, civil engineering, computer engineering, electrical engineering, and mechanical engineering are accredited by the Engineering Accreditation Commission of ABET (111 Market Place, Suite 1050, Baltimore, Maryland 21202-4012; phone: 410-347-7700). All teacher preparation programs are accredited by the Council for the Accreditation of Educator Preparation (www.caepnet.org) and the Indiana Department Education/Office of Educator Licensing and Development (www.doe.ingov/licensing). The Ketner School of Business, Bachelor of Science in business administration program is accredited by the Accreditation Council for Business Schools and

Programs (www.acbsp.org). Associate degree programs in accounting and business administration are also accredited.

Effective July 29, 2014, the Doctor of Physical Therapy Program at Trine University has been granted candidate for accreditation status by the Commission on Accreditation in Physical Therapy Education (1111 North Fairfax Street, Alexandria, Virginia, 22314; phone: 703-706-3245; e-mail: accreditation@apta.org). Candidate for accreditation is a pre-accreditation status of affiliation with the Commission on Accreditation in Physical Therapy Education that indicates that the program may matriculate students in technical/professional courses and that the program is progressing toward accreditation. Candidate for accreditation is not an accreditation status nor does it assure eventual accreditation.

Enhanced Learning

Trine's Innovation One provides opportunities for students to work with business and industry and even manage startup companies. Innovation One, located in the Jim and Joan Bock Center for Innovation and Biomedical Engineering, is an incubator for creativity, invention, and design that enhances education through experiential learning and fosters economic development for supporting new and existing businesses.

Off-Campus Programs

Trine's Employment Resource Center works with many diverse companies to provide co-op and internship opportunities. Semesters of classroom study are alternated with professional work experience, which can give students a competitive edge in the job market and offset college expenses. Often, co-ops and internships launch careers as they lead to full-time employment.

Academic Facilities

The John G. Best Hall of Science, home of the Jannen School of Arts & Sciences, contains classrooms and science laboratories. A $6.6 million, 26,000 square-foot addition opened in January 2017, housing seven laboratories, twelve offices and group study spaces.

The Jim and Joan Bock Center for Innovation and Biomedical Engineering houses laboratories to support the Allen School of Engineering & Technology and Innovation One (i1), an incubator for technology and business. Experiential learning for students in all majors is also available through i1.

The Thomas L. Fawick Hall of Engineering, home to the Allen School of Engineering & Technology, features classrooms and laboratories, all providing student access to technology from day one.

The Perry T. Ford Memorial Building, home of the Ketner School of Business, boasts technology-rich classrooms and a design that mimics a contemporary business setting.

The T. Furth Center for Performing Arts is home to Trine's music program and the Ryan Concert Hall is the venue for a variety of concerts, which include university instrumental and vocal ensembles, as well as nationally known entertainers.

The Rick L. and Vicki L. James University Center is the hub for student activity, including a library stocked with plenty of computers, Fabiani Theatre, WEAX radio station, fitness center, and the newly expanded Whitney Commons dining hall.

William D. Shambaugh Hall, home of the Franks School of Education, offers a juvenile literature and school curriculum collection, kits, and audio-visual resource materials, as well as workspace and materials to support education students.

The Charles and Nancy Taylor Hall of Humanities houses the Department of Humanities & Communication as well as classrooms, the Wells Gallery, the Humanities Institute, the Fine Arts Library, and Wells Theater, home of the university's drama club.

Costs

Tuition for the academic year (two semesters) in 2017–18 is $31,080 ($33,560 for engineering). Room and standard meal plan (nineteen meals per week) for the academic year cost $9,300 (double occupancy).

Financial Aid

Financial aid may be awarded in the form of scholarships, grants, loans, or campus employment. Trine requires the Free Application for Federal Student Aid (FAFSA) and recommends its submission by March 1.

Trine stands out in this area because:

- Ninety-six percent of undergraduate students receive some form of financial aid.
- More than $25 million is awarded in institutional aid.
- Average financial aid per student is $27,000.
- The school has been recognized for graduating students with the least amount of debt.

Faculty

Trine has a full-time faculty of 97 members; most have doctoral degrees and professional experience.

Student Government

The student senate is organized for the purpose of providing funding and formulating policies for campus organizations. Representatives to the senate are elected by each class.

Admission Requirements

Graduation from an approved high school or equivalent preparation is required for admission. Selection is made without regard to race, religion, or gender. Applicants are required to take the ACT or SAT prior to approval for admission. Applicants' high school grade point average and class rank are also important factors for admission.

Graduates of community or junior colleges and students who have attended other colleges and universities are eligible for transfer. Counselors work closely with those who wish to transfer to ensure a smooth transition to Trine. Credit may be allowed in subjects that parallel Trine programs, provided the student earned a grade of C or better in the course.

Application and Information

Trine University's online application is free and available at www.trine.edu. The university admits applicants on the basis of scholastic achievement and academic potential. Admission decisions are made on a rolling basis. Applicants are notified of their status within two weeks of receipt of their application, high school record, and test scores. Transfer students must also submit an official copy of their college transcript(s).

Interested students and their parents are encouraged to visit the campus. Arrangements can be made by contacting the Office of Admission.

For additional information, students should call or write:

Office of Admission
Trine University
One University Avenue
Angola, Indiana 46703-1764
Phone: 260-665-4100
800-347-4878
E-mail: admit@trine.edu
Website: www.trine.edu
www.facebook.com/trineadmissions
www.youtube/trineuniversity

Trine University provides a safe and comfortable environment for learning and intellectual growth as well as for athletics and diverse activities.

TRUMAN STATE UNIVERSITY

KIRKSVILLE, MISSOURI

★ To read more about this school, visit http://petersons.to/trumanstateuniversity

The University

Truman has forged a national reputation for offering an exceptionally high-quality undergraduate education at a competitive price. For the twentieth consecutive year, *U.S. News & World Report* has ranked Truman as the number one public institution in the Midwest offering bachelor's and master's degrees. In addition, Truman is recognized by *Consumer's Digest* as the number-one best value public college.

A commitment to student achievement and learning is at the core of everything Truman does. This commitment is evidenced by faculty and staff members who recognize the importance of providing students with the opportunity to interact with their professors both in and out of the classroom. With class sizes averaging around 20 students and 90 percent having fewer than 40 students, scholars find ample opportunity to ask questions of professors as well as interact with their multitalented peers. Truman's academic environment is enhanced by a student body that achieves at remarkable levels. The 2016 freshman class had an ACT midrange of 25 to 30 and 90 percent had high school GPAs of 3.25 or higher. In addition, numerous opportunities exist for students to engage in undergraduate research. Each year, approximately 1,200 students work alongside professors on University research projects, gaining confidence, knowledge, and skill in their chosen disciplines. The University offers these students the opportunity to present the results of their research at the annual Student Research Conference. In addition, selected students travel to the National Undergraduate Research Symposium to present their research findings. Undergraduate research stipends are also available.

Students wishing to attend Truman to become a teacher must first complete a bachelor's degree in an academic discipline and then apply for admission into professional study at the master's level to obtain a Master of Arts in Education (M.A.E). Through this program, certification can be achieved for elementary education, middle school education, secondary education, and special education.

With more than 240 University organizations available to students, encompassing service, Greek, honorary, professional, religious, social, political, and recreational influences, Truman students have tremendous opportunities to become involved while enrolled at the University. Truman's Student Activities Board provides special guests such as Kid President, comic acts such as Vanessa Bayer and Adam Devine, and musical artists like Andy Grammer, Lee Brice, and Misterwives. Admission to all varsity athletic events is free to students; Truman theater productions, and Lyceum Series events are offered for $5 per show. Recent theater productions have included *The Woman in Black*, *Seussical*, and *Hamlet*.

Location

Truman is located in Kirksville, a town of approximately 17,000 nestled in the northeast corner of Missouri. The town square, located within walking distance of the Truman campus, provides a connection to Kirksville's past. A multiplex movie theater is located on the town square; local merchants operate specialized gift, book, and clothing stores; and several restaurants offer a wide selection of American and international cuisine.

The Kirksville Aquatic Center is a great place to have fun and get fit. This indoor/outdoor pool complex offers a variety of activities, classes, and programs designed to appeal to people of all ages. The complex includes a six-lane indoor swimming pool, perfect for swimming, relaxing, or playing a game of water-basketball. The outdoor pool is designed with a zero-depth entry, a 1-meter diving board, and four 25-yard outdoor lap lanes as well as a 20-foot water slide.

The northeast region of Missouri is also home to Thousand Hills State Park. A 3,252-acre state park and 573-acre lake for camping, hiking, biking, fishing, swimming, boating, and waterskiing is located within 10 minutes of the Truman campus.

Majors and Degrees

Undergraduate degrees offered by Truman include the Bachelor of Arts (B.A.), Bachelor of Science (B.S.), Bachelor of Music: Performance (B.M.), Bachelor of Fine Arts (B.F.A.), and Bachelor of Science in Nursing (B.S.N.). Truman offers more than forty areas of study in the following disciplines: accounting, agricultural science, athletic training, art, art history, biology, business administration, chemistry, classics, communication, communication disorders, computer science, creative writing, economics, English, exercise science, French, German, health science, history, interdisciplinary studies, justice systems, linguistics, mathematics, music, music: performance, nursing, philosophy and religion, physics, political science, psychology, Romance languages, Russian, sociology/anthropology, Spanish, statistics, and theatre.

Professional paths include but are not limited to dentistry, engineering, law, medicine, optometry, pharmacy, physical therapy, and veterinary medicine.

Academic Programs

Truman is Missouri's premier liberal arts and sciences university and the only highly selective public institution in the state. The Liberal Studies Program is the heart of Truman's curriculum and is intended to serve as a foundation for all major programs of study offered by the University. Truman's mission is to offer an exemplary undergraduate education, grounded in the liberal arts and sciences, in the context of a public institution of higher learning. Truman seeks to provide the kind of education in the liberal arts and sciences that has historically been offered only at private colleges. The program is a blend of two intellectual traditions in higher education, one that emphasizes the traditional thought and learning of the culture, as reflected in the classical works produced by it, and the other that emphasizes personal investigation and freedom of discovery. The philosophy behind the Liberal Studies Program is based on a commitment that Truman has made to provide students with essential skills needed for lifelong learning, breadth across the traditional liberal arts and sciences through exposure to various discipline-based modes of inquiry, and interconnecting perspectives that stress interdisciplinary thinking and integration as well as linkage to other cultures and experiences. All students graduating from Truman must complete 63 or more credit hours in liberal arts and sciences courses.

Truman also offers an especially challenging Honors Scholar Program. This program provides students with the opportunity to select the most rigorous honors courses to satisfy the liberal arts component of their respective programs. Students who successfully complete this program benefit from an even richer academic experience and also receive special recognition at graduation and distinction on their academic transcripts. Departmental honors are also available in several disciplines.

Off-Campus Programs

Each year, approximately 400 Truman students participate in enriching and life-changing study-abroad experiences. Truman's own study-abroad programs, combined with programs offered through Truman's membership in the College Consortium for International Studies, International Student Exchange Program, AustraLearn, and the Council on International Educational Exchange, provide students with study-abroad opportunities in more than sixty countries worldwide, including Australia, China, England, Finland, France, Italy, Russia, Spain, and Thailand.

In cooperation with the Washington Center for Internships and Academic Seminars, Truman offers a wide variety of experiential internships in Washington, D.C. Included are work-experience opportunities in such areas as public administration, the fine and performing arts, foreign affairs/diplomacy, government affairs, criminal justice, international relations, health and human services, environmental policy, business administration, and communications as well as other areas. Placement sites include nonprofit groups, media organizations, the State Department, Congress, museums, and much more.

Truman requires internships in education, health science, and exercise science and annually offers internship opportunities with the Missouri State Legislature. In recent years, students have completed internships with United States senators, the governor of Missouri, business and industry managers, zoos, broadcast and print media professionals, accountants, advertising agencies, physical therapists, musicians, artists, and the United States Supreme Court. In the 2015 fall semester, Truman had three interns at the White House.

Academic Facilities

The Truman campus is beautifully situated on an expanse of 140 acres near downtown Kirksville. Featured among the forty facilities on campus is Pickler Memorial Library. This 460,116-volume facility provides a state-of-the-art library resource for students and faculty members alike. Materials not available in Pickler Memorial Library can be obtained through the Interlibrary Loan Office and MOBIUS.

Recent improvements to campus facilities include the expansion of the Pershing Building with the new health sciences wing. Facility improvements included the new Fontaine C. Piper Movement Analysis Lab, a human performance lab, an expanded clinic for communication disorders, athletic training rooms, and a brand-new nursing simulation center. The renovations to the Student Union Building included an expanded Center for Student Involvement, new technology, mural restoration, and a completely renovated university bookstore.

Truman has been measuring its energy consumption and is implementing appropriate measures to lower it. Solar panels are located on five different buildings across campus. During the 2014–15 academic year, Truman saw a reduction of 113.5 tons of CO_2 emissions producing 108 kW of useable energy from these panels. Efforts to manage the consumption of natural resources is also a priority and the University is proud to have been named a Tree Campus USA site by the Arbor Day Foundation.

Residence halls provide comfortable and enriching living environments for students. Most of the halls have been renovated within the last five years. All residence halls offer lounges, kitchenettes, laundry facilities, high-speed internet (including wireless), cable TV, and many other amenities. Students can eat in dining halls or in the food court–style dining in the Student Union Building, which was renovated and reopened in fall 2016.

Additional campus facilities include a student media center with a TV studio, a radio station, print media production facilities, a biofeedback laboratory, an organic chemistry lab, an analytical chemistry lab, an observatory, a greenhouse, a 5,000-seat football stadium, a soccer field, tennis courts, softball and baseball diamonds, a 3,000-seat arena with three basketball courts, an Olympic-size swimming pool, a multicultural affairs center, a writing center, a student success center, and a career center.

Costs

Tuition for Missouri residents for the 2016–17 academic year was $7,152; out-of-state tuition was $13,636. Room and board totals for both Missouri residents and nonresidents average $8,558. Additional fees included a $325 freshman orientation fee, an annual $90 activities fee, a $54 Student Health Center fee, an annual $116 athletic fee, a $34 technology fee, a $10 environmental sustainability fee, a $130 parking fee for those with a vehicle, and the costs of books and personal expenses.

Financial Aid

Truman offers automatic scholarships ranging from $500 to $5,000. Competitive scholarship awards vary from $500 up to full tuition, room and board, plus a $4,000 study-abroad stipend. The application for admission also serves as the application for the automatic and competitive scholarship programs.

Several scholarships are awarded to students for excellence in music, theatre, debate/forensics, or art. These scholarships are available for instrumental or vocal music; acting or dramatic production; speech or debate; and studio art or art history. Of special interest to piano students is the Truman Piano Fellowship Competition.

The National Collegiate Athletic Association and the University authorize a limited number of grants to outstanding athletes. The value of this aid may vary with each individual recipient.

Truman accepts the Free Application for Federal Student Aid (FAFSA) and participates in all Federal Title IV financial aid programs. Financial aid estimates are available upon request.

Faculty

Truman State University is committed to teaching the academically talented undergraduate student. The University has 332 full-time faculty members and 66 part-time faculty members. Of these, 98 percent teach undergraduates and graduate teaching assistants only teach 1 percent of classes. Most major graduate institutions are represented among the Truman faculty, including Harvard, Princeton, Yale, Brown, Cornell, Oxford, and the Sorbonne. The student-faculty ratio at Truman is 16:1.

Student Government

Student Senate is the official elected governing body of the Student Association, representing approximately 5,800 students. Its mission is to represent the views of the Student Association in the formulation of the University policy through legislation and membership on all University committees; to facilitate communication and mutual understanding among the Student Association, faculty and staff members, and administration; to maintain a cohesive vision for the future of the University; and to actively participate in the fulfillment of the University's mission as an exemplary public liberal arts and sciences university.

Admission Requirements

Admission to Truman is competitive. Each applicant is evaluated for admission based upon academic and cocurricular record, ACT or SAT results, and the admission essay. Truman requires the following high school core: 4 units of English, 3 units of mathematics (4 recommended), 3 units of social studies/history, 3 units of natural science, 1 unit of fine arts, and 2 units of the same foreign language.

Application and Information

The priority application date for admission is December 1. Students who have applied by this date are considered for all applicable competitive scholarships. Applications are processed on a rolling basis. There is no application fee. Students may apply online at the University's website. Truman also accepts the Common Application.

For further information or to schedule a campus visit, students should contact:

Admission Office
Ruth W. Towne Museum and Visitors Center
Truman State University
100 East Normal
Kirksville, Missouri 63501
Phone: 660-785-4114
800-892-7792
Fax: 660-785-7456
E-mail: admissions@truman.edu
Website: http://admissions.truman.edu

Pickler Memorial Library is a state-of-the-art resource for the whole campus.

COLLEGE CLOSE-UPS

UNIVERSITY OF CALIFORNIA SAN DIEGO

UC San Diego

SAN DIEGO, CALIFORNIA

The University

Situated on a sunny cliff overlooking the Pacific Ocean, the University of California San Diego is a place that has reimagined the traditional path to knowledge. Established in 1960, UC San Diego is a public research university that has been shaped by exceptional scholars who aren't afraid to make waves—from creating the world's first algae-based surfboard to developing wireless health-monitoring tattoos and printing 3-D blood vessels.

The 1,200-acre campus is located in the La Jolla neighborhood of San Diego, Calif., in the heart of one of the most densely concentrated innovation hubs in the nation. The campus is consistently ranked among the top 10 best public universities in the nation and top 15 in the world for research, teaching, public service, and post-graduation career prospects.

UC San Diego academic programs, taught by highly-regarded scholars, prepare students to stand out and lead change. The university is organized into six undergraduate residential colleges, three graduate schools, and two professional medical schools. The campus is also home to Scripps Institution of Oceanography, one of the first centers dedicated to ocean, earth, and atmospheric science research; and UC San Diego Health, the region's only academic health system.

Over the last 50 years, 16 Nobel laureates have taught on campus. Over 160 current faculty are members of one or more of the prestigious national academies, while numerous others have garnered such awards as the McArthur Fellowship, National Medal of Science, Pulitzer Prize, Fields Medal, and Academy Award.

UC San Diego's more than 175,000 alumni include National Medal of Science honoree J. Craig Venter, one of the first to sequence the human genome; Kate Rubins, NASA astronaut who recently conducted human health studies in space; Nathan East, one of the most recorded bassists in history; Nick Woodman, founder and CEO of GoPro; and Guy "Bud" Tribble, who managed the original Macintosh software development team.

UC San Diego is committed to creating a climate of respect and understanding. Through innovative programs, the campus opens doors to higher education for first generation students and those from underserved communities. The university was recently named first in the nation among peer institutions for enrolling and graduating the most low-income students. In addition, UC San Diego graduates the largest percentage of women with STEM degrees, and has been named one of the top 10 most LGBTQ-friendly universities.

Students are invited to engage in open dialogue, develop leadership skills, and learn about social issues at six campus community centers. In addition, students can take part in numerous cultural events and celebrations of diversity, from Raza Awareness Week to the annual UC San Diego Powwow and Martin Luther King Jr. Parade and Day of Service.

Majors and Degrees

The campus offers more than 100 undergraduate degree programs spanning five academic divisions, as well as master's and doctoral degree programs in 60 academic departments. A complete list of undergraduate degree programs can be found at http://ucsd.edu/academics-detail.html.

Academic Programs

The college system at UC San Diego is a unique university structure that personalizes the delivery of services to undergraduate students. The colleges are residential neighborhoods on campus with their own residence facilities, staff, traditions and general education requirements. Every UC San Diego undergraduate is assigned to one of six colleges when they are admitted to UC San Diego.

Furthermore, college assignments are NOT based on major. Students may select from the full range of available majors regardless of College assignment.

A student-centered university, UC San Diego offers supplemental learning, tutoring, and career development programs to prepare students to thrive academically. Through services offered at the Teaching + Learning Commons, students develop transferable skills, participate in peer-facilitated study groups, and are matched with experiential learning projects.

In addition, nearly a dozen makerspaces and incubators offer resources, training, and mentorship opportunities to help students launch their big ideas. At The Basement, students gain business guidance and funding ideas from alumni and industry mentors. For hands-on projects, the EnVision Arts and Engineering Maker Studio contains tools to design, fabricate, and prototype, including 3-D printers, welding stations, and laser cutters.

Students apply their learning outside the classroom through faculty-mentored research, service learning projects, study abroad and professional internships. Undergraduates can explore opportunities through the Research Experience and Applied Learning Portal, get matched with real-world training opportunities through the Academic Internship Program, and become immersed in the culture of another country through the Study Abroad Office.

Costs

For the 2017–18 academic years, tuition and fees for California residents is $14,230; nonresidents pay a supplemental tuition of $28,014. The estimated cost of on-campus housing and meals is $13,254. Books and supplies are estimated at $1,198.

Financial Aid

For prospective students and their families, budgeting, costs and how to pay for college can seem complicated. UC San Diego offers information and advising to help students understand the big picture and the bottom line. Students may utilize a wide array of grants, loans, scholarships, veteran's benefits, work-study, and other means to finance their education.

Student Life

Life at UC San Diego is far from ordinary. The university was named among the top academic surfing schools in the nation by The Inertia and features a competitive surf team, classes on the physics of surfing as well as opportunities to learn how to ride the salty swells.

When students aren't immersed in the sea, they unwind at one of dozens of campuswide events, including Triton Fest, a month-long fall kickoff experience that has featured a haunted trail, go-kart racing, and outdoor movie night; Winter Game Fest, the largest student-run gaming festival on the West Coast; and the Sun God Festival, a day-long carnival and concert.

The university features 600 student organizations on campus, ranging from academic-focused and pre-professional groups to social and cultural clubs as well as spiritual and service groups. There are also more than 40 Greek organizations focused on academic excellence, service and leadership. In addition, UC San Diego students are very active in their community through a number of co-curricular community service programs; more than 90 student organizations have a primary focus on service. On average, nearly 20,000 UC San Diego students complete more than 3 million hours of change-making community service each year.

UC San Diego's Triton Athletics includes 23 competitive sports teams, which have garnered 30 national championship titles. Facilities include a 5,000-seat arena, ballpark, aquatic center with two Olympic-sized pools, and a state-of-the-art athletic training center. Students can also take part in 30 intramural sports leagues, choose from hundreds of recreation classes, and venture into the wild with the campus's Outback Adventures.

All UC San Diego undergraduates can find their community thanks to the college system. Each of the university's six colleges have distinct neighborhoods, traditions, and educational requirements. Students bond over shared classes and annual events, from the summertime watermelon drop—a fruity physics experiment—to the 1960s-inspired Muirstock concert and the annual chocolate festival.

In addition, transfer students can choose to live in the Village Apartments, comprised of 13 buildings dedicated to transfer student housing, including two high rises with ocean views; while graduate students have the option to reside in one of six housing communities on or nearby campus, with amenities for couples and students with children.

Admission Requirements

UC San Diego looks for students at the freshman level who are well-prepared to succeed in a rigorous and challenging academic setting. Admission is highly competitive and applicants must exceed the minimum requirements. Every application, including the personal insight questions, is reviewed by a minimum of two individuals.

In addition to the 14 factors that are detailed on the University of California admissions website, freshman applicants must earn a high school diploma (or equivalent); complete a rigorous array of college preparatory classes with a C grade or better (detailed on the university's website); earn a GPA of 3.0 or better (California residents) or 3.4 or better (nonresidents); submit scores from either ACT Plus Writing, SAT Reasoning Test with critical reading, math, and writing; answers to UC San Diego's Personal Insight Questions; and a portfolio for students who want to major in history, literature, music, philosophy, theatre and dance, and visual arts. Meeting these requirements does not guarantee admission. Students admitted to UC San Diego exceed UC admission requirements.

Application and Information

The University of California application (available online) must be submitted by November 30. In December, applicants will receive an email that confirms receipt of their application. In January, applicants will receive instructions on how to log into UC San Diego's application status portal. The FAFSA or California Dream Act application must be filed by March 2. Freshman admission decisions will be posted by the end of March.

UC San Diego receives more than 80,000 freshman applications each year. Successful applicants must exceed minimum UC admission requirements. Enrollment goals are established annually. The campus does not select students on the basis of academic major or choice of UC San Diego undergraduate college.

For more information, prospective students may contact:

Office of Admissions
University of California San Diego
9500 Gilman Drive
La Jolla, California 92093
Phone: 858-534-4831
Fax: 858-534-5629
E-mail:
Website: www.ucsd.edu

UC San Diego Geisel Library

COLLEGE CLOSE-UPS

UNIVERSITY OF COLORADO AT BOULDER

BOULDER, COLORADO

★ For more information, visit http://petersons.to/uofcoloradoboulder

The University

The University of Colorado Boulder (CU Boulder) is a dynamic community of scholars and learners situated on one of the most spectacular college campuses in the country. CU Boulder is one of thirty-four U.S. public institutions belonging to the prestigious Association of American Universities (AAU) and has an established reputation for world-class teaching, research and service to the global society.

At the cornerstone of the university experience are CU Boulder's innovative academic programs, hands-on opportunities, and rigorous course work that will prepare students for a complex global society. Within the supportive learning community, students will interact with world-renowned faculty—which include Nobel laureates, MacArthur Genius Grant fellows, U.S. Professor of the Year awardees, and National Medal of Science winners—who listen, question and help students refine their ideas to develop a broad understanding of the world, strong leadership skills, and an enhanced ability to think critically.

CU Boulder offers more than 90 undergraduate and graduate programs; 84 bachelor's majors; 33 concurrent bachelor's/master's degree programs; more 30 minors and 25 certificate programs; 11 research institutes and nearly 90 research centers. More than 2,000 undergraduate students are directly involved in faculty research.

With hands-on experience, world-class education and the ability to think critically, globally, and creatively, CU Boulder graduates benefit from a strong salary potential, high employment rates and the opportunity to find and excel in a career they are passionate about.

Location

Students at CU Boulder get to live in spectacular surroundings and learn in a campus environment of extraordinary opportunities.

The city of Boulder is a fitting home for this institution. It's known as the smartest city in the nation (MarketWatch, 2015), the number-one city in which to start a business (*Forbes*, 2015), the second-most innovative tech hub in the U.S. (*Forbes*, 2015), and the top metro area for female entrepreneurship (*Fast Company*, 2015). The city is known as one of the best places to live because of its beautiful setting, its 45,000 acres of open space, and its lively atmosphere.

Home to approximately 100,000 residents, Boulder has a mild, dry climate with more than 300 days of sunshine per year. Over 300 miles of bike lanes, bike paths, bike routes, designated shoulders and paths in and around Boulder, as well as a convenient bus system, provide excellent options for getting around town.

Majors and Degrees

CU Boulder has eight colleges, schools, and programs. Amongst them, CU Boulder offers more than 3,800 academic courses across 150 fields of study, enabling students to create an academic experience that is unique.

College of Arts and Sciences: The oldest and largest college at CU Boulder and intellectual core of the university, conducting research, scholarship, creative work, and education in more than 60 fields. CU Boulder's research generates new knowledge, solving some of the world's most critical problems. The College offers 50 majors, 25 minors, and 10 certificate programs; there are 10 different residential academic programs available to students during their first year of studies.

College of Engineering and Applied Science: The top-ranked engineering programs in Colorado and the entire Rocky Mountain region are found in this college, with a full range of degree programs that emphasize hands-on, active learning, and a tradition of research excellence. Engineers Without Borders began at CU in 2000, and has since grown to 206 chapters in 34 countries.

College of Media, Communication and Information: Students learn and prepare to be leaders in the ever-changing information society. CMCI students and faculty think across boundaries, innovate around emerging problems, and create culture that transcends convention. CU offers six student media outlets and four affiliated centers and labs.

College of Music: CU Boulder is the home of one of the country's top public music programs. A talented and active faculty of musicians, composers, and scholars teach an impressive series of programs, ranging from performance to music theory. The college offers 7 degree plans and more than 23 fields of study. The College of Music's library contains more than 150,000 volumes, scores, recordings, and periodicals.

Leeds School of Business: Students can earn undergraduate, master's and doctoral degrees from the top-ranked Colorado business school, also one of the best business schools in the Rocky Mountain and Midwest regions. Leeds has several points of pride: 88 percent of internships are paid; 94 percent of 2015 graduates were in a job within three months of graduation; and about 200 students annually take part in the Leeds First-Year Global Experience program (offered in 10 countries); and eight global initiative programs give students the opportunity to travel and learn about international business.

School of Education: CU Boulder is a proud national leader in the field of education, working professionally with colleagues and communities to deliver outstanding undergraduate and graduate programs for classroom teachers and future scholars alike. More than half of the college's alumni teach in Colorado public schools. Students log many hours of field experience and in turn, 98.5 percent of teacher licensure graduates are employed or in graduate school within a year.

Program in Environmental Design (ENVD): This program fosters an innovative interdisciplinary education to prepare students for practice and advanced study in numerous design-based fields, as well as to apply design thinking to a variety of other possible careers. ENVD houses a state-of-the-art design fabrication lab that includes woodworking tools, and metal welding and shaping equipment.

Preprofessional Study Programs in Health and Law: These programs prepare undergraduate students for future advanced education in their field of interest through specialized advising, resources, and networking opportunities—all of which help to determine if it is the right fit.

Academic Programs

CU Boulder offers students a wealth of opportunities to engage in hands-on learning and scholarly research in fields as diverse as literature and biology. Programs include the Undergraduate Research Opportunities program, which funds research projects and scholarly and creative work; the Engineering Active Learning Program, which gives students the chance to gain hands-on engineering experience while forging professional connections through internships; the Biological Sciences Initiative Scholars in STEM Undergraduate Research, which helps students gain research experience as paid research assistants; and the Herbst Program of Humanities for engineering students, a unique program that encourages engineering students to develop thinking skills that incorporate humanities disciplines.

A group of programs, referred to as Top Scholars, is designed to enhance the educational opportunities for high-achieving students who are seeking the challenge of becoming more critical and analytical thinkers.

The CU LEAD Alliance and Scholarship Program is a set of academic learning. LEAD stands for Leadership, Excellence, Achievement and Diversity, and the students, faculty, and staff in these communities work together to help students from diverse and underrepresented backgrounds succeed at CU Boulder.

Off-Campus Programs

Studying abroad is a unique opportunity for students to learn from other cultures, enhance their resumes, travel the world, and grow as individuals. Education Abroad gives students the chance to earn academic credit while taking classes in another country. The Education Abroad Office administers 400 CU Boulder sponsored programs in 65 countries. More than 1,300 students study through CU Boulder programs annually.

Costs

Estimated tuition, fees, on-campus housing (double room), and meals (19 per week) for the 2016–17 academic year for Colorado residents ranges from $26,921 to $31,745, based on course of study. The totals for nonresidents ranges from $50,469 to $53,565, based on course of study.

In April 2016, the University of Colorado Board of Regents approved a four-year guarantee of tuition and mandatory fee costs for undergraduate resident students. The purpose of this guarantee is to provide financial predictability for students and families. The CU Boulder Guarantee will allow students and families to understand not just first-year tuition and mandatory fee costs, but what these will cost in four years.

Financial Aid

Approximately 15,000 undergraduate students received over $255 million in federal, state, and university aid in 2014–15. Of that total, almost $100 million was in the form of grants, scholarships and work-study. Prospective students are encouraged to complete the Free Application for Federal Student Aid (FAFSA) by February 15 to ensure full consideration for limited funds. The FAFSA is available starting October 1 for the 2017–18 academic year and must be completed each year. Incoming students are automatically considered for some scholarships, but more are available via the CU Boulder Scholarship Application between October 1 and February 15.

Faculty

CU Boulder and its nationally and internationally ranked faculty have built a global reputation for outstanding teaching, research, and creative work across more than 150 academic fields. CU Boulder faculty members are leaders in their fields, but are also dedicated to working closely with undergraduate students. Among faculty members, there are: the 2004 and 2013 National Professor of the Year; 5 Nobel Laureates; 8 recipients of MacArthur Fellowships (also known as the Genius Grant); 19 Rhodes Scholars;89 faculty who are part of the National Academies of Science, Arts and Sciences, Engineering, or Education; and more than 100 Fulbright fellows. The student to faculty ratio is 18:1.

Student Life

Estimated CU Boulder's inclusive community offers many ways to get involved and make lifelong friends. CU Boulder has one of the most active college campuses in the nation, where recreation, sports, and student groups play a key role in the campus experience. More than 3,500 students are enrolled in Residential Academic Programs and Living and Learning communities. CU Boulder has 33 competitive club sports, including crew, hockey, snowboarding, and swimming, while 12+ intramural sports provide opportunity for campus competition in sports like broomball, inner-tube water polo, and flag football.

Students also have the opportunity to serve the greater good through volunteerism and civic engagement, whether it's around the world or across the street. More than 2,000 students serve through Volunteer Resource Center programs.

Admission Requirements

CU Boulder's mission is to enroll an incoming class of highly qualified, intellectually curious, and actively involved students who have demonstrated high levels of maturity and personal integrity as well as a commitment to serving their communities. While admission is competitive, applicants will be considered on an individual basis relative to a prediction of academic success in the college to which they apply.

The primary factor in admission decisions is academic achievement: classroom performance in core academic and prerequisite courses, the rigor of those courses, and the best combination of scores on the SAT or ACT.

While academics and test scores play a large role in admission decisions, secondary factors, such as school and community involvement, also help assess the overall qualities of an applicant.

Application and Information

Materials needed for application include the online application, a $50 application fee, a personal essay and writing supplement, a letter of recommendation, high school transcript or equivalency, and SAT or ACT scores. The Early Action deadline is November 15 and the regular decision deadline is January 15.

Office of Admissions
University of Colorado at Boulder
552 UCB
Boulder, Colorado 80309
Phone: 303-492-6301
Fax: 303-492-7115
E-mail:
Website: http://www.colorado.edu

THE UNIVERSITY OF LYNCHBURG

LYNCHBURG, VIRGINIA

University *of* Lynchburg

The College

The University of Lynchburg is a vibrant learning community where students are empowered to discover their abilities and passions, connect with professors and the community, and achieve more than they dreamed possible. Formerly known as Lynchburg College (LC), a name change to the University of Lynchburg will go into effect in the fall of 2018. In claiming its university status, Lynchburg remains committed to its student-centered approach to instruction and has expanded on its institutional priority for active, engaged, and relevant learning opportunities across disciplines and throughout the University's curricula.

A fully accredited, coeducational, residential university affiliated with the Christian Church (Disciples of Christ), The University of Lynchburg offers 40 undergraduate majors, 57 minors, and 15 pre-professional programs, all supported by a strong liberal arts foundation. The University's graduate studies program includes two doctoral degrees and 17 master's programs. The University of Lynchburg is nationally recognized by such publications as The Princeton Review's The Best 376 Colleges: 2016 edition, *U.S. News & World Report* (Best Regional Universities category and Best Colleges for Veterans in the South), and the John Templeton Foundation's Honor Roll of Character-Building Colleges. Lynchburg is one of the 40 colleges and universities featured in Loren Pope's *Colleges That Change Lives.*

The University of Lynchburg is home to 2,800 undergraduate and graduate students, representing 38 states and 19 foreign countries. The University community is largely residential with 75 percent of the full-time undergraduate student body living on campus.

Located in the heart of Lynchburg, Virginia on 250 acres, the beautifully landscaped campus is a showplace. Set against a backdrop of the majestic Blue Ridge Mountains, the campus comprises more than 40 buildings, many of Georgian-style architecture. Buildings form an elliptical pattern with Hopwood Hall at the east end of campus and Snidow Chapel at the west end, symbolically linking the principles of faith and reason, the vision of Dr. Josephus Hopwood, the University's founder. The Drysdale Student Center is the hub for student activities with dining options, fitness room, club and student organization meeting space, the Campus Store, and Veterans Center.

The University community is a busy place, with a wide variety of activities including service and honor organizations, such as the national Bonner Leader Program; more than 100 clubs and organizations; 12 fraternities and sororities; and opportunities to participate in dramatic productions, student publications, religious activities, and musical performances. The Outdoor Leadership Program provides adventure-based leadership and team-building opportunities for individuals and groups. Community service (www.lynchburg.edu/volunteering-and-service) is a distinguishing feature of University of Lynchburg students, staff, and faculty, who last year contributed more than 70,000 volunteer hours to the community. The University has been on the President's Higher Education Community Service Honor Roll for the past seven years.

The University of Lynchburg encourages students to develop and maintain a sustainable lifestyle and supports sustainability initiatives on campus that include recycling, climate commitment, a community bike project, energy upgrades, and free bus rides for students.

The intercollegiate athletic program (www.lynchburgsports.com/landing/index) provides opportunities for men and women to compete in 21 sports in the NCAA Division III and the Old Dominion Athletic Conference (ODAC). In 2014, Lynchburg's women's soccer team won the NCAA Division III championship, bringing home the first team national championship in the history of the institution. Lynchburg students can also play a variety of intramural and club sports. The Turner Athletic Facility includes exercise and fitness areas, a dance studio, and one of the top exercise physiology labs in Virginia.

Shellenberger Field, named for Lynchburg's legendary soccer coach, is state-of-the-art with artificial turf, an eight-lane track, night lighting, and a 3,000-spectator capacity stadium with chair and bleacher seating. The field hosts men's and women's soccer, lacrosse, track and field, field hockey, and intramural and club sports. Moon Field is home to Lynchburg's softball team and the track and field events of javelin, hammer, shot put, and discus. Fox Field is one of the best baseball fields in the ODAC, with batting cages, a press box, and seating for up to 1,000 spectators.

Location

The University of Lynchburg (www.lynchburg.edu) is located in central Virginia, 100 miles from Richmond, Virginia, 180 miles southwest of Washington, D.C., and 50 miles east of Roanoke. Air, bus, and railroad transportation place Lynchburg within easy reach of any urban center. Greater Lynchburg is a growing business and industrial center with a population of more than 240,000. The city is noted for its climate, culture, historic landmarks, and proximity to the Blue Ridge Mountains.

Majors and Degrees

The University of Lynchburg offers the bachelor of arts degree in: accounting, art (graphic design or studio art), athletic training, business administration, communication studies (convergent journalism, social influence, electronic media or public relations), economics (financial or general), English (literature or writing), French, history, international relations, liberal arts studies, management, marketing, music (instrumental or vocal education, instrumental or vocal performance), philosophy, political science, religious studies, sociology (cultural studies, deviance and crime, human services), Spanish, sports management, and theater. The Bachelor of Science degree is offered in: biology, biomedical science, chemistry, computer science, environmental science, exercise physiology, health promotion, human development and learning (elementary education or special education), mathematics, nursing, physics, and psychology. More information is available at www.lynchburg.edu/majors-and-minors.

Pre-professional and professional courses are available in art therapy, dentistry, engineering, forestry and wildlife management, law, library science, medicine, ministry and ministry-related occupations, museum studies, occupational therapy, optometry, pharmacy, physical therapy, and veterinary medicine.

Academic Programs

To be eligible for a degree, a student must complete at least 124 semester hours of college-level academic work with a grade point average of at least 2.0 or higher on all work undertaken in the major field.

The curriculum at the University of Lynchburg is divided into two general areas: general education requirements and the major, providing students with breadth and depth of study. General education requirements are selected from the broad disciplines of world literature, fine arts, philosophy, religious studies, mathematics, history, social science, laboratory science, foreign languages, and health and movement science. Additional hours are available for students to explore coursework in free elective hours of their choice or students may devote their free elective hours to a minor.

The University's Westover Honors Program (www.lynchburg.edu/academics/westover-honors-program) is designed to attract, stimulate, challenge, and fulfill academically gifted students through a challenging curriculum that promotes intellectual curiosity and independent thinking and places strong emphasis on creative problem solving.

Off-Campus Programs

Lynchburg students are encouraged to engage in foreign-study programs, particularly Lynchburg's study-abroad program (www.lynchburg.edu/study-abroad).

More than 1,000 internships (www.lynchburg.edu/career-services) are available locally, nationally, and internationally, and are integral parts of a Lynchburg education. As members of the Tri-College Consortium of Virginia, Lynchburg College, Randolph College, and Sweet Briar College maintain cooperative relationships for sharing facilities and offerings.

Academic Facilities

The University of Lynchburg has 23 computer labs with both PCs and Macs. New students may bring a computer of their own or utilize one of the many available on campus. All students are assigned an e-mail account and have access to the internet. All residence hall rooms are wired for network access and the intranet, which serves the University community. Wireless internet access is available in most areas of the campus.

The University has several active learning classrooms where students can write on the walls, collaborate in the cloud with the help of Chromecast-enabled monitors, and easily rearrange the room thanks to wheeled tables and chairs.

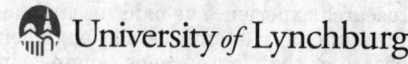

The Hobbs-Sigler Science Center provides an outstanding learning environment for students studying biology, chemistry, physics, biomedical sciences, environmental science, psychology, mathematics, and computer science. A cadaver lab, cutting-edge research labs, online weather station, GIS and remote sensing software, and digitizer are just some of the learning tools available. This facility is also used during the summer by the Virginia Governor's School for Math and Science to provide programming for selected high school students.

Schewel Hall, a $12-million classroom and laboratory facility, houses the School of Business and Economics, the Communication Studies program, foreign languages, and performing arts. This 67,000 square-foot facility includes technology-based classrooms, computer laboratories, and specialized teaching-learning settings, including a model stock exchange room, a digital darkroom, and a multimedia development center with television and recording studios. Sydnor Performance Hall provides an excellent venue for concerts, lectures, and other programs, with seating for 250 people.

The Daura Gallery (www.lynchburg.edu/daura-gallery) is the major repository of more than 1,000 works of Pierre Daura, the Catalan-American artist for whom the Gallery is named. Each year, The Daura Gallery features traveling exhibitions throughout the academic year and is the site for the Senior Art Show where selected student works are exhibited.

The Claytor Nature Study Center located on nearly 500 acres in nearby Bedford County provides an outdoor classroom and laboratory for hands-on, field-based environmental study and research. Donated to the institution by the late A. Boyd Claytor III, a member of the Lynchburg Board of Trustees, the property features lakes, woodlands, wetlands, grasslands, rare plants, formal gardens, a primitive campground, and three miles of hiking trails. The land is now managed for environmental conservation and restoration through agreements with the Virginia Outdoors Foundation and the USDA's Natural Resources Conservation Service. The A. Boyd Claytor III Education and Research Facility, a 7,700 square-foot multipurpose building, offers Lynchburg students and regional K–12 students and teachers an ideal location for learning with seminar, laboratory, classroom, conference, and retreat space.

The Belk Astronomical Observatory sits at one of the highest points of the Claytor Center property (approximately 960 feet above sea level) and is one of the most publicly accessible dark sky observatories in Virginia. The observatory features an RC Optical Systems 20-inch (0.51 meter) Truss Ritchey-Chrétien telescope with a 177-square-foot dome housing, and an observation deck equipped with 12 piers for mounting smaller telescopes. The control room is equipped with instrumentation that allows Lynchburg to conduct extensive stellar and planetary research and pursue astronomical research with other regional colleges and universities.

The Chandler Eco-Lodge, a 16-bed facility at Claytor, provides overnight accommodations for students and researchers who wish to study outside the classroom. The 2,100 square-foot lodge is built with energy-efficiency and low-impact design and includes a constructed wetland to handle wastewater.

Costs

Total charges for resident students for the 2017–18 session were $47,570: $36,720 tuition, $9,880 room and board, and $970 student fees (www.lynchburg.edu/undergraduate-admission/tuition-fees).

Financial Aid

The University of Lynchburg administers a financial aid program of more than $40 million annually. These resources are awarded to students for meritorious achievement and/or for demonstrated need. The University of Lynchburg offers academic scholarships (www.lynchburg.edu/financial-aid/scholarships) that range from $10,000 to $21,000 and are based on performance and accomplishments at the high school or community university level. In addition, the University offers scholarship competitions with awards ranging from $1,000 to $5,000, which are awarded in conjunction with other academic scholarships. The competitions are based upon academic performance, leadership, community service and talent. These awards are renewable each year until the student graduates, as long as the recipient maintains a qualifying minimum academic average each year. Students are identified to receive these scholarships through the admission application; no separate application is necessary. Free early aid estimates are available for students. More than 98 percent of last year's entering class received academic and/or need-based financial aid. The average amount of aid received was $32,000.

To determine eligibility for need-based financial aid, the student should complete the Free Application for Federal Student Aid (FAFSA), which may be obtained at most high schools and at the University. The FAFSA results determine the student's eligibility for federally funded grants and loans and other support such as work-study opportunities. In addition, students from Virginia are eligible to apply for the Virginia Tuition Assistance grant.

Faculty

The University of Lynchburg's faculty members are outstanding scholars who are leaders in their disciplines. Of the 190 full-time members, 83 percent hold the doctorate or terminal degree in their fields. The student-faculty ratio is 11:1, which allows for personal attention and student-faculty collaborative research, both of which are essential to the Lynchburg experience. While Lynchburg faculty are involved in various research and writing projects, University policy requires that teaching is to be their top priority.

Admission Requirements

A candidate for admission to the University of Lynchburg (www.lynchburg.edu/undergraduate-admission) should be a graduate of an approved secondary school with a minimum of 16 academic units or the equivalent, as shown by examination. It is required that the academic work include major emphases in the areas of English, foreign language, social science, natural sciences, and mathematics. An applicant must demonstrate above-average academic ability in all areas of study, as admission is competitive. In support of the record, a student must present satisfactory scores on the ACT or SAT (critical reading and math scores are used to determine admission decisions and merit scholarship awards). It is recommended that all students have a personal interview and visit the campus beginning the spring semester of their junior year or during their senior year. Enrollment Office hours during the academic year are 9 a.m. to 5 p.m. Monday through Friday and 10 a.m. to noon on Saturday during the academic year.

Application and Information

The University operates on an early semester calendar. The first semester begins in late August and ends before Christmas, and the second semester runs from mid-January to early May. An optional winter term abroad is also offered.

Early decision admission applications must be received by November 15 (www.lynchburg.edu/undergraduate-admission/freshman-application-steps); notification of acceptance is made by December 15. All other applications are processed on a rolling admissions basis. Applicants are notified of the status of their application usually within two to four weeks of the date their application file is completed.

For information, students should contact:

Sharon Walters-Bower, Director of Admissions
The University of Lynchburg
1501 Lakeside Drive
Lynchburg, Virginia 24501
Phone: 434-544-8300
800-426-8101 (toll-free)
Fax: 434-544-8653
E-mail: admissions@lynchburg.edu
Website: http://www.lynchburg.edu

The $12 million expansion of the Drysdale Student Center has added a total of 72,000 square-feet and includes a welcome center, a fitness center, meeting rooms, multicultural center, a Commons space, veterans' lounge, dance and aerobics space, a game room, and additional food options.

UNIVERSITY OF ALASKA FAIRBANKS

FAIRBANKS, ALASKA

★ To read more about this school, visit http://petersons.to/universityofalaskafairbanks

UAF UNIVERSITY OF ALASKA FAIRBANKS

The University

The University of Alaska Fairbanks (UAF) draws students into a welcoming community, offering inspiring and transformational educational challenges—from the personal to the global—in the vast natural laboratory that is Alaska. Founded in 1917, UAF is Alaska's top teaching and research university. Total enrollment is nearly 10,000 students; 83 percent are from Alaska, with the rest coming from the United States and 48 other countries.

The 2,250-acre Fairbanks campus, located near the middle of Alaska, offers limitless opportunities for activity and recreation. Academic buildings and residences make up the core of campus, and just beyond are miles of trails, two lakes, and a boreal forest research and recreational area. Most of the UAF's research institutes, including the Geophysical Institute and the International Arctic Research Center, are clustered on the West Ridge, with incredible views of the Tanana Valley and Alaska Range. The university's Agricultural and Forestry Experiment Station is on campus, as are a Cooperative Fish and Wildlife Research Unit and various state and federal agencies and laboratories. The Margaret Murie Building, with 100,000 square feet of life science classrooms and laboratories, opened its doors to students and researchers in 2013. A new six-story engineering building, currently under construction, will double the space available for College of Engineering and Mines labs, classrooms, and offices.

The Student Recreation Center and Patty Center house a variety of sports and physical activity facilities, including multipurpose areas for aerobics, badminton, calisthenics, dance, gymnastics, judo, karate, tennis, and volleyball; a rifle and pistol range; courts for handball, racquetball, and squash; an elevated 200-meter, three-lane jogging track; a swimming pool; weight-training and modern fitness equipment areas; an ice arena for recreational skating and hockey; a three-story indoor climbing wall; and an outdoor rock/ice climbing wall.

The student union, the William Ransom Wood Center, is the focus of numerous activities for students and faculty members. The center houses meeting and exhibit rooms, lounges and television areas, student government offices, campus information, a pub, bowling alley, games room, cafeteria, snack bar, and an espresso bar. A major expansion of the Wood Center dining facilities was completed in fall 2014.

Intercollegiate athletics include men's and women's basketball, cross-country running and skiing, men's ice hockey, and women's volleyball and swim teams. The university also has an outstanding rifle team that has produced several Olympic athletes and earned 10 NCAA championships.

Location

The campus of the University of Alaska Fairbanks is situated on a ridge overlooking the Tanana River valley and the city of Fairbanks. With a population of more than 99,000 in the metro area, Fairbanks is a major trade center for outlying towns and villages in Interior Alaska. The city is connected to the rest of the state and the lower 48 states by air and highway. Municipal bus service is available between downtown Fairbanks, the surrounding area, and campus. A convenient shuttle bus service is available on campus. UAF students can also ride the city bus for free.

Fairbanks offers the amenities of larger cities while maintaining the atmosphere of a smaller, more personal town. Denali National Park and Preserve and other vast wilderness areas are close at hand, and Anchorage is 350 miles south via the Parks Highway. Members of the Fairbanks and UAF communities unite to perform in the Fairbanks Symphony, Arctic Chamber Orchestra, and many other musical and theatrical programs.

Majors and Degrees

The University of Alaska Fairbanks awards occupational endorsements, certificates, A.A., A.S., A.A.S., B.A., B.A.S., B.A.A.S., B.B.A., B.E.M., B.F.A., B.M., and B.S. degrees in accounting; accounting technician; administrative assistant; airframe; airframe and powerplant; Alaska Native studies; anthropology; applied accounting; applied business; applied business management; apprenticeship technologies; art; automotive technology; aviation maintenance; basic carpentry; biological sciences; bookkeeping technician; business administration; chemistry; child development and family studies; civil engineering; communication; community health; computer engineering; computer science; construction management; construction trades technology; culinary arts and hospitality; diesel/heavy equipment; dental assistant; digital journalism; drafting technology; early childhood education; earth science; electrical engineering; elementary education; English; environmental studies; Eskimo (Inupiaq and Yup'ik); ethnobotany; facility maintenance; film and performing arts; financial services representative; fire science; fisheries; fisheries and ocean sciences; foreign languages; general science; geography; geological engineering; geoscience; health care reimbursement; high latitude range management; history; homeland security; homeland security and emergency management; human services; information technology specialist; instrumentation technology; interdisciplinary studies; Japanese studies; justice; law enforcement academy; linguistics; mathematics; mechanical engineering; medical assistant; medical billing; medical coding; medical/dental reception; medical office reception; mining engineering; mining mill operations; music; Native language education; natural resources management (including forestry); northern studies; nurse aide; paralegal studies; paramedicine; petroleum engineering; physics; political science; powerplant; pre-nursing qualifications; process technology; professional piloting; psychology; rural development; rural human services; rural surface water quality testing; rural utilities business management; rural waste management and spill response; safety, health, and environmental awareness technology; secondary education; social work; sustainable energy; tribal justice; tribal management; welding (entry level); wildland fire science; wildlife biology and conservation; Yup'ik language and culture; and Yup'ik language proficiency.

Academic Programs

The academic year is divided into two semesters; registration begins in early April for the fall semester and in November for the spring semester. In addition, there are three-week, six-week, and 12-week summer sessions and two-week between-semester sessions in January and May.

The university is organized into the colleges of Engineering and Mines, Fisheries and Ocean Sciences, Liberal Arts, Natural Science and Mathematics, Rural and Community Development, and the schools of Education, Management, and Natural Resources and Extension. A minimum of 120 credits must be completed for the four-year baccalaureate degree programs.

Students who receive scores of 3 or higher on most of the College Board's Advanced Placement tests may be awarded credit by the university. Students graduating from any school offering the International Baccalaureate Programme should review a comprehensive list of transfer credits available at http://catalog.uaf.edu/getting-started/transferring-credits/. Enrolled students may challenge courses for credit by successfully completing College-Level Examination Program examinations or by completing locally prepared examinations. Requests for advanced placement credit and credit by examination are coordinated through the Office of Admissions and the Registrar.

The Office of Undergraduate Research and Scholarly Activity supports and develops UAF's diverse and robust programs to engage undergraduate students in research and creative scholarship. URSA helps students pursue research from a single credit of first-year seminar to independent scholarly investigations or a senior thesis.

The Honors Program is for highly motivated undergraduate students who wish to acquire an advanced understanding of the natural and social sciences, arts, and humanities. Prospective honors students need a minimum ACT plus writing composite score of 27 or a minimum combined SAT score of 1300.

Off-Campus Programs

The university maintains active exchange programs with universities around the world. Membership in the UArctic's north2north exchange program gives UAF students an extensive array of opportunities throughout the circumpolar North. Additional study programs and internships are available through affiliates maintaining sites in numerous countries. UAF is also a member of the National Student Exchange, participating with more than 200 colleges and universities throughout the United States, in U.S. territories, and at 10 locations in Canada.

Academic Facilities

The Fine Arts Complex features a 480-seat theater, a 1,072-seat concert hall, FM public radio (KUAC) and educational television (PBS) studios, an art gallery, and the Elmer E. Rasmuson Library. The library collection contains more than 1.75 million items, including many in the prestigious Alaska and Polar Regions Collection and Archives. Electronic catalogs provide access to collections in 11,000 libraries nationwide.

Students have free use of the university's academic computing facilities and wireless network in labs, classrooms, dorm rooms, and other campus locations.

The University of Alaska Museum of the North attracts nearly 100,000 visitors each year to Interior Alaska and is located on the Fairbanks campus. The museum collects, preserves, and exhibits materials from Alaska and the North.

Costs

In 2016–17, tuition and fees were $7,798 annually for full-time (30 credits) students. Nonresident students will pay $23,055 annually for 30 credits of tuition. Generally, to qualify as a resident, a student must show proof they have been living in Alaska for two years. Residents of Alaska, and of cities having sister-city agreements with any Alaska city, as well as military, veteran and their dependents are eligible for resident tuition rates.

The approximate annual cost for books and supplies is $2,000. A double-occupancy residence hall room on campus and a meal plan cost $8,530 per academic year during the 2016–17 academic year. All costs are subject to change.

If the student lives in a Western Undergraduate Exchange state (http://www.uaf.edu/admissions/other/wue), tuition is approximately 1.5 times that of an Alaska resident.

Financial Aid

A large portion of financial aid is derived from the Alaska Supplemental Education Loan Program, which is available to all students attending UAF, regardless of residency. Three kinds of aid are available: grants and scholarships (which need not be repaid), loans, and part-time employment. Inquiries should be sent by e-mail to the Financial Aid Office at uaf-financialaid@alaska.edu. Academic merit and service scholarships are one-year scholarships ranging from $1,000–$15,000 that are awarded by the Office of Admissions and the Registrar. To apply, students should submit for review a scholarship application, an application for admission, a high school transcript, and test scores. Questions about this scholarship should be directed to the Office of Admissions and the Registrar. The deadline for University of Alaska and UAF-funded scholarships is February 15. Prospective students should check the financial aid website (www.uaf.edu/finaid/) for information about grants, loans, other aid, and applicable due dates.

Faculty

Seventy-seven percent of full-time faculty members and 50 percent of part-time faculty hold doctoral or terminal degrees, and many are engaged in research. In keeping with university policy, faculty members provide academic counseling for students. The combination of a student-faculty ratio of 12:1 and ready access to instructors for help outside of class leads to an excellent educational experience for students.

Admission Requirements

For admission to a baccalaureate program, applicants must be high school graduates with a GPA of at least 2.5 with 16 credits of high school core curriculum and a cumulative grade point average of at least 3.0. A GPA between 2.5 and 3.0 requires an ACT plus writing score of 18 or SAT score of 955. Transfer students must also have a minimum grade point average of 2.0 in all previous college work.

Applicants for a major in a scientific or technical field may be required to present a higher grade point average and to have completed specific background courses before being accepted into the major department.

Application and Information

The application deadlines are May 1 for the summer semester, June 15 for the fall semester, and November 1 for the spring semester. A $50 application fee is required when the application is submitted. Applicants are notified of the admission decision once all application materials have been received.

For more information, applicants should contact:

Office of Admissions and the Registrar
University of Alaska Fairbanks
P.O. Box 757480
Fairbanks, Alaska 99775-7480
Phone: 907-474-7500
800-478-1823 (toll-free)
E-mail: admissions@uaf.edu
Website: http://www.uaf.edu/admissions

Students make their way across campus on a November afternoon.

COLLEGE CLOSE-UPS

UNIVERSITY OF CALGARY

CALGARY, ALBERTA, CANADA

★ To read more about this school, visit http://petersons.to/universityofcalgary

The University

Located in Canada's fourth largest city, the University of Calgary (popularly known as UCalgary) is home to more than 30,000 students, including a diverse population of more than 3,000 international students. From 2013–15, UCalgary was the #1 ranked young university in Canada (as determined by both QS and *Times Higher Education*). In 2015, QS upgraded the ranking to make UCalgary the #1 young university in North America. And in 2016, *Times Higher Education* ranked UCalgary as one of the top 200 most globally oriented universities in the world.

UCalgary offers small classes with an average undergraduate student to instructor ratio of 23:1. The university's 14 faculties include the Cumming School of Medicine, the Faculty of Arts, the Faculty of Environmental Design, the Faculty of Graduate Studies, Haskayne School of Business, the Faculty of Kinesiology, the Faculty of Law, the Faculty of Nursing, the Faculty of Science, the Faculty of Social Work, the Faculty of Veterinary Medicine, Schulich School of Engineering, and the Werklund School of Education.

But what sets UCalgary apart are the enhanced student experiences. From the day students arrive on campus, they're able to participate in a wide variety of activities such as hands-on learning programs, unique research opportunities, and leadership development seminars.

UCalgary stands out among Canadian universities in how it actively engages students in leadership development in all areas—the arts, athletics, science, medicine, engineering, volunteerism, and business. It's also a leader in sustainability with its set of values embraced by the campus through teaching, leadership and campus operations.

Location

UCalgary's main campus is located on 526 park-like acres minutes from downtown Calgary. The Canadian Rocky Mountains are just an hour's drive away. UCalgary's world-class location puts students in close proximity to some of the best hiking and skiing in the world, not to mention biking, rock climbing, kayaking, and more.

Majors and Degrees

UCalgary's 14 faculties grant degrees up to the doctoral level in most disciplines. UCalgary offers undergraduate programs in the following areas: accounting; actuarial science; ancient and medieval history; anthropology; applied chemistry; archaeology; architecture; art history; astrophysics; biochemistry; bioinformatics; biological sciences; biomechanics; biomedical sciences; business process management; business technology management; Canadian studies; cellular, molecular, and microbial biology; chemical engineering; chemical physics; chemistry; civil engineering; classical and early Christian studies; communication, media, and film; communications studies; community rehabilitation and disability studies; computer science; dance; development studies; drama; earth science; East Asian language studies; East Asian studies; economics; ecology; education; electrical engineering; energy engineering; energy management; English; entrepreneurship and innovation; environmental science; exercise and health physiology; finance; film studies; French; general commerce; geography; geology; geomatics engineering; geophysics; German; Greek and Roman studies; health and society; history; human resources and organizational dynamics; international business; international Indigenous studies; international relations; Italian studies; kinesiology; Latin American studies; law; law and society; leadership in pedagogy and coaching; linguistics; linguistics and language; marketing; mathematics (general); mathematics (applied); mathematics (pure); mechanical engineering; medicine; mind sciences in kinesiology; music; natural sciences; neuroscience; nursing; oil and gas engineering; operations management; personal finance planning; petroleum land management; philosophy; physics; plant biology; political science; psychology; religious studies; risk management: insurance and finance; risk management and insurance; Russian; social work; sociology; software engineering; Spanish; statistics; supply chain management; tourism management; tourism management and marketing; urban studies; veterinary medicine; visual studies; women's studies; and zoology.

Academic Programs

As a comprehensive academic and research institution, UCalgary inspires and supports discovery, creativity and innovation across all disciplines. Through the Taylor Institute for Teaching and Learning, the university will take the lead in educational innovation by researching the most effective methods for engaging students, by supporting faculty to be the best teachers they can be, and by providing some of the most innovative learning spaces available in North America.

UCalgary has numerous programs and services provided on campus to help students achieve success, including Career Services, the Faith and Spirituality Centre, International Student Services, Student Accessibility Services, the Student Success Centre, Students' Union, the Welcome Centre, the Native Centre, and the Women's Resource Centre.

Academic Facilities

The campus has been expanding almost without interruption since 1966. Marking the completion of the university's largest capital expansion ever, several new buildings have opened including the Taylor Institute for Teaching and Learning, the Crowsnest and Aurora Hall residence buildings, as well as a major renovation to the Canadian Natural Resources Limited Engineering Complex.

The libraries at UCalgary contain more than 7.8 million items, which means there are all the materials and resources students need to start their next essay or research project.

As one of the principal research facilities within UCalgary's Department of Physics and Astronomy, the Rothney Astrophysical Observatory is one of Canada's best-equipped astronomical teaching facilities, providing university students with the opportunity to use research-grade telescopes.

Costs

Undergraduate tuition for the 2017–18 academic year is Can$5,386 for full-time Canadian students. The rate for full-time international students is Can$19,562.78. First-year residence costs with a meal plan is Can$7,893. More specific information regarding tuition and fees is available online at http://www.ucalgary.ca/pubs/calendar/current/p.html.

Financial Aid

Domestic UCalgary students may be eligible for a government student loan. Student loans are intended to supplement student and family resources and are based on financial need.

Each year, UCalgary also gives undergraduate students over $15 million in scholarships and awards. Further details and deadlines for these opportunities can be found online at ucalgary.ca/future-students.

Student Life

With a young vibrant campus community, UCalgary offers unforgettable celebrations and events, top-notch recreation facilities, extensive student services, and endless opportunities to meet new people.

UCalgary offers a variety of on-campus housing options in secured buildings. Whether students come from Canberra or Canterbury, they have a guaranteed home on campus for the first two years if they enter directly from high school and apply for residence by May 1. The university also offers various meals plans to suit individual needs, and fully-furnished rooms include features such as Wi-Fi, all utilities, access to student tutoring services, and more.

At UCalgary, everyone is a Dino. Students are encouraged to show their school pride at sporting events and beyond. Student fees include access to all the Active Living facilities and students also receive a discount on rentals from the Outdoor Centre, the largest facility of its kind in North America. Students can re-energize, create, and maintain a healthy, active lifestyle with access to the university's world-class health and recreation facilities.

The University Theatre hosts more than 175 events annually, including academic productions from the School of Creative and Performing Arts. Touring concerts and outside companies also enjoy frequent access to this spacious, well-designed theatre.

The SU Wellness Centre on campus provides an extensive list of services including family medicine, massage therapy, chiropractic, nutrition, dental services, personal counselling, and a walk-in clinic.

Admission Requirements

The UCalgary admissions process can be completed online. Eligible applicants must complete, or be in the process of completing grade 12 (or the equivalent level of schooling). Students should select their first- and second-choice programs, and ensure they meet the program requirements. For more information, visit ucalgary.ca/future-students/undergraduate/apply.

Students must also submit official transcripts and other required documents. Deadlines vary depending on a variety of factors that are provided on the university's website.

To learn more about the university's international admission process, please visit ucalgary.ca/future-students. English is the official language of instruction at UCalgary. All applicants must demonstrate English language proficiency to be considered for admission. To view UCalgary's English language proficiency requirements, please visit ucalgary.ca/future-students.

Academically qualified applicants who don't meet UCalgary's English language proficiency requirement may apply to the International Foundations Program (IFP). Please note that not all degree programs offer this option. Visit ucalgary.ca/future-students/undergraduate/international for details.

International students entering an undergraduate program at UCalgary are required to obtain a study permit before beginning classes. Students must receive an offer of admission before applying for a study permit. International Student Services (ISS) provides support services and customized advising for all international students at UCalgary. Prospective students can visit http://www.ucalgary.ca/iss for more information about ISS. Any questions about the application process should be emailed to the Regulated Canadian Immigration Consultant in ISS at international.advice@ucalgary.ca.

Application and Information

UCalgary accepts undergraduate applications annually from October 1 to March 1. Applicants are allowed to change and resubmit their application form as many times as they want until the submission deadline of March 1. Applicants can also apply for scholarships and awards using the online submission process until the deadline of March 1. Once students submit all of the required documents, they can track the status of the application using the school's online portal. Upon receiving an offer of admission, students can also use the online portal to accept their offer, pay the admission deposit, and register for courses.

For more information, prospective students should contact:

Kaili Xu. Assistant Registrar, Undergraduate Admission
University of Calgary
2500 University Drive, NW
Calgary, Alberta T2N 1N4
Canada
Phone: 403-210-7625
E-mail: future.students@ucalgary.ca
Website: http://www.ucalgary.ca/future-students

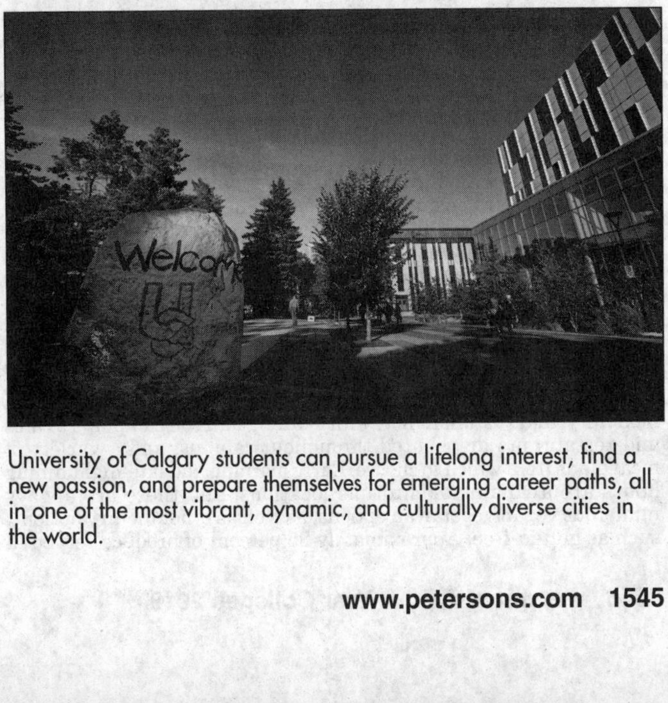

University of Calgary students can pursue a lifelong interest, find a new passion, and prepare themselves for emerging career paths, all in one of the most vibrant, dynamic, and culturally diverse cities in the world.

UNIVERSITY OF CALIFORNIA, SANTA CRUZ

SANTA CRUZ, CALIFORNIA

UNIVERSITY OF CALIFORNIA SANTA CRUZ

★ For more information, visit http://petersons.to/usantacruz

The University

Since its opening in 1965, the University of California, Santa Cruz (UCSC) has combined the depth and rigor of a major research university with the intimacy of a small, liberal arts college. A distinctive aspect of the undergraduate experience is the residential college system, in which each student is affiliated with one of UCSC's 10 residential colleges, providing an integrated learning/living environment, advising, and curricular and co-curricular opportunities and events.

The campus enrolls approximately 17,000 undergraduates and 1,800 graduate students. Undergraduates pursue bachelor's degrees in 66 majors in the Divisions of the Arts, Humanities, Physical and Biological Sciences, and Social Sciences, plus the Jack Baskin School of Engineering. Graduate students work toward graduate certificates, master's degrees, or doctoral degrees in 41 academic programs.

UCSC's undergraduate student body is ethnically, socioeconomically, and geographically diverse. Ethnic composition is as follows: African American 3.9 percent, American Indian 0.9 percent, Asian/Asian American/Pacific Islander 26.6 percent, Chicano/Latino 30.4 percent, European American 33.0 percent, international 3.6 percent, not stated 1.6 percent. Approximately 20 percent of undergraduates enroll at UCSC as transfer students, mostly from California community colleges.

UCSC is a public doctoral university accredited by the WASC Senior College and University Commission (WSCUC).

Students at UCSC enjoy an active social environment, with over 150 student organizations, 27 Greek letter organizations (social clubs only, no fraternity or sorority housing available), numerous academic and pre-professional organizations, honors societies such as Phi Beta Kappa and Golden Key International Honour Society, concerts, plays, two on-campus art galleries, and much more. Students may also participate in the student government body, the Student Union Assembly, with numerous subcommittees, and they may also participate in student government opportunities at the residential colleges.

UCSC students also enjoy many opportunities for sports and recreation, with a broad range of activities so that everyone can be involved. The campus hosts NCAA Division III teams in men's/women's basketball, cross-country, soccer, swimming/diving, tennis, track and field, and volleyball, plus women's golf. UCSC also has numerous competitive and noncompetitive sports clubs and hosts a popular intramural program. UCSC's world-famous recreation program includes an enormous range of activities, from wilderness excursions to wine tasting. With the incomparable opportunities afforded by its beautiful seaside location near the Monterey Bay Marine Sanctuary, off-campus opportunities for year-round water sports and mountain biking abound.

About 99 percent of freshmen and 53 percent of undergraduates live in University-sponsored housing, which is mostly on-campus in the residential colleges. Incoming freshmen who meet all deadlines receive a two-year housing guarantee, and incoming transfers receive a one-year guarantee. Off-campus students receive assistance finding rentals in the community through the campus Community Rentals Program. The campus is committed to the health and safety of its residents, with police and fire stations on campus and the Student Health Center, which provides medical, counseling, and psychological services. Family Student Housing in two-bedroom apartments on campus is also available to qualifying undergraduates.

The campus's award-winning dining program emphasizes quality, flexibility, and sustainability, with 5 dining halls on campus, 12 cafés and restaurants distributed throughout campus, and a variety of meal plans from which to choose. Early morning and late-night dining hours are available at multiple locations, and there are always numerous vegan/vegetarian options, as well as other dietary options, such as gluten-free. Approximately 25 percent of produce served in the dining halls is organic, with much of it coming from local providers, such as UCSC's own organic Farm and Garden.

Student support services offered by UCSC include opportunities for academic support, such as advising, tutoring, the Academic Excellence (ACE) program, and Modified Supplemental Instruction (a unique program in which successful students mentor other students in highly challenging classes). Students may also wish to connect with UCSC's resource centers and other groups on campus, which include the African American Resource Center, the American Indian Resource Center, the Asian American/Pacific Islander Resource Center, the Chicano/Latino Resource Center, the Disability Resource Center, the Lionel Cantú GLBTIQQA Center, the Women's Center, and Services for Transfer and Re-entry Students (STARS).

Location

Few locations are as inspiring as Santa Cruz, where opportunities and convenience are combined with magnificent natural beauty. UCSC features a spectacular campus with redwood forests, panoramic views of the Monterey Bay, and open meadows. It is also the nearest University of California campus to Silicon Valley, which provides visiting professors and lecturers, as well as fantastic opportunities for internships and future employment at companies such as Adobe Systems, Apple, Facebook, and Google.

UCSC is 1.5 hours by car from San Francisco, about a mile from the beach, and a short bus ride away from downtown Santa Cruz, with shops, restaurants, and movie theaters. It is also next to the Monterey Bay National Marine Sanctuary, with unique opportunities to study marine life in diverse ecosystems such as kelp forests. Santa Cruz's Mediterranean climate is mild, averaging 300 sunny days a year (according to Santa Cruz County officials). The Santa Cruz area contains thousands of acres of protected forest land that offers ample opportunities for hiking, photography, and nature viewing.

Majors and Degrees

Undergraduate majors (concentrations listed in parentheses): Anthropology*; Applied Physics; Art; Art and Design: Games and Playable Media; Biochemistry and Molecular Biology; Biology* (Bioeducation); Business Management Economics; Chemistry* (Biochemistry, Environmental Chemistry); Classical Studies*; Cognitive Science; Community Studies; Earth Sciences* (Environmental Geology, Ocean Sciences, Planetary Sciences, Science Education); Earth Sciences/Anthropology; Ecology and Evolution; Economics*; Economics/Mathematics; Environmental Studies (Agroecology and Sustainable Food Systems); Environmental Studies/Biology; Environmental Studies/Earth Sciences; Environmental Studies/Economics); Feminist Studies (Culture, Power, and Representation; Law, Politics, and Social Change; Science, Technology, and Medicine; Sexuality Studies); Film and Digital Media* (Critical Studies, Integrated Critical Practice, Production); German Studies; Global Economics; History* (Americas and Africa, Asia and the Islamic World, Europe); History of Art and Visual Culture* (Religion and Visual Culture); Human Biology; Italian Studies*; Jewish Studies*; Language Studies* (Chinese, French, German, Italian, Japanese, Spanish); Latin American and Latino Studies*; Latin American and Latino Studies/Politics; Latin American and Latino Studies/Sociology; Legal Studies*; Linguistics* (Theoretical Linguistics); Literature* (Creative Writing, French Literature, German Literature, Greek and Latin Literatures, Italian Literature, Spanish/Latin American/Latino Literatures); Marine Biology; Mathematics* (Computational Mathematics, Mathematics Education, Pure Mathematics); Molecular, Cell, and Developmental Biology; Music; Neuroscience; Philosophy*; Physics*; Physics (Astrophysics); Physics Education; Plant Sciences; Politics*; Psychology; Sociology*; Spanish Studies (Languages and Linguistics, Literature and Culture); and Theater Arts* (Dance, Design and Technology, Drama).

Jack Baskin School of Engineering:
Bioengineering (Assistive Technology: Cognitive/Perceptual, Assistive Technology: Motor, Bioelectronics, Biomolecular); Bioinformatics*; Computer Engineering* (Computer Systems, Digital Hardware, Networks, Robotics and Control, Systems Programming); Computer Science*; Computer Science: Computer Game Design; Electrical Engineering* (Communications, Signals, Systems, and Controls; Electronics/Optics); Network and Digital Technology; Robotics Engineering; and Technology and Information Management.
Minor offered

Minors only are available in: astrophysics, dance, East Asian studies, education, electronic music, global information and social enterprise studies, history of consciousness, jazz, STEM education, sustainability studies, applied mathematics, and statistics.

Students may be interested in UCSC's 3+3 B.A./J.D. program, a unique agreement with UC Hastings College of the Law in San Francisco that enables students to earn their B.A. and law degree in six years rather than seven. The human biology B.S. program, designed for students who wish to apply to medical school, and the computer science: computer game design program are also highly regarded, popular programs at UCSC.

UCSC also offers the UCSC College Scholars Program, an intensive honors program for well-prepared students who enroll as freshmen. Specific degree requirements and other advising for prospective students is available at admissions.ucsc.edu/majors.

Off-Campus Programs

UCSC offers many opportunities for co-curricular engagement through internships, volunteer opportunities, and undergraduate research (a full listing is available at https://ugr.ue.ucsc.edu/). The UC Education Abroad Program also offers study opportunities that undergraduates pursue as part of their regular academic program at over 100 institutions in more than 40 countries around the world. UCSC professors also regularly invite undergraduates to participate in their labs and scholarly research, and many students help their professors and other campus researchers co-publish scholarly works. Many internships and field study opportunities carry credit or are paid.

Academic Facilities

Facilities at UCSC include two major libraries, numerous research facilities, arts and performing arts facilities, and recreational/athletic facilities. UCSC is home to the following research centers: UC Observatories/Lick Observatory, Center for Biomolecular Science and Engineering, Center for Agroecology and Sustainable Food Systems, Institute of Geophysics and Planetary Physics, Santa Cruz Institute for Particle Physics, Institute of Marine Sciences, California Institute for Quantitative Biosciences, Institute for the Biology of Stem Cells, Center for information Technology Research in the Interest of Society, Chicano/Latino Research Center, and the NASA University Affiliated Research Center.

Costs

For the 2016–17 academic year, tuition and fees totaled $13,557. Housing and food for on-campus students was estimated at $15,384. Books and supplies are estimated at $1,473. Campus health insurance is mandatory unless proof of insurance is shown. Tuition and fees are subject to change. Updated figures can be found at financialaid.ucsc.edu/cost.shtml.

Financial Aid

The UCSC Financial Aid and Scholarship Office is committed to minimizing financial barriers to support students in achieving their educational goals. Each year, the office assists more than 12,000 students or about 7 out of every 10 undergraduates with scholarships, grants, loans, and/or part-time employment opportunities. They also assist graduate students with federal student loans. These resources, totaling over $260 million, help make UCSC's extraordinary learning facilities affordable to students and families.

To recognize outstanding undergraduate students, UCSC awards about $3 million in scholarships to about 1,500 students per year. The Career Center manages numerous student employment opportunities, both on-campus and off-campus.

Specific financial aid information and publications is available at financialaid.ucsc.edu.

Faculty

UCSC has 567 full-time and 253 part-time faculty members; 804 out of 820 have doctorates, or another terminal degree. No UCSC faculty members are in stand-alone graduate/professional programs—all teach undergraduates. UCSC's student/faculty ratio is 19:1. Additional information on UCSC's faculty is available at admissions.ucsc.edu/academics/learning-from-the-best.html.

Admission Requirements

The admission and selection process for freshmen and transfer students at UCSC reflects the academic rigor and preparation needed for admission to a major research institution. All types of students are welcome to apply, including out-of-state and international students. Applications for the coming fall are accepted through the month of November of the previous year, through an online application process. No on-campus interview is required. Additional details are available at admissions.ucsc.edu.

Contact Information

University of California Santa Cruz Admissions
1156 High Street
Santa Cruz, California 95064
Phone: 831-459-4008 (for students who have not yet applied)
Phone: 831-459-2131 (for students who have applied)
E-mail: admissions@ucsc.edu
Website: admissions.ucsc.edu
facebook.com/ucscadmissions
instagram.com/ucscadmissions
twitter.com/ucsc_admission
admissions.ucsc.edu/#virtualtour

COLLEGE CLOSE-UPS

UNIVERSITY OF CENTRAL FLORIDA

ORLANDO, FLORIDA

UNIVERSITY OF CENTRAL FLORIDA

The University

The University of Central Florida (UCF) is a comprehensive research university with over 64,000 students. As one of the nation's fastest-growing and largest universities, UCF enrolls an academically talented and diverse student body representing all fifty states and more than 120 countries. The University offers educational and research programs that complement the regional economy, with strong components in aerospace engineering, business, education, film, health, hospitality management, medicine, nursing, and social sciences. UCF's programs in communication and the fine arts help to meet the cultural and recreational needs of a growing metropolitan area. The University also offers many graduate programs leading to master's and doctoral degrees, including a doctorate of physical therapy. The UCF College of Medicine offers the M.D. degree.

UCF is accredited by the Commission on Colleges of the Southern Association of Colleges and Schools. In addition, a number of scientific, professional, and academic bodies confer accreditation in specific disciplines and groups of disciplines.

UCF has established extensive partnerships with businesses and industries in the central Florida area and beyond that provide students with exceptional research and learning experiences. These partnerships bring practical learning environments to UCF students through co-op, internship programs, and joint curriculum development strategies.

The on-campus and campus-affiliated housing facilities include traditional residence halls, apartment-style options, and Greek housing that accommodates approximately 11,500 students. In addition, several thousand students live in apartments located within walking distance of the campus.

Students participate in approximately 600 student organizations, including special-interest clubs, multicultural organizations, fraternities and sororities, honor societies, and academic and preprofessional organizations. The Office of Student Involvement schedules a wide array of extracurricular programs, including concerts, movies, and guest speakers.

The University of Central Florida is a member of the NCAA and competes in the American Athletic Conference (AAC). All teams compete on the NCAA Division I level. UCF's men's teams compete in intercollegiate baseball, basketball, football, golf, soccer, and tennis. Women's teams compete in basketball, cross-country, golf, rowing, soccer, softball, tennis, track and field, and volleyball. Intercollegiate coed club activities include championship cheerleading, crew, and waterskiing teams. The University offers an extensive intramural sports program.

Location

The University of Central Florida is located on 1,415 acres approximately 13 miles east of downtown Orlando. In addition to the academic programs offered on the Orlando campus, upper-division students can work toward a degree at ten locations around the central Florida area.

Majors and Degrees

The University offers the degrees of Bachelor of Applied Science, Bachelor of Arts, Bachelor of Design, Bachelor of Fine Arts, Bachelor of Music, Bachelor of Music Education, Bachelor of Science, Bachelor of Science in Business Administration, Bachelor of Science in Education, Bachelor of Science in Engineering, Bachelor of Science in Nursing, Bachelor of Social Work, and Bachelor of Science in Social Sciences. These degrees are available in the colleges listed below, with majors or areas of specialization as indicated.

The College of Arts and Humanities offers degrees in art, architecture, digital media, English, film, French, history, humanities and cultural studies, Latin American studies, music, music education, philosophy, photography, religion and cultural studies, Spanish, theatre studies, and writing and rhetoric.

The College of Business Administration offers degrees in accounting, business economics, economics, finance, integrated business, management, marketing, and real estate.

The College of Education and Human Performance offers degrees in art education, early childhood development and education, elementary education, English language arts education, world languages education, mathematics education, science education, social science education, sport and exercise science, and technical education and industry training.

The College of Engineering and Computer Science offers degrees in aerospace engineering, civil engineering, computer engineering, computer science, construction engineering, electrical engineering, environmental engineering, industrial engineering, information technology, and mechanical engineering.

The College of Health and Public Affairs offers degrees in athletic training, communication sciences and disorders, criminal justice, health informatics and information management, health services administration, health sciences, legal studies, public administration, and social work.

The College of Medicine and the Burnett School of Biomedical Sciences offers degrees in biomedical sciences, biotechnology, and medical laboratory sciences.

The College of Nursing offers degrees in nursing.

The College of Optics and Photonics offers degrees in photonic science and engineering.

The College of Sciences offers degrees in advertising/public relations, anthropology, biology, chemistry, communication and conflict, forensic science, human communication, international and global studies, journalism, mathematics, physics, political science, psychology, radio/television, sociology, social sciences, and statistics.

The Rosen College of Hospitality Management offers degrees in entertainment management, event management, hospitality management, and restaurant and foodservice management.

The College of Undergraduate Studies offers degrees in Interdisciplinary Studies.

Preprofessional programs are offered in chiropractic, dentistry, law, medicine, optometry, osteopathy, pharmacy, podiatry, and veterinary medicine.

Academic Programs

UCF provides a total education through a core curriculum of 36 hours of general education courses. In addition to fulfilling the general education requirement, each student must complete the necessary major and/or minor requirements to reach the minimum of 120 semester hours necessary for graduation.

Several special programs help students reach their academic and leadership potential. The Burnett Honors College at UCF encourages students to achieve academic excellence through small classes and interactive symposia. The innovative LEAD Scholars Academy fosters leadership and service commitment through a comprehensive student development program. The Major Exploration Program (MEP) helps entering freshmen define their career goals and develop an academic strategy to reach those goals. The University also offers online courses and degree programs.

UCF offers Air Force and Army ROTC programs.

Off-Campus Programs

Career Services and Experiential Learning provides comprehensive and coordinated career development, enhances academic study, and builds ongoing partnerships with employers and the community. The Department of Modern Languages offers summer study-abroad programs. Courses are available in the subject areas of language (all levels), art, and civilization. UCF is also a participant in the National Student Exchange Consortium.

Academic Facilities

In addition to the academic programs offered on the Orlando campus, upper division students can work toward a degree at ten campuses located throughout Central Florida. These regional campuses work cooperatively with local state colleges to provide all four years of course work in many academic areas. The library houses over 1.8 million print volumes and subscribes to more than 50,600 periodicals and journals (49,000 in electronic format). Students have access to an online computer catalog that provides information on the collections of the State University System libraries. An extensive online network of more than 600 computers (both PC and Mac) cover the campus. The Institute for Simulation and Training gives students the opportunity to pursue undergraduate research. The College of Optics and Photonics allows faculty members and students to work directly with industry personnel in conducting basic and applied research at the regional and national levels. The Central Florida Research Park, adjacent to the UCF campus, houses more than 125 high-technology firms and agencies. This proximity fosters relationships between industry and the University, which strengthens the academic programs at UCF.

Costs

For Florida residents, the cost of tuition and fees in 2016–17, based on a full-time course load, was $6,368 for the year; for out-of-state residents, the cost was $22,466. Room and board were approximately $9,764 per year, books and supplies cost approximately $1,152.

Financial Aid

Financial aid is awarded according to each student's demonstrated financial need in relation to college costs and may include grants, loans, scholarships, and part-time employment. Programs based upon need include the Federal Perkins Loan, Federal Pell Grant, Florida Student Assistance Grant, Federal Work-Study, Florida College Career Work-Study Program, and Federal Stafford Student Loan. To qualify for these programs, students must complete the Free Application for Federal Student Aid (FAFSA). The priority application deadline is December 1. Seventy-six percent of UCF students receive some form of financial assistance.

Faculty

The University's teaching faculty consists of 2,012 full-time members and adjunct members. Eighty-two percent of the full-time faculty members hold a doctoral or terminal degree. Undergraduate instruction is given primarily by the full-time and adjunct faculty members; graduate students play a minor role in undergraduate instruction. Students are assigned to a faculty adviser in their area of specialization for assistance in academic matters. The student-faculty ratio is 29.5:1.

Student Government

UCF's Student Government Association provides an opportunity for students to become involved at UCF. Every UCF student is encouraged to voice his or her opinion through senate representatives. Student Government is divided into three branches—the student-elected executive branch, the student-elected legislative branch, and the appointed judicial branch. Student Government is responsible for the allocation of all activity and service fees paid by students as a part of their tuition. This money goes toward student services, including the online Macintosh lab, homecoming activities, campus activities board, legal services, and funding for clubs and organizations. Admission is free to all events directly sponsored by the Student Government.

Admission Requirements

A freshman applicant is a student with fewer than 12 hours of college course work after high school graduation. The most important criteria in the admission decision for these applicants are the high school academic record, rigor of course work, grade point average, grade trends, and SAT or ACT test scores. UCF operates on a rolling admission basis. Students are generally notified of their initial admission decision within two to three weeks after receipt of the application and all official supporting documents. If the number of qualified applicants exceeds the number that the University is permitted to enroll, a waiting list is established.

All applicants must have earned a minimum of 18 high school academic units (yearlong courses that are not remedial in nature). These include 4 units of English (3 must include substantial writing), 4 units of mathematics at or above algebra I, 3 units of natural science (2 must include a laboratory), 3 units of social science, 2 units of one world language, and 2 units of academic electives. Grades in honors, International Baccalaureate, Advanced Placement, AICE, dual-enrollment, pre-AP, pre-IB, and pre-AICE courses are given additional weight in the GPA computation. Students must meet the Florida Department of Education minimum eligibility to be considered for admission. Applicants should understand that the satisfaction of minimum requirements does not guarantee admission to UCF.

Admission requirements for transfer applicants vary by the number of college credit hours the student has successfully completed prior to enrolling at UCF. Complete details are available at http://admissions.ucf.edu/transfer. A transfer credit summary evaluation is provided to students once they are offered admission to UCF.

Application and Information

Students are encouraged to apply several months in advance. Transfers can apply online at http://admissions.ucf.edu and freshmen can apply at http://admissions.ucf.edu or through the Common Application. It is recommended that freshman students apply early during the fall semester of their senior year. Applications are accepted up to one year prior to the start of the term for which enrollment is desired. Priority application deadlines are May 1 for the fall term (July 1 for transfers), November 1 for the spring term, and March 1 for the summer term.

The Campus Visit Experience, which includes an information session and a campus tour, is offered Monday through Friday at 10 and 2 (except holidays). Students can sign up for a campus visit online at http://admissions.ucf.edu.

For more information, contact:

Office of Undergraduate Admissions
University of Central Florida
P.O. Box 160111
Orlando, Florida 32816-0111
Phone: 407-823-3000
E-mail: admission@ucf.edu
Website: http://www.ucf.edu

The Charging Knight symbolizes UCF's excellence in academics, partnerships, and athletics.

COLLEGE CLOSE-UPS

UNIVERSITY OF DENVER

DENVER, COLORADO

The University

Since its founding in 1864—2014 marked a sesquicentennial celebration of 150 years of tradition and legacy—the University of Denver (DU) has grown into one of the West's premier private universities, blending the friendliness and personal attention of a small liberal arts college with the resources and intellectual diversity of an advanced research institution. As the oldest private university in the Rocky Mountain region, the University is home to not only a top-ranked undergraduate program, but also to a number of world-renowned research centers and professional programs, including the Josef Korbel School of International Studies, the Sturm College of Law, and the Daniels College of Business.

The 125-acre campus brings together 5,758 traditional undergraduate students and 6,039 graduate students from 50 states and over 90 countries. In an environment that prizes innovation, cross-disciplinary study, and adventurous learning partnerships, students embark on a personalized educational journey inspired and framed by a spirit of exploration and openness.

Whatever their backgrounds and majors, DU students are engaged and active, taking advantage of the region's many recreation and cultural opportunities—everything from world-class skiing and white-water rafting to award-winning professional theater at the Denver Center for the Performing Arts and alternative music shows at Red Rocks Amphitheatre. On campus, students attend performances at the three-venue Newman Center for the Performing Arts and cheer for the 17 varsity teams that compete in NCAA Division I Athletics at the Ritchie Center for Sports & Wellness. DU has claimed many athletic successes over the years including 8 national hockey titles, 1 lacrosse title, and 23 national championship skiing titles.

The University of Denver is accredited by the North Central Association of Colleges and Schools. The Carnegie Foundation classifies the University of Denver as a Doctoral/Research University–Extensive.

Location

Located just eight miles from bustling downtown Denver and mere minutes from the Rocky Mountain foothills, the University of Denver's tree-shaded campus is surrounded by pleasant urban neighborhoods offering coffee shops, retail stores, and diverse restaurants. The institution is located along a light-rail line and major bus lines, providing access to the city's arts districts, shopping centers, sports arenas, and an extensive network of parks. DU students can ride all public transportation for free, using their University-supplied CollegePass smart cards.

Majors and Degrees

The University of Denver offers 12 bachelor's degrees in over 100 programs of study, including the arts, business, computer science, engineering, humanities, international studies, mathematics, natural sciences, and social sciences. Students who are interested in pre-professional programs can choose from law, medical, dental, and veterinary programs that prepare them for professional study beyond their undergraduate degree.

In addition, the University offers 4+1 and 3+2 dual-degree programs that allow students to complete both a bachelor's and master's degree in five years or less. These dual-degree programs are offered in education, social work, computer science, engineering, business, art history, international studies, public policy, and geographic information science. There is also a six-year B.A. or B.S./J.D. program in conjunction with DU's Sturm College of Law.

Academic Programs

Undergraduate programs at the University—which operates on the quarter system—emphasize experiential, dynamic, and cross-disciplinary learning, providing students with the culture and tools to create a positive impact and make meaningful, lasting contributions to their communities and professions.

First-year students enroll in a First-Year Seminar. Limited to 20 students, these seminars focus on a topic that reflects the professor's research interests. This professor, who serves as a mentor throughout the student's first year, introduces the class to university-level work and inquiry, while also advising students on everything from time management to University procedures. The seminar is complemented by a two-quarter writing sequence that trains students to conduct research, construct arguments, and write persuasively for the academic setting. The University's emphasis on writing continues throughout the next three years, with upper-division writing-intensive classes across the disciplines. By the time they graduate, DU students have developed the communication skills that are essential for career success.

Undergraduate students also complete foundations courses in mathematics and computer science, the arts and humanities, natural sciences, and social sciences. DU's Common Curriculum ensures students have a wide base of knowledge upon graduation.

Because the University believes in the value of hands-on learning, students are encouraged to collaborate with faculty members and peers on research projects and creative endeavors. Through the Partners in Scholarship (PinS) program, DU sponsors student work through grants that fund field studies, research trips, and special materials. At year's end, students share their research and findings at a special symposium for their peers.

Thanks to opportunities like these, the University's academic programs earn high marks from students. In a recent National Survey of Student Engagement (NSSE), first-year students and seniors at 546 participating U.S. colleges and universities reported their satisfaction with their own campus. National results revealed that DU students reported significantly higher levels of satisfaction than the average of students at all other participating doctoral-extensive schools for level of academic challenge, involvement in active and collaborative learning, interaction with faculty members, and enriched educational experiences.

Off-Campus Programs

To groom students for the challenges of global citizenship, the University of Denver sponsors Cherrington Global Scholars, a for-credit program that aims to send every eligible junior and senior abroad for at least a quarter of study. The University believes so strongly in this opportunity to expand understanding and foster connections that it ensures qualifying students pay no more for the experience than for a quarter spent on campus. The University budgets about $10 million each year in support of this outstanding program. On average, 70 percent of all DU students participate in study-abroad programs, one of the highest percentages in the nation.

Academic Facilities

In the last decade, the University has invested over $500 million in new buildings and learning centers to ensure that students can prepare for the challenges awaiting them after graduation. These include the Robert and Judi Newman Center for the Performing Arts, home to the University's celebrated Lamont School of Music and host to a performing arts series known for its adventurous offerings; the Daniels College of Business, which houses eleven case-style meeting rooms, nine seminar classrooms, and an Advanced Technology Center; the Knoebel School of Hospitality Management, home to a full-production kitchen, a beverage-management center, a 120-person dining hall, a student-run coffee shop, and a student-faculty-staff commons; and the Anderson Academic Commons, which serves as the new library and hub of the University with a central campus location, multimedia software support services, and a full complement of individual and group study areas and rooms. Construction was recently completed on the Daniel Felix Ritchie School of Engineering and Computer Science, which allows dramatic expansion of both current programming and new STEM initiatives, including the Knoebel Center for the Study of Aging.

Other facilities support the University's commitment to community living and wellness, such as the Nelson Residence Hall which features suites, common kitchens on each floor, a central courtyard, a grand dining hall, and an outdoor dining patio. The Ritchie Center for Sports and Wellness brings students and members of the Denver community together to work out, try new sports, and watch the Pioneer athletic teams. With a state-of-the-art fitness center, a natatorium, a field house, two ice arenas, a gymnastics venue, a lacrosse stadium, a newly remodeled soccer stadium, and a tennis pavilion, the Ritchie Center complex supports the active lifestyle DU students value.

Nagel Residence Hall serves as a campus gathering place, welcoming students and faculty at its food court, providing numerous locations for group study sessions, and offering studio space for students wanting to explore their artistic side. In keeping with the University's far-reaching sustainability initiative, the green building is LEED certified, meaning it uses key resources more efficiently than conventional buildings.

In recent years the University also completed construction on a spectacular new home for both the Morgridge College of Education and the Marsico Institute for Early Learning and Literacy. The influential institute serves as a regional and national nucleus for research and policy analysis on issues related to improving learning environments for young children.

Costs

For the 2017–18 academic year, tuition will be $47,520, fees are estimated at $1,149, and on-campus room and board costs are $12,564, for a total of $61,233. Because the University of Denver is a private institution, costs are the same for in-state and out-of-state students.

Financial Aid

The University of Denver offers two types of financial assistance to students: need-based aid, which includes scholarships, grants, loans, and work-study based on financial need; and merit-based awards, which include scholarships based on merit or special talent. Each year, the Financial Aid office awards over $130 million in need- and merit-based assistance to undergraduate students. About 85 percent of full-time DU undergraduates receive some form of financial assistance.

To recognize achievement in the classroom, the sports arena, leadership, and in music, theatre, and art, the University sponsors a number of merit- and talent-based scholarships. Although the requirements vary from scholarship to scholarship, most are renewable each year if the student maintains a specified minimum GPA. More information regarding scholarships can be found at http://www.du.edu/financialaid.

Need-based financial aid is computed using a number of factors, including family income, assets, size, and the number of family members attending college at the same time. DU utilizes both the CSS PROFILE and the Free Application for Federal Student Aid (FAFSA) to determine need-based aid. Need-based awards generally combine scholarships, grants, loans, and work-study opportunities from a variety of federal, state, and institutional sources. The financial aid offer may also include any competitive scholarships the student has been awarded at the point of admission. To help determine how much need- and merit-based aid might be available to a prospective student and his or her family, DU offers access to a comprehensive net price calculator, found at www.du.edu/estimator.

The priority deadline for applying for financial aid is November 15 for Early Action and Early Decision I applicants, and February 1 for Regular Decision and Early Decision II applicants. Because financial aid funds are limited, students who complete their financial aid applications in a timely manner are more likely to maximize financial aid resources. The student's financial aid package cannot be determined until he or she is officially admitted to DU. More information on applying for financial aid at DU is available at http://www.du.edu/financialaid.

Faculty

DU professors teach more than 99 percent of undergraduate courses, ensuring students work closely with faculty members and the intensity of the learning environment is maximized. The average class size is 21 students; 87 percent of undergraduate classes have fewer than 30 students and 96 percent of classes have fewer than 50 students.

Committed teachers, innovative researchers, and prolific publishers, University of Denver professors often include undergraduate students in their research projects and fieldwork. It is not uncommon for an undergraduate student to share publication credit with a professor or to participate in groundbreaking research with tangible, transformational benefits for humankind.

Student Government

At the University of Denver, the student population is represented by the Undergraduate Student Government (USG), whose elected representatives participate in the University's legislative process and communicate student issues to the administration. In addition, USG oversees the allocation of the student activities fee and the licensing of DU's 100-plus student organizations. In the past few years this group has worked extensively on issues ranging from sustainability to diversity and academic affairs to spirit on campus.

USG includes senators from each major, each geographic area (on-campus, off-campus), and each class (senior, junior, etc.). The USG Executive Board includes an advisor, graduate advisor, president, vice president, and a cabinet of members.

Admission Requirements

Admission to the University of Denver is selective. Students are evaluated individually on the basis of their academic record, test scores, essay, and recommendations. In making its admission decisions, the University seeks to foster an academic community of geographically, ethnically, and economically diverse learners. The admission committee seeks students who are committed to integrity, innovation, inclusiveness, leadership, academic excellence, and community engagement.

Applicants are required to submit either the Common Application or the DU Pioneer Application—both are posted on the DU website. In addition, applicants are required to submit their high school transcripts, scores from either the SAT or ACT (DU uses the superscore system), an essay, and a high school counselor recommendation. Students may also submit a teacher recommendation, although it is not required.

Application and Information

The University of Denver offers four application programs for first-year domestic students seeking fall quarter admission. Early Action (deadline of November 1) is a nonbinding program leading to an admission decision in mid-December. Early Decision I (also a November 1 deadline) is a binding program leading to an admission decision in early December. Regular Decision and Early Decision II (deadline of January 15 for both), which are nonbinding and binding respectively, are the final admission programs for fall quarter consideration. Regular Decision applicants and Early Decision II applicants receive their admission decision in early to mid-March.

To learn more about the University of Denver, students should contact:

Undergraduate Admission
University of Denver
2197 South University Boulevard
Denver, Colorado, 80208-9401
United States
Phone: 303-871-2036
E-mail: admission@du.edu
Website: http://www.du.edu/admission
http://www.youtube.com/uofdenver
http://www.facebook.com/uofdenveradmission
http://twitter.com/uofdenver

University of Denver

UNIVERSITY OF DUBUQUE

DUBUQUE, IOWA

UNIVERSITY *of* DUBUQUE

★ To read more about this school, visit http://petersons.to/universityofdubuque

A Tradition of Professional and Theological Training

The University of Dubuque (UD) is a private, Presbyterian professional university that combines a broad study of liberal arts with hands-on experience. Students gain specialized knowledge and master particular skills within their major. Students develop critical abilities that serve them well in adapting to a changing world.

Located about 175 miles from Chicago, the University has been known throughout its 165-year history as one of the nation's best small Christian universities.

UD is one of the most diverse campuses in the Midwest, representing students from 43 states and 22 countries, and it is a college of community where Christian commitment, intellectual integrity, and academic excellence are the basis for learning. Students can adjust their mix of liberal arts and professional training in ways that suit their learning styles and that help achieve both personal and professional goals. More information, is available online at http://www.dbq.edu/campuslife/officeofstudentlife/.

Campus Setting and Surrounding Area

Situated on the Mississippi River where the borders of Wisconsin, Illinois, and Iowa meet, UD is located in Iowa's first city, Dubuque. This central location puts UD students within easy driving distance of cities such as Chicago, Illinois; Des Moines, Iowa; Madison, Wisconsin; and Rochester, Minnesota.

A lively cultural scene, Dubuque is home to the National Mississippi River Museum and Aquarium, the Dubuque Museum of Art, the Grand Opera House, the Dubuque Symphony Orchestra, and a variety of shops, restaurants, and event venues. The city boasts miles of trails for walking, hiking, biking, and many Mississippi waterway and byway activities.

Surrounded by comfortable green spaces within a historic city, UD students enjoy the benefits of modern facilities. Since 1998, the University has invested over $250 million into new construction and renovations that integrate contemporary green spaces within historic architecture.

Required Freshman Courses

The first-year curriculum orients students into the rigor of upper-level course work, while building a community of new friends through the experiences they share with their peers. With the support of an enthusiastic community, new UD students are challenged to build upon their gifts through academic inquiry, social interactions, and spiritual exploration as they discover their place within a diverse campus community. Students and faculty together explore topics that influence global cultures within the context of the University's Christian tradition.

Undergraduate and Graduate Degrees at a Glance

The University of Dubuque developed Diamond, an education model that focuses all classroom learning around four key principles: academics, stewardship, vocation, and community and character. These features of Diamond set the standards for committed faculty and staff involvement, exciting and relevant course content, and inspirational spiritual guidance. Diamond helps students reach their full potential by promoting an environment that is student centered and individually focused. Students are prepared to manage change by building confidence, developing flexibility, and encouraging critical thinking.

The University's fourteen departments outline the academic programs found within each area as well as options for interdisciplinary majors. The University also has options for individually-designed majors and minors through consultation with academic advisers.

Undergraduate degrees within the Bachelor of Arts area of study include: criminal justice; dance; English; fine and performing arts; liberal studies; music; psychology; religious studies; sociology; sports marketing and management; and theatre.

Undergraduate degrees within the bachelor of business administration field of study include: accounting; business administration; computer information systems; computer information technology; human resource management; and marketing.

Undergraduate degrees within the bachelor of science program include: aviation management; biology; communication; computer graphics/interactive media; chemistry; digital forensics; elementary education; environmental science; flight operations; human health science; mathematics; natural and applied science; secondary education; nursing; pre-professional health science; philosophy; physical education; psychology; sociology; teacher education; and wellness and exercise science.

Graduates are eligible for certification where applicable. For example, the Bachelor of Science degree in Flight Operations is centered on a Pilot Training School certified under FAA 14 CFR Part 141, and prepares students for FAA certification (licensing) and ratings.

All students who complete the UD teacher education program are eligible to apply for an Iowa Initial Teacher License.

Students who graduate with their Bachelor of Science in Nursing degree are eligible to take the licensure exam NCLEX (National Council [of State Boards of Nursing] Licensure Examination) to become registered nurses.

The University of Dubuque's academic strengths support and align with several prominent needs for graduate education both in the region and globally. Offered in a traditional semester-long course format, courses are taught by both University of Dubuque faculty as well as subject matter experts who are currently in the work world. Degrees include: Master of Arts in Communication; Master of Business Administration; Accelerated Adult MBA and MAC Degree (LIFE); Master in Physician Assistant Studies; and a Master of Arts in Christian Leadership.

The MBA degree gives students advanced business acumen with courses that integrate communication and knowledge management, finance, human capital, organizational management, and business strategy and modeling.

Research Fellowships

The Joseph and Linda Chlapaty Summer Research Fellowship and Butler Fellowship are two examples of the research opportunities available to UD students. These fellowships help prepare undergraduate students for their postgraduate pursuits, no matter their discipline of study. Each year, over 30 upperclassmen are awarded a fellowship to conduct research over the course of a summer. The University of Dubuque works hard to ensure that these awards cover the costs of research

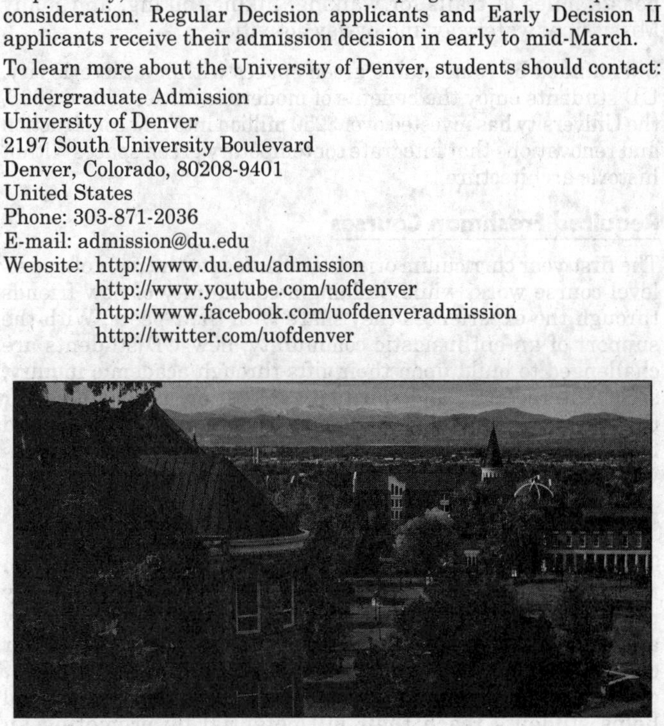

supplies and travel, giving students free reign to explore and inquire within their area of study.

Heeding the Call to Theological Education and Service

The University of Dubuque Theological Seminary (UDTS), a seminary of the Presbyterian Church (U.S.A.), is an ecumenical community, with students and faculty from the Presbyterian Church (U.S.A.), as well as the United Methodist Church, the United Church of Christ, the Reformed Church of America, and a number of other denominations.

The seminary offers the Master of Divinity degree through a residential program and is the only seminary of the Presbyterian Church (U.S.A.) that is accredited to provide a Distance Master of Divinity degree. The seminary is also the only seminary of the Presbyterian Church (U.S.A.) that is part of a university.

Success Center Provides Every Kind of Help

The University's Academic Success Center connects students with the resources to achieve both academic and personal goals.

Services include individual tutoring, writing, disability accommodations, testing services, academic probation support services, English learning labs, math learning labs, peer-assisted learning study groups, and athletic study tables.

Student Life and Community Service

UD has four traditional residence halls for undergraduate students living on campus and six apartment-style buildings for upper-class students. Townhouses are available for seminary and graduate students.

Activities and events planned by over 60 clubs and organizations supplement students' academic life with valuable experience, fun, and friendship. Out-of-classroom programs provide opportunities for vocational growth, leadership training, community service, and personal development. Greek life also thrives at UD through numerous sororities and fraternities.

UD has been recognized nationally for its history of community service throughout the years. Students participate in service projects they plan both in the classroom and through co-curricular programs, fraternities or sororities, and in campus ministry.

Study Abroad Opportunities

UD study-abroad programs bring both long-term (semester) and short-term international experience to students. Students return, even from short study trips, with new knowledge about foreign societies and world viewpoints.

Costs

Tuition (based on a full academic year): $27,400; full-time student fees: $1,300; room and board: $9,124; room only: $4,574.

Academic and Career Guidance, Financial Aid, and ROTC

The University provides academic advising services that empower students to make informed decisions about their academic and professional aspirations. At the beginning of their first year, each student is assigned a Director of Advising who helps them plan their course schedules and enter the University with a platform for success. The University's Center for Vocation and Civic Engagement helps students direct their strengths to real-world experiences outside the college setting. The Center's staff guides students to discover their unique strengths and gifts, providing them with insight into their chosen vocation and directing them toward appropriate internships, potential employers, and possible graduate schools.

Eighty-five percent of UD's students receive financial assistance through scholarships, awards and grants, loans, or work-study programs.

An Army Reserve Officers' Training Corp (ROTC) program is available along with associated merit-based scholarships.

Faculty

UD faculty totals 216. The student-to-faculty ratio is 13:1.

Application Information

All applicants must submit their complete high school transcripts, an essay or personal statement, a letter of recommendation, and a $25 application fee. An average high school GPA of 2.95 is required for first-year students. UD offers rolling admissions.

For further information, prospective students should contact:

Bob Broshous
Dean of Admission
University of Dubuque
2000 University Avenue
Dubuque, Iowa 52001-5009
Phone: 563-589-3199
Fax: 563-589-3690
E-mail: admissns@dbq.edu
Website: http://www.dbq.edu

Heritage Center, the University's fine and performing arts, worship, and campus center, opened in May 2013.

COLLEGE CLOSE-UPS

UNIVERSITY OF GUELPH

GUELPH, ONTARIO, CANADA

The University

The University of Guelph is consistently ranked as one of Canada's top Comprehensive Universities, and as one of the top 500 universities in the world by the **QS World University rankings**. With students from more than 100 countries, U of G is a high-calibre, student-focused university, committed to innovative experiential learning, award-winning research, and a uniquely supportive community. Guelph offers a wide range of programs in the arts, humanities, social sciences, engineering, and the natural sciences. Students can also take advantage of Guelph's cross-disciplinary approach by tailoring degree programs, selecting from professional and applied programs, or specializing in the areas of agriculture and veterinary medicine.

Established in 1964, the University of Guelph is a medium-sized university with a strong campus community, beautiful historical buildings, and green spaces. Guelph has a dedication to four major pillars: food, health, community, and environment. These represent a larger goal of accelerating research that will help people around the world.

On-campus living is guaranteed to all first-semester students, if they apply and submit the deposit by the deadline. Each residence is unique and comfortable, with students being able to choose from more than twenty themed housing options.

Guelph's Athletic Facilities underwent a 170,000 square-foot expansion in 2016, and include a double arena with an Olympic-size ice surface, two pools, a field house and indoor track, aerobic and weight-training gymnasiums, volleyball and basketball courts, six squash courts, events centre, and a climbing wall. Guelph offers 30 varsity sports teams and 17 intramural sports. U of G's intramural program has won the Canadian Intramural Recreation Association Achievement seven times! The University of Guelph aims to become a global leader in promoting healthy living for everyone.

As a learner, students are at the centre of U of G. The Center for New Students assists students with the transition into university and has achieved a 94 percent student retention rate and an 88.8 percent graduate employment rate, both well above the Canadian national average.

Location

The University of Guelph's main campus is located in southwestern Ontario which is an hour from Toronto, Canada's largest city. The city of Guelph has a population of more than 121,000, and is recognized for its environmental sustainability, volunteerism, safety, and its vibrant arts community. The city has all of the amenities of a bigger city, but with a small-town feel. Guelph also offers many dynamic degrees in Toronto at the University of Guelph–Humber, and diploma programs in Ridgetown at the regional campus.

Majors and Degrees

The University of Guelph offers a number of undergraduate degree programs. Programs followed by an asterisk (*) indicate co-operative education degrees which offer students the opportunity to complete three to five paid work terms while completing their degree.

Bachelor of Arts degrees: Anthropology; art history; classical studies; criminal justice and public policy; economics*; English; environmental governance; European studies; food, agriculture, and resource economics; French studies; geography; history; international development; major to be determined; mathematical economics*; mathematical science; music; philosophy; political science; psychology*; sociology; Spanish and Hispanic studies; studio art; and theater studies. In addition, a **Bachelor of Arts and Sciences** degree is available to students who excel in both arts/social sciences and sciences.

Bachelor of Applied Science degrees: Applied human nutrition; child, youth, and family*; and adult development*.

Bachelor of Commerce degrees: Accounting*; food and agricultural business*; hospitality and tourism management*; leadership and organizational management; management economics and finance*; marketing management*; public management*; real estate and housing*; and undeclared (first year only).

Bachelor of Bio-Resource Management degrees: Environmental management and equine management.

The Bachelor of Computing degrees: Computer science* and software engineering*.

Bachelor of Engineering degrees: Biological engineering*; biomedical engineering*; computer engineering*; environmental engineering*; engineering systems and computing*; mechanical engineering*; water resources engineering*; and undeclared (first year only).

Bachelor of Science degrees: Animal biology; biochemistry*; biodiversity; biological science; biological and pharmaceutical chemistry*; biological and medical physics*; bio-medical science; bio-medical toxicology; chemical physics*; chemistry*; environmental biology; environmental geoscience and geomatics; food science*; human kinetics; marine and freshwater biology; mathematical science; microbiology*; molecular biology and genetics; nanoscience*; neuroscience; nutritional and nutraceutical sciences; physical science; physics*; plant science; psychology: brain and cognition; theoretical physics; wildlife biology and conservation; and zoology.

Bachelor of Science in Agriculture degrees: Animal science; crop, horticulture, and turfgrass sciences; honors agriculture; and organic agriculture.

Bachelor of Science in Environmental Sciences degrees: Ecology*; environment and resource management*; environmental economics and policy*; and environmental sciences*.

University of Guelph also offers the **Bachelor of Landscape Architecture** degree, a **Doctor of Veterinary Medicine** degree, and associate diplomas.

University of Guelph–Humber programs include honors degrees in: business administration (accounting; finance; international business; management; marketing or small business management; and entrepreneurship); applied science (early childhood studies; family and community social services; justice studies; kinesiology; or psychology); and applied arts in media studies (journalism; media business or public relations; digital communications; and image arts).

The University of Guelph offers graduate students a unique opportunity to work with faculty and conduct leading-edge research. Graduate programs include: Doctor of Veterinary Medicine, several graduate diploma programs, and more than eighty master's and doctoral degree programs. A full list of graduate programs is available online at uoguelph.ca/graduatestudies.

Academic Programs

The academic year is divided into three semesters: fall (September through December), winter (January through April), and summer (May through August), with the majority of students attending during the fall and winter semesters.

Four-year honors degrees require the completion of eight semesters. Three-year general degrees require the completion of six semesters. A typical full-time semester totals 2.5 credits.

Off-Campus Programs

Guelph encourages students to enrich their learning experience by immersing in another culture to develop a global perspective. The campus attracts nearly 1,000 international students from over 100 countries, maintains 74 exchange programs in 36 countries, and offers six semester-abroad options. More than 600 Guelph students study, research, volunteer, or work each year around the world.

Through the co-op program, over 3,000 students gain relevant work experience, and build professional networks and essential skills. Guelph co-op has one of the highest student enrolments in Ontario. Guelph also offers Open Learning, which provides access to online degree-credit university courses for those students looking to study independently.

Academic Facilities

The University of Guelph library partners with two other universities in the region, providing students with access to millions of print and electronic resources, including world-renowned archival collections in Canadian theatre and Scottish culture. In addition, the Library offers research and writing help, and many other academic support services.

Guelph's faculty receives Can$146.6 million in annual research funding to provide insight into the health and well-being of the global society.

All students receive U of G central login accounts that give them access to university e-mail accounts, campus-wide WiFi, discounted software, and Webadvisor, which manages course selection, grades, and financial accounts.

The campus features North America's largest integrated science teaching and research facility, the Summerlee Science Complex; the art gallery of Guelph; a sculpture park; a covered field house; a Can$44.6-million engineering facility expansion; the Guelph Institute for the Environment; and the Biodiversity Institute of Ontario, which is the world's first center for high-volume DNA barcoding. The campus also includes a 408-acre arboretum that has nearly 5 miles of nature paths.

Costs

Full-time tuition for the 2016–17 academic year ranged from Can$3285 to Can$6087 per semester for Canadian residents, and from Can$10,420 to Can$13,507 per semester for international students. Doctor of Veterinary Medicine tuition was Can$4890 per semester for Canadian residents and Can$30,665 per semester for international students. The cost for international students for two semesters, including tuition and academic fees, health coverage (mandatory), housing, clothing, food, and books, totaled between Can$37,416 and Can$43,591 for all programs except for Doctor of Veterinary Medicine.

Financial Aid

The University of Guelph wholeheartedly believes that an education should be an attainable goal for all qualified students. In 2015–16, Can$18.9 was awarded in merit- and need-based aid to undergraduate students. For international students, Guelph offers merit-based scholarships ranging from Can$2000 to Can$8500, along with needs-based entrance awards ranging from Can$1000 to Can$5000. Students can also seek work-study and part-time jobs on campus. More information can be found online at **uoguelph.ca/registrar/studentfinance**.

Faculty

U of G has approximately 800 full-time professors, 98 percent of which hold a Ph.D. degree or its equivalent, and who all take a genuine interest in the success of every student. The University of Guelph is the first Canadian university to have had its president and provost hold the prestigious 3M National Teaching Fellowship, in addition to 15 other faculty members. Being Canada's top teaching honour, the award recognizes exceptional contributions to teaching and learning. Guelph also has 20 Fellows of the Royal Society of Canada among its researchers.

Student Government

Guelph students are actively involved in dynamic student government groups, including residence council and the Board of Governors. Students are members of the Central Student Association (CSA), the official Guelph student government. In addition, there are more than 200 clubs and organizations on campus that span cultural and religious interests, sports and academics, the arts, and community service. There are also a number of student governments on campus that advocate important social issues.

Admission Requirements

Ontario applicants must present the Ontario Secondary School Diploma (OSSD), with a minimum of six 4U or 4M courses, including specific subject requirements for the chosen degree program. Note: English 4U is required for all degree programs. For those outside Ontario, applicants must complete all requirements for their secondary school graduation diploma, including specific program requirements. The secondary school graduation certificate, which would admit a student to an internationally recognized university in their home country, is normally acceptable for admission, along with completion of specific subject requirements for the degree program chosen (https://admission.uoguelph.ca/international).

Students applying with an International Baccalaureate (IB) diploma should present a minimum score of 28, inclusive of 3 higher level and 3 standard level subjects. Transfer credits may be given for higher level courses with grades of 5 or better, to a maximum of 2.0 credits. Students applying from the United States must have a minimum unweighted grade point average of 3.0, and a combined SAT score of 1100, or ACT score of 24. Among their senior level courses, applicants should also complete specific subject requirements for the chosen program. Applicants who have completed Advanced Placement (AP) examinations with a minimum grade of 4 may receive university credit to a maximum of 2.0 credits, subject to the discretion of the Admissions Committee.

Prospective students should contact Admission Services or see **admission.uoguelph.ca** for applicant deadlines, detailed admission information, and important dates.

Admission information for University of Guelph-Humber is available at **www.guelphhumber.ca**.

Application and Information

For additional information about admissions, academic programs, or events, students should contact:

Admission Services
3rd Floor, University Centre
University of Guelph
Guelph, Ontario N1G 2W1
Canada
Phone: 519-821-2130
519-767-5024 (direct U.S. and international line)
Fax: 519-766-9481
E-mail: internat@uoguelph.ca (International inquiries)
usa@uoguelph.ca (U.S. inquiries)
admission@registrar.uoguelph.ca (Canadian inquiries)
Website: http://admission.uoguelph.ca (main campus)
http://www.guelphhumber.ca (Toronto campus)

The University of Guelph boasts a beautiful campus, with a mix of both modern and traditional buildings, facilities, and lecture halls.

COLLEGE CLOSE-UPS

UNIVERSITY OF HARTFORD

WEST HARTFORD, CONNECTICUT

★ To read more about this school, visit http://petersons.to/universityofhartford

UNIVERSITY OF HARTFORD

The University

The University of Hartford is a fully accredited, independent, nonsectarian institution. The University is composed of seven degree-granting schools and colleges: the College of Arts and Sciences; College of Engineering, Technology, and Architecture; College of Education, Nursing, and Health Professions; Hillyer College; the Barney School of Business; the Hartford Art School; and The Hartt School.

The current full-time undergraduate enrollment is approximately 4,600 men and women. With an average class size of about 20–25 students, each one benefits from additional personalized attention from faculty members. Students can expect to get to know not only their classroom professors, but also all faculty members in their department. Faculty members focus on helping students apply what they learn in the classroom to real-world scenarios and provide the mentoring necessary to push students past perceived limits. A wide range of interests, goals, and backgrounds is found among the students, who represent fifty states and forty countries. There are about 100 organized student groups, including clubs devoted to special interests or to political, professional, religious, or civic activities as well as service learning and community service activities and groups. Intercollegiate (NCAA Division I) and intramural athletics, student publications, and AM and FM radio stations provide further opportunities for extracurricular involvement. In addition, The Hartt School, the Hartford Art School, and the University Players present a variety of concerts, exhibitions, and theatrical productions each year. Recreational and fitness needs of the University community as well as intramural and intercollegiate sports are served by a well-equipped 130,000-square-foot sports center and outdoor athletic facilities.

More than 66 percent of all full-time undergraduates reside on campus. The University offers a wide array of residence halls, from traditional dormitory-style to fully equipped town house–style apartments.

Location

The University is located in the residential suburb of West Hartford. Whether it's to eat at the Cheesecake Factory and catch a movie at Criterion Cinemas, or shop at Ann Taylor or REI, West Hartford is a great place to visit. The Hartford area also boasts an impressive array of entertainment and cultural resources including the Comcast Theatre and the Bushnell Performing Arts Center. The campus is easily accessible by both train and bus and is located about 25 minutes from Bradley International Airport.

Majors and Degrees

About 25 percent of students apply undecided which, at the University of Hartford, is an opportunity to explore many academic interests among the more than 100 areas of study. Students receive support from offices such as Career Services, the Student Success Center, and a Dialogue course which allows them to meet with and learn from other undecided students. The College of Arts and Sciences offers majors in biology, chemistry, chemistry-biology, cinema, communication, computer science, criminal justice, economics, English, history, international studies, Judaic studies, mathematics, philosophy, physics, politics and government, psychology, and sociology.

Within the College of Education, Nursing, and Health Professions, there are majors in early childhood education, elementary education, integrated special education/elementary education, secondary education with a concentration in English or mathematics, health sciences, nursing (for registered nurses only), radiologic technology, respiratory therapy, a combined B.S. in health science, and doctorate in physical therapy (B.S./D.P.T.) program, as well as a combined B.S. in health science and a Master of Science in Prosthetics and Orthotics (B.S./M.S.P.O.) program.

The Hartford Art School offers Bachelor of Fine Arts degrees in ceramics, design, drawing, illustration, painting, photography, printmaking, sculpture, and visual communication as well as a Bachelor of Arts in art history.

At the Hartt School, students can major in actor training, applied music (guitar, orchestral instrument, organ, piano, pre–cantorial studies, and voice), composition, dance (ballet pedagogy or performance emphases), jazz studies, music, music education, music history, music management, music production and technology, music theater, music theory, and performing arts management (interdisciplinary program offered in conjunction with the Barney School of Business). There are also five-year double majors offered within the Hartt School.

Majors for the Bachelor of Science in Business Administration (B.S.B.A.) degree in the Barney School of Business are accounting, economics and finance, entrepreneurial studies, finance and insurance, management, and marketing.

Additional B.S. programs, offered by the College of Engineering, Technology, and Architecture include ABET-EAC accredited programs in electrical, mechanical, civil, computer, and biomedical engineering, and acoustical engineering and music. The newest offering in the mechanical engineering department is a concentration in energy engineering and sustainable design. The most popular B.S.E. options are acoustical engineering and music (interdisciplinary program in conjunction with the Hartt School) and biomedical engineering. In addition, the college offers interdisciplinary B.S.E. options. Technology programs include the Bachelor of Science in architectural engineering technology, audio engineering technology, computer and electronic engineering technology, electronic engineering technology, and the newest technology major, the B.S. in electromechanical engineering technology. The programs in architecture, electronics, and mechanical are ABET-ETAC accredited.

Hillyer College provides the general education course work required to complete most of the University's baccalaureate programs. Particular emphasis is placed on the development of academic skills through small classes and close faculty-student interaction.

University Studies offers the Bachelor of University Studies, a B.A. degree program created for the part-time adult student who typically has previous college experience and seeks to complete a baccalaureate degree. Also offered is a B.A. degree program in multimedia website design and development for full-time undergraduates. Created for students who want to learn how to use and develop multimedia technologies that fit into today's wired world, this program combines courses across several disciplines where students create and use technology with user interaction in mind.

Academic Programs

The University of Hartford enjoys a national reputation for the breadth and depth of its academic programs. As highlighted above, about 100 programs of study are offered through seven schools and colleges. Students are encouraged to sample a variety of academic areas. Those who have special interests can develop interdisciplinary majors that combine courses from the different schools within the University. Academic advisers are assigned to all students to help guide them in curriculum choices, career exploration, and the transition to University life. The University also has a special program to assist students who may be undecided about a major. A reading and writing center provides individual support to help students increase their proficiency in writing, research, reading comprehension, and speed as well as study and test-taking skills. Further help in math is given through the Math Tutoring Lab, which is staffed by full-time faculty members and math majors. Career Services provides vocational counseling and information on occupations, employers, testing, and graduate schools; serves as a reference and credential source; and provides an on-campus recruiting program for graduating students. The Adult

Academic Services Office addresses the needs of the part-time adult learner through courses, programs, and educational counseling. A trained counseling staff is available to assist part-time students in planning their education and resolving their special concerns and needs. Selected students are encouraged to participate in the honors program. Honors students have the opportunity to excel at college and add value to their education at no extra cost. Students in the honors program can enjoy smaller class sizes, special awards and scholarships, honor society membership, and can graduate with an honors degree.

Off-Campus Programs

Intercampus registration through the Hartford Consortium for Higher Education permits University of Hartford students to take certain courses at the School of the Hartford Ballet, Saint Joseph College, and Trinity College. Teaching majors in the College of Education, Nursing, and Health Professions have opportunities for field and/or clinical experiences where applicable. A central internship and cooperative education office is available to custom-tailor work experiences within many of the University's programs. The study-abroad office works with students to arrange international learning experiences that promote cultural exploration and lifelong memories. The University of Hartford has garnered affiliations with schools in more than sixty different countries, making study abroad a vast and popular option on campus.

Academic Facilities

Seven schools and colleges are housed on the main campus. The Harry Jack Gray Center houses the William H. Mortensen Library; the Mildred P. Allen Memorial Library; the Museum of American Political Life; the Harry J. Gray Conference Center; the Joseloff Gallery; the University Bookstore; studios for architecture, art, radio, and television; and the communication department. The library has approximately 600,000 reference items, including books, musical scores, recordings, periodicals, journals, and microfilm units as well as high-speed and wireless Internet access. Extensive resources are also available through the Hartford Consortium for Higher Education, the Hartford Library, and the Interlibrary Loan systems.

The new state-of-the-art Mort and Irma Handel Performing Arts Center, located 5 minutes from the main campus, is a 55,000-square-foot facility that houses five dance studios, four theater rehearsal studios, two black box theaters, a small dining facility, and faculty and staff offices. The Handel Performing Arts Center provides a rehearsal and performance environment for the Hartt School's dancers.

The University of Hartford Computer Center houses the central computer systems and operates a high-performance campus-wide network, which connects all student residential housing, all academic buildings on campus, and the University's remote locations. The University's network is connected via a high-speed telecommunication link to the Internet. The residential network gives each student resident his or her own high-speed Ethernet connection to the campus network and the Internet. All of the University network resources may be accessed on campus in any University facility and off campus by using computers with network connectivity.

Public access computing labs, used by all students of the University, are provided at various locations around the campus. In addition, college-specific labs are available to students. All labs are equipped with microcomputers (both PCs and Macs) and are connected to the campus network and the Internet. Typical microcomputer software includes word processing, spreadsheet, database management, and graphics programs; programming languages; and web browsers for accessing the Internet. Help is available from on-duty lab assistants. In addition to these computer labs, there are specialized computer facilities for instruction and learning. Wireless Internet access is available in all academic buildings, libraries, and dining facilities.

Costs

Tuition for incoming students was $35,036 for the 2016–17 academic year; fees, $2,754; on-campus room costs, $7,774; and board, $4,212. A variety of on-campus housing accommodates the University's residential student population.

Financial Aid

Financial aid for University of Hartford students totals approximately $98 million annually, including student loans. Scholarships, grants, loans, and work-study opportunities are provided through the federal government, private agencies, interested individuals, and University funds. University funds are disbursed based on the college or school in which the student is enrolled, availability of funds, applicant pool, and competition for funds. About 93 percent of new full-time undergraduate students receive some type of University assistance. The average financial aid package for incoming freshman (fall 2015) was $27,748 (this figure includes average gift aid from all sources and average education loans). Partial-tuition scholarships are awarded to entering students who have demonstrated outstanding academic achievement or talent.

Faculty

There are more than 900 full-time and adjunct faculty members. The undergraduate and graduate faculties are essentially the same group, and 79 percent of the members hold the terminal degree in their field. Academic and personal advisory service is readily available. Each new student is assigned to a faculty adviser during summer orientation.

Student Government

The student governing body that represents all full-time students is the Student Government Association, through which students and faculty join in developing and coordinating the co-curricular activities of the University. Students are also represented on all major administrative committees, including the Board of Regents.

Admission Requirements

The Office of Admission considers the quality of the secondary school curriculum, academic performance in secondary school, ACT or SAT results, evidence of a desire to succeed, and leadership qualities shown by academic and extracurricular activities. Auditions, portfolios, and other tests are required of music and art applicants.

Application and Information

The University employs a rolling admission policy. For further information, students should visit the University on the Internet at http://admission.hartford.edu or contact:

Office of Admission
University of Hartford
West Hartford, Connecticut 06117
Phone: 860-768-4296
800-947-4303 (toll-free)
Fax: 860-768-4961
E-mail: admission@hartford.edu
Website: http://admission.hartford.edu

Find yourself here. Your talent will follow.

UNIVERSITY OF MAINE

ORONO, MAINE

★ For more information, visit http://petersons.to/universityofmaine

The University

The University of Maine (UMaine) offers the extensive academic opportunities expected from a major research university, with the close-knit feel of a small college. The University of Maine is Maine's Flagship University, offering the most comprehensive academic experience in the state. There are nearly 100 majors and academic programs, 75 master's degree programs, and 35 doctoral programs. All majors benefit from a strong foundation in the liberal arts. Top students are invited to join the Honors College, one of the country's oldest and most prestigious honors colleges in the nation. UMaine is also the state's only public research university, housing facilities with an international reputation for excellence. UMaine students have extraordinary opportunities to gain real-world experience through research and experiential learning. Undergraduates have the opportunity to collaborate with faculty, conduct fieldwork, and participate in internships around the world. Wildlife ecology majors learn about animal behavior by working in the field with wildlife biologists and black bear cubs. Many engineering students secure co-ops that typically lead to employment immediately after graduation. Education majors have the opportunity to take advantage of urban, rural, and international student-teaching opportunities. There are over 200 student organizations, such as the student investment club that manages a $2.3-million real-money portfolio, Greek Life, Division I athletics, and many more.

Location

There's no place like Maine. UMaine students are surrounded by the great outdoors and have ample opportunity to explore everything the state has to offer. Orono is nestled between the Stillwater and Penobscot rivers. The campus has a traditional New England feel with ivy-covered brick buildings, towering pines, and beautiful fall foliage. Some of the best skiing in the Northeast is within easy driving distance. Beautiful tourist attractions such as Bar Harbor, Acadia National Park, Baxter State Park, and the northern terminus of the Appalachian Trail are just a short drive from campus. The University of Maine is 10 minutes from the city of Bangor, Maine's third-largest city, with its own international airport.

Majors and Degrees

UMaine offers nearly 100 majors and programs across six colleges at the undergraduate level: the College of Education and Human Development; College of Engineering; College of Liberal Arts and Sciences; College of Natural Sciences, Forestry, and Agriculture; the Maine Business School; and the Honors College. In addition, UMaine offers the Explorations program, designed to help undecided students identify a major across the vast academic opportunities available and find the best fit for a degree program. The Division of Lifelong Learning offers online classes, Summer University, Winter Session, and distance-learning opportunities for students who need a flexible class schedule.

Academic Programs

UMaine provides a comprehensive academic and student experience, yielding graduates who are well-educated, well-adjusted, and well-prepared to succeed after graduation and assume leadership roles within their respective careers. The University seeks to foster excellence and innovation through inspired, dedicated teaching by ensuring there is a constant discovery of new knowledge for students. In addition to their major or concentration within their degree programs, University of Maine students benefit from a solid liberal arts foundation. Students develop and refine the qualities needed to fully engage with the world around them, regardless of their academic discipline.

Undergraduate research is a major component of the learning atmosphere. The University of Maine offers students true hands-on research experience, as early as their first year on campus. UMaine is the state's largest research university, providing rich and diverse opportunities for undergraduates to publish findings, travel the globe, and work alongside UMaine's world-class scholars and researchers. The Center for Undergraduate Research connects students with faculty projects applicable to their academic interests and future careers. The abundance of research opportunities also provides students with great mentoring connections between faculty and students that carry benefits beyond the classroom. The skills students develop through research creates applicants who are much more competitive in the workplace and graduate school.

Campus Programs

Students will get a full and enriching college experience at UMaine. The University of Maine hosts many on-campus programs and opportunities for students to explore and meet new people. There are over 200 clubs and organizations for students to get involved in, such as Greek Life, Woodsmen's Team, Robotics Club, Spanish Club, and more. The Campus Activities Board also puts on free events during the school year, including movies, karaoke, game nights, and astronomy shows. Students can join an athletic team or cheer the UMaine Black Bears Division I teams to victory for free during the year.

There are many ways to explore Maine off campus as well through outdoor recreation, music and food festivals, museums, and much more. Bangor, a 10-minute drive from campus, hosts Summer Concerts in the Park, the American Folk Festival, and a state fair.

Through UMaine study-abroad programs, students explore globally while enhancing their education by taking courses, researching or volunteering. UMaine students have traveled to China to study emerging financial markets, to Italy to learn about Renaissance art history, to Turkey to study film, and to Brazil to look at our world's diverse ecosystem.

Academic Facilities

The University of Maine is home to state-of-the-art research facilities, classrooms, and teaching laboratories. Fogler Library is the state's largest library and located in the heart of campus. It houses more than 1.4 million volumes, 1.6 million microforms, and 2.3 million U.S. and Canadian government publications. It's also the archive of papers written by famous UMaine Alumnus Stephen King. Students have access to UMaine's new Capital Markets Training Laboratory with state-of-the-art technology and 12 Bloomberg Terminals that provide hands-on learning in finance. The Virtual Environment and Multimodal Interaction Laboratory (VEMI) is a research facility that combines fully immersive virtual reality with augmented reality technologies in an integrated research and development environment. Students from all interests and majors collaborate in VEMI Lab research in areas such as aging, vision impairment, and virtual realities. The new, multi-million-dollar Innovative Media Research and Commercialization Center (IMRC) and the Wyeth Family Studio Art Center contain facilities for training, research, development, and commercialization. Students have access to many different labs, such as a fabrication studio, electronics lab, audio and video production labs, 3-D printing and design, and prototype production.

The University of Maine is also a cultural hub. It is home to the region's premier performing arts center, the Collins Center for the Arts, as well as several museums and galleries.

Costs

For the 2017–18 academic year, tuition for in-state undergraduate students is estimated at $8,580, and $27,960 for out-of-state residents. Canadian residents and students who qualify for the New England Regional Program (NEBHE) will pay an estimated $13,290 for tuition. The average credit load for full-time students is 15 credit hours per semester or 30 credit hours for the academic year. Required university fees are estimated at $2,322 per year for a full-time student. These fees include a variety of healthcare services and admission to cultural, recreational, and athletic events. Books and supplies cost, on average, about $1,000, and room and board estimated cost is $10,144 for one academic year.

Financial Aid

UMaine requires all financial aid applicants to file the Free Application for Federal Student Aid (FAFSA). The priority deadline to apply for aid is March 1. Awards usually consist of a combination of several types of aid, ranging from grants and scholarships to work-study jobs and student loans. Students are encouraged to apply early in the application cycle to ensure admission in selective academic programs and receive merit scholarships based on high school achievement, as demonstrated by high school rank, grade point average, and standardized test results (SAT and ACT). Additional information on application deadlines and merit scholarships is available online at go.umaine.edu.

Faculty

UMaine is known for its beautiful and vast campus, large student body, and family atmosphere. Students will get to know each other quickly, but even more importantly, so will their professors. UMaine's professors have an open-door policy and encourage students to meet with them outside of class. Undergraduate classes are taught by professors, and many faculty go on to be academic and professional mentors for their students. Students have the opportunity to work alongside UMaine's renowned scholars and scientists in research and other academic ventures.

Student Government

Student Government, Inc. is the independent representative body for UMaine's undergraduate students. An elected president, vice president, and vice president of financial affairs direct and coordinate student clubs and programs at the University of Maine. Student Government works closely with the Office of the Vice President for Student Life and appoints 200 student representatives to various university committees. These students assist with the planning and implementation of residence hall programs, student discipline, athletics, and cultural activities on campus.

Admission Requirements

Admission to the University of Maine is a highly competitive and selective process. Successful applicants hold high scholastic achievement, intellectual curiosity, and extracurricular involvement that promise success at the University of Maine. The holistic selection process looks at the strength of the high school curriculum, grades received, class rank, counselor recommendation, and SAT or ACT scores for admission consideration. Additional information such as essays and community involvement may help the admissions committee evaluate student applications. UMaine recognizes advanced work completed in secondary schools in Advanced Placement tests, honors, or higher education courses. Students who pass examinations may be exempt from certain courses at UMaine.

Application and Information

Applicants may submit electronic or paper versions of the Common Application, the University of Maine System application, or the University of Maine mobile application. Required documents for all applicants include official high school or college transcripts, counselor recommendations, and SAT or ACT scores. Students above the age of 25 do not need to submit SAT or ACT test scores. Students are encouraged to apply by December 1 to ensure admission in selective academic programs and receive merit scholarship–based application review. More information on application deadlines and merit scholarships can be found on the University's website at go.umaine.edu. Applications and all supporting documents (i.e. SAT or ACT scores, transcripts, essays, etc.) should be sent to UMS Processing, P.O. Box 412, Bangor, ME 04402-0412.

For additional information on the application process, prospective students can contact the Office of Admissions at 207-581-1561 or umaineadmissions@maine.edu.

Office of Admissions
5713 Chadbourne Hall
University of Maine
Orono, Maine 04469-5713
Phone: 207-581-1561
Fax: 207-581-1213
E-mail: umaineadmissions@maine.edu
Website: go.umaine.edu
facebook.com/UMaineAdmissions
twitter.com@GoUMaine
instagram.com@university.of.maine
linkedin.com/edu/school?id=18586
pinterest.com/GoUMaine/

The Mall is the heart of the University of Maine campus.

COLLEGE CLOSE-UPS

UNIVERSITY OF MASSACHUSETTS LOWELL

LOWELL, MASSACHUSETTS

★ To read more about this school, visit http://petersons.to/umasslowell

The University

The University of Massachusetts Lowell (UMass Lowell) is a doctoral-level public research university ranked in the top tier of *U.S. News & World Report's* national universities. Founded in 1894, the university is built on a tradition of innovation and entrepreneurship. Extensive partnerships with industry and community advance research, provide public service, and enrich the student experience. UMass Lowell graduates are ready to contribute meaningfully in the workplace, build lives around the principles and passions they develop in college, and make a difference in the world.

The university is part of the University of Massachusetts system and comprises the Francis College of Engineering; the College of Fine Arts, Humanities and Social Sciences (includes the School of Criminology and Justice Studies); the College of Health Sciences (includes the School of Nursing); the Kennedy College of Sciences; the School of Education; the Manning School of Business; and the Honors College. Together, the colleges offer more than 120 bachelor's, 40 master's and 30 doctoral degrees, and a number of certificate programs. All programs are accredited at the highest levels and incorporate vigorous hands-on learning and personalized attention. Students in all undergraduate disciplines who participate in the Honors College and complete its program requirements graduate with a Commonwealth Honors designation on their degrees.

UMass Lowell maintains a student-faculty ratio of 18:1 and focuses on putting the lessons of the classroom into practice in real-world settings through co-ops, internships, service learning, and research. A growing number of interdisciplinary programs, such as the biomedical engineering and technology minor offered jointly by the colleges of Engineering, Sciences, and Health Sciences, reflect emerging fields in the global economy. Dozens of accelerated bachelor's-to-master's programs allow students to earn two degrees in as few as five years. All academic programs are accredited and meet the most rigorous board standards in higher education.

More than 50 percent of undergraduate classes have fewer than 20 students. All first-year students belong to academic learning communities. Optional Living-Learning Communities in the residence halls include: honors, art, music, women in science and engineering, pre-med, business innovation, health professions, DifferenceMakers, criminal justice, creative arts, and veterans. The Centers for Learning offer tutoring and academic support programs. The Career Services and Cooperative Education Center helps students prepare for the transition to the working world. The DifferenceMaker program encourages student teams to address real-world problems through entrepreneurial action and sponsors the annual $25,000 Idea Challenge pitch contest.

The campus community is ethnically, culturally, and economically diverse; students come from 50 states and over 100 countries. Thirty-two percent of undergraduates identify as students of color. The majority of freshmen choose to live in university housing, which includes traditional residence halls, apartments, suites, and a combined conference center and residence hall located downtown. Housing is guaranteed for freshmen and available to most returning and transfer students who want it. More than 250 active student organizations including a gaming group, dance and sport clubs, leadership societies, and a student-run FM radio station. The campus features over a dozen eateries, including Sal's Pizza, Starbucks, Subway, Red Mango, and traditional dining halls. The vibrant campus life includes supporting 17 Division I athletics teams, which compete in the America East and Hockey East conferences. The Campus Recreation Center runs intramural sports, fitness classes, and an outdoor adventure program. The 7,800-seat Tsongas Center at UMass Lowell is a popular venue for national acts and hosts the university's men's hockey team.

Location

The university is clustered along the Merrimack River in Lowell, a city of 110,000 that has gained national attention by successfully leveraging its history, ethnic diversity, and entrepreneurial spirit to create a vital urban center. The site of a unique, urban National Historical Park, Lowell is also home to an acclaimed professional theater company, literary and folk festivals, and numerous restaurants and museums. Lowell is located 25 miles from Boston and Cambridge and within the region's major business corridors, which provide internship and co-op opportunities for students. It is also within easy reach of major outdoor recreational areas via major highways and regional train and bus service.

Majors and Degrees

Dual majors are permitted. Dual B.A./B.S. degrees and bachelor's-to-master's degree programs are available in all fields. Pre-medical, pre-law and other pre-professional advising is available to interested students in all majors. Many of the majors offered have additional program options available, as noted in parentheses below.

The College of Fine Arts, Humanities and Social Sciences offers baccalaureate programs in: American studies; criminal justice and criminology (corrections, homeland security, information technology, police, violence), economics, English (creative writing, journalism and professional writing, literature, theatre arts), fine arts (animation, painting, printmaking, sculpture, photography, graphic design, web design, interactive media), history, legal studies, liberal arts (art history, Asian studies, comparative arts, cultural studies, economics, education, English/literature, environment and society, environmental studies, gender studies, history, languages, legal studies, music, philosophy, political science, psychology, sociology, theatre arts, writing), modern languages (French, Spanish, French/Spanish, Italian/Spanish), music business, music performance (instrumental, vocal), music studies (instrumental, vocal), peace and conflict studies, philosophy (communication and critical thinking), political science, psychology, sociology, and sound recording technology.

The Kennedy College of Sciences offers baccalaureate programs in: biology (bioinformatics, biotechnology, ecology), chemistry (cheminformatics, forensics), computer science (bioinformatics/cheminformatics), environmental science (atmospheric science [meteorology], environmental studies, geoscience), mathematics (applied computational mathematics, bioinformatics, business applications, computer science, probability and statistics, teaching), and physics (general, optics, radiological health).

The James B. Francis College of Engineering offers baccalaureate programs in: biomedical engineering, chemical engineering (biological engineering, computer-aided process design and controls, engineered materials, nanomaterials engineering, nuclear engineering, paper engineering), civil and environmental engineering, electrical and computer engineering, mechanical engineering, and plastics engineering. Engineering programs are accredited by the Accreditation Board for Engineering and Technology, Inc.

The College of Health Sciences and School of Nursing offer baccalaureate programs in: clinical laboratory and nutritional sciences (clinical laboratory sciences, clinical science, medical laboratory science, nutritional science), community health and sustainability (community health, environmental health), exercise physiology, nursing, and public health. A B.S. degree-completion program for RNs is offered through the Division of Online and Continuing Education. Accreditation is by the National Accrediting Agency for Clinical Laboratory Sciences and the National League for Nursing Accrediting Commission.

The Manning School of Business offers baccalaureate programs in: business administration (accounting, corporate finance, entrepreneurship, financial markets, general finance, international business, management, management information systems, marketing, and supply chain/operations management). A one-year M.B.A. is available as a bachelor's-to-master's program. All programs are accredited by the Association to Advance Collegiate Schools of Business (AACSB) International.

The university's School of Education offers a bachelor's degree and widely respected master's and doctoral programs as well as a range of initial certification courses. Undergraduates in STEM majors who are considering teaching can get classroom experience and a teaching minor through UTeach, a national teacher-training program whose only Northeast chapter is at UMass Lowell. Bachelor's-to-master's programs with initial Massachusetts teacher licensure are also available through the Fast Track to Teaching program.

The Division of Online and Continuing Education offers a wide range of programs that are delivered online and on campus in the evening.

Intercollegiate programs in aerospace studies, robotics, and joint military studies are available.

Academic Programs

The university calendar includes two semesters, a three-week intersession in January, and a summer term with two sessions. Full-time undergraduates generally take five courses each semester. A minimum of 120 credits is required for baccalaureate degrees; the minimum credits required for professional degree programs are generally higher. A general education requirement is imposed for all baccalaureate programs. Majors require 30 to 60 credits. Elective course options vary greatly by major. Professional degree program options and requirements follow specific accreditation guidelines. Maximum curricular freedom is permitted in B.A. programs. Qualified students in all majors are invited to join the Honors College. The academic climate is serious, competitive, and requires self-motivation.

Off-Campus Programs

Extensive opportunities for study abroad with credit include faculty-led courses, affiliate programs, exchanges, and more than 120 partnerships with prestigious institutions in 40 countries. Recent faculty-led courses include seminars on health care in Peru; migration in Prague; crime, law, and asset protection in Hong Kong and Macau; Cuban culture and history in Havana; and innovation and entrepreneurship in India. Professional co-ops, internships, and service-learning also take place off campus.

Academic Facilities

The campus is in the midst of a bold expansion. More than a dozen new facilities have opened since 2009, including the Mark and Elisia Saab Emerging Technologies and Innovation Center, the Health and Social Sciences Building (criminal justice and criminology, psychology and nursing), two suite-style residence halls and a townhome-style housing complex, the McGauvran Student Center, and the Pulichino Tong Business Center. A new writing center, a television studio, and a 14,500-square-foot anatomy and physiology lab opened in January 2014. University Crossing, the hub of student services and activities, opened in summer 2014 and connects the university's three campuses to the downtown business and cultural district. Both libraries feature new learning commons with areas for quiet and group study as well as Starbucks cafés.

Costs

The annual costs for 2016–17 for full-time undergraduate residents of Massachusetts were $14,307 per year; for nonresidents of Massachusetts, they were $30,875 per year. Room and board charges were $12,073 per year. Accident insurance is covered by fees; health insurance that meets the comparable benefits established by the state of Massachusetts is required. Books and supplies are estimated at $400 to $800, depending on program. Quoted rates are subject to change.

Financial Aid

UMass Lowell is committed to making higher education accessible to all qualified students. The university participates in federal and state programs, assisting students through grants-in-aid, loans, employment opportunities, and scholarships. The amount of a financial aid award is determined by need, as indicated by the Free Application for Federal Student Aid (FAFSA), which should be filed by March 1. The university awards a growing number of merit-based scholarships. More than $160 million in financial aid was awarded to students in the 2015–16 academic year, meeting approximately 90 percent of need.

Faculty

Faculty members are respected researchers who value their commitment to teaching and extend the learning experience beyond the classroom. There are over 560 full-time faculty members. The part-time day faculty members number approximately 500. Most undergraduate courses are taught by faculty members. Graduate teaching assistants also hold part-time instructional positions, particularly as discussion section leaders and laboratory teaching assistants.

Student Government

The Student Government Association and the Residence Hall Association provide opportunities in student government at the all-campus level. Leadership opportunities are provided in residence halls and student organizations. Students also participate in the disciplinary system and in most university committees.

Admission Requirements

All undergraduate day applicants must have a high school or a general equivalency diploma. Applicants have two application choices: the first is to apply with ACT and/or SAT scores; the second is to apply test-optional. Test-optional applicants need to answer additional supplemental application questions. Admissions standards vary by program. Last year's incoming freshmen had an average GPA of 3.59 and SAT scores of 1171 (reading and math).

Transfer students are considered for fall or spring semester admissions. Transcripts of completed work must be on file prior to acceptance. Depending on the number of transfer credits and college GPA, transfer students who seek admission as matriculating day students may be asked to provide a high school record and SAT scores.

Special-entrance programs that provide nontraditional admissions pathways for international students are available.

Application and Information

UMass Lowell admits students through early action, regular admission, and transfer admission. Entering freshmen are admitted for the fall or spring semesters. The early action deadline for freshmen is November 1; the regular admission deadline is February 1. Applicants to the School of Nursing must apply early action. The preferred deadline for transfer applications is August 15 for the fall and January 7 for the spring. Applicants can apply using the Common Application or the UMass Lowell application; both require an essay and a letter of recommendation. Both applications are available online at www.uml.edu/apply.

For application forms and further information, students should contact:

Office of Undergraduate Admissions
University of Massachusetts Lowell
University Crossing, Suite 420
220 Pawtucket Street
Lowell, Massachusetts 01854
Phone: 978-934-3931
Website: http://www.uml.edu
http://www.facebook.com/umlowell
http://www.twitter.com/umasslowell
http://www.youtube.com/user/umasslowell
http://instagram.com/umasslowell

University Crossing is the hub of student services and activities and connects the university's three campuses to the downtown business and cultural district.
UMass Lowell photo by Jim Higgins

The University of Massachusetts Lowell is an Equal Opportunity/Affirmative Action, Title IX employer.

UNIVERSITY OF NEW ENGLAND

BIDDEFORD AND PORTLAND, MAINE AND TANGIER, MOROCCO

UNE
UNIVERSITY OF NEW ENGLAND
INNOVATION FOR A HEALTHIER PLANET

★ To read more about this school, visit http://petersons.to/une

The University

The University of New England (UNE) is an innovative health sciences university grounded in the liberal arts, with two distinctive coastal Maine campuses and a third campus in Tangier, Morocco. UNE has internationally recognized scholars in the sciences, health, medicine, and humanities; offers more than fifty undergraduate, graduate, and professional degree programs; and is home to Maine's only medical school and the only college of dental medicine in Northern New England. UNE is one of a handful of private universities with a comprehensive health education mission including medicine, pharmacy, dental medicine, nursing, and an array of allied health professions.

UNE's 8,276 students are enrolled in a wide variety of academic programs at the undergraduate, graduate, and professional levels in six colleges: the College of Arts and Sciences, the College of Dental Medicine, the College of Osteopathic Medicine, the College of Pharmacy, the Westbrook College of Health Professions, and the online College of Graduate and Professional Studies. At the undergraduate level, UNE has approximately 2,392 students enrolled, from 31 different states and 16 foreign countries, in more than 40 undergraduate degree programs.

UNE traces its history to 1831 with the founding of Westbrook College, one of Maine's oldest institutions of learning. Today's University represents a union of three unique higher education institutions through the combining of St. Francis College and the New England College of Osteopathic Medicine in 1978 and Westbrook College in 1996.

Location

UNE's Biddeford Campus is located on a beautiful site in Biddeford, Maine, where the Saco River meets the Atlantic Ocean. With more than 4,000 feet of water frontage, enjoying the ocean comes naturally to students. The campus is home to the College of Arts and Sciences and the College of Osteopathic Medicine, which offers the Doctor of Osteopathic Medicine (D.O.). With more than 540 acres, the Biddeford Campus is also home to the Harold Alfond Center for Health Sciences, a modern [illegible]000-square-foot science education facility, the Marine Science Center, and the Harold Alfond Forum.

UNE's quintessential historic New England campus in the city of Portland is home to the College of Dental Medicine, the College of Pharmacy, and the Westbrook College of Health Professions, which offers undergraduate programs in dental hygiene and nursing, among others, and graduate programs in nurse anesthesia, occupational therapy, physical therapy, physician assistant, public health, and social work. The College of Dental Medicine is housed in the state-of-the-art Oral Health Center. The 41-acre Portland Campus is also home to the Center for Global Humanities, the Art Gallery, and the Maine Women Writers Collection.

UNE's third campus is in Tangier, Morocco, and offers students the opportunity to spend a semester or academic year abroad, taking English-language classes in their regular courses of study while discovering the culture of Morocco and the city of Tangier at no additional cost. UNE's campus location offers easy access to downtown, the main beach, and the major cultural activities the city has to offer.

Majors and Degrees

UNE offers highly competitive undergraduate and graduate programs in a variety of areas.

UNE's undergraduate majors include animal behavior, applied exercise science, applied mathematics, applied social and cultural studies, aquaculture and aquarium science, art and design media, art education, athletic training, biochemistry, biological sciences, business, chemistry, communications, dental hygiene, elementary/middle education, English, environmental science, environmental studies, global studies, health, wellness and occupational studies, history, interdisciplinary studies in the humanities, laboratory science, marine affairs, marine entrepreneurship, marine sciences, medical biology (pre-dental medicine, pre-medicine, pre-optometry, pre–physician assistant, and pre–veterinary medicine), neuroscience, nursing, nutrition, political science, pre-pharmacy, pre–physical therapy, psychology, public health, secondary education, social work, sociology, sport and recreation management, and sustainability and business.

Master's degree programs include applied nutrition, athletic training, biological sciences, education, health informatics, marine sciences, nurse anesthesia, occupational therapy, physician assistant, public health, and social work.

Doctorates offered include dental medicine (D.M.D.), education leadership (Ed.D.), osteopathic medicine (D.O.), pharmacy (Pharm.D.), and physical therapy (D.P.T.).

Academic Programs

UNE's academic programs ensure that students have plenty of opportunities for extensive fieldwork, clinical experiences, research, internships, and global experiences at both the undergraduate and graduate levels. All undergraduate programs at UNE have a core curriculum that provides a foundation in the liberal arts. The core reflects the values of each college and is designed to prepare students for living informed, thoughtful, and active lives in a complex and changing society.

The Student Academic Success Center provides a comprehensive array of academic support services including placement testing, courses, workshops, tutoring, and individual consultations. The Office of Career Services provides academic and career exploration assistance, assistance in applying to graduate schools, self-assessment and personal interest exploration, resume help, and information and access to job listings and job fairs.

Off-Campus Programs

UNE is committed to supplementing the traditional learning process with practical applications. All students are encouraged to participate in cooperative education programs, field placements, and practicums. These experiences are required for graduation by most majors and provide valuable learning situations that increase a student's exposure to job-related opportunities. Students also have the opportunity for vibrant study-abroad experiences. Students can enjoy a semester abroad at UNE's Morocco campus or with partner universities in Spain, France, and Iceland for about the same cost as a semester in Maine. Courses are offered in the sciences, humanities, social sciences, business, and the arts and are taught in English by the host university. Faculty-led short-term travel courses offer other exciting opportunities to study abroad.

Student Organizations and Activities

The University offers a variety of cultural and social events and encourages students to become involved in activities, clubs, and sports. Popular interests include scuba diving, skiing, hiking, biking, varsity and intramural sports, swimming, surfing, music, theater, community service, and student leadership development programs. Opportunities for such activities are available at on-campus facilities, including the Campus Center and the Harold Alfond Forum, a 106,000-square-foot facility featuring an ice hockey rink, basketball court, classroom and lab space, fitness center, and multipurpose courts.

UNE's Department of Athletics operates an NCAA Division III varsity athletics program. Varsity sports for men are basketball, cross-country, golf, ice hockey, lacrosse, and soccer. Football will see its first varsity action beginning in 2018. Varsity sports for women are basketball, cross-country, field hockey, ice hockey, lacrosse, rugby, soccer, softball, swimming, and volleyball.

Academic Facilities

Both the Biddeford and Portland Campuses feature buildings with a variety of uses to support the needs of the University community. On the Biddeford Campus, classroom and office spaces are housed in several facilities across campus. Several research facilities are on campus, including the Marine Science Center; the Harold Alfond Center for Health Sciences, with biology and chemistry labs as well as lecture halls, classrooms, a gross anatomy lab, and UNE's medical school facilities; the Pickus Center for Biomedical Research; and Peter and Cécile Morgane Hall, a science center providing additional classrooms and an undergraduate teaching laboratory. The Department of Creative and Fine Arts offers a dedicated building that provides faculty offices and studio space for drawing, painting, printmaking, sculpting, and photography.

On the Portland Campus, Ludcke Auditorium is used for a variety of academic programs. Coleman Dental Hygiene Building houses classroom, clinic, and faculty space. The Blewett Science Center, home to UNE's nursing program, consists of science labs and classrooms. UNE's Interprofessional Simulation and Innovation Center, which provides customized training and education for students and health professionals, is also on the Portland Campus. Proctor Hall is a classroom building and is home to the Proctor Learning and Career Center. The Josephine S. Abplanalp Library houses study space and a computer lab, as well as the Maine Women Writers Collection. The College of Pharmacy is a LEED-certified academic and research facility with teaching and research laboratories and a lecture hall. The College of Dental Medicine has its administration offices in historic Goddard Hall and its clinical home, the Oral Health Center, is a teaching clinic and simulation facility.

Faculty

The personal attention students receive from faculty both in and out of class, and the quality of faculty as experts in their fields are key strengths of the UNE experience. Students appreciate their faculty members as mentors, and trust them as accomplished scholars who impact their fields. From designing coastal trails and restoring wetlands on campus to caring for patients in need, UNE faculty members not only work side-by-side with their students, but are recognized by their peers and other leaders for their expertise. UNE faculty members are national award recipients, Fulbright scholars, authors, and world-class researchers, and they share their knowledge unselfishly with their students.

Costs

The costs for undergraduate students per academic year for 2017–18 are: tuition, $35,240; room and board, $13,580; and fees, $1,280.

Financial Aid

Approximately 98 percent of all full-time students received some form of financial assistance. The average package exceeds $27,000 including scholarships, grants, loans, and employment. The University of New England has an extensive academic scholarship program. Merit awards range from $4,000 to $20,000 per year.

Admission Requirements

Students applying for admission should submit a completed application, a $40 nonrefundable application fee, transcripts of all academic work (high school and college), and scores on either the ACT or SAT. Students who do not use English as their primary language must submit TOEFL scores. Students applying for admission should have completed a curriculum that includes English, mathematics, science, and social sciences. International students must also complete the International Student Supplemental Application. All prospective students are strongly encouraged to visit the University of New England at an open house or for an information session and tour. Information sessions and tours are held daily Monday through Friday; Saturday tours are also available. Prospect students can register for a tour at www.une.edu/visit.

Application and Information

The undergraduate freshman admission application deadlin February 15. Applications received after that date are review on a space-available basis. There is a nonbinding Decembe early action application deadline with a December 31 notificat date. Applications for the spring term are accepted throu December 1.

For application information, students should contact:

University of New England
Office of Undergraduate Admissions
11 Hills Beach Road
Biddeford, Maine 04005
Phone: 207-602-2847
800-477-4863 (toll-free)
Fax: 207-602-5900
E-mail: admissions@une.edu
Website: www.une.edu

With 4,000 feet of water frontage on UNE's Biddeford Campus, students' education and college experiences are enriched both inside and outside the classroom.

UNIVERSITY OF NEW HAMPSHIRE

DURHAM, NEW HAMPSHIRE

★ To read more about this school, visit http://petersons.to/universityofnewhampshire

University of New Hampshire

The University

The University of New Hampshire (UNH) is a top-100 national research institution and the state's flagship public university. Students from all 50 states and 85 countries team with its faculty on some of the world's most ambitious and adventurous research and intellectual efforts.

Work on projects for NASA space missions, finding new ways to assess and prevent sports-related head injuries, the adoption of anti-bullying programs, and a breakthrough in the quest to solve one of the world's oldest mathematical problems all have garnered national attention recently for UNH scholars. It is no surprise that a recent Gallup report found UNH graduates are more likely than those from other large public universities to be thriving in all five elements of well being: financial, physical, community, purpose, and social.

Right from the start, new students feel welcome at UNH. Ninety-six percent of all first-year students and approximately half of UNH's 13,000 undergraduates live on the beautiful Durham campus where classic and modern buildings are clustered around college greens that gradually give way to acres of woods, fields, and farms.

University housing includes residence halls for as few as 100 to as many as 600 students as well as two on-campus apartment complexes. Some halls or floors are focused around a specific theme or learning interest such as honors, engineering, arts, or outdoor experiences. Professional directors and trained resident advisers manage each hall at UNH, organizing programming designed to foster community and healthy habits.

UNH's award-winning culinary experience is evident in its three dining halls where menus focus on healthy eating using fresh local products and can be tailored to suit specific nutritional needs. Other campus food services include cafés and retail sites. Amtrak rail service runs out of The Dairy Bar, a UNH restaurant housed in an historic depot.

The Memorial Union Building (MUB) is the university's community hub with two movie theaters, the UNH Bookstore, a food court, a full-service computer store, game rooms, lounges, meetings and study spaces, and the undergraduate mail center. Holloway Commons (UNH's largest dining hall), the Student Senate Office, the Office of Multicultural Student Affairs, WUNH-FM radio, *The New Hampshire* student newspaper, and more than 200 other student organizations also are based in the MUB.

The University of New Hampshire's rich social and cultural life offers more than 250 student clubs and organizations which sponsor a wide range of activities and lectures, films, exhibitions, master classes, and performances that bring visitors of national and international stature to campus. Most events are free for students.

Every four years, UNH students have unparalleled opportunities to meet candidates on campus during New Hampshire's first-in-the-nation Presidential primary. National debates for both the Republican and Democratic parties have been hosted by UNH.

UNH students embrace the active life. Campus Recreation organizes a broad slate of programs for all skill levels and abilities, allowing students to work on personal fitness goals and have fun through activities like Zumba, cycling, yoga, tai chi, rock climbing, racquetball, skating, swimming, and sailing at facilities on or near campus as well as skiing, snowboarding, hiking, and camping trips in the White Mountains.

More than 20 intramural and club sports for men, women, and co-ed teams reflect the community's diverse interests. The Hamel Student Recreation Center, which includes courts and studios, a fitness center, indoor track, climbing wall, lounge, classrooms, locker rooms, equipment rentals, and saunas, underwent a $30 million expansion to double the fitness space and add wellness classrooms, a kitchen, and an outdoor pool. UNH also has 20 different men's and women's Division I Wildcat sports teams, including Division I-FCS football. Athletic events are well attended and the spirited student-led Cat Pack rouses fans.

Location

Situated not far from the Atlantic coast, Durham is a quintessential college town with restaurants, coffeehouses, a bookstore, pizza shops, and other student hangouts. Popular road trips for students include Boston (about an hour), Portsmouth (about 20 minutes), and the White Mountains (about an hour). There is an Amtrak stop on campus (Downeaster Line) with service between Portland, Maine, and Boston. UNH Wildcat Transit eco-buses run frequently on campus and to nearby towns and shopping areas. UNH also has an urban, nonresidential campus located in downtown Manchester.

Majors and Degrees

When choosing a course of study, students have many options with more than 100 majors in the Colleges of Liberal Arts, Engineering and Physical Sciences, Health and Human Services, Life Sciences and Agriculture, and Business and Economics, as well as at the Thompson School of Applied Science (which offers two-year associate degree programs), and the University of New Hampshire at Manchester.

UNH enjoys a strong reputation in many fields, including biology, business administration, English, communication, engineering, environmental studies, history, hospitality management, kinesiology, marine and animal sciences, performing arts, political science, and psychology. The Peter T. Paul College of Business and Economics offers a distinctive, hands-on first-year experience through its FIRE program. Business administration options include accounting, entrepreneurial venture creation, information systems, international business and economics, management, and a student-designed track. UNH Manchester's bachelor's degree program in data analytics is one of just a handful in the country.

Academic Programs

UNH is committed to the value of a liberal education. The Discovery Program provides students a broad foundation in the liberal arts and an introduction to methods of inquiry through general education courses that cover writing skills, quantitative reasoning, biological and physical sciences, historical perspectives, world cultures, fine and performing arts, social science, humanities, and environment, technology, and society. A senior year capstone experience allows students to reflect on and synthesize their knowledge and skills. Many students begin course work in their major as early as their first year. High-achieving students are invited to join the University Honors Program.

Students are afforded a wide array of research opportunities with UNH's world-class faculty. Aided by generous grants from the university, students work with faculty members or independently, on campus and abroad. More than 1,800 students participate in the annual UNH Undergraduate Research Conference. The Office of Fellowships helps students secure national and international fellowships. UNH students participate in more than 570 programs for study or research abroad.

The university is involved in a wide range of outreach programs with state and industry groups. These partnerships, and Durham's proximity to Boston, Manchester, and Portsmouth provide abundant possibilities for students interested in internships.

Academic Facilities

The Peter T. Paul College of Business and Economics, completed in 2013, features the latest instructional technologies, breakout rooms, an innovative lab for rapid prototyping, and a soaring lobby with study areas and a café. Parsons Hall, a chemistry teaching and research facility, underwent a $50-million renovation in 2009. Dimond Library, the state's only public university research library, offers three grand reading rooms, state-of-the-art adaptive technologies, and online access to its own and other digital academic resources. The Environmental Technology Building, a multidisciplinary science and engineering research facility, focuses on environmental technology development. The Inter Operability Lab (IOL), a leading test facility for data and networking communications, provides jobs for students in an industry setting.

Most of the university's cultural events take place in the Paul Creative Arts Center, home to two theaters, scene and costume shops, a green room, and classrooms. The Newman Dance Studio in New Hampshire hall is equipped for aerial dance. Hamilton Smith Hall, the iconic home of UNH's English Department and other complementary programs, is in the midst of a complete renovation and expansion project.

Costs

The 2016–17 tuition and fees for undergraduate in-state students were $17,624. For out-of-state students, tuition and fees were $31,424. Room (double) and board (unlimited meal plan) cost $10,938.

Financial Aid

Approximately 62 percent of students receive some form of need-based financial assistance from UNH. University merit scholarships ranging from $1,000 to $10,000 are awarded automatically (no additional application required) to selected first-year applicants. Amounts are subject to change. Academic departments may award other scholarships. The university participates in the Federal Pell Grant program, the Federal Supplemental Educational Opportunity Grant program, the Federal Perkins Loan program, the Federal Work-Study Program, and the Federal Stafford Student Loan program. Students seeking financial aid are required to submit the Free Application for Federal Student Aid (FAFSA) by March 1.

Faculty

The University of New Hampshire has 644 full-time and 401 part-time faculty members who are the primary instructors for most undergraduate courses. The student-faculty ratio is 18:1, and 83 percent of classes have fewer than 50 students. The faculty includes recipients of the Pulitzer Prize, Guggenheim awards, MacArthur Fellowships (genius grants), and an unusually high number of Fulbright scholarships. This research productivity has a powerful effect on students.

Student Government

The student senate is a governing body of student officers and senators who represent student opinion to the faculty, staff, administration, and the university community, as well as to the state legislature. Senate committees include areas in academics, residential life, commuters, health and human services, judicial affairs, and community change. They also approve and monitor the rates and uses of all mandatory student fees.

Admission Requirements

Admission to a bachelor's degree program is based upon successful completion of a strong program of college-preparatory course work in secondary school. Primary consideration is given to an applicant's academic record, quality of secondary school course selection, and achievement. Also considered are recommendations, personal essays, additional information, character, initiative, leadership, special talents, and SAT or ACT results.

Most successful applicants present at least 4 years of English and mathematics and 3 or more years of laboratory science, social science, and foreign language. Recommended mathematics preparation includes the equivalent of algebra I, geometry, algebra II, and trigonometry or advanced math. Students who plan to specialize in health, physical sciences, life sciences, engineering, or mathematics should present at least 4 years of mathematics, including trigonometry and laboratory course work in chemistry and/or physics. Students pursuing business-related studies should also have 4 years of mathematics.

All candidates for admission to bachelor's degree programs are required to submit SAT or ACT scores. SAT Subject Tests are not required. A foreign language SAT Subject Test may satisfy the foreign language requirement of the Bachelor of Arts degree programs. Required scores vary by test. International students whose primary language is not English must submit TOEFL or IELTS results. The recommended minimum TOEFL score is 213 (computer-based) or 550 (paper-based) or 80 (Internet-based). The minimum IELTS score is 6.5.

Candidates applying for music programs must make arrangements with the department for an audition (603-862-2404).

Application and Information

High school students may apply for the fall-semester anytime after the start of the senior year and before the February 1 regular decision deadline. Decisions are provided on a continuous basis through March. Admitted first-year students have until May 1 to confirm their intent to enroll at the university. Review of a candidate's application begins when all required materials are received. The Early Action (EA) program allows those who have submitted an application by the November 15 Early Action deadline to receive a response by mid-January. In some cases, the Admission Committee requests senior mid-year grade reports in order to make a final decision. Acceptances made while senior course work is in progress are provisional and subject to verification of satisfactory achievement when final transcripts are reviewed.

Office of Admissions
University of New Hampshire
3 Garrison Avenue
Durham, New Hampshire 03824-3501
Phone: 603-862-1360
Fax: 603-862-0077
Website: http://www.unh.edu/admissions
http://www.facebook.com/universityofnewhampshire (Facebook)
http://www.twitter.com/uofnh (Twitter)
http://www.youtube.com/unhvideo (YouTube)
http://www.instagram.com/uofnh (Instagram)

UNH combines the look and feel of a New England liberal arts college with the academic breadth and depth of a major research university.

UNIVERSITY OF NEW HAVEN

WEST HAVEN, CONNECTICUT

★ To read more about this school, visit http://petersons.to/universityofnewhaven

University *of* New Haven

The University

The University of New Haven's mission is to prepare career-ready graduates for meaningful roles in today's global economy and to nurture the pursuit of lifelong learning. Founded in 1920, the University of New Haven is a private, independent institution focused on combining experience-based learning with liberal arts and sciences. The University is committed to educational innovation, continuous improvement in career and professional education, and support of scholarship and personal development. The main campus moved to its present location in West Haven in 1960 and has since rapidly expanded its programs, facilities, and faculty, attracting a student body that now stands at over 6,800—including the current enrollment of 4,600 full-time undergraduates.

The University is fully accredited by the New England Association of Schools and Colleges (NEASC). Individual programs, departments, and schools hold various forms of national professional accreditation. Seven of the University of New Haven's bachelor's degree programs—chemical, civil, electrical, computer, industrial and systems, mechanical engineering, and computer science—are fully accredited by the Engineering Accreditation Commission of the Accreditation Board for Engineering and Technology, Inc. (EAC/ABET).

The main campus is in West Haven, Connecticut, on a hillside close to Long Island Sound. The University of New Haven also operates four satellite campuses: the Lyme Academy College of Fine Arts in Old Lyme, Connecticut; a graduate business campus in Orange, Connecticut; the M.S. Data Science campus in San Francisco, California; and an international campus in Prato, Italy. Main campus administrative and classroom buildings support the University's four academic colleges: the College of Arts and Sciences, the College of Business, the Tagliatela College of Engineering, and the Henry C. Lee College of Criminal Justice and Forensic Sciences. Following the addition of the Graduate School in 1969, New Haven College was designated a university. Thirty master's degree programs attract full- and part-time graduate students, while just over 100 associate and bachelor's degree programs are available to entering freshmen and transfer students in a great variety of academic disciplines.

Other main campus buildings include the Marvin K. Peterson Library, the Henry C. Lee Institute of Forensic Science, Echlin Hall, the Bayer Hall admissions building, the Campus Bookstore, new residence halls and apartments, and Bartels Hall, the campus center, which houses dining facilities and student activities. The Charger Gymnasium and athletic fields are located on the North Campus, just two short blocks from Maxcy Hall, the main administration building.

The University of New Haven has one of the most respected and successful NCAA Division II athletics programs in the country, with Charger teams combining to make over 120 post-season tournament appearances. The University is a member of the Northeast-10 Conference, one of the most prestigious and celebrated conferences in the nation. The University of New Haven and its student athletes have won numerous conference, regional, and national awards, both athletically and academically. The University offers seventeen varsity sports: men's baseball, basketball, cross-country, football, soccer, indoor and outdoor track and field; and women's basketball, cross-country, field hockey, lacrosse, soccer, softball, tennis, indoor and outdoor track and field, and volleyball.

Over 65 percent of the full-time undergraduate students live on campus in thirteen residence halls. More than 170 clubs and organizations are open to students. Included are student chapters of professional societies, religious organizations, social groups, special-interest clubs, student councils, cultural groups, and fraternities and sororities.

Location

West Haven is contiguous to New Haven. There are theaters that attract star performers from the entertainment world, a harbor and beaches, fine restaurants, museums, and galleries in the area. Numerous social and cultural programs are presented by the many colleges and universities in the area. New Haven is served by a local airport and major railroads, and its location at the junction of two interstate highways places the University of New Haven within easy driving distance of New York, Boston, Cape Cod, and the ski areas of New England.

Majors and Degrees

The College of Arts and Sciences offers a Bachelor of Arts degree in art, communication, English, global studies, graphic design, history, interior design, marine affairs, mathematics, music, music and sound recording, music industry, political science, and psychology; and a Bachelor of Science degree in biology, genetics and biotechnology, dental hygiene, environmental science, marine biology, mathematics, music and sound recording, and nutrition and dietetics.

The College of Business offers the Bachelor of Science degree in accounting, business management, economics, finance, hospitality and tourism management, international business, marketing, and sport management. In addition, the College of Business offers a fast-track study program allowing academically strong students the opportunity to earn a Bachelor of Science degree in business and a Master of Business Administration (M.B.A.) in just four years.

The Tagliatela College of Engineering offers a Bachelor of Science degree in chemical engineering, chemistry, civil engineering, computer engineering, computer science, cyber systems, electrical engineering, general engineering, industrial and systems engineering, and mechanical engineering.

The Henry C. Lee College of Criminal Justice and Forensic Sciences offers a Bachelor of Science degree in criminal justice, fire protection engineering, fire science, forensic science, legal studies, national security studies, and paramedicine.

The Lyme Academy College of Fine Arts offers a Bachelor of Fine Arts degree in drawing, illustration, painting, and sculpture.

Academic Programs

The University of New Haven offers a broad range of programs in both liberal arts and professional areas. Experiential learning is emphasized, and there are diverse and numerous opportunities for internships, cooperative education, independent study, and industrial projects. Certain types of professional experience are required in a number of degree programs. The Center for Learning Resources offers a tutoring service open to all students.

The undergraduate division operates on a 4-1-4 calendar. Credit is given for successful scores on the CLEP, International Baccalaureate, and Advanced Placement examinations. The University honors program provides outstanding study opportunities in most undergraduate disciplines. The residence requirement for all degrees is 30 credit hours.

The University of New Haven believes that all students pursuing a bachelor's degree should develop a common set of skills; its goal is to prepare all graduates for the complex lives they will lead in a changing world. This can best be done through the University Core Curriculum, which consists of a minimum of 40 credit hours in six basic competencies.

Academic Facilities

The Marvin K. Peterson Library contains more than 400,000 volumes in hard copy and provides access to about 20,000 electronic books and 20,000 e-journals from the library website and Voyager online catalog. Databases are available on a wide variety of subjects, with a focus on business, criminal justice/forensic science, engineering, and psychology, as well as general arts and sciences. Through interlibrary loan services, the University community has access to the holdings of more than 8,650 libraries.

Communication majors participate in workshops along with studying sound, film, and television production and radio broadcasting techniques in well-equipped radio/television studios and laboratories. The Tagliatela College of Engineering has modern laboratories and equipment to support its programs. The College of Arts and Sciences maintains art studios, state-of-the-art recording studios, music practice rooms, and science, psychology, and language labs. Hands-on instruction and demonstrations are available in kitchen facilities for students in the hospitality and tourism and the nutrition and dietetics programs. Dental hygiene students gain experience in the Dental Hygiene Clinic.

There are more than a dozen computer labs for student use and teaching on campus. One of these is devoted to forensic computing instruction for the Henry C. Lee College of Criminal Justice and Forensic Sciences.

Costs

Full-time undergraduate tuition for the 2017–18 academic year, including all fees, is $36,770; room and board cost $15,370.

Financial Aid

The University of New Haven offers a comprehensive financial aid program that includes University resources as well as state, federal, and private-aid programs. Approximately 95 percent of full-time undergraduate students receive some form of assistance. Students receive federal aid through the Federal Pell Grant, Federal Supplemental Educational Opportunity Grant, Federal Work-Study, Federal Direct Student Loan, and Federal Direct PLUS loan programs. The University also administers programs sponsored by the state of Connecticut for Connecticut residents attending the University. Some students also qualify for financial aid from other states and from private companies, organizations, and foundations.

Faculty

It is a long-standing University policy that the faculty members teach a mix of undergraduate and graduate courses in order to preserve academic quality at all levels. Faculty members are selected and promoted primarily on the basis of teaching effectiveness, professional qualifications and performance, and contributions to the academic community. No classes are taught by teaching assistants. Some faculty members hold administrative positions and continue to teach. There are over 270 full-time and 400 part-time faculty members, making the student-faculty ratio 16:1. The majority of full-time faculty members (more than 90 percent) hold terminal degrees in their disciplines.

Student Government

The Undergraduate Student Government Association supervises annual expenditures by undergraduate clubs and organizations, directs liaison committees, supports student publications and the student-operated FM radio station, and schedules cultural and social events. Student representatives are elected annually to the University's Board of Governors.

Admission Requirements

To be eligible for admission, one must be a high school graduate or present evidence of equivalent preparation and have submitted all necessary application documents for consideration. The admissions decision is based on an applicant's high school transcript, SAT or ACT results, letter(s) of recommendation, and personal essay. Out-of-state residents are considered for admission on the same basis as in-state residents. The University of New Haven does not discriminate on the basis of age, color, sex, religion, race, sexual orientation, national origin, or disability in admission or treatment of students, administration or distribution of financial aid, or recruitment of employees.

Application and Information

To apply to the University of New Haven, one must submit a completed application via the Common Application (with $50 fee), official records of all academic enrollment, SAT or ACT results, a letter of recommendation (from an academic source), and a personal statement (250–650 words). International students are required to demonstrate proficiency in English and provide documentation of financial support. The University of New Haven is authorized under federal law to enroll nonimmigrant alien students who meet the university's academic and English proficiency standards. Application documents are considered on a rolling admissions basis with the opportunity to apply for early action, early decision, and regular decision.

For more information, contact:

Undergraduate Admissions
University of New Haven
300 Boston Post Road
West Haven, Connecticut 06516
Phone: 203-932-7319
E-mail: admssions@newhaven.edu
Website: http://www.newhaven.edu

Maxcy Hall on the campus of the University of New Haven.

COLLEGE CLOSE-UPS

THE UNIVERSITY OF NORTH CAROLINA WILMINGTON

WILMINGTON, NORTH CAROLINA

★ To read more about this school, visit http://petersons.to/northcarolinawilmington

The University

The University of North Carolina Wilmington (UNCW), a public, comprehensive university, combines a small-college commitment to excellence in teaching with a research university's opportunities for student involvement in significant faculty scholarship. The University provides a personal learning environment that integrates teaching and mentoring with research and service, and promotes cultural diversity, community engagement, and individual growth and development. The school was named among 2016's Best Southeastern Schools by The Princeton Review for the tenth consecutive year, and was ranked among the top 20 Best Regional Universities in the South by *U.S. News & World Report*. UNCW offers 57 bachelor's degrees in 49 majors, 29 graduate degree programs, and four doctoral degrees. The University is accredited by the Commission on Colleges of the Southern Association of Colleges and Schools and is one of the seventeen constituent institutions that compose the public university system in the state of North Carolina.

UNCW enrolls nearly 15,000 students, with approximately 13,914 at the undergraduate level. Moreover, the University has the fourth-highest freshman SAT (critical reading and math only) average (1192), the fourth-highest freshman retention rate (85 percent), and the third-highest six-year graduation rate (70 percent) in the UNC system. With an average GPA of 3.9, incoming students have already demonstrated their motivation and ability to succeed in an academic setting.

At UNCW, students as well as faculty and staff members take full advantage of the University's proximity to the coast and its connections to the community. The internationally respected biology and marine biology programs have created promising research and development opportunities in the biotechnology, pharmacology, and mariculture fields. The Watson College of Education works closely with more than 100 area schools and agencies to improve the quality of public schools in the region. The School of Nursing is housed in a high-tech building equipped with patient simulation labs that replicate clinic, hospital, and home health care settings. The labs prepare students with extensive training prior to their placement in a wide range of clinical-practice experiences.

Campus life is a vibrant part of the UNCW experience. Students can live in one of 12 residential campus communities, with numerous options among residence halls, suites, and apartment buildings. Students enjoy a variety of cutting-edge cuisines at the University's 16 dining locations. Students may participate in more than 270 student organizations, including political, academic, professional, sports, service, ethnic, religious, and student media groups. As a member of NCAA Division I, UNCW fields 20 varsity teams, including men's and women's basketball, cross-country, golf, soccer, swimming and diving, and tennis; women's softball and volleyball; and men's baseball.

Several facilities serve as hubs for the entire campus community. The Fisher Student Center and the Fisher University Union include a two-story bookstore, a 360-seat movie theater, offices for student organizations, student lounges, a large game room, an art exhibition gallery and display spaces, a convenience store, and dining areas. Nearby, Randall Library's technology resource and assistance centers connect students, faculty, and staff to extensive collections of information, both on campus and in the world at large. The Campus Commons features a lake with lighted fountains, a network of sidewalks, a clock tower, and an open-air amphitheater. Monthly exhibitions of paintings, sculptures, and graphic arts are held in a variety of spaces on campus, including Claude Howell Gallery, Randall Library, Cultural Arts Building, Warwick Center, and the Ann Flack Boseman Gallery.

The Department of Campus Recreation offers numerous activities to support students' health and well-being. In 2013, the University completed renovations and expansions to the Student Recreation Center that doubled its original size. The 165,000 square-foot facility includes multipurpose courts; a group exercise room; climbing wall; an elevated, multilane walking and jogging track; a large selection of elliptical trainers, stair climbers, treadmills, and weight machines; and an indoor pool, outdoor leisure pool, and patio deck. Other recreational facilities include the Gazebo Complex, which features four tennis courts, three basketball courts, two volleyball courts, and a softball field; and a natatorium with an eight-lane swimming pool and an adjacent diving tank.

Location

The campus occupies 660 acres in the southeastern part of North Carolina, midway between the Cape Fear River and the Atlantic Ocean. The city of Wilmington is situated on the east bank of the Cape Fear River, about 15 miles from Carolina Beach and 5 miles from Wrightsville Beach. Several main highways lead into the city, and a nearby airport (ILM) provides easy access from the city to other destinations.

Wilmington combines historical beauty and modern convenience. Visitors can visit many art galleries, museums, and historical landmarks; enjoy an evening of theater, music, and nightlife; or visit the city's many shops and restaurants. Ocean breezes and the nearness of the Gulf Stream give Wilmington an enjoyable year-round climate. Nature lovers can go biking, hiking, or bird watching in one of Wilmington's parks or play golf on one of the city's six courses. Wilmington's proximity to the river and the ocean makes it an ideal haven for water lovers, whether they prefer taking a riverboat cruise or spending the day surfing and swimming at the beach.

Majors and Degrees / Academic Programs

The College of Arts and Sciences offers degree programs in Anthropology, Art History, Biology, Chemistry, Communication Studies, Computer Science, Creative Writing, Criminology, English, Environmental Science, Film Studies, French, Geography, Geology, Geosciences, German Studies, History, International Studies, Information Technology, Marine Biology, Mathematics, Music, Music Education, Oceanography, Philosophy and Religion, Physics, Political Science, Psychology, Sociology, Spanish, Statistics, Studio Art, and Theatre.

Degree programs in the College of Health and Human Services include Athletic Training; Exercise Science; Physical Education and Health; Public Health Studies; Recreation, Sport Leadership, and Tourism Management; Recreation Therapy; Clinical Research; Professional Nursing; RN to B.S.N. (online accelerated program), and Social Work.

Degree programs available in the Cameron School of Business include Accounting, Economics, Entrepreneurship and Business Development, Finance, General Business, Human Resources, Information Technology, International Business, Management and Leadership, Management Information Systems, Marketing (Professional Selling or Marketing Strategy), and Operations Management.

Degree programs available in the Watson College of Education include Education of Young Children, Elementary Education, Middle Grades Education, Special Education, and Secondary Education.

Off-Campus Programs

Academic areas across campus sponsor study-abroad programs that are designed to strengthen relationships between the University and the international community, including international students and institutions in other countries. For example, the Cameron School of Business offers an International Master of Business Administration (I.M.B.A.), the Watson College of Education conducts programs in Belize, and the School of Nursing partners with a rural health clinic in Peru. Many of the University's study abroad programs are coordinated by the Office of International Programs. These may last a few weeks, a semester, or an entire academic year; several occur during the summer. The University has developed more than 500 programs in over 50 countries, including Argentina, Ghana, Israel, Thailand, Italy, and China.

The University also coordinates travel experiences that include more than study, such as internships that may consist of a combination of coursework and/or supervised work experience in a government agency, profit or nonprofit agency, or company. Students and recent graduates may work abroad as family caretakers or English language teachers, either in exchange for room and board or for a salary. Volunteer opportunities in other countries may involve healthcare, agriculture, community development, language training, youth camps, or house-building projects.

Academic Facilities

The William Madison Randall Library holds more than 2.1 million items, including more than 1 million books, journals, and government documents; more than 65,000 multimedia items; and a vast microform collection. In addition, the library provides extensive indexes and full texts for thousands of journals and books, including NC LIVE, LexisNexis, Science Direct, and JSTOR. The library's specialized collections include the Rare Book Collection and the Southeastern North Carolina Collection, devoted to publications about or written by residents of the Lower Cape Fear region. In addition, the library is a selective depository for United States government publications and a full depository for North Carolina documents.

Costs

In 2016–17, full-time undergraduate tuition and fees totalled $6,952 per year for in-state residents and $20,920 for nonresidents. Students living on campus can also expect to spend up to $10,060 per academic year on room and board, $1,104 on books and supplies, $1,740 on transportation, $1,608 on health insurance if not covered under another policy, and $1,586 on miscellaneous costs. Room, board, and transportation costs for commuters vary. Students enrolled part-time pay according to the number of credit hours earned each semester; costs vary, depending on the number of credits and whether the student is a resident or nonresident.

Financial Aid

In order to be considered for the maximum amount of financial assistance, prospective students should submit the Free Application for Federal Student Aid (FAFSA) as early as possible; the priority deadline is March 1st. The University awards millions of dollars each year to assist students. Most of this aid is need-based, but a number of merit-based scholarships are available for the most outstanding students.

The University offers several scholarships—including scholarships specifically for incoming freshmen and students enrolled in specific programs—that have been generously donated in honor of individuals or organizations. Award amounts and eligibility criteria vary, but most of these scholarships are renewable as long as the student is enrolled in a degree program and continues to meet the eligibility requirements. For students with exceptional financial need, the University developed the S.O.A.R program designed to help eligible participants reduce student loan debt. The Federal Pell Grant Program and the Federal Supplemental Educational Opportunity Grant (FSEOG) Program, along with several North Carolina state programs, also help offset the cost of attendance for low-income families. Some programs are limited to in-state students only.

Several federal loan programs are available for students who require additional assistance. Loan amount limits are established by the federal government. Some students also participate in federal work-study, which awards money to students who work up to 20 hours per week on campus.

Faculty

The University seeks to attract and maintain a faculty of outstanding individuals who are capable of contributing to the enrichment of its diverse and comprehensive instructional and research programs. Of the nearly 1,000-strong faculty members, approximately 86 percent hold terminal degrees and more than 60 percent are tenured. Faculty members come from all geographic regions of the United States and several foreign countries, bringing a rich variety of educational experiences, training, and scholarly knowledge.

Student Government

The Student Government Association is devoted to the best interests of the University and committed to upholding a high standard of morals and conduct. Student activity fees support the Student Government Association in its objectives and activities. The student body president and class representatives are elected by the student body, and the president appoints an executive board, which includes a chief of staff, treasurer, and secretary.

Admission Requirements

All prospective students must meet the following minimum course requirements for enrollment: 4 units in English; 2 units of the same foreign language; 4 units of mathematics (one for which algebra II is a prerequisite); 3 units in science (including at least 1 unit in biology, 1 unit in the physical sciences, and 1 laboratory course); and 2 units in social science (including 1 unit in United States history).

Prospective students are required to submit the following materials: a completed application for admission, official transcripts from all high schools attended, essay, short answer question on the application, an official SAT or ACT score, letter of recommendation, and a $75 application fee. When reviewing a freshman application, the admissions committee looks carefully at the applicant's academic achievements including rigorous coursework, writing, grade point average, standardized test scores, and extracurricular activities. Students admitted to the University average a combined math and critical reading score of 1260 on the SAT and/or an ACT composite average of 25.

Application and Information

Students applying for early action should have their applications submitted online by November 1 or earlier, and are notified on or around January 20. Regular decision applications must be submitted by February 1; students are notified of the University's decision on or around April 1.

Transfer applicants applying for summer or fall entry must have their applications submitted by March 1, and by October 15 for spring. Decision letters are mailed on a rolling basis.

To receive information and updates about UNCW on a regular basis, students should create a SeaLevel account found on the UNCW website.

Office of Admissions
University of North Carolina Wilmington
601 South College Road
Wilmington, North Carolina 28403-5904
United States
Phone: 910-962-3243
Fax: 910-962-3038
E-mail: admissions@uncw.edu
Website: http://www.uncw.edu/
https://www.facebook.com/UNCWOfficeofAdmissions
https://twitter.com/UNCW_Admissions

The Class of 2020 celebrates their Convocation Ceremony by stopping briefly at UNCW's Clock Tower Lawn for a class photo and to raise the 2020 Class Flag.

UNIVERSITY OF PITTSBURGH AT BRADFORD

BRADFORD, PENNSYLVANIA

University of Pittsburgh Bradford
you can go beyond

★ To read more about this school, visit http://petersons.to/universityofpittsburghatbradford

The University

The University of Pittsburgh at Bradford (Pitt-Bradford) can take students beyond—beyond the classroom by offering internships and research opportunities; beyond the degree by providing a robust Career Services Office and an informal alumni network; beyond 9-to-5 by offering an active student life, a friendly residence-life environment, excellent athletic and cultural facilities, and a wide range of recreational opportunities; beyond place by exposing students to the world and offering many study-abroad opportunities; and beyond students' expectations by giving them a college experience that can transform them.

At Pitt-Bradford, students live and learn on a safe, intimate campus, where they receive individual and personalized attention from committed professors who work at their side. In addition, students earn a degree from the University of Pittsburgh, which commands respect around the world.

Students can work out in a state-of-the-art fitness center or swim in the six-lane swimming pool in the Richard E. and Ruth McDowell Sport and Fitness Center. The building also houses facilities for intercollegiate and intramural athletic events.

The Frame-Westerberg Commons offers a place to eat, gather, and participate in campus life. The building houses the dining hall, where students can help themselves to a wide assortment of meals; a bookstore, which features an after-hours convenience store; offices for many student clubs and organizations; and areas to read or relax.

There are more than sixty clubs and organizations, from the campus radio station and newspaper to academic clubs, honor societies, and fraternities and sororities. Pitt-Bradford competes in Division III of the NCAA and fields six men's teams in baseball, basketball, golf, soccer, swimming, and tennis and seven women's teams in basketball, bowling, soccer, softball, swimming, tennis, and volleyball.

Location

Pitt-Bradford encompasses 317 acres in the foothills of the Allegheny Mountains, only steps from the Allegheny National Forest. Pitt-Bradford also is a short drive from larger cities such as Buffalo, New York (80 miles north); Pittsburgh (160 miles southeast); and Erie, Pennsylvania (90 miles west). Pitt-Bradford can also be reached easily by car and plane.

At Pitt-Bradford, students have many opportunities to participate in co-curricular opportunities in the region, including cross-country and downhill skiing, snowboarding, snowshoeing, ice skating, biking, fishing, hiking, and hunting.

Majors and Degrees

Students may pursue four-year degrees in accounting, applied mathematics; athletic training; biology; biology education 7–12; broadcast communications; business; computer and information technology K–12; business management; chemistry; chemistry education 7–12; computer information systems and technology; criminal justice; early level education PreK–4; economics; energy science and technology; English; English education 7–12; environmental studies; exercise science; general studies; health and physical education K–12; history/political science; hospitality management; interdisciplinary arts; international affairs; mathematics education 7–12; nursing; physical sciences; psychology; public relations; radiological science; social studies education 7–12; sociology; sport and recreation management; and writing.

Pitt-Bradford also offers associate degrees in engineering science, information systems, liberal studies, nursing (RN), and petroleum technology.

Students may also study engineering for up to two years at Pitt-Bradford and then complete a program at the Oakland campus in bioengineering, chemical and petroleum engineering, civil and environmental engineering, electrical and computer engineering, industrial engineering, materials science and engineering, or mechanical engineering.

Pitt-Bradford also provides programs offered in conjunction with the University of Pittsburgh School of Dental Medicine and the Pennsylvania College of Optometry. Students begin their studies at Pitt-Bradford and, after three years, transfer to the appropriate graduate school to complete four more years of study.

Pitt-Bradford also offers the first two years of study leading to the doctorate in pharmacy. Students must complete the program at the Oakland campus, where admission is competitive. The Pittsburgh School of Pharmacy pre-admits some qualified high school seniors, pending completion of the first two years of the pre-professional program at Pitt-Bradford.

The University also has an agreement with Lake Erie College of Osteopathic Medicine (LECOM), which allows qualifying students to continue their education in medicine at LECOM after their third year at Pitt-Bradford. Students who have successfully completed their first year of medical school classes at LECOM will receive their bachelor's degree from Pitt-Bradford. They will then continue at LECOM to finish their medical studies.

Academic Programs

The academic programs stress critical-thinking and communication skills and encourage hands-on learning through field experience, internships, and faculty-student collaboration on research. A Pitt-Bradford bachelor's degree requires 120–128 credit hours (requirements differ slightly among programs). Students need to complete between 60 and 70 credit hours to earn an associate degree.

The accounting major prepares students for the workplace, which has a growing need for accountants. The major also prepares students to earn a master's degree in either professional accountancy or business administration.

The biology program prepares students for careers in health-related professions, education, and research; technical positions in governmental agencies; and careers with food, pharmaceutical, chemical, and biotechnology companies. Most students interested in medicine, dentistry, optometry, pharmacy, osteopathy, physical therapy, occupational therapy, podiatry, chiropractic medicine, veterinary medicine, preclinical dietetics and nutrition, and a variety of careers in health and rehabilitation sciences are biology majors.

Students who choose to major in broadcast communications, English, public relations, or writing are able to work on the award-winning student newspaper, *The Source;* broadcast over the college radio station, WDRQ; and publish original works in the award-winning student literary magazine, *Baily's Beads*. Students also have access to an all-digital television studio and two digital radio facilities.

Students who choose a major in computer information systems and technology will get a broad IT background and gain hands-on lab experiences. Students will learn programming applications, network development, systems design and analysis, web technologies, multimedia applications, database development, and systems administration.

In the criminal justice program, students are able to intern with local and regional police departments, county court and probation offices, and a federal prison. State-of-the-art crime-scene investigatory tools enable students to work a crime scene using many of the same tools as professional law enforcement agents. In the Crime Scene Investigation (CSI) House students can process simulated crime scenes and collect evidence just like the pros.

An education major prepares a student for a career as a teacher in a world of rapid political, economic, scientific, and cultural change. The Education Department seeks to graduate students who have general knowledge and specific content knowledge, as well as sound theory and practice.

The nursing program at Pitt-Bradford offers an Associate of Science degree that can be completed in two years and a Bachelor of Science in Nursing degree that requires two additional years. Students may commence this program upon completion of the associate degree.

In psychology, students gain knowledge in the scientific and theoretical aspects of psychology as well as the application of this knowledge. The major prepares students for graduate work in psychology and related disciplines and for employment in social service agencies, mental health centers, industries, and not-for-profit and governmental agencies.

Students may relocate to another University of Pittsburgh campus to complete academic programs not offered at Pitt-Bradford, but they may earn no more than 70 credits before transferring. All students in the arts and sciences may relocate, provided they are in good standing. Engineering students may relocate if they maintain a grade point average of at least 3.0.

Academic Facilities

In addition to the T. Edward and Tullah Hanley Library on campus, Pitt-Bradford students have online access to the entire University of Pittsburgh library system.

Blaisdell Hall, the fine arts and communication arts building, houses the art, communication arts, interdisciplinary arts, theater, and music programs and features state-of-the-art equipment. Students can find a computer graphics lab, two art studios, a music/theater rehearsal hall, and a radio and television studio. The building also houses a multipurpose theater and serves as the cultural center for the region by housing plays, concerts, lectures, and other arts-related events.

Fisher Hall houses the science programs, such as biology, chemistry, engineering, engineering science and technology, petroleum technology, and physics. The science labs are filled with up-to-date scientific equipment, enabling students to perform a variety of experiments. The building also has two computer-aided learning centers and, on the roof, a campus greenhouse.

In Swarts Hall, students take courses in business, education, sociology, anthropology, psychology, history/political science, languages, English, writing, and criminal justice. The building also houses a nursing suite and multimedia classrooms that can turn a typical class into an audio and visual experience.

There is more to the Richard E. and Ruth McDowell Sport and Fitness Center than sports. The building also houses the athletic training, exercise science, and sport and recreation management programs, along with a human performance lab and an athletic training room.

In the Ceramic Studio, students get their hands dirty—literally. Students have sixteen motorized pottery wheels, a manual kick wheel, a work table, and a kiln to help turn slabs of clay into art.

Costs

For 2016–17, tuition for full-time students was $6,344 per fifteen-week term for Pennsylvania residents and $11,855 for nonresidents. Nursing tuition was $8,127 per term for Pennsylvania residents and $15,117 for nonresidents. Room and board expenses were $4,397 per term. Other costs include an activity fee of $100 per term, a wellness fee of $75 per term, a parking and transportation fee of $40 per term, and a computer fee of $175 per term. Books and supplies cost approximately $500 per term.

Financial Aid

Pitt-Bradford believes that the cost of a college education should not be a deterrent to any student regardless of family financial circumstances. Nearly 99 percent of students who apply for assistance receive some form of financial aid, including grants, scholarships, loans and work-study opportunities administered through the Financial Aid Office. During 2016–17, the average financial aid award was roughly $17,990 for Pennsylvania students and $25,800 for out-of-state students. All aid applicants must submit the Free Application for Federal Student Aid (FAFSA) by March 1 to receive priority consideration. Pennsylvania residents who complete the FAFSA by March 1 are also eligible for Pennsylvania Higher Education Assistance Agency (PHEAA) grants. Students who live outside of Pennsylvania should contact their state agency to learn more about the prerequisites for grants.

The University awards merit-based scholarships to those who demonstrate exceptional academic achievement. The University ROTC program is another possible source of aid. The University encourages veterans to contact the VA about educational benefits.

To learn more about financial assistance, students should contact the Financial Aid Office or visit the financial aid website at http://www.upb.pitt.edu/financialaid.

Faculty

Pitt-Bradford's 74 full-time faculty members hold doctorates and master's degrees from some of the most prestigious universities in the nation, including Cornell, Harvard, Stanford, and the University of Pittsburgh. Teaching is the primary activity of the faculty, and personal attention is emphasized in the classroom. Faculty members welcome the chance to meet with their students and know them by name. The student-faculty ratio is 18:1.

Student Government

Because Pitt-Bradford is a personalized campus, opportunities for leadership abound. Many students become campus leaders as early as their sophomore year. Regardless of students' background or interests, most find many places to become involved at Pitt-Bradford.

The Student Activities Council schedules comedy performances, lectures, art exhibits, movies, and trips to such cities as Toronto, Niagara Falls, Cooperstown, and New York City.

Admission Requirements

The Admissions Committee considers three primary factors in evaluating an applicant's ability to succeed in college work: the high school record, the results of standardized tests (SAT or ACT), and the high school's recommendations. In addition, personal qualifications, extracurricular activities, and potential to contribute to the college community may be taken into consideration.

Application and Information

Pitt-Bradford has a rolling admissions program, and students may apply at any time. All candidates are notified as soon as action is taken on their application.

Candidates for admission should complete and return the paper application with a nonrefundable $45 fee. However, students can apply online at no charge. Students must also submit an official copy of their high school record and scores from either the SAT or ACT. In addition to fulfilling the above requirements, transfer applicants must submit all official college transcripts and must have a minimum cumulative grade point average of 2.0.

The Office of Admissions welcomes campus visits by students and their families; such visits help students arrive at a final decision about Pitt-Bradford. Interviews and tours are scheduled Monday through Friday, 9 a.m. to 3 p.m., and on selected Saturdays. Arrangements can be made by contacting the Office of Admissions or by going online to http://www.upb.pitt.edu/visit.

For application forms, catalogs, and further information, students should contact:

Office of Admissions
University of Pittsburgh at Bradford
300 Campus Drive
Bradford, Pennsylvania 16701-2898
Phone: 814-362-7555
800-872-1787 (toll-free)
Website: http://www.upb.pitt.edu
http://www.facebook.com/PittBradford
https://twitter.com/PittBradford
http://www.instagram.com/upittbradford
http://www.snapchat.com/add/upittbradford

Criminal justice students at Pitt-Bradford enhance their investigative skills while examining a "crime scene" at the Crime Scene Investigation House on campus.

UNIVERSITY OF REDLANDS

REDLANDS, CALIFORNIA

UNIVERSITY OF Redlands

★ To read more about this school, visit http://petersons.to/universityofredlands

The University

For more than 100 years, the University of Redlands has offered its students a tradition of a superior liberal arts and sciences education. Its outstanding faculty provides students with extraordinary opportunities for learning and growth through close, informal interaction. These relationships are the foundation of the University's close-knit community.

The College of Arts and Sciences enrolls more than 2,400 students. Sixty percent of the freshman class comes from California and the remainder from 44 states and 44 countries of citizenship. In addition to a strong academic program in the liberal arts, sciences, pre-professional programs, and the arts, students benefit from many extracurricular programs, including music, drama, dance, and athletics. Internships are available for students in many academic programs. The School of Music and the Department of Theatre Arts provide a rich selection of cultural events throughout the year. Prominent speakers are invited to the campus each year to give major addresses and participate in classes and public discussion groups. Additional social functions are organized by the Office of Student Life and individual residence halls. Students also have the opportunity to join local nonresidential fraternities and sororities or any of the over 120 clubs offered. Students are encouraged to take advantage of ready access to personalized advice and support in the areas of career and personal counseling and academic support.

Seventy percent of students live on campus in residence halls that offer a variety of accommodations including single gender, coed by separate wings, and coed by alternate suites.

The University of Redlands is one of a select number of schools that has a chapter of Phi Beta Kappa, the nation's oldest and most prestigious academic honor society. In addition, 21 Redlands students have been awarded Fulbright awards within the past nine years.

The University of Redlands offers master's programs in the fields of business, communicative disorders, education, geographic information systems, and music. The School of Education offers a Doctorate in Leadership for Educational Justice (Ed.D.).

Location

The University is located in the city of Redlands in Southern California, within an hour's drive of the beach, mountains, and deserts, allowing students to take full advantage of the outdoors. Overlooking the 160-acre campus are the two highest mountains in Southern California, Mt. San Gorgonio and Mt. San Bernardino. Redlands has a population of 70,000 and is situated at an elevation of 1,500 feet. Metropolitan Los Angeles to the west and Palm Springs to the east are both about an hour's drive away by freeway.

Majors and Degrees

The degree can be earned in the academic areas of accounting, Asian studies, biochemistry and molecular biology; biology; business administration; chemistry; communication sciences and disorders; computer science; creative writing; economics; 3-2 engineering program; English; environmental science; environmental studies; financial economics; French; German; global business; history; international relations; Johnston Center for Integrative Studies; Latin American studies; liberal studies; managerial studies; mathematics; media and visual culture studies; philosophy; physics; political science; psychology; public policy; race and ethnic studies; religious studies; sociology and anthropology; Spanish; studio art; theatre arts; theatre business; and women, gender, and sexuality studies. Minors are offered in art history, astronomy, human-animal studies, physical education and athletics, and spatial studies. The professional degree of Bachelor of Music (B.M.) is offered by the School of Music. Primary and secondary credentials are granted by the School of Education. Strong integrated programs of study in pre-law and pre-health are available and advise students for pre-professional development.

Academic Programs

Academic majors are offered in the spirit of a liberal arts program, with an emphasis on developing the whole student. In addition to the standard academic program, study abroad programs, independent study, and an honors program are offered to provide greater diversity.

A liberal arts education exposes students to a wide variety of academic disciplines. Typically, such exposure carries no underlying theme but is distributed among broad categories such as the humanities, arts, social sciences, and natural sciences. The University of Redlands requires students to take courses that emphasize competence in writing, computing, problem solving, and creative skills—all of which are fundamental to a lifetime of learning and career development. In addition, first-year students participate in a seminar that integrates the academic program and helps build close relationships between students and faculty members. The overriding emphasis of this innovative curriculum is a thorough investigation of human values as they affect the individual and society. An examination of the worth of the individual, respect for nature and life, free inquiry, and the understanding of other cultures are a few of the topics covered through various courses. The University hopes that this experience will broaden each student's understanding and better equip them to deal with today's dynamic society.

The Johnston Center for Integrative Studies provides a nontraditional approach for a select group of highly motivated students. Johnston Center students are exempt from most of the academic structure of Redlands and instead negotiate their entire course of study with a faculty and peer committee. Drawing from the Redlands curriculum as well as from courses created each semester by the Johnston community, each student proposes an individually designed general studies program and an area of concentration. Course performance is evaluated in a narrative format rather than with letter grades. These students live in the Johnston Center Complex, a living and learning community that includes student rooms, faculty offices, classrooms, and space for weekly community meetings. Students who are enrolled in the Johnston Center are expected to contribute to the life of the center's community.

The academic calendar divides the school year into a 4-4-1 plan, providing a fall semester, a spring semester, and a May term. The four classes taken in the fall semester are completed prior to the third Friday in December. The spring semester begins in January and runs through April. The four-week May term offers students the chance to pursue one subject in depth. Extensive off-campus opportunities, including internships, study abroad, and on-campus independent study, are available.

Academic Facilities

The institution has facilities with a mix of Greek, Spanish, and modern Californian architecture. The ground floor of the Armacost Library includes rooms for collaboration and learning, the Fletcher Jones Computing Center, a student study area, the Bulldog Café, and an Internet lounge. Other facilities include the Stauffer Complex for Science, Mathematics, and Environmental Studies; and the Center for the Arts, featuring the Glen Wallichs Theatre, Frederick Loewe Performance Hall, and an art gallery. The library houses 400,000 publications and online databases such as Dialog, ABI/INFORM, PsychLIT, ERIC, Wilson Indexes, and the Music Index.

Costs

Tuition for 2016–17 was $46,570, and room and board costs were $13,480.

Financial Aid

More than 90 percent of Redlands students receive some sort of financial aid. Financial aid is merit- and need-based. Students seeking financial assistance should submit the Free Application for Federal Student Aid (FAFSA) by March 2. Forms can be found online at www.fafsa.gov. Academic scholarships are also available based on grades and test scores. In 2015, the Richard and Virginia Hunsaker Scholarship award was presented to its first recipients. This scholarship program is awarded to approximately 8 incoming freshmen annually and recognizes exceptional applicants who exhibit outstanding academic achievement, leadership, and contributions to their schools and communities. Talent Awards of up to $3,000 may be given to students who submit additional work in studio art, creative writing, and theatre arts, and awards of up to $10,000 may be given to students auditioning for the School of Music.

Faculty

The wide variety of academic backgrounds represented in the faculty provides students with an excellent opportunity to live and work in an atmosphere of intellectual inquiry. Academic advising is handled by faculty members, and all students are assigned an adviser in the area of their major interest. Students will find faculty members to be passionate about their work and their students. Classes are rarely taught in a lecture style but rather in a discussion-based narrative including the original thoughts of the students.

Student Government

Authority and responsibility for student government is delegated to the Associated Students of the University of Redlands (ASUR) by the President and the faculty to make possible genuine participation by students in the governance of the University. The organization is composed of all students in the college, and its officers are chosen by the student body. More than 60 positions of representation are open to students on faculty, administrative, trustee, and alumni committees. Among other activities and responsibilities, the student government finances and operates a student-union complex, on-campus shuttle, information center, vending program, convocation series, radio station, and weekly newspaper.

Admission Requirements

Graduation from an accredited high school or the equivalent is necessary for admission. While no single academics schedule is required, it is strongly recommended that students take a college preparatory curriculum. This includes 4 years of English, 3 years of math (including algebra), 3 years of social science, 2 to 3 years of a foreign language, and 2 to 3 years of science, including 2 years of a lab science. An average grade of at least B should have been maintained in the high school program. Applicants are requested to submit the results of the SAT or the ACT. It is recommended that students should submit all scores from these tests as they are super-scored. SAT Subject Tests are not required. Standardized test scores are not required of transfers who bring at least 24 transferable units to the University. International students, for whom English is not their first language, must submit the results from any of the following exams: TOEFL, IELTS, PTE-A, iTEP, University of Cambridge ESOL examinations, or the International Baccalaureate Higher Level English exam.

Transfer students should have maintained a minimum 2.8 grade point average and may transfer up to 66 units of credit from a community college and 96 units from a four-year institution.

All students must submit their application using the Common Application. This can be found online at commonapp.org. The application fee is $50.

Application and Information

Freshmen admissions applications are processed in two phases and on a space-available basis. Those wishing to be considered for Early Action or Early Decision should apply by November 15. Students wanting to apply for Regular Decision should submit their application by January 15. Transfer applicants should apply by March 1 for priority fall semester admission or November 1 for spring semester admission. Applications made after this date are considered on a space-available basis.

Further inquiries should be addressed to:

Office of Admissions
University of Redlands
P.O. Box 3080
Redlands, California 92373-0999
Phone: 800-455-5064 (toll-free)
Fax: 909-335-4089
E-mail: admissions@redlands.edu
Website: http://www.redlands.edu

The University of Redlands against the backdrop of the majestic San Gorgonio Mountain.

COLLEGE CLOSE-UPS

UNIVERSITY OF SAN FRANCISCO

SAN FRANCISCO, CALIFORNIA

★ To read more about this school, visit http://petersons.to/universityofsanfrancisco

UNIVERSITY OF SAN FRANCISCO
CHANGE THE WORLD FROM HERE

The University

The University of San Francisco—a premier, private Jesuit university—reflects the diverse and dynamic city that surrounds it. The University of San Francisco (USF) provides students from all backgrounds an education that is intensely personalized, intellectually inspiring, and designed expressly to help them change the world for the better. USF enrolls 6,782 undergraduate and 4,046 graduate students.

USF offers over 100 undergraduate and graduate degree programs and boasts an ever-expanding network of 105,900 alumni who live in all 50 states, six US territories, and 129 countries. The school's 55-acre campus, in the geographic heart of San Francisco, overlooks downtown to the east and the Pacific Ocean to the west. It puts students right in the middle of everything San Francisco has to offer.

USF is one of the most diverse university campuses in the United States. Living and learning in a community that comprises students from 49 states and 94 other countries is a unique opportunity. All undergraduates, freshmen, and transfer students who enter with 40 or fewer college credits must live on campus for their first two semesters at USF, unless they live within a 40-mile radius of campus. More than 90 percent of the incoming freshmen live on campus.

The University offers four on-campus residence halls, one off-campus residence hall, and two on-campus apartment-style residences. Housing for freshmen and under-21 students is in Gillson, Hayes-Healy, Lone Mountain, and Fromm. Housing for upper-division students ages 21+ is in Loyola Village (apartment-style living for upper-division and graduate students); Pedro Arrupe Hall, located 12 blocks from the USF campus; and Fulton House, a single-family home and cottage. Each residence hall has laundry facilities, study rooms, community kitchens, television lounges, and 24-hour front desk staff.

The Koret Health and Recreation Center is an exciting complex that provides facilities for exercise, racquetball, court games, weight training, massage, personal training, and various aquatic activities in an Olympic-size pool. Fitness interval training, spin, yoga, Pilates mat, and Zumba are just some of the free classes offered at Koret. Outdoor adventures include horseback riding, sailing, skiing/snowboarding, and sea kayaking. Intramural and club sports include basketball, soccer, flag football, sailing, table tennis, karate, lacrosse, rugby, water polo, Ultimate (Frisbee), and volleyball. NCAA Division I sports include baseball, basketball, cross-country, golf, soccer, tennis, track and field, and women's volleyball and sand volleyball.

University dining venues are located all over campus and are within walking distance of the residence halls and classrooms. The Market Café offers a food court experience with a variety of choices, including global, vegan, homestyle classics, and vegetarian options. Other dining options include Wolf & Kettle Café, Outtahere Café, Crossroads Café, Club Ed in the School of Education, and Kendrick Café in the Law School.

Location

USF's 55-acre campus is located in the heart one of the world's most dynamic cities, just minutes from the Financial District, Golden Gate Park, Fisherman's Wharf, and the Pacific Ocean. The hilltop campus offers panoramic views of downtown. Students take advantage of the opportunities available in San Francisco including concerts, museums, theater, dining, the ballet, opera, and major sporting events. The city also offers a wide range of research, community involvement, and employment opportunities.

Majors and Degrees

The College of Arts and Sciences offers both B.A. and B.S. degrees. The School of Management offers B.S. degrees. The School of Nursing and Health Professions offers a direct-entry, four-year B.S. in Nursing for qualified high school and transfer applicants. Major programs include: accounting, advertising, architecture and community design, art history/arts management, Asian studies, biology, business administration, chemistry, communication studies, comparative literature and culture, computer science, critical diversity studies, data science, design, economics, English, entrepreneurship and innovation, environmental science, environmental studies, finance, fine arts, French studies, health studies, history, hospitality management, international business, international studies, Japanese studies, kinesiology, Latin American studies, marketing, management, mathematics, media studies, nursing, organizational behavior and leadership, performing arts and social justice, philosophy, physics, politics, psychology, sociology, Spanish, theology and religious studies, and urban studies.

USF has 77 minors and offers special programs that enhance the learning experience at USF. Special programs include astronomy; African history; Asia Pacific studies; Catholic studies and social thought; ethnic studies; film studies; honors program in the humanities; journalism; Judaic studies; Latino/a and Chicano/a Studies; Middle Eastern studies; neuroscience; 4+3 dual degrees in law, premedical, and other pre-professional health studies; public relations; a five-year dual-degree teacher preparation program that results in teacher certification at the elementary or secondary level; and the School of Management honors cohort program.

Academic Programs

The University of San Francisco delivers a well-rounded education that prepares students not only for successful careers but also for fulfilling lives. A baccalaureate degree is issued upon the successful completion of a 128-unit curriculum. The curriculum consists of 44 units of core courses chosen from six specified categories in addition to 80–85 units that are divided among departmental major requirements and electives. An honors program is available for select students seeking a strong academic challenge. The academic year is based on the two-semester system, with summer sessions and a winter intersession also available.

USF honors advanced placement credits, as certified by the College Board's Advanced Placement Program exams and the International Baccalaureate program. The University also cooperates with the College-Level Examination Program (CLEP). Students in the College of Arts and Sciences can also accelerate the traditional undergraduate process and earn a bachelor's degree in three years with a combination of advanced placement credits and an academically rigorous schedule.

The USF Pre-Professional Health Committee serves to guide and recommend students to medical and dental professional schools as well as to schools for pharmacy, optometry, veterinary medicine, and podiatry. A student may complete the premedical or other pre–health science requirements as part of, or in addition to, the requirements of an academic major. The Pre-Professional Health Committee assists students with the application process, collects and mails recommendations to professional schools, conducts interviews in preparation for application, and endorses approved candidates via a committee letter of recommendation sent to all professional schools selected by the student.

The St. Ignatius Institute offers a core curriculum based on the great books of Western civilization and an emphasis on critical analysis to promote the common good. Any undergraduate student at the University, regardless of major, may take courses through the Institute to meet core curriculum requirements. The University also offers Army ROTC. ROTC scholarships are available for qualified applicants and continuing students.

Off-Campus Programs

The USF Center for Global Education offers over 130 semester-long programs including:

- Exchange programs with Jesuit and Catholic-affiliated universities in Argentina, Australia, Brazil, Chile, China, Colombia, Ecuador, England, France, Greece, Ireland, Japan, Korea, Mexico, Netherlands, Peru, Philippines, Spain, Taiwan, Turkey, and Uruguay.

- Internship-specific programs in a broad range of fields including arts, business, hospitality, international relations, Field study programs focused on global issues such as sustainable development, public health, human rights, and climate change.

Academic Facilities

USF students have access to Gleeson Library's 2.1 million holdings and to Lo Schiavo Center for Science and Innovation, which houses a digital lecture hall, ample space for collaborative learning, and labs for chemistry, toxicology, advanced biotechnology, and mathematics. Cowell Hall, the base for nursing classes and the Nursing Skills Laboratory, also includes the Instructional Media Center. Malloy Hall, headquarters for the School of Management, houses an additional computer laboratory and special seminar rooms. Kalmanovitz Hall houses all programs in the humanities and social sciences and features state-of-the-art classrooms, a rooftop sculpture garden, and seventeen laboratories for language, writing, media, and psychology.

Costs

Tuition for the 2016–17 school year was $44,040. Room and board were $13,990 for the academic year.

Financial Aid

A variety of financial aid programs are available at the University, including scholarships, grants, loans, and campus employment opportunities. Domestic students who wish to be considered for financial aid must file the Free Application for Federal Student Aid (FAFSA) and College Scholarship Service Profile (CSS) by February 15. More than two thirds of all USF students receive some type of financial aid.

In addition to need-based financial aid, the University has a generous academic scholarship program based on the applicant's high school record and test scores. Eligible students are identified during the admission process and can apply as early action, early decision, or regular action applicants. Scholarship recipients are expected to maintain a competitive GPA while enrolled at USF.

Faculty

The University has 1,245 full- and part-time faculty members; 93 percent of full-time faculty hold doctoral or terminal degrees in the fields they teach. The central focus of faculty is on classroom teaching and working with students on research.

USF fosters a close relationship between students and faculty members. This is reflected in the small classes (fewer than 25 students), the low student-to-faculty ratio (14:1), and the faculty members' availability for advising. Classes are not taught by student teachers or teachers' assistants

Student Clubs and Organizations

Undergraduates keep busy by participating in over 100 on-campus, student-run associations, including fraternities, sororities, honor societies, and clubs. Among these are the oldest continuously performing theater group west of the Mississippi River, an entire consortium of culturally focused organizations, and a relationship with over 250 community service organizations. Students also participate in a whole host of Campus Activities Board sponsored events including Spring Carnival, Campus Movie Fest, and Late Nights@Crossroads.

Because all USF students are encouraged to give back to the community and to change the world in ways both small and large, the Leo T. McCarthy Center for Public Service and the Common Good forms partnerships between local communities and USF. Students participate in service-learning projects that include socially just urban design, outreach to underprivileged children in local schools, and habitat restoration.

All undergraduates are members of the Associated Students of the University of San Francisco (ASUSF). ASUSF is the official representative body of undergraduate students at USF. The ASUSF government has three functions: to represent the official student viewpoint, to recommend policies, and to fund activities and services. ASUSF consists of three branches: the executive branch, the Student Senate, and the Student Court. The Senate comprises an executive board and student senators.

Admission Requirements

The University seeks students who are sincerely interested in pursuing a well-rounded education and who hope to make a positive difference in the world. The admission process is selective, and each application is reviewed individually. To enhance the quality and diversity of its student body, USF welcomes men and women of all races, nationalities, and religious beliefs—or no religious belief—to apply. Eligibility is based on high school course work and GPA, the application essay, an academic recommendation, extracurricular involvement, and test scores. Domestic applicants are required to submit SAT or ACT test scores. International applicants are required to submit TOEFL or IELTS test scores; however, if an international applicant submits sufficient SAT or ACT test scores, the TOEFL or IELTS may be waived.

Application and Information

A completed application includes the application form, the application fee, a personal essay, all academic transcripts, standardized test scores, and one letter of recommendation. For the fall semester, the application deadlines are November 15 for early action and early decision (freshmen only) and January 15 for regular action (freshmen and transfers).

Inquiries should be addressed to:

Office of Admission
University of San Francisco
2130 Fulton Street
San Francisco, California 94117-1080
Phone: 415-422-6563
800-CALL-USF (toll-free outside California)
Fax: 415-422-2217
E-mail: admission@usfca.edu
Website: http://www.usfca.edu
http://www.facebook.com/University.of.San.Francisco
http://twitter.com/USFCA
http://www.youtube.com/usfcalifornia

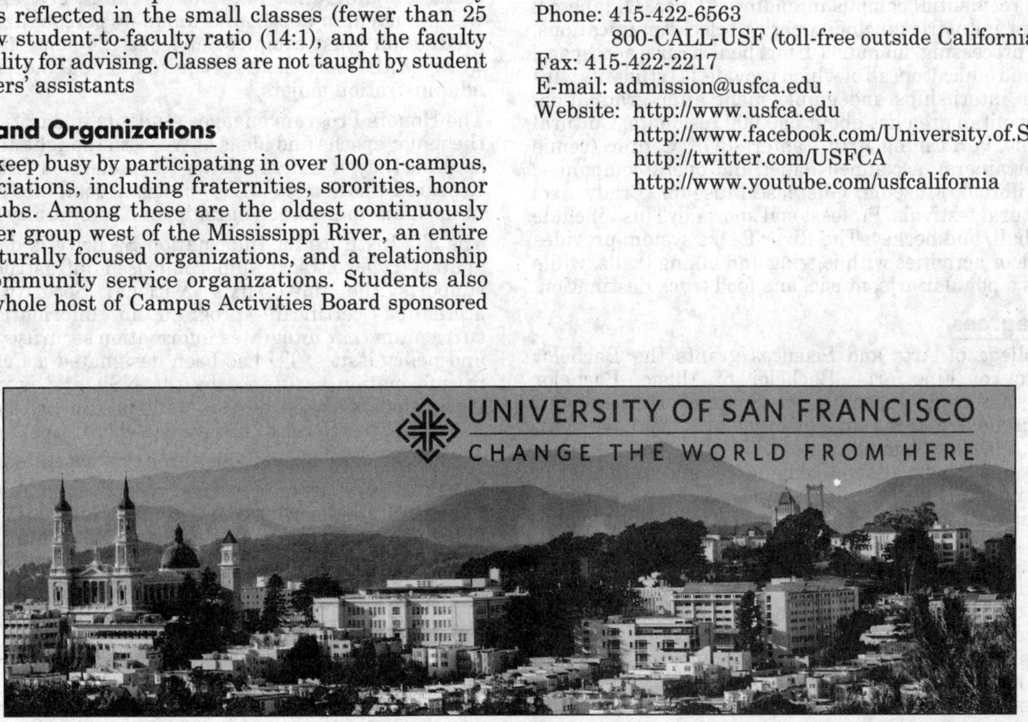

THE UNIVERSITY OF TULSA

TULSA, OKLAHOMA

The University

The University of Tulsa (TU) is a private, comprehensive degree-granting university that provides high-quality education in the arts, humanities, sciences, engineering, business, education, applied health sciences, and law. Fully accredited by the North Central Association of Colleges and Universities, TU comprises the Kendall College of Arts and Sciences, the Collins College of Business, the College of Engineering and Natural Sciences, the Oxley College of Health Sciences, the College of Law, and a Graduate School.

The university is an NCAA Division IA participant currently in the American Athletic Conference. TU, which maintains a covenant relationship with the Presbyterian Church (U.S.A.), is a force for good locally, through its True Blue Neighbors initiatives (with more than 70,000 volunteer hours per year), as well as through various student programs that include projects such as locally producing assistive devices for the disabled and working on international projects that provide self-sustaining sources of energy and hot water.

TU's 11:1 student-faculty ratio, average class size of 23, and emphasis on individual attention anchor an educational culture where students receive both rigorous challenges and comprehensive support. In 2016, TU graduates had a 93 percent placement rate in full-time jobs or graduate/professional schools.

Extracurricular opportunities include intramural sports, special interest clubs, preprofessional organizations, national fraternities and sororities, community service organizations, student government, departmental honorary groups, and campus ministries.

Total fall 2016 enrollment was 4,563, with 3,406 undergraduates and 811 graduate and 346 law students. The ratio of men to women is 57:43, 17 percent of the students are multicultural, and 26 percent international. TU's diverse student population comes from Oklahoma, 29 states and the District of Columbia, and 73 countries.

Based on academic reputation and other factors, the *U.S. News & World Report*'s *2016 Best Colleges* ranks TU eighty-sixth among doctoral/research universities in the United States.

Location

TU is a 220-acre residential campus in midtown Tulsa, Oklahoma. Tulsa's prominent industries include energy, telecommunications, technology, data processing, manufacturing, health care, aerospace, transportation, and education, all of which provide TU students with opportunities for internships and employment after graduation. The Tulsa metropolitan area has about 550,000 residents. Cultural assets include the Performing Arts Center, BOK Center (venue for popular entertainers), acclaimed ballet and opera companies, a symphony, Philbrook Museum, Gilcrease Museum, Brady Arts District, and cultural festivals. Professional sports in Tulsa include baseball, basketball, and hockey. The River Parks system provides facilities for outdoor activities with jogging and biking trails, while Guthrie Green is a popular arts, music, and food truck destination.

Majors and Degrees

The Kendall College of Arts and Sciences grants the Bachelor of Arts, Bachelor of Fine Arts, Bachelor of Music, Bachelor of Music Education, and Bachelor of Science degrees with majors in anthropology, art, art history, arts management, Chinese studies, classics, communication, creative writing, deaf education, economics, education (elementary and secondary), English, environmental policy, film studies, French, German, history, music, musical theatre, organizational studies, philosophy, political science, psychology, religion, Russian studies, sociology, Spanish, theatre, women's and gender studies, and self-designed majors. Minors include most disciplines as well as advertising, Chinese, dance, early childhood intervention, film scoring, Latin, and Russian. Interdisciplinary certificate programs offer a way for students to focus their interests in advertising, African American studies, classics, creative writing, international studies, journalism studies, Judaic studies, museum studies, political philosophy, and visual studies.

The Collins College of Business awards the Bachelor of Science in Business Administration degree in accounting, economics, energy management, finance, management, management information systems, and marketing; and a Bachelor of Science in international business and language. Minors are available in most disciplines plus business administration (for non-majors), coaching, healthcare informatics, and international business (for business majors only). Certificate programs are available in accounting, finance, management information systems, not-for-profit administration, and sports administration. Management majors may choose specializations in business law, entrepreneurship and family business management, or human resource management. The college is home to several specialized centers, including the Energy Management Program, Family Owned Business Institute, the Genave King Rogers Center for Business Law, and the Williams Risk Management Center.

The Oxley College of Health Sciences offers the Bachelor of Science degree in nursing, athletic training, exercise and sport science, and a Bachelor of Arts degree in speech pathology.

The College of Engineering and Natural Sciences offers the Bachelor of Science degree in applied mathematics, biochemistry, biogeosciences, biological science (options in pre-medicine, pre-dentistry, and pre–veterinary science), chemical engineering, chemistry, computer science, computer simulation and gaming, earth and environmental science, electrical and computer engineering, electrical engineering, engineering physics, geology, geophysics, information technology, mathematics, mechanical engineering, petroleum engineering, and physics. Minors are available in the science and computational science disciplines. The college features state-of-the-art research facilities for all majors. Since 1995, more than 50 TU engineering students have received the prestigious Barry M. Goldwater Scholarship, the nation's premier award for undergraduate students in engineering, math, or science.

Academic Programs

The Tulsa Curriculum links a broad, humanities-based core and writing-across-the-curriculum approach for all students with a highly flexible group of majors, minors, concentrations, and certificate programs. TU students can receive an education that is well-rounded, in-depth, and uniquely personalized. Candidates for graduation must complete at least 124 semester hours of course work, with more hours required of engineering and business administration majors.

The Honors Program engages students in a critical examination of the major epochs and ideas of Western thought and culture through careful study of primary texts. The acclaimed Tulsa Undergraduate Research Challenge (TURC) program combines advanced research in most disciplines, scholarship, and community service.

The TU Institute for Information Security is developing defenses against cyber-attacks and comprised infrastructure. The center supports the university's National Security Agency (NSA)–accredited certificate program in information assurance, a curriculum that integrates information security with computer law and policy issues. TU has been designated a Center of Excellence in information assurance by the NSA and is one of six pioneer institutions selected by the National Science Foundation for the Federal Cyber Service Initiative (Cyber Corps).

Air Force ROTC is available through a satellite program.

Qualified students may receive credit through Advanced Placement testing. Students who complete the International Baccalaureate diploma can receive up to 30 college credit hours.

The University of Tulsa operates on a semester calendar. The fall term begins in late August and the spring term in mid-January.

Off-Campus Programs

The university is supportive of study-abroad and internship experiences. The Center for Global Education helps students locate the perfect program, whether for TU credit or as an intern or volunteer. Students choose from hundreds of opportunities offered around the world through a direct exchange with an international university, an affiliate-sponsored program, or as part of a faculty-led course. Internship opportunities are also available in Tulsa and throughout the nation.

Academic Facilities

TU's libraries, historic McFarlin Library and Mabee Legal Information Center, house more than 4 million items. McFarlin holdings include over 920,000 volumes, 620,000 titles, 120,000 e-books, 40,000 electronic periodicals, 7,500 videos, and 10,000 recordings. McFarlin's special collections rare book holdings number over 125,000 volumes and are internationally recognized, particularly for holdings of Native American history and law, along with nineteenth- and twentieth-century Irish, English, and American literature. McFarlin is home to the papers of 2001 Nobel Laureate V. S. Naipaul. The 12,000 square-foot Academic Technology Center annex was dedicated in 2009, adding computer labs, a coffee shop, and restored reading rooms.

The College of Engineering and Natural Sciences added J. Newton Rayzor Hall, a $14-million home for the Tandy School of Computer Science and Department of Electrical Engineering with 24 integrated classrooms and state-of-the-art teaching/research laboratories; and Stephenson Hall, the 38,600 square-foot home for the Department of Mechanical Engineering and McDougall School of Petroleum Engineering. The university's flagship Keplinger Hall is undergoing renovation. Additional research facilities are housed at Tulsa's North Campus where government- and industry-funded research consortia explore innovations and solve problems faced by the petroleum industry while fostering student learning.

Helmerich Hall, which houses the Collins College of Business, includes innovative learning spaces such as the Williams Students Services Center and Studio Blue. The Williams Risk Management Center combines the latest in trading-floor technology and advanced study in risk management theories and techniques.

The Roxana Rózsa and Robert Eugene Lorton Performance Center houses the School of Music and the Department of Film Studies. The 77,000 square-foot facility includes a 600-seat concert hall, specialized rehearsal and practice rooms, and a film production suite with postproduction editing and scoring capabilities.

Most recently, the Oxley College of Health Sciences moved to downtown Tulsa, occupying 50,000 square feet of the building at 1215 South Boulder. To accommodate travel between the main campus and the college, the university will operate continuous shuttle routes for students, faculty, and staff. The new building expands TU's downtown presence, which also includes the Henry Zarrow Center for Art and Education in the Brady Arts District.

The Donald W. Reynolds Center is the campus arena and convocation center, home for TU basketball and volleyball, and includes cutting-edge facilities for video editing and training.

The Allen Chapman Student Union offers dining options and meeting spaces. Meals and snacks are also available in the Pat Case Dining Center, the Collins Fitness Center, and the McFarlin Library Café.

The 29,000 square-foot Case Athletic Complex is home to the Golden Hurricane football program and adjoins the H. A. Chapman Stadium where players enjoy one of the nation's elite college football training and playing environments.

The university's 34-acre sports and recreation complex features a 64,000 square-foot fitness center, the Michael Case Tennis Center, track, NCAA soccer and softball fields, and intramural fields.

TU manages the city's Gilcrease Museum, home to the world's largest collection of art and artifacts of the American West. The two entities have expanded into Tulsa's Brady Arts District to open the Henry Zarrow Center for Art and Education, providing classes and studio space. In 2014, the university opened the Helmerich Center for American Research at Gilcrease Museum to house the museum's library and archive. Visiting faculty, students, and scholars from around the world visit the 25,000 square-foot facility to conduct research and present symposia on their research topics.

Costs

For 2017–18, the typical cost for students living on campus is $52,625, including $40,484 for tuition, $11,116 for room and board, and fees of $1,025. Additional miscellaneous expenses (including books) average about $4,500 per year.

Financial Aid

In 2016, 94 percent of entering students received some form of financial aid (including grants, scholarships, work-study, and loans). TU offers a limited number of highly competitive Presidential Scholarships that cover full tuition, room, and board. All applicants may be considered for a range of University scholarships based on academic merit. Performance scholarships are available in music and theater by audition. The University of Tulsa participates in National Merit and National Achievement Scholarship Corporation's Finalist program and the National Hispanic Scholar Program. Applicants for aid should submit the Free Application for Federal Student Aid (FAFSA) by January 15 for priority consideration.

Faculty

The University has 348 full-time faculty members, with 96 percent having earned the highest degree in their field of study. The faculty is primarily a teaching faculty, although most of its members are also involved in funded research or publishing activities.

Admission Requirements

The University of Tulsa seeks students whose academic background indicates potential for success in the university's rigorous academic environment. Performance in high school college-preparatory subjects and scores on the SAT or ACT are key factors in the admission evaluation, but each applicant is reviewed holistically. Each applicant's counselor recommendation; extracurricular activities; and indicators of leadership, creativity, and focus are all taken into consideration. Campus visits and interviews are highly recommended but not required.

Application and Information

TU has a nonbinding, early action freshman admission plan with an application deadline of November 1. Decisions are mailed within five weeks. Applications received after November 1 are reviewed under a rolling admission process with notifications made on an ongoing basis in early January.

An application, high school transcript, ACT or SAT score results, and a guidance counselor recommendation are required. TU accepts the Common Application or its own online or paper application form. TU adheres to the national Candidate's Reply Date of May 1.

For more information, students should contact:

Office of Undergraduate Admission
The University of Tulsa
800 South Tucker Drive
Tulsa, Oklahoma 74104-3189
Phone: 918-631-2307 (in Tulsa)
800-331-3050 (toll-free)
Fax: 918-631-5008
E-mail: admission@utulsa.edu
Website: https://admission.utulsa.edu

Bayless Plaza is home to the iconic Kendall Bell.

UNITED STATES MERCHANT MARINE ACADEMY

KINGS POINT, NEW YORK

★ For more information, visit http://petersons.to/merchantmarineacademy

The Academy

The United States Merchant Marine Academy is a federal service academy that educates individuals for careers as licensed Merchant Marine officers. Graduates serve America's marine transportation and defense needs. With 95 percent of the world's products transported over water, these leaders are vital to the effective operation of our merchant fleet for both commercial and military transport during war and peace.

The Academy is known for providing rigorous education and training. In fact, its bachelor degree program has more credit hours than programs in any other federal service academy. This challenging coursework is augmented by the Academy's Sea Year experience, which affords midshipmen (students) the opportunity to acquire hands-on, real-world experiences aboard working commercial vessels sailing to ports around the world. Midshipmen who master this demanding curriculum earn three credentials: a Bachelor of Science degree, a United States Coast Guard license, and an officer's commission in the United States armed forces.

Upon graduation, every graduate has a service obligation that offers more career options than any other federal academy. Graduates can work five years in the U.S. maritime industry and serve eight years as an officer in a reserve unit of any branch of the armed forces. Alternatively, they can choose to serve five years of active duty in any branch of the armed forces.

Academy graduates are highly sought after as officers in the military and the merchant marine. U.S. Merchant Marine graduates play a key role in the maritime industry, which is vital to America's economy and continued prosperity. The most important element in a productive merchant fleet and a strong transportation industry is people—men and women who can lead with integrity, honor, intelligence, dedication, and competence. The U.S. Merchant Marine Academy ensures that such people are available to the nation as shipboard officers and as leaders in the transportation field who will meet the challenges of the present and the future.

The Academy's Regiment of Midshipmen numbers approximately 950 young men and women who represent every state of the Union as well as U.S. Trust Territories and Possessions. The size of the student body contributes to a true sense of camaraderie among the members of the Regiment and permits the Academy to maintain an excellent student-teacher ratio.

The United States Merchant Marine Academy is accredited by the Middle States Commission on Higher Education (MSCHE), 3624 Market Street, Philadelphia, Pennsylvania 19104; 267-284-5000, http://www.msche.org.

Location

The United States Merchant Marine Academy is located in Kings Point, New York in the northeastern region of the United States. It's situated on Long Island's "Gold Coast" neighborhood and provides a stunning view of New York City's skyline.

The academy's 82-acre campus features the beautiful American Merchant Marine Museum, a swimming pool along the waterfront, numerous academic buildings including Gibbs Hall, with its state-of-the-art engineering and science laboratories, Yocum Sailing Center, and an interfaith chapel.

Degree Programs

A sound college education is the foundation for every profession in our society and the mariner's profession is no exception. The academic curriculum at the Academy provides each midshipman with the broad college education required for a Bachelor of Science degree, a U. S. Coast Guard License as Merchant Marine Officer, and a Commission as Ensign in the Navy Reserve.

As part of the Bachelor of Science curriculum, midshipmen complete core courses, courses in their majors, and elective courses as well as hands-on experience at sea. Core courses provide in-depth knowledge in the following academic and professional areas: comparative literature and history, English, leadership and ethics, mathematics, and naval science.

The Academy offers the following five majors:

Marine Transportation—emphasizes nautical science and maritime business management.

Maritime Logistics and Security—emphasizes nautical science, managing complex maritime and intermodal supply chains, security challenges facing the marine transportation system.

Marine Engineering—emphasizes shipboard engineering operations.

Marine Engineering Systems—emphasizes design of shipboard systems and machinery.

Marine Engineering and Shipyard Management—emphasizes the management of shipyards, and the production and repair of marine vehicles.

The Academy challenges its midshipmen intellectually and physically. Freshman students make the transition from high school graduate to Academy midshipman. In their first few months, they learn many new terms, the quality of endurance, how to perform under pressure, and most importantly, how to successfully manage time. During sophomore year, and again during junior year, midshipmen are sent to sea for practical shipboard training. Aboard ship, sailing the trade routes of the world, they learn the value of self-reliance and initiative as they gain firsthand experience in the mariner's environment. In senior year, they fine-tune the skills learned in the classroom and at sea as they prepare to enter the professional world.

Career Opportunities

Graduates of the United States Merchant Marine Academy are fully equipped to take advantage of the many career opportunities that await them. They typically build their careers and fulfill the service obligation at sea or ashore as Merchant Marine officers and commission as Ensign in the Navy Reserve, or apply to any branch of the armed forces as active duty officers.

Employers are eager to hire them because of their exemplary character, hands-on experience, leadership and problem-solving skills, professional expertise, and self-discipline. Nearly 100 percent of the Academy's graduates secure well-paying jobs within three to six months of graduation.

Students acquire the tools to achieve long-term career success. A Standard and Poor's report ranked the United States Merchant Marine Academy eighteenth among the top 550 colleges and universities whose alumni include directors of U.S. companies, presidents, and vice presidents (in proportion to total number of graduates).

Facilities

The campus includes multiple buildings, including state-of-the-art classrooms and labs, dining facilities, recently renovated barracks (dorms), and recreational and physical fitness buildings. There are also extensive waterfront facilities and activities.

The Academy library is dedicated to providing information and services to further the education process at Kings Point by offering resources in a variety of formats from traditional to high tech. Easy access to resources quickly provides the reference, research, and reading material needed to support the curriculum.

Costs and Financial Aid

The federal government covers the cost of tuition, books, room and board, and uniforms. Midshipmen pay for an Academy-approved personal laptop, activity fees, licensing fees, personal and transportation expenses, and personal services (such as tailoring, laundry, personal grooming, etc.).

The Academy doesn't offer traditional institutional aid such as scholarships. However, all students, no matter their income levels, are eligible for federal financial aid. They can also seek scholarships from private sources.

Faculty

Faculty members are highly skilled teachers, mentors, and scholars. They help create a supportive, stimulating, and rigorous learning environment where students can reach their full potential.

Student Life

The Academy's 950 midshipmen lead regimented yet interesting and enjoyable lives. During the academic year, they follow a daily schedule Monday through Friday which includes meal times, room inspections, classes, athletics, and study time. On Friday afternoons and Saturday mornings they participate in inspections and regimental parades.

Midshipmen have access to more than 40 registered student organizations that host a variety of events and programs. They can also take on leadership roles such as campus activities board member, morale or diversity training officer, or petty officer. They can also participate in 27 varsity and intramural sports, including basketball, baseball, cross-country, football, lacrosse, swimming, track and field, volleyball, and wresting.

There are also plenty of opportunities to venture off campus to enjoy the culture of New York City and Long Island.

Admission Requirements

To be eligible to enter the Academy, candidates must be at least 17 years of age and no older than 25; be a citizen of the United States; meet the physical, security, suitability, and character requirements necessary for commission in the U.S. Navy Reserve; obtain a Congressional nomination to the Academy; submit a completed application; and qualify scholastically.

Candidates should pursue studies in high school that will prepare them for the Academy's rigorous program. Candidates must have satisfactorily completed their high school education at an accredited secondary school or its equivalent. They must have earned at least 16 units of credit: 4 units must be in English; 3 units in mathematics (from algebra, trigonometry, pre-calculus, and/or calculus); and 1 unit in physics or chemistry with a laboratory. The Academy strongly recommends that candidates take four years of mathematics and both physics and chemistry. Courses in mechanical drawing and machine shop are also desirable.

All candidates are required to take either the SAT or ACT test. The current minimum qualifying scores for the SAT Reasoning Test (taken after March 2016) are 30 Reading and 580 for Math. The current minimum qualifying scores for the ACT are 24 English and 24 Math and applicants must also achieve a minimum composite score of 23. Each of the three minimum scores must be achieved individually in order to meet the Academy's minimum test score requirements.

Satisfactory completion of the Candidate Fitness Assessment (CFA) is required for admission. Passing results must be received in the Admissions Office by the 1 March application deadline. The CFA is a test of strength, agility, speed and endurance. The examination may be administered by a J/ROTC instructor, physical education teacher, coach, or any commissioned/noncommissioned officer other than a parent/guardian.

Candidates must be nominated to the Academy by a U.S. Representative or Senator. The ideal time for a candidate to apply for a nomination is in May of junior year in high school.

Application and Information

Students may begin applying to the Academy on June 1 of their junior year of high school. The application deadline is March 1 of the year they wish to enter the Academy. U.S. candidates for admission to the Academy must apply online; however, all documents must be mailed, e-mailed or faxed and received in the Admissions Office by March 1. Documents cannot be uploaded onto the web portal.

For more information, prospective candidates may contact:
Admissions Office
United States Merchant Marine Academy
300 Steamboat Road
Kings Point, New York 11024
United States
Phone: 866-546-4778
Fax: 516-773-5390
E-mail: admissions@usmma.edu
Website: https://www.usmma.edu/

UTICA COLLEGE

UTICA, NEW YORK

UTICA COLLEGE

The College

A private, independent college founded in 1946, Utica College (UC) is known for its excellent academic programs, outstanding faculty, personal attention, and diverse student population. The hallmarks of Utica College's academic programs are the integration of liberal and professional studies and a strong emphasis on internships, research, and other experiential learning opportunities, but UC is best known for the close, personal relationship students have with both faculty and staff members. More than 4,000 undergraduate and graduate students attend UC, including students from a wide variety of socioeconomic and cultural backgrounds. While most students come from New York, New England, and the middle Atlantic states, students are drawn to UC from all parts of the United States, and there is a growing international student population.

Utica College offers a broad selection of undergraduate majors, minors, and special programs, as well as graduate programs in rapidly growing professions such as cybersecurity, financial crime, physical therapy, and health care administration. UC also offers a robust selection of study-abroad opportunities as well as preprofessional programs and an honors program.

In fall of 2016, Utica College ushered in a new era for college affordability, reducing the cost of undergraduate tuition and fees by 42 percent for all new and returning students in the on-campus undergraduate program. The 2017–18 published price of tuition and fees will be $20,676, and when the average room and board of $10,834 is added in, the approximate total cost of attendance will be $31,510 per year, before financial aid.

Located in a suburban residential area of Utica, New York, Utica College's modern, 128-acre campus offers excellent learning, living, and recreational facilities. Half of UC's students live on campus in residence halls that feature a variety of housing options, modern amenities, and lounges for studying or relaxing with friends. Freshmen primarily live in North and South Halls, which offer double- and triple-occupancy rooms. Dining options on campus satisfy a wide variety of tastes, including American and international cuisines, vegetarian meals, a large salad bar, and lighter fare such as burgers and pizza. Students enjoy a range of dining venues, from the main dining commons in Strebel Student Center to convenient cafés in the Library and academic buildings and a Subway sandwich shop on campus.

Whether students live on or off campus, they can take advantage of more than eighty student organizations, focusing on community service, music, theater, and politics as well as fraternities, sororities, and major-related clubs that provide opportunities for students to organize academic and career-related events. Students can write for the student newspaper, work at the College's radio station, submit entries for the literary magazine, or work on the yearbook. Students also have the opportunity to enjoy lectures, concerts, poetry readings, art exhibits, plays, and nationally recognized speakers.

Utica College offers twenty-six NCAA Division III varsity sports, including men's baseball, basketball, cross-country, football, golf, ice hockey, lacrosse, soccer, swimming and diving, tennis, and track and field; and women's basketball, cross-country, field hockey, golf, ice hockey, lacrosse, soccer, softball, swimming and diving, tennis, track and field, volleyball, and water polo. UC also offers club sports and a wide variety of intramural opportunities. Utica College is a member of the Empire 8 Athletic Conference and the Eastern College Athletic Conference. Nearly a third of all UC students participate in at least one Division III intercollegiate sport, and more than 45 percent are active in intramural or nonvarsity club sports.

Athletic facilities include the 1,200-seat multisport Gaetano Stadium with a state-of-the-art field turf synthetic grass playing surface; the Clark Athletic Center, which contains a large gymnasium, racquetball courts, a swimming pool, saunas, a recently renovated 6,400-square-foot free-weight room and fully equipped fitness facility, and the Todd and Jen Hutton Sports and Recreation Center, a 135,000-square-foot multi-sport dome that is the largest facility of its kind in North America. Ice hockey games are played at the recently upgraded Utica Memorial Auditorium, a 4,000-seat arena in downtown Utica, featuring pro-style hockey locker rooms and training facilities.

Location

The city of Utica is located in the heart of the historic Mohawk Valley in the center of New York State. Just 90 miles west of Albany and 50 miles east of Syracuse, Utica has a thriving arts community, beautiful parks, and expanding shopping centers featuring national retailers. Utica College is conveniently located just 10 minutes from the nearest bus and Amtrak station, and only 50 miles east of Hancock International Airport in Syracuse. There are numerous recreational facilities, including a municipal ski slope and an excellent golf course less than a mile from the Utica College campus. Other nearby recreational opportunities include tennis, swimming, boating, fishing, hiking, and camping.

Academic Programs

Utica College offers undergraduate degree programs in accounting, animal behavior, biochemistry, biology, business economics, chemistry, communication and media, computer science, construction management, criminal justice, cyber-security and information assurance, economics, English, foreign language, fraud and financial crime investigation, geoscience, government and politics, health studies, health studies–management, history, international studies, journalism studies, liberal studies, management, mathematics, neuroscience, nursing (traditional, RN to B.S.N., and accelerated), occupational therapy, philosophy, physical therapy, physics, psychobiology, psychology, psychology–child life, public relations, public relations/journalism studies, risk management and insurance, sociology and anthropology, sports management, teacher education, therapeutic recreation, and wellness and adventure education. Preprofessional programs include dentistry, law, medicine, optometry, podiatry, and veterinary medicine.

Occupational therapy and physical therapy majors earn a bachelor's degree in health studies with direct entry into UC's graduate programs, as long as academic requirements are met. Utica College offers a master's degree in occupational therapy and a doctorate in physical therapy (D.P.T.).

A complete list of programs, including undergraduate minors, can be found online at www.utica.edu/programs.

For those students who are undecided, professionals in the Office of Student Success, Career Services, and Residence Life facilitate exploratory programs, academic advising, and career counseling.

Utica College offers the Higher Education Opportunity Program (HEOP), the Collegiate Science and Technology Entry Program (CSTEP), and Summer Institute, which serves as an academic bridge between high school and college.

Off-Campus Programs

UC's study-abroad programs give students opportunities to widen their global perspectives through exchange programs with universities in Spain, Italy, Poland, Finland, Hungary, Peru, Scotland, and Wales, as well as American College in Dublin, Ireland, among other options. Special study-abroad opportunities include the College's annual forensic anthropology field school in Albania as well as learning experiences in London and elsewhere.

Students are encouraged to complete internships and field placements to gain professional experience with businesses and organizations while they are earning college credit. Utica College's cooperative education program allows students to earn money while gaining professional experience.

Academic Facilities

The Frank E. Gannett Memorial Library includes a collection of some 172,000 volumes, 800 serial subscriptions, hundreds of online journals, and other resources, as well as the new Kelly Teaching and Learning Center, which contains the College's Writing and Math Centers. Located on the lower level of the library are the Media Center, computer labs, the Edith Langley Barrett Fine Art Gallery, and a large concourse—the site of special events, such as musical recitals, receptions, and guest lectures.

Along with smart classrooms and faculty offices, UC's main academic complex features advanced new laboratories for biology, chemistry, and zoology, plus a fully functional trading room to support learning in business and economics. F. Eugene Romano Hall provides state-of-the-art classroom, laboratory, and clinical space, as well as learning technology for students in the health sciences. The Economic Crime, Justice Studies, and Cybersecurity Building supports cutting-edge research and advanced learning at both the undergraduate and graduate levels in these very dynamic disciplines. The Professor Raymond Simon Convergence Media Center features a high-definition broadcast facility, control room, and edit suite.

In addition to wireless Internet available across campus, Utica College maintains computer laboratories with both Windows and Macintosh computers.

Costs

In the fall of 2016, Utica College's "Bold Move For Tomorrow" affordability initiative took effect, reducing the tuition price by 42 percent, with a substantial reduction in room and board costs. For 2017–18, tuition will be $20,676. Average room and board costs will be $10,834. Student activity and technology fees will total $550. Books and supplies average $1,400 per year.

Financial Aid

Keeping quality, private education affordable is central to Utica College's mission. More than 90 percent of UC freshmen typically receive financial aid. The College also awards numerous merit scholarships.

Almost every federal and state financial aid program is available through Utica College. Students apply for institutional and governmental financial aid by filing the Free Application for Federal Student Aid (FAFSA).

Faculty

Utica College's faculty is diverse, energetic, accomplished, and devoted to their students. The vast majority of faculty members have earned their Ph.D. or other terminal degree, and while many are involved in research, the primary focus of faculty members is teaching. The typical class size is 20 students, the student-faculty ratio is 11:1, and all faculty members are involved in assisting students with their academic planning.

Student Government

One of Utica College's strongest traditions is student participation in the College's governance structure. Students may serve on a number of student governing bodies, and students also serve on all standing committees of the College.

Admission Requirements

Utica College admits students who can best benefit from the educational opportunities the College offers. The Admission Committee gives each application individual attention, and the potential for a student's success at UC is measured primarily by an evaluation of past academic performance, scholastic ability, and personal characteristics. Freshman applicants must have completed 16 academic units, including 4 years of English. Students should follow a college-preparatory program, including 3 units of mathematics, 3 units of science, 2 units of foreign language, and 3 units of social studies.

Application and Information

Students may apply for fall, spring, or summer admission. Materials required include a completed Utica College application form, official high school or college transcripts, one letter of recommendation, a personal statement, and a $40 application fee. Utica College is test-optional and therefore does not require SAT or ACT scores, with the exception of the programs listed below. A personal interview for all applications is strongly suggested.

Occupational therapy, physical therapy, nursing, and joint health professions program applicants must submit SAT or ACT scores. International students must complete the international student application form. The application fee is waived for students who apply to HEOP or CSTEP; however, SAT or ACT scores are required to be considered for either program.

The College offers three admissions programs: early decision, early action, and rolling admissions.

Additional admissions information can be found online at http://www.utica.edu/admissions.

Inquiries should be sent to:

Office of Undergraduate Admissions
Utica College
1600 Burrstone Road
Utica, New York 13502-4892
Phone: 315-792-3006
800-782-8884 (toll-free)
E-mail: admiss@utica.edu
Website: http://www.utica.edu
http://www.facebook.com/UticaCollegeAdmissions
http://twitter.com/uticacollege

The Hutton Sports and Recreation Center, the largest facility of its kind in North America, supports UC's 26 intercollegiate athletic programs; several academic programs, including the Wellness and Adventure Education major; and various campus-wide wellness and fitness initiatives.

COLLEGE CLOSE-UPS

VANDERBILT UNIVERSITY

NASHVILLE, TENNESSEE

The University

In 1873, on the heels of the Civil War, "Commodore" Cornelius Vanderbilt gave $1 million to the university that now bears his name, with the hope that it would "contribute to strengthening the ties which should exist between all sections of our common country." Since then, Vanderbilt has consistently enrolled intelligent and talented students and challenged them daily to expand their intellectual horizons in an inclusive environment based on open inquiry and respect. Vanderbilt's comprehensive interdisciplinary approach to education allows students to pursue a wide array of academic and curricular interests outside of their main focus of study, and the University's Opportunity Vanderbilt financial aid program ensures that Vanderbilt is often cited among the country's best values.

Consistently ranked among the top 20 universities in the country by *U.S. News & World Report,* Vanderbilt is a private research university that features four undergraduate schools and six graduate and professional schools. Each year, 1,600 first-year students join the University, bringing the total undergraduate population to approximately 6,900 students. Vanderbilt students come from across the country and around the world, and represent a rich diversity of backgrounds. Among undergraduates, 7.2 percent are international students, 36.3 percent are minority students, and 65 percent receive some type of financial assistance.

Vanderbilt's 8:1 student-faculty ratio gives students access to faculty members of prominence in every area of academic study. More than 50 percent of undergraduates collaborate with professors on research spanning almost every academic field, including natural and social sciences, humanities, engineering, and education. Faculty members share their perspectives as instructors and advisers with the goal of providing a challenging, comprehensive education that encourages broad perspectives and critical thinking.

A park-like campus located in the heart of Nashville, Vanderbilt offers a top-ranked residential experience for its undergraduates, nearly all of whom live on campus all four years. First-year students live and learn on The Martha Rivers Ingram Commons, a collection of ten residence halls, or Houses, clustered along one side of campus. The Ingram Commons incorporates more than just bricks and mortar. Faculty members—including the dean of The Commons and faculty heads of house—and their families live there, facilitating easy and meaningful interactions between students and professors. Frequent educational and social programming at The Commons invites students and faculty to explore current events and social issues. After their first year, students have many housing options, including apartment-style living and two new residential colleges, Warren and Moore.

Vanderbilt students take full advantage of student life in over 420 student organizations, a full range of study-abroad programs, Division I Athletics, and a variety of internship opportunities.

Location

Vanderbilt University is located in Nashville, the capital of Tennessee. Ranked one of the Best Places to Go in 2017 by *Frommer's Travel Guide*, Nashville boasts a rich mosaic of cultures, vibrant arts, business, health, and technology sectors, and an array of recreational opportunities. Nashville hosts thousands of live concerts each year in every conceivable genre and is recognized as a top college city in America and an excellent location for businesses. Nashville's booming cultural scene, striking natural beauty, and thriving economy attract people from around the world.

Majors and Degrees

College of Arts and Science: African American and Diaspora Studies; American Studies; Anthropology; Art; Asian Studies; Biochemistry and Chemical Biology; Biological Sciences; Chemistry; Cinema and Media Arts; Classical Civilizations; Classical Languages; Classics; Communication of Science and Technology; Communication Studies; Earth and Environmental Sciences; Ecology, Evolution, and Organismal Biology; Economics; Economics and History; English; Environmental Sociology; European Studies; French; French and European Studies; German; German and European Studies; History; History of Art; Italian and European Studies; Jewish Studies; Latin American Studies; Latino and Latina Studies; Mathematics; Medicine, Health, and Society; Molecular and Cellular Biology; Neuroscience; Philosophy; Physics; Political Science; Psychology; Public Policy Studies; Religious Studies; Russian; Russian and European Studies; Sociology; Spanish; Spanish and European Studies; Spanish and Portuguese; Spanish, Portuguese, and European Studies; Theater; and Women's and Gender Studies.

Blair School of Music: Composition; Musical Arts; Musical Arts/Teacher Education; and Performance.

School of Engineering: Biomedical Engineering; Chemical Engineering; Civil Engineering; Computer Engineering; Computer Science; Electrical Engineering; Engineering Science; and Mechanical Engineering.

Peabody College of Education and Human Development: Child Development; Child Studies; Cognitive Studies; Early Childhood and Elementary Education; Human and Organizational Development; Secondary Education; and Special Education.

Graduate/Professional Schools: Divinity School; Graduate School; Law School; Owen Graduate School of Management; School of Medicine; and School of Nursing.

Pre-professional advising is available for undergraduate students interested in pursuing graduate degrees in architecture, business, law, or health professions.

Academic Programs

Students apply for admission to one of four undergraduate schools: the College of Arts and Science, the School of Engineering, Peabody College of Education and Human Development, or the Blair School of Music. In all four schools, honors programs and opportunities for research, independent study, and internships are available. About 30 percent of undergraduate students pursue double majors within or across the four undergraduate schools, and about half add an optional minor.

The College of Arts and Science offers a wide spectrum of courses in the humanities, social sciences, and natural sciences, and has majors in 50 departments and interdisciplinary areas. Students in A&S achieve both breadth and depth in their education by satisfying a set of liberal arts and science courses through AXLE (Achieving eXcellence in Liberal Education), and by completing at least one major.

The Blair School of Music offers conservatory-level music training in a strong liberal arts environment. Vanderbilt is one of only four top-twenty universities in the nation to offer an accredited undergraduate school of music, and the only one whose school of music is solely for undergraduates. The curriculum combines intensive musical training with liberal arts studies and students take approximately one-third of their courses outside of the music school. The Blair School also offers a music minor and a wide variety of courses, private instruction, and performing organizations for non-majors.

For more than 125 years, the School of Engineering has educated engineers for practice in industry, government, consulting, teaching, and research careers. In addition to technical courses, each student's program includes a rich complement of course work in the humanities and social sciences, resulting in a balanced foundation for future achievement and the assumption of leadership roles in their chosen fields. All programs leading to a Bachelor of Engineering degree are ABET-accredited, and students can earn a Bachelor of Science degree while majoring in Computer Science or Engineering Science.

Ranked one of the top seven graduate schools of education (according to *U.S. News & World Report*) for fifteen consecutive years, Peabody College offers degree programs in education and human development. The degree reflects a strong liberal arts foundation combined with a solid program of pre-professional courses and a multitude of internship and practicum opportunities. All undergraduates must complete requirements in communications, the humanities, mathematics, the natural sciences, and the social sciences. Moreover, students have an abundance of field experiences throughout their four years.

Regardless of school or major, the academic experience at Vanderbilt goes well beyond the traditional classroom. Across all four undergraduate schools, students engage in hands-on learning that complements and furthers their academic experience at Vanderbilt. Immersion Vanderbilt calls for each undergraduate student to participate in an intensive learning experience that takes place in and beyond the classroom and culminates in the creation of a final project. Students will engage in a civic and professional, creative expression, international, or research immersion experience.

Off-Campus Programs

Study-abroad programs allow students to immerse themselves in languages and cultures around the world. Vanderbilt offers more than 120 programs in countries such as Argentina, Australia, Austria, Chile, China, Cuba, Czech Republic, Denmark, the Dominican Republic, Egypt, England, France, Israel, Italy, Japan, Russia, Singapore, South Africa, and Spain. In these Vanderbilt-approved programs, students receive direct credit for their courses, and the cost of tuition is usually the same as for study on campus in Nashville. In addition, any scholarships, grants, or loans a student has been awarded apply to Vanderbilt study-abroad programs. Students may also participate in programs sponsored by other universities by working with an adviser.

Academic Facilities

The newest academic facilities on campus are the Engineering and Science Building and the adjacent Innovation Pavilion. The Engineering and Science Building is a 230,000 square-foot, seven-story teaching and research building designed to foster project teamwork and promote interdisciplinary research. Right next door in the Innovation Pavilion is the Wond'ry, Vanderbilt's new epicenter for innovation and entrepreneurship. Through collaborative work environments, maker spaces, and curricular programming, the Wond'ry is the place where abstract ideas are transformed into concrete realities that will make differences in people's lives.

Costs

The estimated costs for 2017–18 include: tuition, $46,498; housing, $10,114; meals, $5,372; books and supplies, $1,294; student activities and recreation fee, $1,164; personal expenses allowance, $2,850; first-year experience fee, $765; new student transcript fee, $30; engineering lab fee*, $650; and engineering laptop allowance*, $1,500. Travel allowances are variable. *The engineering laptop allowance and laboratory fee apply to engineering students only. First-year engineering students are required to either purchase a laptop from Vanderbilt or provide their own computer that meets published requirements.

Financial Aid

Through Opportunity Vanderbilt, the University makes three important commitments reflecting a strong dedication to making a Vanderbilt education possible: Vanderbilt is need-blind for all U.S. citizens and eligible non-citizens; Vanderbilt meets 100 percent of demonstrated need for all admitted students; and Vanderbilt's financial aid packages do not include loans. These three commitments combined place Vanderbilt among a small number of universities to adopt such progressive policies. Need-based aid is awarded according to the evaluation of the FAFSA and the CSS/Financial Aid PROFILE.

Vanderbilt also awards merit-based scholarships to selected first-year applicants who demonstrate exceptional accomplishment and intellectual promise. Three signature scholarship programs comprise the majority of these honor scholarships: the Ingram Scholarship Program, the Cornelius Vanderbilt Scholarship Program, and the Chancellor's Scholarship Program. All three scholarship programs require a separate application in addition to the application for admission.

In the 2016–17 school year, 65 percent of Vanderbilt undergraduates received some type of financial assistance.

Faculty

Vanderbilt University has 1,421 full-time faculty members. All undergraduate faculty members teach undergraduate students and many also serve as research mentors and academic advisers. A low student-faculty ratio provides for an intimate academic experience between students and professors who are recognized nationally and worldwide for their research. Ninety-one percent of classes have fewer than 50 students.

Student Government

The Vanderbilt Student Government (VSG) provides students with an opportunity to participate actively in maintaining a high quality of life on campus. It works with student organizations to bring nationally prominent speakers to campus and provides an interesting and diverse array of programming throughout the year. A vital part of life at Vanderbilt is the honor system, governed entirely by students through representatives on the Honor Council. Each year, a senior is selected as a Young Alumni Trustee of the University's Board of Trust.

Admission Requirements

Vanderbilt uses a holistic admissions process—there are no cutoffs based on standardized testing or grade point averages. The Admissions Committee evaluates students' academic records, test scores (either the SAT or ACT is required), extracurricular involvement, counselor and teacher recommendations, and personal essay. Applicants to the Blair School of Music are required to submit a separate application and a prescreening video, and selected applicants are invited to an on-campus audition.

Vanderbilt seeks students with high standards of scholarship and character. Most competitive applicants have a strong academic profile—including excellent grades in the context of a rigorous course load, strong test scores, and positive academic letters of recommendation. In addition, most successful applicants demonstrate significant levels of engagement and leadership outside the classroom.

Application and Information

Students whose first choice is Vanderbilt may apply under one of Vanderbilt's early decision plans. Applications are due by November 1 for Early Decision I and by January 1 for Early Decision II; notification is made by December 15 for Early Decision I and by February 15 for Early Decision II. Regular Decision applications are due January 1 and admission decisions are available by April 1. The priority application deadline for students seeking transfer admission is March 15 for the following fall semester entry.

Office of Undergraduate Admissions
Vanderbilt University
2305 West End Avenue
Nashville, Tennessee 37203-1727
Phone: 615-322-2561
800-288-0432 (toll-free)
E-mail: admissions@vanderbilt.edu
Website: admissions.vanderbilt.edu
facebook.com/vanderbiltadmissions
twitter.com/vanderbiltu
instagram.com/vanderbiltadmissions
vanderbiltadmissions.tumblr.com

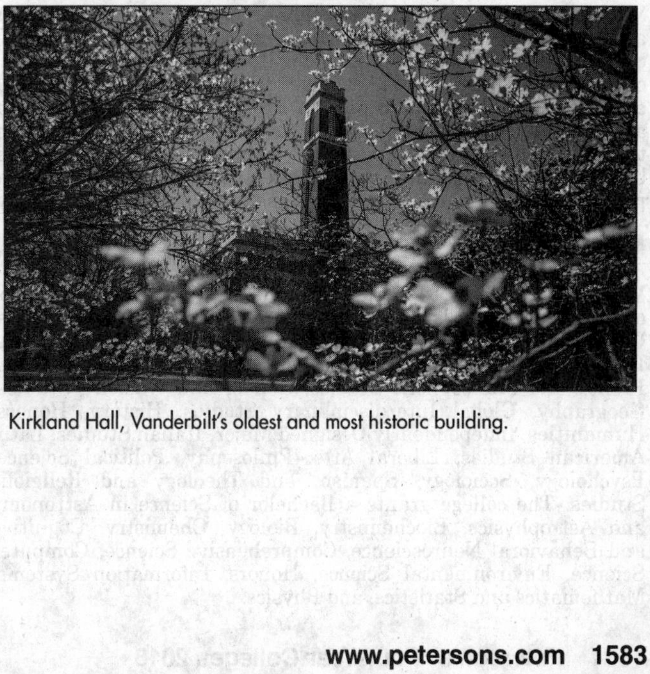

Kirkland Hall, Vanderbilt's oldest and most historic building.

COLLEGE CLOSE-UPS

VILLANOVA UNIVERSITY

VILLANOVA, PENNSYLVANIA

★ To read more about this school, visit http://petersons.to/villanovauniversity

VILLANOVA UNIVERSITY

The University

Since 1842, Villanova University's Augustinian Catholic intellectual tradition has been the cornerstone of an academic community in which students learn to think critically, act compassionately, and succeed while serving others. Villanova enrolls more than 10,500 undergraduate, graduate, and law students in the College of Liberal Arts and Sciences, the Villanova School of Business, the College of Engineering, the College of Nursing, the College of Professional Studies, and the Villanova University Charles Widger School of Law. As students grow intellectually, Villanova prepares them to become ethical leaders who create positive change everywhere life takes them.

Villanova offers nearly 90 majors and minors and features more than 265 student organizations and 36 national honor societies on campus. Undergraduate full-time enrollment is 6,999; total University enrollment is 10,842.

Located just 12 miles (20 kilometers) west of Philadelphia, Villanova's picturesque campus has 65 buildings, including 26 residence halls. Award-winning dining services are available in three residence dining halls and 16 à la carte eateries, all with many culinary options. Students have access to several athletic and fitness facilities on campus, including the Davis Center for Athletics, which features state-of-the-art cardio machines, weight equipment, and free weights. Group exercise classes, including yoga and Pilates, are also offered regularly. Villanova has 56 club and intramural sports on campus, and nearly 25 percent of the student body participates in varsity or club athletics.

To help facilitate the transition to college life, first-year students are encouraged to join a themed Learning Community. Community members live in the same residence halls, take their year-long Augustine and Culture Seminar together, and participate in co-curricular activities. These activities typically include lectures, plays, themed dinners, rich cultural events, and engaging trips. Through Learning Communities, students form deeper, often lifelong relationships with their classmates and professors, and become more intensely engaged in their studies.

Location

Villanova students reap all the benefits of living within the beautiful and tranquil Philadelphia Main Line suburb, while the University's convenient proximity to Philadelphia also provides endless opportunities to complement campus life with cultural, recreational, and social activities found only in a vibrant major metropolitan area. Whether it's visiting world-class art and science museums, touring historic sites, sampling the impressive restaurant scene, browsing through countless stores and shops, or cheering on local professional sports teams, there is something for everyone to enjoy.

Majors and Degrees

Villanova's College of Liberal Arts and Sciences grants a Bachelor of Arts in Arab and Islamic Studies, Art History, Classical Studies, Communication, Criminology, Cultural Studies, Economics, Education (Secondary), English, Environmental Studies, French and Francophone Studies, Gender and Women's Studies, Geography, Global Interdisciplinary Studies, History, Honors, Humanities, Independently Designed Major, Italian Studies, Latin American Studies, Liberal Arts, Philosophy, Political Science, Psychology, Sociology, Spanish, and Theology and Religious Studies. The college grants a Bachelor of Science in Astronomy and Astrophysics, Biochemistry, Biology, Chemistry, Cognitive and Behavioral Neuroscience, Comprehensive Science, Computer Science, Environmental Science, Honors, Information Systems, Mathematics and Statistics, and Physics.

Villanova School of Business (VSB) offers a Bachelor of Business Administration in Accountancy, Economics, Finance, Management, Management Information Systems, and Marketing. VSB also offers co-majors in Business Analytics, International Business and Real Estate.

Through the College of Engineering, Villanova grants a Bachelor of Science in Chemical Engineering, Civil Engineering, Computer Engineering, Electrical Engineering, and Mechanical Engineering.

Villanova offers a Bachelor of Science in Nursing through the College of Nursing and also offers the following Health Science Affiliation programs: Jefferson School of Health Professions of Thomas Jefferson University, Doctor of Physical Therapy and Master of Science in Occupational Therapy; Pennsylvania College of Optometry at Salus University, Doctor of Optometry; and University of Pennsylvania School of Dental Medicine, Doctor of Dental Medicine.

Villanova offers a comprehensive four-year Honors Program of challenging seminars, research opportunities, service projects, and cultural and social events designed to bring together exceptional students and dedicated faculty. In addition, accelerated bachelor's/master's degree programs are available in the following areas: Applied Statistics, B.A./J.D., Biology, Chemical Engineering, Chemistry, Civil Engineering, Classical Studies, Communication, Computer Engineering, Computing Science Education, Electrical Engineering, Human Resource Development, Liberal Studies, Mathematics, Mechanical Engineering, Nursing, Political Science, Psychology, Public Administration, Software Engineering, and Theology.

Academic Programs

Villanova, through the College of Liberal Arts and Sciences, is one of the few institutions in the country that offers an undergraduate program in Astronomy and Astrophysics, and is one of only 18 Catholic colleges or universities in the nation to have a chapter of Phi Beta Kappa, the prestigious liberal arts and sciences honor society. It also is home to the Waterhouse Institute for the Study of Communication and Society—the only institute of its kind in the United States—which provides students with opportunities to explore the ethical dimensions of communication.

Highly ranked nationally, the Villanova School of Business is home to the Applied Finance Lab, where students have access to many of the real-time technologies available to Wall Street traders. The Clay Center at VSB assists students with important decisions regarding course selections, major and minors, and international experiences, and it helps coordinate internships and co-ops, which often lead to full-time job offers.

The College of Engineering, ranked among the best engineering programs in the nation, is home to three research units: the Center for Advanced Communications, the Center for Nonlinear Dynamics and Control, and the Center for the Advancement of Sustainability in Engineering. The Villanova Center for Engineering Education and Research houses state-of-the-art instructional and research labs, including the Multidisciplinary Design Lab and the 10,000-square-foot Structural Engineering Teaching and Research Laboratory.

The College of Nursing, designated a Center for Excellence in Nursing Education by the National League for Nursing, is housed in an advanced facility that features a 200-seat auditorium and a 200-seat lecture hall; future-oriented clinical simulation labs for health assessment, adult health, maternal/child health, anesthesia, and critical care; simulation labs for standardized patient observation and testing; a center for nursing research and scholarship; places for prayer and reflection; space for global health studies and international student activities; and areas for student, faculty, and alumni events and social interaction.

Naval and Marine Reserve Officers Training Corps (ROTC) programs are available on campus. Villanova has had an NROTC program for more than 50 years, and it is structured to complement a normal college lifestyle. Midshipmen are encouraged to participate fully in their academic programs as well as in extracurricular activities.

Off-Campus Programs

Villanova has a rich study abroad program. Each year, approximately 775 students take advantage of international study opportunities in nearly 35 nations, including Ireland, Switzerland, Peru, England, France, Germany, Italy, China, Chile, Russia, Poland, Thailand, Spain, Australia, Rwanda, the West Indies, Madagascar, and Samoa.

Academic Facilities

Villanova's state-of-the-art classrooms and labs are complemented with a vast array of learning and career resources. Falvey Memorial Library contains more than 1,000,000 items and offers access to numerous databases. It is also home to the Idea Accelerator, a cutting-edge facility open to all students that promotes a multidisciplinary approach to generating and advancing new ideas. The Office of Learning Support Services assists students with learning disabilities, neurologically based disorders, and chronic illnesses. The Career Center helps students set and reach their professional development goals; 96.5 percent of the Villanova Class of 2016 was employed or enrolled in graduate school within six months of degree completion. Approximately 10,000 jobs are posted on Villanova's job boards each year, and the average starting salary for recent graduates is $59,010.

Technology is widely available at Villanova. All residence halls are connected to the campus network. Students can participate in learning experiences across campus; receive curricular advising services; and access tests, webcasts, and library reserves online. Through Villanova's student portal, they can keep track of deadlines, class schedules, and financial aid information. Villanova's technology also provides easy access to meal plans, parking registration, laundry reservations, voting processes, ride sharing/carpooling, and basketball ticket lotteries. Students and parents can also sign up for NOVA Alert, the University's emergency notification system.

Costs

For the 2016–17 academic year, the average tuition was $48,610, and room and board were $13,093.

Financial Aid

For the 2016–17 freshman class, 88 percent of those eligible for need-based assistance received Villanova Grants. More than $18.7 million in Villanova Grants was accepted, with an average award amount of $27,672. The average assistance package for students with demonstrated need (combining grants, scholarships, loans, and student employment) was $37,731.

Villanova offers a Presidential Scholarship program to attract academic, civic, and cultural leaders who represent diverse intellectual, social, racial, and economic backgrounds, including students from families in which few or no members have attended college. Successful candidates are awarded this renewable scholarship—which covers tuition, general fee, room and board, and books—for eight consecutive semesters.

Faculty

Villanova has more than 625 full-time faculty members; nearly 85 percent of them hold doctoral degrees. The student-to-faculty ratio is 12:1 and the average class size is 22.

Student Government

Empowering the Villanova student body since 1925, the Student Government Association (SGA) has three branches (administrative, community, and student relations) and twelve committees. The SGA provides opportunities for student leaders to serve the Villanova community as liaisons, representatives, and student senators.

Admission Requirements

Admission to Villanova is competitive. In addition to attracting academically talented, well-rounded students, Villanova seeks applicants who are compassionate and want to transform the world and make it a better place.

Villanova is a Common Application member institution. Prospective students are also required to complete the Villanova Supplement for Undergraduate Admission and submit an official high school transcript and Common Application School Report. Applicants must have their standardized test scores (SAT or ACT) reported directly by the College Board or ACT.

In the Villanova admissions process, high school performance is an extremely important selectivity factor. Each student's high school record, GPA, and class rank, along with each student's demonstration of character and personal abilities, are carefully considered. Extracurricular and volunteer activities are helpful to applicants in this regard. Another important factor is the personal essay. Since interviews are not part of the admission process, a well-crafted essay is essential for prospective students to explain who they are and why they should be selected to become Villanovans. (A recommendation from the secondary school counselor is also carefully considered.)

Prospective students who are not from the United States are encouraged to apply for admission to Villanova. Non-native English speakers must take the TOEFL or IELTS evaluations and have scores reported directly from the College Board. Villanova's International Student Services Office supports enrolled international students in areas including immigration rights and responsibilities; educational, social, and personal counseling; cultural adjustment issues; and campus and community activities.

Transferring to Villanova is possible, but selective. A completed transfer application, official transcripts from each postsecondary school attended, and a completed Dean of Students Transfer Evaluation form are required.

Application and Information

The deadline for early action and health affiliation program applications is November 1; regular decision deadline is January 15.

Villanova Office of University Admission
800 Lancaster Avenue
Villanova, Pennsylvania 19085-1672
Phone: 610-519-4000
Fax: 610-519-6450
E-mail: gotovu@villanova.edu
Website: http://www.villanova.edu
http://virtualvisit.villanova.edu (virtual visit)

St. Thomas of Villanova Church, Villanova University.

WALNUT HILL COLLEGE

PHILADELPHIA, PENNSYLVANIA

Walnut Hill College
Founded in 1974 as The Restaurant School

★ For more information, visit http://petersons.to/the-restaurant-school-at-walnut-hill-college

The College

Established in 1974 as The Restaurant School, Walnut Hill College is dedicated to inspiring the future of the restaurant and hotel industry through dynamic, timely, and insightful training with an emphasis on service to its students. Walnut Hill College combines both intensive classroom training and practical experience so that students can use their knowledge while they learn.

A student's education is cultivated by the College's philosophy that hands-on training is an essential part of the educational process. This approach has multiple benefits—it enhances learning abilities, creates marketable skills and experience for a resume, brings education to life, and most importantly, puts the student at the center of it all.

Walnut Hill College is accredited by the Accrediting Commission of Career Schools and Colleges of Technology, certified for veterans' training by the Veterans Administration, approved by the United States Department of Justice to grant student visas, and recognized as a Professional Management Development Partner of the Educational Foundation of the National Restaurant Association.

There is a diverse population at Walnut Hill College, with students coming from all over the United States and abroad, and ranging in age from the high school graduate to the adult who is changing careers.

Whether at a celebrity chef's cooking demonstration, dinner and a tour at a notable restaurant or hotel, or a winery tour and tasting, students at Walnut Hill College are exposed to the very best Philadelphia has to offer. Students will find a vibrant campus culture with daily activities and special events sponsored by the College's numerous student clubs. The Student Culinary Team has won several major competitions in recent years, both nationally and internationally. Activities are both educational and fun, combining opportunities to learn and to establish camaraderie and professional development. Events are listed on the school's website, posted to social media channels, and sent to students in a daily e-mail blast.

Location

Philadelphia is a great place to live and learn. As the fifth largest city in the United States, Philadelphia has much to offer and is a city of firsts: the first public library, the first college, and the first zoo—all in a first-class setting.

Walnut Hill College is located in the University City section of Philadelphia, neighboring both the University of Pennsylvania and Drexel University. Located just across the Schuylkill River from Center City, University City has a wonderful college-town ambiance. Restaurants, museums, shops, and theaters abound, with many local merchants offering discounts to students. The Amtrak train station is within walking distance of the campus, and the airport is just 20 minutes away by car.

Diversity thrives in this city of neighborhoods, which includes Center City, complete with its bustling shopping and business district; Chinatown, with its exotic restaurants and shops; South Philadelphia, with its famed Italian Market and trendy East Passyunk Square eateries; and the ever-eclectic South Street, with its blocks of restaurants, galleries, shops, and entertainment. The Historic District is also noteworthy, as the birthplace of the nation and home to a waterfront that features an exciting nightlife.

Philadelphia is rich in culture and heritage. Students will find world-class art and science museums, theaters that feature major Broadway shows and renowned regional productions, and musical performances that include everything from jazz to pop to the internationally acclaimed Philadelphia Orchestra.

Majors and Degrees

The College offers associate and bachelor's degrees in four majors: Hotel Management (95.5 A.S. or 186.5 B.S. credits), Restaurant Management (99.5 A.S. or 189 B.S. credits), Culinary Arts (96.5 A.S. or 194 B.S. credits), and Pastry Arts (94 A.S. or 187.5 B.S. credits). Each major provides students with overall knowledge of the inner workings of a fine restaurant or hotel. Beyond that, the programs help students to develop the day-to-day skills and specific knowledge required for careers as restaurant managers, culinary chefs, pastry chefs, hotel managers, and restaurateurs. In partnership with the Educational Foundation of the National Restaurant Association, the College's curriculum includes up to eight nationally recognized food service and hospitality management courses. Upon successful completion of the courses and the certification exam, students receive national certification.

Academic Programs

All students must successfully complete six 10-week terms to be awarded an Associate of Science degree or twelve 10-week terms to be awarded a Bachelor of Science degree in their field of study. Each academic year consists of three terms. A student must fulfill the required term hours in a major as well as the basic requirements of the core curriculum. All students are required to participate in special service programs prior to graduating.

Off-Campus Programs

Walnut Hill College was one of the first schools in the country to offer travel experiences as part of its curriculum. Culinary and Pastry Arts students participate in an eight-day tour of France, while Hotel and Restaurant Management students go on an eight-day Orlando resort tour and cruise through the Bahamas. In addition, a trip to England is part of the capstone program for all baccalaureate students. These travel experiences enhance both the students' training and resumes.

Academic Facilities

Walnut Hill College is proud to offer one of the most dynamic hands-on learning opportunities in the country. The dining experience, situated in the breathtakingly restored 1855 Allison Mansion, turns into a unique gastronomic event with the addition of four themed restaurants. The Italian Trattoria is a casual restaurant that serves classic, handmade pasta presentations in an Italian terrace setting.

Guests looking for more variety can choose to dine in the main restaurant, the International Bistro, and enjoy a continental menu under the twinkling lights of the European Courtyard.

American cuisine is presented in an innovative new style in the American Heartland restaurant. Identified by its signature mural of a farm with a bright blue sky and cornfields, this restaurant allows guests to explore some of America's best cooking within the comfort of a country dining or veranda setting.

Most notable is the elegant Great Chefs restaurant. The dining room features all-white decor with glittering mirrors and thousands of glass balls—along with a menu inspired by the world's greatest chefs. Guests enjoy high-end cuisine and service in a striking, modern space.

The mansion also houses the Student Resource Center, featuring computer lab stations and the Alumni Library, which includes thousands of books, magazines, and DVDs on cooking, management, and wine. The building also has a student conference room and a wine lab.

Early each morning, Pastry Arts students enter the kitchen classrooms to prepare buttery croissants, crisp French baguettes, and glistening pastries for the on-campus Pastry Shop. Meanwhile, Culinary Arts students busily prepare different kinds of pasta, salads, soups, and entrées for lunch service in the European Courtyard.

Student learning takes place in two buildings on campus: Allison Mansion and the Center for Hospitality Studies. Together they boast six state-of-the-art kitchen classrooms, four lecture halls, and the College's purchasing center and school store.

On-campus student support services enhance the educational experience. The College's Offices of Admissions, Financial Aid, and Independent Student Housing are located in Hunter Hall, a turn-of-the-century masterpiece adorned with magnificent carved mahogany, marble, and fireplaces.

Costs

Tuition for students who start in September 2017 is $6,550 per academic term for the full-time program. Technology and lab fees cost $1,070 per term. Equipment and uniform fees vary by degree program. Students interested in on-campus housing may contact the College for information on housing costs.

Financial Aid

Financial aid programs are available for those who qualify. It is recommended that students apply early. The College participates in the Federal Pell Grant, the Pennsylvania PHEAA State Grant, the subsidized Federal Stafford Student Loan, and parents' Federal PLUS Loan, in addition to other alternative loans. Financial aid officers assist students and their families with the creation of a personal plan that outlines expenses and identifies financial resources available to incoming students. For more specific information, students may contact the College.

Faculty

Learning comes to life under the guiding hands and encouragement of the highly trained and technically skilled faculty. The faculty members are seasoned professionals, having logged numerous years of experience in restaurants and food service. Students gain professional insight through their instruction, giving them a competitive edge upon entering the hospitality field. The chefs and instructors are committed to helping students achieve academic, personal, and career success. They continuously keep pace with current trends in the hospitality industry and convey their professional dedication and work ethic to their students.

Admissions Requirements

The admissions process typically begins with a visit to the College. At that time, prospective students and their families tour the campus, watch hands-on classes in action, and get a feel for campus life.

An application for admission to the College is available to any individual with a high school diploma or its equivalent who has an interest in developing a career in the fine dining, food service, or hospitality field. Applicants are evaluated on their educational background and demonstrated or stated interest in their chosen field. In addition to the application, prospective students must submit two reference letters, a high school transcript, a passing grade on an entrance exam, and a personal essay. High school juniors and seniors may contact the College for information on the Early Decision program.

Application and Information

Walnut Hill College practices rolling admission; qualified applicants are accepted at any time. Applications for admission must be submitted with a $50 application fee and a $150 registration fee. Prospective students should contact:

Office of Admissions
Walnut Hill College
4207 Walnut Street
Philadelphia, Pennsylvania 19104
United States
Phone: 215-222-4200 Ext. 3011
877-925-6884 Ext. 3011 (toll-free)
Fax: 215-222-2811
Email: info@walnuthillcollege.edu
Website: http://www.walnuthillcollege.edu

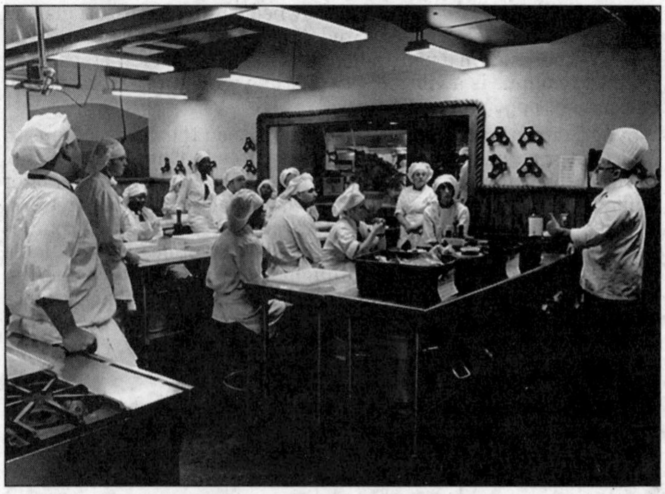

Students at Walnut Hill College receive instruction and hands-on training from our expert chef instructors.

WAYNE STATE UNIVERSITY

DETROIT, MICHIGAN

★ For more information, visit http://petersons.to/waynestateu

The University

While some colleges offer a semester in the city, Wayne State University (WSU) offers every day in Detroit. The 200-acre traditional and high-tech campus is in the heart of Midtown, offering unparalleled access to cultural experiences, community involvement, and corporate career opportunities.

Wayne State students get more than a diploma—they get hands-on experience that helps them soar into a bright future. More than 27,000 students come from every U.S. state and nearly 80 countries to form Michigan's most diverse campus, where education is not confined to the classroom. Wayne State's standing as a premier urban research university results in plenty of opportunities for students to get into the lab and explore, as early as their first year. The city of Detroit is rich with opportunity for experiential learning in a range of fields. Whether students are looking for an internship or a full-time job, WSU can help them find their best match.

For those interested in continuing their studies, Wayne State's renowned graduate school offers certificates as well as master's, doctoral, and professional degrees in hundreds of fields: law, medicine, business, social work, and more.

Upon graduation, Wayne State Warriors automatically become part of an alumni network that's 260,000 strong and stretches across the globe, eager to help fellow Warriors with career opportunities and camaraderie.

Wayne State is a nationally recognized urban center of excellence in research, having received the Carnegie Foundation's highest classifications for research and community engagement, with annual research expenditures of more than $218 million.

WSU offers an immersive educational experience where students work alongside people from different countries, cultures, and socioeconomic backgrounds in a microcosm of today's interconnected world. WSU students gain a distinct advantage as they prepare to build successful careers in the complex global marketplace.

Location

Wayne State is located in Midtown Detroit, the city center and one of the country's fastest growing neighborhoods. The campus features 200 acres of green space, walking paths, and state-of-the-art facilities surrounded by renowned cultural institutions and industry-leading employers. Students benefit from a traditional college experience in a nontraditional setting. Just a few steps away from the campus is a vibrant city bustling with entertainment and enrichment opportunities.

Wayne State students can enroll in courses on the main campus in Midtown or on one of five satellite campuses in Clinton Township, Farmington Hills, Livonia, and Warren. Satellite campuses offer students the convenience of taking classes close to home or work, and at a variety of times. Both undergraduate and graduate courses and degree programs in a wide range of disciplines are available at satellite campuses and are taught by WSU faculty members, providing off-campus students with the same academic experience as those in Midtown.

Majors and Degrees

Whether students come to campus knowing exactly what they want to do with their lives or are searching for their purpose, Wayne State stands ready with hundreds of undergraduate program options (wayne.edu/programs) in the following schools and colleges:

Mike Ilitch School of Business: With a move to a new state-of-the-art building in the heart of The District Detroit on the horizon, the Mike Ilitch School of Business prepares students for challenging and rewarding careers. Entrepreneurial programming and collaboration with the region's business community are two reasons why the Ilitch School is consistently named a best business school by The Princeton Review.

College of Education: With an urban focus and mission behind its commitment to excellence, inclusion, and social justice, the College of Education offers degree programs in 37 program areas. Many are award winning and have received national recognition for their innovative, field-based practices. WSU teacher certification graduates are hired soon after graduation and typically remain in the metro Detroit area, although alumni can be found in countries around the globe.

College of Engineering: Wayne State's engineering curriculum leads the nation in game-changing fields such as electric-drive vehicle technology and alternative energy. Students learn from faculty experts who engineer the physical world at all levels, from nanoscale biomedical innovations to colossal manufacturing plants. Ninety-four percent of 2015 graduates were employed within six months of graduation.

College of Fine, Performing, and Communication Arts (CFPCA): CFPCA students benefit from seamless access to Detroit's cultural riches such as museums and theaters. Equally important are numerous internship opportunities in industry, advertising, PR, and journalism. Alumni include a Pulitzer prize-winning journalist and recipients of and nominees for the Grammy, Emmy, Tony, Golden Globe, Obie, Screen Actors Guild, and Caldecott awards.

College of Liberal Arts and Sciences (CLAS): With 19 departments and more than 40 degree programs, CLAS is the largest and most comprehensive of Wayne State's schools and colleges, producing well-rounded students with a passion for lifelong learning and the skills to succeed at whatever they choose to do. It's where the humanities meets history, where Plato meets plate tectonics, and where students come for the richest educational experience on campus.

College of Nursing: The College of Nursing is committed to providing a world-class educational experience through B.S.N., M.S.N., Ph.D., D.N.P., and graduate certificate programs. A dedication to student success and a state-of-the-art learning environment combine to produce graduates who are prepared to be nurse leaders in research, education, and practice. Faculty and students serve Detroit's diverse populations while promoting community and urban health.

Eugene Applebaum College of Pharmacy and Health Sciences (EACPHS): Devoted to educating the modern health care team, EACPHS offers more than 25 degrees and certificates through 11 academic programs. Its learning environment extends beyond the classroom into underserved communities and hospitals. At EACPHS, students are well prepared to respond effectively in a rapidly changing health care system in their respective health care fields.

School of Social Work: Consistent with its long history of identifying and addressing emerging social issues, the School of Social Work has risen to the challenges of 21st century society, applying technology to cutting-edge research and evidence-based practices, training practitioners within a global context, and marshaling the social and health sciences in interdisciplinary programs that approach complex issues of economic, behavioral, and social well-being from multiple perspectives.

Academic Programs

Academic excellence and pioneering research are central to the university's mission and a primary reason why graduate and undergraduate students alike choose to attend. Wayne State is one of the 50 largest public universities in the nation and a member of the University Research Corridor along with the University of Michigan and Michigan State University, generating 95 percent of research in the state and supporting economic growth throughout Michigan.

WSU's centers and institutes play an integral role in the university's emphasis on encouraging innovative scholarship, providing service to society, and strengthening its performance as a nationally recognized research university. WSU's centers and institutes embrace the multidisciplinary nature of scholarship and research within the university, and expand university boundaries by fostering collaborations with government, industry and organizations to enhance economic growth and the quality of life locally, nationally and globally.

The university's Office of Diversity and Inclusion is a unique resource dedicated to supporting students, faculty, and the entire university community. This committed group of individuals is focused on sustaining Wayne State's inclusive campus and can provide assistance on a number of issues.

Off-Campus Programs

Wayne State students have the opportunity to apply their learning for the betterment of the community and the city as a whole. WSU and its active student body take pride in being a key player in the city's unique urban Renaissance. From student startups to service learning, students make a meaningful impact on the city they call home.

Costs

Wayne State students are assessed tuition each semester based on their residency, credit hours, year in school, division status, academic program, and school or college. Updated information is available at wayne.edu/tuition.

Financial Aid

A range of resources, including grants, scholarships, work-study, and several types of loans are available to help students finance their WSU education. All applicants should file the annual Free Application for Federal Student Aid (FAFSA) early to help determine eligibility. New undergraduates will be considered for a merit award when their admissions application is received. Students may qualify for other specialized types of financial aid based on a variety of factors.

Faculty

WSU faculty members are renowned for innovation and expertise in their fields, crafting hands-on curricula to take students out of the classroom and into the real world.

Student Life

WSU offers hundreds of student organizations that sponsor everything from cultural celebrations and political debates to volunteer events. Comfortable and convenient student housing offers numerous amenities and plenty of space for studying and socializing.

With nearly 20 collegiate teams, Wayne State Warriors compete in most major sports, from football to fencing (wsuathletics.com). Students flock to the Warrior Zone cheering section, and can get in the game themselves at the Mort Harris Recreation and Fitness Center on campus, with its full gym, sport courts, three-lane track, 30-foot rock wall, and access to intramural and club sports.

Application and Information

WSU delivers an exemplary education to students who want to go beyond the books and make a difference. Interested students can apply using the university application or Common Application. Transcripts are also required and there is a $25 application fee. Students can submit their SAT score using the WSU code 1898 or ACT score using the WSU code 2064. Those who plan to major in music, theater, or dance should schedule an audition and/or interview with the department.

All application materials for students who plan to start classes in the fall are due by August 1. Deadline for winter semester is December 1, and for spring/summer semester is April 1. Applicants should receive an admission decision within two to three weeks after submitting all required materials.

Wayne State University
42 West Warren Avenue
P.O. Box 02759
Detroit, Michigan 48202
Phone: 313-577-2100
Fax: 313-577-7536
E-mail: studentservice@wayne.edu
Website: wayne.edu

COLLEGE CLOSE-UPS

At Wayne State University, students prepare for a bright future led by esteemed faculty members in company with a diverse collection of classmates. They do so on a bustling urban campus within walking distance of world-class cultural, entertainment and experiential learning opportunities.

WEBB INSTITUTE

GLEN COVE, NEW YORK

Webb Institute

Webb was founded by the great, entrepreneurial nineteenth-century shipbuilder William H. Webb in 1889. Since its inception, the following traditions have made the Webb experience an unparalleled one:

- A full-tuition scholarship is given to every enrolled student who is a U.S. citizen or permanent resident.
- All students graduate with a dual Bachelor of Science degree in Naval Architecture and Marine Engineering.
- Paid internships are provided for all students in every academic year, giving every student approximately eight months of work experience in the marine industry prior to graduation.
- Upon graduating, students have a 100 percent job placement rate or graduate school acceptance rate.
- With just 90 students, faculty are accessible (8:1 student-to-faculty ratio), and the opportunities for leadership, extra-curricular activities, hands-on experiences, intercollegiate sports, etc. are limitless.
- Located only an hour from New York City, students are provided with unlimited opportunities to take advantage of what the city offers.
- Students are governed by an Honor Code System.

Location

Webb is located in Glen Cove on Long Island's North Shore, about an hour from New York City. Convenient train service from Glen Cove to New York City brings a variety of cultural, educational, and recreational activities within reach of Webb students.

Academic Program

All students at Webb graduate with a dual Bachelor of Science degree in Naval Architecture and Marine Engineering, which encompasses several engineering disciplines. Webb's 146-credit curriculum is based on a systems approach to engineering and provides each student with rich experiences in mathematics, engineering, naval architecture, and design. Students also take one humanities course in each semester as part of the mission not only to offer a first-rate engineering education but also to encourage development of the whole person and lifelong learning. The depth and quality of this rigorous curriculum is made to ensure that all graduates are prepared to pursue careers in the maritime industry or beyond or to continue their education in premier graduate programs. Each semester includes at least one course in naval architecture or marine engineering that serves to tie the program together from the beginning to end.

Webb's academic experience also includes the following unique programs:

- The Classroom Experience—Each of the four classes at Webb has its own classroom, which includes a lecture area in the front, and individual work stations in the back. This environment encourages students to work collaboratively as well as to help one another.
- Winter Work Term—Between the fall and spring semesters, all students take part in a practical work term. These eight-week winter work terms provide students with first-hand experiences in the industry and encourage attitudes and work habits that contribute to a sense of professional excellence. Students have pursued Winter Work Term experiences in each of the seven continents.
- Monday Lecture Series—In addition to formal courses, all students attend Webb's weekly Monday Lectures, during which invited speakers discuss a variety of topics from the technical to historic to current events. The weekly lecture is designed to expand Webb students' education in both technical and non-technical subject areas.
- Zeien Lecture Series—Twice per year, the Webb community and invited guests congregate for a special evening presentation as part of the Zeien Lecture Series, which brings noted individuals from industry, academia, the arts, and government to Webb's campus to share their stories, experiences, insights, and knowledge.
- Senior Thesis—During the junior year, Webb students, under the guidance of members of the faculty, choose a topic for their senior thesis, a requirement for graduation. This process includes developing an approach and presenting a formal proposal for consideration and approval of the faculty. Throughout their last year and a half at Webb, the students conduct research, perform tests, study data, and write their theses, ultimately presenting them to the Webb community at the end of their senior year.
- University of Southampton Exchange Program (SOTON)—Students are given the opportunity to enrich their study of naval architecture and marine engineering as well as to experience the rich culture of Great Britain and Europe with Webb's University of Southampton Exchange Program. Webb students are invited to this premier university during their first semester of sophomore year, and selected students from Southampton are invited to join the Webb administration, faculty, staff and student body in the Spring.

Facilities

Webb's 26-acre ocean-front campus, the former estate of Herbert L. Pratt, includes beautiful historic buildings as well as unique and state-of-the-art facilities. These facilities include:

Haeberle Lab—Houses several state-of-the-art laboratories that are designed to help students further explore and master naval architecture and marine engineering. These laboratories include marine engineering, mechanical engineering, materials testing and structural engineering, electrical engineering, aerodynamics, and hydrodynamics.

The Robinson Model Basin—Built in 1947, the basin houses a shop model towing tank and an instrumentation room. The 93-foot-long model tank is used for student coursework, academic instruction, consulting work, and research for the US Navy. The tank features a full-height viewing window which allows for observations to be made above and below the water line.

The Machine Shop and Carpenter Shop—The shops house various tools available for student use. The woodshop has a table saw, compound mitre saw, jointer, bandsaw, drill press, a suite of hand power tools, and the Webb model cutter, a ShopBot three-axis CNC router. Webb's Machine Shop houses a set of MIG, TIG, and arc-welding stations, lathes and milling machines (including a CNC mill), as well as saws grinders, drill presses, and many smaller items typically found in a shop. It also contains an aluminum shop for cold forming aluminum sheets.

Goldbach Boathouse—Located on Webb's private beach and pier, the boathouse stores supplies for the fleet of 420s, Boston Whalers, rowing sculls, windsurfers, and kayaks.

The Livingston Library—Contains extensive resources in naval architecture, marine engineering, science and general engineering, as well as collections in literature, social sciences, and the arts.

The Couch Computer Lab—The lab includes several multi-core processing computers that support the use of high-end engineering software for Finite Element Analysis (FEA), computational fluid dynamics, and physicist-based modeling and simulation. The lab also has printing and plotting capabilities, including 3-D printing.

The Advanced Learning Classroom (ALC)—The state-of-the-art ALC was designed to support new learning technologies together with distance learning capabilities. The classroom is outfitted with a video conferencing system, cameras, speakers, and microphones that support the receipt and delivery of lectures from remote and local participants, as well as remote collaboration with industry and academia.

Costs

All U.S. citizens and permanent residents who are enrolled at Webb Institute receive a scholarship covering the full cost of tuition. Students must pay for room, board, and an annual fee. The room and board charge is $14,750 for 2017–18, and the annual fee is $425. Noncitizens are charged tuition of $48,350 in addition to the room and board charge and annual fee. Freshmen are required to purchase a laptop through Webb Institute.

Financial Aid

In addition to the full-tuition scholarship for all U.S. citizens and permanent residents enrolled at Webb, students can be awarded internal scholarships for their other costs. Approximately a quarter of the student body are awarded additional need-based and non-need-based scholarships annually. The required winter work internship in the industry during the months of January and February provides income for students that assists in covering additional expenses. Supplementary aid opportunities are available through the Federal Pell Grant, Federal Stafford Student Loan Program, and other external scholarship programs. Students requiring financial assistance must submit the Free Application for Federal Student Aid (FAFSA) two weeks after submitting their application.

Faculty

Webb Institute has an inspiring faculty with extensive industry experience whose primary commitment at Webb is teaching. In addition to being involved in campus life, many members of the faculty possess professional engineer's licenses and engage in sponsored research programs, consult for commercial firms, do research, create reports, and present papers at conferences. Classes are limited to 28 students, and with a student-faculty ratio of 8:1, are also very accessible. Each student is assigned a faculty advisor upon enrolling at Webb, and faculty members also serve as mentors for the students' senior thesis projects.

Student Government and Honor Code

The Student Organization (SO) at Webb is highly active in student administrative, social, and educational affairs. It is supplemented by an Honor Council and Honor Code. Together, these entities provide students with a high degree of responsibility for student life activities. Students also serve on many faculty committees and attend Board Meetings.

Admissions Requirements

To be considered for admission to Webb Institute, applicants must submit the following:

- Webb Institute Application
- A nonrefundable application fee (fee waivers available)
- Secondary School Report Form and Official High School or College Transcript
- The following official standardized test scores:
  - SAT or ACT (SAT Code: 2970, ACT Code: 2987)
  - SAT Subject Test: Math Level 1 or Math Level 2
  - SAT Subject Test: Physics or Chemistry
- Two letters of recommendation from teachers
- To be considered for the Webb Institute full-tuition scholarship, a copy of the applicant's birth certificate, valid U.S. passport, or U.S. Permanent Resident card

Application Process

Admission to Webb is a highly personalized and holistic process. To be considered for admission, prospective students must submit their applications and accompanying documents by the following deadlines: Early Decision, October 15 or regular decision, February 15.

The Admissions Committee will review every application, and select students with diverse perspectives who value intellectual rigor, curiosity, and integrity to be finalists. Finalists are then invited to take part in an overnight experience, during which they are interviewed by the president of the college and a faculty member. A portion of these finalists are accepted to Webb's freshman class.

Transfer applicants are reviewed on an individual basis in the context of the entire applicant pool. Their requirements for admission are, therefore, the same. However, it is important to note that Webb does not accept college credits from other institutions or from AP exams. Regardless of previous college coursework or scores on AP exams, all students enter Webb as first-semester freshmen.

Contact Information:

Webb Institute
Office of Admissions and Student Affairs
298 Crescent Beach Road
Glen Cove, New York 11542
Phone: 516-671-8355
E-mail: admissions@webb.edu
Website: http://www.webb.edu

Webb Institute is located approximately 25 miles east of Manhattan, directly on the Long Island Sound.

WENTWORTH INSTITUTE OF TECHNOLOGY

BOSTON, MASSACHUSETTS

WENTWORTH
INSTITUTE OF TECHNOLOGY

★ To read more about this school, visit http://petersons.to/wentworthinstituteoftechnology

The Institute

Wentworth Institute of Technology was founded in 1904 to provide education in technology. Today, Wentworth has a current undergraduate full-time enrollment of approximately 3,900 men and women. The education acquired at Wentworth enables graduates to assume creative and responsible careers in business and industry. Wentworth is located on a 31-acre campus on Huntington Avenue in Boston.

Wentworth provides dormitory and suite-style residence halls on campus for men and women. Students in the residence halls are on a full meal plan with a full cafeteria, snack bar, and convenience store options on campus. Students living in a suite-style residence hall may prepare their own meals in their kitchen space.

Career counseling and placement assistance are available to all alumni and to students who have completed at least one semester of study at the Institute. While many graduates of Wentworth are employed in the Boston area, alumni have secured positions throughout the United States and abroad.

In addition to Wentworth's undergraduate programs, master's degree programs are awarded in applied computer science, architecture, civil engineering, construction management, facility management, and technology management.

Location

Boston is the educational center of New England. It is a city of charm, tradition, and elegance—a major center of art, science, music, history, medicine, and education. Wentworth is situated near the heart of Boston and is surrounded by institutions that provide the cultural advantages for which the city is famous. The Museum of Fine Arts, with its store of art treasures, is diagonally across the street, and admission is free to any student with a Wentworth ID card. Symphony Hall is just a few blocks away. The Harvard Medical School, the New England Conservatory of Music, Emmanuel College, Simmons College, Massachusetts College of Pharmacy and Health Sciences University, Massachusetts College of Art and Design, Roxbury Community College, and Northeastern University are among the many educational institutions within a few blocks of the campus.

Majors and Degrees

Degree programs are offered in the fields of applied mathematics, architecture, business management, computer science, construction management, design, and engineering. Bachelor of Science (B.S.) degrees are awarded in the following majors: applied mathematics, architecture, biological engineering, biomedical engineering, business management (optional concentrations in entrepreneurship or technology project management), civil engineering, computer engineering, computer information systems, computer networking, computer science, construction management, electromechanical engineering, electrical engineering, engineering (interdisciplinary), industrial design, interior design, and mechanical engineering. Baccalaureate degrees in architecture and interior design are designated as first professional degrees. Completion of a Wentworth baccalaureate degree usually requires four years (five years for the electromechanical engineering degree; applied mathematics is a three-year program with a four-year option).

Academic Programs

At Wentworth, college-level study in technological fundamentals and principles is combined with appropriate laboratory, field, and studio experience. Students apply theory to practical problems, and they acquire skills and techniques by using, operating, and controlling equipment and instruments that are particular to their area of specialization. In addition, study in the social sciences and humanities provides a balanced understanding of the world in which graduates work. Wentworth's programs of study are more practical than theoretical in approach, and the Institute's academic requirements demand extensive time and effort.

During the first two years of study in a degree program at Wentworth, students lay the foundation for more advanced study in the third and fourth (and fifth, where applicable) years. While nearly all majors allow continuous study from the freshman through the senior year, the architecture major requires a petition for acceptance to the baccalaureate program during the sophomore year.

All bachelor's degree programs are conducted as cooperative (co-op) education programs: upon entering their third year, students alternate semesters of academic study at Wentworth with semester-long periods of employment in industry. Two semesters of co-op employment are required; one additional (summer) semester of co-op is optional. Both students and the companies that hire them are enthusiastic about the co-op program and agree that it is a mutually valuable experience.

Off-Campus Programs

Students have the option to study abroad in Wentworth's established programs in Germany and Ireland. As part of various programs and classes, Wentworth students have also traveled to many destinations, such as Nicaragua, the United Kingdom, Italy, Austria, the Czech Republic, Russia, and throughout Scandinavia.

Wentworth's membership in the Colleges of the Fenway (COF) gives students the intimacy of a small college community and the resources of a major university. The COF consortium members are Emmanuel College, Massachusetts College of Art and Design, Massachusetts College of Pharmacy and Health Sciences University, Simmons College, Wentworth Institute of Technology, and Wheelock College. The consortium offers the benefits of cross-registration and access to social events, intramural teams, dance and theater troupes, a chorus and orchestra, professional activities, libraries, and campus facilities at five other colleges within walking distance of one another. The COF's Global Education Opportunities Center provides access to exchange programs and overseas institutions as well as cross-registration for faculty-led travel courses.

Academic Facilities

Wentworth's thirty buildings house classrooms, studios, laboratories, administrative offices, and other facilities. Beatty Hall houses the Flanagan Campus Center, Schumann Fitness Center, Alumni Library, cafeteria, computer center, classrooms, recreation room, and office space. State-of-the-art laboratories, such as the Center for Sciences and Biomedical Engineering and the Manufacturing Center, are situated throughout the campus.

Costs

For 2017–18, tuition is $32,954, books and supplies are approximately $1,500, and the average room and board cost is approximately $13,850 (this figure varies according to accommodation). Tuition includes a brand new laptop that is outfitted with the complete suite of software used in the student's academic program.

Financial Aid

Merit-based scholarships are awarded to accepted students. Wentworth also provides federal and state financial assistance, such as Federal Pell and Federal Supplemental Educational Opportunity Grants, Federal Perkins Loans, Federal Work-Study Program awards, Gilbert Matching Grants, and Massachusetts No-Interest Loans, to students with financial need in accordance with federal and state guidelines.

Wentworth participates in the Federal Direct Lending program. As a result, students are eligible to borrow under the Federal Direct Stafford Student Loan program and parents may borrow under the Federal Direct PLUS program. Individuals participating in these programs borrow money directly from the federal government rather than through lending institutions.

In addition to these need-based programs, Wentworth also participates in the MEFA loan program sponsored by the Massachusetts Educational Financing Authority. Wentworth offers several payment options through payment plans and alternative loan financing.

To apply for financial aid, new students should complete the Free Application for Federal Student Aid (FAFSA) by March 1. Applications received after that date are considered as funds allow.

Faculty

Wentworth's faculty includes 145 full-time and 165 part-time members. The primary responsibility of every faculty member is teaching. Although professors may engage in some research and related work, student development remains the central mission of Wentworth's faculty. Upon entering Wentworth, every student is assigned a faculty adviser.

Student Government

Wentworth's Student Government performs an essential function as the official representative of the student body. Its purposes are to receive and express student opinion, to advance the best interests of the student body with the administration and faculty and with other institutions and associations, to support all extracurricular activities of the student body, and to serve as a bond between the student body and the faculty to foster cooperation and understanding. The Student Government is made up of elected representatives from each class section and the officers elected by the student body at large. The Student Government sponsors social functions and student organizations and serves as an advocate for student concerns.

Admission Requirements

Applicants must be graduates of secondary schools (or have passed the GED test) and must meet specific entrance requirements. All programs require four years of English, a laboratory science, and mathematics through algebra II in a college-preparatory program. Both the electromechanical engineering and the computer science programs require a background in precalculus or trigonometry. All programs require the submission of SAT or ACT scores. International students and transfers are welcome.

Application and Information

Students are admitted to Wentworth for September and January enrollment. Notification of admission is made on a rolling basis. The preferred method for applying is online at http://www.wit.edu/apply. The online application fee is $50. An application form, the application fee, transcripts from the secondary school and any colleges previously attended, SAT or ACT scores, a personal statement, and a letter of recommendation should be sent to:

Admissions Office
Wentworth Institute of Technology
550 Huntington Avenue
Boston, Massachusetts 02115
Phone: 617-989-4000
800-556-0610 (toll-free)
Fax: 617-989-4010
E-mail: admissions@wit.edu
Website: http://www.wit.edu
http://twitter.com/WITadmissions
http://facebook.com/wentworthadmissions

WESTERN CONNECTICUT STATE UNIVERSITY

DANBURY, CONNECTICUT

★ To read more about this school, visit http://petersons.to/westernconnecticutstateuniversity

The University

Western Connecticut State University (WCSU) in Danbury, Connecticut, is a mid-size, academically rich, affordably priced public university conveniently located just off Interstate 84 on Connecticut's border with New York State. Comprising four schools and a graduate studies division, it has an enrollment of close to 6,000 students.

The university has progressed from its beginnings as a small teacher-training school in 1903, through more than a century of program development and multimillion-dollar infrastructure expansion to become the respected, full-service university it is today.

Two Campuses, Each Unique

Only an hour north of New York City, the school's traditional Midtown campus is complemented by the sweeping landscapes of the campus at Westside. Though separated by a short drive, the two are totally in sync with one another. Students develop leadership skills in more than 80 clubs, organizations, and residence hall associations, and participate in activities ranging from sports to fundraisers to carnivals and festivals on whichever campus they're held.

The 35-acre Midtown campus is home to stately Old Main, the school's original structure, which was built in 1904. On the whole, however, Midtown's varied architecture tells a modern story. From the construction of Fairfield Hall in the 1920s, to the nearly $100-million infrastructure infusion that culminated in the "green," technology-rich, LEED-certified Science Building in 2006, Midtown's history has mirrored the extraordinary changes and growth of America's 20th century.

Westside's 364-acre campus boasts a large sports complex and a wide range of beautifully designed campus buildings, including the recently opened 130,000-square-foot Visual and Performing Arts Center (VPAC), home to the School of Visual and Performing Arts. With its state-of-the-art performance, studio, recording, and classroom facilities, the center draws audiences from all over to its productions.

Collegedegreesearch.net, a Web-based search engine, rated VPAC ninth on its list of the nation's "25 Most Amazing Campus Arts Centers." *Connecticut Magazine* called it the best college performing arts venue in the state for 2015. "It is rare that the moment you walk into a theater or concert hall a standing ovation seems in order, but that's the case," stated the magazine. "The main theater and separate acoustically designed musical hall are, in a word, breathtaking."

Great Programs, Accomplished Faculty, and Endless Opportunity

Students at Western gain the foundational knowledge, professional training, critical-thinking, and communication skills essential to compete successfully in today's competitive job market. Experienced professors who understand the present-day applications of their discipline prepare students in 39 programs. Majors, concentrations, and options add up to 90 choices of paths students can follow to a bachelor's degree.

Testimonials Confirm the Value of a Western Degree

"She is exceptional....She leads by example, provides forward momentum for the business, and is an absolute asset," wrote one employer to Western's Career Center about a recent WCSU-grad hire. The center provides guidance and services to students preparing to enter the job market. Other employers send comments such as "He has far exceeded his peers, and our expectations," and "She has been the lead on several projects. Wish I had five more like her!"

Graduates themselves agree. Sam Kantrow '09, a popular on-air meteorologist at WTNH News 8 (New Haven, Connecticut), praised the groundbreaking meteorology program he pursued at Western. "Without the knowledge provided by WCSU, I never would have acquired the skill set needed to succeed on the air in a top-30 television market," he said.

Opportunities to Go Beyond the Campus

The faculty members at Western make the most of the university's location by providing their students with off-campus experiences. Eye-opening visits to world-famous museums in New York City for art majors, tours of Wall Street firms for business students, doing field research locally and abroad as scientists-in-training—these are learning events where the classroom is the world.

On their own, as well, WCSU students enjoy proximity to the attractions of the tri-state area. Growing their independence, they take day trips to New York's Broadway or Greenwich Village, or head out to historic cities like Boston.

Aware of being where so many giants of commerce, entertainment, and global geopolitics meet or make their headquarters, students aim for internships, jobs, and future careers at the many corporations and organizations headquartered from Manhattan on up—some located in or close to Danbury!

Cory Paris '14, a political science major, transferred to WCSU from a college in Kansas, attracted by the many opportunities the region holds. "Being just an hour from New York allowed me to pursue an internship with the Clinton Global Initiative in Manhattan," said Paris, who was later offered a role with that organization.

The World Comes to Western

Over the years, many well-known artists, lecturers, and performers have found Western a great university at which to speak or perform. Oscar-winning actors have appeared, as have famous sports figures, jazz musicians, scientists, and writers. The university has even been host to powerful politicians and world leaders.

"Meeting His Holiness the Dalai Lama at Western and attending his talks about compassion was so memorable for me," said Sheldon Poole, a student in Western's respected Kathwari Honors Program. Poole graduated with a degree in political science. The event he refers to drew audiences from everywhere and culminated, through the generosity of the Dalai Lama, in the establishment of Western's Center for Compassion, Creativity, and Innovation.

Brittany Chengeri '15, a community health major, emphasized how her instructors helped her develop the confidence to participate in a health volunteer program in Africa while studying at WCSU. "I couldn't have asked for more encouraging, dedicated professors and advisers," she said.

Campus Life and Local Attractions

Students who choose to live on campus at Western are housed in six residence halls, three per campus. Safe, with 24/7 University Police presence and full security systems, accommodations range from classic dorm-style living to full apartments for up to five. Midtown's Student Center offers dining facilities, lounges, rec rooms, a bookstore selling various supplies, and various rooms where clubs and organizations have meetings and events. At Westside, the recently built Campus Center provides similar facilities.

Students may have their cars on campus, where there is free, safe, and well-lighted parking. Continuous complimentary shuttle service is available between campuses and to the Danbury Fair Mall, one of the region's largest indoor malls. Buses, trains, and taxis offer additional options for traveling off campus to cities such as New York.

Danbury's many restaurants are known for their various distinctive cuisines. Several are located just a short walk from Midtown or quick ride down beautiful University Avenue at Westside. For movie lovers, choices range from art films to blockbusters at the nearby Danbury Lowes 16-theater complex, the Cinema in neighboring Bethel, or theaters just minutes over the border in New York.

Outdoors, there are several area hiking trails and the glorious nature walk at Westside's own Nature Preserve. Beautiful nearby Candlewood Lake, the state's largest body of fresh water, offers picnicking, hiking and seasonal water sports.

Students Get Involved and Get Productive

From the Adventure Club to the Zeta Beta Tau (ZBT) fraternity, a broad range of clubs and organizations at WCSU bring together individuals with common interests to participate in memory- and friendship-making experiences. Often these include community outreach projects that lead to character and leadership building as well as personal satisfaction. Opportunities to network are inherently part of these experiences. Students are introduced to new challenges and often discover talents they didn't know they had.

Western encourages participation in all areas of collegiate life, supporting student interest in myriad topics from preservation of the natural environment on a global scale—for example, in WCSU's chapter of Jane Goodall's Roots and Shoots organization—to performance groups such the university's dance, acting, and puppetry clubs.

Athletics, club sports and personal fitness are also a great part of the Western experience. About 350 students participate in intercollegiate team sports. With Colonial Chuck as their mascot and spirited fans to cheer them on, WCSU's Colonials meet challengers on home courts and fields, in the 2,500-seat stadium of the Athletic Complex, or away at rival schools. There are men's teams compete in baseball, basketball, football, lacrosse, soccer, and tennis; women's teams compete in basketball, field hockey, lacrosse, soccer softball, swimming, tennis, and volleyball.

In addition, Westside's 80,000-square-foot O'Neill Center houses a pool, arena, courts, and workout facilities for students to participate in numerous intramural and club sports. At Midtown, the WesternRec program and Colonial Fitness Zone provide perfect venues for participation in intramural sports, attending special events and meeting the challenge of staying fit.

Bright Futures Begin at Western

Spirited, talented, and full of promise, students at Western respond to the many opportunities the university offers them. As the future opens on ever-expanding vistas of career and personal possibilities, discovering and developing the unique potential of each of its students will continue to remain priority one for WCSU.

Costs

As part of the Connecticut State Colleges & Universities system, Western provides a high-quality private university education at an exceptionally reasonable public school cost. In the 2016–17 academic year, in-state tuition and fees totaled $5,837 per semester. Tuition and fees for Students in the New England Regional Student Program totaled $7,141 per semester. For other out-of-state students, tuition and fees totaled $12,268 per semester. Books, laboratory fees, health insurance, and personal expenses are not included in these estimates.

Housing costs range from $3,205 to $5,001 per semester. Meal plans range from $$1,287 to $2,527 per semester.

Financial Aid

Western Connecticut State University offers financial aid to help qualified students meet their educational expenses. The staff of Financial Aid and Student Employment is available to assist students in determining their eligibility for the various sources of aid available.

For more information, students should contact the Financial Aid Office at 203-837-8580 or wcsufinancialaid@wcsu.edu.

Admission Requirements

Western requires that candidates for admission have a high school diploma from an accredited secondary school or an equivalency diploma. General Educational Development (GED) scores must be converted into a State of Connecticut Equivalency Diploma. Each applicant is assessed individually, but the following guidelines must also be met: SAT (1000 guideline), ACT also accepted; top one-third rank in graduating class; and a B- average in 4 years of English, 3 years math (algebra 1, geometry, algebra 2), 2 years social sciences, including U.S. history, 2 years of laboratory sciences, and 2 to 3 years of foreign language (3 recommended). Nursing, education, and business applicants may have higher requirements. Auditions are required for applicants to the Department of Music.

Applicants must submit the completed application form, a $50 nonrefundable application fee, SAT or ACT test scores, and official high school transcript or equivalency diploma.

Application and Information

For those applying for the fall semester, notification of admission begins on December 1 and continues on a rolling basis. A reply to an offer of admission must be received by May 1. Rolling admissions for the spring semester begins on October 1. Note that although most freshmen enter WSCU in the fall, roughly 10 percent enter in other semesters.

For more information, students should contact:

Undergraduate Admissions Office
Western Connecticut State University
181 White Street
Danbury, Connecticut 06810
Phone: 203-837-9000
877-837-WCSU (toll-free)
E-mail: admissions@wcsu.edu
Website: http://www.wcsu.edu
http://www.facebook.com/WestConn
http://twitter.com/West

COLLEGE CLOSE-UPS

WESTMONT COLLEGE

SANTA BARBARA, CALIFORNIA

WESTMONT

COLLEGE CLOSE-UPS

The College

Westmont College encourages deeper thinking and wider impact through the depth of a major and the breadth of the liberal arts. Nationally ranked for rigorous academics, this Santa Barbara Christian college fosters a deep love of God. Professors care deeply about students and teach critical thinking and communication skills that prepare them for fulfilling lives of leadership and service. Education occurs outside the classroom through a vital residential community, athletics, off-campus programs, and local and international service projects. Students grow in all areas of their lives and become the best version of themselves.

Westmont's 1,200 students come from 40 states and 19 countries, with the highest percentage from California. About 61 percent are women, 36 percent are from an ethnic or diverse background, and 2 percent are international students. Ninety-five percent live in the six residence halls on campus or the apartment complex off campus. Produce from the Westmont Garden and outdoor seating enhance dining in Kerr Student Center. Alumni enter a wide variety of professions and vocations and pursue professional and graduate programs at the world's finest research universities, including UCLA, Stanford, Harvard, Yale, Princeton, Cambridge, the University of Chicago, and many others.

A member of the National Association of Intercollegiate Athletics and the Golden State Athletic Conference, Westmont offers intercollegiate sports for men and women in basketball, cross-country, soccer, tennis, and track and field. Men also compete in intercollegiate baseball, club polo, club rugby, club soccer, club volleyball, club Ultimate (Frisbee), and club golf. Women participate in intercollegiate volleyball, club polo, club cheer, and club golf. The intramural program offers a wide variety of activities.

Students choose from numerous clubs and organizations (student newspaper, literary magazine, yearbook, choral and music ensembles, intercultural clubs, political organizations, theater productions, community service groups, and Christian outreach programs) or start their own. Chapel offers speakers and programs that inspire and challenge students to grow in their relationship with Christ. Attendance at this integral part of a Westmont education is required three days a week.

Location

Westmont's wooded, 111-acre campus sits in the foothills of Santa Barbara, between the ascending peaks of the Santa Ynez Mountains and the vast expanse of the Pacific Ocean. Students enjoy the beach and mountain trails year-round. Just minutes from campus, Santa Barbara provides a wealth of history, culture, theaters, libraries, community concerts, and other civic offerings.

Majors and Degrees

Westmont awards Bachelor of Arts (B.A.) and Bachelor of Science (B.S.) degrees in more than 100 academic majors, minors, and programs, including: alternative major, art, art history, biology, chemistry, communication studies, computer science, economics and business, education, engineering physics, English, English and modern languages, European studies, French, history, kinesiology, liberal studies, mathematics, music, philosophy, physics, political science, psychology, religious studies, social science, sociology and anthropology, Spanish, and theater arts.

WASC Senior College and University Commission and the National Association of Schools of Music accredit Westmont's programs. The teacher-preparation program, approved by the California Commission for Teacher Preparation and Licensing, awards single-subject or multiple-subject credentials.

Pre-professional programs include athletic training, dentistry, engineering, law, medicine, ministry and missionary studies, pharmacy, physical therapy, and veterinary studies.

Academic Programs

All majors and programs of study feature thought-provoking and inspiring ways to integrate belief, thought, and action to reach a deeper, more accurate understanding of the world. Westmont demonstrates its commitment to academic freedom in courses that demand students' best critical thinking and through a range of opportunities and organizations that explore significant ideas and issues. Students consider issues of science and religion through the Pascal Society and attend lectures in the humanities sponsored by the Erasmus Society. As an exclusively undergraduate college, Westmont seeks to actively engage students in research projects. Professors, staff members, and alumni want to help students grow through their questions toward an ever-deeper faith.

Off-Campus Programs

Semester-long programs off campus that feature Westmont professors include **Westmont in Cairo**, where students live in the heart of the Arab world in a developing megalopolis pulsating with energy, people, and life. **Westmont Downtown** focuses on social entrepreneurship, with students participating in internships 20 hours a week in downtown Santa Barbara. **Westmont in East Asia** addresses contemporary world issues and globalization in Seoul, Shanghai, and Singapore. **Westmont in England**, offered every other year, combines travel and residential study in the British Isles for students of literature. **Westmont in Europe** provides the broadest geographical scope. Through **Westmont in Jerusalem**, students experience the city's many cultures, study its tangled history, and marvel at its rich traditions. Students attending **Westmont in Mexico** gain skills for effective cross-cultural living, experience international ministry, and improve their Spanish language abilities. **Westmont in Northern Europe** explores conflict and peacemaking in London, Berlin, and Northern Ireland. **Westmont in San Francisco** explores American urban society and offers 20-hour-per-week internships. **Global Health Semester in Uganda** provides students majoring in medicine or public health opportunities for international field placement at a local organization. Students may also choose from numerous Westmont-approved programs such as semesters in France and Spain for language study; semesters on the continents of Africa, Asia, South America, and Australia in a variety of disciplines; and programs throughout the world sponsored by the Council for Christian Colleges and Universities. Domestic programs in Washington, D.C. highlight national political processes and incorporate internships in justice, journalism, and national, international, and economic policy. Through the Consortium Visitor Program, students study at any of the Christian College Consortium's 12 other member colleges.

Academic Facilities

Westmont has added new buildings in recent years: Adams Center for the Visual Arts, which includes a museum, art studios, classrooms, and offices; Winter Hall for Science and Mathematics with labs, a lecture hall, classrooms and offices; the Westmont Observatory with the powerful Keck Telescope; and the Global Leadership Center, which opens in fall 2017 with additional student housing and a meeting center. The tri-level Roger John Voskuyl Library, named for Westmont's third president, provides resources and services for faculty, staff, students, and the local community with 237,000 books, media items, music scores, and microforms; 300 print periodical titles; 105 online databases with access to 12,000 online periodicals; and use of the Gold Coast Library Network, Camino, and Interlibrary Loan Services. The library features a computer lab with 27 dual-platform iMacs and a Learning Commons brings together library, technology, and other campus services to foster collaborative and creative work and social interaction. The library also houses student support services: Academic Advising and Disability Services, Writer's Corner, and Information Technology. The college's network features both wired and wireless components, with wireless coverage extending through all campus buildings and most outdoor areas and a total Internet bandwidth of 135 Mb/s. Students receive Westmont Google Apps accounts that provide e-mail, a calendar, document sharing, and four gigabytes of storage per student. Porter Theatre contains state-of-the-art equipment for dramatic productions and concerts. The Mericos H. Whittier Science Building (with recently renovated labs) and Winter Hall for Science and Mathematics house the college's science program and equipment, including an ultracentrifuge, a liquid scintillation counter for measuring radioactivity, physiographic units, and other equipment for advanced physiological studies. The Music Building provides offices for professors and practice space for students.

Costs

Tuition and fees for 2017–18 are $42,890, and room and board for the academic year are $13,886. Books and personal expenses cost about $3,000.

Financial Aid

Westmont provides generous financial aid and encourages all students to apply regardless of their financial resources. The net cost to attend is usually much less than the published tuition, fees, and living expenses. Eighty-five percent of students receive some form of financial assistance from Westmont, ranging from $6,000 to full tuition; the college commits $22.4 million to financial aid. After submitting the Free Application for Federal Student Aid (FAFSA), students may also be eligible for generous state grants, aid from federal programs, institutional grants, loans, and work-study programs. Westmont's Augustinian Scholarship and Honors Program offers significant scholarships (up to full tuition) to first-year applicants selected from those who apply early action, a nonbinding process. The college's merit scholarships recognize impressive academic achievement by entering first-year students: President's Scholarship, $21,000; Ruth Kerr Scholarship: $18,000; Wallace L. Emerson Scholarship, $15,000; Founders Scholarship, $12,500; and the Warrior Academic Award. Transfer students may be eligible for scholarships ranging from $9,000 to $15,000. Westmont also gives awards to students who demonstrate strength in art, music, theater arts, dance, cultural diversity, and athletics.

Faculty

Westmont's outstanding Christian professors provide rigorous training in every area of human knowledge. They know students' names, spend time with them outside of class, and care deeply about who they become. Committed to teaching and to scholarly work in their field, Westmont professors also discuss how their faith informs their learning. With 93 full-time and 54 part-time professors, the student-faculty ratio is 12:1, and the average class size is 18. Ninety-six percent of tenure-track faculty members hold a terminal degree. Although professors focus on teaching, many engage in research, write books, and publish articles in leading journals and periodicals.

Student Government

The Westmont College Student Association (WCSA) is an entirely self-governing body. Students elect their own WCSA representatives, who are responsible for organizing social, cultural, and educational activities. They actively participate in and are voting members on many faculty committees, and they allocate the student budget to various clubs and organizations. Westmont Student Ministries, another student-managed organization, organizes on- and off-campus ministries and mission opportunities.

Admission Requirements

Westmont selects candidates for admission based on evidence that they're prepared for Westmont's academic stimulation and spiritual vitality. All applicants must submit one academic letter of recommendation, official high school or college transcripts, and official SAT or ACT scores. A pastoral/character reference is optional. An interview is strongly encouraged. Transfer students from an accredited two- or four-year college or university or a Bible college or university accredited by the American Association of Bible Colleges are evaluated on their achievement in solid, transferable course work, personal areas covered by the application (as stated above), and the quality of the written responses. They must also submit high school records.

Application and Information

Students may enroll at Westmont at the beginning of either the fall or spring semester. The college offers an Early Action plan: submit applications for Early Action 1 by October 15 and for Early Action 2 by November 15. Westmont mails notifications by December 1 and January 1, respectively. The priority deadline for regular decision is February 15 for first-year applicants and March 15 for transfers. Westmont sends notifications on a rolling basis. Submit applications online using the Westmont Application or the Common Application with an application fee of $50. The Office of Admission encourages prospective students to complete the application process as early as possible.

Prospective students are encouraged to visit any time and stay overnight in the residence halls, attend classes and chapel, speak with professors or coaches, audition for a music program, share a portfolio with the art department, interview with an admissions counselor, and eat meals with Westmont students. Several Preview Day events occur each semester. Westmont seeks to enroll a well-rounded and balanced first-year class and create a dynamic and culturally and traditionally diverse community of learners possessing a variety of attributes, accomplishments, backgrounds, and interests.

For more information regarding admissions students should contact:

Office of Admission
Westmont College
955 La Paz Road
Santa Barbara, California 93108
Phone: 800-777-9011 (toll-free)
Fax: 805-565-6234
E-mail: admissions@westmont.edu
Website: http://www.westmont.edu/
http://www.facebook.com/westmont
http://twitter.com/westmontnews

Nestled in the beautiful hills of Santa Barbara, California, Westmont is home to 1,200 undergraduate scholars, all seeking to engage the academy, church, and world.

WEST VIRGINIA WESLEYAN COLLEGE

BUCKHANNON, WEST VIRGINIA

WEST VIRGINIA WESLEYAN

The College

Founded in 1890, West Virginia Wesleyan College is a coeducational, residential, liberal arts college in Buckhannon, West Virginia. The College has an enrollment of 1,400 undergraduate students from thirty-five states and twenty-one countries. The average class size is 19 and the student-faculty ratio is 14:1. More than 80 percent of the faculty members hold the highest degree in their respective teaching field. Each fall, West Virginia Wesleyan enrolls approximately 415 freshmen and 50 transfers. Fifty percent of students originate from West Virginia, and the ratio of men to women is 1:1. Approximately 17 percent of the students are minority or international students. More than 85 percent of students live on campus, and housing is required for all four years of study. Housing options include residence halls, suites, on-campus apartments, and campus-adjacent residence units.

Among the many services available to students is the Learning Center, which provides comprehensive learning resources for all students, as well as robust services for students with diagnosed learning differences and is one of the foremost programs of its type in the country.

In addition to challenging academic curriculum and innovative technology, Wesleyan offers a balanced and comprehensive student-life program. Co-curricular activities include twenty-two NCAA Division II varsity sports, intramurals, and outdoor recreation adventures. More than seventy campus organizations include vocal and instrumental musical ensembles, theatre arts, dance, community service, clubs, special interest groups, Greek life, and spiritual and religious life programming. On-campus media opportunities include a campus radio station, student newspaper, and yearbook. The student-run Bobcat Entertainment Board schedules cultural and social entertainment every week during the academic year.

Location

Situated in the foothills of the Allegheny Mountains, Wesleyan's picturesque 100-acre campus is located in the historic town of Buckhannon, West Virginia. Buckhannon is located two hours south of Pittsburgh, Pennsylvania, and 90 minutes north of Charleston, West Virginia. It is easily accessible by interstate highways. Buckhannon has been included in Norman Crampton's book, *The Top 100 Best Small Towns in America* and *The 120 Best College Towns in America*. Students are drawn to the attractive and friendly setting and the many restaurants, social events, and outdoor adventures available within a short distance from campus.

Majors and Degrees

The College awards Bachelor of Arts, Bachelor of Science, Bachelor of Science in Nursing, and Bachelor of Music Education degrees, in addition to a number of master's-level degrees. Majors include: accounting, art, arts administration, athletic training, biology, business administration, five-year bachelor's + master's in business administration, chemistry, Christian formation, communication studies, computer information science, computer science, criminal justice, economics, education (combined elementary/secondary, elementary, or secondary), engineering 3-2, English (literature, education, or writing), environmental science, environmental studies, exercise science, gender studies, graphic design, history, international business, international studies, management, marketing, mathematics, music (applied or theory), music education, musical theatre, nursing, painting and drawing, philosophy, physics, political science, psychology, public relations, religion, sociology, sport business, and theatre arts.

Preprofessional study programs are offered in dentistry, law, medicine, optometry, pharmacy, physical therapy, and veterinary medicine. The degrees are determined by the content of the student's program.

West Virginia Wesleyan also offers the following master's degrees: Master of Science in Athletic Training, Master of Business Administration, Master of Fine Arts in Creative Writing, Master of Education, and Master of Science in Nursing.

Academic Programs

Students are required to complete 120 credit hours of course work to become eligible for graduation. Approximately one third of those hours are taken in a student's major, one third in the general studies curriculum requirement, and one third in electives. The general studies and elective courses are taken to develop and enhance a student's worldview.

Wesleyan operates on a traditional semester system. The optional May Term is a three-week intensive period of study giving students the opportunity to earn three credit hours. International travel opportunities are popular options during May Term.

The honors program is offered for superior students who meet the specific requirements and are willing to commit themselves to a rigorous and enriching curriculum that affirms the highest ideals of a liberal arts institution. Challenging classes and cultural outings are an integral part of the honors program and are offered throughout the academic year.

Advanced credit is available for students who achieve required scores on Advanced Placement exams, International Baccalaureate exams, and CLEP tests.

New students are assigned a faculty adviser who assists with course selection and student concerns. All first-year students are required to successfully complete a four-hour First Year Seminar course. In addition to helping students adapt to college life, the First Year Seminar courses are topical and apply credit toward a general studies requirement.

Off-Campus Programs

Study abroad is highly encouraged and is an important part of the Wesleyan student's experience. In the recent past, students have studied in such countries as Australia, Austria, Bolivia, Bulgaria, England, Ireland, Italy, Kenya, Korea, Spain, and Wales, but there are a number of other countries in which students may study. Internships are required for many majors and highly encouraged for others. They are available locally, as well as in cities such as Pittsburgh, New York, Washington, D.C., and others around the globe. These off-campus opportunities can be taken for a complete semester, during the May Term, or during the summer.

Academic Facilities

Wesleyan's twenty-four buildings, including eleven modern residence hall units, house some of the most impressive facilities in the region. Residence hall facilities include Fleming Hall, which was completely remodeled in 2008; Dunn Hall, a new residence hall that opened to students in 2011; and Doney Hall (single rooms) that opened in 2013. Other recent campus construction includes the Virginia Thomas Law Center for the Performing Arts and the Reemsnyder Research Center for the sciences. A brand-new wellness center with Nautilus equipment, full cardio theater, separate workout rooms, and locker room facilities opened in 2012. In 2014 the College opened a new Welcome Center and over the next five years will remodel every major academic classroom through funding received from a Title III grant program. This $10-million grant also provides for a Student Success Center and Center for Teaching and Learning, providing Wesleyan unparalleled support services.

The Annie Merner Pfeiffer Library houses more than 105,000 volumes, 700 periodicals, and 10,000 media materials. More than 220 million additional resources worldwide can be accessed through a number of online databases from students' own residence halls 24 hours a day. Located in the center of the campus is Wesley Chapel, the largest sanctuary in West Virginia, and the Martin Religious Center. The Benedum Campus and Community Center houses a convenience store, bookstore, swimming pool, the Cat's Claw restaurant, the campus radio station, and student services offices.

The Rockefeller Health and Physical Education Center includes a main gymnasium that seats 3,700, an intramural gymnasium, weight-training rooms, and an indoor Astroturf training and recreational area. Other key campus buildings include Christopher Hall of Science and the adjacent Reemsnyder Research Center, which houses state-of-the-art laboratories and classrooms to complement the Christopher's planetarium, herbarium, and greenhouse; Loar Hall, which includes a 165-seat recital hall and state-of-the-art computer music lab; Middleton Hall, which houses the admission offices and department of nursing; Haymond Hall of Science; and the Lynch-Raine Administration Building.

Costs

The College's 2017–18 tuition and fees will be $30,752 and room and board will be $8,436. Wesleyan offers a 10-month interest-free payment plan.

Financial Aid

Wesleyan allocates nearly $15 million each year to help supplement the financial needs of students and their families. Merit scholarships are available for students who demonstrate excellence in the classroom, as well as those who demonstrate talent in the arts and athletics. Scholarship opportunities are available for students who have a strong commitment to community service and for those who have a comprehensive co-curricular resume. A variety of need-based programs are also available, including government grants and loans, institutional grants, and student employment. All students and their families should file the Free Application for Federal Student Aid by February 15. The institutional code for West Virginia Wesleyan is 003830.

Faculty

The faculty members at Wesleyan have a primary goal of teaching and advising. More than 80 percent of the full-time faculty members hold the highest degree in their respective fields. With a 13:1 student-faculty ratio, classes are small, and personal attention is evident in all departments. Not only are faculty members teachers and advisers, but they are also mentors and friends.

Student Government

The Student Senate is structured to encourage and promote student participation. The four peer-elected officers are elected by their respective classes or representative student organizations. Student Senate meets biweekly, along with faculty members, administration, and staff members, and is recognized as the driving force behind many initiatives and decisions on campus.

Admission Requirements

Wesleyan seeks students who have proven academic credentials, combined with achievements and talents that enhance the quality of life on campus. Students are selected by the Office of Admission on the basis of their high school transcripts, college entrance exam results, letters of recommendation, campus interviews, and other supportive information. All applicants must take the SAT or ACT and submit secondary school transcripts from all schools attended, along with the application for admission. Candidates are considered on an individual basis without regard to race, color, national origin, sex, sexual orientation, age, disability, or religious affiliation. Essays and campus interviews are strongly encouraged and may be required in some instances.

Transfer students from accredited institutions are considered for admission. All official college transcripts must be submitted, along with high school transcripts and college entrance exam results.

Applicants who complete their secondary education through an alternative program (e.g., home schooling) must present evidence that they have been adequately prepared for college work to be considered for admission. SAT or ACT results are also required.

Application and Information

Applicants must submit an application for admission, official transcripts, and ACT or SAT scores. The application review period opens each year on September 1. Applying online is free of charge at http://apply.wvwc.edu. Wesleyan is also a Common Application school and applicants may apply free of charge. A paper application is also available and can be submitted along with a $35 nonrefundable fee. Admission decisions are made on a rolling basis, and students are notified within three weeks of receipt of all required documents. The preferred application deadline is March 1 for the fall semester, and December 1 for the spring semester. Applicants who wish to be considered for merit scholarships must apply before March 1. Interviews, campus tours, faculty and staff appointments, and class visits are encouraged and may be arranged through the Office of Admission.

For additional information, students should contact:

Office of Admission
West Virginia Wesleyan College
59 College Avenue
Buckhannon, West Virginia 26201
Phone: 304-473-8510
800-722-9933 (toll-free)
E-mail: admission@wvwc.edu
Website: http://www.wvwc.edu

The Central Campus Green is one of many outdoor gathering spaces where students meet, study, and pass through on their way to classes and co-curricular activities.

WHEATON COLLEGE
WHEATON, ILLINOIS

Wheaton College
For Christ and His Kingdom

The College

Ranked by *U.S. News & World Report* as one of the nation's top liberal arts colleges, Wheaton College attracts exceptional students from all fifty states and more than ninety countries. An interdenominational Christian liberal arts college, Wheaton takes the pursuit of faith and learning seriously. In addition to upholding an academically rigorous curriculum, Wheaton is committed to being a community that fearlessly pursues God's truth; invests in developing whole, well-rounded students; and prepares its graduates to lead lives that make a difference in the world.

The student body at Wheaton College consists of approximately 2,400 undergraduates (including 150+ students in the Conservatory of Music), approximately 80 percent of which come from outside Illinois.

Wheaton College's nearly 160-year history demonstrates the benefits of stable leadership in private Christian higher education—it has had only 8 presidents since it was founded in 1860. Wheaton has been faithful to its original precepts, and its legacy is shown in the lives of its graduates. Many distinguished graduate schools currently enroll Wheaton graduates, including Notre Dame, Princeton, SMU, Yale, and the Universities of Chicago and Missouri–Kansas City; several of the Big Ten music schools; and the A.R.T./MXAT Institute for Advanced Theater Training at Harvard. Wheaton alumni also excel in a wealth of endeavors around the world, with many holding positions in business and finance, government and foreign service, teaching, ministry, law, medicine, and the arts. Wheaton graduates actively contribute to their communities and churches, and no matter what position they hold, they strive to make a difference in the world around them.

Wheaton offers a rich, life-changing education, with graduates trained for life, not just jobs. Students are taught to think, reason, and express themselves effectively. They are equipped to attain knowledge and measure it against the truth of God's word, understand the importance of service, and value faith that embraces both theological accuracy and actively living it out. Developing strong, life-long relationships—with classmates, professors, and Jesus Christ—is a priority. Graduates are well-positioned for whatever they want to pursue and prepared to face the challenges of life. The Wheaton experience is distinctive, and living and learning at Wheaton is extraordinary. As a visiting lecturer recently observed, "I was so impressed by the enthusiasm of the Wheaton students to shape the world, and to make it a better place. And they are approaching this goal in practical ways. Some colleges are full of dour cynics. Wheaton is the opposite—brimming with optimists!"

Location

Wheaton's 80-acre campus is located in a residential suburb (population 55,000) 25 miles west of Chicago. The educational and cultural features of the Chicago metropolitan area are easily accessible by train and regularly visited by students.

Majors and Degrees

Wheaton grants the Bachelor of Arts and Bachelor of Science degrees and, through the Wheaton Conservatory of Music, the Bachelor of Music and Bachelor of Music Education degrees.

The following majors are available in the arts and sciences: ancient languages, anthropology, applied health science, archaeology, art, biblical and theological studies, biology, business/economics, chemistry, Christian education and ministry, communication, computer science, economics, education, English, environmental studies, geology, history, interdisciplinary studies, international relations, mathematics, modern languages (French, German, and Spanish), music, philosophy, physics, political science, psychology, sociology, and urban studies.

The Wheaton Conservatory of Music offers a full range of professional music majors, including composition, education, history/literature, performance, music with elective studies in an outside field, and music with an emphasis in a music-related field (such as media/film music, pedagogy, conducting, and collaborative piano). Students seeking these professional music degrees are accepted directly into the program by audition.

An on-campus program in military science leads to a commission in the U.S. Army at graduation. In addition to the majors offered, Wheaton has programs leading to teacher certification and to athletic training certification as well as programs preparing students for careers in business, health professions, law, and ministry.

Academic Programs

Wheaton's academic curriculum combines with artistic, athletic, religious, service, and social activities to achieve a lively interaction of faith, learning, and living. Because of the College's strong commitment to developing effective servant/leaders for society worldwide and the church, there is a particularly strong integration of faith and learning in all degree programs. A new general education curriculum, Christ at the Core, implemented in fall '16, brings a well-rounded, Christ-centered academic experience while allowing increased freedom and flexibility among cohorts.

Students must demonstrate competence (either by examination or by taking prescribed courses) in foreign language, mathematics, speech, and writing. All students must complete area requirements in applied health science, art, biblical studies, history, literature, music, natural science, philosophy, and social science. A student may be granted advanced placement or college credit on the basis of examination (including SAT Subject Tests, AP, or IB).

Wheaton offers ten natural science majors—applied health science, biology, chemistry, computer science, environmental studies, geology, liberal arts engineering, liberal arts nursing, mathematics, and physics—in six academic departments. Also, 3-2 programs are offered in engineering and nursing, alongside a five-year cooperative engineering program with Illinois Institute of Technology and other engineering schools. The Wheaton faculty members engage the study of science authoritatively, enthusiastically, and creatively in the classrooms and laboratories and beyond the campus. They are creative and offer more than two dozen general education courses in the natural sciences as well as the majors listed above. The programming includes the use of state-of-the-art technologies and techniques on the main Wheaton campus, cutting edge geological and biological studies in a large science station in the scientifically rich area of the Black Hills of South Dakota, and marine biology studies in Belize.

Off-Campus Programs

Wheaton offers a variety of off-campus opportunities to enhance students' programs of study. The Wheaton Passage program is a popular experience available to new students at the College's Northwoods Campus in the wilderness of northern Wisconsin prior to orientation. Another program, Human Needs and Global Resources (HNGR), combines classroom study with a six-month, field-based, service-learning internship in the Global South. A similar program in urban studies, Wheaton in Chicago, focuses on urban issues in U.S. cities and includes a semester living in College-owned housing in urban Chicago.

Other special summer programs for credit include field study at the Wheaton College Science Station in the Black Hills of South Dakota; working with youth at HoneyRock Camp; interdisciplinary study in East Asia; the study of English literature in England; language study in France, Germany, and Spain; the Wheaton in the Holy Lands program, involving biblical and archaeological studies; the Arts in London program, which includes course work in music, theater, and art; and an international study program based in England and the Netherlands, offering courses in economics, political science, and psychology. Wheaton is a member of the Council of Christian Colleges and Universities, based in Washington, D.C. The council's activities increase students' learning opportunities by bringing special programs to campus and by providing off-campus study.

Off-campus programs include American Studies in Washington, D.C.; the Washington Journalism Center in Washington, D.C.; the Los Angeles Film Studies Center; the Contemporary Music Center in Martha's Vineyard; Latin American Studies in Costa Rica; Middle East Studies in Cairo; the Australia Studies Center; China Studies Program; the Scholar's Semester in Oxford; Russia Studies Program; and Uganda Studies Program. Wheaton has also recently affiliated with the International Sustainable Development Studies Institute in Thailand. In addition, Wheaton's membership in the Christian College Consortium allows students a semester of study at one of the other twelve consortium colleges.

Cooperative programs in social science are available at American and Drew Universities, and students may participate in a European seminar conducted by Gordon College.

Academic Facilities

An $80-million science and mathematics facility opened in fall 2010. The 128,000-square-feet of space includes eight teaching labs and research space designed to promote collaborative teacher-student research.

In 2009, an $11 million renovation of Adams Hall added art gallery and studio space. Edman Chapel, often the venue for concerts by world-class musicians, has undergone a $9 million renovation that added rehearsal space, including a large rehearsal room named for alum John Nelson, former conductor of Ensemble Orchestral de Paris. A new Admissions Welcome Center building and the new Armerding Center for Music and the Arts will open Fall of 2017, with the new Concert Hall to follow.

In 2008, Wheaton's Memorial Student Center reopened after an extensive renovation to house the Wheaton Center for Faith, Politics and Economics. The facility provides classroom, research, and public discussion space geared toward the study of economics, politics, and values in business, government, and ministry. Other recent additions to campus facilities include the Todd Beamer Student Center (2004); the Wade Center (2001), which houses the books and papers of seven British authors, including C. S. Lewis and J. R. R. Tolkien; and the Sports and Recreation Complex (2000).

Costs

Tuition for the 2017–18 year is $35,190; room and board for the year are $9,806. The Wheaton Fund subsidizes students' education expenses by nearly a third.

Financial Aid

Realizing that a private college education is a sizable investment, Wheaton is committed to providing the necessary need-based financial aid so students can attend. Last year Wheaton awarded over $30 million in grants and scholarships.

The average need-based aid package for freshmen is about $22,000 and some merit aid is also available. The Center for Vocation and Career helps students to secure part-time jobs, as well as future employment, including Canvas to engage sophomores, employer recruiting, job fairs, professional development, and Wheaton in Network (WiN) alumni networking resources for upperclass students.

Faculty

Over 97 percent of Wheaton's 203 full-time faculty members hold earned doctorates, and more than one third graduated from the top twenty-five graduate schools as designated in *U.S. News & World Report*. The professors' primary commitment as educators and advisers is enriched by their considerable research, publishing, and artistic activities. In addition, the professors are active Christians who strive to show how a profound commitment to God's word structures a vision of all of life, including intellectual life. They are dedicated to honoring a Christian perspective and to modeling Christ's love to their students.

All undergraduate courses are taught by faculty members.

To ensure a rich range of perspectives and expertise, every department at Wheaton has at least 3 full-time professors, and most have 5 to 10. The student-faculty ratio is 11:1.

Student Government

Student Government ensures a student voice in institutional affairs and provides a wide range of opportunities to develop leadership abilities. Student Government's vision is "To further the educational, spiritual, and relational development of the Wheaton College community as elected servant leaders representing student initiative, concern, creativity, and enthusiasm."

Besides Student Government, there are over forty academic, cultural, social justice, and entertainment student groups on campus. In addition, the Office of Christian Outreach provides opportunities for student ministry through student-run mission trips and ministries in urban and suburban Chicago.

Admission Requirements

Wheaton is a selective college that seeks to enroll students who evidence a vital Christian experience, high moral character, personal integrity, social concern, strong academic ability and motivation, and the desire to pursue Christian higher education as defined in the aims and objectives of the College. These qualities are evaluated by consideration of each applicant's academic record, autobiographical essays, test scores, recommendations, optional interview, and participation in extracurricular activities. For students applying to the Conservatory of Music, strong consideration is given to the evaluation of the required audition.

Applicants must have a high school diploma or the equivalent, and at the time of graduation should have completed a college-preparatory curriculum with a minimum of 18 acceptable units.

Satisfactory scores on the SAT or on the ACT examination are required of all applicants to the freshman class. The middle 50 percent range of scores for those admitted is 27–32 (ACT) and 1190–1390 composite score (old SAT) or 1260–1440 (new SAT).

Application and Information

An application packet, complete with detailed instructions and requirements, can be obtained from the Admissions Office or online. For early action (nonbinding), students seeking admission in the fall term should apply to either the College of Arts and Sciences or the Conservatory of Music by November 1. The regular action deadline is January 10; the transfer application deadline is March 1. An admissions counselor can provide more information about Wheaton in general or the application process in particular.

Further information is available from:

Admissions Office
Wheaton College
501 College Avenue
Wheaton, Illinois 60187
Phone: 630-752-5005
800-222-2419
E-mail: admissions@wheaton.edu
Website: wheaton.edu
wheaton.edu/connect

Historic Blanchard Hall overlooks Wheaton's front of campus.

WHITTIER COLLEGE

WHITTIER, CALIFORNIA

★ For more information, visit http://petersons.to/whittiercollege

The College

Whittier College is a private, four-year liberal arts college located in Whittier, California. The school—which has an enrollment of over 1,600 students—offers small class sizes, personalized degree programs, and ample opportunities for real-world learning experiences.

Whittier has earned a reputation for providing a high-quality liberal arts education. The Princeton Review recently named Whittier as one of the country's best institutions for undergraduate education, and it included Whittier in the 2016 edition of "The Best 380 Colleges." Whittier is also among 200 schools listed in "Colleges of Distinction," a national college guidebook that showcases colleges that offer engaged students, great teaching, a vibrant community, and successful outcomes.

Whittier takes on the liberal arts in a distinctly West Coast way—with a fresh eye toward how ideas intersect across disciplines. The College places an emphasis on providing students with a truly interdisciplinary liberal arts education. Whittier students are encouraged to think critically and to learn about other perspectives and cultures through cross-curricular courses and experiential learning activities such as internships and study-abroad opportunities.

The value of a Whittier College education lies in Whittier's core mission: to prepare students from diverse backgrounds for success in a complex global society. Whittier's approach to education produces graduates with skills that are highly valued by employers and graduate schools alike.

With a low faculty-to-student ratio, Whittier students receive the one-on-one attention that helps them stay focused and on-track. Because there are no impacted majors or programs, students can choose their major freely without the stress of competing for a spot.

Eighty-nine percent of Whittier graduates complete their degree in four years. With access to hundreds of semester courses and an interim term, Whittier students can fulfill major requirements without delays.

Whittier College is accredited by the Western Association of Schools and Colleges (WASC).

Location

Whittier College is located in the heart of Southern California, between the vibrant city of Los Angeles and scenic Orange County. Whittier students and professors take full advantage of the region's incomparable geography, culture, and industry, and use it as an extended classroom.

Southern California offers a wide array of recreation, entertainment, educational, and professional opportunities. The region is home to many of the nation's and the world's leading cultural and industry influencers. Hollywood's production studios, Anaheim's theme parks, and the South Bay's aerospace industry are all a short drive from Whittier College.

Just a few blocks from the College, Uptown Whittier boasts cafes and restaurants, a movie theater, a farmer's market, and dozens more shops for students to explore and enjoy.

Majors and Degrees

Students at Whittier College may choose from 31 majors in 23 disciplines, including anthropology, history, mathematics, political science, economics, English, and business administration.

Programs of study include: anthropology, art (art history, studio art, or studio/art history tracks), biochemistry, biology, business administration (accounting, finance, international business, management, or marketing concentrations), chemistry, child development, Chinese, economics (business economics, general distributive, or pre-professional economics options), engineering 3-2 (chemistry, mathematics, physics, or science and letters options), English (creative writing emphasis available), environmental science (environmental studies or environmental science tracks), French, global and cultural studies (culture, geographical area, issues, or national/transnational institutions options), history, kinesiology and nutrition science (pre–physical therapy or sports management emphasis), mathematics (teaching credential emphasis available), mathematics–business, music, applied philosophy, philosophy, physics (astronomy emphasis available), political science (international relations track available), psychology, religious studies, social work, sociology, Spanish, and theatre and communication arts (design and technology or performance emphasis).

Whittier College also provides students with opportunities to pursue self-designed majors through its Whittier Scholars Program (WSP). WSP students work closely with faculty members to develop a highly personalized course of study in specific areas of interest. This program culminates in the research, presentation, and defense of senior projects. Approximately 12 percent of Whittier students participate in WSP.

Academic Programs

In addition to completing the required course work for their major, all Whittier students are required to complete six hours of course work each in the areas of natural science, social science, fine arts, and humanities. The College's paired classes help students see the interconnectedness of ideas. Students take at least two paired classes while at Whittier, and in these classes they explore subjects that intersect in provocative ways.

All Whittier College students are required to complete several specialized courses designed to help them improve and refine their writing skills. The required writing course work begins with a first-year writing seminar and culminates in a paper-in-the-major, which each student completes during his or her senior year of study. The paper-in-the-major, which is developed with the guidance of a faculty member, is often used as a writing sample by students applying to graduate programs.

Whittier provides a wide range of services and programs designed to help new students adjust to college life. All first-year students participate in a linked class, two courses that are taken together during the first semester. These small classes of no more than 16 students help to create a common intellectual experience. In addition, each student is assigned a faculty mentor to provide advising and mentoring during their first semester. They also have a peer mentor who connects them to the College.

First-year students also live in close proximity; they are placed in three residence halls, forming a residential community. Resident Advisers in these communities will intentionally coordinate programs that will assist students in their transition to college. Additional activities, such as orientation and pre-orientation, also play a key role in ensuring student success.

Off-Campus Programs

Because Whittier College is located within driving distance to Los Angeles and Orange County, students have access to a wide range of internships with companies in industries ranging from entertainment to business. Whittier students have completed internships with Sony Pictures, Merrill Lynch, the J. Paul Getty Museum, EMI Music Publishing, New Line Cinema, First Heritage Bank, Southern California Edison, and the U.S. Department of Education.

Students may also choose to gain hands-on work experience through one of Whittier's many partnerships with community and government organizations such as the Boys and Girls Club of Whittier. Students in fields such as education, child psychology, and social work can participate in work-study programs at Broadoaks Children's School, Whittier's private, nonprofit demonstration school.

Whittier College provides many opportunities for students interested in learning about other cultures. Each student may choose to spend a semester, a year, or a summer living and studying in a variety of locations around the world. Whittier also offers several study-abroad opportunities through its faculty-led JanTerm and MayTerm programs. Past and upcoming study-abroad opportunities include a course on managing multinational corporations in Mexico; a study of Islamic culture in Morocco; an examination of race, religion, and gender in South America; and an anthropology course in Tanzania.

Academic Facilities

The campus boasts an eclectic mix of historic architecture and state-of-the art amenities including a 400-seat performing arts center, an art gallery, an outdoor amphitheater, a recently upgraded library, a 7,000-seat sports stadium, and a new aquatics center. The College opened a new Science & Learning Center in fall 2016.

Costs

For the 2017–18 academic year, tuition is $45,730 with fees of $590. The cost of a double room is $7,414 and the 15-flex meal plan is $6,296.

Financial Aid

Scholarships and financial aid are available, and over 90 percent of Whittier students receive a combination of grants, scholarships, and loans. More than $8.5 million in aid was awarded to Whittier students in 2016–17. Students will automatically be considered for a wide range of academic awards when they apply. In addition, there are talent scholarships in art, music, and theater that students can pursue without having to major or even minor in those academic disciplines.

Faculty

At Whittier, professors, students, and staff support each other and come together to share in the thrill of discovery, the joy of learning, and the gratification that comes with contributing to society. Students work with professors and staff to tap into their unique abilities, talents, and aspirations. Together, they design a complete college experience that combines academics, internships, fellowships, and service learning.

The College's full-time faculty numbers 109. The average class size is 19, with a student-faculty ratio of 12:1.

Student Life

Students interested in getting involved in extracurricular activities can choose from a wide variety of options. Whittier is home to more than 70 academic, cultural, political, and general-interest clubs and organizations, as well as several service-oriented fraternities and sororities, called societies at Whittier. The school also has a student newspaper, yearbook, literary magazine, video production studio, and radio station. Through the Leadership Experience and Programs (LEAP) Office, there are opportunities for involvement in student government, community service, and a number of programs dedicated to helping students develop their leadership skills.

Whittier is home to 22 intercollegiate sports teams, including men's and women's basketball, cross-country, track and field, swimming and diving, water polo, soccer, lacrosse, golf, and tennis. Whittier also offers men's baseball and football and women's volleyball.

Admission Requirements

Students interested in applying to Whittier College must submit a completed application (available at www.commonapp.org), a $50 application fee, transcripts, SAT I or ACT scores (test optional for students with a cumulative GPA of 3.0 and higher), a personal statement/essay, counselor evaluation, and letter of recommendation from a current or former teacher. Students interested in transferring to Whittier from another college or university must also submit college transcripts and letters of recommendation from two former or current professors.

Application and Information

Students are encouraged to apply early to ensure consideration for the fullest range of scholarship opportunities. Applications are reviewed on a rolling basis as they are completed.

The application filing date for Early Action candidates (nonbinding early deadline) is November 15. The priority application filing date for Regular Decision candidates is February 1 and the deadline for financial aid applicants to file the Free Application for Federal Student Aid (FAFSA) and for California Residents to apply for the Cal Grant Program is March 2.

Whittier College Admission Office
13406 East Philadelphia Street
P.O. Box 634
Whittier, California 90608
United States
Phone: 562-907-4238
888-200-0369 (toll-free)
Fax: 562-907-4870
E-mail: admissions@whittier.edu
Website: https://www.whittier.edu
https://www.facebook.com/WhittierCollege
https://twitter.com/whittiercollege

WILKES UNIVERSITY

WILKES-BARRE, PENNSYLVANIA

The University

Wilkes University offers the opportunities of a large university and the personal attention of a small institution. Its unique program mix and variety of extracurricular activities let students build their educational experience to suit their goals and interests.

Students may notice something unexpected: professors genuinely interested in their thoughts and aspirations. All Wilkes students have opportunities to gain real-world experience, whether starting a business, conducting research, or using high-tech instruments that even graduate students at other institutions rarely touch.

Located at the foothills of the Pocono Mountains, along the shore of the Susquehanna River and within walking distance of downtown Wilkes-Barre, Pennsylvania, Wilkes University is a private, comprehensive institution with more than 2,400 undergraduate students.

The University includes the College of Arts, Humanities, and Social Sciences; the College of Science and Engineering; the Nesbitt School of Pharmacy; the Passan School of Nursing; the Sidhu School of Business and Leadership; the School of Education; and University College (for undecided students). Wilkes offers bachelor's and master's degrees in the humanities, social and natural sciences, engineering, business administration, nursing, and education as well as the Master of Fine Arts, Doctor of Pharmacy, Doctor of Education, and Doctor of Nursing Practice degrees.

The Wilkes campus features a parklike quadrangle surrounded by modern classroom buildings and historic nineteenth-century mansions that have been restored as student residences and academic buildings. Facilities include the Cohen Science Center, a sports and conference center, and a newly renovated home for the business school.

Programs provide students with a liberal arts foundation that cultivates independent thinking and prepares them for professional life or for graduate or professional school. Academic advising integrated with career planning is stressed, and hands-on experiences are provided in laboratory, internship, and cooperative education settings. Free tutorial services are available to all students.

The University is accredited by the Middle States Association of Colleges and Schools and has specialized accreditation in the sciences, engineering, nursing, education, and business. Ninety-seven percent of students are employed or attending graduate/professional school within one year of receiving their degrees.

First-year students enrolling prior to May 1 are guaranteed housing, and all students may have cars on campus. Campus housing is available for all four years. Residence halls include modern, multifloor buildings and historic mansions.

Student activities complement academic life. Intercollegiate athletics encompass 22 Division III sports, including swimming and women's ice hockey. Men's ice hockey will begin in 2018. More than 70 clubs and organizations recognize student achievement and provide opportunities for leadership development, professional growth, and community service. The award-winning e-mentor program links current students with incoming freshmen to ease the transition to college life.

Location

Wilkes-Barre is a medium-sized city of about 43,000. Nearby recreational facilities include Pocono Mountain ski resorts; PNC Field, home of a Triple A baseball team; the Mohegan Sun Arena, home to a professional hockey team; golf courses; state parks; tennis courts; and harness racing.

The University is located in the historic district, which features a performing arts center, the Wilkes University/King's College Barnes and Noble bookstore, a fourteen-screen movie complex, and numerous shops and restaurants. Other offerings include art galleries, ethnic and community festivals, and libraries and museums. The city is approximately 2 hours from New York City and Philadelphia.

Wilkes-Barre lies near the intersection of Interstates 80, 81, and 476 and within 6 hours of Washington, D.C. and Boston. The Wilkes-Barre/Scranton International Airport is about 20 minutes from campus.

Majors and Degrees

Wilkes University offers Bachelor of Arts, Bachelor of Business Administration, and Bachelor of Science degrees. Majors offered are: accounting; applied and engineering sciences; biochemistry; biology; chemistry; communication studies; computer information systems; computer science; criminology; digital design and media art; earth and environmental sciences; electrical engineering; education (elementary and early childhood, middle-level, secondary with a subject-area major, and special education certification); engineering management; English; entrepreneurship; environmental engineering; finance; geology; history; hospitality leadership; international studies; management; marketing; mathematics; mechanical engineering; medical laboratory sciences; musical theatre; neuroscience; nursing; philosophy; physics; political science; psychology; public administration; sociology; Spanish; sports management; and theatre arts. Wilkes also offers a guaranteed-seat pharmacy program.

Premedical and prelaw preparation programs are strong. Other preprofessional programs include dentistry, occupational therapy, optometry, physical therapy, physician assistant, podiatry, and veterinary science. A full-time director of health sciences and student success advises students who wish to continue study in a professional health-care field. The University offers an affiliated program in medicine with the Penn State College of Medicine at Hershey; in optometry with the Pennsylvania College of Optometry and the State University of New York (SUNY) College of Optometry; in podiatry with Temple University School of Podiatric Medicine; in occupational therapy with Temple University; in physical therapy with Drexel University, Temple University, and Widener University; and in medical technology/medical laboratory sciences with Robert Packer Hospital.

Academic Programs

Through a rigorous curriculum that emphasizes hands-on experience, Wilkes helps prepare students in all majors to adapt to a technologically and socially evolving world. To graduate, students must complete a core curriculum from 120 to 136 credits, depending on their major.

The University operates on a dual-semester calendar, with optional summer sessions and a January intersession. Advanced Placement test credits, College Level Examination Program (CLEP) credits, and International Baccalaureate (I.B.) credits are accepted.

Off-Campus Programs

A cooperative education (internship) program is available to all students, with credit applicable in most majors. Many government offices and private businesses in northeastern Pennsylvania, as well as in New York City, Philadelphia, Harrisburg, and Washington, D.C., employ Wilkes students. A study-abroad adviser works with interested students, placing them in the situation best suited to their academic pursuits. Students have recently attended programs in Costa Rica, England, Spain, Tanzania, and Uganda.

Academic Facilities

The Cohen Science Center and clinical nursing simulation center opened in 2013. The modern Eugene S. Farley Library offers wireless Internet access and areas for both independent study and group collaboration. Complete laboratory facilities are available for biology, chemistry, earth and environmental sciences, engineering, nursing, pharmacy, and psychology. Student-produced programming is broadcast from WCLH-FM and a television studio.

The Dorothy Dickson Darte Center contains a 500-seat main theater and a 45-seat black box theater. A new NeuroTraining and Research Center is located in Breiseth Hall.

Costs

For the 2016–17 academic year, tuition and fees were $33,570 per year, and room and board were $13,632. Books cost approximately $900 per year.

Financial Aid

Financial aid is available to students who demonstrate quality academic ability and/or financial need, as verified by the Free Application for Federal Student Aid (FAFSA). Merit-based and need-based aid is available for qualified students. Scholarships ranging from $13,000 to $19,000 per year are available to students based on academic ability, regardless of financial need. Approximately 90 percent of students receive some type of financial assistance.

Faculty

Wilkes University has a nationally recruited full-time faculty of 173 members, approximately 90 percent of whom have earned Ph.D.'s or terminal degrees in their chosen field. Faculty evaluation criteria emphasize teaching excellence and effective advising, while recognizing continued scholarly activities. The student-faculty ratio is 15:1.

Admission Requirements

SAT or ACT scores are required. In cases where a student has taken the examination more than once, scores from the highest testing in each category are used. Freshman applicants should either have completed or be in the process of completing a college-preparatory course of study, including 3 to 4 years of mathematics, social studies, science, and English. Additional courses should be elected in academic subjects according to individual interests. Acceptable electives include foreign language and computing, among others. Students who have not followed this pattern may still qualify for admission if there is other strong evidence of preparation for college work. Letters of recommendation are not required but may be submitted. Students intending to pursue a major in pharmacy should have completed algebra I and II, geometry, and trigonometry prior to enrollment. Students intending to major in nursing should have completed courses in biology and chemistry. An audition is required for all prospective musical theatre and theatre arts students. Transfer students must submit a transcript from every college previously attended.

Wilkes University is an Equal Opportunity/Affirmative Action institution. No applicant shall be denied admission to the University because of race, color, gender, religion, national or ethnic origin, sexual orientation, or handicap.

Application and Information

Applications for admission should be completed early in the senior year of secondary school. Applications are reviewed after all of the student's credentials have been received. Notification of the University's decision reaches the student two to four weeks after the application file is complete. Priority deadline for all applications is March 1; applications for the Guaranteed Seat Pharmacy Program must be received by February 1. Other health science programs may have additional deadlines.

Contact the Admissions Office for more information.

Admissions Office
Wilkes University
84 West South Street
Wilkes-Barre, Pennsylvania 18766
Phone: 570-408-4400
800-945-5378 Ext. 4400 (toll-free)
Website: http://www.wilkes.edu

The Sidhu School of Business and Leadership's home includes a financial trading room, complete with stock ticker.

WORCESTER POLYTECHNIC INSTITUTE

WORCESTER, MASSACHUSETTS

★ To read more about this school, visit http://petersons.to/wpi

COLLEGE CLOSE-UPS

The University

Following its founding motto of "Theory and Practice," Worcester Polytechnic Institute (WPI) offers a unique project-based curriculum that prepares students to take on the world's great challenges. Students not only take rigorous classes, but also complete distinctive hands-on projects that address real issues in communities across the globe. In addition, small classes, one-on-one interaction with professors, non-punitive grading, and a spirit of innovation and teamwork encourage students to think creatively, collaborate across disciplines, and put their ideas into practice.

WPI has been widely recognized for its research-based academic programs and the success of its graduates. It is consistently ranked among the top national universities by *U.S. News & World Report* and the Princeton Review. The *Wall Street Journal* ranked WPI No. 1 for faculty combining research and teaching. According to the National Association of Colleges and Employers, the starting salaries of WPI graduates are 32 percent higher than those of many other college graduates. WPI was also ranked sixteenth in the nation for return on investment by Payscale.com and was recently ranked twenty-ninth on the Princeton Review's 2015 list of "Top 50 Colleges that Pay You Back." The Princeton Review also ranks WPI No. 1 for the best study-abroad program.

Top-tier employers seek out WPI graduates for their real-world experience and ability to work collaboratively. More than 90 percent of students are in full-time jobs or attending graduate school within several months of graduation. Students are recruited by leading organizations such as Amazon Robotics, Pfizer, General Electric, Fidelity Investments, Johnson & Johnson, and Tesla. Each year, WPI graduates are accepted at many prestigious graduate schools, including MIT, Yale, Johns Hopkins, and Tufts University Medical School.

While many students attend WPI for its top-notch engineering and science programs, about 20 percent of students enter undeclared. WPI encourages students to explore their passions first and foremost. WPI provides a comprehensive academic advising program and a wide array of academic support services, including a robust career services center that was recently ranked seventeenth in the nation by the Princeton Review.

Location

With its beautiful architecture, grassy quad, and ivy-covered walls, WPI provides a traditional New England campus situated on 95 acres in a hilltop residential neighborhood. Students stop and chat with faculty members on tree-lined paths, study by the fountain in Reunion Plaza, grab a coffee at the Rubin Campus Center, and watch live entertainment at the Goat's Head restaurant.

Home to nine other colleges and universities and more than 38,000 college students, Worcester is a true college town. It is ranked ninth on *Forbes*' list of "America's Most Livable Cities" and ninth on *Businessweek*'s list of "Best Cities for Gen Ys." Late-night diners, clubs, museums, concert venues, and theaters are just minutes from WPI. Boston is less than an hour away by commuter rail, and major attractions in the region, including New York, Cape Cod, Providence, and the Berkshires, are easily accessible. There is also skiing and snowboarding at nearby Wachusett Mountain.

Majors and Degrees

WPI offers Bachelor of Science (B.S.) and Bachelor of Art (B.A.) degrees, as well as a combined B.S./M.S. program that enables students to begin studying toward, or even complete, a master's degree in their senior year. Students can major in a wide variety of engineering and science disciplines, as well as subject areas in the humanities and arts, social sciences, and business. They can also design their own majors or choose from interdisciplinary programs such as interactive media and game development, bioinformatics and computational biology, and robotics engineering (WPI's was the first undergraduate program in robotics in the nation). Additional information is available online at wpi.edu/academics.

WPI also offers preprofessional programs in dentistry, law, medicine, and veterinary medicine; see wpi.edu/+prehealth. The university also offers teacher licensure (wpi.edu/+teach).

Academic Programs

At WPI, most students take three courses during each of the four 7-week terms (two in the fall and two in the spring). Classes aim to provide a balance between academic content and hands-on projects and group work. WPI's academic program also encourages collaboration, not competition—students can get grades of A, B, C, or no credit, but do not receive failing grades.

Regardless of their majors, all students must meet a humanities and arts requirement that encourages them to broaden their thinking and explore new areas of performance, creativity, and culture by taking courses in disciplines such as music, art, theatre, foreign language, history, and literature.

Paid internships and co-ops are available to advance education and earn income. Hundreds of opportunities are available each year with global companies like Boston Scientific, ExxonMobil, General Electric, and SpaceX. *U.S. News & World Report* cited WPI's internship/co-ops as 1 of 17 programs to look for.

WPI Projects Program

Projects are at the heart of the WPI curriculum. First-year students gain an introduction to project work through an optional Great Problems Seminar, which focuses on themes of current global importance. All students complete a junior-year project in which they work with a team to address a real-world problem at the intersection of science, technology, and society—from designing bicycle paths in WPI's hometown of Worcester to creating an ambulance-dispatch system in Venice. As seniors, students undertake an intensive capstone project related to their major field of study.

Through WPI's Global Projects Program, over 60 percent of undergraduates complete at least one project off campus and overseas at more than 40 project centers around the world, including centers in Thailand, Australia, South Africa, Nova Scotia, Switzerland, and all over the United States. Students immerse themselves in other cultures while working to solve real-world problems in partnership with government, corporate, and nonprofit sponsors.

Students, alumni, and employers praise WPI's project model for helping students develop professional and personal skills including strategically managing projects, problem solving, teamwork, communication, and leadership abilities, as well as increased global awareness and enriched personal lives. WPI's off-campus programs were recently recognized by the Princeton Review, which ranked WPI first for most popular study abroad program in its 2016 edition of the best colleges. Additional information is available at admissions.wpi.edu/+global.

Academic Facilities

There are many teaching, research, and project facilities available to undergraduates at WPI.

The Foisie Innovation Studio, slated to open in 2018, will be a state-of-the-art innovation space suited for WPI's distinctive hands-on collaborative problem-solving. The Studio will contain a robotics lab, high-tech classrooms, and makerspaces—communal inventing workspaces. The Center for Innovation and Entrepreneurship will help students find paths to commercialization for their projects.

In addition, undergraduates have access to over 40 state-of-the-art research centers and laboratories, including two atomic-force microscopes, medical imaging laboratories, a fire science laboratory, a laser holography lab, a computer music lab, a satellite navigation lab, and a research library with over half a million print and digital resources.

The Life Sciences and Bioengineering Center at Gateway Park is a state-of-the-art 130,000 square-foot facility for research and teaching in biology and biotechnology, biomedical engineering, chemistry and biochemistry, and chemical engineering.

WPI also has an exceptional computer and networking infrastructure, including hundreds of computers in open-access 24/7 labs, powerful UNIX workstations, access to specialized scientific and engineering software, and a campuswide high-speed data network.

Costs

For 2016–17, full-time tuition for first-year undergraduates was $46,364. Room and board charges are $13,736.

Financial Aid

Approximately 97 percent of students at WPI receive financial assistance in the form of need- and merit-based aid. Need-based aid includes financial aid packages, on-campus jobs, and loan programs. More information is available from WPI's Office of Student Aid & Financial Literacy at wpi.edu/+finaid.

All admitted applicants to WPI are also considered for academic scholarships based upon academic performance, standardized test scores, leadership, extracurricular involvement, and community service. More information is available at wpi.edu/+scholarships.

Faculty

WPI's 534 full- and part-time faculty members are passionate teachers as well as committed researchers and scholars with world-class credentials. They are leading contributors to the fields of bioengineering, cybersecurity, robotics, energy and sustainability, materials science, and more. Thirteen members of the current faculty are Fulbright Scholars and 22 have won the CAREER Award, the National Science Foundation's most prestigious honor for young faculty members.

With a 13:1 student-faculty ratio, WPI facilitates small classes where students have ample opportunity to join discussions, work in teams, and interact with professors, as evidenced by the *Wall Street Journal* ranking WPI number one in "Faculty That Best Combine Scholarly Research and Classroom Instruction." WPI ranks number one for student-faculty interaction (National Survey of Student Engagement), and *U.S. News & World Report* ranks WPI as a top-50 college among national universities for faculty resources, including salary, class size, and student-faculty ratio.

Student Activities

At WPI, students work hard but play hard too—undergraduates at all levels take part in more than 200 clubs and organizations, ranging from music and theater ensembles to cultural and religious organizations, community service clubs, and professional groups.

WPI "gets Greek life right," according to BestCollegesOnline.com—more than 30 percent of students participate in one of the 19 fraternities and sororities on campus, performing over 20,000 hours of community service per year. The Student Government Association also gives a voice to undergraduates within WPI's close-knit community.

More than 80 percent of students are involved in sports programs, including twenty varsity (NCAA Division III) athletics teams and nearly forty club and intramural sports. Students also work out at the university's state-of-the art sports and recreation center, one of the finest university athletic facilities in the Northeast, built in 2012 and featuring a four-court gymnasium, indoor jogging track, racquetball and squash courts, and competition pool. The Rec Center is also a reflection of WPI's commitment to support the environment with its green design and sustainable attributes.

Admission Requirements

WPI has high standards for applicants and looks for more than just outstanding academic performance. They take care to admit students who will thrive at the university. These students tend to be creative and curious; like to work in teams; are comfortable making their own decisions; love math and science but feel just as passionate about literature, music, movies, and the arts; and are ready to make a positive impact on the world around them.

As a test-optional university, applicants are not required to submit SAT or ACT scores. WPI will accept scores if they are sent, but admission decisions will not be influenced by the exclusion of standardized test scores. Full admissions requirements can be found at admissions.wpi.edu.

Application and Information

The Common Application is the only way to apply to WPI. The deadline for Early Action round 1 is November 1, with notification by December 20. The deadline for Early Action round 2 is January 1, with notification by February 10. The regular decision deadline is February 1, with notification by April 1. More information is available at admissions.wpi.edu/apply.

Students are encouraged to visit the WPI campus to learn more about the university, see its facilities, and hear firsthand about the WPI experience. Many students call the visit to campus the most influential decision on determining their fit at WPI. Students can also view an interactive online tour at wpi.edu/+tour.

To schedule a visit or request more information, students should contact:

Undergraduate Admissions
Bartlett Center
Worcester Polytechnic Institute
100 Institute Road
Worcester, Massachusetts 01609-2280
Phone: 508-831-5286
Fax: 508-831-5875
E-mail: admissions@wpi.edu
Website: admissions.wpi.edu
Facebook: facebook.com/WPI
Instagram: instagram.com/WPI
Twitter: twitter.com/WPI

WPI is situated on a 95-acre campus, 40 miles west of Boston in a residential section of Worcester, Massachusetts, the second largest city in New England and home to nine colleges.

COLLEGE CLOSE-UPS

Indexes

Majors

ACCOUNTING
Abilene Christian U (TX)
Academy Coll (MN)
Adams State U (CO)
Adelphi U (NY)
Alabama State U (AL)
Albany State U (GA)
Albertus Magnus Coll (CT)
Albion Coll (MI)
Albright Coll (PA)
Alcorn State U (MS)
Alderson Broaddus U (WV)
Alfred U (NY)
Alma Coll (MI)
Alvernia U (PA)
American Intl Coll (MA)
American Public U System (WV)
American U (DC)
The American U in Cairo (Egypt)
The American U in Dubai (United Arab Emirates)
Anderson U (IN)
Anderson U (SC)
Andrews U (MI)
Angelo State U (TX)
Appalachian State U (NC)
Aquinas Coll (MI)
Arcadia U (PA)
Arizona State U at the Tempe campus (AZ)
Arizona State U at the West campus (AZ)
Arkansas Tech U (AR)
Asbury U (KY)
Ashland U (OH)
Assumption Coll (MA)
Athens State U (AL)
Auburn U (AL)
Auburn U at Montgomery (AL)
Augsburg Coll (MN)
Augustana Coll (IL)
Augustana U (SD)
Augusta U (GA)
Aurora U (IL)
Austin Peay State U (TN)
Averett U (VA)
Avila U (MO)
Azusa Pacific U (CA)
Baker U (KS)
Baldwin Wallace U (OH)
Ball State U (IN)
Barry U (FL)
Baruch Coll of the City U of New York (NY)
Bayamón Central U (PR)
Baylor U (TX)
Bay Path U (MA)
Belhaven U (MS)
Bellarmine U (KY)
Belmont Abbey Coll (NC)
Belmont U (TN)
Bemidji State U (MN)
Benedictine Coll (KS)
Bentley U (MA)
Berkeley Coll–New York City Campus (NY)
Berkeley Coll–Woodland Park Campus (NJ)
Berry Coll (GA)
Bethel Coll (IN)
Bethune-Cookman U (FL)
Binghamton U, State U of New York (NY)
Biola U (CA)
Bishop's U (QC, Canada)
Blackburn Coll (IL)
Black Hills State U (SD)
Bloomfield Coll (NJ)
Bloomsburg U of Pennsylvania (PA)
Bluefield Coll (VA)
Bluefield State Coll (WV)
Bluffton U (OH)
Boise State U (ID)
Boston Coll (MA)
Boston U (MA)
Bowie State U (MD)
Bowling Green State U (OH)
Bradley U (IL)
Brenau U (GA)
Brescia U (KY)
Brewton-Parker Coll (GA)
Briar Cliff U (IA)
Bridgewater State U (MA)
Brigham Young U–Idaho (ID)
Brooklyn Coll of the City U of New York (NY)
Bryant U (RI)
Buena Vista U (IA)
Butler U (IN)
Cabrini U (PA)
Cairn U (PA)
Caldwell U (NJ)
California Baptist U (CA)
California Lutheran U (CA)
California State U, Dominguez Hills (CA)
California State U, East Bay (CA)
California State U, Fresno (CA)
California State U, Fullerton (CA)
California State U, Long Beach (CA)
California State U, Northridge (CA)
California State U, San Bernardino (CA)
California State U, San Marcos (CA)
California State U, Stanislaus (CA)
Calumet Coll of Saint Joseph (IN)
Calvin Coll (MI)
Cameron U (OK)
Campbellsville U (KY)
Canisius Coll (NY)
Capital U (OH)
Cardinal Stritch U (WI)
Caribbean U (PR)
Carlow U (PA)
Carroll Coll (MT)
Carson-Newman U (TN)
Carthage Coll (WI)
Case Western Reserve U (OH)
Catawba Coll (NC)
The Catholic U of America (DC)
Cedar Crest Coll (PA)
Cedarville U (OH)
Centenary Coll of Louisiana (LA)
Centenary U (NJ)
Central Baptist Coll (AR)
Central Connecticut State U (CT)
Central Methodist U (MO)
Central Michigan U (MI)
Central Penn Coll (PA)
Central State U (OH)
Central Washington U (WA)
Champlain Coll (VT)
Chapman U (CA)
Charleston Southern U (SC)
Chatham U (PA)
Chestnut Hill Coll (PA)
Chowan U (NC)
Christian Brothers U (TN)
Christopher Newport U (VA)
Claremont McKenna Coll (CA)
Clark Atlanta U (GA)
Clarke U (IA)
Clayton State U (GA)
Clemson U (SC)
Cleveland State U (OH)
Coastal Carolina U (SC)
Coe Coll (IA)
CollAmerica–Fort Collins (CO)
The Coll at Brockport, State U of New York (NY)
Coll of Charleston (SC)
The Coll of Idaho (ID)
The Coll of New Jersey (NJ)
Coll of Saint Benedict (MN)
The Coll of Saint Rose (NY)
The Coll of St. Scholastica (MN)
Coll of Staten Island of the City U of New York (NY)
Coll of the Holy Cross (MA)
Coll of the Ozarks (MO)
The Coll of Westchester (NY)
The Coll of William and Mary (VA)
Colorado Christian U (CO)
Colorado Mesa U (CO)
Colorado State U (CO)
Columbia Coll (MO)
Columbus State U (GA)
Concordia Coll (MN)
Concordia Coll–New York (NY)
Concordia U (QC, Canada)
Concordia U Chicago (IL)
Concordia U, Nebraska (NE)
Concordia U, St. Paul (MN)
Concordia U Wisconsin (WI)
Converse Coll (SC)
Corban U (OR)
Cornerstone U (MI)
Creighton U (NE)
Culver-Stockton Coll (MO)
Curry Coll (MA)
Daemen Coll (NY)
Dakota State U (SD)
Dalhousie U (NS, Canada)
Dallas Baptist U (TX)
Dalton State Coll (GA)
Davenport U, Grand Rapids (MI)
Defiance Coll (OH)
DeSales U (PA)
Dixie State U (UT)
Doane U (NE)
Dominican Coll (NY)
Dominican U (IL)
Drake U (IA)
Drexel U (PA)
Drury U (MO)
Duquesne U (PA)
East Central U (OK)
Eastern Illinois U (IL)
Eastern Mennonite U (VA)
Eastern Michigan U (MI)
Eastern Nazarene Coll (MA)
Eastern Washington U (WA)
East Tennessee State U (TN)
East Texas Baptist U (TX)
Edgewood Coll (WI)
Elizabeth City State U (NC)
Elizabethtown Coll (PA)
Elmira Coll (NY)
Elms Coll (MA)
Elon U (NC)
Emmanuel Coll (MA)
Emory & Henry Coll (VA)
Emory U (GA)
Emporia State U (KS)
Endicott Coll (MA)
Eureka Coll (IL)
Fairfield U (CT)
Fairleigh Dickinson U, Coll at Florham (NJ)
Fairleigh Dickinson U, Metropolitan Campus (NJ)
Faulkner U (AL)
Fayetteville State U (NC)
Felician U (NJ)
Fisher Coll (MA)
Fitchburg State U (MA)
Flagler Coll (FL)
Florida Ag and Mech U (FL)
Florida Atlantic U (FL)
Florida Gulf Coast U (FL)
Florida Intl U (FL)
Florida National U (FL)
Florida Southern Coll (FL)
Florida State U (FL)
Fordham U (NY)
Fort Lewis Coll (CO)
Framingham State U (MA)
Franciscan U of Steubenville (OH)
Francis Marion U (SC)
Franklin Coll (IN)
Franklin Pierce U (NH)
Freed-Hardeman U (TN)
Fresno Pacific U (CA)
Friends U (KS)
Frostburg State U (MD)
Furman U (SC)
Gallaudet U (DC)
Gannon U (PA)
Geneva Coll (PA)
George Fox U (OR)
Georgetown Coll (KY)
Georgetown U (DC)
The George Washington U (DC)
Georgia Coll & State U (GA)
Georgian Court U (NJ)
Georgia Southern U (GA)
Georgia Southwestern State U (GA)
Georgia State U (GA)
Gonzaga U (WA)
Gordon Coll (MA)
Goshen Coll (IN)
Governors State U (IL)
Grace Coll (IN)
Graceland U (IA)
Grambling State U (LA)
Grand Valley State U (MI)
Grand View U (IA)
Greenville Coll (IL)
Grove City Coll (PA)
Guilford Coll (NC)
Gwynedd Mercy U (PA)
Hamline U (MN)
Hampton U (VA)
Hannibal-LaGrange U (MO)
Harding U (AR)
Hardin-Simmons U (TX)
Harris-Stowe State U (MO)
Hartwick Coll (NY)
HEC Montreal (QC, Canada)
Heidelberg U (OH)
Henderson State U (AR)
Hendrix Coll (AR)
High Point U (NC)
Hilbert Coll (NY)
Hillsdale Coll (MI)
Hofstra U (NY)
Holy Family U (PA)
Holy Names U (CA)
Hood Coll (MD)
Hope Coll (MI)
Houghton Coll (NY)
Houston Baptist U (TX)
Howard Payne U (TX)
Hult Intl Business School (United Kingdom)
Hunter Coll of the City U of New York (NY)
Huntingdon Coll (AL)
Huntington U (IN)
Husson U (ME)
Huston-Tillotson U (TX)
Idaho State U (ID)
Illinois Coll (IL)
Illinois State U (IL)
Illinois Wesleyan U (IL)
Immaculata U (PA)
Indiana State U (IN)
Indiana U of Pennsylvania (PA)
Inter American U of Puerto Rico, Aguadilla Campus (PR)
Inter American U of Puerto Rico, Barranquitas Campus (PR)
Inter American U of Puerto Rico, Bayamón Campus (PR)
Inter American U of Puerto Rico, Fajardo Campus (PR)
Inter American U of Puerto Rico, Guayama Campus (PR)
Inter American U of Puerto Rico, Metropolitan Campus (PR)
Inter American U of Puerto Rico, Ponce Campus (PR)
Inter American U of Puerto Rico, San Germán Campus (PR)
Iona Coll (NY)
Iowa State U of Science and Technology (IA)
Ithaca Coll (NY)
Jackson State U (MS)
Jacksonville State U (AL)
Jacksonville U (FL)
James Madison U (VA)
John Brown U (AR)
John Carroll U (OH)
Judson U (IL)
Juniata Coll (PA)
Kansas State U (KS)
Kansas Wesleyan U (KS)
Kean U (NJ)
Kennesaw State U (GA)
Kent State U (OH)
Kentucky Wesleyan Coll (KY)
Keuka Coll (NY)
King's Coll (PA)
King U (TN)
Kuyper Coll (MI)
LaGrange Coll (GA)
Lake Erie Coll (OH)
Lamar U (TX)
Langston U (OK)
La Roche Coll (PA)
La Salle U (PA)
Lasell Coll (MA)
Lebanon Valley Coll (PA)
Lee U (TN)
Lehigh U (PA)
Lehman Coll of the City U of New York (NY)
Le Moyne Coll (NY)
LeTourneau U (TX)
Lewis U (IL)
Liberty U (VA)
Limestone Coll (SC)
Lincoln U (MO)
Lincoln U (PA)
Lindenwood U (MO)
Linfield Coll (OR)
Lipscomb U (TN)
Lock Haven U of Pennsylvania (PA)
Loras Coll (IA)
Louisiana Coll (LA)
Louisiana State U and A&M Coll (LA)
Louisiana Tech U (LA)
Lourdes U (OH)
Loyola Marymount U (CA)
Loyola U Chicago (IL)
Loyola U Maryland (MD)
Loyola U New Orleans (LA)
Lubbock Christian U (TX)
Luther Coll (IA)
Lycoming Coll (PA)
Lynchburg Coll (VA)
MacMurray Coll (IL)
Madonna U (MI)
Malone U (OH)
Manchester U (IN)
Manhattan Coll (NY)
Manhattanville Coll (NY)
Mansfield U of Pennsylvania (PA)
Maranatha Baptist U (WI)
Marian U (IN)
Marian U (WI)
Marietta Coll (OH)
Marist Coll (NY)
Marshall U (WV)
Maryville U of Saint Louis (MO)
Marywood U (PA)
Massachusetts Coll of Liberal Arts (MA)
The Master's U (CA)
McKendree U (IL)
McMurry U (TX)
McNeese State U (LA)
Medgar Evers Coll of the City U of New York (NY)
Menlo Coll (CA)
Mercer U, Macon (GA)
Mercy Coll (NY)
Mercyhurst U (PA)
Meredith Coll (NC)
Merrimack Coll (MA)
Messiah Coll (PA)
Metropolitan State U of Denver (CO)
Miami U (OH)
Michigan State U (MI)
Michigan Technological U (MI)
MidAmerica Nazarene U (KS)
Milligan Coll (TN)
Millikin U (IL)
Millsaps Coll (MS)
Minnesota State U Mankato (MN)
Minnesota State U Moorhead (MN)
Minot State U (ND)
Misericordia U (PA)
Mississippi State U (MS)
Mississippi Valley State U (MS)
Missouri Baptist U (MO)
Missouri State U (MO)
Missouri Valley Coll (MO)
Missouri Western State U (MO)
Molloy Coll (NY)
Monmouth Coll (IL)
Montana State U Billings (MT)
Montclair State U (NJ)
Moravian Coll (PA)

Morehead State U (KY)
Mount Allison U (NB, Canada)
Mount Aloysius Coll (PA)
Mount Marty Coll (SD)
Mount Mary U (WI)
Mount Mercy U (IA)
Mount St. Joseph U (OH)
Mount Saint Mary Coll (NY)
Mount Saint Mary's U (CA)
Mount St. Mary's U (MD)
Mount Vernon Nazarene U (OH)
Muhlenberg Coll (PA)
Murray State U (KY)
Muskingum U (OH)
National U (CA)
Nazareth Coll of Rochester (NY)
Nebraska Wesleyan U (NE)
Neumann U (PA)
Newberry Coll (SC)
New England Coll (NH)
New Jersey City U (NJ)
Newman U (KS)
New Mexico Highlands U (NM)
New Mexico State U (NM)
New York Inst of Technology (NY)
Niagara U (NY)
Nichols Coll (MA)
North Carolina Central U (NC)
North Carolina State U (NC)
North Carolina Wesleyan Coll (NC)
North Central Coll (IL)
North Dakota State U (ND)
Northeastern Illinois U (IL)
Northeastern State U (OK)
Northeastern U (MA)
Northern Arizona U (AZ)
Northern Illinois U (IL)
Northern Kentucky U (KY)
Northern State U (SD)
North Greenville U (SC)
Northwest Christian U (OR)
Northwestern Coll (IA)
Northwestern Oklahoma State U (OK)
Northwestern State U of Louisiana (LA)
Northwest Missouri State U (MO)
Northwest U (WA)
Northwood U, Michigan Campus (MI)
Nova Southeastern U (FL)
Nyack Coll (NY)
Ohio Dominican U (OH)
The Ohio State U (OH)
Ohio U (OH)
Ohio Valley U (WV)
Ohio Wesleyan U (OH)
Oklahoma Baptist U (OK)
Oklahoma Christian U (OK)
Oklahoma City U (OK)
Oklahoma State U (OK)
Old Dominion U (VA)
Olivet Nazarene U (IL)
Oral Roberts U (OK)
Oregon State U (OR)
Otterbein U (OH)
Ouachita Baptist U (AR)
Our Lady of the Lake U of San Antonio (TX)
Pace U (NY)
Pace U, Pleasantville Campus (NY)
Palm Beach Atlantic U (FL)
Peirce Coll (PA)
Penn State Abington (PA)
Penn State Altoona (PA)
Penn State Beaver (PA)
Penn State Berks (PA)
Penn State Brandywine (PA)
Penn State DuBois (PA)
Penn State Erie, The Behrend Coll (PA)
Penn State Fayette, The Eberly Campus (PA)
Penn State Greater Allegheny (PA)
Penn State Hazleton (PA)
Penn State Lehigh Valley (PA)
Penn State Mont Alto (PA)
Penn State New Kensington (PA)
Penn State Schuylkill (PA)
Penn State Shenango (PA)
Penn State U Park (PA)
Penn State Wilkes-Barre (PA)
Penn State Worthington Scranton (PA)
Penn State York (PA)
Pennsylvania Coll of Technology (PA)
Pepperdine U, Malibu (CA)
Pittsburg State U (KS)
Plymouth State U (NH)
Point Loma Nazarene U (CA)
Point Park U (PA)
Point U (GA)
Portland State U (OR)
Prairie View A&M U (TX)
Providence Coll (RI)
Purdue U (IN)
Purdue U Northwest (IN)
Queens Coll of the City U of New York (NY)
Quinnipiac U (CT)
Radford U (VA)
Ramapo Coll of New Jersey (NJ)
Randolph-Macon Coll (VA)
Rasmussen Coll Bloomington (MN)
Rasmussen Coll Brooklyn Park (MN)
Rasmussen Coll Eagan (MN)
Rasmussen Coll Fargo (ND)
Rasmussen Coll Fort Myers (FL)
Rasmussen Coll Kansas City/ Overland Park (KS)
Rasmussen Coll Lake Elmo/ Woodbury (MN)
Rasmussen Coll Land O' Lakes (FL)
Rasmussen Coll Mankato (MN)
Rasmussen Coll Moorhead (MN)
Rasmussen Coll New Port Richey (FL)
Rasmussen Coll Ocala (FL)
Rasmussen Coll Rockford (IL)
Rasmussen Coll St. Cloud (MN)
Rasmussen Coll Tampa/Brandon (FL)
Rasmussen Coll Topeka (KS)
Redeemer U Coll (ON, Canada)
Regent U (VA)
Regis U (CO)
Rhode Island Coll (RI)
Robert Morris U (PA)
Robert Morris U Illinois (IL)
Roberts Wesleyan Coll (NY)
Rochester Inst of Technology (NY)
Rockford U (IL)
Rocky Mountain Coll (MT)
Roger Williams U (RI)
Rosemont Coll (PA)
Rutgers U–Camden (NJ)
Rutgers U–Newark (NJ)
Rutgers U–New Brunswick (NJ)
Sacred Heart U (CT)
The Sage Colls (NY)
Saginaw Valley State U (MI)
St. Ambrose U (IA)
Saint Anselm Coll (NH)
Saint Augustine's U (NC)
St. Bonaventure U (NY)
St. Catherine U (MN)
St. Cloud State U (MN)
St. Edward's U (TX)
Saint Francis U (PA)
St. Gregory's U, Shawnee (OK)
St. John Fisher Coll (NY)
Saint John's U (MN)
St. John's U (NY)
St. Joseph's Coll, Long Island Campus (NY)
St. Joseph's Coll, New York (NY)
Saint Joseph's U (PA)
Saint Leo U (FL)
Saint Louis U (MO)
Saint Louis U–Madrid Campus (Spain)
Saint Martin's U (WA)
Saint Mary-of-the-Woods Coll (IN)
Saint Mary's Coll (IN)
Saint Mary's Coll of California (CA)
Saint Mary's U of Minnesota (MN)
Saint Michael's Coll (VT)
St. Norbert Coll (WI)
Saint Peter's U (NJ)
St. Thomas Aquinas Coll (NY)
St. Thomas U (FL)
Saint Vincent Coll (PA)
Salisbury U (MD)
Salve Regina U (RI)
Samford U (AL)
Sam Houston State U (TX)
San Diego State U (CA)
San Francisco State U (CA)
Santa Clara U (CA)
Schreiner U (TX)
Scripps Coll (CA)
Seattle Pacific U (WA)
Seattle U (WA)
Seton Hill U (PA)
Shawnee State U (OH)
Shaw U (NC)
Shepherd U (WV)
Shippensburg U of Pennsylvania (PA)
Shorter U (GA)
Siena Coll (NY)
Silver Lake Coll of the Holy Family (WI)
Simpson Coll (IA)
Simpson U (CA)
Slippery Rock U of Pennsylvania (PA)
South Carolina State U (SC)
Southeastern Louisiana U (LA)
Southeastern Oklahoma State U (OK)
Southeastern U (FL)
Southeast Missouri State U (MO)
Southern Arkansas U–Magnolia (AR)
Southern Connecticut State U (CT)
Southern Illinois U Carbondale (IL)
Southern Illinois U Edwardsville (IL)
Southern Methodist U (TX)
Southern New Hampshire U (NH)
Southern Oregon U (OR)
Southern Utah U (UT)
Southwest Baptist U (MO)
Southwestern Adventist U (TX)
Southwestern Assemblies of God U (TX)
Southwestern Coll (KS)
Spalding U (KY)
Spring Hill Coll (AL)
State U of New York at Fredonia (NY)
State U of New York at New Paltz (NY)
State U of New York at Oswego (NY)
State U of New York at Plattsburgh (NY)
State U of New York Coll at Geneseo (NY)
State U of New York Coll at Old Westbury (NY)
State U of New York Polytechnic Inst (NY)
Stephen F. Austin State U (TX)
Stevenson U (MD)
Stonehill Coll (MA)
Stratford U, Falls Church (VA)
Stratford U, Glen Allen (VA)
Stratford U, Woodbridge (VA)
Suffolk U (MA)
Sullivan U (KY)
Susquehanna U (PA)
Syracuse U (NY)
Tarleton State U (TX)
Taylor U (IN)
Temple U (PA)
Tennessee State U (TN)
Tennessee Wesleyan U (TN)
Texas A&M Intl U (TX)
Texas A&M U (TX)
Texas A&M U–Central Texas (TX)
Texas A&M U–Commerce (TX)
Texas A&M U–Corpus Christi (TX)
Texas A&M U–Kingsville (TX)
Texas Christian U (TX)
Texas Lutheran U (TX)
Texas State U (TX)
Texas Tech U (TX)
Texas Wesleyan U (TX)
Texas Woman's U (TX)
Thomas Edison State U (NJ)
Thomas More Coll (KY)
Thomas U (GA)
Tiffin U (OH)
Towson U (MD)
Transylvania U (KY)
Trevecca Nazarene U (TN)
Trine U (IN)
Trinity Christian Coll (IL)
Trinity U (TX)
Troy U (AL)
Truman State U (MO)
Tulane U (LA)
Union Coll (KY)
Union Coll (NE)
Union U (TN)
United States Intl U–Africa (Kenya)
Universidad Adventista de las Antillas (PR)
Université de Sherbrooke (QC, Canada)
U at Albany, State U of New York (NY)
U at Buffalo, the State U of New York (NY)
The U of Akron (OH)
The U of Alabama (AL)
The U of Alabama at Birmingham (AL)
The U of Alabama in Huntsville (AL)
U of Alaska Fairbanks (AK)
The U of Arizona (AZ)
U of Arkansas (AR)
U of Bridgeport (CT)
U of Central Arkansas (AR)
U of Central Florida (FL)
U of Charleston (WV)
U of Cincinnati (OH)
U of Colorado Boulder (CO)
U of Dayton (OH)
U of Delaware (DE)
U of Denver (CO)
U of Detroit Mercy (MI)
U of Dubuque (IA)
U of Evansville (IN)
The U of Findlay (OH)
U of Florida (FL)
U of Georgia (GA)
U of Great Falls (MT)
U of Guelph (ON, Canada)
U of Hartford (CT)
U of Hawaii at Manoa (HI)
U of Houston (TX)
U of Houston–Clear Lake (TX)
U of Houston–Downtown (TX)
U of Idaho (ID)
U of Illinois at Chicago (IL)
U of Illinois at Springfield (IL)
U of Indianapolis (IN)
U of Jamestown (ND)
The U of Kansas (KS)
U of Kentucky (KY)
U of La Verne (CA)
U of Lethbridge (AB, Canada)
U of Louisiana at Monroe (LA)
U of Louisville (KY)
U of Maine (ME)
U of Mary Hardin-Baylor (TX)
U of Maryland, Coll Park (MD)
U of Maryland U Coll (MD)
U of Massachusetts Amherst (MA)
U of Massachusetts Dartmouth (MA)
U of Miami (FL)
U of Michigan–Dearborn (MI)
U of Michigan–Flint (MI)
U of Minnesota, Crookston (MN)
U of Minnesota, Duluth (MN)
U of Minnesota, Twin Cities Campus (MN)
U of Missouri–Kansas City (MO)
U of Missouri–St. Louis (MO)
U of Mobile (AL)
U of Montevallo (AL)
U of Mount Union (OH)
U of Nevada, Las Vegas (NV)
U of Nevada, Reno (NV)
U of New Haven (CT)
U of New Orleans (LA)
U of North Alabama (AL)
U of North Carolina at Asheville (NC)
The U of North Carolina at Charlotte (NC)
The U of North Carolina at Greensboro (NC)
The U of North Carolina at Pembroke (NC)
U of North Dakota (ND)
U of Northern Iowa (IA)
U of North Florida (FL)
U of North Georgia (GA)
U of North Texas (TX)
U of Northwestern Ohio (OH)
U of Notre Dame (IN)
U of Oklahoma (OK)
U of Oregon (OR)
U of Pennsylvania (PA)
U of Pittsburgh (PA)
U of Pittsburgh at Bradford (PA)
U of Pittsburgh at Greensburg (PA)
U of Pittsburgh at Johnstown (PA)
U of Puerto Rico in Bayamón (PR)
U of Regina (SK, Canada)
U of Rhode Island (RI)
U of Richmond (VA)
U of St. Francis (IL)
U of Saint Francis (IN)
U of Saint Joseph (CT)
U of Saint Mary (KS)
U of St. Thomas (MN)
U of St. Thomas (TX)
U of San Diego (CA)
U of San Francisco (CA)
U of Saskatchewan (SK, Canada)
The U of Scranton (PA)
U of South Alabama (AL)
U of South Carolina (SC)
The U of South Dakota (SD)
U of Southern California (CA)
U of Southern Indiana (IN)
U of Southern Maine (ME)
U of Southern Mississippi (MS)
U of South Florida (FL)
U of South Florida, St. Petersburg (FL)
U of South Florida Sarasota-Manatee (FL)
The U of Tampa (FL)
The U of Tennessee (TN)
The U of Tennessee at Martin (TN)
The U of Texas at Austin (TX)
The U of Texas at Dallas (TX)
The U of Texas at El Paso (TX)
The U of Texas at San Antonio (TX)
The U of Texas of the Permian Basin (TX)
The U of Texas Rio Grande Valley (TX)
U of the Cumberlands (KY)
U of the Incarnate Word (TX)
U of the Potomac (DC)
U of the Southwest (NM)
U of the Virgin Islands (VI)
The U of Toledo (OH)
U of Toronto (ON, Canada)
The U of Tulsa (OK)
U of Utah (UT)
The U of Virginia's Coll at Wise (VA)
U of Washington (WA)
U of Washington, Bothell (WA)
U of Washington, Tacoma (WA)
U of Waterloo (ON, Canada)
The U of West Alabama (AL)
U of West Georgia (GA)
U of Windsor (ON, Canada)
U of Wisconsin–Eau Claire (WI)
U of Wisconsin–Green Bay (WI)
U of Wisconsin–La Crosse (WI)
U of Wisconsin–Madison (WI)
U of Wisconsin–Milwaukee (WI)
U of Wisconsin–Parkside (WI)
U of Wisconsin–Platteville (WI)
U of Wisconsin–Stevens Point (WI)
U of Wisconsin–Superior (WI)
U of Wisconsin–Whitewater (WI)
Upper Iowa U (IA)
Utah State U (UT)
Utah Valley U (UT)
Utica Coll (NY)
Valdosta State U (GA)
Valparaiso U (IN)
Villanova U (PA)
Virginia Commonwealth U (VA)
Virginia Polytechnic Inst and State U (VA)
Virginia State U (VA)
Virginia Union U (VA)
Viterbo U (WI)
Wagner Coll (NY)
Wake Forest U (NC)
Walla Walla U (WA)
Walsh Coll of Accountancy and Business Administration (MI)
Walsh U (OH)
Wartburg Coll (IA)
Washburn U (KS)
Washington & Jefferson Coll (PA)
Washington State U (WA)
Washington State U–Global Campus (WA)
Washington State U–Tri-Cities (WA)
Washington State U–Vancouver (WA)
Washington U in St. Louis (MO)
Waynesburg U (PA)
Wayne State U (MI)
Webber Intl U (FL)

Weber State U (UT)
Webster U (MO)
Wesleyan Coll (GA)
West Chester U of Pennsylvania (PA)
Western Carolina U (NC)
Western Connecticut State U (CT)
Western Illinois U (IL)
Western Intl U (AZ)
Western Kentucky U (KY)
Western Michigan U (MI)
Western New England U (MA)
Western State Colorado U (CO)
Western Washington U (WA)
Westminster Coll (PA)
Westminster Coll (UT)
West Texas A&M U (TX)
West Virginia U (WV)
West Virginia U Inst of Technology (WV)
West Virginia Wesleyan Coll (WV)
Wheeling Jesuit U (WV)
Whitworth U (WA)
Wichita State U (KS)
Widener U (PA)
Wilkes U (PA)
William Jewell Coll (MO)
William Paterson U of New Jersey (NJ)
William Penn U (IA)
William Woods U (MO)
Wilmington U (DE)
Wilson Coll (PA)
Wingate U (NC)
Winona State U (MN)
Wittenberg U (OH)
Wofford Coll (SC)
Woodbury U (CA)
Wright State U (OH)
Wright State U–Lake Campus (OH)
Xavier U of Louisiana (LA)
York Coll of Pennsylvania (PA)
York Coll of the City U of New York (NY)
Youngstown State U (OH)

ACCOUNTING AND BUSINESS/MANAGEMENT
Canisius Coll (NY)
Carver Coll (GA)
Chaminade U of Honolulu (HI)
Chestnut Hill Coll (PA)
East Carolina U (NC)
Eastern Nazarene Coll (MA)
EDP U of Puerto Rico (PR)
EDP U of Puerto Rico–San Sebastian (PR)
Emory U (GA)
Hope Coll (MI)
Husson U (ME)
Maranatha Baptist U (WI)
Mercy Coll (NY)
Northcentral U (CA)
Rasmussen Coll Fort Myers (FL)
Rasmussen Coll Green Bay (WI)
Rasmussen Coll Land O' Lakes (FL)
Rasmussen Coll New Port Richey (FL)
Rasmussen Coll Ocala (FL)
Rasmussen Coll Tampa/Brandon (FL)
Rasmussen Coll Wausau (WI)
Rocky Mountain Coll (MT)
Santa Clara U (CA)
Sierra Nevada Coll (NV)
Spalding U (KY)
U of Great Falls (MT)
Walla Walla U (WA)
Washington and Lee U (VA)
Western State Colorado U (CO)

ACCOUNTING AND COMPUTER SCIENCE
Fordham U (NY)
Grove City Coll (PA)
Saint Mary-of-the-Woods Coll (IN)

ACCOUNTING AND FINANCE
Bentley U (MA)
Bethel U (MN)
Boise State U (ID)
Bridgewater State U (MA)
Bucknell U (PA)
Clarkson U (NY)
DEREE - The American Coll of Greece (Greece)
Drake U (IA)
East Central U (OK)
Eastern Nazarene Coll (MA)
Eastern U (PA)
Elmira Coll (NY)
Ferris State U (MI)
Granite State Coll (NH)
Hiram Coll (OH)
Holy Family U (PA)
Northwest U (WA)
Ohio Christian U (OH)
Saint Francis U (PA)
Southern New Hampshire U (NH)
U of North Dakota (ND)
U of Southern Maine (ME)
U of Waterloo (ON, Canada)
U of Windsor (ON, Canada)
Western New England U (MA)
Western State Colorado U (CO)

ACCOUNTING RELATED
Bentley U (MA)
Brigham Young U (UT)
Eastern Michigan U (MI)
Eastern Nazarene Coll (MA)
Gwynedd Mercy U (PA)
Maryville U of Saint Louis (MO)
McDaniel Coll (MD)
North Dakota State U (ND)
Rocky Mountain Coll (MT)
Saint Mary's Coll of California (CA)
State U of New York at New Paltz (NY)
State U of New York at Oswego (NY)
Washington State U (WA)

ACCOUNTING TECHNOLOGY AND BOOKKEEPING
Ferris State U (MI)
Missouri Valley Coll (MO)
Rowan U (NJ)
St. Edward's U (TX)
The U of Akron (OH)

ACOUSTICS
Columbia Coll Chicago (IL)

ACTING
Acad of Art U (CA)
Anderson U (SC)
Arcadia U (PA)
Ashland U (OH)
Augsburg Coll (MN)
Baldwin Wallace U (OH)
Barry U (FL)
Baylor U (TX)
Belmont U (TN)
Bennington Coll (VT)
Boston U (MA)
Bradley U (IL)
Brigham Young U (UT)
California Baptist U (CA)
California State U, Long Beach (CA)
Central Michigan U (MI)
Central Washington U (WA)
Chapman U (CA)
Coll of the Ozarks (MO)
Columbia Coll Chicago (IL)
Dalhousie U (NS, Canada)
Drake U (IA)
Elon U (NC)
Emerson Coll (MA)
Emory & Henry Coll (VA)
Florida Southern Coll (FL)
Florida State U (FL)
Freed-Hardeman U (TN)
Gannon U (PA)
Hofstra U (NY)
Illinois Wesleyan U (IL)
Ithaca Coll (NY)
Kean U (NJ)
Keene State Coll (NH)
Lindenwood U (MO)
Lipscomb U (TN)
Marymount Manhattan Coll (NY)
Michigan State U (MI)
Nebraska Wesleyan U (NE)
Ohio U (OH)
Oklahoma City U (OK)
Oral Roberts U (OK)
Pace U (NY)
Penn State Abington (PA)
Penn State Altoona (PA)
Penn State Beaver (PA)
Penn State Berks (PA)
Penn State Brandywine (PA)
Penn State DuBois (PA)
Penn State Erie, The Behrend Coll (PA)
Penn State Fayette, The Eberly Campus (PA)
Penn State Greater Allegheny (PA)
Penn State Hazleton (PA)
Penn State Lehigh Valley (PA)
Penn State Mont Alto (PA)
Penn State New Kensington (PA)
Penn State Schuylkill (PA)
Penn State Shenango (PA)
Penn State U Park (PA)
Penn State Wilkes-Barre (PA)
Penn State Worthington Scranton (PA)
Penn State York (PA)
Pepperdine U, Malibu (CA)
Purdue U (IN)
Rhode Island Coll (RI)
St. Edward's U (TX)
Seton Hill U (PA)
Shenandoah U (VA)
Stevenson U (MD)
Syracuse U (NY)
Temple U (PA)
Texas Christian U (TX)
Towson U (MD)
Trinity U (TX)
U of Hartford (CT)
U of Lethbridge (AB, Canada)
U of Maryland, Baltimore County (MD)
U of Miami (FL)
U of Nevada, Las Vegas (NV)
U of Northern Iowa (IA)
U of Regina (SK, Canada)
U of Southern California (CA)
The U of Texas at Austin (TX)
The U of the Arts (PA)
U of Washington (WA)
U of Windsor (ON, Canada)
Webster U (MO)
Western Michigan U (MI)
Whitworth U (WA)
Wright State U (OH)

ACTUARIAL SCIENCE
Anderson U (SC)
Appalachian State U (NC)
Arcadia U (PA)
Arizona State U at the Tempe campus (AZ)
Ashland U (OH)
Assumption Coll (MA)
Aurora U (IL)
Ball State U (IN)
Baruch Coll of the City U of New York (NY)
Bellarmine U (KY)
Bentley U (MA)
Bowling Green State U (OH)
Bradley U (IL)
Brigham Young U (UT)
Bryant U (RI)
Butler U (IN)
California Baptist U (CA)
Calvin Coll (MI)
Carnegie Mellon U (PA)
Central Michigan U (MI)
Central Washington U (WA)
Concordia U (QC, Canada)
Concordia U Wisconsin (WI)
Drake U (IA)
Eastern Michigan U (MI)
Ferris State U (MI)
Georgia State U (GA)
Grace Coll (IN)
Hartwick Coll (NY)
High Point U (NC)
Indiana U Northwest (IN)
Indiana U South Bend (IN)
Lebanon Valley Coll (PA)
Maryville U of Saint Louis (MO)
Michigan State U (MI)
Milwaukee School of Eng (WI)
Mount Mercy U (IA)
Niagara U (NY)
North Central Coll (IL)
Northwestern Coll (IA)
The Ohio State U (OH)
Ohio U (OH)
Olivet Nazarene U (IL)
Penn State Abington (PA)
Penn State Altoona (PA)
Penn State Beaver (PA)
Penn State Berks (PA)
Penn State Brandywine (PA)
Penn State DuBois (PA)
Penn State Erie, The Behrend Coll (PA)
Penn State Fayette, The Eberly Campus (PA)
Penn State Greater Allegheny (PA)
Penn State Hazleton (PA)
Penn State Lehigh Valley (PA)
Penn State Mont Alto (PA)
Penn State New Kensington (PA)
Penn State Schuylkill (PA)
Penn State Shenango (PA)
Penn State Wilkes-Barre (PA)
Penn State Worthington Scranton (PA)
Penn State York (PA)
Purdue U (IN)
Queens Coll of the City U of New York (NY)
Roanoke Coll (VA)
Robert Morris U (PA)
St. John's U (NY)
Saint Joseph's U (PA)
Saint Mary's U of Minnesota (MN)
Siena Coll (NY)
Simon Fraser U (BC, Canada)
Simpson Coll (IA)
Temple U (PA)
Texas Christian U (TX)
Université de Montréal (QC, Canada)
U at Albany, State U of New York (NY)
U of California, Santa Barbara (CA)
U of Maine at Farmington (ME)
U of Michigan–Flint (MI)
U of Pennsylvania (PA)
U of Regina (SK, Canada)
U of St. Thomas (MN)
The U of Texas at Dallas (TX)
The U of Texas at San Antonio (TX)
U of Toronto (ON, Canada)
U of Waterloo (ON, Canada)
U of Wisconsin–Madison (WI)
U of Wisconsin–Milwaukee (WI)
Valparaiso U (IN)
Wartburg Coll (IA)
Western New England U (MA)

ADMINISTRATIVE ASSISTANT AND SECRETARIAL SCIENCE
Bayamón Central U (PR)
Campbellsville U (KY)
East Central U (OK)
EDP U of Puerto Rico (PR)
EDP U of Puerto Rico–San Sebastian (PR)
Faith Baptist Bible Coll and Theological Sem (IA)
Idaho State U (ID)
Northwest Missouri State U (MO)
Tennessee State U (TN)
Universidad Adventista de las Antillas (PR)
The U of North Carolina at Greensboro (NC)
Valdosta State U (GA)
Weber State U (UT)

ADULT AND CONTINUING EDUCATION
Auburn U (AL)
Eastern Illinois U (IL)
Eastern Washington U (WA)
Houston Baptist U (TX)
Louisiana State U and A&M Coll (LA)
Tennessee State U (TN)
U of Georgia (GA)
U of Regina (SK, Canada)
U of San Francisco (CA)
U of the Fraser Valley (BC, Canada)
Welch Coll (TN)

ADULT AND CONTINUING EDUCATION ADMINISTRATION
Concordia Coll–New York (NY)
Penn State Abington (PA)
Penn State Altoona (PA)
Penn State Beaver (PA)
Penn State Berks (PA)
Penn State Brandywine (PA)
Penn State DuBois (PA)
Penn State Erie, The Behrend Coll (PA)
Penn State Fayette, The Eberly Campus (PA)
Penn State Greater Allegheny (PA)
Penn State Hazleton (PA)
Penn State Lehigh Valley (PA)
Penn State Mont Alto (PA)
Penn State New Kensington (PA)
Penn State Schuylkill (PA)
Penn State Shenango (PA)
Penn State U Park (PA)
Penn State Wilkes-Barre (PA)
Penn State Worthington Scranton (PA)
Penn State York (PA)

ADULT DEVELOPMENT AND AGING
Goddard Coll (VT)
Madonna U (MI)
Rhode Island Coll (RI)
St. Thomas U (NB, Canada)
U of Guelph (ON, Canada)
York Coll of the City U of New York (NY)

ADULT HEALTH NURSING
Concordia Coll–New York (NY)
King U (TN)
Pennsylvania Coll of Technology (PA)
U of Rochester (NY)
Worcester State U (MA)

ADVERTISING
Acad of Art U (CA)
Adams State U (CO)
The American U in Dubai (United Arab Emirates)
Appalachian State U (NC)
Ball State U (IN)
Barry U (FL)
Bowling Green State U (OH)
Bradley U (IL)
Brigham Young U (UT)
California State U, East Bay (CA)
California State U, Fullerton (CA)
Central Michigan U (MI)
Columbia Coll Chicago (IL)
Drake U (IA)
Eastern Nazarene Coll (MA)
Emerson Coll (MA)
Fashion Inst of Technology (NY)
Ferris State U (MI)
Franklin Pierce U (NH)
Gannon U (PA)
Grand Valley State U (MI)
Hampton U (VA)
Harding U (AR)
Iona Coll (NY)
Iowa State U of Science and Technology (IA)
Kent State U (OH)
Lamar U (TX)
Lindenwood U (MO)
Loyola U Chicago (IL)
Michigan State U (MI)
Minneapolis Coll of Art and Design (MN)
Minnesota State U Moorhead (MN)
Murray State U (KY)
New York Inst of Technology (NY)
Northwest Missouri State U (MO)
Oklahoma Christian U (OK)
Pace U (NY)
Pace U, Pleasantville Campus (NY)
Penn State Abington (PA)
Penn State Altoona (PA)
Penn State Beaver (PA)
Penn State Berks (PA)
Penn State Brandywine (PA)
Penn State DuBois (PA)
Penn State Erie, The Behrend Coll (PA)
Penn State Fayette, The Eberly Campus (PA)
Penn State Greater Allegheny (PA)
Penn State Hazleton (PA)
Penn State Lehigh Valley (PA)
Penn State Mont Alto (PA)
Penn State New Kensington (PA)
Penn State Schuylkill (PA)
Penn State Shenango (PA)
Penn State U Park (PA)
Penn State Wilkes-Barre (PA)
Penn State Worthington Scranton (PA)
Penn State York (PA)
Pepperdine U, Malibu (CA)

Portland State U (OR)
Quinnipiac U (CT)
Ringling Coll of Art and Design (FL)
Rochester Inst of Technology (NY)
Rowan U (NJ)
St. Cloud State U (MN)
St. John's U (NY)
Sam Houston State U (TX)
San Diego State U (CA)
South Dakota State U (SD)
Southern Methodist U (TX)
Suffolk U (MA)
Syracuse U (NY)
Temple U (PA)
Texas Christian U (TX)
Texas State U (TX)
Texas Tech U (TX)
Texas Wesleyan U (TX)
Union U (TN)
The U of Alabama (AL)
U of Central Florida (FL)
U of Florida (FL)
U of Georgia (GA)
U of Houston (TX)
U of Idaho (ID)
U of Miami (FL)
U of Oklahoma (OK)
U of Oregon (OR)
U of San Francisco (CA)
U of South Carolina (SC)
U of Southern Indiana (IN)
U of Southern Mississippi (MS)
The U of Tennessee (TN)
The U of Texas at Austin (TX)
Washington U in St. Louis (MO)
Waynesburg U (PA)
Webster U (MO)
Wesleyan Coll (GA)
Western Kentucky U (KY)
Western Michigan U (MI)
Western New England U (MA)
Widener U (PA)
Youngstown State U (OH)

AERONAUTICAL/AEROSPACE ENGINEERING TECHNOLOGY
Bowling Green State U (OH)
Embry-Riddle Aeronautical U–Worldwide (FL)
Idaho State U (ID)
LeTourneau U (TX)
Purdue U (IN)
Saint Louis U–Madrid Campus (Spain)
Utah State U (UT)

AERONAUTICS/AVIATION/AEROSPACE SCIENCE AND TECHNOLOGY
American Public U System (WV)
Arizona State U at the Polytechnic campus (AZ)
Averett U (VA)
Bowling Green State U (OH)
Bridgewater State U (MA)
Elizabeth City State U (NC)
Embry-Riddle Aeronautical U–Daytona (FL)
Embry-Riddle Aeronautical U–Prescott (AZ)
Embry-Riddle Aeronautical U–Worldwide (FL)
Florida Inst of Technology (FL)
Henderson State U (AR)
Indiana State U (IN)
Kansas State U (KS)
Kent State U (OH)
LeTourneau U (TX)
Lewis U (IL)
Liberty U (VA)
Louisiana Tech U (LA)
Metropolitan State U of Denver (CO)
The Ohio State U (OH)
Ohio U (OH)
Oklahoma State U (OK)
Polk State Coll (FL)
Saint Louis U (MO)
South Dakota State U (SD)
Texas A&M U–Central Texas (TX)
Texas Lutheran U (TX)
U of Minnesota, Crookston (MN)
U of North Texas (TX)
U of Oklahoma (OK)
Vaughn Coll of Aeronautics and Technology (NY)
Walla Walla U (WA)

AEROSPACE, AERONAUTICAL AND ASTRONAUTICAL/SPACE ENGINEERING
Arizona State U at the Tempe campus (AZ)
Auburn U (AL)
California Polytechnic State U, San Luis Obispo (CA)
California State Polytechnic U, Pomona (CA)
California State U, Long Beach (CA)
Case Western Reserve U (OH)
Clarkson U (NY)
Concordia U (QC, Canada)
Eastern Nazarene Coll (MA)
Embry-Riddle Aeronautical U–Daytona (FL)
Embry-Riddle Aeronautical U–Prescott (AZ)
Florida Inst of Technology (FL)
Georgia Inst of Technology (GA)
Iowa State U of Science and Technology (IA)
Kent State U (OH)
Massachusetts Inst of Technology (MA)
Mississippi State U (MS)
Missouri U of Science and Technology (MO)
New Mexico State U (NM)
North Carolina State U (NC)
The Ohio State U (OH)
Oklahoma State U (OK)
Penn State Abington (PA)
Penn State Altoona (PA)
Penn State Beaver (PA)
Penn State Berks (PA)
Penn State Brandywine (PA)
Penn State DuBois (PA)
Penn State Erie, The Behrend Coll (PA)
Penn State Fayette, The Eberly Campus (PA)
Penn State Greater Allegheny (PA)
Penn State Hazleton (PA)
Penn State Lehigh Valley (PA)
Penn State Mont Alto (PA)
Penn State New Kensington (PA)
Penn State Schuylkill (PA)
Penn State Shenango (PA)
Penn State U Park (PA)
Penn State Wilkes-Barre (PA)
Penn State Worthington Scranton (PA)
Penn State York (PA)
Purdue U (IN)
Rensselaer Polytechnic Inst (NY)
Rochester Inst of Technology (NY)
Saint Louis U (MO)
San Diego State U (CA)
Southern New Hampshire U (NH)
Stanford U (CA)
Syracuse U (NY)
Texas A&M U (TX)
United States Air Force Acad (CO)
U at Buffalo, the State U of New York (NY)
The U of Alabama (AL)
The U of Alabama in Huntsville (AL)
The U of Arizona (AZ)
U of California, Davis (CA)
U of California, Irvine (CA)
U of California, Los Angeles (CA)
U of California, San Diego (CA)
U of Central Florida (FL)
U of Cincinnati (OH)
U of Colorado Boulder (CO)
U of Florida (FL)
The U of Kansas (KS)
U of Maryland, Coll Park (MD)
U of Miami (FL)
U of Michigan (MI)
U of Minnesota, Twin Cities Campus (MN)
U of Notre Dame (IN)
U of Oklahoma (OK)
U of Southern California (CA)
The U of Tennessee (TN)
The U of Texas at Austin (TX)
U of Toronto (ON, Canada)
U of Virginia (VA)
U of Washington (WA)
Utah State U (UT)
Virginia Polytechnic Inst and State U (VA)
Western Michigan U (MI)
West Virginia U (WV)
West Virginia U Inst of Technology (WV)
Wichita State U (KS)
Worcester Polytechnic Inst (MA)

AEROSPACE GROUND EQUIPMENT TECHNOLOGY
Liberty U (VA)

AFRICAN AMERICAN/BLACK STUDIES
Amherst Coll (MA)
Arizona State U at the Tempe campus (AZ)
Bates Coll (ME)
Berea Coll (KY)
Binghamton U, State U of New York (NY)
Bowling Green State U (OH)
Brandeis U (MA)
Cabrini U (PA)
California State U, Dominguez Hills (CA)
California State U, East Bay (CA)
California State U, Fresno (CA)
California State U, Fullerton (CA)
California State U, Long Beach (CA)
California State U, Northridge (CA)
City Coll of the City U of New York (NY)
Claremont McKenna Coll (CA)
Clemson U (SC)
Cleveland State U (OH)
Coe Coll (IA)
Colby Coll (ME)
The Coll at Brockport, State U of New York (NY)
Coll of Charleston (SC)
The Coll of New Jersey (NJ)
Coll of Staten Island of the City U of New York (NY)
The Coll of William and Mary (VA)
The Coll of Wooster (OH)
Columbia U (NY)
Columbia U, School of General Studies (NY)
Cornell U (NY)
Dartmouth Coll (NH)
Denison U (OH)
DePauw U (IN)
Dominican U (IL)
Drew U (NJ)
Earlham Coll (IN)
East Carolina U (NC)
Eastern Illinois U (IL)
Eastern Michigan U (MI)
Emory U (GA)
Florida Ag and Mech U (FL)
Fordham U (NY)
Georgia State U (GA)
Gettysburg Coll (PA)
Guilford Coll (NC)
Hamilton Coll (NY)
Hampshire Coll (MA)
Harvard U (MA)
Hobart and William Smith Colls (NY)
Hunter Coll of the City U of New York (NY)
Indiana State U (IN)
Indiana U Bloomington (IN)
Indiana U Northwest (IN)
Indiana U–Purdue U Indianapolis (IN)
Johns Hopkins U (MD)
Kent State U (OH)
Knox Coll (IL)
Lake Forest Coll (IL)
Lehman Coll of the City U of New York (NY)
Loyola Marymount U (CA)
Loyola U Chicago (IL)
Luther Coll (IA)
Mercer U, Macon (GA)
Metropolitan State U of Denver (CO)
Miami U (OH)
Morehouse Coll (GA)
Mount Holyoke Coll (MA)
Northeastern U (MA)
Northwestern U (IL)
Oberlin Coll (OH)
The Ohio State U (OH)
Ohio U (OH)
Ohio Wesleyan U (OH)
Old Dominion U (VA)
Penn State Abington (PA)
Penn State Altoona (PA)
Penn State Beaver (PA)
Penn State Berks (PA)
Penn State Brandywine (PA)
Penn State DuBois (PA)
Penn State Erie, The Behrend Coll (PA)
Penn State Fayette, The Eberly Campus (PA)
Penn State Greater Allegheny (PA)
Penn State Hazleton (PA)
Penn State Lehigh Valley (PA)
Penn State Mont Alto (PA)
Penn State New Kensington (PA)
Penn State Schuylkill (PA)
Penn State Shenango (PA)
Penn State U Park (PA)
Penn State Wilkes-Barre (PA)
Penn State Worthington Scranton (PA)
Penn State York (PA)
Pitzer Coll (CA)
Pomona Coll (CA)
Portland State U (OR)
Princeton U (NJ)
Purdue U (IN)
Queens Coll of the City U of New York (NY)
Ramapo Coll of New Jersey (NJ)
Rhode Island Coll (RI)
Rhodes Coll (TN)
Rutgers U–Camden (NJ)
Rutgers U–Newark (NJ)
Saint Louis U (MO)
San Diego State U (CA)
San Francisco State U (CA)
Scripps Coll (CA)
Smith Coll (MA)
Sonoma State U (CA)
Southern Illinois U Carbondale (IL)
Southern Methodist U (TX)
Stanford U (CA)
State U of New York at New Paltz (NY)
State U of New York Coll at Cortland (NY)
State U of New York Coll at Geneseo (NY)
Stony Brook U, State U of New York (NY)
Swarthmore Coll (PA)
Syracuse U (NY)
Temple U (PA)
Tufts U (MA)
U at Albany, State U of New York (NY)
U at Buffalo, the State U of New York (NY)
The U of Alabama (AL)
The U of Alabama at Birmingham (AL)
The U of Arizona (AZ)
U of California, Davis (CA)
U of California, Irvine (CA)
U of California, Los Angeles (CA)
U of California, Riverside (CA)
U of California, Santa Barbara (CA)
U of Central Arkansas (AR)
U of Cincinnati (OH)
U of Delaware (DE)
U of Florida (FL)
U of Georgia (GA)
U of Illinois at Chicago (IL)
The U of Kansas (KS)
U of Louisville (KY)
U of Maryland, Baltimore County (MD)
U of Maryland, Coll Park (MD)
U of Massachusetts Amherst (MA)
U of Massachusetts Boston (MA)
U of Miami (FL)
U of Michigan (MI)
U of Michigan–Dearborn (MI)
U of Michigan–Flint (MI)
U of Minnesota, Twin Cities Campus (MN)
U of Nevada, Las Vegas (NV)
The U of North Carolina at Chapel Hill (NC)
The U of North Carolina at Charlotte (NC)
The U of North Carolina at Greensboro (NC)
U of Northern Colorado (CO)
U of Notre Dame (IN)
U of Oklahoma (OK)
U of Pennsylvania (PA)
U of Pittsburgh (PA)
U of Rhode Island (RI)
U of Rochester (NY)
U of South Carolina (SC)
U of Southern California (CA)
U of South Florida (FL)
The U of Texas at Austin (TX)
The U of Toledo (OH)
U of Virginia (VA)
U of Wisconsin–Madison (WI)
U of Wisconsin–Milwaukee (WI)
Vanderbilt U (TN)
Virginia Commonwealth U (VA)
Washington U in St. Louis (MO)
Wayne State U (MI)
Wesleyan U (CT)
Western Michigan U (MI)
Wheaton Coll (MA)
William Paterson U of New Jersey (NJ)
York Coll of the City U of New York (NY)

AFRICAN LANGUAGES
U of California, Los Angeles (CA)
U of Wisconsin–Madison (WI)

AFRICAN STUDIES
Agnes Scott Coll (GA)
Augustana Coll (IL)
Bard Coll (NY)
Barnard Coll (NY)
Bowdoin Coll (ME)
Bowling Green State U (OH)
Brooklyn Coll of the City U of New York (NY)
Carleton Coll (MN)
The Coll of Wooster (OH)
Columbia U, School of General Studies (NY)
Connecticut Coll (CT)
Dartmouth Coll (NH)
Davidson Coll (NC)
Dickinson Coll (PA)
Emory U (GA)
Fordham U (NY)
Franklin & Marshall Coll (PA)
Hampshire Coll (MA)
Haverford Coll (PA)
Hobart and William Smith Colls (NY)
Hofstra U (NY)
Illinois Wesleyan U (IL)
Kennesaw State U (GA)
Kentucky State U (KY)
Lehigh U (PA)
Lincoln U (PA)
Middlebury Coll (VT)
Northwestern U (IL)
The Ohio State U (OH)
Ohio U (OH)
Portland State U (OR)
Rowan U (NJ)
Rutgers U–New Brunswick (NJ)
Sarah Lawrence Coll (NY)
Simmons Coll (MA)
Tennessee State U (TN)
Tufts U (MA)
Tulane U (LA)
Union Coll (NY)
United States Military Acad (NY)
U of Chicago (IL)
The U of Kansas (KS)
U of Pennsylvania (PA)
U of Richmond (VA)
U of Toronto (ON, Canada)
Vassar Coll (NY)
Washington U in St. Louis (MO)
Willamette U (OR)

AGRIBUSINESS
Abilene Christian U (TX)
Adams State U (CO)
American U of Beirut (Lebanon)
Andrews U (MI)
Angelo State U (TX)
Arkansas Tech U (AR)
Brigham Young U (UT)
Colorado State U (CO)
Delaware Valley U (PA)
Florida Ag and Mech U (FL)
Greenville Coll (IL)
Iowa State U of Science and Technology (IA)
Kent State U at Tuscarawas (OH)
Mississippi State U (MS)

Missouri State U (MO)
Morrisville State Coll (NY)
New Mexico State U (NM)
North Carolina State U (NC)
North Dakota State U (ND)
Northwest Missouri State U (MO)
Penn State Abington (PA)
Penn State Altoona (PA)
Penn State Beaver (PA)
Penn State Berks (PA)
Penn State Brandywine (PA)
Penn State DuBois (PA)
Penn State Erie, The Behrend Coll (PA)
Penn State Fayette, The Eberly Campus (PA)
Penn State Greater Allegheny (PA)
Penn State Hazleton (PA)
Penn State Lehigh Valley (PA)
Penn State Mont Alto (PA)
Penn State New Kensington (PA)
Penn State Schuylkill (PA)
Penn State Shenango (PA)
Penn State U Park (PA)
Penn State Wilkes-Barre (PA)
Penn State Worthington Scranton (PA)
Penn State York (PA)
Sam Houston State U (TX)
South Carolina State U (SC)
South Dakota State U (SD)
Southeast Missouri State U (MO)
Stephen F. Austin State U (TX)
Tarleton State U (TX)
Texas A&M U (TX)
Texas A&M U–Commerce (TX)
Texas A&M U–Kingsville (TX)
Texas State U (TX)
U of Arkansas (AR)
U of Central Missouri (MO)
U of Delaware (DE)
U of Georgia (GA)
U of Idaho (ID)
U of Minnesota, Crookston (MN)
U of Saskatchewan (SK, Canada)
U of Wisconsin–Platteville (WI)
Vermont Tech Coll (VT)
Washington State U (WA)
West Texas A&M U (TX)

AGRICULTURAL AND DOMESTIC ANIMAL SERVICES RELATED
Saint Mary-of-the-Woods Coll (IN)
Tarleton State U (TX)

AGRICULTURAL AND EXTENSION EDUCATION
Colorado State U (CO)
Louisiana State U and A&M Coll (LA)
New Mexico State U (NM)
North Carolina State U (NC)
Northwestern Oklahoma State U (OK)
The Ohio State U (OH)
Penn State Abington (PA)
Penn State Altoona (PA)
Penn State Beaver (PA)
Penn State Berks (PA)
Penn State Brandywine (PA)
Penn State DuBois (PA)
Penn State Erie, The Behrend Coll (PA)
Penn State Fayette, The Eberly Campus (PA)
Penn State Greater Allegheny (PA)
Penn State Hazleton (PA)
Penn State Lehigh Valley (PA)
Penn State Mont Alto (PA)
Penn State New Kensington (PA)
Penn State Schuylkill (PA)
Penn State Shenango (PA)
Penn State Wilkes-Barre (PA)
Penn State Worthington Scranton (PA)
Penn State York (PA)
Tarleton State U (TX)
U of Arkansas (AR)
U of Georgia (GA)
The U of Tennessee (TN)

AGRICULTURAL AND FOOD PRODUCTS PROCESSING
Angelo State U (TX)
Dalhousie U (NS, Canada)
Kansas State U (KS)
Morningside Coll (IA)
The Ohio State U (OH)
Texas A&M U (TX)
U of Florida (FL)
Washington State U (WA)

AGRICULTURAL AND HORTICULTURAL PLANT BREEDING
U of Georgia (GA)
Washington State U (WA)

AGRICULTURAL BUSINESS AND MANAGEMENT
Alcorn State U (MS)
Arizona State U at the Polytechnic campus (AZ)
Brigham Young U (UT)
Brigham Young U–Idaho (ID)
California Polytechnic State U, San Luis Obispo (CA)
California State Polytechnic U, Pomona (CA)
California State U, Chico (CA)
California State U, Fresno (CA)
Clemson U (SC)
Coll of the Ozarks (MO)
Colorado Mesa U (CO)
Florida Southern Coll (FL)
Iowa State U of Science and Technology (IA)
Kansas State U (KS)
Lincoln U (MO)
Louisiana State U and A&M Coll (LA)
Louisiana Tech U (LA)
Michigan State U (MI)
Missouri Valley Coll (MO)
Montana State U (MT)
The Ohio State U (OH)
Oklahoma State U (OK)
Oregon State U (OR)
Purdue U (IN)
Southern Arkansas U–Magnolia (AR)
State U of New York Coll of Agriculture and Technology at Cobleskill (NY)
Texas A&M U (TX)
Texas Tech U (TX)
The U of Arizona (AZ)
U of Delaware (DE)
U of Guelph (ON, Canada)
U of Louisiana at Monroe (LA)
U of Nebraska at Kearney (NE)
U of Northwestern Ohio (OH)
The U of Tennessee (TN)
The U of Tennessee at Martin (TN)
U of the Fraser Valley (BC, Canada)
U of Wisconsin–Madison (WI)
Upper Iowa U (IA)
Utah State U (UT)
Washington State U (WA)
West Texas A&M U (TX)

AGRICULTURAL BUSINESS AND MANAGEMENT RELATED
Penn State New Kensington (PA)
U of California, Davis (CA)
U of Minnesota, Twin Cities Campus (MN)
Utah State U (UT)

AGRICULTURAL BUSINESS TECHNOLOGY
Brigham Young U–Idaho (ID)
The U of Arizona (AZ)
U of Minnesota, Crookston (MN)
U of Wisconsin–Platteville (WI)

AGRICULTURAL COMMUNICATION/ JOURNALISM
Auburn U (AL)
California Polytechnic State U, San Luis Obispo (CA)
Kansas State U (KS)
North Dakota State U (ND)
The Ohio State U (OH)
Oklahoma State U (OK)
Purdue U (IN)
Sam Houston State U (TX)
South Dakota State U (SD)
Texas A&M U (TX)
Texas Tech U (TX)
U of Georgia (GA)
U of Idaho (ID)
U of Wisconsin–Madison (WI)
Washington State U (WA)
West Texas A&M U (TX)

AGRICULTURAL ECONOMICS
Alcorn State U (MS)
Auburn U (AL)
Brigham Young U (UT)
Brigham Young U–Idaho (ID)
Clemson U (SC)
Colorado State U (CO)
Cornell U (NY)
Kansas State U (KS)
Mississippi State U (MS)
North Dakota State U (ND)
The Ohio State U (OH)
Oklahoma State U (OK)
Oregon State U (OR)
Purdue U (IN)
South Dakota State U (SD)
Southern Illinois U Carbondale (IL)
Tarleton State U (TX)
Texas A&M U (TX)
Texas Tech U (TX)
U of Florida (FL)
U of Georgia (GA)
U of Guelph (ON, Canada)
U of Idaho (ID)
U of Kentucky (KY)
U of Maryland, Coll Park (MD)
U of Massachusetts Amherst (MA)
U of Saskatchewan (SK, Canada)
U of Wisconsin–Madison (WI)
Utah State U (UT)
Virginia Polytechnic Inst and State U (VA)
Washington State U (WA)
West Virginia U (WV)

AGRICULTURAL ENGINEERING
Auburn U (AL)
California Polytechnic State U, San Luis Obispo (CA)
Clemson U (SC)
Cornell U (NY)
Dalhousie U (NS, Canada)
Florida Ag and Mech U (FL)
Iowa State U of Science and Technology (IA)
Kansas State U (KS)
Michigan State U (MI)
Missouri U of Science and Technology (MO)
North Carolina State U (NC)
North Dakota State U (ND)
The Ohio State U (OH)
Oklahoma State U (OK)
Oregon State U (OR)
Penn State Abington (PA)
Penn State Beaver (PA)
Penn State Brandywine (PA)
Penn State DuBois (PA)
Penn State Erie, The Behrend Coll (PA)
Penn State Fayette, The Eberly Campus (PA)
Penn State Greater Allegheny (PA)
Penn State Hazleton (PA)
Penn State Lehigh Valley (PA)
Penn State Mont Alto (PA)
Penn State New Kensington (PA)
Penn State Schuylkill (PA)
Penn State Shenango (PA)
Penn State U Park (PA)
Penn State Wilkes-Barre (PA)
Penn State Worthington Scranton (PA)
Penn State York (PA)
Purdue U (IN)
Rutgers U–New Brunswick (NJ)
South Dakota State U (SD)
Texas A&M U (TX)
U of Arkansas (AR)
U of California, Los Angeles (CA)
U of Georgia (GA)
U of Hawaii at Manoa (HI)
U of Maine (ME)
U of Maryland, Coll Park (MD)
The U of Tennessee (TN)
U of Wisconsin–Madison (WI)
Utah State U (UT)
Walla Walla U (WA)
Washington State U (WA)

AGRICULTURAL/FARM SUPPLIES RETAILING AND WHOLESALING
Tarleton State U (TX)
Texas A&M U (TX)

AGRICULTURAL MECHANICS AND EQUIPMENT TECHNOLOGY
Washington State U (WA)

AGRICULTURAL MECHANIZATION
California Polytechnic State U, San Luis Obispo (CA)
Iowa State U of Science and Technology (IA)
Kansas State U (KS)
Montana State U (MT)
Montana State U–Northern (MT)
North Carolina State U (NC)
North Dakota State U (ND)
Penn State Abington (PA)
Penn State Altoona (PA)
Penn State Beaver (PA)
Penn State Berks (PA)
Penn State Brandywine (PA)
Penn State DuBois (PA)
Penn State Erie, The Behrend Coll (PA)
Penn State Fayette, The Eberly Campus (PA)
Penn State Greater Allegheny (PA)
Penn State Hazleton (PA)
Penn State Lehigh Valley (PA)
Penn State Mont Alto (PA)
Penn State New Kensington (PA)
Penn State Schuylkill (PA)
Penn State Shenango (PA)
Penn State Wilkes-Barre (PA)
Penn State Worthington Scranton (PA)
Penn State York (PA)
Purdue U (IN)
Sam Houston State U (TX)
South Dakota State U (SD)
Stephen F. Austin State U (TX)
Tarleton State U (TX)
U of Idaho (ID)
U of Minnesota, Crookston (MN)
Washington State U (WA)

AGRICULTURAL POWER MACHINERY OPERATION
U of Minnesota, Crookston (MN)

AGRICULTURAL PRODUCTION
South Dakota State U (SD)
Stephen F. Austin State U (TX)
Washington State U (WA)

AGRICULTURAL PRODUCTION RELATED
Tarleton State U (TX)

AGRICULTURAL PUBLIC SERVICES RELATED
Oklahoma State U (OK)
South Dakota State U (SD)
U of Kentucky (KY)

AGRICULTURAL TEACHER EDUCATION
Arkansas Tech U (AR)
Auburn U (AL)
California Polytechnic State U, San Luis Obispo (CA)
California State Polytechnic U, Pomona (CA)
California State U, Fresno (CA)
Clemson U (SC)
Coll of the Ozarks (MO)
Colorado State U (CO)
Iowa State U of Science and Technology (IA)
Kansas State U (KS)
Louisiana State U and A&M Coll (LA)
Louisiana Tech U (LA)
Mississippi State U (MS)
Missouri State U (MO)
Montana State U (MT)
New Mexico State U (NM)
North Carolina State U (NC)
North Dakota State U (ND)
Northwest Missouri State U (MO)
The Ohio State U (OH)
Oklahoma State U (OK)
Penn State U Park (PA)
Purdue U (IN)
Sam Houston State U (TX)
South Dakota State U (SD)
Southeast Missouri State U (MO)
Southern Arkansas U–Magnolia (AR)
State U of New York at Oswego (NY)
Tarleton State U (TX)
U of Arkansas (AR)
U of Delaware (DE)
U of Florida (FL)
U of Georgia (GA)
U of Idaho (ID)
U of Minnesota, Twin Cities Campus (MN)
The U of Tennessee at Martin (TN)
U of Wisconsin–Platteville (WI)
Utah State U (UT)
Washington State U (WA)
West Virginia U (WV)

AGRICULTURE
Alcorn State U (MS)
American U of Beirut (Lebanon)
Angelo State U (TX)
Auburn U (AL)
Austin Peay State U (TN)
Berea Coll (KY)
Brigham Young U–Idaho (ID)
California State U, Stanislaus (CA)
Cameron U (OK)
Cornell U (NY)
Dalhousie U (NS, Canada)
Dickinson State U (ND)
Florida Ag and Mech U (FL)
Hampshire Coll (MA)
Illinois State U (IL)
Iowa State U of Science and Technology (IA)
Kentucky State U (KY)
Lincoln U (MO)
McNeese State U (LA)
Mississippi State U (MS)
Missouri State U (MO)
Montana State U (MT)
Morehead State U (KY)
New Mexico State U (NM)
North Carolina State U (NC)
North Dakota State U (ND)
Northwestern Oklahoma State U (OK)
Northwest Missouri State U (MO)
Oregon State U (OR)
Penn State Abington (PA)
Penn State Altoona (PA)
Penn State Beaver (PA)
Penn State Berks (PA)
Penn State Brandywine (PA)
Penn State DuBois (PA)
Penn State Erie, The Behrend Coll (PA)
Penn State Fayette, The Eberly Campus (PA)
Penn State Greater Allegheny (PA)
Penn State Hazleton (PA)
Penn State Lehigh Valley (PA)
Penn State Mont Alto (PA)
Penn State New Kensington (PA)
Penn State Schuylkill (PA)
Penn State Shenango (PA)
Penn State U Park (PA)
Penn State Wilkes-Barre (PA)
Penn State Worthington Scranton (PA)
Penn State York (PA)
Prairie View A&M U (TX)
Purdue U (IN)
Rutgers U–New Brunswick (NJ)
Sam Houston State U (TX)
South Dakota State U (SD)
Southern Arkansas U–Magnolia (AR)
Southern Illinois U Carbondale (IL)
Southern Utah U (UT)
Stephen F. Austin State U (TX)
Tarleton State U (TX)
Tennessee State U (TN)
Texas A&M U (TX)
Texas A&M U–Commerce (TX)
Texas A&M U–Kingsville (TX)
Texas State U (TX)
Texas Tech U (TX)
Truman State U (MO)
U of Delaware (DE)
U of Georgia (GA)
U of Lethbridge (AB, Canada)

U of Maryland, Coll Park (MD)
The U of Tennessee at Martin (TN)
U of Vermont (VT)
Utah State U (UT)
Virginia State U (VA)
Washington State U (WA)
Western Illinois U (IL)
Western Kentucky U (KY)
West Texas A&M U (TX)

AGRICULTURE AND AGRICULTURE OPERATIONS RELATED
California State U, Stanislaus (CA)
Coll of the Atlantic (ME)
Emmanuel Coll (GA)
Murray State U (KY)
The Ohio State U (OH)
Penn State U Park (PA)
Tarleton State U (TX)
The U of Arizona (AZ)
U of California, Davis (CA)
U of Kentucky (KY)
U of Nevada, Reno (NV)
U of Saskatchewan (SK, Canada)

AGROECOLOGY AND SUSTAINABLE AGRICULTURE
Central State U (OH)
Dalhousie U (NS, Canada)
The Evergreen State Coll (WA)
Goshen Coll (IN)
Green Mountain Coll (VT)
Guilford Coll (NC)
Prescott Coll (AZ)
Purdue U (IN)
Unity Coll (ME)
U of Idaho (ID)
U of Maine (ME)
U of Massachusetts Amherst (MA)
U of Minnesota, Crookston (MN)
U of New Hampshire (NH)
Washington State U (WA)

AGRONOMY AND CROP SCIENCE
Auburn U (AL)
Brigham Young U–Idaho (ID)
California Polytechnic State U, San Luis Obispo (CA)
California State U, Fresno (CA)
Coll of the Ozarks (MO)
Dalhousie U (NS, Canada)
Delaware Valley U (PA)
Iowa State U of Science and Technology (IA)
Kansas State U (KS)
Mississippi State U (MS)
Missouri State U (MO)
New Mexico State U (NM)
North Carolina State U (NC)
Northwest Missouri State U (MO)
The Ohio State U (OH)
Oregon State U (OR)
Penn State Abington (PA)
Penn State Altoona (PA)
Penn State Beaver (PA)
Penn State Berks (PA)
Penn State Brandywine (PA)
Penn State DuBois (PA)
Penn State Erie, The Behrend Coll (PA)
Penn State Fayette, The Eberly Campus (PA)
Penn State Greater Allegheny (PA)
Penn State Hazleton (PA)
Penn State Mont Alto (PA)
Penn State New Kensington (PA)
Penn State Shenango (PA)
Penn State Wilkes-Barre (PA)
Penn State Worthington Scranton (PA)
Penn State York (PA)
Purdue U (IN)
South Dakota State U (SD)
State U of New York Coll of Agriculture and Technology at Cobleskill (NY)
Tarleton State U (TX)
Texas A&M U (TX)
Texas A&M U–Kingsville (TX)
U of Arkansas (AR)
U of Georgia (GA)
U of Guelph (ON, Canada)
U of Kentucky (KY)
U of Minnesota, Crookston (MN)
U of Saskatchewan (SK, Canada)
The U of Tennessee at Martin (TN)
U of Vermont (VT)
U of Wisconsin–Madison (WI)
U of Wisconsin–Platteville (WI)
Utah State U (UT)
Virginia Polytechnic Inst and State U (VA)
Washington State U (WA)
West Texas A&M U (TX)

AIR AND SPACE OPERATIONS TECHNOLOGY
Embry-Riddle Aeronautical U–Daytona (FL)

AIRCRAFT POWERPLANT TECHNOLOGY
Embry-Riddle Aeronautical U–Daytona (FL)
Embry-Riddle Aeronautical U–Worldwide (FL)
Idaho State U (ID)

AIR FORCE ROTC/AIR SCIENCE
Elms Coll (MA)

AIRFRAME MECHANICS AND AIRCRAFT MAINTENANCE TECHNOLOGY
Kansas State U (KS)
Southeastern Oklahoma State U (OK)
Vaughn Coll of Aeronautics and Technology (NY)

AIRLINE FLIGHT ATTENDANT
California Baptist U (CA)

AIRLINE PILOT AND FLIGHT CREW
Acad emy Coll (MN)
Auburn U (AL)
Baylor U (TX)
Bridgewater State U (MA)
California Baptist U (CA)
Central Washington U (WA)
Eastern Michigan U (MI)
Embry-Riddle Aeronautical U–Daytona (FL)
Embry-Riddle Aeronautical U–Prescott (AZ)
Farmingdale State Coll (NY)
Indiana State U (IN)
Jacksonville U (FL)
Kansas State U (KS)
LeTourneau U (TX)
Purdue U (IN)
Rocky Mountain Coll (MT)
Southeastern Oklahoma State U (OK)
Tarleton State U (TX)
Texas A&M U–Central Texas (TX)
U of Dubuque (IA)
U of Louisiana at Monroe (LA)
U of Minnesota, Crookston (MN)
U of North Dakota (ND)
Utah Valley U (UT)
Western Michigan U (MI)
Westminster Coll (UT)

AIR TRAFFIC CONTROL
Arizona State U at the Polytechnic campus (AZ)
Embry-Riddle Aeronautical U–Daytona (FL)
Embry-Riddle Aeronautical U–Prescott (AZ)
Hampton U (VA)
LeTourneau U (TX)
Lewis U (IL)
Southern New Hampshire U (NH)
U of North Dakota (ND)

AIR TRANSPORTATION RELATED
California Baptist U (CA)
Florida Inst of Technology (FL)
Inter American U of Puerto Rico, Bayamón Campus (PR)
U of North Dakota (ND)

ALLIED HEALTH AND MEDICAL ASSISTING SERVICES RELATED
Cedarville U (OH)
Coll of Saint Elizabeth (NJ)
The Ohio State U (OH)
The Ohio State U at Lima (OH)
Ramapo Coll of New Jersey (NJ)
Widener U (PA)

ALLIED HEALTH DIAGNOSTIC, INTERVENTION, AND TREATMENT PROFESSIONS RELATED
Cox Coll (MO)
Fairleigh Dickinson U, Coll at Florham (NJ)
Fairleigh Dickinson U, Metropolitan Campus (NJ)
Georgian Court U (NJ)
Hofstra U (NY)
Immaculata U (PA)
Millersville U of Pennsylvania (PA)
Point Loma Nazarene U (CA)
Rutgers U–Newark (NJ)
Rutgers U–New Brunswick (NJ)
Tennessee Wesleyan U (TN)
Thomas Edison State U (NJ)
U of Arkansas for Medical Sciences (AR)
U of Nebraska at Kearney (NE)
The U of North Carolina at Charlotte (NC)
Weber State U (UT)

AMERICAN GOVERNMENT AND POLITICS
Arizona Christian U (AZ)
Belmont Abbey Coll (NC)
Bridgewater State U (MA)
Drury U (MO)
Emmanuel Coll (MA)
Emory & Henry Coll (VA)
Fitchburg State U (MA)
Gallaudet U (DC)
La Salle U (PA)
Lenoir-Rhyne U (NC)
The Master's U (CA)
Misericordia U (PA)
Oklahoma Christian U (OK)
United States Military Acad (NY)
The U of Akron (OH)
Wayland Baptist U (TX)
Western Michigan U (MI)

AMERICAN HISTORY
Charleston Southern U (SC)
Florida Coll (FL)
Gettysburg Coll (PA)
Howard Payne U (TX)
Keene State Coll (NH)
Morningside Coll (IA)
United States Air Force Acad (CO)
United States Military Acad (NY)
U of Washington, Tacoma (WA)

AMERICAN INDIAN/NATIVE AMERICAN STUDIES
Arizona State U at the Tempe campus (AZ)
Augsburg Coll (MN)
Bemidji State U (MN)
Black Hills State U (SD)
California State U, East Bay (CA)
Colgate U (NY)
Concordia U (QC, Canada)
Dartmouth Coll (NH)
East Central U (OK)
The Evergreen State Coll (WA)
Fort Lewis Coll (CO)
Hampshire Coll (MA)
Humboldt State U (CA)
Inst of American Indian Arts (NM)
Northeastern State U (OK)
Northern Arizona U (AZ)
Northland Coll (WI)
Northwest U (WA)
Portland State U (OR)
St. Thomas U (NB, Canada)
San Diego State U (CA)
San Francisco State U (CA)
Sonoma State U (CA)
South Dakota State U (SD)
Stanford U (CA)
Trent U (ON, Canada)
U of Alaska Fairbanks (AK)
The U of Arizona (AZ)
U of California, Davis (CA)
U of California, Los Angeles (CA)
U of California, Riverside (CA)
U of Hawaii at Manoa (HI)
U of Lethbridge (AB, Canada)
U of Minnesota, Duluth (MN)
U of Minnesota, Morris (MN)
U of Minnesota, Twin Cities Campus (MN)
The U of North Carolina at Pembroke (NC)
U of North Dakota (ND)
U of Oklahoma (OK)
U of Regina (SK, Canada)
U of Saskatchewan (SK, Canada)
U of Science and Arts of Oklahoma (OK)
The U of South Dakota (SD)
U of Toronto (ON, Canada)
U of Washington (WA)
U of Wisconsin–Eau Claire (WI)
U of Wisconsin–Green Bay (WI)
Western New England U (MA)

AMERICAN LITERATURE
U of California, Los Angeles (CA)
Washington U in St. Louis (MO)
Whittier Coll (CA)

AMERICAN NATIVE/NATIVE AMERICAN EDUCATION
The Coll of St. Scholastica (MN)
Northeastern State U (OK)
U of Lethbridge (AB, Canada)
U of Regina (SK, Canada)

AMERICAN NATIVE/NATIVE AMERICAN LANGUAGES
Bemidji State U (MN)
U of Alaska Fairbanks (AK)
U of Minnesota, Twin Cities Campus (MN)
U of Regina (SK, Canada)

AMERICAN SIGN LANGUAGE (ASL)
Augustana U (SD)
California State U, Sacramento (CA)
Gardner-Webb U (NC)
Lamar U (TX)
Liberty U (VA)
Madonna U (MI)
Northeastern U (MA)
Rochester Inst of Technology (NY)
St. Catherine U (MN)
U of Houston (TX)
U of Rochester (NY)
Utah Valley U (UT)
William Woods U (MO)

AMERICAN STUDIES
Albright Coll (PA)
American U (DC)
Amherst Coll (MA)
Arizona State U at the West campus (AZ)
Ashland U (OH)
Augustana U (SD)
Austin Coll (TX)
Bard Coll (NY)
Barnard Coll (NY)
Bates Coll (ME)
Baylor U (TX)
Bennington Coll (VT)
Bethany Lutheran Coll (MN)
Boston U (MA)
Bowling Green State U (OH)
Brandeis U (MA)
Brooklyn Coll of the City U of New York (NY)
Bryant U (RI)
Cabrini U (PA)
California State Polytechnic U, Pomona (CA)
California State U, Fullerton (CA)
California State U, Long Beach (CA)
California State U, San Bernardino (CA)
Carleton Coll (MN)
Case Western Reserve U (OH)
Chowan U (NC)
Christopher Newport U (VA)
Claremont McKenna Coll (CA)
Coe Coll (IA)
Colby Coll (ME)
Coll of Coastal Georgia (GA)
Coll of Staten Island of the City U of New York (NY)
The Coll of William and Mary (VA)
Columbia Coll (MO)
Columbia U (NY)
Columbia U, School of General Studies (NY)
Connecticut Coll (CT)
Cornell U (NY)
Creighton U (NE)
Dickinson Coll (PA)
Dominican U (IL)
Eckerd Coll (FL)
Elmira Coll (NY)
Emmanuel Coll (MA)
Emory U (GA)
Fairfield U (CT)
Fordham U (NY)
Franklin & Marshall Coll (PA)
Franklin Pierce U (NH)
George Fox U (OR)
Georgetown Coll (KY)
Georgetown U (DC)
The George Washington U (DC)
Gettysburg Coll (PA)
Goucher Coll (MD)
Hamilton Coll (NY)
Hampshire Coll (MA)
Hendrix Coll (AR)
Hillsdale Coll (MI)
Hobart and William Smith Colls (NY)
Hofstra U (NY)
Illinois Wesleyan U (IL)
Indiana U Bloomington (IN)
Kansas State U (KS)
Keene State Coll (NH)
Kent State U (OH)
Kentucky Wesleyan Coll (KY)
Kenyon Coll (OH)
Knox Coll (IL)
Lafayette Coll (PA)
Lake Forest Coll (IL)
La Salle U (PA)
Lehman Coll of the City U of New York (NY)
Lenoir-Rhyne U (NC)
Lesley U (MA)
Lindsey Wilson Coll (KY)
Lipscomb U (TN)
Lycoming Coll (PA)
Manhattanville Coll (NY)
Marist Coll (NY)
Miami U (OH)
Middlebury Coll (VT)
Mount Allison U (NB, Canada)
Mount Saint Mary's U (CA)
Muhlenberg Coll (PA)
Muskingum U (OH)
Nazareth Coll of Rochester (NY)
Northwestern U (IL)
Occidental Coll (CA)
Oklahoma State U (OK)
Oregon State U (OR)
Pace U (NY)
Pace U, Pleasantville Campus (NY)
Penn State Abington (PA)
Penn State Berks (PA)
Penn State Brandywine (PA)
Penn State Erie, The Behrend Coll (PA)
Penn State Harrisburg (PA)
Penn State Lehigh Valley (PA)
Penn State Schuylkill (PA)
Penn State Worthington Scranton (PA)
Penn State York (PA)
Pitzer Coll (CA)
Pomona Coll (CA)
Providence Coll (RI)
Purdue U (IN)
Queens Coll of the City U of New York (NY)
Ramapo Coll of New Jersey (NJ)
Reed Coll (OR)
Roger Williams U (RI)
Rollins Coll (FL)
Rowan U (NJ)
Rutgers U–Newark (NJ)
Rutgers U–New Brunswick (NJ)
St. Cloud State U (MN)
Saint Francis U (PA)
St. John Fisher Coll (NY)
Saint Louis U (MO)
Saint Mary's Coll of California (CA)
Saint Michael's Coll (VT)
St. Olaf Coll (MN)
Saint Peter's U (NJ)
Salve Regina U (RI)
San Francisco State U (CA)
Scripps Coll (CA)
Sewanee: The U of the South (TN)
Siena Coll (NY)
Skidmore Coll (NY)
Smith Coll (MA)
Sonoma State U (CA)
Stanford U (CA)
State U of New York at Oswego (NY)

State U of New York Coll at Geneseo (NY)
State U of New York Coll at Old Westbury (NY)
Stonehill Coll (MA)
Stony Brook U, State U of New York (NY)
Temple U (PA)
Tennessee Wesleyan U (TN)
Texas State U (TX)
Towson U (MD)
Tufts U (MA)
Tulane U (LA)
Union Coll (NY)
U at Buffalo, the State U of New York (NY)
The U of Alabama (AL)
U of Arkansas (AR)
U of California, Davis (CA)
U of Dayton (OH)
U of Hawaii at Manoa (HI)
The U of Kansas (KS)
U of Maryland, Baltimore County (MD)
U of Maryland, Coll Park (MD)
U of Massachusetts Boston (MA)
U of Massachusetts Lowell (MA)
U of Miami (FL)
U of Michigan (MI)
U of Michigan–Dearborn (MI)
U of Minnesota, Twin Cities Campus (MN)
U of Missouri–Kansas City (MO)
U of Mount Union (OH)
The U of North Carolina at Chapel Hill (NC)
U of Notre Dame (IN)
U of Pennsylvania (PA)
U of Pittsburgh at Greensburg (PA)
U of Richmond (VA)
U of Rochester (NY)
U of San Francisco (CA)
U of Southern California (CA)
U of Southern Mississippi (MS)
U of South Florida (FL)
The U of Texas at Austin (TX)
The U of Texas at Dallas (TX)
The U of Texas at San Antonio (TX)
The U of Toledo (OH)
U of Toronto (ON, Canada)
U of Washington, Bothell (WA)
U of Washington, Tacoma (WA)
Ursinus Coll (PA)
Utah State U (UT)
Valparaiso U (IN)
Vanderbilt U (TN)
Vassar Coll (NY)
Virginia Wesleyan Coll (VA)
Washington Coll (MD)
Washington State U (WA)
Washington U in St. Louis (MO)
Wesleyan U (CT)
Western Connecticut State U (CT)
Western Washington U (WA)
Wheaton Coll (MA)
Wheelock Coll (MA)
Whitworth U (WA)
Williams Coll (MA)
Wittenberg U (OH)

ANALYTICAL CHEMISTRY
North Central Coll (IL)
West Chester U of Pennsylvania (PA)

ANATOMY
Andrews U (MI)
Minnesota State U Mankato (MN)
Tulane U (LA)

ANCIENT/CLASSICAL GREEK
Amherst Coll (MA)
Augustana Coll (IL)
Bard Coll (NY)
Barnard Coll (NY)
Baylor U (TX)
Boston U (MA)
Brigham Young U (UT)
Bryn Mawr Coll (PA)
California State U, Long Beach (CA)
Canisius Coll (NY)
Carleton Coll (MN)
Columbia U (NY)
Dartmouth Coll (NH)
DePauw U (IN)
Duquesne U (PA)
Emory U (GA)
Franklin & Marshall Coll (PA)
Gettysburg Coll (PA)
Hampden-Sydney Coll (VA)
Hillsdale Coll (MI)
Hobart and William Smith Colls (NY)
Hunter Coll of the City U of New York (NY)
Indiana U Bloomington (IN)
Kalamazoo Coll (MI)
Kenyon Coll (OH)
Knox Coll (IL)
Lawrence U (WI)
Loyola U Chicago (IL)
Loyola U New Orleans (LA)
Monmouth Coll (IL)
Mount Allison U (NB, Canada)
Mount Holyoke Coll (MA)
Multnomah U (OR)
Randolph Coll (VA)
Randolph-Macon Coll (VA)
Rice U (TX)
Rutgers U–New Brunswick (NJ)
St. Olaf Coll (MN)
Samford U (AL)
Santa Clara U (CA)
Sewanee: The U of the South (TN)
Smith Coll (MA)
Southwestern U (TX)
Stanford U (CA)
Swarthmore Coll (PA)
Tufts U (MA)
U of California, Los Angeles (CA)
U of Georgia (GA)
U of Miami (FL)
U of Michigan (MI)
The U of North Carolina at Greensboro (NC)
U of Notre Dame (IN)
U of Richmond (VA)
The U of Texas at Austin (TX)
U of Vermont (VT)
U of Washington (WA)
Wabash Coll (IN)
Wake Forest U (NC)
Washington U in St. Louis (MO)
Whitman Coll (WA)

ANCIENT NEAR EASTERN AND BIBLICAL LANGUAGES
Baylor U (TX)
Belmont U (TN)
Carson-Newman U (TN)
Columbia Intl U (SC)
Concordia U Chicago (IL)
Concordia U Irvine (CA)
Concordia U Wisconsin (WI)
Houston Baptist U (TX)
Howard Payne U (TX)
Luther Coll (IA)
The Master's U (CA)
Northwest U (WA)
Oklahoma Baptist U (OK)
Toccoa Falls Coll (GA)
Union U (TN)
U of Toronto (ON, Canada)
U of Valley Forge (PA)
U of Washington (WA)
Walla Walla U (WA)

ANCIENT STUDIES
Bates Coll (ME)
Boston U (MA)
Bowdoin Coll (ME)
Colby Coll (ME)
Columbia U (NY)
Columbia U, School of General Studies (NY)
Concordia U (QC, Canada)
Eckerd Coll (FL)
Emory U (GA)
Lehigh U (PA)
Loyola Marymount U (CA)
Mount Holyoke Coll (MA)
Ohio Wesleyan U (OH)
Purdue U (IN)
Rollins Coll (FL)
Saint Joseph's U (PA)
St. Olaf Coll (MN)
Santa Clara U (CA)
Southwestern Assemblies of God U (TX)
Université de Montréal (QC, Canada)
The U of Kansas (KS)
U of Maryland, Baltimore County (MD)
U of Miami (FL)
U of Michigan (MI)
U of Richmond (VA)
The U of Texas at Austin (TX)
Vanderbilt U (TN)
Washington U in St. Louis (MO)
Wesleyan U (CT)
Wheaton Coll (MA)

ANIMAL-ASSISTED THERAPY
Aurora U (IL)
Averett U (VA)
Carroll Coll (MT)
State U of New York Coll of Agriculture and Technology at Cobleskill (NY)

ANIMAL BEHAVIOR AND ETHOLOGY
Bucknell U (PA)
Canisius Coll (NY)
Franklin & Marshall Coll (PA)
Hampshire Coll (MA)
Indiana U Bloomington (IN)
U of New England (ME)
U of Toronto (ON, Canada)

ANIMAL GENETICS
Clemson U (SC)
Dartmouth Coll (NH)
Jacksonville State U (AL)
Ohio Wesleyan U (OH)
Rutgers U–New Brunswick (NJ)
U of Toronto (ON, Canada)

ANIMAL HEALTH
Brigham Young U–Idaho (ID)
Dalhousie U (NS, Canada)
U of Georgia (GA)

ANIMAL/LIVESTOCK HUSBANDRY AND PRODUCTION
Dalhousie U (NS, Canada)
Rutgers U–New Brunswick (NJ)
Tarleton State U (TX)
Texas A&M U (TX)

ANIMAL NUTRITION
Dalhousie U (NS, Canada)
U of Georgia (GA)

ANIMAL PHYSIOLOGY
California State U, Fresno (CA)
Minnesota State U Mankato (MN)
Rutgers U–New Brunswick (NJ)
Sonoma State U (CA)
The U of Akron (OH)
U of Toronto (ON, Canada)
Utah State U (UT)

ANIMAL SCIENCES
Abilene Christian U (TX)
Angelo State U (TX)
Auburn U (AL)
Becker Coll (MA)
Berry Coll (GA)
Brigham Young U–Idaho (ID)
California Polytechnic State U, San Luis Obispo (CA)
California State Polytechnic U, Pomona (CA)
California State U, Chico (CA)
California State U, Fresno (CA)
Clemson U (SC)
Coll of the Ozarks (MO)
Colorado State U (CO)
Cornell U (NY)
Delaware Valley U (PA)
Iowa State U of Science and Technology (IA)
Kansas State U (KS)
Langston U (OK)
Louisiana State U and A&M Coll (LA)
Louisiana Tech U (LA)
Lubbock Christian U (TX)
Michigan State U (MI)
Mississippi State U (MS)
Missouri State U (MO)
Montana State U (MT)
Morrisville State Coll (NY)
New Mexico State U (NM)
North Carolina State U (NC)
North Dakota State U (ND)
Northwest Missouri State U (MO)
The Ohio State U (OH)
Oklahoma State U (OK)
Oregon State U (OR)
Penn State Abington (PA)
Penn State Altoona (PA)
Penn State Beaver (PA)
Penn State Berks (PA)
Penn State Brandywine (PA)
Penn State DuBois (PA)
Penn State Erie, The Behrend Coll (PA)
Penn State Fayette, The Eberly Campus (PA)
Penn State Greater Allegheny (PA)
Penn State Hazleton (PA)
Penn State Lehigh Valley (PA)
Penn State Mont Alto (PA)
Penn State New Kensington (PA)
Penn State Schuylkill (PA)
Penn State Shenango (PA)
Penn State U Park (PA)
Penn State Wilkes-Barre (PA)
Penn State Worthington Scranton (PA)
Penn State York (PA)
Purdue U (IN)
Rutgers U–New Brunswick (NJ)
Sam Houston State U (TX)
South Dakota State U (SD)
Southern Illinois U Carbondale (IL)
Stephen F. Austin State U (TX)
Tarleton State U (TX)
Tennessee State U (TN)
Texas A&M U (TX)
Texas A&M U–Commerce (TX)
Texas A&M U–Kingsville (TX)
Texas State U (TX)
Texas Tech U (TX)
The U of Arizona (AZ)
U of Arkansas (AR)
U of California, Davis (CA)
U of Delaware (DE)
U of Denver (CO)
The U of Findlay (OH)
U of Florida (FL)
U of Georgia (GA)
U of Guelph (ON, Canada)
U of Hawaii at Manoa (HI)
U of Idaho (ID)
U of Kentucky (KY)
U of Maine (ME)
U of Maryland, Coll Park (MD)
U of Massachusetts Amherst (MA)
U of Minnesota, Crookston (MN)
U of Minnesota, Twin Cities Campus (MN)
U of New Hampshire (NH)
U of Rhode Island (RI)
U of Saskatchewan (SK, Canada)
The U of Tennessee (TN)
The U of Tennessee at Martin (TN)
U of Vermont (VT)
U of Wisconsin–Madison (WI)
U of Wisconsin–Platteville (WI)
Utah State U (UT)
Virginia Polytechnic Inst and State U (VA)
Washington State U (WA)
West Texas A&M U (TX)
West Virginia U (WV)

ANIMAL SCIENCES RELATED
Dalhousie U (NS, Canada)
Delaware Valley U (PA)
Penn State Abington (PA)
Penn State Beaver (PA)
Penn State Brandywine (PA)
Penn State DuBois (PA)
Penn State Erie, The Behrend Coll (PA)
Penn State Fayette, The Eberly Campus (PA)
Penn State Greater Allegheny (PA)
Penn State Hazleton (PA)
Penn State Lehigh Valley (PA)
Penn State Mont Alto (PA)
Penn State New Kensington (PA)
Penn State Schuylkill (PA)
Penn State Shenango (PA)
Penn State Wilkes-Barre (PA)
Penn State Worthington Scranton (PA)
Penn State York (PA)
U of California, Davis (CA)

ANIMATION, INTERACTIVE TECHNOLOGY, VIDEO GRAPHICS AND SPECIAL EFFECTS
Acad of Art U (CA)
American Acad of Art (IL)
Becker Coll (MA)
Bennington Coll (VT)
Bradley U (IL)
Brigham Young U (UT)
California Coll of the Arts (CA)
Cleveland Inst of Art (OH)
Cogswell Polytechnical Coll (CA)
Coll of the Atlantic (ME)
Columbia Coll Chicago (IL)
Columbus Coll of Art & Design (OH)
Concordia U (QC, Canada)
Davenport U, Grand Rapids (MI)
DigiPen Inst of Technology (WA)
Eastern Michigan U (MI)
East Tennessee State U (TN)
Emily Carr U of Art + Design (BC, Canada)
Fashion Inst of Technology (NY)
Ferris State U (MI)
Gulf Coast State Coll (FL)
Huntington U (IN)
Kansas City Art Inst (MO)
Laguna Coll of Art & Design (CA)
Lawrence Technological U (MI)
Loyola Marymount U (CA)
Massachusetts Coll of Art and Design (MA)
Milwaukee Inst of Art and Design (WI)
Minneapolis Coll of Art and Design (MN)
Missouri Western State U (MO)
Mount Ida Coll (MA)
New England Inst of Technology (RI)
New Mexico State U (NM)
North Central Coll (IL)
Northeastern U (MA)
Pennsylvania Coll of Art & Design (PA)
Point Park U (PA)
Regent U (VA)
Ringling Coll of Art and Design (FL)
Rochester Inst of Technology (NY)
Sam Houston State U (TX)
Savannah Coll of Art and Design (GA)
School of the Art Inst of Chicago (IL)
State U of New York Coll of Technology at Alfred (NY)
U of Lethbridge (AB, Canada)
The U of the Arts (PA)
U of the Incarnate Word (TX)
Villa Maria Coll (NY)
Webster U (MO)

ANTHROPOLOGY
Adelphi U (NY)
Agnes Scott Coll (GA)
Albion Coll (MI)
Alma Coll (MI)
American U (DC)
The American U in Cairo (Egypt)
Amherst Coll (MA)
Antioch Coll, Yellow Springs (OH)
Appalachian State U (NC)
Arizona State U at the Tempe campus (AZ)
Auburn U (AL)
Augustana Coll (IL)
Augustana U (SD)
Augusta U (GA)
Austin Coll (TX)
Ball State U (IN)
Bard Coll (NY)
Barnard Coll (NY)
Bates Coll (ME)
Baylor U (TX)
Beloit Coll (WI)
Bennington Coll (VT)
Binghamton U, State U of New York (NY)
Biola U (CA)
Bloomsburg U of Pennsylvania (PA)
Boise State U (ID)
Boston U (MA)
Bowdoin Coll (ME)
Brandeis U (MA)
Bridgewater State U (MA)
Brooklyn Coll of the City U of New York (NY)
Bryn Mawr Coll (PA)
Bucknell U (PA)
Buffalo State Coll, State U of New York (NY)
Butler U (IN)

California State Polytechnic U, Pomona (CA)
California State U, Bakersfield (CA)
California State U, Chico (CA)
California State U, Dominguez Hills (CA)
California State U, East Bay (CA)
California State U, Fresno (CA)
California State U, Fullerton (CA)
California State U, Long Beach (CA)
California State U, Northridge (CA)
California State U, Sacramento (CA)
California State U, San Bernardino (CA)
California State U, San Marcos (CA)
California State U, Stanislaus (CA)
California U of Pennsylvania (PA)
Canisius Coll (NY)
Carleton Coll (MN)
Case Western Reserve U (OH)
The Catholic U of America (DC)
Central Connecticut State U (CT)
Central Michigan U (MI)
Central Washington U (WA)
City Coll of the City U of New York (NY)
Clarion U of Pennsylvania (PA)
Clemson U (SC)
Cleveland State U (OH)
Colby Coll (ME)
Colgate U (NY)
The Coll at Brockport, State U of New York (NY)
Coll of Charleston (SC)
The Coll of Idaho (ID)
Coll of the Holy Cross (MA)
The Coll of William and Mary (VA)
The Coll of Wooster (OH)
The Colorado Coll (CO)
Colorado State U (CO)
Columbia U (NY)
Columbia U, School of General Studies (NY)
Concordia U (QC, Canada)
Connecticut Coll (CT)
Cornell Coll (IA)
Cornell U (NY)
Creighton U (NE)
Dalhousie U (NS, Canada)
Dartmouth Coll (NH)
Davidson Coll (NC)
Denison U (OH)
DePauw U (IN)
Dickinson Coll (PA)
Drake U (IA)
Drew U (NJ)
Drexel U (PA)
Earlham Coll (IN)
East Carolina U (NC)
Eastern Michigan U (MI)
Eastern Washington U (WA)
East Tennessee State U (TN)
Eckerd Coll (FL)
Elon U (NC)
Emory U (GA)
Florida Atlantic U (FL)
Florida Gulf Coast U (FL)
Fordham U (NY)
Fort Lewis Coll (CO)
Franciscan U of Steubenville (OH)
Franklin & Marshall Coll (PA)
Franklin Pierce U (NH)
Furman U (SC)
Georgetown U (DC)
The George Washington U (DC)
Georgia Southern U (GA)
Georgia State U (GA)
Gettysburg Coll (PA)
Grand Valley State U (MI)
Grinnell Coll (IA)
Hamilton Coll (NY)
Hamline U (MN)
Hampshire Coll (MA)
Hanover Coll (IN)
Hartwick Coll (NY)
Harvard U (MA)
Haverford Coll (PA)
Hawai`i Pacific U (HI)
Hendrix Coll (AR)
Hobart and William Smith Colls (NY)
Hofstra U (NY)
Humboldt State U (CA)
Hunter Coll of the City U of New York (NY)
Idaho State U (ID)
Illinois State U (IL)
Illinois Wesleyan U (IL)
Indiana State U (IN)
Indiana U Bloomington (IN)
Indiana U Northwest (IN)
Indiana U of Pennsylvania (PA)
Indiana U–Purdue U Indianapolis (IN)
Indiana U South Bend (IN)
Inter American U of Puerto Rico, San Germán Campus (PR)
Iowa State U of Science and Technology (IA)
Ithaca Coll (NY)
Jacksonville State U (AL)
James Madison U (VA)
Johns Hopkins U (MD)
Juniata Coll (PA)
Kansas State U (KS)
Kennesaw State U (GA)
Kent State U (OH)
Kenyon Coll (OH)
Knox Coll (IL)
Kutztown U of Pennsylvania (PA)
Lafayette Coll (PA)
Lake Forest Coll (IL)
Lawrence U (WI)
Lee U (TN)
Lehigh U (PA)
Lehman Coll of the City U of New York (NY)
Lincoln U (PA)
Lindenwood U (MO)
Linfield Coll (OR)
Longwood U (VA)
Louisiana State U and A&M Coll (LA)
Loyola U Chicago (IL)
Luther Coll (IA)
Macalester Coll (MN)
Massachusetts Inst of Technology (MA)
McMaster U (ON, Canada)
Mercyhurst U (PA)
Metropolitan State U of Denver (CO)
Miami U (OH)
Michigan State U (MI)
Michigan Technological U (MI)
Millersville U of Pennsylvania (PA)
Minnesota State U Mankato (MN)
Minnesota State U Moorhead (MN)
Mississippi State U (MS)
Missouri State U (MO)
Monmouth Coll (IL)
Monmouth U (NJ)
Montana State U (MT)
Montclair State U (NJ)
Mount Allison U (NB, Canada)
Mount Holyoke Coll (MA)
Muhlenberg Coll (PA)
Muskingum U (OH)
Nazareth Coll of Rochester (NY)
New Coll of Florida (FL)
New Mexico State U (NM)
North Carolina State U (NC)
North Central Coll (IL)
North Dakota State U (ND)
Northeastern Illinois U (IL)
Northern Arizona U (AZ)
Northern Illinois U (IL)
Northern Kentucky U (KY)
Northwestern U (IL)
Oberlin Coll (OH)
The Ohio State U (OH)
Ohio U (OH)
Oklahoma Baptist U (OK)
Oregon State U (OR)
Pacific Lutheran U (WA)
Penn State Abington (PA)
Penn State Altoona (PA)
Penn State Beaver (PA)
Penn State Berks (PA)
Penn State Brandywine (PA)
Penn State DuBois (PA)
Penn State Erie, The Behrend Coll (PA)
Penn State Fayette, The Eberly Campus (PA)
Penn State Greater Allegheny (PA)
Penn State Hazleton (PA)
Penn State Lehigh Valley (PA)
Penn State Mont Alto (PA)
Penn State New Kensington (PA)
Penn State Schuylkill (PA)
Penn State Shenango (PA)
Penn State U Park (PA)
Penn State Wilkes-Barre (PA)
Penn State Worthington Scranton (PA)
Penn State York (PA)
Pitzer Coll (CA)
Pomona Coll (CA)
Portland State U (OR)
Princeton U (NJ)
Purchase Coll, State U of New York (NY)
Purdue U (IN)
Queens Coll of the City U of New York (NY)
Radford U (VA)
Reed Coll (OR)
Rhode Island Coll (RI)
Rhodes Coll (TN)
Rice U (TX)
Ripon Coll (WI)
Rockford U (IL)
Rollins Coll (FL)
Rutgers U–Newark (NJ)
Rutgers U–New Brunswick (NJ)
St. Cloud State U (MN)
Saint Francis U (PA)
St. John Fisher Coll (NY)
St. John's U (NY)
Saint Louis U (MO)
Saint Louis U–Madrid Campus (Spain)
Saint Martin's U (WA)
Saint Mary's Coll of California (CA)
St. Mary's Coll of Maryland (MD)
St. Thomas U (NB, Canada)
Saint Vincent Coll (PA)
San Diego State U (CA)
San Francisco State U (CA)
Santa Clara U (CA)
Sarah Lawrence Coll (NY)
Scripps Coll (CA)
Seattle U (WA)
Sewanee: The U of the South (TN)
Skidmore Coll (NY)
Smith Coll (MA)
Sonoma State U (CA)
Southern Connecticut State U (CT)
Southern Illinois U Carbondale (IL)
Southern Illinois U Edwardsville (IL)
Southern Methodist U (TX)
Southern Oregon U (OR)
Southern Utah U (UT)
Southwestern U (TX)
Stanford U (CA)
State U of New York at New Paltz (NY)
State U of New York at Oswego (NY)
State U of New York at Plattsburgh (NY)
State U of New York Coll at Cortland (NY)
State U of New York Coll at Geneseo (NY)
State U of New York Coll at Potsdam (NY)
Stony Brook U, State U of New York (NY)
Susquehanna U (PA)
Sweet Briar Coll (VA)
Syracuse U (NY)
Temple U (PA)
Texas A&M U (TX)
Texas Christian U (TX)
Texas State U (TX)
Texas Tech U (TX)
Transylvania U (KY)
Trent U (ON, Canada)
Trinity U (TX)
Troy U (AL)
Tufts U (MA)
Tulane U (LA)
Union Coll (NY)
Université de Montréal (QC, Canada)
U at Albany, State U of New York (NY)
U at Buffalo, the State U of New York (NY)
The U of Akron (OH)
The U of Alabama (AL)
The U of Alabama at Birmingham (AL)
U of Alaska Fairbanks (AK)
The U of Arizona (AZ)
U of Arkansas (AR)
U of California, Davis (CA)
U of California, Irvine (CA)
U of California, Los Angeles (CA)
U of California, Riverside (CA)
U of California, San Diego (CA)
U of California, Santa Barbara (CA)
U of Central Florida (FL)
U of Chicago (IL)
U of Colorado Boulder (CO)
U of Colorado Colorado Springs (CO)
U of Colorado Denver (CO)
U of Delaware (DE)
U of Denver (CO)
U of Florida (FL)
U of Georgia (GA)
U of Guelph (ON, Canada)
U of Hawaii at Manoa (HI)
U of Houston (TX)
U of Houston–Clear Lake (TX)
U of Idaho (ID)
U of Illinois at Chicago (IL)
U of Indianapolis (IN)
The U of Kansas (KS)
U of Kentucky (KY)
U of King's Coll (NS, Canada)
U of La Verne (CA)
U of Lethbridge (AB, Canada)
U of Louisville (KY)
U of Maine (ME)
U of Maryland, Baltimore County (MD)
U of Maryland, Coll Park (MD)
U of Mary Washington (VA)
U of Massachusetts Amherst (MA)
U of Massachusetts Boston (MA)
U of Miami (FL)
U of Michigan (MI)
U of Michigan–Dearborn (MI)
U of Michigan–Flint (MI)
U of Minnesota, Duluth (MN)
U of Minnesota, Morris (MN)
U of Minnesota, Twin Cities Campus (MN)
U of Missouri–St. Louis (MO)
U of Nevada, Las Vegas (NV)
U of Nevada, Reno (NV)
U of New Hampshire (NH)
U of North Carolina at Asheville (NC)
The U of North Carolina at Chapel Hill (NC)
The U of North Carolina at Charlotte (NC)
The U of North Carolina at Greensboro (NC)
The U of North Carolina Wilmington (NC)
U of North Dakota (ND)
U of Northern Colorado (CO)
U of Northern Iowa (IA)
U of North Florida (FL)
U of North Texas (TX)
U of Notre Dame (IN)
U of Oklahoma (OK)
U of Oregon (OR)
U of Pennsylvania (PA)
U of Pittsburgh (PA)
U of Pittsburgh at Greensburg (PA)
U of Regina (SK, Canada)
U of Rhode Island (RI)
U of Richmond (VA)
U of Rochester (NY)
U of San Diego (CA)
U of Saskatchewan (SK, Canada)
U of South Alabama (AL)
U of South Carolina (SC)
The U of South Dakota (SD)
U of Southern California (CA)
U of Southern Indiana (IN)
U of Southern Mississippi (MS)
U of South Florida (FL)
U of South Florida, St. Petersburg (FL)
The U of Tennessee (TN)
The U of Texas at Austin (TX)
The U of Texas at El Paso (TX)
The U of Texas at San Antonio (TX)
The U of Texas Rio Grande Valley (TX)
U of the Fraser Valley (BC, Canada)
The U of Toledo (OH)
U of Toronto (ON, Canada)
The U of Tulsa (OK)
U of Utah (UT)
U of Vermont (VT)
U of Virginia (VA)
U of Washington (WA)
U of Waterloo (ON, Canada)
U of West Georgia (GA)
U of Wisconsin–Madison (WI)
U of Wisconsin–Milwaukee (WI)
Ursinus Coll (PA)
Utah State U (UT)
Vanderbilt U (TN)
Vassar Coll (NY)
Virginia Commonwealth U (VA)
Wagner Coll (NY)
Wake Forest U (NC)
Washburn U (KS)
Washington Coll (MD)
Washington State U (WA)
Washington State U–Vancouver (WA)
Washington U in St. Louis (MO)
Wayne State U (MI)
Weber State U (UT)
Wells Coll (NY)
Wesleyan U (CT)
West Chester U of Pennsylvania (PA)
Western Carolina U (NC)
Western Connecticut State U (CT)
Western Illinois U (IL)
Western Kentucky U (KY)
Western Michigan U (MI)
Western Oregon U (OR)
Western State Colorado U (CO)
Western Washington U (WA)
Westmont Coll (CA)
Wheaton Coll (IL)
Wheaton Coll (MA)
Whitman Coll (WA)
Whittier Coll (CA)
Wichita State U (KS)
Widener U (PA)
Willamette U (OR)
William Paterson U of New Jersey (NJ)
William Peace U (NC)
Williams Coll (MA)
Wright State U (OH)
Wright State U–Lake Campus (OH)
York Coll of the City U of New York (NY)
Youngstown State U (OH)

ANTHROPOLOGY RELATED
Bridgewater State U (MA)
Butler U (IN)
California Baptist U (CA)
U of Michigan (MI)
Ursinus Coll (PA)
Western Washington U (WA)

APPAREL AND ACCESSORIES MARKETING
Stephens Coll (MO)
U of Rhode Island (RI)
Woodbury U (CA)

APPAREL AND TEXTILE MANUFACTURING
Acad of Art U (CA)
Fashion Inst of Technology (NY)
FIDM/Fashion Inst of Design & Merchandising, Los Angeles Campus (CA)
Michigan State U (MI)

APPAREL AND TEXTILE MARKETING MANAGEMENT
Acad of Art U (CA)
Auburn U (AL)
Central Washington U (WA)
Colorado State U (CO)
Savannah Coll of Art and Design (GA)
South Dakota State U (SD)
U of the Incarnate Word (TX)
Wayne State U (MI)

APPAREL AND TEXTILES
Appalachian State U (NC)
Auburn U (AL)
Bowling Green State U (OH)
California State Polytechnic U, Pomona (CA)
California State U, Long Beach (CA)
East Carolina U (NC)
Framingham State U (MA)
Georgia Southern U (GA)

Illinois State U (IL)
Indiana State U (IN)
Indiana U Bloomington (IN)
Iowa State U of Science and Technology (IA)
Jacksonville State U (AL)
Kansas State U (KS)
Lamar U (TX)
Liberty U (VA)
Lipscomb U (TN)
Louisiana State U and A&M Coll (LA)
Michigan State U (MI)
Missouri State U (MO)
New Mexico State U (NM)
North Dakota State U (ND)
Northern Illinois U (IL)
The Ohio State U (OH)
Ohio U (OH)
Oregon State U (OR)
Rhode Island School of Design (RI)
Seattle Pacific U (WA)
Southern Illinois U Carbondale (IL)
Texas A&M U–Kingsville (TX)
The U of Akron (OH)
The U of Alabama (AL)
U of Arkansas (AR)
U of California, Davis (CA)
U of Delaware (DE)
U of Georgia (GA)
U of Hawaii at Manoa (HI)
U of Idaho (ID)
U of Kentucky (KY)
U of Minnesota, Twin Cities Campus (MN)
The U of North Carolina at Greensboro (NC)
U of Northern Iowa (IA)
U of Rhode Island (RI)
U of Southern Mississippi (MS)
The U of Texas at Austin (TX)
U of Wisconsin–Madison (WI)
U of Wisconsin–Stout (WI)
Virginia Polytechnic Inst and State U (VA)
Washington State U (WA)
Western Kentucky U (KY)

APPAREL AND TEXTILES RELATED
Savannah Coll of Art and Design (GA)
Stephens Coll (MO)

APPLIED AND PROFESSIONAL ETHICS
Carnegie Mellon U (PA)
Carson-Newman U (TN)
Drexel U (PA)
Mount Saint Mary's U (CA)
Nazarene Bible Coll (CO)
Simpson Coll (IA)
U of Michigan–Flint (MI)
Ursinus Coll (PA)
Western Michigan U (MI)

APPLIED BEHAVIOR ANALYSIS
Florida Inst of Technology (FL)
Saint Joseph's U (PA)
Spalding U (KY)
U of North Texas (TX)
Western Michigan U (MI)

APPLIED ECONOMICS
Allegheny Coll (PA)
Augsburg Coll (MN)
Binghamton U, State U of New York (NY)
Bowling Green State U (OH)
Brigham Young U (UT)
Bryant U (RI)
The Coll of St. Scholastica (MN)
Concordia U (QC, Canada)
Farmingdale State Coll (NY)
HEC Montreal (QC, Canada)
Ithaca Coll (NY)
Penn State Abington (PA)
Penn State Beaver (PA)
Penn State Brandywine (PA)
Penn State DuBois (PA)
Penn State Erie, The Behrend Coll (PA)
Penn State Fayette, The Eberly Campus (PA)
Penn State Greater Allegheny (PA)
Penn State Hazleton (PA)
Penn State Lehigh Valley (PA)
Penn State Mont Alto (PA)
Penn State New Kensington (PA)
Penn State Schuylkill (PA)
Penn State Shenango (PA)
Penn State Wilkes-Barre (PA)
Penn State Worthington Scranton (PA)
Penn State York (PA)
The U of Akron (OH)
The U of Arizona (AZ)
U of Massachusetts Amherst (MA)
U of Minnesota, Twin Cities Campus (MN)
U of Northern Iowa (IA)
U of San Francisco (CA)
U of Waterloo (ON, Canada)
Ursinus Coll (PA)
Wabash Coll (IN)

APPLIED HORTICULTURE/ HORTICULTURAL BUSINESS SERVICES RELATED
Delaware Valley U (PA)
Morrisville State Coll (NY)
North Dakota State U (ND)
U of Rhode Island (RI)

APPLIED HORTICULTURE/ HORTICULTURE OPERATIONS
Colorado State U (CO)
Farmingdale State Coll (NY)
Kent State U at Salem (OH)
North Carolina State U (NC)
South Dakota State U (SD)
Texas A&M U (TX)
U of Maine (ME)
U of Massachusetts Amherst (MA)

APPLIED LINGUISTICS
Caldwell U (NJ)
Corban U (OR)
Mid-Atlantic Christian U (NC)
Portland State U (OR)
U of Idaho (ID)

APPLIED MATHEMATICS
Alderson Broaddus U (WV)
American U (DC)
American U of Beirut (Lebanon)
Arizona State U at the West campus (AZ)
Auburn U (AL)
Augustana Coll (IL)
Baylor U (TX)
Biola U (CA)
Bloomfield Coll (NJ)
Boise State U (ID)
Bowie State U (MD)
Brescia U (KY)
Brigham Young U–Idaho (ID)
Bryant U (RI)
California State U, East Bay (CA)
California State U, Fullerton (CA)
California State U, Long Beach (CA)
Carnegie Mellon U (PA)
Carroll Coll (MT)
Case Western Reserve U (OH)
Central Michigan U (MI)
Charleston Southern U (SC)
Christopher Newport U (VA)
Clarkson U (NY)
Coastal Carolina U (SC)
Colgate U (NY)
The Coll of Idaho (ID)
Columbia U (NY)
Columbia U, School of General Studies (NY)
East Central U (OK)
Elizabethtown Coll (PA)
Elon U (NC)
Emmaus Bible Coll (IA)
Emory U (GA)
Endicott Coll (MA)
Farmingdale State Coll (NY)
Ferris State U (MI)
Fitchburg State U (MA)
Florida Inst of Technology (FL)
Fresno Pacific U (CA)
Geneva Coll (PA)
The George Washington U (DC)
Georgia Inst of Technology (GA)
Grand View U (IA)
Hampden-Sydney Coll (VA)
Harvard U (MA)
Hillsdale Coll (MI)
Humboldt State U (CA)
Indiana U South Bend (IN)
Inter American U of Puerto Rico, San Germán Campus (PR)
Iona Coll (NY)
Johns Hopkins U (MD)
Kennesaw State U (GA)
Kent State U (OH)
Kettering U (MI)
La Salle U (PA)
Lasell Coll (MA)
Lee U (TN)
Lehigh U (PA)
Lipscomb U (TN)
Loyola Marymount U (CA)
Loyola U Maryland (MD)
Marist Coll (NY)
Mary Baldwin U (VA)
Maryville U of Saint Louis (MO)
The Master's U (CA)
McMaster U (ON, Canada)
Millsaps Coll (MS)
Missouri U of Science and Technology (MO)
Mount Allison U (NB, Canada)
New Coll of Florida (FL)
New York City Coll of Technology of the City U of New York (NY)
North Carolina State U (NC)
North Central Coll (IL)
Northern Illinois U (IL)
Northwestern U (IL)
Ohio U (OH)
Penn State Harrisburg (PA)
Purdue U (IN)
Quinnipiac U (CT)
Rice U (TX)
Robert Morris U (PA)
Roger Williams U (RI)
Rutgers U–Newark (NJ)
Saginaw Valley State U (MI)
Saint Mary's Coll (IN)
St. Thomas Aquinas Coll (NY)
San Diego State U (CA)
San Francisco State U (CA)
Simon Fraser U (BC, Canada)
Sonoma State U (CA)
State U of New York at Oswego (NY)
State U of New York Coll at Geneseo (NY)
State U of New York Polytechnic Inst (NY)
Stevenson U (MD)
Stony Brook U, State U of New York (NY)
Syracuse U (NY)
Temple U (PA)
Texas A&M U (TX)
Texas State U (TX)
Thomas Edison State U (NJ)
Trent U (ON, Canada)
Trevecca Nazarene U (TN)
Tufts U (MA)
United States Air Force Acad (CO)
Université de Montréal (QC, Canada)
U at Buffalo, the State U of New York (NY)
The U of Akron (OH)
U of California, Davis (CA)
U of California, Los Angeles (CA)
U of California, San Diego (CA)
U of Colorado Boulder (CO)
The U of Findlay (OH)
U of Georgia (GA)
U of Houston–Downtown (TX)
U of Idaho (ID)
U of Jamestown (ND)
U of Massachusetts Lowell (MA)
U of Miami (FL)
U of New England (ME)
U of New Hampshire (NH)
U of New Haven (CT)
The U of North Carolina at Chapel Hill (NC)
U of North Florida (FL)
U of Pittsburgh (PA)
U of Pittsburgh at Bradford (PA)
U of Pittsburgh at Greensburg (PA)
U of Rochester (NY)
The U of Scranton (PA)
U of South Carolina Aiken (SC)
The U of Tennessee at Chattanooga (TN)
The U of Texas at El Paso (TX)
U of the Virgin Islands (VI)
U of Toronto (ON, Canada)
The U of Tulsa (OK)
U of Utah (UT)
U of Waterloo (ON, Canada)
U of Windsor (ON, Canada)
U of Wisconsin–Madison (WI)
U of Wisconsin–Milwaukee (WI)
U of Wisconsin–Stout (WI)
Valdosta State U (GA)
Washington State U (WA)
Washington U in St. Louis (MO)
Weber State U (UT)
Wentworth Inst of Technology (MA)
Wesleyan Coll (GA)
Western Michigan U (MI)
Western Washington U (WA)
Wheaton Coll (IL)
William Penn U (IA)

APPLIED MATHEMATICS RELATED
Arizona State U at the Tempe campus (AZ)
Averett U (VA)
Belmont U (TN)
Berea Coll (KY)
Bucknell U (PA)
Elizabethtown Coll (PA)
Georgia Inst of Technology (GA)
Inter American U of Puerto Rico, Bayamón Campus (PR)
Inter American U of Puerto Rico, Metropolitan Campus (PR)
Keene State Coll (NH)
Louisiana Coll (LA)
Lycoming Coll (PA)
Mount St. Joseph U (OH)
Temple U (PA)
U of California, Santa Barbara (CA)
U of Washington (WA)
U of Waterloo (ON, Canada)
U of Wisconsin–Milwaukee (WI)
Whitworth U (WA)
Willamette U (OR)

APPLIED PSYCHOLOGY
Arizona State U at the Polytechnic campus (AZ)
Armstrong State U (GA)
Belhaven U (MS)
Bryant U (RI)
Carson-Newman U (TN)
Christian Brothers U (TN)
Farmingdale State Coll (NY)
Judson U (IL)
Kansas Wesleyan U (KS)
Loyola U Chicago (IL)
Morrisville State Coll (NY)
Mount Saint Mary's U (CA)
Multnomah U (OR)
Pace U (NY)
Pace U, Pleasantville Campus (NY)
State U of New York Coll of Technology at Canton (NY)
United States Military Acad (NY)
U of Michigan–Flint (MI)

AQUACULTURE
Auburn U (AL)
Clemson U (SC)
Dalhousie U (NS, Canada)
U of New England (ME)

AQUATIC BIOLOGY/ LIMNOLOGY
Florida Inst of Technology (FL)
Gannon U (PA)
State U of New York Coll of Environmental Science and Forestry (NY)
Texas State U (TX)
U of South Carolina (SC)
Western Michigan U (MI)

ARABIC
American U (DC)
American U of Beirut (Lebanon)
Bard Coll (NY)
Baylor U (TX)
Binghamton U, State U of New York (NY)
California U of Pennsylvania (PA)
Dartmouth Coll (NH)
Emory U (GA)
Georgetown U (DC)
Lebanese American U (Lebanon)
Michigan State U (MI)
Middlebury Coll (VT)
Montclair State U (NJ)
The Ohio State U (OH)
Portland State U (OR)
Tufts U (MA)
United States Military Acad (NY)
U of California, Los Angeles (CA)
U of Cincinnati (OH)
U of Georgia (GA)
U of Maryland, Coll Park (MD)
U of Notre Dame (IN)
U of Oklahoma (OK)
The U of Texas at Austin (TX)
U of Toronto (ON, Canada)
Washington U in St. Louis (MO)
Western Kentucky U (KY)

ARCHEOLOGY
The American U in Cairo (Egypt)
American U of Beirut (Lebanon)
The American U of Rome (Italy)
Biola U (CA)
Boston U (MA)
Bowdoin Coll (ME)
Bridgewater State U (MA)
Bryn Mawr Coll (PA)
Coll of Charleston (SC)
The Coll of Wooster (OH)
Columbia U (NY)
Columbia U, School of General Studies (NY)
Cornell Coll (IA)
Cornell U (NY)
Dartmouth Coll (NH)
Dickinson Coll (PA)
Franklin Pierce U (NH)
The George Washington U (DC)
Hamilton Coll (NY)
Haverford Coll (PA)
Hunter Coll of the City U of New York (NY)
Johns Hopkins U (MD)
Lawrence U (WI)
Mercyhurst U (PA)
Oberlin Coll (OH)
Penn State Abington (PA)
Penn State Altoona (PA)
Penn State Beaver (PA)
Penn State Berks (PA)
Penn State Brandywine (PA)
Penn State DuBois (PA)
Penn State Erie, The Behrend Coll (PA)
Penn State Fayette, The Eberly Campus (PA)
Penn State Greater Allegheny (PA)
Penn State Hazleton (PA)
Penn State Lehigh Valley (PA)
Penn State Mont Alto (PA)
Penn State New Kensington (PA)
Penn State Schuylkill (PA)
Penn State Shenango (PA)
Penn State U Park (PA)
Penn State Wilkes-Barre (PA)
Penn State Worthington Scranton (PA)
Penn State York (PA)
Saint Mary's Coll of California (CA)
Simon Fraser U (BC, Canada)
Stanford U (CA)
State U of New York Coll at Potsdam (NY)
Sweet Briar Coll (VA)
Tufts U (MA)
Université de Montréal (QC, Canada)
U of Cincinnati (OH)
U of Evansville (IN)
U of Indianapolis (IN)
U of Lethbridge (AB, Canada)
The U of North Carolina at Chapel Hill (NC)
U of Saskatchewan (SK, Canada)
U of Southern California (CA)
The U of Texas at Austin (TX)
U of Toronto (ON, Canada)
U of Wisconsin–La Crosse (WI)
Washington U in St. Louis (MO)
Wesleyan U (CT)
Western Washington U (WA)
Wheaton Coll (IL)

ARCHITECTURAL AND BUILDING SCIENCES
Georgia Inst of Technology (GA)
Lawrence Technological U (MI)
Pennsylvania Coll of Technology (PA)
Savannah Coll of Art and Design (GA)
U of Massachusetts Amherst (MA)
Washington U in St. Louis (MO)

ARCHITECTURAL DRAFTING AND CAD/CADD
Acad of Art U (CA)

ARCHITECTURAL ENGINEERING
Andrews U (MI)
Auburn U (AL)
California Polytechnic State U, San Luis Obispo (CA)
Drexel U (PA)
Kansas State U (KS)
Lawrence Technological U (MI)
Milwaukee School of Eng (WI)
Missouri U of Science and Technology (MO)
Oklahoma State U (OK)
Penn State Abington (PA)
Penn State Altoona (PA)
Penn State Beaver (PA)
Penn State Berks (PA)
Penn State Brandywine (PA)
Penn State DuBois (PA)
Penn State Erie, The Behrend Coll (PA)
Penn State Fayette, The Eberly Campus (PA)
Penn State Greater Allegheny (PA)
Penn State Hazleton (PA)
Penn State Lehigh Valley (PA)
Penn State Mont Alto (PA)
Penn State New Kensington (PA)
Penn State Schuylkill (PA)
Penn State Shenango (PA)
Penn State U Park (PA)
Penn State Wilkes-Barre (PA)
Penn State Worthington Scranton (PA)
Penn State York (PA)
Rutgers U–New Brunswick (NJ)
Tennessee State U (TN)
Texas A&M U–Kingsville (TX)
Tufts U (MA)
The U of Alabama (AL)
U of Cincinnati (OH)
U of Colorado Boulder (CO)
U of Detroit Mercy (MI)
The U of Kansas (KS)
U of Miami (FL)
U of Oklahoma (OK)
The U of Texas at Austin (TX)
Worcester Polytechnic Inst (MA)

ARCHITECTURAL ENGINEERING TECHNOLOGY
Bluefield State Coll (WV)
Farmingdale State Coll (NY)
Fitchburg State U (MA)
Indiana U–Purdue U Indianapolis (IN)
New England Inst of Technology (RI)
Purdue U (IN)
Seminole State Coll of Florida (FL)
State U of New York Coll of Technology at Alfred (NY)
U of Hartford (CT)
U of Southern Mississippi (MS)
Vermont Tech Coll (VT)
Washington U in St. Louis (MO)

ARCHITECTURAL HISTORY AND CRITICISM
Boston U (MA)
Coll of the Holy Cross (MA)
Columbia U, School of General Studies (NY)
Cornell U (NY)
Savannah Coll of Art and Design (GA)
Syracuse U (NY)
The U of Kansas (KS)
U of Miami (FL)
U of San Diego (CA)
The U of Texas at Austin (TX)
U of Virginia (VA)

ARCHITECTURAL TECHNOLOGY
Indiana State U (IN)
Lawrence Technological U (MI)
New York City Coll of Technology of the City U of New York (NY)
New York Inst of Technology (NY)
Washington U in St. Louis (MO)
Western Kentucky U (KY)

ARCHITECTURE
Acad of Art U (CA)
The American U in Dubai (United Arab Emirates)
American U of Beirut (Lebanon)
Andrews U (MI)
Arizona State U at the Tempe campus (AZ)
Auburn U (AL)
Ball State U (IN)
Barnard Coll (NY)
Benedictine Coll (KS)
Bennington Coll (VT)
Boston Architectural Coll (MA)
California Baptist U (CA)
California Coll of the Arts (CA)
California Polytechnic State U, San Luis Obispo (CA)
California State Polytechnic U, Pomona (CA)
Carnegie Mellon U (PA)
The Catholic U of America (DC)
City Coll of the City U of New York (NY)
Clemson U (SC)
Columbia U (NY)
Columbia U, School of General Studies (NY)
Cooper Union for the Advancement of Science and Art (NY)
Cornell Coll (IA)
Cornell U (NY)
Dalhousie U (NS, Canada)
Drexel U (PA)
Drury U (MO)
Dunwoody Coll of Technology (MN)
Florida Ag and Mech U (FL)
Florida Atlantic U (FL)
Florida Intl U (FL)
Georgia Inst of Technology (GA)
Hampshire Coll (MA)
Hampton U (VA)
Hobart and William Smith Colls (NY)
Inter American U of Puerto Rico, San Germán Campus (PR)
Iowa State U of Science and Technology (IA)
Ithaca Coll (NY)
Judson U (IL)
Kean U (NJ)
Keene State Coll (NH)
Kennesaw State U (GA)
Kent State U (OH)
Lebanese American U (Lebanon)
Lehigh U (PA)
Louisiana State U and A&M Coll (LA)
Louisiana Tech U (LA)
Marywood U (PA)
Massachusetts Coll of Art and Design (MA)
Massachusetts Inst of Technology (MA)
Miami U (OH)
Middlebury Coll (VT)
Mississippi State U (MS)
New York Inst of Technology (NY)
North Carolina State U (NC)
Northeastern U (MA)
The Ohio State U (OH)
Oklahoma State U (OK)
Penn State U Park (PA)
Polytechnic U of Puerto Rico (PR)
Portland State U (OR)
Prairie View A&M U (TX)
Pratt Inst (NY)
Princeton U (NJ)
Rensselaer Polytechnic Inst (NY)
Rhode Island School of Design (RI)
Rice U (TX)
Roger Williams U (RI)
Sarah Lawrence Coll (NY)
Smith Coll (MA)
South Dakota State U (SD)
Southern Illinois U Carbondale (IL)
State U of New York Coll of Technology at Alfred (NY)
Syracuse U (NY)
Temple U (PA)
Texas A&M U (TX)
Texas Tech U (TX)
Tulane U (LA)
Université de Montréal (QC, Canada)
U at Buffalo, the State U of New York (NY)
The U of Arizona (AZ)
U of Arkansas (AR)
U of California, Los Angeles (CA)
U of Central Florida (FL)
U of Cincinnati (OH)
U of Colorado Denver (CO)
U of Detroit Mercy (MI)
U of Florida (FL)
U of Hawaii at Manoa (HI)
U of Houston (TX)
U of Idaho (ID)
U of Illinois at Chicago (IL)
The U of Kansas (KS)
U of Kentucky (KY)
U of Maryland, Coll Park (MD)
U of Massachusetts Amherst (MA)
U of Miami (FL)
U of Michigan (MI)
U of Minnesota, Twin Cities Campus (MN)
U of Missouri–Kansas City (MO)
U of Nevada, Las Vegas (NV)
The U of North Carolina at Charlotte (NC)
U of Notre Dame (IN)
U of Oklahoma (OK)
U of Oregon (OR)
U of Pennsylvania (PA)
U of San Francisco (CA)
U of Southern California (CA)
The U of Tennessee (TN)
The U of Texas at Austin (TX)
The U of Texas at San Antonio (TX)
U of Toronto (ON, Canada)
U of Utah (UT)
U of Virginia (VA)
U of Washington (WA)
U of Waterloo (ON, Canada)
U of Wisconsin–Milwaukee (WI)
Virginia Polytechnic Inst and State U (VA)
Washington State U (WA)
Washington U in St. Louis (MO)
Wentworth Inst of Technology (MA)
Woodbury U (CA)

ARCHITECTURE RELATED
Case Western Reserve U (OH)
Columbia U (NY)
Connecticut Coll (CT)
Eugene Lang Coll of Liberal Arts (NY)
Lipscomb U (TN)
Mount Holyoke Coll (MA)
Parsons School of Design (NY)
School of the Art Inst of Chicago (IL)
The U of Arizona (AZ)
U of Illinois at Chicago (IL)
U of Utah (UT)
Washington U in St. Louis (MO)

AREA STUDIES RELATED
Augsburg Coll (MN)
Boston U (MA)
Bridgewater State U (MA)
Eastern Michigan U (MI)
Gannon U (PA)
Gettysburg Coll (PA)
Hofstra U (NY)
Illinois Wesleyan U (IL)
Lake Forest Coll (IL)
Lycoming Coll (PA)
Millersville U of Pennsylvania (PA)
Nevada State Coll (NV)
Northeastern State U (OK)
Northwestern U (IL)
Queens Coll of the City U of New York (NY)
Ramapo Coll of New Jersey (NJ)
Stanford U (CA)
State U of New York at Plattsburgh (NY)
U of Alaska Fairbanks (AK)
U of California, Santa Barbara (CA)
U of Michigan–Dearborn (MI)
U of Oklahoma (OK)
U of Pittsburgh (PA)
U of Virginia (VA)
U of Washington (WA)
Utah State U (UT)
Virginia Commonwealth U (VA)
Washington U in St. Louis (MO)
Williams Coll (MA)

ARMY ROTC/MILITARY SCIENCE
Jacksonville State U (AL)
Jacksonville U (FL)
Minnesota State U Mankato (MN)
Northwest U (WA)

ARMY ROTC, MILITARY SCIENCE AND OPERATIONS RELATED
Calvary U (MO)
Western Kentucky U (KY)

ART
Alabama State U (AL)
Albany State U (GA)
Albertus Magnus Coll (CT)
Albion Coll (MI)
Albright Coll (PA)
Alfred U (NY)
Allegheny Coll (PA)
Alma Coll (MI)
Alverno Coll (WI)
American Acad of Art (IL)
The American U in Cairo (Egypt)
Andrews U (MI)
Appalachian State U (NC)
Aquinas Coll (MI)
Arcadia U (PA)
Arizona State U at the Tempe campus (AZ)
Arkansas Tech U (AR)
Armstrong State U (GA)
Athens State U (AL)
Auburn U at Montgomery (AL)
Augustana Coll (IL)
Augustana U (SD)
Aurora U (IL)
Austin Coll (TX)
Austin Peay State U (TN)
Averett U (VA)
Avila U (MO)
Baldwin Wallace U (OH)
Ball State U (IN)
Bates Coll (ME)
Baylor U (TX)
Belhaven U (MS)
Belmont U (TN)
Bemidji State U (MN)
Benedictine Coll (KS)
Berea Coll (KY)
Berry Coll (GA)
Bethany Lutheran Coll (MN)
Bethel Coll (IN)
Bethel U (MN)
Binghamton U, State U of New York (NY)
Biola U (CA)
Bishop's U (QC, Canada)
Blackburn Coll (IL)
Black Hills State U (SD)
Bluefield Coll (VA)
Bluffton U (OH)
Bowie State U (MD)
Bowling Green State U (OH)
Bradley U (IL)
Brescia U (KY)
Briar Cliff U (IA)
Brigham Young U–Idaho (ID)
Brooklyn Coll of the City U of New York (NY)
Bucknell U (PA)
Buena Vista U (IA)
Buffalo State Coll, State U of New York (NY)
Caldwell U (NJ)
California Coll of the Arts (CA)
California Lutheran U (CA)
California State Polytechnic U, Pomona (CA)
California State U, Bakersfield (CA)
California State U, Chico (CA)
California State U, Dominguez Hills (CA)
California State U, Fresno (CA)
California State U, Fullerton (CA)
California State U, Long Beach (CA)
California State U, Monterey Bay (CA)
California State U, Northridge (CA)
California State U, Sacramento (CA)
California State U, San Bernardino (CA)
California State U, Stanislaus (CA)
California U of Pennsylvania (PA)
Calvin Coll (MI)
Cameron U (OK)
Campbellsville U (KY)
Capital U (OH)
Cardinal Stritch U (WI)
Carnegie Mellon U (PA)
Carson-Newman U (TN)
The Catholic U of America (DC)
Cedar Crest Coll (PA)
Centenary Coll of Louisiana (LA)
Central Connecticut State U (CT)
Central Michigan U (MI)
Central State U (OH)
Central Washington U (WA)
Chapman U (CA)
City Coll of the City U of New York (NY)
Clarion U of Pennsylvania (PA)
Clark Atlanta U (GA)
Clemson U (SC)
Cleveland State U (OH)
Coe Coll (IA)
Colby Coll (ME)
Colby-Sawyer Coll (NH)
Colgate U (NY)
The Coll at Brockport, State U of New York (NY)
The Coll of Idaho (ID)
The Coll of New Jersey (NJ)
Coll of Saint Benedict (MN)
Coll of Saint Elizabeth (NJ)
Coll of Saint Mary (NE)
The Coll of St. Scholastica (MN)
Coll of the Atlantic (ME)
The Coll of William and Mary (VA)
Colorado Mesa U (CO)
Columbia Coll (MO)
Concordia Coll (MN)
Concordia Coll–New York (NY)
Concordia U Chicago (IL)
Concordia U Irvine (CA)
Concordia U, Nebraska (NE)
Concordia U, St. Paul (MN)
Concordia U Wisconsin (WI)
Converse Coll (SC)
Cornell Coll (IA)
Creighton U (NE)
Culver-Stockton Coll (MO)
Daemen Coll (NY)
Dallas Baptist U (TX)
Davidson Coll (NC)
Denison U (OH)
Dickinson State U (ND)
Doane U (NE)
Dominican U of California (CA)
Drake U (IA)
Earlham Coll (IN)
East Central U (OK)
Eastern Illinois U (IL)
Eastern Mennonite U (VA)
Eastern Michigan U (MI)
Eastern Oregon U (OR)
East Tennessee State U (TN)
Edgewood Coll (WI)
Elmira Coll (NY)
Elon U (NC)
Emporia State U (KS)
Eureka Coll (IL)
Evangel U (MO)
The Evergreen State Coll (WA)
Fayetteville State U (NC)
Felician U (NJ)
Florida Atlantic U (FL)
Florida Gulf Coast U (FL)
Florida Intl U (FL)
Fort Lewis Coll (CO)
Framingham State U (MA)
Francis Marion U (SC)
Franklin Pierce U (NH)
Freed-Hardeman U (TN)
Friends U (KS)
Furman U (SC)
Gardner-Webb U (NC)
George Fox U (OR)
The George Washington U (DC)
Georgia Coll & State U (GA)
Georgian Court U (NJ)
Georgia Southern U (GA)
Georgia Southwestern State U (GA)
Gettysburg Coll (PA)
Goddard Coll (VT)
Gonzaga U (WA)
Gordon Coll (MA)
Goshen Coll (IN)
Governors State U (IL)
Grace Coll (IN)
Graceland U (IA)

Green Mountain Coll (VT)
Greenville Coll (IL)
Grinnell Coll (IA)
Guilford Coll (NC)
Hampton U (VA)
Hannibal-LaGrange U (MO)
Hanover Coll (IN)
Hartwick Coll (NY)
Haverford Coll (PA)
Henderson State U (AR)
Hendrix Coll (AR)
Hillsdale Coll (MI)
Hiram Coll (OH)
Hobart and William Smith Colls (NY)
Hollins U (VA)
Holy Cross Coll (IN)
Hood Coll (MD)
Houghton Coll (NY)
Howard Payne U (TX)
Humboldt State U (CA)
Hunter Coll of the City U of New York (NY)
Huntington U (IN)
Idaho State U (ID)
Illinois Coll (IL)
Illinois State U (IL)
Illinois Wesleyan U (IL)
Indiana State U (IN)
Indiana U Bloomington (IN)
Indiana U East (IN)
Indiana U Kokomo (IN)
Indiana U of Pennsylvania (PA)
Indiana U South Bend (IN)
Indiana U Southeast (IN)
Inter American U of Puerto Rico, San Germán Campus (PR)
Iowa State U of Science and Technology (IA)
Ithaca Coll (NY)
Jacksonville State U (AL)
Jacksonville U (FL)
James Madison U (VA)
Judson U (IL)
Juniata Coll (PA)
Kalamazoo Coll (MI)
Kansas State U (KS)
Kean U (NJ)
Kennesaw State U (GA)
Kentucky Wesleyan Coll (KY)
Knox Coll (IL)
Lafayette Coll (PA)
Laguna Coll of Art & Design (CA)
Lake Forest Coll (IL)
Lebanon Valley Coll (PA)
Lehigh U (PA)
Lehman Coll of the City U of New York (NY)
Lesley U (MA)
Lewis & Clark Coll (OR)
Lewis U (IL)
Lindenwood U (MO)
Linfield Coll (OR)
Lock Haven U of Pennsylvania (PA)
Louisiana Tech U (LA)
Lourdes U (OH)
Loyola U Maryland (MD)
Luther Coll (IA)
Lycoming Coll (PA)
Lynchburg Coll (VA)
Lyon Coll (AR)
Macalester Coll (MN)
MacMurray Coll (IL)
Manchester U (IN)
Marian U (IN)
Marietta Coll (OH)
Marist Coll (NY)
Marshall U (WV)
Mary Baldwin U (VA)
Marylhurst U (OR)
Marymount Manhattan Coll (NY)
Massachusetts Coll of Liberal Arts (MA)
McDaniel Coll (MD)
McKendree U (IL)
McMaster U (ON, Canada)
McNeese State U (LA)
Mercer U, Macon (GA)
Mercyhurst U (PA)
Metropolitan State U of Denver (CO)
Miami U (OH)
Michigan State U (MI)
Millersville U of Pennsylvania (PA)
Minnesota State U Mankato (MN)
Minnesota State U Moorhead (MN)
Minot State U (ND)
Mississippi Valley State U (MS)
Missouri State U (MO)
Missouri Valley Coll (MO)
Monmouth Coll (IL)
Monmouth U (NJ)
Montana State U (MT)
Montana State U Billings (MT)
Montclair State U (NJ)
Moravian Coll (PA)
Morehouse Coll (GA)
Mount Mary U (WI)
Mount Mercy U (IA)
Mount St. Joseph U (OH)
Mount Saint Mary's U (CA)
Mount St. Mary's U (MD)
Mount Vernon Nazarene U (OH)
Muhlenberg Coll (PA)
Muskingum U (OH)
Nazareth Coll of Rochester (NY)
Nebraska Wesleyan U (NE)
Newberry Coll (SC)
New England Coll (NH)
New Jersey City U (NJ)
Newman U (KS)
New Mexico Highlands U (NM)
North Carolina Central U (NC)
North Central Coll (IL)
North Dakota State U (ND)
Northeastern Illinois U (IL)
Northeastern State U (OK)
Northeastern U (MA)
Northern Illinois U (IL)
Northern State U (SD)
Northwestern Coll (IA)
Northwestern U (IL)
Oakland City U (IN)
Oberlin Coll (OH)
Occidental Coll (CA)
Ohio Dominican U (OH)
The Ohio State U (OH)
Ohio U (OH)
Oklahoma Baptist U (OK)
Oklahoma Christian U (OK)
Oklahoma City U (OK)
Oklahoma State U (OK)
Old Dominion U (VA)
Olivet Nazarene U (IL)
Oral Roberts U (OK)
Oregon State U (OR)
Otterbein U (OH)
Our Lady of the Lake U of San Antonio (TX)
Parsons School of Design (NY)
Penn State Abington (PA)
Penn State Altoona (PA)
Penn State Beaver (PA)
Penn State Berks (PA)
Penn State Brandywine (PA)
Penn State DuBois (PA)
Penn State Erie, The Behrend Coll (PA)
Penn State Fayette, The Eberly Campus (PA)
Penn State Greater Allegheny (PA)
Penn State Hazleton (PA)
Penn State Lehigh Valley (PA)
Penn State Mont Alto (PA)
Penn State New Kensington (PA)
Penn State Schuylkill (PA)
Penn State Shenango (PA)
Penn State U Park (PA)
Penn State Wilkes-Barre (PA)
Penn State Worthington Scranton (PA)
Penn State York (PA)
Pepperdine U, Malibu (CA)
Piedmont Coll (GA)
Pittsburg State U (KS)
Pitzer Coll (CA)
Plymouth State U (NH)
Pomona Coll (CA)
Portland State U (OR)
Pratt Inst (NY)
Purchase Coll, State U of New York (NY)
Radford U (VA)
Randolph Coll (VA)
Redeemer U Coll (ON, Canada)
Reed Coll (OR)
Regis U (CO)
Rhodes Coll (TN)
Rice U (TX)
Ripon Coll (WI)
Roanoke Coll (VA)
Roberts Wesleyan Coll (NY)
Rockford U (IL)
Rocky Mountain Coll (MT)
Roger Williams U (RI)
Rollins Coll (FL)
Rowan U (NJ)
Rutgers U–Camden (NJ)
Rutgers U–Newark (NJ)
Rutgers U–New Brunswick (NJ)
Sacred Heart U (CT)
Saginaw Valley State U (MI)
St. Ambrose U (IA)
St. Andrews U (NC)
Saint Anselm Coll (NH)
St. Catherine U (MN)
St. Cloud State U (MN)
St. Edward's U (TX)
Saint John's U (MN)
Saint Joseph's U (PA)
Saint Louis U–Madrid Campus (Spain)
Saint Mary's Coll (IN)
Saint Mary's Coll of California (CA)
St. Mary's Coll of Maryland (MD)
Saint Michael's Coll (VT)
St. Norbert Coll (WI)
St. Olaf Coll (MN)
Saint Peter's U (NJ)
St. Thomas Aquinas Coll (NY)
Salisbury U (MD)
Samford U (AL)
Sam Houston State U (TX)
San Diego State U (CA)
San Francisco State U (CA)
School of the Art Inst of Chicago (IL)
Scripps Coll (CA)
Seattle Pacific U (WA)
Shawnee State U (OH)
Shepherd U (WV)
Shippensburg U of Pennsylvania (PA)
Shorter U (GA)
Sierra Nevada Coll (NV)
Silver Lake Coll of the Holy Family (WI)
Simmons Coll (MA)
Simon Fraser U (BC, Canada)
Simpson Coll (IA)
Skidmore Coll (NY)
Slippery Rock U of Pennsylvania (PA)
Smith Coll (MA)
Sonoma State U (CA)
Southeastern Louisiana U (LA)
Southeastern Oklahoma State U (OK)
Southeast Missouri State U (MO)
Southern Arkansas U–Magnolia (AR)
Southern Illinois U Carbondale (IL)
Southern Illinois U Edwardsville (IL)
Southern Oregon U (OR)
Southern Utah U (UT)
Southwest Baptist U (MO)
Spelman Coll (GA)
Stanford U (CA)
State U of New York at Fredonia (NY)
State U of New York at Oswego (NY)
State U of New York at Plattsburgh (NY)
State U of New York Coll at Old Westbury (NY)
State U of New York Empire State Coll (NY)
Stephen F. Austin State U (TX)
Sterling Coll (KS)
Stony Brook U, State U of New York (NY)
Susquehanna U (PA)
Tarleton State U (TX)
Taylor U (IN)
Temple U (PA)
Tennessee State U (TN)
Texas A&M U–Corpus Christi (TX)
Texas Lutheran U (TX)
Texas State U (TX)
Texas Tech U (TX)
Texas Woman's U (TX)
Tiffin U (OH)
Towson U (MD)
Transylvania U (KY)
Trinity U (TX)
Troy U (AL)
Truman State U (MO)
Tulane U (LA)
Union Coll (NE)
Union U (TN)
Université de Montréal (QC, Canada)
U at Albany, State U of New York (NY)
U at Buffalo, the State U of New York (NY)
The U of Alabama at Birmingham (AL)
The U of Alabama in Huntsville (AL)
U of Alaska Fairbanks (AK)
U of Arkansas (AR)
U of California, Los Angeles (CA)
U of California, Riverside (CA)
U of California, San Diego (CA)
U of Central Arkansas (AR)
U of Central Florida (FL)
U of Charleston (WV)
U of Delaware (DE)
U of Denver (CO)
U of Evansville (IN)
The U of Findlay (OH)
U of Georgia (GA)
U of Great Falls (MT)
U of Hawaii at Manoa (HI)
U of Houston (TX)
U of Idaho (ID)
U of Indianapolis (IN)
U of Jamestown (ND)
U of La Verne (CA)
U of Lethbridge (AB, Canada)
U of Maine at Farmington (ME)
U of Maine at Presque Isle (ME)
U of Massachusetts Boston (MA)
U of Miami (FL)
U of Michigan (MI)
U of Minnesota, Duluth (MN)
U of Minnesota, Twin Cities Campus (MN)
U of Missouri–Kansas City (MO)
U of Mobile (AL)
The U of Montana Western (MT)
U of Montevallo (AL)
U of Nebraska at Kearney (NE)
U of Nevada, Las Vegas (NV)
U of Nevada, Reno (NV)
U of New Hampshire (NH)
U of North Alabama (AL)
U of North Carolina at Asheville (NC)
The U of North Carolina at Charlotte (NC)
The U of North Carolina at Greensboro (NC)
U of North Dakota (ND)
U of Northern Iowa (IA)
U of North Florida (FL)
U of North Georgia (GA)
U of North Texas (TX)
U of Oregon (OR)
U of Pikeville (KY)
U of Puget Sound (WA)
U of Saint Mary (KS)
U of San Diego (CA)
U of San Francisco (CA)
U of Science and Arts of Oklahoma (OK)
U of South Alabama (AL)
The U of South Dakota (SD)
U of Southern California (CA)
U of Southern Indiana (IN)
U of South Florida (FL)
U of South Florida, St. Petersburg (FL)
The U of Tampa (FL)
The U of Tennessee at Chattanooga (TN)
The U of Texas at Austin (TX)
The U of Texas at San Antonio (TX)
The U of Texas of the Permian Basin (TX)
The U of Texas Rio Grande Valley (TX)
U of the Incarnate Word (TX)
U of the Pacific (CA)
U of Utah (UT)
U of Virginia (VA)
The U of Virginia's Coll at Wise (VA)
U of Washington (WA)
U of West Georgia (GA)
U of Windsor (ON, Canada)
U of Wisconsin–Eau Claire (WI)
U of Wisconsin–Green Bay (WI)
U of Wisconsin–La Crosse (WI)
U of Wisconsin–Madison (WI)
U of Wisconsin–Milwaukee (WI)
U of Wisconsin–Parkside (WI)
U of Wisconsin–Platteville (WI)
U of Wisconsin–Whitewater (WI)
Upper Iowa U (IA)
Ursinus Coll (PA)
Utah State U (UT)
Valdosta State U (GA)
Valley City State U (ND)
Valparaiso U (IN)
Virginia Polytechnic Inst and State U (VA)
Virginia Wesleyan Coll (VA)
Viterbo U (WI)
Wabash Coll (IN)
Wagner Coll (NY)
Walla Walla U (WA)
Walsh U (OH)
Wartburg Coll (IA)
Washburn U (KS)
Washington & Jefferson Coll (PA)
Washington Coll (MD)
Washington U in St. Louis (MO)
Watkins Coll of Art, Design, & Film (TN)
Wayland Baptist U (TX)
Waynesburg U (PA)
Wayne State Coll (NE)
Wayne State U (MI)
Weber State U (UT)
Webster U (MO)
Wells Coll (NY)
West Chester U of Pennsylvania (PA)
Western Carolina U (NC)
Western Connecticut State U (CT)
Western Illinois U (IL)
Western Michigan U (MI)
Western Oregon U (OR)
Western State Colorado U (CO)
Western Washington U (WA)
Westfield State U (MA)
Westminster Coll (UT)
Westmont Coll (CA)
West Texas A&M U (TX)
West Virginia State U (WV)
West Virginia U (WV)
West Virginia Wesleyan Coll (WV)
Wheaton Coll (IL)
Whitman Coll (WA)
Whittier Coll (CA)
Whitworth U (WA)
Willamette U (OR)
William Jewell Coll (MO)
William Paterson U of New Jersey (NJ)
Williams Baptist Coll (AR)
Williams Coll (MA)
William Woods U (MO)
Wilson Coll (PA)
Winona State U (MN)
Winthrop U (SC)
Wittenberg U (OH)
Wright State U (OH)
Wright State U–Lake Campus (OH)
Xavier U of Louisiana (LA)
York Coll of the City U of New York (NY)
Youngstown State U (OH)

ART HISTORY, CRITICISM AND CONSERVATION

Acad of Art U (CA)
Adams State U (CO)
Adelphi U (NY)
Agnes Scott Coll (GA)
Albertus Magnus Coll (CT)
Albion Coll (MI)
Allegheny Coll (PA)
American U (DC)
American U of Beirut (Lebanon)
The American U of Paris (France)
The American U of Rome (Italy)
Aquinas Coll (MI)
Arcadia U (PA)
Assumption Coll (MA)
Augsburg Coll (MN)
Augustana Coll (IL)
Baker U (KS)
Bard Coll (NY)
Barnard Coll (NY)
Baylor U (TX)
Belmont U (TN)
Beloit Coll (WI)
Bennington Coll (VT)
Binghamton U, State U of New York (NY)

Bloomsburg U of Pennsylvania (PA)
Boise State U (ID)
Boston Coll (MA)
Boston U (MA)
Bowdoin Coll (ME)
Bowling Green State U (OH)
Bradley U (IL)
Brandeis U (MA)
Bridgewater State U (MA)
Brooklyn Coll of the City U of New York (NY)
Bryn Mawr Coll (PA)
Bucknell U (PA)
Buffalo State Coll, State U of New York (NY)
California State Polytechnic U, Pomona (CA)
California State U, Dominguez Hills (CA)
California State U, East Bay (CA)
California State U, Fullerton (CA)
California State U, Long Beach (CA)
California State U, Stanislaus (CA)
Calvary U (MO)
Canisius Coll (NY)
Carleton Coll (MN)
Carthage Coll (WI)
Case Western Reserve U (OH)
The Catholic U of America (DC)
Centre Coll (KY)
Chapman U (CA)
Chatham U (PA)
City Coll of the City U of New York (NY)
Clarke U (IA)
Clark U (MA)
Coastal Carolina U (SC)
Coe Coll (IA)
Colby Coll (ME)
Colby-Sawyer Coll (NH)
Coll of Charleston (SC)
The Coll of New Jersey (NJ)
Coll of the Holy Cross (MA)
The Coll of William and Mary (VA)
The Coll of Wooster (OH)
The Colorado Coll (CO)
Columbia Coll Chicago (IL)
Columbia U (NY)
Columbia U, School of General Studies (NY)
Columbus Coll of Art & Design (OH)
Concordia U (QC, Canada)
Connecticut Coll (CT)
Converse Coll (SC)
Cornell Coll (IA)
Cornell U (NY)
Dartmouth Coll (NH)
Denison U (OH)
DePauw U (IN)
DEREE - The American Coll of Greece (Greece)
Dominican U (IL)
Dominican U of California (CA)
Drake U (IA)
Drew U (NJ)
Drury U (MO)
Duquesne U (PA)
East Carolina U (NC)
Eastern Michigan U (MI)
Eastern Washington U (WA)
Elon U (NC)
Emory U (GA)
Fairfield U (CT)
Ferris State U (MI)
Flagler Coll (FL)
Florida Intl U (FL)
Florida Southern Coll (FL)
Florida State U (FL)
Fordham U (NY)
Franklin & Marshall Coll (PA)
Furman U (SC)
Gallaudet U (DC)
Georgetown U (DC)
The George Washington U (DC)
Gettysburg Coll (PA)
Goucher Coll (MD)
Grand Valley State U (MI)
Hamilton Coll (NY)
Hamline U (MN)
Hampshire Coll (MA)
Hanover Coll (IN)
Hartwick Coll (NY)
Harvard U (MA)
Haverford Coll (PA)
Hiram Coll (OH)
Hobart and William Smith Colls (NY)
Hofstra U (NY)
Hollins U (VA)
Hope Coll (MI)
Humboldt State U (CA)
Hunter Coll of the City U of New York (NY)
Indiana U Bloomington (IN)
Indiana U–Purdue U Indianapolis (IN)
Ithaca Coll (NY)
Jacksonville U (FL)
James Madison U (VA)
John Carroll U (OH)
Johns Hopkins U (MD)
Juniata Coll (PA)
Kalamazoo Coll (MI)
Kansas City Art Inst (MO)
Kean U (NJ)
Kennesaw State U (GA)
Kent State U (OH)
Kenyon Coll (OH)
Knox Coll (IL)
Kutztown U of Pennsylvania (PA)
Lafayette Coll (PA)
Lake Forest Coll (IL)
La Salle U (PA)
Lawrence U (WI)
Lebanon Valley Coll (PA)
Lehigh U (PA)
Lehman Coll of the City U of New York (NY)
Lewis & Clark Coll (OR)
Lindenwood U (MO)
Lourdes U (OH)
Loyola Marymount U (CA)
Loyola U Chicago (IL)
Loyola U Maryland (MD)
Lycoming Coll (PA)
Manhattanville Coll (NY)
Mansfield U of Pennsylvania (PA)
Marist Coll (NY)
Maryland Inst Coll of Art (MD)
Marymount Manhattan Coll (NY)
Massachusetts Coll of Art and Design (MA)
McDaniel Coll (MD)
McMaster U (ON, Canada)
Merrimack Coll (MA)
Messiah Coll (PA)
Miami U (OH)
Michigan State U (MI)
Middlebury Coll (VT)
Millsaps Coll (MS)
Mills Coll (CA)
Minnesota State U Mankato (MN)
Missouri State U (MO)
Mount Allison U (NB, Canada)
Mount Holyoke Coll (MA)
Muhlenberg Coll (PA)
Nazareth Coll of Rochester (NY)
New Coll of Florida (FL)
The New School–Parsons Paris (France)
Niagara U (NY)
North Carolina State U (NC)
North Central Coll (IL)
Northern Illinois U (IL)
Northwestern U (IL)
Oberlin Coll (OH)
The Ohio State U (OH)
Ohio U (OH)
Ohio Wesleyan U (OH)
Old Dominion U (VA)
Pace U (NY)
Pacific Lutheran U (WA)
Penn State Abington (PA)
Penn State Altoona (PA)
Penn State Beaver (PA)
Penn State Berks (PA)
Penn State Brandywine (PA)
Penn State DuBois (PA)
Penn State Erie, The Behrend Coll (PA)
Penn State Fayette, The Eberly Campus (PA)
Penn State Greater Allegheny (PA)
Penn State Hazleton (PA)
Penn State Lehigh Valley (PA)
Penn State Mont Alto (PA)
Penn State New Kensington (PA)
Penn State Schuylkill (PA)
Penn State Shenango (PA)
Penn State U Park (PA)
Penn State Wilkes-Barre (PA)
Penn State Worthington Scranton (PA)
Penn State York (PA)
Pepperdine U, Malibu (CA)
Pitzer Coll (CA)
Plymouth State U (NH)
Pomona Coll (CA)
Portland State U (OR)
Pratt Inst (NY)
Princeton U (NJ)
Principia Coll (IL)
Providence Coll (RI)
Purchase Coll, State U of New York (NY)
Purdue U (IN)
Queens Coll of the City U of New York (NY)
Randolph Coll (VA)
Randolph-Macon Coll (VA)
Regis U (CO)
Rhode Island Coll (RI)
Rice U (TX)
Roanoke Coll (VA)
Rockford U (IL)
Roger Williams U (RI)
Rollins Coll (FL)
Rosemont Coll (PA)
Rutgers U–New Brunswick (NJ)
St. Bonaventure U (NY)
St. Catherine U (MN)
St. Cloud State U (MN)
Saint Louis U (MO)
Saint Louis U–Madrid Campus (Spain)
Saint Mary's Coll of California (CA)
St. Mary's Coll of Maryland (MD)
St. Olaf Coll (MN)
Saint Peter's U (NJ)
Saint Vincent Coll (PA)
Salve Regina U (RI)
San Diego State U (CA)
San Francisco Art Inst (CA)
Santa Clara U (CA)
Sarah Lawrence Coll (NY)
Savannah Coll of Art and Design (GA)
School of the Art Inst of Chicago (IL)
Scripps Coll (CA)
Seattle U (WA)
Seton Hill U (PA)
Sewanee: The U of the South (TN)
Skidmore Coll (NY)
Smith Coll (MA)
Sonoma State U (CA)
Southern Connecticut State U (CT)
Southern Methodist U (TX)
Southern Utah U (UT)
Southwestern U (TX)
Stanford U (CA)
State U of New York at Fredonia (NY)
State U of New York at New Paltz (NY)
State U of New York Coll at Cortland (NY)
State U of New York Coll at Geneseo (NY)
State U of New York Coll at Potsdam (NY)
Stephen F. Austin State U (TX)
Stonehill Coll (MA)
Stony Brook U, State U of New York (NY)
Susquehanna U (PA)
Swarthmore Coll (PA)
Sweet Briar Coll (VA)
Syracuse U (NY)
Temple U (PA)
Texas Christian U (TX)
Texas State U (TX)
Thomas More Coll (KY)
Towson U (MD)
Transylvania U (KY)
Trinity U (TX)
Truman State U (MO)
Tufts U (MA)
Tulane U (LA)
Université de Montréal (QC, Canada)
U at Albany, State U of New York (NY)
U at Buffalo, the State U of New York (NY)
The U of Akron (OH)
The U of Alabama (AL)
The U of Arizona (AZ)
U of California, Davis (CA)
U of California, Irvine (CA)
U of California, Los Angeles (CA)
U of California, Riverside (CA)
U of California, San Diego (CA)
U of California, Santa Barbara (CA)
U of Chicago (IL)
U of Cincinnati (OH)
U of Colorado Boulder (CO)
U of Dayton (OH)
U of Delaware (DE)
U of Denver (CO)
U of Evansville (IN)
U of Florida (FL)
U of Georgia (GA)
U of Guelph (ON, Canada)
U of Hartford (CT)
U of Houston (TX)
U of Illinois at Chicago (IL)
The U of Kansas (KS)
U of Kentucky (KY)
U of La Verne (CA)
U of Lethbridge (AB, Canada)
U of Louisville (KY)
U of Maine (ME)
U of Maryland, Coll Park (MD)
U of Mary Washington (VA)
U of Massachusetts Amherst (MA)
U of Massachusetts Dartmouth (MA)
U of Miami (FL)
U of Michigan (MI)
U of Michigan–Dearborn (MI)
U of Michigan–Flint (MI)
U of Minnesota, Duluth (MN)
U of Minnesota, Morris (MN)
U of Minnesota, Twin Cities Campus (MN)
U of Missouri–Kansas City (MO)
U of Missouri–St. Louis (MO)
U of Nevada, Las Vegas (NV)
U of Nevada, Reno (NV)
U of New Orleans (LA)
U of North Carolina at Asheville (NC)
The U of North Carolina at Chapel Hill (NC)
The U of North Carolina at Charlotte (NC)
The U of North Carolina at Greensboro (NC)
The U of North Carolina Wilmington (NC)
U of Northern Iowa (IA)
U of North Florida (FL)
U of North Texas (TX)
U of Notre Dame (IN)
U of Oklahoma (OK)
U of Oregon (OR)
U of Pennsylvania (PA)
U of Pittsburgh (PA)
U of Regina (SK, Canada)
U of Rhode Island (RI)
U of Richmond (VA)
U of Rochester (NY)
U of Saint Francis (IN)
U of Saint Joseph (CT)
U of St. Thomas (MN)
U of San Diego (CA)
U of San Francisco (CA)
U of Saskatchewan (SK, Canada)
U of South Carolina (SC)
U of Southern California (CA)
U of South Florida (FL)
The U of Tennessee (TN)
The U of Texas at Austin (TX)
The U of Texas at San Antonio (TX)
U of the Pacific (CA)
The U of Toledo (OH)
The U of Tulsa (OK)
U of Utah (UT)
U of Vermont (VT)
U of Washington (WA)
U of Waterloo (ON, Canada)
U of Windsor (ON, Canada)
U of Wisconsin–Madison (WI)
U of Wisconsin–Milwaukee (WI)
U of Wisconsin–Superior (WI)
Ursinus Coll (PA)
Vanderbilt U (TN)
Vassar Coll (NY)
Villanova U (PA)
Virginia Commonwealth U (VA)
Wake Forest U (NC)
Walsh U (OH)
Washburn U (KS)
Washington and Lee U (VA)
Washington U in St. Louis (MO)
Wayne State U (MI)
Webster U (MO)
Wells Coll (NY)
Wesleyan Coll (GA)
Wesleyan U (CT)
Western Kentucky U (KY)
Western Michigan U (MI)
Western Washington U (WA)
West Virginia U (WV)
Wheaton Coll (MA)
Whitman Coll (WA)
Whitworth U (WA)
Willamette U (OR)
William Paterson U of New Jersey (NJ)
Williams Coll (MA)
Winthrop U (SC)
Wittenberg U (OH)
Wofford Coll (SC)
Wright State U (OH)
Wright State U–Lake Campus (OH)
York Coll of the City U of New York (NY)
Youngstown State U (OH)

ARTIFICIAL INTELLIGENCE
U of Advancing Technology (AZ)
U of Georgia (GA)
U of Windsor (ON, Canada)

ARTS, ENTERTAINMENT, AND MEDIA MANAGEMENT
Anderson U (IN)
Belmont U (TN)
Butler U (IN)
Champlain Coll (VT)
Columbia Coll Chicago (IL)
Concordia U, Nebraska (NE)
Dean Coll (MA)
Dixie State U (UT)
Drexel U (PA)
Drury U (MO)
Elon U (NC)
Judson U (IL)
Kansas Wesleyan U (KS)
National U (CA)
St. Edward's U (TX)
Schreiner U (TX)
Shenandoah U (VA)
State U of New York at Fredonia (NY)
Stonehill Coll (MA)
U of Central Florida (FL)
The U of Findlay (OH)
U of Kentucky (KY)
U of North Alabama (AL)
The U of Tulsa (OK)
U of Wisconsin–Green Bay (WI)
Western New England U (MA)
Whitworth U (WA)

ARTS, ENTERTAINMENT, AND MEDIA MANAGEMENT RELATED
Belmont U (TN)
Loyola U New Orleans (LA)
The New School–Parsons Paris (France)
U of Southern California (CA)

ART TEACHER EDUCATION
Acad of Art U (CA)
Adams State U (CO)
Adelphi U (NY)
Albright Coll (PA)
Alfred U (NY)
Alverno Coll (WI)
Anderson U (SC)
Andrews U (MI)
Appalachian State U (NC)
Arkansas Tech U (AR)
Armstrong State U (GA)
Asbury U (KY)
Ashland U (OH)
Augustana Coll (IL)
Augustana U (SD)
Averett U (VA)
Baker U (KS)
Baylor U (TX)
Belmont U (TN)
Beloit Coll (WI)
Bemidji State U (MN)
Benedictine Coll (KS)
Berea Coll (KY)
Berry Coll (GA)
Bethel Coll (IN)
Bethel U (MN)

Bishop's U (QC, Canada)
Boise State U (ID)
Boston U (MA)
Bowling Green State U (OH)
Bradley U (IL)
Brenau U (GA)
Brescia U (KY)
Bridgewater State U (MA)
Brigham Young U–Idaho (ID)
Brooklyn Coll of the City U of New York (NY)
Buena Vista U (IA)
Buffalo State Coll, State U of New York (NY)
California Lutheran U (CA)
California State U, Long Beach (CA)
Calvin Coll (MI)
Campbellsville U (KY)
Capital U (OH)
Carlow U (PA)
Carson-Newman U (TN)
Case Western Reserve U (OH)
Central Connecticut State U (CT)
Central Michigan U (MI)
Central State U (OH)
City Coll of the City U of New York (NY)
Clarke U (IA)
Coe Coll (IA)
Colby-Sawyer Coll (NH)
The Coll of New Jersey (NJ)
Coll of Saint Mary (NE)
Coll of the Ozarks (MO)
Colorado State U (CO)
Columbus State U (GA)
Concordia Coll (MN)
Concordia U (QC, Canada)
Concordia U Chicago (IL)
Concordia U, Nebraska (NE)
Concordia U, St. Paul (MN)
Concordia U Wisconsin (WI)
Converse Coll (SC)
Culver-Stockton Coll (MO)
Daemen Coll (NY)
Dickinson State U (ND)
East Carolina U (NC)
East Central U (OK)
Eastern Michigan U (MI)
Eastern Washington U (WA)
Edgewood Coll (WI)
Elizabeth City State U (NC)
Elmira Coll (NY)
Emory & Henry Coll (VA)
Escuela de Artes Plasticas y Dise&nno de Puerto Rico (PR)
Evangel U (MO)
Fayetteville State U (NC)
Ferris State U (MI)
Flagler Coll (FL)
Florida Intl U (FL)
Florida Southern Coll (FL)
Framingham State U (MA)
Francis Marion U (SC)
Franklin Pierce U (NH)
Friends U (KS)
Gallaudet U (DC)
Georgia State U (GA)
Goddard Coll (VT)
Goshen Coll (IN)
Grace Coll (IN)
Graceland U (IA)
Grand Valley State U (MI)
Green Mountain Coll (VT)
Hampton U (VA)
Hannibal-LaGrange U (MO)
Harding U (AR)
Hardin-Simmons U (TX)
Henderson State U (AR)
Hofstra U (NY)
Holy Family U (PA)
Hope Coll (MI)
Houghton Coll (NY)
Houston Baptist U (TX)
Howard Payne U (TX)
Humboldt State U (CA)
Huntington U (IN)
Indiana State U (IN)
Indiana U Bloomington (IN)
Indiana U–Purdue U Indianapolis (IN)
Indiana U South Bend (IN)
Inter American U of Puerto Rico, San Germán Campus (PR)
Ithaca Coll (NY)
Jacksonville U (FL)
Kansas State U (KS)
Kennesaw State U (GA)
Kent State U (OH)
Kentucky Wesleyan Coll (KY)
Kutztown U of Pennsylvania (PA)
Lawrence U (WI)
Lee U (TN)
Lehman Coll of the City U of New York (NY)
Lincoln U (MO)
Lindenwood U (MO)
Lindsey Wilson Coll (KY)
Lipscomb U (TN)
Louisiana Coll (LA)
Louisiana Tech U (LA)
Lubbock Christian U (TX)
Manchester U (IN)
Manhattanville Coll (NY)
Maryland Inst Coll of Art (MD)
Maryville U of Saint Louis (MO)
Marywood U (PA)
Massachusetts Coll of Art and Design (MA)
McKendree U (IL)
McMurry U (TX)
Mercyhurst U (PA)
Meredith Coll (NC)
Messiah Coll (PA)
Miami U (OH)
Michigan State U (MI)
Millikin U (IL)
Minnesota State U Mankato (MN)
Minnesota State U Moorhead (MN)
Minot State U (ND)
Missouri State U (MO)
Missouri Western State U (MO)
Molloy Coll (NY)
Montana State U Billings (MT)
Morningside Coll (IA)
Mount Mary U (WI)
Mount Mercy U (IA)
Mount St. Joseph U (OH)
Mount Vernon Nazarene U (OH)
Muskingum U (OH)
Nazareth Coll of Rochester (NY)
New Jersey City U (NJ)
North Central Coll (IL)
Northeastern State U (OK)
Northern Illinois U (IL)
Northern State U (SD)
Northwestern Coll (IA)
Northwest Missouri State U (MO)
Nova Southeastern U (FL)
Ohio Dominican U (OH)
The Ohio State U (OH)
Ohio Wesleyan U (OH)
Oral Roberts U (OK)
Otterbein U (OH)
Ouachita Baptist U (AR)
Palm Beach Atlantic U (FL)
Penn State Abington (PA)
Penn State Altoona (PA)
Penn State Beaver (PA)
Penn State Berks (PA)
Penn State Brandywine (PA)
Penn State DuBois (PA)
Penn State Erie, The Behrend Coll (PA)
Penn State Fayette, The Eberly Campus (PA)
Penn State Greater Allegheny (PA)
Penn State Hazleton (PA)
Penn State Lehigh Valley (PA)
Penn State Mont Alto (PA)
Penn State New Kensington (PA)
Penn State Schuylkill (PA)
Penn State Shenango (PA)
Penn State U Park (PA)
Penn State Wilkes-Barre (PA)
Penn State Worthington Scranton (PA)
Penn State York (PA)
Piedmont Coll (GA)
Plymouth State U (NH)
Point Loma Nazarene U (CA)
Pratt Inst (NY)
Purdue U (IN)
Queens Coll of the City U of New York (NY)
Rhode Island Coll (RI)
Rocky Mountain Coll (MT)
Saginaw Valley State U (MI)
St. Ambrose U (IA)
St. Catherine U (MN)
St. Cloud State U (MN)
St. Edward's U (TX)
Saint Joseph's U (PA)
Saint Louis U–Madrid Campus (Spain)
Saint Mary-of-the-Woods Coll (IN)
Saint Michael's Coll (VT)
Saint Vincent Coll (PA)
School of the Art Inst of Chicago (IL)
Seton Hill U (PA)
Shawnee State U (OH)
Silver Lake Coll of the Holy Family (WI)
Simpson Coll (IA)
South Carolina State U (SC)
Southeastern Oklahoma State U (OK)
Southeast Missouri State U (MO)
Southern Arkansas U–Magnolia (AR)
Southern Connecticut State U (CT)
Southern Utah U (UT)
Southwest Baptist U (MO)
State U of New York at New Paltz (NY)
Syracuse U (NY)
Taylor U (IN)
Temple U (PA)
Texas Christian U (TX)
Texas Lutheran U (TX)
Thomas More Coll (KY)
Towson U (MD)
Transylvania U (KY)
Trinity Christian Coll (IL)
Union Coll (NE)
Union U (TN)
The U of Akron (OH)
The U of Arizona (AZ)
U of Central Florida (FL)
U of Central Missouri (MO)
U of Denver (CO)
U of Evansville (IN)
The U of Findlay (OH)
U of Florida (FL)
U of Great Falls (MT)
U of Illinois at Chicago (IL)
U of Indianapolis (IN)
The U of Kansas (KS)
U of Kentucky (KY)
U of Lethbridge (AB, Canada)
U of Maine (ME)
U of Mary Hardin-Baylor (TX)
U of Maryland, Coll Park (MD)
U of Massachusetts Dartmouth (MA)
U of Michigan–Flint (MI)
U of Minnesota, Duluth (MN)
The U of Montana Western (MT)
The U of North Carolina at Greensboro (NC)
The U of North Carolina at Pembroke (NC)
U of North Florida (FL)
U of North Georgia (GA)
U of Regina (SK, Canada)
U of St. Francis (IL)
U of Saint Francis (IN)
U of South Carolina (SC)
The U of South Dakota (SD)
U of Southern Maine (ME)
The U of Tennessee at Chattanooga (TN)
The U of Texas at Austin (TX)
The U of Texas at El Paso (TX)
U of the Cumberlands (KY)
U of Vermont (VT)
U of Windsor (ON, Canada)
U of Wisconsin–La Crosse (WI)
U of Wisconsin–Madison (WI)
U of Wisconsin–Milwaukee (WI)
U of Wisconsin–Stout (WI)
U of Wisconsin–Superior (WI)
U of Wisconsin–Whitewater (WI)
Upper Iowa U (IA)
Utah Valley U (UT)
Valdosta State U (GA)
Valley City State U (ND)
Valparaiso U (IN)
Virginia Commonwealth U (VA)
Virginia Wesleyan Coll (VA)
Viterbo U (WI)
Walla Walla U (WA)
Wartburg Coll (IA)
Washburn U (KS)
Washington & Jefferson Coll (PA)
Washington U in St. Louis (MO)
Wayne State Coll (NE)
Weber State U (UT)
Western Carolina U (NC)
Western Michigan U (MI)
Western State Colorado U (CO)
Western Washington U (WA)
Westfield State U (MA)
Westmont Coll (CA)
West Virginia Wesleyan Coll (WV)
Whitworth U (WA)
Williams Baptist Coll (AR)
William Woods U (MO)
Winona State U (MN)
Xavier U of Louisiana (LA)
Youngstown State U (OH)

ART THERAPY

Albertus Magnus Coll (CT)
Alverno Coll (WI)
Arcadia U (PA)
Capital U (OH)
Carlow U (PA)
Cedar Crest Coll (PA)
Chowan U (NC)
Concordia U Chicago (IL)
Concordia U, Nebraska (NE)
Converse Coll (SC)
Edgewood Coll (WI)
Emmanuel Coll (MA)
Harding U (AR)
Houston Baptist U (TX)
Kansas Wesleyan U (KS)
Lesley U (MA)
Lipscomb U (TN)
Marywood U (PA)
Mercyhurst U (PA)
Millikin U (IL)
Mount Mary U (WI)
Nazareth Coll of Rochester (NY)
Prescott Coll (AZ)
St. Thomas Aquinas Coll (NY)
Seton Hill U (PA)
Sierra Nevada Coll (NV)
Taylor U (IN)
U of Indianapolis (IN)
U of Saint Francis (IN)
U of Wisconsin–Superior (WI)
West Virginia Wesleyan Coll (WV)

ASIAN AMERICAN STUDIES

Arizona State U at the Tempe campus (AZ)
Binghamton U, State U of New York (NY)
California State U, East Bay (CA)
California State U, Fullerton (CA)
California State U, Long Beach (CA)
California State U, Northridge (CA)
Columbia U (NY)
Pitzer Coll (CA)
Pomona Coll (CA)
San Francisco State U (CA)
Scripps Coll (CA)
Stanford U (CA)
U of California, Davis (CA)
U of California, Irvine (CA)
U of California, Los Angeles (CA)
U of California, Riverside (CA)
U of California, Santa Barbara (CA)
U of Denver (CO)
U of Southern California (CA)

ASIAN HISTORY

Gettysburg Coll (PA)
U of Washington, Tacoma (WA)

ASIAN STUDIES

Amherst Coll (MA)
Arizona State U at the Tempe campus (AZ)
Augustana Coll (IL)
Austin Coll (TX)
Bard Coll (NY)
Barnard Coll (NY)
Baylor U (TX)
Belmont U (TN)
Bennington Coll (VT)
Berea Coll (KY)
Binghamton U, State U of New York (NY)
Boston U (MA)
Bowdoin Coll (ME)
Bowling Green State U (OH)
California State U, Chico (CA)
California State U, Long Beach (CA)
California State U, Sacramento (CA)
Calvin Coll (MI)
Carleton Coll (MN)
Case Western Reserve U (OH)
City Coll of the City U of New York (NY)
Claremont McKenna Coll (CA)
Clark U (MA)
Coe Coll (IA)
Colgate U (NY)
Coll of the Holy Cross (MA)
The Colorado Coll (CO)
Cornell U (NY)
Dartmouth Coll (NH)
Elms Coll (MA)
Florida Intl U (FL)
Florida State U (FL)
Furman U (SC)
The George Washington U (DC)
Gonzaga U (WA)
Hamilton Coll (NY)
Hobart and William Smith Colls (NY)
Illinois Wesleyan U (IL)
Indiana U of Pennsylvania (PA)
John Carroll U (OH)
Kean U (NJ)
Kennesaw State U (GA)
Kenyon Coll (OH)
Knox Coll (IL)
Lake Forest Coll (IL)
Lehigh U (PA)
Loyola Marymount U (CA)
Macalester Coll (MN)
Manhattanville Coll (NY)
Marietta Coll (OH)
McDaniel Coll (MD)
Mount Holyoke Coll (MA)
Nazareth Coll of Rochester (NY)
Northeastern U (MA)
Northwestern U (IL)
Ohio U (OH)
Old Dominion U (VA)
Pace U (NY)
Penn State U Park (PA)
Pepperdine U, Malibu (CA)
Pitzer Coll (CA)
Pomona Coll (CA)
Purdue U (IN)
Randolph-Macon Coll (VA)
Rice U (TX)
Rollins Coll (FL)
St. John's U (NY)
Saint Joseph's U (PA)
St. Mary's Coll of Maryland (MD)
St. Olaf Coll (MN)
San Diego State U (CA)
Sarah Lawrence Coll (NY)
Scripps Coll (CA)
Seattle U (WA)
Sewanee: The U of the South (TN)
Skidmore Coll (NY)
State U of New York at New Paltz (NY)
Stony Brook U, State U of New York (NY)
Swarthmore Coll (PA)
Temple U (PA)
Texas State U (TX)
Trinity U (TX)
Tufts U (MA)
Tulane U (LA)
Union Coll (NY)
Université de Montréal (QC, Canada)
U at Albany, State U of New York (NY)
U at Buffalo, the State U of New York (NY)
U of California, Riverside (CA)
U of California, Santa Barbara (CA)
U of Cincinnati (OH)
U of Colorado Boulder (CO)
U of Delaware (DE)
U of Hawaii at Manoa (HI)
U of Louisville (KY)
U of Maryland, Baltimore County (MD)
U of Maryland U Coll (MD)
U of Massachusetts Boston (MA)
U of Michigan (MI)
U of Mount Union (OH)
U of Nevada, Las Vegas (NV)
The U of North Carolina at Chapel Hill (NC)
U of Northern Colorado (CO)
U of Oregon (OR)
U of Puget Sound (WA)
U of Richmond (VA)
U of San Francisco (CA)

The U of Texas at Austin (TX)
The U of Toledo (OH)
U of Toronto (ON, Canada)
U of Utah (UT)
U of Vermont (VT)
U of Washington (WA)
U of Wisconsin–Madison (WI)
Utah State U (UT)
Vanderbilt U (TN)
Vassar Coll (NY)
Washington State U (WA)
Washington U in St. Louis (MO)
Western Kentucky U (KY)
Wheaton Coll (MA)
Whitman Coll (WA)
Willamette U (OR)
William Paterson U of New Jersey (NJ)
Williams Coll (MA)

ASIAN STUDIES (EAST)
Austin Coll (TX)
Bates Coll (ME)
Binghamton U, State U of New York (NY)
Boston U (MA)
Brandeis U (MA)
Bryn Mawr Coll (PA)
Bucknell U (PA)
Colby Coll (ME)
Columbia U (NY)
Columbia U, School of General Studies (NY)
Connecticut Coll (CT)
Davidson Coll (NC)
Denison U (OH)
DePauw U (IN)
Dickinson Coll (PA)
Emory U (GA)
The George Washington U (DC)
Gettysburg Coll (PA)
Grand Valley State U (MI)
Hamline U (MN)
Hampshire Coll (MA)
Harvard U (MA)
Haverford Coll (PA)
Hofstra U (NY)
Indiana U Bloomington (IN)
John Carroll U (OH)
Johns Hopkins U (MD)
Kalamazoo Coll (MI)
Lawrence U (WI)
Lewis & Clark Coll (OR)
Miami U (OH)
Middlebury Coll (VT)
Minnesota State U Moorhead (MN)
Mount Holyoke Coll (MA)
New Coll of Florida (FL)
North Central Coll (IL)
Oberlin Coll (OH)
Occidental Coll (CA)
Ohio Wesleyan U (OH)
Penn State Abington (PA)
Penn State Altoona (PA)
Penn State Beaver (PA)
Penn State Berks (PA)
Penn State Brandywine (PA)
Penn State DuBois (PA)
Penn State Erie, The Behrend Coll (PA)
Penn State Fayette, The Eberly Campus (PA)
Penn State Greater Allegheny (PA)
Penn State Hazleton (PA)
Penn State Lehigh Valley (PA)
Penn State Mont Alto (PA)
Penn State New Kensington (PA)
Penn State Schuylkill (PA)
Penn State Shenango (PA)
Penn State Worthington Scranton (PA)
Penn State York (PA)
Portland State U (OR)
Princeton U (NJ)
Queens Coll of the City U of New York (NY)
Rutgers U–New Brunswick (NJ)
Simmons Coll (MA)
Smith Coll (MA)
Stanford U (CA)
Trinity U (TX)
Tufts U (MA)
United States Military Acad (NY)
Université de Montréal (QC, Canada)
U at Albany, State U of New York (NY)
The U of Arizona (AZ)
U of Bridgeport (CT)
U of California, Davis (CA)
U of California, Irvine (CA)
U of Pennsylvania (PA)
U of Rochester (NY)
U of Southern California (CA)
U of Toronto (ON, Canada)
Ursinus Coll (PA)
Valparaiso U (IN)
Washington U in St. Louis (MO)
Wayne State U (MI)
Wesleyan U (CT)
Western Washington U (WA)
Willamette U (OR)
Wittenberg U (OH)

ASIAN STUDIES (SOUTH)
Binghamton U, State U of New York (NY)
Columbia U, School of General Studies (NY)
Concordia U (QC, Canada)
Gettysburg Coll (PA)
Hampshire Coll (MA)
Indiana U Bloomington (IN)
Middlebury Coll (VT)
Mount Holyoke Coll (MA)
U of Pennsylvania (PA)
U of Toronto (ON, Canada)
U of Washington (WA)

ASIAN STUDIES (SOUTHEAST)
Tufts U (MA)
U of Washington (WA)

ASIAN STUDIES (URAL-ALTAIC AND CENTRAL)
Indiana U Bloomington (IN)

ASTRONOMY
Amherst Coll (MA)
Ball State U (IN)
Barnard Coll (NY)
Baylor U (TX)
Benedictine Coll (KS)
Bennington Coll (VT)
Boston U (MA)
Brigham Young U (UT)
Bryn Mawr Coll (PA)
Case Western Reserve U (OH)
Central Michigan U (MI)
Colgate U (NY)
Columbia U (NY)
Columbia U, School of General Studies (NY)
Cornell U (NY)
Dartmouth Coll (NH)
Drake U (IA)
Embry-Riddle Aeronautical U–Prescott (AZ)
Franklin & Marshall Coll (PA)
Hampshire Coll (MA)
Haverford Coll (PA)
Indiana U Bloomington (IN)
Lehigh U (PA)
Lycoming Coll (PA)
Minnesota State U Mankato (MN)
Mount Holyoke Coll (MA)
Northern Arizona U (AZ)
Northwestern U (IL)
The Ohio State U (OH)
Ohio Wesleyan U (OH)
Penn State Abington (PA)
Penn State Altoona (PA)
Penn State Beaver (PA)
Penn State Berks (PA)
Penn State Brandywine (PA)
Penn State DuBois (PA)
Penn State Erie, The Behrend Coll (PA)
Penn State Fayette, The Eberly Campus (PA)
Penn State Greater Allegheny (PA)
Penn State Hazleton (PA)
Penn State Lehigh Valley (PA)
Penn State Mont Alto (PA)
Penn State New Kensington (PA)
Penn State Schuylkill (PA)
Penn State Shenango (PA)
Penn State U Park (PA)
Penn State Wilkes-Barre (PA)
Penn State Worthington Scranton (PA)
Penn State York (PA)
Pomona Coll (CA)
Rice U (TX)
San Diego State U (CA)
San Francisco State U (CA)
Smith Coll (MA)
State U of New York at New Paltz (NY)
Stonehill Coll (MA)
Stony Brook U, State U of New York (NY)
Swarthmore Coll (PA)
Tufts U (MA)
Union Coll (NY)
The U of Arizona (AZ)
U of Colorado Boulder (CO)
U of Florida (FL)
U of Georgia (GA)
U of Hawaii at Manoa (HI)
The U of Kansas (KS)
U of Maryland, Coll Park (MD)
U of Massachusetts Amherst (MA)
U of Michigan (MI)
U of Oklahoma (OK)
U of Pittsburgh (PA)
U of Southern California (CA)
The U of Texas at Austin (TX)
The U of Toledo (OH)
U of Virginia (VA)
U of Washington (WA)
Valdosta State U (GA)
Valparaiso U (IN)
Vassar Coll (NY)
Villanova U (PA)
Wayne State U (MI)
Wesleyan U (CT)
Whitman Coll (WA)
Williams Coll (MA)
Youngstown State U (OH)

ASTRONOMY AND ASTROPHYSICS RELATED
Butler U (IN)
Coll of Charleston (SC)
Emory U (GA)
Florida Inst of Technology (FL)
Harvard U (MA)
Texas Christian U (TX)
Whitman Coll (WA)

ASTROPHYSICS
Agnes Scott Coll (GA)
Barnard Coll (NY)
Baylor U (TX)
Boston U (MA)
California Inst of Technology (CA)
Carnegie Mellon U (PA)
Colgate U (NY)
Columbia U (NY)
Columbia U, School of General Studies (NY)
Franklin & Marshall Coll (PA)
Haverford Coll (PA)
Lehigh U (PA)
Lycoming Coll (PA)
McMaster U (ON, Canada)
Michigan State U (MI)
Ohio U (OH)
Ohio Wesleyan U (OH)
Princeton U (NJ)
Rice U (TX)
Rutgers U–New Brunswick (NJ)
San Francisco State U (CA)
Swarthmore Coll (PA)
Tufts U (MA)
United States Military Acad (NY)
U of California, Los Angeles (CA)
U of Cincinnati (OH)
U of Hawaii at Manoa (HI)
U of Minnesota, Twin Cities Campus (MN)
U of Oklahoma (OK)
U of Wisconsin–Madison (WI)
Villanova U (PA)
Whitman Coll (WA)
Williams Coll (MA)

ATHLETIC TRAINING
Alfred U (NY)
Alma Coll (MI)
Alvernia U (PA)
Anderson U (IN)
Anderson U (SC)
Appalachian State U (NC)
Aquinas Coll (MI)
Ashland U (OH)
Augustana U (SD)
Aurora U (IL)
Averett U (VA)
Azusa Pacific U (CA)
Baldwin Wallace U (OH)
Ball State U (IN)
Baylor U (TX)
Benedictine Coll (KS)
Bethel Coll (KS)
Bethel U (MN)
Boston U (MA)
Bowling Green State U (OH)
Bridgewater Coll (VA)
Bridgewater State U (MA)
Brigham Young U (UT)
Buena Vista U (IA)
California State U, East Bay (CA)
California State U, Fullerton (CA)
California State U, Long Beach (CA)
California State U, Northridge (CA)
California U of Pennsylvania (PA)
Canisius Coll (NY)
Capital U (OH)
Carthage Coll (WI)
Catawba Coll (NC)
Cedarville U (OH)
Central Connecticut State U (CT)
Central Methodist U (MO)
Central Michigan U (MI)
Chapman U (CA)
Clarke U (IA)
Coe Coll (IA)
Colby-Sawyer Coll (NH)
The Coll at Brockport, State U of New York (NY)
Coll of Charleston (SC)
Colorado Mesa U (CO)
Concordia U Irvine (CA)
Concordia U Wisconsin (WI)
Concord U (WV)
Culver-Stockton Coll (MO)
Defiance Coll (OH)
DePauw U (IN)
Dominican Coll (NY)
Duquesne U (PA)
East Carolina U (NC)
East Central U (OK)
Eastern Illinois U (IL)
Eastern Michigan U (MI)
Eastern U (PA)
Eastern Washington U (WA)
East Stroudsburg U of Pennsylvania (PA)
East Texas Baptist U (TX)
Emory & Henry Coll (VA)
Emporia State U (KS)
Endicott Coll (MA)
Florida Gulf Coast U (FL)
Florida Southern Coll (FL)
Florida State U (FL)
Fort Lewis Coll (CO)
Franklin Coll (IN)
Frostburg State U (MD)
Gardner-Webb U (NC)
George Fox U (OR)
Georgetown Coll (KY)
Georgia Coll & State U (GA)
Georgia Southern U (GA)
Graceland U (IA)
Grand Valley State U (MI)
Harding U (AR)
Hardin-Simmons U (TX)
Heidelberg U (OH)
Hofstra U (NY)
Hope Coll (MI)
Houston Baptist U (TX)
Howard Payne U (TX)
Huntington U (IN)
Illinois State U (IL)
Immaculata U (PA)
Indiana State U (IN)
Indiana U Bloomington (IN)
Indiana U of Pennsylvania (PA)
Iowa State U of Science and Technology (IA)
Ithaca Coll (NY)
James Madison U (VA)
Kansas State U (KS)
Kean U (NJ)
Keene State Coll (NH)
Kent State U (OH)
King's Coll (PA)
King U (TN)
Lasell Coll (MA)
Lees-McRae Coll (NC)
Lee U (TN)
Lewis U (IL)
Liberty U (VA)
Limestone Coll (SC)
Lindenwood U (MO)
Linfield Coll (OR)
Longwood U (VA)
Loras Coll (IA)
Louisiana Coll (LA)
Louisiana State U and A&M Coll (LA)
Lubbock Christian U (TX)
Luther Coll (IA)
Lynchburg Coll (VA)
Manchester U (IN)
Marietta Coll (OH)
Marist Coll (NY)
Marshall U (WV)
Marywood U (PA)
Massachusetts Coll of Liberal Arts (MA)
McKendree U (IL)
McMurry U (TX)
McNeese State U (LA)
Mercyhurst U (PA)
Merrimack Coll (MA)
Messiah Coll (PA)
Miami U (OH)
Michigan State U (MI)
MidAmerica Nazarene U (KS)
Millikin U (IL)
Minnesota State U Moorhead (MN)
Minot State U (ND)
Missouri State U (MO)
Missouri Valley Coll (MO)
Montclair State U (NJ)
Mount St. Joseph U (OH)
Muskingum U (OH)
Nebraska Wesleyan U (NE)
Neumann U (PA)
New Mexico State U (NM)
North Carolina Central U (NC)
North Central Coll (IL)
Northern Illinois U (IL)
Northern Kentucky U (KY)
Northwestern Coll (IA)
The Ohio State U (OH)
Ohio U (OH)
Oklahoma Baptist U (OK)
Olivet Nazarene U (IL)
Otterbein U (OH)
Palm Beach Atlantic U (FL)
Penn State U Park (PA)
Piedmont Coll (GA)
Plymouth State U (NH)
Point Loma Nazarene U (CA)
Quinnipiac U (CT)
Radford U (VA)
Roanoke Coll (VA)
Rowan U (NJ)
Saginaw Valley State U (MI)
Saint Augustine's U (NC)
Saint Louis U–Madrid Campus (Spain)
Salisbury U (MD)
Samford U (AL)
Sam Houston State U (TX)
San Diego State U (CA)
Shawnee State U (OH)
Simpson Coll (IA)
Slippery Rock U of Pennsylvania (PA)
South Dakota State U (SD)
Southeastern Louisiana U (LA)
Southeast Missouri State U (MO)
Southern Arkansas U–Magnolia (AR)
Southern Connecticut State U (CT)
Southern Utah U (UT)
Southwest Baptist U (MO)
Southwestern Coll (KS)
State U of New York Coll at Cortland (NY)
Sterling Coll (KS)
Stony Brook U, State U of New York (NY)
Tabor Coll (KS)
Temple U (PA)
Texas A&M U–Corpus Christi (TX)
Texas Christian U (TX)
Texas Lutheran U (TX)
Texas State U (TX)
Texas Wesleyan U (TX)
Thomas More Coll (KY)
Tiffin U (OH)
Towson U (MD)
Troy U (AL)
Truman State U (MO)
Tusculum Coll (TN)
Union Coll (KY)
Union U (TN)
Université de Sherbrooke (QC, Canada)
The U of Akron (OH)

The U of Alabama (AL)
U of Central Arkansas (AR)
U of Central Florida (FL)
U of Charleston (WV)
U of Cincinnati (OH)
U of Delaware (DE)
U of Evansville (IN)
U of Florida (FL)
U of Georgia (GA)
U of Idaho (ID)
U of Indianapolis (IN)
The U of Kansas (KS)
U of La Verne (CA)
U of Maine (ME)
U of Maine at Presque Isle (ME)
U of Miami (FL)
U of Michigan (MI)
U of Minnesota, Duluth (MN)
U of Mobile (AL)
U of Mount Union (OH)
U of Nevada, Las Vegas (NV)
U of New England (ME)
U of New Hampshire (NH)
The U of North Carolina at Charlotte (NC)
The U of North Carolina at Pembroke (NC)
The U of North Carolina Wilmington (NC)
U of North Dakota (ND)
U of Northern Colorado (CO)
U of North Florida (FL)
U of Pittsburgh at Bradford (PA)
U of Southern Maine (ME)
U of Southern Mississippi (MS)
The U of Tampa (FL)
The U of Tennessee at Martin (TN)
The U of Texas at Austin (TX)
The U of Texas of the Permian Basin (TX)
U of the Incarnate Word (TX)
The U of Toledo (OH)
The U of Tulsa (OK)
U of Utah (UT)
U of Vermont (VT)
The U of West Alabama (AL)
U of Wisconsin–Eau Claire (WI)
U of Wisconsin–La Crosse (WI)
U of Wisconsin–Madison (WI)
U of Wisconsin–Milwaukee (WI)
U of Wisconsin–Stevens Point (WI)
Upper Iowa U (IA)
Valdosta State U (GA)
Valley City State U (ND)
Washburn U (KS)
Washington State U (WA)
Waynesburg U (PA)
Wayne State Coll (NE)
Weber State U (UT)
Welch Coll (TN)
West Chester U of Pennsylvania (PA)
Western Carolina U (NC)
Western Illinois U (IL)
Western Michigan U (MI)
Westfield State U (MA)
West Texas A&M U (TX)
West Virginia Wesleyan Coll (WV)
Wheeling Jesuit U (WV)
Whitworth U (WA)
Wichita State U (KS)
William Paterson U of New Jersey (NJ)
William Woods U (MO)
Wingate U (NC)
Winona State U (MN)
Wright State U (OH)
Wright State U–Lake Campus (OH)
Youngstown State U (OH)

ATMOSPHERIC CHEMISTRY AND CLIMATOLOGY
Rutgers U–New Brunswick (NJ)

ATMOSPHERIC SCIENCES AND METEOROLOGY
The Coll at Brockport, State U of New York (NY)
Cornell U (NY)
Dalhousie U (NS, Canada)
Embry-Riddle Aeronautical U–Daytona (FL)
Embry-Riddle Aeronautical U–Prescott (AZ)
Florida State U (FL)
Iowa State U of Science and Technology (IA)
Jackson State U (MS)
Millersville U of Pennsylvania (PA)
North Carolina State U (NC)
Northern Illinois U (IL)
The Ohio State U (OH)
Ohio U (OH)
Penn State Abington (PA)
Penn State Altoona (PA)
Penn State Beaver (PA)
Penn State Berks (PA)
Penn State Brandywine (PA)
Penn State DuBois (PA)
Penn State Erie, The Behrend Coll (PA)
Penn State Fayette, The Eberly Campus (PA)
Penn State Greater Allegheny (PA)
Penn State Hazleton (PA)
Penn State Lehigh Valley (PA)
Penn State Mont Alto (PA)
Penn State New Kensington (PA)
Penn State Schuylkill (PA)
Penn State Shenango (PA)
Penn State U Park (PA)
Penn State Wilkes-Barre (PA)
Penn State Worthington Scranton (PA)
Penn State York (PA)
Plymouth State U (NH)
Purdue U (IN)
Rutgers U–New Brunswick (NJ)
St. Cloud State U (MN)
Saint Louis U (MO)
State U of New York at Oswego (NY)
State U of New York Maritime Coll (NY)
Stony Brook U, State U of New York (NY)
Texas A&M U (TX)
United States Air Force Acad (CO)
U at Albany, State U of New York (NY)
U of California, Davis (CA)
The U of Kansas (KS)
U of Louisiana at Monroe (LA)
U of Louisville (KY)
U of Maryland, Coll Park (MD)
U of Massachusetts Lowell (MA)
U of Miami (FL)
U of Michigan (MI)
U of Nevada, Reno (NV)
U of North Carolina at Asheville (NC)
U of North Dakota (ND)
U of Utah (UT)
U of Washington (WA)
U of Waterloo (ON, Canada)
U of Wisconsin–Madison (WI)
Valparaiso U (IN)
Western Connecticut State U (CT)

ATMOSPHERIC SCIENCES AND METEOROLOGY RELATED
East Carolina U (NC)
U of California, Los Angeles (CA)

ATOMIC/MOLECULAR PHYSICS
Columbia U (NY)
San Diego State U (CA)
U of Waterloo (ON, Canada)

AUDIOLOGY
American U of Beirut (Lebanon)
Biola U (CA)
California State U, Long Beach (CA)
Cleveland State U (OH)
Northwestern U (IL)
The Ohio State U (OH)
Stephen F. Austin State U (TX)
Université de Montréal (QC, Canada)
U of Montevallo (AL)
Western Michigan U (MI)

AUDIOLOGY AND SPEECH-LANGUAGE PATHOLOGY
Adelphi U (NY)
Andrews U (MI)
Auburn U (AL)
Auburn U at Montgomery (AL)
Augustana U (SD)
Ball State U (IN)
Biola U (CA)
Bloomsburg U of Pennsylvania (PA)
Bluffton U (OH)
Boston U (MA)
Bowling Green State U (OH)
Brescia U (KY)
Brooklyn Coll of the City U of New York (NY)
Buffalo State Coll, State U of New York (NY)
California State U, East Bay (CA)
California State U, Fresno (CA)
California State U, Long Beach (CA)
California State U, Sacramento (CA)
Calvin Coll (MI)
The Coll of Idaho (ID)
The Coll of Saint Rose (NY)
East Carolina U (NC)
Elmira Coll (NY)
Emerson Coll (MA)
The George Washington U (DC)
Hardin-Simmons U (TX)
Hofstra U (NY)
Hunter Coll of the City U of New York (NY)
Idaho State U (ID)
Illinois State U (IL)
Indiana State U (IN)
Indiana U Bloomington (IN)
Indiana U of Pennsylvania (PA)
Iona Coll (NY)
Ithaca Coll (NY)
Kent State U (OH)
Lehman Coll of the City U of New York (NY)
Longwood U (VA)
Louisiana State U and A&M Coll (LA)
Louisiana Tech U (LA)
Marymount Manhattan Coll (NY)
Marywood U (PA)
Mercy Coll (NY)
Miami U (OH)
Minnesota State U Mankato (MN)
Minnesota State U Moorhead (MN)
Missouri State U (MO)
Murray State U (KY)
Nazareth Coll of Rochester (NY)
Northeastern State U (OK)
Northwestern U (IL)
The Ohio State U (OH)
Ohio U (OH)
Old Dominion U (VA)
Purdue U (IN)
St. Cloud State U (MN)
St. John's U (NY)
South Carolina State U (SC)
Southeastern Louisiana U (LA)
Southern Connecticut State U (CT)
Southern Illinois U Edwardsville (IL)
State U of New York at Fredonia (NY)
State U of New York at Plattsburgh (NY)
State U of New York Coll at Cortland (NY)
Stockton U (NJ)
Temple U (PA)
Tennessee State U (TN)
Texas Woman's U (TX)
Towson U (MD)
Université de Montréal (QC, Canada)
U at Buffalo, the State U of New York (NY)
The U of Alabama (AL)
U of Arkansas (AR)
U of Central Arkansas (AR)
U of Central Florida (FL)
U of Florida (FL)
U of Kentucky (KY)
U of Louisiana at Monroe (LA)
U of Minnesota, Twin Cities Campus (MN)
The U of North Carolina at Greensboro (NC)
U of Northern Colorado (CO)
U of North Texas (TX)
U of Pittsburgh (PA)
U of Southern Mississippi (MS)
U of South Florida (FL)
The U of Tennessee (TN)
The U of Texas at Austin (TX)
The U of Texas at Dallas (TX)
The U of Texas at El Paso (TX)
U of the Pacific (CA)
The U of Tulsa (OK)
U of Utah (UT)
U of Virginia (VA)
U of Wisconsin–Madison (WI)
U of Wisconsin–Milwaukee (WI)
U of Wisconsin–Stevens Point (WI)
Utah State U (UT)
Washington State U (WA)
Washington State U–Spokane (WA)
West Chester U of Pennsylvania (PA)
Western Michigan U (MI)
Western Washington U (WA)
West Virginia U (WV)

AUDIOVISUAL COMMUNICATIONS TECHNOLOGIES RELATED
Husson U (ME)
Webster U (MO)

AUDITING
Bradley U (IL)
Carlow U (PA)
Davenport U, Grand Rapids (MI)
Inter American U of Puerto Rico, Bayamón Campus (PR)

AUTOBODY/COLLISION AND REPAIR TECHNOLOGY
Idaho State U (ID)
Pennsylvania Coll of Technology (PA)

AUTOMOBILE/AUTOMOTIVE MECHANICS TECHNOLOGY
Brigham Young U–Idaho (ID)
Idaho State U (ID)
Montana State U–Northern (MT)
Morrisville State Coll (NY)
New England Inst of Technology (RI)
U of Northwestern Ohio (OH)
Walla Walla U (WA)
Weber State U (UT)

AUTOMOTIVE ENGINEERING TECHNOLOGY
Ferris State U (MI)
Indiana State U (IN)
Minnesota State U Mankato (MN)
Pennsylvania Coll of Technology (PA)
Pittsburg State U (KS)
Southern Illinois U Carbondale (IL)
Weber State U (UT)
Western Washington U (WA)

AVIATION/AIRWAY MANAGEMENT
Auburn U (AL)
Averett U (VA)
Baylor U (TX)
Bridgewater State U (MA)
California Baptist U (CA)
Central Washington U (WA)
Dixie State U (UT)
Eastern Michigan U (MI)
Embry-Riddle Aeronautical U–Prescott (AZ)
Embry-Riddle Aeronautical U–Worldwide (FL)
Farmingdale State Coll (NY)
Florida Inst of Technology (FL)
Hallmark U (TX)
Hampton U (VA)
Indiana State U (IN)
Inter American U of Puerto Rico, Bayamón Campus (PR)
Jacksonville U (FL)
LeTourneau U (TX)
Lewis U (IL)
Liberty U (VA)
Louisiana Tech U (LA)
Lynn U (FL)
Marywood U (PA)
Metropolitan State U of Denver (CO)
Minnesota State U Mankato (MN)
The Ohio State U (OH)
Ohio U (OH)
Purdue U (IN)
Rocky Mountain Coll (MT)
Saint Louis U–Madrid Campus (Spain)
South Dakota State U (SD)
Southern Illinois U Carbondale (IL)
Southern New Hampshire U (NH)
Tarleton State U (TX)
Texas A&M U–Central Texas (TX)
Thomas Edison State U (NJ)
U of Dubuque (IA)
U of North Dakota (ND)
U of the Fraser Valley (BC, Canada)
Vaughn Coll of Aeronautics and Technology (NY)
Western Michigan U (MI)
Westminster Coll (UT)
West Virginia U Inst of Technology (WV)
Wilmington U (DE)

AVIONICS MAINTENANCE TECHNOLOGY
Lewis U (IL)
Pennsylvania Coll of Technology (PA)
Southern Illinois U Carbondale (IL)
Vaughn Coll of Aeronautics and Technology (NY)
Western Michigan U (MI)

AYURVEDIC MEDICINE
Maharishi U of Management (IA)

BAKING AND PASTRY ARTS
New England Culinary Inst (VT)

BALLET
Brigham Young U (UT)
Friends U (KS)
Indiana U Bloomington (IN)
Marymount Manhattan Coll (NY)
Texas Christian U (TX)
U of Utah (UT)

BANKING AND FINANCIAL SUPPORT SERVICES
Brescia U (KY)
Buena Vista U (IA)
Hardin-Simmons U (TX)
Husson U (ME)
Saint Peter's U (NJ)
Sam Houston State U (TX)
State U of New York Coll of Agriculture and Technology at Cobleskill (NY)
Stephen F. Austin State U (TX)
U of North Florida (FL)
U of the Incarnate Word (TX)
Youngstown State U (OH)

BEHAVIORAL ASPECTS OF HEALTH
Goddard Coll (VT)
Taylor U (IN)
U of Southern California (CA)
The U of Texas at Austin (TX)

BEHAVIORAL SCIENCES
Ambrose U (AB, Canada)
Andrews U (MI)
Athens State U (AL)
Bemidji State U (MN)
California Baptist U (CA)
California State U, Dominguez Hills (CA)
Carnegie Mellon U (PA)
Carver Coll (GA)
Central Washington U (WA)
Chaminade U of Honolulu (HI)
Columbia Southern U (AL)
Concordia Coll–New York (NY)
Concordia U Irvine (CA)
Concordia U, Nebraska (NE)
Duquesne U (PA)
Evangel U (MO)
George Fox U (OR)
Goddard Coll (VT)
Inter American U of Puerto Rico, San Germán Campus (PR)
Johns Hopkins U (MD)
Metropolitan State U of Denver (CO)
Minnesota State U Mankato (MN)
Missouri Baptist U (MO)
Nova Southeastern U (FL)
Point Park U (PA)
Purdue U Northwest (IN)
Saint Augustine's U (NC)
St. Cloud State U (MN)
Sterling Coll (KS)
Tabor Coll (KS)
Tennessee Wesleyan U (TN)
Trevecca Nazarene U (TN)
Tufts U (MA)
United States Air Force Acad (CO)
U of Houston–Clear Lake (TX)

The U of Kansas (KS)
U of La Verne (CA)
U of Maine at Fort Kent (ME)
U of Wisconsin–Green Bay (WI)
Walsh U (OH)
Western Intl U (AZ)
Widener U (PA)
Wilmington U (DE)
York Coll of Pennsylvania (PA)

BIBLICAL STUDIES
Abilene Christian U (TX)
Alaska Bible Coll (AK)
Amridge U (AL)
Anderson U (IN)
Anderson U (SC)
Andrews U (MI)
Arizona Christian U (AZ)
Arlington Baptist Coll (TX)
Asbury U (KY)
Austin Graduate School of Theology (TX)
Azusa Pacific U (CA)
The Baptist Coll of Florida (FL)
Baptist U of the Americas (TX)
Barclay Coll (KS)
Belhaven U (MS)
Belmont U (TN)
Bethel Coll (IN)
Bethel U (MN)
Biola U (CA)
Bluefield Coll (VA)
Blue Mountain Coll (MS)
Bluffton U (OH)
Bryan Coll (TN)
Cairn U (PA)
California Baptist U (CA)
Calvary U (MO)
Calvin Coll (MI)
Campbellsville U (KY)
Canisius Coll (NY)
Carolina Christian Coll (NC)
Carson-Newman U (TN)
Carver Coll (GA)
Cedarville U (OH)
Central Baptist Coll (AR)
Coll of the Ozarks (MO)
Corban U (OR)
Cornerstone U (MI)
Crandall U (NB, Canada)
Criswell Coll (TX)
Dallas Baptist U (TX)
Dallas Christian Coll (TX)
Davis Coll (NY)
Eastern Mennonite U (VA)
Eastern U (PA)
East Texas Baptist U (TX)
Ecclesia Coll (AR)
Emmaus Bible Coll (IA)
Evangel U (MO)
Faith Baptist Bible Coll and Theological Sem (IA)
Faulkner U (AL)
Florida Coll (FL)
Freed-Hardeman U (TN)
Fresno Pacific U (CA)
Gardner-Webb U (NC)
Geneva Coll (PA)
George Fox U (OR)
Global U (MO)
Goshen Coll (IN)
Grace Coll (IN)
Hannibal-LaGrange U (MO)
Harding U (AR)
Hardin-Simmons U (TX)
Hobe Sound Bible Coll (FL)
Hope Intl U (CA)
Houghton Coll (NY)
Houston Baptist U (TX)
Howard Payne U (TX)
Huntington U (IN)
Johnson U (TN)
Johnson U Florida (FL)
Judson U (IL)
Kentucky Mountain Bible Coll (KY)
King U (TN)
Kuyper Coll (MI)
Lee U (TN)
LeTourneau U (TX)
Liberty U (VA)
Lincoln Christian U (IL)
Lipscomb U (TN)
Louisiana Coll (LA)
Lubbock Christian U (TX)
Luther Rice Coll & Sem (GA)
Malone U (OH)
Maranatha Baptist U (WI)
Master's Coll and Sem (ON, Canada)
The Master's U (CA)
Messenger Coll (TX)
Messiah Coll (PA)
MidAmerica Nazarene U (KS)
Mid-Atlantic Christian U (NC)
Milligan Coll (TN)
Mount Vernon Nazarene U (OH)
Multnomah U (OR)
Nazarene Bible Coll (CO)
North Greenville U (SC)
Northwest Christian U (OR)
Northwest U (WA)
Nyack Coll (NY)
Ohio Valley U (WV)
Oklahoma Baptist U (OK)
Oklahoma Christian U (OK)
Oral Roberts U (OK)
Ouachita Baptist U (AR)
Palm Beach Atlantic U (FL)
Piedmont Intl U (NC)
Point Loma Nazarene U (CA)
Point U (GA)
Redeemer U Coll (ON, Canada)
Roberts Wesleyan Coll (NY)
Saint Louis Christian Coll (MO)
Shiloh U (IA)
Simpson U (CA)
Southeastern Bible Coll (AL)
Southeastern U (FL)
Southwest Baptist U (MO)
Southwestern Assemblies of God U (TX)
Taylor U (IN)
Theological U of the Caribbean (PR)
Toccoa Falls Coll (GA)
Trinity Baptist Coll (FL)
Truett McConnell U (GA)
Union Coll (NE)
Union U (TN)
Université de Montréal (QC, Canada)
The U of Findlay (OH)
U of Minnesota, Twin Cities Campus (MN)
U of Valley Forge (PA)
Waynesburg U (PA)
Welch Coll (TN)
Wheaton Coll (IL)
Whitworth U (WA)
Williamson Coll (TN)

BILINGUAL AND MULTILINGUAL EDUCATION
Boise State U (ID)
Boston U (MA)
Brooklyn Coll of the City U of New York (NY)
California State U, Stanislaus (CA)
Calvin Coll (MI)
Canisius Coll (NY)
Goddard Coll (VT)
Houston Baptist U (TX)
Loyola U Chicago (IL)
Nevada State Coll (NV)
Northeastern Illinois U (IL)
Our Lady of the Lake U of San Antonio (TX)
Southwestern Assemblies of God U (TX)
State U of New York Coll at Old Westbury (NY)
Texas A&M Intl U (TX)
Texas Christian U (TX)
Texas Wesleyan U (TX)
U of Delaware (DE)
U of Regina (SK, Canada)
U of San Francisco (CA)
The U of Texas at San Antonio (TX)
U of the Southwest (NM)
Western Illinois U (IL)
York Coll of the City U of New York (NY)

BIOCHEMICAL ENGINEERING
Christian Brothers U (TN)
U of Colorado Boulder (CO)
U of Georgia (GA)

BIOCHEMISTRY
Abilene Christian U (TX)
Adams State U (CO)
Adelphi U (NY)
Agnes Scott Coll (GA)
Albion Coll (MI)
Albright Coll (PA)
Allegheny Coll (PA)
Alma Coll (MI)
Alvernia U (PA)
American Intl Coll (MA)
American U (DC)
Anderson U (IN)
Andrews U (MI)
Arizona State U at the Tempe campus (AZ)
Armstrong State U (GA)
Asbury U (KY)
Auburn U (AL)
Augustana Coll (IL)
Augustana U (SD)
Austin Coll (TX)
Azusa Pacific U (CA)
Barnard Coll (NY)
Bates Coll (ME)
Baylor U (TX)
Beloit Coll (WI)
Benedictine Coll (KS)
Berry Coll (GA)
Binghamton U, State U of New York (NY)
Biola U (CA)
Bishop's U (QC, Canada)
Boston Coll (MA)
Bowdoin Coll (ME)
Bowling Green State U (OH)
Bradley U (IL)
Brandeis U (MA)
Bridgewater Coll (VA)
Bridgewater State U (MA)
Bryant U (RI)
Bucknell U (PA)
Butler U (IN)
California Lutheran U (CA)
California Polytechnic State U, San Luis Obispo (CA)
California State U, Chico (CA)
California State U, Dominguez Hills (CA)
California State U, East Bay (CA)
California State U, Fullerton (CA)
California State U, Long Beach (CA)
California State U, Northridge (CA)
California State U, San Marcos (CA)
Calvin Coll (MI)
Canisius Coll (NY)
Capital U (OH)
Carson-Newman U (TN)
Case Western Reserve U (OH)
The Catholic U of America (DC)
Cedar Crest Coll (PA)
Centenary Coll of Louisiana (LA)
Central Connecticut State U (CT)
Central Michigan U (MI)
Central Washington U (WA)
Chaminade U of Honolulu (HI)
Chapman U (CA)
Charleston Southern U (SC)
Chatham U (PA)
Chestnut Hill Coll (PA)
Christian Brothers U (TN)
Christopher Newport U (VA)
City Coll of the City U of New York (NY)
Claremont McKenna Coll (CA)
Clarke U (IA)
Clark U (MA)
Clemson U (SC)
Coastal Carolina U (SC)
Coe Coll (IA)
Colby Coll (ME)
Colgate U (NY)
The Coll at Brockport, State U of New York (NY)
Coll of Mount Saint Vincent (NY)
Coll of Saint Benedict (MN)
Coll of Saint Elizabeth (NJ)
The Coll of Saint Rose (NY)
The Coll of St. Scholastica (MN)
Coll of Staten Island of the City U of New York (NY)
The Coll of Wooster (OH)
The Colorado Coll (CO)
Colorado State U (CO)
Columbia U (NY)
Columbia U, School of General Studies (NY)
Connecticut Coll (CT)
Converse Coll (SC)
Cornell Coll (IA)
Curry Coll (MA)
Daemen Coll (NY)
Dartmouth Coll (NH)
Denison U (OH)
DePauw U (IN)
DeSales U (PA)
Dickinson Coll (PA)
Doane U (NE)
Dominican U (IL)
Drake U (IA)
Drew U (NJ)
Duquesne U (PA)
Earlham Coll (IN)
East Carolina U (NC)
Eastern Mennonite U (VA)
Eastern Michigan U (MI)
Eastern Nazarene Coll (MA)
Eastern U (PA)
East Stroudsburg U of Pennsylvania (PA)
Eckerd Coll (FL)
Elizabethtown Coll (PA)
Elon U (NC)
Emmanuel Coll (MA)
Fairfield U (CT)
Fairleigh Dickinson U, Coll at Florham (NJ)
Fairleigh Dickinson U, Metropolitan Campus (NJ)
Faulkner U (AL)
Ferris State U (MI)
Florida Gulf Coast U (FL)
Florida Inst of Technology (FL)
Florida State U (FL)
Fort Lewis Coll (CO)
Franklin & Marshall Coll (PA)
Freed-Hardeman U (TN)
Furman U (SC)
Gannon U (PA)
Geneva Coll (PA)
George Fox U (OR)
Georgetown Coll (KY)
Georgetown U (DC)
Georgia Inst of Technology (GA)
Georgian Court U (NJ)
Gettysburg Coll (PA)
Gonzaga U (WA)
Grand View U (IA)
Grinnell Coll (IA)
Grove City Coll (PA)
Hamilton Coll (NY)
Hamline U (MN)
Hanover Coll (IN)
Harding U (AR)
Hartwick Coll (NY)
Harvard U (MA)
Haverford Coll (PA)
Hawai`i Pacific U (HI)
High Point U (NC)
Hillsdale Coll (MI)
Hiram Coll (OH)
Hobart and William Smith Colls (NY)
Hofstra U (NY)
Holy Family U (PA)
Hood Coll (MD)
Houghton Coll (NY)
Humboldt State U (CA)
Huntingdon Coll (AL)
Idaho State U (ID)
Illinois State U (IL)
Indiana U Bloomington (IN)
Indiana U East (IN)
Indiana U Kokomo (IN)
Indiana U Northwest (IN)
Indiana U of Pennsylvania (PA)
Indiana U South Bend (IN)
Iona Coll (NY)
Iowa State U of Science and Technology (IA)
Ithaca Coll (NY)
John Brown U (AR)
Judson U (IL)
Juniata Coll (PA)
Kansas State U (KS)
Kennesaw State U (GA)
Kenyon Coll (OH)
Kettering U (MI)
Keuka Coll (NY)
King U (TN)
Knox Coll (IL)
Kutztown U of Pennsylvania (PA)
Lafayette Coll (PA)
LaGrange Coll (GA)
Lamar U (TX)
La Roche Coll (PA)
La Salle U (PA)
Lawrence Technological U (MI)
Lawrence U (WI)
Lee U (TN)
Lehigh U (PA)
Lehman Coll of the City U of New York (NY)
Le Moyne Coll (NY)
Lewis & Clark Coll (OR)
Lewis U (IL)
Liberty U (VA)
Lipscomb U (TN)
Loras Coll (IA)
Louisiana State U and A&M Coll (LA)
Loyola Marymount U (CA)
Loyola U Chicago (IL)
Loyola U New Orleans (LA)
Lubbock Christian U (TX)
Madonna U (MI)
Malone U (OH)
Manchester U (IN)
Manhattan Coll (NY)
Manhattanville Coll (NY)
Mansfield U of Pennsylvania (PA)
Marietta Coll (OH)
Marist Coll (NY)
Mary Baldwin U (VA)
Marymount U (VA)
Maryville U of Saint Louis (MO)
McMaster U (ON, Canada)
McMurry U (TX)
Mercer U, Macon (GA)
Mercyhurst U (PA)
Merrimack Coll (MA)
Messiah Coll (PA)
Miami U (OH)
Michigan State U (MI)
Middlebury Coll (VT)
Millsaps Coll (MS)
Mills Coll (CA)
Minnesota State U Mankato (MN)
Misericordia U (PA)
Mississippi State U (MS)
Missouri Baptist U (MO)
Missouri Western State U (MO)
Monmouth Coll (IL)
Montclair State U (NJ)
Moravian Coll (PA)
Mount Allison U (NB, Canada)
Mount Holyoke Coll (MA)
Mount Mercy U (IA)
Mount St. Joseph U (OH)
Mount Saint Mary's U (CA)
Mount St. Mary's U (MD)
Muhlenberg Coll (PA)
Nazareth Coll of Rochester (NY)
New Coll of Florida (FL)
Newman U (KS)
New Mexico State U (NM)
Niagara U (NY)
North Carolina State U (NC)
North Central Coll (IL)
Northeastern U (MA)
Northwestern Coll (IA)
Northwestern U (IL)
Oberlin Coll (OH)
Occidental Coll (CA)
The Ohio State U (OH)
Oklahoma Baptist U (OK)
Oklahoma Christian U (OK)
Oklahoma City U (OK)
Oklahoma State U (OK)
Old Dominion U (VA)
Oral Roberts U (OK)
Otterbein U (OH)
Pace U (NY)
Pace U, Pleasantville Campus (NY)
Penn State Abington (PA)
Penn State Altoona (PA)
Penn State Beaver (PA)
Penn State Berks (PA)
Penn State Brandywine (PA)
Penn State DuBois (PA)
Penn State Erie, The Behrend Coll (PA)
Penn State Fayette, The Eberly Campus (PA)
Penn State Greater Allegheny (PA)
Penn State Hazleton (PA)
Penn State Lehigh Valley (PA)
Penn State Mont Alto (PA)
Penn State New Kensington (PA)
Penn State Schuylkill (PA)
Penn State Shenango (PA)
Penn State U Park (PA)
Penn State Wilkes-Barre (PA)
Penn State Worthington Scranton (PA)
Penn State York (PA)

Pitzer Coll (CA)
Point Loma Nazarene U (CA)
Portland State U (OR)
Providence Coll (RI)
Purchase Coll, State U of New York (NY)
Purdue U (IN)
Quinnipiac U (CT)
Ramapo Coll of New Jersey (NJ)
Reed Coll (OR)
Regis U (CO)
Rice U (TX)
Ripon Coll (WI)
Roanoke Coll (VA)
Roberts Wesleyan Coll (NY)
Rochester Inst of Technology (NY)
Rockford U (IL)
Rockhurst U (MO)
Roger Williams U (RI)
Rollins Coll (FL)
Rose-Hulman Inst of Technology (IN)
Rosemont Coll (PA)
Rowan U (NJ)
Rutgers U–New Brunswick (NJ)
Sacred Heart U (CT)
The Sage Colls (NY)
Saginaw Valley State U (MI)
Saint Anselm Coll (NH)
St. Bonaventure U (NY)
St. Catherine U (MN)
St. Edward's U (TX)
Saint John's U (MN)
Saint Joseph's U (PA)
Saint Louis U (MO)
Saint Mary's Coll of California (CA)
St. Mary's Coll of Maryland (MD)
Saint Mary's U of Minnesota (MN)
Saint Michael's Coll (VT)
Saint Peter's U (NJ)
Saint Vincent Coll (PA)
Samford U (AL)
San Francisco State U (CA)
Santa Clara U (CA)
Schreiner U (TX)
Scripps Coll (CA)
Seattle Pacific U (WA)
Seattle U (WA)
Seton Hill U (PA)
Sewanee: The U of the South (TN)
Siena Coll (NY)
Simon Fraser U (BC, Canada)
Simpson Coll (IA)
Smith Coll (MA)
South Dakota State U (SD)
Southern Methodist U (TX)
Southern Oregon U (OR)
Southwestern Adventist U (TX)
Southwestern Coll (KS)
Southwestern U (TX)
Spelman Coll (GA)
Spring Hill Coll (AL)
State U of New York at Fredonia (NY)
State U of New York at New Paltz (NY)
State U of New York at Oswego (NY)
State U of New York at Plattsburgh (NY)
State U of New York Coll at Geneseo (NY)
State U of New York Coll at Old Westbury (NY)
State U of New York Coll at Potsdam (NY)
Stephen F. Austin State U (TX)
Stevens Inst of Technology (NJ)
Stevenson U (MD)
Stockton U (NJ)
Stonehill Coll (MA)
Stony Brook U, State U of New York (NY)
Susquehanna U (PA)
Swarthmore Coll (PA)
Syracuse U (NY)
Tabor Coll (KS)
Taylor U (IN)
Temple U (PA)
Texas A&M U (TX)
Texas Christian U (TX)
Texas State U (TX)
Texas Tech U (TX)
Texas Wesleyan U (TX)
Texas Woman's U (TX)
Thomas More Coll (KY)
Trent U (ON, Canada)
Trinity Christian Coll (IL)
Trinity U (TX)
Tufts U (MA)
Tulane U (LA)
Union Coll (NY)
United States Air Force Acad (CO)
Université de Montréal (QC, Canada)
Université de Sherbrooke (QC, Canada)
U at Albany, State U of New York (NY)
U at Buffalo, the State U of New York (NY)
The U of Akron (OH)
The U of Arizona (AZ)
U of California, Los Angeles (CA)
U of California, Riverside (CA)
U of California, San Diego (CA)
U of Charleston (WV)
U of Cincinnati (OH)
U of Colorado Boulder (CO)
U of Colorado Colorado Springs (CO)
U of Dayton (OH)
U of Delaware (DE)
U of Denver (CO)
U of Detroit Mercy (MI)
U of Evansville (IN)
U of Guelph (ON, Canada)
U of Hawaii at Manoa (HI)
U of Houston (TX)
U of Idaho (ID)
U of Illinois at Chicago (IL)
U of Illinois at Springfield (IL)
U of Jamestown (ND)
The U of Kansas (KS)
U of King's Coll (NS, Canada)
U of Lethbridge (AB, Canada)
U of Maine (ME)
U of Mary Hardin-Baylor (TX)
U of Maryland, Coll Park (MD)
U of Massachusetts Boston (MA)
U of Miami (FL)
U of Michigan (MI)
U of Michigan–Dearborn (MI)
U of Michigan–Flint (MI)
U of Minnesota, Duluth (MN)
U of Minnesota, Twin Cities Campus (MN)
U of Missouri–St. Louis (MO)
U of Mount Union (OH)
U of Nevada, Las Vegas (NV)
U of Nevada, Reno (NV)
U of New England (ME)
U of New Hampshire (NH)
U of New Haven (CT)
The U of North Carolina at Greensboro (NC)
U of Northern Iowa (IA)
U of North Texas (TX)
U of Notre Dame (IN)
U of Oklahoma (OK)
U of Oregon (OR)
U of Pennsylvania (PA)
U of Puget Sound (WA)
U of Regina (SK, Canada)
U of Saint Joseph (CT)
U of St. Thomas (MN)
U of St. Thomas (TX)
U of San Diego (CA)
U of Saskatchewan (SK, Canada)
The U of Scranton (PA)
U of Southern California (CA)
U of Southern Indiana (IN)
The U of Tampa (FL)
The U of Texas at Austin (TX)
The U of Texas at Dallas (TX)
The U of Texas at San Antonio (TX)
U of the Incarnate Word (TX)
U of the Pacific (CA)
The U of Toledo (OH)
U of Toronto (ON, Canada)
The U of Tulsa (OK)
U of Vermont (VT)
U of Washington (WA)
U of Washington, Bothell (WA)
U of Waterloo (ON, Canada)
U of Windsor (ON, Canada)
U of Wisconsin–La Crosse (WI)
U of Wisconsin–Madison (WI)
U of Wisconsin–Milwaukee (WI)
U of Wisconsin–Stevens Point (WI)
Ursinus Coll (PA)
Valparaiso U (IN)
Vassar Coll (NY)
Villanova U (PA)
Virginia Polytechnic Inst and State U (VA)
Viterbo U (WI)
Wabash Coll (IN)
Walla Walla U (WA)
Wartburg Coll (IA)
Washburn U (KS)
Washington & Jefferson Coll (PA)
Washington and Lee U (VA)
Washington State U (WA)
Washington U in St. Louis (MO)
Weber State U (UT)
Wells Coll (NY)
West Chester U of Pennsylvania (PA)
Western Kentucky U (KY)
Western Michigan U (MI)
Western State Colorado U (CO)
Western Washington U (WA)
Westminster Coll (PA)
West Virginia U (WV)
Wheaton Coll (MA)
Whitman Coll (WA)
Whittier Coll (CA)
Widener U (PA)
Wilkes U (PA)
William Jewell Coll (MO)
Winona State U (MN)
Worcester Polytechnic Inst (MA)
Wright State U (OH)
Wright State U–Lake Campus (OH)
Xavier U of Louisiana (LA)
Youngstown State U (OH)

BIOCHEMISTRY AND MOLECULAR BIOLOGY

Anderson U (SC)
Bellarmine U (KY)
Belmont U (TN)
Bethel Coll (IN)
Boston U (MA)
Bryn Mawr Coll (PA)
California State U, Long Beach (CA)
Carroll Coll (MT)
Centre Coll (KY)
Connecticut Coll (CT)
Culver-Stockton Coll (MO)
Dalhousie U (NS, Canada)
The Evergreen State Coll (WA)
Florida Southern Coll (FL)
Goucher Coll (MD)
Harding U (AR)
Hardin-Simmons U (TX)
Hendrix Coll (AR)
Hope Coll (MI)
Houston Baptist U (TX)
Lebanon Valley Coll (PA)
Lincoln U (PA)
Linfield Coll (OR)
Michigan State U (MI)
Michigan Technological U (MI)
Middlebury Coll (VT)
Minnesota State U Moorhead (MN)
Nebraska Wesleyan U (NE)
North Dakota State U (ND)
Oregon State U (OR)
Purdue U (IN)
Rhodes Coll (TN)
Simmons Coll (MA)
Université de Montréal (QC, Canada)
U of California, Irvine (CA)
U of Georgia (GA)
U of Maryland, Baltimore County (MD)
U of Massachusetts Amherst (MA)
U of Minnesota, Duluth (MN)
U of New Hampshire (NH)
U of Regina (SK, Canada)
U of Waterloo (ON, Canada)
Whitman Coll (WA)
Wilson Coll (PA)
Wittenberg U (OH)

BIOCHEMISTRY, BIOPHYSICS AND MOLECULAR BIOLOGY RELATED

Amherst Coll (MA)
Blackburn Coll (IL)
California Baptist U (CA)
Indiana U Kokomo (IN)
Rensselaer Polytechnic Inst (NY)
Sweet Briar Coll (VA)
Towson U (MD)
U of Miami (FL)
U of Waterloo (ON, Canada)
Wichita State U (KS)

BIOENGINEERING AND BIOMEDICAL ENGINEERING

Alabama State U (AL)
Alfred U (NY)
Arizona State U at the Tempe campus (AZ)
Binghamton U, State U of New York (NY)
Boston U (MA)
Bucknell U (PA)
California Baptist U (CA)
California Inst of Technology (CA)
California Polytechnic State U, San Luis Obispo (CA)
California State U, Long Beach (CA)
Carnegie Mellon U (PA)
Case Western Reserve U (OH)
The Catholic U of America (DC)
Central Michigan U (MI)
City Coll of the City U of New York (NY)
Clemson U (SC)
The Coll of New Jersey (NJ)
Colorado School of Mines (CO)
Colorado State U (CO)
Columbia U (NY)
Dalhousie U (NS, Canada)
Drexel U (PA)
Duquesne U (PA)
Eastern Nazarene Coll (MA)
Elon U (NC)
Endicott Coll (MA)
Fairfield U (CT)
Florida Gulf Coast U (FL)
Florida Inst of Technology (FL)
Florida Intl U (FL)
Gannon U (PA)
Georgia Inst of Technology (GA)
Harding U (AR)
Harvard U (MA)
Hofstra U (NY)
Indiana U–Purdue U Indianapolis (IN)
Johns Hopkins U (MD)
Lawrence Technological U (MI)
Lehigh U (PA)
LeTourneau U (TX)
Louisiana State U and A&M Coll (LA)
Louisiana Tech U (LA)
Loyola U Chicago (IL)
Massachusetts Inst of Technology (MA)
Miami U (OH)
Michigan Technological U (MI)
Milwaukee School of Eng (WI)
Mississippi State U (MS)
North Carolina State U (NC)
Northwestern U (IL)
The Ohio State U (OH)
Oral Roberts U (OK)
Oregon State U (OR)
Penn State Abington (PA)
Penn State Altoona (PA)
Penn State Beaver (PA)
Penn State Berks (PA)
Penn State Brandywine (PA)
Penn State DuBois (PA)
Penn State Erie, The Behrend Coll (PA)
Penn State Fayette, The Eberly Campus (PA)
Penn State Greater Allegheny (PA)
Penn State Hazleton (PA)
Penn State Lehigh Valley (PA)
Penn State Mont Alto (PA)
Penn State New Kensington (PA)
Penn State Schuylkill (PA)
Penn State Shenango (PA)
Penn State U Park (PA)
Penn State Wilkes-Barre (PA)
Penn State Worthington Scranton (PA)
Penn State York (PA)
Purdue U (IN)
Rensselaer Polytechnic Inst (NY)
Rice U (TX)
Rochester Inst of Technology (NY)
Rose-Hulman Inst of Technology (IN)
Rowan U (NJ)
Rutgers U–New Brunswick (NJ)
Saint Louis U (MO)
Saint Louis U–Madrid Campus (Spain)
Santa Clara U (CA)
Stanford U (CA)
Stevens Inst of Technology (NJ)
Stony Brook U, State U of New York (NY)
Syracuse U (NY)
Temple U (PA)
Texas A&M U (TX)
Tufts U (MA)
Tulane U (LA)
Union Coll (NY)
U at Buffalo, the State U of New York (NY)
The U of Akron (OH)
The U of Alabama at Birmingham (AL)
The U of Arizona (AZ)
U of Arkansas (AR)
U of California, Davis (CA)
U of California, Irvine (CA)
U of California, Riverside (CA)
U of California, San Diego (CA)
U of Cincinnati (OH)
U of Colorado Denver (CO)
U of Delaware (DE)
U of Florida (FL)
U of Guelph (ON, Canada)
U of Houston (TX)
U of Illinois at Chicago (IL)
U of Louisville (KY)
U of Maine (ME)
U of Massachusetts Amherst (MA)
U of Massachusetts Dartmouth (MA)
U of Massachusetts Lowell (MA)
U of Miami (FL)
U of Michigan (MI)
U of Michigan–Dearborn (MI)
U of Minnesota, Twin Cities Campus (MN)
U of Nevada, Reno (NV)
U of New Hampshire (NH)
U of North Texas (TX)
U of Oklahoma (OK)
U of Pennsylvania (PA)
U of Pittsburgh (PA)
U of Rhode Island (RI)
U of Rochester (NY)
U of South Carolina (SC)
U of Southern California (CA)
The U of Tennessee (TN)
The U of Texas at Austin (TX)
The U of Texas at Dallas (TX)
The U of Texas at San Antonio (TX)
U of the Pacific (CA)
The U of Toledo (OH)
U of Toronto (ON, Canada)
U of Utah (UT)
U of Vermont (VT)
U of Virginia (VA)
U of Washington (WA)
U of Waterloo (ON, Canada)
U of Wisconsin–Madison (WI)
Vanderbilt U (TN)
Virginia Commonwealth U (VA)
Walla Walla U (WA)
Washington State U (WA)
Washington U in St. Louis (MO)
Wayne State U (MI)
Wentworth Inst of Technology (MA)
Western New England U (MA)
West Virginia U (WV)
Wichita State U (KS)
Widener U (PA)
Worcester Polytechnic Inst (MA)
Wright State U (OH)
Wright State U–Lake Campus (OH)

BIOETHICS/MEDICAL ETHICS

Houston Baptist U (TX)
U of Miami (FL)
U of Richmond (VA)
U of Rochester (NY)

BIOINFORMATICS

Arizona State U at the Tempe campus (AZ)
Baylor U (TX)
California State U, San Bernardino (CA)
Canisius Coll (NY)
Dalhousie U (NS, Canada)
Davenport U, Grand Rapids (MI)
Gannon U (PA)
Inter American U of Puerto Rico, Bayamón Campus (PR)
Iowa State U of Science and Technology (IA)

Kettering U (MI)
Lebanese American U (Lebanon)
Loyola U Chicago (IL)
Michigan Technological U (MI)
New York City Coll of Technology of the City U of New York (NY)
Portland State U (OR)
Ramapo Coll of New Jersey (NJ)
Rensselaer Polytechnic Inst (NY)
Rochester Inst of Technology (NY)
Rowan U (NJ)
St. Bonaventure U (NY)
St. Edward's U (TX)
Saint Vincent Coll (PA)
Stevens Inst of Technology (NJ)
Trinity Christian Coll (IL)
Université de Montréal (QC, Canada)
U at Buffalo, the State U of New York (NY)
The U of Arizona (AZ)
U of California, Irvine (CA)
U of Denver (CO)
U of Georgia (GA)
U of Maryland, Baltimore County (MD)
U of Pennsylvania (PA)
U of Pittsburgh (PA)
U of St. Thomas (TX)
U of Saskatchewan (SK, Canada)
U of Waterloo (ON, Canada)
U of Windsor (ON, Canada)
Virginia Commonwealth U (VA)
Wheaton Coll (MA)
Whitworth U (WA)

BIOLOGICAL AND BIOMEDICAL SCIENCES RELATED

Alvernia U (PA)
Bethel U (MN)
Biola U (CA)
Boston U (MA)
Central Michigan U (MI)
Central Washington U (WA)
Charleston Southern U (SC)
Christopher Newport U (VA)
Cornell U (NY)
Dakota State U (SD)
Gordon State Coll (GA)
Grand Valley State U (MI)
Guilford Coll (NC)
Hiram Coll (OH)
Holy Names U (CA)
Indiana U Bloomington (IN)
Indiana U East (IN)
Kent State U (OH)
King U (TN)
Mount Aloysius Coll (PA)
New York Inst of Technology (NY)
Oklahoma City U (OK)
Our Lady of the Lake Coll (LA)
Penn State Abington (PA)
Penn State Altoona (PA)
Penn State Beaver (PA)
Penn State Berks (PA)
Penn State Brandywine (PA)
Penn State DuBois (PA)
Penn State Erie, The Behrend Coll (PA)
Penn State Fayette, The Eberly Campus (PA)
Penn State Greater Allegheny (PA)
Penn State Hazleton (PA)
Penn State Lehigh Valley (PA)
Penn State Mont Alto (PA)
Penn State New Kensington (PA)
Penn State Schuylkill (PA)
Penn State Shenango (PA)
Penn State U Park (PA)
Penn State Wilkes-Barre (PA)
Penn State Worthington Scranton (PA)
Penn State York (PA)
Rochester Inst of Technology (NY)
Rutgers U–Newark (NJ)
The Sage Colls (NY)
Saint Mary's Coll of California (CA)
Swarthmore Coll (PA)
Trevecca Nazarene U (TN)
Union Coll (NY)
U of Cincinnati (OH)
U of Maryland U Coll (MD)
U of Michigan (MI)
U of New Hampshire (NH)
U of North Dakota (ND)
U of Puerto Rico in Bayamón (PR)
U of Wisconsin–Parkside (WI)
Utah State U (UT)
Washington U in St. Louis (MO)
Western State Colorado U (CO)
Whitman Coll (WA)

BIOLOGICAL AND PHYSICAL SCIENCES

Adelphi U (NY)
Alaska Pacific U (AK)
Alfred U (NY)
Alice Lloyd Coll (KY)
Allegheny Coll (PA)
Alvernia U (PA)
Arcadia U (PA)
Averett U (VA)
Baldwin Wallace U (OH)
Bemidji State U (MN)
Bennington Coll (VT)
Bishop's U (QC, Canada)
Bluefield State Coll (WV)
Bryn Athyn Coll of the New Church (PA)
Buena Vista U (IA)
California State U, Fresno (CA)
Calumet Coll of Saint Joseph (IN)
Calvin Coll (MI)
Charleston Southern U (SC)
Clarion U of Pennsylvania (PA)
Coll of Saint Benedict (MN)
Coll of the Atlantic (ME)
Colorado Christian U (CO)
Concordia U Chicago (IL)
Dominican U (IL)
Drexel U (PA)
Eastern Michigan U (MI)
Eastern Nazarene Coll (MA)
East Stroudsburg U of Pennsylvania (PA)
Elmira Coll (NY)
Emory U (GA)
Eugene Lang Coll of Liberal Arts (NY)
Eureka Coll (IL)
The Evergreen State Coll (WA)
Fairleigh Dickinson U, Metropolitan Campus (NJ)
Fordham U (NY)
Gettysburg Coll (PA)
Grace Coll (IN)
Grand Valley State U (MI)
Houghton Coll (NY)
Huntington U (IN)
Indiana U Kokomo (IN)
Indiana U of Pennsylvania (PA)
Indiana U–Purdue U Indianapolis (IN)
Iowa Wesleyan U (IA)
John Carroll U (OH)
Johns Hopkins U (MD)
Johnson C. Smith U (NC)
Keene State Coll (NH)
King's Coll (PA)
King U (TN)
Le Moyne Coll (NY)
Mansfield U of Pennsylvania (PA)
Maryville U of Saint Louis (MO)
The Master's U (CA)
McMaster U (ON, Canada)
Michigan State U (MI)
Minnesota State U Mankato (MN)
Mississippi State U (MS)
Mount Allison U (NB, Canada)
New Coll of Florida (FL)
North Carolina Wesleyan Coll (NC)
North Central Coll (IL)
Northwestern U (IL)
Northwest Missouri State U (MO)
Penn State Abington (PA)
Penn State Altoona (PA)
Penn State Beaver (PA)
Penn State Berks (PA)
Penn State Brandywine (PA)
Penn State DuBois (PA)
Penn State Erie, The Behrend Coll (PA)
Penn State Fayette, The Eberly Campus (PA)
Penn State Greater Allegheny (PA)
Penn State Hazleton (PA)
Penn State Lehigh Valley (PA)
Penn State Mont Alto (PA)
Penn State New Kensington (PA)
Penn State Schuylkill (PA)
Penn State Shenango (PA)
Penn State U Park (PA)
Penn State Wilkes-Barre (PA)
Penn State Worthington Scranton (PA)
Penn State York (PA)
Philander Smith Coll (AR)
Portland State U (OR)
Purdue U (IN)
Quinnipiac U (CT)
Ramapo Coll of New Jersey (NJ)
Roberts Wesleyan Coll (NY)
Rockford U (IL)
Saint Anselm Coll (NH)
St. Gregory's U, Shawnee (OK)
Saint John's U (MN)
Saint Louis U–Madrid Campus (Spain)
St. Mary's Coll of Maryland (MD)
St. Norbert Coll (WI)
Saint Peter's U (NJ)
Sam Houston State U (TX)
San Francisco State U (CA)
Sierra Nevada Coll (NV)
Simon Fraser U (BC, Canada)
Southern Arkansas U–Magnolia (AR)
Spalding U (KY)
State U of New York at Fredonia (NY)
Stony Brook U, State U of New York (NY)
Texas State U (TX)
Texas Tech U (TX)
Thomas Edison State U (NJ)
Trent U (ON, Canada)
Troy U (AL)
Union Coll (NY)
Union U (TN)
The U of Alabama at Birmingham (AL)
U of Alaska Fairbanks (AK)
U of Central Arkansas (AR)
U of Denver (CO)
U of Georgia (GA)
U of Houston–Downtown (TX)
U of Massachusetts Amherst (MA)
U of Northern Iowa (IA)
U of Notre Dame (IN)
U of Oregon (OR)
U of Pittsburgh (PA)
U of Puget Sound (WA)
U of Regina (SK, Canada)
U of Southern Indiana (IN)
U of Southern Mississippi (MS)
U of South Florida (FL)
The U of Texas at San Antonio (TX)
U of Waterloo (ON, Canada)
The U of West Alabama (AL)
U of Windsor (ON, Canada)
U of Wisconsin–Platteville (WI)
U of Wisconsin–Stevens Point (WI)
U of Wisconsin–Superior (WI)
Upper Iowa U (IA)
Ursinus Coll (PA)
Virginia Commonwealth U (VA)
Walsh U (OH)
Washington State U (WA)
Washington State U–Tri-Cities (WA)
Washington U in St. Louis (MO)
Wesleyan U (CT)
Western Washington U (WA)

BIOLOGICAL/BIOSYSTEMS ENGINEERING

Auburn U (AL)
Iowa State U of Science and Technology (IA)
The U of Arizona (AZ)
U of Arkansas (AR)
U of Florida (FL)
U of Georgia (GA)
U of Guelph (ON, Canada)
U of Idaho (ID)

BIOLOGY/BIOLOGICAL SCIENCES

Abilene Christian U (TX)
Adams State U (CO)
Adelphi U (NY)
Agnes Scott Coll (GA)
Alabama State U (AL)
Albany State U (GA)
Albertus Magnus Coll (CT)
Albion Coll (MI)
Albright Coll (PA)
Alcorn State U (MS)
Alderson Broaddus U (WV)
Alfred U (NY)
Alice Lloyd Coll (KY)
Allegheny Coll (PA)
Alma Coll (MI)
Alvernia U (PA)
Alverno Coll (WI)
Ambrose U (AB, Canada)
American Intl Coll (MA)
American U (DC)
The American U in Cairo (Egypt)
American U of Beirut (Lebanon)
Amherst Coll (MA)
Anderson U (IN)
Anderson U (SC)
Andrews U (MI)
Angelo State U (TX)
Appalachian State U (NC)
Aquinas Coll (MI)
Arcadia U (PA)
Arizona Christian U (AZ)
Arizona State U at the Polytechnic campus (AZ)
Arizona State U at the Tempe campus (AZ)
Arizona State U at the West campus (AZ)
Arkansas Tech U (AR)
Armstrong State U (GA)
Asbury U (KY)
Ashland U (OH)
Assumption Coll (MA)
Athens State U (AL)
Auburn U (AL)
Auburn U at Montgomery (AL)
Augsburg Coll (MN)
Augustana Coll (IL)
Augustana U (SD)
Augusta U (GA)
Aurora U (IL)
Austin Coll (TX)
Austin Peay State U (TN)
Averett U (VA)
Avila U (MO)
Azusa Pacific U (CA)
Baker U (KS)
Baldwin Wallace U (OH)
Ball State U (IN)
Bard Coll (NY)
Barnard Coll (NY)
Barry U (FL)
Barton Coll (NC)
Bates Coll (ME)
Bayamón Central U (PR)
Baylor U (TX)
Bay Path U (MA)
Becker Coll (MA)
Belhaven U (MS)
Bellarmine U (KY)
Belmont Abbey Coll (NC)
Belmont U (TN)
Beloit Coll (WI)
Bemidji State U (MN)
Benedictine Coll (KS)
Bennett Coll (NC)
Bennington Coll (VT)
Berea Coll (KY)
Berry Coll (GA)
Bethany Lutheran Coll (MN)
Bethel Coll (IN)
Bethel Coll (KS)
Bethel U (MN)
Bethune-Cookman U (FL)
Binghamton U, State U of New York (NY)
Biola U (CA)
Bishop's U (QC, Canada)
Blackburn Coll (IL)
Black Hills State U (SD)
Bloomfield Coll (NJ)
Bloomsburg U of Pennsylvania (PA)
Bluefield Coll (VA)
Blue Mountain Coll (MS)
Bluffton U (OH)
Boise State U (ID)
Boston Coll (MA)
Boston U (MA)
Bowdoin Coll (ME)
Bowie State U (MD)
Bowling Green State U (OH)
Bradley U (IL)
Brandeis U (MA)
Brenau U (GA)
Brescia U (KY)
Brewton-Parker Coll (GA)
Briar Cliff U (IA)
Bridgewater Coll (VA)
Bridgewater State U (MA)
Brigham Young U–Idaho (ID)
Brooklyn Coll of the City U of New York (NY)
Bryan Coll (TN)
Bryant U (RI)
Bryn Athyn Coll of the New Church (PA)
Bryn Mawr Coll (PA)
Bucknell U (PA)
Buena Vista U (IA)
Buffalo State Coll, State U of New York (NY)
Butler U (IN)
Cabrini U (PA)
Caldwell U (NJ)
California Baptist U (CA)
California Inst of Technology (CA)
California Lutheran U (CA)
California Polytechnic State U, San Luis Obispo (CA)
California State Polytechnic U, Pomona (CA)
California State U, Bakersfield (CA)
California State U, Chico (CA)
California State U, Dominguez Hills (CA)
California State U, East Bay (CA)
California State U, Fresno (CA)
California State U, Fullerton (CA)
California State U, Long Beach (CA)
California State U, Monterey Bay (CA)
California State U, Northridge (CA)
California State U, Sacramento (CA)
California State U, San Bernardino (CA)
California State U, San Marcos (CA)
California State U, Stanislaus (CA)
California U of Pennsylvania (PA)
Calvin Coll (MI)
Cameron U (OK)
Campbellsville U (KY)
Canisius Coll (NY)
Capital U (OH)
Cardinal Stritch U (WI)
Carleton Coll (MN)
Carlow U (PA)
Carnegie Mellon U (PA)
Carroll Coll (MT)
Carson-Newman U (TN)
Carthage Coll (WI)
Case Western Reserve U (OH)
Catawba Coll (NC)
The Catholic U of America (DC)
Cazenovia Coll (NY)
Cedar Crest Coll (PA)
Cedarville U (OH)
Centenary Coll of Louisiana (LA)
Centenary U (NJ)
Central Baptist Coll (AR)
Central Connecticut State U (CT)
Central Methodist U (MO)
Central Michigan U (MI)
Central State U (OH)
Central Washington U (WA)
Centre Coll (KY)
Chaminade U of Honolulu (HI)
Chapman U (CA)
Charleston Southern U (SC)
Chatham U (PA)
Chestnut Hill Coll (PA)
Chowan U (NC)
Christian Brothers U (TN)
Christopher Newport U (VA)
The Citadel, The Military Coll of South Carolina (SC)
City Coll of the City U of New York (NY)
Claremont McKenna Coll (CA)
Clarion U of Pennsylvania (PA)
Clark Atlanta U (GA)
Clarke U (IA)
Clarkson U (NY)
Clark U (MA)
Clayton State U (GA)
Clemson U (SC)
Cleveland State U (OH)
Coastal Carolina U (SC)
Coe Coll (IA)
Colby Coll (ME)
Colby-Sawyer Coll (NH)
Colgate U (NY)
The Coll at Brockport, State U of New York (NY)
Coll of Charleston (SC)

Coll of Coastal Georgia (GA)
The Coll of Idaho (ID)
Coll of Mount Saint Vincent (NY)
The Coll of New Jersey (NJ)
Coll of Saint Benedict (MN)
Coll of Saint Elizabeth (NJ)
Coll of Saint Mary (NE)
The Coll of Saint Rose (NY)
The Coll of St. Scholastica (MN)
Coll of Staten Island of the City U of New York (NY)
Coll of the Atlantic (ME)
Coll of the Holy Cross (MA)
The Coll of William and Mary (VA)
The Coll of Wooster (OH)
Colorado Christian U (CO)
Colorado Mesa U (CO)
Colorado State U (CO)
Columbia Coll (MO)
Columbia U (NY)
Columbia U, School of General Studies (NY)
Columbus State U (GA)
Concordia Coll (MN)
Concordia Coll–New York (NY)
Concordia U (QC, Canada)
Concordia U Chicago (IL)
Concordia U Irvine (CA)
Concordia U, Nebraska (NE)
Concordia U, St. Paul (MN)
Concordia U Wisconsin (WI)
Concord U (WV)
Connecticut Coll (CT)
Converse Coll (SC)
Cornell Coll (IA)
Cornell U (NY)
Cornerstone U (MI)
Crandall U (NB, Canada)
Creighton U (NE)
Culver-Stockton Coll (MO)
Curry Coll (MA)
Daemen Coll (NY)
Dalhousie U (NS, Canada)
Dallas Baptist U (TX)
Dalton State Coll (GA)
Dartmouth Coll (NH)
Davidson Coll (NC)
Defiance Coll (OH)
Delaware Valley U (PA)
Denison U (OH)
DePauw U (IN)
DeSales U (PA)
Dickinson Coll (PA)
Dickinson State U (ND)
Dixie State U (UT)
Doane U (NE)
Dominican Coll (NY)
Dominican U (IL)
Dominican U of California (CA)
Drake U (IA)
Drew U (NJ)
Drexel U (PA)
Drury U (MO)
Duquesne U (PA)
Earlham Coll (IN)
East Carolina U (NC)
East Central U (OK)
Eastern Illinois U (IL)
Eastern Mennonite U (VA)
Eastern Michigan U (MI)
Eastern Nazarene Coll (MA)
Eastern Oregon U (OR)
Eastern U (PA)
Eastern Washington U (WA)
East Georgia State Coll (GA)
East Stroudsburg U of Pennsylvania (PA)
East Tennessee State U (TN)
East Texas Baptist U (TX)
Eckerd Coll (FL)
Edgewood Coll (WI)
Elizabeth City State U (NC)
Elizabethtown Coll (PA)
Elmira Coll (NY)
Elms Coll (MA)
Elon U (NC)
Emmanuel Coll (GA)
Emmanuel Coll (MA)
Emory & Henry Coll (VA)
Emory U (GA)
Emporia State U (KS)
Eureka Coll (IL)
Evangel U (MO)
The Evergreen State Coll (WA)
Fairfield U (CT)
Fairleigh Dickinson U, Coll at Florham (NJ)
Fairleigh Dickinson U, Metropolitan Campus (NJ)
Farmingdale State Coll (NY)
Faulkner U (AL)
Fayetteville State U (NC)
Felician U (NJ)
Ferris State U (MI)
Fisher Coll (MA)
Fitchburg State U (MA)
Florida Ag and Mech U (FL)
Florida Atlantic U (FL)
Florida Gulf Coast U (FL)
Florida Inst of Technology (FL)
Florida Intl U (FL)
Florida Southern Coll (FL)
Fordham U (NY)
Framingham State U (MA)
Franciscan U of Steubenville (OH)
Francis Marion U (SC)
Franklin & Marshall Coll (PA)
Franklin Coll (IN)
Franklin Pierce U (NH)
Freed-Hardeman U (TN)
Fresno Pacific U (CA)
Friends U (KS)
Frostburg State U (MD)
Furman U (SC)
Gallaudet U (DC)
Gannon U (PA)
Gardner-Webb U (NC)
Geneva Coll (PA)
George Fox U (OR)
Georgetown Coll (KY)
Georgetown U (DC)
The George Washington U (DC)
Georgia Coll & State U (GA)
Georgia Gwinnett Coll (GA)
Georgia Inst of Technology (GA)
Georgian Court U (NJ)
Georgia Southern U (GA)
Georgia Southwestern State U (GA)
Georgia State U (GA)
Gettysburg Coll (PA)
Gonzaga U (WA)
Gordon Coll (MA)
Goshen Coll (IN)
Goucher Coll (MD)
Governors State U (IL)
Grace Coll (IN)
Graceland U (IA)
Grambling State U (LA)
Grand Valley State U (MI)
Grand View U (IA)
Great Basin Coll (NV)
Green Mountain Coll (VT)
Greenville Coll (IL)
Grinnell Coll (IA)
Grove City Coll (PA)
Guilford Coll (NC)
Gwynedd Mercy U (PA)
Hamilton Coll (NY)
Hamline U (MN)
Hampden-Sydney Coll (VA)
Hampshire Coll (MA)
Hampton U (VA)
Hannibal-LaGrange U (MO)
Hanover Coll (IN)
Harding U (AR)
Hardin-Simmons U (TX)
Harrisburg U of Science and Technology (PA)
Harris-Stowe State U (MO)
Hartwick Coll (NY)
Harvard U (MA)
Harvey Mudd Coll (CA)
Haverford Coll (PA)
Hawai`i Pacific U (HI)
Heidelberg U (OH)
Henderson State U (AR)
Hendrix Coll (AR)
High Point U (NC)
Hillsdale Coll (MI)
Hiram Coll (OH)
Hobart and William Smith Colls (NY)
Hofstra U (NY)
Hollins U (VA)
Holy Cross Coll (IN)
Holy Family U (PA)
Holy Names U (CA)
Hood Coll (MD)
Hope Coll (MI)
Houghton Coll (NY)
Houston Baptist U (TX)
Howard Payne U (TX)
Humboldt State U (CA)
Hunter Coll of the City U of New York (NY)
Huntingdon Coll (AL)
Huntington U (IN)
Husson U (ME)
Huston-Tillotson U (TX)
Idaho State U (ID)
Illinois Coll (IL)
Illinois State U (IL)
Illinois Wesleyan U (IL)
Immaculata U (PA)
Indiana State U (IN)
Indiana U Bloomington (IN)
Indiana U East (IN)
Indiana U Kokomo (IN)
Indiana U Northwest (IN)
Indiana U of Pennsylvania (PA)
Indiana U–Purdue U Indianapolis (IN)
Indiana U South Bend (IN)
Indiana U Southeast (IN)
Inter American U of Puerto Rico, Aguadilla Campus (PR)
Inter American U of Puerto Rico, Barranquitas Campus (PR)
Inter American U of Puerto Rico, Bayamón Campus (PR)
Inter American U of Puerto Rico, Fajardo Campus (PR)
Inter American U of Puerto Rico, Guayama Campus (PR)
Inter American U of Puerto Rico, Metropolitan Campus (PR)
Inter American U of Puerto Rico, Ponce Campus (PR)
Inter American U of Puerto Rico, San Germán Campus (PR)
Iona Coll (NY)
Iowa State U of Science and Technology (IA)
Iowa Wesleyan U (IA)
Ithaca Coll (NY)
Jackson State U (MS)
Jacksonville State U (AL)
Jacksonville U (FL)
James Madison U (VA)
John Brown U (AR)
John Carroll U (OH)
Johns Hopkins U (MD)
Johnson C. Smith U (NC)
Judson U (IL)
Juniata Coll (PA)
Kalamazoo Coll (MI)
Kansas State U (KS)
Kansas Wesleyan U (KS)
Kean U (NJ)
Keene State Coll (NH)
Kennesaw State U (GA)
Kent State U (OH)
Kent State U at Stark (OH)
Kentucky State U (KY)
Kentucky Wesleyan Coll (KY)
Kenyon Coll (OH)
Kettering U (MI)
Keuka Coll (NY)
King's Coll (PA)
The King's U (AB, Canada)
King U (TN)
Knox Coll (IL)
Kutztown U of Pennsylvania (PA)
Lafayette Coll (PA)
LaGrange Coll (GA)
Lake Erie Coll (OH)
Lake Forest Coll (IL)
Lamar U (TX)
Lane Coll (TN)
Langston U (OK)
La Roche Coll (PA)
La Salle U (PA)
Lawrence U (WI)
Lebanese American U (Lebanon)
Lebanon Valley Coll (PA)
Lees-McRae Coll (NC)
Lee U (TN)
Lehigh U (PA)
Lehman Coll of the City U of New York (NY)
Le Moyne Coll (NY)
Lenoir-Rhyne U (NC)
LeTourneau U (TX)
Lewis & Clark Coll (OR)
Lewis U (IL)
Liberty U (VA)
Life U (GA)
Limestone Coll (SC)
Lincoln U (MO)
Lincoln U (PA)
Lindenwood U (MO)
Lindsey Wilson Coll (KY)
Linfield Coll (OR)
Lipscomb U (TN)
Lock Haven U of Pennsylvania (PA)
Logan U (MO)
Longwood U (VA)
Loras Coll (IA)
Louisiana Coll (LA)
Louisiana State U and A&M Coll (LA)
Louisiana State U at Alexandria (LA)
Louisiana Tech U (LA)
Lourdes U (OH)
Loyola Marymount U (CA)
Loyola U Chicago (IL)
Loyola U Maryland (MD)
Loyola U New Orleans (LA)
Lubbock Christian U (TX)
Luther Coll (IA)
Lycoming Coll (PA)
Lynchburg Coll (VA)
Lynn U (FL)
Lyon Coll (AR)
Macalester Coll (MN)
MacMurray Coll (IL)
Madonna U (MI)
Malone U (OH)
Manchester U (IN)
Manhattan Coll (NY)
Manhattanville Coll (NY)
Mansfield U of Pennsylvania (PA)
Maranatha Baptist U (WI)
Marian U (IN)
Marian U (WI)
Marietta Coll (OH)
Marist Coll (NY)
Marshall U (WV)
Mary Baldwin U (VA)
Marymount California U (CA)
Marymount Manhattan Coll (NY)
Marymount U (VA)
Maryville U of Saint Louis (MO)
Marywood U (PA)
Massachusetts Coll of Liberal Arts (MA)
Massachusetts Inst of Technology (MA)
The Master's U (CA)
McDaniel Coll (MD)
McKendree U (IL)
McMaster U (ON, Canada)
McMurry U (TX)
McNeese State U (LA)
Medgar Evers Coll of the City U of New York (NY)
Mercer U, Macon (GA)
Mercy Coll (NY)
Mercy Coll of Ohio (OH)
Mercyhurst U (PA)
Meredith Coll (NC)
Merrimack Coll (MA)
Messiah Coll (PA)
Metropolitan State U of Denver (CO)
Miami Dade Coll (FL)
Miami U (OH)
Michigan State U (MI)
Michigan Technological U (MI)
MidAmerica Nazarene U (KS)
Mid-Atlantic Christian U (NC)
Middlebury Coll (VT)
Millersville U of Pennsylvania (PA)
Milligan Coll (TN)
Millikin U (IL)
Millsaps Coll (MS)
Mills Coll (CA)
Minnesota State U Mankato (MN)
Minnesota State U Moorhead (MN)
Minot State U (ND)
Misericordia U (PA)
Mississippi State U (MS)
Mississippi Valley State U (MS)
Missouri Baptist U (MO)
Missouri State U (MO)
Missouri U of Science and Technology (MO)
Missouri Valley Coll (MO)
Missouri Western State U (MO)
Molloy Coll (NY)
Monmouth Coll (IL)
Monmouth U (NJ)
Montana State U (MT)
Montana State U Billings (MT)
Montana State U–Northern (MT)
Montana Tech of The U of Montana (MT)
Montclair State U (NJ)
Moravian Coll (PA)
Morehead State U (KY)
Morehouse Coll (GA)
Morningside Coll (IA)
Morris Coll (SC)
Mount Allison U (NB, Canada)
Mount Aloysius Coll (PA)
Mount Holyoke Coll (MA)
Mount Ida Coll (MA)
Mount Marty Coll (SD)
Mount Mary U (WI)
Mount Mercy U (IA)
Mount St. Joseph U (OH)
Mount Saint Mary Coll (NY)
Mount Saint Mary's U (CA)
Mount St. Mary's U (MD)
Mount Vernon Nazarene U (OH)
Muhlenberg Coll (PA)
Murray State U (KY)
National U (CA)
Nazareth Coll of Rochester (NY)
Nebraska Wesleyan U (NE)
Neumann U (PA)
Nevada State Coll (NV)
Newberry Coll (SC)
New Coll of Florida (FL)
New England Coll (NH)
New Jersey City U (NJ)
Newman U (KS)
New Mexico Highlands U (NM)
New Mexico Inst of Mining and Technology (NM)
New Mexico State U (NM)
New York Inst of Technology (NY)
Niagara U (NY)
North Carolina Central U (NC)
North Carolina State U (NC)
North Carolina Wesleyan Coll (NC)
North Central Coll (IL)
North Dakota State U (ND)
Northeastern Illinois U (IL)
Northeastern State U (OK)
Northeastern U (MA)
Northern Arizona U (AZ)
Northern Illinois U (IL)
Northern Kentucky U (KY)
Northern State U (SD)
North Greenville U (SC)
Northland Coll (WI)
Northwest Christian U (OR)
Northwestern Coll (IA)
Northwestern Oklahoma State U (OK)
Northwestern State U of Louisiana (LA)
Northwestern U (IL)
Northwest Missouri State U (MO)
Northwest U (WA)
Nova Southeastern U (FL)
Nyack Coll (NY)
Oakland City U (IN)
Oberlin Coll (OH)
Occidental Coll (CA)
Ohio Dominican U (OH)
The Ohio State U (OH)
The Ohio State U at Lima (OH)
Ohio U (OH)
Ohio Wesleyan U (OH)
Oklahoma Baptist U (OK)
Oklahoma Christian U (OK)
Oklahoma City U (OK)
Oklahoma State U (OK)
Old Dominion U (VA)
Olivet Nazarene U (IL)
Oral Roberts U (OK)
Oregon State U (OR)
Otterbein U (OH)
Ouachita Baptist U (AR)
Our Lady of the Lake Coll (LA)
Our Lady of the Lake U of San Antonio (TX)
Pace U (NY)
Pace U, Pleasantville Campus (NY)
Pacific Lutheran U (WA)
Paine Coll (GA)
Palm Beach Atlantic U (FL)
Penn State Abington (PA)
Penn State Altoona (PA)
Penn State Beaver (PA)
Penn State Berks (PA)
Penn State Brandywine (PA)
Penn State DuBois (PA)
Penn State Erie, The Behrend Coll (PA)

Penn State Fayette, The Eberly Campus (PA)
Penn State Greater Allegheny (PA)
Penn State Hazleton (PA)
Penn State Lehigh Valley (PA)
Penn State Mont Alto (PA)
Penn State New Kensington (PA)
Penn State Schuylkill (PA)
Penn State Shenango (PA)
Penn State U Park (PA)
Penn State Wilkes-Barre (PA)
Penn State Worthington Scranton (PA)
Penn State York (PA)
Pepperdine U, Malibu (CA)
Philander Smith Coll (AR)
Piedmont Coll (GA)
Pine Manor Coll (MA)
Pittsburg State U (KS)
Pitzer Coll (CA)
Plymouth State U (NH)
Point Loma Nazarene U (CA)
Point Park U (PA)
Point U (GA)
Pomona Coll (CA)
Portland State U (OR)
Prairie View A&M U (TX)
Principia Coll (IL)
Providence Coll (RI)
Purchase Coll, State U of New York (NY)
Purdue U (IN)
Purdue U Northwest (IN)
Queens Coll of the City U of New York (NY)
Quinnipiac U (CT)
Radford U (VA)
Ramapo Coll of New Jersey (NJ)
Randolph Coll (VA)
Randolph-Macon Coll (VA)
Redeemer U Coll (ON, Canada)
Reed Coll (OR)
Regis Coll (MA)
Regis U (CO)
Rensselaer Polytechnic Inst (NY)
Rhode Island Coll (RI)
Rhodes Coll (TN)
Rice U (TX)
Ripon Coll (WI)
Roanoke Coll (VA)
Robert Morris U (PA)
Roberts Wesleyan Coll (NY)
Rochester Inst of Technology (NY)
Rockford U (IL)
Rockhurst U (MO)
Rocky Mountain Coll (MT)
Rogers State U (OK)
Roger Williams U (RI)
Rollins Coll (FL)
Rose-Hulman Inst of Technology (IN)
Rosemont Coll (PA)
Rowan U (NJ)
Rust Coll (MS)
Rutgers U–Camden (NJ)
Rutgers U–Newark (NJ)
Rutgers U–New Brunswick (NJ)
Sacred Heart U (CT)
The Sage Colls (NY)
Saginaw Valley State U (MI)
St. Ambrose U (IA)
St. Andrews U (NC)
Saint Anselm Coll (NH)
Saint Augustine's U (NC)
St. Bonaventure U (NY)
St. Catherine U (MN)
St. Cloud State U (MN)
St. Edward's U (TX)
Saint Francis U (PA)
St. Gregory's U, Shawnee (OK)
St. John Fisher Coll (NY)
Saint John's U (MN)
St. John's U (NY)
St. Joseph's Coll, Long Island Campus (NY)
St. Joseph's Coll, New York (NY)
Saint Joseph's U (PA)
Saint Leo U (FL)
Saint Louis U (MO)
Saint Martin's U (WA)
Saint Mary-of-the-Woods Coll (IN)
Saint Mary's Coll (IN)
Saint Mary's Coll of California (CA)
St. Mary's Coll of Maryland (MD)
Saint Mary's U of Minnesota (MN)
Saint Michael's Coll (VT)
St. Norbert Coll (WI)
St. Olaf Coll (MN)
St. Petersburg Coll (FL)
Saint Peter's U (NJ)
St. Thomas Aquinas Coll (NY)
St. Thomas U (FL)
Saint Vincent Coll (PA)
Salisbury U (MD)
Salve Regina U (RI)
Samford U (AL)
Sam Houston State U (TX)
San Diego State U (CA)
San Francisco State U (CA)
Santa Clara U (CA)
Sarah Lawrence Coll (NY)
Schreiner U (TX)
Scripps Coll (CA)
Seattle Pacific U (WA)
Seattle U (WA)
Seton Hill U (PA)
Sewanee: The U of the South (TN)
Shawnee State U (OH)
Shaw U (NC)
Shenandoah U (VA)
Shepherd U (WV)
Shippensburg U of Pennsylvania (PA)
Shorter U (GA)
Siena Coll (NY)
Silver Lake Coll of the Holy Family (WI)
Simmons Coll (MA)
Simon Fraser U (BC, Canada)
Simpson Coll (IA)
Simpson U (CA)
Skidmore Coll (NY)
Slippery Rock U of Pennsylvania (PA)
Smith Coll (MA)
Sonoma State U (CA)
South Carolina State U (SC)
South Dakota State U (SD)
Southeastern Louisiana U (LA)
Southeastern Oklahoma State U (OK)
Southeastern U (FL)
Southeast Missouri State U (MO)
Southern Arkansas U–Magnolia (AR)
Southern Connecticut State U (CT)
Southern Illinois U Carbondale (IL)
Southern Illinois U Edwardsville (IL)
Southern Methodist U (TX)
Southern Oregon U (OR)
Southern Utah U (UT)
Southwest Baptist U (MO)
Southwestern Adventist U (TX)
Southwestern Coll (KS)
Southwestern U (TX)
Spelman Coll (GA)
Spring Hill Coll (AL)
Stanford U (CA)
State U of New York at Fredonia (NY)
State U of New York at New Paltz (NY)
State U of New York at Oswego (NY)
State U of New York at Plattsburgh (NY)
State U of New York Coll at Cortland (NY)
State U of New York Coll at Geneseo (NY)
State U of New York Coll at Old Westbury (NY)
State U of New York Coll at Potsdam (NY)
State U of New York Polytechnic Inst (NY)
Stephen F. Austin State U (TX)
Stephens Coll (MO)
Sterling Coll (KS)
Stevens Inst of Technology (NJ)
Stevenson U (MD)
Stockton U (NJ)
Stonehill Coll (MA)
Stony Brook U, State U of New York (NY)
Suffolk U (MA)
Susquehanna U (PA)
Swarthmore Coll (PA)
Sweet Briar Coll (VA)
Syracuse U (NY)
Tabor Coll (KS)
Tarleton State U (TX)
Taylor U (IN)
Temple U (PA)
Tennessee State U (TN)
Tennessee Wesleyan U (TN)
Texas A&M Intl U (TX)
Texas A&M U (TX)
Texas A&M U–Commerce (TX)
Texas A&M U–Corpus Christi (TX)
Texas A&M U–Kingsville (TX)
Texas Christian U (TX)
Texas Coll (TX)
Texas Lutheran U (TX)
Texas State U (TX)
Texas Tech U (TX)
Texas Wesleyan U (TX)
Texas Woman's U (TX)
Thomas More Coll (KY)
Thomas U (GA)
Toccoa Falls Coll (GA)
Towson U (MD)
Transylvania U (KY)
Trent U (ON, Canada)
Trevecca Nazarene U (TN)
Trine U (IN)
Trinity Christian Coll (IL)
Trinity U (TX)
Troy U (AL)
Truett McConnell U (GA)
Truman State U (MO)
Tufts U (MA)
Tulane U (LA)
Tusculum Coll (TN)
Union Coll (KY)
Union Coll (NE)
Union Coll (NY)
Union U (TN)
United States Air Force Acad (CO)
United States Military Acad (NY)
Universidad Adventista de las Antillas (PR)
Université de Montréal (QC, Canada)
Université de Sherbrooke (QC, Canada)
U at Albany, State U of New York (NY)
U at Buffalo, the State U of New York (NY)
The U of Akron (OH)
The U of Alabama (AL)
The U of Alabama at Birmingham (AL)
The U of Alabama in Huntsville (AL)
U of Alaska Fairbanks (AK)
The U of Arizona (AZ)
U of Arkansas (AR)
U of Bridgeport (CT)
U of California, Davis (CA)
U of California, Irvine (CA)
U of California, Los Angeles (CA)
U of California, Riverside (CA)
U of California, San Diego (CA)
U of California, Santa Barbara (CA)
U of Central Arkansas (AR)
U of Central Florida (FL)
U of Central Missouri (MO)
U of Charleston (WV)
U of Chicago (IL)
U of Cincinnati (OH)
U of Colorado Colorado Springs (CO)
U of Colorado Denver (CO)
U of Dayton (OH)
U of Delaware (DE)
U of Denver (CO)
U of Detroit Mercy (MI)
U of Dubuque (IA)
U of Evansville (IN)
The U of Findlay (OH)
U of Florida (FL)
U of Georgia (GA)
U of Great Falls (MT)
U of Guelph (ON, Canada)
U of Hartford (CT)
U of Hawaii at Manoa (HI)
U of Houston (TX)
U of Houston–Clear Lake (TX)
U of Houston–Downtown (TX)
U of Idaho (ID)
U of Illinois at Chicago (IL)
U of Illinois at Springfield (IL)
U of Indianapolis (IN)
U of Jamestown (ND)
The U of Kansas (KS)
U of Kentucky (KY)
U of King's Coll (NS, Canada)
U of La Verne (CA)
U of Lethbridge (AB, Canada)
U of Louisiana at Monroe (LA)
U of Louisville (KY)
U of Maine (ME)
U of Maine at Farmington (ME)
U of Maine at Fort Kent (ME)
U of Maine at Presque Isle (ME)
U of Mary Hardin-Baylor (TX)
U of Maryland, Baltimore County (MD)
U of Maryland, Coll Park (MD)
U of Mary Washington (VA)
U of Massachusetts Amherst (MA)
U of Massachusetts Boston (MA)
U of Massachusetts Dartmouth (MA)
U of Massachusetts Lowell (MA)
U of Miami (FL)
U of Michigan (MI)
U of Michigan–Dearborn (MI)
U of Michigan–Flint (MI)
U of Minnesota, Crookston (MN)
U of Minnesota, Duluth (MN)
U of Minnesota, Morris (MN)
U of Minnesota, Twin Cities Campus (MN)
U of Missouri–Kansas City (MO)
U of Missouri–St. Louis (MO)
U of Mobile (AL)
The U of Montana Western (MT)
U of Montevallo (AL)
U of Mount Union (OH)
U of Nebraska at Kearney (NE)
U of Nevada, Las Vegas (NV)
U of Nevada, Reno (NV)
U of New England (ME)
U of New Hampshire (NH)
U of New Hampshire at Manchester (NH)
U of New Haven (CT)
U of New Orleans (LA)
U of North Alabama (AL)
U of North Carolina at Asheville (NC)
The U of North Carolina at Chapel Hill (NC)
The U of North Carolina at Charlotte (NC)
The U of North Carolina at Greensboro (NC)
The U of North Carolina at Pembroke (NC)
The U of North Carolina Wilmington (NC)
U of North Dakota (ND)
U of Northern Colorado (CO)
U of Northern Iowa (IA)
U of North Florida (FL)
U of North Georgia (GA)
U of North Texas (TX)
U of Notre Dame (IN)
U of Oregon (OR)
U of Pennsylvania (PA)
U of Pikeville (KY)
U of Pittsburgh (PA)
U of Pittsburgh at Bradford (PA)
U of Pittsburgh at Greensburg (PA)
U of Pittsburgh at Johnstown (PA)
U of Puerto Rico in Bayamón (PR)
U of Puget Sound (WA)
U of Regina (SK, Canada)
U of Rhode Island (RI)
U of Richmond (VA)
U of Rochester (NY)
U of St. Francis (IL)
U of Saint Francis (IN)
U of Saint Joseph (CT)
U of Saint Mary (KS)
U of St. Thomas (MN)
U of St. Thomas (TX)
U of San Diego (CA)
U of San Francisco (CA)
U of Saskatchewan (SK, Canada)
U of Science and Arts of Oklahoma (OK)
The U of Scranton (PA)
U of South Carolina (SC)
U of South Carolina Aiken (SC)
The U of South Dakota (SD)
U of Southern California (CA)
U of Southern Indiana (IN)
U of Southern Maine (ME)
U of Southern Mississippi (MS)
U of South Florida (FL)
U of South Florida, St. Petersburg (FL)
U of South Florida Sarasota-Manatee (FL)
The U of Tampa (FL)
The U of Tennessee (TN)
The U of Tennessee at Chattanooga (TN)
The U of Tennessee at Martin (TN)
The U of Texas at Austin (TX)
The U of Texas at Dallas (TX)
The U of Texas at El Paso (TX)
The U of Texas at San Antonio (TX)
The U of Texas of the Permian Basin (TX)
The U of Texas Rio Grande Valley (TX)
U of the Cumberlands (KY)
U of the Fraser Valley (BC, Canada)
U of the Incarnate Word (TX)
U of the Pacific (CA)
U of the Southwest (NM)
U of the Virgin Islands (VI)
The U of Toledo (OH)
U of Toronto (ON, Canada)
The U of Tulsa (OK)
U of Utah (UT)
U of Vermont (VT)
U of Virginia (VA)
The U of Virginia's Coll at Wise (VA)
U of Washington (WA)
U of Washington, Bothell (WA)
U of Waterloo (ON, Canada)
The U of West Alabama (AL)
U of West Georgia (GA)
U of Windsor (ON, Canada)
U of Wisconsin–Eau Claire (WI)
U of Wisconsin–Green Bay (WI)
U of Wisconsin–La Crosse (WI)
U of Wisconsin–Madison (WI)
U of Wisconsin–Milwaukee (WI)
U of Wisconsin–Platteville (WI)
U of Wisconsin–Stevens Point (WI)
U of Wisconsin–Superior (WI)
U of Wisconsin–Whitewater (WI)
Upper Iowa U (IA)
Ursinus Coll (PA)
Utah State U (UT)
Utah Valley U (UT)
Utica Coll (NY)
Valdosta State U (GA)
Valley City State U (ND)
Valparaiso U (IN)
Vanderbilt U (TN)
Vassar Coll (NY)
Villanova U (PA)
Virginia Commonwealth U (VA)
Virginia Military Inst (VA)
Virginia Polytechnic Inst and State U (VA)
Virginia State U (VA)
Virginia Union U (VA)
Virginia Wesleyan Coll (VA)
Viterbo U (WI)
Wabash Coll (IN)
Wagner Coll (NY)
Wake Forest U (NC)
Waldorf U (IA)
Walla Walla U (WA)
Walsh U (OH)
Wartburg Coll (IA)
Washburn U (KS)
Washington & Jefferson Coll (PA)
Washington and Lee U (VA)
Washington Coll (MD)
Washington State U (WA)
Washington State U–Vancouver (WA)
Washington U in St. Louis (MO)
Wayland Baptist U (TX)
Waynesburg U (PA)
Wayne State Coll (NE)
Wayne State U (MI)
Webster U (MO)
Wells Coll (NY)
Wesleyan Coll (GA)
Wesleyan U (CT)
West Chester U of Pennsylvania (PA)
Western Carolina U (NC)
Western Connecticut State U (CT)
Western Illinois U (IL)
Western Kentucky U (KY)
Western Michigan U (MI)
Western New England U (MA)
Western Oregon U (OR)
Western State Colorado U (CO)

Western Washington U (WA)
Westfield State U (MA)
Westminster Coll (PA)
Westminster Coll (UT)
Westmont Coll (CA)
West Texas A&M U (TX)
West Virginia State U (WV)
West Virginia U (WV)
West Virginia Wesleyan Coll (WV)
Wheaton Coll (IL)
Wheaton Coll (MA)
Wheeling Jesuit U (WV)
Whitman Coll (WA)
Whittier Coll (CA)
Whitworth U (WA)
Wichita State U (KS)
Widener U (PA)
Wilkes U (PA)
Willamette U (OR)
William Jewell Coll (MO)
William Paterson U of New Jersey (NJ)
William Peace U (NC)
William Penn U (IA)
Williams Baptist Coll (AR)
Williams Coll (MA)
William Woods U (MO)
Wilson Coll (PA)
Wingate U (NC)
Winona State U (MN)
Winthrop U (SC)
Wittenberg U (OH)
Wofford Coll (SC)
Worcester Polytechnic Inst (MA)
Worcester State U (MA)
Wright State U (OH)
Xavier U of Louisiana (LA)
York Coll of Pennsylvania (PA)
York Coll of the City U of New York (NY)
Youngstown State U (OH)

BIOLOGY/BIOTECHNOLOGY LABORATORY TECHNICIAN

Cleveland State U (OH)
Davenport U, Grand Rapids (MI)
McMaster U (ON, Canada)
Penn State Abington (PA)
Penn State Altoona (PA)
Penn State Beaver (PA)
Penn State Berks (PA)
Penn State Brandywine (PA)
Penn State DuBois (PA)
Penn State Erie, The Behrend Coll (PA)
Penn State Fayette, The Eberly Campus (PA)
Penn State Greater Allegheny (PA)
Penn State Hazleton (PA)
Penn State Lehigh Valley (PA)
Penn State Mont Alto (PA)
Penn State New Kensington (PA)
Penn State Schuylkill (PA)
Penn State Shenango (PA)
Penn State U Park (PA)
Penn State Wilkes-Barre (PA)
Penn State Worthington Scranton (PA)
Penn State York (PA)
St. Cloud State U (MN)
State U of New York at Fredonia (NY)
U of New Haven (CT)
Washburn U (KS)
York Coll of the City U of New York (NY)

BIOLOGY TEACHER EDUCATION

Abilene Christian U (TX)
Adams State U (CO)
Albion Coll (MI)
Alvernia U (PA)
Arizona Christian U (AZ)
Arkansas Tech U (AR)
Ashland U (OH)
Augustana Coll (IL)
Averett U (VA)
Ball State U (IN)
Baylor U (TX)
Bay Path U (MA)
Bethel Coll (IN)
Bethune-Cookman U (FL)
Biola U (CA)
Bishop's U (QC, Canada)
Blackburn Coll (IL)
Bluefield Coll (VA)
Blue Mountain Coll (MS)
Boise State U (ID)
Bowling Green State U (OH)
Bradley U (IL)
Brewton-Parker Coll (GA)
Bridgewater State U (MA)
Brigham Young U–Idaho (ID)
Brooklyn Coll of the City U of New York (NY)
Bryan Coll (TN)
Buena Vista U (IA)
Cabrini U (PA)
California State U, Long Beach (CA)
Calvin Coll (MI)
Campbellsville U (KY)
Canisius Coll (NY)
Carroll Coll (MT)
Cedarville U (OH)
Central Methodist U (MO)
Central Michigan U (MI)
Central Washington U (WA)
City Coll of the City U of New York (NY)
The Coll of New Jersey (NJ)
Coll of Saint Mary (NE)
The Coll of Saint Rose (NY)
Coll of Staten Island of the City U of New York (NY)
Coll of the Ozarks (MO)
Colorado State U (CO)
Concordia Coll (MN)
Concordia U Chicago (IL)
Concordia U, St. Paul (MN)
Corban U (OR)
Cornerstone U (MI)
Culver-Stockton Coll (MO)
Daemen Coll (NY)
Dakota State U (SD)
Dallas Baptist U (TX)
Daytona State Coll (FL)
Dickinson State U (ND)
Dixie State U (UT)
Dominican Coll (NY)
East Central U (OK)
Eastern Michigan U (MI)
Eastern Nazarene Coll (MA)
Eastern Washington U (WA)
East Texas Baptist U (TX)
Edgewood Coll (WI)
Elizabeth City State U (NC)
Elmira Coll (NY)
Emory & Henry Coll (VA)
Evangel U (MO)
Faulkner U (AL)
Ferris State U (MI)
Fitchburg State U (MA)
Florida Inst of Technology (FL)
Florida Southern Coll (FL)
Florida SouthWestern State Coll (FL)
Fort Lewis Coll (CO)
Franklin Coll (IN)
Friends U (KS)
Gordon State Coll (GA)
Goshen Coll (IN)
Grace Coll (IN)
Grand Valley State U (MI)
Green Mountain Coll (VT)
Greenville Coll (IL)
Grove City Coll (PA)
Gwynedd Mercy U (PA)
Harding U (AR)
Hofstra U (NY)
Holy Family U (PA)
Hope Coll (MI)
Houston Baptist U (TX)
Howard Payne U (TX)
Hunter Coll of the City U of New York (NY)
Huntingdon Coll (AL)
Huntington U (IN)
Illinois State U (IL)
Indiana U Bloomington (IN)
Indiana U Northwest (IN)
Indiana U South Bend (IN)
Indiana U Southeast (IN)
Inter American U of Puerto Rico, Aguadilla Campus (PR)
Inter American U of Puerto Rico, Barranquitas Campus (PR)
Inter American U of Puerto Rico, Fajardo Campus (PR)
Inter American U of Puerto Rico, Metropolitan Campus (PR)
Inter American U of Puerto Rico, Ponce Campus (PR)
Inter American U of Puerto Rico, San Germán Campus (PR)
Iona Coll (NY)
Ithaca Coll (NY)
Juniata Coll (PA)
Kansas Wesleyan U (KS)
Kennesaw State U (GA)
Keuka Coll (NY)
King U (TN)
Lee U (TN)
Le Moyne Coll (NY)
Lincoln U (MO)
Lindenwood U (MO)
Lindsey Wilson Coll (KY)
Lipscomb U (TN)
Louisiana Coll (LA)
Louisiana Tech U (LA)
Madonna U (MI)
Manchester U (IN)
Manhattanville Coll (NY)
Maranatha Baptist U (WI)
Marist Coll (NY)
Marywood U (PA)
McMurry U (TX)
Mercyhurst U (PA)
Merrimack Coll (MA)
Messiah Coll (PA)
Miami Dade Coll (FL)
Miami U (OH)
Michigan State U (MI)
MidAmerica Nazarene U (KS)
Millikin U (IL)
Minnesota State U Moorhead (MN)
Minot State U (ND)
Misericordia U (PA)
Missouri State U (MO)
Montana State U Billings (MT)
Morningside Coll (IA)
Morris Coll (SC)
Mount Mary U (WI)
Mount Vernon Nazarene U (OH)
Nazareth Coll of Rochester (NY)
Nevada State Coll (NV)
Niagara U (NY)
North Dakota State U (ND)
Northwestern Coll (IA)
Northwest Missouri State U (MO)
Northwest U (WA)
Oakland City U (IN)
Ohio Dominican U (OH)
Ohio Wesleyan U (OH)
Pace U (NY)
Pace U, Pleasantville Campus (NY)
Palm Beach Atlantic U (FL)
Pittsburg State U (KS)
Point Park U (PA)
Providence Coll (RI)
Queens Coll of the City U of New York (NY)
Rhode Island Coll (RI)
Roberts Wesleyan Coll (NY)
Rocky Mountain Coll (MT)
Rust Coll (MS)
Saginaw Valley State U (MI)
St. Catherine U (MN)
St. Edward's U (TX)
Saint Francis U (PA)
St. Gregory's U, Shawnee (OK)
St. John Fisher Coll (NY)
St. John's U (NY)
St. Joseph's Coll, Long Island Campus (NY)
St. Joseph's Coll, New York (NY)
Saint Joseph's U (PA)
Saint Mary's U of Minnesota (MN)
St. Petersburg Coll (FL)
Salve Regina U (RI)
Schreiner U (TX)
Seattle U (WA)
Seton Hill U (PA)
Southeastern U (FL)
Southern Utah U (UT)
Southwest Baptist U (MO)
Southwestern Adventist U (TX)
Spring Hill Coll (AL)
State U of New York at New Paltz (NY)
State U of New York at Plattsburgh (NY)
State U of New York Coll at Cortland (NY)
State U of New York Coll at Old Westbury (NY)
State U of New York Coll at Potsdam (NY)
Syracuse U (NY)
Texas Wesleyan U (TX)
Trevecca Nazarene U (TN)
Trinity Christian Coll (IL)
Union Coll (KY)
Union Coll (NE)
Universidad Adventista de las Antillas (PR)
U of California, Irvine (CA)
U of Charleston (WV)
U of Delaware (DE)
U of Dubuque (IA)
U of Evansville (IN)
The U of Findlay (OH)
U of Great Falls (MT)
U of Illinois at Chicago (IL)
U of Jamestown (ND)
U of Louisiana at Monroe (LA)
U of Maine (ME)
U of Maine at Farmington (ME)
U of Mary Hardin-Baylor (TX)
U of Maryland, Baltimore County (MD)
U of Mobile (AL)
The U of Montana Western (MT)
The U of North Carolina at Greensboro (NC)
U of Pittsburgh at Johnstown (PA)
U of Regina (SK, Canada)
The U of South Dakota (SD)
The U of Tennessee at Martin (TN)
U of Waterloo (ON, Canada)
U of Windsor (ON, Canada)
U of Wisconsin–Superior (WI)
Utah State U (UT)
Utah Valley U (UT)
Utica Coll (NY)
Valley City State U (ND)
Valparaiso U (IN)
Virginia Union U (VA)
Viterbo U (WI)
Washburn U (KS)
Washington U in St. Louis (MO)
Waynesburg U (PA)
Wayne State Coll (NE)
Weber State U (UT)
Welch Coll (TN)
Western Michigan U (MI)
Western State Colorado U (CO)
Western Washington U (WA)
Westfield State U (MA)
Widener U (PA)
William Woods U (MO)
Wingate U (NC)
Winona State U (MN)
Xavier U of Louisiana (LA)
York Coll of Pennsylvania (PA)
Youngstown State U (OH)

BIOMATHEMATICS, BIOINFORMATICS, AND COMPUTATIONAL BIOLOGY RELATED

Florida Inst of Technology (FL)
Florida State U (FL)
Harvey Mudd Coll (CA)
U of California, Los Angeles (CA)
Walsh U (OH)
Washington U in St. Louis (MO)
Worcester Polytechnic Inst (MA)

BIOMEDICAL SCIENCES

Adventist U of Health Sciences (FL)
Antioch Coll, Yellow Springs (OH)
Auburn U (AL)
Bradley U (IL)
Bridgewater State U (MA)
Brigham Young U (UT)
Central Michigan U (MI)
Central Washington U (WA)
Christian Brothers U (TN)
City Coll of the City U of New York (NY)
Coll of the Ozarks (MO)
Colorado State U (CO)
Concordia Coll–New York (NY)
Concordia U Wisconsin (WI)
Edgewood Coll (WI)
Fitchburg State U (MA)
Florida Inst of Technology (FL)
Hiram Coll (OH)
Inter American U of Puerto Rico, Metropolitan Campus (PR)
Inter American U of Puerto Rico, Ponce Campus (PR)
Keuka Coll (NY)
Lewis U (IL)
Liberty U (VA)
Lynchburg Coll (VA)
Madonna U (MI)
Marist Coll (NY)
Marymount Manhattan Coll (NY)
Maryville U of Saint Louis (MO)
McMurry U (TX)
Morehead State U (KY)
Multnomah U (OR)
North Carolina Central U (NC)
North Carolina Wesleyan Coll (NC)
Northern Arizona U (AZ)
The Ohio State U (OH)
Oklahoma City U (OK)
Our Lady of the Lake Coll (LA)
Rochester Inst of Technology (NY)
Rowan U (NJ)
Rutgers U–New Brunswick (NJ)
St. Cloud State U (MN)
St. Gregory's U, Shawnee (OK)
Saint Leo U (FL)
St. Louis Coll of Pharmacy (MO)
Saint Louis U (MO)
Sam Houston State U (TX)
Slippery Rock U of Pennsylvania (PA)
State U of New York at Fredonia (NY)
Susquehanna U (PA)
Tarleton State U (TX)
Texas A&M U (TX)
Texas A&M U–Corpus Christi (TX)
Texas A&M U–Kingsville (TX)
Trent U (ON, Canada)
Troy U (AL)
Union Coll (NE)
Université de Montréal (QC, Canada)
U at Buffalo, the State U of New York (NY)
U of California, Riverside (CA)
U of Central Florida (FL)
U of Colorado Denver (CO)
U of Georgia (GA)
U of Guelph (ON, Canada)
U of Michigan–Flint (MI)
U of Minnesota, Duluth (MN)
U of New England (ME)
U of New Hampshire (NH)
U of Northern Iowa (IA)
U of Pennsylvania (PA)
U of Saskatchewan (SK, Canada)
U of South Alabama (AL)
U of South Carolina Aiken (SC)
The U of South Dakota (SD)
U of South Florida (FL)
The U of Texas at Austin (TX)
The U of Texas Rio Grande Valley (TX)
U of Washington, Tacoma (WA)
Washington State U (WA)
Western Michigan U (MI)

BIOMEDICAL TECHNOLOGY

Andrews U (MI)
California State U, East Bay (CA)
Cleveland State U (OH)
Indiana U–Purdue U Indianapolis (IN)
Rutgers U–Camden (NJ)

BIOMETRY/BIOMETRICS

Carnegie Mellon U (PA)
Cornell U (NY)
Rutgers U–New Brunswick (NJ)
Stanford U (CA)
U of Delaware (DE)

BIOPHYSICS

Andrews U (MI)
Arizona State U at the Tempe campus (AZ)
Augsburg Coll (MN)
Brandeis U (MA)
Brigham Young U (UT)
Carnegie Mellon U (PA)
Claremont McKenna Coll (CA)
Columbia U (NY)
Columbia U, School of General Studies (NY)
Elon U (NC)
Emory U (GA)
Haverford Coll (PA)
Iowa State U of Science and Technology (IA)
Johns Hopkins U (MD)
Lipscomb U (TN)
Loyola U Chicago (IL)
Miami U (OH)
Northeastern U (MA)

Regent U (VA)
Scripps Coll (CA)
Southern Methodist U (TX)
State U of New York Coll at Geneseo (NY)
Syracuse U (NY)
Temple U (PA)
U at Buffalo, the State U of New York (NY)
U of California, Los Angeles (CA)
U of California, San Diego (CA)
U of Michigan (MI)
U of Pennsylvania (PA)
U of San Diego (CA)
The U of Scranton (PA)
U of Southern California (CA)
U of Southern Indiana (IN)
U of Toronto (ON, Canada)
Walla Walla U (WA)
Washington & Jefferson Coll (PA)
Washington U in St. Louis (MO)
Whitman Coll (WA)
Whitworth U (WA)

BIOPSYCHOLOGY
Augsburg Coll (MN)
Bucknell U (PA)
Carnegie Mellon U (PA)
Columbia U (NY)
Geneva Coll (PA)
Grand Valley State U (MI)
Immaculata U (PA)
Liberty U (VA)
Life U (GA)
Messiah Coll (PA)
Monmouth Coll (IL)
Morningside Coll (IA)
Mount Allison U (NB, Canada)
Nebraska Wesleyan U (NE)
New Coll of Florida (FL)
Ohio Dominican U (OH)
Spring Hill Coll (AL)
Tufts U (MA)
U of California, Santa Barbara (CA)
U of Guelph (ON, Canada)
U of Pittsburgh at Johnstown (PA)
Viterbo U (WI)
Wagner Coll (NY)
Washington U in St. Louis (MO)

BIOSTATISTICS
Emmanuel Coll (MA)
Saint Louis U (MO)
Simmons Coll (MA)
Tulane U (LA)
U of Georgia (GA)
The U of North Carolina at Chapel Hill (NC)

BIOTECHNOLOGY
Alma Coll (MI)
Ashland U (OH)
Assumption Coll (MA)
Auburn U (AL)
Bay Path U (MA)
California State Polytechnic U, Pomona (CA)
California State U, San Marcos (CA)
Calvin Coll (MI)
Central Baptist Coll (AR)
City Coll of the City U of New York (NY)
Colorado State U (CO)
East Stroudsburg U of Pennsylvania (PA)
Elizabethtown Coll (PA)
Endicott Coll (MA)
Ferris State U (MI)
Fitchburg State U (MA)
Florida Gulf Coast U (FL)
Florida Southern Coll (FL)
Grand View U (IA)
Hunter Coll of the City U of New York (NY)
Indiana U Bloomington (IN)
Indiana U East (IN)
Indiana U–Purdue U Indianapolis (IN)
Inter American U of Puerto Rico, Aguadilla Campus (PR)
Inter American U of Puerto Rico, Barranquitas Campus (PR)
Inter American U of Puerto Rico, Bayamón Campus (PR)
Inter American U of Puerto Rico, Guayama Campus (PR)
Inter American U of Puerto Rico, Ponce Campus (PR)
James Madison U (VA)
Kennesaw State U (GA)
Kent State U (OH)
Manhattan Coll (NY)
Marywood U (PA)
Massachusetts Coll of Liberal Arts (MA)
Missouri Baptist U (MO)
Missouri Western State U (MO)
Montana State U (MT)
New York Inst of Technology (NY)
North Dakota State U (ND)
Oregon State U (OR)
Plymouth State U (NH)
Point Park U (PA)
Rochester Inst of Technology (NY)
Rutgers U–New Brunswick (NJ)
Simpson U (CA)
South Dakota State U (SD)
Southeastern Oklahoma State U (OK)
State U of New York Coll of Agriculture and Technology at Cobleskill (NY)
State U of New York Coll of Environmental Science and Forestry (NY)
Stevenson U (MD)
Syracuse U (NY)
Tufts U (MA)
U at Buffalo, the State U of New York (NY)
U of California, Davis (CA)
U of California, San Diego (CA)
U of Central Florida (FL)
U of Georgia (GA)
U of Hawaii at Manoa (HI)
U of Houston (TX)
U of Houston–Downtown (TX)
The U of Kansas (KS)
U of Kentucky (KY)
U of Lethbridge (AB, Canada)
U of Nevada, Reno (NV)
U of New Hampshire at Manchester (NH)
The U of North Carolina at Pembroke (NC)
U of Saskatchewan (SK, Canada)
U of Waterloo (ON, Canada)
U of Windsor (ON, Canada)
Utah Valley U (UT)
Washington State U (WA)
West Texas A&M U (TX)
William Peterson U of New Jersey (NJ)
Worcester State U (MA)
York Coll of the City U of New York (NY)

BLOOD BANK TECHNOLOGY
Boston U (MA)
Rasmussen Coll St. Cloud (MN)

BOTANY/PLANT BIOLOGY
Andrews U (MI)
Auburn U (AL)
Bennington Coll (VT)
California State U, Long Beach (CA)
Coll of the Atlantic (ME)
Colorado State U (CO)
Connecticut Coll (CT)
Dalhousie U (NS, Canada)
Goddard Coll (VT)
Humboldt State U (CA)
Iowa State U of Science and Technology (IA)
Kent State U (OH)
Miami U (OH)
Michigan State U (MI)
North Carolina State U (NC)
North Dakota State U (ND)
The Ohio State U (OH)
Ohio U (OH)
Ohio Wesleyan U (OH)
Oklahoma State U (OK)
Oregon State U (OR)
Purdue U (IN)
Rutgers U–Newark (NJ)
St. Cloud State U (MN)
San Francisco State U (CA)
Sonoma State U (CA)
Southern Illinois U Carbondale (IL)
The U of Akron (OH)
U of California, Davis (CA)
U of California, Irvine (CA)
U of California, Riverside (CA)
U of Florida (FL)
U of Georgia (GA)
U of Great Falls (MT)
U of Hawaii at Manoa (HI)
U of Maine (ME)
U of Oklahoma (OK)
The U of Texas at Austin (TX)
The U of Texas at El Paso (TX)
U of Toronto (ON, Canada)
U of Vermont (VT)
U of Washington (WA)
U of Wisconsin–Madison (WI)
U of Wisconsin–Superior (WI)
Utah State U (UT)
Utah Valley U (UT)
Washington State U (WA)
Weber State U (UT)

BOTANY/PLANT BIOLOGY RELATED
Dalhousie U (NS, Canada)
Frostburg State U (MD)
U of Hawaii at Manoa (HI)
U of Minnesota, Twin Cities Campus (MN)

BRASS INSTRUMENTS
Houghton Coll (NY)
Liberty U (VA)
San Francisco Conservatory of Music (CA)
The U of Kansas (KS)
U of Southern California (CA)
Vanderbilt U (TN)
Youngstown State U (OH)

BROADCAST JOURNALISM
Auburn U (AL)
Barry U (FL)
Belmont U (TN)
Bemidji State U (MN)
Biola U (CA)
Bluffton U (OH)
Bowie State U (MD)
Bowling Green State U (OH)
Brigham Young U (UT)
Brooklyn Coll of the City U of New York (NY)
Buffalo State Coll, State U of New York (NY)
California State U, East Bay (CA)
California State U, Long Beach (CA)
Cameron U (OK)
Central State U (OH)
Central Washington U (WA)
Chapman U (CA)
The Coll at Brockport, State U of New York (NY)
Concordia U Chicago (IL)
Drake U (IA)
Elon U (NC)
Emerson Coll (MA)
Evangel U (MO)
Gettysburg Coll (PA)
Gonzaga U (WA)
Goshen Coll (IN)
Grand View U (IA)
Hampton U (VA)
Hannibal-LaGrange U (MO)
Harding U (AR)
Humboldt State U (CA)
Huntington U (IN)
Ithaca Coll (NY)
Kuyper Coll (MI)
Langston U (OK)
Lincoln U (PA)
Louisiana Coll (LA)
Manchester U (IN)
Marywood U (PA)
Massachusetts Coll of Liberal Arts (MA)
Minnesota State U Moorhead (MN)
Morrisville State Coll (NY)
Mount Vernon Nazarene U (OH)
Northern Kentucky U (KY)
North Greenville U (SC)
Ohio U (OH)
Ohio Wesleyan U (OH)
Oklahoma Christian U (OK)
Oklahoma City U (OK)
Point Loma Nazarene U (CA)
Point Park U (PA)
Quinnipiac U (CT)
Rust Coll (MS)
St. Cloud State U (MN)
State U of New York at Oswego (NY)
Suffolk U (MA)
Syracuse U (NY)
Trevecca Nazarene U (TN)
Union U (TN)
U of Georgia (GA)
U of La Verne (CA)
U of Miami (FL)
U of North Texas (TX)
U of Oklahoma (OK)
The U of Scranton (PA)
U of South Carolina (SC)
U of Southern California (CA)
The U of Texas at El Paso (TX)
U of Wisconsin–Superior (WI)
Wartburg Coll (IA)
Western Kentucky U (KY)
West Texas A&M U (TX)

BUILDING/CONSTRUCTION FINISHING, MANAGEMENT, AND INSPECTION RELATED
California State U, Long Beach (CA)
Minnesota State U Mankato (MN)
Pratt Inst (NY)
Weber State U (UT)

BUILDING/CONSTRUCTION SITE MANAGEMENT
Pennsylvania Coll of Technology (PA)
Southern Utah U (UT)
The U of Texas at San Antonio (TX)

BUILDING CONSTRUCTION TECHNOLOGY
U of Massachusetts Amherst (MA)

BUSINESS ADMINISTRATION AND MANAGEMENT
Abilene Christian U (TX)
Academy Coll (MN)
Adams State U (CO)
Adelphi U (NY)
Agnes Scott Coll (GA)
Alabama State U (AL)
Alaska Pacific U (AK)
Albany State U (GA)
Albertus Magnus Coll (CT)
Albion Coll (MI)
Albright Coll (PA)
Alcorn State U (MS)
Alderson Broaddus U (WV)
Alfred U (NY)
Alice Lloyd Coll (KY)
Alliant Intl U–San Diego (CA)
Alma Coll (MI)
Alvernia U (PA)
Alverno Coll (WI)
Ambrose U (AB, Canada)
American Intl Coll (MA)
American Public U System (WV)
American U (DC)
American U in Bulgaria (Bulgaria)
The American U in Cairo (Egypt)
The American U in Dubai (United Arab Emirates)
American U of Beirut (Lebanon)
The American U of Paris (France)
The American U of Rome (Italy)
Amridge U (AL)
Anderson U (IN)
Anderson U (SC)
Angelo State U (TX)
Antioch U Los Angeles (CA)
Antioch U Midwest (OH)
Appalachian State U (NC)
Aquinas Coll (MI)
Aquinas Coll (TN)
Arcadia U (PA)
Arizona Christian U (AZ)
Arizona State U at the Polytechnic campus (AZ)
Arizona State U at the Tempe campus (AZ)
Arizona State U at the West campus (AZ)
Arkansas Tech U (AR)
Ashland U (OH)
Assumption Coll (MA)
Athens State U (AL)
Auburn U (AL)
Auburn U at Montgomery (AL)
Augsburg Coll (MN)
Augustana Coll (IL)
Augustana U (SD)
Augusta U (GA)
Aurora U (IL)
Austin Coll (TX)
Averett U (VA)
Avila U (MO)
Azusa Pacific U (CA)
Bainbridge State Coll (GA)
Baldwin Wallace U (OH)
The Baptist Coll of Florida (FL)
Baptist U of the Americas (TX)
Barclay Coll (KS)
Barry U (FL)
Barton Coll (NC)
Baruch Coll of the City U of New York (NY)
Bayamón Central U (PR)
Baylor U (TX)
Bay Path U (MA)
Beacon Coll (FL)
Becker Coll (MA)
Belhaven U (MS)
Belmont Abbey Coll (NC)
Bemidji State U (MN)
Benedictine Coll (KS)
Bennett Coll (NC)
Bentley U (MA)
Berea Coll (KY)
Berkeley Coll–New York City Campus (NY)
Berkeley Coll–White Plains Campus (NY)
Berkeley Coll–Woodland Park Campus (NJ)
Berry Coll (GA)
Bethany Lutheran Coll (MN)
Bethel Coll (IN)
Bethel U (MN)
Bethune-Cookman U (FL)
Binghamton U, State U of New York (NY)
Biola U (CA)
Bishop's U (QC, Canada)
Black Hills State U (SD)
Bloomfield Coll (NJ)
Bloomsburg U of Pennsylvania (PA)
Bluefield Coll (VA)
Bluefield State Coll (WV)
Blue Mountain Coll (MS)
Bluffton U (OH)
Boise State U (ID)
Boston Coll (MA)
Boston U (MA)
Bowie State U (MD)
Bowling Green State U (OH)
Bowling Green State U–Firelands Coll (OH)
Bradley U (IL)
Brandman U (CA)
Brewton-Parker Coll (GA)
Briar Cliff U (IA)
Bridgewater Coll (VA)
Bridgewater State U (MA)
Brigham Young U–Idaho (ID)
Bryan Coll (TN)
Bryant U (RI)
Bucknell U (PA)
Buena Vista U (IA)
Buffalo State Coll, State U of New York (NY)
Cabrini U (PA)
Cairn U (PA)
Caldwell U (NJ)
California Lutheran U (CA)
California Polytechnic State U, San Luis Obispo (CA)
California State Polytechnic U, Pomona (CA)
California State U, Bakersfield (CA)
California State U, Dominguez Hills (CA)
California State U, East Bay (CA)
California State U, Fresno (CA)
California State U, Fullerton (CA)
California State U, Long Beach (CA)
California State U Maritime Acad (CA)
California State U, Monterey Bay (CA)
California State U, Northridge (CA)
California State U, Sacramento (CA)
California State U, San Bernardino (CA)
California State U, San Marcos (CA)
California State U, Stanislaus (CA)
California U of Pennsylvania (PA)

Calumet Coll of Saint Joseph (IN)
Calvary U (MO)
Calvin Coll (MI)
Cameron U (OK)
Campbellsville U (KY)
Canisius Coll (NY)
Capital U (OH)
Cardinal Stritch U (WI)
Caribbean U (PR)
Carlow U (PA)
Carroll Coll (MT)
Carson-Newman U (TN)
Carthage Coll (WI)
Case Western Reserve U (OH)
Catawba Coll (NC)
The Catholic U of America (DC)
Cazenovia Coll (NY)
Cedar Crest Coll (PA)
Cedarville U (OH)
Centenary Coll of Louisiana (LA)
Centenary U (NJ)
Central Baptist Coll (AR)
Central Connecticut State U (CT)
Central Methodist U (MO)
Central Michigan U (MI)
Central Penn Coll (PA)
Central Washington U (WA)
Chaminade U of Honolulu (HI)
Champlain Coll (VT)
Chapman U (CA)
Charleston Southern U (SC)
Charter Oak State Coll (CT)
Chatham U (PA)
Chestnut Hill Coll (PA)
Chowan U (NC)
Christian Brothers U (TN)
Christopher Newport U (VA)
The Citadel, The Military Coll of South Carolina (SC)
City Coll of the City U of New York (NY)
City Vision U (MO)
Clarion U of Pennsylvania (PA)
Clark Atlanta U (GA)
Clarke U (IA)
Clarkson U (NY)
Clark U (MA)
Clayton State U (GA)
Clemson U (SC)
Cleveland State U (OH)
Coastal Carolina U (SC)
Coe Coll (IA)
Colby-Sawyer Coll (NH)
CollAmerica–Fort Collins (CO)
The Coll at Brockport, State U of New York (NY)
Coll of Business and Technology–Main Campus (FL)
Coll of Business and Technology–Miami Gardens (FL)
Coll of Charleston (SC)
Coll of Coastal Georgia (GA)
The Coll of Idaho (ID)
The Coll of New Jersey (NJ)
Coll of Saint Benedict (MN)
Coll of Saint Elizabeth (NJ)
Coll of Saint Mary (NE)
The Coll of Saint Rose (NY)
The Coll of St. Scholastica (MN)
Coll of the Ozarks (MO)
The Coll of Westchester (NY)
The Coll of William and Mary (VA)
Colorado Christian U (CO)
Colorado State U (CO)
Columbia Coll (MO)
Columbia Southern U (AL)
Columbus State U (GA)
Concordia Coll (MN)
Concordia Coll–New York (NY)
Concordia U (QC, Canada)
Concordia U Chicago (IL)
Concordia U Irvine (CA)
Concordia U, St. Paul (MN)
Concordia U Wisconsin (WI)
Concord U (WV)
Converse Coll (SC)
Corban U (OR)
Cornerstone U (MI)
Crandall U (NB, Canada)
Creighton U (NE)
Culver-Stockton Coll (MO)
Curry Coll (MA)
Daemen Coll (NY)
Dakota State U (SD)
Dalhousie U (NS, Canada)
Dallas Baptist U (TX)
Dallas Christian Coll (TX)
Dalton State Coll (GA)
Davenport U, Grand Rapids (MI)
Daytona State Coll (FL)
Dean Coll (MA)
Defiance Coll (OH)
Delaware Valley U (PA)
DEREE - The American Coll of Greece (Greece)
Dickinson State U (ND)
Dixie State U (UT)
Doane U (NE)
Dominican Coll (NY)
Dominican U (IL)
Dominican U of California (CA)
Drake U (IA)
Drew U (NJ)
Drury U (MO)
Dunwoody Coll of Technology (MN)
East Carolina U (NC)
East Central U (OK)
Eastern Illinois U (IL)
Eastern Mennonite U (VA)
Eastern Michigan U (MI)
Eastern Nazarene Coll (MA)
Eastern U (PA)
Eastern Washington U (WA)
East Stroudsburg U of Pennsylvania (PA)
East Tennessee State U (TN)
East Texas Baptist U (TX)
Ecclesia Coll (AR)
Eckerd Coll (FL)
Edgewood Coll (WI)
EDP U of Puerto Rico (PR)
EDP U of Puerto Rico–San Sebastian (PR)
Elizabeth City State U (NC)
Elizabethtown Coll (PA)
Elmira Coll (NY)
Elms Coll (MA)
Elon U (NC)
Embry-Riddle Aeronautical U–Worldwide (FL)
Emmanuel Coll (MA)
Emmaus Bible Coll (IA)
Emory & Henry Coll (VA)
Emory U (GA)
Emporia State U (KS)
Endicott Coll (MA)
Eureka Coll (IL)
Evangel U (MO)
Excelsior Coll (NY)
Fairfield U (CT)
Fairleigh Dickinson U, Coll at Florham (NJ)
Fairleigh Dickinson U, Metropolitan Campus (NJ)
Farmingdale State Coll (NY)
Faulkner U (AL)
Fayetteville State U (NC)
Felician U (NJ)
Fisher Coll (MA)
Fitchburg State U (MA)
Flagler Coll (FL)
Florida Ag and Mech U (FL)
Florida Atlantic U (FL)
Florida Coll (FL)
Florida Inst of Technology (FL)
Florida Intl U (FL)
Florida National U (FL)
Florida Southern Coll (FL)
Florida State U (FL)
Fordham U (NY)
Fort Lewis Coll (CO)
Franciscan U of Steubenville (OH)
Francis Marion U (SC)
Franklin & Marshall Coll (PA)
Franklin Pierce U (NH)
Freed-Hardeman U (TN)
Friends U (KS)
Frostburg State U (MD)
Furman U (SC)
Gallaudet U (DC)
Gannon U (PA)
Gardner-Webb U (NC)
Geneva Coll (PA)
George Fox U (OR)
Georgetown Coll (KY)
Georgetown U (DC)
The George Washington U (DC)
Georgia Coll & State U (GA)
Georgia Inst of Technology (GA)
Georgia Military Coll (GA)
Georgian Court U (NJ)
Georgia Southern U (GA)
Georgia Southwestern State U (GA)
Georgia State U (GA)
Gettysburg Coll (PA)
Gonzaga U (WA)
Gordon Coll (MA)
Gordon State Coll (GA)
Goshen Coll (IN)
Goucher Coll (MD)
Governors State U (IL)
Grace Coll (IN)
Graceland U (IA)
Grambling State U (LA)
Grand View U (IA)
Granite State Coll (NH)
Great Basin Coll (NV)
Green Mountain Coll (VT)
Greenville Coll (IL)
Grove City Coll (PA)
Guilford Coll (NC)
Gwynedd Mercy U (PA)
Hallmark U (TX)
Hamline U (MN)
Hampton U (VA)
Hannibal-LaGrange U (MO)
Harding U (AR)
Hardin-Simmons U (TX)
Harris-Stowe State U (MO)
Hartwick Coll (NY)
Hawai`i Pacific U (HI)
HEC Montreal (QC, Canada)
Heidelberg U (OH)
High Point U (NC)
Hilbert Coll (NY)
Hiram Coll (OH)
Hofstra U (NY)
Holy Cross Coll (IN)
Holy Family U (PA)
Holy Names U (CA)
Hood Coll (MD)
Hope Coll (MI)
Hope Intl U (CA)
Houghton Coll (NY)
Houston Baptist U (TX)
Howard Payne U (TX)
Hult Intl Business School (United Kingdom)
Humboldt State U (CA)
Huntingdon Coll (AL)
Huntington U (IN)
Husson U (ME)
Huston-Tillotson U (TX)
Idaho State U (ID)
Illinois Coll (IL)
Illinois State U (IL)
Illinois Wesleyan U (IL)
Immaculata U (PA)
Indiana State U (IN)
Indiana U of Pennsylvania (PA)
Inter American U of Puerto Rico, Barranquitas Campus (PR)
Inter American U of Puerto Rico, Fajardo Campus (PR)
Inter American U of Puerto Rico, Guayama Campus (PR)
Inter American U of Puerto Rico, Ponce Campus (PR)
Inter American U of Puerto Rico, San Germán Campus (PR)
Iona Coll (NY)
Iowa State U of Science and Technology (IA)
Iowa Wesleyan U (IA)
Ithaca Coll (NY)
Jackson State U (MS)
Jacksonville State U (AL)
Jacksonville U (FL)
James Madison U (VA)
John Brown U (AR)
John Carroll U (OH)
Johnson C. Smith U (NC)
Johnson U (TN)
Johnson U Florida (FL)
John Wesley U (NC)
Judson U (IL)
Kansas State U (KS)
Kansas Wesleyan U (KS)
Kean U (NJ)
Keene State Coll (NH)
Kennesaw State U (GA)
Kent State U (OH)
Kent State U at Ashtabula (OH)
Kent State U at Geauga (OH)
Kent State U at Salem (OH)
Kent State U at Stark (OH)
Kent State U at Trumbull (OH)
Kent State U at Tuscarawas (OH)
Kentucky State U (KY)
Kentucky Wesleyan Coll (KY)
Kettering U (MI)
Keuka Coll (NY)
The King's Coll (NY)
King's Coll (PA)
The King's U (AB, Canada)
King U (TN)
Kutztown U of Pennsylvania (PA)
Kuyper Coll (MI)
LaGrange Coll (GA)
Lake Erie Coll (OH)
Lane Coll (TN)
Langston U (OK)
La Salle U (PA)
Lasell Coll (MA)
Lawrence Technological U (MI)
Lebanese American U (Lebanon)
Lebanon Valley Coll (PA)
Lees-McRae Coll (NC)
Lee U (TN)
Lehman Coll of the City U of New York (NY)
Lenoir-Rhyne U (NC)
Lesley U (MA)
LeTourneau U (TX)
Lewis U (IL)
Liberty U (VA)
Limestone Coll (SC)
Lincoln Coll (IL)
Lincoln Coll–Normal (IL)
Lincoln U (CA)
Lincoln U (MO)
Lincoln U (PA)
Lindenwood U (MO)
Lindsey Wilson Coll (KY)
Linfield Coll (OR)
Lipscomb U (TN)
Lock Haven U of Pennsylvania (PA)
Longwood U (VA)
Loras Coll (IA)
Louisiana Coll (LA)
Louisiana State U and A&M Coll (LA)
Louisiana State U at Alexandria (LA)
Louisiana Tech U (LA)
Lourdes U (OH)
Loyola U Chicago (IL)
Loyola U New Orleans (LA)
Lubbock Christian U (TX)
Luther Coll (IA)
Lycoming Coll (PA)
Lynchburg Coll (VA)
Lynn U (FL)
Lyon Coll (AR)
MacMurray Coll (IL)
Madonna U (MI)
Maharishi U of Management (IA)
Malone U (OH)
Manchester U (IN)
Manhattanville Coll (NY)
Mansfield U of Pennsylvania (PA)
Maranatha Baptist U (WI)
Marian U (IN)
Marian U (WI)
Marietta Coll (OH)
Marist Coll (NY)
Marshall U (WV)
Mary Baldwin U (VA)
Marylhurst U (OR)
Marymount California U (CA)
Marymount Manhattan Coll (NY)
Marymount U (VA)
Maryville U of Saint Louis (MO)
Marywood U (PA)
Massachusetts Coll of Liberal Arts (MA)
The Master's U (CA)
McDaniel Coll (MD)
McKendree U (IL)
McMaster U (ON, Canada)
McMurry U (TX)
McNeese State U (LA)
Mercy Coll (NY)
Mercyhurst U (PA)
Meredith Coll (NC)
Merrimack Coll (MA)
Messenger Coll (TX)
Messiah Coll (PA)
Metropolitan State U of Denver (CO)
Miami U (OH)
Michigan State U (MI)
Michigan Technological U (MI)
MidAmerica Nazarene U (KS)
Mid-Atlantic Christian U (NC)
Midland Coll (TX)
Millersville U of Pennsylvania (PA)
Milligan Coll (TN)
Millikin U (IL)
Millsaps Coll (MS)
Milwaukee School of Eng (WI)
Minnesota State U Mankato (MN)
Minnesota State U Moorhead (MN)
Minot State U (ND)
Misericordia U (PA)
Mississippi State U (MS)
Mississippi Valley State U (MS)
Missouri Baptist U (MO)
Missouri State U (MO)
Missouri U of Science and Technology (MO)
Missouri Valley Coll (MO)
Missouri Western State U (MO)
Molloy Coll (NY)
Monmouth Coll (IL)
Monmouth U (NJ)
Montana State U Billings (MT)
Montana State U–Northern (MT)
Montclair State U (NJ)
Moravian Coll (PA)
Morehead State U (KY)
Morehouse Coll (GA)
Morningside Coll (IA)
Morris Coll (SC)
Morrisville State Coll (NY)
Mount Allison U (NB, Canada)
Mount Aloysius Coll (PA)
Mount Ida Coll (MA)
Mount Marty Coll (SD)
Mount Mary U (WI)
Mount Mercy U (IA)
Mount St. Joseph U (OH)
Mount Saint Mary Coll (NY)
Mount Saint Mary's U (CA)
Mount Vernon Nazarene U (OH)
Muhlenberg Coll (PA)
Murray State U (KY)
Muskingum U (OH)
National Louis U (IL)
National Paralegal Coll (AZ)
National U (CA)
Nazareth Coll of Rochester (NY)
Nebraska Wesleyan U (NE)
Neumann U (PA)
Nevada State Coll (NV)
Newberry Coll (SC)
New England Coll (NH)
New England Inst of Technology (RI)
New Jersey City U (NJ)
Newman U (KS)
New Mexico Highlands U (NM)
New Mexico Inst of Mining and Technology (NM)
New Mexico State U (NM)
New York Inst of Technology (NY)
Niagara U (NY)
Nichols Coll (MA)
North American U (TX)
North Carolina Central U (NC)
North Carolina State U (NC)
North Carolina Wesleyan Coll (NC)
North Central Coll (IL)
Northcentral U (CA)
North Dakota State U (ND)
Northeastern Illinois U (IL)
Northeastern State U (OK)
Northeastern U (MA)
Northern Arizona U (AZ)
Northern Illinois U (IL)
Northern Kentucky U (KY)
North Greenville U (SC)
Northland Coll (WI)
Northwest Christian U (OR)
Northwestern Coll (IA)
Northwestern Oklahoma State U (OK)
Northwestern State U of Louisiana (LA)
Northwest Missouri State U (MO)
Northwest U (WA)
Northwood U, Michigan Campus (MI)
Nova Southeastern U (FL)
Nyack Coll (NY)
Oakland City U (IN)
Ohio Christian U (OH)
Ohio Dominican U (OH)
The Ohio State U (OH)
The Ohio State U at Lima (OH)
The Ohio State U at Marion (OH)
The Ohio State U–Mansfield Campus (OH)

The Ohio State U–Newark Campus (OH)
Ohio U (OH)
Ohio U–Eastern (OH)
Ohio Valley U (WV)
Ohio Wesleyan U (OH)
Oklahoma Christian U (OK)
Oklahoma City U (OK)
Oklahoma State U (OK)
Old Dominion U (VA)
Olivet Nazarene U (IL)
Oral Roberts U (OK)
Oregon State U (OR)
Otterbein U (OH)
Ouachita Baptist U (AR)
Our Lady of the Lake U of San Antonio (TX)
Pace U (NY)
Pacific Lutheran U (WA)
Pacific States U (CA)
Paine Coll (GA)
Palm Beach Atlantic U (FL)
Peirce Coll (PA)
Penn State Beaver (PA)
Penn State Brandywine (PA)
Penn State DuBois (PA)
Penn State Erie, The Behrend Coll (PA)
Penn State Fayette, The Eberly Campus (PA)
Penn State Greater Allegheny (PA)
Penn State Harrisburg (PA)
Penn State Hazleton (PA)
Penn State Mont Alto (PA)
Penn State New Kensington (PA)
Penn State Shenango (PA)
Penn State Wilkes-Barre (PA)
Penn State Worthington Scranton (PA)
Penn State York (PA)
Pennsylvania Coll of Technology (PA)
Pepperdine U, Malibu (CA)
Philander Smith Coll (AR)
Piedmont Coll (GA)
Pine Manor Coll (MA)
Pittsburgh Tech Coll (PA)
Plymouth State U (NH)
Point Loma Nazarene U (CA)
Point Park U (PA)
Point U (GA)
Polk State Coll (FL)
Polytechnic U of Puerto Rico (PR)
Portland State U (OR)
Prairie View A&M U (TX)
Principia Coll (IL)
Providence Coll (RI)
Purdue U (IN)
Purdue U Northwest (IN)
Quinnipiac U (CT)
Radford U (VA)
Ramapo Coll of New Jersey (NJ)
Rasmussen Coll Bloomington (MN)
Rasmussen Coll Brooklyn Park (MN)
Rasmussen Coll Eagan (MN)
Rasmussen Coll Fargo (ND)
Rasmussen Coll Fort Myers (FL)
Rasmussen Coll Kansas City/ Overland Park (KS)
Rasmussen Coll Lake Elmo/ Woodbury (MN)
Rasmussen Coll Land O' Lakes (FL)
Rasmussen Coll Mankato (MN)
Rasmussen Coll Moorhead (MN)
Rasmussen Coll New Port Richey (FL)
Rasmussen Coll Ocala (FL)
Rasmussen Coll Rockford (IL)
Rasmussen Coll St. Cloud (MN)
Rasmussen Coll Tampa/Brandon (FL)
Rasmussen Coll Topeka (KS)
Redeemer U Coll (ON, Canada)
Regent U (VA)
Regis U (CO)
Rensselaer Polytechnic Inst (NY)
Rhode Island Coll (RI)
Rhodes Coll (TN)
Rice U (TX)
Ripon Coll (WI)
Roanoke Coll (VA)
Robert Morris U (PA)
Robert Morris U Illinois (IL)
Roberts Wesleyan Coll (NY)
Rochester Inst of Technology (NY)
Rockford U (IL)
Rockhurst U (MO)
Rocky Mountain Coll (MT)
Rogers State U (OK)
Roger Williams U (RI)
Rollins Coll (FL)
Rosemont Coll (PA)
Rowan U (NJ)
Royal Military Coll of Canada (ON, Canada)
Rust Coll (MS)
Rutgers U–Camden (NJ)
Rutgers U–Newark (NJ)
Rutgers U–New Brunswick (NJ)
Sacred Heart U (CT)
The Sage Colls (NY)
Saginaw Valley State U (MI)
St. Andrews U (NC)
Saint Augustine's U (NC)
St. Bonaventure U (NY)
St. Catherine U (MN)
St. Cloud State U (MN)
St. Edward's U (TX)
Saint Francis U (PA)
St. Gregory's U, Shawnee (OK)
St. John Fisher Coll (NY)
Saint John's U (MN)
St. John's U (NY)
St. Joseph's Coll, Long Island Campus (NY)
St. Joseph's Coll, New York (NY)
Saint Joseph's U (PA)
Saint Leo U (FL)
Saint Louis U (MO)
Saint Louis U–Madrid Campus (Spain)
Saint Martin's U (WA)
Saint Mary-of-the-Woods Coll (IN)
Saint Mary's Coll (IN)
Saint Mary's Coll of California (CA)
Saint Michael's Coll (VT)
St. Norbert Coll (WI)
St. Petersburg Coll (FL)
Saint Peter's U (NJ)
St. Thomas Aquinas Coll (NY)
St. Thomas U (FL)
Saint Vincent Coll (PA)
Salisbury U (MD)
Salve Regina U (RI)
Samford U (AL)
Sam Houston State U (TX)
San Diego State U (CA)
San Francisco State U (CA)
Schreiner U (TX)
Seattle Pacific U (WA)
Seattle U (WA)
Seminole State Coll of Florida (FL)
Seton Hill U (PA)
Shawnee State U (OH)
Shaw U (NC)
Shenandoah U (VA)
Shepherd U (WV)
Shippensburg U of Pennsylvania (PA)
Shorter U (GA)
Sierra Nevada Coll (NV)
Silver Lake Coll of the Holy Family (WI)
Simmons Coll (MA)
Simon Fraser U (BC, Canada)
Simpson Coll (IA)
Simpson U (CA)
Slippery Rock U of Pennsylvania (PA)
Sonoma State U (CA)
South Carolina State U (SC)
Southeastern Louisiana U (LA)
Southeastern Oklahoma State U (OK)
Southeastern U (FL)
Southeast Missouri State U (MO)
Southern Arkansas U–Magnolia (AR)
Southern Connecticut State U (CT)
Southern Illinois U Carbondale (IL)
Southern Illinois U Edwardsville (IL)
Southern Methodist U (TX)
Southern New Hampshire U (NH)
Southern Oregon U (OR)
Southern Utah U (UT)
Southwest Baptist U (MO)
Southwestern Assemblies of God U (TX)
Southwestern Coll (KS)
Spring Hill Coll (AL)
State U of New York at Fredonia (NY)
State U of New York at New Paltz (NY)
State U of New York at Oswego (NY)
State U of New York at Plattsburgh (NY)
State U of New York Coll at Geneseo (NY)
State U of New York Coll at Old Westbury (NY)
State U of New York Coll at Potsdam (NY)
State U of New York Coll of Technology at Alfred (NY)
State U of New York Coll of Technology at Canton (NY)
State U of New York Polytechnic Inst (NY)
Stephen F. Austin State U (TX)
Sterling Coll (KS)
Stevens Inst of Technology (NJ)
Stevenson U (MD)
Stockton U (NJ)
Stonehill Coll (MA)
Stony Brook U, State U of New York (NY)
Stratford U, Alexandria (VA)
Stratford U, Falls Church (VA)
Stratford U, Glen Allen (VA)
Stratford U, Newport News (VA)
Stratford U, Virginia Beach (VA)
Stratford U, Woodbridge (VA)
Suffolk U (MA)
Sullivan U (KY)
Susquehanna U (PA)
Syracuse U (NY)
Tarleton State U (TX)
Taylor U (IN)
Tennessee State U (TN)
Tennessee Wesleyan U (TN)
Texas A&M Intl U (TX)
Texas A&M U (TX)
Texas A&M U–Central Texas (TX)
Texas A&M U–Commerce (TX)
Texas A&M U–Corpus Christi (TX)
Texas A&M U–Kingsville (TX)
Texas Coll (TX)
Texas Lutheran U (TX)
Texas State U (TX)
Texas Tech U (TX)
Texas Wesleyan U (TX)
Texas Woman's U (TX)
Thomas Edison State U (NJ)
Thomas More Coll (KY)
Thomas U (GA)
Tiffin U (OH)
Toccoa Falls Coll (GA)
Towson U (MD)
Trent U (ON, Canada)
Trevecca Nazarene U (TN)
Trine U (IN)
Trinity U (TX)
Troy U (AL)
Truett McConnell U (GA)
Truman State U (MO)
Tulane U (LA)
Tusculum Coll (TN)
Union Coll (KY)
Union Coll (NE)
Union Inst & U (OH)
Union U (TN)
United States Air Force Acad (CO)
United States Intl U–Africa (Kenya)
United States Military Acad (NY)
Universidad Adventista de las Antillas (PR)
Université de Sherbrooke (QC, Canada)
U at Albany, State U of New York (NY)
U at Buffalo, the State U of New York (NY)
The U of Akron (OH)
The U of Alabama (AL)
The U of Alabama at Birmingham (AL)
The U of Alabama in Huntsville (AL)
U of Alaska Fairbanks (AK)
U of Arkansas (AR)
U of California, Irvine (CA)
U of California, Riverside (CA)
U of Central Arkansas (AR)
U of Central Florida (FL)
U of Central Missouri (MO)
U of Charleston (WV)
U of Colorado Boulder (CO)
U of Colorado Colorado Springs (CO)
U of Colorado Denver (CO)
U of Denver (CO)
U of Detroit Mercy (MI)
U of Dubuque (IA)
U of Evansville (IN)
The U of Findlay (OH)
U of Florida (FL)
U of Georgia (GA)
U of Great Falls (MT)
U of Hartford (CT)
U of Hawaii at Manoa (HI)
U of Houston (TX)
U of Houston–Clear Lake (TX)
U of Houston–Downtown (TX)
U of Idaho (ID)
U of Illinois at Chicago (IL)
U of Illinois at Springfield (IL)
U of Jamestown (ND)
The U of Kansas (KS)
U of La Verne (CA)
U of Lethbridge (AB, Canada)
U of Louisiana at Monroe (LA)
U of Maine (ME)
U of Maine at Fort Kent (ME)
U of Management and Technology (VA)
U of Mary Hardin-Baylor (TX)
U of Maryland U Coll (MD)
U of Mary Washington (VA)
U of Massachusetts Amherst (MA)
U of Massachusetts Boston (MA)
U of Massachusetts Lowell (MA)
U of Miami (FL)
U of Michigan (MI)
U of Michigan–Dearborn (MI)
U of Michigan–Flint (MI)
U of Minnesota, Crookston (MN)
U of Minnesota, Duluth (MN)
U of Minnesota, Morris (MN)
U of Missouri–Kansas City (MO)
U of Missouri–St. Louis (MO)
U of Mobile (AL)
The U of Montana Western (MT)
U of Montevallo (AL)
U of Mount Union (OH)
U of Nebraska at Kearney (NE)
U of Nevada, Las Vegas (NV)
U of Nevada, Reno (NV)
U of New England (ME)
U of New Hampshire (NH)
U of New Hampshire at Manchester (NH)
U of New Haven (CT)
U of New Orleans (LA)
U of North Alabama (AL)
U of North Carolina at Asheville (NC)
The U of North Carolina at Chapel Hill (NC)
The U of North Carolina at Charlotte (NC)
The U of North Carolina at Greensboro (NC)
The U of North Carolina at Pembroke (NC)
The U of North Carolina Wilmington (NC)
U of North Dakota (ND)
U of Northern Colorado (CO)
U of Northern Iowa (IA)
U of North Florida (FL)
U of North Georgia (GA)
U of Northwestern Ohio (OH)
U of Oklahoma (OK)
U of Pennsylvania (PA)
U of Pikeville (KY)
U of Pittsburgh at Bradford (PA)
U of Pittsburgh at Greensburg (PA)
U of Pittsburgh at Johnstown (PA)
U of Puget Sound (WA)
U of Regina (SK, Canada)
U of Rhode Island (RI)
U of Richmond (VA)
U of St. Francis (IL)
U of Saint Francis (IN)
U of Saint Joseph (CT)
U of Saint Mary (KS)
U of St. Thomas (MN)
U of St. Thomas (TX)
U of San Diego (CA)
U of San Francisco (CA)
U of Saskatchewan (SK, Canada)
The U of Scranton (PA)
U of South Alabama (AL)
U of South Carolina (SC)
U of South Carolina Aiken (SC)
The U of South Dakota (SD)
U of Southern California (CA)
U of Southern Indiana (IN)
U of Southern Maine (ME)
U of Southern Mississippi (MS)
U of South Florida (FL)
U of South Florida, St. Petersburg (FL)
U of South Florida Sarasota-Manatee (FL)
The U of Tampa (FL)
The U of Tennessee (TN)
The U of Tennessee at Chattanooga (TN)
The U of Tennessee at Martin (TN)
The U of Texas at Austin (TX)
The U of Texas at El Paso (TX)
The U of Texas at San Antonio (TX)
The U of Texas of the Permian Basin (TX)
The U of Texas Rio Grande Valley (TX)
U of the Cumberlands (KY)
U of the Fraser Valley (BC, Canada)
U of the Incarnate Word (TX)
U of the Pacific (CA)
U of the Potomac (DC)
U of the Southwest (NM)
U of the Virgin Islands (VI)
U of the West (CA)
The U of Toledo (OH)
U of Toronto (ON, Canada)
The U of Tulsa (OK)
U of Utah (UT)
U of Valley Forge (PA)
U of Vermont (VT)
The U of Virginia's Coll at Wise (VA)
U of Washington (WA)
U of Washington, Bothell (WA)
U of Washington, Tacoma (WA)
U of Waterloo (ON, Canada)
The U of West Alabama (AL)
U of West Georgia (GA)
U of Windsor (ON, Canada)
U of Wisconsin–Eau Claire (WI)
U of Wisconsin–Green Bay (WI)
U of Wisconsin–La Crosse (WI)
U of Wisconsin–Madison (WI)
U of Wisconsin–Parkside (WI)
U of Wisconsin–Stevens Point (WI)
U of Wisconsin–Stout (WI)
U of Wisconsin–Superior (WI)
U of Wisconsin–Whitewater (WI)
Upper Iowa U (IA)
Ursinus Coll (PA)
Utah State U (UT)
Utah Valley U (UT)
Utica Coll (NY)
Valdosta State U (GA)
Valley City State U (ND)
Vermont Tech Coll (VT)
Villa Maria Coll (NY)
Villanova U (PA)
Virginia Polytechnic Inst and State U (VA)
Virginia State U (VA)
Virginia Wesleyan Coll (VA)
Viterbo U (WI)
Wagner Coll (NY)
Waldorf U (IA)
Walla Walla U (WA)
Walsh Coll of Accountancy and Business Administration (MI)
Walsh U (OH)
Wartburg Coll (IA)
Washburn U (KS)
Washington and Lee U (VA)
Washington Coll (MD)
Washington State U (WA)
Washington State U–Global Campus (WA)
Washington State U–Spokane (WA)
Washington State U–Tri-Cities (WA)
Washington State U–Vancouver (WA)
Washington U in St. Louis (MO)
Wayland Baptist U (TX)
Waynesburg U (PA)
Wayne State Coll (NE)
Webber Intl U (FL)

Weber State U (UT)
Webster U (MO)
Welch Coll (TN)
Wells Coll (NY)
Wesleyan Coll (GA)
West Chester U of Pennsylvania (PA)
Western Carolina U (NC)
Western Connecticut State U (CT)
Western Illinois U (IL)
Western Intl U (AZ)
Western Kentucky U (KY)
Western Michigan U (MI)
Western New England U (MA)
Western State Colorado U (CO)
Western Washington U (WA)
Westfield State U (MA)
Westminster Coll (PA)
West Texas A&M U (TX)
West Virginia State U (WV)
West Virginia U (WV)
West Virginia U Inst of Technology (WV)
West Virginia Wesleyan Coll (WV)
Wheeling Jesuit U (WV)
Whittier Coll (CA)
Whitworth U (WA)
Wichita State U (KS)
Widener U (PA)
Wilkes U (PA)
William Jewell Coll (MO)
William Paterson U of New Jersey (NJ)
William Peace U (NC)
Williams Baptist Coll (AR)
William Woods U (MO)
Wilmington U (DE)
Wilson Coll (PA)
Wingate U (NC)
Winona State U (MN)
Winthrop U (SC)
Wittenberg U (OH)
Woodbury U (CA)
Worcester Polytechnic Inst (MA)
Worcester State U (MA)
Wright State U (OH)
Xavier U of Louisiana (LA)
York Coll of Pennsylvania (PA)
York Coll of the City U of New York (NY)
Youngstown State U (OH)

BUSINESS ADMINISTRATION, MANAGEMENT AND OPERATIONS RELATED

Adams State U (CO)
Albany State U (GA)
Alverno Coll (WI)
Augsburg Coll (MN)
Austin Coll (TX)
Bay Path U (MA)
Blackburn Coll (IL)
Bowling Green State U (OH)
Brenau U (GA)
California State U, San Bernardino (CA)
Calumet Coll of Saint Joseph (IN)
Capital U (OH)
Cardinal Stritch U (WI)
Carnegie Mellon U (PA)
Cazenovia Coll (NY)
Central Michigan U (MI)
Central Washington U (WA)
Charleston Southern U (SC)
Clayton State U (GA)
Coll of Central Florida (FL)
Colorado Christian U (CO)
Colorado Mesa U (CO)
Cornerstone U (MI)
Davenport U, Grand Rapids (MI)
Dixie State U (UT)
Dominican U of California (CA)
Eastern Oregon U (OR)
Embry-Riddle Aeronautical U–Daytona (FL)
Embry-Riddle Aeronautical U–Prescott (AZ)
Embry-Riddle Aeronautical U–Worldwide (FL)
Florida Inst of Technology (FL)
Florida Keys Comm Coll (FL)
Florida SouthWestern State Coll (FL)
Gettysburg Coll (PA)
Grace Coll (IN)
Gulf Coast State Coll (FL)
Hallmark U (TX)
Hofstra U (NY)
Houston Baptist U (TX)
Howard Payne U (TX)
Huntingdon Coll (AL)
Inter American U of Puerto Rico, Metropolitan Campus (PR)
Jacksonville U (FL)
Judson U (IL)
Kettering U (MI)
La Roche Coll (PA)
Le Moyne Coll (NY)
Limestone Coll (SC)
Lincoln Christian U (IL)
Lincoln Coll of New England, Southington (CT)
Malone U (OH)
Mercer U, Macon (GA)
Miami Dade Coll (FL)
Millikin U (IL)
Missouri Baptist U (MO)
Missouri State U (MO)
Morris Coll (SC)
Morrisville State Coll (NY)
North Dakota State U (ND)
Northwest U (WA)
Pennsylvania Coll of Technology (PA)
Pensacola State Coll (FL)
Polk State Coll (FL)
Prescott Coll (AZ)
St. Petersburg Coll (FL)
St. Thomas U (FL)
Shenandoah U (VA)
Siena Coll (NY)
South Florida State Coll (FL)
Spring Hill Coll (AL)
State U of New York at New Paltz (NY)
Texas Tech U (TX)
Thomas Edison State U (NJ)
The U of Alabama at Birmingham (AL)
U of Charleston (WV)
U of Houston–Clear Lake (TX)
U of Illinois at Springfield (IL)
U of Louisville (KY)
U of Maine at Farmington (ME)
U of Maryland, Baltimore County (MD)
U of Maryland U Coll (MD)
U of Miami (FL)
U of Michigan–Dearborn (MI)
U of North Georgia (GA)
U of Pennsylvania (PA)
U of Puerto Rico in Bayamón (PR)
U of Southern Maine (ME)
The U of Texas at Austin (TX)
U of Waterloo (ON, Canada)
Viterbo U (WI)
Washington U in St. Louis (MO)
Waynesburg U (PA)
Western New England U (MA)
Widener U (PA)
Williamson Coll (TN)
Woodbury U (CA)

BUSINESS AND PERSONAL/ FINANCIAL SERVICES MARKETING

Dixie State U (UT)
Lindenwood U (MO)
Walla Walla U (WA)

BUSINESS AUTOMATION/ TECHNOLOGY/DATA ENTRY

East Carolina U (NC)
Mount Vernon Nazarene U (OH)
The U of Tampa (FL)

BUSINESS/COMMERCE

Adams State U (CO)
Alice Lloyd Coll (KY)
Alvernia U (PA)
American Coll of Thessaloniki (Greece)
Anderson U (SC)
Asbury U (KY)
Auburn U at Montgomery (AL)
Austin Coll (TX)
Austin Peay State U (TN)
Avila U (MO)
Baker U (KS)
Ball State U (IN)
Bayamón Central U (PR)
Baylor U (TX)
Bellarmine U (KY)
Belmont U (TN)
Bethel Coll (IN)
Bethel Coll (KS)
Bloomsburg U of Pennsylvania (PA)
Boise State U (ID)
Bowling Green State U (OH)
Brandeis U (MA)
Brenau U (GA)
Brescia U (KY)
Bryn Athyn Coll of the New Church (PA)
Bucknell U (PA)
California Baptist U (CA)
California State U, Dominguez Hills (CA)
Canisius Coll (NY)
Cardinal Stritch U (WI)
Caribbean U (PR)
The Catholic U of America (DC)
Central State U (OH)
Champlain Coll (VT)
Christian Brothers U (TN)
Clayton State U (GA)
Coll of Central Florida (FL)
Coll of Coastal Georgia (GA)
Colorado Mesa U (CO)
Columbia Coll (MO)
Columbus State U (GA)
Concordia U, Nebraska (NE)
Dalhousie U (NS, Canada)
Davenport U, Grand Rapids (MI)
Dickinson State U (ND)
Drake U (IA)
Drexel U (PA)
Earlham Coll (IN)
East Central U (OK)
Eastern Michigan U (MI)
Eastern Nazarene Coll (MA)
East Texas Baptist U (TX)
Edgewood Coll (WI)
The Evergreen State Coll (WA)
Faulkner U (AL)
Florida State U (FL)
Framingham State U (MA)
Franklin Coll (IN)
Georgia Gwinnett Coll (GA)
Goshen Coll (IN)
Grace Coll (IN)
Grand Valley State U (MI)
HEC Montreal (QC, Canada)
Henderson State U (AR)
Hofstra U (NY)
Hollins U (VA)
Holy Cross Coll (IN)
Houston Baptist U (TX)
Howard Payne U (TX)
Hult Intl Business School (United Kingdom)
Humacao Comm Coll (PR)
Huntingdon Coll (AL)
Husson U (ME)
Idaho State U (ID)
Indiana U Bloomington (IN)
Indiana U East (IN)
Indiana U Kokomo (IN)
Indiana U Northwest (IN)
Indiana U of Pennsylvania (PA)
Indiana U–Purdue U Indianapolis (IN)
Indiana U South Bend (IN)
Indiana U Southeast (IN)
Iowa State U of Science and Technology (IA)
Iowa Wesleyan U (IA)
Ithaca Coll (NY)
Jacksonville U (FL)
John Brown U (AR)
Johns Hopkins U (MD)
Juniata Coll (PA)
Kalamazoo Coll (MI)
Kansas State U (KS)
Kendall Coll (IL)
Kentucky State U (KY)
Lamar U (TX)
La Salle U (PA)
Lasell Coll (MA)
LIM Coll (NY)
Limestone Coll (SC)
Lourdes U (OH)
Loyola U Maryland (MD)
Manchester U (IN)
Marymount Manhattan Coll (NY)
Maryville U of Saint Louis (MO)
Massachusetts Inst of Technology (MA)
McMurry U (TX)
Medgar Evers Coll of the City U of New York (NY)
Mercer U, Macon (GA)
Metropolitan Coll of New York (NY)
MidAmerica Nazarene U (KS)
Missouri State U (MO)
Montana State U (MT)
Montana State U Billings (MT)
Montana Tech of The U of Montana (MT)
Morehead State U (KY)
Mount Allison U (NB, Canada)
Mount Mercy U (IA)
Mount St. Mary's U (MD)
Mount Vernon Nazarene U (OH)
Multnomah U (OR)
Murray State U (KY)
New Mexico State U (NM)
Niagara U (NY)
Nichols Coll (MA)
Northeastern Illinois U (IL)
Northeastern U (MA)
Northern Illinois U (IL)
Northern Kentucky U (KY)
Northwest Christian U (OR)
The Ohio State U (OH)
The Ohio State U at Lima (OH)
The Ohio State U at Marion (OH)
The Ohio State U–Mansfield Campus (OH)
The Ohio State U–Newark Campus (OH)
Ohio Valley U (WV)
Ohio Wesleyan U (OH)
Oklahoma Christian U (OK)
Pace U (NY)
Pace U, Pleasantville Campus (NY)
Penn State Abington (PA)
Penn State Altoona (PA)
Penn State Berks (PA)
Penn State Lehigh Valley (PA)
Penn State Schuylkill (PA)
Pittsburg State U (KS)
Plymouth State U (NH)
Purdue U Northwest (IN)
Randolph Coll (VA)
Regis Coll (MA)
Rochester Inst of Technology (NY)
Saginaw Valley State U (MI)
Saint Anselm Coll (NH)
Saint Mary's Coll of California (CA)
St. Thomas U (FL)
Saint Vincent Coll (PA)
Sam Houston State U (TX)
Schreiner U (TX)
Seattle Pacific U (WA)
Seattle U (WA)
Skidmore Coll (NY)
Southeastern U (FL)
Southern Arkansas U–Magnolia (AR)
Southwestern U (TX)
Spalding U (KY)
State U of New York at New Paltz (NY)
State U of New York at Plattsburgh (NY)
State U of New York Empire State Coll (NY)
Stephen F. Austin State U (TX)
Stratford U, Alexandria (VA)
Sullivan U (KY)
Sweet Briar Coll (VA)
Tabor Coll (KS)
Tarleton State U (TX)
Temple U (PA)
Texas A&M U–Commerce (TX)
Texas A&M U–Kingsville (TX)
Texas Tech U (TX)
Transylvania U (KY)
Trinity Christian Coll (IL)
The U of Akron (OH)
The U of Arizona (AZ)
U of Arkansas (AR)
U of Bridgeport (CT)
U of Central Arkansas (AR)
U of Central Florida (FL)
U of Delaware (DE)
U of Denver (CO)
U of Georgia (GA)
U of Hawaii at Manoa (HI)
U of Houston–Clear Lake (TX)
U of Houston–Downtown (TX)
The U of Kansas (KS)
U of Kentucky (KY)
U of Maine at Fort Kent (ME)
U of Maryland, Coll Park (MD)
U of Massachusetts Dartmouth (MA)
U of Nevada, Reno (NV)
U of North Texas (TX)
U of Notre Dame (IN)
U of Oregon (OR)
U of Pittsburgh (PA)
U of Regina (SK, Canada)
U of Rhode Island (RI)
U of Rochester (NY)
U of Saint Francis (IN)
U of San Francisco (CA)
U of Science and Arts of Oklahoma (OK)
U of South Alabama (AL)
The U of South Dakota (SD)
U of South Florida (FL)
U of South Florida, St. Petersburg (FL)
U of South Florida Sarasota-Manatee (FL)
The U of Texas at Austin (TX)
The U of Texas at Dallas (TX)
The U of Texas at San Antonio (TX)
U of the Southwest (NM)
The U of Tulsa (OK)
U of Utah (UT)
U of Virginia (VA)
U of Windsor (ON, Canada)
U of Wisconsin–Milwaukee (WI)
U of Wisconsin–Platteville (WI)
U of Wisconsin–Whitewater (WI)
Utah State U (UT)
Villa Maria Coll (NY)
Virginia Commonwealth U (VA)
Wake Forest U (NC)
Waldorf U (IA)
Walsh Coll of Accountancy and Business Administration (MI)
Washburn U (KS)
Washington & Jefferson Coll (PA)
Washington State U (WA)
Washington U in St. Louis (MO)
Webber Intl U (FL)
Welch Coll (TN)
Western Intl U (AZ)
Western New England U (MA)
Western Oregon U (OR)
Western Washington U (WA)
Westmont Coll (CA)
West Texas A&M U (TX)
West Virginia U (WV)
West Virginia U Inst of Technology (WV)
Wright State U (OH)
Wright State U–Lake Campus (OH)
Youngstown State U (OH)

BUSINESS/CORPORATE COMMUNICATIONS

Aquinas Coll (MI)
Augustana U (SD)
Bentley U (MA)
Bryant U (RI)
Calvin Coll (MI)
Central Penn Coll (PA)
Chestnut Hill Coll (PA)
Christian Brothers U (TN)
Concordia U Chicago (IL)
Concordia U, Nebraska (NE)
Duquesne U (PA)
Elon U (NC)
Holy Names U (CA)
Lycoming Coll (PA)
Marietta Coll (OH)
MidAmerica Nazarene U (KS)
Morningside Coll (IA)
National U (CA)
Nichols Coll (MA)
North Dakota State U (ND)
Penn State Abington (PA)
Point Loma Nazarene U (CA)
Rockhurst U (MO)
Saint Leo U (FL)
Stephen F. Austin State U (TX)
Stevenson U (MD)
Trinity Christian Coll (IL)
U of Houston (TX)
U of New England (ME)
Walsh U (OH)

BUSINESS FAMILY AND CONSUMER SCIENCES/ HUMAN SCIENCES

Brigham Young U (UT)
The Ohio State U (OH)
U of Houston (TX)
Virginia Polytechnic Inst and State U (VA)

BUSINESS, MANAGEMENT, AND MARKETING RELATED
Adelphi U (NY)
Alfred U (NY)
American U (DC)
Arizona State U at the Polytechnic campus (AZ)
Arizona State U at the Tempe campus (AZ)
Arizona State U at the West campus (AZ)
Arlington Baptist Coll (TX)
Athens State U (AL)
Baylor U (TX)
Bentley U (MA)
Bowling Green State U (OH)
Bridgewater State U (MA)
California State U, Dominguez Hills (CA)
Central Baptist Coll (AR)
Concordia Coll–New York (NY)
Corban U (OR)
Duquesne U (PA)
Eastern Nazarene Coll (MA)
Eastern U (PA)
FIDM/Fashion Inst of Design & Merchandising, Los Angeles Campus (CA)
FIDM/Fashion Inst of Design & Merchandising, San Francisco Campus (CA)
Hamline U (MN)
Hofstra U (NY)
Howard Payne U (TX)
Lehigh U (PA)
Loyola U Chicago (IL)
Mercyhurst U (PA)
Messiah Coll (PA)
Missouri U of Science and Technology (MO)
Morrisville State Coll (NY)
Multnomah U (OR)
Nebraska Wesleyan U (NE)
Neumann U (PA)
Penn State U Park (PA)
Point Park U (PA)
Polytechnic U of Puerto Rico (PR)
Purdue U Northwest (IN)
Roberts Wesleyan Coll (NY)
Saint Anselm Coll (NH)
Saint Mary's U of Minnesota (MN)
Seton Hill U (PA)
Sierra Nevada Coll (NV)
Skidmore Coll (NY)
Southern New Hampshire U (NH)
Southwestern Coll (KS)
State U of New York at Plattsburgh (NY)
State U of New York Coll of Agriculture and Technology at Cobleskill (NY)
State U of New York Coll of Technology at Alfred (NY)
State U of New York Coll of Technology at Canton (NY)
State U of New York Maritime Coll (NY)
Susquehanna U (PA)
Trevecca Nazarene U (TN)
Troy U (AL)
U of Minnesota, Crookston (MN)
U of Southern Mississippi (MS)
U of the Southwest (NM)
U of Wisconsin–Stout (WI)
U of Wisconsin–Whitewater (WI)
Utica Coll (NY)
Walla Walla U (WA)
Western State Colorado U (CO)
Worcester Polytechnic Inst (MA)

BUSINESS/MANAGERIAL ECONOMICS
Allegheny Coll (PA)
Anderson U (IN)
Andrews U (MI)
Arcadia U (PA)
Arkansas Tech U (AR)
Armstrong State U (GA)
Auburn U (AL)
Ball State U (IN)
Bard Coll (NY)
Baruch Coll of the City U of New York (NY)
Baylor U (TX)
Belmont U (TN)
Beloit Coll (WI)
Bentley U (MA)
Berry Coll (GA)
Bishop's U (QC, Canada)
Boise State U (ID)
Boston Coll (MA)
Bowling Green State U (OH)
Bradley U (IL)
Bryant U (RI)
Buena Vista U (IA)
California Inst of Technology (CA)
California State U, East Bay (CA)
California State U, Fullerton (CA)
California State U, Long Beach (CA)
Campbellsville U (KY)
Canisius Coll (NY)
Capital U (OH)
Carson-Newman U (TN)
Cedarville U (OH)
Central Washington U (WA)
Chapman U (CA)
Charleston Southern U (SC)
Chatham U (PA)
Clarion U of Pennsylvania (PA)
Clark Atlanta U (GA)
Cleveland State U (OH)
Coastal Carolina U (SC)
Coll of Mount Saint Vincent (NY)
The Coll of Saint Rose (NY)
Coll of the Ozarks (MO)
The Coll of Wooster (OH)
Converse Coll (SC)
Duquesne U (PA)
Eastern Michigan U (MI)
Eastern Washington U (WA)
East Tennessee State U (TN)
Fordham U (NY)
Fort Lewis Coll (CO)
Francis Marion U (SC)
Georgetown Coll (KY)
The George Washington U (DC)
Georgia Coll & State U (GA)
Georgia Inst of Technology (GA)
Georgia Southern U (GA)
Georgia State U (GA)
Gonzaga U (WA)
Grambling State U (LA)
Grand Valley State U (MI)
Green Mountain Coll (VT)
Grove City Coll (PA)
Hampden-Sydney Coll (VA)
HEC Montreal (QC, Canada)
High Point U (NC)
Hofstra U (NY)
Hope Coll (MI)
Huntington U (IN)
Husson U (ME)
Illinois Coll (IL)
Inter American U of Puerto Rico, Bayamón Campus (PR)
Inter American U of Puerto Rico, Metropolitan Campus (PR)
Inter American U of Puerto Rico, San Germán Campus (PR)
Iowa State U of Science and Technology (IA)
Ithaca Coll (NY)
Jackson State U (MS)
Jacksonville U (FL)
James Madison U (VA)
Kennesaw State U (GA)
Kent State U (OH)
Kentucky Wesleyan Coll (KY)
Lake Forest Coll (IL)
Lamar U (TX)
Lehigh U (PA)
Lewis U (IL)
Limestone Coll (SC)
Lipscomb U (TN)
Louisiana State U and A&M Coll (LA)
Louisiana Tech U (LA)
Loyola U Chicago (IL)
Loyola U New Orleans (LA)
Marshall U (WV)
Mary Baldwin U (VA)
Marymount Manhattan Coll (NY)
Miami U (OH)
Mississippi State U (MS)
Missouri Valley Coll (MO)
Montana State U Billings (MT)
Morehead State U (KY)
Mount Allison U (NB, Canada)
Niagara U (NY)
Nichols Coll (MA)
North Carolina State U (NC)
Northern Arizona U (AZ)
Northern Kentucky U (KY)
Northern State U (SD)
Northwest Missouri State U (MO)
Northwood U, Michigan Campus (MI)
The Ohio State U (OH)
The Ohio State U at Lima (OH)
The Ohio State U at Marion (OH)
The Ohio State U–Mansfield Campus (OH)
The Ohio State U–Newark Campus (OH)
Ohio U (OH)
Ohio Wesleyan U (OH)
Oklahoma State U (OK)
Old Dominion U (VA)
Otterbein U (OH)
Pace U (NY)
Pace U, Pleasantville Campus (NY)
Patrick Henry Coll (VA)
Penn State Abington (PA)
Penn State Altoona (PA)
Penn State Beaver (PA)
Penn State Berks (PA)
Penn State Brandywine (PA)
Penn State DuBois (PA)
Penn State Erie, The Behrend Coll (PA)
Penn State Fayette, The Eberly Campus (PA)
Penn State Greater Allegheny (PA)
Penn State Hazleton (PA)
Penn State Lehigh Valley (PA)
Penn State Mont Alto (PA)
Penn State New Kensington (PA)
Penn State Schuylkill (PA)
Penn State Shenango (PA)
Penn State Wilkes-Barre (PA)
Penn State Worthington Scranton (PA)
Penn State York (PA)
Point Loma Nazarene U (CA)
Quinnipiac U (CT)
Saginaw Valley State U (MI)
Saint Anselm Coll (NH)
Saint Louis U (MO)
Saint Peter's U (NJ)
Salisbury U (MD)
Samford U (AL)
Sam Houston State U (TX)
Seattle U (WA)
Shenandoah U (VA)
Shorter U (GA)
Sonoma State U (CA)
South Carolina State U (SC)
Southern Connecticut State U (CT)
Southern Illinois U Carbondale (IL)
Southern Illinois U Edwardsville (IL)
Spring Hill Coll (AL)
State U of New York at Plattsburgh (NY)
State U of New York Coll at Potsdam (NY)
Stephen F. Austin State U (TX)
Tarleton State U (TX)
Taylor U (IN)
Tennessee State U (TN)
Texas State U (TX)
Troy U (AL)
Union Coll (NY)
Union U (TN)
The U of Alabama (AL)
The U of Alabama at Birmingham (AL)
The U of Alabama in Huntsville (AL)
The U of Arizona (AZ)
U of Arkansas (AR)
U of California, Irvine (CA)
U of California, Los Angeles (CA)
U of California, Riverside (CA)
U of Central Florida (FL)
U of Dayton (OH)
U of Denver (CO)
U of Georgia (GA)
U of Guelph (ON, Canada)
U of Idaho (ID)
U of Indianapolis (IN)
U of Kentucky (KY)
U of Lethbridge (AB, Canada)
U of Louisville (KY)
U of Maine at Farmington (ME)
U of Mary Hardin-Baylor (TX)
U of Miami (FL)
U of Nevada, Reno (NV)
U of North Alabama (AL)
The U of North Carolina at Charlotte (NC)
The U of North Carolina at Greensboro (NC)
U of North Dakota (ND)
U of North Florida (FL)
U of North Texas (TX)
U of Oklahoma (OK)
U of Pittsburgh at Johnstown (PA)
U of Rochester (NY)
U of San Diego (CA)
U of San Francisco (CA)
U of Saskatchewan (SK, Canada)
U of South Carolina (SC)
U of Southern Mississippi (MS)
U of South Florida, St. Petersburg (FL)
The U of Tennessee (TN)
The U of Tennessee at Martin (TN)
The U of Texas at San Antonio (TX)
The U of Texas of the Permian Basin (TX)
U of the Incarnate Word (TX)
U of West Georgia (GA)
U of Windsor (ON, Canada)
U of Wisconsin–Superior (WI)
Utica Coll (NY)
Valdosta State U (GA)
Villanova U (PA)
Virginia Commonwealth U (VA)
Virginia Polytechnic Inst and State U (VA)
Virginia State U (VA)
Washburn U (KS)
Washington State U (WA)
Washington U in St. Louis (MO)
Weber State U (UT)
West Chester U of Pennsylvania (PA)
Western Kentucky U (KY)
Western Michigan U (MI)
Western State Colorado U (CO)
Westminster Coll (UT)
Westmont Coll (CA)
West Texas A&M U (TX)
West Virginia U (WV)
West Virginia Wesleyan Coll (WV)
Wheaton Coll (IL)
Wichita State U (KS)
Widener U (PA)
Wofford Coll (SC)
Wright State U (OH)
Wright State U–Lake Campus (OH)
Youngstown State U (OH)

BUSINESS OPERATIONS SUPPORT AND SECRETARIAL SERVICES RELATED
State U of New York at New Paltz (NY)

BUSINESS STATISTICS
Baylor U (TX)
Bryant U (RI)
Ferris State U (MI)
HEC Montreal (QC, Canada)
Loyola U New Orleans (LA)
Marian U (IN)
Maryville U of Saint Louis (MO)
Southern Oregon U (OR)
U of Central Missouri (MO)
U of Denver (CO)
The U of Tennessee (TN)
The U of Tulsa (OK)

BUSINESS TEACHER EDUCATION
Adams State U (CO)
Alfred U (NY)
Arizona Christian U (AZ)
Arkansas Tech U (AR)
Auburn U (AL)
Avila U (MO)
Baylor U (TX)
Bethune-Cookman U (FL)
Black Hills State U (SD)
Bluefield Coll (VA)
Bowling Green State U (OH)
Buena Vista U (IA)
Buffalo State Coll, State U of New York (NY)
California State U, Dominguez Hills (CA)
Campbellsville U (KY)
Canisius Coll (NY)
Carson-Newman U (TN)
Coll of Saint Mary (NE)
Concordia Coll (MN)
Concordia U Wisconsin (WI)
Corban U (OR)
Dakota State U (SD)
Dickinson State U (ND)
Doane U (NE)
East Carolina U (NC)
East Central U (OK)
Eastern Michigan U (MI)
Eastern Nazarene Coll (MA)
Eastern Washington U (WA)
Edgewood Coll (WI)
Emmanuel Coll (GA)
Emory & Henry Coll (VA)
Evangel U (MO)
Fayetteville State U (NC)
Ferris State U (MI)
Friends U (KS)
Goshen Coll (IN)
Grace Coll (IN)
Hampton U (VA)
Hannibal-LaGrange U (MO)
Hardin-Simmons U (TX)
Henderson State U (AR)
Hofstra U (NY)
Howard Payne U (TX)
Illinois State U (IL)
Immaculata U (PA)
Indiana State U (IN)
Lee U (TN)
Lehman Coll of the City U of New York (NY)
LeTourneau U (TX)
Lincoln U (MO)
Lindenwood U (MO)
Louisiana Coll (LA)
Louisiana Tech U (LA)
Maranatha Baptist U (WI)
McKendree U (IL)
Mercyhurst U (PA)
Minot State U (ND)
Mississippi State U (MS)
Missouri Baptist U (MO)
Missouri State U (MO)
Montana State U–Northern (MT)
Morehead State U (KY)
Mount Vernon Nazarene U (OH)
Nazareth Coll of Rochester (NY)
Niagara U (NY)
Northwestern Coll (IA)
Northwest Missouri State U (MO)
Oakland City U (IN)
Ohio Wesleyan U (OH)
Oral Roberts U (OK)
Robert Morris U (PA)
Rust Coll (MS)
St. Petersburg Coll (FL)
Saint Vincent Coll (PA)
Sam Houston State U (TX)
South Carolina State U (SC)
Southern Arkansas U–Magnolia (AR)
Southern Utah U (UT)
Southwestern Adventist U (TX)
Tennessee State U (TN)
Thomas More Coll (KY)
Trevecca Nazarene U (TN)
Trinity Christian Coll (IL)
Union Coll (NE)
Union U (TN)
U of Central Arkansas (AR)
U of Central Missouri (MO)
U of Indianapolis (IN)
U of Lethbridge (AB, Canada)
U of Minnesota, Twin Cities Campus (MN)
The U of Montana Western (MT)
U of Nebraska at Kearney (NE)
The U of North Carolina at Greensboro (NC)
U of Northern Iowa (IA)
U of Regina (SK, Canada)
U of Southern Mississippi (MS)
The U of Tennessee at Martin (TN)
U of Wisconsin–Superior (WI)
U of Wisconsin–Whitewater (WI)
Upper Iowa U (IA)
Utah State U (UT)
Utah Valley U (UT)
Utica Coll (NY)
Valley City State U (ND)
Virginia Union U (VA)
Viterbo U (WI)
Walla Walla U (WA)
Wayland Baptist U (TX)
Wayne State Coll (NE)
Weber State U (UT)
Western Kentucky U (KY)
Western Michigan U (MI)
Winona State U (MN)

CAD/CADD DRAFTING/ DESIGN TECHNOLOGY
Acad of Art U (CA)
Eastern Michigan U (MI)
Idaho State U (ID)
Murray State U (KY)

CANADIAN STUDIES
Dalhousie U (NS, Canada)
Mount Allison U (NB, Canada)
Trent U (ON, Canada)
U of Lethbridge (AB, Canada)
U of Toronto (ON, Canada)
U of Washington (WA)
U of Waterloo (ON, Canada)
Western Washington U (WA)

CARDIOVASCULAR TECHNOLOGY
Louisiana State U Health Sciences Center (LA)
Piedmont Coll (GA)
Weber State U (UT)

CARIBBEAN STUDIES
Brooklyn Coll of the City U of New York (NY)
Columbia U, School of General Studies (NY)
Hofstra U (NY)
Northwestern U (IL)

CASINO MANAGEMENT
Central Michigan U (MI)

CELL AND MOLECULAR BIOLOGY
Adams State U (CO)
Augusta U (GA)
Bennington Coll (VT)
Binghamton U, State U of New York (NY)
Bradley U (IL)
Bridgewater State U (MA)
Bryant U (RI)
Bucknell U (PA)
Canisius Coll (NY)
Cedarville U (OH)
Central Washington U (WA)
Christopher Newport U (VA)
The Colorado Coll (CO)
Concordia U (QC, Canada)
Florida State U (FL)
Fort Lewis Coll (CO)
Grand Valley State U (MI)
Harvard U (MA)
Illinois State U (IL)
John Jay Coll of Criminal Justice of the City U of New York (NY)
Johns Hopkins U (MD)
Liberty U (VA)
Limestone Coll (SC)
Marymount U (VA)
Missouri State U (MO)
Northeastern State U (OK)
Ohio U (OH)
Oklahoma City U (OK)
Purdue U (IN)
Seattle Pacific U (WA)
Seattle U (WA)
Texas A&M U (TX)
Texas Tech U (TX)
The U of Arizona (AZ)
U of California, Irvine (CA)
U of California, Los Angeles (CA)
U of Colorado Boulder (CO)
U of Hawaii at Manoa (HI)
U of Michigan (MI)
U of Regina (SK, Canada)
U of Rhode Island (RI)
The U of Tennessee at Martin (TN)
The U of Texas at Austin (TX)
U of Washington (WA)
U of Wisconsin–Superior (WI)
Western Washington U (WA)

CELL BIOLOGY AND ANATOMICAL SCIENCES RELATED
Rutgers U–New Brunswick (NJ)
Tulane U (LA)
U of Mary Hardin-Baylor (TX)
Washington & Jefferson Coll (PA)

CELL BIOLOGY AND ANATOMY
Dallas Baptist U (TX)
Huntingdon Coll (AL)
U of Saskatchewan (SK, Canada)
Western State Colorado U (CO)

CELL BIOLOGY AND HISTOLOGY
Beloit Coll (WI)
California State U, Dominguez Hills (CA)
California State U, Fresno (CA)
California State U, Long Beach (CA)
California State U, San Marcos (CA)
The Coll of Saint Rose (NY)
Humboldt State U (CA)
Johns Hopkins U (MD)
Mansfield U of Pennsylvania (PA)
Montana State U (MT)
Northwestern U (IL)
Rutgers U–New Brunswick (NJ)
San Francisco State U (CA)
Sonoma State U (CA)
Tulane U (LA)
U of California, Davis (CA)
U of California, San Diego (CA)
U of Georgia (GA)
U of Minnesota, Duluth (MN)
U of Minnesota, Twin Cities Campus (MN)
Western Washington U (WA)

CELTIC LANGUAGES
U of Notre Dame (IN)

CERAMIC ARTS AND CERAMICS
Adams State U (CO)
Alfred U (NY)
Anderson U (SC)
Aquinas Coll (MI)
Arcadia U (PA)
Bennington Coll (VT)
Bowling Green State U (OH)
Bradley U (IL)
Brigham Young U (UT)
California Coll of the Arts (CA)
California State U, East Bay (CA)
California State U, Long Beach (CA)
Central Washington U (WA)
Cleveland Inst of Art (OH)
Coll of the Atlantic (ME)
Coll of the Ozarks (MO)
Columbia Coll (MO)
Concordia U (QC, Canada)
Emily Carr U of Art + Design (BC, Canada)
Franklin Pierce U (NH)
Hofstra U (NY)
Inter American U of Puerto Rico, San Germán Campus (PR)
Kansas City Art Inst (MO)
Maryland Inst Coll of Art (MD)
Marywood U (PA)
Massachusetts Coll of Art and Design (MA)
Minnesota State U Mankato (MN)
New Hampshire Inst of Art (NH)
Ohio U (OH)
Pratt Inst (NY)
Providence Coll (RI)
Rhode Island Coll (RI)
Rhode Island School of Design (RI)
Rochester Inst of Technology (NY)
Rutgers U–New Brunswick (NJ)
Salve Regina U (RI)
School of the Art Inst of Chicago (IL)
Seton Hill U (PA)
State U of New York at New Paltz (NY)
Syracuse U (NY)
Temple U (PA)
Texas Christian U (TX)
The U of Akron (OH)
U of Hartford (CT)
The U of Kansas (KS)
U of Massachusetts Dartmouth (MA)
U of Miami (FL)
U of Michigan (MI)
U of Oregon (OR)
U of Regina (SK, Canada)
The U of Texas at El Paso (TX)
U of Washington (WA)
Washington U in St. Louis (MO)
Western State Colorado U (CO)
Western Washington U (WA)

CERAMIC SCIENCES AND ENGINEERING
Alfred U (NY)
Missouri U of Science and Technology (MO)
Rutgers U–New Brunswick (NJ)

CHEMICAL AND BIOMOLECULAR ENGINEERING
Johns Hopkins U (MD)
Massachusetts Inst of Technology (MA)
Milwaukee School of Eng (WI)
Stony Brook U, State U of New York (NY)
U of Chicago (IL)
U of Washington (WA)

CHEMICAL ENGINEERING
American U of Beirut (Lebanon)
Arizona State U at the Tempe campus (AZ)
Auburn U (AL)
Bucknell U (PA)
California Baptist U (CA)
California Inst of Technology (CA)
California State Polytechnic U, Pomona (CA)
California State U, Long Beach (CA)
Calvin Coll (MI)
Carnegie Mellon U (PA)
Case Western Reserve U (OH)
Christian Brothers U (TN)
City Coll of the City U of New York (NY)
Clarkson U (NY)
Clemson U (SC)
Cleveland State U (OH)
Colorado School of Mines (CO)
Colorado State U (CO)
Columbia U (NY)
Cooper Union for the Advancement of Science and Art (NY)
Cornell U (NY)
Dalhousie U (NS, Canada)
Drexel U (PA)
Elon U (NC)
Florida Ag and Mech U (FL)
Florida Inst of Technology (FL)
Georgia Inst of Technology (GA)
Hampton U (VA)
Iowa State U of Science and Technology (IA)
Johns Hopkins U (MD)
Kansas State U (KS)
Kettering U (MI)
Lafayette Coll (PA)
Lamar U (TX)
Lehigh U (PA)
Louisiana Coll (LA)
Louisiana State U and A&M Coll (LA)
Louisiana Tech U (LA)
Manhattan Coll (NY)
Massachusetts Inst of Technology (MA)
McMaster U (ON, Canada)
Miami U (OH)
Michigan State U (MI)
Michigan Technological U (MI)
Mississippi State U (MS)
Missouri U of Science and Technology (MO)
Montana State U (MT)
New Mexico Inst of Mining and Technology (NM)
New Mexico State U (NM)
North Carolina State U (NC)
Northeastern U (MA)
Northwestern U (IL)
The Ohio State U (OH)
Ohio U (OH)
Oklahoma State U (OK)
Oregon State U (OR)
Pace U (NY)
Penn State Abington (PA)
Penn State Altoona (PA)
Penn State Beaver (PA)
Penn State Berks (PA)
Penn State Brandywine (PA)
Penn State DuBois (PA)
Penn State Erie, The Behrend Coll (PA)
Penn State Fayette, The Eberly Campus (PA)
Penn State Greater Allegheny (PA)
Penn State Hazleton (PA)
Penn State Lehigh Valley (PA)
Penn State Mont Alto (PA)
Penn State New Kensington (PA)
Penn State Schuylkill (PA)
Penn State Shenango (PA)
Penn State U Park (PA)
Penn State Wilkes-Barre (PA)
Penn State Worthington Scranton (PA)
Penn State York (PA)
Polytechnic U of Puerto Rico (PR)
Prairie View A&M U (TX)
Princeton U (NJ)
Purdue U (IN)
Rensselaer Polytechnic Inst (NY)
Rice U (TX)
Rochester Inst of Technology (NY)
Rose-Hulman Inst of Technology (IN)
Rowan U (NJ)
Royal Military Coll of Canada (ON, Canada)
Rutgers U–New Brunswick (NJ)
Saint Louis U–Madrid Campus (Spain)
South Dakota School of Mines and Technology (SD)
Stanford U (CA)
Stevens Inst of Technology (NJ)
Syracuse U (NY)
Texas A&M U (TX)
Texas A&M U–Kingsville (TX)
Texas Tech U (TX)
Trine U (IN)
Tufts U (MA)
Tulane U (LA)
United States Military Acad (NY)
Université de Montréal (QC, Canada)
Université de Sherbrooke (QC, Canada)
U at Buffalo, the State U of New York (NY)
The U of Akron (OH)
The U of Alabama (AL)
The U of Alabama in Huntsville (AL)
The U of Arizona (AZ)
U of Arkansas (AR)
U of California, Davis (CA)
U of California, Irvine (CA)
U of California, Los Angeles (CA)
U of California, Riverside (CA)
U of California, San Diego (CA)
U of California, Santa Barbara (CA)
U of Cincinnati (OH)
U of Colorado Boulder (CO)
U of Dayton (OH)
U of Delaware (DE)
U of Florida (FL)
U of Houston (TX)
U of Idaho (ID)
U of Illinois at Chicago (IL)
The U of Kansas (KS)
U of Kentucky (KY)
U of Louisville (KY)
U of Maine (ME)
U of Maryland, Baltimore County (MD)
U of Maryland, Coll Park (MD)
U of Massachusetts Amherst (MA)
U of Massachusetts Lowell (MA)
U of Michigan (MI)
U of Minnesota, Duluth (MN)
U of Minnesota, Twin Cities Campus (MN)
U of Nevada, Reno (NV)
U of New Hampshire (NH)
U of New Haven (CT)
U of North Dakota (ND)
U of Notre Dame (IN)
U of Oklahoma (OK)
U of Pennsylvania (PA)
U of Pittsburgh (PA)
U of Pittsburgh at Johnstown (PA)
U of Rhode Island (RI)
U of Rochester (NY)
U of Saskatchewan (SK, Canada)
U of South Alabama (AL)
U of South Carolina (SC)
U of Southern California (CA)
U of South Florida (FL)
The U of Tennessee (TN)
The U of Tennessee at Chattanooga (TN)
The U of Texas at Austin (TX)
The U of Texas at San Antonio (TX)
The U of Toledo (OH)
U of Toronto (ON, Canada)
The U of Tulsa (OK)
U of Utah (UT)
U of Virginia (VA)
U of Washington (WA)
U of Waterloo (ON, Canada)
U of Wisconsin–Madison (WI)
U of Wisconsin–Stevens Point (WI)
Vanderbilt U (TN)
Villanova U (PA)
Virginia Commonwealth U (VA)
Virginia Polytechnic Inst and State U (VA)
Washington and Lee U (VA)
Washington State U (WA)
Washington U in St. Louis (MO)
Wayne State U (MI)
Western Michigan U (MI)
West Virginia U (WV)
West Virginia U Inst of Technology (WV)
Widener U (PA)
Worcester Polytechnic Inst (MA)
Youngstown State U (OH)

CHEMICAL ENGINEERING RELATED
State U of New York Coll of Environmental Science and Forestry (NY)

CHEMICAL ENGINEERING TECHNOLOGY
United States Military Acad (NY)

CHEMICAL PHYSICS
Adams State U (CO)
Augustana U (SD)
Bowdoin Coll (ME)
Carnegie Mellon U (PA)
Centre Coll (KY)
Columbia U, School of General Studies (NY)
Hamilton Coll (NY)
Harvard U (MA)
Hendrix Coll (AR)
Lewis U (IL)
Michigan State U (MI)
Saginaw Valley State U (MI)
Simon Fraser U (BC, Canada)
Susquehanna U (PA)
Swarthmore Coll (PA)
U of Guelph (ON, Canada)
U of Waterloo (ON, Canada)

CHEMICAL TECHNOLOGY
Inter American U of Puerto Rico, Guayama Campus (PR)
U of Regina (SK, Canada)

CHEMISTRY
Abilene Christian U (TX)
Adams State U (CO)
Adelphi U (NY)
Agnes Scott Coll (GA)
Alabama State U (AL)
Albany State U (GA)
Albertus Magnus Coll (CT)
Albion Coll (MI)
Albright Coll (PA)
Alcorn State U (MS)
Alderson Broaddus U (WV)
Alfred U (NY)
Allegheny Coll (PA)
Alma Coll (MI)
Alvernia U (PA)
Alverno Coll (WI)
American Intl Coll (MA)
American U (DC)
The American U in Cairo (Egypt)
American U of Beirut (Lebanon)
Amherst Coll (MA)
Anderson U (IN)
Andrews U (MI)
Angelo State U (TX)
Appalachian State U (NC)
Aquinas Coll (MI)
Arcadia U (PA)
Arizona State U at the Tempe campus (AZ)
Arkansas Tech U (AR)
Armstrong State U (GA)
Asbury U (KY)
Ashland U (OH)
Assumption Coll (MA)
Athens State U (AL)
Auburn U (AL)

Auburn U at Montgomery (AL)
Augsburg Coll (MN)
Augustana Coll (IL)
Augustana U (SD)
Augusta U (GA)
Austin Coll (TX)
Austin Peay State U (TN)
Averett U (VA)
Azusa Pacific U (CA)
Baker U (KS)
Baldwin Wallace U (OH)
Ball State U (IN)
Bard Coll (NY)
Barnard Coll (NY)
Barry U (FL)
Barton Coll (NC)
Bates Coll (ME)
Bayamón Central U (PR)
Baylor U (TX)
Belhaven U (MS)
Bellarmine U (KY)
Belmont U (TN)
Beloit Coll (WI)
Bemidji State U (MN)
Benedictine Coll (KS)
Bennett Coll (NC)
Bennington Coll (VT)
Berea Coll (KY)
Berry Coll (GA)
Bethany Lutheran Coll (MN)
Bethel Coll (IN)
Bethel Coll (KS)
Bethel U (MN)
Bethune-Cookman U (FL)
Binghamton U, State U of New York (NY)
Biola U (CA)
Bishop's U (QC, Canada)
Blackburn Coll (IL)
Black Hills State U (SD)
Bloomfield Coll (NJ)
Bloomsburg U of Pennsylvania (PA)
Bluefield Coll (VA)
Bluffton U (OH)
Boise State U (ID)
Boston Coll (MA)
Boston U (MA)
Bowdoin Coll (ME)
Bowling Green State U (OH)
Bradley U (IL)
Brandeis U (MA)
Brescia U (KY)
Briar Cliff U (IA)
Bridgewater Coll (VA)
Bridgewater State U (MA)
Brigham Young U–Idaho (ID)
Brooklyn Coll of the City U of New York (NY)
Bryn Mawr Coll (PA)
Bucknell U (PA)
Buena Vista U (IA)
Buffalo State Coll, State U of New York (NY)
Butler U (IN)
Cabrini U (PA)
Caldwell U (NJ)
California Baptist U (CA)
California Inst of Technology (CA)
California Lutheran U (CA)
California Polytechnic State U, San Luis Obispo (CA)
California State Polytechnic U, Pomona (CA)
California State U, Bakersfield (CA)
California State U, Chico (CA)
California State U, Dominguez Hills (CA)
California State U, East Bay (CA)
California State U, Fresno (CA)
California State U, Fullerton (CA)
California State U, Long Beach (CA)
California State U, Northridge (CA)
California State U, Sacramento (CA)
California State U, San Bernardino (CA)
California State U, San Marcos (CA)
California State U, Stanislaus (CA)
California U of Pennsylvania (PA)
Calvin Coll (MI)
Cameron U (OK)
Campbellsville U (KY)
Canisius Coll (NY)
Capital U (OH)
Cardinal Stritch U (WI)
Carleton Coll (MN)
Carlow U (PA)
Carnegie Mellon U (PA)
Carroll Coll (MT)
Carson-Newman U (TN)
Carthage Coll (WI)
Case Western Reserve U (OH)
Catawba Coll (NC)
The Catholic U of America (DC)
Cedar Crest Coll (PA)
Cedarville U (OH)
Centenary Coll of Louisiana (LA)
Central Connecticut State U (CT)
Central Methodist U (MO)
Central Michigan U (MI)
Central State U (OH)
Central Washington U (WA)
Centre Coll (KY)
Chapman U (CA)
Charleston Southern U (SC)
Chatham U (PA)
Chestnut Hill Coll (PA)
Christian Brothers U (TN)
Christopher Newport U (VA)
The Citadel, The Military Coll of South Carolina (SC)
City Coll of the City U of New York (NY)
Claremont McKenna Coll (CA)
Clarion U of Pennsylvania (PA)
Clark Atlanta U (GA)
Clarke U (IA)
Clarkson U (NY)
Clark U (MA)
Clayton State U (GA)
Clemson U (SC)
Cleveland State U (OH)
Coastal Carolina U (SC)
Coe Coll (IA)
Colby Coll (ME)
Colgate U (NY)
The Coll at Brockport, State U of New York (NY)
Coll of Charleston (SC)
The Coll of Idaho (ID)
Coll of Mount Saint Vincent (NY)
The Coll of New Jersey (NJ)
Coll of Saint Benedict (MN)
Coll of Saint Elizabeth (NJ)
Coll of Saint Mary (NE)
The Coll of Saint Rose (NY)
The Coll of St. Scholastica (MN)
Coll of Staten Island of the City U of New York (NY)
Coll of the Holy Cross (MA)
Coll of the Ozarks (MO)
The Coll of William and Mary (VA)
The Coll of Wooster (OH)
The Colorado Coll (CO)
Colorado Mesa U (CO)
Colorado School of Mines (CO)
Colorado State U (CO)
Columbia Coll (MO)
Columbia U (NY)
Columbia U, School of General Studies (NY)
Columbus State U (GA)
Concordia Coll (MN)
Concordia U (QC, Canada)
Concordia U Chicago (IL)
Concordia U Irvine (CA)
Concordia U, Nebraska (NE)
Concordia U, St. Paul (MN)
Concord U (WV)
Connecticut Coll (CT)
Converse Coll (SC)
Cornell Coll (IA)
Cornell U (NY)
Creighton U (NE)
Dalhousie U (NS, Canada)
Dalton State Coll (GA)
Dartmouth Coll (NH)
Davidson Coll (NC)
Delaware Valley U (PA)
Denison U (OH)
DePauw U (IN)
DeSales U (PA)
Dickinson Coll (PA)
Dickinson State U (ND)
Doane U (NE)
Dominican U (IL)
Dominican U of California (CA)
Drake U (IA)
Drew U (NJ)
Drexel U (PA)
Drury U (MO)
Duquesne U (PA)
Earlham Coll (IN)
East Carolina U (NC)
East Central U (OK)
Eastern Illinois U (IL)
Eastern Mennonite U (VA)
Eastern Michigan U (MI)
Eastern Nazarene Coll (MA)
Eastern U (PA)
Eastern Washington U (WA)
East Stroudsburg U of Pennsylvania (PA)
East Tennessee State U (TN)
East Texas Baptist U (TX)
Eckerd Coll (FL)
Edgewood Coll (WI)
Elizabeth City State U (NC)
Elizabethtown Coll (PA)
Elmira Coll (NY)
Elms Coll (MA)
Elon U (NC)
Emmanuel Coll (MA)
Emory & Henry Coll (VA)
Emory U (GA)
Emporia State U (KS)
Eureka Coll (IL)
Evangel U (MO)
Fairfield U (CT)
Fairleigh Dickinson U, Coll at Florham (NJ)
Fairleigh Dickinson U, Metropolitan Campus (NJ)
Fayetteville State U (NC)
Ferris State U (MI)
Fitchburg State U (MA)
Florida Ag and Mech U (FL)
Florida Atlantic U (FL)
Florida Gulf Coast U (FL)
Florida Inst of Technology (FL)
Florida Intl U (FL)
Florida Southern Coll (FL)
Florida State U (FL)
Fordham U (NY)
Fort Lewis Coll (CO)
Framingham State U (MA)
Franciscan U of Steubenville (OH)
Francis Marion U (SC)
Franklin & Marshall Coll (PA)
Franklin Coll (IN)
Freed-Hardeman U (TN)
Fresno Pacific U (CA)
Friends U (KS)
Frostburg State U (MD)
Furman U (SC)
Gallaudet U (DC)
Gannon U (PA)
Gardner-Webb U (NC)
Geneva Coll (PA)
George Fox U (OR)
Georgetown Coll (KY)
Georgetown U (DC)
The George Washington U (DC)
Georgia Coll & State U (GA)
Georgia Gwinnett Coll (GA)
Georgia Inst of Technology (GA)
Georgian Court U (NJ)
Georgia Southern U (GA)
Georgia Southwestern State U (GA)
Georgia State U (GA)
Gettysburg Coll (PA)
Gonzaga U (WA)
Gordon Coll (MA)
Goshen Coll (IN)
Goucher Coll (MD)
Governors State U (IL)
Graceland U (IA)
Grambling State U (LA)
Grand Valley State U (MI)
Greenville Coll (IL)
Grinnell Coll (IA)
Grove City Coll (PA)
Guilford Coll (NC)
Hamilton Coll (NY)
Hamline U (MN)
Hampden-Sydney Coll (VA)
Hampshire Coll (MA)
Hampton U (VA)
Hanover Coll (IN)
Harding U (AR)
Hardin-Simmons U (TX)
Hartwick Coll (NY)
Harvard U (MA)
Harvey Mudd Coll (CA)
Haverford Coll (PA)
Heidelberg U (OH)
Henderson State U (AR)
Hendrix Coll (AR)
High Point U (NC)
Hillsdale Coll (MI)
Hiram Coll (OH)
Hobart and William Smith Colls (NY)
Hofstra U (NY)
Hollins U (VA)
Hood Coll (MD)
Hope Coll (MI)
Houghton Coll (NY)
Houston Baptist U (TX)
Howard Payne U (TX)
Humboldt State U (CA)
Hunter Coll of the City U of New York (NY)
Huntingdon Coll (AL)
Huntington U (IN)
Huston-Tillotson U (TX)
Idaho State U (ID)
Illinois Coll (IL)
Illinois State U (IL)
Illinois Wesleyan U (IL)
Immaculata U (PA)
Indiana State U (IN)
Indiana U Bloomington (IN)
Indiana U Kokomo (IN)
Indiana U Northwest (IN)
Indiana U of Pennsylvania (PA)
Indiana U–Purdue U Indianapolis (IN)
Indiana U South Bend (IN)
Indiana U Southeast (IN)
Inter American U of Puerto Rico, Metropolitan Campus (PR)
Inter American U of Puerto Rico, San Germán Campus (PR)
Iona Coll (NY)
Iowa State U of Science and Technology (IA)
Ithaca Coll (NY)
Jackson State U (MS)
Jacksonville State U (AL)
Jacksonville U (FL)
James Madison U (VA)
John Brown U (AR)
John Carroll U (OH)
Johns Hopkins U (MD)
Johnson C. Smith U (NC)
Judson U (IL)
Juniata Coll (PA)
Kalamazoo Coll (MI)
Kansas State U (KS)
Kansas Wesleyan U (KS)
Kean U (NJ)
Keene State Coll (NH)
Kennesaw State U (GA)
Kent State U (OH)
Kentucky State U (KY)
Kentucky Wesleyan Coll (KY)
Kenyon Coll (OH)
Kettering U (MI)
King's Coll (PA)
The King's U (AB, Canada)
King U (TN)
Knox Coll (IL)
Kutztown U of Pennsylvania (PA)
Lafayette Coll (PA)
LaGrange Coll (GA)
Lake Erie Coll (OH)
Lake Forest Coll (IL)
Lamar U (TX)
Lane Coll (TN)
Langston U (OK)
La Roche Coll (PA)
La Salle U (PA)
Lawrence Technological U (MI)
Lawrence U (WI)
Lebanese American U (Lebanon)
Lebanon Valley Coll (PA)
Lee U (TN)
Lehigh U (PA)
Lehman Coll of the City U of New York (NY)
Le Moyne Coll (NY)
Lenoir-Rhyne U (NC)
LeTourneau U (TX)
Lewis & Clark Coll (OR)
Lewis U (IL)
Liberty U (VA)
Limestone Coll (SC)
Lincoln U (MO)
Lincoln U (PA)
Lindenwood U (MO)
Linfield Coll (OR)
Lipscomb U (TN)
Lock Haven U of Pennsylvania (PA)
Longwood U (VA)
Loras Coll (IA)
Louisiana Coll (LA)
Louisiana State U and A&M Coll (LA)
Louisiana Tech U (LA)
Loyola Marymount U (CA)
Loyola U Chicago (IL)
Loyola U Maryland (MD)
Loyola U New Orleans (LA)
Lubbock Christian U (TX)
Luther Coll (IA)
Lycoming Coll (PA)
Lynchburg Coll (VA)
Lyon Coll (AR)
Macalester Coll (MN)
Madonna U (MI)
Malone U (OH)
Manchester U (IN)
Manhattan Coll (NY)
Manhattanville Coll (NY)
Mansfield U of Pennsylvania (PA)
Marian U (IN)
Marian U (WI)
Marietta Coll (OH)
Marist Coll (NY)
Marshall U (WV)
Mary Baldwin U (VA)
Maryville U of Saint Louis (MO)
Massachusetts Coll of Liberal Arts (MA)
Massachusetts Inst of Technology (MA)
McDaniel Coll (MD)
McKendree U (IL)
McMaster U (ON, Canada)
McMurry U (TX)
McNeese State U (LA)
MCPHS U (MA)
Mercer U, Macon (GA)
Mercyhurst U (PA)
Meredith Coll (NC)
Merrimack Coll (MA)
Messiah Coll (PA)
Metropolitan State U of Denver (CO)
Miami U (OH)
Michigan State U (MI)
Michigan Technological U (MI)
MidAmerica Nazarene U (KS)
Middlebury Coll (VT)
Millersville U of Pennsylvania (PA)
Milligan Coll (TN)
Millikin U (IL)
Millsaps Coll (MS)
Mills Coll (CA)
Minnesota State U Mankato (MN)
Minnesota State U Moorhead (MN)
Minot State U (ND)
Misericordia U (PA)
Mississippi State U (MS)
Mississippi Valley State U (MS)
Missouri Baptist U (MO)
Missouri State U (MO)
Missouri U of Science and Technology (MO)
Missouri Western State U (MO)
Monmouth Coll (IL)
Monmouth U (NJ)
Montana State U (MT)
Montana State U Billings (MT)
Montana Tech of The U of Montana (MT)
Montclair State U (NJ)
Moravian Coll (PA)
Morehead State U (KY)
Morehouse Coll (GA)
Morningside Coll (IA)
Mount Allison U (NB, Canada)
Mount Holyoke Coll (MA)
Mount Marty Coll (SD)
Mount Mary U (WI)
Mount Mercy U (IA)
Mount St. Joseph U (OH)
Mount Saint Mary Coll (NY)
Mount Saint Mary's U (CA)
Mount St. Mary's U (MD)
Mount Vernon Nazarene U (OH)
Muhlenberg Coll (PA)
Murray State U (KY)
Muskingum U (OH)
Nazareth Coll of Rochester (NY)
Nebraska Wesleyan U (NE)
Newberry Coll (SC)
New Coll of Florida (FL)
New Jersey City U (NJ)
Newman U (KS)
New Mexico Highlands U (NM)

New Mexico Inst of Mining and Technology (NM)
New Mexico State U (NM)
New York Inst of Technology (NY)
Niagara U (NY)
North Carolina Central U (NC)
North Carolina State U (NC)
North Carolina Wesleyan Coll (NC)
North Central Coll (IL)
North Dakota State U (ND)
Northeastern Illinois U (IL)
Northeastern State U (OK)
Northeastern U (MA)
Northern Arizona U (AZ)
Northern Illinois U (IL)
Northern Kentucky U (KY)
Northern State U (SD)
Northland Coll (WI)
Northwestern Coll (IA)
Northwestern Oklahoma State U (OK)
Northwestern U (IL)
Northwest Missouri State U (MO)
Nova Southeastern U (FL)
Oberlin Coll (OH)
Occidental Coll (CA)
Ohio Dominican U (OH)
The Ohio State U (OH)
Ohio U (OH)
Ohio Wesleyan U (OH)
Oklahoma Baptist U (OK)
Oklahoma Christian U (OK)
Oklahoma State U (OK)
Old Dominion U (VA)
Olivet Nazarene U (IL)
Oral Roberts U (OK)
Oregon State U (OR)
Otterbein U (OH)
Ouachita Baptist U (AR)
Our Lady of the Lake U of San Antonio (TX)
Pace U (NY)
Pace U, Pleasantville Campus (NY)
Pacific Lutheran U (WA)
Paine Coll (GA)
Penn State Abington (PA)
Penn State Altoona (PA)
Penn State Beaver (PA)
Penn State Berks (PA)
Penn State Brandywine (PA)
Penn State DuBois (PA)
Penn State Erie, The Behrend Coll (PA)
Penn State Fayette, The Eberly Campus (PA)
Penn State Greater Allegheny (PA)
Penn State Hazleton (PA)
Penn State Lehigh Valley (PA)
Penn State Mont Alto (PA)
Penn State New Kensington (PA)
Penn State Schuylkill (PA)
Penn State Shenango (PA)
Penn State U Park (PA)
Penn State Wilkes-Barre (PA)
Penn State Worthington Scranton (PA)
Penn State York (PA)
Pepperdine U, Malibu (CA)
Philander Smith Coll (AR)
Piedmont Coll (GA)
Pittsburg State U (KS)
Pitzer Coll (CA)
Plymouth State U (NH)
Point Loma Nazarene U (CA)
Pomona Coll (CA)
Portland State U (OR)
Prairie View A&M U (TX)
Princeton U (NJ)
Principia Coll (IL)
Providence Coll (RI)
Purchase Coll, State U of New York (NY)
Purdue U (IN)
Purdue U Northwest (IN)
Queens Coll of the City U of New York (NY)
Quinnipiac U (CT)
Radford U (VA)
Ramapo Coll of New Jersey (NJ)
Randolph Coll (VA)
Randolph-Macon Coll (VA)
Redeemer U Coll (ON, Canada)
Reed Coll (OR)
Regis U (CO)
Rensselaer Polytechnic Inst (NY)
Rhode Island Coll (RI)
Rhodes Coll (TN)
Rice U (TX)
Ripon Coll (WI)
Roanoke Coll (VA)
Roberts Wesleyan Coll (NY)
Rochester Inst of Technology (NY)
Rockford U (IL)
Rockhurst U (MO)
Rocky Mountain Coll (MT)
Roger Williams U (RI)
Rollins Coll (FL)
Rose-Hulman Inst of Technology (IN)
Rosemont Coll (PA)
Rowan U (NJ)
Royal Military Coll of Canada (ON, Canada)
Rust Coll (MS)
Rutgers U–Camden (NJ)
Rutgers U–Newark (NJ)
Rutgers U–New Brunswick (NJ)
Sacred Heart U (CT)
The Sage Colls (NY)
Saginaw Valley State U (MI)
St. Ambrose U (IA)
Saint Anselm Coll (NH)
Saint Augustine's U (NC)
St. Bonaventure U (NY)
St. Catherine U (MN)
St. Cloud State U (MN)
St. Edward's U (TX)
Saint Francis U (PA)
St. John Fisher Coll (NY)
Saint John's U (MN)
St. John's U (NY)
St. Joseph's Coll, Long Island Campus (NY)
St. Joseph's Coll, New York (NY)
Saint Joseph's U (PA)
Saint Louis U (MO)
Saint Louis U–Madrid Campus (Spain)
Saint Martin's U (WA)
Saint Mary's Coll (IN)
Saint Mary's Coll of California (CA)
St. Mary's Coll of Maryland (MD)
Saint Mary's U of Minnesota (MN)
Saint Michael's Coll (VT)
St. Norbert Coll (WI)
St. Olaf Coll (MN)
Saint Peter's U (NJ)
St. Thomas U (FL)
Saint Vincent Coll (PA)
Salisbury U (MD)
Salve Regina U (RI)
Samford U (AL)
Sam Houston State U (TX)
San Diego State U (CA)
San Francisco State U (CA)
Santa Clara U (CA)
Sarah Lawrence Coll (NY)
Schreiner U (TX)
Scripps Coll (CA)
Seattle Pacific U (WA)
Seattle U (WA)
Seton Hill U (PA)
Sewanee: The U of the South (TN)
Shawnee State U (OH)
Shaw U (NC)
Shenandoah U (VA)
Shepherd U (WV)
Shippensburg U of Pennsylvania (PA)
Shorter U (GA)
Siena Coll (NY)
Simmons Coll (MA)
Simon Fraser U (BC, Canada)
Simpson Coll (IA)
Skidmore Coll (NY)
Slippery Rock U of Pennsylvania (PA)
Smith Coll (MA)
Sonoma State U (CA)
South Carolina State U (SC)
South Dakota School of Mines and Technology (SD)
South Dakota State U (SD)
Southeastern Louisiana U (LA)
Southeastern Oklahoma State U (OK)
Southeast Missouri State U (MO)
Southern Arkansas U–Magnolia (AR)
Southern Connecticut State U (CT)
Southern Illinois U Carbondale (IL)
Southern Illinois U Edwardsville (IL)
Southern Methodist U (TX)
Southern Oregon U (OR)
Southern Utah U (UT)
Southwest Baptist U (MO)
Southwestern Adventist U (TX)
Southwestern Coll (KS)
Southwestern U (TX)
Spelman Coll (GA)
Spring Hill Coll (AL)
Stanford U (CA)
State U of New York at Fredonia (NY)
State U of New York at New Paltz (NY)
State U of New York at Oswego (NY)
State U of New York at Plattsburgh (NY)
State U of New York Coll at Cortland (NY)
State U of New York Coll at Geneseo (NY)
State U of New York Coll at Old Westbury (NY)
State U of New York Coll at Potsdam (NY)
State U of New York Coll of Environmental Science and Forestry (NY)
Stephen F. Austin State U (TX)
Stevens Inst of Technology (NJ)
Stevenson U (MD)
Stockton U (NJ)
Stonehill Coll (MA)
Stony Brook U, State U of New York (NY)
Susquehanna U (PA)
Swarthmore Coll (PA)
Sweet Briar Coll (VA)
Syracuse U (NY)
Tabor Coll (KS)
Tarleton State U (TX)
Taylor U (IN)
Temple U (PA)
Tennessee State U (TN)
Tennessee Wesleyan U (TN)
Texas A&M Intl U (TX)
Texas A&M U (TX)
Texas A&M U–Commerce (TX)
Texas A&M U–Corpus Christi (TX)
Texas A&M U–Kingsville (TX)
Texas Christian U (TX)
Texas Lutheran U (TX)
Texas State U (TX)
Texas Tech U (TX)
Texas Wesleyan U (TX)
Texas Woman's U (TX)
Thomas More Coll (KY)
Towson U (MD)
Transylvania U (KY)
Trent U (ON, Canada)
Trevecca Nazarene U (TN)
Trine U (IN)
Trinity Christian Coll (IL)
Trinity U (TX)
Troy U (AL)
Truman State U (MO)
Tufts U (MA)
Tulane U (LA)
Tusculum Coll (TN)
Union Coll (KY)
Union Coll (NE)
Union Coll (NY)
Union U (TN)
United States Air Force Acad (CO)
United States Military Acad (NY)
Université de Montréal (QC, Canada)
Université de Sherbrooke (QC, Canada)
U at Albany, State U of New York (NY)
U at Buffalo, the State U of New York (NY)
The U of Akron (OH)
The U of Alabama (AL)
The U of Alabama at Birmingham (AL)
The U of Alabama in Huntsville (AL)
U of Alaska Fairbanks (AK)
The U of Arizona (AZ)
U of Arkansas (AR)
U of California, Davis (CA)
U of California, Irvine (CA)
U of California, Los Angeles (CA)
U of California, Riverside (CA)
U of California, San Diego (CA)
U of California, Santa Barbara (CA)
U of Central Arkansas (AR)
U of Central Florida (FL)
U of Central Missouri (MO)
U of Charleston (WV)
U of Chicago (IL)
U of Cincinnati (OH)
U of Colorado Boulder (CO)
U of Colorado Colorado Springs (CO)
U of Colorado Denver (CO)
U of Dayton (OH)
U of Delaware (DE)
U of Denver (CO)
U of Detroit Mercy (MI)
U of Dubuque (IA)
U of Evansville (IN)
The U of Findlay (OH)
U of Florida (FL)
U of Georgia (GA)
U of Great Falls (MT)
U of Guelph (ON, Canada)
U of Hartford (CT)
U of Hawaii at Manoa (HI)
U of Houston (TX)
U of Houston–Clear Lake (TX)
U of Houston–Downtown (TX)
U of Idaho (ID)
U of Illinois at Chicago (IL)
U of Illinois at Springfield (IL)
U of Jamestown (ND)
The U of Kansas (KS)
U of Kentucky (KY)
U of King's Coll (NS, Canada)
U of La Verne (CA)
U of Lethbridge (AB, Canada)
U of Louisville (KY)
U of Maine (ME)
U of Mary Hardin-Baylor (TX)
U of Maryland, Baltimore County (MD)
U of Maryland, Coll Park (MD)
U of Mary Washington (VA)
U of Massachusetts Amherst (MA)
U of Massachusetts Boston (MA)
U of Massachusetts Dartmouth (MA)
U of Massachusetts Lowell (MA)
U of Miami (FL)
U of Michigan (MI)
U of Michigan–Dearborn (MI)
U of Michigan–Flint (MI)
U of Minnesota, Duluth (MN)
U of Minnesota, Morris (MN)
U of Minnesota, Twin Cities Campus (MN)
U of Missouri–Kansas City (MO)
U of Missouri–St. Louis (MO)
U of Montevallo (AL)
U of Mount Union (OH)
U of Nebraska at Kearney (NE)
U of Nevada, Las Vegas (NV)
U of Nevada, Reno (NV)
U of New England (ME)
U of New Hampshire (NH)
U of New Haven (CT)
U of New Orleans (LA)
U of North Alabama (AL)
U of North Carolina at Asheville (NC)
The U of North Carolina at Chapel Hill (NC)
The U of North Carolina at Charlotte (NC)
The U of North Carolina at Greensboro (NC)
The U of North Carolina at Pembroke (NC)
The U of North Carolina Wilmington (NC)
U of North Dakota (ND)
U of Northern Colorado (CO)
U of Northern Iowa (IA)
U of North Florida (FL)
U of North Georgia (GA)
U of North Texas (TX)
U of Notre Dame (IN)
U of Oklahoma (OK)
U of Oregon (OR)
U of Pennsylvania (PA)
U of Pikeville (KY)
U of Pittsburgh (PA)
U of Pittsburgh at Bradford (PA)
U of Pittsburgh at Greensburg (PA)
U of Pittsburgh at Johnstown (PA)
U of Puget Sound (WA)
U of Regina (SK, Canada)
U of Rhode Island (RI)
U of Richmond (VA)
U of Rochester (NY)
U of Saint Francis (IN)
U of Saint Joseph (CT)
U of Saint Mary (KS)
U of St. Thomas (MN)
U of St. Thomas (TX)
U of San Diego (CA)
U of San Francisco (CA)
U of Saskatchewan (SK, Canada)
U of Science and Arts of Oklahoma (OK)
The U of Scranton (PA)
U of South Alabama (AL)
U of South Carolina (SC)
U of South Carolina Aiken (SC)
The U of South Dakota (SD)
U of Southern California (CA)
U of Southern Indiana (IN)
U of Southern Maine (ME)
U of Southern Mississippi (MS)
U of South Florida (FL)
The U of Tampa (FL)
The U of Tennessee (TN)
The U of Tennessee at Chattanooga (TN)
The U of Tennessee at Martin (TN)
The U of Texas at Austin (TX)
The U of Texas at Dallas (TX)
The U of Texas at El Paso (TX)
The U of Texas at San Antonio (TX)
The U of Texas of the Permian Basin (TX)
The U of Texas Rio Grande Valley (TX)
U of the Cumberlands (KY)
U of the Fraser Valley (BC, Canada)
U of the Incarnate Word (TX)
U of the Pacific (CA)
U of the Virgin Islands (VI)
The U of Toledo (OH)
The U of Tulsa (OK)
U of Utah (UT)
U of Vermont (VT)
U of Virginia (VA)
The U of Virginia's Coll at Wise (VA)
U of Washington (WA)
U of Washington, Bothell (WA)
U of Waterloo (ON, Canada)
The U of West Alabama (AL)
U of West Georgia (GA)
U of Windsor (ON, Canada)
U of Wisconsin–Eau Claire (WI)
U of Wisconsin–Green Bay (WI)
U of Wisconsin–La Crosse (WI)
U of Wisconsin–Madison (WI)
U of Wisconsin–Milwaukee (WI)
U of Wisconsin–Parkside (WI)
U of Wisconsin–Platteville (WI)
U of Wisconsin–Stevens Point (WI)
U of Wisconsin–Superior (WI)
U of Wisconsin–Whitewater (WI)
Upper Iowa U (IA)
Ursinus Coll (PA)
Utah State U (UT)
Utah Valley U (UT)
Utica Coll (NY)
Valdosta State U (GA)
Valley City State U (ND)
Valparaiso U (IN)
Vanderbilt U (TN)
Vassar Coll (NY)
Villanova U (PA)
Virginia Commonwealth U (VA)
Virginia Military Inst (VA)
Virginia Polytechnic Inst and State U (VA)
Virginia State U (VA)
Virginia Union U (VA)
Virginia Wesleyan Coll (VA)
Viterbo U (WI)
Wabash Coll (IN)
Wagner Coll (NY)
Wake Forest U (NC)
Walla Walla U (WA)
Walsh U (OH)
Wartburg Coll (IA)
Washburn U (KS)
Washington & Jefferson Coll (PA)
Washington and Lee U (VA)
Washington Coll (MD)
Washington State U (WA)
Washington U in St. Louis (MO)
Wayland Baptist U (TX)

Waynesburg U (PA)
Wayne State Coll (NE)
Wayne State U (MI)
Weber State U (UT)
Wells Coll (NY)
Wesleyan Coll (GA)
Wesleyan U (CT)
West Chester U of Pennsylvania (PA)
Western Carolina U (NC)
Western Connecticut State U (CT)
Western Illinois U (IL)
Western Kentucky U (KY)
Western Michigan U (MI)
Western New England U (MA)
Western Oregon U (OR)
Western State Colorado U (CO)
Western Washington U (WA)
Westfield State U (MA)
Westminster Coll (PA)
Westminster Coll (UT)
Westmont Coll (CA)
West Texas A&M U (TX)
West Virginia State U (WV)
West Virginia U (WV)
West Virginia U Inst of Technology (WV)
West Virginia Wesleyan Coll (WV)
Wheaton Coll (IL)
Wheaton Coll (MA)
Wheeling Jesuit U (WV)
Whitman Coll (WA)
Whittier Coll (CA)
Whitworth U (WA)
Wichita State U (KS)
Widener U (PA)
Wilkes U (PA)
Willamette U (OR)
William Jewell Coll (MO)
William Paterson U of New Jersey (NJ)
Williams Coll (MA)
Wilson Coll (PA)
Wingate U (NC)
Winona State U (MN)
Winthrop U (SC)
Wittenberg U (OH)
Wofford Coll (SC)
Worcester Polytechnic Inst (MA)
Worcester State U (MA)
Wright State U (OH)
Xavier U of Louisiana (LA)
York Coll of Pennsylvania (PA)
York Coll of the City U of New York (NY)
Youngstown State U (OH)

CHEMISTRY RELATED

Alvernia U (PA)
Boston U (MA)
Bridgewater Coll (VA)
Bridgewater State U (MA)
Carnegie Mellon U (PA)
Case Western Reserve U (OH)
Chatham U (PA)
Coll of Charleston (SC)
Dartmouth Coll (NH)
Duquesne U (PA)
Eastern Nazarene Coll (MA)
Eastern Oregon U (OR)
Eastern U (PA)
East Stroudsburg U of Pennsylvania (PA)
Ferris State U (MI)
Florida Inst of Technology (FL)
Florida State U (FL)
Harvard U (MA)
Inter American U of Puerto Rico, Bayamón Campus (PR)
Kansas Wesleyan U (KS)
Keene State Coll (NH)
LeTourneau U (TX)
Mercer U, Macon (GA)
Michigan Technological U (MI)
Mount St. Joseph U (OH)
Palm Beach Atlantic U (FL)
Rhode Island Coll (RI)
Saginaw Valley State U (MI)
Saint Anselm Coll (NH)
Saint Mary's Coll of California (CA)
Saint Vincent Coll (PA)
Sam Houston State U (TX)
Stony Brook U, State U of New York (NY)
Taylor U (IN)
Union Coll (KY)
U at Buffalo, the State U of New York (NY)
U of California, Santa Barbara (CA)
U of Chicago (IL)
U of Denver (CO)
U of Houston–Downtown (TX)
U of Notre Dame (IN)
The U of Scranton (PA)
U of Southern Mississippi (MS)
U of the Pacific (CA)
U of Wisconsin–Eau Claire (WI)
U of Wisconsin–Milwaukee (WI)
Washington U in St. Louis (MO)
Wayne State U (MI)
Western Illinois U (IL)
Western Michigan U (MI)
Western State Colorado U (CO)
West Virginia Wesleyan Coll (WV)
Whitman Coll (WA)

CHEMISTRY TEACHER EDUCATION

Adams State U (CO)
Albion Coll (MI)
Alvernia U (PA)
Ashland U (OH)
Augustana Coll (IL)
Ball State U (IN)
Baylor U (TX)
Bethel Coll (IN)
Bethune-Cookman U (FL)
Bishop's U (QC, Canada)
Bluefield Coll (VA)
Boston U (MA)
Bowling Green State U (OH)
Bradley U (IL)
Brigham Young U–Idaho (ID)
Brooklyn Coll of the City U of New York (NY)
Buena Vista U (IA)
Cabrini U (PA)
Calvin Coll (MI)
Campbellsville U (KY)
Canisius Coll (NY)
Carroll Coll (MT)
Cedarville U (OH)
Central Methodist U (MO)
Central Michigan U (MI)
Central Washington U (WA)
City Coll of the City U of New York (NY)
The Coll of New Jersey (NJ)
Coll of Saint Mary (NE)
Coll of Staten Island of the City U of New York (NY)
Coll of the Ozarks (MO)
Colorado State U (CO)
Concordia Coll (MN)
Concordia U Chicago (IL)
Concordia U, St. Paul (MN)
Dickinson State U (ND)
East Central U (OK)
Eastern Michigan U (MI)
Eastern Nazarene Coll (MA)
Eastern Washington U (WA)
Edgewood Coll (WI)
Elizabeth City State U (NC)
Elmira Coll (NY)
Emory & Henry Coll (VA)
Evangel U (MO)
Ferris State U (MI)
Florida Inst of Technology (FL)
Fort Lewis Coll (CO)
Franklin Coll (IN)
Goshen Coll (IN)
Grand Valley State U (MI)
Greenville Coll (IL)
Grove City Coll (PA)
Hofstra U (NY)
Holy Family U (PA)
Hope Coll (MI)
Huntingdon Coll (AL)
Huntington U (IN)
Indiana U Bloomington (IN)
Indiana U Northwest (IN)
Indiana U South Bend (IN)
Inter American U of Puerto Rico, Metropolitan Campus (PR)
Inter American U of Puerto Rico, San Germán Campus (PR)
Ithaca Coll (NY)
Juniata Coll (PA)
Kansas Wesleyan U (KS)
Kent State U (OH)
King U (TN)
Lee U (TN)
Le Moyne Coll (NY)
Lincoln U (MO)
Lindenwood U (MO)
Lipscomb U (TN)
Louisiana Tech U (LA)
Madonna U (MI)
Manchester U (IN)
Manhattanville Coll (NY)
Marist Coll (NY)
McMurry U (TX)
Mercyhurst U (PA)
Merrimack Coll (MA)
Messiah Coll (PA)
Miami Dade Coll (FL)
Miami U (OH)
Michigan State U (MI)
Millikin U (IL)
Minnesota State U Moorhead (MN)
Minot State U (ND)
Misericordia U (PA)
Missouri State U (MO)
Montana State U Billings (MT)
Morningside Coll (IA)
Mount Marty Coll (SD)
Mount Mary U (WI)
Mount Vernon Nazarene U (OH)
Nazareth Coll of Rochester (NY)
Niagara U (NY)
North Dakota State U (ND)
Northwest Missouri State U (MO)
Ohio Dominican U (OH)
Ohio Wesleyan U (OH)
Pace U (NY)
Pace U, Pleasantville Campus (NY)
Pepperdine U, Malibu (CA)
Pittsburg State U (KS)
Providence Coll (RI)
Queens Coll of the City U of New York (NY)
Rhode Island Coll (RI)
Roberts Wesleyan Coll (NY)
Saginaw Valley State U (MI)
St. Catherine U (MN)
St. Cloud State U (MN)
St. Edward's U (TX)
Saint Francis U (PA)
St. John Fisher Coll (NY)
St. Joseph's Coll, Long Island Campus (NY)
St. Joseph's Coll, New York (NY)
Saint Joseph's U (PA)
Saint Mary's U of Minnesota (MN)
Schreiner U (TX)
Seattle U (WA)
Seton Hill U (PA)
South Dakota State U (SD)
Southern Utah U (UT)
Southwest Baptist U (MO)
Southwestern Adventist U (TX)
State U of New York at New Paltz (NY)
State U of New York at Plattsburgh (NY)
State U of New York Coll at Cortland (NY)
State U of New York Coll at Old Westbury (NY)
State U of New York Coll at Potsdam (NY)
Syracuse U (NY)
Transylvania U (KY)
Trevecca Nazarene U (TN)
Trinity Christian Coll (IL)
Union Coll (KY)
Union Coll (NE)
U of California, San Diego (CA)
U of Delaware (DE)
U of Dubuque (IA)
U of Evansville (IN)
U of Great Falls (MT)
U of Illinois at Chicago (IL)
U of Jamestown (ND)
U of Louisiana at Monroe (LA)
U of Maine (ME)
U of Maine at Farmington (ME)
U of Mary Hardin-Baylor (TX)
U of Maryland, Baltimore County (MD)
U of Michigan–Dearborn (MI)
U of Pittsburgh at Johnstown (PA)
U of Regina (SK, Canada)
U of St. Thomas (MN)
The U of Tennessee at Martin (TN)
U of Waterloo (ON, Canada)
U of Windsor (ON, Canada)
U of Wisconsin–Superior (WI)
U of Wisconsin–Whitewater (WI)
Utah State U (UT)
Utah Valley U (UT)
Utica Coll (NY)
Valley City State U (ND)
Valparaiso U (IN)
Virginia Union U (VA)
Viterbo U (WI)
Washburn U (KS)
Washington U in St. Louis (MO)
Waynesburg U (PA)
Wayne State Coll (NE)
Weber State U (UT)
Western Michigan U (MI)
Western State Colorado U (CO)
Western Washington U (WA)
Westfield State U (MA)
Widener U (PA)
Winona State U (MN)
Xavier U of Louisiana (LA)

CHILD-CARE AND SUPPORT SERVICES MANAGEMENT

Brigham Young U (UT)
Chestnut Hill Coll (PA)
Ferris State U (MI)
Idaho State U (ID)
National Louis U (IL)
Newberry Coll (SC)
Rust Coll (MS)
Seton Hill U (PA)
State U of New York Coll of Agriculture and Technology at Cobleskill (NY)
Texas Tech U (TX)
Union Inst & U (OH)
The U of Texas Rio Grande Valley (TX)
U of the Fraser Valley (BC, Canada)

CHILD-CARE PROVISION

Brigham Young U (UT)
Southeastern Oklahoma State U (OK)
Wayne State Coll (NE)

CHILD DEVELOPMENT

Albertus Magnus Coll (CT)
Alcorn State U (MS)
Alliant Intl U–San Diego (CA)
Appalachian State U (NC)
Auburn U (AL)
Bennington Coll (VT)
Bowling Green State U (OH)
Brigham Young U (UT)
Brigham Young U–Idaho (ID)
California State U, East Bay (CA)
California State U, Fresno (CA)
California State U, Long Beach (CA)
California State U, Northridge (CA)
California State U, Sacramento (CA)
Cameron U (OK)
Carson-Newman U (TN)
Central Michigan U (MI)
Coll of the Ozarks (MO)
Concordia U, St. Paul (MN)
East Carolina U (NC)
Eastern Washington U (WA)
East Tennessee State U (TN)
Goddard Coll (VT)
Hampton U (VA)
Hannibal-LaGrange U (MO)
Harding U (AR)
Henderson State U (AR)
Humboldt State U (CA)
Iowa State U of Science and Technology (IA)
Kansas State U (KS)
Kuyper Coll (MI)
Lesley U (MA)
Louisiana Tech U (LA)
Madonna U (MI)
Meredith Coll (NC)
Michigan State U (MI)
Milligan Coll (TN)
Minnesota State U Mankato (MN)
Missouri Baptist U (MO)
Mount Saint Mary's U (CA)
Oklahoma Christian U (OK)
Olivet Nazarene U (IL)
Point Loma Nazarene U (CA)
Point U (GA)
Portland State U (OR)
Quinnipiac U (CT)
St. Bonaventure U (NY)
St. Cloud State U (MN)
Seton Hill U (PA)
Texas Tech U (TX)
Texas Woman's U (TX)
Trent U (ON, Canada)
Tufts U (MA)
Union Inst & U (OH)
The U of Akron (OH)
U of Alaska Fairbanks (AK)
U of Guelph (ON, Canada)
U of La Verne (CA)
U of Nevada, Reno (NV)
The U of North Carolina at Greensboro (NC)
U of Saint Joseph (CT)
U of Saint Mary (KS)
The U of Tennessee at Martin (TN)
The U of Texas at Dallas (TX)
U of Virginia (VA)
Vanderbilt U (TN)
Weber State U (UT)
Western Michigan U (MI)
West Virginia U (WV)
Wheelock Coll (MA)
Whittier Coll (CA)
Youngstown State U (OH)

CHILDREN'S AND ADOLESCENT LITERATURE

Central Michigan U (MI)

CHINESE

Ball State U (IN)
Bard Coll (NY)
Bates Coll (ME)
Beloit Coll (WI)
Bennington Coll (VT)
Boston U (MA)
Brooklyn Coll of the City U of New York (NY)
Bryant U (RI)
California State U, Long Beach (CA)
Calvin Coll (MI)
Carnegie Mellon U (PA)
Case Western Reserve U (OH)
Colgate U (NY)
Coll of the Holy Cross (MA)
Concordia Coll (MN)
Dartmouth Coll (NH)
Davidson Coll (NC)
Emory U (GA)
Georgetown U (DC)
The George Washington U (DC)
Grinnell Coll (IA)
Hamilton Coll (NY)
Hobart and William Smith Colls (NY)
Hofstra U (NY)
Hunter Coll of the City U of New York (NY)
Lawrence U (WI)
Lehigh U (PA)
Macalester Coll (MN)
Messiah Coll (PA)
Michigan State U (MI)
Middlebury Coll (VT)
Nazareth Coll of Rochester (NY)
New Coll of Florida (FL)
North Central Coll (IL)
Occidental Coll (CA)
The Ohio State U (OH)
Penn State U Park (PA)
Pomona Coll (CA)
Portland State U (OR)
Queens Coll of the City U of New York (NY)
Reed Coll (OR)
Rutgers U–New Brunswick (NJ)
San Francisco State U (CA)
Sarah Lawrence Coll (NY)
Scripps Coll (CA)
Stanford U (CA)
Swarthmore Coll (PA)
Trinity U (TX)
Tufts U (MA)
Union Coll (NY)
United States Military Acad (NY)
U of California, Davis (CA)
U of California, Los Angeles (CA)
U of California, San Diego (CA)
U of California, Santa Barbara (CA)
U of Colorado Boulder (CO)
U of Georgia (GA)
U of Hawaii at Manoa (HI)
U of Houston (TX)
U of Kentucky (KY)
U of Maryland, Coll Park (MD)
U of Massachusetts Amherst (MA)
U of North Georgia (GA)

U of Notre Dame (IN)
U of Oklahoma (OK)
U of Oregon (OR)
U of Pittsburgh (PA)
U of Puget Sound (WA)
U of Regina (SK, Canada)
U of Rhode Island (RI)
U of Utah (UT)
U of Vermont (VT)
U of Washington (WA)
U of Wisconsin–Madison (WI)
Vassar Coll (NY)
Wake Forest U (NC)
Washington State U (WA)
Washington U in St. Louis (MO)
Western Kentucky U (KY)
Western Washington U (WA)
Whittier Coll (CA)
Williams Coll (MA)
Wofford Coll (SC)

CHINESE STUDIES
Ball State U (IN)
The Coll of William and Mary (VA)
Drew U (NJ)
Gettysburg Coll (PA)
Pacific Lutheran U (WA)
U at Albany, State U of New York (NY)
U of California, Irvine (CA)
U of Minnesota, Duluth (MN)
U of North Dakota (ND)
U of Richmond (VA)
The U of Tulsa (OK)
U of Washington (WA)
Willamette U (OR)

CHRISTIAN STUDIES
Ambrose U (AB, Canada)
Anderson U (SC)
Bluefield Coll (VA)
Bryan Coll (TN)
California Baptist U (CA)
Canisius Coll (NY)
The Coll of St. Scholastica (MN)
Coll of the Holy Cross (MA)
Concordia U Wisconsin (WI)
Ecclesia Coll (AR)
Gordon Coll (MA)
Hardin-Simmons U (TX)
Hillsdale Coll (MI)
Houston Baptist U (TX)
Iowa Wesleyan U (IA)
Lee U (TN)
Liberty U (VA)
Louisiana Coll (LA)
Loyola U Chicago (IL)
Loyola U New Orleans (LA)
Marian U (IN)
McMurry U (TX)
Mercer U, Macon (GA)
Missouri Baptist U (MO)
Oklahoma Baptist U (OK)
Ouachita Baptist U (AR)
Point Loma Nazarene U (CA)
Roanoke Coll (VA)
St. Edward's U (TX)
Saint Mary's U of Minnesota (MN)
St. Thomas U (NB, Canada)
Simpson U (CA)
Southwestern Coll (KS)
Stonehill Coll (MA)
Tabor Coll (KS)
Tennessee Wesleyan U (TN)
Texas Wesleyan U (TX)
Toccoa Falls Coll (GA)
Truett McConnell U (GA)
U of Dubuque (IA)
U of Mary Hardin-Baylor (TX)
U of the Cumberlands (KY)
Whitworth U (WA)

CINEMATOGRAPHY AND FILM/VIDEO PRODUCTION
Acad of Art U (CA)
American U (DC)
Anderson U (IN)
Belmont U (TN)
Bennington Coll (VT)
Binghamton U, State U of New York (NY)
Biola U (CA)
Brigham Young U (UT)
Brooklyn Coll of the City U of New York (NY)
California State U, Long Beach (CA)
California State U, Northridge (CA)
Central Washington U (WA)
Chapman U (CA)
City Coll of the City U of New York (NY)
Clayton State U (GA)
Cleveland State U (OH)
Columbia Coll Chicago (IL)
Columbus Coll of Art & Design (OH)
Concordia U (QC, Canada)
Cornerstone U (MI)
Drexel U (PA)
Eastern Washington U (WA)
Emerson Coll (MA)
Emily Carr U of Art + Design (BC, Canada)
The Evergreen State Coll (WA)
Fairleigh Dickinson U, Coll at Florham (NJ)
Fashion Inst of Technology (NY)
FIDM/Fashion Inst of Design & Merchandising, Los Angeles Campus (CA)
Fitchburg State U (MA)
George Fox U (OR)
Goshen Coll (IN)
Hunter Coll of the City U of New York (NY)
Inst of American Indian Arts (NM)
Ithaca Coll (NY)
John Brown U (AR)
John Paul the Great Catholic U (CA)
Keene State Coll (NH)
Liberty U (VA)
Loyola Marymount U (CA)
Loyola U New Orleans (LA)
Lynn U (FL)
Maharishi U of Management (IA)
Massachusetts Coll of Art and Design (MA)
Messiah Coll (PA)
Miami Dade Coll (FL)
Minneapolis Coll of Art and Design (MN)
Montana State U (MT)
Montclair State U (NJ)
Mount Saint Mary's U (CA)
New England Inst of Technology (RI)
New Mexico Highlands U (NM)
New Mexico State U (NM)
New York Film Acad (CA)
Ohio U (OH)
Oklahoma City U (OK)
Pace U, Pleasantville Campus (NY)
Palm Beach Atlantic U (FL)
Point Park U (PA)
Pratt Inst (NY)
Purchase Coll, State U of New York (NY)
Quinnipiac U (CT)
Regent U (VA)
Ringling Coll of Art and Design (FL)
Rochester Inst of Technology (NY)
Rutgers U–Newark (NJ)
San Francisco Art Inst (CA)
Savannah Coll of Art and Design (GA)
School of the Art Inst of Chicago (IL)
Southern Illinois U Carbondale (IL)
Southern Methodist U (TX)
Southwestern Assemblies of God U (TX)
Stanford U (CA)
Stevenson U (MD)
Syracuse U (NY)
Temple U (PA)
Université de Montréal (QC, Canada)
U of Advancing Technology (AZ)
U of Central Arkansas (AR)
U of Central Florida (FL)
U of Illinois at Chicago (IL)
U of Miami (FL)
U of North Carolina School of the Arts (NC)
The U of North Carolina Wilmington (NC)
U of Regina (SK, Canada)
U of Rhode Island (RI)
U of Southern California (CA)
Villa Maria Coll (NY)
Virginia Commonwealth U (VA)
Walla Walla U (WA)
Wayne State U (MI)
Webster U (MO)
Wilmington U (DE)

CITY/URBAN, COMMUNITY AND REGIONAL PLANNING
Appalachian State U (NC)
Arizona State U at the Tempe campus (AZ)
Ball State U (IN)
Bridgewater State U (MA)
Buffalo State Coll, State U of New York (NY)
California Polytechnic State U, San Luis Obispo (CA)
California State Polytechnic U, Pomona (CA)
Concordia U (QC, Canada)
Cornell U (NY)
Dalhousie U (NS, Canada)
East Carolina U (NC)
Eastern Michigan U (MI)
Eastern Washington U (WA)
Florida Atlantic U (FL)
Frostburg State U (MD)
Indiana U of Pennsylvania (PA)
Iowa State U of Science and Technology (IA)
Jacksonville U (FL)
Massachusetts Inst of Technology (MA)
Miami U (OH)
Michigan State U (MI)
Minnesota State U Mankato (MN)
Missouri State U (MO)
The Ohio State U (OH)
Parsons School of Design (NY)
Plymouth State U (NH)
Portland State U (OR)
Rowan U (NJ)
St. Cloud State U (MN)
South Dakota State U (SD)
Temple U (PA)
Texas A&M U (TX)
Texas State U (TX)
Tufts U (MA)
The U of Akron (OH)
The U of Arizona (AZ)
U of California, Davis (CA)
U of Cincinnati (OH)
U of Georgia (GA)
U of Missouri–Kansas City (MO)
U of New Hampshire (NH)
U of San Francisco (CA)
U of Saskatchewan (SK, Canada)
The U of Texas at Austin (TX)
U of Virginia (VA)
U of Washington (WA)
U of Waterloo (ON, Canada)
West Chester U of Pennsylvania (PA)
Western Michigan U (MI)
Westfield State U (MA)

CIVIL ENGINEERING
The American U in Dubai (United Arab Emirates)
American U of Beirut (Lebanon)
Angelo State U (TX)
Arizona State U at the Tempe campus (AZ)
Auburn U (AL)
Boise State U (ID)
Bradley U (IL)
Bucknell U (PA)
California Baptist U (CA)
California Polytechnic State U, San Luis Obispo (CA)
California State Polytechnic U, Pomona (CA)
California State U, Chico (CA)
California State U, Fresno (CA)
California State U, Long Beach (CA)
California State U, Northridge (CA)
California State U, Sacramento (CA)
Calvin Coll (MI)
Caribbean U (PR)
Carnegie Mellon U (PA)
Carroll Coll (MT)
Case Western Reserve U (OH)
The Catholic U of America (DC)
Central Connecticut State U (CT)
Christian Brothers U (TN)
The Citadel, The Military Coll of South Carolina (SC)
City Coll of the City U of New York (NY)
Clarkson U (NY)
Clemson U (SC)
Cleveland State U (OH)
The Coll of New Jersey (NJ)
Colorado School of Mines (CO)
Colorado State U (CO)
Columbia U (NY)
Concordia U (QC, Canada)
Cooper Union for the Advancement of Science and Art (NY)
Cornell U (NY)
Drexel U (PA)
Florida Ag and Mech U (FL)
Florida Atlantic U (FL)
Florida Gulf Coast U (FL)
Florida Inst of Technology (FL)
Florida Intl U (FL)
George Fox U (OR)
The George Washington U (DC)
Georgia Inst of Technology (GA)
Georgia Southern U (GA)
Gonzaga U (WA)
Hofstra U (NY)
Idaho State U (ID)
Iowa State U of Science and Technology (IA)
Jackson State U (MS)
Johns Hopkins U (MD)
Kansas State U (KS)
Kennesaw State U (GA)
King's Coll (PA)
Lafayette Coll (PA)
Lamar U (TX)
Lawrence Technological U (MI)
Lebanese American U (Lebanon)
Lehigh U (PA)
LeTourneau U (TX)
Lipscomb U (TN)
Louisiana State U and A&M Coll (LA)
Louisiana Tech U (LA)
Loyola Marymount U (CA)
Manhattan Coll (NY)
Massachusetts Inst of Technology (MA)
McMaster U (ON, Canada)
Merrimack Coll (MA)
Michigan State U (MI)
Michigan Technological U (MI)
Milwaukee School of Eng (WI)
Minnesota State U Mankato (MN)
Mississippi State U (MS)
Missouri U of Science and Technology (MO)
Montana State U (MT)
Montana Tech of The U of Montana (MT)
New Mexico Inst of Mining and Technology (NM)
New Mexico State U (NM)
North Carolina State U (NC)
North Dakota State U (ND)
Northeastern U (MA)
Northern Arizona U (AZ)
Northwestern U (IL)
The Ohio State U (OH)
Ohio U (OH)
Oklahoma State U (OK)
Old Dominion U (VA)
Oregon State U (OR)
Penn State Abington (PA)
Penn State Altoona (PA)
Penn State Beaver (PA)
Penn State Berks (PA)
Penn State Brandywine (PA)
Penn State DuBois (PA)
Penn State Erie, The Behrend Coll (PA)
Penn State Fayette, The Eberly Campus (PA)
Penn State Greater Allegheny (PA)
Penn State Harrisburg (PA)
Penn State Hazleton (PA)
Penn State Lehigh Valley (PA)
Penn State Mont Alto (PA)
Penn State New Kensington (PA)
Penn State Schuylkill (PA)
Penn State Shenango (PA)
Penn State U Park (PA)
Penn State Wilkes-Barre (PA)
Penn State Worthington Scranton (PA)
Penn State York (PA)
Polytechnic U of Puerto Rico (PR)
Portland State U (OR)
Prairie View A&M U (TX)
Princeton U (NJ)
Purdue U (IN)
Purdue U Northwest (IN)
Quinnipiac U (CT)
Rensselaer Polytechnic Inst (NY)
Rice U (TX)
Rockhurst U (MO)
Roger Williams U (RI)
Rose-Hulman Inst of Technology (IN)
Rowan U (NJ)
Royal Military Coll of Canada (ON, Canada)
Rutgers U–New Brunswick (NJ)
Saint Louis U (MO)
Saint Louis U–Madrid Campus (Spain)
Saint Martin's U (WA)
San Diego State U (CA)
San Francisco State U (CA)
Santa Clara U (CA)
Seattle U (WA)
South Carolina State U (SC)
South Dakota School of Mines and Technology (SD)
South Dakota State U (SD)
Southern Illinois U Carbondale (IL)
Southern Illinois U Edwardsville (IL)
Southern Methodist U (TX)
Stanford U (CA)
State U of New York Polytechnic Inst (NY)
Stevens Inst of Technology (NJ)
Stony Brook U, State U of New York (NY)
Syracuse U (NY)
Tarleton State U (TX)
Temple U (PA)
Tennessee State U (TN)
Texas A&M U (TX)
Texas A&M U–Kingsville (TX)
Texas Tech U (TX)
Trine U (IN)
Tufts U (MA)
United States Air Force Acad (CO)
United States Coast Guard Acad (CT)
United States Military Acad (NY)
Université de Sherbrooke (QC, Canada)
U at Buffalo, the State U of New York (NY)
The U of Akron (OH)
The U of Alabama (AL)
The U of Alabama at Birmingham (AL)
The U of Alabama in Huntsville (AL)
U of Alaska Fairbanks (AK)
The U of Arizona (AZ)
U of Arkansas (AR)
U of California, Davis (CA)
U of California, Irvine (CA)
U of California, Los Angeles (CA)
U of Central Florida (FL)
U of Cincinnati (OH)
U of Colorado Boulder (CO)
U of Colorado Denver (CO)
U of Dayton (OH)
U of Delaware (DE)
U of Detroit Mercy (MI)
U of Evansville (IN)
U of Florida (FL)
U of Georgia (GA)
U of Hartford (CT)
U of Hawaii at Manoa (HI)
U of Houston (TX)
U of Idaho (ID)
U of Illinois at Chicago (IL)
The U of Kansas (KS)
U of Kentucky (KY)
U of Louisville (KY)
U of Maine (ME)
U of Maryland, Coll Park (MD)
U of Massachusetts Amherst (MA)
U of Massachusetts Dartmouth (MA)
U of Massachusetts Lowell (MA)
U of Miami (FL)
U of Michigan (MI)
U of Minnesota, Duluth (MN)
U of Minnesota, Twin Cities Campus (MN)
U of Missouri–Kansas City (MO)
U of Missouri–St. Louis (MO)
U of Mount Union (OH)
U of Nevada, Las Vegas (NV)

U of Nevada, Reno (NV)
U of New Hampshire (NH)
U of New Haven (CT)
U of New Orleans (LA)
The U of North Carolina at Charlotte (NC)
U of North Dakota (ND)
U of North Florida (FL)
U of Notre Dame (IN)
U of Oklahoma (OK)
U of Pittsburgh (PA)
U of Pittsburgh at Johnstown (PA)
U of Rhode Island (RI)
U of Saskatchewan (SK, Canada)
U of South Alabama (AL)
U of South Carolina (SC)
U of Southern California (CA)
U of South Florida (FL)
The U of Tennessee (TN)
The U of Tennessee at Chattanooga (TN)
The U of Texas at Austin (TX)
The U of Texas at El Paso (TX)
The U of Texas at San Antonio (TX)
The U of Texas Rio Grande Valley (TX)
U of the Pacific (CA)
The U of Toledo (OH)
U of Toronto (ON, Canada)
U of Utah (UT)
U of Vermont (VT)
U of Virginia (VA)
U of Washington (WA)
U of Waterloo (ON, Canada)
U of Windsor (ON, Canada)
U of Wisconsin–Madison (WI)
U of Wisconsin–Milwaukee (WI)
U of Wisconsin–Platteville (WI)
Ursinus Coll (PA)
Utah State U (UT)
Valparaiso U (IN)
Vanderbilt U (TN)
Villanova U (PA)
Virginia Military Inst (VA)
Virginia Polytechnic Inst and State U (VA)
Walla Walla U (WA)
Washington State U (WA)
Washington State U–Tri-Cities (WA)
Wayne State U (MI)
Wentworth Inst of Technology (MA)
Western Kentucky U (KY)
Western Michigan U (MI)
Western New England U (MA)
West Texas A&M U (TX)
West Virginia U (WV)
West Virginia U Inst of Technology (WV)
Widener U (PA)
William Jewell Coll (MO)
Worcester Polytechnic Inst (MA)
Youngstown State U (OH)

CIVIL ENGINEERING RELATED

California Polytechnic State U, San Luis Obispo (CA)
Embry-Riddle Aeronautical U–Daytona (FL)
U of Southern California (CA)

CIVIL ENGINEERING TECHNOLOGY

Bluefield State Coll (WV)
Central Connecticut State U (CT)
Fairleigh Dickinson U, Metropolitan Campus (NJ)
Georgia Southern U (GA)
Idaho State U (ID)
Indiana State U (IN)
Kennesaw State U (GA)
Lincoln U (MO)
Metropolitan State U of Denver (CO)
Montana State U–Northern (MT)
Murray State U (KY)
Oklahoma State U Inst of Technology (OK)
Pennsylvania Coll of Technology (PA)
Point Park U (PA)
Rochester Inst of Technology (NY)
South Carolina State U (SC)
State U of New York Coll of Technology at Canton (NY)
State U of New York Polytechnic Inst (NY)
Temple U (PA)
United States Military Acad (NY)
U of Houston–Downtown (TX)
U of Maine (ME)
U of Massachusetts Lowell (MA)
The U of North Carolina at Charlotte (NC)
Youngstown State U (OH)

CLASSICAL, ANCIENT MEDITERRANEAN AND NEAR EASTERN STUDIES AND ARCHAEOLOGY

Bard Coll (NY)
Bowdoin Coll (ME)
Butler U (IN)
Calvin Coll (MI)
Colgate U (NY)
Columbia U (NY)
Emory U (GA)
Hampshire Coll (MA)
Hanover Coll (IN)
Kalamazoo Coll (MI)
Lycoming Coll (PA)
Randolph-Macon Coll (VA)
Saint Anselm Coll (NH)
Swarthmore Coll (PA)
Syracuse U (NY)
U of California, Davis (CA)
U of California, Irvine (CA)
U of California, Los Angeles (CA)
U of Georgia (GA)
U of Illinois at Chicago (IL)
U of Michigan (MI)
U of St. Thomas (MN)
U of Toronto (ON, Canada)

CLASSICS AND CLASSICAL LANGUAGES

Agnes Scott Coll (GA)
Amherst Coll (MA)
Asbury U (KY)
Assumption Coll (MA)
Augustana Coll (IL)
Augustana U (SD)
Austin Coll (TX)
Ball State U (IN)
Barnard Coll (NY)
Baylor U (TX)
Beloit Coll (WI)
Binghamton U, State U of New York (NY)
Bishop's U (QC, Canada)
Boston Coll (MA)
Boston U (MA)
Bowdoin Coll (ME)
Bowling Green State U (OH)
Brandeis U (MA)
Brooklyn Coll of the City U of New York (NY)
Bryn Mawr Coll (PA)
Bucknell U (PA)
Carleton Coll (MN)
Carroll Coll (MT)
Carthage Coll (WI)
Case Western Reserve U (OH)
The Catholic U of America (DC)
Centre Coll (KY)
Christendom Coll (VA)
Christopher Newport U (VA)
Claremont McKenna Coll (CA)
Clark U (MA)
Colby Coll (ME)
Colgate U (NY)
Coll of Charleston (SC)
Coll of Saint Benedict (MN)
Coll of the Holy Cross (MA)
The Coll of William and Mary (VA)
The Coll of Wooster (OH)
The Colorado Coll (CO)
Columbia U (NY)
Columbia U, School of General Studies (NY)
Concordia U (QC, Canada)
Connecticut Coll (CT)
Cornell Coll (IA)
Cornell U (NY)
Creighton U (NE)
Dalhousie U (NS, Canada)
Dartmouth Coll (NH)
Davidson Coll (NC)
Denison U (OH)
DePauw U (IN)
Dickinson Coll (PA)
Drew U (NJ)
Duquesne U (PA)
Earlham Coll (IN)
Emory U (GA)
The Evergreen State Coll (WA)
Fordham U (NY)
Franciscan U of Steubenville (OH)
Franklin & Marshall Coll (PA)
Furman U (SC)
Georgetown U (DC)
The George Washington U (DC)
Gettysburg Coll (PA)
Gonzaga U (WA)
Grand Valley State U (MI)
Grinnell Coll (IA)
Hamilton Coll (NY)
Hampden-Sydney Coll (VA)
Hanover Coll (IN)
Harvard U (MA)
Haverford Coll (PA)
Hendrix Coll (AR)
Hillsdale Coll (MI)
Hobart and William Smith Colls (NY)
Hofstra U (NY)
Hollins U (VA)
Hope Coll (MI)
Houston Baptist U (TX)
Hunter Coll of the City U of New York (NY)
Illinois Wesleyan U (IL)
Indiana U Bloomington (IN)
John Carroll U (OH)
Johns Hopkins U (MD)
Kenyon Coll (OH)
Knox Coll (IL)
Lawrence U (WI)
Lehigh U (PA)
Lehman Coll of the City U of New York (NY)
Lewis & Clark Coll (OR)
Loyola U Chicago (IL)
Loyola U Maryland (MD)
Luther Coll (IA)
Macalester Coll (MN)
Manhattan Coll (NY)
McMaster U (ON, Canada)
Mercer U, Macon (GA)
Miami U (OH)
Middlebury Coll (VT)
Millsaps Coll (MS)
Monmouth Coll (IL)
Montclair State U (NJ)
Mount Allison U (NB, Canada)
Mount Holyoke Coll (MA)
North Central Coll (IL)
Northwestern U (IL)
Oberlin Coll (OH)
The Ohio State U (OH)
Ohio U (OH)
Ohio Wesleyan U (OH)
Pacific Lutheran U (WA)
Penn State Abington (PA)
Penn State Altoona (PA)
Penn State Beaver (PA)
Penn State Berks (PA)
Penn State Brandywine (PA)
Penn State DuBois (PA)
Penn State Erie, The Behrend Coll (PA)
Penn State Fayette, The Eberly Campus (PA)
Penn State Greater Allegheny (PA)
Penn State Hazleton (PA)
Penn State Lehigh Valley (PA)
Penn State Mont Alto (PA)
Penn State New Kensington (PA)
Penn State Schuylkill (PA)
Penn State Shenango (PA)
Penn State U Park (PA)
Penn State Wilkes-Barre (PA)
Penn State Worthington Scranton (PA)
Penn State York (PA)
Pitzer Coll (CA)
Pomona Coll (CA)
Princeton U (NJ)
Queens Coll of the City U of New York (NY)
Randolph Coll (VA)
Randolph-Macon Coll (VA)
Reed Coll (OR)
Rhodes Coll (TN)
Rice U (TX)
Rockford U (IL)
Rutgers U–Newark (NJ)
Rutgers U–New Brunswick (NJ)
Saint Anselm Coll (NH)
St. Bonaventure U (NY)
Saint John's U (MN)
Saint Louis U (MO)
Saint Louis U–Madrid Campus (Spain)
Saint Michael's Coll (VT)
St. Olaf Coll (MN)
Saint Peter's U (NJ)
Samford U (AL)
San Diego State U (CA)
San Francisco State U (CA)
Santa Clara U (CA)
Sarah Lawrence Coll (NY)
Scripps Coll (CA)
Sewanee: The U of the South (TN)
Siena Coll (NY)
Skidmore Coll (NY)
Smith Coll (MA)
Southwestern U (TX)
Stanford U (CA)
Swarthmore Coll (PA)
Sweet Briar Coll (VA)
Syracuse U (NY)
Temple U (PA)
Texas A&M U (TX)
Texas Tech U (TX)
Transylvania U (KY)
Trent U (ON, Canada)
Trinity U (TX)
Truman State U (MO)
Tufts U (MA)
Tulane U (LA)
Union Coll (NY)
Université de Montréal (QC, Canada)
U at Buffalo, the State U of New York (NY)
The U of Akron (OH)
The U of Arizona (AZ)
U of Arkansas (AR)
U of California, Irvine (CA)
U of California, San Diego (CA)
U of California, Santa Barbara (CA)
U of Chicago (IL)
U of Cincinnati (OH)
U of Colorado Boulder (CO)
U of Evansville (IN)
U of Florida (FL)
U of Georgia (GA)
U of Guelph (ON, Canada)
U of Hawaii at Manoa (HI)
U of Illinois at Chicago (IL)
The U of Kansas (KS)
U of Kentucky (KY)
U of King's Coll (NS, Canada)
U of Maryland, Coll Park (MD)
U of Mary Washington (VA)
U of Massachusetts Amherst (MA)
U of Massachusetts Boston (MA)
U of Miami (FL)
U of Michigan (MI)
U of Minnesota, Twin Cities Campus (MN)
U of New Hampshire (NH)
U of North Carolina at Asheville (NC)
The U of North Carolina at Chapel Hill (NC)
The U of North Carolina at Greensboro (NC)
U of North Dakota (ND)
U of Notre Dame (IN)
U of Oklahoma (OK)
U of Oregon (OR)
U of Pennsylvania (PA)
U of Pittsburgh (PA)
U of Puget Sound (WA)
U of Regina (SK, Canada)
U of Rhode Island (RI)
U of Rochester (NY)
U of St. Thomas (MN)
The U of Scranton (PA)
U of South Carolina (SC)
U of Southern California (CA)
U of South Florida (FL)
The U of Tennessee (TN)
The U of Texas at Austin (TX)
U of the Pacific (CA)
U of Toronto (ON, Canada)
U of Utah (UT)
U of Vermont (VT)
U of Virginia (VA)
U of Washington (WA)
U of Waterloo (ON, Canada)
U of Windsor (ON, Canada)
U of Wisconsin–Madison (WI)
U of Wisconsin–Milwaukee (WI)
Valparaiso U (IN)
Vanderbilt U (TN)
Vassar Coll (NY)
Villanova U (PA)
Virginia Wesleyan Coll (VA)
Wabash Coll (IN)
Wake Forest U (NC)
Washington and Lee U (VA)
Washington State U (WA)
Washington U in St. Louis (MO)
Wayne State U (MI)
Wesleyan U (CT)
Wheaton Coll (MA)
Whitman Coll (WA)
Willamette U (OR)
Williams Coll (MA)
Wright State U (OH)

CLASSICS AND CLASSICAL LANGUAGES RELATED

Austin Coll (TX)
California State U, Long Beach (CA)
Columbia U, School of General Studies (NY)
Eckerd Coll (FL)
Elmira Coll (NY)
Gonzaga U (WA)
Lawrence U (WI)
Lee U (TN)
Loyola U New Orleans (LA)
New Coll of Florida (FL)
Ohio U (OH)
Rutgers U–Newark (NJ)
Tulane U (LA)
U of California, Los Angeles (CA)
Wheaton Coll (IL)
Wheaton Coll (MA)

CLINICAL, COUNSELING AND APPLIED PSYCHOLOGY RELATED

Goddard Coll (VT)
Grace Coll (IN)
Lincoln U (PA)

CLINICAL LABORATORY SCIENCE/MEDICAL TECHNOLOGY

Anderson U (IN)
Andrews U (MI)
Arkansas Tech U (AR)
Armstrong State U (GA)
Auburn U (AL)
Augustana U (SD)
Augusta U (GA)
Austin Peay State U (TN)
Ball State U (IN)
Barry U (FL)
Baylor U (TX)
Bellarmine U (KY)
Bemidji State U (MN)
Bethune-Cookman U (FL)
Blackburn Coll (IL)
Blue Mountain Coll (MS)
Bowling Green State U (OH)
Bradley U (IL)
Brescia U (KY)
Brigham Young U (UT)
Caldwell U (NJ)
California State U, Dominguez Hills (CA)
Campbellsville U (KY)
Canisius Coll (NY)
The Catholic U of America (DC)
The Coll at Brockport, State U of New York (NY)
Coll of Saint Elizabeth (NJ)
Coll of Saint Mary (NE)
The Coll of Saint Rose (NY)
Coll of Staten Island of the City U of New York (NY)
Coll of the Ozarks (MO)
Dixie State U (UT)
East Carolina U (NC)
East Central U (OK)
Eastern Illinois U (IL)
Eastern Mennonite U (VA)
Eastern Michigan U (MI)
East Stroudsburg U of Pennsylvania (PA)
Elmira Coll (NY)
Evangel U (MO)
Fairleigh Dickinson U, Coll at Florham (NJ)
Fairleigh Dickinson U, Metropolitan Campus (NJ)
Farmingdale State Coll (NY)
Ferris State U (MI)
Florida Gulf Coast U (FL)
Gannon U (PA)

The George Washington U (DC)
Georgian Court U (NJ)
Graceland U (IA)
Grand Valley State U (MI)
Hartwick Coll (NY)
Henderson State U (AR)
Holy Family U (PA)
Houghton Coll (NY)
Idaho State U (ID)
Illinois Coll (IL)
Illinois State U (IL)
Indiana State U (IN)
Indiana U of Pennsylvania (PA)
Indiana U–Purdue U Indianapolis (IN)
Indiana U South Bend (IN)
Indiana U Southeast (IN)
Inter American U of Puerto Rico, Metropolitan Campus (PR)
Inter American U of Puerto Rico, San Germán Campus (PR)
Jacksonville U (FL)
Kansas State U (KS)
Kean U (NJ)
Kent State U (OH)
Keuka Coll (NY)
King's Coll (PA)
King U (TN)
Lebanon Valley Coll (PA)
Lincoln U (MO)
Louisiana Coll (LA)
Louisiana State U at Alexandria (LA)
Louisiana State U Health Sciences Center (LA)
Louisiana Tech U (LA)
Lubbock Christian U (TX)
Malone U (OH)
Manchester U (IN)
Mansfield U of Pennsylvania (PA)
Marian U (IN)
Marist Coll (NY)
Marshall U (WV)
Mary Baldwin U (VA)
Maryville U of Saint Louis (MO)
Marywood U (PA)
McNeese State U (LA)
Mercy Coll (NY)
Miami U (OH)
Michigan State U (MI)
Michigan Technological U (MI)
Minnesota State U Mankato (MN)
Minnesota State U Moorhead (MN)
Minot State U (ND)
Misericordia U (PA)
Mississippi State U (MS)
Missouri State U (MO)
Missouri Western State U (MO)
Monmouth U (NJ)
Morningside Coll (IA)
Mount Marty Coll (SD)
Mount Mercy U (IA)
Mount Vernon Nazarene U (OH)
Muskingum U (OH)
National U (CA)
Nazareth Coll of Rochester (NY)
North Dakota State U (ND)
Northeastern State U (OK)
Northern Illinois U (IL)
Northern State U (SD)
Northwestern Coll (IA)
Northwest Missouri State U (MO)
The Ohio State U (OH)
Oklahoma Christian U (OK)
Old Dominion U (VA)
Oral Roberts U (OK)
Our Lady of the Lake Coll (LA)
Pittsburg State U (KS)
Purdue U (IN)
Ramapo Coll of New Jersey (NJ)
Roberts Wesleyan Coll (NY)
Rochester Inst of Technology (NY)
Rockhurst U (MO)
Rutgers U–Camden (NJ)
Rutgers U–Newark (NJ)
Rutgers U–New Brunswick (NJ)
Saginaw Valley State U (MI)
St. Catherine U (MN)
St. Cloud State U (MN)
Saint Francis U (PA)
St. John's U (NY)
St. Joseph's Coll, Long Island Campus (NY)
St. Joseph's Coll, New York (NY)
Saint Louis U (MO)
Saint Mary-of-the-Woods Coll (IN)
Saint Mary's U of Minnesota (MN)
St. Thomas Aquinas Coll (NY)
Salisbury U (MD)
Salve Regina U (RI)
Sam Houston State U (TX)
Seton Hill U (PA)
South Dakota State U (SD)
Southeast Missouri State U (MO)
Southern Arkansas U–Magnolia (AR)
Southwest Baptist U (MO)
Southwestern Adventist U (TX)
Spencerian Coll (KY)
State U of New York at Fredonia (NY)
State U of New York at Plattsburgh (NY)
Stevenson U (MD)
Stony Brook U, State U of New York (NY)
Tarleton State U (TX)
Tennessee State U (TN)
Texas State U (TX)
Texas Woman's U (TX)
Thomas More Coll (KY)
Union Coll (NE)
Union U (TN)
U at Buffalo, the State U of New York (NY)
The U of Akron (OH)
The U of Alabama at Birmingham (AL)
U of Arkansas for Medical Sciences (AR)
U of Bridgeport (CT)
U of Central Arkansas (AR)
U of Central Florida (FL)
U of Central Missouri (MO)
U of Cincinnati (OH)
U of Delaware (DE)
U of Evansville (IN)
The U of Findlay (OH)
U of Hartford (CT)
U of Hawaii at Manoa (HI)
U of Illinois at Springfield (IL)
U of Indianapolis (IN)
U of Jamestown (ND)
The U of Kansas (KS)
U of Kentucky (KY)
U of Louisiana at Monroe (LA)
U of Maine (ME)
U of Mary Hardin-Baylor (TX)
U of Massachusetts Dartmouth (MA)
U of Michigan–Flint (MI)
U of Mount Union (OH)
U of New England (ME)
The U of North Carolina at Chapel Hill (NC)
The U of North Carolina at Greensboro (NC)
U of North Dakota (ND)
U of North Texas (TX)
U of Regina (SK, Canada)
U of Rhode Island (RI)
U of St. Francis (IL)
U of Saint Francis (IN)
The U of South Dakota (SD)
U of Southern Mississippi (MS)
U of South Florida (FL)
The U of Tennessee (TN)
The U of Texas at Austin (TX)
The U of Texas at El Paso (TX)
The U of Texas Rio Grande Valley (TX)
The U of Toledo (OH)
U of Utah (UT)
U of Vermont (VT)
The U of Virginia's Coll at Wise (VA)
U of Washington (WA)
U of Wisconsin–La Crosse (WI)
U of Wisconsin–Milwaukee (WI)
U of Wisconsin–Stevens Point (WI)
Utah State U (UT)
Virginia Commonwealth U (VA)
Wake Forest U (NC)
Walla Walla U (WA)
Walsh U (OH)
Wartburg Coll (IA)
Washburn U (KS)
Wayne State U (MI)
Weber State U (UT)
Western Connecticut State U (CT)
Western Illinois U (IL)
Western Kentucky U (KY)
West Virginia U (WV)
Wichita State U (KS)
Wilkes U (PA)
Winona State U (MN)
Wright State U (OH)
Wright State U–Lake Campus (OH)
York Coll of Pennsylvania (PA)
York Coll of the City U of New York (NY)
Youngstown State U (OH)

CLINICAL/MEDICAL LABORATORY SCIENCE AND ALLIED PROFESSIONS RELATED

Allen Coll (IA)
Auburn U (AL)
Blackburn Coll (IL)
Bloomfield Coll (NJ)
The Coll of Idaho (ID)
Gwynedd Mercy U (PA)
Hunter Coll of the City U of New York (NY)
Misericordia U (PA)
Rutgers U–Newark (NJ)
Rutgers U–New Brunswick (NJ)
Saint Louis U (MO)
U of Massachusetts Lowell (MA)
U of Minnesota, Twin Cities Campus (MN)

CLINICAL/MEDICAL LABORATORY TECHNOLOGY

American U of Beirut (Lebanon)
Auburn U (AL)
Auburn U at Montgomery (AL)
Barry U (FL)
Bismarck State Coll (ND)
Boston U (MA)
California State U, East Bay (CA)
Clarion U of Pennsylvania (PA)
Northern State U (SD)
Penn State DuBois (PA)
Rhode Island Coll (RI)
St. Thomas Aquinas Coll (NY)
Sonoma State U (CA)
U of Missouri–Kansas City (MO)
U of Science and Arts of Oklahoma (OK)
Viterbo U (WI)
Weber State U (UT)
York Coll of the City U of New York (NY)

CLINICAL/MEDICAL SOCIAL WORK

New Mexico Highlands U (NM)

CLINICAL NURSE SPECIALIST

LeTourneau U (TX)
The U of Texas at Austin (TX)

CLINICAL NUTRITION

Kent State U (OH)
La Salle U (PA)
Life U (GA)
Messiah Coll (PA)
Southern Illinois U Edwardsville (IL)
U of North Dakota (ND)

CLINICAL PSYCHOLOGY

Augsburg Coll (MN)
Biola U (CA)
Eastern Nazarene Coll (MA)
Faulkner U (AL)
Goddard Coll (VT)
Redeemer U Coll (ON, Canada)
Sam Houston State U (TX)
Simon Fraser U (BC, Canada)
Tennessee State U (TN)
Tufts U (MA)
U of Mary Hardin-Baylor (TX)
The U of Texas at Austin (TX)
U of Windsor (ON, Canada)
Western State Colorado U (CO)

COGNITIVE PSYCHOLOGY AND PSYCHOLINGUISTICS

Dartmouth Coll (NH)
Emory U (GA)
Fitchburg State U (MA)
Lawrence U (WI)
Northwestern U (IL)
Scripps Coll (CA)
State U of New York at Oswego (NY)
Tulane U (LA)
U of California, San Diego (CA)
Vassar Coll (NY)
Washington U in St. Louis (MO)
Welch Coll (TN)

COGNITIVE SCIENCE

California State U, Fresno (CA)
California State U, Stanislaus (CA)
Canisius Coll (NY)
Carnegie Mellon U (PA)
Case Western Reserve U (OH)
George Fox U (OR)
Hampshire Coll (MA)
Indiana U Bloomington (IN)
Johns Hopkins U (MD)
Lawrence U (WI)
Lehigh U (PA)
Massachusetts Inst of Technology (MA)
Millsaps Coll (MS)
Occidental Coll (CA)
Pomona Coll (CA)
Rensselaer Polytechnic Inst (NY)
Sarah Lawrence Coll (NY)
Simmons Coll (MA)
Simon Fraser U (BC, Canada)
State U of New York at Oswego (NY)
Susquehanna U (PA)
United States Military Acad (NY)
Université de Montréal (QC, Canada)
U of California, Irvine (CA)
U of California, Los Angeles (CA)
U of Delaware (DE)
U of Evansville (IN)
U of Georgia (GA)
U of Michigan (MI)
U of Pennsylvania (PA)
U of Richmond (VA)
U of Southern California (CA)
The U of Texas at Dallas (TX)
Vanderbilt U (TN)
Virginia Polytechnic Inst and State U (VA)

COLLEGE STUDENT COUNSELING AND PERSONNEL SERVICES

Bowling Green State U (OH)
U of Georgia (GA)

COMMERCIAL AND ADVERTISING ART

Acad of Art U (CA)
American Acad of Art (IL)
Arcadia U (PA)
Ashland U (OH)
Bemidji State U (MN)
Biola U (CA)
Black Hills State U (SD)
Boise State U (ID)
Bowling Green State U (OH)
Buena Vista U (IA)
Buffalo State Coll, State U of New York (NY)
California Coll of the Arts (CA)
California State U, East Bay (CA)
California State U, Fresno (CA)
California State U, Long Beach (CA)
California U of Pennsylvania (PA)
Carson-Newman U (TN)
Centenary U (NJ)
Clark U (MA)
The Coll of New Jersey (NJ)
The Coll of Saint Rose (NY)
The Coll of Westchester (NY)
Columbia Coll Chicago (IL)
Columbus Coll of Art & Design (OH)
Concordia U Chicago (IL)
Concordia U Wisconsin (WI)
Dominican U (IL)
Drake U (IA)
Fashion Inst of Technology (NY)
Franklin Pierce U (NH)
Graceland U (IA)
Hampton U (VA)
Iowa State U of Science and Technology (IA)
Jacksonville U (FL)
Keene State Coll (NH)
Kent State U (OH)
Kutztown U of Pennsylvania (PA)
Laguna Coll of Art & Design (CA)
Lewis U (IL)
Lipscomb U (TN)
Louisiana Coll (LA)
Louisiana Tech U (LA)
Lycoming Coll (PA)
Marietta Coll (OH)
Marymount Manhattan Coll (NY)
Massachusetts Coll of Art and Design (MA)
Mercy Coll (NY)
Miami U (OH)
Millikin U (IL)
Minneapolis Coll of Art and Design (MN)
Minnesota State U Mankato (MN)
Minnesota State U Moorhead (MN)
Montana State U–Northern (MT)
New York City Coll of Technology of the City U of New York (NY)
New York Inst of Technology (NY)
Northern Kentucky U (KY)
Oklahoma Christian U (OK)
O'More Coll of Design (TN)
Oral Roberts U (OK)
Pennsylvania Coll of Art & Design (PA)
Pennsylvania Coll of Technology (PA)
Portland State U (OR)
Pratt Inst (NY)
Purchase Coll, State U of New York (NY)
Rochester Inst of Technology (NY)
Rutgers U–New Brunswick (NJ)
St. Norbert Coll (WI)
St. Thomas Aquinas Coll (NY)
Sam Houston State U (TX)
Seattle U (WA)
Seton Hill U (PA)
Southeastern U (FL)
Southwest Baptist U (MO)
State U of New York at Fredonia (NY)
State U of New York at Oswego (NY)
Syracuse U (NY)
U of Advancing Technology (AZ)
U of Central Missouri (MO)
U of Cincinnati (OH)
U of Indianapolis (IN)
U of Minnesota, Duluth (MN)
U of New Haven (CT)
U of North Georgia (GA)
U of San Francisco (CA)
The U of Tennessee (TN)
The U of Texas at El Paso (TX)
The U of the Arts (PA)
U of the Pacific (CA)
U of Wisconsin–Stevens Point (WI)
Upper Iowa U (IA)
Walla Walla U (WA)
Wartburg Coll (IA)
Washington U in St. Louis (MO)
Waynesburg U (PA)
Weber State U (UT)
Woodbury U (CA)
York Coll of Pennsylvania (PA)

COMMERCIAL PHOTOGRAPHY

Appalachian State U (NC)
Fashion Inst of Technology (NY)
Nossi Coll of Art (TN)
Rochester Inst of Technology (NY)

COMMUNICATION

Albion Coll (MI)
Alvernia U (PA)
Arizona Christian U (AZ)
Asbury U (KY)
Ashland U (OH)
Averett U (VA)
Bethany Lutheran Coll (MN)
Bethel U (MN)
Biola U (CA)
Blackburn Coll (IL)
Boston Coll (MA)
Boston U (MA)
Bradley U (IL)
Brigham Young U–Idaho (ID)
California State U, Northridge (CA)
Carlow U (PA)
Cazenovia Coll (NY)
Centenary Coll of Louisiana (LA)
Centenary U (NJ)
Central Washington U (WA)
Cleveland State U (OH)
The Coll of New Jersey (NJ)
Coll of the Ozarks (MO)
Colorado Christian U (CO)
Concordia Coll (MN)
Concordia U Irvine (CA)
Cornell U (NY)
Dallas Baptist U (TX)

DEREE - The American Coll of Greece (Greece)
DeSales U (PA)
Dominican Coll (NY)
Eastern Illinois U (IL)
Edgewood Coll (WI)
Florida Coll (FL)
Florida Inst of Technology (FL)
Fordham U (NY)
Franciscan U of Steubenville (OH)
Frostburg State U (MD)
Geneva Coll (PA)
Gonzaga U (WA)
Goshen Coll (IN)
Grace Coll (IN)
Granite State Coll (NH)
Hannibal-LaGrange U (MO)
Hardin-Simmons U (TX)
Hawai`i Pacific U (HI)
Henderson State U (AR)
High Point U (NC)
Hiram Coll (OH)
Holy Cross Coll (IN)
Huntingdon Coll (AL)
Huntington U (IN)
Inter American U of Puerto Rico, Ponce Campus (PR)
Jacksonville State U (AL)
John Brown U (AR)
Kansas Wesleyan U (KS)
King U (TN)
Kutztown U of Pennsylvania (PA)
Lake Forest Coll (IL)
Lamar U (TX)
La Salle U (PA)
Lasell Coll (MA)
Le Moyne Coll (NY)
Lenoir-Rhyne U (NC)
Liberty U (VA)
Limestone Coll (SC)
Lincoln Christian U (IL)
Lynn U (FL)
Marist Coll (NY)
Marymount Manhattan Coll (NY)
Marymount U (VA)
Massachusetts Coll of Liberal Arts (MA)
Milligan Coll (TN)
Misericordia U (PA)
National Louis U (IL)
New Mexico State U (NM)
New York Inst of Technology (NY)
Northwest Christian U (OR)
Northwest Missouri State U (MO)
Nyack Coll (NY)
Oakland City U (IN)
Oklahoma City U (OK)
Paine Coll (GA)
Pepperdine U, Malibu (CA)
Portland State U (OR)
Purdue U (IN)
Randolph-Macon Coll (VA)
Regent U (VA)
Regis Coll (MA)
Roanoke Coll (VA)
Rowan U (NJ)
Sacred Heart U (CT)
Saint Anselm Coll (NH)
St. John Fisher Coll (NY)
Saint Joseph's U (PA)
Saint Louis U (MO)
Saint Louis U–Madrid Campus (Spain)
Saint Martin's U (WA)
Saint Mary's Coll (IN)
Simpson Coll (IA)
Southeastern U (FL)
Southwestern Coll (KS)
Spalding U (KY)
Spring Hill Coll (AL)
Susquehanna U (PA)
Tarleton State U (TX)
Tennessee Wesleyan U (TN)
Texas A&M U (TX)
Texas A&M U–Kingsville (TX)
Thomas More Coll (KY)
Toccoa Falls Coll (GA)
Towson U (MD)
Trinity U (TX)
U of California, Santa Barbara (CA)
U of Colorado Colorado Springs (CO)
U of Delaware (DE)
U of Evansville (IN)
U of Houston–Clear Lake (TX)
U of Houston–Downtown (TX)
U of Illinois at Chicago (IL)
U of Illinois at Springfield (IL)
U of Maine (ME)
U of Mary Hardin-Baylor (TX)
U of Massachusetts Amherst (MA)
U of Massachusetts Boston (MA)
U of Michigan–Flint (MI)
U of Minnesota, Crookston (MN)
U of Mobile (AL)
U of Mount Union (OH)
U of North Dakota (ND)
U of Saint Francis (IN)
U of San Diego (CA)
The U of Tampa (FL)
The U of Tennessee at Chattanooga (TN)
The U of Texas at San Antonio (TX)
The U of Texas of the Permian Basin (TX)
U of Utah (UT)
U of Wisconsin–Eau Claire (WI)
U of Wisconsin–Green Bay (WI)
U of Wisconsin–Stevens Point (WI)
U of Wisconsin–Whitewater (WI)
Washington State U–Vancouver (WA)
Wesleyan Coll (GA)
Westminster Coll (PA)
Whitworth U (WA)
Wichita State U (KS)
William Peace U (NC)
William Penn U (IA)
Wingate U (NC)
Woodbury U (CA)
Youngstown State U (OH)

COMMUNICATION AND JOURNALISM RELATED

The American U in Dubai (United Arab Emirates)
Auburn U (AL)
Augustana Coll (IL)
Berry Coll (GA)
Bowling Green State U (OH)
Brigham Young U (UT)
California Lutheran U (CA)
Carlow U (PA)
Chestnut Hill Coll (PA)
Clarke U (IA)
Concordia U (QC, Canada)
Dalhousie U (NS, Canada)
Dominican Coll (NY)
Dominican U of California (CA)
Drexel U (PA)
Eastern Nazarene Coll (MA)
Endicott Coll (MA)
Farmingdale State Coll (NY)
Florida Inst of Technology (FL)
Friends U (KS)
Hannibal-LaGrange U (MO)
Immaculata U (PA)
Lake Erie Coll (OH)
Lehman Coll of the City U of New York (NY)
Madonna U (MI)
Malone U (OH)
Manhattanville Coll (NY)
Mary Baldwin U (VA)
McMaster U (ON, Canada)
Mercer U, Macon (GA)
Merrimack Coll (MA)
Minot State U (ND)
Morehead State U (KY)
Newberry Coll (SC)
The Ohio State U (OH)
Oklahoma Christian U (OK)
Our Lady of the Lake U of San Antonio (TX)
Penn State Abington (PA)
Penn State Altoona (PA)
Penn State Beaver (PA)
Penn State Berks (PA)
Penn State Brandywine (PA)
Penn State DuBois (PA)
Penn State Erie, The Behrend Coll (PA)
Penn State Fayette, The Eberly Campus (PA)
Penn State Greater Allegheny (PA)
Penn State Hazleton (PA)
Penn State Lehigh Valley (PA)
Penn State Mont Alto (PA)
Penn State New Kensington (PA)
Penn State Schuylkill (PA)
Penn State Shenango (PA)
Penn State U Park (PA)
Penn State Wilkes-Barre (PA)
Penn State Worthington Scranton (PA)
Penn State York (PA)
Point Park U (PA)
Quinnipiac U (CT)
Rosemont Coll (PA)
Saint Mary's Coll of California (CA)
Southeastern Oklahoma State U (OK)
State U of New York Polytechnic Inst (NY)
Sterling Coll (KS)
Trevecca Nazarene U (TN)
U of Miami (FL)
U of Minnesota, Duluth (MN)
U of Minnesota, Twin Cities Campus (MN)
U of Wisconsin–Green Bay (WI)
Virginia Polytechnic Inst and State U (VA)
Washington U in St. Louis (MO)
Webster U (MO)
West Virginia U (WV)

COMMUNICATION AND MEDIA RELATED

Acad of Art U (CA)
Adelphi U (NY)
Albion Coll (MI)
American U of Beirut (Lebanon)
Arcadia U (PA)
Ashland U (OH)
Auburn U (AL)
Austin Coll (TX)
Belmont U (TN)
Bennington Coll (VT)
Biola U (CA)
Butler U (IN)
Cameron U (OK)
Canisius Coll (NY)
Carthage Coll (WI)
The Coll of Saint Rose (NY)
Columbia Intl U (SC)
Concordia U (QC, Canada)
Curry Coll (MA)
DeSales U (PA)
Eastern Mennonite U (VA)
Elon U (NC)
Emory U (GA)
Fairleigh Dickinson U, Metropolitan Campus (NJ)
Florida State U (FL)
Gardner-Webb U (NC)
Georgetown Coll (KY)
Granite State Coll (NH)
Greenville Coll (IL)
Hood Coll (MD)
Houghton Coll (NY)
Hult Intl Business School (United Kingdom)
Judson U (IL)
Kennesaw State U (GA)
King's Coll (PA)
Lane Coll (TN)
La Roche Coll (PA)
Lasell Coll (MA)
Lees-McRae Coll (NC)
Loyola U Chicago (IL)
Lycoming Coll (PA)
Lynn U (FL)
Marymount Manhattan Coll (NY)
Milligan Coll (TN)
Missouri Baptist U (MO)
Molloy Coll (NY)
Montclair State U (NJ)
Morehead State U (KY)
Neumann U (PA)
Nevada State Coll (NV)
Newberry Coll (SC)
Northeastern Illinois U (IL)
Northeastern U (MA)
Northwestern U (IL)
Oklahoma City U (OK)
Pace U (NY)
Pace U, Pleasantville Campus (NY)
Penn State Erie, The Behrend Coll (PA)
Rochester Inst of Technology (NY)
Roger Williams U (RI)
Rollins Coll (FL)
St. Thomas U (FL)
Salve Regina U (RI)
Southern Methodist U (TX)
Southwestern Coll (KS)
Stanford U (CA)
Taylor U (IN)
Trent U (ON, Canada)
Unity Coll (ME)
Université de Sherbrooke (QC, Canada)
U of Central Missouri (MO)
U of Colorado Boulder (CO)
U of Miami (FL)
U of Mobile (AL)
U of North Georgia (GA)
The U of Texas at Dallas (TX)
The U of West Alabama (AL)
U of Wisconsin–Superior (WI)
Virginia Wesleyan Coll (VA)
Waldorf U (IA)
Walsh U (OH)
Washington & Jefferson Coll (PA)
Wheelock Coll (MA)

COMMUNICATION DISORDERS SCIENCES AND SERVICES RELATED

Ouachita Baptist U (AR)
St. Cloud State U (MN)
Saint Mary's Coll (IN)
U of New Hampshire (NH)

COMMUNICATION SCIENCES AND DISORDERS

Appalachian State U (NC)
Arizona State U at the Tempe campus (AZ)
Auburn U (AL)
Augustana Coll (IL)
Baldwin Wallace U (OH)
Baylor U (TX)
Biola U (CA)
Bowling Green State U (OH)
Bridgewater State U (MA)
Butler U (IN)
California State U, Chico (CA)
California State U, Fresno (CA)
California State U, Fullerton (CA)
California State U, Long Beach (CA)
California State U, Northridge (CA)
California U of Pennsylvania (PA)
Case Western Reserve U (OH)
Central Michigan U (MI)
Eastern Illinois U (IL)
Elms Coll (MA)
Emerson Coll (MA)
Governors State U (IL)
Hampton U (VA)
Harding U (AR)
Jacksonville U (FL)
Kansas State U (KS)
Lamar U (TX)
La Salle U (PA)
Lebanon Valley Coll (PA)
Maryville U of Saint Louis (MO)
Minnesota State U Mankato (MN)
Minot State U (ND)
Mount Vernon Nazarene U (OH)
Northern Illinois U (IL)
Northwestern U (IL)
Our Lady of the Lake U of San Antonio (TX)
Pace U (NY)
Penn State Abington (PA)
Penn State Altoona (PA)
Penn State Beaver (PA)
Penn State Berks (PA)
Penn State Brandywine (PA)
Penn State DuBois (PA)
Penn State Erie, The Behrend Coll (PA)
Penn State Fayette, The Eberly Campus (PA)
Penn State Greater Allegheny (PA)
Penn State Hazleton (PA)
Penn State Lehigh Valley (PA)
Penn State Mont Alto (PA)
Penn State New Kensington (PA)
Penn State Schuylkill (PA)
Penn State Shenango (PA)
Penn State U Park (PA)
Penn State Wilkes-Barre (PA)
Penn State Worthington Scranton (PA)
Penn State York (PA)
Portland State U (OR)
Queens Coll of the City U of New York (NY)
Radford U (VA)
Rhode Island Coll (RI)
St. Cloud State U (MN)
Saint Louis U (MO)
Saint Mary's Coll (IN)
Samford U (AL)
San Diego State U (CA)
San Francisco State U (CA)
Shaw U (NC)
Southeast Missouri State U (MO)
Southern Illinois U Carbondale (IL)
State U of New York at Fredonia (NY)
State U of New York at New Paltz (NY)
Stephen F. Austin State U (TX)
Syracuse U (NY)
Texas A&M Intl U (TX)
Texas A&M U–Kingsville (TX)
Texas State U (TX)
Truman State U (MO)
The U of Akron (OH)
The U of Arizona (AZ)
U of Cincinnati (OH)
U of Colorado Boulder (CO)
U of Georgia (GA)
U of Houston (TX)
The U of Kansas (KS)
U of Maine (ME)
U of Maryland, Coll Park (MD)
U of Massachusetts Amherst (MA)
U of Minnesota, Duluth (MN)
U of Nebraska at Kearney (NE)
U of North Dakota (ND)
U of Oklahoma Health Sciences Center (OK)
U of Oregon (OR)
U of Rhode Island (RI)
U of South Alabama (AL)
The U of South Dakota (SD)
U of South Florida Sarasota-Manatee (FL)
The U of Texas at Austin (TX)
The U of Texas Rio Grande Valley (TX)
U of Vermont (VT)
U of Wisconsin–Eau Claire (WI)
U of Wisconsin–Stevens Point (WI)
U of Wisconsin–Whitewater (WI)
Wayne State U (MI)
Western Carolina U (NC)
Western Illinois U (IL)
Western Kentucky U (KY)
Western Washington U (WA)
West Texas A&M U (TX)
Wichita State U (KS)
William Paterson U of New Jersey (NJ)
Winthrop U (SC)
Worcester State U (MA)
Xavier U of Louisiana (LA)

COMMUNICATIONS TECHNOLOGIES AND SUPPORT SERVICES RELATED

Alverno Coll (WI)
Becker Coll (MA)
Chestnut Hill Coll (PA)
Framingham State U (MA)
Lesley U (MA)
Minot State U (ND)
Salve Regina U (RI)
U of Windsor (ON, Canada)
U of Wisconsin–Platteville (WI)

COMMUNICATIONS TECHNOLOGY

Eastern Michigan U (MI)
Inter American U of Puerto Rico, Bayamón Campus (PR)
Messiah Coll (PA)
York Coll of the City U of New York (NY)

COMMUNITY HEALTH AND PREVENTIVE MEDICINE

Bowling Green State U (OH)
Canisius Coll (NY)
Carroll Coll (MT)
Florida Gulf Coast U (FL)
Georgia Coll & State U (GA)
Governors State U (IL)
Hofstra U (NY)
Indiana U Bloomington (IN)
Mansfield U of Pennsylvania (PA)
Minnesota State U Moorhead (MN)
Moravian Coll (PA)
Murray State U (KY)
National U (CA)
Ohio U–Eastern (OH)
Pine Manor Coll (MA)
Portland State U (OR)
Tufts U (MA)
U of Florida (FL)

U of the Incarnate Word (TX)
U of Wisconsin–Eau Claire (WI)
U of Wisconsin–La Crosse (WI)
Western Kentucky U (KY)

COMMUNITY HEALTH SERVICES COUNSELING

Becker Coll (MA)
Canisius Coll (NY)
Carroll Coll (MT)
Central Michigan U (MI)
Cornerstone U (MI)
Eastern Washington U (WA)
Indiana State U (IN)
James Madison U (VA)
Johnson C. Smith U (NC)
Morris Coll (SC)
New Mexico State U (NM)
Northeastern Illinois U (IL)
Northern Illinois U (IL)
Ohio U (OH)
Rhode Island Coll (RI)
Texas A&M U (TX)
The U of Arizona (AZ)
U of Central Arkansas (AR)
The U of Kansas (KS)
U of Maine at Farmington (ME)
U of Massachusetts Lowell (MA)
U of Michigan–Dearborn (MI)
U of Pennsylvania (PA)
Western Connecticut State U (CT)
Western Washington U (WA)
Whitworth U (WA)
Worcester State U (MA)
Wright State U (OH)
Wright State U–Lake Campus (OH)
Youngstown State U (OH)

COMMUNITY ORGANIZATION AND ADVOCACY

Allegheny Coll (PA)
Alverno Coll (WI)
Arizona State U at the Downtown Phoenix campus (AZ)
Bemidji State U (MN)
Bryant U (RI)
Central Michigan U (MI)
Elmira Coll (NY)
Emory & Henry Coll (VA)
Goddard Coll (VT)
Mercer U, Macon (GA)
Metropolitan Coll of New York (NY)
Montana State U–Northern (MT)
Nazareth Coll of Rochester (NY)
New Mexico State U (NM)
Northern State U (SD)
Northland Coll (WI)
Northwestern U (IL)
Providence Coll (RI)
Rockhurst U (MO)
Southern Arkansas U–Magnolia (AR)
State U of New York Empire State Coll (NY)
U of Alaska Fairbanks (AK)
U of Hartford (CT)
U of Massachusetts Boston (MA)
U of Saint Mary (KS)
The U of Texas at El Paso (TX)
West Virginia U Inst of Technology (WV)

COMMUNITY PSYCHOLOGY

Clayton State U (GA)
Goddard Coll (VT)
Montana State U Billings (MT)
Northwestern U (IL)
Rogers State U (OK)
U of Miami (FL)
U of New Haven (CT)
U of Saint Mary (KS)
U of Washington, Bothell (WA)

COMPARATIVE LITERATURE

The American U in Cairo (Egypt)
The American U of Paris (France)
Barnard Coll (NY)
Barry U (FL)
Beloit Coll (WI)
Binghamton U, State U of New York (NY)
Bishop's U (QC, Canada)
Boston U (MA)
Brandeis U (MA)
Brooklyn Coll of the City U of New York (NY)
Bryn Mawr Coll (PA)
California State U, Fullerton (CA)
California State U, Long Beach (CA)
Case Western Reserve U (OH)
Chowan U (NC)
City Coll of the City U of New York (NY)
Clark U (MA)
Coll of the Atlantic (ME)
Coll of the Holy Cross (MA)
The Coll of Wooster (OH)
The Colorado Coll (CO)
Columbia U (NY)
Columbia U, School of General Studies (NY)
Cornell U (NY)
Dalhousie U (NS, Canada)
Dartmouth Coll (NH)
Earlham Coll (IN)
Eckerd Coll (FL)
Emory U (GA)
Fordham U (NY)
Franklin Pierce U (NH)
Georgetown U (DC)
Gettysburg Coll (PA)
Goddard Coll (VT)
Graceland U (IA)
Hamilton Coll (NY)
Harvard U (MA)
Haverford Coll (PA)
Hillsdale Coll (MI)
Hobart and William Smith Colls (NY)
Hofstra U (NY)
Houghton Coll (NY)
Hunter Coll of the City U of New York (NY)
Indiana U Bloomington (IN)
Inter American U of Puerto Rico, San Germán Campus (PR)
John Carroll U (OH)
Lycoming Coll (PA)
Manchester U (IN)
McMaster U (ON, Canada)
Middlebury Coll (VT)
Minnesota State U Mankato (MN)
Mount Allison U (NB, Canada)
New Coll of Florida (FL)
Northwestern U (IL)
Northwest U (WA)
Oberlin Coll (OH)
The Ohio State U (OH)
Ohio Wesleyan U (OH)
Penn State Abington (PA)
Penn State Altoona (PA)
Penn State Beaver (PA)
Penn State Berks (PA)
Penn State Brandywine (PA)
Penn State DuBois (PA)
Penn State Erie, The Behrend Coll (PA)
Penn State Fayette, The Eberly Campus (PA)
Penn State Greater Allegheny (PA)
Penn State Hazleton (PA)
Penn State Lehigh Valley (PA)
Penn State Mont Alto (PA)
Penn State New Kensington (PA)
Penn State Schuylkill (PA)
Penn State Shenango (PA)
Penn State U Park (PA)
Penn State Wilkes-Barre (PA)
Penn State Worthington Scranton (PA)
Penn State York (PA)
Princeton U (NJ)
Purchase Coll, State U of New York (NY)
Purdue U (IN)
Queens Coll of the City U of New York (NY)
Quinnipiac U (CT)
Ramapo Coll of New Jersey (NJ)
Reed Coll (OR)
Rockford U (IL)
Rutgers U–New Brunswick (NJ)
St. Catherine U (MN)
Saint Francis U (PA)
Saint Mary's Coll of California (CA)
San Diego State U (CA)
San Francisco State U (CA)
Smith Coll (MA)
Sonoma State U (CA)
Stanford U (CA)
State U of New York Coll at Geneseo (NY)
State U of New York Coll at Old Westbury (NY)
Stony Brook U, State U of New York (NY)
Swarthmore Coll (PA)
Syracuse U (NY)
Tufts U (MA)
Université de Montréal (QC, Canada)
U of California, Davis (CA)
U of California, Irvine (CA)
U of California, Los Angeles (CA)
U of California, San Diego (CA)
U of California, Santa Barbara (CA)
U of Chicago (IL)
U of Delaware (DE)
U of Georgia (GA)
U of La Verne (CA)
U of Massachusetts Amherst (MA)
U of Michigan (MI)
U of Minnesota, Twin Cities Campus (MN)
The U of North Carolina at Chapel Hill (NC)
U of Oregon (OR)
U of Pennsylvania (PA)
U of Pittsburgh at Greensburg (PA)
U of Pittsburgh at Johnstown (PA)
U of Rochester (NY)
U of St. Thomas (MN)
U of San Francisco (CA)
U of South Carolina (SC)
U of Southern California (CA)
The U of Texas at Austin (TX)
U of Toronto (ON, Canada)
U of Utah (UT)
U of Virginia (VA)
U of Washington (WA)
U of Wisconsin–Madison (WI)
U of Wisconsin–Milwaukee (WI)
Washington U in St. Louis (MO)
Willamette U (OR)
Williams Coll (MA)

COMPUTATIONAL AND APPLIED MATHEMATICS

American Public U System (WV)
Bryant U (RI)
Columbia Coll Chicago (IL)
Harrisburg U of Science and Technology (PA)
Purdue U (IN)
Saint Mary's Coll (IN)
U of Notre Dame (IN)
U of Southern California (CA)
The U of Texas at Austin (TX)
Virginia Polytechnic Inst and State U (VA)

COMPUTATIONAL BIOLOGY

Case Western Reserve U (OH)
Colby Coll (ME)
Lipscomb U (TN)
Massachusetts Inst of Technology (MA)

COMPUTATIONAL MATHEMATICS

Arizona State U at the Tempe campus (AZ)
Asbury U (KY)
Brooklyn Coll of the City U of New York (NY)
California Inst of Technology (CA)
Carnegie Mellon U (PA)
Christopher Newport U (VA)
Coll of Saint Benedict (MN)
Embry-Riddle Aeronautical U–Daytona (FL)
Loyola U New Orleans (LA)
McKendree U (IL)
Michigan State U (MI)
Rochester Inst of Technology (NY)
Saint John's U (MN)
Siena Coll (NY)
Simmons Coll (MA)
Southwestern U (TX)
Stevens Inst of Technology (NJ)
U of California, Davis (CA)
U of California, Los Angeles (CA)
U of Washington (WA)
U of Waterloo (ON, Canada)

COMPUTATIONAL SCIENCE

American U (DC)
Anderson U (IN)
Canisius Coll (NY)
Hood Coll (MD)
Siena Coll (NY)
Stockton U (NJ)
U of Michigan–Dearborn (MI)
The U of Tennessee at Chattanooga (TN)
The U of Texas at Austin (TX)
The U of Texas Rio Grande Valley (TX)
U of Wisconsin–Stevens Point (WI)
Washington State U (WA)
Washington State U–Global Campus (WA)
Washington State U–Vancouver (WA)
Winona State U (MN)

COMPUTER AND INFORMATION SCIENCES

Academy Coll (MN)
Adelphi U (NY)
Albany State U (GA)
Alcorn State U (MS)
Alverno Coll (WI)
American U (DC)
American U in Bulgaria (Bulgaria)
Anderson U (SC)
Andrews U (MI)
Angelo State U (TX)
Aquinas Coll (MI)
Arcadia U (PA)
Arizona State U at the Tempe campus (AZ)
Arkansas Tech U (AR)
Armstrong State U (GA)
Assumption Coll (MA)
Athens State U (AL)
Auburn U (AL)
Augusta U (GA)
Austin Coll (TX)
Avila U (MO)
Ball State U (IN)
Barnard Coll (NY)
Beacon Coll (FL)
Becker Coll (MA)
Bellarmine U (KY)
Belmont U (TN)
Bennett Coll (NC)
Bennington Coll (VT)
Bentley U (MA)
Berea Coll (KY)
Bethel U (MN)
Binghamton U, State U of New York (NY)
Bishop's U (QC, Canada)
Bloomfield Coll (NJ)
Bluefield State Coll (WV)
Boston Coll (MA)
Bowie State U (MD)
Bowling Green State U (OH)
Bradley U (IL)
Brandman U (CA)
Brewton-Parker Coll (GA)
Brooklyn Coll of the City U of New York (NY)
Bryant U (RI)
Bucknell U (PA)
Butler U (IN)
Cairn U (PA)
Caldwell U (NJ)
California Lutheran U (CA)
California State U, Fresno (CA)
California U of Pennsylvania (PA)
Carroll Coll (MT)
Catawba Coll (NC)
The Catholic U of America (DC)
Central Connecticut State U (CT)
Central State U (OH)
Champlain Coll (VT)
Chapman U (CA)
Chestnut Hill Coll (PA)
Chowan U (NC)
The Citadel, The Military Coll of South Carolina (SC)
Clarion U of Pennsylvania (PA)
Clark Atlanta U (GA)
Clarke U (IA)
Clemson U (SC)
Cleveland State U (OH)
Coastal Carolina U (SC)
The Coll at Brockport, State U of New York (NY)
Coll of Charleston (SC)
The Coll of New Jersey (NJ)
The Coll of St. Scholastica (MN)
The Coll of William and Mary (VA)
Colorado Christian U (CO)
Colorado Mesa U (CO)
Colorado State U (CO)
Columbia Coll (MO)
Columbus State U (GA)
Concordia U Chicago (IL)
Cornell U (NY)
Curry Coll (MA)
Dakota State U (SD)
Dallas Baptist U (TX)
DEREE - The American Coll of Greece (Greece)
Dickinson Coll (PA)
Dickinson State U (ND)
Dixie State U (UT)
Doane U (NE)
Dominican Coll (NY)
Earlham Coll (IN)
East Central U (OK)
Eastern Michigan U (MI)
Eastern Oregon U (OR)
Eastern Washington U (WA)
East Stroudsburg U of Pennsylvania (PA)
East Tennessee State U (TN)
Edgewood Coll (WI)
Elizabethtown Coll (PA)
Elms Coll (MA)
Elon U (NC)
Emmanuel Coll (GA)
Emmaus Bible Coll (IA)
Emporia State U (KS)
The Evergreen State Coll (WA)
Fairfield U (CT)
Fairleigh Dickinson U, Coll at Florham (NJ)
Faulkner U (AL)
Felician U (NJ)
Fisher Coll (MA)
Fitchburg State U (MA)
Florida Ag and Mech U (FL)
Florida Atlantic U (FL)
Florida Gulf Coast U (FL)
Florida Intl U (FL)
Fordham U (NY)
Framingham State U (MA)
Franciscan U of Steubenville (OH)
Francis Marion U (SC)
Franklin & Marshall Coll (PA)
Franklin Coll (IN)
Freed-Hardeman U (TN)
Friends U (KS)
Gallaudet U (DC)
Gannon U (PA)
Gardner-Webb U (NC)
Geneva Coll (PA)
George Fox U (OR)
Georgetown Coll (KY)
The George Washington U (DC)
Georgia Inst of Technology (GA)
Georgia Southern U (GA)
Georgia State U (GA)
Goucher Coll (MD)
Grand Valley State U (MI)
Grand View U (IA)
Greenville Coll (IL)
Guilford Coll (NC)
Hamilton Coll (NY)
Hannibal-LaGrange U (MO)
Harrisburg U of Science and Technology (PA)
Hartwick Coll (NY)
Henderson State U (AR)
Hope Coll (MI)
Howard Payne U (TX)
Husson U (ME)
Huston-Tillotson U (TX)
Indiana State U (IN)
Indiana U of Pennsylvania (PA)
Inter American U of Puerto Rico, Barranquitas Campus (PR)
Inter American U of Puerto Rico, Fajardo Campus (PR)
Ithaca Coll (NY)
Jackson State U (MS)
Jacksonville State U (AL)
Jacksonville U (FL)
James Madison U (VA)
John Jay Coll of Criminal Justice of the City U of New York (NY)
Johns Hopkins U (MD)
Johnson C. Smith U (NC)
Juniata Coll (PA)
Kalamazoo Coll (MI)
Kansas State U (KS)
Kean U (NJ)
Keene State Coll (NH)
Kennesaw State U (GA)
Kent State U (OH)
Kentucky State U (KY)
Kentucky Wesleyan Coll (KY)

King's Coll (PA)
Kutztown U of Pennsylvania (PA)
Kuyper Coll (MI)
Lamar U (TX)
Lane Coll (TN)
La Roche Coll (PA)
La Salle U (PA)
Lebanon Valley Coll (PA)
Lehman Coll of the City U of New York (NY)
Le Moyne Coll (NY)
Lenoir-Rhyne U (NC)
Liberty U (VA)
Lincoln U (PA)
Lindenwood U (MO)
Lock Haven U of Pennsylvania (PA)
Loyola Marymount U (CA)
Loyola U Chicago (IL)
Loyola U New Orleans (LA)
Lubbock Christian U (TX)
Macalester Coll (MN)
Mansfield U of Pennsylvania (PA)
Marist Coll (NY)
Marshall U (WV)
Massachusetts Coll of Liberal Arts (MA)
The Master's U (CA)
McDaniel Coll (MD)
McMurry U (TX)
Mercy Coll (NY)
Mercyhurst U (PA)
Metropolitan State U of Denver (CO)
Miami Dade Coll (FL)
Miami U (OH)
Michigan State U (MI)
Millersville U of Pennsylvania (PA)
Milligan Coll (TN)
Mills Coll (CA)
Minot State U (ND)
Misericordia U (PA)
Mississippi State U (MS)
Missouri Western State U (MO)
Molloy Coll (NY)
Monmouth U (NJ)
Montana State U–Northern (MT)
Montclair State U (NJ)
Morehead State U (KY)
Morehouse Coll (GA)
Morrisville State Coll (NY)
Mount St. Joseph U (OH)
Mount St. Mary's U (MD)
Neumann U (PA)
New England Coll (NH)
New England Inst of Technology (RI)
New Jersey City U (NJ)
New Mexico Highlands U (NM)
New Mexico State U (NM)
New York Inst of Technology (NY)
Niagara U (NY)
North American U (TX)
North Carolina Wesleyan Coll (NC)
Northeastern U (MA)
Northern Kentucky U (KY)
Northwestern U (IL)
Northwest Missouri State U (MO)
Northwood U, Michigan Campus (MI)
Nova Southeastern U (FL)
The Ohio State U (OH)
Ohio U (OH)
Oklahoma Baptist U (OK)
Oklahoma City U (OK)
Oklahoma State U (OK)
Old Dominion U (VA)
Oral Roberts U (OK)
Our Lady of the Lake U of San Antonio (TX)
Pace U (NY)
Pace U, Pleasantville Campus (NY)
Palm Beach Atlantic U (FL)
Penn State Abington (PA)
Penn State Altoona (PA)
Penn State Beaver (PA)
Penn State Berks (PA)
Penn State Brandywine (PA)
Penn State DuBois (PA)
Penn State Erie, The Behrend Coll (PA)
Penn State Fayette, The Eberly Campus (PA)
Penn State Greater Allegheny (PA)
Penn State Harrisburg (PA)
Penn State Hazleton (PA)
Penn State Lehigh Valley (PA)
Penn State Mont Alto (PA)
Penn State New Kensington (PA)
Penn State Schuylkill (PA)
Penn State Shenango (PA)
Penn State U Park (PA)
Penn State Wilkes-Barre (PA)
Penn State Worthington Scranton (PA)
Penn State York (PA)
Pittsburg State U (KS)
Polytechnic U of Puerto Rico (PR)
Portland State U (OR)
Prairie View A&M U (TX)
Principia Coll (IL)
Ramapo Coll of New Jersey (NJ)
Regis U (CO)
Rhode Island Coll (RI)
Rice U (TX)
Roanoke Coll (VA)
Rochester Inst of Technology (NY)
Roger Williams U (RI)
Rollins Coll (FL)
Rutgers U–Camden (NJ)
Rutgers U–Newark (NJ)
Sacred Heart U (CT)
Saginaw Valley State U (MI)
Saint Augustine's U (NC)
St. Catherine U (MN)
St. Edward's U (TX)
St. John Fisher Coll (NY)
St. John's U (NY)
Saint Joseph's U (PA)
Saint Leo U (FL)
Saint Louis U (MO)
Saint Louis U–Madrid Campus (Spain)
Saint Mary-of-the-Woods Coll (IN)
St. Mary's Coll of Maryland (MD)
St. Norbert Coll (WI)
Saint Peter's U (NJ)
St. Thomas Aquinas Coll (NY)
St. Thomas U (FL)
Saint Vincent Coll (PA)
Salisbury U (MD)
Sam Houston State U (TX)
Shaw U (NC)
Shepherd U (WV)
Shippensburg U of Pennsylvania (PA)
Shorter U (GA)
Siena Coll (NY)
Sierra Nevada Coll (NV)
Simmons Coll (MA)
Simpson Coll (IA)
Skidmore Coll (NY)
Slippery Rock U of Pennsylvania (PA)
South Carolina State U (SC)
South Dakota State U (SD)
Southeastern Oklahoma State U (OK)
Southeast Missouri State U (MO)
Southern Arkansas U–Magnolia (AR)
Southern Illinois U Edwardsville (IL)
Southern New Hampshire U (NH)
Southern Utah U (UT)
Southwest Baptist U (MO)
Southwestern U (TX)
Spelman Coll (GA)
Spring Hill Coll (AL)
State U of New York at New Paltz (NY)
State U of New York at Plattsburgh (NY)
State U of New York Coll at Old Westbury (NY)
Stephen F. Austin State U (TX)
Sterling Coll (KS)
Stevenson U (MD)
Stony Brook U, State U of New York (NY)
Suffolk U (MA)
Swarthmore Coll (PA)
Syracuse U (NY)
Tarleton State U (TX)
Temple U (PA)
Tennessee Wesleyan U (TN)
Texas A&M U–Central Texas (TX)
Texas A&M U–Commerce (TX)
Texas A&M U–Kingsville (TX)
Texas Christian U (TX)
Texas State U (TX)
Texas Tech U (TX)
Texas Woman's U (TX)
Tiffin U (OH)
Transylvania U (KY)
Trinity Christian Coll (IL)
Trinity U (TX)
Troy U (AL)
Truman State U (MO)
Tufts U (MA)
Tulane U (LA)
Union Coll (NE)
Union Coll (NY)
United States Military Acad (NY)
U at Albany, State U of New York (NY)
The U of Alabama (AL)
The U of Alabama at Birmingham (AL)
The U of Alabama in Huntsville (AL)
U of Alaska Fairbanks (AK)
The U of Arizona (AZ)
U of Arkansas (AR)
U of California, Irvine (CA)
U of California, Los Angeles (CA)
U of Central Arkansas (AR)
U of Central Florida (FL)
U of Central Missouri (MO)
U of Cincinnati (OH)
U of Colorado Denver (CO)
U of Dayton (OH)
U of Delaware (DE)
U of Denver (CO)
U of Dubuque (IA)
The U of Findlay (OH)
U of Florida (FL)
U of Great Falls (MT)
U of Hartford (CT)
U of Hawaii at Manoa (HI)
U of Houston (TX)
U of Houston–Clear Lake (TX)
U of Houston–Downtown (TX)
The U of Kansas (KS)
U of Kentucky (KY)
U of La Verne (CA)
U of Mary Hardin-Baylor (TX)
U of Maryland, Coll Park (MD)
U of Maryland U Coll (MD)
U of Mary Washington (VA)
U of Massachusetts Boston (MA)
U of Massachusetts Dartmouth (MA)
U of Michigan (MI)
U of Michigan–Dearborn (MI)
U of Mobile (AL)
U of Nebraska at Kearney (NE)
U of Nevada, Reno (NV)
U of New Hampshire (NH)
U of New Haven (CT)
U of North Alabama (AL)
U of North Dakota (ND)
U of North Florida (FL)
U of North Georgia (GA)
U of North Texas (TX)
U of Notre Dame (IN)
U of Oregon (OR)
U of Pikeville (KY)
U of Pittsburgh at Greensburg (PA)
U of Puerto Rico in Bayamón (PR)
U of Rhode Island (RI)
U of Richmond (VA)
U of Saint Mary (KS)
U of San Francisco (CA)
U of South Carolina (SC)
The U of South Dakota (SD)
U of Southern Indiana (IN)
U of Southern Mississippi (MS)
U of South Florida (FL)
The U of Tampa (FL)
The U of Texas at Austin (TX)
The U of Texas at San Antonio (TX)
The U of Texas of the Permian Basin (TX)
U of the Fraser Valley (BC, Canada)
U of the Incarnate Word (TX)
U of Vermont (VT)
U of Virginia (VA)
The U of Virginia's Coll at Wise (VA)
U of Washington, Bothell (WA)
U of Washington, Tacoma (WA)
U of West Georgia (GA)
U of Windsor (ON, Canada)
U of Wisconsin–Eau Claire (WI)
U of Wisconsin–La Crosse (WI)
U of Wisconsin–Madison (WI)
U of Wisconsin–Milwaukee (WI)
U of Wisconsin–Platteville (WI)
U of Wisconsin–Stevens Point (WI)
U of Wisconsin–Superior (WI)
U of Wisconsin–Whitewater (WI)
Utah State U (UT)
Utica Coll (NY)
Valdosta State U (GA)
Valley City State U (ND)
Vassar Coll (NY)
Virginia Commonwealth U (VA)
Virginia Polytechnic Inst and State U (VA)
Virginia Union U (VA)
Wake Forest U (NC)
Walsh Coll of Accountancy and Business Administration (MI)
Wartburg Coll (IA)
Washburn U (KS)
Washington State U (WA)
Washington State U–Tri-Cities (WA)
Washington State U–Vancouver (WA)
Washington U in St. Louis (MO)
Waynesburg U (PA)
Wayne State Coll (NE)
Wayne State U (MI)
Webber Intl U (FL)
Weber State U (UT)
Webster U (MO)
West Chester U of Pennsylvania (PA)
Western Illinois U (IL)
Western Kentucky U (KY)
Western Michigan U (MI)
Western Washington U (WA)
Westminster Coll (PA)
Westminster Coll (UT)
West Texas A&M U (TX)
West Virginia U Inst of Technology (WV)
West Virginia Wesleyan Coll (WV)
Wheeling Jesuit U (WV)
Widener U (PA)
Wilkes U (PA)
Willamette U (OR)
William Paterson U of New Jersey (NJ)
William Penn U (IA)
Williams Baptist Coll (AR)
Worcester State U (MA)
Wright State U (OH)
Wright State U–Lake Campus (OH)
Xavier U of Louisiana (LA)
Youngstown State U (OH)

COMPUTER AND INFORMATION SCIENCES AND SUPPORT SERVICES RELATED

Amridge U (AL)
Arizona State U at the West campus (AZ)
Cabrini U (PA)
Coll of Staten Island of the City U of New York (NY)
Ferris State U (MI)
Hilbert Coll (NY)
Hofstra U (NY)
Indiana U–Purdue U Indianapolis (IN)
Inter American U of Puerto Rico, Guayama Campus (PR)
Lehigh U (PA)
Limestone Coll (SC)
Missouri U of Science and Technology (MO)
Morrisville State Coll (NY)
Northern Kentucky U (KY)
St. Bonaventure U (NY)
State U of New York Coll of Agriculture and Technology at Cobleskill (NY)
Syracuse U (NY)
Talladega Coll (AL)
United States Military Acad (NY)
U at Albany, State U of New York (NY)
U of Great Falls (MT)
U of Mount Union (OH)
U of Northern Iowa (IA)
U of Notre Dame (IN)
U of Pittsburgh (PA)
U of the Potomac (DC)
U of Washington, Bothell (WA)
Utah State U (UT)
Valley City State U (ND)
Washington U in St. Louis (MO)

COMPUTER AND INFORMATION SCIENCES RELATED

California State U, Dominguez Hills (CA)
California State U, Monterey Bay (CA)
Carnegie Mellon U (PA)
Coll of Charleston (SC)
The Colorado Coll (CO)
Columbia U, School of General Studies (NY)
Eastern Illinois U (IL)
Granite State Coll (NH)
Gwynedd Mercy U (PA)
Limestone Coll (SC)
Mercer U, Macon (GA)
Missouri State U (MO)
Northern Kentucky U (KY)
Temple U (PA)
Université de Sherbrooke (QC, Canada)
U of Great Falls (MT)
U of Northern Iowa (IA)
U of Windsor (ON, Canada)
U of Wisconsin–Stout (WI)
Wagner Coll (NY)
West Virginia U (WV)

COMPUTER AND INFORMATION SYSTEMS SECURITY

Anderson U (IN)
Bay Path U (MA)
Central Penn Coll (PA)
Central Washington U (WA)
Charter Oak State Coll (CT)
Columbia Southern U (AL)
Dakota State U (SD)
Davenport U, Grand Rapids (MI)
Donnelly Coll (KS)
Drexel U (PA)
East Stroudsburg U of Pennsylvania (PA)
Excelsior Coll (NY)
Ferris State U (MI)
Frostburg State U (MD)
Hallmark U (TX)
Hilbert Coll (NY)
Immaculata U (PA)
Kennesaw State U (GA)
LeTourneau U (TX)
Lewis U (IL)
Limestone Coll (SC)
Lindenwood U (MO)
Lipscomb U (TN)
Loyola U Chicago (IL)
Marshall U (WV)
Marywood U (PA)
Mercy Coll (NY)
Mount St. Mary's U (MD)
Oklahoma State U Inst of Technology (OK)
Pennsylvania Coll of Technology (PA)
Rasmussen Coll Blaine (MN)
Rasmussen Coll Bloomington (MN)
Rasmussen Coll Brooklyn Park (MN)
Rasmussen Coll Eagan (MN)
Rasmussen Coll Fargo (ND)
Rasmussen Coll Fort Myers (FL)
Rasmussen Coll Green Bay (WI)
Rasmussen Coll Kansas City/Overland Park (KS)
Rasmussen Coll Lake Elmo/Woodbury (MN)
Rasmussen Coll Land O' Lakes (FL)
Rasmussen Coll Mankato (MN)
Rasmussen Coll Moorhead (MN)
Rasmussen Coll New Port Richey (FL)
Rasmussen Coll Ocala (FL)
Rasmussen Coll St. Cloud (MN)
Rasmussen Coll Tampa/Brandon (FL)
Rasmussen Coll Topeka (KS)
Rasmussen Coll Wausau (WI)
Rochester Inst of Technology (NY)
St. Ambrose U (IA)
St. John's U (NY)
Saint Leo U (FL)
Sam Houston State U (TX)
Southeast Missouri State U (MO)
State U of New York Coll of Technology at Alfred (NY)

State U of New York Polytechnic Inst (NY)
Stevens Inst of Technology (NJ)
Sullivan U (KY)
U of Advancing Technology (AZ)
U of Cincinnati (OH)
U of Colorado Colorado Springs (CO)
U of Great Falls (MT)
U of Illinois at Springfield (IL)
U of Maryland U Coll (MD)
U of Miami (FL)
U of Michigan–Dearborn (MI)
U of Saint Francis (IN)
U of St. Thomas (MN)
U of South Alabama (AL)
The U of Tampa (FL)
The U of Texas at Austin (TX)
The U of Texas at San Antonio (TX)
U of the Potomac (DC)
The U of Tulsa (OK)
Walla Walla U (WA)
Weber State U (UT)
Wilmington U (DE)

COMPUTER ENGINEERING
The American U in Dubai (United Arab Emirates)
American U of Beirut (Lebanon)
Anderson U (IN)
Arizona State U at the Tempe campus (AZ)
Auburn U (AL)
Bellarmine U (KY)
Bethune-Cookman U (FL)
Binghamton U, State U of New York (NY)
Boston U (MA)
Bowling Green State U (OH)
Bradley U (IL)
Brigham Young U–Idaho (ID)
Bucknell U (PA)
California Baptist U (CA)
California Polytechnic State U, San Luis Obispo (CA)
California State Polytechnic U, Pomona (CA)
California State U, Chico (CA)
California State U, Fresno (CA)
California State U, Fullerton (CA)
California State U, Long Beach (CA)
California State U, Northridge (CA)
California State U, Sacramento (CA)
California State U, San Bernardino (CA)
Capital U (OH)
Case Western Reserve U (OH)
Cedarville U (OH)
Central Michigan U (MI)
Christian Brothers U (TN)
Christopher Newport U (VA)
Clarkson U (NY)
Clemson U (SC)
Cleveland State U (OH)
The Coll of New Jersey (NJ)
Colorado State U (CO)
Columbia U (NY)
Concordia U (QC, Canada)
DigiPen Inst of Technology (WA)
Drexel U (PA)
Eastern Nazarene Coll (MA)
Elizabethtown Coll (PA)
Elon U (NC)
Embry-Riddle Aeronautical U–Daytona (FL)
Embry-Riddle Aeronautical U–Prescott (AZ)
Fairfield U (CT)
Florida Ag and Mech U (FL)
Florida Atlantic U (FL)
Florida Inst of Technology (FL)
Florida Intl U (FL)
George Fox U (OR)
The George Washington U (DC)
Georgia Inst of Technology (GA)
Gonzaga U (WA)
Hanover Coll (IN)
Harding U (AR)
Hofstra U (NY)
Indiana U–Purdue U Indianapolis (IN)
Inter American U of Puerto Rico, Bayamón Campus (PR)
Iowa State U of Science and Technology (IA)
Jackson State U (MS)
Johns Hopkins U (MD)
Johnson C. Smith U (NC)
Kansas State U (KS)
Kettering U (MI)
Lawrence Technological U (MI)
Lebanese American U (Lebanon)
Lehigh U (PA)
LeTourneau U (TX)
Lewis U (IL)
Liberty U (VA)
Lipscomb U (TN)
Louisiana State U and A&M Coll (LA)
Loyola U Chicago (IL)
Manhattan Coll (NY)
McMaster U (ON, Canada)
Miami U (OH)
Michigan State U (MI)
Michigan Technological U (MI)
Milwaukee School of Eng (WI)
Minnesota State U Mankato (MN)
Mississippi State U (MS)
Missouri U of Science and Technology (MO)
Montana State U (MT)
New England Inst of Technology (RI)
North Carolina State U (NC)
North Dakota State U (ND)
Northeastern U (MA)
Northwestern U (IL)
The Ohio State U (OH)
Oklahoma Christian U (OK)
Oklahoma State U (OK)
Old Dominion U (VA)
Oral Roberts U (OK)
Penn State Abington (PA)
Penn State Altoona (PA)
Penn State Beaver (PA)
Penn State Berks (PA)
Penn State Brandywine (PA)
Penn State DuBois (PA)
Penn State Erie, The Behrend Coll (PA)
Penn State Fayette, The Eberly Campus (PA)
Penn State Greater Allegheny (PA)
Penn State Hazleton (PA)
Penn State Lehigh Valley (PA)
Penn State Mont Alto (PA)
Penn State New Kensington (PA)
Penn State Schuylkill (PA)
Penn State Shenango (PA)
Penn State U Park (PA)
Penn State Wilkes-Barre (PA)
Penn State Worthington Scranton (PA)
Penn State York (PA)
Polytechnic U of Puerto Rico (PR)
Portland State U (OR)
Prairie View A&M U (TX)
Princeton U (NJ)
Purdue U (IN)
Purdue U Northwest (IN)
Rice U (TX)
Rochester Inst of Technology (NY)
Roger Williams U (RI)
Rose-Hulman Inst of Technology (IN)
Royal Military Coll of Canada (ON, Canada)
Rutgers U–New Brunswick (NJ)
St. Cloud State U (MN)
Saint Louis U (MO)
Saint Louis U–Madrid Campus (Spain)
San Diego State U (CA)
San Francisco State U (CA)
Santa Clara U (CA)
Shepherd U (WV)
South Dakota School of Mines and Technology (SD)
Southern Illinois U Carbondale (IL)
Southern Illinois U Edwardsville (IL)
Southern Methodist U (TX)
State U of New York at New Paltz (NY)
Stevens Inst of Technology (NJ)
Stony Brook U, State U of New York (NY)
Suffolk U (MA)
Syracuse U (NY)
Taylor U (IN)
Texas A&M U (TX)
Texas Tech U (TX)
Trine U (IN)
Tufts U (MA)
Université de Sherbrooke (QC, Canada)
U at Buffalo, the State U of New York (NY)
The U of Akron (OH)
The U of Alabama in Huntsville (AL)
U of Alaska Fairbanks (AK)
U of Arkansas (AR)
U of Bridgeport (CT)
U of California, Irvine (CA)
U of California, Los Angeles (CA)
U of California, Riverside (CA)
U of California, San Diego (CA)
U of California, Santa Barbara (CA)
U of Central Florida (FL)
U of Cincinnati (OH)
U of Colorado Boulder (CO)
U of Colorado Colorado Springs (CO)
U of Dayton (OH)
U of Delaware (DE)
U of Denver (CO)
U of Evansville (IN)
U of Florida (FL)
U of Georgia (GA)
U of Guelph (ON, Canada)
U of Hartford (CT)
U of Houston (TX)
U of Houston–Clear Lake (TX)
U of Idaho (ID)
U of Illinois at Chicago (IL)
U of Indianapolis (IN)
The U of Kansas (KS)
U of Kentucky (KY)
U of La Verne (CA)
U of Louisville (KY)
U of Maine (ME)
U of Maryland, Baltimore County (MD)
U of Maryland, Coll Park (MD)
U of Massachusetts Amherst (MA)
U of Massachusetts Boston (MA)
U of Massachusetts Dartmouth (MA)
U of Massachusetts Lowell (MA)
U of Miami (FL)
U of Michigan (MI)
U of Michigan–Dearborn (MI)
U of Minnesota, Twin Cities Campus (MN)
U of Nevada, Las Vegas (NV)
U of Nevada, Reno (NV)
U of New Hampshire (NH)
U of New Haven (CT)
The U of North Carolina at Charlotte (NC)
U of North Texas (TX)
U of Notre Dame (IN)
U of Oklahoma (OK)
U of Pennsylvania (PA)
U of Pittsburgh (PA)
U of Pittsburgh at Johnstown (PA)
U of Rhode Island (RI)
U of St. Thomas (MN)
U of Saskatchewan (SK, Canada)
The U of Scranton (PA)
U of South Alabama (AL)
U of South Carolina (SC)
U of Southern California (CA)
U of South Florida (FL)
The U of Tennessee (TN)
The U of Texas at Dallas (TX)
The U of Texas at San Antonio (TX)
The U of Texas Rio Grande Valley (TX)
U of the Pacific (CA)
The U of Toledo (OH)
U of Toronto (ON, Canada)
The U of Tulsa (OK)
U of Utah (UT)
U of Virginia (VA)
U of Washington (WA)
U of Washington, Bothell (WA)
U of Waterloo (ON, Canada)
U of Wisconsin–Madison (WI)
U of Wisconsin–Milwaukee (WI)
U of Wisconsin–Stout (WI)
Utah State U (UT)
Valparaiso U (IN)
Vanderbilt U (TN)
Villanova U (PA)
Virginia Commonwealth U (VA)
Virginia Polytechnic Inst and State U (VA)
Virginia State U (VA)
Walla Walla U (WA)
Washington State U (WA)
Washington U in St. Louis (MO)
Weber State U (UT)
Wentworth Inst of Technology (MA)
Western Michigan U (MI)
Western New England U (MA)
West Virginia U (WV)
West Virginia U Inst of Technology (WV)
Wichita State U (KS)
Wright State U (OH)
Wright State U–Lake Campus (OH)
Xavier U of Louisiana (LA)
York Coll of Pennsylvania (PA)

COMPUTER ENGINEERING RELATED
Auburn U (AL)

COMPUTER ENGINEERING TECHNOLOGIES RELATED
Inter American U of Puerto Rico, Bayamón Campus (PR)
U of Guelph (ON, Canada)

COMPUTER ENGINEERING TECHNOLOGY
Arizona State U at the Polytechnic campus (AZ)
California State U, Long Beach (CA)
California U of Pennsylvania (PA)
Central Connecticut State U (CT)
Central Washington U (WA)
Eastern Michigan U (MI)
Farmingdale State Coll (NY)
Indiana State U (IN)
Indiana U–Purdue U Indianapolis (IN)
Kennesaw State U (GA)
LeTourneau U (TX)
Minnesota State U Mankato (MN)
Missouri Western State U (MO)
New York City Coll of Technology of the City U of New York (NY)
Prairie View A&M U (TX)
Rochester Inst of Technology (NY)
Sam Houston State U (TX)
Shawnee State U (OH)
State U of New York Coll of Technology at Alfred (NY)
State U of New York Polytechnic Inst (NY)
U of Cincinnati (OH)
U of Hartford (CT)
U of Houston (TX)
U of Houston–Downtown (TX)
U of Southern Mississippi (MS)
Utah State U (UT)
Vermont Tech Coll (VT)
Weber State U (UT)

COMPUTER GRAPHICS
Acad of Art U (CA)
Bowie State U (MD)
Brooklyn Coll of the City U of New York (NY)
California State U, East Bay (CA)
Champlain Coll (VT)
Coll of the Atlantic (ME)
Concordia U (QC, Canada)
Dakota State U (SD)
Dixie State U (UT)
Great Basin Coll (NV)
Lindenwood U (MO)
Los Angeles Film School (CA)
Pratt Inst (NY)
Purdue U (IN)
Purdue U Northwest (IN)
Rochester Inst of Technology (NY)
Rogers State U (OK)
School of the Art Inst of Chicago (IL)
Southern New Hampshire U (NH)
State U of New York at Fredonia (NY)
Texas A&M U (TX)
U of Advancing Technology (AZ)
U of Dubuque (IA)
U of Great Falls (MT)
U of Houston (TX)
U of Mary Hardin-Baylor (TX)
U of Miami (FL)
U of Pennsylvania (PA)
Walsh U (OH)
Whitworth U (WA)
Wilmington U (DE)

COMPUTER HARDWARE ENGINEERING
Auburn U (AL)
Utah Valley U (UT)

COMPUTER HARDWARE TECHNOLOGY
U of Advancing Technology (AZ)

COMPUTER/INFORMATION TECHNOLOGY SERVICES ADMINISTRATION RELATED
Berkeley Coll–New York City Campus (NY)
Berkeley Coll–Woodland Park Campus (NJ)
Bloomsburg U of Pennsylvania (PA)
Champlain Coll (VT)
Chestnut Hill Coll (PA)
Concordia U, St. Paul (MN)
Dalhousie U (NS, Canada)
DeSales U (PA)
Friends U (KS)
Great Basin Coll (NV)
Gulf Coast State Coll (FL)
Holy Names U (CA)
Lake Erie Coll (OH)
Limestone Coll (SC)
Marywood U (PA)
Missouri State U (MO)
Point Park U (PA)
Robert Morris U (PA)
St. Joseph's Coll, Long Island Campus (NY)
St. Joseph's Coll, New York (NY)
St. Petersburg Coll (FL)
Southwestern Coll (KS)
The U of Findlay (OH)
U of Great Falls (MT)
U of Maryland, Baltimore County (MD)
U of Northern Iowa (IA)
Washington U in St. Louis (MO)

COMPUTER INSTALLATION AND REPAIR TECHNOLOGY
Inter American U of Puerto Rico, Bayamón Campus (PR)

COMPUTER PROGRAMMING
Andrews U (MI)
Arcadia U (PA)
Bishop's U (QC, Canada)
Caribbean U (PR)
Champlain Coll (VT)
Cogswell Polytechnical Coll (CA)
Davenport U, Grand Rapids (MI)
EDP U of Puerto Rico (PR)
Farmingdale State Coll (NY)
Franklin Pierce U (NH)
Gannon U (PA)
Hardin-Simmons U (TX)
Husson U (ME)
Inter American U of Puerto Rico, San Germán Campus (PR)
La Salle U (PA)
Le Moyne Coll (NY)
Limestone Coll (SC)
Missouri Valley Coll (MO)
Morrisville State Coll (NY)
New England Inst of Technology (RI)
Saint Francis U (PA)
Southeast Missouri State U (MO)
Southwestern Coll (KS)
Tufts U (MA)
Université de Sherbrooke (QC, Canada)
U of Advancing Technology (AZ)
The U of Akron (OH)
U of Great Falls (MT)
U of Michigan–Dearborn (MI)
U of Mount Union (OH)
Walla Walla U (WA)
Youngstown State U (OH)

COMPUTER PROGRAMMING RELATED
Curry Coll (MA)
The U of Akron (OH)

COMPUTER PROGRAMMING (SPECIFIC APPLICATIONS)
Acad of Art U (CA)
Central Penn Coll (PA)
DigiPen Inst of Technology (WA)
Kennesaw State U (GA)

State U of New York Coll of Technology at Alfred (NY)
U of Washington, Bothell (WA)
U of Windsor (ON, Canada)

COMPUTER SCIENCE
Abilene Christian U (TX)
Academy Coll (MN)
Adams State U (CO)
Alabama State U (AL)
Albright Coll (PA)
Alderson Broaddus U (WV)
Allegheny Coll (PA)
Alma Coll (MI)
American Coll of Thessaloniki (Greece)
The American U in Cairo (Egypt)
American U of Beirut (Lebanon)
The American U of Paris (France)
Amherst Coll (MA)
Anderson U (IN)
Andrews U (MI)
Appalachian State U (NC)
Arcadia U (PA)
Arizona State U at the Tempe campus (AZ)
Ashland U (OH)
Athens State U (AL)
Auburn U at Montgomery (AL)
Augsburg Coll (MN)
Augustana Coll (IL)
Augustana U (SD)
Aurora U (IL)
Austin Coll (TX)
Austin Peay State U (TN)
Azusa Pacific U (CA)
Baker U (KS)
Baldwin Wallace U (OH)
Bard Coll (NY)
Barry U (FL)
Baylor U (TX)
Belhaven U (MS)
Beloit Coll (WI)
Bemidji State U (MN)
Benedictine Coll (KS)
Bennett Coll (NC)
Bennington Coll (VT)
Bethune-Cookman U (FL)
Binghamton U, State U of New York (NY)
Biola U (CA)
Bishop's U (QC, Canada)
Blackburn Coll (IL)
Bloomfield Coll (NJ)
Bloomsburg U of Pennsylvania (PA)
Boise State U (ID)
Boston Coll (MA)
Boston U (MA)
Bowdoin Coll (ME)
Bradley U (IL)
Brandeis U (MA)
Bridgewater Coll (VA)
Bridgewater State U (MA)
Brigham Young U–Idaho (ID)
Bryn Mawr Coll (PA)
Buena Vista U (IA)
California Baptist U (CA)
California Inst of Technology (CA)
California Lutheran U (CA)
California Polytechnic State U, San Luis Obispo (CA)
California State Polytechnic U, Pomona (CA)
California State U, Bakersfield (CA)
California State U, Chico (CA)
California State U, Dominguez Hills (CA)
California State U, East Bay (CA)
California State U, Fresno (CA)
California State U, Fullerton (CA)
California State U, Long Beach (CA)
California State U, Northridge (CA)
California State U, Sacramento (CA)
California State U, San Bernardino (CA)
California State U, San Marcos (CA)
California State U, Stanislaus (CA)
Calvary U (MO)
Calvin Coll (MI)
Cameron U (OK)
Canisius Coll (NY)
Capital U (OH)
Cardinal Stritch U (WI)
Carleton Coll (MN)
Carnegie Mellon U (PA)
Carroll Coll (MT)
Carson-Newman U (TN)
Carthage Coll (WI)
Case Western Reserve U (OH)
The Catholic U of America (DC)
Cedarville U (OH)
Central Methodist U (MO)
Central Michigan U (MI)
Central State U (OH)
Central Washington U (WA)
Centre Coll (KY)
Champlain Coll (VT)
Chapman U (CA)
Charleston Southern U (SC)
Christian Brothers U (TN)
Christopher Newport U (VA)
City Coll of the City U of New York (NY)
Clark Atlanta U (GA)
Clarkson U (NY)
Clark U (MA)
Clayton State U (GA)
Coe Coll (IA)
Colby Coll (ME)
Colgate U (NY)
CollAmerica–Fort Collins (CO)
Coll of Saint Benedict (MN)
The Coll of Saint Rose (NY)
Coll of Staten Island of the City U of New York (NY)
Coll of the Holy Cross (MA)
Coll of the Ozarks (MO)
The Coll of Wooster (OH)
Colorado School of Mines (CO)
Columbia Coll (MO)
Columbia U (NY)
Columbia U, School of General Studies (NY)
Concordia Coll (MN)
Concordia U (QC, Canada)
Concordia U, St. Paul (MN)
Concordia U Wisconsin (WI)
Connecticut Coll (CT)
Cornell Coll (IA)
Cornell U (NY)
Creighton U (NE)
Dalhousie U (NS, Canada)
Dallas Baptist U (TX)
Dartmouth Coll (NH)
Denison U (OH)
DePauw U (IN)
DeSales U (PA)
Dixie State U (UT)
Doane U (NE)
Dominican U (IL)
Drake U (IA)
Drew U (NJ)
Drexel U (PA)
Drury U (MO)
Dunwoody Coll of Technology (MN)
Duquesne U (PA)
East Carolina U (NC)
Eastern Mennonite U (VA)
Eastern Michigan U (MI)
Eckerd Coll (FL)
Elizabeth City State U (NC)
Elon U (NC)
Embry-Riddle Aeronautical U–Daytona (FL)
Embry-Riddle Aeronautical U–Prescott (AZ)
Emory U (GA)
Endicott Coll (MA)
Evangel U (MO)
Fairleigh Dickinson U, Metropolitan Campus (NJ)
Faulkner U (AL)
Fayetteville State U (NC)
Felician U (NJ)
Fitchburg State U (MA)
Florida Inst of Technology (FL)
Florida Southern Coll (FL)
Fordham U (NY)
Franciscan U of Steubenville (OH)
Franklin Coll (IN)
Franklin Pierce U (NH)
Frostburg State U (MD)
Furman U (SC)
Gannon U (PA)
Gardner-Webb U (NC)
Georgetown U (DC)
The George Washington U (DC)
Georgia Coll & State U (GA)
Georgia Southwestern State U (GA)
Georgia State U (GA)
Gettysburg Coll (PA)
Gonzaga U (WA)
Gordon Coll (MA)
Goshen Coll (IN)
Goucher Coll (MD)
Governors State U (IL)
Graceland U (IA)
Grambling State U (LA)
Grand View U (IA)
Grinnell Coll (IA)
Grove City Coll (PA)
Hampden-Sydney Coll (VA)
Hampshire Coll (MA)
Hampton U (VA)
Hanover Coll (IN)
Harding U (AR)
Hartwick Coll (NY)
Harvard U (MA)
Harvey Mudd Coll (CA)
Haverford Coll (PA)
Hawai`i Pacific U (HI)
Heidelberg U (OH)
Hendrix Coll (AR)
High Point U (NC)
Hiram Coll (OH)
Hobart and William Smith Colls (NY)
Hofstra U (NY)
Holy Cross Coll (IN)
Hood Coll (MD)
Houghton Coll (NY)
Humboldt State U (CA)
Hunter Coll of the City U of New York (NY)
Huntington U (IN)
Huston-Tillotson U (TX)
Idaho State U (ID)
Illinois Coll (IL)
Illinois State U (IL)
Illinois Wesleyan U (IL)
Indiana U Bloomington (IN)
Indiana U Kokomo (IN)
Indiana U Northwest (IN)
Indiana U–Purdue U Indianapolis (IN)
Indiana U South Bend (IN)
Indiana U Southeast (IN)
Inter American U of Puerto Rico, Aguadilla Campus (PR)
Inter American U of Puerto Rico, Bayamón Campus (PR)
Inter American U of Puerto Rico, Metropolitan Campus (PR)
Inter American U of Puerto Rico, Ponce Campus (PR)
Inter American U of Puerto Rico, San Germán Campus (PR)
Iona Coll (NY)
Iowa State U of Science and Technology (IA)
Ithaca Coll (NY)
John Carroll U (OH)
Kennesaw State U (GA)
Kettering U (MI)
King's Coll (PA)
The King's U (AB, Canada)
King U (TN)
Knox Coll (IL)
Lafayette Coll (PA)
Lake Forest Coll (IL)
Langston U (OK)
La Roche Coll (PA)
La Salle U (PA)
Lawrence Technological U (MI)
Lawrence U (WI)
Lebanese American U (Lebanon)
Lehigh U (PA)
Lehman Coll of the City U of New York (NY)
LeTourneau U (TX)
Lewis & Clark Coll (OR)
Lewis U (IL)
Limestone Coll (SC)
Lindenwood U (MO)
Linfield Coll (OR)
Lipscomb U (TN)
Longwood U (VA)
Loras Coll (IA)
Louisiana Coll (LA)
Louisiana State U and A&M Coll (LA)
Louisiana Tech U (LA)
Loyola U Maryland (MD)
Luther Coll (IA)
Lynchburg Coll (VA)
Madonna U (MI)
Maharishi U of Management (IA)
Malone U (OH)
Manchester U (IN)
Manhattan Coll (NY)
Manhattanville Coll (NY)
Mansfield U of Pennsylvania (PA)
Marietta Coll (OH)
Marist Coll (NY)
Marywood U (PA)
Massachusetts Coll of Liberal Arts (MA)
Massachusetts Inst of Technology (MA)
McKendree U (IL)
McMaster U (ON, Canada)
McNeese State U (LA)
Mercer U, Macon (GA)
Mercy Coll (NY)
Mercyhurst U (PA)
Meredith Coll (NC)
Merrimack Coll (MA)
Messiah Coll (PA)
Metropolitan State U of Denver (CO)
Michigan Technological U (MI)
Middlebury Coll (VT)
Milligan Coll (TN)
Millsaps Coll (MS)
Mills Coll (CA)
Minnesota State U Moorhead (MN)
Minot State U (ND)
Mississippi Valley State U (MS)
Missouri State U (MO)
Missouri U of Science and Technology (MO)
Missouri Valley Coll (MO)
Monmouth Coll (IL)
Montana State U (MT)
Montana Tech of The U of Montana (MT)
Moravian Coll (PA)
Mount Allison U (NB, Canada)
Mount Holyoke Coll (MA)
Mount St. Joseph U (OH)
Mount Vernon Nazarene U (OH)
Murray State U (KY)
Muskingum U (OH)
National U (CA)
New Coll of Florida (FL)
New England Inst of Technology (RI)
New Mexico Inst of Mining and Technology (NM)
North Carolina State U (NC)
North Central Coll (IL)
Northcentral U (CA)
North Dakota State U (ND)
Northeastern Illinois U (IL)
Northeastern State U (OK)
Northeastern U (MA)
Northern Arizona U (AZ)
Northern Illinois U (IL)
Northwestern Coll (IA)
Northwestern Oklahoma State U (OK)
Northwestern U (IL)
Nova Southeastern U (FL)
Nyack Coll (NY)
Oberlin Coll (OH)
Ohio Dominican U (OH)
The Ohio State U (OH)
Ohio U (OH)
Ohio Wesleyan U (OH)
Oklahoma Baptist U (OK)
Oklahoma Christian U (OK)
Olivet Nazarene U (IL)
Oral Roberts U (OK)
Oregon State U (OR)
Ouachita Baptist U (AR)
Pace U (NY)
Pace U, Pleasantville Campus (NY)
Pacific Lutheran U (WA)
Pacific States U (CA)
Palm Beach Atlantic U (FL)
Penn State Erie, The Behrend Coll (PA)
Philander Smith Coll (AR)
Plymouth State U (NH)
Polytechnic U of Puerto Rico (PR)
Pomona Coll (CA)
Portland State U (OR)
Prairie View A&M U (TX)
Providence Coll (RI)
Purdue U (IN)
Purdue U Northwest (IN)
Queens Coll of the City U of New York (NY)
Quinnipiac U (CT)
Radford U (VA)
Randolph-Macon Coll (VA)
Rasmussen Coll Blaine (MN)
Rasmussen Coll Bloomington (MN)
Rasmussen Coll Brooklyn Park (MN)
Rasmussen Coll Eagan (MN)
Rasmussen Coll Fargo (ND)
Rasmussen Coll Fort Myers (FL)
Rasmussen Coll Green Bay (WI)
Rasmussen Coll Lake Elmo/ Woodbury (MN)
Rasmussen Coll Land O' Lakes (FL)
Rasmussen Coll Mankato (MN)
Rasmussen Coll Moorhead (MN)
Rasmussen Coll New Port Richey (FL)
Rasmussen Coll Ocala (FL)
Rasmussen Coll St. Cloud (MN)
Rasmussen Coll Tampa/Brandon (FL)
Rasmussen Coll Topeka (KS)
Rasmussen Coll Wausau (WI)
Redeemer U Coll (ON, Canada)
Reed Coll (OR)
Regent U (VA)
Regis U (CO)
Rensselaer Polytechnic Inst (NY)
Renton Tech Coll (WA)
Rhodes Coll (TN)
Roanoke Coll (VA)
Rochester Inst of Technology (NY)
Rockford U (IL)
Rocky Mountain Coll (MT)
Roger Williams U (RI)
Rose-Hulman Inst of Technology (IN)
Rowan U (NJ)
Royal Military Coll of Canada (ON, Canada)
Rust Coll (MS)
Saginaw Valley State U (MI)
St. Ambrose U (IA)
Saint Anselm Coll (NH)
Saint Augustine's U (NC)
St. Bonaventure U (NY)
St. Cloud State U (MN)
St. Edward's U (TX)
Saint Francis U (PA)
Saint John's U (MN)
Saint Louis U (MO)
Saint Martin's U (WA)
Saint Mary's U of Minnesota (MN)
Saint Michael's Coll (VT)
St. Norbert Coll (WI)
St. Olaf Coll (MN)
St. Thomas U (FL)
Samford U (AL)
San Diego State U (CA)
San Francisco State U (CA)
Sarah Lawrence Coll (NY)
Scripps Coll (CA)
Seattle U (WA)
Seton Hill U (PA)
Sewanee: The U of the South (TN)
Shaw U (NC)
Silver Lake Coll of the Holy Family (WI)
Simon Fraser U (BC, Canada)
Simpson Coll (IA)
Smith Coll (MA)
Sonoma State U (CA)
South Dakota School of Mines and Technology (SD)
Southeastern Louisiana U (LA)
Southern Connecticut State U (CT)
Southern Illinois U Carbondale (IL)
Southern Illinois U Edwardsville (IL)
Southern Methodist U (TX)
Southern New Hampshire U (NH)
Southern Oregon U (OR)
Southern Utah U (UT)
Southwest Baptist U (MO)
Southwestern Adventist U (TX)
Southwestern Coll (KS)
Spelman Coll (GA)
Stanford U (CA)
State U of New York at Fredonia (NY)
State U of New York at Oswego (NY)
State U of New York Coll at Old Westbury (NY)
State U of New York Coll at Potsdam (NY)

Stevens Inst of Technology (NJ)
Stonehill Coll (MA)
Suffolk U (MA)
Susquehanna U (PA)
Tarleton State U (TX)
Taylor U (IN)
Tennessee State U (TN)
Texas A&M U (TX)
Texas Coll (TX)
Texas Lutheran U (TX)
Texas State U (TX)
Texas Wesleyan U (TX)
Tiffin U (OH)
Towson U (MD)
Trent U (ON, Canada)
Trine U (IN)
Trinity Christian Coll (IL)
Tufts U (MA)
Tulane U (LA)
Tusculum Coll (TN)
Union Coll (NE)
Union U (TN)
United States Air Force Acad (CO)
Universidad Adventista de las Antillas (PR)
Université de Montréal (QC, Canada)
Université de Sherbrooke (QC, Canada)
U at Albany, State U of New York (NY)
U at Buffalo, the State U of New York (NY)
U of Advancing Technology (AZ)
The U of Akron (OH)
U of Alaska Fairbanks (AK)
The U of Arizona (AZ)
U of Bridgeport (CT)
U of California, Irvine (CA)
U of California, Riverside (CA)
U of California, San Diego (CA)
U of California, Santa Barbara (CA)
U of Chicago (IL)
U of Colorado Boulder (CO)
U of Colorado Colorado Springs (CO)
U of Dayton (OH)
U of Delaware (DE)
U of Denver (CO)
U of Detroit Mercy (MI)
U of Evansville (IN)
The U of Findlay (OH)
U of Georgia (GA)
U of Great Falls (MT)
U of Guelph (ON, Canada)
U of Hawaii at Manoa (HI)
U of Houston–Clear Lake (TX)
U of Idaho (ID)
U of Illinois at Chicago (IL)
U of Illinois at Springfield (IL)
U of Indianapolis (IN)
U of Jamestown (ND)
U of King's Coll (NS, Canada)
U of La Verne (CA)
U of Lethbridge (AB, Canada)
U of Louisiana at Monroe (LA)
U of Maine (ME)
U of Maine at Farmington (ME)
U of Maine at Fort Kent (ME)
U of Management and Technology (VA)
U of Mary Hardin-Baylor (TX)
U of Maryland, Baltimore County (MD)
U of Massachusetts Amherst (MA)
U of Massachusetts Lowell (MA)
U of Miami (FL)
U of Michigan–Flint (MI)
U of Minnesota, Duluth (MN)
U of Minnesota, Morris (MN)
U of Minnesota, Twin Cities Campus (MN)
U of Missouri–Kansas City (MO)
U of Missouri–St. Louis (MO)
U of Nevada, Las Vegas (NV)
U of Nevada, Reno (NV)
U of New Hampshire at Manchester (NH)
U of New Haven (CT)
U of New Orleans (LA)
U of North Carolina at Asheville (NC)
The U of North Carolina at Chapel Hill (NC)
The U of North Carolina at Charlotte (NC)
The U of North Carolina at Greensboro (NC)
The U of North Carolina at Pembroke (NC)
The U of North Carolina Wilmington (NC)
U of Northern Iowa (IA)
U of Oklahoma (OK)
U of Pittsburgh (PA)
U of Pittsburgh at Bradford (PA)
U of Pittsburgh at Johnstown (PA)
U of Puget Sound (WA)
U of Regina (SK, Canada)
U of Rochester (NY)
U of St. Francis (IL)
U of St. Thomas (MN)
U of St. Thomas (TX)
U of San Diego (CA)
U of San Francisco (CA)
U of Saskatchewan (SK, Canada)
The U of Scranton (PA)
U of South Alabama (AL)
U of Southern California (CA)
U of Southern Indiana (IN)
U of Southern Maine (ME)
The U of Tennessee (TN)
The U of Tennessee at Chattanooga (TN)
The U of Tennessee at Martin (TN)
The U of Texas at Dallas (TX)
The U of Texas at El Paso (TX)
The U of Texas Rio Grande Valley (TX)
U of the Pacific (CA)
U of the Virgin Islands (VI)
U of Toronto (ON, Canada)
The U of Tulsa (OK)
U of Utah (UT)
U of Vermont (VT)
U of Washington (WA)
U of Washington, Bothell (WA)
U of Waterloo (ON, Canada)
U of Windsor (ON, Canada)
U of Wisconsin–Green Bay (WI)
U of Wisconsin–Milwaukee (WI)
U of Wisconsin–Parkside (WI)
U of Wisconsin–Superior (WI)
Ursinus Coll (PA)
Utah Valley U (UT)
Valparaiso U (IN)
Vanderbilt U (TN)
Villanova U (PA)
Virginia Military Inst (VA)
Virginia Polytechnic Inst and State U (VA)
Virginia State U (VA)
Virginia Wesleyan Coll (VA)
Wagner Coll (NY)
Walla Walla U (WA)
Walsh U (OH)
Wartburg Coll (IA)
Washington and Lee U (VA)
Washington Coll (MD)
Washington State U (WA)
Washington State U–Tri-Cities (WA)
Washington State U–Vancouver (WA)
Washington U in St. Louis (MO)
Wayland Baptist U (TX)
Weber State U (UT)
Webster U (MO)
Wells Coll (NY)
Wentworth Inst of Technology (MA)
Wesleyan U (CT)
Western Carolina U (NC)
Western Connecticut State U (CT)
Western Michigan U (MI)
Western New England U (MA)
Western Oregon U (OR)
Western State Colorado U (CO)
Westfield State U (MA)
Westminster Coll (PA)
Westminster Coll (UT)
Westmont Coll (CA)
West Texas A&M U (TX)
West Virginia State U (WV)
West Virginia U (WV)
West Virginia U Inst of Technology (WV)
West Virginia Wesleyan Coll (WV)
Wheaton Coll (IL)
Wheaton Coll (MA)
Whitworth U (WA)
Widener U (PA)
Willamette U (OR)
William Penn U (IA)
Williams Coll (MA)
Winona State U (MN)
Wittenberg U (OH)
Wofford Coll (SC)
Worcester Polytechnic Inst (MA)
Xavier U of Louisiana (LA)
York Coll of Pennsylvania (PA)
York Coll of the City U of New York (NY)
Youngstown State U (OH)

COMPUTER SOFTWARE AND MEDIA APPLICATIONS RELATED

Acad of Art U (CA)
Champlain Coll (VT)
Coll of Charleston (SC)
Duquesne U (PA)
Florida State U (FL)
Holy Names U (CA)
LeTourneau U (TX)
Limestone Coll (SC)
Loyola U Chicago (IL)
Morrisville State Coll (NY)
Pace U, Pleasantville Campus (NY)
State U of New York Coll of Agriculture and Technology at Cobleskill (NY)
U of Denver (CO)
U of Great Falls (MT)
U of Wisconsin–Stout (WI)
Worcester Polytechnic Inst (MA)

COMPUTER SOFTWARE ENGINEERING

Allegheny Coll (PA)
Arizona State U at the Polytechnic campus (AZ)
Auburn U (AL)
Baldwin Wallace U (OH)
Bowling Green State U (OH)
California Baptist U (CA)
Clarkson U (NY)
Concordia U (QC, Canada)
Dalhousie U (NS, Canada)
DigiPen Inst of Technology (WA)
Drexel U (PA)
Embry-Riddle Aeronautical U–Daytona (FL)
Embry-Riddle Aeronautical U–Prescott (AZ)
Fairfield U (CT)
Florida Inst of Technology (FL)
Iowa State U of Science and Technology (IA)
Kennesaw State U (GA)
Lawrence Technological U (MI)
Loyola U Chicago (IL)
Miami U (OH)
Michigan Technological U (MI)
Milwaukee School of Eng (WI)
Monmouth U (NJ)
Montana Tech of The U of Montana (MT)
Nova Southeastern U (FL)
Ohio Dominican U (OH)
Oklahoma City U (OK)
Penn State Erie, The Behrend Coll (PA)
Point Loma Nazarene U (CA)
Quinnipiac U (CT)
Robert Morris U (PA)
Rochester Inst of Technology (NY)
Rose-Hulman Inst of Technology (IN)
Shippensburg U of Pennsylvania (PA)
State U of New York at Oswego (NY)
Stevens Inst of Technology (NJ)
U of California, Irvine (CA)
U of Detroit Mercy (MI)
U of Guelph (ON, Canada)
U of Miami (FL)
U of Minnesota, Crookston (MN)
U of Northern Colorado (CO)
U of Regina (SK, Canada)
The U of Texas at Dallas (TX)
U of Toronto (ON, Canada)
U of Waterloo (ON, Canada)
U of Wisconsin–Platteville (WI)
Utah Valley U (UT)
Vermont Tech Coll (VT)
Washington State U (WA)
Wichita State U (KS)
William Penn U (IA)

COMPUTER SOFTWARE TECHNOLOGY

Cogswell Polytechnical Coll (CA)
Farmingdale State Coll (NY)
Sam Houston State U (TX)
U of Advancing Technology (AZ)

COMPUTER SYSTEMS ANALYSIS

Arizona State U at the Polytechnic campus (AZ)
Arkansas Tech U (AR)
Baldwin Wallace U (OH)
California Polytechnic State U, San Luis Obispo (CA)
Concordia U (QC, Canada)
Davenport U, Grand Rapids (MI)
HEC Montreal (QC, Canada)
Kent State U (OH)
Pittsburg State U (KS)
Rochester Inst of Technology (NY)
Saginaw Valley State U (MI)
St. Ambrose U (IA)
Seattle Pacific U (WA)
Shippensburg U of Pennsylvania (PA)
Southern New Hampshire U (NH)
Taylor U (IN)
Texas Christian U (TX)
Tiffin U (OH)
U of Advancing Technology (AZ)
U of Denver (CO)
U of Great Falls (MT)
U of Houston (TX)
U of Illinois at Springfield (IL)
U of Minnesota, Twin Cities Campus (MN)
U of North Dakota (ND)
U of Vermont (VT)
U of Washington, Bothell (WA)
West Virginia U Inst of Technology (WV)

COMPUTER SYSTEMS NETWORKING AND TELECOMMUNICATIONS

Baldwin Wallace U (OH)
Bayamón Central U (PR)
Bloomfield Coll (NJ)
Boise State U (ID)
California State U, East Bay (CA)
Champlain Coll (VT)
Chowan U (NC)
Concordia U (QC, Canada)
Davenport U, Grand Rapids (MI)
EDP U of Puerto Rico (PR)
EDP U of Puerto Rico–San Sebastian (PR)
Ferris State U (MI)
Idaho State U (ID)
Illinois State U (IL)
Inter American U of Puerto Rico, Aguadilla Campus (PR)
Inter American U of Puerto Rico, Bayamón Campus (PR)
Inter American U of Puerto Rico, Ponce Campus (PR)
Iona Coll (NY)
Johns Hopkins U (MD)
Kansas State U (KS)
Kean U (NJ)
Lindenwood U (MO)
Montana Tech of The U of Montana (MT)
Morrisville State Coll (NY)
Mount Vernon Nazarene U (OH)
Northwestern Oklahoma State U (OK)
Ohio U (OH)
Pennsylvania Coll of Technology (PA)
Rochester Inst of Technology (NY)
Stevenson U (MD)
Tiffin U (OH)
The U of Akron (OH)
U of Great Falls (MT)
U of Minnesota, Duluth (MN)
U of Minnesota, Twin Cities Campus (MN)
The U of North Carolina at Greensboro (NC)
U of Pennsylvania (PA)
U of Toronto (ON, Canada)
U of Wisconsin–Stout (WI)
Utah Valley U (UT)
Virginia Union U (VA)
Weber State U (UT)
Wentworth Inst of Technology (MA)
Western Illinois U (IL)
Western State Colorado U (CO)

COMPUTER TEACHER EDUCATION

Abilene Christian U (TX)
Arkansas Tech U (AR)
Baylor U (TX)
Bishop's U (QC, Canada)
Bowling Green State U (OH)
Buena Vista U (IA)
Colorado State U (CO)
Concordia U Chicago (IL)
Dakota State U (SD)
Dallas Baptist U (TX)
Eastern Michigan U (MI)
Edgewood Coll (WI)
Howard Payne U (TX)
McMurry U (TX)
Michigan State U (MI)
Utica Coll (NY)
Western Washington U (WA)

COMPUTER TECHNOLOGY/ COMPUTER SYSTEMS TECHNOLOGY

Colorado State U (CO)
Daytona State Coll (FL)
Excelsior Coll (NY)
Florida Atlantic U (FL)
New England Inst of Technology (RI)
Pittsburgh Tech Coll (PA)
Point Loma Nazarene U (CA)
Rensselaer Polytechnic Inst (NY)
Wayne State U (MI)

CONDENSED MATTER AND MATERIALS PHYSICS

Kansas Wesleyan U (KS)
Michigan Technological U (MI)
Rowan U (NJ)

CONDUCTING

Chapman U (CA)
McMurry U (TX)
The New School Coll of Performing Arts (NY)
Union Coll (NE)
The U of Texas at Austin (TX)

CONSERVATION BIOLOGY

Boston U (MA)
Bryant U (RI)
Cedar Crest Coll (PA)
Florida Inst of Technology (FL)
Grove City Coll (PA)
Prescott Coll (AZ)
Seattle U (WA)
State U of New York Coll of Environmental Science and Forestry (NY)
U of Idaho (ID)
U of Wisconsin–Madison (WI)

CONSTRUCTION ENGINEERING

The American U in Cairo (Egypt)
American U of Beirut (Lebanon)
Arizona State U at the Tempe campus (AZ)
Bowling Green State U (OH)
Bradley U (IL)
California State U, Long Beach (CA)
Concordia U (QC, Canada)
Iowa State U of Science and Technology (IA)
Kennesaw State U (GA)
Lamar U (TX)
National U (CA)
North Carolina State U (NC)
North Dakota State U (ND)
Oregon State U (OR)
Purdue U (IN)
Southern New Hampshire U (NH)
Texas A&M U–Commerce (TX)
Texas Tech U (TX)
The U of Alabama (AL)
Washington State U (WA)

CONSTRUCTION ENGINEERING TECHNOLOGY

Bemidji State U (MN)
Bowling Green State U (OH)
Bradley U (IL)
California Baptist U (CA)
California State Polytechnic U, Pomona (CA)
California State U, Chico (CA)

California State U, Fresno (CA)
California State U, Long Beach (CA)
California State U, Sacramento (CA)
Central Michigan U (MI)
Colorado Mesa U (CO)
Fairleigh Dickinson U, Metropolitan Campus (NJ)
Farmingdale State Coll (NY)
Fitchburg State U (MA)
Florida Ag and Mech U (FL)
Florida Inst of Technology (FL)
Florida Intl U (FL)
Georgia Southern U (GA)
Kansas State U (KS)
Louisiana Tech U (LA)
Michigan State U (MI)
Missouri Western State U (MO)
Montana State U (MT)
The Ohio State U (OH)
Oklahoma State U (OK)
Pittsburg State U (KS)
Prairie View A&M U (TX)
Purdue U Northwest (IN)
Sam Houston State U (TX)
San Diego State U (CA)
Seminole State Coll of Florida (FL)
South Dakota State U (SD)
Southern Illinois U Edwardsville (IL)
Tarleton State U (TX)
Texas A&M U (TX)
Texas State U (TX)
The U of Akron (OH)
U of Florida (FL)
U of Houston (TX)
U of Nevada, Las Vegas (NV)
U of North Florida (FL)
U of North Texas (TX)
The U of Toledo (OH)
Wayne State U (MI)
Western Carolina U (NC)
Western Kentucky U (KY)

CONSTRUCTION MANAGEMENT
Appalachian State U (NC)
Arizona State U at the Tempe campus (AZ)
Ball State U (IN)
Boise State U (ID)
Bradley U (IL)
Brigham Young U–Idaho (ID)
California State U, Fresno (CA)
California State U, Northridge (CA)
Central Connecticut State U (CT)
Central Washington U (WA)
Clemson U (SC)
Colorado State U (CO)
Drexel U (PA)
Dunwoody Coll of Technology (MN)
Eastern Michigan U (MI)
Ferris State U (MI)
Illinois State U (IL)
Indiana State U (IN)
John Brown U (AR)
Kennesaw State U (GA)
Kent State U (OH)
Lawrence Technological U (MI)
Louisiana State U and A&M Coll (LA)
Michigan State U (MI)
Michigan Technological U (MI)
Milwaukee School of Eng (WI)
Minnesota State U Moorhead (MN)
Mississippi State U (MS)
Missouri State U (MO)
Montana Tech of The U of Montana (MT)
National U (CA)
New England Inst of Technology (RI)
North Dakota State U (ND)
Northern Kentucky U (KY)
The Ohio State U (OH)
Pittsburg State U (KS)
Roger Williams U (RI)
State U of New York Coll of Environmental Science and Forestry (NY)
State U of New York Coll of Technology at Alfred (NY)
U of Louisiana at Monroe (LA)
U of Minnesota, Twin Cities Campus (MN)
U of Nevada, Las Vegas (NV)
U of Northern Iowa (IA)
U of Oklahoma (OK)
U of Wisconsin–Stout (WI)
Utah Valley U (UT)
Vermont Tech Coll (VT)
Virginia Polytechnic Inst and State U (VA)
Washington State U (WA)
Wentworth Inst of Technology (MA)
Western Carolina U (NC)
Western Illinois U (IL)
Western Nevada Coll (NV)

CONSTRUCTION TRADES
Utica Coll (NY)

CONSTRUCTION TRADES RELATED
Weber State U (UT)

CONSUMER ECONOMICS
Louisiana Tech U (LA)
South Dakota State U (SD)
U of Georgia (GA)
U of Kentucky (KY)
The U of Tennessee (TN)
U of Utah (UT)

CONSUMER MERCHANDISING/ RETAILING MANAGEMENT
Acad of Art U (CA)
Bradley U (IL)
HEC Montreal (QC, Canada)
Madonna U (MI)
Oregon State U (OR)
Purdue U (IN)
San Francisco State U (CA)
Savannah Coll of Art and Design (GA)
Simmons Coll (MA)
Syracuse U (NY)

CONSUMER SERVICES AND ADVOCACY
Carson-Newman U (TN)
Tennessee State U (TN)
Texas State U (TX)

CORRECTIONS
Adams State U (CO)
Bowling Green State U (OH)
California State U, East Bay (CA)
California State U, Stanislaus (CA)
California U of Pennsylvania (PA)
Jacksonville State U (AL)
John Jay Coll of Criminal Justice of the City U of New York (NY)
Langston U (OK)
Lincoln Coll–Normal (IL)
Mercyhurst U (PA)
Minnesota State U Mankato (MN)
Missouri Valley Coll (MO)
Southeast Missouri State U (MO)
Stephen F. Austin State U (TX)
Texas State U (TX)
Tiffin U (OH)
Tulane U (LA)
U of Great Falls (MT)
U of Minnesota, Crookston (MN)
U of Pittsburgh (PA)
Washburn U (KS)
Weber State U (UT)
Western Oregon U (OR)
Youngstown State U (OH)

CORRECTIONS ADMINISTRATION
Inter American U of Puerto Rico, Barranquitas Campus (PR)
U of Great Falls (MT)

CORRECTIONS AND CRIMINAL JUSTICE RELATED
Albany State U (GA)
Anderson U (SC)
Averett U (VA)
Bethune-Cookman U (FL)
Cameron U (OK)
Cedarville U (OH)
Corban U (OR)
Emporia State U (KS)
Eureka Coll (IL)
John Jay Coll of Criminal Justice of the City U of New York (NY)
Keene State Coll (NH)
La Roche Coll (PA)
Limestone Coll (SC)
Morrisville State Coll (NY)
Muskingum U (OH)
Newberry Coll (SC)
Northwestern Coll (IA)
Rasmussen Coll Bloomington (MN)
Rasmussen Coll Brooklyn Park (MN)
Rasmussen Coll Eagan (MN)
Rasmussen Coll Fargo (ND)
Rasmussen Coll Fort Myers (FL)
Rasmussen Coll Kansas City/ Overland Park (KS)
Rasmussen Coll Lake Elmo/ Woodbury (MN)
Rasmussen Coll Land O' Lakes (FL)
Rasmussen Coll Mankato (MN)
Rasmussen Coll Moorhead (MN)
Rasmussen Coll New Port Richey (FL)
Rasmussen Coll Ocala (FL)
Rasmussen Coll St. Cloud (MN)
Rasmussen Coll Tampa/Brandon (FL)
Rasmussen Coll Topeka (KS)
Robert Morris U (PA)
Roger Williams U (RI)
Saint Mary's U of Minnesota (MN)
Sam Houston State U (TX)
Southern New Hampshire U (NH)
State U of New York Coll of Technology at Canton (NY)
The U of Alabama at Birmingham (AL)
U of Alaska Fairbanks (AK)
U of Great Falls (MT)
U of Michigan–Flint (MI)
U of Saint Joseph (CT)
Vincennes U (IN)
Weber State U (UT)

COSTUME DESIGN
Acad of Art U (CA)
Marymount Manhattan Coll (NY)
Stephens Coll (MO)
Webster U (MO)

COUNSELING PSYCHOLOGY
Arizona Christian U (AZ)
Averett U (VA)
Avila U (MO)
Cornerstone U (MI)
Delaware Valley U (PA)
Eastern Nazarene Coll (MA)
Eastern Washington U (WA)
Ecclesia Coll (AR)
Emmanuel Coll (MA)
Emmaus Bible Coll (IA)
Faulkner U (AL)
Fort Lewis Coll (CO)
Hobe Sound Bible Coll (FL)
Hope Intl U (CA)
Lesley U (MA)
Mid-Atlantic Christian U (NC)
Morningside Coll (IA)
Mount Saint Mary's U (CA)
Newman U (KS)
Northwestern U (IL)
Point U (GA)
Prescott Coll (AZ)
Saint Leo U (FL)
Southwestern Assemblies of God U (TX)
Tarleton State U (TX)
Toccoa Falls Coll (GA)
U of Chicago (IL)
U of Georgia (GA)
U of Jamestown (ND)
Wayne State Coll (NE)
Wheelock Coll (MA)

COUNSELOR EDUCATION/ SCHOOL COUNSELING AND GUIDANCE
Bowling Green State U (OH)
Buena Vista U (IA)
East Central U (OK)
St. Cloud State U (MN)
Sam Houston State U (TX)
Tarleton State U (TX)
Université de Sherbrooke (QC, Canada)
U of Georgia (GA)
The U of South Dakota (SD)
U of Windsor (ON, Canada)

CRAFTS, FOLK ART AND ARTISANRY
Bowling Green State U (OH)
Bridgewater State U (MA)
Brigham Young U (UT)
Kent State U (OH)
Kutztown U of Pennsylvania (PA)
Malone U (OH)
Oregon Coll of Art and Craft (OR)
Rochester Inst of Technology (NY)
The U of the Arts (PA)
Virginia Commonwealth U (VA)

CREATIVE WRITING
Adams State U (CO)
Agnes Scott Coll (GA)
Albion Coll (MI)
Allegheny Coll (PA)
The American U of Paris (France)
Anderson U (SC)
Arcadia U (PA)
Arkansas Tech U (AR)
Asbury U (KY)
Ashland U (OH)
Augsburg Coll (MN)
Augustana Coll (IL)
Austin Coll (TX)
Baldwin Wallace U (OH)
Bard Coll (NY)
Belhaven U (MS)
Beloit Coll (WI)
Bennington Coll (VT)
Berry Coll (GA)
Binghamton U, State U of New York (NY)
Biola U (CA)
Blackburn Coll (IL)
Bowie State U (MD)
Bowling Green State U (OH)
Brandeis U (MA)
Briar Cliff U (IA)
Bridgewater State U (MA)
Brooklyn Coll of the City U of New York (NY)
Bucknell U (PA)
Butler U (IN)
California Baptist U (CA)
California Coll of the Arts (CA)
California State U, East Bay (CA)
California State U, Long Beach (CA)
Calvary U (MO)
Canisius Coll (NY)
Capital U (OH)
Carlow U (PA)
Carnegie Mellon U (PA)
Carson-Newman U (TN)
Catawba Coll (NC)
Central Michigan U (MI)
Central Washington U (WA)
Chapman U (CA)
Chatham U (PA)
Christian Brothers U (TN)
City Coll of the City U of New York (NY)
Coe Coll (IA)
Colby Coll (ME)
Colby-Sawyer Coll (NH)
The Coll of Idaho (ID)
Coll of the Atlantic (ME)
Colorado Christian U (CO)
The Colorado Coll (CO)
Colorado State U (CO)
Columbia Coll Chicago (IL)
Columbia U (NY)
Columbia U, School of General Studies (NY)
Concordia U (QC, Canada)
Converse Coll (SC)
Corban U (OR)
Cornell Coll (IA)
Dartmouth Coll (NH)
Denison U (OH)
Dixie State U (UT)
Dominican U of California (CA)
Eastern Michigan U (MI)
Eastern Nazarene Coll (MA)
Eckerd Coll (FL)
Emerson Coll (MA)
Emily Carr U of Art + Design (BC, Canada)
Emory & Henry Coll (VA)
Emory U (GA)
Fairleigh Dickinson U, Coll at Florham (NJ)
Florida Southern Coll (FL)
Florida State U (FL)
Franklin & Marshall Coll (PA)
Franklin Coll (IN)
Franklin Pierce U (NH)
Gettysburg Coll (PA)
Goddard Coll (VT)
Green Mountain Coll (VT)
Hamilton Coll (NY)
Hamline U (MN)
Hampshire Coll (MA)
Hiram Coll (OH)
Hofstra U (NY)
Houghton Coll (NY)
Inst of American Indian Arts (NM)
Ithaca Coll (NY)
Johns Hopkins U (MD)
Kansas City Art Inst (MO)
Knox Coll (IL)
Lasell Coll (MA)
Lee U (TN)
Lehman Coll of the City U of New York (NY)
Linfield Coll (OR)
Loras Coll (IA)
Loyola U Maryland (MD)
Loyola U New Orleans (LA)
Lubbock Christian U (TX)
Lycoming Coll (PA)
Malone U (OH)
Massachusetts Coll of Liberal Arts (MA)
Massachusetts Inst of Technology (MA)
McMurry U (TX)
Mercer U, Macon (GA)
Miami U (OH)
Minnesota State U Mankato (MN)
Morehead State U (KY)
Mount St. Joseph U (OH)
Murray State U (KY)
New England Coll (NH)
New Hampshire Inst of Art (NH)
North Central Coll (IL)
Northland Coll (WI)
Oberlin Coll (OH)
Ohio U (OH)
Ohio Wesleyan U (OH)
Oklahoma Christian U (OK)
Pepperdine U, Malibu (CA)
Pratt Inst (NY)
Providence Coll (RI)
Purchase Coll, State U of New York (NY)
Purdue U (IN)
Randolph Coll (VA)
Redeemer U Coll (ON, Canada)
Rhode Island Coll (RI)
Ringling Coll of Art and Design (FL)
Roanoke Coll (VA)
Rocky Mountain Coll (MT)
Roger Williams U (RI)
Saginaw Valley State U (MI)
St. Bonaventure U (NY)
St. Catherine U (MN)
Saint Mary-of-the-Woods Coll (IN)
Saint Mary's Coll (IN)
St. Thomas Aquinas Coll (NY)
San Francisco State U (CA)
Sarah Lawrence Coll (NY)
School of the Art Inst of Chicago (IL)
Seattle U (WA)
Seton Hill U (PA)
Sierra Nevada Coll (NV)
Southern Methodist U (TX)
Southern New Hampshire U (NH)
Southern Oregon U (OR)
Southwestern Coll (KS)
Spalding U (KY)
State U of New York at Oswego (NY)
State U of New York Coll at Potsdam (NY)
Stephen F. Austin State U (TX)
Stephens Coll (MO)
Susquehanna U (PA)
Sweet Briar Coll (VA)
Texas Christian U (TX)
Texas Wesleyan U (TX)
Truman State U (MO)
Université de Montréal (QC, Canada)
The U of Arizona (AZ)
U of California, Riverside (CA)
U of California, San Diego (CA)
U of Cincinnati (OH)
U of Denver (CO)
U of Evansville (IN)
The U of Findlay (OH)
U of Great Falls (MT)
U of Houston (TX)
U of Idaho (ID)
U of La Verne (CA)

U of Maine at Farmington (ME)
U of Miami (FL)
U of Michigan (MI)
U of Mount Union (OH)
The U of North Carolina Wilmington (NC)
U of Pittsburgh (PA)
U of Pittsburgh at Bradford (PA)
U of Pittsburgh at Greensburg (PA)
U of Pittsburgh at Johnstown (PA)
U of Regina (SK, Canada)
U of St. Thomas (MN)
U of Southern California (CA)
The U of Texas at Austin (TX)
The U of Texas at El Paso (TX)
The U of the Arts (PA)
U of Windsor (ON, Canada)
Valparaiso U (IN)
Villa Maria Coll (NY)
Waldorf U (IA)
Washington U in St. Louis (MO)
Waynesburg U (PA)
Weber State U (UT)
Wells Coll (NY)
Western Michigan U (MI)
Western New England U (MA)
Western State Colorado U (CO)
Western Washington U (WA)
West Virginia Wesleyan Coll (WV)
Wheaton Coll (MA)
Wichita State U (KS)

CRIMINALISTICS AND CRIMINAL SCIENCE
Alabama State U (AL)
Bay Path U (MA)
Florida Gulf Coast U (FL)
Inter American U of Puerto Rico, Metropolitan Campus (PR)
Inter American U of Puerto Rico, Ponce Campus (PR)
Saint Leo U (FL)
Seattle U (WA)
Tiffin U (OH)
Weber State U (UT)

CRIMINAL JUSTICE/LAW ENFORCEMENT ADMINISTRATION
Abilene Christian U (TX)
Adams State U (CO)
Albertus Magnus Coll (CT)
Alfred U (NY)
Alvernia U (PA)
American Public U System (WV)
Anderson U (IN)
Anderson U (SC)
Arcadia U (PA)
Arizona State U at the Downtown Phoenix campus (AZ)
Arizona State U at the West campus (AZ)
Athens State U (AL)
Austin Peay State U (TN)
Averett U (VA)
Barton Coll (NC)
Bay Path U (MA)
Becker Coll (MA)
Belhaven U (MS)
Bemidji State U (MN)
Berkeley Coll–New York City Campus (NY)
Berkeley Coll–White Plains Campus (NY)
Berkeley Coll–Woodland Park Campus (NJ)
Blackburn Coll (IL)
Bluefield Coll (VA)
Boise State U (ID)
Bowie State U (MD)
Bowling Green State U (OH)
Bradley U (IL)
Briar Cliff U (IA)
Buffalo State Coll, State U of New York (NY)
California Baptist U (CA)
California Lutheran U (CA)
California State U, Bakersfield (CA)
California State U, East Bay (CA)
California State U, Long Beach (CA)
California State U, Sacramento (CA)
Calvary U (MO)
Campbellsville U (KY)
Canisius Coll (NY)
Carthage Coll (WI)
Catawba Coll (NC)
Central Penn Coll (PA)
Chestnut Hill Coll (PA)
The Citadel, The Military Coll of South Carolina (SC)
Clarion U of Pennsylvania (PA)
Coll of Coastal Georgia (GA)
The Coll of New Jersey (NJ)
The Coll of Saint Rose (NY)
Columbia Coll (MO)
Concordia U Wisconsin (WI)
Corban U (OR)
Culver-Stockton Coll (MO)
Dalton State Coll (GA)
Delaware Valley U (PA)
Drexel U (PA)
Eastern Nazarene Coll (MA)
East Tennessee State U (TN)
East Texas Baptist U (TX)
Elmira Coll (NY)
Elms Coll (MA)
Emmanuel Coll (GA)
Evangel U (MO)
Fairleigh Dickinson U, Metropolitan Campus (NJ)
Fayetteville State U (NC)
Felician U (NJ)
Ferris State U (MI)
Florida National U (FL)
Florida SouthWestern State Coll (FL)
Franklin Pierce U (NH)
The George Washington U (DC)
Georgia Coll & State U (GA)
Georgia Southwestern State U (GA)
Graceland U (IA)
Grand Valley State U (MI)
Grand View U (IA)
Greenville Coll (IL)
Hampton U (VA)
Hannibal-LaGrange U (MO)
Harris-Stowe State U (MO)
Hartwick Coll (NY)
Hawai`i Pacific U (HI)
Huntingdon Coll (AL)
Husson U (ME)
Huston-Tillotson U (TX)
Indiana U East (IN)
Inter American U of Puerto Rico, Guayama Campus (PR)
Iona Coll (NY)
Jacksonville State U (AL)
John Jay Coll of Criminal Justice of the City U of New York (NY)
Kansas Wesleyan U (KS)
Kean U (NJ)
Keuka Coll (NY)
Lake Erie Coll (OH)
Lees-McRae Coll (NC)
Limestone Coll (SC)
Lincoln Coll (IL)
Lincoln Coll–Normal (IL)
Lincoln Coll of New England, Southington (CT)
Lincoln U (MO)
Lindsey Wilson Coll (KY)
Lock Haven U of Pennsylvania (PA)
Lubbock Christian U (TX)
Lynn U (FL)
MacMurray Coll (IL)
Mansfield U of Pennsylvania (PA)
Marist Coll (NY)
Marymount California U (CA)
Marymount U (VA)
Marywood U (PA)
Mercy Coll (NY)
Merrimack Coll (MA)
Michigan State U (MI)
MidAmerica Nazarene U (KS)
Mississippi Valley State U (MS)
Missouri Valley Coll (MO)
Morris Coll (SC)
Mount Aloysius Coll (PA)
Mount Ida Coll (MA)
Mount Mary U (WI)
Mount Mercy U (IA)
Mount Vernon Nazarene U (OH)
Muskingum U (OH)
National U (CA)
Nevada State Coll (NV)
New England Coll (NH)
New England Inst of Technology (RI)
Newman U (KS)
New York Inst of Technology (NY)
North Carolina Wesleyan Coll (NC)
Northcentral U (CA)
Northeastern State U (OK)
North Greenville U (SC)
Northwest Christian U (OR)
Northwest U (WA)
Ohio U–Eastern (OH)
Ohio U–Zanesville (OH)
Oklahoma City U (OK)
Olivet Nazarene U (IL)
Pace U (NY)
Pace U, Pleasantville Campus (NY)
Penn State Abington (PA)
Penn State Altoona (PA)
Penn State Beaver (PA)
Penn State Berks (PA)
Penn State Brandywine (PA)
Penn State DuBois (PA)
Penn State Erie, The Behrend Coll (PA)
Penn State Fayette, The Eberly Campus (PA)
Penn State Greater Allegheny (PA)
Penn State Hazleton (PA)
Penn State Lehigh Valley (PA)
Penn State Mont Alto (PA)
Penn State New Kensington (PA)
Penn State Schuylkill (PA)
Penn State Shenango (PA)
Penn State U Park (PA)
Penn State Wilkes-Barre (PA)
Penn State Worthington Scranton (PA)
Penn State York (PA)
Piedmont Coll (GA)
Portland State U (OR)
Regent U (VA)
Roberts Wesleyan Coll (NY)
Rochester Inst of Technology (NY)
Rockhurst U (MO)
Rogers State U (OK)
Roger Williams U (RI)
Rutgers U–New Brunswick (NJ)
Sacred Heart U (CT)
Saint Augustine's U (NC)
St. Cloud State U (MN)
Saint Francis U (PA)
St. John's U (NY)
St. Joseph's Coll, Long Island Campus (NY)
St. Joseph's Coll, New York (NY)
St. Thomas Aquinas Coll (NY)
St. Thomas U (FL)
Salve Regina U (RI)
Sam Houston State U (TX)
San Francisco State U (CA)
Shenandoah U (VA)
Simpson Coll (IA)
Sonoma State U (CA)
South Carolina State U (SC)
Southwest Baptist U (MO)
State U of New York at Fredonia (NY)
State U of New York at Oswego (NY)
State U of New York Coll of Technology at Canton (NY)
Sterling Coll (KS)
Stevenson U (MD)
Talladega Coll (AL)
Tarleton State U (TX)
Tennessee State U (TN)
Thomas U (GA)
Tiffin U (OH)
Trevecca Nazarene U (TN)
Trine U (IN)
Trinity Christian Coll (IL)
Tusculum Coll (TN)
Union Coll (KY)
Union Inst & U (OH)
U at Albany, State U of New York (NY)
U of Central Missouri (MO)
U of Colorado Colorado Springs (CO)
U of Colorado Denver (CO)
U of Dayton (OH)
The U of Findlay (OH)
U of Georgia (GA)
U of Great Falls (MT)
U of Guelph (ON, Canada)
U of Louisville (KY)
U of Maine at Presque Isle (ME)
U of Management and Technology (VA)
U of Mary Hardin-Baylor (TX)
U of Massachusetts Lowell (MA)
U of Minnesota, Crookston (MN)
U of Missouri–Kansas City (MO)
U of New Haven (CT)
U of North Alabama (AL)
U of Northern Iowa (IA)
U of Oklahoma (OK)
U of Pittsburgh at Bradford (PA)
U of Pittsburgh at Greensburg (PA)
U of Regina (SK, Canada)
U of St. Francis (IL)
U of South Alabama (AL)
U of South Carolina (SC)
The U of South Dakota (SD)
The U of Tennessee at Chattanooga (TN)
The U of Tennessee at Martin (TN)
The U of Texas at El Paso (TX)
U of the Incarnate Word (TX)
U of the Southwest (NM)
U of Wisconsin–Parkside (WI)
Utah Valley U (UT)
Utica Coll (NY)
Villanova U (PA)
Virginia Commonwealth U (VA)
Viterbo U (WI)
Waldorf U (IA)
Washburn U (KS)
Waynesburg U (PA)
Webber Intl U (FL)
Western Illinois U (IL)
Western Oregon U (OR)
Westminster Coll (PA)
West Virginia U Inst of Technology (WV)
West Virginia Wesleyan Coll (WV)
Widener U (PA)
William Peace U (NC)
Wilmington U (DE)
Wingate U (NC)
York Coll of Pennsylvania (PA)
Youngstown State U (OH)

CRIMINAL JUSTICE/POLICE SCIENCE
Armstrong State U (GA)
Bemidji State U (MN)
Bowling Green State U (OH)
California State U, East Bay (CA)
Caribbean U (PR)
Colorado Mesa U (CO)
Columbia Southern U (AL)
East Central U (OK)
Eastern Nazarene Coll (MA)
Ferris State U (MI)
Gwynedd Mercy U (PA)
Heidelberg U (OH)
Hilbert Coll (NY)
Idaho State U (ID)
Inter American U of Puerto Rico, Metropolitan Campus (PR)
Inter American U of Puerto Rico, San Germán Campus (PR)
Jacksonville State U (AL)
John Jay Coll of Criminal Justice of the City U of New York (NY)
MacMurray Coll (IL)
Malone U (OH)
Marian U (WI)
Minnesota State U Mankato (MN)
Northern State U (SD)
Northwestern Oklahoma State U (OK)
Oklahoma Baptist U (OK)
Oklahoma City U (OK)
Rowan U (NJ)
St. Gregory's U, Shawnee (OK)
Sam Houston State U (TX)
Southern Utah U (UT)
Stephen F. Austin State U (TX)
Texas A&M Intl U (TX)
Texas State U (TX)
Université de Montréal (QC, Canada)
U of Great Falls (MT)
U of Hartford (CT)
U of Pittsburgh at Greensburg (PA)
U of Regina (SK, Canada)
U of the Virgin Islands (VI)
U of Toronto (ON, Canada)
U of Washington, Tacoma (WA)
U of Wisconsin–Superior (WI)
Washington State U (WA)
Washington State U–Global Campus (WA)
Washington State U–Vancouver (WA)
Weber State U (UT)
Western Connecticut State U (CT)
Western Oregon U (OR)

CRIMINAL JUSTICE/SAFETY
Adelphi U (NY)
Alabama State U (AL)
Albany State U (GA)
Alcorn State U (MS)
American Intl Coll (MA)
American Public U System (WV)
American U (DC)
Angelo State U (TX)
Antioch U Los Angeles (CA)
Appalachian State U (NC)
Athens State U (AL)
Auburn U at Montgomery (AL)
Augusta U (GA)
Aurora U (IL)
Baldwin Wallace U (OH)
Ball State U (IN)
Bellarmine U (KY)
Belmont Abbey Coll (NC)
Bethel Coll (IN)
Bloomsburg U of Pennsylvania (PA)
Bluefield State Coll (WV)
Blue Mountain Coll (MS)
Bluffton U (OH)
Boston U (MA)
Bowling Green State U (OH)
Bowling Green State U–Firelands Coll (OH)
Brandman U (CA)
Bridgewater State U (MA)
Bryan Coll (TN)
Buena Vista U (IA)
Cairn U (PA)
Caldwell U (NJ)
California State U, Chico (CA)
California State U, Dominguez Hills (CA)
California State U, Fresno (CA)
California State U, Fullerton (CA)
California State U, San Bernardino (CA)
California State U, Stanislaus (CA)
California U of Pennsylvania (PA)
Calumet Coll of Saint Joseph (IN)
Cardinal Stritch U (WI)
Cazenovia Coll (NY)
Centenary U (NJ)
Central Methodist U (MO)
Central Penn Coll (PA)
Central State U (OH)
Central Washington U (WA)
Chaminade U of Honolulu (HI)
Champlain Coll (VT)
Charleston Southern U (SC)
Chowan U (NC)
Clark Atlanta U (GA)
Clayton State U (GA)
The Coll at Brockport, State U of New York (NY)
Coll of Coastal Georgia (GA)
Coll of the Ozarks (MO)
Colorado Mesa U (CO)
Columbus State U (GA)
Concordia U, Nebraska (NE)
Concordia U, St. Paul (MN)
Curry Coll (MA)
Dallas Baptist U (TX)
Davenport U, Grand Rapids (MI)
Defiance Coll (OH)
DeSales U (PA)
Dixie State U (UT)
Dominican Coll (NY)
East Carolina U (NC)
Eastern Nazarene Coll (MA)
East Stroudsburg U of Pennsylvania (PA)
Edgewood Coll (WI)
Elizabeth City State U (NC)
Endicott Coll (MA)
Faulkner U (AL)
Fisher Coll (MA)
Fitchburg State U (MA)
Florida Ag and Mech U (FL)
Florida Atlantic U (FL)
Florida Gulf Coast U (FL)
Florida Intl U (FL)
Freed-Hardeman U (TN)
Friends U (KS)
Frostburg State U (MD)
Gannon U (PA)
Georgia Gwinnett Coll (GA)
Georgian Court U (NJ)
Georgia Southern U (GA)
Georgia State U (GA)
Gonzaga U (WA)
Governors State U (IL)
Grace Coll (IN)

Grambling State U (LA)
Grand View U (IA)
Granite State Coll (NH)
Guilford Coll (NC)
Hamline U (MN)
Harding U (AR)
Hardin-Simmons U (TX)
Harris-Stowe State U (MO)
Henderson State U (AR)
High Point U (NC)
Hilbert Coll (NY)
Holy Family U (PA)
Hood Coll (MD)
Husson U (ME)
Huston-Tillotson U (TX)
Illinois State U (IL)
Immaculata U (PA)
Indiana U Bloomington (IN)
Indiana U Kokomo (IN)
Indiana U Northwest (IN)
Indiana U–Purdue U Indianapolis (IN)
Indiana U South Bend (IN)
Indiana U Southeast (IN)
Inter American U of Puerto Rico, Aguadilla Campus (PR)
Inter American U of Puerto Rico, Barranquitas Campus (PR)
Inter American U of Puerto Rico, Fajardo Campus (PR)
Inter American U of Puerto Rico, Metropolitan Campus (PR)
Inter American U of Puerto Rico, Ponce Campus (PR)
Iowa State U of Science and Technology (IA)
Iowa Wesleyan U (IA)
Jackson State U (MS)
Kennesaw State U (GA)
Kent State U (OH)
Kent State U at Ashtabula (OH)
Kent State U at East Liverpool (OH)
Kent State U at Salem (OH)
Kent State U at Stark (OH)
Kent State U at Trumbull (OH)
Kent State U at Tuscarawas (OH)
Kentucky State U (KY)
Kentucky Wesleyan Coll (KY)
King's Coll (PA)
King U (TN)
Kutztown U of Pennsylvania (PA)
Lamar U (TX)
Lane Coll (TN)
La Roche Coll (PA)
La Salle U (PA)
Lasell Coll (MA)
Lenoir-Rhyne U (NC)
Lewis U (IL)
Liberty U (VA)
Limestone Coll (SC)
Lincoln U (PA)
Lindenwood U (MO)
Lipscomb U (TN)
Longwood U (VA)
Loras Coll (IA)
Louisiana Coll (LA)
Louisiana State U at Alexandria (LA)
Lourdes U (OH)
Loyola U Chicago (IL)
Madonna U (MI)
Manchester U (IN)
Marshall U (WV)
McNeese State U (LA)
Mercer U, Macon (GA)
Mercyhurst U (PA)
Messiah Coll (PA)
Metropolitan State U of Denver (CO)
Michigan State U (MI)
Minnesota State U Moorhead (MN)
Minot State U (ND)
Missouri Baptist U (MO)
Missouri Western State U (MO)
Molloy Coll (NY)
Monmouth U (NJ)
Montana State U Billings (MT)
Mount Marty Coll (SD)
Mount Vernon Nazarene U (OH)
Murray State U (KY)
Neumann U (PA)
New Jersey City U (NJ)
New Mexico Highlands U (NM)
New Mexico State U (NM)
North Carolina Central U (NC)
North Dakota State U (ND)
Northeastern Illinois U (IL)
Northeastern U (MA)
Northern Kentucky U (KY)
Northwestern State U of Louisiana (LA)
Northwest U (WA)
Nova Southeastern U (FL)
Nyack Coll (NY)
Oakland City U (IN)
Ohio Christian U (OH)
Our Lady of the Lake U of San Antonio (TX)
Penn State Abington (PA)
Penn State Altoona (PA)
Penn State Erie, The Behrend Coll (PA)
Penn State Fayette, The Eberly Campus (PA)
Penn State Harrisburg (PA)
Penn State Schuylkill (PA)
Penn State Wilkes-Barre (PA)
Pittsburg State U (KS)
Plymouth State U (NH)
Point Park U (PA)
Point U (GA)
Polk State Coll (FL)
Prairie View A&M U (TX)
Quinnipiac U (CT)
Radford U (VA)
Regis Coll (MA)
Rhode Island Coll (RI)
Roanoke Coll (VA)
Rochester Inst of Technology (NY)
Rosemont Coll (PA)
Rowan U (NJ)
Royal Roads U (BC, Canada)
Rutgers U–Camden (NJ)
Rutgers U–Newark (NJ)
Sacred Heart U (CT)
Saginaw Valley State U (MI)
St. Ambrose U (IA)
Saint Anselm Coll (NH)
St. Edward's U (TX)
Saint Leo U (FL)
Saint Louis U (MO)
Saint Martin's U (WA)
Saint Peter's U (NJ)
St. Thomas U (FL)
Samford U (AL)
Sam Houston State U (TX)
San Diego State U (CA)
Seattle U (WA)
Seton Hill U (PA)
Shaw U (NC)
Shippensburg U of Pennsylvania (PA)
Southeastern Louisiana U (LA)
Southeastern Oklahoma State U (OK)
Southeastern U (FL)
Southern Arkansas U–Magnolia (AR)
Southern Illinois U Edwardsville (IL)
Southwestern Assemblies of God U (TX)
Southwestern Coll (KS)
State U of New York at Plattsburgh (NY)
State U of New York Coll at Potsdam (NY)
Sullivan U (KY)
Tarleton State U (TX)
Temple U (PA)
Tennessee Wesleyan U (TN)
Texas A&M U–Central Texas (TX)
Texas A&M U–Commerce (TX)
Texas A&M U–Kingsville (TX)
Texas Christian U (TX)
Texas Coll (TX)
Texas State U (TX)
Texas Wesleyan U (TX)
Texas Woman's U (TX)
Thomas More Coll (KY)
Troy U (AL)
Truett McConnell U (GA)
Truman State U (MO)
The U of Akron (OH)
The U of Alabama (AL)
U of Arkansas (AR)
U of Bridgeport (CT)
U of Central Florida (FL)
U of Cincinnati (OH)
U of Detroit Mercy (MI)
U of Evansville (IN)
U of Great Falls (MT)
U of Houston–Downtown (TX)
U of Illinois at Chicago (IL)
U of Illinois at Springfield (IL)
U of Jamestown (ND)
U of Louisiana at Monroe (LA)
U of Maryland U Coll (MD)
U of Massachusetts Boston (MA)
U of Michigan–Dearborn (MI)
U of Mount Union (OH)
U of Nebraska at Kearney (NE)
U of Nevada, Las Vegas (NV)
The U of North Carolina at Charlotte (NC)
The U of North Carolina at Pembroke (NC)
U of North Dakota (ND)
U of Northern Colorado (CO)
U of North Florida (FL)
U of North Georgia (GA)
U of North Texas (TX)
U of Pikeville (KY)
U of Regina (SK, Canada)
U of Saint Francis (IN)
The U of Scranton (PA)
The U of South Dakota (SD)
U of Southern Indiana (IN)
U of Southern Mississippi (MS)
The U of Texas at San Antonio (TX)
The U of Texas of the Permian Basin (TX)
The U of Texas Rio Grande Valley (TX)
U of the Cumberlands (KY)
U of the Fraser Valley (BC, Canada)
U of the Incarnate Word (TX)
The U of Toledo (OH)
U of Valley Forge (PA)
The U of Virginia's Coll at Wise (VA)
U of Wisconsin–Eau Claire (WI)
U of Wisconsin–Milwaukee (WI)
U of Wisconsin–Platteville (WI)
U of Wisconsin–Superior (WI)
Valdosta State U (GA)
Virginia State U (VA)
Virginia Wesleyan Coll (VA)
Viterbo U (WI)
Waldorf U (IA)
Wayne State Coll (NE)
Wayne State U (MI)
Weber State U (UT)
West Chester U of Pennsylvania (PA)
Western Carolina U (NC)
Western Michigan U (MI)
Western New England U (MA)
Westfield State U (MA)
Westminster Coll (UT)
West Texas A&M U (TX)
West Virginia State U (WV)
Wheeling Jesuit U (WV)
Wichita State U (KS)
Wilkes U (PA)
William Paterson U of New Jersey (NJ)
William Woods U (MO)
Winona State U (MN)
Worcester State U (MA)
Youngstown State U (OH)

CRIMINOLOGY
Adams State U (CO)
Albright Coll (PA)
Alderson Broaddus U (WV)
Arcadia U (PA)
Assumption Coll (MA)
Auburn U (AL)
Avila U (MO)
Barry U (FL)
Benedictine Coll (KS)
Biola U (CA)
Butler U (IN)
Cabrini U (PA)
California State U, Fresno (CA)
California State U, San Marcos (CA)
California State U, Stanislaus (CA)
Capital U (OH)
Carlow U (PA)
Cedar Crest Coll (PA)
Centenary U (NJ)
Central Connecticut State U (CT)
Chatham U (PA)
Cleveland State U (OH)
The Coll of New Jersey (NJ)
Concordia U Chicago (IL)
Dominican U (IL)
Drexel U (PA)
Drury U (MO)
Eastern Michigan U (MI)
Eastern U (PA)
Eastern Washington U (WA)
Emmanuel Coll (MA)
Fairleigh Dickinson U, Coll at Florham (NJ)
Flagler Coll (FL)
Florida Southern Coll (FL)
Florida State U (FL)
Framingham State U (MA)
Geneva Coll (PA)
Gonzaga U (WA)
Hamline U (MN)
Hofstra U (NY)
Howard Payne U (TX)
Husson U (ME)
Indiana State U (IN)
Indiana U of Pennsylvania (PA)
John Jay Coll of Criminal Justice of the City U of New York (NY)
Johnson C. Smith U (NC)
Lasell Coll (MA)
Lebanon Valley Coll (PA)
Lees-McRae Coll (NC)
Le Moyne Coll (NY)
LeTourneau U (TX)
Loyola U New Orleans (LA)
Lycoming Coll (PA)
Lynchburg Coll (VA)
Mary Baldwin U (VA)
Maryville U of Saint Louis (MO)
Meredith Coll (NC)
Mississippi State U (MS)
Missouri State U (MO)
Mount St. Joseph U (OH)
Mount Saint Mary Coll (NY)
Mount Saint Mary's U (CA)
Mount St. Mary's U (MD)
Niagara U (NY)
North Carolina State U (NC)
Northern Arizona U (AZ)
Ohio Dominican U (OH)
The Ohio State U (OH)
The Ohio State U at Marion (OH)
The Ohio State U–Mansfield Campus (OH)
Ohio U (OH)
Old Dominion U (VA)
Regis U (CO)
St. Cloud State U (MN)
St. Edward's U (TX)
Saint Francis U (PA)
St. John Fisher Coll (NY)
Saint Joseph's U (PA)
Saint Mary-of-the-Woods Coll (IN)
St. Thomas U (NB, Canada)
Saint Vincent Coll (PA)
Simon Fraser U (BC, Canada)
Slippery Rock U of Pennsylvania (PA)
Southern Oregon U (OR)
Spring Hill Coll (AL)
State U of New York Coll at Cortland (NY)
State U of New York Coll at Old Westbury (NY)
Stockton U (NJ)
Stonehill Coll (MA)
Tabor Coll (KS)
Texas A&M U–Kingsville (TX)
Thomas U (GA)
Université de Montréal (QC, Canada)
The U of Akron (OH)
U of California, Irvine (CA)
U of Delaware (DE)
U of Denver (CO)
U of Florida (FL)
U of Houston–Clear Lake (TX)
U of La Verne (CA)
U of Maryland, Coll Park (MD)
U of Massachusetts Dartmouth (MA)
U of Miami (FL)
U of Minnesota, Duluth (MN)
U of Minnesota, Twin Cities Campus (MN)
U of Missouri–Kansas City (MO)
U of Missouri–St. Louis (MO)
U of Mount Union (OH)
U of Nevada, Reno (NV)
U of New Hampshire (NH)
The U of North Carolina Wilmington (NC)
U of Northern Iowa (IA)
U of Saint Mary (KS)
U of St. Thomas (MN)
U of St. Thomas (TX)
U of Southern Maine (ME)
U of South Florida (FL)
U of South Florida, St. Petersburg (FL)
U of South Florida Sarasota-Manatee (FL)
The U of Tampa (FL)
The U of Texas at Dallas (TX)
The U of Texas of the Permian Basin (TX)
U of Toronto (ON, Canada)
U of West Georgia (GA)
U of Windsor (ON, Canada)
U of Wisconsin–Whitewater (WI)
Upper Iowa U (IA)
Valparaiso U (IN)
Virginia Union U (VA)
Virginia Wesleyan Coll (VA)
Walsh U (OH)
Western Kentucky U (KY)
Western State Colorado U (CO)
West Virginia U (WV)
William Penn U (IA)
Wittenberg U (OH)
Wright State U (OH)
Wright State U–Lake Campus (OH)

CRISIS/EMERGENCY/DISASTER MANAGEMENT
Adelphi U (NY)
American Public U System (WV)
Arkansas Tech U (AR)
Embry-Riddle Aeronautical U–Worldwide (FL)
Immaculata U (PA)
Kansas Wesleyan U (KS)
North Dakota State U (ND)
Northwest Missouri State U (MO)
Ohio Christian U (OH)
Pennsylvania Coll of Technology (PA)
Saint Louis U (MO)
Southeast Missouri State U (MO)
State U of New York Coll of Technology at Canton (NY)
Truckee Meadows Comm Coll (NV)
Union Inst & U (OH)
U at Albany, State U of New York (NY)
U of Alaska Fairbanks (AK)
U of Northern Iowa (IA)
U of North Texas (TX)
Waldorf U (IA)

CRITICAL INFRASTRUCTURE PROTECTION
Anderson U (SC)
Excelsior Coll (NY)
Idaho State U (ID)

CROP PRODUCTION
Delaware Valley U (PA)
North Dakota State U (ND)
U of Minnesota, Crookston (MN)
Washington State U (WA)

CULINARY ARTS
Coll of the Ozarks (MO)
Drexel U (PA)
Kendall Coll (IL)
New England Culinary Inst (VT)
Southern New Hampshire U (NH)

CULINARY ARTS RELATED
U of Nevada, Las Vegas (NV)
U of North Alabama (AL)

CULINARY SCIENCE
The Culinary Inst of America (NY)
Iowa State U of Science and Technology (IA)
Mississippi State U (MS)

CULTURAL ANTHROPOLOGY
Arcadia U (PA)
Eugene Lang Coll of Liberal Arts (NY)
Webster U (MO)

CULTURAL RESOURCE MANAGEMENT AND POLICY ANALYSIS
California State U, Dominguez Hills (CA)
U of Georgia (GA)
U of Waterloo (ON, Canada)

CULTURAL STUDIES/ CRITICAL THEORY AND ANALYSIS
American Public U System (WV)
The American U in Dubai (United Arab Emirates)
Arizona State U at the West campus (AZ)
Bryant U (RI)
Goddard Coll (VT)
Howard Payne U (TX)
Northern Arizona U (AZ)
Rollins Coll (FL)
The U of Tampa (FL)
Western Kentucky U (KY)
Willamette U (OR)

CURRICULUM AND INSTRUCTION
Albertus Magnus Coll (CT)
Curry Coll (MA)
Eastern Washington U (WA)
Franklin Pierce U (NH)
Lasell Coll (MA)
Randolph Coll (VA)
Sam Houston State U (TX)
Tarleton State U (TX)
The U of South Dakota (SD)
The U of Texas at Austin (TX)
Utah State U (UT)
Welch Coll (TN)

CUSTOMER SERVICE MANAGEMENT
Drexel U (PA)
Ohio U (OH)
Southwest Baptist U (MO)

CYBER/COMPUTER FORENSICS AND COUNTERTERRORISM
Bloomsburg U of Pennsylvania (PA)
Champlain Coll (VT)
Chestnut Hill Coll (PA)
Christian Brothers U (TN)
Davenport U, Grand Rapids (MI)
Embry-Riddle Aeronautical U–Prescott (AZ)
Excelsior Coll (NY)
Farmingdale State Coll (NY)
Kansas Wesleyan U (KS)
National U (CA)
Northeastern State U (OK)
Pensacola State Coll (FL)
Regent U (VA)
Robert Morris U (PA)
Roger Williams U (RI)
Sullivan U (KY)
U of the Incarnate Word (TX)
U of the Potomac (DC)

CYBER/ELECTRONIC OPERATIONS AND WARFARE
Excelsior Coll (NY)
LeTourneau U (TX)
Maryville U of Saint Louis (MO)

CYTOTECHNOLOGY
Barry U (FL)
Edgewood Coll (WI)
Illinois Coll (IL)
Indiana U–Purdue U Indianapolis (IN)
Marian U (WI)
Marshall U (WV)
Saint Louis U (MO)
Saint Mary's U of Minnesota (MN)
State U of New York at Plattsburgh (NY)
U of Arkansas for Medical Sciences (AR)
U of North Dakota (ND)
U of North Texas (TX)

CZECH
The U of Texas at Austin (TX)

DAIRY HUSBANDRY AND PRODUCTION
Morrisville State Coll (NY)
U of Vermont (VT)

DAIRY SCIENCE
California Polytechnic State U, San Luis Obispo (CA)
Delaware Valley U (PA)
Iowa State U of Science and Technology (IA)
Morrisville State Coll (NY)
South Dakota State U (SD)
U of Georgia (GA)
U of New Hampshire (NH)
U of Wisconsin–Madison (WI)
Utah State U (UT)
Virginia Polytechnic Inst and State U (VA)

DANCE
Adelphi U (NY)
Agnes Scott Coll (GA)
Alabama State U (AL)
Amherst Coll (MA)
Anderson U (IN)
Anderson U (SC)
Appalachian State U (NC)
Arizona State U at the Tempe campus (AZ)
Ball State U (IN)
Bard Coll (NY)
Barnard Coll (NY)
Bates Coll (ME)
Belhaven U (MS)
Beloit Coll (WI)
Bennington Coll (VT)
Bowling Green State U (OH)
Brenau U (GA)
Brigham Young U–Idaho (ID)
Butler U (IN)
California State U, East Bay (CA)
California State U, Fresno (CA)
California State U, Fullerton (CA)
California State U, Long Beach (CA)
California State U, Sacramento (CA)
Case Western Reserve U (OH)
Cedar Crest Coll (PA)
Chapman U (CA)
The Coll at Brockport, State U of New York (NY)
Coll of Charleston (SC)
The Colorado Coll (CO)
Colorado State U (CO)
Columbia Coll Chicago (IL)
Columbia U (NY)
Columbia U, School of General Studies (NY)
Concordia U (QC, Canada)
Connecticut Coll (CT)
Dean Coll (MA)
Denison U (OH)
DEREE - The American Coll of Greece (Greece)
DeSales U (PA)
Dickinson Coll (PA)
Dominican U of California (CA)
East Carolina U (NC)
Eastern Michigan U (MI)
Elon U (NC)
Emory U (GA)
Florida Southern Coll (FL)
Florida State U (FL)
Fordham U (NY)
Franklin & Marshall Coll (PA)
The George Washington U (DC)
Georgian Court U (NJ)
Goucher Coll (MD)
Grand Valley State U (MI)
Hamilton Coll (NY)
Hampshire Coll (MA)
Hobart and William Smith Colls (NY)
Hofstra U (NY)
Hollins U (VA)
Hope Coll (MI)
Hunter Coll of the City U of New York (NY)
Idaho State U (ID)
Indiana U Bloomington (IN)
Jacksonville U (FL)
Johnson C. Smith U (NC)
The Juilliard School (NY)
Keene State Coll (NH)
Kennesaw State U (GA)
Kent State U (OH)
Kenyon Coll (OH)
La Roche Coll (PA)
Lehman Coll of the City U of New York (NY)
Lindenwood U (MO)
Loyola Marymount U (CA)
Loyola U Chicago (IL)
Manhattanville Coll (NY)
Marymount Manhattan Coll (NY)
Mercyhurst U (PA)
Meredith Coll (NC)
Messiah Coll (PA)
Middlebury Coll (VT)
Mills Coll (CA)
Missouri Valley Coll (MO)
Montclair State U (NJ)
Mount Holyoke Coll (MA)
Muhlenberg Coll (PA)
Nazareth Coll of Rochester (NY)
New Mexico State U (NM)
Northwestern U (IL)
Nova Southeastern U (FL)
Oberlin Coll (OH)
The Ohio State U (OH)
Ohio U (OH)
Oklahoma City U (OK)
Oral Roberts U (OK)
Pace U (NY)
Palm Beach Atlantic U (FL)
Pitzer Coll (CA)
Point Park U (PA)
Pomona Coll (CA)
Purchase Coll, State U of New York (NY)
Radford U (VA)
Randolph Coll (VA)
Reed Coll (OR)
Rhode Island Coll (RI)
Rockford U (IL)
Roger Williams U (RI)
Rutgers U–New Brunswick (NJ)
St. Gregory's U, Shawnee (OK)
Saint Louis U–Madrid Campus (Spain)
Saint Mary's Coll of California (CA)
St. Olaf Coll (MN)
Sam Houston State U (TX)
San Diego State U (CA)
San Francisco State U (CA)
Sarah Lawrence Coll (NY)
Scripps Coll (CA)
Seton Hill U (PA)
Shenandoah U (VA)
Simon Fraser U (BC, Canada)
Skidmore Coll (NY)
Slippery Rock U of Pennsylvania (PA)
Smith Coll (MA)
Southern Methodist U (TX)
Southern Utah U (UT)
State U of New York at Fredonia (NY)
State U of New York Coll at Potsdam (NY)
Stephen F. Austin State U (TX)
Stephens Coll (MO)
Swarthmore Coll (PA)
Sweet Briar Coll (VA)
Temple U (PA)
Texas Christian U (TX)
Texas State U (TX)
Texas Tech U (TX)
Texas Woman's U (TX)
Towson U (MD)
Troy U (AL)
Tulane U (LA)
U at Buffalo, the State U of New York (NY)
The U of Akron (OH)
The U of Alabama (AL)
The U of Arizona (AZ)
U of California, Irvine (CA)
U of California, Los Angeles (CA)
U of California, San Diego (CA)
U of California, Santa Barbara (CA)
U of Cincinnati (OH)
U of Colorado Boulder (CO)
U of Florida (FL)
U of Georgia (GA)
U of Hartford (CT)
U of Hawaii at Manoa (HI)
U of Houston (TX)
U of Idaho (ID)
The U of Kansas (KS)
U of Maryland, Baltimore County (MD)
U of Maryland, Coll Park (MD)
U of Massachusetts Amherst (MA)
U of Michigan (MI)
U of Michigan–Flint (MI)
U of Minnesota, Twin Cities Campus (MN)
U of Missouri–Kansas City (MO)
U of Nevada, Las Vegas (NV)
The U of North Carolina at Charlotte (NC)
The U of North Carolina at Greensboro (NC)
U of North Carolina School of the Arts (NC)
U of North Texas (TX)
U of Oklahoma (OK)
U of Oregon (OR)
U of Richmond (VA)
U of Rochester (NY)
U of Saint Francis (IN)
U of South Carolina (SC)
U of Southern California (CA)
U of Southern Mississippi (MS)
U of South Florida (FL)
The U of Tampa (FL)
The U of Texas at Austin (TX)
The U of Texas Rio Grande Valley (TX)
The U of the Arts (PA)
U of Utah (UT)
U of Washington (WA)
U of Wisconsin–Madison (WI)
U of Wisconsin–Milwaukee (WI)
U of Wisconsin–Stevens Point (WI)
Ursinus Coll (PA)
Utah State U (UT)
Utah Valley U (UT)
Valdosta State U (GA)
Virginia Commonwealth U (VA)
Washington U in St. Louis (MO)
Wayne State U (MI)
Weber State U (UT)
Webster U (MO)
Wells Coll (NY)
Wesleyan U (CT)
Western Kentucky U (KY)
Western Michigan U (MI)
Western Oregon U (OR)
Western Washington U (WA)
Westminster Coll (UT)
West Texas A&M U (TX)
Winthrop U (SC)
Wittenberg U (OH)
Wright State U (OH)
Wright State U–Lake Campus (OH)

DANCE RELATED
Anderson U (IN)
Brigham Young U (UT)
California State U, Long Beach (CA)
Drexel U (PA)
Marymount Manhattan Coll (NY)
Western Michigan U (MI)
Youngstown State U (OH)

DANISH
U of Washington (WA)

DATA MODELING/ WAREHOUSING AND DATABASE ADMINISTRATION
Bryant U (RI)
Central Washington U (WA)
Limestone Coll (SC)
Pennsylvania Coll of Technology (PA)
Rochester Inst of Technology (NY)
U of Michigan (MI)

DATA PROCESSING AND DATA PROCESSING TECHNOLOGY
Bemidji State U (MN)
California State U, San Marcos (CA)
Central Baptist Coll (AR)
Dickinson State U (ND)
U of Advancing Technology (AZ)
U of Arkansas (AR)
U of Southern Mississippi (MS)

DEAF STUDIES
California State U, Northridge (CA)
Coll of the Holy Cross (MA)
Columbia Coll Chicago (IL)
Nevada State Coll (NV)
Towson U (MD)
U of Valley Forge (PA)

DEMOGRAPHY AND POPULATION
Université de Montréal (QC, Canada)

DENTAL HYGIENE
Allen Coll (IA)
Augusta U (GA)
Ball State U (IN)
Clayton State U (GA)
Dalhousie U (NS, Canada)
Dixie State U (UT)
Eastern Washington U (WA)
East Tennessee State U (TN)
Farmingdale State Coll (NY)
Georgia Highlands Coll (GA)
Idaho State U (ID)
Indiana U Northwest (IN)
Indiana U South Bend (IN)
Lewis U (IL)
Louisiana State U Health Sciences Center (LA)
MCPHS U (MA)
Minnesota State U Mankato (MN)
Mount Ida Coll (MA)
Northern Arizona U (AZ)
The Ohio State U (OH)
The Ohio State U at Lima (OH)
Old Dominion U (VA)
Pennsylvania Coll of Technology (PA)
Rhode Island Coll (RI)
St. Petersburg Coll (FL)
Southern Illinois U Carbondale (IL)
State U of New York Coll of Technology at Canton (NY)
Tennessee State U (TN)
Texas Woman's U (TX)
Tyler Jr Coll (TX)
U of Arkansas for Medical Sciences (AR)
U of Bridgeport (CT)
U of Detroit Mercy (MI)
U of Hawaii at Manoa (HI)
U of Louisiana at Monroe (LA)
U of Louisville (KY)
U of Michigan (MI)
U of Minnesota, Twin Cities Campus (MN)
U of Missouri–Kansas City (MO)
U of New England (ME)
U of New Haven (CT)
The U of North Carolina at Chapel Hill (NC)
U of Oklahoma Health Sciences Center (OK)
U of Pittsburgh (PA)
The U of South Dakota (SD)
U of Southern California (CA)
U of Southern Indiana (IN)
U of Washington (WA)
Utah Valley U (UT)
Vermont Tech Coll (VT)
Virginia Commonwealth U (VA)
Weber State U (UT)
Western Kentucky U (KY)
West Virginia U (WV)
Wichita State U (KS)
Youngstown State U (OH)

DENTAL LABORATORY TECHNOLOGY
Boston U (MA)

DENTAL SERVICES AND ALLIED PROFESSIONS RELATED
Indiana U–Purdue U Indianapolis (IN)

DESIGN AND APPLIED ARTS RELATED
Alverno Coll (WI)
Antioch U Los Angeles (CA)
Arizona State U at the Tempe campus (AZ)
Asbury U (KY)
Auburn U (AL)
Augsburg Coll (MN)
Azusa Pacific U (CA)
Bemidji State U (MN)
Berkeley Coll–Woodland Park Campus (NJ)
Buffalo State Coll, State U of New York (NY)
Butler U (IN)
California Coll of the Arts (CA)
Centenary U (NJ)
Columbia U, School of General Studies (NY)
Concordia U (QC, Canada)
Converse Coll (SC)
Drexel U (PA)
Eugene Lang Coll of Liberal Arts (NY)
Farmingdale State Coll (NY)
Fashion Inst of Technology (NY)
Ferris State U (MI)
Franklin Pierce U (NH)
Hampshire Coll (MA)

Harding U (AR)
Hofstra U (NY)
Houston Baptist U (TX)
Inter American U of Puerto Rico, San Germán Campus (PR)
Iowa State U of Science and Technology (IA)
Laguna Coll of Art & Design (CA)
Mansfield U of Pennsylvania (PA)
Maryland Inst Coll of Art (MD)
McMurry U (TX)
Merrimack Coll (MA)
Minnesota State U Mankato (MN)
Montclair State U (NJ)
The New School–Parsons Paris (France)
New York Inst of Technology (NY)
Parsons School of Design (NY)
Penn State Altoona (PA)
Penn State Berks (PA)
Penn State U Park (PA)
Portland State U (OR)
Pratt Inst (NY)
Roberts Wesleyan Coll (NY)
St. Cloud State U (MN)
School of the Art Inst of Chicago (IL)
Schreiner U (TX)
Shawnee State U (OH)
Southern Methodist U (TX)
State U of New York at Fredonia (NY)
Syracuse U (NY)
U of California, Los Angeles (CA)
The U of Findlay (OH)
U of Illinois at Chicago (IL)
U of Oregon (OR)
U of Wisconsin–Stout (WI)
Washington U in St. Louis (MO)
Western Washington U (WA)

DESIGN AND VISUAL COMMUNICATIONS
Albright Coll (PA)
American U (DC)
The American U in Dubai (United Arab Emirates)
Anderson U (IN)
Auburn U (AL)
Barton Coll (NC)
Bellarmine U (KY)
Belmont U (TN)
Bennington Coll (VT)
Biola U (CA)
Boise State U (ID)
Bowling Green State U (OH)
Bowling Green State U–Firelands Coll (OH)
Bryant U (RI)
Buffalo State Coll, State U of New York (NY)
California Coll of the Arts (CA)
California State U, Chico (CA)
California State U, Monterey Bay (CA)
Carnegie Mellon U (PA)
Cazenovia Coll (NY)
Cedarville U (OH)
Central Connecticut State U (CT)
Coll of the Ozarks (MO)
Columbia Coll Chicago (IL)
Concordia U, St. Paul (MN)
Drury U (MO)
EDP U of Puerto Rico (PR)
Emily Carr U of Art + Design (BC, Canada)
Endicott Coll (MA)
Escuela de Artes Plasticas y Dise&nno de Puerto Rico (PR)
Eugene Lang Coll of Liberal Arts (NY)
Farmingdale State Coll (NY)
Ferris State U (MI)
Houghton Coll (NY)
Indiana U Bloomington (IN)
Inter American U of Puerto Rico, Metropolitan Campus (PR)
Iowa State U of Science and Technology (IA)
Iowa Wesleyan U (IA)
Jacksonville U (FL)
Kean U (NJ)
Laguna Coll of Art & Design (CA)
La Roche Coll (PA)
Lawrence Technological U (MI)
Lees-McRae Coll (NC)
Lehigh U (PA)
Lewis U (IL)
LIM Coll (NY)
Linfield Coll (OR)
Loyola U Chicago (IL)
Loyola U New Orleans (LA)
Lubbock Christian U (TX)
Madonna U (MI)
Marymount U (VA)
Massachusetts Coll of Art and Design (MA)
Memphis Coll of Art (TN)
Millersville U of Pennsylvania (PA)
Milwaukee Inst of Art and Design (WI)
Missouri State U (MO)
Mount St. Joseph U (OH)
Muskingum U (OH)
Nazareth Coll of Rochester (NY)
Nevada State Coll (NV)
New Hampshire Inst of Art (NH)
New Mexico Highlands U (NM)
New York City Coll of Technology of the City U of New York (NY)
North Carolina State U (NC)
Northern Arizona U (AZ)
Northwest Coll of Art & Design (WA)
The Ohio State U (OH)
Oral Roberts U (OK)
Oregon State U (OR)
Parsons School of Design (NY)
Purdue U (IN)
Radford U (VA)
Rensselaer Polytechnic Inst (NY)
Robert Morris U (PA)
Rochester Inst of Technology (NY)
Saginaw Valley State U (MI)
Saint Mary-of-the-Woods Coll (IN)
San Francisco State U (CA)
Savannah Coll of Art and Design (GA)
School of the Art Inst of Chicago (IL)
Seattle Pacific U (WA)
Southern Illinois U Carbondale (IL)
Stevenson U (MD)
Syracuse U (NY)
Texas Christian U (TX)
Texas State U (TX)
U of Advancing Technology (AZ)
U of Arkansas (AR)
U of Cincinnati (OH)
U of Dayton (OH)
U of Evansville (IN)
U of Hartford (CT)
The U of Kansas (KS)
U of Mary Hardin-Baylor (TX)
U of Maryland, Baltimore County (MD)
U of Massachusetts Dartmouth (MA)
U of Michigan–Flint (MI)
U of North Texas (TX)
U of Notre Dame (IN)
U of Oklahoma (OK)
U of Pittsburgh at Johnstown (PA)
U of Saint Francis (IN)
U of San Francisco (CA)
The U of Tennessee at Martin (TN)
The U of Texas at Austin (TX)
U of Washington (WA)
U of Wisconsin–Green Bay (WI)
U of Wisconsin–Stevens Point (WI)
Utah Valley U (UT)
Viterbo U (WI)
Washington U in St. Louis (MO)
Watkins Coll of Art, Design, & Film (TN)
Weber State U (UT)
Western Washington U (WA)
West Virginia U (WV)
Wilmington U (DE)

DESKTOP PUBLISHING AND DIGITAL IMAGING DESIGN
California Baptist U (CA)
Chowan U (NC)
EDP U of Puerto Rico (PR)
La Salle U (PA)
New England Inst of Technology (RI)
O'More Coll of Design (TN)
Rochester Inst of Technology (NY)
Wilmington U (DE)

DEVELOPMENTAL AND CHILD PSYCHOLOGY
Antioch U Midwest (OH)
Bay Path U (MA)
Boston Coll (MA)
Bridgewater State U (MA)
Brooklyn Coll of the City U of New York (NY)
California State U, Bakersfield (CA)
California State U, East Bay (CA)
California State U, Stanislaus (CA)
Carson-Newman U (TN)
Cornerstone U (MI)
Eastern Nazarene Coll (MA)
Eastern Washington U (WA)
East Texas Baptist U (TX)
Emmanuel Coll (MA)
Fitchburg State U (MA)
Hampton U (VA)
Humboldt State U (CA)
LeTourneau U (TX)
Mills Coll (CA)
Minnesota State U Mankato (MN)
Mount Saint Mary's U (CA)
Quinnipiac U (CT)
Saint Leo U (FL)
Sarah Lawrence Coll (NY)
Sonoma State U (CA)
Texas Christian U (TX)
Tufts U (MA)
Université de Montréal (QC, Canada)
U of Detroit Mercy (MI)
U of Georgia (GA)
U of Minnesota, Twin Cities Campus (MN)
U of Saint Francis (IN)
U of Windsor (ON, Canada)
U of Wisconsin–Green Bay (WI)
Utica Coll (NY)
Vanderbilt U (TN)
Western Washington U (WA)
Wheelock Coll (MA)

DEVELOPMENTAL BIOLOGY AND EMBRYOLOGY
U of California, Santa Barbara (CA)

DEVELOPMENT ECONOMICS AND INTERNATIONAL DEVELOPMENT
Calvin Coll (MI)
Clark U (MA)
Dalhousie U (NS, Canada)
Georgia Southern U (GA)
Houghton Coll (NY)
Messiah Coll (PA)
Penn State Altoona (PA)
Penn State Berks (PA)
Point Loma Nazarene U (CA)
Seattle Pacific U (WA)
U of California, Los Angeles (CA)
U of Dayton (OH)
U of Guelph (ON, Canada)
U of King's Coll (NS, Canada)
U of Richmond (VA)
U of St. Thomas (TX)
U of San Francisco (CA)
U of the Fraser Valley (BC, Canada)
U of Vermont (VT)

DIAGNOSTIC MEDICAL SONOGRAPHY AND ULTRASOUND TECHNOLOGY
Adventist U of Health Sciences (FL)
Dalhousie U (NS, Canada)
The George Washington U (DC)
Lewis U (IL)
Marian U (WI)
Misericordia U (PA)
Newman U (KS)
Nova Southeastern U (FL)
Regis Coll (MA)
Rhode Island Coll (RI)
Rochester Inst of Technology (NY)
Seattle U (WA)
U of Arkansas for Medical Sciences (AR)
U of Charleston (WV)
The U of Findlay (OH)
U of Oklahoma Health Sciences Center (OK)
Washburn U (KS)
Weber State U (UT)

DIESEL MECHANICS TECHNOLOGY
Idaho State U (ID)
Montana State U–Northern (MT)
U of Northwestern Ohio (OH)

DIETETICS
Abilene Christian U (TX)
Andrews U (MI)
Appalachian State U (NC)
Ashland U (OH)
Ball State U (IN)
Bowling Green State U (OH)
Bradley U (IL)
Buffalo State Coll, State U of New York (NY)
California Polytechnic State U, San Luis Obispo (CA)
California State Polytechnic U, Pomona (CA)
California State U, Chico (CA)
California State U, Fresno (CA)
California State U, Long Beach (CA)
California State U, San Bernardino (CA)
Carson-Newman U (TN)
Case Western Reserve U (OH)
Central Michigan U (MI)
Central Washington U (WA)
Coll of Saint Elizabeth (NJ)
Coll of the Ozarks (MO)
Dominican U (IL)
East Carolina U (NC)
Eastern Michigan U (MI)
Florida Intl U (FL)
Georgia State U (GA)
Harding U (AR)
Idaho State U (ID)
Illinois State U (IL)
Immaculata U (PA)
Indiana State U (IN)
Iowa State U of Science and Technology (IA)
Jacksonville State U (AL)
Kansas State U (KS)
Keene State Coll (NH)
Lebanese American U (Lebanon)
Lehman Coll of the City U of New York (NY)
Life U (GA)
Lipscomb U (TN)
Louisiana Tech U (LA)
Mansfield U of Pennsylvania (PA)
Marshall U (WV)
Marywood U (PA)
Meredith Coll (NC)
Miami U (OH)
Michigan State U (MI)
Minnesota State U Mankato (MN)
Missouri State U (MO)
Mount Mary U (WI)
New Mexico State U (NM)
North Dakota State U (ND)
Northeastern State U (OK)
Northern Illinois U (IL)
Northwest Missouri State U (MO)
The Ohio State U (OH)
Olivet Nazarene U (IL)
Ouachita Baptist U (AR)
Point Loma Nazarene U (CA)
Purdue U (IN)
Queens Coll of the City U of New York (NY)
Rutgers U–New Brunswick (NJ)
St. Catherine U (MN)
Saint Louis U (MO)
San Diego State U (CA)
San Francisco State U (CA)
Seton Hill U (PA)
Simmons Coll (MA)
South Dakota State U (SD)
Texas A&M U–Kingsville (TX)
Texas Christian U (TX)
Texas Tech U (TX)
The U of Akron (OH)
The U of Alabama (AL)
U of Central Missouri (MO)
U of Cincinnati (OH)
U of Dayton (OH)
U of Delaware (DE)
U of Florida (FL)
U of Georgia (GA)
U of Illinois at Chicago (IL)
U of New Haven (CT)
U of North Dakota (ND)
U of Northern Colorado (CO)
U of North Florida (FL)
U of Oklahoma Health Sciences Center (OK)
U of Pittsburgh (PA)
U of Rhode Island (RI)
U of Southern Mississippi (MS)
The U of Tennessee at Martin (TN)
The U of Texas at San Antonio (TX)
U of Vermont (VT)
U of Wisconsin–Stevens Point (WI)
U of Wisconsin–Stout (WI)
Viterbo U (WI)
Wayne State U (MI)
West Chester U of Pennsylvania (PA)
Western Carolina U (NC)
Western Illinois U (IL)
Youngstown State U (OH)

DIETETICS AND CLINICAL NUTRITION SERVICES RELATED
Bowling Green State U (OH)
Coll of Saint Benedict (MN)
Madonna U (MI)
Saint John's U (MN)
Texas Christian U (TX)
Western Michigan U (MI)

DIGITAL ARTS
Acad of Art U (CA)
Antioch Coll, Yellow Springs (OH)
Arizona State U at the Tempe campus (AZ)
Ashland U (OH)
Austin Coll (TX)
Bethany Lutheran Coll (MN)
Blackburn Coll (IL)
Bowling Green State U (OH)
Champlain Coll (VT)
Concordia U (QC, Canada)
Daemen Coll (NY)
DeSales U (PA)
Escuela de Artes Plasticas y Dise&nno de Puerto Rico (PR)
Florida Southern Coll (FL)
Georgian Court U (NJ)
Greenville Coll (IL)
Hamline U (MN)
Kansas Wesleyan U (KS)
Kennesaw State U (GA)
King U (TN)
Kutztown U of Pennsylvania (PA)
Lake Erie Coll (OH)
La Salle U (PA)
Lubbock Christian U (TX)
Marymount California U (CA)
Marymount Manhattan Coll (NY)
Memphis Coll of Art (TN)
Northeastern U (MA)
Pacific Northwest Coll of Art (OR)
Pennsylvania Coll of Art & Design (PA)
Rhode Island Coll (RI)
Roberts Wesleyan Coll (NY)
San Francisco Art Inst (CA)
Sarah Lawrence Coll (NY)
Southwestern Coll (KS)
State U of New York Coll at Potsdam (NY)
Tiffin U (OH)
Trinity Christian Coll (IL)
U of Advancing Technology (AZ)
U of Central Florida (FL)
U of Florida (FL)
U of Massachusetts Dartmouth (MA)
U of North Carolina at Asheville (NC)
U of Saint Francis (IN)
U of Southern California (CA)
The U of Tampa (FL)
The U of Texas at Austin (TX)
The U of Toledo (OH)
U of Wisconsin–Stout (WI)
U of Wisconsin–Whitewater (WI)

DIGITAL COMMUNICATION AND MEDIA/MULTIMEDIA
Abilene Christian U (TX)
Acad of Art U (CA)
Alma Coll (MI)
The American U in Dubai (United Arab Emirates)
Anderson U (SC)
Arcadia U (PA)
Ashland U (OH)
Baldwin Wallace U (OH)
Ball State U (IN)
Baylor U (TX)
Bennington Coll (VT)
Bethany Lutheran Coll (MN)
Bowling Green State U (OH)
Bradley U (IL)

Butler U (IN)
California Coll of the Arts (CA)
California Lutheran U (CA)
California State U, Dominguez Hills (CA)
Calvin Coll (MI)
Canisius Coll (NY)
Carson-Newman U (TN)
Cedar Crest Coll (PA)
Cedarville U (OH)
Central Washington U (WA)
Clarkson U (NY)
Cleveland State U (OH)
Columbia Coll Chicago (IL)
Columbia Intl U (SC)
Concordia Coll–New York (NY)
Concordia U Wisconsin (WI)
Corban U (OR)
Cornerstone U (MI)
Dallas Baptist U (TX)
Dixie State U (UT)
Eastern Mennonite U (VA)
Endicott Coll (MA)
Eugene Lang Coll of Liberal Arts (NY)
The Evergreen State Coll (WA)
Fitchburg State U (MA)
Florida Atlantic U (FL)
Georgia Inst of Technology (GA)
Georgian Court U (NJ)
Georgia Southern U (GA)
Granite State Coll (NH)
Harding U (AR)
Hawai`i Pacific U (HI)
Hilbert Coll (NY)
Howard Payne U (TX)
Huntington U (IN)
Indiana U Bloomington (IN)
Indiana U Kokomo (IN)
Indiana U–Purdue U Indianapolis (IN)
Indiana U South Bend (IN)
Inter American U of Puerto Rico, Bayamón Campus (PR)
Juniata Coll (PA)
Keene State Coll (NH)
Kent State U (OH)
Kutztown U of Pennsylvania (PA)
Lawrence Technological U (MI)
Lebanon Valley Coll (PA)
Lee U (TN)
Lewis U (IL)
Liberty U (VA)
Limestone Coll (SC)
Lincoln U (PA)
Lindenwood U (MO)
Loyola U Chicago (IL)
Lubbock Christian U (TX)
Lycoming Coll (PA)
Lynn U (FL)
Manhattanville Coll (NY)
Marywood U (PA)
Messiah Coll (PA)
Miami U (OH)
Minnesota State U Moorhead (MN)
Mount Marty Coll (SD)
Mount Mercy U (IA)
Muskingum U (OH)
National U (CA)
New York Inst of Technology (NY)
North Greenville U (SC)
Ohio U (OH)
Oregon State U (OR)
Point Park U (PA)
Rensselaer Polytechnic Inst (NY)
Rochester Inst of Technology (NY)
Saginaw Valley State U (MI)
St. Bonaventure U (NY)
St. Edward's U (TX)
St. John Fisher Coll (NY)
San Diego State U (CA)
Savannah Coll of Art and Design (GA)
School of the Art Inst of Chicago (IL)
Seattle U (WA)
Simpson Coll (IA)
Southeastern U (FL)
Southern Oregon U (OR)
Southwestern Coll (KS)
State U of New York at New Paltz (NY)
Stevenson U (MD)
Taylor U (IN)
Texas A&M U (TX)
Texas State U (TX)
Tiffin U (OH)
Trevecca Nazarene U (TN)
U of Advancing Technology (AZ)
U of Denver (CO)
U of Detroit Mercy (MI)
U of Georgia (GA)
U of Idaho (ID)
U of Maine (ME)
U of Miami (FL)
U of Northern Iowa (IA)
U of North Georgia (GA)
U of Rochester (NY)
U of Saskatchewan (SK, Canada)
The U of Scranton (PA)
The U of Tampa (FL)
U of the Incarnate Word (TX)
U of Toronto (ON, Canada)
U of Valley Forge (PA)
U of Waterloo (ON, Canada)
Valparaiso U (IN)
Villa Maria Coll (NY)
Walsh U (OH)
Washington State U (WA)
Washington State U–Tri-Cities (WA)
Washington State U–Vancouver (WA)
Webster U (MO)
Westminster Coll (PA)
West Texas A&M U (TX)
Wilkes U (PA)

DIRECTING AND THEATRICAL PRODUCTION

Anderson U (SC)
Augsburg Coll (MN)
Baldwin Wallace U (OH)
Belmont U (TN)
Bennington Coll (VT)
Binghamton U, State U of New York (NY)
Boston U (MA)
Bradley U (IL)
Brigham Young U (UT)
California State U, Long Beach (CA)
Columbia Coll Chicago (IL)
Drake U (IA)
Emory & Henry Coll (VA)
Hofstra U (NY)
Keene State Coll (NH)
Lipscomb U (TN)
Marymount Manhattan Coll (NY)
Nebraska Wesleyan U (NE)
Pace U (NY)
Pepperdine U, Malibu (CA)
Texas Christian U (TX)
U of Chicago (IL)
U of Miami (FL)
The U of the Arts (PA)
U of Washington (WA)
Webster U (MO)

DISABILITY STUDIES

Aurora U (IL)

DISPUTE RESOLUTION

Life U (GA)

DIVINITY/MINISTRY

Anderson U (SC)
Azusa Pacific U (CA)
Barclay Coll (KS)
Belmont U (TN)
Bethel Coll (IN)
Biola U (CA)
Bluefield Coll (VA)
Calvary U (MO)
Campbellsville U (KY)
Carson-Newman U (TN)
Corban U (OR)
Davis Coll (NY)
Eastern Nazarene Coll (MA)
Ecclesia Coll (AR)
Faith Baptist Bible Coll and Theological Sem (IA)
Faulkner U (AL)
Global U (MO)
Houston Baptist U (TX)
Huntington U (IN)
Johnson U (TN)
John Wesley U (NC)
Judson U (IL)
Kansas Wesleyan U (KS)
Kuyper Coll (MI)
Master's Coll and Sem (ON, Canada)
The Master's U (CA)
Messenger Coll (TX)
Nazarene Bible Coll (CO)
Northwest U (WA)
Ohio Christian U (OH)
Oklahoma Baptist U (OK)
Piedmont Intl U (NC)
Providence Coll (RI)
Regent U (VA)
Roberts Wesleyan Coll (NY)
Shiloh U (IA)
Shorter U (GA)
Southwestern Assemblies of God U (TX)
Toccoa Falls Coll (GA)
Trevecca Nazarene U (TN)
U of Valley Forge (PA)
Williams Baptist Coll (AR)

DOCUMENTARY PRODUCTION

Columbia Coll Chicago (IL)
High Point U (NC)
Ithaca Coll (NY)
Mount Saint Mary's U (CA)
U at Albany, State U of New York (NY)

DRAFTING AND DESIGN TECHNOLOGY

Acad of Art U (CA)
East Carolina U (NC)
East Central U (OK)
Montana State U–Northern (MT)
Sam Houston State U (TX)
Trine U (IN)
Weber State U (UT)
Western Michigan U (MI)

DRAFTING/DESIGN ENGINEERING TECHNOLOGIES RELATED

Central Michigan U (MI)
Weber State U (UT)

DRAMA AND DANCE TEACHER EDUCATION

Adams State U (CO)
Austin Coll (TX)
Belmont U (TN)
Bishop's U (QC, Canada)
Boise State U (ID)
Brenau U (GA)
Bridgewater State U (MA)
Catawba Coll (NC)
Central Connecticut State U (CT)
Central Washington U (WA)
Coll of the Ozarks (MO)
Columbus State U (GA)
East Carolina U (NC)
East Texas Baptist U (TX)
Edgewood Coll (WI)
Emerson Coll (MA)
Faulkner U (AL)
Hardin-Simmons U (TX)
Hofstra U (NY)
Hope Coll (MI)
Howard Payne U (TX)
Jacksonville U (FL)
Keene State Coll (NH)
Lees-McRae Coll (NC)
Lee U (TN)
Lipscomb U (TN)
Lubbock Christian U (TX)
Meredith Coll (NC)
Missouri Baptist U (MO)
Montclair State U (NJ)
Ohio Wesleyan U (OH)
Piedmont Coll (GA)
Point Park U (PA)
St. Catherine U (MN)
St. Edward's U (TX)
Southern Utah U (UT)
Southwestern Assemblies of God U (TX)
State U of New York Coll at Potsdam (NY)
Trevecca Nazarene U (TN)
The U of Akron (OH)
U of Evansville (IN)
U of Lethbridge (AB, Canada)
The U of North Carolina at Greensboro (NC)
U of Regina (SK, Canada)
The U of South Dakota (SD)
U of Windsor (ON, Canada)
U of Wisconsin–Whitewater (WI)
Utah Valley U (UT)
Valparaiso U (IN)
Viterbo U (WI)
Washington U in St. Louis (MO)
Wayne State Coll (NE)
Weber State U (UT)
Western Washington U (WA)

DRAMATIC/THEATER ARTS

Abilene Christian U (TX)
Adelphi U (NY)
Agnes Scott Coll (GA)
Alabama State U (AL)
Albertus Magnus Coll (CT)
Albion Coll (MI)
Albright Coll (PA)
Alfred U (NY)
Allegheny Coll (PA)
Alma Coll (MI)
Alvernia U (PA)
American Intl Coll (MA)
American U (DC)
The American U in Cairo (Egypt)
Amherst Coll (MA)
Anderson U (SC)
Angelo State U (TX)
Appalachian State U (NC)
Aquinas Coll (MI)
Arizona State U at the Tempe campus (AZ)
Armstrong State U (GA)
Asbury U (KY)
Ashland U (OH)
Auburn U (AL)
Augsburg Coll (MN)
Augustana Coll (IL)
Augustana U (SD)
Aurora U (IL)
Austin Peay State U (TN)
Averett U (VA)
Avila U (MO)
Baker U (KS)
Ball State U (IN)
Bard Coll (NY)
Barnard Coll (NY)
Barry U (FL)
Barton Coll (NC)
Bates Coll (ME)
Baylor U (TX)
Belhaven U (MS)
Bellarmine U (KY)
Belmont U (TN)
Beloit Coll (WI)
Bemidji State U (MN)
Benedictine Coll (KS)
Bennington Coll (VT)
Berea Coll (KY)
Bethany Lutheran Coll (MN)
Bethel Coll (IN)
Bethel U (MN)
Binghamton U, State U of New York (NY)
Biola U (CA)
Bishop's U (QC, Canada)
Blackburn Coll (IL)
Bloomsburg U of Pennsylvania (PA)
Bluefield Coll (VA)
Boise State U (ID)
Boston Coll (MA)
Boston U (MA)
Bowling Green State U (OH)
Bradley U (IL)
Brandeis U (MA)
Briar Cliff U (IA)
Bridgewater State U (MA)
Brigham Young U–Idaho (ID)
Bryan Coll (TN)
Bucknell U (PA)
Buffalo State Coll, State U of New York (NY)
Butler U (IN)
California Baptist U (CA)
California Lutheran U (CA)
California Polytechnic State U, San Luis Obispo (CA)
California State Polytechnic U, Pomona (CA)
California State U, Bakersfield (CA)
California State U, Dominguez Hills (CA)
California State U, East Bay (CA)
California State U, Fresno (CA)
California State U, Fullerton (CA)
California State U, Long Beach (CA)
California State U, Northridge (CA)
California State U, Sacramento (CA)
California State U, San Bernardino (CA)
California State U, Stanislaus (CA)
California U of Pennsylvania (PA)
Calvary U (MO)
Capital U (OH)
Cardinal Stritch U (WI)
Carleton Coll (MN)
Carnegie Mellon U (PA)
Carroll Coll (MT)
Carson-Newman U (TN)
Carthage Coll (WI)
Case Western Reserve U (OH)
Catawba Coll (NC)
The Catholic U of America (DC)
Cedar Crest Coll (PA)
Cedarville U (OH)
Centenary Coll of Louisiana (LA)
Central Connecticut State U (CT)
Central Methodist U (MO)
Centre Coll (KY)
Chapman U (CA)
Chowan U (NC)
Christopher Newport U (VA)
City Coll of the City U of New York (NY)
Claremont McKenna Coll (CA)
Clarion U of Pennsylvania (PA)
Clarke U (IA)
Clark U (MA)
Cleveland State U (OH)
Coastal Carolina U (SC)
Coe Coll (IA)
Colby Coll (ME)
Colgate U (NY)
The Coll at Brockport, State U of New York (NY)
Coll of Charleston (SC)
The Coll of Idaho (ID)
Coll of Saint Benedict (MN)
Coll of Staten Island of the City U of New York (NY)
Coll of the Holy Cross (MA)
Coll of the Ozarks (MO)
The Coll of William and Mary (VA)
The Coll of Wooster (OH)
The Colorado Coll (CO)
Colorado Mesa U (CO)
Colorado State U (CO)
Columbia Coll Chicago (IL)
Columbia U (NY)
Columbia U, School of General Studies (NY)
Columbus State U (GA)
Concordia Coll (MN)
Concordia U (QC, Canada)
Concordia U Chicago (IL)
Concordia U Irvine (CA)
Concordia U, Nebraska (NE)
Concordia U, St. Paul (MN)
Connecticut Coll (CT)
Converse Coll (SC)
Cornell Coll (IA)
Cornell U (NY)
Creighton U (NE)
Culver-Stockton Coll (MO)
Daemen Coll (NY)
Dalhousie U (NS, Canada)
Dartmouth Coll (NH)
Davidson Coll (NC)
Dean Coll (MA)
Denison U (OH)
DePauw U (IN)
DeSales U (PA)
Dickinson Coll (PA)
Dickinson State U (ND)
Dixie State U (UT)
Dominican U (IL)
Drake U (IA)
Drew U (NJ)
Drury U (MO)
Duquesne U (PA)
Earlham Coll (IN)
East Carolina U (NC)
East Central U (OK)
Eastern Illinois U (IL)
Eastern Mennonite U (VA)
Eastern Michigan U (MI)
Eastern Nazarene Coll (MA)
Eastern Oregon U (OR)
Eastern Washington U (WA)
East Stroudsburg U of Pennsylvania (PA)
East Tennessee State U (TN)
East Texas Baptist U (TX)
Eckerd Coll (FL)
Edgewood Coll (WI)
Elizabethtown Coll (PA)
Elmira Coll (NY)
Elms Coll (MA)

Elon U (NC)
Emerson Coll (MA)
Emory & Henry Coll (VA)
Emory U (GA)
Emporia State U (KS)
Eugene Lang Coll of Liberal Arts (NY)
Eureka Coll (IL)
The Evergreen State Coll (WA)
Fairfield U (CT)
Fairleigh Dickinson U, Coll at Florham (NJ)
Faulkner U (AL)
Fitchburg State U (MA)
Flagler Coll (FL)
Florida Ag and Mech U (FL)
Florida Atlantic U (FL)
Florida Gulf Coast U (FL)
Florida Intl U (FL)
Florida Southern Coll (FL)
Florida State U (FL)
Fordham U (NY)
Fort Lewis Coll (CO)
Franciscan U of Steubenville (OH)
Francis Marion U (SC)
Franklin & Marshall Coll (PA)
Franklin Coll (IN)
Franklin Pierce U (NH)
Friends U (KS)
Frostburg State U (MD)
Furman U (SC)
Gannon U (PA)
Gardner-Webb U (NC)
George Fox U (OR)
Georgetown Coll (KY)
The George Washington U (DC)
Georgia Coll & State U (GA)
Georgia Southern U (GA)
Georgia Southwestern State U (GA)
Gettysburg Coll (PA)
Gonzaga U (WA)
Gordon Coll (MA)
Goshen Coll (IN)
Goucher Coll (MD)
Governors State U (IL)
Grace Coll (IN)
Graceland U (IA)
Grand Valley State U (MI)
Grand View U (IA)
Grinnell Coll (IA)
Guilford Coll (NC)
Hamilton Coll (NY)
Hamline U (MN)
Hampshire Coll (MA)
Hampton U (VA)
Hannibal-LaGrange U (MO)
Hanover Coll (IN)
Harding U (AR)
Hardin-Simmons U (TX)
Hartwick Coll (NY)
Heidelberg U (OH)
Henderson State U (AR)
Hendrix Coll (AR)
High Point U (NC)
Hillsdale Coll (MI)
Hiram Coll (OH)
Hofstra U (NY)
Hollins U (VA)
Hope Coll (MI)
Howard Payne U (TX)
Humboldt State U (CA)
Hunter Coll of the City U of New York (NY)
Huntington U (IN)
Idaho State U (ID)
Illinois Coll (IL)
Illinois State U (IL)
Illinois Wesleyan U (IL)
Indiana State U (IN)
Indiana U Bloomington (IN)
Indiana U Northwest (IN)
Indiana U of Pennsylvania (PA)
Indiana U South Bend (IN)
Iowa State U of Science and Technology (IA)
Ithaca Coll (NY)
Jacksonville State U (AL)
Jacksonville U (FL)
James Madison U (VA)
The Juilliard School (NY)
Kalamazoo Coll (MI)
Kansas State U (KS)
Kansas Wesleyan U (KS)
Kean U (NJ)
Kennesaw State U (GA)
Kent State U (OH)
Kentucky Wesleyan Coll (KY)
Kenyon Coll (OH)
King's Coll (PA)
Knox Coll (IL)
Lafayette Coll (PA)
LaGrange Coll (GA)
Lake Forest Coll (IL)
Lamar U (TX)
Lawrence U (WI)
Lees-McRae Coll (NC)
Lehigh U (PA)
Lehman Coll of the City U of New York (NY)
Le Moyne Coll (NY)
Lenoir-Rhyne U (NC)
Lewis & Clark Coll (OR)
Lewis U (IL)
Liberty U (VA)
Limestone Coll (SC)
Lincoln Coll (IL)
Lindenwood U (MO)
Linfield Coll (OR)
Lipscomb U (TN)
Lock Haven U of Pennsylvania (PA)
Louisiana Coll (LA)
Louisiana State U and A&M Coll (LA)
Loyola Marymount U (CA)
Loyola U Chicago (IL)
Loyola U New Orleans (LA)
Luther Coll (IA)
Lycoming Coll (PA)
Lynchburg Coll (VA)
Lynn U (FL)
Lyon Coll (AR)
Macalester Coll (MN)
Manchester U (IN)
Marietta Coll (OH)
Marymount Manhattan Coll (NY)
Marywood U (PA)
Massachusetts Inst of Technology (MA)
McDaniel Coll (MD)
McMaster U (ON, Canada)
McMurry U (TX)
Mercer U, Macon (GA)
Meredith Coll (NC)
Merrimack Coll (MA)
Messiah Coll (PA)
Metropolitan State U of Denver (CO)
Miami U (OH)
Michigan State U (MI)
Middlebury Coll (VT)
Millikin U (IL)
Mills Coll (CA)
Minnesota State U Mankato (MN)
Minnesota State U Moorhead (MN)
Missouri Baptist U (MO)
Missouri State U (MO)
Missouri Valley Coll (MO)
Missouri Western State U (MO)
Molloy Coll (NY)
Monmouth Coll (IL)
Montana State U Billings (MT)
Montclair State U (NJ)
Morehead State U (KY)
Morehouse Coll (GA)
Morningside Coll (IA)
Mount Allison U (NB, Canada)
Mount Holyoke Coll (MA)
Mount Marty Coll (SD)
Mount Vernon Nazarene U (OH)
Muhlenberg Coll (PA)
Murray State U (KY)
Muskingum U (OH)
Nazareth Coll of Rochester (NY)
Nebraska Wesleyan U (NE)
Newberry Coll (SC)
New Coll of Florida (FL)
New England Coll (NH)
New Mexico State U (NM)
The New School Coll of Performing Arts (NY)
Niagara U (NY)
North Carolina Central U (NC)
North Carolina Wesleyan Coll (NC)
North Central Coll (IL)
North Dakota State U (ND)
Northeastern State U (OK)
Northeastern U (MA)
Northern Arizona U (AZ)
Northern Illinois U (IL)
Northern Kentucky U (KY)
Northern State U (SD)
North Greenville U (SC)
Northwestern Coll (IA)
Northwestern State U of Louisiana (LA)
Northwestern U (IL)
Northwest Missouri State U (MO)
Northwest U (WA)
Nova Southeastern U (FL)
Oberlin Coll (OH)
Occidental Coll (CA)
The Ohio State U (OH)
The Ohio State U at Lima (OH)
Ohio U (OH)
Ohio Wesleyan U (OH)
Oklahoma Baptist U (OK)
Oklahoma Christian U (OK)
Oklahoma City U (OK)
Oklahoma State U (OK)
Old Dominion U (VA)
Oral Roberts U (OK)
Otterbein U (OH)
Ouachita Baptist U (AR)
Our Lady of the Lake U of San Antonio (TX)
Pacific Lutheran U (WA)
Palm Beach Atlantic U (FL)
Pepperdine U, Malibu (CA)
Piedmont Coll (GA)
Pitzer Coll (CA)
Plymouth State U (NH)
Point Park U (PA)
Pomona Coll (CA)
Portland State U (OR)
Prairie View A&M U (TX)
Principia Coll (IL)
Providence Coll (RI)
Purchase Coll, State U of New York (NY)
Purdue U (IN)
Queens Coll of the City U of New York (NY)
Quinnipiac U (CT)
Radford U (VA)
Ramapo Coll of New Jersey (NJ)
Randolph Coll (VA)
Randolph-Macon Coll (VA)
Redeemer U Coll (ON, Canada)
Reed Coll (OR)
Rhode Island Coll (RI)
Rhodes Coll (TN)
Ripon Coll (WI)
Roanoke Coll (VA)
Rockford U (IL)
Rocky Mountain Coll (MT)
Roger Williams U (RI)
Rowan U (NJ)
Rutgers U–Camden (NJ)
Rutgers U–Newark (NJ)
Rutgers U–New Brunswick (NJ)
Sacred Heart U (CT)
The Sage Colls (NY)
Saginaw Valley State U (MI)
St. Ambrose U (IA)
St. Bonaventure U (NY)
St. Catherine U (MN)
St. Cloud State U (MN)
St. Edward's U (TX)
St. Gregory's U, Shawnee (OK)
Saint John's U (MN)
St. John's U (NY)
Saint Louis U (MO)
Saint Louis U–Madrid Campus (Spain)
Saint Martin's U (WA)
Saint Mary's Coll (IN)
Saint Mary's Coll of California (CA)
St. Mary's Coll of Maryland (MD)
Saint Mary's U of Minnesota (MN)
Saint Michael's Coll (VT)
St. Norbert Coll (WI)
St. Olaf Coll (MN)
Salisbury U (MD)
Salve Regina U (RI)
Sam Houston State U (TX)
San Diego State U (CA)
San Francisco State U (CA)
Santa Clara U (CA)
Sarah Lawrence Coll (NY)
Savannah Coll of Art and Design (GA)
Schreiner U (TX)
Scripps Coll (CA)
Seattle Pacific U (WA)
Seattle U (WA)
Seton Hill U (PA)
Sewanee: The U of the South (TN)
Shorter U (GA)
Simon Fraser U (BC, Canada)
Simpson Coll (IA)
Skidmore Coll (NY)
Slippery Rock U of Pennsylvania (PA)
Smith Coll (MA)
Sonoma State U (CA)
South Carolina State U (SC)
South Dakota State U (SD)
Southeastern Oklahoma State U (OK)
Southeast Missouri State U (MO)
Southern Arkansas U–Magnolia (AR)
Southern Connecticut State U (CT)
Southern Illinois U Carbondale (IL)
Southern Illinois U Edwardsville (IL)
Southern Methodist U (TX)
Southern Oregon U (OR)
Southern Utah U (UT)
Southwest Baptist U (MO)
Southwestern Assemblies of God U (TX)
Southwestern Coll (KS)
Southwestern U (TX)
Spelman Coll (GA)
Spring Hill Coll (AL)
Stanford U (CA)
State U of New York at Fredonia (NY)
State U of New York at New Paltz (NY)
State U of New York at Oswego (NY)
State U of New York at Plattsburgh (NY)
State U of New York Coll at Geneseo (NY)
State U of New York Coll at Potsdam (NY)
Stephen F. Austin State U (TX)
Stephens Coll (MO)
Sterling Coll (KS)
Stevenson U (MD)
Stony Brook U, State U of New York (NY)
Suffolk U (MA)
Susquehanna U (PA)
Swarthmore Coll (PA)
Sweet Briar Coll (VA)
Syracuse U (NY)
Tabor Coll (KS)
Tarleton State U (TX)
Tennessee Wesleyan U (TN)
Texas A&M U (TX)
Texas A&M U–Commerce (TX)
Texas A&M U–Kingsville (TX)
Texas Christian U (TX)
Texas Lutheran U (TX)
Texas State U (TX)
Texas Tech U (TX)
Texas Woman's U (TX)
Thomas More Coll (KY)
Towson U (MD)
Transylvania U (KY)
Trevecca Nazarene U (TN)
Trinity U (TX)
Truman State U (MO)
Tufts U (MA)
Tulane U (LA)
Union U (TN)
U at Albany, State U of New York (NY)
U at Buffalo, the State U of New York (NY)
The U of Akron (OH)
The U of Alabama (AL)
The U of Alabama at Birmingham (AL)
The U of Arizona (AZ)
U of Arkansas (AR)
U of California, Irvine (CA)
U of California, Los Angeles (CA)
U of California, Riverside (CA)
U of California, San Diego (CA)
U of California, Santa Barbara (CA)
U of Central Arkansas (AR)
U of Central Florida (FL)
U of Central Missouri (MO)
U of Cincinnati (OH)
U of Colorado Boulder (CO)
U of Colorado Denver (CO)
U of Dayton (OH)
U of Denver (CO)
U of Detroit Mercy (MI)
U of Evansville (IN)
The U of Findlay (OH)
U of Florida (FL)
U of Georgia (GA)
U of Guelph (ON, Canada)
U of Hawaii at Manoa (HI)
U of Houston (TX)
U of Idaho (ID)
U of Illinois at Chicago (IL)
U of Indianapolis (IN)
U of Jamestown (ND)
The U of Kansas (KS)
U of Kentucky (KY)
U of King's Coll (NS, Canada)
U of La Verne (CA)
U of Lethbridge (AB, Canada)
U of Louisville (KY)
U of Maine (ME)
U of Maryland, Baltimore County (MD)
U of Maryland, Coll Park (MD)
U of Massachusetts Amherst (MA)
U of Massachusetts Boston (MA)
U of Miami (FL)
U of Michigan (MI)
U of Michigan–Flint (MI)
U of Minnesota, Duluth (MN)
U of Minnesota, Morris (MN)
U of Minnesota, Twin Cities Campus (MN)
U of Missouri–Kansas City (MO)
U of Missouri–St. Louis (MO)
U of Mobile (AL)
U of Montevallo (AL)
U of Mount Union (OH)
U of Nebraska at Kearney (NE)
U of Nevada, Las Vegas (NV)
U of Nevada, Reno (NV)
U of New Hampshire (NH)
U of New Haven (CT)
U of New Orleans (LA)
U of North Alabama (AL)
U of North Carolina at Asheville (NC)
The U of North Carolina at Chapel Hill (NC)
The U of North Carolina at Charlotte (NC)
The U of North Carolina at Greensboro (NC)
The U of North Carolina at Pembroke (NC)
U of North Carolina School of the Arts (NC)
The U of North Carolina Wilmington (NC)
U of North Dakota (ND)
U of Northern Colorado (CO)
U of Northern Iowa (IA)
U of North Texas (TX)
U of Notre Dame (IN)
U of Oklahoma (OK)
U of Oregon (OR)
U of Pennsylvania (PA)
U of Pittsburgh (PA)
U of Pittsburgh at Johnstown (PA)
U of Puget Sound (WA)
U of Regina (SK, Canada)
U of Rhode Island (RI)
U of Richmond (VA)
U of Saint Mary (KS)
U of St. Thomas (TX)
U of San Diego (CA)
U of Saskatchewan (SK, Canada)
U of Science and Arts of Oklahoma (OK)
The U of Scranton (PA)
U of South Alabama (AL)
U of South Carolina (SC)
The U of South Dakota (SD)
U of Southern California (CA)
U of Southern Indiana (IN)
U of Southern Maine (ME)
U of Southern Mississippi (MS)
U of South Florida (FL)
The U of Tampa (FL)
The U of Tennessee (TN)
The U of Tennessee at Chattanooga (TN)
The U of Tennessee at Martin (TN)
The U of Texas at Austin (TX)
The U of Texas at El Paso (TX)
The U of Texas Rio Grande Valley (TX)
U of the Cumberlands (KY)
U of the Fraser Valley (BC, Canada)
U of the Incarnate Word (TX)
U of the Pacific (CA)
The U of Toledo (OH)

The U of Tulsa (OK)
U of Utah (UT)
U of Vermont (VT)
U of Virginia (VA)
The U of Virginia's Coll at Wise (VA)
U of Washington (WA)
U of Waterloo (ON, Canada)
U of West Georgia (GA)
U of Windsor (ON, Canada)
U of Wisconsin–Eau Claire (WI)
U of Wisconsin–Green Bay (WI)
U of Wisconsin–La Crosse (WI)
U of Wisconsin–Madison (WI)
U of Wisconsin–Milwaukee (WI)
U of Wisconsin–Parkside (WI)
U of Wisconsin–Stevens Point (WI)
U of Wisconsin–Superior (WI)
U of Wisconsin–Whitewater (WI)
Ursinus Coll (PA)
Utah State U (UT)
Utah Valley U (UT)
Valdosta State U (GA)
Valparaiso U (IN)
Vanderbilt U (TN)
Vassar Coll (NY)
Virginia Commonwealth U (VA)
Virginia Polytechnic Inst and State U (VA)
Virginia Union U (VA)
Virginia Wesleyan Coll (VA)
Viterbo U (WI)
Wabash Coll (IN)
Wagner Coll (NY)
Wake Forest U (NC)
Waldorf U (IA)
Washburn U (KS)
Washington and Lee U (VA)
Washington Coll (MD)
Washington State U (WA)
Washington U in St. Louis (MO)
Wayland Baptist U (TX)
Wayne State Coll (NE)
Wayne State U (MI)
Weber State U (UT)
Webster U (MO)
Wells Coll (NY)
Wesleyan Coll (GA)
Wesleyan U (CT)
West Chester U of Pennsylvania (PA)
Western Carolina U (NC)
Western Connecticut State U (CT)
Western Illinois U (IL)
Western Kentucky U (KY)
Western Oregon U (OR)
Western State Colorado U (CO)
Western Washington U (WA)
Westfield State U (MA)
Westminster Coll (PA)
Westminster Coll (UT)
Westmont Coll (CA)
West Texas A&M U (TX)
West Virginia U (WV)
West Virginia Wesleyan Coll (WV)
Whitman Coll (WA)
Whittier Coll (CA)
Whitworth U (WA)
Wichita State U (KS)
Wilkes U (PA)
Willamette U (OR)
William Jewell Coll (MO)
William Peace U (NC)
Williams Coll (MA)
William Woods U (MO)
Winona State U (MN)
Winthrop U (SC)
Wittenberg U (OH)
Wofford Coll (SC)
Wright State U (OH)
Wright State U–Lake Campus (OH)
York Coll of Pennsylvania (PA)
York Coll of the City U of New York (NY)
Youngstown State U (OH)

DRAMATIC/THEATER ARTS AND STAGECRAFT RELATED

Adams State U (CO)
Benedictine Coll (KS)
Brigham Young U (UT)
Catawba Coll (NC)
Charleston Southern U (SC)
Coastal Carolina U (SC)
Columbia Coll Chicago (IL)
Dalhousie U (NS, Canada)
Drake U (IA)
Fayetteville State U (NC)
Indiana U South Bend (IN)
Lee U (TN)
Lindenwood U (MO)
Nebraska Wesleyan U (NE)
Pepperdine U, Malibu (CA)
Saint Augustine's U (NC)
St. Cloud State U (MN)
Seton Hill U (PA)
Southern Illinois U Carbondale (IL)
Southwestern Coll (KS)
Syracuse U (NY)
U of Miami (FL)
U of Michigan–Flint (MI)
U of Northern Colorado (CO)
U of Southern California (CA)
Webster U (MO)
Western Kentucky U (KY)
Western Michigan U (MI)
Wheaton Coll (MA)

DRAWING

Adams State U (CO)
Albany State U (GA)
American Acad of Art (IL)
Aquinas Coll (MI)
Bennington Coll (VT)
Biola U (CA)
Bowling Green State U (OH)
Bradley U (IL)
Brigham Young U (UT)
Buffalo State Coll, State U of New York (NY)
California Coll of the Arts (CA)
California State U, East Bay (CA)
California State U, Long Beach (CA)
Carson-Newman U (TN)
Central Washington U (WA)
Cleveland Inst of Art (OH)
Coll of the Atlantic (ME)
Colorado State U (CO)
Columbus State U (GA)
Concord U (WV)
Dixie State U (UT)
Drake U (IA)
Emily Carr U of Art + Design (BC, Canada)
Ferris State U (MI)
Georgia State U (GA)
Grace Coll (IN)
Inter American U of Puerto Rico, San Germán Campus (PR)
Laguna Coll of Art & Design (CA)
Lewis U (IL)
Lindenwood U (MO)
Maryland Inst Coll of Art (MD)
Milwaukee Inst of Art and Design (WI)
Minneapolis Coll of Art and Design (MN)
Minnesota State U Mankato (MN)
Mount Allison U (NB, Canada)
New England Coll (NH)
Portland State U (OR)
Pratt Inst (NY)
Providence Coll (RI)
Rutgers U–New Brunswick (NJ)
Sarah Lawrence Coll (NY)
School of the Art Inst of Chicago (IL)
Seton Hill U (PA)
Sonoma State U (CA)
State U of New York at Fredonia (NY)
U of Hartford (CT)
U of Michigan (MI)
U of New Haven (CT)
U of Regina (SK, Canada)
U of San Francisco (CA)
The U of Texas at El Paso (TX)
U of Windsor (ON, Canada)
Washington U in St. Louis (MO)
Western Washington U (WA)
West Virginia Wesleyan Coll (WV)

DUTCH/FLEMISH

Weber State U (UT)

EARLY CHILDHOOD EDUCATION

Adams State U (CO)
Alabama State U (AL)
Albany State U (GA)
Alma Coll (MI)
Alvernia U (PA)
Antioch U Midwest (OH)
Arcadia U (PA)
Arizona State U at the Tempe campus (AZ)
Arkansas Tech U (AR)
Arlington Baptist Coll (TX)
Armstrong State U (GA)
Auburn U (AL)
Augusta U (GA)
Baldwin Wallace U (OH)
Ball State U (IN)
Barton Coll (NC)
Bayamón Central U (PR)
Baylor U (TX)
Bay Path U (MA)
Becker Coll (MA)
Belmont U (TN)
Berry Coll (GA)
Bethel Coll (IN)
Bloomsburg U of Pennsylvania (PA)
Boise State U (ID)
Boston U (MA)
Bradley U (IL)
Brandman U (CA)
Brewton-Parker Coll (GA)
Bridgewater State U (MA)
Brigham Young U (UT)
Brigham Young U–Idaho (ID)
Brooklyn Coll of the City U of New York (NY)
Bucknell U (PA)
Butler U (IN)
California Baptist U (CA)
California State U, Chico (CA)
California State U, Dominguez Hills (CA)
California State U, San Bernardino (CA)
California State U, San Marcos (CA)
California State U, Stanislaus (CA)
California U of Pennsylvania (PA)
Calvin Coll (MI)
Cameron U (OK)
Canisius Coll (NY)
Capital U (OH)
Cardinal Stritch U (WI)
Carlow U (PA)
Carson-Newman U (TN)
The Catholic U of America (DC)
Cazenovia Coll (NY)
Cedar Crest Coll (PA)
Cedarville U (OH)
Central Baptist Coll (AR)
Central Methodist U (MO)
Central Michigan U (MI)
Central State U (OH)
Central Washington U (WA)
Chaminade U of Honolulu (HI)
Champlain Coll (VT)
Charleston Southern U (SC)
Chatham U (PA)
Chestnut Hill Coll (PA)
Christian Brothers U (TN)
City Coll of the City U of New York (NY)
Clarion U of Pennsylvania (PA)
Clark Atlanta U (GA)
Clemson U (SC)
Cleveland State U (OH)
Coastal Carolina U (SC)
Colby-Sawyer Coll (NH)
Coll of Central Florida (FL)
Coll of Charleston (SC)
Coll of Coastal Georgia (GA)
The Coll of New Jersey (NJ)
The Coll of Saint Rose (NY)
Coll of the Ozarks (MO)
Colorado State U (CO)
Columbia Coll Chicago (IL)
Columbus State U (GA)
Concordia Coll–New York (NY)
Concordia U Chicago (IL)
Concordia U, Nebraska (NE)
Concordia U, St. Paul (MN)
Curry Coll (MA)
Daemen Coll (NY)
DeSales U (PA)
Dominican U (IL)
Duquesne U (PA)
East Central U (OK)
Eastern Michigan U (MI)
Eastern Nazarene Coll (MA)
Eastern Oregon U (OR)
Eastern U (PA)
Eastern Washington U (WA)
East Stroudsburg U of Pennsylvania (PA)
Edgewood Coll (WI)
Elizabethtown Coll (PA)
Elon U (NC)
Endicott Coll (MA)
Evangel U (MO)
Faulkner U (AL)
Fayetteville State U (NC)
Fitchburg State U (MA)
Florida Ag and Mech U (FL)
Florida Atlantic U (FL)
Florida Gulf Coast U (FL)
Florida Intl U (FL)
Florida State U (FL)
Fort Lewis Coll (CO)
Framingham State U (MA)
Francis Marion U (SC)
Freed-Hardeman U (TN)
Frostburg State U (MD)
Gannon U (PA)
Georgia Coll & State U (GA)
Georgia Gwinnett Coll (GA)
Gordon Coll (MA)
Gordon State Coll (GA)
Governors State U (IL)
Granite State Coll (NH)
Grove City Coll (PA)
Gwynedd Mercy U (PA)
Hannibal-LaGrange U (MO)
Harding U (AR)
Hardin-Simmons U (TX)
Harris-Stowe State U (MO)
Hiram Coll (OH)
Hofstra U (NY)
Holy Family U (PA)
Hood Coll (MD)
Idaho State U (ID)
Illinois Coll (IL)
Illinois State U (IL)
Indiana U Bloomington (IN)
Indiana U Kokomo (IN)
Indiana U of Pennsylvania (PA)
Inter American U of Puerto Rico, San Germán Campus (PR)
Iona Coll (NY)
Iowa State U of Science and Technology (IA)
Iowa Wesleyan U (IA)
Judson U (IL)
Keene State Coll (NH)
Kendall Coll (IL)
Kennesaw State U (GA)
Kent State U (OH)
Kent State U at Salem (OH)
Kent State U at Tuscarawas (OH)
King's Coll (PA)
Kutztown U of Pennsylvania (PA)
LaGrange Coll (GA)
Lake Erie Coll (OH)
La Salle U (PA)
Lasell Coll (MA)
Lebanon Valley Coll (PA)
Lees-McRae Coll (NC)
Lee U (TN)
Limestone Coll (SC)
Lindenwood U (MO)
Lock Haven U of Pennsylvania (PA)
Louisiana State U and A&M Coll (LA)
Louisiana Tech U (LA)
Lourdes U (OH)
Loyola U Chicago (IL)
Lubbock Christian U (TX)
Lynn U (FL)
Madonna U (MI)
Malone U (OH)
Maranatha Baptist U (WI)
Marian U (WI)
Marywood U (PA)
McMurry U (TX)
McNeese State U (LA)
Merrimack Coll (MA)
Messiah Coll (PA)
Miami Dade Coll (FL)
Miami U (OH)
Michigan State U (MI)
Millersville U of Pennsylvania (PA)
Milligan Coll (TN)
Millikin U (IL)
Minnesota State U Moorhead (MN)
Misericordia U (PA)
Missouri Baptist U (MO)
Missouri State U (MO)
Missouri Valley Coll (MO)
Missouri Western State U (MO)
Morehead State U (KY)
Morehouse Coll (GA)
Morris Coll (SC)
Mount Aloysius Coll (PA)
Mount Ida Coll (MA)
Mount St. Joseph U (OH)
Mount Saint Mary Coll (NY)
Mount Vernon Nazarene U (OH)
Murray State U (KY)
Muskingum U (OH)
National Louis U (IL)
National U (CA)
Newberry Coll (SC)
New Jersey City U (NJ)
Newman U (KS)
New Mexico State U (NM)
Northeastern Illinois U (IL)
Northeastern State U (OK)
Northern Arizona U (AZ)
Northern Illinois U (IL)
North Greenville U (SC)
Northwest Christian U (OR)
Northwestern Oklahoma State U (OK)
Northwestern State U of Louisiana (LA)
Nyack Coll (NY)
Oakland City U (IN)
Ohio Christian U (OH)
Ohio Dominican U (OH)
Ohio U (OH)
Ohio U–Eastern (OH)
Ohio Wesleyan U (OH)
Oklahoma Baptist U (OK)
Oklahoma Christian U (OK)
Oklahoma City U (OK)
Oral Roberts U (OK)
Ouachita Baptist U (AR)
Penn State U Park (PA)
Piedmont Intl U (NC)
Pine Manor Coll (MA)
Plymouth State U (NH)
Point U (GA)
Prescott Coll (AZ)
Purdue U (IN)
Purdue U Northwest (IN)
Regent U (VA)
Rhode Island Coll (RI)
Ripon Coll (WI)
Roberts Wesleyan Coll (NY)
Rockford U (IL)
Rowan U (NJ)
St. Ambrose U (IA)
Saint Vincent Coll (PA)
Salisbury U (MD)
Salve Regina U (RI)
San Diego State U (CA)
San Francisco State U (CA)
Schreiner U (TX)
Shawnee State U (OH)
Shippensburg U of Pennsylvania (PA)
Silver Lake Coll of the Holy Family (WI)
Slippery Rock U of Pennsylvania (PA)
South Carolina State U (SC)
South Dakota State U (SD)
Southeastern Louisiana U (LA)
Southern Arkansas U–Magnolia (AR)
Southern Connecticut State U (CT)
Southern Illinois U Carbondale (IL)
Southern Illinois U Edwardsville (IL)
Southern New Hampshire U (NH)
Southwest Baptist U (MO)
Southwestern Coll (KS)
Spalding U (KY)
Spring Hill Coll (AL)
State Coll of Florida Manatee-Sarasota (FL)
State U of New York Coll at Geneseo (NY)
State U of New York Coll at Old Westbury (NY)
State U of New York Coll at Potsdam (NY)
Stephens Coll (MO)
Stevenson U (MD)
Stonehill Coll (MA)
Susquehanna U (PA)
Tennessee Wesleyan U (TN)
Texas Christian U (TX)
Thomas U (GA)
Towson U (MD)
Trevecca Nazarene U (TN)
Tufts U (MA)
Union Coll (NE)
The U of Akron (OH)
The U of Alabama (AL)

The U of Alabama at Birmingham (AL)
U of Arkansas (AR)
U of Central Florida (FL)
U of Colorado Colorado Springs (CO)
U of Dayton (OH)
U of Delaware (DE)
U of Georgia (GA)
U of Hartford (CT)
U of Hawaii at Manoa (HI)
The U of Kansas (KS)
U of Kentucky (KY)
U of Maine at Farmington (ME)
U of Massachusetts Boston (MA)
U of Michigan–Dearborn (MI)
U of Minnesota, Crookston (MN)
U of Missouri–Kansas City (MO)
U of Missouri–St. Louis (MO)
U of Mobile (AL)
The U of Montana Western (MT)
U of Mount Union (OH)
U of Nevada, Las Vegas (NV)
The U of North Carolina at Chapel Hill (NC)
The U of North Carolina at Greensboro (NC)
U of North Dakota (ND)
U of Northern Colorado (CO)
U of North Florida (FL)
U of North Georgia (GA)
U of Oklahoma (OK)
U of Regina (SK, Canada)
U of Science and Arts of Oklahoma (OK)
The U of Scranton (PA)
U of South Alabama (AL)
U of South Carolina Aiken (SC)
U of Southern Indiana (IN)
U of South Florida (FL)
The U of Tennessee at Chattanooga (TN)
U of the Virgin Islands (VI)
The U of Tulsa (OK)
U of Valley Forge (PA)
U of Vermont (VT)
U of Wisconsin–Parkside (WI)
U of Wisconsin–Stevens Point (WI)
U of Wisconsin–Stout (WI)
U of Wisconsin–Whitewater (WI)
Valdosta State U (GA)
Vanderbilt U (TN)
Walsh U (OH)
Wayland Baptist U (TX)
Wayne State Coll (NE)
Weber State U (UT)
Webster U (MO)
Welch Coll (TN)
Wells Coll (NY)
West Chester U of Pennsylvania (PA)
Western Kentucky U (KY)
Western Michigan U (MI)
Western Washington U (WA)
Wheaton Coll (MA)
Wheelock Coll (MA)
Widener U (PA)
William Paterson U of New Jersey (NJ)
Wilmington U (DE)
Worcester State U (MA)
Wright State U (OH)
Wright State U–Lake Campus (OH)
Xavier U of Louisiana (LA)
York Coll of Pennsylvania (PA)
Youngstown State U (OH)

EARTH SCIENCE EDUCATION
Albion Coll (MI)
Ball State U (IN)
Boise State U (ID)
Brigham Young U–Idaho (ID)
Calvin Coll (MI)
Central Michigan U (MI)
Florida Inst of Technology (FL)
Minnesota State U Moorhead (MN)
Pace U (NY)
Pace U, Pleasantville Campus (NY)
Queens Coll of the City U of New York (NY)
State U of New York Coll at Potsdam (NY)
Syracuse U (NY)
U of Maine at Farmington (ME)
U of Michigan–Flint (MI)
Western Michigan U (MI)
Western Washington U (WA)
Winona State U (MN)

EAST ASIAN LANGUAGES
Arizona State U at the Tempe campus (AZ)
Austin Coll (TX)
Columbia U (NY)
Eckerd Coll (FL)
Indiana U Bloomington (IN)
Smith Coll (MA)
U of Georgia (GA)
The U of Kansas (KS)
U of Pennsylvania (PA)
U of Puget Sound (WA)
U of Southern California (CA)
The U of Texas at Austin (TX)
Washington and Lee U (VA)

EAST ASIAN LANGUAGES RELATED
Boston U (MA)
Columbia U, School of General Studies (NY)
Dartmouth Coll (NH)
Northwestern U (IL)
U of Chicago (IL)
U of Florida (FL)
U of Minnesota, Twin Cities Campus (MN)
Washington U in St. Louis (MO)

ECOLOGY
Augusta U (GA)
Barry U (FL)
Beloit Coll (WI)
Bemidji State U (MN)
Bennington Coll (VT)
Brigham Young U–Idaho (ID)
Bryant U (RI)
California State U, Dominguez Hills (CA)
California State U, East Bay (CA)
California State U, Fresno (CA)
California State U, Long Beach (CA)
California State U, San Marcos (CA)
Central Washington U (WA)
Christian Brothers U (TN)
Clark U (MA)
Coll of the Ozarks (MO)
Colorado State U (CO)
Concordia Coll–New York (NY)
Concordia U (QC, Canada)
Dartmouth Coll (NH)
Defiance Coll (OH)
The Evergreen State Coll (WA)
Fort Lewis Coll (CO)
Georgetown Coll (KY)
Iowa State U of Science and Technology (IA)
Jacksonville State U (AL)
Lawrence U (WI)
Le Moyne Coll (NY)
Manchester U (IN)
Medgar Evers Coll of the City U of New York (NY)
Minnesota State U Mankato (MN)
Molloy Coll (NY)
New Mexico State U (NM)
Northwestern U (IL)
Oberlin Coll (OH)
Ohio U (OH)
Oklahoma State U (OK)
Olivet Nazarene U (IL)
Prescott Coll (AZ)
Princeton U (NJ)
Rice U (TX)
Rutgers U–New Brunswick (NJ)
St. Cloud State U (MN)
Salisbury U (MD)
San Diego State U (CA)
San Francisco State U (CA)
Seattle Pacific U (WA)
Siena Coll (NY)
Sierra Nevada Coll (NV)
Sonoma State U (CA)
State U of New York at Plattsburgh (NY)
Stony Brook U, State U of New York (NY)
Susquehanna U (PA)
Tufts U (MA)
Tulane U (LA)
Université de Sherbrooke (QC, Canada)
The U of Akron (OH)
U of California, Los Angeles (CA)
U of California, San Diego (CA)
U of California, Santa Barbara (CA)
U of Delaware (DE)
U of Denver (CO)
U of Georgia (GA)
U of Guelph (ON, Canada)
U of Maryland, Coll Park (MD)
U of Minnesota, Twin Cities Campus (MN)
U of Northern Iowa (IA)
U of North Texas (TX)
U of Pittsburgh (PA)
U of Pittsburgh at Johnstown (PA)
U of Saskatchewan (SK, Canada)
U of Waterloo (ON, Canada)
Utah State U (UT)
Washington Coll (MD)
Washington U in St. Louis (MO)

ECOLOGY AND EVOLUTIONARY BIOLOGY
Angelo State U (TX)
Bradley U (IL)
Case Western Reserve U (OH)
Colby Coll (ME)
The Colorado Coll (CO)
Columbia U, School of General Studies (NY)
Purdue U (IN)
The U of Arizona (AZ)
U of California, Irvine (CA)
U of Colorado Boulder (CO)
U of Michigan (MI)
U of Pittsburgh (PA)
The U of Texas at Austin (TX)
Vanderbilt U (TN)

ECOLOGY, EVOLUTION, SYSTEMATICS AND POPULATION BIOLOGY RELATED
Hofstra U (NY)
The Ohio State U (OH)
U of California, Davis (CA)
U of Colorado Boulder (CO)
U of Guelph (ON, Canada)
U of Regina (SK, Canada)
U of Washington (WA)

E-COMMERCE
Bloomfield Coll (NJ)
Harrisburg U of Science and Technology (PA)
Lewis U (IL)
Limestone Coll (SC)
Maryville U of Saint Louis (MO)
Seattle U (WA)
Towson U (MD)
Trevecca Nazarene U (TN)
The U of Akron (OH)
U of La Verne (CA)
U of Pennsylvania (PA)
The U of Scranton (PA)
U of the Incarnate Word (TX)
The U of Toledo (OH)
U of Toronto (ON, Canada)
Washington State U (WA)
Western Michigan U (MI)
Winthrop U (SC)

ECONOMETRICS AND QUANTITATIVE ECONOMICS
Baldwin Wallace U (OH)
Bowdoin Coll (ME)
Bucknell U (PA)
Carnegie Mellon U (PA)
Colgate U (NY)
The Colorado Coll (CO)
Drexel U (PA)
Hampden-Sydney Coll (VA)
High Point U (NC)
Hofstra U (NY)
Providence Coll (RI)
Scripps Coll (CA)
Southern Methodist U (TX)
State U of New York at Oswego (NY)
U of California, Irvine (CA)
U of California, Santa Barbara (CA)
U of Dayton (OH)
U of Guelph (ON, Canada)
U of Minnesota, Twin Cities Campus (MN)
U of Northern Iowa (IA)
U of Rhode Island (RI)
Wake Forest U (NC)
Weber State U (UT)
Western Kentucky U (KY)
Youngstown State U (OH)

ECONOMICS
Adams State U (CO)
Adelphi U (NY)
Agnes Scott Coll (GA)
Albion Coll (MI)
Albright Coll (PA)
Allegheny Coll (PA)
Alma Coll (MI)
American U (DC)
American U in Bulgaria (Bulgaria)
The American U in Cairo (Egypt)
The American U in Dubai (United Arab Emirates)
American U of Beirut (Lebanon)
Amherst Coll (MA)
Andrews U (MI)
Appalachian State U (NC)
Aquinas Coll (MI)
Arizona State U at the Tempe campus (AZ)
Armstrong State U (GA)
Ashland U (OH)
Assumption Coll (MA)
Auburn U (AL)
Auburn U at Montgomery (AL)
Augsburg Coll (MN)
Augustana Coll (IL)
Augustana U (SD)
Austin Coll (TX)
Baker U (KS)
Baldwin Wallace U (OH)
Bard Coll (NY)
Barnard Coll (NY)
Barry U (FL)
Baruch Coll of the City U of New York (NY)
Bates Coll (ME)
Baylor U (TX)
Bellarmine U (KY)
Beloit Coll (WI)
Bemidji State U (MN)
Benedictine Coll (KS)
Berea Coll (KY)
Bethel Coll (IN)
Bethel U (MN)
Binghamton U, State U of New York (NY)
Bishop's U (QC, Canada)
Bloomsburg U of Pennsylvania (PA)
Bluffton U (OH)
Boise State U (ID)
Boston Coll (MA)
Boston U (MA)
Bowdoin Coll (ME)
Bowie State U (MD)
Bowling Green State U (OH)
Bradley U (IL)
Brandeis U (MA)
Bridgewater Coll (VA)
Bridgewater State U (MA)
Brigham Young U–Idaho (ID)
Brooklyn Coll of the City U of New York (NY)
Bryant U (RI)
Bryn Mawr Coll (PA)
Bucknell U (PA)
Buffalo State Coll, State U of New York (NY)
Butler U (IN)
Caldwell U (NJ)
California Inst of Technology (CA)
California Lutheran U (CA)
California Polytechnic State U, San Luis Obispo (CA)
California State Polytechnic U, Pomona (CA)
California State U, Bakersfield (CA)
California State U, Chico (CA)
California State U, East Bay (CA)
California State U, Fresno (CA)
California State U, Fullerton (CA)
California State U, Long Beach (CA)
California State U, Northridge (CA)
California State U, Sacramento (CA)
California State U, San Bernardino (CA)
California State U, San Marcos (CA)
California State U, Stanislaus (CA)
Calvin Coll (MI)
Campbellsville U (KY)
Canisius Coll (NY)
Capital U (OH)
Carleton Coll (MN)
Carnegie Mellon U (PA)
Carthage Coll (WI)
Case Western Reserve U (OH)
Catawba Coll (NC)
The Catholic U of America (DC)
Centenary Coll of Louisiana (LA)
Central Connecticut State U (CT)
Central Methodist U (MO)
Central Michigan U (MI)
Central State U (OH)
Central Washington U (WA)
Centre Coll (KY)
Charleston Southern U (SC)
Chowan U (NC)
Christopher Newport U (VA)
City Coll of the City U of New York (NY)
Claremont McKenna Coll (CA)
Clarion U of Pennsylvania (PA)
Clark U (MA)
Clemson U (SC)
Cleveland State U (OH)
Coastal Carolina U (SC)
Coe Coll (IA)
Colby Coll (ME)
Colgate U (NY)
Coll of Charleston (SC)
Coll of Mount Saint Vincent (NY)
The Coll of New Jersey (NJ)
Coll of Saint Benedict (MN)
Coll of Staten Island of the City U of New York (NY)
Coll of the Atlantic (ME)
Coll of the Holy Cross (MA)
The Coll of William and Mary (VA)
The Coll of Wooster (OH)
Colorado Christian U (CO)
The Colorado Coll (CO)
Colorado School of Mines (CO)
Colorado State U (CO)
Columbia U (NY)
Columbia U, School of General Studies (NY)
Concordia U (QC, Canada)
Concordia U Irvine (CA)
Concordia U Wisconsin (WI)
Connecticut Coll (CT)
Converse Coll (SC)
Cornell Coll (IA)
Cornell U (NY)
Cornerstone U (MI)
Creighton U (NE)
Dalhousie U (NS, Canada)
Dartmouth Coll (NH)
Davidson Coll (NC)
Denison U (OH)
DePauw U (IN)
DEREE - The American Coll of Greece (Greece)
DeSales U (PA)
Dickinson Coll (PA)
Doane U (NE)
Dominican U (IL)
Drew U (NJ)
Drexel U (PA)
Drury U (MO)
Duquesne U (PA)
Earlham Coll (IN)
East Carolina U (NC)
Eastern Illinois U (IL)
Eastern Mennonite U (VA)
Eastern Michigan U (MI)
Eastern Oregon U (OR)
Eastern Washington U (WA)
East Stroudsburg U of Pennsylvania (PA)
East Tennessee State U (TN)
Eckerd Coll (FL)
Edgewood Coll (WI)
Elizabethtown Coll (PA)
Elmira Coll (NY)
Elon U (NC)
Emmanuel Coll (MA)
Emory & Henry Coll (VA)
Emory U (GA)
Emporia State U (KS)
Eugene Lang Coll of Liberal Arts (NY)
Fairfield U (CT)
Fairleigh Dickinson U, Coll at Florham (NJ)
Fairleigh Dickinson U, Metropolitan Campus (NJ)
Fitchburg State U (MA)
Flagler Coll (FL)

Florida Ag and Mech U (FL)
Florida Atlantic U (FL)
Florida Gulf Coast U (FL)
Florida Intl U (FL)
Florida Southern Coll (FL)
Florida State U (FL)
Fordham U (NY)
Fort Lewis Coll (CO)
Framingham State U (MA)
Franciscan U of Steubenville (OH)
Francis Marion U (SC)
Franklin & Marshall Coll (PA)
Franklin Coll (IN)
Frostburg State U (MD)
Furman U (SC)
Gardner-Webb U (NC)
George Fox U (OR)
Georgetown Coll (KY)
Georgetown U (DC)
The George Washington U (DC)
Georgia Southern U (GA)
Georgia State U (GA)
Gettysburg Coll (PA)
Gonzaga U (WA)
Gordon Coll (MA)
Goucher Coll (MD)
Governors State U (IL)
Graceland U (IA)
Grand Valley State U (MI)
Grinnell Coll (IA)
Grove City Coll (PA)
Guilford Coll (NC)
Hamilton Coll (NY)
Hamline U (MN)
Hampden-Sydney Coll (VA)
Hampshire Coll (MA)
Hampton U (VA)
Hanover Coll (IN)
Harding U (AR)
Hardin-Simmons U (TX)
Hartwick Coll (NY)
Harvard U (MA)
Haverford Coll (PA)
Heidelberg U (OH)
Hendrix Coll (AR)
Hillsdale Coll (MI)
Hiram Coll (OH)
Hobart and William Smith Colls (NY)
Hofstra U (NY)
Hollins U (VA)
Hood Coll (MD)
Hope Coll (MI)
Humboldt State U (CA)
Hunter Coll of the City U of New York (NY)
Huntington U (IN)
Idaho State U (ID)
Illinois Coll (IL)
Illinois State U (IL)
Illinois Wesleyan U (IL)
Indiana State U (IN)
Indiana U Bloomington (IN)
Indiana U Northwest (IN)
Indiana U of Pennsylvania (PA)
Indiana U–Purdue U Indianapolis (IN)
Indiana U South Bend (IN)
Indiana U Southeast (IN)
Inter American U of Puerto Rico, San Germán Campus (PR)
Iona Coll (NY)
Iowa State U of Science and Technology (IA)
Ithaca Coll (NY)
Jacksonville State U (AL)
Jacksonville U (FL)
James Madison U (VA)
John Carroll U (OH)
John Jay Coll of Criminal Justice of the City U of New York (NY)
Johns Hopkins U (MD)
Johnson C. Smith U (NC)
Juniata Coll (PA)
Kalamazoo Coll (MI)
Kansas State U (KS)
Kean U (NJ)
Keene State Coll (NH)
Kenyon Coll (OH)
King's Coll (PA)
King U (TN)
Knox Coll (IL)
Lafayette Coll (PA)
Lake Forest Coll (IL)
La Salle U (PA)
Lawrence U (WI)
Lebanese American U (Lebanon)
Lebanon Valley Coll (PA)
Lehman Coll of the City U of New York (NY)
Le Moyne Coll (NY)
Lenoir-Rhyne U (NC)
Lewis & Clark Coll (OR)
Limestone Coll (SC)
Lincoln U (CA)
Lindenwood U (MO)
Linfield Coll (OR)
Longwood U (VA)
Loras Coll (IA)
Louisiana State U and A&M Coll (LA)
Loyola Marymount U (CA)
Loyola U Maryland (MD)
Loyola U New Orleans (LA)
Lubbock Christian U (TX)
Luther Coll (IA)
Lycoming Coll (PA)
Lynchburg Coll (VA)
Lyon Coll (AR)
Macalester Coll (MN)
Manchester U (IN)
Manhattan Coll (NY)
Manhattanville Coll (NY)
Marietta Coll (OH)
Marist Coll (NY)
Marshall U (WV)
Mary Baldwin U (VA)
Marymount U (VA)
Massachusetts Inst of Technology (MA)
McDaniel Coll (MD)
McKendree U (IL)
McMaster U (ON, Canada)
Mercer U, Macon (GA)
Meredith Coll (NC)
Merrimack Coll (MA)
Messiah Coll (PA)
Metropolitan State U of Denver (CO)
Miami U (OH)
Michigan State U (MI)
Michigan Technological U (MI)
Middlebury Coll (VT)
Millersville U of Pennsylvania (PA)
Milligan Coll (TN)
Millsaps Coll (MS)
Mills Coll (CA)
Minnesota State U Mankato (MN)
Minnesota State U Moorhead (MN)
Mississippi State U (MS)
Missouri State U (MO)
Missouri U of Science and Technology (MO)
Missouri Valley Coll (MO)
Missouri Western State U (MO)
Monmouth Coll (IL)
Montana State U (MT)
Montclair State U (NJ)
Moravian Coll (PA)
Morehouse Coll (GA)
Mount Allison U (NB, Canada)
Mount Holyoke Coll (MA)
Mount St. Mary's U (MD)
Muhlenberg Coll (PA)
Murray State U (KY)
Muskingum U (OH)
Nazareth Coll of Rochester (NY)
Nebraska Wesleyan U (NE)
Nevada State Coll (NV)
New Coll of Florida (FL)
New Jersey City U (NJ)
New Mexico State U (NM)
Niagara U (NY)
Nichols Coll (MA)
North Central Coll (IL)
North Dakota State U (ND)
Northeastern Illinois U (IL)
Northeastern U (MA)
Northern Illinois U (IL)
Northern State U (SD)
Northwestern Coll (IA)
Northwestern U (IL)
Northwest Missouri State U (MO)
Oberlin Coll (OH)
Occidental Coll (CA)
Ohio Dominican U (OH)
The Ohio State U (OH)
Ohio U (OH)
Ohio Wesleyan U (OH)
Oklahoma City U (OK)
Oklahoma State U (OK)
Old Dominion U (VA)
Olivet Nazarene U (IL)
Oregon State U (OR)
Otterbein U (OH)
Our Lady of the Lake U of San Antonio (TX)
Pace U (NY)
Pace U, Pleasantville Campus (NY)
Pacific Lutheran U (WA)
Penn State Abington (PA)
Penn State Altoona (PA)
Penn State Beaver (PA)
Penn State Berks (PA)
Penn State Brandywine (PA)
Penn State DuBois (PA)
Penn State Erie, The Behrend Coll (PA)
Penn State Fayette, The Eberly Campus (PA)
Penn State Greater Allegheny (PA)
Penn State Hazleton (PA)
Penn State Lehigh Valley (PA)
Penn State Mont Alto (PA)
Penn State New Kensington (PA)
Penn State Schuylkill (PA)
Penn State Shenango (PA)
Penn State U Park (PA)
Penn State Wilkes-Barre (PA)
Penn State Worthington Scranton (PA)
Penn State York (PA)
Pepperdine U, Malibu (CA)
Pittsburg State U (KS)
Pitzer Coll (CA)
Point Park U (PA)
Pomona Coll (CA)
Portland State U (OR)
Princeton U (NJ)
Principia Coll (IL)
Providence Coll (RI)
Purchase Coll, State U of New York (NY)
Purdue U (IN)
Queens Coll of the City U of New York (NY)
Quinnipiac U (CT)
Radford U (VA)
Ramapo Coll of New Jersey (NJ)
Randolph Coll (VA)
Randolph-Macon Coll (VA)
Reed Coll (OR)
Regis U (CO)
Rensselaer Polytechnic Inst (NY)
Rhode Island Coll (RI)
Rhodes Coll (TN)
Rice U (TX)
Ripon Coll (WI)
Roanoke Coll (VA)
Robert Morris U (PA)
Rochester Inst of Technology (NY)
Rockford U (IL)
Rockhurst U (MO)
Roger Williams U (RI)
Rollins Coll (FL)
Rose-Hulman Inst of Technology (IN)
Rowan U (NJ)
Rutgers U–Camden (NJ)
Rutgers U–Newark (NJ)
Rutgers U–New Brunswick (NJ)
Sacred Heart U (CT)
Saginaw Valley State U (MI)
St. Ambrose U (IA)
Saint Anselm Coll (NH)
St. Catherine U (MN)
St. Cloud State U (MN)
St. Edward's U (TX)
Saint Francis U (PA)
St. John Fisher Coll (NY)
Saint John's U (MN)
St. John's U (NY)
Saint Joseph's U (PA)
Saint Leo U (FL)
Saint Louis U–Madrid Campus (Spain)
Saint Mary's Coll (IN)
Saint Mary's Coll of California (CA)
St. Mary's Coll of Maryland (MD)
Saint Michael's Coll (VT)
St. Norbert Coll (WI)
St. Olaf Coll (MN)
Saint Peter's U (NJ)
St. Thomas U (FL)
St. Thomas U (NB, Canada)
Saint Vincent Coll (PA)
Salisbury U (MD)
Salve Regina U (RI)
San Diego State U (CA)
San Francisco State U (CA)
Santa Clara U (CA)
Sarah Lawrence Coll (NY)
Scripps Coll (CA)
Seattle Pacific U (WA)
Seattle U (WA)
Seton Hill U (PA)
Sewanee: The U of the South (TN)
Shepherd U (WV)
Shippensburg U of Pennsylvania (PA)
Shorter U (GA)
Siena Coll (NY)
Simmons Coll (MA)
Simon Fraser U (BC, Canada)
Simpson Coll (IA)
Skidmore Coll (NY)
Smith Coll (MA)
Sonoma State U (CA)
South Dakota State U (SD)
Southeast Missouri State U (MO)
Southern Connecticut State U (CT)
Southern Illinois U Carbondale (IL)
Southern Illinois U Edwardsville (IL)
Southern Methodist U (TX)
Southern New Hampshire U (NH)
Southern Oregon U (OR)
Southern Utah U (UT)
Southwestern U (TX)
Spelman Coll (GA)
Stanford U (CA)
State U of New York at Fredonia (NY)
State U of New York at New Paltz (NY)
State U of New York at Oswego (NY)
State U of New York at Plattsburgh (NY)
State U of New York Coll at Cortland (NY)
State U of New York Coll at Geneseo (NY)
State U of New York Coll at Potsdam (NY)
Stephen F. Austin State U (TX)
Stockton U (NJ)
Stonehill Coll (MA)
Stony Brook U, State U of New York (NY)
Suffolk U (MA)
Susquehanna U (PA)
Swarthmore Coll (PA)
Sweet Briar Coll (VA)
Syracuse U (NY)
Tarleton State U (TX)
Taylor U (IN)
Temple U (PA)
Texas A&M U (TX)
Texas A&M U–Central Texas (TX)
Texas A&M U–Corpus Christi (TX)
Texas Christian U (TX)
Texas Lutheran U (TX)
Texas State U (TX)
Texas Tech U (TX)
Thomas More Coll (KY)
Towson U (MD)
Transylvania U (KY)
Trent U (ON, Canada)
Trinity U (TX)
Troy U (AL)
Truman State U (MO)
Tufts U (MA)
Tulane U (LA)
Union Coll (NY)
Union U (TN)
United States Air Force Acad (CO)
United States Military Acad (NY)
Université de Montréal (QC, Canada)
U at Albany, State U of New York (NY)
U at Buffalo, the State U of New York (NY)
The U of Akron (OH)
U of Alaska Fairbanks (AK)
The U of Arizona (AZ)
U of Arkansas (AR)
U of California, Davis (CA)
U of California, Irvine (CA)
U of California, Los Angeles (CA)
U of California, Riverside (CA)
U of California, San Diego (CA)
U of California, Santa Barbara (CA)
U of Central Arkansas (AR)
U of Central Florida (FL)
U of Central Missouri (MO)
U of Chicago (IL)
U of Cincinnati (OH)
U of Colorado Boulder (CO)
U of Colorado Colorado Springs (CO)
U of Colorado Denver (CO)
U of Dayton (OH)
U of Delaware (DE)
U of Denver (CO)
U of Detroit Mercy (MI)
U of Evansville (IN)
The U of Findlay (OH)
U of Florida (FL)
U of Georgia (GA)
U of Guelph (ON, Canada)
U of Hartford (CT)
U of Hawaii at Manoa (HI)
U of Houston (TX)
U of Idaho (ID)
U of Illinois at Chicago (IL)
U of Illinois at Springfield (IL)
The U of Kansas (KS)
U of Kentucky (KY)
U of King's Coll (NS, Canada)
U of La Verne (CA)
U of Lethbridge (AB, Canada)
U of Louisville (KY)
U of Maine (ME)
U of Maryland, Baltimore County (MD)
U of Maryland, Coll Park (MD)
U of Mary Washington (VA)
U of Massachusetts Amherst (MA)
U of Massachusetts Boston (MA)
U of Massachusetts Dartmouth (MA)
U of Massachusetts Lowell (MA)
U of Miami (FL)
U of Michigan (MI)
U of Michigan–Dearborn (MI)
U of Michigan–Flint (MI)
U of Minnesota, Duluth (MN)
U of Minnesota, Morris (MN)
U of Minnesota, Twin Cities Campus (MN)
U of Missouri–Kansas City (MO)
U of Missouri–St. Louis (MO)
U of Mount Union (OH)
U of Nebraska at Kearney (NE)
U of Nevada, Las Vegas (NV)
U of New Hampshire (NH)
U of New Haven (CT)
U of North Carolina at Asheville (NC)
The U of North Carolina at Chapel Hill (NC)
The U of North Carolina at Charlotte (NC)
The U of North Carolina at Greensboro (NC)
The U of North Carolina Wilmington (NC)
U of North Dakota (ND)
U of Northern Colorado (CO)
U of Northern Iowa (IA)
U of North Florida (FL)
U of North Texas (TX)
U of Notre Dame (IN)
U of Oklahoma (OK)
U of Oregon (OR)
U of Pennsylvania (PA)
U of Pittsburgh (PA)
U of Pittsburgh at Bradford (PA)
U of Pittsburgh at Johnstown (PA)
U of Puget Sound (WA)
U of Regina (SK, Canada)
U of Rhode Island (RI)
U of Richmond (VA)
U of Rochester (NY)
U of St. Thomas (MN)
U of St. Thomas (TX)
U of San Diego (CA)
U of San Francisco (CA)
U of Saskatchewan (SK, Canada)
U of Science and Arts of Oklahoma (OK)
The U of Scranton (PA)
U of South Carolina (SC)
The U of South Dakota (SD)
U of Southern California (CA)
U of Southern Indiana (IN)
U of Southern Maine (ME)
U of South Florida (FL)
U of South Florida, St. Petersburg (FL)
The U of Tampa (FL)
The U of Tennessee (TN)

The U of Tennessee at Chattanooga (TN)
The U of Tennessee at Martin (TN)
The U of Texas at Austin (TX)
The U of Texas at Dallas (TX)
The U of Texas at El Paso (TX)
The U of Texas Rio Grande Valley (TX)
U of the Fraser Valley (BC, Canada)
U of the Pacific (CA)
The U of Toledo (OH)
U of Toronto (ON, Canada)
The U of Tulsa (OK)
U of Utah (UT)
U of Vermont (VT)
U of Virginia (VA)
The U of Virginia's Coll at Wise (VA)
U of Washington (WA)
U of Waterloo (ON, Canada)
U of West Georgia (GA)
U of Windsor (ON, Canada)
U of Wisconsin–Eau Claire (WI)
U of Wisconsin–Green Bay (WI)
U of Wisconsin–La Crosse (WI)
U of Wisconsin–Madison (WI)
U of Wisconsin–Milwaukee (WI)
U of Wisconsin–Parkside (WI)
U of Wisconsin–Platteville (WI)
U of Wisconsin–Stevens Point (WI)
U of Wisconsin–Superior (WI)
U of Wisconsin–Whitewater (WI)
Ursinus Coll (PA)
Utah State U (UT)
Utah Valley U (UT)
Utica Coll (NY)
Valparaiso U (IN)
Vanderbilt U (TN)
Vassar Coll (NY)
Villanova U (PA)
Virginia Military Inst (VA)
Virginia Polytechnic Inst and State U (VA)
Wabash Coll (IN)
Wagner Coll (NY)
Wake Forest U (NC)
Walla Walla U (WA)
Washburn U (KS)
Washington & Jefferson Coll (PA)
Washington and Lee U (VA)
Washington Coll (MD)
Washington State U (WA)
Washington State U–Global Campus (WA)
Washington U in St. Louis (MO)
Wayne State U (MI)
Weber State U (UT)
Webster U (MO)
Wells Coll (NY)
Wesleyan Coll (GA)
Wesleyan U (CT)
Western Connecticut State U (CT)
Western Illinois U (IL)
Western Kentucky U (KY)
Western Michigan U (MI)
Western New England U (MA)
Western Oregon U (OR)
Western State Colorado U (CO)
Western Washington U (WA)
Westfield State U (MA)
Westminster Coll (UT)
Westmont Coll (CA)
West Virginia State U (WV)
West Virginia U (WV)
West Virginia Wesleyan Coll (WV)
Wheaton Coll (IL)
Wheaton Coll (MA)
Whitman Coll (WA)
Whittier Coll (CA)
Whitworth U (WA)
Wichita State U (KS)
Widener U (PA)
Willamette U (OR)
William Jewell Coll (MO)
William Paterson U of New Jersey (NJ)
Williams Coll (MA)
Winona State U (MN)
Wittenberg U (OH)
Wofford Coll (SC)
Worcester Polytechnic Inst (MA)
Worcester State U (MA)
Wright State U (OH)
Wright State U–Lake Campus (OH)
York Coll of Pennsylvania (PA)
York Coll of the City U of New York (NY)
Youngstown State U (OH)

ECONOMICS RELATED
American Intl Coll (MA)
Augsburg Coll (MN)
Central Washington U (WA)
Centre Coll (KY)
Colorado Christian U (CO)
The Colorado Coll (CO)
Columbia U, School of General Studies (NY)
Emory & Henry Coll (VA)
Florida Southern Coll (FL)
Lindenwood U (MO)
Muhlenberg Coll (PA)
Regis U (CO)
U of Delaware (DE)
U of Detroit Mercy (MI)
U of Maine (ME)
U of Minnesota, Duluth (MN)
U of Regina (SK, Canada)
U of Richmond (VA)
U of Wisconsin–Whitewater (WI)
Valparaiso U (IN)
Washington & Jefferson Coll (PA)
Wayne State U (MI)
Western Washington U (WA)
Westminster Coll (PA)
Whitworth U (WA)
Wittenberg U (OH)

EDUCATION
Albertus Magnus Coll (CT)
Alma Coll (MI)
Alverno Coll (WI)
Anderson U (IN)
Andrews U (MI)
Arcadia U (PA)
Arlington Baptist Coll (TX)
Ashland U (OH)
Auburn U (AL)
Augsburg Coll (MN)
Avila U (MO)
The Baptist Coll of Florida (FL)
Barnard Coll (NY)
Barry U (FL)
Baylor U (TX)
Bay Path U (MA)
Becker Coll (MA)
Belmont Abbey Coll (NC)
Beloit Coll (WI)
Bemidji State U (MN)
Bennington Coll (VT)
Berea Coll (KY)
Bethel Coll (IN)
Bethune-Cookman U (FL)
Biola U (CA)
Bishop's U (QC, Canada)
Bloomfield Coll (NJ)
Bluefield Coll (VA)
Bowdoin Coll (ME)
Bowie State U (MD)
Bowling Green State U (OH)
Bowling Green State U–Firelands Coll (OH)
Bradley U (IL)
Brandeis U (MA)
Brenau U (GA)
Brewton-Parker Coll (GA)
Briar Cliff U (IA)
Brooklyn Coll of the City U of New York (NY)
Bucknell U (PA)
Cabrini U (PA)
Canisius Coll (NY)
Carson-Newman U (TN)
The Catholic U of America (DC)
Cedar Crest Coll (PA)
Centenary U (NJ)
Central Methodist U (MO)
Central Washington U (WA)
Chapman U (CA)
Chowan U (NC)
Christian Brothers U (TN)
City Coll of the City U of New York (NY)
Clark Atlanta U (GA)
Clark U (MA)
Coe Coll (IA)
Colby Coll (ME)
Colgate U (NY)
Coll of Mount Saint Vincent (NY)
Coll of Saint Mary (NE)
Coll of the Atlantic (ME)
The Colorado Coll (CO)
Concordia Coll (MN)
Concordia Coll–New York (NY)
Concordia U (QC, Canada)
Concordia U Chicago (IL)
Concordia U, St. Paul (MN)
Concordia U Wisconsin (WI)
Concord U (WV)
Converse Coll (SC)
Corban U (OR)
Crandall U (NB, Canada)
Curry Coll (MA)
Dallas Christian Coll (TX)
Defiance Coll (OH)
Dominican Coll (NY)
Duquesne U (PA)
Eastern Nazarene Coll (MA)
Eastern Washington U (WA)
East Texas Baptist U (TX)
Elms Coll (MA)
Elon U (NC)
Emory U (GA)
Eureka Coll (IL)
The Evergreen State Coll (WA)
Felician U (NJ)
Fitchburg State U (MA)
Florida Gulf Coast U (FL)
Fordham U (NY)
Franklin Pierce U (NH)
Furman U (SC)
Gallaudet U (DC)
Gardner-Webb U (NC)
Georgia Southern U (GA)
Gettysburg Coll (PA)
Goddard Coll (VT)
Goshen Coll (IN)
Graceland U (IA)
Guilford Coll (NC)
Hampshire Coll (MA)
Hampton U (VA)
Hannibal-LaGrange U (MO)
Hardin-Simmons U (TX)
Harris-Stowe State U (MO)
Haverford Coll (PA)
Heidelberg U (OH)
Hiram Coll (OH)
Humboldt State U (CA)
Huntington U (IN)
Huston-Tillotson U (TX)
Illinois Coll (IL)
Illinois Wesleyan U (IL)
Inter American U of Puerto Rico, San Germán Campus (PR)
Iowa State U of Science and Technology (IA)
Iowa Wesleyan U (IA)
Jacksonville State U (AL)
Jacksonville U (FL)
John Carroll U (OH)
Juniata Coll (PA)
Kent State U (OH)
Knox Coll (IL)
Lake Forest Coll (IL)
Langston U (OK)
Lasell Coll (MA)
Lebanese American U (Lebanon)
Lesley U (MA)
Liberty U (VA)
Limestone Coll (SC)
Lindenwood U (MO)
Lindsey Wilson Coll (KY)
Lipscomb U (TN)
Loyola U Maryland (MD)
Macalester Coll (MN)
Manchester U (IN)
Manhattan Coll (NY)
Manhattanville Coll (NY)
Mansfield U of Pennsylvania (PA)
Marian U (IN)
Marietta Coll (OH)
Massachusetts Coll of Liberal Arts (MA)
The Master's U (CA)
Mercyhurst U (PA)
Merrimack Coll (MA)
Miami Dade Coll (FL)
Michigan State U (MI)
Milligan Coll (TN)
Millsaps Coll (MS)
Minnesota State U Mankato (MN)
Mississippi Valley State U (MS)
Missouri Baptist U (MO)
Missouri Valley Coll (MO)
Monmouth U (NJ)
Montana State U Billings (MT)
Mount Marty Coll (SD)
Mount Mary U (WI)
Mount St. Joseph U (OH)
Mount Saint Mary's U (CA)
Mount Vernon Nazarene U (OH)
Muskingum U (OH)
Nazareth Coll of Rochester (NY)
Neumann U (PA)
Nevada State Coll (NV)
New England Coll (NH)
Newman U (KS)
New Mexico State U (NM)
Niagara U (NY)
North Carolina State U (NC)
North Carolina Wesleyan Coll (NC)
North Central Coll (IL)
Northeastern U (MA)
Northern Illinois U (IL)
Northern State U (SD)
Northwestern U (IL)
Northwest U (WA)
Nova Southeastern U (FL)
Ohio Christian U (OH)
Ohio Dominican U (OH)
Ohio Wesleyan U (OH)
Oklahoma Baptist U (OK)
Oklahoma City U (OK)
Oregon State U (OR)
Otterbein U (OH)
Pacific Lutheran U (WA)
Piedmont Coll (GA)
Purdue U (IN)
Quinnipiac U (CT)
Redeemer U Coll (ON, Canada)
Regent U (VA)
Regis U (CO)
Rhodes Coll (TN)
Ripon Coll (WI)
Rockford U (IL)
Roger Williams U (RI)
Rosemont Coll (PA)
Rowan U (NJ)
Sacred Heart U (CT)
Saginaw Valley State U (MI)
St. Ambrose U (IA)
St. Catherine U (MN)
St. Cloud State U (MN)
Saint Francis U (PA)
St. Joseph's Coll, New York (NY)
Saint Louis U (MO)
Saint Martin's U (WA)
Saint Michael's Coll (VT)
St. Thomas Aquinas Coll (NY)
St. Thomas U (NB, Canada)
Schreiner U (TX)
Seattle Pacific U (WA)
Shawnee State U (OH)
Simmons Coll (MA)
Simon Fraser U (BC, Canada)
Simpson Coll (IA)
Skidmore Coll (NY)
Smith Coll (MA)
Southern New Hampshire U (NH)
Southwestern Assemblies of God U (TX)
Southwestern U (TX)
Spalding U (KY)
State U of New York at Fredonia (NY)
State U of New York at Oswego (NY)
State U of New York at Plattsburgh (NY)
State U of New York Coll at Geneseo (NY)
State U of New York Empire State Coll (NY)
Stonehill Coll (MA)
Syracuse U (NY)
Tabor Coll (KS)
Tarleton State U (TX)
Taylor U (IN)
Tennessee State U (TN)
Tennessee Wesleyan U (TN)
Texas Lutheran U (TX)
Texas Wesleyan U (TX)
Tiffin U (OH)
Trent U (ON, Canada)
Trine U (IN)
Trinity Christian Coll (IL)
Tufts U (MA)
Union U (TN)
Université de Montréal (QC, Canada)
Université de Sherbrooke (QC, Canada)
U of Arkansas (AR)
U of California, Irvine (CA)
U of Central Missouri (MO)
U of Charleston (WV)
U of Colorado Denver (CO)
U of Detroit Mercy (MI)
U of Georgia (GA)
U of Hawaii at Manoa (HI)
U of Indianapolis (IN)
U of Lethbridge (AB, Canada)
U of Massachusetts Amherst (MA)
U of Massachusetts Boston (MA)
U of Miami (FL)
U of Michigan–Dearborn (MI)
U of Michigan–Flint (MI)
U of Minnesota, Duluth (MN)
U of Missouri–St. Louis (MO)
U of Nevada, Las Vegas (NV)
U of North Texas (TX)
U of Oregon (OR)
U of Pittsburgh at Greensburg (PA)
U of Pittsburgh at Johnstown (PA)
U of Regina (SK, Canada)
U of Saint Francis (IN)
U of Saint Mary (KS)
U of St. Thomas (TX)
U of San Francisco (CA)
U of Saskatchewan (SK, Canada)
The U of South Dakota (SD)
The U of Texas at San Antonio (TX)
U of the Pacific (CA)
U of Toronto (ON, Canada)
The U of Tulsa (OK)
U of Utah (UT)
U of Vermont (VT)
U of Washington, Bothell (WA)
U of Washington, Tacoma (WA)
U of Windsor (ON, Canada)
U of Wisconsin–Green Bay (WI)
U of Wisconsin–Milwaukee (WI)
U of Wisconsin–Platteville (WI)
U of Wisconsin–Stevens Point (WI)
U of Wisconsin–Superior (WI)
Upper Iowa U (IA)
Valley City State U (ND)
Vanderbilt U (TN)
Vassar Coll (NY)
Viterbo U (WI)
Wagner Coll (NY)
Walsh U (OH)
Washburn U (KS)
Washington & Jefferson Coll (PA)
Washington State U (WA)
Washington State U–Vancouver (WA)
Washington U in St. Louis (MO)
Webster U (MO)
Welch Coll (TN)
Wells Coll (NY)
Westminster Coll (PA)
Westmont Coll (CA)
West Texas A&M U (TX)
West Virginia Wesleyan Coll (WV)
Wheeling Jesuit U (WV)
Wheelock Coll (MA)
Whitworth U (WA)
Wilkes U (PA)
William Peace U (NC)
Williams Baptist Coll (AR)
William Woods U (MO)
Winona State U (MN)
Wittenberg U (OH)
Xavier U of Louisiana (LA)
Youngstown State U (OH)

EDUCATIONAL ADMINISTRATION AND SUPERVISION RELATED
Canisius Coll (NY)
Philander Smith Coll (AR)

EDUCATIONAL ASSESSMENT, EVALUATION, AND RESEARCH RELATED
Blackburn Coll (IL)
Penn State Altoona (PA)
Penn State Berks (PA)
Penn State U Park (PA)

EDUCATIONAL EVALUATION AND RESEARCH
U of Georgia (GA)

EDUCATIONAL, INSTRUCTIONAL, AND CURRICULUM SUPERVISION
Canisius Coll (NY)
Millikin U (IL)
Nevada State Coll (NV)
Sam Houston State U (TX)

EDUCATIONAL/INSTRUCTIONAL TECHNOLOGY
Acad of Art U (CA)
Bayamón Central U (PR)
Bowling Green State U (OH)
Bridgewater State U (MA)
Canisius Coll (NY)
Eastern Washington U (WA)
Inter American U of Puerto Rico, Barranquitas Campus (PR)
Jackson State U (MS)
Jacksonville State U (AL)
LeTourneau U (TX)
Nevada State Coll (NV)
St. Cloud State U (MN)
Sam Houston State U (TX)
U of Georgia (GA)
U of Michigan–Dearborn (MI)
Wayne State U (MI)
Western Oregon U (OR)
Widener U (PA)
Wilmington U (DE)

EDUCATIONAL LEADERSHIP AND ADMINISTRATION
Avila U (MO)
Canisius Coll (NY)
Dallas Baptist U (TX)
Eastern Washington U (WA)
Jacksonville State U (AL)
St. Cloud State U (MN)
Sam Houston State U (TX)
Tarleton State U (TX)
Tennessee State U (TN)
U of Georgia (GA)
U of Minnesota, Crookston (MN)
U of San Francisco (CA)
The U of Texas at Austin (TX)
Welch Coll (TN)

EDUCATIONAL PSYCHOLOGY
Jacksonville State U (AL)
Mississippi State U (MS)
Saint Vincent Coll (PA)
Tarleton State U (TX)
Université de Montréal (QC, Canada)
U of Georgia (GA)
U of Pittsburgh (PA)
The U of Texas at Austin (TX)

EDUCATIONAL STATISTICS AND RESEARCH METHODS
Bucknell U (PA)

EDUCATIONAL SYSTEM ADMINISTRATION AND SUPERINTENDENCY
Western Illinois U (IL)

EDUCATION (MULTIPLE LEVELS)
Adams State U (CO)
Anderson U (SC)
Arcadia U (PA)
Assumption Coll (MA)
Augustana U (SD)
Austin Peay State U (TN)
Averett U (VA)
Biola U (CA)
Bowling Green State U (OH)
Canisius Coll (NY)
Central State U (OH)
Coll of Charleston (SC)
Coll of Coastal Georgia (GA)
Coll of Saint Elizabeth (NJ)
Coll of Saint Mary (NE)
The Coll of St. Scholastica (MN)
Columbia Intl U (SC)
Columbia U (NY)
Concordia U Chicago (IL)
Concordia U, Nebraska (NE)
Concordia U Wisconsin (WI)
Crandall U (NB, Canada)
Dominican U (IL)
Eastern Nazarene Coll (MA)
Eastern Washington U (WA)
Emory & Henry Coll (VA)
Felician U (NJ)
Florida Southern Coll (FL)
Frostburg State U (MD)
Gannon U (PA)
Gardner-Webb U (NC)
Geneva Coll (PA)
Goddard Coll (VT)
Gwynedd Mercy U (PA)
Hamline U (MN)
Harding U (AR)
Hofstra U (NY)
Huston-Tillotson U (TX)
Illinois Coll (IL)
Ithaca Coll (NY)
John Carroll U (OH)
Lindenwood U (MO)
Manchester U (IN)
Manhattan Coll (NY)
Marian U (IN)
Martin Luther Coll (MN)
Merrimack Coll (MA)
Missouri Baptist U (MO)
Mount Mary U (WI)
Mount Saint Mary Coll (NY)
New England Coll (NH)
Niagara U (NY)
North American U (TX)
Northland Coll (WI)
Northwestern Coll (IA)
Nyack Coll (NY)
Ohio Wesleyan U (OH)
Piedmont Coll (GA)
Redeemer U Coll (ON, Canada)
Saint Augustine's U (NC)
St. Cloud State U (MN)
Saint Mary-of-the-Woods Coll (IN)
Samford U (AL)
Shawnee State U (OH)
Slippery Rock U of Pennsylvania (PA)
Spalding U (KY)
Spelman Coll (GA)
Stockton U (NJ)
Tarleton State U (TX)
Tennessee Wesleyan U (TN)
Texas A&M U–Central Texas (TX)
Texas Lutheran U (TX)
Troy U (AL)
U of Great Falls (MT)
U of Louisville (KY)
U of Maine at Fort Kent (ME)
U of Michigan–Flint (MI)
U of Minnesota, Duluth (MN)
The U of Montana Western (MT)
U of North Alabama (AL)
U of Puerto Rico in Bayamón (PR)
U of Saskatchewan (SK, Canada)
U of South Florida, St. Petersburg (FL)
The U of Tennessee at Martin (TN)
U of the Southwest (NM)
The U of West Alabama (AL)
U of Windsor (ON, Canada)
Utah State U (UT)
Virginia Union U (VA)
Virginia Wesleyan Coll (VA)
Wake Forest U (NC)
Walla Walla U (WA)
Washington U in St. Louis (MO)
Wayland Baptist U (TX)
Western Kentucky U (KY)
West Virginia Wesleyan Coll (WV)
William Jewell Coll (MO)

EDUCATION RELATED
Albany State U (GA)
Arcadia U (PA)
Arizona State U at the Polytechnic campus (AZ)
Arizona State U at the Tempe campus (AZ)
Arizona State U at the West campus (AZ)
Becker Coll (MA)
Blackburn Coll (IL)
Bowling Green State U (OH)
Brigham Young U (UT)
California State Polytechnic U, Pomona (CA)
Central State U (OH)
Colorado Christian U (CO)
Concordia U, St. Paul (MN)
Eastern Oregon U (OR)
Edgewood Coll (WI)
Elmira Coll (NY)
Grace Coll (IN)
Indiana U Bloomington (IN)
Jackson State U (MS)
Lee U (TN)
Lindsey Wilson Coll (KY)
Louisiana Coll (LA)
Mercer U, Macon (GA)
Messenger Coll (TX)
Mount Holyoke Coll (MA)
Nazarene Bible Coll (CO)
Northwest Missouri State U (MO)
Piedmont Coll (GA)
Point Park U (PA)
Prescott Coll (AZ)
Saginaw Valley State U (MI)
Saint Mary-of-the-Woods Coll (IN)
Saint Mary's U of Minnesota (MN)
St. Petersburg Coll (FL)
Shaw U (NC)
Southern New Hampshire U (NH)
State U of New York at New Paltz (NY)
Swarthmore Coll (PA)
Thomas More Coll (KY)
Towson U (MD)
Union Coll (NE)
U of Maine at Presque Isle (ME)
U of Miami (FL)
U of Minnesota, Duluth (MN)
U of Minnesota, Twin Cities Campus (MN)
U of Nevada, Reno (NV)
U of Northern Iowa (IA)
U of South Alabama (AL)
U of Washington (WA)
U of Waterloo (ON, Canada)
Vanderbilt U (TN)
Waldorf U (IA)

EDUCATION (SPECIFIC LEVELS AND METHODS) RELATED
Appalachian State U (NC)
Bayamón Central U (PR)
Brigham Young U (UT)
Cairn U (PA)
Concordia Coll–New York (NY)
Eastern Nazarene Coll (MA)
Emory & Henry Coll (VA)
Immaculata U (PA)
Inter American U of Puerto Rico, Metropolitan Campus (PR)
Inter American U of Puerto Rico, San Germán Campus (PR)
Lenoir-Rhyne U (NC)
Lynchburg Coll (VA)
Rowan U (NJ)
St. Cloud State U (MN)
Washington U in St. Louis (MO)
Weber State U (UT)
Western Washington U (WA)

EDUCATION (SPECIFIC SUBJECT AREAS) RELATED
Anderson U (SC)
Appalachian State U (NC)
Augsburg Coll (MN)
Averett U (VA)
Avila U (MO)
Bayamón Central U (PR)
Baylor U (TX)
Bowling Green State U (OH)
Brigham Young U (UT)
Cairn U (PA)
Eastern Michigan U (MI)
Eastern Nazarene Coll (MA)
Florida Inst of Technology (FL)
Gardner-Webb U (NC)
Graceland U (IA)
Gwynedd Mercy U (PA)
Indiana U Bloomington (IN)
Louisiana Tech U (LA)
Madonna U (MI)
Marywood U (PA)
Minot State U (ND)
Mississippi State U (MS)
Missouri State U (MO)
Missouri Western State U (MO)
Murray State U (KY)
Northwest Missouri State U (MO)
Old Dominion U (VA)
Piedmont Coll (GA)
Pittsburg State U (KS)
Plymouth State U (NH)
Point Park U (PA)
Union Coll (NE)
U of Kentucky (KY)
U of Lethbridge (AB, Canada)
U of Minnesota, Duluth (MN)
U of New Hampshire (NH)
U of Regina (SK, Canada)
The U of Texas at Austin (TX)
U of Wisconsin–Eau Claire (WI)
U of Wisconsin–Stout (WI)
Utah State U (UT)
Wartburg Coll (IA)
Wayne State Coll (NE)
Weber State U (UT)
Western Washington U (WA)
William Woods U (MO)

ELECTRICAL AND ELECTRONIC ENGINEERING TECHNOLOGIES RELATED
Embry-Riddle Aeronautical U–Prescott (AZ)
Excelsior Coll (NY)
LeTourneau U (TX)
Penn State Berks (PA)
Pennsylvania Coll of Technology (PA)
Point Park U (PA)
Rochester Inst of Technology (NY)
Southern Illinois U Carbondale (IL)
Vaughn Coll of Aeronautics and Technology (NY)
Virginia State U (VA)
Wayne State U (MI)
West Virginia U Inst of Technology (WV)

ELECTRICAL AND ELECTRONICS ENGINEERING
American Public U System (WV)
The American U in Cairo (Egypt)
The American U in Dubai (United Arab Emirates)
American U of Beirut (Lebanon)
Anderson U (IN)
Arizona State U at the Tempe campus (AZ)
Arkansas Tech U (AR)
Auburn U (AL)
Baylor U (TX)
Binghamton U, State U of New York (NY)
Bloomsburg U of Pennsylvania (PA)
Boise State U (ID)
Boston U (MA)
Bradley U (IL)
Bucknell U (PA)
California Inst of Technology (CA)
California Polytechnic State U, San Luis Obispo (CA)
California State Polytechnic U, Pomona (CA)
California State U, Chico (CA)
California State U, Fresno (CA)
California State U, Fullerton (CA)
California State U, Long Beach (CA)
California State U, Northridge (CA)
California State U, Sacramento (CA)
Calvin Coll (MI)
Caribbean U (PR)
Carnegie Mellon U (PA)
Case Western Reserve U (OH)
The Catholic U of America (DC)
Cedarville U (OH)
Central Michigan U (MI)
Christian Brothers U (TN)
Christopher Newport U (VA)
The Citadel, The Military Coll of South Carolina (SC)
City Coll of the City U of New York (NY)
Clarkson U (NY)
Clemson U (SC)
Cleveland State U (OH)
The Coll of New Jersey (NJ)
Colorado School of Mines (CO)
Colorado State U (CO)
Columbia U (NY)
Concordia U (QC, Canada)
Cooper Union for the Advancement of Science and Art (NY)
Cornell U (NY)
Dalhousie U (NS, Canada)
Dominican U (IL)
Drexel U (PA)
Eastern Nazarene Coll (MA)
Eastern Washington U (WA)
Embry-Riddle Aeronautical U–Daytona (FL)
Embry-Riddle Aeronautical U–Prescott (AZ)
Fairfield U (CT)
Fairleigh Dickinson U, Metropolitan Campus (NJ)
Florida Ag and Mech U (FL)
Florida Atlantic U (FL)
Florida Inst of Technology (FL)
Florida Intl U (FL)
Franklin W. Olin Coll of Eng (MA)
Gannon U (PA)
George Fox U (OR)
The George Washington U (DC)
Georgia Inst of Technology (GA)
Georgia Southern U (GA)
Gonzaga U (WA)
Grove City Coll (PA)
Hampton U (VA)
Hanover Coll (IN)
Harding U (AR)
Hofstra U (NY)
Idaho State U (ID)
Indiana U–Purdue U Indianapolis (IN)
Inter American U of Puerto Rico, Bayamón Campus (PR)
Iowa State U of Science and Technology (IA)
Jackson State U (MS)
Jacksonville U (FL)
Johns Hopkins U (MD)
Kansas State U (KS)
Kennesaw State U (GA)
Kettering U (MI)
Lafayette Coll (PA)
Lamar U (TX)
Lawrence Technological U (MI)
Lebanese American U (Lebanon)
Lehigh U (PA)
LeTourneau U (TX)
Liberty U (VA)
Louisiana State U and A&M Coll (LA)
Louisiana Tech U (LA)
Loyola Marymount U (CA)
Manhattan Coll (NY)
Marshall U (WV)
Massachusetts Inst of Technology (MA)
McMaster U (ON, Canada)
Merrimack Coll (MA)
Miami U (OH)
Michigan State U (MI)
Michigan Technological U (MI)
Milligan Coll (TN)
Milwaukee School of Eng (WI)
Minnesota State U Mankato (MN)
Mississippi State U (MS)
Missouri U of Science and Technology (MO)
Montana State U (MT)
Montana Tech of The U of Montana (MT)
Mount Vernon Nazarene U (OH)
National U (CA)
New England Inst of Technology (RI)
New Mexico Highlands U (NM)
New Mexico Inst of Mining and Technology (NM)
New Mexico State U (NM)
New York Inst of Technology (NY)
North Carolina State U (NC)
North Dakota State U (ND)
Northeastern U (MA)
Northern Arizona U (AZ)
Northern Illinois U (IL)
Northwestern U (IL)
The Ohio State U (OH)
Ohio U (OH)
Oklahoma Christian U (OK)
Oklahoma State U (OK)
Old Dominion U (VA)
Oral Roberts U (OK)
Oregon State U (OR)
Penn State Abington (PA)
Penn State Altoona (PA)
Penn State Beaver (PA)
Penn State Berks (PA)
Penn State Brandywine (PA)
Penn State DuBois (PA)
Penn State Erie, The Behrend Coll (PA)
Penn State Fayette, The Eberly Campus (PA)
Penn State Greater Allegheny (PA)
Penn State Harrisburg (PA)
Penn State Hazleton (PA)
Penn State Lehigh Valley (PA)
Penn State Mont Alto (PA)
Penn State New Kensington (PA)
Penn State Schuylkill (PA)
Penn State Shenango (PA)
Penn State U Park (PA)
Penn State Wilkes-Barre (PA)
Penn State Worthington Scranton (PA)
Penn State York (PA)
Polytechnic U of Puerto Rico (PR)
Portland State U (OR)
Prairie View A&M U (TX)

Princeton U (NJ)
Purdue U (IN)
Purdue U Northwest (IN)
Rensselaer Polytechnic Inst (NY)
Rice U (TX)
Rochester Inst of Technology (NY)
Rockhurst U (MO)
Roger Williams U (RI)
Rose-Hulman Inst of Technology (IN)
Rowan U (NJ)
Royal Military Coll of Canada (ON, Canada)
Rutgers U–New Brunswick (NJ)
Saginaw Valley State U (MI)
St. Cloud State U (MN)
Saint Louis U (MO)
Saint Louis U–Madrid Campus (Spain)
San Diego State U (CA)
San Francisco State U (CA)
Santa Clara U (CA)
Seattle Pacific U (WA)
Seattle U (WA)
Shippensburg U of Pennsylvania (PA)
South Dakota School of Mines and Technology (SD)
South Dakota State U (SD)
Southern Illinois U Carbondale (IL)
Southern Illinois U Edwardsville (IL)
Southern Methodist U (TX)
Stanford U (CA)
State U of New York at New Paltz (NY)
State U of New York at Oswego (NY)
State U of New York Maritime Coll (NY)
State U of New York Polytechnic Inst (NY)
Stevens Inst of Technology (NJ)
Stony Brook U, State U of New York (NY)
Suffolk U (MA)
Syracuse U (NY)
Tarleton State U (TX)
Temple U (PA)
Tennessee State U (TN)
Texas A&M U (TX)
Texas A&M U–Kingsville (TX)
Texas State U (TX)
Texas Tech U (TX)
Trine U (IN)
Tufts U (MA)
Tulane U (LA)
Union Coll (NY)
United States Air Force Acad (CO)
United States Coast Guard Acad (CT)
United States Military Acad (NY)
Université de Sherbrooke (QC, Canada)
U at Buffalo, the State U of New York (NY)
The U of Akron (OH)
The U of Alabama (AL)
The U of Alabama at Birmingham (AL)
The U of Alabama in Huntsville (AL)
U of Alaska Fairbanks (AK)
U of Arkansas (AR)
U of Bridgeport (CT)
U of California, Davis (CA)
U of California, Irvine (CA)
U of California, Los Angeles (CA)
U of California, Riverside (CA)
U of California, San Diego (CA)
U of California, Santa Barbara (CA)
U of Central Florida (FL)
U of Cincinnati (OH)
U of Colorado Boulder (CO)
U of Colorado Colorado Springs (CO)
U of Colorado Denver (CO)
U of Dayton (OH)
U of Delaware (DE)
U of Denver (CO)
U of Detroit Mercy (MI)
U of Evansville (IN)
U of Florida (FL)
U of Georgia (GA)
U of Hartford (CT)
U of Hawaii at Manoa (HI)
U of Houston (TX)
U of Idaho (ID)
U of Illinois at Chicago (IL)
The U of Kansas (KS)
U of Kentucky (KY)
U of Louisville (KY)
U of Maine (ME)
U of Maryland, Coll Park (MD)
U of Massachusetts Amherst (MA)
U of Massachusetts Boston (MA)
U of Massachusetts Dartmouth (MA)
U of Massachusetts Lowell (MA)
U of Miami (FL)
U of Michigan (MI)
U of Michigan–Dearborn (MI)
U of Minnesota, Duluth (MN)
U of Minnesota, Twin Cities Campus (MN)
U of Missouri–Kansas City (MO)
U of Missouri–St. Louis (MO)
U of Nevada, Las Vegas (NV)
U of Nevada, Reno (NV)
U of New Hampshire (NH)
U of New Haven (CT)
U of New Orleans (LA)
The U of North Carolina at Charlotte (NC)
U of North Dakota (ND)
U of North Florida (FL)
U of North Texas (TX)
U of Notre Dame (IN)
U of Oklahoma (OK)
U of Pennsylvania (PA)
U of Pittsburgh (PA)
U of Pittsburgh at Johnstown (PA)
U of Regina (SK, Canada)
U of Rhode Island (RI)
U of Rochester (NY)
U of St. Thomas (MN)
U of San Diego (CA)
U of Saskatchewan (SK, Canada)
The U of Scranton (PA)
U of South Alabama (AL)
U of South Carolina (SC)
U of Southern California (CA)
U of Southern Maine (ME)
U of South Florida (FL)
The U of Tennessee (TN)
The U of Tennessee at Chattanooga (TN)
The U of Texas at Austin (TX)
The U of Texas at Dallas (TX)
The U of Texas at El Paso (TX)
The U of Texas at San Antonio (TX)
The U of Texas Rio Grande Valley (TX)
U of the Pacific (CA)
The U of Toledo (OH)
U of Toronto (ON, Canada)
The U of Tulsa (OK)
U of Utah (UT)
U of Vermont (VT)
U of Virginia (VA)
U of Washington (WA)
U of Washington, Bothell (WA)
U of Waterloo (ON, Canada)
U of Windsor (ON, Canada)
U of Wisconsin–Madison (WI)
U of Wisconsin–Milwaukee (WI)
U of Wisconsin–Platteville (WI)
Ursinus Coll (PA)
Utah State U (UT)
Valparaiso U (IN)
Vanderbilt U (TN)
Villanova U (PA)
Virginia Commonwealth U (VA)
Virginia Military Inst (VA)
Virginia Polytechnic Inst and State U (VA)
Walla Walla U (WA)
Washington State U (WA)
Washington State U–Global Campus (WA)
Washington State U–Tri-Cities (WA)
Washington State U–Vancouver (WA)
Washington U in St. Louis (MO)
Wayne State U (MI)
Weber State U (UT)
Wentworth Inst of Technology (MA)
Western Carolina U (NC)
Western Kentucky U (KY)
Western Michigan U (MI)
Western New England U (MA)
Western Washington U (WA)
Westminster Coll (PA)
West Texas A&M U (TX)
West Virginia U (WV)
West Virginia U Inst of Technology (WV)
Wichita State U (KS)
Widener U (PA)
Wilkes U (PA)
Worcester Polytechnic Inst (MA)
Wright State U (OH)
Wright State U–Lake Campus (OH)
York Coll of Pennsylvania (PA)
Youngstown State U (OH)

ELECTRICAL, ELECTRONIC AND COMMUNICATIONS ENGINEERING TECHNOLOGY

Arizona State U at the Polytechnic campus (AZ)
Bluefield State Coll (WV)
Bowling Green State U (OH)
Brigham Young U–Idaho (ID)
Buffalo State Coll, State U of New York (NY)
California State Polytechnic U, Pomona (CA)
California State U, Long Beach (CA)
California U of Pennsylvania (PA)
Central Connecticut State U (CT)
Central Washington U (WA)
Cleveland State U (OH)
Daytona State Coll (FL)
Eastern Michigan U (MI)
Fairleigh Dickinson U, Metropolitan Campus (NJ)
Farmingdale State Coll (NY)
Ferris State U (MI)
Fitchburg State U (MA)
Florida Ag and Mech U (FL)
Georgia Southern U (GA)
Hampton U (VA)
Idaho State U (ID)
Indiana State U (IN)
Indiana U–Purdue U Indianapolis (IN)
Inter American U of Puerto Rico, Aguadilla Campus (PR)
Inter American U of Puerto Rico, San Germán Campus (PR)
Jacksonville State U (AL)
Kennesaw State U (GA)
LeTourneau U (TX)
Louisiana Tech U (LA)
Metropolitan State U of Denver (CO)
Miami Dade Coll (FL)
Michigan Technological U (MI)
Minnesota State U Mankato (MN)
Missouri Western State U (MO)
Nevada State Coll (NV)
New York City Coll of Technology of the City U of New York (NY)
Northern Kentucky U (KY)
Northwestern State U of Louisiana (LA)
Oklahoma State U (OK)
Penn State Erie, The Behrend Coll (PA)
Pittsburg State U (KS)
Prairie View A&M U (TX)
Purdue U (IN)
Purdue U Northwest (IN)
St. Cloud State U (MN)
Sam Houston State U (TX)
South Carolina State U (SC)
South Dakota State U (SD)
State U of New York Coll of Technology at Alfred (NY)
State U of New York Coll of Technology at Canton (NY)
State U of New York Polytechnic Inst (NY)
Texas A&M U (TX)
Texas A&M U–Corpus Christi (TX)
Troy U (AL)
The U of Akron (OH)
U of Central Missouri (MO)
U of Cincinnati (OH)
U of Dayton (OH)
U of Hartford (CT)
U of Houston (TX)
U of Maine (ME)
U of Massachusetts Lowell (MA)
U of New Hampshire at Manchester (NH)
The U of North Carolina at Charlotte (NC)
U of North Texas (TX)
U of Puerto Rico in Bayamón (PR)
U of Southern Mississippi (MS)
U of Wisconsin–Green Bay (WI)
Valencia Coll (FL)
Vaughn Coll of Aeronautics and Technology (NY)
Vermont Tech Coll (VT)
Wayne State U (MI)
Weber State U (UT)
Western Carolina U (NC)
Western Washington U (WA)
Youngstown State U (OH)

ELECTRICAL, ELECTRONICS AND COMMUNICATIONS ENGINEERING RELATED

The U of Arizona (AZ)
U of Miami (FL)

ELECTROMECHANICAL AND INSTRUMENTATION AND MAINTENANCE TECHNOLOGIES RELATED

Excelsior Coll (NY)

ELECTROMECHANICAL ENGINEERING

Hanover Coll (IN)
Wentworth Inst of Technology (MA)

ELECTROMECHANICAL TECHNOLOGY

Buffalo State Coll, State U of New York (NY)
Excelsior Coll (NY)
Murray State U (KY)
Purdue U Northwest (IN)
Rochester Inst of Technology (NY)
U of Northern Iowa (IA)
The U of Toledo (OH)
Vermont Tech Coll (VT)
Wayne State U (MI)

ELEMENTARY AND MIDDLE SCHOOL ADMINISTRATION/ PRINCIPALSHIP

Berea Coll (KY)
Charleston Southern U (SC)
The Ohio State U (OH)
The Ohio State U at Lima (OH)
The Ohio State U at Marion (OH)
The Ohio State U–Mansfield Campus (OH)
The Ohio State U–Newark Campus (OH)
Philander Smith Coll (AR)

ELEMENTARY EDUCATION

Abilene Christian U (TX)
Alabama State U (AL)
Alcorn State U (MS)
Alderson Broaddus U (WV)
Alfred U (NY)
Alice Lloyd Coll (KY)
Alma Coll (MI)
Alverno Coll (WI)
American U (DC)
American U of Beirut (Lebanon)
Anderson U (IN)
Anderson U (SC)
Andrews U (MI)
Appalachian State U (NC)
Aquinas Coll (TN)
Arcadia U (PA)
Arizona Christian U (AZ)
Arizona State U at the Polytechnic campus (AZ)
Arizona State U at the Tempe campus (AZ)
Arizona State U at the West campus (AZ)
Arkansas Tech U (AR)
Arlington Baptist Coll (TX)
Asbury U (KY)
Ashland U (OH)
Athens State U (AL)
Auburn U (AL)
Auburn U at Montgomery (AL)
Augsburg Coll (MN)
Augustana Coll (IL)
Augustana U (SD)
Aurora U (IL)
Austin Coll (TX)
Avila U (MO)
Baker U (KS)
Ball State U (IN)
The Baptist Coll of Florida (FL)
Barclay Coll (KS)
Barry U (FL)
Barton Coll (NC)
Bayamón Central U (PR)
Baylor U (TX)
Bay Path U (MA)
Becker Coll (MA)
Belhaven U (MS)
Bellarmine U (KY)
Belmont Abbey Coll (NC)
Belmont U (TN)
Beloit Coll (WI)
Bemidji State U (MN)
Benedictine Coll (KS)
Bennett Coll (NC)
Bethany Lutheran Coll (MN)
Bethel Coll (IN)
Bethel Coll (KS)
Bethel U (MN)
Bethune-Cookman U (FL)
Biola U (CA)
Bishop's U (QC, Canada)
Blackburn Coll (IL)
Black Hills State U (SD)
Bluefield Coll (VA)
Bluefield State Coll (WV)
Blue Mountain Coll (MS)
Bluffton U (OH)
Boise State U (ID)
Boston Coll (MA)
Boston U (MA)
Bowie State U (MD)
Bowling Green State U (OH)
Bradley U (IL)
Brenau U (GA)
Brescia U (KY)
Briar Cliff U (IA)
Bridgewater State U (MA)
Brigham Young U–Idaho (ID)
Brooklyn Coll of the City U of New York (NY)
Bryan Coll (TN)
Bryn Athyn Coll of the New Church (PA)
Bucknell U (PA)
Buena Vista U (IA)
Buffalo State Coll, State U of New York (NY)
Butler U (IN)
Cabrini U (PA)
Cairn U (PA)
Caldwell U (NJ)
California U of Pennsylvania (PA)
Calumet Coll of Saint Joseph (IN)
Calvary U (MO)
Calvin Coll (MI)
Cameron U (OK)
Campbellsville U (KY)
Canisius Coll (NY)
Cardinal Stritch U (WI)
Caribbean U (PR)
Carroll Coll (MT)
Carson-Newman U (TN)
Carthage Coll (WI)
Catawba Coll (NC)
The Catholic U of America (DC)
Cedar Crest Coll (PA)
Centenary U (NJ)
Central Connecticut State U (CT)
Central Methodist U (MO)
Central Michigan U (MI)
Central Washington U (WA)
Chaminade U of Honolulu (HI)
Champlain Coll (VT)
Charleston Southern U (SC)
Chatham U (PA)
Chestnut Hill Coll (PA)
Chowan U (NC)
City Coll of the City U of New York (NY)
Clarion U of Pennsylvania (PA)
Clarke U (IA)
Clark U (MA)
Clemson U (SC)
Coastal Carolina U (SC)
Coe Coll (IA)
Coll of Charleston (SC)
Coll of Mount Saint Vincent (NY)
The Coll of New Jersey (NJ)
Coll of Saint Benedict (MN)
Coll of Saint Mary (NE)
The Coll of Saint Rose (NY)
The Coll of St. Scholastica (MN)
Coll of Staten Island of the City U of New York (NY)
Coll of the Atlantic (ME)
Coll of the Ozarks (MO)
Colorado Christian U (CO)
Concordia Coll (MN)

Concordia Coll–New York (NY)
Concordia U (QC, Canada)
Concordia U Chicago (IL)
Concordia U, Nebraska (NE)
Concordia U, St. Paul (MN)
Concordia U Wisconsin (WI)
Concord U (WV)
Converse Coll (SC)
Corban U (OR)
Cornell Coll (IA)
Cornerstone U (MI)
Creighton U (NE)
Culver-Stockton Coll (MO)
Curry Coll (MA)
Daemen Coll (NY)
Dakota State U (SD)
Dallas Baptist U (TX)
Dalton State Coll (GA)
Daytona State Coll (FL)
Defiance Coll (OH)
DeSales U (PA)
Dickinson State U (ND)
Dixie State U (UT)
Doane U (NE)
Dominican Coll (NY)
Dominican U (IL)
Donnelly Coll (KS)
Drake U (IA)
Drexel U (PA)
Drury U (MO)
East Carolina U (NC)
East Central U (OK)
Eastern Illinois U (IL)
Eastern Michigan U (MI)
Eastern Nazarene Coll (MA)
East Texas Baptist U (TX)
Edgewood Coll (WI)
Elizabeth City State U (NC)
Elmira Coll (NY)
Elon U (NC)
Emmanuel Coll (GA)
Emmanuel Coll (MA)
Emmaus Bible Coll (IA)
Emporia State U (KS)
Endicott Coll (MA)
Eureka Coll (IL)
Evangel U (MO)
Faith Baptist Bible Coll and Theological Sem (IA)
Faulkner U (AL)
Fayetteville State U (NC)
Felician U (NJ)
Ferris State U (MI)
Fitchburg State U (MA)
Flagler Coll (FL)
Florida Ag and Mech U (FL)
Florida Atlantic U (FL)
Florida Coll (FL)
Florida Gulf Coast U (FL)
Florida Intl U (FL)
Florida Southern Coll (FL)
Florida SouthWestern State Coll (FL)
Fordham U (NY)
Fort Lewis Coll (CO)
Framingham State U (MA)
Franciscan U of Steubenville (OH)
Francis Marion U (SC)
Franklin Coll (IN)
Franklin Pierce U (NH)
Freed-Hardeman U (TN)
Friends U (KS)
Frostburg State U (MD)
Furman U (SC)
Gardner-Webb U (NC)
Geneva Coll (PA)
George Fox U (OR)
Georgetown Coll (KY)
Georgian Court U (NJ)
Georgia Southern U (GA)
Georgia Southwestern State U (GA)
Gettysburg Coll (PA)
Goddard Coll (VT)
Gonzaga U (WA)
Gordon Coll (MA)
Gordon State Coll (GA)
Goshen Coll (IN)
Goucher Coll (MD)
Governors State U (IL)
Grace Coll (IN)
Graceland U (IA)
Grambling State U (LA)
Grand Valley State U (MI)
Grand View U (IA)
Granite State Coll (NH)
Great Basin Coll (NV)
Green Mountain Coll (VT)
Greenville Coll (IL)
Guilford Coll (NC)
Gwynedd Mercy U (PA)
Hamline U (MN)
Hampton U (VA)
Hannibal-LaGrange U (MO)
Hanover Coll (IN)
Harding U (AR)
Harris-Stowe State U (MO)
Hawai`i Pacific U (HI)
Heidelberg U (OH)
High Point U (NC)
Hobe Sound Bible Coll (FL)
Hofstra U (NY)
Holy Cross Coll (IN)
Holy Family U (PA)
Hope Coll (MI)
Hope Intl U (CA)
Houghton Coll (NY)
Houston Baptist U (TX)
Howard Payne U (TX)
Humboldt State U (CA)
Hunter Coll of the City U of New York (NY)
Huntingdon Coll (AL)
Huntington U (IN)
Husson U (ME)
Huston-Tillotson U (TX)
Idaho State U (ID)
Illinois Coll (IL)
Illinois State U (IL)
Illinois Wesleyan U (IL)
Indiana State U (IN)
Indiana U Bloomington (IN)
Indiana U East (IN)
Indiana U Kokomo (IN)
Indiana U Northwest (IN)
Indiana U–Purdue U Indianapolis (IN)
Indiana U South Bend (IN)
Indiana U Southeast (IN)
Inter American U of Puerto Rico, Aguadilla Campus (PR)
Inter American U of Puerto Rico, Barranquitas Campus (PR)
Inter American U of Puerto Rico, Fajardo Campus (PR)
Inter American U of Puerto Rico, Guayama Campus (PR)
Inter American U of Puerto Rico, Metropolitan Campus (PR)
Inter American U of Puerto Rico, Ponce Campus (PR)
Inter American U of Puerto Rico, San Germán Campus (PR)
Iona Coll (NY)
Iowa State U of Science and Technology (IA)
Iowa Wesleyan U (IA)
Jackson State U (MS)
Jacksonville State U (AL)
Jacksonville U (FL)
John Brown U (AR)
John Carroll U (OH)
Johnson U (TN)
Johnson U Florida (FL)
John Wesley U (NC)
Judson U (IL)
Kansas State U (KS)
Kansas Wesleyan U (KS)
Kean U (NJ)
Keene State Coll (NH)
Kennesaw State U (GA)
Kentucky Mountain Bible Coll (KY)
Kentucky State U (KY)
Kentucky Wesleyan Coll (KY)
Keuka Coll (NY)
King's Coll (PA)
The King's U (AB, Canada)
Knox Coll (IL)
Kuyper Coll (MI)
Langston U (OK)
La Roche Coll (PA)
Lasell Coll (MA)
Lees-McRae Coll (NC)
Lee U (TN)
Le Moyne Coll (NY)
Lenoir-Rhyne U (NC)
Lesley U (MA)
LeTourneau U (TX)
Lewis U (IL)
Liberty U (VA)
Limestone Coll (SC)
Lincoln U (MO)
Lindenwood U (MO)
Lindsey Wilson Coll (KY)
Linfield Coll (OR)
Lipscomb U (TN)
Loras Coll (IA)
Louisiana Coll (LA)
Louisiana State U and A&M Coll (LA)
Louisiana State U at Alexandria (LA)
Louisiana Tech U (LA)
Loyola U Chicago (IL)
Loyola U Maryland (MD)
Luther Coll (IA)
Lynchburg Coll (VA)
Lynn U (FL)
Madonna U (MI)
Maharishi U of Management (IA)
Manchester U (IN)
Manhattan Coll (NY)
Manhattanville Coll (NY)
Mansfield U of Pennsylvania (PA)
Maranatha Baptist U (WI)
Marian U (IN)
Marian U (WI)
Marietta Coll (OH)
Marshall U (WV)
Martin Luther Coll (MN)
Marymount U (VA)
Maryville U of Saint Louis (MO)
Marywood U (PA)
The Master's U (CA)
McKendree U (IL)
McMurry U (TX)
McNeese State U (LA)
Medgar Evers Coll of the City U of New York (NY)
Mercer U, Macon (GA)
Mercyhurst U (PA)
Merrimack Coll (MA)
Messiah Coll (PA)
Michigan State U (MI)
MidAmerica Nazarene U (KS)
Mid-Atlantic Christian U (NC)
Millikin U (IL)
Minnesota State U Mankato (MN)
Minnesota State U Moorhead (MN)
Minot State U (ND)
Mississippi State U (MS)
Mississippi Valley State U (MS)
Missouri Baptist U (MO)
Missouri State U (MO)
Missouri Valley Coll (MO)
Missouri Western State U (MO)
Molloy Coll (NY)
Monmouth Coll (IL)
Montana State U (MT)
Montana State U Billings (MT)
Montana State U–Northern (MT)
Morehead State U (KY)
Morningside Coll (IA)
Morris Coll (SC)
Mount Marty Coll (SD)
Mount Mercy U (IA)
Mount Saint Mary's U (CA)
Mount St. Mary's U (MD)
Multnomah U (OR)
Murray State U (KY)
National Louis U (IL)
National U (CA)
Nazareth Coll of Rochester (NY)
Neumann U (PA)
Nevada State Coll (NV)
Newberry Coll (SC)
New England Coll (NH)
New Jersey City U (NJ)
Newman U (KS)
New Mexico Highlands U (NM)
New Mexico State U (NM)
Niagara U (NY)
North Carolina Central U (NC)
North Carolina State U (NC)
North Carolina Wesleyan Coll (NC)
North Central Coll (IL)
Northcentral U (CA)
Northeastern Illinois U (IL)
Northeastern State U (OK)
Northern Arizona U (AZ)
Northern Illinois U (IL)
Northern Kentucky U (KY)
Northern State U (SD)
North Greenville U (SC)
Northwest Christian U (OR)
Northwestern Coll (IA)
Northwestern Oklahoma State U (OK)
Northwestern State U of Louisiana (LA)
Northwest Missouri State U (MO)
Northwest U (WA)
Nova Southeastern U (FL)
Nyack Coll (NY)
Oakland City U (IN)
The Ohio State U (OH)
The Ohio State U at Lima (OH)
The Ohio State U at Marion (OH)
The Ohio State U–Mansfield Campus (OH)
The Ohio State U–Newark Campus (OH)
Ohio U–Zanesville (OH)
Ohio Valley U (WV)
Ohio Wesleyan U (OH)
Oklahoma Baptist U (OK)
Oklahoma Christian U (OK)
Oklahoma City U (OK)
Oklahoma State U (OK)
Olivet Nazarene U (IL)
Oral Roberts U (OK)
Otterbein U (OH)
Pace U (NY)
Pace U, Pleasantville Campus (NY)
Paine Coll (GA)
Palm Beach Atlantic U (FL)
Penn State Abington (PA)
Penn State Altoona (PA)
Penn State Beaver (PA)
Penn State Berks (PA)
Penn State Brandywine (PA)
Penn State DuBois (PA)
Penn State Erie, The Behrend Coll (PA)
Penn State Fayette, The Eberly Campus (PA)
Penn State Greater Allegheny (PA)
Penn State Harrisburg (PA)
Penn State Hazleton (PA)
Penn State Lehigh Valley (PA)
Penn State Mont Alto (PA)
Penn State New Kensington (PA)
Penn State Schuylkill (PA)
Penn State Shenango (PA)
Penn State U Park (PA)
Penn State Wilkes-Barre (PA)
Penn State Worthington Scranton (PA)
Penn State York (PA)
Piedmont Intl U (NC)
Pittsburg State U (KS)
Plymouth State U (NH)
Point Loma Nazarene U (CA)
Point Park U (PA)
Prescott Coll (AZ)
Purdue U (IN)
Purdue U Northwest (IN)
Queens Coll of the City U of New York (NY)
Redeemer U Coll (ON, Canada)
Regis U (CO)
Rhode Island Coll (RI)
Ripon Coll (WI)
Robert Morris U (PA)
Rockford U (IL)
Rockhurst U (MO)
Rocky Mountain Coll (MT)
Roger Williams U (RI)
Rollins Coll (FL)
Rosemont Coll (PA)
Rowan U (NJ)
Rust Coll (MS)
Sacred Heart U (CT)
The Sage Colls (NY)
Saginaw Valley State U (MI)
St. Ambrose U (IA)
St. Andrews U (NC)
Saint Anselm Coll (NH)
St. Bonaventure U (NY)
St. Catherine U (MN)
St. Cloud State U (MN)
Saint Francis U (PA)
St. Gregory's U, Shawnee (OK)
St. John Fisher Coll (NY)
Saint John's U (MN)
St. John's U (NY)
St. Joseph's Coll, Long Island Campus (NY)
St. Joseph's Coll, New York (NY)
Saint Joseph's U (PA)
Saint Leo U (FL)
Saint Martin's U (WA)
Saint Mary-of-the-Woods Coll (IN)
Saint Mary's Coll (IN)
Saint Mary's U of Minnesota (MN)
Saint Michael's Coll (VT)
St. Norbert Coll (WI)
St. Petersburg Coll (FL)
Saint Peter's U (NJ)
St. Thomas Aquinas Coll (NY)
St. Thomas U (FL)
Salisbury U (MD)
Salve Regina U (RI)
Samford U (AL)
Schreiner U (TX)
Seton Hill U (PA)
Shaw U (NC)
Shepherd U (WV)
Shorter U (GA)
Silver Lake Coll of the Holy Family (WI)
Simmons Coll (MA)
Simpson Coll (IA)
Skidmore Coll (NY)
South Carolina State U (SC)
Southeastern Louisiana U (LA)
Southeastern Oklahoma State U (OK)
Southeastern U (FL)
Southeast Missouri State U (MO)
Southern Connecticut State U (CT)
Southern Illinois U Carbondale (IL)
Southern Illinois U Edwardsville (IL)
Southern New Hampshire U (NH)
Southern Utah U (UT)
South Florida State Coll (FL)
Southwest Baptist U (MO)
Southwestern Adventist U (TX)
Southwestern Assemblies of God U (TX)
Southwestern Coll (KS)
Spalding U (KY)
Spring Hill Coll (AL)
State U of New York at Fredonia (NY)
State U of New York at New Paltz (NY)
State U of New York at Oswego (NY)
State U of New York at Plattsburgh (NY)
State U of New York Coll at Cortland (NY)
State U of New York Coll at Geneseo (NY)
State U of New York Coll at Old Westbury (NY)
State U of New York Coll at Potsdam (NY)
Sterling Coll (KS)
Stevenson U (MD)
Stonehill Coll (MA)
Tabor Coll (KS)
Tarleton State U (TX)
Taylor U (IN)
Temple U (PA)
Tennessee State U (TN)
Tennessee Wesleyan U (TN)
Texas Christian U (TX)
Texas Coll (TX)
Texas Lutheran U (TX)
Thomas More Coll (KY)
Toccoa Falls Coll (GA)
Towson U (MD)
Transylvania U (KY)
Trent U (ON, Canada)
Trevecca Nazarene U (TN)
Trine U (IN)
Trinity Baptist Coll (FL)
Trinity Christian Coll (IL)
Trinity Coll of Florida (FL)
Troy U (AL)
Truett McConnell U (GA)
Tufts U (MA)
Union Coll (KY)
Union Coll (NE)
Union Inst & U (OH)
Union U (TN)
Universidad Adventista de las Antillas (PR)
Université de Montréal (QC, Canada)
Université de Sherbrooke (QC, Canada)
The U of Alabama (AL)
The U of Alabama at Birmingham (AL)
The U of Alabama in Huntsville (AL)
U of Alaska Fairbanks (AK)
The U of Arizona (AZ)
U of Arkansas (AR)
U of Central Florida (FL)
U of Central Missouri (MO)

U of Charleston (WV)
U of Colorado Colorado Springs (CO)
U of Delaware (DE)
U of Detroit Mercy (MI)
U of Dubuque (IA)
U of Evansville (IN)
The U of Findlay (OH)
U of Florida (FL)
U of Georgia (GA)
U of Great Falls (MT)
U of Hartford (CT)
U of Hawaii at Manoa (HI)
U of Idaho (ID)
U of Illinois at Chicago (IL)
U of Indianapolis (IN)
U of Jamestown (ND)
The U of Kansas (KS)
U of Kentucky (KY)
U of Louisiana at Monroe (LA)
U of Louisville (KY)
U of Maine (ME)
U of Maine at Farmington (ME)
U of Maine at Presque Isle (ME)
U of Mary Hardin-Baylor (TX)
U of Maryland, Coll Park (MD)
U of Miami (FL)
U of Michigan (MI)
U of Michigan–Dearborn (MI)
U of Michigan–Flint (MI)
U of Minnesota, Crookston (MN)
U of Minnesota, Morris (MN)
U of Minnesota, Twin Cities Campus (MN)
U of Missouri–Kansas City (MO)
U of Missouri–St. Louis (MO)
U of Mobile (AL)
The U of Montana Western (MT)
U of Montevallo (AL)
U of Nebraska at Kearney (NE)
U of Nevada, Las Vegas (NV)
U of Nevada, Reno (NV)
U of New England (ME)
U of New Orleans (LA)
U of North Alabama (AL)
The U of North Carolina at Chapel Hill (NC)
The U of North Carolina at Charlotte (NC)
The U of North Carolina at Greensboro (NC)
The U of North Carolina at Pembroke (NC)
The U of North Carolina Wilmington (NC)
U of North Dakota (ND)
U of Northern Colorado (CO)
U of Northern Iowa (IA)
U of North Florida (FL)
U of Oklahoma (OK)
U of Pennsylvania (PA)
U of Pikeville (KY)
U of Pittsburgh at Bradford (PA)
U of Pittsburgh at Johnstown (PA)
U of Regina (SK, Canada)
U of Rhode Island (RI)
U of St. Francis (IL)
U of Saint Francis (IN)
U of Saint Mary (KS)
U of St. Thomas (TX)
U of San Francisco (CA)
U of Science and Arts of Oklahoma (OK)
The U of Scranton (PA)
U of South Alabama (AL)
U of South Carolina (SC)
U of South Carolina Aiken (SC)
The U of South Dakota (SD)
U of Southern Indiana (IN)
U of Southern Mississippi (MS)
U of South Florida (FL)
U of South Florida, St. Petersburg (FL)
U of South Florida Sarasota-Manatee (FL)
The U of Tampa (FL)
The U of Tennessee at Martin (TN)
The U of Texas at San Antonio (TX)
U of the Cumberlands (KY)
U of the Incarnate Word (TX)
U of the Southwest (NM)
U of the Virgin Islands (VI)
The U of Tulsa (OK)
U of Utah (UT)
U of Vermont (VT)
U of West Georgia (GA)
U of Windsor (ON, Canada)
U of Wisconsin–Eau Claire (WI)
U of Wisconsin–La Crosse (WI)
U of Wisconsin–Madison (WI)
U of Wisconsin–Parkside (WI)
U of Wisconsin–Platteville (WI)
U of Wisconsin–Stevens Point (WI)
U of Wisconsin–Superior (WI)
U of Wisconsin–Whitewater (WI)
Upper Iowa U (IA)
Utah State U (UT)
Utah Valley U (UT)
Utica Coll (NY)
Valley City State U (ND)
Valparaiso U (IN)
Vanderbilt U (TN)
Virginia Union U (VA)
Virginia Wesleyan Coll (VA)
Viterbo U (WI)
Wagner Coll (NY)
Waldorf U (IA)
Walla Walla U (WA)
Wartburg Coll (IA)
Washburn U (KS)
Washington State U (WA)
Washington State U–Tri-Cities (WA)
Washington State U–Vancouver (WA)
Washington U in St. Louis (MO)
Wayland Baptist U (TX)
Waynesburg U (PA)
Wayne State Coll (NE)
Wayne State U (MI)
Webber Intl U (FL)
Weber State U (UT)
Webster U (MO)
Welch Coll (TN)
Wells Coll (NY)
Wesleyan Coll (GA)
Western Carolina U (NC)
Western Connecticut State U (CT)
Western Illinois U (IL)
Western Kentucky U (KY)
Western Michigan U (MI)
Western New England U (MA)
Western Washington U (WA)
Westfield State U (MA)
Westminster Coll (PA)
Westminster Coll (UT)
Westmont Coll (CA)
West Virginia State U (WV)
West Virginia U (WV)
West Virginia Wesleyan Coll (WV)
Wheaton Coll (IL)
Wheaton Coll (MA)
Wheelock Coll (MA)
Whitworth U (WA)
Wichita State U (KS)
Widener U (PA)
Wilkes U (PA)
William Jewell Coll (MO)
William Paterson U of New Jersey (NJ)
William Penn U (IA)
Williams Baptist Coll (AR)
William Woods U (MO)
Wilmington U (DE)
Wilson Coll (PA)
Wingate U (NC)
Winona State U (MN)
Winthrop U (SC)
Worcester State U (MA)
Wright State U–Lake Campus (OH)
Xavier U of Louisiana (LA)
York Coll of the City U of New York (NY)
Youngstown State U (OH)

EMERGENCY MEDICAL TECHNOLOGY (EMT PARAMEDIC)

Brigham Young U–Idaho (ID)
Central Washington U (WA)
Columbia Southern U (AL)
Concordia U Chicago (IL)
Creighton U (NE)
The George Washington U (DC)
U of Arkansas for Medical Sciences (AR)
U of Maryland, Baltimore County (MD)
U of New Haven (CT)
U of South Alabama (AL)
U of Washington (WA)
Western Carolina U (NC)

ENERGY MANAGEMENT AND SYSTEMS TECHNOLOGY

Creighton U (NE)
Excelsior Coll (NY)
Ferris State U (MI)
Fitchburg State U (MA)
Idaho State U (ID)
Illinois State U (IL)
State Coll of Florida Manatee-Sarasota (FL)
Unity Coll (ME)
Vermont Tech Coll (VT)

ENGINEERING

Abilene Christian U (TX)
Albion Coll (MI)
Arizona State U at the Polytechnic campus (AZ)
Auburn U (AL)
Augsburg Coll (MN)
Baldwin Wallace U (OH)
Ball State U (IN)
Barry U (FL)
Bates Coll (ME)
Baylor U (TX)
Beloit Coll (WI)
Benedictine Coll (KS)
Bethany Lutheran Coll (MN)
Bethel Coll (IN)
Binghamton U, State U of New York (NY)
Biola U (CA)
Boston U (MA)
Buffalo State Coll, State U of New York (NY)
California Baptist U (CA)
California Inst of Technology (CA)
California State Polytechnic U, Pomona (CA)
California State U, Long Beach (CA)
Calvin Coll (MI)
Carnegie Mellon U (PA)
Carthage Coll (WI)
Case Western Reserve U (OH)
The Catholic U of America (DC)
Clarkson U (NY)
Clark U (MA)
Coll of Staten Island of the City U of New York (NY)
Coll of the Ozarks (MO)
Colorado School of Mines (CO)
Cooper Union for the Advancement of Science and Art (NY)
Cornell U (NY)
Dalhousie U (NS, Canada)
Dartmouth Coll (NH)
Daytona State Coll (FL)
Dominican U (IL)
Drexel U (PA)
East Carolina U (NC)
East Central U (OK)
Eastern Mennonite U (VA)
Eastern Nazarene Coll (MA)
Elizabethtown Coll (PA)
Elon U (NC)
Embry-Riddle Aeronautical U–Daytona (FL)
Florida Inst of Technology (FL)
Franklin W. Olin Coll of Eng (MA)
Frostburg State U (MD)
Geneva Coll (PA)
George Fox U (OR)
The George Washington U (DC)
Gonzaga U (WA)
Grand Valley State U (MI)
Hanover Coll (IN)
Harvard U (MA)
Harvey Mudd Coll (CA)
Hope Coll (MI)
Indiana U Bloomington (IN)
Indiana U–Purdue U Indianapolis (IN)
Inter American U of Puerto Rico, San Germán Campus (PR)
Iowa State U of Science and Technology (IA)
Jacksonville U (FL)
James Madison U (VA)
John Brown U (AR)
Johns Hopkins U (MD)
Lafayette Coll (PA)
LaGrange Coll (GA)
LeTourneau U (TX)
Loyola U Maryland (MD)
Manchester U (IN)
Manhattan Coll (NY)
Marshall U (WV)
McNeese State U (LA)
Mercer U, Macon (GA)
Messiah Coll (PA)
Miami U (OH)
Michigan State U (MI)
Michigan Technological U (MI)
Milwaukee School of Eng (WI)
Missouri U of Science and Technology (MO)
Montana State U (MT)
Montana Tech of The U of Montana (MT)
New Mexico Highlands U (NM)
North Carolina State U (NC)
Northeastern U (MA)
Northland Coll (WI)
Northwestern U (IL)
The Ohio State U (OH)
Oklahoma Christian U (OK)
Old Dominion U (VA)
Olivet Nazarene U (IL)
Oral Roberts U (OK)
Pacific Lutheran U (WA)
Princeton U (NJ)
Purdue U Northwest (IN)
Quinnipiac U (CT)
Rensselaer Polytechnic Inst (NY)
Robert Morris U (PA)
Rochester Inst of Technology (NY)
Roger Williams U (RI)
Rutgers U–Camden (NJ)
Rutgers U–Newark (NJ)
Saginaw Valley State U (MI)
Saint Anselm Coll (NH)
Saint Augustine's U (NC)
St. Cloud State U (MN)
Saint Francis U (PA)
Saint Louis U (MO)
Saint Louis U–Madrid Campus (Spain)
Saint Mary's Coll of California (CA)
Saint Vincent Coll (PA)
San Diego State U (CA)
Sarah Lawrence Coll (NY)
Schreiner U (TX)
Seattle Pacific U (WA)
Seattle U (WA)
Spelman Coll (GA)
Stanford U (CA)
State U of New York Polytechnic Inst (NY)
Stevens Inst of Technology (NJ)
Stony Brook U, State U of New York (NY)
Swarthmore Coll (PA)
Tarleton State U (TX)
Temple U (PA)
Tennessee State U (TN)
Texas Christian U (TX)
Tufts U (MA)
United States Air Force Acad (CO)
U at Buffalo, the State U of New York (NY)
The U of Akron (OH)
U of California, Irvine (CA)
U of California, San Diego (CA)
U of Cincinnati (OH)
U of Colorado Boulder (CO)
U of Delaware (DE)
U of Denver (CO)
U of Detroit Mercy (MI)
U of Georgia (GA)
U of Hartford (CT)
U of Hawaii at Manoa (HI)
U of Maryland, Baltimore County (MD)
U of Miami (FL)
U of Michigan (MI)
U of Missouri–Kansas City (MO)
U of Nevada, Las Vegas (NV)
U of New Haven (CT)
U of North Carolina at Asheville (NC)
U of Oklahoma (OK)
U of Pittsburgh at Johnstown (PA)
U of Regina (SK, Canada)
U of Rochester (NY)
U of San Diego (CA)
U of Southern Indiana (IN)
The U of Tennessee at Chattanooga (TN)
The U of Tennessee at Martin (TN)
U of the Incarnate Word (TX)
U of Toronto (ON, Canada)
U of Utah (UT)
U of Virginia (VA)
U of Windsor (ON, Canada)
U of Wisconsin–Platteville (WI)
Vaughn Coll of Aeronautics and Technology (NY)
Wake Forest U (NC)
Walla Walla U (WA)
Wartburg Coll (IA)
Washington U in St. Louis (MO)
Weber State U (UT)
Wells Coll (NY)
Wentworth Inst of Technology (MA)
Western Illinois U (IL)
Widener U (PA)
Wilkes U (PA)
Wright State U (OH)
Youngstown State U (OH)

ENGINEERING CHEMISTRY

Washington and Lee U (VA)

ENGINEERING FIELDS RELATED

California State U, Chico (CA)

ENGINEERING/INDUSTRIAL MANAGEMENT

Arizona State U at the Tempe campus (AZ)
Bowling Green State U (OH)
California State U, Long Beach (CA)
Christian Brothers U (TN)
Claremont McKenna Coll (CA)
Clarkson U (NY)
Columbia U (NY)
Eastern Michigan U (MI)
Fort Lewis Coll (CO)
Grove City Coll (PA)
Iowa State U of Science and Technology (IA)
Kansas State U (KS)
Kennesaw State U (GA)
McMaster U (ON, Canada)
Miami U (OH)
Michigan Technological U (MI)
Missouri State U (MO)
Missouri U of Science and Technology (MO)
Morehead State U (KY)
New York Inst of Technology (NY)
Pittsburg State U (KS)
Purdue U (IN)
Purdue U Northwest (IN)
Saginaw Valley State U (MI)
Stanford U (CA)
State U of New York Coll of Technology at Canton (NY)
Stevens Inst of Technology (NJ)
Texas State U (TX)
United States Merchant Marine Acad (NY)
United States Military Acad (NY)
The U of Arizona (AZ)
U of Illinois at Chicago (IL)
U of Management and Technology (VA)
The U of Scranton (PA)
The U of Tennessee at Chattanooga (TN)
The U of Texas at Austin (TX)
U of the Incarnate Word (TX)
U of the Pacific (CA)
U of Vermont (VT)
Washburn U (KS)
Western Michigan U (MI)
Widener U (PA)
Wilkes U (PA)

ENGINEERING MECHANICS

Carroll Coll (MT)
Columbia U (NY)
Johns Hopkins U (MD)
Lehigh U (PA)
The U of Texas at Austin (TX)
U of Windsor (ON, Canada)
U of Wisconsin–Madison (WI)
Virginia Polytechnic Inst and State U (VA)

ENGINEERING PHYSICS/ APPLIED PHYSICS

Adams State U (CO)
Arkansas Tech U (AR)
Augustana Coll (IL)
Augustana U (SD)
Belmont U (TN)
Bemidji State U (MN)
Biola U (CA)
California Inst of Technology (CA)

Case Western Reserve U (OH)
Central Washington U (WA)
Christian Brothers U (TN)
Colorado School of Mines (CO)
Colorado State U (CO)
Columbia U (NY)
Cornell U (NY)
Dartmouth Coll (NH)
Doane U (NE)
Eastern Michigan U (MI)
Eastern Nazarene Coll (MA)
Elon U (NC)
Embry-Riddle Aeronautical U–Daytona (FL)
Fordham U (NY)
Fort Lewis Coll (CO)
Goshen Coll (IN)
Grace Coll (IN)
Hanover Coll (IN)
Henderson State U (AR)
Jacksonville U (FL)
John Carroll U (OH)
Juniata Coll (PA)
Kansas Wesleyan U (KS)
Kettering U (MI)
Lehigh U (PA)
LeTourneau U (TX)
Linfield Coll (OR)
Loras Coll (IA)
Loyola Marymount U (CA)
McMaster U (ON, Canada)
Miami U (OH)
Morehouse Coll (GA)
Morningside Coll (IA)
Murray State U (KY)
New Mexico State U (NM)
Northeastern State U (OK)
The Ohio State U (OH)
Oral Roberts U (OK)
Otterbein U (OH)
Point Loma Nazarene U (CA)
Providence Coll (RI)
Randolph Coll (VA)
Randolph-Macon Coll (VA)
Rensselaer Polytechnic Inst (NY)
Rose-Hulman Inst of Technology (IN)
St. Ambrose U (IA)
Saint Louis U (MO)
Saint Louis U–Madrid Campus (Spain)
Saint Mary's U of Minnesota (MN)
Samford U (AL)
Santa Clara U (CA)
Southeast Missouri State U (MO)
Stephen F. Austin State U (TX)
Stevens Inst of Technology (NJ)
Syracuse U (NY)
Tarleton State U (TX)
Taylor U (IN)
Trevecca Nazarene U (TN)
Tufts U (MA)
U at Buffalo, the State U of New York (NY)
U of California, San Diego (CA)
U of Colorado Boulder (CO)
U of Illinois at Chicago (IL)
The U of Kansas (KS)
U of Maine (ME)
U of Massachusetts Boston (MA)
U of Michigan (MI)
U of Nevada, Reno (NV)
U of Oklahoma (OK)
U of Pittsburgh (PA)
U of Saskatchewan (SK, Canada)
U of the Pacific (CA)
The U of Tulsa (OK)
U of Wisconsin–Madison (WI)
U of Wisconsin–Platteville (WI)
Washington and Lee U (VA)
Westminster Coll (PA)
Westmont Coll (CA)
Whittier Coll (CA)
Whitworth U (WA)
Worcester Polytechnic Inst (MA)
Wright State U (OH)

ENGINEERING RELATED
Agnes Scott Coll (GA)
Alfred U (NY)
Auburn U (AL)
Benedictine Coll (KS)
California State U, Chico (CA)
California State U, Long Beach (CA)
Claremont McKenna Coll (CA)
The Coll of Idaho (ID)
Eastern Illinois U (IL)
Gettysburg Coll (PA)
Indiana U–Purdue U Indianapolis (IN)
Lehigh U (PA)
Madonna U (MI)
Maryville U of Saint Louis (MO)
Massachusetts Maritime Acad (MA)
Mississippi State U (MS)
Morehead State U (KY)
Northwestern U (IL)
The Ohio State U (OH)
Ohio Wesleyan U (OH)
Oregon State U (OR)
Penn State Altoona (PA)
Penn State Berks (PA)
Penn State U Park (PA)
Polytechnic U of Puerto Rico (PR)
Principia Coll (IL)
Purdue U (IN)
Rochester Inst of Technology (NY)
Rose-Hulman Inst of Technology (IN)
State U of New York at Oswego (NY)
State U of New York Polytechnic Inst (NY)
Stevens Inst of Technology (NJ)
Tufts U (MA)
U at Albany, State U of New York (NY)
The U of Alabama in Huntsville (AL)
U of California, Davis (CA)
U of Colorado Colorado Springs (CO)
U of Delaware (DE)
U of Maryland, Coll Park (MD)
U of Miami (FL)
U of Michigan–Dearborn (MI)
U of New Hampshire (NH)
U of Pennsylvania (PA)
The U of Virginia's Coll at Wise (VA)
U of Washington (WA)
U of Waterloo (ON, Canada)
U of Wisconsin–Madison (WI)
Washington U in St. Louis (MO)
Waynesburg U (PA)
Western Michigan U (MI)
Wheaton Coll (IL)
York Coll of Pennsylvania (PA)

ENGINEERING-RELATED TECHNOLOGIES
Rochester Inst of Technology (NY)
United States Merchant Marine Acad (NY)

ENGINEERING SCIENCE
Bethel U (MN)
California Polytechnic State U, San Luis Obispo (CA)
Carroll Coll (MT)
Coastal Carolina U (SC)
The Coll of New Jersey (NJ)
Colorado State U (CO)
Concordia U, St. Paul (MN)
Emory U (GA)
Hanover Coll (IN)
Hofstra U (NY)
Lincoln U (PA)
Morehouse Coll (GA)
Muskingum U (OH)
Northwestern U (IL)
Ohio Wesleyan U (OH)
Penn State Abington (PA)
Penn State Altoona (PA)
Penn State Beaver (PA)
Penn State Berks (PA)
Penn State Brandywine (PA)
Penn State DuBois (PA)
Penn State Erie, The Behrend Coll (PA)
Penn State Fayette, The Eberly Campus (PA)
Penn State Greater Allegheny (PA)
Penn State Hazleton (PA)
Penn State Lehigh Valley (PA)
Penn State Mont Alto (PA)
Penn State New Kensington (PA)
Penn State Schuylkill (PA)
Penn State Shenango (PA)
Penn State U Park (PA)
Penn State Wilkes-Barre (PA)
Penn State Worthington Scranton (PA)
Penn State York (PA)
Rensselaer Polytechnic Inst (NY)
Rutgers U–New Brunswick (NJ)
St. Thomas Aquinas Coll (NY)
Simon Fraser U (BC, Canada)
Smith Coll (MA)
Sonoma State U (CA)
Southern Utah U (UT)
Sweet Briar Coll (VA)
Trinity U (TX)
Tufts U (MA)
Tulane U (LA)
U of California, San Diego (CA)
U of Mary Hardin-Baylor (TX)
U of Miami (FL)
U of Michigan (MI)
U of Michigan–Flint (MI)
U of Pittsburgh (PA)
U of Pittsburgh at Bradford (PA)
U of Rochester (NY)
U of South Carolina (SC)
U of Toronto (ON, Canada)
Vanderbilt U (TN)
Wartburg Coll (IA)
Wheeling Jesuit U (WV)
Wright State U (OH)
Wright State U–Lake Campus (OH)

ENGINEERING TECHNOLOGIES AND ENGINEERING RELATED
Ball State U (IN)
Bowling Green State U (OH)
California State U Maritime Acad (CA)
Cameron U (OK)
East Carolina U (NC)
East Central U (OK)
Eastern Washington U (WA)
Elizabeth City State U (NC)
Embry-Riddle Aeronautical U–Prescott (AZ)
Excelsior Coll (NY)
Keene State Coll (NH)
New York Inst of Technology (NY)
Northeastern State U (OK)
Old Dominion U (VA)
Pennsylvania Coll of Technology (PA)
Pittsburg State U (KS)
Rogers State U (OK)
Shawnee State U (OH)
U of Hartford (CT)
The U of North Carolina at Charlotte (NC)
The U of West Alabama (AL)

ENGINEERING TECHNOLOGY
Austin Peay State U (TN)
Berry Coll (GA)
Buffalo State Coll, State U of New York (NY)
California State Polytechnic U, Pomona (CA)
California State U, Long Beach (CA)
California U of Pennsylvania (PA)
Drexel U (PA)
East Tennessee State U (TN)
Grambling State U (LA)
Illinois State U (IL)
Indiana State U (IN)
Kansas State U (KS)
Kennesaw State U (GA)
Kent State U (OH)
Kent State U at Tuscarawas (OH)
Lawrence Technological U (MI)
Lenoir-Rhyne U (NC)
Morehead State U (KY)
New Mexico State U (NM)
New York Inst of Technology (NY)
Northern Illinois U (IL)
St. Cloud State U (MN)
Southeastern Louisiana U (LA)
Southeast Missouri State U (MO)
Southern Illinois U Carbondale (IL)
Southern Utah U (UT)
Tarleton State U (TX)
Temple U (PA)
Texas A&M U (TX)
Texas State U (TX)
U of Delaware (DE)
U of Hartford (CT)
U of North Alabama (AL)
U of Rochester (NY)
The U of Texas Rio Grande Valley (TX)
The U of West Alabama (AL)
U of Wisconsin–Stout (WI)
Walla Walla U (WA)
Wentworth Inst of Technology (MA)
Western Carolina U (NC)
Western Illinois U (IL)
West Texas A&M U (TX)
West Virginia U Inst of Technology (WV)
Wichita State U (KS)
William Penn U (IA)
Youngstown State U (OH)

ENGLISH
Abilene Christian U (TX)
Adams State U (CO)
Adelphi U (NY)
Agnes Scott Coll (GA)
Alabama State U (AL)
Albany State U (GA)
Albertus Magnus Coll (CT)
Albion Coll (MI)
Albright Coll (PA)
Alcorn State U (MS)
Alfred U (NY)
Alice Lloyd Coll (KY)
Allegheny Coll (PA)
Alma Coll (MI)
Alvernia U (PA)
Alverno Coll (WI)
American Coll of Thessaloniki (Greece)
American Intl Coll (MA)
American Public U System (WV)
The American U in Cairo (Egypt)
American U of Beirut (Lebanon)
Amherst Coll (MA)
Anderson U (IN)
Anderson U (SC)
Andrews U (MI)
Angelo State U (TX)
Appalachian State U (NC)
Aquinas Coll (MI)
Aquinas Coll (TN)
Arcadia U (PA)
Arizona State U at the Polytechnic campus (AZ)
Arizona State U at the Tempe campus (AZ)
Arizona State U at the West campus (AZ)
Arkansas Tech U (AR)
Armstrong State U (GA)
Asbury U (KY)
Ashland U (OH)
Assumption Coll (MA)
Athens State U (AL)
Auburn U (AL)
Auburn U at Montgomery (AL)
Augsburg Coll (MN)
Augustana Coll (IL)
Augustana U (SD)
Augusta U (GA)
Aurora U (IL)
Austin Coll (TX)
Austin Peay State U (TN)
Averett U (VA)
Avila U (MO)
Azusa Pacific U (CA)
Baker U (KS)
Baldwin Wallace U (OH)
Ball State U (IN)
Bard Coll (NY)
Barnard Coll (NY)
Barry U (FL)
Barton Coll (NC)
Baruch Coll of the City U of New York (NY)
Bates Coll (ME)
Bayamón Central U (PR)
Baylor U (TX)
Belhaven U (MS)
Bellarmine U (KY)
Belmont Abbey Coll (NC)
Belmont U (TN)
Beloit Coll (WI)
Bemidji State U (MN)
Benedictine Coll (KS)
Bennett Coll (NC)
Bennington Coll (VT)
Bentley U (MA)
Berea Coll (KY)
Berry Coll (GA)
Bethany Lutheran Coll (MN)
Bethel Coll (IN)
Bethel Coll (KS)
Bethel U (MN)
Bethune-Cookman U (FL)
Binghamton U, State U of New York (NY)
Biola U (CA)
Bishop's U (QC, Canada)
Blackburn Coll (IL)
Black Hills State U (SD)
Bloomfield Coll (NJ)
Bloomsburg U of Pennsylvania (PA)
Bluefield Coll (VA)
Blue Mountain Coll (MS)
Bluffton U (OH)
Boise State U (ID)
Boston Coll (MA)
Boston U (MA)
Bowdoin Coll (ME)
Bowie State U (MD)
Bowling Green State U (OH)
Bradley U (IL)
Brandeis U (MA)
Brenau U (GA)
Brescia U (KY)
Brewton-Parker Coll (GA)
Briar Cliff U (IA)
Bridgewater Coll (VA)
Bridgewater State U (MA)
Brigham Young U–Idaho (ID)
Brooklyn Coll of the City U of New York (NY)
Bryan Coll (TN)
Bryant U (RI)
Bryn Athyn Coll of the New Church (PA)
Bryn Mawr Coll (PA)
Bucknell U (PA)
Buena Vista U (IA)
Buffalo State Coll, State U of New York (NY)
Butler U (IN)
Cabrini U (PA)
Cairn U (PA)
Caldwell U (NJ)
California Baptist U (CA)
California Inst of Technology (CA)
California Lutheran U (CA)
California Polytechnic State U, San Luis Obispo (CA)
California State Polytechnic U, Pomona (CA)
California State U, Bakersfield (CA)
California State U, Chico (CA)
California State U, Dominguez Hills (CA)
California State U, East Bay (CA)
California State U, Fresno (CA)
California State U, Fullerton (CA)
California State U, Long Beach (CA)
California State U, Northridge (CA)
California State U, Sacramento (CA)
California State U, San Bernardino (CA)
California State U, San Marcos (CA)
California State U, Stanislaus (CA)
California U of Pennsylvania (PA)
Calumet Coll of Saint Joseph (IN)
Calvary U (MO)
Calvin Coll (MI)
Cameron U (OK)
Campbellsville U (KY)
Canisius Coll (NY)
Capital U (OH)
Cardinal Stritch U (WI)
Carleton Coll (MN)
Carlow U (PA)
Carnegie Mellon U (PA)
Carroll Coll (MT)
Carson-Newman U (TN)
Carthage Coll (WI)
Case Western Reserve U (OH)
Catawba Coll (NC)
The Catholic U of America (DC)
Cazenovia Coll (NY)
Cedar Crest Coll (PA)
Cedarville U (OH)
Centenary Coll of Louisiana (LA)
Centenary U (NJ)
Central Baptist Coll (AR)
Central Connecticut State U (CT)
Central Methodist U (MO)
Central Michigan U (MI)
Central State U (OH)
Central Washington U (WA)
Centre Coll (KY)
Chaminade U of Honolulu (HI)
Chapman U (CA)

Charleston Southern U (SC)
Chatham U (PA)
Chestnut Hill Coll (PA)
Chowan U (NC)
Christendom Coll (VA)
Christian Brothers U (TN)
Christopher Newport U (VA)
The Citadel, The Military Coll of South Carolina (SC)
City Coll of the City U of New York (NY)
Claremont McKenna Coll (CA)
Clarion U of Pennsylvania (PA)
Clark Atlanta U (GA)
Clarke U (IA)
Clark U (MA)
Clayton State U (GA)
Clemson U (SC)
Cleveland State U (OH)
Coastal Carolina U (SC)
Coe Coll (IA)
Colby Coll (ME)
Colgate U (NY)
The Coll at Brockport, State U of New York (NY)
Coll of Charleston (SC)
The Coll of Idaho (ID)
Coll of Mount Saint Vincent (NY)
The Coll of New Jersey (NJ)
Coll of Saint Benedict (MN)
Coll of Saint Elizabeth (NJ)
Coll of Saint Mary (NE)
The Coll of Saint Rose (NY)
The Coll of St. Scholastica (MN)
Coll of Staten Island of the City U of New York (NY)
Coll of the Atlantic (ME)
Coll of the Holy Cross (MA)
Coll of the Ozarks (MO)
The Coll of William and Mary (VA)
The Coll of Wooster (OH)
Colorado Christian U (CO)
The Colorado Coll (CO)
Colorado Mesa U (CO)
Colorado State U (CO)
Columbia Coll (MO)
Columbia Intl U (SC)
Columbia U (NY)
Columbia U, School of General Studies (NY)
Columbus State U (GA)
Concordia Coll (MN)
Concordia Coll–New York (NY)
Concordia U (QC, Canada)
Concordia U Chicago (IL)
Concordia U Irvine (CA)
Concordia U, Nebraska (NE)
Concordia U, St. Paul (MN)
Concordia U Wisconsin (WI)
Concord U (WV)
Connecticut Coll (CT)
Converse Coll (SC)
Corban U (OR)
Cornell Coll (IA)
Cornell U (NY)
Crandall U (NB, Canada)
Creighton U (NE)
Culver-Stockton Coll (MO)
Curry Coll (MA)
Daemen Coll (NY)
Dalhousie U (NS, Canada)
Dallas Baptist U (TX)
Dalton State Coll (GA)
Dartmouth Coll (NH)
Davidson Coll (NC)
Dean Coll (MA)
Defiance Coll (OH)
Delaware Valley U (PA)
Denison U (OH)
DePauw U (IN)
DEREE - The American Coll of Greece (Greece)
DeSales U (PA)
Dickinson Coll (PA)
Dickinson State U (ND)
Dixie State U (UT)
Doane U (NE)
Dominican Coll (NY)
Dominican U (IL)
Dominican U of California (CA)
Drake U (IA)
Drew U (NJ)
Drury U (MO)
Duquesne U (PA)
Earlham Coll (IN)
East Carolina U (NC)
East Central U (OK)
Eastern Illinois U (IL)
Eastern Mennonite U (VA)
Eastern Michigan U (MI)
Eastern Nazarene Coll (MA)
Eastern Oregon U (OR)
Eastern Washington U (WA)
East Stroudsburg U of Pennsylvania (PA)
East Tennessee State U (TN)
East Texas Baptist U (TX)
Eckerd Coll (FL)
Edgewood Coll (WI)
Elizabeth City State U (NC)
Elizabethtown Coll (PA)
Elmira Coll (NY)
Elms Coll (MA)
Elon U (NC)
Emmanuel Coll (GA)
Emory & Henry Coll (VA)
Emory U (GA)
Emporia State U (KS)
Endicott Coll (MA)
Eureka Coll (IL)
Evangel U (MO)
The Evergreen State Coll (WA)
Fairfield U (CT)
Fairleigh Dickinson U, Coll at Florham (NJ)
Fairleigh Dickinson U, Metropolitan Campus (NJ)
Faulkner U (AL)
Fayetteville State U (NC)
Felician U (NJ)
Fitchburg State U (MA)
Flagler Coll (FL)
Florida Ag and Mech U (FL)
Florida Atlantic U (FL)
Florida Gulf Coast U (FL)
Florida Intl U (FL)
Florida State U (FL)
Fordham U (NY)
Fort Lewis Coll (CO)
Framingham State U (MA)
Franciscan U of Steubenville (OH)
Francis Marion U (SC)
Franklin & Marshall Coll (PA)
Franklin Coll (IN)
Franklin Pierce U (NH)
Freed-Hardeman U (TN)
Fresno Pacific U (CA)
Friends U (KS)
Frostburg State U (MD)
Furman U (SC)
Gallaudet U (DC)
Gardner-Webb U (NC)
Geneva Coll (PA)
George Fox U (OR)
Georgetown Coll (KY)
Georgetown U (DC)
The George Washington U (DC)
Georgia Coll & State U (GA)
Georgia Gwinnett Coll (GA)
Georgian Court U (NJ)
Georgia Southern U (GA)
Georgia Southwestern State U (GA)
Georgia State U (GA)
Gettysburg Coll (PA)
Gonzaga U (WA)
Gordon Coll (MA)
Gordon State Coll (GA)
Goshen Coll (IN)
Goucher Coll (MD)
Governors State U (IL)
Grace Coll (IN)
Graceland U (IA)
Grambling State U (LA)
Grand Valley State U (MI)
Grand View U (IA)
Granite State Coll (NH)
Great Basin Coll (NV)
Green Mountain Coll (VT)
Greenville Coll (IL)
Grinnell Coll (IA)
Guilford Coll (NC)
Gwynedd Mercy U (PA)
Hamilton Coll (NY)
Hamline U (MN)
Hampden-Sydney Coll (VA)
Hampshire Coll (MA)
Hampton U (VA)
Hannibal-LaGrange U (MO)
Hanover Coll (IN)
Harding U (AR)
Hardin-Simmons U (TX)
Hartwick Coll (NY)
Harvard U (MA)
Haverford Coll (PA)
Hawai`i Pacific U (HI)
Heidelberg U (OH)
Henderson State U (AR)
Hendrix Coll (AR)
High Point U (NC)
Hilbert Coll (NY)
Hillsdale Coll (MI)
Hiram Coll (OH)
Hobart and William Smith Colls (NY)
Hofstra U (NY)
Hollins U (VA)
Holy Cross Coll (IN)
Holy Family U (PA)
Holy Names U (CA)
Hood Coll (MD)
Hope Coll (MI)
Hope Intl U (CA)
Houghton Coll (NY)
Houston Baptist U (TX)
Howard Payne U (TX)
Humboldt State U (CA)
Hunter Coll of the City U of New York (NY)
Huntingdon Coll (AL)
Huntington U (IN)
Husson U (ME)
Huston-Tillotson U (TX)
Idaho State U (ID)
Illinois Coll (IL)
Illinois State U (IL)
Immaculata U (PA)
Indiana State U (IN)
Indiana U Bloomington (IN)
Indiana U East (IN)
Indiana U Kokomo (IN)
Indiana U Northwest (IN)
Indiana U of Pennsylvania (PA)
Indiana U–Purdue U Indianapolis (IN)
Indiana U South Bend (IN)
Indiana U Southeast (IN)
Inter American U of Puerto Rico, Metropolitan Campus (PR)
Inter American U of Puerto Rico, San Germán Campus (PR)
Iona Coll (NY)
Iowa State U of Science and Technology (IA)
Ithaca Coll (NY)
Jackson State U (MS)
Jacksonville State U (AL)
Jacksonville U (FL)
James Madison U (VA)
John Brown U (AR)
John Carroll U (OH)
John Jay Coll of Criminal Justice of the City U of New York (NY)
Johns Hopkins U (MD)
Johnson C. Smith U (NC)
Judson U (IL)
Juniata Coll (PA)
Kalamazoo Coll (MI)
Kansas State U (KS)
Kansas Wesleyan U (KS)
Kean U (NJ)
Keene State Coll (NH)
Kennesaw State U (GA)
Kent State U (OH)
Kent State U at Ashtabula (OH)
Kent State U at East Liverpool (OH)
Kent State U at Geauga (OH)
Kent State U at Salem (OH)
Kent State U at Stark (OH)
Kent State U at Trumbull (OH)
Kent State U at Tuscarawas (OH)
Kentucky State U (KY)
Kentucky Wesleyan Coll (KY)
Kenyon Coll (OH)
Keuka Coll (NY)
The King's Coll (NY)
King's Coll (PA)
The King's U (AB, Canada)
King U (TN)
Knox Coll (IL)
Kutztown U of Pennsylvania (PA)
Lafayette Coll (PA)
LaGrange Coll (GA)
Lake Erie Coll (OH)
Lake Forest Coll (IL)
Lamar U (TX)
Lane Coll (TN)
Langston U (OK)
La Roche Coll (PA)
La Salle U (PA)
Lasell Coll (MA)
Lawrence Technological U (MI)
Lawrence U (WI)
Lebanese American U (Lebanon)
Lebanon Valley Coll (PA)
Lees-McRae Coll (NC)
Lee U (TN)
Lehigh U (PA)
Lehman Coll of the City U of New York (NY)
Le Moyne Coll (NY)
Lenoir-Rhyne U (NC)
Lesley U (MA)
LeTourneau U (TX)
Lewis & Clark Coll (OR)
Lewis U (IL)
Liberty U (VA)
Limestone Coll (SC)
Lincoln U (MO)
Lincoln U (PA)
Lindenwood U (MO)
Lindsey Wilson Coll (KY)
Lipscomb U (TN)
Lock Haven U of Pennsylvania (PA)
Longwood U (VA)
Loras Coll (IA)
Louisiana Coll (LA)
Louisiana State U and A&M Coll (LA)
Louisiana State U at Alexandria (LA)
Louisiana Tech U (LA)
Lourdes U (OH)
Loyola Marymount U (CA)
Loyola U Chicago (IL)
Loyola U Maryland (MD)
Lubbock Christian U (TX)
Luther Coll (IA)
Lycoming Coll (PA)
Lynchburg Coll (VA)
Lyon Coll (AR)
Macalester Coll (MN)
MacMurray Coll (IL)
Madonna U (MI)
Maharishi U of Management (IA)
Malone U (OH)
Manchester U (IN)
Manhattan Coll (NY)
Manhattanville Coll (NY)
Mansfield U of Pennsylvania (PA)
Maranatha Baptist U (WI)
Marian U (IN)
Marian U (WI)
Marietta Coll (OH)
Marist Coll (NY)
Marshall U (WV)
Mary Baldwin U (VA)
Marylhurst U (OR)
Marymount Manhattan Coll (NY)
Marymount U (VA)
Maryville U of Saint Louis (MO)
Marywood U (PA)
Massachusetts Coll of Liberal Arts (MA)
Massachusetts Inst of Technology (MA)
The Master's U (CA)
McDaniel Coll (MD)
McKendree U (IL)
McMaster U (ON, Canada)
McMurry U (TX)
McNeese State U (LA)
Mercer U, Macon (GA)
Mercy Coll (NY)
Mercyhurst U (PA)
Meredith Coll (NC)
Merrimack Coll (MA)
Messiah Coll (PA)
Metropolitan State U of Denver (CO)
Miami U (OH)
Michigan State U (MI)
Michigan Technological U (MI)
MidAmerica Nazarene U (KS)
Millersville U of Pennsylvania (PA)
Milligan Coll (TN)
Millikin U (IL)
Millsaps Coll (MS)
Mills Coll (CA)
Minnesota State U Mankato (MN)
Minnesota State U Moorhead (MN)
Minot State U (ND)
Misericordia U (PA)
Mississippi State U (MS)
Mississippi Valley State U (MS)
Missouri Baptist U (MO)
Missouri State U (MO)
Missouri U of Science and Technology (MO)
Missouri Valley Coll (MO)
Missouri Western State U (MO)
Molloy Coll (NY)
Monmouth Coll (IL)
Monmouth U (NJ)
Montana State U (MT)
Montana State U Billings (MT)
Montclair State U (NJ)
Moravian Coll (PA)
Morehead State U (KY)
Morehouse Coll (GA)
Morningside Coll (IA)
Morris Coll (SC)
Mount Allison U (NB, Canada)
Mount Aloysius Coll (PA)
Mount Holyoke Coll (MA)
Mount Ida Coll (MA)
Mount Marty Coll (SD)
Mount Mary U (WI)
Mount Mercy U (IA)
Mount St. Joseph U (OH)
Mount Saint Mary Coll (NY)
Mount Saint Mary's U (CA)
Mount St. Mary's U (MD)
Mount Vernon Nazarene U (OH)
Muhlenberg Coll (PA)
Multnomah U (OR)
Murray State U (KY)
Muskingum U (OH)
National U (CA)
Nazareth Coll of Rochester (NY)
Nebraska Wesleyan U (NE)
Neumann U (PA)
Nevada State Coll (NV)
Newberry Coll (SC)
New Coll of Florida (FL)
New Jersey City U (NJ)
Newman U (KS)
New Mexico Highlands U (NM)
New Mexico State U (NM)
New York Inst of Technology (NY)
Niagara U (NY)
Nichols Coll (MA)
North Carolina Central U (NC)
North Carolina State U (NC)
North Carolina Wesleyan Coll (NC)
North Central Coll (IL)
North Dakota State U (ND)
Northeastern Illinois U (IL)
Northeastern State U (OK)
Northeastern U (MA)
Northern Arizona U (AZ)
Northern Illinois U (IL)
Northern Kentucky U (KY)
Northern State U (SD)
North Greenville U (SC)
Northland Coll (WI)
Northwest Christian U (OR)
Northwestern Coll (IA)
Northwestern Oklahoma State U (OK)
Northwestern State U of Louisiana (LA)
Northwestern U (IL)
Northwest Missouri State U (MO)
Northwest U (WA)
Nova Southeastern U (FL)
Nyack Coll (NY)
Oakland City U (IN)
Oberlin Coll (OH)
Occidental Coll (CA)
Ohio Christian U (OH)
Ohio Dominican U (OH)
The Ohio State U (OH)
The Ohio State U at Lima (OH)
The Ohio State U at Marion (OH)
The Ohio State U–Mansfield Campus (OH)
The Ohio State U–Newark Campus (OH)
Ohio U (OH)
Ohio Wesleyan U (OH)
Oklahoma Christian U (OK)
Oklahoma City U (OK)
Oklahoma State U (OK)
Old Dominion U (VA)
Olivet Nazarene U (IL)
Oral Roberts U (OK)
Oregon State U (OR)
Otterbein U (OH)
Ouachita Baptist U (AR)
Our Lady of the Lake U of San Antonio (TX)
Pace U (NY)
Pace U, Pleasantville Campus (NY)

Pacific Lutheran U (WA)
Paine Coll (GA)
Palm Beach Atlantic U (FL)
Penn State Abington (PA)
Penn State Altoona (PA)
Penn State Beaver (PA)
Penn State Berks (PA)
Penn State Brandywine (PA)
Penn State DuBois (PA)
Penn State Erie, The Behrend Coll (PA)
Penn State Fayette, The Eberly Campus (PA)
Penn State Greater Allegheny (PA)
Penn State Harrisburg (PA)
Penn State Hazleton (PA)
Penn State Lehigh Valley (PA)
Penn State Mont Alto (PA)
Penn State New Kensington (PA)
Penn State Schuylkill (PA)
Penn State Shenango (PA)
Penn State U Park (PA)
Penn State Wilkes-Barre (PA)
Penn State Worthington Scranton (PA)
Penn State York (PA)
Pepperdine U, Malibu (CA)
Philander Smith Coll (AR)
Piedmont Coll (GA)
Pine Manor Coll (MA)
Pittsburg State U (KS)
Pitzer Coll (CA)
Plymouth State U (NH)
Point Loma Nazarene U (CA)
Point Park U (PA)
Point U (GA)
Pomona Coll (CA)
Portland State U (OR)
Prairie View A&M U (TX)
Princeton U (NJ)
Principia Coll (IL)
Providence Coll (RI)
Purdue U (IN)
Purdue U Northwest (IN)
Queens Coll of the City U of New York (NY)
Quinnipiac U (CT)
Radford U (VA)
Randolph Coll (VA)
Randolph-Macon Coll (VA)
Redeemer U Coll (ON, Canada)
Reed Coll (OR)
Regent U (VA)
Regis Coll (MA)
Regis U (CO)
Rhode Island Coll (RI)
Rhodes Coll (TN)
Rice U (TX)
Ripon Coll (WI)
Roanoke Coll (VA)
Robert Morris U (PA)
Roberts Wesleyan Coll (NY)
Rockford U (IL)
Rockhurst U (MO)
Rocky Mountain Coll (MT)
Roger Williams U (RI)
Rollins Coll (FL)
Rosemont Coll (PA)
Rowan U (NJ)
Royal Military Coll of Canada (ON, Canada)
Rust Coll (MS)
Rutgers U–Camden (NJ)
Rutgers U–Newark (NJ)
Rutgers U–New Brunswick (NJ)
Sacred Heart U (CT)
The Sage Colls (NY)
Saginaw Valley State U (MI)
St. Ambrose U (IA)
St. Andrews U (NC)
Saint Anselm Coll (NH)
Saint Augustine's U (NC)
St. Bonaventure U (NY)
St. Catherine U (MN)
St. Cloud State U (MN)
St. Edward's U (TX)
Saint Francis U (PA)
St. Gregory's U, Shawnee (OK)
St. John Fisher Coll (NY)
Saint John's U (MN)
St. John's U (NY)
St. Joseph's Coll, Long Island Campus (NY)
St. Joseph's Coll, New York (NY)
Saint Joseph's U (PA)
Saint Leo U (FL)
Saint Louis U (MO)
Saint Louis U–Madrid Campus (Spain)
Saint Martin's U (WA)
Saint Mary-of-the-Woods Coll (IN)
Saint Mary's Coll (IN)
Saint Mary's Coll of California (CA)
St. Mary's Coll of Maryland (MD)
Saint Michael's Coll (VT)
St. Norbert Coll (WI)
St. Olaf Coll (MN)
Saint Peter's U (NJ)
St. Thomas Aquinas Coll (NY)
St. Thomas U (FL)
St. Thomas U (NB, Canada)
Saint Vincent Coll (PA)
Salisbury U (MD)
Salve Regina U (RI)
Samford U (AL)
Sam Houston State U (TX)
San Diego State U (CA)
San Francisco State U (CA)
Santa Clara U (CA)
Schreiner U (TX)
Scripps Coll (CA)
Seattle Pacific U (WA)
Seattle U (WA)
Seton Hill U (PA)
Sewanee: The U of the South (TN)
Shawnee State U (OH)
Shaw U (NC)
Shenandoah U (VA)
Shepherd U (WV)
Shippensburg U of Pennsylvania (PA)
Shorter U (GA)
Siena Coll (NY)
Sierra Nevada Coll (NV)
Silver Lake Coll of the Holy Family (WI)
Simmons Coll (MA)
Simon Fraser U (BC, Canada)
Simpson Coll (IA)
Simpson U (CA)
Skidmore Coll (NY)
Slippery Rock U of Pennsylvania (PA)
Smith Coll (MA)
Sonoma State U (CA)
South Carolina State U (SC)
South Dakota State U (SD)
Southeastern Louisiana U (LA)
Southeastern Oklahoma State U (OK)
Southeastern U (FL)
Southeast Missouri State U (MO)
Southern Arkansas U–Magnolia (AR)
Southern Connecticut State U (CT)
Southern Illinois U Carbondale (IL)
Southern Illinois U Edwardsville (IL)
Southern Methodist U (TX)
Southern New Hampshire U (NH)
Southern Oregon U (OR)
Southern Utah U (UT)
Southwest Baptist U (MO)
Southwestern Adventist U (TX)
Southwestern Assemblies of God U (TX)
Southwestern U (TX)
Spelman Coll (GA)
Spring Hill Coll (AL)
Stanford U (CA)
State U of New York at Fredonia (NY)
State U of New York at New Paltz (NY)
State U of New York at Oswego (NY)
State U of New York at Plattsburgh (NY)
State U of New York Coll at Cortland (NY)
State U of New York Coll at Geneseo (NY)
State U of New York Coll at Potsdam (NY)
Stephen F. Austin State U (TX)
Stephens Coll (MO)
Sterling Coll (KS)
Stevens Inst of Technology (NJ)
Stevenson U (MD)
Stockton U (NJ)
Stonehill Coll (MA)
Stony Brook U, State U of New York (NY)
Suffolk U (MA)
Susquehanna U (PA)
Swarthmore Coll (PA)
Sweet Briar Coll (VA)
Syracuse U (NY)
Tabor Coll (KS)
Tarleton State U (TX)
Taylor U (IN)
Temple U (PA)
Tennessee State U (TN)
Tennessee Wesleyan U (TN)
Texas A&M Intl U (TX)
Texas A&M U (TX)
Texas A&M U–Central Texas (TX)
Texas A&M U–Commerce (TX)
Texas A&M U–Corpus Christi (TX)
Texas A&M U–Kingsville (TX)
Texas Christian U (TX)
Texas Coll (TX)
Texas Lutheran U (TX)
Texas State U (TX)
Texas Tech U (TX)
Texas Wesleyan U (TX)
Texas Woman's U (TX)
Thomas More Coll (KY)
Thomas U (GA)
Tiffin U (OH)
Toccoa Falls Coll (GA)
Towson U (MD)
Transylvania U (KY)
Trent U (ON, Canada)
Trevecca Nazarene U (TN)
Trinity Christian Coll (IL)
Trinity U (TX)
Troy U (AL)
Truett McConnell U (GA)
Truman State U (MO)
Tufts U (MA)
Tulane U (LA)
Tusculum Coll (TN)
Union Coll (KY)
Union Coll (NE)
Union Coll (NY)
Union U (TN)
United States Air Force Acad (CO)
United States Military Acad (NY)
Université de Montréal (QC, Canada)
Université de Sherbrooke (QC, Canada)
U at Albany, State U of New York (NY)
U at Buffalo, the State U of New York (NY)
The U of Akron (OH)
The U of Alabama (AL)
The U of Alabama at Birmingham (AL)
The U of Alabama in Huntsville (AL)
U of Alaska Fairbanks (AK)
The U of Arizona (AZ)
U of Arkansas (AR)
U of Bridgeport (CT)
U of California, Davis (CA)
U of California, Irvine (CA)
U of California, Los Angeles (CA)
U of California, Riverside (CA)
U of California, San Diego (CA)
U of California, Santa Barbara (CA)
U of Central Arkansas (AR)
U of Central Florida (FL)
U of Central Missouri (MO)
U of Charleston (WV)
U of Chicago (IL)
U of Cincinnati (OH)
U of Colorado Boulder (CO)
U of Colorado Colorado Springs (CO)
U of Colorado Denver (CO)
U of Dayton (OH)
U of Delaware (DE)
U of Denver (CO)
U of Detroit Mercy (MI)
U of Dubuque (IA)
U of Evansville (IN)
U of Florida (FL)
U of Georgia (GA)
U of Great Falls (MT)
U of Guelph (ON, Canada)
U of Hartford (CT)
U of Hawaii at Manoa (HI)
U of Houston (TX)
U of Houston–Clear Lake (TX)
U of Houston–Downtown (TX)
U of Idaho (ID)
U of Illinois at Chicago (IL)
U of Illinois at Springfield (IL)
U of Indianapolis (IN)
U of Jamestown (ND)
The U of Kansas (KS)
U of Kentucky (KY)
U of King's Coll (NS, Canada)
U of La Verne (CA)
U of Lethbridge (AB, Canada)
U of Louisiana at Monroe (LA)
U of Louisville (KY)
U of Maine (ME)
U of Maine at Farmington (ME)
U of Maine at Fort Kent (ME)
U of Maine at Presque Isle (ME)
U of Mary Hardin-Baylor (TX)
U of Maryland, Baltimore County (MD)
U of Maryland, Coll Park (MD)
U of Maryland U Coll (MD)
U of Mary Washington (VA)
U of Massachusetts Amherst (MA)
U of Massachusetts Boston (MA)
U of Massachusetts Dartmouth (MA)
U of Massachusetts Lowell (MA)
U of Miami (FL)
U of Michigan (MI)
U of Michigan–Dearborn (MI)
U of Michigan–Flint (MI)
U of Minnesota, Duluth (MN)
U of Minnesota, Morris (MN)
U of Minnesota, Twin Cities Campus (MN)
U of Missouri–Kansas City (MO)
U of Missouri–St. Louis (MO)
U of Mobile (AL)
The U of Montana Western (MT)
U of Montevallo (AL)
U of Mount Union (OH)
U of Nebraska at Kearney (NE)
U of Nevada, Las Vegas (NV)
U of Nevada, Reno (NV)
U of New England (ME)
U of New Hampshire (NH)
U of New Hampshire at Manchester (NH)
U of New Haven (CT)
U of New Orleans (LA)
U of North Alabama (AL)
U of North Carolina at Asheville (NC)
The U of North Carolina at Chapel Hill (NC)
The U of North Carolina at Charlotte (NC)
The U of North Carolina at Greensboro (NC)
The U of North Carolina at Pembroke (NC)
The U of North Carolina Wilmington (NC)
U of North Dakota (ND)
U of Northern Colorado (CO)
U of Northern Iowa (IA)
U of North Florida (FL)
U of North Georgia (GA)
U of North Texas (TX)
U of Notre Dame (IN)
U of Oklahoma (OK)
U of Oregon (OR)
U of Pennsylvania (PA)
U of Pikeville (KY)
U of Pittsburgh at Bradford (PA)
U of Pittsburgh at Greensburg (PA)
U of Pittsburgh at Johnstown (PA)
U of Puget Sound (WA)
U of Regina (SK, Canada)
U of Rhode Island (RI)
U of Richmond (VA)
U of Rochester (NY)
U of St. Francis (IL)
U of Saint Francis (IN)
U of Saint Joseph (CT)
U of Saint Mary (KS)
U of St. Thomas (MN)
U of St. Thomas (TX)
U of San Diego (CA)
U of San Francisco (CA)
U of Saskatchewan (SK, Canada)
U of Science and Arts of Oklahoma (OK)
The U of Scranton (PA)
U of South Alabama (AL)
U of South Carolina (SC)
U of South Carolina Aiken (SC)
The U of South Dakota (SD)
U of Southern California (CA)
U of Southern Indiana (IN)
U of Southern Maine (ME)
U of Southern Mississippi (MS)
U of South Florida (FL)
U of South Florida, St. Petersburg (FL)
U of South Florida Sarasota-Manatee (FL)
The U of Tampa (FL)
The U of Tennessee (TN)
The U of Tennessee at Chattanooga (TN)
The U of Tennessee at Martin (TN)
The U of Texas at Austin (TX)
The U of Texas at El Paso (TX)
The U of Texas at San Antonio (TX)
The U of Texas of the Permian Basin (TX)
The U of Texas Rio Grande Valley (TX)
U of the Cumberlands (KY)
U of the Fraser Valley (BC, Canada)
U of the Incarnate Word (TX)
U of the Pacific (CA)
U of the Southwest (NM)
U of the Virgin Islands (VI)
U of the West (CA)
The U of Toledo (OH)
U of Toronto (ON, Canada)
The U of Tulsa (OK)
U of Utah (UT)
U of Valley Forge (PA)
U of Vermont (VT)
U of Virginia (VA)
The U of Virginia's Coll at Wise (VA)
U of Washington (WA)
U of Waterloo (ON, Canada)
The U of West Alabama (AL)
U of West Georgia (GA)
U of Windsor (ON, Canada)
U of Wisconsin–Eau Claire (WI)
U of Wisconsin–Green Bay (WI)
U of Wisconsin–La Crosse (WI)
U of Wisconsin–Madison (WI)
U of Wisconsin–Milwaukee (WI)
U of Wisconsin–Parkside (WI)
U of Wisconsin–Platteville (WI)
U of Wisconsin–Stevens Point (WI)
U of Wisconsin–Superior (WI)
U of Wisconsin–Whitewater (WI)
Upper Iowa U (IA)
Ursinus Coll (PA)
Utah State U (UT)
Utah Valley U (UT)
Utica Coll (NY)
Valdosta State U (GA)
Valley City State U (ND)
Valparaiso U (IN)
Vanderbilt U (TN)
Vassar Coll (NY)
Villanova U (PA)
Virginia Commonwealth U (VA)
Virginia Military Inst (VA)
Virginia Polytechnic Inst and State U (VA)
Virginia State U (VA)
Virginia Union U (VA)
Virginia Wesleyan Coll (VA)
Viterbo U (WI)
Wabash Coll (IN)
Wagner Coll (NY)
Wake Forest U (NC)
Waldorf U (IA)
Walla Walla U (WA)
Walsh U (OH)
Wartburg Coll (IA)
Washburn U (KS)
Washington & Jefferson Coll (PA)
Washington and Lee U (VA)
Washington Coll (MD)
Washington State U (WA)
Washington State U–Tri-Cities (WA)
Washington State U–Vancouver (WA)
Washington U in St. Louis (MO)
Wayland Baptist U (TX)
Waynesburg U (PA)
Wayne State Coll (NE)
Wayne State U (MI)
Weber State U (UT)
Webster U (MO)
Welch Coll (TN)
Wells Coll (NY)
Wesleyan Coll (GA)
Wesleyan U (CT)

West Chester U of Pennsylvania (PA)
Western Carolina U (NC)
Western Connecticut State U (CT)
Western Illinois U (IL)
Western Kentucky U (KY)
Western Michigan U (MI)
Western New England U (MA)
Western Oregon U (OR)
Western State Colorado U (CO)
Western Washington U (WA)
Westfield State U (MA)
Westminster Coll (PA)
Westminster Coll (UT)
Westmont Coll (CA)
West Texas A&M U (TX)
West Virginia State U (WV)
West Virginia U (WV)
West Virginia Wesleyan Coll (WV)
Wheaton Coll (IL)
Wheaton Coll (MA)
Wheeling Jesuit U (WV)
Whitman Coll (WA)
Whittier Coll (CA)
Whitworth U (WA)
Wichita State U (KS)
Widener U (PA)
Wilkes U (PA)
Willamette U (OR)
William Jewell Coll (MO)
William Paterson U of New Jersey (NJ)
William Peace U (NC)
William Penn U (IA)
Williams Baptist Coll (AR)
Williams Coll (MA)
William Woods U (MO)
Wilson Coll (PA)
Wingate U (NC)
Winona State U (MN)
Winthrop U (SC)
Wittenberg U (OH)
Wofford Coll (SC)
Worcester State U (MA)
Wright State U (OH)
Wright State U–Lake Campus (OH)
Xavier U of Louisiana (LA)
York Coll of Pennsylvania (PA)
York Coll of the City U of New York (NY)
Youngstown State U (OH)

ENGLISH AS A SECOND/ FOREIGN LANGUAGE (TEACHING)
American U (DC)
Augsburg Coll (MN)
Bayamón Central U (PR)
Bethel Coll (IN)
Bethel U (MN)
Brigham Young U (UT)
California State U, Stanislaus (CA)
Calvin Coll (MI)
Carroll Coll (MT)
The Catholic U of America (DC)
Concordia U (QC, Canada)
Concordia U, Nebraska (NE)
Concordia U, St. Paul (MN)
Concordia U Wisconsin (WI)
Davis Coll (NY)
Doane U (NE)
Eastern Washington U (WA)
Gardner-Webb U (NC)
Goshen Coll (IN)
Granite State Coll (NH)
Hawai`i Pacific U (HI)
Houghton Coll (NY)
Huntington U (IN)
Inter American U of Puerto Rico, Aguadilla Campus (PR)
Inter American U of Puerto Rico, Barranquitas Campus (PR)
Inter American U of Puerto Rico, Fajardo Campus (PR)
Inter American U of Puerto Rico, Guayama Campus (PR)
Inter American U of Puerto Rico, Metropolitan Campus (PR)
Inter American U of Puerto Rico, Ponce Campus (PR)
Inter American U of Puerto Rico, San Germán Campus (PR)
Kent State U (OH)
Lee U (TN)
Le Moyne Coll (NY)
Liberty U (VA)
Minnesota State U Moorhead (MN)
Molloy Coll (NY)
Multnomah U (OR)
Nevada State Coll (NV)
Niagara U (NY)
Northwest U (WA)
Nyack Coll (NY)
Oklahoma Christian U (OK)
Oklahoma City U (OK)
Queens Coll of the City U of New York (NY)
Roberts Wesleyan Coll (NY)
Saint Joseph's U (PA)
Salisbury U (MD)
Simmons Coll (MA)
Tarleton State U (TX)
Union U (TN)
The U of Findlay (OH)
U of Georgia (GA)
U of Hawaii at Manoa (HI)
U of Northern Iowa (IA)
The U of Texas at San Antonio (TX)
Winona State U (MN)

ENGLISH LANGUAGE AND LITERATURE RELATED
Binghamton U, State U of New York (NY)
Columbia U, School of General Studies (NY)
Concordia Coll–New York (NY)
Dakota State U (SD)
Doane U (NE)
Drexel U (PA)
Eastern Nazarene Coll (MA)
Eastern U (PA)
Emmanuel Coll (MA)
Fort Lewis Coll (CO)
Harvard U (MA)
Hofstra U (NY)
Loyola U New Orleans (LA)
Middlebury Coll (VT)
Milligan Coll (TN)
Ohio U (OH)
Patrick Henry Coll (VA)
Rowan U (NJ)
Saint Leo U (FL)
Saint Mary's Coll of California (CA)
Saint Mary's U of Minnesota (MN)
Southeastern U (FL)
State U of New York Empire State Coll (NY)
U of Great Falls (MT)
U of Michigan (MI)
U of Pennsylvania (PA)
Viterbo U (WI)
Washington U in St. Louis (MO)
Webster U (MO)
Wesleyan U (CT)
Western Kentucky U (KY)

ENGLISH/LANGUAGE ARTS TEACHER EDUCATION
Abilene Christian U (TX)
Adams State U (CO)
Albion Coll (MI)
Alice Lloyd Coll (KY)
Alvernia U (PA)
Alverno Coll (WI)
Anderson U (IN)
Anderson U (SC)
Appalachian State U (NC)
Aquinas Coll (MI)
Aquinas Coll (TN)
Arizona Christian U (AZ)
Arkansas Tech U (AR)
Arlington Baptist Coll (TX)
Armstrong State U (GA)
Auburn U (AL)
Augustana Coll (IL)
Averett U (VA)
The Baptist Coll of Florida (FL)
Barry U (FL)
Bayamón Central U (PR)
Baylor U (TX)
Bennett Coll (NC)
Bethel Coll (IN)
Bethel U (MN)
Bethune-Cookman U (FL)
Bishop's U (QC, Canada)
Blackburn Coll (IL)
Bluefield Coll (VA)
Blue Mountain Coll (MS)
Boise State U (ID)
Boston U (MA)
Bowling Green State U (OH)
Bradley U (IL)
Brewton-Parker Coll (GA)
Bridgewater State U (MA)
Brigham Young U–Idaho (ID)
Brooklyn Coll of the City U of New York (NY)
Bryan Coll (TN)
Buena Vista U (IA)
Buffalo State Coll, State U of New York (NY)
Cabrini U (PA)
Cairn U (PA)
California State U, Long Beach (CA)
Cameron U (OK)
Campbellsville U (KY)
Canisius Coll (NY)
Capital U (OH)
Carroll Coll (MT)
The Catholic U of America (DC)
Cedarville U (OH)
Central Michigan U (MI)
Central Washington U (WA)
Charleston Southern U (SC)
The Coll of New Jersey (NJ)
Coll of Saint Mary (NE)
The Coll of Saint Rose (NY)
Coll of Staten Island of the City U of New York (NY)
Coll of the Ozarks (MO)
Colorado Christian U (CO)
Colorado State U (CO)
Columbus State U (GA)
Concordia U Chicago (IL)
Corban U (OR)
Cornerstone U (MI)
Culver-Stockton Coll (MO)
Daemen Coll (NY)
Dakota State U (SD)
Dallas Baptist U (TX)
Dickinson State U (ND)
Dixie State U (UT)
Dominican Coll (NY)
Duquesne U (PA)
East Carolina U (NC)
East Central U (OK)
Eastern Michigan U (MI)
Eastern Washington U (WA)
East Texas Baptist U (TX)
Edgewood Coll (WI)
Elizabeth City State U (NC)
Elmira Coll (NY)
Emmanuel Coll (GA)
Emory & Henry Coll (VA)
Faith Baptist Bible Coll and Theological Sem (IA)
Faulkner U (AL)
Ferris State U (MI)
Fitchburg State U (MA)
Flagler Coll (FL)
Florida Ag and Mech U (FL)
Florida Atlantic U (FL)
Florida Southern Coll (FL)
Florida SouthWestern State Coll (FL)
Fort Lewis Coll (CO)
Franklin Coll (IN)
Friends U (KS)
Gardner-Webb U (NC)
Goddard Coll (VT)
Gordon State Coll (GA)
Goshen Coll (IN)
Grace Coll (IN)
Grambling State U (LA)
Grand Valley State U (MI)
Grand View U (IA)
Granite State Coll (NH)
Green Mountain Coll (VT)
Greenville Coll (IL)
Grove City Coll (PA)
Gwynedd Mercy U (PA)
Hannibal-LaGrange U (MO)
Harding U (AR)
Hardin-Simmons U (TX)
Hiram Coll (OH)
Hobe Sound Bible Coll (FL)
Hofstra U (NY)
Holy Family U (PA)
Hope Coll (MI)
Houston Baptist U (TX)
Howard Payne U (TX)
Huntingdon Coll (AL)
Huntington U (IN)
Husson U (ME)
Indiana U Bloomington (IN)
Indiana U Northwest (IN)
Indiana U–Purdue U Indianapolis (IN)
Indiana U South Bend (IN)
Inter American U of Puerto Rico, San Germán Campus (PR)
Iona Coll (NY)
Ithaca Coll (NY)
John Brown U (AR)
Juniata Coll (PA)
Kansas Wesleyan U (KS)
Kennesaw State U (GA)
Keuka Coll (NY)
King U (TN)
Lee U (TN)
Le Moyne Coll (NY)
LeTourneau U (TX)
Limestone Coll (SC)
Lincoln U (MO)
Lipscomb U (TN)
Louisiana Coll (LA)
Louisiana Tech U (LA)
Madonna U (MI)
Malone U (OH)
Manchester U (IN)
Manhattanville Coll (NY)
Maranatha Baptist U (WI)
Marian U (WI)
Marist Coll (NY)
Marywood U (PA)
McMurry U (TX)
Mercyhurst U (PA)
Merrimack Coll (MA)
Messiah Coll (PA)
Miami U (OH)
MidAmerica Nazarene U (KS)
Millikin U (IL)
Minnesota State U Moorhead (MN)
Minot State U (ND)
Misericordia U (PA)
Missouri State U (MO)
Missouri Western State U (MO)
Montana State U Billings (MT)
Montana State U–Northern (MT)
Morningside Coll (IA)
Morris Coll (SC)
Mount Marty Coll (SD)
Mount Mary U (WI)
Mount Vernon Nazarene U (OH)
National U (CA)
Nazareth Coll of Rochester (NY)
Nebraska Wesleyan U (NE)
Nevada State Coll (NV)
Niagara U (NY)
North Dakota State U (ND)
Northeastern State U (OK)
North Greenville U (SC)
Northwestern Coll (IA)
Northwestern Oklahoma State U (OK)
Northwest Missouri State U (MO)
Northwest U (WA)
Nova Southeastern U (FL)
Nyack Coll (NY)
Oakland City U (IN)
Ohio Dominican U (OH)
The Ohio State U at Lima (OH)
The Ohio State U at Marion (OH)
The Ohio State U–Mansfield Campus (OH)
The Ohio State U–Newark Campus (OH)
Oklahoma Baptist U (OK)
Oklahoma Christian U (OK)
Oklahoma City U (OK)
Oral Roberts U (OK)
Pace U (NY)
Pace U, Pleasantville Campus (NY)
Palm Beach Atlantic U (FL)
Pepperdine U, Malibu (CA)
Piedmont Coll (GA)
Piedmont Intl U (NC)
Pittsburg State U (KS)
Point Park U (PA)
Providence Coll (RI)
Purdue U (IN)
Queens Coll of the City U of New York (NY)
Rhode Island Coll (RI)
Roberts Wesleyan Coll (NY)
Rocky Mountain Coll (MT)
Roger Williams U (RI)
Rust Coll (MS)
Saginaw Valley State U (MI)
St. Ambrose U (IA)
St. Catherine U (MN)
St. Edward's U (TX)
Saint Francis U (PA)
St. Gregory's U, Shawnee (OK)
St. John Fisher Coll (NY)
St. John's U (NY)
St. Joseph's Coll, Long Island Campus (NY)
St. Joseph's Coll, New York (NY)
Saint Mary's U of Minnesota (MN)
Samford U (AL)
Schreiner U (TX)
Seattle Pacific U (WA)
Seton Hill U (PA)
Shaw U (NC)
Simpson U (CA)
Slippery Rock U of Pennsylvania (PA)
Southeastern Louisiana U (LA)
Southeastern Oklahoma State U (OK)
Southeastern U (FL)
Southeast Missouri State U (MO)
Southern New Hampshire U (NH)
Southern Utah U (UT)
Southwest Baptist U (MO)
Southwestern Adventist U (TX)
Southwestern Assemblies of God U (TX)
Southwestern Coll (KS)
Spring Hill Coll (AL)
State U of New York at New Paltz (NY)
State U of New York at Plattsburgh (NY)
State U of New York Coll at Potsdam (NY)
Syracuse U (NY)
Taylor U (IN)
Temple U (PA)
Texas Christian U (TX)
Texas Wesleyan U (TX)
Tiffin U (OH)
Toccoa Falls Coll (GA)
Trevecca Nazarene U (TN)
Trinity Christian Coll (IL)
Union Coll (KY)
Union Coll (NE)
The U of Akron (OH)
U of Central Florida (FL)
U of Delaware (DE)
U of Dubuque (IA)
U of Evansville (IN)
The U of Findlay (OH)
U of Georgia (GA)
U of Great Falls (MT)
U of Idaho (ID)
U of Illinois at Chicago (IL)
U of Indianapolis (IN)
U of Jamestown (ND)
U of Lethbridge (AB, Canada)
U of Louisiana at Monroe (LA)
U of Maine (ME)
U of Maine at Farmington (ME)
U of Mary Hardin-Baylor (TX)
U of Michigan–Flint (MI)
U of Mobile (AL)
The U of Montana Western (MT)
The U of North Carolina at Greensboro (NC)
The U of North Carolina at Pembroke (NC)
U of Oklahoma (OK)
U of Pittsburgh at Johnstown (PA)
U of Regina (SK, Canada)
U of St. Francis (IL)
U of St. Thomas (MN)
The U of South Dakota (SD)
U of South Florida (FL)
The U of Tennessee at Chattanooga (TN)
The U of Tennessee at Martin (TN)
U of Vermont (VT)
U of Windsor (ON, Canada)
U of Wisconsin–Superior (WI)
U of Wisconsin–Whitewater (WI)
Utah Valley U (UT)
Utica Coll (NY)
Valley City State U (ND)
Valparaiso U (IN)
Virginia Union U (VA)
Viterbo U (WI)
Washburn U (KS)
Washington U in St. Louis (MO)
Wayland Baptist U (TX)
Waynesburg U (PA)
Wayne State Coll (NE)
Weber State U (UT)
Webster U (MO)
Welch Coll (TN)
Western Carolina U (NC)
Western Michigan U (MI)
Western State Colorado U (CO)

Western Washington U (WA)
Westfield State U (MA)
Westmont Coll (CA)
West Virginia Wesleyan Coll (WV)
Widener U (PA)
William Woods U (MO)
Wilmington U (DE)
Wingate U (NC)
Winona State U (MN)
York Coll of Pennsylvania (PA)
Youngstown State U (OH)

ENGLISH LITERATURE (BRITISH AND COMMONWEALTH)
Ambrose U (AB, Canada)
American U of Beirut (Lebanon)
Bennington Coll (VT)
Concordia U (QC, Canada)
Gannon U (PA)
Hunter Coll of the City U of New York (NY)
Marian U (WI)
Pace U (NY)
Saint Mary's Coll (IN)
Université de Montréal (QC, Canada)
U of Pittsburgh (PA)
Washington U in St. Louis (MO)
Whittier Coll (CA)

ENTOMOLOGY
Cornell U (NY)
Iowa State U of Science and Technology (IA)
Michigan State U (MI)
The Ohio State U (OH)
Oklahoma State U (OK)
Purdue U (IN)
Texas A&M U (TX)
U of California, Davis (CA)
U of California, Riverside (CA)
U of Delaware (DE)
U of Florida (FL)
U of Georgia (GA)
U of Wisconsin–Madison (WI)
Utah State U (UT)
Washington State U (WA)

ENTREPRENEURIAL AND SMALL BUSINESS RELATED
Fairleigh Dickinson U, Coll at Florham (NJ)
Fairleigh Dickinson U, Metropolitan Campus (NJ)
Fashion Inst of Technology (NY)
Florida State U (FL)
Lipscomb U (TN)
Loyola U Chicago (IL)
New York Inst of Technology (NY)
Penn State U Park (PA)
State U of New York at Plattsburgh (NY)
U of St. Thomas (MN)

ENTREPRENEURSHIP
American Public U System (WV)
The American U of Paris (France)
Anderson U (IN)
Arizona State U at the Tempe campus (AZ)
Ashland U (OH)
Auburn U at Montgomery (AL)
Avila U (MO)
Baldwin Wallace U (OH)
Ball State U (IN)
Baylor U (TX)
Bay Path U (MA)
Binghamton U, State U of New York (NY)
Bradley U (IL)
Brigham Young U (UT)
Bryant U (RI)
Buena Vista U (IA)
Butler U (IN)
California Baptist U (CA)
California State U, Dominguez Hills (CA)
California State U, Fullerton (CA)
Canisius Coll (NY)
Central Michigan U (MI)
Clarkson U (NY)
Cogswell Polytechnical Coll (CA)
Coll of the Atlantic (ME)
Dalhousie U (NS, Canada)
Dallas Baptist U (TX)
Drexel U (PA)
Duquesne U (PA)
East Central U (OK)
Eastern Michigan U (MI)
Eastern U (PA)
Elon U (NC)
Endicott Coll (MA)
Fairleigh Dickinson U, Coll at Florham (NJ)
Gannon U (PA)
George Fox U (OR)
Governors State U (IL)
Grace Coll (IN)
Grove City Coll (PA)
Hampshire Coll (MA)
HEC Montreal (QC, Canada)
High Point U (NC)
Hofstra U (NY)
Hult Intl Business School (United Kingdom)
Husson U (ME)
Inter American U of Puerto Rico, Aguadilla Campus (PR)
Inter American U of Puerto Rico, Barranquitas Campus (PR)
Inter American U of Puerto Rico, Bayamón Campus (PR)
Inter American U of Puerto Rico, Metropolitan Campus (PR)
Inter American U of Puerto Rico, Ponce Campus (PR)
Inter American U of Puerto Rico, San Germán Campus (PR)
Iowa State U of Science and Technology (IA)
Jackson State U (MS)
Jacksonville U (FL)
John Paul the Great Catholic U (CA)
Juniata Coll (PA)
Kansas State U (KS)
Kennesaw State U (GA)
Kent State U (OH)
Lake Erie Coll (OH)
Lamar U (TX)
Lasell Coll (MA)
Lenoir-Rhyne U (NC)
Lincoln Coll (IL)
Lincoln Coll–Normal (IL)
Lindenwood U (MO)
Lipscomb U (TN)
Loyola Marymount U (CA)
Lynn U (FL)
Marymount Manhattan Coll (NY)
Menlo Coll (CA)
Mercy Coll (NY)
Millikin U (IL)
Missouri State U (MO)
Morrisville State Coll (NY)
Northeastern State U (OK)
Northeastern U (MA)
Northern Kentucky U (KY)
Northland Coll (WI)
Northwood U, Michigan Campus (MI)
Oklahoma State U (OK)
Pace U (NY)
Pace U, Pleasantville Campus (NY)
Point Loma Nazarene U (CA)
Quinnipiac U (CT)
Rollins Coll (FL)
Rowan U (NJ)
Royal Roads U (BC, Canada)
St. Edward's U (TX)
Saint Louis U (MO)
Saint Louis U–Madrid Campus (Spain)
Saint Mary's U of Minnesota (MN)
Samford U (AL)
Sam Houston State U (TX)
Seton Hill U (PA)
Shenandoah U (VA)
Shippensburg U of Pennsylvania (PA)
Sierra Nevada Coll (NV)
South Dakota State U (SD)
Suffolk U (MA)
Syracuse U (NY)
Temple U (PA)
Texas Christian U (TX)
Trine U (IN)
Trinity Christian Coll (IL)
The U of Arizona (AZ)
U of Central Arkansas (AR)
U of Dayton (OH)
U of Hartford (CT)
U of Hawaii at Manoa (HI)
U of Houston (TX)
U of Illinois at Chicago (IL)
U of Indianapolis (IN)
U of Miami (FL)
U of Michigan–Flint (MI)
U of Minnesota, Crookston (MN)
U of Minnesota, Duluth (MN)
U of Nevada, Las Vegas (NV)
U of New England (ME)
The U of North Carolina at Greensboro (NC)
The U of North Carolina at Pembroke (NC)
U of North Dakota (ND)
U of North Texas (TX)
U of Pittsburgh at Bradford (PA)
U of Regina (SK, Canada)
U of St. Francis (IL)
U of St. Thomas (MN)
U of San Francisco (CA)
The U of South Dakota (SD)
U of South Florida, St. Petersburg (FL)
The U of Tampa (FL)
The U of Texas at San Antonio (TX)
The U of Texas Rio Grande Valley (TX)
The U of Toledo (OH)
U of Utah (UT)
U of Vermont (VT)
U of Washington (WA)
U of Wisconsin–Whitewater (WI)
Virginia Union U (VA)
Washington State U (WA)
Washington U in St. Louis (MO)
Waynesburg U (PA)
Western Carolina U (NC)
Western Kentucky U (KY)
Western Michigan U (MI)
Western New England U (MA)
Western State Colorado U (CO)
West Virginia U (WV)
Wichita State U (KS)
Wilkes U (PA)
Wittenberg U (OH)
York Coll of Pennsylvania (PA)

ENVIRONMENTAL BIOLOGY
Arcadia U (PA)
Barnard Coll (NY)
Beloit Coll (WI)
Bennington Coll (VT)
Blackburn Coll (IL)
Boston U (MA)
Bridgewater State U (MA)
California State Polytechnic U, Pomona (CA)
Cazenovia Coll (NY)
Cedar Crest Coll (PA)
Central Methodist U (MO)
Central Washington U (WA)
Chowan U (NC)
Christopher Newport U (VA)
Colby Coll (ME)
Colgate U (NY)
Coll of the Atlantic (ME)
Columbia U (NY)
Columbia U, School of General Studies (NY)
Cornerstone U (MI)
East Stroudsburg U of Pennsylvania (PA)
Elizabethtown Coll (PA)
Ferris State U (MI)
Fitchburg State U (MA)
Fort Lewis Coll (CO)
Franklin Pierce U (NH)
Friends U (KS)
Grace Coll (IN)
Greenville Coll (IL)
Heidelberg U (OH)
Houghton Coll (NY)
Humboldt State U (CA)
Inter American U of Puerto Rico, Bayamón Campus (PR)
Iona Coll (NY)
Jacksonville State U (AL)
Liberty U (VA)
Lindenwood U (MO)
Manchester U (IN)
The Master's U (CA)
McDaniel Coll (MD)
Michigan State U (MI)
Minnesota State U Mankato (MN)
Monmouth U (NJ)
Northern Arizona U (AZ)
Northwestern Coll (IA)
Otterbein U (OH)
Plymouth State U (NH)
Roberts Wesleyan Coll (NY)
St. Cloud State U (MN)
Saint Mary's U of Minnesota (MN)
Sewanee: The U of the South (TN)
State U of New York Coll at Cortland (NY)
State U of New York Coll of Environmental Science and Forestry (NY)
Texas A&M U (TX)
Tulane U (LA)
Unity Coll (ME)
U of Dayton (OH)
U of Guelph (ON, Canada)
U of La Verne (CA)
U of Mount Union (OH)
U of Pittsburgh at Johnstown (PA)
U of Regina (SK, Canada)
U of Saskatchewan (SK, Canada)
The U of Tennessee at Martin (TN)
U of Windsor (ON, Canada)
Viterbo U (WI)
Washington U in St. Louis (MO)
Western State Colorado U (CO)
Wingate U (NC)

ENVIRONMENTAL CHEMISTRY
Beloit Coll (WI)
Central Washington U (WA)
Colby Coll (ME)
Columbia U, School of General Studies (NY)
Lawrence Technological U (MI)
Rhode Island Coll (RI)
Roberts Wesleyan Coll (NY)
St. Edward's U (TX)
U of Georgia (GA)

ENVIRONMENTAL DESIGN/ ARCHITECTURE
Arizona State U at the Tempe campus (AZ)
Auburn U (AL)
Ball State U (IN)
Bennington Coll (VT)
Boston Architectural Coll (MA)
Bowling Green State U (OH)
Coll of the Atlantic (ME)
Cornell U (NY)
Dalhousie U (NS, Canada)
Delaware Valley U (PA)
Florida Atlantic U (FL)
Green Mountain Coll (VT)
Marywood U (PA)
Montana State U (MT)
North Carolina State U (NC)
North Dakota State U (ND)
Rutgers U–New Brunswick (NJ)
Stony Brook U, State U of New York (NY)
U at Buffalo, the State U of New York (NY)
U of Colorado Boulder (CO)
U of Georgia (GA)
U of Hawaii at Manoa (HI)
U of Houston (TX)
U of Massachusetts Amherst (MA)
U of Minnesota, Twin Cities Campus (MN)
U of Missouri–Kansas City (MO)
U of Oklahoma (OK)
U of Pennsylvania (PA)
The U of Texas at Austin (TX)

ENVIRONMENTAL EDUCATION
Coll of the Atlantic (ME)
Juniata Coll (PA)
Prescott Coll (AZ)
Sonoma State U (CA)

ENVIRONMENTAL ENGINEERING TECHNOLOGY
Bowling Green State U (OH)
California State U, Long Beach (CA)
City Coll of the City U of New York (NY)
Kennesaw State U (GA)
North Carolina State U (NC)
Shawnee State U (OH)
Tufts U (MA)
United States Military Acad (NY)
The U of Findlay (OH)
U of Guelph (ON, Canada)
U of Wisconsin–Green Bay (WI)
U of Wisconsin–Whitewater (WI)

ENVIRONMENTAL/ ENVIRONMENTAL HEALTH ENGINEERING
Arizona State U at the Polytechnic campus (AZ)
Bucknell U (PA)
California Inst of Technology (CA)
California Polytechnic State U, San Luis Obispo (CA)
Central State U (OH)
Clarkson U (NY)
Clemson U (SC)
Colorado School of Mines (CO)
Colorado State U (CO)
Columbia U (NY)
Cornell U (NY)
Dalhousie U (NS, Canada)
Drexel U (PA)
East Central U (OK)
Elon U (NC)
Florida Gulf Coast U (FL)
Florida Intl U (FL)
Gannon U (PA)
The George Washington U (DC)
Georgia Inst of Technology (GA)
Humboldt State U (CA)
Johns Hopkins U (MD)
Kennesaw State U (GA)
Lafayette Coll (PA)
Lehigh U (PA)
Louisiana State U and A&M Coll (LA)
Loyola U Chicago (IL)
Manhattan Coll (NY)
Massachusetts Inst of Technology (MA)
Michigan Technological U (MI)
Missouri U of Science and Technology (MO)
Montana Tech of The U of Montana (MT)
New Mexico Inst of Mining and Technology (NM)
North Carolina State U (NC)
Northern Arizona U (AZ)
Northwestern U (IL)
The Ohio State U (OH)
Oral Roberts U (OK)
Oregon State U (OR)
Penn State Abington (PA)
Penn State Altoona (PA)
Penn State Beaver (PA)
Penn State Berks (PA)
Penn State Brandywine (PA)
Penn State DuBois (PA)
Penn State Erie, The Behrend Coll (PA)
Penn State Fayette, The Eberly Campus (PA)
Penn State Greater Allegheny (PA)
Penn State Harrisburg (PA)
Penn State Hazleton (PA)
Penn State Lehigh Valley (PA)
Penn State Mont Alto (PA)
Penn State New Kensington (PA)
Penn State Schuylkill (PA)
Penn State Shenango (PA)
Penn State U Park (PA)
Penn State Wilkes-Barre (PA)
Penn State Worthington Scranton (PA)
Penn State York (PA)
Polytechnic U of Puerto Rico (PR)
Purdue U (IN)
Rensselaer Polytechnic Inst (NY)
Rice U (TX)
Roger Williams U (RI)
San Diego State U (CA)
Seattle U (WA)
South Dakota School of Mines and Technology (SD)
Southern Methodist U (TX)
Stanford U (CA)
State U of New York Coll of Environmental Science and Forestry (NY)
Stevens Inst of Technology (NJ)
Suffolk U (MA)
Syracuse U (NY)
Tarleton State U (TX)
Taylor U (IN)
Temple U (PA)
Texas A&M U–Kingsville (TX)
Texas Tech U (TX)
Tufts U (MA)
Tulane U (LA)
United States Air Force Acad (CO)

United States Military Acad (NY)
U at Buffalo, the State U of New York (NY)
The U of Alabama (AL)
U of California, Irvine (CA)
U of California, Riverside (CA)
U of Central Florida (FL)
U of Cincinnati (OH)
U of Colorado Boulder (CO)
U of Delaware (DE)
U of Florida (FL)
U of Georgia (GA)
U of Miami (FL)
U of Michigan (MI)
U of Minnesota, Twin Cities Campus (MN)
U of Nevada, Reno (NV)
U of North Dakota (ND)
U of Notre Dame (IN)
U of Oklahoma (OK)
U of Pennsylvania (PA)
U of Pittsburgh (PA)
U of Regina (SK, Canada)
U of Saskatchewan (SK, Canada)
U of Southern California (CA)
The U of Texas at Austin (TX)
U of Vermont (VT)
U of Waterloo (ON, Canada)
U of Windsor (ON, Canada)
U of Wisconsin–Platteville (WI)
Utah State U (UT)
West Texas A&M U (TX)
Wilkes U (PA)
Worcester Polytechnic Inst (MA)

ENVIRONMENTAL HEALTH

American U of Beirut (Lebanon)
Baylor U (TX)
Boise State U (ID)
Bowling Green State U (OH)
California State U, Northridge (CA)
Central Michigan U (MI)
Colorado State U (CO)
Dickinson State U (ND)
Drury U (MO)
East Carolina U (NC)
East Central U (OK)
East Tennessee State U (TN)
Illinois State U (IL)
Indiana U Bloomington (IN)
Mississippi Valley State U (MS)
Ohio U (OH)
State U of New York Coll of Environmental Science and Forestry (NY)
U of Georgia (GA)
U of Massachusetts Lowell (MA)
The U of North Carolina at Chapel Hill (NC)
U of Regina (SK, Canada)
U of Washington (WA)
West Chester U of Pennsylvania (PA)
Western Carolina U (NC)
Western Kentucky U (KY)
Willamette U (OR)
York Coll of the City U of New York (NY)

ENVIRONMENTAL PSYCHOLOGY

Embry-Riddle Aeronautical U–Daytona (FL)

ENVIRONMENTAL SCIENCE

Abilene Christian U (TX)
Albion Coll (MI)
Albright Coll (PA)
Alderson Broaddus U (WV)
Allegheny Coll (PA)
Alverno Coll (WI)
American Public U System (WV)
American U (DC)
The American U of Paris (France)
Antioch Coll, Yellow Springs (OH)
Appalachian State U (NC)
Arizona State U at the West campus (AZ)
Arkansas Tech U (AR)
Ashland U (OH)
Assumption Coll (MA)
Auburn U (AL)
Auburn U at Montgomery (AL)
Averett U (VA)
Ball State U (IN)
Barnard Coll (NY)
Bayamón Central U (PR)
Baylor U (TX)
Bellarmine U (KY)
Belmont U (TN)
Bennington Coll (VT)
Berry Coll (GA)
Bethel U (MN)
Bethune-Cookman U (FL)
Biola U (CA)
Boston U (MA)
Bradley U (IL)
Briar Cliff U (IA)
Bridgewater Coll (VA)
Brigham Young U (UT)
Bryant U (RI)
Bucknell U (PA)
Buena Vista U (IA)
California Baptist U (CA)
California Lutheran U (CA)
California State U, Fresno (CA)
California State U, Long Beach (CA)
California State U, Monterey Bay (CA)
California U of Pennsylvania (PA)
Calvin Coll (MI)
Canisius Coll (NY)
Capital U (OH)
Carthage Coll (WI)
Catawba Coll (NC)
Cedarville U (OH)
Central Methodist U (MO)
Central Michigan U (MI)
Central Washington U (WA)
Chatham U (PA)
Chestnut Hill Coll (PA)
Clarion U of Pennsylvania (PA)
Clarkson U (NY)
Cleveland State U (OH)
Coe Coll (IA)
Colby Coll (ME)
Colgate U (NY)
The Coll at Brockport, State U of New York (NY)
The Colorado Coll (CO)
Colorado Mesa U (CO)
Columbia Coll (MO)
Columbia U, School of General Studies (NY)
Concordia U (QC, Canada)
Concordia U Chicago (IL)
Concordia U, Nebraska (NE)
Creighton U (NE)
Dalhousie U (NS, Canada)
Dallas Baptist U (TX)
DEREE - The American Coll of Greece (Greece)
Dickinson Coll (PA)
Dickinson State U (ND)
Dominican U (IL)
Drake U (IA)
Drexel U (PA)
Drury U (MO)
Duquesne U (PA)
Earlham Coll (IN)
Eastern Nazarene Coll (MA)
Eastern U (PA)
Eastern Washington U (WA)
Edgewood Coll (WI)
Elon U (NC)
Emory & Henry Coll (VA)
Endicott Coll (MA)
Eureka Coll (IL)
The Evergreen State Coll (WA)
Fairleigh Dickinson U, Metropolitan Campus (NJ)
Flagler Coll (FL)
Florida Ag and Mech U (FL)
Florida Inst of Technology (FL)
Florida State U (FL)
Fordham U (NY)
Framingham State U (MA)
Franklin & Marshall Coll (PA)
Freed-Hardeman U (TN)
Frostburg State U (MD)
Gannon U (PA)
Gardner-Webb U (NC)
Geneva Coll (PA)
Georgia Coll & State U (GA)
Georgia Gwinnett Coll (GA)
Gettysburg Coll (PA)
Gonzaga U (WA)
Goshen Coll (IN)
Grace Coll (IN)
Hardin-Simmons U (TX)
Hartwick Coll (NY)
Hawai`i Pacific U (HI)
Heidelberg U (OH)
Hollins U (VA)
Humboldt State U (CA)
Hunter Coll of the City U of New York (NY)
Husson U (ME)
Idaho State U (ID)
Indiana U Bloomington (IN)
Indiana U–Purdue U Indianapolis (IN)
Inter American U of Puerto Rico, Bayamón Campus (PR)
Inter American U of Puerto Rico, Ponce Campus (PR)
Inter American U of Puerto Rico, San Germán Campus (PR)
Iowa State U of Science and Technology (IA)
Johns Hopkins U (MD)
Juniata Coll (PA)
Kennesaw State U (GA)
Keuka Coll (NY)
King's Coll (PA)
Kutztown U of Pennsylvania (PA)
Lake Erie Coll (OH)
Lamar U (TX)
La Salle U (PA)
Lebanon Valley Coll (PA)
Lewis U (IL)
Lincoln Coll (IL)
Lincoln U (MO)
Lincoln U (PA)
Linfield Coll (OR)
Lipscomb U (TN)
Longwood U (VA)
Louisiana State U and A&M Coll (LA)
Lourdes U (OH)
Loyola Marymount U (CA)
Loyola U Chicago (IL)
Loyola U New Orleans (LA)
Lynchburg Coll (VA)
Madonna U (MI)
Marietta Coll (OH)
Marshall U (WV)
Marylhurst U (OR)
Maryville U of Saint Louis (MO)
Marywood U (PA)
Massachusetts Coll of Liberal Arts (MA)
Massachusetts Maritime Acad (MA)
McDaniel Coll (MD)
McMurry U (TX)
Merrimack Coll (MA)
Messiah Coll (PA)
Metropolitan State U of Denver (CO)
Miami U (OH)
Michigan State U (MI)
Michigan Technological U (MI)
Mills Coll (CA)
Monmouth Coll (IL)
Montana State U (MT)
Moravian Coll (PA)
Mount Ida Coll (MA)
Muhlenberg Coll (PA)
Muskingum U (OH)
Nazareth Coll of Rochester (NY)
Nevada State Coll (NV)
New England Coll (NH)
New Mexico State U (NM)
North Carolina State U (NC)
Northeastern U (MA)
Northern Arizona U (AZ)
Northern Kentucky U (KY)
Northwestern U (IL)
Northwest U (WA)
Nova Southeastern U (FL)
Ohio Dominican U (OH)
The Ohio State U (OH)
Oklahoma State U (OK)
Oregon State U (OR)
Pace U (NY)
Pace U, Pleasantville Campus (NY)
Piedmont Coll (GA)
Pitzer Coll (CA)
Point Loma Nazarene U (CA)
Queens Coll of the City U of New York (NY)
Ramapo Coll of New Jersey (NJ)
Randolph Coll (VA)
Regis U (CO)
Rensselaer Polytechnic Inst (NY)
Rhodes Coll (TN)
Rochester Inst of Technology (NY)
Rocky Mountain Coll (MT)
Roger Williams U (RI)
Royal Roads U (BC, Canada)
Rutgers U–New Brunswick (NJ)
Saint Francis U (PA)
Saint Louis U (MO)
Saint Louis U–Madrid Campus (Spain)
St. Norbert Coll (WI)
Saint Vincent Coll (PA)
Salisbury U (MD)
Samford U (AL)
Sam Houston State U (TX)
San Diego State U (CA)
Santa Clara U (CA)
Scripps Coll (CA)
Seattle U (WA)
Siena Coll (NY)
Sierra Nevada Coll (NV)
Simmons Coll (MA)
Simon Fraser U (BC, Canada)
Simpson Coll (IA)
Skidmore Coll (NY)
South Dakota State U (SD)
Southeast Missouri State U (MO)
Southern Illinois U Edwardsville (IL)
Southern Methodist U (TX)
Southern New Hampshire U (NH)
State U of New York Coll at Cortland (NY)
State U of New York Coll of Environmental Science and Forestry (NY)
Stephen F. Austin State U (TX)
Stevenson U (MD)
Stonehill Coll (MA)
Suffolk U (MA)
Sweet Briar Coll (VA)
Tarleton State U (TX)
Taylor U (IN)
Temple U (PA)
Texas A&M U (TX)
Texas A&M U–Commerce (TX)
Texas A&M U–Corpus Christi (TX)
Texas Christian U (TX)
Texas State U (TX)
Thomas More Coll (KY)
Trinity Christian Coll (IL)
Troy U (AL)
Tusculum Coll (TN)
United States Military Acad (NY)
Unity Coll (ME)
U at Albany, State U of New York (NY)
The U of Alabama (AL)
The U of Arizona (AZ)
U of Arkansas (AR)
U of California, Irvine (CA)
U of California, Los Angeles (CA)
U of California, Riverside (CA)
U of Delaware (DE)
U of Denver (CO)
U of Dubuque (IA)
U of Evansville (IN)
U of Florida (FL)
U of Georgia (GA)
U of Guelph (ON, Canada)
U of Hawaii at Manoa (HI)
U of Houston (TX)
U of Houston–Clear Lake (TX)
U of Idaho (ID)
U of Illinois at Chicago (IL)
U of La Verne (CA)
U of Lethbridge (AB, Canada)
U of Maine (ME)
U of Maine at Farmington (ME)
U of Maine at Presque Isle (ME)
U of Maryland, Baltimore County (MD)
U of Maryland, Coll Park (MD)
U of Massachusetts Amherst (MA)
U of Massachusetts Boston (MA)
U of Massachusetts Lowell (MA)
U of Michigan–Dearborn (MI)
U of Michigan–Flint (MI)
U of Minnesota, Duluth (MN)
U of Minnesota, Twin Cities Campus (MN)
The U of Montana Western (MT)
U of Mount Union (OH)
U of New England (ME)
U of New Hampshire (NH)
U of New Haven (CT)
The U of North Carolina at Chapel Hill (NC)
The U of North Carolina at Pembroke (NC)
The U of North Carolina Wilmington (NC)
U of Northern Iowa (IA)
U of Notre Dame (IN)
U of Oklahoma (OK)
U of Oregon (OR)
U of Rochester (NY)
U of St. Francis (IL)
U of Saint Francis (IN)
U of St. Thomas (MN)
U of St. Thomas (TX)
U of San Diego (CA)
U of San Francisco (CA)
U of Saskatchewan (SK, Canada)
The U of Scranton (PA)
U of South Carolina (SC)
U of Southern California (CA)
U of Southern Indiana (IN)
U of Southern Maine (ME)
U of South Florida (FL)
U of South Florida, St. Petersburg (FL)
The U of Tennessee at Chattanooga (TN)
The U of Texas at San Antonio (TX)
The U of Texas Rio Grande Valley (TX)
U of the Incarnate Word (TX)
The U of Toledo (OH)
U of Vermont (VT)
U of Virginia (VA)
U of Washington (WA)
U of Washington, Bothell (WA)
U of Washington, Tacoma (WA)
U of Waterloo (ON, Canada)
U of Windsor (ON, Canada)
U of Wisconsin–Green Bay (WI)
U of Wisconsin–Madison (WI)
U of Wisconsin–Milwaukee (WI)
U of Wisconsin–Stout (WI)
U of Wisconsin–Whitewater (WI)
Upper Iowa U (IA)
Utah Valley U (UT)
Valparaiso U (IN)
Vassar Coll (NY)
Villanova U (PA)
Walla Walla U (WA)
Walsh U (OH)
Wartburg Coll (IA)
Washington & Jefferson Coll (PA)
Washington Coll (MD)
Washington State U (WA)
Washington State U–Tri-Cities (WA)
Washington State U–Vancouver (WA)
Washington U in St. Louis (MO)
Wayland Baptist U (TX)
Wayne State U (MI)
Western Carolina U (NC)
Western Washington U (WA)
Westfield State U (MA)
Westminster Coll (PA)
West Texas A&M U (TX)
West Virginia Wesleyan Coll (WV)
Wheaton Coll (IL)
Wheaton Coll (MA)
Whittier Coll (CA)
Willamette U (OR)
Williams Coll (MA)
Wilmington U (DE)
Wilson Coll (PA)
Winthrop U (SC)
Wittenberg U (OH)
Wright State U (OH)
Wright State U–Lake Campus (OH)
Youngstown State U (OH)

ENVIRONMENTAL STUDIES

Adelphi U (NY)
Albion Coll (MI)
Alfred U (NY)
Allegheny Coll (PA)
Alma Coll (MI)
American U (DC)
The American U of Paris (France)
Amherst Coll (MA)
Appalachian State U (NC)
Arizona State U at the Tempe campus (AZ)
Augsburg Coll (MN)
Augustana Coll (IL)
Austin Coll (TX)
Bard Coll (NY)
Bates Coll (ME)
Baylor U (TX)
Bellarmine U (KY)
Beloit Coll (WI)
Bemidji State U (MN)

Bennington Coll (VT)
Bethel U (MN)
Binghamton U, State U of New York (NY)
Bishop's U (QC, Canada)
Blackburn Coll (IL)
Black Hills State U (SD)
Boise State U (ID)
Boston Coll (MA)
Bowdoin Coll (ME)
Bowling Green State U (OH)
Brandeis U (MA)
Brooklyn Coll of the City U of New York (NY)
Bryant U (RI)
Bucknell U (PA)
California State U, East Bay (CA)
California State U, Monterey Bay (CA)
California State U, Sacramento (CA)
California State U, San Marcos (CA)
Calvin Coll (MI)
Canisius Coll (NY)
Carleton Coll (MN)
Carroll Coll (MT)
Carthage Coll (WI)
Case Western Reserve U (OH)
Catawba Coll (NC)
Central Michigan U (MI)
Central Washington U (WA)
Centre Coll (KY)
Chaminade U of Honolulu (HI)
Champlain Coll (VT)
Chatham U (PA)
Christopher Newport U (VA)
Claremont McKenna Coll (CA)
Clarke U (IA)
Cleveland State U (OH)
Coe Coll (IA)
Colby Coll (ME)
Colby-Sawyer Coll (NH)
Colgate U (NY)
The Coll of Idaho (ID)
Coll of Saint Benedict (MN)
Coll of the Atlantic (ME)
Coll of the Holy Cross (MA)
The Coll of William and Mary (VA)
The Colorado Coll (CO)
Columbia Southern U (AL)
Columbia U (NY)
Concordia Coll (MN)
Concordia U, Nebraska (NE)
Concordia U Wisconsin (WI)
Connecticut Coll (CT)
Cornell Coll (IA)
Dalhousie U (NS, Canada)
Dartmouth Coll (NH)
Davidson Coll (NC)
Denison U (OH)
DePauw U (IN)
DEREE - The American Coll of Greece (Greece)
Dickinson Coll (PA)
Doane U (NE)
Drake U (IA)
Drew U (NJ)
Drexel U (PA)
Drury U (MO)
Earlham Coll (IN)
Eastern Mennonite U (VA)
Eastern Nazarene Coll (MA)
Eckerd Coll (FL)
Elon U (NC)
Emory & Henry Coll (VA)
Emory U (GA)
Eugene Lang Coll of Liberal Arts (NY)
Eureka Coll (IL)
The Evergreen State Coll (WA)
Fairfield U (CT)
Florida Ag and Mech U (FL)
Florida Gulf Coast U (FL)
Florida Intl U (FL)
Florida Southern Coll (FL)
Fort Lewis Coll (CO)
Franklin & Marshall Coll (PA)
Franklin Pierce U (NH)
Furman U (SC)
Georgetown U (DC)
The George Washington U (DC)
Gettysburg Coll (PA)
Goddard Coll (VT)
Gonzaga U (WA)
Goucher Coll (MD)
Grace Coll (IN)
Green Mountain Coll (VT)
Guilford Coll (NC)
Hamilton Coll (NY)
Hamline U (MN)
Hampshire Coll (MA)
Hampton U (VA)
Harvard U (MA)
Hawai`i Pacific U (HI)
Heidelberg U (OH)
Hendrix Coll (AR)
Hiram Coll (OH)
Hobart and William Smith Colls (NY)
Hofstra U (NY)
Hollins U (VA)
Hood Coll (MD)
Humboldt State U (CA)
Huston-Tillotson U (TX)
Illinois Coll (IL)
Illinois Wesleyan U (IL)
Indiana U Bloomington (IN)
Indiana U South Bend (IN)
Inter American U of Puerto Rico, San Germán Campus (PR)
Iowa State U of Science and Technology (IA)
Ithaca Coll (NY)
Jacksonville U (FL)
John Carroll U (OH)
Johns Hopkins U (MD)
Juniata Coll (PA)
Kansas Wesleyan U (KS)
Keene State Coll (NH)
King's Coll (PA)
The King's U (AB, Canada)
Knox Coll (IL)
Lake Forest Coll (IL)
La Salle U (PA)
Lasell Coll (MA)
Lawrence U (WI)
Lehigh U (PA)
Le Moyne Coll (NY)
Lenoir-Rhyne U (NC)
Lesley U (MA)
Lewis & Clark Coll (OR)
Linfield Coll (OR)
Louisiana Tech U (LA)
Loyola U Chicago (IL)
Loyola U New Orleans (LA)
Luther Coll (IA)
Lynchburg Coll (VA)
Lynn U (FL)
Macalester Coll (MN)
Maharishi U of Management (IA)
Malone U (OH)
Manchester U (IN)
Manhattanville Coll (NY)
Mansfield U of Pennsylvania (PA)
Marietta Coll (OH)
Marymount Manhattan Coll (NY)
Maryville U of Saint Louis (MO)
Massachusetts Coll of Liberal Arts (MA)
McDaniel Coll (MD)
McKendree U (IL)
McMaster U (ON, Canada)
Meredith Coll (NC)
Michigan State U (MI)
Middlebury Coll (VT)
Millikin U (IL)
Mills Coll (CA)
Minnesota State U Mankato (MN)
Minnesota State U Moorhead (MN)
Montana State U Billings (MT)
Moravian Coll (PA)
Mount Allison U (NB, Canada)
Mount Holyoke Coll (MA)
Mount St. Mary's U (MD)
Muskingum U (OH)
New Coll of Florida (FL)
New Mexico Highlands U (NM)
New Mexico Inst of Mining and Technology (NM)
The New School for Public Engagement (NY)
North Carolina Wesleyan Coll (NC)
North Central Coll (IL)
Northeastern Illinois U (IL)
Northeastern U (MA)
Northern Arizona U (AZ)
Northern Illinois U (IL)
Northern State U (SD)
Northland Coll (WI)
Northwestern U (IL)
Oberlin Coll (OH)
Occidental Coll (CA)
The Ohio State U (OH)
Ohio U (OH)
Ohio Wesleyan U (OH)
Oklahoma City U (OK)
Pace U (NY)
Pace U, Pleasantville Campus (NY)
Pacific Lutheran U (WA)
Penn State Altoona (PA)
Penn State U Park (PA)
Plymouth State U (NH)
Pomona Coll (CA)
Portland State U (OR)
Prescott Coll (AZ)
Principia Coll (IL)
Purchase Coll, State U of New York (NY)
Queens Coll of the City U of New York (NY)
Ramapo Coll of New Jersey (NJ)
Randolph Coll (VA)
Randolph-Macon Coll (VA)
Redeemer U Coll (ON, Canada)
Reed Coll (OR)
Regis U (CO)
Ripon Coll (WI)
Roanoke Coll (VA)
Robert Morris U (PA)
Rocky Mountain Coll (MT)
Rollins Coll (FL)
Rowan U (NJ)
Rutgers U–New Brunswick (NJ)
The Sage Colls (NY)
Saint Anselm Coll (NH)
St. Bonaventure U (NY)
St. Edward's U (TX)
Saint Francis U (PA)
Saint John's U (MN)
St. John's U (NY)
Saint Joseph's U (PA)
Saint Louis U (MO)
St. Mary's Coll of Maryland (MD)
Saint Michael's Coll (VT)
St. Olaf Coll (MN)
St. Thomas U (FL)
St. Thomas U (NB, Canada)
Saint Vincent Coll (PA)
Salve Regina U (RI)
San Diego State U (CA)
San Francisco State U (CA)
Santa Clara U (CA)
Sarah Lawrence Coll (NY)
Seattle U (WA)
Sewanee: The U of the South (TN)
Shenandoah U (VA)
Shepherd U (WV)
Shippensburg U of Pennsylvania (PA)
Shorter U (GA)
Siena Coll (NY)
Skidmore Coll (NY)
Smith Coll (MA)
Sonoma State U (CA)
Southern Methodist U (TX)
Southern New Hampshire U (NH)
Southern Oregon U (OR)
Southwestern U (TX)
Spelman Coll (GA)
Stanford U (CA)
State U of New York at Fredonia (NY)
State U of New York at Plattsburgh (NY)
State U of New York Coll at Cortland (NY)
State U of New York Coll at Potsdam (NY)
State U of New York Coll of Agriculture and Technology at Cobleskill (NY)
State U of New York Coll of Environmental Science and Forestry (NY)
Stockton U (NJ)
Stonehill Coll (MA)
Stony Brook U, State U of New York (NY)
Susquehanna U (PA)
Sweet Briar Coll (VA)
Tarleton State U (TX)
Temple U (PA)
Tennessee Wesleyan U (TN)
Texas A&M U (TX)
Trent U (ON, Canada)
Trine U (IN)
Trinity U (TX)
Tufts U (MA)
Tulane U (LA)
Tusculum Coll (TN)
United States Military Acad (NY)
Université de Sherbrooke (QC, Canada)
The U of Arizona (AZ)
U of California, Davis (CA)
U of California, Irvine (CA)
U of California, San Diego (CA)
U of California, Santa Barbara (CA)
U of Central Arkansas (AR)
U of Chicago (IL)
U of Cincinnati (OH)
U of Colorado Boulder (CO)
U of Delaware (DE)
U of Denver (CO)
U of Dubuque (IA)
U of Evansville (IN)
U of Guelph (ON, Canada)
U of Illinois at Springfield (IL)
U of Indianapolis (IN)
The U of Kansas (KS)
U of Kentucky (KY)
U of Maine at Farmington (ME)
U of Maine at Fort Kent (ME)
U of Maine at Presque Isle (ME)
U of Maryland, Baltimore County (MD)
U of Massachusetts Lowell (MA)
U of Michigan (MI)
U of Michigan–Dearborn (MI)
U of Minnesota, Duluth (MN)
U of Minnesota, Morris (MN)
U of Missouri–Kansas City (MO)
U of Nevada, Las Vegas (NV)
U of New England (ME)
U of New Haven (CT)
U of North Carolina at Asheville (NC)
The U of North Carolina at Chapel Hill (NC)
The U of North Carolina at Pembroke (NC)
The U of North Carolina Wilmington (NC)
U of North Georgia (GA)
U of Oklahoma (OK)
U of Oregon (OR)
U of Pennsylvania (PA)
U of Pittsburgh at Bradford (PA)
U of Pittsburgh at Johnstown (PA)
U of Regina (SK, Canada)
U of Rhode Island (RI)
U of Richmond (VA)
U of Rochester (NY)
U of St. Thomas (MN)
U of St. Thomas (TX)
U of San Diego (CA)
U of San Francisco (CA)
U of Southern California (CA)
U of Southern Indiana (IN)
U of Southern Maine (ME)
The U of Tampa (FL)
The U of Tennessee at Martin (TN)
U of the Pacific (CA)
The U of Toledo (OH)
U of Toronto (ON, Canada)
The U of Tulsa (OK)
U of Utah (UT)
U of Vermont (VT)
The U of Virginia's Coll at Wise (VA)
U of Washington (WA)
U of Washington, Bothell (WA)
U of Washington, Tacoma (WA)
U of Waterloo (ON, Canada)
U of Windsor (ON, Canada)
U of Wisconsin–Green Bay (WI)
U of Wisconsin–Madison (WI)
Ursinus Coll (PA)
Vassar Coll (NY)
Villanova U (PA)
Virginia Commonwealth U (VA)
Virginia Polytechnic Inst and State U (VA)
Virginia Wesleyan Coll (VA)
Walla Walla U (WA)
Washington & Jefferson Coll (PA)
Washington and Lee U (VA)
Washington Coll (MD)
Washington U in St. Louis (MO)
Waynesburg U (PA)
Wells Coll (NY)
Wesleyan Coll (GA)
Wesleyan U (CT)
Western Michigan U (MI)
Western State Colorado U (CO)
Western Washington U (WA)
Westminster Coll (UT)
Wheelock Coll (MA)
Whitman Coll (WA)
Whittier Coll (CA)
Widener U (PA)
William Paterson U of New Jersey (NJ)
William Peace U (NC)
Williams Coll (MA)
Wofford Coll (SC)

ENVIRONMENTAL TOXICOLOGY

Clarkson U (NY)
U of California, Davis (CA)

EPIDEMIOLOGY

Indiana U Bloomington (IN)
U of Georgia (GA)
U of Rochester (NY)

EQUESTRIAN STUDIES

Asbury U (KY)
Averett U (VA)
Becker Coll (MA)
Centenary U (NJ)
Colorado State U (CO)
Delaware Valley U (PA)
Emory & Henry Coll (VA)
Houghton Coll (NY)
Lake Erie Coll (OH)
North Dakota State U (ND)
Otterbein U (OH)
Rocky Mountain Coll (MT)
Rutgers U–New Brunswick (NJ)
Saint Mary-of-the-Woods Coll (IN)
Savannah Coll of Art and Design (GA)
Stephens Coll (MO)
The U of Findlay (OH)
The U of Montana Western (MT)
West Texas A&M U (TX)
Wilson Coll (PA)

ETHICS

Bridgewater State U (MA)
Carroll Coll (MT)
Drake U (IA)
Southeastern Baptist Theological Sem (NC)
Syracuse U (NY)
U of Evansville (IN)
U of Washington, Bothell (WA)

ETHNIC, CULTURAL MINORITY, GENDER, AND GROUP STUDIES RELATED

Albion Coll (MI)
Allegheny Coll (PA)
American U (DC)
The American U of Paris (France)
Beloit Coll (WI)
Bethel U (MN)
Boise State U (ID)
Bowdoin Coll (ME)
Bowling Green State U (OH)
California Polytechnic State U, San Luis Obispo (CA)
California State Polytechnic U, Pomona (CA)
California State U, Chico (CA)
California State U, Stanislaus (CA)
Central Michigan U (MI)
Chatham U (PA)
Christian Brothers U (TN)
The Colorado Coll (CO)
Columbia Coll Chicago (IL)
Columbia U, School of General Studies (NY)
Cornell Coll (IA)
Davidson Coll (NC)
Emmanuel Coll (MA)
The Evergreen State Coll (WA)
Grinnell Coll (IA)
Hampshire Coll (MA)
Indiana U Bloomington (IN)
Indiana U South Bend (IN)
John Jay Coll of Criminal Justice of the City U of New York (NY)
Lawrence U (WI)
Mills Coll (CA)
Mount Holyoke Coll (MA)
New Coll of Florida (FL)
Northeastern Illinois U (IL)
The Ohio State U (OH)
Saint Michael's Coll (VT)
San Diego State U (CA)
Santa Clara U (CA)
Sarah Lawrence Coll (NY)
Skidmore Coll (NY)

Stanford U (CA)
Stonehill Coll (MA)
U at Buffalo, the State U of New York (NY)
U of California, Irvine (CA)
U of Chicago (IL)
U of Colorado Colorado Springs (CO)
U of Denver (CO)
U of Hawaii at Manoa (HI)
U of Houston (TX)
U of Illinois at Chicago (IL)
U of Kentucky (KY)
U of Minnesota, Duluth (MN)
U of Pittsburgh (PA)
U of Southern California (CA)
U of Utah (UT)
U of Washington, Tacoma (WA)
Washington State U (WA)
Washington U in St. Louis (MO)
Wayne State U (MI)
Wesleyan U (CT)
Western Kentucky U (KY)
Westfield State U (MA)
Whitman Coll (WA)
Williams Coll (MA)

ETHNIC STUDIES
Arizona State U at the West campus (AZ)
Colorado State U (CO)
Edgewood Coll (WI)
Goddard Coll (VT)
Kansas State U (KS)
Lewis & Clark Coll (OR)
Messiah Coll (PA)
Minnesota State U Moorhead (MN)
Oregon State U (OR)
St. Olaf Coll (MN)
Sarah Lawrence Coll (NY)
U of Colorado Boulder (CO)
U of Colorado Denver (CO)
U of Oregon (OR)
U of San Diego (CA)
The U of Texas at Austin (TX)
Willamette U (OR)

EUROPEAN HISTORY
Charleston Southern U (SC)
Gettysburg Coll (PA)
Howard Payne U (TX)
Keene State Coll (NH)
U of Idaho (ID)
U of Washington, Tacoma (WA)

EUROPEAN STUDIES
American U in Bulgaria (Bulgaria)
Amherst Coll (MA)
Barnard Coll (NY)
Bennington Coll (VT)
Boston U (MA)
Bowling Green State U (OH)
Brandeis U (MA)
Canisius Coll (NY)
Carnegie Mellon U (PA)
Dalhousie U (NS, Canada)
Emory & Henry Coll (VA)
Fort Lewis Coll (CO)
Georgetown Coll (KY)
The George Washington U (DC)
Gettysburg Coll (PA)
Gonzaga U (WA)
Hampshire Coll (MA)
Hillsdale Coll (MI)
Hobart and William Smith Colls (NY)
Loyola Marymount U (CA)
Middlebury Coll (VT)
Millsaps Coll (MS)
New Coll of Florida (FL)
Ohio U (OH)
Pepperdine U, Malibu (CA)
Portland State U (OR)
Rutgers U–New Brunswick (NJ)
Saint Joseph's U (PA)
Saint Mary's Coll of California (CA)
San Diego State U (CA)
Scripps Coll (CA)
Seattle Pacific U (WA)
Stony Brook U, State U of New York (NY)
Texas State U (TX)
Trinity U (TX)
Tufts U (MA)
United States Military Acad (NY)
U of California, Irvine (CA)
U of California, Los Angeles (CA)
U of Delaware (DE)
U of Guelph (ON, Canada)
The U of Kansas (KS)
U of King's Coll (NS, Canada)
U of Minnesota, Morris (MN)
The U of North Carolina at Chapel Hill (NC)
U of Richmond (VA)
U of South Carolina (SC)
The U of Texas at Austin (TX)
U of Toronto (ON, Canada)
U of Vermont (VT)
U of Washington (WA)
Vanderbilt U (TN)
Washington U in St. Louis (MO)
Webster U (MO)

EUROPEAN STUDIES (WESTERN)
Bates Coll (ME)
Illinois Wesleyan U (IL)
Seattle U (WA)
Tufts U (MA)
Willamette U (OR)

EVOLUTIONARY BIOLOGY
Bennington Coll (VT)
Case Western Reserve U (OH)
Coll of the Atlantic (ME)
Columbia U, School of General Studies (NY)
Dartmouth Coll (NH)
Harvard U (MA)
Rice U (TX)
Rutgers U–New Brunswick (NJ)
Stony Brook U, State U of New York (NY)
Tulane U (LA)

EXECUTIVE ASSISTANT/ EXECUTIVE SECRETARY
Bowling Green State U (OH)
Caribbean U (PR)
U of Puerto Rico in Bayamón (PR)

EXERCISE PHYSIOLOGY
Anderson U (SC)
Auburn U (AL)
Baldwin Wallace U (OH)
Baylor U (TX)
Biola U (CA)
Brigham Young U–Idaho (ID)
Brooklyn Coll of the City U of New York (NY)
California Baptist U (CA)
Central Washington U (WA)
Chestnut Hill Coll (PA)
Coll of Charleston (SC)
The Coll of St. Scholastica (MN)
Concordia U Wisconsin (WI)
East Carolina U (NC)
Faulkner U (AL)
Fitchburg State U (MA)
Florida Southern Coll (FL)
Gonzaga U (WA)
Gordon Coll (MA)
Lynchburg Coll (VA)
Merrimack Coll (MA)
Northwest Christian U (OR)
Ohio U (OH)
Ohio U–Eastern (OH)
Saint Francis U (PA)
Shenandoah U (VA)
Skidmore Coll (NY)
State U of New York Coll at Potsdam (NY)
U at Buffalo, the State U of New York (NY)
U of California, Davis (CA)
U of California, Irvine (CA)
U of Colorado Colorado Springs (CO)
U of Dayton (OH)
U of Delaware (DE)
U of Florida (FL)
U of Massachusetts Amherst (MA)
U of Miami (FL)
U of Minnesota, Twin Cities Campus (MN)
U of Southern Maine (ME)
The U of Toledo (OH)
Ursinus Coll (PA)
Washington State U (WA)
Washington State U–Spokane (WA)
West Virginia U (WV)

EXPERIMENTAL PSYCHOLOGY
Armstrong State U (GA)
Purdue U (IN)
Redeemer U Coll (ON, Canada)
Saint Leo U (FL)
Tiffin U (OH)
Tufts U (MA)
U of California, Santa Barbara (CA)
U of Chicago (IL)
U of Mary Hardin-Baylor (TX)
U of Michigan (MI)
U of Rochester (NY)
U of South Carolina (SC)

FACILITIES PLANNING AND MANAGEMENT
Eastern Michigan U (MI)
Missouri State U (MO)
New England Inst of Technology (RI)
New York City Coll of Technology of the City U of New York (NY)

FAMILY AND COMMUNITY SERVICES
Andrews U (MI)
Bowling Green State U (OH)
Coll of the Ozarks (MO)
East Carolina U (NC)
Harding U (AR)
Iowa State U of Science and Technology (IA)
John Brown U (AR)
La Roche Coll (PA)
Messiah Coll (PA)
Michigan State U (MI)
Mount St. Mary's U (MD)
Oklahoma Baptist U (OK)
Oklahoma Christian U (OK)
Stevenson U (MD)
Texas Tech U (TX)
Toccoa Falls Coll (GA)
Union U (TN)
U of Florida (FL)
U of Maryland, Coll Park (MD)
U of Miami (FL)
U of Michigan–Dearborn (MI)
U of Northern Iowa (IA)
U of Wisconsin–Madison (WI)
Youngstown State U (OH)

FAMILY AND CONSUMER ECONOMICS RELATED
Andrews U (MI)
Bowling Green State U (OH)
Brigham Young U (UT)
California State U, Fresno (CA)
California State U, Sacramento (CA)
Carson-Newman U (TN)
Minnesota State U Mankato (MN)
Tennessee State U (TN)
U of Hawaii at Manoa (HI)
U of Minnesota, Twin Cities Campus (MN)
U of Nebraska at Kearney (NE)
U of Northern Iowa (IA)
U of Wisconsin–Stevens Point (WI)
Utah State U (UT)
Virginia State U (VA)

FAMILY AND CONSUMER SCIENCES/HOME ECONOMICS TEACHER EDUCATION
Baylor U (TX)
Bowling Green State U (OH)
Bradley U (IL)
Carson-Newman U (TN)
Central Washington U (WA)
Colorado State U (CO)
East Carolina U (NC)
East Central U (OK)
Georgia Southern U (GA)
Hampton U (VA)
Harding U (AR)
Immaculata U (PA)
Iowa State U of Science and Technology (IA)
Jacksonville State U (AL)
Langston U (OK)
Louisiana Tech U (LA)
Messiah Coll (PA)
Minnesota State U Mankato (MN)
Missouri State U (MO)
New Mexico State U (NM)
North Dakota State U (ND)
Northern Illinois U (IL)
The Ohio State U (OH)
The Ohio State U at Lima (OH)
Ohio U (OH)
Pittsburg State U (KS)
Queens Coll of the City U of New York (NY)
St. Catherine U (MN)
Seton Hill U (PA)
South Dakota State U (SD)
Southeast Missouri State U (MO)
Southern Utah U (UT)
Syracuse U (NY)
The U of Akron (OH)
U of Central Arkansas (AR)
U of Georgia (GA)
U of Saskatchewan (SK, Canada)
The U of Tennessee at Martin (TN)
U of Wisconsin–Stevens Point (WI)
U of Wisconsin–Stout (WI)
Utah State U (UT)
Virginia Polytechnic Inst and State U (VA)
Wayne State Coll (NE)
Western Kentucky U (KY)
Western Michigan U (MI)
Winthrop U (SC)

FAMILY AND CONSUMER SCIENCES/HUMAN SCIENCES
Auburn U (AL)
Ball State U (IN)
Baylor U (TX)
Berea Coll (KY)
Bowling Green State U (OH)
Bradley U (IL)
Bridgewater Coll (VA)
Brigham Young U (UT)
Brigham Young U–Idaho (ID)
California State U, East Bay (CA)
California State U, Long Beach (CA)
California State U, Northridge (CA)
Carson-Newman U (TN)
Central Washington U (WA)
Coll of the Atlantic (ME)
Coll of the Ozarks (MO)
Colorado State U (CO)
Cornell U (NY)
Eastern Illinois U (IL)
East Tennessee State U (TN)
Harding U (AR)
Henderson State U (AR)
Idaho State U (ID)
Illinois State U (IL)
Indiana State U (IN)
Indiana U of Pennsylvania (PA)
Iowa State U of Science and Technology (IA)
Jacksonville State U (AL)
Kansas State U (KS)
Liberty U (VA)
Lipscomb U (TN)
Louisiana State U and A&M Coll (LA)
Madonna U (MI)
The Master's U (CA)
Meredith Coll (NC)
Miami U (OH)
Minnesota State U Mankato (MN)
Mississippi State U (MS)
Montana State U (MT)
Montclair State U (NJ)
New Mexico Highlands U (NM)
North Carolina Central U (NC)
Northeastern State U (OK)
Northwestern State U of Louisiana (LA)
Olivet Nazarene U (IL)
Pittsburg State U (KS)
Prairie View A&M U (TX)
Purdue U (IN)
Queens Coll of the City U of New York (NY)
Rutgers U–New Brunswick (NJ)
St. Catherine U (MN)
Sam Houston State U (TX)
San Francisco State U (CA)
Seattle Pacific U (WA)
Seton Hill U (PA)
Shepherd U (WV)
South Carolina State U (SC)
Southeastern Louisiana U (LA)
Southeast Missouri State U (MO)
Southern Utah U (UT)
Tarleton State U (TX)
Texas A&M U–Kingsville (TX)
Texas Tech U (TX)
Texas Woman's U (TX)
The U of Alabama (AL)
U of Arkansas (AR)
U of California, San Diego (CA)
U of Central Arkansas (AR)
U of Central Missouri (MO)
U of Georgia (GA)
U of Kentucky (KY)
U of Montevallo (AL)
U of North Alabama (AL)
The U of North Carolina at Greensboro (NC)
U of Saint Joseph (CT)
The U of Tennessee at Martin (TN)
The U of Texas at Austin (TX)
Washington State U (WA)
Wayne State Coll (NE)
Youngstown State U (OH)

FAMILY AND CONSUMER SCIENCES/HUMAN SCIENCES BUSINESS SERVICES RELATED
Brigham Young U (UT)

FAMILY AND CONSUMER SCIENCES/HUMAN SCIENCES COMMUNICATION
U of Georgia (GA)

FAMILY AND CONSUMER SCIENCES/HUMAN SCIENCES RELATED
Auburn U (AL)
California State U, Long Beach (CA)

FAMILY PRACTICE NURSING
Grand Valley State U (MI)
Michigan State U (MI)
Pace U (NY)
Pace U, Pleasantville Campus (NY)
The U of Texas at Austin (TX)
The U of Virginia's Coll at Wise (VA)
U of Windsor (ON, Canada)

FAMILY PSYCHOLOGY
Arizona Christian U (AZ)
Corban U (OR)
Cornerstone U (MI)
Goddard Coll (VT)
Kansas Wesleyan U (KS)

FAMILY RESOURCE MANAGEMENT
Arizona State U at the Tempe campus (AZ)
Brigham Young U (UT)
Iowa State U of Science and Technology (IA)
New Mexico State U (NM)
The Ohio State U (OH)
The Ohio State U at Lima (OH)
Ohio U (OH)
Texas Tech U (TX)
The U of Alabama (AL)
U of Georgia (GA)

FAMILY SYSTEMS
Anderson U (IN)
Bowling Green State U (OH)
Central Michigan U (MI)
Central Washington U (WA)
Lipscomb U (TN)
Lubbock Christian U (TX)
Mid-Atlantic Christian U (NC)
Towson U (MD)
The U of Akron (OH)
U of Southern Mississippi (MS)
Weber State U (UT)
Western Michigan U (MI)

FARM AND RANCH MANAGEMENT
Colorado State U (CO)
Iowa State U of Science and Technology (IA)
Lake Erie Coll (OH)
Purdue U (IN)
Tarleton State U (TX)
Texas A&M U (TX)
Texas Christian U (TX)
U of Minnesota, Crookston (MN)

FASHION AND FABRIC CONSULTING
Acad of Art U (CA)

FASHION/APPAREL DESIGN
Acad of Art U (CA)
Baylor U (TX)
Bennington Coll (VT)
Bowling Green State U (OH)
Brenau U (GA)

Buffalo State Coll, State U of New York (NY)
Cairn U (PA)
California Coll of the Arts (CA)
Carson-Newman U (TN)
Cazenovia Coll (NY)
Centenary U (NJ)
Clark Atlanta U (GA)
Columbia Coll Chicago (IL)
Columbus Coll of Art & Design (OH)
Dalhousie U (NS, Canada)
Dominican U (IL)
Drexel U (PA)
EDP U of Puerto Rico (PR)
Escuela de Artes Plasticas y Dise&nno de Puerto Rico (PR)
Eugene Lang Coll of Liberal Arts (NY)
Fashion Inst of Technology (NY)
Ferris State U (MI)
FIDM/Fashion Inst of Design & Merchandising, Los Angeles Campus (CA)
Hampton U (VA)
Indiana U Bloomington (IN)
Iowa State U of Science and Technology (IA)
Jacksonville U (FL)
Kent State U (OH)
Lasell Coll (MA)
Lebanese American U (Lebanon)
Lindenwood U (MO)
Marist Coll (NY)
Marymount U (VA)
Massachusetts Coll of Art and Design (MA)
Meredith Coll (NC)
Michigan State U (MI)
Montclair State U (NJ)
Mount Ida Coll (MA)
Mount Mary U (WI)
The New School–Parsons Paris (France)
O'More Coll of Design (TN)
Parsons School of Design (NY)
Pratt Inst (NY)
Purdue U (IN)
St. Catherine U (MN)
Savannah Coll of Art and Design (GA)
School of the Art Inst of Chicago (IL)
Stephens Coll (MO)
Stevenson U (MD)
Syracuse U (NY)
Texas Tech U (TX)
Texas Woman's U (TX)
U of Cincinnati (OH)
U of Delaware (DE)
U of North Texas (TX)
U of the Incarnate Word (TX)
Villa Maria Coll (NY)
Virginia Commonwealth U (VA)
Washington U in St. Louis (MO)
Western Michigan U (MI)
Woodbury U (CA)

FASHION MERCHANDISING
Acad of Art U (CA)
Ashland U (OH)
Baylor U (TX)
Berkeley Coll–New York City Campus (NY)
Berkeley Coll–White Plains Campus (NY)
Berkeley Coll–Woodland Park Campus (NJ)
Bowling Green State U (OH)
Brenau U (GA)
Buffalo State Coll, State U of New York (NY)
California State U, Long Beach (CA)
Carson-Newman U (TN)
Cazenovia Coll (NY)
Central Michigan U (MI)
Dominican U (IL)
East Central U (OK)
Eastern Michigan U (MI)
Fashion Inst of Technology (NY)
Fisher Coll (MA)
Hampton U (VA)
Harding U (AR)
Immaculata U (PA)
Indiana U of Pennsylvania (PA)
Kent State U (OH)
Lasell Coll (MA)
LIM Coll (NY)
Lipscomb U (TN)
Louisiana State U and A&M Coll (LA)
Lynn U (FL)
Marymount Manhattan Coll (NY)
Marymount U (VA)
Mercyhurst U (PA)
Meredith Coll (NC)
Mount Ida Coll (MA)
Mount Mary U (WI)
Northwood U, Michigan Campus (MI)
Olivet Nazarene U (IL)
O'More Coll of Design (TN)
St. Catherine U (MN)
Sam Houston State U (TX)
Southern New Hampshire U (NH)
Stephen F. Austin State U (TX)
Stevenson U (MD)
Texas Christian U (TX)
Texas State U (TX)
Texas Tech U (TX)
Texas Woman's U (TX)
U of Bridgeport (CT)
U of Central Missouri (MO)
U of Georgia (GA)
U of North Texas (TX)
The U of Tennessee at Martin (TN)
Utah State U (UT)
Western Michigan U (MI)
Woodbury U (CA)
Youngstown State U (OH)

FIBER, TEXTILE AND WEAVING ARTS
Adams State U (CO)
Bowling Green State U (OH)
California Coll of the Arts (CA)
California State U, Long Beach (CA)
Coll of the Ozarks (MO)
Colorado State U (CO)
Cornell U (NY)
Kansas City Art Inst (MO)
Maryland Inst Coll of Art (MD)
Massachusetts Coll of Art and Design (MA)
Rhode Island School of Design (RI)
Savannah Coll of Art and Design (GA)
School of the Art Inst of Chicago (IL)
Syracuse U (NY)
Temple U (PA)
The U of Kansas (KS)
U of Massachusetts Dartmouth (MA)
U of Michigan (MI)
U of Oregon (OR)
Western Washington U (WA)

FILIPINO/TAGALOG
U of Hawaii at Manoa (HI)

FILM/CINEMA/VIDEO STUDIES
The American U in Cairo (Egypt)
The American U of Paris (France)
The American U of Rome (Italy)
Augsburg Coll (MN)
Baldwin Wallace U (OH)
Bard Coll (NY)
Barnard Coll (NY)
Belhaven U (MS)
Bennington Coll (VT)
Biola U (CA)
Bishop's U (QC, Canada)
Boston Coll (MA)
Boston U (MA)
Bowling Green State U (OH)
Brandeis U (MA)
Brigham Young U (UT)
Brooklyn Coll of the City U of New York (NY)
California Baptist U (CA)
California Coll of the Arts (CA)
California State U, Long Beach (CA)
California State U, Northridge (CA)
California State U, Sacramento (CA)
Carleton Coll (MN)
Carson-Newman U (TN)
Central Washington U (WA)
Champlain Coll (VT)
Chapman U (CA)
Claremont McKenna Coll (CA)
Clark U (MA)
Coe Coll (IA)
Coll of Staten Island of the City U of New York (NY)
The Colorado Coll (CO)
Columbia U (NY)
Columbia U, School of General Studies (NY)
Concordia U (QC, Canada)
Connecticut Coll (CT)
Cornell U (NY)
Dartmouth Coll (NH)
Denison U (OH)
DeSales U (PA)
Dominican U (IL)
Eastern Michigan U (MI)
Eastern Washington U (WA)
Eckerd Coll (FL)
Emerson Coll (MA)
Emory U (GA)
Eugene Lang Coll of Liberal Arts (NY)
The Evergreen State Coll (WA)
Fashion Inst of Technology (NY)
Florida State U (FL)
Georgia State U (GA)
Grace Coll (IN)
Grand Valley State U (MI)
Hamilton Coll (NY)
Houston Baptist U (TX)
Hunter Coll of the City U of New York (NY)
Huntington U (IN)
Ithaca Coll (NY)
Jacksonville U (FL)
Johns Hopkins U (MD)
Judson U (IL)
Keene State Coll (NH)
Kenyon Coll (OH)
Lafayette Coll (PA)
Marymount Manhattan Coll (NY)
McDaniel Coll (MD)
Memphis Coll of Art (TN)
Miami U (OH)
Middlebury Coll (VT)
Minnesota State U Moorhead (MN)
Morehouse Coll (GA)
Mount Holyoke Coll (MA)
Muhlenberg Coll (PA)
National U (CA)
Northwestern U (IL)
Northwest U (WA)
The Ohio State U (OH)
Pace U (NY)
Pace U, Pleasantville Campus (NY)
Penn State Abington (PA)
Penn State Altoona (PA)
Penn State Beaver (PA)
Penn State Berks (PA)
Penn State Brandywine (PA)
Penn State DuBois (PA)
Penn State Erie, The Behrend Coll (PA)
Penn State Fayette, The Eberly Campus (PA)
Penn State Greater Allegheny (PA)
Penn State Hazleton (PA)
Penn State Lehigh Valley (PA)
Penn State Mont Alto (PA)
Penn State New Kensington (PA)
Penn State Schuylkill (PA)
Penn State Shenango (PA)
Penn State U Park (PA)
Penn State Wilkes-Barre (PA)
Penn State Worthington Scranton (PA)
Penn State York (PA)
Pepperdine U, Malibu (CA)
Pitzer Coll (CA)
Purchase Coll, State U of New York (NY)
Purdue U (IN)
Queens Coll of the City U of New York (NY)
Quinnipiac U (CT)
Rhode Island Coll (RI)
Rutgers U–New Brunswick (NJ)
Saint Augustine's U (NC)
St. Cloud State U (MN)
San Francisco State U (CA)
Sarah Lawrence Coll (NY)
School of the Art Inst of Chicago (IL)
Seattle U (WA)
Simon Fraser U (BC, Canada)
Smith Coll (MA)
Southeastern U (FL)
Southwestern Coll (KS)
Stanford U (CA)
State U of New York at Fredonia (NY)
Stephens Coll (MO)
Stevenson U (MD)
Temple U (PA)
Tufts U (MA)
Université de Montréal (QC, Canada)
U at Buffalo, the State U of New York (NY)
U of Alaska Fairbanks (AK)
The U of Arizona (AZ)
U of California, Davis (CA)
U of California, Irvine (CA)
U of California, Los Angeles (CA)
U of California, San Diego (CA)
U of California, Santa Barbara (CA)
U of Chicago (IL)
U of Colorado Boulder (CO)
U of Denver (CO)
U of Georgia (GA)
U of Hartford (CT)
The U of Kansas (KS)
U of Mary Hardin-Baylor (TX)
U of Maryland, Coll Park (MD)
U of Michigan (MI)
U of Nevada, Las Vegas (NV)
U of Oklahoma (OK)
U of Oregon (OR)
U of Pennsylvania (PA)
U of Pikeville (KY)
U of Pittsburgh (PA)
U of Regina (SK, Canada)
U of Richmond (VA)
U of Rochester (NY)
U of Southern California (CA)
The U of Tampa (FL)
The U of the Arts (PA)
The U of Toledo (OH)
The U of Tulsa (OK)
U of Utah (UT)
U of Vermont (VT)
U of Waterloo (ON, Canada)
U of Windsor (ON, Canada)
U of Wisconsin–Milwaukee (WI)
Vanderbilt U (TN)
Vassar Coll (NY)
Washington U in St. Louis (MO)
Watkins Coll of Art, Design, & Film (TN)
Wayne State U (MI)
Webster U (MO)
Wells Coll (NY)
Wesleyan U (CT)
Wheaton Coll (MA)
Whitman Coll (WA)
Wright State U (OH)
Wright State U–Lake Campus (OH)

FILM/VIDEO AND PHOTOGRAPHIC ARTS RELATED
Arizona State U at the Tempe campus (AZ)
Brigham Young U (UT)
Calvary U (MO)
Chatham U (PA)
Cleveland State U (OH)
Coe Coll (IA)
Coll of the Atlantic (ME)
Columbus Coll of Art & Design (OH)
Fairfield U (CT)
Hampshire Coll (MA)
Hollins U (VA)
Kansas City Art Inst (MO)
La Roche Coll (PA)
Maryland Inst Coll of Art (MD)
Mount Saint Mary's U (CA)
Nossi Coll of Art (TN)
Oklahoma City U (OK)
Portland State U (OR)
Pratt Inst (NY)
Rhode Island School of Design (RI)
Saint Joseph's U (PA)
School of the Art Inst of Chicago (IL)
Scripps Coll (CA)
Swarthmore Coll (PA)
U of Illinois at Chicago (IL)
U of Minnesota, Twin Cities Campus (MN)
Western Michigan U (MI)
Woodbury U (CA)

FINANCE
Abilene Christian U (TX)
Adams State U (CO)
Adelphi U (NY)
Alabama State U (AL)
Albertus Magnus Coll (CT)
Albion Coll (MI)
Albright Coll (PA)
Alfred U (NY)
Alma Coll (MI)
American U (DC)
The American U in Dubai (United Arab Emirates)
Anderson U (IN)
Angelo State U (TX)
Appalachian State U (NC)
Aquinas Coll (TN)
Arcadia U (PA)
Arizona State U at the Tempe campus (AZ)
Ashland U (OH)
Auburn U (AL)
Auburn U at Montgomery (AL)
Augsburg Coll (MN)
Augusta U (GA)
Aurora U (IL)
Austin Coll (TX)
Austin Peay State U (TN)
Avila U (MO)
Baldwin Wallace U (OH)
Ball State U (IN)
Barry U (FL)
Baruch Coll of the City U of New York (NY)
Bayamón Central U (PR)
Baylor U (TX)
Bellarmine U (KY)
Benedictine Coll (KS)
Bentley U (MA)
Berry Coll (GA)
Binghamton U, State U of New York (NY)
Bishop's U (QC, Canada)
Boise State U (ID)
Boston Coll (MA)
Bowling Green State U (OH)
Bradley U (IL)
Brescia U (KY)
Bridgewater State U (MA)
Brigham Young U–Idaho (ID)
Bryant U (RI)
Butler U (IN)
Cabrini U (PA)
California State U, Bakersfield (CA)
California State U, Dominguez Hills (CA)
California State U, East Bay (CA)
California State U, Fresno (CA)
California State U, Long Beach (CA)
California State U, Northridge (CA)
California State U, San Marcos (CA)
California State U, Stanislaus (CA)
Canisius Coll (NY)
Carnegie Mellon U (PA)
Carroll Coll (MT)
Case Western Reserve U (OH)
The Catholic U of America (DC)
Cedarville U (OH)
Centenary U (NJ)
Central Connecticut State U (CT)
Central Michigan U (MI)
Central Penn Coll (PA)
Central Washington U (WA)
Charleston Southern U (SC)
Christopher Newport U (VA)
Clarion U of Pennsylvania (PA)
Clemson U (SC)
Cleveland State U (OH)
Coastal Carolina U (SC)
The Coll at Brockport, State U of New York (NY)
Coll of Charleston (SC)
The Coll of Saint Rose (NY)
The Coll of St. Scholastica (MN)
The Coll of William and Mary (VA)
Colorado Christian U (CO)
Colorado State U (CO)
Columbia Coll (MO)
Columbus State U (GA)
Concordia Coll (MN)
Concordia U (QC, Canada)
Concordia U, St. Paul (MN)
Converse Coll (SC)
Corban U (OR)
Cornerstone U (MI)

Creighton U (NE)
Culver-Stockton Coll (MO)
Dakota State U (SD)
Dalhousie U (NS, Canada)
Dallas Baptist U (TX)
Davenport U, Grand Rapids (MI)
DEREE - The American Coll of Greece (Greece)
DeSales U (PA)
Dickinson State U (ND)
Dixie State U (UT)
Dominican U (IL)
Drake U (IA)
Drexel U (PA)
Drury U (MO)
Duquesne U (PA)
East Carolina U (NC)
East Central U (OK)
Eastern Illinois U (IL)
Eastern Michigan U (MI)
Eastern Washington U (WA)
East Tennessee State U (TN)
Elon U (NC)
Endicott Coll (MA)
Excelsior Coll (NY)
Fairfield U (CT)
Fairleigh Dickinson U, Coll at Florham (NJ)
Fairleigh Dickinson U, Metropolitan Campus (NJ)
Fayetteville State U (NC)
Ferris State U (MI)
Fisher Coll (MA)
Fitchburg State U (MA)
Flagler Coll (FL)
Florida Atlantic U (FL)
Florida Gulf Coast U (FL)
Florida Intl U (FL)
Florida State U (FL)
Fordham U (NY)
Fort Lewis Coll (CO)
Framingham State U (MA)
Franciscan U of Steubenville (OH)
Francis Marion U (SC)
Franklin Pierce U (NH)
Freed-Hardeman U (TN)
Friends U (KS)
Gannon U (PA)
Gardner-Webb U (NC)
George Fox U (OR)
Georgetown Coll (KY)
Georgetown U (DC)
The George Washington U (DC)
Georgian Court U (NJ)
Georgia Southern U (GA)
Georgia State U (GA)
Gonzaga U (WA)
Gordon Coll (MA)
Grace Coll (IN)
Grand Valley State U (MI)
Grove City Coll (PA)
Hamline U (MN)
Hampton U (VA)
Harding U (AR)
Hardin-Simmons U (TX)
HEC Montreal (QC, Canada)
High Point U (NC)
Hillsdale Coll (MI)
Hofstra U (NY)
Holy Family U (PA)
Houston Baptist U (TX)
Howard Payne U (TX)
Hult Intl Business School (United Kingdom)
Husson U (ME)
Idaho State U (ID)
Illinois Coll (IL)
Illinois State U (IL)
Immaculata U (PA)
Indiana State U (IN)
Indiana U of Pennsylvania (PA)
Inter American U of Puerto Rico, Bayamón Campus (PR)
Inter American U of Puerto Rico, Metropolitan Campus (PR)
Inter American U of Puerto Rico, Ponce Campus (PR)
Inter American U of Puerto Rico, San Germán Campus (PR)
Iona Coll (NY)
Iowa State U of Science and Technology (IA)
Ithaca Coll (NY)
Jackson State U (MS)
Jacksonville State U (AL)
Jacksonville U (FL)
James Madison U (VA)
John Carroll U (OH)
Juniata Coll (PA)
Kansas State U (KS)
Kean U (NJ)
Kennesaw State U (GA)
Kent State U (OH)
The King's Coll (NY)
King's Coll (PA)
King U (TN)
Lake Erie Coll (OH)
Lake Forest Coll (IL)
Lamar U (TX)
La Roche Coll (PA)
La Salle U (PA)
Lasell Coll (MA)
Lebanon Valley Coll (PA)
Lehigh U (PA)
Le Moyne Coll (NY)
Lenoir-Rhyne U (NC)
LeTourneau U (TX)
Lewis U (IL)
Lincoln U (PA)
Lindenwood U (MO)
Linfield Coll (OR)
Loras Coll (IA)
Louisiana State U and A&M Coll (LA)
Louisiana Tech U (LA)
Loyola Marymount U (CA)
Loyola U Chicago (IL)
Loyola U Maryland (MD)
Loyola U New Orleans (LA)
Lubbock Christian U (TX)
Malone U (OH)
Manchester U (IN)
Manhattan Coll (NY)
Manhattanville Coll (NY)
Marian U (IN)
Marian U (WI)
Marietta Coll (OH)
Marshall U (WV)
Marymount Manhattan Coll (NY)
Massachusetts Inst of Technology (MA)
The Master's U (CA)
McMurry U (TX)
McNeese State U (LA)
Menlo Coll (CA)
Mercer U, Macon (GA)
Merrimack Coll (MA)
Metropolitan State U of Denver (CO)
Miami U (OH)
Michigan State U (MI)
Michigan Technological U (MI)
Minnesota State U Mankato (MN)
Minnesota State U Moorhead (MN)
Minot State U (ND)
Mississippi State U (MS)
Missouri State U (MO)
Missouri Valley Coll (MO)
Missouri Western State U (MO)
Molloy Coll (NY)
Montana State U Billings (MT)
Morehead State U (KY)
Mount Mercy U (IA)
Mount St. Joseph U (OH)
Mount Vernon Nazarene U (OH)
Murray State U (KY)
National U (CA)
Nazareth Coll of Rochester (NY)
New England Coll (NH)
New Jersey City U (NJ)
New Mexico Highlands U (NM)
New Mexico State U (NM)
New York Inst of Technology (NY)
Nichols Coll (MA)
North Central Coll (IL)
North Dakota State U (ND)
Northeastern Illinois U (IL)
Northeastern State U (OK)
Northeastern U (MA)
Northern Arizona U (AZ)
Northern Illinois U (IL)
Northern Kentucky U (KY)
Northern State U (SD)
Northwest Missouri State U (MO)
Northwood U, Michigan Campus (MI)
Nova Southeastern U (FL)
Ohio Dominican U (OH)
The Ohio State U (OH)
Ohio U (OH)
Oklahoma Baptist U (OK)
Oklahoma Christian U (OK)
Oklahoma City U (OK)
Oklahoma State U (OK)
Old Dominion U (VA)
Oral Roberts U (OK)
Oregon State U (OR)
Otterbein U (OH)
Our Lady of the Lake U of San Antonio (TX)
Pace U (NY)
Pace U, Pleasantville Campus (NY)
Palm Beach Atlantic U (FL)
Penn State Abington (PA)
Penn State Altoona (PA)
Penn State Beaver (PA)
Penn State Berks (PA)
Penn State Brandywine (PA)
Penn State DuBois (PA)
Penn State Erie, The Behrend Coll (PA)
Penn State Fayette, The Eberly Campus (PA)
Penn State Greater Allegheny (PA)
Penn State Harrisburg (PA)
Penn State Hazleton (PA)
Penn State Lehigh Valley (PA)
Penn State Mont Alto (PA)
Penn State New Kensington (PA)
Penn State Schuylkill (PA)
Penn State Shenango (PA)
Penn State U Park (PA)
Penn State Wilkes-Barre (PA)
Penn State Worthington Scranton (PA)
Penn State York (PA)
Pepperdine U, Malibu (CA)
Pittsburg State U (KS)
Plymouth State U (NH)
Point Loma Nazarene U (CA)
Polytechnic U of Puerto Rico (PR)
Portland State U (OR)
Prairie View A&M U (TX)
Providence Coll (RI)
Queens Coll of the City U of New York (NY)
Quinnipiac U (CT)
Radford U (VA)
Regis U (CO)
Rhode Island Coll (RI)
Robert Morris U (PA)
Rochester Inst of Technology (NY)
Rockford U (IL)
Roger Williams U (RI)
Rosemont Coll (PA)
Rowan U (NJ)
Rutgers U–Camden (NJ)
Rutgers U–Newark (NJ)
Rutgers U–New Brunswick (NJ)
Sacred Heart U (CT)
Saginaw Valley State U (MI)
St. Ambrose U (IA)
Saint Anselm Coll (NH)
St. Bonaventure U (NY)
St. Cloud State U (MN)
St. Edward's U (TX)
Saint Francis U (PA)
St. Gregory's U, Shawnee (OK)
St. John Fisher Coll (NY)
St. John's U (NY)
Saint Joseph's U (PA)
Saint Louis U (MO)
Saint Louis U–Madrid Campus (Spain)
Saint Mary's U of Minnesota (MN)
St. Thomas Aquinas Coll (NY)
St. Thomas U (FL)
Saint Vincent Coll (PA)
Salisbury U (MD)
Salve Regina U (RI)
Samford U (AL)
Sam Houston State U (TX)
San Diego State U (CA)
San Francisco State U (CA)
Santa Clara U (CA)
Schreiner U (TX)
Seattle U (WA)
Shippensburg U of Pennsylvania (PA)
Siena Coll (NY)
Sierra Nevada Coll (NV)
Simmons Coll (MA)
Southeastern Louisiana U (LA)
Southeastern Oklahoma State U (OK)
Southeastern U (FL)
Southeast Missouri State U (MO)
Southern Connecticut State U (CT)
Southern Illinois U Carbondale (IL)
Southern Methodist U (TX)
Southern Utah U (UT)
Southwest Baptist U (MO)
Southwestern Adventist U (TX)
Southwestern Coll (KS)
State U of New York at Fredonia (NY)
State U of New York at New Paltz (NY)
State U of New York at Oswego (NY)
State U of New York at Plattsburgh (NY)
State U of New York Coll at Old Westbury (NY)
State U of New York Coll of Technology at Canton (NY)
Stephen F. Austin State U (TX)
Stonehill Coll (MA)
Suffolk U (MA)
Susquehanna U (PA)
Syracuse U (NY)
Tarleton State U (TX)
Taylor U (IN)
Temple U (PA)
Tennessee Wesleyan U (TN)
Texas A&M Intl U (TX)
Texas A&M U (TX)
Texas A&M U–Central Texas (TX)
Texas A&M U–Commerce (TX)
Texas A&M U–Corpus Christi (TX)
Texas A&M U–Kingsville (TX)
Texas Christian U (TX)
Texas Lutheran U (TX)
Texas State U (TX)
Texas Tech U (TX)
Texas Wesleyan U (TX)
Texas Woman's U (TX)
Thomas Edison State U (NJ)
Tiffin U (OH)
Trinity Christian Coll (IL)
Trinity U (TX)
Tulane U (LA)
Union U (TN)
Université de Sherbrooke (QC, Canada)
The U of Alabama (AL)
The U of Alabama at Birmingham (AL)
The U of Alabama in Huntsville (AL)
The U of Arizona (AZ)
U of Arkansas (AR)
U of Bridgeport (CT)
U of Central Arkansas (AR)
U of Central Florida (FL)
U of Central Missouri (MO)
U of Charleston (WV)
U of Cincinnati (OH)
U of Colorado Boulder (CO)
U of Dayton (OH)
U of Delaware (DE)
U of Denver (CO)
U of Evansville (IN)
The U of Findlay (OH)
U of Florida (FL)
U of Georgia (GA)
U of Guelph (ON, Canada)
U of Hartford (CT)
U of Hawaii at Manoa (HI)
U of Houston (TX)
U of Houston–Clear Lake (TX)
U of Houston–Downtown (TX)
U of Idaho (ID)
U of Illinois at Chicago (IL)
The U of Kansas (KS)
U of Kentucky (KY)
U of Lethbridge (AB, Canada)
U of Louisiana at Monroe (LA)
U of Louisville (KY)
U of Maine (ME)
U of Mary Hardin-Baylor (TX)
U of Maryland, Coll Park (MD)
U of Maryland U Coll (MD)
U of Massachusetts Amherst (MA)
U of Massachusetts Dartmouth (MA)
U of Miami (FL)
U of Michigan–Dearborn (MI)
U of Michigan–Flint (MI)
U of Minnesota, Duluth (MN)
U of Minnesota, Twin Cities Campus (MN)
U of Missouri–St. Louis (MO)
U of Montevallo (AL)
U of Mount Union (OH)
U of Nevada, Las Vegas (NV)
U of Nevada, Reno (NV)
U of New Haven (CT)
U of New Orleans (LA)
U of North Alabama (AL)
The U of North Carolina at Charlotte (NC)
The U of North Carolina at Greensboro (NC)
U of North Dakota (ND)
U of Northern Iowa (IA)
U of North Florida (FL)
U of North Georgia (GA)
U of North Texas (TX)
U of Notre Dame (IN)
U of Oklahoma (OK)
U of Pennsylvania (PA)
U of Pittsburgh (PA)
U of Pittsburgh at Johnstown (PA)
U of Puerto Rico in Bayamón (PR)
U of Regina (SK, Canada)
U of Rhode Island (RI)
U of St. Francis (IL)
U of Saint Francis (IN)
U of St. Thomas (MN)
U of St. Thomas (TX)
U of San Diego (CA)
U of San Francisco (CA)
U of Saskatchewan (SK, Canada)
The U of Scranton (PA)
U of South Alabama (AL)
U of South Carolina (SC)
The U of South Dakota (SD)
U of Southern Indiana (IN)
U of Southern Maine (ME)
U of Southern Mississippi (MS)
U of South Florida (FL)
U of South Florida, St. Petersburg (FL)
U of South Florida Sarasota-Manatee (FL)
The U of Tampa (FL)
The U of Tennessee (TN)
The U of Tennessee at Martin (TN)
The U of Texas at Austin (TX)
The U of Texas at Dallas (TX)
The U of Texas at El Paso (TX)
The U of Texas at San Antonio (TX)
The U of Texas of the Permian Basin (TX)
The U of Texas Rio Grande Valley (TX)
U of the Incarnate Word (TX)
The U of Toledo (OH)
U of Toronto (ON, Canada)
The U of Tulsa (OK)
U of Utah (UT)
U of Washington (WA)
U of Washington, Tacoma (WA)
The U of West Alabama (AL)
U of West Georgia (GA)
U of Windsor (ON, Canada)
U of Wisconsin–Eau Claire (WI)
U of Wisconsin–La Crosse (WI)
U of Wisconsin–Madison (WI)
U of Wisconsin–Milwaukee (WI)
U of Wisconsin–Superior (WI)
U of Wisconsin–Whitewater (WI)
Utah State U (UT)
Utah Valley U (UT)
Valdosta State U (GA)
Valparaiso U (IN)
Villanova U (PA)
Virginia Polytechnic Inst and State U (VA)
Virginia Union U (VA)
Viterbo U (WI)
Wagner Coll (NY)
Wake Forest U (NC)
Walla Walla U (WA)
Walsh Coll of Accountancy and Business Administration (MI)
Walsh U (OH)
Wartburg Coll (IA)
Washburn U (KS)
Washington State U (WA)
Washington State U–Vancouver (WA)
Washington U in St. Louis (MO)
Waynesburg U (PA)
Wayne State U (MI)
Webber Intl U (FL)
Weber State U (UT)
Webster U (MO)
West Chester U of Pennsylvania (PA)
Western Carolina U (NC)
Western Connecticut State U (CT)
Western Illinois U (IL)
Western Kentucky U (KY)

Western Michigan U (MI)
Western New England U (MA)
Western Washington U (WA)
Westminster Coll (UT)
West Texas A&M U (TX)
West Virginia U (WV)
Whitworth U (WA)
Wichita State U (KS)
Wilkes U (PA)
William Paterson U of New Jersey (NJ)
Wilmington U (DE)
Wingate U (NC)
Winona State U (MN)
Wittenberg U (OH)
Wofford Coll (SC)
Wright State U (OH)
Wright State U–Lake Campus (OH)
York Coll of Pennsylvania (PA)
Youngstown State U (OH)

FINANCE AND FINANCIAL MANAGEMENT SERVICES RELATED
Brenau U (GA)
Columbia U, School of General Studies (NY)
Dominican Coll (NY)
Hofstra U (NY)
Immaculata U (PA)
James Madison U (VA)
Minot State U (ND)
Saint Mary's Coll of California (CA)
Simmons Coll (MA)
State U of New York at New Paltz (NY)
U of Northern Iowa (IA)
The U of Tampa (FL)
Virginia Commonwealth U (VA)
Westminster Coll (UT)

FINANCIAL FORENSICS AND FRAUD INVESTIGATION
Canisius Coll (NY)
Champlain Coll (VT)
Embry-Riddle Aeronautical U–Prescott (AZ)
Hilbert Coll (NY)
John Jay Coll of Criminal Justice of the City U of New York (NY)
Mount St. Mary's U (MD)

FINANCIAL MATHEMATICS
American U (DC)
Anderson U (IN)
Asbury U (KY)
Blackburn Coll (IL)
Carnegie Mellon U (PA)
Concordia Coll (MN)
Hofstra U (NY)
Knox Coll (IL)
Lee U (TN)
LeTourneau U (TX)
Lindenwood U (MO)
Mount St. Joseph U (OH)
Purdue U (IN)
Trinity U (TX)
U of California, Los Angeles (CA)
U of Cincinnati (OH)
U of Kentucky (KY)
U of Mount Union (OH)

FINANCIAL PLANNING AND SERVICES
Baylor U (TX)
Berkeley Coll–New York City Campus (NY)
Berkeley Coll–Woodland Park Campus (NJ)
Bethel Coll (IN)
Brigham Young U (UT)
Bryant U (RI)
Central Michigan U (MI)
The Coll of Saint Rose (NY)
Kansas State U (KS)
Lubbock Christian U (TX)
Maryville U of Saint Louis (MO)
Marywood U (PA)
Purdue U (IN)
Roger Williams U (RI)
Saint Joseph's U (PA)
San Diego State U (CA)
Southern Methodist U (TX)
State U of New York Coll of Technology at Alfred (NY)
Temple U (PA)
The U of Akron (OH)
U of Jamestown (ND)
U of Minnesota, Duluth (MN)
U of Mount Union (OH)
U of Wisconsin–Madison (WI)
Utah Valley U (UT)
Western Michigan U (MI)
Widener U (PA)
William Paterson U of New Jersey (NJ)
Youngstown State U (OH)

FINE AND STUDIO ARTS MANAGEMENT
Aquinas Coll (MI)
Baldwin Wallace U (OH)
Belhaven U (MS)
Bellarmine U (KY)
Bennett Coll (NC)
Bishop's U (QC, Canada)
Bluefield Coll (VA)
Brenau U (GA)
Buena Vista U (IA)
Butler U (IN)
California State U, East Bay (CA)
Chatham U (PA)
Coll of Charleston (SC)
The Coll of Idaho (ID)
Columbia Coll Chicago (IL)
Concordia U Chicago (IL)
Culver-Stockton Coll (MO)
Daemen Coll (NY)
Dickinson State U (ND)
Eastern Michigan U (MI)
Fashion Inst of Technology (NY)
Fort Lewis Coll (CO)
Indiana U Bloomington (IN)
Ithaca Coll (NY)
Lake Erie Coll (OH)
Lasell Coll (MA)
Lenoir-Rhyne U (NC)
Lipscomb U (TN)
Mary Baldwin U (VA)
Marywood U (PA)
Massachusetts Coll of Liberal Arts (MA)
Mercyhurst U (PA)
Messiah Coll (PA)
Miami U (OH)
Minot State U (ND)
North Carolina State U (NC)
Parsons School of Design (NY)
Purchase Coll, State U of New York (NY)
Randolph-Macon Coll (VA)
Ringling Coll of Art and Design (FL)
Saint Vincent Coll (PA)
Seton Hill U (PA)
Simmons Coll (MA)
Spring Hill Coll (AL)
State U of New York at Fredonia (NY)
Syracuse U (NY)
The U of North Carolina at Greensboro (NC)
U of San Francisco (CA)
The U of Tulsa (OK)
U of Waterloo (ON, Canada)
U of Wisconsin–Stevens Point (WI)
Upper Iowa U (IA)
Viterbo U (WI)
Wagner Coll (NY)
Wartburg Coll (IA)
Waynesburg U (PA)
Westminster Coll (UT)
Whitworth U (WA)

FINE ARTS RELATED
Acad of Art U (CA)
Adelphi U (NY)
Alfred U (NY)
Allegheny Coll (PA)
Ball State U (IN)
Binghamton U, State U of New York (NY)
Bowdoin Coll (ME)
Bowling Green State U (OH)
California State U, Long Beach (CA)
Cleveland Inst of Art (OH)
The Coll of Saint Rose (NY)
Columbia Coll Chicago (IL)
Columbus Coll of Art & Design (OH)
DeSales U (PA)
Elmira Coll (NY)
Grand Valley State U (MI)
Grand View U (IA)
Hampden-Sydney Coll (VA)
Hampshire Coll (MA)
Huntingdon Coll (AL)
Jacksonville U (FL)
Kansas Wesleyan U (KS)
Kentucky Wesleyan Coll (KY)
Kenyon Coll (OH)
Lake Erie Coll (OH)
Lindenwood U (MO)
Loyola U Maryland (MD)
Madonna U (MI)
Manhattanville Coll (NY)
Maryland Inst Coll of Art (MD)
Monmouth U (NJ)
The Ohio State U (OH)
Oklahoma City U (OK)
Oregon Coll of Art and Craft (OR)
Pratt Inst (NY)
Providence Coll (RI)
Purchase Coll, State U of New York (NY)
Rhode Island School of Design (RI)
Rutgers U–Newark (NJ)
St. John's U (NY)
School of the Art Inst of Chicago (IL)
Seattle U (WA)
Seton Hill U (PA)
Skidmore Coll (NY)
Spelman Coll (GA)
Stevens Inst of Technology (NJ)
The U of Akron (OH)
U of California, Los Angeles (CA)
U of Denver (CO)
U of Hartford (CT)
U of Maryland, Baltimore County (MD)
U of Mary Washington (VA)
U of Massachusetts Lowell (MA)
U of Michigan (MI)
U of Regina (SK, Canada)
The U of the Arts (PA)
U of Washington (WA)
U of Wisconsin–Milwaukee (WI)
Ursinus Coll (PA)
Washington State U–Vancouver (WA)
Widener U (PA)

FINE/STUDIO ARTS
Abilene Christian U (TX)
Acad of Art U (CA)
Agnes Scott Coll (GA)
Albertus Magnus Coll (CT)
Albion Coll (MI)
Alfred U (NY)
Allegheny Coll (PA)
American U (DC)
The American U in Dubai (United Arab Emirates)
American U of Beirut (Lebanon)
The American U of Paris (France)
The American U of Rome (Italy)
Amherst Coll (MA)
Angelo State U (TX)
Antioch Coll, Yellow Springs (OH)
Appalachian State U (NC)
Aquinas Coll (MI)
Arcadia U (PA)
Asbury U (KY)
Ashland U (OH)
Assumption Coll (MA)
Auburn U (AL)
Augsburg Coll (MN)
Baker U (KS)
Baldwin Wallace U (OH)
Bard Coll (NY)
Barton Coll (NC)
Baylor U (TX)
Beacon Coll (FL)
Bellarmine U (KY)
Belmont U (TN)
Beloit Coll (WI)
Bemidji State U (MN)
Bennington Coll (VT)
Bethany Lutheran Coll (MN)
Bethel Coll (IN)
Bethel Coll (KS)
Bethel U (MN)
Binghamton U, State U of New York (NY)
Biola U (CA)
Bishop's U (QC, Canada)
Bloomsburg U of Pennsylvania (PA)
Boston Coll (MA)
Bowdoin Coll (ME)
Bowling Green State U (OH)
Bradley U (IL)
Brandeis U (MA)
Brenau U (GA)
Bridgewater Coll (VA)
Bridgewater State U (MA)
Brigham Young U (UT)
Brigham Young U–Idaho (ID)
Brooklyn Coll of the City U of New York (NY)
Bryn Mawr Coll (PA)
Bucknell U (PA)
Buffalo State Coll, State U of New York (NY)
Caldwell U (NJ)
California Coll of the Arts (CA)
California Polytechnic State U, San Luis Obispo (CA)
California State U, East Bay (CA)
California State U, Fullerton (CA)
California State U, Long Beach (CA)
California State U, Stanislaus (CA)
Calvin Coll (MI)
Canisius Coll (NY)
Carleton Coll (MN)
Carlow U (PA)
Carthage Coll (WI)
Cazenovia Coll (NY)
Cedarville U (OH)
Centenary Coll of Louisiana (LA)
Central Michigan U (MI)
Central Washington U (WA)
Centre Coll (KY)
Chapman U (CA)
Chatham U (PA)
Chestnut Hill Coll (PA)
Chowan U (NC)
Christian Brothers U (TN)
Christopher Newport U (VA)
Clarke U (IA)
Clark U (MA)
Coastal Carolina U (SC)
Coe Coll (IA)
Colby Coll (ME)
Colby-Sawyer Coll (NH)
Coll of Charleston (SC)
The Coll of Idaho (ID)
The Coll of New Jersey (NJ)
Coll of Saint Benedict (MN)
Coll of Staten Island of the City U of New York (NY)
Coll of the Holy Cross (MA)
The Coll of Wooster (OH)
The Colorado Coll (CO)
Colorado State U (CO)
Columbia Coll Chicago (IL)
Columbia U, School of General Studies (NY)
Concordia U (QC, Canada)
Concordia U, Nebraska (NE)
Concordia U, St. Paul (MN)
Concord U (WV)
Connecticut Coll (CT)
Converse Coll (SC)
Cooper Union for the Advancement of Science and Art (NY)
Cornell U (NY)
Creighton U (NE)
Culver-Stockton Coll (MO)
Curry Coll (MA)
Daemen Coll (NY)
Dartmouth Coll (NH)
Denison U (OH)
DePauw U (IN)
Dickinson Coll (PA)
Dominican U (IL)
Drake U (IA)
Drury U (MO)
East Carolina U (NC)
Eastern Washington U (WA)
Elizabeth City State U (NC)
Elizabethtown Coll (PA)
Elms Coll (MA)
Emily Carr U of Art + Design (BC, Canada)
Emmanuel Coll (MA)
Emory & Henry Coll (VA)
Emory U (GA)
Endicott Coll (MA)
Eugene Lang Coll of Liberal Arts (NY)
The Evergreen State Coll (WA)
Fairfield U (CT)
Fashion Inst of Technology (NY)
Ferris State U (MI)
Flagler Coll (FL)
Florida Ag and Mech U (FL)
Florida Intl U (FL)
Florida Southern Coll (FL)
Florida State U (FL)
Franklin & Marshall Coll (PA)
Franklin Pierce U (NH)
Frostburg State U (MD)
Furman U (SC)
Gallaudet U (DC)
Gardner-Webb U (NC)
Georgetown Coll (KY)
Georgetown U (DC)
The George Washington U (DC)
Gettysburg Coll (PA)
Gonzaga U (WA)
Gordon Coll (MA)
Goucher Coll (MD)
Graceland U (IA)
Grand View U (IA)
Green Mountain Coll (VT)
Grinnell Coll (IA)
Hamilton Coll (NY)
Hamline U (MN)
Hampden-Sydney Coll (VA)
Harding U (AR)
Hardin-Simmons U (TX)
High Point U (NC)
Hobart and William Smith Colls (NY)
Hofstra U (NY)
Holy Cross Coll (IN)
Holy Family U (PA)
Hope Coll (MI)
Houston Baptist U (TX)
Howard Payne U (TX)
Humboldt State U (CA)
Hunter Coll of the City U of New York (NY)
Huntingdon Coll (AL)
Huntington U (IN)
Illinois State U (IL)
Indiana State U (IN)
Indiana U Bloomington (IN)
Indiana U Kokomo (IN)
Indiana U Northwest (IN)
Indiana U of Pennsylvania (PA)
Indiana U–Purdue U Indianapolis (IN)
Indiana U South Bend (IN)
Indiana U Southeast (IN)
Inst of American Indian Arts (NM)
Ithaca Coll (NY)
Jacksonville U (FL)
Judson U (IL)
Juniata Coll (PA)
Kansas State U (KS)
Kean U (NJ)
Keene State Coll (NH)
Kent State U (OH)
Kentucky State U (KY)
Kenyon Coll (OH)
Knox Coll (IL)
Kutztown U of Pennsylvania (PA)
Lafayette Coll (PA)
Laguna Coll of Art & Design (CA)
Lamar U (TX)
Lawrence U (WI)
Lebanese American U (Lebanon)
Lee U (TN)
Lewis & Clark Coll (OR)
Liberty U (VA)
Limestone Coll (SC)
Lincoln U (MO)
Lincoln U (PA)
Lindenwood U (MO)
Lindsey Wilson Coll (KY)
Linfield Coll (OR)
Lipscomb U (TN)
Lock Haven U of Pennsylvania (PA)
Louisiana Coll (LA)
Louisiana State U and A&M Coll (LA)
Loyola Marymount U (CA)
Loyola U Chicago (IL)
Loyola U New Orleans (LA)
Lubbock Christian U (TX)
Lycoming Coll (PA)
Maharishi U of Management (IA)
Manchester U (IN)
Manhattanville Coll (NY)
Marian U (IN)
Marietta Coll (OH)
Marist Coll (NY)
Marylhurst U (OR)
Marymount Manhattan Coll (NY)
Marymount U (VA)
Maryville U of Saint Louis (MO)
Massachusetts Coll of Art and Design (MA)
McMurry U (TX)
Memphis Coll of Art (TN)

Mercyhurst U (PA)
Meredith Coll (NC)
Messiah Coll (PA)
Middlebury Coll (VT)
Milligan Coll (TN)
Millikin U (IL)
Millsaps Coll (MS)
Mills Coll (CA)
Milwaukee Inst of Art and Design (WI)
Minneapolis Coll of Art and Design (MN)
Minnesota State U Mankato (MN)
Missouri Western State U (MO)
Molloy Coll (NY)
Montana State U (MT)
Morehead State U (KY)
Morningside Coll (IA)
Mount Allison U (NB, Canada)
Mount Holyoke Coll (MA)
Mount St. Joseph U (OH)
Muhlenberg Coll (PA)
Murray State U (KY)
Nazareth Coll of Rochester (NY)
New Coll of Florida (FL)
New England Coll (NH)
New Hampshire Inst of Art (NH)
New Mexico State U (NM)
Northeastern U (MA)
Northern Arizona U (AZ)
Northern Illinois U (IL)
Northern Kentucky U (KY)
North Greenville U (SC)
Northland Coll (WI)
Northwestern State U of Louisiana (LA)
Northwest Missouri State U (MO)
Nova Southeastern U (FL)
Oberlin Coll (OH)
The Ohio State U (OH)
Ohio U (OH)
Ohio Wesleyan U (OH)
Oklahoma Baptist U (OK)
Oklahoma City U (OK)
Oral Roberts U (OK)
Ouachita Baptist U (AR)
Pace U (NY)
Pacific Lutheran U (WA)
Pacific Northwest Coll of Art (OR)
Palm Beach Atlantic U (FL)
Parsons School of Design (NY)
Pennsylvania Coll of Art & Design (PA)
Piedmont Coll (GA)
Pitzer Coll (CA)
Plymouth State U (NH)
Pratt Inst (NY)
Prescott Coll (AZ)
Principia Coll (IL)
Providence Coll (RI)
Purdue U (IN)
Queens Coll of the City U of New York (NY)
Randolph Coll (VA)
Randolph-Macon Coll (VA)
Reed Coll (OR)
Rice U (TX)
Ringling Coll of Art and Design (FL)
Rochester Inst of Technology (NY)
Roger Williams U (RI)
Rosemont Coll (PA)
The Sage Colls (NY)
Saginaw Valley State U (MI)
St. Ambrose U (IA)
St. Catherine U (MN)
St. Cloud State U (MN)
Saint John's U (MN)
St. Joseph's Coll, Long Island Campus (NY)
Saint Louis U (MO)
Saint Louis U–Madrid Campus (Spain)
St. Mary's Coll of Maryland (MD)
Saint Mary's U of Minnesota (MN)
Saint Peter's U (NJ)
St. Thomas Aquinas Coll (NY)
Saint Vincent Coll (PA)
Salisbury U (MD)
Salve Regina U (RI)
Sam Houston State U (TX)
San Diego State U (CA)
Santa Clara U (CA)
Sarah Lawrence Coll (NY)
School of the Art Inst of Chicago (IL)
Scripps Coll (CA)
Seattle U (WA)
Seton Hill U (PA)
Sewanee: The U of the South (TN)
Shawnee State U (OH)
Shorter U (GA)
Siena Coll (NY)
Sierra Nevada Coll (NV)
Simpson Coll (IA)
Smith Coll (MA)
Sonoma State U (CA)
South Carolina State U (SC)
South Dakota State U (SD)
Southern Arkansas U–Magnolia (AR)
Southern Connecticut State U (CT)
Southern Illinois U Carbondale (IL)
Southern Illinois U Edwardsville (IL)
Southern Methodist U (TX)
Southern Utah U (UT)
Southwestern U (TX)
Spalding U (KY)
Spring Hill Coll (AL)
Stanford U (CA)
State U of New York at Fredonia (NY)
State U of New York Coll at Cortland (NY)
State U of New York Coll at Potsdam (NY)
Stockton U (NJ)
Stonehill Coll (MA)
Suffolk U (MA)
Susquehanna U (PA)
Swarthmore Coll (PA)
Sweet Briar Coll (VA)
Syracuse U (NY)
Tabor Coll (KS)
Tarleton State U (TX)
Texas A&M Intl U (TX)
Texas A&M U–Commerce (TX)
Texas A&M U–Kingsville (TX)
Texas Christian U (TX)
Texas State U (TX)
Thomas More Coll (KY)
Towson U (MD)
Trinity Christian Coll (IL)
Truman State U (MO)
Tufts U (MA)
Tulane U (LA)
Union Coll (NE)
Union Coll (NY)
Unity Coll (ME)
U at Buffalo, the State U of New York (NY)
The U of Akron (OH)
The U of Alabama (AL)
The U of Arizona (AZ)
U of California, Davis (CA)
U of California, Irvine (CA)
U of California, Riverside (CA)
U of California, San Diego (CA)
U of California, Santa Barbara (CA)
U of Central Florida (FL)
U of Central Missouri (MO)
U of Cincinnati (OH)
U of Colorado Boulder (CO)
U of Colorado Denver (CO)
U of Dayton (OH)
U of Delaware (DE)
U of Florida (FL)
U of Georgia (GA)
U of Great Falls (MT)
U of Guelph (ON, Canada)
U of Houston–Clear Lake (TX)
U of Idaho (ID)
U of Illinois at Chicago (IL)
U of Illinois at Springfield (IL)
U of Indianapolis (IN)
U of Jamestown (ND)
The U of Kansas (KS)
U of Kentucky (KY)
U of La Verne (CA)
U of Lethbridge (AB, Canada)
U of Louisiana at Monroe (LA)
U of Louisville (KY)
U of Maine (ME)
U of Maine at Presque Isle (ME)
U of Mary Hardin-Baylor (TX)
U of Maryland, Baltimore County (MD)
U of Maryland, Coll Park (MD)
U of Massachusetts Amherst (MA)
U of Miami (FL)
U of Michigan–Flint (MI)
U of Minnesota, Duluth (MN)
U of Minnesota, Morris (MN)
U of Missouri–Kansas City (MO)
U of Missouri–St. Louis (MO)
U of Mount Union (OH)
U of New Hampshire (NH)
U of New Haven (CT)
U of New Orleans (LA)
U of North Carolina at Asheville (NC)
The U of North Carolina at Chapel Hill (NC)
The U of North Carolina at Charlotte (NC)
The U of North Carolina at Greensboro (NC)
The U of North Carolina at Pembroke (NC)
The U of North Carolina Wilmington (NC)
U of Northern Colorado (CO)
U of Northern Iowa (IA)
U of North Florida (FL)
U of North Texas (TX)
U of Notre Dame (IN)
U of Oklahoma (OK)
U of Oregon (OR)
U of Pennsylvania (PA)
U of Pittsburgh (PA)
U of Regina (SK, Canada)
U of Rhode Island (RI)
U of Richmond (VA)
U of Rochester (NY)
U of Saint Francis (IN)
U of St. Thomas (TX)
U of San Francisco (CA)
U of Saskatchewan (SK, Canada)
U of Science and Arts of Oklahoma (OK)
U of South Carolina (SC)
U of South Carolina Aiken (SC)
U of Southern California (CA)
U of Southern Maine (ME)
U of Southern Mississippi (MS)
U of South Florida (FL)
The U of Tennessee (TN)
The U of Texas at Austin (TX)
The U of Texas at El Paso (TX)
The U of Texas at San Antonio (TX)
The U of the Arts (PA)
U of the Cumberlands (KY)
U of the Fraser Valley (BC, Canada)
U of the Incarnate Word (TX)
U of the Pacific (CA)
The U of Tulsa (OK)
U of Vermont (VT)
U of Waterloo (ON, Canada)
U of Windsor (ON, Canada)
U of Wisconsin–Stevens Point (WI)
U of Wisconsin–Superior (WI)
Vanderbilt U (TN)
Vassar Coll (NY)
Virginia Union U (VA)
Viterbo U (WI)
Wake Forest U (NC)
Walla Walla U (WA)
Washington and Lee U (VA)
Washington State U (WA)
Washington State U–Tri-Cities (WA)
Washington U in St. Louis (MO)
Watkins Coll of Art, Design, & Film (TN)
Wayland Baptist U (TX)
Webster U (MO)
Wells Coll (NY)
Wesleyan Coll (GA)
Wesleyan U (CT)
West Chester U of Pennsylvania (PA)
Western Carolina U (NC)
Western Illinois U (IL)
Western Kentucky U (KY)
Western Michigan U (MI)
Western State Colorado U (CO)
Westminster Coll (PA)
Westminster Coll (UT)
West Texas A&M U (TX)
West Virginia Wesleyan Coll (WV)
Whitman Coll (WA)
Whitworth U (WA)
Wichita State U (KS)
Willamette U (OR)
William Paterson U of New Jersey (NJ)
Williams Baptist Coll (AR)
Wittenberg U (OH)
Wright State U–Lake Campus (OH)
York Coll of Pennsylvania (PA)
Youngstown State U (OH)

FIRE PREVENTION AND SAFETY TECHNOLOGY

Athens State U (AL)
Oklahoma State U (OK)
U of New Haven (CT)

FIRE PROTECTION RELATED

The U of Akron (OH)

FIRE SCIENCE/FIREFIGHTING

Coll of the Ozarks (MO)
Columbia Southern U (AL)
Embry-Riddle Aeronautical U–Worldwide (FL)
Hampton U (VA)
Idaho State U (ID)
John Jay Coll of Criminal Justice of the City U of New York (NY)
Madonna U (MI)
New Jersey City U (NJ)
Providence Coll (RI)
U of Florida (FL)
U of New Haven (CT)
Utah Valley U (UT)

FIRE SERVICES ADMINISTRATION

Albany State U (GA)
American Public U System (WV)
Bowling Green State U (OH)
Colorado State U (CO)
Columbia Southern U (AL)
Eastern Oregon U (OR)
East Georgia State Coll (GA)
Fayetteville State U (NC)
Holy Family U (PA)
John Jay Coll of Criminal Justice of the City U of New York (NY)
Lewis U (IL)
Lindenwood U (MO)
St. Thomas U (FL)
Southern Illinois U Carbondale (IL)
U of Cincinnati (OH)
The U of North Carolina at Charlotte (NC)
Waldorf U (IA)
Western Illinois U (IL)
Western Oregon U (OR)

FISHING AND FISHERIES SCIENCES AND MANAGEMENT

Colorado State U (CO)
Humboldt State U (CA)
Iowa State U of Science and Technology (IA)
Mansfield U of Pennsylvania (PA)
Michigan State U (MI)
The Ohio State U (OH)
Oregon State U (OR)
Purdue U (IN)
Texas A&M U (TX)
U of Alaska Fairbanks (AK)
U of Idaho (ID)
U of Minnesota, Twin Cities Campus (MN)
U of Rhode Island (RI)
The U of Tennessee at Martin (TN)

FLIGHT INSTRUCTION

South Dakota State U (SD)
U of North Dakota (ND)

FOLKLORE

Goddard Coll (VT)
Indiana U Bloomington (IN)
U of Oregon (OR)

FOODS AND NUTRITION RELATED

California State U, Long Beach (CA)
Samford U (AL)
Schoolcraft Coll (MI)
U of Guelph (ON, Canada)
U of Minnesota, Twin Cities Campus (MN)
Utah State U (UT)

FOOD SCIENCE

American U of Beirut (Lebanon)
Auburn U (AL)
Bay Path U (MA)
California Polytechnic State U, San Luis Obispo (CA)
California State Polytechnic U, Pomona (CA)
Clarke U (IA)
Clemson U (SC)
Cornell U (NY)
Dalhousie U (NS, Canada)
Delaware Valley U (PA)
Dominican U (IL)
Framingham State U (MA)
Iowa State U of Science and Technology (IA)
Kansas State U (KS)
Michigan State U (MI)
Mississippi State U (MS)
Mount Mary U (WI)
North Carolina State U (NC)
North Dakota State U (ND)
The Ohio State U (OH)
Oklahoma State U (OK)
Oregon State U (OR)
Penn State Abington (PA)
Penn State Altoona (PA)
Penn State Beaver (PA)
Penn State Berks (PA)
Penn State Brandywine (PA)
Penn State DuBois (PA)
Penn State Erie, The Behrend Coll (PA)
Penn State Fayette, The Eberly Campus (PA)
Penn State Greater Allegheny (PA)
Penn State Hazleton (PA)
Penn State Lehigh Valley (PA)
Penn State Mont Alto (PA)
Penn State New Kensington (PA)
Penn State Schuylkill (PA)
Penn State Shenango (PA)
Penn State U Park (PA)
Penn State Wilkes-Barre (PA)
Penn State Worthington Scranton (PA)
Penn State York (PA)
Purdue U (IN)
Rutgers U–New Brunswick (NJ)
Simmons Coll (MA)
South Dakota State U (SD)
Texas Tech U (TX)
U of Arkansas (AR)
U of California, Davis (CA)
U of Delaware (DE)
U of Florida (FL)
U of Georgia (GA)
U of Guelph (ON, Canada)
U of Idaho (ID)
U of Kentucky (KY)
U of Maine (ME)
U of Maryland, Coll Park (MD)
U of Massachusetts Amherst (MA)
U of Minnesota, Twin Cities Campus (MN)
U of Saskatchewan (SK, Canada)
The U of Tennessee (TN)
U of Wisconsin–Madison (WI)
Virginia Polytechnic Inst and State U (VA)
Washington State U (WA)
Western Michigan U (MI)

FOOD SCIENCE AND TECHNOLOGY RELATED

Appalachian State U (NC)
North Dakota State U (ND)
Virginia Polytechnic Inst and State U (VA)

FOOD SERVICE SYSTEMS ADMINISTRATION

Dominican U (IL)
Lamar U (TX)
Lipscomb U (TN)
The Ohio State U (OH)
Ohio U (OH)
Point Loma Nazarene U (CA)
Rochester Inst of Technology (NY)
Sam Houston State U (TX)
Simmons Coll (MA)
The U of North Carolina at Greensboro (NC)
U of Wisconsin–Stout (WI)
Western Michigan U (MI)

FOODS, NUTRITION, AND WELLNESS

Alcorn State U (MS)
Andrews U (MI)
Arizona State U at the Downtown Phoenix campus (AZ)
Auburn U (AL)
Bluffton U (OH)
Bowling Green State U (OH)

Bradley U (IL)
Brooklyn Coll of the City U of New York (NY)
California State U, Fresno (CA)
Carson-Newman U (TN)
Cedar Crest Coll (PA)
Coll of the Ozarks (MO)
Dominican U (IL)
Framingham State U (MA)
Georgia Southern U (GA)
Goddard Coll (VT)
Hunter Coll of the City U of New York (NY)
Indiana State U (IN)
Indiana U of Pennsylvania (PA)
Iowa State U of Science and Technology (IA)
Ithaca Coll (NY)
Jacksonville State U (AL)
James Madison U (VA)
Lehman Coll of the City U of New York (NY)
Life U (GA)
Lincoln U (MO)
Madonna U (MI)
Minnesota State U Mankato (MN)
Montclair State U (NJ)
Morrisville State Coll (NY)
Murray State U (KY)
New Mexico State U (NM)
The New School for Public Engagement (NY)
Northern Illinois U (IL)
The Ohio State U (OH)
Ohio U (OH)
Oklahoma State U (OK)
Oregon State U (OR)
Point Loma Nazarene U (CA)
Prairie View A&M U (TX)
Radford U (VA)
St. Catherine U (MN)
Samford U (AL)
Sam Houston State U (TX)
Seattle Pacific U (WA)
South Carolina State U (SC)
State U of New York at Plattsburgh (NY)
Stephen F. Austin State U (TX)
Syracuse U (NY)
Texas A&M U (TX)
Texas State U (TX)
Texas Woman's U (TX)
Université de Montréal (QC, Canada)
The U of Akron (OH)
U of Arkansas (AR)
U of Central Arkansas (AR)
U of Delaware (DE)
U of Georgia (GA)
U of Idaho (ID)
U of Kentucky (KY)
U of Nevada, Reno (NV)
The U of North Carolina at Chapel Hill (NC)
U of Saint Joseph (CT)
The U of Tennessee (TN)
The U of Texas at Austin (TX)
U of Toronto (ON, Canada)
Virginia Polytechnic Inst and State U (VA)
Waldorf U (IA)
Washington State U (WA)
Wayne State U (MI)
Western Illinois U (IL)
Youngstown State U (OH)

FOOD TECHNOLOGY AND PROCESSING

Brigham Young U (UT)
Iowa State U of Science and Technology (IA)
New Mexico State U (NM)
State U of New York Coll of Agriculture and Technology at Cobleskill (NY)
Tennessee State U (TN)

FOREIGN LANGUAGES AND LITERATURES

Arkansas Tech U (AR)
Assumption Coll (MA)
Auburn U (AL)
Auburn U at Montgomery (AL)
Augustana U (SD)
Austin Peay State U (TN)
Benedictine Coll (KS)
Bennington Coll (VT)
Bloomsburg U of Pennsylvania (PA)
California Polytechnic State U, San Luis Obispo (CA)
Cameron U (OK)
Central Methodist U (MO)
The Citadel, The Military Coll of South Carolina (SC)
Clarion U of Pennsylvania (PA)
Clemson U (SC)
Coll of Coastal Georgia (GA)
Colorado State U (CO)
Duquesne U (PA)
East Carolina U (NC)
Eastern Illinois U (IL)
East Tennessee State U (TN)
Elmira Coll (NY)
Elon U (NC)
Emporia State U (KS)
The Evergreen State Coll (WA)
Framingham State U (MA)
Francis Marion U (SC)
Frostburg State U (MD)
Gannon U (PA)
Georgia Coll & State U (GA)
Georgia Inst of Technology (GA)
Gordon Coll (MA)
Grace Coll (IN)
Hamilton Coll (NY)
Jackson State U (MS)
James Madison U (VA)
Juniata Coll (PA)
Kansas State U (KS)
Kenyon Coll (OH)
Knox Coll (IL)
Lake Erie Coll (OH)
Lamar U (TX)
Lewis & Clark Coll (OR)
Lock Haven U of Pennsylvania (PA)
Longwood U (VA)
Louisiana Coll (LA)
Lycoming Coll (PA)
Manchester U (IN)
Marshall U (WV)
Massachusetts Inst of Technology (MA)
McNeese State U (LA)
Mercyhurst U (PA)
Mississippi State U (MS)
Missouri Western State U (MO)
Monmouth U (NJ)
Montana State U (MT)
New Coll of Florida (FL)
New Mexico State U (NM)
North Carolina State U (NC)
Northern Arizona U (AZ)
Old Dominion U (VA)
Pace U (NY)
Penn State Berks (PA)
Penn State Lehigh Valley (PA)
Piedmont Coll (GA)
Pitzer Coll (CA)
Plymouth State U (NH)
Principia Coll (IL)
Purdue U Northwest (IN)
Radford U (VA)
Roger Williams U (RI)
Rutgers U–New Brunswick (NJ)
St. Mary's Coll of Maryland (MD)
Saint Peter's U (NJ)
Samford U (AL)
Scripps Coll (CA)
Slippery Rock U of Pennsylvania (PA)
South Carolina State U (SC)
Southern Illinois U Carbondale (IL)
Southern Illinois U Edwardsville (IL)
Stanford U (CA)
State U of New York Coll at Old Westbury (NY)
Stephen F. Austin State U (TX)
Stockton U (NJ)
Stonehill Coll (MA)
Suffolk U (MA)
Syracuse U (NY)
Texas A&M U (TX)
Texas Tech U (TX)
Towson U (MD)
Tufts U (MA)
Tulane U (LA)
Union Coll (NE)
Union Coll (NY)
Union U (TN)
The U of Alabama (AL)
The U of Alabama at Birmingham (AL)
The U of Alabama in Huntsville (AL)
U of Alaska Fairbanks (AK)
U of California, Riverside (CA)
U of California, San Diego (CA)
U of Dayton (OH)
U of Delaware (DE)
U of Florida (FL)
U of Hartford (CT)
U of Houston (TX)
U of Idaho (ID)
U of Louisiana at Monroe (LA)
U of Maine (ME)
U of Maryland, Baltimore County (MD)
U of Mary Washington (VA)
U of Massachusetts Lowell (MA)
U of Minnesota, Twin Cities Campus (MN)
U of Missouri–Kansas City (MO)
U of Missouri–St. Louis (MO)
U of Montevallo (AL)
U of New Orleans (LA)
U of North Alabama (AL)
The U of North Carolina at Chapel Hill (NC)
The U of North Carolina at Greensboro (NC)
U of Northern Colorado (CO)
U of North Georgia (GA)
U of Puget Sound (WA)
U of Saskatchewan (SK, Canada)
The U of Scranton (PA)
U of South Alabama (AL)
U of Southern Mississippi (MS)
U of South Florida, St. Petersburg (FL)
The U of Tennessee (TN)
The U of Tennessee at Chattanooga (TN)
The U of Texas at San Antonio (TX)
The U of Virginia's Coll at Wise (VA)
U of Wisconsin–Platteville (WI)
Utica Coll (NY)
Virginia Commonwealth U (VA)
Washington Coll (MD)
Washington State U (WA)
Wayne State Coll (NE)
Wayne State U (MI)
Webster U (MO)
West Chester U of Pennsylvania (PA)
Western Illinois U (IL)
Western Washington U (WA)
West Virginia U (WV)
Wichita State U (KS)
Widener U (PA)
Winthrop U (SC)
Wright State U (OH)
Youngstown State U (OH)

FOREIGN LANGUAGES RELATED

Arizona State U at the Tempe campus (AZ)
Augustana U (SD)
Augusta U (GA)
Averett U (VA)
Binghamton U, State U of New York (NY)
Clemson U (SC)
Georgia Southern U (GA)
Indiana State U (IN)
Kennesaw State U (GA)
Miami U (OH)
Northeastern U (MA)
Occidental Coll (CA)
Purchase Coll, State U of New York (NY)
Saint Mary's Coll of California (CA)
United States Military Acad (NY)
U of Alaska Fairbanks (AK)
U of California, Los Angeles (CA)
U of Delaware (DE)
U of Hawaii at Manoa (HI)
U of Lethbridge (AB, Canada)
U of West Georgia (GA)
Wayne State U (MI)
Western Washington U (WA)

FOREIGN LANGUAGE TEACHER EDUCATION

Arkansas Tech U (AR)
Ashland U (OH)
Auburn U (AL)
Baylor U (TX)
Boston U (MA)
Bowling Green State U (OH)
Buffalo State Coll, State U of New York (NY)
Calvin Coll (MI)
Central Methodist U (MO)
Coll of Staten Island of the City U of New York (NY)
Concordia Coll (MN)
Eastern Michigan U (MI)
Elmira Coll (NY)
Florida Southern Coll (FL)
Gardner-Webb U (NC)
Grand Valley State U (MI)
Hofstra U (NY)
Iona Coll (NY)
Manchester U (IN)
Mercyhurst U (PA)
Messiah Coll (PA)
Miami U (OH)
Nazareth Coll of Rochester (NY)
Ohio Wesleyan U (OH)
Oral Roberts U (OK)
Pace U, Pleasantville Campus (NY)
Penn State Abington (PA)
Penn State Altoona (PA)
Penn State Beaver (PA)
Penn State Berks (PA)
Penn State Brandywine (PA)
Penn State DuBois (PA)
Penn State Erie, The Behrend Coll (PA)
Penn State Fayette, The Eberly Campus (PA)
Penn State Greater Allegheny (PA)
Penn State Mont Alto (PA)
Penn State Shenango (PA)
Penn State U Park (PA)
Penn State Worthington Scranton (PA)
Penn State York (PA)
Piedmont Coll (GA)
Providence Coll (RI)
Queens Coll of the City U of New York (NY)
Rhode Island Coll (RI)
Roger Williams U (RI)
Saint Francis U (PA)
Seton Hill U (PA)
Southeast Missouri State U (MO)
State U of New York Coll at Old Westbury (NY)
Temple U (PA)
Université de Montréal (QC, Canada)
U of Central Florida (FL)
U of Dayton (OH)
The U of Findlay (OH)
U of Georgia (GA)
U of Maine (ME)
U of Mary Hardin-Baylor (TX)
U of Minnesota, Duluth (MN)
U of Nevada, Reno (NV)
U of Oklahoma (OK)
The U of South Dakota (SD)
U of South Florida (FL)
The U of Tennessee at Chattanooga (TN)
U of Vermont (VT)
U of Windsor (ON, Canada)
Valparaiso U (IN)
Vanderbilt U (TN)
Virginia Wesleyan Coll (VA)
Wayne State Coll (NE)
Youngstown State U (OH)

FORENSIC CHEMISTRY

Alabama State U (AL)
Arizona State U at the West campus (AZ)
Ashland U (OH)
Bowling Green State U (OH)
Chestnut Hill Coll (PA)
Emmanuel Coll (MA)
Lamar U (TX)
LeTourneau U (TX)
Loyola U New Orleans (LA)
Maryville U of Saint Louis (MO)
MidAmerica Nazarene U (KS)
Missouri Baptist U (MO)
Mount Mercy U (IA)
Palm Beach Atlantic U (FL)
St. Edward's U (TX)
U of Rhode Island (RI)
U of Saint Francis (IN)
Western Carolina U (NC)
Western New England U (MA)

FORENSIC PSYCHOLOGY

Bay Path U (MA)
Canisius Coll (NY)
The Coll of Saint Rose (NY)
Embry-Riddle Aeronautical U–Prescott (AZ)
Faulkner U (AL)
Florida Inst of Technology (FL)
John Jay Coll of Criminal Justice of the City U of New York (NY)
Oklahoma Baptist U (OK)
St. Ambrose U (IA)
Tiffin U (OH)
U of New Haven (CT)
Walla Walla U (WA)
Western State Colorado U (CO)

FORENSIC SCIENCE AND TECHNOLOGY

Alvernia U (PA)
American Public U System (WV)
Bay Path U (MA)
Becker Coll (MA)
Bluefield Coll (VA)
Bryant U (RI)
Buffalo State Coll, State U of New York (NY)
Cedar Crest Coll (PA)
Cedarville U (OH)
Chaminade U of Honolulu (HI)
Chestnut Hill Coll (PA)
The Coll of Saint Rose (NY)
Columbia Coll (MO)
Defiance Coll (OH)
Dixie State U (UT)
Eastern Nazarene Coll (MA)
Embry-Riddle Aeronautical U–Prescott (AZ)
Farmingdale State Coll (NY)
Fayetteville State U (NC)
Friends U (KS)
Gannon U (PA)
Hilbert Coll (NY)
Hofstra U (NY)
Husson U (ME)
Indiana U–Purdue U Indianapolis (IN)
Inter American U of Puerto Rico, Aguadilla Campus (PR)
Inter American U of Puerto Rico, Bayamón Campus (PR)
Inter American U of Puerto Rico, Ponce Campus (PR)
Jacksonville State U (AL)
John Jay Coll of Criminal Justice of the City U of New York (NY)
King U (TN)
Lewis U (IL)
Liberty U (VA)
Loyola U Chicago (IL)
Lynn U (FL)
Madonna U (MI)
Marian U (WI)
Mercyhurst U (PA)
Mount Ida Coll (MA)
Mount Marty Coll (SD)
Newman U (KS)
New Mexico Highlands U (NM)
Pace U (NY)
Penn State Altoona (PA)
Penn State Berks (PA)
Penn State U Park (PA)
Piedmont Coll (GA)
Point Park U (PA)
Roberts Wesleyan Coll (NY)
Roger Williams U (RI)
The Sage Colls (NY)
St. Andrews U (NC)
Saint Augustine's U (NC)
St. Edward's U (TX)
Saint Francis U (PA)
Saint Louis U (MO)
St. Thomas Aquinas Coll (NY)
Sam Houston State U (TX)
Seton Hill U (PA)
Simpson Coll (IA)
State U of New York Coll of Technology at Alfred (NY)
Syracuse U (NY)
Texas A&M U (TX)
Thomas More Coll (KY)
Tiffin U (OH)
Towson U (MD)
Trine U (IN)
U of Central Florida (FL)
The U of Findlay (OH)
U of Great Falls (MT)

U of Maryland U Coll (MD)
U of New Haven (CT)
U of North Dakota (ND)
The U of Scranton (PA)
U of Southern Mississippi (MS)
The U of Tampa (FL)
U of Toronto (ON, Canada)
U of Windsor (ON, Canada)
U of Wisconsin–Platteville (WI)
Utah Valley U (UT)
Virginia Commonwealth U (VA)
Washburn U (KS)
Waynesburg U (PA)
Weber State U (UT)
Western New England U (MA)
West Virginia U (WV)
West Virginia U Inst of Technology (WV)
Wichita State U (KS)
York Coll of Pennsylvania (PA)
Youngstown State U (OH)

FOREST ENGINEERING
Oregon State U (OR)

FOREST/FOREST RESOURCES MANAGEMENT
Clemson U (SC)
Elizabethtown Coll (PA)
North Carolina State U (NC)
State U of New York Coll of Environmental Science and Forestry (NY)
Stephen F. Austin State U (TX)
U of Idaho (ID)
U of Toronto (ON, Canada)
West Virginia U (WV)
Whitman Coll (WA)

FORESTRY
Albright Coll (PA)
Beloit Coll (WI)
California Polytechnic State U, San Luis Obispo (CA)
Coll of Saint Benedict (MN)
Georgia Southern U (GA)
Humboldt State U (CA)
Iowa State U of Science and Technology (IA)
Lenoir-Rhyne U (NC)
Louisiana Tech U (LA)
Michigan State U (MI)
Michigan Technological U (MI)
Mississippi State U (MS)
New Mexico Highlands U (NM)
The Ohio State U (OH)
Purdue U (IN)
Saint John's U (MN)
Southern Illinois U Carbondale (IL)
State U of New York Coll of Environmental Science and Forestry (NY)
Stephen F. Austin State U (TX)
Texas A&M U (TX)
U of Florida (FL)
U of Georgia (GA)
U of Maine (ME)
U of Nevada, Reno (NV)
U of New Hampshire (NH)
The U of Tennessee (TN)
U of Toronto (ON, Canada)
U of Vermont (VT)
U of Wisconsin–Stevens Point (WI)
Utah State U (UT)
Virginia Polytechnic Inst and State U (VA)
Washington State U (WA)

FORESTRY RELATED
Northland Coll (WI)
Northwest Missouri State U (MO)
U of Minnesota, Twin Cities Campus (MN)
U of Wisconsin–Parkside (WI)
Utah State U (UT)

FOREST SCIENCES AND BIOLOGY
Auburn U (AL)
Colorado State U (CO)
Iowa State U of Science and Technology (IA)
Northern Arizona U (AZ)
Penn State Abington (PA)
Penn State Altoona (PA)
Penn State Beaver (PA)
Penn State Berks (PA)
Penn State Brandywine (PA)
Penn State DuBois (PA)
Penn State Erie, The Behrend Coll (PA)
Penn State Fayette, The Eberly Campus (PA)
Penn State Greater Allegheny (PA)
Penn State Hazleton (PA)
Penn State Lehigh Valley (PA)
Penn State Mont Alto (PA)
Penn State New Kensington (PA)
Penn State Schuylkill (PA)
Penn State Shenango (PA)
Penn State U Park (PA)
Penn State Wilkes-Barre (PA)
Penn State Worthington Scranton (PA)
Penn State York (PA)
Sewanee: The U of the South (TN)
State U of New York Coll of Environmental Science and Forestry (NY)
U of Georgia (GA)
U of Idaho (ID)
U of Kentucky (KY)
U of Maine (ME)
U of Wisconsin–Madison (WI)

FOREST TECHNOLOGY
Penn State Abington (PA)
Penn State Altoona (PA)
Penn State Beaver (PA)
Penn State Berks (PA)
Penn State Brandywine (PA)
Penn State DuBois (PA)
Penn State Erie, The Behrend Coll (PA)
Penn State Fayette, The Eberly Campus (PA)
Penn State Greater Allegheny (PA)
Penn State Hazleton (PA)
Penn State Lehigh Valley (PA)
Penn State Mont Alto (PA)
Penn State New Kensington (PA)
Penn State Schuylkill (PA)
Penn State Shenango (PA)
Penn State Wilkes-Barre (PA)
Penn State Worthington Scranton (PA)
Penn State York (PA)

FRANCHISING
Northwood U, Michigan Campus (MI)
St. Catherine U (MN)

FRENCH
Adelphi U (NY)
Agnes Scott Coll (GA)
Albion Coll (MI)
Albright Coll (PA)
Allegheny Coll (PA)
Alma Coll (MI)
American U (DC)
Amherst Coll (MA)
Andrews U (MI)
Aquinas Coll (MI)
Arcadia U (PA)
Arizona State U at the Tempe campus (AZ)
Armstrong State U (GA)
Asbury U (KY)
Ashland U (OH)
Assumption Coll (MA)
Auburn U (AL)
Augsburg Coll (MN)
Augustana Coll (IL)
Augustana U (SD)
Austin Coll (TX)
Baker U (KS)
Baldwin Wallace U (OH)
Ball State U (IN)
Bard Coll (NY)
Barnard Coll (NY)
Barry U (FL)
Bates Coll (ME)
Baylor U (TX)
Belmont U (TN)
Beloit Coll (WI)
Benedictine Coll (KS)
Bennington Coll (VT)
Berea Coll (KY)
Berry Coll (GA)
Binghamton U, State U of New York (NY)
Bishop's U (QC, Canada)
Boise State U (ID)
Boston Coll (MA)
Boston U (MA)
Bowdoin Coll (ME)
Bowling Green State U (OH)
Bradley U (IL)
Bridgewater Coll (VA)
Brooklyn Coll of the City U of New York (NY)
Bryant U (RI)
Bryn Mawr Coll (PA)
Bucknell U (PA)
Buffalo State Coll, State U of New York (NY)
Butler U (IN)
Cabrini U (PA)
California Lutheran U (CA)
California State U, Chico (CA)
California State U, East Bay (CA)
California State U, Fresno (CA)
California State U, Fullerton (CA)
California State U, Long Beach (CA)
California State U, Northridge (CA)
California State U, Sacramento (CA)
California State U, San Bernardino (CA)
Calvin Coll (MI)
Canisius Coll (NY)
Capital U (OH)
Carleton Coll (MN)
Carnegie Mellon U (PA)
Carroll Coll (MT)
Carthage Coll (WI)
Case Western Reserve U (OH)
The Catholic U of America (DC)
Centenary Coll of Louisiana (LA)
Central Connecticut State U (CT)
Central Michigan U (MI)
Central Washington U (WA)
Centre Coll (KY)
Chapman U (CA)
Chestnut Hill Coll (PA)
Christopher Newport U (VA)
City Coll of the City U of New York (NY)
Claremont McKenna Coll (CA)
Clarion U of Pennsylvania (PA)
Clark Atlanta U (GA)
Clark U (MA)
Cleveland State U (OH)
Coe Coll (IA)
Colby Coll (ME)
Colgate U (NY)
The Coll at Brockport, State U of New York (NY)
Coll of Charleston (SC)
Coll of Coastal Georgia (GA)
Coll of Mount Saint Vincent (NY)
Coll of Saint Benedict (MN)
Coll of the Holy Cross (MA)
The Coll of William and Mary (VA)
The Coll of Wooster (OH)
The Colorado Coll (CO)
Colorado State U (CO)
Columbia U (NY)
Columbia U, School of General Studies (NY)
Columbus State U (GA)
Concordia Coll (MN)
Concordia U (QC, Canada)
Connecticut Coll (CT)
Cornell Coll (IA)
Cornell U (NY)
Creighton U (NE)
Daemen Coll (NY)
Dalhousie U (NS, Canada)
Dartmouth Coll (NH)
Davidson Coll (NC)
Denison U (OH)
DePauw U (IN)
Dickinson Coll (PA)
Doane U (NE)
Dominican U (IL)
Drew U (NJ)
Drury U (MO)
Earlham Coll (IN)
Eastern Michigan U (MI)
Eastern Washington U (WA)
Eckerd Coll (FL)
Edgewood Coll (WI)
Elizabethtown Coll (PA)
Elon U (NC)
Emory & Henry Coll (VA)
Fairfield U (CT)
Fairleigh Dickinson U, Coll at Florham (NJ)
Fairleigh Dickinson U, Metropolitan Campus (NJ)
Florida Atlantic U (FL)
Florida Intl U (FL)
Fordham U (NY)
Franciscan U of Steubenville (OH)
Franklin & Marshall Coll (PA)
Franklin Coll (IN)
Furman U (SC)
Gardner-Webb U (NC)
Georgetown Coll (KY)
Georgetown U (DC)
The George Washington U (DC)
Georgia Southern U (GA)
Georgia State U (GA)
Gettysburg Coll (PA)
Gonzaga U (WA)
Gordon Coll (MA)
Goucher Coll (MD)
Grace Coll (IN)
Grand Valley State U (MI)
Grinnell Coll (IA)
Grove City Coll (PA)
Guilford Coll (NC)
Hamilton Coll (NY)
Hampden-Sydney Coll (VA)
Hanover Coll (IN)
Harding U (AR)
Hartwick Coll (NY)
Haverford Coll (PA)
Hendrix Coll (AR)
High Point U (NC)
Hillsdale Coll (MI)
Hiram Coll (OH)
Hobart and William Smith Colls (NY)
Hofstra U (NY)
Hollins U (VA)
Hood Coll (MD)
Hope Coll (MI)
Humboldt State U (CA)
Hunter Coll of the City U of New York (NY)
Idaho State U (ID)
Illinois Coll (IL)
Illinois State U (IL)
Illinois Wesleyan U (IL)
Indiana U Bloomington (IN)
Indiana U Northwest (IN)
Indiana U–Purdue U Indianapolis (IN)
Indiana U South Bend (IN)
Indiana U Southeast (IN)
Iona Coll (NY)
Iowa State U of Science and Technology (IA)
Ithaca Coll (NY)
Jacksonville State U (AL)
Jacksonville U (FL)
John Carroll U (OH)
Johns Hopkins U (MD)
Johnson C. Smith U (NC)
Juniata Coll (PA)
Kalamazoo Coll (MI)
Keene State Coll (NH)
Kent State U (OH)
Kenyon Coll (OH)
King's Coll (PA)
King U (TN)
Knox Coll (IL)
Lafayette Coll (PA)
Lake Erie Coll (OH)
Lake Forest Coll (IL)
Lane Coll (TN)
Lawrence U (WI)
Lebanon Valley Coll (PA)
Lee U (TN)
Lehigh U (PA)
Lehman Coll of the City U of New York (NY)
Le Moyne Coll (NY)
Lewis & Clark Coll (OR)
Lincoln U (PA)
Lindenwood U (MO)
Linfield Coll (OR)
Lipscomb U (TN)
Louisiana Coll (LA)
Louisiana State U and A&M Coll (LA)
Louisiana Tech U (LA)
Loyola Marymount U (CA)
Loyola U Chicago (IL)
Loyola U Maryland (MD)
Loyola U New Orleans (LA)
Luther Coll (IA)
Lycoming Coll (PA)
Lynchburg Coll (VA)
Macalester Coll (MN)
Manchester U (IN)
Manhattan Coll (NY)
Manhattanville Coll (NY)
Marist Coll (NY)
McDaniel Coll (MD)
McMaster U (ON, Canada)
Mercer U, Macon (GA)
Merrimack Coll (MA)
Messiah Coll (PA)
Miami U (OH)
Michigan State U (MI)
Middlebury Coll (VT)
Millersville U of Pennsylvania (PA)
Minnesota State U Mankato (MN)
Missouri State U (MO)
Monmouth Coll (IL)
Montclair State U (NJ)
Moravian Coll (PA)
Morehead State U (KY)
Morehouse Coll (GA)
Mount Allison U (NB, Canada)
Mount Holyoke Coll (MA)
Mount Saint Mary's U (CA)
Mount St. Mary's U (MD)
Muhlenberg Coll (PA)
Murray State U (KY)
Muskingum U (OH)
Nazareth Coll of Rochester (NY)
Nebraska Wesleyan U (NE)
New Coll of Florida (FL)
Niagara U (NY)
North Carolina State U (NC)
North Central Coll (IL)
North Dakota State U (ND)
Northeastern Illinois U (IL)
Northern Illinois U (IL)
Northern Kentucky U (KY)
Northern State U (SD)
Northwestern U (IL)
Oberlin Coll (OH)
Occidental Coll (CA)
The Ohio State U (OH)
Ohio U (OH)
Ohio Wesleyan U (OH)
Oklahoma City U (OK)
Oklahoma State U (OK)
Oral Roberts U (OK)
Oregon State U (OR)
Otterbein U (OH)
Pacific Lutheran U (WA)
Penn State Abington (PA)
Penn State Altoona (PA)
Penn State Beaver (PA)
Penn State Berks (PA)
Penn State Brandywine (PA)
Penn State DuBois (PA)
Penn State Erie, The Behrend Coll (PA)
Penn State Fayette, The Eberly Campus (PA)
Penn State Greater Allegheny (PA)
Penn State Hazleton (PA)
Penn State Lehigh Valley (PA)
Penn State Mont Alto (PA)
Penn State New Kensington (PA)
Penn State Schuylkill (PA)
Penn State Shenango (PA)
Penn State U Park (PA)
Penn State Wilkes-Barre (PA)
Penn State Worthington Scranton (PA)
Penn State York (PA)
Pepperdine U, Malibu (CA)
Pittsburg State U (KS)
Plymouth State U (NH)
Point Loma Nazarene U (CA)
Pomona Coll (CA)
Portland State U (OR)
Princeton U (NJ)
Principia Coll (IL)
Providence Coll (RI)
Purchase Coll, State U of New York (NY)
Purdue U (IN)
Queens Coll of the City U of New York (NY)
Randolph Coll (VA)
Randolph-Macon Coll (VA)
Redeemer U Coll (ON, Canada)
Reed Coll (OR)
Regis U (CO)
Rhode Island Coll (RI)
Rhodes Coll (TN)
Rice U (TX)
Roanoke Coll (VA)
Rockford U (IL)
Rockhurst U (MO)
Royal Military Coll of Canada (ON, Canada)

Rutgers U–Camden (NJ)
Rutgers U–Newark (NJ)
Rutgers U–New Brunswick (NJ)
Saginaw Valley State U (MI)
St. Ambrose U (IA)
Saint Anselm Coll (NH)
St. Catherine U (MN)
St. Cloud State U (MN)
St. Edward's U (TX)
St. John Fisher Coll (NY)
Saint John's U (MN)
St. John's U (NY)
Saint Joseph's U (PA)
Saint Louis U (MO)
Saint Louis U–Madrid Campus (Spain)
Saint Mary's Coll of California (CA)
Saint Michael's Coll (VT)
St. Norbert Coll (WI)
St. Olaf Coll (MN)
St. Thomas U (NB, Canada)
Saint Vincent Coll (PA)
Salisbury U (MD)
Salve Regina U (RI)
Samford U (AL)
Sam Houston State U (TX)
San Diego State U (CA)
San Francisco State U (CA)
Santa Clara U (CA)
Sarah Lawrence Coll (NY)
Scripps Coll (CA)
Seattle U (WA)
Sewanee: The U of the South (TN)
Shippensburg U of Pennsylvania (PA)
Siena Coll (NY)
Simmons Coll (MA)
Simon Fraser U (BC, Canada)
Simpson Coll (IA)
Skidmore Coll (NY)
Slippery Rock U of Pennsylvania (PA)
Smith Coll (MA)
Sonoma State U (CA)
South Dakota State U (SD)
Southern Connecticut State U (CT)
Southern Methodist U (TX)
Southern Oregon U (OR)
Southern Utah U (UT)
Southwestern U (TX)
Spelman Coll (GA)
Stanford U (CA)
State U of New York at Fredonia (NY)
State U of New York at New Paltz (NY)
State U of New York at Oswego (NY)
State U of New York at Plattsburgh (NY)
State U of New York Coll at Cortland (NY)
State U of New York Coll at Geneseo (NY)
State U of New York Coll at Potsdam (NY)
Stonehill Coll (MA)
Stony Brook U, State U of New York (NY)
Suffolk U (MA)
Susquehanna U (PA)
Swarthmore Coll (PA)
Sweet Briar Coll (VA)
Syracuse U (NY)
Temple U (PA)
Tennessee State U (TN)
Tennessee Wesleyan U (TN)
Texas A&M U (TX)
Texas Christian U (TX)
Texas State U (TX)
Texas Tech U (TX)
Transylvania U (KY)
Trent U (ON, Canada)
Trinity U (TX)
Truman State U (MO)
Tufts U (MA)
Tulane U (LA)
Union Coll (NE)
Union Coll (NY)
Union U (TN)
United States Military Acad (NY)
Université de Montréal (QC, Canada)
Université de Sherbrooke (QC, Canada)
U at Buffalo, the State U of New York (NY)
The U of Akron (OH)
The U of Arizona (AZ)
U of Arkansas (AR)
U of California, Davis (CA)
U of California, Irvine (CA)
U of California, Los Angeles (CA)
U of California, Riverside (CA)
U of California, San Diego (CA)
U of California, Santa Barbara (CA)
U of Central Arkansas (AR)
U of Central Florida (FL)
U of Central Missouri (MO)
U of Cincinnati (OH)
U of Colorado Boulder (CO)
U of Colorado Denver (CO)
U of Dayton (OH)
U of Denver (CO)
U of Evansville (IN)
U of Florida (FL)
U of Georgia (GA)
U of Hawaii at Manoa (HI)
U of Houston (TX)
U of Idaho (ID)
U of Illinois at Chicago (IL)
U of Indianapolis (IN)
U of Jamestown (ND)
The U of Kansas (KS)
U of Kentucky (KY)
U of King's Coll (NS, Canada)
U of La Verne (CA)
U of Louisville (KY)
U of Maine (ME)
U of Maine at Fort Kent (ME)
U of Maryland, Coll Park (MD)
U of Massachusetts Amherst (MA)
U of Massachusetts Boston (MA)
U of Massachusetts Dartmouth (MA)
U of Miami (FL)
U of Michigan (MI)
U of Michigan–Dearborn (MI)
U of Michigan–Flint (MI)
U of Minnesota, Duluth (MN)
U of Minnesota, Morris (MN)
U of Minnesota, Twin Cities Campus (MN)
U of Mount Union (OH)
U of Nebraska at Kearney (NE)
U of Nevada, Las Vegas (NV)
U of Nevada, Reno (NV)
U of New Hampshire (NH)
U of North Alabama (AL)
U of North Carolina at Asheville (NC)
The U of North Carolina at Charlotte (NC)
The U of North Carolina at Greensboro (NC)
The U of North Carolina Wilmington (NC)
U of North Dakota (ND)
U of North Texas (TX)
U of Notre Dame (IN)
U of Oklahoma (OK)
U of Oregon (OR)
U of Pennsylvania (PA)
U of Pittsburgh (PA)
U of Puget Sound (WA)
U of Regina (SK, Canada)
U of Rhode Island (RI)
U of Richmond (VA)
U of Rochester (NY)
U of St. Thomas (MN)
U of St. Thomas (TX)
U of San Diego (CA)
U of San Francisco (CA)
U of Saskatchewan (SK, Canada)
The U of Scranton (PA)
U of South Carolina (SC)
The U of South Dakota (SD)
U of Southern California (CA)
U of Southern Indiana (IN)
U of Southern Maine (ME)
U of South Florida (FL)
The U of Tennessee (TN)
The U of Tennessee at Martin (TN)
The U of Texas at Austin (TX)
The U of Texas at El Paso (TX)
U of the Pacific (CA)
The U of Toledo (OH)
U of Toronto (ON, Canada)
The U of Tulsa (OK)
U of Utah (UT)
U of Vermont (VT)
U of Virginia (VA)
The U of Virginia's Coll at Wise (VA)
U of Washington (WA)
U of Waterloo (ON, Canada)
U of Windsor (ON, Canada)
U of Wisconsin–Eau Claire (WI)
U of Wisconsin–Green Bay (WI)
U of Wisconsin–La Crosse (WI)
U of Wisconsin–Madison (WI)
U of Wisconsin–Milwaukee (WI)
U of Wisconsin–Stevens Point (WI)
U of Wisconsin–Whitewater (WI)
Ursinus Coll (PA)
Utah State U (UT)
Valdosta State U (GA)
Valparaiso U (IN)
Vanderbilt U (TN)
Vassar Coll (NY)
Villanova U (PA)
Virginia Polytechnic Inst and State U (VA)
Virginia Wesleyan Coll (VA)
Wabash Coll (IN)
Wake Forest U (NC)
Walla Walla U (WA)
Walsh U (OH)
Washburn U (KS)
Washington & Jefferson Coll (PA)
Washington and Lee U (VA)
Washington Coll (MD)
Washington State U (WA)
Washington U in St. Louis (MO)
Weber State U (UT)
Webster U (MO)
Wesleyan Coll (GA)
West Chester U of Pennsylvania (PA)
Western Carolina U (NC)
Western Kentucky U (KY)
Western Michigan U (MI)
Western Washington U (WA)
Westminster Coll (PA)
Westmont Coll (CA)
Wheaton Coll (IL)
Wheaton Coll (MA)
Wheeling Jesuit U (WV)
Whitman Coll (WA)
Whittier Coll (CA)
Whitworth U (WA)
Widener U (PA)
Willamette U (OR)
William Jewell Coll (MO)
Williams Coll (MA)
Wittenberg U (OH)
Wofford Coll (SC)
Wright State U (OH)
Wright State U–Lake Campus (OH)
Xavier U of Louisiana (LA)
York Coll of the City U of New York (NY)

FRENCH AS A SECOND/ FOREIGN LANGUAGE (TEACHING)

Bishop's U (QC, Canada)
Saginaw Valley State U (MI)
U of Toronto (ON, Canada)
U of Windsor (ON, Canada)

FRENCH LANGUAGE TEACHER EDUCATION

Albion Coll (MI)
Ashland U (OH)
Auburn U (AL)
Augustana Coll (IL)
Austin Coll (TX)
Boise State U (ID)
Bradley U (IL)
Brooklyn Coll of the City U of New York (NY)
California Lutheran U (CA)
Calvin Coll (MI)
Canisius Coll (NY)
The Catholic U of America (DC)
Central Michigan U (MI)
Central Washington U (WA)
Colorado State U (CO)
Concordia Coll (MN)
Daemen Coll (NY)
Eastern Michigan U (MI)
Eastern Washington U (WA)
Edgewood Coll (WI)
Elmira Coll (NY)
Emory & Henry Coll (VA)
Franklin Coll (IN)
Gardner-Webb U (NC)
Grace Coll (IN)
Grand Valley State U (MI)
Grove City Coll (PA)
Harding U (AR)
Hofstra U (NY)
Holy Family U (PA)
Hope Coll (MI)
Indiana U South Bend (IN)
Iona Coll (NY)
Ithaca Coll (NY)
Juniata Coll (PA)
King U (TN)
Lee U (TN)
Le Moyne Coll (NY)
Lindenwood U (MO)
Lipscomb U (TN)
Louisiana Coll (LA)
Louisiana Tech U (LA)
Manchester U (IN)
Manhattanville Coll (NY)
Marist Coll (NY)
Merrimack Coll (MA)
Messiah Coll (PA)
Miami U (OH)
Michigan State U (MI)
Missouri State U (MO)
Missouri Western State U (MO)
Niagara U (NY)
North Dakota State U (ND)
Ohio U (OH)
Ohio Wesleyan U (OH)
Pittsburg State U (KS)
Providence Coll (RI)
Queens Coll of the City U of New York (NY)
Rhode Island Coll (RI)
St. Catherine U (MN)
St. John Fisher Coll (NY)
Saint Joseph's U (PA)
Salve Regina U (RI)
Southern Utah U (UT)
State U of New York at Plattsburgh (NY)
State U of New York Coll at Cortland (NY)
State U of New York Coll at Potsdam (NY)
Université de Montréal (QC, Canada)
The U of Akron (OH)
U of Delaware (DE)
U of Evansville (IN)
U of Illinois at Chicago (IL)
U of Indianapolis (IN)
U of Lethbridge (AB, Canada)
U of Maine (ME)
U of Michigan–Flint (MI)
The U of North Carolina at Greensboro (NC)
U of Regina (SK, Canada)
U of St. Thomas (MN)
The U of South Dakota (SD)
The U of Tennessee at Martin (TN)
U of Toronto (ON, Canada)
U of Waterloo (ON, Canada)
U of Windsor (ON, Canada)
U of Wisconsin–Whitewater (WI)
Valparaiso U (IN)
Washburn U (KS)
Washington U in St. Louis (MO)
Weber State U (UT)
Western Illinois U (IL)
Western Michigan U (MI)
Western Washington U (WA)
Widener U (PA)
Xavier U of Louisiana (LA)

FRENCH STUDIES

American U (DC)
Arcadia U (PA)
Bard Coll (NY)
Barnard Coll (NY)
Bowdoin Coll (ME)
Brandeis U (MA)
Carleton Coll (MN)
Case Western Reserve U (OH)
Coe Coll (IA)
The Colorado Coll (CO)
Columbia U (NY)
Columbia U, School of General Studies (NY)
Emory & Henry Coll (VA)
Emory U (GA)
Fordham U (NY)
Lewis & Clark Coll (OR)
Linfield Coll (OR)
Mills Coll (CA)
Moravian Coll (PA)
Rhode Island Coll (RI)
Saint Joseph's U (PA)
Skidmore Coll (NY)
Smith Coll (MA)
Suffolk U (MA)
U of Guelph (ON, Canada)
U of New Hampshire (NH)
U of North Florida (FL)
The U of Scranton (PA)
U of Waterloo (ON, Canada)
U of Windsor (ON, Canada)
Wagner Coll (NY)
Wesleyan U (CT)
Wheaton Coll (MA)

FUNERAL DIRECTION/ SERVICE

Wayne State U (MI)

FUNERAL SERVICE AND MORTUARY SCIENCE

Gannon U (PA)
Lincoln Coll of New England, Southington (CT)
Mount Ida Coll (MA)
Point Park U (PA)
St. John's U (NY)
Southern Illinois U Carbondale (IL)
U of Minnesota, Twin Cities Campus (MN)

FURNITURE DESIGN AND MANUFACTURING

Rhode Island School of Design (RI)

GAME AND INTERACTIVE MEDIA DESIGN

Abilene Christian U (TX)
Acad of Art U (CA)
Arkansas Tech U (AR)
Becker Coll (MA)
Bradley U (IL)
Cardinal Stritch U (WI)
Champlain Coll (VT)
Cleveland Inst of Art (OH)
Cogswell Polytechnical Coll (CA)
Columbia Coll Chicago (IL)
Dakota State U (SD)
DeSales U (PA)
Drexel U (PA)
Freed-Hardeman U (TN)
Grand View U (IA)
Indiana U Bloomington (IN)
Inter American U of Puerto Rico, Bayamón Campus (PR)
Kennesaw State U (GA)
Laguna Coll of Art & Design (CA)
Marist Coll (NY)
Maryland Inst Coll of Art (MD)
Memphis Coll of Art (TN)
New England Inst of Technology (RI)
Oklahoma Christian U (OK)
Quinnipiac U (CT)
Ringling Coll of Art and Design (FL)
Rochester Inst of Technology (NY)
St. Edward's U (TX)
Sarah Lawrence Coll (NY)
Savannah Coll of Art and Design (GA)
Shawnee State U (OH)
Southern Arkansas U–Magnolia (AR)
Southwestern Coll (KS)
U of California, Irvine (CA)
U of Denver (CO)
U of Saint Francis (IN)
U of Southern California (CA)
The U of Texas at Dallas (TX)
U of Wisconsin–Whitewater (WI)
Webster U (MO)
William Peace U (NC)
Wilmington U (DE)

GAY/LESBIAN STUDIES

Bennington Coll (VT)
Bryant U (RI)
Cornell U (NY)
Hampshire Coll (MA)
Mills Coll (CA)
Sarah Lawrence Coll (NY)

GENERAL STUDIES

Albertus Magnus Coll (CT)
Alfred U (NY)
Ambrose U (AB, Canada)
American Public U System (WV)
Antioch U Midwest (OH)
Aquinas Coll (MI)
Austin Coll (TX)
Austin Peay State U (TN)
Ball State U (IN)

Bethel Coll (IN)
Bluefield State Coll (WV)
Boise State U (ID)
Brenau U (GA)
Brewton-Parker Coll (GA)
Buffalo State Coll, State U of New York (NY)
California State U, San Bernardino (CA)
California State U, San Marcos (CA)
Calumet Coll of Saint Joseph (IN)
Cameron U (OK)
The Catholic U of America (DC)
Centenary U (NJ)
Champlain Coll (VT)
Colorado Christian U (CO)
Columbia Coll (MO)
Columbia Coll Chicago (IL)
Columbia Intl U (SC)
Concordia U Chicago (IL)
Concordia U, St. Paul (MN)
Concordia U Wisconsin (WI)
Concord U (WV)
Cornell U (NY)
Cornerstone U (MI)
Dean Coll (MA)
Drexel U (PA)
East Carolina U (NC)
East Central U (OK)
Eastern Nazarene Coll (MA)
East Tennessee State U (TN)
Emory & Henry Coll (VA)
Emporia State U (KS)
Excelsior Coll (NY)
Fairfield U (CT)
Fairleigh Dickinson U, Coll at Florham (NJ)
Fairleigh Dickinson U, Metropolitan Campus (NJ)
Ferris State U (MI)
Florida Inst of Technology (FL)
Fort Lewis Coll (CO)
Georgia Southern U (GA)
Granite State Coll (NH)
Hampton U (VA)
Harding U (AR)
Henderson State U (AR)
Holy Family U (PA)
Howard Payne U (TX)
Idaho State U (ID)
Illinois State U (IL)
Iowa State U of Science and Technology (IA)
Jacksonville U (FL)
Kansas Wesleyan U (KS)
Keene State Coll (NH)
Kent State U (OH)
Kent State U at Ashtabula (OH)
Kent State U at East Liverpool (OH)
Kent State U at Geauga (OH)
Kent State U at Salem (OH)
Kent State U at Stark (OH)
Kent State U at Trumbull (OH)
Kent State U at Tuscarawas (OH)
Kentucky Wesleyan Coll (KY)
Kutztown U of Pennsylvania (PA)
LaGrange Coll (GA)
Lamar U (TX)
La Roche Coll (PA)
La Salle U (PA)
Lasell Coll (MA)
Lee U (TN)
Lewis U (IL)
Liberty U (VA)
Lincoln Christian U (IL)
Lindenwood U (MO)
Lipscomb U (TN)
Louisiana Tech U (LA)
Loyola U Chicago (IL)
Madonna U (MI)
Marshall U (WV)
Marywood U (PA)
McNeese State U (LA)
Minot State U (ND)
Misericordia U (PA)
Mississippi Valley State U (MS)
Missouri Baptist U (MO)
Missouri Valley Coll (MO)
Molloy Coll (NY)
Montana Tech of The U of Montana (MT)
Morehead State U (KY)
Mount Marty Coll (SD)
Mount Mary U (WI)
Mount St. Joseph U (OH)
Murray State U (KY)
National U (CA)
New Mexico Inst of Mining and Technology (NM)
New Mexico State U (NM)
North Carolina Wesleyan Coll (NC)
Northeastern State U (OK)
Northern Kentucky U (KY)
North Greenville U (SC)
Northwestern Oklahoma State U (OK)
Northwestern State U of Louisiana (LA)
Northwestern U (IL)
Northwest U (WA)
Nova Southeastern U (FL)
Oakland City U (IN)
The Ohio State U (OH)
Ohio Wesleyan U (OH)
Oklahoma State U (OK)
Palm Beach Atlantic U (FL)
Pepperdine U, Malibu (CA)
Providence Coll (RI)
Roberts Wesleyan Coll (NY)
Sacred Heart U (CT)
Saginaw Valley State U (MI)
St. John's Coll (NM)
Saint Louis U (MO)
Samford U (AL)
Sam Houston State U (TX)
San Diego State U (CA)
Seattle Pacific U (WA)
Seton Hill U (PA)
Shawnee State U (OH)
Shenandoah U (VA)
Shepherd U (WV)
Shorter U (GA)
Simmons Coll (MA)
Simon Fraser U (BC, Canada)
Slippery Rock U of Pennsylvania (PA)
South Dakota State U (SD)
Southeastern Louisiana U (LA)
Southeastern Oklahoma State U (OK)
Southeastern U (FL)
Southeast Missouri State U (MO)
Southern Arkansas U–Magnolia (AR)
Southern New Hampshire U (NH)
Southern Utah U (UT)
Southwestern Adventist U (TX)
Southwestern Assemblies of God U (TX)
Southwestern Coll (KS)
Spalding U (KY)
Spring Hill Coll (AL)
State U of New York at New Paltz (NY)
State U of New York Coll of Technology at Alfred (NY)
State U of New York Maritime Coll (NY)
State U of New York Polytechnic Inst (NY)
Tarleton State U (TX)
Temple U (PA)
Texas A&M U–Commerce (TX)
Texas Christian U (TX)
Texas State U (TX)
Texas Tech U (TX)
Texas Woman's U (TX)
Tiffin U (OH)
Toccoa Falls Coll (GA)
Trevecca Nazarene U (TN)
Trinity Coll of Florida (FL)
Union Coll (NE)
United States Air Force Acad (CO)
U of Bridgeport (CT)
U of Central Florida (FL)
U of Charleston (WV)
U of Delaware (DE)
U of Hartford (CT)
U of Idaho (ID)
U of Kentucky (KY)
U of Lethbridge (AB, Canada)
U of Louisiana at Monroe (LA)
U of Management and Technology (VA)
U of Mary Hardin-Baylor (TX)
U of Massachusetts Amherst (MA)
U of Miami (FL)
U of Michigan (MI)
U of Michigan–Dearborn (MI)
U of Missouri–Kansas City (MO)
U of Mobile (AL)
U of Nebraska at Kearney (NE)
U of Nevada, Reno (NV)
U of North Dakota (ND)
U of Northern Iowa (IA)
U of North Georgia (GA)
U of North Texas (TX)
U of St. Thomas (TX)
U of South Florida (FL)
U of South Florida Sarasota-Manatee (FL)
The U of Tampa (FL)
The U of Tennessee at Martin (TN)
The U of Texas at San Antonio (TX)
U of the Cumberlands (KY)
U of the Fraser Valley (BC, Canada)
U of the Southwest (NM)
U of the West (CA)
The U of Toledo (OH)
U of Washington (WA)
U of Washington, Bothell (WA)
U of Washington, Tacoma (WA)
U of Wisconsin–Stevens Point (WI)
Ursinus Coll (PA)
Western Kentucky U (KY)
Western Washington U (WA)
West Texas A&M U (TX)
West Virginia State U (WV)
West Virginia U (WV)
West Virginia U Inst of Technology (WV)
Wheeling Jesuit U (WV)
Wichita State U (KS)
Widener U (PA)
Wilmington U (DE)
York Coll of Pennsylvania (PA)
Youngstown State U (OH)

GENETICS

Cedar Crest Coll (PA)
Iowa State U of Science and Technology (IA)
New Mexico State U (NM)
North Carolina State U (NC)
Ohio Wesleyan U (OH)
Purdue U (IN)
U of California, Davis (CA)
U of California, Irvine (CA)
U of Georgia (GA)
U of New Hampshire (NH)
U of Wisconsin–Madison (WI)
Washington State U (WA)

GENETICS RELATED

The George Washington U (DC)

GENOME SCIENCES/ GENOMICS

Northwestern Coll (IA)

GEOCHEMISTRY

Bowling Green State U (OH)
Bridgewater State U (MA)
California Inst of Technology (CA)
Columbia U (NY)
Grand Valley State U (MI)
State U of New York at Fredonia (NY)
State U of New York at New Paltz (NY)
State U of New York at Oswego (NY)
State U of New York Coll at Cortland (NY)
State U of New York Coll at Geneseo (NY)
U of Waterloo (ON, Canada)
Washington U in St. Louis (MO)
Western Michigan U (MI)
Whitman Coll (WA)

GEOGRAPHIC INFORMATION SCIENCE AND CARTOGRAPHY

Arizona State U at the Tempe campus (AZ)
Auburn U at Montgomery (AL)
Binghamton U, State U of New York (NY)
Brigham Young U (UT)
Central Michigan U (MI)
Central Washington U (WA)
East Central U (OK)
Kennesaw State U (GA)
Michigan State U (MI)
Northwest Missouri State U (MO)
The Ohio State U (OH)
Oklahoma State U (OK)
Radford U (VA)
Rowan U (NJ)
Slippery Rock U of Pennsylvania (PA)
South Dakota State U (SD)
Stephen F. Austin State U (TX)
Texas A&M U (TX)
Texas State U (TX)
United States Military Acad (NY)
U at Buffalo, the State U of New York (NY)
The U of Akron (OH)
The U of Arizona (AZ)
U of Cincinnati (OH)
U of Lethbridge (AB, Canada)
U of Minnesota, Duluth (MN)
U of North Alabama (AL)
U of Oklahoma (OK)
The U of Texas at Dallas (TX)
U of Utah (UT)
U of Wisconsin–Eau Claire (WI)
U of Wisconsin–Madison (WI)
Western Kentucky U (KY)

GEOGRAPHY

Adams State U (CO)
Appalachian State U (NC)
Aquinas Coll (MI)
Arizona State U at the Tempe campus (AZ)
Auburn U (AL)
Augustana Coll (IL)
Ball State U (IN)
Bemidji State U (MN)
Bishop's U (QC, Canada)
Boston U (MA)
Bowling Green State U (OH)
Bridgewater State U (MA)
Bucknell U (PA)
Buffalo State Coll, State U of New York (NY)
California State Polytechnic U, Pomona (CA)
California State U, Chico (CA)
California State U, Dominguez Hills (CA)
California State U, East Bay (CA)
California State U, Fresno (CA)
California State U, Fullerton (CA)
California State U, Long Beach (CA)
California State U, Northridge (CA)
California State U, Sacramento (CA)
California State U, San Bernardino (CA)
California State U, Stanislaus (CA)
California U of Pennsylvania (PA)
Calvin Coll (MI)
Carthage Coll (WI)
Central Connecticut State U (CT)
Central Michigan U (MI)
Central State U (OH)
Central Washington U (WA)
City Coll of the City U of New York (NY)
Clark U (MA)
Colgate U (NY)
Coll of Staten Island of the City U of New York (NY)
Concordia U (QC, Canada)
Concordia U Chicago (IL)
Concordia U, Nebraska (NE)
Concord U (WV)
Dartmouth Coll (NH)
East Carolina U (NC)
Eastern Illinois U (IL)
Eastern Michigan U (MI)
Eastern Washington U (WA)
East Tennessee State U (TN)
Emory & Henry Coll (VA)
Fayetteville State U (NC)
Fitchburg State U (MA)
Florida Atlantic U (FL)
Florida Intl U (FL)
Florida State U (FL)
Framingham State U (MA)
Frostburg State U (MD)
The George Washington U (DC)
Georgia Coll & State U (GA)
Georgia Southern U (GA)
Grand Valley State U (MI)
Harrisburg U of Science and Technology (PA)
Hofstra U (NY)
Humboldt State U (CA)
Hunter Coll of the City U of New York (NY)
Illinois State U (IL)
Indiana State U (IN)
Indiana U Bloomington (IN)
Indiana U of Pennsylvania (PA)
Indiana U–Purdue U Indianapolis (IN)
Indiana U Southeast (IN)
Jacksonville State U (AL)
Jacksonville U (FL)
James Madison U (VA)
Johns Hopkins U (MD)
Kansas State U (KS)
Keene State Coll (NH)
Kennesaw State U (GA)
Kent State U (OH)
Kutztown U of Pennsylvania (PA)
Lehman Coll of the City U of New York (NY)
Louisiana State U and A&M Coll (LA)
Louisiana Tech U (LA)
Macalester Coll (MN)
Marshall U (WV)
McMaster U (ON, Canada)
Miami U (OH)
Michigan State U (MI)
Middlebury Coll (VT)
Millersville U of Pennsylvania (PA)
Minnesota State U Mankato (MN)
Missouri State U (MO)
Montclair State U (NJ)
Mount Allison U (NB, Canada)
Mount Holyoke Coll (MA)
New Mexico State U (NM)
Northeastern Illinois U (IL)
Northeastern State U (OK)
Northern Arizona U (AZ)
Northern Illinois U (IL)
Northern Kentucky U (KY)
Northwestern U (IL)
Northwest Missouri State U (MO)
The Ohio State U (OH)
Ohio U (OH)
Ohio Wesleyan U (OH)
Oklahoma State U (OK)
Old Dominion U (VA)
Olivet Nazarene U (IL)
Penn State Abington (PA)
Penn State Altoona (PA)
Penn State Beaver (PA)
Penn State Berks (PA)
Penn State Brandywine (PA)
Penn State DuBois (PA)
Penn State Erie, The Behrend Coll (PA)
Penn State Fayette, The Eberly Campus (PA)
Penn State Greater Allegheny (PA)
Penn State Hazleton (PA)
Penn State Lehigh Valley (PA)
Penn State Mont Alto (PA)
Penn State New Kensington (PA)
Penn State Schuylkill (PA)
Penn State Shenango (PA)
Penn State U Park (PA)
Penn State Wilkes-Barre (PA)
Penn State Worthington Scranton (PA)
Penn State York (PA)
Pittsburg State U (KS)
Plymouth State U (NH)
Portland State U (OR)
Rhode Island Coll (RI)
Rowan U (NJ)
Rutgers U–New Brunswick (NJ)
Saginaw Valley State U (MI)
St. Cloud State U (MN)
Salisbury U (MD)
Samford U (AL)
Sam Houston State U (TX)
San Diego State U (CA)
San Francisco State U (CA)
Sarah Lawrence Coll (NY)
Shippensburg U of Pennsylvania (PA)
Simon Fraser U (BC, Canada)
Slippery Rock U of Pennsylvania (PA)
Sonoma State U (CA)
South Dakota State U (SD)
Southern Connecticut State U (CT)
Southern Illinois U Carbondale (IL)
Southern Illinois U Edwardsville (IL)
State U of New York at New Paltz (NY)
State U of New York at Plattsburgh (NY)
State U of New York Coll at Cortland (NY)

State U of New York Coll at Geneseo (NY)
Stephen F. Austin State U (TX)
Syracuse U (NY)
Taylor U (IN)
Texas A&M U (TX)
Texas Christian U (TX)
Texas State U (TX)
Texas Tech U (TX)
Towson U (MD)
Trent U (ON, Canada)
United States Air Force Acad (CO)
United States Military Acad (NY)
Université de Montréal (QC, Canada)
U at Albany, State U of New York (NY)
U at Buffalo, the State U of New York (NY)
The U of Akron (OH)
The U of Alabama (AL)
U of Alaska Fairbanks (AK)
The U of Arizona (AZ)
U of Arkansas (AR)
U of California, Los Angeles (CA)
U of California, Santa Barbara (CA)
U of Central Arkansas (AR)
U of Central Missouri (MO)
U of Chicago (IL)
U of Cincinnati (OH)
U of Colorado Boulder (CO)
U of Colorado Colorado Springs (CO)
U of Colorado Denver (CO)
U of Delaware (DE)
U of Denver (CO)
U of Florida (FL)
U of Georgia (GA)
U of Guelph (ON, Canada)
U of Hawaii at Manoa (HI)
U of Houston–Clear Lake (TX)
U of Idaho (ID)
The U of Kansas (KS)
U of Kentucky (KY)
U of Lethbridge (AB, Canada)
U of Louisville (KY)
U of Maine at Farmington (ME)
U of Maryland, Baltimore County (MD)
U of Maryland, Coll Park (MD)
U of Mary Washington (VA)
U of Massachusetts Amherst (MA)
U of Miami (FL)
U of Minnesota, Duluth (MN)
U of Minnesota, Twin Cities Campus (MN)
U of Missouri–Kansas City (MO)
U of Nebraska at Kearney (NE)
U of Nevada, Reno (NV)
U of New Hampshire (NH)
U of North Alabama (AL)
The U of North Carolina at Chapel Hill (NC)
The U of North Carolina at Charlotte (NC)
The U of North Carolina at Greensboro (NC)
The U of North Carolina Wilmington (NC)
U of North Dakota (ND)
U of Northern Colorado (CO)
U of Northern Iowa (IA)
U of North Texas (TX)
U of Oklahoma (OK)
U of Oregon (OR)
U of Pittsburgh at Johnstown (PA)
U of Regina (SK, Canada)
U of Richmond (VA)
U of St. Thomas (MN)
U of Saskatchewan (SK, Canada)
U of South Alabama (AL)
U of South Carolina (SC)
U of Southern California (CA)
U of Southern Mississippi (MS)
U of South Florida (FL)
The U of Tennessee (TN)
The U of Tennessee at Martin (TN)
The U of Texas at Austin (TX)
The U of Texas at El Paso (TX)
The U of Texas at San Antonio (TX)
U of the Fraser Valley (BC, Canada)
The U of Toledo (OH)
U of Toronto (ON, Canada)
U of Vermont (VT)
U of Washington (WA)
U of Waterloo (ON, Canada)
U of West Georgia (GA)
U of Wisconsin–Eau Claire (WI)
U of Wisconsin–La Crosse (WI)
U of Wisconsin–Madison (WI)
U of Wisconsin–Milwaukee (WI)
U of Wisconsin–Parkside (WI)
U of Wisconsin–Platteville (WI)
U of Wisconsin–Stevens Point (WI)
U of Wisconsin–Whitewater (WI)
Utah State U (UT)
Valparaiso U (IN)
Vassar Coll (NY)
Villanova U (PA)
Virginia Polytechnic Inst and State U (VA)
Wayne State Coll (NE)
Weber State U (UT)
West Chester U of Pennsylvania (PA)
Western Carolina U (NC)
Western Illinois U (IL)
Western Kentucky U (KY)
Western Michigan U (MI)
Western Oregon U (OR)
Western Washington U (WA)
West Virginia U (WV)
William Paterson U of New Jersey (NJ)
Worcester State U (MA)
Wright State U (OH)
Wright State U–Lake Campus (OH)
Youngstown State U (OH)

GEOGRAPHY RELATED

Arkansas Tech U (AR)
Bridgewater State U (MA)
Brigham Young U (UT)
Central Washington U (WA)
Emory & Henry Coll (VA)
Mount Ida Coll (MA)
Ohio U (OH)
Temple U (PA)
U of California, Los Angeles (CA)

GEOGRAPHY TEACHER EDUCATION

Bishop's U (QC, Canada)
Calvin Coll (MI)
Ferris State U (MI)
Grand Valley State U (MI)
Michigan State U (MI)
Rhode Island Coll (RI)
Université de Montréal (QC, Canada)
U of Delaware (DE)
The U of Tennessee at Martin (TN)
U of Windsor (ON, Canada)
U of Wisconsin–Whitewater (WI)
Valparaiso U (IN)
Wayne State Coll (NE)
Weber State U (UT)

GEOLOGICAL AND EARTH SCIENCES/GEOSCIENCES RELATED

Allegheny Coll (PA)
Boston U (MA)
Bridgewater State U (MA)
Brigham Young U (UT)
California State U, Chico (CA)
California State U, Dominguez Hills (CA)
California State U, Fullerton (CA)
Cedarville U (OH)
Central Washington U (WA)
Earlham Coll (IN)
Eckerd Coll (FL)
Georgia Inst of Technology (GA)
Hamilton Coll (NY)
Harrisburg U of Science and Technology (PA)
Lehigh U (PA)
Minnesota State U Moorhead (MN)
Muskingum U (OH)
Old Dominion U (VA)
Oregon State U (OR)
Penn State Abington (PA)
Penn State Altoona (PA)
Penn State Beaver (PA)
Penn State Berks (PA)
Penn State Brandywine (PA)
Penn State DuBois (PA)
Penn State Erie, The Behrend Coll (PA)
Penn State Fayette, The Eberly Campus (PA)
Penn State Greater Allegheny (PA)
Penn State Hazleton (PA)
Penn State Lehigh Valley (PA)
Penn State Mont Alto (PA)
Penn State New Kensington (PA)
Penn State Schuylkill (PA)
Penn State Shenango (PA)
Penn State U Park (PA)
Penn State Wilkes-Barre (PA)
Penn State Worthington Scranton (PA)
Penn State York (PA)
Princeton U (NJ)
Rocky Mountain Coll (MT)
Salisbury U (MD)
Stanford U (CA)
Texas A&M U (TX)
Texas Christian U (TX)
Towson U (MD)
Union Coll (NY)
U at Buffalo, the State U of New York (NY)
U of Guelph (ON, Canada)
U of Miami (FL)
U of Pittsburgh (PA)
U of Rhode Island (RI)
U of Utah (UT)
U of Washington (WA)
Utica Coll (NY)
Western State Colorado U (CO)
Western Washington U (WA)
Whitman Coll (WA)

GEOLOGICAL/GEOPHYSICAL ENGINEERING

Colorado School of Mines (CO)
Michigan Technological U (MI)
Missouri U of Science and Technology (MO)
Montana Tech of The U of Montana (MT)
Rutgers U–Newark (NJ)
South Dakota School of Mines and Technology (SD)
Tufts U (MA)
U of Alaska Fairbanks (AK)
U of California, Los Angeles (CA)
U of Michigan (MI)
U of Minnesota, Twin Cities Campus (MN)
U of Nevada, Reno (NV)
U of North Dakota (ND)
U of Rochester (NY)
U of Saskatchewan (SK, Canada)
The U of Texas at Austin (TX)
U of Toronto (ON, Canada)
U of Utah (UT)
U of Waterloo (ON, Canada)
U of Wisconsin–Madison (WI)

GEOLOGY/EARTH SCIENCE

Adams State U (CO)
Albion Coll (MI)
Alfred U (NY)
Allegheny Coll (PA)
American U of Beirut (Lebanon)
Amherst Coll (MA)
Angelo State U (TX)
Appalachian State U (NC)
Arkansas Tech U (AR)
Ashland U (OH)
Auburn U (AL)
Augustana Coll (IL)
Austin Peay State U (TN)
Ball State U (IN)
Bates Coll (ME)
Baylor U (TX)
Beloit Coll (WI)
Bemidji State U (MN)
Binghamton U, State U of New York (NY)
Bloomsburg U of Pennsylvania (PA)
Boise State U (ID)
Boston Coll (MA)
Boston U (MA)
Bowdoin Coll (ME)
Bowling Green State U (OH)
Bridgewater State U (MA)
Brigham Young U–Idaho (ID)
Brooklyn Coll of the City U of New York (NY)
Bryn Mawr Coll (PA)
Bucknell U (PA)
Buffalo State Coll, State U of New York (NY)
California Inst of Technology (CA)
California Lutheran U (CA)
California Polytechnic State U, San Luis Obispo (CA)
California State Polytechnic U, Pomona (CA)
California State U, Bakersfield (CA)
California State U, Chico (CA)
California State U, East Bay (CA)
California State U, Fresno (CA)
California State U, Fullerton (CA)
California State U, Long Beach (CA)
California State U, Northridge (CA)
California State U, Sacramento (CA)
California State U, San Bernardino (CA)
California State U, Stanislaus (CA)
California U of Pennsylvania (PA)
Calvin Coll (MI)
Carleton Coll (MN)
Case Western Reserve U (OH)
Cedarville U (OH)
Centenary Coll of Louisiana (LA)
Central Connecticut State U (CT)
Central Michigan U (MI)
Central State U (OH)
Central Washington U (WA)
City Coll of the City U of New York (NY)
Clarion U of Pennsylvania (PA)
Clark U (MA)
Clemson U (SC)
Colby Coll (ME)
Colgate U (NY)
The Coll at Brockport, State U of New York (NY)
Coll of Charleston (SC)
The Coll of William and Mary (VA)
The Coll of Wooster (OH)
The Colorado Coll (CO)
Colorado Mesa U (CO)
Colorado State U (CO)
Columbia U (NY)
Columbia U, School of General Studies (NY)
Columbus State U (GA)
Concordia U Chicago (IL)
Concord U (WV)
Cornell Coll (IA)
Dalhousie U (NS, Canada)
Dartmouth Coll (NH)
Denison U (OH)
DePauw U (IN)
Dickinson Coll (PA)
Drexel U (PA)
East Carolina U (NC)
Eastern Illinois U (IL)
Eastern Michigan U (MI)
Eastern Washington U (WA)
East Stroudsburg U of Pennsylvania (PA)
East Tennessee State U (TN)
Elizabeth City State U (NC)
Emporia State U (KS)
Florida Atlantic U (FL)
Florida Intl U (FL)
Florida State U (FL)
Fort Lewis Coll (CO)
Framingham State U (MA)
Franklin & Marshall Coll (PA)
Frostburg State U (MD)
Furman U (SC)
The George Washington U (DC)
Georgia Southern U (GA)
Georgia Southwestern State U (GA)
Georgia State U (GA)
Grand Valley State U (MI)
Guilford Coll (NC)
Hamilton Coll (NY)
Hanover Coll (IN)
Hardin-Simmons U (TX)
Hartwick Coll (NY)
Harvard U (MA)
Haverford Coll (PA)
Hobart and William Smith Colls (NY)
Hofstra U (NY)
Hope Coll (MI)
Humboldt State U (CA)
Idaho State U (ID)
Illinois State U (IL)
Indiana State U (IN)
Indiana U Bloomington (IN)
Indiana U Northwest (IN)
Indiana U of Pennsylvania (PA)
Indiana U–Purdue U Indianapolis (IN)
Iowa State U of Science and Technology (IA)
Jackson State U (MS)
Jacksonville State U (AL)
James Madison U (VA)
Johns Hopkins U (MD)
Kansas State U (KS)
Kean U (NJ)
Kent State U (OH)
Kutztown U of Pennsylvania (PA)
Lafayette Coll (PA)
Lamar U (TX)
La Salle U (PA)
Lawrence U (WI)
Lehman Coll of the City U of New York (NY)
Lock Haven U of Pennsylvania (PA)
Louisiana State U and A&M Coll (LA)
Louisiana Tech U (LA)
Macalester Coll (MN)
Marietta Coll (OH)
Marshall U (WV)
Massachusetts Inst of Technology (MA)
McMaster U (ON, Canada)
Mercyhurst U (PA)
Miami U (OH)
Michigan State U (MI)
Michigan Technological U (MI)
Middlebury Coll (VT)
Millersville U of Pennsylvania (PA)
Millsaps Coll (MS)
Minnesota State U Mankato (MN)
Minot State U (ND)
Mississippi State U (MS)
Missouri State U (MO)
Missouri U of Science and Technology (MO)
Montana State U (MT)
Montclair State U (NJ)
Moravian Coll (PA)
Morehead State U (KY)
Mount Allison U (NB, Canada)
Mount Holyoke Coll (MA)
Murray State U (KY)
Muskingum U (OH)
New Jersey City U (NJ)
New Mexico Highlands U (NM)
New Mexico Inst of Mining and Technology (NM)
New Mexico State U (NM)
North Carolina State U (NC)
North Dakota State U (ND)
Northeastern Illinois U (IL)
Northeastern U (MA)
Northern Arizona U (AZ)
Northern Illinois U (IL)
Northern Kentucky U (KY)
Northland Coll (WI)
Northwestern U (IL)
Northwest Missouri State U (MO)
Oberlin Coll (OH)
Occidental Coll (CA)
The Ohio State U (OH)
Ohio U (OH)
Ohio Wesleyan U (OH)
Oklahoma State U (OK)
Olivet Nazarene U (IL)
Pacific Lutheran U (WA)
Penn State Abington (PA)
Penn State Altoona (PA)
Penn State Beaver (PA)
Penn State Berks (PA)
Penn State Brandywine (PA)
Penn State DuBois (PA)
Penn State Erie, The Behrend Coll (PA)
Penn State Fayette, The Eberly Campus (PA)
Penn State Greater Allegheny (PA)
Penn State Hazleton (PA)
Penn State Lehigh Valley (PA)
Penn State Mont Alto (PA)
Penn State New Kensington (PA)
Penn State Schuylkill (PA)
Penn State Shenango (PA)
Penn State U Park (PA)
Penn State Wilkes-Barre (PA)
Penn State Worthington Scranton (PA)
Penn State York (PA)
Piedmont Coll (GA)
Pomona Coll (CA)
Portland State U (OR)
Purdue U (IN)

Queens Coll of the City U of New York (NY)
Radford U (VA)
Rensselaer Polytechnic Inst (NY)
Rice U (TX)
Rocky Mountain Coll (MT)
Rutgers U–Newark (NJ)
Rutgers U–New Brunswick (NJ)
St. Cloud State U (MN)
Saint Louis U (MO)
St. Norbert Coll (WI)
Sam Houston State U (TX)
San Diego State U (CA)
San Francisco State U (CA)
Scripps Coll (CA)
Sewanee: The U of the South (TN)
Shawnee State U (OH)
Shippensburg U of Pennsylvania (PA)
Skidmore Coll (NY)
Slippery Rock U of Pennsylvania (PA)
Smith Coll (MA)
Sonoma State U (CA)
South Dakota School of Mines and Technology (SD)
Southern Connecticut State U (CT)
Southern Illinois U Carbondale (IL)
Southern Methodist U (TX)
Southern Oregon U (OR)
Southern Utah U (UT)
Stanford U (CA)
State U of New York at Fredonia (NY)
State U of New York at New Paltz (NY)
State U of New York at Oswego (NY)
State U of New York at Plattsburgh (NY)
State U of New York Coll at Cortland (NY)
State U of New York Coll at Geneseo (NY)
State U of New York Coll at Potsdam (NY)
Stephen F. Austin State U (TX)
Stockton U (NJ)
Stony Brook U, State U of New York (NY)
Susquehanna U (PA)
Syracuse U (NY)
Tarleton State U (TX)
Temple U (PA)
Texas A&M U (TX)
Texas A&M U–Corpus Christi (TX)
Texas A&M U–Kingsville (TX)
Texas Christian U (TX)
Texas Tech U (TX)
Towson U (MD)
Trinity U (TX)
Tufts U (MA)
Tulane U (LA)
Union Coll (NY)
Université de Montréal (QC, Canada)
U at Buffalo, the State U of New York (NY)
The U of Akron (OH)
The U of Alabama (AL)
U of Alaska Fairbanks (AK)
The U of Arizona (AZ)
U of Arkansas (AR)
U of California, Davis (CA)
U of California, Irvine (CA)
U of California, Los Angeles (CA)
U of California, Riverside (CA)
U of California, San Diego (CA)
U of California, Santa Barbara (CA)
U of Central Missouri (MO)
U of Cincinnati (OH)
U of Colorado Boulder (CO)
U of Dayton (OH)
U of Delaware (DE)
U of Florida (FL)
U of Georgia (GA)
U of Hawaii at Manoa (HI)
U of Houston (TX)
U of Houston–Downtown (TX)
U of Idaho (ID)
U of Illinois at Chicago (IL)
U of Indianapolis (IN)
The U of Kansas (KS)
U of Kentucky (KY)
U of King's Coll (NS, Canada)
U of Maine (ME)
U of Maine at Farmington (ME)
U of Maryland, Coll Park (MD)
U of Massachusetts Amherst (MA)
U of Massachusetts Boston (MA)
U of Massachusetts Lowell (MA)
U of Miami (FL)
U of Michigan (MI)
U of Michigan–Dearborn (MI)
U of Minnesota, Duluth (MN)
U of Minnesota, Morris (MN)
U of Minnesota, Twin Cities Campus (MN)
U of Missouri–Kansas City (MO)
U of Mount Union (OH)
U of Nevada, Las Vegas (NV)
U of Nevada, Reno (NV)
U of New Hampshire (NH)
U of New Orleans (LA)
The U of North Carolina at Chapel Hill (NC)
The U of North Carolina at Charlotte (NC)
The U of North Carolina at Greensboro (NC)
The U of North Carolina Wilmington (NC)
U of North Dakota (ND)
U of Northern Colorado (CO)
U of Northern Iowa (IA)
U of Oklahoma (OK)
U of Oregon (OR)
U of Pennsylvania (PA)
U of Pittsburgh (PA)
U of Pittsburgh at Johnstown (PA)
U of Puget Sound (WA)
U of Regina (SK, Canada)
U of Rhode Island (RI)
U of Rochester (NY)
U of St. Thomas (MN)
U of Saskatchewan (SK, Canada)
U of South Alabama (AL)
U of South Carolina (SC)
The U of South Dakota (SD)
U of Southern California (CA)
U of Southern Indiana (IN)
U of Southern Maine (ME)
U of Southern Mississippi (MS)
U of South Florida (FL)
The U of Tennessee (TN)
The U of Tennessee at Chattanooga (TN)
The U of Tennessee at Martin (TN)
The U of Texas at Austin (TX)
The U of Texas at Dallas (TX)
The U of Texas at El Paso (TX)
The U of Texas at San Antonio (TX)
The U of Texas of the Permian Basin (TX)
U of the Pacific (CA)
U of Toledo (OH)
The U of Tulsa (OK)
U of Utah (UT)
U of Vermont (VT)
U of Washington (WA)
U of Waterloo (ON, Canada)
U of West Georgia (GA)
U of Windsor (ON, Canada)
U of Wisconsin–Eau Claire (WI)
U of Wisconsin–Green Bay (WI)
U of Wisconsin–Madison (WI)
U of Wisconsin–Milwaukee (WI)
U of Wisconsin–Parkside (WI)
U of Wisconsin–Stevens Point (WI)
Utah State U (UT)
Utah Valley U (UT)
Valdosta State U (GA)
Valparaiso U (IN)
Vanderbilt U (TN)
Vassar Coll (NY)
Virginia Polytechnic Inst and State U (VA)
Virginia Wesleyan Coll (VA)
Wartburg Coll (IA)
Washington and Lee U (VA)
Washington State U (WA)
Washington State U–Tri-Cities (WA)
Washington State U–Vancouver (WA)
Washington U in St. Louis (MO)
Wayland Baptist U (TX)
Wayne State U (MI)
Weber State U (UT)
West Chester U of Pennsylvania (PA)
Western Carolina U (NC)
Western Connecticut State U (CT)
Western Illinois U (IL)
Western Kentucky U (KY)
Western Michigan U (MI)
Western State Colorado U (CO)
Western Washington U (WA)
Westminster Coll (UT)
West Virginia U (WV)
Wheaton Coll (IL)
Whitman Coll (WA)
Wichita State U (KS)
Wilkes U (PA)
William Paterson U of New Jersey (NJ)
Williams Coll (MA)
Winona State U (MN)
Wittenberg U (OH)
Wright State U (OH)
York Coll of the City U of New York (NY)
Youngstown State U (OH)

GEOPHYSICS AND SEISMOLOGY

Baylor U (TX)
Boise State U (ID)
Boston Coll (MA)
Boston U (MA)
Bowling Green State U (OH)
California Inst of Technology (CA)
Eastern Michigan U (MI)
Michigan Technological U (MI)
Missouri U of Science and Technology (MO)
New Mexico Inst of Mining and Technology (NM)
Rice U (TX)
Southern Methodist U (TX)
Stanford U (CA)
State U of New York at Fredonia (NY)
State U of New York Coll at Geneseo (NY)
Texas A&M U (TX)
The U of Akron (OH)
U of California, Los Angeles (CA)
U of California, Riverside (CA)
U of California, Santa Barbara (CA)
U of Chicago (IL)
U of Houston (TX)
U of Nevada, Reno (NV)
U of Oklahoma (OK)
U of Saskatchewan (SK, Canada)
U of South Carolina (SC)
The U of Texas at Austin (TX)
The U of Texas at El Paso (TX)
The U of Tulsa (OK)
U of Utah (UT)
U of Washington (WA)
U of Waterloo (ON, Canada)
Washington U in St. Louis (MO)
Western Michigan U (MI)
Western Washington U (WA)
Whitman Coll (WA)

GERIATRIC NURSING

Keuka Coll (NY)

GERMAN

Agnes Scott Coll (GA)
Albion Coll (MI)
Allegheny Coll (PA)
Alma Coll (MI)
American U (DC)
Amherst Coll (MA)
Aquinas Coll (MI)
Arizona State U at the Tempe campus (AZ)
Auburn U (AL)
Augsburg Coll (MN)
Augustana Coll (IL)
Augustana U (SD)
Austin Coll (TX)
Baker U (KS)
Baldwin Wallace U (OH)
Ball State U (IN)
Bard Coll (NY)
Barnard Coll (NY)
Bates Coll (ME)
Baylor U (TX)
Belmont U (TN)
Beloit Coll (WI)
Bemidji State U (MN)
Berea Coll (KY)
Berry Coll (GA)
Binghamton U, State U of New York (NY)
Bishop's U (QC, Canada)
Boise State U (ID)
Boston Coll (MA)
Boston U (MA)
Bowdoin Coll (ME)
Bowling Green State U (OH)
Brooklyn Coll of the City U of New York (NY)
Bryn Mawr Coll (PA)
Bucknell U (PA)
Butler U (IN)
California Lutheran U (CA)
California State U, Chico (CA)
California State U, Long Beach (CA)
Calvin Coll (MI)
Canisius Coll (NY)
Carleton Coll (MN)
Carnegie Mellon U (PA)
Carthage Coll (WI)
Case Western Reserve U (OH)
The Catholic U of America (DC)
Central Connecticut State U (CT)
Central Michigan U (MI)
Central Washington U (WA)
Centre Coll (KY)
Christopher Newport U (VA)
Coe Coll (IA)
Colby Coll (ME)
Colgate U (NY)
Coll of Charleston (SC)
Coll of Saint Benedict (MN)
Coll of the Holy Cross (MA)
The Coll of William and Mary (VA)
The Coll of Wooster (OH)
The Colorado Coll (CO)
Colorado State U (CO)
Columbia U (NY)
Columbia U, School of General Studies (NY)
Concordia Coll (MN)
Concordia U Wisconsin (WI)
Converse Coll (SC)
Cornell Coll (IA)
Cornell U (NY)
Creighton U (NE)
Dalhousie U (NS, Canada)
Dartmouth Coll (NH)
Davidson Coll (NC)
Denison U (OH)
DePauw U (IN)
Dickinson Coll (PA)
Doane U (NE)
Drew U (NJ)
Drury U (MO)
Earlham Coll (IN)
Eastern Michigan U (MI)
Elizabethtown Coll (PA)
Fairfield U (CT)
Fordham U (NY)
Franciscan U of Steubenville (OH)
Franklin & Marshall Coll (PA)
Furman U (SC)
Georgetown U (DC)
The George Washington U (DC)
Georgia Southern U (GA)
Georgia State U (GA)
Gettysburg Coll (PA)
Gordon Coll (MA)
Grinnell Coll (IA)
Guilford Coll (NC)
Hamline U (MN)
Hampden-Sydney Coll (VA)
Hanover Coll (IN)
Hartwick Coll (NY)
Harvard U (MA)
Haverford Coll (PA)
Heidelberg U (OH)
Hendrix Coll (AR)
Hillsdale Coll (MI)
Hofstra U (NY)
Hood Coll (MD)
Hope Coll (MI)
Hunter Coll of the City U of New York (NY)
Idaho State U (ID)
Illinois Coll (IL)
Illinois State U (IL)
Illinois Wesleyan U (IL)
Indiana U–Purdue U Indianapolis (IN)
Indiana U South Bend (IN)
Indiana U Southeast (IN)
Iowa State U of Science and Technology (IA)
Ithaca Coll (NY)
Jacksonville State U (AL)
John Carroll U (OH)
Johns Hopkins U (MD)
Juniata Coll (PA)
Kalamazoo Coll (MI)
Kent State U (OH)
Kenyon Coll (OH)
Knox Coll (IL)
Lafayette Coll (PA)
Lawrence U (WI)
Lebanon Valley Coll (PA)
Lehigh U (PA)
Lenoir-Rhyne U (NC)
Lewis & Clark Coll (OR)
Linfield Coll (OR)
Lipscomb U (TN)
Loyola U Maryland (MD)
Luther Coll (IA)
Lycoming Coll (PA)
Macalester Coll (MN)
McDaniel Coll (MD)
McMaster U (ON, Canada)
Mercer U, Macon (GA)
Messiah Coll (PA)
Miami U (OH)
Michigan State U (MI)
Middlebury Coll (VT)
Millersville U of Pennsylvania (PA)
Minnesota State U Mankato (MN)
Minot State U (ND)
Missouri State U (MO)
Montclair State U (NJ)
Moravian Coll (PA)
Mount Allison U (NB, Canada)
Mount St. Mary's U (MD)
Murray State U (KY)
Muskingum U (OH)
Nazareth Coll of Rochester (NY)
Nebraska Wesleyan U (NE)
New Coll of Florida (FL)
North Central Coll (IL)
Northern Illinois U (IL)
Northern Kentucky U (KY)
Northern State U (SD)
Northwestern U (IL)
Oberlin Coll (OH)
The Ohio State U (OH)
Ohio U (OH)
Ohio Wesleyan U (OH)
Oklahoma State U (OK)
Oregon State U (OR)
Pacific Lutheran U (WA)
Penn State Abington (PA)
Penn State Altoona (PA)
Penn State Beaver (PA)
Penn State Berks (PA)
Penn State Brandywine (PA)
Penn State DuBois (PA)
Penn State Erie, The Behrend Coll (PA)
Penn State Fayette, The Eberly Campus (PA)
Penn State Greater Allegheny (PA)
Penn State Hazleton (PA)
Penn State Lehigh Valley (PA)
Penn State Mont Alto (PA)
Penn State New Kensington (PA)
Penn State Schuylkill (PA)
Penn State Shenango (PA)
Penn State U Park (PA)
Penn State Wilkes-Barre (PA)
Penn State Worthington Scranton (PA)
Penn State York (PA)
Pomona Coll (CA)
Portland State U (OR)
Princeton U (NJ)
Purdue U (IN)
Queens Coll of the City U of New York (NY)
Randolph-Macon Coll (VA)
Reed Coll (OR)
Rhodes Coll (TN)
Rice U (TX)
Rutgers U–Camden (NJ)
Rutgers U–Newark (NJ)
Rutgers U–New Brunswick (NJ)
St. Cloud State U (MN)
Saint John's U (MN)
Saint Joseph's U (PA)
Saint Louis U (MO)
Saint Louis U–Madrid Campus (Spain)
Saint Mary's Coll of California (CA)
St. Norbert Coll (WI)
St. Olaf Coll (MN)
Samford U (AL)
Sam Houston State U (TX)
San Diego State U (CA)
San Francisco State U (CA)
Santa Clara U (CA)

Sarah Lawrence Coll (NY)
Scripps Coll (CA)
Sewanee: The U of the South (TN)
Simpson Coll (IA)
Skidmore Coll (NY)
Smith Coll (MA)
South Dakota State U (SD)
Southern Connecticut State U (CT)
Southern Methodist U (TX)
Southwestern U (TX)
State U of New York at Oswego (NY)
State U of New York Coll at Cortland (NY)
Stony Brook U, State U of New York (NY)
Susquehanna U (PA)
Swarthmore Coll (PA)
Syracuse U (NY)
Temple U (PA)
Texas A&M U (TX)
Texas Christian U (TX)
Texas State U (TX)
Texas Tech U (TX)
Transylvania U (KY)
Trent U (ON, Canada)
Trinity U (TX)
Truman State U (MO)
Tufts U (MA)
Tulane U (LA)
Union Coll (NE)
Union Coll (NY)
United States Military Acad (NY)
Université de Montréal (QC, Canada)
U at Buffalo, the State U of New York (NY)
The U of Arizona (AZ)
U of Arkansas (AR)
U of California, Davis (CA)
U of California, Los Angeles (CA)
U of California, San Diego (CA)
U of California, Santa Barbara (CA)
U of Central Missouri (MO)
U of Chicago (IL)
U of Cincinnati (OH)
U of Dayton (OH)
U of Denver (CO)
U of Evansville (IN)
U of Florida (FL)
U of Georgia (GA)
U of Hawaii at Manoa (HI)
U of Indianapolis (IN)
U of Jamestown (ND)
U of Kentucky (KY)
U of King's Coll (NS, Canada)
U of Lethbridge (AB, Canada)
U of Maryland, Coll Park (MD)
U of Miami (FL)
U of Michigan (MI)
U of Minnesota, Duluth (MN)
U of Mount Union (OH)
U of Nebraska at Kearney (NE)
U of Nevada, Las Vegas (NV)
U of New Hampshire (NH)
U of North Alabama (AL)
U of North Carolina at Asheville (NC)
The U of North Carolina at Charlotte (NC)
The U of North Carolina at Greensboro (NC)
The U of North Carolina Wilmington (NC)
U of North Dakota (ND)
U of North Texas (TX)
U of Notre Dame (IN)
U of Oregon (OR)
U of Pennsylvania (PA)
U of Pittsburgh (PA)
U of Puget Sound (WA)
U of Regina (SK, Canada)
U of Rhode Island (RI)
U of Rochester (NY)
U of St. Thomas (MN)
The U of Scranton (PA)
U of South Carolina (SC)
The U of South Dakota (SD)
U of Southern Indiana (IN)
U of South Florida (FL)
The U of Tennessee (TN)
The U of Texas at Austin (TX)
The U of Texas at El Paso (TX)
U of the Pacific (CA)
The U of Toledo (OH)
U of Toronto (ON, Canada)
The U of Tulsa (OK)
U of Utah (UT)
U of Virginia (VA)
U of Waterloo (ON, Canada)
U of Windsor (ON, Canada)
U of Wisconsin–La Crosse (WI)
U of Wisconsin–Stevens Point (WI)
U of Wisconsin–Whitewater (WI)
Ursinus Coll (PA)
Utah State U (UT)
Valparaiso U (IN)
Vanderbilt U (TN)
Vassar Coll (NY)
Virginia Polytechnic Inst and State U (VA)
Virginia Wesleyan Coll (VA)
Wabash Coll (IN)
Wake Forest U (NC)
Wartburg Coll (IA)
Washburn U (KS)
Washington & Jefferson Coll (PA)
Washington and Lee U (VA)
Washington Coll (MD)
Washington State U (WA)
Washington U in St. Louis (MO)
Wayne State U (MI)
Weber State U (UT)
Webster U (MO)
West Chester U of Pennsylvania (PA)
Western Carolina U (NC)
Western Kentucky U (KY)
Western Michigan U (MI)
Western Oregon U (OR)
Western Washington U (WA)
Wheaton Coll (IL)
Wheaton Coll (MA)
Whitman Coll (WA)
Willamette U (OR)
Williams Coll (MA)
Wittenberg U (OH)
Wofford Coll (SC)
Wright State U (OH)
Wright State U–Lake Campus (OH)

GERMANIC LANGUAGES
Eastern Michigan U (MI)
Grand Valley State U (MI)
Indiana U Bloomington (IN)
Jacksonville U (FL)
U of Colorado Boulder (CO)
The U of Kansas (KS)
U of Oklahoma (OK)
The U of Texas at Austin (TX)
U of Washington (WA)
U of Wisconsin–Eau Claire (WI)
U of Wisconsin–Green Bay (WI)
U of Wisconsin–Madison (WI)
U of Wisconsin–Milwaukee (WI)
Washington U in St. Louis (MO)

GERMANIC LANGUAGES RELATED
Calvin Coll (MI)
Columbia U, School of General Studies (NY)
U of Minnesota, Twin Cities Campus (MN)

GERMAN LANGUAGE TEACHER EDUCATION
Albion Coll (MI)
Auburn U (AL)
Augustana Coll (IL)
Boise State U (ID)
California Lutheran U (CA)
Calvin Coll (MI)
Canisius Coll (NY)
The Catholic U of America (DC)
Colorado State U (CO)
Concordia Coll (MN)
Concordia U Wisconsin (WI)
Eastern Michigan U (MI)
Grand Valley State U (MI)
Hofstra U (NY)
Hope Coll (MI)
Hunter Coll of the City U of New York (NY)
Indiana U South Bend (IN)
Ithaca Coll (NY)
Messiah Coll (PA)
Miami U (OH)
Michigan State U (MI)
Minot State U (ND)
Missouri State U (MO)
Montclair State U (NJ)
Ohio U (OH)
Ohio Wesleyan U (OH)
Saint Joseph's U (PA)
Southern Utah U (UT)
U of Delaware (DE)
U of Evansville (IN)
U of Illinois at Chicago (IL)
U of Lethbridge (AB, Canada)
The U of North Carolina at Greensboro (NC)
U of St. Thomas (MN)
The U of South Dakota (SD)
The U of Tennessee at Martin (TN)
U of Windsor (ON, Canada)
U of Wisconsin–Whitewater (WI)
Valparaiso U (IN)
Washburn U (KS)
Washington U in St. Louis (MO)
Western Michigan U (MI)
Western Washington U (WA)

GERMAN STUDIES
American U (DC)
Bard Coll (NY)
Barnard Coll (NY)
Brandeis U (MA)
Case Western Reserve U (OH)
Coe Coll (IA)
The Coll of Wooster (OH)
Columbia U (NY)
Connecticut Coll (CT)
Cornell U (NY)
Emory U (GA)
Fordham U (NY)
Franklin & Marshall Coll (PA)
Hamilton Coll (NY)
Ithaca Coll (NY)
Kutztown U of Pennsylvania (PA)
Lewis & Clark Coll (OR)
Linfield Coll (OR)
Moravian Coll (PA)
Mount Holyoke Coll (MA)
North Carolina State U (NC)
Pomona Coll (CA)
Smith Coll (MA)
Stanford U (CA)
Université de Montréal (QC, Canada)
U of California, Irvine (CA)
U of California, Riverside (CA)
U of Illinois at Chicago (IL)
U of Massachusetts Amherst (MA)
U of Pittsburgh (PA)
U of Richmond (VA)
The U of Scranton (PA)
U of Windsor (ON, Canada)
Wesleyan U (CT)
Wheaton Coll (MA)

GERONTOLOGY
Alfred U (NY)
Barton Coll (NC)
Bethune-Cookman U (FL)
Bishop's U (QC, Canada)
Bowling Green State U (OH)
California State U, East Bay (CA)
California State U, Sacramento (CA)
California U of Pennsylvania (PA)
Canisius Coll (NY)
Case Western Reserve U (OH)
Gwynedd Mercy U (PA)
Ithaca Coll (NY)
John Carroll U (OH)
Madonna U (MI)
McMaster U (ON, Canada)
Miami U (OH)
Minnesota State U Moorhead (MN)
Missouri State U (MO)
Mount Saint Mary's U (CA)
Niagara U (NY)
Quinnipiac U (CT)
St. Bonaventure U (NY)
St. Cloud State U (MN)
St. Thomas U (NB, Canada)
San Diego State U (CA)
State Coll of Florida Manatee-Sarasota (FL)
U of Maryland U Coll (MD)
U of Massachusetts Boston (MA)
U of Northern Iowa (IA)
U of North Texas (TX)
U of Regina (SK, Canada)
U of Southern California (CA)
U of South Florida (FL)
York Coll of the City U of New York (NY)
Youngstown State U (OH)

GOLF COURSE OPERATION AND GROUNDS MANAGEMENT
U of the Incarnate Word (TX)

GRAPHIC AND PRINTING EQUIPMENT OPERATION/ PRODUCTION
Chowan U (NC)
Georgia Southern U (GA)
Western Illinois U (IL)

GRAPHIC COMMUNICATIONS
Arizona State U at the Polytechnic campus (AZ)
Bradley U (IL)
California Polytechnic State U, San Luis Obispo (CA)
Chowan U (NC)
Eastern Washington U (WA)
Grand View U (IA)
Illinois State U (IL)
Murray State U (KY)
New England Inst of Technology (RI)
Rochester Inst of Technology (NY)
Roger Williams U (RI)
Sam Houston State U (TX)
School of the Art Inst of Chicago (IL)
The U of Findlay (OH)
U of Maryland U Coll (MD)
U of North Dakota (ND)
U of Northern Iowa (IA)
Walla Walla U (WA)

GRAPHIC COMMUNICATIONS RELATED
Bowling Green State U (OH)
Rasmussen Coll Aurora (IL)
Rasmussen Coll Blaine (MN)
Rasmussen Coll Bloomington (MN)
Rasmussen Coll Brooklyn Park (MN)
Rasmussen Coll Eagan (MN)
Rasmussen Coll Fargo (ND)
Rasmussen Coll Fort Myers (FL)
Rasmussen Coll Green Bay (WI)
Rasmussen Coll Lake Elmo/ Woodbury (MN)
Rasmussen Coll Land O' Lakes (FL)
Rasmussen Coll Mankato (MN)
Rasmussen Coll Mokena/Tinley Park (IL)
Rasmussen Coll New Port Richey (FL)
Rasmussen Coll Ocala (FL)
Rasmussen Coll Rockford (IL)
Rasmussen Coll Romeoville/Joliet (IL)
Rasmussen Coll St. Cloud (MN)
Rasmussen Coll Tampa/Brandon (FL)
Rasmussen Coll Wausau (WI)
U of Wisconsin–Stout (WI)

GRAPHIC DESIGN
Abilene Christian U (TX)
Acad of Art U (CA)
Adams State U (CO)
Albertus Magnus Coll (CT)
Alderson Broaddus U (WV)
American Acad of Art (IL)
American U (DC)
The American U in Dubai (United Arab Emirates)
American U of Beirut (Lebanon)
Anderson U (SC)
Appalachian State U (NC)
Arizona State U at the Tempe campus (AZ)
Arkansas Tech U (AR)
Assumption Coll (MA)
Auburn U (AL)
Augsburg Coll (MN)
Augustana Coll (IL)
Baker U (KS)
Baldwin Wallace U (OH)
Becker Coll (MA)
Belhaven U (MS)
Berkeley Coll–Woodland Park Campus (NJ)
Bethel Coll (IN)
Bethel U (MN)
Bluffton U (OH)
Boise State U (ID)
Boston U (MA)
Bradley U (IL)
Brescia U (KY)
Briar Cliff U (IA)
Bridgewater State U (MA)
Brigham Young U (UT)
Cabrini U (PA)
Caldwell U (NJ)
California State Polytechnic U, Pomona (CA)
California State U, Dominguez Hills (CA)
California State U, Fresno (CA)
California State U, Long Beach (CA)
California State U, Sacramento (CA)
California U of Pennsylvania (PA)
Calvin Coll (MI)
Cardinal Stritch U (WI)
Carson-Newman U (TN)
Carthage Coll (WI)
Cedarville U (OH)
Centenary U (NJ)
Central Michigan U (MI)
Central Washington U (WA)
Champlain Coll (VT)
Chapman U (CA)
Chatham U (PA)
Chowan U (NC)
City Coll of the City U of New York (NY)
Clarke U (IA)
Cleveland Inst of Art (OH)
Coastal Carolina U (SC)
Colby-Sawyer Coll (NH)
Coll of the Ozarks (MO)
Colorado Mesa U (CO)
Colorado State U (CO)
Columbia Coll (MO)
Columbia Coll Chicago (IL)
Concordia U Irvine (CA)
Concordia U, Nebraska (NE)
Concordia U Wisconsin (WI)
Concord U (WV)
Creative Center (NE)
Creighton U (NE)
Culver-Stockton Coll (MO)
Curry Coll (MA)
Daemen Coll (NY)
Defiance Coll (OH)
DEREE - The American Coll of Greece (Greece)
Dixie State U (UT)
Doane U (NE)
Dominican U of California (CA)
Drake U (IA)
Drexel U (PA)
East Central U (OK)
Eastern Washington U (WA)
East Stroudsburg U of Pennsylvania (PA)
Edgewood Coll (WI)
Elizabeth City State U (NC)
Emmanuel Coll (MA)
Emory & Henry Coll (VA)
Endicott Coll (MA)
Eugene Lang Coll of Liberal Arts (NY)
Fashion Inst of Technology (NY)
Ferris State U (MI)
FIDM/Fashion Inst of Design & Merchandising, Los Angeles Campus (CA)
FIDM/Fashion Inst of Design & Merchandising, San Francisco Campus (CA)
Fitchburg State U (MA)
Flagler Coll (FL)
Florida Ag and Mech U (FL)
Florida State U (FL)
Georgia Southern U (GA)
Grace Coll (IN)
Grand View U (IA)
Harding U (AR)
Hardin-Simmons U (TX)
High Point U (NC)
Holy Family U (PA)
Huntington U (IN)
Inter American U of Puerto Rico, San Germán Campus (PR)
Iowa State U of Science and Technology (IA)
John Brown U (AR)
Judson U (IL)
Kansas City Art Inst (MO)
Kansas Wesleyan U (KS)
Keene State Coll (NH)
Kentucky Wesleyan Coll (KY)

Laguna Coll of Art & Design (CA)
Lamar U (TX)
Lasell Coll (MA)
Lebanese American U (Lebanon)
Lenoir-Rhyne U (NC)
Liberty U (VA)
Limestone Coll (SC)
Louisiana Coll (LA)
Madonna U (MI)
Malone U (OH)
Mansfield U of Pennsylvania (PA)
Marian U (WI)
Marietta Coll (OH)
Maryland Inst Coll of Art (MD)
Marymount Manhattan Coll (NY)
Maryville U of Saint Louis (MO)
Marywood U (PA)
Memphis Coll of Art (TN)
Mercer U, Macon (GA)
Mercyhurst U (PA)
Meredith Coll (NC)
Michigan State U (MI)
MidAmerica Nazarene U (KS)
Milligan Coll (TN)
Milwaukee Inst of Art and Design (WI)
Minnesota State U Moorhead (MN)
Missouri Western State U (MO)
Montana State U–Northern (MT)
Montclair State U (NJ)
Morningside Coll (IA)
Mount Ida Coll (MA)
Mount Mary U (WI)
Mount Mercy U (IA)
Mount St. Joseph U (OH)
Mount Vernon Nazarene U (OH)
Newberry Coll (SC)
North Carolina State U (NC)
North Central Coll (IL)
Northeastern U (MA)
Northland Coll (WI)
Northwestern Coll (IA)
Nossi Coll of Art (TN)
Ohio U (OH)
Oklahoma Baptist U (OK)
O'More Coll of Design (TN)
Oral Roberts U (OK)
Ouachita Baptist U (AR)
Pacific Northwest Coll of Art (OR)
Palm Beach Atlantic U (FL)
Parsons School of Design (NY)
Penn State Abington (PA)
Penn State Altoona (PA)
Penn State Beaver (PA)
Penn State Berks (PA)
Penn State Brandywine (PA)
Penn State DuBois (PA)
Penn State Erie, The Behrend Coll (PA)
Penn State Fayette, The Eberly Campus (PA)
Penn State Greater Allegheny (PA)
Penn State Hazleton (PA)
Penn State Lehigh Valley (PA)
Penn State Mont Alto (PA)
Penn State New Kensington (PA)
Penn State Schuylkill (PA)
Penn State Shenango (PA)
Penn State U Park (PA)
Penn State Wilkes-Barre (PA)
Penn State Worthington Scranton (PA)
Penn State York (PA)
Pennsylvania Coll of Art & Design (PA)
Pensacola State Coll (FL)
Plymouth State U (NH)
Point Loma Nazarene U (CA)
Portland State U (OR)
Prairie View A&M U (TX)
Pratt Inst (NY)
Queens Coll of the City U of New York (NY)
Rhode Island Coll (RI)
Rhode Island School of Design (RI)
Ringling Coll of Art and Design (FL)
Robert Morris U Illinois (IL)
Rochester Inst of Technology (NY)
The Sage Colls (NY)
Saginaw Valley State U (MI)
St. Edward's U (TX)
St. John's U (NY)
Saint Mary's U of Minnesota (MN)
St. Norbert Coll (WI)
St. Thomas Aquinas Coll (NY)
Saint Vincent Coll (PA)
Salve Regina U (RI)
Samford U (AL)
San Diego State U (CA)
School of the Art Inst of Chicago (IL)
Schreiner U (TX)
Simpson Coll (IA)
South Dakota State U (SD)
Southeastern U (FL)
Southern New Hampshire U (NH)
Southern Utah U (UT)
Spring Hill Coll (AL)
State U of New York at New Paltz (NY)
State U of New York Coll of Technology at Canton (NY)
Stephens Coll (MO)
Stonehill Coll (MA)
Susquehanna U (PA)
Tabor Coll (KS)
Taylor U (IN)
Temple U (PA)
Texas Christian U (TX)
Trinity Christian Coll (IL)
Union Coll (NE)
The U of Akron (OH)
U of Bridgeport (CT)
U of Denver (CO)
U of Florida (FL)
U of Hartford (CT)
U of Houston (TX)
U of Illinois at Chicago (IL)
U of Mary Hardin-Baylor (TX)
U of Miami (FL)
U of Michigan (MI)
U of Minnesota, Twin Cities Campus (MN)
U of Nevada, Las Vegas (NV)
U of New Haven (CT)
U of North Dakota (ND)
U of Northern Iowa (IA)
U of San Francisco (CA)
U of South Florida, St. Petersburg (FL)
The U of Tampa (FL)
The U of Tennessee at Martin (TN)
The U of the Arts (PA)
U of the Incarnate Word (TX)
U of Wisconsin–Parkside (WI)
U of Wisconsin–Stout (WI)
Villa Maria Coll (NY)
Virginia Commonwealth U (VA)
Walla Walla U (WA)
Walsh U (OH)
Washington U in St. Louis (MO)
Wayne State Coll (NE)
Weber State U (UT)
Western Michigan U (MI)
Western State Colorado U (CO)
West Texas A&M U (TX)
Wichita State U (KS)
William Woods U (MO)
Youngstown State U (OH)

GREENHOUSE MANAGEMENT
U of Minnesota, Crookston (MN)

HEALTH AND MEDICAL ADMINISTRATIVE SERVICES RELATED
Brenau U (GA)
Concordia Coll–New York (NY)
Concordia U, St. Paul (MN)
DEREE - The American Coll of Greece (Greece)
Eastern Oregon U (OR)
Indiana U East (IN)
Indiana U Kokomo (IN)
Indiana U Northwest (IN)
Indiana U South Bend (IN)
Indiana U Southeast (IN)
Mount Mercy U (IA)
National Louis U (IL)
Northeastern U (MA)
Pennsylvania Coll of Technology (PA)
State U of New York Coll of Technology at Canton (NY)
U of Detroit Mercy (MI)
Washburn U (KS)
Weber State U (UT)
Western Michigan U (MI)
Wheeling Jesuit U (WV)

HEALTH AND PHYSICAL EDUCATION/FITNESS
Austin Peay State U (TN)
Averett U (VA)
Baker U (KS)
Baldwin Wallace U (OH)
Baylor U (TX)
Berea Coll (KY)
Bethel Coll (KS)
Biola U (CA)
Blackburn Coll (IL)
Black Hills State U (SD)
Bluffton U (OH)
Boise State U (ID)
Bridgewater Coll (VA)
Bryan Coll (TN)
California Polytechnic State U, San Luis Obispo (CA)
California State Polytechnic U, Pomona (CA)
California State U, Chico (CA)
California State U, Dominguez Hills (CA)
California State U, Fullerton (CA)
California State U, Monterey Bay (CA)
California State U, San Bernardino (CA)
California State U, San Marcos (CA)
California State U, Stanislaus (CA)
Cameron U (OK)
Capital U (OH)
Carroll Coll (MT)
Catawba Coll (NC)
Charleston Southern U (SC)
Cleveland State U (OH)
Coll of the Ozarks (MO)
The Coll of William and Mary (VA)
Concordia Coll (MN)
Concordia U Irvine (CA)
Concordia U, Nebraska (NE)
Concordia U, St. Paul (MN)
Concordia U Wisconsin (WI)
Dallas Baptist U (TX)
Dean Coll (MA)
Doane U (NE)
Eastern Michigan U (MI)
Eastern Oregon U (OR)
Eastern Washington U (WA)
East Tennessee State U (TN)
East Texas Baptist U (TX)
Emory & Henry Coll (VA)
Emory U (GA)
Evangel U (MO)
Florida Ag and Mech U (FL)
Freed-Hardeman U (TN)
Friends U (KS)
Gardner-Webb U (NC)
George Fox U (OR)
Georgia Southern U (GA)
Grand View U (IA)
Hanover Coll (IN)
Hillsdale Coll (MI)
Houghton Coll (NY)
Howard Payne U (TX)
Husson U (ME)
Indiana U Bloomington (IN)
Indiana U of Pennsylvania (PA)
Iowa State U of Science and Technology (IA)
Iowa Wesleyan U (IA)
Ithaca Coll (NY)
Jacksonville State U (AL)
Jacksonville U (FL)
James Madison U (VA)
Keene State Coll (NH)
Lee U (TN)
Liberty U (VA)
Linfield Coll (OR)
Louisiana Coll (LA)
Louisiana Tech U (LA)
Lubbock Christian U (TX)
Luther Coll (IA)
Lynchburg Coll (VA)
Marian U (IN)
Marywood U (PA)
The Master's U (CA)
McDaniel Coll (MD)
MidAmerica Nazarene U (KS)
Milligan Coll (TN)
Minnesota State U Moorhead (MN)
Missouri Western State U (MO)
Monmouth Coll (IL)
Monmouth U (NJ)
Montana State U Billings (MT)
Morehead State U (KY)
Morehouse Coll (GA)
Muskingum U (OH)
New England Coll (NH)
North Carolina Central U (NC)
Northern Illinois U (IL)
Northwestern State U of Louisiana (LA)
Northwest U (WA)
Oakland City U (IN)
The Ohio State U (OH)
Ohio U (OH)
Oklahoma Baptist U (OK)
Oral Roberts U (OK)
Palm Beach Atlantic U (FL)
Philander Smith Coll (AR)
Plymouth State U (NH)
Point Loma Nazarene U (CA)
Randolph Coll (VA)
Redeemer U Coll (ON, Canada)
Rhode Island Coll (RI)
Rocky Mountain Coll (MT)
Rowan U (NJ)
St. Catherine U (MN)
St. Gregory's U, Shawnee (OK)
Saint Mary's Coll of California (CA)
Sam Houston State U (TX)
San Diego State U (CA)
Shawnee State U (OH)
Slippery Rock U of Pennsylvania (PA)
South Carolina State U (SC)
South Dakota State U (SD)
Southeast Missouri State U (MO)
Southwest Baptist U (MO)
Southwestern Adventist U (TX)
Sterling Coll (KS)
Syracuse U (NY)
Tabor Coll (KS)
Tarleton State U (TX)
Tennessee Wesleyan U (TN)
Texas A&M U–Kingsville (TX)
Texas Christian U (TX)
Truman State U (MO)
Union Coll (NE)
U of Arkansas (AR)
U of Delaware (DE)
The U of Findlay (OH)
U of Georgia (GA)
U of Great Falls (MT)
U of Hawaii at Manoa (HI)
The U of Kansas (KS)
U of Louisville (KY)
U of Massachusetts Boston (MA)
U of Michigan (MI)
U of Mobile (AL)
The U of Montana Western (MT)
U of Montevallo (AL)
U of New Orleans (LA)
The U of North Carolina at Chapel Hill (NC)
The U of North Carolina at Charlotte (NC)
The U of North Carolina at Pembroke (NC)
The U of North Carolina Wilmington (NC)
U of Northern Iowa (IA)
U of Regina (SK, Canada)
U of St. Thomas (MN)
U of San Francisco (CA)
U of Science and Arts of Oklahoma (OK)
U of Southern Maine (ME)
U of Southern Mississippi (MS)
The U of Tampa (FL)
The U of Tennessee at Martin (TN)
The U of Texas at Austin (TX)
U of the Cumberlands (KY)
U of Toronto (ON, Canada)
U of Utah (UT)
U of Windsor (ON, Canada)
U of Wisconsin–La Crosse (WI)
U of Wisconsin–Stevens Point (WI)
U of Wisconsin–Superior (WI)
Ursinus Coll (PA)
Utah Valley U (UT)
Valley City State U (ND)
Valparaiso U (IN)
Walla Walla U (WA)
Walsh U (OH)
Wayland Baptist U (TX)
Weber State U (UT)
Welch Coll (TN)
West Chester U of Pennsylvania (PA)
Western Washington U (WA)
Westfield State U (MA)
West Texas A&M U (TX)
West Virginia State U (WV)
West Virginia U (WV)
West Virginia Wesleyan Coll (WV)
Whittier Coll (CA)
Wingate U (NC)
Youngstown State U (OH)

HEALTH AND PHYSICAL EDUCATION RELATED
Adelphi U (NY)
Arizona State U at the Downtown Phoenix campus (AZ)
Averett U (VA)
Avila U (MO)
Bloomsburg U of Pennsylvania (PA)
Bowling Green State U (OH)
Brewton-Parker Coll (GA)
Bridgewater State U (MA)
California State U, Long Beach (CA)
Coe Coll (IA)
Concordia U Wisconsin (WI)
Cornell Coll (IA)
East Carolina U (NC)
Ithaca Coll (NY)
Limestone Coll (SC)
Lock Haven U of Pennsylvania (PA)
Mount Vernon Nazarene U (OH)
North Greenville U (SC)
Regis Coll (MA)
Saint Mary's Coll of California (CA)
South Dakota State U (SD)
Texas Lutheran U (TX)
Union Coll (NE)
U of Wisconsin–Superior (WI)
Valdosta State U (GA)
Wayne State Coll (NE)
Weber State U (UT)

HEALTH AND WELLNESS
Antioch U Midwest (OH)
Arizona State U at the Downtown Phoenix campus (AZ)
Arizona State U at the West campus (AZ)
Bowling Green State U (OH)
Canisius Coll (NY)
Chatham U (PA)
Creighton U (NE)
Culver-Stockton Coll (MO)
Daemen Coll (NY)
DeSales U (PA)
Georgetown Coll (KY)
Goddard Coll (VT)
Granite State Coll (NH)
Huntingdon Coll (AL)
Indiana U Kokomo (IN)
Indiana U South Bend (IN)
Jacksonville State U (AL)
Johnson C. Smith U (NC)
Keene State Coll (NH)
Lamar U (TX)
Lenoir-Rhyne U (NC)
Maryville U of Saint Louis (MO)
Missouri Baptist U (MO)
Mount St. Joseph U (OH)
New York Inst of Technology (NY)
North Dakota State U (ND)
North Greenville U (SC)
Northwest U (WA)
Point Loma Nazarene U (CA)
Prairie View A&M U (TX)
Purdue U (IN)
Rhode Island Coll (RI)
Sam Houston State U (TX)
Slippery Rock U of Pennsylvania (PA)
State U of New York Coll at Potsdam (NY)
Texas A&M U (TX)
Texas Woman's U (TX)
Towson U (MD)
Union Coll (KY)
U of Houston (TX)
U of Saint Francis (IN)
The U of Texas at San Antonio (TX)
The U of Texas Rio Grande Valley (TX)
U of West Georgia (GA)
U of Wisconsin–La Crosse (WI)
U of Wisconsin–Stout (WI)
U of Wisconsin–Superior (WI)
Viterbo U (WI)

HEALTH COMMUNICATION
Ashland U (OH)
Cornerstone U (MI)
Grand Valley State U (MI)
Juniata Coll (PA)
North Dakota State U (ND)
Ohio U–Eastern (OH)
San Diego State U (CA)

Southeast Missouri State U (MO)
U of Houston (TX)
Winona State U (MN)

HEALTH/HEALTH-CARE ADMINISTRATION
Adams State U (CO)
Adventist U of Health Sciences (FL)
Alma Coll (MI)
Appalachian State U (NC)
Arcadia U (PA)
Arizona State U at the Downtown Phoenix campus (AZ)
Arizona State U at the Polytechnic campus (AZ)
Arizona State U at the West campus (AZ)
Auburn U (AL)
Augustana U (SD)
Baldwin Wallace U (OH)
Barton Coll (NC)
Belhaven U (MS)
Berkeley Coll–New York City Campus (NY)
Berkeley Coll–White Plains Campus (NY)
Berkeley Coll–Woodland Park Campus (NJ)
Black Hills State U (SD)
Bluefield State Coll (WV)
Bluffton U (OH)
Bowling Green State U (OH)
Brigham Young U–Idaho (ID)
Butler U (IN)
Caldwell U (NJ)
California Baptist U (CA)
California State U, Dominguez Hills (CA)
California State U, Long Beach (CA)
Carlow U (PA)
Central Michigan U (MI)
Central Penn Coll (PA)
Charter Oak State Coll (CT)
Chestnut Hill Coll (PA)
Coastal Carolina U (SC)
CollAmerica–Fort Collins (CO)
The Coll of Westchester (NY)
Columbia Coll (MO)
Columbia Southern U (AL)
Concordia U Chicago (IL)
Concordia U Irvine (CA)
Concordia U, St. Paul (MN)
Concordia U Wisconsin (WI)
Converse Coll (SC)
Creighton U (NE)
Dallas Baptist U (TX)
Davenport U, Grand Rapids (MI)
Drexel U (PA)
East Carolina U (NC)
East Central U (OK)
Eastern Michigan U (MI)
Eastern Washington U (WA)
Elms Coll (MA)
Fayetteville State U (NC)
Ferris State U (MI)
Fisher Coll (MA)
Florida Ag and Mech U (FL)
Florida Atlantic U (FL)
Florida Intl U (FL)
Florida Southern Coll (FL)
Gannon U (PA)
Gardner-Webb U (NC)
Granite State Coll (NH)
Harding U (AR)
Harris-Stowe State U (MO)
Heidelberg U (OH)
Idaho State U (ID)
Immaculata U (PA)
Indiana U–Purdue U Indianapolis (IN)
Iona Coll (NY)
Ithaca Coll (NY)
Jackson State U (MS)
James Madison U (VA)
King U (TN)
Langston U (OK)
Lebanon Valley Coll (PA)
Lee U (TN)
Lehman Coll of the City U of New York (NY)
LeTourneau U (TX)
Lewis U (IL)
Liberty U (VA)
Limestone Coll (SC)
Lincoln Coll–Normal (IL)
Lindenwood U (MO)
Lourdes U (OH)
Loyola U Chicago (IL)
Madonna U (MI)
Malone U (OH)
Maria Coll (NY)
Marian U (WI)
Mary Baldwin U (VA)
Marywood U (PA)
Mercy Coll of Health Sciences (IA)
Mercy Coll of Ohio (OH)
Metropolitan State U of Denver (CO)
Midland Coll (TX)
Minnesota State U Moorhead (MN)
Misericordia U (PA)
Mississippi State U (MS)
Missouri Baptist U (MO)
Montana State U Billings (MT)
Mount Mercy U (IA)
Muskingum U (OH)
National U (CA)
Nebraska Methodist Coll (NE)
Newberry Coll (SC)
New England Coll (NH)
New England Inst of Technology (RI)
Northwood U, Michigan Campus (MI)
Ohio U (OH)
Ohio U–Eastern (OH)
Our Lady of the Lake Coll (LA)
Our Lady of the Lake U of San Antonio (TX)
Peirce Coll (PA)
Penn State Abington (PA)
Penn State Altoona (PA)
Penn State Beaver (PA)
Penn State Berks (PA)
Penn State Brandywine (PA)
Penn State DuBois (PA)
Penn State Erie, The Behrend Coll (PA)
Penn State Fayette, The Eberly Campus (PA)
Penn State Greater Allegheny (PA)
Penn State Hazleton (PA)
Penn State Lehigh Valley (PA)
Penn State Mont Alto (PA)
Penn State New Kensington (PA)
Penn State Schuylkill (PA)
Penn State Shenango (PA)
Penn State U Park (PA)
Penn State Wilkes-Barre (PA)
Penn State Worthington Scranton (PA)
Penn State York (PA)
Pennsylvania Coll of Health Sciences (PA)
Piedmont Coll (GA)
Providence Coll (RI)
Rasmussen Coll Aurora (IL)
Rasmussen Coll Blaine (MN)
Rasmussen Coll Bloomington (MN)
Rasmussen Coll Brooklyn Park (MN)
Rasmussen Coll Eagan (MN)
Rasmussen Coll Fargo (ND)
Rasmussen Coll Fort Myers (FL)
Rasmussen Coll Green Bay (WI)
Rasmussen Coll Kansas City/ Overland Park (KS)
Rasmussen Coll Lake Elmo/ Woodbury (MN)
Rasmussen Coll Land O' Lakes (FL)
Rasmussen Coll Mankato (MN)
Rasmussen Coll Mokena/Tinley Park (IL)
Rasmussen Coll Moorhead (MN)
Rasmussen Coll New Port Richey (FL)
Rasmussen Coll Ocala (FL)
Rasmussen Coll Rockford (IL)
Rasmussen Coll Romeoville/Joliet (IL)
Rasmussen Coll St. Cloud (MN)
Rasmussen Coll Tampa/Brandon (FL)
Rasmussen Coll Topeka (KS)
Rasmussen Coll Wausau (WI)
Regent U (VA)
Regis U (CO)
Rhode Island Coll (RI)
Roberts Wesleyan Coll (NY)
Roger Williams U (RI)
Saint Leo U (FL)
Saint Louis U (MO)
Saint Mary-of-the-Woods Coll (IN)
Saint Peter's U (NJ)
St. Vincent's Coll (CT)
Salve Regina U (RI)
Sam Houston State U (TX)
Shippensburg U of Pennsylvania (PA)
Simpson Coll (IA)
Simpson U (CA)
Southeast Missouri State U (MO)
Southern Illinois U Carbondale (IL)
Southwestern Coll (KS)
State U of New York Coll of Technology at Canton (NY)
Stonehill Coll (MA)
Stratford U, Alexandria (VA)
Stratford U, Falls Church (VA)
Stratford U, Glen Allen (VA)
Stratford U, Newport News (VA)
Stratford U, Virginia Beach (VA)
Stratford U, Woodbridge (VA)
Tennessee State U (TN)
Texas State U (TX)
Thomas More Coll (KY)
Tiffin U (OH)
Towson U (MD)
Trevecca Nazarene U (TN)
The U of Alabama at Birmingham (AL)
U of Central Florida (FL)
U of Dubuque (IA)
U of Evansville (IN)
U of Great Falls (MT)
U of Houston–Clear Lake (TX)
U of Kentucky (KY)
U of La Verne (CA)
U of Management and Technology (VA)
U of Maryland U Coll (MD)
U of Massachusetts Dartmouth (MA)
U of Miami (FL)
U of Michigan–Dearborn (MI)
U of Michigan–Flint (MI)
U of Minnesota, Crookston (MN)
U of Minnesota, Duluth (MN)
U of Minnesota, Twin Cities Campus (MN)
U of Mount Union (OH)
U of Nevada, Las Vegas (NV)
U of New Hampshire (NH)
The U of North Carolina at Chapel Hill (NC)
U of North Florida (FL)
U of Northwestern Ohio (OH)
U of Pennsylvania (PA)
U of Rhode Island (RI)
U of St. Francis (IL)
U of Saint Francis (IN)
The U of Scranton (PA)
U of Southern Indiana (IN)
U of South Florida (FL)
The U of Texas at Dallas (TX)
The U of Texas at El Paso (TX)
U of the Potomac (DC)
U of Virginia (VA)
U of Wisconsin–Eau Claire (WI)
Upper Iowa U (IA)
Valdosta State U (GA)
Valparaiso U (IN)
Viterbo U (WI)
Waldorf U (IA)
Washington U in St. Louis (MO)
Waynesburg U (PA)
Weber State U (UT)
Western Carolina U (NC)
Western Illinois U (IL)
Western Kentucky U (KY)
West Virginia U Inst of Technology (WV)
Wichita State U (KS)
Winona State U (MN)

HEALTH INFORMATION/ MEDICAL RECORDS ADMINISTRATION
Alabama State U (AL)
Arkansas Tech U (AR)
Augusta U (GA)
Boise State U (ID)
Bowling Green State U (OH)
Charter Oak State Coll (CT)
Coll of Coastal Georgia (GA)
The Coll of St. Scholastica (MN)
Dakota State U (SD)
Dalhousie U (NS, Canada)
Davenport U, Grand Rapids (MI)
Duquesne U (PA)
East Carolina U (NC)
East Central U (OK)
Eastern Washington U (WA)
Fairleigh Dickinson U, Metropolitan Campus (NJ)
Ferris State U (MI)
Fisher Coll (MA)
Florida Ag and Mech U (FL)
Georgian Court U (NJ)
Gordon State Coll (GA)
Granite State Coll (NH)
Illinois State U (IL)
Indiana U Northwest (IN)
Indiana U–Purdue U Indianapolis (IN)
Indiana U Southeast (IN)
Kean U (NJ)
Louisiana Tech U (LA)
Metropolitan Coll of New York (NY)
Missouri Western State U (MO)
The Ohio State U (OH)
The Ohio State U at Lima (OH)
Peirce Coll (PA)
Pennsylvania Coll of Technology (PA)
Rasmussen Coll Aurora (IL)
Rasmussen Coll Blaine (MN)
Rasmussen Coll Bloomington (MN)
Rasmussen Coll Brooklyn Park (MN)
Rasmussen Coll Eagan (MN)
Rasmussen Coll Fargo (ND)
Rasmussen Coll Fort Myers (FL)
Rasmussen Coll Green Bay (WI)
Rasmussen Coll Kansas City/ Overland Park (KS)
Rasmussen Coll Lake Elmo/ Woodbury (MN)
Rasmussen Coll Land O' Lakes (FL)
Rasmussen Coll Mankato (MN)
Rasmussen Coll Mokena/Tinley Park (IL)
Rasmussen Coll Moorhead (MN)
Rasmussen Coll New Port Richey (FL)
Rasmussen Coll Ocala (FL)
Rasmussen Coll Rockford (IL)
Rasmussen Coll Romeoville/Joliet (IL)
Rasmussen Coll St. Cloud (MN)
Rasmussen Coll Tampa/Brandon (FL)
Rasmussen Coll Topeka (KS)
Rasmussen Coll Wausau (WI)
Regis U (CO)
Rutgers U–New Brunswick (NJ)
Saint Louis U (MO)
State U of New York Polytechnic Inst (NY)
Stephens Coll (MO)
Stratford U, Alexandria (VA)
Stratford U, Falls Church (VA)
Stratford U, Glen Allen (VA)
Stratford U, Newport News (VA)
Stratford U, Virginia Beach (VA)
Stratford U, Woodbridge (VA)
Sullivan U (KY)
Tennessee State U (TN)
Texas State U (TX)
Thomas Edison State U (NJ)
Trevecca Nazarene U (TN)
The U of Alabama at Birmingham (AL)
U of Arkansas for Medical Sciences (AR)
U of Central Florida (FL)
U of Cincinnati (OH)
U of Detroit Mercy (MI)
U of Illinois at Chicago (IL)
The U of Kansas (KS)
U of Maine at Farmington (ME)
U of Pittsburgh (PA)
The U of Toledo (OH)
U of Washington (WA)
U of Wisconsin–Green Bay (WI)
U of Wisconsin–Parkside (WI)
Weber State U (UT)
Western Carolina U (NC)
Western Kentucky U (KY)

HEALTH INFORMATION/ MEDICAL RECORDS TECHNOLOGY
Davenport U, Grand Rapids (MI)
East Central U (OK)
Excelsior Coll (NY)
Fisher Coll (MA)
Idaho State U (ID)
Resurrection U (IL)
St. John's U (NY)
U of Saint Mary (KS)

HEALTH/MEDICAL PHYSICS
Belmont U (TN)
Bloomsburg U of Pennsylvania (PA)
Cabarrus Coll of Health Sciences (NC)
California State U, Dominguez Hills (CA)
California State U, Northridge (CA)
Oregon State U (OR)
U of Guelph (ON, Canada)
U of Nevada, Las Vegas (NV)

HEALTH/MEDICAL PREPARATORY PROGRAMS RELATED
Abilene Christian U (TX)
Allegheny Coll (PA)
Arizona State U at the Downtown Phoenix campus (AZ)
Arizona State U at the West campus (AZ)
Asbury U (KY)
Aurora U (IL)
Avila U (MO)
Baylor U (TX)
Blackburn Coll (IL)
Bloomsburg U of Pennsylvania (PA)
Cleveland State U (OH)
Corban U (OR)
Cornerstone U (MI)
Duquesne U (PA)
Eastern Nazarene Coll (MA)
Emory & Henry Coll (VA)
Frostburg State U (MD)
Gannon U (PA)
Grace Coll (IN)
Grove City Coll (PA)
Guilford Coll (NC)
Hofstra U (NY)
Iowa State U of Science and Technology (IA)
Ithaca Coll (NY)
Kansas Wesleyan U (KS)
Kent State U (OH)
Kent State U at Ashtabula (OH)
Lee U (TN)
Le Moyne Coll (NY)
Lenoir-Rhyne U (NC)
Lipscomb U (TN)
Lock Haven U of Pennsylvania (PA)
Louisiana Coll (LA)
Lubbock Christian U (TX)
Madonna U (MI)
Marshall U (WV)
Maryville U of Saint Louis (MO)
Mercer U, Macon (GA)
Mercyhurst U (PA)
Meredith Coll (NC)
Northern Illinois U (IL)
Oregon State U (OR)
Point Park U (PA)
Saginaw Valley State U (MI)
St. Cloud State U (MN)
Seattle Pacific U (WA)
Seattle U (WA)
Southwestern Coll (KS)
The U of Findlay (OH)
U of Michigan–Flint (MI)
U of Regina (SK, Canada)
U of South Alabama (AL)
U of Waterloo (ON, Canada)
U of Wisconsin–Parkside (WI)
Utica Coll (NY)
Valley City State U (ND)
Weber State U (UT)
Western Washington U (WA)

HEALTH/MEDICAL PSYCHOLOGY
Averett U (VA)
Bridgewater State U (MA)
Faulkner U (AL)
Greenville Coll (IL)
Kansas Wesleyan U (KS)
MCPHS U (MA)
U of Mary Hardin-Baylor (TX)

HEALTH OCCUPATIONS TEACHER EDUCATION
Northwest U (WA)

HEALTH POLICY ANALYSIS
Brandeis U (MA)
Mount Saint Mary's U (CA)

HEALTH PROFESSIONS RELATED
Alvernia U (PA)
Armstrong State U (GA)
Athens State U (AL)
Azusa Pacific U (CA)
Baldwin Wallace U (OH)
Boise State U (ID)
Boston U (MA)
Bowling Green State U (OH)
Bradley U (IL)
California State U, East Bay (CA)
California State U, Fresno (CA)
California State U, Long Beach (CA)
California State U, Sacramento (CA)
Caribbean U (PR)
Clemson U (SC)
Cleveland State U (OH)
Concordia Coll–New York (NY)
Cornell U (NY)
Curry Coll (MA)
Dalhousie U (NS, Canada)
Eastern Nazarene Coll (MA)
East Tennessee State U (TN)
Elizabethtown Coll (PA)
Elmira Coll (NY)
Excelsior Coll (NY)
Ferris State U (MI)
Fisher Coll (MA)
Furman U (SC)
Gannon U (PA)
Georgetown U (DC)
Gettysburg Coll (PA)
Inter American U of Puerto Rico, Ponce Campus (PR)
King's Coll (PA)
King U (TN)
Lock Haven U of Pennsylvania (PA)
Manchester U (IN)
Maryville U of Saint Louis (MO)
Marywood U (PA)
MCPHS U (MA)
Merrimack Coll (MA)
Milligan Coll (TN)
Minnesota State U Mankato (MN)
Molloy Coll (NY)
Morrisville State Coll (NY)
Mount St. Mary's U (MD)
Muskingum U (OH)
New Jersey City U (NJ)
Newman U (KS)
New York Inst of Technology (NY)
Northeastern State U (OK)
Northern Illinois U (IL)
Nova Southeastern U (FL)
The Ohio State U (OH)
Old Dominion U (VA)
Point Park U (PA)
Purdue U (IN)
Randolph Coll (VA)
The Sage Colls (NY)
Saint Augustine's U (NC)
St. John's U (NY)
St. Joseph's Coll, Long Island Campus (NY)
St. Joseph's Coll, New York (NY)
Saint Joseph's U (PA)
Saint Mary-of-the-Woods Coll (IN)
Samford U (AL)
San Francisco State U (CA)
Sonoma State U (CA)
Southern Methodist U (TX)
State U of New York Coll at Cortland (NY)
Stephens Coll (MO)
Tennessee Wesleyan U (TN)
Thomas Edison State U (NJ)
The U of Alabama (AL)
U of Bridgeport (CT)
U of Central Arkansas (AR)
U of Charleston (WV)
U of Cincinnati (OH)
U of Delaware (DE)
U of Hartford (CT)
U of Louisiana at Monroe (LA)
U of Maryland, Baltimore County (MD)
U of Nevada, Reno (NV)
U of New England (ME)
The U of North Carolina Wilmington (NC)
U of Northern Iowa (IA)
U of Pennsylvania (PA)
U of Pittsburgh (PA)
The U of Tennessee at Martin (TN)
The U of Texas at El Paso (TX)
U of Waterloo (ON, Canada)
U of Wisconsin–Parkside (WI)
U of Wisconsin–Stevens Point (WI)
Walla Walla U (WA)
Washington U in St. Louis (MO)
Wayne State U (MI)
West Virginia State U (WV)
Worcester State U (MA)
Youngstown State U (OH)

HEALTH SERVICES ADMINISTRATION
Anderson U (SC)
Arizona State U at the Downtown Phoenix campus (AZ)
Arizona State U at the West campus (AZ)
Bentley U (MA)
Chapman U (CA)
Florida National U (FL)
Indiana U Northwest (IN)
Indiana U–Purdue U Indianapolis (IN)
Indiana U South Bend (IN)
Inter American U of Puerto Rico, Ponce Campus (PR)
McNeese State U (LA)
Northeastern State U (OK)
Robert Morris U (PA)
St. Petersburg Coll (FL)
State Coll of Florida Manatee-Sarasota (FL)
U of Detroit Mercy (MI)
U of New Orleans (LA)
U of San Francisco (CA)
U of Washington, Tacoma (WA)

HEALTH SERVICES/ALLIED HEALTH/HEALTH SCIENCES
Adventist U of Health Sciences (FL)
Albion Coll (MI)
Alvernia U (PA)
American Intl Coll (MA)
Aultman Coll of Nursing and Health Sciences (OH)
Bay Path U (MA)
Biola U (CA)
Boston U (MA)
Bradley U (IL)
Brenau U (GA)
Brigham Young U–Idaho (ID)
Butler U (IN)
California Baptist U (CA)
California State U, Chico (CA)
California State U, Dominguez Hills (CA)
California State U, Fullerton (CA)
California State U, Northridge (CA)
California State U, San Bernardino (CA)
Canisius Coll (NY)
Carroll Coll (MT)
Central Baptist Coll (AR)
Chowan U (NC)
Clayton State U (GA)
Colby-Sawyer Coll (NH)
The Coll at Brockport, State U of New York (NY)
The Coll of Idaho (ID)
The Coll of St. Scholastica (MN)
Coll of the Ozarks (MO)
Colorado Christian U (CO)
Columbus State U (GA)
Dalhousie U (NS, Canada)
East Texas Baptist U (TX)
The Evergreen State Coll (WA)
Fairleigh Dickinson U, Coll at Florham (NJ)
Florida Ag and Mech U (FL)
Florida Gulf Coast U (FL)
Friends U (KS)
Graceland U (IA)
Granite State Coll (NH)
Heidelberg U (OH)
Hendrix Coll (AR)
Hofstra U (NY)
Husson U (ME)
Idaho State U (ID)
Kentucky Wesleyan Coll (KY)
Lebanon Valley Coll (PA)
Lee U (TN)
LeTourneau U (TX)
Lincoln U (CA)
Lincoln U (PA)
Madonna U (MI)
Maria Coll (NY)
Marian U (IN)
Mary Baldwin U (VA)
Marywood U (PA)
McKendree U (IL)
Mercy Coll (NY)
Mercy Coll of Health Sciences (IA)
Mercy Coll of Ohio (OH)
Mercyhurst U (PA)
Merrimack Coll (MA)
Messiah Coll (PA)
Miami Dade Coll (FL)
Milligan Coll (TN)
Misericordia U (PA)
Monmouth U (NJ)
National U (CA)
Nebraska Methodist Coll (NE)
Northern Kentucky U (KY)
Northwestern State U of Louisiana (LA)
Pace U (NY)
Pace U, Pleasantville Campus (NY)
Pennsylvania Coll of Health Sciences (PA)
Piedmont Coll (GA)
Purdue U Northwest (IN)
Quinnipiac U (CT)
Rhode Island Coll (RI)
Rutgers U–Newark (NJ)
The Sage Colls (NY)
Saginaw Valley State U (MI)
St. Cloud State U (MN)
Saint Joseph's U (PA)
Saint Louis U (MO)
St. Luke's Coll (IA)
Sam Houston State U (TX)
San Diego State U (CA)
Southeast Missouri State U (MO)
Spalding U (KY)
Spelman Coll (GA)
Spring Hill Coll (AL)
Stephen F. Austin State U (TX)
Stockton U (NJ)
Stonehill Coll (MA)
Stony Brook U, State U of New York (NY)
Stratford U, Alexandria (VA)
Stratford U, Newport News (VA)
Stratford U, Virginia Beach (VA)
Stratford U, Woodbridge (VA)
Texas Woman's U (TX)
Towson U (MD)
Union Coll (NE)
U of Central Florida (FL)
U of Colorado Colorado Springs (CO)
U of Florida (FL)
U of Hartford (CT)
U of Kentucky (KY)
U of Miami (FL)
U of Michigan–Flint (MI)
U of Minnesota, Crookston (MN)
U of Missouri–Kansas City (MO)
U of Northern Colorado (CO)
U of North Florida (FL)
U of Oklahoma Health Sciences Center (OK)
U of San Francisco (CA)
The U of South Dakota (SD)
U of Southern California (CA)
U of Southern Mississippi (MS)
U of South Florida (FL)
U of South Florida, St. Petersburg (FL)
The U of Tampa (FL)
The U of Texas at Dallas (TX)
The U of Texas Rio Grande Valley (TX)
U of the Incarnate Word (TX)
U of Utah (UT)
U of Washington, Bothell (WA)
Valparaiso U (IN)
Washington U in St. Louis (MO)
Weber State U (UT)
West Chester U of Pennsylvania (PA)
Western Kentucky U (KY)
Western New England U (MA)
Westminster Coll (UT)
West Texas A&M U (TX)
West Virginia Wesleyan Coll (WV)
Wheaton Coll (IL)
Whitworth U (WA)
Widener U (PA)
William Paterson U of New Jersey (NJ)
Wilmington U (DE)
Youngstown State U (OH)

HEALTH TEACHER EDUCATION
Auburn U (AL)
Augsburg Coll (MN)
Averett U (VA)
Bemidji State U (MN)
Bethel U (MN)
Bluefield Coll (VA)
Bowling Green State U (OH)
Bridgewater State U (MA)
Brooklyn Coll of the City U of New York (NY)
California State U, Stanislaus (CA)
Campbellsville U (KY)
Capital U (OH)
Central Michigan U (MI)
Concordia U, St. Paul (MN)
Defiance Coll (OH)
East Carolina U (NC)
Eastern Illinois U (IL)
Eastern Washington U (WA)
East Stroudsburg U of Pennsylvania (PA)
Elon U (NC)
Gardner-Webb U (NC)
Graceland U (IA)
Grand Valley State U (MI)
Hampton U (VA)
Harding U (AR)
Heidelberg U (OH)
Hofstra U (NY)
Houghton Coll (NY)
Hunter Coll of the City U of New York (NY)
Idaho State U (ID)
Illinois State U (IL)
Indiana U Bloomington (IN)
Inter American U of Puerto Rico, Barranquitas Campus (PR)
Inter American U of Puerto Rico, San Germán Campus (PR)
Iowa State U of Science and Technology (IA)
Iowa Wesleyan U (IA)
Ithaca Coll (NY)
Jacksonville State U (AL)
Kansas Wesleyan U (KS)
Kent State U (OH)
Lee U (TN)
Lehman Coll of the City U of New York (NY)
Linfield Coll (OR)
McKendree U (IL)
Michigan State U (MI)
Minnesota State U Mankato (MN)
Minnesota State U Moorhead (MN)
Missouri Baptist U (MO)
Missouri Valley Coll (MO)
Montana State U Billings (MT)
Montana State U–Northern (MT)
Montclair State U (NJ)
Morehead State U (KY)
Murray State U (KY)
Muskingum U (OH)
New Mexico Highlands U (NM)
North Carolina Central U (NC)
North Dakota State U (ND)
Northern Illinois U (IL)
Northern State U (SD)
Northwestern Oklahoma State U (OK)
Ohio Wesleyan U (OH)
Oral Roberts U (OK)
Otterbein U (OH)
Portland State U (OR)
Purdue U (IN)
Rhode Island Coll (RI)
St. Cloud State U (MN)
Salisbury U (MD)
Sam Houston State U (TX)
South Dakota State U (SD)
Southern Oregon U (OR)
Southwest Baptist U (MO)
State U of New York at Oswego (NY)
State U of New York Coll at Cortland (NY)
Tennessee State U (TN)
Troy U (AL)
Union Coll (KY)
The U of Akron (OH)
The U of Alabama at Birmingham (AL)
U of Charleston (WV)
U of Cincinnati (OH)
The U of Findlay (OH)
U of Great Falls (MT)
U of Kentucky (KY)
U of Maine at Farmington (ME)
U of Maryland, Coll Park (MD)
The U of Montana Western (MT)
U of Mount Union (OH)
U of Nevada, Las Vegas (NV)
The U of North Carolina at Greensboro (NC)
U of Regina (SK, Canada)
The U of South Dakota (SD)
U of the Cumberlands (KY)
U of Toronto (ON, Canada)
U of Windsor (ON, Canada)
U of Wisconsin–La Crosse (WI)
Utah State U (UT)
Utah Valley U (UT)
Valley City State U (ND)
Virginia Commonwealth U (VA)
Washington State U (WA)
Wayne State U (MI)
Western Connecticut State U (CT)
Western Michigan U (MI)
West Virginia Wesleyan Coll (WV)
William Penn U (IA)
Winona State U (MN)
York Coll of the City U of New York (NY)
Youngstown State U (OH)

HEAVY EQUIPMENT MAINTENANCE TECHNOLOGY
Ferris State U (MI)

HEBREW
Baruch Coll of the City U of New York (NY)
Binghamton U, State U of New York (NY)
Brandeis U (MA)
Brigham Young U (UT)
Brooklyn Coll of the City U of New York (NY)
Concordia U Wisconsin (WI)
Dartmouth Coll (NH)
Hofstra U (NY)
Hunter Coll of the City U of New York (NY)
Lehman Coll of the City U of New York (NY)
Multnomah U (OR)
The Ohio State U (OH)
Queens Coll of the City U of New York (NY)
U of Cincinnati (OH)
The U of Texas at Austin (TX)
Washington U in St. Louis (MO)

HIGHER EDUCATION/HIGHER EDUCATION ADMINISTRATION
U of Georgia (GA)

HISPANIC-AMERICAN, PUERTO RICAN, AND MEXICAN-AMERICAN/CHICANO STUDIES
Arizona State U at the Tempe campus (AZ)
Boston Coll (MA)
Bowling Green State U (OH)
Brooklyn Coll of the City U of New York (NY)
California State U, Dominguez Hills (CA)
California State U, East Bay (CA)
California State U, Fresno (CA)
California State U, Fullerton (CA)
California State U, Long Beach (CA)
California State U, Northridge (CA)
Claremont McKenna Coll (CA)
The Colorado Coll (CO)
Columbia U (NY)
Columbia U, School of General Studies (NY)
Dartmouth Coll (NH)
Gettysburg Coll (PA)
Hunter Coll of the City U of New York (NY)
Lewis & Clark Coll (OR)
Loyola Marymount U (CA)
McMaster U (ON, Canada)

Metropolitan State U of Denver (CO)
Mills Coll (CA)
Our Lady of the Lake U of San Antonio (TX)
Pepperdine U, Malibu (CA)
Pitzer Coll (CA)
Pomona Coll (CA)
Rutgers U–Newark (NJ)
Rutgers U–New Brunswick (NJ)
San Diego State U (CA)
San Francisco State U (CA)
Scripps Coll (CA)
Sonoma State U (CA)
Southern Methodist U (TX)
Stanford U (CA)
Trent U (ON, Canada)
Tulane U (LA)
Université de Montréal (QC, Canada)
U at Albany, State U of New York (NY)
The U of Arizona (AZ)
U of California, Davis (CA)
U of California, Irvine (CA)
U of California, Riverside (CA)
U of California, Santa Barbara (CA)
U of Michigan (MI)
U of Minnesota, Twin Cities Campus (MN)
U of Northern Colorado (CO)
The U of Scranton (PA)
U of Southern California (CA)
The U of Texas at Austin (TX)
The U of Texas at El Paso (TX)
The U of Texas at San Antonio (TX)
The U of Texas Rio Grande Valley (TX)
Vanderbilt U (TN)
Wheaton Coll (MA)

HISPANIC AND LATIN AMERICAN LANGUAGES
Boston U (MA)
Hamilton Coll (NY)
Loyola U New Orleans (LA)
Molloy Coll (NY)
Pacific Lutheran U (WA)
Purdue U (IN)
Roger Williams U (RI)
Saint Louis U–Madrid Campus (Spain)
The U of Texas at Austin (TX)
U of Washington, Tacoma (WA)

HISTORIC PRESERVATION AND CONSERVATION
Coll of Charleston (SC)
Roger Williams U (RI)
Salve Regina U (RI)
Savannah Coll of Art and Design (GA)
Southeast Missouri State U (MO)
U of Delaware (DE)
U of Georgia (GA)
U of Mary Washington (VA)
The U of Texas at Austin (TX)

HISTORY
Abilene Christian U (TX)
Adams State U (CO)
Adelphi U (NY)
Agnes Scott Coll (GA)
Alabama State U (AL)
Albany State U (GA)
Albertus Magnus Coll (CT)
Albion Coll (MI)
Albright Coll (PA)
Alcorn State U (MS)
Alfred U (NY)
Alice Lloyd Coll (KY)
Allegheny Coll (PA)
Alma Coll (MI)
Alvernia U (PA)
Alverno Coll (WI)
Ambrose U (AB, Canada)
American Intl Coll (MA)
American Public U System (WV)
American U (DC)
American U in Bulgaria (Bulgaria)
The American U in Cairo (Egypt)
American U of Beirut (Lebanon)
The American U of Paris (France)
Amherst Coll (MA)
Anderson U (IN)
Anderson U (SC)
Andrews U (MI)
Angelo State U (TX)
Antioch Coll, Yellow Springs (OH)
Appalachian State U (NC)
Aquinas Coll (MI)
Aquinas Coll (TN)
Arcadia U (PA)
Arizona State U at the Polytechnic campus (AZ)
Arizona State U at the Tempe campus (AZ)
Arizona State U at the West campus (AZ)
Arkansas Tech U (AR)
Armstrong State U (GA)
Asbury U (KY)
Ashland U (OH)
Assumption Coll (MA)
Athens State U (AL)
Auburn U (AL)
Auburn U at Montgomery (AL)
Augsburg Coll (MN)
Augustana Coll (IL)
Augustana U (SD)
Augusta U (GA)
Aurora U (IL)
Austin Coll (TX)
Austin Peay State U (TN)
Averett U (VA)
Avila U (MO)
Azusa Pacific U (CA)
Baker U (KS)
Baldwin Wallace U (OH)
Ball State U (IN)
Bard Coll (NY)
Barnard Coll (NY)
Barry U (FL)
Barton Coll (NC)
Baruch Coll of the City U of New York (NY)
Bates Coll (ME)
Baylor U (TX)
Belhaven U (MS)
Bellarmine U (KY)
Belmont Abbey Coll (NC)
Belmont U (TN)
Beloit Coll (WI)
Bemidji State U (MN)
Benedictine Coll (KS)
Bennington Coll (VT)
Bentley U (MA)
Berea Coll (KY)
Berry Coll (GA)
Bethany Lutheran Coll (MN)
Bethel Coll (IN)
Bethel Coll (KS)
Bethel U (MN)
Binghamton U, State U of New York (NY)
Biola U (CA)
Bishop's U (QC, Canada)
Blackburn Coll (IL)
Black Hills State U (SD)
Bloomfield Coll (NJ)
Bloomsburg U of Pennsylvania (PA)
Bluefield Coll (VA)
Blue Mountain Coll (MS)
Bluffton U (OH)
Boise State U (ID)
Boston Coll (MA)
Boston U (MA)
Bowdoin Coll (ME)
Bowie State U (MD)
Bowling Green State U (OH)
Bradley U (IL)
Brandeis U (MA)
Brenau U (GA)
Brescia U (KY)
Brewton-Parker Coll (GA)
Briar Cliff U (IA)
Bridgewater Coll (VA)
Bridgewater State U (MA)
Brigham Young U–Idaho (ID)
Brooklyn Coll of the City U of New York (NY)
Bryan Coll (TN)
Bryant U (RI)
Bryn Athyn Coll of the New Church (PA)
Bryn Mawr Coll (PA)
Bucknell U (PA)
Buena Vista U (IA)
Buffalo State Coll, State U of New York (NY)
Butler U (IN)
Cabrini U (PA)
Caldwell U (NJ)
California Baptist U (CA)
California Inst of Technology (CA)
California Lutheran U (CA)
California Polytechnic State U, San Luis Obispo (CA)
California State Polytechnic U, Pomona (CA)
California State U, Bakersfield (CA)
California State U, Chico (CA)
California State U, Dominguez Hills (CA)
California State U, East Bay (CA)
California State U, Fresno (CA)
California State U, Fullerton (CA)
California State U, Long Beach (CA)
California State U, Northridge (CA)
California State U, Sacramento (CA)
California State U, San Bernardino (CA)
California State U, San Marcos (CA)
California State U, Stanislaus (CA)
California U of Pennsylvania (PA)
Calvary U (MO)
Calvin Coll (MI)
Cameron U (OK)
Campbellsville U (KY)
Canisius Coll (NY)
Capital U (OH)
Cardinal Stritch U (WI)
Carleton Coll (MN)
Carlow U (PA)
Carnegie Mellon U (PA)
Carroll Coll (MT)
Carson-Newman U (TN)
Carthage Coll (WI)
Case Western Reserve U (OH)
Catawba Coll (NC)
The Catholic U of America (DC)
Cedar Crest Coll (PA)
Cedarville U (OH)
Centenary Coll of Louisiana (LA)
Centenary U (NJ)
Central Baptist Coll (AR)
Central Connecticut State U (CT)
Central Methodist U (MO)
Central Michigan U (MI)
Central State U (OH)
Central Washington U (WA)
Centre Coll (KY)
Chapman U (CA)
Charleston Southern U (SC)
Chatham U (PA)
Chestnut Hill Coll (PA)
Chowan U (NC)
Christendom Coll (VA)
Christian Brothers U (TN)
Christopher Newport U (VA)
The Citadel, The Military Coll of South Carolina (SC)
City Coll of the City U of New York (NY)
Claremont McKenna Coll (CA)
Clarion U of Pennsylvania (PA)
Clark Atlanta U (GA)
Clarke U (IA)
Clarkson U (NY)
Clark U (MA)
Clayton State U (GA)
Clemson U (SC)
Cleveland State U (OH)
Coastal Carolina U (SC)
Coe Coll (IA)
Colby Coll (ME)
Colgate U (NY)
The Coll at Brockport, State U of New York (NY)
Coll of Charleston (SC)
The Coll of Idaho (ID)
Coll of Mount Saint Vincent (NY)
The Coll of New Jersey (NJ)
Coll of Saint Benedict (MN)
Coll of Saint Elizabeth (NJ)
The Coll of Saint Rose (NY)
The Coll of St. Scholastica (MN)
Coll of Staten Island of the City U of New York (NY)
Coll of the Holy Cross (MA)
Coll of the Ozarks (MO)
The Coll of William and Mary (VA)
The Coll of Wooster (OH)
The Colorado Coll (CO)
Colorado Mesa U (CO)
Colorado State U (CO)
Columbia Coll (MO)
Columbia U (NY)
Columbia U, School of General Studies (NY)
Columbus State U (GA)
Concordia Coll (MN)
Concordia Coll–New York (NY)
Concordia U (QC, Canada)
Concordia U Chicago (IL)
Concordia U Irvine (CA)
Concordia U, Nebraska (NE)
Concordia U, St. Paul (MN)
Concordia U Wisconsin (WI)
Concord U (WV)
Connecticut Coll (CT)
Converse Coll (SC)
Corban U (OR)
Cornell Coll (IA)
Cornell U (NY)
Cornerstone U (MI)
Crandall U (NB, Canada)
Creighton U (NE)
Culver-Stockton Coll (MO)
Daemen Coll (NY)
Dalhousie U (NS, Canada)
Dallas Baptist U (TX)
Dalton State Coll (GA)
Dartmouth Coll (NH)
Davidson Coll (NC)
Dean Coll (MA)
Defiance Coll (OH)
Denison U (OH)
DePauw U (IN)
DEREE - The American Coll of Greece (Greece)
DeSales U (PA)
Dickinson Coll (PA)
Dickinson State U (ND)
Dixie State U (UT)
Doane U (NE)
Dominican Coll (NY)
Dominican U (IL)
Dominican U of California (CA)
Drake U (IA)
Drew U (NJ)
Drexel U (PA)
Drury U (MO)
Duquesne U (PA)
Earlham Coll (IN)
East Carolina U (NC)
East Central U (OK)
Eastern Illinois U (IL)
Eastern Mennonite U (VA)
Eastern Michigan U (MI)
Eastern Nazarene Coll (MA)
Eastern Oregon U (OR)
Eastern U (PA)
Eastern Washington U (WA)
East Stroudsburg U of Pennsylvania (PA)
East Tennessee State U (TN)
East Texas Baptist U (TX)
Eckerd Coll (FL)
Edgewood Coll (WI)
Elizabeth City State U (NC)
Elizabethtown Coll (PA)
Elmira Coll (NY)
Elms Coll (MA)
Elon U (NC)
Emmanuel Coll (MA)
Emory & Henry Coll (VA)
Emory U (GA)
Emporia State U (KS)
Endicott Coll (MA)
Eugene Lang Coll of Liberal Arts (NY)
Eureka Coll (IL)
Evangel U (MO)
Excelsior Coll (NY)
Fairfield U (CT)
Fairleigh Dickinson U, Coll at Florham (NJ)
Fairleigh Dickinson U, Metropolitan Campus (NJ)
Faulkner U (AL)
Fayetteville State U (NC)
Felician U (NJ)
Ferris State U (MI)
Fitchburg State U (MA)
Flagler Coll (FL)
Florida Ag and Mech U (FL)
Florida Atlantic U (FL)
Florida Coll (FL)
Florida Gulf Coast U (FL)
Florida Intl U (FL)
Florida Southern Coll (FL)
Florida State U (FL)
Fordham U (NY)
Fort Lewis Coll (CO)
Framingham State U (MA)
Franciscan U of Steubenville (OH)
Francis Marion U (SC)
Franklin & Marshall Coll (PA)
Franklin Coll (IN)
Franklin Pierce U (NH)
Freed-Hardeman U (TN)
Fresno Pacific U (CA)
Friends U (KS)
Frostburg State U (MD)
Furman U (SC)
Gannon U (PA)
Gardner-Webb U (NC)
Geneva Coll (PA)
George Fox U (OR)
Georgetown Coll (KY)
Georgetown U (DC)
The George Washington U (DC)
Georgia Coll & State U (GA)
Georgia Gwinnett Coll (GA)
Georgian Court U (NJ)
Georgia Southern U (GA)
Georgia Southwestern State U (GA)
Georgia State U (GA)
Gettysburg Coll (PA)
Goddard Coll (VT)
Gonzaga U (WA)
Gordon Coll (MA)
Gordon State Coll (GA)
Goshen Coll (IN)
Goucher Coll (MD)
Governors State U (IL)
Grace Coll (IN)
Graceland U (IA)
Grambling State U (LA)
Grand Valley State U (MI)
Grand View U (IA)
Granite State Coll (NH)
Green Mountain Coll (VT)
Greenville Coll (IL)
Grinnell Coll (IA)
Grove City Coll (PA)
Guilford Coll (NC)
Gwynedd Mercy U (PA)
Hamilton Coll (NY)
Hamline U (MN)
Hampden-Sydney Coll (VA)
Hampshire Coll (MA)
Hampton U (VA)
Hannibal-LaGrange U (MO)
Hanover Coll (IN)
Harding U (AR)
Hardin-Simmons U (TX)
Hartwick Coll (NY)
Harvard U (MA)
Haverford Coll (PA)
Hawai`i Pacific U (HI)
Heidelberg U (OH)
Henderson State U (AR)
Hendrix Coll (AR)
High Point U (NC)
Hillsdale Coll (MI)
Hiram Coll (OH)
Hobart and William Smith Colls (NY)
Hofstra U (NY)
Hollins U (VA)
Holy Cross Coll (IN)
Holy Family U (PA)
Holy Names U (CA)
Hood Coll (MD)
Hope Coll (MI)
Houghton Coll (NY)
Houston Baptist U (TX)
Howard Payne U (TX)
Humboldt State U (CA)
Hunter Coll of the City U of New York (NY)
Huntingdon Coll (AL)
Huntington U (IN)
Huston-Tillotson U (TX)
Idaho State U (ID)
Illinois Coll (IL)
Illinois State U (IL)
Illinois Wesleyan U (IL)
Immaculata U (PA)
Indiana State U (IN)
Indiana U Bloomington (IN)
Indiana U East (IN)
Indiana U Northwest (IN)
Indiana U of Pennsylvania (PA)
Indiana U–Purdue U Indianapolis (IN)
Indiana U South Bend (IN)
Indiana U Southeast (IN)

Inter American U of Puerto Rico, San Germán Campus (PR)
Iona Coll (NY)
Iowa State U of Science and Technology (IA)
Ithaca Coll (NY)
Jackson State U (MS)
Jacksonville State U (AL)
Jacksonville U (FL)
James Madison U (VA)
John Brown U (AR)
John Carroll U (OH)
John Jay Coll of Criminal Justice of the City U of New York (NY)
Johns Hopkins U (MD)
Johnson C. Smith U (NC)
Judson U (IL)
Juniata Coll (PA)
Kalamazoo Coll (MI)
Kansas State U (KS)
Kansas Wesleyan U (KS)
Kean U (NJ)
Keene State Coll (NH)
Kennesaw State U (GA)
Kent State U (OH)
Kent State U at Stark (OH)
Kentucky Wesleyan Coll (KY)
Kenyon Coll (OH)
Keuka Coll (NY)
King's Coll (PA)
The King's U (AB, Canada)
King U (TN)
Knox Coll (IL)
Kutztown U of Pennsylvania (PA)
Lafayette Coll (PA)
LaGrange Coll (GA)
Lake Erie Coll (OH)
Lake Forest Coll (IL)
Lamar U (TX)
Lane Coll (TN)
La Roche Coll (PA)
La Salle U (PA)
Lasell Coll (MA)
Lawrence U (WI)
Lebanese American U (Lebanon)
Lebanon Valley Coll (PA)
Lees-McRae Coll (NC)
Lee U (TN)
Lehigh U (PA)
Lehman Coll of the City U of New York (NY)
Le Moyne Coll (NY)
Lenoir-Rhyne U (NC)
Lewis & Clark Coll (OR)
Lewis U (IL)
Liberty U (VA)
Limestone Coll (SC)
Lincoln U (MO)
Lincoln U (PA)
Lindenwood U (MO)
Lindsey Wilson Coll (KY)
Linfield Coll (OR)
Lipscomb U (TN)
Lock Haven U of Pennsylvania (PA)
Longwood U (VA)
Loras Coll (IA)
Louisiana Coll (LA)
Louisiana State U and A&M Coll (LA)
Louisiana State U at Alexandria (LA)
Louisiana Tech U (LA)
Lourdes U (OH)
Loyola Marymount U (CA)
Loyola U Chicago (IL)
Loyola U Maryland (MD)
Loyola U New Orleans (LA)
Lubbock Christian U (TX)
Luther Coll (IA)
Lycoming Coll (PA)
Lynchburg Coll (VA)
Lyon Coll (AR)
Macalester Coll (MN)
Madonna U (MI)
Malone U (OH)
Manchester U (IN)
Manhattan Coll (NY)
Manhattanville Coll (NY)
Mansfield U of Pennsylvania (PA)
Marian U (IN)
Marian U (WI)
Marietta Coll (OH)
Marist Coll (NY)
Marshall U (WV)
Mary Baldwin U (VA)
Marymount U (VA)
Maryville U of Saint Louis (MO)
Marywood U (PA)
Massachusetts Coll of Liberal Arts (MA)
Massachusetts Inst of Technology (MA)
The Master's U (CA)
McDaniel Coll (MD)
McKendree U (IL)
McMaster U (ON, Canada)
McMurry U (TX)
McNeese State U (LA)
Mercer U, Macon (GA)
Mercy Coll (NY)
Mercyhurst U (PA)
Meredith Coll (NC)
Merrimack Coll (MA)
Messiah Coll (PA)
Metropolitan State U of Denver (CO)
Miami U (OH)
Michigan State U (MI)
Michigan Technological U (MI)
MidAmerica Nazarene U (KS)
Middlebury Coll (VT)
Millersville U of Pennsylvania (PA)
Milligan Coll (TN)
Millikin U (IL)
Millsaps Coll (MS)
Mills Coll (CA)
Minnesota State U Mankato (MN)
Minnesota State U Moorhead (MN)
Minot State U (ND)
Misericordia U (PA)
Mississippi State U (MS)
Mississippi Valley State U (MS)
Missouri Baptist U (MO)
Missouri State U (MO)
Missouri U of Science and Technology (MO)
Missouri Valley Coll (MO)
Missouri Western State U (MO)
Molloy Coll (NY)
Monmouth Coll (IL)
Monmouth U (NJ)
Montana State U (MT)
Montana State U Billings (MT)
Montclair State U (NJ)
Moravian Coll (PA)
Morehead State U (KY)
Morehouse Coll (GA)
Morningside Coll (IA)
Morris Coll (SC)
Mount Allison U (NB, Canada)
Mount Holyoke Coll (MA)
Mount Marty Coll (SD)
Mount Mary U (WI)
Mount Mercy U (IA)
Mount St. Joseph U (OH)
Mount Saint Mary Coll (NY)
Mount Saint Mary's U (CA)
Mount St. Mary's U (MD)
Mount Vernon Nazarene U (OH)
Muhlenberg Coll (PA)
Multnomah U (OR)
Murray State U (KY)
Muskingum U (OH)
National U (CA)
Nazareth Coll of Rochester (NY)
Nebraska Wesleyan U (NE)
Nevada State Coll (NV)
Newberry Coll (SC)
New Coll of Florida (FL)
New England Coll (NH)
New Jersey City U (NJ)
Newman U (KS)
New Mexico Highlands U (NM)
New Mexico State U (NM)
Niagara U (NY)
North Carolina Central U (NC)
North Carolina State U (NC)
North Carolina Wesleyan Coll (NC)
North Central Coll (IL)
North Dakota State U (ND)
Northeastern Illinois U (IL)
Northeastern State U (OK)
Northeastern U (MA)
Northern Arizona U (AZ)
Northern Illinois U (IL)
Northern Kentucky U (KY)
Northern State U (SD)
North Greenville U (SC)
Northland Coll (WI)
Northwest Christian U (OR)
Northwestern Coll (IA)
Northwestern Oklahoma State U (OK)
Northwestern State U of Louisiana (LA)
Northwestern U (IL)
Northwest Missouri State U (MO)
Northwest U (WA)
Nova Southeastern U (FL)
Nyack Coll (NY)
Oakland City U (IN)
Oberlin Coll (OH)
Occidental Coll (CA)
Ohio Christian U (OH)
Ohio Dominican U (OH)
The Ohio State U (OH)
The Ohio State U at Lima (OH)
The Ohio State U at Marion (OH)
The Ohio State U–Mansfield Campus (OH)
The Ohio State U–Newark Campus (OH)
Ohio U (OH)
Ohio Valley U (WV)
Ohio Wesleyan U (OH)
Oklahoma Baptist U (OK)
Oklahoma Christian U (OK)
Oklahoma City U (OK)
Oklahoma State U (OK)
Old Dominion U (VA)
Olivet Nazarene U (IL)
Oral Roberts U (OK)
Oregon State U (OR)
Otterbein U (OH)
Ouachita Baptist U (AR)
Our Lady of the Lake U of San Antonio (TX)
Pace U (NY)
Pace U, Pleasantville Campus (NY)
Pacific Lutheran U (WA)
Paine Coll (GA)
Palm Beach Atlantic U (FL)
Patrick Henry Coll (VA)
Penn State Abington (PA)
Penn State Altoona (PA)
Penn State Beaver (PA)
Penn State Berks (PA)
Penn State Brandywine (PA)
Penn State DuBois (PA)
Penn State Erie, The Behrend Coll (PA)
Penn State Fayette, The Eberly Campus (PA)
Penn State Greater Allegheny (PA)
Penn State Hazleton (PA)
Penn State Lehigh Valley (PA)
Penn State Mont Alto (PA)
Penn State New Kensington (PA)
Penn State Schuylkill (PA)
Penn State Shenango (PA)
Penn State U Park (PA)
Penn State Wilkes-Barre (PA)
Penn State Worthington Scranton (PA)
Penn State York (PA)
Pepperdine U, Malibu (CA)
Piedmont Coll (GA)
Pittsburg State U (KS)
Pitzer Coll (CA)
Plymouth State U (NH)
Point Loma Nazarene U (CA)
Point Park U (PA)
Point U (GA)
Pomona Coll (CA)
Portland State U (OR)
Prairie View A&M U (TX)
Princeton U (NJ)
Principia Coll (IL)
Providence Coll (RI)
Purchase Coll, State U of New York (NY)
Purdue U (IN)
Purdue U Northwest (IN)
Queens Coll of the City U of New York (NY)
Quinnipiac U (CT)
Radford U (VA)
Ramapo Coll of New Jersey (NJ)
Randolph Coll (VA)
Randolph-Macon Coll (VA)
Redeemer U Coll (ON, Canada)
Reed Coll (OR)
Regent U (VA)
Regis U (CO)
Rhode Island Coll (RI)
Rhodes Coll (TN)
Rice U (TX)
Ripon Coll (WI)
Roanoke Coll (VA)
Roberts Wesleyan Coll (NY)
Rockford U (IL)
Rockhurst U (MO)
Rocky Mountain Coll (MT)
Rogers State U (OK)
Roger Williams U (RI)
Rollins Coll (FL)
Rosemont Coll (PA)
Rowan U (NJ)
Royal Military Coll of Canada (ON, Canada)
Rutgers U–Camden (NJ)
Rutgers U–Newark (NJ)
Rutgers U–New Brunswick (NJ)
Sacred Heart U (CT)
The Sage Colls (NY)
Saginaw Valley State U (MI)
St. Ambrose U (IA)
Saint Anselm Coll (NH)
Saint Augustine's U (NC)
St. Bonaventure U (NY)
St. Catherine U (MN)
St. Cloud State U (MN)
St. Edward's U (TX)
Saint Francis U (PA)
St. Gregory's U, Shawnee (OK)
St. John Fisher Coll (NY)
Saint John's U (MN)
St. John's U (NY)
St. Joseph's Coll, Long Island Campus (NY)
St. Joseph's Coll, New York (NY)
Saint Joseph's U (PA)
Saint Leo U (FL)
Saint Louis U (MO)
Saint Louis U–Madrid Campus (Spain)
Saint Martin's U (WA)
Saint Mary's Coll (IN)
Saint Mary's Coll of California (CA)
St. Mary's Coll of Maryland (MD)
Saint Mary's U of Minnesota (MN)
Saint Michael's Coll (VT)
St. Norbert Coll (WI)
St. Olaf Coll (MN)
Saint Peter's U (NJ)
St. Thomas Aquinas Coll (NY)
St. Thomas U (FL)
St. Thomas U (NB, Canada)
Saint Vincent Coll (PA)
Salisbury U (MD)
Salve Regina U (RI)
Samford U (AL)
Sam Houston State U (TX)
San Diego State U (CA)
San Francisco State U (CA)
Santa Clara U (CA)
Sarah Lawrence Coll (NY)
Schreiner U (TX)
Scripps Coll (CA)
Seattle Pacific U (WA)
Seattle U (WA)
Seton Hill U (PA)
Sewanee: The U of the South (TN)
Shawnee State U (OH)
Shenandoah U (VA)
Shepherd U (WV)
Shippensburg U of Pennsylvania (PA)
Shorter U (GA)
Siena Coll (NY)
Silver Lake Coll of the Holy Family (WI)
Simmons Coll (MA)
Simon Fraser U (BC, Canada)
Simpson Coll (IA)
Simpson U (CA)
Skidmore Coll (NY)
Slippery Rock U of Pennsylvania (PA)
Smith Coll (MA)
Sonoma State U (CA)
South Carolina State U (SC)
South Dakota State U (SD)
Southeastern Louisiana U (LA)
Southeastern Oklahoma State U (OK)
Southeastern U (FL)
Southeast Missouri State U (MO)
Southern Arkansas U–Magnolia (AR)
Southern Connecticut State U (CT)
Southern Illinois U Carbondale (IL)
Southern Illinois U Edwardsville (IL)
Southern Methodist U (TX)
Southern New Hampshire U (NH)
Southern Oregon U (OR)
Southern Utah U (UT)
Southwest Baptist U (MO)
Southwestern Adventist U (TX)
Southwestern Assemblies of God U (TX)
Southwestern Coll (KS)
Southwestern U (TX)
Spelman Coll (GA)
Spring Hill Coll (AL)
Stanford U (CA)
State U of New York at Fredonia (NY)
State U of New York at New Paltz (NY)
State U of New York at Oswego (NY)
State U of New York at Plattsburgh (NY)
State U of New York Coll at Cortland (NY)
State U of New York Coll at Geneseo (NY)
State U of New York Coll at Old Westbury (NY)
State U of New York Coll at Potsdam (NY)
State U of New York Empire State Coll (NY)
Stephen F. Austin State U (TX)
Sterling Coll (KS)
Stevens Inst of Technology (NJ)
Stevenson U (MD)
Stockton U (NJ)
Stonehill Coll (MA)
Stony Brook U, State U of New York (NY)
Suffolk U (MA)
Susquehanna U (PA)
Swarthmore Coll (PA)
Sweet Briar Coll (VA)
Syracuse U (NY)
Tabor Coll (KS)
Tarleton State U (TX)
Taylor U (IN)
Temple U (PA)
Tennessee State U (TN)
Tennessee Wesleyan U (TN)
Texas A&M Intl U (TX)
Texas A&M U (TX)
Texas A&M U–Central Texas (TX)
Texas A&M U–Commerce (TX)
Texas A&M U–Corpus Christi (TX)
Texas A&M U–Kingsville (TX)
Texas Christian U (TX)
Texas Lutheran U (TX)
Texas State U (TX)
Texas Tech U (TX)
Texas Wesleyan U (TX)
Texas Woman's U (TX)
Thomas More Coll (KY)
Tiffin U (OH)
Toccoa Falls Coll (GA)
Towson U (MD)
Transylvania U (KY)
Trent U (ON, Canada)
Trevecca Nazarene U (TN)
Trinity Christian Coll (IL)
Trinity U (TX)
Troy U (AL)
Truett McConnell U (GA)
Truman State U (MO)
Tufts U (MA)
Tulane U (LA)
Tusculum Coll (TN)
Union Coll (KY)
Union Coll (NE)
Union Coll (NY)
Union U (TN)
United States Air Force Acad (CO)
Universidad Adventista de las Antillas (PR)
Université de Montréal (QC, Canada)
Université de Sherbrooke (QC, Canada)
U at Albany, State U of New York (NY)
U at Buffalo, the State U of New York (NY)
The U of Akron (OH)
The U of Alabama (AL)
The U of Alabama at Birmingham (AL)
The U of Alabama in Huntsville (AL)
U of Alaska Fairbanks (AK)
The U of Arizona (AZ)

U of Arkansas (AR)
U of California, Davis (CA)
U of California, Irvine (CA)
U of California, Los Angeles (CA)
U of California, Riverside (CA)
U of California, San Diego (CA)
U of California, Santa Barbara (CA)
U of Central Arkansas (AR)
U of Central Florida (FL)
U of Central Missouri (MO)
U of Charleston (WV)
U of Chicago (IL)
U of Cincinnati (OH)
U of Colorado Boulder (CO)
U of Colorado Colorado Springs (CO)
U of Colorado Denver (CO)
U of Dayton (OH)
U of Delaware (DE)
U of Denver (CO)
U of Detroit Mercy (MI)
U of Evansville (IN)
The U of Findlay (OH)
U of Florida (FL)
U of Georgia (GA)
U of Great Falls (MT)
U of Guelph (ON, Canada)
U of Hartford (CT)
U of Hawaii at Manoa (HI)
U of Houston (TX)
U of Houston–Clear Lake (TX)
U of Houston–Downtown (TX)
U of Idaho (ID)
U of Illinois at Chicago (IL)
U of Illinois at Springfield (IL)
U of Indianapolis (IN)
U of Jamestown (ND)
The U of Kansas (KS)
U of Kentucky (KY)
U of King's Coll (NS, Canada)
U of La Verne (CA)
U of Lethbridge (AB, Canada)
U of Louisiana at Monroe (LA)
U of Louisville (KY)
U of Maine (ME)
U of Maine at Farmington (ME)
U of Maine at Presque Isle (ME)
U of Mary Hardin-Baylor (TX)
U of Maryland, Baltimore County (MD)
U of Maryland, Coll Park (MD)
U of Maryland U Coll (MD)
U of Mary Washington (VA)
U of Massachusetts Amherst (MA)
U of Massachusetts Boston (MA)
U of Massachusetts Dartmouth (MA)
U of Massachusetts Lowell (MA)
U of Miami (FL)
U of Michigan (MI)
U of Michigan–Dearborn (MI)
U of Michigan–Flint (MI)
U of Minnesota, Duluth (MN)
U of Minnesota, Morris (MN)
U of Minnesota, Twin Cities Campus (MN)
U of Missouri–Kansas City (MO)
U of Missouri–St. Louis (MO)
U of Mobile (AL)
The U of Montana Western (MT)
U of Montevallo (AL)
U of Mount Union (OH)
U of Nebraska at Kearney (NE)
U of Nevada, Las Vegas (NV)
U of Nevada, Reno (NV)
U of New England (ME)
U of New Hampshire (NH)
U of New Hampshire at Manchester (NH)
U of New Haven (CT)
U of New Orleans (LA)
U of North Alabama (AL)
U of North Carolina at Asheville (NC)
The U of North Carolina at Chapel Hill (NC)
The U of North Carolina at Charlotte (NC)
The U of North Carolina at Greensboro (NC)
The U of North Carolina at Pembroke (NC)
The U of North Carolina Wilmington (NC)
U of North Dakota (ND)
U of Northern Colorado (CO)
U of Northern Iowa (IA)
U of North Florida (FL)
U of North Georgia (GA)
U of North Texas (TX)
U of Notre Dame (IN)
U of Oklahoma (OK)
U of Oregon (OR)
U of Pennsylvania (PA)
U of Pikeville (KY)
U of Pittsburgh (PA)
U of Pittsburgh at Bradford (PA)
U of Pittsburgh at Johnstown (PA)
U of Puget Sound (WA)
U of Regina (SK, Canada)
U of Rhode Island (RI)
U of Richmond (VA)
U of Rochester (NY)
U of St. Francis (IL)
U of Saint Francis (IN)
U of Saint Joseph (CT)
U of Saint Mary (KS)
U of St. Thomas (MN)
U of St. Thomas (TX)
U of San Diego (CA)
U of San Francisco (CA)
U of Saskatchewan (SK, Canada)
U of Science and Arts of Oklahoma (OK)
The U of Scranton (PA)
U of South Alabama (AL)
U of South Carolina (SC)
U of South Carolina Aiken (SC)
The U of South Dakota (SD)
U of Southern California (CA)
U of Southern Indiana (IN)
U of Southern Maine (ME)
U of Southern Mississippi (MS)
U of South Florida (FL)
U of South Florida, St. Petersburg (FL)
U of South Florida Sarasota-Manatee (FL)
The U of Tampa (FL)
The U of Tennessee (TN)
The U of Tennessee at Chattanooga (TN)
The U of Tennessee at Martin (TN)
The U of Texas at Austin (TX)
The U of Texas at Dallas (TX)
The U of Texas at El Paso (TX)
The U of Texas at San Antonio (TX)
The U of Texas of the Permian Basin (TX)
The U of Texas Rio Grande Valley (TX)
U of the Cumberlands (KY)
U of the Fraser Valley (BC, Canada)
U of the Incarnate Word (TX)
U of the Pacific (CA)
U of the Southwest (NM)
The U of Toledo (OH)
U of Toronto (ON, Canada)
The U of Tulsa (OK)
U of Utah (UT)
U of Vermont (VT)
U of Virginia (VA)
The U of Virginia's Coll at Wise (VA)
U of Washington (WA)
U of Washington, Tacoma (WA)
U of Waterloo (ON, Canada)
The U of West Alabama (AL)
U of West Georgia (GA)
U of Windsor (ON, Canada)
U of Wisconsin–Eau Claire (WI)
U of Wisconsin–Green Bay (WI)
U of Wisconsin–La Crosse (WI)
U of Wisconsin–Madison (WI)
U of Wisconsin–Milwaukee (WI)
U of Wisconsin–Parkside (WI)
U of Wisconsin–Platteville (WI)
U of Wisconsin–Stevens Point (WI)
U of Wisconsin–Superior (WI)
U of Wisconsin–Whitewater (WI)
Ursinus Coll (PA)
Utah State U (UT)
Utah Valley U (UT)
Utica Coll (NY)
Valdosta State U (GA)
Valley City State U (ND)
Valparaiso U (IN)
Vanderbilt U (TN)
Vassar Coll (NY)
Villanova U (PA)
Virginia Commonwealth U (VA)
Virginia Military Inst (VA)
Virginia Polytechnic Inst and State U (VA)
Virginia State U (VA)
Virginia Union U (VA)
Virginia Wesleyan Coll (VA)
Wabash Coll (IN)
Wagner Coll (NY)
Wake Forest U (NC)
Waldorf U (IA)
Walla Walla U (WA)
Walsh U (OH)
Wartburg Coll (IA)
Washburn U (KS)
Washington & Jefferson Coll (PA)
Washington and Lee U (VA)
Washington Coll (MD)
Washington State U (WA)
Washington State U–Tri-Cities (WA)
Washington State U–Vancouver (WA)
Washington U in St. Louis (MO)
Wayland Baptist U (TX)
Waynesburg U (PA)
Wayne State Coll (NE)
Wayne State U (MI)
Weber State U (UT)
Webster U (MO)
Welch Coll (TN)
Wells Coll (NY)
Wesleyan Coll (GA)
Wesleyan U (CT)
West Chester U of Pennsylvania (PA)
Western Carolina U (NC)
Western Connecticut State U (CT)
Western Illinois U (IL)
Western Kentucky U (KY)
Western Michigan U (MI)
Western New England U (MA)
Western Oregon U (OR)
Western State Colorado U (CO)
Western Washington U (WA)
Westfield State U (MA)
Westminster Coll (PA)
Westminster Coll (UT)
Westmont Coll (CA)
West Texas A&M U (TX)
West Virginia State U (WV)
West Virginia U (WV)
West Virginia U Inst of Technology (WV)
West Virginia Wesleyan Coll (WV)
Wheaton Coll (IL)
Wheaton Coll (MA)
Wheeling Jesuit U (WV)
Whitman Coll (WA)
Whittier Coll (CA)
Whitworth U (WA)
Wichita State U (KS)
Widener U (PA)
Wilkes U (PA)
Willamette U (OR)
William Jewell Coll (MO)
William Paterson U of New Jersey (NJ)
William Penn U (IA)
Williams Baptist Coll (AR)
Williams Coll (MA)
William Woods U (MO)
Wingate U (NC)
Winona State U (MN)
Winthrop U (SC)
Wittenberg U (OH)
Wofford Coll (SC)
Woodbury U (CA)
Worcester State U (MA)
Wright State U (OH)
Xavier U of Louisiana (LA)
York Coll of Pennsylvania (PA)
York Coll of the City U of New York (NY)
Youngstown State U (OH)

HISTORY AND PHILOSOPHY OF SCIENCE AND TECHNOLOGY

Bard Coll (NY)
California Inst of Technology (CA)
Case Western Reserve U (OH)
Dalhousie U (NS, Canada)
Georgia Inst of Technology (GA)
Harvard U (MA)
Johns Hopkins U (MD)
Stevens Inst of Technology (NJ)
U of Chicago (IL)
U of Oklahoma (OK)
U of Pennsylvania (PA)
U of Pittsburgh (PA)
U of Toronto (ON, Canada)
U of Washington (WA)
U of Wisconsin–Madison (WI)

HISTORY RELATED

The American U of Paris (France)
Bentley U (MA)
Bridgewater Coll (VA)
Bridgewater State U (MA)
Bryn Athyn Coll of the New Church (PA)
Chaminade U of Honolulu (HI)
Harvard U (MA)
Indiana U Kokomo (IN)
Lebanon Valley Coll (PA)
LeTourneau U (TX)
Mercyhurst U (PA)
The Ohio State U (OH)
The Ohio State U at Lima (OH)
The Ohio State U at Marion (OH)
The Ohio State U–Mansfield Campus (OH)
The Ohio State U–Newark Campus (OH)
Purdue U Northwest (IN)
Saint Mary's U of Minnesota (MN)
United States Air Force Acad (CO)
United States Military Acad (NY)
U at Albany, State U of New York (NY)
U of California, Santa Barbara (CA)
U of Southern California (CA)
U of Washington (WA)
U of Washington, Tacoma (WA)
Vanderbilt U (TN)
Virginia Wesleyan Coll (VA)
Viterbo U (WI)
Woodbury U (CA)

HISTORY TEACHER EDUCATION

Abilene Christian U (TX)
Albion Coll (MI)
Appalachian State U (NC)
Aquinas Coll (TN)
Armstrong State U (GA)
Auburn U (AL)
Augustana Coll (IL)
Biola U (CA)
Bishop's U (QC, Canada)
Bluefield Coll (VA)
Boise State U (ID)
Bowling Green State U (OH)
Bradley U (IL)
Brewton-Parker Coll (GA)
Brigham Young U–Idaho (ID)
Bryan Coll (TN)
Buena Vista U (IA)
Calvin Coll (MI)
Campbellsville U (KY)
Carroll Coll (MT)
The Catholic U of America (DC)
Central Michigan U (MI)
Central Washington U (WA)
Charleston Southern U (SC)
The Coll of New Jersey (NJ)
Coll of Staten Island of the City U of New York (NY)
Coll of the Ozarks (MO)
Colorado Christian U (CO)
Concordia U Chicago (IL)
Concordia U Wisconsin (WI)
Cornerstone U (MI)
Culver-Stockton Coll (MO)
Dallas Baptist U (TX)
Dickinson State U (ND)
Dominican Coll (NY)
Dominican U (IL)
East Central U (OK)
Eastern Michigan U (MI)
Eastern Nazarene Coll (MA)
East Texas Baptist U (TX)
Elizabeth City State U (NC)
Emory & Henry Coll (VA)
Evangel U (MO)
Faith Baptist Bible Coll and Theological Sem (IA)
Faulkner U (AL)
Ferris State U (MI)
Fitchburg State U (MA)
Florida Southern Coll (FL)
Friends U (KS)
Gardner-Webb U (NC)
Gordon State Coll (GA)
Grand Valley State U (MI)
Greenville Coll (IL)
Gwynedd Mercy U (PA)
Hannibal-LaGrange U (MO)
Hardin-Simmons U (TX)
Hobe Sound Bible Coll (FL)
Holy Family U (PA)
Hope Coll (MI)
Houston Baptist U (TX)
Howard Payne U (TX)
Huntingdon Coll (AL)
Inter American U of Puerto Rico, Metropolitan Campus (PR)
Inter American U of Puerto Rico, San Germán Campus (PR)
Ithaca Coll (NY)
Kansas Wesleyan U (KS)
Keene State Coll (NH)
King U (TN)
Lee U (TN)
LeTourneau U (TX)
Lindenwood U (MO)
Lipscomb U (TN)
Manchester U (IN)
Maranatha Baptist U (WI)
McKendree U (IL)
McMurry U (TX)
Merrimack Coll (MA)
Michigan State U (MI)
MidAmerica Nazarene U (KS)
Minot State U (ND)
Missouri State U (MO)
Montana State U Billings (MT)
Morningside Coll (IA)
Mount Marty Coll (SD)
Mount Mary U (WI)
Mount Vernon Nazarene U (OH)
Nazareth Coll of Rochester (NY)
Nevada State Coll (NV)
North Dakota State U (ND)
Oakland City U (IN)
Ohio Wesleyan U (OH)
Piedmont Coll (GA)
Pittsburg State U (KS)
Providence Coll (RI)
Rhode Island Coll (RI)
Rocky Mountain Coll (MT)
Roger Williams U (RI)
Saginaw Valley State U (MI)
St. Ambrose U (IA)
St. Edward's U (TX)
Saint Francis U (PA)
St. John Fisher Coll (NY)
Saint Joseph's U (PA)
Salve Regina U (RI)
Samford U (AL)
Schreiner U (TX)
Southern Utah U (UT)
Spring Hill Coll (AL)
Texas Lutheran U (TX)
Texas Wesleyan U (TX)
Tiffin U (OH)
Toccoa Falls Coll (GA)
Trevecca Nazarene U (TN)
Trinity Christian Coll (IL)
Union Coll (NE)
Universidad Adventista de las Antillas (PR)
The U of Akron (OH)
U of Delaware (DE)
U of Great Falls (MT)
U of Illinois at Chicago (IL)
U of Jamestown (ND)
U of Maine (ME)
U of Mary Hardin-Baylor (TX)
U of Michigan–Flint (MI)
U of Mobile (AL)
The U of Montana Western (MT)
U of Pittsburgh at Johnstown (PA)
The U of South Dakota (SD)
The U of Tennessee at Martin (TN)
U of Windsor (ON, Canada)
U of Wisconsin–Superior (WI)
U of Wisconsin–Whitewater (WI)
Utah Valley U (UT)
Utica Coll (NY)
Valley City State U (ND)
Valparaiso U (IN)
Virginia Union U (VA)
Wartburg Coll (IA)
Washburn U (KS)
Washington U in St. Louis (MO)
Wayne State Coll (NE)
Weber State U (UT)
Welch Coll (TN)
Western Michigan U (MI)
Western State Colorado U (CO)
Western Washington U (WA)
Westfield State U (MA)

Widener U (PA)
William Woods U (MO)
Wingate U (NC)
Xavier U of Louisiana (LA)

HOLOCAUST AND RELATED STUDIES
Keene State Coll (NH)

HOME FURNISHINGS AND EQUIPMENT INSTALLATION
Brigham Young U (UT)

HOMELAND SECURITY
American Public U System (WV)
Anderson U (SC)
Angelo State U (TX)
Central Penn Coll (PA)
Columbia Southern U (AL)
DeSales U (PA)
Embry-Riddle Aeronautical U–Daytona (FL)
Excelsior Coll (NY)
Mercy Coll (NY)
Monmouth U (NJ)
National U (CA)
Northcentral U (CA)
Northeastern State U (OK)
Saint Leo U (FL)
Slippery Rock U of Pennsylvania (PA)
State Coll of Florida Manatee-Sarasota (FL)
State U of New York Coll of Technology at Canton (NY)
Tulane U (LA)
The U of Arizona (AZ)
U of Management and Technology (VA)
U of New Hampshire at Manchester (NH)
Waldorf U (IA)

HOMELAND SECURITY, LAW ENFORCEMENT, FIREFIGHTING AND PROTECTIVE SERVICES RELATED
Anderson U (SC)
Chestnut Hill Coll (PA)
Clayton State U (GA)
Eastern Michigan U (MI)
Florida Atlantic U (FL)
Florida SouthWestern State Coll (FL)
Idaho State U (ID)
Lewis U (IL)
Madonna U (MI)
Marian U (WI)
Massachusetts Maritime Acad (MA)
Miami Dade Coll (FL)
Neumann U (PA)
North Dakota State U (ND)
Northwestern Oklahoma State U (OK)
Oklahoma State U–Oklahoma City (OK)
Penn State Altoona (PA)
Penn State Berks (PA)
Penn State U Park (PA)
Point Park U (PA)
Roberts Wesleyan Coll (NY)
St. Petersburg Coll (FL)
Thomas Edison State U (NJ)
Tiffin U (OH)
Union Coll (KY)
The U of West Alabama (AL)
Virginia Commonwealth U (VA)
Washburn U (KS)
Western Illinois U (IL)

HOMELAND SECURITY RELATED
King U (TN)

HORSE HUSBANDRY/EQUINE SCIENCE AND MANAGEMENT
Averett U (VA)
Becker Coll (MA)
Delaware Valley U (PA)
Feather River Coll (CA)
Morrisville State Coll (NY)
Saint Mary-of-the-Woods Coll (IN)
Tiffin U (OH)
U of Guelph (ON, Canada)
U of Kentucky (KY)
U of Minnesota, Crookston (MN)
U of New Hampshire (NH)
Vermont Tech Coll (VT)
William Woods U (MO)

HORTICULTURAL SCIENCE
Auburn U (AL)
Brigham Young U–Idaho (ID)
California State U, Fresno (CA)
Clemson U (SC)
Coll of the Ozarks (MO)
Colorado State U (CO)
Delaware Valley U (PA)
Iowa State U of Science and Technology (IA)
Kansas State U (KS)
Michigan State U (MI)
Mississippi State U (MS)
Missouri State U (MO)
Montana State U (MT)
Morrisville State Coll (NY)
New Mexico State U (NM)
North Carolina State U (NC)
Northwest Missouri State U (MO)
Oklahoma State U (OK)
Oregon State U (OR)
Penn State Abington (PA)
Penn State Altoona (PA)
Penn State Beaver (PA)
Penn State Berks (PA)
Penn State Brandywine (PA)
Penn State DuBois (PA)
Penn State Erie, The Behrend Coll (PA)
Penn State Fayette, The Eberly Campus (PA)
Penn State Greater Allegheny (PA)
Penn State Hazleton (PA)
Penn State Lehigh Valley (PA)
Penn State Mont Alto (PA)
Penn State New Kensington (PA)
Penn State Schuylkill (PA)
Penn State Shenango (PA)
Penn State Wilkes-Barre (PA)
Penn State Worthington Scranton (PA)
Penn State York (PA)
Purdue U (IN)
Sam Houston State U (TX)
Stephen F. Austin State U (TX)
Tarleton State U (TX)
Temple U (PA)
U of Cincinnati (OH)
U of Florida (FL)
U of Georgia (GA)
U of Idaho (ID)
U of Minnesota, Crookston (MN)
U of Saskatchewan (SK, Canada)
U of Vermont (VT)
U of Wisconsin–Madison (WI)
U of Wisconsin–Platteville (WI)
Utah State U (UT)
Virginia Polytechnic Inst and State U (VA)
Washington State U (WA)
Washington State U–Tri-Cities (WA)

HOSPITAL AND HEALTH-CARE FACILITIES ADMINISTRATION
American Intl Coll (MA)
Avila U (MO)
Black Hills State U (SD)
Champlain Coll (VT)
Clayton State U (GA)
Governors State U (IL)
Ithaca Coll (NY)
Metropolitan Coll of New York (NY)
Newman U (KS)
New York City Coll of Technology of the City U of New York (NY)
St. Joseph's Coll, Long Island Campus (NY)
St. Joseph's Coll, New York (NY)
Saint Joseph's U (PA)
Tiffin U (OH)
The U of Alabama (AL)
U of Oklahoma (OK)
U of St. Francis (IL)
The U of South Dakota (SD)
The U of Toledo (OH)
U of Wisconsin–Milwaukee (WI)
Youngstown State U (OH)

HOSPITALITY ADMINISTRATION
American Public U System (WV)
Appalachian State U (NC)
Arkansas Tech U (AR)
Ashland U (OH)
Auburn U (AL)
Beacon Coll (FL)
Boston U (MA)
Bowling Green State U (OH)
Bradley U (IL)
Buffalo State Coll, State U of New York (NY)
California State Polytechnic U, Pomona (CA)
Cardinal Stritch U (WI)
Central Connecticut State U (CT)
Central Michigan U (MI)
Coll of Charleston (SC)
Coll of the Ozarks (MO)
Colorado Mesa U (CO)
Columbia Southern U (AL)
Concordia U, St. Paul (MN)
Concord U (WV)
Dallas Baptist U (TX)
East Carolina U (NC)
Eastern Michigan U (MI)
East Stroudsburg U of Pennsylvania (PA)
Endicott Coll (MA)
Fairleigh Dickinson U, Coll at Florham (NJ)
Fairleigh Dickinson U, Metropolitan Campus (NJ)
Ferris State U (MI)
Fisher Coll (MA)
Flagler Coll (FL)
Florida Atlantic U (FL)
Florida Intl U (FL)
Florida State U (FL)
Georgia State U (GA)
Grand Valley State U (MI)
Granite State Coll (NH)
Husson U (ME)
Indiana U Kokomo (IN)
Indiana U of Pennsylvania (PA)
Iowa State U of Science and Technology (IA)
James Madison U (VA)
Kansas State U (KS)
Kendall Coll (IL)
Kent State U (OH)
Kent State U at Ashtabula (OH)
Lasell Coll (MA)
Lebanese American U (Lebanon)
Lynn U (FL)
Madonna U (MI)
Marywood U (PA)
Mercyhurst U (PA)
Metropolitan State U of Denver (CO)
Michigan State U (MI)
Missouri State U (MO)
Montclair State U (NJ)
Morrisville State Coll (NY)
New Mexico State U (NM)
New York City Coll of Technology of the City U of New York (NY)
Nichols Coll (MA)
North Carolina Central U (NC)
North Dakota State U (ND)
Northern Arizona U (AZ)
Northwestern State U of Louisiana (LA)
Northwood U, Michigan Campus (MI)
The Ohio State U (OH)
Oklahoma State U (OK)
Oregon State U (OR)
Philander Smith Coll (AR)
Purdue U Northwest (IN)
Robert Morris U (PA)
Rochester Inst of Technology (NY)
Rutgers U–Camden (NJ)
St. John's U (NY)
St. Joseph's Coll, Long Island Campus (NY)
St. Joseph's Coll, New York (NY)
Saint Leo U (FL)
St. Thomas U (FL)
San Diego State U (CA)
San Francisco State U (CA)
Seton Hill U (PA)
South Dakota State U (SD)
Southern New Hampshire U (NH)
Southern Utah U (UT)
Stephen F. Austin State U (TX)
Stockton U (NJ)
Stratford U (MD)
Stratford U, Woodbridge (VA)
Sullivan U (KY)
Syracuse U (NY)
Temple U (PA)
Tiffin U (OH)
U of Central Florida (FL)
U of Delaware (DE)
U of Denver (CO)
The U of Findlay (OH)
U of Kentucky (KY)
U of Massachusetts Amherst (MA)
U of Nevada, Las Vegas (NV)
U of New Hampshire (NH)
U of New Haven (CT)
U of New Orleans (LA)
The U of North Carolina at Greensboro (NC)
U of North Texas (TX)
U of Pittsburgh at Bradford (PA)
U of San Francisco (CA)
U of South Alabama (AL)
U of South Carolina (SC)
U of South Florida (FL)
U of South Florida Sarasota-Manatee (FL)
U of the Potomac (DC)
U of the Virgin Islands (VI)
U of Wisconsin–Stout (WI)
Utah Valley U (UT)
Virginia State U (VA)
Washington State U (WA)
Washington State U–Global Campus (WA)
Washington State U–Tri-Cities (WA)
Washington State U–Vancouver (WA)
Webber Intl U (FL)
Western Carolina U (NC)
Western Illinois U (IL)
Western Kentucky U (KY)
West Virginia U (WV)
York Coll of Pennsylvania (PA)
Youngstown State U (OH)

HOSPITALITY ADMINISTRATION RELATED
Auburn U (AL)
California State U, Dominguez Hills (CA)
California State U, Fullerton (CA)
DEREE - The American Coll of Greece (Greece)
Morrisville State Coll (NY)
Penn State Abington (PA)
Penn State Altoona (PA)
Penn State Beaver (PA)
Penn State Berks (PA)
Penn State Brandywine (PA)
Penn State DuBois (PA)
Penn State Erie, The Behrend Coll (PA)
Penn State Fayette, The Eberly Campus (PA)
Penn State Greater Allegheny (PA)
Penn State Hazleton (PA)
Penn State Lehigh Valley (PA)
Penn State Mont Alto (PA)
Penn State New Kensington (PA)
Penn State Schuylkill (PA)
Penn State Shenango (PA)
Penn State U Park (PA)
Penn State Wilkes-Barre (PA)
Penn State Worthington Scranton (PA)
Penn State York (PA)
Southern Illinois U Carbondale (IL)
U of Central Florida (FL)
U of Nevada, Las Vegas (NV)
U of Southern Mississippi (MS)
Widener U (PA)

HOSPITALITY AND RECREATION MARKETING
Ferris State U (MI)
Grace Coll (IN)
Husson U (ME)
Rochester Inst of Technology (NY)
Saint Joseph's U (PA)

HOTEL/MOTEL ADMINISTRATION
Ashland U (OH)
Auburn U (AL)
Bethune-Cookman U (FL)
Buffalo State Coll, State U of New York (NY)
California State U, Long Beach (CA)
Concord U (WV)
Cornell U (NY)
Drexel U (PA)
Ferris State U (MI)
Georgia Southern U (GA)
Grand Valley State U (MI)
Hampton U (VA)
Husson U (ME)
Inter American U of Puerto Rico, Aguadilla Campus (PR)
Inter American U of Puerto Rico, Ponce Campus (PR)
Kansas State U (KS)
Keuka Coll (NY)
The Ohio State U (OH)
Pace U (NY)
Purdue U (IN)
Rochester Inst of Technology (NY)
Royal Roads U (BC, Canada)
St. Thomas U (FL)
Southern Oregon U (OR)
State U of New York at Plattsburgh (NY)
Texas Tech U (TX)
United States Intl U–Africa (Kenya)
U of Central Missouri (MO)
U of Delaware (DE)
U of Denver (CO)
U of Guelph (ON, Canada)
U of Houston (TX)
U of New Haven (CT)
U of San Francisco (CA)
U of Southern Mississippi (MS)
The U of Tennessee (TN)
Virginia Polytechnic Inst and State U (VA)
Washington State U (WA)
Widener U (PA)

HOTEL, MOTEL, AND RESTAURANT MANAGEMENT
Endicott Coll (MA)
New York Inst of Technology (NY)
Niagara U (NY)

HOUSING AND HUMAN ENVIRONMENTS
Harding U (AR)
Missouri State U (MO)
Ohio U (OH)
Oklahoma State U (OK)
The U of Akron (OH)
U of Georgia (GA)
U of Minnesota, Twin Cities Campus (MN)
Utah State U (UT)

HOUSING AND HUMAN ENVIRONMENTS RELATED
U of Nevada, Reno (NV)

HUMAN BIOLOGY
Biola U (CA)
Hamline U (MN)
Indiana U–Purdue U Indianapolis (IN)
Scripps Coll (CA)
U of California, Irvine (CA)
U of California, Los Angeles (CA)
The U of Kansas (KS)
U of Southern California (CA)
U of Wisconsin–Green Bay (WI)

HUMAN COMPUTER INTERACTION
DigiPen Inst of Technology (WA)
Milwaukee School of Eng (WI)
Savannah Coll of Art and Design (GA)
Stony Brook U, State U of New York (NY)
U of Advancing Technology (AZ)
U of Guelph (ON, Canada)
Whitworth U (WA)

HUMAN DEVELOPMENT AND FAMILY STUDIES
Abilene Christian U (TX)
Antioch U Midwest (OH)
Auburn U (AL)
Baylor U (TX)
Bowling Green State U (OH)
Brigham Young U (UT)
California State U, East Bay (CA)
California State U, Long Beach (CA)
California State U, San Bernardino (CA)
California State U, San Marcos (CA)
Colorado State U (CO)

Concordia U, St. Paul (MN)
Connecticut Coll (CT)
Cornell U (NY)
Cornerstone U (MI)
Eckerd Coll (FL)
Freed-Hardeman U (TN)
Georgia Southern U (GA)
Hope Intl U (CA)
Howard Payne U (TX)
Indiana State U (IN)
Indiana U of Pennsylvania (PA)
John Brown U (AR)
Kansas State U (KS)
Kent State U (OH)
Kent State U at Salem (OH)
Kent State U at Stark (OH)
Kentucky State U (KY)
Lamar U (TX)
Lesley U (MA)
Liberty U (VA)
Miami U (OH)
Missouri State U (MO)
New Mexico State U (NM)
Niagara U (NY)
North Dakota State U (ND)
Northern Illinois U (IL)
Nova Southeastern U (FL)
The Ohio State U (OH)
Ohio U (OH)
Oklahoma State U (OK)
Oregon State U (OR)
Penn State Abington (PA)
Penn State Altoona (PA)
Penn State Beaver (PA)
Penn State Berks (PA)
Penn State Brandywine (PA)
Penn State DuBois (PA)
Penn State Erie, The Behrend Coll (PA)
Penn State Fayette, The Eberly Campus (PA)
Penn State Greater Allegheny (PA)
Penn State Harrisburg (PA)
Penn State Hazleton (PA)
Penn State Lehigh Valley (PA)
Penn State Mont Alto (PA)
Penn State New Kensington (PA)
Penn State Schuylkill (PA)
Penn State Shenango (PA)
Penn State U Park (PA)
Penn State Wilkes-Barre (PA)
Penn State Worthington Scranton (PA)
Penn State York (PA)
Purdue U (IN)
Purdue U Northwest (IN)
Rockford U (IL)
St. Joseph's Coll, Long Island Campus (NY)
St. Joseph's Coll, New York (NY)
Samford U (AL)
Seattle Pacific U (WA)
South Dakota State U (SD)
State U of New York at Oswego (NY)
State U of New York at Plattsburgh (NY)
Stephens Coll (MO)
Syracuse U (NY)
Temple U (PA)
Texas A&M U–Kingsville (TX)
Texas State U (TX)
Texas Tech U (TX)
Texas Woman's U (TX)
The U of Alabama (AL)
The U of Arizona (AZ)
U of Arkansas (AR)
U of California, Davis (CA)
U of Colorado Denver (CO)
U of Georgia (GA)
U of Guelph (ON, Canada)
U of Houston (TX)
U of Idaho (ID)
U of Kentucky (KY)
U of Maine (ME)
U of Nevada, Reno (NV)
U of New Hampshire (NH)
The U of North Carolina at Greensboro (NC)
U of North Texas (TX)
U of Rhode Island (RI)
U of St. Thomas (MN)
The U of Tennessee (TN)
The U of Texas at Austin (TX)
The U of Texas of the Permian Basin (TX)
U of Utah (UT)
U of Vermont (VT)
U of Waterloo (ON, Canada)
U of Wisconsin–Madison (WI)
Utah State U (UT)
Virginia Polytechnic Inst and State U (VA)
Washington State U (WA)
Washington State U–Global Campus (WA)
Washington State U–Vancouver (WA)
Westminster Coll (PA)
Wheelock Coll (MA)
Youngstown State U (OH)

HUMAN DEVELOPMENT AND FAMILY STUDIES RELATED
American Public U System (WV)
Auburn U (AL)
Ball State U (IN)
Binghamton U, State U of New York (NY)
Bowling Green State U (OH)
Clemson U (SC)
Harding U (AR)
Hope Intl U (CA)
LaGrange Coll (GA)
Merrimack Coll (MA)
The U of Alabama (AL)
U of Valley Forge (PA)
Washington State U–Vancouver (WA)

HUMANITIES
Adelphi U (NY)
Albertus Magnus Coll (CT)
Antioch U Midwest (OH)
Aquinas Coll (TN)
Athens State U (AL)
Baptist U of the Americas (TX)
Bard Coll (NY)
Baylor U (TX)
Belhaven U (MS)
Bemidji State U (MN)
Bennington Coll (VT)
Bethel Coll (IN)
Biola U (CA)
Bishop's U (QC, Canada)
Bluefield State Coll (WV)
Bradley U (IL)
Brigham Young U–Idaho (ID)
Bucknell U (PA)
Buffalo State Coll, State U of New York (NY)
California State Polytechnic U, Pomona (CA)
California State U, Chico (CA)
California State U, Monterey Bay (CA)
California State U, Northridge (CA)
California State U, Sacramento (CA)
California State U, San Bernardino (CA)
Chaminade U of Honolulu (HI)
Charleston Southern U (SC)
Chowan U (NC)
Clarkson U (NY)
Coastal Carolina U (SC)
Coll of Saint Benedict (MN)
Coll of Saint Mary (NE)
The Coll of St. Scholastica (MN)
Columbia Intl U (SC)
Concordia Coll (MN)
Concordia U (QC, Canada)
Concordia U Irvine (CA)
Concordia U Wisconsin (WI)
Corban U (OR)
Cornerstone U (MI)
Dominican Coll (NY)
Dominican U of California (CA)
Drexel U (PA)
Eastern Washington U (WA)
Eckerd Coll (FL)
Emory U (GA)
The Evergreen State Coll (WA)
Excelsior Coll (NY)
Fairleigh Dickinson U, Coll at Florham (NJ)
Fairleigh Dickinson U, Metropolitan Campus (NJ)
Faulkner U (AL)
Felician U (NJ)
Florida Inst of Technology (FL)
Florida Southern Coll (FL)
Florida State U (FL)
Fort Lewis Coll (CO)
Franciscan U of Steubenville (OH)
Fresno Pacific U (CA)
The George Washington U (DC)
Goddard Coll (VT)
Harding U (AR)
Harrison Middleton U (AZ)
Hawai`i Pacific U (HI)
Holy Family U (PA)
Holy Names U (CA)
Houghton Coll (NY)
Hunter Coll of the City U of New York (NY)
Indiana U East (IN)
Indiana U Kokomo (IN)
Inter American U of Puerto Rico, Metropolitan Campus (PR)
Jacksonville U (FL)
John Carroll U (OH)
John Jay Coll of Criminal Justice of the City U of New York (NY)
Johnson U Florida (FL)
Juniata Coll (PA)
Kansas State U (KS)
Kent State U (OH)
The King's Coll (NY)
Lasell Coll (MA)
Lawrence Technological U (MI)
Lee U (TN)
Lesley U (MA)
Loyola Marymount U (CA)
Lubbock Christian U (TX)
Maranatha Baptist U (WI)
Marshall U (WV)
Marymount Manhattan Coll (NY)
Michigan State U (MI)
Milligan Coll (TN)
Minnesota State U Mankato (MN)
Montclair State U (NJ)
Mount Allison U (NB, Canada)
Muskingum U (OH)
New Coll of Florida (FL)
North Central Coll (IL)
Northland Coll (WI)
Northwestern Coll (IA)
Northwestern U (IL)
Northwest Missouri State U (MO)
Nova Southeastern U (FL)
Oakland City U (IN)
The Ohio State U (OH)
Ohio Wesleyan U (OH)
Oklahoma Baptist U (OK)
Our Lady of the Lake Coll (LA)
Penn State Harrisburg (PA)
Plymouth State U (NH)
Point U (GA)
Portland State U (OR)
Providence Coll (RI)
Purchase Coll, State U of New York (NY)
Purdue U (IN)
Roberts Wesleyan Coll (NY)
Rockford U (IL)
Roger Williams U (RI)
Rollins Coll (FL)
The Sage Colls (NY)
St. Andrews U (NC)
Saint John's U (MN)
Saint Mary-of-the-Woods Coll (IN)
Saint Mary's Coll (IN)
St. Norbert Coll (WI)
Saint Peter's U (NJ)
St. Thomas Aquinas Coll (NY)
Sam Houston State U (TX)
San Diego State U (CA)
San Francisco State U (CA)
Scripps Coll (CA)
Seattle U (WA)
Sierra Nevada Coll (NV)
Simon Fraser U (BC, Canada)
Spalding U (KY)
State U of New York Coll at Old Westbury (NY)
Stevens Inst of Technology (NJ)
Tennessee State U (TN)
Thomas Edison State U (NJ)
Thomas More Coll (KY)
Thomas U (GA)
Trent U (ON, Canada)
Trinity U (TX)
Union Coll (NY)
United States Air Force Acad (CO)
United States Military Acad (NY)
U at Buffalo, the State U of New York (NY)
The U of Akron (OH)
U of Bridgeport (CT)
U of California, Irvine (CA)
U of California, Riverside (CA)
U of Central Florida (FL)
U of Chicago (IL)
U of Colorado Boulder (CO)
U of Houston–Clear Lake (TX)
U of Houston–Downtown (TX)
The U of Kansas (KS)
U of Lethbridge (AB, Canada)
U of Louisville (KY)
U of Massachusetts Amherst (MA)
U of Michigan (MI)
U of Michigan–Dearborn (MI)
U of Mobile (AL)
U of New Hampshire (NH)
U of New Hampshire at Manchester (NH)
U of Northern Iowa (IA)
U of Oklahoma (OK)
U of Oregon (OR)
U of Pennsylvania (PA)
U of Pittsburgh (PA)
U of Pittsburgh at Bradford (PA)
U of Pittsburgh at Greensburg (PA)
U of Pittsburgh at Johnstown (PA)
U of Regina (SK, Canada)
U of Richmond (VA)
U of San Diego (CA)
U of Southern Maine (ME)
U of South Florida (FL)
The U of Tennessee at Chattanooga (TN)
The U of Texas at Austin (TX)
The U of Texas at San Antonio (TX)
The U of Texas of the Permian Basin (TX)
U of the Virgin Islands (VI)
The U of Toledo (OH)
U of Toronto (ON, Canada)
U of Washington (WA)
U of Washington, Bothell (WA)
U of Washington, Tacoma (WA)
U of Wisconsin–Green Bay (WI)
Valparaiso U (IN)
Villanova U (PA)
Virginia Wesleyan Coll (VA)
Wabash Coll (IN)
Walla Walla U (WA)
Washington Coll (MD)
Washington State U (WA)
Washington State U–Global Campus (WA)
Washington State U–Tri-Cities (WA)
Washington State U–Vancouver (WA)
Washington U in St. Louis (MO)
Webster U (MO)
Welch Coll (TN)
Wesleyan U (CT)
Western Oregon U (OR)
Western Washington U (WA)
Wheelock Coll (MA)
Widener U (PA)
Willamette U (OR)
Wofford Coll (SC)
Worcester Polytechnic Inst (MA)

HUMAN NUTRITION
Baylor U (TX)
Bridgewater Coll (VA)
Case Western Reserve U (OH)
Cedar Crest Coll (PA)
Central Washington U (WA)
Colorado State U (CO)
Kansas State U (KS)
Metropolitan State U of Denver (CO)
The Ohio State U (OH)
Penn State Abington (PA)
Penn State Altoona (PA)
Penn State Beaver (PA)
Penn State Berks (PA)
Penn State Brandywine (PA)
Penn State DuBois (PA)
Penn State Erie, The Behrend Coll (PA)
Penn State Fayette, The Eberly Campus (PA)
Penn State Greater Allegheny (PA)
Penn State Hazleton (PA)
Penn State Lehigh Valley (PA)
Penn State Mont Alto (PA)
Penn State New Kensington (PA)
Penn State Schuylkill (PA)
Penn State Shenango (PA)
Penn State U Park (PA)
Penn State Wilkes-Barre (PA)
Penn State Worthington Scranton (PA)
Penn State York (PA)
Prairie View A&M U (TX)
Rochester Inst of Technology (NY)
Southern Utah U (UT)
State Coll of Florida Manatee-Sarasota (FL)
Syracuse U (NY)
Tarleton State U (TX)
Université de Montréal (QC, Canada)
U of Dayton (OH)
U of Guelph (ON, Canada)
U of Houston (TX)
U of Kentucky (KY)
Washington State U (WA)

HUMAN RESOURCES DEVELOPMENT
Blackburn Coll (IL)
Hawai`i Pacific U (HI)
Houghton Coll (NY)
LeTourneau U (TX)
Limestone Coll (SC)
Nichols Coll (MA)
Northern Kentucky U (KY)
The Ohio State U (OH)
Southwestern Coll (KS)
Texas A&M U (TX)
U of Arkansas (AR)
U of Houston (TX)
U of Wisconsin–Milwaukee (WI)
Washington State U–Vancouver (WA)

HUMAN RESOURCES MANAGEMENT
Alvernia U (PA)
Anderson U (SC)
Antioch U Midwest (OH)
Athens State U (AL)
Auburn U (AL)
Auburn U at Montgomery (AL)
Avila U (MO)
Baldwin Wallace U (OH)
Ball State U (IN)
Barton Coll (NC)
Bayamón Central U (PR)
Baylor U (TX)
Belhaven U (MS)
Bishop's U (QC, Canada)
Black Hills State U (SD)
Boston Coll (MA)
Bowling Green State U (OH)
Bradley U (IL)
Brenau U (GA)
Brescia U (KY)
Briar Cliff U (IA)
Brigham Young U (UT)
Bryant U (RI)
Buena Vista U (IA)
Cabrini U (PA)
California State U, East Bay (CA)
California State U, Fresno (CA)
California State U, Long Beach (CA)
Canisius Coll (NY)
Cardinal Stritch U (WI)
The Catholic U of America (DC)
Central Baptist Coll (AR)
Central Michigan U (MI)
Central Washington U (WA)
Chestnut Hill Coll (PA)
The Coll of Saint Rose (NY)
Columbia Coll (MO)
Columbia Southern U (AL)
Concordia U (QC, Canada)
Concordia U, St. Paul (MN)
Converse Coll (SC)
Davenport U, Grand Rapids (MI)
DeSales U (PA)
Dickinson State U (ND)
East Central U (OK)
Eastern Washington U (WA)
Faulkner U (AL)
Ferris State U (MI)
Fisher Coll (MA)
Florida Intl U (FL)
Friends U (KS)
The George Washington U (DC)
Georgia Southwestern State U (GA)
Granite State Coll (NH)
Gwynedd Mercy U (PA)
HEC Montreal (QC, Canada)
Holy Family U (PA)
Holy Names U (CA)

Houghton Coll (NY)
Huntington U (IN)
Idaho State U (ID)
Indiana State U (IN)
Indiana U of Pennsylvania (PA)
Inter American U of Puerto Rico, Aguadilla Campus (PR)
Inter American U of Puerto Rico, Barranquitas Campus (PR)
Inter American U of Puerto Rico, Bayamón Campus (PR)
Inter American U of Puerto Rico, Fajardo Campus (PR)
Inter American U of Puerto Rico, Guayama Campus (PR)
Inter American U of Puerto Rico, Metropolitan Campus (PR)
Inter American U of Puerto Rico, Ponce Campus (PR)
Inter American U of Puerto Rico, San Germán Campus (PR)
John Carroll U (OH)
Juniata Coll (PA)
King's Coll (PA)
Lake Erie Coll (OH)
Lamar U (TX)
La Salle U (PA)
Le Moyne Coll (NY)
LeTourneau U (TX)
Lewis U (IL)
Limestone Coll (SC)
Lindenwood U (MO)
Lipscomb U (TN)
Louisiana Tech U (LA)
Lourdes U (OH)
Loyola U Chicago (IL)
Lynchburg Coll (VA)
Madonna U (MI)
Mansfield U of Pennsylvania (PA)
Marian U (WI)
Marymount Manhattan Coll (NY)
McKendree U (IL)
Mercyhurst U (PA)
Michigan State U (MI)
MidAmerica Nazarene U (KS)
Mount Mercy U (IA)
Nazareth Coll of Rochester (NY)
New York Inst of Technology (NY)
Nichols Coll (MA)
North Central Coll (IL)
Northcentral U (CA)
Northeastern Illinois U (IL)
The Ohio State U (OH)
Ohio U (OH)
Ohio Valley U (WV)
Otterbein U (OH)
Our Lady of the Lake U of San Antonio (TX)
Pace U (NY)
Pace U, Pleasantville Campus (NY)
Peirce Coll (PA)
Point Park U (PA)
Portland State U (OR)
Quinnipiac U (CT)
Rasmussen Coll Bloomington (MN)
Rasmussen Coll Brooklyn Park (MN)
Rasmussen Coll Eagan (MN)
Rasmussen Coll Fort Myers (FL)
Rasmussen Coll Kansas City/ Overland Park (KS)
Rasmussen Coll Lake Elmo/ Woodbury (MN)
Rasmussen Coll Land O' Lakes (FL)
Rasmussen Coll Mankato (MN)
Rasmussen Coll Moorhead (MN)
Rasmussen Coll New Port Richey (FL)
Rasmussen Coll Ocala (FL)
Rasmussen Coll Tampa/Brandon (FL)
Rasmussen Coll Topeka (KS)
Regis U (CO)
Rhode Island Coll (RI)
Roberts Wesleyan Coll (NY)
Rowan U (NJ)
Rutgers U–New Brunswick (NJ)
Saint Francis U (PA)
Saint Joseph's U (PA)
Saint Mary-of-the-Woods Coll (IN)
Saint Mary's U of Minnesota (MN)
Sam Houston State U (TX)
San Diego State U (CA)
Seton Hill U (PA)
Silver Lake Coll of the Holy Family (WI)
Simpson U (CA)
Southwestern Assemblies of God U (TX)
State U of New York at Oswego (NY)
State U of New York Coll of Technology at Alfred (NY)
Stephen F. Austin State U (TX)
Sullivan U (KY)
Tarleton State U (TX)
Temple U (PA)
Tennessee Wesleyan U (TN)
Texas A&M U–Central Texas (TX)
Texas Woman's U (TX)
Thomas Edison State U (NJ)
Tiffin U (OH)
The U of Akron (OH)
The U of Arizona (AZ)
U of Dubuque (IA)
The U of Findlay (OH)
U of Georgia (GA)
U of Guelph (ON, Canada)
U of Hawaii at Manoa (HI)
U of Idaho (ID)
U of Lethbridge (AB, Canada)
U of Maryland U Coll (MD)
U of Miami (FL)
U of Michigan–Dearborn (MI)
U of Michigan–Flint (MI)
U of Minnesota, Duluth (MN)
U of Minnesota, Twin Cities Campus (MN)
The U of North Carolina at Chapel Hill (NC)
U of North Dakota (ND)
U of Pennsylvania (PA)
U of Regina (SK, Canada)
U of St. Francis (IL)
U of St. Thomas (MN)
U of Saskatchewan (SK, Canada)
The U of Scranton (PA)
U of Southern Mississippi (MS)
The U of Tennessee (TN)
The U of Tennessee at Martin (TN)
The U of Texas at San Antonio (TX)
U of the Incarnate Word (TX)
The U of Toledo (OH)
U of Valley Forge (PA)
U of Washington (WA)
U of Waterloo (ON, Canada)
U of Windsor (ON, Canada)
U of Wisconsin–Whitewater (WI)
Utah State U (UT)
Valley City State U (ND)
Washington State U (WA)
Washington U in St. Louis (MO)
Weber State U (UT)
Webster U (MO)
Western Illinois U (IL)
Western Intl U (AZ)
Western Washington U (WA)
Westminster Coll (PA)
Wichita State U (KS)
William Penn U (IA)
Wilmington U (DE)
Winona State U (MN)
Wright State U (OH)
Wright State U–Lake Campus (OH)
Youngstown State U (OH)

HUMAN RESOURCES MANAGEMENT AND SERVICES RELATED

Albertus Magnus Coll (CT)
Carlow U (PA)
Grand Valley State U (MI)
Immaculata U (PA)
Menlo Coll (CA)
Oakland City U (IN)
Simpson U (CA)
Stevens Inst of Technology (NJ)
U of Mount Union (OH)
U of Oklahoma (OK)
U of Pittsburgh (PA)
Western Michigan U (MI)
Widener U (PA)

HUMAN SERVICES

Albertus Magnus Coll (CT)
Anderson U (SC)
Antioch U Midwest (OH)
Arcadia U (PA)
Beacon Coll (FL)
Bethel Coll (IN)
Black Hills State U (SD)
California State U, Dominguez Hills (CA)
California State U, Fullerton (CA)
California State U, Monterey Bay (CA)
California State U, San Bernardino (CA)
Calumet Coll of Saint Joseph (IN)
Carson-Newman U (TN)
Cazenovia Coll (NY)
Central Washington U (WA)
Chestnut Hill Coll (PA)
Columbia Coll (MO)
Doane U (NE)
Dominican U (IL)
East Tennessee State U (TN)
Elon U (NC)
Emmanuel Coll (MA)
Fisher Coll (MA)
Fitchburg State U (MA)
Geneva Coll (PA)
The George Washington U (DC)
Gordon State Coll (GA)
Graceland U (IA)
Grand View U (IA)
Granite State Coll (NH)
Gwynedd Mercy U (PA)
Hardin-Simmons U (TX)
Hilbert Coll (NY)
Holy Names U (CA)
Iowa Wesleyan U (IA)
Judson U (IL)
Kennesaw State U (GA)
Kentucky Wesleyan Coll (KY)
Lasell Coll (MA)
Lees-McRae Coll (NC)
Lenoir-Rhyne U (NC)
Lesley U (MA)
LeTourneau U (TX)
Liberty U (VA)
Lincoln Christian U (IL)
Lincoln Coll (IL)
Lincoln Coll of New England, Southington (CT)
Lincoln U (PA)
Lindsey Wilson Coll (KY)
Loyola U Chicago (IL)
Marian U (WI)
Mercer U, Macon (GA)
Metropolitan State U of Denver (CO)
Missouri Baptist U (MO)
Missouri Valley Coll (MO)
Mount Ida Coll (MA)
Mount Marty Coll (SD)
Mount Saint Mary Coll (NY)
New York City Coll of Technology of the City U of New York (NY)
Northeastern U (MA)
Nova Southeastern U (FL)
Quinnipiac U (CT)
St. Joseph's Coll, Long Island Campus (NY)
St. Joseph's Coll, New York (NY)
Saint Mary-of-the-Woods Coll (IN)
Saint Mary's U of Minnesota (MN)
St. Thomas U (FL)
Seton Hill U (PA)
Southeastern U (FL)
Southwest Baptist U (MO)
Southwestern Assemblies of God U (TX)
Spelman Coll (GA)
State U of New York Coll at Cortland (NY)
Syracuse U (NY)
Tennessee Wesleyan U (TN)
Texas A&M U–Kingsville (TX)
Thomas Edison State U (NJ)
Towson U (MD)
U of Bridgeport (CT)
U of Delaware (DE)
U of Great Falls (MT)
U of Hartford (CT)
U of Massachusetts Boston (MA)
U of Minnesota, Morris (MN)
U of Nevada, Las Vegas (NV)
U of North Georgia (GA)
U of North Texas (TX)
U of Oregon (OR)
The U of Scranton (PA)
U of South Florida (FL)
U of the Cumberlands (KY)
Upper Iowa U (IA)
Virginia Wesleyan Coll (VA)
Wayland Baptist U (TX)
Waynesburg U (PA)
Western Washington U (WA)
William Penn U (IA)
Wingate U (NC)

HYDROLOGY AND WATER RESOURCES SCIENCE

The Coll at Brockport, State U of New York (NY)
Heidelberg U (OH)
Humboldt State U (CA)
Northland Coll (WI)
Rensselaer Polytechnic Inst (NY)
Tarleton State U (TX)
The U of Arizona (AZ)
U of California, Davis (CA)
U of California, Santa Barbara (CA)
The U of Texas at Austin (TX)
U of Toronto (ON, Canada)
U of Wisconsin–Stevens Point (WI)
Western Michigan U (MI)

ILLUSTRATION

Acad of Art U (CA)
American Acad of Art (IL)
Arcadia U (PA)
Boise State U (ID)
Brigham Young U (UT)
California Coll of the Arts (CA)
California State U, Long Beach (CA)
Cleveland Inst of Art (OH)
Columbia Coll Chicago (IL)
Columbus Coll of Art & Design (OH)
Emily Carr U of Art + Design (BC, Canada)
Eugene Lang Coll of Liberal Arts (NY)
Fashion Inst of Technology (NY)
Ferris State U (MI)
Grace Coll (IN)
John Brown U (AR)
Kansas City Art Inst (MO)
Laguna Coll of Art & Design (CA)
Lawrence Technological U (MI)
Maryland Inst Coll of Art (MD)
Marywood U (PA)
Memphis Coll of Art (TN)
Minneapolis Coll of Art and Design (MN)
New Hampshire Inst of Art (NH)
Nossi Coll of Art (TN)
Pacific Northwest Coll of Art (OR)
Parsons School of Design (NY)
Pennsylvania Coll of Art & Design (PA)
Pratt Inst (NY)
Rhode Island School of Design (RI)
Ringling Coll of Art and Design (FL)
Rochester Inst of Technology (NY)
St. John's U (NY)
Savannah Coll of Art and Design (GA)
School of the Art Inst of Chicago (IL)
Syracuse U (NY)
U of Hartford (CT)
The U of Kansas (KS)
U of Massachusetts Dartmouth (MA)
U of Michigan (MI)
U of New Haven (CT)
U of San Francisco (CA)
The U of the Arts (PA)
Virginia Commonwealth U (VA)
Washington U in St. Louis (MO)

INDUSTRIAL AND ORGANIZATIONAL PSYCHOLOGY

Albright Coll (PA)
Avila U (MO)
Baldwin Wallace U (OH)
Baruch Coll of the City U of New York (NY)
Bridgewater State U (MA)
Brooklyn Coll of the City U of New York (NY)
California State U, East Bay (CA)
Canisius Coll (NY)
Concordia U Irvine (CA)
Embry-Riddle Aeronautical U–Prescott (AZ)
Excelsior Coll (NY)
Faulkner U (AL)
Fitchburg State U (MA)
Fort Lewis Coll (CO)
Holy Family U (PA)
Ithaca Coll (NY)
Maryville U of Saint Louis (MO)
Marywood U (PA)
Morningside Coll (IA)
Multnomah U (OR)
Northwest Missouri State U (MO)
Saint Mary's Coll of California (CA)
United States Military Acad (NY)
U of Georgia (GA)
U of St. Francis (IL)
The U of Tennessee at Martin (TN)
Washington U in St. Louis (MO)

INDUSTRIAL AND PHYSICAL PHARMACY AND COSMETIC SCIENCES

The U of Toledo (OH)

INDUSTRIAL AND PRODUCT DESIGN

Acad of Art U (CA)
Appalachian State U (NC)
Arizona State U at the Tempe campus (AZ)
Auburn U (AL)
California Coll of the Arts (CA)
California State U, Long Beach (CA)
Carnegie Mellon U (PA)
Cedarville U (OH)
Clemson U (SC)
Cleveland Inst of Art (OH)
Columbia Coll Chicago (IL)
Columbus Coll of Art & Design (OH)
Drexel U (PA)
Emily Carr U of Art + Design (BC, Canada)
Escuela de Artes Plasticas y Dise&nno de Puerto Rico (PR)
Eugene Lang Coll of Liberal Arts (NY)
Fashion Inst of Technology (NY)
Ferris State U (MI)
FIDM/Fashion Inst of Design & Merchandising, Los Angeles Campus (CA)
Georgia Inst of Technology (GA)
Iowa State U of Science and Technology (IA)
Kean U (NJ)
Lawrence Technological U (MI)
Maryland Inst Coll of Art (MD)
Massachusetts Coll of Art and Design (MA)
Metropolitan State U of Denver (CO)
Milwaukee Inst of Art and Design (WI)
Montclair State U (NJ)
North Carolina State U (NC)
The Ohio State U (OH)
Parsons School of Design (NY)
Pennsylvania Coll of Technology (PA)
Pratt Inst (NY)
Purdue U (IN)
Rhode Island School of Design (RI)
Rochester Inst of Technology (NY)
San Francisco State U (CA)
Savannah Coll of Art and Design (GA)
Stanford U (CA)
Syracuse U (NY)
Université de Montréal (QC, Canada)
U of Bridgeport (CT)
U of Cincinnati (OH)
U of Houston (TX)
U of Illinois at Chicago (IL)
The U of Kansas (KS)
U of Michigan (MI)
U of Minnesota, Twin Cities Campus (MN)
The U of the Arts (PA)
U of Washington (WA)
U of Wisconsin–Stout (WI)
Virginia Polytechnic Inst and State U (VA)
Walla Walla U (WA)
Wentworth Inst of Technology (MA)
Western Washington U (WA)

INDUSTRIAL ENGINEERING

American U of Beirut (Lebanon)
Arizona State U at the Tempe campus (AZ)
Auburn U (AL)
Binghamton U, State U of New York (NY)
Bradley U (IL)
California Baptist U (CA)

California Polytechnic State U, San Luis Obispo (CA)
California State Polytechnic U, Pomona (CA)
California State U, East Bay (CA)
California State U, Long Beach (CA)
Caribbean U (PR)
Clemson U (SC)
Columbia U (NY)
Concordia U (QC, Canada)
Dalhousie U (NS, Canada)
Eastern Nazarene Coll (MA)
Elizabethtown Coll (PA)
Florida Ag and Mech U (FL)
Francis Marion U (SC)
Gannon U (PA)
Georgia Inst of Technology (GA)
Hofstra U (NY)
Inter American U of Puerto Rico, Bayamón Campus (PR)
Iowa State U of Science and Technology (IA)
Kansas State U (KS)
Kent State U (OH)
Kettering U (MI)
Lamar U (TX)
Lawrence Technological U (MI)
Lebanese American U (Lebanon)
Lehigh U (PA)
Liberty U (VA)
Louisiana State U and A&M Coll (LA)
Louisiana Tech U (LA)
McMaster U (ON, Canada)
Milwaukee School of Eng (WI)
Mississippi State U (MS)
Missouri U of Science and Technology (MO)
Montana State U (MT)
New Mexico State U (NM)
North Carolina State U (NC)
North Dakota State U (ND)
Northeastern U (MA)
Northern Illinois U (IL)
Northwestern U (IL)
The Ohio State U (OH)
Ohio U (OH)
Oklahoma State U (OK)
Oregon State U (OR)
Penn State Abington (PA)
Penn State Altoona (PA)
Penn State Beaver (PA)
Penn State Berks (PA)
Penn State Brandywine (PA)
Penn State DuBois (PA)
Penn State Erie, The Behrend Coll (PA)
Penn State Fayette, The Eberly Campus (PA)
Penn State Greater Allegheny (PA)
Penn State Hazleton (PA)
Penn State Lehigh Valley (PA)
Penn State Mont Alto (PA)
Penn State New Kensington (PA)
Penn State Schuylkill (PA)
Penn State Shenango (PA)
Penn State U Park (PA)
Penn State Wilkes-Barre (PA)
Penn State Worthington Scranton (PA)
Penn State York (PA)
Polytechnic U of Puerto Rico (PR)
Purdue U (IN)
Quinnipiac U (CT)
Rensselaer Polytechnic Inst (NY)
Rochester Inst of Technology (NY)
Rutgers U–New Brunswick (NJ)
St. Ambrose U (IA)
St. Cloud State U (MN)
South Carolina State U (SC)
South Dakota School of Mines and Technology (SD)
Southern Illinois U Edwardsville (IL)
Stanford U (CA)
State U of New York Maritime Coll (NY)
Tennessee State U (TN)
Texas A&M U (TX)
Texas A&M U–Commerce (TX)
Texas A&M U–Kingsville (TX)
Texas State U (TX)
Texas Tech U (TX)
U at Buffalo, the State U of New York (NY)
The U of Alabama in Huntsville (AL)
The U of Arizona (AZ)
U of Arkansas (AR)
U of Central Florida (FL)
U of Houston (TX)
U of Illinois at Chicago (IL)
U of Louisville (KY)
U of Massachusetts Amherst (MA)
U of Miami (FL)
U of Michigan (MI)
U of Michigan–Dearborn (MI)
U of Minnesota, Duluth (MN)
U of Minnesota, Twin Cities Campus (MN)
U of New Haven (CT)
U of Oklahoma (OK)
U of Pittsburgh (PA)
U of Regina (SK, Canada)
U of Rhode Island (RI)
U of San Diego (CA)
U of South Carolina Aiken (SC)
U of Southern California (CA)
U of South Florida (FL)
The U of Tennessee (TN)
The U of Texas at Austin (TX)
The U of Texas at El Paso (TX)
U of Toronto (ON, Canada)
U of Vermont (VT)
U of Washington (WA)
U of Windsor (ON, Canada)
U of Wisconsin–Madison (WI)
U of Wisconsin–Milwaukee (WI)
U of Wisconsin–Platteville (WI)
Virginia Polytechnic Inst and State U (VA)
Wayne State U (MI)
Western Michigan U (MI)
Western New England U (MA)
West Virginia U (WV)
Wichita State U (KS)
Worcester Polytechnic Inst (MA)
Youngstown State U (OH)

INDUSTRIAL PRODUCTION TECHNOLOGIES RELATED
Bowling Green State U (OH)
Central Washington U (WA)
Ferris State U (MI)
Georgia Southern U (GA)
Kennesaw State U (GA)
Millersville U of Pennsylvania (PA)
Mississippi State U (MS)
Missouri State U (MO)
Northwest Missouri State U (MO)
Pennsylvania Coll of Technology (PA)
Saginaw Valley State U (MI)
Tarleton State U (TX)
Valdosta State U (GA)
Wayne State Coll (NE)

INDUSTRIAL RADIOLOGIC TECHNOLOGY
Briar Cliff U (IA)
Concordia U Wisconsin (WI)

INDUSTRIAL SAFETY TECHNOLOGY
Central Washington U (WA)
Mansfield U of Pennsylvania (PA)
Northeastern State U (OK)
U of Houston–Downtown (TX)

INDUSTRIAL TECHNOLOGY
Ball State U (IN)
Bemidji State U (MN)
Black Hills State U (SD)
Bowling Green State U (OH)
Buffalo State Coll, State U of New York (NY)
California Polytechnic State U, San Luis Obispo (CA)
California State U, Fresno (CA)
California State U, Long Beach (CA)
Central Connecticut State U (CT)
Central State U (OH)
Central Washington U (WA)
Clarion U of Pennsylvania (PA)
Dunwoody Coll of Technology (MN)
East Carolina U (NC)
Eastern Illinois U (IL)
Eastern Michigan U (MI)
Elizabeth City State U (NC)
Farmingdale State Coll (NY)
Ferris State U (MI)
Fitchburg State U (MA)
Illinois State U (IL)
Indiana State U (IN)
Jackson State U (MS)
Jacksonville State U (AL)
Lamar U (TX)
Millersville U of Pennsylvania (PA)
Mississippi State U (MS)
Mississippi Valley State U (MS)
Montana State U–Northern (MT)
Northern Illinois U (IL)
Northwestern State U of Louisiana (LA)
Ohio U (OH)
Pittsburg State U (KS)
Roger Williams U (RI)
Sam Houston State U (TX)
South Carolina State U (SC)
Southeastern Louisiana U (LA)
Southeast Missouri State U (MO)
Southern Illinois U Carbondale (IL)
Tarleton State U (TX)
Tennessee State U (TN)
Texas A&M U–Commerce (TX)
Texas A&M U–Kingsville (TX)
Texas State U (TX)
U of Dayton (OH)
U of Idaho (ID)
U of Massachusetts Lowell (MA)
U of North Dakota (ND)
U of Northern Iowa (IA)
U of Southern Maine (ME)
U of Southern Mississippi (MS)
The U of Texas of the Permian Basin (TX)
Vincennes U (IN)
Washington State U (WA)
Western Kentucky U (KY)
Western Washington U (WA)
West Virginia U Inst of Technology (WV)
William Penn U (IA)

INFORMATICS
American Coll of Thessaloniki (Greece)
Arizona State U at the Tempe campus (AZ)
Brigham Young U–Idaho (ID)
Dominican U (IL)
Drexel U (PA)
Faulkner U (AL)
Goshen Coll (IN)
Indiana U Bloomington (IN)
Indiana U East (IN)
Indiana U Kokomo (IN)
Indiana U Northwest (IN)
Indiana U–Purdue U Indianapolis (IN)
Indiana U South Bend (IN)
Indiana U Southeast (IN)
King U (TN)
Liberty U (VA)
Université de Montréal (QC, Canada)
U at Buffalo, the State U of New York (NY)
U of California, Irvine (CA)
U of Michigan (MI)
U of Washington (WA)

INFORMATION RESOURCES MANAGEMENT
Abilene Christian U (TX)
Athens State U (AL)
Chestnut Hill Coll (PA)
Lewis U (IL)
Lipscomb U (TN)
Lubbock Christian U (TX)
Michigan State U (MI)
Mount St. Mary's U (MD)
Rasmussen Coll Land O' Lakes (FL)
Rasmussen Coll New Port Richey (FL)
Rasmussen Coll Ocala (FL)
Rasmussen Coll Tampa/Brandon (FL)
Salve Regina U (RI)
U of California, Irvine (CA)
U of Wisconsin–Eau Claire (WI)
Western Michigan U (MI)
Wilmington U (DE)

INFORMATION SCIENCE/ STUDIES
Adelphi U (NY)
Alabama State U (AL)
Albany State U (GA)
Albertus Magnus Coll (CT)
Albright Coll (PA)
Anderson U (IN)
Andrews U (MI)
Armstrong State U (GA)
Ashland U (OH)
Averett U (VA)
Barry U (FL)
Baruch Coll of the City U of New York (NY)
Bemidji State U (MN)
Bethune-Cookman U (FL)
Boise State U (ID)
Bowling Green State U (OH)
Bradley U (IL)
Brewton-Parker Coll (GA)
Brooklyn Coll of the City U of New York (NY)
Buffalo State Coll, State U of New York (NY)
California Lutheran U (CA)
California State U, East Bay (CA)
California State U, Northridge (CA)
California State U, Stanislaus (CA)
Campbellsville U (KY)
Carnegie Mellon U (PA)
Carson-Newman U (TN)
Case Western Reserve U (OH)
Chowan U (NC)
Christopher Newport U (VA)
Clarion U of Pennsylvania (PA)
Clayton State U (GA)
Clemson U (SC)
Coastal Carolina U (SC)
The Coll at Brockport, State U of New York (NY)
Coll of Charleston (SC)
Coll of Staten Island of the City U of New York (NY)
Colorado State U (CO)
Columbia U, School of General Studies (NY)
Concord U (WV)
Dakota State U (SD)
Davenport U, Grand Rapids (MI)
Doane U (NE)
Drexel U (PA)
East Carolina U (NC)
Elizabethtown Coll (PA)
Elon U (NC)
Emporia State U (KS)
Excelsior Coll (NY)
Fordham U (NY)
Friends U (KS)
Frostburg State U (MD)
Gallaudet U (DC)
George Fox U (OR)
Georgia Southern U (GA)
Goshen Coll (IN)
Grambling State U (LA)
Grand Valley State U (MI)
Grand View U (IA)
Hampton U (VA)
Harris-Stowe State U (MO)
HEC Montreal (QC, Canada)
Heidelberg U (OH)
Idaho State U (ID)
Illinois Coll (IL)
Immaculata U (PA)
Inter American U of Puerto Rico, Ponce Campus (PR)
Inter American U of Puerto Rico, San Germán Campus (PR)
Jacksonville U (FL)
James Madison U (VA)
Kansas State U (KS)
Kennesaw State U (GA)
King U (TN)
Lenoir-Rhyne U (NC)
LeTourneau U (TX)
Limestone Coll (SC)
Lincoln U (MO)
Lipscomb U (TN)
Luther Coll (IA)
Mansfield U of Pennsylvania (PA)
Marietta Coll (OH)
McKendree U (IL)
Medgar Evers Coll of the City U of New York (NY)
Mercer U, Macon (GA)
Mercy Coll (NY)
Mercyhurst U (PA)
Minnesota State U Mankato (MN)
Minnesota State U Moorhead (MN)
Missouri U of Science and Technology (MO)
Molloy Coll (NY)
Murray State U (KY)
Newman U (KS)
New Mexico Highlands U (NM)
New York City Coll of Technology of the City U of New York (NY)
Northeastern U (MA)
Northern Kentucky U (KY)
Northwestern Coll (IA)
Northwestern Oklahoma State U (OK)
Northwestern State U of Louisiana (LA)
Northwestern U (IL)
The Ohio State U (OH)
Oklahoma Baptist U (OK)
Oklahoma Christian U (OK)
Olivet Nazarene U (IL)
Pace U (NY)
Penn State Abington (PA)
Penn State Altoona (PA)
Penn State Beaver (PA)
Penn State Berks (PA)
Penn State Brandywine (PA)
Penn State DuBois (PA)
Penn State Erie, The Behrend Coll (PA)
Penn State Fayette, The Eberly Campus (PA)
Penn State Greater Allegheny (PA)
Penn State Harrisburg (PA)
Penn State Lehigh Valley (PA)
Penn State Mont Alto (PA)
Penn State New Kensington (PA)
Penn State Schuylkill (PA)
Penn State Shenango (PA)
Penn State U Park (PA)
Penn State Wilkes-Barre (PA)
Penn State Worthington Scranton (PA)
Penn State York (PA)
Portland State U (OR)
Prairie View A&M U (TX)
Quinnipiac U (CT)
Radford U (VA)
Ramapo Coll of New Jersey (NJ)
Robert Morris U (PA)
Rutgers U–Newark (NJ)
Rutgers U–New Brunswick (NJ)
The Sage Colls (NY)
St. Cloud State U (MN)
St. Joseph's Coll, Long Island Campus (NY)
St. Joseph's Coll, New York (NY)
Saint Joseph's U (PA)
Saint Michael's Coll (VT)
Saint Peter's U (NJ)
St. Thomas Aquinas Coll (NY)
St. Thomas U (FL)
Salisbury U (MD)
San Francisco State U (CA)
Silver Lake Coll of the Holy Family (WI)
Simmons Coll (MA)
Slippery Rock U of Pennsylvania (PA)
Southeastern Oklahoma State U (OK)
Southern Illinois U Carbondale (IL)
State U of New York at Fredonia (NY)
State U of New York at Oswego (NY)
State U of New York Coll at Old Westbury (NY)
State U of New York Polytechnic Inst (NY)
Stevenson U (MD)
Stockton U (NJ)
Stony Brook U, State U of New York (NY)
Suffolk U (MA)
Susquehanna U (PA)
Syracuse U (NY)
Tarleton State U (TX)
Texas A&M Intl U (TX)
Texas A&M U–Central Texas (TX)
Texas A&M U–Commerce (TX)
Texas Lutheran U (TX)
Texas Tech U (TX)
Towson U (MD)
Tufts U (MA)
Tulane U (LA)
Union U (TN)
Université de Sherbrooke (QC, Canada)
U at Albany, State U of New York (NY)

U of Cincinnati (OH)
U of Colorado Boulder (CO)
U of Great Falls (MT)
U of Hartford (CT)
U of Houston (TX)
U of Illinois at Chicago (IL)
U of Kentucky (KY)
U of Management and Technology (VA)
U of Mary Hardin-Baylor (TX)
U of Maryland, Baltimore County (MD)
U of Maryland, Coll Park (MD)
U of Maryland U Coll (MD)
U of Massachusetts Lowell (MA)
U of Miami (FL)
U of Michigan (MI)
U of Michigan–Flint (MI)
U of Nevada, Las Vegas (NV)
U of New Haven (CT)
The U of North Carolina at Chapel Hill (NC)
U of North Texas (TX)
U of Oklahoma (OK)
U of Pittsburgh (PA)
U of St. Thomas (MN)
U of San Francisco (CA)
The U of Scranton (PA)
U of South Alabama (AL)
U of South Carolina (SC)
U of South Florida (FL)
The U of Texas at Austin (TX)
The U of Texas at El Paso (TX)
The U of Texas of the Permian Basin (TX)
The U of Texas Rio Grande Valley (TX)
U of the Pacific (CA)
The U of Toledo (OH)
The U of Tulsa (OK)
U of Utah (UT)
U of Vermont (VT)
U of Washington, Bothell (WA)
U of Wisconsin–Green Bay (WI)
U of Wisconsin–Milwaukee (WI)
U of Wisconsin–Superior (WI)
Utah State U (UT)
Utah Valley U (UT)
Valdosta State U (GA)
Virginia Commonwealth U (VA)
Virginia Polytechnic Inst and State U (VA)
Wayne State Coll (NE)
Wayne State U (MI)
Weber State U (UT)
Webster U (MO)
Wentworth Inst of Technology (MA)
Westfield State U (MA)
West Virginia Wesleyan Coll (WV)
Widener U (PA)
Wilkes U (PA)
York Coll of the City U of New York (NY)

INFORMATION TECHNOLOGY
Abilene Christian U (TX)
American Public U System (WV)
Anderson U (SC)
Arkansas Tech U (AR)
Augusta U (GA)
Austin Peay State U (TN)
Baylor U (TX)
Bluefield Coll (VA)
Bluffton U (OH)
Boise State U (ID)
Bradley U (IL)
Brandman U (CA)
Brigham Young U (UT)
Brigham Young U–Idaho (ID)
Bryant U (RI)
Cabrini U (PA)
Cairn U (PA)
Caldwell U (NJ)
California Baptist U (CA)
California State U, Dominguez Hills (CA)
California State U, Fullerton (CA)
California State U, San Bernardino (CA)
California State U, Stanislaus (CA)
Cameron U (OK)
Central Michigan U (MI)
Central Penn Coll (PA)
Central Washington U (WA)
Christopher Newport U (VA)
Clayton State U (GA)
Coastal Carolina U (SC)
The Coll of Saint Rose (NY)
Coll of the Ozarks (MO)
Columbia Southern U (AL)
Columbus State U (GA)
Cornell U (NY)
Creighton U (NE)
Daytona State Coll (FL)
DEREE - The American Coll of Greece (Greece)
DeSales U (PA)
Dixie State U (UT)
Duquesne U (PA)
East Carolina U (NC)
Fairleigh Dickinson U, Metropolitan Campus (NJ)
Ferris State U (MI)
Florida Ag and Mech U (FL)
Florida Intl U (FL)
Frostburg State U (MD)
Furman U (SC)
Georgia Gwinnett Coll (GA)
Georgia Southwestern State U (GA)
Governors State U (IL)
Grace Coll (IN)
Granite State Coll (NH)
Harding U (AR)
Humboldt State U (CA)
Illinois State U (IL)
Indiana State U (IN)
Inter American U of Puerto Rico, Bayamón Campus (PR)
Johnson C. Smith U (NC)
Juniata Coll (PA)
Kansas Wesleyan U (KS)
Kennesaw State U (GA)
Kentucky State U (KY)
La Roche Coll (PA)
La Salle U (PA)
Lawrence Technological U (MI)
Lee U (TN)
Lehigh U (PA)
Liberty U (VA)
Life U (GA)
Limestone Coll (SC)
Lincoln U (PA)
Lindenwood U (MO)
Lipscomb U (TN)
Loyola U Chicago (IL)
Marian U (WI)
Marymount U (VA)
McKendree U (IL)
McMurry U (TX)
Merrimack Coll (MA)
Miami Dade Coll (FL)
Misericordia U (PA)
Missouri Baptist U (MO)
Missouri Western State U (MO)
Montclair State U (NJ)
Morrisville State Coll (NY)
Mount Aloysius Coll (PA)
Mount Marty Coll (SD)
Mount Saint Mary Coll (NY)
Murray State U (KY)
New England Inst of Technology (RI)
New Mexico Inst of Mining and Technology (NM)
New Mexico State U (NM)
New York Inst of Technology (NY)
Northern Kentucky U (KY)
Northwest U (WA)
Oklahoma State U (OK)
Olympic Coll (WA)
Peirce Coll (PA)
Plymouth State U (NH)
Point Loma Nazarene U (CA)
Point Park U (PA)
Purdue U (IN)
Purdue U Northwest (IN)
Regent U (VA)
Rensselaer Polytechnic Inst (NY)
Robert Morris U Illinois (IL)
Rochester Inst of Technology (NY)
Saint Joseph's U (PA)
Saint Louis U (MO)
Saint Louis U–Madrid Campus (Spain)
San Diego State U (CA)
Seminole State Coll of Florida (FL)
Simmons Coll (MA)
Slippery Rock U of Pennsylvania (PA)
State U of New York Coll of Agriculture and Technology at Cobleskill (NY)
State U of New York Coll of Technology at Canton (NY)
Stephen F. Austin State U (TX)
Stevens Inst of Technology (NJ)
Stratford U, Alexandria (VA)
Stratford U, Falls Church (VA)
Stratford U, Glen Allen (VA)
Stratford U, Newport News (VA)
Stratford U, Virginia Beach (VA)
Stratford U, Woodbridge (VA)
Sullivan U (KY)
Tarleton State U (TX)
Temple U (PA)
Texas Christian U (TX)
Thomas Edison State U (NJ)
Thomas More Coll (KY)
Tiffin U (OH)
Towson U (MD)
Trevecca Nazarene U (TN)
Tusculum Coll (TN)
Union Coll (KY)
United States Intl U–Africa (Kenya)
United States Military Acad (NY)
Université de Sherbrooke (QC, Canada)
U of Central Florida (FL)
U of Cincinnati (OH)
U of Denver (CO)
U of Great Falls (MT)
U of Houston–Clear Lake (TX)
U of Jamestown (ND)
The U of Kansas (KS)
U of Management and Technology (VA)
U of Massachusetts Boston (MA)
U of Missouri–Kansas City (MO)
U of New Hampshire (NH)
U of New Hampshire at Manchester (NH)
The U of North Carolina at Pembroke (NC)
The U of North Carolina Wilmington (NC)
U of North Texas (TX)
U of St. Francis (IL)
U of Saint Mary (KS)
U of San Francisco (CA)
U of South Alabama (AL)
U of South Florida (FL)
U of South Florida Sarasota-Manatee (FL)
The U of Texas at Dallas (TX)
The U of Toledo (OH)
The U of Tulsa (OK)
U of Washington (WA)
U of Washington, Tacoma (WA)
U of Wisconsin–Stevens Point (WI)
U of Wisconsin–Whitewater (WI)
Vermont Tech Coll (VT)
Walsh Coll of Accountancy and Business Administration (MI)
Washington & Jefferson Coll (PA)
Western Illinois U (IL)
Western Intl U (AZ)
Western Kentucky U (KY)
Western New England U (MA)
William Paterson U of New Jersey (NJ)
William Penn U (IA)
Wilmington U (DE)
Youngstown State U (OH)

INFORMATION TECHNOLOGY PROJECT MANAGEMENT
Arizona State U at the Polytechnic campus (AZ)
Davenport U, Grand Rapids (MI)
LeTourneau U (TX)
Michigan State U (MI)
National U (CA)
Pace U (NY)
Pace U, Pleasantville Campus (NY)

INORGANIC CHEMISTRY
Central Connecticut State U (CT)

INSTRUMENTATION TECHNOLOGY
Great Basin Coll (NV)
Oklahoma State U Inst of Technology (OK)

INSURANCE
Appalachian State U (NC)
Baylor U (TX)
Bowling Green State U (OH)
Bradley U (IL)
Butler U (IN)
Ferris State U (MI)
Gallaudet U (DC)
Gannon U (PA)
Georgia State U (GA)
Hilbert Coll (NY)
Idaho State U (ID)
Illinois State U (IL)
Illinois Wesleyan U (IL)
Indiana State U (IN)
Mississippi State U (MS)
Missouri State U (MO)
Northwood U, Michigan Campus (MI)
Ohio Dominican U (OH)
The Ohio State U (OH)
St. John's U (NY)
Saint Joseph's U (PA)
Southern Methodist U (TX)
U of Central Arkansas (AR)
U of Cincinnati (OH)
U of Georgia (GA)
U of Hartford (CT)
U of Houston–Downtown (TX)
U of Louisiana at Monroe (LA)
U of Minnesota, Twin Cities Campus (MN)
U of North Texas (TX)
U of Pennsylvania (PA)
U of Saint Francis (IN)
U of South Carolina (SC)
U of Wisconsin–La Crosse (WI)
U of Wisconsin–Madison (WI)
Washington State U (WA)
William Penn U (IA)

INTELLIGENCE
Coastal Carolina U (SC)
Excelsior Coll (NY)
Mercyhurst U (PA)

INTERCULTURAL/ MULTICULTURAL AND DIVERSITY STUDIES
Biola U (CA)
Calvary U (MO)
Columbia Intl U (SC)
Concordia U (QC, Canada)
Evangel U (MO)
The Evergreen State Coll (WA)
Goddard Coll (VT)
Judson U (IL)
Macalester Coll (MN)
MidAmerica Nazarene U (KS)
Missouri Valley Coll (MO)
Northwest U (WA)
Nyack Coll (NY)
St. Catherine U (MN)
Trevecca Nazarene U (TN)
U of Mobile (AL)
U of Regina (SK, Canada)
U of the Incarnate Word (TX)
Villanova U (PA)
Western Oregon U (OR)
Whitworth U (WA)
Wofford Coll (SC)
Wright State U (OH)
Wright State U–Lake Campus (OH)

INTERDISCIPLINARY STUDIES
Agnes Scott Coll (GA)
Albright Coll (PA)
Alfred U (NY)
The American U of Rome (Italy)
Amherst Coll (MA)
Auburn U (AL)
Auburn U at Montgomery (AL)
Averett U (VA)
Ball State U (IN)
Bard Coll (NY)
Barnard Coll (NY)
Bay Path U (MA)
Beloit Coll (WI)
Berry Coll (GA)
Bethel Coll (IN)
Biola U (CA)
Blackburn Coll (IL)
Bloomsburg U of Pennsylvania (PA)
Bluefield Coll (VA)
Boston Coll (MA)
Bryn Athyn Coll of the New Church (PA)
Bucknell U (PA)
California Lutheran U (CA)
California State U, Bakersfield (CA)
California State U, East Bay (CA)
California State U, Long Beach (CA)
Calvin Coll (MI)
Carleton Coll (MN)
Carson-Newman U (TN)
Centenary Coll of Louisiana (LA)
Central Methodist U (MO)
Chowan U (NC)
Christian Brothers U (TN)
Clark U (MA)
Coe Coll (IA)
Coll of Coastal Georgia (GA)
Coll of the Atlantic (ME)
Coll of the Ozarks (MO)
The Coll of William and Mary (VA)
The Coll of Wooster (OH)
Connecticut Coll (CT)
Corban U (OR)
Cornell Coll (IA)
Crandall U (NB, Canada)
DePauw U (IN)
Doane U (NE)
Drexel U (PA)
Earlham Coll (IN)
East Stroudsburg U of Pennsylvania (PA)
Eckerd Coll (FL)
Elms Coll (MA)
Emerson Coll (MA)
Fairleigh Dickinson U, Metropolitan Campus (NJ)
FIDM/Fashion Inst of Design & Merchandising, Los Angeles Campus (CA)
FIDM/Fashion Inst of Design & Merchandising, San Francisco Campus (CA)
Florida Ag and Mech U (FL)
Florida Inst of Technology (FL)
Geneva Coll (PA)
George Fox U (OR)
Georgetown U (DC)
The George Washington U (DC)
Georgian Court U (NJ)
Gettysburg Coll (PA)
Goddard Coll (VT)
Goshen Coll (IN)
Green Mountain Coll (VT)
Grinnell Coll (IA)
Hamilton Coll (NY)
Harrisburg U of Science and Technology (PA)
Harris-Stowe State U (MO)
Hendrix Coll (AR)
Hollins U (VA)
Houghton Coll (NY)
Houston Baptist U (TX)
Huston-Tillotson U (TX)
Illinois Coll (IL)
Indiana U Bloomington (IN)
Indiana U East (IN)
Indiana U Kokomo (IN)
Indiana U Northwest (IN)
Indiana U–Purdue U Indianapolis (IN)
Indiana U South Bend (IN)
Indiana U Southeast (IN)
Iowa State U of Science and Technology (IA)
Ithaca Coll (NY)
Jacksonville U (FL)
John Carroll U (OH)
Johns Hopkins U (MD)
Kalamazoo Coll (MI)
Keuka Coll (NY)
King U (TN)
Kuyper Coll (MI)
Lees-McRae Coll (NC)
Lehman Coll of the City U of New York (NY)
Liberty U (VA)
Life U (GA)
Lipscomb U (TN)
Lynchburg Coll (VA)
Lynn U (FL)
Maranatha Baptist U (WI)
Martin Luther Coll (MN)
Marymount Manhattan Coll (NY)
Massachusetts Coll of Liberal Arts (MA)
Merrimack Coll (MA)
MidAmerica Nazarene U (KS)
Millersville U of Pennsylvania (PA)
Mills Coll (CA)
Minneapolis Coll of Art and Design (MN)
Minnesota State U Moorhead (MN)
Misericordia U (PA)
Mount Allison U (NB, Canada)
Mount Saint Mary Coll (NY)

Mount Saint Mary's U (CA)
National U (CA)
Nebraska Wesleyan U (NE)
North Dakota State U (ND)
Northern Arizona U (AZ)
North Greenville U (SC)
Northland Coll (WI)
Northwestern U (IL)
Northwest U (WA)
Nyack Coll (NY)
Oberlin Coll (OH)
Ohio Christian U (OH)
Ohio Dominican U (OH)
Oklahoma Baptist U (OK)
Pennsylvania Coll of Technology (PA)
Piedmont Coll (GA)
Purdue U Northwest (IN)
Queens Coll of the City U of New York (NY)
Rhode Island Coll (RI)
Rhodes Coll (TN)
Ripon Coll (WI)
Roanoke Coll (VA)
Rochester Inst of Technology (NY)
Rutgers U–New Brunswick (NJ)
St. Andrews U (NC)
St. Cloud State U (MN)
Saint Mary's Coll of California (CA)
St. Thomas U (NB, Canada)
Shiloh U (IA)
Siena Coll (NY)
Sierra Nevada Coll (NV)
Simpson Coll (IA)
Slippery Rock U of Pennsylvania (PA)
Smith Coll (MA)
Sonoma State U (CA)
South Dakota School of Mines and Technology (SD)
Southern Oregon U (OR)
Southwestern Coll (KS)
Stanford U (CA)
State U of New York at Fredonia (NY)
State U of New York Coll at Potsdam (NY)
Sterling Coll (KS)
Stevenson U (MD)
Sweet Briar Coll (VA)
Syracuse U (NY)
Tarleton State U (TX)
Tennessee Wesleyan U (TN)
Texas Christian U (TX)
Towson U (MD)
Trent U (ON, Canada)
Trinity Baptist Coll (FL)
Union Coll (KY)
Université de Montréal (QC, Canada)
Université de Sherbrooke (QC, Canada)
U at Albany, State U of New York (NY)
The U of Alabama (AL)
The U of Arizona (AZ)
U of Arkansas (AR)
U of Bridgeport (CT)
U of California, San Diego (CA)
U of California, Santa Barbara (CA)
U of Central Florida (FL)
U of Colorado Colorado Springs (CO)
U of Evansville (IN)
U of Hartford (CT)
U of Kentucky (KY)
U of Michigan–Flint (MI)
U of Minnesota, Duluth (MN)
U of Mount Union (OH)
U of North Alabama (AL)
U of North Dakota (ND)
U of North Florida (FL)
U of Oklahoma (OK)
U of Puget Sound (WA)
U of Saint Francis (IN)
U of Saint Mary (KS)
U of San Francisco (CA)
U of Science and Arts of Oklahoma (OK)
U of South Alabama (AL)
The U of Tennessee at Chattanooga (TN)
The U of Tennessee at Martin (TN)
The U of Texas at Dallas (TX)
The U of Texas at El Paso (TX)
U of the Fraser Valley (BC, Canada)
U of the Pacific (CA)
The U of Tulsa (OK)
U of Vermont (VT)
The U of Virginia's Coll at Wise (VA)
U of Washington, Tacoma (WA)
U of Waterloo (ON, Canada)
The U of West Alabama (AL)
Vassar Coll (NY)
Virginia Polytechnic Inst and State U (VA)
Virginia State U (VA)
Virginia Wesleyan Coll (VA)
Wayne State Coll (NE)
Wesleyan Coll (GA)
Western Oregon U (OR)
Western State Colorado U (CO)
Western Washington U (WA)
William Woods U (MO)
Wittenberg U (OH)
Woodbury U (CA)

INTERIOR ARCHITECTURE

Auburn U (AL)
Benedictine Coll (KS)
Boston Architectural Coll (MA)
Bowling Green State U (OH)
California Coll of the Arts (CA)
Chatham U (PA)
Indiana State U (IN)
La Roche Coll (PA)
Lawrence Technological U (MI)
Lebanese American U (Lebanon)
Louisiana State U and A&M Coll (LA)
Louisiana Tech U (LA)
Miami U (OH)
Milwaukee Inst of Art and Design (WI)
Mississippi State U (MS)
Rhode Island School of Design (RI)
Sam Houston State U (TX)
School of the Art Inst of Chicago (IL)
Stephen F. Austin State U (TX)
Syracuse U (NY)
Texas Tech U (TX)
U of Houston (TX)
U of Nevada, Las Vegas (NV)
U of New Haven (CT)
U of North Texas (TX)
U of Oregon (OR)
U of Southern Mississippi (MS)
The U of Texas at San Antonio (TX)
Woodbury U (CA)

INTERIOR DESIGN

Abilene Christian U (TX)
Acad of Art U (CA)
The American U in Dubai (United Arab Emirates)
Anderson U (SC)
Appalachian State U (NC)
Arizona State U at the Tempe campus (AZ)
Auburn U (AL)
Baylor U (TX)
Bay Path U (MA)
Berkeley Coll–Woodland Park Campus (NJ)
Brenau U (GA)
Brigham Young U–Idaho (ID)
California State U, Fresno (CA)
California State U, Long Beach (CA)
California State U, Sacramento (CA)
Carson-Newman U (TN)
Cazenovia Coll (NY)
Chaminade U of Honolulu (HI)
Cleveland Inst of Art (OH)
Colorado State U (CO)
Columbia Coll Chicago (IL)
Columbus Coll of Art & Design (OH)
Concordia U Wisconsin (WI)
Converse Coll (SC)
Design Inst of San Diego (CA)
Drexel U (PA)
Dunwoody Coll of Technology (MN)
East Carolina U (NC)
Eastern Michigan U (MI)
East Tennessee State U (TN)
EDP U of Puerto Rico (PR)
Endicott Coll (MA)
Eugene Lang Coll of Liberal Arts (NY)
Fashion Inst of Technology (NY)
Ferris State U (MI)
FIDM/Fashion Inst of Design & Merchandising, Los Angeles Campus (CA)
FIDM/Fashion Inst of Design & Merchandising, San Francisco Campus (CA)
Florida Intl U (FL)
Florida State U (FL)
Georgia Southern U (GA)
Hampton U (VA)
Harding U (AR)
High Point U (NC)
Illinois State U (IL)
Indiana U Bloomington (IN)
Indiana U of Pennsylvania (PA)
Indiana U–Purdue U Indianapolis (IN)
Iowa State U of Science and Technology (IA)
Judson U (IL)
Kansas State U (KS)
Kean U (NJ)
Kent State U (OH)
Lebanese American U (Lebanon)
Marist Coll (NY)
Maryland Inst Coll of Art (MD)
Marylhurst U (OR)
Marymount U (VA)
Maryville U of Saint Louis (MO)
Marywood U (PA)
Mercyhurst U (PA)
Meredith Coll (NC)
Michigan State U (MI)
Mount Ida Coll (MA)
Mount Mary U (WI)
New England Inst of Technology (RI)
New York Inst of Technology (NY)
North Dakota State U (ND)
Northern Arizona U (AZ)
The Ohio State U (OH)
Oklahoma Christian U (OK)
Olivet Nazarene U (IL)
O'More Coll of Design (TN)
Oregon State U (OR)
Parsons School of Design (NY)
Polytechnic U of Puerto Rico (PR)
Pratt Inst (NY)
Purdue U (IN)
Ringling Coll of Art and Design (FL)
Rochester Inst of Technology (NY)
The Sage Colls (NY)
Samford U (AL)
San Diego State U (CA)
San Francisco State U (CA)
Savannah Coll of Art and Design (GA)
Seattle Pacific U (WA)
Seminole State Coll of Florida (FL)
South Dakota State U (SD)
Southern Illinois U Carbondale (IL)
Suffolk U (MA)
Texas Christian U (TX)
Texas State U (TX)
Université de Montréal (QC, Canada)
The U of Alabama (AL)
U of Arkansas (AR)
U of Bridgeport (CT)
U of Central Arkansas (AR)
U of Central Missouri (MO)
U of Charleston (WV)
U of Cincinnati (OH)
U of Florida (FL)
U of Idaho (ID)
U of Kentucky (KY)
U of Minnesota, Twin Cities Campus (MN)
The U of North Carolina at Greensboro (NC)
U of Northern Iowa (IA)
U of Oklahoma (OK)
The U of Tennessee (TN)
The U of Tennessee at Chattanooga (TN)
The U of Tennessee at Martin (TN)
The U of Texas at Austin (TX)
U of the Incarnate Word (TX)
U of Wisconsin–Madison (WI)
U of Wisconsin–Stevens Point (WI)
U of Wisconsin–Stout (WI)
Utah State U (UT)
Valdosta State U (GA)
Villa Maria Coll (NY)
Virginia Commonwealth U (VA)
Virginia Polytechnic Inst and State U (VA)
Washington State U (WA)
Washington State U–Spokane (WA)
Watkins Coll of Art, Design, & Film (TN)
Wentworth Inst of Technology (MA)
Western Carolina U (NC)
Western Michigan U (MI)

INTERMEDIA/MULTIMEDIA

Augusta U (GA)
Bennington Coll (VT)
Biola U (CA)
Calumet Coll of Saint Joseph (IN)
City Coll of the City U of New York (NY)
The Coll of New Jersey (NJ)
Columbia Coll Chicago (IL)
Concordia U (QC, Canada)
Emerson Coll (MA)
The Evergreen State Coll (WA)
Indiana U of Pennsylvania (PA)
Jacksonville U (FL)
Laguna Coll of Art & Design (CA)
Luther Coll (IA)
Marist Coll (NY)
Maryland Inst Coll of Art (MD)
Massachusetts Coll of Art and Design (MA)
McMaster U (ON, Canada)
Mills Coll (CA)
Minneapolis Coll of Art and Design (MN)
Missouri State U (MO)
Pacific Northwest Coll of Art (OR)
Providence Coll (RI)
Purchase Coll, State U of New York (NY)
Ramapo Coll of New Jersey (NJ)
Rochester Inst of Technology (NY)
School of the Art Inst of Chicago (IL)
State U of New York at Fredonia (NY)
State U of New York Coll of Technology at Alfred (NY)
Tufts U (MA)
U of Hartford (CT)
U of Maine at Farmington (ME)
U of Oregon (OR)
U of Regina (SK, Canada)
The U of the Arts (PA)
U of the Incarnate Word (TX)
The U of Toledo (OH)
Weber State U (UT)
Western Washington U (WA)

INTERNATIONAL AGRICULTURE

Cornell U (NY)
Dalhousie U (NS, Canada)
Iowa State U of Science and Technology (IA)
Tarleton State U (TX)
U of California, Davis (CA)
Utah State U (UT)

INTERNATIONAL AND COMPARATIVE EDUCATION

Avila U (MO)

INTERNATIONAL AND INTERCULTURAL COMMUNICATION

The American U of Paris (France)
Becker Coll (MA)
Linfield Coll (OR)
Michigan Technological U (MI)
Pepperdine U, Malibu (CA)
Saint Louis U–Madrid Campus (Spain)
U of Valley Forge (PA)

INTERNATIONAL BUSINESS/TRADE/COMMERCE

Adams State U (CO)
Albertus Magnus Coll (CT)
Albright Coll (PA)
Alverno Coll (WI)
American Intl Coll (MA)
The American U of Paris (France)
The American U of Rome (Italy)
Anderson U (IN)
Anderson U (SC)
Angelo State U (TX)
Appalachian State U (NC)
Aquinas Coll (MI)
Arcadia U (PA)
Assumption Coll (MA)
Auburn U (AL)
Auburn U at Montgomery (AL)
Augsburg Coll (MN)
Augustana Coll (IL)
Austin Coll (TX)
Avila U (MO)
Baker U (KS)
Baldwin Wallace U (OH)
Ball State U (IN)
Barry U (FL)
Baruch Coll of the City U of New York (NY)
Baylor U (TX)
Belmont U (TN)
Benedictine Coll (KS)
Berkeley Coll–New York City Campus (NY)
Berkeley Coll–Woodland Park Campus (NJ)
Berry Coll (GA)
Bethune-Cookman U (FL)
Binghamton U, State U of New York (NY)
Biola U (CA)
Bishop's U (QC, Canada)
Boise State U (ID)
Bowling Green State U (OH)
Bradley U (IL)
Bridgewater State U (MA)
Brooklyn Coll of the City U of New York (NY)
Bryant U (RI)
Bucknell U (PA)
Buena Vista U (IA)
Butler U (IN)
Caldwell U (NJ)
California State U, Dominguez Hills (CA)
California State U, Fresno (CA)
California State U, Fullerton (CA)
California State U, Long Beach (CA)
California State U, San Marcos (CA)
Canisius Coll (NY)
Cardinal Stritch U (WI)
Carnegie Mellon U (PA)
The Catholic U of America (DC)
Cedarville U (OH)
Central Michigan U (MI)
Chaminade U of Honolulu (HI)
Champlain Coll (VT)
Chatham U (PA)
Chestnut Hill Coll (PA)
Clarion U of Pennsylvania (PA)
Cleveland State U (OH)
The Coll at Brockport, State U of New York (NY)
Coll of Charleston (SC)
The Coll of Idaho (ID)
Columbia Coll (MO)
Concordia Coll (MN)
Concordia Coll–New York (NY)
Concordia U (QC, Canada)
Concordia U Wisconsin (WI)
Converse Coll (SC)
Cornell Coll (IA)
Cornerstone U (MI)
Creighton U (NE)
Dalhousie U (NS, Canada)
Davenport U, Grand Rapids (MI)
Denison U (OH)
DEREE - The American Coll of Greece (Greece)
DeSales U (PA)
Dickinson Coll (PA)
Dickinson State U (ND)
Dominican U (IL)
Drake U (IA)
Drexel U (PA)
Duquesne U (PA)
East Central U (OK)
Eastern Mennonite U (VA)
Eastern Michigan U (MI)
Eastern U (PA)
Eckerd Coll (FL)
Elizabethtown Coll (PA)
Elms Coll (MA)
Elon U (NC)
Embry-Riddle Aeronautical U–Prescott (AZ)
Emory & Henry Coll (VA)
Endicott Coll (MA)
Excelsior Coll (NY)
Fairfield U (CT)

Farmingdale State Coll (NY)
Felician U (NJ)
Florida Atlantic U (FL)
Florida Inst of Technology (FL)
Florida Intl U (FL)
Fordham U (NY)
Fort Lewis Coll (CO)
Franciscan U of Steubenville (OH)
Fresno Pacific U (CA)
Friends U (KS)
Gannon U (PA)
Gardner-Webb U (NC)
George Fox U (OR)
Georgetown U (DC)
The George Washington U (DC)
Georgian Court U (NJ)
Georgia Southern U (GA)
Gettysburg Coll (PA)
Gonzaga U (WA)
Graceland U (IA)
Grand Valley State U (MI)
Grove City Coll (PA)
Hamline U (MN)
Harding U (AR)
HEC Montreal (QC, Canada)
High Point U (NC)
Hilbert Coll (NY)
Hillsdale Coll (MI)
Hofstra U (NY)
Holy Family U (PA)
Houston Baptist U (TX)
Husson U (ME)
Illinois State U (IL)
Illinois Wesleyan U (IL)
Indiana U of Pennsylvania (PA)
Iona Coll (NY)
Iowa State U of Science and Technology (IA)
Ithaca Coll (NY)
Jacksonville U (FL)
James Madison U (VA)
John Brown U (AR)
John Carroll U (OH)
Juniata Coll (PA)
Kean U (NJ)
Kennesaw State U (GA)
King's Coll (PA)
Kuyper Coll (MI)
Lake Erie Coll (OH)
La Roche Coll (PA)
La Salle U (PA)
Lasell Coll (MA)
Lebanon Valley Coll (PA)
Lenoir-Rhyne U (NC)
LeTourneau U (TX)
Lewis U (IL)
LIM Coll (NY)
Lincoln U (CA)
Lindenwood U (MO)
Linfield Coll (OR)
Lipscomb U (TN)
Louisiana State U and A&M Coll (LA)
Loyola U Chicago (IL)
Loyola U New Orleans (LA)
Lynn U (FL)
Madonna U (MI)
Mansfield U of Pennsylvania (PA)
Marietta Coll (OH)
Marshall U (WV)
Marymount Manhattan Coll (NY)
Maryville U of Saint Louis (MO)
Marywood U (PA)
Massachusetts Coll of Liberal Arts (MA)
Massachusetts Maritime Acad (MA)
Menlo Coll (CA)
Mercer U, Macon (GA)
Merrimack Coll (MA)
Messiah Coll (PA)
Millikin U (IL)
Minnesota State U Mankato (MN)
Minot State U (ND)
Monmouth Coll (IL)
Monmouth U (NJ)
Moravian Coll (PA)
Mount Allison U (NB, Canada)
Mount Mercy U (IA)
Mount Saint Mary's U (CA)
Mount Vernon Nazarene U (OH)
Muskingum U (OH)
Nazareth Coll of Rochester (NY)
Nebraska Wesleyan U (NE)
Neumann U (PA)
New Mexico State U (NM)
New York Inst of Technology (NY)
Nichols Coll (MA)
North Central Coll (IL)
Northeastern State U (OK)
Northeastern U (MA)
Northern State U (SD)
North Greenville U (SC)
Northwest Missouri State U (MO)
Northwood U, Michigan Campus (MI)
The Ohio State U (OH)
Ohio U (OH)
Ohio Wesleyan U (OH)
Oklahoma Baptist U (OK)
Oklahoma State U (OK)
Olivet Nazarene U (IL)
Oral Roberts U (OK)
Otterbein U (OH)
Pace U (NY)
Pace U, Pleasantville Campus (NY)
Palm Beach Atlantic U (FL)
Penn State DuBois (PA)
Penn State Erie, The Behrend Coll (PA)
Penn State Harrisburg (PA)
Penn State Lehigh Valley (PA)
Penn State Schuylkill (PA)
Pepperdine U, Malibu (CA)
Pittsburg State U (KS)
Queens Coll of the City U of New York (NY)
Quinnipiac U (CT)
Ramapo Coll of New Jersey (NJ)
Rhode Island Coll (RI)
Rhodes Coll (TN)
Rochester Inst of Technology (NY)
Roger Williams U (RI)
Rollins Coll (FL)
Rosemont Coll (PA)
Saginaw Valley State U (MI)
St. Ambrose U (IA)
Saint Anselm Coll (NH)
St. Catherine U (MN)
St. Cloud State U (MN)
St. Edward's U (TX)
Saint Francis U (PA)
Saint Joseph's U (PA)
Saint Louis U (MO)
Saint Louis U–Madrid Campus (Spain)
Saint Mary's Coll of California (CA)
Saint Mary's U of Minnesota (MN)
St. Norbert Coll (WI)
St. Petersburg Coll (FL)
Saint Peter's U (NJ)
St. Thomas U (FL)
Saint Vincent Coll (PA)
Salisbury U (MD)
Samford U (AL)
Sam Houston State U (TX)
San Diego State U (CA)
San Francisco State U (CA)
Seattle U (WA)
Seton Hill U (PA)
Sierra Nevada Coll (NV)
Simpson Coll (IA)
Southeastern U (FL)
Southeast Missouri State U (MO)
Southern New Hampshire U (NH)
Southwestern Adventist U (TX)
Spring Hill Coll (AL)
State Coll of Florida Manatee-Sarasota (FL)
State U of New York at New Paltz (NY)
State U of New York at Plattsburgh (NY)
Stephen F. Austin State U (TX)
Stonehill Coll (MA)
Suffolk U (MA)
Susquehanna U (PA)
Tarleton State U (TX)
Taylor U (IN)
Temple U (PA)
Texas A&M U–Central Texas (TX)
Texas A&M U–Kingsville (TX)
Texas Christian U (TX)
Texas Tech U (TX)
Tiffin U (OH)
Trevecca Nazarene U (TN)
Trinity U (TX)
Union Coll (NE)
United States Intl U–Africa (Kenya)
U at Buffalo, the State U of New York (NY)
The U of Akron (OH)
U of Arkansas (AR)
U of Bridgeport (CT)
U of Cincinnati (OH)
U of Dayton (OH)
U of Delaware (DE)
U of Denver (CO)
U of Evansville (IN)
The U of Findlay (OH)
U of Georgia (GA)
U of Hawaii at Manoa (HI)
U of Houston–Downtown (TX)
U of Indianapolis (IN)
U of Jamestown (ND)
U of La Verne (CA)
U of Lethbridge (AB, Canada)
U of Mary Hardin-Baylor (TX)
U of Maryland, Coll Park (MD)
U of Miami (FL)
U of Michigan–Flint (MI)
U of Minnesota, Twin Cities Campus (MN)
U of Mount Union (OH)
U of Nevada, Las Vegas (NV)
U of Nevada, Reno (NV)
The U of North Carolina at Charlotte (NC)
The U of North Carolina at Greensboro (NC)
U of North Florida (FL)
U of Pennsylvania (PA)
U of Pittsburgh (PA)
U of Regina (SK, Canada)
U of Rhode Island (RI)
U of St. Francis (IL)
U of St. Thomas (MN)
U of San Diego (CA)
U of San Francisco (CA)
The U of Scranton (PA)
U of South Carolina (SC)
U of Southern California (CA)
U of Southern Mississippi (MS)
U of South Florida (FL)
U of South Florida, St. Petersburg (FL)
The U of Tampa (FL)
The U of Tennessee at Martin (TN)
The U of Texas at Dallas (TX)
The U of Texas at San Antonio (TX)
The U of Texas Rio Grande Valley (TX)
U of the Incarnate Word (TX)
U of the Potomac (DC)
U of the Southwest (NM)
The U of Toledo (OH)
The U of Tulsa (OK)
U of Waterloo (ON, Canada)
U of Wisconsin–Eau Claire (WI)
U of Wisconsin–La Crosse (WI)
U of Wisconsin–Madison (WI)
U of Wisconsin–Whitewater (WI)
Utica Coll (NY)
Valdosta State U (GA)
Valparaiso U (IN)
Villanova U (PA)
Waldorf U (IA)
Walla Walla U (WA)
Wartburg Coll (IA)
Washington & Jefferson Coll (PA)
Washington State U (WA)
Washington U in St. Louis (MO)
Waynesburg U (PA)
Wayne State U (MI)
Wesleyan Coll (GA)
West Chester U of Pennsylvania (PA)
Western Kentucky U (KY)
Western New England U (MA)
Western Washington U (WA)
Westminster Coll (PA)
Westminster Coll (UT)
Whitworth U (WA)
Wichita State U (KS)
Widener U (PA)
William Paterson U of New Jersey (NJ)
Wright State U (OH)

INTERNATIONAL ECONOMICS

Albion Coll (MI)
The American U of Paris (France)
Austin Coll (TX)
Belmont U (TN)
Bryant U (RI)
Carthage Coll (WI)
The Coll of Idaho (ID)
The Colorado Coll (CO)
Elon U (NC)
Fitchburg State U (MA)
Georgetown U (DC)
Georgia State U (GA)
Gettysburg Coll (PA)
HEC Montreal (QC, Canada)
John Carroll U (OH)
La Salle U (PA)
Lawrence U (WI)
Rhodes Coll (TN)
Rockford U (IL)
St. Catherine U (MN)
Salve Regina U (RI)
State U of New York at Oswego (NY)
Texas Christian U (TX)
Texas Tech U (TX)
Trinity U (TX)
U of Puget Sound (WA)
U of Richmond (VA)
U of West Georgia (GA)
Valparaiso U (IN)
Washington U in St. Louis (MO)
Weber State U (UT)
Youngstown State U (OH)

INTERNATIONAL FINANCE

The American U of Paris (France)
Brigham Young U (UT)
The Catholic U of America (DC)
HEC Montreal (QC, Canada)
Lenoir-Rhyne U (NC)
Texas Christian U (TX)
Washington U in St. Louis (MO)

INTERNATIONAL/GLOBAL STUDIES

Abilene Christian U (TX)
Adelphi U (NY)
Albertus Magnus Coll (CT)
Albion Coll (MI)
Alfred U (NY)
The American U of Rome (Italy)
Appalachian State U (NC)
Arcadia U (PA)
Arizona State U at the Tempe campus (AZ)
Arkansas Tech U (AR)
Assumption Coll (MA)
Auburn U at Montgomery (AL)
Baker U (KS)
Baldwin Wallace U (OH)
Bard Coll (NY)
Belhaven U (MS)
Benedictine Coll (KS)
Bennington Coll (VT)
Bentley U (MA)
Boston Coll (MA)
Bowling Green State U (OH)
Brandeis U (MA)
Brigham Young U–Idaho (ID)
Bryant U (RI)
Bryn Mawr Coll (PA)
California Baptist U (CA)
Carnegie Mellon U (PA)
Case Western Reserve U (OH)
Cazenovia Coll (NY)
Cedar Crest Coll (PA)
Cedarville U (OH)
Central Connecticut State U (CT)
Centre Coll (KY)
Chatham U (PA)
Chestnut Hill Coll (PA)
City Coll of the City U of New York (NY)
Colby Coll (ME)
Coll of Charleston (SC)
The Coll of St. Scholastica (MN)
Coll of Staten Island of the City U of New York (NY)
Coll of the Holy Cross (MA)
Colorado Christian U (CO)
Colorado State U (CO)
Columbia Intl U (SC)
Concordia Coll (MN)
Concordia Coll–New York (NY)
Concordia U Irvine (CA)
Concordia U, Nebraska (NE)
Culver-Stockton Coll (MO)
Davis Coll (NY)
Doane U (NE)
Dominican U of California (CA)
Drexel U (PA)
East Texas Baptist U (TX)
Emmanuel Coll (MA)
Endicott Coll (MA)
Eugene Lang Coll of Liberal Arts (NY)
The Evergreen State Coll (WA)
Flagler Coll (FL)
Framingham State U (MA)
Frostburg State U (MD)
Gannon U (PA)
George Fox U (OR)
Georgia Inst of Technology (GA)
Goddard Coll (VT)
Greenville Coll (IL)
Hamline U (MN)
Hampshire Coll (MA)
Hanover Coll (IN)
Harding U (AR)
Hartwick Coll (NY)
Hawai`i Pacific U (HI)
Hofstra U (NY)
Hood Coll (MD)
Hope Coll (MI)
Illinois Wesleyan U (IL)
John Brown U (AR)
Juniata Coll (PA)
Kenyon Coll (OH)
Knox Coll (IL)
Lebanon Valley Coll (PA)
Lehigh U (PA)
Le Moyne Coll (NY)
LeTourneau U (TX)
Louisiana State U and A&M Coll (LA)
Luther Coll (IA)
Macalester Coll (MN)
Malone U (OH)
Manchester U (IN)
Manhattanville Coll (NY)
Marymount Manhattan Coll (NY)
Maryville U of Saint Louis (MO)
McKendree U (IL)
Mercyhurst U (PA)
Meredith Coll (NC)
Michigan State U (MI)
Minnesota State U Moorhead (MN)
Missouri State U (MO)
Missouri Western State U (MO)
Monmouth Coll (IL)
Morehead State U (KY)
Morningside Coll (IA)
Mount Mary U (WI)
Multnomah U (OR)
National U (CA)
Nebraska Wesleyan U (NE)
New Coll of Florida (FL)
The New School for Public Engagement (NY)
North Carolina State U (NC)
North Central Coll (IL)
North Dakota State U (ND)
Northwest U (WA)
The Ohio State U (OH)
Oregon State U (OR)
Pace U, Pleasantville Campus (NY)
Pacific Lutheran U (WA)
Pepperdine U, Malibu (CA)
Pitzer Coll (CA)
Point Loma Nazarene U (CA)
Point Park U (PA)
Providence Coll (RI)
Randolph Coll (VA)
Randolph-Macon Coll (VA)
Regent U (VA)
Rockford U (IL)
Roger Williams U (RI)
Saginaw Valley State U (MI)
St. Bonaventure U (NY)
St. Edward's U (TX)
Saint Leo U (FL)
Saint Mary's Coll (IN)
Saint Mary's U of Minnesota (MN)
St. Norbert Coll (WI)
St. Thomas U (FL)
Salisbury U (MD)
Salve Regina U (RI)
Samford U (AL)
Sarah Lawrence Coll (NY)
Scripps Coll (CA)
Seattle U (WA)
Sewanee: The U of the South (TN)
Shippensburg U of Pennsylvania (PA)
Sierra Nevada Coll (NV)
South Dakota State U (SD)
Southeast Missouri State U (MO)
Southern Methodist U (TX)
Spelman Coll (GA)
State U of New York Coll at Cortland (NY)
State U of New York Coll at Potsdam (NY)
Susquehanna U (PA)
Tabor Coll (KS)

Tarleton State U (TX)
Temple U (PA)
Tennessee Wesleyan U (TN)
Texas A&M U (TX)
Texas State U (TX)
Texas Tech U (TX)
Thomas More Coll (KY)
United States Air Force Acad (CO)
Université de Montréal (QC, Canada)
U at Albany, State U of New York (NY)
The U of Arizona (AZ)
U of California, Irvine (CA)
U of California, Los Angeles (CA)
U of California, Riverside (CA)
U of California, Santa Barbara (CA)
U of Central Arkansas (AR)
U of Central Florida (FL)
U of Colorado Boulder (CO)
U of Colorado Denver (CO)
U of Dayton (OH)
U of Florida (FL)
U of Illinois at Springfield (IL)
The U of Kansas (KS)
U of Kentucky (KY)
U of La Verne (CA)
U of Maine at Farmington (ME)
U of Maryland, Baltimore County (MD)
U of Michigan (MI)
U of New England (ME)
U of New Haven (CT)
U of New Orleans (LA)
The U of North Carolina at Charlotte (NC)
The U of North Carolina Wilmington (NC)
U of North Dakota (ND)
U of Northern Colorado (CO)
U of Northern Iowa (IA)
U of North Florida (FL)
U of North Texas (TX)
U of Notre Dame (IN)
U of Oklahoma (OK)
U of Oregon (OR)
U of Pennsylvania (PA)
U of Regina (SK, Canada)
U of Saint Joseph (CT)
U of Saskatchewan (SK, Canada)
U of South Alabama (AL)
The U of South Dakota (SD)
U of Southern California (CA)
The U of Tampa (FL)
The U of Texas at Austin (TX)
U of Utah (UT)
U of Washington, Bothell (WA)
U of Washington, Tacoma (WA)
U of Waterloo (ON, Canada)
U of Wisconsin–Madison (WI)
U of Wisconsin–Milwaukee (WI)
U of Wisconsin–Platteville (WI)
U of Wisconsin–Stevens Point (WI)
U of Wisconsin–Whitewater (WI)
Valparaiso U (IN)
Villanova U (PA)
Virginia Polytechnic Inst and State U (VA)
Washington & Jefferson Coll (PA)
Webster U (MO)
Western Carolina U (NC)
Western Michigan U (MI)
Western New England U (MA)
Westminster Coll (PA)
West Virginia State U (WV)
Whitman Coll (WA)
Whittier Coll (CA)
Willamette U (OR)
William Peace U (NC)
Winona State U (MN)
Wright State U (OH)
Wright State U–Lake Campus (OH)

INTERNATIONAL MARKETING

Fashion Inst of Technology (NY)
Husson U (ME)
Oklahoma Baptist U (OK)
Oral Roberts U (OK)
Pace U, Pleasantville Campus (NY)
Texas Christian U (TX)
U of Northern Iowa (IA)

INTERNATIONAL POLICY ANALYSIS

Southern Methodist U (TX)
Waynesburg U (PA)

INTERNATIONAL PUBLIC HEALTH

Allegheny Coll (PA)
American U (DC)
Bethel Coll (IN)
California Baptist U (CA)
Mercer U, Macon (GA)
Union Coll (NE)
U of Southern California (CA)

INTERNATIONAL RELATIONS AND AFFAIRS

Agnes Scott Coll (GA)
Allegheny Coll (PA)
Alverno Coll (WI)
American Coll of Thessaloniki (Greece)
American Intl Coll (MA)
American Public U System (WV)
American U (DC)
American U in Bulgaria (Bulgaria)
The American U in Dubai (United Arab Emirates)
The American U of Rome (Italy)
Aquinas Coll (MI)
Augsburg Coll (MN)
Augustana U (SD)
Austin Coll (TX)
Azusa Pacific U (CA)
Barry U (FL)
Baylor U (TX)
Belmont U (TN)
Beloit Coll (WI)
Bennington Coll (VT)
Berry Coll (GA)
Bethel U (MN)
Bethune-Cookman U (FL)
Binghamton U, State U of New York (NY)
Bishop's U (QC, Canada)
Boston U (MA)
Bowling Green State U (OH)
Bradley U (IL)
Brenau U (GA)
Bridgewater Coll (VA)
Bridgewater State U (MA)
Bryant U (RI)
Bucknell U (PA)
Butler U (IN)
California Lutheran U (CA)
California State U, Chico (CA)
California State U, East Bay (CA)
California State U, Long Beach (CA)
California State U, Monterey Bay (CA)
California State U, San Marcos (CA)
Calvin Coll (MI)
Canisius Coll (NY)
Capital U (OH)
Carleton Coll (MN)
Carnegie Mellon U (PA)
Carroll Coll (MT)
Case Western Reserve U (OH)
Centenary U (NJ)
Central Michigan U (MI)
Chaminade U of Honolulu (HI)
Chatham U (PA)
City Coll of the City U of New York (NY)
Claremont McKenna Coll (CA)
Clark U (MA)
Cleveland State U (OH)
Colgate U (NY)
The Coll at Brockport, State U of New York (NY)
The Coll of Idaho (ID)
The Coll of New Jersey (NJ)
The Coll of William and Mary (VA)
The Coll of Wooster (OH)
Concordia Coll–New York (NY)
Connecticut Coll (CT)
Cornell Coll (IA)
Creighton U (NE)
Dalhousie U (NS, Canada)
Denison U (OH)
Dickinson Coll (PA)
Dominican U (IL)
Drake U (IA)
Drew U (NJ)
Drury U (MO)
Duquesne U (PA)
Eastern Michigan U (MI)
Eastern Washington U (WA)
East Tennessee State U (TN)
Eckerd Coll (FL)
Edgewood Coll (WI)
Elmira Coll (NY)
Elon U (NC)
Embry-Riddle Aeronautical U–Prescott (AZ)
Emmanuel Coll (MA)
Emory U (GA)
Excelsior Coll (NY)
Fairfield U (CT)
Fairleigh Dickinson U, Metropolitan Campus (NJ)
Fitchburg State U (MA)
Florida Intl U (FL)
Florida State U (FL)
Fordham U (NY)
Francis Marion U (SC)
Georgetown U (DC)
The George Washington U (DC)
Georgia Inst of Technology (GA)
Georgia Southern U (GA)
Gettysburg Coll (PA)
Gonzaga U (WA)
Gordon Coll (MA)
Goucher Coll (MD)
Graceland U (IA)
Grand Valley State U (MI)
Hamilton Coll (NY)
Hampden-Sydney Coll (VA)
Hampshire Coll (MA)
Heidelberg U (OH)
Hendrix Coll (AR)
High Point U (NC)
Hobart and William Smith Colls (NY)
Hollins U (VA)
Holy Names U (CA)
Howard Payne U (TX)
Hult Intl Business School (United Kingdom)
Idaho State U (ID)
Illinois Coll (IL)
Illinois Wesleyan U (IL)
Immaculata U (PA)
Indiana U Bloomington (IN)
Indiana U East (IN)
Indiana U of Pennsylvania (PA)
Indiana U–Purdue U Indianapolis (IN)
Indiana U Southeast (IN)
Iona Coll (NY)
Iowa State U of Science and Technology (IA)
Jacksonville U (FL)
James Madison U (VA)
John Carroll U (OH)
Johns Hopkins U (MD)
Juniata Coll (PA)
Kennesaw State U (GA)
Kent State U (OH)
Knox Coll (IL)
Lafayette Coll (PA)
Lake Forest Coll (IL)
La Roche Coll (PA)
La Salle U (PA)
Lawrence U (WI)
Lebanese American U (Lebanon)
Lehigh U (PA)
Lenoir-Rhyne U (NC)
Lewis & Clark Coll (OR)
Lewis U (IL)
Liberty U (VA)
Lindenwood U (MO)
Linfield Coll (OR)
Lock Haven U of Pennsylvania (PA)
Loras Coll (IA)
Loyola Marymount U (CA)
Loyola U Chicago (IL)
Lynchburg Coll (VA)
Manhattan Coll (NY)
Marshall U (WV)
Mary Baldwin U (VA)
Marymount Manhattan Coll (NY)
McKendree U (IL)
Mercer U, Macon (GA)
Mercy Coll (NY)
Meredith Coll (NC)
Miami U (OH)
Michigan State U (MI)
Middlebury Coll (VT)
Mills Coll (CA)
Minnesota State U Mankato (MN)
Morningside Coll (IA)
Mount Allison U (NB, Canada)
Mount Holyoke Coll (MA)
Mount Mercy U (IA)
Mount St. Mary's U (MD)
Muhlenberg Coll (PA)
Murray State U (KY)
Muskingum U (OH)
Nazareth Coll of Rochester (NY)
Newberry Coll (SC)
Niagara U (NY)
Northeastern U (MA)
Northern Arizona U (AZ)
Northern Kentucky U (KY)
Northwestern U (IL)
Nova Southeastern U (FL)
Occidental Coll (CA)
The Ohio State U (OH)
Ohio U (OH)
Ohio Wesleyan U (OH)
Oklahoma Baptist U (OK)
Old Dominion U (VA)
Oral Roberts U (OK)
Otterbein U (OH)
Penn State Abington (PA)
Penn State Altoona (PA)
Penn State Beaver (PA)
Penn State Berks (PA)
Penn State Brandywine (PA)
Penn State DuBois (PA)
Penn State Erie, The Behrend Coll (PA)
Penn State Fayette, The Eberly Campus (PA)
Penn State Greater Allegheny (PA)
Penn State Hazleton (PA)
Penn State Lehigh Valley (PA)
Penn State Mont Alto (PA)
Penn State New Kensington (PA)
Penn State Schuylkill (PA)
Penn State Shenango (PA)
Penn State U Park (PA)
Penn State Wilkes-Barre (PA)
Penn State Worthington Scranton (PA)
Penn State York (PA)
Pomona Coll (CA)
Portland State U (OR)
Quinnipiac U (CT)
Redeemer U Coll (ON, Canada)
Reed Coll (OR)
Rhodes Coll (TN)
Roanoke Coll (VA)
Rochester Inst of Technology (NY)
Rockhurst U (MO)
Roger Williams U (RI)
Rollins Coll (FL)
Saginaw Valley State U (MI)
Saint Anselm Coll (NH)
St. Catherine U (MN)
St. Cloud State U (MN)
Saint Francis U (PA)
St. John Fisher Coll (NY)
Saint Joseph's U (PA)
Saint Louis U (MO)
Saint Mary's Coll of California (CA)
Saint Michael's Coll (VT)
St. Norbert Coll (WI)
St. Thomas U (NB, Canada)
Samford U (AL)
San Diego State U (CA)
San Francisco State U (CA)
Seton Hill U (PA)
Shawnee State U (OH)
Shaw U (NC)
Simmons Coll (MA)
Simpson Coll (IA)
Skidmore Coll (NY)
Sonoma State U (CA)
Southern Oregon U (OR)
Southwestern Adventist U (TX)
Southwestern U (TX)
Spelman Coll (GA)
Spring Hill Coll (AL)
Stanford U (CA)
State U of New York at New Paltz (NY)
State U of New York at Oswego (NY)
State U of New York Coll at Cortland (NY)
State U of New York Coll at Geneseo (NY)
Sweet Briar Coll (VA)
Syracuse U (NY)
Taylor U (IN)
Temple U (PA)
Texas Christian U (TX)
Texas State U (TX)
Tiffin U (OH)
Towson U (MD)
Trent U (ON, Canada)
Trinity U (TX)
Tufts U (MA)
Tulane U (LA)
United States Intl U–Africa (Kenya)
United States Military Acad (NY)
The U of Alabama (AL)
U of Arkansas (AR)
U of Bridgeport (CT)
U of California, Davis (CA)
U of Chicago (IL)
U of Cincinnati (OH)
U of Delaware (DE)
U of Denver (CO)
U of Evansville (IN)
U of Georgia (GA)
U of Hartford (CT)
U of Idaho (ID)
U of Indianapolis (IN)
U of La Verne (CA)
U of Maine (ME)
U of Mary Washington (VA)
U of Massachusetts Boston (MA)
U of Miami (FL)
U of Minnesota, Duluth (MN)
U of Minnesota, Twin Cities Campus (MN)
U of Mount Union (OH)
U of Nebraska at Kearney (NE)
U of Nevada, Reno (NV)
U of New Hampshire (NH)
U of North Georgia (GA)
U of Pennsylvania (PA)
U of Pittsburgh at Bradford (PA)
U of Richmond (VA)
U of Rochester (NY)
U of St. Thomas (MN)
U of St. Thomas (TX)
U of San Diego (CA)
U of San Francisco (CA)
The U of Scranton (PA)
U of South Carolina (SC)
U of Southern California (CA)
U of Southern Indiana (IN)
U of Southern Mississippi (MS)
U of South Florida (FL)
The U of Tennessee at Martin (TN)
U of the Incarnate Word (TX)
U of the Pacific (CA)
The U of Toledo (OH)
U of Toronto (ON, Canada)
U of Virginia (VA)
U of Waterloo (ON, Canada)
U of West Georgia (GA)
U of Windsor (ON, Canada)
U of Wisconsin–Parkside (WI)
U of Wisconsin–Stevens Point (WI)
U of Wisconsin–Superior (WI)
Ursinus Coll (PA)
Utica Coll (NY)
Valparaiso U (IN)
Vassar Coll (NY)
Virginia Military Inst (VA)
Virginia Polytechnic Inst and State U (VA)
Virginia Wesleyan Coll (VA)
Wagner Coll (NY)
Walsh U (OH)
Wartburg Coll (IA)
Washington Coll (MD)
Washington State U (WA)
Washington U in St. Louis (MO)
Webster U (MO)
Wells Coll (NY)
Wesleyan Coll (GA)
Western Kentucky U (KY)
Western Oregon U (OR)
Westminster Coll (PA)
West Virginia Wesleyan Coll (WV)
Wheaton Coll (IL)
Wheaton Coll (MA)
Wheeling Jesuit U (WV)
Whitworth U (WA)
Widener U (PA)
Wilkes U (PA)
William Jewell Coll (MO)
Wilson Coll (PA)
Wittenberg U (OH)
Worcester Polytechnic Inst (MA)
York Coll of Pennsylvania (PA)

INTERNATIONAL RELATIONS AND NATIONAL SECURITY RELATED

Arcadia U (PA)
San Diego State U (CA)
U of Mount Union (OH)
Virginia Polytechnic Inst and State U (VA)

INVESTMENTS AND SECURITIES
Lynn U (FL)
Marymount Manhattan Coll (NY)
U of North Dakota (ND)
U of Northern Iowa (IA)

IRANIAN LANGUAGES
U of Maryland, Coll Park (MD)
The U of Texas at Austin (TX)

IRISH STUDIES
Bard Coll (NY)
Canisius Coll (NY)

ISLAMIC STUDIES
Boston Coll (MA)
Connecticut Coll (CT)
The Ohio State U (OH)
Sarah Lawrence Coll (NY)
Swarthmore Coll (PA)
The U of Texas at Austin (TX)
U of Washington (WA)
Villanova U (PA)
Washington U in St. Louis (MO)

ITALIAN
The American U of Rome (Italy)
Arizona State U at the Tempe campus (AZ)
Bard Coll (NY)
Barnard Coll (NY)
Bennington Coll (VT)
Binghamton U, State U of New York (NY)
Bishop's U (QC, Canada)
Boston Coll (MA)
Brooklyn Coll of the City U of New York (NY)
Bryn Mawr Coll (PA)
Cabrini U (PA)
California State U, Long Beach (CA)
Central Connecticut State U (CT)
Coll of Staten Island of the City U of New York (NY)
Coll of the Holy Cross (MA)
The Colorado Coll (CO)
Columbia U (NY)
Columbia U, School of General Studies (NY)
Concordia U (QC, Canada)
Cornell U (NY)
Dartmouth Coll (NH)
Dominican U (IL)
Drew U (NJ)
Fairfield U (CT)
Florida Intl U (FL)
Fordham U (NY)
Georgetown U (DC)
Gettysburg Coll (PA)
Gonzaga U (WA)
Haverford Coll (PA)
Hofstra U (NY)
Hunter Coll of the City U of New York (NY)
Indiana U Bloomington (IN)
Iona Coll (NY)
Ithaca Coll (NY)
Johns Hopkins U (MD)
Lake Erie Coll (OH)
Lehman Coll of the City U of New York (NY)
Loyola U Chicago (IL)
Marist Coll (NY)
Middlebury Coll (VT)
Montclair State U (NJ)
Mount Holyoke Coll (MA)
Nazareth Coll of Rochester (NY)
Northwestern U (IL)
The Ohio State U (OH)
Penn State Abington (PA)
Penn State Altoona (PA)
Penn State Beaver (PA)
Penn State Berks (PA)
Penn State Brandywine (PA)
Penn State DuBois (PA)
Penn State Erie, The Behrend Coll (PA)
Penn State Fayette, The Eberly Campus (PA)
Penn State Greater Allegheny (PA)
Penn State Hazleton (PA)
Penn State Lehigh Valley (PA)
Penn State Mont Alto (PA)
Penn State New Kensington (PA)
Penn State Schuylkill (PA)
Penn State Shenango (PA)
Penn State U Park (PA)
Penn State Wilkes-Barre (PA)
Penn State Worthington Scranton (PA)
Penn State York (PA)
Pepperdine U, Malibu (CA)
Providence Coll (RI)
Queens Coll of the City U of New York (NY)
Rutgers U–Newark (NJ)
Rutgers U–New Brunswick (NJ)
St. John's U (NY)
Saint Joseph's U (PA)
Saint Mary's Coll of California (CA)
San Francisco State U (CA)
Santa Clara U (CA)
Sarah Lawrence Coll (NY)
Scripps Coll (CA)
Smith Coll (MA)
Southern Connecticut State U (CT)
Stanford U (CA)
Stony Brook U, State U of New York (NY)
Susquehanna U (PA)
Syracuse U (NY)
Temple U (PA)
Tufts U (MA)
Tulane U (LA)
U at Buffalo, the State U of New York (NY)
The U of Arizona (AZ)
U of California, Davis (CA)
U of California, Los Angeles (CA)
U of California, San Diego (CA)
U of Colorado Boulder (CO)
U of Delaware (DE)
U of Denver (CO)
U of Georgia (GA)
U of Houston (TX)
U of Illinois at Chicago (IL)
U of Maryland, Coll Park (MD)
U of Massachusetts Amherst (MA)
U of Massachusetts Boston (MA)
U of Michigan (MI)
U of Minnesota, Twin Cities Campus (MN)
U of New Hampshire (NH)
U of Notre Dame (IN)
U of Oklahoma (OK)
U of Oregon (OR)
U of Pennsylvania (PA)
U of Pittsburgh (PA)
U of Rhode Island (RI)
The U of Scranton (PA)
U of Southern California (CA)
U of South Florida (FL)
The U of Tennessee (TN)
The U of Texas at Austin (TX)
U of Toronto (ON, Canada)
U of Virginia (VA)
U of Washington (WA)
U of Windsor (ON, Canada)
U of Wisconsin–Madison (WI)
U of Wisconsin–Milwaukee (WI)
Vassar Coll (NY)
Villanova U (PA)
Washington U in St. Louis (MO)
York Coll of the City U of New York (NY)
Youngstown State U (OH)

ITALIAN STUDIES
Arcadia U (PA)
Assumption Coll (MA)
Bard Coll (NY)
Boston U (MA)
The Colorado Coll (CO)
Columbia U (NY)
Columbia U, School of General Studies (NY)
Connecticut Coll (CT)
Dalhousie U (NS, Canada)
Dickinson Coll (PA)
Emory U (GA)
Fordham U (NY)
Merrimack Coll (MA)
Miami U (OH)
Purdue U (IN)
Saint Joseph's U (PA)
Scripps Coll (CA)
Southern Methodist U (TX)
Tufts U (MA)
Tulane U (LA)
Université de Montréal (QC, Canada)
U of California, Santa Barbara (CA)
U of Richmond (VA)
U of San Diego (CA)
The U of Scranton (PA)
The U of Texas at Austin (TX)
U of Vermont (VT)
U of Windsor (ON, Canada)
Wesleyan U (CT)
Wheaton Coll (MA)

JAPANESE
Ball State U (IN)
Bard Coll (NY)
Bates Coll (ME)
Beloit Coll (WI)
Bennington Coll (VT)
Boston U (MA)
California State U, Fullerton (CA)
California State U, Long Beach (CA)
California State U, Monterey Bay (CA)
Calvin Coll (MI)
Carnegie Mellon U (PA)
Central Washington U (WA)
Colgate U (NY)
Dartmouth Coll (NH)
Eastern Michigan U (MI)
Elizabethtown Coll (PA)
Emory U (GA)
Georgetown U (DC)
Gettysburg Coll (PA)
Hobart and William Smith Colls (NY)
Hofstra U (NY)
Lawrence U (WI)
Linfield Coll (OR)
Macalester Coll (MN)
McMaster U (ON, Canada)
Michigan State U (MI)
Middlebury Coll (VT)
Murray State U (KY)
North Central Coll (IL)
Occidental Coll (CA)
The Ohio State U (OH)
Penn State Abington (PA)
Penn State Altoona (PA)
Penn State Beaver (PA)
Penn State Berks (PA)
Penn State Brandywine (PA)
Penn State DuBois (PA)
Penn State Erie, The Behrend Coll (PA)
Penn State Fayette, The Eberly Campus (PA)
Penn State Greater Allegheny (PA)
Penn State Hazleton (PA)
Penn State Lehigh Valley (PA)
Penn State Mont Alto (PA)
Penn State New Kensington (PA)
Penn State Schuylkill (PA)
Penn State Shenango (PA)
Penn State U Park (PA)
Penn State Wilkes-Barre (PA)
Penn State Worthington Scranton (PA)
Penn State York (PA)
Pomona Coll (CA)
Portland State U (OR)
Purdue U (IN)
San Diego State U (CA)
San Francisco State U (CA)
Sarah Lawrence Coll (NY)
Scripps Coll (CA)
Stanford U (CA)
Swarthmore Coll (PA)
Temple U (PA)
Tufts U (MA)
U of Alaska Fairbanks (AK)
U of California, Davis (CA)
U of California, Irvine (CA)
U of California, Los Angeles (CA)
U of California, San Diego (CA)
U of California, Santa Barbara (CA)
U of Colorado Boulder (CO)
The U of Findlay (OH)
U of Georgia (GA)
U of Hawaii at Manoa (HI)
U of Kentucky (KY)
U of Maryland, Coll Park (MD)
U of Massachusetts Amherst (MA)
U of Mount Union (OH)
The U of North Carolina at Charlotte (NC)
U of Notre Dame (IN)
U of Oklahoma (OK)
U of Oregon (OR)
U of Pittsburgh (PA)
U of Puget Sound (WA)
U of Regina (SK, Canada)
U of Rochester (NY)
U of San Francisco (CA)
U of the Pacific (CA)
U of Vermont (VT)
U of Washington (WA)
U of Wisconsin–Madison (WI)
Vassar Coll (NY)
Wake Forest U (NC)
Washington State U (WA)
Washington U in St. Louis (MO)
Western Michigan U (MI)
Western Washington U (WA)
Williams Coll (MA)

JAPANESE STUDIES
Case Western Reserve U (OH)
Earlham Coll (IN)
Gettysburg Coll (PA)
Hofstra U (NY)
Hope Coll (MI)
Linfield Coll (OR)
U at Albany, State U of New York (NY)
U of San Francisco (CA)
U of Washington (WA)
U of Wisconsin–Whitewater (WI)
Willamette U (OR)

JAZZ/JAZZ STUDIES
Ashland U (OH)
Bard Coll (NY)
Bennington Coll (VT)
Brigham Young U (UT)
Butler U (IN)
Capital U (OH)
Central State U (OH)
Central Washington U (WA)
City Coll of the City U of New York (NY)
Concordia U (QC, Canada)
Drake U (IA)
Eugene Lang Coll of Liberal Arts (NY)
Florida State U (FL)
Hampton U (VA)
Hofstra U (NY)
Hope Coll (MI)
Ithaca Coll (NY)
Jacksonville U (FL)
Liberty U (VA)
Limestone Coll (SC)
Lincoln Coll (IL)
Loyola U New Orleans (LA)
Michigan State U (MI)
Minnesota State U Moorhead (MN)
The New School Coll of Performing Arts (NY)
North Carolina Central U (NC)
North Central Coll (IL)
Northwestern U (IL)
Oberlin Coll (OH)
The Ohio State U (OH)
Rutgers U–New Brunswick (NJ)
St. Cloud State U (MN)
Shenandoah U (VA)
Temple U (PA)
Université de Montréal (QC, Canada)
The U of Akron (OH)
U of Hartford (CT)
U of Maryland, Baltimore County (MD)
U of Miami (FL)
U of Michigan (MI)
U of Missouri–Kansas City (MO)
U of North Carolina at Asheville (NC)
The U of North Carolina at Greensboro (NC)
U of Northern Iowa (IA)
U of North Florida (FL)
U of North Texas (TX)
U of Oregon (OR)
U of Rochester (NY)
U of Southern California (CA)
The U of Texas at Austin (TX)
U of Washington (WA)
Webster U (MO)
Western Michigan U (MI)
Whitman Coll (WA)
Youngstown State U (OH)

JEWISH/JUDAIC STUDIES
American U (DC)
Arizona State U at the Tempe campus (AZ)
Bard Coll (NY)
Barnard Coll (NY)
Bennington Coll (VT)
Binghamton U, State U of New York (NY)
Brooklyn Coll of the City U of New York (NY)
California State U, Northridge (CA)
City Coll of the City U of New York (NY)
Clark U (MA)
Coll of Charleston (SC)
Concordia U (QC, Canada)
Dickinson Coll (PA)
Emory U (GA)
Florida Atlantic U (FL)
The George Washington U (DC)
Gettysburg Coll (PA)
Hofstra U (NY)
Hunter Coll of the City U of New York (NY)
Indiana U Bloomington (IN)
Lehman Coll of the City U of New York (NY)
Muhlenberg Coll (PA)
Northeastern U (MA)
Oberlin Coll (OH)
The Ohio State U (OH)
Penn State Abington (PA)
Penn State Altoona (PA)
Penn State Beaver (PA)
Penn State Berks (PA)
Penn State Brandywine (PA)
Penn State DuBois (PA)
Penn State Erie, The Behrend Coll (PA)
Penn State Fayette, The Eberly Campus (PA)
Penn State Greater Allegheny (PA)
Penn State Hazleton (PA)
Penn State Lehigh Valley (PA)
Penn State Mont Alto (PA)
Penn State New Kensington (PA)
Penn State Schuylkill (PA)
Penn State Shenango (PA)
Penn State U Park (PA)
Penn State Wilkes-Barre (PA)
Penn State Worthington Scranton (PA)
Penn State York (PA)
Piedmont Intl U (NC)
Purdue U (IN)
Queens Coll of the City U of New York (NY)
Rutgers U–New Brunswick (NJ)
San Diego State U (CA)
San Francisco State U (CA)
Scripps Coll (CA)
Syracuse U (NY)
Temple U (PA)
Tufts U (MA)
Tulane U (LA)
U at Buffalo, the State U of New York (NY)
The U of Arizona (AZ)
U of California, Los Angeles (CA)
U of California, San Diego (CA)
U of Chicago (IL)
U of Colorado Boulder (CO)
U of Florida (FL)
U of Hartford (CT)
The U of Kansas (KS)
U of Maryland, Coll Park (MD)
U of Massachusetts Amherst (MA)
U of Miami (FL)
U of Michigan (MI)
U of Minnesota, Twin Cities Campus (MN)
U of Oklahoma (OK)
U of Oregon (OR)
U of Pennsylvania (PA)
U of Southern California (CA)
The U of Texas at Austin (TX)
U of Washington (WA)
U of Wisconsin–Madison (WI)
U of Wisconsin–Milwaukee (WI)
Vanderbilt U (TN)
Vassar Coll (NY)
Washington U in St. Louis (MO)

JOURNALISM
Acad of Art U (CA)
Alderson Broaddus U (WV)
American U (DC)
American U in Bulgaria (Bulgaria)
The American U in Cairo (Egypt)
The American U in Dubai (United Arab Emirates)

The American U of Paris (France)
Andrews U (MI)
Angelo State U (TX)
Appalachian State U (NC)
Arizona State U at the Downtown Phoenix campus (AZ)
Arkansas Tech U (AR)
Asbury U (KY)
Ashland U (OH)
Auburn U (AL)
Augustana U (SD)
Averett U (VA)
Ball State U (IN)
Barry U (FL)
Baruch Coll of the City U of New York (NY)
Bayamón Central U (PR)
Baylor U (TX)
Belmont U (TN)
Bemidji State U (MN)
Benedictine Coll (KS)
Bethel U (MN)
Biola U (CA)
Boston U (MA)
Bowling Green State U (OH)
Bradley U (IL)
Brigham Young U (UT)
Brooklyn Coll of the City U of New York (NY)
Buffalo State Coll, State U of New York (NY)
Butler U (IN)
California Baptist U (CA)
California Lutheran U (CA)
California Polytechnic State U, San Luis Obispo (CA)
California State U, Chico (CA)
California State U, Dominguez Hills (CA)
California State U, East Bay (CA)
California State U, Fresno (CA)
California State U, Fullerton (CA)
California State U, Long Beach (CA)
California State U, Northridge (CA)
California State U, Sacramento (CA)
Campbellsville U (KY)
Canisius Coll (NY)
Cedarville U (OH)
Central Connecticut State U (CT)
Central Michigan U (MI)
Central State U (OH)
Central Washington U (WA)
Chatham U (PA)
Cleveland State U (OH)
The Coll of New Jersey (NJ)
The Coll of St. Scholastica (MN)
Coll of the Ozarks (MO)
Colorado State U (CO)
Columbia Coll Chicago (IL)
Concordia U (QC, Canada)
Concordia U Chicago (IL)
Concordia U, St. Paul (MN)
Concord U (WV)
Corban U (OR)
Cornerstone U (MI)
Creighton U (NE)
Doane U (NE)
Dominican U (IL)
Drake U (IA)
Drury U (MO)
Duquesne U (PA)
East Central U (OK)
Eastern Illinois U (IL)
Eastern Michigan U (MI)
Eastern Nazarene Coll (MA)
Eastern Washington U (WA)
Elon U (NC)
Emerson Coll (MA)
Flagler Coll (FL)
Florida Ag and Mech U (FL)
Franklin Coll (IN)
Franklin Pierce U (NH)
Freed-Hardeman U (TN)
Gannon U (PA)
Gardner-Webb U (NC)
George Fox U (OR)
The George Washington U (DC)
Georgia Coll & State U (GA)
Georgia Southern U (GA)
Georgia State U (GA)
Gettysburg Coll (PA)
Gonzaga U (WA)
Goshen Coll (IN)
Grace Coll (IN)
Grand Valley State U (MI)
Grand View U (IA)
Hampton U (VA)
Harding U (AR)
Henderson State U (AR)
Hofstra U (NY)
Humboldt State U (CA)
Huntington U (IN)
Illinois State U (IL)
Indiana U Bloomington (IN)
Indiana U of Pennsylvania (PA)
Indiana U–Purdue U Indianapolis (IN)
Indiana U Southeast (IN)
Iona Coll (NY)
Iowa State U of Science and Technology (IA)
Ithaca Coll (NY)
Kansas State U (KS)
Keene State Coll (NH)
Kennesaw State U (GA)
Kent State U (OH)
Lebanese American U (Lebanon)
Lee U (TN)
Lehigh U (PA)
Lewis U (IL)
Liberty U (VA)
Lincoln U (MO)
Lincoln U (PA)
Lindenwood U (MO)
Louisiana Coll (LA)
Louisiana Tech U (LA)
Loyola U Chicago (IL)
Loyola U New Orleans (LA)
Lubbock Christian U (TX)
Madonna U (MI)
Marietta Coll (OH)
Marshall U (WV)
Massachusetts Coll of Liberal Arts (MA)
Mercer U, Macon (GA)
Messiah Coll (PA)
Metropolitan State U of Denver (CO)
Miami U (OH)
Michigan State U (MI)
Minnesota State U Mankato (MN)
Minnesota State U Moorhead (MN)
Missouri State U (MO)
Montclair State U (NJ)
Mount Mercy U (IA)
Mount Saint Mary's U (CA)
Mount Vernon Nazarene U (OH)
Murray State U (KY)
Muskingum U (OH)
New England Coll (NH)
New Mexico State U (NM)
North Central Coll (IL)
Northeastern State U (OK)
Northeastern U (MA)
Northern Arizona U (AZ)
Northern Illinois U (IL)
Northern Kentucky U (KY)
North Greenville U (SC)
Northwestern Coll (IA)
Northwestern U (IL)
The Ohio State U (OH)
Ohio U (OH)
Ohio Wesleyan U (OH)
Oklahoma Baptist U (OK)
Oklahoma Christian U (OK)
Otterbein U (OH)
Pace U, Pleasantville Campus (NY)
Palm Beach Atlantic U (FL)
Patrick Henry Coll (VA)
Penn State Abington (PA)
Penn State Altoona (PA)
Penn State Beaver (PA)
Penn State Berks (PA)
Penn State Brandywine (PA)
Penn State DuBois (PA)
Penn State Erie, The Behrend Coll (PA)
Penn State Fayette, The Eberly Campus (PA)
Penn State Greater Allegheny (PA)
Penn State Hazleton (PA)
Penn State Lehigh Valley (PA)
Penn State Mont Alto (PA)
Penn State New Kensington (PA)
Penn State Schuylkill (PA)
Penn State Shenango (PA)
Penn State U Park (PA)
Penn State Wilkes-Barre (PA)
Penn State Worthington Scranton (PA)
Penn State York (PA)
Pepperdine U, Malibu (CA)
Point Loma Nazarene U (CA)
Point Park U (PA)
Purchase Coll, State U of New York (NY)
Quinnipiac U (CT)
Radford U (VA)
Rochester Inst of Technology (NY)
Rowan U (NJ)
Rust Coll (MS)
Rutgers U–Newark (NJ)
Rutgers U–New Brunswick (NJ)
St. Ambrose U (IA)
Saint Augustine's U (NC)
St. Bonaventure U (NY)
St. Catherine U (MN)
St. Cloud State U (MN)
Saint Francis U (PA)
St. John's U (NY)
St. Joseph's Coll, Long Island Campus (NY)
St. Joseph's Coll, New York (NY)
St. Thomas Aquinas Coll (NY)
St. Thomas U (NB, Canada)
Samford U (AL)
Sam Houston State U (TX)
San Diego State U (CA)
San Francisco State U (CA)
Seattle U (WA)
Seton Hill U (PA)
Shippensburg U of Pennsylvania (PA)
South Dakota State U (SD)
Southern Arkansas U–Magnolia (AR)
Southern Connecticut State U (CT)
Southern Illinois U Carbondale (IL)
Southern Methodist U (TX)
Southwestern Adventist U (TX)
Southwestern Coll (KS)
Spring Hill Coll (AL)
State U of New York at New Paltz (NY)
State U of New York at Oswego (NY)
State U of New York at Plattsburgh (NY)
Stony Brook U, State U of New York (NY)
Suffolk U (MA)
Syracuse U (NY)
Taylor U (IN)
Temple U (PA)
Texas A&M U–Commerce (TX)
Texas Christian U (TX)
Texas State U (TX)
Texas Tech U (TX)
Texas Wesleyan U (TX)
Tiffin U (OH)
Trent U (ON, Canada)
Trevecca Nazarene U (TN)
Troy U (AL)
Union U (TN)
United States Intl U–Africa (Kenya)
U at Albany, State U of New York (NY)
The U of Alabama (AL)
U of Alaska Fairbanks (AK)
The U of Arizona (AZ)
U of Arkansas (AR)
U of Bridgeport (CT)
U of Central Arkansas (AR)
U of Central Florida (FL)
U of Central Missouri (MO)
U of Cincinnati (OH)
U of Denver (CO)
The U of Findlay (OH)
U of Florida (FL)
U of Georgia (GA)
U of Hawaii at Manoa (HI)
U of Houston (TX)
U of Idaho (ID)
The U of Kansas (KS)
U of Kentucky (KY)
U of King's Coll (NS, Canada)
U of La Verne (CA)
U of Maine (ME)
U of Maryland, Coll Park (MD)
U of Massachusetts Amherst (MA)
U of Miami (FL)
U of Minnesota, Duluth (MN)
U of Minnesota, Twin Cities Campus (MN)
U of Nebraska at Kearney (NE)
U of Nevada, Reno (NV)
The U of North Carolina at Chapel Hill (NC)
U of Northern Colorado (CO)
U of North Texas (TX)
U of Oklahoma (OK)
U of Oregon (OR)
U of Pittsburgh at Greensburg (PA)
U of Pittsburgh at Johnstown (PA)
U of Regina (SK, Canada)
U of Rhode Island (RI)
U of Richmond (VA)
U of South Carolina (SC)
U of Southern California (CA)
U of Southern Indiana (IN)
U of Southern Mississippi (MS)
The U of Tennessee (TN)
The U of Texas at Austin (TX)
The U of Texas at El Paso (TX)
U of the Cumberlands (KY)
U of the Incarnate Word (TX)
U of Washington (WA)
U of West Georgia (GA)
U of Wisconsin–Eau Claire (WI)
U of Wisconsin–Madison (WI)
U of Wisconsin–Superior (WI)
U of Wisconsin–Whitewater (WI)
Utah State U (UT)
Utica Coll (NY)
Walla Walla U (WA)
Wartburg Coll (IA)
Washington and Lee U (VA)
Washington U in St. Louis (MO)
Waynesburg U (PA)
Wayne State U (MI)
Weber State U (UT)
Webster U (MO)
Western Illinois U (IL)
Western Kentucky U (KY)
Western Michigan U (MI)
Western Washington U (WA)
West Texas A&M U (TX)
West Virginia U (WV)
Whitworth U (WA)
Youngstown State U (OH)

JOURNALISM RELATED

Abilene Christian U (TX)
Arizona State U at the Downtown Phoenix campus (AZ)
Bennett Coll (NC)
Bowling Green State U (OH)
California State U, Long Beach (CA)
Calvary U (MO)
Central Michigan U (MI)
Concordia Coll (MN)
Fairfield U (CT)
Florida Inst of Technology (FL)
Kentucky State U (KY)
Marymount Manhattan Coll (NY)
Missouri Baptist U (MO)
Oklahoma State U (OK)
Simpson Coll (IA)
Southeastern U (FL)
Syracuse U (NY)
The U of Akron (OH)
U of California, Irvine (CA)
U of Colorado Boulder (CO)
U of Georgia (GA)
Webster U (MO)
Western Washington U (WA)
Westminster Coll (PA)
Wilson Coll (PA)

JUVENILE CORRECTIONS

Harris-Stowe State U (MO)
Prairie View A&M U (TX)

KEYBOARD INSTRUMENTS

Abilene Christian U (TX)
Anderson U (SC)
Andrews U (MI)
Ashland U (OH)
Baldwin Wallace U (OH)
Barry U (FL)
Boston U (MA)
Bowling Green State U (OH)
Brigham Young U (UT)
California Baptist U (CA)
Calvary U (MO)
Campbellsville U (KY)
Capital U (OH)
Carson-Newman U (TN)
The Catholic U of America (DC)
Central Washington U (WA)
Chapman U (CA)
Coll of the Ozarks (MO)
Converse Coll (SC)
Dallas Baptist U (TX)
Drake U (IA)
East Central U (OK)
Eastern Nazarene Coll (MA)
East Texas Baptist U (TX)
Furman U (SC)
Hardin-Simmons U (TX)
Heidelberg U (OH)
Hope Coll (MI)
Houghton Coll (NY)
Houston Baptist U (TX)
Howard Payne U (TX)
Illinois Wesleyan U (IL)
Ithaca Coll (NY)
Jacksonville U (FL)
Lawrence U (WI)
Liberty U (VA)
Lipscomb U (TN)
Madonna U (MI)
The Master's U (CA)
Mount Allison U (NB, Canada)
The New School Coll of Performing Arts (NY)
Northwestern U (IL)
Nyack Coll (NY)
Oberlin Coll (OH)
The Ohio State U (OH)
Ohio U (OH)
Oklahoma City U (OK)
Oral Roberts U (OK)
Ouachita Baptist U (AR)
Palm Beach Atlantic U (FL)
Point Loma Nazarene U (CA)
Roberts Wesleyan Coll (NY)
St. Cloud State U (MN)
Samford U (AL)
San Francisco Conservatory of Music (CA)
Shenandoah U (VA)
Shorter U (GA)
Southeastern U (FL)
Southern Methodist U (TX)
State U of New York at Fredonia (NY)
Syracuse U (NY)
Texas Christian U (TX)
Union U (TN)
The U of Akron (OH)
U of Cincinnati (OH)
U of Delaware (DE)
The U of Kansas (KS)
U of Miami (FL)
U of Southern California (CA)
The U of Tennessee at Martin (TN)
U of the Pacific (CA)
The U of Tulsa (OK)
U of Washington (WA)
Valparaiso U (IN)
Vanderbilt U (TN)
Walla Walla U (WA)
Weber State U (UT)
Western Michigan U (MI)
Whitworth U (WA)
Wichita State U (KS)
Willamette U (OR)
Xavier U of Louisiana (LA)
Youngstown State U (OH)

KINDERGARTEN/PRESCHOOL EDUCATION

Arcadia U (PA)
Ashland U (OH)
Athens State U (AL)
Barry U (FL)
Bayamón Central U (PR)
Baylor U (TX)
Black Hills State U (SD)
Bluefield Coll (VA)
Bluffton U (OH)
Bowie State U (MD)
Bowling Green State U (OH)
Bucknell U (PA)
Buffalo State Coll, State U of New York (NY)
Cabrini U (PA)
Cairn U (PA)
California Polytechnic State U, San Luis Obispo (CA)
Carson-Newman U (TN)
Catawba Coll (NC)
Central Connecticut State U (CT)
Central Methodist U (MO)
Concordia U (QC, Canada)
Concordia U Wisconsin (WI)
Concord U (WV)
Converse Coll (SC)
East Carolina U (NC)
Eastern Illinois U (IL)
Eastern Nazarene Coll (MA)
Elizabeth City State U (NC)

Evangel U (MO)
Furman U (SC)
Georgia State U (GA)
Hampton U (VA)
Humboldt State U (CA)
Hunter Coll of the City U of New York (NY)
Illinois State U (IL)
Inter American U of Puerto Rico, Aguadilla Campus (PR)
Inter American U of Puerto Rico, Barranquitas Campus (PR)
Inter American U of Puerto Rico, Guayama Campus (PR)
Inter American U of Puerto Rico, Metropolitan Campus (PR)
Inter American U of Puerto Rico, Ponce Campus (PR)
Inter American U of Puerto Rico, San Germán Campus (PR)
Jacksonville State U (AL)
John Carroll U (OH)
Kean U (NJ)
Lees-McRae Coll (NC)
Lesley U (MA)
Louisiana Tech U (LA)
Mansfield U of Pennsylvania (PA)
Marshall U (WV)
Martin Luther Coll (MN)
Michigan State U (MI)
Minnesota State U Mankato (MN)
Mississippi Valley State U (MS)
New Jersey City U (NJ)
New Mexico Highlands U (NM)
North Carolina Central U (NC)
Northern Illinois U (IL)
Northern Kentucky U (KY)
Northwestern Oklahoma State U (OK)
Ohio Wesleyan U (OH)
Oklahoma Baptist U (OK)
Oklahoma Christian U (OK)
Olivet Nazarene U (IL)
Philander Smith Coll (AR)
Piedmont Coll (GA)
Piedmont Intl U (NC)
St. Catherine U (MN)
St. Cloud State U (MN)
St. Thomas Aquinas Coll (NY)
Shaw U (NC)
Southeastern Oklahoma State U (OK)
State U of New York at Fredonia (NY)
State U of New York Coll at Cortland (NY)
State U of New York Coll of Agriculture and Technology at Cobleskill (NY)
Susquehanna U (PA)
Tennessee State U (TN)
Thomas U (GA)
Tufts U (MA)
Union U (TN)
Université de Montréal (QC, Canada)
Université de Sherbrooke (QC, Canada)
The U of Arizona (AZ)
U of Arkansas (AR)
U of Central Arkansas (AR)
U of Georgia (GA)
U of Great Falls (MT)
U of Maine at Farmington (ME)
U of Maryland, Coll Park (MD)
U of Minnesota, Crookston (MN)
U of Minnesota, Duluth (MN)
U of Minnesota, Twin Cities Campus (MN)
The U of North Carolina at Charlotte (NC)
The U of North Carolina at Pembroke (NC)
The U of North Carolina Wilmington (NC)
U of Northern Iowa (IA)
U of Regina (SK, Canada)
The U of Tennessee at Martin (TN)
The U of Toledo (OH)
U of Vermont (VT)
U of Windsor (ON, Canada)
U of Wisconsin–Stevens Point (WI)
Utah State U (UT)
Virginia Union U (VA)
Wagner Coll (NY)
Walsh U (OH)
Wartburg Coll (IA)
Western Carolina U (NC)
Westfield State U (MA)
West Virginia Wesleyan Coll (WV)
Widener U (PA)
Williams Baptist Coll (AR)

KINESIOLOGY AND EXERCISE SCIENCE

Adams State U (CO)
Albion Coll (MI)
Alderson Broaddus U (WV)
American Public U System (WV)
Anderson U (SC)
Angelo State U (TX)
Appalachian State U (NC)
Arizona State U at the Downtown Phoenix campus (AZ)
Asbury U (KY)
Auburn U at Montgomery (AL)
Augsburg Coll (MN)
Augustana U (SD)
Augusta U (GA)
Aurora U (IL)
Avila U (MO)
Baker U (KS)
Ball State U (IN)
Barry U (FL)
Barton Coll (NC)
Baylor U (TX)
Becker Coll (MA)
Belhaven U (MS)
Bellarmine U (KY)
Belmont U (TN)
Berea Coll (KY)
Berry Coll (GA)
Bethel Coll (IN)
Bethel U (MN)
Biola U (CA)
Bluefield Coll (VA)
Blue Mountain Coll (MS)
Boise State U (ID)
Bridgewater State U (MA)
Brigham Young U (UT)
Buffalo State Coll, State U of New York (NY)
Cabrini U (PA)
California Baptist U (CA)
California Lutheran U (CA)
California State U, Chico (CA)
California State U, East Bay (CA)
California State U, Long Beach (CA)
California State U, Northridge (CA)
California State U, Sacramento (CA)
California State U, San Marcos (CA)
Calvin Coll (MI)
Capital U (OH)
Carson-Newman U (TN)
Catawba Coll (NC)
Cedarville U (OH)
Central Baptist Coll (AR)
Central Connecticut State U (CT)
Central Michigan U (MI)
Central Washington U (WA)
Chatham U (PA)
Chowan U (NC)
The Citadel, The Military Coll of South Carolina (SC)
Coastal Carolina U (SC)
Colby-Sawyer Coll (NH)
The Coll at Brockport, State U of New York (NY)
The Coll of Idaho (ID)
Colorado Mesa U (CO)
Colorado State U (CO)
Columbus State U (GA)
Concordia U (QC, Canada)
Concordia U Chicago (IL)
Concordia U, Nebraska (NE)
Concordia U, St. Paul (MN)
Corban U (OR)
Cornell Coll (IA)
Cornerstone U (MI)
Creighton U (NE)
Dakota State U (SD)
Dalhousie U (NS, Canada)
Defiance Coll (OH)
DePauw U (IN)
DeSales U (PA)
Dickinson State U (ND)
Drury U (MO)
East Central U (OK)
Eastern Illinois U (IL)
Eastern Mennonite U (VA)
Eastern Michigan U (MI)
Eastern U (PA)
Eastern Washington U (WA)
East Stroudsburg U of Pennsylvania (PA)
East Texas Baptist U (TX)
Elon U (NC)
Emmanuel Coll (GA)
Endicott Coll (MA)
Eureka Coll (IL)
Fitchburg State U (MA)
Florida Atlantic U (FL)
Florida Gulf Coast U (FL)
Florida State U (FL)
Franklin Coll (IN)
Freed-Hardeman U (TN)
Frostburg State U (MD)
Gannon U (PA)
Georgetown Coll (KY)
The George Washington U (DC)
Georgia Coll & State U (GA)
Georgia Gwinnett Coll (GA)
Georgian Court U (NJ)
Georgia Southern U (GA)
Gonzaga U (WA)
Goshen Coll (IN)
Grace Coll (IN)
Grand View U (IA)
Greenville Coll (IL)
Grove City Coll (PA)
Guilford Coll (NC)
Hamline U (MN)
Hannibal-LaGrange U (MO)
Hanover Coll (IN)
Harding U (AR)
Hardin-Simmons U (TX)
High Point U (NC)
Hillsdale Coll (MI)
Hiram Coll (OH)
Hope Coll (MI)
Houston Baptist U (TX)
Humboldt State U (CA)
Huntingdon Coll (AL)
Huntington U (IN)
Husson U (ME)
Huston-Tillotson U (TX)
Illinois State U (IL)
Immaculata U (PA)
Indiana State U (IN)
Indiana U Bloomington (IN)
Indiana U–Purdue U Indianapolis (IN)
Iowa State U of Science and Technology (IA)
Iowa Wesleyan U (IA)
Ithaca Coll (NY)
Jacksonville State U (AL)
Jacksonville U (FL)
John Brown U (AR)
Kansas State U (KS)
Kansas Wesleyan U (KS)
Kennesaw State U (GA)
Kent State U (OH)
Kentucky State U (KY)
Kentucky Wesleyan Coll (KY)
King's Coll (PA)
Kuyper Coll (MI)
LaGrange Coll (GA)
Lamar U (TX)
La Roche Coll (PA)
Lasell Coll (MA)
Lebanon Valley Coll (PA)
Lee U (TN)
Lenoir-Rhyne U (NC)
LeTourneau U (TX)
Lewis U (IL)
Liberty U (VA)
Life U (GA)
Lincoln Coll (IL)
Lindenwood U (MO)
Linfield Coll (OR)
Lipscomb U (TN)
Longwood U (VA)
Loras Coll (IA)
Louisiana Coll (LA)
Malone U (OH)
Manchester U (IN)
Marian U (IN)
Marian U (WI)
Marshall U (WV)
Maryville U of Saint Louis (MO)
The Master's U (CA)
McDaniel Coll (MD)
McKendree U (IL)
McMaster U (ON, Canada)
McMurry U (TX)
McNeese State U (LA)
Mercy Coll (NY)
Meredith Coll (NC)
Miami U (OH)
Michigan State U (MI)
Michigan Technological U (MI)
MidAmerica Nazarene U (KS)
Minnesota State U Moorhead (MN)
Missouri Baptist U (MO)
Missouri State U (MO)
Missouri Valley Coll (MO)
Monmouth Coll (IL)
Montclair State U (NJ)
Morehead State U (KY)
Morrisville State Coll (NY)
Mount Vernon Nazarene U (OH)
Murray State U (KY)
Nebraska Wesleyan U (NE)
New Mexico State U (NM)
North Carolina Wesleyan Coll (NC)
North Central Coll (IL)
North Dakota State U (ND)
Northeastern State U (OK)
Northern Arizona U (AZ)
Northwestern Coll (IA)
Nova Southeastern U (FL)
Occidental Coll (CA)
Ohio Dominican U (OH)
The Ohio State U (OH)
Oklahoma Baptist U (OK)
Oklahoma State U (OK)
Olivet Nazarene U (IL)
Oral Roberts U (OK)
Oregon State U (OR)
Ouachita Baptist U (AR)
Our Lady of the Lake U of San Antonio (TX)
Pacific Lutheran U (WA)
Palm Beach Atlantic U (FL)
Penn State Abington (PA)
Penn State Altoona (PA)
Penn State Beaver (PA)
Penn State Berks (PA)
Penn State Brandywine (PA)
Penn State DuBois (PA)
Penn State Erie, The Behrend Coll (PA)
Penn State Fayette, The Eberly Campus (PA)
Penn State Greater Allegheny (PA)
Penn State Hazleton (PA)
Penn State Lehigh Valley (PA)
Penn State Mont Alto (PA)
Penn State New Kensington (PA)
Penn State Schuylkill (PA)
Penn State Shenango (PA)
Penn State U Park (PA)
Penn State Wilkes-Barre (PA)
Penn State Worthington Scranton (PA)
Penn State York (PA)
Pepperdine U, Malibu (CA)
Piedmont Coll (GA)
Pittsburg State U (KS)
Plymouth State U (NH)
Point U (GA)
Prairie View A&M U (TX)
Purdue U (IN)
Queens Coll of the City U of New York (NY)
Redeemer U Coll (ON, Canada)
Regis U (CO)
Rice U (TX)
Roanoke Coll (VA)
Roberts Wesleyan Coll (NY)
Rockford U (IL)
Rocky Mountain Coll (MT)
Rutgers U–New Brunswick (NJ)
Saginaw Valley State U (MI)
Saint Augustine's U (NC)
St. Cloud State U (MN)
St. Edward's U (TX)
St. Gregory's U, Shawnee (OK)
Saint Louis U (MO)
Saint Mary's Coll of California (CA)
St. Olaf Coll (MN)
Salisbury U (MD)
Samford U (AL)
Sam Houston State U (TX)
San Diego State U (CA)
San Francisco State U (CA)
Schreiner U (TX)
Seattle Pacific U (WA)
Seattle U (WA)
Seton Hill U (PA)
Shaw U (NC)
Shippensburg U of Pennsylvania (PA)
Simmons Coll (MA)
Simon Fraser U (BC, Canada)
Simpson Coll (IA)
Sonoma State U (CA)
Southeastern U (FL)
Southern Arkansas U–Magnolia (AR)
Southern Illinois U Carbondale (IL)
Southern Illinois U Edwardsville (IL)
Southern Utah U (UT)
Southwest Baptist U (MO)
Southwestern Adventist U (TX)
Southwestern U (TX)
State U of New York Coll at Cortland (NY)
Stephen F. Austin State U (TX)
Stockton U (NJ)
Syracuse U (NY)
Tabor Coll (KS)
Tarleton State U (TX)
Taylor U (IN)
Temple U (PA)
Tennessee Wesleyan U (TN)
Texas A&M Intl U (TX)
Texas A&M U (TX)
Texas A&M U–Commerce (TX)
Texas A&M U–Corpus Christi (TX)
Texas A&M U–Kingsville (TX)
Texas Lutheran U (TX)
Texas State U (TX)
Texas Tech U (TX)
Texas Wesleyan U (TX)
Texas Woman's U (TX)
Towson U (MD)
Transylvania U (KY)
Trent U (ON, Canada)
Trinity Christian Coll (IL)
Troy U (AL)
Truett McConnell U (GA)
Truman State U (MO)
Tusculum Coll (TN)
Union Coll (KY)
Union Coll (NE)
Union U (TN)
United States Military Acad (NY)
United States Sports Acad (AL)
Université de Montréal (QC, Canada)
Université de Sherbrooke (QC, Canada)
U of Central Arkansas (AR)
U of Dayton (OH)
U of Delaware (DE)
U of Dubuque (IA)
U of Evansville (IN)
U of Georgia (GA)
U of Guelph (ON, Canada)
U of Hawaii at Manoa (HI)
U of Houston (TX)
U of Houston–Clear Lake (TX)
U of Illinois at Chicago (IL)
U of Illinois at Springfield (IL)
U of Indianapolis (IN)
U of Jamestown (ND)
The U of Kansas (KS)
U of La Verne (CA)
U of Lethbridge (AB, Canada)
U of Louisiana at Monroe (LA)
U of Mary Hardin-Baylor (TX)
U of Maryland, Coll Park (MD)
U of Michigan (MI)
U of Minnesota, Duluth (MN)
U of Mount Union (OH)
U of Nevada, Las Vegas (NV)
U of New England (ME)
U of New Hampshire (NH)
The U of North Carolina at Greensboro (NC)
The U of North Carolina Wilmington (NC)
U of North Dakota (ND)
U of Northern Colorado (CO)
U of North Texas (TX)
U of Oklahoma (OK)
U of Pittsburgh at Bradford (PA)
U of Puget Sound (WA)
U of Regina (SK, Canada)
U of Rhode Island (RI)
U of San Francisco (CA)
U of Saskatchewan (SK, Canada)
The U of Scranton (PA)
U of South Carolina (SC)
U of South Carolina Aiken (SC)
U of Southern Indiana (IN)
The U of Tennessee (TN)
The U of Tennessee at Chattanooga (TN)

The U of Texas at Austin (TX)
The U of Texas at San Antonio (TX)
The U of Texas of the Permian Basin (TX)
The U of Texas Rio Grande Valley (TX)
U of the Fraser Valley (BC, Canada)
U of the Incarnate Word (TX)
U of the Pacific (CA)
The U of Toledo (OH)
The U of Tulsa (OK)
U of Utah (UT)
U of Vermont (VT)
U of Virginia (VA)
U of Waterloo (ON, Canada)
The U of West Alabama (AL)
U of Windsor (ON, Canada)
U of Wisconsin–Eau Claire (WI)
U of Wisconsin–La Crosse (WI)
U of Wisconsin–Madison (WI)
U of Wisconsin–Milwaukee (WI)
U of Wisconsin–Parkside (WI)
U of Wisconsin–Superior (WI)
Upper Iowa U (IA)
Valparaiso U (IN)
Viterbo U (WI)
Wake Forest U (NC)
Walla Walla U (WA)
Walsh U (OH)
Washington State U (WA)
Waynesburg U (PA)
Webster U (MO)
Western Illinois U (IL)
Western Kentucky U (KY)
Western Michigan U (MI)
Western Oregon U (OR)
Western State Colorado U (CO)
Western Washington U (WA)
Westmont Coll (CA)
West Texas A&M U (TX)
West Virginia Wesleyan Coll (WV)
Wheeling Jesuit U (WV)
Whittier Coll (CA)
Whitworth U (WA)
Wichita State U (KS)
Willamette U (OR)
William Paterson U of New Jersey (NJ)
William Penn U (IA)
William Woods U (MO)
Wingate U (NC)
Winona State U (MN)
Wright State U (OH)
Wright State U–Lake Campus (OH)
Youngstown State U (OH)

KINESIOTHERAPY
Boston U (MA)
Bridgewater State U (MA)
California State U, Long Beach (CA)
Shaw U (NC)

KNOWLEDGE MANAGEMENT
Framingham State U (MA)
Saint Joseph's U (PA)
Syracuse U (NY)

KOREAN
Brigham Young U (UT)
The Ohio State U (OH)
U of California, Irvine (CA)
U of California, Los Angeles (CA)
U of Hawaii at Manoa (HI)
U of Washington (WA)

KOREAN STUDIES
U of Washington (WA)

LABOR AND INDUSTRIAL RELATIONS
Bowling Green State U (OH)
Clarion U of Pennsylvania (PA)
Cleveland State U (OH)
Cornell U (NY)
Ithaca Coll (NY)
McMaster U (ON, Canada)
Penn State Abington (PA)
Penn State Altoona (PA)
Penn State Beaver (PA)
Penn State Berks (PA)
Penn State Brandywine (PA)
Penn State DuBois (PA)
Penn State Erie, The Behrend Coll (PA)
Penn State Fayette, The Eberly Campus (PA)
Penn State Greater Allegheny (PA)
Penn State Hazleton (PA)
Penn State Lehigh Valley (PA)
Penn State Mont Alto (PA)
Penn State New Kensington (PA)
Penn State Schuylkill (PA)
Penn State Shenango (PA)
Penn State U Park (PA)
Penn State Wilkes-Barre (PA)
Penn State Worthington Scranton (PA)
Penn State York (PA)
Rutgers U–New Brunswick (NJ)
Saint Francis U (PA)
San Francisco State U (CA)
State U of New York at Fredonia (NY)
State U of New York Coll at Old Westbury (NY)
State U of New York Empire State Coll (NY)
Université de Montréal (QC, Canada)
U of Bridgeport (CT)
U of Massachusetts Boston (MA)
U of Minnesota, Twin Cities Campus (MN)
U of Toronto (ON, Canada)
Wayne State U (MI)

LABOR STUDIES
California State U, Dominguez Hills (CA)
Eastern Michigan U (MI)
Goddard Coll (VT)
Hofstra U (NY)
Indiana U Bloomington (IN)
Indiana U Kokomo (IN)
Indiana U Northwest (IN)
Indiana U–Purdue U Indianapolis (IN)
Indiana U South Bend (IN)
Queens Coll of the City U of New York (NY)
U of Windsor (ON, Canada)

LANDSCAPE ARCHITECTURE
Acad of Art U (CA)
American U of Beirut (Lebanon)
Arizona State U at the Tempe campus (AZ)
Ball State U (IN)
Boston Architectural Coll (MA)
California Polytechnic State U, San Luis Obispo (CA)
California State Polytechnic U, Pomona (CA)
Clemson U (SC)
Coll of the Atlantic (ME)
Colorado State U (CO)
Cornell U (NY)
Iowa State U of Science and Technology (IA)
Louisiana State U and A&M Coll (LA)
Michigan State U (MI)
Mississippi State U (MS)
North Dakota State U (ND)
Northeastern U (MA)
The Ohio State U (OH)
Oklahoma State U (OK)
Penn State Brandywine (PA)
Penn State Lehigh Valley (PA)
Penn State Schuylkill (PA)
Penn State U Park (PA)
Penn State Wilkes-Barre (PA)
Purdue U (IN)
Rutgers U–New Brunswick (NJ)
South Dakota State U (SD)
State U of New York Coll of Environmental Science and Forestry (NY)
Temple U (PA)
Texas A&M U (TX)
Texas Tech U (TX)
Université de Montréal (QC, Canada)
U of Arkansas (AR)
U of California, Davis (CA)
U of Delaware (DE)
U of Florida (FL)
U of Georgia (GA)
U of Idaho (ID)
U of Kentucky (KY)
U of Maryland, Coll Park (MD)
U of Massachusetts Amherst (MA)
U of Nevada, Las Vegas (NV)
U of Oregon (OR)
U of Rhode Island (RI)
The U of Texas at Austin (TX)
U of Washington (WA)
U of Wisconsin–Madison (WI)
Utah State U (UT)
Virginia Polytechnic Inst and State U (VA)
Washington State U (WA)
West Virginia U (WV)

LANDSCAPING AND GROUNDSKEEPING
Andrews U (MI)
Mississippi State U (MS)
Oklahoma State U (OK)
Penn State Abington (PA)
Penn State Altoona (PA)
Penn State Beaver (PA)
Penn State Berks (PA)
Penn State Brandywine (PA)
Penn State DuBois (PA)
Penn State Erie, The Behrend Coll (PA)
Penn State Fayette, The Eberly Campus (PA)
Penn State Greater Allegheny (PA)
Penn State Hazleton (PA)
Penn State Lehigh Valley (PA)
Penn State Mont Alto (PA)
Penn State New Kensington (PA)
Penn State Schuylkill (PA)
Penn State Shenango (PA)
Penn State U Park (PA)
Penn State Wilkes-Barre (PA)
Penn State Worthington Scranton (PA)
Penn State York (PA)
State U of New York Coll of Agriculture and Technology at Cobleskill (NY)
U of Minnesota, Crookston (MN)
Washington State U (WA)

LAND USE PLANNING AND MANAGEMENT
California State U, Bakersfield (CA)
Central Michigan U (MI)
Marietta Coll (OH)
Metropolitan State U of Denver (CO)
Montana State U (MT)
U of Saskatchewan (SK, Canada)
West Virginia U (WV)

LANGUAGE INTERPRETATION AND TRANSLATION
Brigham Young U (UT)
Concordia U (QC, Canada)
Grace Coll (IN)
Kent State U (OH)
Lebanese American U (Lebanon)
Northwestern Coll (IA)
Oklahoma State U–Oklahoma City (OK)
Université de Montréal (QC, Canada)
The U of Texas Rio Grande Valley (TX)

LASER AND OPTICAL ENGINEERING
U of Central Florida (FL)
U of Rochester (NY)

LATIN
Amherst Coll (MA)
Augustana Coll (IL)
Austin Coll (TX)
Bard Coll (NY)
Barnard Coll (NY)
Baylor U (TX)
Binghamton U, State U of New York (NY)
Boston U (MA)
Bowling Green State U (OH)
Bryn Mawr Coll (PA)
Canisius Coll (NY)
Carleton Coll (MN)
The Catholic U of America (DC)
Colgate U (NY)
Dartmouth Coll (NH)
DePauw U (IN)
Duquesne U (PA)
Emory U (GA)
Fordham U (NY)
Franklin & Marshall Coll (PA)
Furman U (SC)
Gettysburg Coll (PA)
Hampden-Sydney Coll (VA)
Haverford Coll (PA)
Hillsdale Coll (MI)
Hobart and William Smith Colls (NY)
Hofstra U (NY)
Hunter Coll of the City U of New York (NY)
John Carroll U (OH)
Kalamazoo Coll (MI)
Kenyon Coll (OH)
Knox Coll (IL)
Lawrence U (WI)
Lehman Coll of the City U of New York (NY)
Loyola U Chicago (IL)
Loyola U Maryland (MD)
Loyola U New Orleans (LA)
Mercer U, Macon (GA)
Missouri State U (MO)
Monmouth Coll (IL)
Montclair State U (NJ)
Mount Allison U (NB, Canada)
Mount Holyoke Coll (MA)
Oberlin Coll (OH)
Randolph Coll (VA)
Randolph-Macon Coll (VA)
Rice U (TX)
Rockford U (IL)
Rutgers U–New Brunswick (NJ)
Saint Joseph's U (PA)
Saint Mary's Coll of California (CA)
St. Olaf Coll (MN)
Samford U (AL)
Santa Clara U (CA)
Sarah Lawrence Coll (NY)
Sewanee: The U of the South (TN)
Smith Coll (MA)
Southwestern U (TX)
Swarthmore Coll (PA)
Trinity U (TX)
Tufts U (MA)
Tulane U (LA)
U of California, Los Angeles (CA)
U of Georgia (GA)
U of Miami (FL)
U of Michigan (MI)
The U of North Carolina at Greensboro (NC)
U of Richmond (VA)
U of St. Thomas (MN)
The U of Texas at Austin (TX)
U of Toronto (ON, Canada)
U of Vermont (VT)
U of Washington (WA)
U of Windsor (ON, Canada)
U of Wisconsin–Madison (WI)
Virginia Wesleyan Coll (VA)
Wabash Coll (IN)
Wake Forest U (NC)
Washington U in St. Louis (MO)
West Chester U of Pennsylvania (PA)
Western Michigan U (MI)
Westminster Coll (PA)
Whitman Coll (WA)
Wright State U (OH)
Wright State U–Lake Campus (OH)

LATIN AMERICAN AND CARIBBEAN STUDIES
Coll of Charleston (SC)
Linfield Coll (OR)
Mount Holyoke Coll (MA)
Rollins Coll (FL)
Union Coll (NY)
U of Georgia (GA)
U of Michigan (MI)
U of Wisconsin–Madison (WI)
U of Wisconsin–Milwaukee (WI)

LATIN AMERICAN STUDIES
Adelphi U (NY)
Albion Coll (MI)
Albright Coll (PA)
American U (DC)
Arizona State U at the West campus (AZ)
Assumption Coll (MA)
Bard Coll (NY)
Barnard Coll (NY)
Bates Coll (ME)
Baylor U (TX)
Bennington Coll (VT)
Binghamton U, State U of New York (NY)
Boston U (MA)
Bowdoin Coll (ME)
Bowling Green State U (OH)
Brandeis U (MA)
Bucknell U (PA)
California State U, Chico (CA)
California State U, East Bay (CA)
California State U, Fullerton (CA)
California State U, Northridge (CA)
Canisius Coll (NY)
Carleton Coll (MN)
City Coll of the City U of New York (NY)
Colby Coll (ME)
Colgate U (NY)
Coll of the Holy Cross (MA)
The Coll of William and Mary (VA)
Columbia U (NY)
Columbia U, School of General Studies (NY)
Connecticut Coll (CT)
Cornell Coll (IA)
Dartmouth Coll (NH)
Davidson Coll (NC)
Denison U (OH)
Dickinson Coll (PA)
Earlham Coll (IN)
Emory U (GA)
Flagler Coll (FL)
Fordham U (NY)
The George Washington U (DC)
Gettysburg Coll (PA)
Gonzaga U (WA)
Hamline U (MN)
Hampshire Coll (MA)
Haverford Coll (PA)
Hobart and William Smith Colls (NY)
Hofstra U (NY)
Hood Coll (MD)
Hunter Coll of the City U of New York (NY)
Illinois Wesleyan U (IL)
John Jay Coll of Criminal Justice of the City U of New York (NY)
Johns Hopkins U (MD)
Knox Coll (IL)
Lake Forest Coll (IL)
Lehman Coll of the City U of New York (NY)
Macalester Coll (MN)
McMaster U (ON, Canada)
Miami U (OH)
Middlebury Coll (VT)
Millsaps Coll (MS)
Oberlin Coll (OH)
Occidental Coll (CA)
Ohio U (OH)
Ohio Wesleyan U (OH)
Pace U (NY)
Penn State Abington (PA)
Penn State Altoona (PA)
Penn State Beaver (PA)
Penn State Berks (PA)
Penn State Brandywine (PA)
Penn State DuBois (PA)
Penn State Erie, The Behrend Coll (PA)
Penn State Fayette, The Eberly Campus (PA)
Penn State Greater Allegheny (PA)
Penn State Hazleton (PA)
Penn State Lehigh Valley (PA)
Penn State Mont Alto (PA)
Penn State New Kensington (PA)
Penn State Schuylkill (PA)
Penn State Shenango (PA)
Penn State U Park (PA)
Penn State Wilkes-Barre (PA)
Penn State Worthington Scranton (PA)
Penn State York (PA)
Pepperdine U, Malibu (CA)
Pomona Coll (CA)
Portland State U (OR)
Prescott Coll (AZ)
Queens Coll of the City U of New York (NY)
Rhode Island Coll (RI)
Rhodes Coll (TN)
Rice U (TX)
Rutgers U–New Brunswick (NJ)
St. Cloud State U (MN)
Saint Louis U (MO)
Saint Mary's Coll of California (CA)
St. Olaf Coll (MN)
Samford U (AL)
San Diego State U (CA)
Sarah Lawrence Coll (NY)

Scripps Coll (CA)
Seattle Pacific U (WA)
Smith Coll (MA)
Southern Methodist U (TX)
Southwestern U (TX)
Stanford U (CA)
State U of New York at New Paltz (NY)
State U of New York at Plattsburgh (NY)
Swarthmore Coll (PA)
Syracuse U (NY)
Temple U (PA)
Texas Tech U (TX)
Trinity U (TX)
Tufts U (MA)
Tulane U (LA)
United States Military Acad (NY)
U at Albany, State U of New York (NY)
The U of Alabama (AL)
The U of Arizona (AZ)
U of California, Los Angeles (CA)
U of California, Riverside (CA)
U of California, San Diego (CA)
U of Central Florida (FL)
U of Chicago (IL)
U of Delaware (DE)
U of Denver (CO)
U of Idaho (ID)
U of Illinois at Chicago (IL)
The U of Kansas (KS)
U of Kentucky (KY)
U of Louisville (KY)
U of Miami (FL)
U of Minnesota, Duluth (MN)
U of Minnesota, Morris (MN)
U of Nevada, Las Vegas (NV)
The U of North Carolina at Chapel Hill (NC)
The U of North Carolina at Charlotte (NC)
U of Oregon (OR)
U of Pennsylvania (PA)
U of Richmond (VA)
U of San Francisco (CA)
U of South Carolina (SC)
The U of Texas at Austin (TX)
The U of Texas at El Paso (TX)
U of Toronto (ON, Canada)
U of Utah (UT)
U of Vermont (VT)
U of Washington (WA)
U of Wisconsin–Eau Claire (WI)
Vanderbilt U (TN)
Vassar Coll (NY)
Villanova U (PA)
Washington Coll (MD)
Washington U in St. Louis (MO)
Wesleyan U (CT)
Westminster Coll (UT)
Whittier Coll (CA)
Willamette U (OR)
William Paterson U of New Jersey (NJ)

LATIN TEACHER EDUCATION
Boston U (MA)
Brigham Young U (UT)
Duquesne U (PA)
Miami U (OH)
Missouri State U (MO)
Montclair State U (NJ)
Ohio Wesleyan U (OH)
U of Delaware (DE)
Western Michigan U (MI)

LAY MINISTRY
Arizona Christian U (AZ)
Bethel Coll (IN)
Bethel U (MN)
Huntingdon Coll (AL)
Point Loma Nazarene U (CA)
Saint Mary's U of Minnesota (MN)
Southeastern Bible Coll (AL)
Trevecca Nazarene U (TN)
U of Saint Francis (IN)
U of St. Thomas (MN)

LEARNING SCIENCES
Purdue U (IN)
The U of Arizona (AZ)

LEGAL ASSISTANT/ PARALEGAL
Bay Path U (MA)
Boston U (MA)
Champlain Coll (VT)
Clayton State U (GA)
Coll of Saint Mary (NE)
Concordia U Wisconsin (WI)
Daemen Coll (NY)
Davenport U, Grand Rapids (MI)
East Central U (OK)
Eastern Michigan U (MI)
Elms Coll (MA)
Florida Gulf Coast U (FL)
Gannon U (PA)
Grand Valley State U (MI)
Hamline U (MN)
Hampton U (VA)
Hilbert Coll (NY)
Husson U (ME)
Idaho State U (ID)
Illinois State U (IL)
Indiana U–Purdue U Indianapolis (IN)
Kent State U (OH)
Lake Erie Coll (OH)
Lewis U (IL)
Liberty U (VA)
Loyola U Chicago (IL)
Madonna U (MI)
Maryville U of Saint Louis (MO)
Mercy Coll (NY)
Minnesota State U Moorhead (MN)
Morehead State U (KY)
Mount St. Joseph U (OH)
National U (CA)
New York City Coll of Technology of the City U of New York (NY)
Nova Southeastern U (FL)
Peirce Coll (PA)
Pennsylvania Coll of Technology (PA)
Quinnipiac U (CT)
Regent U (VA)
Roger Williams U (RI)
Saint Mary-of-the-Woods Coll (IN)
St. Petersburg Coll (FL)
Samford U (AL)
Southern Illinois U Carbondale (IL)
State U of New York Coll of Technology at Canton (NY)
Stephen F. Austin State U (TX)
Stevenson U (MD)
Suffolk U (MA)
Sullivan U (KY)
Texas A&M U–Commerce (TX)
Texas Wesleyan U (TX)
Texas Woman's U (TX)
Tiffin U (OH)
U of Central Florida (FL)
U of Great Falls (MT)
U of Hartford (CT)
U of Houston–Clear Lake (TX)
U of La Verne (CA)
U of North Georgia (GA)
U of Southern Mississippi (MS)
The U of Tennessee at Chattanooga (TN)
The U of Toledo (OH)
Valdosta State U (GA)
Washburn U (KS)
Western Kentucky U (KY)
William Woods U (MO)
Winona State U (MN)

LEGAL PROFESSIONS AND STUDIES RELATED
Armstrong State U (GA)
Ball State U (IN)
Bay Path U (MA)
Berkeley Coll–New York City Campus (NY)
Berkeley Coll–Woodland Park Campus (NJ)
Brenau U (GA)
California U of Pennsylvania (PA)
Drexel U (PA)
John Jay Coll of Criminal Justice of the City U of New York (NY)
Maryville U of Saint Louis (MO)
Montclair State U (NJ)
Ramapo Coll of New Jersey (NJ)
Roger Williams U (RI)
St. John's U (NY)
Syracuse U (NY)
Temple U (PA)
Tulane U (LA)
The U of Arizona (AZ)
U of Illinois at Springfield (IL)
U of Pennsylvania (PA)
The U of Tulsa (OK)
Western Michigan U (MI)
William Woods U (MO)

LEGAL STUDIES
Adams State U (CO)
Alderson Broaddus U (WV)
American Public U System (WV)
American U (DC)
Amherst Coll (MA)
Anderson U (SC)
Arizona State U at the Tempe campus (AZ)
Bay Path U (MA)
Bethany Lutheran Coll (MN)
Blackburn Coll (IL)
Brandman U (CA)
Brenau U (GA)
Bridgewater State U (MA)
Central Michigan U (MI)
Central Penn Coll (PA)
Coll of the Atlantic (ME)
Culver-Stockton Coll (MO)
DeSales U (PA)
Dickinson Coll (PA)
Doane U (NE)
Dominican U (IL)
Elms Coll (MA)
Emory & Henry Coll (VA)
Faulkner U (AL)
Florida National U (FL)
Hamline U (MN)
Hampshire Coll (MA)
Harding U (AR)
Houston Baptist U (TX)
Illinois State U (IL)
John Jay Coll of Criminal Justice of the City U of New York (NY)
Kentucky Wesleyan Coll (KY)
Lasell Coll (MA)
Lipscomb U (TN)
Mercy Coll (NY)
Morehead State U (KY)
Mount St. Joseph U (OH)
National Paralegal Coll (AZ)
Nazareth Coll of Rochester (NY)
Northeastern State U (OK)
Northwestern U (IL)
Northwest U (WA)
Oberlin Coll (OH)
Point Park U (PA)
Quinnipiac U (CT)
St. John Fisher Coll (NY)
St. John's U (NY)
Saint Joseph's U (PA)
Saint Louis U (MO)
Samford U (AL)
Scripps Coll (CA)
Southeastern U (FL)
State U of New York at Fredonia (NY)
Stevenson U (MD)
Thomas More Coll (KY)
United States Air Force Acad (CO)
United States Military Acad (NY)
Université de Montréal (QC, Canada)
Université de Sherbrooke (QC, Canada)
U of Denver (CO)
U of Detroit Mercy (MI)
U of Hartford (CT)
The U of Kansas (KS)
U of Maryland U Coll (MD)
U of Massachusetts Amherst (MA)
U of Miami (FL)
U of New Haven (CT)
U of Pittsburgh (PA)
The U of Texas at San Antonio (TX)
U of Washington (WA)
U of Washington, Tacoma (WA)
U of Windsor (ON, Canada)
U of Wisconsin–Madison (WI)
U of Wisconsin–Superior (WI)
Webster U (MO)
Western New England U (MA)
William Paterson U of New Jersey (NJ)
Wilmington U (DE)
Winona State U (MN)

LIBERAL ARTS AND SCIENCES AND HUMANITIES RELATED
The American U in Dubai (United Arab Emirates)
Anderson U (IN)
Anderson U (SC)
Antioch Coll, Yellow Springs (OH)
Armstrong State U (GA)
Auburn U (AL)
Augsburg Coll (MN)
Becker Coll (MA)
Belhaven U (MS)
Bishop's U (QC, Canada)
Blue Mountain Coll (MS)
Brigham Young U (UT)
Bryan Coll (TN)
Butler U (IN)
California Polytechnic State U, San Luis Obispo (CA)
California State U, Dominguez Hills (CA)
Carnegie Mellon U (PA)
Centre Coll (KY)
Coll of Saint Mary (NE)
The Colorado Coll (CO)
Concordia Coll (MN)
Drexel U (PA)
Duquesne U (PA)
Fairfield U (CT)
Florida Atlantic U (FL)
Georgia Coll & State U (GA)
Goddard Coll (VT)
Hampshire Coll (MA)
Hobe Sound Bible Coll (FL)
Hofstra U (NY)
Indiana U Bloomington (IN)
Indiana U East (IN)
Indiana U Kokomo (IN)
Indiana U Northwest (IN)
Indiana U–Purdue U Indianapolis (IN)
Indiana U South Bend (IN)
Indiana U Southeast (IN)
Johns Hopkins U (MD)
Kansas Wesleyan U (KS)
Kent State U at Ashtabula (OH)
Kent State U at East Liverpool (OH)
Kent State U at Geauga (OH)
Kent State U at Salem (OH)
Kent State U at Stark (OH)
Kent State U at Trumbull (OH)
Kent State U at Tuscarawas (OH)
The King's Coll (NY)
Lewis & Clark Coll (OR)
Loyola U New Orleans (LA)
Malone U (OH)
Marymount California U (CA)
Missouri Baptist U (MO)
Molloy Coll (NY)
Mount Aloysius Coll (PA)
New Coll of Florida (FL)
North Carolina State U (NC)
Ohio U (OH)
Oklahoma City U (OK)
Pepperdine U, Malibu (CA)
Prescott Coll (AZ)
Saint Anselm Coll (NH)
St. John's Coll (NM)
Saint Louis U (MO)
Saint Mary's Coll of California (CA)
Seattle U (WA)
Southern Methodist U (TX)
Southern New Hampshire U (NH)
Stevens Inst of Technology (NJ)
Truett McConnell U (GA)
Tulane U (LA)
Union Coll (NE)
The U of Akron (OH)
U of California, Los Angeles (CA)
U of California, Santa Barbara (CA)
U of Maine at Farmington (ME)
U of Maryland U Coll (MD)
U of Mary Washington (VA)
U of Massachusetts Amherst (MA)
U of Oklahoma (OK)
U of Rhode Island (RI)
The U of Texas at Austin (TX)
The U of Texas at San Antonio (TX)
U of Utah (UT)
U of Wisconsin–Milwaukee (WI)
U of Wisconsin–Platteville (WI)
U of Wisconsin–Whitewater (WI)
Valdosta State U (GA)
Vassar Coll (NY)
Walsh U (OH)
Wayland Baptist U (TX)
Western Illinois U (IL)
Westminster Coll (UT)
West Virginia U Inst of Technology (WV)
Wheeling Jesuit U (WV)
Worcester Polytechnic Inst (MA)

LIBERAL ARTS AND SCIENCES/LIBERAL STUDIES
Abilene Christian U (TX)
Adams State U (CO)
Alaska Pacific U (AK)
Albion Coll (MI)
Alcorn State U (MS)
Alvernia U (PA)
Alverno Coll (WI)
American Intl Coll (MA)
American U (DC)
Amridge U (AL)
Antioch U Los Angeles (CA)
Antioch U Midwest (OH)
Antioch U Santa Barbara (CA)
Antioch U Seattle (WA)
Appalachian State U (NC)
Aquinas Coll (MI)
Arcadia U (PA)
Arizona State U at the Polytechnic campus (AZ)
Ashland U (OH)
Athens State U (AL)
Augsburg Coll (MN)
Augustana Coll (IL)
Augustana U (SD)
Aurora U (IL)
Austin Peay State U (TN)
Averett U (VA)
Azusa Pacific U (CA)
Ball State U (IN)
Barry U (FL)
Barton Coll (NC)
Baruch Coll of the City U of New York (NY)
Bay Path U (MA)
Beacon Coll (FL)
Becker Coll (MA)
Bellarmine U (KY)
Belmont Abbey Coll (NC)
Belmont U (TN)
Bemidji State U (MN)
Benedictine Coll (KS)
Bennington Coll (VT)
Bentley U (MA)
Bethany Lutheran Coll (MN)
Bethel Coll (IN)
Bethune-Cookman U (FL)
Biola U (CA)
Bishop's U (QC, Canada)
Bluefield Coll (VA)
Bowling Green State U (OH)
Bowling Green State U–Firelands Coll (OH)
Bradley U (IL)
Brandman U (CA)
Brescia U (KY)
Bridgewater Coll (VA)
Brigham Young U (UT)
Brigham Young U–Idaho (ID)
Bryan Coll (TN)
Bryant U (RI)
Buffalo State Coll, State U of New York (NY)
Cabrini U (PA)
Cairn U (PA)
California Baptist U (CA)
California Lutheran U (CA)
California Polytechnic State U, San Luis Obispo (CA)
California State Polytechnic U, Pomona (CA)
California State U, Bakersfield (CA)
California State U, Chico (CA)
California State U, Dominguez Hills (CA)
California State U, East Bay (CA)
California State U, Fresno (CA)
California State U, Fullerton (CA)
California State U, Long Beach (CA)
California State U, Monterey Bay (CA)
California State U, Northridge (CA)
California State U, Sacramento (CA)
California State U, San Bernardino (CA)
California State U, San Marcos (CA)
California State U, Stanislaus (CA)
California U of Pennsylvania (PA)
Canisius Coll (NY)
Carlow U (PA)
Carnegie Mellon U (PA)
Carson-Newman U (TN)
The Catholic U of America (DC)

Cazenovia Coll (NY)
Cedarville U (OH)
Central Baptist Coll (AR)
Central Michigan U (MI)
Champlain Coll (VT)
Chapman U (CA)
Charter Oak State Coll (CT)
Chatham U (PA)
Chestnut Hill Coll (PA)
Christian Brothers U (TN)
Clarion U of Pennsylvania (PA)
Clarke U (IA)
Clarkson U (NY)
Clayton State U (GA)
Cleveland State U (OH)
Coastal Carolina U (SC)
Coe Coll (IA)
The Coll at Brockport, State U of New York (NY)
Coll of Mount Saint Vincent (NY)
Coll of Saint Benedict (MN)
The Coll of Saint Rose (NY)
Coll of the Atlantic (ME)
Colorado Christian U (CO)
Colorado Mesa U (CO)
Colorado State U (CO)
Columbia Coll Chicago (IL)
Columbia Intl U (SC)
Columbus State U (GA)
Concordia Coll–New York (NY)
Concordia U Irvine (CA)
Concordia U Wisconsin (WI)
Corban U (OR)
Cornell Coll (IA)
Cornell U (NY)
Culver-Stockton Coll (MO)
Curry Coll (MA)
Daemen Coll (NY)
Dakota State U (SD)
Dean Coll (MA)
Defiance Coll (OH)
DeSales U (PA)
Dickinson State U (ND)
Dominican U of California (CA)
Drexel U (PA)
Duquesne U (PA)
East Carolina U (NC)
Eastern Illinois U (IL)
Eastern Mennonite U (VA)
Eastern Nazarene Coll (MA)
Eastern Oregon U (OR)
East Tennessee State U (TN)
Elmira Coll (NY)
Elms Coll (MA)
Elon U (NC)
Emmanuel Coll (MA)
Emory & Henry Coll (VA)
Emory U (GA)
Endicott Coll (MA)
Eugene Lang Coll of Liberal Arts (NY)
Eureka Coll (IL)
The Evergreen State Coll (WA)
Excelsior Coll (NY)
Faulkner U (AL)
Fayetteville State U (NC)
Felician U (NJ)
Fisher Coll (MA)
Fitchburg State U (MA)
Flagler Coll (FL)
Florida Atlantic U (FL)
Florida Coll (FL)
Florida Gulf Coast U (FL)
Florida Intl U (FL)
Florida National U (FL)
Fort Lewis Coll (CO)
Framingham State U (MA)
Francis Marion U (SC)
Franklin Pierce U (NH)
Friends U (KS)
Frostburg State U (MD)
Gannon U (PA)
Georgetown U (DC)
The George Washington U (DC)
Gettysburg Coll (PA)
Gonzaga U (WA)
Governors State U (IL)
Graceland U (IA)
Grand Valley State U (MI)
Grand View U (IA)
Granite State Coll (NH)
Green Mountain Coll (VT)
Greenville Coll (IL)
Hannibal-LaGrange U (MO)
Harris-Stowe State U (MO)
Harvard U (MA)
Hofstra U (NY)
Holy Cross Coll (IN)
Holy Names U (CA)
Hope Intl U (CA)
Houghton Coll (NY)
Houston Baptist U (TX)
Howard Payne U (TX)
Humboldt State U (CA)
Huntington U (IN)
Husson U (ME)
Illinois Coll (IL)
Illinois State U (IL)
Illinois Wesleyan U (IL)
Immaculata U (PA)
Indiana State U (IN)
Indiana U Bloomington (IN)
Indiana U of Pennsylvania (PA)
Iona Coll (NY)
Iowa State U of Science and Technology (IA)
Ithaca Coll (NY)
Jacksonville U (FL)
James Madison U (VA)
Johns Hopkins U (MD)
Johnson C. Smith U (NC)
Juniata Coll (PA)
Kentucky State U (KY)
Keuka Coll (NY)
Kutztown U of Pennsylvania (PA)
Langston U (OK)
La Roche Coll (PA)
Lenoir-Rhyne U (NC)
Lesley U (MA)
Lewis U (IL)
Liberty U (VA)
Limestone Coll (SC)
Lincoln Coll–Normal (IL)
Lincoln U (MO)
Lincoln U (PA)
Lindenwood U (MO)
Lock Haven U of Pennsylvania (PA)
Longwood U (VA)
Loras Coll (IA)
Louisiana Coll (LA)
Louisiana State U and A&M Coll (LA)
Louisiana State U at Alexandria (LA)
Loyola Marymount U (CA)
Loyola U Chicago (IL)
Lynn U (FL)
Manchester U (IN)
Manhattan Coll (NY)
Manhattanville Coll (NY)
Mansfield U of Pennsylvania (PA)
Maria Coll (NY)
Marian U (WI)
Marietta Coll (OH)
Marist Coll (NY)
Mary Baldwin U (VA)
Marymount California U (CA)
Marymount Manhattan Coll (NY)
Marymount U (VA)
Maryville U of Saint Louis (MO)
Massachusetts Coll of Liberal Arts (MA)
Massachusetts Inst of Technology (MA)
The Master's U (CA)
McNeese State U (LA)
Mercy Coll (NY)
Mercy Coll of Health Sciences (IA)
Merrimack Coll (MA)
Miami U (OH)
Michigan Technological U (MI)
Middlebury Coll (VT)
Mississippi State U (MS)
Monmouth Coll (IL)
Montana State U (MT)
Montana State U Billings (MT)
Montana State U–Northern (MT)
Montana Tech of The U of Montana (MT)
Morris Coll (SC)
Mount Allison U (NB, Canada)
Mount Aloysius Coll (PA)
Mount Ida Coll (MA)
Mount Marty Coll (SD)
Mount Mary U (WI)
Mount St. Joseph U (OH)
Mount Saint Mary's U (CA)
Murray State U (KY)
National Louis U (IL)
Neumann U (PA)
Nevada State Coll (NV)
Newman U (KS)
New Mexico Highlands U (NM)
New Mexico State U (NM)
New Saint Andrews Coll (ID)
The New School for Public Engagement (NY)
Niagara U (NY)
North Carolina State U (NC)
North Carolina Wesleyan Coll (NC)
North Central Coll (IL)
Northeastern Illinois U (IL)
Northern Arizona U (AZ)
Northern Illinois U (IL)
Northern Kentucky U (KY)
North Greenville U (SC)
Northwestern Coll (IA)
Northwestern State U of Louisiana (LA)
Northwestern U (IL)
Ohio U–Eastern (OH)
Ohio Valley U (WV)
Oklahoma Christian U (OK)
Oklahoma City U (OK)
Oklahoma State U (OK)
Olivet Nazarene U (IL)
Oral Roberts U (OK)
Oregon State U (OR)
Pace U (NY)
Pace U, Pleasantville Campus (NY)
Parsons School of Design (NY)
Patrick Henry Coll (VA)
Penn State Abington (PA)
Penn State Altoona (PA)
Penn State Beaver (PA)
Penn State Berks (PA)
Penn State Brandywine (PA)
Penn State DuBois (PA)
Penn State Erie, The Behrend Coll (PA)
Penn State Fayette, The Eberly Campus (PA)
Penn State Greater Allegheny (PA)
Penn State Lehigh Valley (PA)
Penn State Mont Alto (PA)
Penn State New Kensington (PA)
Penn State Schuylkill (PA)
Penn State Shenango (PA)
Penn State U Park (PA)
Penn State Wilkes-Barre (PA)
Penn State Worthington Scranton (PA)
Penn State York (PA)
Pepperdine U, Malibu (CA)
Pittsburg State U (KS)
Point Loma Nazarene U (CA)
Point Park U (PA)
Portland State U (OR)
Providence Coll (RI)
Purchase Coll, State U of New York (NY)
Purdue U Northwest (IN)
Quinnipiac U (CT)
Ramapo Coll of New Jersey (NJ)
Randolph Coll (VA)
Regis U (CO)
Rhode Island Coll (RI)
Roberts Wesleyan Coll (NY)
Rochester Inst of Technology (NY)
Rogers State U (OK)
Roger Williams U (RI)
Rowan U (NJ)
Rutgers U–Camden (NJ)
Rutgers U–New Brunswick (NJ)
The Sage Colls (NY)
St. Cloud State U (MN)
St. Edward's U (TX)
St. Gregory's U, Shawnee (OK)
St. John Fisher Coll (NY)
St. John's Coll (MD)
St. John's Coll (NM)
Saint John's U (MN)
St. John's U (NY)
St. Joseph's Coll, Long Island Campus (NY)
St. Joseph's Coll, New York (NY)
Saint Joseph's U (PA)
St. Louis Coll of Pharmacy (MO)
Saint Mary-of-the-Woods Coll (IN)
Saint Mary's Coll of California (CA)
St. Olaf Coll (MN)
Saint Peter's U (NJ)
St. Thomas U (FL)
Saint Vincent Coll (PA)
Salisbury U (MD)
Salve Regina U (RI)
San Diego State U (CA)
San Francisco State U (CA)
Santa Clara U (CA)
Sarah Lawrence Coll (NY)
Schreiner U (TX)
Seattle Pacific U (WA)
Seattle U (WA)
Shaw U (NC)
Shenandoah U (VA)
Shippensburg U of Pennsylvania (PA)
Shorter U (GA)
Simon Fraser U (BC, Canada)
Simpson U (CA)
Skidmore Coll (NY)
Soka U of America (CA)
Sonoma State U (CA)
South Dakota State U (SD)
Southeastern U (FL)
Southern Connecticut State U (CT)
Southern Illinois U Carbondale (IL)
Southern Illinois U Edwardsville (IL)
Southern Oregon U (OR)
Southwestern Coll (KS)
Spalding U (KY)
Spring Hill Coll (AL)
State U of New York at Fredonia (NY)
State U of New York at New Paltz (NY)
State U of New York at Plattsburgh (NY)
State U of New York Coll at Old Westbury (NY)
Stephen F. Austin State U (TX)
Stevens Inst of Technology (NJ)
Stockton U (NJ)
Sweet Briar Coll (VA)
Syracuse U (NY)
Tarleton State U (TX)
Temple U (PA)
Tennessee State U (TN)
Texas A&M U–Central Texas (TX)
Texas A&M U–Commerce (TX)
Texas Coll (TX)
Texas Tech U (TX)
Texas Wesleyan U (TX)
Thomas Aquinas Coll (CA)
Thomas Edison State U (NJ)
Thomas More Coll (KY)
Thomas U (GA)
Trent U (ON, Canada)
Trine U (IN)
Troy U (AL)
Tufts U (MA)
Tulane U (LA)
Union Coll (KY)
Union Coll (NY)
U at Albany, State U of New York (NY)
The U of Akron (OH)
U of Alaska Fairbanks (AK)
U of Bridgeport (CT)
U of California, Riverside (CA)
U of California, Santa Barbara (CA)
U of Central Arkansas (AR)
U of Chicago (IL)
U of Cincinnati (OH)
U of Delaware (DE)
U of Detroit Mercy (MI)
U of Dubuque (IA)
U of Evansville (IN)
U of Georgia (GA)
U of Hartford (CT)
U of Hawaii at Manoa (HI)
U of Houston (TX)
U of Illinois at Springfield (IL)
The U of Kansas (KS)
U of La Verne (CA)
U of Lethbridge (AB, Canada)
U of Louisville (KY)
U of Maine (ME)
U of Maine at Farmington (ME)
U of Maine at Fort Kent (ME)
U of Maine at Presque Isle (ME)
U of Mary Washington (VA)
U of Massachusetts Dartmouth (MA)
U of Massachusetts Lowell (MA)
U of Michigan–Dearborn (MI)
U of Missouri–St. Louis (MO)
The U of Montana Western (MT)
U of Nevada, Las Vegas (NV)
U of New England (ME)
U of New Haven (CT)
U of North Carolina at Asheville (NC)
The U of North Carolina at Chapel Hill (NC)
The U of North Carolina at Greensboro (NC)
U of Northern Iowa (IA)
U of Notre Dame (IN)
U of Oklahoma (OK)
U of Pennsylvania (PA)
U of Pittsburgh (PA)
U of Pittsburgh at Bradford (PA)
U of Regina (SK, Canada)
U of Rochester (NY)
U of St. Francis (IL)
U of Saint Francis (IN)
U of Saint Mary (KS)
U of St. Thomas (TX)
U of San Diego (CA)
U of San Francisco (CA)
The U of Scranton (PA)
U of South Carolina (SC)
U of South Carolina Aiken (SC)
The U of South Dakota (SD)
U of Southern Indiana (IN)
U of Southern Maine (ME)
The U of Tampa (FL)
The U of Texas at Austin (TX)
U of the Incarnate Word (TX)
The U of Toledo (OH)
The U of Tulsa (OK)
U of Vermont (VT)
U of Virginia (VA)
The U of Virginia's Coll at Wise (VA)
U of Waterloo (ON, Canada)
U of Wisconsin–Eau Claire (WI)
U of Wisconsin–Green Bay (WI)
U of Wisconsin–Parkside (WI)
U of Wisconsin–Whitewater (WI)
Utah State U (UT)
Utica Coll (NY)
Villanova U (PA)
Virginia State U (VA)
Viterbo U (WI)
Walsh U (OH)
Washburn U (KS)
Washington Coll (MD)
Washington State U (WA)
Washington U in St. Louis (MO)
Weber State U (UT)
Wesleyan U (CT)
West Chester U of Pennsylvania (PA)
Western Carolina U (NC)
Western Connecticut State U (CT)
Western Illinois U (IL)
Western New England U (MA)
Western Washington U (WA)
Westfield State U (MA)
Westmont Coll (CA)
West Virginia U (WV)
Whittier Coll (CA)
Wichita State U (KS)
Wilkes U (PA)
Willamette U (OR)
William Jewell Coll (MO)
William Paterson U of New Jersey (NJ)
William Peace U (NC)
Williams Baptist Coll (AR)
Wingate U (NC)
Wittenberg U (OH)
York Coll of the City U of New York (NY)

LIBRARY AND INFORMATION SCIENCE
Clarion U of Pennsylvania (PA)
Emory & Henry Coll (VA)
Kutztown U of Pennsylvania (PA)
St. Cloud State U (MN)
Sam Houston State U (TX)
Southern Connecticut State U (CT)
U of Southern Mississippi (MS)

LIBRARY SCIENCE RELATED
U of Great Falls (MT)

LICENSED PRACTICAL/ VOCATIONAL NURSE TRAINING
Campbellsville U (KY)
Lindenwood U (MO)
York Coll of Pennsylvania (PA)

LINGUISTIC AND COMPARATIVE LANGUAGE STUDIES RELATED
Appalachian State U (NC)
Boston U (MA)
Brigham Young U (UT)
Indiana U Bloomington (IN)
Iowa State U of Science and Technology (IA)

U of California, Los Angeles (CA)
U of California, Santa Barbara (CA)
U of Kentucky (KY)
U of Southern California (CA)

LINGUISTICS
Baylor U (TX)
Bethel U (MN)
Binghamton U, State U of New York (NY)
Biola U (CA)
Boston U (MA)
Brandeis U (MA)
Brooklyn Coll of the City U of New York (NY)
Bryn Mawr Coll (PA)
Bucknell U (PA)
California State U, Dominguez Hills (CA)
California State U, Fresno (CA)
California State U, Fullerton (CA)
California State U, Monterey Bay (CA)
California State U, Northridge (CA)
Calvin Coll (MI)
Carleton Coll (MN)
Carnegie Mellon U (PA)
Carson-Newman U (TN)
Cedarville U (OH)
City Coll of the City U of New York (NY)
Cleveland State U (OH)
The Coll of William and Mary (VA)
Columbia U (NY)
Concordia U (QC, Canada)
Cornell U (NY)
Dartmouth Coll (NH)
Eastern Michigan U (MI)
Emory U (GA)
Florida Atlantic U (FL)
Georgetown U (DC)
Georgia State U (GA)
Gordon Coll (MA)
Hampshire Coll (MA)
Harvard U (MA)
Hofstra U (NY)
Indiana U Bloomington (IN)
Iowa State U of Science and Technology (IA)
Lawrence U (WI)
Lehman Coll of the City U of New York (NY)
Macalester Coll (MN)
Massachusetts Inst of Technology (MA)
McMaster U (ON, Canada)
Miami U (OH)
Michigan State U (MI)
Mid-Atlantic Christian U (NC)
Montclair State U (NJ)
Northeastern U (MA)
Northwestern U (IL)
The Ohio State U (OH)
Ohio U (OH)
Pitzer Coll (CA)
Pomona Coll (CA)
Portland State U (OR)
Purdue U (IN)
Queens Coll of the City U of New York (NY)
Reed Coll (OR)
Rice U (TX)
Rutgers U–New Brunswick (NJ)
Saint Joseph's U (PA)
San Diego State U (CA)
Scripps Coll (CA)
Seattle Pacific U (WA)
Simon Fraser U (BC, Canada)
Southern Illinois U Carbondale (IL)
Stanford U (CA)
State U of New York at Oswego (NY)
Stony Brook U, State U of New York (NY)
Swarthmore Coll (PA)
Syracuse U (NY)
Temple U (PA)
Truman State U (MO)
Tulane U (LA)
Université de Montréal (QC, Canada)
U at Albany, State U of New York (NY)
U at Buffalo, the State U of New York (NY)
U of Alaska Fairbanks (AK)
The U of Arizona (AZ)
U of California, Davis (CA)
U of California, Irvine (CA)
U of California, Los Angeles (CA)
U of California, Riverside (CA)
U of California, San Diego (CA)
U of California, Santa Barbara (CA)
U of Chicago (IL)
U of Colorado Boulder (CO)
U of Delaware (DE)
U of Florida (FL)
U of Georgia (GA)
U of Houston (TX)
The U of Kansas (KS)
U of Kentucky (KY)
U of King's Coll (NS, Canada)
U of Maryland, Coll Park (MD)
U of Massachusetts Amherst (MA)
U of Michigan (MI)
U of Michigan–Flint (MI)
U of Minnesota, Duluth (MN)
U of Minnesota, Twin Cities Campus (MN)
U of Nevada, Las Vegas (NV)
U of New Hampshire (NH)
The U of North Carolina at Chapel Hill (NC)
U of North Texas (TX)
U of Oklahoma (OK)
U of Oregon (OR)
U of Pennsylvania (PA)
U of Pittsburgh (PA)
U of Regina (SK, Canada)
U of Rochester (NY)
U of Saskatchewan (SK, Canada)
U of Southern California (CA)
U of Southern Maine (ME)
The U of Texas at Austin (TX)
The U of Texas at El Paso (TX)
The U of Toledo (OH)
U of Toronto (ON, Canada)
U of Washington (WA)
U of Wisconsin–Madison (WI)
U of Wisconsin–Milwaukee (WI)
Ursinus Coll (PA)
Washington State U (WA)
Washington U in St. Louis (MO)
Wayne State U (MI)
Western Washington U (WA)

LITERATURE
American U (DC)
Antioch Coll, Yellow Springs (OH)
Bryant U (RI)
Calvin Coll (MI)
Carson-Newman U (TN)
Central Michigan U (MI)
Colorado Christian U (CO)
Concordia U, St. Paul (MN)
Dixie State U (UT)
Eugene Lang Coll of Liberal Arts (NY)
Florida Southern Coll (FL)
Grove City Coll (PA)
Huntington U (IN)
Linfield Coll (OR)
Lipscomb U (TN)
Loyola U New Orleans (LA)
Lubbock Christian U (TX)
Marymount Manhattan Coll (NY)
Massachusetts Coll of Liberal Arts (MA)
New Coll of Florida (FL)
Occidental Coll (CA)
Saint Mary's U of Minnesota (MN)
Southwestern Coll (KS)
Stevens Inst of Technology (NJ)
The U of Findlay (OH)
U of Michigan–Flint (MI)
The U of Texas at Dallas (TX)
Washington U in St. Louis (MO)

LITERATURE RELATED
Colorado Christian U (CO)

LIVESTOCK MANAGEMENT
The Ohio State U (OH)
Tarleton State U (TX)

LOGIC
Carnegie Mellon U (PA)
U of Pennsylvania (PA)

LOGISTICS, MATERIALS, AND SUPPLY CHAIN MANAGEMENT
Albany State U (GA)
American Public U System (WV)
Anderson U (SC)
Athens State U (AL)
Auburn U (AL)
Baylor U (TX)
Binghamton U, State U of New York (NY)
Bloomfield Coll (NJ)
Bloomsburg U of Pennsylvania (PA)
Boise State U (ID)
Bowling Green State U (OH)
Bradley U (IL)
Brigham Young U (UT)
Bryant U (RI)
California State U, Dominguez Hills (CA)
Central Michigan U (MI)
Central Washington U (WA)
Clarkson U (NY)
Clayton State U (GA)
Concordia U (QC, Canada)
DEREE - The American Coll of Greece (Greece)
DeSales U (PA)
Duquesne U (PA)
Eastern Michigan U (MI)
Embry-Riddle Aeronautical U–Worldwide (FL)
Florida Inst of Technology (FL)
Gannon U (PA)
Georgia Southern U (GA)
HEC Montreal (QC, Canada)
Hofstra U (NY)
Iowa State U of Science and Technology (IA)
Kennesaw State U (GA)
Lehigh U (PA)
Lincoln Coll (IL)
Lincoln Coll–Normal (IL)
Miami Dade Coll (FL)
Michigan State U (MI)
Missouri State U (MO)
Murray State U (KY)
Niagara U (NY)
Northeastern State U (OK)
Northeastern U (MA)
Northwood U, Michigan Campus (MI)
The Ohio State U (OH)
Penn State Beaver (PA)
Penn State Brandywine (PA)
Penn State Fayette, The Eberly Campus (PA)
Penn State Greater Allegheny (PA)
Penn State Hazleton (PA)
Penn State Lehigh Valley (PA)
Penn State New Kensington (PA)
Penn State Schuylkill (PA)
Penn State Shenango (PA)
Penn State U Park (PA)
Penn State York (PA)
Portland State U (OR)
Rutgers U–Newark (NJ)
Rutgers U–New Brunswick (NJ)
St. Thomas U (FL)
Shippensburg U of Pennsylvania (PA)
Southeastern Louisiana U (LA)
Syracuse U (NY)
Texas A&M U (TX)
Texas Christian U (TX)
Texas Tech U (TX)
Tiffin U (OH)
Truckee Meadows Comm Coll (NV)
United States Merchant Marine Acad (NY)
U of Arkansas (AR)
The U of Findlay (OH)
The U of Kansas (KS)
U of Maryland, Coll Park (MD)
U of Massachusetts Amherst (MA)
U of Michigan–Dearborn (MI)
U of Northern Iowa (IA)
U of North Texas (TX)
U of Pittsburgh (PA)
U of Puerto Rico in Bayamón (PR)
U of Rhode Island (RI)
U of St. Francis (IL)
The U of Tennessee (TN)
The U of Texas at Austin (TX)
The U of Texas at Dallas (TX)
The U of Texas Rio Grande Valley (TX)
The U of Toledo (OH)
U of Washington (WA)
U of Wisconsin–Platteville (WI)
U of Wisconsin–Stout (WI)
U of Wisconsin–Whitewater (WI)
Weber State U (UT)
Western Illinois U (IL)
Western Michigan U (MI)
West Virginia U (WV)
Wright State U (OH)
Wright State U–Lake Campus (OH)
York Coll of Pennsylvania (PA)

LONG TERM CARE ADMINISTRATION
Bowling Green State U (OH)
Weber State U (UT)

MACHINE TOOL TECHNOLOGY
Idaho State U (ID)

MAGNETIC RESONANCE IMAGING (MRI) TECHNOLOGY
Saint Louis U (MO)
Weber State U (UT)

MANAGEMENT INFORMATION SYSTEMS
Adams State U (CO)
Albany State U (GA)
The American U of Paris (France)
Angelo State U (TX)
Appalachian State U (NC)
Arcadia U (PA)
Auburn U (AL)
Auburn U at Montgomery (AL)
Augsburg Coll (MN)
Augustana U (SD)
Augusta U (GA)
Avila U (MO)
Azusa Pacific U (CA)
Ball State U (IN)
Barry U (FL)
Bayamón Central U (PR)
Baylor U (TX)
Belmont U (TN)
Binghamton U, State U of New York (NY)
Biola U (CA)
Bishop's U (QC, Canada)
Boston Coll (MA)
Bowling Green State U (OH)
Bradley U (IL)
Briar Cliff U (IA)
Bridgewater Coll (VA)
Bridgewater State U (MA)
Bryant U (RI)
Butler U (IN)
California State U, East Bay (CA)
California State U, Fresno (CA)
California State U, Long Beach (CA)
Calvin Coll (MI)
Canisius Coll (NY)
Carson-Newman U (TN)
Catawba Coll (NC)
Cedarville U (OH)
Central Baptist Coll (AR)
Central Connecticut State U (CT)
Central Michigan U (MI)
Central Washington U (WA)
Charleston Southern U (SC)
Clarkson U (NY)
Cleveland State U (OH)
Colorado Christian U (CO)
Colorado Mesa U (CO)
Colorado State U (CO)
Columbia Coll (MO)
Columbus State U (GA)
Concordia U (QC, Canada)
Concordia U Chicago (IL)
Concordia U, Nebraska (NE)
Corban U (OR)
Cornerstone U (MI)
Dallas Baptist U (TX)
Dalton State Coll (GA)
DEREE - The American Coll of Greece (Greece)
DeSales U (PA)
Dominican Coll (NY)
Drexel U (PA)
Drury U (MO)
East Carolina U (NC)
East Central U (OK)
Eastern Michigan U (MI)
Eastern Washington U (WA)
Edgewood Coll (WI)
Excelsior Coll (NY)
Fairfield U (CT)
Faulkner U (AL)
Fayetteville State U (NC)
Felician U (NJ)
Florida Atlantic U (FL)
Florida Inst of Technology (FL)
Florida Intl U (FL)
Fordham U (NY)
Francis Marion U (SC)
Gannon U (PA)
Gardner-Webb U (NC)
George Fox U (OR)
Georgia Southern U (GA)
Gonzaga U (WA)
Governors State U (IL)
Grace Coll (IN)
Graceland U (IA)
Grand View U (IA)
Greenville Coll (IL)
Hardin-Simmons U (TX)
Harris-Stowe State U (MO)
HEC Montreal (QC, Canada)
Henderson State U (AR)
Hofstra U (NY)
Holy Family U (PA)
Howard Payne U (TX)
Husson U (ME)
Illinois Coll (IL)
Illinois State U (IL)
Immaculata U (PA)
Indiana State U (IN)
Indiana U of Pennsylvania (PA)
Inter American U of Puerto Rico, Aguadilla Campus (PR)
Inter American U of Puerto Rico, Barranquitas Campus (PR)
Iona Coll (NY)
Iowa State U of Science and Technology (IA)
Jacksonville U (FL)
Lamar U (TX)
La Salle U (PA)
Le Moyne Coll (NY)
Lewis U (IL)
Lincoln U (CA)
Linfield Coll (OR)
Loras Coll (IA)
Louisiana Tech U (LA)
Loyola Marymount U (CA)
Loyola U Chicago (IL)
Luther Coll (IA)
Madonna U (MI)
Marshall U (WV)
Maryville U of Saint Louis (MO)
Massachusetts Coll of Liberal Arts (MA)
The Master's U (CA)
McMurry U (TX)
Mercer U, Macon (GA)
Miami U (OH)
Michigan Technological U (MI)
Millikin U (IL)
Minot State U (ND)
Mississippi State U (MS)
Missouri State U (MO)
Morehead State U (KY)
Morrisville State Coll (NY)
Mount Ida Coll (MA)
Mount Mercy U (IA)
Mount Vernon Nazarene U (OH)
National Louis U (IL)
National U (CA)
Newman U (KS)
New Mexico Highlands U (NM)
North Dakota State U (ND)
Northeastern State U (OK)
Northeastern U (MA)
Northern Arizona U (AZ)
Northern Illinois U (IL)
Northern Kentucky U (KY)
Northern State U (SD)
Northwest Missouri State U (MO)
Northwood U, Michigan Campus (MI)
The Ohio State U (OH)
Ohio U (OH)
Oklahoma Baptist U (OK)
Old Dominion U (VA)
Olivet Nazarene U (IL)
Oral Roberts U (OK)
Oregon State U (OR)
Penn State Abington (PA)
Penn State Altoona (PA)
Penn State Beaver (PA)
Penn State Berks (PA)
Penn State Brandywine (PA)
Penn State DuBois (PA)
Penn State Erie, The Behrend Coll (PA)
Penn State Fayette, The Eberly Campus (PA)
Penn State Greater Allegheny (PA)
Penn State Harrisburg (PA)
Penn State Hazleton (PA)

Penn State Lehigh Valley (PA)
Penn State Mont Alto (PA)
Penn State New Kensington (PA)
Penn State Schuylkill (PA)
Penn State Shenango (PA)
Penn State U Park (PA)
Penn State Wilkes-Barre (PA)
Penn State Worthington Scranton (PA)
Penn State York (PA)
Point Loma Nazarene U (CA)
Prairie View A&M U (TX)
Rhode Island Coll (RI)
Robert Morris U (PA)
Rochester Inst of Technology (NY)
Rockford U (IL)
Roger Williams U (RI)
Rowan U (NJ)
Rutgers U–Newark (NJ)
St. Catherine U (MN)
Saint Francis U (PA)
St. Gregory's U, Shawnee (OK)
St. John's U (NY)
Saint Joseph's U (PA)
Saint Louis U (MO)
Saint Mary's Coll (IN)
Sam Houston State U (TX)
Santa Clara U (CA)
Schreiner U (TX)
Seattle Pacific U (WA)
Seton Hill U (PA)
Shawnee State U (OH)
Simon Fraser U (BC, Canada)
Simpson Coll (IA)
Southeastern U (FL)
Southwestern Coll (KS)
State U of New York at Plattsburgh (NY)
State U of New York Coll at Old Westbury (NY)
Stevenson U (MD)
Tarleton State U (TX)
Texas A&M Intl U (TX)
Texas A&M U (TX)
Texas A&M U–Central Texas (TX)
Texas A&M U–Commerce (TX)
Texas A&M U–Corpus Christi (TX)
Texas A&M U–Kingsville (TX)
Thomas More Coll (KY)
The U of Akron (OH)
The U of Alabama (AL)
The U of Alabama at Birmingham (AL)
The U of Alabama in Huntsville (AL)
The U of Arizona (AZ)
U of Arkansas (AR)
U of Bridgeport (CT)
U of Central Arkansas (AR)
U of Central Missouri (MO)
U of Colorado Boulder (CO)
U of Dayton (OH)
U of Delaware (DE)
U of Denver (CO)
U of Detroit Mercy (MI)
U of Georgia (GA)
U of Hartford (CT)
U of Hawaii at Manoa (HI)
U of Houston (TX)
U of Houston–Downtown (TX)
U of Idaho (ID)
U of Jamestown (ND)
The U of Kansas (KS)
U of Lethbridge (AB, Canada)
U of Louisiana at Monroe (LA)
U of Louisville (KY)
U of Mary Hardin-Baylor (TX)
U of Massachusetts Dartmouth (MA)
U of Michigan–Dearborn (MI)
U of Missouri–St. Louis (MO)
U of Nevada, Las Vegas (NV)
U of North Alabama (AL)
The U of North Carolina at Charlotte (NC)
U of Northern Iowa (IA)
U of North Texas (TX)
U of Notre Dame (IN)
U of Oklahoma (OK)
U of Pennsylvania (PA)
U of Puget Sound (WA)
U of Saint Francis (IN)
U of San Francisco (CA)
U of Southern Mississippi (MS)
U of South Florida (FL)
U of South Florida, St. Petersburg (FL)
The U of Tennessee at Martin (TN)
The U of Texas at Austin (TX)
The U of Texas at San Antonio (TX)
The U of Texas Rio Grande Valley (TX)
U of the Cumberlands (KY)
U of the Incarnate Word (TX)
U of the Virgin Islands (VI)
The U of Tulsa (OK)
U of Washington (WA)
The U of West Alabama (AL)
U of West Georgia (GA)
U of Wisconsin–Green Bay (WI)
U of Wisconsin–La Crosse (WI)
U of Wisconsin–Madison (WI)
U of Wisconsin–Milwaukee (WI)
Upper Iowa U (IA)
Valley City State U (ND)
Villanova U (PA)
Virginia State U (VA)
Virginia Union U (VA)
Viterbo U (WI)
Wake Forest U (NC)
Walla Walla U (WA)
Washington State U (WA)
Washington State U–Global Campus (WA)
Washington State U–Vancouver (WA)
Wayne State U (MI)
Weber State U (UT)
Western Carolina U (NC)
Western Connecticut State U (CT)
Western Kentucky U (KY)
Western New England U (MA)
Western State Colorado U (CO)
Western Washington U (WA)
West Texas A&M U (TX)
West Virginia U (WV)
Wichita State U (KS)
William Woods U (MO)
Winona State U (MN)
Worcester Polytechnic Inst (MA)
Wright State U (OH)
Wright State U–Lake Campus (OH)
York Coll of Pennsylvania (PA)
York Coll of the City U of New York (NY)
Youngstown State U (OH)

MANAGEMENT INFORMATION SYSTEMS AND SERVICES RELATED

Bowling Green State U (OH)
Buena Vista U (IA)
Cardinal Stritch U (WI)
DeSales U (PA)
Fordham U (NY)
Montana Tech of The U of Montana (MT)
Newberry Coll (SC)
Purdue U Northwest (IN)
Rogers State U (OK)
Southeastern U (FL)
Temple U (PA)
Tiffin U (OH)
U of Pittsburgh (PA)
Western New England U (MA)
Westminster Coll (UT)
Widener U (PA)

MANAGEMENT SCIENCE

American Intl Coll (MA)
Arizona State U at the Tempe campus (AZ)
Auburn U (AL)
Averett U (VA)
Becker Coll (MA)
Bridgewater State U (MA)
Brigham Young U–Idaho (ID)
Bryant U (RI)
California State U, Northridge (CA)
The Catholic U of America (DC)
Centenary U (NJ)
Central Methodist U (MO)
Dalhousie U (NS, Canada)
Denison U (OH)
Duquesne U (PA)
Eastern Illinois U (IL)
Elon U (NC)
Faulkner U (AL)
Fitchburg State U (MA)
Grand Valley State U (MI)
Great Basin Coll (NV)
Hamline U (MN)
Hardin-Simmons U (TX)
HEC Montreal (QC, Canada)
Illinois State U (IL)
Jacksonville U (FL)
La Roche Coll (PA)
La Salle U (PA)
Lehigh U (PA)
Lenoir-Rhyne U (NC)
LeTourneau U (TX)
Loras Coll (IA)
Louisiana State U and A&M Coll (LA)
Louisiana Tech U (LA)
Lourdes U (OH)
Manhattan Coll (NY)
Marian U (IN)
McKendree U (IL)
Miami U (OH)
National Louis U (IL)
Northern Illinois U (IL)
Oklahoma Baptist U (OK)
Oral Roberts U (OK)
Point Loma Nazarene U (CA)
Portland State U (OR)
Rocky Mountain Coll (MT)
Rutgers U–New Brunswick (NJ)
St. Ambrose U (IA)
St. Gregory's U, Shawnee (OK)
Salve Regina U (RI)
Siena Coll (NY)
Simon Fraser U (BC, Canada)
Southeastern Oklahoma State U (OK)
Southern Illinois U Carbondale (IL)
Southwestern Assemblies of God U (TX)
State U of New York at Oswego (NY)
Texas Wesleyan U (TX)
Trinity U (TX)
United States Coast Guard Acad (CT)
The U of Alabama (AL)
U of Arkansas (AR)
U of California, San Diego (CA)
U of Delaware (DE)
U of Florida (FL)
U of Great Falls (MT)
U of Illinois at Chicago (IL)
The U of Kansas (KS)
U of Kentucky (KY)
U of Maryland, Coll Park (MD)
U of Miami (FL)
U of Missouri–St. Louis (MO)
U of Notre Dame (IN)
U of St. Francis (IL)
U of South Carolina (SC)
The U of Tennessee at Martin (TN)
The U of Texas at Austin (TX)
The U of Texas at San Antonio (TX)
U of the Fraser Valley (BC, Canada)
U of the Southwest (NM)
U of Washington, Tacoma (WA)
Valparaiso U (IN)
Vaughn Coll of Aeronautics and Technology (NY)
Virginia Polytechnic Inst and State U (VA)
Wake Forest U (NC)
Washington State U (WA)
Western Kentucky U (KY)
Western Michigan U (MI)
William Paterson U of New Jersey (NJ)

MANAGEMENT SCIENCES AND QUANTITATIVE METHODS RELATED

Arkansas Tech U (AR)
Canisius Coll (NY)
HEC Montreal (QC, Canada)
Indiana State U (IN)
Inter American U of Puerto Rico, Metropolitan Campus (PR)
Massachusetts Inst of Technology (MA)
Mercer U, Macon (GA)
Miami U (OH)
Pace U (NY)
Penn State Lehigh Valley (PA)
Penn State Schuylkill (PA)
Purdue U (IN)
Rutgers U–New Brunswick (NJ)
U of North Texas (TX)
U of Pennsylvania (PA)
The U of South Dakota (SD)
The U of Texas at Austin (TX)

MANUFACTURING ENGINEERING

Arizona State U at the Polytechnic campus (AZ)
Boston U (MA)
Bradley U (IL)
Brigham Young U (UT)
California Polytechnic State U, San Luis Obispo (CA)
California State Polytechnic U, Pomona (CA)
California State U, Northridge (CA)
Central State U (OH)
Dunwoody Coll of Technology (MN)
Ferris State U (MI)
Georgia Southern U (GA)
Hofstra U (NY)
Miami U (OH)
National U (CA)
North Dakota State U (ND)
Northwestern U (IL)
Oregon State U (OR)
Robert Morris U (PA)
Savannah Coll of Art and Design (GA)
Southern Illinois U Edwardsville (IL)
Texas State U (TX)
U of Detroit Mercy (MI)
U of Michigan–Dearborn (MI)
U of Southern Indiana (IN)
The U of Texas Rio Grande Valley (TX)
U of Toronto (ON, Canada)
U of Wisconsin–Milwaukee (WI)
U of Wisconsin–Stout (WI)
Virginia State U (VA)
Washington State U (WA)
Washington State U–Vancouver (WA)
Western Washington U (WA)
Wichita State U (KS)

MANUFACTURING ENGINEERING TECHNOLOGY

Arizona State U at the Polytechnic campus (AZ)
Berea Coll (KY)
Bradley U (IL)
California State U, Long Beach (CA)
Central Connecticut State U (CT)
Central Michigan U (MI)
Central Washington U (WA)
East Carolina U (NC)
Eastern Michigan U (MI)
Farmingdale State Coll (NY)
Fitchburg State U (MA)
Idaho State U (ID)
Indiana State U (IN)
Missouri Western State U (MO)
Morehead State U (KY)
Murray State U (KY)
Northern Kentucky U (KY)
Pennsylvania Coll of Technology (PA)
Pittsburg State U (KS)
Purdue U (IN)
Rochester Inst of Technology (NY)
Sam Houston State U (TX)
Tarleton State U (TX)
Texas A&M U (TX)
Texas State U (TX)
The U of Akron (OH)
U of Northern Iowa (IA)
U of Southern Indiana (IN)
U of Wisconsin–Platteville (WI)
Wayne State U (MI)
Weber State U (UT)
Western Carolina U (NC)
Western Kentucky U (KY)
Western Michigan U (MI)
Western Washington U (WA)

MARINE BIOLOGY AND BIOLOGICAL OCEANOGRAPHY

Alabama State U (AL)
Auburn U (AL)
Barry U (FL)
Bemidji State U (MN)
Boston U (MA)
California State U, Long Beach (CA)
Coastal Carolina U (SC)
Coll of Charleston (SC)
Coll of the Atlantic (ME)
Dalhousie U (NS, Canada)
East Stroudsburg U of Pennsylvania (PA)
Eckerd Coll (FL)
Fairleigh Dickinson U, Coll at Florham (NJ)
Fairleigh Dickinson U, Metropolitan Campus (NJ)
Florida Inst of Technology (FL)
Florida Intl U (FL)
Florida Southern Coll (FL)
Gettysburg Coll (PA)
Hampton U (VA)
Hawai`i Pacific U (HI)
Humboldt State U (CA)
Jacksonville State U (AL)
Jacksonville U (FL)
Monmouth U (NJ)
Montclair State U (NJ)
New Coll of Florida (FL)
Northeastern U (MA)
Northwest Missouri State U (MO)
Nova Southeastern U (FL)
Prescott Coll (AZ)
Roger Williams U (RI)
Rollins Coll (FL)
Rutgers U–New Brunswick (NJ)
Saint Francis U (PA)
Samford U (AL)
San Francisco State U (CA)
Sonoma State U (CA)
Southwestern Coll (KS)
Spring Hill Coll (AL)
Stockton U (NJ)
Stony Brook U, State U of New York (NY)
Texas A&M U (TX)
Troy U (AL)
Unity Coll (ME)
The U of Alabama (AL)
U of California, Los Angeles (CA)
U of California, Santa Barbara (CA)
U of Delaware (DE)
U of Georgia (GA)
U of Guelph (ON, Canada)
U of Hawaii at Manoa (HI)
U of King's Coll (NS, Canada)
U of Miami (FL)
U of Mobile (AL)
U of New England (ME)
U of New Haven (CT)
U of North Alabama (AL)
The U of North Carolina Wilmington (NC)
U of Rhode Island (RI)
U of South Carolina (SC)
U of Southern Mississippi (MS)
The U of Tampa (FL)
The U of Texas Rio Grande Valley (TX)
U of the Virgin Islands (VI)
The U of West Alabama (AL)
Waynesburg U (PA)
Western Washington U (WA)
Whitman Coll (WA)

MARINE MAINTENANCE AND SHIP REPAIR TECHNOLOGY

California State U Maritime Acad (CA)

MARINE SCIENCE/MERCHANT MARINE OFFICER

Hampton U (VA)
Jacksonville U (FL)
Massachusetts Maritime Acad (MA)
State U of New York Maritime Coll (NY)
Texas A&M U (TX)
United States Merchant Marine Acad (NY)
U of South Carolina (SC)

MARINE SCIENCES

California State U, Monterey Bay (CA)
Goshen Coll (IN)
Texas A&M U (TX)
U of Maine (ME)
The U of Texas at Austin (TX)

MARINE TRANSPORTATION RELATED

United States Merchant Marine Acad (NY)

MARITIME STUDIES

Coll of the Atlantic (ME)

DEREE - The American Coll of Greece (Greece)
Texas A&M U (TX)

MARKETING/MARKETING MANAGEMENT

Abilene Christian U (TX)
Adams State U (CO)
Adelphi U (NY)
Alabama State U (AL)
Albany State U (GA)
Albertus Magnus Coll (CT)
Albright Coll (PA)
Alderson Broaddus U (WV)
Alfred U (NY)
Alma Coll (MI)
Alvernia U (PA)
American Intl Coll (MA)
American Public U System (WV)
The American U of Paris (France)
Anderson U (IN)
Anderson U (SC)
Andrews U (MI)
Angelo State U (TX)
Appalachian State U (NC)
Aquinas Coll (TN)
Arcadia U (PA)
Arizona State U at the Tempe campus (AZ)
Asbury U (KY)
Ashland U (OH)
Assumption Coll (MA)
Auburn U (AL)
Auburn U at Montgomery (AL)
Augsburg Coll (MN)
Augusta U (GA)
Aurora U (IL)
Austin Peay State U (TN)
Averett U (VA)
Avila U (MO)
Azusa Pacific U (CA)
Baldwin Wallace U (OH)
Ball State U (IN)
Barry U (FL)
Bayamón Central U (PR)
Baylor U (TX)
Bay Path U (MA)
Becker Coll (MA)
Benedictine Coll (KS)
Bentley U (MA)
Berkeley Coll–New York City Campus (NY)
Berkeley Coll–White Plains Campus (NY)
Berkeley Coll–Woodland Park Campus (NJ)
Berry Coll (GA)
Binghamton U, State U of New York (NY)
Biola U (CA)
Bishop's U (QC, Canada)
Blackburn Coll (IL)
Black Hills State U (SD)
Bluffton U (OH)
Boise State U (ID)
Boston Coll (MA)
Bowie State U (MD)
Bowling Green State U (OH)
Bradley U (IL)
Brenau U (GA)
Bridgewater State U (MA)
Bryant U (RI)
Bucknell U (PA)
Buena Vista U (IA)
Butler U (IN)
Cabrini U (PA)
Caldwell U (NJ)
California Baptist U (CA)
California Lutheran U (CA)
California State U, Dominguez Hills (CA)
California State U, East Bay (CA)
California State U, Fresno (CA)
California State U, Fullerton (CA)
California State U, Long Beach (CA)
California State U, Northridge (CA)
California State U, Sacramento (CA)
California State U, San Marcos (CA)
California State U, Stanislaus (CA)
Calvary U (MO)
Campbellsville U (KY)
Canisius Coll (NY)
Capital U (OH)
Cardinal Stritch U (WI)
Caribbean U (PR)
Carnegie Mellon U (PA)
Carson-Newman U (TN)
Carthage Coll (WI)
Case Western Reserve U (OH)
Catawba Coll (NC)
The Catholic U of America (DC)
Cedarville U (OH)
Centenary U (NJ)
Central Baptist Coll (AR)
Central Connecticut State U (CT)
Central Michigan U (MI)
Central Penn Coll (PA)
Central Washington U (WA)
Champlain Coll (VT)
Charleston Southern U (SC)
Chatham U (PA)
Chestnut Hill Coll (PA)
Chowan U (NC)
Christopher Newport U (VA)
Clarion U of Pennsylvania (PA)
Clayton State U (GA)
Clemson U (SC)
Cleveland State U (OH)
Coastal Carolina U (SC)
The Coll at Brockport, State U of New York (NY)
Coll of Charleston (SC)
The Coll of Saint Rose (NY)
The Coll of St. Scholastica (MN)
Coll of the Ozarks (MO)
The Coll of William and Mary (VA)
Colorado Christian U (CO)
Colorado State U (CO)
Columbia Coll (MO)
Columbia Coll Chicago (IL)
Columbia Southern U (AL)
Columbus State U (GA)
Concordia U (QC, Canada)
Concordia U Chicago (IL)
Concordia U, Nebraska (NE)
Concordia U, St. Paul (MN)
Concordia U Wisconsin (WI)
Converse Coll (SC)
Cornerstone U (MI)
Creighton U (NE)
Culver-Stockton Coll (MO)
Dakota State U (SD)
Dalhousie U (NS, Canada)
Dallas Baptist U (TX)
Dalton State Coll (GA)
Davenport U, Grand Rapids (MI)
DEREE - The American Coll of Greece (Greece)
DeSales U (PA)
Dominican Coll (NY)
Dominican U (IL)
Drake U (IA)
Drexel U (PA)
Drury U (MO)
Duquesne U (PA)
East Carolina U (NC)
East Central U (OK)
Eastern Illinois U (IL)
Eastern Michigan U (MI)
Eastern Nazarene Coll (MA)
Eastern Washington U (WA)
East Tennessee State U (TN)
East Texas Baptist U (TX)
Elms Coll (MA)
Elon U (NC)
Emerson Coll (MA)
Emmanuel Coll (MA)
Emporia State U (KS)
Endicott Coll (MA)
Evangel U (MO)
Excelsior Coll (NY)
Fairfield U (CT)
Fairleigh Dickinson U, Coll at Florham (NJ)
Fairleigh Dickinson U, Metropolitan Campus (NJ)
Fayetteville State U (NC)
Felician U (NJ)
Fisher Coll (MA)
Fitchburg State U (MA)
Florida Atlantic U (FL)
Florida Gulf Coast U (FL)
Florida Inst of Technology (FL)
Florida Intl U (FL)
Fordham U (NY)
Fort Lewis Coll (CO)
Framingham State U (MA)
Franciscan U of Steubenville (OH)
Francis Marion U (SC)
Franklin Pierce U (NH)
Freed-Hardeman U (TN)
Fresno Pacific U (CA)
Friends U (KS)
Gannon U (PA)
Gardner-Webb U (NC)
George Fox U (OR)
Georgetown Coll (KY)
Georgetown U (DC)
The George Washington U (DC)
Georgia Coll & State U (GA)
Georgian Court U (NJ)
Georgia Southern U (GA)
Georgia Southwestern State U (GA)
Georgia State U (GA)
Gonzaga U (WA)
Goshen Coll (IN)
Grace Coll (IN)
Grambling State U (LA)
Grand Valley State U (MI)
Grand View U (IA)
Granite State Coll (NH)
Greenville Coll (IL)
Grove City Coll (PA)
Hamline U (MN)
Hampton U (VA)
Hannibal-LaGrange U (MO)
Harding U (AR)
Hardin-Simmons U (TX)
HEC Montreal (QC, Canada)
High Point U (NC)
Hillsdale Coll (MI)
Hofstra U (NY)
Holy Family U (PA)
Holy Names U (CA)
Houston Baptist U (TX)
Howard Payne U (TX)
Hult Intl Business School (United Kingdom)
Huntington U (IN)
Husson U (ME)
Idaho State U (ID)
Illinois State U (IL)
Immaculata U (PA)
Indiana State U (IN)
Indiana U of Pennsylvania (PA)
Inter American U of Puerto Rico, Aguadilla Campus (PR)
Inter American U of Puerto Rico, Bayamón Campus (PR)
Inter American U of Puerto Rico, Fajardo Campus (PR)
Inter American U of Puerto Rico, Metropolitan Campus (PR)
Inter American U of Puerto Rico, Ponce Campus (PR)
Inter American U of Puerto Rico, San Germán Campus (PR)
Iona Coll (NY)
Iowa State U of Science and Technology (IA)
Ithaca Coll (NY)
Jackson State U (MS)
Jacksonville State U (AL)
Jacksonville U (FL)
James Madison U (VA)
John Brown U (AR)
John Carroll U (OH)
Judson U (IL)
Juniata Coll (PA)
Kansas State U (KS)
Kansas Wesleyan U (KS)
Kean U (NJ)
Kennesaw State U (GA)
Kent State U (OH)
Kent State U at Stark (OH)
Keuka Coll (NY)
King's Coll (PA)
King U (TN)
Lake Erie Coll (OH)
Lamar U (TX)
La Roche Coll (PA)
La Salle U (PA)
Lasell Coll (MA)
Lehigh U (PA)
Le Moyne Coll (NY)
Lenoir-Rhyne U (NC)
LeTourneau U (TX)
Lewis U (IL)
LIM Coll (NY)
Limestone Coll (SC)
Lindenwood U (MO)
Linfield Coll (OR)
Lipscomb U (TN)
Loras Coll (IA)
Louisiana State U and A&M Coll (LA)
Louisiana Tech U (LA)
Loyola Marymount U (CA)
Loyola U Chicago (IL)
Loyola U New Orleans (LA)
Lubbock Christian U (TX)
Lynchburg Coll (VA)
Lynn U (FL)
MacMurray Coll (IL)
Madonna U (MI)
Malone U (OH)
Manchester U (IN)
Manhattan Coll (NY)
Manhattanville Coll (NY)
Mansfield U of Pennsylvania (PA)
Maranatha Baptist U (WI)
Marian U (IN)
Marian U (WI)
Marietta Coll (OH)
Marshall U (WV)
Marymount Manhattan Coll (NY)
Maryville U of Saint Louis (MO)
Marywood U (PA)
Massachusetts Coll of Liberal Arts (MA)
McKendree U (IL)
McMurry U (TX)
McNeese State U (LA)
Menlo Coll (CA)
Mercer U, Macon (GA)
Mercy Coll (NY)
Mercyhurst U (PA)
Merrimack Coll (MA)
Messiah Coll (PA)
Metropolitan State U of Denver (CO)
Miami U (OH)
Michigan State U (MI)
Michigan Technological U (MI)
MidAmerica Nazarene U (KS)
Millikin U (IL)
Minnesota State U Mankato (MN)
Minot State U (ND)
Mississippi State U (MS)
Missouri Baptist U (MO)
Missouri State U (MO)
Missouri Valley Coll (MO)
Missouri Western State U (MO)
Molloy Coll (NY)
Montana State U (MT)
Montana State U Billings (MT)
Morehead State U (KY)
Mount Mary U (WI)
Mount Mercy U (IA)
Mount Saint Mary's U (CA)
Mount Vernon Nazarene U (OH)
Murray State U (KY)
Muskingum U (OH)
Nazareth Coll of Rochester (NY)
Neumann U (PA)
New England Coll (NH)
New Mexico Highlands U (NM)
New Mexico State U (NM)
New York Inst of Technology (NY)
Niagara U (NY)
Nichols Coll (MA)
North Carolina Wesleyan Coll (NC)
North Central Coll (IL)
Northcentral U (CA)
North Dakota State U (ND)
Northeastern Illinois U (IL)
Northeastern State U (OK)
Northeastern U (MA)
Northern Arizona U (AZ)
Northern Illinois U (IL)
Northern Kentucky U (KY)
Northern State U (SD)
North Greenville U (SC)
Northwest Missouri State U (MO)
Northwest U (WA)
Northwood U, Michigan Campus (MI)
Nova Southeastern U (FL)
The Ohio State U (OH)
Ohio U (OH)
Ohio Valley U (WV)
Oklahoma Baptist U (OK)
Oklahoma Christian U (OK)
Oklahoma City U (OK)
Oklahoma State U (OK)
Old Dominion U (VA)
Olivet Nazarene U (IL)
Oral Roberts U (OK)
Oregon State U (OR)
Otterbein U (OH)
Pace U (NY)
Pace U, Pleasantville Campus (NY)
Palm Beach Atlantic U (FL)
Penn State Abington (PA)
Penn State Altoona (PA)
Penn State Beaver (PA)
Penn State Berks (PA)
Penn State Brandywine (PA)
Penn State DuBois (PA)
Penn State Erie, The Behrend Coll (PA)
Penn State Fayette, The Eberly Campus (PA)
Penn State Greater Allegheny (PA)
Penn State Harrisburg (PA)
Penn State Hazleton (PA)
Penn State Lehigh Valley (PA)
Penn State Mont Alto (PA)
Penn State New Kensington (PA)
Penn State Schuylkill (PA)
Penn State Shenango (PA)
Penn State U Park (PA)
Penn State Wilkes-Barre (PA)
Penn State Worthington Scranton (PA)
Penn State York (PA)
Pittsburg State U (KS)
Plymouth State U (NH)
Point Loma Nazarene U (CA)
Point U (GA)
Polytechnic U of Puerto Rico (PR)
Portland State U (OR)
Prairie View A&M U (TX)
Providence Coll (RI)
Quinnipiac U (CT)
Radford U (VA)
Rasmussen Coll Bloomington (MN)
Rasmussen Coll Brooklyn Park (MN)
Rasmussen Coll Eagan (MN)
Rasmussen Coll Fort Myers (FL)
Rasmussen Coll Kansas City/ Overland Park (KS)
Rasmussen Coll Lake Elmo/ Woodbury (MN)
Rasmussen Coll Land O' Lakes (FL)
Rasmussen Coll Mankato (MN)
Rasmussen Coll Moorhead (MN)
Rasmussen Coll New Port Richey (FL)
Rasmussen Coll Ocala (FL)
Rasmussen Coll St. Cloud (MN)
Rasmussen Coll Tampa/Brandon (FL)
Rasmussen Coll Topeka (KS)
Redeemer U Coll (ON, Canada)
Regis U (CO)
Rhode Island Coll (RI)
Robert Morris U (PA)
Roberts Wesleyan Coll (NY)
Rochester Inst of Technology (NY)
Rockford U (IL)
Roger Williams U (RI)
Rosemont Coll (PA)
Rowan U (NJ)
Rutgers U–Camden (NJ)
Rutgers U–Newark (NJ)
Rutgers U–New Brunswick (NJ)
Sacred Heart U (CT)
Saginaw Valley State U (MI)
St. Ambrose U (IA)
St. Bonaventure U (NY)
St. Catherine U (MN)
St. Cloud State U (MN)
St. Edward's U (TX)
Saint Francis U (PA)
St. Gregory's U, Shawnee (OK)
St. John's U (NY)
St. Joseph's Coll, Long Island Campus (NY)
St. Joseph's Coll, New York (NY)
Saint Joseph's U (PA)
Saint Leo U (FL)
Saint Louis U (MO)
Saint Mary-of-the-Woods Coll (IN)
Saint Mary's U of Minnesota (MN)
Saint Peter's U (NJ)
St. Thomas Aquinas Coll (NY)
St. Thomas U (FL)
Saint Vincent Coll (PA)
Salisbury U (MD)
Salve Regina U (RI)
Samford U (AL)
Sam Houston State U (TX)
San Diego State U (CA)
San Francisco State U (CA)
Santa Clara U (CA)
Schreiner U (TX)
Seattle U (WA)
Seton Hill U (PA)

Shippensburg U of Pennsylvania (PA)
Siena Coll (NY)
Simmons Coll (MA)
Simpson Coll (IA)
South Carolina State U (SC)
Southeastern Louisiana U (LA)
Southeastern Oklahoma State U (OK)
Southeastern U (FL)
Southeast Missouri State U (MO)
Southern Connecticut State U (CT)
Southern Illinois U Carbondale (IL)
Southern Methodist U (TX)
Southern New Hampshire U (NH)
Southern Oregon U (OR)
Southern Utah U (UT)
Southwest Baptist U (MO)
Southwestern Adventist U (TX)
Southwestern Assemblies of God U (TX)
Southwestern Coll (KS)
Spring Hill Coll (AL)
State U of New York at Fredonia (NY)
State U of New York at New Paltz (NY)
State U of New York at Oswego (NY)
State U of New York at Plattsburgh (NY)
State U of New York Coll at Old Westbury (NY)
Stephen F. Austin State U (TX)
Stonehill Coll (MA)
Suffolk U (MA)
Susquehanna U (PA)
Syracuse U (NY)
Tarleton State U (TX)
Taylor U (IN)
Temple U (PA)
Tennessee Wesleyan U (TN)
Texas A&M U (TX)
Texas A&M U–Central Texas (TX)
Texas A&M U–Commerce (TX)
Texas A&M U–Corpus Christi (TX)
Texas A&M U–Kingsville (TX)
Texas Christian U (TX)
Texas State U (TX)
Texas Tech U (TX)
Texas Wesleyan U (TX)
Texas Woman's U (TX)
Thomas Edison State U (NJ)
Tiffin U (OH)
Trevecca Nazarene U (TN)
Trine U (IN)
Trinity Christian Coll (IL)
Trinity U (TX)
Tulane U (LA)
Union Coll (KY)
Union U (TN)
Université de Sherbrooke (QC, Canada)
The U of Akron (OH)
The U of Alabama (AL)
The U of Alabama at Birmingham (AL)
The U of Alabama in Huntsville (AL)
The U of Arizona (AZ)
U of Arkansas (AR)
U of Bridgeport (CT)
U of Central Arkansas (AR)
U of Central Florida (FL)
U of Central Missouri (MO)
U of Charleston (WV)
U of Cincinnati (OH)
U of Colorado Boulder (CO)
U of Dayton (OH)
U of Delaware (DE)
U of Denver (CO)
U of Dubuque (IA)
U of Evansville (IN)
The U of Findlay (OH)
U of Florida (FL)
U of Georgia (GA)
U of Great Falls (MT)
U of Guelph (ON, Canada)
U of Hawaii at Manoa (HI)
U of Houston (TX)
U of Houston–Clear Lake (TX)
U of Houston–Downtown (TX)
U of Idaho (ID)
U of Illinois at Chicago (IL)
U of Indianapolis (IN)
U of Jamestown (ND)
The U of Kansas (KS)
U of Kentucky (KY)
U of La Verne (CA)
U of Lethbridge (AB, Canada)
U of Louisiana at Monroe (LA)
U of Louisville (KY)
U of Maine (ME)
U of Mary Hardin-Baylor (TX)
U of Maryland, Coll Park (MD)
U of Maryland U Coll (MD)
U of Massachusetts Amherst (MA)
U of Massachusetts Dartmouth (MA)
U of Miami (FL)
U of Michigan–Dearborn (MI)
U of Michigan–Flint (MI)
U of Minnesota, Crookston (MN)
U of Minnesota, Duluth (MN)
U of Minnesota, Twin Cities Campus (MN)
U of Missouri–St. Louis (MO)
U of Montevallo (AL)
U of Mount Union (OH)
U of Nevada, Las Vegas (NV)
U of Nevada, Reno (NV)
U of New Haven (CT)
U of New Orleans (LA)
U of North Alabama (AL)
The U of North Carolina at Charlotte (NC)
U of North Dakota (ND)
U of Northern Iowa (IA)
U of North Florida (FL)
U of North Georgia (GA)
U of North Texas (TX)
U of Northwestern Ohio (OH)
U of Notre Dame (IN)
U of Oklahoma (OK)
U of Pennsylvania (PA)
U of Pittsburgh (PA)
U of Puerto Rico in Bayamón (PR)
U of Regina (SK, Canada)
U of Rhode Island (RI)
U of St. Francis (IL)
U of Saint Francis (IN)
U of St. Thomas (MN)
U of St. Thomas (TX)
U of San Diego (CA)
U of San Francisco (CA)
U of Saskatchewan (SK, Canada)
The U of Scranton (PA)
U of South Alabama (AL)
U of South Carolina (SC)
The U of South Dakota (SD)
U of Southern Indiana (IN)
U of Southern Maine (ME)
U of Southern Mississippi (MS)
U of South Florida (FL)
U of South Florida, St. Petersburg (FL)
U of South Florida Sarasota-Manatee (FL)
The U of Tampa (FL)
The U of Tennessee (TN)
The U of Tennessee at Martin (TN)
The U of Texas at Austin (TX)
The U of Texas at Dallas (TX)
The U of Texas at El Paso (TX)
The U of Texas at San Antonio (TX)
The U of Texas of the Permian Basin (TX)
The U of Texas Rio Grande Valley (TX)
U of the Incarnate Word (TX)
U of the Virgin Islands (VI)
The U of Toledo (OH)
The U of Tulsa (OK)
U of Utah (UT)
U of Washington (WA)
U of Washington, Tacoma (WA)
The U of West Alabama (AL)
U of West Georgia (GA)
U of Windsor (ON, Canada)
U of Wisconsin–Eau Claire (WI)
U of Wisconsin–La Crosse (WI)
U of Wisconsin–Madison (WI)
U of Wisconsin–Milwaukee (WI)
U of Wisconsin–Parkside (WI)
U of Wisconsin–Superior (WI)
U of Wisconsin–Whitewater (WI)
Upper Iowa U (IA)
Utah State U (UT)
Utah Valley U (UT)
Valdosta State U (GA)
Valparaiso U (IN)
Villanova U (PA)
Virginia Commonwealth U (VA)
Virginia Polytechnic Inst and State U (VA)
Virginia State U (VA)
Virginia Union U (VA)
Viterbo U (WI)
Walla Walla U (WA)
Walsh Coll of Accountancy and Business Administration (MI)
Walsh U (OH)
Wartburg Coll (IA)
Washburn U (KS)
Washington State U (WA)
Washington State U–Vancouver (WA)
Washington U in St. Louis (MO)
Waynesburg U (PA)
Wayne State U (MI)
Webber Intl U (FL)
Weber State U (UT)
Webster U (MO)
Western Carolina U (NC)
Western Connecticut State U (CT)
Western Illinois U (IL)
Western Kentucky U (KY)
Western Michigan U (MI)
Western New England U (MA)
Western State Colorado U (CO)
Western Washington U (WA)
Westminster Coll (PA)
Westminster Coll (UT)
West Texas A&M U (TX)
West Virginia U (WV)
West Virginia Wesleyan Coll (WV)
Whitworth U (WA)
Wichita State U (KS)
Widener U (PA)
Wilkes U (PA)
William Paterson U of New Jersey (NJ)
Wilmington U (DE)
Wingate U (NC)
Winona State U (MN)
Wittenberg U (OH)
Woodbury U (CA)
Wright State U (OH)
Wright State U–Lake Campus (OH)
Xavier U of Louisiana (LA)
York Coll of Pennsylvania (PA)
York Coll of the City U of New York (NY)
Youngstown State U (OH)

MARKETING RELATED
The American U in Dubai (United Arab Emirates)
Anderson U (IN)
Bowling Green State U (OH)
Colorado Christian U (CO)
Duquesne U (PA)
Eastern Nazarene Coll (MA)
Eastern U (PA)
Lourdes U (OH)
Mary Baldwin U (VA)
Mount Mercy U (IA)
Mount St. Joseph U (OH)
Newberry Coll (SC)
Niagara U (NY)
Northwood U, Michigan Campus (MI)
Our Lady of the Lake U of San Antonio (TX)
Saginaw Valley State U (MI)
Saint Louis U–Madrid Campus (Spain)
State U of New York at New Paltz (NY)
Stephens Coll (MO)
Stevenson U (MD)
U of Michigan–Dearborn (MI)
U of Minnesota, Duluth (MN)
U of Southern Mississippi (MS)
U of South Florida (FL)
Washington U in St. Louis (MO)
Western Carolina U (NC)
Western Michigan U (MI)
Western New England U (MA)

MARKETING RESEARCH
Ashland U (OH)
Bowling Green State U (OH)
Fashion Inst of Technology (NY)
Husson U (ME)
Ithaca Coll (NY)
Mercyhurst U (PA)
U of Georgia (GA)

MARRIAGE AND FAMILY THERAPY/COUNSELING
DeSales U (PA)
Johnson U (TN)
Johnson U Florida (FL)
Oklahoma Baptist U (OK)
Piedmont Intl U (NC)
U of Mobile (AL)

MASSAGE THERAPY
Idaho State U (ID)

MASS COMMUNICATION/ MEDIA
Adams State U (CO)
Albany State U (GA)
Albion Coll (MI)
Alcorn State U (MS)
Alderson Broaddus U (WV)
Allegheny Coll (PA)
American Intl Coll (MA)
American U (DC)
American U in Bulgaria (Bulgaria)
The American U in Cairo (Egypt)
Andrews U (MI)
Arcadia U (PA)
Ashland U (OH)
Auburn U (AL)
Augustana Coll (IL)
Austin Coll (TX)
Austin Peay State U (TN)
Baker U (KS)
Baldwin Wallace U (OH)
Barry U (FL)
Barton Coll (NC)
Belmont U (TN)
Beloit Coll (WI)
Bemidji State U (MN)
Benedictine Coll (KS)
Bentley U (MA)
Berea Coll (KY)
Bethel Coll (KS)
Bethel U (MN)
Bethune-Cookman U (FL)
Black Hills State U (SD)
Bloomsburg U of Pennsylvania (PA)
Bluefield Coll (VA)
Boise State U (ID)
Bowie State U (MD)
Brenau U (GA)
Briar Cliff U (IA)
Bridgewater Coll (VA)
Bryant U (RI)
Buena Vista U (IA)
Buffalo State Coll, State U of New York (NY)
California Lutheran U (CA)
California State U, Bakersfield (CA)
California State U, East Bay (CA)
California State U, Fresno (CA)
California State U, Long Beach (CA)
California State U, Sacramento (CA)
California State U, San Marcos (CA)
Calvary U (MO)
Calvin Coll (MI)
Campbellsville U (KY)
Carson-Newman U (TN)
Cedar Crest Coll (PA)
Centenary U (NJ)
Central Connecticut State U (CT)
Chestnut Hill Coll (PA)
City Coll of the City U of New York (NY)
Clark U (MA)
Colby-Sawyer Coll (NH)
Coll of Mount Saint Vincent (NY)
The Coll of Wooster (OH)
Colorado Mesa U (CO)
Columbia Intl U (SC)
Concordia U (QC, Canada)
Concordia U, St. Paul (MN)
Concordia U Wisconsin (WI)
Concord U (WV)
Crandall U (NB, Canada)
Culver-Stockton Coll (MO)
Defiance Coll (OH)
Denison U (OH)
DePauw U (IN)
Dixie State U (UT)
Drake U (IA)
East Central U (OK)
Eastern Nazarene Coll (MA)
East Tennessee State U (TN)
East Texas Baptist U (TX)
Elizabethtown Coll (PA)
Emerson Coll (MA)
Emmanuel Coll (GA)
Emory & Henry Coll (VA)
Endicott Coll (MA)
Eugene Lang Coll of Liberal Arts (NY)
The Evergreen State Coll (WA)
Felician U (NJ)
Fisher Coll (MA)
Flagler Coll (FL)
Florida Gulf Coast U (FL)
Florida Intl U (FL)
Florida Southern Coll (FL)
Fordham U (NY)
Francis Marion U (SC)
Franklin Pierce U (NH)
Freed-Hardeman U (TN)
Frostburg State U (MD)
Gardner-Webb U (NC)
The George Washington U (DC)
Gonzaga U (WA)
Goucher Coll (MD)
Governors State U (IL)
Grambling State U (LA)
Grand View U (IA)
Green Mountain Coll (VT)
Greenville Coll (IL)
Hampton U (VA)
Hanover Coll (IN)
Hawai`i Pacific U (HI)
Heidelberg U (OH)
Hobart and William Smith Colls (NY)
Hofstra U (NY)
Hollins U (VA)
Holy Family U (PA)
Houston Baptist U (TX)
Hunter Coll of the City U of New York (NY)
Huntington U (IN)
Huston-Tillotson U (TX)
Illinois Coll (IL)
Illinois State U (IL)
Indiana U Bloomington (IN)
Iona Coll (NY)
Iowa State U of Science and Technology (IA)
Ithaca Coll (NY)
Jackson State U (MS)
Jacksonville U (FL)
John Carroll U (OH)
Johnson C. Smith U (NC)
Johnson U (TN)
Kuyper Coll (MI)
Lehman Coll of the City U of New York (NY)
LeTourneau U (TX)
Lindenwood U (MO)
Lindsey Wilson Coll (KY)
Linfield Coll (OR)
Lipscomb U (TN)
Lock Haven U of Pennsylvania (PA)
Loras Coll (IA)
Louisiana Coll (LA)
Louisiana State U and A&M Coll (LA)
Louisiana State U at Alexandria (LA)
Lubbock Christian U (TX)
Macalester Coll (MN)
Manchester U (IN)
Mansfield U of Pennsylvania (PA)
Marylhurst U (OR)
Maryville U of Saint Louis (MO)
Massachusetts Inst of Technology (MA)
The Master's U (CA)
McNeese State U (LA)
Mercer U, Macon (GA)
Mercy Coll (NY)
Meredith Coll (NC)
Miami U (OH)
Michigan State U (MI)
MidAmerica Nazarene U (KS)
Minnesota State U Mankato (MN)
Minnesota State U Moorhead (MN)
Mississippi Valley State U (MS)
Missouri State U (MO)
Missouri Valley Coll (MO)
Morris Coll (SC)
Mount Saint Mary Coll (NY)
Muskingum U (OH)
New England Coll (NH)
Newman U (KS)
The New School for Public Engagement (NY)
North Carolina Central U (NC)

North Greenville U (SC)
Northwestern Oklahoma State U (OK)
Oklahoma Baptist U (OK)
Oklahoma Christian U (OK)
Oklahoma City U (OK)
Olivet Nazarene U (IL)
Ouachita Baptist U (AR)
Pace U (NY)
Palm Beach Atlantic U (FL)
Piedmont Coll (GA)
Point Loma Nazarene U (CA)
Point Park U (PA)
Pomona Coll (CA)
Principia Coll (IL)
Queens Coll of the City U of New York (NY)
Quinnipiac U (CT)
Rhode Island Coll (RI)
Robert Morris U (PA)
Roberts Wesleyan Coll (NY)
Rutgers U–New Brunswick (NJ)
St. Catherine U (MN)
St. Cloud State U (MN)
Saint Francis U (PA)
Saint Mary-of-the-Woods Coll (IN)
Saint Michael's Coll (VT)
St. Norbert Coll (WI)
St. Thomas Aquinas Coll (NY)
St. Thomas U (FL)
Sam Houston State U (TX)
Scripps Coll (CA)
Shaw U (NC)
Sonoma State U (CA)
South Carolina State U (SC)
Southern Illinois U Edwardsville (IL)
Spalding U (KY)
State U of New York at Fredonia (NY)
State U of New York at Oswego (NY)
Stephen F. Austin State U (TX)
Stephens Coll (MO)
Suffolk U (MA)
Temple U (PA)
Tennessee State U (TN)
Texas State U (TX)
Texas Tech U (TX)
Texas Wesleyan U (TX)
Towson U (MD)
Trevecca Nazarene U (TN)
Tufts U (MA)
Tulane U (LA)
Union Coll (KY)
Union U (TN)
Université de Montréal (QC, Canada)
U at Albany, State U of New York (NY)
U of Bridgeport (CT)
U of California, San Diego (CA)
U of Charleston (WV)
U of Colorado Boulder (CO)
U of Denver (CO)
U of Georgia (GA)
U of Houston (TX)
U of Jamestown (ND)
U of Louisiana at Monroe (LA)
U of Maine (ME)
U of Mary Hardin-Baylor (TX)
U of Maryland, Baltimore County (MD)
U of Miami (FL)
U of Michigan–Dearborn (MI)
U of Missouri–Kansas City (MO)
U of Missouri–St. Louis (MO)
U of Nebraska at Kearney (NE)
U of Nevada, Las Vegas (NV)
U of New Hampshire at Manchester (NH)
U of North Alabama (AL)
U of North Carolina at Asheville (NC)
The U of North Carolina at Chapel Hill (NC)
The U of North Carolina at Greensboro (NC)
The U of North Carolina at Pembroke (NC)
U of North Florida (FL)
U of Oregon (OR)
U of Pittsburgh (PA)
U of Pittsburgh at Greensburg (PA)
U of Pittsburgh at Johnstown (PA)
U of St. Francis (IL)
U of San Francisco (CA)
U of Southern Indiana (IN)
U of Southern Maine (ME)
U of South Florida (FL)
U of South Florida, St. Petersburg (FL)
The U of Tennessee at Chattanooga (TN)
The U of Texas at El Paso (TX)
The U of Texas Rio Grande Valley (TX)
U of the Incarnate Word (TX)
U of Toronto (ON, Canada)
U of Washington, Bothell (WA)
U of Washington, Tacoma (WA)
U of Wisconsin–Eau Claire (WI)
U of Wisconsin–Milwaukee (WI)
U of Wisconsin–Superior (WI)
Upper Iowa U (IA)
Ursinus Coll (PA)
Valdosta State U (GA)
Valley City State U (ND)
Vassar Coll (NY)
Villanova U (PA)
Virginia Commonwealth U (VA)
Virginia State U (VA)
Virginia Union U (VA)
Virginia Wesleyan Coll (VA)
Walla Walla U (WA)
Wartburg Coll (IA)
Washburn U (KS)
Washington State U (WA)
Wayland Baptist U (TX)
Wayne State Coll (NE)
Webster U (MO)
Western New England U (MA)
Westminster Coll (PA)
Whitworth U (WA)
Widener U (PA)
Wilson Coll (PA)
Winona State U (MN)
Winthrop U (SC)
Worcester State U (MA)
Wright State U (OH)
Xavier U of Louisiana (LA)
York Coll of Pennsylvania (PA)

MATERIALS CHEMISTRY
United States Air Force Acad (CO)

MATERIALS ENGINEERING
Alfred U (NY)
Arizona State U at the Tempe campus (AZ)
Auburn U (AL)
Boise State U (ID)
California Inst of Technology (CA)
California Polytechnic State U, San Luis Obispo (CA)
California State U, Long Beach (CA)
Case Western Reserve U (OH)
Clemson U (SC)
Cornell U (NY)
Drexel U (PA)
Georgia Inst of Technology (GA)
Iowa State U of Science and Technology (IA)
Johns Hopkins U (MD)
Lehigh U (PA)
Massachusetts Inst of Technology (MA)
McMaster U (ON, Canada)
Michigan State U (MI)
Michigan Technological U (MI)
New Mexico Inst of Mining and Technology (NM)
North Carolina State U (NC)
Northwestern U (IL)
The Ohio State U (OH)
Purdue U (IN)
Rensselaer Polytechnic Inst (NY)
Rice U (TX)
U at Albany, State U of New York (NY)
The U of Alabama at Birmingham (AL)
U of California, Davis (CA)
U of California, Irvine (CA)
U of California, Los Angeles (CA)
U of Florida (FL)
U of Idaho (ID)
U of Kentucky (KY)
U of Maryland, Coll Park (MD)
U of Michigan (MI)
U of Minnesota, Twin Cities Campus (MN)
U of North Texas (TX)
U of Pennsylvania (PA)
U of Pittsburgh (PA)
The U of Tennessee (TN)
The U of Texas at Austin (TX)
U of Toronto (ON, Canada)
U of Utah (UT)
U of Washington (WA)
U of Windsor (ON, Canada)
U of Wisconsin–Eau Claire (WI)
U of Wisconsin–Madison (WI)
U of Wisconsin–Milwaukee (WI)
Virginia Polytechnic Inst and State U (VA)
Washington State U (WA)
Winona State U (MN)
Wright State U (OH)
Wright State U–Lake Campus (OH)

MATERIALS SCIENCE
Carnegie Mellon U (PA)
Case Western Reserve U (OH)
Columbia U (NY)
Johns Hopkins U (MD)
McMaster U (ON, Canada)
Northwestern U (IL)
The Ohio State U (OH)
Penn State Abington (PA)
Penn State Altoona (PA)
Penn State Beaver (PA)
Penn State Berks (PA)
Penn State Brandywine (PA)
Penn State DuBois (PA)
Penn State Erie, The Behrend Coll (PA)
Penn State Fayette, The Eberly Campus (PA)
Penn State Greater Allegheny (PA)
Penn State Hazleton (PA)
Penn State Lehigh Valley (PA)
Penn State Mont Alto (PA)
Penn State New Kensington (PA)
Penn State Schuylkill (PA)
Penn State Shenango (PA)
Penn State U Park (PA)
Penn State Wilkes-Barre (PA)
Penn State Worthington Scranton (PA)
Penn State York (PA)
Rice U (TX)
Stanford U (CA)
The U of Arizona (AZ)
U of California, Los Angeles (CA)
U of California, Riverside (CA)
U of Georgia (GA)
U of Pennsylvania (PA)
U of Toronto (ON, Canada)
U of Wisconsin–Eau Claire (WI)

MATERNAL AND CHILD HEALTH
Union Inst & U (OH)

MATHEMATICAL BIOLOGY
Averett U (VA)
LeTourneau U (TX)
U of Houston (TX)
U of Idaho (ID)
U of Pittsburgh (PA)

MATHEMATICAL STATISTICS AND PROBABILITY
Albion Coll (MI)
Calvin Coll (MI)
Carnegie Mellon U (PA)
Concordia Coll–New York (NY)
Concordia U (QC, Canada)
Purdue U (IN)
U of Miami (FL)
U of the Incarnate Word (TX)

MATHEMATICS
Abilene Christian U (TX)
Adams State U (CO)
Adelphi U (NY)
Agnes Scott Coll (GA)
Alabama State U (AL)
Albany State U (GA)
Albertus Magnus Coll (CT)
Albion Coll (MI)
Albright Coll (PA)
Alcorn State U (MS)
Alfred U (NY)
Allegheny Coll (PA)
Alma Coll (MI)
Alvernia U (PA)
Alverno Coll (WI)
American U (DC)
American U in Bulgaria (Bulgaria)
The American U in Cairo (Egypt)
American U of Beirut (Lebanon)
Amherst Coll (MA)
Anderson U (IN)
Anderson U (SC)
Andrews U (MI)
Angelo State U (TX)
Antioch U Midwest (OH)
Appalachian State U (NC)
Aquinas Coll (MI)
Arcadia U (PA)
Arizona State U at the Tempe campus (AZ)
Arkansas Tech U (AR)
Armstrong State U (GA)
Asbury U (KY)
Ashland U (OH)
Assumption Coll (MA)
Athens State U (AL)
Auburn U (AL)
Auburn U at Montgomery (AL)
Augsburg Coll (MN)
Augustana Coll (IL)
Augustana U (SD)
Augusta U (GA)
Aurora U (IL)
Austin Coll (TX)
Austin Peay State U (TN)
Averett U (VA)
Avila U (MO)
Azusa Pacific U (CA)
Baker U (KS)
Baldwin Wallace U (OH)
Ball State U (IN)
Bard Coll (NY)
Barnard Coll (NY)
Barry U (FL)
Barton Coll (NC)
Baruch Coll of the City U of New York (NY)
Bates Coll (ME)
Baylor U (TX)
Belhaven U (MS)
Bellarmine U (KY)
Belmont Abbey Coll (NC)
Belmont U (TN)
Beloit Coll (WI)
Bemidji State U (MN)
Benedictine Coll (KS)
Bennett Coll (NC)
Bennington Coll (VT)
Bentley U (MA)
Berea Coll (KY)
Berry Coll (GA)
Bethany Lutheran Coll (MN)
Bethel Coll (IN)
Bethel Coll (KS)
Bethel U (MN)
Bethune-Cookman U (FL)
Binghamton U, State U of New York (NY)
Biola U (CA)
Bishop's U (QC, Canada)
Blackburn Coll (IL)
Black Hills State U (SD)
Bloomsburg U of Pennsylvania (PA)
Bluefield Coll (VA)
Blue Mountain Coll (MS)
Bluffton U (OH)
Boise State U (ID)
Boston Coll (MA)
Boston U (MA)
Bowdoin Coll (ME)
Bowie State U (MD)
Bowling Green State U (OH)
Bradley U (IL)
Brandeis U (MA)
Briar Cliff U (IA)
Bridgewater Coll (VA)
Bridgewater State U (MA)
Brooklyn Coll of the City U of New York (NY)
Bryan Coll (TN)
Bryn Mawr Coll (PA)
Bucknell U (PA)
Buena Vista U (IA)
Buffalo State Coll, State U of New York (NY)
Butler U (IN)
Cabrini U (PA)
Cairn U (PA)
Caldwell U (NJ)
California Baptist U (CA)
California Inst of Technology (CA)
California Lutheran U (CA)
California Polytechnic State U, San Luis Obispo (CA)
California State Polytechnic U, Pomona (CA)
California State U, Bakersfield (CA)
California State U, Chico (CA)
California State U, Dominguez Hills (CA)
California State U, East Bay (CA)
California State U, Fresno (CA)
California State U, Fullerton (CA)
California State U, Long Beach (CA)
California State U, Monterey Bay (CA)
California State U, Northridge (CA)
California State U, Sacramento (CA)
California State U, San Bernardino (CA)
California State U, San Marcos (CA)
California State U, Stanislaus (CA)
California U of Pennsylvania (PA)
Calvary U (MO)
Calvin Coll (MI)
Cameron U (OK)
Campbellsville U (KY)
Capital U (OH)
Cardinal Stritch U (WI)
Carleton Coll (MN)
Carlow U (PA)
Carnegie Mellon U (PA)
Carroll Coll (MT)
Carson-Newman U (TN)
Carthage Coll (WI)
Case Western Reserve U (OH)
Catawba Coll (NC)
The Catholic U of America (DC)
Cedar Crest Coll (PA)
Cedarville U (OH)
Centenary Coll of Louisiana (LA)
Centenary U (NJ)
Central Connecticut State U (CT)
Central Methodist U (MO)
Central Michigan U (MI)
Central State U (OH)
Central Washington U (WA)
Centre Coll (KY)
Chapman U (CA)
Charleston Southern U (SC)
Chatham U (PA)
Chestnut Hill Coll (PA)
Chowan U (NC)
Christendom Coll (VA)
Christian Brothers U (TN)
Christopher Newport U (VA)
The Citadel, The Military Coll of South Carolina (SC)
City Coll of the City U of New York (NY)
Claremont McKenna Coll (CA)
Clarion U of Pennsylvania (PA)
Clark Atlanta U (GA)
Clarke U (IA)
Clarkson U (NY)
Clark U (MA)
Clayton State U (GA)
Clemson U (SC)
Cleveland State U (OH)
Coe Coll (IA)
Colby Coll (ME)
Colgate U (NY)
The Coll at Brockport, State U of New York (NY)
Coll of Charleston (SC)
Coll of Coastal Georgia (GA)
The Coll of Idaho (ID)
Coll of Mount Saint Vincent (NY)
The Coll of New Jersey (NJ)
Coll of Saint Benedict (MN)
Coll of Saint Elizabeth (NJ)
Coll of Saint Mary (NE)
The Coll of Saint Rose (NY)
The Coll of St. Scholastica (MN)
Coll of Staten Island of the City U of New York (NY)
Coll of the Holy Cross (MA)
Coll of the Ozarks (MO)
The Coll of William and Mary (VA)
The Coll of Wooster (OH)
The Colorado Coll (CO)
Colorado Mesa U (CO)
Colorado School of Mines (CO)
Colorado State U (CO)
Columbia Coll (MO)
Columbia U (NY)
Columbia U, School of General Studies (NY)

Columbus State U (GA)
Concordia Coll (MN)
Concordia Coll–New York (NY)
Concordia U (QC, Canada)
Concordia U Chicago (IL)
Concordia U Irvine (CA)
Concordia U, Nebraska (NE)
Concordia U, St. Paul (MN)
Concordia U Wisconsin (WI)
Concord U (WV)
Connecticut Coll (CT)
Converse Coll (SC)
Corban U (OR)
Cornell Coll (IA)
Cornell U (NY)
Cornerstone U (MI)
Creighton U (NE)
Culver-Stockton Coll (MO)
Daemen Coll (NY)
Dalhousie U (NS, Canada)
Dallas Baptist U (TX)
Dalton State Coll (GA)
Dartmouth Coll (NH)
Davidson Coll (NC)
Defiance Coll (OH)
Denison U (OH)
DePauw U (IN)
DeSales U (PA)
Dickinson Coll (PA)
Dickinson State U (ND)
Dixie State U (UT)
Doane U (NE)
Dominican Coll (NY)
Dominican U (IL)
Drake U (IA)
Drew U (NJ)
Drexel U (PA)
Drury U (MO)
Duquesne U (PA)
Earlham Coll (IN)
East Carolina U (NC)
East Central U (OK)
Eastern Illinois U (IL)
Eastern Mennonite U (VA)
Eastern Michigan U (MI)
Eastern Nazarene Coll (MA)
Eastern Oregon U (OR)
Eastern U (PA)
Eastern Washington U (WA)
East Stroudsburg U of Pennsylvania (PA)
East Tennessee State U (TN)
East Texas Baptist U (TX)
Eckerd Coll (FL)
Edgewood Coll (WI)
Elizabeth City State U (NC)
Elizabethtown Coll (PA)
Elmira Coll (NY)
Elms Coll (MA)
Elon U (NC)
Emmanuel Coll (GA)
Emmanuel Coll (MA)
Emory & Henry Coll (VA)
Emory U (GA)
Emporia State U (KS)
Endicott Coll (MA)
Eureka Coll (IL)
Evangel U (MO)
Fairfield U (CT)
Fairleigh Dickinson U, Coll at Florham (NJ)
Fairleigh Dickinson U, Metropolitan Campus (NJ)
Faulkner U (AL)
Fayetteville State U (NC)
Felician U (NJ)
Fitchburg State U (MA)
Florida Ag and Mech U (FL)
Florida Atlantic U (FL)
Florida Gulf Coast U (FL)
Florida Inst of Technology (FL)
Florida Intl U (FL)
Florida Southern Coll (FL)
Florida State U (FL)
Fordham U (NY)
Fort Lewis Coll (CO)
Framingham State U (MA)
Franciscan U of Steubenville (OH)
Francis Marion U (SC)
Franklin & Marshall Coll (PA)
Franklin Coll (IN)
Franklin Pierce U (NH)
Freed-Hardeman U (TN)
Fresno Pacific U (CA)
Friends U (KS)
Frostburg State U (MD)
Furman U (SC)
Gallaudet U (DC)
Gannon U (PA)
Gardner-Webb U (NC)
George Fox U (OR)
Georgetown Coll (KY)
Georgetown U (DC)
The George Washington U (DC)
Georgia Coll & State U (GA)
Georgia Gwinnett Coll (GA)
Georgian Court U (NJ)
Georgia Southern U (GA)
Georgia Southwestern State U (GA)
Georgia State U (GA)
Gettysburg Coll (PA)
Gonzaga U (WA)
Gordon Coll (MA)
Gordon State Coll (GA)
Goshen Coll (IN)
Goucher Coll (MD)
Governors State U (IL)
Grace Coll (IN)
Graceland U (IA)
Grand Valley State U (MI)
Greenville Coll (IL)
Grinnell Coll (IA)
Grove City Coll (PA)
Guilford Coll (NC)
Gwynedd Mercy U (PA)
Hamilton Coll (NY)
Hamline U (MN)
Hampden-Sydney Coll (VA)
Hampshire Coll (MA)
Hampton U (VA)
Hannibal-LaGrange U (MO)
Hanover Coll (IN)
Harding U (AR)
Hardin-Simmons U (TX)
Harris-Stowe State U (MO)
Hartwick Coll (NY)
Harvard U (MA)
Harvey Mudd Coll (CA)
Haverford Coll (PA)
Hawai`i Pacific U (HI)
Heidelberg U (OH)
Henderson State U (AR)
Hendrix Coll (AR)
High Point U (NC)
Hillsdale Coll (MI)
Hiram Coll (OH)
Hobart and William Smith Colls (NY)
Hofstra U (NY)
Hollins U (VA)
Holy Family U (PA)
Hood Coll (MD)
Hope Coll (MI)
Houghton Coll (NY)
Houston Baptist U (TX)
Howard Payne U (TX)
Humboldt State U (CA)
Hunter Coll of the City U of New York (NY)
Huntingdon Coll (AL)
Huntington U (IN)
Huston-Tillotson U (TX)
Idaho State U (ID)
Illinois Coll (IL)
Illinois State U (IL)
Illinois Wesleyan U (IL)
Immaculata U (PA)
Indiana State U (IN)
Indiana U Bloomington (IN)
Indiana U East (IN)
Indiana U Kokomo (IN)
Indiana U Northwest (IN)
Indiana U of Pennsylvania (PA)
Indiana U–Purdue U Indianapolis (IN)
Indiana U South Bend (IN)
Indiana U Southeast (IN)
Inter American U of Puerto Rico, Bayamón Campus (PR)
Inter American U of Puerto Rico, Metropolitan Campus (PR)
Inter American U of Puerto Rico, San Germán Campus (PR)
Iona Coll (NY)
Iowa State U of Science and Technology (IA)
Ithaca Coll (NY)
Jackson State U (MS)
Jacksonville State U (AL)
Jacksonville U (FL)
James Madison U (VA)
John Brown U (AR)
John Carroll U (OH)
Johns Hopkins U (MD)
Johnson C. Smith U (NC)
Judson U (IL)
Juniata Coll (PA)
Kalamazoo Coll (MI)
Kansas State U (KS)
Kansas Wesleyan U (KS)
Kean U (NJ)
Keene State Coll (NH)
Kennesaw State U (GA)
Kent State U (OH)
Kent State U at Stark (OH)
Kentucky State U (KY)
Kentucky Wesleyan Coll (KY)
Kenyon Coll (OH)
Keuka Coll (NY)
King's Coll (PA)
King U (TN)
Knox Coll (IL)
Kutztown U of Pennsylvania (PA)
Lafayette Coll (PA)
LaGrange Coll (GA)
Lake Erie Coll (OH)
Lake Forest Coll (IL)
Lamar U (TX)
Lane Coll (TN)
Langston U (OK)
La Roche Coll (PA)
La Salle U (PA)
Lawrence Technological U (MI)
Lawrence U (WI)
Lebanese American U (Lebanon)
Lebanon Valley Coll (PA)
Lee U (TN)
Lehigh U (PA)
Lehman Coll of the City U of New York (NY)
Le Moyne Coll (NY)
Lenoir-Rhyne U (NC)
LeTourneau U (TX)
Lewis & Clark Coll (OR)
Lewis U (IL)
Liberty U (VA)
Limestone Coll (SC)
Lincoln U (MO)
Lincoln U (PA)
Lindenwood U (MO)
Linfield Coll (OR)
Lipscomb U (TN)
Lock Haven U of Pennsylvania (PA)
Longwood U (VA)
Loras Coll (IA)
Louisiana Coll (LA)
Louisiana State U and A&M Coll (LA)
Louisiana State U at Alexandria (LA)
Louisiana Tech U (LA)
Loyola Marymount U (CA)
Loyola U Chicago (IL)
Loyola U Maryland (MD)
Loyola U New Orleans (LA)
Lubbock Christian U (TX)
Luther Coll (IA)
Lycoming Coll (PA)
Lynchburg Coll (VA)
Lyon Coll (AR)
Macalester Coll (MN)
Madonna U (MI)
Maharishi U of Management (IA)
Malone U (OH)
Manchester U (IN)
Manhattan Coll (NY)
Manhattanville Coll (NY)
Mansfield U of Pennsylvania (PA)
Marian U (IN)
Marian U (WI)
Marietta Coll (OH)
Marist Coll (NY)
Marshall U (WV)
Mary Baldwin U (VA)
Marymount U (VA)
Maryville U of Saint Louis (MO)
Marywood U (PA)
Massachusetts Coll of Liberal Arts (MA)
Massachusetts Inst of Technology (MA)
The Master's U (CA)
McDaniel Coll (MD)
McKendree U (IL)
McMaster U (ON, Canada)
McMurry U (TX)
McNeese State U (LA)
Mercer U, Macon (GA)
Mercy Coll (NY)
Mercyhurst U (PA)
Meredith Coll (NC)
Merrimack Coll (MA)
Messiah Coll (PA)
Metropolitan State U of Denver (CO)
Miami U (OH)
Michigan State U (MI)
Michigan Technological U (MI)
MidAmerica Nazarene U (KS)
Middlebury Coll (VT)
Millersville U of Pennsylvania (PA)
Milligan Coll (TN)
Millikin U (IL)
Millsaps Coll (MS)
Mills Coll (CA)
Minnesota State U Mankato (MN)
Minnesota State U Moorhead (MN)
Minot State U (ND)
Misericordia U (PA)
Mississippi State U (MS)
Mississippi Valley State U (MS)
Missouri Baptist U (MO)
Missouri State U (MO)
Missouri Valley Coll (MO)
Missouri Western State U (MO)
Molloy Coll (NY)
Monmouth Coll (IL)
Monmouth U (NJ)
Montana State U (MT)
Montana State U Billings (MT)
Montana State U–Northern (MT)
Montana Tech of The U of Montana (MT)
Montclair State U (NJ)
Moravian Coll (PA)
Morehead State U (KY)
Morehouse Coll (GA)
Morningside Coll (IA)
Morris Coll (SC)
Mount Allison U (NB, Canada)
Mount Holyoke Coll (MA)
Mount Marty Coll (SD)
Mount Mary U (WI)
Mount Mercy U (IA)
Mount St. Joseph U (OH)
Mount Saint Mary Coll (NY)
Mount Saint Mary's U (CA)
Mount St. Mary's U (MD)
Mount Vernon Nazarene U (OH)
Muhlenberg Coll (PA)
Murray State U (KY)
Muskingum U (OH)
National U (CA)
Nazareth Coll of Rochester (NY)
Nebraska Wesleyan U (NE)
Nevada State Coll (NV)
Newberry Coll (SC)
New Coll of Florida (FL)
New Jersey City U (NJ)
Newman U (KS)
New Mexico Highlands U (NM)
New Mexico Inst of Mining and Technology (NM)
New Mexico State U (NM)
Niagara U (NY)
Nichols Coll (MA)
North Carolina Central U (NC)
North Carolina State U (NC)
North Carolina Wesleyan Coll (NC)
North Central Coll (IL)
North Dakota State U (ND)
Northeastern Illinois U (IL)
Northeastern State U (OK)
Northeastern U (MA)
Northern Arizona U (AZ)
Northern Illinois U (IL)
Northern Kentucky U (KY)
Northern State U (SD)
North Greenville U (SC)
Northland Coll (WI)
Northwest Christian U (OR)
Northwestern Coll (IA)
Northwestern Oklahoma State U (OK)
Northwestern State U of Louisiana (LA)
Northwestern U (IL)
Northwest Missouri State U (MO)
Northwest U (WA)
Nyack Coll (NY)
Oakland City U (IN)
Oberlin Coll (OH)
Occidental Coll (CA)
Ohio Dominican U (OH)
The Ohio State U (OH)
Ohio U (OH)
Ohio Wesleyan U (OH)
Oklahoma Baptist U (OK)
Oklahoma Christian U (OK)
Oklahoma City U (OK)
Oklahoma State U (OK)
Old Dominion U (VA)
Olivet Nazarene U (IL)
Oral Roberts U (OK)
Oregon State U (OR)
Otterbein U (OH)
Ouachita Baptist U (AR)
Our Lady of the Lake U of San Antonio (TX)
Pace U (NY)
Pace U, Pleasantville Campus (NY)
Pacific Lutheran U (WA)
Paine Coll (GA)
Palm Beach Atlantic U (FL)
Penn State Abington (PA)
Penn State Altoona (PA)
Penn State Beaver (PA)
Penn State Berks (PA)
Penn State Brandywine (PA)
Penn State DuBois (PA)
Penn State Erie, The Behrend Coll (PA)
Penn State Fayette, The Eberly Campus (PA)
Penn State Greater Allegheny (PA)
Penn State Hazleton (PA)
Penn State Lehigh Valley (PA)
Penn State Mont Alto (PA)
Penn State New Kensington (PA)
Penn State Schuylkill (PA)
Penn State Shenango (PA)
Penn State U Park (PA)
Penn State Wilkes-Barre (PA)
Penn State Worthington Scranton (PA)
Penn State York (PA)
Pepperdine U, Malibu (CA)
Philander Smith Coll (AR)
Piedmont Coll (GA)
Pittsburg State U (KS)
Pitzer Coll (CA)
Plymouth State U (NH)
Point Loma Nazarene U (CA)
Pomona Coll (CA)
Portland State U (OR)
Prairie View A&M U (TX)
Princeton U (NJ)
Principia Coll (IL)
Providence Coll (RI)
Purchase Coll, State U of New York (NY)
Purdue U (IN)
Purdue U Northwest (IN)
Queens Coll of the City U of New York (NY)
Quinnipiac U (CT)
Radford U (VA)
Ramapo Coll of New Jersey (NJ)
Randolph Coll (VA)
Randolph-Macon Coll (VA)
Redeemer U Coll (ON, Canada)
Reed Coll (OR)
Regent U (VA)
Regis U (CO)
Rensselaer Polytechnic Inst (NY)
Rhode Island Coll (RI)
Rhodes Coll (TN)
Rice U (TX)
Ripon Coll (WI)
Roanoke Coll (VA)
Roberts Wesleyan Coll (NY)
Rochester Inst of Technology (NY)
Rockford U (IL)
Rockhurst U (MO)
Rocky Mountain Coll (MT)
Roger Williams U (RI)
Rollins Coll (FL)
Rose-Hulman Inst of Technology (IN)
Rosemont Coll (PA)
Rowan U (NJ)
Rust Coll (MS)
Rutgers U–Camden (NJ)
Rutgers U–Newark (NJ)
Rutgers U–New Brunswick (NJ)
Sacred Heart U (CT)
Saginaw Valley State U (MI)
St. Ambrose U (IA)
Saint Anselm Coll (NH)
Saint Augustine's U (NC)
St. Bonaventure U (NY)
St. Catherine U (MN)
St. Cloud State U (MN)
St. Edward's U (TX)

Saint Francis U (PA)
St. Gregory's U, Shawnee (OK)
St. John Fisher Coll (NY)
Saint John's U (MN)
St. John's U (NY)
St. Joseph's Coll, Long Island Campus (NY)
St. Joseph's Coll, New York (NY)
Saint Joseph's U (PA)
Saint Leo U (FL)
Saint Louis U (MO)
Saint Louis U–Madrid Campus (Spain)
Saint Martin's U (WA)
Saint Mary-of-the-Woods Coll (IN)
Saint Mary's Coll (IN)
Saint Mary's Coll of California (CA)
St. Mary's Coll of Maryland (MD)
Saint Mary's U of Minnesota (MN)
Saint Michael's Coll (VT)
St. Norbert Coll (WI)
St. Olaf Coll (MN)
Saint Peter's U (NJ)
St. Thomas Aquinas Coll (NY)
St. Thomas U (FL)
St. Thomas U (NB, Canada)
Saint Vincent Coll (PA)
Salisbury U (MD)
Salve Regina U (RI)
Samford U (AL)
Sam Houston State U (TX)
San Diego State U (CA)
San Francisco State U (CA)
Santa Clara U (CA)
Sarah Lawrence Coll (NY)
Schreiner U (TX)
Scripps Coll (CA)
Seattle Pacific U (WA)
Seattle U (WA)
Seton Hill U (PA)
Sewanee: The U of the South (TN)
Shawnee State U (OH)
Shaw U (NC)
Shenandoah U (VA)
Shepherd U (WV)
Shippensburg U of Pennsylvania (PA)
Shorter U (GA)
Siena Coll (NY)
Silver Lake Coll of the Holy Family (WI)
Simmons Coll (MA)
Simon Fraser U (BC, Canada)
Simpson Coll (IA)
Simpson U (CA)
Skidmore Coll (NY)
Slippery Rock U of Pennsylvania (PA)
Smith Coll (MA)
Sonoma State U (CA)
South Carolina State U (SC)
South Dakota School of Mines and Technology (SD)
South Dakota State U (SD)
Southeastern Louisiana U (LA)
Southeastern Oklahoma State U (OK)
Southeastern U (FL)
Southeast Missouri State U (MO)
Southern Arkansas U–Magnolia (AR)
Southern Connecticut State U (CT)
Southern Illinois U Carbondale (IL)
Southern Illinois U Edwardsville (IL)
Southern Methodist U (TX)
Southern New Hampshire U (NH)
Southern Oregon U (OR)
Southern Utah U (UT)
Southwest Baptist U (MO)
Southwestern Adventist U (TX)
Southwestern Assemblies of God U (TX)
Southwestern Coll (KS)
Southwestern U (TX)
Spelman Coll (GA)
Spring Hill Coll (AL)
Stanford U (CA)
State U of New York at Fredonia (NY)
State U of New York at New Paltz (NY)
State U of New York at Oswego (NY)
State U of New York at Plattsburgh (NY)
State U of New York Coll at Cortland (NY)
State U of New York Coll at Geneseo (NY)
State U of New York Coll at Old Westbury (NY)
State U of New York Coll at Potsdam (NY)
Stephen F. Austin State U (TX)
Sterling Coll (KS)
Stevens Inst of Technology (NJ)
Stockton U (NJ)
Stonehill Coll (MA)
Stony Brook U, State U of New York (NY)
Suffolk U (MA)
Susquehanna U (PA)
Swarthmore Coll (PA)
Sweet Briar Coll (VA)
Syracuse U (NY)
Tabor Coll (KS)
Tarleton State U (TX)
Taylor U (IN)
Temple U (PA)
Tennessee State U (TN)
Tennessee Wesleyan U (TN)
Texas A&M Intl U (TX)
Texas A&M U (TX)
Texas A&M U–Central Texas (TX)
Texas A&M U–Commerce (TX)
Texas A&M U–Corpus Christi (TX)
Texas A&M U–Kingsville (TX)
Texas Christian U (TX)
Texas Coll (TX)
Texas Lutheran U (TX)
Texas State U (TX)
Texas Tech U (TX)
Texas Wesleyan U (TX)
Texas Woman's U (TX)
Thomas More Coll (KY)
Towson U (MD)
Transylvania U (KY)
Trent U (ON, Canada)
Trevecca Nazarene U (TN)
Trine U (IN)
Trinity Christian Coll (IL)
Trinity U (TX)
Troy U (AL)
Truman State U (MO)
Tufts U (MA)
Tulane U (LA)
Tusculum Coll (TN)
Union Coll (KY)
Union Coll (NE)
Union Coll (NY)
Union U (TN)
United States Air Force Acad (CO)
United States Military Acad (NY)
Université de Montréal (QC, Canada)
Université de Sherbrooke (QC, Canada)
U at Albany, State U of New York (NY)
U at Buffalo, the State U of New York (NY)
The U of Akron (OH)
The U of Alabama (AL)
The U of Alabama at Birmingham (AL)
The U of Alabama in Huntsville (AL)
U of Alaska Fairbanks (AK)
The U of Arizona (AZ)
U of Arkansas (AR)
U of Bridgeport (CT)
U of California, Davis (CA)
U of California, Irvine (CA)
U of California, Los Angeles (CA)
U of California, Riverside (CA)
U of California, San Diego (CA)
U of California, Santa Barbara (CA)
U of Central Arkansas (AR)
U of Central Florida (FL)
U of Central Missouri (MO)
U of Chicago (IL)
U of Cincinnati (OH)
U of Colorado Boulder (CO)
U of Colorado Colorado Springs (CO)
U of Colorado Denver (CO)
U of Dayton (OH)
U of Delaware (DE)
U of Denver (CO)
U of Detroit Mercy (MI)
U of Dubuque (IA)
U of Evansville (IN)
The U of Findlay (OH)
U of Florida (FL)
U of Georgia (GA)
U of Great Falls (MT)
U of Hartford (CT)
U of Hawaii at Manoa (HI)
U of Houston (TX)
U of Houston–Clear Lake (TX)
U of Houston–Downtown (TX)
U of Idaho (ID)
U of Illinois at Chicago (IL)
U of Illinois at Springfield (IL)
U of Indianapolis (IN)
U of Jamestown (ND)
The U of Kansas (KS)
U of Kentucky (KY)
U of King's Coll (NS, Canada)
U of La Verne (CA)
U of Lethbridge (AB, Canada)
U of Louisiana at Monroe (LA)
U of Louisville (KY)
U of Maine (ME)
U of Maine at Farmington (ME)
U of Maine at Presque Isle (ME)
U of Mary Hardin-Baylor (TX)
U of Maryland, Baltimore County (MD)
U of Maryland, Coll Park (MD)
U of Mary Washington (VA)
U of Massachusetts Amherst (MA)
U of Massachusetts Boston (MA)
U of Massachusetts Dartmouth (MA)
U of Massachusetts Lowell (MA)
U of Miami (FL)
U of Michigan (MI)
U of Michigan–Dearborn (MI)
U of Michigan–Flint (MI)
U of Minnesota, Duluth (MN)
U of Minnesota, Morris (MN)
U of Minnesota, Twin Cities Campus (MN)
U of Missouri–Kansas City (MO)
U of Missouri–St. Louis (MO)
U of Mobile (AL)
The U of Montana Western (MT)
U of Montevallo (AL)
U of Mount Union (OH)
U of Nebraska at Kearney (NE)
U of Nevada, Las Vegas (NV)
U of Nevada, Reno (NV)
U of New England (ME)
U of New Hampshire (NH)
U of New Haven (CT)
U of New Orleans (LA)
U of North Alabama (AL)
U of North Carolina at Asheville (NC)
The U of North Carolina at Chapel Hill (NC)
The U of North Carolina at Charlotte (NC)
The U of North Carolina at Greensboro (NC)
The U of North Carolina at Pembroke (NC)
The U of North Carolina Wilmington (NC)
U of North Dakota (ND)
U of Northern Colorado (CO)
U of Northern Iowa (IA)
U of North Florida (FL)
U of North Georgia (GA)
U of North Texas (TX)
U of Notre Dame (IN)
U of Oklahoma (OK)
U of Oregon (OR)
U of Pennsylvania (PA)
U of Pikeville (KY)
U of Pittsburgh (PA)
U of Pittsburgh at Johnstown (PA)
U of Puget Sound (WA)
U of Regina (SK, Canada)
U of Rhode Island (RI)
U of Richmond (VA)
U of Rochester (NY)
U of St. Francis (IL)
U of Saint Francis (IN)
U of Saint Joseph (CT)
U of Saint Mary (KS)
U of St. Thomas (MN)
U of St. Thomas (TX)
U of San Diego (CA)
U of San Francisco (CA)
U of Saskatchewan (SK, Canada)
U of Science and Arts of Oklahoma (OK)
The U of Scranton (PA)
U of South Carolina (SC)
The U of South Dakota (SD)
U of Southern California (CA)
U of Southern Indiana (IN)
U of Southern Maine (ME)
U of Southern Mississippi (MS)
U of South Florida (FL)
The U of Tampa (FL)
The U of Tennessee (TN)
The U of Tennessee at Chattanooga (TN)
The U of Tennessee at Martin (TN)
The U of Texas at Austin (TX)
The U of Texas at Dallas (TX)
The U of Texas at El Paso (TX)
The U of Texas at San Antonio (TX)
The U of Texas of the Permian Basin (TX)
The U of Texas Rio Grande Valley (TX)
U of the Cumberlands (KY)
U of the Fraser Valley (BC, Canada)
U of the Incarnate Word (TX)
U of the Pacific (CA)
U of the Virgin Islands (VI)
The U of Toledo (OH)
The U of Tulsa (OK)
U of Utah (UT)
U of Vermont (VT)
U of Virginia (VA)
The U of Virginia's Coll at Wise (VA)
U of Washington (WA)
U of Washington, Bothell (WA)
U of Waterloo (ON, Canada)
The U of West Alabama (AL)
U of West Georgia (GA)
U of Windsor (ON, Canada)
U of Wisconsin–Eau Claire (WI)
U of Wisconsin–Green Bay (WI)
U of Wisconsin–La Crosse (WI)
U of Wisconsin–Madison (WI)
U of Wisconsin–Milwaukee (WI)
U of Wisconsin–Parkside (WI)
U of Wisconsin–Platteville (WI)
U of Wisconsin–Stevens Point (WI)
U of Wisconsin–Superior (WI)
U of Wisconsin–Whitewater (WI)
Upper Iowa U (IA)
Ursinus Coll (PA)
Utah State U (UT)
Utah Valley U (UT)
Utica Coll (NY)
Valdosta State U (GA)
Valley City State U (ND)
Valparaiso U (IN)
Vanderbilt U (TN)
Vassar Coll (NY)
Villanova U (PA)
Virginia Commonwealth U (VA)
Virginia Military Inst (VA)
Virginia Polytechnic Inst and State U (VA)
Virginia State U (VA)
Virginia Union U (VA)
Virginia Wesleyan Coll (VA)
Viterbo U (WI)
Wabash Coll (IN)
Wagner Coll (NY)
Wake Forest U (NC)
Walla Walla U (WA)
Walsh U (OH)
Wartburg Coll (IA)
Washburn U (KS)
Washington & Jefferson Coll (PA)
Washington and Lee U (VA)
Washington Coll (MD)
Washington State U (WA)
Washington State U–Tri-Cities (WA)
Washington U in St. Louis (MO)
Wayland Baptist U (TX)
Waynesburg U (PA)
Wayne State Coll (NE)
Wayne State U (MI)
Weber State U (UT)
Webster U (MO)
Wells Coll (NY)
Wesleyan Coll (GA)
Wesleyan U (CT)
West Chester U of Pennsylvania (PA)
Western Carolina U (NC)
Western Connecticut State U (CT)
Western Illinois U (IL)
Western Kentucky U (KY)
Western Michigan U (MI)
Western New England U (MA)
Western Oregon U (OR)
Western State Colorado U (CO)
Western Washington U (WA)
Westfield State U (MA)
Westminster Coll (PA)
Westminster Coll (UT)
Westmont Coll (CA)
West Texas A&M U (TX)
West Virginia State U (WV)
West Virginia U (WV)
West Virginia U Inst of Technology (WV)
West Virginia Wesleyan Coll (WV)
Wheaton Coll (IL)
Wheaton Coll (MA)
Wheeling Jesuit U (WV)
Whitman Coll (WA)
Whittier Coll (CA)
Whitworth U (WA)
Wichita State U (KS)
Widener U (PA)
Wilkes U (PA)
Willamette U (OR)
William Jewell Coll (MO)
William Paterson U of New Jersey (NJ)
William Penn U (IA)
Williams Coll (MA)
William Woods U (MO)
Wilson Coll (PA)
Wingate U (NC)
Winona State U (MN)
Winthrop U (SC)
Wittenberg U (OH)
Wofford Coll (SC)
Worcester Polytechnic Inst (MA)
Worcester State U (MA)
Wright State U (OH)
Wright State U–Lake Campus (OH)
Xavier U of Louisiana (LA)
York Coll of Pennsylvania (PA)
York Coll of the City U of New York (NY)
Youngstown State U (OH)

MATHEMATICS AND COMPUTER SCIENCE

Anderson U (IN)
Bennington Coll (VT)
Biola U (CA)
Bowdoin Coll (ME)
Brescia U (KY)
Bryan Coll (TN)
Calvin Coll (MI)
Chestnut Hill Coll (PA)
Christian Brothers U (TN)
Colgate U (NY)
The Colorado Coll (CO)
Dominican U (IL)
Eastern Illinois U (IL)
Emory U (GA)
Grace Coll (IN)
Hampden-Sydney Coll (VA)
Hofstra U (NY)
Immaculata U (PA)
Ithaca Coll (NY)
Lawrence Technological U (MI)
Lawrence U (WI)
LeTourneau U (TX)
Lewis & Clark Coll (OR)
Loyola U Chicago (IL)
Manchester U (IN)
Massachusetts Inst of Technology (MA)
Mount Allison U (NB, Canada)
Palm Beach Atlantic U (FL)
Pepperdine U, Malibu (CA)
Purdue U (IN)
Redeemer U Coll (ON, Canada)
Rochester Inst of Technology (NY)
Saint Francis U (PA)
Saint Mary's Coll (IN)
Saint Mary's Coll of California (CA)
Santa Clara U (CA)
Southern Oregon U (OR)
Stanford U (CA)
Temple U (PA)
Tufts U (MA)
U at Albany, State U of New York (NY)
The U of Akron (OH)
U of California, Irvine (CA)
The U of Findlay (OH)
U of Illinois at Chicago (IL)

U of Massachusetts Amherst (MA)
U of Massachusetts Dartmouth (MA)
U of Oregon (OR)
U of Regina (SK, Canada)
U of St. Francis (IL)
The U of Tampa (FL)
The U of Texas at Austin (TX)
U of Vermont (VT)
U of Waterloo (ON, Canada)
U of Windsor (ON, Canada)
Washington U in St. Louis (MO)
Western Washington U (WA)
Wheaton Coll (MA)
Whitman Coll (WA)

MATHEMATICS AND STATISTICS

Canisius Coll (NY)
Colby Coll (ME)
Dakota State U (SD)
Emory U (GA)
The Evergreen State Coll (WA)
Luther Coll (IA)
Reed Coll (OR)
U of Notre Dame (IN)
U of South Alabama (AL)
U of Washington, Tacoma (WA)

MATHEMATICS AND STATISTICS RELATED

Anderson U (IN)
Carnegie Mellon U (PA)
Columbia U, School of General Studies (NY)
Emory U (GA)
Hofstra U (NY)
Lycoming Coll (PA)
Montana Tech of The U of Montana (MT)
Ohio U (OH)
Purchase Coll, State U of New York (NY)
St. Joseph's Coll, Long Island Campus (NY)
St. Joseph's Coll, New York (NY)
Saint Mary's Coll (IN)
Saint Mary's Coll of California (CA)
Seattle Pacific U (WA)
Tulane U (LA)
U of Missouri–Kansas City (MO)
The U of North Carolina at Charlotte (NC)
U of Notre Dame (IN)
U of Pittsburgh (PA)
U of Regina (SK, Canada)
U of Rochester (NY)
Western State Colorado U (CO)
Worcester Polytechnic Inst (MA)

MATHEMATICS RELATED

Agnes Scott Coll (GA)
Berry Coll (GA)
Carnegie Mellon U (PA)
Eastern Nazarene Coll (MA)
Grambling State U (LA)
Seton Hill U (PA)
Temple U (PA)
United States Military Acad (NY)
U of California, Los Angeles (CA)
U of Miami (FL)
U of Pittsburgh (PA)
U of Washington (WA)
U of Waterloo (ON, Canada)
Wheelock Coll (MA)

MATHEMATICS TEACHER EDUCATION

Abilene Christian U (TX)
Adams State U (CO)
Albion Coll (MI)
Alice Lloyd Coll (KY)
Alvernia U (PA)
Anderson U (IN)
Anderson U (SC)
Arizona Christian U (AZ)
Arkansas Tech U (AR)
Armstrong State U (GA)
Auburn U (AL)
Augustana Coll (IL)
Averett U (VA)
Bayamón Central U (PR)
Baylor U (TX)
Bennett Coll (NC)
Berry Coll (GA)
Bethel Coll (IN)
Bethel U (MN)
Biola U (CA)
Bishop's U (QC, Canada)
Blackburn Coll (IL)
Black Hills State U (SD)
Bluefield Coll (VA)
Blue Mountain Coll (MS)
Boise State U (ID)
Boston U (MA)
Bowdoin Coll (ME)
Bowie State U (MD)
Bowling Green State U (OH)
Bradley U (IL)
Brigham Young U–Idaho (ID)
Brooklyn Coll of the City U of New York (NY)
Bryan Coll (TN)
Buena Vista U (IA)
Buffalo State Coll, State U of New York (NY)
Cabrini U (PA)
Cairn U (PA)
California Baptist U (CA)
California Lutheran U (CA)
California State U, Long Beach (CA)
Calvin Coll (MI)
Cameron U (OK)
Campbellsville U (KY)
Canisius Coll (NY)
Capital U (OH)
Carroll Coll (MT)
The Catholic U of America (DC)
Cedarville U (OH)
Central Michigan U (MI)
Central Washington U (WA)
Charleston Southern U (SC)
City Coll of the City U of New York (NY)
Clemson U (SC)
The Coll of New Jersey (NJ)
Coll of Saint Mary (NE)
The Coll of Saint Rose (NY)
Coll of Staten Island of the City U of New York (NY)
Coll of the Ozarks (MO)
Colorado State U (CO)
Columbus State U (GA)
Concordia Coll (MN)
Concordia U Chicago (IL)
Concordia U, St. Paul (MN)
Corban U (OR)
Cornerstone U (MI)
Culver-Stockton Coll (MO)
Curry Coll (MA)
Daemen Coll (NY)
Dakota State U (SD)
Dallas Baptist U (TX)
Daytona State Coll (FL)
Dickinson State U (ND)
Dixie State U (UT)
Dominican Coll (NY)
Duquesne U (PA)
East Carolina U (NC)
East Central U (OK)
Eastern Michigan U (MI)
Eastern Washington U (WA)
East Texas Baptist U (TX)
Edgewood Coll (WI)
Elizabeth City State U (NC)
Elmira Coll (NY)
Emmanuel Coll (GA)
Emory & Henry Coll (VA)
Faulkner U (AL)
Felician U (NJ)
Ferris State U (MI)
Fitchburg State U (MA)
Florida Ag and Mech U (FL)
Florida Atlantic U (FL)
Florida Inst of Technology (FL)
Florida Southern Coll (FL)
Florida SouthWestern State Coll (FL)
Franklin Coll (IN)
Friends U (KS)
Gardner-Webb U (NC)
Geneva Coll (PA)
Gordon State Coll (GA)
Goshen Coll (IN)
Grace Coll (IN)
Grambling State U (LA)
Grand Valley State U (MI)
Greenville Coll (IL)
Grove City Coll (PA)
Gwynedd Mercy U (PA)
Hannibal-LaGrange U (MO)
Harding U (AR)
Hardin-Simmons U (TX)
Hobe Sound Bible Coll (FL)
Hofstra U (NY)
Holy Family U (PA)
Hope Coll (MI)
Houston Baptist U (TX)
Howard Payne U (TX)
Hunter Coll of the City U of New York (NY)
Huntingdon Coll (AL)
Huntington U (IN)
Indiana U Bloomington (IN)
Indiana U Northwest (IN)
Indiana U South Bend (IN)
Indiana U Southeast (IN)
Inter American U of Puerto Rico, Metropolitan Campus (PR)
Inter American U of Puerto Rico, San Germán Campus (PR)
Iona Coll (NY)
Ithaca Coll (NY)
Jackson State U (MS)
John Brown U (AR)
Juniata Coll (PA)
Kansas Wesleyan U (KS)
Keene State Coll (NH)
Kennesaw State U (GA)
Kent State U (OH)
Keuka Coll (NY)
King U (TN)
LaGrange Coll (GA)
Lee U (TN)
Le Moyne Coll (NY)
LeTourneau U (TX)
Limestone Coll (SC)
Lindenwood U (MO)
Lindsey Wilson Coll (KY)
Lipscomb U (TN)
Louisiana Coll (LA)
Louisiana Tech U (LA)
Loyola U Chicago (IL)
Madonna U (MI)
Manchester U (IN)
Manhattanville Coll (NY)
Maranatha Baptist U (WI)
Marist Coll (NY)
Marywood U (PA)
McMurry U (TX)
Mercyhurst U (PA)
Merrimack Coll (MA)
Messiah Coll (PA)
Miami Dade Coll (FL)
Miami U (OH)
Michigan State U (MI)
MidAmerica Nazarene U (KS)
Millikin U (IL)
Minnesota State U Moorhead (MN)
Minot State U (ND)
Misericordia U (PA)
Missouri State U (MO)
Montana State U Billings (MT)
Morningside Coll (IA)
Morris Coll (SC)
Mount Marty Coll (SD)
Mount Mary U (WI)
Mount Vernon Nazarene U (OH)
National U (CA)
Nazareth Coll of Rochester (NY)
Nevada State Coll (NV)
New York City Coll of Technology of the City U of New York (NY)
Niagara U (NY)
North Carolina State U (NC)
North Dakota State U (ND)
Northeastern State U (OK)
North Greenville U (SC)
Northwestern Oklahoma State U (OK)
Northwestern U (IL)
Northwest Missouri State U (MO)
Northwest U (WA)
Nova Southeastern U (FL)
Nyack Coll (NY)
Oakland City U (IN)
Ohio Dominican U (OH)
Ohio Valley U (WV)
Ohio Wesleyan U (OH)
Oklahoma Baptist U (OK)
Oklahoma Christian U (OK)
Oral Roberts U (OK)
Pace U (NY)
Pace U, Pleasantville Campus (NY)
Palm Beach Atlantic U (FL)
Pepperdine U, Malibu (CA)
Piedmont Coll (GA)
Pittsburg State U (KS)
Plymouth State U (NH)
Point Park U (PA)
Providence Coll (RI)
Queens Coll of the City U of New York (NY)
Regis Coll (MA)
Rhode Island Coll (RI)
Roberts Wesleyan Coll (NY)
Rocky Mountain Coll (MT)
Roger Williams U (RI)
Rust Coll (MS)
Saginaw Valley State U (MI)
St. Ambrose U (IA)
St. Catherine U (MN)
St. Edward's U (TX)
Saint Francis U (PA)
St. Gregory's U, Shawnee (OK)
St. John Fisher Coll (NY)
St. John's U (NY)
St. Joseph's Coll, Long Island Campus (NY)
St. Joseph's Coll, New York (NY)
Saint Mary's U of Minnesota (MN)
St. Petersburg Coll (FL)
Salve Regina U (RI)
Schreiner U (TX)
Seattle U (WA)
Seton Hill U (PA)
Shawnee State U (OH)
Shorter U (GA)
Simpson U (CA)
Southeastern Oklahoma State U (OK)
Southeastern U (FL)
Southeast Missouri State U (MO)
Southern New Hampshire U (NH)
Southern Utah U (UT)
Southwest Baptist U (MO)
Southwestern Assemblies of God U (TX)
Southwestern Coll (KS)
Spring Hill Coll (AL)
State U of New York at New Paltz (NY)
State U of New York Coll at Cortland (NY)
State U of New York Coll at Old Westbury (NY)
State U of New York Coll at Potsdam (NY)
Syracuse U (NY)
Taylor U (IN)
Temple U (PA)
Texas Christian U (TX)
Texas Lutheran U (TX)
Texas Wesleyan U (TX)
Trevecca Nazarene U (TN)
Trine U (IN)
Trinity Christian Coll (IL)
Union Coll (KY)
Union Coll (NE)
Universidad Adventista de las Antillas (PR)
Université de Montréal (QC, Canada)
The U of Akron (OH)
U of California, San Diego (CA)
U of Central Arkansas (AR)
U of Central Florida (FL)
U of Delaware (DE)
U of Detroit Mercy (MI)
U of Dubuque (IA)
U of Evansville (IN)
The U of Findlay (OH)
U of Georgia (GA)
U of Great Falls (MT)
U of Hartford (CT)
U of Illinois at Chicago (IL)
U of Indianapolis (IN)
U of Jamestown (ND)
U of Lethbridge (AB, Canada)
U of Louisiana at Monroe (LA)
U of Maine (ME)
U of Maine at Farmington (ME)
U of Mary Hardin-Baylor (TX)
U of Michigan–Dearborn (MI)
U of Michigan–Flint (MI)
U of Minnesota, Duluth (MN)
U of Mobile (AL)
The U of Montana Western (MT)
U of New Hampshire (NH)
The U of North Carolina at Greensboro (NC)
The U of North Carolina at Pembroke (NC)
U of Northern Iowa (IA)
U of North Florida (FL)
U of Oklahoma (OK)
U of Pittsburgh at Johnstown (PA)
U of Regina (SK, Canada)
U of St. Francis (IL)
U of St. Thomas (MN)
The U of South Dakota (SD)
U of Southern Maine (ME)
U of South Florida (FL)
The U of Tennessee at Chattanooga (TN)
The U of Tennessee at Martin (TN)
The U of Tulsa (OK)
U of Vermont (VT)
U of Waterloo (ON, Canada)
U of Windsor (ON, Canada)
U of Wisconsin–Superior (WI)
U of Wisconsin–Whitewater (WI)
Utah State U (UT)
Utah Valley U (UT)
Utica Coll (NY)
Valley City State U (ND)
Valparaiso U (IN)
Vincennes U (IN)
Virginia Union U (VA)
Viterbo U (WI)
Walsh U (OH)
Wartburg Coll (IA)
Washburn U (KS)
Washington U in St. Louis (MO)
Waynesburg U (PA)
Wayne State Coll (NE)
Weber State U (UT)
Western Carolina U (NC)
Western Michigan U (MI)
Western State Colorado U (CO)
Western Washington U (WA)
Westfield State U (MA)
Westmont Coll (CA)
West Virginia Wesleyan Coll (WV)
Widener U (PA)
William Woods U (MO)
Wilmington U (DE)
Wingate U (NC)
Winona State U (MN)
York Coll of Pennsylvania (PA)
Youngstown State U (OH)

MECHANICAL DRAFTING AND CAD/CADD

Indiana U–Purdue U Indianapolis (IN)

MECHANICAL ENGINEERING

Alfred U (NY)
The American U in Cairo (Egypt)
The American U in Dubai (United Arab Emirates)
American U of Beirut (Lebanon)
Anderson U (IN)
Andrews U (MI)
Arizona State U at the Tempe campus (AZ)
Arkansas Tech U (AR)
Auburn U (AL)
Baylor U (TX)
Benedictine Coll (KS)
Binghamton U, State U of New York (NY)
Boise State U (ID)
Boston U (MA)
Bradley U (IL)
Bucknell U (PA)
California Baptist U (CA)
California Inst of Technology (CA)
California Polytechnic State U, San Luis Obispo (CA)
California State Polytechnic U, Pomona (CA)
California State U, Chico (CA)
California State U, Fresno (CA)
California State U, Fullerton (CA)
California State U, Long Beach (CA)
California State U Maritime Acad (CA)
California State U, Northridge (CA)
California State U, Sacramento (CA)
Calvin Coll (MI)
Carnegie Mellon U (PA)
Case Western Reserve U (OH)
The Catholic U of America (DC)
Cedarville U (OH)
Central Connecticut State U (CT)
Central Michigan U (MI)
Christian Brothers U (TN)
The Citadel, The Military Coll of South Carolina (SC)
City Coll of the City U of New York (NY)
Clarkson U (NY)

Clemson U (SC)
Cleveland State U (OH)
The Coll of New Jersey (NJ)
Colorado School of Mines (CO)
Colorado State U (CO)
Columbia U (NY)
Concordia U (QC, Canada)
Cooper Union for the Advancement of Science and Art (NY)
Cornell U (NY)
Drexel U (PA)
Eastern Nazarene Coll (MA)
Eastern Washington U (WA)
Embry-Riddle Aeronautical U–Daytona (FL)
Embry-Riddle Aeronautical U–Prescott (AZ)
Fairfield U (CT)
Florida Ag and Mech U (FL)
Florida Atlantic U (FL)
Florida Inst of Technology (FL)
Florida Intl U (FL)
Franklin W. Olin Coll of Eng (MA)
Gannon U (PA)
George Fox U (OR)
The George Washington U (DC)
Georgia Inst of Technology (GA)
Georgia Southern U (GA)
Gonzaga U (WA)
Grove City Coll (PA)
Hanover Coll (IN)
Harding U (AR)
Hofstra U (NY)
Idaho State U (ID)
Indiana U–Purdue U Indianapolis (IN)
Inter American U of Puerto Rico, Bayamón Campus (PR)
Iowa State U of Science and Technology (IA)
Jacksonville U (FL)
Johns Hopkins U (MD)
Kansas State U (KS)
Kennesaw State U (GA)
Kettering U (MI)
King's Coll (PA)
Lafayette Coll (PA)
Lamar U (TX)
Lawrence Technological U (MI)
Lebanese American U (Lebanon)
Lehigh U (PA)
LeTourneau U (TX)
Liberty U (VA)
Lipscomb U (TN)
Louisiana State U and A&M Coll (LA)
Louisiana Tech U (LA)
Loyola Marymount U (CA)
Manhattan Coll (NY)
Marshall U (WV)
Massachusetts Inst of Technology (MA)
McMaster U (ON, Canada)
Merrimack Coll (MA)
Miami U (OH)
Michigan State U (MI)
Michigan Technological U (MI)
Milligan Coll (TN)
Milwaukee School of Eng (WI)
Minnesota State U Mankato (MN)
Mississippi State U (MS)
Missouri U of Science and Technology (MO)
Montana State U (MT)
Montana Tech of The U of Montana (MT)
Mount Vernon Nazarene U (OH)
New England Inst of Technology (RI)
New Mexico Inst of Mining and Technology (NM)
New Mexico State U (NM)
New York Inst of Technology (NY)
North Carolina State U (NC)
North Dakota State U (ND)
Northeastern U (MA)
Northern Arizona U (AZ)
Northern Illinois U (IL)
Northwestern U (IL)
The Ohio State U (OH)
Ohio U (OH)
Oklahoma Christian U (OK)
Oklahoma State U (OK)
Old Dominion U (VA)
Oral Roberts U (OK)
Oregon State U (OR)
Penn State Abington (PA)
Penn State Altoona (PA)
Penn State Beaver (PA)
Penn State Berks (PA)
Penn State Brandywine (PA)
Penn State DuBois (PA)
Penn State Erie, The Behrend Coll (PA)
Penn State Fayette, The Eberly Campus (PA)
Penn State Greater Allegheny (PA)
Penn State Harrisburg (PA)
Penn State Hazleton (PA)
Penn State Lehigh Valley (PA)
Penn State Mont Alto (PA)
Penn State New Kensington (PA)
Penn State Schuylkill (PA)
Penn State Shenango (PA)
Penn State U Park (PA)
Penn State Wilkes-Barre (PA)
Penn State Worthington Scranton (PA)
Penn State York (PA)
Polytechnic U of Puerto Rico (PR)
Portland State U (OR)
Prairie View A&M U (TX)
Princeton U (NJ)
Purdue U (IN)
Purdue U Northwest (IN)
Quinnipiac U (CT)
Rensselaer Polytechnic Inst (NY)
Rice U (TX)
Rochester Inst of Technology (NY)
Rockhurst U (MO)
Roger Williams U (RI)
Rose-Hulman Inst of Technology (IN)
Rowan U (NJ)
Royal Military Coll of Canada (ON, Canada)
Rutgers U–New Brunswick (NJ)
Saginaw Valley State U (MI)
St. Cloud State U (MN)
Saint Louis U (MO)
Saint Louis U–Madrid Campus (Spain)
Saint Martin's U (WA)
San Diego State U (CA)
San Francisco State U (CA)
Santa Clara U (CA)
Seattle U (WA)
South Dakota School of Mines and Technology (SD)
South Dakota State U (SD)
Southern Illinois U Carbondale (IL)
Southern Illinois U Edwardsville (IL)
Southern Methodist U (TX)
Southern New Hampshire U (NH)
Stanford U (CA)
State U of New York at New Paltz (NY)
State U of New York Maritime Coll (NY)
State U of New York Polytechnic Inst (NY)
Stevens Inst of Technology (NJ)
Stony Brook U, State U of New York (NY)
Syracuse U (NY)
Temple U (PA)
Tennessee State U (TN)
Texas A&M U (TX)
Texas A&M U–Corpus Christi (TX)
Texas A&M U–Kingsville (TX)
Texas Tech U (TX)
Trine U (IN)
Tufts U (MA)
Union Coll (NY)
United States Air Force Acad (CO)
United States Coast Guard Acad (CT)
United States Military Acad (NY)
Université de Sherbrooke (QC, Canada)
U at Buffalo, the State U of New York (NY)
The U of Akron (OH)
The U of Alabama (AL)
The U of Alabama at Birmingham (AL)
The U of Alabama in Huntsville (AL)
U of Alaska Fairbanks (AK)
The U of Arizona (AZ)
U of Arkansas (AR)
U of Bridgeport (CT)
U of California, Davis (CA)
U of California, Irvine (CA)
U of California, Los Angeles (CA)
U of California, Riverside (CA)
U of California, San Diego (CA)
U of California, Santa Barbara (CA)
U of Central Florida (FL)
U of Cincinnati (OH)
U of Colorado Boulder (CO)
U of Colorado Colorado Springs (CO)
U of Colorado Denver (CO)
U of Dayton (OH)
U of Delaware (DE)
U of Denver (CO)
U of Evansville (IN)
U of Florida (FL)
U of Georgia (GA)
U of Guelph (ON, Canada)
U of Hartford (CT)
U of Hawaii at Manoa (HI)
U of Houston (TX)
U of Idaho (ID)
U of Illinois at Chicago (IL)
U of Indianapolis (IN)
U of Jamestown (ND)
The U of Kansas (KS)
U of Kentucky (KY)
U of Louisville (KY)
U of Maine (ME)
U of Maryland, Baltimore County (MD)
U of Maryland, Coll Park (MD)
U of Massachusetts Amherst (MA)
U of Massachusetts Dartmouth (MA)
U of Massachusetts Lowell (MA)
U of Miami (FL)
U of Michigan (MI)
U of Michigan–Dearborn (MI)
U of Michigan–Flint (MI)
U of Minnesota, Duluth (MN)
U of Minnesota, Twin Cities Campus (MN)
U of Missouri–Kansas City (MO)
U of Missouri–St. Louis (MO)
U of Mount Union (OH)
U of Nevada, Las Vegas (NV)
U of Nevada, Reno (NV)
U of New Hampshire (NH)
U of New Haven (CT)
U of New Orleans (LA)
The U of North Carolina at Charlotte (NC)
U of North Dakota (ND)
U of North Florida (FL)
U of North Texas (TX)
U of Notre Dame (IN)
U of Oklahoma (OK)
U of Pennsylvania (PA)
U of Pittsburgh (PA)
U of Pittsburgh at Johnstown (PA)
U of Rhode Island (RI)
U of Rochester (NY)
U of St. Thomas (MN)
U of San Diego (CA)
U of Saskatchewan (SK, Canada)
U of South Alabama (AL)
U of South Carolina (SC)
U of Southern California (CA)
U of Southern Indiana (IN)
U of Southern Maine (ME)
U of South Florida (FL)
The U of Tennessee (TN)
The U of Tennessee at Chattanooga (TN)
The U of Texas at Austin (TX)
The U of Texas at Dallas (TX)
The U of Texas at El Paso (TX)
The U of Texas at San Antonio (TX)
The U of Texas of the Permian Basin (TX)
The U of Texas Rio Grande Valley (TX)
U of the Pacific (CA)
The U of Toledo (OH)
U of Toronto (ON, Canada)
The U of Tulsa (OK)
U of Utah (UT)
U of Vermont (VT)
U of Virginia (VA)
U of Washington (WA)
U of Washington, Bothell (WA)
U of Waterloo (ON, Canada)
U of Windsor (ON, Canada)
U of Wisconsin–Madison (WI)
U of Wisconsin–Milwaukee (WI)
U of Wisconsin–Platteville (WI)
Ursinus Coll (PA)
Utah State U (UT)
Valparaiso U (IN)
Vanderbilt U (TN)
Villanova U (PA)
Virginia Commonwealth U (VA)
Virginia Military Inst (VA)
Virginia Polytechnic Inst and State U (VA)
Walla Walla U (WA)
Washington State U (WA)
Washington State U–Global Campus (WA)
Washington State U–Tri-Cities (WA)
Washington State U–Vancouver (WA)
Washington U in St. Louis (MO)
Wayne State U (MI)
Wentworth Inst of Technology (MA)
Western Illinois U (IL)
Western Kentucky U (KY)
Western Michigan U (MI)
Western New England U (MA)
West Texas A&M U (TX)
West Virginia U (WV)
West Virginia U Inst of Technology (WV)
Wichita State U (KS)
Widener U (PA)
Wilkes U (PA)
William Penn U (IA)
Worcester Polytechnic Inst (MA)
Wright State U (OH)
Wright State U–Lake Campus (OH)
York Coll of Pennsylvania (PA)
Youngstown State U (OH)

MECHANICAL ENGINEERING/ MECHANICAL TECHNOLOGY

Arizona State U at the Polytechnic campus (AZ)
Bluefield State Coll (WV)
Bowling Green State U (OH)
Buffalo State Coll, State U of New York (NY)
California State U, Long Beach (CA)
California State U, Sacramento (CA)
Central Connecticut State U (CT)
Central Michigan U (MI)
Central Washington U (WA)
Colorado Mesa U (CO)
Eastern Michigan U (MI)
Eastern Washington U (WA)
Fairleigh Dickinson U, Metropolitan Campus (NJ)
Farmingdale State Coll (NY)
Ferris State U (MI)
Georgia Southern U (GA)
Idaho State U (ID)
Kennesaw State U (GA)
LeTourneau U (TX)
Metropolitan State U of Denver (CO)
Michigan Technological U (MI)
Montana State U (MT)
New York City Coll of Technology of the City U of New York (NY)
Oklahoma State U (OK)
Penn State Erie, The Behrend Coll (PA)
Pennsylvania Coll of Technology (PA)
Pittsburg State U (KS)
Point Park U (PA)
Purdue U (IN)
Purdue U Northwest (IN)
South Carolina State U (SC)
State U of New York Coll of Technology at Alfred (NY)
State U of New York Polytechnic Inst (NY)
Tarleton State U (TX)
Texas A&M U–Corpus Christi (TX)
United States Military Acad (NY)
The U of Akron (OH)
U of Dayton (OH)
U of Hartford (CT)
U of Houston (TX)
U of Maine (ME)
U of New Hampshire at Manchester (NH)
The U of North Carolina at Charlotte (NC)
U of North Texas (TX)
The U of Toledo (OH)
U of Wisconsin–Green Bay (WI)
Virginia State U (VA)
Wayne State U (MI)
Weber State U (UT)
Youngstown State U (OH)

MECHANICAL ENGINEERING TECHNOLOGIES RELATED

Cleveland State U (OH)
Indiana State U (IN)
Indiana U–Purdue U Indianapolis (IN)
LeTourneau U (TX)
Pennsylvania Coll of Technology (PA)
Purdue U Northwest (IN)
State U of New York Coll of Technology at Canton (NY)
U of Massachusetts Lowell (MA)
Vaughn Coll of Aeronautics and Technology (NY)

MECHANIC AND REPAIR TECHNOLOGIES RELATED

Inter American U of Puerto Rico, Guayama Campus (PR)

MECHANICS AND REPAIR

Idaho State U (ID)

MECHATRONICS, ROBOTICS, AND AUTOMATION ENGINEERING

California U of Pennsylvania (PA)
Lawrence Technological U (MI)
Lebanese American U (Lebanon)
Simon Fraser U (BC, Canada)
Southern Illinois U Edwardsville (IL)
U of Detroit Mercy (MI)
U of Washington (WA)
Worcester Polytechnic Inst (MA)

MEDICAL ANTHROPOLOGY

Creighton U (NE)
U of Miami (FL)
Washington U in St. Louis (MO)

MEDICAL/CLINICAL ASSISTANT

Idaho State U (ID)

MEDICAL/HEALTH MANAGEMENT AND CLINICAL ASSISTANT

Davenport U, Grand Rapids (MI)
Nebraska Methodist Coll (NE)
Stratford U, Woodbridge (VA)
The U of Texas at Dallas (TX)

MEDICAL ILLUSTRATION

Arcadia U (PA)
Cleveland Inst of Art (OH)
Iowa State U of Science and Technology (IA)
Rochester Inst of Technology (NY)

MEDICAL INFORMATICS

American U of Beirut (Lebanon)
Idaho State U (ID)
Mercy Coll of Health Sciences (IA)
Montana Tech of The U of Montana (MT)
Simmons Coll (MA)
State U of New York at Plattsburgh (NY)
U of South Alabama (AL)
U of Waterloo (ON, Canada)
Western Michigan U (MI)

MEDICAL MICROBIOLOGY AND BACTERIOLOGY

Adams State U (CO)
Auburn U (AL)
Bowling Green State U (OH)
California Polytechnic State U, San Luis Obispo (CA)
Dalhousie U (NS, Canada)
Humboldt State U (CA)
Minnesota State U Mankato (MN)
Mississippi State U (MS)
Montana State U (MT)
New Mexico State U (NM)
Ohio Wesleyan U (OH)
Penn State Abington (PA)
Penn State Altoona (PA)
Penn State Beaver (PA)
Penn State Berks (PA)
Penn State Brandywine (PA)
Penn State DuBois (PA)

Penn State Erie, The Behrend Coll (PA)
Penn State Fayette, The Eberly Campus (PA)
Penn State Greater Allegheny (PA)
Penn State Hazleton (PA)
Penn State Lehigh Valley (PA)
Penn State Mont Alto (PA)
Penn State New Kensington (PA)
Penn State Schuylkill (PA)
Penn State Shenango (PA)
Penn State U Park (PA)
Penn State Wilkes-Barre (PA)
Penn State Worthington Scranton (PA)
Penn State York (PA)
Quinnipiac U (CT)
Rutgers U–New Brunswick (NJ)
San Francisco State U (CA)
Sonoma State U (CA)
Université de Montréal (QC, Canada)
Université de Sherbrooke (QC, Canada)
U of California, San Diego (CA)
U of Delaware (DE)
U of Florida (FL)
U of Kentucky (KY)
U of King's Coll (NS, Canada)
U of Minnesota, Twin Cities Campus (MN)
U of Saskatchewan (SK, Canada)
U of South Florida (FL)
The U of Texas at El Paso (TX)
U of Toronto (ON, Canada)
U of Vermont (VT)
U of Wisconsin–La Crosse (WI)
Utah State U (UT)
Wagner Coll (NY)
Xavier U of Louisiana (LA)

MEDICAL OFFICE ASSISTANT
Concordia U Wisconsin (WI)

MEDICAL RADIOLOGIC TECHNOLOGY
Armstrong State U (GA)
Augusta U (GA)
Averett U (VA)
Avila U (MO)
Bellarmine U (KY)
Bloomsburg U of Pennsylvania (PA)
Boise State U (ID)
California State U, Long Beach (CA)
Clarion U of Pennsylvania (PA)
Concordia U Wisconsin (WI)
Creighton U (NE)
Emory U (GA)
Fairleigh Dickinson U, Coll at Florham (NJ)
Grand Valley State U (MI)
Gwynedd Mercy U (PA)
Idaho State U (ID)
Indiana U Kokomo (IN)
Indiana U Northwest (IN)
Indiana U–Purdue U Indianapolis (IN)
Indiana U South Bend (IN)
Inter American U of Puerto Rico, San Germán Campus (PR)
Kent State U at Salem (OH)
La Roche Coll (PA)
MCPHS U (MA)
Minot State U (ND)
Misericordia U (PA)
Morehead State U (KY)
Mount Aloysius Coll (PA)
Mount Marty Coll (SD)
National U (CA)
New York City Coll of Technology of the City U of New York (NY)
North Central Coll (IL)
The Ohio State U (OH)
Saint Louis U (MO)
Southern Illinois U Carbondale (IL)
Texas State U (TX)
U of Arkansas for Medical Sciences (AR)
U of Central Arkansas (AR)
U of Hartford (CT)
U of Michigan–Flint (MI)
U of Nevada, Las Vegas (NV)
The U of North Carolina at Chapel Hill (NC)
U of Oklahoma Health Sciences Center (OK)
U of St. Francis (IL)
U of Southern Indiana (IN)
U of Vermont (VT)
U of Wisconsin–La Crosse (WI)
Valencia Coll (FL)
Wayne State U (MI)
Weber State U (UT)

MEDICAL STAFF SERVICES TECHNOLOGY
Converse Coll (SC)

MEDICINAL AND PHARMACEUTICAL CHEMISTRY
King U (TN)
Michigan Technological U (MI)
U of California, San Diego (CA)
U of Dayton (OH)
U of Guelph (ON, Canada)
U of Michigan (MI)

MEDIEVAL AND RENAISSANCE STUDIES
Augsburg Coll (MN)
Bard Coll (NY)
Barnard Coll (NY)
Binghamton U, State U of New York (NY)
The Catholic U of America (DC)
Cleveland State U (OH)
The Coll of William and Mary (VA)
Columbia U (NY)
Cornell Coll (IA)
Dickinson Coll (PA)
Fordham U (NY)
Georgetown U (DC)
Hanover Coll (IN)
Mount Allison U (NB, Canada)
Mount Holyoke Coll (MA)
New Coll of Florida (FL)
The Ohio State U (OH)
Ohio Wesleyan U (OH)
Penn State Abington (PA)
Penn State Altoona (PA)
Penn State Beaver (PA)
Penn State Berks (PA)
Penn State Brandywine (PA)
Penn State DuBois (PA)
Penn State Erie, The Behrend Coll (PA)
Penn State Fayette, The Eberly Campus (PA)
Penn State Greater Allegheny (PA)
Penn State Hazleton (PA)
Penn State Lehigh Valley (PA)
Penn State Mont Alto (PA)
Penn State New Kensington (PA)
Penn State Schuylkill (PA)
Penn State Shenango (PA)
Penn State U Park (PA)
Penn State Wilkes-Barre (PA)
Penn State Worthington Scranton (PA)
Penn State York (PA)
Pomona Coll (CA)
Purdue U (IN)
Rutgers U–New Brunswick (NJ)
Saint Louis U (MO)
St. Olaf Coll (MN)
Sewanee: The U of the South (TN)
Smith Coll (MA)
Southern Methodist U (TX)
Swarthmore Coll (PA)
Tulane U (LA)
Université de Montréal (QC, Canada)
U at Albany, State U of New York (NY)
U of California, Santa Barbara (CA)
U of Chicago (IL)
U of Michigan (MI)
U of Notre Dame (IN)
U of Oregon (OR)
U of Regina (SK, Canada)
U of Saskatchewan (SK, Canada)
U of Waterloo (ON, Canada)
Ursinus Coll (PA)
Vassar Coll (NY)
Washington and Lee U (VA)

MEETING AND EVENT PLANNING
Central Michigan U (MI)
Coll of the Ozarks (MO)
Fisher Coll (MA)
Grace Coll (IN)
Iowa State U of Science and Technology (IA)
Lasell Coll (MA)
Lynn U (FL)
Stephens Coll (MO)
U of Central Florida (FL)

MENTAL AND SOCIAL HEALTH SERVICES AND ALLIED PROFESSIONS RELATED
Clarion U of Pennsylvania (PA)
Northern Kentucky U (KY)
Old Dominion U (VA)
Pennsylvania Coll of Technology (PA)
Roger Williams U (RI)
Southwestern Assemblies of God U (TX)
Washburn U (KS)

MENTAL HEALTH COUNSELING
Canisius Coll (NY)
Faulkner U (AL)
Goddard Coll (VT)
Iona Coll (NY)
St. Cloud State U (MN)

MERCHANDISING, SALES, AND MARKETING OPERATIONS RELATED (GENERAL)
Dalhousie U (NS, Canada)
Eastern Michigan U (MI)
Georgia State U (GA)
Lincoln U (MO)
U of Hartford (CT)
Virginia Union U (VA)
Washington U in St. Louis (MO)

MERCHANDISING, SALES, AND MARKETING OPERATIONS RELATED (SPECIALIZED)
Baylor U (TX)
Fashion Inst of Technology (NY)
High Point U (NC)
Saint Joseph's U (PA)

METAL AND JEWELRY ARTS
Acad of Art U (CA)
Adams State U (CO)
Arcadia U (PA)
Bowling Green State U (OH)
California Coll of the Arts (CA)
California State U, Long Beach (CA)
Central Washington U (WA)
Cleveland Inst of Art (OH)
Colorado State U (CO)
Ferris State U (MI)
Hofstra U (NY)
Massachusetts Coll of Art and Design (MA)
Memphis Coll of Art (TN)
Pratt Inst (NY)
Rhode Island Coll (RI)
Rhode Island School of Design (RI)
Rochester Inst of Technology (NY)
Savannah Coll of Art and Design (GA)
School of the Art Inst of Chicago (IL)
Seton Hill U (PA)
State U of New York at New Paltz (NY)
Syracuse U (NY)
Temple U (PA)
The U of Akron (OH)
The U of Kansas (KS)
U of Massachusetts Dartmouth (MA)
U of Michigan (MI)
U of Oregon (OR)
Western State Colorado U (CO)

METALLURGICAL ENGINEERING
Colorado School of Mines (CO)
LeTourneau U (TX)
Missouri U of Science and Technology (MO)
Montana Tech of The U of Montana (MT)
South Dakota School of Mines and Technology (SD)
The U of Alabama (AL)
U of Nevada, Reno (NV)
The U of Texas at El Paso (TX)
U of Toronto (ON, Canada)
U of Utah (UT)

METEOROLOGY
Central Michigan U (MI)
Dalhousie U (NS, Canada)
Florida Inst of Technology (FL)
Florida State U (FL)
Iowa State U of Science and Technology (IA)
Metropolitan State U of Denver (CO)
Northland Coll (WI)
Rutgers U–New Brunswick (NJ)
U of Hawaii at Manoa (HI)
U of Miami (FL)
The U of North Carolina at Charlotte (NC)
U of Oklahoma (OK)
U of South Alabama (AL)
U of the Incarnate Word (TX)
U of Wisconsin–Milwaukee (WI)
Virginia Polytechnic Inst and State U (VA)
Western Illinois U (IL)
Western Kentucky U (KY)

MICROBIOLOGICAL SCIENCES AND IMMUNOLOGY RELATED
Dalhousie U (NS, Canada)
Université de Montréal (QC, Canada)
U of California, Los Angeles (CA)

MICROBIOLOGY
Arizona State U at the Tempe campus (AZ)
Auburn U (AL)
Bowling Green State U (OH)
Brigham Young U (UT)
California State U, Chico (CA)
California State U, Dominguez Hills (CA)
California State U, Long Beach (CA)
Central Washington U (WA)
Clemson U (SC)
Colorado State U (CO)
Concordia U Chicago (IL)
Idaho State U (ID)
Indiana U Bloomington (IN)
Inter American U of Puerto Rico, Aguadilla Campus (PR)
Inter American U of Puerto Rico, Bayamón Campus (PR)
Inter American U of Puerto Rico, Ponce Campus (PR)
Inter American U of Puerto Rico, San Germán Campus (PR)
Iowa State U of Science and Technology (IA)
Kansas State U (KS)
Louisiana State U and A&M Coll (LA)
Miami U (OH)
Michigan State U (MI)
North Carolina State U (NC)
North Dakota State U (ND)
Northern Arizona U (AZ)
Northwestern State U of Louisiana (LA)
The Ohio State U (OH)
Ohio U (OH)
Oklahoma State U (OK)
Oregon State U (OR)
Rutgers U–New Brunswick (NJ)
San Diego State U (CA)
South Dakota State U (SD)
Southern Illinois U Carbondale (IL)
Texas A&M U (TX)
Texas State U (TX)
Texas Tech U (TX)
Université de Montréal (QC, Canada)
The U of Akron (OH)
The U of Alabama (AL)
The U of Arizona (AZ)
U of California, Davis (CA)
U of California, Santa Barbara (CA)
U of Georgia (GA)
U of Guelph (ON, Canada)
U of Hawaii at Manoa (HI)
U of Idaho (ID)
The U of Kansas (KS)
U of Maine (ME)
U of Maryland, Coll Park (MD)
U of Massachusetts Amherst (MA)
U of Michigan (MI)
U of Michigan–Dearborn (MI)
U of Oklahoma (OK)
U of Pittsburgh (PA)
U of Rhode Island (RI)
The U of Texas at Austin (TX)
U of Toronto (ON, Canada)
U of Vermont (VT)
U of Washington (WA)
U of Wisconsin–La Crosse (WI)
U of Wisconsin–Madison (WI)
U of Wisconsin–Milwaukee (WI)
Washington State U (WA)
Weber State U (UT)

MICROBIOLOGY AND IMMUNOLOGY
Purdue U (IN)
U of California, Irvine (CA)
U of Miami (FL)
U of Nevada, Reno (NV)
U of Saskatchewan (SK, Canada)
The U of Texas at San Antonio (TX)
West Virginia U (WV)

MIDDLE/NEAR EASTERN AND SEMITIC LANGUAGES
Indiana U Bloomington (IN)
Pepperdine U, Malibu (CA)
U of Pennsylvania (PA)
The U of Texas at Austin (TX)

MIDDLE/NEAR EASTERN AND SEMITIC LANGUAGES RELATED
Columbia U, School of General Studies (NY)
U of Chicago (IL)
U of Michigan (MI)
U of Washington (WA)
Wayne State U (MI)

MIDDLE SCHOOL EDUCATION
Albany State U (GA)
Albertus Magnus Coll (CT)
Alice Lloyd Coll (KY)
Alvernia U (PA)
Alverno Coll (WI)
Appalachian State U (NC)
Arcadia U (PA)
Arkansas Tech U (AR)
Arlington Baptist Coll (TX)
Armstrong State U (GA)
Asbury U (KY)
Ashland U (OH)
Augusta U (GA)
Austin Coll (TX)
Avila U (MO)
Baker U (KS)
Baldwin Wallace U (OH)
Barton Coll (NC)
Bayamón Central U (PR)
Bellarmine U (KY)
Belmont U (TN)
Berea Coll (KY)
Berry Coll (GA)
Bethel Coll (IN)
Black Hills State U (SD)
Bloomsburg U of Pennsylvania (PA)
Bluefield Coll (VA)
Bluffton U (OH)
Bowling Green State U (OH)
Brenau U (GA)
Brescia U (KY)
Brewton-Parker Coll (GA)
California U of Pennsylvania (PA)
Capital U (OH)
Carlow U (PA)
Carson-Newman U (TN)
Catawba Coll (NC)
Cedarville U (OH)
Central Methodist U (MO)
Central State U (OH)
Champlain Coll (VT)
Clarion U of Pennsylvania (PA)
Clark U (MA)
Clayton State U (GA)
Cleveland State U (OH)
Coastal Carolina U (SC)
Coll of Charleston (SC)
Coll of Coastal Georgia (GA)
Coll of the Atlantic (ME)
Columbus State U (GA)
Concordia Coll–New York (NY)
Concordia U, Nebraska (NE)
Concordia U, St. Paul (MN)
Concordia U Wisconsin (WI)
Duquesne U (PA)
East Carolina U (NC)
Eastern Illinois U (IL)
Eastern Nazarene Coll (MA)
Eastern U (PA)

East Stroudsburg U of Pennsylvania (PA)
Elizabeth City State U (NC)
Elizabethtown Coll (PA)
Elon U (NC)
Emmanuel Coll (GA)
Evangel U (MO)
Fayetteville State U (NC)
Fitchburg State U (MA)
Florida Inst of Technology (FL)
Francis Marion U (SC)
Freed-Hardeman U (TN)
Gannon U (PA)
Gardner-Webb U (NC)
Georgetown Coll (KY)
Georgia Coll & State U (GA)
Georgia Southern U (GA)
Georgia Southwestern State U (GA)
Gettysburg Coll (PA)
Goddard Coll (VT)
Gordon Coll (MA)
Gordon State Coll (GA)
Grand Valley State U (MI)
Granite State Coll (NH)
Grove City Coll (PA)
Hampton U (VA)
Harding U (AR)
Harris-Stowe State U (MO)
Henderson State U (AR)
High Point U (NC)
Hiram Coll (OH)
Huntington U (IN)
Illinois State U (IL)
Indiana U of Pennsylvania (PA)
Ithaca Coll (NY)
Jacksonville State U (AL)
Johnson U (TN)
Kennesaw State U (GA)
Kent State U (OH)
Kent State U at Geauga (OH)
Kent State U at Stark (OH)
Kentucky Wesleyan Coll (KY)
Kutztown U of Pennsylvania (PA)
La Salle U (PA)
Lee U (TN)
Lenoir-Rhyne U (NC)
Lesley U (MA)
Lewis U (IL)
Lincoln U (MO)
Lindenwood U (MO)
Lindsey Wilson Coll (KY)
Lipscomb U (TN)
Lock Haven U of Pennsylvania (PA)
Louisiana Tech U (LA)
Lourdes U (OH)
Lubbock Christian U (TX)
Malone U (OH)
Manchester U (IN)
Manhattan Coll (NY)
Marian U (WI)
Maryville U of Saint Louis (MO)
The Master's U (CA)
McMurry U (TX)
Mercer U, Macon (GA)
Merrimack Coll (MA)
Messiah Coll (PA)
Miami U (OH)
Michigan State U (MI)
MidAmerica Nazarene U (KS)
Millersville U of Pennsylvania (PA)
Misericordia U (PA)
Missouri Baptist U (MO)
Missouri State U (MO)
Missouri Valley Coll (MO)
Morehead State U (KY)
Mount Aloysius Coll (PA)
Mount Mary U (WI)
Mount Mercy U (IA)
Mount St. Joseph U (OH)
Mount Vernon Nazarene U (OH)
Murray State U (KY)
Muskingum U (OH)
Newberry Coll (SC)
North Carolina Central U (NC)
North Carolina State U (NC)
North Carolina Wesleyan Coll (NC)
Northern Kentucky U (KY)
Northwest Christian U (OR)
Northwest Missouri State U (MO)
Ohio Christian U (OH)
Ohio Dominican U (OH)
The Ohio State U (OH)
The Ohio State U at Lima (OH)
The Ohio State U at Marion (OH)
The Ohio State U–Mansfield Campus (OH)
The Ohio State U–Newark Campus (OH)
Ohio U–Eastern (OH)
Ohio Wesleyan U (OH)
Otterbein U (OH)
Ouachita Baptist U (AR)
Piedmont Coll (GA)
Point U (GA)
Rockhurst U (MO)
St. Cloud State U (MN)
Saint Leo U (FL)
Saint Vincent Coll (PA)
Schreiner U (TX)
Shippensburg U of Pennsylvania (PA)
Shorter U (GA)
South Carolina State U (SC)
Southeastern Louisiana U (LA)
Southeast Missouri State U (MO)
Southern Arkansas U–Magnolia (AR)
Southern Illinois U Edwardsville (IL)
Southwest Baptist U (MO)
Spalding U (KY)
State U of New York Coll at Cortland (NY)
State U of New York Coll at Old Westbury (NY)
Stevenson U (MD)
Tarleton State U (TX)
Temple U (PA)
Texas Lutheran U (TX)
Thomas More Coll (KY)
Thomas U (GA)
Toccoa Falls Coll (GA)
Towson U (MD)
Transylvania U (KY)
Trinity Christian Coll (IL)
Truett McConnell U (GA)
Union Coll (KY)
The U of Akron (OH)
U of Central Arkansas (AR)
U of Central Missouri (MO)
U of Cincinnati (OH)
U of Dayton (OH)
The U of Findlay (OH)
U of Georgia (GA)
U of Great Falls (MT)
The U of Kansas (KS)
U of Kentucky (KY)
U of Maryland, Coll Park (MD)
U of Minnesota, Duluth (MN)
U of Missouri–Kansas City (MO)
U of Mount Union (OH)
The U of North Carolina at Chapel Hill (NC)
The U of North Carolina at Charlotte (NC)
The U of North Carolina at Greensboro (NC)
The U of North Carolina at Pembroke (NC)
The U of North Carolina Wilmington (NC)
U of North Dakota (ND)
U of Northern Iowa (IA)
U of North Florida (FL)
U of North Georgia (GA)
U of Pikeville (KY)
U of Regina (SK, Canada)
U of St. Thomas (MN)
The U of Scranton (PA)
U of South Carolina (SC)
U of South Carolina Aiken (SC)
The U of Tennessee at Chattanooga (TN)
The U of Texas at San Antonio (TX)
U of the Cumberlands (KY)
U of Valley Forge (PA)
U of Vermont (VT)
Valdosta State U (GA)
Virginia Wesleyan Coll (VA)
Walsh U (OH)
Washington U in St. Louis (MO)
Wayland Baptist U (TX)
Wayne State Coll (NE)
Webster U (MO)
West Chester U of Pennsylvania (PA)
Western Carolina U (NC)
West Virginia Wesleyan Coll (WV)
Wilkes U (PA)
Wilmington U (DE)
Wingate U (NC)
Wright State U (OH)
Wright State U–Lake Campus (OH)
Xavier U of Louisiana (LA)
Youngstown State U (OH)

MILITARY AND STRATEGIC LEADERSHIP
Excelsior Coll (NY)

MILITARY APPLIED SCIENCES RELATED
United States Military Acad (NY)

MILITARY HISTORY
American Public U System (WV)
Hawai`i Pacific U (HI)
Rogers State U (OK)
United States Air Force Acad (CO)
United States Military Acad (NY)

MILITARY INSTALLATION MANAGEMENT
American Public U System (WV)

MILITARY SCIENCE, LEADERSHIP AND OPERATIONAL ART RELATED
Dixie State U (UT)

MILITARY STUDIES
Excelsior Coll (NY)
United States Air Force Acad (CO)

MILITARY TECHNOLOGIES AND APPLIED SCIENCES RELATED
Alcorn State U (MS)

MINING AND MINERAL ENGINEERING
Colorado School of Mines (CO)
Missouri U of Science and Technology (MO)
Montana Tech of The U of Montana (MT)
New Mexico Inst of Mining and Technology (NM)
Penn State Abington (PA)
Penn State Altoona (PA)
Penn State Beaver (PA)
Penn State Berks (PA)
Penn State Brandywine (PA)
Penn State DuBois (PA)
Penn State Erie, The Behrend Coll (PA)
Penn State Fayette, The Eberly Campus (PA)
Penn State Greater Allegheny (PA)
Penn State Hazleton (PA)
Penn State Lehigh Valley (PA)
Penn State Mont Alto (PA)
Penn State New Kensington (PA)
Penn State Schuylkill (PA)
Penn State Shenango (PA)
Penn State U Park (PA)
Penn State Wilkes-Barre (PA)
Penn State Worthington Scranton (PA)
Penn State York (PA)
South Dakota School of Mines and Technology (SD)
Southern Illinois U Carbondale (IL)
U of Alaska Fairbanks (AK)
The U of Arizona (AZ)
U of Kentucky (KY)
U of Nevada, Reno (NV)
U of Toronto (ON, Canada)
U of Utah (UT)
Virginia Polytechnic Inst and State U (VA)
West Virginia U (WV)

MINING TECHNOLOGY
Bluefield State Coll (WV)

MISSIONARY STUDIES AND MISSIOLOGY
Anderson U (SC)
Arizona Christian U (AZ)
Asbury U (KY)
Bethel Coll (IN)
Biola U (CA)
California Baptist U (CA)
Calvary U (MO)
Carson-Newman U (TN)
Cedarville U (OH)
Central Baptist Coll (AR)
City Vision U (MO)
Concordia U, St. Paul (MN)
Concordia U Wisconsin (WI)
Corban U (OR)
Cornerstone U (MI)
Dallas Baptist U (TX)
Eastern U (PA)
East Texas Baptist U (TX)
Emmaus Bible Coll (IA)
Faith Baptist Bible Coll and Theological Sem (IA)
Faulkner U (AL)
Freed-Hardeman U (TN)
Gardner-Webb U (NC)
Geneva Coll (PA)
Global U (MO)
Grace Coll (IN)
Harding U (AR)
Hobe Sound Bible Coll (FL)
Hope Intl U (CA)
Huntington U (IN)
Johnson U (TN)
Johnson U Florida (FL)
Kentucky Mountain Bible Coll (KY)
Kuyper Coll (MI)
Lee U (TN)
LeTourneau U (TX)
Lincoln Christian U (IL)
Lipscomb U (TN)
Lubbock Christian U (TX)
Maranatha Baptist U (WI)
Messenger Coll (TX)
MidAmerica Nazarene U (KS)
Mid-Atlantic Christian U (NC)
Mount Vernon Nazarene U (OH)
Multnomah U (OR)
North Greenville U (SC)
Northwest Christian U (OR)
Northwest U (WA)
Ohio Christian U (OH)
Oklahoma Christian U (OK)
Olivet Nazarene U (IL)
Oral Roberts U (OK)
Ouachita Baptist U (AR)
Palm Beach Atlantic U (FL)
Piedmont Intl U (NC)
Simpson U (CA)
Southeastern U (FL)
Southwest Baptist U (MO)
Southwestern Assemblies of God U (TX)
Toccoa Falls Coll (GA)
Trinity Baptist Coll (FL)
Trinity Coll of Florida (FL)
Truett McConnell U (GA)
U of the Cumberlands (KY)
U of Valley Forge (PA)
Wayland Baptist U (TX)
Welch Coll (TN)

MODELING, VIRTUAL ENVIRONMENTS AND SIMULATION
Cogswell Polytechnical Coll (CA)
DigiPen Inst of Technology (WA)
Lipscomb U (TN)
Pennsylvania Coll of Technology (PA)
U of Colorado Colorado Springs (CO)
U of Idaho (ID)
U of Southern California (CA)

MODERN GREEK
Colgate U (NY)
Columbia U (NY)
Concordia U Wisconsin (WI)
Furman U (SC)
John Carroll U (OH)
Lehman Coll of the City U of New York (NY)
Oberlin Coll (OH)
The Ohio State U (OH)
Tufts U (MA)
Tulane U (LA)
U of Michigan (MI)
U of Toronto (ON, Canada)
Wright State U (OH)
Wright State U–Lake Campus (OH)

MODERN LANGUAGES
Beloit Coll (WI)
Bemidji State U (MN)
Bishop's U (QC, Canada)
Clark U (MA)
Coll of Mount Saint Vincent (NY)
The Coll of William and Mary (VA)
Cornell Coll (IA)
Fordham U (NY)
Gettysburg Coll (PA)
Hampton U (VA)
McMaster U (ON, Canada)
Metropolitan State U of Denver (CO)
Minnesota State U Mankato (MN)
Mount Allison U (NB, Canada)
Nazareth Coll of Rochester (NY)
Purchase Coll, State U of New York (NY)
Saint Francis U (PA)
Saint Mary's Coll of California (CA)
Saint Michael's Coll (VT)
Saint Peter's U (NJ)
St. Thomas Aquinas Coll (NY)
Trent U (ON, Canada)
Université de Montréal (QC, Canada)
U of Toronto (ON, Canada)
U of Windsor (ON, Canada)
Virginia Military Inst (VA)
Walla Walla U (WA)
Walsh U (OH)
Washington U in St. Louis (MO)
Westmont Coll (CA)
Widener U (PA)

MOLECULAR BIOCHEMISTRY
Clarkson U (NY)
Simon Fraser U (BC, Canada)
U of California, Davis (CA)
U of Richmond (VA)
Wesleyan U (CT)

MOLECULAR BIOLOGY
Alverno Coll (WI)
Arizona State U at the Tempe campus (AZ)
Assumption Coll (MA)
Auburn U (AL)
Beloit Coll (WI)
Blackburn Coll (IL)
Boston U (MA)
California Lutheran U (CA)
California State U, Fresno (CA)
Central Connecticut State U (CT)
Chestnut Hill Coll (PA)
Claremont McKenna Coll (CA)
Clarion U of Pennsylvania (PA)
Clark U (MA)
Coe Coll (IA)
Colby Coll (ME)
Colgate U (NY)
Coll of the Ozarks (MO)
The Coll of Wooster (OH)
Dartmouth Coll (NH)
Florida Inst of Technology (FL)
Gettysburg Coll (PA)
Goshen Coll (IN)
Grove City Coll (PA)
Hampton U (VA)
Humboldt State U (CA)
Johns Hopkins U (MD)
Kenyon Coll (OH)
Lawrence Technological U (MI)
Lehigh U (PA)
McMaster U (ON, Canada)
Messiah Coll (PA)
Millikin U (IL)
Montclair State U (NJ)
Muskingum U (OH)
Northwestern U (IL)
Pitzer Coll (CA)
Pomona Coll (CA)
Princeton U (NJ)
Rollins Coll (FL)
Rutgers U–New Brunswick (NJ)
San Francisco State U (CA)
Scripps Coll (CA)
Simon Fraser U (BC, Canada)
Tulane U (LA)
U at Albany, State U of New York (NY)
U of California, San Diego (CA)
U of California, Santa Barbara (CA)
U of Denver (CO)
U of Guelph (ON, Canada)
U of Idaho (ID)
The U of Kansas (KS)
U of Maine (ME)
U of Michigan (MI)
U of Michigan–Flint (MI)
U of North Dakota (ND)
U of Pittsburgh (PA)
U of Puget Sound (WA)
The U of Scranton (PA)
The U of Texas at Dallas (TX)
U of Toronto (ON, Canada)
U of Vermont (VT)
U of Wisconsin–Eau Claire (WI)
U of Wisconsin–Madison (WI)
U of Wisconsin–Parkside (WI)

Vanderbilt U (TN)
Wayland Baptist U (TX)
Wells Coll (NY)
Westminster Coll (PA)
Whitman Coll (WA)
William Jewell Coll (MO)

MOLECULAR GENETICS
Michigan State U (MI)
The Ohio State U (OH)
Rutgers U–New Brunswick (NJ)
Texas A&M U (TX)
U of Guelph (ON, Canada)
U of Vermont (VT)
Washington State U (WA)

MOLECULAR PHARMACOLOGY
The U of Scranton (PA)

MONTESSORI TEACHER EDUCATION
Canisius Coll (NY)

MOVEMENT THERAPY AND MOVEMENT EDUCATION
Eastern Nazarene Coll (MA)
Texas Christian U (TX)
U of Vermont (VT)

MULTICULTURAL EDUCATION
Fort Lewis Coll (CO)
Goddard Coll (VT)
U of St. Thomas (TX)

MULTI/INTERDISCIPLINARY STUDIES RELATED
Abilene Christian U (TX)
Adams State U (CO)
Adelphi U (NY)
Agnes Scott Coll (GA)
Albion Coll (MI)
Albright Coll (PA)
Allegheny Coll (PA)
Alverno Coll (WI)
American U (DC)
Anderson U (IN)
Angelo State U (TX)
Arcadia U (PA)
Arizona State U at the Downtown Phoenix campus (AZ)
Arizona State U at the Polytechnic campus (AZ)
Arizona State U at the Tempe campus (AZ)
Arizona State U at the West campus (AZ)
Arkansas Tech U (AR)
Athens State U (AL)
Austin Coll (TX)
Baldwin Wallace U (OH)
Barton Coll (NC)
Bates Coll (ME)
Baylor U (TX)
Belmont U (TN)
Bennett Coll (NC)
Bennington Coll (VT)
Berea Coll (KY)
Berry Coll (GA)
Bethel U (MN)
Binghamton U, State U of New York (NY)
Bloomfield Coll (NJ)
Bluffton U (OH)
Boise State U (ID)
Boston U (MA)
Bowdoin Coll (ME)
Bowling Green State U (OH)
Brandeis U (MA)
Bryn Athyn Coll of the New Church (PA)
Bryn Mawr Coll (PA)
Bucknell U (PA)
Buena Vista U (IA)
Buffalo State Coll, State U of New York (NY)
Cabarrus Coll of Health Sciences (NC)
Caldwell U (NJ)
California Baptist U (CA)
California Inst of Integral Studies (CA)
California Inst of Technology (CA)
California Lutheran U (CA)
California Polytechnic State U, San Luis Obispo (CA)
California State U, Dominguez Hills (CA)
California State U, Long Beach (CA)
California State U, Monterey Bay (CA)
California State U, San Bernardino (CA)
California State U, San Marcos (CA)
California State U, Stanislaus (CA)
Calvary U (MO)
Cameron U (OK)
Capital U (OH)
Carroll Coll (MT)
Catawba Coll (NC)
Cedarville U (OH)
Central Connecticut State U (CT)
Central Washington U (WA)
Chestnut Hill Coll (PA)
Christopher Newport U (VA)
Claremont McKenna Coll (CA)
Clarkson U (NY)
Cleveland State U (OH)
Colby Coll (ME)
Coll of Charleston (SC)
The Coll of Idaho (ID)
The Coll of New Jersey (NJ)
Coll of Saint Benedict (MN)
Coll of Saint Elizabeth (NJ)
The Coll of William and Mary (VA)
The Coll of Wooster (OH)
The Colorado Coll (CO)
Columbia Coll Chicago (IL)
Concord U (WV)
Cornell Coll (IA)
Cornerstone U (MI)
The Culinary Inst of America (NY)
Curry Coll (MA)
Dalhousie U (NS, Canada)
Dallas Baptist U (TX)
Dallas Christian Coll (TX)
Dartmouth Coll (NH)
Davidson Coll (NC)
Delaware Valley U (PA)
DePauw U (IN)
Dickinson State U (ND)
Dixie State U (UT)
Earlham Coll (IN)
Eastern Illinois U (IL)
Eastern Mennonite U (VA)
Eastern Michigan U (MI)
Eastern Washington U (WA)
East Tennessee State U (TN)
East Texas Baptist U (TX)
Edgewood Coll (WI)
Embry-Riddle Aeronautical U–Daytona (FL)
Embry-Riddle Aeronautical U–Prescott (AZ)
Emmanuel Coll (MA)
Emory U (GA)
Emporia State U (KS)
The Evergreen State Coll (WA)
Florida Inst of Technology (FL)
Florida Intl U (FL)
Florida Southern Coll (FL)
Franklin & Marshall Coll (PA)
Freed-Hardeman U (TN)
Gannon U (PA)
Georgetown Coll (KY)
Georgetown U (DC)
Georgia Inst of Technology (GA)
Georgian Court U (NJ)
Georgia State U (GA)
Goucher Coll (MD)
Granite State Coll (NH)
Greenville Coll (IL)
Guilford Coll (NC)
Hamline U (MN)
Hampshire Coll (MA)
Harris-Stowe State U (MO)
Hawai`i Pacific U (HI)
High Point U (NC)
Hood Coll (MD)
Hope Coll (MI)
Howard Payne U (TX)
Humboldt State U (CA)
Idaho State U (ID)
Illinois Wesleyan U (IL)
Immaculata U (PA)
Indiana State U (IN)
Indiana U–Purdue U Indianapolis (IN)
Iowa State U of Science and Technology (IA)
Ithaca Coll (NY)
Jackson State U (MS)
Jacksonville U (FL)
John Brown U (AR)
Juniata Coll (PA)
Kalamazoo Coll (MI)
Keene State Coll (NH)
Kennesaw State U (GA)
Kentucky Wesleyan Coll (KY)
Kenyon Coll (OH)
Knox Coll (IL)
Lake Erie Coll (OH)
Lamar U (TX)
Lane Coll (TN)
Lasell Coll (MA)
Lebanon Valley Coll (PA)
Lee U (TN)
LeTourneau U (TX)
Lewis U (IL)
Liberty U (VA)
Louisiana State U and A&M Coll (LA)
Lourdes U (OH)
Loyola Marymount U (CA)
Loyola U Chicago (IL)
Loyola U Maryland (MD)
Luther Coll (IA)
Lycoming Coll (PA)
Macalester Coll (MN)
Manchester U (IN)
Manhattan Coll (NY)
Marian U (WI)
Mary Baldwin U (VA)
Marylhurst U (OR)
McDaniel Coll (MD)
McMurry U (TX)
Mercer U, Macon (GA)
Mercyhurst U (PA)
Meredith Coll (NC)
Messiah Coll (PA)
Miami U (OH)
Michigan State U (MI)
Millikin U (IL)
Millsaps Coll (MS)
Minnesota State U Moorhead (MN)
Mississippi State U (MS)
Missouri Baptist U (MO)
Missouri Western State U (MO)
Monmouth U (NJ)
Montana State U Billings (MT)
Montclair State U (NJ)
Morrisville State Coll (NY)
Mount Holyoke Coll (MA)
Mount Mary U (WI)
Mount Mercy U (IA)
Mount St. Mary's U (MD)
National Louis U (IL)
Newman U (KS)
New York Inst of Technology (NY)
North Central Coll (IL)
Northeastern State U (OK)
Northern Illinois U (IL)
Northwest Christian U (OR)
Northwestern Oklahoma State U (OK)
Northwestern State U of Louisiana (LA)
Northwestern U (IL)
Northwest U (WA)
The Ohio State U (OH)
Ohio Wesleyan U (OH)
Old Dominion U (VA)
Otterbein U (OH)
Our Lady of the Lake U of San Antonio (TX)
Pace U (NY)
Pacific Lutheran U (WA)
Palm Beach Atlantic U (FL)
Penn State Erie, The Behrend Coll (PA)
Penn State Harrisburg (PA)
Pepperdine U, Malibu (CA)
Pittsburg State U (KS)
Plymouth State U (NH)
Point Park U (PA)
Prairie View A&M U (TX)
Prescott Coll (AZ)
Princeton U (NJ)
Providence Coll (RI)
Radford U (VA)
Regis Coll (MA)
Regis U (CO)
Rice U (TX)
Robert Morris U (PA)
Robert Morris U Illinois (IL)
Rogers State U (OK)
Roger Williams U (RI)
Rollins Coll (FL)
Rowan U (NJ)
Rutgers U–Camden (NJ)
Rutgers U–Newark (NJ)
Rutgers U–New Brunswick (NJ)
Saginaw Valley State U (MI)
Saint Anselm Coll (NH)
St. Cloud State U (MN)
Saint John's U (MN)
Saint Martin's U (WA)
Saint Mary's Coll of California (CA)
St. Mary's Coll of Maryland (MD)
Salisbury U (MD)
Samford U (AL)
Sam Houston State U (TX)
San Diego State U (CA)
San Francisco State U (CA)
Scripps Coll (CA)
Sewanee: The U of the South (TN)
Shippensburg U of Pennsylvania (PA)
Simmons Coll (MA)
Slippery Rock U of Pennsylvania (PA)
Sonoma State U (CA)
Southeastern Oklahoma State U (OK)
Southeast Missouri State U (MO)
Southern Arkansas U–Magnolia (AR)
Southern Illinois U Carbondale (IL)
Southern Methodist U (TX)
Southern Utah U (UT)
Southwestern Adventist U (TX)
Spelman Coll (GA)
State U of New York Empire State Coll (NY)
Stephen F. Austin State U (TX)
Stephens Coll (MO)
Stevens Inst of Technology (NJ)
Stonehill Coll (MA)
Stony Brook U, State U of New York (NY)
Syracuse U (NY)
Tarleton State U (TX)
Taylor U (IN)
Temple U (PA)
Tennessee Wesleyan U (TN)
Texas A&M U (TX)
Texas A&M U–Central Texas (TX)
Texas A&M U–Commerce (TX)
Texas A&M U–Kingsville (TX)
Texas State U (TX)
Texas Tech U (TX)
Texas Wesleyan U (TX)
Texas Woman's U (TX)
Thomas Edison State U (NJ)
Thomas More Coll (KY)
Towson U (MD)
Trevecca Nazarene U (TN)
Trinity U (TX)
Truett McConnell U (GA)
Truman State U (MO)
Tulane U (LA)
Tusculum Coll (TN)
U at Albany, State U of New York (NY)
U at Buffalo, the State U of New York (NY)
The U of Akron (OH)
The U of Alabama in Huntsville (AL)
U of Alaska Fairbanks (AK)
U of California, Davis (CA)
U of California, Irvine (CA)
U of California, Los Angeles (CA)
U of California, Santa Barbara (CA)
U of Central Arkansas (AR)
U of Cincinnati (OH)
U of Colorado Boulder (CO)
U of Colorado Denver (CO)
U of Denver (CO)
U of Florida (FL)
U of Houston (TX)
U of Houston–Clear Lake (TX)
U of Houston–Downtown (TX)
U of Idaho (ID)
U of Kentucky (KY)
U of King's Coll (NS, Canada)
U of Lethbridge (AB, Canada)
U of Maine (ME)
U of Maine at Farmington (ME)
U of Maryland, Baltimore County (MD)
U of Maryland, Coll Park (MD)
U of Maryland U Coll (MD)
U of Mary Washington (VA)
U of Massachusetts Amherst (MA)
U of Massachusetts Boston (MA)
U of Massachusetts Dartmouth (MA)
U of Michigan (MI)
U of Michigan–Dearborn (MI)
U of Michigan–Flint (MI)
U of Minnesota, Crookston (MN)
U of Minnesota, Duluth (MN)
U of Minnesota, Morris (MN)
U of Minnesota, Twin Cities Campus (MN)
U of Missouri–St. Louis (MO)
U of Montevallo (AL)
U of Nevada, Las Vegas (NV)
U of New Hampshire (NH)
U of New Orleans (LA)
The U of North Carolina at Pembroke (NC)
U of North Dakota (ND)
U of Northern Colorado (CO)
U of North Texas (TX)
U of Pikeville (KY)
U of Pittsburgh (PA)
U of Richmond (VA)
U of Rochester (NY)
U of St. Francis (IL)
U of Saint Joseph (CT)
U of Saint Mary (KS)
The U of South Dakota (SD)
U of Southern California (CA)
U of Southern Mississippi (MS)
The U of Tennessee (TN)
The U of Texas at Austin (TX)
The U of Texas at San Antonio (TX)
The U of Texas of the Permian Basin (TX)
The U of Texas Rio Grande Valley (TX)
U of Virginia (VA)
U of Washington, Bothell (WA)
U of Washington, Tacoma (WA)
U of Waterloo (ON, Canada)
The U of West Alabama (AL)
U of Wisconsin–Green Bay (WI)
U of Wisconsin–Milwaukee (WI)
U of Wisconsin–Platteville (WI)
U of Wisconsin–Stevens Point (WI)
U of Wisconsin–Superior (WI)
U of Wisconsin–Whitewater (WI)
Ursinus Coll (PA)
Utah State U (UT)
Utah Valley U (UT)
Valparaiso U (IN)
Vanderbilt U (TN)
Vassar Coll (NY)
Villanova U (PA)
Virginia Commonwealth U (VA)
Virginia Union U (VA)
Virginia Wesleyan Coll (VA)
Viterbo U (WI)
Washburn U (KS)
Washington & Jefferson Coll (PA)
Washington and Lee U (VA)
Washington Coll (MD)
Washington State U (WA)
Washington U in St. Louis (MO)
Waynesburg U (PA)
Western Kentucky U (KY)
Western Michigan U (MI)
Western Washington U (WA)
Westminster Coll (PA)
West Texas A&M U (TX)
West Virginia U (WV)
West Virginia U Inst of Technology (WV)
Wheaton Coll (IL)
Wheaton Coll (MA)
Wheeling Jesuit U (WV)
Wichita State U (KS)
Wilkes U (PA)
William Jewell Coll (MO)
Winona State U (MN)
Woodbury U (CA)
Wright State U (OH)
Wright State U–Lake Campus (OH)

MUSEUM STUDIES
Beloit Coll (WI)
Central Washington U (WA)
Coll of the Atlantic (ME)
Concordia Coll (MN)
Inst of American Indian Arts (NM)
Juniata Coll (PA)
Middlebury Coll (VT)
Randolph Coll (VA)
Tusculum Coll (TN)
U of Saint Francis (IN)
Walsh U (OH)

MUSIC

Abilene Christian U (TX)
Adams State U (CO)
Adelphi U (NY)
Agnes Scott Coll (GA)
Alabama State U (AL)
Albany State U (GA)
Albion Coll (MI)
Albright Coll (PA)
Alcorn State U (MS)
Allegheny Coll (PA)
Alma Coll (MI)
Alverno Coll (WI)
Ambrose U (AB, Canada)
American U (DC)
Amherst Coll (MA)
Anderson U (SC)
Andrews U (MI)
Angelo State U (TX)
Aquinas Coll (MI)
Arizona State U at the Tempe campus (AZ)
Arkansas Tech U (AR)
Arlington Baptist Coll (TX)
Armstrong State U (GA)
Asbury U (KY)
Ashland U (OH)
Assumption Coll (MA)
Auburn U (AL)
Augsburg Coll (MN)
Augustana Coll (IL)
Augustana U (SD)
Augusta U (GA)
Aurora U (IL)
Austin Coll (TX)
Austin Peay State U (TN)
Averett U (VA)
Avila U (MO)
Azusa Pacific U (CA)
Baker U (KS)
Baldwin Wallace U (OH)
Ball State U (IN)
Baptist U of the Americas (TX)
Bard Coll (NY)
Barnard Coll (NY)
Baruch Coll of the City U of New York (NY)
Bates Coll (ME)
Baylor U (TX)
Belhaven U (MS)
Bellarmine U (KY)
Belmont U (TN)
Bemidji State U (MN)
Benedictine Coll (KS)
Bennett Coll (NC)
Bennington Coll (VT)
Berea Coll (KY)
Berry Coll (GA)
Bethany Lutheran Coll (MN)
Bethel Coll (IN)
Bethel U (MN)
Binghamton U, State U of New York (NY)
Biola U (CA)
Bishop's U (QC, Canada)
Blackburn Coll (IL)
Black Hills State U (SD)
Bloomsburg U of Pennsylvania (PA)
Bluefield Coll (VA)
Blue Mountain Coll (MS)
Bluffton U (OH)
Boise State U (ID)
Boston Coll (MA)
Boston U (MA)
Bowdoin Coll (ME)
Bowling Green State U (OH)
Bradley U (IL)
Brandeis U (MA)
Brenau U (GA)
Briar Cliff U (IA)
Bridgewater State U (MA)
Brigham Young U–Idaho (ID)
Brooklyn Coll of the City U of New York (NY)
Bryan Coll (TN)
Bryn Mawr Coll (PA)
Bucknell U (PA)
Buffalo State Coll, State U of New York (NY)
Butler U (IN)
Cairn U (PA)
Caldwell U (NJ)
California Baptist U (CA)
California Lutheran U (CA)
California Polytechnic State U, San Luis Obispo (CA)
California State Polytechnic U, Pomona (CA)
California State U, Bakersfield (CA)
California State U, Chico (CA)
California State U, Dominguez Hills (CA)
California State U, East Bay (CA)
California State U, Fresno (CA)
California State U, Fullerton (CA)
California State U, Long Beach (CA)
California State U, Monterey Bay (CA)
California State U, Northridge (CA)
California State U, Sacramento (CA)
California State U, San Bernardino (CA)
California State U, San Marcos (CA)
California State U, Stanislaus (CA)
Calvin Coll (MI)
Cameron U (OK)
Campbellsville U (KY)
Capital U (OH)
Carleton Coll (MN)
Carnegie Mellon U (PA)
Carson-Newman U (TN)
Carthage Coll (WI)
Case Western Reserve U (OH)
Catawba Coll (NC)
The Catholic U of America (DC)
Cedarville U (OH)
Centenary Coll of Louisiana (LA)
Central Baptist Coll (AR)
Central Connecticut State U (CT)
Central Methodist U (MO)
Central Michigan U (MI)
Central Washington U (WA)
Centre Coll (KY)
Chapman U (CA)
Charleston Southern U (SC)
Chatham U (PA)
Chestnut Hill Coll (PA)
Chowan U (NC)
City Coll of the City U of New York (NY)
Clark Atlanta U (GA)
Clark U (MA)
Cleveland State U (OH)
Coastal Carolina U (SC)
Coe Coll (IA)
Colby Coll (ME)
Colgate U (NY)
Coll of Charleston (SC)
The Coll of Idaho (ID)
The Coll of New Jersey (NJ)
Coll of Saint Benedict (MN)
The Coll of Saint Rose (NY)
Coll of Staten Island of the City U of New York (NY)
Coll of the Atlantic (ME)
Coll of the Holy Cross (MA)
Coll of the Ozarks (MO)
The Coll of William and Mary (VA)
The Coll of Wooster (OH)
Colorado Christian U (CO)
The Colorado Coll (CO)
Colorado Mesa U (CO)
Colorado State U (CO)
Columbia Coll Chicago (IL)
Columbia U (NY)
Columbia U, School of General Studies (NY)
Columbus State U (GA)
Concordia Coll (MN)
Concordia Coll–New York (NY)
Concordia U (QC, Canada)
Concordia U Chicago (IL)
Concordia U, Nebraska (NE)
Concordia U, St. Paul (MN)
Concordia U Wisconsin (WI)
Connecticut Coll (CT)
Converse Coll (SC)
Corban U (OR)
Cornell Coll (IA)
Cornell U (NY)
Cornerstone U (MI)
Creighton U (NE)
Culver-Stockton Coll (MO)
Dalhousie U (NS, Canada)
Dallas Baptist U (TX)
Dartmouth Coll (NH)
Davidson Coll (NC)
Denison U (OH)
DePauw U (IN)
DEREE - The American Coll of Greece (Greece)
Dickinson Coll (PA)
Dickinson State U (ND)
Dixie State U (UT)
Doane U (NE)
Dominican U (IL)
Dominican U of California (CA)
Drake U (IA)
Drew U (NJ)
Drury U (MO)
Duquesne U (PA)
Earlham Coll (IN)
East Carolina U (NC)
East Central U (OK)
Eastern Illinois U (IL)
Eastern Mennonite U (VA)
Eastern Michigan U (MI)
Eastern Nazarene Coll (MA)
Eastern Oregon U (OR)
Eastern U (PA)
Eastern Washington U (WA)
East Tennessee State U (TN)
East Texas Baptist U (TX)
Eckerd Coll (FL)
Edgewood Coll (WI)
Elizabeth City State U (NC)
Elizabethtown Coll (PA)
Elmira Coll (NY)
Elms Coll (MA)
Elon U (NC)
Emmanuel Coll (GA)
Emory U (GA)
Emporia State U (KS)
Eureka Coll (IL)
Evangel U (MO)
Fairfield U (CT)
Faulkner U (AL)
Fayetteville State U (NC)
Felician U (NJ)
Florida Ag and Mech U (FL)
Florida Atlantic U (FL)
Florida Coll (FL)
Florida Intl U (FL)
Florida Southern Coll (FL)
Florida State U (FL)
Fordham U (NY)
Fort Lewis Coll (CO)
Francis Marion U (SC)
Franklin & Marshall Coll (PA)
Franklin Pierce U (NH)
Freed-Hardeman U (TN)
Fresno Pacific U (CA)
Friends U (KS)
Frostburg State U (MD)
Furman U (SC)
Gardner-Webb U (NC)
Geneva Coll (PA)
George Fox U (OR)
The George Washington U (DC)
Georgia Coll & State U (GA)
Georgia Southern U (GA)
Georgia Southwestern State U (GA)
Gettysburg Coll (PA)
Gonzaga U (WA)
Gordon Coll (MA)
Goshen Coll (IN)
Goucher Coll (MD)
Graceland U (IA)
Grambling State U (LA)
Grand Valley State U (MI)
Grand View U (IA)
Greenville Coll (IL)
Grinnell Coll (IA)
Grove City Coll (PA)
Guilford Coll (NC)
Hamilton Coll (NY)
Hamline U (MN)
Hampshire Coll (MA)
Hampton U (VA)
Hannibal-LaGrange U (MO)
Hanover Coll (IN)
Harding U (AR)
Hardin-Simmons U (TX)
Hartwick Coll (NY)
Harvard U (MA)
Haverford Coll (PA)
Heidelberg U (OH)
Henderson State U (AR)
Hendrix Coll (AR)
High Point U (NC)
Hillsdale Coll (MI)
Hiram Coll (OH)
Hobart and William Smith Colls (NY)
Hofstra U (NY)
Hollins U (VA)
Holy Names U (CA)
Hood Coll (MD)
Hope Coll (MI)
Houghton Coll (NY)
Houston Baptist U (TX)
Humboldt State U (CA)
Hunter Coll of the City U of New York (NY)
Huntington U (IN)
Huston-Tillotson U (TX)
Idaho State U (ID)
Illinois Coll (IL)
Illinois State U (IL)
Illinois Wesleyan U (IL)
Immaculata U (PA)
Indiana State U (IN)
Indiana U of Pennsylvania (PA)
Indiana U South Bend (IN)
Indiana U Southeast (IN)
Inter American U of Puerto Rico, San Germán Campus (PR)
Iowa State U of Science and Technology (IA)
Iowa Wesleyan U (IA)
Ithaca Coll (NY)
Jacksonville State U (AL)
Jacksonville U (FL)
John Brown U (AR)
Johns Hopkins U (MD)
Johnson C. Smith U (NC)
The Juilliard School (NY)
Kalamazoo Coll (MI)
Kansas State U (KS)
Kansas Wesleyan U (KS)
Kean U (NJ)
Keene State Coll (NH)
Kennesaw State U (GA)
Kent State U (OH)
Kentucky State U (KY)
Kenyon Coll (OH)
The King's U (AB, Canada)
King U (TN)
Knox Coll (IL)
Kutztown U of Pennsylvania (PA)
Lafayette Coll (PA)
LaGrange Coll (GA)
Lake Forest Coll (IL)
Lamar U (TX)
Lane Coll (TN)
Langston U (OK)
Lawrence U (WI)
Lee U (TN)
Lehigh U (PA)
Lehman Coll of the City U of New York (NY)
Lenoir-Rhyne U (NC)
Lewis & Clark Coll (OR)
Lewis U (IL)
Liberty U (VA)
Limestone Coll (SC)
Lincoln U (PA)
Lindenwood U (MO)
Linfield Coll (OR)
Lipscomb U (TN)
Lock Haven U of Pennsylvania (PA)
Loras Coll (IA)
Louisiana Coll (LA)
Louisiana State U and A&M Coll (LA)
Louisiana Tech U (LA)
Loyola Marymount U (CA)
Loyola U Chicago (IL)
Loyola U New Orleans (LA)
Lubbock Christian U (TX)
Luther Coll (IA)
Lycoming Coll (PA)
Lynchburg Coll (VA)
Lyon Coll (AR)
Macalester Coll (MN)
Madonna U (MI)
Malone U (OH)
Manchester U (IN)
Manhattanville Coll (NY)
Mansfield U of Pennsylvania (PA)
Marian U (IN)
Marian U (WI)
Marietta Coll (OH)
Marylhurst U (OR)
Massachusetts Coll of Liberal Arts (MA)
Massachusetts Inst of Technology (MA)
The Master's U (CA)
McDaniel Coll (MD)
McKendree U (IL)
McMaster U (ON, Canada)
McMurry U (TX)
Mercer U, Macon (GA)
Mercyhurst U (PA)
Meredith Coll (NC)
Messenger Coll (TX)
Messiah Coll (PA)
Metropolitan State U of Denver (CO)
Miami U (OH)
Michigan State U (MI)
MidAmerica Nazarene U (KS)
Middlebury Coll (VT)
Millersville U of Pennsylvania (PA)
Milligan Coll (TN)
Millikin U (IL)
Millsaps Coll (MS)
Mills Coll (CA)
Minnesota State U Mankato (MN)
Minnesota State U Moorhead (MN)
Minot State U (ND)
Mississippi State U (MS)
Mississippi Valley State U (MS)
Missouri Baptist U (MO)
Missouri State U (MO)
Missouri Valley Coll (MO)
Missouri Western State U (MO)
Molloy Coll (NY)
Monmouth Coll (IL)
Monmouth U (NJ)
Montana State U (MT)
Montana State U Billings (MT)
Montclair State U (NJ)
Moravian Coll (PA)
Morehead State U (KY)
Morehouse Coll (GA)
Morningside Coll (IA)
Mount Allison U (NB, Canada)
Mount Holyoke Coll (MA)
Mount Marty Coll (SD)
Mount Mercy U (IA)
Mount St. Joseph U (OH)
Mount Saint Mary's U (CA)
Mount Vernon Nazarene U (OH)
Muhlenberg Coll (PA)
Murray State U (KY)
Muskingum U (OH)
Nazareth Coll of Rochester (NY)
Nebraska Wesleyan U (NE)
Newberry Coll (SC)
New Coll of Florida (FL)
New Jersey City U (NJ)
New Mexico Highlands U (NM)
North Carolina Central U (NC)
North Central Coll (IL)
North Dakota State U (ND)
Northeastern Illinois U (IL)
Northeastern State U (OK)
Northeastern U (MA)
Northern Arizona U (AZ)
Northern Illinois U (IL)
Northern Kentucky U (KY)
Northern State U (SD)
North Greenville U (SC)
Northwestern Coll (IA)
Northwestern Oklahoma State U (OK)
Northwestern U (IL)
Northwest Missouri State U (MO)
Northwest U (WA)
Nova Southeastern U (FL)
Nyack Coll (NY)
Oakland City U (IN)
Oberlin Coll (OH)
Occidental Coll (CA)
The Ohio State U (OH)
Ohio Wesleyan U (OH)
Oklahoma Baptist U (OK)
Oklahoma Christian U (OK)
Oklahoma City U (OK)
Oklahoma State U (OK)
Olivet Nazarene U (IL)
Oral Roberts U (OK)
Oregon State U (OR)
Otterbein U (OH)
Ouachita Baptist U (AR)
Our Lady of the Lake U of San Antonio (TX)
Pacific Lutheran U (WA)
Palm Beach Atlantic U (FL)
Penn State Altoona (PA)
Penn State Beaver (PA)
Penn State Berks (PA)
Penn State Brandywine (PA)
Penn State DuBois (PA)
Penn State Greater Allegheny (PA)
Penn State Hazleton (PA)
Penn State Mont Alto (PA)

Penn State New Kensington (PA)
Penn State Shenango (PA)
Penn State U Park (PA)
Penn State Wilkes-Barre (PA)
Penn State Worthington Scranton (PA)
Penn State York (PA)
Pepperdine U, Malibu (CA)
Piedmont Coll (GA)
Pitzer Coll (CA)
Plymouth State U (NH)
Point Loma Nazarene U (CA)
Point U (GA)
Pomona Coll (CA)
Portland State U (OR)
Prairie View A&M U (TX)
Princeton U (NJ)
Principia Coll (IL)
Providence Coll (RI)
Radford U (VA)
Ramapo Coll of New Jersey (NJ)
Randolph-Macon Coll (VA)
Redeemer U Coll (ON, Canada)
Reed Coll (OR)
Regis U (CO)
Rhode Island Coll (RI)
Rhodes Coll (TN)
Rice U (TX)
Ripon Coll (WI)
Roanoke Coll (VA)
Roberts Wesleyan Coll (NY)
Rockford U (IL)
Rocky Mountain Coll (MT)
Rollins Coll (FL)
Rowan U (NJ)
Rutgers U–Camden (NJ)
Rutgers U–Newark (NJ)
Rutgers U–New Brunswick (NJ)
Saginaw Valley State U (MI)
St. Ambrose U (IA)
Saint Augustine's U (NC)
St. Catherine U (MN)
St. Cloud State U (MN)
Saint John's U (MN)
Saint Joseph's U (PA)
Saint Louis U (MO)
Saint Louis U–Madrid Campus (Spain)
Saint Martin's U (WA)
Saint Mary-of-the-Woods Coll (IN)
Saint Mary's Coll (IN)
Saint Mary's Coll of California (CA)
St. Mary's Coll of Maryland (MD)
Saint Mary's U of Minnesota (MN)
Saint Michael's Coll (VT)
St. Norbert Coll (WI)
St. Olaf Coll (MN)
Saint Vincent Coll (PA)
Salisbury U (MD)
Salve Regina U (RI)
Samford U (AL)
Sam Houston State U (TX)
San Diego State U (CA)
San Francisco State U (CA)
Santa Clara U (CA)
Sarah Lawrence Coll (NY)
Schreiner U (TX)
Scripps Coll (CA)
Seattle Pacific U (WA)
Seattle U (WA)
Seton Hill U (PA)
Sewanee: The U of the South (TN)
Shaw U (NC)
Shepherd U (WV)
Shorter U (GA)
Silver Lake Coll of the Holy Family (WI)
Simmons Coll (MA)
Simon Fraser U (BC, Canada)
Simpson Coll (IA)
Simpson U (CA)
Slippery Rock U of Pennsylvania (PA)
Smith Coll (MA)
Sonoma State U (CA)
South Dakota State U (SD)
Southeastern Oklahoma State U (OK)
Southeastern U (FL)
Southeast Missouri State U (MO)
Southern Arkansas U–Magnolia (AR)
Southern Connecticut State U (CT)
Southern Illinois U Carbondale (IL)
Southern Illinois U Edwardsville (IL)
Southern Methodist U (TX)
Southern Oregon U (OR)
Southern Utah U (UT)
Southwest Baptist U (MO)
Southwestern Adventist U (TX)
Southwestern Coll (KS)
Southwestern U (TX)
Spelman Coll (GA)
Stanford U (CA)
State U of New York at Fredonia (NY)
State U of New York at New Paltz (NY)
State U of New York at Oswego (NY)
State U of New York at Plattsburgh (NY)
State U of New York Coll at Geneseo (NY)
State U of New York Coll at Potsdam (NY)
Stephen F. Austin State U (TX)
Sterling Coll (KS)
Stony Brook U, State U of New York (NY)
Susquehanna U (PA)
Swarthmore Coll (PA)
Sweet Briar Coll (VA)
Syracuse U (NY)
Talladega Coll (AL)
Tarleton State U (TX)
Taylor U (IN)
Temple U (PA)
Tennessee State U (TN)
Tennessee Wesleyan U (TN)
Texas A&M Intl U (TX)
Texas A&M U (TX)
Texas A&M U–Commerce (TX)
Texas A&M U–Corpus Christi (TX)
Texas A&M U–Kingsville (TX)
Texas Christian U (TX)
Texas Coll (TX)
Texas Lutheran U (TX)
Texas State U (TX)
Texas Tech U (TX)
Texas Wesleyan U (TX)
Texas Woman's U (TX)
Tiffin U (OH)
Toccoa Falls Coll (GA)
Towson U (MD)
Trinity Baptist Coll (FL)
Trinity Christian Coll (IL)
Trinity U (TX)
Troy U (AL)
Truett McConnell U (GA)
Truman State U (MO)
Tufts U (MA)
Tulane U (LA)
Union Coll (NE)
Union U (TN)
Université de Montréal (QC, Canada)
U at Albany, State U of New York (NY)
U at Buffalo, the State U of New York (NY)
The U of Akron (OH)
The U of Alabama (AL)
The U of Alabama at Birmingham (AL)
The U of Alabama in Huntsville (AL)
U of Alaska Fairbanks (AK)
The U of Arizona (AZ)
U of Bridgeport (CT)
U of California, Davis (CA)
U of California, Irvine (CA)
U of California, Los Angeles (CA)
U of California, Riverside (CA)
U of California, San Diego (CA)
U of California, Santa Barbara (CA)
U of Central Arkansas (AR)
U of Central Missouri (MO)
U of Chicago (IL)
U of Cincinnati (OH)
U of Colorado Boulder (CO)
U of Colorado Denver (CO)
U of Dayton (OH)
U of Delaware (DE)
U of Denver (CO)
U of Evansville (IN)
U of Florida (FL)
U of Georgia (GA)
U of Guelph (ON, Canada)
U of Hartford (CT)
U of Hawaii at Manoa (HI)
U of Houston (TX)
U of Illinois at Chicago (IL)
U of Indianapolis (IN)
U of Jamestown (ND)
The U of Kansas (KS)
U of King's Coll (NS, Canada)
U of La Verne (CA)
U of Lethbridge (AB, Canada)
U of Louisville (KY)
U of Maine (ME)
U of Maine at Farmington (ME)
U of Mary Hardin-Baylor (TX)
U of Maryland, Baltimore County (MD)
U of Maryland, Coll Park (MD)
U of Mary Washington (VA)
U of Massachusetts Amherst (MA)
U of Massachusetts Boston (MA)
U of Massachusetts Dartmouth (MA)
U of Massachusetts Lowell (MA)
U of Miami (FL)
U of Michigan (MI)
U of Michigan–Flint (MI)
U of Minnesota, Duluth (MN)
U of Minnesota, Morris (MN)
U of Minnesota, Twin Cities Campus (MN)
U of Missouri–Kansas City (MO)
U of Missouri–St. Louis (MO)
U of Mobile (AL)
U of Montevallo (AL)
U of Mount Union (OH)
U of Nebraska at Kearney (NE)
U of Nevada, Las Vegas (NV)
U of Nevada, Reno (NV)
U of New Hampshire (NH)
U of New Haven (CT)
U of New Orleans (LA)
U of North Alabama (AL)
U of North Carolina at Asheville (NC)
The U of North Carolina at Chapel Hill (NC)
The U of North Carolina at Charlotte (NC)
The U of North Carolina at Greensboro (NC)
The U of North Carolina at Pembroke (NC)
The U of North Carolina Wilmington (NC)
U of North Dakota (ND)
U of Northern Colorado (CO)
U of Northern Iowa (IA)
U of North Texas (TX)
U of Notre Dame (IN)
U of Oklahoma (OK)
U of Oregon (OR)
U of Pennsylvania (PA)
U of Pittsburgh (PA)
U of Puget Sound (WA)
U of Regina (SK, Canada)
U of Rhode Island (RI)
U of Richmond (VA)
U of Rochester (NY)
U of St. Francis (IL)
U of St. Thomas (MN)
U of St. Thomas (TX)
U of San Diego (CA)
U of Saskatchewan (SK, Canada)
U of Science and Arts of Oklahoma (OK)
U of South Alabama (AL)
U of South Carolina (SC)
The U of South Dakota (SD)
U of Southern California (CA)
U of Southern Maine (ME)
U of Southern Mississippi (MS)
The U of Tampa (FL)
The U of Tennessee (TN)
The U of Tennessee at Chattanooga (TN)
The U of Tennessee at Martin (TN)
The U of Texas at Austin (TX)
The U of Texas at El Paso (TX)
The U of Texas at San Antonio (TX)
The U of Texas of the Permian Basin (TX)
U of the Cumberlands (KY)
U of the Incarnate Word (TX)
U of the Pacific (CA)
The U of Toledo (OH)
The U of Tulsa (OK)
U of Utah (UT)
U of Vermont (VT)
U of Virginia (VA)
U of Washington (WA)
U of Waterloo (ON, Canada)
U of Windsor (ON, Canada)
U of Wisconsin–Eau Claire (WI)
U of Wisconsin–Green Bay (WI)
U of Wisconsin–La Crosse (WI)
U of Wisconsin–Madison (WI)
U of Wisconsin–Milwaukee (WI)
U of Wisconsin–Parkside (WI)
U of Wisconsin–Platteville (WI)
U of Wisconsin–Stevens Point (WI)
U of Wisconsin–Superior (WI)
U of Wisconsin–Whitewater (WI)
Utah State U (UT)
Utah Valley U (UT)
Valdosta State U (GA)
Valley City State U (ND)
Valparaiso U (IN)
Vanderbilt U (TN)
Vassar Coll (NY)
Villa Maria Coll (NY)
Virginia Polytechnic Inst and State U (VA)
Virginia State U (VA)
Virginia Union U (VA)
Virginia Wesleyan Coll (VA)
Viterbo U (WI)
Wabash Coll (IN)
Wagner Coll (NY)
Wake Forest U (NC)
Waldorf U (IA)
Walla Walla U (WA)
Walsh U (OH)
Wartburg Coll (IA)
Washburn U (KS)
Washington & Jefferson Coll (PA)
Washington and Lee U (VA)
Washington Coll (MD)
Washington State U (WA)
Washington U in St. Louis (MO)
Wayland Baptist U (TX)
Wayne State Coll (NE)
Wayne State U (MI)
Weber State U (UT)
Webster U (MO)
Welch Coll (TN)
Wesleyan Coll (GA)
West Chester U of Pennsylvania (PA)
Western Carolina U (NC)
Western Connecticut State U (CT)
Western Michigan U (MI)
Western Oregon U (OR)
Western State Colorado U (CO)
Western Washington U (WA)
Westfield State U (MA)
Westminster Coll (PA)
Westminster Coll (UT)
Westmont Coll (CA)
West Texas A&M U (TX)
West Virginia U (WV)
West Virginia Wesleyan Coll (WV)
Wheaton Coll (IL)
Wheaton Coll (MA)
Whitman Coll (WA)
Whittier Coll (CA)
Whitworth U (WA)
Wichita State U (KS)
Willamette U (OR)
William Jewell Coll (MO)
William Paterson U of New Jersey (NJ)
Williams Baptist Coll (AR)
Williams Coll (MA)
Wingate U (NC)
Winona State U (MN)
Winthrop U (SC)
Wittenberg U (OH)
Wright State U (OH)
Wright State U–Lake Campus (OH)
Xavier U of Louisiana (LA)
York Coll of Pennsylvania (PA)
York Coll of the City U of New York (NY)
Youngstown State U (OH)

MUSICAL THEATER
American U (DC)
Anderson U (SC)
Aurora U (IL)
Blackburn Coll (IL)
Brenau U (GA)
Central Michigan U (MI)
Central Washington U (WA)
Clarke U (IA)
Columbia Coll Chicago (IL)
Converse Coll (SC)
Creighton U (NE)
Culver-Stockton Coll (MO)
Elon U (NC)
Emory & Henry Coll (VA)
Faulkner U (AL)
Florida Southern Coll (FL)
Indiana U Bloomington (IN)
Kansas Wesleyan U (KS)
LaGrange Coll (GA)
Lees-McRae Coll (NC)
Limestone Coll (SC)
Lindenwood U (MO)
Loyola U New Orleans (LA)
Marywood U (PA)
Messiah Coll (PA)
Millikin U (IL)
Missouri Baptist U (MO)
Nebraska Wesleyan U (NE)
The New School for Public Engagement (NY)
North Central Coll (IL)
Pace U (NY)
Rhode Island Coll (RI)
Shenandoah U (VA)
Southwestern Coll (KS)
Sweet Briar Coll (VA)
Syracuse U (NY)
Taylor U (IN)
Texas Christian U (TX)
Texas State U (TX)
U at Buffalo, the State U of New York (NY)
The U of Arizona (AZ)
U of California, Irvine (CA)
U of Michigan (MI)
U of Mobile (AL)
U of North Dakota (ND)
U of Oklahoma (OK)
The U of Tampa (FL)
The U of the Arts (PA)
Viterbo U (WI)
Wayland Baptist U (TX)
Weber State U (UT)
Western Michigan U (MI)
West Texas A&M U (TX)
William Peace U (NC)

MUSIC HISTORY, LITERATURE, AND THEORY
American U (DC)
Baldwin Wallace U (OH)
Baylor U (TX)
Bennington Coll (VT)
Bowling Green State U (OH)
Bridgewater Coll (VA)
Brigham Young U (UT)
Bucknell U (PA)
Cairn U (PA)
California State U, Long Beach (CA)
Calvin Coll (MI)
The Catholic U of America (DC)
The Coll of Wooster (OH)
Concordia Coll–New York (NY)
Converse Coll (SC)
Dalhousie U (NS, Canada)
Eastern Nazarene Coll (MA)
Eugene Lang Coll of Liberal Arts (NY)
Hofstra U (NY)
Jacksonville U (FL)
Lehigh U (PA)
Liberty U (VA)
McMaster U (ON, Canada)
Mount Allison U (NB, Canada)
Nazareth Coll of Rochester (NY)
New Coll of Florida (FL)
Northwestern U (IL)
Oberlin Coll (OH)
The Ohio State U (OH)
Ohio U (OH)
Ouachita Baptist U (AR)
Randolph Coll (VA)
Rice U (TX)
St. Bonaventure U (NY)
St. Cloud State U (MN)
Sarah Lawrence Coll (NY)
Skidmore Coll (NY)
State U of New York at Fredonia (NY)
Syracuse U (NY)
Temple U (PA)
Tufts U (MA)
The U of Akron (OH)
U of California, Los Angeles (CA)
U of California, San Diego (CA)
U of Cincinnati (OH)
U of Delaware (DE)
U of Hartford (CT)

U of Idaho (ID)
U of Kentucky (KY)
U of Michigan (MI)
The U of North Carolina at Greensboro (NC)
U of Regina (SK, Canada)
U of the Pacific (CA)
U of Toronto (ON, Canada)
U of Vermont (VT)
U of Washington (WA)
U of Windsor (ON, Canada)
Ursinus Coll (PA)
Washington U in St. Louis (MO)
Western Washington U (WA)
Wheaton Coll (IL)
Whitman Coll (WA)
Wright State U (OH)
Wright State U–Lake Campus (OH)
Youngstown State U (OH)

MUSIC MANAGEMENT
Anderson U (IN)
Anderson U (SC)
Appalachian State U (NC)
Augsburg Coll (MN)
Belmont U (TN)
Berry Coll (GA)
Boise State U (ID)
Bradley U (IL)
Capital U (OH)
Chowan U (NC)
Columbia Coll Chicago (IL)
Concordia U, St. Paul (MN)
Dallas Baptist U (TX)
DePauw U (IN)
Drake U (IA)
Drexel U (PA)
Eastern Nazarene Coll (MA)
Edgewood Coll (WI)
Elizabeth City State U (NC)
Ferris State U (MI)
Florida Atlantic U (FL)
Florida Southern Coll (FL)
Francis Marion U (SC)
Gardner-Webb U (NC)
Geneva Coll (PA)
Greenville Coll (IL)
Grove City Coll (PA)
Hardin-Simmons U (TX)
Heidelberg U (OH)
Hofstra U (NY)
Huntington U (IN)
Jacksonville U (FL)
Judson U (IL)
Kentucky Wesleyan Coll (KY)
Lamar U (TX)
Lebanon Valley Coll (PA)
Lee U (TN)
Lewis U (IL)
Liberty U (VA)
Lindenwood U (MO)
Loyola U New Orleans (LA)
Lubbock Christian U (TX)
Madonna U (MI)
Mansfield U of Pennsylvania (PA)
The Master's U (CA)
Messiah Coll (PA)
Milligan Coll (TN)
Minnesota State U Mankato (MN)
Minnesota State U Moorhead (MN)
Missouri Baptist U (MO)
Murray State U (KY)
Nazareth Coll of Rochester (NY)
Northwest Christian U (OR)
Northwest U (WA)
Oklahoma City U (OK)
Simmons Coll (MA)
South Carolina State U (SC)
Southeastern U (FL)
Southern Oregon U (OR)
State U of New York at Fredonia (NY)
State U of New York Coll at Potsdam (NY)
Syracuse U (NY)
Trevecca Nazarene U (TN)
Union U (TN)
U of Evansville (IN)
U of Hartford (CT)
U of Idaho (ID)
U of New Haven (CT)
U of Puget Sound (WA)
U of Southern California (CA)
U of Southern Mississippi (MS)
The U of the Arts (PA)
U of the Incarnate Word (TX)
U of the Pacific (CA)
Villa Maria Coll (NY)
Western State Colorado U (CO)
Winona State U (MN)

MUSICOLOGY AND ETHNOMUSICOLOGY
Bennington Coll (VT)
Boston U (MA)
Bowling Green State U (OH)
Converse Coll (SC)
East Tennessee State U (TN)
Liberty U (VA)
Northwestern U (IL)
Roger Williams U (RI)
Tufts U (MA)
Université de Montréal (QC, Canada)
U of California, Los Angeles (CA)
U of Denver (CO)
The U of Kansas (KS)

MUSIC PEDAGOGY
Anderson U (SC)
Baylor U (TX)
Brigham Young U (UT)
Calvary U (MO)
Cedarville U (OH)
Eastern Nazarene Coll (MA)
Holy Names U (CA)
Huntington U (IN)
Lawrence U (WI)
Liberty U (VA)
Maranatha Baptist U (WI)
Michigan State U (MI)
MidAmerica Nazarene U (KS)
St. Cloud State U (MN)
Samford U (AL)
Temple U (PA)
Union Coll (NE)
U of Maryland, Baltimore County (MD)
U of Oklahoma (OK)
The U of Tennessee at Martin (TN)
Viterbo U (WI)
Weber State U (UT)
Wheaton Coll (IL)
Willamette U (OR)

MUSIC PERFORMANCE
Adams State U (CO)
Albion Coll (MI)
Alcorn State U (MS)
Allegheny Coll (PA)
Anderson U (IN)
Appalachian State U (NC)
Aquinas Coll (MI)
Arizona State U at the Tempe campus (AZ)
Augsburg Coll (MN)
Augustana Coll (IL)
Augusta U (GA)
Avila U (MO)
Baldwin Wallace U (OH)
Baylor U (TX)
Belmont U (TN)
Bennington Coll (VT)
Berry Coll (GA)
Bethel Coll (IN)
Bethel U (MN)
Bethune-Cookman U (FL)
Binghamton U, State U of New York (NY)
Biola U (CA)
Black Hills State U (SD)
Boise State U (ID)
Boston U (MA)
Bowling Green State U (OH)
Bradley U (IL)
Brenau U (GA)
Brooklyn Coll of the City U of New York (NY)
Bucknell U (PA)
Buena Vista U (IA)
Butler U (IN)
California Baptist U (CA)
California State U, Fullerton (CA)
California State U, Long Beach (CA)
California State U, Stanislaus (CA)
Calvary U (MO)
Calvin Coll (MI)
Canisius Coll (NY)
Capital U (OH)
Cardinal Stritch U (WI)
Carnegie Mellon U (PA)
Carson-Newman U (TN)
Catawba Coll (NC)
The Catholic U of America (DC)
Cedarville U (OH)
Central Methodist U (MO)
Central State U (OH)
Central Washington U (WA)
Chapman U (CA)
Charleston Southern U (SC)
Christopher Newport U (VA)
City Coll of the City U of New York (NY)
Clarke U (IA)
Coe Coll (IA)
The Coll of St. Scholastica (MN)
The Coll of Wooster (OH)
Colorado Christian U (CO)
Colorado State U (CO)
Columbia Coll Chicago (IL)
Columbus State U (GA)
Concordia Coll (MN)
Concordia Coll–New York (NY)
Concordia U (QC, Canada)
Concordia U Chicago (IL)
Converse Coll (SC)
Corban U (OR)
Cornerstone U (MI)
Dalhousie U (NS, Canada)
Dallas Baptist U (TX)
DePauw U (IN)
Drake U (IA)
Duquesne U (PA)
Eastern Michigan U (MI)
Eastern Nazarene Coll (MA)
Elon U (NC)
Emory & Henry Coll (VA)
Florida Gulf Coast U (FL)
Florida Southern Coll (FL)
Fort Lewis Coll (CO)
Friends U (KS)
Gardner-Webb U (NC)
Georgia Southern U (GA)
Georgia State U (GA)
Gonzaga U (WA)
Gordon Coll (MA)
Grove City Coll (PA)
Hamline U (MN)
Hardin-Simmons U (TX)
Henderson State U (AR)
Hofstra U (NY)
Holy Names U (CA)
Hope Coll (MI)
Houghton Coll (NY)
Houston Baptist U (TX)
Howard Payne U (TX)
Huntingdon Coll (AL)
Huntington U (IN)
Idaho State U (ID)
Illinois State U (IL)
Illinois Wesleyan U (IL)
Immaculata U (PA)
Indiana State U (IN)
Indiana U Bloomington (IN)
Indiana U of Pennsylvania (PA)
Indiana U South Bend (IN)
Inter American U of Puerto Rico, Metropolitan Campus (PR)
Ithaca Coll (NY)
Jackson State U (MS)
Jacksonville U (FL)
James Madison U (VA)
Judson U (IL)
The Juilliard School (NY)
Kansas Wesleyan U (KS)
Kean U (NJ)
Keene State Coll (NH)
Kennesaw State U (GA)
Kentucky State U (KY)
Kentucky Wesleyan Coll (KY)
LaGrange Coll (GA)
Lawrence U (WI)
Lebanon Valley Coll (PA)
Lee U (TN)
Lenoir-Rhyne U (NC)
Liberty U (VA)
Limestone Coll (SC)
Lipscomb U (TN)
Louisiana Coll (LA)
Louisiana State U and A&M Coll (LA)
Louisiana Tech U (LA)
Loyola U New Orleans (LA)
Lynn U (FL)
Madonna U (MI)
Manchester U (IN)
Mansfield U of Pennsylvania (PA)
Maranatha Baptist U (WI)
Marian U (IN)
Marywood U (PA)
McNeese State U (LA)
Mercer U, Macon (GA)
Mercyhurst U (PA)
Messiah Coll (PA)
Miami U (OH)
Michigan State U (MI)
MidAmerica Nazarene U (KS)
Millikin U (IL)
Minnesota State U Moorhead (MN)
Missouri Baptist U (MO)
Missouri State U (MO)
Montclair State U (NJ)
Morningside Coll (IA)
Mount Allison U (NB, Canada)
Mount Vernon Nazarene U (OH)
Nazareth Coll of Rochester (NY)
Nebraska Wesleyan U (NE)
Newberry Coll (SC)
New Mexico State U (NM)
The New School Coll of Performing Arts (NY)
Northern Arizona U (AZ)
North Greenville U (SC)
Northwestern State U of Louisiana (LA)
Northwestern U (IL)
Nyack Coll (NY)
The Ohio State U (OH)
Ohio U (OH)
Ohio Wesleyan U (OH)
Oklahoma Baptist U (OK)
Oklahoma City U (OK)
Old Dominion U (VA)
Olivet Nazarene U (IL)
Oral Roberts U (OK)
Otterbein U (OH)
Ouachita Baptist U (AR)
Palm Beach Atlantic U (FL)
Penn State U Park (PA)
Piedmont Coll (GA)
Pittsburg State U (KS)
Point Loma Nazarene U (CA)
Portland State U (OR)
Queens Coll of the City U of New York (NY)
Randolph Coll (VA)
Rhode Island Coll (RI)
Rice U (TX)
Rockford U (IL)
Rocky Mountain Coll (MT)
Rowan U (NJ)
Rutgers U–New Brunswick (NJ)
St. Cloud State U (MN)
Saint Mary's U of Minnesota (MN)
St. Olaf Coll (MN)
Saint Vincent Coll (PA)
Samford U (AL)
Sam Houston State U (TX)
San Diego State U (CA)
San Francisco State U (CA)
Seton Hill U (PA)
Shenandoah U (VA)
Simpson Coll (IA)
Slippery Rock U of Pennsylvania (PA)
Southeastern Louisiana U (LA)
Southeastern Oklahoma State U (OK)
Southeastern U (FL)
Southern Methodist U (TX)
Southwestern Adventist U (TX)
Southwestern Assemblies of God U (TX)
Southwestern Coll (KS)
State U of New York Coll at Potsdam (NY)
Susquehanna U (PA)
Syracuse U (NY)
Tarleton State U (TX)
Temple U (PA)
Texas A&M U–Kingsville (TX)
Texas Christian U (TX)
Texas State U (TX)
Toccoa Falls Coll (GA)
Transylvania U (KY)
Trevecca Nazarene U (TN)
Trinity U (TX)
Truman State U (MO)
Tulane U (LA)
Union Coll (NE)
Union U (TN)
Université de Montréal (QC, Canada)
U at Buffalo, the State U of New York (NY)
The U of Akron (OH)
U of Alaska Fairbanks (AK)
The U of Arizona (AZ)
U of Arkansas (AR)
U of California, Irvine (CA)
U of Central Arkansas (AR)
U of Central Florida (FL)
U of Cincinnati (OH)
U of Colorado Boulder (CO)
U of Dayton (OH)
U of Delaware (DE)
U of Denver (CO)
U of Evansville (IN)
U of Georgia (GA)
U of Hartford (CT)
U of Houston (TX)
U of Idaho (ID)
U of Indianapolis (IN)
U of Jamestown (ND)
The U of Kansas (KS)
U of Kentucky (KY)
U of Louisiana at Monroe (LA)
U of Maine (ME)
U of Mary Hardin-Baylor (TX)
U of Maryland, Baltimore County (MD)
U of Maryland, Coll Park (MD)
U of Massachusetts Amherst (MA)
U of Massachusetts Lowell (MA)
U of Miami (FL)
U of Michigan (MI)
U of Michigan–Flint (MI)
U of Minnesota, Duluth (MN)
U of Missouri–Kansas City (MO)
U of Mount Union (OH)
U of Nevada, Reno (NV)
The U of North Carolina at Chapel Hill (NC)
The U of North Carolina at Charlotte (NC)
The U of North Carolina at Greensboro (NC)
The U of North Carolina at Pembroke (NC)
U of North Carolina School of the Arts (NC)
The U of North Carolina Wilmington (NC)
U of North Dakota (ND)
U of Northern Iowa (IA)
U of North Florida (FL)
U of North Georgia (GA)
U of North Texas (TX)
U of Oregon (OR)
U of Puget Sound (WA)
U of Rochester (NY)
U of St. Francis (IL)
U of St. Thomas (MN)
The U of South Dakota (SD)
U of Southern California (CA)
U of Southern Maine (ME)
U of South Florida (FL)
The U of Tampa (FL)
The U of Tennessee at Martin (TN)
The U of Texas at Austin (TX)
The U of the Arts (PA)
The U of Tulsa (OK)
U of Valley Forge (PA)
U of Vermont (VT)
U of Washington (WA)
U of West Georgia (GA)
U of Windsor (ON, Canada)
U of Wisconsin–Madison (WI)
U of Wisconsin–Stevens Point (WI)
U of Wisconsin–Superior (WI)
Utah Valley U (UT)
Valdosta State U (GA)
Valparaiso U (IN)
Virginia Commonwealth U (VA)
Virginia Union U (VA)
Viterbo U (WI)
Walla Walla U (WA)
Wartburg Coll (IA)
Washburn U (KS)
Washington State U (WA)
Wayland Baptist U (TX)
Weber State U (UT)
Webster U (MO)
Welch Coll (TN)
West Chester U of Pennsylvania (PA)
Western Carolina U (NC)
Western Connecticut State U (CT)
Western Illinois U (IL)
Western Kentucky U (KY)
Western Michigan U (MI)
Western Washington U (WA)
Wheaton Coll (IL)
Whitman Coll (WA)
Wichita State U (KS)

Willamette U (OR)
William Jewell Coll (MO)
William Paterson U of New Jersey (NJ)
William Penn U (IA)
Wright State U (OH)
Wright State U–Lake Campus (OH)
Xavier U of Louisiana (LA)
Youngstown State U (OH)

MUSIC RELATED
Alverno Coll (WI)
Ball State U (IN)
Bellarmine U (KY)
Belmont U (TN)
Bethel Coll (KS)
Biola U (CA)
Bowling Green State U (OH)
Brigham Young U (UT)
Capital U (OH)
Carnegie Mellon U (PA)
Coll of the Ozarks (MO)
Colorado Christian U (CO)
Columbia Coll Chicago (IL)
Concordia U Irvine (CA)
Cornerstone U (MI)
Duquesne U (PA)
Eastern Nazarene Coll (MA)
Friends U (KS)
Greenville Coll (IL)
Grove City Coll (PA)
Hampton U (VA)
Illinois Wesleyan U (IL)
Indiana U Bloomington (IN)
Indiana U South Bend (IN)
Jacksonville U (FL)
Kent State U at Stark (OH)
Lipscomb U (TN)
McKendree U (IL)
Mercer U, Macon (GA)
Messiah Coll (PA)
Milligan Coll (TN)
Missouri Western State U (MO)
Morehead State U (KY)
Murray State U (KY)
Northwestern U (IL)
Northwest U (WA)
Palm Beach Atlantic U (FL)
Saint Mary's U of Minnesota (MN)
School of the Art Inst of Chicago (IL)
Tiffin U (OH)
Trevecca Nazarene U (TN)
Truett McConnell U (GA)
U of Delaware (DE)
U of Denver (CO)
U of Hartford (CT)
U of Lethbridge (AB, Canada)
U of Massachusetts Lowell (MA)
U of Miami (FL)
U of Minnesota, Duluth (MN)
U of North Carolina at Asheville (NC)
U of Northern Iowa (IA)
U of Southern California (CA)
The U of Tulsa (OK)
U of Washington (WA)
Valparaiso U (IN)
Vanderbilt U (TN)
Wesleyan U (CT)
Western Illinois U (IL)
Western Kentucky U (KY)
West Virginia U (WV)
Wheaton Coll (IL)
Wichita State U (KS)

MUSIC TEACHER EDUCATION
Abilene Christian U (TX)
Adams State U (CO)
Adelphi U (NY)
Alabama State U (AL)
Albany State U (GA)
Albion Coll (MI)
Alderson Broaddus U (WV)
Alma Coll (MI)
Alverno Coll (WI)
Anderson U (IN)
Anderson U (SC)
Andrews U (MI)
Appalachian State U (NC)
Aquinas Coll (MI)
Arizona State U at the Tempe campus (AZ)
Arkansas Tech U (AR)
Arlington Baptist Coll (TX)
Armstrong State U (GA)
Asbury U (KY)
Ashland U (OH)
Auburn U (AL)
Augsburg Coll (MN)
Augustana Coll (IL)
Augustana U (SD)
Augusta U (GA)
Baker U (KS)
Baldwin Wallace U (OH)
Ball State U (IN)
The Baptist Coll of Florida (FL)
Baylor U (TX)
Belmont U (TN)
Beloit Coll (WI)
Bemidji State U (MN)
Benedictine Coll (KS)
Berea Coll (KY)
Berry Coll (GA)
Bethel Coll (IN)
Bethel U (MN)
Bethune-Cookman U (FL)
Biola U (CA)
Bishop's U (QC, Canada)
Bluefield Coll (VA)
Blue Mountain Coll (MS)
Bluffton U (OH)
Boise State U (ID)
Boston U (MA)
Bowling Green State U (OH)
Bradley U (IL)
Brenau U (GA)
Bridgewater State U (MA)
Brigham Young U–Idaho (ID)
Brooklyn Coll of the City U of New York (NY)
Bryan Coll (TN)
Bucknell U (PA)
Buena Vista U (IA)
Buffalo State Coll, State U of New York (NY)
Butler U (IN)
California Baptist U (CA)
California Lutheran U (CA)
California State U, Fresno (CA)
California State U, Fullerton (CA)
Calvary U (MO)
Calvin Coll (MI)
Cameron U (OK)
Campbellsville U (KY)
Capital U (OH)
Carson-Newman U (TN)
Carthage Coll (WI)
Case Western Reserve U (OH)
Catawba Coll (NC)
Cedarville U (OH)
Central Connecticut State U (CT)
Central Methodist U (MO)
Central State U (OH)
Central Washington U (WA)
Chapman U (CA)
Charleston Southern U (SC)
Chestnut Hill Coll (PA)
Chowan U (NC)
City Coll of the City U of New York (NY)
Clarion U of Pennsylvania (PA)
Clarke U (IA)
Coe Coll (IA)
The Coll of New Jersey (NJ)
The Coll of Saint Rose (NY)
Coll of the Ozarks (MO)
The Coll of Wooster (OH)
Colorado Christian U (CO)
Colorado State U (CO)
Columbus State U (GA)
Concordia Coll (MN)
Concordia U Chicago (IL)
Concordia U, Nebraska (NE)
Concordia U, St. Paul (MN)
Concordia U Wisconsin (WI)
Converse Coll (SC)
Corban U (OR)
Cornell Coll (IA)
Cornerstone U (MI)
Culver-Stockton Coll (MO)
Dallas Baptist U (TX)
DePauw U (IN)
Dickinson State U (ND)
Dixie State U (UT)
Drake U (IA)
Duquesne U (PA)
East Carolina U (NC)
East Central U (OK)
Eastern Michigan U (MI)
Eastern Nazarene Coll (MA)
Eastern Washington U (WA)
East Texas Baptist U (TX)
Edgewood Coll (WI)
Elon U (NC)
Emmanuel Coll (GA)
Emmaus Bible Coll (IA)
Emory & Henry Coll (VA)
Emporia State U (KS)
Evangel U (MO)
Faith Baptist Bible Coll and Theological Sem (IA)
Faulkner U (AL)
Florida Ag and Mech U (FL)
Florida Atlantic U (FL)
Florida Southern Coll (FL)
Fort Lewis Coll (CO)
Fresno Pacific U (CA)
Friends U (KS)
Furman U (SC)
Gardner-Webb U (NC)
Geneva Coll (PA)
George Fox U (OR)
Georgia Coll & State U (GA)
Georgia Southern U (GA)
Gettysburg Coll (PA)
Gonzaga U (WA)
Gordon Coll (MA)
Goshen Coll (IN)
Graceland U (IA)
Grand Valley State U (MI)
Grand View U (IA)
Greenville Coll (IL)
Grove City Coll (PA)
Hampton U (VA)
Hannibal-LaGrange U (MO)
Harding U (AR)
Hardin-Simmons U (TX)
Hartwick Coll (NY)
Heidelberg U (OH)
Hobe Sound Bible Coll (FL)
Hofstra U (NY)
Hope Coll (MI)
Houghton Coll (NY)
Houston Baptist U (TX)
Howard Payne U (TX)
Humboldt State U (CA)
Huntingdon Coll (AL)
Huntington U (IN)
Idaho State U (ID)
Illinois State U (IL)
Illinois Wesleyan U (IL)
Immaculata U (PA)
Indiana U Bloomington (IN)
Indiana U South Bend (IN)
Inter American U of Puerto Rico, San Germán Campus (PR)
Iowa State U of Science and Technology (IA)
Ithaca Coll (NY)
Jackson State U (MS)
Jacksonville State U (AL)
Jacksonville U (FL)
John Brown U (AR)
Kansas State U (KS)
Kansas Wesleyan U (KS)
Kean U (NJ)
Keene State Coll (NH)
Kennesaw State U (GA)
Kent State U (OH)
Kentucky State U (KY)
Kentucky Wesleyan Coll (KY)
King U (TN)
Kutztown U of Pennsylvania (PA)
Langston U (OK)
Lawrence U (WI)
Lebanon Valley Coll (PA)
Lee U (TN)
Lenoir-Rhyne U (NC)
Limestone Coll (SC)
Lindenwood U (MO)
Lipscomb U (TN)
Loras Coll (IA)
Louisiana Coll (LA)
Louisiana State U and A&M Coll (LA)
Louisiana Tech U (LA)
Loyola U New Orleans (LA)
Lubbock Christian U (TX)
Lynchburg Coll (VA)
Madonna U (MI)
Malone U (OH)
Manchester U (IN)
Manhattanville Coll (NY)
Mansfield U of Pennsylvania (PA)
Maranatha Baptist U (WI)
Marian U (IN)
Marietta Coll (OH)
Marywood U (PA)
The Master's U (CA)
McKendree U (IL)
McMaster U (ON, Canada)
Mercer U, Macon (GA)
Mercyhurst U (PA)
Meredith Coll (NC)
Messiah Coll (PA)
Metropolitan State U of Denver (CO)
Miami U (OH)
Michigan State U (MI)
MidAmerica Nazarene U (KS)
Milligan Coll (TN)
Millikin U (IL)
Minnesota State U Mankato (MN)
Minnesota State U Moorhead (MN)
Minot State U (ND)
Mississippi State U (MS)
Mississippi Valley State U (MS)
Missouri Baptist U (MO)
Missouri State U (MO)
Missouri Western State U (MO)
Molloy Coll (NY)
Montana State U (MT)
Montana State U Billings (MT)
Morningside Coll (IA)
Mount Marty Coll (SD)
Mount Mercy U (IA)
Mount Vernon Nazarene U (OH)
Muskingum U (OH)
Nazareth Coll of Rochester (NY)
Nebraska Wesleyan U (NE)
Newberry Coll (SC)
New Jersey City U (NJ)
New Mexico State U (NM)
North Central Coll (IL)
North Dakota State U (ND)
Northeastern State U (OK)
Northern Arizona U (AZ)
Northern Illinois U (IL)
Northern Kentucky U (KY)
Northern State U (SD)
North Greenville U (SC)
Northwestern Coll (IA)
Northwestern Oklahoma State U (OK)
Northwestern State U of Louisiana (LA)
Northwestern U (IL)
Northwest Missouri State U (MO)
Northwest U (WA)
Nyack Coll (NY)
Oberlin Coll (OH)
Ohio Christian U (OH)
The Ohio State U (OH)
Ohio Wesleyan U (OH)
Oklahoma Baptist U (OK)
Oklahoma Christian U (OK)
Oklahoma State U (OK)
Olivet Nazarene U (IL)
Oral Roberts U (OK)
Otterbein U (OH)
Ouachita Baptist U (AR)
Pacific Lutheran U (WA)
Palm Beach Atlantic U (FL)
Penn State U Park (PA)
Pepperdine U, Malibu (CA)
Piedmont Coll (GA)
Piedmont Intl U (NC)
Pittsburg State U (KS)
Plymouth State U (NH)
Point Loma Nazarene U (CA)
Providence Coll (RI)
Queens Coll of the City U of New York (NY)
Rhode Island Coll (RI)
Ripon Coll (WI)
Roberts Wesleyan Coll (NY)
Rocky Mountain Coll (MT)
Rowan U (NJ)
Rutgers U–New Brunswick (NJ)
Saginaw Valley State U (MI)
St. Ambrose U (IA)
St. Catherine U (MN)
St. Cloud State U (MN)
Saint Mary's Coll (IN)
Saint Mary's U of Minnesota (MN)
St. Norbert Coll (WI)
St. Olaf Coll (MN)
Salve Regina U (RI)
Samford U (AL)
Sam Houston State U (TX)
San Diego State U (CA)
Schreiner U (TX)
Seton Hill U (PA)
Shenandoah U (VA)
Shorter U (GA)
Silver Lake Coll of the Holy Family (WI)
Simpson Coll (IA)
Simpson U (CA)
Sonoma State U (CA)
South Carolina State U (SC)
South Dakota State U (SD)
Southeastern Oklahoma State U (OK)
Southeastern U (FL)
Southeast Missouri State U (MO)
Southern Arkansas U–Magnolia (AR)
Southern Methodist U (TX)
Southern New Hampshire U (NH)
Southern Utah U (UT)
Southwest Baptist U (MO)
Southwestern Assemblies of God U (TX)
Southwestern Coll (KS)
State U of New York at Fredonia (NY)
State U of New York Coll at Potsdam (NY)
Sterling Coll (KS)
Susquehanna U (PA)
Syracuse U (NY)
Tabor Coll (KS)
Tarleton State U (TX)
Taylor U (IN)
Temple U (PA)
Texas Christian U (TX)
Texas Lutheran U (TX)
Texas Wesleyan U (TX)
Toccoa Falls Coll (GA)
Towson U (MD)
Transylvania U (KY)
Trevecca Nazarene U (TN)
Trinity Christian Coll (IL)
Trinity U (TX)
Truett McConnell U (GA)
Union Coll (NE)
Union U (TN)
The U of Akron (OH)
The U of Alabama (AL)
The U of Arizona (AZ)
U of Central Florida (FL)
U of Central Missouri (MO)
U of Cincinnati (OH)
U of Colorado Boulder (CO)
U of Dayton (OH)
U of Delaware (DE)
U of Evansville (IN)
U of Florida (FL)
U of Georgia (GA)
U of Hartford (CT)
U of Idaho (ID)
U of Indianapolis (IN)
U of Jamestown (ND)
The U of Kansas (KS)
U of Kentucky (KY)
U of Lethbridge (AB, Canada)
U of Louisville (KY)
U of Maine (ME)
U of Mary Hardin-Baylor (TX)
U of Maryland, Coll Park (MD)
U of Miami (FL)
U of Michigan (MI)
U of Michigan–Flint (MI)
U of Minnesota, Duluth (MN)
U of Minnesota, Twin Cities Campus (MN)
U of Missouri–Kansas City (MO)
U of Missouri–St. Louis (MO)
U of Mobile (AL)
The U of Montana Western (MT)
U of Mount Union (OH)
U of Nevada, Reno (NV)
The U of North Carolina at Greensboro (NC)
The U of North Carolina at Pembroke (NC)
U of North Dakota (ND)
U of Northern Colorado (CO)
U of Northern Iowa (IA)
U of North Florida (FL)
U of North Georgia (GA)
U of Oklahoma (OK)
U of Oregon (OR)
U of Puget Sound (WA)
U of Regina (SK, Canada)
U of Rochester (NY)
U of St. Francis (IL)
U of St. Thomas (MN)
U of St. Thomas (TX)
U of Saskatchewan (SK, Canada)
U of South Carolina (SC)
U of South Carolina Aiken (SC)
The U of South Dakota (SD)

U of Southern Maine (ME)
U of Southern Mississippi (MS)
U of South Florida (FL)
The U of Tampa (FL)
The U of Tennessee at Chattanooga (TN)
The U of Tennessee at Martin (TN)
The U of Texas at Austin (TX)
U of the Cumberlands (KY)
U of the Incarnate Word (TX)
U of the Pacific (CA)
U of the Virgin Islands (VI)
U of Toronto (ON, Canada)
The U of Tulsa (OK)
U of Valley Forge (PA)
U of Vermont (VT)
U of Washington (WA)
U of West Georgia (GA)
U of Windsor (ON, Canada)
U of Wisconsin–Green Bay (WI)
U of Wisconsin–Madison (WI)
U of Wisconsin–Milwaukee (WI)
U of Wisconsin–Stevens Point (WI)
U of Wisconsin–Superior (WI)
Utah State U (UT)
Utah Valley U (UT)
Valley City State U (ND)
Valparaiso U (IN)
Vanderbilt U (TN)
Viterbo U (WI)
Waldorf U (IA)
Walla Walla U (WA)
Wartburg Coll (IA)
Washburn U (KS)
Wayland Baptist U (TX)
Wayne State Coll (NE)
Weber State U (UT)
Webster U (MO)
Welch Coll (TN)
Western Carolina U (NC)
Western Connecticut State U (CT)
Western Michigan U (MI)
Western State Colorado U (CO)
Western Washington U (WA)
Westfield State U (MA)
Westminster Coll (PA)
West Virginia Wesleyan Coll (WV)
Wheaton Coll (IL)
Whitworth U (WA)
Wichita State U (KS)
Williams Baptist Coll (AR)
Wingate U (NC)
Winona State U (MN)
Winthrop U (SC)
Wright State U (OH)
Wright State U–Lake Campus (OH)
Xavier U of Louisiana (LA)
York Coll of Pennsylvania (PA)
Youngstown State U (OH)

MUSIC TECHNOLOGY
American U (DC)
Bethune-Cookman U (FL)
California U of Pennsylvania (PA)
Carnegie Mellon U (PA)
Cogswell Polytechnical Coll (CA)
The Coll of Saint Rose (NY)
Columbia Coll Chicago (IL)
Connecticut Coll (CT)
Culver-Stockton Coll (MO)
Edgewood Coll (WI)
Elon U (NC)
Indiana U–Purdue U Indianapolis (IN)
Keene State Coll (NH)
LaGrange Coll (GA)
Lebanon Valley Coll (PA)
Mercy Coll (NY)
Northwest Christian U (OR)
San Francisco Conservatory of Music (CA)
Shenandoah U (VA)
Stevens Inst of Technology (NJ)
Syracuse U (NY)
Transylvania U (KY)
Trinity Christian Coll (IL)
Université de Montréal (QC, Canada)
U of Denver (CO)
U of Maryland, Baltimore County (MD)
U of Michigan (MI)
U of New Haven (CT)
U of North Carolina at Asheville (NC)
U of Northern Iowa (IA)
U of St. Francis (IL)
U of Saint Francis (IN)
U of Valley Forge (PA)
Utah Valley U (UT)
Western Michigan U (MI)

MUSIC THEORY AND COMPOSITION
Acad of Art U (CA)
Adams State U (CO)
Anderson U (IN)
Arizona State U at the Tempe campus (AZ)
Augustana Coll (IL)
Baldwin Wallace U (OH)
Baylor U (TX)
Belmont U (TN)
Bennington Coll (VT)
Biola U (CA)
Boise State U (ID)
Boston U (MA)
Bowling Green State U (OH)
Bradley U (IL)
Brooklyn Coll of the City U of New York (NY)
Bucknell U (PA)
Butler U (IN)
California Baptist U (CA)
California State U, Long Beach (CA)
Calvin Coll (MI)
Capital U (OH)
Carnegie Mellon U (PA)
Carson-Newman U (TN)
The Catholic U of America (DC)
Cedarville U (OH)
Central Michigan U (MI)
Central Washington U (WA)
Chapman U (CA)
City Coll of the City U of New York (NY)
Coe Coll (IA)
Coll of the Ozarks (MO)
The Coll of Wooster (OH)
Colorado State U (CO)
Columbia Coll Chicago (IL)
Concordia Coll (MN)
Concordia U (QC, Canada)
Concordia U Chicago (IL)
Dalhousie U (NS, Canada)
Dallas Baptist U (TX)
DePauw U (IN)
DigiPen Inst of Technology (WA)
Eastern Nazarene Coll (MA)
Florida State U (FL)
Gardner-Webb U (NC)
Georgia Southern U (GA)
Hardin-Simmons U (TX)
Hofstra U (NY)
Hope Coll (MI)
Houghton Coll (NY)
Illinois Wesleyan U (IL)
Ithaca Coll (NY)
Jacksonville U (FL)
Keene State Coll (NH)
Lawrence U (WI)
Lewis & Clark Coll (OR)
Lipscomb U (TN)
Loyola U New Orleans (LA)
Lynn U (FL)
Madonna U (MI)
Manchester U (IN)
Michigan State U (MI)
Minnesota State U Moorhead (MN)
Newberry Coll (SC)
The New School Coll of Performing Arts (NY)
Northwestern U (IL)
Northwest U (WA)
Nyack Coll (NY)
Oberlin Coll (OH)
The Ohio State U (OH)
Ohio U (OH)
Oklahoma Baptist U (OK)
Oklahoma City U (OK)
Olivet Nazarene U (IL)
Oral Roberts U (OK)
Ouachita Baptist U (AR)
Palm Beach Atlantic U (FL)
Pepperdine U, Malibu (CA)
Point Loma Nazarene U (CA)
Randolph Coll (VA)
Rice U (TX)
Rowan U (NJ)
St. Cloud State U (MN)
St. Olaf Coll (MN)
Samford U (AL)
Sam Houston State U (TX)
San Francisco Conservatory of Music (CA)
Shenandoah U (VA)
Southern Methodist U (TX)
State U of New York Coll at Potsdam (NY)
Susquehanna U (PA)
Syracuse U (NY)
Taylor U (IN)
Temple U (PA)
Texas Christian U (TX)
Trevecca Nazarene U (TN)
Trinity U (TX)
Tufts U (MA)
Tulane U (LA)
Université de Montréal (QC, Canada)
The U of Akron (OH)
U of California, Santa Barbara (CA)
U of Central Missouri (MO)
U of Cincinnati (OH)
U of Dayton (OH)
U of Delaware (DE)
U of Denver (CO)
U of Georgia (GA)
U of Idaho (ID)
The U of Kansas (KS)
U of Maryland, Baltimore County (MD)
U of Miami (FL)
U of Michigan (MI)
U of Minnesota, Duluth (MN)
U of Missouri–Kansas City (MO)
The U of North Carolina at Greensboro (NC)
U of Northern Iowa (IA)
U of North Texas (TX)
U of Oregon (OR)
U of Regina (SK, Canada)
U of Rochester (NY)
U of Southern California (CA)
The U of Texas at Austin (TX)
The U of the Arts (PA)
U of the Pacific (CA)
The U of Tulsa (OK)
U of Washington (WA)
U of West Georgia (GA)
U of Windsor (ON, Canada)
Valparaiso U (IN)
Vanderbilt U (TN)
Virginia Union U (VA)
Wartburg Coll (IA)
Washington State U (WA)
Washington U in St. Louis (MO)
Webster U (MO)
Western Connecticut State U (CT)
Western Michigan U (MI)
Western Washington U (WA)
Wheaton Coll (IL)
Whitman Coll (WA)
Wichita State U (KS)
Willamette U (OR)
William Jewell Coll (MO)
Youngstown State U (OH)

MUSIC THERAPY
Alverno Coll (WI)
Appalachian State U (NC)
Arizona State U at the Tempe campus (AZ)
Augsburg Coll (MN)
Baldwin Wallace U (OH)
Belmont U (TN)
Charleston Southern U (SC)
The Coll of Wooster (OH)
Colorado State U (CO)
Concordia U, Nebraska (NE)
Concordia U Wisconsin (WI)
Converse Coll (SC)
Drury U (MO)
Duquesne U (PA)
Eastern Michigan U (MI)
Edgewood Coll (WI)
Elizabethtown Coll (PA)
Florida State U (FL)
Georgia Coll & State U (GA)
Immaculata U (PA)
Loyola U New Orleans (LA)
Marylhurst U (OR)
Maryville U of Saint Louis (MO)
Marywood U (PA)
Mercyhurst U (PA)
Molloy Coll (NY)
Montclair State U (NJ)
Nazareth Coll of Rochester (NY)
Saint Mary-of-the-Woods Coll (IN)
Sam Houston State U (TX)
Seattle Pacific U (WA)
Seton Hill U (PA)
Shenandoah U (VA)
Slippery Rock U of Pennsylvania (PA)
Southern Methodist U (TX)
State U of New York at Fredonia (NY)
Temple U (PA)
U of Dayton (OH)
U of Evansville (IN)
U of Georgia (GA)
The U of Kansas (KS)
U of Louisville (KY)
U of Miami (FL)
U of Minnesota, Twin Cities Campus (MN)
U of Missouri–Kansas City (MO)
U of North Dakota (ND)
U of the Incarnate Word (TX)
U of the Pacific (CA)
Utah State U (UT)
Wartburg Coll (IA)
Western Michigan U (MI)
Willamette U (OR)

NANOTECHNOLOGY
Excelsior Coll (NY)
U of Guelph (ON, Canada)
U of Wisconsin–Platteville (WI)
Virginia Polytechnic Inst and State U (VA)

NATIONAL SECURITY POLICY
Anderson U (IN)
Angelo State U (TX)
Baldwin Wallace U (OH)
Excelsior Coll (NY)
U of New Haven (CT)
U of North Georgia (GA)

NATURAL RESOURCE ECONOMICS
Baldwin Wallace U (OH)
Juniata Coll (PA)
Malone U (OH)
Michigan State U (MI)
New Mexico State U (NM)
U of Guelph (ON, Canada)
U of New Hampshire (NH)
U of Rhode Island (RI)
U of Saskatchewan (SK, Canada)
The U of Tennessee (TN)

NATURAL RESOURCE RECREATION AND TOURISM
Unity Coll (ME)
U of Georgia (GA)
U of Idaho (ID)

NATURAL RESOURCES AND CONSERVATION RELATED
Bowling Green State U (OH)
California Polytechnic State U, San Luis Obispo (CA)
Mount Mercy U (IA)
Northland Coll (WI)
Penn State Abington (PA)
Penn State Altoona (PA)
Penn State Beaver (PA)
Penn State Berks (PA)
Penn State Brandywine (PA)
Penn State DuBois (PA)
Penn State Erie, The Behrend Coll (PA)
Penn State Fayette, The Eberly Campus (PA)
Penn State Greater Allegheny (PA)
Penn State Hazleton (PA)
Penn State Lehigh Valley (PA)
Penn State Mont Alto (PA)
Penn State New Kensington (PA)
Penn State Schuylkill (PA)
Penn State Shenango (PA)
Penn State U Park (PA)
Penn State Wilkes-Barre (PA)
Penn State Worthington Scranton (PA)
Penn State York (PA)
Prescott Coll (AZ)
State U of New York Coll of Technology at Canton (NY)
U of Alaska Fairbanks (AK)
U of California, Davis (CA)
U of Wisconsin–Platteville (WI)
U of Wisconsin–Stevens Point (WI)
Utah State U (UT)

NATURAL RESOURCES/ CONSERVATION
Central Michigan U (MI)
Clemson U (SC)
Colorado State U (CO)
Cornell U (NY)
The Evergreen State Coll (WA)
Grand Valley State U (MI)
Green Mountain Coll (VT)
Humboldt State U (CA)
Kent State U (OH)
Louisiana Tech U (LA)
Lubbock Christian U (TX)
Manchester U (IN)
Mississippi State U (MS)
Montana State U (MT)
Morrisville State Coll (NY)
Muskingum U (OH)
North Carolina State U (NC)
The Ohio State U (OH)
Penn State Abington (PA)
Penn State Altoona (PA)
Penn State Beaver (PA)
Penn State Berks (PA)
Penn State Brandywine (PA)
Penn State DuBois (PA)
Penn State Erie, The Behrend Coll (PA)
Penn State Fayette, The Eberly Campus (PA)
Penn State Greater Allegheny (PA)
Penn State Hazleton (PA)
Penn State Lehigh Valley (PA)
Penn State Mont Alto (PA)
Penn State New Kensington (PA)
Penn State Schuylkill (PA)
Penn State Shenango (PA)
Penn State U Park (PA)
Penn State Wilkes-Barre (PA)
Penn State Worthington Scranton (PA)
Penn State York (PA)
Purdue U (IN)
Rutgers U–New Brunswick (NJ)
Sewanee: The U of the South (TN)
Southeastern Oklahoma State U (OK)
State U of New York at Plattsburgh (NY)
State U of New York Coll of Environmental Science and Forestry (NY)
Texas A&M U (TX)
Texas Tech U (TX)
Towson U (MD)
Tusculum Coll (TN)
U of Alaska Fairbanks (AK)
The U of Arizona (AZ)
U of California, Davis (CA)
U of Georgia (GA)
U of Kentucky (KY)
U of Maryland, Coll Park (MD)
U of Maryland U Coll (MD)
U of Massachusetts Amherst (MA)
U of Michigan (MI)
U of Michigan–Dearborn (MI)
U of Minnesota, Crookston (MN)
U of Nevada, Reno (NV)
U of New Hampshire (NH)
U of Vermont (VT)
U of Wisconsin–Stevens Point (WI)
Upper Iowa U (IA)
Washington State U (WA)
Washington U in St. Louis (MO)

NATURAL RESOURCES/ CONSERVATION RELATED
Colby Coll (ME)
Miami U (OH)
Northland Coll (WI)
Sierra Nevada Coll (NV)
Stanford U (CA)
State U of New York Coll of Agriculture and Technology at Cobleskill (NY)
U of Michigan–Flint (MI)
Wheeling Jesuit U (WV)

NATURAL RESOURCES LAW ENFORCEMENT AND PROTECTIVE SERVICES
Texas Tech U (TX)
Unity Coll (ME)
U of Minnesota, Crookston (MN)

NATURAL RESOURCES MANAGEMENT AND POLICY
Alaska Pacific U (AK)
Alderson Broaddus U (WV)

Angelo State U (TX)
Auburn U (AL)
Bowling Green State U (OH)
Bryant U (RI)
Clark U (MA)
Colorado State U (CO)
Dominican U of California (CA)
Humboldt State U (CA)
Iowa State U of Science and Technology (IA)
Kansas State U (KS)
Louisiana State U and A&M Coll (LA)
Marist Coll (NY)
Michigan Technological U (MI)
Morrisville State Coll (NY)
New Mexico Highlands U (NM)
North Carolina State U (NC)
North Dakota State U (ND)
The Ohio State U (OH)
Oregon State U (OR)
Purdue U (IN)
Rochester Inst of Technology (NY)
Rocky Mountain Coll (MT)
Royal Roads U (BC, Canada)
South Dakota State U (SD)
State U of New York Coll of Environmental Science and Forestry (NY)
U of Delaware (DE)
U of Guelph (ON, Canada)
U of Hawaii at Manoa (HI)
U of La Verne (CA)
U of Miami (FL)
U of Minnesota, Crookston (MN)
U of Nevada, Reno (NV)
U of Rhode Island (RI)
The U of Tennessee at Martin (TN)
U of Wisconsin–Stevens Point (WI)
Washington State U (WA)
Washington U in St. Louis (MO)
Western Carolina U (NC)

NATURAL RESOURCES MANAGEMENT AND POLICY RELATED
Great Basin Coll (NV)
Humboldt State U (CA)
Morrisville State Coll (NY)
The Ohio State U (OH)
Rutgers U–New Brunswick (NJ)
St. Petersburg Coll (FL)
U of Saskatchewan (SK, Canada)
The U of Tennessee at Martin (TN)

NATURAL SCIENCES
American Public U System (WV)
Arcadia U (PA)
Athens State U (AL)
Azusa Pacific U (CA)
Bayamón Central U (PR)
Bemidji State U (MN)
Benedictine Coll (KS)
Bethel Coll (KS)
Bishop's U (QC, Canada)
California State U, Dominguez Hills (CA)
California State U, Fresno (CA)
Calvin Coll (MI)
Carthage Coll (WI)
Case Western Reserve U (OH)
Christian Brothers U (TN)
Colgate U (NY)
Coll of Saint Benedict (MN)
Coll of Saint Mary (NE)
The Coll of St. Scholastica (MN)
Coll of the Atlantic (ME)
Colorado State U (CO)
Concordia Coll (MN)
Concordia U Chicago (IL)
Concordia U, Nebraska (NE)
Daemen Coll (NY)
Dallas Baptist U (TX)
Defiance Coll (OH)
Doane U (NE)
Dominican U (IL)
Edgewood Coll (WI)
Elms Coll (MA)
The Evergreen State Coll (WA)
Excelsior Coll (NY)
Felician U (NJ)
Fordham U (NY)
Fresno Pacific U (CA)
Georgian Court U (NJ)
Harrisburg U of Science and Technology (PA)
Hofstra U (NY)
Houghton Coll (NY)
Humboldt State U (CA)
Indiana U East (IN)
Inter American U of Puerto Rico, Metropolitan Campus (PR)
Inter American U of Puerto Rico, San Germán Campus (PR)
Johns Hopkins U (MD)
Judson U (IL)
Juniata Coll (PA)
Kansas State U (KS)
Lesley U (MA)
Logan U (MO)
Loyola Marymount U (CA)
Madonna U (MI)
The Master's U (CA)
Minnesota State U Mankato (MN)
Mount Allison U (NB, Canada)
Mount St. Joseph U (OH)
Mount Saint Mary Coll (NY)
Muhlenberg Coll (PA)
New Coll of Florida (FL)
Oklahoma Baptist U (OK)
Pepperdine U, Malibu (CA)
St. Cloud State U (MN)
Saint John's U (MN)
Saint Peter's U (NJ)
St. Thomas Aquinas Coll (NY)
Saint Vincent Coll (PA)
Shorter U (GA)
State U of New York Coll at Geneseo (NY)
State U of New York Coll at Potsdam (NY)
Temple U (PA)
Trent U (ON, Canada)
U of Detroit Mercy (MI)
U of La Verne (CA)
U of Pennsylvania (PA)
U of Pittsburgh at Greensburg (PA)
U of Pittsburgh at Johnstown (PA)
U of Puget Sound (WA)
U of Science and Arts of Oklahoma (OK)
U of Washington (WA)
U of Wisconsin–Stevens Point (WI)
Virginia Wesleyan Coll (VA)
Washington U in St. Louis (MO)
Western Oregon U (OR)

NAVAL ARCHITECTURE AND MARINE ENGINEERING
Massachusetts Maritime Acad (MA)
State U of New York Maritime Coll (NY)
Stevens Inst of Technology (NJ)
Texas A&M U (TX)
United States Coast Guard Acad (CT)
United States Merchant Marine Acad (NY)
U of Michigan (MI)
U of New Orleans (LA)
Webb Inst (NY)

NAVY/MARINE CORPS ROTC/ NAVAL SCIENCE
Hampton U (VA)
Jacksonville U (FL)

NEAR AND MIDDLE EASTERN STUDIES
American U (DC)
The American U in Cairo (Egypt)
The American U in Dubai (United Arab Emirates)
The American U of Paris (France)
Bard Coll (NY)
Boston U (MA)
Brandeis U (MA)
Claremont McKenna Coll (CA)
Colgate U (NY)
Columbia Intl U (SC)
Columbia U (NY)
Columbia U, School of General Studies (NY)
Cornell U (NY)
Dartmouth Coll (NH)
Dickinson Coll (PA)
Emory & Henry Coll (VA)
Emory U (GA)
Fordham U (NY)
The George Washington U (DC)
Hampshire Coll (MA)
Harvard U (MA)
Hood Coll (MD)
Johns Hopkins U (MD)
McDaniel Coll (MD)
Middlebury Coll (VT)
Mount Holyoke Coll (MA)
Oberlin Coll (OH)
Pomona Coll (CA)
Portland State U (OR)
Princeton U (NJ)
Queens Coll of the City U of New York (NY)
Rutgers U–New Brunswick (NJ)
Sarah Lawrence Coll (NY)
Scripps Coll (CA)
Smith Coll (MA)
Swarthmore Coll (PA)
Syracuse U (NY)
Texas State U (TX)
Trinity U (TX)
Tufts U (MA)
United States Military Acad (NY)
The U of Arizona (AZ)
U of California, Santa Barbara (CA)
U of Massachusetts Amherst (MA)
U of Michigan (MI)
U of Richmond (VA)
The U of Texas at Austin (TX)
The U of Toledo (OH)
U of Toronto (ON, Canada)
U of Utah (UT)
Washington U in St. Louis (MO)
Williams Coll (MA)

NETWORK AND SYSTEM ADMINISTRATION
Central Connecticut State U (CT)
Central Penn Coll (PA)
Champlain Coll (VT)
Kansas Wesleyan U (KS)
Michigan Technological U (MI)
Regis U (CO)
Rochester Inst of Technology (NY)
Simmons Coll (MA)
U of Great Falls (MT)
Walsh U (OH)

NEUROBIOLOGY AND ANATOMY
Andrews U (MI)
Georgetown U (DC)
Harvard U (MA)
New Coll of Florida (FL)
Purdue U (IN)
U of California, Davis (CA)
U of California, Irvine (CA)
U of Washington (WA)

NEUROBIOLOGY AND BEHAVIOR
Fitchburg State U (MA)
St. Edward's U (TX)

NEUROBIOLOGY AND NEUROSCIENCES RELATED
U of Southern California (CA)
Ursinus Coll (PA)
Wesleyan Coll (GA)

NEUROSCIENCE
Adelphi U (NY)
Agnes Scott Coll (GA)
Allegheny Coll (PA)
American U (DC)
Amherst Coll (MA)
Augustana Coll (IL)
Baldwin Wallace U (OH)
Barnard Coll (NY)
Bates Coll (ME)
Baylor U (TX)
Bay Path U (MA)
Belmont U (TN)
Binghamton U, State U of New York (NY)
Bishop's U (QC, Canada)
Boston U (MA)
Bowdoin Coll (ME)
Bowling Green State U (OH)
Brandeis U (MA)
Bucknell U (PA)
California Inst of Technology (CA)
Carnegie Mellon U (PA)
Carthage Coll (WI)
Cedar Crest Coll (PA)
Centenary Coll of Louisiana (LA)
Central Michigan U (MI)
Christopher Newport U (VA)
Claremont McKenna Coll (CA)
Clark U (MA)
Coe Coll (IA)
Colby Coll (ME)
Colgate U (NY)
The Coll of William and Mary (VA)
The Coll of Wooster (OH)
The Colorado Coll (CO)
Colorado State U (CO)
Columbia U, School of General Studies (NY)
Concordia U (QC, Canada)
Connecticut Coll (CT)
Creighton U (NE)
Dalhousie U (NS, Canada)
Dickinson Coll (PA)
Dominican U (IL)
Drake U (IA)
Drew U (NJ)
Earlham Coll (IN)
Emmanuel Coll (MA)
Emory U (GA)
Fordham U (NY)
Franklin & Marshall Coll (PA)
Furman U (SC)
Georgia State U (GA)
Hamilton Coll (NY)
Hampshire Coll (MA)
High Point U (NC)
Hiram Coll (OH)
Hofstra U (NY)
Indiana U Bloomington (IN)
Indiana U–Purdue U Indianapolis (IN)
Indiana U Southeast (IN)
John Carroll U (OH)
Johns Hopkins U (MD)
Kenyon Coll (OH)
King's Coll (PA)
King U (TN)
Knox Coll (IL)
Lake Forest Coll (IL)
Lawrence U (WI)
Lebanon Valley Coll (PA)
Lehigh U (PA)
Loras Coll (IA)
Luther Coll (IA)
Macalester Coll (MN)
Marymount Manhattan Coll (NY)
Massachusetts Inst of Technology (MA)
Mercer U, Macon (GA)
Miami U (OH)
Michigan State U (MI)
Middlebury Coll (VT)
Moravian Coll (PA)
Morehead State U (KY)
Mount Holyoke Coll (MA)
Mount St. Joseph U (OH)
Muhlenberg Coll (PA)
Muskingum U (OH)
Northeastern U (MA)
Northwestern U (IL)
Oberlin Coll (OH)
The Ohio State U (OH)
Ohio U (OH)
Ohio Wesleyan U (OH)
Pitzer Coll (CA)
Pomona Coll (CA)
Princeton U (NJ)
Regis Coll (MA)
Regis U (CO)
Rhodes Coll (TN)
Rice U (TX)
Saginaw Valley State U (MI)
Saint Louis U (MO)
Saint Michael's Coll (VT)
Santa Clara U (CA)
Scripps Coll (CA)
Skidmore Coll (NY)
Smith Coll (MA)
State U of New York Coll at Geneseo (NY)
Stonehill Coll (MA)
Syracuse U (NY)
Temple U (PA)
Texas Christian U (TX)
Transylvania U (KY)
Trinity U (TX)
Tulane U (LA)
Union Coll (NY)
Université de Montréal (QC, Canada)
The U of Alabama at Birmingham (AL)
The U of Arizona (AZ)
U of California, Riverside (CA)
U of Chicago (IL)
U of Cincinnati (OH)
U of Colorado Boulder (CO)
U of Delaware (DE)
U of Evansville (IN)
U of Georgia (GA)
U of Illinois at Chicago (IL)
U of King's Coll (NS, Canada)
U of Lethbridge (AB, Canada)
U of Miami (FL)
U of Michigan (MI)
U of Minnesota, Twin Cities Campus (MN)
U of Mount Union (OH)
U of Nevada, Reno (NV)
U of New England (ME)
U of New Hampshire (NH)
U of Notre Dame (IN)
U of Pennsylvania (PA)
U of Pittsburgh (PA)
U of Rochester (NY)
U of St. Thomas (MN)
U of San Diego (CA)
The U of Scranton (PA)
U of Southern California (CA)
The U of Texas at Austin (TX)
The U of Texas at Dallas (TX)
U of Windsor (ON, Canada)
Ursinus Coll (PA)
Vanderbilt U (TN)
Villanova U (PA)
Virginia Polytechnic Inst and State U (VA)
Wartburg Coll (IA)
Washington & Jefferson Coll (PA)
Washington and Lee U (VA)
Washington State U (WA)
Washington State U–Vancouver (WA)
Washington U in St. Louis (MO)
Western New England U (MA)
Western Washington U (WA)
Westminster Coll (PA)
Westminster Coll (UT)
Westmont Coll (CA)
Wheaton Coll (MA)
Wilkes U (PA)
Willamette U (OR)

NONPROFIT MANAGEMENT
Arizona State U at the Downtown Phoenix campus (AZ)
Aurora U (IL)
Austin Coll (TX)
Austin Peay State U (TN)
Bryant U (RI)
City Vision U (MO)
Cleveland State U (OH)
Columbia Intl U (SC)
Concordia U Chicago (IL)
Concordia U Irvine (CA)
Cornerstone U (MI)
Dalhousie U (NS, Canada)
Donnelly Coll (KS)
Duquesne U (PA)
Fairleigh Dickinson U, Metropolitan Campus (NJ)
Fresno Pacific U (CA)
Friends U (KS)
Gettysburg Coll (PA)
Grace Coll (IN)
Granite State Coll (NH)
Hardin-Simmons U (TX)
High Point U (NC)
Huntington U (IN)
Johnson U Florida (FL)
LaGrange Coll (GA)
Lenoir-Rhyne U (NC)
LeTourneau U (TX)
Mercy Coll (NY)
Missouri Valley Coll (MO)
Moravian Coll (PA)
Morningside Coll (IA)
Point Loma Nazarene U (CA)
Rogers State U (OK)
Tiffin U (OH)
Toccoa Falls Coll (GA)
Trevecca Nazarene U (TN)
U of Denver (CO)
U of Georgia (GA)
U of Minnesota, Twin Cities Campus (MN)
William Jewell Coll (MO)
Williamson Coll (TN)

NORWEGIAN
Brigham Young U (UT)
Pacific Lutheran U (WA)
St. Olaf Coll (MN)
U of North Dakota (ND)
U of Washington (WA)

NUCLEAR AND INDUSTRIAL RADIOLOGIC TECHNOLOGIES RELATED
Manhattan Coll (NY)

NUCLEAR ENGINEERING
Georgia Inst of Technology (GA)
Idaho State U (ID)
Massachusetts Inst of Technology (MA)
Missouri U of Science and Technology (MO)
North Carolina State U (NC)
Oregon State U (OR)
Penn State Abington (PA)
Penn State Altoona (PA)
Penn State Beaver (PA)
Penn State Berks (PA)
Penn State Brandywine (PA)
Penn State DuBois (PA)
Penn State Erie, The Behrend Coll (PA)
Penn State Fayette, The Eberly Campus (PA)
Penn State Greater Allegheny (PA)
Penn State Hazleton (PA)
Penn State Lehigh Valley (PA)
Penn State Mont Alto (PA)
Penn State New Kensington (PA)
Penn State Schuylkill (PA)
Penn State Shenango (PA)
Penn State U Park (PA)
Penn State Wilkes-Barre (PA)
Penn State Worthington Scranton (PA)
Penn State York (PA)
Purdue U (IN)
Rensselaer Polytechnic Inst (NY)
South Carolina State U (SC)
Texas A&M U (TX)
United States Military Acad (NY)
U of Florida (FL)
U of Massachusetts Lowell (MA)
U of Michigan (MI)
The U of Tennessee (TN)
U of Wisconsin–Madison (WI)

NUCLEAR ENGINEERING TECHNOLOGY
Excelsior Coll (NY)
Idaho State U (ID)
United States Military Acad (NY)

NUCLEAR MEDICAL TECHNOLOGY
Adventist U of Health Sciences (FL)
Allen Coll (IA)
Augusta U (GA)
Barry U (FL)
Cedar Crest Coll (PA)
Dalhousie U (NS, Canada)
East Central U (OK)
Ferris State U (MI)
Indiana U of Pennsylvania (PA)
Indiana U–Purdue U Indianapolis (IN)
Lewis U (IL)
Manhattan Coll (NY)
MCPHS U (MA)
Molloy Coll (NY)
North Central Coll (IL)
Old Dominion U (VA)
Regis Coll (MA)
Rhode Island Coll (RI)
Robert Morris U (PA)
St. Cloud State U (MN)
Saint Louis U (MO)
Saint Mary's U of Minnesota (MN)
U at Buffalo, the State U of New York (NY)
The U of Alabama at Birmingham (AL)
U of Arkansas for Medical Sciences (AR)
U of Central Arkansas (AR)
U of Cincinnati (OH)
The U of Findlay (OH)
U of Nevada, Las Vegas (NV)
U of Oklahoma Health Sciences Center (OK)
U of St. Francis (IL)
U of the Incarnate Word (TX)
U of Vermont (VT)
U of Wisconsin–La Crosse (WI)
Weber State U (UT)
York Coll of Pennsylvania (PA)

NUCLEAR/NUCLEAR POWER TECHNOLOGY
U of North Texas (TX)

NUCLEAR PHYSICS
Arkansas Tech U (AR)

NURSE MIDWIFE/NURSING MIDWIFERY
McMaster U (ON, Canada)
U of Toronto (ON, Canada)

NURSING ADMINISTRATION
Augsburg Coll (MN)
Huntington U (IN)
Nebraska Wesleyan U (NE)
Northwest Christian U (OR)
Nova Southeastern U (FL)
U of San Francisco (CA)

NURSING EDUCATION
Excelsior Coll (NY)

NURSING PRACTICE
Benedictine Coll (KS)
Bluefield Coll (VA)
Brenau U (GA)
Christian Brothers U (TN)
Concordia Coll–New York (NY)
Concordia U, St. Paul (MN)
Eastern U (PA)
Hiram Coll (OH)
Lebanese American U (Lebanon)
Louisiana Coll (LA)
Misericordia U (PA)
Sentara Coll of Health Sciences (VA)
Stratford U, Glen Allen (VA)
The U of Texas at Austin (TX)
William Penn U (IA)

NURSING SCIENCE
American U of Beirut (Lebanon)
Averett U (VA)
Carson-Newman U (TN)
Cedar Crest Coll (PA)
Coll of Saint Elizabeth (NJ)
Dixie State U (UT)
Duquesne U (PA)
EDP U of Puerto Rico (PR)
EDP U of Puerto Rico–San Sebastian (PR)
Holy Names U (CA)
Inter American U of Puerto Rico, Barranquitas Campus (PR)
Kean U (NJ)
Millersville U of Pennsylvania (PA)
Monmouth U (NJ)
New Jersey City U (NJ)
Ohio Christian U (OH)
The Ohio State U (OH)
Oklahoma City U (OK)
Pensacola State Coll (FL)
Rutgers U–Newark (NJ)
Rutgers U–New Brunswick (NJ)
Sacred Heart U (CT)
Saint Louis U–Madrid Campus (Spain)
Saint Peter's U (NJ)
Siena Coll (NY)
Texas A&M U–Central Texas (TX)
U of California, Irvine (CA)
U of Illinois at Chicago (IL)
U of Pittsburgh at Johnstown (PA)
The U of Texas at Austin (TX)
U of the Cumberlands (KY)
Wayne State U (MI)

NUTRITION SCIENCES
American U of Beirut (Lebanon)
Auburn U (AL)
Boston U (MA)
Bowling Green State U (OH)
California Baptist U (CA)
Canisius Coll (NY)
Case Western Reserve U (OH)
Central Washington U (WA)
Coll of Saint Benedict (MN)
Concordia Coll (MN)
Cornell U (NY)
Drexel U (PA)
Goddard Coll (VT)
Huntington Coll of Health Sciences (TN)
Iowa State U of Science and Technology (IA)
La Salle U (PA)
Lebanese American U (Lebanon)
Louisiana State U and A&M Coll (LA)
McNeese State U (LA)
Merrimack Coll (MA)
Michigan State U (MI)
North Carolina State U (NC)
The Ohio State U (OH)
Pepperdine U, Malibu (CA)
Purdue U (IN)
Rutgers U–New Brunswick (NJ)
The Sage Colls (NY)
Saint John's U (MN)
Simmons Coll (MA)
Southern Illinois U Carbondale (IL)
Syracuse U (NY)
Texas Tech U (TX)
Texas Woman's U (TX)
Université de Montréal (QC, Canada)
The U of Arizona (AZ)
U of California, Davis (CA)
U of Cincinnati (OH)
U of Delaware (DE)
U of Florida (FL)
U of Georgia (GA)
U of Guelph (ON, Canada)
U of Hawaii at Manoa (HI)
U of Illinois at Chicago (IL)
U of Massachusetts Amherst (MA)
U of Massachusetts Lowell (MA)
U of Minnesota, Twin Cities Campus (MN)
U of Nevada, Las Vegas (NV)
U of Nevada, Reno (NV)
U of New Hampshire (NH)
The U of North Carolina at Greensboro (NC)
U of Northern Colorado (CO)
U of Oklahoma Health Sciences Center (OK)
U of Saint Francis (IN)
U of Saskatchewan (SK, Canada)
U of Southern Indiana (IN)
The U of Texas at Austin (TX)
U of the Incarnate Word (TX)
U of Vermont (VT)
U of Wisconsin–Madison (WI)
U of Wisconsin–Milwaukee (WI)
U of Wisconsin–Stevens Point (WI)

OCCUPATIONAL HEALTH AND INDUSTRIAL HYGIENE
California State U, Fresno (CA)
Grand Valley State U (MI)
Illinois State U (IL)
Montana Tech of The U of Montana (MT)
Ohio U (OH)

OCCUPATIONAL SAFETY AND HEALTH TECHNOLOGY
Bayamón Central U (PR)
California State U, Fresno (CA)
Central Washington U (WA)
Columbia Southern U (AL)
Embry-Riddle Aeronautical U–Daytona (FL)
Embry-Riddle Aeronautical U–Worldwide (FL)
Grand Valley State U (MI)
Indiana State U (IN)
Indiana U of Pennsylvania (PA)
Jacksonville State U (AL)
Keene State Coll (NH)
Marshall U (WV)
Millersville U of Pennsylvania (PA)
Murray State U (KY)
Pittsburg State U (KS)
Rochester Inst of Technology (NY)
Slippery Rock U of Pennsylvania (PA)
Southeastern Louisiana U (LA)
Southeastern Oklahoma State U (OK)
Southwest Baptist U (MO)
U of Central Missouri (MO)
U of Houston–Downtown (TX)
U of Wisconsin–Whitewater (WI)
Waldorf U (IA)

OCCUPATIONAL THERAPIST ASSISTANT
Idaho State U (ID)
Rutgers U–Newark (NJ)

OCCUPATIONAL THERAPY
Alabama State U (AL)
American Intl Coll (MA)
Bay Path U (MA)
Brenau U (GA)
Calvin Coll (MI)
Carthage Coll (WI)
Coll of Saint Benedict (MN)
Concordia U Wisconsin (WI)
Dalhousie U (NS, Canada)
Dominican Coll (NY)
Dominican U of California (CA)
Duquesne U (PA)
Eastern Michigan U (MI)
Eastern Washington U (WA)
Elizabethtown Coll (PA)
Gannon U (PA)
Grand Valley State U (MI)
Illinois Coll (IL)
Ithaca Coll (NY)
Keuka Coll (NY)
Louisiana Coll (LA)
McKendree U (IL)
Mount Mary U (WI)
Nazareth Coll of Rochester (NY)
Penn State Mont Alto (PA)
Quinnipiac U (CT)
Sacred Heart U (CT)
Saginaw Valley State U (MI)
St. Catherine U (MN)
Saint Francis U (PA)
Saint John's U (MN)
Saint Louis U (MO)
Saint Vincent Coll (PA)
Shawnee State U (OH)
Spalding U (KY)
Towson U (MD)
Université de Montréal (QC, Canada)
U at Buffalo, the State U of New York (NY)
U of New England (ME)
U of New Hampshire (NH)
The U of Scranton (PA)
U of Southern California (CA)
U of Southern Indiana (IN)
U of Wisconsin–Milwaukee (WI)
Wartburg Coll (IA)
Western Michigan U (MI)
West Virginia U (WV)
Worcester State U (MA)
York Coll of the City U of New York (NY)

OCEAN ENGINEERING
California State U, Long Beach (CA)
Florida Atlantic U (FL)
Florida Inst of Technology (FL)
Texas A&M U (TX)
U of New Hampshire (NH)
U of Rhode Island (RI)
Virginia Polytechnic Inst and State U (VA)

OCEANOGRAPHY (CHEMICAL AND PHYSICAL)
Coll of the Atlantic (ME)
Dalhousie U (NS, Canada)
Elizabeth City State U (NC)
Florida Inst of Technology (FL)
Hawai`i Pacific U (HI)
Humboldt State U (CA)
Kutztown U of Pennsylvania (PA)
Louisiana State U and A&M Coll (LA)
Millersville U of Pennsylvania (PA)
North Carolina State U (NC)
United States Coast Guard Acad (CT)
U of Miami (FL)
U of Michigan (MI)
The U of North Carolina Wilmington (NC)
U of South Carolina (SC)
U of Southern Mississippi (MS)
U of Washington (WA)
Whitman Coll (WA)

OFFICE MANAGEMENT
Adams State U (CO)
Bowling Green State U (OH)
Clayton State U (GA)
East Central U (OK)
Eastern Michigan U (MI)
Indiana State U (IN)
Inter American U of Puerto Rico, Aguadilla Campus (PR)
Inter American U of Puerto Rico, Barranquitas Campus (PR)
Inter American U of Puerto Rico, Fajardo Campus (PR)
Inter American U of Puerto Rico, Guayama Campus (PR)
Inter American U of Puerto Rico, Metropolitan Campus (PR)
Inter American U of Puerto Rico, Ponce Campus (PR)
Inter American U of Puerto Rico, San Germán Campus (PR)
Loyola U Chicago (IL)
Maranatha Baptist U (WI)
Morrisville State Coll (NY)
National U (CA)
Point Loma Nazarene U (CA)
Southwest Baptist U (MO)
Tarleton State U (TX)
Texas A&M U–Central Texas (TX)
Union Coll (KY)
U of Central Missouri (MO)
U of South Carolina (SC)
Valley City State U (ND)

OFFICE OCCUPATIONS AND CLERICAL SERVICES
East Central U (OK)

OPERATIONS MANAGEMENT
Arizona State U at the Polytechnic campus (AZ)
Auburn U (AL)
Avila U (MO)
Ball State U (IN)
Bismarck State Coll (ND)
Boise State U (ID)
Boston Coll (MA)
Bowling Green State U (OH)
California State U, Dominguez Hills (CA)
California State U, Long Beach (CA)
California State U, Stanislaus (CA)
Carnegie Mellon U (PA)
Central Connecticut State U (CT)
Central Michigan U (MI)
Cleveland State U (OH)
Concordia U (QC, Canada)
Drexel U (PA)
Excelsior Coll (NY)
Ferris State U (MI)
Florida SouthWestern State Coll (FL)
Fort Lewis Coll (CO)
Gonzaga U (WA)
Governors State U (IL)
Granite State Coll (NH)
Indiana U–Purdue U Indianapolis (IN)
Inter American U of Puerto Rico, Bayamón Campus (PR)
Inter American U of Puerto Rico, Metropolitan Campus (PR)
Inter American U of Puerto Rico, Ponce Campus (PR)
Lamar U (TX)
Le Moyne Coll (NY)
Louisiana Tech U (LA)
Loyola U Chicago (IL)
Marian U (WI)
Miami U (OH)
Minnesota State U Moorhead (MN)
Mount Mercy U (IA)
Northeastern State U (OK)
Northern Illinois U (IL)
Oakland City U (IN)
The Ohio State U (OH)
Oregon State U (OR)
Purdue U Northwest (IN)
Rhode Island Coll (RI)
Roger Williams U (RI)
Saginaw Valley State U (MI)
Sam Houston State U (TX)
San Diego State U (CA)
South Dakota State U (SD)
Southern New Hampshire U (NH)
Southwestern Coll (KS)
Thomas Edison State U (NJ)
Trine U (IN)
The U of Akron (OH)
The U of Arizona (AZ)
U of Cincinnati (OH)
U of Dayton (OH)
U of Delaware (DE)
U of Houston (TX)
U of Indianapolis (IN)
U of Massachusetts Amherst (MA)
U of Massachusetts Dartmouth (MA)

U of Minnesota, Crookston (MN)
U of Minnesota, Twin Cities Campus (MN)
U of Nebraska at Kearney (NE)
The U of North Carolina at Charlotte (NC)
U of North Dakota (ND)
U of North Texas (TX)
U of Pennsylvania (PA)
U of St. Thomas (MN)
U of Saskatchewan (SK, Canada)
The U of Scranton (PA)
U of Southern Indiana (IN)
The U of Toledo (OH)
U of Utah (UT)
U of Wisconsin–Madison (WI)
U of Wisconsin–Milwaukee (WI)
U of Wisconsin–Stout (WI)
U of Wisconsin–Whitewater (WI)
Utah State U (UT)
Utah Valley U (UT)
Washington State U (WA)
Washington State U–Global Campus (WA)
Washington State U–Tri-Cities (WA)
Washington State U–Vancouver (WA)
Washington U in St. Louis (MO)
Wentworth Inst of Technology (MA)
Western Washington U (WA)
Widener U (PA)
Youngstown State U (OH)

OPERATIONS RESEARCH
Bowling Green State U (OH)
Bryant U (RI)
California State U, Fullerton (CA)
Canisius Coll (NY)
Carnegie Mellon U (PA)
Columbia U (NY)
Cornell U (NY)
HEC Montreal (QC, Canada)
Princeton U (NJ)
Southern Methodist U (TX)
United States Air Force Acad (CO)
United States Coast Guard Acad (CT)
United States Military Acad (NY)
U of Toronto (ON, Canada)
U of Washington (WA)
U of Waterloo (ON, Canada)

OPHTHALMIC AND OPTOMETRIC SUPPORT SERVICES AND ALLIED PROFESSIONS RELATED
Tennessee Wesleyan U (TN)

OPHTHALMIC TECHNOLOGY
U of Arkansas for Medical Sciences (AR)

OPTICAL SCIENCES
The Ohio State U (OH)
Saginaw Valley State U (MI)
The U of Arizona (AZ)
U of Rochester (NY)
Western Washington U (WA)

ORGANIC CHEMISTRY
Concordia U (QC, Canada)
U of California, Santa Barbara (CA)

ORGANIZATIONAL BEHAVIOR
Bluffton U (OH)
Bowling Green State U (OH)
Central Baptist Coll (AR)
Coe Coll (IA)
The Coll of St. Scholastica (MN)
Concordia U Chicago (IL)
Eastern Mennonite U (VA)
Edgewood Coll (WI)
Greenville Coll (IL)
High Point U (NC)
Manhattan Coll (NY)
Mount St. Joseph U (OH)
National U (CA)
Northern Kentucky U (KY)
Northwestern U (IL)
Nyack Coll (NY)
Oral Roberts U (OK)
Palm Beach Atlantic U (FL)
Penn State Abington (PA)
Penn State Altoona (PA)
Penn State Beaver (PA)
Penn State Berks (PA)
Penn State Brandywine (PA)
Penn State DuBois (PA)
Penn State Erie, The Behrend Coll (PA)
Penn State Fayette, The Eberly Campus (PA)
Penn State Greater Allegheny (PA)
Penn State Harrisburg (PA)
Penn State Hazleton (PA)
Penn State Lehigh Valley (PA)
Penn State Mont Alto (PA)
Penn State New Kensington (PA)
Penn State Schuylkill (PA)
Penn State Shenango (PA)
Penn State U Park (PA)
Penn State Wilkes-Barre (PA)
Penn State Worthington Scranton (PA)
Penn State York (PA)
Philander Smith Coll (AR)
Pitzer Coll (CA)
Robert Morris U (PA)
Saint Joseph's U (PA)
Saint Louis U (MO)
Santa Clara U (CA)
Scripps Coll (CA)
Simpson U (CA)
Union Coll (NE)
United States Military Acad (NY)
U of Cincinnati (OH)
U of Michigan (MI)
U of North Texas (TX)
U of Oklahoma (OK)
U of Richmond (VA)
U of St. Francis (IL)
U of San Francisco (CA)
U of the Incarnate Word (TX)
The U of Tulsa (OK)
Waldorf U (IA)
Wayne State U (MI)
Wilmington U (DE)

ORGANIZATIONAL COMMUNICATION
Albion Coll (MI)
Aquinas Coll (MI)
Assumption Coll (MA)
Bloomsburg U of Pennsylvania (PA)
Bradley U (IL)
Brigham Young U (UT)
Buena Vista U (IA)
Butler U (IN)
Calvin Coll (MI)
Capital U (OH)
Cleveland State U (OH)
Concordia U, Nebraska (NE)
Creighton U (NE)
Dixie State U (UT)
Emmanuel Coll (GA)
Fairleigh Dickinson U, Metropolitan Campus (NJ)
Florida Coll (FL)
Florida Southern Coll (FL)
George Fox U (OR)
Howard Payne U (TX)
Idaho State U (ID)
Lewis U (IL)
Lubbock Christian U (TX)
Marian U (WI)
McKendree U (IL)
Missouri State U (MO)
Montana State U Billings (MT)
Murray State U (KY)
Muskingum U (OH)
North Central Coll (IL)
Northwest Missouri State U (MO)
Northwest U (WA)
Ohio U–Eastern (OH)
Pepperdine U, Malibu (CA)
Providence Coll (RI)
St. Ambrose U (IA)
Shorter U (GA)
Southeast Missouri State U (MO)
Southern New Hampshire U (NH)
Suffolk U (MA)
Trevecca Nazarene U (TN)
The U of Akron (OH)
U of Idaho (ID)
U of Mount Union (OH)
The U of Texas at Austin (TX)
Viterbo U (WI)
Weber State U (UT)
Western Kentucky U (KY)
Western Michigan U (MI)
Wheeling Jesuit U (WV)

ORGANIZATIONAL LEADERSHIP
Anderson U (IN)
Anderson U (SC)
Arizona State U at the Polytechnic campus (AZ)
Auburn U at Montgomery (AL)
Averett U (VA)
Avila U (MO)
Bay Path U (MA)
Belhaven U (MS)
Bethel Coll (IN)
Blackburn Coll (IL)
Brandman U (CA)
Brenau U (GA)
Cabrini U (PA)
California Baptist U (CA)
Calvary U (MO)
Cardinal Stritch U (WI)
Central Washington U (WA)
Chestnut Hill Coll (PA)
Cleveland State U (OH)
Columbia Southern U (AL)
Creighton U (NE)
Eastern U (PA)
Eureka Coll (IL)
Fisher Coll (MA)
Florida Inst of Technology (FL)
Hilbert Coll (NY)
La Salle U (PA)
Lewis U (IL)
Lincoln Christian U (IL)
Lincoln Coll (IL)
Lincoln Coll–Normal (IL)
Lipscomb U (TN)
Louisiana Coll (LA)
Lubbock Christian U (TX)
McNeese State U (LA)
MidAmerica Nazarene U (KS)
Missouri Baptist U (MO)
National U (CA)
North Carolina Wesleyan Coll (NC)
Ohio Christian U (OH)
Olympic Coll (WA)
Oral Roberts U (OK)
Point U (GA)
Providence Coll (RI)
Purdue U (IN)
Regent U (VA)
Saint Louis U (MO)
St. Thomas U (FL)
Salve Regina U (RI)
Samford U (AL)
Seattle U (WA)
Southeastern Louisiana U (LA)
Southeastern U (FL)
Southwestern Coll (KS)
Spring Hill Coll (AL)
Syracuse U (NY)
Toccoa Falls Coll (GA)
Trinity Coll of Florida (FL)
Union Inst & U (OH)
U of Dayton (OH)
U of Evansville (IN)
U of Houston (TX)
U of Louisiana at Monroe (LA)
U of Maine at Farmington (ME)
U of Northern Iowa (IA)
U of Wisconsin–Platteville (WI)
Valdosta State U (GA)
Viterbo U (WI)
Western Kentucky U (KY)
Wheeling Jesuit U (WV)
Woodbury U (CA)
Wright State U (OH)
Wright State U–Lake Campus (OH)

ORNAMENTAL HORTICULTURE
California State U, Fresno (CA)
Delaware Valley U (PA)
Morrisville State Coll (NY)
The Ohio State U (OH)
Tarleton State U (TX)
Texas A&M U (TX)
U of Arkansas (AR)

ORTHOPTICS
St. Catherine U (MN)

ORTHOTICS/PROSTHETICS
Concordia U, St. Paul (MN)
St. Petersburg Coll (FL)
U of Washington (WA)

OUTDOOR EDUCATION
Huntington U (IN)
Liberty U (VA)
Messiah Coll (PA)
Murray State U (KY)
Northland Coll (WI)
Prescott Coll (AZ)
Sierra Nevada Coll (NV)
Toccoa Falls Coll (GA)
Unity Coll (ME)

PACIFIC AREA/PACIFIC RIM STUDIES
Central Washington U (WA)
Hawai`i Pacific U (HI)
U of Hawaii at Manoa (HI)

PACKAGING SCIENCE
Clemson U (SC)
Indiana State U (IN)
Michigan State U (MI)
U of Wisconsin–Stout (WI)

PAINTING
Adams State U (CO)
American Acad of Art (IL)
Anderson U (SC)
Aquinas Coll (MI)
Arcadia U (PA)
Bennington Coll (VT)
Biola U (CA)
Boston U (MA)
Bowling Green State U (OH)
Bradley U (IL)
Brigham Young U (UT)
Buffalo State Coll, State U of New York (NY)
California Coll of the Arts (CA)
California State U, East Bay (CA)
California State U, Long Beach (CA)
Carson-Newman U (TN)
Central Washington U (WA)
Cleveland Inst of Art (OH)
Coe Coll (IA)
Coll of the Ozarks (MO)
Colorado State U (CO)
Columbia Coll (MO)
Concordia U (QC, Canada)
Dixie State U (UT)
Drake U (IA)
Emily Carr U of Art + Design (BC, Canada)
Escuela de Artes Plasticas y Dise&nno de Puerto Rico (PR)
Ferris State U (MI)
Harding U (AR)
Hofstra U (NY)
Inter American U of Puerto Rico, San Germán Campus (PR)
Kansas City Art Inst (MO)
Laguna Coll of Art & Design (CA)
Lewis U (IL)
Maryland Inst Coll of Art (MD)
Marywood U (PA)
Massachusetts Coll of Art and Design (MA)
Memphis Coll of Art (TN)
Milwaukee Inst of Art and Design (WI)
Minneapolis Coll of Art and Design (MN)
Pacific Northwest Coll of Art (OR)
Pratt Inst (NY)
Providence Coll (RI)
Rhode Island Coll (RI)
Rhode Island School of Design (RI)
Rochester Inst of Technology (NY)
Rutgers U–New Brunswick (NJ)
St. Ambrose U (IA)
Salve Regina U (RI)
San Francisco Art Inst (CA)
Sarah Lawrence Coll (NY)
Savannah Coll of Art and Design (GA)
School of the Art Inst of Chicago (IL)
Seton Hill U (PA)
State U of New York at New Paltz (NY)
Syracuse U (NY)
Temple U (PA)
Texas Christian U (TX)
U of Hartford (CT)
U of Houston (TX)
U of Illinois at Chicago (IL)
The U of Kansas (KS)
U of Massachusetts Dartmouth (MA)
U of Miami (FL)
U of New Haven (CT)
U of Oregon (OR)
U of Regina (SK, Canada)
U of San Francisco (CA)
The U of Tampa (FL)
The U of the Arts (PA)
U of Washington (WA)
U of Windsor (ON, Canada)
Virginia Commonwealth U (VA)
Washington U in St. Louis (MO)
Western State Colorado U (CO)
Western Washington U (WA)
West Virginia Wesleyan Coll (WV)
Youngstown State U (OH)

PALEONTOLOGY
Bowling Green State U (OH)

PALLIATIVE CARE NURSING
Madonna U (MI)

PAPER SCIENCE AND ENGINEERING
U of Wisconsin–Stevens Point (WI)
Western Michigan U (MI)

PARASITOLOGY
Bowling Green State U (OH)

PARKS, RECREATION AND LEISURE
Alaska Pacific U (AK)
Alcorn State U (MS)
Arizona State U at the Downtown Phoenix campus (AZ)
Asbury U (KY)
Aurora U (IL)
Bemidji State U (MN)
Bethune-Cookman U (FL)
Biola U (CA)
Black Hills State U (SD)
Bowling Green State U (OH)
Bridgewater State U (MA)
California Polytechnic State U, San Luis Obispo (CA)
California State U, Chico (CA)
California State U, East Bay (CA)
California State U, Fresno (CA)
California State U, Long Beach (CA)
California State U, Northridge (CA)
California State U, Sacramento (CA)
Campbellsville U (KY)
Catawba Coll (NC)
Central Michigan U (MI)
Central State U (OH)
Concordia U (QC, Canada)
Dalhousie U (NS, Canada)
East Carolina U (NC)
East Central U (OK)
Eastern Washington U (WA)
Elon U (NC)
Emporia State U (KS)
Evangel U (MO)
Fort Lewis Coll (CO)
Frostburg State U (MD)
Georgia Coll & State U (GA)
Georgia Southern U (GA)
Gordon Coll (MA)
Graceland U (IA)
Grambling State U (LA)
Green Mountain Coll (VT)
Houghton Coll (NY)
Humboldt State U (CA)
Huntington U (IN)
Indiana U Bloomington (IN)
Ithaca Coll (NY)
Jacksonville State U (AL)
Kutztown U of Pennsylvania (PA)
Limestone Coll (SC)
Lindenwood U (MO)
Lindsey Wilson Coll (KY)
Manchester U (IN)
Messiah Coll (PA)
Metropolitan State U of Denver (CO)
Michigan State U (MI)
Minnesota State U Mankato (MN)
Missouri State U (MO)
Missouri Valley Coll (MO)
Morris Coll (SC)
Newberry Coll (SC)
New England Coll (NH)
New Mexico Highlands U (NM)
Northern Arizona U (AZ)
North Greenville U (SC)
The Ohio State U (OH)
Ohio U (OH)
Oklahoma Baptist U (OK)
Oklahoma State U (OK)
Olivet Nazarene U (IL)
Oregon State U (OR)
Pittsburg State U (KS)

Radford U (VA)
Rhode Island Coll (RI)
St. Andrews U (NC)
St. Thomas Aquinas Coll (NY)
Salisbury U (MD)
San Diego State U (CA)
San Francisco State U (CA)
Shaw U (NC)
Shepherd U (WV)
Shorter U (GA)
Simpson U (CA)
Southeastern Oklahoma State U (OK)
Southeast Missouri State U (MO)
Southern Connecticut State U (CT)
Southern Illinois U Carbondale (IL)
Southern Utah U (UT)
Southwest Baptist U (MO)
State U of New York Coll at Cortland (NY)
Tennessee State U (TN)
Texas A&M U (TX)
U of Arkansas (AR)
U of Central Missouri (MO)
U of Georgia (GA)
U of Minnesota, Duluth (MN)
U of Minnesota, Twin Cities Campus (MN)
U of Nebraska at Kearney (NE)
U of Nevada, Las Vegas (NV)
The U of North Carolina at Greensboro (NC)
U of Northern Iowa (IA)
U of South Alabama (AL)
The U of South Dakota (SD)
U of Southern Mississippi (MS)
U of Utah (UT)
U of Waterloo (ON, Canada)
Upper Iowa U (IA)
Utah State U (UT)
Virginia Wesleyan Coll (VA)
Washington State U (WA)
Western State Colorado U (CO)
Western Washington U (WA)
Wingate U (NC)
York Coll of Pennsylvania (PA)

PARKS, RECREATION AND LEISURE FACILITIES MANAGEMENT
Appalachian State U (NC)
Arkansas Tech U (AR)
Belmont Abbey Coll (NC)
Brigham Young U–Idaho (ID)
California State U, Fresno (CA)
California State U, Sacramento (CA)
California U of Pennsylvania (PA)
Central Michigan U (MI)
Central Washington U (WA)
Clemson U (SC)
The Coll at Brockport, State U of New York (NY)
Coll of the Ozarks (MO)
Colorado State U (CO)
Concord U (WV)
Eastern Illinois U (IL)
Eastern Michigan U (MI)
Eastern Washington U (WA)
East Stroudsburg U of Pennsylvania (PA)
Florida Intl U (FL)
Franklin Pierce U (NH)
Hannibal-LaGrange U (MO)
Henderson State U (AR)
Humboldt State U (CA)
Husson U (ME)
Illinois State U (IL)
Indiana State U (IN)
Kansas State U (KS)
Kean U (NJ)
Kent State U (OH)
Lock Haven U of Pennsylvania (PA)
Marshall U (WV)
Minnesota State U Mankato (MN)
Missouri Valley Coll (MO)
Missouri Western State U (MO)
Mount Marty Coll (SD)
New England Coll (NH)
New Mexico Highlands U (NM)
North Carolina Central U (NC)
North Carolina State U (NC)
Northwest Missouri State U (MO)
Old Dominion U (VA)
Oral Roberts U (OK)
Penn State Abington (PA)
Penn State Altoona (PA)
Penn State Beaver (PA)
Penn State Berks (PA)
Penn State Brandywine (PA)
Penn State DuBois (PA)
Penn State Erie, The Behrend Coll (PA)
Penn State Fayette, The Eberly Campus (PA)
Penn State Greater Allegheny (PA)
Penn State Hazleton (PA)
Penn State Lehigh Valley (PA)
Penn State Mont Alto (PA)
Penn State New Kensington (PA)
Penn State Schuylkill (PA)
Penn State Shenango (PA)
Penn State U Park (PA)
Penn State Wilkes-Barre (PA)
Penn State Worthington Scranton (PA)
Penn State York (PA)
St. Joseph's Coll, Long Island Campus (NY)
St. Joseph's Coll, New York (NY)
Slippery Rock U of Pennsylvania (PA)
South Dakota State U (SD)
State U of New York Coll at Cortland (NY)
Texas A&M U (TX)
Texas State U (TX)
Thomas U (GA)
Trine U (IN)
Union Coll (KY)
Union U (TN)
U of Delaware (DE)
U of Florida (FL)
U of Idaho (ID)
U of Maine (ME)
U of Minnesota, Crookston (MN)
U of New Hampshire (NH)
The U of North Carolina Wilmington (NC)
U of North Dakota (ND)
U of Northern Colorado (CO)
U of North Texas (TX)
U of St. Francis (IL)
U of Vermont (VT)
U of Waterloo (ON, Canada)
U of West Georgia (GA)
U of Wisconsin–La Crosse (WI)
Wayland Baptist U (TX)
Western Carolina U (NC)
Western Illinois U (IL)
Western Kentucky U (KY)
Western Michigan U (MI)
Western State Colorado U (CO)
West Virginia State U (WV)
West Virginia U (WV)
Winona State U (MN)

PARKS, RECREATION AND LEISURE FACILITIES MANAGEMENT RELATED
Emmaus Bible Coll (IA)

PARKS, RECREATION, LEISURE, AND FITNESS STUDIES RELATED
Belhaven U (MS)
Brigham Young U (UT)
New England Coll (NH)
Plymouth State U (NH)
Trinity Christian Coll (IL)
U of North Alabama (AL)
U of Waterloo (ON, Canada)
Utah State U (UT)
Western State Colorado U (CO)

PASTORAL COUNSELING AND SPECIALIZED MINISTRIES RELATED
Bethel Coll (IN)
Brescia U (KY)
Calvary U (MO)
Davis Coll (NY)
John Brown U (AR)
Judson U (IL)
Lee U (TN)
Lipscomb U (TN)
Madonna U (MI)
Malone U (OH)
Maranatha Baptist U (WI)
Multnomah U (OR)
Nazarene Bible Coll (CO)
Ouachita Baptist U (AR)

PASTORAL STUDIES/ COUNSELING
The Baptist Coll of Florida (FL)
Barclay Coll (KS)
Biola U (CA)
Calvary U (MO)
Campbellsville U (KY)
Concordia U Wisconsin (WI)
Corban U (OR)
Davis Coll (NY)
Dominican U (IL)
Eastern Nazarene Coll (MA)
East Texas Baptist U (TX)
Emmanuel Coll (GA)
Faith Baptist Bible Coll and Theological Sem (IA)
Gardner-Webb U (NC)
George Fox U (OR)
Greenville Coll (IL)
Houghton Coll (NY)
Johnson U Florida (FL)
John Wesley U (NC)
Kentucky Mountain Bible Coll (KY)
Kuyper Coll (MI)
Lee U (TN)
Liberty U (VA)
Louisiana Coll (LA)
Loyola U Chicago (IL)
Maranatha Baptist U (WI)
Marian U (IN)
The Master's U (CA)
Messenger Coll (TX)
MidAmerica Nazarene U (KS)
Milligan Coll (TN)
Mount St. Joseph U (OH)
Mount Vernon Nazarene U (OH)
Multnomah U (OR)
Newman U (KS)
Northwest Christian U (OR)
Northwest U (WA)
Olivet Nazarene U (IL)
Oral Roberts U (OK)
Ouachita Baptist U (AR)
Providence Coll (RI)
Saint Francis U (PA)
St. Gregory's U, Shawnee (OK)
St. Thomas U (FL)
Simpson U (CA)
Southwest Baptist U (MO)
Southwestern Assemblies of God U (TX)
Theological U of the Caribbean (PR)
Trinity Baptist Coll (FL)
Trinity Coll of Florida (FL)
U of Mary Hardin-Baylor (TX)
U of Saint Mary (KS)
U of St. Thomas (TX)
U of the Incarnate Word (TX)
U of Valley Forge (PA)
Walsh U (OH)
Welch Coll (TN)
Williams Baptist Coll (AR)

PATHOLOGIST ASSISTANT
Wayne State U (MI)

PATHOLOGY/EXPERIMENTAL PATHOLOGY
Penn State Berks (PA)

PEACE STUDIES AND CONFLICT RESOLUTION
Bennington Coll (VT)
Bethel U (MN)
Butler U (IN)
California State U, Dominguez Hills (CA)
Chapman U (CA)
Clark U (MA)
Colgate U (NY)
Coll of Saint Benedict (MN)
The Coll of St. Scholastica (MN)
Creighton U (NE)
DePauw U (IN)
Earlham Coll (IN)
Eastern Mennonite U (VA)
Gettysburg Coll (PA)
Goddard Coll (VT)
Goshen Coll (IN)
Goucher Coll (MD)
Guilford Coll (NC)
Hamline U (MN)
Hampshire Coll (MA)
Haverford Coll (PA)
John Carroll U (OH)
Juniata Coll (PA)
Kent State U (OH)
Manchester U (IN)
Manhattan Coll (NY)
Messiah Coll (PA)
Nazareth Coll of Rochester (NY)
Pace U (NY)
Regis U (CO)
Saint Anselm Coll (NH)
Saint John's U (MN)
Salisbury U (MD)
Swarthmore Coll (PA)
Tufts U (MA)
U of Massachusetts Lowell (MA)
The U of North Carolina at Chapel Hill (NC)
The U of North Carolina at Greensboro (NC)
U of St. Thomas (MN)
U of Toronto (ON, Canada)
U of Utah (UT)
U of Wisconsin–Superior (WI)
Ursinus Coll (PA)
Wartburg Coll (IA)
Whitworth U (WA)
Willamette U (OR)

PEDIATRIC NURSING
Youngstown State U (OH)

PERCUSSION INSTRUMENTS
Central Washington U (WA)
Eastern Nazarene Coll (MA)
Houghton Coll (NY)
Lawrence U (WI)
Mount Allison U (NB, Canada)
Northwestern U (IL)
Oberlin Coll (OH)
Oklahoma Christian U (OK)
San Francisco Conservatory of Music (CA)
State U of New York at Fredonia (NY)
Syracuse U (NY)
The U of Kansas (KS)
U of Southern California (CA)
U of Washington (WA)
Vanderbilt U (TN)
Xavier U of Louisiana (LA)
Youngstown State U (OH)

PERFUSION TECHNOLOGY
Carlow U (PA)

PERSONALITY PSYCHOLOGY
Goddard Coll (VT)
Pace U, Pleasantville Campus (NY)

PETROLEUM ENGINEERING
The American U in Cairo (Egypt)
Colorado School of Mines (CO)
Lebanese American U (Lebanon)
Louisiana State U and A&M Coll (LA)
Marietta Coll (OH)
Missouri U of Science and Technology (MO)
Montana Tech of The U of Montana (MT)
New Mexico Inst of Mining and Technology (NM)
Penn State Abington (PA)
Penn State Altoona (PA)
Penn State Beaver (PA)
Penn State Berks (PA)
Penn State Brandywine (PA)
Penn State DuBois (PA)
Penn State Erie, The Behrend Coll (PA)
Penn State Fayette, The Eberly Campus (PA)
Penn State Greater Allegheny (PA)
Penn State Hazleton (PA)
Penn State Lehigh Valley (PA)
Penn State Mont Alto (PA)
Penn State New Kensington (PA)
Penn State Schuylkill (PA)
Penn State Shenango (PA)
Penn State U Park (PA)
Penn State Wilkes-Barre (PA)
Penn State Worthington Scranton (PA)
Penn State York (PA)
Saint Francis U (PA)
Slippery Rock U of Pennsylvania (PA)
Stanford U (CA)
Texas A&M U (TX)
Texas A&M U–Kingsville (TX)
Texas Tech U (TX)
U of Alaska Fairbanks (AK)
U of Houston (TX)
The U of Kansas (KS)
U of North Dakota (ND)
U of Oklahoma (OK)
U of Regina (SK, Canada)
The U of Texas at Austin (TX)
The U of Texas of the Permian Basin (TX)
U of Toronto (ON, Canada)
The U of Tulsa (OK)
West Virginia U (WV)

PETROLEUM TECHNOLOGY
American U of Beirut (Lebanon)
Mercyhurst U (PA)
Muskingum U (OH)

PHARMACEUTICAL MARKETING AND MANAGEMENT
DeSales U (PA)
Western New England U (MA)

PHARMACEUTICAL SCIENCES
Belmont U (TN)
Cedarville U (OH)
Cleveland State U (OH)
Duquesne U (PA)
Lebanese American U (Lebanon)
Université de Montréal (QC, Canada)
U of California, Irvine (CA)
U of Georgia (GA)
U of Michigan (MI)
U of Pittsburgh (PA)
The U of Texas at Austin (TX)
West Virginia Wesleyan Coll (WV)

PHARMACEUTICS AND DRUG DESIGN
The Ohio State U (OH)
Purdue U (IN)
Temple U (PA)
U of Rhode Island (RI)
The U of Toledo (OH)
West Chester U of Pennsylvania (PA)

PHARMACOLOGY
Georgia Southern U (GA)
McMaster U (ON, Canada)
Stony Brook U, State U of New York (NY)
U of California, Santa Barbara (CA)
U of Saskatchewan (SK, Canada)

PHARMACOLOGY AND TOXICOLOGY
U at Buffalo, the State U of New York (NY)
U of Wisconsin–Madison (WI)

PHARMACOLOGY AND TOXICOLOGY RELATED
The George Washington U (DC)
MCPHS U (MA)
Mount Ida Coll (MA)
U at Buffalo, the State U of New York (NY)

PHARMACY
Butler U (IN)
The Coll of Idaho (ID)
Dalhousie U (NS, Canada)
Drake U (IA)
Eastern Nazarene Coll (MA)
Manchester U (IN)
MCPHS U (MA)
Northeastern U (MA)
The Ohio State U (OH)
St. John's U (NY)
Saint Vincent Coll (PA)
Samford U (AL)
South Dakota State U (SD)
Université de Montréal (QC, Canada)
U of Cincinnati (OH)
U of Delaware (DE)
U of Georgia (GA)
The U of Kansas (KS)
U of Kentucky (KY)
U of Louisiana at Monroe (LA)
U of Oklahoma Health Sciences Center (OK)
U of Saskatchewan (SK, Canada)
The U of Texas at Austin (TX)
U of the Pacific (CA)
The U of Toledo (OH)
U of Toronto (ON, Canada)
Washington State U (WA)
Washington State U–Spokane (WA)

PHARMACY ADMINISTRATION AND PHARMACY POLICY AND REGULATORY AFFAIRS
Drake U (IA)
U of Michigan (MI)

PHARMACY, PHARMACEUTICAL SCIENCES, AND ADMINISTRATION RELATED
Dalhousie U (NS, Canada)
Duquesne U (PA)
Francis Marion U (SC)
MCPHS U (MA)
North Dakota State U (ND)

PHILOSOPHY
Adelphi U (NY)
Agnes Scott Coll (GA)
Albertus Magnus Coll (CT)
Albion Coll (MI)
Albright Coll (PA)
Alfred U (NY)
Allegheny Coll (PA)
Alma Coll (MI)
Alvernia U (PA)
Alverno Coll (WI)
American Public U System (WV)
American U (DC)
The American U in Cairo (Egypt)
American U of Beirut (Lebanon)
The American U of Paris (France)
Amherst Coll (MA)
Angelo State U (TX)
Antioch Coll, Yellow Springs (OH)
Appalachian State U (NC)
Aquinas Coll (MI)
Aquinas Coll (TN)
Arcadia U (PA)
Arizona State U at the Tempe campus (AZ)
Asbury U (KY)
Ashland U (OH)
Assumption Coll (MA)
Auburn U (AL)
Augsburg Coll (MN)
Augustana Coll (IL)
Augustana U (SD)
Aurora U (IL)
Austin Coll (TX)
Austin Peay State U (TN)
Azusa Pacific U (CA)
Baker U (KS)
Baldwin Wallace U (OH)
Ball State U (IN)
Bard Coll (NY)
Barnard Coll (NY)
Barry U (FL)
Baruch Coll of the City U of New York (NY)
Bates Coll (ME)
Bayamón Central U (PR)
Baylor U (TX)
Belhaven U (MS)
Bellarmine U (KY)
Belmont U (TN)
Beloit Coll (WI)
Bemidji State U (MN)
Benedictine Coll (KS)
Bennington Coll (VT)
Bentley U (MA)
Berea Coll (KY)
Bethel Coll (IN)
Bethel U (MN)
Binghamton U, State U of New York (NY)
Biola U (CA)
Bishop's U (QC, Canada)
Bloomfield Coll (NJ)
Bloomsburg U of Pennsylvania (PA)
Boise State U (ID)
Boston Coll (MA)
Boston U (MA)
Bowdoin Coll (ME)
Bowling Green State U (OH)
Bradley U (IL)
Brandeis U (MA)
Bridgewater State U (MA)
Brooklyn Coll of the City U of New York (NY)
Bryn Mawr Coll (PA)
Bucknell U (PA)
Buffalo State Coll, State U of New York (NY)
Butler U (IN)
Cabrini U (PA)
California Baptist U (CA)
California Inst of Technology (CA)
California Lutheran U (CA)
California Polytechnic State U, San Luis Obispo (CA)
California State Polytechnic U, Pomona (CA)
California State U, Bakersfield (CA)
California State U, Chico (CA)
California State U, Dominguez Hills (CA)
California State U, East Bay (CA)
California State U, Fresno (CA)
California State U, Fullerton (CA)
California State U, Long Beach (CA)
California State U, Northridge (CA)
California State U, Sacramento (CA)
California State U, San Bernardino (CA)
California State U, Stanislaus (CA)
California U of Pennsylvania (PA)
Calvin Coll (MI)
Canisius Coll (NY)
Capital U (OH)
Carleton Coll (MN)
Carlow U (PA)
Carnegie Mellon U (PA)
Carroll Coll (MT)
Carson-Newman U (TN)
Carthage Coll (WI)
Case Western Reserve U (OH)
The Catholic U of America (DC)
Centenary Coll of Louisiana (LA)
Central Connecticut State U (CT)
Central Methodist U (MO)
Central Michigan U (MI)
Centre Coll (KY)
Chapman U (CA)
Christendom Coll (VA)
Christopher Newport U (VA)
City Coll of the City U of New York (NY)
Claremont McKenna Coll (CA)
Clarion U of Pennsylvania (PA)
Clark Atlanta U (GA)
Clarke U (IA)
Clark U (MA)
Clayton State U (GA)
Clemson U (SC)
Cleveland State U (OH)
Coastal Carolina U (SC)
Coe Coll (IA)
Colby Coll (ME)
Colgate U (NY)
The Coll at Brockport, State U of New York (NY)
Coll of Charleston (SC)
The Coll of Idaho (ID)
Coll of Mount Saint Vincent (NY)
The Coll of New Jersey (NJ)
Coll of Saint Benedict (MN)
The Coll of St. Scholastica (MN)
Coll of Staten Island of the City U of New York (NY)
Coll of the Atlantic (ME)
Coll of the Holy Cross (MA)
The Coll of William and Mary (VA)
The Coll of Wooster (OH)
The Colorado Coll (CO)
Colorado State U (CO)
Columbia Coll (MO)
Columbia U (NY)
Columbia U, School of General Studies (NY)
Concordia Coll (MN)
Concordia Coll–New York (NY)
Concordia U (QC, Canada)
Concordia U Chicago (IL)
Connecticut Coll (CT)
Converse Coll (SC)
Cornell Coll (IA)
Cornell U (NY)
Creighton U (NE)
Curry Coll (MA)
Dalhousie U (NS, Canada)
Dallas Baptist U (TX)
Dartmouth Coll (NH)
Davidson Coll (NC)
Denison U (OH)
DePauw U (IN)
DEREE - The American Coll of Greece (Greece)
DeSales U (PA)
Dickinson Coll (PA)
Doane U (NE)
Dominican U (IL)
Drake U (IA)
Drew U (NJ)
Drexel U (PA)
Drury U (MO)
Duquesne U (PA)
Earlham Coll (IN)
East Carolina U (NC)
Eastern Illinois U (IL)
Eastern Michigan U (MI)
Eastern U (PA)
Eastern Washington U (WA)
East Stroudsburg U of Pennsylvania (PA)
East Tennessee State U (TN)
Eckerd Coll (FL)
Elizabethtown Coll (PA)
Elon U (NC)
Emmanuel Coll (MA)
Emory & Henry Coll (VA)
Emory U (GA)
Eugene Lang Coll of Liberal Arts (NY)
The Evergreen State Coll (WA)
Fairfield U (CT)
Fairleigh Dickinson U, Coll at Florham (NJ)
Fairleigh Dickinson U, Metropolitan Campus (NJ)
Felician U (NJ)
Florida Atlantic U (FL)
Florida Gulf Coast U (FL)
Florida Intl U (FL)
Florida Southern Coll (FL)
Fordham U (NY)
Fort Lewis Coll (CO)
Franciscan U of Steubenville (OH)
Franklin & Marshall Coll (PA)
Franklin Coll (IN)
Freed-Hardeman U (TN)
Frostburg State U (MD)
Furman U (SC)
Gallaudet U (DC)
Gannon U (PA)
Geneva Coll (PA)
George Fox U (OR)
Georgetown Coll (KY)
Georgetown U (DC)
The George Washington U (DC)
Georgia Coll & State U (GA)
Georgia Southern U (GA)
Georgia State U (GA)
Gettysburg Coll (PA)
Gonzaga U (WA)
Gordon Coll (MA)
Goucher Coll (MD)
Grand Valley State U (MI)
Green Mountain Coll (VT)
Greenville Coll (IL)
Grinnell Coll (IA)
Grove City Coll (PA)
Guilford Coll (NC)
Gwynedd Mercy U (PA)
Hamilton Coll (NY)
Hamline U (MN)
Hampden-Sydney Coll (VA)
Hampshire Coll (MA)
Hanover Coll (IN)
Hardin-Simmons U (TX)
Hartwick Coll (NY)
Harvard U (MA)
Haverford Coll (PA)
Heidelberg U (OH)
Hendrix Coll (AR)
High Point U (NC)
Hillsdale Coll (MI)
Hiram Coll (OH)
Hobart and William Smith Colls (NY)
Hofstra U (NY)
Hollins U (VA)
Holy Names U (CA)
Hood Coll (MD)
Hope Coll (MI)
Houghton Coll (NY)
Houston Baptist U (TX)
Howard Payne U (TX)
Humboldt State U (CA)
Hunter Coll of the City U of New York (NY)
Huntington U (IN)
Idaho State U (ID)
Illinois Coll (IL)
Illinois State U (IL)
Illinois Wesleyan U (IL)
Indiana State U (IN)
Indiana U Bloomington (IN)
Indiana U Northwest (IN)
Indiana U of Pennsylvania (PA)
Indiana U–Purdue U Indianapolis (IN)
Indiana U South Bend (IN)
Indiana U Southeast (IN)
Iona Coll (NY)
Iowa State U of Science and Technology (IA)
Ithaca Coll (NY)
Jacksonville U (FL)
John Brown U (AR)
John Carroll U (OH)
John Jay Coll of Criminal Justice of the City U of New York (NY)
Johns Hopkins U (MD)
Juniata Coll (PA)
Kalamazoo Coll (MI)
Kansas State U (KS)
Kansas Wesleyan U (KS)
Kennesaw State U (GA)
Kent State U (OH)
Kenyon Coll (OH)
King's Coll (PA)
The King's U (AB, Canada)
King U (TN)
Knox Coll (IL)
Kutztown U of Pennsylvania (PA)
Lafayette Coll (PA)
Lake Forest Coll (IL)
La Salle U (PA)
Lawrence U (WI)
Lebanese American U (Lebanon)
Lebanon Valley Coll (PA)
Lee U (TN)
Lehigh U (PA)
Lehman Coll of the City U of New York (NY)
Le Moyne Coll (NY)
Lenoir-Rhyne U (NC)
Lewis & Clark Coll (OR)
Lewis U (IL)
Liberty U (VA)
Lincoln Christian U (IL)
Lincoln U (PA)
Lindenwood U (MO)
Linfield Coll (OR)
Lipscomb U (TN)
Lock Haven U of Pennsylvania (PA)
Loras Coll (IA)
Louisiana Coll (LA)
Louisiana State U and A&M Coll (LA)
Loyola Marymount U (CA)
Loyola U Chicago (IL)
Loyola U Maryland (MD)
Loyola U New Orleans (LA)
Luther Coll (IA)
Lycoming Coll (PA)
Lynchburg Coll (VA)
Macalester Coll (MN)
Malone U (OH)
Manchester U (IN)
Manhattan Coll (NY)
Manhattanville Coll (NY)
Mansfield U of Pennsylvania (PA)
Marian U (IN)
Marietta Coll (OH)
Marist Coll (NY)
Marymount U (VA)
Marywood U (PA)
Massachusetts Coll of Liberal Arts (MA)
Massachusetts Inst of Technology (MA)
McDaniel Coll (MD)
McKendree U (IL)
McMaster U (ON, Canada)
Mercer U, Macon (GA)
Mercyhurst U (PA)
Merrimack Coll (MA)
Messiah Coll (PA)
Metropolitan State U of Denver (CO)
Miami U (OH)
Michigan State U (MI)
Middlebury Coll (VT)
Millersville U of Pennsylvania (PA)
Millikin U (IL)
Millsaps Coll (MS)
Mills Coll (CA)
Minnesota State U Mankato (MN)
Minnesota State U Moorhead (MN)
Misericordia U (PA)
Mississippi State U (MS)
Missouri State U (MO)
Missouri U of Science and Technology (MO)
Missouri Valley Coll (MO)
Missouri Western State U (MO)
Molloy Coll (NY)
Monmouth Coll (IL)
Montana State U (MT)
Montclair State U (NJ)
Moravian Coll (PA)
Morehead State U (KY)
Morehouse Coll (GA)
Morningside Coll (IA)
Mount Allison U (NB, Canada)
Mount Holyoke Coll (MA)
Mount Mary U (WI)
Mount Mercy U (IA)
Mount Saint Mary's U (CA)
Mount St. Mary's U (MD)
Mount Vernon Nazarene U (OH)
Muhlenberg Coll (PA)
Muskingum U (OH)
Nazareth Coll of Rochester (NY)
Nebraska Wesleyan U (NE)
New Coll of Florida (FL)
New England Coll (NH)
New Jersey City U (NJ)
Newman U (KS)
New Mexico State U (NM)
Niagara U (NY)
North Carolina State U (NC)
North Central Coll (IL)
North Dakota State U (ND)
Northeastern Illinois U (IL)
Northeastern U (MA)
Northern Arizona U (AZ)
Northern Illinois U (IL)
Northern Kentucky U (KY)
Northwestern Coll (IA)
Northwestern U (IL)
Northwest Missouri State U (MO)
Northwest U (WA)
Nova Southeastern U (FL)
Nyack Coll (NY)
Oberlin Coll (OH)
Occidental Coll (CA)
Ohio Dominican U (OH)
The Ohio State U (OH)
Ohio U (OH)
Ohio Wesleyan U (OH)
Oklahoma Baptist U (OK)
Oklahoma City U (OK)
Oklahoma State U (OK)
Old Dominion U (VA)
Olivet Nazarene U (IL)
Oregon State U (OR)
Otterbein U (OH)
Ouachita Baptist U (AR)
Pacific Lutheran U (WA)
Paine Coll (GA)
Palm Beach Atlantic U (FL)
Penn State Abington (PA)
Penn State Altoona (PA)
Penn State Beaver (PA)
Penn State Berks (PA)
Penn State Brandywine (PA)
Penn State DuBois (PA)
Penn State Erie, The Behrend Coll (PA)
Penn State Fayette, The Eberly Campus (PA)
Penn State Greater Allegheny (PA)
Penn State Hazleton (PA)
Penn State Lehigh Valley (PA)
Penn State Mont Alto (PA)
Penn State New Kensington (PA)
Penn State Schuylkill (PA)
Penn State Shenango (PA)
Penn State U Park (PA)
Penn State Wilkes-Barre (PA)
Penn State Worthington Scranton (PA)
Penn State York (PA)
Pepperdine U, Malibu (CA)
Piedmont Coll (GA)
Pitzer Coll (CA)
Plymouth State U (NH)
Point Loma Nazarene U (CA)
Pomona Coll (CA)
Portland State U (OR)
Princeton U (NJ)
Principia Coll (IL)
Providence Coll (RI)
Purchase Coll, State U of New York (NY)
Purdue U (IN)
Purdue U Northwest (IN)
Queens Coll of the City U of New York (NY)
Quinnipiac U (CT)

Randolph Coll (VA)
Randolph-Macon Coll (VA)
Redeemer U Coll (ON, Canada)
Reed Coll (OR)
Regis U (CO)
Rensselaer Polytechnic Inst (NY)
Rhode Island Coll (RI)
Rhodes Coll (TN)
Rice U (TX)
Ripon Coll (WI)
Roanoke Coll (VA)
Rochester Inst of Technology (NY)
Rockford U (IL)
Rockhurst U (MO)
Roger Williams U (RI)
Rollins Coll (FL)
Rosemont Coll (PA)
Rutgers U–Camden (NJ)
Rutgers U–Newark (NJ)
Rutgers U–New Brunswick (NJ)
Sacred Heart U (CT)
St. Ambrose U (IA)
Saint Anselm Coll (NH)
St. Bonaventure U (NY)
St. Catherine U (MN)
St. Cloud State U (MN)
St. Edward's U (TX)
Saint Francis U (PA)
St. Gregory's U, Shawnee (OK)
St. John Fisher Coll (NY)
Saint John's U (MN)
St. John's U (NY)
Saint Joseph's U (PA)
Saint Louis U (MO)
Saint Louis U–Madrid Campus (Spain)
Saint Mary's Coll (IN)
Saint Mary's Coll of California (CA)
St. Mary's Coll of Maryland (MD)
Saint Mary's U of Minnesota (MN)
Saint Michael's Coll (VT)
St. Norbert Coll (WI)
St. Olaf Coll (MN)
Saint Peter's U (NJ)
St. Thomas Aquinas Coll (NY)
St. Thomas U (NB, Canada)
Saint Vincent Coll (PA)
Salisbury U (MD)
Salve Regina U (RI)
Samford U (AL)
Sam Houston State U (TX)
San Diego State U (CA)
San Francisco State U (CA)
Santa Clara U (CA)
Sarah Lawrence Coll (NY)
Scripps Coll (CA)
Seattle Pacific U (WA)
Seattle U (WA)
Sewanee: The U of the South (TN)
Siena Coll (NY)
Simmons Coll (MA)
Simon Fraser U (BC, Canada)
Simpson Coll (IA)
Skidmore Coll (NY)
Slippery Rock U of Pennsylvania (PA)
Smith Coll (MA)
Sonoma State U (CA)
Southeast Missouri State U (MO)
Southern Connecticut State U (CT)
Southern Illinois U Carbondale (IL)
Southern Illinois U Edwardsville (IL)
Southern Methodist U (TX)
Southern Utah U (UT)
Southwestern U (TX)
Spelman Coll (GA)
Spring Hill Coll (AL)
Stanford U (CA)
State U of New York at Fredonia (NY)
State U of New York at New Paltz (NY)
State U of New York at Oswego (NY)
State U of New York at Plattsburgh (NY)
State U of New York Coll at Cortland (NY)
State U of New York Coll at Geneseo (NY)
State U of New York Coll at Old Westbury (NY)
State U of New York Coll at Potsdam (NY)
Stephen F. Austin State U (TX)
Stevens Inst of Technology (NJ)
Stonehill Coll (MA)
Stony Brook U, State U of New York (NY)
Suffolk U (MA)
Susquehanna U (PA)
Swarthmore Coll (PA)
Sweet Briar Coll (VA)
Syracuse U (NY)
Taylor U (IN)
Temple U (PA)
Texas A&M U (TX)
Texas Christian U (TX)
Texas Lutheran U (TX)
Texas State U (TX)
Texas Tech U (TX)
Thomas More Coll (KY)
Toccoa Falls Coll (GA)
Towson U (MD)
Transylvania U (KY)
Trent U (ON, Canada)
Trinity Christian Coll (IL)
Trinity U (TX)
Tufts U (MA)
Tulane U (LA)
Union Coll (NY)
Union U (TN)
United States Air Force Acad (CO)
United States Military Acad (NY)
Université de Montréal (QC, Canada)
Université de Sherbrooke (QC, Canada)
U at Albany, State U of New York (NY)
U at Buffalo, the State U of New York (NY)
The U of Akron (OH)
The U of Alabama (AL)
The U of Alabama at Birmingham (AL)
The U of Alabama in Huntsville (AL)
U of Alaska Fairbanks (AK)
The U of Arizona (AZ)
U of Arkansas (AR)
U of California, Davis (CA)
U of California, Irvine (CA)
U of California, Los Angeles (CA)
U of California, Riverside (CA)
U of California, San Diego (CA)
U of California, Santa Barbara (CA)
U of Central Arkansas (AR)
U of Central Florida (FL)
U of Chicago (IL)
U of Cincinnati (OH)
U of Colorado Boulder (CO)
U of Colorado Colorado Springs (CO)
U of Colorado Denver (CO)
U of Dayton (OH)
U of Delaware (DE)
U of Denver (CO)
U of Detroit Mercy (MI)
U of Dubuque (IA)
U of Evansville (IN)
The U of Findlay (OH)
U of Florida (FL)
U of Georgia (GA)
U of Guelph (ON, Canada)
U of Hartford (CT)
U of Hawaii at Manoa (HI)
U of Houston (TX)
U of Houston–Downtown (TX)
U of Idaho (ID)
U of Illinois at Chicago (IL)
U of Illinois at Springfield (IL)
U of Indianapolis (IN)
The U of Kansas (KS)
U of Kentucky (KY)
U of King's Coll (NS, Canada)
U of La Verne (CA)
U of Lethbridge (AB, Canada)
U of Louisville (KY)
U of Maine (ME)
U of Maryland, Baltimore County (MD)
U of Maryland, Coll Park (MD)
U of Massachusetts Amherst (MA)
U of Massachusetts Boston (MA)
U of Massachusetts Dartmouth (MA)
U of Massachusetts Lowell (MA)
U of Miami (FL)
U of Michigan (MI)
U of Michigan–Dearborn (MI)
U of Michigan–Flint (MI)
U of Minnesota, Duluth (MN)
U of Minnesota, Morris (MN)
U of Minnesota, Twin Cities Campus (MN)
U of Missouri–Kansas City (MO)
U of Missouri–St. Louis (MO)
U of Mount Union (OH)
U of Nebraska at Kearney (NE)
U of Nevada, Las Vegas (NV)
U of Nevada, Reno (NV)
U of New Hampshire (NH)
U of New Orleans (LA)
U of North Carolina at Asheville (NC)
The U of North Carolina at Chapel Hill (NC)
The U of North Carolina at Charlotte (NC)
The U of North Carolina at Greensboro (NC)
U of North Dakota (ND)
U of Northern Colorado (CO)
U of Northern Iowa (IA)
U of North Florida (FL)
U of North Texas (TX)
U of Notre Dame (IN)
U of Oklahoma (OK)
U of Oregon (OR)
U of Pennsylvania (PA)
U of Pittsburgh (PA)
U of Puget Sound (WA)
U of Regina (SK, Canada)
U of Rhode Island (RI)
U of Richmond (VA)
U of Rochester (NY)
U of Saint Francis (IN)
U of Saint Joseph (CT)
U of St. Thomas (MN)
U of St. Thomas (TX)
U of San Diego (CA)
U of San Francisco (CA)
U of Saskatchewan (SK, Canada)
The U of Scranton (PA)
U of South Alabama (AL)
U of South Carolina (SC)
The U of South Dakota (SD)
U of Southern California (CA)
U of Southern Indiana (IN)
U of Southern Maine (ME)
U of Southern Mississippi (MS)
U of South Florida (FL)
The U of Tampa (FL)
The U of Tennessee (TN)
The U of Tennessee at Martin (TN)
The U of Texas at Austin (TX)
The U of Texas at El Paso (TX)
The U of Texas at San Antonio (TX)
The U of Texas Rio Grande Valley (TX)
U of the Fraser Valley (BC, Canada)
U of the Incarnate Word (TX)
U of the Pacific (CA)
The U of Toledo (OH)
The U of Tulsa (OK)
U of Utah (UT)
U of Vermont (VT)
U of Virginia (VA)
U of Washington (WA)
U of Waterloo (ON, Canada)
U of West Georgia (GA)
U of Windsor (ON, Canada)
U of Wisconsin–Eau Claire (WI)
U of Wisconsin–Green Bay (WI)
U of Wisconsin–La Crosse (WI)
U of Wisconsin–Madison (WI)
U of Wisconsin–Milwaukee (WI)
U of Wisconsin–Parkside (WI)
U of Wisconsin–Platteville (WI)
U of Wisconsin–Stevens Point (WI)
Ursinus Coll (PA)
Utah State U (UT)
Utah Valley U (UT)
Utica Coll (NY)
Valparaiso U (IN)
Vanderbilt U (TN)
Vassar Coll (NY)
Villanova U (PA)
Virginia Commonwealth U (VA)
Virginia Polytechnic Inst and State U (VA)
Virginia Wesleyan Coll (VA)
Viterbo U (WI)
Wabash Coll (IN)
Wagner Coll (NY)
Wake Forest U (NC)
Walla Walla U (WA)
Walsh U (OH)
Wartburg Coll (IA)
Washburn U (KS)
Washington & Jefferson Coll (PA)
Washington and Lee U (VA)
Washington Coll (MD)
Washington State U (WA)
Washington U in St. Louis (MO)
Wayne State U (MI)
Weber State U (UT)
Webster U (MO)
Wells Coll (NY)
Wesleyan U (CT)
West Chester U of Pennsylvania (PA)
Western Carolina U (NC)
Western Michigan U (MI)
Western New England U (MA)
Western Oregon U (OR)
Western Washington U (WA)
Westminster Coll (PA)
Westminster Coll (UT)
Westmont Coll (CA)
West Virginia U (WV)
West Virginia Wesleyan Coll (WV)
Wheaton Coll (IL)
Wheaton Coll (MA)
Wheeling Jesuit U (WV)
Whitman Coll (WA)
Whittier Coll (CA)
Whitworth U (WA)
Wichita State U (KS)
Wilkes U (PA)
Willamette U (OR)
William Jewell Coll (MO)
William Paterson U of New Jersey (NJ)
Williams Coll (MA)
Wilson Coll (PA)
Wittenberg U (OH)
Wofford Coll (SC)
Wright State U (OH)
Wright State U–Lake Campus (OH)
Xavier U of Louisiana (LA)
York Coll of Pennsylvania (PA)
York Coll of the City U of New York (NY)
Youngstown State U (OH)

PHILOSOPHY AND RELIGIOUS STUDIES
Arizona State U at the West campus (AZ)
Berry Coll (GA)
Bethune-Cookman U (FL)
Central Washington U (WA)
Christian Brothers U (TN)
Coll of the Ozarks (MO)
Concordia Coll–New York (NY)
Flagler Coll (FL)
Goddard Coll (VT)
Hillsdale Coll (MI)
LaGrange Coll (GA)
Marist Coll (NY)
Marymount Manhattan Coll (NY)
Muskingum U (OH)
Oklahoma City U (OK)
Pace U (NY)
Pace U, Pleasantville Campus (NY)
Point Loma Nazarene U (CA)
St. Andrews U (NC)
St. Joseph's Coll, Long Island Campus (NY)
St. Joseph's Coll, New York (NY)
Southwestern Coll (KS)
Stockton U (NJ)
U of Maine at Farmington (ME)
Valdosta State U (GA)

PHILOSOPHY AND RELIGIOUS STUDIES RELATED
Barton Coll (NC)
Berry Coll (GA)
Bethune-Cookman U (FL)
Bridgewater Coll (VA)
Butler U (IN)
Eastern Mennonite U (VA)
Eastern Nazarene Coll (MA)
Elmira Coll (NY)
Eureka Coll (IL)
Florida Ag and Mech U (FL)
Friends U (KS)
Graceland U (IA)
Hendrix Coll (AR)
Holy Names U (CA)
Iowa Wesleyan U (IA)
James Madison U (VA)
Juniata Coll (PA)
Lyon Coll (AR)
Millsaps Coll (MS)
Newberry Coll (SC)
Northwest U (WA)
Ouachita Baptist U (AR)
Radford U (VA)
Roberts Wesleyan Coll (NY)
Rocky Mountain Coll (MT)
Rowan U (NJ)
Samford U (AL)
San Francisco State U (CA)
Shawnee State U (OH)
Shaw U (NC)
State U of New York at Oswego (NY)
Sterling Coll (KS)
Syracuse U (NY)
Truman State U (MO)
Union U (TN)
U of Mary Washington (VA)
The U of North Carolina at Pembroke (NC)
The U of North Carolina Wilmington (NC)
U of Notre Dame (IN)
The U of Tennessee at Chattanooga (TN)
Ursinus Coll (PA)
Washington U in St. Louis (MO)
West Virginia Wesleyan Coll (WV)
William Jewell Coll (MO)
Winthrop U (SC)

PHILOSOPHY RELATED
Butler U (IN)
Coll of Staten Island of the City U of New York (NY)
Lewis U (IL)
Loyola U New Orleans (LA)
Mount Vernon Nazarene U (OH)
The U of Arizona (AZ)
U of Massachusetts Boston (MA)
U of Pennsylvania (PA)
U of Southern California (CA)
Washington U in St. Louis (MO)

PHOTOGRAPHIC AND FILM/VIDEO TECHNOLOGY
Coll of the Ozarks (MO)
Husson U (ME)
Rochester Inst of Technology (NY)
St. John's U (NY)
Wilmington U (DE)

PHOTOGRAPHY
Adams State U (CO)
Albertus Magnus Coll (CT)
American Acad of Art (IL)
Aquinas Coll (MI)
Arcadia U (PA)
Bard Coll (NY)
Barry U (FL)
Bennington Coll (VT)
Bowling Green State U (OH)
Bradley U (IL)
Bridgewater State U (MA)
Buffalo State Coll, State U of New York (NY)
California Baptist U (CA)
California Coll of the Arts (CA)
California State U, East Bay (CA)
California State U, Long Beach (CA)
California State U, Sacramento (CA)
Calvary U (MO)
Cardinal Stritch U (WI)
Carson-Newman U (TN)
Cazenovia Coll (NY)
Central Washington U (WA)
Chatham U (PA)
Cleveland Inst of Art (OH)
Coe Coll (IA)
Colorado State U (CO)
Columbia Coll (MO)
Columbia Coll Chicago (IL)
Columbus Coll of Art & Design (OH)
Concordia U (QC, Canada)
Concordia U Wisconsin (WI)
Dixie State U (UT)
Dominican U (IL)
Drexel U (PA)
Eastern Mennonite U (VA)
Emily Carr U of Art + Design (BC, Canada)
Endicott Coll (MA)
Eugene Lang Coll of Liberal Arts (NY)

Ferris State U (MI)
Fitchburg State U (MA)
Freed-Hardeman U (TN)
Gallaudet U (DC)
Goddard Coll (VT)
Grace Coll (IN)
Grand Valley State U (MI)
Grand View U (IA)
Hampton U (VA)
Hofstra U (NY)
Inter American U of Puerto Rico, San Germán Campus (PR)
Ithaca Coll (NY)
John Brown U (AR)
Judson U (IL)
Kansas City Art Inst (MO)
Kansas Wesleyan U (KS)
King U (TN)
Louisiana Tech U (LA)
Maryland Inst Coll of Art (MD)
Marymount Manhattan Coll (NY)
Marywood U (PA)
Massachusetts Coll of Art and Design (MA)
Memphis Coll of Art (TN)
Milwaukee Inst of Art and Design (WI)
Minneapolis Coll of Art and Design (MN)
Morningside Coll (IA)
Mount Allison U (NB, Canada)
New Hampshire Inst of Art (NH)
Northern Arizona U (AZ)
Ohio U (OH)
Oklahoma City U (OK)
Pacific Northwest Coll of Art (OR)
Parsons School of Design (NY)
Pennsylvania Coll of Art & Design (PA)
Point Park U (PA)
Pratt Inst (NY)
Providence Coll (RI)
Purchase Coll, State U of New York (NY)
Purdue U (IN)
Rhode Island Coll (RI)
Rhode Island School of Design (RI)
Ringling Coll of Art and Design (FL)
Rutgers U–New Brunswick (NJ)
St. Edward's U (TX)
St. John's U (NY)
Salve Regina U (RI)
Sam Houston State U (TX)
San Francisco Art Inst (CA)
Sarah Lawrence Coll (NY)
Savannah Coll of Art and Design (GA)
School of the Art Inst of Chicago (IL)
Seattle U (WA)
State U of New York at New Paltz (NY)
Syracuse U (NY)
Temple U (PA)
Texas Christian U (TX)
Texas State U (TX)
The U of Akron (OH)
U of Central Florida (FL)
U of Central Missouri (MO)
U of Dayton (OH)
U of Hartford (CT)
U of Houston (TX)
U of Illinois at Chicago (IL)
U of La Verne (CA)
U of Massachusetts Dartmouth (MA)
U of Miami (FL)
U of Oregon (OR)
The U of the Arts (PA)
U of Washington (WA)
Villa Maria Coll (NY)
Virginia Commonwealth U (VA)
Washington U in St. Louis (MO)
Watkins Coll of Art, Design, & Film (TN)
Weber State U (UT)
Western State Colorado U (CO)
Western Washington U (WA)
Youngstown State U (OH)

PHOTOJOURNALISM

Barton Coll (NC)
Bradley U (IL)
Central Michigan U (MI)
Minnesota State U Moorhead (MN)
Ohio U (OH)
Point Park U (PA)
Rochester Inst of Technology (NY)
St. John's U (NY)
Sierra Nevada Coll (NV)
Syracuse U (NY)
U of Miami (FL)
Walla Walla U (WA)
Western Kentucky U (KY)

PHYSICAL AND BIOLOGICAL ANTHROPOLOGY

U of Washington (WA)

PHYSICAL CHEMISTRY

LeTourneau U (TX)
Rice U (TX)

PHYSICAL EDUCATION TEACHING AND COACHING

Adams State U (CO)
Adelphi U (NY)
Alabama State U (AL)
Albany State U (GA)
Alderson Broaddus U (WV)
Alice Lloyd Coll (KY)
Anderson U (IN)
Appalachian State U (NC)
Aquinas Coll (MI)
Arkansas Tech U (AR)
Armstrong State U (GA)
Asbury U (KY)
Athens State U (AL)
Auburn U (AL)
Augsburg Coll (MN)
Augustana U (SD)
Augusta U (GA)
Aurora U (IL)
Austin Coll (TX)
Azusa Pacific U (CA)
Ball State U (IN)
Barry U (FL)
Barton Coll (NC)
Bayamón Central U (PR)
Baylor U (TX)
Bemidji State U (MN)
Benedictine Coll (KS)
Bethel Coll (IN)
Bethel U (MN)
Bethune-Cookman U (FL)
Biola U (CA)
Blackburn Coll (IL)
Bluefield Coll (VA)
Blue Mountain Coll (MS)
Boise State U (ID)
Boston U (MA)
Bowling Green State U (OH)
Brewton-Parker Coll (GA)
Briar Cliff U (IA)
Bridgewater State U (MA)
Brooklyn Coll of the City U of New York (NY)
Bryan Coll (TN)
Buena Vista U (IA)
Cairn U (PA)
California Lutheran U (CA)
California State U, Bakersfield (CA)
California State U, East Bay (CA)
California State U, Fresno (CA)
California State U, Long Beach (CA)
California State U, Stanislaus (CA)
Calvin Coll (MI)
Campbellsville U (KY)
Canisius Coll (NY)
Capital U (OH)
Caribbean U (PR)
Carroll Coll (MT)
Carson-Newman U (TN)
Carthage Coll (WI)
Catawba Coll (NC)
Cedarville U (OH)
Central Baptist Coll (AR)
Central Connecticut State U (CT)
Central Methodist U (MO)
Central Michigan U (MI)
Central Washington U (WA)
Charleston Southern U (SC)
Chowan U (NC)
The Citadel, The Military Coll of South Carolina (SC)
Coastal Carolina U (SC)
Coe Coll (IA)
The Coll at Brockport, State U of New York (NY)
Coll of Charleston (SC)
The Coll of Idaho (ID)
The Coll of New Jersey (NJ)
Coll of the Ozarks (MO)
Columbus State U (GA)
Concordia Coll (MN)
Concordia U Chicago (IL)
Concordia U, Nebraska (NE)
Concordia U, St. Paul (MN)
Concordia U Wisconsin (WI)
Concord U (WV)
Corban U (OR)
Cornell Coll (IA)
Cornerstone U (MI)
Culver-Stockton Coll (MO)
Dakota State U (SD)
Dallas Baptist U (TX)
Defiance Coll (OH)
Denison U (OH)
DePauw U (IN)
DeSales U (PA)
Dickinson State U (ND)
Doane U (NE)
Drury U (MO)
East Carolina U (NC)
Eastern Mennonite U (VA)
Eastern Michigan U (MI)
Eastern Nazarene Coll (MA)
East Stroudsburg U of Pennsylvania (PA)
East Texas Baptist U (TX)
Elizabeth City State U (NC)
Elms Coll (MA)
Elon U (NC)
Emory & Henry Coll (VA)
Endicott Coll (MA)
Evangel U (MO)
Faulkner U (AL)
Fayetteville State U (NC)
Florida Ag and Mech U (FL)
Florida Intl U (FL)
Fort Lewis Coll (CO)
Franklin Coll (IN)
Fresno Pacific U (CA)
Friends U (KS)
Frostburg State U (MD)
Gallaudet U (DC)
Gardner-Webb U (NC)
Georgia Southern U (GA)
Georgia Southwestern State U (GA)
Georgia State U (GA)
Gettysburg Coll (PA)
Gonzaga U (WA)
Goshen Coll (IN)
Graceland U (IA)
Grambling State U (LA)
Grand Valley State U (MI)
Grand View U (IA)
Greenville Coll (IL)
Hampton U (VA)
Hannibal-LaGrange U (MO)
Hardin-Simmons U (TX)
Heidelberg U (OH)
Henderson State U (AR)
High Point U (NC)
Hofstra U (NY)
Hope Coll (MI)
Houghton Coll (NY)
Houston Baptist U (TX)
Howard Payne U (TX)
Humboldt State U (CA)
Hunter Coll of the City U of New York (NY)
Huntingdon Coll (AL)
Huntington U (IN)
Husson U (ME)
Huston-Tillotson U (TX)
Idaho State U (ID)
Illinois Coll (IL)
Illinois State U (IL)
Indiana State U (IN)
Inter American U of Puerto Rico, Aguadilla Campus (PR)
Inter American U of Puerto Rico, Guayama Campus (PR)
Inter American U of Puerto Rico, Metropolitan Campus (PR)
Inter American U of Puerto Rico, San Germán Campus (PR)
Iowa Wesleyan U (IA)
Ithaca Coll (NY)
Jackson State U (MS)
Jacksonville State U (AL)
Jacksonville U (FL)
John Carroll U (OH)
Judson U (IL)
Kean U (NJ)
Keene State Coll (NH)
Kennesaw State U (GA)
Kent State U (OH)
Kentucky State U (KY)
Kentucky Wesleyan Coll (KY)
King U (TN)
Lane Coll (TN)
Langston U (OK)
Lees-McRae Coll (NC)
LeTourneau U (TX)
Limestone Coll (SC)
Lincoln U (MO)
Lindenwood U (MO)
Lindsey Wilson Coll (KY)
Linfield Coll (OR)
Lipscomb U (TN)
Louisiana Coll (LA)
Louisiana State U and A&M Coll (LA)
Louisiana Tech U (LA)
Lubbock Christian U (TX)
Madonna U (MI)
Manchester U (IN)
Manhattan Coll (NY)
Maranatha Baptist U (WI)
Marshall U (WV)
Marywood U (PA)
The Master's U (CA)
McKendree U (IL)
McMurry U (TX)
McNeese State U (LA)
Meredith Coll (NC)
Messiah Coll (PA)
Michigan State U (MI)
MidAmerica Nazarene U (KS)
Millikin U (IL)
Minnesota State U Mankato (MN)
Minnesota State U Moorhead (MN)
Minot State U (ND)
Mississippi State U (MS)
Mississippi Valley State U (MS)
Missouri Baptist U (MO)
Missouri State U (MO)
Missouri Valley Coll (MO)
Monmouth Coll (IL)
Montana State U Billings (MT)
Montclair State U (NJ)
Morehead State U (KY)
Muskingum U (OH)
Nebraska Wesleyan U (NE)
New England Coll (NH)
New Mexico Highlands U (NM)
New Mexico State U (NM)
North Central Coll (IL)
North Dakota State U (ND)
Northeastern Illinois U (IL)
Northeastern State U (OK)
Northern Illinois U (IL)
Northern Kentucky U (KY)
Northern State U (SD)
Northwestern Coll (IA)
Northwestern Oklahoma State U (OK)
Northwestern State U of Louisiana (LA)
Northwest Missouri State U (MO)
Nova Southeastern U (FL)
Oakland City U (IN)
The Ohio State U (OH)
Ohio U (OH)
Ohio Valley U (WV)
Oklahoma Baptist U (OK)
Oklahoma Christian U (OK)
Oklahoma City U (OK)
Oklahoma State U (OK)
Old Dominion U (VA)
Olivet Nazarene U (IL)
Oral Roberts U (OK)
Otterbein U (OH)
Ouachita Baptist U (AR)
Palm Beach Atlantic U (FL)
Piedmont Intl U (NC)
Pittsburg State U (KS)
Purdue U (IN)
Queens Coll of the City U of New York (NY)
Radford U (VA)
Redeemer U Coll (ON, Canada)
Rhode Island Coll (RI)
Ripon Coll (WI)
Roanoke Coll (VA)
Roberts Wesleyan Coll (NY)
Rockford U (IL)
Rocky Mountain Coll (MT)
Rowan U (NJ)
The Sage Colls (NY)
Saginaw Valley State U (MI)
St. Andrews U (NC)
St. Bonaventure U (NY)
St. Catherine U (MN)
St. Cloud State U (MN)
St. Edward's U (TX)
Salisbury U (MD)
Sam Houston State U (TX)
San Francisco State U (CA)
Schreiner U (TX)
Shenandoah U (VA)
Simpson Coll (IA)
Slippery Rock U of Pennsylvania (PA)
Sonoma State U (CA)
South Carolina State U (SC)
Southeastern Louisiana U (LA)
Southeastern Oklahoma State U (OK)
Southeast Missouri State U (MO)
Southern Arkansas U–Magnolia (AR)
Southern Oregon U (OR)
Southern Utah U (UT)
Southwest Baptist U (MO)
Southwestern Assemblies of God U (TX)
Southwestern Coll (KS)
State U of New York Coll at Cortland (NY)
Sterling Coll (KS)
Syracuse U (NY)
Tabor Coll (KS)
Tarleton State U (TX)
Taylor U (IN)
Tennessee State U (TN)
Texas Christian U (TX)
Texas Lutheran U (TX)
Towson U (MD)
Transylvania U (KY)
Trevecca Nazarene U (TN)
Trine U (IN)
Trinity Christian Coll (IL)
Union Coll (KY)
Union Coll (NE)
Union U (TN)
United States Sports Acad (AL)
Université de Montréal (QC, Canada)
Université de Sherbrooke (QC, Canada)
The U of Akron (OH)
The U of Alabama (AL)
The U of Alabama at Birmingham (AL)
U of Central Arkansas (AR)
U of Central Florida (FL)
U of Central Missouri (MO)
U of Dubuque (IA)
U of Great Falls (MT)
U of Idaho (ID)
U of Indianapolis (IN)
U of Jamestown (ND)
The U of Kansas (KS)
U of Kentucky (KY)
U of Lethbridge (AB, Canada)
U of Louisiana at Monroe (LA)
U of Maine (ME)
U of Maine at Presque Isle (ME)
U of Mary Hardin-Baylor (TX)
U of Maryland, Coll Park (MD)
U of Minnesota, Duluth (MN)
U of Missouri–St. Louis (MO)
U of Mobile (AL)
The U of Montana Western (MT)
U of Mount Union (OH)
U of Nebraska at Kearney (NE)
The U of North Carolina at Greensboro (NC)
The U of North Carolina at Pembroke (NC)
U of Northern Iowa (IA)
U of North Florida (FL)
U of North Georgia (GA)
U of Pittsburgh (PA)
U of Pittsburgh at Bradford (PA)
U of Regina (SK, Canada)
U of St. Thomas (MN)
U of San Francisco (CA)
U of Saskatchewan (SK, Canada)
U of South Alabama (AL)
U of South Carolina (SC)
U of Southern Indiana (IN)
U of Southern Mississippi (MS)
U of South Florida (FL)
The U of Tampa (FL)
The U of Texas at Austin (TX)
U of the Cumberlands (KY)
U of the Incarnate Word (TX)
U of the Southwest (NM)
U of Vermont (VT)
The U of West Alabama (AL)

U of West Georgia (GA)
U of Windsor (ON, Canada)
U of Wisconsin–Madison (WI)
U of Wisconsin–Platteville (WI)
U of Wisconsin–Stevens Point (WI)
U of Wisconsin–Superior (WI)
U of Wisconsin–Whitewater (WI)
Upper Iowa U (IA)
Utah State U (UT)
Utah Valley U (UT)
Valdosta State U (GA)
Valley City State U (ND)
Valparaiso U (IN)
Virginia State U (VA)
Waldorf U (IA)
Walla Walla U (WA)
Walsh U (OH)
Wartburg Coll (IA)
Washburn U (KS)
Wayland Baptist U (TX)
Wayne State Coll (NE)
Wayne State U (MI)
Weber State U (UT)
Welch Coll (TN)
Western Carolina U (NC)
Western Illinois U (IL)
Western Kentucky U (KY)
Western Michigan U (MI)
Western State Colorado U (CO)
Western Washington U (WA)
Westfield State U (MA)
Westmont Coll (CA)
West Virginia U (WV)
West Virginia U Inst of Technology (WV)
West Virginia Wesleyan Coll (WV)
Whitworth U (WA)
William Paterson U of New Jersey (NJ)
William Penn U (IA)
Williams Baptist Coll (AR)
William Woods U (MO)
Wingate U (NC)
Winona State U (MN)
Winthrop U (SC)
Wright State U (OH)
Wright State U–Lake Campus (OH)
Xavier U of Louisiana (LA)
York Coll of the City U of New York (NY)
Youngstown State U (OH)

PHYSICAL FITNESS TECHNICIAN
Averett U (VA)
Central Methodist U (MO)
Trevecca Nazarene U (TN)

PHYSICAL SCIENCES
Anderson U (IN)
Arizona State U at the Tempe campus (AZ)
Arkansas Tech U (AR)
Bemidji State U (MN)
Bennington Coll (VT)
Bethany Lutheran Coll (MN)
Biola U (CA)
Black Hills State U (SD)
California State U, East Bay (CA)
California State U, Sacramento (CA)
California State U, Stanislaus (CA)
California U of Pennsylvania (PA)
Calvin Coll (MI)
Chowan U (NC)
Coe Coll (IA)
Colgate U (NY)
Colorado Mesa U (CO)
Concordia U Chicago (IL)
Concordia U, Nebraska (NE)
Dakota State U (SD)
Defiance Coll (OH)
Doane U (NE)
Emporia State U (KS)
The Evergreen State Coll (WA)
Florida Inst of Technology (FL)
Graceland U (IA)
Hampshire Coll (MA)
Hampton U (VA)
Juniata Coll (PA)
Kansas State U (KS)
Lincoln U (PA)
The Master's U (CA)
McMaster U (ON, Canada)
Michigan State U (MI)
Minnesota State U Mankato (MN)
Minot State U (ND)
Montana Tech of The U of Montana (MT)
Morrisville State Coll (NY)
Mount Vernon Nazarene U (OH)
Muhlenberg Coll (PA)
New Mexico Inst of Mining and Technology (NM)
Northwestern State U of Louisiana (LA)
Olivet Nazarene U (IL)
Otterbein U (OH)
Penn State Erie, The Behrend Coll (PA)
Purdue U Northwest (IN)
Ripon Coll (WI)
Rowan U (NJ)
St. Cloud State U (MN)
St. John's U (NY)
Saint Michael's Coll (VT)
Saint Vincent Coll (PA)
Salisbury U (MD)
Sam Houston State U (TX)
San Diego State U (CA)
San Francisco State U (CA)
Seattle Pacific U (WA)
Seattle U (WA)
Southern Utah U (UT)
Suffolk U (MA)
Trent U (ON, Canada)
Trine U (IN)
United States Military Acad (NY)
U of California, Riverside (CA)
U of Chicago (IL)
U of Dayton (OH)
U of Guelph (ON, Canada)
U of Maryland, Coll Park (MD)
U of North Dakota (ND)
U of Pittsburgh (PA)
U of Pittsburgh at Bradford (PA)
U of Southern California (CA)
U of Southern Maine (ME)
The U of Texas Rio Grande Valley (TX)
U of the Pacific (CA)
U of Utah (UT)
U of Wisconsin–Superior (WI)
Villanova U (PA)
Washburn U (KS)
Washington State U (WA)
Washington State U–Tri-Cities (WA)
Wesleyan U (CT)
Western Kentucky U (KY)
Westfield State U (MA)
Wheeling Jesuit U (WV)
Worcester State U (MA)
Wright State U (OH)
Wright State U–Lake Campus (OH)
Youngstown State U (OH)

PHYSICAL SCIENCES RELATED
Bowling Green State U (OH)
The Coll of St. Scholastica (MN)
Eastern Michigan U (MI)
Rochester Inst of Technology (NY)
Saginaw Valley State U (MI)
State U of New York Empire State Coll (NY)
Stevens Inst of Technology (NJ)
Stony Brook U, State U of New York (NY)
Union Coll (NY)
The U of Alabama in Huntsville (AL)
U of California, Davis (CA)
U of Mary Washington (VA)
U of Massachusetts Lowell (MA)
U of Miami (FL)
U of North Alabama (AL)
The U of North Carolina at Chapel Hill (NC)
U of Utah (UT)
Wayne State U (MI)
Wheelock Coll (MA)

PHYSICAL THERAPY
American Intl Coll (MA)
Andrews U (MI)
Armstrong State U (GA)
Bellarmine U (KY)
Biola U (CA)
Bowling Green State U (OH)
California State U, Fresno (CA)
Coll of Saint Benedict (MN)
Concordia U (QC, Canada)
Concordia U Wisconsin (WI)
Dalhousie U (NS, Canada)
Dominican U (IL)
Duquesne U (PA)
Eastern Nazarene Coll (MA)
Grand Valley State U (MI)
Hampton U (VA)
Ithaca Coll (NY)
Langston U (OK)
Loyola U Chicago (IL)
Maryville U of Saint Louis (MO)
Mount Saint Mary Coll (NY)
Muskingum U (OH)
Nazareth Coll of Rochester (NY)
Northeastern U (MA)
Northern Illinois U (IL)
Quinnipiac U (CT)
Sacred Heart U (CT)
St. Cloud State U (MN)
Saint Francis U (PA)
Saint John's U (MN)
Saint Vincent Coll (PA)
Simmons Coll (MA)
Tarleton State U (TX)
Tennessee State U (TN)
Université de Montréal (QC, Canada)
The U of Akron (OH)
U of Hartford (CT)
U of Minnesota, Morris (MN)
The U of Scranton (PA)
The U of Tennessee at Chattanooga (TN)

PHYSICAL THERAPY TECHNOLOGY
Idaho State U (ID)
Union Coll (NE)

PHYSICIAN ASSISTANT
Butler U (IN)
Cleveland State U (OH)
DeSales U (PA)
Duquesne U (PA)
Gannon U (PA)
The George Washington U (DC)
Grand Valley State U (MI)
Pennsylvania Coll of Technology (PA)
Quinnipiac U (CT)
Rochester Inst of Technology (NY)
Saint Francis U (PA)
St. John's U (NY)
Saint Vincent Coll (PA)
Seton Hill U (PA)
Southern Illinois U Carbondale (IL)
Union Coll (NE)
U of Kentucky (KY)
The U of South Dakota (SD)
U of Washington (WA)
Wagner Coll (NY)
York Coll of the City U of New York (NY)

PHYSICS
Abilene Christian U (TX)
Adams State U (CO)
Adelphi U (NY)
Agnes Scott Coll (GA)
Alabama State U (AL)
Albion Coll (MI)
Albright Coll (PA)
Alfred U (NY)
Allegheny Coll (PA)
Alma Coll (MI)
American U (DC)
The American U in Cairo (Egypt)
American U of Beirut (Lebanon)
Amherst Coll (MA)
Anderson U (IN)
Andrews U (MI)
Angelo State U (TX)
Appalachian State U (NC)
Aquinas Coll (MI)
Arizona State U at the Tempe campus (AZ)
Arkansas Tech U (AR)
Armstrong State U (GA)
Ashland U (OH)
Auburn U (AL)
Augsburg Coll (MN)
Augustana Coll (IL)
Augustana U (SD)
Augusta U (GA)
Austin Coll (TX)
Austin Peay State U (TN)
Azusa Pacific U (CA)
Baker U (KS)
Baldwin Wallace U (OH)
Ball State U (IN)
Bard Coll (NY)
Barnard Coll (NY)
Bates Coll (ME)
Baylor U (TX)
Bellarmine U (KY)
Belmont U (TN)
Beloit Coll (WI)
Bemidji State U (MN)
Benedictine Coll (KS)
Bennington Coll (VT)
Berea Coll (KY)
Berry Coll (GA)
Bethel U (MN)
Binghamton U, State U of New York (NY)
Biola U (CA)
Bishop's U (QC, Canada)
Bloomsburg U of Pennsylvania (PA)
Bluffton U (OH)
Boise State U (ID)
Boston Coll (MA)
Boston U (MA)
Bowdoin Coll (ME)
Bowling Green State U (OH)
Bradley U (IL)
Brandeis U (MA)
Bridgewater Coll (VA)
Bridgewater State U (MA)
Brigham Young U–Idaho (ID)
Brooklyn Coll of the City U of New York (NY)
Bryn Mawr Coll (PA)
Bucknell U (PA)
Buena Vista U (IA)
Buffalo State Coll, State U of New York (NY)
Butler U (IN)
California Inst of Technology (CA)
California Lutheran U (CA)
California Polytechnic State U, San Luis Obispo (CA)
California State Polytechnic U, Pomona (CA)
California State U, Bakersfield (CA)
California State U, Chico (CA)
California State U, Dominguez Hills (CA)
California State U, East Bay (CA)
California State U, Fresno (CA)
California State U, Fullerton (CA)
California State U, Long Beach (CA)
California State U, Northridge (CA)
California State U, Sacramento (CA)
California State U, San Bernardino (CA)
California State U, Stanislaus (CA)
California U of Pennsylvania (PA)
Calvin Coll (MI)
Cameron U (OK)
Canisius Coll (NY)
Carleton Coll (MN)
Carnegie Mellon U (PA)
Carroll Coll (MT)
Carson-Newman U (TN)
Carthage Coll (WI)
Case Western Reserve U (OH)
The Catholic U of America (DC)
Cedarville U (OH)
Central Connecticut State U (CT)
Central Methodist U (MO)
Central Michigan U (MI)
Central Washington U (WA)
Centre Coll (KY)
Chatham U (PA)
Christian Brothers U (TN)
The Citadel, The Military Coll of South Carolina (SC)
City Coll of the City U of New York (NY)
Claremont McKenna Coll (CA)
Clarion U of Pennsylvania (PA)
Clark Atlanta U (GA)
Clarkson U (NY)
Clark U (MA)
Clemson U (SC)
Cleveland State U (OH)
Coastal Carolina U (SC)
Coe Coll (IA)
Colby Coll (ME)
Colgate U (NY)
The Coll at Brockport, State U of New York (NY)
Coll of Charleston (SC)
The Coll of Idaho (ID)
The Coll of New Jersey (NJ)
Coll of Saint Benedict (MN)
Coll of Staten Island of the City U of New York (NY)
Coll of the Holy Cross (MA)
The Coll of William and Mary (VA)
The Coll of Wooster (OH)
The Colorado Coll (CO)
Colorado Mesa U (CO)
Colorado State U (CO)
Columbia U (NY)
Columbia U, School of General Studies (NY)
Concordia Coll (MN)
Concordia U (QC, Canada)
Concordia U Irvine (CA)
Concordia U, Nebraska (NE)
Connecticut Coll (CT)
Cornell Coll (IA)
Cornell U (NY)
Creighton U (NE)
Dalhousie U (NS, Canada)
Dartmouth Coll (NH)
Davidson Coll (NC)
Denison U (OH)
DePauw U (IN)
Dickinson Coll (PA)
Doane U (NE)
Drake U (IA)
Drew U (NJ)
Drury U (MO)
Duquesne U (PA)
Earlham Coll (IN)
East Carolina U (NC)
East Central U (OK)
Eastern Illinois U (IL)
Eastern Michigan U (MI)
Eastern Nazarene Coll (MA)
Eastern Washington U (WA)
East Stroudsburg U of Pennsylvania (PA)
East Tennessee State U (TN)
Eckerd Coll (FL)
Edgewood Coll (WI)
Elizabeth City State U (NC)
Elizabethtown Coll (PA)
Elon U (NC)
Emory & Henry Coll (VA)
Emory U (GA)
Emporia State U (KS)
Fairfield U (CT)
Fairleigh Dickinson U, Metropolitan Campus (NJ)
Florida Ag and Mech U (FL)
Florida Atlantic U (FL)
Florida Inst of Technology (FL)
Florida Intl U (FL)
Florida State U (FL)
Fordham U (NY)
Francis Marion U (SC)
Franklin & Marshall Coll (PA)
Frostburg State U (MD)
Furman U (SC)
Geneva Coll (PA)
Georgetown Coll (KY)
Georgetown U (DC)
The George Washington U (DC)
Georgia Coll & State U (GA)
Georgia Inst of Technology (GA)
Georgia Southern U (GA)
Georgia State U (GA)
Gettysburg Coll (PA)
Gonzaga U (WA)
Gordon Coll (MA)
Goshen Coll (IN)
Goucher Coll (MD)
Grand Valley State U (MI)
Greenville Coll (IL)
Grinnell Coll (IA)
Grove City Coll (PA)
Guilford Coll (NC)
Hamilton Coll (NY)
Hamline U (MN)
Hampden-Sydney Coll (VA)
Hampshire Coll (MA)
Hampton U (VA)
Hanover Coll (IN)
Harding U (AR)
Hardin-Simmons U (TX)
Hartwick Coll (NY)
Harvard U (MA)
Harvey Mudd Coll (CA)
Haverford Coll (PA)
Henderson State U (AR)
Hendrix Coll (AR)
High Point U (NC)
Hillsdale Coll (MI)
Hiram Coll (OH)

Hobart and William Smith Colls (NY)
Hofstra U (NY)
Hollins U (VA)
Hope Coll (MI)
Houghton Coll (NY)
Houston Baptist U (TX)
Humboldt State U (CA)
Hunter Coll of the City U of New York (NY)
Idaho State U (ID)
Illinois Coll (IL)
Illinois State U (IL)
Illinois Wesleyan U (IL)
Indiana State U (IN)
Indiana U Bloomington (IN)
Indiana U of Pennsylvania (PA)
Indiana U–Purdue U Indianapolis (IN)
Indiana U South Bend (IN)
Indiana U Southeast (IN)
Iona Coll (NY)
Iowa State U of Science and Technology (IA)
Ithaca Coll (NY)
Jackson State U (MS)
Jacksonville State U (AL)
Jacksonville U (FL)
James Madison U (VA)
John Carroll U (OH)
Johns Hopkins U (MD)
Juniata Coll (PA)
Kalamazoo Coll (MI)
Kansas State U (KS)
Kansas Wesleyan U (KS)
Kennesaw State U (GA)
Kent State U (OH)
Kentucky Wesleyan Coll (KY)
Kenyon Coll (OH)
Kettering U (MI)
King's Coll (PA)
King U (TN)
Knox Coll (IL)
Kutztown U of Pennsylvania (PA)
Lafayette Coll (PA)
Lake Forest Coll (IL)
Lamar U (TX)
Lane Coll (TN)
Lawrence Technological U (MI)
Lawrence U (WI)
Lebanon Valley Coll (PA)
Lehigh U (PA)
Lehman Coll of the City U of New York (NY)
Le Moyne Coll (NY)
Lenoir-Rhyne U (NC)
Lewis & Clark Coll (OR)
Lewis U (IL)
Lincoln U (MO)
Lincoln U (PA)
Linfield Coll (OR)
Lipscomb U (TN)
Lock Haven U of Pennsylvania (PA)
Longwood U (VA)
Louisiana State U and A&M Coll (LA)
Louisiana Tech U (LA)
Loyola Marymount U (CA)
Loyola U Chicago (IL)
Loyola U Maryland (MD)
Loyola U New Orleans (LA)
Luther Coll (IA)
Lycoming Coll (PA)
Lynchburg Coll (VA)
Macalester Coll (MN)
Manchester U (IN)
Manhattan Coll (NY)
Marietta Coll (OH)
Marshall U (WV)
Mary Baldwin U (VA)
Massachusetts Coll of Liberal Arts (MA)
Massachusetts Inst of Technology (MA)
McDaniel Coll (MD)
McMaster U (ON, Canada)
McMurry U (TX)
Mercer U, Macon (GA)
Merrimack Coll (MA)
Messiah Coll (PA)
Metropolitan State U of Denver (CO)
Miami U (OH)
Michigan State U (MI)
Michigan Technological U (MI)
MidAmerica Nazarene U (KS)
Middlebury Coll (VT)
Millersville U of Pennsylvania (PA)
Millikin U (IL)
Millsaps Coll (MS)
Minnesota State U Mankato (MN)
Minnesota State U Moorhead (MN)
Minot State U (ND)
Mississippi State U (MS)
Missouri State U (MO)
Missouri U of Science and Technology (MO)
Monmouth Coll (IL)
Montana State U (MT)
Montclair State U (NJ)
Moravian Coll (PA)
Morehead State U (KY)
Morehouse Coll (GA)
Morningside Coll (IA)
Mount Allison U (NB, Canada)
Mount Holyoke Coll (MA)
Muhlenberg Coll (PA)
Murray State U (KY)
Muskingum U (OH)
Nebraska Wesleyan U (NE)
New Coll of Florida (FL)
New Jersey City U (NJ)
New Mexico Highlands U (NM)
New Mexico Inst of Mining and Technology (NM)
New Mexico State U (NM)
North Carolina Central U (NC)
North Carolina State U (NC)
North Central Coll (IL)
North Dakota State U (ND)
Northeastern Illinois U (IL)
Northeastern U (MA)
Northern Arizona U (AZ)
Northern Illinois U (IL)
Northern Kentucky U (KY)
Northwestern U (IL)
Oberlin Coll (OH)
Occidental Coll (CA)
The Ohio State U (OH)
Ohio U (OH)
Ohio Wesleyan U (OH)
Oklahoma Baptist U (OK)
Oklahoma City U (OK)
Oklahoma State U (OK)
Old Dominion U (VA)
Oral Roberts U (OK)
Oregon State U (OR)
Otterbein U (OH)
Ouachita Baptist U (AR)
Pace U, Pleasantville Campus (NY)
Pacific Lutheran U (WA)
Paine Coll (GA)
Penn State Abington (PA)
Penn State Altoona (PA)
Penn State Beaver (PA)
Penn State Berks (PA)
Penn State Brandywine (PA)
Penn State DuBois (PA)
Penn State Erie, The Behrend Coll (PA)
Penn State Fayette, The Eberly Campus (PA)
Penn State Greater Allegheny (PA)
Penn State Hazleton (PA)
Penn State Lehigh Valley (PA)
Penn State Mont Alto (PA)
Penn State New Kensington (PA)
Penn State Schuylkill (PA)
Penn State Shenango (PA)
Penn State U Park (PA)
Penn State Wilkes-Barre (PA)
Penn State Worthington Scranton (PA)
Penn State York (PA)
Pepperdine U, Malibu (CA)
Piedmont Coll (GA)
Pittsburg State U (KS)
Pitzer Coll (CA)
Point Loma Nazarene U (CA)
Pomona Coll (CA)
Portland State U (OR)
Princeton U (NJ)
Principia Coll (IL)
Purchase Coll, State U of New York (NY)
Purdue U (IN)
Purdue U Northwest (IN)
Queens Coll of the City U of New York (NY)
Radford U (VA)
Ramapo Coll of New Jersey (NJ)
Randolph Coll (VA)
Randolph-Macon Coll (VA)
Reed Coll (OR)
Regis U (CO)
Rensselaer Polytechnic Inst (NY)
Rhode Island Coll (RI)
Rhodes Coll (TN)
Rice U (TX)
Roanoke Coll (VA)
Roberts Wesleyan Coll (NY)
Rockhurst U (MO)
Rocky Mountain Coll (MT)
Rollins Coll (FL)
Rose-Hulman Inst of Technology (IN)
Rowan U (NJ)
Royal Military Coll of Canada (ON, Canada)
Rutgers U–Camden (NJ)
Rutgers U–Newark (NJ)
Rutgers U–New Brunswick (NJ)
Saginaw Valley State U (MI)
Saint Anselm Coll (NH)
St. Bonaventure U (NY)
St. Catherine U (MN)
St. Cloud State U (MN)
St. John Fisher Coll (NY)
Saint John's U (MN)
St. John's U (NY)
Saint Joseph's U (PA)
Saint Louis U (MO)
Saint Mary's Coll (IN)
Saint Mary's Coll of California (CA)
St. Mary's Coll of Maryland (MD)
Saint Mary's U of Minnesota (MN)
Saint Michael's Coll (VT)
St. Norbert Coll (WI)
St. Olaf Coll (MN)
Saint Peter's U (NJ)
St. Thomas U (FL)
Saint Vincent Coll (PA)
Salisbury U (MD)
Samford U (AL)
Sam Houston State U (TX)
San Diego State U (CA)
San Francisco State U (CA)
Santa Clara U (CA)
Sarah Lawrence Coll (NY)
Scripps Coll (CA)
Seattle Pacific U (WA)
Seattle U (WA)
Sewanee: The U of the South (TN)
Shippensburg U of Pennsylvania (PA)
Siena Coll (NY)
Simmons Coll (MA)
Simon Fraser U (BC, Canada)
Simpson Coll (IA)
Skidmore Coll (NY)
Slippery Rock U of Pennsylvania (PA)
Smith Coll (MA)
Sonoma State U (CA)
South Carolina State U (SC)
South Dakota School of Mines and Technology (SD)
South Dakota State U (SD)
Southeastern Louisiana U (LA)
Southeast Missouri State U (MO)
Southern Arkansas U–Magnolia (AR)
Southern Connecticut State U (CT)
Southern Illinois U Carbondale (IL)
Southern Illinois U Edwardsville (IL)
Southern Methodist U (TX)
Southwestern U (TX)
Spelman Coll (GA)
Stanford U (CA)
State U of New York at Fredonia (NY)
State U of New York at New Paltz (NY)
State U of New York at Oswego (NY)
State U of New York at Plattsburgh (NY)
State U of New York Coll at Cortland (NY)
State U of New York Coll at Geneseo (NY)
State U of New York Coll at Potsdam (NY)
Stephen F. Austin State U (TX)
Stevens Inst of Technology (NJ)
Stockton U (NJ)
Stonehill Coll (MA)
Stony Brook U, State U of New York (NY)
Suffolk U (MA)
Susquehanna U (PA)
Swarthmore Coll (PA)
Sweet Briar Coll (VA)
Syracuse U (NY)
Tarleton State U (TX)
Taylor U (IN)
Temple U (PA)
Tennessee State U (TN)
Texas A&M U (TX)
Texas A&M U–Central Texas (TX)
Texas A&M U–Commerce (TX)
Texas A&M U–Kingsville (TX)
Texas Christian U (TX)
Texas Lutheran U (TX)
Texas State U (TX)
Texas Tech U (TX)
Thomas More Coll (KY)
Towson U (MD)
Transylvania U (KY)
Trent U (ON, Canada)
Trevecca Nazarene U (TN)
Trinity U (TX)
Troy U (AL)
Truman State U (MO)
Tufts U (MA)
Tulane U (LA)
Union Coll (NE)
Union Coll (NY)
Union U (TN)
United States Air Force Acad (CO)
United States Military Acad (NY)
Université de Montréal (QC, Canada)
Université de Sherbrooke (QC, Canada)
U at Albany, State U of New York (NY)
U at Buffalo, the State U of New York (NY)
The U of Akron (OH)
The U of Alabama (AL)
The U of Alabama at Birmingham (AL)
The U of Alabama in Huntsville (AL)
U of Alaska Fairbanks (AK)
The U of Arizona (AZ)
U of Arkansas (AR)
U of California, Davis (CA)
U of California, Irvine (CA)
U of California, Los Angeles (CA)
U of California, Riverside (CA)
U of California, San Diego (CA)
U of California, Santa Barbara (CA)
U of Central Arkansas (AR)
U of Central Florida (FL)
U of Central Missouri (MO)
U of Chicago (IL)
U of Cincinnati (OH)
U of Colorado Boulder (CO)
U of Colorado Colorado Springs (CO)
U of Colorado Denver (CO)
U of Dayton (OH)
U of Delaware (DE)
U of Denver (CO)
U of Evansville (IN)
U of Florida (FL)
U of Georgia (GA)
U of Guelph (ON, Canada)
U of Hartford (CT)
U of Hawaii at Manoa (HI)
U of Houston (TX)
U of Houston–Clear Lake (TX)
U of Idaho (ID)
U of Illinois at Chicago (IL)
U of Indianapolis (IN)
The U of Kansas (KS)
U of Kentucky (KY)
U of King's Coll (NS, Canada)
U of La Verne (CA)
U of Lethbridge (AB, Canada)
U of Louisville (KY)
U of Maine (ME)
U of Maryland, Baltimore County (MD)
U of Maryland, Coll Park (MD)
U of Mary Washington (VA)
U of Massachusetts Amherst (MA)
U of Massachusetts Boston (MA)
U of Massachusetts Dartmouth (MA)
U of Massachusetts Lowell (MA)
U of Miami (FL)
U of Michigan (MI)
U of Michigan–Dearborn (MI)
U of Michigan–Flint (MI)
U of Minnesota, Duluth (MN)
U of Minnesota, Morris (MN)
U of Minnesota, Twin Cities Campus (MN)
U of Missouri–Kansas City (MO)
U of Missouri–St. Louis (MO)
U of Mount Union (OH)
U of Nebraska at Kearney (NE)
U of Nevada, Las Vegas (NV)
U of Nevada, Reno (NV)
U of New Hampshire (NH)
U of New Orleans (LA)
U of North Alabama (AL)
U of North Carolina at Asheville (NC)
The U of North Carolina at Chapel Hill (NC)
The U of North Carolina at Charlotte (NC)
The U of North Carolina at Greensboro (NC)
The U of North Carolina at Pembroke (NC)
The U of North Carolina Wilmington (NC)
U of North Dakota (ND)
U of Northern Colorado (CO)
U of Northern Iowa (IA)
U of North Florida (FL)
U of North Georgia (GA)
U of North Texas (TX)
U of Notre Dame (IN)
U of Oklahoma (OK)
U of Oregon (OR)
U of Pennsylvania (PA)
U of Pittsburgh (PA)
U of Puget Sound (WA)
U of Regina (SK, Canada)
U of Rhode Island (RI)
U of Richmond (VA)
U of Rochester (NY)
U of St. Thomas (MN)
U of San Diego (CA)
U of San Francisco (CA)
U of Saskatchewan (SK, Canada)
U of Science and Arts of Oklahoma (OK)
The U of Scranton (PA)
U of South Alabama (AL)
U of South Carolina (SC)
The U of South Dakota (SD)
U of Southern California (CA)
U of Southern Maine (ME)
U of Southern Mississippi (MS)
U of South Florida (FL)
The U of Tampa (FL)
The U of Tennessee (TN)
The U of Tennessee at Chattanooga (TN)
The U of Texas at Austin (TX)
The U of Texas at Dallas (TX)
The U of Texas at El Paso (TX)
The U of Texas at San Antonio (TX)
The U of Texas Rio Grande Valley (TX)
U of the Cumberlands (KY)
U of the Fraser Valley (BC, Canada)
U of the Pacific (CA)
The U of Toledo (OH)
The U of Tulsa (OK)
U of Utah (UT)
U of Vermont (VT)
U of Virginia (VA)
U of Washington (WA)
U of Waterloo (ON, Canada)
U of West Georgia (GA)
U of Windsor (ON, Canada)
U of Wisconsin–Eau Claire (WI)
U of Wisconsin–La Crosse (WI)
U of Wisconsin–Madison (WI)
U of Wisconsin–Milwaukee (WI)
U of Wisconsin–Parkside (WI)
U of Wisconsin–Stevens Point (WI)
U of Wisconsin–Whitewater (WI)
Ursinus Coll (PA)
Utah State U (UT)
Utah Valley U (UT)
Utica Coll (NY)
Valdosta State U (GA)
Valparaiso U (IN)
Vanderbilt U (TN)
Vassar Coll (NY)
Villanova U (PA)
Virginia Commonwealth U (VA)
Virginia Military Inst (VA)

Virginia Polytechnic Inst and State U (VA)
Wabash Coll (IN)
Wagner Coll (NY)
Wake Forest U (NC)
Walla Walla U (WA)
Wartburg Coll (IA)
Washburn U (KS)
Washington & Jefferson Coll (PA)
Washington and Lee U (VA)
Washington Coll (MD)
Washington State U (WA)
Washington U in St. Louis (MO)
Wayne State U (MI)
Weber State U (UT)
Wells Coll (NY)
Wesleyan U (CT)
West Chester U of Pennsylvania (PA)
Western Illinois U (IL)
Western Kentucky U (KY)
Western Michigan U (MI)
Western State Colorado U (CO)
Western Washington U (WA)
Westminster Coll (PA)
Westminster Coll (UT)
Westmont Coll (CA)
West Texas A&M U (TX)
West Virginia U (WV)
West Virginia Wesleyan Coll (WV)
Wheaton Coll (IL)
Wheaton Coll (MA)
Wheeling Jesuit U (WV)
Whitman Coll (WA)
Whittier Coll (CA)
Whitworth U (WA)
Wichita State U (KS)
Widener U (PA)
Wilkes U (PA)
Willamette U (OR)
William Jewell Coll (MO)
Williams Coll (MA)
Winona State U (MN)
Wittenberg U (OH)
Wofford Coll (SC)
Worcester Polytechnic Inst (MA)
Wright State U (OH)
Wright State U–Lake Campus (OH)
Xavier U of Louisiana (LA)
York Coll of the City U of New York (NY)
Youngstown State U (OH)

PHYSICS RELATED
Albion Coll (MI)
Arcadia U (PA)
Augsburg Coll (MN)
Berry Coll (GA)
Bridgewater Coll (VA)
Bridgewater State U (MA)
Brigham Young U (UT)
California State U, San Marcos (CA)
Christopher Newport U (VA)
Coll of Saint Benedict (MN)
The Coll of Wooster (OH)
Drexel U (PA)
Embry-Riddle Aeronautical U–Daytona (FL)
Embry-Riddle Aeronautical U–Prescott (AZ)
Emory U (GA)
Florida Inst of Technology (FL)
Fort Lewis Coll (CO)
Francis Marion U (SC)
Lawrence Technological U (MI)
Rensselaer Polytechnic Inst (NY)
Rutgers U–Newark (NJ)
Saint John's U (MN)
Saint Mary's U of Minnesota (MN)
Southern Arkansas U–Magnolia (AR)
Southwestern U (TX)
U of California, Davis (CA)
U of California, Irvine (CA)
U of Dayton (OH)
U of Minnesota, Duluth (MN)
U of Notre Dame (IN)
U of Regina (SK, Canada)
U of Rhode Island (RI)
U of Rochester (NY)
Wheeling Jesuit U (WV)
Whitman Coll (WA)

PHYSICS TEACHER EDUCATION
Abilene Christian U (TX)
Albion Coll (MI)
Anderson U (IN)
Auburn U (AL)
Augustana Coll (IL)
Ball State U (IN)
Bishop's U (QC, Canada)
Bowdoin Coll (ME)
Bowling Green State U (OH)
Bradley U (IL)
Brigham Young U–Idaho (ID)
Brooklyn Coll of the City U of New York (NY)
Buena Vista U (IA)
Canisius Coll (NY)
Cedarville U (OH)
Central Methodist U (MO)
Central Michigan U (MI)
City Coll of the City U of New York (NY)
The Coll of New Jersey (NJ)
Coll of Staten Island of the City U of New York (NY)
Colorado State U (CO)
Concordia Coll (MN)
East Central U (OK)
Eastern Michigan U (MI)
Eastern Nazarene Coll (MA)
Eastern Washington U (WA)
Emory & Henry Coll (VA)
Florida Inst of Technology (FL)
Goshen Coll (IN)
Grand Valley State U (MI)
Greenville Coll (IL)
Grove City Coll (PA)
Hofstra U (NY)
Hope Coll (MI)
Indiana U Bloomington (IN)
Indiana U South Bend (IN)
Ithaca Coll (NY)
Juniata Coll (PA)
Kansas Wesleyan U (KS)
Kennesaw State U (GA)
King U (TN)
Le Moyne Coll (NY)
Lincoln U (MO)
Lipscomb U (TN)
Louisiana Tech U (LA)
Madonna U (MI)
Manchester U (IN)
Merrimack Coll (MA)
Messiah Coll (PA)
Miami Dade Coll (FL)
Michigan State U (MI)
Minnesota State U Moorhead (MN)
Minot State U (ND)
Missouri State U (MO)
Morningside Coll (IA)
Mount Vernon Nazarene U (OH)
Muskingum U (OH)
North Dakota State U (ND)
Northwest U (WA)
Ohio Wesleyan U (OH)
Pittsburg State U (KS)
Providence Coll (RI)
Queens Coll of the City U of New York (NY)
Rhode Island Coll (RI)
Roberts Wesleyan Coll (NY)
Saginaw Valley State U (MI)
St. John Fisher Coll (NY)
St. John's U (NY)
Saint Joseph's U (PA)
Saint Mary's U of Minnesota (MN)
Saint Vincent Coll (PA)
Seattle U (WA)
Southwestern Adventist U (TX)
State U of New York at New Paltz (NY)
State U of New York Coll at Cortland (NY)
State U of New York Coll at Potsdam (NY)
Syracuse U (NY)
Trevecca Nazarene U (TN)
Union Coll (NE)
U of California, San Diego (CA)
U of Central Missouri (MO)
U of Delaware (DE)
U of Evansville (IN)
U of Illinois at Chicago (IL)
U of Maine at Farmington (ME)
U of Maryland, Baltimore County (MD)
U of Regina (SK, Canada)
U of St. Thomas (MN)
The U of South Dakota (SD)
U of Waterloo (ON, Canada)
U of Windsor (ON, Canada)
U of Wisconsin–Whitewater (WI)
Utah State U (UT)
Utica Coll (NY)
Valparaiso U (IN)
Washington U in St. Louis (MO)
Weber State U (UT)
Western Michigan U (MI)
Winona State U (MN)

PHYSIOLOGICAL PSYCHOLOGY/ PSYCHOBIOLOGY
Albright Coll (PA)
Arcadia U (PA)
Averett U (VA)
Binghamton U, State U of New York (NY)
Centre Coll (KY)
Florida Atlantic U (FL)
Holy Family U (PA)
Holy Names U (CA)
Houghton Coll (NY)
Mills Coll (CA)
Mount Allison U (NB, Canada)
Oberlin Coll (OH)
Pace U, Pleasantville Campus (NY)
Quinnipiac U (CT)
Ripon Coll (WI)
Saint Mary's Coll of California (CA)
Swarthmore Coll (PA)
U of California, Los Angeles (CA)
U of California, Santa Barbara (CA)
U of Colorado Denver (CO)
U of Michigan (MI)
Vassar Coll (NY)
Washington Coll (MD)
Wesleyan U (CT)

PHYSIOLOGY
Brigham Young U (UT)
California State U, Long Beach (CA)
California State U, San Marcos (CA)
Emmanuel Coll (MA)
Gonzaga U (WA)
Michigan State U (MI)
Oklahoma Baptist U (OK)
Oklahoma State U (OK)
Seattle Pacific U (WA)
Southern Illinois U Carbondale (IL)
The U of Arizona (AZ)
U of California, Los Angeles (CA)
U of California, Santa Barbara (CA)
U of Colorado Boulder (CO)
U of Minnesota, Twin Cities Campus (MN)
U of Oregon (OR)
U of Saskatchewan (SK, Canada)
U of Washington (WA)

PLANETARY ASTRONOMY AND SCIENCE
California Inst of Technology (CA)
Florida Inst of Technology (FL)
Stonehill Coll (MA)
U of Waterloo (ON, Canada)

PLANT GENETICS
Purdue U (IN)

PLANT NURSERY MANAGEMENT
Colorado State U (CO)
Washington State U (WA)

PLANT PATHOLOGY/ PHYTOPATHOLOGY
New Mexico State U (NM)
The Ohio State U (OH)
U of Georgia (GA)
U of Wisconsin–Madison (WI)

PLANT PROTECTION AND INTEGRATED PEST MANAGEMENT
California State Polytechnic U, Pomona (CA)
Colorado State U (CO)
Iowa State U of Science and Technology (IA)
U of Delaware (DE)
U of Georgia (GA)
U of Hawaii at Manoa (HI)
Washington State U (WA)

PLANT SCIENCES
Auburn U (AL)
California State U, Fresno (CA)
Cornell U (NY)
Dalhousie U (NS, Canada)
Louisiana State U and A&M Coll (LA)
Louisiana Tech U (LA)
Montana State U (MT)
The Ohio State U (OH)
Penn State U Park (PA)
Rutgers U–New Brunswick (NJ)
Southern Illinois U Carbondale (IL)
State U of New York Coll of Agriculture and Technology at Cobleskill (NY)
State U of New York Coll of Environmental Science and Forestry (NY)
Texas Tech U (TX)
The U of Arizona (AZ)
U of Delaware (DE)
U of Florida (FL)
U of Guelph (ON, Canada)
U of Massachusetts Amherst (MA)
U of Minnesota, Crookston (MN)
U of Minnesota, Twin Cities Campus (MN)
The U of Tennessee (TN)
U of Vermont (VT)
Utah State U (UT)
Washington State U (WA)

PLANT SCIENCES RELATED
Auburn U (AL)
U of Hawaii at Manoa (HI)
Utah State U (UT)
West Virginia U (WV)

PLASTICS AND POLYMER ENGINEERING TECHNOLOGY
Eastern Michigan U (MI)
Ferris State U (MI)
Pennsylvania Coll of Technology (PA)
Pittsburg State U (KS)
Shawnee State U (OH)
Weber State U (UT)
Western Washington U (WA)

PLAYWRITING AND SCREENWRITING
Acad of Art U (CA)
Bennington Coll (VT)
Brigham Young U (UT)
Central Washington U (WA)
Chapman U (CA)
Columbia Coll Chicago (IL)
Concordia U (QC, Canada)
Drexel U (PA)
Emerson Coll (MA)
Emory U (GA)
Judson U (IL)
Loyola Marymount U (CA)
Marymount Manhattan Coll (NY)
Ohio U (OH)
Point Park U (PA)
Purchase Coll, State U of New York (NY)
Université de Montréal (QC, Canada)
U of Southern California (CA)
The U of the Arts (PA)

POLISH
U of Illinois at Chicago (IL)
U of Michigan (MI)
U of Pittsburgh (PA)
U of Wisconsin–Madison (WI)

POLITICAL COMMUNICATION
Emerson Coll (MA)
Florida Southern Coll (FL)
Nebraska Wesleyan U (NE)
Regent U (VA)
St. Thomas U (NB, Canada)
Suffolk U (MA)
Université de Montréal (QC, Canada)
U of Washington (WA)
Weber State U (UT)

POLITICAL ECONOMY
Antioch Coll, Yellow Springs (OH)
Augsburg Coll (MN)
Eastern Oregon U (OR)
The Evergreen State Coll (WA)
Hillsdale Coll (MI)
Rhodes Coll (TN)
Rollins Coll (FL)
Université de Montréal (QC, Canada)
U of Southern California (CA)
The U of Texas at Dallas (TX)
U of Washington, Bothell (WA)
U of Washington, Tacoma (WA)
Williams Coll (MA)

POLITICAL SCIENCE AND GOVERNMENT
Abilene Christian U (TX)
Adelphi U (NY)
Agnes Scott Coll (GA)
Alabama State U (AL)
Albany State U (GA)
Albertus Magnus Coll (CT)
Albion Coll (MI)
Albright Coll (PA)
Alcorn State U (MS)
Alderson Broaddus U (WV)
Alfred U (NY)
Allegheny Coll (PA)
Alma Coll (MI)
Alvernia U (PA)
Alverno Coll (WI)
American Intl Coll (MA)
American Public U System (WV)
American U (DC)
The American U in Cairo (Egypt)
American U of Beirut (Lebanon)
The American U of Paris (France)
Amherst Coll (MA)
Anderson U (IN)
Andrews U (MI)
Angelo State U (TX)
Appalachian State U (NC)
Aquinas Coll (MI)
Arcadia U (PA)
Arizona State U at the Polytechnic campus (AZ)
Arizona State U at the Tempe campus (AZ)
Arizona State U at the West campus (AZ)
Arkansas Tech U (AR)
Armstrong State U (GA)
Asbury U (KY)
Ashland U (OH)
Assumption Coll (MA)
Athens State U (AL)
Auburn U (AL)
Auburn U at Montgomery (AL)
Augsburg Coll (MN)
Augustana Coll (IL)
Augustana U (SD)
Augusta U (GA)
Aurora U (IL)
Austin Coll (TX)
Austin Peay State U (TN)
Averett U (VA)
Avila U (MO)
Azusa Pacific U (CA)
Baldwin Wallace U (OH)
Ball State U (IN)
Bard Coll (NY)
Barnard Coll (NY)
Barry U (FL)
Barton Coll (NC)
Baruch Coll of the City U of New York (NY)
Bates Coll (ME)
Baylor U (TX)
Belhaven U (MS)
Bellarmine U (KY)
Belmont U (TN)
Beloit Coll (WI)
Bemidji State U (MN)
Benedictine Coll (KS)
Bennett Coll (NC)
Bennington Coll (VT)
Berea Coll (KY)
Berry Coll (GA)
Bethel U (MN)
Bethune-Cookman U (FL)
Binghamton U, State U of New York (NY)
Biola U (CA)
Bishop's U (QC, Canada)
Blackburn Coll (IL)
Black Hills State U (SD)
Bloomfield Coll (NJ)
Bloomsburg U of Pennsylvania (PA)
Boise State U (ID)
Boston Coll (MA)
Boston U (MA)
Bowdoin Coll (ME)
Bowie State U (MD)
Bowling Green State U (OH)
Bradley U (IL)
Brescia U (KY)

Brewton-Parker Coll (GA)
Briar Cliff U (IA)
Bridgewater Coll (VA)
Bridgewater State U (MA)
Brigham Young U–Idaho (ID)
Brooklyn Coll of the City U of New York (NY)
Bryan Coll (TN)
Bryant U (RI)
Bryn Mawr Coll (PA)
Bucknell U (PA)
Buena Vista U (IA)
Buffalo State Coll, State U of New York (NY)
Butler U (IN)
Cabrini U (PA)
Caldwell U (NJ)
California Baptist U (CA)
California Inst of Technology (CA)
California Lutheran U (CA)
California Polytechnic State U, San Luis Obispo (CA)
California State Polytechnic U, Pomona (CA)
California State U, Bakersfield (CA)
California State U, Chico (CA)
California State U, Dominguez Hills (CA)
California State U, East Bay (CA)
California State U, Fresno (CA)
California State U, Fullerton (CA)
California State U, Long Beach (CA)
California State U, Northridge (CA)
California State U, Sacramento (CA)
California State U, San Bernardino (CA)
California State U, San Marcos (CA)
California State U, Stanislaus (CA)
California U of Pennsylvania (PA)
Calvary U (MO)
Calvin Coll (MI)
Cameron U (OK)
Campbellsville U (KY)
Canisius Coll (NY)
Capital U (OH)
Cardinal Stritch U (WI)
Carleton Coll (MN)
Carlow U (PA)
Carroll Coll (MT)
Carson-Newman U (TN)
Carthage Coll (WI)
Case Western Reserve U (OH)
Catawba Coll (NC)
The Catholic U of America (DC)
Cedar Crest Coll (PA)
Cedarville U (OH)
Centenary Coll of Louisiana (LA)
Centenary U (NJ)
Central Connecticut State U (CT)
Central Methodist U (MO)
Central Michigan U (MI)
Central State U (OH)
Central Washington U (WA)
Centre Coll (KY)
Chapman U (CA)
Charleston Southern U (SC)
Chatham U (PA)
Chestnut Hill Coll (PA)
Christendom Coll (VA)
Christopher Newport U (VA)
The Citadel, The Military Coll of South Carolina (SC)
City Coll of the City U of New York (NY)
Claremont McKenna Coll (CA)
Clarion U of Pennsylvania (PA)
Clark Atlanta U (GA)
Clarkson U (NY)
Clark U (MA)
Clayton State U (GA)
Clemson U (SC)
Cleveland State U (OH)
Coastal Carolina U (SC)
Coe Coll (IA)
Colby Coll (ME)
Colgate U (NY)
The Coll at Brockport, State U of New York (NY)
Coll of Charleston (SC)
The Coll of Idaho (ID)
The Coll of New Jersey (NJ)
Coll of Saint Benedict (MN)
The Coll of Saint Rose (NY)
Coll of Staten Island of the City U of New York (NY)
Coll of the Holy Cross (MA)
The Coll of William and Mary (VA)
The Coll of Wooster (OH)
Colorado Christian U (CO)
The Colorado Coll (CO)
Colorado Mesa U (CO)
Colorado State U (CO)
Columbia Coll (MO)
Columbia U (NY)
Columbia U, School of General Studies (NY)
Columbus State U (GA)
Concordia Coll (MN)
Concordia U (QC, Canada)
Concordia U Chicago (IL)
Concordia U Irvine (CA)
Concordia U Wisconsin (WI)
Concord U (WV)
Connecticut Coll (CT)
Converse Coll (SC)
Corban U (OR)
Cornell Coll (IA)
Cornell U (NY)
Creighton U (NE)
Culver-Stockton Coll (MO)
Daemen Coll (NY)
Dalhousie U (NS, Canada)
Dallas Baptist U (TX)
Dartmouth Coll (NH)
Davidson Coll (NC)
Denison U (OH)
DePauw U (IN)
DeSales U (PA)
Dickinson Coll (PA)
Dickinson State U (ND)
Doane U (NE)
Dominican U (IL)
Dominican U of California (CA)
Drake U (IA)
Drew U (NJ)
Drexel U (PA)
Drury U (MO)
Duquesne U (PA)
Earlham Coll (IN)
East Carolina U (NC)
East Central U (OK)
Eastern Illinois U (IL)
Eastern Michigan U (MI)
Eastern U (PA)
Eastern Washington U (WA)
East Stroudsburg U of Pennsylvania (PA)
East Tennessee State U (TN)
East Texas Baptist U (TX)
Eckerd Coll (FL)
Edgewood Coll (WI)
Elizabeth City State U (NC)
Elizabethtown Coll (PA)
Elmira Coll (NY)
Elon U (NC)
Emmanuel Coll (MA)
Emory & Henry Coll (VA)
Emory U (GA)
Emporia State U (KS)
Endicott Coll (MA)
Eugene Lang Coll of Liberal Arts (NY)
Evangel U (MO)
The Evergreen State Coll (WA)
Fairfield U (CT)
Fairleigh Dickinson U, Coll at Florham (NJ)
Fairleigh Dickinson U, Metropolitan Campus (NJ)
Fayetteville State U (NC)
Felician U (NJ)
Ferris State U (MI)
Fitchburg State U (MA)
Flagler Coll (FL)
Florida Ag and Mech U (FL)
Florida Atlantic U (FL)
Florida Gulf Coast U (FL)
Florida Intl U (FL)
Florida Southern Coll (FL)
Florida State U (FL)
Fordham U (NY)
Fort Lewis Coll (CO)
Framingham State U (MA)
Franciscan U of Steubenville (OH)
Francis Marion U (SC)
Franklin & Marshall Coll (PA)
Franklin Coll (IN)
Franklin Pierce U (NH)
Freed-Hardeman U (TN)
Friends U (KS)
Frostburg State U (MD)
Furman U (SC)
Gannon U (PA)
Gardner-Webb U (NC)
Geneva Coll (PA)
George Fox U (OR)
Georgetown Coll (KY)
Georgetown U (DC)
The George Washington U (DC)
Georgia Coll & State U (GA)
Georgia Gwinnett Coll (GA)
Georgia Southern U (GA)
Georgia Southwestern State U (GA)
Georgia State U (GA)
Gettysburg Coll (PA)
Gonzaga U (WA)
Gordon Coll (MA)
Goucher Coll (MD)
Governors State U (IL)
Grace Coll (IN)
Grambling State U (LA)
Grand Valley State U (MI)
Grand View U (IA)
Grinnell Coll (IA)
Grove City Coll (PA)
Guilford Coll (NC)
Hamilton Coll (NY)
Hamline U (MN)
Hampden-Sydney Coll (VA)
Hampshire Coll (MA)
Hampton U (VA)
Hanover Coll (IN)
Harding U (AR)
Hardin-Simmons U (TX)
Harris-Stowe State U (MO)
Hartwick Coll (NY)
Harvard U (MA)
Haverford Coll (PA)
Hawai`i Pacific U (HI)
Heidelberg U (OH)
Henderson State U (AR)
Hendrix Coll (AR)
High Point U (NC)
Hilbert Coll (NY)
Hillsdale Coll (MI)
Hiram Coll (OH)
Hobart and William Smith Colls (NY)
Hofstra U (NY)
Hollins U (VA)
Holy Family U (PA)
Hood Coll (MD)
Hope Coll (MI)
Houghton Coll (NY)
Houston Baptist U (TX)
Howard Payne U (TX)
Humboldt State U (CA)
Hunter Coll of the City U of New York (NY)
Huntingdon Coll (AL)
Huntington U (IN)
Huston-Tillotson U (TX)
Idaho State U (ID)
Illinois Coll (IL)
Illinois State U (IL)
Illinois Wesleyan U (IL)
Immaculata U (PA)
Indiana State U (IN)
Indiana U Bloomington (IN)
Indiana U East (IN)
Indiana U Northwest (IN)
Indiana U of Pennsylvania (PA)
Indiana U–Purdue U Indianapolis (IN)
Indiana U South Bend (IN)
Indiana U Southeast (IN)
Inter American U of Puerto Rico, Metropolitan Campus (PR)
Inter American U of Puerto Rico, San Germán Campus (PR)
Iona Coll (NY)
Iowa State U of Science and Technology (IA)
Ithaca Coll (NY)
Jackson State U (MS)
Jacksonville State U (AL)
Jacksonville U (FL)
James Madison U (VA)
John Brown U (AR)
John Carroll U (OH)
John Jay Coll of Criminal Justice of the City U of New York (NY)
Johns Hopkins U (MD)
Johnson C. Smith U (NC)
Juniata Coll (PA)
Kalamazoo Coll (MI)
Kansas State U (KS)
Kean U (NJ)
Keene State Coll (NH)
Kennesaw State U (GA)
Kent State U (OH)
Kentucky State U (KY)
Kentucky Wesleyan Coll (KY)
Kenyon Coll (OH)
King's Coll (PA)
King U (TN)
Knox Coll (IL)
Kutztown U of Pennsylvania (PA)
Lafayette Coll (PA)
LaGrange Coll (GA)
Lake Erie Coll (OH)
Lake Forest Coll (IL)
Lamar U (TX)
La Roche Coll (PA)
La Salle U (PA)
Lawrence U (WI)
Lebanese American U (Lebanon)
Lebanon Valley Coll (PA)
Lee U (TN)
Lehigh U (PA)
Lehman Coll of the City U of New York (NY)
Le Moyne Coll (NY)
Lenoir-Rhyne U (NC)
LeTourneau U (TX)
Lewis & Clark Coll (OR)
Lewis U (IL)
Liberty U (VA)
Lincoln U (MO)
Lincoln U (PA)
Lindenwood U (MO)
Linfield Coll (OR)
Lipscomb U (TN)
Lock Haven U of Pennsylvania (PA)
Longwood U (VA)
Loras Coll (IA)
Louisiana State U and A&M Coll (LA)
Louisiana Tech U (LA)
Loyola Marymount U (CA)
Loyola U Chicago (IL)
Loyola U Maryland (MD)
Loyola U New Orleans (LA)
Luther Coll (IA)
Lycoming Coll (PA)
Lynchburg Coll (VA)
Lynn U (FL)
Lyon Coll (AR)
Macalester Coll (MN)
Malone U (OH)
Manchester U (IN)
Manhattan Coll (NY)
Manhattanville Coll (NY)
Mansfield U of Pennsylvania (PA)
Marian U (IN)
Marietta Coll (OH)
Marist Coll (NY)
Marshall U (WV)
Mary Baldwin U (VA)
Marymount Manhattan Coll (NY)
Marymount U (VA)
Massachusetts Coll of Liberal Arts (MA)
Massachusetts Inst of Technology (MA)
The Master's U (CA)
McDaniel Coll (MD)
McKendree U (IL)
McMaster U (ON, Canada)
McMurry U (TX)
McNeese State U (LA)
Mercer U, Macon (GA)
Mercy Coll (NY)
Mercyhurst U (PA)
Meredith Coll (NC)
Merrimack Coll (MA)
Messiah Coll (PA)
Metropolitan State U of Denver (CO)
Miami U (OH)
Michigan State U (MI)
Middlebury Coll (VT)
Millersville U of Pennsylvania (PA)
Milligan Coll (TN)
Millikin U (IL)
Millsaps Coll (MS)
Mills Coll (CA)
Minnesota State U Mankato (MN)
Minnesota State U Moorhead (MN)
Mississippi State U (MS)
Mississippi Valley State U (MS)
Missouri State U (MO)
Missouri Valley Coll (MO)
Missouri Western State U (MO)
Molloy Coll (NY)
Monmouth Coll (IL)
Monmouth U (NJ)
Montana State U (MT)
Montclair State U (NJ)
Moravian Coll (PA)
Morehead State U (KY)
Morehouse Coll (GA)
Morningside Coll (IA)
Morris Coll (SC)
Mount Allison U (NB, Canada)
Mount Holyoke Coll (MA)
Mount Mercy U (IA)
Mount Saint Mary Coll (NY)
Mount Saint Mary's U (CA)
Mount St. Mary's U (MD)
Mount Vernon Nazarene U (OH)
Muhlenberg Coll (PA)
Murray State U (KY)
Muskingum U (OH)
National U (CA)
Nazareth Coll of Rochester (NY)
Nebraska Wesleyan U (NE)
Neumann U (PA)
Newberry Coll (SC)
New Coll of Florida (FL)
New England Coll (NH)
New Jersey City U (NJ)
New Mexico Highlands U (NM)
New Mexico State U (NM)
New York Inst of Technology (NY)
Niagara U (NY)
North Carolina Central U (NC)
North Carolina State U (NC)
North Carolina Wesleyan Coll (NC)
North Central Coll (IL)
North Dakota State U (ND)
Northeastern Illinois U (IL)
Northeastern State U (OK)
Northeastern U (MA)
Northern Arizona U (AZ)
Northern Illinois U (IL)
Northern Kentucky U (KY)
Northern State U (SD)
North Greenville U (SC)
Northwestern Coll (IA)
Northwestern Oklahoma State U (OK)
Northwestern U (IL)
Northwest Missouri State U (MO)
Northwest U (WA)
Nova Southeastern U (FL)
Oberlin Coll (OH)
Occidental Coll (CA)
Ohio Christian U (OH)
Ohio Dominican U (OH)
The Ohio State U (OH)
The Ohio State U–Newark Campus (OH)
Ohio U (OH)
Ohio Wesleyan U (OH)
Oklahoma Baptist U (OK)
Oklahoma City U (OK)
Oklahoma State U (OK)
Old Dominion U (VA)
Olivet Nazarene U (IL)
Oral Roberts U (OK)
Oregon State U (OR)
Otterbein U (OH)
Ouachita Baptist U (AR)
Pace U (NY)
Pace U, Pleasantville Campus (NY)
Pacific Lutheran U (WA)
Palm Beach Atlantic U (FL)
Patrick Henry Coll (VA)
Penn State Abington (PA)
Penn State Altoona (PA)
Penn State Beaver (PA)
Penn State Berks (PA)
Penn State Brandywine (PA)
Penn State DuBois (PA)
Penn State Erie, The Behrend Coll (PA)
Penn State Fayette, The Eberly Campus (PA)
Penn State Greater Allegheny (PA)
Penn State Hazleton (PA)
Penn State Lehigh Valley (PA)
Penn State Mont Alto (PA)
Penn State New Kensington (PA)
Penn State Schuylkill (PA)
Penn State Shenango (PA)
Penn State U Park (PA)
Penn State Wilkes-Barre (PA)
Penn State Worthington Scranton (PA)

Penn State York (PA)
Pepperdine U, Malibu (CA)
Philander Smith Coll (AR)
Piedmont Coll (GA)
Pine Manor Coll (MA)
Pittsburg State U (KS)
Pitzer Coll (CA)
Plymouth State U (NH)
Point Loma Nazarene U (CA)
Point Park U (PA)
Pomona Coll (CA)
Portland State U (OR)
Prairie View A&M U (TX)
Princeton U (NJ)
Principia Coll (IL)
Providence Coll (RI)
Purchase Coll, State U of New York (NY)
Purdue U (IN)
Purdue U Northwest (IN)
Queens Coll of the City U of New York (NY)
Quinnipiac U (CT)
Radford U (VA)
Ramapo Coll of New Jersey (NJ)
Randolph Coll (VA)
Randolph-Macon Coll (VA)
Redeemer U Coll (ON, Canada)
Reed Coll (OR)
Regis U (CO)
Rhode Island Coll (RI)
Rhodes Coll (TN)
Rice U (TX)
Ripon Coll (WI)
Roanoke Coll (VA)
Rochester Inst of Technology (NY)
Rockford U (IL)
Rockhurst U (MO)
Rocky Mountain Coll (MT)
Roger Williams U (RI)
Rollins Coll (FL)
Rosemont Coll (PA)
Rowan U (NJ)
Rust Coll (MS)
Rutgers U–Camden (NJ)
Rutgers U–Newark (NJ)
Rutgers U–New Brunswick (NJ)
Sacred Heart U (CT)
The Sage Colls (NY)
Saginaw Valley State U (MI)
St. Ambrose U (IA)
Saint Anselm Coll (NH)
Saint Augustine's U (NC)
St. Bonaventure U (NY)
St. Catherine U (MN)
St. Cloud State U (MN)
St. Edward's U (TX)
Saint Francis U (PA)
St. Gregory's U, Shawnee (OK)
St. John Fisher Coll (NY)
Saint John's U (MN)
St. John's U (NY)
St. Joseph's Coll, Long Island Campus (NY)
St. Joseph's Coll, New York (NY)
Saint Joseph's U (PA)
Saint Leo U (FL)
Saint Louis U (MO)
Saint Martin's U (WA)
Saint Mary's Coll (IN)
Saint Mary's Coll of California (CA)
St. Mary's Coll of Maryland (MD)
Saint Michael's Coll (VT)
St. Norbert Coll (WI)
St. Olaf Coll (MN)
Saint Peter's U (NJ)
St. Thomas U (FL)
St. Thomas U (NB, Canada)
Saint Vincent Coll (PA)
Salisbury U (MD)
Salve Regina U (RI)
Samford U (AL)
Sam Houston State U (TX)
San Diego State U (CA)
San Francisco State U (CA)
Santa Clara U (CA)
Sarah Lawrence Coll (NY)
Schreiner U (TX)
Scripps Coll (CA)
Seattle Pacific U (WA)
Seattle U (WA)
Seton Hill U (PA)
Sewanee: The U of the South (TN)
Shaw U (NC)
Shenandoah U (VA)
Shepherd U (WV)
Shippensburg U of Pennsylvania (PA)
Siena Coll (NY)
Simmons Coll (MA)
Simon Fraser U (BC, Canada)
Simpson Coll (IA)
Simpson U (CA)
Skidmore Coll (NY)
Slippery Rock U of Pennsylvania (PA)
Smith Coll (MA)
Sonoma State U (CA)
South Carolina State U (SC)
South Dakota State U (SD)
Southeastern Louisiana U (LA)
Southeastern Oklahoma State U (OK)
Southeast Missouri State U (MO)
Southern Connecticut State U (CT)
Southern Illinois U Carbondale (IL)
Southern Illinois U Edwardsville (IL)
Southern Methodist U (TX)
Southern New Hampshire U (NH)
Southern Oregon U (OR)
Southern Utah U (UT)
Southwest Baptist U (MO)
Southwestern U (TX)
Spelman Coll (GA)
Spring Hill Coll (AL)
Stanford U (CA)
State U of New York at Fredonia (NY)
State U of New York at New Paltz (NY)
State U of New York at Oswego (NY)
State U of New York at Plattsburgh (NY)
State U of New York Coll at Cortland (NY)
State U of New York Coll at Geneseo (NY)
State U of New York Coll at Potsdam (NY)
Stephen F. Austin State U (TX)
Stockton U (NJ)
Stonehill Coll (MA)
Stony Brook U, State U of New York (NY)
Suffolk U (MA)
Susquehanna U (PA)
Swarthmore Coll (PA)
Sweet Briar Coll (VA)
Syracuse U (NY)
Tarleton State U (TX)
Taylor U (IN)
Temple U (PA)
Tennessee State U (TN)
Texas A&M Intl U (TX)
Texas A&M U (TX)
Texas A&M U–Central Texas (TX)
Texas A&M U–Commerce (TX)
Texas A&M U–Corpus Christi (TX)
Texas A&M U–Kingsville (TX)
Texas Christian U (TX)
Texas Lutheran U (TX)
Texas State U (TX)
Texas Tech U (TX)
Texas Wesleyan U (TX)
Texas Woman's U (TX)
Thomas More Coll (KY)
Thomas U (GA)
Towson U (MD)
Transylvania U (KY)
Trent U (ON, Canada)
Trinity U (TX)
Troy U (AL)
Truman State U (MO)
Tufts U (MA)
Tulane U (LA)
Tusculum Coll (TN)
Union Coll (NY)
Union U (TN)
United States Air Force Acad (CO)
United States Coast Guard Acad (CT)
United States Military Acad (NY)
Université de Montréal (QC, Canada)
U at Albany, State U of New York (NY)
U at Buffalo, the State U of New York (NY)
The U of Akron (OH)
The U of Alabama (AL)
The U of Alabama at Birmingham (AL)
The U of Alabama in Huntsville (AL)
U of Alaska Fairbanks (AK)
The U of Arizona (AZ)
U of Arkansas (AR)
U of California, Davis (CA)
U of California, Irvine (CA)
U of California, Los Angeles (CA)
U of California, Riverside (CA)
U of California, San Diego (CA)
U of California, Santa Barbara (CA)
U of Central Arkansas (AR)
U of Central Florida (FL)
U of Central Missouri (MO)
U of Charleston (WV)
U of Chicago (IL)
U of Cincinnati (OH)
U of Colorado Boulder (CO)
U of Colorado Colorado Springs (CO)
U of Colorado Denver (CO)
U of Dayton (OH)
U of Delaware (DE)
U of Denver (CO)
U of Detroit Mercy (MI)
U of Evansville (IN)
The U of Findlay (OH)
U of Florida (FL)
U of Georgia (GA)
U of Great Falls (MT)
U of Hartford (CT)
U of Hawaii at Manoa (HI)
U of Houston (TX)
U of Houston–Downtown (TX)
U of Idaho (ID)
U of Illinois at Chicago (IL)
U of Illinois at Springfield (IL)
U of Indianapolis (IN)
U of Jamestown (ND)
The U of Kansas (KS)
U of Kentucky (KY)
U of King's Coll (NS, Canada)
U of La Verne (CA)
U of Lethbridge (AB, Canada)
U of Louisiana at Monroe (LA)
U of Louisville (KY)
U of Maine (ME)
U of Maine at Farmington (ME)
U of Maine at Presque Isle (ME)
U of Mary Hardin-Baylor (TX)
U of Maryland, Baltimore County (MD)
U of Maryland, Coll Park (MD)
U of Maryland U Coll (MD)
U of Mary Washington (VA)
U of Massachusetts Amherst (MA)
U of Massachusetts Boston (MA)
U of Massachusetts Dartmouth (MA)
U of Massachusetts Lowell (MA)
U of Miami (FL)
U of Michigan (MI)
U of Michigan–Dearborn (MI)
U of Michigan–Flint (MI)
U of Minnesota, Duluth (MN)
U of Minnesota, Morris (MN)
U of Minnesota, Twin Cities Campus (MN)
U of Missouri–Kansas City (MO)
U of Missouri–St. Louis (MO)
U of Mobile (AL)
U of Montevallo (AL)
U of Mount Union (OH)
U of Nebraska at Kearney (NE)
U of Nevada, Las Vegas (NV)
U of Nevada, Reno (NV)
U of New England (ME)
U of New Hampshire (NH)
U of New Hampshire at Manchester (NH)
U of New Haven (CT)
U of New Orleans (LA)
U of North Alabama (AL)
U of North Carolina at Asheville (NC)
The U of North Carolina at Chapel Hill (NC)
The U of North Carolina at Charlotte (NC)
The U of North Carolina at Greensboro (NC)
The U of North Carolina at Pembroke (NC)
The U of North Carolina Wilmington (NC)
U of North Dakota (ND)
U of Northern Colorado (CO)
U of Northern Iowa (IA)
U of North Florida (FL)
U of North Georgia (GA)
U of North Texas (TX)
U of Notre Dame (IN)
U of Oklahoma (OK)
U of Oregon (OR)
U of Pennsylvania (PA)
U of Pittsburgh (PA)
U of Pittsburgh at Bradford (PA)
U of Pittsburgh at Greensburg (PA)
U of Pittsburgh at Johnstown (PA)
U of Puget Sound (WA)
U of Regina (SK, Canada)
U of Rhode Island (RI)
U of Richmond (VA)
U of Rochester (NY)
U of St. Francis (IL)
U of Saint Francis (IN)
U of Saint Mary (KS)
U of St. Thomas (MN)
U of St. Thomas (TX)
U of San Diego (CA)
U of San Francisco (CA)
U of Saskatchewan (SK, Canada)
U of Science and Arts of Oklahoma (OK)
The U of Scranton (PA)
U of South Alabama (AL)
U of South Carolina (SC)
U of South Carolina Aiken (SC)
The U of South Dakota (SD)
U of Southern California (CA)
U of Southern Indiana (IN)
U of Southern Maine (ME)
U of Southern Mississippi (MS)
U of South Florida (FL)
U of South Florida, St. Petersburg (FL)
The U of Tampa (FL)
The U of Tennessee (TN)
The U of Tennessee at Chattanooga (TN)
The U of Tennessee at Martin (TN)
The U of Texas at Austin (TX)
The U of Texas at Dallas (TX)
The U of Texas at El Paso (TX)
The U of Texas at San Antonio (TX)
The U of Texas of the Permian Basin (TX)
The U of Texas Rio Grande Valley (TX)
U of the Cumberlands (KY)
U of the Fraser Valley (BC, Canada)
U of the Incarnate Word (TX)
U of the Pacific (CA)
The U of Toledo (OH)
U of Toronto (ON, Canada)
The U of Tulsa (OK)
U of Utah (UT)
U of Vermont (VT)
U of Virginia (VA)
The U of Virginia's Coll at Wise (VA)
U of Washington (WA)
U of Waterloo (ON, Canada)
U of West Georgia (GA)
U of Windsor (ON, Canada)
U of Wisconsin–Eau Claire (WI)
U of Wisconsin–Green Bay (WI)
U of Wisconsin–La Crosse (WI)
U of Wisconsin–Madison (WI)
U of Wisconsin–Milwaukee (WI)
U of Wisconsin–Parkside (WI)
U of Wisconsin–Platteville (WI)
U of Wisconsin–Stevens Point (WI)
U of Wisconsin–Superior (WI)
U of Wisconsin–Whitewater (WI)
Ursinus Coll (PA)
Utah State U (UT)
Utah Valley U (UT)
Utica Coll (NY)
Valdosta State U (GA)
Valparaiso U (IN)
Vanderbilt U (TN)
Vassar Coll (NY)
Villanova U (PA)
Virginia Commonwealth U (VA)
Virginia Polytechnic Inst and State U (VA)
Virginia State U (VA)
Virginia Union U (VA)
Virginia Wesleyan Coll (VA)
Wabash Coll (IN)
Wagner Coll (NY)
Wake Forest U (NC)
Walsh U (OH)
Wartburg Coll (IA)
Washburn U (KS)
Washington & Jefferson Coll (PA)
Washington and Lee U (VA)
Washington Coll (MD)
Washington State U (WA)
Washington State U–Vancouver (WA)
Washington U in St. Louis (MO)
Wayne State Coll (NE)
Wayne State U (MI)
Weber State U (UT)
Webster U (MO)
Wells Coll (NY)
Wesleyan Coll (GA)
Wesleyan U (CT)
West Chester U of Pennsylvania (PA)
Western Carolina U (NC)
Western Connecticut State U (CT)
Western Illinois U (IL)
Western Kentucky U (KY)
Western Michigan U (MI)
Western New England U (MA)
Western Oregon U (OR)
Western State Colorado U (CO)
Western Washington U (WA)
Westfield State U (MA)
Westminster Coll (PA)
Westminster Coll (UT)
Westmont Coll (CA)
West Texas A&M U (TX)
West Virginia State U (WV)
West Virginia U (WV)
West Virginia U Inst of Technology (WV)
West Virginia Wesleyan Coll (WV)
Wheaton Coll (IL)
Wheaton Coll (MA)
Wheeling Jesuit U (WV)
Whitman Coll (WA)
Whittier Coll (CA)
Whitworth U (WA)
Wichita State U (KS)
Widener U (PA)
Wilkes U (PA)
Willamette U (OR)
William Jewell Coll (MO)
William Paterson U of New Jersey (NJ)
Williams Coll (MA)
Wilmington U (DE)
Wingate U (NC)
Winona State U (MN)
Winthrop U (SC)
Wittenberg U (OH)
Wofford Coll (SC)
Wright State U (OH)
Wright State U–Lake Campus (OH)
Xavier U of Louisiana (LA)
York Coll of Pennsylvania (PA)
York Coll of the City U of New York (NY)
Youngstown State U (OH)

POLITICAL SCIENCE AND GOVERNMENT RELATED

American U in Bulgaria (Bulgaria)
The American U of Paris (France)
Belmont U (TN)
Bethel Coll (IN)
Blackburn Coll (IL)
Brandeis U (MA)
Buena Vista U (IA)
Capital U (OH)
Colorado Christian U (CO)
Columbia U, School of General Studies (NY)
Emory & Henry Coll (VA)
Georgetown Coll (KY)
Goddard Coll (VT)
McDaniel Coll (MD)
Muhlenberg Coll (PA)
Our Lady of the Lake U of San Antonio (TX)
Saint Mary's Coll of California (CA)
Saint Mary's U of Minnesota (MN)
Shenandoah U (VA)
U of California, Davis (CA)
U of Guelph (ON, Canada)
U of Northern Iowa (IA)
U of Washington (WA)
U of Wisconsin–Whitewater (WI)
Western Michigan U (MI)

Wheelock Coll (MA)
Whitman Coll (WA)
William Peace U (NC)

POLYMER CHEMISTRY
Pittsburg State U (KS)
The U of Akron (OH)
U of Wisconsin–Stevens Point (WI)

POLYMER/PLASTICS ENGINEERING
Auburn U (AL)
Case Western Reserve U (OH)
Penn State Erie, The Behrend Coll (PA)
The U of Akron (OH)
U of Massachusetts Lowell (MA)
U of Southern Mississippi (MS)
U of Wisconsin–Stout (WI)
Western Washington U (WA)

POLYSOMNOGRAPHY
Stony Brook U, State U of New York (NY)

PORTUGUESE
Brooklyn Coll of the City U of New York (NY)
Florida Intl U (FL)
Georgetown U (DC)
Indiana U Bloomington (IN)
The Ohio State U (OH)
Rhode Island Coll (RI)
Rutgers U–New Brunswick (NJ)
Smith Coll (MA)
Tulane U (LA)
United States Military Acad (NY)
U of California, Los Angeles (CA)
U of California, Santa Barbara (CA)
U of Florida (FL)
U of Massachusetts Amherst (MA)
U of Massachusetts Dartmouth (MA)
The U of Texas at Austin (TX)
U of Toronto (ON, Canada)
U of Wisconsin–Madison (WI)

POULTRY SCIENCE
Auburn U (AL)
Mississippi State U (MS)
North Carolina State U (NC)
Stephen F. Austin State U (TX)
Texas A&M U (TX)
U of Arkansas (AR)
U of Georgia (GA)
U of Wisconsin–Madison (WI)
Virginia Polytechnic Inst and State U (VA)

PRACTICAL NURSING, VOCATIONAL NURSING AND NURSING ASSISTANTS RELATED
Caribbean U (PR)
St. Joseph's Coll, Long Island Campus (NY)
St. Joseph's Coll, New York (NY)

PRE-CHIROPRACTIC
Ashland U (OH)
Augustana U (SD)
Millikin U (IL)
U of Regina (SK, Canada)
Viterbo U (WI)
Weber State U (UT)

PRE-DENTISTRY STUDIES
Abilene Christian U (TX)
Albertus Magnus Coll (CT)
Allegheny Coll (PA)
American U (DC)
Anderson U (IN)
Arcadia U (PA)
Ashland U (OH)
Auburn U (AL)
Augustana U (SD)
Baldwin Wallace U (OH)
Ball State U (IN)
Barry U (FL)
Boise State U (ID)
Boston U (MA)
Bowling Green State U (OH)
Bradley U (IL)
Buffalo State Coll, State U of New York (NY)
California State U, East Bay (CA)
Calvin Coll (MI)
Campbellsville U (KY)
Carthage Coll (WI)
Cedar Crest Coll (PA)
Chapman U (CA)
City Coll of the City U of New York (NY)
Clark U (MA)
Clemson U (SC)
Coe Coll (IA)
Coll of Mount Saint Vincent (NY)
Coll of Saint Benedict (MN)
Concordia U Chicago (IL)
Dalhousie U (NS, Canada)
Defiance Coll (OH)
Drake U (IA)
Eastern Nazarene Coll (MA)
Elmira Coll (NY)
Evangel U (MO)
Florida Southern Coll (FL)
Fordham U (NY)
Franklin Pierce U (NH)
Furman U (SC)
Gardner-Webb U (NC)
The George Washington U (DC)
Georgia Southern U (GA)
Gettysburg Coll (PA)
Graceland U (IA)
Grand Valley State U (MI)
Hamline U (MN)
Hampton U (VA)
Heidelberg U (OH)
Hobart and William Smith Colls (NY)
Hofstra U (NY)
Houghton Coll (NY)
Illinois Coll (IL)
Iowa State U of Science and Technology (IA)
Iowa Wesleyan U (IA)
Jacksonville U (FL)
John Carroll U (OH)
Keuka Coll (NY)
King's Coll (PA)
Lawrence U (WI)
Lehigh U (PA)
Le Moyne Coll (NY)
Limestone Coll (SC)
Lindenwood U (MO)
Lindsey Wilson Coll (KY)
Lipscomb U (TN)
Lubbock Christian U (TX)
MacMurray Coll (IL)
Madonna U (MI)
Manchester U (IN)
Maryville U of Saint Louis (MO)
Mercyhurst U (PA)
Millikin U (IL)
Minnesota State U Mankato (MN)
Missouri Valley Coll (MO)
Mount Allison U (NB, Canada)
Mount Mercy U (IA)
Mount Vernon Nazarene U (OH)
Muskingum U (OH)
Nazareth Coll of Rochester (NY)
Newman U (KS)
North Central Coll (IL)
Northern State U (SD)
Northwestern Oklahoma State U (OK)
The Ohio State U (OH)
Ohio Wesleyan U (OH)
Ouachita Baptist U (AR)
Quinnipiac U (CT)
Rhode Island Coll (RI)
Ripon Coll (WI)
Roberts Wesleyan Coll (NY)
Rochester Inst of Technology (NY)
Rockford U (IL)
Rutgers U–New Brunswick (NJ)
Saginaw Valley State U (MI)
Saint Anselm Coll (NH)
St. Catherine U (MN)
St. Cloud State U (MN)
Saint Francis U (PA)
Saint John's U (MN)
Saint Michael's Coll (VT)
St. Thomas U (FL)
Simpson Coll (IA)
Sonoma State U (CA)
State U of New York at Oswego (NY)
State U of New York Coll at Cortland (NY)
State U of New York Coll at Geneseo (NY)
State U of New York Coll of Environmental Science and Forestry (NY)
Stevens Inst of Technology (NJ)
Susquehanna U (PA)
Syracuse U (NY)
Tarleton State U (TX)
Texas Wesleyan U (TX)
Trinity U (TX)
Union Coll (NE)
Union U (TN)
Université de Montréal (QC, Canada)
U of Bridgeport (CT)
U of Central Missouri (MO)
U of Dayton (OH)
U of Illinois at Chicago (IL)
U of Indianapolis (IN)
U of Maryland, Coll Park (MD)
U of Massachusetts Amherst (MA)
U of Minnesota, Morris (MN)
U of New England (ME)
U of Pittsburgh at Johnstown (PA)
U of Regina (SK, Canada)
U of St. Francis (IL)
U of San Francisco (CA)
The U of Tampa (FL)
The U of Tennessee at Martin (TN)
U of Windsor (ON, Canada)
U of Wisconsin–Parkside (WI)
Upper Iowa U (IA)
Utah State U (UT)
Utica Coll (NY)
Valley City State U (ND)
Virginia Wesleyan Coll (VA)
Viterbo U (WI)
Wagner Coll (NY)
Walla Walla U (WA)
Walsh U (OH)
Washburn U (KS)
Washington Coll (MD)
Washington U in St. Louis (MO)
Waynesburg U (PA)
Weber State U (UT)
Wells Coll (NY)
Westminster Coll (PA)
Westmont Coll (CA)
West Virginia Wesleyan Coll (WV)
Whitworth U (WA)
Widener U (PA)
Williams Baptist Coll (AR)
Youngstown State U (OH)

PRE-ENGINEERING
Anderson U (SC)
Asbury U (KY)
Augustana U (SD)
Azusa Pacific U (CA)
Baldwin Wallace U (OH)
Canisius Coll (NY)
Cedarville U (OH)
Drake U (IA)
Eastern Nazarene Coll (MA)
Freed-Hardeman U (TN)
Hamline U (MN)
Houghton Coll (NY)
Inter American U of Puerto Rico, San Germán Campus (PR)
Le Moyne Coll (NY)
Ouachita Baptist U (AR)
Roberts Wesleyan Coll (NY)
Scripps Coll (CA)
Simpson Coll (IA)
Spring Hill Coll (AL)
U of Lethbridge (AB, Canada)
The U of Scranton (PA)
U of the Cumberlands (KY)
U of Wisconsin–Parkside (WI)
Ursinus Coll (PA)
Valley City State U (ND)
Viterbo U (WI)
Wagner Coll (NY)
Waynesburg U (PA)
West Texas A&M U (TX)

PRE-LAW STUDIES
Abilene Christian U (TX)
Albertus Magnus Coll (CT)
Albright Coll (PA)
Allegheny Coll (PA)
Anderson U (IN)
Andrews U (MI)
Arcadia U (PA)
Ashland U (OH)
Auburn U (AL)
Augustana U (SD)
Azusa Pacific U (CA)
Ball State U (IN)
Bard Coll (NY)
Barry U (FL)
Baylor U (TX)
Becker Coll (MA)
Bemidji State U (MN)
Bennington Coll (VT)
Binghamton U, State U of New York (NY)
Biola U (CA)
Bowling Green State U (OH)
Bryant U (RI)
Buffalo State Coll, State U of New York (NY)
California State U, Dominguez Hills (CA)
California State U, Fresno (CA)
Calvin Coll (MI)
Campbellsville U (KY)
Carthage Coll (WI)
Cedar Crest Coll (PA)
Cedarville U (OH)
Champlain Coll (VT)
City Coll of the City U of New York (NY)
Clark U (MA)
Coe Coll (IA)
Coll of Mount Saint Vincent (NY)
Coll of Saint Benedict (MN)
The Coll of Saint Rose (NY)
Coll of the Ozarks (MO)
Colorado Christian U (CO)
Concordia Coll–New York (NY)
Concordia U Chicago (IL)
Concordia U Wisconsin (WI)
Corban U (OR)
Dalhousie U (NS, Canada)
Defiance Coll (OH)
DeSales U (PA)
Dominican U (IL)
Drake U (IA)
Eastern Nazarene Coll (MA)
Elmira Coll (NY)
Emmanuel Coll (GA)
Emory & Henry Coll (VA)
Evangel U (MO)
Florida Inst of Technology (FL)
Florida Southern Coll (FL)
Fordham U (NY)
Franklin Pierce U (NH)
Fresno Pacific U (CA)
Furman U (SC)
Gardner-Webb U (NC)
The George Washington U (DC)
Gettysburg Coll (PA)
Grand View U (IA)
Hamline U (MN)
Hampton U (VA)
Hartwick Coll (NY)
Heidelberg U (OH)
Hobart and William Smith Colls (NY)
Hofstra U (NY)
Houghton Coll (NY)
Howard Payne U (TX)
Huntington U (IN)
Illinois Coll (IL)
Iowa State U of Science and Technology (IA)
Ithaca Coll (NY)
Jacksonville U (FL)
John Carroll U (OH)
Judson U (IL)
Keuka Coll (NY)
King's Coll (PA)
King U (TN)
Lasell Coll (MA)
Lawrence U (WI)
Le Moyne Coll (NY)
Limestone Coll (SC)
Lindenwood U (MO)
Lindsey Wilson Coll (KY)
Lipscomb U (TN)
Louisiana Coll (LA)
MacMurray Coll (IL)
Madonna U (MI)
Manchester U (IN)
Mansfield U of Pennsylvania (PA)
Massachusetts Coll of Liberal Arts (MA)
The Master's U (CA)
Michigan State U (MI)
Millikin U (IL)
Minnesota State U Mankato (MN)
Mississippi Valley State U (MS)
Missouri Valley Coll (MO)
Mount Allison U (NB, Canada)
Mount Ida Coll (MA)
Mount Mercy U (IA)
Mount Vernon Nazarene U (OH)
Muskingum U (OH)
National U (CA)
Nazareth Coll of Rochester (NY)
New England Coll (NH)
Newman U (KS)
North Central Coll (IL)
Northern Arizona U (AZ)
Northern State U (SD)
Northwestern Oklahoma State U (OK)
Nova Southeastern U (FL)
Ohio Wesleyan U (OH)
Oklahoma Christian U (OK)
Oklahoma City U (OK)
Ouachita Baptist U (AR)
Palm Beach Atlantic U (FL)
Quinnipiac U (CT)
Rensselaer Polytechnic Inst (NY)
Rhode Island Coll (RI)
Ripon Coll (WI)
Roberts Wesleyan Coll (NY)
Rochester Inst of Technology (NY)
Rockford U (IL)
Rutgers U–New Brunswick (NJ)
Saginaw Valley State U (MI)
Saint Anselm Coll (NH)
St. Catherine U (MN)
St. Cloud State U (MN)
Saint Francis U (PA)
Saint John's U (MN)
Saint Michael's Coll (VT)
St. Thomas U (FL)
Sarah Lawrence Coll (NY)
Seton Hill U (PA)
Simpson Coll (IA)
Smith Coll (MA)
Sonoma State U (CA)
Southern Oregon U (OR)
State U of New York at Fredonia (NY)
State U of New York at Oswego (NY)
State U of New York Coll at Cortland (NY)
State U of New York Coll at Geneseo (NY)
State U of New York Coll of Environmental Science and Forestry (NY)
Stevens Inst of Technology (NJ)
Susquehanna U (PA)
Syracuse U (NY)
Trine U (IN)
Trinity U (TX)
Union Coll (NE)
Union U (TN)
Université de Montréal (QC, Canada)
U of Bridgeport (CT)
The U of Findlay (OH)
U of Indianapolis (IN)
U of Maryland, Coll Park (MD)
U of Minnesota, Morris (MN)
U of Pittsburgh at Greensburg (PA)
U of Pittsburgh at Johnstown (PA)
U of Regina (SK, Canada)
U of St. Francis (IL)
The U of Tampa (FL)
U of Windsor (ON, Canada)
U of Wisconsin–Parkside (WI)
U of Wisconsin–Superior (WI)
Utah State U (UT)
Utica Coll (NY)
Valley City State U (ND)
Viterbo U (WI)
Wagner Coll (NY)
Walla Walla U (WA)
Washburn U (KS)
Washington Coll (MD)
Wayland Baptist U (TX)
Waynesburg U (PA)
Weber State U (UT)
Wells Coll (NY)
Western State Colorado U (CO)
Westminster Coll (PA)
Westmont Coll (CA)
West Texas A&M U (TX)
West Virginia Wesleyan Coll (WV)
Whittier Coll (CA)
Whitworth U (WA)
William Peace U (NC)
Williams Baptist Coll (AR)
Wingate U (NC)
Xavier U of Louisiana (LA)
Youngstown State U (OH)

PREMEDICAL STUDIES
Abilene Christian U (TX)
Alaska Pacific U (AK)

Albertus Magnus Coll (CT)
Allegheny Coll (PA)
American U (DC)
Anderson U (IN)
Andrews U (MI)
Arcadia U (PA)
Arizona State U at the Downtown Phoenix campus (AZ)
Arizona State U at the West campus (AZ)
Ashland U (OH)
Auburn U (AL)
Augustana Coll (IL)
Augustana U (SD)
Averett U (VA)
Avila U (MO)
Baldwin Wallace U (OH)
Ball State U (IN)
Bard Coll (NY)
Barry U (FL)
Bemidji State U (MN)
Bennington Coll (VT)
Binghamton U, State U of New York (NY)
Bluffton U (OH)
Boise State U (ID)
Boston U (MA)
Bowling Green State U (OH)
Bradley U (IL)
Bryant U (RI)
Buffalo State Coll, State U of New York (NY)
California State U, East Bay (CA)
Calvin Coll (MI)
Campbellsville U (KY)
Caribbean U (PR)
Carthage Coll (WI)
Cedar Crest Coll (PA)
Chapman U (CA)
City Coll of the City U of New York (NY)
Clark U (MA)
Clemson U (SC)
Coe Coll (IA)
Coll of Mount Saint Vincent (NY)
Coll of Saint Benedict (MN)
Colorado Christian U (CO)
Concordia U Chicago (IL)
Dalhousie U (NS, Canada)
Defiance Coll (OH)
Dominican U (IL)
Drake U (IA)
Earlham Coll (IN)
Eastern Nazarene Coll (MA)
Elmira Coll (NY)
Evangel U (MO)
Florida Southern Coll (FL)
Fordham U (NY)
Franklin Pierce U (NH)
Fresno Pacific U (CA)
Furman U (SC)
Gardner-Webb U (NC)
The George Washington U (DC)
Georgia Southern U (GA)
Gettysburg Coll (PA)
Graceland U (IA)
Grand Valley State U (MI)
Hamline U (MN)
Hampton U (VA)
Hartwick Coll (NY)
Heidelberg U (OH)
Hobart and William Smith Colls (NY)
Hofstra U (NY)
Houghton Coll (NY)
Huntington U (IN)
Illinois Coll (IL)
Immaculata U (PA)
Indiana U–Purdue U Indianapolis (IN)
Iowa State U of Science and Technology (IA)
Iowa Wesleyan U (IA)
Ithaca Coll (NY)
Jacksonville U (FL)
John Carroll U (OH)
Keuka Coll (NY)
King's Coll (PA)
King U (TN)
La Salle U (PA)
Lawrence U (WI)
Lehigh U (PA)
Le Moyne Coll (NY)
Lenoir-Rhyne U (NC)
Limestone Coll (SC)
Lindenwood U (MO)
Lindsey Wilson Coll (KY)
Lipscomb U (TN)
Lubbock Christian U (TX)
MacMurray Coll (IL)
Madonna U (MI)
Manchester U (IN)
Maryville U of Saint Louis (MO)
Massachusetts Coll of Liberal Arts (MA)
The Master's U (CA)
MCPHS U (MA)
Mercer U, Macon (GA)
Mercy Coll of Health Sciences (IA)
Miami U (OH)
Michigan State U (MI)
Millikin U (IL)
Minnesota State U Mankato (MN)
Missouri Valley Coll (MO)
Mount Allison U (NB, Canada)
Mount Mercy U (IA)
Mount St. Joseph U (OH)
Mount Vernon Nazarene U (OH)
Muskingum U (OH)
Nazareth Coll of Rochester (NY)
Nevada State Coll (NV)
Newman U (KS)
North Carolina Wesleyan Coll (NC)
North Central Coll (IL)
Northern State U (SD)
Northwestern Oklahoma State U (OK)
Northwestern U (IL)
Ohio Wesleyan U (OH)
Oklahoma City U (OK)
Ouachita Baptist U (AR)
Pacific Lutheran U (WA)
Penn State Abington (PA)
Penn State Altoona (PA)
Penn State Beaver (PA)
Penn State Berks (PA)
Penn State Brandywine (PA)
Penn State DuBois (PA)
Penn State Erie, The Behrend Coll (PA)
Penn State Fayette, The Eberly Campus (PA)
Penn State Greater Allegheny (PA)
Penn State Hazleton (PA)
Penn State Lehigh Valley (PA)
Penn State Mont Alto (PA)
Penn State New Kensington (PA)
Penn State Schuylkill (PA)
Penn State Shenango (PA)
Penn State U Park (PA)
Penn State Wilkes-Barre (PA)
Penn State Worthington Scranton (PA)
Penn State York (PA)
Quinnipiac U (CT)
Rensselaer Polytechnic Inst (NY)
Rhode Island Coll (RI)
Ripon Coll (WI)
Roberts Wesleyan Coll (NY)
Rochester Inst of Technology (NY)
Rockford U (IL)
Rutgers U–New Brunswick (NJ)
Saginaw Valley State U (MI)
St. Andrews U (NC)
Saint Anselm Coll (NH)
St. Catherine U (MN)
St. Cloud State U (MN)
Saint Francis U (PA)
Saint John's U (MN)
Saint Michael's Coll (VT)
St. Thomas Aquinas Coll (NY)
St. Thomas U (FL)
Samford U (AL)
Sarah Lawrence Coll (NY)
Simpson Coll (IA)
Smith Coll (MA)
Sonoma State U (CA)
Southeastern U (FL)
Southern Oregon U (OR)
State U of New York at Fredonia (NY)
State U of New York at Oswego (NY)
State U of New York Coll at Cortland (NY)
State U of New York Coll at Geneseo (NY)
State U of New York Coll of Environmental Science and Forestry (NY)
Stevens Inst of Technology (NJ)
Susquehanna U (PA)
Syracuse U (NY)
Tarleton State U (TX)
Texas Lutheran U (TX)
Trine U (IN)
Trinity U (TX)
Union Coll (NE)
Union U (TN)
Université de Montréal (QC, Canada)
Université de Sherbrooke (QC, Canada)
The U of Akron (OH)
U of Arkansas (AR)
U of Bridgeport (CT)
U of Central Missouri (MO)
U of Dayton (OH)
U of Hartford (CT)
U of Indianapolis (IN)
U of Massachusetts Amherst (MA)
U of Minnesota, Morris (MN)
U of New England (ME)
U of Notre Dame (IN)
U of Pittsburgh at Johnstown (PA)
U of Regina (SK, Canada)
U of St. Francis (IL)
U of San Francisco (CA)
The U of Tampa (FL)
The U of Tennessee at Martin (TN)
U of Windsor (ON, Canada)
U of Wisconsin–Milwaukee (WI)
U of Wisconsin–Parkside (WI)
Upper Iowa U (IA)
Utah State U (UT)
Utica Coll (NY)
Valley City State U (ND)
Virginia Wesleyan Coll (VA)
Viterbo U (WI)
Wagner Coll (NY)
Walla Walla U (WA)
Walsh U (OH)
Washburn U (KS)
Washington Coll (MD)
Washington U in St. Louis (MO)
Waynesburg U (PA)
Weber State U (UT)
Wells Coll (NY)
West Chester U of Pennsylvania (PA)
Westminster Coll (PA)
Westmont Coll (CA)
West Virginia Wesleyan Coll (WV)
Whittier Coll (CA)
Whitworth U (WA)
Widener U (PA)
Williams Baptist Coll (AR)
Wingate U (NC)
Xavier U of Louisiana (LA)
Youngstown State U (OH)

PRENURSING STUDIES

Allegheny Coll (PA)
Arizona State U at the Downtown Phoenix campus (AZ)
Averett U (VA)
Baylor U (TX)
Berry Coll (GA)
Biola U (CA)
Brigham Young U (UT)
California State U, Fullerton (CA)
Cedarville U (OH)
Central Washington U (WA)
Cleveland State U (OH)
The Coll of Idaho (ID)
Concordia U Chicago (IL)
Eastern Nazarene Coll (MA)
Gettysburg Coll (PA)
Hardin-Simmons U (TX)
Houghton Coll (NY)
Jacksonville U (FL)
La Salle U (PA)
Limestone Coll (SC)
Lindenwood U (MO)
Lipscomb U (TN)
Lubbock Christian U (TX)
Madonna U (MI)
Missouri Baptist U (MO)
Missouri Valley Coll (MO)
Mount St. Joseph U (OH)
Nevada State Coll (NV)
Oklahoma City U (OK)
Ouachita Baptist U (AR)
Purdue U Northwest (IN)
St. Thomas U (FL)
Seattle U (WA)
Simpson Coll (IA)
State U of New York Coll at Geneseo (NY)
Tennessee Wesleyan U (TN)
U of Michigan–Flint (MI)

PRE-OCCUPATIONAL THERAPY

Ashland U (OH)
Augustana U (SD)
Bradley U (IL)
Cornerstone U (MI)
Lubbock Christian U (TX)
Millikin U (IL)
Mount Vernon Nazarene U (OH)
Pace U (NY)
Trevecca Nazarene U (TN)
The U of Findlay (OH)
U of Regina (SK, Canada)
Walsh U (OH)

PRE-OPTOMETRY

Ashland U (OH)
Augustana U (SD)
Calvin Coll (MI)
Lehigh U (PA)
Le Moyne Coll (NY)
Madonna U (MI)
Millikin U (IL)
Pace U (NY)
Rhode Island Coll (RI)
Simpson Coll (IA)
Université de Montréal (QC, Canada)
U of Regina (SK, Canada)
U of Wisconsin–Parkside (WI)
Viterbo U (WI)

PRE-PHARMACY STUDIES

Allegheny Coll (PA)
Ashland U (OH)
Auburn U (AL)
Augustana U (SD)
Baldwin Wallace U (OH)
Barry U (FL)
Butler U (IN)
Calvin Coll (MI)
Chapman U (CA)
Clemson U (SC)
Coll of Saint Benedict (MN)
Dalhousie U (NS, Canada)
Dominican U (IL)
Eastern Nazarene Coll (MA)
Emmanuel Coll (GA)
Emory & Henry Coll (VA)
Gardner-Webb U (NC)
Georgia Southern U (GA)
Gettysburg Coll (PA)
Hamline U (MN)
Houghton Coll (NY)
Huntington U (IN)
Husson U (ME)
Indiana U–Purdue U Indianapolis (IN)
King's Coll (PA)
King U (TN)
Le Moyne Coll (NY)
Limestone Coll (SC)
Lindsey Wilson Coll (KY)
Lipscomb U (TN)
Louisiana Coll (LA)
Lubbock Christian U (TX)
Manchester U (IN)
Millikin U (IL)
Missouri Valley Coll (MO)
Mount Allison U (NB, Canada)
Mount Vernon Nazarene U (OH)
Muskingum U (OH)
Ouachita Baptist U (AR)
Roberts Wesleyan Coll (NY)
St. Cloud State U (MN)
Saint John's U (MN)
Saint Michael's Coll (VT)
Simpson Coll (IA)
Tarleton State U (TX)
Union U (TN)
Université de Montréal (QC, Canada)
U of Central Missouri (MO)
U of Charleston (WV)
U of Minnesota, Morris (MN)
U of New England (ME)
U of Regina (SK, Canada)
U of St. Francis (IL)
The U of Tennessee at Martin (TN)
U of the Incarnate Word (TX)
U of Windsor (ON, Canada)
U of Wisconsin–Parkside (WI)
Valley City State U (ND)
Viterbo U (WI)
Walsh U (OH)
Washburn U (KS)
Washington State U (WA)
Washington U in St. Louis (MO)
Weber State U (UT)
Westmont Coll (CA)
West Virginia Wesleyan Coll (WV)
Wingate U (NC)
Youngstown State U (OH)

PRE-PHYSICAL THERAPY

Anderson U (SC)
Asbury U (KY)
Ashland U (OH)
Augustana U (SD)
Becker Coll (MA)
Blue Mountain Coll (MS)
Bradley U (IL)
California Baptist U (CA)
Calvin Coll (MI)
Hamline U (MN)
Iowa Wesleyan U (IA)
Kansas Wesleyan U (KS)
Lubbock Christian U (TX)
Massachusetts Coll of Liberal Arts (MA)
Merrimack Coll (MA)
Millikin U (IL)
Mount St. Joseph U (OH)
Mount Vernon Nazarene U (OH)
Pace U (NY)
Rockford U (IL)
Saint Mary's U of Minnesota (MN)
Simpson Coll (IA)
Trevecca Nazarene U (TN)
Université de Montréal (QC, Canada)
U of Dayton (OH)
The U of Findlay (OH)
U of Kentucky (KY)
U of Mary Hardin-Baylor (TX)
U of Regina (SK, Canada)
U of Wisconsin–Parkside (WI)
Viterbo U (WI)
Walsh U (OH)
Weber State U (UT)
Western Washington U (WA)

PRE-THEOLOGY/PRE-MINISTERIAL STUDIES

Alderson Broaddus U (WV)
Ashland U (OH)
Augustana U (SD)
Calvin Coll (MI)
Coll of Saint Benedict (MN)
Columbia Intl U (SC)
Concordia Coll–New York (NY)
Concordia U Chicago (IL)
Corban U (OR)
Doane U (NE)
Eastern Nazarene Coll (MA)
Ecclesia Coll (AR)
Emmaus Bible Coll (IA)
Geneva Coll (PA)
King U (TN)
Kuyper Coll (MI)
Lee U (TN)
Manchester U (IN)
Martin Luther Coll (MN)
Mid-Atlantic Christian U (NC)
Mount Allison U (NB, Canada)
Nyack Coll (NY)
Ohio Wesleyan U (OH)
Oral Roberts U (OK)
Point U (GA)
Saint John's U (MN)
Shorter U (GA)
Simpson Coll (IA)
Southeastern U (FL)
Tabor Coll (KS)
Tennessee Wesleyan U (TN)
U of Indianapolis (IN)
Washburn U (KS)
Waynesburg U (PA)
Westmont Coll (CA)
Williamson Coll (TN)

PRE-VETERINARY STUDIES

Abilene Christian U (TX)
Albertus Magnus Coll (CT)
Allegheny Coll (PA)
American U (DC)
Anderson U (IN)
Andrews U (MI)
Arcadia U (PA)
Ashland U (OH)
Auburn U (AL)
Augustana U (SD)
Baldwin Wallace U (OH)
Ball State U (IN)
Barry U (FL)
Becker Coll (MA)

Bemidji State U (MN)
Binghamton U, State U of New York (NY)
Boise State U (ID)
Bradley U (IL)
Buffalo State Coll, State U of New York (NY)
California State U, East Bay (CA)
Calvin Coll (MI)
Campbellsville U (KY)
Carthage Coll (WI)
Cedar Crest Coll (PA)
Chapman U (CA)
City Coll of the City U of New York (NY)
Clark U (MA)
Clemson U (SC)
Coe Coll (IA)
Coll of Saint Benedict (MN)
Coll of the Atlantic (ME)
Concordia Coll–New York (NY)
Dalhousie U (NS, Canada)
Defiance Coll (OH)
Drake U (IA)
Eastern Nazarene Coll (MA)
Elmira Coll (NY)
Emory & Henry Coll (VA)
Evangel U (MO)
Florida Southern Coll (FL)
Fordham U (NY)
Franklin Pierce U (NH)
Furman U (SC)
Gardner-Webb U (NC)
Georgia Southern U (GA)
Gettysburg Coll (PA)
Grand Valley State U (MI)
Hamline U (MN)
Hampton U (VA)
Hartwick Coll (NY)
Heidelberg U (OH)
Hobart and William Smith Colls (NY)
Hofstra U (NY)
Houghton Coll (NY)
Illinois Coll (IL)
Indiana U–Purdue U Indianapolis (IN)
Iowa State U of Science and Technology (IA)
Iowa Wesleyan U (IA)
Jacksonville U (FL)
John Carroll U (OH)
Keuka Coll (NY)
King's Coll (PA)
King U (TN)
Lawrence U (WI)
Le Moyne Coll (NY)
Limestone Coll (SC)
Lindenwood U (MO)
Lindsey Wilson Coll (KY)
Lipscomb U (TN)
Lubbock Christian U (TX)
MacMurray Coll (IL)
Madonna U (MI)
Manchester U (IN)
Maryville U of Saint Louis (MO)
Mercy Coll (NY)
Mercyhurst U (PA)
Michigan State U (MI)
Millikin U (IL)
Minnesota State U Mankato (MN)
Missouri Valley Coll (MO)
Montana State U (MT)
Mount Allison U (NB, Canada)
Mount Mercy U (IA)
Mount Vernon Nazarene U (OH)
Muskingum U (OH)
Nazareth Coll of Rochester (NY)
Newman U (KS)
North Central Coll (IL)
Northwest Missouri State U (MO)
Ohio Wesleyan U (OH)
Ouachita Baptist U (AR)
Penn State U Park (PA)
Purdue U Northwest (IN)
Quinnipiac U (CT)
Rhode Island Coll (RI)
Ripon Coll (WI)
Roberts Wesleyan Coll (NY)
Rochester Inst of Technology (NY)
Rockford U (IL)
St. Andrews U (NC)
St. Catherine U (MN)
St. Cloud State U (MN)
Saint Francis U (PA)
Saint John's U (MN)
Simpson Coll (IA)
Sonoma State U (CA)
State U of New York at Fredonia (NY)
State U of New York at Oswego (NY)
State U of New York Coll at Geneseo (NY)
State U of New York Coll of Environmental Science and Forestry (NY)
State U of New York Coll of Technology at Canton (NY)
Susquehanna U (PA)
Syracuse U (NY)
Tarleton State U (TX)
Trinity U (TX)
Université de Montréal (QC, Canada)
The U of Arizona (AZ)
U of Bridgeport (CT)
U of Central Missouri (MO)
U of Delaware (DE)
The U of Findlay (OH)
U of Illinois at Chicago (IL)
U of Indianapolis (IN)
U of Maryland, Coll Park (MD)
U of Massachusetts Amherst (MA)
U of Minnesota, Crookston (MN)
U of Minnesota, Morris (MN)
U of Nevada, Reno (NV)
U of Pittsburgh at Johnstown (PA)
U of Regina (SK, Canada)
U of St. Francis (IL)
U of San Francisco (CA)
The U of Tampa (FL)
The U of Tennessee at Martin (TN)
U of Wisconsin–Parkside (WI)
Upper Iowa U (IA)
Utah State U (UT)
Utica Coll (NY)
Valley City State U (ND)
Virginia Wesleyan Coll (VA)
Viterbo U (WI)
Walla Walla U (WA)
Walsh U (OH)
Washburn U (KS)
Washington Coll (MD)
Washington U in St. Louis (MO)
Waynesburg U (PA)
Weber State U (UT)
Wells Coll (NY)
Westminster Coll (PA)
Westmont Coll (CA)
West Virginia Wesleyan Coll (WV)
Whitworth U (WA)
Widener U (PA)
Wingate U (NC)
Youngstown State U (OH)

PRINTING MANAGEMENT

Coll of the Ozarks (MO)
Ferris State U (MI)
Pittsburg State U (KS)
Rochester Inst of Technology (NY)
U of Minnesota, Duluth (MN)

PRINTMAKING

Adams State U (CO)
Aquinas Coll (MI)
Arcadia U (PA)
Bennington Coll (VT)
Boston U (MA)
Bowling Green State U (OH)
Bradley U (IL)
Brigham Young U (UT)
Buffalo State Coll, State U of New York (NY)
California Coll of the Arts (CA)
California State U, East Bay (CA)
California State U, Long Beach (CA)
Cleveland Inst of Art (OH)
Columbia Coll (MO)
Concordia U (QC, Canada)
Drake U (IA)
Emily Carr U of Art + Design (BC, Canada)
Escuela de Artes Plasticas y Dise&nno de Puerto Rico (PR)
Ferris State U (MI)
Inter American U of Puerto Rico, San Germán Campus (PR)
Kansas City Art Inst (MO)
Laguna Coll of Art & Design (CA)
Maryland Inst Coll of Art (MD)
Massachusetts Coll of Art and Design (MA)
Milwaukee Inst of Art and Design (WI)
Minneapolis Coll of Art and Design (MN)
Mount Allison U (NB, Canada)
Ohio U (OH)
Pacific Northwest Coll of Art (OR)
Pratt Inst (NY)
Providence Coll (RI)
Purchase Coll, State U of New York (NY)
Rhode Island Coll (RI)
Rhode Island School of Design (RI)
Rutgers U–New Brunswick (NJ)
San Francisco Art Inst (CA)
Sarah Lawrence Coll (NY)
Savannah Coll of Art and Design (GA)
School of the Art Inst of Chicago (IL)
Seton Hill U (PA)
Sonoma State U (CA)
State U of New York at New Paltz (NY)
Syracuse U (NY)
Temple U (PA)
Texas Christian U (TX)
U of Hartford (CT)
The U of Kansas (KS)
U of Miami (FL)
U of Michigan (MI)
U of Oregon (OR)
U of Regina (SK, Canada)
U of San Francisco (CA)
The U of Texas at El Paso (TX)
The U of the Arts (PA)
U of Windsor (ON, Canada)
Washington U in St. Louis (MO)
Western State Colorado U (CO)
Youngstown State U (OH)

PROFESSIONAL, TECHNICAL, BUSINESS, AND SCIENTIFIC WRITING

Albion Coll (MI)
Arizona State U at the Polytechnic campus (AZ)
Baylor U (TX)
Blackburn Coll (IL)
Boise State U (ID)
Bowling Green State U (OH)
Brescia U (KY)
Carnegie Mellon U (PA)
Cedarville U (OH)
Chatham U (PA)
Concordia U, St. Paul (MN)
Dixie State U (UT)
Eastern Michigan U (MI)
Eastern Washington U (WA)
Emory & Henry Coll (VA)
Excelsior Coll (NY)
Fitchburg State U (MA)
Iowa State U of Science and Technology (IA)
James Madison U (VA)
Juniata Coll (PA)
King U (TN)
Lubbock Christian U (TX)
Madonna U (MI)
Massachusetts Coll of Liberal Arts (MA)
Miami U (OH)
Michigan State U (MI)
Missouri State U (MO)
Montana Tech of The U of Montana (MT)
Mount Mary U (WI)
New Mexico Inst of Mining and Technology (NM)
Penn State Berks (PA)
Penn State Lehigh Valley (PA)
Purdue U (IN)
Saginaw Valley State U (MI)
Saint Leo U (FL)
St. Thomas U (FL)
San Francisco State U (CA)
Savannah Coll of Art and Design (GA)
Tarleton State U (TX)
Taylor U (IN)
Texas Tech U (TX)
U of Hartford (CT)
U of Houston–Downtown (TX)
U of North Texas (TX)
U of South Florida Sarasota-Manatee (FL)
U of Washington (WA)
U of Wisconsin–Stout (WI)
Valparaiso U (IN)
Walsh U (OH)
Weber State U (UT)
Winthrop U (SC)
York Coll of Pennsylvania (PA)
Youngstown State U (OH)

PROJECT MANAGEMENT

Davenport U, Grand Rapids (MI)
Huntington U (IN)
Malone U (OH)
Minnesota State U Moorhead (MN)
Northcentral U (CA)
U of the Incarnate Word (TX)
Wentworth Inst of Technology (MA)

PROTECTIVE SERVICES OPERATIONS

Embry-Riddle Aeronautical U–Worldwide (FL)

PSYCHIATRIC/MENTAL HEALTH SERVICES TECHNOLOGY

Columbia Southern U (AL)

PSYCHOLOGY

Abilene Christian U (TX)
Adams State U (CO)
Adelphi U (NY)
Agnes Scott Coll (GA)
Alabama State U (AL)
Alaska Pacific U (AK)
Albany State U (GA)
Albertus Magnus Coll (CT)
Albion Coll (MI)
Albright Coll (PA)
Alcorn State U (MS)
Alderson Broaddus U (WV)
Alfred U (NY)
Allegheny Coll (PA)
Alliant Intl U–San Diego (CA)
Alma Coll (MI)
Alvernia U (PA)
Alverno Coll (WI)
American Intl Coll (MA)
American Public U System (WV)
American U (DC)
The American U in Cairo (Egypt)
American U of Beirut (Lebanon)
The American U of Paris (France)
Amherst Coll (MA)
Anderson U (IN)
Anderson U (SC)
Andrews U (MI)
Angelo State U (TX)
Antioch Coll, Yellow Springs (OH)
Appalachian State U (NC)
Aquinas Coll (MI)
Aquinas Coll (TN)
Arcadia U (PA)
Arizona Christian U (AZ)
Arizona State U at the Tempe campus (AZ)
Arizona State U at the West campus (AZ)
Arkansas Tech U (AR)
Armstrong State U (GA)
Asbury U (KY)
Ashland U (OH)
Assumption Coll (MA)
Athens State U (AL)
Auburn U (AL)
Auburn U at Montgomery (AL)
Augsburg Coll (MN)
Augustana Coll (IL)
Augustana U (SD)
Augusta U (GA)
Aurora U (IL)
Austin Coll (TX)
Austin Peay State U (TN)
Averett U (VA)
Avila U (MO)
Azusa Pacific U (CA)
Baker U (KS)
Baldwin Wallace U (OH)
Ball State U (IN)
Barclay Coll (KS)
Bard Coll (NY)
Barnard Coll (NY)
Barry U (FL)
Barton Coll (NC)
Baruch Coll of the City U of New York (NY)
Bates Coll (ME)
Bayamón Central U (PR)
Baylor U (TX)
Bay Path U (MA)
Beacon Coll (FL)
Becker Coll (MA)
Belhaven U (MS)
Bellarmine U (KY)
Belmont Abbey Coll (NC)
Belmont U (TN)
Beloit Coll (WI)
Bemidji State U (MN)
Benedictine Coll (KS)
Bennett Coll (NC)
Bennington Coll (VT)
Berea Coll (KY)
Berry Coll (GA)
Bethany Lutheran Coll (MN)
Bethel Coll (IN)
Bethel Coll (KS)
Bethel U (MN)
Bethune-Cookman U (FL)
Binghamton U, State U of New York (NY)
Biola U (CA)
Bishop's U (QC, Canada)
Blackburn Coll (IL)
Black Hills State U (SD)
Bloomfield Coll (NJ)
Bloomsburg U of Pennsylvania (PA)
Bluefield Coll (VA)
Blue Mountain Coll (MS)
Bluffton U (OH)
Boise State U (ID)
Boston Coll (MA)
Boston U (MA)
Bowie State U (MD)
Bowling Green State U (OH)
Bradley U (IL)
Brandeis U (MA)
Brandman U (CA)
Brescia U (KY)
Brewton-Parker Coll (GA)
Briar Cliff U (IA)
Bridgewater Coll (VA)
Bridgewater State U (MA)
Brigham Young U–Idaho (ID)
Brooklyn Coll of the City U of New York (NY)
Bryan Coll (TN)
Bryant U (RI)
Bryn Athyn Coll of the New Church (PA)
Bryn Mawr Coll (PA)
Bucknell U (PA)
Buena Vista U (IA)
Buffalo State Coll, State U of New York (NY)
Butler U (IN)
Cabrini U (PA)
Cairn U (PA)
Caldwell U (NJ)
California Baptist U (CA)
California Lutheran U (CA)
California Polytechnic State U, San Luis Obispo (CA)
California State Polytechnic U, Pomona (CA)
California State U, Bakersfield (CA)
California State U, Chico (CA)
California State U, Dominguez Hills (CA)
California State U, East Bay (CA)
California State U, Fresno (CA)
California State U, Fullerton (CA)
California State U, Long Beach (CA)
California State U, Monterey Bay (CA)
California State U, Northridge (CA)
California State U, Sacramento (CA)
California State U, San Bernardino (CA)
California State U, San Marcos (CA)
California State U, Stanislaus (CA)
California U of Pennsylvania (PA)
Calumet Coll of Saint Joseph (IN)
Calvin Coll (MI)
Cameron U (OK)
Campbellsville U (KY)
Canisius Coll (NY)
Capital U (OH)
Cardinal Stritch U (WI)
Carleton Coll (MN)
Carlow U (PA)
Carnegie Mellon U (PA)
Carroll Coll (MT)
Carson-Newman U (TN)

Carthage Coll (WI)
Case Western Reserve U (OH)
Catawba Coll (NC)
The Catholic U of America (DC)
Cazenovia Coll (NY)
Cedar Crest Coll (PA)
Cedarville U (OH)
Centenary Coll of Louisiana (LA)
Centenary U (NJ)
Central Baptist Coll (AR)
Central Connecticut State U (CT)
Central Methodist U (MO)
Central Michigan U (MI)
Central State U (OH)
Central Washington U (WA)
Centre Coll (KY)
Chaminade U of Honolulu (HI)
Champlain Coll (VT)
Chapman U (CA)
Charleston Southern U (SC)
Charter Oak State Coll (CT)
Chatham U (PA)
Chestnut Hill Coll (PA)
Chowan U (NC)
Christian Brothers U (TN)
Christopher Newport U (VA)
The Citadel, The Military Coll of South Carolina (SC)
City Coll of the City U of New York (NY)
Claremont McKenna Coll (CA)
Clarion U of Pennsylvania (PA)
Clark Atlanta U (GA)
Clarke U (IA)
Clarkson U (NY)
Clark U (MA)
Clemson U (SC)
Cleveland State U (OH)
Coastal Carolina U (SC)
Coe Coll (IA)
Colby Coll (ME)
Colby-Sawyer Coll (NH)
Colgate U (NY)
The Coll at Brockport, State U of New York (NY)
Coll of Charleston (SC)
Coll of Coastal Georgia (GA)
The Coll of Idaho (ID)
Coll of Mount Saint Vincent (NY)
The Coll of New Jersey (NJ)
Coll of Saint Benedict (MN)
Coll of Saint Elizabeth (NJ)
Coll of Saint Mary (NE)
The Coll of Saint Rose (NY)
The Coll of St. Scholastica (MN)
Coll of Staten Island of the City U of New York (NY)
Coll of the Atlantic (ME)
Coll of the Holy Cross (MA)
Coll of the Ozarks (MO)
The Coll of William and Mary (VA)
The Coll of Wooster (OH)
Colorado Christian U (CO)
The Colorado Coll (CO)
Colorado Mesa U (CO)
Colorado State U (CO)
Columbia Coll (MO)
Columbia Intl U (SC)
Columbia U (NY)
Columbia U, School of General Studies (NY)
Columbus State U (GA)
Concordia Coll (MN)
Concordia Coll–New York (NY)
Concordia U (QC, Canada)
Concordia U Chicago (IL)
Concordia U Irvine (CA)
Concordia U, Nebraska (NE)
Concordia U, St. Paul (MN)
Concordia U Wisconsin (WI)
Concord U (WV)
Connecticut Coll (CT)
Converse Coll (SC)
Corban U (OR)
Cornell Coll (IA)
Cornell U (NY)
Cornerstone U (MI)
Crandall U (NB, Canada)
Creighton U (NE)
Culver-Stockton Coll (MO)
Curry Coll (MA)
Daemen Coll (NY)
Dalhousie U (NS, Canada)
Dallas Baptist U (TX)
Dallas Christian Coll (TX)
Dartmouth Coll (NH)
Davidson Coll (NC)
Dean Coll (MA)
Defiance Coll (OH)
Denison U (OH)
DePauw U (IN)
DEREE - The American Coll of Greece (Greece)
DeSales U (PA)
Dickinson Coll (PA)
Dickinson State U (ND)
Dixie State U (UT)
Doane U (NE)
Dominican Coll (NY)
Dominican U (IL)
Dominican U of California (CA)
Drake U (IA)
Drew U (NJ)
Drexel U (PA)
Drury U (MO)
Duquesne U (PA)
Earlham Coll (IN)
East Carolina U (NC)
East Central U (OK)
Eastern Illinois U (IL)
Eastern Mennonite U (VA)
Eastern Michigan U (MI)
Eastern Nazarene Coll (MA)
Eastern Oregon U (OR)
Eastern U (PA)
Eastern Washington U (WA)
East Stroudsburg U of Pennsylvania (PA)
East Tennessee State U (TN)
East Texas Baptist U (TX)
Eckerd Coll (FL)
Edgewood Coll (WI)
Elizabeth City State U (NC)
Elizabethtown Coll (PA)
Elmira Coll (NY)
Elms Coll (MA)
Elon U (NC)
Emmanuel Coll (GA)
Emmanuel Coll (MA)
Emory & Henry Coll (VA)
Emory U (GA)
Emporia State U (KS)
Endicott Coll (MA)
Eugene Lang Coll of Liberal Arts (NY)
Eureka Coll (IL)
Evangel U (MO)
The Evergreen State Coll (WA)
Excelsior Coll (NY)
Fairfield U (CT)
Fairleigh Dickinson U, Coll at Florham (NJ)
Fairleigh Dickinson U, Metropolitan Campus (NJ)
Faulkner U (AL)
Fayetteville State U (NC)
Felician U (NJ)
Fisher Coll (MA)
Fitchburg State U (MA)
Flagler Coll (FL)
Florida Ag and Mech U (FL)
Florida Atlantic U (FL)
Florida Gulf Coast U (FL)
Florida Inst of Technology (FL)
Florida Intl U (FL)
Florida National U (FL)
Florida Southern Coll (FL)
Florida State U (FL)
Fordham U (NY)
Fort Lewis Coll (CO)
Framingham State U (MA)
Franciscan U of Steubenville (OH)
Francis Marion U (SC)
Franklin & Marshall Coll (PA)
Franklin Coll (IN)
Franklin Pierce U (NH)
Freed-Hardeman U (TN)
Fresno Pacific U (CA)
Friends U (KS)
Frostburg State U (MD)
Furman U (SC)
Gallaudet U (DC)
Gannon U (PA)
Gardner-Webb U (NC)
Geneva Coll (PA)
George Fox U (OR)
Georgetown Coll (KY)
Georgetown U (DC)
The George Washington U (DC)
Georgia Gwinnett Coll (GA)
Georgian Court U (NJ)
Georgia Southern U (GA)
Georgia Southwestern State U (GA)
Georgia State U (GA)
Gettysburg Coll (PA)
Goddard Coll (VT)
Gonzaga U (WA)
Gordon Coll (MA)
Goshen Coll (IN)
Goucher Coll (MD)
Governors State U (IL)
Grace Coll (IN)
Graceland U (IA)
Grambling State U (LA)
Grand Valley State U (MI)
Grand View U (IA)
Granite State Coll (NH)
Green Mountain Coll (VT)
Greenville Coll (IL)
Grinnell Coll (IA)
Grove City Coll (PA)
Guilford Coll (NC)
Gwynedd Mercy U (PA)
Hamilton Coll (NY)
Hamline U (MN)
Hampden-Sydney Coll (VA)
Hampshire Coll (MA)
Hampton U (VA)
Hannibal-LaGrange U (MO)
Hanover Coll (IN)
Harding U (AR)
Hardin-Simmons U (TX)
Hartwick Coll (NY)
Harvard U (MA)
Haverford Coll (PA)
Hawai`i Pacific U (HI)
Heidelberg U (OH)
Henderson State U (AR)
Hendrix Coll (AR)
High Point U (NC)
Hilbert Coll (NY)
Hillsdale Coll (MI)
Hiram Coll (OH)
Hobart and William Smith Colls (NY)
Hofstra U (NY)
Hollins U (VA)
Holy Cross Coll (IN)
Holy Family U (PA)
Holy Names U (CA)
Hood Coll (MD)
Hope Coll (MI)
Hope Intl U (CA)
Houghton Coll (NY)
Houston Baptist U (TX)
Howard Payne U (TX)
Humboldt State U (CA)
Hunter Coll of the City U of New York (NY)
Huntingdon Coll (AL)
Huntington U (IN)
Husson U (ME)
Huston-Tillotson U (TX)
Idaho State U (ID)
Illinois Coll (IL)
Illinois State U (IL)
Illinois Wesleyan U (IL)
Immaculata U (PA)
Indiana State U (IN)
Indiana U Bloomington (IN)
Indiana U East (IN)
Indiana U Kokomo (IN)
Indiana U Northwest (IN)
Indiana U of Pennsylvania (PA)
Indiana U–Purdue U Indianapolis (IN)
Indiana U South Bend (IN)
Indiana U Southeast (IN)
Inter American U of Puerto Rico, Aguadilla Campus (PR)
Inter American U of Puerto Rico, Fajardo Campus (PR)
Inter American U of Puerto Rico, Metropolitan Campus (PR)
Inter American U of Puerto Rico, Ponce Campus (PR)
Inter American U of Puerto Rico, San Germán Campus (PR)
Iona Coll (NY)
Iowa State U of Science and Technology (IA)
Iowa Wesleyan U (IA)
Ithaca Coll (NY)
Jackson State U (MS)
Jacksonville State U (AL)
Jacksonville U (FL)
James Madison U (VA)
John Brown U (AR)
John Carroll U (OH)
Johns Hopkins U (MD)
Johnson C. Smith U (NC)
John Wesley U (NC)
Judson U (IL)
Juniata Coll (PA)
Kalamazoo Coll (MI)
Kansas State U (KS)
Kansas Wesleyan U (KS)
Kean U (NJ)
Keene State Coll (NH)
Kennesaw State U (GA)
Kent State U (OH)
Kent State U at Ashtabula (OH)
Kent State U at East Liverpool (OH)
Kent State U at Geauga (OH)
Kent State U at Salem (OH)
Kent State U at Stark (OH)
Kent State U at Trumbull (OH)
Kent State U at Tuscarawas (OH)
Kentucky State U (KY)
Kentucky Wesleyan Coll (KY)
Kenyon Coll (OH)
Keuka Coll (NY)
King's Coll (PA)
The King's U (AB, Canada)
King U (TN)
Knox Coll (IL)
Kutztown U of Pennsylvania (PA)
Lafayette Coll (PA)
LaGrange Coll (GA)
Lake Erie Coll (OH)
Lake Forest Coll (IL)
Lamar U (TX)
Langston U (OK)
La Roche Coll (PA)
La Salle U (PA)
Lasell Coll (MA)
Lawrence Technological U (MI)
Lawrence U (WI)
Lebanese American U (Lebanon)
Lebanon Valley Coll (PA)
Lees-McRae Coll (NC)
Lee U (TN)
Lehigh U (PA)
Lehman Coll of the City U of New York (NY)
Le Moyne Coll (NY)
Lenoir-Rhyne U (NC)
LeTourneau U (TX)
Lewis & Clark Coll (OR)
Lewis U (IL)
Liberty U (VA)
Life U (GA)
Limestone Coll (SC)
Lincoln Christian U (IL)
Lincoln U (MO)
Lincoln U (PA)
Lindenwood U (MO)
Lindsey Wilson Coll (KY)
Linfield Coll (OR)
Lipscomb U (TN)
Lock Haven U of Pennsylvania (PA)
Longwood U (VA)
Loras Coll (IA)
Louisiana Coll (LA)
Louisiana State U and A&M Coll (LA)
Louisiana State U at Alexandria (LA)
Louisiana Tech U (LA)
Lourdes U (OH)
Loyola Marymount U (CA)
Loyola U Chicago (IL)
Loyola U Maryland (MD)
Lubbock Christian U (TX)
Luther Coll (IA)
Lycoming Coll (PA)
Lynchburg Coll (VA)
Lynn U (FL)
Lyon Coll (AR)
Macalester Coll (MN)
MacMurray Coll (IL)
Madonna U (MI)
Malone U (OH)
Manchester U (IN)
Manhattan Coll (NY)
Manhattanville Coll (NY)
Mansfield U of Pennsylvania (PA)
Maria Coll (NY)
Marian U (IN)
Marian U (WI)
Marietta Coll (OH)
Marist Coll (NY)
Marshall U (WV)
Mary Baldwin U (VA)
Marylhurst U (OR)
Marymount California U (CA)
Marymount Manhattan Coll (NY)
Marymount U (VA)
Maryville U of Saint Louis (MO)
Marywood U (PA)
Massachusetts Coll of Liberal Arts (MA)
McDaniel Coll (MD)
McKendree U (IL)
McMaster U (ON, Canada)
McMurry U (TX)
McNeese State U (LA)
Medgar Evers Coll of the City U of New York (NY)
Menlo Coll (CA)
Mercer U, Macon (GA)
Mercy Coll (NY)
Mercyhurst U (PA)
Meredith Coll (NC)
Merrimack Coll (MA)
Messiah Coll (PA)
Metropolitan State U of Denver (CO)
Miami U (OH)
Michigan State U (MI)
Michigan Technological U (MI)
MidAmerica Nazarene U (KS)
Middlebury Coll (VT)
Millersville U of Pennsylvania (PA)
Milligan Coll (TN)
Millikin U (IL)
Millsaps Coll (MS)
Mills Coll (CA)
Minnesota State U Mankato (MN)
Minnesota State U Moorhead (MN)
Minot State U (ND)
Misericordia U (PA)
Mississippi State U (MS)
Missouri Baptist U (MO)
Missouri State U (MO)
Missouri U of Science and Technology (MO)
Missouri Valley Coll (MO)
Missouri Western State U (MO)
Molloy Coll (NY)
Monmouth Coll (IL)
Monmouth U (NJ)
Montana State U (MT)
Montana State U Billings (MT)
Montclair State U (NJ)
Moravian Coll (PA)
Morehead State U (KY)
Morehouse Coll (GA)
Morningside Coll (IA)
Mount Allison U (NB, Canada)
Mount Aloysius Coll (PA)
Mount Holyoke Coll (MA)
Mount Ida Coll (MA)
Mount Marty Coll (SD)
Mount Mary U (WI)
Mount Mercy U (IA)
Mount St. Joseph U (OH)
Mount Saint Mary Coll (NY)
Mount Saint Mary's U (CA)
Mount St. Mary's U (MD)
Mount Vernon Nazarene U (OH)
Muhlenberg Coll (PA)
Multnomah U (OR)
Muskingum U (OH)
National Louis U (IL)
National U (CA)
Nazareth Coll of Rochester (NY)
Nebraska Wesleyan U (NE)
Neumann U (PA)
Nevada State Coll (NV)
Newberry Coll (SC)
New Coll of Florida (FL)
New England Coll (NH)
New Jersey City U (NJ)
Newman U (KS)
New Mexico Highlands U (NM)
New Mexico Inst of Mining and Technology (NM)
New Mexico State U (NM)
The New School for Public Engagement (NY)
New York Inst of Technology (NY)
Nichols Coll (MA)
North Carolina Central U (NC)
North Carolina State U (NC)
North Carolina Wesleyan Coll (NC)
North Central Coll (IL)
Northcentral U (CA)
North Dakota State U (ND)
Northeastern Illinois U (IL)
Northeastern State U (OK)
Northeastern U (MA)
Northern Arizona U (AZ)
Northern Illinois U (IL)

Northern Kentucky U (KY)
Northern State U (SD)
North Greenville U (SC)
Northland Coll (WI)
Northwest Christian U (OR)
Northwestern Coll (IA)
Northwestern Oklahoma State U (OK)
Northwestern State U of Louisiana (LA)
Northwestern U (IL)
Northwest Missouri State U (MO)
Northwest U (WA)
Nova Southeastern U (FL)
Nyack Coll (NY)
Oakland City U (IN)
Oberlin Coll (OH)
Occidental Coll (CA)
Ohio Christian U (OH)
Ohio Dominican U (OH)
The Ohio State U (OH)
The Ohio State U at Lima (OH)
The Ohio State U at Marion (OH)
The Ohio State U–Mansfield Campus (OH)
The Ohio State U–Newark Campus (OH)
Ohio U (OH)
Ohio Valley U (WV)
Ohio Wesleyan U (OH)
Oklahoma Baptist U (OK)
Oklahoma Christian U (OK)
Oklahoma City U (OK)
Oklahoma State U (OK)
Old Dominion U (VA)
Olivet Nazarene U (IL)
Oral Roberts U (OK)
Oregon State U (OR)
Otterbein U (OH)
Ouachita Baptist U (AR)
Our Lady of the Lake U of San Antonio (TX)
Pace U (NY)
Pace U, Pleasantville Campus (NY)
Pacific Lutheran U (WA)
Paine Coll (GA)
Palm Beach Atlantic U (FL)
Penn State Abington (PA)
Penn State Altoona (PA)
Penn State Beaver (PA)
Penn State Berks (PA)
Penn State Brandywine (PA)
Penn State DuBois (PA)
Penn State Erie, The Behrend Coll (PA)
Penn State Fayette, The Eberly Campus (PA)
Penn State Greater Allegheny (PA)
Penn State Harrisburg (PA)
Penn State Hazleton (PA)
Penn State Lehigh Valley (PA)
Penn State Mont Alto (PA)
Penn State New Kensington (PA)
Penn State Schuylkill (PA)
Penn State Shenango (PA)
Penn State U Park (PA)
Penn State Wilkes-Barre (PA)
Penn State Worthington Scranton (PA)
Penn State York (PA)
Pepperdine U, Malibu (CA)
Philander Smith Coll (AR)
Piedmont Coll (GA)
Pine Manor Coll (MA)
Pittsburg State U (KS)
Pitzer Coll (CA)
Plymouth State U (NH)
Point Loma Nazarene U (CA)
Point Park U (PA)
Point U (GA)
Pomona Coll (CA)
Portland State U (OR)
Prairie View A&M U (TX)
Prescott Coll (AZ)
Princeton U (NJ)
Providence Coll (RI)
Purchase Coll, State U of New York (NY)
Purdue U (IN)
Purdue U Northwest (IN)
Queens Coll of the City U of New York (NY)
Quinnipiac U (CT)
Radford U (VA)
Ramapo Coll of New Jersey (NJ)
Randolph Coll (VA)
Randolph-Macon Coll (VA)
Redeemer U Coll (ON, Canada)
Reed Coll (OR)
Regent U (VA)
Regis Coll (MA)
Regis U (CO)
Rensselaer Polytechnic Inst (NY)
Rhode Island Coll (RI)
Rhodes Coll (TN)
Rice U (TX)
Ripon Coll (WI)
Roanoke Coll (VA)
Robert Morris U (PA)
Robert Morris U Illinois (IL)
Roberts Wesleyan Coll (NY)
Rochester Inst of Technology (NY)
Rockford U (IL)
Rockhurst U (MO)
Rocky Mountain Coll (MT)
Roger Williams U (RI)
Rollins Coll (FL)
Rosemont Coll (PA)
Rowan U (NJ)
Royal Military Coll of Canada (ON, Canada)
Rutgers U–Camden (NJ)
Rutgers U–Newark (NJ)
Rutgers U–New Brunswick (NJ)
Sacred Heart U (CT)
The Sage Colls (NY)
Saginaw Valley State U (MI)
St. Ambrose U (IA)
St. Andrews U (NC)
Saint Anselm Coll (NH)
Saint Augustine's U (NC)
St. Bonaventure U (NY)
St. Catherine U (MN)
St. Cloud State U (MN)
St. Edward's U (TX)
Saint Francis U (PA)
St. Gregory's U, Shawnee (OK)
St. John Fisher Coll (NY)
Saint John's U (MN)
St. John's U (NY)
St. Joseph's Coll, Long Island Campus (NY)
St. Joseph's Coll, New York (NY)
Saint Joseph's U (PA)
Saint Leo U (FL)
Saint Louis U (MO)
Saint Louis U–Madrid Campus (Spain)
Saint Martin's U (WA)
Saint Mary-of-the-Woods Coll (IN)
Saint Mary's Coll (IN)
Saint Mary's Coll of California (CA)
St. Mary's Coll of Maryland (MD)
Saint Mary's U of Minnesota (MN)
Saint Michael's Coll (VT)
St. Norbert Coll (WI)
St. Olaf Coll (MN)
Saint Peter's U (NJ)
St. Thomas Aquinas Coll (NY)
St. Thomas U (FL)
St. Thomas U (NB, Canada)
Saint Vincent Coll (PA)
Salisbury U (MD)
Salve Regina U (RI)
Samford U (AL)
Sam Houston State U (TX)
San Diego State U (CA)
San Francisco State U (CA)
Santa Clara U (CA)
Sarah Lawrence Coll (NY)
Schreiner U (TX)
Scripps Coll (CA)
Seattle Pacific U (WA)
Seattle U (WA)
Seton Hill U (PA)
Sewanee: The U of the South (TN)
Shawnee State U (OH)
Shaw U (NC)
Shenandoah U (VA)
Shepherd U (WV)
Shippensburg U of Pennsylvania (PA)
Shorter U (GA)
Siena Coll (NY)
Sierra Nevada Coll (NV)
Silver Lake Coll of the Holy Family (WI)
Simmons Coll (MA)
Simon Fraser U (BC, Canada)
Simpson Coll (IA)
Simpson U (CA)
Skidmore Coll (NY)
Slippery Rock U of Pennsylvania (PA)
Smith Coll (MA)
Sonoma State U (CA)
South Carolina State U (SC)
South Dakota State U (SD)
Southeastern Louisiana U (LA)
Southeastern Oklahoma State U (OK)
Southeastern U (FL)
Southeast Missouri State U (MO)
Southern Arkansas U–Magnolia (AR)
Southern Connecticut State U (CT)
Southern Illinois U Carbondale (IL)
Southern Illinois U Edwardsville (IL)
Southern Methodist U (TX)
Southern New Hampshire U (NH)
Southern Oregon U (OR)
Southern Utah U (UT)
Southwest Baptist U (MO)
Southwestern Adventist U (TX)
Southwestern Coll (KS)
Southwestern U (TX)
Spalding U (KY)
Spelman Coll (GA)
Spring Hill Coll (AL)
Stanford U (CA)
State U of New York at Fredonia (NY)
State U of New York at New Paltz (NY)
State U of New York at Oswego (NY)
State U of New York at Plattsburgh (NY)
State U of New York Coll at Cortland (NY)
State U of New York Coll at Geneseo (NY)
State U of New York Coll at Old Westbury (NY)
State U of New York Coll at Potsdam (NY)
State U of New York Empire State Coll (NY)
State U of New York Polytechnic Inst (NY)
Stephen F. Austin State U (TX)
Stephens Coll (MO)
Stevenson U (MD)
Stockton U (NJ)
Stonehill Coll (MA)
Stony Brook U, State U of New York (NY)
Suffolk U (MA)
Susquehanna U (PA)
Swarthmore Coll (PA)
Sweet Briar Coll (VA)
Syracuse U (NY)
Tabor Coll (KS)
Tarleton State U (TX)
Taylor U (IN)
Temple U (PA)
Tennessee State U (TN)
Tennessee Wesleyan U (TN)
Texas A&M Intl U (TX)
Texas A&M U (TX)
Texas A&M U–Central Texas (TX)
Texas A&M U–Commerce (TX)
Texas A&M U–Corpus Christi (TX)
Texas A&M U–Kingsville (TX)
Texas Christian U (TX)
Texas Lutheran U (TX)
Texas State U (TX)
Texas Tech U (TX)
Texas Wesleyan U (TX)
Texas Woman's U (TX)
Thomas More Coll (KY)
Thomas U (GA)
Tiffin U (OH)
Towson U (MD)
Transylvania U (KY)
Trent U (ON, Canada)
Trevecca Nazarene U (TN)
Trine U (IN)
Trinity Christian Coll (IL)
Trinity Coll of Florida (FL)
Trinity U (TX)
Troy U (AL)
Truett McConnell U (GA)
Truman State U (MO)
Tufts U (MA)
Tulane U (LA)
Tusculum Coll (TN)
Union Coll (KY)
Union Coll (NE)
Union Coll (NY)
Union Inst & U (OH)
Union U (TN)
United States Intl U–Africa (Kenya)
Universidad Adventista de las Antillas (PR)
Université de Montréal (QC, Canada)
Université de Sherbrooke (QC, Canada)
U at Albany, State U of New York (NY)
U at Buffalo, the State U of New York (NY)
The U of Akron (OH)
The U of Alabama (AL)
The U of Alabama at Birmingham (AL)
The U of Alabama in Huntsville (AL)
U of Alaska Fairbanks (AK)
The U of Arizona (AZ)
U of Arkansas (AR)
U of Bridgeport (CT)
U of California, Davis (CA)
U of California, Irvine (CA)
U of California, Los Angeles (CA)
U of California, Riverside (CA)
U of California, San Diego (CA)
U of California, Santa Barbara (CA)
U of Central Arkansas (AR)
U of Central Florida (FL)
U of Central Missouri (MO)
U of Charleston (WV)
U of Cincinnati (OH)
U of Colorado Boulder (CO)
U of Colorado Colorado Springs (CO)
U of Colorado Denver (CO)
U of Dayton (OH)
U of Delaware (DE)
U of Denver (CO)
U of Detroit Mercy (MI)
U of Dubuque (IA)
U of Evansville (IN)
The U of Findlay (OH)
U of Florida (FL)
U of Georgia (GA)
U of Great Falls (MT)
U of Guelph (ON, Canada)
U of Hartford (CT)
U of Hawaii at Manoa (HI)
U of Houston (TX)
U of Houston–Clear Lake (TX)
U of Houston–Downtown (TX)
U of Idaho (ID)
U of Illinois at Chicago (IL)
U of Illinois at Springfield (IL)
U of Indianapolis (IN)
U of Jamestown (ND)
The U of Kansas (KS)
U of Kentucky (KY)
U of King's Coll (NS, Canada)
U of La Verne (CA)
U of Lethbridge (AB, Canada)
U of Louisiana at Monroe (LA)
U of Louisville (KY)
U of Maine (ME)
U of Maine at Farmington (ME)
U of Maine at Presque Isle (ME)
U of Mary Hardin-Baylor (TX)
U of Maryland, Baltimore County (MD)
U of Maryland, Coll Park (MD)
U of Maryland U Coll (MD)
U of Mary Washington (VA)
U of Massachusetts Amherst (MA)
U of Massachusetts Boston (MA)
U of Massachusetts Dartmouth (MA)
U of Massachusetts Lowell (MA)
U of Miami (FL)
U of Michigan–Dearborn (MI)
U of Michigan–Flint (MI)
U of Minnesota, Duluth (MN)
U of Minnesota, Morris (MN)
U of Minnesota, Twin Cities Campus (MN)
U of Missouri–Kansas City (MO)
U of Missouri–St. Louis (MO)
U of Mobile (AL)
The U of Montana Western (MT)
U of Montevallo (AL)
U of Mount Union (OH)
U of Nebraska at Kearney (NE)
U of Nevada, Las Vegas (NV)
U of Nevada, Reno (NV)
U of New England (ME)
U of New Hampshire (NH)
U of New Hampshire at Manchester (NH)
U of New Haven (CT)
U of New Orleans (LA)
U of North Alabama (AL)
U of North Carolina at Asheville (NC)
The U of North Carolina at Chapel Hill (NC)
The U of North Carolina at Charlotte (NC)
The U of North Carolina at Greensboro (NC)
The U of North Carolina at Pembroke (NC)
The U of North Carolina Wilmington (NC)
U of North Dakota (ND)
U of Northern Colorado (CO)
U of Northern Iowa (IA)
U of North Florida (FL)
U of North Georgia (GA)
U of North Texas (TX)
U of Notre Dame (IN)
U of Oklahoma (OK)
U of Oregon (OR)
U of Pennsylvania (PA)
U of Pikeville (KY)
U of Pittsburgh (PA)
U of Pittsburgh at Bradford (PA)
U of Pittsburgh at Greensburg (PA)
U of Pittsburgh at Johnstown (PA)
U of Puget Sound (WA)
U of Regina (SK, Canada)
U of Rhode Island (RI)
U of Richmond (VA)
U of Rochester (NY)
U of St. Francis (IL)
U of Saint Joseph (CT)
U of Saint Mary (KS)
U of St. Thomas (MN)
U of St. Thomas (TX)
U of San Diego (CA)
U of San Francisco (CA)
U of Saskatchewan (SK, Canada)
U of Science and Arts of Oklahoma (OK)
The U of Scranton (PA)
U of South Alabama (AL)
U of South Carolina Aiken (SC)
The U of South Dakota (SD)
U of Southern California (CA)
U of Southern Indiana (IN)
U of Southern Maine (ME)
U of Southern Mississippi (MS)
U of South Florida (FL)
U of South Florida, St. Petersburg (FL)
U of South Florida Sarasota-Manatee (FL)
The U of Tampa (FL)
The U of Tennessee (TN)
The U of Tennessee at Chattanooga (TN)
The U of Tennessee at Martin (TN)
The U of Texas at Austin (TX)
The U of Texas at Dallas (TX)
The U of Texas at El Paso (TX)
The U of Texas at San Antonio (TX)
The U of Texas of the Permian Basin (TX)
The U of Texas Rio Grande Valley (TX)
U of the Cumberlands (KY)
U of the Fraser Valley (BC, Canada)
U of the Incarnate Word (TX)
U of the Pacific (CA)
U of the Southwest (NM)
U of the Virgin Islands (VI)
U of the West (CA)
The U of Toledo (OH)
The U of Tulsa (OK)
U of Utah (UT)
U of Valley Forge (PA)
U of Vermont (VT)
U of Virginia (VA)
The U of Virginia's Coll at Wise (VA)
U of Washington (WA)
U of Washington, Tacoma (WA)
U of Waterloo (ON, Canada)
The U of West Alabama (AL)
U of West Georgia (GA)
U of Windsor (ON, Canada)
U of Wisconsin–Eau Claire (WI)

U of Wisconsin–Green Bay (WI)
U of Wisconsin–La Crosse (WI)
U of Wisconsin–Madison (WI)
U of Wisconsin–Milwaukee (WI)
U of Wisconsin–Parkside (WI)
U of Wisconsin–Platteville (WI)
U of Wisconsin–Stevens Point (WI)
U of Wisconsin–Stout (WI)
U of Wisconsin–Superior (WI)
U of Wisconsin–Whitewater (WI)
Upper Iowa U (IA)
Ursinus Coll (PA)
Utah State U (UT)
Utah Valley U (UT)
Utica Coll (NY)
Valdosta State U (GA)
Valley City State U (ND)
Valparaiso U (IN)
Vanderbilt U (TN)
Villa Maria Coll (NY)
Villanova U (PA)
Virginia Commonwealth U (VA)
Virginia Military Inst (VA)
Virginia Polytechnic Inst and State U (VA)
Virginia State U (VA)
Virginia Union U (VA)
Virginia Wesleyan Coll (VA)
Viterbo U (WI)
Wabash Coll (IN)
Wagner Coll (NY)
Wake Forest U (NC)
Waldorf U (IA)
Walla Walla U (WA)
Walsh U (OH)
Wartburg Coll (IA)
Washburn U (KS)
Washington & Jefferson Coll (PA)
Washington and Lee U (VA)
Washington Coll (MD)
Washington State U (WA)
Washington State U–Global Campus (WA)
Washington State U–Tri-Cities (WA)
Washington State U–Vancouver (WA)
Washington U in St. Louis (MO)
Wayland Baptist U (TX)
Waynesburg U (PA)
Wayne State Coll (NE)
Wayne State U (MI)
Weber State U (UT)
Webster U (MO)
Wells Coll (NY)
Wesleyan Coll (GA)
Wesleyan U (CT)
West Chester U of Pennsylvania (PA)
Western Carolina U (NC)
Western Connecticut State U (CT)
Western Illinois U (IL)
Western Kentucky U (KY)
Western Michigan U (MI)
Western New England U (MA)
Western Oregon U (OR)
Western State Colorado U (CO)
Westfield State U (MA)
Westminster Coll (PA)
Westminster Coll (UT)
Westmont Coll (CA)
West Texas A&M U (TX)
West Virginia State U (WV)
West Virginia U (WV)
West Virginia U Inst of Technology (WV)
West Virginia Wesleyan Coll (WV)
Wheaton Coll (IL)
Wheaton Coll (MA)
Wheeling Jesuit U (WV)
Whitman Coll (WA)
Whittier Coll (CA)
Whitworth U (WA)
Wichita State U (KS)
Widener U (PA)
Wilkes U (PA)
Willamette U (OR)
William Jewell Coll (MO)
William Paterson U of New Jersey (NJ)
William Peace U (NC)
William Penn U (IA)
Williams Baptist Coll (AR)
Williams Coll (MA)
William Woods U (MO)
Wilmington U (DE)
Wilson Coll (PA)
Wingate U (NC)
Winona State U (MN)
Winthrop U (SC)
Wittenberg U (OH)
Wofford Coll (SC)
Woodbury U (CA)
Worcester Polytechnic Inst (MA)
Worcester State U (MA)
Wright State U (OH)
Wright State U–Lake Campus (OH)
Xavier U of Louisiana (LA)
York Coll of Pennsylvania (PA)
York Coll of the City U of New York (NY)
Youngstown State U (OH)

PSYCHOLOGY RELATED
Adams State U (CO)
Augsburg Coll (MN)
Becker Coll (MA)
Buena Vista U (IA)
Butler U (IN)
Canisius Coll (NY)
Central Baptist Coll (AR)
Eastern Nazarene Coll (MA)
Faulkner U (AL)
Kansas Wesleyan U (KS)
Kean U (NJ)
Madonna U (MI)
Marist Coll (NY)
National U (CA)
Prescott Coll (AZ)
Rhode Island Coll (RI)
Saint Mary's Coll of California (CA)
State U of New York at Oswego (NY)
State U of New York Coll of Agriculture and Technology at Cobleskill (NY)
Swarthmore Coll (PA)
Tiffin U (OH)
The U of North Carolina at Greensboro (NC)
Western State Colorado U (CO)

PSYCHOLOGY TEACHER EDUCATION
Albion Coll (MI)
Boise State U (ID)
Bradley U (IL)
Brigham Young U (UT)
California Lutheran U (CA)
Campbellsville U (KY)
Lee U (TN)
Ohio Wesleyan U (OH)
Pittsburg State U (KS)
Rocky Mountain Coll (MT)
U of Delaware (DE)
U of Michigan–Flint (MI)
U of Wisconsin–Whitewater (WI)
Valparaiso U (IN)
Wayne State Coll (NE)
Weber State U (UT)
Widener U (PA)

PUBLIC ADMINISTRATION
Alfred U (NY)
American U of Beirut (Lebanon)
Auburn U (AL)
Baldwin Wallace U (OH)
Baruch Coll of the City U of New York (NY)
Bayamón Central U (PR)
Baylor U (TX)
Biola U (CA)
Blackburn Coll (IL)
Bowling Green State U (OH)
Buena Vista U (IA)
California Baptist U (CA)
California Lutheran U (CA)
California State U, Bakersfield (CA)
California State U, Chico (CA)
California State U, Dominguez Hills (CA)
California State U, East Bay (CA)
California State U, Fresno (CA)
California State U, Fullerton (CA)
Calvin Coll (MI)
Capital U (OH)
Catawba Coll (NC)
Cedarville U (OH)
Central Methodist U (MO)
Cleveland State U (OH)
Colorado Mesa U (CO)
Columbia Coll (MO)
Concordia U (QC, Canada)
Doane U (NE)
Eastern Michigan U (MI)
Eastern Washington U (WA)
Elon U (NC)
Evangel U (MO)
The Evergreen State Coll (WA)
Flagler Coll (FL)
Florida Atlantic U (FL)
Florida Intl U (FL)
Grand Valley State U (MI)
Harding U (AR)
Heidelberg U (OH)
Henderson State U (AR)
Indiana U Bloomington (IN)
Indiana U Kokomo (IN)
Indiana U Northwest (IN)
Indiana U–Purdue U Indianapolis (IN)
Iowa State U of Science and Technology (IA)
Jacksonville U (FL)
James Madison U (VA)
John Carroll U (OH)
John Jay Coll of Criminal Justice of the City U of New York (NY)
Johns Hopkins U (MD)
Kean U (NJ)
Kentucky State U (KY)
Kutztown U of Pennsylvania (PA)
La Salle U (PA)
Lewis U (IL)
Lincoln U (MO)
Lindenwood U (MO)
Lipscomb U (TN)
Louisiana Coll (LA)
Metropolitan Coll of New York (NY)
Miami U (OH)
MidAmerica Nazarene U (KS)
Millsaps Coll (MS)
Minnesota State U Mankato (MN)
Mississippi Valley State U (MS)
Missouri State U (MO)
Missouri Valley Coll (MO)
Mount Ida Coll (MA)
Muskingum U (OH)
National U (CA)
Northern Arizona U (AZ)
Northern State U (SD)
Northwest Missouri State U (MO)
Nova Southeastern U (FL)
The Ohio State U (OH)
Ohio Wesleyan U (OH)
Plymouth State U (NH)
Point Park U (PA)
Regent U (VA)
Regis U (CO)
Rhode Island Coll (RI)
Rogers State U (OK)
Roger Williams U (RI)
Saginaw Valley State U (MI)
St. Cloud State U (MN)
Saint Francis U (PA)
St. John's U (NY)
St. Thomas U (FL)
Samford U (AL)
Sam Houston State U (TX)
San Diego State U (CA)
Seattle U (WA)
Shaw U (NC)
Shippensburg U of Pennsylvania (PA)
Silver Lake Coll of the Holy Family (WI)
Southern New Hampshire U (NH)
Stephen F. Austin State U (TX)
Syracuse U (NY)
Tennessee State U (TN)
Texas State U (TX)
U at Albany, State U of New York (NY)
The U of Arizona (AZ)
U of Central Arkansas (AR)
U of Central Florida (FL)
U of Georgia (GA)
U of Guelph (ON, Canada)
U of Houston–Clear Lake (TX)
The U of Kansas (KS)
U of La Verne (CA)
U of Lethbridge (AB, Canada)
U of Maine at Fort Kent (ME)
U of Maryland U Coll (MD)
U of Michigan–Flint (MI)
U of Missouri–St. Louis (MO)
U of Nevada, Las Vegas (NV)
U of New Haven (CT)
The U of North Carolina at Pembroke (NC)
U of North Dakota (ND)
U of Northern Iowa (IA)
U of Oklahoma (OK)
U of Oregon (OR)
U of Pittsburgh (PA)
U of San Francisco (CA)
U of Saskatchewan (SK, Canada)
The U of Tennessee (TN)
The U of Tennessee at Martin (TN)
The U of Texas at San Antonio (TX)
U of Toronto (ON, Canada)
U of Wisconsin–Green Bay (WI)
U of Wisconsin–La Crosse (WI)
U of Wisconsin–Stevens Point (WI)
U of Wisconsin–Whitewater (WI)
Upper Iowa U (IA)
Wagner Coll (NY)
Washburn U (KS)
Wayne State U (MI)
Western Oregon U (OR)
West Texas A&M U (TX)
Wilkes U (PA)
Willamette U (OR)
Winona State U (MN)

PUBLIC ADMINISTRATION AND SOCIAL SERVICE PROFESSIONS RELATED
Coll of Coastal Georgia (GA)
Emory & Henry Coll (VA)
The Evergreen State Coll (WA)
Jacksonville State U (AL)
Milligan Coll (TN)
National Louis U (IL)
Northeastern Illinois U (IL)
Prescott Coll (AZ)
Rutgers U–Newark (NJ)
San Diego State U (CA)
State U of New York Empire State Coll (NY)
Trevecca Nazarene U (TN)
Troy U (AL)
U of Colorado Denver (CO)
U of Detroit Mercy (MI)

PUBLIC/APPLIED HISTORY
Arkansas Tech U (AR)
Baldwin Wallace U (OH)
Cairn U (PA)
Central Michigan U (MI)
Concordia U (QC, Canada)
Emory & Henry Coll (VA)
Flagler Coll (FL)
Goshen Coll (IN)
North Dakota State U (ND)
Rhode Island Coll (RI)
Western Michigan U (MI)

PUBLIC FINANCE
Husson U (ME)
Niagara U (NY)

PUBLIC HEALTH
Agnes Scott Coll (GA)
Allen Coll (IA)
American Intl Coll (MA)
American Public U System (WV)
American U (DC)
Arcadia U (PA)
Arizona State U at the Downtown Phoenix campus (AZ)
Augustana Coll (IL)
Austin Coll (TX)
Baldwin Wallace U (OH)
Belmont U (TN)
Bluffton U (OH)
Bowling Green State U (OH)
Caldwell U (NJ)
California State U, Long Beach (CA)
Calvin Coll (MI)
Central Washington U (WA)
Colby-Sawyer Coll (NH)
The Coll of New Jersey (NJ)
The Coll of Saint Rose (NY)
Curry Coll (MA)
Dominican U of California (CA)
Drexel U (PA)
East Stroudsburg U of Pennsylvania (PA)
East Tennessee State U (TN)
Elon U (NC)
Excelsior Coll (NY)
Ferris State U (MI)
Fort Lewis Coll (CO)
Franklin Pierce U (NH)
Gannon U (PA)
Hawai`i Pacific U (HI)
Hunter Coll of the City U of New York (NY)
Indiana U of Pennsylvania (PA)
Indiana U–Purdue U Indianapolis (IN)
Johns Hopkins U (MD)
Kent State U (OH)
Kent State U at Trumbull (OH)
Langston U (OK)
La Salle U (PA)
Marian U (IN)
Marshall U (WV)
Marymount Manhattan Coll (NY)
Mercer U, Macon (GA)
Mercy Coll of Health Sciences (IA)
Mercyhurst U (PA)
Meredith Coll (NC)
Merrimack Coll (MA)
Miami U (OH)
Minnesota State U Mankato (MN)
Missouri Western State U (MO)
Montclair State U (NJ)
Muhlenberg Coll (PA)
Muskingum U (OH)
Northern Arizona U (AZ)
The Ohio State U (OH)
Ohio U (OH)
Oregon State U (OR)
Portland State U (OR)
Regis Coll (MA)
Roger Williams U (RI)
Rutgers U–New Brunswick (NJ)
Saint Francis U (PA)
Saint Louis U (MO)
Saint Louis U–Madrid Campus (Spain)
Samford U (AL)
Sam Houston State U (TX)
Santa Clara U (CA)
Slippery Rock U of Pennsylvania (PA)
Southern Connecticut State U (CT)
State U of New York Coll at Old Westbury (NY)
Syracuse U (NY)
Tarleton State U (TX)
Texas A&M U (TX)
Tufts U (MA)
U at Albany, State U of New York (NY)
The U of Arizona (AZ)
U of Arkansas (AR)
U of Colorado Denver (CO)
U of Evansville (IN)
U of Florida (FL)
U of Georgia (GA)
U of Hawaii at Manoa (HI)
U of Kentucky (KY)
U of Lethbridge (AB, Canada)
U of Louisville (KY)
U of Massachusetts Amherst (MA)
U of Massachusetts Lowell (MA)
U of Miami (FL)
U of Nevada, Las Vegas (NV)
U of New England (ME)
The U of North Carolina at Charlotte (NC)
U of North Texas (TX)
U of Rochester (NY)
U of Saint Joseph (CT)
U of Southern Mississippi (MS)
U of South Florida (FL)
The U of Tampa (FL)
The U of Texas at Austin (TX)
The U of Texas at San Antonio (TX)
U of the Cumberlands (KY)
U of Washington (WA)
Valparaiso U (IN)
Wartburg Coll (IA)
Wayne State U (MI)
Weber State U (UT)
Westminster Coll (UT)
West Virginia U (WV)
William Paterson U of New Jersey (NJ)
Youngstown State U (OH)

PUBLIC HEALTH/COMMUNITY NURSING
Capital U (OH)
Northern Illinois U (IL)
U of Miami (FL)
Walla Walla U (WA)

PUBLIC HEALTH EDUCATION AND PROMOTION
American U (DC)
Appalachian State U (NC)
Arizona State U at the Downtown Phoenix campus (AZ)

Barton Coll (NC)
Baylor U (TX)
California Baptist U (CA)
California State U, Long Beach (CA)
Central Michigan U (MI)
Central Washington U (WA)
Coastal Carolina U (SC)
Colby-Sawyer Coll (NH)
Coll of Charleston (SC)
Dalhousie U (NS, Canada)
East Carolina U (NC)
Eastern Washington U (WA)
Georgia Southern U (GA)
Inter American U of Puerto Rico, Ponce Campus (PR)
Ithaca Coll (NY)
Kennesaw State U (GA)
Liberty U (VA)
Lynchburg Coll (VA)
Malone U (OH)
Marymount U (VA)
Montana State U–Northern (MT)
New Mexico State U (NM)
North Carolina Central U (NC)
Oklahoma State U (OK)
Plymouth State U (NH)
Purdue U (IN)
Simmons Coll (MA)
Southeastern Louisiana U (LA)
Southern Illinois U Edwardsville (IL)
State U of New York Coll of Technology at Canton (NY)
Temple U (PA)
Texas State U (TX)
U of Arkansas (AR)
U of Georgia (GA)
U of Michigan–Dearborn (MI)
U of Minnesota, Duluth (MN)
U of Mount Union (OH)
U of North Carolina at Asheville (NC)
The U of North Carolina at Greensboro (NC)
The U of North Carolina Wilmington (NC)
U of North Dakota (ND)
U of North Texas (TX)
U of St. Thomas (MN)
The U of Scranton (PA)
The U of Texas at Austin (TX)
The U of Toledo (OH)
U of Wisconsin–La Crosse (WI)
Walla Walla U (WA)
Weber State U (UT)
West Chester U of Pennsylvania (PA)
Western Illinois U (IL)
Winona State U (MN)

PUBLIC HEALTH RELATED
Franklin & Marshall Coll (PA)
Hampshire Coll (MA)
Henderson State U (AR)
Indiana U Bloomington (IN)
Lourdes U (OH)
Shenandoah U (VA)
Stockton U (NJ)
U of California, Irvine (CA)
U of Maryland, Coll Park (MD)
U of Michigan (MI)
U of Michigan–Flint (MI)
U of South Carolina (SC)
Utah State U (UT)

PUBLIC POLICY ANALYSIS
Albion Coll (MI)
Arizona State U at the Downtown Phoenix campus (AZ)
Bennington Coll (VT)
Bentley U (MA)
Brigham Young U (UT)
Bryant U (RI)
Carnegie Mellon U (PA)
Central Washington U (WA)
Chatham U (PA)
Coll of the Atlantic (ME)
The Coll of William and Mary (VA)
Concordia U, St. Paul (MN)
Cornell U (NY)
Dickinson Coll (PA)
Elon U (NC)
The George Washington U (DC)
Georgia Inst of Technology (GA)
Georgia State U (GA)
Hamilton Coll (NY)
Hampshire Coll (MA)
Hobart and William Smith Colls (NY)
Hofstra U (NY)
Howard Payne U (TX)
Jacksonville U (FL)
Johns Hopkins U (MD)
Massachusetts Coll of Liberal Arts (MA)
Michigan State U (MI)
Mills Coll (CA)
Morehead State U (KY)
Muskingum U (OH)
New Coll of Florida (FL)
Northwestern U (IL)
Olivet Nazarene U (IL)
Penn State Harrisburg (PA)
Pomona Coll (CA)
Princeton U (NJ)
Rice U (TX)
Rochester Inst of Technology (NY)
The Sage Colls (NY)
St. Cloud State U (MN)
St. Mary's Coll of Maryland (MD)
Saint Peter's U (NJ)
Saint Vincent Coll (PA)
Sarah Lawrence Coll (NY)
Scripps Coll (CA)
Southern Methodist U (TX)
Stanford U (CA)
State U of New York Empire State Coll (NY)
Suffolk U (MA)
Susquehanna U (PA)
Trevecca Nazarene U (TN)
U at Albany, State U of New York (NY)
U of California, Riverside (CA)
U of Chicago (IL)
U of Delaware (DE)
U of Denver (CO)
U of Michigan (MI)
The U of North Carolina at Chapel Hill (NC)
U of Pennsylvania (PA)
U of Pittsburgh at Greensburg (PA)
U of Rhode Island (RI)
U of Saint Joseph (CT)
The U of Texas at Austin (TX)
The U of Texas at Dallas (TX)
U of Virginia (VA)
Vanderbilt U (TN)
Virginia Polytechnic Inst and State U (VA)
Wagner Coll (NY)
Washington & Jefferson Coll (PA)
Washington State U (WA)
Washington State U–Vancouver (WA)

PUBLIC RELATIONS, ADVERTISING, AND APPLIED COMMUNICATION
Anderson U (IN)
Anderson U (SC)
Belmont U (TN)
Biola U (CA)
Bluffton U (OH)
Bradley U (IL)
Butler U (IN)
California Baptist U (CA)
California State U, Dominguez Hills (CA)
Cardinal Stritch U (WI)
Dallas Baptist U (TX)
Endicott Coll (MA)
Flagler Coll (FL)
Florida Inst of Technology (FL)
Florida Southern Coll (FL)
Goshen Coll (IN)
Houghton Coll (NY)
Howard Payne U (TX)
Kansas Wesleyan U (KS)
Kennesaw State U (GA)
Lake Erie Coll (OH)
Loyola U New Orleans (LA)
Lynn U (FL)
Marymount Manhattan Coll (NY)
Massachusetts Coll of Liberal Arts (MA)
Messiah Coll (PA)
Minnesota State U Moorhead (MN)
Muskingum U (OH)
National U (CA)
New York Inst of Technology (NY)
Ohio Dominican U (OH)
Oklahoma City U (OK)
Pepperdine U, Malibu (CA)
Point Park U (PA)
Rhode Island Coll (RI)
Seattle U (WA)
Simpson Coll (IA)
Taylor U (IN)
Texas Christian U (TX)
U of Colorado Boulder (CO)
The U of Findlay (OH)
U of Kentucky (KY)
U of Mount Union (OH)
The U of Scranton (PA)
The U of Tampa (FL)
West Texas A&M U (TX)
William Jewell Coll (MO)

PUBLIC RELATIONS, ADVERTISING, AND APPLIED COMMUNICATION RELATED
Abilene Christian U (TX)
Alma Coll (MI)
Brigham Young U (UT)
Buena Vista U (IA)
Butler U (IN)
California Lutheran U (CA)
The Coll of St. Scholastica (MN)
Columbia Coll (MO)
Duquesne U (PA)
Fairfield U (CT)
Grace Coll (IN)
Lipscomb U (TN)
Loyola U Chicago (IL)
Marietta Coll (OH)
Marywood U (PA)
Metropolitan State U of Denver (CO)
Missouri Western State U (MO)
Morrisville State Coll (NY)
Muskingum U (OH)
Northern Arizona U (AZ)
Oklahoma City U (OK)
Oklahoma State U (OK)
Pepperdine U, Malibu (CA)
Rochester Inst of Technology (NY)
Royal Roads U (BC, Canada)
St. John's U (NY)
Saint Mary's U of Minnesota (MN)
Spring Hill Coll (AL)
U of Central Arkansas (AR)
The U of Tampa (FL)
U of Vermont (VT)
Virginia Polytechnic Inst and State U (VA)
Virginia State U (VA)
Weber State U (UT)
Western Michigan U (MI)

PUBLIC RELATIONS/IMAGE MANAGEMENT
Alderson Broaddus U (WV)
Andrews U (MI)
Appalachian State U (NC)
Auburn U (AL)
Avila U (MO)
Baldwin Wallace U (OH)
Barry U (FL)
Belmont U (TN)
Biola U (CA)
Bowie State U (MD)
Bowling Green State U (OH)
Bradley U (IL)
Buffalo State Coll, State U of New York (NY)
California Lutheran U (CA)
California State U, Dominguez Hills (CA)
California State U, East Bay (CA)
California State U, Fresno (CA)
California State U, Fullerton (CA)
California State U, Long Beach (CA)
Capital U (OH)
Carroll Coll (MT)
Central Michigan U (MI)
Central Washington U (WA)
Champlain Coll (VT)
Chapman U (CA)
Chatham U (PA)
Cleveland State U (OH)
Coe Coll (IA)
Columbia Coll Chicago (IL)
Dominican U (IL)
Drake U (IA)
Eastern Illinois U (IL)
Eastern Michigan U (MI)
Emerson Coll (MA)
Ferris State U (MI)
Florida Ag and Mech U (FL)
Freed-Hardeman U (TN)
Georgia Southern U (GA)
Gonzaga U (WA)
Greenville Coll (IL)
Hampton U (VA)
Harding U (AR)
Heidelberg U (OH)
Hofstra U (NY)
Hood Coll (MD)
Huntington U (IN)
Illinois State U (IL)
Inter American U of Puerto Rico, Ponce Campus (PR)
Iona Coll (NY)
Iowa State U of Science and Technology (IA)
Ithaca Coll (NY)
Keene State Coll (NH)
Kent State U (OH)
La Salle U (PA)
Lee U (TN)
Lewis U (IL)
Lipscomb U (TN)
Loras Coll (IA)
Louisiana Coll (LA)
Mansfield U of Pennsylvania (PA)
The Master's U (CA)
Miami U (OH)
Minnesota State U Mankato (MN)
Minnesota State U Moorhead (MN)
Missouri Baptist U (MO)
Missouri Valley Coll (MO)
Monmouth Coll (IL)
Montana State U Billings (MT)
Mount Mercy U (IA)
Mount Saint Mary Coll (NY)
Mount Vernon Nazarene U (OH)
Murray State U (KY)
New England Coll (NH)
North Dakota State U (ND)
Northern Kentucky U (KY)
Northwestern Coll (IA)
Ohio U–Zanesville (OH)
Oklahoma Christian U (OK)
Olivet Nazarene U (IL)
Palm Beach Atlantic U (FL)
Point Park U (PA)
Quinnipiac U (CT)
Rochester Inst of Technology (NY)
Rowan U (NJ)
St. Ambrose U (IA)
St. Cloud State U (MN)
Saint Francis U (PA)
San Diego State U (CA)
South Dakota State U (SD)
Southeastern U (FL)
Southern Methodist U (TX)
State U of New York at Oswego (NY)
Stephens Coll (MO)
Suffolk U (MA)
Syracuse U (NY)
Taylor U (IN)
Texas Christian U (TX)
Texas State U (TX)
Texas Tech U (TX)
Tiffin U (OH)
Union U (TN)
The U of Akron (OH)
The U of Alabama (AL)
U of Central Missouri (MO)
U of Florida (FL)
U of Georgia (GA)
U of Houston (TX)
U of Idaho (ID)
U of Miami (FL)
U of Northern Iowa (IA)
U of Oregon (OR)
U of Pittsburgh at Bradford (PA)
U of Rhode Island (RI)
U of South Carolina (SC)
U of Southern California (CA)
The U of Tennessee (TN)
The U of Texas at Austin (TX)
U of Toronto (ON, Canada)
Utica Coll (NY)
Walla Walla U (WA)
Wartburg Coll (IA)
Washington and Lee U (VA)
Wayne State U (MI)
Weber State U (UT)
Webster U (MO)
Western Kentucky U (KY)
Western New England U (MA)
Westminster Coll (PA)
West Virginia Wesleyan Coll (WV)
William Penn U (IA)
York Coll of Pennsylvania (PA)

PUBLISHING
Belmont U (TN)
Emerson Coll (MA)
Graceland U (IA)
Rochester Inst of Technology (NY)

PURCHASING, PROCUREMENT/ ACQUISITIONS AND CONTRACTS MANAGEMENT
Arizona State U at the Tempe campus (AZ)
Athens State U (AL)
California State U, East Bay (CA)
Central Michigan U (MI)
The U of Alabama in Huntsville (AL)
U of Houston–Downtown (TX)
U of the Potomac (DC)

QUALITY CONTROL AND SAFETY TECHNOLOGIES RELATED
Madonna U (MI)

QUALITY CONTROL TECHNOLOGY
Bowling Green State U (OH)
California State U, Long Beach (CA)
Tarleton State U (TX)

RADIATION BIOLOGY
Suffolk U (MA)

RADIATION PROTECTION/ HEALTH PHYSICS TECHNOLOGY
Indiana U–Purdue U Indianapolis (IN)
Lewis U (IL)
Thomas Edison State U (NJ)

RADIO AND TELEVISION
Appalachian State U (NC)
Ashland U (OH)
Auburn U (AL)
Barry U (FL)
Bemidji State U (MN)
Biola U (CA)
Boston U (MA)
Bowling Green State U (OH)
Bradley U (IL)
Brooklyn Coll of the City U of New York (NY)
Buffalo State Coll, State U of New York (NY)
Butler U (IN)
California State U, Fresno (CA)
California State U, Fullerton (CA)
California State U, Long Beach (CA)
California State U, Monterey Bay (CA)
Columbia Coll Chicago (IL)
Cornerstone U (MI)
Drake U (IA)
Eastern Nazarene Coll (MA)
Elon U (NC)
Emerson Coll (MA)
Evangel U (MO)
Franklin Pierce U (NH)
The George Washington U (DC)
Georgia Southern U (GA)
Gonzaga U (WA)
Grand Valley State U (MI)
Hofstra U (NY)
Iona Coll (NY)
Ithaca Coll (NY)
Lebanese American U (Lebanon)
Lewis U (IL)
Marietta Coll (OH)
Marist Coll (NY)
The Master's U (CA)
Minot State U (ND)
Missouri Baptist U (MO)
Montclair State U (NJ)
Murray State U (KY)
North Central Coll (IL)
Northern Arizona U (AZ)
Northwestern U (IL)
Ohio U (OH)
Oklahoma Christian U (OK)
Pepperdine U, Malibu (CA)
Point Park U (PA)
Rowan U (NJ)
St. Ambrose U (IA)

St. Cloud State U (MN)
Sam Houston State U (TX)
San Diego State U (CA)
San Francisco State U (CA)
Savannah Coll of Art and Design (GA)
Southeastern U (FL)
Southern Illinois U Carbondale (IL)
Southwestern Coll (KS)
State U of New York at Fredonia (NY)
Syracuse U (NY)
Texas A&M U–Commerce (TX)
Texas State U (TX)
Texas Tech U (TX)
Texas Wesleyan U (TX)
Troy U (AL)
Union U (TN)
The U of Akron (OH)
The U of Alabama (AL)
U of Central Florida (FL)
U of Central Missouri (MO)
U of Cincinnati (OH)
U of Dayton (OH)
U of Florida (FL)
U of Houston (TX)
U of Kentucky (KY)
U of Miami (FL)
U of Montevallo (AL)
U of North Texas (TX)
U of Pittsburgh at Bradford (PA)
U of Southern Indiana (IN)
The U of Texas at Austin (TX)
U of the Incarnate Word (TX)
U of Wisconsin–Superior (WI)
Walla Walla U (WA)
Wartburg Coll (IA)
Waynesburg U (PA)
Wayne State U (MI)
Weber State U (UT)
Western Illinois U (IL)
Western Kentucky U (KY)
Westminster Coll (PA)
William Penn U (IA)
Youngstown State U (OH)

RADIO AND TELEVISION BROADCASTING TECHNOLOGY
Coll of the Ozarks (MO)
Emerson Coll (MA)
Ferris State U (MI)
Gannon U (PA)
Gardner-Webb U (NC)
La Salle U (PA)
Lincoln Coll (IL)
New England Inst of Technology (RI)
New York Inst of Technology (NY)
Suffolk U (MA)
Wilmington U (DE)

RADIOLOGIC TECHNOLOGY/ SCIENCE
Adventist U of Health Sciences (FL)
Austin Peay State U (TN)
Bluefield State Coll (WV)
Central Penn Coll (PA)
Colorado Mesa U (CO)
Cox Coll (MO)
Dalhousie U (NS, Canada)
Friends U (KS)
The George Washington U (DC)
Gwynedd Mercy U (PA)
Henderson State U (AR)
Holy Family U (PA)
Indiana U Northwest (IN)
Inter American U of Puerto Rico, Aguadilla Campus (PR)
Inter American U of Puerto Rico, Barranquitas Campus (PR)
Inter American U of Puerto Rico, Ponce Campus (PR)
Inter American U of Puerto Rico, San Germán Campus (PR)
Lewis U (IL)
Manhattan Coll (NY)
Marian U (WI)
Marshall U (WV)
McNeese State U (LA)
MCPHS U (MA)
Missouri State U (MO)
Nebraska Methodist Coll (NE)
North Dakota State U (ND)
Northern Kentucky U (KY)
Northwestern State U of Louisiana (LA)
Northwest Missouri State U (MO)
The Ohio State U (OH)
Quinnipiac U (CT)
Regis Coll (MA)
Rhode Island Coll (RI)
St. John's U (NY)
St. Vincent's Coll (CT)
Spencerian Coll (KY)
U of Charleston (WV)
U of Jamestown (ND)
U of Louisiana at Monroe (LA)
U of Oklahoma Health Sciences Center (OK)
U of Pittsburgh at Bradford (PA)
U of St. Francis (IL)
U of South Alabama (AL)
U of Southern Indiana (IN)
U of Toronto (ON, Canada)
Virginia Commonwealth U (VA)
Weber State U (UT)
Widener U (PA)
York Coll of Pennsylvania (PA)

RADIOLOGIST ASSISTANT
Weber State U (UT)

RADIO, TELEVISION, AND DIGITAL COMMUNICATION RELATED
Asbury U (KY)
Ashland U (OH)
Brigham Young U (UT)
Central Michigan U (MI)
Clark Atlanta U (GA)
Dallas Baptist U (TX)
Drake U (IA)
Emerson Coll (MA)
Hofstra U (NY)
Louisiana Coll (LA)
Madonna U (MI)
North Dakota State U (ND)
Rogers State U (OK)
San Francisco State U (CA)
Spring Hill Coll (AL)
State U of New York Coll of Agriculture and Technology at Cobleskill (NY)
Texas Christian U (TX)
Towson U (MD)
U of Advancing Technology (AZ)
The U of Akron (OH)
Washington State U (WA)
Western Carolina U (NC)
William Penn U (IA)

RANGE SCIENCE AND MANAGEMENT
Colorado State U (CO)
Humboldt State U (CA)
New Mexico State U (NM)
North Dakota State U (ND)
Oregon State U (OR)
South Dakota State U (SD)
Tarleton State U (TX)
Texas A&M U (TX)
U of Idaho (ID)
U of Nevada, Reno (NV)
Utah State U (UT)
Washington State U (WA)

READING TEACHER EDUCATION
Aquinas Coll (MI)
Baylor U (TX)
Canisius Coll (NY)
Concordia U Chicago (IL)
Eastern Michigan U (MI)
Eastern Washington U (WA)
Goddard Coll (VT)
Grand Valley State U (MI)
Harding U (AR)
Iowa Wesleyan U (IA)
Michigan State U (MI)
St. Cloud State U (MN)
Sam Houston State U (TX)
State U of New York Coll at Cortland (NY)
Tennessee State U (TN)
Texas A&M Intl U (TX)
Texas Wesleyan U (TX)
U of Central Missouri (MO)
U of Georgia (GA)
U of Great Falls (MT)
Upper Iowa U (IA)
William Penn U (IA)
Wingate U (NC)

REAL ESTATE
Baruch Coll of the City U of New York (NY)
Baylor U (TX)
Bowling Green State U (OH)
California State U, Dominguez Hills (CA)
California State U, East Bay (CA)
California State U, Fresno (CA)
Central Michigan U (MI)
Clarion U of Pennsylvania (PA)
Colorado State U (CO)
Drexel U (PA)
Florida Atlantic U (FL)
Florida Intl U (FL)
Georgia State U (GA)
Inter American U of Puerto Rico, Metropolitan Campus (PR)
Menlo Coll (CA)
Minnesota State U Mankato (MN)
Mississippi State U (MS)
The Ohio State U (OH)
Portland State U (OR)
St. Cloud State U (MN)
San Diego State U (CA)
Southern Methodist U (TX)
Syracuse U (NY)
Temple U (PA)
Texas Christian U (TX)
The U of Akron (OH)
U of Central Florida (FL)
U of Cincinnati (OH)
U of Denver (CO)
U of Florida (FL)
U of Georgia (GA)
U of Guelph (ON, Canada)
U of Miami (FL)
U of Nevada, Las Vegas (NV)
U of Northern Iowa (IA)
U of North Texas (TX)
U of Pennsylvania (PA)
U of St. Thomas (MN)
U of San Diego (CA)
U of South Carolina (SC)
U of Southern California (CA)
The U of Texas at El Paso (TX)
The U of Texas at San Antonio (TX)
U of West Georgia (GA)
U of Wisconsin–Madison (WI)
U of Wisconsin–Milwaukee (WI)
U of Wisconsin–Stout (WI)
Villanova U (PA)
Virginia Commonwealth U (VA)
Virginia Polytechnic Inst and State U (VA)
Washington State U (WA)

RECORDING ARTS TECHNOLOGY
Acad of Art U (CA)
American U (DC)
Belmont U (TN)
Butler U (IN)
Columbia Coll Chicago (IL)
Elon U (NC)
Greenville Coll (IL)
Husson U (ME)
Indiana U Bloomington (IN)
Ithaca Coll (NY)
Loyola Marymount U (CA)
Malone U (OH)
Michigan Technological U (MI)
New England Inst of Technology (RI)
Northwest U (WA)
Savannah Coll of Art and Design (GA)
State U of New York at Fredonia (NY)
Texas State U (TX)
York Coll of Pennsylvania (PA)

REGIONAL STUDIES
The Colorado Coll (CO)
Columbia U, School of General Studies (NY)
Houghton Coll (NY)
Mercer U, Macon (GA)
Prescott Coll (AZ)
U of Regina (SK, Canada)
U of Saskatchewan (SK, Canada)
Washington U in St. Louis (MO)

REGISTERED NURSING, NURSING ADMINISTRATION, NURSING RESEARCH AND CLINICAL NURSING RELATED
Bethel Coll (IN)
Cardinal Stritch U (WI)
Cleveland State U (OH)
Excelsior Coll (NY)
Jacksonville U (FL)
Louisiana Coll (LA)
Molloy Coll (NY)
Moravian Coll (PA)
Neumann U (PA)
Northwest U (WA)
Rasmussen Coll Ocala School of Nursing (FL)
Rowan U (NJ)
Tabor Coll (KS)
Union Coll (KY)
U of California, Los Angeles (CA)
U of Massachusetts Dartmouth (MA)
U of Miami (FL)
The U of Texas at Austin (TX)
Wheaton Coll (IL)

REGISTERED NURSING/ REGISTERED NURSE
Abilene Christian U (TX)
Adams State U (CO)
Adelphi U (NY)
Adventist U of Health Sciences (FL)
Albany State U (GA)
Alcorn State U (MS)
Alderson Broaddus U (WV)
Allen Coll (IA)
Alma Coll (MI)
Alvernia U (PA)
Alverno Coll (WI)
American Intl Coll (MA)
American Public U System (WV)
American U of Beirut (Lebanon)
Anderson U (IN)
Anderson U (SC)
Andrews U (MI)
Angelo State U (TX)
Appalachian State U (NC)
Aquinas Coll (TN)
Arizona State U at the Downtown Phoenix campus (AZ)
Arkansas Tech U (AR)
Armstrong State U (GA)
Auburn U (AL)
Auburn U at Montgomery (AL)
Augustana U (SD)
Augusta U (GA)
Aultman Coll of Nursing and Health Sciences (OH)
Aurora U (IL)
Austin Peay State U (TN)
Avila U (MO)
Azusa Pacific U (CA)
Baker U (KS)
Baldwin Wallace U (OH)
Ball State U (IN)
Barry U (FL)
Barton Coll (NC)
Bayamón Central U (PR)
Baylor U (TX)
Becker Coll (MA)
Belhaven U (MS)
Bellarmine U (KY)
Bellin Coll (WI)
Belmont U (TN)
Bemidji State U (MN)
Berea Coll (KY)
Berkeley Coll–Woodland Park Campus (NJ)
Berry Coll (GA)
Bethel Coll (IN)
Bethel Coll (KS)
Bethel U (MN)
Bethune-Cookman U (FL)
Binghamton U, State U of New York (NY)
Biola U (CA)
Bloomfield Coll (NJ)
Bloomsburg U of Pennsylvania (PA)
Bluefield State Coll (WV)
Bluffton U (OH)
Boise State U (ID)
Boston Coll (MA)
Bowie State U (MD)
Bowling Green State U (OH)
Bowling Green State U–Firelands Coll (OH)
Bradley U (IL)
Brandman U (CA)
Briar Cliff U (IA)
Brigham Young U–Idaho (ID)
Cabarrus Coll of Health Sciences (NC)
Caldwell U (NJ)
California Baptist U (CA)
California State U, Bakersfield (CA)
California State U, Chico (CA)
California State U, Dominguez Hills (CA)
California State U, East Bay (CA)
California State U, Fresno (CA)
California State U, Long Beach (CA)
California State U, Monterey Bay (CA)
California State U, Northridge (CA)
California State U, Sacramento (CA)
California State U, San Bernardino (CA)
California State U, San Marcos (CA)
California State U, Stanislaus (CA)
California U of Pennsylvania (PA)
Calvin Coll (MI)
Campbellsville U (KY)
Capital U (OH)
Cardinal Stritch U (WI)
Carlow U (PA)
Carroll Coll (MT)
Carson-Newman U (TN)
Case Western Reserve U (OH)
The Catholic U of America (DC)
Cedar Crest Coll (PA)
Cedarville U (OH)
Central Connecticut State U (CT)
Central Methodist U (MO)
Central Penn Coll (PA)
Chaminade U of Honolulu (HI)
Charleston Southern U (SC)
Chatham U (PA)
The Citadel, The Military Coll of South Carolina (SC)
Clarion U of Pennsylvania (PA)
Clarke U (IA)
Clayton State U (GA)
Clemson U (SC)
Cleveland State U (OH)
Coastal Carolina U (SC)
Coe Coll (IA)
Colby-Sawyer Coll (NH)
The Coll at Brockport, State U of New York (NY)
Coll of Central Florida (FL)
Coll of Coastal Georgia (GA)
Coll of Mount Saint Vincent (NY)
The Coll of New Jersey (NJ)
Coll of Saint Benedict (MN)
Coll of Saint Mary (NE)
The Coll of St. Scholastica (MN)
Coll of Staten Island of the City U of New York (NY)
Coll of the Ozarks (MO)
Colorado Mesa U (CO)
Columbus State U (GA)
Concordia Coll (MN)
Concordia U Irvine (CA)
Concordia U Wisconsin (WI)
Cox Coll (MO)
Creighton U (NE)
Culver-Stockton Coll (MO)
Curry Coll (MA)
Daemen Coll (NY)
Dalhousie U (NS, Canada)
Dalton State Coll (GA)
Davenport U, Grand Rapids (MI)
Daytona State Coll (FL)
Defiance Coll (OH)
DeSales U (PA)
Dickinson State U (ND)
Dixie State U (UT)
Dominican Coll (NY)
Dominican U (IL)
Dominican U of California (CA)
Drexel U (PA)
Duquesne U (PA)
East Carolina U (NC)
East Central U (OK)
Eastern Illinois U (IL)
Eastern Mennonite U (VA)
Eastern Michigan U (MI)
Eastern U (PA)
Eastern Washington U (WA)
East Stroudsburg U of Pennsylvania (PA)
East Tennessee State U (TN)
East Texas Baptist U (TX)
Edgewood Coll (WI)

Elmira Coll (NY)
Elms Coll (MA)
Emory U (GA)
Emporia State U (KS)
Endicott Coll (MA)
Fairfield U (CT)
Fairleigh Dickinson U, Metropolitan Campus (NJ)
Farmingdale State Coll (NY)
Fayetteville State U (NC)
Felician U (NJ)
Ferris State U (MI)
Fisher Coll (MA)
Fitchburg State U (MA)
Florida Ag and Mech U (FL)
Florida Atlantic U (FL)
Florida Intl U (FL)
Florida National U (FL)
Florida Southern Coll (FL)
Florida SouthWestern State Coll (FL)
Framingham State U (MA)
Franciscan U of Steubenville (OH)
Francis Marion U (SC)
Freed-Hardeman U (TN)
Frostburg State U (MD)
Gannon U (PA)
Gardner-Webb U (NC)
George Fox U (OR)
Georgetown U (DC)
Georgia Coll & State U (GA)
Georgia Gwinnett Coll (GA)
Georgia Highlands Coll (GA)
Georgian Court U (NJ)
Georgia Southern U (GA)
Georgia Southwestern State U (GA)
Georgia State U (GA)
Goldfarb School of Nursing at Barnes-Jewish Coll (MO)
Gonzaga U (WA)
Gordon State Coll (GA)
Goshen Coll (IN)
Governors State U (IL)
Graceland U (IA)
Grand Valley State U (MI)
Grand View U (IA)
Granite State Coll (NH)
Great Basin Coll (NV)
Gulf Coast State Coll (FL)
Gwynedd Mercy U (PA)
Hampton U (VA)
Hannibal-LaGrange U (MO)
Harding U (AR)
Hardin-Simmons U (TX)
Hartwick Coll (NY)
Hawai`i Pacific U (HI)
Henderson State U (AR)
Holy Family U (PA)
Holy Names U (CA)
Hood Coll (MD)
Hope Coll (MI)
Houston Baptist U (TX)
Howard Payne U (TX)
Humacao Comm Coll (PR)
Hunter Coll of the City U of New York (NY)
Husson U (ME)
Idaho State U (ID)
Illinois State U (IL)
Illinois Wesleyan U (IL)
Immaculata U (PA)
Indiana State U (IN)
Indiana U Bloomington (IN)
Indiana U East (IN)
Indiana U Kokomo (IN)
Indiana U Northwest (IN)
Indiana U of Pennsylvania (PA)
Indiana U–Purdue U Indianapolis (IN)
Indiana U South Bend (IN)
Indiana U Southeast (IN)
Inter American U of Puerto Rico, Aguadilla Campus (PR)
Inter American U of Puerto Rico, Bayamón Campus (PR)
Inter American U of Puerto Rico, Guayama Campus (PR)
Inter American U of Puerto Rico, Metropolitan Campus (PR)
Inter American U of Puerto Rico, Ponce Campus (PR)
Inter American U of Puerto Rico, San Germán Campus (PR)
Iowa Wesleyan U (IA)
Jacksonville State U (AL)
Jacksonville U (FL)
James Madison U (VA)
John Brown U (AR)
Johns Hopkins U (MD)
Kansas Wesleyan U (KS)
Keene State Coll (NH)
Kennesaw State U (GA)
Kent State U (OH)
Kent State U at Ashtabula (OH)
Kent State U at East Liverpool (OH)
Kent State U at Geauga (OH)
Kent State U at Salem (OH)
Kent State U at Stark (OH)
Kent State U at Trumbull (OH)
Kent State U at Tuscarawas (OH)
Kentucky State U (KY)
Keuka Coll (NY)
King U (TN)
Kuyper Coll (MI)
LaGrange Coll (GA)
Lakeview Coll of Nursing (IL)
Lamar U (TX)
Langston U (OK)
La Roche Coll (PA)
La Salle U (PA)
Lawrence Technological U (MI)
Lees-McRae Coll (NC)
Lee U (TN)
Lehman Coll of the City U of New York (NY)
Le Moyne Coll (NY)
Lenoir-Rhyne U (NC)
Lewis U (IL)
Liberty U (VA)
Lincoln Coll of New England, Southington (CT)
Lincoln U (MO)
Lincoln U (PA)
Lindsey Wilson Coll (KY)
Linfield Coll (OR)
Lipscomb U (TN)
Lock Haven U of Pennsylvania (PA)
Longwood U (VA)
Louisiana State U at Alexandria (LA)
Lourdes U (OH)
Loyola U Chicago (IL)
Loyola U New Orleans (LA)
Lubbock Christian U (TX)
Luther Coll (IA)
Lynchburg Coll (VA)
MacMurray Coll (IL)
Madonna U (MI)
Malone U (OH)
Mansfield U of Pennsylvania (PA)
Maranatha Baptist U (WI)
Maria Coll (NY)
Marian U (IN)
Marian U (WI)
Marshall U (WV)
Marymount U (VA)
Maryville U of Saint Louis (MO)
Marywood U (PA)
McKendree U (IL)
McMaster U (ON, Canada)
McMurry U (TX)
McNeese State U (LA)
MCPHS U (MA)
Medgar Evers Coll of the City U of New York (NY)
Mercer U, Macon (GA)
Mercy Coll (NY)
Mercy Coll of Health Sciences (IA)
Mercy Coll of Ohio (OH)
Mercyhurst U (PA)
Messiah Coll (PA)
Metropolitan State U of Denver (CO)
Miami Dade Coll (FL)
Michigan State U (MI)
MidAmerica Nazarene U (KS)
Milligan Coll (TN)
Millikin U (IL)
Milwaukee School of Eng (WI)
Minnesota State U Mankato (MN)
Minnesota State U Moorhead (MN)
Minot State U (ND)
Misericordia U (PA)
Missouri State U (MO)
Missouri Valley Coll (MO)
Missouri Western State U (MO)
Molloy Coll (NY)
Monmouth U (NJ)
Montana State U (MT)
Montana State U–Northern (MT)
Montana Tech of The U of Montana (MT)
Montclair State U (NJ)
Moravian Coll (PA)
Morehead State U (KY)
Morningside Coll (IA)
Morrisville State Coll (NY)
Mount Aloysius Coll (PA)
Mount Carmel Coll of Nursing (OH)
Mount Marty Coll (SD)
Mount Mary U (WI)
Mount Mercy U (IA)
Mount St. Joseph U (OH)
Mount Saint Mary Coll (NY)
Mount Saint Mary's U (CA)
Mount Vernon Nazarene U (OH)
Murray State U (KY)
Muskingum U (OH)
National U (CA)
Nazareth Coll of Rochester (NY)
Nebraska Methodist Coll (NE)
Nebraska Wesleyan U (NE)
Nevada State Coll (NV)
Newberry Coll (SC)
New England Inst of Technology (RI)
Newman U (KS)
New Mexico Highlands U (NM)
New Mexico State U (NM)
New York City Coll of Technology of the City U of New York (NY)
New York Inst of Technology (NY)
Niagara U (NY)
North Carolina Central U (NC)
North Dakota State U (ND)
Northeastern State U (OK)
Northeastern U (MA)
Northern Arizona U (AZ)
Northern Illinois U (IL)
Northern Kentucky U (KY)
Northwestern Coll (IA)
Northwestern Oklahoma State U (OK)
Northwestern State U of Louisiana (LA)
Northwest Missouri State U (MO)
Northwest U (WA)
Nova Southeastern U (FL)
Nyack Coll (NY)
The Ohio State U (OH)
The Ohio State U at Lima (OH)
The Ohio State U at Marion (OH)
The Ohio State U–Mansfield Campus (OH)
Ohio U (OH)
Ohio U–Eastern (OH)
Oklahoma Baptist U (OK)
Oklahoma Christian U (OK)
Oklahoma State U (OK)
Old Dominion U (VA)
Olivet Nazarene U (IL)
Olympic Coll (WA)
Oral Roberts U (OK)
Otterbein U (OH)
Our Lady of the Lake Coll (LA)
Pace U (NY)
Pace U, Pleasantville Campus (NY)
Pacific Lutheran U (WA)
Palm Beach Atlantic U (FL)
Penn State Abington (PA)
Penn State Altoona (PA)
Penn State Beaver (PA)
Penn State Berks (PA)
Penn State Brandywine (PA)
Penn State DuBois (PA)
Penn State Erie, The Behrend Coll (PA)
Penn State Fayette, The Eberly Campus (PA)
Penn State Greater Allegheny (PA)
Penn State Harrisburg (PA)
Penn State Hazleton (PA)
Penn State Lehigh Valley (PA)
Penn State Mont Alto (PA)
Penn State New Kensington (PA)
Penn State Schuylkill (PA)
Penn State Shenango (PA)
Penn State U Park (PA)
Penn State Wilkes-Barre (PA)
Penn State Worthington Scranton (PA)
Penn State York (PA)
Pennsylvania Coll of Health Sciences (PA)
Pensacola State Coll (FL)
Piedmont Coll (GA)
Pittsburg State U (KS)
Plymouth State U (NH)
Point Loma Nazarene U (CA)
Polk State Coll (FL)
Prairie View A&M U (TX)
Purdue U (IN)
Purdue U Northwest (IN)
Quinnipiac U (CT)
Radford U (VA)
Ramapo Coll of New Jersey (NJ)
Rasmussen Coll Fort Myers (FL)
Rasmussen Coll Land O' Lakes (FL)
Rasmussen Coll New Port Richey (FL)
Rasmussen Coll Tampa/Brandon (FL)
Regent U (VA)
Regis Coll (MA)
Regis U (CO)
Research Coll of Nursing (MO)
Resurrection U (IL)
Rhode Island Coll (RI)
Robert Morris U (PA)
Robert Morris U Illinois (IL)
Roberts Wesleyan Coll (NY)
Rockford U (IL)
Rockhurst U (MO)
Rogers State U (OK)
Rowan U (NJ)
Rutgers U–Camden (NJ)
Rutgers U–Newark (NJ)
Rutgers U–New Brunswick (NJ)
Sacred Heart U (CT)
The Sage Colls (NY)
Saginaw Valley State U (MI)
St. Ambrose U (IA)
Saint Anthony Coll of Nursing (IL)
St. Catherine U (MN)
St. Cloud State U (MN)
Saint Francis Medical Center Coll of Nursing (IL)
Saint Francis U (PA)
St. Gregory's U, Shawnee (OK)
St. John Fisher Coll (NY)
Saint John's U (MN)
St. Joseph's Coll, New York (NY)
Saint Louis U (MO)
St. Luke's Coll (IA)
Saint Martin's U (WA)
Saint Mary's Coll (IN)
St. Olaf Coll (MN)
St. Petersburg Coll (FL)
St. Thomas U (FL)
St. Vincent's Coll (CT)
Salisbury U (MD)
Salve Regina U (RI)
Samford U (AL)
Sam Houston State U (TX)
Samuel Merritt U (CA)
San Diego State U (CA)
San Francisco State U (CA)
Seattle Pacific U (WA)
Seattle U (WA)
Sentara Coll of Health Sciences (VA)
Shawnee State U (OH)
Shenandoah U (VA)
Shepherd U (WV)
Shorter U (GA)
Silver Lake Coll of the Holy Family (WI)
Simmons Coll (MA)
Simpson U (CA)
Slippery Rock U of Pennsylvania (PA)
Sonoma State U (CA)
South Dakota State U (SD)
Southeastern U (FL)
Southeast Missouri State U (MO)
Southern Arkansas U–Magnolia (AR)
Southern Connecticut State U (CT)
Southern Illinois U Edwardsville (IL)
Southern Oregon U (OR)
Southern Utah U (UT)
South Florida State Coll (FL)
Southwest Baptist U (MO)
Southwestern Adventist U (TX)
Southwestern Coll (KS)
Spalding U (KY)
Spring Hill Coll (AL)
State Coll of Florida Manatee-Sarasota (FL)
State U of New York at Plattsburgh (NY)
State U of New York Coll of Technology at Alfred (NY)
State U of New York Coll of Technology at Canton (NY)
State U of New York Empire State Coll (NY)
State U of New York Polytechnic Inst (NY)
Stephen F. Austin State U (TX)
Stevenson U (MD)
Stockton U (NJ)
Stony Brook U, State U of New York (NY)
Stratford U, Falls Church (VA)
Stratford U, Woodbridge (VA)
Sullivan U (KY)
Tarleton State U (TX)
Temple U (PA)
Tennessee State U (TN)
Tennessee Wesleyan U (TN)
Texas A&M Intl U (TX)
Texas A&M U–Commerce (TX)
Texas Christian U (TX)
Texas Lutheran U (TX)
Texas State U (TX)
Texas Woman's U (TX)
Thomas Edison State U (NJ)
Thomas More Coll (KY)
Thomas U (GA)
Towson U (MD)
Trent U (ON, Canada)
Trevecca Nazarene U (TN)
Trinity Christian Coll (IL)
Troy U (AL)
Truett McConnell U (GA)
Truman State U (MO)
Tusculum Coll (TN)
Union Coll (KY)
Union Coll (NE)
Union U (TN)
Universidad Adventista de las Antillas (PR)
Université de Montréal (QC, Canada)
Université de Sherbrooke (QC, Canada)
U at Buffalo, the State U of New York (NY)
The U of Akron (OH)
The U of Alabama (AL)
The U of Alabama at Birmingham (AL)
The U of Alabama in Huntsville (AL)
The U of Arizona (AZ)
U of Arkansas (AR)
U of Arkansas for Medical Sciences (AR)
U of Bridgeport (CT)
U of Central Arkansas (AR)
U of Central Florida (FL)
U of Central Missouri (MO)
U of Charleston (WV)
U of Cincinnati (OH)
U of Colorado Colorado Springs (CO)
U of Colorado Denver (CO)
U of Delaware (DE)
U of Detroit Mercy (MI)
U of Dubuque (IA)
U of Evansville (IN)
The U of Findlay (OH)
U of Florida (FL)
U of Hartford (CT)
U of Hawaii at Manoa (HI)
U of Houston (TX)
U of Houston–Clear Lake (TX)
U of Illinois at Chicago (IL)
U of Jamestown (ND)
The U of Kansas (KS)
U of Kentucky (KY)
U of Lethbridge (AB, Canada)
U of Louisiana at Monroe (LA)
U of Louisville (KY)
U of Maine (ME)
U of Maine at Fort Kent (ME)
U of Mary Hardin-Baylor (TX)
U of Maryland U Coll (MD)
U of Mary Washington (VA)
U of Massachusetts Amherst (MA)
U of Massachusetts Boston (MA)
U of Massachusetts Lowell (MA)
U of Miami (FL)
U of Michigan (MI)
U of Michigan–Flint (MI)
U of Minnesota, Twin Cities Campus (MN)
U of Missouri–Kansas City (MO)
U of Missouri–St. Louis (MO)
U of Mobile (AL)
U of Mount Union (OH)

U of Nevada, Las Vegas (NV)
U of Nevada, Reno (NV)
U of New England (ME)
U of New Hampshire (NH)
U of North Alabama (AL)
The U of North Carolina at Chapel Hill (NC)
The U of North Carolina at Charlotte (NC)
The U of North Carolina at Greensboro (NC)
The U of North Carolina at Pembroke (NC)
The U of North Carolina Wilmington (NC)
U of North Dakota (ND)
U of Northern Colorado (CO)
U of North Florida (FL)
U of North Georgia (GA)
U of Oklahoma Health Sciences Center (OK)
U of Pennsylvania (PA)
U of Pikeville (KY)
U of Pittsburgh (PA)
U of Pittsburgh at Bradford (PA)
U of Regina (SK, Canada)
U of Rhode Island (RI)
U of Rochester (NY)
U of St. Francis (IL)
U of Saint Francis (IN)
U of Saint Joseph (CT)
U of Saint Mary (KS)
U of San Francisco (CA)
U of Saskatchewan (SK, Canada)
The U of Scranton (PA)
U of South Alabama (AL)
U of South Carolina (SC)
U of South Carolina Aiken (SC)
U of Southern Indiana (IN)
U of Southern Maine (ME)
U of Southern Mississippi (MS)
U of South Florida (FL)
The U of Tampa (FL)
The U of Tennessee (TN)
The U of Tennessee at Chattanooga (TN)
The U of Tennessee at Martin (TN)
The U of Texas at Austin (TX)
The U of Texas at El Paso (TX)
The U of Texas of the Permian Basin (TX)
The U of Texas Rio Grande Valley (TX)
U of the Fraser Valley (BC, Canada)
U of the Incarnate Word (TX)
U of the Virgin Islands (VI)
The U of Toledo (OH)
U of Toronto (ON, Canada)
The U of Tulsa (OK)
U of Vermont (VT)
U of Virginia (VA)
U of Washington (WA)
U of Washington, Bothell (WA)
U of Washington, Tacoma (WA)
U of West Georgia (GA)
U of Windsor (ON, Canada)
U of Wisconsin–Eau Claire (WI)
U of Wisconsin–Green Bay (WI)
U of Wisconsin–Madison (WI)
U of Wisconsin–Milwaukee (WI)
U of Wisconsin–Parkside (WI)
Utah Valley U (UT)
Utica Coll (NY)
Valdosta State U (GA)
Valparaiso U (IN)
Villanova U (PA)
Vincennes U (IN)
Virginia Commonwealth U (VA)
Viterbo U (WI)
Wagner Coll (NY)
Walla Walla U (WA)
Walsh U (OH)
Washburn U (KS)
Washington State U (WA)
Washington State U–Spokane (WA)
Washington State U–Tri-Cities (WA)
Washington State U–Vancouver (WA)
Wayland Baptist U (TX)
Waynesburg U (PA)
Weber State U (UT)
Webster U (MO)
Wesleyan Coll (GA)
West Chester U of Pennsylvania (PA)
Western Carolina U (NC)
Western Connecticut State U (CT)
Western Illinois U (IL)
Western Kentucky U (KY)
Western Michigan U (MI)
Western Washington U (WA)
Westfield State U (MA)
Westminster Coll (UT)
West Texas A&M U (TX)
West Virginia U (WV)
West Virginia U Inst of Technology (WV)
West Virginia Wesleyan Coll (WV)
Wheeling Jesuit U (WV)
Whitworth U (WA)
Wichita State U (KS)
Widener U (PA)
Wilkes U (PA)
William Jewell Coll (MO)
William Paterson U of New Jersey (NJ)
Wilmington U (DE)
Wingate U (NC)
Winona State U (MN)
Wittenberg U (OH)
Worcester State U (MA)
Wright State U (OH)
Wright State U–Lake Campus (OH)
York Coll of Pennsylvania (PA)
York Coll of the City U of New York (NY)
Youngstown State U (OH)

REHABILITATION AND THERAPEUTIC PROFESSIONS RELATED

Alabama State U (AL)
Assumption Coll (MA)
Boston U (MA)
Coll of Saint Mary (NE)
East Stroudsburg U of Pennsylvania (PA)
Georgian Court U (NJ)
Ithaca Coll (NY)
Lock Haven U of Pennsylvania (PA)
Montana State U Billings (MT)
Penn State Abington (PA)
Penn State Altoona (PA)
Penn State Beaver (PA)
Penn State Berks (PA)
Penn State Brandywine (PA)
Penn State DuBois (PA)
Penn State Erie, The Behrend Coll (PA)
Penn State Fayette, The Eberly Campus (PA)
Penn State Greater Allegheny (PA)
Penn State Hazleton (PA)
Penn State Lehigh Valley (PA)
Penn State Mont Alto (PA)
Penn State New Kensington (PA)
Penn State Schuylkill (PA)
Penn State Shenango (PA)
Penn State U Park (PA)
Penn State Wilkes-Barre (PA)
Penn State Worthington Scranton (PA)
Penn State York (PA)
Prescott Coll (AZ)
Rutgers U–Newark (NJ)
Rutgers U–New Brunswick (NJ)
Southern Illinois U Carbondale (IL)
Thomas U (GA)
Troy U (AL)
Université de Montréal (QC, Canada)
U of Massachusetts Lowell (MA)
U of Waterloo (ON, Canada)

REHABILITATION SCIENCE

Arkansas Tech U (AR)
Boston U (MA)
Marshall U (WV)
New England Inst of Technology (RI)
Stephen F. Austin State U (TX)
U of Maine at Farmington (ME)
U of North Dakota (ND)
U of North Texas (TX)
U of Pittsburgh (PA)
The U of Texas Rio Grande Valley (TX)
U of the Incarnate Word (TX)

RELIGIOUS EDUCATION

Andrews U (MI)
Asbury U (KY)
Ashland U (OH)
Barclay Coll (KS)
Belmont Abbey Coll (NC)
Benedictine Coll (KS)
Biola U (CA)
Bryan Coll (TN)
Campbellsville U (KY)
Cedarville U (OH)
Columbia Intl U (SC)
Concordia Coll–New York (NY)
Concordia U Chicago (IL)
Concordia U Irvine (CA)
Concordia U, Nebraska (NE)
Concordia U, St. Paul (MN)
Corban U (OR)
Dallas Baptist U (TX)
Defiance Coll (OH)
Eastern Nazarene Coll (MA)
Edgewood Coll (WI)
Faith Baptist Bible Coll and Theological Sem (IA)
Florida Coll (FL)
Franciscan U of Steubenville (OH)
Gardner-Webb U (NC)
Global U (MO)
Hannibal-LaGrange U (MO)
Harding U (AR)
Heritage Bible Coll (NC)
Houghton Coll (NY)
Howard Payne U (TX)
Inter American U of Puerto Rico, Fajardo Campus (PR)
John Carroll U (OH)
Kentucky Mountain Bible Coll (KY)
Kuyper Coll (MI)
Lee U (TN)
Lindsey Wilson Coll (KY)
Louisiana Coll (LA)
Loyola U Chicago (IL)
Loyola U New Orleans (LA)
Malone U (OH)
Marian U (IN)
Master's Coll and Sem (ON, Canada)
The Master's U (CA)
McMaster U (ON, Canada)
Messenger Coll (TX)
Messiah Coll (PA)
Morris Coll (SC)
Mount Vernon Nazarene U (OH)
Multnomah U (OR)
Muskingum U (OH)
Nazarene Bible Coll (CO)
Northwestern Coll (IA)
Northwest U (WA)
Oklahoma Christian U (OK)
Olivet Nazarene U (IL)
Oral Roberts U (OK)
Piedmont Intl U (NC)
Saint Louis Christian Coll (MO)
Saint Mary's U of Minnesota (MN)
Seattle Pacific U (WA)
Simpson U (CA)
Southwest Baptist U (MO)
Sterling Coll (KS)
Taylor U (IN)
Theological U of the Caribbean (PR)
Toccoa Falls Coll (GA)
Universidad Adventista de las Antillas (PR)
U of Dayton (OH)
The U of Findlay (OH)
U of Valley Forge (PA)
Wayland Baptist U (TX)
Welch Coll (TN)
Wheaton Coll (IL)
Williams Baptist Coll (AR)

RELIGIOUS/SACRED MUSIC

Anderson U (IN)
Aquinas Coll (MI)
Arizona Christian U (AZ)
Asbury U (KY)
Barclay Coll (KS)
Baylor U (TX)
Bethany Lutheran Coll (MN)
Bluefield Coll (VA)
Blue Mountain Coll (MS)
Bowling Green State U (OH)
Calvary U (MO)
Calvin Coll (MI)
Campbellsville U (KY)
Carson-Newman U (TN)
Central Baptist Coll (AR)
Charleston Southern U (SC)
Coll of the Ozarks (MO)
Columbia Intl U (SC)
Concordia Coll–New York (NY)
Concordia U Chicago (IL)
Concordia U, Nebraska (NE)
Concordia U, St. Paul (MN)
Concordia U Wisconsin (WI)
Corban U (OR)
Dallas Baptist U (TX)
Drake U (IA)
East Central U (OK)
Eastern Nazarene Coll (MA)
East Texas Baptist U (TX)
Emmanuel Coll (GA)
Evangel U (MO)
Faith Baptist Bible Coll and Theological Sem (IA)
Franciscan U of Steubenville (OH)
Furman U (SC)
Gardner-Webb U (NC)
Greenville Coll (IL)
Hardin-Simmons U (TX)
Hope Intl U (CA)
Howard Payne U (TX)
Huntington U (IN)
Jacksonville U (FL)
John Brown U (AR)
Johnson U (TN)
Johnson U Florida (FL)
Judson U (IL)
Kentucky Mountain Bible Coll (KY)
Kentucky Wesleyan Coll (KY)
Kuyper Coll (MI)
Lee U (TN)
Lenoir-Rhyne U (NC)
Liberty U (VA)
Louisiana Coll (LA)
Madonna U (MI)
Malone U (OH)
Maranatha Baptist U (WI)
Marian U (IN)
The Master's U (CA)
Messenger Coll (TX)
MidAmerica Nazarene U (KS)
Missouri Baptist U (MO)
Mount Vernon Nazarene U (OH)
Multnomah U (OR)
North Greenville U (SC)
Northwest Christian U (OR)
Northwest U (WA)
Nyack Coll (NY)
Oakland City U (IN)
Ohio Christian U (OH)
Oklahoma Baptist U (OK)
Oklahoma City U (OK)
Olivet Nazarene U (IL)
Oral Roberts U (OK)
Ouachita Baptist U (AR)
Piedmont Intl U (NC)
Point Loma Nazarene U (CA)
St. Olaf Coll (MN)
Samford U (AL)
Seton Hill U (PA)
Shenandoah U (VA)
Shorter U (GA)
Southeastern U (FL)
Southwestern Assemblies of God U (TX)
Texas Christian U (TX)
Trevecca Nazarene U (TN)
Truett McConnell U (GA)
Union U (TN)
U of Mary Hardin-Baylor (TX)
U of Mobile (AL)
U of the Cumberlands (KY)
U of Valley Forge (PA)
Wartburg Coll (IA)
Wayland Baptist U (TX)
Welch Coll (TN)
Williams Baptist Coll (AR)

RELIGIOUS STUDIES

Agnes Scott Coll (GA)
Albertus Magnus Coll (CT)
Albion Coll (MI)
Albright Coll (PA)
Allegheny Coll (PA)
Alma Coll (MI)
Alvernia U (PA)
Alverno Coll (WI)
American Public U System (WV)
Amherst Coll (MA)
Anderson U (IN)
Andrews U (MI)
Appalachian State U (NC)
Aquinas Coll (MI)
Arizona State U at the Tempe campus (AZ)
Arlington Baptist Coll (TX)
Ashland U (OH)
Athens State U (AL)
Augsburg Coll (MN)
Augustana Coll (IL)
Augustana U (SD)
Aurora U (IL)
Austin Coll (TX)
Averett U (VA)
Avila U (MO)
Azusa Pacific U (CA)
Baker U (KS)
Baldwin Wallace U (OH)
Ball State U (IN)
Baptist U of the Americas (TX)
Bard Coll (NY)
Barnard Coll (NY)
Baruch Coll of the City U of New York (NY)
Bates Coll (ME)
Bayamón Central U (PR)
Baylor U (TX)
Belmont U (TN)
Beloit Coll (WI)
Bemidji State U (MN)
Berea Coll (KY)
Bethany Lutheran Coll (MN)
Bethel Coll (KS)
Biola U (CA)
Bishop's U (QC, Canada)
Bloomfield Coll (NJ)
Bluefield Coll (VA)
Boston U (MA)
Bowdoin Coll (ME)
Bradley U (IL)
Brewton-Parker Coll (GA)
Brooklyn Coll of the City U of New York (NY)
Bryn Mawr Coll (PA)
Bucknell U (PA)
Butler U (IN)
Cabrini U (PA)
Cairn U (PA)
California Lutheran U (CA)
California State U, Bakersfield (CA)
California State U, East Bay (CA)
California State U, Fresno (CA)
California State U, Fullerton (CA)
California State U, Long Beach (CA)
California State U, Northridge (CA)
California State U, Sacramento (CA)
Calumet Coll of Saint Joseph (IN)
Calvin Coll (MI)
Campbellsville U (KY)
Canisius Coll (NY)
Capital U (OH)
Cardinal Stritch U (WI)
Carleton Coll (MN)
Carson-Newman U (TN)
Carthage Coll (WI)
Case Western Reserve U (OH)
Catawba Coll (NC)
The Catholic U of America (DC)
Centenary Coll of Louisiana (LA)
Central Methodist U (MO)
Central Michigan U (MI)
Central Washington U (WA)
Centre Coll (KY)
Chaminade U of Honolulu (HI)
Chapman U (CA)
Charleston Southern U (SC)
Chowan U (NC)
Claremont McKenna Coll (CA)
Clark Atlanta U (GA)
Clarke U (IA)
Cleveland State U (OH)
Coe Coll (IA)
Colby Coll (ME)
Colgate U (NY)
Coll of Charleston (SC)
The Coll of Idaho (ID)
Coll of Mount Saint Vincent (NY)
The Coll of St. Scholastica (MN)
Coll of the Holy Cross (MA)
The Coll of William and Mary (VA)
The Coll of Wooster (OH)
Colorado Christian U (CO)
The Colorado Coll (CO)
Columbia U (NY)
Columbia U, School of General Studies (NY)
Concordia Coll (MN)
Concordia Coll–New York (NY)

Concordia U (QC, Canada)
Concordia U Chicago (IL)
Concordia U Irvine (CA)
Concordia U Wisconsin (WI)
Connecticut Coll (CT)
Converse Coll (SC)
Corban U (OR)
Cornell Coll (IA)
Cornell U (NY)
Crandall U (NB, Canada)
Criswell Coll (TX)
Culver-Stockton Coll (MO)
Daemen Coll (NY)
Dalhousie U (NS, Canada)
Dartmouth Coll (NH)
Davidson Coll (NC)
Defiance Coll (OH)
Denison U (OH)
DePauw U (IN)
Dickinson Coll (PA)
Doane U (NE)
Dominican U of California (CA)
Drake U (IA)
Drew U (NJ)
Drury U (MO)
Earlham Coll (IN)
Eastern Nazarene Coll (MA)
East Texas Baptist U (TX)
Eckerd Coll (FL)
Edgewood Coll (WI)
Elizabethtown Coll (PA)
Elms Coll (MA)
Elon U (NC)
Emmanuel Coll (MA)
Emory & Henry Coll (VA)
Emory U (GA)
The Evergreen State Coll (WA)
Fairfield U (CT)
Felician U (NJ)
Florida Intl U (FL)
Florida Southern Coll (FL)
Fordham U (NY)
Franklin & Marshall Coll (PA)
Franklin Coll (IN)
Furman U (SC)
Gardner-Webb U (NC)
Georgetown Coll (KY)
The George Washington U (DC)
Georgian Court U (NJ)
Georgia State U (GA)
Gettysburg Coll (PA)
Goddard Coll (VT)
Gonzaga U (WA)
Goshen Coll (IN)
Goucher Coll (MD)
Graceland U (IA)
Grand View U (IA)
Greenville Coll (IL)
Grinnell Coll (IA)
Grove City Coll (PA)
Guilford Coll (NC)
Hamilton Coll (NY)
Hamline U (MN)
Hampden-Sydney Coll (VA)
Hampshire Coll (MA)
Hampton U (VA)
Hartwick Coll (NY)
Harvard U (MA)
Haverford Coll (PA)
Heidelberg U (OH)
Hendrix Coll (AR)
High Point U (NC)
Hillsdale Coll (MI)
Hiram Coll (OH)
Hobart and William Smith Colls (NY)
Hofstra U (NY)
Hollins U (VA)
Holy Family U (PA)
Holy Names U (CA)
Hood Coll (MD)
Hope Coll (MI)
Hope Intl U (CA)
Houghton Coll (NY)
Humboldt State U (CA)
Hunter Coll of the City U of New York (NY)
Huntingdon Coll (AL)
Huntington U (IN)
Illinois Coll (IL)
Illinois Wesleyan U (IL)
Indiana U Bloomington (IN)
Indiana U of Pennsylvania (PA)
Indiana U–Purdue U Indianapolis (IN)
Inter American U of Puerto Rico, Metropolitan Campus (PR)
Iona Coll (NY)
Iowa State U of Science and Technology (IA)
John Carroll U (OH)
Johnson U (TN)
Johnson U Florida (FL)
Juniata Coll (PA)
Kalamazoo Coll (MI)
Kansas Wesleyan U (KS)
Kentucky Wesleyan Coll (KY)
Kenyon Coll (OH)
The King's Coll (NY)
King U (TN)
Lafayette Coll (PA)
LaGrange Coll (GA)
Lake Forest Coll (IL)
Lane Coll (TN)
La Roche Coll (PA)
La Salle U (PA)
Lawrence U (WI)
Lebanon Valley Coll (PA)
Lees-McRae Coll (NC)
Lehigh U (PA)
Le Moyne Coll (NY)
Lenoir-Rhyne U (NC)
Lewis & Clark Coll (OR)
Lewis U (IL)
Liberty U (VA)
Lincoln U (PA)
Linfield Coll (OR)
Loras Coll (IA)
Lourdes U (OH)
Loyola U Maryland (MD)
Loyola U New Orleans (LA)
Luther Coll (IA)
Lycoming Coll (PA)
Lynchburg Coll (VA)
Macalester Coll (MN)
Madonna U (MI)
Manchester U (IN)
Manhattan Coll (NY)
Manhattanville Coll (NY)
Marist Coll (NY)
Marymount U (VA)
Marywood U (PA)
The Master's U (CA)
McDaniel Coll (MD)
McKendree U (IL)
McMaster U (ON, Canada)
Medgar Evers Coll of the City U of New York (NY)
Mercyhurst U (PA)
Meredith Coll (NC)
Merrimack Coll (MA)
Messenger Coll (TX)
Miami U (OH)
Michigan State U (MI)
MidAmerica Nazarene U (KS)
Middlebury Coll (VT)
Millsaps Coll (MS)
Missouri State U (MO)
Missouri Valley Coll (MO)
Molloy Coll (NY)
Monmouth Coll (IL)
Montclair State U (NJ)
Moravian Coll (PA)
Morehouse Coll (GA)
Morningside Coll (IA)
Mount Allison U (NB, Canada)
Mount Holyoke Coll (MA)
Mount Marty Coll (SD)
Mount Mercy U (IA)
Mount St. Joseph U (OH)
Mount Saint Mary's U (CA)
Mount Vernon Nazarene U (OH)
Muhlenberg Coll (PA)
Muskingum U (OH)
Nazareth Coll of Rochester (NY)
Nebraska Wesleyan U (NE)
New Coll of Florida (FL)
Niagara U (NY)
North Carolina State U (NC)
North Carolina Wesleyan Coll (NC)
North Central Coll (IL)
Northeastern U (MA)
Northland Coll (WI)
Northwestern Coll (IA)
Northwestern U (IL)
Northwest U (WA)
Nyack Coll (NY)
Oakland City U (IN)
Oberlin Coll (OH)
Occidental Coll (CA)
The Ohio State U (OH)
Ohio U (OH)
Ohio Valley U (WV)
Ohio Wesleyan U (OH)
Oklahoma Baptist U (OK)
Oklahoma Christian U (OK)
Oklahoma City U (OK)
Olivet Nazarene U (IL)
Oregon State U (OR)
Otterbein U (OH)
Our Lady of the Lake U of San Antonio (TX)
Pacific Lutheran U (WA)
Paine Coll (GA)
Penn State Abington (PA)
Penn State Altoona (PA)
Penn State Beaver (PA)
Penn State Berks (PA)
Penn State Brandywine (PA)
Penn State DuBois (PA)
Penn State Erie, The Behrend Coll (PA)
Penn State Fayette, The Eberly Campus (PA)
Penn State Greater Allegheny (PA)
Penn State Hazleton (PA)
Penn State Lehigh Valley (PA)
Penn State Mont Alto (PA)
Penn State New Kensington (PA)
Penn State Schuylkill (PA)
Penn State Shenango (PA)
Penn State Wilkes-Barre (PA)
Penn State Worthington Scranton (PA)
Penn State York (PA)
Pepperdine U, Malibu (CA)
Philander Smith Coll (AR)
Piedmont Coll (GA)
Pitzer Coll (CA)
Pomona Coll (CA)
Portland State U (OR)
Princeton U (NJ)
Principia Coll (IL)
Providence Coll (RI)
Purdue U (IN)
Queens Coll of the City U of New York (NY)
Randolph Coll (VA)
Randolph-Macon Coll (VA)
Redeemer U Coll (ON, Canada)
Reed Coll (OR)
Regis U (CO)
Rhodes Coll (TN)
Rice U (TX)
Ripon Coll (WI)
Roanoke Coll (VA)
Roberts Wesleyan Coll (NY)
Rollins Coll (FL)
Rosemont Coll (PA)
Rutgers U–New Brunswick (NJ)
Saint Francis U (PA)
St. John Fisher Coll (NY)
Saint Joseph's U (PA)
Saint Leo U (FL)
Saint Martin's U (WA)
Saint Mary's Coll (IN)
Saint Mary's Coll of California (CA)
St. Mary's Coll of Maryland (MD)
Saint Michael's Coll (VT)
St. Norbert Coll (WI)
St. Olaf Coll (MN)
Saint Peter's U (NJ)
St. Thomas Aquinas Coll (NY)
St. Thomas U (FL)
St. Thomas U (NB, Canada)
Salve Regina U (RI)
Samford U (AL)
San Diego State U (CA)
Santa Clara U (CA)
Sarah Lawrence Coll (NY)
Schreiner U (TX)
Scripps Coll (CA)
Seattle U (WA)
Seton Hill U (PA)
Sewanee: The U of the South (TN)
Shenandoah U (VA)
Shorter U (GA)
Siena Coll (NY)
Simpson Coll (IA)
Skidmore Coll (NY)
Smith Coll (MA)
Southern Methodist U (TX)
Southwest Baptist U (MO)
Southwestern Adventist U (TX)
Southwestern U (TX)
Spelman Coll (GA)
Spring Hill Coll (AL)
Stanford U (CA)
State U of New York Coll at Old Westbury (NY)
Stonehill Coll (MA)
Stony Brook U, State U of New York (NY)
Susquehanna U (PA)
Swarthmore Coll (PA)
Sweet Briar Coll (VA)
Syracuse U (NY)
Temple U (PA)
Tennessee Wesleyan U (TN)
Texas Christian U (TX)
Texas Coll (TX)
Texas Wesleyan U (TX)
Thomas More Coll (KY)
Towson U (MD)
Transylvania U (KY)
Trevecca Nazarene U (TN)
Trinity U (TX)
Tufts U (MA)
Tulane U (LA)
Union Coll (KY)
Union Coll (NY)
Union U (TN)
Université de Montréal (QC, Canada)
U at Albany, State U of New York (NY)
The U of Alabama (AL)
The U of Arizona (AZ)
U of Bridgeport (CT)
U of California, Davis (CA)
U of California, Irvine (CA)
U of California, Los Angeles (CA)
U of California, Riverside (CA)
U of California, San Diego (CA)
U of California, Santa Barbara (CA)
U of Central Arkansas (AR)
U of Central Florida (FL)
U of Colorado Boulder (CO)
U of Dayton (OH)
U of Denver (CO)
U of Detroit Mercy (MI)
U of Dubuque (IA)
U of Florida (FL)
U of Georgia (GA)
U of Great Falls (MT)
U of Hawaii at Manoa (HI)
U of Houston (TX)
U of Indianapolis (IN)
U of Jamestown (ND)
The U of Kansas (KS)
U of King's Coll (NS, Canada)
U of La Verne (CA)
U of Lethbridge (AB, Canada)
U of Miami (FL)
U of Michigan (MI)
U of Minnesota, Twin Cities Campus (MN)
U of Mobile (AL)
U of Mount Union (OH)
U of North Carolina at Asheville (NC)
The U of North Carolina at Chapel Hill (NC)
The U of North Carolina at Charlotte (NC)
The U of North Carolina at Greensboro (NC)
U of North Dakota (ND)
U of Northern Iowa (IA)
U of North Florida (FL)
U of North Texas (TX)
U of Oklahoma (OK)
U of Oregon (OR)
U of Pennsylvania (PA)
U of Pikeville (KY)
U of Pittsburgh (PA)
U of Puget Sound (WA)
U of Regina (SK, Canada)
U of Richmond (VA)
U of Rochester (NY)
U of Saint Joseph (CT)
U of St. Thomas (MN)
U of San Diego (CA)
U of San Francisco (CA)
U of Saskatchewan (SK, Canada)
The U of Scranton (PA)
U of South Carolina (SC)
U of Southern California (CA)
U of Southern Mississippi (MS)
U of South Florida (FL)
The U of Tennessee (TN)
The U of Texas at Austin (TX)
U of the Incarnate Word (TX)
U of the Pacific (CA)
The U of Toledo (OH)
The U of Tulsa (OK)
U of Utah (UT)
U of Vermont (VT)
U of Virginia (VA)
U of Washington (WA)
U of Waterloo (ON, Canada)
U of Wisconsin–Eau Claire (WI)
U of Wisconsin–Madison (WI)
U of Wisconsin–Milwaukee (WI)
Ursinus Coll (PA)
Vanderbilt U (TN)
Vassar Coll (NY)
Villanova U (PA)
Virginia Commonwealth U (VA)
Virginia Wesleyan Coll (VA)
Viterbo U (WI)
Wabash Coll (IN)
Wake Forest U (NC)
Walla Walla U (WA)
Wartburg Coll (IA)
Washburn U (KS)
Washington and Lee U (VA)
Washington State U (WA)
Washington U in St. Louis (MO)
Webster U (MO)
Wesleyan Coll (GA)
Wesleyan U (CT)
Western Kentucky U (KY)
Western Michigan U (MI)
Westminster Coll (PA)
Westmont Coll (CA)
West Virginia Wesleyan Coll (WV)
Wheaton Coll (MA)
Whitman Coll (WA)
Whittier Coll (CA)
Whitworth U (WA)
Willamette U (OR)
William Jewell Coll (MO)
Williams Baptist Coll (AR)
Williams Coll (MA)
Wilson Coll (PA)
Wingate U (NC)
Wittenberg U (OH)
Wofford Coll (SC)
Wright State U (OH)
Wright State U–Lake Campus (OH)
Youngstown State U (OH)

RELIGIOUS STUDIES RELATED
Agnes Scott Coll (GA)
Belmont U (TN)
Bryn Athyn Coll of the New Church (PA)
Colorado Christian U (CO)
Newberry Coll (SC)
Webster U (MO)

RESEARCH AND DEVELOPMENT MANAGEMENT
Oregon State U (OR)

RESEARCH AND EXPERIMENTAL PSYCHOLOGY RELATED
Bowdoin Coll (ME)
Gannon U (PA)
Georgia Coll & State U (GA)
Georgia Inst of Technology (GA)
Loyola U New Orleans (LA)
Mount Saint Mary's U (CA)
Mount St. Mary's U (MD)
Murray State U (KY)
Niagara U (NY)
U of Michigan–Flint (MI)
U of North Georgia (GA)
Vassar Coll (NY)

RESEARCH METHODOLOGY AND QUANTITATIVE METHODS
Bryant U (RI)
Walsh U (OH)

RESORT MANAGEMENT
Coastal Carolina U (SC)
Florida Gulf Coast U (FL)
Green Mountain Coll (VT)
Lasell Coll (MA)
Morrisville State Coll (NY)
Rochester Inst of Technology (NY)
Sierra Nevada Coll (NV)

RESPIRATORY CARE THERAPY
Armstrong State U (GA)
Augusta U (GA)
Ball State U (IN)
Bellarmine U (KY)
Boise State U (ID)
Bowling Green State U (OH)
Bowling Green State U–Firelands Coll (OH)

Canisius Coll (NY)
Cardinal Stritch U (WI)
Concordia U, St. Paul (MN)
Dakota State U (SD)
Dalhousie U (NS, Canada)
Fairleigh Dickinson U, Coll at Florham (NJ)
Florida Ag and Mech U (FL)
Florida SouthWestern State Coll (FL)
Gannon U (PA)
Georgia State U (GA)
Gwynedd Mercy U (PA)
Indiana U of Pennsylvania (PA)
Indiana U–Purdue U Indianapolis (IN)
Marshall U (WV)
Missouri State U (MO)
Nebraska Methodist Coll (NE)
North Dakota State U (ND)
Northern Kentucky U (KY)
Nova Southeastern U (FL)
The Ohio State U (OH)
Rutgers U–Newark (NJ)
St. Catherine U (MN)
Salisbury U (MD)
Shenandoah U (VA)
Stony Brook U, State U of New York (NY)
Tennessee State U (TN)
Texas State U (TX)
Universidad Adventista de las Antillas (PR)
The U of Akron (OH)
The U of Alabama at Birmingham (AL)
U of Cincinnati (OH)
U of Hartford (CT)
U of Indianapolis (IN)
The U of Kansas (KS)
The U of North Carolina at Charlotte (NC)
U of South Alabama (AL)
U of Southern Indiana (IN)
The U of Toledo (OH)
U of Waterloo (ON, Canada)
Valencia Coll (FL)
Weber State U (UT)
Wheeling Jesuit U (WV)
York Coll of Pennsylvania (PA)
Youngstown State U (OH)

RESPIRATORY THERAPY TECHNICIAN
Dalhousie U (NS, Canada)
Florida National U (FL)
Rhode Island Coll (RI)

RESTAURANT, CULINARY, AND CATERING MANAGEMENT
Bowling Green State U (OH)
New England Culinary Inst (VT)
Pennsylvania Coll of Technology (PA)

RESTAURANT/FOOD SERVICES MANAGEMENT
Central Washington U (WA)
Colorado State U (CO)
The Culinary Inst of America (NY)
Kennesaw State U (GA)
Morrisville State Coll (NY)
The Ohio State U (OH)
Rochester Inst of Technology (NY)
Stratford U (MD)
Stratford U, Alexandria (VA)
Stratford U, Falls Church (VA)
Stratford U, Glen Allen (VA)
Stratford U, Virginia Beach (VA)
The U of Alabama (AL)
U of Central Florida (FL)
U of Nevada, Las Vegas (NV)
U of San Francisco (CA)

RETAILING
American Public U System (WV)
Bowling Green State U (OH)
Central Washington U (WA)
Fisher Coll (MA)
Lamar U (TX)
U of Minnesota, Twin Cities Campus (MN)
U of South Carolina (SC)
U of Wisconsin–Madison (WI)

RETAIL MANAGEMENT
Columbia Coll Chicago (IL)
The U of Arizona (AZ)
U of Arkansas (AR)
U of North Texas (TX)

RHETORIC AND COMPOSITION
Albany State U (GA)
Ashland U (OH)
Auburn U (AL)
Bates Coll (ME)
Bemidji State U (MN)
Bethel Coll (IN)
Black Hills State U (SD)
Bowling Green State U (OH)
Brigham Young U (UT)
California State U, East Bay (CA)
California State U, Fresno (CA)
California State U, Fullerton (CA)
California State U, Long Beach (CA)
Calvin Coll (MI)
Carson-Newman U (TN)
Carthage Coll (WI)
Clark Atlanta U (GA)
Clemson U (SC)
Coe Coll (IA)
Coll of Saint Benedict (MN)
Columbus State U (GA)
Cornell Coll (IA)
Denison U (OH)
Drake U (IA)
Duquesne U (PA)
East Central U (OK)
East Tennessee State U (TN)
East Texas Baptist U (TX)
Emerson Coll (MA)
Evangel U (MO)
Ferris State U (MI)
The George Washington U (DC)
Georgia Coll & State U (GA)
Georgia Southern U (GA)
Gonzaga U (WA)
Graceland U (IA)
Humboldt State U (CA)
Illinois Coll (IL)
Ithaca Coll (NY)
Jackson State U (MS)
Lehman Coll of the City U of New York (NY)
Lipscomb U (TN)
Louisiana Tech U (LA)
Manchester U (IN)
Marietta Coll (OH)
Marshall U (WV)
The Master's U (CA)
McKendree U (IL)
Metropolitan State U of Denver (CO)
Minnesota State U Mankato (MN)
Mississippi Valley State U (MS)
Missouri Valley Coll (MO)
North Central Coll (IL)
Northeastern Illinois U (IL)
Northern State U (SD)
Northwestern Coll (IA)
Northwestern Oklahoma State U (OK)
Northwestern U (IL)
Ohio U (OH)
Oklahoma Baptist U (OK)
Oklahoma Christian U (OK)
Old Dominion U (VA)
Ouachita Baptist U (AR)
Portland State U (OR)
St. Catherine U (MN)
St. Cloud State U (MN)
Saint John's U (MN)
St. John's U (NY)
St. Joseph's Coll, Long Island Campus (NY)
St. Joseph's Coll, New York (NY)
Shippensburg U of Pennsylvania (PA)
Southern Illinois U Edwardsville (IL)
State U of New York Coll at Cortland (NY)
Stephen F. Austin State U (TX)
Tarleton State U (TX)
Texas A&M U–Commerce (TX)
Texas State U (TX)
Texas Tech U (TX)
Trinity U (TX)
Union U (TN)
U at Albany, State U of New York (NY)
U of Central Florida (FL)
U of Central Missouri (MO)
U of Cincinnati (OH)
U of Kentucky (KY)
U of Minnesota, Morris (MN)
U of Minnesota, Twin Cities Campus (MN)
U of Montevallo (AL)
U of Nebraska at Kearney (NE)
U of North Texas (TX)
U of Pittsburgh (PA)
U of Rhode Island (RI)
U of Richmond (VA)
The U of South Dakota (SD)
The U of Texas at Austin (TX)
The U of Texas at El Paso (TX)
U of Utah (UT)
U of Waterloo (ON, Canada)
U of Wisconsin–Superior (WI)
Utah State U (UT)
Wabash Coll (IN)
Walla Walla U (WA)
West Chester U of Pennsylvania (PA)
West Virginia Wesleyan Coll (WV)
Whitworth U (WA)
Willamette U (OR)
York Coll of the City U of New York (NY)
Youngstown State U (OH)

RHETORIC AND COMPOSITION/WRITING RELATED
Augsburg Coll (MN)
Pepperdine U, Malibu (CA)
Syracuse U (NY)

ROBOTICS TECHNOLOGY
Alcorn State U (MS)
Central Connecticut State U (CT)
Idaho State U (ID)
Indiana State U (IN)
U of Advancing Technology (AZ)

ROMANCE LANGUAGES
Beloit Coll (WI)
Bowdoin Coll (ME)
Bryn Mawr Coll (PA)
Carleton Coll (MN)
City Coll of the City U of New York (NY)
Colgate U (NY)
Dartmouth Coll (NH)
DePauw U (IN)
Emory U (GA)
Gettysburg Coll (PA)
Harvard U (MA)
Haverford Coll (PA)
Hunter Coll of the City U of New York (NY)
Iowa State U of Science and Technology (IA)
Johns Hopkins U (MD)
Loyola Marymount U (CA)
Merrimack Coll (MA)
Mount Allison U (NB, Canada)
Mount Holyoke Coll (MA)
Oberlin Coll (OH)
Pomona Coll (CA)
Rockford U (IL)
St. Thomas Aquinas Coll (NY)
Truman State U (MO)
Tufts U (MA)
U of Georgia (GA)
U of Illinois at Chicago (IL)
U of Maryland, Coll Park (MD)
U of Michigan (MI)
U of Notre Dame (IN)
U of Oregon (OR)
U of Toronto (ON, Canada)
U of Washington (WA)
Vanderbilt U (TN)
Washington and Lee U (VA)
Washington U in St. Louis (MO)
Wesleyan U (CT)
William Jewell Coll (MO)

ROMANCE LANGUAGES RELATED
Boston U (MA)
Bryn Mawr Coll (PA)
U of Chicago (IL)
U of Lethbridge (AB, Canada)
U of Maine (ME)
U of Michigan–Flint (MI)
U of Nevada, Las Vegas (NV)
The U of North Carolina at Chapel Hill (NC)
U of Pennsylvania (PA)
Wheeling Jesuit U (WV)

RURAL SOCIOLOGY
U of Wisconsin–Madison (WI)

RUSSIAN
American U (DC)
Amherst Coll (MA)
Arizona State U at the Tempe campus (AZ)
Bard Coll (NY)
Barnard Coll (NY)
Baylor U (TX)
Beloit Coll (WI)
Boston Coll (MA)
Boston U (MA)
Bowdoin Coll (ME)
Bowling Green State U (OH)
Brooklyn Coll of the City U of New York (NY)
Bryn Mawr Coll (PA)
Bucknell U (PA)
Carleton Coll (MN)
Carnegie Mellon U (PA)
Central Washington U (WA)
Colgate U (NY)
Coll of the Holy Cross (MA)
Columbia U (NY)
Columbia U, School of General Studies (NY)
Cornell Coll (IA)
Cornell U (NY)
Dalhousie U (NS, Canada)
Dartmouth Coll (NH)
Dickinson Coll (PA)
Emory U (GA)
Georgetown U (DC)
The George Washington U (DC)
Goucher Coll (MD)
Grinnell Coll (IA)
Haverford Coll (PA)
Hofstra U (NY)
Hunter Coll of the City U of New York (NY)
Juniata Coll (PA)
Kent State U (OH)
Lawrence U (WI)
Lehman Coll of the City U of New York (NY)
Luther Coll (IA)
Macalester Coll (MN)
McMaster U (ON, Canada)
Michigan State U (MI)
Middlebury Coll (VT)
New Coll of Florida (FL)
Oberlin Coll (OH)
The Ohio State U (OH)
Ohio U (OH)
Penn State Abington (PA)
Penn State Altoona (PA)
Penn State Beaver (PA)
Penn State Berks (PA)
Penn State Brandywine (PA)
Penn State DuBois (PA)
Penn State Erie, The Behrend Coll (PA)
Penn State Fayette, The Eberly Campus (PA)
Penn State Greater Allegheny (PA)
Penn State Hazleton (PA)
Penn State Lehigh Valley (PA)
Penn State Mont Alto (PA)
Penn State New Kensington (PA)
Penn State Schuylkill (PA)
Penn State Shenango (PA)
Penn State U Park (PA)
Penn State Wilkes-Barre (PA)
Penn State Worthington Scranton (PA)
Penn State York (PA)
Pomona Coll (CA)
Portland State U (OR)
Purdue U (IN)
Queens Coll of the City U of New York (NY)
Reed Coll (OR)
Rutgers U–New Brunswick (NJ)
Saint Louis U (MO)
St. Olaf Coll (MN)
San Diego State U (CA)
Sarah Lawrence Coll (NY)
Scripps Coll (CA)
Seattle Pacific U (WA)
Sewanee: The U of the South (TN)
Smith Coll (MA)
Swarthmore Coll (PA)
Syracuse U (NY)
Texas A&M U (TX)
Trinity U (TX)
Truman State U (MO)
Tufts U (MA)
Tulane U (LA)
United States Military Acad (NY)
The U of Arizona (AZ)
U of California, Davis (CA)
U of California, Los Angeles (CA)
U of California, San Diego (CA)
U of Denver (CO)
U of Florida (FL)
U of Georgia (GA)
U of Hawaii at Manoa (HI)
U of Illinois at Chicago (IL)
U of Kentucky (KY)
U of King's Coll (NS, Canada)
U of Maryland, Coll Park (MD)
U of Michigan (MI)
U of Minnesota, Twin Cities Campus (MN)
U of New Hampshire (NH)
U of Notre Dame (IN)
U of Oklahoma (OK)
U of Pennsylvania (PA)
U of Pittsburgh (PA)
U of Rochester (NY)
U of Saskatchewan (SK, Canada)
U of South Carolina (SC)
U of Southern California (CA)
U of South Florida (FL)
The U of Tennessee (TN)
The U of Texas at Austin (TX)
U of Toronto (ON, Canada)
U of Utah (UT)
U of Vermont (VT)
U of Washington (WA)
U of Waterloo (ON, Canada)
U of Wisconsin–Madison (WI)
U of Wisconsin–Milwaukee (WI)
Vanderbilt U (TN)
Vassar Coll (NY)
Virginia Polytechnic Inst and State U (VA)
Wake Forest U (NC)
Washington State U (WA)
West Chester U of Pennsylvania (PA)
Wheaton Coll (MA)
Willamette U (OR)
Williams Coll (MA)

RUSSIAN, CENTRAL EUROPEAN, EAST EUROPEAN AND EURASIAN STUDIES
Bowdoin Coll (ME)
Florida State U (FL)
Pomona Coll (CA)
Portland State U (OR)
San Diego State U (CA)
Tufts U (MA)
U of Toronto (ON, Canada)
Washington U in St. Louis (MO)
Wayne State U (MI)
Wittenberg U (OH)

RUSSIAN STUDIES
American U (DC)
Bard Coll (NY)
Boston Coll (MA)
Bowling Green State U (OH)
Brandeis U (MA)
Carleton Coll (MN)
Carnegie Mellon U (PA)
Colby Coll (ME)
Colgate U (NY)
The Coll of Wooster (OH)
The Colorado Coll (CO)
Columbia U (NY)
Columbia U, School of General Studies (NY)
Cornell Coll (IA)
Dalhousie U (NS, Canada)
Dartmouth Coll (NH)
DePauw U (IN)
Emory U (GA)
The George Washington U (DC)
Grand Valley State U (MI)
Hamilton Coll (NY)
Hobart and William Smith Colls (NY)
Iowa State U of Science and Technology (IA)
Lafayette Coll (PA)
Lawrence U (WI)
McMaster U (ON, Canada)
Middlebury Coll (VT)

Mount Holyoke Coll (MA)
Muhlenberg Coll (PA)
Oberlin Coll (OH)
Rhodes Coll (TN)
St. Olaf Coll (MN)
Scripps Coll (CA)
Smith Coll (MA)
Syracuse U (NY)
Texas Tech U (TX)
Tufts U (MA)
Tulane U (LA)
United States Military Acad (NY)
U of Alaska Fairbanks (AK)
U of California, Los Angeles (CA)
U of California, Riverside (CA)
U of California, San Diego (CA)
U of Colorado Boulder (CO)
U of Delaware (DE)
The U of Kansas (KS)
U of Maryland, Coll Park (MD)
U of Massachusetts Amherst (MA)
U of Michigan (MI)
U of Oregon (OR)
U of Richmond (VA)
U of Rochester (NY)
The U of Texas at Austin (TX)
U of Toronto (ON, Canada)
The U of Tulsa (OK)
U of Vermont (VT)
U of Waterloo (ON, Canada)
Washington and Lee U (VA)
Washington U in St. Louis (MO)
Wesleyan U (CT)
Wheaton Coll (MA)

SALES AND MARKETING/ MARKETING AND DISTRIBUTION TEACHER EDUCATION
Bowling Green State U (OH)
Central Washington U (WA)
Eastern Michigan U (MI)
Fayetteville State U (NC)
North Carolina State U (NC)
State U of New York at Oswego (NY)
U of Wisconsin–Stout (WI)
Utah State U (UT)
Western Michigan U (MI)

SALES, DISTRIBUTION, AND MARKETING OPERATIONS
Avila U (MO)
Baylor U (TX)
Bentley U (MA)
Black Hills State U (SD)
Bowling Green State U (OH)
Dalton State Coll (GA)
Hampton U (VA)
Harding U (AR)
HEC Montreal (QC, Canada)
Husson U (ME)
Kennesaw State U (GA)
Missouri Valley Coll (MO)
Quinnipiac U (CT)
St. Catherine U (MN)
Sam Houston State U (TX)
Seton Hill U (PA)
Syracuse U (NY)
Texas A&M U (TX)
The U of Akron (OH)
U of Houston (TX)
U of Minnesota, Twin Cities Campus (MN)
U of Pennsylvania (PA)
U of Wisconsin–Stout (WI)
U of Wisconsin–Superior (WI)
West Chester U of Pennsylvania (PA)

SANSKRIT AND CLASSICAL INDIAN LANGUAGES
Harvard U (MA)

SCANDINAVIAN LANGUAGES
Augustana Coll (IL)
Luther Coll (IA)
Southern Utah U (UT)
The U of Texas at Austin (TX)

SCANDINAVIAN STUDIES
American U (DC)
Concordia Coll (MN)
Pacific Lutheran U (WA)
U of California, Los Angeles (CA)
U of Washington (WA)
U of Wisconsin–Madison (WI)

SCHOOL LIBRARIAN/SCHOOL LIBRARY MEDIA
The Coll of St. Scholastica (MN)
East Central U (OK)
U of Great Falls (MT)

SCHOOL PSYCHOLOGY
Eastern Washington U (WA)
Kansas Wesleyan U (KS)
Northwest U (WA)
Sam Houston State U (TX)
Tarleton State U (TX)
Texas A&M U–Central Texas (TX)

SCIENCE TEACHER EDUCATION
Abilene Christian U (TX)
Adams State U (CO)
Albany State U (GA)
Albion Coll (MI)
Alfred U (NY)
Alice Lloyd Coll (KY)
Alverno Coll (WI)
Andrews U (MI)
Aquinas Coll (MI)
Arcadia U (PA)
Arizona Christian U (AZ)
Arkansas Tech U (AR)
Armstrong State U (GA)
Ashland U (OH)
Auburn U (AL)
Ball State U (IN)
Bayamón Central U (PR)
Baylor U (TX)
Bemidji State U (MN)
Biola U (CA)
Bishop's U (QC, Canada)
Blackburn Coll (IL)
Black Hills State U (SD)
Bluefield Coll (VA)
Boston U (MA)
Bowie State U (MD)
Bowling Green State U (OH)
Bradley U (IL)
Brewton-Parker Coll (GA)
Brigham Young U (UT)
Buena Vista U (IA)
Buffalo State Coll, State U of New York (NY)
California Lutheran U (CA)
Calvin Coll (MI)
Campbellsville U (KY)
Canisius Coll (NY)
Capital U (OH)
Catawba Coll (NC)
Cedarville U (OH)
Central Methodist U (MO)
Central Michigan U (MI)
Central Washington U (WA)
Charleston Southern U (SC)
City Coll of the City U of New York (NY)
Clemson U (SC)
Coe Coll (IA)
Coll of Saint Mary (NE)
Coll of the Atlantic (ME)
Colorado State U (CO)
Columbus State U (GA)
Concordia Coll–New York (NY)
Concordia U Chicago (IL)
Concordia U Wisconsin (WI)
Cornerstone U (MI)
Dallas Baptist U (TX)
Defiance Coll (OH)
Dickinson State U (ND)
Dixie State U (UT)
Doane U (NE)
East Carolina U (NC)
East Central U (OK)
Eastern Illinois U (IL)
Eastern Michigan U (MI)
Eastern Nazarene Coll (MA)
Eastern Washington U (WA)
Edgewood Coll (WI)
Elizabethtown Coll (PA)
Elon U (NC)
Evangel U (MO)
Faulkner U (AL)
Florida Ag and Mech U (FL)
Florida Atlantic U (FL)
Florida Inst of Technology (FL)
Florida SouthWestern State Coll (FL)
Gettysburg Coll (PA)
Goshen Coll (IN)
Graceland U (IA)
Grand Valley State U (MI)
Hannibal-LaGrange U (MO)
Harding U (AR)
Hardin-Simmons U (TX)
Heidelberg U (OH)
Hobe Sound Bible Coll (FL)
Hofstra U (NY)
Hope Coll (MI)
Houston Baptist U (TX)
Hunter Coll of the City U of New York (NY)
Huntingdon Coll (AL)
Huntington U (IN)
Indiana State U (IN)
Indiana U South Bend (IN)
Inter American U of Puerto Rico, Metropolitan Campus (PR)
Inter American U of Puerto Rico, San Germán Campus (PR)
Ithaca Coll (NY)
Juniata Coll (PA)
Keene State Coll (NH)
Kent State U (OH)
Le Moyne Coll (NY)
LeTourneau U (TX)
Lindenwood U (MO)
Louisiana Coll (LA)
Loyola U Chicago (IL)
Madonna U (MI)
Malone U (OH)
Manchester U (IN)
Maranatha Baptist U (WI)
Marian U (WI)
Marywood U (PA)
The Master's U (CA)
McKendree U (IL)
Mercyhurst U (PA)
Merrimack Coll (MA)
Miami Dade Coll (FL)
Miami U (OH)
Michigan State U (MI)
Mid-Atlantic Christian U (NC)
Minnesota State U Mankato (MN)
Minot State U (ND)
Missouri Baptist U (MO)
Missouri State U (MO)
Missouri Valley Coll (MO)
Montana State U (MT)
Montana State U Billings (MT)
Montana State U–Northern (MT)
Morningside Coll (IA)
Mount Mary U (WI)
Mount Mercy U (IA)
Mount Vernon Nazarene U (OH)
Nebraska Wesleyan U (NE)
Nevada State Coll (NV)
New Mexico Highlands U (NM)
North Carolina State U (NC)
North Dakota State U (ND)
Northeastern State U (OK)
Northland Coll (WI)
Northwestern Oklahoma State U (OK)
Northwest Missouri State U (MO)
Ohio Dominican U (OH)
Oklahoma Baptist U (OK)
Oklahoma Christian U (OK)
Olivet Nazarene U (IL)
Oral Roberts U (OK)
Otterbein U (OH)
Ouachita Baptist U (AR)
Piedmont Coll (GA)
Plymouth State U (NH)
Rhode Island Coll (RI)
Rocky Mountain Coll (MT)
Saginaw Valley State U (MI)
St. Cloud State U (MN)
Saint Francis U (PA)
St. Petersburg Coll (FL)
Shawnee State U (OH)
Southeast Missouri State U (MO)
Southern Illinois U Edwardsville (IL)
Southern New Hampshire U (NH)
Southern Utah U (UT)
Southwest Baptist U (MO)
State U of New York at Fredonia (NY)
State U of New York at New Paltz (NY)
State U of New York at Oswego (NY)
State U of New York Coll at Cortland (NY)
State U of New York Coll at Old Westbury (NY)
Tarleton State U (TX)
Taylor U (IN)
Temple U (PA)
Texas Christian U (TX)
Tiffin U (OH)
Trine U (IN)
Union Coll (KY)
Union Coll (NE)
Union U (TN)
The U of Akron (OH)
U of Central Arkansas (AR)
U of Central Florida (FL)
U of Charleston (WV)
U of Dayton (OH)
U of Dubuque (IA)
The U of Findlay (OH)
U of Georgia (GA)
U of Great Falls (MT)
U of Indianapolis (IN)
U of Kentucky (KY)
U of Lethbridge (AB, Canada)
U of Maine (ME)
U of Mary Hardin-Baylor (TX)
U of Michigan–Dearborn (MI)
U of Minnesota, Duluth (MN)
The U of Montana Western (MT)
U of Nevada, Las Vegas (NV)
The U of North Carolina at Greensboro (NC)
The U of North Carolina at Pembroke (NC)
U of North Dakota (ND)
U of North Florida (FL)
U of Notre Dame (IN)
U of Oklahoma (OK)
U of Pittsburgh at Johnstown (PA)
U of Regina (SK, Canada)
U of St. Francis (IL)
U of St. Thomas (MN)
The U of South Dakota (SD)
U of South Florida (FL)
The U of Tennessee at Chattanooga (TN)
The U of Tennessee at Martin (TN)
U of Toronto (ON, Canada)
U of Vermont (VT)
U of Windsor (ON, Canada)
U of Wisconsin–Eau Claire (WI)
U of Wisconsin–La Crosse (WI)
U of Wisconsin–Stout (WI)
U of Wisconsin–Superior (WI)
Upper Iowa U (IA)
Utah State U (UT)
Utah Valley U (UT)
Valley City State U (ND)
Valparaiso U (IN)
Vincennes U (IN)
Viterbo U (WI)
Walsh U (OH)
Washington U in St. Louis (MO)
Wayland Baptist U (TX)
Waynesburg U (PA)
Wayne State Coll (NE)
Weber State U (UT)
Webster U (MO)
Western Carolina U (NC)
Western Michigan U (MI)
Western State Colorado U (CO)
Westfield State U (MA)
Widener U (PA)
William Penn U (IA)
Wilmington U (DE)
Winona State U (MN)
Wright State U (OH)
Wright State U–Lake Campus (OH)
Xavier U of Louisiana (LA)
York Coll of Pennsylvania (PA)
Youngstown State U (OH)

SCIENCE TECHNOLOGIES
Baylor U (TX)
Excelsior Coll (NY)

SCIENCE TECHNOLOGIES RELATED
Arizona State U at the Downtown Phoenix campus (AZ)
Arizona State U at the Polytechnic campus (AZ)
Bridgewater State U (MA)
Excelsior Coll (NY)
Kean U (NJ)
Madonna U (MI)
North Carolina State U (NC)
Northern Arizona U (AZ)
The U of Arizona (AZ)
U of Wisconsin–Stout (WI)
Willamette U (OR)

SCIENCE, TECHNOLOGY AND SOCIETY
Arizona State U at the Polytechnic campus (AZ)
Arizona State U at the Tempe campus (AZ)
Butler U (IN)
California State Polytechnic U, Pomona (CA)
Claremont McKenna Coll (CA)
Colby Coll (ME)
Cornell U (NY)
Dalhousie U (NS, Canada)
Eastern Michigan U (MI)
Farmingdale State Coll (NY)
Georgetown U (DC)
Georgia Inst of Technology (GA)
James Madison U (VA)
Lehigh U (PA)
Massachusetts Inst of Technology (MA)
Morrisville State Coll (NY)
North Carolina State U (NC)
Northwestern U (IL)
Penn State U Park (PA)
Pitzer Coll (CA)
Pomona Coll (CA)
Rensselaer Polytechnic Inst (NY)
Rutgers U–Newark (NJ)
St. Thomas U (NB, Canada)
Sarah Lawrence Coll (NY)
Scripps Coll (CA)
Stanford U (CA)
Texas Tech U (TX)
Tufts U (MA)
U of King's Coll (NS, Canada)
U of Puget Sound (WA)
U of Washington, Bothell (WA)
U of Windsor (ON, Canada)
Vanderbilt U (TN)
Vassar Coll (NY)
Washington U in St. Louis (MO)
Wesleyan U (CT)
Worcester Polytechnic Inst (MA)

SCULPTURE
Aquinas Coll (MI)
Bennington Coll (VT)
Binghamton U, State U of New York (NY)
Biola U (CA)
Boston U (MA)
Bowling Green State U (OH)
Bradley U (IL)
Brigham Young U (UT)
Buffalo State Coll, State U of New York (NY)
California Coll of the Arts (CA)
California State U, East Bay (CA)
California State U, Long Beach (CA)
Central Washington U (WA)
Cleveland Inst of Art (OH)
Colorado State U (CO)
Concordia U (QC, Canada)
Dixie State U (UT)
Dominican U (IL)
Drake U (IA)
Emily Carr U of Art + Design (BC, Canada)
Escuela de Artes Plasticas y Dise&nno de Puerto Rico (PR)
Ferris State U (MI)
Inter American U of Puerto Rico, San Germán Campus (PR)
Kansas City Art Inst (MO)
Laguna Coll of Art & Design (CA)
Maryland Inst Coll of Art (MD)
Marywood U (PA)
Massachusetts Coll of Art and Design (MA)
Milwaukee Inst of Art and Design (WI)
Minneapolis Coll of Art and Design (MN)
Minnesota State U Mankato (MN)
Mount Allison U (NB, Canada)
Ohio U (OH)
Pacific Northwest Coll of Art (OR)
Portland State U (OR)
Pratt Inst (NY)
Providence Coll (RI)
Rhode Island Coll (RI)
Rhode Island School of Design (RI)
Rochester Inst of Technology (NY)
Rutgers U–New Brunswick (NJ)
St. Cloud State U (MN)

San Francisco Art Inst (CA)
Sarah Lawrence Coll (NY)
Savannah Coll of Art and Design (GA)
School of the Art Inst of Chicago (IL)
Seton Hill U (PA)
Sonoma State U (CA)
State U of New York at New Paltz (NY)
Syracuse U (NY)
Temple U (PA)
Texas Christian U (TX)
The U of Akron (OH)
U of Hartford (CT)
U of Houston (TX)
The U of Kansas (KS)
U of Massachusetts Dartmouth (MA)
U of Miami (FL)
U of Michigan (MI)
U of New Haven (CT)
U of Oregon (OR)
U of Regina (SK, Canada)
The U of Texas at El Paso (TX)
The U of the Arts (PA)
U of Washington (WA)
U of Windsor (ON, Canada)
Virginia Commonwealth U (VA)
Washington U in St. Louis (MO)
Western State Colorado U (CO)

SECONDARY EDUCATION
Abilene Christian U (TX)
Alabama State U (AL)
Albertus Magnus Coll (CT)
Albright Coll (PA)
Alderson Broaddus U (WV)
Alfred U (NY)
Alice Lloyd Coll (KY)
Alma Coll (MI)
American U (DC)
Andrews U (MI)
Arcadia U (PA)
Arizona Christian U (AZ)
Arizona State U at the Polytechnic campus (AZ)
Arizona State U at the Tempe campus (AZ)
Arizona State U at the West campus (AZ)
Ashland U (OH)
Auburn U (AL)
Auburn U at Montgomery (AL)
Augsburg Coll (MN)
Augustana U (SD)
Aurora U (IL)
Austin Coll (TX)
Baker U (KS)
Baylor U (TX)
Bellarmine U (KY)
Belmont U (TN)
Beloit Coll (WI)
Bemidji State U (MN)
Benedictine Coll (KS)
Berry Coll (GA)
Bethel Coll (IN)
Biola U (CA)
Bishop's U (QC, Canada)
Blackburn Coll (IL)
Black Hills State U (SD)
Bluefield Coll (VA)
Boston Coll (MA)
Bowdoin Coll (ME)
Bowie State U (MD)
Bradley U (IL)
Brewton-Parker Coll (GA)
Briar Cliff U (IA)
Bucknell U (PA)
Buffalo State Coll, State U of New York (NY)
Butler U (IN)
Caldwell U (NJ)
Calvary U (MO)
Calvin Coll (MI)
Campbellsville U (KY)
Canisius Coll (NY)
Cardinal Stritch U (WI)
Caribbean U (PR)
Carroll Coll (MT)
Carson-Newman U (TN)
Carthage Coll (WI)
The Catholic U of America (DC)
Cedar Crest Coll (PA)
Centenary U (NJ)
Central Baptist Coll (AR)
Central Methodist U (MO)
Central State U (OH)
Chaminade U of Honolulu (HI)
Champlain Coll (VT)
Charleston Southern U (SC)
The Citadel, The Military Coll of South Carolina (SC)
City Coll of the City U of New York (NY)
Clarke U (IA)
Clark U (MA)
Clemson U (SC)
Coe Coll (IA)
Coll of Charleston (SC)
The Coll of New Jersey (NJ)
Coll of Saint Benedict (MN)
Coll of Saint Mary (NE)
The Coll of Saint Rose (NY)
Coll of the Atlantic (ME)
Concordia U Chicago (IL)
Concordia U, Nebraska (NE)
Concordia U, St. Paul (MN)
Concordia U Wisconsin (WI)
Concord U (WV)
Converse Coll (SC)
Corban U (OR)
Cornell Coll (IA)
Daytona State Coll (FL)
Defiance Coll (OH)
Delaware Valley U (PA)
DeSales U (PA)
Dixie State U (UT)
Dominican Coll (NY)
Dominican U (IL)
Drake U (IA)
Drexel U (PA)
Eastern Nazarene Coll (MA)
Elmira Coll (NY)
Elon U (NC)
Emmanuel Coll (MA)
Emmaus Bible Coll (IA)
Emporia State U (KS)
Endicott Coll (MA)
Evangel U (MO)
Felician U (NJ)
Fitchburg State U (MA)
Florida Gulf Coast U (FL)
Fordham U (NY)
Fort Lewis Coll (CO)
Franklin Pierce U (NH)
Freed-Hardeman U (TN)
Furman U (SC)
Gardner-Webb U (NC)
Gettysburg Coll (PA)
Gonzaga U (WA)
Gordon Coll (MA)
Goshen Coll (IN)
Graceland U (IA)
Grambling State U (LA)
Grand Valley State U (MI)
Grand View U (IA)
Granite State Coll (NH)
Great Basin Coll (NV)
Guilford Coll (NC)
Hamline U (MN)
Hampton U (VA)
Hannibal-LaGrange U (MO)
Harding U (AR)
Harris-Stowe State U (MO)
Heidelberg U (OH)
High Point U (NC)
Hofstra U (NY)
Houghton Coll (NY)
Humboldt State U (CA)
Hunter Coll of the City U of New York (NY)
Huntington U (IN)
Husson U (ME)
Huston-Tillotson U (TX)
Idaho State U (ID)
Illinois Coll (IL)
Indiana U Bloomington (IN)
Indiana U East (IN)
Indiana U Kokomo (IN)
Indiana U Northwest (IN)
Indiana U South Bend (IN)
Indiana U Southeast (IN)
Inter American U of Puerto Rico, San Germán Campus (PR)
Iona Coll (NY)
Iowa State U of Science and Technology (IA)
Ithaca Coll (NY)
Jacksonville State U (AL)
Jacksonville U (FL)
John Carroll U (OH)
Judson U (IL)
Kansas State U (KS)
Kansas Wesleyan U (KS)
Keene State Coll (NH)
Keuka Coll (NY)
The King's U (AB, Canada)
Knox Coll (IL)
Kutztown U of Pennsylvania (PA)
Kuyper Coll (MI)
Lake Erie Coll (OH)
Langston U (OK)
La Salle U (PA)
Lasell Coll (MA)
Lawrence U (WI)
Le Moyne Coll (NY)
Lesley U (MA)
LeTourneau U (TX)
Lewis U (IL)
Lindsey Wilson Coll (KY)
Lock Haven U of Pennsylvania (PA)
Lourdes U (OH)
Loyola U Chicago (IL)
Lubbock Christian U (TX)
Maharishi U of Management (IA)
Manchester U (IN)
Manhattanville Coll (NY)
Mansfield U of Pennsylvania (PA)
Marian U (IN)
Marian U (WI)
Marietta Coll (OH)
Marshall U (WV)
The Master's U (CA)
McMurry U (TX)
McNeese State U (LA)
Mercyhurst U (PA)
Merrimack Coll (MA)
Michigan State U (MI)
MidAmerica Nazarene U (KS)
Minnesota State U Mankato (MN)
Mississippi State U (MS)
Mississippi Valley State U (MS)
Missouri Baptist U (MO)
Missouri State U (MO)
Missouri U of Science and Technology (MO)
Missouri Valley Coll (MO)
Molloy Coll (NY)
Monmouth U (NJ)
Montana State U Billings (MT)
Mount Aloysius Coll (PA)
Mount Marty Coll (SD)
Mount Mercy U (IA)
Mount Saint Mary Coll (NY)
Mount Saint Mary's U (CA)
National U (CA)
Nazareth Coll of Rochester (NY)
Nevada State Coll (NV)
New England Coll (NH)
Newman U (KS)
New Mexico State U (NM)
North Central Coll (IL)
Northcentral U (CA)
Northern Kentucky U (KY)
Northern State U (SD)
Northland Coll (WI)
Northwest Christian U (OR)
Northwestern Coll (IA)
Northwestern Oklahoma State U (OK)
Northwestern State U of Louisiana (LA)
Northwestern U (IL)
Northwest U (WA)
Nova Southeastern U (FL)
Ohio U (OH)
Ohio Valley U (WV)
Ohio Wesleyan U (OH)
Oklahoma Christian U (OK)
Oklahoma City U (OK)
Oklahoma State U (OK)
Otterbein U (OH)
Ouachita Baptist U (AR)
Penn State Abington (PA)
Penn State Altoona (PA)
Penn State Beaver (PA)
Penn State Berks (PA)
Penn State Brandywine (PA)
Penn State DuBois (PA)
Penn State Erie, The Behrend Coll (PA)
Penn State Fayette, The Eberly Campus (PA)
Penn State Greater Allegheny (PA)
Penn State Hazleton (PA)
Penn State Lehigh Valley (PA)
Penn State Mont Alto (PA)
Penn State New Kensington (PA)
Penn State Schuylkill (PA)
Penn State Shenango (PA)
Penn State U Park (PA)
Penn State Wilkes-Barre (PA)
Penn State Worthington Scranton (PA)
Penn State York (PA)
Piedmont Coll (GA)
Polytechnic U of Puerto Rico (PR)
Prescott Coll (AZ)
Providence Coll (RI)
Purdue U Northwest (IN)
Rhode Island Coll (RI)
Ripon Coll (WI)
Rockford U (IL)
Rockhurst U (MO)
Rocky Mountain Coll (MT)
Roger Williams U (RI)
St. Ambrose U (IA)
Saint Anselm Coll (NH)
St. Catherine U (MN)
St. Cloud State U (MN)
Saint Francis U (PA)
Saint John's U (MN)
Saint Joseph's U (PA)
Saint Leo U (FL)
Saint Michael's Coll (VT)
St. Thomas Aquinas Coll (NY)
St. Thomas U (FL)
Salve Regina U (RI)
Sam Houston State U (TX)
Shepherd U (WV)
Simmons Coll (MA)
Simpson Coll (IA)
Slippery Rock U of Pennsylvania (PA)
Southern Connecticut State U (CT)
Southwestern Assemblies of God U (TX)
Spalding U (KY)
Spring Hill Coll (AL)
State U of New York at Fredonia (NY)
State U of New York at Oswego (NY)
State U of New York Coll at Cortland (NY)
State U of New York Coll at Old Westbury (NY)
Stonehill Coll (MA)
Susquehanna U (PA)
Tabor Coll (KS)
Tarleton State U (TX)
Taylor U (IN)
Temple U (PA)
Tennessee Wesleyan U (TN)
Texas Christian U (TX)
Thomas More Coll (KY)
Thomas U (GA)
Toccoa Falls Coll (GA)
Trent U (ON, Canada)
Trine U (IN)
Trinity Baptist Coll (FL)
Troy U (AL)
Union Inst & U (OH)
Union U (TN)
Unity Coll (ME)
Universidad Adventista de las Antillas (PR)
Université de Montréal (QC, Canada)
Université de Sherbrooke (QC, Canada)
The U of Alabama (AL)
The U of Alabama at Birmingham (AL)
The U of Alabama in Huntsville (AL)
U of Alaska Fairbanks (AK)
U of Central Missouri (MO)
U of Cincinnati (OH)
U of Dayton (OH)
U of Detroit Mercy (MI)
U of Dubuque (IA)
U of Great Falls (MT)
U of Hartford (CT)
U of Hawaii at Manoa (HI)
U of Idaho (ID)
U of Indianapolis (IN)
The U of Kansas (KS)
U of Louisiana at Monroe (LA)
U of Maine (ME)
U of Maine at Farmington (ME)
U of Maine at Presque Isle (ME)
U of Maryland, Coll Park (MD)
U of Michigan (MI)
U of Michigan–Dearborn (MI)
U of Minnesota, Morris (MN)
U of Missouri–Kansas City (MO)
U of Missouri–St. Louis (MO)
The U of Montana Western (MT)
U of Nevada, Las Vegas (NV)
U of New England (ME)
U of New Orleans (LA)
U of North Alabama (AL)
The U of North Carolina at Greensboro (NC)
U of North Dakota (ND)
U of North Florida (FL)
U of Pittsburgh at Bradford (PA)
U of Pittsburgh at Johnstown (PA)
U of Regina (SK, Canada)
U of Rhode Island (RI)
U of St. Thomas (TX)
U of San Francisco (CA)
U of Saskatchewan (SK, Canada)
The U of Scranton (PA)
U of South Alabama (AL)
U of South Carolina Aiken (SC)
The U of South Dakota (SD)
The U of Tampa (FL)
The U of Tennessee at Chattanooga (TN)
U of the Cumberlands (KY)
U of the Southwest (NM)
The U of Toledo (OH)
U of Valley Forge (PA)
U of Vermont (VT)
U of Windsor (ON, Canada)
U of Wisconsin–Parkside (WI)
U of Wisconsin–Stevens Point (WI)
Utah State U (UT)
Utica Coll (NY)
Valley City State U (ND)
Valparaiso U (IN)
Vanderbilt U (TN)
Villanova U (PA)
Virginia Polytechnic Inst and State U (VA)
Virginia Wesleyan Coll (VA)
Wagner Coll (NY)
Waldorf U (IA)
Walsh U (OH)
Wartburg Coll (IA)
Washington U in St. Louis (MO)
Waynesburg U (PA)
Wayne State U (MI)
Webster U (MO)
Welch Coll (TN)
Wells Coll (NY)
Western Connecticut State U (CT)
Western New England U (MA)
Western Oregon U (OR)
Westmont Coll (CA)
West Virginia State U (WV)
West Virginia Wesleyan Coll (WV)
Wheaton Coll (IL)
Wheaton Coll (MA)
Whitworth U (WA)
Wichita State U (KS)
William Jewell Coll (MO)
William Paterson U of New Jersey (NJ)
William Penn U (IA)
William Woods U (MO)
Xavier U of Louisiana (LA)
York Coll of the City U of New York (NY)
Youngstown State U (OH)

SECONDARY SCHOOL ADMINISTRATION/ PRINCIPALSHIP
Charleston Southern U (SC)

SECURITIES SERVICES ADMINISTRATION
American Public U System (WV)
Dean Coll (MA)
John Jay Coll of Criminal Justice of the City U of New York (NY)
St. John's U (NY)
Saint Louis U (MO)
Slippery Rock U of Pennsylvania (PA)
Southwestern Coll (KS)
Washburn U (KS)

SECURITY AND LOSS PREVENTION
Farmingdale State Coll (NY)

SELLING SKILLS AND SALES
Ball State U (IN)
Bradley U (IL)
High Point U (NC)
Purdue U (IN)
St. Catherine U (MN)

Weber State U (UT)
William Paterson U of New Jersey (NJ)

SIGN LANGUAGE INTERPRETATION AND TRANSLATION
Augustana U (SD)
Bethel Coll (IN)
Bloomsburg U of Pennsylvania (PA)
Columbia Coll Chicago (IL)
Framingham State U (MA)
Gallaudet U (DC)
Goshen Coll (IN)
Idaho State U (ID)
Indiana U–Purdue U Indianapolis (IN)
Kent State U (OH)
MacMurray Coll (IL)
Madonna U (MI)
Mount Aloysius Coll (PA)
Rochester Inst of Technology (NY)
Troy U (AL)
U of Cincinnati (OH)
U of Louisville (KY)
U of New Hampshire at Manchester (NH)
U of Northern Colorado (CO)
U of North Florida (FL)
Valdosta State U (GA)
Western Oregon U (OR)
William Woods U (MO)

SLAVIC, BALTIC, AND ALBANIAN LANGUAGES RELATED
Rutgers U–Newark (NJ)

SLAVIC LANGUAGES
Boston Coll (MA)
Columbia U (NY)
Columbia U, School of General Studies (NY)
Harvard U (MA)
Indiana U Bloomington (IN)
Northwestern U (IL)
Princeton U (NJ)
Stanford U (CA)
U of California, Los Angeles (CA)
U of California, Santa Barbara (CA)
U of Chicago (IL)
U of Illinois at Chicago (IL)
The U of Kansas (KS)
U of Pittsburgh (PA)
U of Toronto (ON, Canada)
U of Virginia (VA)
U of Washington (WA)
Wayne State U (MI)

SLAVIC STUDIES
Barnard Coll (NY)
Baylor U (TX)
Columbia U, School of General Studies (NY)
Connecticut Coll (CT)
Lawrence U (WI)
Northwestern U (IL)
U of Waterloo (ON, Canada)

SMALL BUSINESS ADMINISTRATION
Adams State U (CO)
Arcadia U (PA)
Avila U (MO)
Bradley U (IL)
Brenau U (GA)
Carson-Newman U (TN)
Chowan U (NC)
Dalhousie U (NS, Canada)
Florida Inst of Technology (FL)
Florida Southern Coll (FL)
Hilbert Coll (NY)
Huntington U (IN)
Husson U (ME)
Lincoln U (CA)
North Central Coll (IL)
Ohio Wesleyan U (OH)
Rocky Mountain Coll (MT)
Saint Joseph's U (PA)
The U of Scranton (PA)

SOCIAL AND PHILOSOPHICAL FOUNDATIONS OF EDUCATION
Dickinson Coll (PA)
Eastern Washington U (WA)
Goddard Coll (VT)
Hope Intl U (CA)
Northwestern U (IL)
Transylvania U (KY)
Washington U in St. Louis (MO)

SOCIAL PSYCHOLOGY
Augsburg Coll (MN)
Bennington Coll (VT)
Brigham Young U (UT)
Clarion U of Pennsylvania (PA)
Eastern Nazarene Coll (MA)
Florida Atlantic U (FL)
Goddard Coll (VT)
Grand Valley State U (MI)
Lawrence U (WI)
Maryville U of Saint Louis (MO)
Northwest Missouri State U (MO)
Penn State Abington (PA)
U of California, Irvine (CA)
U of Wisconsin–Superior (WI)
Western Michigan U (MI)

SOCIAL SCIENCES
Adelphi U (NY)
Albertus Magnus Coll (CT)
Alverno Coll (WI)
American Intl Coll (MA)
American U (DC)
Andrews U (MI)
Aquinas Coll (MI)
Arizona State U at the West campus (AZ)
Asbury U (KY)
Ashland U (OH)
Athens State U (AL)
Azusa Pacific U (CA)
Ball State U (IN)
Belhaven U (MS)
Bemidji State U (MN)
Benedictine Coll (KS)
Bennington Coll (VT)
Berry Coll (GA)
Bethany Lutheran Coll (MN)
Bethel U (MN)
Binghamton U, State U of New York (NY)
Biola U (CA)
Bishop's U (QC, Canada)
Black Hills State U (SD)
Bluefield State Coll (WV)
Bluffton U (OH)
Boise State U (ID)
Bowling Green State U (OH)
Brandman U (CA)
Brescia U (KY)
Brewton-Parker Coll (GA)
Caldwell U (NJ)
California Lutheran U (CA)
California State U, Monterey Bay (CA)
California State U, Sacramento (CA)
California State U, San Bernardino (CA)
California State U, San Marcos (CA)
California State U, Stanislaus (CA)
California U of Pennsylvania (PA)
Calvin Coll (MI)
Campbellsville U (KY)
Canisius Coll (NY)
Carthage Coll (WI)
Cazenovia Coll (NY)
Central Connecticut State U (CT)
Central Michigan U (MI)
Central Washington U (WA)
Chaminade U of Honolulu (HI)
Charleston Southern U (SC)
Clarkson U (NY)
Cleveland State U (OH)
Colgate U (NY)
Coll of Mount Saint Vincent (NY)
Coll of Saint Benedict (MN)
The Coll of St. Scholastica (MN)
Colorado Christian U (CO)
Colorado Mesa U (CO)
Concordia Coll–New York (NY)
Corban U (OR)
Daemen Coll (NY)
Defiance Coll (OH)
Dickinson State U (ND)
Doane U (NE)
Dominican Coll (NY)
Eastern Mennonite U (VA)
Eastern Michigan U (MI)
Edgewood Coll (WI)
Elizabethtown Coll (PA)
Elmira Coll (NY)
Emporia State U (KS)
Excelsior Coll (NY)
Faulkner U (AL)
Florida Atlantic U (FL)
Florida Southern Coll (FL)
Florida State U (FL)
Frostburg State U (MD)
Gardner-Webb U (NC)
Gettysburg Coll (PA)
Governors State U (IL)
Grand Valley State U (MI)
Granite State Coll (NH)
Great Basin Coll (NV)
Hampton U (VA)
Harding U (AR)
Harvard U (MA)
Hope Intl U (CA)
Howard Payne U (TX)
Humboldt State U (CA)
Ithaca Coll (NY)
Jacksonville U (FL)
Johns Hopkins U (MD)
Johnson C. Smith U (NC)
Kansas State U (KS)
Kentucky State U (KY)
Keuka Coll (NY)
The King's U (AB, Canada)
Lake Erie Coll (OH)
La Salle U (PA)
Lesley U (MA)
Liberty U (VA)
Lock Haven U of Pennsylvania (PA)
Loyola U New Orleans (LA)
Manchester U (IN)
Manhattanville Coll (NY)
Mansfield U of Pennsylvania (PA)
Marylhurst U (OR)
Marywood U (PA)
McKendree U (IL)
Mercy Coll (NY)
Mercyhurst U (PA)
Michigan State U (MI)
Michigan Technological U (MI)
MidAmerica Nazarene U (KS)
Minnesota State U Mankato (MN)
Minot State U (ND)
Misericordia U (PA)
Missouri Baptist U (MO)
Morehead State U (KY)
Mount Mary U (WI)
Mount Saint Mary Coll (NY)
Mount Saint Mary's U (CA)
Muhlenberg Coll (PA)
National Louis U (IL)
National U (CA)
Nazareth Coll of Rochester (NY)
New Coll of Florida (FL)
Niagara U (NY)
North Central Coll (IL)
North Dakota State U (ND)
Northern Kentucky U (KY)
Northwestern Oklahoma State U (OK)
Oklahoma Baptist U (OK)
Olivet Nazarene U (IL)
Oregon State U (OR)
Our Lady of the Lake U of San Antonio (TX)
Pace U (NY)
Pace U, Pleasantville Campus (NY)
Piedmont Coll (GA)
Plymouth State U (NH)
Point Loma Nazarene U (CA)
Point U (GA)
Portland State U (OR)
Providence Coll (RI)
Quinnipiac U (CT)
Radford U (VA)
Ramapo Coll of New Jersey (NJ)
Regis U (CO)
Robert Morris U (PA)
Rockford U (IL)
Rogers State U (OK)
Roger Williams U (RI)
Royal Military Coll of Canada (ON, Canada)
Rust Coll (MS)
The Sage Colls (NY)
St. Andrews U (NC)
St. Catherine U (MN)
St. Cloud State U (MN)
St. Gregory's U, Shawnee (OK)
Saint John's U (MN)
St. John's U (NY)
St. Joseph's Coll, Long Island Campus (NY)
St. Joseph's Coll, New York (NY)
Saint Mary's Coll of California (CA)
Saint Peter's U (NJ)
St. Thomas Aquinas Coll (NY)
Salisbury U (MD)
San Diego State U (CA)
Sarah Lawrence Coll (NY)
Shawnee State U (OH)
Shorter U (GA)
South Carolina State U (SC)
Southeast Missouri State U (MO)
Southern Arkansas U–Magnolia (AR)
Southern Illinois U Carbondale (IL)
Southern New Hampshire U (NH)
Southern Oregon U (OR)
Southwestern Adventist U (TX)
Spalding U (KY)
Spring Hill Coll (AL)
State U of New York Coll at Old Westbury (NY)
State U of New York Empire State Coll (NY)
Stevens Inst of Technology (NJ)
Thomas Edison State U (NJ)
Thomas U (GA)
Towson U (MD)
Trent U (ON, Canada)
Trine U (IN)
Troy U (AL)
Union Coll (NY)
United States Air Force Acad (CO)
Université de Montréal (QC, Canada)
U at Buffalo, the State U of New York (NY)
The U of Akron (OH)
U of Bridgeport (CT)
U of California, Irvine (CA)
U of Central Florida (FL)
U of Chicago (IL)
U of Denver (CO)
U of Detroit Mercy (MI)
U of Great Falls (MT)
U of Houston–Downtown (TX)
U of La Verne (CA)
U of Lethbridge (AB, Canada)
U of Maine at Fort Kent (ME)
U of Maryland U Coll (MD)
U of Massachusetts Boston (MA)
U of Michigan (MI)
U of Michigan–Dearborn (MI)
U of Michigan–Flint (MI)
U of Minnesota, Morris (MN)
U of Mobile (AL)
U of Montevallo (AL)
U of Nevada, Las Vegas (NV)
U of North Alabama (AL)
U of North Dakota (ND)
U of North Texas (TX)
U of Oregon (OR)
U of Pennsylvania (PA)
U of Pittsburgh (PA)
U of Pittsburgh at Bradford (PA)
U of Pittsburgh at Greensburg (PA)
U of Pittsburgh at Johnstown (PA)
U of Regina (SK, Canada)
U of St. Thomas (MN)
U of Southern California (CA)
U of Southern Indiana (IN)
U of South Florida (FL)
U of South Florida, St. Petersburg (FL)
U of South Florida Sarasota-Manatee (FL)
The U of Texas Rio Grande Valley (TX)
U of the Pacific (CA)
U of the Southwest (NM)
U of the Virgin Islands (VI)
U of Utah (UT)
U of Washington (WA)
U of Windsor (ON, Canada)
U of Wisconsin–Platteville (WI)
U of Wisconsin–Stevens Point (WI)
U of Wisconsin–Stout (WI)
U of Wisconsin–Superior (WI)
U of Wisconsin–Whitewater (WI)
Upper Iowa U (IA)
Utica Coll (NY)
Valley City State U (ND)
Valparaiso U (IN)
Vanderbilt U (TN)
Virginia Wesleyan Coll (VA)
Viterbo U (WI)
Wartburg Coll (IA)
Washington State U (WA)
Washington State U–Global Campus (WA)
Washington State U–Tri-Cities (WA)
Washington State U–Vancouver (WA)
Washington U in St. Louis (MO)
Wayland Baptist U (TX)
Waynesburg U (PA)
Wayne State Coll (NE)
Western Connecticut State U (CT)
Western Kentucky U (KY)
Western Oregon U (OR)
Westmont Coll (CA)
West Texas A&M U (TX)
Whittier Coll (CA)
Widener U (PA)
Wilson Coll (PA)

SOCIAL SCIENCES RELATED
Bloomsburg U of Pennsylvania (PA)
Boston U (MA)
Bowling Green State U (OH)
California Polytechnic State U, San Luis Obispo (CA)
California U of Pennsylvania (PA)
Central Michigan U (MI)
Clarion U of Pennsylvania (PA)
Cleveland State U (OH)
Colby-Sawyer Coll (NH)
The Coll of Idaho (ID)
Coll of Staten Island of the City U of New York (NY)
Concordia U (QC, Canada)
Curry Coll (MA)
Eastern Oregon U (OR)
Elmira Coll (NY)
The Evergreen State Coll (WA)
Georgetown U (DC)
Gettysburg Coll (PA)
Hamline U (MN)
Hilbert Coll (NY)
Indiana U of Pennsylvania (PA)
John Jay Coll of Criminal Justice of the City U of New York (NY)
Kalamazoo Coll (MI)
Loyola U Maryland (MD)
Marywood U (PA)
Millersville U of Pennsylvania (PA)
Monmouth U (NJ)
Mount Aloysius Coll (PA)
Mount Holyoke Coll (MA)
Mount Mary U (WI)
New Mexico Highlands U (NM)
North Central Coll (IL)
Northwestern U (IL)
Pace U (NY)
Plymouth State U (NH)
Prescott Coll (AZ)
Purchase Coll, State U of New York (NY)
Rutgers U–New Brunswick (NJ)
Saint Mary's Coll of California (CA)
Simon Fraser U (BC, Canada)
Skidmore Coll (NY)
State U of New York Polytechnic Inst (NY)
Towson U (MD)
Union Coll (NE)
The U of Alabama at Birmingham (AL)
U of Denver (CO)
U of La Verne (CA)
U of Maine at Presque Isle (ME)
U of Massachusetts Amherst (MA)
U of New England (ME)
U of Pittsburgh (PA)
U of Regina (SK, Canada)
U of Rhode Island (RI)
U of Rochester (NY)
U of Southern Maine (ME)
The U of Tennessee at Chattanooga (TN)
The U of Texas at San Antonio (TX)
U of Washington, Tacoma (WA)
U of Waterloo (ON, Canada)
U of Wisconsin–Green Bay (WI)
Ursinus Coll (PA)
Washington U in St. Louis (MO)
Wesleyan U (CT)
Whitman Coll (WA)
Williams Coll (MA)

SOCIAL SCIENCE TEACHER EDUCATION
Auburn U (AL)
Baylor U (TX)
Biola U (CA)
Blackburn Coll (IL)
Blue Mountain Coll (MS)

Boise State U (ID)
Bowling Green State U (OH)
Bradley U (IL)
Brigham Young U (UT)
Buena Vista U (IA)
California Lutheran U (CA)
Campbellsville U (KY)
Carroll Coll (MT)
Central Methodist U (MO)
Central Washington U (WA)
Chowan U (NC)
Coll of Saint Mary (NE)
Concordia U Chicago (IL)
Corban U (OR)
Dickinson State U (ND)
Dixie State U (UT)
Dominican Coll (NY)
Eastern Illinois U (IL)
Eastern Michigan U (MI)
Eastern Washington U (WA)
Emmanuel Coll (GA)
Emporia State U (KS)
Faulkner U (AL)
Fayetteville State U (NC)
Ferris State U (MI)
Flagler Coll (FL)
Florida Ag and Mech U (FL)
Florida Atlantic U (FL)
Florida Southern Coll (FL)
Gardner-Webb U (NC)
Henderson State U (AR)
Holy Family U (PA)
Jackson State U (MS)
Knox Coll (IL)
Lincoln U (MO)
Lindenwood U (MO)
Lindsey Wilson Coll (KY)
Manchester U (IN)
Mansfield U of Pennsylvania (PA)
Marywood U (PA)
Mercyhurst U (PA)
Michigan State U (MI)
Millikin U (IL)
Minot State U (ND)
Missouri Valley Coll (MO)
Montana State U (MT)
Montana State U Billings (MT)
Montana State U–Northern (MT)
Mount St. Mary's U (MD)
Nebraska Wesleyan U (NE)
Northwest Missouri State U (MO)
Ohio Dominican U (OH)
Rhode Island Coll (RI)
Rust Coll (MS)
Saginaw Valley State U (MI)
St. Ambrose U (IA)
Saint Mary's U of Minnesota (MN)
Shawnee State U (OH)
Simpson U (CA)
Southeastern U (FL)
Southern Utah U (UT)
Southwest Baptist U (MO)
Union Coll (NE)
U of Central Florida (FL)
U of Delaware (DE)
U of Detroit Mercy (MI)
U of Great Falls (MT)
U of Maine at Farmington (ME)
U of Mobile (AL)
The U of North Carolina at Greensboro (NC)
U of North Dakota (ND)
U of Northern Iowa (IA)
The U of South Dakota (SD)
U of South Florida (FL)
U of Utah (UT)
U of Wisconsin–Superior (WI)
U of Wisconsin–Whitewater (WI)
Upper Iowa U (IA)
Utica Coll (NY)
Valley City State U (ND)
Valparaiso U (IN)
Wartburg Coll (IA)
Washington U in St. Louis (MO)
Wayne State Coll (NE)
Weber State U (UT)
Western Michigan U (MI)
Western State Colorado U (CO)
Westmont Coll (CA)
William Penn U (IA)
Wilmington U (DE)
Winona State U (MN)
Youngstown State U (OH)

SOCIAL STUDIES TEACHER EDUCATION

Abilene Christian U (TX)
Adams State U (CO)
Alice Lloyd Coll (KY)
Alvernia U (PA)
Alverno Coll (WI)
Anderson U (IN)
Anderson U (SC)
Aquinas Coll (MI)
Arizona Christian U (AZ)
Arkansas Tech U (AR)
Augustana U (SD)
Averett U (VA)
Ball State U (IN)
The Baptist Coll of Florida (FL)
Barton Coll (NC)
Baylor U (TX)
Bethel Coll (IN)
Bethel U (MN)
Bethune-Cookman U (FL)
Biola U (CA)
Blackburn Coll (IL)
Bluefield Coll (VA)
Boston U (MA)
Bowling Green State U (OH)
Bradley U (IL)
Brigham Young U–Idaho (ID)
Brooklyn Coll of the City U of New York (NY)
Buffalo State Coll, State U of New York (NY)
Cabrini U (PA)
Cairn U (PA)
Calvin Coll (MI)
Cameron U (OK)
Campbellsville U (KY)
Canisius Coll (NY)
Capital U (OH)
Carroll Coll (MT)
Cedarville U (OH)
Central Michigan U (MI)
Charleston Southern U (SC)
City Coll of the City U of New York (NY)
Cleveland State U (OH)
The Coll of Saint Rose (NY)
Colorado State U (CO)
Columbus State U (GA)
Concordia Coll (MN)
Concordia U, St. Paul (MN)
Corban U (OR)
Cornerstone U (MI)
Daemen Coll (NY)
Duquesne U (PA)
East Carolina U (NC)
Eastern Michigan U (MI)
Eastern Washington U (WA)
East Texas Baptist U (TX)
Elmira Coll (NY)
Ferris State U (MI)
Franklin Coll (IN)
Gannon U (PA)
Geneva Coll (PA)
Goshen Coll (IN)
Grace Coll (IN)
Grambling State U (LA)
Grand Valley State U (MI)
Granite State Coll (NH)
Green Mountain Coll (VT)
Grove City Coll (PA)
Harding U (AR)
Hardin-Simmons U (TX)
Hiram Coll (OH)
Hofstra U (NY)
Holy Family U (PA)
Hope Coll (MI)
Houston Baptist U (TX)
Howard Payne U (TX)
Huntingdon Coll (AL)
Huntington U (IN)
Huston-Tillotson U (TX)
Indiana State U (IN)
Indiana U Bloomington (IN)
Indiana U Northwest (IN)
Indiana U–Purdue U Indianapolis (IN)
Indiana U South Bend (IN)
Indiana U Southeast (IN)
Inter American U of Puerto Rico, Barranquitas Campus (PR)
Inter American U of Puerto Rico, Metropolitan Campus (PR)
Inter American U of Puerto Rico, San Germán Campus (PR)
Iona Coll (NY)
Ithaca Coll (NY)
John Brown U (AR)
Juniata Coll (PA)
Kennesaw State U (GA)
Kent State U (OH)
Keuka Coll (NY)
LaGrange Coll (GA)
Le Moyne Coll (NY)
LeTourneau U (TX)
Louisiana Coll (LA)
Louisiana Tech U (LA)
Madonna U (MI)
Malone U (OH)
Manchester U (IN)
Manhattanville Coll (NY)
Mansfield U of Pennsylvania (PA)
Maranatha Baptist U (WI)
Marian U (WI)
Marist Coll (NY)
Merrimack Coll (MA)
Messiah Coll (PA)
Miami U (OH)
Michigan State U (MI)
MidAmerica Nazarene U (KS)
Minnesota State U Mankato (MN)
Minnesota State U Moorhead (MN)
Misericordia U (PA)
Morris Coll (SC)
Mount Mary U (WI)
Mount Vernon Nazarene U (OH)
Nazareth Coll of Rochester (NY)
Niagara U (NY)
North Dakota State U (ND)
Northeastern State U (OK)
North Greenville U (SC)
Northland Coll (WI)
Northwest U (WA)
Nova Southeastern U (FL)
Nyack Coll (NY)
Ohio Wesleyan U (OH)
Oklahoma Baptist U (OK)
Oklahoma Christian U (OK)
Oral Roberts U (OK)
Ouachita Baptist U (AR)
Pace U (NY)
Pace U, Pleasantville Campus (NY)
Penn State Harrisburg (PA)
Plymouth State U (NH)
Purdue U (IN)
Queens Coll of the City U of New York (NY)
Roberts Wesleyan Coll (NY)
Rocky Mountain Coll (MT)
St. Catherine U (MN)
St. Edward's U (TX)
Saint Francis U (PA)
St. Gregory's U, Shawnee (OK)
St. John Fisher Coll (NY)
St. John's U (NY)
St. Joseph's Coll, Long Island Campus (NY)
St. Joseph's Coll, New York (NY)
Saint Mary-of-the-Woods Coll (IN)
St. Olaf Coll (MN)
St. Thomas U (FL)
Simmons Coll (MA)
Southeastern Louisiana U (LA)
Southeastern Oklahoma State U (OK)
Southeast Missouri State U (MO)
Southern New Hampshire U (NH)
Southwestern Adventist U (TX)
Southwestern Assemblies of God U (TX)
Spring Hill Coll (AL)
State U of New York at New Paltz (NY)
State U of New York Coll at Cortland (NY)
State U of New York Coll at Old Westbury (NY)
State U of New York Coll at Potsdam (NY)
Syracuse U (NY)
Taylor U (IN)
Temple U (PA)
Texas Christian U (TX)
Texas Lutheran U (TX)
Trine U (IN)
Union Coll (KY)
Universidad Adventista de las Antillas (PR)
The U of Akron (OH)
U of Central Arkansas (AR)
U of Charleston (WV)
U of Delaware (DE)
U of Detroit Mercy (MI)
U of Evansville (IN)
The U of Findlay (OH)
U of Georgia (GA)
U of Great Falls (MT)
U of Indianapolis (IN)
U of Kentucky (KY)
U of Lethbridge (AB, Canada)
U of Louisiana at Monroe (LA)
U of Maine (ME)
U of Michigan–Dearborn (MI)
U of Michigan–Flint (MI)
U of Minnesota, Duluth (MN)
The U of North Carolina at Greensboro (NC)
The U of North Carolina at Pembroke (NC)
U of Northern Colorado (CO)
U of Oklahoma (OK)
U of Pittsburgh at Johnstown (PA)
U of Regina (SK, Canada)
U of St. Francis (IL)
U of St. Thomas (MN)
The U of Tennessee at Chattanooga (TN)
U of the Cumberlands (KY)
U of Vermont (VT)
U of Wisconsin–Eau Claire (WI)
U of Wisconsin–La Crosse (WI)
U of Wisconsin–Superior (WI)
U of Wisconsin–Whitewater (WI)
Utah State U (UT)
Utica Coll (NY)
Virginia Wesleyan Coll (VA)
Viterbo U (WI)
Washington U in St. Louis (MO)
Wayland Baptist U (TX)
Waynesburg U (PA)
Weber State U (UT)
Western Carolina U (NC)
Western Michigan U (MI)
Widener U (PA)
Xavier U of Louisiana (LA)
York Coll of Pennsylvania (PA)
Youngstown State U (OH)

SOCIAL WORK

Abilene Christian U (TX)
Adams State U (CO)
Adelphi U (NY)
Albany State U (GA)
Albertus Magnus Coll (CT)
Alcorn State U (MS)
Alvernia U (PA)
Anderson U (IN)
Andrews U (MI)
Angelo State U (TX)
Appalachian State U (NC)
Arizona State U at the Downtown Phoenix campus (AZ)
Arizona State U at the West campus (AZ)
Asbury U (KY)
Ashland U (OH)
Auburn U (AL)
Augsburg Coll (MN)
Augusta U (GA)
Aurora U (IL)
Austin Peay State U (TN)
Avila U (MO)
Azusa Pacific U (CA)
Ball State U (IN)
Barton Coll (NC)
Bayamón Central U (PR)
Baylor U (TX)
Belhaven U (MS)
Belmont U (TN)
Bemidji State U (MN)
Bennett Coll (NC)
Bethel Coll (KS)
Bethel U (MN)
Biola U (CA)
Bloomsburg U of Pennsylvania (PA)
Bluffton U (OH)
Boise State U (ID)
Bowie State U (MD)
Bowling Green State U (OH)
Bowling Green State U–Firelands Coll (OH)
Bradley U (IL)
Brandman U (CA)
Brescia U (KY)
Briar Cliff U (IA)
Bridgewater State U (MA)
Brigham Young U–Idaho (ID)
Buena Vista U (IA)
Buffalo State Coll, State U of New York (NY)
Cabrini U (PA)
Cairn U (PA)
California State U, East Bay (CA)
California State U, Fresno (CA)
California State U, Long Beach (CA)
California State U, Sacramento (CA)
California State U, San Bernardino (CA)
California U of Pennsylvania (PA)
Calvin Coll (MI)
Campbellsville U (KY)
Capital U (OH)
Caribbean U (PR)
Carlow U (PA)
Carthage Coll (WI)
The Catholic U of America (DC)
Cedar Crest Coll (PA)
Cedarville U (OH)
Centenary U (NJ)
Central Baptist Coll (AR)
Central Connecticut State U (CT)
Central Michigan U (MI)
Central State U (OH)
Champlain Coll (VT)
Chapman U (CA)
Chatham U (PA)
Christopher Newport U (VA)
Clark Atlanta U (GA)
Clarke U (IA)
Cleveland State U (OH)
The Coll at Brockport, State U of New York (NY)
The Coll of Saint Rose (NY)
The Coll of St. Scholastica (MN)
Coll of Staten Island of the City U of New York (NY)
Coll of the Ozarks (MO)
Colorado Mesa U (CO)
Colorado State U (CO)
Concordia Coll (MN)
Concordia Coll–New York (NY)
Concordia U Chicago (IL)
Concordia U Wisconsin (WI)
Concord U (WV)
Cornerstone U (MI)
Creighton U (NE)
Daemen Coll (NY)
Dalhousie U (NS, Canada)
Dalton State Coll (GA)
Defiance Coll (OH)
Dominican Coll (NY)
East Carolina U (NC)
East Central U (OK)
Eastern Mennonite U (VA)
Eastern Michigan U (MI)
Eastern Nazarene Coll (MA)
Eastern U (PA)
Eastern Washington U (WA)
East Stroudsburg U of Pennsylvania (PA)
East Tennessee State U (TN)
Elizabeth City State U (NC)
Elizabethtown Coll (PA)
Elms Coll (MA)
Evangel U (MO)
Fayetteville State U (NC)
Ferris State U (MI)
Florida Ag and Mech U (FL)
Florida Atlantic U (FL)
Florida Gulf Coast U (FL)
Florida Intl U (FL)
Florida State U (FL)
Fordham U (NY)
Franciscan U of Steubenville (OH)
Franklin Pierce U (NH)
Freed-Hardeman U (TN)
Fresno Pacific U (CA)
Frostburg State U (MD)
Gannon U (PA)
George Fox U (OR)
Georgian Court U (NJ)
Georgia State U (GA)
Gordon Coll (MA)
Goshen Coll (IN)
Governors State U (IL)
Graceland U (IA)
Grambling State U (LA)
Grand Valley State U (MI)
Grand View U (IA)
Great Basin Coll (NV)
Greenville Coll (IL)
Hampton U (VA)
Hannibal-LaGrange U (MO)
Harding U (AR)
Hardin-Simmons U (TX)
Hawai`i Pacific U (HI)
Henderson State U (AR)
Hood Coll (MD)
Hope Coll (MI)

Howard Payne U (TX)
Humboldt State U (CA)
Huntington U (IN)
Idaho State U (ID)
Illinois State U (IL)
Immaculata U (PA)
Indiana State U (IN)
Indiana U Bloomington (IN)
Indiana U East (IN)
Indiana U Northwest (IN)
Indiana U–Purdue U Indianapolis (IN)
Indiana U South Bend (IN)
Inter American U of Puerto Rico, Aguadilla Campus (PR)
Inter American U of Puerto Rico, Fajardo Campus (PR)
Inter American U of Puerto Rico, Metropolitan Campus (PR)
Iona Coll (NY)
Jackson State U (MS)
Jacksonville State U (AL)
James Madison U (VA)
Johnson C. Smith U (NC)
Juniata Coll (PA)
Kansas State U (KS)
Kentucky State U (KY)
Keuka Coll (NY)
King U (TN)
Kutztown U of Pennsylvania (PA)
Kuyper Coll (MI)
Lamar U (TX)
La Salle U (PA)
Lebanese American U (Lebanon)
Lehman Coll of the City U of New York (NY)
Lewis U (IL)
Liberty U (VA)
Limestone Coll (SC)
Lincoln U (MO)
Lindenwood U (MO)
Lipscomb U (TN)
Lock Haven U of Pennsylvania (PA)
Longwood U (VA)
Loras Coll (IA)
Louisiana Coll (LA)
Louisiana State U and A&M Coll (LA)
Lourdes U (OH)
Loyola U Chicago (IL)
Lubbock Christian U (TX)
Luther Coll (IA)
MacMurray Coll (IL)
Madonna U (MI)
Malone U (OH)
Manchester U (IN)
Mansfield U of Pennsylvania (PA)
Marian U (WI)
Marist Coll (NY)
Marshall U (WV)
Mary Baldwin U (VA)
Marywood U (PA)
McDaniel Coll (MD)
McMaster U (ON, Canada)
Medgar Evers Coll of the City U of New York (NY)
Mercy Coll (NY)
Mercyhurst U (PA)
Meredith Coll (NC)
Messiah Coll (PA)
Metropolitan State U of Denver (CO)
Miami U (OH)
Michigan State U (MI)
Millersville U of Pennsylvania (PA)
Milligan Coll (TN)
Millikin U (IL)
Minnesota State U Mankato (MN)
Minnesota State U Moorhead (MN)
Minot State U (ND)
Misericordia U (PA)
Mississippi State U (MS)
Mississippi Valley State U (MS)
Missouri State U (MO)
Missouri Western State U (MO)
Molloy Coll (NY)
Monmouth U (NJ)
Montclair State U (NJ)
Morehead State U (KY)
Mount Mary U (WI)
Mount Mercy U (IA)
Mount St. Joseph U (OH)
Mount Saint Mary Coll (NY)
Mount Saint Mary's U (CA)
Mount Vernon Nazarene U (OH)
Murray State U (KY)
Nazareth Coll of Rochester (NY)
Nebraska Wesleyan U (NE)
Neumann U (PA)
New Mexico State U (NM)
Niagara U (NY)
North Carolina Central U (NC)
North Carolina State U (NC)
Northeastern Illinois U (IL)
Northeastern State U (OK)
Northern Arizona U (AZ)
Northern Kentucky U (KY)
Northwestern Coll (IA)
Northwestern Oklahoma State U (OK)
Northwestern State U of Louisiana (LA)
Nyack Coll (NY)
Ohio Dominican U (OH)
The Ohio State U (OH)
Ohio U (OH)
Olivet Nazarene U (IL)
Oral Roberts U (OK)
Our Lady of the Lake U of San Antonio (TX)
Pacific Lutheran U (WA)
Philander Smith Coll (AR)
Pittsburg State U (KS)
Plymouth State U (NH)
Point Loma Nazarene U (CA)
Portland State U (OR)
Prairie View A&M U (TX)
Providence Coll (RI)
Purdue U Northwest (IN)
Radford U (VA)
Ramapo Coll of New Jersey (NJ)
Redeemer U Coll (ON, Canada)
Regis Coll (MA)
Rhode Island Coll (RI)
Roberts Wesleyan Coll (NY)
Rockford U (IL)
Rust Coll (MS)
Rutgers U–Camden (NJ)
Rutgers U–Newark (NJ)
Rutgers U–New Brunswick (NJ)
Sacred Heart U (CT)
Saginaw Valley State U (MI)
Saint Anselm Coll (NH)
St. Catherine U (MN)
St. Cloud State U (MN)
St. Edward's U (TX)
Saint Francis U (PA)
Saint Leo U (FL)
Saint Louis U (MO)
Saint Martin's U (WA)
Saint Mary's Coll (IN)
St. Olaf Coll (MN)
St. Thomas U (NB, Canada)
Salisbury U (MD)
Salve Regina U (RI)
San Diego State U (CA)
San Francisco State U (CA)
Seattle U (WA)
Seton Hill U (PA)
Shaw U (NC)
Shepherd U (WV)
Shippensburg U of Pennsylvania (PA)
Siena Coll (NY)
Simmons Coll (MA)
Skidmore Coll (NY)
Slippery Rock U of Pennsylvania (PA)
South Carolina State U (SC)
Southeastern Louisiana U (LA)
Southeastern U (FL)
Southeast Missouri State U (MO)
Southern Arkansas U–Magnolia (AR)
Southern Connecticut State U (CT)
Southern Illinois U Carbondale (IL)
Southern Illinois U Edwardsville (IL)
Southwest Baptist U (MO)
Southwestern Assemblies of God U (TX)
Spalding U (KY)
State U of New York at Fredonia (NY)
State U of New York at Plattsburgh (NY)
State U of New York Coll at Cortland (NY)
Stephen F. Austin State U (TX)
Stockton U (NJ)
Stony Brook U, State U of New York (NY)
Syracuse U (NY)
Tabor Coll (KS)
Tarleton State U (TX)
Taylor U (IN)
Temple U (PA)
Tennessee State U (TN)
Texas A&M U–Central Texas (TX)
Texas A&M U–Commerce (TX)
Texas A&M U–Kingsville (TX)
Texas Christian U (TX)
Texas Coll (TX)
Texas State U (TX)
Texas Tech U (TX)
Texas Woman's U (TX)
Thomas U (GA)
Trent U (ON, Canada)
Trevecca Nazarene U (TN)
Trinity Christian Coll (IL)
Troy U (AL)
Union Coll (KY)
Union Coll (NE)
Union Inst & U (OH)
Union U (TN)
Université de Montréal (QC, Canada)
Université de Sherbrooke (QC, Canada)
U at Albany, State U of New York (NY)
The U of Akron (OH)
The U of Alabama (AL)
The U of Alabama at Birmingham (AL)
U of Alaska Fairbanks (AK)
U of Arkansas (AR)
U of Central Florida (FL)
U of Central Missouri (MO)
U of Cincinnati (OH)
U of Detroit Mercy (MI)
The U of Findlay (OH)
U of Georgia (GA)
U of Hawaii at Manoa (HI)
U of Houston–Clear Lake (TX)
U of Houston–Downtown (TX)
U of Illinois at Chicago (IL)
U of Illinois at Springfield (IL)
U of Indianapolis (IN)
The U of Kansas (KS)
U of Kentucky (KY)
U of Louisiana at Monroe (LA)
U of Louisville (KY)
U of Maine (ME)
U of Maine at Presque Isle (ME)
U of Mary Hardin-Baylor (TX)
U of Maryland, Baltimore County (MD)
U of Michigan–Flint (MI)
U of Minnesota, Duluth (MN)
U of Missouri–St. Louis (MO)
U of Montevallo (AL)
U of Nebraska at Kearney (NE)
U of Nevada, Las Vegas (NV)
U of Nevada, Reno (NV)
U of New England (ME)
U of New Hampshire (NH)
U of North Alabama (AL)
The U of North Carolina at Charlotte (NC)
The U of North Carolina at Greensboro (NC)
The U of North Carolina at Pembroke (NC)
The U of North Carolina Wilmington (NC)
U of North Dakota (ND)
U of Northern Iowa (IA)
U of North Florida (FL)
U of North Texas (TX)
U of Oklahoma (OK)
U of Pikeville (KY)
U of Pittsburgh (PA)
U of Regina (SK, Canada)
U of St. Francis (IL)
U of Saint Francis (IN)
U of Saint Joseph (CT)
U of St. Thomas (MN)
U of South Alabama (AL)
U of South Carolina (SC)
The U of South Dakota (SD)
U of Southern Indiana (IN)
U of Southern Maine (ME)
U of Southern Mississippi (MS)
U of South Florida (FL)
The U of Tennessee (TN)
The U of Tennessee at Chattanooga (TN)
The U of Tennessee at Martin (TN)
The U of Texas at Austin (TX)
The U of Texas at El Paso (TX)
The U of Texas of the Permian Basin (TX)
The U of Texas Rio Grande Valley (TX)
U of the Fraser Valley (BC, Canada)
U of the Virgin Islands (VI)
The U of Toledo (OH)
U of Utah (UT)
U of Valley Forge (PA)
U of Vermont (VT)
U of Washington (WA)
U of Washington, Tacoma (WA)
U of Waterloo (ON, Canada)
U of Windsor (ON, Canada)
U of Wisconsin–Eau Claire (WI)
U of Wisconsin–Green Bay (WI)
U of Wisconsin–Madison (WI)
U of Wisconsin–Milwaukee (WI)
U of Wisconsin–Superior (WI)
U of Wisconsin–Whitewater (WI)
Utah State U (UT)
Utah Valley U (UT)
Valparaiso U (IN)
Virginia Commonwealth U (VA)
Virginia State U (VA)
Virginia Union U (VA)
Virginia Wesleyan Coll (VA)
Viterbo U (WI)
Walla Walla U (WA)
Wartburg Coll (IA)
Washburn U (KS)
Washington State U (WA)
Wayne State U (MI)
Weber State U (UT)
West Chester U of Pennsylvania (PA)
Western Carolina U (NC)
Western Connecticut State U (CT)
Western Illinois U (IL)
Western Kentucky U (KY)
Western Michigan U (MI)
Western New England U (MA)
Westfield State U (MA)
West Texas A&M U (TX)
West Virginia State U (WV)
West Virginia U (WV)
Wheelock Coll (MA)
Whittier Coll (CA)
Wichita State U (KS)
Widener U (PA)
William Woods U (MO)
Winona State U (MN)
Winthrop U (SC)
Wright State U (OH)
Wright State U–Lake Campus (OH)
York Coll of the City U of New York (NY)
Youngstown State U (OH)

SOCIAL WORK RELATED

Davenport U, Grand Rapids (MI)
Eastern Washington U (WA)

SOCIOLOGY

Abilene Christian U (TX)
Adelphi U (NY)
Agnes Scott Coll (GA)
Albany State U (GA)
Albertus Magnus Coll (CT)
Albion Coll (MI)
Albright Coll (PA)
Alcorn State U (MS)
Alfred U (NY)
Alma Coll (MI)
Alverno Coll (WI)
American Intl Coll (MA)
American Public U System (WV)
American U (DC)
The American U in Cairo (Egypt)
Amherst Coll (MA)
Anderson U (IN)
Andrews U (MI)
Angelo State U (TX)
Appalachian State U (NC)
Aquinas Coll (MI)
Arcadia U (PA)
Arizona State U at the Tempe campus (AZ)
Arizona State U at the West campus (AZ)
Arkansas Tech U (AR)
Asbury U (KY)
Ashland U (OH)
Assumption Coll (MA)
Athens State U (AL)
Auburn U (AL)
Auburn U at Montgomery (AL)
Augsburg Coll (MN)
Augustana Coll (IL)
Augustana U (SD)
Augusta U (GA)
Aurora U (IL)
Austin Coll (TX)
Austin Peay State U (TN)
Averett U (VA)
Avila U (MO)
Azusa Pacific U (CA)
Baker U (KS)
Baldwin Wallace U (OH)
Ball State U (IN)
Bard Coll (NY)
Barnard Coll (NY)
Barry U (FL)
Baruch Coll of the City U of New York (NY)
Bates Coll (ME)
Baylor U (TX)
Bellarmine U (KY)
Belmont U (TN)
Beloit Coll (WI)
Bemidji State U (MN)
Benedictine Coll (KS)
Bennington Coll (VT)
Berea Coll (KY)
Bethany Lutheran Coll (MN)
Bethel Coll (IN)
Bethune-Cookman U (FL)
Binghamton U, State U of New York (NY)
Biola U (CA)
Bishop's U (QC, Canada)
Black Hills State U (SD)
Bloomfield Coll (NJ)
Bloomsburg U of Pennsylvania (PA)
Boise State U (ID)
Boston Coll (MA)
Boston U (MA)
Bowdoin Coll (ME)
Bowie State U (MD)
Bowling Green State U (OH)
Bradley U (IL)
Brandeis U (MA)
Brandman U (CA)
Brewton-Parker Coll (GA)
Bridgewater Coll (VA)
Bridgewater State U (MA)
Brigham Young U–Idaho (ID)
Brooklyn Coll of the City U of New York (NY)
Bryant U (RI)
Bryn Mawr Coll (PA)
Bucknell U (PA)
Buena Vista U (IA)
Buffalo State Coll, State U of New York (NY)
Butler U (IN)
Cabrini U (PA)
Caldwell U (NJ)
California Baptist U (CA)
California Lutheran U (CA)
California Polytechnic State U, San Luis Obispo (CA)
California State Polytechnic U, Pomona (CA)
California State U, Bakersfield (CA)
California State U, Dominguez Hills (CA)
California State U, East Bay (CA)
California State U, Fresno (CA)
California State U, Fullerton (CA)
California State U, Long Beach (CA)
California State U, Northridge (CA)
California State U, Sacramento (CA)
California State U, San Bernardino (CA)
California State U, San Marcos (CA)
California State U, Stanislaus (CA)
Calvin Coll (MI)
Cameron U (OK)
Campbellsville U (KY)
Canisius Coll (NY)
Capital U (OH)
Cardinal Stritch U (WI)
Carleton Coll (MN)
Carlow U (PA)
Carroll Coll (MT)
Carson-Newman U (TN)
Carthage Coll (WI)
Case Western Reserve U (OH)
Catawba Coll (NC)

The Catholic U of America (DC)
Centenary Coll of Louisiana (LA)
Centenary U (NJ)
Central Connecticut State U (CT)
Central Methodist U (MO)
Central Michigan U (MI)
Central State U (OH)
Central Washington U (WA)
Chapman U (CA)
Charleston Southern U (SC)
Chestnut Hill Coll (PA)
Christopher Newport U (VA)
City Coll of the City U of New York (NY)
Clarion U of Pennsylvania (PA)
Clark Atlanta U (GA)
Clarkson U (NY)
Clark U (MA)
Clayton State U (GA)
Clemson U (SC)
Cleveland State U (OH)
Coastal Carolina U (SC)
Coe Coll (IA)
Colby Coll (ME)
Colby-Sawyer Coll (NH)
Colgate U (NY)
The Coll at Brockport, State U of New York (NY)
Coll of Charleston (SC)
Coll of Mount Saint Vincent (NY)
The Coll of New Jersey (NJ)
Coll of Saint Benedict (MN)
Coll of Saint Elizabeth (NJ)
Coll of the Holy Cross (MA)
The Coll of William and Mary (VA)
The Coll of Wooster (OH)
The Colorado Coll (CO)
Colorado Mesa U (CO)
Colorado State U (CO)
Columbia Coll (MO)
Columbia U (NY)
Columbia U, School of General Studies (NY)
Columbus State U (GA)
Concordia Coll (MN)
Concordia Coll–New York (NY)
Concordia U (QC, Canada)
Concordia U Chicago (IL)
Concordia U, St. Paul (MN)
Concord U (WV)
Connecticut Coll (CT)
Converse Coll (SC)
Cornell Coll (IA)
Cornell U (NY)
Crandall U (NB, Canada)
Creighton U (NE)
Curry Coll (MA)
Dalhousie U (NS, Canada)
Dallas Baptist U (TX)
Dartmouth Coll (NH)
Davidson Coll (NC)
Dean Coll (MA)
Denison U (OH)
DePauw U (IN)
DEREE - The American Coll of Greece (Greece)
Dickinson Coll (PA)
Dixie State U (UT)
Doane U (NE)
Dominican U (IL)
Drake U (IA)
Drew U (NJ)
Drexel U (PA)
Drury U (MO)
Duquesne U (PA)
Earlham Coll (IN)
East Carolina U (NC)
East Central U (OK)
Eastern Illinois U (IL)
Eastern Michigan U (MI)
Eastern Nazarene Coll (MA)
Eastern U (PA)
Eastern Washington U (WA)
East Stroudsburg U of Pennsylvania (PA)
East Tennessee State U (TN)
East Texas Baptist U (TX)
Eckerd Coll (FL)
Edgewood Coll (WI)
Elizabeth City State U (NC)
Elizabethtown Coll (PA)
Elms Coll (MA)
Elon U (NC)
Emmanuel Coll (MA)
Emory & Henry Coll (VA)
Emory U (GA)
Emporia State U (KS)
Eugene Lang Coll of Liberal Arts (NY)
Eureka Coll (IL)
Evangel U (MO)
The Evergreen State Coll (WA)
Fairfield U (CT)
Fairleigh Dickinson U, Coll at Florham (NJ)
Fairleigh Dickinson U, Metropolitan Campus (NJ)
Fayetteville State U (NC)
Ferris State U (MI)
Fitchburg State U (MA)
Flagler Coll (FL)
Florida Ag and Mech U (FL)
Florida Atlantic U (FL)
Florida Gulf Coast U (FL)
Florida Intl U (FL)
Florida State U (FL)
Fordham U (NY)
Fort Lewis Coll (CO)
Framingham State U (MA)
Franciscan U of Steubenville (OH)
Francis Marion U (SC)
Franklin & Marshall Coll (PA)
Franklin Coll (IN)
Franklin Pierce U (NH)
Friends U (KS)
Frostburg State U (MD)
Furman U (SC)
Gallaudet U (DC)
Gardner-Webb U (NC)
Geneva Coll (PA)
George Fox U (OR)
Georgetown Coll (KY)
Georgetown U (DC)
The George Washington U (DC)
Georgia Coll & State U (GA)
Georgia Southern U (GA)
Georgia Southwestern State U (GA)
Georgia State U (GA)
Gettysburg Coll (PA)
Goddard Coll (VT)
Gonzaga U (WA)
Gordon Coll (MA)
Goshen Coll (IN)
Goucher Coll (MD)
Grace Coll (IN)
Grambling State U (LA)
Grand Valley State U (MI)
Greenville Coll (IL)
Grinnell Coll (IA)
Grove City Coll (PA)
Guilford Coll (NC)
Hamilton Coll (NY)
Hamline U (MN)
Hampshire Coll (MA)
Hampton U (VA)
Hannibal-LaGrange U (MO)
Hanover Coll (IN)
Hardin-Simmons U (TX)
Harris-Stowe State U (MO)
Hartwick Coll (NY)
Harvard U (MA)
Haverford Coll (PA)
Hawai`i Pacific U (HI)
Henderson State U (AR)
Hendrix Coll (AR)
High Point U (NC)
Hillsdale Coll (MI)
Hiram Coll (OH)
Hobart and William Smith Colls (NY)
Hofstra U (NY)
Hollins U (VA)
Holy Family U (PA)
Holy Names U (CA)
Hood Coll (MD)
Hope Coll (MI)
Houghton Coll (NY)
Howard Payne U (TX)
Humboldt State U (CA)
Hunter Coll of the City U of New York (NY)
Huntington U (IN)
Huston-Tillotson U (TX)
Idaho State U (ID)
Illinois Coll (IL)
Illinois State U (IL)
Illinois Wesleyan U (IL)
Immaculata U (PA)
Indiana U Bloomington (IN)
Indiana U East (IN)
Indiana U Kokomo (IN)
Indiana U Northwest (IN)
Indiana U of Pennsylvania (PA)
Indiana U–Purdue U Indianapolis (IN)
Indiana U South Bend (IN)
Indiana U Southeast (IN)
Inter American U of Puerto Rico, Metropolitan Campus (PR)
Inter American U of Puerto Rico, Ponce Campus (PR)
Inter American U of Puerto Rico, San Germán Campus (PR)
Iona Coll (NY)
Iowa State U of Science and Technology (IA)
Ithaca Coll (NY)
Jackson State U (MS)
Jacksonville State U (AL)
Jacksonville U (FL)
James Madison U (VA)
John Carroll U (OH)
John Jay Coll of Criminal Justice of the City U of New York (NY)
Johns Hopkins U (MD)
Juniata Coll (PA)
Kansas State U (KS)
Kansas Wesleyan U (KS)
Kean U (NJ)
Keene State Coll (NH)
Kennesaw State U (GA)
Kent State U at Ashtabula (OH)
Kent State U at Stark (OH)
Kentucky Wesleyan Coll (KY)
Kenyon Coll (OH)
Keuka Coll (NY)
King's Coll (PA)
The King's U (AB, Canada)
Knox Coll (IL)
Kutztown U of Pennsylvania (PA)
Lafayette Coll (PA)
LaGrange Coll (GA)
Lake Forest Coll (IL)
Lamar U (TX)
Lane Coll (TN)
Langston U (OK)
La Roche Coll (PA)
La Salle U (PA)
Lasell Coll (MA)
Lebanon Valley Coll (PA)
Lee U (TN)
Lehigh U (PA)
Lehman Coll of the City U of New York (NY)
Le Moyne Coll (NY)
Lenoir-Rhyne U (NC)
Lewis U (IL)
Lincoln U (MO)
Lincoln U (PA)
Lindenwood U (MO)
Linfield Coll (OR)
Lock Haven U of Pennsylvania (PA)
Longwood U (VA)
Loras Coll (IA)
Louisiana State U and A&M Coll (LA)
Louisiana Tech U (LA)
Lourdes U (OH)
Loyola Marymount U (CA)
Loyola U Chicago (IL)
Loyola U Maryland (MD)
Loyola U New Orleans (LA)
Luther Coll (IA)
Lycoming Coll (PA)
Lynchburg Coll (VA)
Macalester Coll (MN)
Madonna U (MI)
Manchester U (IN)
Manhattan Coll (NY)
Manhattanville Coll (NY)
Marian U (IN)
Marshall U (WV)
Mary Baldwin U (VA)
Marymount Manhattan Coll (NY)
Marymount U (VA)
Maryville U of Saint Louis (MO)
Marywood U (PA)
Massachusetts Coll of Liberal Arts (MA)
McDaniel Coll (MD)
McKendree U (IL)
McMaster U (ON, Canada)
McMurry U (TX)
McNeese State U (LA)
Mercer U, Macon (GA)
Mercy Coll (NY)
Mercyhurst U (PA)
Meredith Coll (NC)
Merrimack Coll (MA)
Messiah Coll (PA)
Metropolitan State U of Denver (CO)
Miami U (OH)
Michigan State U (MI)
MidAmerica Nazarene U (KS)
Middlebury Coll (VT)
Millersville U of Pennsylvania (PA)
Milligan Coll (TN)
Millikin U (IL)
Mills Coll (CA)
Minnesota State U Mankato (MN)
Minnesota State U Moorhead (MN)
Minot State U (ND)
Mississippi State U (MS)
Mississippi Valley State U (MS)
Missouri State U (MO)
Missouri Valley Coll (MO)
Missouri Western State U (MO)
Molloy Coll (NY)
Monmouth Coll (IL)
Monmouth U (NJ)
Montana State U (MT)
Montana State U Billings (MT)
Montclair State U (NJ)
Moravian Coll (PA)
Morehead State U (KY)
Morehouse Coll (GA)
Morris Coll (SC)
Mount Allison U (NB, Canada)
Mount Holyoke Coll (MA)
Mount Mercy U (IA)
Mount St. Joseph U (OH)
Mount Saint Mary Coll (NY)
Mount Saint Mary's U (CA)
Mount St. Mary's U (MD)
Muhlenberg Coll (PA)
Murray State U (KY)
Muskingum U (OH)
National U (CA)
Nazareth Coll of Rochester (NY)
Nebraska Wesleyan U (NE)
Newberry Coll (SC)
New Coll of Florida (FL)
New England Coll (NH)
New Jersey City U (NJ)
Newman U (KS)
New Mexico State U (NM)
New York Inst of Technology (NY)
Niagara U (NY)
North Carolina State U (NC)
North Carolina Wesleyan Coll (NC)
North Central Coll (IL)
North Dakota State U (ND)
Northeastern Illinois U (IL)
Northeastern State U (OK)
Northeastern U (MA)
Northern Arizona U (AZ)
Northern Illinois U (IL)
Northern Kentucky U (KY)
Northern State U (SD)
Northland Coll (WI)
Northwestern Coll (IA)
Northwestern Oklahoma State U (OK)
Northwestern U (IL)
Northwest Missouri State U (MO)
Nova Southeastern U (FL)
Nyack Coll (NY)
Oberlin Coll (OH)
Occidental Coll (CA)
Ohio Dominican U (OH)
The Ohio State U (OH)
The Ohio State U at Marion (OH)
The Ohio State U–Mansfield Campus (OH)
The Ohio State U–Newark Campus (OH)
Ohio U (OH)
Ohio Wesleyan U (OH)
Oklahoma Baptist U (OK)
Oklahoma City U (OK)
Oklahoma State U (OK)
Old Dominion U (VA)
Olivet Nazarene U (IL)
Oregon State U (OR)
Otterbein U (OH)
Ouachita Baptist U (AR)
Our Lady of the Lake U of San Antonio (TX)
Pacific Lutheran U (WA)
Paine Coll (GA)
Penn State Abington (PA)
Penn State Altoona (PA)
Penn State Beaver (PA)
Penn State Berks (PA)
Penn State Brandywine (PA)
Penn State DuBois (PA)
Penn State Erie, The Behrend Coll (PA)
Penn State Fayette, The Eberly Campus (PA)
Penn State Greater Allegheny (PA)
Penn State Harrisburg (PA)
Penn State Hazleton (PA)
Penn State Lehigh Valley (PA)
Penn State Mont Alto (PA)
Penn State New Kensington (PA)
Penn State Schuylkill (PA)
Penn State Shenango (PA)
Penn State U Park (PA)
Penn State Wilkes-Barre (PA)
Penn State Worthington Scranton (PA)
Penn State York (PA)
Pepperdine U, Malibu (CA)
Philander Smith Coll (AR)
Piedmont Coll (GA)
Pittsburg State U (KS)
Pitzer Coll (CA)
Point Loma Nazarene U (CA)
Point U (GA)
Pomona Coll (CA)
Portland State U (OR)
Prairie View A&M U (TX)
Princeton U (NJ)
Providence Coll (RI)
Purchase Coll, State U of New York (NY)
Purdue U (IN)
Purdue U Northwest (IN)
Queens Coll of the City U of New York (NY)
Quinnipiac U (CT)
Radford U (VA)
Ramapo Coll of New Jersey (NJ)
Randolph Coll (VA)
Randolph-Macon Coll (VA)
Redeemer U Coll (ON, Canada)
Reed Coll (OR)
Regis U (CO)
Rhode Island Coll (RI)
Rice U (TX)
Ripon Coll (WI)
Roanoke Coll (VA)
Rockford U (IL)
Rocky Mountain Coll (MT)
Rollins Coll (FL)
Rosemont Coll (PA)
Rowan U (NJ)
Rust Coll (MS)
Rutgers U–Camden (NJ)
Rutgers U–Newark (NJ)
Rutgers U–New Brunswick (NJ)
Sacred Heart U (CT)
The Sage Colls (NY)
Saginaw Valley State U (MI)
St. Ambrose U (IA)
Saint Anselm Coll (NH)
Saint Augustine's U (NC)
St. Bonaventure U (NY)
St. Catherine U (MN)
St. Cloud State U (MN)
St. Edward's U (TX)
Saint Francis U (PA)
St. John Fisher Coll (NY)
Saint John's U (MN)
St. John's U (NY)
St. Joseph's Coll, Long Island Campus (NY)
St. Joseph's Coll, New York (NY)
Saint Joseph's U (PA)
Saint Leo U (FL)
Saint Louis U (MO)
Saint Louis U–Madrid Campus (Spain)
Saint Mary's Coll (IN)
Saint Mary's Coll of California (CA)
St. Mary's Coll of Maryland (MD)
Saint Mary's U of Minnesota (MN)
Saint Michael's Coll (VT)
St. Norbert Coll (WI)
Saint Peter's U (NJ)
St. Thomas U (NB, Canada)
Saint Vincent Coll (PA)
Salisbury U (MD)
Salve Regina U (RI)
Samford U (AL)
Sam Houston State U (TX)
San Diego State U (CA)
San Francisco State U (CA)
Santa Clara U (CA)
Sarah Lawrence Coll (NY)
Scripps Coll (CA)
Seattle Pacific U (WA)

Seattle U (WA)
Seton Hill U (PA)
Shawnee State U (OH)
Shaw U (NC)
Shenandoah U (VA)
Shepherd U (WV)
Shippensburg U of Pennsylvania (PA)
Shorter U (GA)
Siena Coll (NY)
Simmons Coll (MA)
Simon Fraser U (BC, Canada)
Simpson Coll (IA)
Skidmore Coll (NY)
Smith Coll (MA)
Sonoma State U (CA)
South Carolina State U (SC)
South Dakota State U (SD)
Southeastern Louisiana U (LA)
Southeastern Oklahoma State U (OK)
Southern Connecticut State U (CT)
Southern Illinois U Carbondale (IL)
Southern Illinois U Edwardsville (IL)
Southern Methodist U (TX)
Southern Oregon U (OR)
Southern Utah U (UT)
Southwest Baptist U (MO)
Southwestern U (TX)
Spelman Coll (GA)
Spring Hill Coll (AL)
Stanford U (CA)
State U of New York at Fredonia (NY)
State U of New York at New Paltz (NY)
State U of New York at Oswego (NY)
State U of New York at Plattsburgh (NY)
State U of New York Coll at Cortland (NY)
State U of New York Coll at Geneseo (NY)
State U of New York Coll at Old Westbury (NY)
State U of New York Coll at Potsdam (NY)
State U of New York Polytechnic Inst (NY)
Stephen F. Austin State U (TX)
Stockton U (NJ)
Stonehill Coll (MA)
Stony Brook U, State U of New York (NY)
Suffolk U (MA)
Susquehanna U (PA)
Sweet Briar Coll (VA)
Syracuse U (NY)
Tarleton State U (TX)
Taylor U (IN)
Temple U (PA)
Tennessee State U (TN)
Tennessee Wesleyan U (TN)
Texas A&M Intl U (TX)
Texas A&M U (TX)
Texas A&M U–Central Texas (TX)
Texas A&M U–Commerce (TX)
Texas A&M U–Corpus Christi (TX)
Texas A&M U–Kingsville (TX)
Texas Christian U (TX)
Texas Coll (TX)
Texas Lutheran U (TX)
Texas State U (TX)
Texas Tech U (TX)
Texas Wesleyan U (TX)
Texas Woman's U (TX)
Thomas More Coll (KY)
Thomas U (GA)
Transylvania U (KY)
Trent U (ON, Canada)
Trevecca Nazarene U (TN)
Trinity U (TX)
Troy U (AL)
Truman State U (MO)
Tufts U (MA)
Tulane U (LA)
Union Coll (KY)
Union Coll (NY)
Union U (TN)
United States Military Acad (NY)
Université de Montréal (QC, Canada)
U at Albany, State U of New York (NY)
U at Buffalo, the State U of New York (NY)
The U of Akron (OH)
The U of Alabama (AL)
The U of Alabama at Birmingham (AL)
The U of Alabama in Huntsville (AL)
U of Alaska Fairbanks (AK)
The U of Arizona (AZ)
U of Arkansas (AR)
U of California, Davis (CA)
U of California, Irvine (CA)
U of California, Los Angeles (CA)
U of California, Riverside (CA)
U of California, San Diego (CA)
U of California, Santa Barbara (CA)
U of Central Arkansas (AR)
U of Central Florida (FL)
U of Central Missouri (MO)
U of Chicago (IL)
U of Cincinnati (OH)
U of Colorado Boulder (CO)
U of Colorado Colorado Springs (CO)
U of Colorado Denver (CO)
U of Dayton (OH)
U of Delaware (DE)
U of Denver (CO)
U of Detroit Mercy (MI)
U of Dubuque (IA)
U of Evansville (IN)
The U of Findlay (OH)
U of Florida (FL)
U of Georgia (GA)
U of Great Falls (MT)
U of Guelph (ON, Canada)
U of Hartford (CT)
U of Hawaii at Manoa (HI)
U of Houston (TX)
U of Houston–Clear Lake (TX)
U of Houston–Downtown (TX)
U of Idaho (ID)
U of Illinois at Chicago (IL)
U of Indianapolis (IN)
The U of Kansas (KS)
U of Kentucky (KY)
U of King's Coll (NS, Canada)
U of La Verne (CA)
U of Lethbridge (AB, Canada)
U of Louisiana at Monroe (LA)
U of Louisville (KY)
U of Maine (ME)
U of Mary Hardin-Baylor (TX)
U of Maryland, Baltimore County (MD)
U of Maryland, Coll Park (MD)
U of Mary Washington (VA)
U of Massachusetts Amherst (MA)
U of Massachusetts Boston (MA)
U of Massachusetts Dartmouth (MA)
U of Massachusetts Lowell (MA)
U of Miami (FL)
U of Michigan (MI)
U of Michigan–Dearborn (MI)
U of Michigan–Flint (MI)
U of Minnesota, Duluth (MN)
U of Minnesota, Morris (MN)
U of Minnesota, Twin Cities Campus (MN)
U of Missouri–Kansas City (MO)
U of Missouri–St. Louis (MO)
U of Mobile (AL)
U of Montevallo (AL)
U of Mount Union (OH)
U of Nebraska at Kearney (NE)
U of Nevada, Las Vegas (NV)
U of Nevada, Reno (NV)
U of New England (ME)
U of New Hampshire (NH)
U of New Orleans (LA)
U of North Alabama (AL)
U of North Carolina at Asheville (NC)
The U of North Carolina at Chapel Hill (NC)
The U of North Carolina at Charlotte (NC)
The U of North Carolina at Greensboro (NC)
The U of North Carolina at Pembroke (NC)
The U of North Carolina Wilmington (NC)
U of North Dakota (ND)
U of Northern Colorado (CO)
U of Northern Iowa (IA)
U of North Florida (FL)
U of North Georgia (GA)
U of North Texas (TX)
U of Notre Dame (IN)
U of Oklahoma (OK)
U of Oregon (OR)
U of Pennsylvania (PA)
U of Pikeville (KY)
U of Pittsburgh (PA)
U of Pittsburgh at Bradford (PA)
U of Pittsburgh at Johnstown (PA)
U of Puget Sound (WA)
U of Regina (SK, Canada)
U of Rhode Island (RI)
U of Richmond (VA)
U of Saint Francis (IN)
U of St. Thomas (MN)
U of San Diego (CA)
U of San Francisco (CA)
U of Saskatchewan (SK, Canada)
U of Science and Arts of Oklahoma (OK)
The U of Scranton (PA)
U of South Alabama (AL)
U of South Carolina (SC)
U of South Carolina Aiken (SC)
The U of South Dakota (SD)
U of Southern California (CA)
U of Southern Indiana (IN)
U of Southern Maine (ME)
U of Southern Mississippi (MS)
U of South Florida (FL)
The U of Tampa (FL)
The U of Tennessee (TN)
The U of Tennessee at Martin (TN)
The U of Texas at Austin (TX)
The U of Texas at Dallas (TX)
The U of Texas at El Paso (TX)
The U of Texas at San Antonio (TX)
The U of Texas of the Permian Basin (TX)
The U of Texas Rio Grande Valley (TX)
U of the Fraser Valley (BC, Canada)
U of the Incarnate Word (TX)
U of the Pacific (CA)
U of Toledo (OH)
U of Toronto (ON, Canada)
The U of Tulsa (OK)
U of Utah (UT)
U of Vermont (VT)
U of Virginia (VA)
The U of Virginia's Coll at Wise (VA)
U of Washington (WA)
U of Waterloo (ON, Canada)
The U of West Alabama (AL)
U of West Georgia (GA)
U of Windsor (ON, Canada)
U of Wisconsin–Eau Claire (WI)
U of Wisconsin–La Crosse (WI)
U of Wisconsin–Madison (WI)
U of Wisconsin–Milwaukee (WI)
U of Wisconsin–Parkside (WI)
U of Wisconsin–Stevens Point (WI)
U of Wisconsin–Superior (WI)
U of Wisconsin–Whitewater (WI)
Upper Iowa U (IA)
Ursinus Coll (PA)
Utah State U (UT)
Utica Coll (NY)
Valparaiso U (IN)
Vanderbilt U (TN)
Vassar Coll (NY)
Villanova U (PA)
Virginia Commonwealth U (VA)
Virginia Polytechnic Inst and State U (VA)
Virginia State U (VA)
Virginia Wesleyan Coll (VA)
Viterbo U (WI)
Wagner Coll (NY)
Wake Forest U (NC)
Walla Walla U (WA)
Walsh U (OH)
Wartburg Coll (IA)
Washburn U (KS)
Washington & Jefferson Coll (PA)
Washington Coll (MD)
Washington State U (WA)
Washington State U–Vancouver (WA)
Wayland Baptist U (TX)
Waynesburg U (PA)
Wayne State Coll (NE)
Wayne State U (MI)
Weber State U (UT)
Webster U (MO)
Wells Coll (NY)
Wesleyan U (CT)
West Chester U of Pennsylvania (PA)
Western Carolina U (NC)
Western Connecticut State U (CT)
Western Illinois U (IL)
Western Kentucky U (KY)
Western Michigan U (MI)
Western New England U (MA)
Western Oregon U (OR)
Western State Colorado U (CO)
Westfield State U (MA)
Westminster Coll (PA)
Westminster Coll (UT)
Westmont Coll (CA)
West Texas A&M U (TX)
West Virginia State U (WV)
West Virginia U (WV)
West Virginia Wesleyan Coll (WV)
Wheaton Coll (IL)
Wheaton Coll (MA)
Whitman Coll (WA)
Whittier Coll (CA)
Whitworth U (WA)
Wichita State U (KS)
Widener U (PA)
Wilkes U (PA)
Willamette U (OR)
William Paterson U of New Jersey (NJ)
William Penn U (IA)
Williams Coll (MA)
Wilson Coll (PA)
Wingate U (NC)
Winona State U (MN)
Winthrop U (SC)
Wittenberg U (OH)
Wofford Coll (SC)
Worcester State U (MA)
Wright State U (OH)
Wright State U–Lake Campus (OH)
Xavier U of Louisiana (LA)
York Coll of Pennsylvania (PA)
York Coll of the City U of New York (NY)
Youngstown State U (OH)

SOCIOLOGY AND ANTHROPOLOGY
Albion Coll (MI)
American U of Beirut (Lebanon)
Centre Coll (KY)
Coll of Staten Island of the City U of New York (NY)
Fairfield U (CT)
Goddard Coll (VT)
Goucher Coll (MD)
Governors State U (IL)
High Point U (NC)
Keene State Coll (NH)
Lewis & Clark Coll (OR)
Millsaps Coll (MS)
Pace U (NY)
Rochester Inst of Technology (NY)
Roger Williams U (RI)
St. Olaf Coll (MN)
Spelman Coll (GA)
Swarthmore Coll (PA)
Transylvania U (KY)
U of Illinois at Springfield (IL)
U of Maine at Farmington (ME)
U of Massachusetts Dartmouth (MA)
The U of Montana Western (MT)
Ursinus Coll (PA)
Valdosta State U (GA)
Washington and Lee U (VA)
Wofford Coll (SC)

SOIL CHEMISTRY AND PHYSICS
The U of Tennessee (TN)

SOIL SCIENCE AND AGRONOMY
California Polytechnic State U, San Luis Obispo (CA)
Colorado State U (CO)
Michigan State U (MI)
New Mexico State U (NM)
North Dakota State U (ND)
Oklahoma State U (OK)
Penn State Abington (PA)
Penn State Altoona (PA)
Penn State Beaver (PA)
Penn State Berks (PA)
Penn State Brandywine (PA)
Penn State DuBois (PA)
Penn State Erie, The Behrend Coll (PA)
Penn State Fayette, The Eberly Campus (PA)
Penn State Greater Allegheny (PA)
Penn State Hazleton (PA)
Penn State Lehigh Valley (PA)
Penn State Mont Alto (PA)
Penn State New Kensington (PA)
Penn State Schuylkill (PA)
Penn State Shenango (PA)
Penn State Wilkes-Barre (PA)
Penn State Worthington Scranton (PA)
Penn State York (PA)
Purdue U (IN)
U of California, Davis (CA)
U of Florida (FL)
U of Georgia (GA)
U of Saskatchewan (SK, Canada)
The U of Tennessee at Martin (TN)
U of Wisconsin–Madison (WI)
U of Wisconsin–Stevens Point (WI)
Utah State U (UT)
Washington State U (WA)

SOIL SCIENCES RELATED
Brigham Young U (UT)
Clemson U (SC)
North Carolina State U (NC)
U of Georgia (GA)
U of Hawaii at Manoa (HI)

SOMATIC BODYWORK
Goddard Coll (VT)

SOMATIC BODYWORK RELATED
Goddard Coll (VT)

SOUTH ASIAN LANGUAGES
Northwestern U (IL)
U of Chicago (IL)
U of Washington (WA)

SOUTHEAST ASIAN LANGUAGES
Harvard U (MA)

SPANISH
Abilene Christian U (TX)
Adams State U (CO)
Adelphi U (NY)
Agnes Scott Coll (GA)
Albany State U (GA)
Albertus Magnus Coll (CT)
Albion Coll (MI)
Albright Coll (PA)
Alfred U (NY)
Allegheny Coll (PA)
Alma Coll (MI)
American U (DC)
Amherst Coll (MA)
Anderson U (IN)
Anderson U (SC)
Andrews U (MI)
Angelo State U (TX)
Aquinas Coll (MI)
Arcadia U (PA)
Arizona State U at the Tempe campus (AZ)
Arizona State U at the West campus (AZ)
Armstrong State U (GA)
Asbury U (KY)
Ashland U (OH)
Assumption Coll (MA)
Auburn U (AL)
Auburn U at Montgomery (AL)
Augsburg Coll (MN)
Augustana Coll (IL)
Augustana U (SD)
Aurora U (IL)
Austin Coll (TX)
Azusa Pacific U (CA)
Baker U (KS)
Baldwin Wallace U (OH)
Ball State U (IN)
Baptist U of the Americas (TX)
Bard Coll (NY)
Barnard Coll (NY)
Barry U (FL)
Barton Coll (NC)
Baruch Coll of the City U of New York (NY)

Bates Coll (ME)
Baylor U (TX)
Bellarmine U (KY)
Belmont U (TN)
Beloit Coll (WI)
Bemidji State U (MN)
Benedictine Coll (KS)
Bennington Coll (VT)
Bentley U (MA)
Berea Coll (KY)
Berry Coll (GA)
Bethel U (MN)
Binghamton U, State U of New York (NY)
Biola U (CA)
Bishop's U (QC, Canada)
Blackburn Coll (IL)
Black Hills State U (SD)
Blue Mountain Coll (MS)
Bluffton U (OH)
Boise State U (ID)
Boston Coll (MA)
Boston U (MA)
Bowdoin Coll (ME)
Bowling Green State U (OH)
Bradley U (IL)
Brescia U (KY)
Briar Cliff U (IA)
Bridgewater Coll (VA)
Bridgewater State U (MA)
Brooklyn Coll of the City U of New York (NY)
Bryan Coll (TN)
Bryant U (RI)
Bryn Mawr Coll (PA)
Bucknell U (PA)
Buena Vista U (IA)
Buffalo State Coll, State U of New York (NY)
Butler U (IN)
Cabrini U (PA)
Caldwell U (NJ)
California Baptist U (CA)
California Lutheran U (CA)
California State Polytechnic U, Pomona (CA)
California State U, Bakersfield (CA)
California State U, Dominguez Hills (CA)
California State U, East Bay (CA)
California State U, Fresno (CA)
California State U, Fullerton (CA)
California State U, Long Beach (CA)
California State U, Monterey Bay (CA)
California State U, Northridge (CA)
California State U, Sacramento (CA)
California State U, San Bernardino (CA)
California State U, San Marcos (CA)
California State U, Stanislaus (CA)
California U of Pennsylvania (PA)
Calvin Coll (MI)
Canisius Coll (NY)
Capital U (OH)
Cardinal Stritch U (WI)
Carleton Coll (MN)
Carnegie Mellon U (PA)
Carroll Coll (MT)
Carson-Newman U (TN)
Carthage Coll (WI)
Case Western Reserve U (OH)
Catawba Coll (NC)
The Catholic U of America (DC)
Cedarville U (OH)
Central Connecticut State U (CT)
Central Michigan U (MI)
Central Washington U (WA)
Centre Coll (KY)
Chapman U (CA)
Charleston Southern U (SC)
Chestnut Hill Coll (PA)
Christopher Newport U (VA)
City Coll of the City U of New York (NY)
Claremont McKenna Coll (CA)
Clarion U of Pennsylvania (PA)
Clark Atlanta U (GA)
Clarke U (IA)
Clark U (MA)
Clemson U (SC)
Cleveland State U (OH)
Coastal Carolina U (SC)
Coe Coll (IA)
Colby Coll (ME)
Colgate U (NY)
The Coll at Brockport, State U of New York (NY)
Coll of Charleston (SC)
Coll of Coastal Georgia (GA)
The Coll of Idaho (ID)
Coll of Mount Saint Vincent (NY)
The Coll of New Jersey (NJ)
Coll of Saint Benedict (MN)
The Coll of St. Scholastica (MN)
Coll of Staten Island of the City U of New York (NY)
Coll of the Holy Cross (MA)
Coll of the Ozarks (MO)
The Coll of Wooster (OH)
The Colorado Coll (CO)
Colorado Mesa U (CO)
Colorado State U (CO)
Columbia U (NY)
Columbus State U (GA)
Concordia Coll (MN)
Concordia U (QC, Canada)
Concordia U Chicago (IL)
Concordia U, Nebraska (NE)
Concordia U Wisconsin (WI)
Connecticut Coll (CT)
Converse Coll (SC)
Cornell Coll (IA)
Cornell U (NY)
Cornerstone U (MI)
Creighton U (NE)
Daemen Coll (NY)
Dalhousie U (NS, Canada)
Dartmouth Coll (NH)
Davidson Coll (NC)
Denison U (OH)
DePauw U (IN)
DeSales U (PA)
Dickinson Coll (PA)
Dickinson State U (ND)
Dixie State U (UT)
Doane U (NE)
Dominican U (IL)
Drew U (NJ)
Drury U (MO)
Duquesne U (PA)
Earlham Coll (IN)
Eastern Mennonite U (VA)
Eastern Michigan U (MI)
Eastern U (PA)
Eastern Washington U (WA)
East Stroudsburg U of Pennsylvania (PA)
Eckerd Coll (FL)
Edgewood Coll (WI)
Elizabethtown Coll (PA)
Elms Coll (MA)
Elon U (NC)
Emmanuel Coll (MA)
Emory & Henry Coll (VA)
Emory U (GA)
Evangel U (MO)
Fairfield U (CT)
Fairleigh Dickinson U, Coll at Florham (NJ)
Fairleigh Dickinson U, Metropolitan Campus (NJ)
Fayetteville State U (NC)
Ferris State U (MI)
Flagler Coll (FL)
Florida Atlantic U (FL)
Florida Intl U (FL)
Florida Southern Coll (FL)
Fordham U (NY)
Fort Lewis Coll (CO)
Framingham State U (MA)
Franciscan U of Steubenville (OH)
Franklin & Marshall Coll (PA)
Franklin Coll (IN)
Freed-Hardeman U (TN)
Fresno Pacific U (CA)
Friends U (KS)
Furman U (SC)
Gallaudet U (DC)
Gardner-Webb U (NC)
George Fox U (OR)
Georgetown Coll (KY)
Georgetown U (DC)
The George Washington U (DC)
Georgian Court U (NJ)
Georgia State U (GA)
Gettysburg Coll (PA)
Gonzaga U (WA)
Gordon Coll (MA)
Goshen Coll (IN)
Goucher Coll (MD)
Grace Coll (IN)
Graceland U (IA)
Grand Valley State U (MI)
Grand View U (IA)
Greenville Coll (IL)
Grinnell Coll (IA)
Grove City Coll (PA)
Guilford Coll (NC)
Hamline U (MN)
Hampden-Sydney Coll (VA)
Hanover Coll (IN)
Harding U (AR)
Hardin-Simmons U (TX)
Hartwick Coll (NY)
Haverford Coll (PA)
Heidelberg U (OH)
Henderson State U (AR)
Hendrix Coll (AR)
High Point U (NC)
Hillsdale Coll (MI)
Hiram Coll (OH)
Hobart and William Smith Colls (NY)
Hofstra U (NY)
Hollins U (VA)
Holy Names U (CA)
Hood Coll (MD)
Hope Coll (MI)
Houghton Coll (NY)
Houston Baptist U (TX)
Howard Payne U (TX)
Humboldt State U (CA)
Hunter Coll of the City U of New York (NY)
Idaho State U (ID)
Illinois Coll (IL)
Illinois State U (IL)
Illinois Wesleyan U (IL)
Immaculata U (PA)
Indiana U Bloomington (IN)
Indiana U East (IN)
Indiana U Northwest (IN)
Indiana U of Pennsylvania (PA)
Indiana U–Purdue U Indianapolis (IN)
Indiana U South Bend (IN)
Indiana U Southeast (IN)
Inter American U of Puerto Rico, Metropolitan Campus (PR)
Iona Coll (NY)
Iowa State U of Science and Technology (IA)
Ithaca Coll (NY)
Jacksonville State U (AL)
Jacksonville U (FL)
John Brown U (AR)
John Carroll U (OH)
John Jay Coll of Criminal Justice of the City U of New York (NY)
Johns Hopkins U (MD)
Johnson C. Smith U (NC)
Juniata Coll (PA)
Kalamazoo Coll (MI)
Kean U (NJ)
Keene State Coll (NH)
Kent State U (OH)
Kentucky State U (KY)
Kentucky Wesleyan Coll (KY)
Kenyon Coll (OH)
King's Coll (PA)
King U (TN)
Knox Coll (IL)
Kutztown U of Pennsylvania (PA)
Lafayette Coll (PA)
LaGrange Coll (GA)
Lake Erie Coll (OH)
Lake Forest Coll (IL)
La Salle U (PA)
Lawrence U (WI)
Lebanon Valley Coll (PA)
Lee U (TN)
Lehigh U (PA)
Lehman Coll of the City U of New York (NY)
Le Moyne Coll (NY)
Lenoir-Rhyne U (NC)
Lewis & Clark Coll (OR)
Lewis U (IL)
Liberty U (VA)
Lincoln U (MO)
Lincoln U (PA)
Lindenwood U (MO)
Linfield Coll (OR)
Lipscomb U (TN)
Lock Haven U of Pennsylvania (PA)
Loras Coll (IA)
Louisiana Coll (LA)
Louisiana State U and A&M Coll (LA)
Louisiana Tech U (LA)
Loyola Marymount U (CA)
Loyola U Chicago (IL)
Loyola U Maryland (MD)
Loyola U New Orleans (LA)
Luther Coll (IA)
Lycoming Coll (PA)
Lynchburg Coll (VA)
Lyon Coll (AR)
Macalester Coll (MN)
Madonna U (MI)
Manchester U (IN)
Manhattan Coll (NY)
Manhattanville Coll (NY)
Marian U (IN)
Marian U (WI)
Marietta Coll (OH)
Marist Coll (NY)
Marywood U (PA)
McDaniel Coll (MD)
McKendree U (IL)
McMurry U (TX)
Mercer U, Macon (GA)
Mercy Coll (NY)
Meredith Coll (NC)
Merrimack Coll (MA)
Messiah Coll (PA)
Miami U (OH)
Michigan State U (MI)
Middlebury Coll (VT)
Millersville U of Pennsylvania (PA)
Milligan Coll (TN)
Millikin U (IL)
Millsaps Coll (MS)
Mills Coll (CA)
Minnesota State U Mankato (MN)
Minnesota State U Moorhead (MN)
Minot State U (ND)
Missouri State U (MO)
Monmouth Coll (IL)
Montana State U Billings (MT)
Montclair State U (NJ)
Moravian Coll (PA)
Morehead State U (KY)
Morehouse Coll (GA)
Morningside Coll (IA)
Mount Allison U (NB, Canada)
Mount Holyoke Coll (MA)
Mount Mary U (WI)
Mount Saint Mary Coll (NY)
Mount Saint Mary's U (CA)
Mount St. Mary's U (MD)
Mount Vernon Nazarene U (OH)
Muhlenberg Coll (PA)
Murray State U (KY)
Muskingum U (OH)
National U (CA)
Nazareth Coll of Rochester (NY)
Nebraska Wesleyan U (NE)
Newberry Coll (SC)
New Coll of Florida (FL)
New Jersey City U (NJ)
New Mexico Highlands U (NM)
Niagara U (NY)
North Carolina Central U (NC)
North Carolina State U (NC)
North Central Coll (IL)
North Dakota State U (ND)
Northeastern Illinois U (IL)
Northeastern State U (OK)
Northeastern U (MA)
Northern Arizona U (AZ)
Northern Illinois U (IL)
Northern Kentucky U (KY)
Northern State U (SD)
North Greenville U (SC)
Northwestern Coll (IA)
Northwestern U (IL)
Northwest Missouri State U (MO)
Oberlin Coll (OH)
Occidental Coll (CA)
The Ohio State U (OH)
Ohio U (OH)
Ohio Wesleyan U (OH)
Oklahoma Baptist U (OK)
Oklahoma Christian U (OK)
Oklahoma City U (OK)
Oklahoma State U (OK)
Olivet Nazarene U (IL)
Oral Roberts U (OK)
Oregon State U (OR)
Otterbein U (OH)
Ouachita Baptist U (AR)
Our Lady of the Lake U of San Antonio (TX)
Pace U (NY)
Pace U, Pleasantville Campus (NY)
Penn State Abington (PA)
Penn State Altoona (PA)
Penn State Beaver (PA)
Penn State Berks (PA)
Penn State Brandywine (PA)
Penn State DuBois (PA)
Penn State Erie, The Behrend Coll (PA)
Penn State Fayette, The Eberly Campus (PA)
Penn State Greater Allegheny (PA)
Penn State Hazleton (PA)
Penn State Lehigh Valley (PA)
Penn State Mont Alto (PA)
Penn State New Kensington (PA)
Penn State Schuylkill (PA)
Penn State Shenango (PA)
Penn State U Park (PA)
Penn State Wilkes-Barre (PA)
Penn State Worthington Scranton (PA)
Penn State York (PA)
Pepperdine U, Malibu (CA)
Piedmont Coll (GA)
Pittsburg State U (KS)
Pitzer Coll (CA)
Plymouth State U (NH)
Point Loma Nazarene U (CA)
Pomona Coll (CA)
Portland State U (OR)
Princeton U (NJ)
Principia Coll (IL)
Providence Coll (RI)
Purchase Coll, State U of New York (NY)
Queens Coll of the City U of New York (NY)
Quinnipiac U (CT)
Ramapo Coll of New Jersey (NJ)
Randolph Coll (VA)
Randolph-Macon Coll (VA)
Reed Coll (OR)
Regis U (CO)
Rhode Island Coll (RI)
Rhodes Coll (TN)
Rice U (TX)
Ripon Coll (WI)
Roanoke Coll (VA)
Roberts Wesleyan Coll (NY)
Rockford U (IL)
Rockhurst U (MO)
Rollins Coll (FL)
Rosemont Coll (PA)
Rowan U (NJ)
Rutgers U–Camden (NJ)
Rutgers U–Newark (NJ)
Rutgers U–New Brunswick (NJ)
Sacred Heart U (CT)
Saginaw Valley State U (MI)
St. Ambrose U (IA)
Saint Anselm Coll (NH)
St. Bonaventure U (NY)
St. Catherine U (MN)
St. Cloud State U (MN)
St. Edward's U (TX)
Saint Francis U (PA)
St. John Fisher Coll (NY)
Saint John's U (MN)
St. John's U (NY)
St. Joseph's Coll, Long Island Campus (NY)
St. Joseph's Coll, New York (NY)
Saint Joseph's U (PA)
Saint Louis U (MO)
Saint Louis U–Madrid Campus (Spain)
Saint Mary's Coll (IN)
Saint Mary's Coll of California (CA)
Saint Mary's U of Minnesota (MN)
Saint Michael's Coll (VT)
St. Norbert Coll (WI)
St. Olaf Coll (MN)
Saint Peter's U (NJ)
St. Thomas Aquinas Coll (NY)
St. Thomas U (NB, Canada)
Saint Vincent Coll (PA)
Salisbury U (MD)
Salve Regina U (RI)
Samford U (AL)
Sam Houston State U (TX)
San Diego State U (CA)
San Francisco State U (CA)
Santa Clara U (CA)
Sarah Lawrence Coll (NY)
Scripps Coll (CA)

Seattle U (WA)
Seton Hill U (PA)
Sewanee: The U of the South (TN)
Shenandoah U (VA)
Shepherd U (WV)
Shippensburg U of Pennsylvania (PA)
Shorter U (GA)
Siena Coll (NY)
Simmons Coll (MA)
Simpson Coll (IA)
Simpson U (CA)
Skidmore Coll (NY)
Slippery Rock U of Pennsylvania (PA)
Smith Coll (MA)
Sonoma State U (CA)
South Dakota State U (SD)
Southeastern Louisiana U (LA)
Southeastern Oklahoma State U (OK)
Southern Arkansas U–Magnolia (AR)
Southern Connecticut State U (CT)
Southern Methodist U (TX)
Southern Oregon U (OR)
Southern Utah U (UT)
Southwest Baptist U (MO)
Southwestern U (TX)
Spelman Coll (GA)
Spring Hill Coll (AL)
Stanford U (CA)
State U of New York at Fredonia (NY)
State U of New York at New Paltz (NY)
State U of New York at Oswego (NY)
State U of New York at Plattsburgh (NY)
State U of New York Coll at Cortland (NY)
State U of New York Coll at Geneseo (NY)
State U of New York Coll at Old Westbury (NY)
State U of New York Coll at Potsdam (NY)
Stonehill Coll (MA)
Stony Brook U, State U of New York (NY)
Suffolk U (MA)
Susquehanna U (PA)
Swarthmore Coll (PA)
Sweet Briar Coll (VA)
Syracuse U (NY)
Tarleton State U (TX)
Taylor U (IN)
Temple U (PA)
Tennessee State U (TN)
Tennessee Wesleyan U (TN)
Texas A&M Intl U (TX)
Texas A&M U (TX)
Texas A&M U–Commerce (TX)
Texas A&M U–Corpus Christi (TX)
Texas A&M U–Kingsville (TX)
Texas Christian U (TX)
Texas Lutheran U (TX)
Texas State U (TX)
Texas Tech U (TX)
Texas Wesleyan U (TX)
Thomas More Coll (KY)
Transylvania U (KY)
Trinity Christian Coll (IL)
Trinity U (TX)
Troy U (AL)
Truman State U (MO)
Tufts U (MA)
Tulane U (LA)
Union Coll (NE)
Union Coll (NY)
Union U (TN)
United States Military Acad (NY)
Universidad Adventista de las Antillas (PR)
U at Albany, State U of New York (NY)
U at Buffalo, the State U of New York (NY)
The U of Akron (OH)
The U of Alabama (AL)
The U of Arizona (AZ)
U of Arkansas (AR)
U of California, Davis (CA)
U of California, Irvine (CA)
U of California, Los Angeles (CA)
U of California, Riverside (CA)
U of California, San Diego (CA)
U of California, Santa Barbara (CA)
U of Central Arkansas (AR)
U of Central Florida (FL)
U of Central Missouri (MO)
U of Cincinnati (OH)
U of Colorado Boulder (CO)
U of Colorado Colorado Springs (CO)
U of Colorado Denver (CO)
U of Dayton (OH)
U of Delaware (DE)
U of Denver (CO)
U of Evansville (IN)
The U of Findlay (OH)
U of Florida (FL)
U of Georgia (GA)
U of Guelph (ON, Canada)
U of Hawaii at Manoa (HI)
U of Houston (TX)
U of Houston–Downtown (TX)
U of Idaho (ID)
U of Illinois at Chicago (IL)
U of Indianapolis (IN)
U of Jamestown (ND)
The U of Kansas (KS)
U of Kentucky (KY)
U of King's Coll (NS, Canada)
U of La Verne (CA)
U of Louisville (KY)
U of Maine (ME)
U of Mary Hardin-Baylor (TX)
U of Maryland, Coll Park (MD)
U of Massachusetts Amherst (MA)
U of Massachusetts Boston (MA)
U of Massachusetts Dartmouth (MA)
U of Miami (FL)
U of Michigan (MI)
U of Michigan–Dearborn (MI)
U of Michigan–Flint (MI)
U of Minnesota, Duluth (MN)
U of Minnesota, Morris (MN)
U of Minnesota, Twin Cities Campus (MN)
U of Mount Union (OH)
U of Nebraska at Kearney (NE)
U of Nevada, Las Vegas (NV)
U of Nevada, Reno (NV)
U of New Hampshire (NH)
U of North Alabama (AL)
U of North Carolina at Asheville (NC)
The U of North Carolina at Charlotte (NC)
The U of North Carolina at Greensboro (NC)
The U of North Carolina at Pembroke (NC)
The U of North Carolina Wilmington (NC)
U of North Dakota (ND)
U of Northern Colorado (CO)
U of Northern Iowa (IA)
U of North Florida (FL)
U of North Texas (TX)
U of Notre Dame (IN)
U of Oklahoma (OK)
U of Oregon (OR)
U of Pennsylvania (PA)
U of Pikeville (KY)
U of Pittsburgh (PA)
U of Pittsburgh at Greensburg (PA)
U of Puget Sound (WA)
U of Regina (SK, Canada)
U of Rhode Island (RI)
U of Richmond (VA)
U of Rochester (NY)
U of Saint Joseph (CT)
U of St. Thomas (MN)
U of St. Thomas (TX)
U of San Diego (CA)
U of San Francisco (CA)
U of Saskatchewan (SK, Canada)
The U of Scranton (PA)
U of South Carolina (SC)
The U of South Dakota (SD)
U of Southern California (CA)
U of Southern Indiana (IN)
U of South Florida (FL)
The U of Tampa (FL)
The U of Tennessee (TN)
The U of Tennessee at Martin (TN)
The U of Texas at Austin (TX)
The U of Texas at El Paso (TX)
The U of Texas at San Antonio (TX)
The U of Texas of the Permian Basin (TX)
The U of Texas Rio Grande Valley (TX)
U of the Cumberlands (KY)
U of the Incarnate Word (TX)
U of the Pacific (CA)
The U of Toledo (OH)
U of Toronto (ON, Canada)
The U of Tulsa (OK)
U of Utah (UT)
U of Vermont (VT)
U of Virginia (VA)
The U of Virginia's Coll at Wise (VA)
U of Washington (WA)
U of Waterloo (ON, Canada)
U of Windsor (ON, Canada)
U of Wisconsin–Eau Claire (WI)
U of Wisconsin–Green Bay (WI)
U of Wisconsin–La Crosse (WI)
U of Wisconsin–Madison (WI)
U of Wisconsin–Milwaukee (WI)
U of Wisconsin–Parkside (WI)
U of Wisconsin–Stevens Point (WI)
U of Wisconsin–Whitewater (WI)
Ursinus Coll (PA)
Utah State U (UT)
Utah Valley U (UT)
Valdosta State U (GA)
Valley City State U (ND)
Valparaiso U (IN)
Vanderbilt U (TN)
Vassar Coll (NY)
Villanova U (PA)
Virginia Polytechnic Inst and State U (VA)
Virginia Wesleyan Coll (VA)
Viterbo U (WI)
Wabash Coll (IN)
Wagner Coll (NY)
Wake Forest U (NC)
Walla Walla U (WA)
Walsh U (OH)
Wartburg Coll (IA)
Washburn U (KS)
Washington & Jefferson Coll (PA)
Washington and Lee U (VA)
Washington Coll (MD)
Washington State U (WA)
Washington U in St. Louis (MO)
Wayland Baptist U (TX)
Wayne State Coll (NE)
Weber State U (UT)
Webster U (MO)
Wells Coll (NY)
Wesleyan Coll (GA)
West Chester U of Pennsylvania (PA)
Western Carolina U (NC)
Western Connecticut State U (CT)
Western Kentucky U (KY)
Western Michigan U (MI)
Western Oregon U (OR)
Western State Colorado U (CO)
Westfield State U (MA)
Westminster Coll (PA)
Westmont Coll (CA)
West Texas A&M U (TX)
Wheaton Coll (IL)
Wheeling Jesuit U (WV)
Whitman Coll (WA)
Whittier Coll (CA)
Whitworth U (WA)
Widener U (PA)
Wilkes U (PA)
Willamette U (OR)
William Jewell Coll (MO)
William Paterson U of New Jersey (NJ)
Williams Coll (MA)
Wilson Coll (PA)
Winona State U (MN)
Wittenberg U (OH)
Wofford Coll (SC)
Worcester State U (MA)
Wright State U (OH)
Xavier U of Louisiana (LA)
York Coll of Pennsylvania (PA)
York Coll of the City U of New York (NY)
Youngstown State U (OH)

SPANISH AND IBERIAN STUDIES

Austin Coll (TX)
Bard Coll (NY)
Bowdoin Coll (ME)
Brandeis U (MA)
Coe Coll (IA)
Emory & Henry Coll (VA)
Fordham U (NY)
Saint Louis U–Madrid Campus (Spain)
Wabash Coll (IN)
Wesleyan U (CT)

SPANISH LANGUAGE TEACHER EDUCATION

Abilene Christian U (TX)
Adams State U (CO)
Albion Coll (MI)
Anderson U (IN)
Ashland U (OH)
Auburn U (AL)
Augustana Coll (IL)
Bayamón Central U (PR)
Baylor U (TX)
Bethel U (MN)
Bishop's U (QC, Canada)
Blackburn Coll (IL)
Blue Mountain Coll (MS)
Boise State U (ID)
Brigham Young U–Idaho (ID)
Brooklyn Coll of the City U of New York (NY)
Bryan Coll (TN)
Buena Vista U (IA)
California Lutheran U (CA)
Calvin Coll (MI)
Canisius Coll (NY)
Carroll Coll (MT)
The Catholic U of America (DC)
Cedarville U (OH)
Central Michigan U (MI)
Central Washington U (WA)
Charleston Southern U (SC)
Coll of Saint Mary (NE)
Coll of Staten Island of the City U of New York (NY)
Coll of the Ozarks (MO)
Colorado State U (CO)
Concordia Coll (MN)
Concordia U Wisconsin (WI)
Cornerstone U (MI)
Daemen Coll (NY)
Eastern Michigan U (MI)
Eastern Washington U (WA)
Edgewood Coll (WI)
Elmira Coll (NY)
Evangel U (MO)
Franklin Coll (IN)
Friends U (KS)
Gardner-Webb U (NC)
Georgia Southern U (GA)
Goshen Coll (IN)
Grace Coll (IN)
Grand Valley State U (MI)
Greenville Coll (IL)
Grove City Coll (PA)
Harding U (AR)
Hardin-Simmons U (TX)
Hofstra U (NY)
Holy Family U (PA)
Hope Coll (MI)
Houston Baptist U (TX)
Howard Payne U (TX)
Indiana U–Purdue U Indianapolis (IN)
Indiana U South Bend (IN)
Inter American U of Puerto Rico, Aguadilla Campus (PR)
Inter American U of Puerto Rico, Barranquitas Campus (PR)
Inter American U of Puerto Rico, Metropolitan Campus (PR)
Inter American U of Puerto Rico, San Germán Campus (PR)
Iona Coll (NY)
Ithaca Coll (NY)
Kentucky Wesleyan Coll (KY)
King U (TN)
Lee U (TN)
Le Moyne Coll (NY)
Lewis U (IL)
Lindenwood U (MO)
Lipscomb U (TN)
Louisiana Coll (LA)
Lubbock Christian U (TX)
Manchester U (IN)
Manhattanville Coll (NY)
Marian U (WI)
Marist Coll (NY)
Marywood U (PA)
McMurry U (TX)
Merrimack Coll (MA)
Messiah Coll (PA)
Miami U (OH)
Michigan State U (MI)
Minnesota State U Moorhead (MN)
Minot State U (ND)
Missouri Western State U (MO)
Montana State U Billings (MT)
Morningside Coll (IA)
Mount Mary U (WI)
Mount Vernon Nazarene U (OH)
Niagara U (NY)
North Dakota State U (ND)
Northeastern State U (OK)
North Greenville U (SC)
Northwest Missouri State U (MO)
Ohio U (OH)
Ohio Wesleyan U (OH)
Oklahoma Baptist U (OK)
Oral Roberts U (OK)
Our Lady of the Lake U of San Antonio (TX)
Pace U (NY)
Piedmont Coll (GA)
Pittsburg State U (KS)
Providence Coll (RI)
Queens Coll of the City U of New York (NY)
Rhode Island Coll (RI)
Roberts Wesleyan Coll (NY)
Saginaw Valley State U (MI)
St. Ambrose U (IA)
St. Catherine U (MN)
St. Edward's U (TX)
St. John Fisher Coll (NY)
St. John's U (NY)
St. Joseph's Coll, Long Island Campus (NY)
St. Joseph's Coll, New York (NY)
Saint Joseph's U (PA)
Saint Mary's U of Minnesota (MN)
Salve Regina U (RI)
Southern Utah U (UT)
Spring Hill Coll (AL)
State U of New York at New Paltz (NY)
State U of New York Coll at Cortland (NY)
State U of New York Coll at Old Westbury (NY)
State U of New York Coll at Potsdam (NY)
Syracuse U (NY)
Taylor U (IN)
Texas Wesleyan U (TX)
Trinity Christian Coll (IL)
The U of Akron (OH)
U of Delaware (DE)
U of Evansville (IN)
The U of Findlay (OH)
U of Illinois at Chicago (IL)
U of Indianapolis (IN)
U of Maine (ME)
U of Mary Hardin-Baylor (TX)
U of Michigan–Flint (MI)
U of Nevada, Las Vegas (NV)
The U of North Carolina at Greensboro (NC)
U of St. Thomas (MN)
The U of South Dakota (SD)
The U of Tennessee at Martin (TN)
U of the Cumberlands (KY)
U of Wisconsin–Whitewater (WI)
Utah Valley U (UT)
Valley City State U (ND)
Valparaiso U (IN)
Viterbo U (WI)
Washburn U (KS)
Washington U in St. Louis (MO)
Weber State U (UT)
Western Carolina U (NC)
Western Illinois U (IL)
Western Michigan U (MI)
Western State Colorado U (CO)
Widener U (PA)
Winona State U (MN)
Xavier U of Louisiana (LA)
York Coll of Pennsylvania (PA)
Youngstown State U (OH)

SPECIAL EDUCATION

Adams State U (CO)
Alabama State U (AL)
Albany State U (GA)
Alma Coll (MI)
Anderson U (SC)

Arizona State U at the Polytechnic campus (AZ)
Arizona State U at the Tempe campus (AZ)
Arizona State U at the West campus (AZ)
Armstrong State U (GA)
Asbury U (KY)
Ashland U (OH)
Athens State U (AL)
Auburn U (AL)
Auburn U at Montgomery (AL)
Augsburg Coll (MN)
Augustana U (SD)
Augusta U (GA)
Aurora U (IL)
Austin Peay State U (TN)
Avila U (MO)
Barry U (FL)
Barton Coll (NC)
Bayamón Central U (PR)
Baylor U (TX)
Bellarmine U (KY)
Benedictine Coll (KS)
Bennett Coll (NC)
Black Hills State U (SD)
Bloomsburg U of Pennsylvania (PA)
Bluffton U (OH)
Boise State U (ID)
Boston U (MA)
Bowie State U (MD)
Bowling Green State U (OH)
Brescia U (KY)
Bridgewater State U (MA)
Brigham Young U (UT)
Buena Vista U (IA)
Buffalo State Coll, State U of New York (NY)
Cabrini U (PA)
California U of Pennsylvania (PA)
Calvin Coll (MI)
Capital U (OH)
Caribbean U (PR)
Carson-Newman U (TN)
Carthage Coll (WI)
Cedarville U (OH)
Centenary U (NJ)
Central State U (OH)
Central Washington U (WA)
Christian Brothers U (TN)
Clemson U (SC)
Cleveland State U (OH)
Coastal Carolina U (SC)
Coll of Charleston (SC)
The Coll of New Jersey (NJ)
The Coll of Saint Rose (NY)
Colorado Christian U (CO)
Columbus State U (GA)
Concordia U Chicago (IL)
Concordia U, Nebraska (NE)
Concord U (WV)
Converse Coll (SC)
Curry Coll (MA)
Daemen Coll (NY)
Doane U (NE)
Dominican Coll (NY)
East Carolina U (NC)
East Central U (OK)
Eastern Illinois U (IL)
Eastern Nazarene Coll (MA)
Eastern Washington U (WA)
East Tennessee State U (TN)
Elizabeth City State U (NC)
Elon U (NC)
Evangel U (MO)
Felician U (NJ)
Fitchburg State U (MA)
Flagler Coll (FL)
Florida Atlantic U (FL)
Florida Gulf Coast U (FL)
Florida Intl U (FL)
Freed-Hardeman U (TN)
Furman U (SC)
Geneva Coll (PA)
Georgia Coll & State U (GA)
Georgia Gwinnett Coll (GA)
Georgia Southern U (GA)
Georgia Southwestern State U (GA)
Gonzaga U (WA)
Goshen Coll (IN)
Goucher Coll (MD)
Grace Coll (IN)
Grand Valley State U (MI)
Greenville Coll (IL)
Grove City Coll (PA)
Hampton U (VA)
Heidelberg U (OH)
High Point U (NC)
Holy Family U (PA)
Houghton Coll (NY)
Houston Baptist U (TX)
Huntington U (IN)
Idaho State U (ID)
Illinois State U (IL)
Indiana State U (IN)
Indiana U Bloomington (IN)
Indiana U of Pennsylvania (PA)
Indiana U South Bend (IN)
Indiana U Southeast (IN)
Inter American U of Puerto Rico, Barranquitas Campus (PR)
Inter American U of Puerto Rico, Fajardo Campus (PR)
Inter American U of Puerto Rico, Metropolitan Campus (PR)
Inter American U of Puerto Rico, Ponce Campus (PR)
Inter American U of Puerto Rico, San Germán Campus (PR)
Jackson State U (MS)
Jacksonville State U (AL)
Jacksonville U (FL)
John Carroll U (OH)
Kean U (NJ)
Kent State U (OH)
Keuka Coll (NY)
Kutztown U of Pennsylvania (PA)
Lake Erie Coll (OH)
Langston U (OK)
Lebanon Valley Coll (PA)
Lee U (TN)
Le Moyne Coll (NY)
Lesley U (MA)
Lewis U (IL)
Liberty U (VA)
Lindenwood U (MO)
Lipscomb U (TN)
Louisiana Coll (LA)
Louisiana Tech U (LA)
Loyola U Chicago (IL)
Loyola U Maryland (MD)
MacMurray Coll (IL)
Manchester U (IN)
Manhattan Coll (NY)
Mansfield U of Pennsylvania (PA)
Marian U (IN)
Marymount U (VA)
Marywood U (PA)
Medgar Evers Coll of the City U of New York (NY)
Mercyhurst U (PA)
Merrimack Coll (MA)
Metropolitan State U of Denver (CO)
Miami Dade Coll (FL)
Miami U (OH)
Michigan State U (MI)
Millersville U of Pennsylvania (PA)
Minnesota State U Moorhead (MN)
Mississippi State U (MS)
Missouri State U (MO)
Missouri Valley Coll (MO)
Monmouth U (NJ)
Montana State U Billings (MT)
Morehead State U (KY)
Morningside Coll (IA)
Mount Marty Coll (SD)
Mount St. Joseph U (OH)
Mount Vernon Nazarene U (OH)
Murray State U (KY)
Muskingum U (OH)
National U (CA)
Nazareth Coll of Rochester (NY)
Nebraska Wesleyan U (NE)
Nevada State Coll (NV)
New England Coll (NH)
New Jersey City U (NJ)
New Mexico Highlands U (NM)
New Mexico State U (NM)
Niagara U (NY)
North Carolina Wesleyan Coll (NC)
Northeastern Illinois U (IL)
Northern Arizona U (AZ)
Northern Kentucky U (KY)
Northern State U (SD)
Northwestern Oklahoma State U (OK)
Oakland City U (IN)
Ohio Dominican U (OH)
The Ohio State U (OH)
Ohio U (OH)
Oklahoma Baptist U (OK)
Oklahoma City U (OK)
Olivet Nazarene U (IL)
Oral Roberts U (OK)
Our Lady of the Lake U of San Antonio (TX)
Pace U (NY)
Pace U, Pleasantville Campus (NY)
Penn State Abington (PA)
Penn State Altoona (PA)
Penn State Beaver (PA)
Penn State Berks (PA)
Penn State Brandywine (PA)
Penn State DuBois (PA)
Penn State Erie, The Behrend Coll (PA)
Penn State Fayette, The Eberly Campus (PA)
Penn State Greater Allegheny (PA)
Penn State Hazleton (PA)
Penn State Lehigh Valley (PA)
Penn State Mont Alto (PA)
Penn State New Kensington (PA)
Penn State Schuylkill (PA)
Penn State Shenango (PA)
Penn State U Park (PA)
Penn State Wilkes-Barre (PA)
Penn State Worthington Scranton (PA)
Penn State York (PA)
Providence Coll (RI)
Rhode Island Coll (RI)
Roberts Wesleyan Coll (NY)
Rockford U (IL)
Rowan U (NJ)
Saginaw Valley State U (MI)
St. Bonaventure U (NY)
St. Cloud State U (MN)
St. Edward's U (TX)
Saint Francis U (PA)
St. John Fisher Coll (NY)
St. John's U (NY)
St. Joseph's Coll, Long Island Campus (NY)
St. Joseph's Coll, New York (NY)
Saint Joseph's U (PA)
Saint Martin's U (WA)
Saint Mary-of-the-Woods Coll (IN)
St. Petersburg Coll (FL)
St. Thomas Aquinas Coll (NY)
Salve Regina U (RI)
Sam Houston State U (TX)
Seattle Pacific U (WA)
Shawnee State U (OH)
Simmons Coll (MA)
Slippery Rock U of Pennsylvania (PA)
South Carolina State U (SC)
Southeastern U (FL)
Southeast Missouri State U (MO)
Southern Connecticut State U (CT)
Southern Illinois U Carbondale (IL)
Southern Illinois U Edwardsville (IL)
Spalding U (KY)
State U of New York at Plattsburgh (NY)
State U of New York Coll at Geneseo (NY)
State U of New York Coll at Old Westbury (NY)
Tennessee State U (TN)
Texas A&M Intl U (TX)
Texas Christian U (TX)
Towson U (MD)
Trevecca Nazarene U (TN)
Trinity Baptist Coll (FL)
Trinity Christian Coll (IL)
Tusculum Coll (TN)
Union Inst & U (OH)
Union U (TN)
Université de Montréal (QC, Canada)
Université de Sherbrooke (QC, Canada)
The U of Akron (OH)
The U of Alabama (AL)
The U of Arizona (AZ)
U of Arkansas (AR)
U of Central Missouri (MO)
U of Cincinnati (OH)
U of Dayton (OH)
U of Delaware (DE)
U of Detroit Mercy (MI)
U of Evansville (IN)
The U of Findlay (OH)
U of Florida (FL)
U of Georgia (GA)
U of Great Falls (MT)
U of Hartford (CT)
U of Hawaii at Manoa (HI)
U of Kentucky (KY)
U of Lethbridge (AB, Canada)
U of Maine at Farmington (ME)
U of Maryland, Coll Park (MD)
U of Michigan–Dearborn (MI)
U of Minnesota, Twin Cities Campus (MN)
U of Missouri–St. Louis (MO)
U of Mount Union (OH)
U of Nebraska at Kearney (NE)
U of Nevada, Las Vegas (NV)
The U of North Carolina at Charlotte (NC)
The U of North Carolina at Greensboro (NC)
The U of North Carolina at Pembroke (NC)
The U of North Carolina Wilmington (NC)
U of Northern Colorado (CO)
U of North Florida (FL)
U of Oklahoma (OK)
U of St. Francis (IL)
U of Saint Francis (IN)
U of Saint Joseph (CT)
U of South Alabama (AL)
U of South Carolina Aiken (SC)
The U of South Dakota (SD)
U of Southern Mississippi (MS)
U of South Florida (FL)
The U of Tennessee (TN)
The U of Tennessee at Chattanooga (TN)
The U of Tennessee at Martin (TN)
The U of Texas at Austin (TX)
The U of Texas at San Antonio (TX)
U of the Cumberlands (KY)
U of the Pacific (CA)
U of the Southwest (NM)
The U of Toledo (OH)
U of Utah (UT)
The U of West Alabama (AL)
U of West Georgia (GA)
U of Windsor (ON, Canada)
U of Wisconsin–Eau Claire (WI)
U of Wisconsin–Madison (WI)
U of Wisconsin–Milwaukee (WI)
U of Wisconsin–Parkside (WI)
U of Wisconsin–Stevens Point (WI)
U of Wisconsin–Stout (WI)
U of Wisconsin–Superior (WI)
U of Wisconsin–Whitewater (WI)
Utah State U (UT)
Valdosta State U (GA)
Vanderbilt U (TN)
Vincennes U (IN)
Virginia Union U (VA)
Virginia Wesleyan Coll (VA)
Walsh U (OH)
Waynesburg U (PA)
Wayne State Coll (NE)
Wayne State U (MI)
Weber State U (UT)
Webster U (MO)
West Chester U of Pennsylvania (PA)
Western Carolina U (NC)
Western Illinois U (IL)
Western Kentucky U (KY)
Westfield State U (MA)
Westminster Coll (UT)
West Virginia Wesleyan Coll (WV)
Wheelock Coll (MA)
Whitworth U (WA)
Widener U (PA)
William Paterson U of New Jersey (NJ)
William Penn U (IA)
William Woods U (MO)
Winona State U (MN)
Winthrop U (SC)
Youngstown State U (OH)

SPECIAL EDUCATION–EARLY CHILDHOOD

Aurora U (IL)
Bowling Green State U (OH)
Canisius Coll (NY)
Cazenovia Coll (NY)
Clarion U of Pennsylvania (PA)
Daytona State Coll (FL)
Eastern Washington U (WA)
East Stroudsburg U of Pennsylvania (PA)
Edgewood Coll (WI)
Elmira Coll (NY)
Gwynedd Mercy U (PA)
Harding U (AR)
Henderson State U (AR)
Hope Coll (MI)
Indiana U of Pennsylvania (PA)
Inter American U of Puerto Rico, Aguadilla Campus (PR)
Inter American U of Puerto Rico, Ponce Campus (PR)
Judson U (IL)
Juniata Coll (PA)
Keuka Coll (NY)
Lewis U (IL)
Lindenwood U (MO)
Lock Haven U of Pennsylvania (PA)
Missouri Baptist U (MO)
Nevada State Coll (NV)
Prescott Coll (AZ)
Roberts Wesleyan Coll (NY)
Shippensburg U of Pennsylvania (PA)
Silver Lake Coll of the Holy Family (WI)
State U of New York Coll at Geneseo (NY)
Syracuse U (NY)
The U of Akron (OH)
U of Maine at Farmington (ME)
U of Mount Union (OH)
U of Vermont (VT)
Western Washington U (WA)
Winona State U (MN)
York Coll of Pennsylvania (PA)

SPECIAL EDUCATION–ELEMENTARY SCHOOL

Abilene Christian U (TX)
Alvernia U (PA)
Ball State U (IN)
Canisius Coll (NY)
Granite State Coll (NH)
La Salle U (PA)
Molloy Coll (NY)
Neumann U (PA)
Niagara U (NY)
Northcentral U (CA)
Rhode Island Coll (RI)
Shawnee State U (OH)
Syracuse U (NY)
Towson U (MD)
U of Mount Union (OH)
Weber State U (UT)

SPECIAL EDUCATION–GIFTED AND TALENTED

Canisius Coll (NY)
Grand Valley State U (MI)
U of Great Falls (MT)

SPECIAL EDUCATION–INDIVIDUALS WHO ARE DEVELOPMENTALLY DELAYED

Millikin U (IL)
Saint Mary-of-the-Woods Coll (IN)

SPECIAL EDUCATION–INDIVIDUALS WITH AUTISM

Inter American U of Puerto Rico, Ponce Campus (PR)
Nevada State Coll (NV)

SPECIAL EDUCATION–INDIVIDUALS WITH EMOTIONAL DISTURBANCES

Central Michigan U (MI)
Eastern Michigan U (MI)
Grand Valley State U (MI)
Hope Coll (MI)
Morningside Coll (IA)
U of Detroit Mercy (MI)
Western Michigan U (MI)

SPECIAL EDUCATION–INDIVIDUALS WITH HEARING IMPAIRMENTS

Barton Coll (NC)
Boston U (MA)
Bowling Green State U (OH)
Canisius Coll (NY)
The Coll of New Jersey (NJ)
Converse Coll (SC)
Eastern Michigan U (MI)
Flagler Coll (FL)
Grand Valley State U (MI)
MacMurray Coll (IL)
Michigan State U (MI)
Minot State U (ND)
Texas Christian U (TX)

The U of North Carolina at Greensboro (NC)
U of North Florida (FL)
U of Science and Arts of Oklahoma (OK)
U of Southern Mississippi (MS)
The U of Tulsa (OK)
Utah Valley U (UT)

SPECIAL EDUCATION–INDIVIDUALS WITH INTELLECTUAL DISABILITIES
Bowling Green State U (OH)
Bradley U (IL)
Brenau U (GA)
Central Michigan U (MI)
Eastern Michigan U (MI)
Grand Valley State U (MI)
Manchester U (IN)
Minot State U (ND)
Morningside Coll (IA)
Silver Lake Coll of the Holy Family (WI)
Walsh U (OH)

SPECIAL EDUCATION–INDIVIDUALS WITH MULTIPLE DISABILITIES
Adventist U of Health Sciences (FL)
Ball State U (IN)
Bowling Green State U (OH)
Bradley U (IL)
Dominican Coll (NY)
Grand Valley State U (MI)
Missouri Baptist U (MO)
Northwest Missouri State U (MO)
The U of Akron (OH)
The U of North Carolina Wilmington (NC)
Walsh U (OH)
Wright State U (OH)
Wright State U–Lake Campus (OH)

SPECIAL EDUCATION–INDIVIDUALS WITH ORTHOPEDIC AND OTHER PHYSICAL HEALTH IMPAIRMENTS
Eastern Michigan U (MI)
Grand Valley State U (MI)
U of Puerto Rico in Bayamón (PR)

SPECIAL EDUCATION–INDIVIDUALS WITH SPECIFIC LEARNING DISABILITIES
Appalachian State U (NC)
Aquinas Coll (MI)
Baldwin Wallace U (OH)
Bethune-Cookman U (FL)
Bowling Green State U (OH)
Bradley U (IL)
Canisius Coll (NY)
Cornerstone U (MI)
Hope Coll (MI)
Judson U (IL)
Malone U (OH)
Michigan State U (MI)
Northeastern State U (OK)
Northwestern U (IL)
Prescott Coll (AZ)
Silver Lake Coll of the Holy Family (WI)
State U of New York at Plattsburgh (NY)
U of Detroit Mercy (MI)
Western Michigan U (MI)
West Virginia Wesleyan Coll (WV)

SPECIAL EDUCATION–INDIVIDUALS WITH SPEECH/LANGUAGE IMPAIRMENTS
Armstrong State U (GA)
Baylor U (TX)
Brooklyn Coll of the City U of New York (NY)
Buffalo State Coll, State U of New York (NY)
Eastern Michigan U (MI)
Elmira Coll (NY)
Emerson Coll (MA)
Ithaca Coll (NY)
Louisiana Tech U (LA)
Minot State U (ND)
New Mexico State U (NM)
Pace U (NY)
State U of New York Coll at Cortland (NY)
The U of North Carolina at Greensboro (NC)

SPECIAL EDUCATION–INDIVIDUALS WITH VISION IMPAIRMENTS
Eastern Michigan U (MI)
Kutztown U of Pennsylvania (PA)

SPECIAL EDUCATION–JUNIOR HIGH/MIDDLE SCHOOL
Clarion U of Pennsylvania (PA)
East Stroudsburg U of Pennsylvania (PA)
La Salle U (PA)

SPECIAL EDUCATION RELATED
Auburn U (AL)
Bowling Green State U (OH)
Canisius Coll (NY)
Catawba Coll (NC)
Clarion U of Pennsylvania (PA)
Dakota State U (SD)
East Carolina U (NC)
Eastern Nazarene Coll (MA)
Hood Coll (MD)
Kean U (NJ)
Lee U (TN)
Lincoln U (MO)
Minot State U (ND)
Purdue U (IN)
Saint Mary-of-the-Woods Coll (IN)
Southeastern Oklahoma State U (OK)
Southern New Hampshire U (NH)
Talladega Coll (AL)
The U of North Carolina at Charlotte (NC)
U of Southern Indiana (IN)

SPECIAL EDUCATION–SECONDARY SCHOOL
Abilene Christian U (TX)
Canisius Coll (NY)
Molloy Coll (NY)
Nevada State Coll (NV)
Niagara U (NY)
Oklahoma City U (OK)
Rhode Island Coll (RI)

SPECIAL PRODUCTS MARKETING
Buffalo State Coll, State U of New York (NY)
Central Washington U (WA)
Dominican U (IL)
Fashion Inst of Technology (NY)
Rochester Inst of Technology (NY)
Saint Joseph's U (PA)
Stephen F. Austin State U (TX)
U of North Texas (TX)

SPEECH COMMUNICATION AND RHETORIC
Abilene Christian U (TX)
Alabama State U (AL)
Albertus Magnus Coll (CT)
Albright Coll (PA)
Alfred U (NY)
Allegheny Coll (PA)
Alma Coll (MI)
Alverno Coll (WI)
American U (DC)
The American U of Rome (Italy)
Appalachian State U (NC)
Aquinas Coll (MI)
Arizona State U at the Downtown Phoenix campus (AZ)
Arizona State U at the Polytechnic campus (AZ)
Arizona State U at the Tempe campus (AZ)
Arizona State U at the West campus (AZ)
Arkansas Tech U (AR)
Ashland U (OH)
Auburn U at Montgomery (AL)
Augsburg Coll (MN)
Augustana U (SD)
Augusta U (GA)
Aurora U (IL)
Austin Coll (TX)
Avila U (MO)
Azusa Pacific U (CA)
Baldwin Wallace U (OH)
Ball State U (IN)
Barry U (FL)
Baylor U (TX)
Belhaven U (MS)
Bellarmine U (KY)
Belmont U (TN)
Bethany Lutheran Coll (MN)
Bethel Coll (IN)
Bethune-Cookman U (FL)
Biola U (CA)
Blackburn Coll (IL)
Bluffton U (OH)
Boise State U (ID)
Bowling Green State U (OH)
Brewton-Parker Coll (GA)
Bridgewater State U (MA)
Brooklyn Coll of the City U of New York (NY)
Bryan Coll (TN)
Bryant U (RI)
Buena Vista U (IA)
Buffalo State Coll, State U of New York (NY)
Cabrini U (PA)
Caldwell U (NJ)
California Baptist U (CA)
California Polytechnic State U, San Luis Obispo (CA)
California State Polytechnic U, Pomona (CA)
California State U, Dominguez Hills (CA)
California State U, Fresno (CA)
California State U, Fullerton (CA)
California State U, Sacramento (CA)
California State U, San Marcos (CA)
California State U, Stanislaus (CA)
California U of Pennsylvania (PA)
Calvin Coll (MI)
Capital U (OH)
Cardinal Stritch U (WI)
Carthage Coll (WI)
Catawba Coll (NC)
The Catholic U of America (DC)
Cedar Crest Coll (PA)
Cedarville U (OH)
Central Methodist U (MO)
Central Michigan U (MI)
Chaminade U of Honolulu (HI)
Champlain Coll (VT)
Chapman U (CA)
Chatham U (PA)
Christopher Newport U (VA)
Clarkson U (NY)
Clayton State U (GA)
Cleveland State U (OH)
Coastal Carolina U (SC)
Coe Coll (IA)
The Coll at Brockport, State U of New York (NY)
Coll of Charleston (SC)
Coll of Saint Elizabeth (NJ)
The Coll of St. Scholastica (MN)
Coll of Staten Island of the City U of New York (NY)
The Coll of Wooster (OH)
Colorado State U (CO)
Columbia Coll (MO)
Concordia Coll (MN)
Concordia U Chicago (IL)
Concordia U, Nebraska (NE)
Corban U (OR)
Cornerstone U (MI)
Creighton U (NE)
Culver-Stockton Coll (MO)
Dallas Baptist U (TX)
Dickinson State U (ND)
Dixie State U (UT)
Dominican U (IL)
Duquesne U (PA)
East Carolina U (NC)
East Central U (OK)
Eastern Michigan U (MI)
Eastern Oregon U (OR)
Eastern U (PA)
Eastern Washington U (WA)
East Stroudsburg U of Pennsylvania (PA)
Ecclesia Coll (AR)
Eckerd Coll (FL)
Elizabeth City State U (NC)
Elon U (NC)
Embry-Riddle Aeronautical U–Daytona (FL)
Embry-Riddle Aeronautical U–Worldwide (FL)
Emerson Coll (MA)
Emmanuel Coll (MA)
Emporia State U (KS)
Eureka Coll (IL)
Fairfield U (CT)
Fairleigh Dickinson U, Coll at Florham (NJ)
Fayetteville State U (NC)
Felician U (NJ)
Ferris State U (MI)
Fitchburg State U (MA)
Florida Atlantic U (FL)
Florida Gulf Coast U (FL)
Florida Intl U (FL)
Freed-Hardeman U (TN)
Furman U (SC)
Gallaudet U (DC)
George Fox U (OR)
Georgia Southern U (GA)
Georgia State U (GA)
Gonzaga U (WA)
Gordon Coll (MA)
Governors State U (IL)
Grace Coll (IN)
Grand Valley State U (MI)
Greenville Coll (IL)
Grove City Coll (PA)
Gwynedd Mercy U (PA)
Hamline U (MN)
Hampshire Coll (MA)
Hannibal-LaGrange U (MO)
Harding U (AR)
Hardin-Simmons U (TX)
Hillsdale Coll (MI)
Hofstra U (NY)
Hope Coll (MI)
Houghton Coll (NY)
Howard Payne U (TX)
Huntington U (IN)
Illinois State U (IL)
Indiana State U (IN)
Indiana U Bloomington (IN)
Indiana U East (IN)
Indiana U Kokomo (IN)
Indiana U Northwest (IN)
Indiana U of Pennsylvania (PA)
Indiana U–Purdue U Indianapolis (IN)
Indiana U South Bend (IN)
Indiana U Southeast (IN)
Iona Coll (NY)
Iowa State U of Science and Technology (IA)
Jacksonville State U (AL)
Jacksonville U (FL)
James Madison U (VA)
Judson U (IL)
Juniata Coll (PA)
Kansas State U (KS)
Kansas Wesleyan U (KS)
Kean U (NJ)
Keene State Coll (NH)
Kennesaw State U (GA)
Kent State U (OH)
Kent State U at Ashtabula (OH)
Kent State U at East Liverpool (OH)
Kent State U at Salem (OH)
Kent State U at Stark (OH)
Kent State U at Trumbull (OH)
Kent State U at Tuscarawas (OH)
Kentucky Wesleyan Coll (KY)
Keuka Coll (NY)
Kuyper Coll (MI)
Lawrence Technological U (MI)
Lee U (TN)
Lewis & Clark Coll (OR)
Liberty U (VA)
Linfield Coll (OR)
Longwood U (VA)
Louisiana Coll (LA)
Louisiana State U and A&M Coll (LA)
Loyola Marymount U (CA)
Loyola U Chicago (IL)
Loyola U Maryland (MD)
Luther Coll (IA)
Lynchburg Coll (VA)
Manchester U (IN)
Manhattanville Coll (NY)
Mansfield U of Pennsylvania (PA)
Marian U (IN)
Marian U (WI)
Marietta Coll (OH)
Marymount Manhattan Coll (NY)
McDaniel Coll (MD)
McKendree U (IL)
Mercer U, Macon (GA)
Mercyhurst U (PA)
Meredith Coll (NC)
Messiah Coll (PA)
Michigan State U (MI)
Millersville U of Pennsylvania (PA)
Millikin U (IL)
Millsaps Coll (MS)
Minnesota State U Moorhead (MN)
Mississippi State U (MS)
Missouri State U (MO)
Missouri Valley Coll (MO)
Missouri Western State U (MO)
Molloy Coll (NY)
Monmouth Coll (IL)
Monmouth U (NJ)
Montclair State U (NJ)
Mount Mary U (WI)
Mount Mercy U (IA)
Mount St. Joseph U (OH)
Mount St. Mary's U (MD)
Mount Vernon Nazarene U (OH)
Muskingum U (OH)
Nazareth Coll of Rochester (NY)
Nebraska Wesleyan U (NE)
New Mexico Highlands U (NM)
North Carolina State U (NC)
North Central Coll (IL)
Northeastern State U (OK)
Northeastern U (MA)
Northern Arizona U (AZ)
Northern Illinois U (IL)
Northern Kentucky U (KY)
Northwest Christian U (OR)
Northwestern State U of Louisiana (LA)
Northwestern U (IL)
Northwest Missouri State U (MO)
Nova Southeastern U (FL)
The Ohio State U (OH)
Ohio U (OH)
Oklahoma Baptist U (OK)
Olivet Nazarene U (IL)
Oral Roberts U (OK)
Oregon State U (OR)
Ouachita Baptist U (AR)
Pace U, Pleasantville Campus (NY)
Pacific Lutheran U (WA)
Palm Beach Atlantic U (FL)
Penn State Abington (PA)
Penn State Altoona (PA)
Penn State Beaver (PA)
Penn State Berks (PA)
Penn State Brandywine (PA)
Penn State DuBois (PA)
Penn State Erie, The Behrend Coll (PA)
Penn State Fayette, The Eberly Campus (PA)
Penn State Greater Allegheny (PA)
Penn State Harrisburg (PA)
Penn State Hazleton (PA)
Penn State Lehigh Valley (PA)
Penn State Mont Alto (PA)
Penn State New Kensington (PA)
Penn State Schuylkill (PA)
Penn State Shenango (PA)
Penn State U Park (PA)
Penn State Wilkes-Barre (PA)
Penn State Worthington Scranton (PA)
Penn State York (PA)
Pepperdine U, Malibu (CA)
Pine Manor Coll (MA)
Pittsburg State U (KS)
Plymouth State U (NH)
Point Loma Nazarene U (CA)
Prairie View A&M U (TX)
Purchase Coll, State U of New York (NY)
Purdue U Northwest (IN)
Radford U (VA)
Ramapo Coll of New Jersey (NJ)
Randolph Coll (VA)
Regis U (CO)
Rensselaer Polytechnic Inst (NY)
Rhode Island Coll (RI)
Ripon Coll (WI)
Robert Morris U (PA)
Roberts Wesleyan Coll (NY)
Rochester Inst of Technology (NY)
Rockhurst U (MO)
Rocky Mountain Coll (MT)
Rosemont Coll (PA)
Rutgers U–New Brunswick (NJ)
Sacred Heart U (CT)
Saginaw Valley State U (MI)
Saint Anselm Coll (NH)
St. Gregory's U, Shawnee (OK)
St. John's U (NY)
Saint Joseph's U (PA)
Saint Mary's Coll (IN)
Saint Mary's Coll of California (CA)

St. Norbert Coll (WI)
Saint Peter's U (NJ)
Saint Vincent Coll (PA)
Salisbury U (MD)
Samford U (AL)
Sam Houston State U (TX)
San Diego State U (CA)
San Francisco State U (CA)
Santa Clara U (CA)
Schreiner U (TX)
Seattle Pacific U (WA)
Seattle U (WA)
Seton Hill U (PA)
Shenandoah U (VA)
Shepherd U (WV)
Simmons Coll (MA)
Simon Fraser U (BC, Canada)
Simpson U (CA)
Slippery Rock U of Pennsylvania (PA)
Sonoma State U (CA)
South Dakota State U (SD)
Southeastern Louisiana U (LA)
Southeastern Oklahoma State U (OK)
Southeast Missouri State U (MO)
Southern Connecticut State U (CT)
Southern Illinois U Edwardsville (IL)
Southern Oregon U (OR)
Southern Utah U (UT)
Southwest Baptist U (MO)
Southwestern Assemblies of God U (TX)
Southwestern Coll (KS)
Southwestern U (TX)
Spalding U (KY)
State U of New York at New Paltz (NY)
State U of New York at Plattsburgh (NY)
State U of New York Coll at Cortland (NY)
State U of New York Coll at Old Westbury (NY)
State U of New York Coll at Potsdam (NY)
Stockton U (NJ)
Stonehill Coll (MA)
Suffolk U (MA)
Susquehanna U (PA)
Syracuse U (NY)
Tabor Coll (KS)
Tarleton State U (TX)
Taylor U (IN)
Texas Christian U (TX)
Texas Lutheran U (TX)
Thomas U (GA)
Tiffin U (OH)
Trevecca Nazarene U (TN)
Trine U (IN)
Trinity Christian Coll (IL)
Trinity U (TX)
Troy U (AL)
Truman State U (MO)
U at Albany, State U of New York (NY)
U at Buffalo, the State U of New York (NY)
The U of Akron (OH)
The U of Alabama (AL)
The U of Alabama at Birmingham (AL)
The U of Alabama in Huntsville (AL)
U of Alaska Fairbanks (AK)
The U of Arizona (AZ)
U of Arkansas (AR)
U of California, Davis (CA)
U of Central Florida (FL)
U of Cincinnati (OH)
U of Colorado Boulder (CO)
U of Colorado Denver (CO)
U of Dayton (OH)
U of Delaware (DE)
U of Denver (CO)
U of Detroit Mercy (MI)
U of Georgia (GA)
U of Hartford (CT)
U of Hawaii at Manoa (HI)
U of Houston (TX)
U of Illinois at Chicago (IL)
U of Indianapolis (IN)
U of Jamestown (ND)
The U of Kansas (KS)
U of Kentucky (KY)
U of La Verne (CA)
U of Louisville (KY)
U of Mary Hardin-Baylor (TX)
U of Maryland, Coll Park (MD)
U of Maryland U Coll (MD)
U of Miami (FL)
U of Michigan (MI)
U of Michigan–Dearborn (MI)
U of Minnesota, Duluth (MN)
U of Missouri–St. Louis (MO)
U of Nevada, Las Vegas (NV)
U of Nevada, Reno (NV)
U of New Hampshire (NH)
U of New Haven (CT)
U of North Alabama (AL)
The U of North Carolina at Chapel Hill (NC)
The U of North Carolina at Charlotte (NC)
The U of North Carolina at Greensboro (NC)
The U of North Carolina Wilmington (NC)
U of Northern Colorado (CO)
U of Northern Iowa (IA)
U of Oklahoma (OK)
U of Pennsylvania (PA)
U of Pikeville (KY)
U of Puget Sound (WA)
U of Rhode Island (RI)
U of St. Thomas (TX)
U of San Francisco (CA)
U of Science and Arts of Oklahoma (OK)
The U of Scranton (PA)
U of South Alabama (AL)
U of South Carolina Aiken (SC)
U of Southern California (CA)
U of Southern Maine (ME)
U of Southern Mississippi (MS)
U of South Florida (FL)
The U of Tennessee (TN)
The U of Tennessee at Chattanooga (TN)
The U of Texas at Austin (TX)
The U of Texas Rio Grande Valley (TX)
U of the Cumberlands (KY)
U of the Incarnate Word (TX)
U of the Pacific (CA)
U of the Virgin Islands (VI)
The U of Toledo (OH)
The U of Tulsa (OK)
The U of Virginia's Coll at Wise (VA)
U of Washington (WA)
U of Waterloo (ON, Canada)
U of Wisconsin–La Crosse (WI)
U of Wisconsin–Madison (WI)
U of Wisconsin–Milwaukee (WI)
U of Wisconsin–Platteville (WI)
U of Wisconsin–Stevens Point (WI)
U of Wisconsin–Whitewater (WI)
Utica Coll (NY)
Valdosta State U (GA)
Valparaiso U (IN)
Vanderbilt U (TN)
Virginia Polytechnic Inst and State U (VA)
Wake Forest U (NC)
Waldorf U (IA)
Wartburg Coll (IA)
Washburn U (KS)
Washington U in St. Louis (MO)
Wayland Baptist U (TX)
Waynesburg U (PA)
Wayne State Coll (NE)
Wayne State U (MI)
Webber Intl U (FL)
Weber State U (UT)
Webster U (MO)
Western Carolina U (NC)
Western Connecticut State U (CT)
Western Illinois U (IL)
Western Kentucky U (KY)
Western Michigan U (MI)
Western New England U (MA)
Westfield State U (MA)
Westminster Coll (UT)
Westmont Coll (CA)
West Texas A&M U (TX)
West Virginia State U (WV)
West Virginia Wesleyan Coll (WV)
Wheaton Coll (IL)
Whitman Coll (WA)
Whitworth U (WA)
Wichita State U (KS)
Wilkes U (PA)
Willamette U (OR)
William Jewell Coll (MO)
William Paterson U of New Jersey (NJ)
William Peace U (NC)
William Woods U (MO)
Wingate U (NC)
Winona State U (MN)
Wittenberg U (OH)
Woodbury U (CA)
Worcester State U (MA)
Wright State U (OH)
Wright State U–Lake Campus (OH)
York Coll of Pennsylvania (PA)
Youngstown State U (OH)

SPEECH-LANGUAGE PATHOLOGY

Abilene Christian U (TX)
Biola U (CA)
Brooklyn Coll of the City U of New York (NY)
Clarion U of Pennsylvania (PA)
Cleveland State U (OH)
Duquesne U (PA)
Eastern Michigan U (MI)
Eastern Washington U (WA)
East Stroudsburg U of Pennsylvania (PA)
Emerson Coll (MA)
Geneva Coll (PA)
Harding U (AR)
Inter American U of Puerto Rico, Aguadilla Campus (PR)
Inter American U of Puerto Rico, Fajardo Campus (PR)
Inter American U of Puerto Rico, Ponce Campus (PR)
Jackson State U (MS)
James Madison U (VA)
Lehman Coll of the City U of New York (NY)
Loyola U Maryland (MD)
Marshall U (WV)
Marymount Manhattan Coll (NY)
Maryville U of Saint Louis (MO)
Minnesota State U Moorhead (MN)
Molloy Coll (NY)
Nazareth Coll of Rochester (NY)
Nevada State Coll (NV)
Northwestern U (IL)
Nova Southeastern U (FL)
Oklahoma State U (OK)
Rockhurst U (MO)
St. Cloud State U (MN)
San Diego State U (CA)
Texas Christian U (TX)
Trinity Christian Coll (IL)
U of Central Missouri (MO)
U of Montevallo (AL)
U of Nevada, Reno (NV)
U of Northern Iowa (IA)
U of Oklahoma Health Sciences Center (OK)
U of Science and Arts of Oklahoma (OK)
The U of Toledo (OH)
U of West Georgia (GA)
Valdosta State U (GA)
Xavier U of Louisiana (LA)

SPEECH-LANGUAGE PATHOLOGY ASSISTANT

Caribbean U (PR)

SPEECH TEACHER EDUCATION

Albion Coll (MI)
Anderson U (IN)
Arkansas Tech U (AR)
Augustana U (SD)
Austin Coll (TX)
Bemidji State U (MN)
Boise State U (ID)
Bowling Green State U (OH)
Brigham Young U (UT)
Brooklyn Coll of the City U of New York (NY)
Buena Vista U (IA)
Capital U (OH)
Carroll Coll (MT)
Central Michigan U (MI)
Colorado State U (CO)
Cornerstone U (MI)
Culver-Stockton Coll (MO)
Dallas Baptist U (TX)
East Texas Baptist U (TX)
Evangel U (MO)
Friends U (KS)
Harding U (AR)
Hardin-Simmons U (TX)
Houston Baptist U (TX)
Howard Payne U (TX)
Kansas Wesleyan U (KS)
Lee U (TN)
Louisiana Tech U (LA)
Northwestern Coll (IA)
Northwest U (WA)
Oklahoma City U (OK)
Saginaw Valley State U (MI)
St. Ambrose U (IA)
St. Catherine U (MN)
St. Cloud State U (MN)
Southwest Baptist U (MO)
Southwestern Coll (KS)
Trevecca Nazarene U (TN)
U of Indianapolis (IN)
U of Mary Hardin-Baylor (TX)
U of Michigan–Flint (MI)
The U of North Carolina at Greensboro (NC)
The U of South Dakota (SD)
U of the Cumberlands (KY)
U of Windsor (ON, Canada)
Wartburg Coll (IA)
Wayne State Coll (NE)
William Jewell Coll (MO)

SPORT AND FITNESS ADMINISTRATION/ MANAGEMENT

Abilene Christian U (TX)
Adelphi U (NY)
Albertus Magnus Coll (CT)
Alcorn State U (MS)
Alderson Broaddus U (WV)
Alice Lloyd Coll (KY)
Alvernia U (PA)
American Intl Coll (MA)
American Public U System (WV)
Anderson U (IN)
Arcadia U (PA)
Arizona State U at the Downtown Phoenix campus (AZ)
Asbury U (KY)
Athens State U (AL)
Augustana U (SD)
Aurora U (IL)
Averett U (VA)
Baker U (KS)
Baldwin Wallace U (OH)
Ball State U (IN)
Barclay Coll (KS)
Barry U (FL)
Barton Coll (NC)
Becker Coll (MA)
Belhaven U (MS)
Bellarmine U (KY)
Belmont Abbey Coll (NC)
Belmont U (TN)
Bemidji State U (MN)
Berry Coll (GA)
Bethel Coll (IN)
Blackburn Coll (IL)
Black Hills State U (SD)
Bluffton U (OH)
Bowling Green State U (OH)
Brenau U (GA)
Bridgewater State U (MA)
Buena Vista U (IA)
Caldwell U (NJ)
California U of Pennsylvania (PA)
Calvin Coll (MI)
Canisius Coll (NY)
Cardinal Stritch U (WI)
Carthage Coll (WI)
Catawba Coll (NC)
Cazenovia Coll (NY)
Cedarville U (OH)
Centenary U (NJ)
Central Methodist U (MO)
Central Michigan U (MI)
Chowan U (NC)
The Citadel, The Military Coll of South Carolina (SC)
Clarke U (IA)
Clayton State U (GA)
Cleveland State U (OH)
Coastal Carolina U (SC)
Colby-Sawyer Coll (NH)
The Coll at Brockport, State U of New York (NY)
The Coll of Idaho (ID)
Colorado Mesa U (CO)
Columbia Coll (MO)
Columbia Coll Chicago (IL)
Concordia Coll–New York (NY)
Concordia U Chicago (IL)
Concordia U, St. Paul (MN)
Concordia U Wisconsin (WI)
Corban U (OR)
Cornerstone U (MI)
Culver-Stockton Coll (MO)
Dallas Baptist U (TX)
Davenport U, Grand Rapids (MI)
Dean Coll (MA)
Defiance Coll (OH)
DEREE - The American Coll of Greece (Greece)
DeSales U (PA)
Drexel U (PA)
Eastern Mennonite U (VA)
Eastern Michigan U (MI)
Eastern Nazarene Coll (MA)
East Stroudsburg U of Pennsylvania (PA)
East Tennessee State U (TN)
East Texas Baptist U (TX)
Ecclesia Coll (AR)
Elms Coll (MA)
Elon U (NC)
Emmanuel Coll (GA)
Emmanuel Coll (MA)
Emory & Henry Coll (VA)
Endicott Coll (MA)
Farmingdale State Coll (NY)
Faulkner U (AL)
Fisher Coll (MA)
Fitchburg State U (MA)
Flagler Coll (FL)
Florida Inst of Technology (FL)
Florida Southern Coll (FL)
Fort Lewis Coll (CO)
Franklin Pierce U (NH)
Fresno Pacific U (CA)
Friends U (KS)
Gannon U (PA)
Gardner-Webb U (NC)
Geneva Coll (PA)
Georgetown Coll (KY)
Georgia Southern U (GA)
Gonzaga U (WA)
Grace Coll (IN)
Grand View U (IA)
Greenville Coll (IL)
Guilford Coll (NC)
Hamline U (MN)
Hampton U (VA)
Harding U (AR)
Hardin-Simmons U (TX)
Hilbert Coll (NY)
Hillsdale Coll (MI)
Holy Family U (PA)
Houston Baptist U (TX)
Howard Payne U (TX)
Huntingdon Coll (AL)
Huntington U (IN)
Husson U (ME)
Inter American U of Puerto Rico, Metropolitan Campus (PR)
Ithaca Coll (NY)
Jacksonville State U (AL)
Jacksonville U (FL)
Johnson C. Smith U (NC)
Judson U (IL)
Kansas Wesleyan U (KS)
Kennesaw State U (GA)
Kent State U (OH)
Kentucky Wesleyan Coll (KY)
King U (TN)
Lake Erie Coll (OH)
Lamar U (TX)
Lasell Coll (MA)
Lees-McRae Coll (NC)
Lee U (TN)
Lenoir-Rhyne U (NC)
LeTourneau U (TX)
Lewis U (IL)
Liberty U (VA)
Limestone Coll (SC)
Lincoln Coll (IL)
Lincoln Coll–Normal (IL)
Lindenwood U (MO)
Lipscomb U (TN)
Lock Haven U of Pennsylvania (PA)
Loras Coll (IA)
Louisiana State U and A&M Coll (LA)
Lubbock Christian U (TX)
Lynchburg Coll (VA)
Lynn U (FL)
MacMurray Coll (IL)

Madonna U (MI)
Malone U (OH)
Manchester U (IN)
Maranatha Baptist U (WI)
Marian U (IN)
Marian U (WI)
Marietta Coll (OH)
Maryville U of Saint Louis (MO)
McKendree U (IL)
Menlo Coll (CA)
Merrimack Coll (MA)
Messiah Coll (PA)
Miami U (OH)
Michigan Technological U (MI)
MidAmerica Nazarene U (KS)
Millikin U (IL)
Minnesota State U Mankato (MN)
Minot State U (ND)
Misericordia U (PA)
Mississippi Valley State U (MS)
Missouri Baptist U (MO)
Missouri Valley Coll (MO)
Montana State U (MT)
Montana State U Billings (MT)
Morehead State U (KY)
Mount Ida Coll (MA)
Mount St. Joseph U (OH)
Mount St. Mary's U (MD)
Mount Vernon Nazarene U (OH)
Muskingum U (OH)
Nebraska Wesleyan U (NE)
Neumann U (PA)
Newberry Coll (SC)
New England Coll (NH)
Niagara U (NY)
Nichols Coll (MA)
North Carolina State U (NC)
North Central Coll (IL)
North Dakota State U (ND)
Northern Kentucky U (KY)
Northern State U (SD)
North Greenville U (SC)
Northwestern Coll (IA)
Northwood U, Michigan Campus (MI)
Nova Southeastern U (FL)
Ohio Dominican U (OH)
The Ohio State U (OH)
Oklahoma Baptist U (OK)
Oklahoma Christian U (OK)
Olivet Nazarene U (IL)
Otterbein U (OH)
Pennsylvania Coll of Technology (PA)
Pepperdine U, Malibu (CA)
Piedmont Coll (GA)
Plymouth State U (NH)
Rice U (TX)
Roanoke Coll (VA)
Robert Morris U (PA)
Rockford U (IL)
Rockhurst U (MO)
Rocky Mountain Coll (MT)
Rogers State U (OK)
Saginaw Valley State U (MI)
St. Ambrose U (IA)
St. Bonaventure U (NY)
St. John Fisher Coll (NY)
St. John's U (NY)
Saint Leo U (FL)
Saint Louis U (MO)
Saint Louis U–Madrid Campus (Spain)
Saint Mary's Coll of California (CA)
St. Thomas Aquinas Coll (NY)
St. Thomas U (FL)
Samford U (AL)
Schreiner U (TX)
Seattle Pacific U (WA)
Seton Hill U (PA)
Shawnee State U (OH)
Shenandoah U (VA)
Simpson Coll (IA)
Southeastern Louisiana U (LA)
Southeastern U (FL)
Southeast Missouri State U (MO)
Southern Illinois U Carbondale (IL)
Southern Methodist U (TX)
Southern New Hampshire U (NH)
Southwest Baptist U (MO)
Southwestern Adventist U (TX)
Southwestern Assemblies of God U (TX)
Southwestern Coll (KS)
State U of New York at Oswego (NY)
Syracuse U (NY)
Taylor U (IN)
Temple U (PA)
Tennessee Wesleyan U (TN)
Texas A&M U (TX)
Texas A&M U–Commerce (TX)
Texas Lutheran U (TX)
Texas State U (TX)
Texas Tech U (TX)
Thomas More Coll (KY)
Tiffin U (OH)
Toccoa Falls Coll (GA)
Towson U (MD)
Trevecca Nazarene U (TN)
Trine U (IN)
Troy U (AL)
Tusculum Coll (TN)
Union Coll (KY)
Union Coll (NE)
Union U (TN)
United States Sports Acad (AL)
The U of Akron (OH)
U of Charleston (WV)
U of Cincinnati (OH)
U of Dayton (OH)
U of Delaware (DE)
U of Dubuque (IA)
The U of Findlay (OH)
U of Florida (FL)
U of Georgia (GA)
U of Houston (TX)
U of Indianapolis (IN)
U of Jamestown (ND)
The U of Kansas (KS)
U of Louisville (KY)
U of Mary Hardin-Baylor (TX)
U of Massachusetts Amherst (MA)
U of Miami (FL)
U of Michigan (MI)
U of Minnesota, Crookston (MN)
U of Minnesota, Twin Cities Campus (MN)
U of Mount Union (OH)
U of Nebraska at Kearney (NE)
U of Nevada, Las Vegas (NV)
U of New Haven (CT)
U of North Florida (FL)
U of Pittsburgh at Bradford (PA)
U of Regina (SK, Canada)
U of Saint Mary (KS)
U of South Carolina (SC)
U of Southern Indiana (IN)
U of Southern Mississippi (MS)
The U of Tampa (FL)
The U of Tennessee (TN)
The U of Texas at Austin (TX)
U of the Cumberlands (KY)
U of the Incarnate Word (TX)
The U of Tulsa (OK)
U of Valley Forge (PA)
U of Windsor (ON, Canada)
U of Wisconsin–Parkside (WI)
Valparaiso U (IN)
Viterbo U (WI)
Waldorf U (IA)
Walla Walla U (WA)
Wartburg Coll (IA)
Washington State U (WA)
Wayland Baptist U (TX)
Wayne State Coll (NE)
Webber Intl U (FL)
Western Carolina U (NC)
Western Michigan U (MI)
Western New England U (MA)
Western State Colorado U (CO)
Westminster Coll (PA)
West Virginia Wesleyan Coll (WV)
Wichita State U (KS)
Widener U (PA)
William Paterson U of New Jersey (NJ)
William Penn U (IA)
William Woods U (MO)
Wilmington U (DE)
Wingate U (NC)
Winthrop U (SC)
Wittenberg U (OH)
York Coll of Pennsylvania (PA)

SPORTS COMMUNICATION
Arizona State U at the Downtown Phoenix campus (AZ)
Ashland U (OH)
Belhaven U (MS)
Bluffton U (OH)
Bradley U (IL)
Butler U (IN)
Clemson U (SC)
Cornerstone U (MI)
Culver-Stockton Coll (MO)
Ferris State U (MI)
Florida Southern Coll (FL)
Grace Coll (IN)
Grand View U (IA)
LeTourneau U (TX)
Louisiana Coll (LA)
Oklahoma State U (OK)
U of Evansville (IN)
Youngstown State U (OH)

SPORTS STUDIES
Bethel Coll (IN)
Bryant U (RI)
Canisius Coll (NY)
Central Michigan U (MI)
Concordia U, St. Paul (MN)
Grace Coll (IN)
Hillsdale Coll (MI)
Huntington U (IN)
Inter American U of Puerto Rico, San Germán Campus (PR)
Lubbock Christian U (TX)
Manhattanville Coll (NY)
National U (CA)
St. Bonaventure U (NY)
Southwestern Coll (KS)
Texas Christian U (TX)
United States Sports Acad (AL)
U of Dubuque (IA)
Western Kentucky U (KY)

STATISTICS
American U (DC)
American U of Beirut (Lebanon)
Amherst Coll (MA)
Arizona State U at the West campus (AZ)
Barnard Coll (NY)
Baruch Coll of the City U of New York (NY)
Baylor U (TX)
Bowling Green State U (OH)
Bryant U (RI)
California Baptist U (CA)
California Polytechnic State U, San Luis Obispo (CA)
California State U, East Bay (CA)
California State U, Fullerton (CA)
California State U, Long Beach (CA)
Carnegie Mellon U (PA)
Case Western Reserve U (OH)
Central Michigan U (MI)
Colorado School of Mines (CO)
Colorado State U (CO)
Columbia U (NY)
Columbia U, School of General Studies (NY)
Concordia U (QC, Canada)
Cornell U (NY)
Dalhousie U (NS, Canada)
Eastern Michigan U (MI)
Elon U (NC)
Emory U (GA)
Florida Intl U (FL)
Florida State U (FL)
The George Washington U (DC)
Grand Valley State U (MI)
Harvard U (MA)
Hunter Coll of the City U of New York (NY)
Idaho State U (ID)
Indiana U Bloomington (IN)
Iowa State U of Science and Technology (IA)
Jackson State U (MS)
Kansas State U (KS)
Lehigh U (PA)
LeTourneau U (TX)
Loyola U Chicago (IL)
Loyola U Maryland (MD)
McMaster U (ON, Canada)
Miami U (OH)
Michigan State U (MI)
Michigan Technological U (MI)
Misericordia U (PA)
Montana State U (MT)
Montana Tech of The U of Montana (MT)
Mount Holyoke Coll (MA)
North Carolina State U (NC)
North Dakota State U (ND)
Northern Kentucky U (KY)
Northwestern U (IL)
Ohio Wesleyan U (OH)
Oklahoma State U (OK)
Penn State Abington (PA)
Penn State Altoona (PA)
Penn State Beaver (PA)
Penn State Berks (PA)
Penn State Brandywine (PA)
Penn State DuBois (PA)
Penn State Erie, The Behrend Coll (PA)
Penn State Fayette, The Eberly Campus (PA)
Penn State Greater Allegheny (PA)
Penn State Hazleton (PA)
Penn State Lehigh Valley (PA)
Penn State Mont Alto (PA)
Penn State New Kensington (PA)
Penn State Schuylkill (PA)
Penn State Shenango (PA)
Penn State U Park (PA)
Penn State Wilkes-Barre (PA)
Penn State Worthington Scranton (PA)
Penn State York (PA)
Reed Coll (OR)
Rice U (TX)
Rochester Inst of Technology (NY)
Rutgers U–New Brunswick (NJ)
St. Cloud State U (MN)
St. John Fisher Coll (NY)
San Diego State U (CA)
San Francisco State U (CA)
Simon Fraser U (BC, Canada)
Sonoma State U (CA)
Southern Methodist U (TX)
Université de Montréal (QC, Canada)
U at Buffalo, the State U of New York (NY)
The U of Akron (OH)
U of California, Davis (CA)
U of California, Los Angeles (CA)
U of California, Riverside (CA)
U of California, Santa Barbara (CA)
U of Central Florida (FL)
U of Chicago (IL)
U of Delaware (DE)
U of Florida (FL)
U of Georgia (GA)
U of Illinois at Chicago (IL)
U of King's Coll (NS, Canada)
U of Maryland, Baltimore County (MD)
U of Michigan (MI)
U of Michigan–Dearborn (MI)
U of Minnesota, Duluth (MN)
U of Minnesota, Morris (MN)
U of Minnesota, Twin Cities Campus (MN)
The U of North Carolina Wilmington (NC)
U of North Florida (FL)
U of Pennsylvania (PA)
U of Pittsburgh (PA)
U of Regina (SK, Canada)
U of Rochester (NY)
U of St. Thomas (MN)
U of Saskatchewan (SK, Canada)
U of South Carolina (SC)
U of South Florida (FL)
The U of Tennessee (TN)
The U of Tennessee at Martin (TN)
The U of Texas at Austin (TX)
The U of Texas at El Paso (TX)
The U of Texas at San Antonio (TX)
U of Vermont (VT)
U of Washington (WA)
U of Waterloo (ON, Canada)
U of Wisconsin–Madison (WI)
Utah State U (UT)
Valparaiso U (IN)
Virginia Polytechnic Inst and State U (VA)
Washington U in St. Louis (MO)
Western Michigan U (MI)
Williams Coll (MA)
Winona State U (MN)
Wright State U (OH)
Wright State U–Lake Campus (OH)
Xavier U of Louisiana (LA)

STATISTICS RELATED
California Baptist U (CA)
Saint Mary's Coll (IN)
U of Evansville (IN)
U of New Hampshire (NH)
U of Northern Iowa (IA)

STRATEGIC INTELLIGENCE
Florida Inst of Technology (FL)
Patrick Henry Coll (VA)

STRINGED INSTRUMENTS
Boston U (MA)
Brigham Young U (UT)
Carnegie Mellon U (PA)
Central Washington U (WA)
Converse Coll (SC)
Eastern Nazarene Coll (MA)
Hardin-Simmons U (TX)
Heidelberg U (OH)
Hope Coll (MI)
Houghton Coll (NY)
Lawrence U (WI)
Liberty U (VA)
Mount Allison U (NB, Canada)
The New School Coll of Performing Arts (NY)
Northwestern U (IL)
Oberlin Coll (OH)
Oklahoma City U (OK)
St. Cloud State U (MN)
San Francisco Conservatory of Music (CA)
Seattle U (WA)
State U of New York at Fredonia (NY)
Syracuse U (NY)
Texas Christian U (TX)
The U of Akron (OH)
The U of Kansas (KS)
U of Southern California (CA)
U of Washington (WA)
Vanderbilt U (TN)
Willamette U (OR)
Xavier U of Louisiana (LA)
Youngstown State U (OH)

STRUCTURAL ENGINEERING
Penn State Harrisburg (PA)
U of California, San Diego (CA)
U of Central Florida (FL)
U of Southern California (CA)
Western Michigan U (MI)

SUBSTANCE ABUSE/ ADDICTION COUNSELING
Alvernia U (PA)
Bay Path U (MA)
City Vision U (MO)
Drexel U (PA)
Kansas Wesleyan U (KS)
Keene State Coll (NH)
Minot State U (ND)
Newman U (KS)
Northwestern State U of Louisiana (LA)
Ohio Christian U (OH)
St. Cloud State U (MN)
Tiffin U (OH)
Union Coll (KY)
U of Central Arkansas (AR)
U of Cincinnati (OH)
U of Detroit Mercy (MI)
U of Great Falls (MT)
U of Lethbridge (AB, Canada)
U of St. Francis (IL)
The U of South Dakota (SD)
Viterbo U (WI)
Washburn U (KS)

SURGICAL TECHNOLOGY
Weber State U (UT)

SURVEYING ENGINEERING
Ferris State U (MI)
Florida Atlantic U (FL)
Michigan Technological U (MI)

SURVEYING TECHNOLOGY
Bismarck State Coll (ND)
East Tennessee State U (TN)
Ferris State U (MI)
Great Basin Coll (NV)
Idaho State U (ID)
Kennesaw State U (GA)
Metropolitan State U of Denver (CO)
New Mexico State U (NM)
The Ohio State U (OH)
Penn State Wilkes-Barre (PA)
Polytechnic U of Puerto Rico (PR)
South Carolina State U (SC)
State U of New York Coll of Technology at Alfred (NY)
Troy U (AL)
The U of Akron (OH)

U of Florida (FL)
U of Maine (ME)
Utah Valley U (UT)

SUSTAINABILITY STUDIES
Alaska Pacific U (AK)
Albion Coll (MI)
Aquinas Coll (MI)
Aurora U (IL)
Bentley U (MA)
Bryant U (RI)
California Baptist U (CA)
Chatham U (PA)
Columbia U, School of General Studies (NY)
Creighton U (NE)
Daemen Coll (NY)
The Evergreen State Coll (WA)
Florida Inst of Technology (FL)
Furman U (SC)
Goddard Coll (VT)
Goshen Coll (IN)
Harris-Stowe State U (MO)
Hartwick Coll (NY)
Hofstra U (NY)
Jacksonville U (FL)
Kean U (NJ)
Lipscomb U (TN)
Messiah Coll (PA)
Miami U (OH)
Montclair State U (NJ)
Mount Ida Coll (MA)
Oregon State U (OR)
Prescott Coll (AZ)
Rensselaer Polytechnic Inst (NY)
Sewanee: The U of the South (TN)
Sierra Nevada Coll (NV)
Stephen F. Austin State U (TX)
Stockton U (NJ)
Stony Brook U, State U of New York (NY)
Toccoa Falls Coll (GA)
Trent U (ON, Canada)
U of Florida (FL)
U of New Hampshire (NH)
U of New Haven (CT)
U of North Alabama (AL)
U of Northern Colorado (CO)
The U of South Dakota (SD)
The U of Texas at Austin (TX)
U of Wisconsin–Parkside (WI)
U of Wisconsin–Platteville (WI)
U of Wisconsin–Stout (WI)
Viterbo U (WI)
Western Washington U (WA)
Worcester Polytechnic Inst (MA)

SWEDISH
Brigham Young U (UT)
U of Washington (WA)

SYSTEM, NETWORKING, AND LAN/WAN MANAGEMENT
Alcorn State U (MS)
Central Washington U (WA)
Dakota State U (SD)
Hallmark U (TX)
Morrisville State Coll (NY)
Rochester Inst of Technology (NY)
State U of New York Coll of Technology at Alfred (NY)
Texas A&M U (TX)
U of Great Falls (MT)

SYSTEMS ENGINEERING
Case Western Reserve U (OH)
Eastern Nazarene Coll (MA)
Ferris State U (MI)
The George Washington U (DC)
Kennesaw State U (GA)
Massachusetts Maritime Acad (MA)
Otterbein U (OH)
Providence Coll (RI)
Rochester Inst of Technology (NY)
Stanford U (CA)
Stevens Inst of Technology (NJ)
Taylor U (IN)
Texas A&M Intl U (TX)
United States Air Force Acad (CO)
United States Merchant Marine Acad (NY)
United States Military Acad (NY)
The U of Arizona (AZ)
U of Florida (FL)
The U of North Carolina at Charlotte (NC)
U of Pennsylvania (PA)
U of Virginia (VA)
U of Waterloo (ON, Canada)
Washington U in St. Louis (MO)

SYSTEMS SCIENCE AND THEORY
Boston U (MA)
Carnegie Mellon U (PA)
James Madison U (VA)
Marshall U (WV)
Purdue U (IN)
Stanford U (CA)
Syracuse U (NY)
United States Military Acad (NY)
Washington U in St. Louis (MO)

TAXATION
Canisius Coll (NY)
Grand Valley State U (MI)

TEACHER ASSISTANT/AIDE
Blackburn Coll (IL)
East Central U (OK)
Waldorf U (IA)

TECHNICAL AND SCIENTIFIC COMMUNICATION
Indiana U–Purdue U Indianapolis (IN)
Iowa State U of Science and Technology (IA)
Lehigh U (PA)
Michigan Technological U (MI)
Missouri U of Science and Technology (MO)

TECHNICAL TEACHER EDUCATION
Athens State U (AL)
Auburn U (AL)
Bowling Green State U (OH)
Central Washington U (WA)
Eastern Illinois U (IL)
Ferris State U (MI)
Montana State U (MT)
The Ohio State U (OH)
Oklahoma State U (OK)
The U of Akron (OH)
U of Arkansas (AR)
U of Georgia (GA)
U of Idaho (ID)
U of Kentucky (KY)
U of Saskatchewan (SK, Canada)
U of Wisconsin–Stout (WI)
Utah State U (UT)
Valley City State U (ND)
Washington State U (WA)
West Virginia U Inst of Technology (WV)
Wright State U (OH)
Wright State U–Lake Campus (OH)

TECHNOLOGY/INDUSTRIAL ARTS TEACHER EDUCATION
Ball State U (IN)
Bemidji State U (MN)
Berea Coll (KY)
Bowling Green State U (OH)
Buffalo State Coll, State U of New York (NY)
Central Connecticut State U (CT)
The Coll of New Jersey (NJ)
Colorado State U (CO)
Dickinson State U (ND)
Eastern Michigan U (MI)
Fitchburg State U (MA)
Georgia Southern U (GA)
Illinois State U (IL)
Indiana State U (IN)
Jackson State U (MS)
Lindenwood U (MO)
Montana State U–Northern (MT)
New Mexico Highlands U (NM)
New York City Coll of Technology of the City U of New York (NY)
North Carolina State U (NC)
The Ohio State U (OH)
Pittsburg State U (KS)
Purdue U (IN)
Rhode Island Coll (RI)
St. Cloud State U (MN)
St. Petersburg Coll (FL)
South Carolina State U (SC)
Southeast Missouri State U (MO)
Southern Utah U (UT)
State U of New York at Oswego (NY)
Union Coll (NE)
U of Northern Iowa (IA)
U of Wisconsin–Platteville (WI)
U of Wisconsin–Stout (WI)
Utah State U (UT)
Valley City State U (ND)
Viterbo U (WI)
Wayland Baptist U (TX)
Wayne State Coll (NE)
Western Michigan U (MI)
Westfield State U (MA)

TELECOMMUNICATIONS MANAGEMENT
St. Thomas U (FL)

TELECOMMUNICATIONS TECHNOLOGY
California State U, East Bay (CA)
Canisius Coll (NY)
Farmingdale State Coll (NY)
Ferris State U (MI)
Kennesaw State U (GA)
Lawrence Technological U (MI)
New York City Coll of Technology of the City U of New York (NY)
Pace U (NY)
Pace U, Pleasantville Campus (NY)
Rochester Inst of Technology (NY)
St. John's U (NY)

TEXTILE SCIENCE
Michigan State U (MI)
U of Georgia (GA)

TEXTILE SCIENCES AND ENGINEERING
Auburn U (AL)
North Carolina State U (NC)

THEATER DESIGN AND TECHNOLOGY
Ashland U (OH)
Baldwin Wallace U (OH)
Baylor U (TX)
Belmont U (TN)
Bennington Coll (VT)
Binghamton U, State U of New York (NY)
Biola U (CA)
Boston U (MA)
Brigham Young U (UT)
Centenary U (NJ)
Central Washington U (WA)
Coe Coll (IA)
Columbia Coll Chicago (IL)
Concordia U (QC, Canada)
Dixie State U (UT)
Doane U (NE)
Elon U (NC)
Emerson Coll (MA)
Fitchburg State U (MA)
Florida Southern Coll (FL)
Freed-Hardeman U (TN)
Gannon U (PA)
Huntington U (IN)
Husson U (ME)
Illinois Wesleyan U (IL)
Ithaca Coll (NY)
Kean U (NJ)
Keene State Coll (NH)
Lindenwood U (MO)
Lipscomb U (TN)
Marymount Manhattan Coll (NY)
Michigan Technological U (MI)
Millikin U (IL)
Nazareth Coll of Rochester (NY)
New York City Coll of Technology of the City U of New York (NY)
North Central Coll (IL)
Oklahoma City U (OK)
Oral Roberts U (OK)
Penn State Abington (PA)
Penn State Altoona (PA)
Penn State Beaver (PA)
Penn State Berks (PA)
Penn State Brandywine (PA)
Penn State DuBois (PA)
Penn State Erie, The Behrend Coll (PA)
Penn State Fayette, The Eberly Campus (PA)
Penn State Greater Allegheny (PA)
Penn State Hazleton (PA)
Penn State Lehigh Valley (PA)
Penn State Mont Alto (PA)
Penn State New Kensington (PA)
Penn State Schuylkill (PA)
Penn State Shenango (PA)
Penn State U Park (PA)
Penn State Wilkes-Barre (PA)
Penn State Worthington Scranton (PA)
Penn State York (PA)
Pepperdine U, Malibu (CA)
Piedmont Coll (GA)
Purchase Coll, State U of New York (NY)
Rhode Island Coll (RI)
Rocky Mountain Coll (MT)
Savannah Coll of Art and Design (GA)
Seton Hill U (PA)
Shenandoah U (VA)
Southwestern Coll (KS)
Stephens Coll (MO)
Syracuse U (NY)
Texas Christian U (TX)
Trinity U (TX)
U of Alaska Fairbanks (AK)
The U of Arizona (AZ)
U of Cincinnati (OH)
The U of Kansas (KS)
U of Lethbridge (AB, Canada)
U of Miami (FL)
U of Michigan (MI)
U of Michigan–Flint (MI)
U of Nevada, Las Vegas (NV)
U of North Carolina School of the Arts (NC)
U of Northern Iowa (IA)
U of North Georgia (GA)
U of Regina (SK, Canada)
U of Southern California (CA)
The U of the Arts (PA)
Western Michigan U (MI)
Western State Colorado U (CO)
Wright State U (OH)
Wright State U–Lake Campus (OH)

THEATER LITERATURE, HISTORY AND CRITICISM
Albertus Magnus Coll (CT)
The American U in Cairo (Egypt)
Averett U (VA)
Bennington Coll (VT)
Bowdoin Coll (ME)
Buena Vista U (IA)
Clark Atlanta U (GA)
Dalhousie U (NS, Canada)
Hiram Coll (OH)
Marymount Manhattan Coll (NY)
Northwestern U (IL)
Saint Mary's Coll of California (CA)
Suffolk U (MA)
Tufts U (MA)
U of Washington (WA)
Washington U in St. Louis (MO)
Western Michigan U (MI)
West Virginia U (WV)

THEATER/THEATER ARTS MANAGEMENT
Berry Coll (GA)
Biola U (CA)
Brooklyn Coll of the City U of New York (NY)
Canisius Coll (NY)
Catawba Coll (NC)
Centenary U (NJ)
Columbia Coll Chicago (IL)
DEREE - The American Coll of Greece (Greece)
Graceland U (IA)
Marymount Manhattan Coll (NY)
Massachusetts Coll of Liberal Arts (MA)
Messiah Coll (PA)
Michigan State U (MI)
MidAmerica Nazarene U (KS)
Nazareth Coll of Rochester (NY)
Ohio U (OH)
Oklahoma City U (OK)
Pace U (NY)
Quinnipiac U (CT)
Regent U (VA)
Rockford U (IL)
St. Cloud State U (MN)
Saint Louis U (MO)
Seton Hill U (PA)
Texas Wesleyan U (TX)
U of Evansville (IN)
U of Miami (FL)
U of New Haven (CT)
U of Regina (SK, Canada)
William Peace U (NC)

THEOLOGICAL AND MINISTERIAL STUDIES RELATED
California Christian Coll (CA)
Concordia U (QC, Canada)
Concordia U, St. Paul (MN)
Cornerstone U (MI)
Hardin-Simmons U (TX)
Hope Intl U (CA)
Howard Payne U (TX)
Huntington U (IN)
Lincoln Christian U (IL)
Lubbock Christian U (TX)
Malone U (OH)
Messenger Coll (TX)
Providence Coll (RI)
Saint Mary-of-the-Woods Coll (IN)
Trinity Coll of Florida (FL)
Union Coll (NE)
Williamson Coll (TN)

THEOLOGY
Ambrose U (AB, Canada)
Anderson U (IN)
Anderson U (SC)
Andrews U (MI)
Aquinas Coll (TN)
Assumption Coll (MA)
Azusa Pacific U (CA)
Bard Coll (NY)
Barry U (FL)
Bellarmine U (KY)
Belmont Abbey Coll (NC)
Benedictine Coll (KS)
Bethel Coll (IN)
Biola U (CA)
Bluefield Coll (VA)
Boston Coll (MA)
Brescia U (KY)
Brewton-Parker Coll (GA)
Briar Cliff U (IA)
Caldwell U (NJ)
Calvary U (MO)
Calvin Coll (MI)
Carlow U (PA)
Carroll Coll (MT)
Christendom Coll (VA)
Coll of Saint Benedict (MN)
Coll of Saint Elizabeth (NJ)
Coll of Saint Mary (NE)
Colorado Christian U (CO)
Concordia U (QC, Canada)
Concordia U Chicago (IL)
Concordia U Irvine (CA)
Concordia U, Nebraska (NE)
Concordia U, St. Paul (MN)
Concordia U Wisconsin (WI)
Corban U (OR)
Creighton U (NE)
DeSales U (PA)
Dominican U (IL)
Duquesne U (PA)
Eastern Mennonite U (VA)
Eastern Nazarene Coll (MA)
Eastern U (PA)
Fordham U (NY)
Franciscan U of Steubenville (OH)
Gannon U (PA)
Georgetown U (DC)
Global U (MO)
Hanover Coll (IN)
Hardin-Simmons U (TX)
Holy Cross Coll (IN)
Holy Trinity Orthodox Sem (NY)
Houghton Coll (NY)
Houston Baptist U (TX)
Howard Payne U (TX)
Huntington U (IN)
Immaculata U (PA)
Johnson U (TN)
Johnson U Florida (FL)
John Wesley U (NC)
Kentucky Mountain Bible Coll (KY)
King's Coll (PA)
The King's U (AB, Canada)
Kuyper Coll (MI)
Lee U (TN)
LeTourneau U (TX)
Liberty U (VA)
Louisiana Coll (LA)
Loyola Marymount U (CA)
Loyola U Chicago (IL)
Marian U (IN)
Marian U (WI)
Martin Luther Coll (MN)
Master's Coll and Sem (ON, Canada)
The Master's U (CA)

MidAmerica Nazarene U (KS)
Morris Coll (SC)
Mount Mary U (WI)
Mount St. Mary's U (MD)
Mount Vernon Nazarene U (OH)
Multnomah U (OR)
Newman U (KS)
Ohio Dominican U (OH)
Olivet Nazarene U (IL)
Oral Roberts U (OK)
Ouachita Baptist U (AR)
Pacific Lutheran U (WA)
Palm Beach Atlantic U (FL)
Piedmont Intl U (NC)
Point Loma Nazarene U (CA)
Providence Coll (RI)
Redeemer U Coll (ON, Canada)
Rockhurst U (MO)
St. Ambrose U (IA)
Saint Anselm Coll (NH)
St. Bonaventure U (NY)
St. Catherine U (MN)
St. Edward's U (TX)
St. Gregory's U, Shawnee (OK)
Saint John's U (MN)
St. John's U (NY)
Saint Louis Christian Coll (MO)
Saint Louis U (MO)
Saint Louis U–Madrid Campus (Spain)
Saint Mary's Coll of California (CA)
Saint Mary's U of Minnesota (MN)
Saint Peter's U (NJ)
St. Thomas U (FL)
Saint Vincent Coll (PA)
Seattle Pacific U (WA)
Silver Lake Coll of the Holy Family (WI)
Southwest Baptist U (MO)
Southwestern Adventist U (TX)
Southwestern Assemblies of God U (TX)
Texas Lutheran U (TX)
Trinity Christian Coll (IL)
Trinity Coll of Florida (FL)
Union Coll (NE)
Union U (TN)
Universidad Adventista de las Antillas (PR)
Université de Montréal (QC, Canada)
U of Chicago (IL)
U of Great Falls (MT)
U of Notre Dame (IN)
U of St. Francis (IL)
U of Saint Francis (IN)
U of Saint Mary (KS)
U of St. Thomas (TX)
U of San Francisco (CA)
U of the Southwest (NM)
U of Valley Forge (PA)
Valparaiso U (IN)
Walla Walla U (WA)
Walsh U (OH)
Wheeling Jesuit U (WV)
Whitworth U (WA)
Williams Baptist Coll (AR)
Xavier U of Louisiana (LA)

THEOLOGY AND RELIGIOUS VOCATIONS RELATED
Abilene Christian U (TX)
Arlington Baptist Coll (TX)
Belmont U (TN)
Cedarville U (OH)
Concordia Coll–New York (NY)
Dallas Baptist U (TX)
Eastern Nazarene Coll (MA)
Ecclesia Coll (AR)
Hobe Sound Bible Coll (FL)
Kentucky Mountain Bible Coll (KY)
Lee U (TN)
LeTourneau U (TX)
Master's Coll and Sem (ON, Canada)
Missouri Baptist U (MO)
Newman U (KS)
Northwest U (WA)
Ouachita Baptist U (AR)
Simpson U (CA)
Southeastern U (FL)
Trevecca Nazarene U (TN)
Trinity Christian Coll (IL)
Union U (TN)
U of St. Thomas (TX)
U of Valley Forge (PA)
Williamson Coll (TN)

THEORETICAL AND MATHEMATICAL PHYSICS
Carnegie Mellon U (PA)
Chapman U (CA)
U at Buffalo, the State U of New York (NY)
U of Guelph (ON, Canada)
Viterbo U (WI)

THERAPEUTIC RECREATION
Brigham Young U (UT)
California State U, East Bay (CA)
Calvin Coll (MI)
Catawba Coll (NC)
Central Michigan U (MI)
Concordia U (QC, Canada)
Dalhousie U (NS, Canada)
East Carolina U (NC)
Eastern Michigan U (MI)
Eastern Washington U (WA)
Grand Valley State U (MI)
Hampton U (VA)
Ithaca Coll (NY)
Longwood U (VA)
Minnesota State U Mankato (MN)
St. Andrews U (NC)
St. Cloud State U (MN)
St. Thomas Aquinas Coll (NY)
Shaw U (NC)
Slippery Rock U of Pennsylvania (PA)
State U of New York Coll at Cortland (NY)
Temple U (PA)
Unity Coll (ME)
The U of North Carolina Wilmington (NC)
U of Southern Maine (ME)
The U of Toledo (OH)
U of Waterloo (ON, Canada)
U of Wisconsin–La Crosse (WI)
U of Wisconsin–Milwaukee (WI)
Utica Coll (NY)
Western Carolina U (NC)

TOOL AND DIE TECHNOLOGY
Utah State U (UT)

TOURISM AND TRAVEL SERVICES MANAGEMENT
Arizona State U at the Downtown Phoenix campus (AZ)
Black Hills State U (SD)
Bowling Green State U (OH)
Central Washington U (WA)
Concord U (WV)
Fisher Coll (MA)
Fort Lewis Coll (CO)
Indiana U–Purdue U Indianapolis (IN)
Niagara U (NY)
Northeastern State U (OK)
Plymouth State U (NH)
St. Cloud State U (MN)
St. Thomas U (FL)
Texas A&M U (TX)
United States Intl U–Africa (Kenya)
U of Guelph (ON, Canada)
U of Hawaii at Manoa (HI)
U of South Carolina (SC)
The U of Texas at San Antonio (TX)

TOURISM AND TRAVEL SERVICES MARKETING
Rochester Inst of Technology (NY)
U of Central Missouri (MO)
Western Michigan U (MI)

TOURISM PROMOTION
Bowling Green State U (OH)

TOXICOLOGY
Ashland U (OH)
Eastern Michigan U (MI)
John Jay Coll of Criminal Justice of the City U of New York (NY)
Nazareth Coll of Rochester (NY)
Penn State Beaver (PA)
Penn State Berks (PA)
Penn State DuBois (PA)
Penn State Fayette, The Eberly Campus (PA)
Penn State Greater Allegheny (PA)
Penn State Hazleton (PA)
Penn State Mont Alto (PA)
Penn State New Kensington (PA)
Penn State Shenango (PA)
Penn State U Park (PA)
Penn State Wilkes-Barre (PA)
Penn State York (PA)
St. John's U (NY)
U of Georgia (GA)
U of Guelph (ON, Canada)
U of Louisiana at Monroe (LA)
U of Saskatchewan (SK, Canada)
U of Toronto (ON, Canada)

TRADE AND INDUSTRIAL TEACHER EDUCATION
Auburn U (AL)
Bemidji State U (MN)
Bowling Green State U (OH)
Buffalo State Coll, State U of New York (NY)
California State U, Long Beach (CA)
California State U, San Bernardino (CA)
Central Washington U (WA)
Fitchburg State U (MA)
Florida Ag and Mech U (FL)
Indiana State U (IN)
Indiana U of Pennsylvania (PA)
Kent State U (OH)
Lindenwood U (MO)
Southern Illinois U Carbondale (IL)
State U of New York at Oswego (NY)
Temple U (PA)
U of Central Florida (FL)
U of Louisville (KY)
U of Saskatchewan (SK, Canada)
U of Southern Maine (ME)
The U of Toledo (OH)
Upper Iowa U (IA)
Valdosta State U (GA)
Virginia State U (VA)
Wayland Baptist U (TX)
Western Kentucky U (KY)
Western Michigan U (MI)

TRANSPORTATION AND HIGHWAY ENGINEERING
U of Toronto (ON, Canada)

TRANSPORTATION AND MATERIALS MOVING RELATED
Lewis U (IL)
Niagara U (NY)
Tennessee State U (TN)
United States Merchant Marine Acad (NY)

TRANSPORTATION/MOBILITY MANAGEMENT
Bridgewater State U (MA)
Embry-Riddle Aeronautical U–Worldwide (FL)
LeTourneau U (TX)
Texas A&M U (TX)
U of North Florida (FL)
U of Pennsylvania (PA)
U of Wisconsin–Superior (WI)

TURF AND TURFGRASS MANAGEMENT
Clemson U (SC)
Delaware Valley U (PA)
New Mexico State U (NM)
North Carolina State U (NC)
North Dakota State U (ND)
The Ohio State U (OH)
Penn State Abington (PA)
Penn State Altoona (PA)
Penn State Beaver (PA)
Penn State Berks (PA)
Penn State Brandywine (PA)
Penn State DuBois (PA)
Penn State Erie, The Behrend Coll (PA)
Penn State Fayette, The Eberly Campus (PA)
Penn State Greater Allegheny (PA)
Penn State Hazleton (PA)
Penn State Lehigh Valley (PA)
Penn State Mont Alto (PA)
Penn State New Kensington (PA)
Penn State Schuylkill (PA)
Penn State Shenango (PA)
Penn State U Park (PA)
Penn State Wilkes-Barre (PA)
Penn State Worthington Scranton (PA)
Penn State York (PA)
Purdue U (IN)
Rutgers U–New Brunswick (NJ)
Texas A&M U (TX)
U of Georgia (GA)
U of Massachusetts Amherst (MA)
U of Minnesota, Crookston (MN)
Washington State U (WA)

TURKISH
The U of Texas at Austin (TX)

UKRAINIAN
U of Saskatchewan (SK, Canada)

URALIC LANGUAGES
U of Washington (WA)

URBAN EDUCATION AND LEADERSHIP
Belmont U (TN)
The Coll of New Jersey (NJ)
U of Delaware (DE)
U of Wisconsin–Milwaukee (WI)

URBAN FORESTRY
U of California, Davis (CA)
U of Minnesota, Crookston (MN)

URBAN MINISTRY
Greenville Coll (IL)

URBAN STUDIES/AFFAIRS
Albertus Magnus Coll (CT)
Albright Coll (PA)
Antioch U Los Angeles (CA)
Aquinas Coll (MI)
Arizona State U at the Downtown Phoenix campus (AZ)
Augsburg Coll (MN)
Barnard Coll (NY)
Boston U (MA)
Bryn Mawr Coll (PA)
Buffalo State Coll, State U of New York (NY)
California State U, Dominguez Hills (CA)
California State U, Northridge (CA)
California State U, Stanislaus (CA)
Canisius Coll (NY)
Cleveland State U (OH)
Coll of Charleston (SC)
Coll of Mount Saint Vincent (NY)
The Coll of Wooster (OH)
Columbia U (NY)
Columbia U, School of General Studies (NY)
Concordia U (QC, Canada)
Eugene Lang Coll of Liberal Arts (NY)
Fordham U (NY)
Furman U (SC)
Hampshire Coll (MA)
Harris-Stowe State U (MO)
Haverford Coll (PA)
Hobart and William Smith Colls (NY)
Hunter Coll of the City U of New York (NY)
Jackson State U (MS)
Lipscomb U (TN)
Loyola Marymount U (CA)
Loyola U Chicago (IL)
Manhattan Coll (NY)
Metropolitan Coll of New York (NY)
Minnesota State U Mankato (MN)
Morehouse Coll (GA)
New Coll of Florida (FL)
New Jersey City U (NJ)
The New School for Public Engagement (NY)
New York Inst of Technology (NY)
Northeastern Illinois U (IL)
Northwestern U (IL)
Ohio U (OH)
Ohio Wesleyan U (OH)
Portland State U (OR)
Purchase Coll, State U of New York (NY)
Queens Coll of the City U of New York (NY)
Rhodes Coll (TN)
Rutgers U–Camden (NJ)
Rutgers U–New Brunswick (NJ)
St. Cloud State U (MN)
Saint Peter's U (NJ)
San Diego State U (CA)
San Francisco State U (CA)
Sarah Lawrence Coll (NY)
Stanford U (CA)
Towson U (MD)
Trinity U (TX)
Tufts U (MA)
Université de Montréal (QC, Canada)
U at Albany, State U of New York (NY)
U of California, Irvine (CA)
U of California, San Diego (CA)
U of Cincinnati (OH)
U of Illinois at Chicago (IL)
U of Lethbridge (AB, Canada)
U of Michigan–Dearborn (MI)
U of Minnesota, Duluth (MN)
U of Minnesota, Twin Cities Campus (MN)
U of Missouri–Kansas City (MO)
U of New Orleans (LA)
U of Pennsylvania (PA)
U of Pittsburgh (PA)
The U of Texas at Austin (TX)
The U of Toledo (OH)
U of Utah (UT)
U of Washington, Tacoma (WA)
U of Wisconsin–Green Bay (WI)
Vassar Coll (NY)
Virginia Commonwealth U (VA)
Virginia Polytechnic Inst and State U (VA)
Washington U in St. Louis (MO)
Wayne State U (MI)
Wheaton Coll (IL)
Worcester State U (MA)
Wright State U (OH)
Wright State U–Lake Campus (OH)

VEHICLE AND VEHICLE PARTS AND ACCESSORIES MARKETING
Northwood U, Michigan Campus (MI)

VETERINARY/ANIMAL HEALTH TECHNOLOGY
Becker Coll (MA)
Brigham Young U (UT)
Michigan State U (MI)
Mississippi State U (MS)
Morehead State U (KY)
Mount Ida Coll (MA)
Murray State U (KY)
North Dakota State U (ND)
Purdue U (IN)
St. Petersburg Coll (FL)
State U of New York Coll of Technology at Canton (NY)
Tarleton State U (TX)
Texas A&M U–Kingsville (TX)
Wilson Coll (PA)

VETERINARY MICROBIOLOGY AND IMMUNOBIOLOGY
Penn State U Park (PA)

VISION SCIENCE/ PHYSIOLOGICAL OPTICS
Indiana U Bloomington (IN)
Providence Coll (RI)
U of the Incarnate Word (TX)

VISUAL AND PERFORMING ARTS
The American U of Rome (Italy)
Antioch Coll, Yellow Springs (OH)
Arizona State U at the Tempe campus (AZ)
Arizona State U at the West campus (AZ)
Austin Coll (TX)
Barnard Coll (NY)
Bennett Coll (NC)
Bennington Coll (VT)
Blackburn Coll (IL)
Bloomfield Coll (NJ)
Blue Mountain Coll (MS)
Boston U (MA)
Bucknell U (PA)
California Baptist U (CA)
California State U, San Marcos (CA)
Cardinal Stritch U (WI)
Cazenovia Coll (NY)
Centenary Coll of Louisiana (LA)
Champlain Coll (VT)
Chowan U (NC)
Clayton State U (GA)
Columbia U (NY)
Columbia U, School of General Studies (NY)
Columbus Coll of Art & Design (OH)
Concordia U (QC, Canada)

DEREE - The American Coll of Greece (Greece)
Drexel U (PA)
East Stroudsburg U of Pennsylvania (PA)
Eckerd Coll (FL)
Emerson Coll (MA)
Emory U (GA)
The Evergreen State Coll (WA)
Fairleigh Dickinson U, Coll at Florham (NJ)
Fairleigh Dickinson U, Metropolitan Campus (NJ)
Fayetteville State U (NC)
Gannon U (PA)
Gettysburg Coll (PA)
Harvard U (MA)
Indiana U of Pennsylvania (PA)
Inter American U of Puerto Rico, San Germán Campus (PR)
Iowa State U of Science and Technology (IA)
Ithaca Coll (NY)
Jackson State U (MS)
Jacksonville U (FL)
Johnson C. Smith U (NC)
Kansas Wesleyan U (KS)
Kennesaw State U (GA)
Kent State U (OH)
Kent State U at Stark (OH)
King U (TN)
LaGrange Coll (GA)
Lebanese American U (Lebanon)
Lees-McRae Coll (NC)
Longwood U (VA)
Manhattanville Coll (NY)
Marian U (IN)
Marshall U (WV)
Mary Baldwin U (VA)
Massachusetts Coll of Liberal Arts (MA)
Michigan Technological U (MI)
MidAmerica Nazarene U (KS)
Mississippi State U (MS)
Missouri State U (MO)
Neumann U (PA)
New Mexico Highlands U (NM)
New Mexico State U (NM)
Northwestern U (IL)
Occidental Coll (CA)
Oregon State U (OR)
Penn State Abington (PA)
Penn State Altoona (PA)
Penn State Beaver (PA)
Penn State Berks (PA)
Penn State Brandywine (PA)
Penn State DuBois (PA)
Penn State Erie, The Behrend Coll (PA)
Penn State Fayette, The Eberly Campus (PA)
Penn State Greater Allegheny (PA)
Penn State Hazleton (PA)
Penn State Lehigh Valley (PA)
Penn State Mont Alto (PA)
Penn State New Kensington (PA)
Penn State Schuylkill (PA)
Penn State Shenango (PA)
Penn State U Park (PA)
Penn State Wilkes-Barre (PA)
Penn State Worthington Scranton (PA)
Penn State York (PA)
Pine Manor Coll (MA)
Point Loma Nazarene U (CA)
Prescott Coll (AZ)
Purchase Coll, State U of New York (NY)
Ramapo Coll of New Jersey (NJ)
Rensselaer Polytechnic Inst (NY)
Rogers State U (OK)
Rutgers U–New Brunswick (NJ)
Saint Augustine's U (NC)
St. Bonaventure U (NY)
St. Gregory's U, Shawnee (OK)
Saint Joseph's U (PA)
Saint Peter's U (NJ)
School of the Art Inst of Chicago (IL)
Southeast Missouri State U (MO)
State U of New York at New Paltz (NY)
State U of New York Coll at Old Westbury (NY)
Stockton U (NJ)
Stonehill Coll (MA)
Suffolk U (MA)
Temple U (PA)
Tennessee Wesleyan U (TN)
Tusculum Coll (TN)
Union Coll (KY)
The U of Arizona (AZ)
U of California, Irvine (CA)
U of Colorado Colorado Springs (CO)
U of Houston–Downtown (TX)
U of Maine at Farmington (ME)
U of Mary Washington (VA)
U of Mount Union (OH)
U of New Haven (CT)
U of Pennsylvania (PA)
U of Pittsburgh at Greensburg (PA)
U of Regina (SK, Canada)
U of St. Francis (IL)
U of Saint Mary (KS)
U of San Francisco (CA)
U of Saskatchewan (SK, Canada)
The U of South Dakota (SD)
U of Southern California (CA)
U of Southern Mississippi (MS)
U of South Florida, St. Petersburg (FL)
The U of Tennessee at Martin (TN)
The U of Texas at Austin (TX)
The U of Texas at Dallas (TX)
U of Toronto (ON, Canada)
U of Utah (UT)
U of Windsor (ON, Canada)
U of Wisconsin–Superior (WI)
Vassar Coll (NY)
Virginia State U (VA)
Virginia Union U (VA)
Wheelock Coll (MA)
Wichita State U (KS)
Wittenberg U (OH)
Worcester State U (MA)
Youngstown State U (OH)

VISUAL AND PERFORMING ARTS RELATED
Adelphi U (NY)
Baldwin Wallace U (OH)
The Baptist Coll of Florida (FL)
Bluffton U (OH)
Brigham Young U (UT)
Cameron U (OK)
Clemson U (SC)
Columbia U, School of General Studies (NY)
Cornell U (NY)
Endicott Coll (MA)
Grambling State U (LA)
Illinois State U (IL)
Illinois Wesleyan U (IL)
Millikin U (IL)
Northwestern Coll (IA)
Oklahoma City U (OK)
Penn State Altoona (PA)
Purchase Coll, State U of New York (NY)
Rice U (TX)
The Sage Colls (NY)
St. Cloud State U (MN)
Saint Mary's Coll of California (CA)
Samford U (AL)
San Francisco Art Inst (CA)
School of the Art Inst of Chicago (IL)
Seton Hill U (PA)
Simon Fraser U (BC, Canada)
State U of New York Coll at Geneseo (NY)
U of California, Davis (CA)
U of California, Los Angeles (CA)
U of Chicago (IL)
U of Cincinnati (OH)
U of Lethbridge (AB, Canada)
U of Michigan (MI)
U of South Florida (FL)
U of Washington (WA)
U of Washington, Bothell (WA)
U of Wisconsin–Green Bay (WI)
Virginia Wesleyan Coll (VA)
Western State Colorado U (CO)

VITICULTURE AND ENOLOGY
California Polytechnic State U, San Luis Obispo (CA)
Cornell U (NY)
Washington State U (WA)
Washington State U–Tri-Cities (WA)

VOCATIONAL REHABILITATION COUNSELING
Bowling Green State U (OH)
East Carolina U (NC)
East Central U (OK)
Emporia State U (KS)
Maryville U of Saint Louis (MO)
U of Wisconsin–Madison (WI)
U of Wisconsin–Stout (WI)
Wright State U (OH)
Wright State U–Lake Campus (OH)

VOICE AND OPERA
Abilene Christian U (TX)
Anderson U (SC)
Andrews U (MI)
Arizona Christian U (AZ)
Baldwin Wallace U (OH)
Barry U (FL)
Bennington Coll (VT)
Biola U (CA)
Black Hills State U (SD)
Bradley U (IL)
Brigham Young U (UT)
Bucknell U (PA)
California Baptist U (CA)
California State U, Long Beach (CA)
Calvary U (MO)
Calvin Coll (MI)
Campbellsville U (KY)
Capital U (OH)
Carnegie Mellon U (PA)
Carson-Newman U (TN)
The Catholic U of America (DC)
Central Washington U (WA)
Chapman U (CA)
Converse Coll (SC)
Dallas Baptist U (TX)
Drake U (IA)
East Central U (OK)
Eastern Nazarene Coll (MA)
East Texas Baptist U (TX)
Furman U (SC)
Hardin-Simmons U (TX)
Heidelberg U (OH)
Hope Coll (MI)
Houghton Coll (NY)
Houston Baptist U (TX)
Howard Payne U (TX)
Illinois Wesleyan U (IL)
Ithaca Coll (NY)
Jacksonville U (FL)
Lawrence U (WI)
Liberty U (VA)
Lincoln Coll (IL)
Lipscomb U (TN)
Loyola U New Orleans (LA)
Madonna U (MI)
The Master's U (CA)
Minnesota State U Mankato (MN)
Mount Allison U (NB, Canada)
The New School Coll of Performing Arts (NY)
Northern State U (SD)
Northwestern U (IL)
Nyack Coll (NY)
Oberlin Coll (OH)
The Ohio State U (OH)
Ohio U (OH)
Oklahoma Baptist U (OK)
Oklahoma Christian U (OK)
Oklahoma City U (OK)
Oral Roberts U (OK)
Ouachita Baptist U (AR)
Palm Beach Atlantic U (FL)
Point Loma Nazarene U (CA)
Roberts Wesleyan Coll (NY)
St. Cloud State U (MN)
Samford U (AL)
San Francisco Conservatory of Music (CA)
Shorter U (GA)
Southeastern U (FL)
Southern Methodist U (TX)
State U of New York at Fredonia (NY)
Syracuse U (NY)
Texas Christian U (TX)
Trinity U (TX)
Union U (TN)
Université de Montréal (QC, Canada)
The U of Akron (OH)
U of Cincinnati (OH)
U of Delaware (DE)
The U of Kansas (KS)
U of Miami (FL)
U of Mobile (AL)
U of Southern California (CA)
The U of Tennessee at Martin (TN)
U of the Pacific (CA)
The U of Tulsa (OK)
U of Washington (WA)
Valparaiso U (IN)
Vanderbilt U (TN)
Washington U in St. Louis (MO)
Weber State U (UT)
Western Michigan U (MI)
Whitworth U (WA)
Willamette U (OR)
Youngstown State U (OH)

WATER QUALITY AND WASTEWATER TREATMENT MANAGEMENT AND RECYCLING TECHNOLOGY
Virginia Polytechnic Inst and State U (VA)

WATER RESOURCES ENGINEERING
Central State U (OH)
U of Guelph (ON, Canada)
U of Nevada, Reno (NV)

WATER, WETLANDS, AND MARINE RESOURCES MANAGEMENT
Colorado State U (CO)
Florida Gulf Coast U (FL)
Texas A&M U (TX)
Texas State U (TX)
U of Minnesota, Crookston (MN)
Western State Colorado U (CO)

WEB/MULTIMEDIA MANAGEMENT AND WEBMASTER
American Public U System (WV)
Georgia Coll & State U (GA)
Limestone Coll (SC)
Morrisville State Coll (NY)
Pepperdine U, Malibu (CA)
Rochester Inst of Technology (NY)
Saint Leo U (FL)
State U of New York Coll of Technology at Alfred (NY)
Trevecca Nazarene U (TN)
U of Great Falls (MT)
U of St. Francis (IL)

WEB PAGE, DIGITAL/ MULTIMEDIA AND INFORMATION RESOURCES DESIGN
Acad of Art U (CA)
American Acad of Art (IL)
Azusa Pacific U (CA)
Beacon Coll (FL)
Belmont U (TN)
Bishop's U (QC, Canada)
Cedarville U (OH)
Central Connecticut State U (CT)
Central Washington U (WA)
Columbia Coll Chicago (IL)
Concordia U (QC, Canada)
Davenport U, Grand Rapids (MI)
Drexel U (PA)
Duquesne U (PA)
Emily Carr U of Art + Design (BC, Canada)
Grace Coll (IN)
Hampshire Coll (MA)
Harding U (AR)
Immaculata U (PA)
Iona Coll (NY)
Iowa Wesleyan U (IA)
Limestone Coll (SC)
Lindenwood U (MO)
Lipscomb U (TN)
Mercyhurst U (PA)
Morrisville State Coll (NY)
Mount St. Joseph U (OH)
New England Inst of Technology (RI)
New York City Coll of Technology of the City U of New York (NY)
Northwest Missouri State U (MO)
Pennsylvania Coll of Technology (PA)
Quinnipiac U (CT)
Rasmussen Coll Bloomington (MN)
Rasmussen Coll Brooklyn Park (MN)
Rasmussen Coll Eagan (MN)
Rasmussen Coll Fort Myers (FL)
Rasmussen Coll Kansas City/ Overland Park (KS)
Rasmussen Coll Lake Elmo/ Woodbury (MN)
Rasmussen Coll Land O' Lakes (FL)
Rasmussen Coll Mankato (MN)
Rasmussen Coll Moorhead (MN)
Rasmussen Coll New Port Richey (FL)
Rasmussen Coll Ocala (FL)
Rasmussen Coll Rockford (IL)
Rasmussen Coll St. Cloud (MN)
Rasmussen Coll Tampa/Brandon (FL)
Rasmussen Coll Topeka (KS)
Rochester Inst of Technology (NY)
Santa Clara U (CA)
School of the Art Inst of Chicago (IL)
Seattle U (WA)
Simmons Coll (MA)
Trevecca Nazarene U (TN)
U of Advancing Technology (AZ)
The U of Arizona (AZ)
The U of Findlay (OH)
U of Georgia (GA)
U of Great Falls (MT)
U of Mount Union (OH)
The U of the Arts (PA)
U of Washington, Bothell (WA)
U of Wisconsin–Stevens Point (WI)
Utah Valley U (UT)
Walla Walla U (WA)
Weber State U (UT)
William Jewell Coll (MO)

WELDING ENGINEERING TECHNOLOGY
LeTourneau U (TX)
Weber State U (UT)

WELDING TECHNOLOGY
Brigham Young U–Idaho (ID)
Idaho State U (ID)
The Ohio State U (OH)
Weber State U (UT)

WILDLIFE BIOLOGY
Adams State U (CO)
Coll of the Atlantic (ME)
Colorado State U (CO)
Friends U (KS)
Frostburg State U (MD)
Kansas State U (KS)
Lees-McRae Coll (NC)
Liberty U (VA)
Ohio U (OH)
St. Cloud State U (MN)
State U of New York Coll of Environmental Science and Forestry (NY)
Texas State U (TX)
Unity Coll (ME)
U of Guelph (ON, Canada)
U of Michigan–Flint (MI)
U of Vermont (VT)
West Texas A&M U (TX)

WILDLIFE, FISH AND WILDLANDS SCIENCE AND MANAGEMENT
Arkansas Tech U (AR)
Auburn U (AL)
Coll of the Ozarks (MO)
Delaware Valley U (PA)
Frostburg State U (MD)
Humboldt State U (CA)
McNeese State U (LA)
Michigan State U (MI)
Michigan Technological U (MI)
Mississippi State U (MS)
Missouri State U (MO)
Missouri Western State U (MO)
Montana State U (MT)
Murray State U (KY)
New Mexico State U (NM)
Northwest Missouri State U (MO)
The Ohio State U (OH)
Oregon State U (OR)
South Dakota State U (SD)
State U of New York Coll of Agriculture and Technology at Cobleskill (NY)
State U of New York Coll of Environmental Science and Forestry (NY)
Stephen F. Austin State U (TX)

Tarleton State U (TX)
Texas A&M U (TX)
Texas A&M U–Commerce (TX)
Texas A&M U–Kingsville (TX)
Unity Coll (ME)
U of Alaska Fairbanks (AK)
U of Delaware (DE)
U of Florida (FL)
U of Georgia (GA)
U of Idaho (ID)
U of Maine (ME)
U of Nevada, Reno (NV)
U of New Hampshire (NH)
U of Rhode Island (RI)
The U of Tennessee (TN)
The U of Tennessee at Martin (TN)
U of Wisconsin–Madison (WI)
U of Wisconsin–Stevens Point (WI)
Utah State U (UT)
Valley City State U (ND)
Washington State U (WA)
West Virginia U (WV)

WOMEN'S STUDIES

Agnes Scott Coll (GA)
Albion Coll (MI)
Albright Coll (PA)
Alverno Coll (WI)
American U (DC)
Amherst Coll (MA)
Appalachian State U (NC)
Arizona State U at the Tempe campus (AZ)
Arizona State U at the West campus (AZ)
Armstrong State U (GA)
Augsburg Coll (MN)
Augustana Coll (IL)
Austin Coll (TX)
Ball State U (IN)
Barnard Coll (NY)
Bates Coll (ME)
Bennington Coll (VT)
Berea Coll (KY)
Bishop's U (QC, Canada)
Bowling Green State U (OH)
Brandeis U (MA)
Brooklyn Coll of the City U of New York (NY)
Bryant U (RI)
Bucknell U (PA)
Butler U (IN)
Cabrini U (PA)
California State U, Fresno (CA)
California State U, Fullerton (CA)
California State U, Long Beach (CA)
California State U, Northridge (CA)
California State U, San Marcos (CA)
Canisius Coll (NY)
Carleton Coll (MN)
Case Western Reserve U (OH)
Central Michigan U (MI)
Chatham U (PA)
City Coll of the City U of New York (NY)
Clark U (MA)
Clemson U (SC)
Cleveland State U (OH)
Coe Coll (IA)
Colby Coll (ME)
Colgate U (NY)
The Coll at Brockport, State U of New York (NY)
Coll of Charleston (SC)
The Coll of New Jersey (NJ)
Coll of Saint Benedict (MN)
The Coll of William and Mary (VA)
The Coll of Wooster (OH)
The Colorado Coll (CO)
Columbia U (NY)
Columbia U, School of General Studies (NY)
Concordia U (QC, Canada)
Concordia U Chicago (IL)
Connecticut Coll (CT)
Cornell Coll (IA)
Dalhousie U (NS, Canada)
Dartmouth Coll (NH)
Denison U (OH)
DePauw U (IN)
Dickinson Coll (PA)
Dominican U (IL)
Dominican U of California (CA)
Drew U (NJ)
Duquesne U (PA)
Earlham Coll (IN)
Eastern Michigan U (MI)
Eastern Washington U (WA)
East Tennessee State U (TN)
Eckerd Coll (FL)
Emory U (GA)
Florida Intl U (FL)
Fordham U (NY)
Fort Lewis Coll (CO)
Georgetown U (DC)
Georgia State U (GA)
Gettysburg Coll (PA)
Goddard Coll (VT)
Goucher Coll (MD)
Grand Valley State U (MI)
Guilford Coll (NC)
Hamilton Coll (NY)
Hamline U (MN)
Hampshire Coll (MA)
Harvard U (MA)
Hobart and William Smith Colls (NY)
Hofstra U (NY)
Hollins U (VA)
Hope Coll (MI)
Hunter Coll of the City U of New York (NY)
Illinois Wesleyan U (IL)
Iowa State U of Science and Technology (IA)
Kalamazoo Coll (MI)
Kansas State U (KS)
Keene State Coll (NH)
Kenyon Coll (OH)
Knox Coll (IL)
Lafayette Coll (PA)
Lehigh U (PA)
Loyola Marymount U (CA)
Loyola U Chicago (IL)
Luther Coll (IA)
Macalester Coll (MN)
Manchester U (IN)
McMaster U (ON, Canada)
Merrimack Coll (MA)
Miami U (OH)
Michigan State U (MI)
Middlebury Coll (VT)
Minnesota State U Mankato (MN)
Minnesota State U Moorhead (MN)
Nazareth Coll of Rochester (NY)
New Jersey City U (NJ)
New Mexico State U (NM)
North Carolina State U (NC)
North Dakota State U (ND)
Northeastern Illinois U (IL)
Northern Arizona U (AZ)
Northland Coll (WI)
Northwestern U (IL)
Oberlin Coll (OH)
The Ohio State U (OH)
Ohio U (OH)
Ohio Wesleyan U (OH)
Old Dominion U (VA)
Oregon State U (OR)
Otterbein U (OH)
Pace U (NY)
Pacific Lutheran U (WA)
Penn State Abington (PA)
Penn State Altoona (PA)
Penn State Beaver (PA)
Penn State Berks (PA)
Penn State Brandywine (PA)
Penn State DuBois (PA)
Penn State Erie, The Behrend Coll (PA)
Penn State Fayette, The Eberly Campus (PA)
Penn State Greater Allegheny (PA)
Penn State Hazleton (PA)
Penn State Lehigh Valley (PA)
Penn State Mont Alto (PA)
Penn State New Kensington (PA)
Penn State Schuylkill (PA)
Penn State Shenango (PA)
Penn State U Park (PA)
Penn State Wilkes-Barre (PA)
Penn State Worthington Scranton (PA)
Penn State York (PA)
Pitzer Coll (CA)
Pomona Coll (CA)
Portland State U (OR)
Prescott Coll (AZ)
Providence Coll (RI)
Purchase Coll, State U of New York (NY)
Purdue U (IN)
Queens Coll of the City U of New York (NY)
Randolph-Macon Coll (VA)
Regis U (CO)
Rhode Island Coll (RI)
Rice U (TX)
Rutgers U–Newark (NJ)
Rutgers U–New Brunswick (NJ)
Sacred Heart U (CT)
St. Bonaventure U (NY)
St. Catherine U (MN)
Saint John's U (MN)
Saint Louis U (MO)
Saint Louis U–Madrid Campus (Spain)
Saint Mary's Coll (IN)
Saint Mary's Coll of California (CA)
St. Olaf Coll (MN)
St. Thomas U (NB, Canada)
San Diego State U (CA)
San Francisco State U (CA)
Santa Clara U (CA)
Sarah Lawrence Coll (NY)
Scripps Coll (CA)
Seattle U (WA)
Sewanee: The U of the South (TN)
Simmons Coll (MA)
Simon Fraser U (BC, Canada)
Smith Coll (MA)
Sonoma State U (CA)
Southwestern U (TX)
Spelman Coll (GA)
Stanford U (CA)
State U of New York at Fredonia (NY)
State U of New York at New Paltz (NY)
State U of New York at Oswego (NY)
State U of New York at Plattsburgh (NY)
State U of New York Coll at Potsdam (NY)
Stony Brook U, State U of New York (NY)
Swarthmore Coll (PA)
Syracuse U (NY)
Texas A&M U (TX)
Towson U (MD)
Trent U (ON, Canada)
Tufts U (MA)
Tulane U (LA)
U at Albany, State U of New York (NY)
The U of Arizona (AZ)
U of California, Davis (CA)
U of California, Riverside (CA)
U of California, San Diego (CA)
U of California, Santa Barbara (CA)
U of Cincinnati (OH)
U of Colorado Boulder (CO)
U of Dayton (OH)
U of Delaware (DE)
U of Florida (FL)
U of Georgia (GA)
U of Hartford (CT)
U of Hawaii at Manoa (HI)
U of Houston–Clear Lake (TX)
U of Illinois at Chicago (IL)
The U of Kansas (KS)
U of King's Coll (NS, Canada)
U of Lethbridge (AB, Canada)
U of Louisville (KY)
U of Maine (ME)
U of Maryland, Baltimore County (MD)
U of Maryland, Coll Park (MD)
U of Massachusetts Amherst (MA)
U of Massachusetts Boston (MA)
U of Massachusetts Dartmouth (MA)
U of Miami (FL)
U of Michigan (MI)
U of Michigan–Dearborn (MI)
U of Minnesota, Duluth (MN)
U of Minnesota, Morris (MN)
U of Minnesota, Twin Cities Campus (MN)
U of Nevada, Las Vegas (NV)
U of Nevada, Reno (NV)
U of New Hampshire (NH)
U of North Carolina at Asheville (NC)
The U of North Carolina at Chapel Hill (NC)
The U of North Carolina at Greensboro (NC)
U of Notre Dame (IN)
U of Oklahoma (OK)
U of Oregon (OR)
U of Pennsylvania (PA)
U of Pittsburgh (PA)
U of Regina (SK, Canada)
U of Rhode Island (RI)
U of Richmond (VA)
U of Rochester (NY)
U of Saint Joseph (CT)
U of St. Thomas (MN)
U of Saskatchewan (SK, Canada)
The U of Scranton (PA)
U of South Carolina (SC)
U of Southern Maine (ME)
U of South Florida (FL)
The U of Texas at Austin (TX)
The U of Texas at San Antonio (TX)
The U of Toledo (OH)
U of Toronto (ON, Canada)
The U of Tulsa (OK)
U of Utah (UT)
U of Vermont (VT)
U of Washington (WA)
U of Waterloo (ON, Canada)
U of Windsor (ON, Canada)
U of Wisconsin–Eau Claire (WI)
U of Wisconsin–La Crosse (WI)
U of Wisconsin–Madison (WI)
U of Wisconsin–Milwaukee (WI)
U of Wisconsin–Whitewater (WI)
Vanderbilt U (TN)
Vassar Coll (NY)
Villanova U (PA)
Virginia Commonwealth U (VA)
Virginia Wesleyan Coll (VA)
Washington State U (WA)
Washington U in St. Louis (MO)
Webster U (MO)
Wells Coll (NY)
Wesleyan Coll (GA)
West Chester U of Pennsylvania (PA)
Western Michigan U (MI)
Wheaton Coll (MA)
Wichita State U (KS)
Willamette U (OR)
William Paterson U of New Jersey (NJ)
Williams Coll (MA)

WOOD SCIENCE AND WOOD PRODUCTS/PULP AND PAPER TECHNOLOGY

North Carolina State U (NC)
Oregon State U (OR)
Purdue U (IN)
State U of New York Coll of Environmental Science and Forestry (NY)
U of Idaho (ID)
U of Maine (ME)
U of Toronto (ON, Canada)
U of Wisconsin–Stevens Point (WI)
West Virginia U (WV)

WOODWIND INSTRUMENTS

Eastern Nazarene Coll (MA)
Houghton Coll (NY)
Lawrence U (WI)
Mount Allison U (NB, Canada)
Northwestern U (IL)
Oberlin Coll (OH)
Oklahoma Christian U (OK)
San Francisco Conservatory of Music (CA)
State U of New York at Fredonia (NY)
The U of Kansas (KS)
U of Michigan (MI)
U of Southern California (CA)
Vanderbilt U (TN)
Xavier U of Louisiana (LA)
Youngstown State U (OH)

WOODWORKING

Rochester Inst of Technology (NY)

WORK AND FAMILY STUDIES

Brigham Young U (UT)
Washington State U (WA)

WRITING

Augustana Coll (IL)
Aurora U (IL)
Baylor U (TX)
Bennington Coll (VT)
Biola U (CA)
Brigham Young U (UT)
Calvin Coll (MI)
Canisius Coll (NY)
Cardinal Stritch U (WI)
Carroll Coll (MT)
Central Washington U (WA)
Champlain Coll (VT)
Columbia U, School of General Studies (NY)
DePauw U (IN)
Drury U (MO)
Eastern Michigan U (MI)
Ferris State U (MI)
Geneva Coll (PA)
Georgia Southern U (GA)
Gettysburg Coll (PA)
Goddard Coll (VT)
Goshen Coll (IN)
Graceland U (IA)
Grand Valley State U (MI)
High Point U (NC)
Houston Baptist U (TX)
Huntington U (IN)
Kansas Wesleyan U (KS)
La Roche Coll (PA)
Lipscomb U (TN)
Lubbock Christian U (TX)
Madonna U (MI)
Marian U (WI)
Massachusetts Coll of Liberal Arts (MA)
Northwest Missouri State U (MO)
Northwest U (WA)
Oral Roberts U (OK)
Pacific Northwest Coll of Art (OR)
Point Loma Nazarene U (CA)
St. Edward's U (TX)
San Diego State U (CA)
Spring Hill Coll (AL)
State U of New York Coll at Potsdam (NY)
U of Central Arkansas (AR)
U of Colorado Denver (CO)
U of Evansville (IN)
The U of Findlay (OH)
U of Great Falls (MT)
U of Jamestown (ND)
U of Michigan–Flint (MI)
U of Mount Union (OH)
The U of Tampa (FL)
The U of Texas at Austin (TX)
U of Washington, Tacoma (WA)
U of Wisconsin–Superior (WI)
Western Michigan U (MI)
William Peace U (NC)

YOUTH MINISTRY

Anderson U (IN)
Anderson U (SC)
Andrews U (MI)
Arizona Christian U (AZ)
Asbury U (KY)
Augsburg Coll (MN)
Bluffton U (OH)
Cairn U (PA)
Calvary U (MO)
Carson-Newman U (TN)
Cedarville U (OH)
Charleston Southern U (SC)
Colorado Christian U (CO)
Columbia Intl U (SC)
Concordia U Wisconsin (WI)
Cornerstone U (MI)
Davis Coll (NY)
Eastern Nazarene Coll (MA)
Eastern U (PA)
East Texas Baptist U (TX)
Emmaus Bible Coll (IA)
Faulkner U (AL)
Florida Southern Coll (FL)
Freed-Hardeman U (TN)
Geneva Coll (PA)
Gordon Coll (MA)
Grace Coll (IN)
Greenville Coll (IL)
Harding U (AR)
Hope Intl U (CA)
Howard Payne U (TX)
Huntington U (IN)
John Brown U (AR)
Judson U (IL)
Kentucky Mountain Bible Coll (KY)
King U (TN)
Kuyper Coll (MI)
Lee U (TN)
LeTourneau U (TX)
Liberty U (VA)
Lincoln Christian U (IL)

Lipscomb U (TN)
Lubbock Christian U (TX)
Malone U (OH)
Maranatha Baptist U (WI)
Master's Coll and Sem (ON, Canada)
Messenger Coll (TX)
MidAmerica Nazarene U (KS)
Mid-Atlantic Christian U (NC)
Mount Vernon Nazarene U (OH)
Multnomah U (OR)
North Greenville U (SC)
Northwest Christian U (OR)
Northwest U (WA)
Nyack Coll (NY)
Ohio Christian U (OH)
Olivet Nazarene U (IL)
Piedmont Intl U (NC)
Point Loma Nazarene U (CA)
Redeemer U Coll (ON, Canada)
Simpson U (CA)
Southwestern Assemblies of God U (TX)
Taylor U (IN)
Toccoa Falls Coll (GA)
Trevecca Nazarene U (TN)
Trinity Coll of Florida (FL)
U of Indianapolis (IN)
U of Valley Forge (PA)

YOUTH SERVICES
Montclair State U (NJ)
Murray State U (KY)
Rhode Island Coll (RI)
Samford U (AL)
Wheelock Coll (MA)

ZOOLOGY/ANIMAL BIOLOGY
Andrews U (MI)
Auburn U (AL)
Bennington Coll (VT)
Berry Coll (GA)
California State U, Long Beach (CA)
Canisius Coll (NY)
Coll of the Atlantic (ME)
Colorado State U (CO)
Dalhousie U (NS, Canada)
Delaware Valley U (PA)
The Evergreen State Coll (WA)
Humboldt State U (CA)
Kent State U (OH)
Kentucky Wesleyan Coll (KY)
Liberty U (VA)
Malone U (OH)
Miami U (OH)
Michigan State U (MI)
Muskingum U (OH)
North Carolina State U (NC)
North Dakota State U (ND)
The Ohio State U (OH)
Ohio U (OH)
Ohio Wesleyan U (OH)
Oklahoma State U (OK)
Olivet Nazarene U (IL)
Oregon State U (OR)
Otterbein U (OH)
Rutgers U–Newark (NJ)
San Diego State U (CA)
San Francisco State U (CA)
Sonoma State U (CA)
Southern Illinois U Carbondale (IL)
State U of New York at Oswego (NY)
Texas A&M U (TX)
Texas Tech U (TX)
The U of Akron (OH)
U of California, Davis (CA)
U of California, Santa Barbara (CA)
U of Florida (FL)
U of Guelph (ON, Canada)
U of Hawaii at Manoa (HI)
U of Maine (ME)
U of New Hampshire (NH)
U of Oklahoma (OK)
The U of Texas at El Paso (TX)
U of Toronto (ON, Canada)
U of Vermont (VT)
U of Wisconsin–Madison (WI)
Utah State U (UT)
Washington State U (WA)
Weber State U (UT)

ZOOLOGY/ANIMAL BIOLOGY RELATED
Beacon Coll (FL)
Canisius Coll (NY)

Entrance Difficulty

This index groups colleges by their own assessment of their entrance difficulty level. The colleges were asked to select the level that most closely corresponds to their entrance difficulty, according to the guidelines below. Institutions for which high school class rank and/or standardized test scores do not apply as admission criteria were asked to select the level that best indicates their entrance difficulty as compared to other institutions.

MOST DIFFICULT

More than 75 percent of the freshmen were in the top 10 percent of their high school class and scored over 1310 on the SAT (critical reading and mathematical combined) or over 29 on the ACT (composite); about 30 percent or fewer of the applicants were accepted.

Amherst Coll (MA)
Barnard Coll (NY)
Bowdoin Coll (ME)
Brandeis U (MA)
Brown U (RI)
Bryn Mawr Coll (PA)
Bucknell U (PA)
California Inst of Technology (CA)
Carnegie Mellon U (PA)
Claremont McKenna Coll (CA)
Colby Coll (ME)
Colgate U (NY)
The Coll of William and Mary (VA)
Columbia U (NY)
Columbia U, School of General Studies (NY)
Cornell U (NY)
Dartmouth Coll (NH)
Duke (NC)
Emory U (GA)
Franklin W. Olin Coll of Eng (MA)
Georgetown U (DC)
Gettysburg Coll (PA)
Harvard U (MA)
Harvey Mudd Coll (CA)
Haverford Coll (PA)
The Juilliard School (NY)
Kenyon Coll (OH)
Lehigh U (PA)
Massachusetts Inst of Technology (MA)
Middlebury Coll (VT)
Northwestern U (IL)
Pomona Coll (CA)
Princeton U (NJ)
Rice U (TX)
Soka U of America (CA)
Stanford U (CA)
Tufts U (MA)
United States Air Force Acad (CO)
U of Chicago (IL)
U of Notre Dame (IN)
U of Pennsylvania (PA)
U of Southern California (CA)
Vanderbilt U (TN)
Washington and Lee U (VA)
Washington U in St. Louis (MO)
Webb Inst (NY)
Wellesley (MA)
Wesleyan U (CT)
Williams Coll (MA)

VERY DIFFICULT

More than 50 percent of the freshmen were in the top 10 percent of their high school class and scored over 1230 on the SAT or over 26 on the ACT; about 60 percent or fewer applicants were accepted.

Allegheny Coll (PA)
American U (DC)
American U in Bulgaria (Bulgaria)
The American U in Cairo (Egypt)
Antioch Coll, Yellow Springs (OH)
Art Center Coll of Design (MA)
Austin Coll (TX)
Babson Coll (MA)
Baruch Coll of the City U of New York (NY)
Bates Coll (ME)
Bennington Coll (VT)
Bentley U (MA)
Binghamton U, State U of New York (NY)
Boston Coll (MA)
Boston U (MA)
California Institute of Arts (CA)
Carleton Coll (MN)
Case Western Reserve U (OH)
Centre Coll (KY)
Chapman U (CA)
Clarkson U (NY)
Clemson U (SC)
The Coll of New Jersey (NJ)
Coll of the Atlantic (ME)
Coll of the Holy Cross (MA)
The Colorado Coll (CO)
Colorado School of Mines (CO)
Connecticut Coll (CT)
Davidson Coll (NC)
Denison U (OH)
Dickinson Coll (PA)
Earlham Coll (IN)
Emerson Coll (MA)
Fairfield U (CT)
Florida State U (FL)
Fordham U (NY)
Franklin & Marshall Coll (PA)
The George Washington U (DC)
Grinnell Coll (IA)
Gustavus Adolphus (MN)
Hamilton Coll (NY)
Hendrix Coll (AR)
Hillsdale Coll (MI)
Hobart and William Smith Colls (NY)
Illinois Wesleyan U (IL)
James Madison U (VA)
Kalamazoo Coll (MI)
Kettering U (MI)
Knox Coll (IL)
Laguna Coll of Art & Design (CA)
Lawrence U (WI)
Lewis & Clark Coll (OR)
Macalester Coll (MN)
Marist Coll (NY)
Maryland Inst Coll of Art (MD)
McMaster U (ON, Canada)
Missouri U of Science and Technology (MO)
Mount Holyoke Coll (MA)
Muhlenberg Coll (PA)
New England Conservatory of Music (MA)
New Coll of Florida (FL)
North Carolina State U (NC)
Northeastern U (MA)
Oberlin Coll (OH)
Occidental Coll (CA)
Oglethorpe (GA)
The Ohio State U (OH)
Ohio Wesleyan U (OH)
Penn State Abington (PA)
Penn State Altoona (PA)
Penn State Berks (PA)
Penn State Erie, The Behrend Coll (PA)
Penn State Harrisburg (PA)
Penn State U Park (PA)
Pepperdine U, Malibu (CA)
Pitzer Coll (CA)
Pratt Inst (NY)
Presbyterian Coll (SC)
Queens Coll of the City U of New York (NY)
Reed Coll (OR)
Rensselaer Polytechnic Inst (NY)
Rhodes Coll (TN)
Rose-Hulman Inst of Technology (IN)
St. Olaf Coll (MN)
San Jose State (CA)
Santa Clara U (CA)
Sarah Lawrence Coll (NY)
School of the Art Inst of Chicago (IL)
Scripps Coll (CA)
Seton Hall (NJ)
Sewanee: The U of the South (TN)
Skidmore Coll (NY)
Smith Coll (MA)
Southwestern U (TX)
Spelman Coll (GA)
State U of New York at New Paltz (NY)
State U of New York Coll of Environmental Science and Forestry (NY)
State U of New York Maritime Coll (NY)
Stevens Inst of Technology (NJ)
Stockton U (NJ)
Stonehill Coll (MA)
Stony Brook U, State U of New York (NY)
Syracuse U (NY)
Texas Christian U (TX)
Thomas Aquinas Coll (CA)
Transylvania U (KY)
Trinity U (TX)
Tulane U (LA)
Union Coll (NY)
United States Coast Guard Acad (CT)
United States Merchant Marine Acad (NY)
United States Naval Acad (MD)
U at Albany, State U of New York (NY)
U of California, Davis (CA)
U of California, Irvine (CA)
U of California, Los Angeles (CA)
U of California, Riverside (CA)
U of California, San Diego (CA)
U of California, Santa Barbara (CA)
U of California, Santa Cruz (CA)
U of Florida (FL)
U of Mary Washington (VA)
U of Miami (FL)
U of Michigan (MI)
The U of North Carolina at Chapel Hill (NC)
U of Pittsburgh (PA)
U of Puerto Rico in Bayamón (PR)
U of Richmond (VA)
U of Rochester (NY)
U of San Diego (CA)
The U of Texas at Dallas (TX)
U of Toronto (ON, Canada)
The U of Tulsa (OK)
U of Virginia (VA)
U of Washington (WA)
U of Western Ontario (ON, Canada)
U of Wisconsin–Madison (WI)
Vassar Coll (NY)
Villanova U (PA)
Wake Forest U (NC)
Washington & Jefferson Coll (PA)
Wheaton Coll (IL)
Wheaton Coll (MA)
Whitman Coll (WA)
Willamette U (OR)
Wofford Coll (SC)
Worcester Polytechnic Inst (MA)

MODERATELY DIFFICULT

More than 75 percent of the freshmen were in the top half of their high school class and scored over 1010 on the SAT or over 18 on the ACT; about 85 percent or fewer of the applicants were accepted.

Abilene Christian U (TX)
Adams State U (CO)
Adelphi U (NY)
Agnes Scott Coll (GA)
Albertus Magnus Coll (CT)

Albion Coll (MI)
Albright Coll (PA)
Alcorn State U (MS)
Alderson Broaddus U (WV)
Alfred U (NY)
Allen Coll (IA)
Alma Coll (MI)
Alvernia U (PA)
Alverno Coll (WI)
American Acad of Art (IL)
The American U of Paris (France)
The American U of Rome (Italy)
Anderson U (IN)
Andrews U (MI)
Angelo State U (TX)
Antioch U Los Angeles (CA)
Antioch U Santa Barbara (CA)
Appalachian State U (NC)
Aquinas Coll (MI)
Arcadia U (PA)
Arizona State U at the Downtown Phoenix campus (AZ)
Arizona State U at the Polytechnic campus (AZ)
Arizona State U at the Tempe campus (AZ)
Arizona State U at the West campus (AZ)
Arkansas State University (AR)
Arkansas Tech U (AR)
Asbury U (KY)
Ashland U (OH)
Assumption Coll (MA)
Auburn U (AL)
Auburn U at Montgomery (AL)
Augsburg Coll (MN)
Augustana Coll (IL)
Augustana U (SD)
Aultman Coll of Nursing and Health Sciences (OH)
Aurora U (IL)
Austin Peay State U (TN)
Ave Maria (FL)
Averett U (VA)
Azusa Pacific U (CA)
Baker U (KS)
Baldwin Wallace U (OH)
Bard Coll (NY)
Barry U (FL)
Baylor U (TX)
Bay Path U (MA)
Beacon Coll (FL)
Becker Coll (MA)
Belhaven U (MS)
Bellarmine U (KY)
Bellin Coll (WI)
Belmont Abbey Coll (NC)
Belmont U (TN)
Bemidji State U (MN)
Benedictine Univ (IL)
Berea Coll (KY)
Berklee Coll of Music (MA)
Berry Coll (GA)
Beth Medrash Govoha (NJ)
Bethany Coll (WV)
Bethel Coll (KS)
Bethel Coll (VA)
Bethany Lutheran Coll (MN)
Bethel U (MN)
Biola U (CA)
Bishop's U (QC, Canada)
Blackburn Coll (IL)
Blessing-Reiman Coll of Nursing & Health Sciences (IL)
Bloomfield Coll (NJ)
Blue Mountain Coll (MS)
Bluffton U (OH)
Boise State U (ID)
Bowling Green State U (OH)
Bradley U (IL)
Brenau U (GA)
Brescia U (KY)
Briar Cliff U (IA)
Bridgewater Coll (VA)
Bridgewater State U (MA)
Brigham Young U (UT)
Brigham Young U–Idaho (ID)
Brooklyn Coll of the City U of New York (NY)
Bryan Coll (TN)
Bryant U (RI)
Buena Vista U (IA)
Buffalo State Coll, State U of New York (NY)
Butler U (IN)
Cabarrus Coll of Health Sciences (NC)
Cabrini U (PA)
Cairn U (PA)
Caldwell U (NJ)
California Baptist U (CA)
California Lutheran U (CA)
California Polytechnic State U, San Luis Obispo (CA)
California State Polytechnic U, Pomona (CA)
California State U, Bakersfield (CA)
California State U, Chico (CA)
California State U, Dominguez Hills (CA)
California State U, East Bay (CA)
California State U, Fullerton (CA)
California State U, Long Beach (CA)
California State U Maritime Acad (CA)
California State U, Monterey Bay (CA)
California State U, Northridge (CA)
California State U, Sacramento (CA)
California State U, San Bernardino (CA)
California State U, San Marcos (CA)
California State U, Stanislaus (CA)
California U of Pennsylvania (PA)
Calvin Coll (MI)
Campbellsville U (KY)
Canisius Coll (NY)
Cape Breton Univ (NS) Canada
Capital U (OH)
Cardinal Stritch U (WI)
Carlos Abizu Univ (FL)
Carroll Coll (MT)
Carson-Newman U (TN)
Carthage Coll (WI)
Catawba Coll (NC)
Cedar Crest Coll (PA)
Cedarville U (OH)
Centenary Coll of Louisiana (LA)
Centenary U (NJ)
Central Coll (IA)
Central Connecticut State U (CT)
Central Methodist U (MO)
Central Michigan U (MI)
Central Washington U (WA)
Chamberlain Coll of Nursing (FL)
Chaminade U of Honolulu (HI)
Champlain Coll (VT)
Charleston Southern U (SC)
Chatham U (PA)
Chestnut Hill Coll (PA)
Christendom Coll (VA)
Christian Brothers U (TN)
Christopher Newport U (VA)
The Citadel, The Military Coll of South Carolina (SC)
City Coll of the City U of New York (NY)
Clark Atlanta U (GA)
Clarke U (IA)
Clark U (MA)
Cleary Univ (MI)
Cleveland Inst of Art (OH)
Cleveland State U (OH)
Coastal Carolina U (SC)
Coe Coll (IA)
Cogswell Polytechnical Coll (CA)
Colby-Sawyer Coll (NH)
The Coll at Brockport, State U of New York (NY)
Coll of Charleston (SC)
The Coll of Idaho (ID)
Coll of Mount Saint Vincent (NY)
The Coll of New Rochelle (NY)
Coll of Saint Benedict (MN)
Coll of Saint Elizabeth (NJ)
The Coll of Saint Rose (NY)
The Coll of St. Scholastica (MN)
Coll of the Ozarks (MO)
The Coll of Wooster (OH)
Colorado Christian U (CO)
Colorado State U (CO)
Columbia Coll (SC)
Columbia Coll Chicago (IL)
Columbia Intl U (SC)
Columbus Coll of Art & Design (OH)
Concordia Coll (AL)
Concordia Coll (MN)
Concordia Coll–New York (NY)
Concordia U (QC, Canada)
Concordia U Chicago (IL)
Concordia U Irvine (CA)
Concordia U, Nebraska (NE)
Concordia U Wisconsin (WI)
Converse Coll (SC)
Corban U (OR)
Cornell Coll (IA)
Cornish Coll (WA)
Covenant Coll (GA)
Conservatorio de Musica (PR)
Creighton U (NE)
The Culinary Inst of America (NY)
Culver-Stockton Coll (MO)
Curry Coll (MA)
Daemen Coll (NY)
Dalhousie U (NS, Canada)
Dallas Baptist U (TX)
Dallas Christian Coll (TX)
Defiance Coll (OH
Delaware State (DE))
Delaware Valley U (PA)
DePaul U ((IL)
DePauw U (IN)
DEREE - The American Coll of Greece (Greece)
DeSales U (PA
Dillard U (LA)
D'Youville Coll (NY)
Dominican U (IL)
Dominican U of California (CA)
Drake U (IA)
Drew U (NJ)
Drexel U (PA)
Drury U (MO)
Duquesne U (PA)
East Carolina U (NC)
Eastern Connecticut State (CT)
Eastern Illinois U (IL)
Eastern Mennonite U (VA)
Eastern Michigan U (MI)
Eastern Nazarene Coll (MA)
Eastern U (PA)
East Stroudsburg U of Pennsylvania (PA)
East Tennessee State U (TN)
East Texas Baptist U (TX)
Eckerd Coll (FL)
Edgewood Coll (WI)
Elizabeth City State U (NC)
Elizabethtown Coll (PA)
Elmhurst Coll (IL)
Elmira Coll (NY)
Elms Coll (MA)
Elon U (NC)
Embry-Riddle Aeronautical U–Daytona (FL)
Embry-Riddle Aeronautical U–Prescott (AZ)
Emily Carr U of Art + Design (BC, Canada)
Endicott Coll (MA)
Erskine Coll (SC)
Escuela de Artes Plasticas y Dise&nno de Puerto Rico (PR)
Evangel U (MO)
The Evergreen State Coll (WA)
Fairleigh Dickinson U, Coll at Florham (NJ)
Fairleigh Dickinson U, Metropolitan Campus (NJ)
Farmingdale State Coll (NY)
Fashion Inst of Technology (NY)
Felician U (NJ)
FIDM/Fashion Inst of Design & Merchandising, Los Angeles Campus (CA)
FIDM/Fashion Inst of Design & Merchandising, San Francisco Campus (CA)
Fisk Univ (TN)
Five Towns Coll (NY)
Fitchburg State U (MA)
Florida Ag and Mech U (FL)
Florida Atlantic U (FL)
Florida Coll (FL)
Florida Gulf Coast U (FL)
Florida Inst of Technology (FL)
Florida Intl U (FL)
Florida National U (FL)
Florida Southern Coll (FL)
Fontbonne Univ (MO)
Fort Lewis Coll (CO)
Framingham State U (MA)

Franciscan U of Steubenville (OH)
Francis Marion U (SC)
Franklin Coll (IN)
Freed-Hardeman U (TN)
Fresno Pacific U (CA)
Friends U (KS)
Frostburg State U (MD)
Furman U (SC)
Gallaudet U (DC)
Gannon U (PA)
Gardner-Webb U (NC)
Geneva Coll (PA)
George Fox U (OR)
Georgetown Coll (KY)
Georgia Coll & State U (GA)
Georgian Court U (NJ)
Georgia Southern U (GA)
Georgia Southwestern State U (GA)
Georgia State U (CA)
Golden Gate Univ (GA)
Goldfarb School of Nursing at Barnes-Jewish Coll (MO)
Gonzaga U (WA)
Gordon Coll (MA)
Goshen Coll (IN)
Goucher Coll (MD)
Governors State U (IL)
Grace Coll (IN)
Graceland U (IA)
Grand Valley State U (MI)
Green Mountain Coll (VT)
Greenville Coll (IL)
Grove City Coll (PA)
Guilford Coll (NC)
Gwynedd Mercy U (PA)
Hallmark U (TX)
Hamline U (MN)
Hampden-Sydney Coll (VA)
Hampshire Coll (MA)
Hampton U (VA)
Hanover Coll (IN)
Harding U (AR)
Hardin-Simmons U (TX)
Hartwick Coll (NY)
Hastings Coll (NE)
Hawai`i Pacific U (HI)
HEC Montreal (QC, Canada)
Heidelberg U (OH)
Helene Fuld Coll of Nursing (NY)
Henderson State U (AR)
High Point U (NC)
Hiram Coll (OH)
Hofstra U (NY)
Hollins U (VA)
Holy Cross Coll (IN)
Holy Names U (CA)
Hood Coll (MD)
Hope Coll (MI)
Hope Intl U (CA)
Houghton Coll (NY)
Houston Baptist U (TX)
Howard Univ (DC)
Howard Payne U (TX)
Hult Intl Business School (United Kingdom)
Humboldt State U (CA)
Hunter Coll of the City U of New York (NY)
Huntington U (IN)
Husson U (ME)
Huston-Tillotson U (TX)
Illinois Coll (IL)
Illinois Inst of Tech (IL)
Illinois State U (IL)
Immaculata U (PA)
Indiana State U (IN)
Indiana U Bloomington (IN)
Indiana U East (IN)
Indiana U–Purdue U Indianapolis (IN)
Indiana U South Bend (IN)
Indiana Wesleyan (IN)
Inter American U of Puerto Rico, Aguadilla Campus (PR)
Inter American U of Puerto Rico, Fajardo Campus (PR)
Inter American U of Puerto Rico, Guayama Campus (PR)
Inter American U of Puerto Rico, Metropolitan Campus (PR)
Inter American U of Puerto Rico, Ponce Campus (PR)
Inter American U of Puerto Rico, San Germán Campus (PR)
Iona Coll (NY)
Iowa State U of Science and Technology (IA)
Iowa Wesleyan U (IA)
Ithaca Coll (NY)
Jacksonville State U (AL)
Jacksonville U (FL)
Jefferson Coll of Health Services (VA)
John Brown U (AR)
John Carroll U (OH)
John Jay Coll of Criminal Justice of the City U of New York (NY)
John Paul the Great Catholic U (CA)
Johnson & Wales (CO)
Johnson & Wales (FL)
Johnson & Wales (RI)
Johnson C. Smith U (NC)
Johnson State Coll (VT)
Johnson U (TN)
John Wesley U (NC)
Judson U (IL)
Juniata Coll (PA)
Kansas City Art Inst (MO)
Kansas Wesleyan U (KS)
Kean U (NJ)
Keene State Coll (NH)
Kennesaw State U (GA)
Kent State U (OH)
Kentucky Wesleyan Coll (KY)
Keuka Coll (NY)
The King's Coll (NY)
King's Coll (PA)
The King's U (AB, Canada)
King U (TN)
Kutztown U of Pennsylvania (PA)
Kuyper Coll (MI)
LaGrange Coll (GA)
Lake Erie Coll (OH)
Lake Forest Coll (IL)
Lakeview Coll of Nursing (IL)
Langston U (OK)
La Salle U (PA)
Lasell Coll (MA)
Lawrence Technological U (MI)
Lebanese American U (Lebanon)
Lebanon Valley Coll (PA)
Lehman Coll of the City U of New York (NY)
Le Moyne Coll (NY)
Lenoir-Rhyne U (NC)
LeTourneau U (TX)
Lewis U (IL)
Lincoln Christian U (IL)
Lindenwood U (MO)
Linfield Coll (OR)
Lipscomb U (TN)
Living Arts Coll (NC)
Lock Haven U of Pennsylvania (PA)
Long Island Univ, Brooklyn (NY)
Long Island Univ, Post (NY)
Longwood U (VA)
Loras Coll (IA)
Louisiana State U at Shreveport (LA)
Louisiana Coll (LA)
Louisiana State U and A&M Coll (LA)
Louisiana State U at Alexandria (LA)
Louisiana Tech U (LA)
Lourdes U (OH)
Loyola U Chicago (IL)
Loyola U Maryland (MD)
Loyola U New Orleans (LA)
Lubbock Christian U (TX)
Luther Coll (IA)
Lycoming Coll (PA)
Lynn U (FL)
Lyon Coll (AR)
MacMurray Coll (IL)
Madonna U (MI)
Maharishi U of Management (IA)
Malone U (OH)
Manchester U (IN)
Manhattan Coll (NY)
Manhattanville Coll (NY)
Mansfield U of Pennsylvania (PA)
Marian U (IN)
Marian U (WI)
Marietta Co (OH)
Marlboro Coll (VT)
Marquette (WI)
Mars Hill Univ (NC)
Marshall U (WV)
Martin Luther Coll (MN)
Mary Baldwin U (VA)
Marymount Manhattan Coll (NY)
Marymount U (VA)
Maryville Coll of Maryville (TN)
Maryville U of Saint Louis (MO)
Marywood U (PA)
Massachusetts Coll of Art and Design (MA)
Massachusetts Coll of Liberal Arts (MA)
Massachusetts Maritime Acad (MA)
The Master's U (CA)
McDaniel Coll (MD)
McKendree U (IL)
McMurry U (TX)
McNeese State U (LA)
Memphis Coll of Art (TN)
Menlo Coll (CA)
Mercer U, Macon (GA)
Mercy Coll (NY)
Mercy Coll of Ohio (OH)
Mercyhurst U (PA)
Meredith Coll (NC)
Merrimack Coll (MA)
Mesivta of Eastern Park Yeshiva (NY)
Messenger Coll (TX)
Messiah Coll (PA)
Metropolitan Coll of New York (NY)
Miami U (OH)
Michigan State U (MI)
Michigan Technological U (MI)
Middle Tennessee State Univ (TN)
Midwestern State Univ (TX)
Millersville U of Pennsylvania (PA)
Milligan Coll (TN)
Millikin U (IL)
Millsaps Coll (MS)
Mills Coll (CA)
Milwaukee Inst of Art and Design (WI)
Milwaukee School of Eng (WI)
Minneapolis Coll of Art and Design (MN)
Minnesota State U Moorhead (MN)
Minot State U (ND)
Misericordia U (PA)
Mississippi Coll (MS)
Mississippi State U (MS)
Mississippi Univ for Women (MS)
Missouri Baptist U (MO)
Missouri Southern State Univ (MO)
Missouri State U (MO)
Molloy Coll (NY)
Monmouth Coll (IL)
Monmouth U (NJ)
Montana State U (MT)
Montana State U–Northern (MT)
Montana Tech of The U of Montana (MT)
Montclair State U (NJ)
Moore Coll of Art & Design (PA)
Moravian Coll (PA)
Morehouse Coll (GA)
Morningside Coll (IA)
Morrisville State Coll (NY)
Mount Allison U (NB, Canada)
Mount Carmel Coll of Nursing (OH)
Mount Ida Coll (MA)
Mount Mary U (WI)
Mount Mercy U (IA)
Mount Saint Mary Coll (NY)
Mount St. Mary's U (MD)
Mount Vernon Nazarene U (OH)
Multnomah U (OR)
Murray State U (KY)
Muskingum U (OH)
Naropa U (CO)
Nazareth Coll of Rochester (NY)
Nebraska Methodist Coll (NE)
Nebraska Wesleyan U (NE)
Neumont Univ (UT)
Newberry Coll (SC)
NewSchool of Arch. & Design (CA)
New England Culinary Inst (VT)
New Hampshire Inst of Art (NH)
New Jersey City U (NJ)
New Jersey Inst of Tech (NJ)
New Mexico Inst of Mining and Technology (NM)
New Mexico State U (NM)

INDEXES

New Saint Andrews Coll (ID)
The New School Coll of Performing Arts (NY)
The New School–Parsons Paris (France)
New York Inst of Technology (NY)
New York School of Interior Design (NY)
Niagara U (NY)
North Carolina Wesleyan Coll (NC)
North Central Coll (IL)
North Dakota State U (ND)
Northeastern State U (OK)
Northern Arizona U (AZ)
Northern Illinois U (IL)
Northland Coll (WI)
Northwest Nazarene Univ (ID)
Northwestern Coll (IA)
Northwestern Oklahoma State U (OK)
Northwestern State U of Louisiana (LA)
Northwest Missouri State U (MO)
Northwest U (WA)
Northwood U, Michigan Campus (MI)
Nova Southeastern U (FL)
Oakland Univ (MI)
Ohio Dominican U (OH)
Ohio Northern Univ (OH)
Ohio U (OH)
Oklahoma Baptist U (OK)
Oklahoma Christian U (OK)
Oklahoma State U (OK)
Old Dominion U (VA)
O'More Coll of Design (TN)
Oral Roberts U (OK)
Oregon Coll of Art and Craft (OR)
Oregon State U (OR)
Otterbein U (OH)
Ouachita Baptist U (AR)
Pace U (NY)
Pace U, Pleasantville Campus (NY)
Pacific Lutheran U (WA)
Pacific Union (CA)
Pacific Univ (OR)
Palm Beach Atlantic U (FL)
Patrick Henry Coll (VA)
Penn State Beaver (PA)
Penn State Brandywine (PA)
Penn State DuBois (PA)
Penn State Fayette, The Eberly Campus (PA)
Penn State Greater Allegheny (PA)
Penn State Hazleton (PA)
Penn State Lehigh Valley (PA)
Penn State Mont Alto (PA)
Penn State New Kensington (PA)
Penn State Schuylkill (PA)
Penn State Shenango (PA)
Penn State Wilkes-Barre (PA)
Penn State Worthington Scranton (PA)
Penn State York (PA)
Pennsylvania Coll of Art & Design (PA)
Pennsylvania Coll of Health Sciences (PA)
Philadelphia Univ (PA)
Phillips Beth Israel School of Nursing (NY)
Piedmont Coll (GA)
Pine Manor Coll (MA)
Plymouth State U (NH)
Point Loma Nazarene U (CA)
Point Park U (PA)
Point U (GA)
Portland State U (OR)
Post Univ (CT)
Prairie View A&M U (TX)
Prescott Coll (AZ)
Principia Coll (IL)
Purchase Coll, State U of New York (NY)
Purdue U (IN)
Purdue U Northwest (IN)
Quincy Univ (IL)
Quinnipiac U (CT)
Ramapo Coll of New Jersey (NJ)
Randolph Coll (VA)
Randolph-Macon Coll (VA)
Ranken Tech Coll (MO)
Regis Coll (MA)
Regis U (CO)
Research Coll of Nursing (MO)
Resurrection U (IL)
Rhode Island Coll (RI)
Rider Univ (NJ)
Ringling Coll of Art and Design (FL)
Ripon Coll (WI)
Roanoke Coll (VA)
Roberts Wesleyan Coll (NY)
Rochester Inst of Technology (NY)
Rockhurst U (MO)
Rocky Mountain Coll (MT)
Rocky Mountain Coll of Art & Design (CO)
Roger Williams U (RI)
Rollins Coll (FL)
Roosevelt U (IL)
Rosemont Coll (PA)
Rowan U (NJ)
Royal Roads U (BC, Canada)
Rutgers U–Camden (NJ)
Rutgers U–Newark (NJ)
Rutgers U–New Brunswick (NJ)
Sacred Heart U (CT)
The Sage Colls (NY)
Saginaw Valley State U (MI)
St. Ambrose U (IA)
St. Andrews U (NC)
Saint Anselm Coll (NH)
Saint Anthony Coll of Nursing (IL)
Saint Augustine's U (NC)
St. Bonaventure U (NY)
St. Catherine U (MN)
St. Cloud State U (MN)
St. Edward's U (TX)
Saint Francis U (PA)
St. John Fisher Coll (NY)
St. John's Coll (MD)
St. John's Coll (NM)
Saint John's U (MN)
St. John's U (NY)
St. Joseph's Coll, Long Island Campus (NY)
St. Joseph's Coll, New York (NY)
Saint Joseph's U (PA)
St. Lawrence U (NY)
Saint Leo U (FL)
St. Louis Coll of Pharmacy (MO)
Saint Louis U–Madrid Campus (Spain)
Saint Martin's U (WA)
Saint Mary's Coll (IN)
Saint Mary's Coll of California (CA)
St. Mary's Coll of Maryland (MD)
St. Mary's U (TX)
Saint Mary's U of Minnesota (MN)
Saint Michael's Coll (VT)
St. Norbert Coll (WI)
Saint Peter's U (NJ)
St. Thomas Aquinas Coll (NY)
St. Thomas U (NB, Canada)
Saint Vincent Coll (PA)
Salem Coll (NC)
Salisbury U (MD)
Salve Regina U (RI)
Samford U (AL)
Sam Houston State U (TX)
San Diego State U (CA)
San Francisco Art Inst (CA)
San Francisco State U (CA)
Savannah Coll of Art and Design (GA)
School of Visual Arts (NY)
Schreiner U (TX)
Seattle Pacific U (WA)
Seattle U (WA)
Seton Hill U (PA)
Shepherd U (WV)
Shorter U (GA)
Siena Coll (NY)
Sierra Nevada Coll (NV)
Simmons Coll (MA)
Simon Fraser U (BC, Canada)
Simpson Coll (IA)
Simpson U (CA)
Slippery Rock U of Pennsylvania (PA)
Sonoma State U (CA)
South Dakota School of Mines and Technology (SD)
Southeastern Louisiana U (LA)
Southeastern Oklahoma State U (OK)
Southeast Missouri State U (MO)
Southern Adventist U (TN)
Southern Arkansas U–Magnolia (AR)
Southern California Institute of Architecture (CA)
Southern California Seminary (CA)
Southern Connecticut State U (CT)
Southern Illinois U Carbondale (IL)
Southern Illinois U Edwardsville (IL)
Southern Methodist U (TX)
Southern New Hampshire U (NH)
Southern Oregon U (OR)
Southern Utah U (UT)
Southwest Baptist U (MO)
Southwestern Adventist U (TX)
Spalding U (KY)
Spring Arbor U (MI)
Spring Hill Coll (AL)
Springfield Coll (MA)
State U of New York at Fredonia (NY)
State U of New York at Oswego (NY)
State U of New York at Plattsburgh (NY)
State U of New York Coll at Cortland (NY)
State U of New York Coll at Geneseo (NY)
State U of New York Coll at Old Westbury (NY)
State U of New York Coll at Potsdam (NY)
State U of New York Coll of Technology at Alfred (NY)
State U of New York Coll of Technology at Delhi (NY)
State U of New York Polytechnic Inst (NY)
Stephen F. Austin State U (TX)
Stephens Coll (MO)
Stetson U (FL)
Stevenson U (MD)
Suffolk U (MA)
Susquehanna U (PA)
Tabor Coll (KS)
Talladega Coll (AL)
Tarleton State U (TX)
Taylor U (IN)
Temple U (PA)
Texas A&M Intl U (TX)
Texas A&M U (TX)
Texas A&M U–Commerce (TX)
Texas A&M U–Corpus Christi (TX)
Texas A&M U–Kingsville (TX)
Texas State U (TX)
Texas Tech U (TX)
Texas Wesleyan U (TX)
Theil Coll (PA)
Thomas More Coll (KY)
Tiffin U (OH)
Toura Coll (NY)
Toccoa Falls Coll (GA)
Towson U (MD)
Trent U (ON, Canada)
Trevecca Nazarene U (TN)
Trine U (IN)
Trinity Baptist Coll (FL)
Trinity Christian Coll (IL)
Troy U (AL)
Truman State U (MO)
Tusculum Coll (TN)
Tuskagee U (AL)
Union Coll (KY)
Union Coll (NE)
Union U (TN)
United States Intl U–Africa (Kenya)
Unity Coll (ME)
Universidad Metropolitana (Puerto Rico)
Université de Montréal (QC, Canada)
Université de Sherbrooke (QC, Canada)
U at Buffalo, the State U of New York (NY)
The U of Akron (OH)
The U of Alabama (AL)
The U of Alabama at Birmingham (AL)
The U of Alabama in Huntsville (AL)
The U of Arizona (AZ)
U of Arkansas (AR)
U of Bridgeport (CT)
U of Calgary (AB, Canada)
U of California–Merced (CA)
U of Central Arkansas (AR)
U of Central Florida (FL)
U of Central Missouri (MO)
U of Charleston (WV)
U of Cincinnati (OH)
U of Colorado Boulder (CO)
U of Colorado Colorado Springs (CO)
U of Colorado Denver (CO)

U of Dallas (TX)
U of Dayton (OH)
U of Delaware (DE)
U of Denver (CO)
U of Detroit Mercy (MI)
U of Dubuque (IA)
U of Evansville (IN)
The U of Findlay (OH)
U of Georgia (GA)
U of Guelph (ON, Canada)
U of Hartford (CT)
U of Hawaii at Manoa (HI)
U of Hawaii-West Oahu (HI)
U of Houston (TX)
U of Idaho (ID)
U of Iowa (IA)
U of Illinois at Chicago (IL)
U of Illinois at Springfield (IL)
U of Indianapolis (IN)
The U of Kansas (KS)
U of Kentucky (KY)
U of King's Coll (NS, Canada)
U of La Verne (CA)
U of Lethbridge (AB, Canada)
U of Louisiana at Lafayette (LA)
U of Louisiana at Monroe (LA)
U of Louisville (KY)
U of Lynchburg (VA)
U of Maine (ME)
U of Maine at Machias (ME)
U of Mary Hardin-Baylor (TX)
U of Maryland, Baltimore County (MD)
U of Maryland, Coll Park (MD)
U of Massachusetts Amherst (MA)
U of Massachusetts Boston (MA)
U of Massachusetts Dartmouth (MA)
U of Massachusetts Lowell (MA)
U of Memphis (TN)
U of Michigan–Dearborn (MI)
U of Michigan–Flint (MI)
U of Minnesota, Duluth (MN)
U of Minnesota, Morris (MN)
U of Minnesota, Twin Cities Campus (MN)
U of Mississippi (MS)
U of Missouri-Columbia (MO)
U of Missouri–Kansas City (MO)
U of Missouri–St. Louis (MO)
U of Mobile (AL)
U of Montana (MT)
U of Montevallo (AL)
U of Mount Union (OH)
U of Nebraska at Kearney (NE)
U of Nebraska at Lincoln (NE)
U of Nevada, Las Vegas (NV)
U of Nevada, Reno (NV)
U of New Brunswick St. John (NB, Canada)
U of New England (ME)
U of New Mexico (NM)
U of New Hampshire (NH)
U of New Hampshire at Manchester (NH)
U of New Haven (CT)
U of New Orleans (LA)
U of North Carolina at Asheville (NC)
The U of North Carolina at Charlotte (NC)
The U of North Carolina at Greensboro (NC)
The U of North Carolina at Pembroke (NC)
The U of North Carolina Wilmington (NC)
U of Northern Colorado (CO)
U of Northern Iowa (IA)
U of North Florida (FL)
U of North Georgia (GA)
U of North Texas (TX)
U of Oklahoma (OK)
U of Oregon (OR)
U of Pittsburgh at Greensburg (PA)
U of Pittsburgh at Johnstown (PA)
U of Portland (OR)
U of Puget Sound (WA)
U of Redlands (CA)
U of Rhode Island (RI)
U of St. Francis (IL)
U of Saint Joseph (CT)
U of Saint Mary (KS)
U of St. Thomas (MN)
U of St. Thomas (TX)
U of San Francisco (CA)
U of Science and Arts of Oklahoma (OK)
The U of Scranton (PA)
U of South Alabama (AL)
U of South Carolina (SC)
U of South Carolina Aiken (SC)
The U of South Dakota (SD)
U of Southern Indiana (IN)
U of Southern Maine (ME)
U of Southern Mississippi (MS)
U of South Florida (FL)
The U of Tampa (FL)
The U of Tennessee (TN)
The U of Tennessee at Chattanooga (TN)
The U of Tennessee at Martin (TN)
The U of Texas at Austin (TX)
The U of Texas at San Antonio (TX)
U of Texas at Tyler (TX)
U of Texas Health Science at Houston (TX)
The U of Texas of the Permian Basin (TX)
The U of the Arts (PA)
U of the Cumberlands (KY)
U of the Incarnate Word (TX)
U of the Pacific (CA)
U of the Sciences (PA)
U of the Southwest (NM)
U of Utah (UT)
U of Vermont (VT)
The U of Virginia's Coll at Wise (VA)
U of Washington, Bothell (WA)
U of Washington, Tacoma (WA)
U of Waterloo (ON, Canada)
U of West Florida (FL)
U of West Georgia (GA)
U of Wisconsin–Eau Claire (WI)
U of Wisconsin–Green Bay (WI)
U of Wisconsin–La Crosse (WI)
U of Wisconsin–Milwaukee (WI)
U of Wisconsin–Parkside (WI)
U of Wisconsin–River Falls (WI)
U of Wisconsin–Stevens Point (WI)
U of Wisconsin–Stout (WI)
U of Wisconsin–Whitewater (WI)
U of Wyoming (WY)
Upper Iowa U (IA)
Ursinus Coll (PA)
Utah State U (UT)
Utica Coll (NY)
Valdosta State U (GA)
Valparaiso U (IN)
Vanguard U (CA)
Vaughn Coll of Aeronautics and Technology (NY)
Vermont Tech Coll (VT)
Virginia Military Inst (VA)
Virginia Polytechnic Inst and State U (VA)
Virginia Union U (VA)
Virginia Wesleyan Coll (VA)
Viterbo U (WI)
Wabash Coll (IN)
Waldorf U (IA)
Walla Walla U (WA)
Walsh U (OH)
Wartburg Coll (IA)
Warner Pacific Coll (OR)
Warren Wilson Coll (NC)
Washington Coll (MD)
Washington State U (WA)
Washington State U–Global Campus (WA)
Washington State U–Spokane (WA)
Washington State U–Tri-Cities (WA)
Washington State U–Vancouver (WA)
Watkins Coll of Art, Design, & Film (TN)
Waynesburg U (PA)
Wayne State U (MI)
Webber Intl U (FL)
Webster U (MO)
Wells Coll (NY)
Wentworth Inst of Technology (MA)
Wesleyan Coll (GA)
West Chester U of Pennsylvania (PA)
Western Carolina U (NC)
Western Connecticut State U (CT)
Western Illinois U (IL)
Western Michigan U (MI)
Western New England U (MA)
Western Oregon U (OR)
Western State Colorado U (CO)
Western Washington U (WA)
Westfield State U (MA)
Westminster Coll (MO)
Westminster Coll (PA)
Westminster Coll (UT)
Westmont Coll (CA)
West Texas A&M U (TX)
West Virginia U (WV)
West Virginia Wesleyan Coll (WV)
Wheeling Jesuit U (WV)
Whittier Coll (CA)
Whitworth U (WA)
Widener U (PA)
Wilkes U (PA)
William Jessup U (CA)
William Jewell Coll (MO)
William Paterson U of New Jersey (NJ)
William Peace U (NC)
William Penn U (IA)
William Woods U (MO)
Wilson Coll (PA)
Wingate U (NC)
Winona State U (MN)
Winthrop U (SC)
Wittenberg U (OH)
Woodbury U (CA)
Worcester State U (MA)
Xavier U of Louisiana (LA)
Yeshiva U (NY)
York Coll of Pennsylvania (PA)
York Coll of the City U of New York (NY)
Young Harris Coll (GA)

MINIMALLY DIFFICULT

Most freshmen were not in the top half of their high school class and scored somewhat below 1010 on the SAT or below 19 on the ACT; up to 95 percent of the applicants were accepted.

Adventist U of Health Sciences (FL)
Alabama State U (AL)
Alaska Bible Coll (AK)
Alaska Pacific U (AK)
Albany State U (GA)
Alliant Intl U–San Diego (CA)
Amberton U (TX)
American Coll of Thessaloniki (Greece)
American Intl Coll (MA)
Amridge U (AL)
Anderson U (SC)
Anna Maria Coll(MA)
Aquinas Coll (TN)
Austin Graduate School of Theology (TX)
Avila U (MO)
Baker Coll (MI)
Barclay Coll (KS)
Barton Coll (NC)
Benedictine Coll (KS)
Bennett Coll (NC)
Berkeley Coll–New York City Campus (NY)
Berkeley Coll–White Plains Campus (NY)
Berkeley Coll–Woodland Park Campus (NJ)
Bethel Coll (IN)
Bethune-Cookman U (FL)
Bloomsburg U of Pennsylvania (PA)
Bowie State U (MD)
Brewton-Parker Coll (GA)
Bryn Athyn Coll of the New Church (PA)
California Inst of Integral Studies (CA)
California State U, Fresno (CA)
Caribbean U (PR)
Carlow U (PA)
Cazenovia Coll (NY)
Central Baptist Coll (AR)
Central Penn Coll (PA)
Central State U (OH)
Chowan U (NC)
Clayton State U (GA)
CollAmerica–Fort Collins (CO)
Coll of Business and Technology–Main Campus (FL)
Coll of Business and Technology–Miami Gardens (FL)
Coll of Coastal Georgia (GA)
Coll of Saint Mary (NE)
The Coll of Westchester (NY)
Colorado Mesa U (CO)

INDEXES

Columbia Coll (MO)
Columbus State U (GA)
Concordia U, St. Paul (MN)
Concord U (WV)
Cornerstone U (MI)
Crandall U (NB, Canada)
Criswell Coll (TX)
Dakota State U (SD)
Davis Coll (NY)
Dean Coll (MA)
DeVry U–Arlington Campus (VA)
DeVry U–Chicago Campus (IL)
DeVry U–Columbus Campus (OH)
DeVry U–Decatur Campus (GA)
DeVry U–Irving Campus (TX)
DeVry U-Kansas City Campus (MO)
DeVRy U–Long Beach Campus (CA)
DeVry U–Midtown Manhattan Campus (NY)
DeVry U–Miramar Campus (FL)
DeVry U–North Brunswick Campus (NJ)
DeVry U–Orlando Campus (FL)
DeVry U–Phoenix Campus (AZ)
Dickinson State U (ND)
DigiPen Inst of Technology (WA)
Dunwoody Coll of Technology (MN)
East Central U (OK)
Eastern Kentucky U (KY)
Eastern Oregon U (OR)
East Georgia State Coll (GA)
EDP U of Puerto Rico–San Sebastian (PR)
Embry-Riddle Aeronautical U–Worldwide (FL)
Emmanuel Coll (GA)
Eureka Coll (IL)
Fairmont State U (WV)
Faith Baptist Bible Coll and Theological Sem (IA)
Faulkner U (AL)
Fayetteville State U (NC)
Ferris State U (MI)
Franklin Pierce U (NH)
Goddard Coll (VT)
Grand View U (IA)
Greensboro Coll (NC)
Hannibal-LaGrange U (MO)
Harrisburg U of Science and Technology (PA)
Helenic Coll (MA)
Heritage Bible Coll (NC)
Hilbert Coll (NY)
Hodges U (FL)
Holy Family U (PA)
Hussian Coll, School of Art (PA)
Idaho State U (ID)
Indiana U Kokomo (IN)
Indiana U Northwest (IN)
Indiana U of Pennsylvania (PA)
Indiana U Southeast (IN)
Jackson State U (MS)
Jamestown Business Coll (NY)
Jarvis Christian Coll(TX)
Johnson U Florida (FL)
Kansas State U (KS)
Kendall Coll (IL)
Kentucky Mountain Bible Coll (KY)
Lamar U (TX)
Lane Coll (TN)
La Roche Coll (PA)
LaSierra U (CA)
Lees-McRae Coll (NC)
LeMoyne–Owen Coll (TN)
Lewis–Clark State Coll (ID)
Liberty U (VA)
Life U (GA)
Limestone Coll (SC)
Lincoln Coll (IL)
Lincoln Coll–Normal (IL)
Lincoln Coll of New England, Southington (CT)
Lincoln U (CA)
Lincoln U (PA)
Lindsey Wilson Coll (KY)
Maria Coll (NY)
Marymount California U (CA)
Metropolitan State U of Denver (CO)
MidAmerica Nazarene U (KS)
Mid-Atlantic Christian U (NC)
Middle Georgia State U (GA)
Mississippi Valley State U (MS)
Missouri Valley Coll (MO)
Mitchell Coll (CT)
Montana State U Billings (MT)
Morehead State U (KY)
Mount Aloysius Coll (PA)
Mount Marty Coll (SD)
Mount St. Joseph U (OH)
National Louis U (IL)
Neumann U (PA)
Nevada State Coll (NV)
New England Coll (NH)
New England Inst of Technology (RI)
Newberry Coll (MA)
Newman U (KS)
New Mexico Highlands U (NM)
North American U (TX)
North Carolina Central U (NC)
Northcentral U (CA)
Northeastern Illinois U (IL)
Northern State U (SD)
North Greenville U (SC)
Northwest Christian U (OR)
Nyack Coll (NY)
Oakland City U (IN)
Ohio Christian U (OH)
Ohio Valley U (WV)
Oklahoma Wesleyan U (OK)
Olivet Nazarene U (IL)
Our Lady of the Lake Coll (LA)
Pacific Northwest Coll of Art (OR)
Paine Coll (GA)
Philander Smith Coll (AR)
Pittsburg State U (KS)
Polytechnic U of Puerto Rico (PR)
Radford U (VA)
Rasmussen Coll Aurora (IL)
Rasmussen Coll Blaine (MN)
Rasmussen Coll Bloomington (MN)
Rasmussen Coll Brooklyn Park (MN)
Rasmussen Coll Eagan (MN)
Rasmussen Coll Fargo (ND)
Rasmussen Coll Fort Myers (FL)
Rasmussen Coll Green Bay (WI)
Rasmussen Coll Kansas City/Overland Park (KS)
Rasmussen Coll Lake Elmo/Woodbury (MN)
Rasmussen Coll Land O' Lakes (FL)
Rasmussen Coll Mankato (MN)
Rasmussen Coll Mokena/Tinley Park (IL)
Rasmussen Coll Moorhead (MN)
Rasmussen Coll New Port Richey (FL)
Rasmussen Coll Ocala (FL)
Rasmussen Coll Ocala School of Nursing (FL)
Rasmussen Coll Rockford (IL)
Rasmussen Coll Romeoville/Joliet (IL)
Rasmussen Coll St. Cloud (MN)
Rasmussen Coll Tampa/Brandon (FL)
Rasmussen Coll Topeka (KS)
Rasmussen Coll Wausau (WI)
Regent U (VA)
Robert Morris U (PA)
Robert Morris U Illinois (IL)
Rust Coll (MS)
St. Gregory's U, Shawnee (OK)
Saint Louis Christian Coll (MO)
St. Luke's Coll (IA)
Saint Mary-of-the-Woods Coll (IN)
San Diego Christian Coll (CA)
Savannah State U (GA)
Shaw U (NC)
Silver Lake Coll of the Holy Family (WI)
South Carolina State U (SC)
South Dakota State U (SD)
Southeastern U (FL)
Southwestern Coll (KS)
Southwestern Oklahoma State (OK)
Spencerian Coll (KY)
State U of New York Coll of Agriculture and Technology at Cobleskill (NY)
State U of New York Coll of Technology at Canton (NY)
Sterling Coll (KS)
Stratford U (MD)
Sullivan U (KY)
Sweet Briar Coll (VA)
Tennessee State U (TN)
Tennessee Wesleyan U (TN)
Texas Woman's U (TX)
Thomas U (GA)
Trociare Coll (NY)
Truett McConnell U (GA)
Universidad Adventista de las Antillas (PR)
Universidad del Turabo (PR)
U of Alaska Fairbanks (AK)
U of Central Oklahoma (OK)
U of Houston–Clear Lake (TX)
U of Jamestown (ND)
U of Maine at Fort Kent (ME)
U of Maine at Presque Isle (ME)
U of Mary (ND)
U of Minnesota, Crookston (MN)
The U of Montana Western (MT)
U of North Alabama (AL)
U of North Dakota (ND)
U of Pittsburgh at Bradford (PA)
U of Regina (SK, Canada)
U of Saint Francis (IN)
U of South Carolina Beaufort (SC)
U of South Carolina Union (SC)
The U of Texas at El Paso (TX)
U of the West (CA)
U of Valley Forge (PA)
The U of West Alabama (AL)
U of Wisconsin–Superior (WI)
Ursuline Coll (OH)
Virginia State U (VA)
Wayland Baptist U (TX)
Western Kentucky U (KY)
West Liberty U (WV)
West Virginia State U (WV)
West Virginia U Inst of Technology (WV)
Wheelock Coll (MA)
Williams Baptist Coll (AR)
Wright State U (OH)
Wright State U–Lake Campus (OH)
Youngstown State U (OH)

NONCOMPETITIVE

Virtually all applicants were accepted regardless of high school rank or test scores.

Academy Coll (MN)
Acad of Art U (CA)
Appalachian Bible Coll (WV)
American Baptist Coll (TN)
American Public U System (WV)
American Samoa Comm Coll (AS)
Antioch U Midwest (OH)
Antioch U Seattle (WA)
Arlington Baptist Coll (TX)
Athens State U (AL)
Bainbridge State Coll (GA)
The Baptist Coll of Florida (FL)
Beulah Heights U (GA)
Beverly Hills Design Institute (CA)
Bismarck State Coll (ND)
Bluefield State Coll (WV)
Boston Architectural Coll (MA)
Bowling Green State U–Firelands Coll (OH)
California Christian Coll (CA)
Calumet Coll of Saint Joseph (IN)
Calvary U (MO)
Cameron U (OK)
Capilano U (BC, Canada)
Carolina Christian Coll (NC)
Carver Coll (GA)
Cascadia Coll (WA)
Cecil Coll (MD)
Charter Oak State Coll (CT)
Chipola Coll
City Vision U (MO)
Clark Coll (WA)
Cleveland U–Kansas City (KS)
CollegeAmerica–Denver (CO)
College of Biblical Studies–Houston (TX)
Coll of Central Florida (FL)
Colorado Mtn College–Glenwood Springs (CO)
Colorado Mtn College–Steamboat Springs(CO)
Columbia Southern U (AL)
Conception Seminary Coll (MO)

Dalton State Coll (GA)
Davenport U, Grand Rapids (MI)
Daytona State Coll (FL)
Dixie State U (UT)
Dominican Coll (NY)
Donnelly Coll (KS)
Ecclesia Coll (AR)
EDP U of Puerto Rico (PR)
Emmaus Bible Coll (IA)
Emporia State U (KS)
Everglades U–Boca Raton (FL)
Everglades U–Maitland (FL)
Everglades U–Sarasota (FL)
Everglades U–Tampa (FL)
Feather River Coll (CA)
Florida Keys Comm Coll (FL)
Florida SouthWestern State Coll (FL)
Georgia Gwinnett Coll (GA)
Georgia Highlands Coll (GA)
Georgia Military Coll (GA)
Glenville State Coll (WV)
Global U (MO)
Grambling State U (LA)
Granite State Coll (NH)
Great Basin Coll (NV)
Gulf Coast State Coll (FL)
Harris-Stowe State U (MO)
Hesston Coll (KS)
Hobe Sound Bible Coll (FL)
Holy Apostles Coll & Seminary
Holy Trinity Orthodox Sem (NY)
Humacao Comm Coll (PR)
Humphreys Coll (CA)
Huntington Coll of Health Sciences (TN)
Jones Coll (FL)
Kent State U at Ashtabula (OH)
Kent State U at East Liverpool (OH)
Kent State U at Geauga (OH)
Kent State U at Salem (OH)
Kent State U at Stark (OH)
Kent State U at Trumbull (OH)
Kent State U at Tuscarawas (OH)
Lincoln U (MO)
Los Angeles Film School (CA)
Luther Rice Coll & Sem (GA)
Maranatha Baptist U (WI)
Marylhurst U (OR)
Maryville State U (ND)
Master's Coll and Sem (ON, Canada)
Medgar Evers Coll of the City U of New York (NY)
Miami Dade Coll (FL)
Midland Coll (TX)
Missouri Western State U (MO)
Morris Coll (SC)
National U (CA)
Nazarene Bible Coll (CO)
New York City Coll of Technology of the City U of New York (NY)
The Ohio State U at Lima (OH)
The Ohio State U at Marion (OH)
The Ohio State U–Mansfield Campus (OH)
The Ohio State U–Newark Campus (OH)
Ohio U–Chillicothe (OH)
Ohio U–Eastern (OH)
Ohio U–Zanesville (OH)
Oklahoma State U Inst of Technology (OK)
Oklahoma State U–Oklahoma City (OK)
Olympic Coll (WA)
Pacific States U (CA)
Palm Beach State Coll (FL)
Peirce Coll (PA)
Pennsylvania Coll of Technology (PA)
Pensacola State Coll (FL)
Piedmont Intl U (NC)
Polk State Coll (FL)
Potomac State Coll of West VA U (WV)
Pueblo Comm Coll (CO)
Renton Tech Coll (WA)
Rocky Mtn Coll (AB, Canada)
Rogers State U (OK)
St. Petersburg Coll (FL)
Schoolcraft Coll (MI)
Seminole State Coll of Florida (FL)
Shawnee State U (OH)
Shiloh U (IA)
Southeastern Baptist Theological Sem (NC)
Southeastern Bible Coll (AL)
Southern Nazarene U (OK)
Southern Vermont Coll (VT)
South Florida State Coll (FL)
Southwestern Assemblies of God U (TX)
State Coll of Florida Manatee-Sarasota (FL)
State U of New York Empire State Coll (NY)
Stratford U, Falls Church (VA)
Sul Ross State U (TX)
Tallahassee Comm Coll (FL)
Thomas Edison State U (NJ)
Trinity Bible Coll (ND)
Trinity Coll of Florida (FL)
Truckee Meadows Comm Coll (NV)
Tyler Jr Coll (TX)
Union Inst & U (OH)
Universidad del Este (PR)
U of Alaska Anchorage, Kenai Penn Coll (AK)
U of Cincinnati Blue Ash Coll (OH)
U of Cincinnati Clermont Coll (OH)
U of Great Falls (MT)
U of Houston–Downtown (TX)
U of Maine at Augusta (ME)
U of Maryland U Coll (MD)
U of Northwestern Ohio (OH)
U of Pikeville (KY)
U of Rio Grande (OH)
The U of Texas Rio Grande Valley (TX)
U of the Potomac (DC)
U of the Virgin Islands (VI)
The U of Toledo (OH)
Utah Valley U (UT)
Valley City State U (ND)
Vincennes U (IN)
Walsh Coll of Accountancy and Business Administration (MI)
Washburn U (KS)
Wayne State Coll (NE)
Weber State U (UT)
Welch Coll (TN)
Western Nevada Coll (NV)
Wichita State U (KS)
Williamson Coll (TN)
Wilmington U (DE)

INDEXES

Cost Ranges

LESS THAN $2000

Colleges with No Room and Board or with Room Only
United States Merchant Marine Acad (NY)

Colleges with Room and Board
Royal Military Coll of Canada (ON, Canada)
Silver Lake Coll of the Holy Family (WI)
United States Military Acad (NY)

$2000–$3999

Colleges with No Room and Board or with Room Only
American Samoa Comm Coll (AS)
Capilano U (BC, Canada)
Cecil Coll (MD)
Georgia Highlands Coll (GA)
Oklahoma State U–Oklahoma City (OK)
Polk State Coll (FL)
St. Petersburg Coll (FL)
Seminole State Coll of Florida (FL)
Shiloh U (IA)
U of South Carolina Union (SC)
Valencia Coll (FL)
Western Nevada Coll (NV)

$4000–$5999

Colleges with No Room and Board or with Room Only
Bowling Green State U–Firelands Coll (OH)
Columbia Southern U (AL)
EDP U of Puerto Rico (PR)
EDP U of Puerto Rico–San Sebastian (PR)
Humacao Comm Coll (PR)
Inter American U of Puerto Rico, Aguadilla Campus (PR)
Inter American U of Puerto Rico, Fajardo Campus (PR)
Nevada State Coll (NV)
Ohio U–Eastern (OH)
U of Toronto (ON, Canada)

$6000–$7999

Colleges with No Room and Board or with Room Only
Bayamón Central U (PR)
City Vision U (MO)
Georgia Military Coll (GA)
Great Basin Coll (NV) **(room only)**
Inter American U of Puerto Rico, Barranquitas Campus (PR)
Inter American U of Puerto Rico, Guayama Campus (PR)
Lehman Coll of the City U of New York (NY)
National Paralegal Coll (AZ)
Pueblo Comm Coll (CO)
State U of New York Empire State Coll (NY)
U of Cincinnati Blue Ash Coll (OH)
U of Lethbridge (AB, Canada)
U of Maryland U Coll (MD)
U of Saskatchewan (SK, Canada)
Western Intl U (AZ)

Colleges with Room and Board
Midland Coll (TX)
Theological U of the Caribbean (PR)

$8000–$9999

Colleges with No Room and Board or with Room Only
American Coll of Thessaloniki (Greece)
Austin Graduate School of Theology (TX)
Baptist U of the Americas (TX) **(room only)**
Criswell Coll (TX)
Embry-Riddle Aeronautical U–Worldwide (FL)
U of Missouri–Kansas City (MO)

Colleges with Room and Board
Inter American U of Puerto Rico, San Germán Campus (PR)
South Florida State Coll (FL)

$10,000–$11,999

Colleges with No Room and Board or with Room Only
Harris-Stowe State U (MO) **(room only)**
Hunter Coll of the City U of New York (NY) **(room only)**
Nazarene Bible Coll (CO)
Northcentral U (CA)
United States Sports Acad (AL)
U of Colorado Denver (CO)
U of Hawaii at Manoa (HI)

Colleges with Room and Board
Dixie State U (UT)
East Central U (OK)
Holy Trinity Orthodox Sem (NY)
Inter American U of Puerto Rico, Bayamón Campus (PR)
Oklahoma State U Inst of Technology (OK)
Universidad Adventista de las Antillas (PR)

$12,000–$13,999

Colleges with No Room and Board or with Room Only
Carolina Christian Coll (NC)
Coll of Business and Technology–Main Campus (FL)
Coll of Business and Technology–Miami Gardens (FL)
Eastern Michigan U (MI)
Louisiana State U Health Sciences Center (LA) **(room only)**
National Louis U (IL)
National U (CA)
Rasmussen Coll Aurora (IL)
Rasmussen Coll Blaine (MN)
Rasmussen Coll Bloomington (MN)
Rasmussen Coll Brooklyn Park (MN)
Rasmussen Coll Eagan (MN)
Rasmussen Coll Fargo (ND)
Rasmussen Coll Fort Myers (FL)
Rasmussen Coll Green Bay (WI)
Rasmussen Coll Kansas City/Overland Park (KS)
Rasmussen Coll Lake Elmo/Woodbury (MN)
Rasmussen Coll Land O' Lakes (FL)
Rasmussen Coll Mankato (MN)
Rasmussen Coll Mokena/Tinley Park (IL)
Rasmussen Coll Moorhead (MN)
Rasmussen Coll New Port Richey (FL)
Rasmussen Coll Ocala (FL)
Rasmussen Coll Ocala School of Nursing (FL)
Rasmussen Coll Rockford (IL)
Rasmussen Coll Romeoville/Joliet (IL)
Rasmussen Coll St. Cloud (MN)
Rasmussen Coll Tampa/Brandon (FL)
Rasmussen Coll Topeka (KS)
Rasmussen Coll Wausau (WI)
Union Inst & U (OH)
U of Northwestern Ohio (OH) **(room only)**
U of the Potomac (DC)
Williamson Coll (TN)

Colleges with Room and Board
Alaska Bible Coll (AK)
American U in Bulgaria (Bulgaria)
Bishop's U (QC, Canada)
Coll of Coastal Georgia (GA)
Concordia U (QC, Canada)
Dalton State Coll (GA)
Dickinson State U (ND)
East Georgia State Coll (GA)
Gordon State Coll (GA)
Hobe Sound Bible Coll (FL)
Idaho State U (ID)
Mississippi Valley State U (MS)
Montana State U Billings (MT)
Montana State U–Northern (MT)
New Mexico Highlands U (NM)
Texas Coll (TX)
U of the Fraser Valley (BC, Canada)

$14,000–$15,999

Colleges with No Room and Board or with Room Only
Lane Coll (TN) **(room only)**
Stratford U, Alexandria (VA)
Stratford U, Newport News (VA)
Stratford U, Virginia Beach (VA)
Stratford U, Woodbridge (VA)
U of New Hampshire at Manchester (NH)

Colleges with Room and Board
Alabama State U (AL)
Albany State U (GA)
The Baptist Coll of Florida (FL)
Black Hills State U (SD)
Calvary U (MO)
Florida Ag and Mech U (FL)
Grambling State U (LA)
Inst of American Indian Arts (NM)
Master's Coll and Sem (ON, Canada)
Minnesota State U Moorhead (MN)
U of Maine at Fort Kent (ME)
U of South Florida, St. Petersburg (FL)
U of the Virgin Islands (VI)
The U of West Alabama (AL)
U of Wisconsin–Green Bay (WI)
U of Wisconsin–Parkside (WI)
Valdosta State U (GA)
Washburn U (KS)

$16,000–$17,999

Colleges with No Room and Board or with Room Only
Academy Coll (MN)
Aultman Coll of Nursing and Health Sciences (OH)
Calumet Coll of Saint Joseph (IN)
Lakeview Coll of Nursing (IL)
Nossi Coll of Art (TN)

Colleges with Room and Board
Austin Peay State U (TN)
East Carolina U (NC)
Florida Intl U (FL)
Iowa State U of Science and Technology (IA)
New Coll of Florida (FL)
Northern State U (SD)
Piedmont Intl U (NC)
Rogers State U (OK)
Texas A&M U–Commerce (TX)
Texas Woman's U (TX)
U of Alaska Fairbanks (AK)
U of Guelph (ON, Canada)
U of Maine at Presque Isle (ME)
U of Northern Iowa (IA)

U of North Georgia (GA)
U of Southern Indiana (IN)
U of Southern Mississippi (MS)
U of South Florida (FL)
The U of Texas at El Paso (TX)
The U of Texas of the Permian Basin (TX)
U of West Georgia (GA)
U of Wisconsin–Stevens Point (WI)

$18,000–$19,999

Colleges with No Room and Board or with Room Only

Adventist U of Health Sciences (FL) **(room only)**
Allen Coll (IA)
Metropolitan Coll of New York (NY)
Mount Carmel Coll of Nursing (OH) **(room only)**
Northwest Coll of Art & Design (WA)
Rosemont Coll (PA)
Spencerian Coll (KY)

Colleges with Room and Board

Ambrose U (AB, Canada)
Ball State U (IN)
California State U, Sacramento (CA)
California State U, San Bernardino (CA)
Central Washington U (WA)
Florida Atlantic U (FL)
Humboldt State U (CA)
The King's U (AB, Canada)
Lamar U (TX)
Louisiana Coll (LA)
Missouri U of Science and Technology (MO)
North American U (TX)
North Carolina State U (NC)
Ohio Christian U (OH)
Rhode Island Coll (RI)
Sam Houston State U (TX)
State U of New York Polytechnic Inst (NY)
Tarleton State U (TX)
Texas A&M Intl U (TX)
Trinity Baptist Coll (FL)
U of Louisville (KY)
U of Maine at Farmington (ME)
U of Nevada, Las Vegas (NV)
U of Nevada, Reno (NV)
U of North Carolina School of the Arts (NC)
U of Northern Colorado (CO)

$20,000–$24,999

Colleges with No Room and Board or with Room Only

Boston Architectural Coll (MA)
Brescia U (KY)
California Inst of Integral Studies (CA)
Chowan U (NC)
The Coll of Westchester (NY)
Design Inst of San Diego (CA)
Dunwoody Coll of Technology (MN)
Goldfarb School of Nursing at Barnes-Jewish Coll (MO)
Mercy Coll of Ohio (OH) **(room only)**
Nebraska Methodist Coll (NE) **(room only)**
Saint Francis Medical Center Coll of Nursing (IL) **(room only)**
St. Luke's Coll (IA)
Thomas U (GA) **(room only)**

Colleges with Room and Board

Arlington Baptist Coll (TX)
Augusta U (GA)
Bridgewater State U (MA)
California Polytechnic State U, San Luis Obispo (CA)
California State Polytechnic U, Pomona (CA)
California State U, East Bay (CA)
California State U Maritime Acad (CA)
Central Baptist Coll (AR)
The Citadel, The Military Coll of South Carolina (SC)
Dalhousie U (NS, Canada)
Davis Coll (NY)
Ecclesia Coll (AR)
Framingham State U (MA)
Lee U (TN)
Lincoln Christian U (IL)
Lincoln Coll of New England, Southington (CT)
Mansfield U of Pennsylvania (PA)
Maranatha Baptist U (WI)
Martin Luther Coll (MN)
Morrisville State Coll (NY)
New Jersey City U (NJ)
Northeastern Illinois U (IL)
Polytechnic U of Puerto Rico (PR)
Purchase Coll, State U of New York (NY)
Queens Coll of the City U of New York (NY)
Rowan U (NJ)
Shawnee State U (OH)
Sonoma State U (CA)
Southern Illinois U Edwardsville (IL)
State U of New York at Fredonia (NY)
Texas A&M U (TX)
Texas State U (TX)
Trinity Coll of Florida (FL)
U at Albany, State U of New York (NY)
The U of Akron (OH)
U of Illinois at Springfield (IL)
The U of North Carolina at Chapel Hill (NC)
U of Pittsburgh at Johnstown (PA)
U of the West (CA)
U of Washington (WA)
U of Washington, Bothell (WA)
U of Washington, Tacoma (WA)
U of Waterloo (ON, Canada)
U of Wisconsin–Milwaukee (WI)
Williams Baptist Coll (AR)

$25,000–$29,999

Colleges with No Room and Board or with Room Only

Berkeley Coll–New York City Campus (NY)
Berkeley Coll–Woodland Park Campus (NJ)
Columbia Coll Chicago (IL)
Creative Center (NE)
New England Inst of Technology (RI)
Pennsylvania Coll of Art & Design (PA)
St. Joseph's Coll, Long Island Campus (NY)
St. Joseph's Coll, New York (NY)

Colleges with Room and Board

Alaska Pacific U (AK)
The American U of Rome (Italy)
Blackburn Coll (IL)
Brewton-Parker Coll (GA)
Central Penn Coll (PA)
The Coll of New Jersey (NJ)
Coll of Saint Mary (NE)
Columbia Coll (MO)
Converse Coll (SC)
Emmaus Bible Coll (IA)
Faulkner U (AL)
Flagler Coll (FL)
Freed-Hardeman U (TN)
Hannibal-LaGrange U (MO)
Husson U (ME)
Johnson C. Smith U (NC)
Life U (GA)
Lourdes U (OH)
Ohio Valley U (WV)
Oklahoma Christian U (OK)
Pennsylvania Coll of Technology (PA)
Pittsburgh Tech Coll (PA)
Saint Augustine's U (NC)
Saint Louis U–Madrid Campus (Spain)
Southwestern Assemblies of God U (TX)
Toccoa Falls Coll (GA)
Truett McConnell U (GA)
Union Coll (NE)
U of Colorado Boulder (CO)
U of Jamestown (ND)
U of Pikeville (KY)
U of Valley Forge (PA)
Vermont Tech Coll (VT)
Virginia Union U (VA)
Welch Coll (TN)

$30,000 AND OVER

Colleges with No Room and Board or with Room Only

The American U of Paris (France)
Berkeley Coll–White Plains Campus (NY) **(room only)**
California Coll of the Arts (CA) **(room only)**
DigiPen Inst of Technology (WA)
FIDM/Fashion Inst of Design & Merchandising, Los Angeles Campus (CA)
FIDM/Fashion Inst of Design & Merchandising, San Francisco Campus (CA)
Ithaca Coll (NY)
John Carroll U (OH)
Laguna Coll of Art & Design (CA) **(room only)**
Milwaukee Inst of Art and Design (WI) **(room only)**
Minneapolis Coll of Art and Design (MN) **(room only)**
Stevenson U (MD) **(room only)**
Walsh U (OH)

Colleges with Room and Board

Acad of Art U (CA)
Agnes Scott Coll (GA)
Albertus Magnus Coll (CT)
Albright Coll (PA)
Alfred U (NY)
Allegheny Coll (PA)
Alvernia U (PA)
American Intl Coll (MA)
Anderson U (IN)
Aquinas Coll (MI)
Arcadia U (PA)
Arizona Christian U (AZ)
Asbury U (KY)
Ashland U (OH)
Augsburg Coll (MN)
Augustana Coll (IL)
Aurora U (IL)
Austin Coll (TX)
Baker U (KS)
Baldwin Wallace U (OH)
Bard Coll (NY)
Barry U (FL)
Barton Coll (NC)
Baylor U (TX)
Bay Path U (MA)
Becker Coll (MA)
Belhaven U (MS)
Bellarmine U (KY)
Belmont U (TN)
Bennington Coll (VT)
Bethel Coll (IN)
Bethel Coll (KS)
Bethel U (MN)
Bloomfield Coll (NJ)
Bluefield Coll (VA)
Bluffton U (OH)
Boston U (MA)
Briar Cliff U (IA)
Bridgewater Coll (VA)
Bryan Coll (TN)
Bryant U (RI)
Bryn Athyn Coll of the New Church (PA)
Bryn Mawr Coll (PA)
Buena Vista U (IA)
Butler U (IN)
Cabrini U (PA)
Cairn U (PA)
California Baptist U (CA)
Canisius Coll (NY)
Capital U (OH)
Carroll Coll (MT)
Carson-Newman U (TN)
Carthage Coll (WI)
Catawba Coll (NC)
Cazenovia Coll (NY)
Cedar Crest Coll (PA)
Cedarville U (OH)
Centenary Coll of Louisiana (LA)
Centenary U (NJ)
Central Methodist U (MO)
Centre Coll (KY)
Chaminade U of Honolulu (HI)
Chapman U (CA)

Chestnut Hill Coll (PA)
Christian Brothers U (TN)
Clarke U (IA)
Cleveland Inst of Art (OH)
Coe Coll (IA)
Colby-Sawyer Coll (NH)
The Coll of Idaho (ID)
Coll of Mount Saint Vincent (NY)
Coll of Saint Elizabeth (NJ)
The Coll of Saint Rose (NY)
Coll of the Atlantic (ME)
Coll of the Holy Cross (MA)
Columbia Intl U (SC)
Columbus Coll of Art & Design (OH)
Concordia Coll–New York (NY)
Concordia U Chicago (IL)
Concordia U Irvine (CA)
Concordia U, Nebraska (NE)
Concordia U, St. Paul (MN)
Concordia U Wisconsin (WI)
Cooper Union for the Advancement of Science and Art (NY)
Corban U (OR)
Cornell Coll (IA)
Cornerstone U (MI)
Creighton U (NE)
The Culinary Inst of America (NY)
Culver-Stockton Coll (MO)
Curry Coll (MA)
Davidson Coll (NC)
Defiance Coll (OH)
DePauw U (IN)
Dominican Coll (NY)
Dominican U (IL)
Dominican U of California (CA)
Drexel U (PA)
Drury U (MO)
Eastern Nazarene Coll (MA)
Eastern U (PA)
Eckerd Coll (FL)
Elizabethtown Coll (PA)
Embry-Riddle Aeronautical U–Daytona (FL)
Embry-Riddle Aeronautical U–Prescott (AZ)
Emerson Coll (MA)
Emmanuel Coll (MA)
Emory U (GA)
Eureka Coll (IL)
Evangel U (MO)
Felician U (NJ)
Fisher Coll (MA)
Florida Inst of Technology (FL)
Franciscan U of Steubenville (OH)
Franklin & Marshall Coll (PA)
Franklin Coll (IN)
Franklin W. Olin Coll of Eng (MA)
Friends U (KS)
Gallaudet U (DC)
Geneva Coll (PA)
George Fox U (OR)
The George Washington U (DC)
Gonzaga U (WA)
Gordon Coll (MA)
Goshen Coll (IN)
Goucher Coll (MD)
Grace Coll (IN)
Graceland U (IA)
Grand View U (IA)
Green Mountain Coll (VT)
Greenville Coll (IL)
Grinnell Coll (IA)
Guilford Coll (NC)
Gwynedd Mercy U (PA)
Hamline U (MN)
Hampden-Sydney Coll (VA)
Hampshire Coll (MA)
Hanover Coll (IN)
Hardin-Simmons U (TX)
Hartwick Coll (NY)
Hawai`i Pacific U (HI)
Heidelberg U (OH)
Hendrix Coll (AR)
High Point U (NC)
Hilbert Coll (NY)
Hobart and William Smith Colls (NY)
Holy Family U (PA)
Holy Names U (CA)
Hood Coll (MD)
Hope Intl U (CA)
Houghton Coll (NY)
Howard Payne U (TX)
Huntingdon Coll (AL)
Huntington U (IN)
Illinois Coll (IL)
Illinois Wesleyan U (IL)
Immaculata U (PA)
Iona Coll (NY)
Judson U (IL)
Juniata Coll (PA)
Kalamazoo Coll (MI)
Kansas City Art Inst (MO)
Kansas Wesleyan U (KS)
Kentucky Wesleyan Coll (KY)
Keuka Coll (NY)
Knox Coll (IL)
Lafayette Coll (PA)
Lake Erie Coll (OH)
Lake Forest Coll (IL)
La Salle U (PA)
Lasell Coll (MA)
Lawrence U (WI)
Lebanon Valley Coll (PA)
Lees-McRae Coll (NC)
Lenoir-Rhyne U (NC)
Lesley U (MA)
LeTourneau U (TX)
Lewis U (IL)
LIM Coll (NY)
Limestone Coll (SC)
Lindsey Wilson Coll (KY)
Linfield Coll (OR)
Lipscomb U (TN)
Loras Coll (IA)
Loyola U Chicago (IL)
Loyola U New Orleans (LA)
Luther Coll (IA)
Lynn U (FL)
Macalester Coll (MN)
MacMurray Coll (IL)
Madonna U (MI)
Malone U (OH)
Manchester U (IN)
Manhattanville Coll (NY)
Marian U (IN)
Marian U (WI)
Marietta Coll (OH)
Mary Baldwin U (VA)
Marymount California U (CA)
Marymount Manhattan Coll (NY)
Marymount U (VA)
Maryville U of Saint Louis (MO)
Massachusetts Inst of Technology (MA)
The Master's U (CA)
McDaniel Coll (MD)
McKendree U (IL)
McMurry U (TX)
MCPHS U (MA)
Menlo Coll (CA)
MidAmerica Nazarene U (KS)
Millsaps Coll (MS)
Milwaukee School of Eng (WI)
Misericordia U (PA)
Missouri Baptist U (MO)
Monmouth Coll (IL)
Monmouth U (NJ)
Moravian Coll (PA)
Morehouse Coll (GA)
Mount Ida Coll (MA)
Mount Marty Coll (SD)
Mount Mary U (WI)
Mount Mercy U (IA)
Mount St. Joseph U (OH)
Mount Saint Mary Coll (NY)
Mount St. Mary's U (MD)
Mount Vernon Nazarene U (OH)
Multnomah U (OR)
Muskingum U (OH)
Nazareth Coll of Rochester (NY)
New England Coll (NH)
New Hampshire Inst of Art (NH)
Nichols Coll (MA)
North Carolina Wesleyan Coll (NC)
Northland Coll (WI)
Northwest Christian U (OR)
Northwestern Coll (IA)
Northwest U (WA)
Northwood U, Michigan Campus (MI)
Nyack Coll (NY)
Oakland City U (IN)
Ohio Dominican U (OH)
Oklahoma Baptist U (OK)
Oklahoma City U (OK)
Oral Roberts U (OK)
Oregon Coll of Art and Craft (OR)
Otterbein U (OH)
Ouachita Baptist U (AR)
Our Lady of the Lake U of San Antonio (TX)
Pacific Lutheran U (WA)
Pacific Northwest Coll of Art (OR)
Palm Beach Atlantic U (FL)
Patrick Henry Coll (VA)
Piedmont Coll (GA)
Point Loma Nazarene U (CA)
Point Park U (PA)
Pratt Inst (NY)
Prescott Coll (AZ)
Princeton U (NJ)
Principia Coll (IL)
Quinnipiac U (CT)
Randolph-Macon Coll (VA)
Regis Coll (MA)
Regis U (CO)
Rensselaer Polytechnic Inst (NY)
Rhodes Coll (TN)
Ripon Coll (WI)
Roanoke Coll (VA)
Robert Morris U Illinois (IL)
Roberts Wesleyan Coll (NY)
Rockford U (IL)
Rocky Mountain Coll (MT)
Roger Williams U (RI)
Rollins Coll (FL)
St. Ambrose U (IA)
Saint Anselm Coll (NH)
St. Edward's U (TX)
St. John Fisher Coll (NY)
St. John's Coll (MD)
St. John's Coll (NM)
Saint Leo U (FL)
Saint Martin's U (WA)
Saint Mary's Coll (IN)
Saint Mary's Coll of California (CA)
Saint Mary's U of Minnesota (MN)
St. Norbert Coll (WI)
St. Olaf Coll (MN)
Samford U (AL)
Schreiner U (TX)
Sewanee: The U of the South (TN)
Shenandoah U (VA)
Shorter U (GA)
Siena Coll (NY)
Sierra Nevada Coll (NV)
Simmons Coll (MA)
Simpson Coll (IA)
Simpson U (CA)
Smith Coll (MA)
Soka U of America (CA)
Southeastern U (FL)
Southern Methodist U (TX)
Southern New Hampshire U (NH)
Southwestern Coll (KS)
Southwestern U (TX)
Stanford U (CA)
Sterling Coll (KS)
Stevens Inst of Technology (NJ)
Suffolk U (MA)
Susquehanna U (PA)
Swarthmore Coll (PA)
Sweet Briar Coll (VA)
Tabor Coll (KS)
Tennessee Wesleyan U (TN)
Texas Lutheran U (TX)
Texas Wesleyan U (TX)
Thomas Aquinas Coll (CA)
Tiffin U (OH)
Transylvania U (KY)
Trevecca Nazarene U (TN)
Trine U (IN)
Trinity U (TX)

Tusculum Coll (TN)
Union Coll (KY)
Union Coll (NY)
Union U (TN)
Unity Coll (ME)
U of California, Davis (CA)
U of Denver (CO)
U of Detroit Mercy (MI)
U of Evansville (IN)
The U of Findlay (OH)
U of Great Falls (MT)
U of Hartford (CT)
U of Indianapolis (IN)
U of La Verne (CA)
U of Mary Hardin-Baylor (TX)
U of Mount Union (OH)
U of Pennsylvania (PA)
U of Puget Sound (WA)
U of Richmond (VA)
U of Rochester (NY)
U of Saint Joseph (CT)
U of Saint Mary (KS)
U of St. Thomas (MN)
U of St. Thomas (TX)
U of San Diego (CA)
U of San Francisco (CA)
The U of the Arts (PA)
U of the Cumberlands (KY)
U of the Incarnate Word (TX)
The U of Tulsa (OK)
Upper Iowa U (IA)
Ursinus Coll (PA)
Valparaiso U (IN)
Vaughn Coll of Aeronautics and Technology (NY)
Virginia Wesleyan Coll (VA)
Viterbo U (WI)
Wabash Coll (IN)
Wake Forest U (NC)
Walla Walla U (WA)
Wartburg Coll (IA)
Washington Coll (MD)
Washington U in St. Louis (MO)
Webber Intl U (FL)
Webb Inst (NY)
Wells Coll (NY)
Wentworth Inst of Technology (MA)
Wesleyan Coll (GA)
Wesleyan U (CT)
Westminster Coll (PA)
Westmont Coll (CA)
Wheaton Coll (MA)
Wheeling Jesuit U (WV)
Wheelock Coll (MA)
Whitman Coll (WA)
Whittier Coll (CA)
Whitworth U (WA)
Willamette U (OR)
William Jewell Coll (MO)
William Peace U (NC)
William Penn U (IA)
William Woods U (MO)
Wilson Coll (PA)
Wingate U (NC)
Wittenberg U (OH)
Wofford Coll (SC)

Advertisers Index

The following schools have provided and paid for a half-page display ad, which appears in the **Profiles** section on or near the page noted in this index.

Alphabetical Listing of Colleges and Universities

INDEXES

INDEXES

INDEXES

INDEXES

INDEXES

INDEXES

INDEXES

Geographic Listing of Close-Ups

Geographic Listing of Close-Ups

INDEXES

INDEXES

NOTES

NOTES